Don Green.

Handbook of Loan Payment Tables

Handbook of Loan Payment Tables

JACK C. ESTES, *Realtor*®
President, Jack C. Estes, Inc.

McGRAW-HILL BOOK COMPANY

New York St. Louis San Francisco Auckland Düsseldorf
Johannesburg Kuala Lumpur London Mexico Montreal
New Delhi Panama Paris São Paulo Singapore
Sydney Tokyo Toronto

Library of Congress Cataloging in Publication Data

Estes, Jack C, date.
  Handbook of loan payment tables.

  1. Interest and usury—Tables, etc.   I. Title.
HG1634.E78   332.8′2′0212   76-208
ISBN 0-07-019682-6

1234567890   VHVH   785432109876

Preface

"How much will my payments be?" is an often asked question.

This book is designed to furnish answers for real estate salespersons, officials of financial institutions, and other professionals who are asked that question. It is also designed to furnish answers for the many members of the public who wish to be informed regarding this vital factor of their economic life.

For over twenty years in real estate as a salesman, sales manager, and broker-owner, the author was faced with answering the above question. Very often, the available rate books did not cover the specific interest rate or amount sought, forcing interpolations, which are often not accurate. Or, if the proper information could be located, it was presented in type too small to read. These problems have increased in recent years by the fluctuating and rapidly-rising interest rates. Rate books just did not keep up with the market.

Upon learning that other brokers and officials of financial institutions were encountering the same problems, the author decided to prepare a complete set of tables to satisfy all present and future needs. The result is this book which provides the following coverage:

1. *Rates:* 329 separate interest rate increments, from 5 to 25.5 percent, in increments of tenths and eighths of a percent
2. *Terms:* From 1 year to 25 years in 1-year increments; then 30, 35, and 40 years
3. *Amounts:* $5, $10, $15, $25, $50, $75, $100; then to $1,000 by $100s; then $1,000 to $50,000 by $1,000s; then $50,000 to $100,000 by $5,000s

With this complete coverage, it truly should be the only such book ever needed.

Repayment of a mortgage or other real estate loan and most long term installment loans can be made by the use of several plans. The most popular is the monthly amortizing plan with level or constant, systematic repayment of both principal and interest, sometimes referred to as a direct reduction loan. In this plan, monthly payments

v

to principal and interest are fixed at the equal, constant payment amount necessary to amortize or fully repay the original loan, with interest, during the term of the loan. In this type of loan, interest is paid only on the unpaid balance of the principal amount as of each payment due date. As the amount of the principal decreases, a smaller amount of interest is charged, therefore a larger percentage of each total monthly payment is available to reduce the principal balance.

All FHA-insured, VA-guaranteed and almost all conventional real estate loans in the United States are amortizing, constant payment loans. The tables in this book are for use with this type of loan, with payments made in arrears (at the end of each payment period), as is the usual practice for payments on mortgages and most other long term installment loans. NOTE: For FHA-insured loans, a mortgage insurance premium (MIP) would be added to the principal and interest payments shown here.

Extreme care has been taken to ensure the accuracy of these tables. Each calculation was computed with "double precision accuracy" (computer programmed to 14 decimals, before rounding). Because of this, you may find some variation from other, less accurate tables. One deviation from absolute accuracy has been made in the rounding procedure. Normally, when computing payments or interest, any half cent or greater would be rounded up, and anything less than a half cent would be dropped. In these tables, any portion of a cent has been rounded up. This was done to ensure that any loan would be fully paid within the time periods specified, without a large lump sum payment at the end. With rounding up of any fraction of a cent, the user can be sure to repay fully the loan within the time period shown.

My sincere thanks to Robert A. Arnold of Computer Sciences Corporation, and Sandor Rosenberg, a computer programmer, whose knowledge and dedication to precision and accuracy have made these tables possible. Also to W. Z. Smith, Jr., Director, Systems, Airline Tariff Publishing Company, for the use of unique printing equipment, which made possible the presentation of these tables in clear, easy-to-read type.

Jack C. Estes

PUBLISHER'S NOTE

The author of these tables died suddenly on December 1, 1975, on the eve of their publication.

Mr. Estes enjoyed a long and successful career in real estate, and he was truly a professional in every sense of the word. His loss will be felt keenly by his associates and by his former students, who number in the thousands. These tables are but one example of his lifelong desire "to find a better way," and to some small degree they will be something of a continuing testimonial to these efforts.

Among Mr. Estes' other published works are *Real Estate License Preparation Course for the Uniform Examinations for Salespersons and Brokers*, coauthored with Dr. John Kokus, Jr., of The American University (McGraw-Hill, 1976), and *Handbook of Interest and Annuity Tables* (McGraw-Hill, 1976).

Handbook
of
Loan
Payment
Tables

5.000%

MONTHLY PAYMENT
REQUIRED TO AMORTIZE A LOAN

TERM	1 Year	2 Years	3 Years	4 Years	5 Years	6 Years	7 Years	8 Years	9 Years	10 Years	11 Years	12 Years	13 Years	14 Years
AMOUNT														
5	.43	.22	.15	.12	.10	.09	.08	.07	.06	.06	.05	.05	.05	.05
10	.86	.44	.30	.24	.19	.17	.15	.13	.12	.11	.10	.10	.09	.09
15	1.29	.66	.45	.35	.29	.25	.22	.19	.18	.16	.15	.14	.14	.13
25	2.15	1.10	.75	.58	.48	.41	.36	.32	.29	.27	.25	.24	.22	.21
50	4.29	2.20	1.50	1.16	.95	.81	.71	.64	.58	.54	.50	.47	.44	.42
75	6.43	3.30	2.25	1.73	1.42	1.21	1.07	.95	.87	.80	.74	.70	.66	.63
100	8.57	4.39	3.00	2.31	1.89	1.62	1.42	1.27	1.16	1.07	.99	.93	.88	.83
200	17.13	8.78	6.00	4.61	3.78	3.23	2.83	2.54	2.31	2.13	1.98	1.85	1.75	1.66
300	25.69	13.17	9.00	6.91	5.67	4.84	4.25	3.80	3.46	3.19	2.96	2.78	2.62	2.49
400	34.25	17.55	11.99	9.22	7.55	6.45	5.66	5.07	4.61	4.25	3.95	3.70	3.50	3.32
500	42.81	21.94	14.99	11.52	9.44	8.06	7.07	6.33	5.76	5.31	4.94	4.63	4.37	4.15
600	51.37	26.33	17.99	13.82	11.33	9.67	8.49	7.60	6.92	6.37	5.92	5.55	5.24	4.98
700	59.93	30.71	20.98	16.13	13.21	11.28	9.90	8.87	8.07	7.43	6.91	6.48	6.12	5.81
800	68.49	35.10	23.98	18.43	15.10	12.89	11.31	10.13	9.22	8.49	7.90	7.40	6.99	6.64
900	77.05	39.49	26.98	20.73	16.99	14.50	12.73	11.40	10.37	9.55	8.88	8.33	7.86	7.46
1000	85.61	43.88	29.98	23.03	18.88	16.11	14.14	12.66	11.52	10.61	9.87	9.25	8.74	8.29
2000	171.22	87.75	59.95	46.06	37.75	32.21	28.27	25.32	23.04	21.22	19.73	18.50	17.47	16.58
3000	256.83	131.62	89.92	69.09	56.62	48.32	42.41	37.98	34.56	31.82	29.60	27.75	26.20	24.87
4000	342.43	175.49	119.89	92.12	75.49	64.42	56.54	50.64	46.07	42.43	39.46	37.00	34.93	33.16
5000	428.04	219.36	149.86	115.15	94.36	80.53	70.67	63.30	57.59	53.04	49.33	46.25	43.66	41.45
6000	513.65	263.23	179.83	138.18	113.23	96.63	84.81	75.96	69.11	63.64	59.19	55.50	52.39	49.74
7000	599.26	307.10	209.80	161.21	132.10	112.74	98.94	88.62	80.63	74.25	69.06	64.75	61.12	58.03
8000	684.86	350.98	239.77	184.24	150.97	128.84	113.08	101.28	92.14	84.86	78.92	74.00	69.85	66.31
9000	770.47	394.85	269.74	207.27	169.85	144.95	127.21	113.94	103.66	95.46	88.79	83.25	78.58	74.60
10000	856.08	438.72	299.71	230.30	188.72	161.05	141.34	126.60	115.18	106.07	98.65	92.49	87.31	82.89
11000	941.69	482.59	329.68	253.33	207.59	177.16	155.48	139.26	126.70	116.68	108.51	101.74	96.04	91.18
12000	1027.29	526.46	359.66	276.36	226.46	193.26	169.61	151.92	138.21	127.28	118.38	110.99	104.77	99.47
13000	1112.90	570.33	389.63	299.39	245.33	209.37	183.75	164.58	149.73	137.89	128.24	120.24	113.50	107.76
14000	1198.51	614.20	419.60	322.42	264.20	225.47	197.88	177.24	161.25	148.50	138.11	129.49	122.23	116.05
15000	1284.12	658.08	449.57	345.44	283.07	241.58	212.01	189.90	172.76	159.10	147.97	138.74	130.96	124.34
16000	1369.72	701.95	479.54	368.47	301.94	257.68	226.15	202.56	184.28	169.71	157.84	147.99	139.69	132.62
17000	1455.33	745.82	509.51	391.50	320.82	273.79	240.28	215.22	195.80	180.32	167.70	157.24	148.43	140.91
18000	1540.94	789.69	539.48	414.53	339.69	289.89	254.42	227.88	207.32	190.92	177.57	166.49	157.16	149.20
19000	1626.55	833.56	569.45	437.56	358.56	306.00	268.55	240.54	218.83	201.53	187.43	175.73	165.89	157.49
20000	1712.15	877.43	599.42	460.59	377.43	322.10	282.68	253.20	230.35	212.14	197.29	184.98	174.62	165.78
21000	1797.76	921.30	629.39	483.62	396.30	338.21	296.82	265.86	241.87	222.74	207.16	194.23	183.35	174.07
22000	1883.37	965.18	659.36	506.65	415.17	354.31	310.95	278.52	253.39	233.35	217.02	203.48	192.08	182.36
23000	1968.98	1009.05	689.34	529.68	434.04	370.42	325.08	291.18	264.90	243.96	226.89	212.73	200.81	190.65
24000	2054.58	1052.92	719.31	552.71	452.91	386.52	339.22	303.84	276.42	254.56	236.75	221.98	209.54	198.93
25000	2140.19	1096.79	749.28	575.74	471.79	402.63	353.35	316.50	287.94	265.17	246.62	231.23	218.27	207.22
26000	2225.80	1140.66	779.25	598.77	490.66	418.73	367.49	329.16	299.45	275.78	256.48	240.48	227.00	215.51
27000	2311.41	1184.53	809.22	621.80	509.53	434.84	381.62	341.82	310.97	286.38	266.35	249.73	235.73	223.80
28000	2397.01	1228.40	839.19	644.83	528.40	450.94	395.75	354.48	322.49	296.99	276.21	258.97	244.46	232.09
29000	2482.62	1272.28	869.16	667.85	547.27	467.05	409.89	367.14	334.01	307.59	286.08	268.22	253.19	240.38
30000	2568.23	1316.15	899.13	690.88	566.14	483.15	424.02	379.80	345.52	318.20	295.94	277.47	261.92	248.67
31000	2653.84	1360.02	929.10	713.91	585.01	499.26	438.16	392.46	357.04	328.81	305.80	286.72	270.65	256.95
32000	2739.44	1403.89	959.07	736.94	603.88	515.36	452.29	405.12	368.56	339.41	315.67	295.97	279.38	265.24
33000	2825.05	1447.76	989.04	759.97	622.76	531.47	466.42	417.78	380.08	350.02	325.53	305.22	288.11	273.53
34000	2910.66	1491.63	1019.02	783.00	641.63	547.57	480.56	430.44	391.59	360.63	335.40	314.47	296.85	281.82
35000	2996.27	1535.50	1048.99	806.03	660.50	563.68	494.69	443.10	403.11	371.23	345.26	323.72	305.58	290.11
36000	3081.87	1579.38	1078.96	829.06	679.37	579.78	508.83	455.76	414.63	381.84	355.13	332.97	314.31	298.40
37000	3167.48	1623.25	1108.93	852.09	698.24	595.89	522.96	468.42	426.14	392.45	364.99	342.21	323.04	306.69
38000	3253.09	1667.12	1138.90	875.12	717.11	611.99	537.09	481.08	437.66	403.05	374.86	351.46	331.77	314.98
39000	3338.70	1710.99	1168.87	898.15	735.98	628.10	551.23	493.74	449.18	413.66	384.72	360.71	340.50	323.26
40000	3424.30	1754.86	1198.84	921.18	754.85	644.20	565.36	506.40	460.70	424.27	394.58	369.96	349.23	331.55
41000	3509.91	1798.73	1228.81	944.21	773.73	660.31	579.50	519.06	472.21	434.87	404.45	379.21	357.96	339.84
42000	3595.52	1842.60	1258.78	967.24	792.60	676.41	593.63	531.72	483.73	445.48	414.31	388.46	366.69	348.13
43000	3681.13	1886.47	1288.75	990.26	811.47	692.52	607.76	544.38	495.25	456.09	424.18	397.71	375.42	356.42
44000	3766.73	1930.35	1318.72	1013.29	830.34	708.62	621.90	557.04	506.77	466.69	434.04	406.96	384.15	364.71
45000	3852.34	1974.22	1348.70	1036.32	849.21	724.73	636.03	569.70	518.28	477.30	443.91	416.21	392.88	373.00
46000	3937.95	2018.09	1378.67	1059.35	868.08	740.83	650.16	582.36	529.80	487.91	453.77	425.45	401.61	381.29
47000	4023.56	2061.96	1408.64	1082.38	886.95	756.94	664.30	595.02	541.32	498.51	463.64	434.70	410.34	389.57
48000	4109.16	2105.83	1438.61	1105.41	905.82	773.04	678.43	607.68	552.83	509.12	473.50	443.95	419.07	397.86
49000	4194.77	2149.70	1468.58	1128.44	924.70	789.15	692.57	620.34	564.35	519.73	483.36	453.20	427.80	406.15
50000	4280.38	2193.57	1498.55	1151.47	943.57	805.25	706.70	633.00	575.87	530.33	493.23	462.45	436.53	414.44
55000	4708.42	2412.93	1648.40	1266.62	1037.92	885.78	777.37	696.30	633.46	583.37	542.55	508.69	480.19	455.88
60000	5136.45	2632.29	1798.26	1381.76	1132.28	966.30	848.04	759.60	691.04	636.40	591.87	554.94	523.84	497.33
65000	5564.49	2851.65	1948.11	1496.91	1226.64	1046.83	918.71	822.90	748.63	689.43	641.20	601.18	567.49	538.77
70000	5992.53	3071.00	2097.97	1612.06	1320.99	1127.35	989.38	886.20	806.21	742.46	690.52	647.43	611.15	580.21
75000	6420.57	3290.36	2247.82	1727.20	1415.35	1207.87	1060.05	949.50	863.80	795.50	739.84	693.67	654.80	621.66
80000	6848.60	3509.72	2397.68	1842.35	1509.70	1288.40	1130.72	1012.80	921.39	848.53	789.16	739.92	698.45	663.10
85000	7276.64	3729.07	2547.53	1957.49	1604.06	1368.92	1201.39	1076.10	978.97	901.56	838.49	786.16	742.11	704.55
90000	7704.68	3948.43	2697.39	2072.64	1698.42	1449.45	1272.06	1139.40	1036.56	954.59	887.81	832.41	785.76	745.99
95000	8132.72	4167.79	2847.24	2187.79	1792.77	1529.97	1342.73	1202.70	1094.15	1007.63	937.13	878.65	829.41	787.43
100000	8560.75	4387.14	2997.09	2302.93	1887.13	1610.50	1413.40	1266.00	1151.73	1060.66	986.45	924.90	873.06	828.88

MONTHLY PAYMENT
REQUIRED TO AMORTIZE A LOAN

5.000%

TERM	15 Years	16 Years	17 Years	18 Years	19 Years	20 Years	21 Years	22 Years	23 Years	24 Years	25 Years	30 Years	35 Years	40 Years
AMOUNT														
5	.04	.04	.04	.04	.04	.04	.04	.04	.04	.03	.03	.03	.03	.03
10	.08	.08	.08	.08	.07	.07	.07	.07	.07	.06	.06	.06	.06	.05
15	.12	.12	.11	.11	.11	.10	.10	.10	.10	.09	.09	.09	.08	.08
25	.20	.19	.19	.18	.18	.17	.17	.16	.16	.15	.15	.14	.13	.13
50	.40	.38	.37	.36	.35	.33	.33	.32	.31	.30	.30	.27	.26	.25
75	.60	.57	.55	.53	.52	.50	.49	.47	.46	.45	.44	.41	.38	.37
100	.80	.76	.73	.71	.69	.66	.65	.63	.62	.60	.59	.54	.51	.49
200	1.59	1.52	1.46	1.41	1.37	1.32	1.29	1.26	1.23	1.20	1.17	1.08	1.01	.97
300	2.38	2.28	2.19	2.11	2.05	1.98	1.93	1.88	1.84	1.80	1.76	1.62	1.52	1.45
400	3.17	3.04	2.92	2.82	2.73	2.64	2.57	2.51	2.45	2.39	2.34	2.15	2.02	1.93
500	3.96	3.79	3.65	3.52	3.41	3.30	3.21	3.13	3.06	2.99	2.93	2.69	2.53	2.42
600	4.75	4.55	4.38	4.22	4.09	3.96	3.86	3.76	3.67	3.59	3.51	3.23	3.03	2.90
700	5.54	5.31	5.11	4.93	4.77	4.62	4.50	4.38	4.28	4.18	4.10	3.76	3.54	3.38
800	6.33	6.07	5.83	5.63	5.45	5.28	5.14	5.01	4.89	4.78	4.68	4.30	4.04	3.86
900	7.12	6.82	6.56	6.33	6.13	5.94	5.78	5.63	5.50	5.38	5.27	4.84	4.55	4.34
1000	7.91	7.58	7.29	7.04	6.81	6.60	6.42	6.26	6.11	5.97	5.85	5.37	5.05	4.83
2000	15.82	15.16	14.58	14.07	13.61	13.20	12.84	12.51	12.21	11.94	11.70	10.74	10.10	9.65
3000	23.73	22.74	21.86	21.10	20.41	19.80	19.26	18.76	18.32	17.91	17.54	16.11	15.15	14.47
4000	31.64	30.31	29.15	28.13	27.22	26.40	25.67	25.02	24.42	23.88	23.39	21.48	20.19	19.29
5000	39.54	37.89	36.44	35.16	34.02	33.00	32.09	31.27	30.53	29.85	29.23	26.85	25.24	24.11
6000	47.45	45.47	43.72	42.19	40.82	39.60	38.51	37.52	36.63	35.82	35.08	32.21	30.29	28.94
7000	55.36	53.04	51.01	49.22	47.62	46.20	44.93	43.77	42.73	41.79	40.93	37.58	35.33	33.76
8000	63.27	60.62	58.30	56.25	54.43	52.80	51.34	50.03	48.84	47.76	46.77	42.95	40.38	38.58
9000	71.18	68.20	65.58	63.28	61.23	59.40	57.76	56.28	54.94	53.73	52.62	48.32	45.43	43.40
10000	79.08	75.77	72.87	70.31	68.03	66.00	64.18	62.53	61.05	59.69	58.46	53.69	50.47	48.22
11000	86.99	83.35	80.16	77.34	74.84	72.60	70.59	68.79	67.15	65.66	64.31	59.06	55.52	53.05
12000	94.90	90.93	87.44	84.37	81.64	79.20	77.01	75.04	73.25	71.63	70.16	64.42	60.57	57.87
13000	102.81	98.50	94.73	91.40	88.44	85.80	83.43	81.29	79.36	77.60	76.00	69.79	65.61	62.69
14000	110.72	106.08	102.02	98.43	95.24	92.40	89.85	87.54	85.46	83.57	81.85	75.16	70.66	67.51
15000	118.62	113.66	109.30	105.46	102.05	99.00	96.26	93.80	91.57	89.54	87.69	80.53	75.71	72.33
16000	126.53	121.23	116.59	112.49	108.85	105.60	102.68	100.05	97.67	95.51	93.54	85.90	80.76	77.16
17000	134.44	128.81	123.88	119.52	115.65	112.20	109.10	106.30	103.77	101.48	99.39	91.26	85.80	81.98
18000	142.35	136.39	131.16	126.55	122.45	118.80	115.51	112.56	109.88	107.45	105.23	96.63	90.85	86.80
19000	150.26	143.96	138.45	133.58	129.26	125.40	121.93	118.81	115.98	113.42	111.08	102.00	95.90	91.62
20000	158.16	151.54	145.74	140.61	136.06	132.00	128.35	125.06	122.09	119.38	116.92	107.37	100.94	96.44
21000	166.07	159.12	153.02	147.64	142.86	138.60	134.77	131.31	128.19	125.35	122.77	112.74	105.99	101.27
22000	173.98	166.69	160.31	154.67	149.67	145.20	141.18	137.57	134.29	131.32	128.61	118.11	111.04	106.09
23000	181.89	174.27	167.60	161.70	156.47	151.79	147.60	143.82	140.40	137.29	134.46	123.47	116.08	110.91
24000	189.80	181.85	174.88	168.73	163.27	158.39	154.02	150.07	146.50	143.26	140.31	128.84	121.13	115.73
25000	197.70	189.43	182.17	175.76	170.07	164.99	160.43	156.33	152.61	149.23	146.15	134.21	126.18	120.55
26000	205.61	197.00	189.46	182.79	176.88	171.59	166.85	162.58	158.71	155.20	152.00	139.58	131.22	125.38
27000	213.52	204.58	196.74	189.82	183.68	178.19	173.27	168.83	164.81	161.17	157.84	144.95	136.27	130.20
28000	221.43	212.16	204.03	196.85	190.48	184.79	179.69	175.08	170.92	167.14	163.69	150.32	141.32	135.02
29000	229.34	219.73	211.32	203.88	197.29	191.39	186.10	181.34	177.02	173.11	169.54	155.68	146.36	139.84
30000	237.24	227.31	218.60	210.92	204.09	197.99	192.52	187.59	183.13	179.07	175.38	161.05	151.41	144.66
31000	245.15	234.89	225.89	217.95	210.89	204.59	198.94	193.84	189.23	185.04	181.23	166.42	156.46	149.49
32000	253.06	242.46	233.17	224.98	217.69	211.19	205.35	200.09	195.33	191.01	187.07	171.79	161.51	154.31
33000	260.97	250.04	240.46	232.01	224.50	217.79	211.77	206.35	201.44	196.98	192.92	177.16	166.55	159.13
34000	268.87	257.62	247.75	239.04	231.30	224.39	218.19	212.60	207.54	202.95	198.77	182.52	171.60	163.95
35000	276.78	265.19	255.03	246.07	238.10	230.99	224.61	218.85	213.65	208.92	204.61	187.89	176.65	168.77
36000	284.69	272.77	262.32	253.10	244.90	237.59	231.02	225.11	219.75	214.89	210.46	193.26	181.69	173.60
37000	292.60	280.35	269.61	260.13	251.71	244.19	237.44	231.36	225.86	220.86	216.30	198.63	186.74	178.42
38000	300.51	287.92	276.89	267.16	258.51	250.79	243.86	237.61	231.96	226.83	222.15	204.00	191.79	183.24
39000	308.41	295.50	284.18	274.19	265.31	257.39	250.28	243.86	238.06	232.80	228.00	209.37	196.83	188.06
40000	316.32	303.08	291.47	281.22	272.12	263.99	256.69	250.12	244.17	238.76	233.84	214.73	201.88	192.88
41000	324.23	310.65	298.75	288.25	278.92	270.59	263.11	256.37	250.27	244.73	239.69	220.10	206.93	197.71
42000	332.14	318.23	306.04	295.28	285.72	277.19	269.53	262.62	256.38	250.70	245.53	225.47	211.97	202.53
43000	340.05	325.81	313.33	302.31	292.52	283.79	275.94	268.88	262.48	256.67	251.38	230.84	217.02	207.35
44000	347.95	333.38	320.61	309.34	299.33	290.39	282.36	275.13	268.58	262.64	257.22	236.21	222.07	212.17
45000	355.86	340.96	327.90	316.37	306.13	296.99	288.78	281.38	274.69	268.61	263.07	241.57	227.11	216.99
46000	363.77	348.54	335.19	323.40	312.93	303.58	295.20	287.63	280.79	274.58	268.92	246.94	232.16	221.82
47000	371.68	356.12	342.47	330.43	319.74	310.18	301.61	293.89	286.90	280.55	274.76	252.31	237.21	226.64
48000	379.59	363.69	349.76	337.46	326.54	316.78	308.03	300.14	293.00	286.52	280.61	257.68	242.26	231.46
49000	387.49	371.27	357.05	344.49	333.34	323.38	314.45	306.39	299.10	292.48	286.45	263.05	247.30	236.28
50000	395.40	378.85	364.33	351.52	340.14	329.98	320.86	312.65	305.21	298.45	292.30	268.42	252.35	241.10
55000	434.94	416.73	400.77	386.67	374.16	362.98	352.95	343.91	335.73	328.30	321.53	295.26	277.58	265.21
60000	474.48	454.61	437.20	421.83	408.17	395.98	385.04	375.17	366.25	358.14	350.76	322.10	302.82	289.32
65000	514.02	492.50	473.63	456.98	442.19	428.98	417.12	406.44	396.77	387.99	379.99	348.94	328.05	313.43
70000	553.56	530.38	510.06	492.13	476.20	461.97	449.21	437.70	427.29	417.83	409.22	375.78	353.29	337.54
75000	593.10	568.27	546.50	527.28	510.21	494.97	481.29	468.97	457.81	447.68	438.45	402.62	378.52	361.65
80000	632.64	606.15	582.93	562.43	544.23	527.97	513.38	500.23	488.33	477.52	467.68	429.46	403.76	385.76
85000	672.18	644.03	619.36	597.58	578.24	560.97	545.47	531.49	518.85	507.37	496.91	456.30	428.99	409.87
90000	711.72	681.92	655.79	632.74	612.25	593.97	577.55	562.76	549.37	537.21	526.14	483.14	454.22	433.98
95000	751.26	719.80	692.23	667.89	646.27	626.96	609.64	594.02	579.89	567.06	555.37	509.99	479.46	458.09
100000	790.80	757.69	728.66	703.04	680.28	659.96	641.72	625.29	610.41	596.90	584.60	536.83	504.69	482.20

MONTHLY PAYMENT
REQUIRED TO AMORTIZE A LOAN

TERM / AMOUNT	1 Year	2 Years	3 Years	4 Years	5 Years	6 Years	7 Years	8 Years	9 Years	10 Years	11 Years	12 Years	13 Years	14 Years
5	.43	.22	.16	.12	.10	.09	.08	.07	.06	.06	.05	.05	.05	.05
10	.86	.44	.31	.24	.19	.17	.15	.13	.12	.11	.10	.10	.09	.09
15	1.29	.66	.46	.35	.29	.25	.22	.20	.18	.16	.15	.14	.14	.13
25	2.15	1.10	.76	.58	.48	.41	.36	.32	.29	.27	.25	.24	.22	.21
50	4.29	2.20	1.51	1.16	.95	.81	.71	.64	.58	.54	.50	.47	.44	.42
75	6.43	3.30	2.26	1.74	1.42	1.22	1.07	.96	.87	.80	.75	.70	.66	.63
100	8.57	4.40	3.01	2.31	1.90	1.62	1.42	1.28	1.16	1.07	1.00	.93	.88	.84
200	17.14	8.79	6.01	4.62	3.79	3.24	2.84	2.55	2.32	2.14	1.99	1.86	1.76	1.67
300	25.70	13.18	9.01	6.93	5.68	4.85	4.26	3.82	3.47	3.20	2.98	2.79	2.64	2.51
400	34.27	17.57	12.01	9.23	7.57	6.47	5.68	5.09	4.63	4.27	3.97	3.72	3.52	3.34
500	42.83	21.96	15.01	11.54	9.46	8.08	7.10	6.36	5.79	5.33	4.96	4.65	4.40	4.18
600	51.40	26.35	18.01	13.85	11.36	9.70	8.51	7.63	6.94	6.40	5.95	5.58	5.27	5.01
700	59.96	30.75	21.02	16.16	13.25	11.31	9.93	8.90	8.10	7.46	6.94	6.51	6.15	5.84
800	68.53	35.14	24.02	18.46	15.14	12.93	11.35	10.17	9.26	8.53	7.94	7.44	7.03	6.68
900	77.09	39.53	27.02	20.77	17.03	14.54	12.77	11.44	10.41	9.59	8.93	8.37	7.91	7.51
1000	85.66	43.92	30.02	23.08	18.92	16.16	14.19	12.71	11.57	10.66	9.92	9.30	8.79	8.35
2000	171.31	87.84	60.04	46.15	37.84	32.31	28.37	25.42	23.14	21.32	19.83	18.60	17.57	16.69
3000	256.96	131.75	90.05	69.23	56.76	48.46	42.55	38.13	34.70	31.97	29.75	27.90	26.35	25.03
4000	342.62	175.67	120.07	92.30	75.67	64.61	56.73	50.84	46.27	42.63	39.66	37.20	35.13	33.37
5000	428.27	219.59	150.08	115.38	94.59	80.76	70.91	63.54	57.83	53.28	49.58	46.50	43.91	41.71
6000	513.92	263.50	180.10	138.45	113.51	96.91	85.09	76.25	69.40	63.94	59.49	55.80	52.69	50.05
7000	599.58	307.42	210.12	161.53	132.42	113.06	99.27	88.96	80.96	74.59	69.40	65.10	61.48	58.39
8000	685.23	351.33	240.13	184.60	151.34	129.22	113.45	101.67	92.53	85.25	79.32	74.40	70.26	66.73
9000	770.88	395.25	270.15	207.68	170.26	145.37	127.63	114.37	104.10	95.90	89.23	83.70	79.04	75.07
10000	856.54	439.17	300.16	230.75	189.18	161.52	141.81	127.08	115.66	106.56	99.15	93.00	87.82	83.41
11000	942.19	483.08	330.18	253.83	208.09	177.67	156.00	139.79	127.23	117.22	109.06	102.30	96.60	91.75
12000	1027.84	527.00	360.19	276.90	227.01	193.82	170.18	152.50	138.79	127.87	118.97	111.59	105.38	100.09
13000	1113.50	570.92	390.21	299.98	245.93	209.97	184.36	165.20	150.36	138.53	128.89	120.89	114.16	108.43
14000	1199.15	614.83	420.23	323.05	264.84	226.12	198.54	177.91	161.92	149.18	138.80	130.19	122.95	116.77
15000	1284.80	658.75	450.24	346.12	283.76	242.28	212.72	190.62	173.49	159.84	148.72	139.49	131.73	125.11
16000	1370.46	702.66	480.26	369.20	302.68	258.43	226.90	203.33	185.05	170.49	158.63	148.79	140.51	133.45
17000	1456.11	746.58	510.27	392.27	321.60	274.58	241.08	216.03	196.62	181.15	168.54	158.09	149.29	141.79
18000	1541.76	790.50	540.29	415.35	340.51	290.73	255.26	228.74	208.19	191.80	178.46	167.39	158.07	150.13
19000	1627.42	834.41	570.31	438.42	359.43	306.88	269.44	241.45	219.75	202.46	188.37	176.69	166.85	158.47
20000	1713.07	878.33	600.32	461.50	378.35	323.03	283.62	254.16	231.32	213.11	198.29	185.99	175.63	166.81
21000	1798.72	922.24	630.34	484.57	397.26	339.18	297.80	266.86	242.88	223.77	208.20	195.29	184.42	175.15
22000	1884.38	966.16	660.35	507.65	416.18	355.33	311.99	279.57	254.45	234.43	218.11	204.59	193.20	183.49
23000	1970.03	1010.08	690.37	530.72	435.10	371.49	326.17	292.28	266.01	245.08	228.03	213.89	201.98	191.83
24000	2055.68	1053.99	720.38	553.80	454.01	387.64	340.35	304.99	277.58	255.74	237.94	223.18	210.76	200.17
25000	2141.34	1097.91	750.40	576.87	472.93	403.79	354.53	317.69	289.14	266.39	247.86	232.48	219.54	208.51
26000	2226.99	1141.83	780.42	599.95	491.85	419.94	368.71	330.40	300.71	277.05	257.77	241.78	228.32	216.85
27000	2312.64	1185.74	810.43	623.02	510.77	436.09	382.89	343.11	312.28	287.70	267.69	251.08	237.11	225.19
28000	2398.30	1229.66	840.45	646.09	529.68	452.24	397.07	355.82	323.84	298.36	277.60	260.38	245.89	233.53
29000	2483.95	1273.57	870.46	669.17	548.60	468.39	411.25	368.52	335.41	309.01	287.51	269.68	254.67	241.87
30000	2569.60	1317.49	900.48	692.24	567.52	484.55	425.43	381.23	346.97	319.67	297.43	278.98	263.45	250.21
31000	2655.26	1361.41	930.50	715.32	586.43	500.70	439.61	393.94	358.54	330.33	307.34	288.28	272.23	258.55
32000	2740.91	1405.32	960.51	738.39	605.35	516.85	453.80	406.65	370.10	340.98	317.26	297.58	281.01	266.89
33000	2826.56	1449.24	990.53	761.47	624.27	533.00	467.98	419.36	381.67	351.64	327.17	306.88	289.79	275.23
34000	2912.22	1493.16	1020.54	784.54	643.19	549.15	482.16	432.06	393.23	362.29	337.08	316.18	298.58	283.57
35000	2997.87	1537.07	1050.56	807.62	662.10	565.30	496.34	444.77	404.80	372.95	347.00	325.48	307.36	291.91
36000	3083.52	1580.99	1080.57	830.69	681.02	581.45	510.52	457.48	416.37	383.60	356.91	334.77	316.14	300.25
37000	3169.18	1624.90	1110.59	853.77	699.94	597.61	524.70	470.19	427.93	394.26	366.83	344.07	324.92	308.59
38000	3254.83	1668.82	1140.61	876.84	718.85	613.76	538.88	482.89	439.50	404.91	376.74	353.37	333.70	316.93
39000	3340.48	1712.74	1170.62	899.92	737.77	629.91	553.06	495.60	451.06	415.57	386.65	362.67	342.48	325.27
40000	3426.14	1756.65	1200.64	922.99	756.69	646.06	567.24	508.31	462.63	426.22	396.57	371.97	351.26	333.62
41000	3511.79	1800.57	1230.65	946.06	775.61	662.21	581.42	521.02	474.19	436.88	406.48	381.27	360.05	341.96
42000	3597.44	1844.48	1260.67	969.14	794.52	678.36	595.60	533.72	485.76	447.54	416.40	390.57	368.83	350.30
43000	3683.10	1888.40	1290.69	992.21	813.44	694.51	609.79	546.43	497.32	458.19	426.31	399.87	377.61	358.64
44000	3768.75	1932.32	1320.70	1015.29	832.36	710.66	623.97	559.14	508.89	468.85	436.22	409.17	386.39	366.98
45000	3854.40	1976.23	1350.72	1038.36	851.27	726.82	638.15	571.85	520.46	479.50	446.14	418.47	395.17	375.32
46000	3940.06	2020.15	1380.73	1061.44	870.19	742.97	652.33	584.55	532.02	490.16	456.05	427.77	403.95	383.66
47000	4025.71	2064.07	1410.75	1084.51	889.11	759.12	666.51	597.26	543.59	500.81	465.97	437.07	412.74	392.00
48000	4111.36	2107.98	1440.76	1107.59	908.02	775.27	680.69	609.97	555.15	511.47	475.88	446.36	421.52	400.34
49000	4197.02	2151.90	1470.78	1130.66	926.94	791.42	694.87	622.68	566.72	522.12	485.80	455.66	430.30	408.68
50000	4282.67	2195.81	1500.80	1153.74	945.86	807.57	709.05	635.38	578.28	532.78	495.71	464.96	439.08	417.02
55000	4710.94	2415.40	1650.87	1269.11	1040.44	888.33	779.96	698.92	636.11	586.06	545.28	511.46	482.99	458.72
60000	5139.20	2634.98	1800.95	1384.48	1135.03	969.09	850.86	762.46	693.94	639.33	594.85	557.95	526.89	500.42
65000	5567.47	2854.56	1951.03	1499.86	1229.62	1049.84	921.77	826.00	751.77	692.61	644.42	604.45	570.80	542.12
70000	5995.74	3074.14	2101.11	1615.23	1324.20	1130.60	992.67	889.54	809.60	745.89	693.99	650.95	614.71	583.82
75000	6424.00	3293.72	2251.19	1730.60	1418.79	1211.36	1063.58	953.07	867.42	799.17	743.56	697.44	658.62	625.52
80000	6852.27	3513.30	2401.27	1845.97	1513.37	1292.11	1134.48	1016.61	925.25	852.44	793.13	743.94	702.52	667.23
85000	7280.54	3732.88	2551.35	1961.35	1607.96	1372.87	1205.39	1080.15	983.08	905.72	842.70	790.43	746.43	708.93
90000	7708.80	3952.46	2701.43	2076.72	1702.54	1453.63	1276.29	1143.69	1040.91	959.00	892.27	836.93	790.34	750.63
95000	8137.07	4172.04	2851.51	2192.09	1797.13	1534.38	1347.19	1207.23	1098.73	1012.28	941.84	883.42	834.25	792.33
100000	8565.34	4391.62	3001.59	2307.47	1891.71	1615.14	1418.10	1270.76	1156.56	1065.55	991.41	929.92	878.15	834.03

TERM AMOUNT	15 Years	16 Years	17 Years	18 Years	19 Years	20 Years	21 Years	22 Years	23 Years	24 Years	25 Years	30 Years	35 Years	40 Years
5	.04	.04	.04	.04	.04	.04	.04	.04	.04	.04	.03	.03	.03	.03
10	.08	.08	.08	.08	.07	.07	.07	.07	.07	.07	.06	.06	.06	.05
15	.12	.12	.12	.11	.11	.10	.10	.10	.10	.10	.09	.09	.08	.08
25	.20	.20	.19	.18	.18	.17	.17	.16	.16	.16	.15	.14	.13	.13
50	.40	.39	.37	.36	.35	.34	.33	.32	.31	.31	.30	.28	.26	.25
75	.60	.58	.56	.54	.52	.50	.49	.48	.47	.46	.45	.41	.39	.37
100	.80	.77	.74	.71	.69	.67	.65	.64	.61	.60	.60	.55	.52	.49
200	1.60	1.53	1.47	1.42	1.38	1.34	1.30	1.27	1.24	1.21	1.19	1.09	1.03	.98
300	2.39	2.29	2.21	2.13	2.06	2.00	1.95	1.90	1.85	1.81	1.78	1.63	1.54	1.47
400	3.19	3.06	2.94	2.84	2.75	2.67	2.59	2.53	2.47	2.42	2.37	2.18	2.05	1.96
500	3.99	3.82	3.68	3.55	3.43	3.33	3.24	3.16	3.09	3.02	2.96	2.72	2.56	2.45
600	4.78	4.58	4.41	4.26	4.12	4.00	3.89	3.79	3.70	3.62	3.55	3.26	3.07	2.94
700	5.58	5.35	5.14	4.96	4.81	4.66	4.54	4.42	4.32	4.22	4.14	3.81	3.58	3.43
800	6.37	6.11	5.88	5.67	5.49	5.33	5.18	5.05	4.93	4.83	4.73	4.35	4.09	3.92
900	7.17	6.87	6.61	6.38	6.18	5.99	5.83	5.68	5.55	5.43	5.32	4.89	4.60	4.40
1000	7.97	7.63	7.35	7.09	6.86	6.66	6.48	6.31	6.17	6.03	5.91	5.43	5.12	4.89
2000	15.93	15.26	14.69	14.17	13.72	13.31	12.95	12.62	12.33	12.06	11.81	10.86	10.23	9.78
3000	23.89	22.89	22.03	21.26	20.58	19.97	19.42	18.93	18.49	18.09	17.72	16.29	15.34	14.67
4000	31.85	30.52	29.37	28.34	27.44	26.62	25.90	25.24	24.65	24.11	23.62	21.72	20.45	19.56
5000	39.81	38.15	36.71	35.43	34.29	33.28	32.37	31.55	30.81	30.14	29.53	27.15	25.56	24.45
6000	47.77	45.78	44.05	42.51	41.15	39.93	38.84	37.86	36.97	36.17	35.43	32.58	30.67	29.34
7000	55.73	53.41	51.39	49.60	48.01	46.59	45.32	44.17	43.13	42.19	41.34	38.01	35.78	34.22
8000	63.69	61.04	58.73	56.68	54.87	53.24	51.79	50.48	49.30	48.22	47.24	43.44	40.89	39.11
9000	71.65	68.67	66.07	63.77	61.72	59.90	58.26	56.79	55.46	54.25	53.14	48.87	46.00	44.00
10000	79.61	76.30	73.41	70.85	68.58	66.55	64.74	63.10	61.62	60.27	59.05	54.30	51.11	48.89
11000	87.57	83.93	80.75	77.93	75.44	73.21	71.21	69.41	67.78	66.30	64.95	59.73	56.22	53.78
12000	95.53	91.56	88.09	85.02	82.30	79.86	77.68	75.72	73.94	72.33	70.06	65.16	61.33	58.67
13000	103.49	99.19	95.43	92.10	89.15	86.52	84.16	82.03	80.10	78.35	76.76	70.59	66.45	63.55
14000	111.45	106.82	102.77	99.19	96.01	93.17	90.63	88.34	86.26	84.38	82.67	76.02	71.56	68.44
15000	119.41	114.45	110.11	106.27	102.87	99.83	97.10	94.65	92.42	90.41	88.57	81.45	76.67	73.33
16000	127.37	122.08	117.45	113.36	109.73	106.48	103.58	100.96	98.59	96.43	94.47	86.88	81.78	78.22
17000	135.33	129.71	124.79	120.44	116.58	113.14	110.05	107.26	104.75	102.46	100.38	92.31	86.89	83.11
18000	143.29	137.34	132.13	127.53	123.44	119.79	116.52	113.57	110.91	108.49	106.28	97.74	92.00	88.00
19000	151.25	144.97	139.47	134.61	130.30	126.45	123.00	119.88	117.07	114.51	112.19	103.17	97.11	92.88
20000	159.21	152.60	146.81	141.69	137.16	133.10	129.47	126.19	123.23	120.54	118.09	108.59	102.22	97.77
21000	167.17	160.23	154.15	148.78	144.01	139.76	135.94	132.50	129.39	126.57	124.00	114.02	107.33	102.66
22000	175.13	167.86	161.49	155.86	150.87	146.41	142.41	138.81	135.55	132.59	129.90	119.45	112.44	107.55
23000	183.09	175.49	168.83	162.95	157.73	153.07	148.89	145.12	141.71	138.62	135.80	124.88	117.55	112.44
24000	191.05	183.12	176.17	170.03	164.59	159.72	155.36	151.43	147.88	144.65	141.71	130.31	122.66	117.33
25000	199.01	190.75	183.51	177.12	171.44	166.38	161.83	157.74	154.04	150.67	147.61	135.74	127.78	122.21
26000	206.97	198.38	190.85	184.20	178.30	173.03	168.31	164.05	160.20	156.70	153.52	141.17	132.89	127.10
27000	214.93	206.01	198.19	191.29	185.16	179.69	174.78	170.36	166.36	162.73	159.42	146.60	138.00	131.99
28000	222.89	213.64	205.53	198.37	192.02	186.34	181.25	176.67	172.52	168.76	165.33	152.03	143.11	136.88
29000	230.85	221.26	212.87	205.45	198.87	193.00	187.73	182.98	178.68	174.78	171.23	157.46	148.22	141.77
30000	238.81	228.89	220.21	212.54	205.73	199.65	194.20	189.29	184.84	180.81	177.13	162.89	153.33	146.66
31000	246.77	236.52	227.55	219.62	212.59	206.31	200.67	195.60	191.00	186.84	183.04	168.32	158.44	151.54
32000	254.73	244.15	234.89	226.71	219.45	212.96	207.15	201.91	197.17	192.86	188.94	173.75	163.55	156.43
33000	262.69	251.78	242.23	233.79	226.30	219.62	213.62	208.22	203.33	198.89	194.85	179.18	168.66	161.32
34000	270.65	259.41	249.57	240.88	233.16	226.27	220.09	214.52	209.49	204.92	200.75	184.61	173.77	166.21
35000	278.61	267.04	256.91	247.96	240.02	232.93	226.57	220.83	215.65	210.94	206.66	190.04	178.88	171.10
36000	286.57	274.67	264.25	255.05	246.88	239.58	233.04	227.14	221.81	216.97	212.56	195.47	183.99	175.99
37000	294.53	282.30	271.59	262.13	253.73	246.24	239.51	233.45	227.97	223.00	218.46	200.90	189.11	180.88
38000	302.49	289.93	278.93	269.21	260.59	252.89	245.99	239.76	234.13	229.02	224.37	206.33	194.22	185.76
39000	310.45	297.56	286.27	276.30	267.45	259.55	252.46	246.07	240.29	235.05	230.27	211.76	199.33	190.65
40000	318.41	305.19	293.61	283.38	274.31	266.20	258.93	252.38	246.46	241.08	236.18	217.18	204.44	195.54
41000	326.37	312.82	300.95	290.47	281.16	272.86	265.41	258.69	252.62	247.10	242.08	222.61	209.55	200.43
42000	334.33	320.45	308.29	297.55	288.02	279.51	271.88	265.00	258.78	253.13	247.99	228.04	214.66	205.32
43000	342.29	328.08	315.63	304.64	294.88	286.17	278.35	271.31	264.94	259.16	253.89	233.47	219.77	210.21
44000	350.25	335.71	322.97	311.72	301.74	292.82	284.82	277.62	271.10	265.18	259.79	238.90	224.88	215.09
45000	358.21	343.34	330.31	318.81	308.59	299.48	291.30	283.93	277.26	271.21	265.70	244.33	229.99	219.98
46000	366.17	350.97	337.65	325.89	315.45	306.13	297.77	290.24	283.42	277.24	271.60	249.76	235.10	224.87
47000	374.13	358.60	344.99	332.97	322.31	312.79	304.24	296.55	289.58	283.26	277.51	255.19	240.21	229.76
48000	382.09	366.23	352.33	340.06	329.17	319.44	310.72	302.86	295.75	289.29	283.41	260.62	245.32	234.65
49000	390.05	373.86	359.67	347.14	336.02	326.10	317.19	309.17	301.91	295.32	289.32	266.05	250.44	239.54
50000	398.01	381.49	367.01	354.23	342.88	332.75	323.66	315.48	308.07	301.34	295.22	271.48	255.55	244.42
55000	437.81	419.64	403.71	389.65	377.17	366.03	356.03	347.02	338.87	331.48	324.74	298.63	281.10	268.87
60000	477.61	457.78	440.41	425.07	411.46	399.30	388.40	378.57	369.68	361.61	354.26	325.77	306.65	293.31
65000	517.41	495.93	477.11	460.49	445.74	432.58	420.76	410.12	400.49	391.75	383.79	352.92	332.21	317.75
70000	557.21	534.08	513.81	495.92	480.03	465.85	453.13	441.66	431.29	421.88	413.31	380.07	357.76	342.19
75000	597.01	572.23	550.51	531.34	514.32	499.12	485.49	473.21	462.10	452.01	442.83	407.22	383.32	366.63
80000	636.82	610.38	587.21	566.76	548.61	532.40	517.86	504.76	492.91	482.15	472.35	434.36	408.87	391.08
85000	676.62	648.52	623.91	602.18	582.89	565.67	550.22	536.30	523.71	512.28	501.87	461.51	434.43	415.52
90000	716.42	686.67	660.61	637.61	617.18	598.95	582.59	567.85	554.52	542.42	531.39	488.66	459.98	439.96
95000	756.22	724.82	697.31	673.03	651.47	632.22	614.96	599.40	585.33	572.55	560.91	515.81	485.53	464.40
100000	796.02	762.97	734.01	708.45	685.76	665.50	647.32	630.95	616.13	602.68	590.44	542.95	511.09	488.84

5.125%

TERM AMOUNT	1 Year	2 Years	3 Years	4 Years	5 Years	6 Years	7 Years	8 Years	9 Years	10 Years	11 Years	12 Years	13 Years	14 Years
5	.43	.22	.16	.12	.10	.09	.08	.07	.06	.06	.05	.05	.05	.05
10	.86	.44	.31	.24	.19	.17	.15	.13	.12	.11	.10	.10	.09	.09
15	1.29	.66	.46	.35	.29	.25	.22	.20	.18	.17	.15	.14	.14	.13
25	2.15	1.10	.76	.58	.48	.41	.36	.32	.29	.27	.25	.24	.22	.21
50	4.29	2.20	1.51	1.16	.95	.81	.71	.64	.58	.54	.50	.47	.44	.42
75	6.43	3.30	2.26	1.74	1.42	1.22	1.07	.96	.87	.81	.75	.70	.66	.63
100	8.57	4.40	3.01	2.31	1.90	1.62	1.42	1.28	1.16	1.07	1.00	.94	.88	.84
200	17.14	8.79	6.01	4.62	3.79	3.24	2.84	2.55	2.32	2.14	1.99	1.87	1.76	1.68
300	25.70	13.18	9.01	6.93	5.68	4.85	4.26	3.82	3.48	3.21	2.98	2.80	2.64	2.51
400	34.27	17.58	12.02	9.24	7.58	6.47	5.68	5.09	4.64	4.27	3.98	3.73	3.52	3.35
500	42.84	21.97	15.02	11.55	9.47	8.09	7.10	6.36	5.79	5.34	4.97	4.66	4.40	4.18
600	51.40	26.36	18.02	13.86	11.36	9.70	8.52	7.64	6.95	6.41	5.96	5.59	5.28	5.02
700	59.97	30.75	21.02	16.17	13.25	11.32	9.94	8.91	8.11	7.47	6.95	6.52	6.16	5.85
800	68.54	35.15	24.03	18.47	15.15	12.94	11.36	10.18	9.27	8.54	7.95	7.45	7.04	6.69
900	77.10	39.54	27.03	20.78	17.04	14.55	12.78	11.45	10.42	9.61	8.94	8.39	7.92	7.52
1000	85.67	43.93	30.03	23.09	18.93	16.17	14.20	12.72	11.58	10.67	9.93	9.32	8.80	8.36
2000	171.33	87.86	60.06	46.18	37.86	32.33	28.39	25.44	23.16	21.34	19.86	18.63	17.59	16.71
3000	257.00	131.79	90.09	69.26	56.79	48.49	42.58	38.16	34.74	32.01	29.78	27.94	26.39	25.06
4000	342.66	175.71	120.11	92.35	75.72	64.66	56.78	50.88	46.32	42.68	39.71	37.25	35.18	33.42
5000	428.33	219.64	150.14	115.43	94.65	80.82	70.97	63.60	57.89	53.34	49.64	46.56	43.98	41.77
6000	513.99	263.57	180.17	138.52	113.58	96.98	85.16	76.32	69.47	64.01	59.56	55.88	52.77	50.12
7000	599.66	307.50	210.19	161.61	132.50	113.15	99.35	89.04	81.05	74.68	69.49	65.19	61.56	58.48
8000	685.32	351.42	240.22	184.69	151.43	129.31	113.55	101.76	92.63	85.35	79.42	74.50	70.36	66.83
9000	770.99	395.35	270.25	207.78	170.36	145.47	127.74	114.48	104.20	96.01	89.34	83.81	79.15	75.18
10000	856.65	439.28	300.28	230.86	189.29	161.63	141.93	127.20	115.78	106.68	99.27	93.12	87.95	83.54
11000	942.32	483.21	330.30	253.95	208.22	177.80	156.12	139.92	127.36	117.35	109.20	102.43	96.74	91.89
12000	1027.98	527.13	360.33	277.04	227.15	193.96	170.32	152.64	138.94	128.02	119.12	111.75	105.54	100.24
13000	1113.65	571.06	390.36	300.12	246.08	210.12	184.51	165.36	150.51	138.69	129.05	121.06	114.33	108.60
14000	1199.31	614.99	420.38	323.21	265.00	226.29	198.70	178.08	162.09	149.35	138.98	130.37	123.12	116.95
15000	1284.98	658.92	450.41	346.29	283.93	242.45	212.90	190.80	173.67	160.02	148.90	139.68	131.92	125.30
16000	1370.64	702.84	480.44	369.38	302.86	258.61	227.09	203.52	185.25	170.69	158.83	148.99	140.71	133.66
17000	1456.31	746.77	510.46	392.47	321.79	274.78	241.28	216.24	196.83	181.36	168.76	158.30	149.51	142.01
18000	1541.97	790.70	540.49	415.55	340.72	290.94	255.47	228.96	208.40	192.02	178.68	167.62	158.30	150.36
19000	1627.64	834.63	570.52	438.64	359.65	307.10	269.67	241.68	219.98	202.69	188.61	176.93	167.10	158.72
20000	1713.30	878.55	600.55	461.72	378.58	323.26	283.86	254.40	231.56	213.36	198.54	186.24	175.89	167.07
21000	1798.97	922.48	630.57	484.81	397.50	339.43	298.05	267.11	243.14	224.03	208.46	195.55	184.68	175.42
22000	1884.63	966.41	660.60	507.90	416.43	355.59	312.24	279.83	254.71	234.70	218.39	204.86	193.48	183.77
23000	1970.29	1010.34	690.63	530.98	435.36	371.75	326.44	292.55	266.29	245.36	228.31	214.17	202.27	192.13
24000	2055.96	1054.26	720.65	554.07	454.29	387.92	340.63	305.27	277.87	256.03	238.24	223.49	211.07	200.48
25000	2141.62	1098.19	750.68	577.15	473.22	404.08	354.82	317.99	289.45	266.70	248.17	232.80	219.86	208.83
26000	2227.29	1142.12	780.71	600.24	492.15	420.24	369.02	330.71	301.02	277.37	258.09	242.11	228.66	217.19
27000	2312.95	1186.04	810.74	623.33	511.08	436.41	383.21	343.43	312.60	288.03	268.02	251.42	237.45	225.54
28000	2398.62	1229.97	840.76	646.41	530.00	452.57	397.40	356.15	324.18	298.70	277.95	260.73	246.24	233.89
29000	2484.28	1273.90	870.79	669.50	548.93	468.73	411.59	368.87	335.76	309.37	287.87	270.05	255.04	242.25
30000	2569.95	1317.83	900.82	692.58	567.86	484.89	425.79	381.59	347.34	320.04	297.80	279.36	263.83	250.60
31000	2655.61	1361.75	930.84	715.67	586.79	501.06	439.98	394.31	358.91	330.71	307.73	288.67	272.63	258.95
32000	2741.28	1405.68	960.87	738.76	605.72	517.22	454.17	407.03	370.49	341.37	317.65	297.98	281.42	267.31
33000	2826.94	1449.61	990.90	761.84	624.65	533.38	468.36	419.75	382.07	352.04	327.58	307.29	290.21	275.66
34000	2912.61	1493.54	1020.92	784.93	643.58	549.55	482.56	432.47	393.65	362.71	337.51	316.60	299.01	284.01
35000	2998.27	1537.46	1050.95	808.01	662.50	565.71	496.75	445.19	405.22	373.38	347.43	325.92	307.80	292.37
36000	3083.94	1581.39	1080.98	831.10	681.43	581.87	510.94	457.91	416.80	384.04	357.36	335.23	316.60	300.72
37000	3169.60	1625.32	1111.01	854.19	700.36	598.04	525.14	470.63	428.38	394.71	367.29	344.54	325.39	309.07
38000	3255.27	1669.25	1141.03	877.27	719.29	614.20	539.33	483.35	439.96	405.38	377.21	353.85	334.19	317.43
39000	3340.93	1713.17	1171.06	900.36	738.22	630.36	553.52	496.07	451.53	416.05	387.14	363.16	342.98	325.78
40000	3426.60	1757.10	1201.09	923.44	757.15	646.52	567.71	508.79	463.11	426.72	397.07	372.47	351.77	334.13
41000	3512.26	1801.03	1231.11	946.53	776.08	662.69	581.91	521.51	474.69	437.38	406.99	381.79	360.57	342.48
42000	3597.93	1844.96	1261.14	969.62	795.00	678.85	596.10	534.22	486.27	448.05	416.92	391.10	369.36	350.84
43000	3683.59	1888.88	1291.17	992.70	813.93	695.01	610.29	546.94	497.84	458.72	426.84	400.41	378.16	359.19
44000	3769.26	1932.81	1321.20	1015.79	832.86	711.18	624.48	559.66	509.42	469.39	436.77	409.72	386.95	367.54
45000	3854.92	1976.74	1351.22	1038.87	851.79	727.34	638.68	572.38	521.00	480.05	446.70	419.03	395.75	375.90
46000	3940.58	2020.67	1381.25	1061.96	870.72	743.50	652.87	585.10	532.58	490.72	456.62	428.34	404.54	384.25
47000	4026.25	2064.59	1411.28	1085.05	889.65	759.67	667.06	597.82	544.16	501.39	466.55	437.66	413.33	392.60
48000	4111.91	2108.52	1441.30	1108.13	908.58	775.83	681.26	610.54	555.73	512.06	476.48	446.97	422.13	400.96
49000	4197.58	2152.45	1471.33	1131.22	927.50	791.99	695.45	623.26	567.31	522.73	486.40	456.28	430.92	409.31
50000	4283.24	2196.37	1501.36	1154.30	946.43	808.15	709.64	635.98	578.89	533.39	496.33	465.59	439.72	417.66
55000	4711.57	2416.01	1651.49	1269.73	1041.08	888.97	780.60	699.58	636.78	586.73	545.96	512.15	483.69	459.43
60000	5139.89	2635.65	1801.63	1385.16	1135.72	969.78	851.57	763.18	694.67	640.07	595.60	558.71	527.66	501.19
65000	5568.22	2855.29	1951.76	1500.59	1230.36	1050.60	922.53	826.77	752.55	693.41	645.23	605.27	571.63	542.96
70000	5996.54	3074.92	2101.90	1616.02	1325.00	1131.41	993.50	890.37	810.44	746.75	694.86	651.83	615.60	584.73
75000	6424.86	3294.56	2252.03	1731.45	1419.65	1212.23	1064.46	953.97	868.33	800.09	744.49	698.39	659.57	626.49
80000	6853.19	3514.20	2402.17	1846.88	1514.29	1293.04	1135.42	1017.57	926.22	853.43	794.13	744.94	703.54	668.26
85000	7281.51	3733.83	2552.30	1962.31	1608.93	1373.86	1206.39	1081.16	984.11	906.76	843.76	791.50	747.52	710.02
90000	7709.83	3953.47	2702.44	2077.74	1703.58	1454.67	1277.35	1144.76	1042.00	960.10	893.39	838.06	791.49	751.79
95000	8138.16	4173.11	2852.57	2193.17	1798.22	1535.49	1348.31	1208.36	1099.88	1013.44	943.02	884.62	835.46	793.56
100000	8566.48	4392.74	3002.71	2308.60	1892.86	1616.30	1419.28	1271.96	1157.77	1066.78	992.66	931.18	879.43	835.32

TERM / AMOUNT	15 Years	16 Years	17 Years	18 Years	19 Years	20 Years	21 Years	22 Years	23 Years	24 Years	25 Years	30 Years	35 Years	40 Years
5	.04	.04	.04	.04	.04	.04	.04	.04	.04	.04	.03	.03	.03	.03
10	.08	.08	.08	.08	.07	.07	.07	.07	.07	.07	.06	.06	.06	.05
15	.12	.12	.12	.11	.11	.11	.10	.10	.10	.10	.09	.09	.08	.08
25	.20	.20	.19	.18	.18	.17	.17	.16	.16	.16	.15	.14	.13	.13
50	.40	.39	.37	.36	.35	.34	.33	.32	.31	.31	.30	.28	.26	.25
75	.60	.58	.56	.54	.52	.51	.49	.48	.47	.46	.45	.41	.39	.37
100	.80	.77	.74	.71	.69	.67	.65	.64	.62	.61	.60	.55	.52	.50
200	1.60	1.53	1.48	1.42	1.38	1.34	1.30	1.27	1.24	1.21	1.19	1.09	1.03	.99
300	2.40	2.30	2.21	2.13	2.07	2.01	1.95	1.90	1.86	1.82	1.78	1.64	1.54	1.48
400	3.19	3.06	2.95	2.84	2.75	2.67	2.60	2.53	2.48	2.42	2.37	2.18	2.06	1.97
500	3.99	3.83	3.68	3.55	3.44	3.34	3.25	3.17	3.09	3.03	2.96	2.73	2.57	2.46
600	4.79	4.59	4.42	4.26	4.13	4.01	3.90	3.80	3.71	3.63	3.56	3.27	3.08	2.95
700	5.59	5.36	5.15	4.97	4.81	4.67	4.55	4.43	4.33	4.23	4.15	3.82	3.59	3.44
800	6.38	6.12	5.89	5.68	5.50	5.34	5.19	5.06	4.95	4.84	4.74	4.36	4.11	3.93
900	7.18	6.88	6.62	6.39	6.19	6.01	5.84	5.70	5.56	5.44	5.33	4.91	4.62	4.42
1000	7.98	7.65	7.36	7.10	6.88	6.67	6.49	6.33	6.18	6.05	5.92	5.45	5.13	4.91
2000	15.95	15.29	14.71	14.20	13.75	13.34	12.98	12.65	12.36	12.09	11.84	10.89	10.26	9.82
3000	23.92	22.93	22.07	21.30	20.62	20.01	19.47	18.98	18.53	18.13	17.76	16.34	15.39	14.72
4000	31.90	30.58	29.42	28.40	27.49	26.68	25.95	25.30	24.71	24.17	23.68	21.78	20.51	19.63
5000	39.87	38.22	36.77	35.50	34.36	33.35	32.44	31.62	30.88	30.21	29.60	27.23	25.64	24.53
6000	47.84	45.86	44.13	42.59	41.23	40.02	38.93	37.95	37.06	36.25	35.52	32.67	30.77	29.44
7000	55.82	53.51	51.48	49.69	48.10	46.69	45.42	44.27	43.23	42.29	41.44	38.12	35.89	34.34
8000	63.79	61.15	58.83	56.79	54.97	53.36	51.90	50.59	49.41	48.34	47.36	43.56	41.02	39.25
9000	71.76	68.79	66.19	63.89	61.85	60.02	58.39	56.92	55.59	54.38	53.28	49.01	46.15	44.15
10000	79.74	76.43	73.54	70.99	68.72	66.69	64.88	63.24	61.76	60.42	59.19	54.45	51.27	49.06
11000	87.71	84.08	80.89	78.08	75.59	73.36	71.36	69.56	67.94	66.46	65.11	59.90	56.40	53.96
12000	95.68	91.72	88.25	85.18	82.46	80.03	77.85	75.89	74.11	72.50	71.03	65.34	61.53	58.87
13000	103.66	99.36	95.60	92.28	89.33	86.70	84.34	82.21	80.29	78.54	76.95	70.79	66.65	63.77
14000	111.63	107.01	102.95	99.38	96.20	93.37	90.83	88.54	86.46	84.58	82.87	76.23	71.78	68.68
15000	119.60	114.65	110.31	106.48	103.07	100.04	97.31	94.86	92.64	90.62	88.79	81.68	76.91	73.58
16000	127.58	122.29	117.66	113.57	109.94	106.71	103.80	101.18	98.81	96.67	94.71	87.12	82.04	78.49
17000	135.55	129.93	125.01	120.67	116.82	113.37	107.51	104.99	102.71	100.63	92.57	87.16	83.39	
18000	143.52	137.58	132.37	127.77	123.69	120.04	116.77	113.83	111.17	108.75	106.55	98.01	92.29	88.30
19000	151.50	145.22	139.72	134.87	130.56	126.71	123.25	120.15	117.34	114.79	112.47	103.46	97.42	93.20
20000	159.47	152.86	147.07	141.97	137.43	133.38	129.75	126.48	123.52	120.83	118.30	108.90	102.54	98.11
21000	167.44	160.51	154.43	149.06	144.30	140.05	136.24	132.80	129.69	126.87	124.30	114.35	107.67	103.01
22000	175.42	168.15	161.78	156.16	151.17	146.72	142.72	139.12	135.87	132.91	130.22	119.79	112.80	107.92
23000	183.39	175.79	169.13	163.26	158.04	153.39	149.21	145.45	142.04	138.95	136.14	125.24	117.92	112.82
24000	191.36	183.43	176.49	170.36	164.91	160.06	155.70	151.77	148.22	145.00	142.06	130.68	123.05	117.73
25000	199.34	191.08	183.84	177.46	171.79	166.73	162.19	158.10	154.40	151.04	147.98	136.13	128.18	122.63
26000	207.31	198.72	191.19	184.55	178.66	173.39	168.67	164.42	160.57	157.08	153.90	141.57	133.30	127.54
27000	215.28	206.36	198.55	191.65	185.53	180.06	175.16	170.74	166.75	163.12	159.82	147.02	138.43	132.44
28000	223.25	214.01	205.90	198.75	192.40	186.73	181.65	177.07	172.92	169.16	165.74	152.46	143.56	137.35
29000	231.23	221.65	213.25	205.85	199.27	193.40	188.13	183.39	179.10	175.20	171.65	157.91	148.68	142.25
30000	239.20	229.29	220.61	212.95	206.14	200.07	194.62	189.71	185.27	181.24	177.57	163.35	153.81	147.16
31000	247.17	236.93	227.96	220.04	213.01	206.74	201.11	196.04	191.45	187.28	183.49	168.80	158.94	152.06
32000	255.15	244.58	235.31	227.14	219.88	213.41	207.60	202.36	197.62	193.33	189.41	174.24	164.07	156.97
33000	263.12	252.22	242.67	234.24	226.76	220.08	214.08	208.68	203.80	199.37	195.33	179.69	169.19	161.87
34000	271.09	259.86	250.02	241.34	233.63	226.74	221.07	215.01	209.98	205.41	201.25	185.13	174.32	166.78
35000	279.07	267.51	257.38	248.44	240.50	233.41	227.06	221.33	216.15	211.45	207.17	190.58	179.45	171.68
36000	287.04	275.15	264.73	255.53	247.37	240.08	233.54	227.65	222.33	217.49	213.09	196.02	184.57	176.59
37000	295.01	282.79	272.08	262.63	254.24	246.75	240.03	233.98	228.50	223.53	219.01	201.47	189.70	181.49
38000	302.99	290.43	279.44	269.73	261.11	253.42	246.52	240.30	234.68	229.57	224.93	206.91	194.83	186.40
39000	310.96	298.08	286.79	276.83	267.98	260.09	253.01	246.63	240.85	235.62	230.84	212.35	199.95	191.30
40000	318.93	305.72	294.14	283.93	274.85	266.76	259.49	252.95	247.03	241.66	236.76	217.80	205.08	196.21
41000	326.91	313.36	301.50	291.02	281.73	273.43	265.98	259.27	253.21	247.70	242.68	223.24	210.21	201.11
42000	334.88	321.01	308.85	298.12	288.60	280.09	272.47	265.60	259.38	253.74	248.60	228.69	215.33	206.02
43000	342.85	328.65	316.20	305.22	295.47	286.76	278.95	271.92	265.56	259.78	254.52	234.13	220.46	210.92
44000	350.83	336.29	323.56	312.32	302.34	293.43	285.44	278.24	271.73	265.82	260.44	239.58	225.59	215.83
45000	358.80	343.93	330.91	319.42	309.21	300.10	291.93	284.57	277.91	271.86	266.36	245.02	230.71	220.73
46000	366.77	351.58	338.26	326.51	316.08	306.77	298.42	290.89	284.08	277.90	272.28	250.47	235.84	225.64
47000	374.75	359.22	345.62	333.61	322.95	313.44	304.90	297.21	290.26	283.95	278.20	255.91	240.97	230.54
48000	382.72	366.86	352.97	340.71	329.82	320.11	311.39	303.54	296.43	289.99	284.12	261.36	246.10	235.45
49000	390.69	374.51	360.32	347.81	336.70	326.78	317.88	309.86	302.61	296.03	290.03	266.80	251.22	240.35
50000	398.67	382.15	367.68	354.91	343.57	333.45	324.37	316.19	308.79	302.07	295.95	272.25	256.35	245.26
55000	438.53	420.36	404.44	390.40	377.92	366.79	356.80	347.80	339.66	332.28	325.55	299.47	281.98	269.78
60000	478.40	458.58	441.21	425.89	412.28	400.13	389.24	379.42	370.54	362.48	355.14	326.70	307.62	294.31
65000	518.26	496.79	477.98	461.38	446.64	433.48	421.67	411.04	401.42	392.69	384.74	353.92	333.25	318.83
70000	558.13	535.01	514.75	496.87	480.99	466.82	454.11	442.66	432.30	422.90	414.33	381.15	358.89	343.36
75000	598.00	573.22	551.51	532.36	515.35	500.17	486.55	474.28	463.18	453.10	443.93	408.37	384.52	367.88
80000	637.86	611.44	588.28	567.85	549.70	533.51	518.98	505.89	494.05	483.31	473.52	435.59	410.16	392.41
85000	677.73	649.65	625.05	603.34	584.06	566.85	551.42	537.51	524.93	513.51	503.12	462.82	435.79	416.93
90000	717.59	687.86	661.81	638.83	618.42	600.20	583.85	569.13	555.81	543.72	532.71	490.04	461.42	441.46
95000	757.46	726.08	698.58	674.32	652.77	633.54	616.29	600.75	586.69	573.93	562.31	517.27	487.06	465.98
100000	797.33	764.29	735.35	709.81	687.13	666.89	648.73	632.37	617.57	604.13	591.90	544.49	512.69	490.51

MONTHLY PAYMENT
REQUIRED TO AMORTIZE A LOAN

TERM AMOUNT	1 Year	2 Years	3 Years	4 Years	5 Years	6 Years	7 Years	8 Years	9 Years	10 Years	11 Years	12 Years	13 Years	14 Years
5	.43	.22	.16	.12	.10	.09	.08	.07	.06	.06	.05	.05	.05	.05
10	.86	.44	.31	.24	.19	.17	.15	.13	.12	.11	.10	.10	.09	.09
15	1.29	.66	.46	.35	.29	.25	.22	.20	.18	.17	.15	.15	.14	.13
25	2.15	1.10	.76	.58	.48	.41	.36	.32	.30	.27	.25	.24	.23	.21
50	4.29	2.20	1.51	1.16	.95	.81	.72	.64	.59	.54	.50	.47	.45	.42
75	6.43	3.30	2.26	1.74	1.43	1.22	1.07	.96	.88	.81	.75	.71	.67	.63
100	8.57	4.40	3.01	2.32	1.90	1.62	1.43	1.28	1.17	1.08	1.00	.94	.89	.84
200	17.14	8.80	6.02	4.63	3.80	3.24	2.85	2.56	2.33	2.15	2.00	1.87	1.77	1.68
300	25.71	13.19	9.02	6.94	5.69	4.86	4.27	3.83	3.49	3.22	2.99	2.81	2.65	2.52
400	34.28	17.59	12.03	9.25	7.59	6.49	5.70	5.11	4.65	4.29	3.99	3.74	3.54	3.36
500	42.85	21.99	15.04	11.57	9.49	8.10	7.12	6.38	5.81	5.36	4.99	4.68	4.42	4.20
600	51.42	26.38	18.04	13.88	11.38	9.72	8.54	7.66	6.97	6.43	5.98	5.61	5.30	5.04
700	59.99	30.78	21.05	16.19	13.28	11.34	9.96	8.93	8.13	7.50	6.98	6.55	6.19	5.88
800	68.56	35.17	24.05	18.50	15.18	12.96	11.39	10.21	9.30	8.57	7.98	7.48	7.07	6.72
900	77.13	39.57	27.06	20.81	17.07	14.58	12.81	11.48	10.46	9.64	8.97	8.42	7.95	7.56
1000	85.70	43.97	30.07	23.13	18.97	16.20	14.23	12.76	11.62	10.71	9.97	9.35	8.84	8.40
2000	171.40	87.93	60.13	46.25	37.93	32.40	28.46	25.52	23.23	21.41	19.93	18.70	17.67	16.79
3000	257.10	131.89	90.19	69.37	56.89	48.60	42.69	38.27	34.85	32.12	29.90	28.05	26.50	25.18
4000	342.80	175.85	120.25	92.49	75.86	64.80	56.92	51.03	46.46	42.82	39.86	37.40	35.34	33.57
5000	428.50	219.81	150.31	115.61	94.82	80.99	71.15	63.78	58.07	53.53	49.82	46.75	44.17	41.96
6000	514.20	263.77	180.37	138.73	113.78	97.19	85.37	76.54	69.69	64.23	59.79	56.10	53.00	50.36
7000	599.90	307.73	210.43	161.85	132.75	113.39	99.60	89.29	81.30	74.94	69.75	65.45	61.83	58.75
8000	685.60	351.69	240.49	184.97	151.71	129.59	113.83	102.05	92.92	85.64	79.72	74.80	70.67	67.14
9000	771.30	395.65	270.55	208.09	170.67	145.79	128.06	114.80	104.53	96.35	89.68	84.15	79.50	75.53
10000	857.00	439.62	300.61	231.21	189.63	161.98	142.29	127.56	116.14	107.05	99.64	93.50	88.33	83.92
11000	942.70	483.58	330.67	254.33	208.60	178.18	156.51	140.31	127.76	117.76	109.61	102.85	97.16	92.32
12000	1028.39	527.54	360.73	277.45	227.56	194.38	170.74	153.07	139.37	128.46	119.57	112.20	106.00	100.71
13000	1114.09	571.50	390.80	300.57	246.52	210.58	184.97	165.82	150.99	139.16	129.53	121.55	114.83	109.10
14000	1199.79	615.46	420.86	323.69	265.49	226.78	199.20	178.58	162.60	149.87	139.50	130.90	123.66	117.49
15000	1285.49	659.42	450.92	346.81	284.45	242.97	213.43	191.34	174.21	160.57	149.46	140.25	132.49	125.88
16000	1371.19	703.38	480.98	369.93	303.41	259.17	227.65	204.09	185.83	171.28	159.43	149.60	141.33	134.28
17000	1456.89	747.34	511.04	393.05	322.38	275.37	241.88	216.85	197.44	181.98	169.39	158.95	150.16	142.67
18000	1542.59	791.30	541.10	416.17	341.34	291.57	256.11	229.60	209.06	192.69	179.35	168.30	158.99	151.06
19000	1628.29	835.26	571.16	439.29	360.30	307.76	270.34	242.36	220.67	203.39	189.32	177.65	167.82	159.45
20000	1713.99	879.23	601.22	462.41	379.26	323.96	284.57	255.11	232.28	214.10	199.28	187.00	176.66	167.84
21000	1799.69	923.19	631.28	485.53	398.23	340.16	298.79	267.87	243.90	224.80	209.25	196.35	185.49	176.24
22000	1885.39	967.15	661.34	508.65	417.19	356.36	313.02	280.62	255.51	235.51	219.21	205.70	194.32	184.63
23000	1971.09	1011.11	691.40	531.77	436.15	372.56	327.25	293.38	267.13	246.21	229.17	215.04	203.15	193.02
24000	2056.78	1055.07	721.46	554.89	455.12	388.75	341.48	306.13	278.74	256.91	239.14	224.39	211.99	201.41
25000	2142.48	1099.03	751.52	578.01	474.08	404.95	355.71	318.89	290.35	267.62	249.10	233.74	220.82	209.80
26000	2228.18	1142.99	781.59	601.13	493.04	421.15	369.93	331.64	301.97	278.32	259.06	243.09	229.65	218.20
27000	2313.88	1186.95	811.65	624.25	512.01	437.35	384.16	344.40	313.58	289.03	269.03	252.44	238.48	226.59
28000	2399.58	1230.91	841.71	647.37	530.97	453.55	398.39	357.15	325.20	299.73	278.99	261.79	247.32	234.98
29000	2485.28	1274.87	871.77	670.49	549.93	469.74	412.62	369.91	336.81	310.44	288.96	271.14	256.15	243.37
30000	2570.98	1318.84	901.83	693.61	568.89	485.94	426.85	382.67	348.42	321.14	298.92	280.49	264.98	251.76
31000	2656.68	1362.80	931.89	716.73	587.86	502.14	441.08	395.42	360.04	331.85	308.88	289.84	273.81	260.16
32000	2742.38	1406.76	961.96	739.85	606.82	518.34	455.30	408.18	371.65	342.55	318.85	299.19	282.65	268.55
33000	2828.08	1450.72	992.01	762.97	625.78	534.53	469.53	420.93	383.27	353.26	328.81	308.54	291.48	276.94
34000	2913.78	1494.68	1022.07	786.09	644.75	550.73	483.76	433.69	394.88	363.96	338.78	317.89	300.31	285.33
35000	2999.48	1538.64	1052.13	809.21	663.71	566.93	497.99	446.44	406.49	374.67	348.74	327.24	309.14	293.72
36000	3085.17	1582.60	1082.19	832.33	682.67	583.13	512.22	459.20	418.11	385.37	358.70	336.59	317.98	302.12
37000	3170.87	1626.56	1112.25	855.45	701.64	599.33	526.44	471.95	429.72	396.07	368.67	345.94	326.81	310.51
38000	3256.57	1670.52	1142.31	878.57	720.60	615.53	540.67	484.71	441.34	406.78	378.63	355.29	335.64	318.90
39000	3342.27	1714.48	1172.38	901.69	739.56	631.72	554.90	497.46	452.95	417.48	388.59	364.64	344.47	327.29
40000	3427.97	1758.45	1202.44	924.81	758.52	647.92	569.13	510.22	464.56	428.19	398.56	373.99	353.31	335.68
41000	3513.67	1802.41	1232.50	947.93	777.49	664.12	583.36	522.97	476.18	438.89	408.52	383.34	362.14	344.08
42000	3599.37	1846.37	1262.56	971.05	796.45	680.32	597.58	535.73	487.79	449.60	418.49	392.69	370.97	352.47
43000	3685.07	1890.33	1292.62	994.17	815.41	696.51	611.81	548.49	499.41	460.30	428.45	402.04	379.81	360.86
44000	3770.77	1934.29	1322.68	1017.29	834.38	712.71	626.04	561.24	511.02	471.01	438.41	411.39	388.64	369.25
45000	3856.47	1978.25	1352.74	1040.41	853.34	728.91	640.27	574.00	522.63	481.71	448.38	420.73	397.47	377.64
46000	3942.17	2022.21	1382.80	1063.53	872.30	745.11	654.50	586.75	534.25	492.42	458.34	430.08	406.30	386.04
47000	4027.87	2066.17	1412.86	1086.65	891.27	761.30	668.72	599.51	545.86	503.12	468.30	439.43	415.14	394.43
48000	4113.56	2110.13	1442.92	1109.77	910.23	777.50	682.95	612.26	557.48	513.82	478.27	448.78	423.97	402.82
49000	4199.26	2154.09	1472.98	1132.89	929.19	793.70	697.18	625.02	569.09	524.53	488.23	458.13	432.80	411.21
50000	4284.96	2198.06	1503.04	1156.01	948.15	809.90	711.41	637.77	580.70	535.23	498.20	467.48	441.63	419.60
55000	4713.46	2417.86	1653.35	1271.61	1042.97	890.89	782.55	701.55	638.77	588.76	548.02	514.23	485.80	461.56
60000	5141.95	2637.67	1803.65	1387.21	1137.79	971.88	853.69	765.33	696.84	642.28	597.83	560.98	529.96	503.52
65000	5570.45	2857.47	1953.96	1502.81	1232.60	1052.87	924.83	829.10	754.91	695.80	647.65	607.73	574.12	545.48
70000	5998.95	3077.28	2104.26	1618.41	1327.42	1133.86	995.97	892.88	812.98	749.33	697.47	654.47	618.28	587.44
75000	6427.44	3297.08	2254.56	1734.01	1422.23	1214.85	1067.11	956.66	871.05	802.85	747.29	701.22	662.45	629.40
80000	6855.94	3516.89	2404.87	1849.61	1517.05	1295.83	1138.25	1020.43	929.12	856.37	797.11	747.97	706.61	671.36
85000	7284.43	3736.69	2555.17	1965.21	1611.86	1376.82	1209.39	1084.21	987.19	909.89	846.93	794.72	750.77	713.32
90000	7712.93	3956.50	2705.47	2080.81	1706.68	1457.81	1280.53	1147.99	1045.26	963.42	896.75	841.46	794.94	755.28
95000	8141.43	4176.30	2855.78	2196.41	1801.49	1538.80	1351.67	1211.76	1103.33	1016.94	946.57	888.21	839.10	797.24
100000	8569.92	4396.11	3006.08	2312.01	1896.30	1619.79	1422.81	1275.54	1161.40	1070.46	996.39	934.96	883.26	839.20

MONTHLY PAYMENT
REQUIRED TO AMORTIZE A LOAN

5.200%

TERM	15 Years	16 Years	17 Years	18 Years	19 Years	20 Years	21 Years	22 Years	23 Years	24 Years	25 Years	30 Years	35 Years	40 Years
AMOUNT														
5	.05	.04	.04	.04	.04	.04	.04	.04	.04	.04	.03	.03	.03	.03
10	.09	.08	.08	.08	.07	.07	.07	.07	.07	.07	.06	.06	.06	.05
15	.13	.12	.12	.11	.11	.11	.10	.10	.10	.10	.09	.09	.08	.08
25	.21	.20	.19	.18	.18	.17	.17	.16	.16	.16	.15	.14	.13	.13
50	.41	.39	.37	.36	.35	.34	.33	.32	.32	.31	.30	.28	.26	.25
75	.61	.58	.56	.54	.52	.51	.49	.48	.47	.46	.45	.42	.39	.38
100	.81	.77	.74	.72	.70	.68	.66	.64	.63	.61	.60	.55	.52	.50
200	1.61	1.54	1.48	1.43	1.39	1.35	1.31	1.28	1.25	1.22	1.20	1.10	1.04	1.00
300	2.41	2.31	2.22	2.15	2.08	2.02	1.96	1.91	1.87	1.83	1.79	1.65	1.56	1.49
400	3.21	3.08	2.96	2.86	2.77	2.69	2.62	2.55	2.49	2.44	2.39	2.20	2.08	1.99
500	4.01	3.85	3.70	3.57	3.46	3.36	3.27	3.19	3.11	3.05	2.99	2.75	2.59	2.48
600	4.81	4.61	4.44	4.29	4.15	4.03	3.92	3.82	3.74	3.66	3.58	3.30	3.11	2.98
700	5.61	5.38	5.18	5.00	4.84	4.70	4.58	4.46	4.36	4.26	4.18	3.85	3.63	3.47
800	6.42	6.15	5.92	5.72	5.53	5.37	5.23	5.10	4.98	4.87	4.78	4.40	4.15	3.97
900	7.22	6.92	6.66	6.43	6.23	6.04	5.88	5.73	5.60	5.48	5.37	4.95	4.66	4.46
1000	8.02	7.69	7.40	7.14	6.92	6.72	6.53	6.37	6.22	6.09	5.97	5.50	5.18	4.96
2000	16.03	15.37	14.79	14.28	13.83	13.43	13.06	12.74	12.44	12.17	11.93	10.99	10.36	9.92
3000	24.04	23.05	22.19	21.42	20.74	20.14	19.59	19.10	18.66	18.26	17.89	16.48	15.53	14.87
4000	32.06	30.74	29.58	28.56	27.65	26.85	26.12	25.47	24.88	24.34	23.86	21.97	20.71	19.83
5000	40.07	38.42	36.97	35.70	34.57	33.56	32.65	31.84	31.10	30.43	29.82	27.46	25.88	24.78
6000	48.08	46.10	44.37	42.84	41.48	40.27	39.18	38.20	37.32	36.51	35.78	32.95	31.06	29.74
7000	56.09	53.78	51.76	49.98	48.39	46.98	45.71	44.57	43.54	42.60	41.75	38.44	36.23	34.69
8000	64.11	61.47	59.15	57.12	55.30	53.69	52.24	50.94	49.76	48.68	47.71	43.93	41.41	39.65
9000	72.12	69.15	66.55	64.25	62.22	60.40	58.77	57.30	55.97	54.77	53.67	49.42	46.58	44.60
10000	80.13	76.83	73.94	71.39	69.13	67.11	65.30	63.67	62.19	60.85	59.64	54.92	51.76	49.56
11000	88.14	84.51	81.34	78.53	76.04	73.82	71.83	70.03	68.41	66.94	65.60	60.41	56.93	54.51
12000	96.16	92.20	88.73	85.67	82.95	80.53	78.36	76.40	74.63	73.02	71.56	65.90	62.11	59.47
13000	104.17	99.88	96.12	92.81	89.87	87.24	84.89	82.77	80.85	79.11	77.52	71.39	67.28	64.42
14000	112.18	107.56	103.52	99.95	96.78	93.95	91.42	89.13	87.07	85.19	83.49	76.88	72.46	69.38
15000	120.19	115.25	110.91	107.09	103.69	100.66	97.95	95.50	93.29	91.28	89.45	82.37	77.63	74.33
16000	128.21	122.93	118.30	114.23	110.60	107.37	104.48	101.87	99.51	97.36	95.41	87.86	82.81	79.29
17000	136.22	130.61	125.70	121.36	117.52	114.08	111.01	108.23	105.72	103.45	101.38	93.35	87.98	84.24
18000	144.23	138.29	133.09	128.50	124.43	120.79	117.53	114.60	111.94	109.53	107.34	98.84	93.16	89.20
19000	152.24	145.98	140.49	135.64	131.34	127.51	124.06	120.96	118.16	115.62	113.30	104.34	98.33	94.15
20000	160.26	153.66	147.88	142.78	138.25	134.22	130.59	127.33	124.38	121.70	119.27	109.83	103.51	99.11
21000	168.27	161.34	155.27	149.92	145.17	140.93	137.12	133.70	130.60	127.79	125.23	115.32	108.68	104.06
22000	176.28	169.02	162.67	157.06	152.08	147.64	143.65	140.06	136.82	133.87	131.19	120.81	113.86	109.02
23000	184.29	176.71	170.06	164.20	158.99	154.35	150.18	146.43	143.04	139.96	137.15	126.30	119.03	113.97
24000	192.31	184.39	177.45	171.34	165.90	161.06	156.71	152.80	149.26	146.04	143.12	131.79	124.21	118.93
25000	200.32	192.07	184.85	178.47	172.82	167.77	163.24	159.16	155.47	152.13	149.08	137.28	129.38	123.88
26000	208.33	199.75	192.24	185.61	179.73	174.48	169.77	165.53	161.69	158.21	155.04	142.77	134.56	128.84
27000	216.34	207.44	199.64	192.75	186.64	181.19	176.30	171.89	167.91	164.30	161.01	148.26	139.73	133.79
28000	224.36	215.12	207.03	199.89	193.55	187.90	182.83	178.26	174.13	170.38	166.97	153.76	144.91	138.75
29000	232.37	222.80	214.42	207.03	200.47	194.61	189.36	184.63	180.35	176.47	172.93	159.25	150.08	143.70
30000	240.38	230.49	221.82	214.17	207.38	201.32	195.89	190.99	186.57	182.55	178.90	164.74	155.26	148.66
31000	248.39	238.17	229.21	221.31	214.29	208.03	202.42	197.36	192.79	188.64	184.86	170.23	160.43	153.62
32000	256.41	245.85	236.60	228.45	221.20	214.74	208.95	203.73	199.01	194.72	190.82	175.72	165.61	158.57
33000	264.42	253.53	244.00	235.58	228.12	221.45	215.48	210.09	205.22	200.81	196.78	181.21	170.78	163.53
34000	272.43	261.22	251.39	242.72	235.03	228.16	222.01	216.46	211.44	206.89	202.75	186.70	175.96	168.48
35000	280.44	268.90	258.79	249.86	241.94	234.87	228.53	222.82	217.66	212.98	208.71	192.19	181.14	173.44
36000	288.46	276.58	266.18	257.00	248.85	241.58	235.06	229.19	223.88	219.06	214.67	197.68	186.31	178.39
37000	296.47	284.26	273.57	264.14	255.77	248.30	241.59	235.56	230.10	225.15	220.64	203.18	191.49	183.35
38000	304.48	291.95	280.97	271.28	262.68	255.01	248.12	241.92	236.32	231.23	226.60	208.67	196.66	188.30
39000	312.49	299.63	288.36	278.42	269.59	261.72	254.65	248.29	242.54	237.32	232.56	214.16	201.84	193.26
40000	320.51	307.31	295.75	285.56	276.50	268.43	261.18	254.66	248.76	243.40	238.53	219.65	207.01	198.21
41000	328.52	315.00	303.15	292.70	283.42	275.14	267.71	261.02	254.97	249.49	244.49	225.14	212.19	203.17
42000	336.53	322.68	310.54	299.83	290.33	281.85	274.24	267.39	261.19	255.57	250.45	230.63	217.36	208.12
43000	344.54	330.36	317.93	306.97	297.24	288.56	280.77	273.76	267.41	261.66	256.41	236.12	222.54	213.08
44000	352.56	338.04	325.33	314.11	304.15	295.27	287.30	280.12	273.63	267.74	262.38	241.61	227.71	218.03
45000	360.57	345.73	332.72	321.25	311.07	301.98	293.83	286.49	279.85	273.83	268.34	247.10	232.89	222.99
46000	368.58	353.41	340.12	328.39	317.98	308.69	300.36	292.85	286.07	279.91	274.30	252.60	238.06	227.94
47000	376.59	361.09	347.51	335.53	324.89	315.40	306.89	299.22	292.29	285.99	280.27	258.09	243.24	232.90
48000	384.61	368.77	354.90	342.67	331.80	322.11	313.42	305.59	298.51	292.08	286.23	263.58	248.41	237.85
49000	392.62	376.46	362.30	349.81	338.72	328.82	319.95	311.95	304.72	298.16	292.19	269.07	253.59	242.81
50000	400.63	384.14	369.69	356.94	345.63	335.53	326.48	318.32	310.94	304.25	298.16	274.56	258.76	247.76
55000	440.69	422.55	406.66	392.64	380.19	369.08	359.12	350.15	342.04	334.67	328.17	302.02	284.64	272.54
60000	480.76	460.97	443.63	428.33	414.75	402.64	391.77	381.98	373.13	365.10	357.79	329.47	310.51	297.32
65000	520.82	499.38	480.60	464.03	449.32	436.19	424.42	413.81	404.22	395.52	387.60	356.93	336.39	322.09
70000	560.88	537.79	517.57	499.72	483.88	469.74	457.06	445.64	435.32	425.95	417.42	384.38	362.27	346.87
75000	600.94	576.21	554.53	535.41	518.44	503.30	489.71	477.48	466.41	456.37	447.23	411.84	388.14	371.64
80000	641.01	614.62	591.50	571.11	553.00	536.85	522.36	509.31	497.51	486.80	477.05	439.29	414.02	396.42
85000	681.07	653.03	628.47	606.80	587.57	570.40	555.01	541.14	528.60	517.22	506.86	466.75	439.89	421.19
90000	721.13	691.45	665.44	642.50	622.13	603.95	587.65	572.97	559.69	547.65	536.68	494.20	465.77	445.97
95000	761.19	729.86	702.41	678.19	656.69	637.51	620.30	604.80	590.79	578.07	566.49	521.66	491.64	470.75
100000	801.26	768.27	739.38	713.88	691.25	671.06	652.95	636.63	621.88	608.49	596.31	549.12	517.52	495.52

MONTHLY PAYMENT
REQUIRED TO AMORTIZE A LOAN

TERM / AMOUNT	1 Year	2 Years	3 Years	4 Years	5 Years	6 Years	7 Years	8 Years	9 Years	10 Years	11 Years	12 Years	13 Years	14 Years
5	.43	.22	.16	.12	.10	.09	.08	.07	.06	.06	.05	.05	.05	.05
10	.86	.44	.31	.24	.19	.17	.15	.13	.12	.11	.10	.10	.09	.09
15	1.29	.66	.46	.35	.29	.25	.22	.20	.18	.17	.15	.15	.14	.13
25	2.15	1.10	.76	.58	.48	.41	.36	.32	.30	.27	.25	.24	.23	.22
50	4.29	2.20	1.51	1.16	.95	.82	.72	.64	.59	.54	.50	.47	.45	.43
75	6.43	3.30	2.26	1.74	1.43	1.22	1.07	.96	.88	.81	.75	.71	.67	.64
100	8.58	4.40	3.01	2.32	1.90	1.63	1.43	1.28	1.17	1.08	1.00	.94	.89	.85
200	17.15	8.80	6.02	4.63	3.80	3.25	2.86	2.56	2.33	2.15	2.00	1.88	1.78	1.69
300	25.72	13.20	9.03	6.95	5.70	4.87	4.28	3.84	3.50	3.22	3.00	2.82	2.66	2.53
400	34.29	17.60	12.04	9.26	7.60	6.49	5.71	5.12	4.66	4.30	4.00	3.75	3.55	3.37
500	42.87	22.00	15.05	11.58	9.50	8.12	7.13	6.39	5.82	5.37	5.00	4.69	4.43	4.21
600	51.44	26.40	18.05	13.89	11.40	9.74	8.56	7.67	6.99	6.44	6.00	5.63	5.32	5.06
700	60.01	30.79	21.06	16.20	13.30	11.36	9.98	8.95	8.15	7.52	7.00	6.57	6.21	5.90
800	68.58	35.19	24.07	18.52	15.19	12.98	11.41	10.23	9.32	8.59	8.00	7.50	7.09	6.74
900	77.15	39.59	27.08	20.83	17.09	14.60	12.83	11.51	10.48	9.66	8.99	8.44	7.98	7.58
1000	85.73	43.99	30.09	23.15	18.99	16.23	14.26	12.78	11.64	10.73	9.99	9.38	8.86	8.42
2000	171.45	87.97	60.17	46.29	37.98	32.45	28.51	25.56	23.28	21.46	19.98	18.75	17.72	16.84
3000	257.17	131.96	90.25	69.43	56.96	48.67	42.76	38.34	34.92	32.19	29.97	28.13	26.58	25.26
4000	342.89	175.94	120.34	92.58	75.95	64.89	57.01	51.12	46.56	42.92	39.96	37.50	35.44	33.68
5000	428.62	219.92	150.42	115.72	94.93	81.11	71.26	63.90	58.20	53.65	49.95	46.88	44.30	42.09
6000	514.34	263.91	180.50	138.86	113.92	97.33	85.52	76.68	69.83	64.38	59.94	56.25	53.15	50.51
7000	600.06	307.89	210.59	162.00	132.91	113.55	99.77	89.46	81.47	75.11	69.93	65.63	62.01	58.93
8000	685.78	351.87	240.67	185.15	151.89	129.77	114.02	102.24	93.11	85.84	79.92	75.00	70.87	67.35
9000	771.50	395.86	270.75	208.29	146.00	146.00	128.27	115.02	104.75	96.57	89.90	84.38	79.73	75.77
10000	857.23	439.84	300.84	231.43	189.86	162.22	142.52	127.80	116.39	107.30	99.89	93.75	88.59	84.18
11000	942.95	483.82	330.92	254.57	208.85	178.44	156.77	140.58	128.03	118.03	109.88	103.13	97.44	92.60
12000	1028.67	527.81	361.00	277.72	227.84	194.66	171.03	153.36	139.66	128.76	119.87	112.50	106.30	101.02
13000	1114.39	571.79	391.09	300.86	246.82	210.88	185.28	166.14	151.30	139.48	129.86	121.88	115.16	109.44
14000	1200.11	615.77	421.17	324.00	265.81	227.10	199.53	178.91	162.94	150.21	139.85	131.25	124.02	117.86
15000	1285.84	659.76	451.25	347.15	284.79	243.32	213.78	191.69	174.58	160.94	149.84	140.63	132.88	126.27
16000	1371.56	703.74	481.34	370.29	303.78	259.54	228.03	204.47	186.22	171.67	159.83	150.00	141.74	134.69
17000	1457.28	747.72	511.42	393.43	322.77	275.76	242.28	217.25	197.86	182.40	169.81	159.38	150.59	143.11
18000	1543.00	791.71	541.50	416.57	341.75	291.99	256.54	230.03	209.49	193.13	179.80	168.75	159.45	151.53
19000	1628.72	835.69	571.59	439.72	360.74	308.21	270.79	242.81	221.13	203.86	189.79	178.13	168.31	159.95
20000	1714.45	879.67	601.67	462.86	379.72	324.43	285.04	255.59	232.77	214.59	199.78	187.50	177.17	168.36
21000	1800.17	923.66	631.75	486.00	398.71	340.65	299.29	268.37	244.41	225.32	209.77	196.88	186.03	176.78
22000	1885.89	967.64	661.84	509.14	417.70	356.87	313.54	281.15	256.05	236.05	219.76	206.25	194.88	185.20
23000	1971.61	1011.62	691.92	532.29	436.68	373.09	327.79	293.93	267.68	246.78	229.75	215.63	203.74	193.62
24000	2057.34	1055.61	722.00	555.43	455.67	389.31	342.05	306.71	279.32	257.51	239.74	225.00	212.60	202.03
25000	2143.06	1099.59	752.09	578.57	474.65	405.53	356.30	319.49	290.96	268.23	249.72	234.38	221.46	210.45
26000	2228.78	1143.57	782.17	601.72	493.64	421.76	370.55	332.27	302.60	278.96	259.71	243.75	230.32	218.87
27000	2314.50	1187.56	812.25	624.86	512.63	437.98	384.80	345.05	314.24	289.69	269.70	253.13	239.18	227.29
28000	2400.22	1231.54	842.34	648.00	531.61	454.20	399.05	357.82	325.88	300.42	279.69	262.50	248.03	235.71
29000	2485.95	1275.52	872.42	671.14	550.60	470.42	413.30	370.60	337.51	311.15	289.68	271.87	256.89	244.12
30000	2571.67	1319.51	902.50	694.29	569.58	486.64	427.56	383.38	349.15	321.88	299.67	281.25	265.75	252.54
31000	2657.39	1363.49	932.59	717.43	588.57	502.86	441.81	396.16	360.79	332.61	309.66	290.62	274.61	260.96
32000	2743.11	1407.48	962.67	740.57	607.56	519.08	456.06	408.94	372.43	343.34	319.65	300.00	283.47	269.38
33000	2828.83	1451.46	992.75	763.71	626.54	535.30	470.31	421.72	384.07	354.07	329.63	309.37	292.32	277.80
34000	2914.56	1495.44	1022.84	786.86	645.53	551.52	484.56	434.50	395.71	364.80	339.62	318.75	301.18	286.21
35000	3000.28	1539.43	1052.92	810.00	664.51	567.75	498.81	447.28	407.34	375.53	349.61	328.12	310.04	294.63
36000	3086.00	1583.41	1083.00	833.14	683.50	583.97	513.07	460.06	418.98	386.26	359.60	337.50	318.90	303.05
37000	3171.72	1627.39	1113.09	856.29	702.49	600.19	527.32	472.84	430.62	396.98	369.59	346.87	327.76	311.47
38000	3257.44	1671.38	1143.17	879.43	721.47	616.41	541.57	485.62	442.26	407.71	379.58	356.25	336.61	319.89
39000	3343.17	1715.36	1173.25	902.57	740.46	632.63	555.82	498.40	453.90	418.44	389.57	365.62	345.47	328.30
40000	3428.89	1759.34	1203.34	925.71	759.44	648.85	570.07	511.18	465.54	429.17	399.56	375.00	354.33	336.72
41000	3514.61	1803.33	1233.42	948.86	778.43	665.07	584.32	523.96	477.17	439.90	409.54	384.37	363.19	345.14
42000	3600.33	1847.31	1263.50	972.00	797.42	681.29	598.58	536.73	488.81	450.63	419.53	393.75	372.05	353.56
43000	3686.05	1891.29	1293.59	995.14	816.40	697.51	612.83	549.51	500.45	461.36	429.52	403.12	380.91	361.98
44000	3771.78	1935.28	1323.67	1018.29	835.39	713.74	627.08	562.29	512.09	472.09	439.51	412.50	389.76	370.39
45000	3857.50	1979.26	1353.75	1041.43	854.37	729.96	641.33	575.07	523.73	482.82	449.50	421.87	398.62	378.81
46000	3943.22	2023.24	1383.84	1064.57	873.36	746.18	655.58	587.85	535.36	493.55	459.49	431.25	407.48	387.23
47000	4028.94	2067.23	1413.92	1087.71	892.35	762.40	669.83	600.63	547.00	504.28	469.48	440.62	416.34	395.65
48000	4114.67	2111.21	1444.00	1110.86	911.33	778.62	684.09	613.41	558.64	515.01	479.47	450.00	425.20	404.06
49000	4200.39	2155.19	1474.09	1134.00	930.32	794.84	698.34	626.19	570.28	525.73	489.45	459.37	434.05	412.48
50000	4286.11	2199.18	1504.17	1157.14	949.30	811.06	712.59	638.97	581.92	536.46	499.44	468.75	442.91	420.90
55000	4714.72	2419.09	1654.58	1272.85	1044.23	892.17	783.85	702.87	640.11	590.11	549.39	515.62	487.20	462.99
60000	5143.33	2639.01	1805.00	1388.57	1139.16	973.27	855.11	766.76	698.30	643.76	599.33	562.49	531.49	505.08
65000	5571.94	2858.93	1955.42	1504.28	1234.09	1054.38	926.36	830.66	756.49	697.40	649.27	609.37	575.79	547.17
70000	6000.55	3078.85	2105.83	1619.99	1329.02	1135.49	997.62	894.55	814.68	751.05	699.22	656.24	620.08	589.26
75000	6429.16	3298.76	2256.25	1735.71	1423.95	1216.59	1068.88	958.45	872.87	804.69	749.16	703.12	664.37	631.35
80000	6857.77	3518.68	2406.67	1851.42	1518.88	1297.70	1140.14	1022.35	931.07	858.34	799.11	749.99	708.66	673.44
85000	7286.38	3738.60	2557.08	1967.14	1613.81	1378.81	1211.40	1086.24	989.26	911.98	849.05	796.86	752.95	715.53
90000	7714.99	3958.51	2707.50	2082.85	1708.74	1459.91	1282.66	1150.14	1047.45	965.63	898.99	843.74	797.24	757.62
95000	8143.60	4178.43	2857.92	2198.56	1803.67	1541.01	1353.91	1214.04	1105.64	1019.28	948.94	890.61	841.53	799.71
100000	8572.21	4398.35	3008.33	2314.28	1898.60	1622.12	1425.17	1277.93	1163.83	1072.92	998.88	937.49	885.82	841.80

TERM	15 Years	16 Years	17 Years	18 Years	19 Years	20 Years	21 Years	22 Years	23 Years	24 Years	25 Years	30 Years	35 Years	40 Years
AMOUNT														
5	.05	.04	.04	.04	.04	.04	.04	.04	.04	.04	.03	.03	.03	.03
10	.09	.08	.08	.08	.07	.07	.07	.07	.07	.07	.06	.06	.06	.05
15	.13	.12	.12	.11	.11	.11	.10	.10	.10	.10	.09	.09	.08	.08
25	.21	.20	.19	.18	.18	.17	.17	.16	.16	.16	.15	.14	.14	.13
50	.41	.39	.38	.36	.35	.34	.33	.32	.32	.31	.30	.28	.27	.25
75	.61	.58	.56	.54	.53	.51	.50	.48	.47	.46	.45	.42	.40	.38
100	.81	.78	.75	.72	.70	.68	.66	.64	.63	.62	.60	.56	.53	.50
200	1.61	1.55	1.49	1.44	1.39	1.35	1.32	1.28	1.25	1.23	1.20	1.11	1.05	1.00
300	2.42	2.32	2.23	2.15	2.09	2.03	1.97	1.92	1.88	1.84	1.80	1.66	1.57	1.50
400	3.22	3.09	2.97	2.87	2.78	2.70	2.63	2.56	2.50	2.45	2.40	2.21	2.09	2.00
500	4.02	3.86	3.72	3.59	3.48	3.37	3.28	3.20	3.13	3.06	3.00	2.77	2.61	2.50
600	4.83	4.63	4.46	4.30	4.17	4.05	3.94	3.84	3.75	3.67	3.60	3.32	3.13	3.00
700	5.63	5.40	5.20	5.02	4.86	4.72	4.60	4.48	4.38	4.28	4.20	3.87	3.65	3.50
800	6.44	6.17	5.94	5.74	5.56	5.40	5.25	5.12	5.00	4.90	4.80	4.42	4.17	4.00
900	7.24	6.94	6.68	6.45	6.25	6.07	5.91	5.76	5.63	5.51	5.40	4.97	4.69	4.49
1000	8.04	7.71	7.43	7.17	6.95	6.74	6.56	6.40	6.25	6.12	6.00	5.53	5.21	4.99
2000	16.08	15.42	14.85	14.34	13.89	13.48	13.12	12.79	12.50	12.23	11.99	11.05	10.42	9.98
3000	24.12	23.13	22.27	21.50	20.83	20.22	19.68	19.19	18.75	18.35	17.98	16.57	15.63	14.97
4000	32.16	30.84	29.69	28.67	27.77	26.96	26.24	25.58	25.00	24.46	23.97	22.09	20.83	19.96
5000	40.20	38.55	37.11	35.84	34.71	33.70	32.79	31.98	31.24	30.58	29.97	27.62	26.04	24.95
6000	48.24	46.26	44.53	43.00	41.65	40.44	39.35	38.37	37.49	36.69	35.96	33.14	31.25	29.94
7000	56.28	53.97	51.95	50.17	48.59	47.17	45.91	44.77	43.74	42.80	41.95	38.66	36.46	34.93
8000	64.32	61.68	59.37	57.33	55.53	53.91	52.47	51.16	49.99	48.92	47.94	44.18	41.66	39.91
9000	72.35	69.39	66.79	64.50	62.47	60.65	59.02	57.56	56.23	55.03	53.94	49.70	46.87	44.90
10000	80.39	77.10	74.21	71.67	69.41	67.39	65.58	63.95	62.48	61.15	59.93	55.23	52.08	49.89
11000	88.43	84.81	81.63	78.83	76.35	74.13	72.14	70.35	68.73	67.26	65.92	60.75	57.29	54.88
12000	96.47	92.52	89.05	86.00	83.29	80.87	78.70	76.74	74.98	73.37	71.91	66.27	62.49	59.87
13000	104.51	100.23	96.47	93.16	90.23	87.60	85.25	83.14	81.22	79.49	77.91	71.79	67.70	64.86
14000	112.55	107.93	103.09	100.33	97.17	94.34	91.81	89.53	87.47	85.60	83.90	77.31	72.91	69.85
15000	120.59	115.64	111.31	107.50	104.11	101.08	98.37	95.93	93.72	91.72	89.89	82.84	78.12	74.84
16000	128.63	123.35	118.74	114.66	111.05	107.82	104.93	102.32	99.97	97.83	95.88	88.36	83.32	79.82
17000	136.66	131.06	126.16	121.83	117.99	114.56	111.48	108.72	106.21	103.94	101.88	93.88	88.53	84.81
18000	144.70	138.77	133.58	128.99	124.93	121.30	118.04	115.11	112.46	110.06	107.87	99.40	93.74	89.80
19000	152.74	146.48	141.00	136.16	131.87	128.04	124.60	121.51	118.71	116.17	113.86	104.92	98.95	94.79
20000	160.78	154.19	148.42	143.33	138.81	134.77	131.16	127.90	124.96	122.29	119.85	110.45	104.15	99.78
21000	168.82	161.90	155.84	150.49	145.75	141.51	137.72	134.30	131.20	128.40	125.85	115.97	109.36	104.77
22000	176.86	169.61	163.26	157.66	152.69	148.25	144.27	140.69	137.45	134.51	131.84	121.49	114.57	109.76
23000	184.90	177.32	170.68	164.82	159.63	154.99	150.83	147.09	143.70	140.63	137.83	127.01	119.78	114.75
24000	192.94	185.03	178.10	171.99	166.57	161.73	157.39	153.48	149.95	146.74	143.82	132.53	124.98	119.73
25000	200.97	192.74	185.52	179.16	173.51	168.47	163.95	159.88	156.20	152.86	149.82	138.06	130.19	124.72
26000	209.01	200.45	192.94	186.32	180.45	175.20	170.50	166.27	162.44	158.97	155.81	143.58	135.40	129.71
27000	217.05	208.16	200.36	193.49	187.39	181.94	177.06	172.67	168.69	165.08	161.80	149.10	140.61	134.70
28000	225.09	215.86	207.78	200.65	194.33	188.68	183.62	179.06	174.94	171.20	167.79	154.62	145.81	139.69
29000	233.13	223.57	215.20	207.82	201.27	195.42	190.18	185.45	181.19	177.31	173.79	160.14	151.02	144.68
30000	241.17	231.28	222.62	214.99	208.21	202.16	196.73	191.85	187.43	183.43	179.78	165.67	156.23	149.67
31000	249.21	238.99	230.04	222.15	215.15	208.90	203.29	198.24	193.68	189.54	185.77	171.19	161.44	154.65
32000	257.25	246.70	237.47	229.32	222.09	215.64	209.85	204.64	199.93	195.65	191.76	176.71	166.64	159.64
33000	265.28	254.41	244.89	236.48	229.03	222.37	216.41	211.03	206.18	201.77	197.76	182.23	171.85	164.63
34000	273.32	262.12	252.31	243.65	235.97	229.11	222.96	217.43	212.42	207.88	203.75	187.75	177.06	169.62
35000	281.36	269.83	259.73	250.82	242.91	235.85	229.52	223.82	218.67	214.00	209.74	193.28	182.27	174.61
36000	289.40	277.54	267.15	257.98	249.85	242.59	236.08	230.22	224.92	220.11	215.73	198.80	187.47	179.60
37000	297.44	285.25	274.57	265.15	256.79	249.33	242.64	236.61	231.17	226.22	221.73	204.32	192.68	184.59
38000	305.48	292.96	281.99	272.31	263.73	256.07	249.20	243.01	237.41	232.34	227.72	209.84	197.89	189.58
39000	313.52	300.67	289.41	279.48	270.67	262.80	255.75	249.40	243.66	238.45	233.71	215.36	203.09	194.56
40000	321.56	308.38	296.83	286.65	277.61	269.54	262.31	255.80	249.91	244.57	239.70	220.89	208.30	199.55
41000	329.59	316.09	304.25	293.81	284.55	276.28	268.87	262.19	256.16	250.68	245.70	226.41	213.51	204.54
42000	337.63	323.79	311.67	300.98	291.49	283.02	275.43	268.59	262.40	256.79	251.69	231.93	218.72	209.53
43000	345.67	331.50	319.09	308.14	298.43	289.76	281.98	274.98	268.65	262.91	257.68	237.45	223.92	214.52
44000	353.71	339.21	326.51	315.31	305.37	296.50	288.54	281.38	274.90	269.02	263.67	242.97	229.13	219.51
45000	361.75	346.92	333.93	322.48	312.31	303.23	295.10	287.77	281.15	275.14	269.67	248.50	234.34	224.50
46000	369.79	354.63	341.35	329.64	319.25	309.97	301.66	294.17	287.40	281.25	275.66	254.02	239.55	229.49
47000	377.83	362.34	348.78	336.81	326.19	316.71	308.21	300.56	293.64	287.37	281.65	259.54	244.75	234.47
48000	385.87	370.05	356.20	343.97	333.13	323.45	314.77	306.96	299.89	293.48	287.64	265.06	249.96	239.46
49000	393.91	377.76	363.62	351.14	340.07	330.19	321.33	313.35	306.14	299.59	293.64	270.58	255.17	244.45
50000	401.94	385.47	371.04	358.31	347.01	336.93	327.89	319.75	312.39	305.71	299.63	276.11	260.38	249.44
55000	442.14	424.02	408.14	394.14	381.71	370.62	360.68	351.72	343.62	336.28	329.59	303.72	286.41	274.38
60000	482.33	462.56	445.24	429.97	416.41	404.31	393.46	383.69	374.86	366.85	359.55	331.33	312.45	299.33
65000	522.53	501.11	482.35	465.80	451.11	438.00	426.25	415.67	406.10	397.42	389.52	358.94	338.49	324.27
70000	562.72	539.65	519.45	501.63	485.81	471.70	459.04	447.64	437.34	427.99	419.48	386.55	364.53	349.21
75000	602.91	578.20	556.55	537.46	520.51	505.39	491.83	479.62	468.58	458.56	449.44	414.16	390.56	374.16
80000	643.11	616.75	593.66	573.29	555.21	539.08	524.62	511.59	499.81	489.13	479.40	441.77	416.60	399.10
85000	683.30	655.29	630.76	609.12	589.91	572.77	557.40	543.56	531.05	519.70	509.37	469.38	442.64	424.04
90000	723.49	693.84	667.86	644.95	624.61	606.46	590.19	575.54	562.29	550.27	539.33	496.99	468.67	448.99
95000	763.69	732.39	704.97	680.78	659.31	640.16	622.98	607.51	593.53	580.84	569.29	524.60	494.71	473.93
100000	803.88	770.93	742.07	716.61	694.01	673.85	655.77	639.49	624.77	611.41	599.25	552.21	520.75	498.88

MONTHLY PAYMENT
REQUIRED TO AMORTIZE A LOAN

TERM	1 Year	2 Years	3 Years	4 Years	5 Years	6 Years	7 Years	8 Years	9 Years	10 Years	11 Years	12 Years	13 Years	14 Years
AMOUNT														
5	.43	.23	.16	.12	.10	.09	.08	.07	.06	.06	.06	.05	.05	.05
10	.86	.45	.31	.24	.20	.17	.15	.13	.12	.11	.11	.10	.09	.09
15	1.29	.67	.46	.35	.29	.25	.22	.20	.18	.17	.16	.15	.14	.13
25	2.15	1.11	.76	.58	.48	.41	.36	.33	.30	.27	.26	.24	.23	.22
50	4.29	2.21	1.51	1.16	.96	.82	.72	.65	.59	.54	.51	.48	.45	.43
75	6.44	3.31	2.26	1.74	1.43	1.22	1.08	.97	.88	.81	.76	.71	.67	.64
100	8.58	4.41	3.02	2.32	1.91	1.63	1.43	1.29	1.17	1.08	1.01	.95	.89	.85
200	17.15	8.81	6.03	4.64	3.81	3.25	2.86	2.57	2.34	2.16	2.01	1.89	1.78	1.69
300	25.73	13.21	9.04	6.95	5.71	4.88	4.29	3.85	3.50	3.23	3.01	2.83	2.67	2.54
400	34.30	17.61	12.05	9.27	7.61	6.50	5.72	5.13	4.67	4.31	4.01	3.77	3.56	3.38
500	42.88	22.01	15.06	11.59	9.51	8.13	7.14	6.41	5.84	5.38	5.01	4.71	4.45	4.23
600	51.45	26.41	18.07	13.90	11.41	9.75	8.57	7.69	7.00	6.46	6.01	5.65	5.34	5.07
700	60.03	30.81	21.08	16.22	13.31	11.38	10.00	8.97	8.17	7.53	7.01	6.59	6.22	5.92
800	68.60	35.21	24.09	18.54	15.21	13.00	11.43	10.25	9.34	8.61	8.02	7.53	7.11	6.76
900	77.18	39.61	27.10	20.85	17.11	14.63	12.85	11.53	10.50	9.68	9.02	8.47	8.00	7.60
1000	85.75	44.01	30.11	23.17	19.01	16.25	14.28	12.81	11.67	10.76	10.02	9.41	8.89	8.45
2000	171.50	88.02	60.22	46.34	38.02	32.49	28.56	25.61	23.33	21.51	20.03	18.81	17.77	16.89
3000	257.24	132.02	90.32	69.50	57.03	48.74	42.83	38.41	34.99	32.27	30.05	28.21	26.66	25.34
4000	342.99	176.03	120.43	92.67	76.04	64.98	57.11	51.22	46.66	43.02	40.06	37.61	35.54	33.78
5000	428.73	220.03	150.53	115.83	95.05	81.23	71.38	64.02	58.32	53.77	50.07	47.01	44.42	42.22
6000	514.48	264.04	180.64	139.00	114.06	97.47	85.66	76.82	69.98	64.53	60.09	56.41	53.31	50.67
7000	600.22	308.05	210.75	162.16	133.07	113.72	99.93	89.63	81.64	75.28	70.10	65.81	62.19	59.11
8000	685.97	352.05	240.85	185.33	152.08	129.96	114.21	102.43	93.31	86.04	80.11	75.21	71.08	67.56
9000	771.71	396.06	270.96	208.49	171.09	146.21	128.48	115.23	104.97	96.79	90.13	84.61	79.96	76.00
10000	857.46	440.06	301.06	231.66	190.09	162.45	142.76	128.04	116.63	107.54	100.14	94.01	88.84	84.44
11000	943.20	484.07	331.17	254.82	209.10	178.69	157.03	140.84	128.29	118.30	110.16	103.41	97.73	92.89
12000	1028.95	528.08	361.27	277.99	228.11	194.94	171.31	153.64	139.96	129.05	120.17	112.81	106.61	101.33
13000	1114.69	572.08	391.38	301.16	247.12	211.18	185.58	166.45	151.62	139.80	130.18	122.21	115.49	109.78
14000	1200.44	616.09	421.49	324.32	266.13	227.43	199.86	179.25	163.28	150.56	140.20	131.61	124.38	118.22
15000	1286.18	660.09	451.59	347.49	285.14	243.67	214.13	192.05	174.94	161.31	150.21	141.01	133.26	126.66
16000	1371.93	704.10	481.70	370.65	304.15	259.92	228.41	204.86	186.61	172.07	160.22	150.41	142.15	135.11
17000	1457.67	748.10	511.80	393.82	323.16	276.16	242.69	217.66	198.27	182.82	170.24	159.81	151.03	143.55
18000	1543.42	792.11	541.91	416.98	342.17	292.41	256.96	230.46	209.93	193.57	180.25	169.21	159.91	151.99
19000	1629.16	836.12	572.01	440.15	361.18	308.65	271.24	243.27	221.59	204.33	190.27	178.61	168.80	160.44
20000	1714.91	880.12	602.12	463.31	380.18	324.89	285.51	256.07	233.26	215.08	200.28	188.01	177.68	168.88
21000	1800.65	924.13	632.23	486.48	399.19	341.14	299.79	268.87	244.92	225.83	210.29	197.41	186.56	177.33
22000	1886.40	968.13	662.33	509.64	418.20	357.38	314.06	281.68	256.58	236.59	220.31	206.81	195.45	185.77
23000	1972.14	1012.14	692.44	532.81	437.21	373.63	328.34	294.48	268.24	247.34	230.32	216.21	204.33	194.21
24000	2057.89	1056.15	722.54	555.98	456.22	389.87	342.61	307.28	279.91	258.10	240.33	225.61	213.22	202.66
25000	2143.63	1100.15	752.65	579.14	475.23	406.12	356.89	320.09	291.57	268.85	250.35	235.01	222.10	211.10
26000	2229.38	1144.16	782.76	602.31	494.24	422.36	371.16	332.89	303.23	279.60	260.36	244.41	230.98	219.55
27000	2315.12	1188.16	812.86	625.47	513.25	438.61	385.44	345.69	314.89	290.36	270.38	253.81	239.87	227.99
28000	2400.87	1232.17	842.97	648.64	532.26	454.85	399.71	358.50	326.56	301.11	280.39	263.21	248.75	236.43
29000	2486.61	1276.18	873.07	671.80	551.27	471.09	413.99	371.30	338.22	311.87	290.40	272.61	257.64	244.88
30000	2572.36	1320.18	903.18	694.97	570.27	487.34	428.26	384.10	349.88	322.62	300.42	282.01	266.52	253.32
31000	2658.10	1364.19	933.28	718.13	589.28	503.58	442.54	396.91	361.54	333.37	310.43	291.41	275.40	261.77
32000	2743.85	1408.19	963.39	741.30	608.29	519.83	456.81	409.71	373.21	344.13	320.44	300.81	284.29	270.21
33000	2829.59	1452.20	993.50	764.46	627.30	536.07	471.09	422.51	384.87	354.88	330.46	310.21	293.17	278.65
34000	2915.34	1496.20	1023.60	787.63	646.31	552.32	485.37	435.32	396.53	365.63	340.47	319.61	302.05	287.10
35000	3001.08	1540.21	1053.71	810.80	665.32	568.56	499.64	448.12	408.19	376.39	350.49	329.01	310.94	295.54
36000	3086.83	1584.22	1083.81	833.96	684.33	584.81	513.92	460.92	419.86	387.14	360.50	338.41	319.82	303.98
37000	3172.57	1628.22	1113.92	857.13	703.34	601.05	528.19	473.72	431.52	397.90	370.51	347.81	328.71	312.43
38000	3258.32	1672.23	1144.02	880.29	722.35	617.29	542.47	486.53	443.18	408.65	380.53	357.21	337.59	320.87
39000	3344.06	1716.23	1174.13	903.46	741.36	633.54	556.74	499.33	454.84	419.40	390.54	366.61	346.47	329.32
40000	3429.81	1760.24	1204.24	926.62	760.36	649.78	571.02	512.13	466.51	430.16	400.55	376.01	355.36	337.76
41000	3515.55	1804.25	1234.34	949.79	779.37	666.03	585.29	524.94	478.17	440.91	410.57	385.41	364.24	346.20
42000	3601.30	1848.25	1264.45	972.95	798.38	682.27	599.57	537.74	489.83	451.66	420.58	394.81	373.12	354.65
43000	3687.04	1892.26	1294.55	996.12	817.39	698.52	613.84	550.54	501.49	462.42	430.59	404.21	382.01	363.09
44000	3772.79	1936.26	1324.66	1019.28	836.40	714.76	628.12	563.35	513.16	473.17	440.61	413.61	390.89	371.54
45000	3858.53	1980.27	1354.76	1042.45	855.41	731.01	642.39	576.15	524.82	483.93	450.62	423.01	399.78	379.98
46000	3944.28	2024.27	1384.87	1065.62	874.42	747.25	656.67	588.95	536.48	494.68	460.64	432.41	408.66	388.42
47000	4030.02	2068.28	1414.98	1088.78	893.43	763.49	670.94	601.76	548.14	505.43	470.65	441.81	417.54	396.87
48000	4115.77	2112.29	1445.08	1111.95	912.44	779.74	685.22	614.56	559.81	516.19	480.66	451.21	426.43	405.31
49000	4201.51	2156.29	1475.19	1135.11	931.45	795.98	699.49	627.36	571.47	526.94	490.68	460.61	435.31	413.76
50000	4287.26	2200.30	1505.29	1158.28	950.45	812.23	713.77	640.17	583.13	537.69	500.69	470.01	444.19	422.20
55000	4715.98	2420.33	1655.82	1274.10	1045.50	893.45	785.15	704.18	641.46	591.46	550.76	517.01	488.61	464.42
60000	5144.71	2640.36	1806.35	1389.93	1140.54	974.67	856.52	768.20	699.76	645.23	600.83	564.01	533.03	506.64
65000	5573.43	2860.39	1956.88	1505.76	1235.59	1055.89	927.90	832.22	758.07	699.00	650.90	611.01	577.45	548.86
70000	6002.16	3080.42	2107.41	1621.59	1330.63	1137.12	999.28	896.23	816.38	752.77	700.97	658.01	621.87	591.08
75000	6430.88	3300.45	2257.94	1737.41	1425.68	1218.34	1070.65	960.25	874.70	806.54	751.03	705.01	666.29	633.30
80000	6859.61	3520.47	2408.47	1853.24	1520.72	1299.56	1142.03	1024.26	933.01	860.31	801.10	752.01	710.71	675.52
85000	7288.33	3740.50	2559.00	1969.07	1615.77	1380.78	1213.41	1088.28	991.32	914.08	851.17	799.01	755.13	717.74
90000	7717.06	3960.53	2709.52	2084.89	1710.81	1462.01	1284.78	1152.30	1049.63	967.85	901.24	846.02	799.55	759.95
95000	8145.78	4180.56	2860.05	2200.72	1805.86	1543.23	1356.16	1216.31	1107.95	1021.62	951.31	893.02	843.97	802.17
100000	8574.51	4400.59	3010.58	2316.55	1900.90	1624.45	1427.54	1280.33	1166.26	1075.38	1001.38	940.02	888.38	844.39

TERM / AMOUNT	15 Years	16 Years	17 Years	18 Years	19 Years	20 Years	21 Years	22 Years	23 Years	24 Years	25 Years	30 Years	35 Years	40 Years
5	.05	.04	.04	.04	.04	.04	.04	.04	.04	.04	.04	.03	.03	.03
10	.09	.08	.08	.08	.07	.07	.07	.07	.07	.07	.07	.06	.06	.06
15	.13	.12	.12	.11	.11	.11	.10	.10	.10	.10	.10	.09	.08	.08
25	.21	.20	.19	.18	.16	.17	.17	.17	.16	.16	.16	.14	.14	.13
50	.41	.39	.38	.36	.35	.34	.33	.33	.32	.31	.31	.28	.27	.26
75	.61	.59	.56	.54	.53	.51	.50	.49	.48	.47	.46	.42	.40	.38
100	.81	.78	.75	.72	.70	.68	.65	.65	.63	.62	.61	.56	.53	.51
200	1.62	1.55	1.49	1.44	1.40	1.36	1.32	1.29	1.26	1.23	1.21	1.12	1.05	1.01
300	2.42	2.33	2.24	2.16	2.10	2.03	1.98	1.93	1.89	1.85	1.81	1.67	1.58	1.51
400	3.23	3.10	2.98	2.88	2.79	2.71	2.64	2.57	2.52	2.46	2.41	2.23	2.10	2.01
500	4.04	3.87	3.73	3.60	3.49	3.39	3.30	3.22	3.14	3.08	3.02	2.78	2.62	2.52
600	4.84	4.65	4.47	4.32	4.19	4.06	3.96	3.86	3.77	3.69	3.62	3.34	3.15	3.02
700	5.65	5.42	5.22	5.04	4.88	4.74	4.62	4.50	4.40	4.31	4.22	3.89	3.67	3.52
800	6.46	6.19	5.96	5.76	5.58	5.42	5.27	5.14	5.03	4.92	4.82	4.45	4.20	4.02
900	7.26	6.97	6.71	6.48	6.28	6.09	5.93	5.79	5.65	5.53	5.42	5.00	4.72	4.53
1000	8.07	7.74	7.45	7.20	6.97	6.77	6.59	6.43	6.28	6.15	6.03	5.56	5.24	5.03
2000	16.14	15.48	14.90	14.39	13.94	13.54	13.18	12.85	12.56	12.29	12.05	11.11	10.48	10.05
3000	24.20	23.21	22.35	21.59	20.91	20.30	19.76	19.28	18.83	18.43	18.07	16.66	15.72	15.07
4000	32.27	30.95	29.80	28.78	27.88	27.07	26.35	25.70	25.11	24.58	24.09	22.22	20.96	20.09
5000	40.33	38.68	37.24	35.97	34.84	33.84	32.93	32.12	31.39	30.72	30.12	27.77	26.20	25.12
6000	48.40	46.42	44.69	43.17	41.81	40.60	39.52	38.55	37.66	36.86	36.14	33.32	31.44	30.14
7000	56.46	54.16	52.14	50.36	48.78	47.37	46.11	44.97	43.94	43.01	42.16	38.88	36.68	35.16
8000	64.53	61.89	59.59	57.55	55.75	54.14	52.69	51.39	50.22	49.15	48.18	44.43	41.92	40.18
9000	72.59	69.63	67.03	64.75	62.71	60.90	59.28	57.82	56.49	55.29	54.20	49.98	47.16	45.21
10000	80.66	77.36	74.48	71.94	69.68	67.67	65.86	64.24	62.77	61.44	60.23	55.54	52.40	50.23
11000	88.72	85.10	81.93	79.13	76.65	74.44	72.45	70.66	69.05	67.58	66.25	61.09	57.64	55.25
12000	96.79	92.84	89.38	86.33	83.62	81.20	79.04	77.09	75.32	73.72	72.27	66.64	62.88	60.27
13000	104.85	100.57	96.82	93.52	90.59	87.97	85.62	83.51	81.60	79.87	78.29	72.19	68.12	65.30
14000	112.92	108.31	104.27	100.71	97.55	94.73	92.21	89.93	87.88	86.01	84.31	77.75	73.36	70.32
15000	120.98	116.04	111.72	107.91	104.52	101.50	98.79	96.36	94.15	92.15	90.34	83.30	78.60	75.34
16000	129.05	123.78	119.17	115.10	111.49	108.27	105.38	102.78	100.43	98.30	96.36	88.85	83.84	80.36
17000	137.11	131.52	126.61	122.29	118.46	115.03	111.97	109.20	106.71	104.44	102.38	94.41	89.08	85.38
18000	145.18	139.25	134.06	129.49	125.42	121.80	118.55	115.63	112.98	110.58	108.40	99.96	94.32	90.41
19000	153.24	146.99	141.51	136.68	132.39	128.57	125.14	122.05	119.26	116.73	114.42	105.51	99.56	95.43
20000	161.31	154.72	148.96	143.87	139.36	135.33	131.72	128.47	125.54	122.87	120.45	111.07	104.80	100.45
21000	169.37	162.46	156.41	151.07	146.33	142.10	138.31	134.90	131.81	129.01	126.47	116.62	110.04	105.47
22000	177.44	170.20	163.85	158.26	153.29	148.87	144.90	141.32	138.09	135.16	132.49	122.17	115.28	110.50
23000	185.50	177.93	171.30	165.45	160.26	155.63	151.48	147.74	144.37	141.30	138.51	127.73	120.52	115.52
24000	193.57	185.67	178.75	172.65	167.23	162.40	158.07	154.17	150.64	147.44	144.53	133.28	125.76	120.54
25000	201.63	193.40	186.20	179.84	174.20	169.17	164.65	160.59	156.92	153.59	150.56	138.83	131.00	125.56
26000	209.70	201.14	193.64	187.03	181.17	175.93	171.24	167.01	163.19	159.73	156.58	144.38	136.24	130.59
27000	217.76	208.88	201.09	194.22	188.13	182.70	177.82	173.44	169.47	165.87	162.60	149.94	141.48	135.61
28000	225.83	216.61	208.54	201.42	195.10	189.46	184.41	179.86	175.75	172.02	168.62	155.49	146.72	140.63
29000	233.89	224.35	215.99	208.61	202.07	196.23	191.00	186.28	182.02	178.16	174.64	161.04	151.96	145.65
30000	241.96	232.08	223.43	215.81	209.04	203.00	197.58	192.71	188.30	184.30	180.67	166.60	157.20	150.67
31000	250.02	239.82	230.88	223.00	216.00	209.76	204.17	199.13	194.58	190.45	186.69	172.15	162.44	155.70
32000	258.09	247.55	238.33	230.19	222.97	216.53	210.75	205.55	200.85	196.59	192.71	177.70	167.68	160.72
33000	266.15	255.29	245.78	237.39	229.94	223.30	217.34	211.98	207.13	202.73	198.73	183.26	172.92	165.74
34000	274.22	263.03	253.22	244.58	236.91	230.06	223.93	218.40	213.41	208.88	204.75	188.81	178.16	170.76
35000	282.28	270.76	260.67	251.77	243.88	236.83	230.51	224.82	219.68	215.02	210.78	194.36	183.40	175.79
36000	290.35	278.50	268.12	258.97	250.84	243.60	237.10	231.25	225.96	221.16	216.80	199.91	188.64	180.81
37000	298.41	286.23	275.57	266.16	257.81	250.36	243.68	237.67	232.24	227.31	222.82	205.47	193.88	185.83
38000	306.48	293.97	283.01	273.35	264.78	257.13	250.27	244.09	238.51	233.45	228.84	211.02	199.12	190.85
39000	314.54	301.71	290.46	280.55	271.75	263.89	256.86	250.52	244.79	239.59	234.86	216.57	204.36	195.88
40000	322.61	309.44	297.91	287.74	278.71	270.66	263.44	256.94	251.07	245.74	240.89	222.13	209.60	200.90
41000	330.67	317.18	305.36	294.93	285.68	277.43	270.03	263.37	257.34	251.88	246.91	227.68	214.84	205.92
42000	338.74	324.91	312.81	302.13	292.65	284.19	276.61	269.79	263.62	258.02	252.93	233.23	220.08	210.94
43000	346.80	332.65	320.25	309.32	299.62	290.96	283.20	276.21	269.90	264.17	258.95	238.79	225.32	215.96
44000	354.87	340.39	327.70	316.51	306.58	297.73	289.79	282.64	276.17	270.31	264.97	244.34	230.56	220.99
45000	362.93	348.12	335.15	323.71	313.55	304.49	296.37	289.06	282.45	276.45	271.00	249.89	235.80	226.01
46000	371.00	355.86	342.60	330.90	320.52	311.26	302.96	295.48	288.73	282.60	277.02	255.45	241.04	231.03
47000	379.06	363.59	350.04	338.09	327.49	318.03	309.54	301.91	295.00	288.74	283.04	261.00	246.28	236.05
48000	387.13	371.33	357.49	345.29	334.46	324.79	316.13	308.33	301.28	294.88	289.06	266.55	251.52	241.08
49000	395.19	379.07	364.94	352.48	341.42	331.56	322.72	314.75	307.55	301.03	295.08	272.10	256.76	246.10
50000	403.26	386.80	372.39	359.67	348.39	338.33	329.30	321.18	313.83	307.17	301.11	277.66	262.00	251.12
55000	443.59	425.48	409.62	395.64	383.23	372.16	362.23	353.29	345.21	337.89	331.22	305.42	288.19	276.23
60000	483.91	464.16	446.86	431.61	418.07	405.99	395.16	385.41	376.60	368.60	361.33	333.19	314.39	301.34
65000	524.24	502.84	484.10	467.57	452.91	439.82	428.09	417.53	407.98	399.32	391.44	360.95	340.59	326.46
70000	564.56	541.52	521.34	503.54	487.75	473.65	461.02	449.64	439.36	430.03	421.54	388.72	366.79	351.57
75000	604.89	580.20	558.58	539.51	522.58	507.49	493.95	481.76	470.74	460.75	451.66	416.48	392.99	376.68
80000	645.21	618.88	595.82	575.47	557.42	541.32	526.88	513.88	502.13	491.47	481.77	444.25	419.19	401.79
85000	685.54	657.56	633.05	611.44	592.26	575.15	559.81	546.00	533.51	522.18	511.88	472.01	445.39	426.90
90000	725.86	696.24	670.29	647.41	627.10	608.98	592.74	578.11	564.89	552.90	541.99	499.78	471.59	452.01
95000	766.19	734.92	707.53	683.37	661.94	642.81	625.67	610.23	596.27	583.62	572.10	527.54	497.79	477.13
100000	806.51	773.60	744.77	719.34	696.78	676.65	658.60	642.35	627.66	614.33	602.21	555.31	523.99	502.24

5.375%

TERM AMOUNT	1 Year	2 Years	3 Years	4 Years	5 Years	6 Years	7 Years	8 Years	9 Years	10 Years	11 Years	12 Years	13 Years	14 Years
5	.43	.23	.16	.12	.10	.09	.08	.07	.06	.06	.06	.05	.05	.05
10	.86	.45	.31	.24	.20	.17	.15	.13	.12	.11	.11	.10	.09	.09
15	1.29	.67	.46	.35	.29	.25	.22	.20	.18	.17	.16	.15	.14	.13
25	2.15	1.11	.76	.58	.48	.41	.36	.33	.30	.27	.26	.24	.23	.22
50	4.29	2.21	1.51	1.16	.96	.82	.72	.65	.59	.54	.51	.48	.45	.43
75	6.44	3.31	2.27	1.74	1.43	1.23	1.08	.97	.88	.81	.76	.71	.67	.64
100	8.58	4.41	3.02	2.32	1.91	1.63	1.44	1.29	1.17	1.08	1.01	.95	.90	.85
200	17.16	8.81	6.03	4.64	3.81	3.26	2.87	2.57	2.34	2.16	2.02	1.89	1.79	1.70
300	25.74	13.22	9.05	6.96	5.72	4.89	4.30	3.86	3.51	3.24	3.02	2.84	2.68	2.55
400	34.32	17.62	12.06	9.28	7.62	6.52	5.73	5.14	4.68	4.32	4.03	3.78	3.57	3.40
500	42.89	22.02	15.07	11.60	9.53	8.14	7.16	6.42	5.85	5.40	5.03	4.72	4.47	4.25
600	51.47	26.43	18.09	13.92	11.43	9.77	8.59	7.71	7.02	6.48	6.04	5.67	5.36	5.09
700	60.05	30.83	21.10	16.24	13.34	11.40	10.02	8.99	8.19	7.56	7.04	6.61	6.25	5.94
800	68.63	35.24	24.12	18.56	15.24	13.03	11.45	10.28	9.36	8.64	8.05	7.56	7.14	6.79
900	77.21	39.64	27.13	20.88	17.14	14.66	12.88	11.56	10.53	9.72	9.05	8.50	8.04	7.64
1000	85.78	44.04	30.14	23.20	19.05	16.28	14.32	12.84	11.70	10.80	10.06	9.44	8.93	8.49
2000	171.56	88.08	60.28	46.40	38.09	32.56	28.63	25.68	23.40	21.59	20.11	18.88	17.85	16.97
3000	257.34	132.12	90.42	69.60	57.14	48.84	42.94	38.52	35.10	32.38	30.16	28.32	26.77	25.45
4000	343.12	176.16	120.56	92.80	76.18	65.12	57.25	51.36	46.80	43.17	40.21	37.76	35.69	33.94
5000	428.90	220.20	150.70	116.00	95.22	81.40	71.56	64.20	58.50	53.96	50.26	47.20	44.62	42.42
6000	514.68	264.24	180.84	139.20	114.27	97.68	85.87	77.04	70.20	64.75	60.31	56.63	53.54	50.90
7000	600.46	308.28	210.98	162.40	133.31	113.96	100.18	89.88	81.90	75.54	70.36	66.07	62.46	59.39
8000	686.24	352.32	241.12	185.60	152.35	130.24	114.49	102.72	93.60	86.33	80.41	75.51	71.38	67.87
9000	772.02	396.36	271.26	208.80	171.40	146.52	128.80	115.56	105.30	97.12	90.47	84.95	80.31	76.35
10000	857.80	440.40	301.40	232.00	190.44	162.80	143.11	128.40	117.00	107.91	100.52	94.39	89.23	84.83
11000	943.58	484.44	331.54	255.20	209.48	179.08	157.42	141.24	128.69	118.70	110.57	103.82	98.15	93.32
12000	1029.36	528.48	361.68	278.40	228.53	195.36	171.73	154.08	140.39	129.49	120.62	113.26	107.07	101.80
13000	1115.14	572.52	391.82	301.60	247.57	211.64	186.05	166.91	152.09	140.29	130.67	122.70	116.00	110.28
14000	1200.92	616.56	421.96	324.80	266.61	227.92	200.36	179.75	163.79	151.08	140.72	132.14	124.92	118.77
15000	1286.70	660.60	452.10	348.00	285.66	244.20	214.67	192.59	175.49	161.87	150.77	141.58	133.84	127.25
16000	1372.48	704.64	482.24	371.20	304.70	260.48	228.98	205.43	187.19	172.66	160.82	151.02	142.76	135.73
17000	1458.26	748.68	512.38	394.40	323.74	276.76	243.29	218.27	198.89	183.45	170.88	160.45	151.68	144.21
18000	1544.03	792.72	542.52	417.60	342.79	293.04	257.60	231.11	210.59	194.24	180.93	169.89	160.61	152.70
19000	1629.81	836.76	572.66	440.80	361.83	309.31	271.91	243.95	222.29	205.03	190.98	179.33	169.53	161.18
20000	1715.59	880.80	602.80	464.00	380.88	325.59	286.22	256.79	233.99	215.82	201.03	188.77	178.45	169.66
21000	1801.37	924.84	632.94	487.20	399.92	341.87	300.53	269.63	245.68	226.61	211.08	198.21	187.37	178.15
22000	1887.15	968.87	663.08	510.40	418.96	358.15	314.84	282.47	257.38	237.40	221.13	207.64	196.30	186.63
23000	1972.93	1012.91	693.21	533.59	438.01	374.43	329.15	295.31	269.08	248.19	231.18	217.08	205.22	195.11
24000	2058.71	1056.95	723.35	556.79	457.05	390.71	343.46	308.15	280.78	258.98	241.23	226.52	214.14	203.60
25000	2144.49	1100.99	753.49	579.99	476.09	406.99	357.77	320.99	292.48	269.77	251.29	235.96	223.06	212.08
26000	2230.27	1145.03	783.63	603.19	495.14	423.27	372.09	333.82	304.18	280.57	261.34	245.40	231.99	220.56
27000	2316.05	1189.07	813.77	626.39	514.18	439.55	386.40	346.66	315.88	291.36	271.39	254.83	240.91	229.04
28000	2401.83	1233.11	843.91	649.59	533.22	455.83	400.71	359.50	327.58	302.15	281.44	264.27	249.83	237.53
29000	2487.61	1277.15	874.05	672.79	552.27	472.11	415.02	372.34	339.28	312.94	291.49	273.71	258.75	246.01
30000	2573.39	1321.19	904.19	695.99	571.31	488.39	429.33	385.18	350.98	323.73	301.54	283.15	267.68	254.49
31000	2659.17	1365.23	934.33	719.19	590.35	504.67	443.64	398.02	362.67	334.52	311.59	292.59	276.60	262.98
32000	2744.95	1409.27	964.47	742.39	609.40	520.95	457.95	410.86	374.37	345.31	321.64	302.03	285.52	271.46
33000	2830.73	1453.31	994.61	765.59	628.44	537.23	472.26	423.70	386.07	356.10	331.70	311.46	294.44	279.94
34000	2916.51	1497.35	1024.75	788.79	647.48	553.51	486.57	436.54	397.77	366.89	341.75	320.90	303.36	288.42
35000	3002.28	1541.39	1054.89	811.99	666.53	569.79	500.88	449.38	409.47	377.68	351.80	330.34	312.29	296.91
36000	3088.06	1585.43	1085.03	835.19	685.57	586.07	515.19	462.22	421.17	388.47	361.85	339.78	321.21	305.39
37000	3173.84	1629.47	1115.17	858.39	704.62	602.34	529.50	475.06	432.87	399.26	371.90	349.22	330.13	313.87
38000	3259.62	1673.51	1145.31	881.59	723.66	618.62	543.81	487.90	444.57	410.06	381.95	358.65	339.05	322.36
39000	3345.40	1717.55	1175.45	904.79	742.70	634.90	558.13	500.73	456.27	420.85	392.00	368.09	347.98	330.84
40000	3431.18	1761.59	1205.59	927.99	761.75	651.18	572.44	513.57	467.97	431.64	402.05	377.53	356.90	339.32
41000	3516.96	1805.63	1235.73	951.19	780.79	667.46	586.75	526.41	479.67	442.43	412.11	386.97	365.82	347.81
42000	3602.74	1849.67	1265.87	974.39	799.83	683.74	601.06	539.25	491.36	453.22	422.16	396.41	374.74	356.29
43000	3688.52	1893.70	1296.01	997.59	818.88	700.02	615.37	552.09	503.06	464.01	432.21	405.85	383.67	364.77
44000	3774.30	1937.74	1326.15	1020.79	837.92	716.30	629.68	564.93	514.76	474.80	442.26	415.28	392.59	373.25
45000	3860.08	1981.78	1356.28	1043.98	856.96	732.58	643.99	577.77	526.46	485.59	452.31	424.72	401.51	381.74
46000	3945.86	2025.82	1386.42	1067.18	876.01	748.86	658.30	590.61	538.16	496.38	462.36	434.16	410.43	390.22
47000	4031.64	2069.86	1416.56	1090.38	895.05	765.14	672.61	603.45	549.86	507.17	472.41	443.60	419.35	398.70
48000	4117.42	2113.90	1446.70	1113.58	914.09	781.42	686.92	616.29	561.56	517.96	482.46	453.04	428.28	407.19
49000	4203.20	2157.94	1476.84	1136.78	933.14	797.70	701.23	629.13	573.26	528.75	492.52	462.47	437.20	415.67
50000	4288.98	2201.98	1506.98	1159.98	952.18	813.98	715.54	641.97	584.96	539.54	502.57	471.91	446.12	424.15
55000	4717.87	2422.18	1657.68	1275.98	1047.40	895.38	787.10	706.16	643.45	593.50	552.82	519.10	490.73	466.57
60000	5146.77	2642.38	1808.38	1391.98	1142.62	976.77	858.65	770.36	701.95	647.45	603.08	566.29	535.35	508.98
65000	5575.67	2862.57	1959.08	1507.98	1237.83	1058.17	930.21	834.55	760.44	701.41	653.33	613.48	579.96	551.40
70000	6004.56	3082.77	2109.77	1623.97	1333.05	1139.57	1001.76	898.75	818.94	755.36	703.59	660.68	624.57	593.81
75000	6433.46	3302.97	2260.47	1739.97	1428.27	1220.96	1073.31	962.95	877.43	809.31	753.85	707.87	669.18	636.23
80000	6862.36	3523.17	2411.17	1855.97	1523.49	1302.36	1144.87	1027.14	935.93	863.27	804.10	755.06	713.79	678.64
85000	7291.26	3743.36	2561.87	1971.97	1618.70	1383.76	1216.42	1091.34	994.42	917.22	854.36	802.25	758.40	721.05
90000	7720.15	3963.56	2712.56	2087.96	1713.92	1465.16	1287.98	1155.53	1052.92	971.18	904.62	849.44	803.02	763.47
95000	8149.05	4183.76	2863.26	2203.96	1809.14	1546.55	1359.53	1219.73	1111.41	1025.13	954.87	896.63	847.63	805.88
100000	8577.95	4403.96	3013.96	2319.96	1904.36	1627.95	1431.08	1283.93	1169.91	1079.08	1005.13	943.82	892.24	848.30

MONTHLY PAYMENT
REQUIRED TO AMORTIZE A LOAN

5.375%

TERM / AMOUNT	15 Years	16 Years	17 Years	18 Years	19 Years	20 Years	21 Years	22 Years	23 Years	24 Years	25 Years	30 Years	35 Years	40 Years
5	.05	.04	.04	.04	.04	.04	.04	.04	.04	.04	.04	.03	.03	.03
10	.09	.08	.08	.08	.08	.07	.07	.07	.07	.07	.07	.06	.06	.06
15	.13	.12	.12	.11	.11	.11	.10	.10	.10	.10	.10	.09	.08	.08
25	.21	.20	.19	.19	.18	.18	.17	.17	.16	.16	.16	.14	.14	.13
50	.41	.39	.38	.37	.36	.35	.34	.33	.32	.31	.31	.28	.27	.26
75	.61	.59	.57	.55	.53	.52	.50	.49	.48	.47	.46	.42	.40	.39
100	.82	.78	.75	.73	.71	.69	.67	.65	.64	.62	.61	.56	.53	.51
200	1.63	1.56	1.50	1.45	1.41	1.37	1.33	1.30	1.27	1.24	1.22	1.12	1.06	1.02
300	2.44	2.34	2.25	2.18	2.11	2.05	1.99	1.94	1.90	1.86	1.82	1.68	1.59	1.53
400	3.25	3.12	3.00	2.90	2.81	2.73	2.66	2.59	2.53	2.48	2.43	2.24	2.12	2.03
500	4.06	3.89	3.75	3.62	3.51	3.41	3.32	3.24	3.17	3.10	3.04	2.80	2.65	2.54
600	4.87	4.67	4.50	4.35	4.21	4.09	3.98	3.88	3.80	3.72	3.64	3.36	3.18	3.05
700	5.68	5.45	5.25	5.07	4.91	4.77	4.64	4.53	4.43	4.34	4.25	3.92	3.71	3.56
800	6.49	6.23	6.00	5.79	5.61	5.45	5.31	5.18	5.06	4.95	4.86	4.48	4.24	4.06
900	7.30	7.00	6.74	6.52	6.31	6.13	5.97	5.82	5.69	5.57	5.46	5.04	4.76	4.57
1000	8.11	7.78	7.49	7.24	7.01	6.81	6.63	6.47	6.33	6.19	6.07	5.60	5.29	5.08
2000	16.21	15.56	14.98	14.47	14.02	13.62	13.26	12.94	12.65	12.38	12.14	11.20	10.58	10.15
3000	24.32	23.33	22.47	21.71	21.03	20.43	19.89	19.40	18.97	18.57	18.20	16.80	15.87	15.22
4000	32.42	31.11	29.96	28.94	28.04	27.24	26.52	25.87	25.29	24.75	24.27	22.40	21.16	20.30
5000	40.53	38.88	37.45	36.18	35.05	34.05	33.15	32.34	31.61	30.94	30.34	28.00	26.45	25.37
6000	48.63	46.66	44.93	43.41	42.06	40.86	39.78	38.80	37.93	37.13	36.40	33.60	31.74	30.44
7000	56.74	54.44	52.42	50.65	49.07	47.66	46.40	45.27	44.25	43.32	42.47	39.20	37.02	35.52
8000	64.84	62.21	59.91	57.88	56.08	54.47	53.03	51.74	50.57	49.50	48.54	44.80	42.31	40.59
9000	72.95	69.99	67.40	65.11	63.09	61.28	59.66	58.20	56.89	55.69	54.60	50.40	47.60	45.66
10000	81.05	77.76	74.89	72.35	70.10	68.09	66.29	64.67	63.21	61.88	60.67	56.00	52.89	50.73
11000	89.16	85.54	82.38	79.58	77.11	74.90	72.92	71.14	69.53	68.06	66.74	61.60	58.18	55.81
12000	97.26	93.32	89.86	86.82	84.12	81.71	79.55	77.60	75.85	74.25	72.80	67.20	63.47	60.88
13000	105.37	101.09	97.35	94.05	91.13	88.52	86.18	84.07	82.17	80.44	78.87	72.80	68.76	65.95
14000	113.47	108.87	104.84	101.29	98.13	95.32	92.80	90.54	88.49	86.63	84.94	78.40	74.04	71.03
15000	121.57	116.64	112.33	108.52	105.14	102.13	99.43	97.00	94.81	92.81	91.00	84.00	79.33	76.10
16000	129.68	124.42	119.82	115.76	112.15	108.94	106.06	103.47	101.13	99.00	97.07	89.60	84.62	81.17
17000	137.78	132.20	127.30	122.99	119.16	115.75	112.69	109.93	107.45	105.19	103.13	95.20	89.91	86.24
18000	145.89	139.97	134.79	130.22	126.17	122.56	119.32	116.40	113.77	111.38	109.20	100.80	95.20	91.32
19000	153.99	147.75	142.28	137.46	133.18	129.37	125.95	122.87	120.09	117.56	115.27	106.40	100.49	96.39
20000	162.10	155.53	149.77	144.69	140.19	136.17	132.57	129.33	126.41	123.75	121.33	112.00	105.78	101.46
21000	170.20	163.30	157.26	151.93	147.20	142.98	139.20	135.80	132.73	129.94	127.40	117.60	111.06	106.54
22000	178.31	171.08	164.75	159.16	154.21	149.79	145.83	142.27	139.05	136.12	133.47	123.20	116.35	111.61
23000	186.41	178.85	172.23	166.40	161.22	156.60	152.46	148.73	145.37	142.31	139.53	128.80	121.64	116.68
24000	194.52	186.63	179.72	173.63	168.23	163.41	159.09	155.20	151.69	148.50	145.60	134.40	126.93	121.76
25000	202.62	194.40	187.21	180.87	175.24	170.22	165.72	161.67	158.01	154.69	151.67	140.00	132.22	126.83
26000	210.73	202.18	194.70	188.10	182.25	177.03	172.35	168.13	164.33	160.87	157.73	145.60	137.51	131.90
27000	218.83	209.96	202.19	195.33	189.26	183.83	178.97	174.60	170.65	167.06	163.80	151.20	142.80	136.97
28000	226.94	217.73	209.67	202.57	196.26	190.64	185.60	181.07	176.97	173.25	169.87	156.80	148.08	142.05
29000	235.04	225.51	217.16	209.80	203.27	197.45	192.23	187.53	183.29	179.44	175.93	162.40	153.37	147.12
30000	243.14	233.28	224.65	217.04	210.28	204.26	198.86	194.00	189.61	185.62	182.00	168.00	158.66	152.19
31000	251.25	241.06	232.14	224.27	217.29	211.07	205.49	200.46	195.93	191.81	188.06	173.60	163.95	157.27
32000	259.35	248.84	239.63	231.51	224.30	217.88	212.12	206.93	202.25	198.00	194.13	179.20	169.24	162.34
33000	267.46	256.61	247.12	238.74	231.31	224.68	218.74	213.40	208.57	204.18	200.20	184.80	174.53	167.41
34000	275.56	264.39	254.60	245.98	238.32	231.49	225.37	219.86	214.89	210.37	206.26	190.40	179.81	172.48
35000	283.67	272.16	262.09	253.21	245.33	238.30	232.00	226.33	221.21	216.56	212.33	195.99	185.10	177.56
36000	291.77	279.94	269.58	260.44	252.34	245.11	238.63	232.80	227.53	222.75	218.40	201.59	190.39	182.63
37000	299.88	287.72	277.07	267.68	259.35	251.92	245.26	239.26	233.85	228.93	224.46	207.19	195.68	187.70
38000	307.98	295.49	284.56	274.91	266.36	258.73	251.89	245.73	240.17	235.12	230.53	212.79	200.97	192.78
39000	316.09	303.27	292.04	282.15	273.37	265.54	258.52	252.20	246.49	241.31	236.60	218.39	206.26	197.85
40000	324.19	311.04	299.53	289.38	280.38	272.34	265.14	258.66	252.81	247.49	242.66	223.99	211.55	202.92
41000	332.30	318.82	307.02	296.62	287.39	279.15	271.77	265.13	259.13	253.68	248.73	229.59	216.83	207.99
42000	340.40	326.60	314.51	303.85	294.39	285.96	278.40	271.60	265.45	259.87	254.80	235.19	222.12	213.07
43000	348.51	334.37	322.00	311.09	301.40	292.77	285.03	278.06	271.77	266.06	260.86	240.79	227.41	218.14
44000	356.61	342.15	329.49	318.32	308.41	299.58	291.66	284.53	278.09	272.24	266.93	246.39	232.70	223.21
45000	364.71	349.92	336.97	325.55	315.42	306.39	298.29	291.00	284.41	278.43	273.00	251.99	237.99	228.29
46000	372.82	357.70	344.46	332.79	322.43	313.19	304.91	297.46	290.73	284.62	279.06	257.59	243.28	233.36
47000	380.92	365.48	351.95	340.02	329.44	320.00	311.54	303.93	297.05	290.81	285.13	263.19	248.57	238.43
48000	389.03	373.25	359.44	347.26	336.45	326.81	318.17	310.39	303.37	296.99	291.19	268.79	253.85	243.51
49000	397.13	381.03	366.93	354.49	343.46	333.62	324.80	316.86	309.69	303.18	297.26	274.39	259.14	248.58
50000	405.24	388.80	374.41	361.73	350.47	340.43	331.43	323.33	316.01	309.37	303.33	279.99	264.43	253.65
55000	445.76	427.68	411.86	397.90	385.52	374.47	364.57	355.66	347.61	340.30	333.66	307.99	290.87	279.02
60000	486.28	466.56	449.30	434.07	420.56	408.51	397.71	387.99	379.21	371.24	363.99	335.99	317.32	304.38
65000	526.81	505.44	486.74	470.24	455.61	442.56	430.86	420.32	410.81	402.18	394.32	363.99	343.76	329.75
70000	567.33	544.32	524.18	506.41	490.65	476.60	464.00	452.65	442.41	433.11	424.66	391.98	370.20	355.11
75000	607.85	583.20	561.62	542.59	525.70	510.64	497.14	484.99	474.01	464.05	454.99	419.98	396.65	380.47
80000	648.38	622.08	599.06	578.76	560.75	544.68	530.28	517.32	505.61	494.98	485.32	447.98	423.09	405.84
85000	688.90	660.96	636.50	614.93	595.79	578.72	563.43	549.65	537.21	525.92	515.65	475.98	449.53	431.20
90000	729.42	699.84	673.94	651.10	630.84	612.77	596.57	581.99	568.81	556.86	545.99	503.98	475.97	456.57
95000	769.95	738.72	711.38	687.28	665.89	646.81	629.71	614.32	600.41	587.79	576.32	531.98	502.42	481.93
100000	810.47	777.60	748.82	723.45	700.93	680.85	662.85	646.65	632.01	618.73	606.65	559.98	528.86	507.30

TERM / AMOUNT	1 Year	2 Years	3 Years	4 Years	5 Years	6 Years	7 Years	8 Years	9 Years	10 Years	11 Years	12 Years	13 Years	14 Years
5	.43	.23	.16	.12	.10	.09	.08	.07	.06	.06	.06	.05	.05	.05
10	.86	.45	.31	.24	.20	.17	.15	.13	.12	.11	.11	.10	.09	.09
15	1.29	.67	.46	.35	.29	.25	.22	.20	.18	.17	.16	.15	.14	.13
25	2.15	1.11	.76	.59	.48	.41	.36	.33	.30	.28	.26	.24	.23	.22
50	4.29	2.21	1.51	1.17	.96	.82	.72	.65	.59	.55	.51	.48	.45	.43
75	6.44	3.31	2.27	1.75	1.43	1.23	1.08	.97	.88	.82	.76	.71	.68	.64
100	8.58	4.41	3.02	2.33	1.91	1.63	1.44	1.29	1.18	1.09	1.01	.95	.90	.85
200	17.16	8.82	6.04	4.65	3.82	3.26	2.87	2.58	2.35	2.17	2.02	1.90	1.79	1.70
300	25.74	13.22	9.05	6.97	5.72	4.89	4.30	3.86	3.52	3.25	3.02	2.84	2.69	2.55
400	34.32	17.63	12.07	9.29	7.63	6.52	5.73	5.15	4.69	4.33	4.03	3.79	3.58	3.40
500	42.90	22.03	15.08	11.61	9.53	8.15	7.17	6.43	5.86	5.41	5.04	4.73	4.47	4.25
600	51.48	26.44	18.10	13.93	11.44	9.78	8.60	7.72	7.03	6.49	6.04	5.68	5.37	5.10
700	60.06	30.84	21.11	16.25	13.34	11.41	10.03	9.00	8.20	7.57	7.05	6.62	6.26	5.95
800	68.64	35.25	24.13	18.57	15.25	13.04	11.46	10.29	9.37	8.65	8.06	7.57	7.15	6.80
900	77.22	39.65	27.14	20.89	17.15	14.67	12.90	11.57	10.55	9.73	9.06	8.51	8.05	7.65
1000	85.80	44.06	30.16	23.22	19.06	16.30	14.33	12.86	11.72	10.81	10.07	9.46	8.94	8.50
2000	171.59	88.11	60.31	46.43	38.12	32.59	28.65	25.71	23.43	21.61	20.13	18.91	17.88	17.00
3000	257.38	132.16	90.46	69.64	57.17	48.88	42.97	38.56	35.14	32.41	30.20	28.36	26.81	25.49
4000	343.17	176.21	120.61	92.85	76.23	65.17	57.30	51.41	46.85	43.22	40.26	37.81	35.75	33.99
5000	428.96	220.26	150.76	116.06	95.28	81.46	71.62	64.26	58.56	54.02	50.32	47.26	44.68	42.48
6000	514.75	264.31	180.91	139.27	114.34	97.75	85.94	77.11	70.27	64.82	60.39	56.71	53.62	50.98
7000	600.54	308.36	211.06	162.48	133.39	114.04	100.26	89.96	81.98	75.63	70.45	66.16	62.55	59.48
8000	686.33	352.41	241.21	185.69	152.45	130.33	114.59	102.81	93.69	86.43	80.52	75.61	71.49	67.97
9000	772.12	396.46	271.36	208.90	171.50	146.63	128.91	115.67	105.41	97.23	90.58	85.06	80.42	76.47
10000	857.91	440.51	301.51	232.11	190.56	162.92	143.23	128.52	117.12	108.04	100.64	94.51	89.36	84.96
11000	943.70	484.56	331.66	255.33	209.61	179.21	157.55	141.37	128.83	118.84	110.71	103.96	98.29	93.46
12000	1029.50	528.61	361.81	278.54	228.67	195.50	171.88	154.22	140.54	129.64	120.77	113.42	107.23	101.96
13000	1115.29	572.66	391.97	301.75	247.72	211.79	186.20	167.07	152.25	140.45	130.83	122.87	116.16	110.45
14000	1201.08	616.72	422.12	324.96	266.78	228.08	200.52	179.92	163.96	151.25	140.90	132.32	125.10	118.95
15000	1286.87	660.77	452.27	348.17	285.83	244.37	214.84	192.77	175.67	162.05	150.96	141.77	134.03	127.44
16000	1372.66	704.82	482.42	371.38	304.89	260.66	229.17	205.62	187.38	172.86	161.03	151.22	142.97	135.94
17000	1458.45	748.87	512.57	394.59	323.94	276.95	243.49	218.48	199.10	183.66	171.09	160.67	151.90	144.44
18000	1544.24	792.92	542.72	417.80	343.00	293.25	257.81	231.33	210.81	194.46	181.15	170.12	160.84	152.93
19000	1630.03	836.97	572.87	441.01	362.05	309.54	272.13	244.18	222.52	205.26	191.22	179.57	169.77	161.43
20000	1715.82	881.02	603.02	464.22	381.11	325.83	286.46	257.03	234.23	216.07	201.28	189.02	178.71	169.92
21000	1801.61	925.07	633.17	487.43	400.16	342.12	300.78	269.88	245.94	226.87	211.34	198.47	187.64	178.42
22000	1887.40	969.12	663.32	510.65	419.22	358.41	315.10	282.73	257.65	237.67	221.41	207.92	196.58	186.92
23000	1973.20	1013.17	693.47	533.86	438.27	374.70	329.43	295.58	269.36	248.48	231.47	217.37	205.51	195.41
24000	2058.99	1057.22	723.62	557.07	457.33	390.99	343.75	308.43	281.07	259.28	241.54	226.83	214.45	203.91
25000	2144.78	1101.27	753.78	580.28	476.38	407.28	358.07	321.29	292.79	270.08	251.60	236.28	223.39	212.40
26000	2230.57	1145.32	783.93	603.49	495.44	423.57	372.39	334.14	304.50	280.89	261.66	245.73	232.32	220.90
27000	2316.36	1189.38	814.08	626.70	514.49	439.87	386.72	346.99	316.21	291.69	271.73	255.18	241.26	229.40
28000	2402.15	1233.43	844.23	649.91	533.55	456.16	401.04	359.84	327.92	302.49	281.79	264.63	250.19	237.89
29000	2487.94	1277.48	874.38	673.12	552.60	472.45	415.36	372.69	339.63	313.30	291.85	274.08	259.13	246.39
30000	2573.73	1321.53	904.53	696.33	571.66	488.74	429.68	385.54	351.34	324.10	301.92	283.53	268.06	254.88
31000	2659.52	1365.58	934.68	719.54	590.71	505.03	444.01	398.39	363.05	334.90	311.98	292.98	277.00	263.38
32000	2745.31	1409.63	964.83	742.75	609.77	521.32	458.33	411.24	374.76	345.71	322.05	302.43	285.93	271.88
33000	2831.10	1453.68	994.98	765.97	628.82	537.61	472.65	424.10	386.47	356.51	332.11	311.88	294.87	280.37
34000	2916.90	1497.73	1025.13	789.18	647.88	553.90	486.97	436.95	398.19	367.31	342.17	321.33	303.80	288.87
35000	3002.69	1541.78	1055.28	812.39	666.93	570.19	501.30	449.80	409.90	378.12	352.24	330.78	312.74	297.36
36000	3088.48	1585.83	1085.43	835.60	685.99	586.49	515.62	462.65	421.61	388.92	362.30	340.24	321.67	305.86
37000	3174.27	1629.88	1115.59	858.81	705.04	602.78	529.94	475.50	433.32	399.72	372.36	349.69	330.61	314.36
38000	3260.06	1673.93	1145.74	882.02	724.10	619.07	544.26	488.35	445.03	410.52	382.43	359.14	339.54	322.85
39000	3345.85	1717.98	1175.89	905.23	743.15	635.36	558.59	501.20	456.74	421.33	392.49	368.59	348.48	331.35
40000	3431.64	1762.03	1206.04	928.44	762.21	651.65	572.91	514.05	468.45	432.13	402.56	378.04	357.41	339.84
41000	3517.43	1806.09	1236.19	951.65	781.26	667.94	587.23	526.91	480.16	442.93	412.62	387.49	366.35	348.34
42000	3603.22	1850.14	1266.34	974.86	800.32	684.23	601.56	539.76	491.88	453.74	422.68	396.94	375.28	356.84
43000	3689.01	1894.19	1296.49	998.07	819.37	700.52	615.88	552.61	503.59	464.54	432.75	406.39	384.22	365.33
44000	3774.80	1938.24	1326.64	1021.29	838.43	716.81	630.20	565.46	515.30	475.34	442.81	415.84	393.15	373.83
45000	3860.60	1982.29	1356.79	1044.50	857.48	733.11	644.52	578.31	527.01	486.15	452.87	425.29	402.09	382.32
46000	3946.39	2026.34	1386.94	1067.71	876.54	749.40	658.85	591.16	538.72	496.95	462.94	434.74	411.02	390.82
47000	4032.18	2070.39	1417.09	1090.92	895.59	765.69	673.17	604.01	550.43	507.75	473.00	444.19	419.96	399.32
48000	4117.97	2114.44	1447.24	1114.13	914.65	781.98	687.49	616.86	562.14	518.56	483.07	453.65	428.89	407.81
49000	4203.76	2158.49	1477.40	1137.34	933.70	798.27	701.81	629.72	573.85	529.36	493.13	463.10	437.83	416.31
50000	4289.55	2202.54	1507.55	1160.55	952.76	814.56	716.14	642.57	585.57	540.16	503.19	472.55	446.77	424.80
55000	4718.50	2422.80	1658.30	1276.61	1048.03	896.02	787.75	706.82	644.12	594.18	553.51	519.80	491.44	467.28
60000	5147.46	2643.05	1809.05	1392.66	1143.31	977.47	859.36	771.08	702.68	648.19	603.83	567.06	536.12	509.76
65000	5576.41	2863.30	1959.81	1508.72	1238.58	1058.93	930.98	835.33	761.23	702.21	654.15	614.31	580.79	552.24
70000	6005.37	3083.56	2110.56	1624.77	1333.86	1140.38	1002.59	899.59	819.79	756.23	704.47	661.56	625.47	594.72
75000	6434.32	3303.81	2261.32	1740.83	1429.13	1221.84	1074.20	963.85	878.35	810.24	754.79	708.82	670.15	637.20
80000	6863.28	3524.06	2412.07	1856.88	1524.41	1303.30	1145.82	1028.10	936.90	864.26	805.11	756.07	714.82	679.68
85000	7292.23	3744.32	2562.82	1972.93	1619.68	1384.75	1217.43	1092.36	995.46	918.27	855.42	803.33	759.50	722.16
90000	7721.19	3964.57	2713.58	2088.99	1714.96	1466.21	1289.04	1156.62	1054.01	972.29	905.74	850.58	804.17	764.64
95000	8150.14	4184.83	2864.33	2205.04	1810.23	1547.66	1360.65	1220.87	1112.57	1026.30	956.06	897.83	848.85	807.12
100000	8579.10	4405.08	3015.09	2321.10	1905.51	1629.12	1432.27	1285.13	1171.13	1080.32	1006.38	945.09	893.53	849.60

TERM	15 Years	16 Years	17 Years	18 Years	19 Years	20 Years	21 Years	22 Years	23 Years	24 Years	25 Years	30 Years	35 Years	40 Years
AMOUNT														
5	.05	.04	.04	.04	.04	.04	.04	.04	.04	.04	.04	.03	.03	.03
10	.09	.08	.08	.08	.08	.07	.07	.07	.07	.07	.07	.06	.06	.06
15	.13	.12	.12	.11	.11	.11	.10	.10	.10	.10	.10	.09	.08	.08
25	.21	.20	.19	.19	.18	.18	.17	.17	.16	.16	.16	.15	.14	.13
50	.41	.39	.38	.37	.36	.35	.34	.33	.32	.32	.31	.29	.27	.26
75	.61	.59	.57	.55	.53	.52	.50	.49	.48	.47	.46	.43	.40	.39
100	.82	.78	.76	.73	.71	.69	.67	.65	.64	.63	.61	.57	.54	.51
200	1.63	1.56	1.51	1.45	1.41	1.37	1.33	1.30	1.27	1.25	1.22	1.13	1.07	1.02
300	2.44	2.34	2.26	2.18	2.11	2.05	2.00	1.95	1.91	1.87	1.83	1.69	1.60	1.53
400	3.25	3.12	3.01	2.90	2.81	2.73	2.66	2.60	2.54	2.49	2.44	2.25	2.13	2.04
500	4.06	3.90	3.76	3.63	3.52	3.42	3.33	3.25	3.17	3.11	3.05	2.81	2.66	2.55
600	4.88	4.68	4.51	4.35	4.22	4.10	3.99	3.89	3.81	3.73	3.65	3.37	3.19	3.06
700	5.69	5.46	5.26	5.08	4.92	4.78	4.65	4.54	4.44	4.35	4.26	3.94	3.72	3.57
800	6.50	6.24	6.01	5.80	5.62	5.46	5.32	5.19	5.07	4.97	4.87	4.50	4.25	4.08
900	7.31	7.02	6.76	6.53	6.33	6.15	5.98	5.84	5.71	5.59	5.48	5.06	4.78	4.59
1000	8.12	7.79	7.51	7.25	7.03	6.83	6.65	6.49	6.34	6.21	6.09	5.62	5.31	5.09
2000	16.24	15.58	15.01	14.50	14.05	13.65	13.29	12.97	12.67	12.41	12.17	11.24	10.61	10.18
3000	24.36	23.37	22.51	21.75	21.07	20.47	19.93	19.45	19.01	18.61	18.25	16.85	15.92	15.27
4000	32.48	31.16	30.01	29.00	28.10	27.30	26.58	25.93	25.34	24.81	24.33	22.47	21.22	20.36
5000	40.59	38.95	37.51	36.25	35.12	34.12	33.22	32.41	31.68	31.01	30.41	28.08	26.53	25.45
6000	48.71	46.74	45.02	43.49	42.14	40.94	39.86	38.89	38.01	37.22	36.49	33.70	31.83	30.54
7000	56.83	54.53	52.52	50.74	49.17	47.76	46.50	45.37	44.35	43.42	42.57	39.31	37.14	35.63
8000	64.95	62.32	60.02	57.99	56.19	54.59	53.15	51.85	50.68	49.62	48.66	44.93	42.44	40.72
9000	73.07	70.11	67.52	65.24	63.21	61.41	59.79	58.33	57.02	55.82	54.74	50.54	47.75	45.81
10000	81.18	77.90	75.02	72.49	70.24	68.23	66.43	64.81	63.35	62.02	60.82	56.16	53.05	50.90
11000	89.30	85.69	82.52	79.73	77.26	75.05	73.07	71.29	69.69	68.23	66.90	61.77	58.36	55.99
12000	97.42	93.48	90.03	86.98	84.28	81.88	79.72	77.77	76.02	74.43	72.98	67.39	63.66	61.08
13000	105.54	101.27	97.53	94.23	91.31	88.70	86.36	84.26	82.35	80.63	79.06	73.00	68.97	66.17
14000	113.66	109.06	105.03	101.48	98.33	95.52	93.00	90.74	88.69	86.83	85.14	78.62	74.27	71.26
15000	121.77	116.85	112.53	108.73	105.35	102.34	99.65	97.22	95.02	93.03	91.22	84.23	79.58	76.35
16000	129.89	124.64	120.03	115.98	112.38	109.17	106.29	103.70	101.36	99.24	97.31	89.85	84.88	81.44
17000	138.01	132.42	127.53	123.22	119.40	115.99	112.93	110.18	107.69	105.44	103.39	95.47	90.19	86.53
18000	146.13	140.21	135.04	130.47	126.42	122.81	119.57	116.66	114.03	111.64	109.47	101.08	95.49	91.62
19000	154.24	148.00	142.54	137.72	133.45	129.63	126.22	123.14	120.36	117.84	115.55	106.70	100.80	96.71
20000	162.36	155.79	150.04	144.97	140.47	136.46	132.86	129.62	126.70	124.04	121.63	112.31	106.10	101.80
21000	170.48	163.58	157.54	152.22	147.49	143.28	139.50	136.10	133.03	130.25	127.71	117.93	111.41	106.89
22000	178.60	171.37	165.04	159.46	154.51	150.10	146.14	142.58	139.37	136.45	133.79	123.54	116.71	111.98
23000	186.72	179.16	172.55	166.71	161.54	156.92	152.79	149.06	145.70	142.65	139.87	129.16	122.02	117.07
24000	194.83	186.95	180.05	173.96	168.56	163.75	159.43	155.54	152.03	148.85	145.96	134.77	127.32	122.16
25000	202.95	194.74	187.55	181.21	175.58	170.57	166.07	162.03	158.37	155.05	152.04	140.39	132.63	127.25
26000	211.07	202.53	195.05	188.46	182.61	177.39	172.71	168.51	164.70	161.26	158.12	146.00	137.93	132.34
27000	219.19	210.32	202.55	195.70	189.63	184.21	179.36	174.99	171.04	167.46	164.20	151.62	143.23	137.43
28000	227.31	218.11	210.05	202.95	196.65	191.04	186.00	181.47	177.37	173.66	170.28	157.23	148.54	142.52
29000	235.42	225.90	217.56	210.20	203.68	197.86	192.64	187.95	183.71	179.86	176.36	162.85	153.84	147.61
30000	243.54	233.69	225.06	217.45	210.70	204.68	199.29	194.43	190.04	186.06	182.44	168.46	159.15	152.70
31000	251.66	241.48	232.56	224.70	217.72	211.50	205.93	200.91	196.38	192.27	188.53	174.08	164.45	157.79
32000	259.78	249.27	240.06	231.95	224.75	218.33	212.57	207.39	202.71	198.47	194.61	179.69	169.76	162.88
33000	267.89	257.05	247.56	239.19	231.77	225.15	219.21	213.87	209.05	204.67	200.69	185.31	175.06	167.97
34000	276.01	264.84	255.06	246.44	238.79	231.97	225.86	220.35	215.38	210.87	206.77	190.93	180.37	173.06
35000	284.13	272.63	262.57	253.69	245.82	238.79	232.50	226.83	221.71	217.07	212.85	196.54	185.67	178.15
36000	292.25	280.42	270.07	260.94	252.84	245.62	239.14	233.31	228.05	223.27	218.93	202.16	190.98	183.24
37000	300.37	288.21	277.57	268.19	259.86	252.44	245.78	239.80	234.38	229.48	225.01	207.77	196.28	188.33
38000	308.48	296.00	285.07	275.43	266.89	259.26	252.43	246.28	240.72	235.68	231.09	213.39	201.59	193.42
39000	316.60	303.79	292.57	282.68	273.91	266.08	259.07	252.76	247.05	241.88	237.18	219.00	206.89	198.51
40000	324.72	311.58	300.08	289.93	280.93	272.91	265.71	259.24	253.39	248.08	243.26	224.62	212.20	203.60
41000	332.84	319.37	307.58	297.18	287.96	279.73	272.36	265.72	259.72	254.28	249.34	230.23	217.50	208.69
42000	340.96	327.16	315.08	304.43	294.98	286.55	279.00	272.20	266.06	260.49	255.42	235.85	222.81	213.78
43000	349.07	334.95	322.58	311.68	302.00	293.37	285.64	278.68	272.39	266.69	261.50	241.46	228.11	218.87
44000	357.19	342.74	330.08	318.92	309.02	300.20	292.28	285.16	278.73	272.89	267.58	247.08	233.42	223.96
45000	365.31	350.53	337.58	326.17	316.05	307.02	298.93	291.64	285.06	279.09	273.66	252.69	238.72	229.05
46000	373.43	358.32	345.09	333.42	323.07	313.84	305.57	298.12	291.39	285.29	279.74	258.31	244.03	234.14
47000	381.54	366.11	352.59	340.67	330.09	320.66	312.21	304.60	297.73	291.50	285.83	263.92	249.33	239.23
48000	389.66	373.90	360.09	347.92	337.12	327.49	318.85	311.08	304.06	297.70	291.91	269.54	254.64	244.32
49000	397.78	381.68	367.59	355.16	344.14	334.31	325.50	317.57	310.40	303.90	297.99	275.16	259.94	249.41
50000	405.90	389.47	375.09	362.41	351.16	341.13	332.14	324.05	316.73	310.10	304.07	280.77	265.25	254.50
55000	446.49	428.42	412.60	398.65	386.28	375.24	365.35	356.45	348.41	341.11	334.48	308.85	291.77	279.95
60000	487.08	467.37	450.11	434.89	421.40	409.36	398.57	388.85	380.08	372.12	364.88	336.92	318.29	305.40
65000	527.67	506.31	487.62	471.13	456.51	443.47	431.78	421.26	411.75	403.13	395.29	365.00	344.82	330.84
70000	568.26	545.26	525.13	507.38	491.63	477.58	464.99	453.66	443.42	434.14	425.70	393.08	371.34	356.29
75000	608.84	584.21	562.64	543.62	526.74	511.69	498.21	486.07	475.10	465.15	456.10	421.15	397.87	381.74
80000	649.43	623.16	600.15	579.86	561.86	545.81	531.42	518.47	506.77	496.16	486.51	449.23	424.39	407.19
85000	690.02	662.10	637.65	616.10	596.97	579.92	564.63	550.87	538.44	527.17	516.92	477.31	450.91	432.64
90000	730.61	701.05	675.16	652.34	632.09	614.03	597.85	583.28	570.12	558.18	547.32	505.38	477.44	458.09
95000	771.20	740.00	712.67	688.58	667.21	648.14	631.06	615.68	601.79	589.19	577.73	533.46	503.96	483.54
100000	811.79	778.94	750.18	724.82	702.32	682.26	664.27	648.09	633.46	620.20	608.13	561.54	530.49	508.99

17

MONTHLY PAYMENT
REQUIRED TO AMORTIZE A LOAN

TERM AMOUNT	1 Year	2 Years	3 Years	4 Years	5 Years	6 Years	7 Years	8 Years	9 Years	10 Years	11 Years	12 Years	13 Years	14 Years
5	.43	.23	.16	.12	.10	.09	.08	.07	.06	.06	.06	.05	.05	.05
10	.86	.45	.31	.24	.20	.17	.15	.13	.12	.11	.11	.10	.09	.09
15	1.29	.67	.46	.35	.29	.25	.22	.20	.18	.17	.16	.15	.14	.13
25	2.15	1.11	.76	.59	.48	.41	.36	.33	.30	.28	.26	.24	.23	.22
50	4.30	2.21	1.51	1.17	.96	.82	.72	.65	.59	.55	.51	.48	.45	.43
75	6.44	3.31	2.27	1.75	1.44	1.23	1.08	.97	.89	.82	.76	.72	.68	.65
100	8.59	4.41	3.02	2.33	1.92	1.64	1.44	1.29	1.18	1.09	1.02	.96	.90	.86
200	17.17	8.82	6.04	4.66	3.83	3.27	2.88	2.58	2.36	2.18	2.03	1.91	1.80	1.71
300	25.76	13.23	9.06	6.98	5.74	4.91	4.32	3.87	3.53	3.26	3.04	2.86	2.70	2.57
400	34.34	17.04	12.08	9.31	7.65	6.54	5.75	5.16	4.71	4.35	4.05	3.81	3.60	3.42
500	42.92	22.05	15.10	11.63	9.56	8.17	7.19	6.45	5.88	5.43	5.06	4.76	4.50	4.28
600	51.51	26.46	18.12	13.96	11.47	9.81	8.63	7.74	7.06	6.52	6.07	5.71	5.40	5.13
700	60.09	30.87	21.14	16.28	13.38	11.44	10.06	9.03	8.24	7.60	7.08	6.66	6.30	5.99
800	68.67	35.28	24.16	18.61	15.29	13.08	11.50	10.32	9.41	8.69	8.10	7.61	7.19	6.84
900	77.26	39.69	27.18	20.94	17.20	14.71	12.94	11.61	10.59	9.77	9.11	8.56	8.09	7.70
1000	85.84	44.10	30.20	23.26	19.11	16.34	14.38	12.90	11.76	10.86	10.12	9.51	8.99	8.55
2000	171.68	88.20	60.40	46.52	38.21	32.68	28.75	25.80	23.52	21.71	20.23	19.01	17.98	17.10
3000	257.52	132.29	90.59	69.77	57.31	49.02	43.12	38.70	35.28	32.56	30.35	28.51	26.97	25.65
4000	343.35	176.39	120.79	93.03	76.41	65.36	57.49	51.60	47.04	43.42	40.46	38.01	35.95	34.20
5000	429.19	220.48	150.98	116.29	95.51	81.69	71.86	64.50	58.80	54.27	50.57	47.51	44.94	42.75
6000	515.03	264.58	181.18	139.54	114.61	98.03	86.23	77.40	70.56	65.12	60.69	57.02	53.93	51.29
7000	600.86	308.67	211.38	162.80	133.71	114.37	100.60	90.30	82.32	75.97	70.80	66.52	62.91	59.84
8000	686.70	352.77	241.57	186.06	152.81	130.71	114.97	103.20	94.08	86.83	80.92	76.02	71.90	68.39
9000	772.54	396.87	271.77	209.31	171.92	147.05	129.34	116.10	105.84	97.68	91.03	85.52	80.89	76.94
10000	858.37	440.96	301.96	232.57	191.02	163.38	143.71	129.00	117.60	108.53	101.14	95.02	89.87	85.49
11000	944.21	485.06	332.16	255.83	210.12	179.72	158.08	141.90	129.36	119.38	111.26	104.52	98.86	94.04
12000	1030.05	529.15	362.36	279.08	229.22	196.06	172.45	154.80	141.12	130.24	121.37	114.03	107.85	102.58
13000	1115.88	573.25	392.55	302.34	248.32	212.40	186.82	167.70	152.88	141.09	131.49	123.53	116.83	111.13
14000	1201.72	617.34	422.75	325.60	267.42	228.74	201.19	180.60	164.64	151.94	141.60	133.03	125.82	119.68
15000	1287.56	661.44	452.94	348.85	286.52	245.07	215.56	193.49	176.40	162.79	151.71	142.53	134.81	128.23
16000	1373.39	705.54	483.14	372.11	305.62	261.41	229.93	206.39	188.16	173.65	161.83	152.03	143.79	136.78
17000	1459.23	749.63	513.34	395.37	324.72	277.75	244.30	219.29	199.92	184.50	171.94	161.53	152.78	145.33
18000	1545.07	793.73	543.53	418.62	343.83	294.09	258.67	232.19	211.68	195.35	182.06	171.04	161.77	153.87
19000	1630.90	837.82	573.73	441.88	362.93	310.42	273.04	245.09	223.44	206.20	192.17	180.54	170.75	162.42
20000	1716.74	881.92	603.92	465.13	382.03	326.76	287.41	257.99	235.20	217.06	202.28	190.04	179.74	170.97
21000	1802.58	926.01	634.12	488.39	401.13	343.10	301.78	270.89	246.96	227.91	212.40	199.54	188.73	179.52
22000	1888.41	970.11	664.31	511.65	420.23	359.44	316.15	283.79	258.72	238.76	222.51	209.04	197.71	188.07
23000	1974.25	1014.21	694.51	534.90	439.33	375.78	330.52	296.69	270.48	249.62	232.63	218.54	206.70	196.61
24000	2060.09	1058.30	724.71	558.16	458.43	392.11	344.89	309.59	282.24	260.47	242.74	228.05	215.69	205.16
25000	2145.92	1102.40	754.90	581.42	477.53	408.45	359.26	322.49	294.00	271.32	252.85	237.55	224.67	213.71
26000	2231.76	1146.49	785.10	604.67	496.64	424.79	373.63	335.39	305.76	282.17	262.97	247.05	233.66	222.26
27000	2317.60	1190.59	815.29	627.93	515.74	441.13	388.00	348.29	317.52	293.03	273.08	256.55	242.65	230.81
28000	2403.44	1234.68	845.49	651.19	534.84	457.47	402.37	361.19	329.28	303.88	283.20	266.05	251.63	239.36
29000	2489.27	1278.78	875.69	674.44	553.94	473.80	416.74	374.09	341.04	314.73	293.31	275.55	260.62	247.90
30000	2575.11	1322.87	905.88	697.70	573.04	490.14	431.11	386.98	352.80	325.58	303.42	285.06	269.61	256.45
31000	2660.95	1366.97	936.08	720.96	592.14	506.48	445.48	399.88	364.56	336.44	313.54	294.56	278.60	265.00
32000	2746.78	1411.07	966.27	744.21	611.24	522.82	459.85	412.78	376.32	347.29	323.65	304.06	287.58	273.55
33000	2832.62	1455.16	996.47	767.47	630.34	539.16	474.22	425.68	388.08	358.14	333.76	313.56	296.57	282.10
34000	2918.46	1499.26	1026.67	790.73	649.44	555.49	488.59	438.58	399.84	368.99	343.88	323.06	305.56	290.65
35000	3004.29	1543.35	1056.86	813.98	668.55	571.83	502.96	451.48	411.60	379.85	353.99	332.57	314.54	299.19
36000	3090.13	1587.45	1087.06	837.24	687.65	588.17	517.33	464.38	423.36	390.70	364.11	342.07	323.53	307.74
37000	3175.97	1631.54	1117.25	860.49	706.75	604.51	531.70	477.28	435.12	401.55	374.22	351.57	332.52	316.29
38000	3261.80	1675.64	1147.45	883.75	725.85	620.84	546.07	490.18	446.88	412.40	384.33	361.07	341.50	324.84
39000	3347.64	1719.74	1177.65	907.01	744.95	637.18	560.44	503.08	458.64	423.26	394.45	370.57	350.49	333.39
40000	3433.48	1763.83	1207.84	930.26	764.05	653.52	574.81	515.98	470.40	434.11	404.56	380.07	359.48	341.94
41000	3519.31	1807.93	1238.04	953.52	783.15	669.86	589.18	528.88	482.16	444.96	414.68	389.58	368.46	350.48
42000	3605.15	1852.02	1268.23	976.78	802.25	686.20	603.55	541.78	493.92	455.82	424.79	399.08	377.45	359.03
43000	3690.99	1896.12	1298.43	1000.03	821.35	702.53	617.92	554.68	505.68	466.67	434.90	408.58	386.44	367.58
44000	3776.82	1940.21	1328.62	1023.29	840.46	718.87	632.29	567.58	517.44	477.52	445.02	418.08	395.42	376.13
45000	3862.66	1984.31	1358.82	1046.55	859.56	735.21	646.66	580.47	529.20	488.37	455.13	427.58	404.41	384.68
46000	3948.50	2028.41	1389.02	1069.80	878.66	751.55	661.03	593.37	540.96	499.23	465.25	437.08	413.40	393.22
47000	4034.33	2072.50	1419.21	1093.06	897.76	767.89	675.40	606.27	552.72	510.08	475.36	446.59	422.38	401.77
48000	4120.17	2116.60	1449.41	1116.32	916.86	784.22	689.77	619.17	564.48	520.93	485.47	456.09	431.37	410.32
49000	4206.01	2160.69	1479.60	1139.57	935.96	800.56	704.14	632.07	576.24	531.78	495.59	465.59	440.36	418.87
50000	4291.84	2204.79	1509.80	1162.83	955.06	816.90	718.51	644.97	588.00	542.64	505.70	475.09	449.34	427.42
55000	4721.03	2425.27	1660.78	1279.11	1050.57	898.59	790.36	709.47	646.80	596.90	556.27	522.60	494.28	470.16
60000	5150.21	2645.74	1811.76	1395.39	1146.07	980.28	862.21	773.96	705.60	651.16	606.84	570.11	539.21	512.90
65000	5579.40	2866.22	1962.74	1511.68	1241.58	1061.97	934.06	838.46	764.40	705.43	657.41	617.62	584.15	555.64
70000	6008.58	3086.70	2113.72	1627.96	1337.09	1143.66	1005.91	902.96	823.20	759.69	707.98	665.13	629.08	598.38
75000	6437.76	3307.18	2264.70	1744.24	1432.59	1225.35	1077.76	967.45	882.00	813.95	758.55	712.63	674.01	641.12
80000	6866.95	3527.66	2415.68	1860.52	1528.10	1307.04	1149.61	1031.95	940.80	868.22	809.12	760.14	718.95	683.87
85000	7296.13	3748.14	2566.66	1976.81	1623.60	1388.73	1221.46	1096.45	999.60	922.48	859.69	807.65	763.88	726.61
90000	7725.32	3968.61	2717.64	2093.09	1719.11	1470.41	1293.31	1160.94	1058.40	976.74	910.26	855.16	808.82	769.35
95000	8154.50	4189.09	2868.62	2209.37	1814.62	1552.10	1365.16	1225.44	1117.20	1031.00	960.83	902.67	853.75	812.09
100000	8583.68	4409.57	3019.60	2325.65	1910.12	1633.79	1437.01	1289.94	1176.00	1085.27	1011.40	950.18	898.68	854.83

TERM	15 Years	16 Years	17 Years	18 Years	19 Years	20 Years	21 Years	22 Years	23 Years	24 Years	25 Years	30 Years	35 Years	40 Years
AMOUNT														
5	.05	.04	.04	.04	.04	.04	.04	.04	.04	.04	.04	.03	.03	.03
10	.09	.08	.08	.08	.08	.07	.07	.07	.07	.07	.07	.06	.06	.06
15	.13	.12	.12	.11	.11	.11	.11	.10	.10	.10	.10	.09	.09	.08
25	.21	.20	.19	.19	.18	.18	.17	.17	.16	.16	.16	.15	.14	.13
50	.41	.40	.38	.37	.36	.35	.34	.33	.32	.32	.31	.29	.27	.26
75	.62	.59	.57	.55	.54	.52	.51	.50	.48	.47	.47	.43	.41	.39
100	.82	.79	.76	.74	.71	.69	.67	.66	.64	.63	.62	.57	.54	.52
200	1.64	1.57	1.52	1.47	1.42	1.38	1.34	1.31	1.28	1.26	1.23	1.14	1.08	1.04
300	2.46	2.36	2.27	2.20	2.13	2.07	2.01	1.97	1.92	1.88	1.85	1.71	1.62	1.55
400	3.27	3.14	3.03	2.93	2.84	2.76	2.68	2.62	2.56	2.51	2.46	2.28	2.15	2.07
500	4.09	3.93	3.78	3.66	3.54	3.44	3.35	3.27	3.20	3.14	3.08	2.84	2.69	2.58
600	4.91	4.71	4.54	4.39	4.25	4.13	4.02	3.93	3.84	3.76	3.69	3.41	3.23	3.10
700	5.72	5.50	5.29	5.12	4.96	4.82	4.69	4.58	4.48	4.39	4.30	3.98	3.76	3.62
800	6.54	6.28	6.05	5.85	5.67	5.51	5.36	5.24	5.12	5.01	4.92	4.55	4.30	4.13
900	7.36	7.06	6.81	6.58	6.38	6.20	6.03	5.89	5.76	5.64	5.53	5.12	4.84	4.65
1000	8.18	7.85	7.56	7.31	7.08	6.88	6.70	6.54	6.40	6.27	6.15	5.68	5.38	5.16
2000	16.35	15.69	15.12	14.61	14.16	13.76	13.40	13.08	12.79	12.53	12.29	11.36	10.75	10.32
3000	24.52	23.53	22.67	21.91	21.24	20.64	20.10	19.62	19.18	18.79	18.43	17.04	16.12	15.48
4000	32.69	31.38	30.23	29.22	28.32	27.52	26.80	26.16	25.58	25.05	24.57	22.72	21.49	20.64
5000	40.86	39.22	37.79	36.52	35.40	34.40	33.50	32.70	31.97	31.31	30.71	28.39	26.86	25.79
6000	49.03	47.06	45.34	43.82	42.48	41.28	40.20	39.24	38.36	37.57	36.85	34.07	32.23	30.95
7000	57.20	54.91	52.90	51.13	49.56	48.16	46.90	45.77	44.76	43.83	42.99	39.75	37.60	36.11
8000	65.37	62.75	60.45	58.43	56.64	55.04	53.60	52.31	51.15	50.09	49.13	45.43	42.97	41.27
9000	73.54	70.59	68.01	65.73	63.71	61.91	60.30	58.85	57.54	56.35	55.27	51.11	48.34	46.42
10000	81.71	78.44	75.57	73.04	70.79	68.79	67.00	65.39	63.93	62.61	61.41	56.78	53.71	51.58
11000	89.88	86.28	83.12	80.34	77.87	75.67	73.70	71.93	70.33	68.87	67.55	62.46	59.08	56.74
12000	98.06	94.12	90.68	87.64	84.95	82.55	80.40	78.47	76.72	75.14	73.70	68.14	64.45	61.90
13000	106.23	101.96	98.23	94.95	92.03	89.43	87.10	85.01	83.11	81.40	79.84	73.82	69.82	67.06
14000	114.40	109.81	105.79	102.25	99.11	96.31	93.80	91.54	89.51	87.66	85.98	79.50	75.19	72.21
15000	122.57	117.65	113.35	109.55	106.19	103.19	100.50	98.08	95.90	93.92	92.12	85.17	80.56	77.37
16000	130.74	125.49	120.90	116.86	113.27	110.07	107.20	104.62	102.29	100.18	98.26	90.85	85.93	82.53
17000	138.91	133.34	128.46	124.16	120.35	116.95	113.90	111.16	108.68	106.44	104.40	96.53	91.30	87.69
18000	147.08	141.18	136.01	131.46	127.42	123.82	120.60	117.70	115.08	112.70	110.54	102.21	96.67	92.84
19000	155.25	149.02	143.57	138.77	134.50	130.70	127.30	124.24	121.47	118.96	116.68	107.88	102.04	98.00
20000	163.42	156.87	151.13	146.07	141.58	137.58	134.00	130.77	127.86	125.22	122.82	113.56	107.41	103.16
21000	171.59	164.71	158.68	153.37	148.66	144.46	140.70	137.31	134.26	131.48	128.96	119.24	112.78	108.32
22000	179.76	172.55	166.24	160.67	155.74	151.34	147.40	143.85	140.65	137.74	135.10	124.92	118.15	113.47
23000	187.93	180.39	173.80	167.98	162.82	158.22	154.10	150.39	147.04	144.01	141.25	130.60	123.52	118.63
24000	196.11	188.24	181.35	175.28	169.90	165.10	160.80	156.93	153.43	150.27	147.39	136.27	128.89	123.79
25000	204.28	196.08	188.91	182.58	176.98	171.98	167.50	163.47	159.83	156.53	153.53	141.95	134.26	128.95
26000	212.45	203.92	196.46	189.89	184.06	178.86	174.20	170.01	166.22	162.79	159.67	147.63	139.63	134.11
27000	220.62	211.77	204.02	197.19	191.13	185.73	180.90	176.54	172.61	169.05	165.81	153.31	145.00	139.26
28000	228.79	219.61	211.58	204.49	198.21	192.61	187.60	183.08	179.01	175.31	171.95	158.99	150.37	144.42
29000	236.96	227.45	219.13	211.80	205.29	199.49	194.30	189.62	185.40	181.57	178.09	164.66	155.74	149.58
30000	245.13	235.30	226.69	219.10	212.37	206.37	201.00	196.16	191.79	187.83	184.23	170.34	161.11	154.74
31000	253.30	243.14	234.24	226.40	219.45	213.25	207.70	202.70	198.18	194.09	190.37	176.02	166.48	159.89
32000	261.47	250.98	241.80	233.71	226.53	220.13	214.40	209.24	204.58	200.35	196.51	181.70	171.85	165.05
33000	269.64	258.83	249.36	241.01	233.61	227.01	221.10	215.78	210.97	206.61	202.65	187.38	177.22	170.21
34000	277.81	266.67	256.91	248.31	240.69	233.89	227.79	222.31	217.36	212.88	208.79	193.05	182.59	175.37
35000	285.98	274.51	264.47	255.62	247.77	240.77	234.49	228.85	223.76	219.14	214.94	198.73	187.96	180.52
36000	294.16	282.35	272.02	262.92	254.84	247.64	241.19	235.39	230.15	225.40	221.08	204.41	193.33	185.68
37000	302.33	290.20	279.58	270.22	261.92	254.52	247.89	241.93	236.54	231.66	227.22	210.09	198.70	190.84
38000	310.50	298.04	287.14	277.53	269.00	261.40	254.59	248.47	242.93	237.92	233.36	215.76	204.07	196.00
39000	318.67	305.88	294.69	284.83	276.08	268.28	261.29	255.01	249.33	244.18	239.50	221.44	209.44	201.16
40000	326.84	313.73	302.25	292.13	283.16	275.16	267.99	261.54	255.72	250.44	245.64	227.12	214.81	206.31
41000	335.01	321.57	309.80	299.43	290.24	282.04	274.69	268.08	262.11	256.70	251.78	232.80	220.18	211.47
42000	343.18	329.41	317.36	306.74	297.32	288.92	281.39	274.62	268.51	262.96	257.92	238.48	225.55	216.63
43000	351.35	337.26	324.92	314.04	304.40	295.80	288.09	281.16	274.90	269.22	264.06	244.15	230.92	221.79
44000	359.52	345.10	332.47	321.34	311.47	302.68	294.79	287.70	281.29	275.48	270.20	249.83	236.29	226.94
45000	367.69	352.94	340.03	328.65	318.55	309.55	301.49	294.24	287.68	281.75	276.34	255.51	241.66	232.10
46000	375.86	360.78	347.59	335.95	325.63	316.43	308.19	300.78	294.08	288.01	282.49	261.19	247.03	237.26
47000	384.03	368.63	355.14	343.25	332.71	323.31	314.89	307.31	300.47	294.27	288.63	266.87	252.40	242.42
48000	392.21	376.47	362.70	350.56	339.79	330.19	321.59	313.85	306.86	300.53	294.77	272.54	257.77	247.57
49000	400.38	384.31	370.25	357.86	346.87	337.07	328.29	320.39	313.26	306.79	300.91	278.22	263.14	252.73
50000	408.55	392.16	377.81	365.16	353.95	343.95	334.99	326.93	319.65	313.05	307.05	283.90	268.51	257.89
55000	449.40	431.37	415.59	401.68	389.34	378.34	368.49	359.62	351.61	344.35	337.75	312.29	295.36	283.68
60000	490.26	470.59	453.37	438.19	424.74	412.74	401.99	392.31	383.58	375.66	368.46	340.68	322.21	309.47
65000	531.11	509.80	491.15	474.71	460.13	447.13	435.49	425.01	415.54	406.96	399.16	369.07	349.07	335.26
70000	571.96	549.02	528.93	511.23	495.53	481.53	468.98	457.70	447.51	438.27	429.87	397.46	375.92	361.04
75000	612.82	588.23	566.71	547.74	530.92	515.92	502.48	490.39	479.47	469.57	460.57	425.85	402.77	386.83
80000	653.67	627.45	604.49	584.26	566.31	550.31	535.98	523.08	511.44	500.88	491.27	454.24	429.62	412.62
85000	694.53	666.66	642.27	620.77	601.71	584.71	569.48	555.78	543.40	532.18	521.98	482.63	456.47	438.41
90000	735.38	705.88	680.05	657.29	637.10	619.10	602.98	588.47	575.36	563.49	552.68	511.02	483.32	464.20
95000	776.23	745.09	717.83	693.81	672.50	653.50	636.48	621.16	607.33	594.79	583.39	539.40	510.17	489.99
100000	817.09	784.31	755.61	730.32	707.89	687.89	669.98	653.85	639.29	626.09	614.09	567.79	537.02	515.78

MONTHLY PAYMENT
REQUIRED TO AMORTIZE A LOAN

TERM AMOUNT	1 Year	2 Years	3 Years	4 Years	5 Years	6 Years	7 Years	8 Years	9 Years	10 Years	11 Years	12 Years	13 Years	14 Years
5	.43	.23	.16	.12	.10	.09	.08	.07	.06	.06	.06	.05	.05	.05
10	.86	.45	.31	.24	.20	.17	.15	.13	.12	.11	.11	.10	.10	.09
15	1.29	.67	.46	.35	.29	.25	.22	.20	.18	.17	.16	.15	.14	.13
25	2.15	1.11	.76	.59	.48	.41	.37	.33	.30	.28	.26	.24	.23	.22
50	4.30	2.21	1.52	1.17	.96	.82	.73	.65	.60	.55	.51	.48	.46	.44
75	6.45	3.32	2.27	1.75	1.44	1.23	1.09	.98	.89	.82	.77	.72	.68	.65
100	8.59	4.42	3.03	2.34	1.92	1.64	1.45	1.30	1.19	1.10	1.02	.96	.91	.87
200	17.18	8.83	6.05	4.67	3.83	3.28	2.89	2.59	2.37	2.19	2.04	1.92	1.81	1.73
300	25.77	13.25	9.08	7.00	5.75	4.92	4.33	3.89	3.55	3.28	3.05	2.87	2.72	2.59
400	34.36	17.66	12.10	9.33	7.66	6.56	5.77	5.18	4.73	4.37	4.07	3.82	3.62	3.45
500	42.95	22.08	15.13	11.66	9.58	8.20	7.21	6.48	5.91	5.46	5.09	4.78	4.52	4.31
600	51.53	26.49	18.15	13.99	11.49	9.84	8.66	7.77	7.09	6.55	6.10	5.74	5.43	5.17
700	60.12	30.90	21.17	16.32	13.41	11.47	10.10	9.07	8.27	7.64	7.12	6.69	6.33	6.03
800	68.71	35.32	24.20	18.65	15.32	13.11	11.54	10.36	9.45	8.73	8.14	7.65	7.24	6.89
900	77.30	39.73	27.22	20.98	17.24	14.75	12.98	11.66	10.63	9.82	9.15	8.60	8.14	7.75
1000	85.89	44.15	30.25	23.31	19.15	16.39	14.42	12.95	11.81	10.91	10.17	9.56	9.04	8.61
2000	171.77	88.29	60.49	46.61	38.30	32.77	28.84	25.90	23.62	21.81	20.33	19.11	18.08	17.21
3000	257.65	132.43	90.73	69.91	57.45	49.16	43.26	38.85	35.43	32.71	30.50	28.66	27.12	25.81
4000	343.54	176.57	120.97	93.21	76.59	65.54	57.68	51.80	47.24	43.61	40.66	38.22	36.16	34.41
5000	429.42	220.71	151.21	116.52	95.74	81.93	72.09	64.74	59.05	54.52	50.83	47.77	45.20	43.01
6000	515.30	264.85	181.45	139.82	114.89	98.31	86.51	77.69	70.86	65.42	60.99	57.32	54.24	51.61
7000	601.18	308.99	211.69	163.12	134.04	114.70	100.93	90.64	82.67	76.32	71.15	66.87	63.27	60.21
8000	687.07	353.13	241.93	186.42	153.18	131.08	115.35	103.59	94.48	87.22	81.32	76.43	72.31	68.81
9000	772.95	397.27	272.17	209.72	172.33	147.47	129.76	116.53	106.29	98.13	91.48	85.98	81.35	77.41
10000	858.83	441.41	302.42	233.03	191.48	163.85	144.18	129.48	118.09	109.03	101.65	95.53	90.39	86.01
11000	944.71	485.55	332.66	256.33	210.63	180.24	158.60	142.43	129.90	119.93	111.81	105.09	99.43	94.61
12000	1030.60	529.69	362.90	279.63	229.77	196.62	173.02	155.38	141.71	130.83	121.98	114.64	108.47	103.21
13000	1116.48	573.83	393.14	302.93	248.92	213.01	187.43	168.32	153.52	141.73	132.14	124.19	117.51	111.81
14000	1202.36	617.97	423.38	326.23	268.07	229.39	201.85	181.27	165.33	152.64	142.30	133.74	126.54	120.42
15000	1288.25	662.11	453.62	349.54	287.22	245.78	216.27	194.22	177.14	163.54	152.47	143.30	135.58	129.02
16000	1374.13	706.25	483.86	372.84	306.36	262.16	230.69	207.17	188.95	174.44	162.63	152.85	144.62	137.62
17000	1460.01	750.40	514.10	396.14	325.51	278.55	245.10	220.11	200.76	185.34	172.80	162.40	153.66	146.22
18000	1545.89	794.54	544.34	419.44	344.66	294.93	259.52	233.06	212.57	196.25	182.96	171.95	162.70	154.82
19000	1631.78	838.68	574.58	442.74	363.80	311.31	273.94	246.01	224.37	207.15	193.13	181.51	171.74	163.42
20000	1717.66	882.82	604.83	466.05	382.95	327.70	288.36	258.96	236.18	218.05	203.29	191.06	180.78	172.02
21000	1803.54	926.96	635.07	489.35	402.10	344.08	302.77	271.90	247.99	228.95	213.45	200.61	189.81	180.62
22000	1889.42	971.10	665.31	512.65	421.25	360.47	317.19	284.85	259.80	239.85	223.62	210.17	198.85	189.22
23000	1975.31	1015.24	695.55	535.95	440.39	376.85	331.61	297.80	271.61	250.76	233.78	219.72	207.89	197.82
24000	2061.19	1059.38	725.79	559.25	459.54	393.24	346.03	310.75	283.42	261.66	243.95	229.27	216.93	206.42
25000	2147.07	1103.52	756.03	582.56	478.69	409.62	360.44	323.69	295.23	272.56	254.11	238.82	225.97	215.02
26000	2232.95	1147.66	786.27	605.86	497.84	426.01	374.86	336.64	307.04	283.46	264.28	248.38	235.01	223.62
27000	2318.84	1191.80	816.51	629.16	516.98	442.39	389.28	349.59	318.85	294.37	274.44	257.93	244.05	232.22
28000	2404.72	1235.94	846.75	652.46	536.13	458.78	403.70	362.54	330.65	305.27	284.60	267.48	253.08	240.83
29000	2490.60	1280.08	876.99	675.77	555.28	475.16	418.11	375.48	342.46	316.17	294.77	277.04	262.12	249.43
30000	2576.49	1324.22	907.24	699.07	574.43	491.55	432.53	388.43	354.27	327.07	304.93	286.59	271.16	258.03
31000	2662.37	1368.36	937.48	722.37	593.57	507.93	446.95	401.38	366.08	337.97	315.10	296.14	280.20	266.63
32000	2748.25	1412.50	967.72	745.67	612.72	524.32	461.37	414.33	377.89	348.88	325.26	305.69	289.24	275.23
33000	2834.13	1456.64	997.96	768.97	631.87	540.70	475.78	427.27	389.70	359.78	335.43	315.25	298.28	283.83
34000	2920.02	1500.79	1028.20	792.28	651.02	557.09	490.20	440.22	401.51	370.68	345.59	324.80	307.32	292.43
35000	3005.90	1544.93	1058.44	815.58	670.16	573.47	504.62	453.17	413.32	381.58	355.75	334.35	316.35	301.03
36000	3091.78	1589.07	1088.68	838.88	689.31	589.86	519.04	466.12	425.13	392.49	365.92	343.90	325.39	309.63
37000	3177.66	1633.21	1118.92	862.18	708.46	606.24	533.45	479.06	436.93	403.39	376.08	353.46	334.43	318.23
38000	3263.55	1677.35	1149.16	885.48	727.60	622.62	547.87	492.01	448.74	414.29	386.25	363.01	343.47	326.83
39000	3349.43	1721.49	1179.41	908.79	746.75	639.01	562.29	504.96	460.55	425.19	396.41	372.56	352.51	335.43
40000	3435.31	1765.63	1209.65	932.09	765.90	655.39	576.71	517.91	472.36	436.09	406.58	382.12	361.55	344.03
41000	3521.20	1809.77	1239.89	955.39	785.05	671.77	591.12	530.85	484.17	447.00	416.74	391.67	370.58	352.63
42000	3607.08	1853.91	1270.13	978.69	804.19	688.16	605.54	543.80	495.98	457.90	426.90	401.22	379.62	361.24
43000	3692.96	1898.05	1300.37	1001.99	823.34	704.55	619.96	556.75	507.79	468.80	437.07	410.77	388.66	369.84
44000	3778.84	1942.19	1330.61	1025.30	842.49	720.93	634.38	569.70	519.60	479.70	447.23	420.33	397.70	378.44
45000	3864.73	1986.33	1360.85	1048.60	861.64	737.32	648.79	582.64	531.41	490.61	457.40	429.88	406.74	387.04
46000	3950.61	2030.47	1391.09	1071.90	880.78	753.70	663.21	595.59	543.21	501.51	467.56	439.43	415.78	395.64
47000	4036.49	2074.61	1421.33	1095.20	899.93	770.09	677.63	608.54	555.02	512.41	477.73	448.98	424.82	404.24
48000	4122.37	2118.75	1451.57	1118.50	919.08	786.47	692.05	621.49	566.83	523.31	487.89	458.54	433.85	412.84
49000	4208.26	2162.89	1481.82	1141.81	938.23	802.86	706.47	634.43	578.64	534.22	498.05	468.09	442.89	421.44
50000	4294.14	2207.03	1512.06	1165.11	957.37	819.24	720.88	647.38	590.45	545.12	508.22	477.64	451.93	430.04
55000	4723.55	2427.74	1663.26	1281.62	1053.11	901.16	792.97	712.12	649.49	599.63	559.04	525.41	497.12	473.04
60000	5152.97	2648.44	1814.47	1398.13	1148.85	983.09	865.06	776.86	708.54	654.14	609.86	573.17	542.32	516.05
65000	5582.38	2869.14	1965.67	1514.64	1244.58	1065.01	937.15	841.59	767.58	708.65	660.68	620.93	587.51	559.05
70000	6011.79	3089.85	2116.88	1631.15	1340.32	1146.94	1009.23	906.33	826.63	763.16	711.50	668.70	632.70	602.06
75000	6441.21	3310.55	2268.08	1747.66	1436.06	1228.86	1081.32	971.07	885.67	817.67	762.32	716.46	677.90	645.06
80000	6870.62	3531.25	2419.29	1864.17	1531.79	1310.78	1153.41	1035.81	944.72	872.18	813.15	764.23	723.09	688.06
85000	7300.03	3751.96	2570.49	1980.68	1627.53	1392.71	1225.50	1100.54	1003.76	926.70	863.97	811.99	768.28	731.07
90000	7729.45	3972.66	2721.70	2097.19	1723.27	1474.63	1297.58	1165.28	1062.81	981.21	914.79	859.75	813.47	774.07
95000	8158.86	4193.36	2872.90	2213.70	1819.00	1556.55	1369.67	1230.02	1121.85	1035.72	965.61	907.52	858.67	817.07
100000	8588.27	4414.06	3024.11	2330.21	1914.74	1638.48	1441.76	1294.76	1180.90	1090.23	1016.43	955.28	903.86	860.08

TERM	15 Years	16 Years	17 Years	18 Years	19 Years	20 Years	21 Years	22 Years	23 Years	24 Years	25 Years	30 Years	35 Years	40 Years
AMOUNT														
5	.05	.04	.04	.04	.04	.04	.04	.04	.04	.04	.04	.03	.03	.03
10	.09	.08	.08	.08	.08	.07	.07	.07	.07	.07	.07	.06	.06	.06
15	.13	.12	.12	.12	.11	.11	.11	.10	.10	.10	.10	.09	.09	.08
25	.21	.20	.20	.19	.18	.18	.17	.17	.17	.16	.16	.15	.14	.14
50	.42	.40	.39	.37	.36	.35	.34	.33	.33	.32	.32	.29	.28	.27
75	.62	.60	.58	.56	.54	.53	.51	.50	.49	.48	.47	.44	.41	.40
100	.83	.79	.77	.74	.72	.70	.68	.66	.65	.64	.63	.58	.55	.53
200	1.65	1.58	1.53	1.48	1.43	1.39	1.36	1.32	1.30	1.27	1.25	1.15	1.09	1.05
300	2.47	2.37	2.29	2.21	2.15	2.09	2.03	1.98	1.94	1.90	1.87	1.73	1.64	1.57
400	3.29	3.16	3.05	2.95	2.86	2.78	2.71	2.64	2.59	2.53	2.49	2.30	2.18	2.10
500	4.12	3.95	3.81	3.68	3.57	3.47	3.38	3.30	3.23	3.17	3.11	2.88	2.72	2.62
600	4.94	4.74	4.57	4.42	4.29	4.17	4.06	3.96	3.88	3.80	3.73	3.45	3.27	3.14
700	5.76	5.53	5.33	5.16	5.00	4.86	4.73	4.62	4.52	4.43	4.35	4.02	3.81	3.66
800	6.58	6.32	6.09	5.89	5.71	5.55	5.41	5.28	5.17	5.06	4.97	4.60	4.35	4.19
900	7.41	7.11	6.85	6.63	6.43	6.25	6.09	5.94	5.81	5.69	5.59	5.17	4.90	4.71
1000	8.23	7.90	7.62	7.36	7.14	6.94	6.76	6.60	6.46	6.33	6.21	5.75	5.44	5.23
2000	16.45	15.80	15.23	14.72	14.27	13.88	13.52	13.20	12.91	12.65	12.41	11.49	10.88	10.46
3000	24.68	23.70	22.84	22.08	21.41	20.81	20.28	19.79	19.36	18.97	18.61	17.23	16.31	15.68
4000	32.90	31.59	30.45	29.44	28.54	27.75	27.03	26.39	25.81	25.29	24.81	22.97	21.75	20.91
5000	41.12	39.49	38.06	36.80	35.68	34.68	33.79	32.99	32.26	31.61	31.01	28.71	27.18	26.13
6000	49.35	47.39	45.67	44.16	42.81	41.62	40.55	39.58	38.71	37.93	37.21	34.45	32.62	31.36
7000	57.57	55.28	53.28	51.51	49.95	48.55	47.30	46.18	45.17	44.25	43.41	40.19	38.06	36.59
8000	65.80	63.18	60.89	58.87	57.08	55.49	54.06	52.78	51.62	50.57	49.61	45.93	43.49	41.81
9000	74.02	71.08	68.50	66.23	64.22	62.42	60.82	59.37	58.07	56.89	55.81	51.67	48.93	47.04
10000	82.24	78.97	76.11	73.59	71.35	69.36	67.57	65.97	64.52	63.21	62.01	57.41	54.36	52.26
11000	90.47	86.87	83.72	80.95	78.49	76.30	74.33	72.57	70.97	69.53	68.21	63.15	59.80	57.49
12000	98.69	94.77	91.33	88.31	85.62	83.23	81.09	79.16	77.42	75.85	74.41	68.89	65.24	62.72
13000	106.92	102.66	98.94	95.66	92.76	90.17	87.85	85.76	83.87	82.17	80.61	74.64	70.67	67.94
14000	115.14	110.56	106.55	103.02	99.89	97.10	94.60	92.35	90.33	88.49	86.82	80.38	76.11	73.17
15000	123.36	118.46	114.16	110.38	107.03	104.04	101.36	98.95	96.78	94.81	93.02	86.12	81.54	78.39
16000	131.59	126.36	121.78	117.74	114.16	110.97	108.12	105.55	103.23	101.13	99.22	91.86	86.98	83.62
17000	139.81	134.25	129.39	125.10	121.30	117.91	114.87	112.14	109.68	107.45	105.42	97.60	92.41	88.85
18000	148.04	142.15	137.00	132.46	128.43	124.84	121.63	118.74	116.13	113.77	111.62	103.34	97.85	94.07
19000	156.26	150.05	144.61	139.81	135.57	131.78	128.39	125.34	122.58	120.09	117.82	109.08	103.29	99.30
20000	164.48	157.94	152.22	147.17	142.70	138.71	135.14	131.93	129.03	126.41	124.02	114.82	108.72	104.52
21000	172.71	165.84	159.83	154.53	149.84	145.65	141.90	138.53	135.49	132.73	130.22	120.56	114.16	109.75
22000	180.93	173.74	167.44	161.89	156.97	152.59	148.66	145.13	141.94	139.05	136.42	126.30	119.59	114.98
23000	189.16	181.63	175.05	169.25	164.11	159.52	155.42	151.72	148.39	145.37	142.62	132.04	125.03	120.20
24000	197.38	189.53	182.66	176.61	171.24	166.46	162.17	158.32	154.84	151.69	148.82	137.78	130.47	125.43
25000	205.60	197.43	190.27	183.97	178.37	173.39	168.93	164.92	161.29	158.01	155.02	143.52	135.90	130.65
26000	213.83	205.32	197.88	191.32	185.51	180.33	175.69	171.51	167.74	164.33	161.22	149.27	141.34	135.88
27000	222.05	213.22	205.49	198.68	192.64	187.26	182.44	178.11	174.19	170.65	167.42	155.01	146.77	141.10
28000	230.28	221.12	213.10	206.04	199.78	194.20	189.20	184.70	180.65	176.97	173.63	160.75	152.21	146.33
29000	238.50	229.02	220.71	213.40	206.91	201.13	195.96	191.30	187.10	183.29	179.83	166.49	157.64	151.56
30000	246.72	236.91	228.32	220.76	214.05	208.07	202.71	197.90	193.55	189.61	186.03	172.23	163.08	156.78
31000	254.95	244.81	235.94	228.12	221.18	215.00	209.47	204.49	200.00	195.93	192.23	177.97	168.52	162.01
32000	263.17	252.71	243.55	235.47	228.32	221.94	216.23	211.09	206.45	202.25	198.43	183.71	173.95	167.23
33000	271.40	260.60	251.16	242.83	235.45	228.88	222.99	217.69	212.90	208.57	204.63	189.45	179.39	172.46
34000	279.62	268.50	258.77	250.19	242.59	235.81	229.74	224.28	219.35	214.89	210.83	195.19	184.82	177.69
35000	287.84	276.40	266.38	257.55	249.72	242.75	236.50	230.88	225.81	221.21	217.03	200.93	190.26	182.91
36000	296.07	284.29	273.99	264.91	256.86	249.68	243.26	237.48	232.26	227.53	223.23	206.67	195.70	188.14
37000	304.29	292.19	281.60	272.27	263.99	256.62	250.01	244.07	238.71	233.85	229.43	212.41	201.13	193.36
38000	312.52	300.09	289.21	279.62	271.13	263.55	256.77	250.67	245.16	240.17	235.63	218.16	206.57	198.59
39000	320.74	307.98	296.82	286.98	278.26	270.49	263.53	257.27	251.61	246.49	241.83	223.90	212.00	203.82
40000	328.96	315.88	304.43	294.34	285.40	277.42	270.28	263.86	258.06	252.81	248.03	229.64	217.44	209.04
41000	337.19	323.78	312.04	301.70	292.53	284.36	277.04	270.46	264.51	259.13	254.24	235.38	222.87	214.27
42000	345.41	331.67	319.65	309.06	299.67	291.29	283.80	277.05	270.97	265.45	260.44	241.12	228.31	219.49
43000	353.64	339.57	327.26	316.42	306.80	298.23	290.55	283.65	277.42	271.77	266.64	246.86	233.75	224.72
44000	361.86	347.47	334.87	323.77	313.94	305.17	297.31	290.25	283.87	278.09	272.84	252.60	239.18	229.95
45000	370.08	355.37	342.48	331.13	321.07	312.10	304.07	296.84	290.32	284.41	279.04	258.34	244.62	235.17
46000	378.31	363.26	350.09	338.49	328.21	319.04	310.83	303.44	296.77	290.73	285.24	264.08	250.05	240.40
47000	386.53	371.16	357.71	345.85	335.34	325.97	317.58	310.04	303.22	297.05	291.44	269.82	255.49	245.62
48000	394.76	379.06	365.32	353.21	342.47	332.91	324.34	316.63	309.68	303.37	297.64	275.56	260.93	250.85
49000	402.98	386.95	372.93	360.57	349.61	339.84	331.10	323.23	316.13	309.69	303.84	281.30	266.36	256.07
50000	411.20	394.85	380.54	367.93	356.74	346.78	337.85	329.83	322.58	316.01	310.04	287.04	271.80	261.30
55000	452.32	434.33	418.59	404.72	392.42	381.46	371.64	362.81	354.84	347.61	341.05	315.75	298.98	287.43
60000	493.44	473.82	456.64	441.51	428.09	416.13	405.42	395.79	387.09	379.21	372.05	344.45	326.16	313.56
65000	534.56	513.30	494.70	478.30	463.77	450.81	439.21	428.77	419.35	410.81	403.05	373.16	353.34	339.69
70000	575.68	552.79	532.75	515.09	499.44	485.49	472.99	461.75	451.61	442.41	434.06	401.86	380.51	365.82
75000	616.80	592.27	570.80	551.89	535.11	520.17	506.78	494.74	483.86	474.01	465.06	430.56	407.69	391.95
80000	657.92	631.76	608.86	588.68	570.79	554.84	540.56	527.72	516.12	505.61	496.06	459.27	434.87	418.08
85000	699.04	671.24	646.91	625.47	606.46	589.52	574.35	560.70	548.38	537.21	527.07	487.97	462.05	444.21
90000	740.16	710.73	684.96	662.26	642.14	624.20	608.13	593.68	580.64	568.82	558.07	516.68	489.23	470.34
95000	781.28	750.21	723.02	699.05	677.81	658.88	641.92	626.67	612.89	600.42	589.08	545.38	516.41	496.47
100000	822.40	789.70	761.07	735.85	713.48	693.55	675.70	659.65	645.15	632.02	620.08	574.08	543.59	522.60

MONTHLY PAYMENT
REQUIRED TO AMORTIZE A LOAN

TERM / AMOUNT	1 Year	2 Years	3 Years	4 Years	5 Years	6 Years	7 Years	8 Years	9 Years	10 Years	11 Years	12 Years	13 Years	14 Years
5	.43	.23	.16	.12	.10	.09	.08	.07	.06	.06	.06	.05	.05	.05
10	.86	.45	.31	.24	.20	.17	.15	.13	.12	.11	.11	.10	.10	.09
15	1.29	.67	.46	.35	.29	.25	.22	.20	.18	.17	.16	.15	.14	.13
25	2.15	1.11	.76	.59	.48	.41	.37	.33	.30	.28	.26	.24	.23	.22
50	4.30	2.21	1.52	1.17	.96	.82	.73	.65	.60	.55	.51	.48	.46	.44
75	6.45	3.32	2.27	1.75	1.44	1.23	1.09	.98	.89	.82	.77	.72	.68	.65
100	8.59	4.42	3.03	2.34	1.92	1.64	1.45	1.30	1.19	1.10	1.02	.96	.91	.87
200	17.18	8.84	6.06	4.67	3.84	3.28	2.89	2.60	2.37	2.19	2.04	1.92	1.82	1.73
300	25.77	13.25	9.08	7.00	5.75	4.92	4.33	3.89	3.55	3.28	3.06	2.87	2.72	2.59
400	34.36	17.67	12.11	9.33	7.67	6.56	5.78	5.19	4.73	4.37	4.08	3.83	3.63	3.45
500	42.95	22.08	15.13	11.66	9.58	8.20	7.22	6.48	5.92	5.46	5.09	4.79	4.53	4.31
600	51.54	26.50	18.16	13.99	11.50	9.84	8.66	7.78	7.10	6.55	6.11	5.74	5.44	5.17
700	60.13	30.91	21.18	16.32	13.42	11.48	10.11	9.08	8.28	7.65	7.13	6.70	6.34	6.03
800	68.72	35.33	24.21	18.66	15.33	13.12	11.55	10.37	9.46	8.74	8.15	7.66	7.25	6.90
900	77.31	39.74	27.23	20.99	17.25	14.76	12.99	11.67	10.64	9.83	9.16	8.61	8.15	7.76
1000	85.90	44.16	30.26	23.32	19.16	16.40	14.43	12.96	11.83	10.92	10.18	9.57	9.06	8.62
2000	171.79	88.31	60.51	46.63	38.32	32.80	28.86	25.92	23.65	21.83	20.36	19.14	18.11	17.23
3000	257.69	132.46	90.76	69.95	57.48	49.19	43.29	38.88	35.47	32.75	30.54	28.70	27.16	25.85
4000	343.58	176.61	121.01	93.26	76.64	65.59	57.72	51.84	47.29	43.66	40.71	38.27	36.21	34.46
5000	429.48	220.76	151.27	116.57	95.80	81.99	72.15	64.80	59.11	54.58	50.89	47.83	45.26	43.07
6000	515.37	264.92	181.52	139.89	114.96	98.38	86.58	77.76	70.93	65.49	61.07	57.40	54.31	51.69
7000	601.26	309.07	211.77	163.20	134.12	114.78	101.01	90.72	82.75	76.41	71.24	66.96	63.37	60.30
8000	687.16	353.22	242.02	186.51	153.28	131.18	115.44	103.68	94.57	87.32	81.42	76.53	72.42	68.92
9000	773.05	397.37	272.28	209.83	172.44	147.57	129.87	116.64	106.40	98.24	91.60	86.09	81.47	77.53
10000	858.95	441.52	302.53	233.14	191.59	163.97	144.30	129.60	118.22	109.15	101.77	95.66	90.52	86.14
11000	944.84	485.68	332.78	256.45	210.75	180.37	158.73	142.56	130.04	120.07	111.95	105.23	99.57	94.76
12000	1030.74	529.83	363.03	279.77	229.91	196.76	173.16	155.52	141.86	130.98	122.13	114.79	108.62	103.37
13000	1116.63	573.98	393.29	303.08	249.07	213.16	187.59	168.48	153.68	141.90	132.30	124.36	117.67	111.99
14000	1202.52	618.13	423.54	326.39	268.23	229.56	202.02	181.44	165.50	152.81	142.48	133.92	126.73	120.60
15000	1288.42	662.28	453.79	349.71	287.39	245.95	216.45	194.40	177.32	163.73	152.66	143.49	135.78	129.21
16000	1374.31	706.43	484.04	373.02	306.55	262.35	230.88	207.36	189.14	174.64	162.83	153.05	144.83	137.83
17000	1460.21	750.59	514.29	396.33	325.71	278.74	245.31	220.32	200.96	185.55	173.01	162.62	153.88	146.44
18000	1546.10	794.74	544.55	419.65	344.87	295.14	259.74	233.28	212.79	196.47	183.19	172.18	162.93	155.05
19000	1631.99	838.89	574.80	442.96	364.02	311.54	274.16	246.24	224.61	207.38	193.37	181.75	171.98	163.67
20000	1717.89	883.04	605.05	466.27	383.18	327.93	288.59	259.20	236.43	218.30	203.54	191.32	181.03	172.28
21000	1803.78	927.19	635.30	489.59	402.34	344.33	303.02	272.16	248.25	229.21	213.72	200.88	190.09	180.90
22000	1889.68	971.35	665.56	512.90	421.50	360.73	317.45	285.12	260.07	240.13	223.90	210.45	199.14	189.51
23000	1975.57	1015.50	695.81	536.22	440.66	377.12	331.88	298.08	271.89	251.04	234.07	220.01	208.19	198.12
24000	2061.46	1059.65	726.06	559.53	459.82	393.52	346.31	311.04	283.71	261.96	244.25	229.58	217.24	206.74
25000	2147.36	1103.80	756.31	582.84	478.98	409.92	360.74	323.99	295.53	272.87	254.43	239.14	226.29	215.35
26000	2233.25	1147.95	786.57	606.16	498.14	426.31	375.17	336.95	307.35	283.79	264.60	248.71	235.34	223.97
27000	2319.15	1192.10	816.82	629.47	517.30	442.71	389.60	349.91	319.18	294.70	274.78	258.27	244.40	232.58
28000	2405.04	1236.26	847.07	652.78	536.45	459.11	404.03	362.87	331.00	305.62	284.96	267.84	253.45	241.19
29000	2490.94	1280.41	877.32	676.10	555.61	475.50	418.46	375.83	342.82	316.53	295.13	277.41	262.50	249.81
30000	2576.83	1324.56	907.57	699.41	574.77	491.90	432.89	388.79	354.64	327.45	305.31	286.97	271.55	258.42
31000	2662.72	1368.71	937.83	722.72	593.93	508.29	447.32	401.75	366.46	338.36	315.49	296.54	280.60	267.03
32000	2748.62	1412.86	968.08	746.04	613.09	524.69	461.75	414.71	378.28	349.27	325.66	306.10	289.65	275.65
33000	2834.51	1457.02	998.33	769.35	632.25	541.09	476.18	427.67	390.10	360.19	335.84	315.67	298.70	284.26
34000	2920.41	1501.17	1028.58	792.66	651.41	557.48	490.61	440.63	401.92	371.10	346.02	325.23	307.76	292.88
35000	3006.30	1545.32	1058.84	815.98	670.57	573.88	505.04	453.59	413.75	382.02	356.20	334.80	316.81	301.49
36000	3092.19	1589.47	1089.09	839.29	689.73	590.28	519.47	466.55	425.57	392.93	366.37	344.36	325.86	310.10
37000	3178.09	1633.62	1119.34	862.60	708.88	606.67	533.89	479.51	437.39	403.85	376.55	353.93	334.91	318.72
38000	3263.98	1677.77	1149.59	885.92	728.04	623.07	548.32	492.47	449.21	414.76	386.73	363.50	343.96	327.33
39000	3349.88	1721.93	1179.85	909.23	747.20	639.47	562.75	505.43	461.03	425.68	396.90	373.06	353.01	335.95
40000	3435.77	1766.08	1210.10	932.54	766.36	655.86	577.18	518.39	472.85	436.59	407.08	382.63	362.06	344.56
41000	3521.67	1810.23	1240.35	955.86	785.52	672.26	591.61	531.35	484.67	447.51	417.26	392.19	371.12	353.17
42000	3607.56	1854.38	1270.60	979.17	804.68	688.66	606.04	544.31	496.49	458.42	427.43	401.76	380.17	361.79
43000	3693.45	1898.53	1300.85	1002.48	823.84	705.05	620.47	557.27	508.31	469.34	437.61	411.32	389.22	370.40
44000	3779.35	1942.69	1331.11	1025.80	843.00	721.45	634.90	570.23	520.14	480.25	447.79	420.89	398.27	379.01
45000	3865.24	1986.84	1361.36	1049.11	862.16	737.85	649.33	583.19	531.96	491.17	457.96	430.45	407.32	387.63
46000	3951.14	2030.99	1391.61	1072.43	881.31	754.24	663.76	596.15	543.78	502.08	468.14	440.02	416.37	396.24
47000	4037.03	2075.14	1421.86	1095.74	900.47	770.64	678.19	609.11	555.60	512.99	478.32	449.59	425.43	404.86
48000	4122.92	2119.29	1452.12	1119.05	919.63	787.03	692.62	622.07	567.42	523.91	488.49	459.15	434.48	413.47
49000	4208.82	2163.44	1482.37	1142.37	938.79	803.43	707.05	635.03	579.24	534.82	498.67	468.72	443.53	422.08
50000	4294.71	2207.60	1512.62	1165.68	957.95	819.83	721.48	647.98	591.06	545.74	508.85	478.28	452.58	430.70
55000	4724.18	2428.36	1663.88	1282.25	1053.75	901.81	793.62	712.78	650.17	600.31	559.73	526.11	497.84	473.77
60000	5153.65	2649.11	1815.14	1398.81	1149.54	983.79	865.77	777.58	709.27	654.89	610.62	573.94	543.09	516.84
65000	5583.13	2869.87	1966.41	1515.38	1245.33	1065.77	937.92	842.38	768.38	709.46	661.50	621.77	588.35	559.91
70000	6012.60	3090.63	2117.67	1631.95	1341.13	1147.76	1010.07	907.18	827.49	764.03	712.39	669.59	633.61	602.98
75000	6442.07	3311.39	2268.93	1748.52	1436.92	1229.74	1082.21	971.97	886.59	818.61	763.27	717.42	678.87	646.06
80000	6871.54	3532.15	2420.19	1865.08	1532.72	1311.72	1154.36	1036.77	945.70	873.18	814.15	765.25	724.12	689.11
85000	7301.01	3752.91	2571.45	1981.65	1628.51	1393.70	1226.51	1101.57	1004.80	927.75	865.04	813.08	769.38	732.18
90000	7730.48	3973.67	2722.71	2098.22	1724.31	1475.69	1298.66	1166.37	1063.91	982.33	915.92	860.90	814.64	775.25
95000	8159.95	4194.43	2873.97	2214.79	1820.10	1557.67	1370.80	1231.17	1123.01	1036.90	966.81	908.73	859.90	818.32
100000	8589.42	4415.19	3025.24	2331.35	1915.90	1639.65	1442.95	1295.96	1182.12	1091.47	1017.69	956.56	905.15	861.39

MONTHLY PAYMENT
REQUIRED TO AMORTIZE A LOAN

5.625%

TERM	15 Years	16 Years	17 Years	18 Years	19 Years	20 Years	21 Years	22 Years	23 Years	24 Years	25 Years	30 Years	35 Years	40 Years
AMOUNT														
5	.05	.04	.04	.04	.04	.04	.04	.04	.04	.04	.04	.03	.03	.03
10	.09	.08	.08	.08	.08	.07	.07	.07	.07	.07	.07	.06	.06	.06
15	.13	.12	.12	.12	.11	.11	.11	.10	.10	.10	.10	.09	.09	.08
25	.21	.20	.20	.19	.18	.18	.17	.17	.17	.16	.16	.15	.14	.14
50	.42	.40	.39	.37	.36	.35	.34	.34	.33	.32	.32	.29	.28	.27
75	.62	.60	.58	.56	.54	.53	.51	.50	.49	.48	.47	.44	.41	.40
100	.83	.80	.77	.74	.72	.70	.68	.67	.65	.64	.63	.58	.55	.53
200	1.65	1.59	1.53	1.48	1.43	1.39	1.36	1.33	1.30	1.27	1.25	1.16	1.10	1.05
300	2.48	2.38	2.29	2.22	2.15	2.09	2.04	1.99	1.94	1.91	1.87	1.73	1.64	1.58
400	3.30	3.17	3.05	2.95	2.86	2.78	2.71	2.65	2.59	2.54	2.49	2.31	2.19	2.10
500	4.12	3.96	3.82	3.69	3.58	3.48	3.39	3.31	3.24	3.17	3.11	2.88	2.73	2.63
600	4.95	4.75	4.58	4.43	4.29	4.17	4.07	3.97	3.88	3.81	3.73	3.46	3.28	3.15
700	5.77	5.54	5.34	5.17	5.01	4.87	4.74	4.63	4.53	4.44	4.36	4.03	3.82	3.68
800	6.59	6.33	6.10	5.90	5.72	5.56	5.42	5.29	5.18	5.07	4.98	4.61	4.37	4.20
900	7.42	7.12	6.87	6.64	6.44	6.26	6.10	5.95	5.82	5.71	5.60	5.19	4.91	4.72
1000	8.24	7.92	7.63	7.38	7.15	6.95	6.78	6.62	6.47	6.34	6.22	5.76	5.46	5.25
2000	16.48	15.83	15.25	14.75	14.30	13.90	13.55	13.23	12.94	12.67	12.44	11.52	10.91	10.49
3000	24.72	23.74	22.88	22.12	21.45	20.85	20.32	19.84	19.40	19.01	18.65	17.27	16.36	15.73
4000	32.95	31.65	30.50	29.49	28.60	27.80	27.09	26.45	25.87	25.34	24.87	23.03	21.81	20.98
5000	41.19	39.56	38.13	36.87	35.75	34.75	33.86	33.06	32.34	31.68	31.08	28.79	27.27	26.22
6000	49.43	47.47	45.75	44.24	42.90	41.70	40.63	39.67	38.80	38.01	37.30	34.54	32.72	31.46
7000	57.67	55.38	53.38	51.61	50.05	48.65	47.40	46.28	45.27	44.35	43.52	40.30	38.17	36.71
8000	65.90	63.29	61.00	58.98	57.20	55.60	54.18	52.89	51.73	50.68	49.73	46.06	43.62	41.95
9000	74.14	71.20	68.62	66.36	64.34	62.55	60.95	59.50	58.20	57.02	55.95	51.81	49.08	47.19
10000	82.38	79.11	76.25	73.73	71.49	69.50	67.72	66.11	64.67	63.35	62.16	57.57	54.53	52.44
11000	90.62	87.02	83.87	81.10	78.64	76.45	74.49	72.73	71.13	69.69	68.38	63.33	59.98	57.68
12000	98.85	94.93	91.50	88.47	85.79	83.40	81.26	79.34	77.60	76.02	74.59	69.08	65.43	62.92
13000	107.09	102.84	99.12	95.84	92.94	90.35	88.03	85.95	86.06	82.36	80.81	74.84	70.09	68.16
14000	115.33	110.75	106.75	103.22	100.09	97.30	94.80	92.56	90.53	88.69	87.03	80.60	76.34	73.41
15000	123.56	118.66	114.37	110.59	107.24	104.25	101.57	99.17	97.00	95.03	93.24	86.35	81.79	78.65
16000	131.80	126.57	121.99	117.96	114.39	111.20	108.35	105.78	103.46	101.36	99.46	92.11	87.24	83.89
17000	140.04	134.48	129.62	125.33	121.53	118.15	115.12	112.39	109.93	107.70	105.67	97.87	92.69	89.14
18000	148.28	142.39	137.24	132.71	128.66	125.10	121.89	119.00	116.40	114.03	111.89	103.62	98.15	94.38
19000	156.51	150.30	144.87	140.08	135.83	132.05	128.66	125.61	122.86	120.37	118.10	109.38	103.60	99.62
20000	164.75	158.21	152.49	147.45	142.98	139.00	135.43	132.22	129.33	126.70	124.32	115.14	109.05	104.87
21000	172.99	166.12	160.12	154.82	150.13	145.95	142.20	138.83	135.79	133.04	130.54	120.89	114.50	110.11
22000	181.23	174.03	167.74	162.19	157.28	152.90	148.97	145.45	142.26	139.37	136.75	126.65	119.96	115.35
23000	189.46	181.94	175.36	169.57	164.43	159.85	155.75	152.06	148.73	145.71	142.97	132.41	125.41	120.59
24000	197.70	189.85	182.99	176.94	171.58	166.80	162.52	158.67	155.19	152.04	149.18	138.16	130.86	125.84
25000	205.94	197.76	190.61	184.31	178.73	173.75	169.29	165.28	161.66	158.38	155.40	143.92	136.31	131.08
26000	214.18	205.68	198.24	191.68	185.87	180.70	176.06	171.89	168.12	164.71	161.61	149.68	141.77	136.32
27000	222.41	213.59	205.86	199.06	193.02	187.65	182.83	178.50	174.59	171.05	167.83	155.43	147.22	141.57
28000	230.65	221.50	213.49	206.43	200.17	194.60	189.60	185.11	181.06	177.38	174.05	161.19	152.67	146.81
29000	238.89	229.41	221.11	213.80	207.32	201.55	196.37	191.72	187.52	183.72	180.26	166.95	158.12	152.05
30000	247.12	237.32	228.73	221.17	214.47	208.49	203.14	198.33	193.99	190.05	186.48	172.70	163.57	157.30
31000	255.36	245.23	236.36	228.54	221.62	215.44	209.92	204.94	200.46	196.39	192.69	178.46	169.03	162.54
32000	263.60	253.14	243.98	235.92	228.77	222.39	216.69	211.56	206.92	202.72	198.91	184.22	174.48	167.78
33000	271.84	261.05	251.61	243.29	235.92	229.34	223.46	218.17	213.39	209.06	205.12	189.97	179.93	173.02
34000	280.07	268.96	259.23	250.66	243.06	236.29	230.23	224.78	219.85	215.39	211.34	195.73	185.38	178.27
35000	288.31	276.87	266.86	258.03	250.21	243.24	237.00	231.39	226.32	221.73	217.56	201.48	190.84	183.51
36000	296.55	284.78	274.48	265.41	257.36	250.19	243.77	238.00	232.79	228.06	223.77	207.24	196.29	188.75
37000	304.79	292.69	282.10	272.78	264.51	257.14	250.54	244.61	239.25	234.40	229.99	213.00	201.74	194.00
38000	313.02	300.60	289.73	280.15	271.66	264.09	257.32	251.22	245.72	240.73	236.20	218.75	207.19	199.24
39000	321.26	308.51	297.35	287.52	278.81	271.04	264.09	257.83	252.18	247.07	242.42	224.51	212.65	204.48
40000	329.50	316.42	304.98	294.90	285.96	277.99	270.86	264.44	258.65	253.40	248.63	230.27	218.10	209.73
41000	337.74	324.33	312.60	302.27	293.11	284.94	277.63	271.05	265.12	259.74	254.85	236.02	223.55	214.97
42000	345.97	332.24	320.23	309.64	300.25	291.89	284.40	277.66	271.58	266.07	261.07	241.78	229.00	220.21
43000	354.21	340.15	327.85	317.01	307.40	298.84	291.17	284.28	278.05	272.41	267.28	247.54	234.45	225.46
44000	362.45	348.06	335.48	324.38	314.55	305.79	297.94	290.89	284.52	278.74	273.50	253.29	239.91	230.70
45000	370.68	355.97	343.10	331.76	321.70	312.74	304.71	297.50	290.98	285.08	279.71	259.05	245.36	235.94
46000	378.92	363.88	350.72	339.13	328.85	319.69	311.49	304.11	297.45	291.41	285.93	264.81	250.81	241.18
47000	387.16	371.79	358.35	346.50	336.00	326.64	318.26	310.72	303.91	297.75	292.15	270.56	256.26	246.43
48000	395.40	379.70	365.97	353.87	343.15	333.59	325.03	317.33	310.38	304.08	298.36	276.32	261.72	251.67
49000	403.63	387.61	373.60	361.25	350.30	340.54	331.80	323.94	316.85	310.42	304.58	282.08	267.17	256.91
50000	411.87	395.52	381.22	368.62	357.45	347.49	338.57	330.55	323.31	316.75	310.79	287.83	272.62	262.16
55000	453.06	435.08	419.34	405.48	393.19	382.24	372.43	363.61	355.64	348.43	341.87	316.62	299.88	288.37
60000	494.24	474.63	457.46	442.34	428.93	416.98	406.28	396.66	387.97	380.10	372.95	345.40	327.14	314.59
65000	535.43	514.18	495.59	479.20	464.68	451.73	440.14	429.72	420.30	411.78	404.03	374.18	354.41	340.80
70000	576.62	553.73	533.71	516.06	500.42	486.48	474.00	462.77	452.64	443.45	435.11	402.96	381.67	367.02
75000	617.80	593.28	571.83	552.92	536.17	521.23	507.85	495.83	484.97	475.13	466.19	431.75	408.93	393.23
80000	658.99	632.84	609.95	589.79	571.91	555.98	541.71	528.88	517.30	506.80	497.26	460.53	436.19	419.45
85000	700.18	672.39	648.07	626.65	607.65	590.73	575.57	561.94	549.63	538.48	528.34	489.31	463.45	445.66
90000	741.36	711.94	686.19	663.51	643.40	625.47	609.42	594.99	581.96	570.15	559.42	518.10	490.71	471.88
95000	782.55	751.49	724.32	700.37	679.14	660.22	643.28	628.04	614.29	601.83	590.50	546.88	517.98	498.09
100000	823.74	791.04	762.44	737.23	714.89	694.97	677.14	661.10	646.62	633.50	621.58	575.66	545.24	524.31

MONTHLY PAYMENT
REQUIRED TO AMORTIZE A LOAN

TERM	1 Year	2 Years	3 Years	4 Years	5 Years	6 Years	7 Years	8 Years	9 Years	10 Years	11 Years	12 Years	13 Years	14 Years
AMOUNT														
5	.43	.23	.16	.12	.10	.09	.08	.07	.06	.06	.06	.05	.05	.05
10	.86	.45	.31	.24	.20	.17	.15	.13	.12	.11	.11	.10	.10	.09
15	1.29	.67	.46	.36	.29	.25	.22	.20	.18	.17	.16	.15	.14	.13
25	2.15	1.11	.76	.59	.48	.42	.37	.33	.30	.28	.26	.25	.23	.22
50	4.30	2.21	1.52	1.17	.96	.83	.73	.65	.60	.55	.52	.49	.46	.44
75	6.45	3.32	2.28	1.76	1.44	1.24	1.09	.98	.89	.83	.77	.73	.69	.65
100	8.60	4.42	3.03	2.34	1.92	1.65	1.45	1.30	1.19	1.10	1.03	.97	.91	.87
200	17.19	8.84	6.06	4.67	3.84	3.29	2.90	2.60	2.38	2.20	2.05	1.93	1.82	1.74
300	25.78	13.26	9.09	7.01	5.76	4.93	4.34	3.90	3.56	3.29	3.07	2.89	2.73	2.60
400	34.38	17.68	12.12	9.34	7.68	6.58	5.79	5.20	4.75	4.39	4.09	3.85	3.64	3.47
500	42.97	22.10	15.15	11.68	9.60	8.22	7.24	6.50	5.93	5.48	5.11	4.81	4.55	4.33
600	51.56	26.52	18.18	14.01	11.52	9.86	8.68	7.80	7.12	6.58	6.13	5.77	5.46	5.20
700	60.16	30.93	21.21	16.35	13.44	11.51	10.13	9.10	8.31	7.67	7.16	6.73	6.37	6.06
800	68.75	35.35	24.23	18.68	15.36	13.15	11.58	10.40	9.49	8.77	8.18	7.69	7.28	6.93
900	77.34	39.77	27.26	21.02	17.28	14.79	13.02	11.70	10.68	9.86	9.20	8.65	8.19	7.79
1000	85.93	44.19	30.29	23.35	19.20	16.44	14.47	13.00	11.86	10.96	10.22	9.61	9.10	8.66
2000	171.86	88.38	60.58	46.70	38.39	32.87	28.94	26.00	23.72	21.91	20.43	19.21	18.19	17.31
3000	257.79	132.56	90.86	70.05	57.59	49.30	43.40	38.99	35.58	32.86	30.65	28.82	27.28	25.97
4000	343.72	176.75	121.15	93.40	76.78	65.73	57.87	51.99	47.44	43.81	40.86	38.42	36.37	34.62
5000	429.65	220.93	151.44	116.74	95.97	82.16	72.33	64.98	59.29	54.76	51.08	48.02	45.46	43.27
6000	515.58	265.12	181.72	140.09	115.17	98.59	86.80	77.98	71.15	65.72	61.29	57.63	54.55	51.93
7000	601.51	309.30	212.01	163.44	134.36	115.03	101.26	90.98	83.01	76.67	71.51	67.23	63.64	60.58
8000	687.43	353.49	242.29	186.79	153.55	131.46	115.73	103.97	94.87	87.62	81.72	76.84	72.73	69.23
9000	773.36	397.68	272.58	210.13	172.75	147.89	130.19	116.97	106.73	98.57	91.94	86.44	81.82	77.89
10000	859.29	441.86	302.87	233.48	191.94	164.32	144.66	129.96	118.58	109.52	102.15	96.04	90.91	86.54
11000	945.22	486.05	333.15	256.83	211.13	180.75	159.12	142.96	130.44	120.48	112.37	105.65	100.00	95.19
12000	1031.15	530.23	363.44	280.18	230.33	197.18	173.59	155.96	142.30	131.43	122.58	115.25	109.09	103.85
13000	1117.08	574.42	393.73	303.53	249.52	213.62	188.05	168.95	154.16	142.38	132.80	124.86	118.18	112.50
14000	1203.01	618.60	424.01	326.87	268.72	230.05	202.52	181.95	166.02	153.33	143.01	134.46	127.27	121.15
15000	1288.93	662.79	454.30	350.22	287.91	246.48	216.98	194.94	177.87	164.28	153.23	144.06	136.36	129.81
16000	1374.86	706.97	484.58	373.57	307.10	262.91	231.45	207.94	189.73	175.24	163.44	153.67	145.45	138.46
17000	1460.79	751.16	514.87	396.92	326.30	279.34	245.91	220.93	201.59	186.19	173.66	163.27	154.54	147.11
18000	1546.72	795.34	545.16	420.26	345.49	295.77	260.38	233.93	213.45	197.14	183.87	172.88	163.63	155.77
19000	1632.65	839.53	575.44	443.61	364.68	312.21	274.84	246.93	225.31	208.09	194.08	182.48	172.72	164.42
20000	1718.58	883.72	605.73	466.96	383.88	328.64	289.31	259.92	237.16	219.04	204.30	192.08	181.81	173.07
21000	1804.51	927.90	636.02	490.31	403.07	345.07	303.77	272.92	249.02	230.00	214.51	201.69	190.90	181.73
22000	1890.43	972.09	666.30	513.66	422.26	361.50	318.24	285.91	260.88	240.95	224.73	211.29	200.00	190.38
23000	1976.36	1016.27	696.59	537.00	441.46	377.93	332.70	298.91	272.74	251.90	234.94	220.90	209.09	199.03
24000	2062.29	1060.46	726.87	560.35	460.65	394.34	347.17	311.91	284.60	262.85	245.16	230.50	218.18	207.69
25000	2148.22	1104.64	757.16	583.70	479.85	410.80	361.63	324.90	296.45	273.80	255.37	240.10	227.27	216.34
26000	2234.15	1148.83	787.45	607.05	499.04	427.23	376.10	337.90	308.31	284.76	265.59	249.71	236.36	224.99
27000	2320.08	1193.02	817.73	630.39	518.23	443.66	390.56	350.89	320.17	295.71	275.80	259.31	245.45	233.65
28000	2406.01	1237.20	848.02	653.74	537.43	460.09	405.03	363.89	332.03	306.66	286.02	268.92	254.54	242.30
29000	2491.93	1281.39	878.30	677.09	556.62	476.52	419.49	376.88	343.89	317.61	296.23	278.52	263.63	250.95
30000	2577.86	1325.57	908.59	700.44	575.81	492.95	433.96	389.88	355.74	328.56	306.45	288.12	272.72	259.61
31000	2663.79	1369.76	938.88	723.78	595.01	509.39	448.43	402.88	367.60	339.52	316.66	297.73	281.81	268.26
32000	2749.72	1413.94	969.16	747.13	614.20	525.82	462.89	415.87	379.46	350.47	326.88	307.33	290.90	276.91
33000	2835.65	1458.13	999.45	770.48	633.39	542.25	477.36	428.87	391.32	361.42	337.09	316.94	299.99	285.57
34000	2921.58	1502.31	1029.74	793.83	652.59	558.68	491.82	441.86	403.17	372.37	347.31	326.54	309.08	294.22
35000	3007.51	1546.50	1060.02	817.18	671.78	575.11	506.29	454.86	415.03	383.32	357.52	336.14	318.17	302.87
36000	3093.43	1590.69	1090.31	840.52	690.98	591.54	520.75	467.86	426.89	394.28	367.74	345.75	327.26	311.53
37000	3179.36	1634.87	1120.59	863.87	710.17	607.98	535.22	480.85	438.75	405.23	377.95	355.35	336.35	320.18
38000	3265.29	1679.06	1150.88	887.22	729.36	624.41	549.68	493.85	450.61	416.18	388.16	364.96	345.44	328.83
39000	3351.22	1723.24	1181.17	910.57	748.56	640.84	564.15	506.84	462.46	427.13	398.38	374.56	354.53	337.49
40000	3437.15	1767.43	1211.45	933.91	767.75	657.27	578.61	519.84	474.32	438.08	408.59	384.16	363.62	346.14
41000	3523.08	1811.61	1241.74	957.26	786.94	673.70	593.08	532.83	486.18	449.04	418.81	393.77	372.71	354.79
42000	3609.01	1855.60	1272.03	980.61	806.14	690.13	607.54	545.83	498.04	459.99	429.02	403.37	381.80	363.45
43000	3694.93	1899.98	1302.31	1003.96	825.33	706.57	622.01	558.83	509.90	470.94	439.24	412.98	390.89	372.10
44000	3780.86	1944.17	1332.60	1027.31	844.52	723.00	636.47	571.82	521.75	481.89	449.45	422.58	399.99	380.75
45000	3866.79	1988.36	1362.88	1050.65	863.72	739.43	650.94	584.82	533.61	492.84	459.67	432.18	409.08	389.41
46000	3952.72	2032.54	1393.17	1074.00	882.91	755.86	665.40	597.81	545.47	503.80	469.88	441.79	418.17	398.06
47000	4038.65	2076.73	1423.46	1097.35	902.10	772.29	679.87	610.81	557.33	514.75	480.10	451.39	427.26	406.71
48000	4124.58	2120.91	1453.74	1120.70	921.30	788.72	694.33	623.81	569.19	525.70	490.31	461.00	436.35	415.37
49000	4210.51	2165.10	1484.03	1144.04	940.49	805.16	708.80	636.80	581.04	536.65	500.53	470.60	445.44	424.02
50000	4296.44	2209.28	1514.31	1167.39	959.69	821.59	723.26	649.80	592.90	547.60	510.74	480.20	454.53	432.67
55000	4726.08	2430.21	1665.75	1284.13	1055.65	903.75	795.59	714.78	652.19	602.36	561.82	528.22	499.98	475.94
60000	5155.72	2651.14	1817.18	1400.87	1151.62	985.90	867.91	779.76	711.48	657.12	612.89	576.24	545.43	519.21
65000	5585.36	2872.07	1968.61	1517.61	1247.59	1068.06	940.24	844.73	770.77	711.88	663.96	624.26	590.88	562.47
70000	6015.01	3092.99	2120.04	1634.35	1343.56	1150.22	1012.57	909.71	830.06	766.64	715.04	672.28	636.34	605.74
75000	6444.65	3313.92	2271.47	1751.08	1439.53	1232.38	1084.89	974.69	889.35	821.40	766.11	720.30	681.79	649.01
80000	6874.29	3534.85	2422.90	1867.82	1535.49	1314.54	1157.22	1039.67	948.64	876.16	817.18	768.32	727.24	692.27
85000	7303.94	3755.78	2574.33	1984.56	1631.46	1396.69	1229.54	1104.65	1007.93	930.92	868.26	816.34	772.69	735.54
90000	7733.58	3976.71	2725.76	2101.30	1727.43	1478.85	1301.87	1169.63	1067.22	985.68	919.33	864.36	818.15	778.81
95000	8163.22	4197.63	2877.19	2218.04	1823.40	1561.01	1374.20	1234.61	1126.51	1040.44	970.40	912.38	863.60	822.07
100000	8592.87	4418.56	3028.62	2334.78	1919.37	1643.17	1446.52	1299.59	1185.80	1095.20	1021.48	960.40	909.05	865.34

TERM / AMOUNT	15 Years	16 Years	17 Years	18 Years	19 Years	20 Years	21 Years	22 Years	23 Years	24 Years	25 Years	30 Years	35 Years	40 Years
5	.05	.04	.04	.04	.04	.04	.04	.04	.04	.04	.04	.03	.03	.03
10	.09	.08	.08	.08	.08	.07	.07	.07	.07	.07	.07	.06	.06	.06
15	.13	.12	.12	.12	.11	.11	.11	.10	.10	.10	.10	.09	.09	.08
25	.21	.20	.20	.19	.18	.18	.18	.17	.17	.16	.16	.15	.14	.14
50	.42	.40	.39	.38	.36	.35	.35	.34	.33	.32	.32	.30	.28	.27
75	.63	.60	.58	.56	.54	.53	.52	.50	.49	.48	.47	.44	.42	.40
100	.83	.80	.77	.75	.72	.70	.69	.67	.66	.64	.63	.59	.56	.53
200	1.66	1.60	1.54	1.49	1.44	1.40	1.37	1.34	1.31	1.28	1.26	1.17	1.11	1.06
300	2.49	2.39	2.30	2.23	2.16	2.10	2.05	2.00	1.96	1.92	1.88	1.75	1.66	1.59
400	3.32	3.19	3.07	2.97	2.88	2.80	2.73	2.67	2.61	2.56	2.51	2.33	2.21	2.12
500	4.14	3.98	3.84	3.71	3.60	3.50	3.41	3.33	3.26	3.19	3.14	2.91	2.76	2.65
600	4.97	4.78	4.60	4.45	4.32	4.20	4.09	4.00	3.91	3.83	3.76	3.49	3.31	3.18
700	5.80	5.57	5.37	5.19	5.04	4.90	4.78	4.66	4.56	4.47	4.39	4.07	3.86	3.71
800	6.63	6.37	6.14	5.94	5.76	5.60	5.46	5.33	5.21	5.11	5.01	4.65	4.41	4.24
900	7.45	7.16	6.90	6.68	6.48	6.30	6.14	5.99	5.86	5.75	5.64	5.23	4.96	4.77
1000	8.28	7.96	7.67	7.42	7.20	7.00	6.82	6.66	6.52	6.38	6.27	5.81	5.51	5.30
2000	16.56	15.91	15.34	14.83	14.39	13.99	13.63	13.31	13.03	12.76	12.53	11.61	11.01	10.59
3000	24.84	23.86	23.00	22.25	21.58	20.98	20.45	19.97	19.54	19.14	18.79	17.42	16.51	15.89
4000	33.11	31.81	30.67	29.66	28.77	27.97	27.26	26.62	26.05	25.52	25.05	23.22	22.01	21.18
5000	41.39	39.76	38.33	37.07	35.96	34.97	34.08	33.28	32.56	31.90	31.31	29.03	27.51	26.48
6000	49.67	47.71	46.00	44.49	43.15	41.96	40.89	39.93	39.07	38.28	37.57	34.83	33.02	31.77
7000	57.95	55.66	53.66	51.90	50.34	48.95	47.71	46.59	45.58	44.66	43.83	40.63	38.52	37.07
8000	66.22	63.61	61.33	59.32	57.53	55.94	54.52	53.24	52.09	51.04	50.09	46.44	44.02	42.36
9000	74.50	71.56	68.99	66.73	64.72	62.94	61.34	59.90	58.60	57.42	56.35	52.24	49.52	47.66
10000	82.78	79.51	76.66	74.14	71.91	69.93	68.15	66.55	65.11	63.80	62.61	58.05	55.02	52.95
11000	91.06	87.47	84.32	81.56	79.11	76.92	74.96	73.21	71.62	70.18	68.87	63.85	60.53	58.24
12000	99.33	95.42	91.99	88.97	86.30	83.91	81.78	79.06	78.13	76.56	75.14	69.65	66.03	63.54
13000	107.61	103.37	99.66	96.39	93.49	90.91	88.59	86.51	84.64	82.94	81.40	75.46	71.53	68.83
14000	115.89	111.32	107.32	103.80	100.68	97.90	95.41	93.17	91.15	89.32	87.66	81.26	77.03	74.13
15000	124.17	119.27	114.99	111.21	107.87	104.89	102.22	99.82	97.66	95.70	93.92	87.07	82.53	79.42
16000	132.44	127.22	122.65	118.63	115.06	111.88	109.04	106.48	104.17	102.00	100.18	92.87	88.03	84.72
17000	140.72	135.17	130.32	126.04	122.25	118.87	115.85	113.13	110.68	108.46	106.44	98.67	93.54	90.01
18000	149.00	143.12	137.98	133.45	129.44	125.87	122.67	119.79	117.19	114.84	112.70	104.48	99.04	95.31
19000	157.27	151.07	145.65	140.87	136.63	132.86	129.48	126.44	123.70	121.22	118.96	110.28	104.54	100.60
20000	165.55	159.02	153.31	148.28	143.82	139.85	136.29	133.10	130.21	127.60	125.22	116.09	110.04	105.89
21000	173.83	166.98	160.98	155.70	151.01	146.84	143.11	139.75	136.72	133.98	131.48	121.89	115.54	111.19
22000	182.11	174.93	168.64	163.11	158.21	153.84	149.92	146.41	143.23	140.38	137.74	127.69	121.05	116.48
23000	190.38	182.88	176.31	170.52	165.40	160.83	156.74	153.06	149.74	146.74	144.01	133.50	126.55	121.78
24000	198.66	190.83	183.98	177.94	172.59	167.82	163.55	159.72	156.25	153.12	150.27	139.30	132.05	127.07
25000	206.94	198.78	191.64	185.35	179.78	174.81	170.37	166.37	162.76	159.50	156.53	145.11	137.55	132.37
26000	215.22	206.73	199.31	192.77	186.97	181.81	177.18	173.02	169.27	165.88	162.79	150.91	143.05	137.66
27000	223.49	214.68	206.97	200.18	194.16	188.80	184.00	179.68	175.78	172.25	169.05	156.71	148.56	142.96
28000	231.77	222.63	214.64	207.59	201.35	195.79	190.81	186.33	182.29	178.63	175.31	162.52	154.06	148.25
29000	240.05	230.58	222.30	215.01	208.54	202.78	197.63	192.99	188.80	185.01	181.57	168.32	159.56	153.54
30000	248.33	238.53	229.97	222.42	215.73	209.77	204.44	199.64	195.31	191.39	187.83	174.13	165.06	158.84
31000	256.60	246.48	237.63	229.84	222.92	216.77	211.25	206.30	201.82	197.77	194.09	179.93	170.56	164.13
32000	264.88	254.44	245.30	237.25	230.12	223.76	218.07	212.95	208.33	204.15	200.35	185.73	176.06	169.43
33000	273.16	262.39	252.96	244.66	237.31	230.75	224.88	219.61	214.85	210.53	206.61	191.54	181.57	174.72
34000	281.43	270.34	260.63	252.08	244.50	237.74	231.70	226.26	221.36	216.91	212.88	197.34	187.07	180.02
35000	289.71	278.29	268.29	259.49	251.69	244.74	238.51	232.92	227.87	223.29	219.14	203.15	192.57	185.31
36000	297.99	286.24	275.96	266.90	258.88	251.73	245.33	239.57	234.38	229.67	225.40	208.95	198.07	190.61
37000	306.27	294.19	283.63	274.32	266.07	258.72	252.14	246.23	240.89	236.05	231.66	214.75	203.57	195.90
38000	314.54	302.14	291.29	281.73	273.26	265.71	258.96	252.88	247.40	242.43	237.92	220.56	209.08	201.19
39000	322.82	310.09	298.96	289.15	280.45	272.71	265.77	259.53	253.91	248.81	244.18	226.36	214.58	206.49
40000	331.10	318.04	306.62	296.56	287.64	279.70	272.58	266.19	260.42	255.19	250.44	232.17	220.08	211.78
41000	339.38	325.99	314.29	303.97	294.83	286.69	279.40	272.84	266.93	261.57	256.70	237.97	225.58	217.08
42000	347.65	333.95	321.95	311.39	302.02	293.68	286.21	279.50	273.44	267.95	262.96	243.77	231.08	222.37
43000	355.93	341.90	329.62	318.80	309.22	300.67	293.03	286.15	279.95	274.33	269.22	249.58	236.59	227.67
44000	364.21	349.85	337.28	326.22	316.41	307.67	299.84	292.81	286.46	280.71	275.48	255.38	242.09	232.96
45000	372.49	357.80	344.95	333.63	323.60	314.66	306.66	299.46	292.97	287.09	281.74	261.19	247.59	238.26
46000	380.76	365.75	352.61	341.04	330.79	321.65	313.47	306.12	299.48	293.47	288.01	266.99	253.09	243.55
47000	389.04	373.70	360.28	348.46	337.98	328.64	320.29	312.77	305.99	299.85	294.27	272.79	258.59	248.85
48000	397.32	381.65	367.95	355.87	345.17	335.64	327.10	319.43	312.50	306.23	300.53	278.60	264.09	254.14
49000	405.60	389.60	375.61	363.28	352.36	342.63	333.92	326.08	319.01	312.61	306.79	284.40	269.60	259.43
50000	413.87	397.55	383.28	370.70	359.55	349.62	340.73	332.74	325.52	318.99	313.05	290.21	275.10	264.73
55000	455.26	437.31	421.60	407.77	395.51	384.58	374.80	366.01	358.07	350.88	344.35	319.23	302.61	291.20
60000	496.65	477.06	459.93	444.84	431.46	419.54	408.87	399.28	390.62	382.78	375.66	348.25	330.12	317.67
65000	538.03	516.82	498.26	481.91	467.42	454.51	442.95	432.55	423.18	414.68	406.96	377.27	357.63	344.15
70000	579.42	556.57	536.58	518.98	503.37	489.47	477.02	465.83	455.73	446.58	438.27	406.29	385.14	370.62
75000	620.81	596.33	574.91	556.05	539.33	524.43	511.09	499.10	488.28	478.48	469.57	435.31	412.65	397.09
80000	662.19	636.08	613.24	593.12	575.28	559.39	545.16	532.37	520.83	510.37	500.88	464.33	440.15	423.56
85000	703.58	675.84	651.57	630.18	611.24	594.35	579.24	565.65	553.38	542.27	532.18	493.35	467.66	450.04
90000	744.97	715.59	689.89	667.25	647.19	629.31	613.31	598.92	585.93	574.17	563.48	522.37	495.17	476.51
95000	786.35	755.35	728.22	704.32	683.15	664.28	647.38	632.19	618.48	606.07	594.79	551.39	522.68	502.98
100000	827.74	795.10	766.55	741.39	719.10	699.24	681.45	665.47	651.04	637.97	626.09	580.41	550.19	529.45

MONTHLY PAYMENT
REQUIRED TO AMORTIZE A LOAN

TERM / AMOUNT	1 Year	2 Years	3 Years	4 Years	5 Years	6 Years	7 Years	8 Years	9 Years	10 Years	11 Years	12 Years	13 Years	14 Years
5	.43	.23	.16	.12	.10	.09	.08	.07	.06	.06	.06	.05	.05	.05
10	.86	.45	.31	.24	.20	.17	.15	.14	.12	.11	.11	.10	.10	.09
15	1.29	.67	.46	.36	.29	.25	.22	.20	.18	.17	.16	.15	.14	.14
25	2.15	1.11	.76	.59	.49	.42	.37	.33	.30	.28	.26	.25	.23	.22
50	4.30	2.22	1.52	1.17	.97	.83	.73	.66	.60	.55	.52	.49	.46	.44
75	6.45	3.32	2.28	1.76	1.45	1.24	1.09	.98	.90	.83	.77	.73	.69	.66
100	8.60	4.43	3.04	2.34	1.93	1.65	1.45	1.31	1.19	1.10	1.03	.97	.92	.87
200	17.20	8.85	6.07	4.68	3.85	3.30	2.90	2.61	2.38	2.20	2.05	1.93	1.83	1.74
300	25.79	13.27	9.10	7.02	5.77	4.94	4.35	3.91	3.57	3.30	3.08	2.89	2.74	2.61
400	34.39	17.69	12.13	9.35	7.69	6.59	5.80	5.21	4.76	4.40	4.10	3.86	3.65	3.48
500	42.98	22.11	15.16	11.69	9.61	8.23	7.25	6.52	5.95	5.49	5.13	4.82	4.56	4.34
600	51.58	26.53	18.19	14.03	11.54	9.88	8.70	7.82	7.13	6.59	6.15	5.78	5.47	5.21
700	60.17	30.95	21.22	16.36	13.46	11.52	10.15	9.12	8.32	7.69	7.17	6.75	6.39	6.08
800	68.77	35.37	24.25	18.70	15.38	13.17	11.60	10.42	9.51	8.79	8.20	7.71	7.30	6.95
900	77.36	39.79	27.28	21.04	17.30	14.81	13.05	11.72	10.70	9.88	9.22	8.67	8.21	7.82
1000	85.96	44.21	30.31	23.38	19.22	16.46	14.49	13.03	11.89	10.98	10.25	9.63	9.12	8.68
2000	171.91	86.42	60.62	46.75	38.44	32.92	28.98	26.05	23.77	21.96	20.49	19.26	18.24	17.36
3000	257.86	132.63	90.93	70.12	57.66	49.37	43.47	39.07	35.65	32.94	30.73	28.89	27.35	26.04
4000	343.81	176.84	121.24	93.49	76.87	65.83	57.96	52.09	47.53	43.91	40.97	38.52	36.47	34.72
5000	429.76	221.05	151.55	116.86	96.09	82.28	72.45	65.11	59.42	54.89	51.21	48.15	45.59	43.40
6000	515.71	265.25	181.86	140.23	115.31	98.74	86.94	78.13	71.30	65.87	61.45	57.78	54.70	52.08
7000	601.67	309.46	212.17	163.60	134.52	115.19	101.43	91.15	83.18	76.84	71.69	67.41	63.82	60.76
8000	687.62	353.67	242.48	186.97	153.74	131.65	115.92	104.17	95.06	87.82	81.93	77.04	72.94	69.44
9000	773.57	397.88	272.78	210.34	172.96	148.10	130.41	117.19	106.95	98.80	92.17	86.67	82.05	78.12
10000	859.52	442.09	303.09	233.71	192.17	164.56	144.90	130.21	118.83	109.77	102.41	96.30	91.17	86.80
11000	945.47	486.29	333.40	257.08	211.39	181.01	159.38	143.23	130.71	120.75	112.65	105.93	100.29	95.48
12000	1031.42	530.50	363.71	280.45	230.61	197.47	173.87	156.25	142.59	131.73	122.89	115.56	109.40	104.16
13000	1117.38	574.71	394.02	303.82	249.82	213.92	188.36	169.27	154.48	142.70	133.13	125.19	118.52	112.84
14000	1203.33	618.92	424.33	327.19	269.04	230.38	202.85	182.29	166.36	153.68	143.37	134.82	127.64	121.52
15000	1289.28	663.13	454.64	350.56	288.26	246.83	217.34	195.31	178.24	164.66	153.61	144.45	136.75	130.20
16000	1375.23	707.33	484.95	373.93	307.47	263.29	231.83	208.33	190.12	175.64	163.85	154.08	145.87	138.88
17000	1461.18	751.54	515.25	397.30	326.69	279.74	246.32	221.35	202.01	186.61	174.09	163.71	154.99	147.56
18000	1547.13	795.75	545.56	420.68	345.91	296.20	260.81	234.37	213.89	197.59	184.33	173.34	164.10	156.24
19000	1633.08	839.96	575.87	444.05	365.12	312.65	275.30	247.39	225.77	208.57	194.57	182.97	173.22	164.92
20000	1719.04	884.17	606.18	467.42	384.34	329.11	289.79	260.41	237.65	219.54	204.81	192.60	182.33	173.60
21000	1804.99	928.37	636.49	490.79	403.56	345.56	304.27	273.43	249.54	230.52	215.05	202.23	191.45	182.28
22000	1890.94	972.58	666.80	514.16	422.77	362.02	318.76	286.45	261.42	241.50	225.29	211.86	200.57	190.96
23000	1976.89	1016.79	697.11	537.53	441.99	378.47	333.25	299.47	273.30	252.47	235.53	221.49	209.68	199.64
24000	2062.84	1061.00	727.42	560.90	461.21	394.93	347.74	312.49	285.18	263.45	245.77	231.12	218.80	208.32
25000	2148.79	1105.21	757.72	584.27	480.42	411.38	362.23	325.51	297.07	274.43	256.01	240.75	227.92	217.00
26000	2234.75	1149.41	788.03	607.64	499.64	427.84	376.72	338.53	308.95	285.40	266.25	250.38	237.03	225.68
27000	2320.70	1193.62	818.34	631.01	518.86	444.29	391.21	351.55	320.83	296.38	276.49	260.00	246.15	234.36
28000	2406.65	1237.83	848.65	654.38	538.07	460.75	405.70	364.57	332.71	307.36	286.73	269.63	255.27	243.04
29000	2492.60	1282.04	878.96	677.75	557.29	477.20	420.19	377.59	344.60	318.34	296.97	279.26	264.38	251.72
30000	2578.55	1326.25	909.27	701.12	576.51	493.66	434.68	390.61	356.48	329.31	307.21	288.89	273.50	260.40
31000	2664.50	1370.45	939.58	724.49	595.72	510.11	449.16	403.63	368.36	340.29	317.45	298.52	282.62	269.08
32000	2750.46	1414.66	969.89	747.86	614.94	526.57	463.65	416.65	380.24	351.27	327.69	308.15	291.73	277.76
33000	2836.41	1458.87	1000.20	771.23	634.16	543.02	478.14	429.67	392.13	362.24	337.93	317.78	300.85	286.44
34000	2922.36	1503.08	1030.50	794.60	653.38	559.48	492.63	442.69	404.01	373.22	348.17	327.41	309.97	295.12
35000	3008.31	1547.29	1060.81	817.98	672.59	575.93	507.12	455.71	415.89	384.20	358.41	337.04	319.08	303.80
36000	3094.26	1591.49	1091.12	841.35	691.81	592.39	521.61	468.73	427.77	395.17	368.65	346.67	328.20	312.48
37000	3180.21	1635.70	1121.43	864.72	711.03	608.84	536.10	481.75	439.66	406.15	378.89	356.30	337.31	321.16
38000	3266.16	1679.91	1151.74	888.09	730.24	625.30	550.59	494.77	451.54	417.13	389.13	365.93	346.43	329.84
39000	3352.12	1724.12	1182.05	911.46	749.46	641.76	565.08	507.79	463.42	428.10	399.37	375.56	355.55	338.51
40000	3438.07	1768.33	1212.36	934.83	768.68	658.21	579.57	520.81	475.30	439.08	409.61	385.19	364.66	347.19
41000	3524.02	1812.53	1242.67	958.20	787.89	674.67	594.05	533.83	487.19	450.06	419.85	394.82	373.78	355.87
42000	3609.97	1856.74	1272.97	981.57	807.11	691.12	608.54	546.85	499.07	461.04	430.09	404.45	382.90	364.55
43000	3695.92	1900.95	1303.28	1004.94	826.33	707.58	623.03	559.87	510.95	472.01	440.33	414.08	392.01	373.23
44000	3781.87	1945.16	1333.59	1028.31	845.54	724.03	637.52	572.89	522.83	482.99	450.57	423.71	401.13	381.91
45000	3867.83	1989.37	1363.90	1051.68	864.76	740.49	652.01	585.91	534.72	493.97	460.81	433.34	410.25	390.59
46000	3953.78	2033.58	1394.21	1075.05	883.98	756.94	666.50	598.93	546.60	504.94	471.05	442.97	419.36	399.27
47000	4039.73	2077.78	1424.52	1098.42	903.19	773.40	680.99	611.95	558.48	515.92	481.29	452.60	428.48	407.95
48000	4125.68	2121.99	1454.83	1121.79	922.41	789.85	695.48	624.97	570.36	526.90	491.53	462.23	437.60	416.63
49000	4211.63	2166.20	1485.14	1145.16	941.63	806.31	709.97	637.99	582.25	537.87	501.77	471.86	446.71	425.31
50000	4297.58	2210.41	1515.44	1168.53	960.84	822.76	724.46	651.01	594.13	548.85	512.01	481.49	455.83	433.99
55000	4727.34	2431.45	1666.99	1285.39	1056.93	905.04	796.90	716.11	653.54	603.74	563.21	529.63	501.41	477.39
60000	5157.10	2652.49	1818.53	1402.24	1153.01	987.31	869.35	781.21	712.95	658.62	614.41	577.78	546.99	520.79
65000	5586.86	2873.53	1970.08	1519.09	1249.09	1069.59	941.79	846.31	772.37	713.50	665.61	625.93	592.58	564.19
70000	6016.61	3094.57	2121.62	1635.95	1345.18	1151.86	1014.24	911.41	831.78	768.39	716.81	674.08	638.16	607.59
75000	6446.37	3315.61	2273.16	1752.80	1441.26	1234.14	1086.68	976.51	891.19	823.27	768.01	722.23	683.74	650.99
80000	6876.13	3536.65	2424.71	1869.65	1537.35	1316.42	1159.13	1041.61	950.60	878.16	819.21	770.37	729.32	694.38
85000	7305.89	3757.69	2576.25	1986.50	1633.43	1398.69	1231.57	1106.71	1010.02	933.04	870.41	818.52	774.91	737.78
90000	7735.65	3978.73	2727.80	2103.36	1729.51	1480.97	1304.02	1171.81	1069.43	987.93	921.61	866.67	820.49	781.18
95000	8165.40	4199.77	2879.34	2220.21	1825.60	1563.24	1376.46	1236.91	1128.84	1042.81	972.81	914.82	866.07	824.58
100000	8595.16	4420.81	3030.88	2337.06	1921.68	1645.52	1448.91	1302.01	1188.25	1097.70	1024.01	962.97	911.65	867.98

TERM	15 Years	16 Years	17 Years	18 Years	19 Years	20 Years	21 Years	22 Years	23 Years	24 Years	25 Years	30 Years	35 Years	40 Years
AMOUNT
5	.05	.04	.04	.04	.04	.04	.04	.04	.04	.04	.04	.03	.03	.03
10	.09	.08	.08	.08	.08	.08	.07	.07	.07	.07	.07	.06	.06	.06
15	.13	.12	.12	.12	.11	.11	.11	.11	.10	.10	.10	.09	.09	.08
25	.21	.20	.20	.19	.19	.18	.18	.17	.17	.17	.16	.15	.14	.14
50	.42	.40	.39	.38	.37	.36	.35	.34	.33	.33	.32	.30	.28	.27
75	.63	.60	.58	.56	.55	.53	.52	.51	.50	.49	.48	.44	.42	.40
100	.84	.80	.77	.75	.73	.71	.69	.67	.66	.65	.63	.59	.56	.54
200	1.67	1.60	1.54	1.49	1.45	1.41	1.37	1.34	1.31	1.29	1.26	1.17	1.11	1.07
300	2.50	2.40	2.31	2.24	2.17	2.11	2.06	2.01	1.97	1.93	1.89	1.76	1.67	1.60
400	3.33	3.20	3.08	2.98	2.89	2.81	2.74	2.68	2.62	2.57	2.52	2.34	2.22	2.14
500	4.16	3.99	3.85	3.73	3.61	3.52	3.43	3.35	3.27	3.21	3.15	2.92	2.77	2.67
600	4.99	4.79	4.62	4.47	4.34	4.22	4.11	4.02	3.93	3.85	3.78	3.51	3.33	3.20
700	5.82	5.59	5.39	5.21	5.06	4.92	4.80	4.68	4.58	4.49	4.41	4.09	3.88	3.74
800	6.65	6.39	6.16	5.96	5.78	5.62	5.48	5.35	5.24	5.13	5.04	4.67	4.43	4.27
900	7.48	7.19	6.93	6.70	6.50	6.32	6.16	6.02	5.89	5.77	5.67	5.26	4.99	4.80
1000	8.31	7.98	7.70	7.45	7.22	7.03	6.85	6.69	6.54	6.41	6.30	5.84	5.54	5.33
2000	16.61	15.96	15.39	14.89	14.44	14.05	13.69	13.37	13.08	12.82	12.59	11.68	11.08	10.66
3000	24.92	23.94	23.08	22.33	21.66	21.07	20.54	20.06	19.62	19.23	18.88	17.51	16.61	15.99
4000	33.22	31.92	30.78	29.77	28.88	28.09	27.38	26.74	26.16	25.64	25.17	23.35	22.15	21.32
5000	41.53	39.90	38.47	37.21	36.10	35.11	34.22	33.42	32.70	32.05	31.46	29.18	27.68	26.65
6000	49.83	47.87	46.16	44.66	43.32	42.13	41.07	40.11	39.24	38.46	37.75	35.02	33.22	31.98
7000	58.13	55.85	53.86	52.10	50.54	49.15	47.91	46.79	45.78	44.87	44.04	40.86	38.75	37.31
8000	66.44	63.83	61.55	59.54	57.76	56.17	54.75	53.48	52.32	51.28	50.33	46.69	44.29	42.64
9000	74.74	71.81	69.24	66.98	64.98	63.19	61.60	60.16	58.86	57.69	56.62	52.53	49.82	47.96
10000	83.05	79.79	76.93	74.42	72.20	70.21	68.44	66.84	65.40	64.10	62.92	58.36	55.36	53.29
11000	91.35	87.76	84.63	81.86	79.42	77.23	75.28	73.53	71.94	70.51	69.21	64.20	60.89	58.62
12000	99.65	95.74	92.32	89.31	86.63	84.26	82.13	80.21	78.48	76.92	75.50	70.03	66.43	63.95
13000	107.96	103.72	100.01	96.75	93.85	91.28	88.97	86.89	85.02	83.33	81.79	75.87	71.96	69.28
14000	116.26	111.70	107.71	104.19	101.07	98.30	95.81	93.58	91.56	89.74	88.08	81.71	77.50	74.61
15000	124.57	119.68	115.40	111.63	108.29	105.32	102.66	100.26	98.10	96.15	94.37	87.54	83.03	79.94
16000	132.87	127.65	123.09	119.07	115.51	112.34	109.50	106.95	104.64	102.56	100.66	93.38	88.57	85.27
17000	141.17	135.63	130.78	126.51	122.73	119.36	116.34	113.63	111.18	108.97	106.95	99.21	94.10	90.60
18000	149.48	143.61	138.48	133.96	129.95	126.38	123.19	120.31	117.72	115.38	113.24	105.05	99.64	95.92
19000	157.78	151.59	146.17	141.40	137.17	133.40	130.03	127.00	124.26	121.79	119.54	110.88	105.17	101.25
20000	166.09	159.57	153.86	148.84	144.39	140.42	136.87	133.68	130.80	128.19	125.83	116.72	110.71	106.58
21000	174.39	167.54	161.56	156.28	151.61	147.44	143.72	140.36	137.34	134.60	132.12	122.56	116.24	111.91
22000	182.70	175.52	169.25	163.72	158.83	154.46	150.56	147.05	143.88	141.01	138.41	128.39	121.70	117.24
23000	191.00	183.50	176.94	171.16	166.04	161.48	157.40	153.73	150.42	147.42	144.70	134.23	127.31	122.57
24000	199.30	191.48	184.63	178.61	173.26	168.51	164.25	160.42	156.96	153.83	150.99	140.06	132.85	127.90
25000	207.61	199.46	192.33	186.05	180.48	175.53	171.09	167.10	163.50	160.24	157.28	145.90	138.38	133.23
26000	215.91	207.43	200.02	193.49	187.70	182.55	177.93	173.78	170.04	166.65	163.57	151.73	143.92	138.56
27000	224.22	215.41	207.71	200.93	194.92	189.57	184.78	180.47	176.58	173.06	169.86	157.57	149.45	143.88
28000	232.52	223.39	215.41	208.37	202.14	196.59	191.62	187.15	183.12	179.47	176.15	163.41	154.99	149.21
29000	240.82	231.37	223.10	215.81	209.36	203.61	198.46	193.84	189.66	185.88	182.45	169.24	160.52	154.54
30000	249.13	239.35	230.79	223.26	216.58	210.63	205.31	200.52	196.20	192.29	188.74	175.08	166.06	159.87
31000	257.43	247.33	238.48	230.70	223.80	217.65	212.15	207.20	202.74	198.70	195.03	180.91	171.59	165.20
32000	265.74	255.30	246.18	238.14	231.02	224.67	218.99	213.89	209.28	205.11	201.32	186.75	177.13	170.53
33000	274.04	263.28	253.87	245.58	238.24	231.69	225.84	220.57	215.82	211.52	207.61	192.58	182.66	175.86
34000	282.34	271.26	261.56	253.02	245.46	238.71	232.68	227.25	222.36	217.93	213.90	198.42	188.20	181.19
35000	290.65	279.24	269.26	260.46	252.67	245.73	239.52	233.94	228.90	224.34	220.19	204.26	193.73	186.52
36000	298.95	287.22	276.95	267.91	259.89	252.76	246.37	240.62	235.44	230.75	226.48	210.09	199.27	191.84
37000	307.26	295.19	284.64	275.35	267.11	259.78	253.21	247.31	241.98	237.16	232.77	215.93	204.80	197.17
38000	315.56	303.17	292.33	282.79	274.33	266.80	260.05	253.99	248.52	243.57	239.07	221.76	210.34	202.50
39000	323.86	311.15	300.03	290.23	281.55	273.82	266.90	260.67	255.06	249.97	245.36	227.60	215.87	207.83
40000	332.17	319.13	307.72	297.67	288.77	280.84	273.74	267.36	261.60	256.38	251.65	233.43	221.41	213.16
41000	340.47	327.11	315.41	305.11	295.99	287.86	280.58	274.04	268.14	262.79	257.94	239.27	226.94	218.49
42000	348.78	335.08	323.11	312.56	303.21	294.88	287.43	280.72	274.68	269.20	264.23	245.11	232.48	223.82
43000	357.08	343.06	330.80	320.00	310.43	301.90	294.27	287.41	281.22	275.61	270.52	250.94	238.01	229.15
44000	365.39	351.04	338.49	327.44	317.65	308.92	301.11	294.09	287.76	282.02	276.81	256.78	243.55	234.48
45000	373.69	359.02	346.18	334.88	324.87	315.94	307.96	300.78	294.30	288.43	283.10	262.61	249.08	239.80
46000	381.99	367.00	353.88	342.32	332.08	322.96	314.80	307.46	300.84	294.84	289.39	268.45	254.62	245.13
47000	390.30	374.97	361.57	349.76	339.30	329.98	321.64	314.14	307.38	301.25	295.69	274.28	260.15	250.46
48000	398.60	382.95	369.26	357.21	346.52	337.01	328.49	320.83	313.92	307.66	301.98	280.12	265.69	255.79
49000	406.91	390.93	376.96	364.65	353.74	344.03	335.33	327.51	320.46	314.07	308.27	285.96	271.22	261.12
50000	415.21	398.91	384.65	372.09	360.96	351.05	342.17	334.20	327.00	320.48	314.56	291.79	276.76	266.45
55000	456.73	438.80	423.11	409.30	397.06	386.15	376.39	367.61	359.70	352.53	346.01	320.97	304.43	293.09
60000	498.25	478.69	461.58	446.51	433.15	421.26	410.61	401.03	392.40	384.57	377.47	350.15	332.11	319.74
65000	539.77	518.58	500.04	483.72	469.25	456.36	444.82	434.45	425.09	416.62	408.92	379.33	359.78	346.38
70000	581.29	558.47	538.51	520.92	505.34	491.46	479.04	467.87	457.79	448.67	440.38	408.51	387.46	373.03
75000	622.81	598.36	576.97	558.13	541.44	526.57	513.26	501.29	490.49	480.72	471.83	437.68	415.13	399.67
80000	664.33	638.25	615.44	595.34	577.53	561.67	547.47	534.71	523.19	512.76	503.29	466.86	442.81	426.32
85000	705.85	678.14	653.90	632.55	613.63	596.78	581.69	568.13	555.89	544.81	534.75	496.04	470.48	452.96
90000	747.37	718.03	692.36	669.76	649.73	631.88	615.91	601.55	588.59	576.86	566.20	525.22	498.16	479.60
95000	788.89	757.92	730.83	706.97	685.82	666.98	650.12	634.97	621.28	608.91	597.66	554.40	525.83	506.25
100000	830.42	797.81	769.29	744.17	721.92	702.09	684.34	668.39	653.99	640.95	629.11	583.58	553.51	532.89

MONTHLY PAYMENT
REQUIRED TO AMORTIZE A LOAN

TERM / AMOUNT	1 Year	2 Years	3 Years	4 Years	5 Years	6 Years	7 Years	8 Years	9 Years	10 Years	11 Years	12 Years	13 Years	14 Years
5	.43	.23	.16	.12	.10	.09	.08	.07	.06	.06	.06	.05	.05	.05
10	.86	.45	.31	.24	.20	.17	.15	.14	.12	.12	.11	.10	.10	.09
15	1.29	.67	.46	.36	.29	.25	.22	.20	.18	.17	.16	.15	.14	.14
25	2.15	1.11	.76	.59	.49	.42	.37	.33	.30	.28	.26	.25	.23	.22
50	4.30	2.22	1.52	1.17	.97	.83	.73	.66	.60	.56	.52	.49	.46	.44
75	6.45	3.32	2.28	1.76	1.45	1.24	1.09	.98	.90	.83	.77	.73	.69	.66
100	8.60	4.43	3.04	2.34	1.93	1.65	1.46	1.31	1.20	1.11	1.03	.97	.92	.88
200	17.20	8.85	6.07	4.68	3.85	3.30	2.91	2.61	2.39	2.21	2.06	1.94	1.83	1.75
300	25.80	13.27	9.10	7.02	5.78	4.95	4.36	3.92	3.58	3.31	3.08	2.90	2.75	2.62
400	34.39	17.70	12.14	9.36	7.70	6.60	5.81	5.22	4.77	4.41	4.11	3.87	3.66	3.49
500	42.99	22.12	15.17	11.70	9.62	8.24	7.26	6.53	5.96	5.51	5.14	4.83	4.58	4.36
600	51.59	26.54	18.20	14.04	11.55	9.89	8.71	7.83	7.15	6.61	6.16	5.80	5.49	5.23
700	60.19	30.97	21.24	16.38	13.47	11.54	10.16	9.14	8.34	7.71	7.19	6.76	6.40	6.10
800	68.78	35.39	24.27	18.72	15.40	13.19	11.62	10.44	9.53	8.81	8.22	7.73	7.32	6.97
900	77.38	39.81	27.30	21.06	17.32	14.84	13.07	11.74	10.72	9.91	9.24	8.69	8.23	7.84
1000	85.98	44.24	30.34	23.40	19.24	16.48	14.52	13.05	11.91	11.01	10.27	9.66	9.15	8.71
2000	171.95	88.47	60.67	46.79	38.48	32.96	29.03	26.09	23.82	22.01	20.54	19.32	18.29	17.42
3000	257.93	132.70	91.00	70.19	57.72	49.44	43.54	39.14	35.73	33.01	30.80	28.97	27.43	26.12
4000	343.90	176.93	121.33	93.58	76.96	65.92	58.06	52.18	47.63	44.01	41.07	38.63	36.58	34.83
5000	429.88	221.16	151.66	116.97	96.20	82.40	72.57	65.23	59.54	55.01	51.33	48.28	45.72	43.54
6000	515.85	265.39	181.99	140.37	115.44	98.88	87.08	78.27	71.45	66.02	61.60	57.94	54.86	52.24
7000	601.83	309.62	212.32	163.76	134.68	115.36	101.60	91.31	83.35	77.02	71.86	67.59	64.00	60.95
8000	687.80	353.85	242.66	187.15	153.92	131.83	116.11	104.36	95.26	88.02	82.13	77.25	73.15	69.65
9000	773.78	398.08	272.99	210.55	173.16	148.31	130.62	117.40	107.17	99.02	92.39	86.90	82.29	78.36
10000	859.75	442.31	303.32	233.94	192.40	164.79	145.13	130.45	119.08	110.02	102.66	96.56	91.43	87.07
11000	945.72	486.54	333.65	257.33	211.64	181.27	159.65	143.49	130.98	121.03	112.92	106.21	100.57	95.77
12000	1031.70	530.77	363.98	280.73	230.88	197.75	174.16	156.54	142.89	132.03	123.19	115.87	109.72	104.48
13000	1117.67	575.00	394.31	304.12	250.12	214.23	188.67	169.58	154.80	143.03	133.45	125.52	118.86	113.19
14000	1203.65	619.23	424.64	327.51	269.36	230.71	203.19	182.62	166.70	154.03	143.72	135.18	128.00	121.89
15000	1289.62	663.46	454.98	350.91	288.60	247.18	217.70	195.67	178.61	165.03	153.99	144.83	137.14	130.60
16000	1375.60	707.69	485.31	374.30	307.84	263.66	232.21	208.71	190.52	176.04	164.25	154.49	146.29	139.30
17000	1461.57	751.92	515.64	397.69	327.08	280.14	246.72	221.76	202.43	187.04	174.52	164.15	155.43	148.01
18000	1547.55	796.15	545.97	421.09	346.32	296.62	261.24	234.80	214.33	198.04	184.78	173.80	164.57	156.72
19000	1633.52	840.39	576.30	444.48	365.56	313.10	275.75	247.85	226.24	209.04	195.05	183.46	173.71	165.42
20000	1719.50	884.62	606.63	467.87	384.80	329.58	290.26	260.89	238.15	220.04	205.31	193.11	182.86	174.13
21000	1805.47	928.85	636.96	491.27	404.04	346.06	304.78	273.93	250.05	231.04	215.58	202.77	192.00	182.83
22000	1891.44	973.08	667.30	514.66	423.28	362.54	319.29	286.98	261.96	242.05	225.84	212.42	201.14	191.54
23000	1977.42	1017.31	697.63	538.05	442.52	379.01	333.80	300.02	273.87	253.05	236.11	222.08	210.28	200.25
24000	2063.39	1061.54	727.96	561.45	461.76	395.49	348.31	313.07	285.78	264.05	246.37	231.73	219.43	208.95
25000	2149.37	1105.77	758.29	584.84	481.00	411.97	362.83	326.11	297.68	275.05	256.64	241.39	228.57	217.66
26000	2235.34	1150.00	788.62	608.23	500.24	428.45	377.34	339.16	309.59	286.05	266.90	251.04	237.71	226.37
27000	2321.32	1194.23	818.95	631.63	519.48	444.93	391.85	352.20	321.50	297.06	277.17	260.70	246.85	235.07
28000	2407.29	1238.46	849.28	655.02	538.72	461.41	406.37	365.24	333.40	308.06	287.43	270.35	256.00	243.78
29000	2493.27	1282.69	879.62	678.41	557.96	477.89	420.88	378.29	345.31	319.06	297.70	280.01	265.14	252.48
30000	2579.24	1326.92	909.95	701.81	577.20	494.36	435.39	391.33	357.22	330.06	307.97	289.66	274.28	261.19
31000	2665.22	1371.15	940.28	725.20	596.44	510.84	449.90	404.38	369.12	341.06	318.23	259.32	283.42	269.90
32000	2751.19	1415.38	970.61	748.60	615.68	527.32	464.42	417.42	381.03	352.07	328.50	308.98	292.57	278.60
33000	2837.16	1459.61	1000.94	771.99	634.92	543.80	478.93	430.47	392.94	363.07	338.76	318.63	301.71	287.31
34000	2923.14	1503.84	1031.27	795.38	654.16	560.28	493.44	443.51	404.85	374.07	349.03	328.29	310.85	296.01
35000	3009.11	1548.07	1061.60	818.78	673.40	576.76	507.96	456.55	416.75	385.07	359.29	337.94	319.99	304.72
36000	3095.09	1592.30	1091.94	842.17	692.64	593.24	522.47	469.60	428.66	396.07	369.56	347.60	329.14	313.43
37000	3181.06	1636.54	1122.27	865.56	711.88	609.71	536.98	482.64	440.57	407.07	379.82	357.25	338.28	322.13
38000	3267.04	1680.77	1152.60	888.96	731.12	626.19	551.49	495.69	452.47	418.08	390.09	366.91	347.42	330.84
39000	3353.01	1725.00	1182.93	912.35	750.36	642.67	566.01	508.73	464.38	429.08	400.35	376.56	356.56	339.55
40000	3438.99	1769.23	1213.26	935.74	769.60	659.15	580.52	521.78	476.29	440.08	410.62	386.22	365.71	348.25
41000	3524.96	1813.46	1243.59	959.14	788.84	675.63	595.03	534.82	488.20	451.08	420.88	395.87	374.85	356.96
42000	3610.94	1857.69	1273.92	982.53	808.08	692.11	609.55	547.86	500.10	462.08	431.15	405.53	383.99	365.66
43000	3696.91	1901.92	1304.26	1005.92	827.32	708.59	624.06	560.91	512.01	473.09	441.42	415.18	393.13	374.37
44000	3782.88	1946.15	1334.59	1029.32	846.56	725.07	638.57	573.95	523.92	484.09	451.68	424.84	402.28	383.08
45000	3868.86	1990.38	1364.92	1052.71	865.80	741.54	653.08	587.00	535.82	495.09	461.95	434.49	411.42	391.78
46000	3954.83	2034.61	1395.25	1076.10	885.04	758.02	667.60	600.04	547.73	506.09	472.21	444.15	420.56	400.49
47000	4040.81	2078.84	1425.58	1099.50	904.28	774.50	682.11	613.09	559.64	517.09	482.48	453.80	429.70	409.20
48000	4126.78	2123.07	1455.91	1122.89	923.52	790.98	696.62	626.13	571.55	528.10	492.74	463.46	438.85	417.90
49000	4212.76	2167.30	1486.24	1146.28	942.76	807.46	711.14	639.17	583.45	539.10	503.01	473.12	447.99	426.61
50000	4298.73	2211.53	1516.58	1169.68	962.00	823.94	725.65	652.22	595.36	550.10	513.27	482.77	457.13	435.31
55000	4728.60	2432.69	1668.23	1286.64	1058.20	906.33	798.21	717.44	654.89	605.11	564.60	531.05	502.85	478.84
60000	5158.48	2653.84	1819.89	1403.61	1154.40	988.72	870.78	782.66	714.43	660.12	615.93	579.32	548.56	522.38
65000	5588.35	2874.99	1971.55	1520.58	1250.60	1071.12	943.34	847.88	773.97	715.13	667.25	627.60	594.27	565.91
70000	6018.22	3096.14	2123.20	1637.55	1346.80	1153.51	1015.91	913.11	833.50	770.14	718.58	675.88	639.98	609.44
75000	6448.09	3317.30	2274.86	1754.51	1443.00	1235.90	1088.47	978.32	893.04	825.15	769.91	724.15	685.70	652.97
80000	6877.97	3538.45	2426.52	1871.48	1539.20	1318.30	1161.03	1043.55	952.57	880.16	821.23	772.43	731.41	696.50
85000	7307.84	3759.60	2578.17	1988.45	1635.40	1400.69	1233.60	1108.77	1012.11	935.16	872.56	820.71	777.12	740.03
90000	7737.71	3980.75	2729.83	2105.41	1731.60	1483.08	1306.16	1173.99	1071.64	990.17	923.89	868.98	822.83	783.56
95000	8167.59	4201.91	2881.49	2222.38	1827.80	1565.48	1378.73	1239.21	1131.18	1045.18	975.21	917.26	868.55	827.09
100000	8597.46	4423.06	3033.14	2339.35	1924.00	1647.87	1451.29	1304.43	1190.71	1100.19	1026.54	965.54	914.26	870.62

TERM AMOUNT	15 Years	16 Years	17 Years	18 Years	19 Years	20 Years	21 Years	22 Years	23 Years	24 Years	25 Years	30 Years	35 Years	40 Years
5	.05	.05	.04	.04	.04	.04	.04	.04	.04	.04	.04	.03	.03	.03
10	.09	.09	.08	.08	.08	.08	.07	.07	.07	.07	.07	.06	.06	.06
15	.13	.13	.12	.12	.11	.11	.11	.11	.10	.10	.10	.09	.09	.09
25	.21	.21	.20	.19	.19	.18	.18	.17	.17	.17	.16	.15	.14	.14
50	.42	.41	.39	.38	.37	.36	.35	.34	.33	.33	.32	.30	.28	.27
75	.63	.61	.58	.57	.55	.53	.52	.51	.50	.49	.48	.45	.42	.41
100	.84	.81	.78	.75	.73	.71	.69	.68	.66	.65	.64	.59	.56	.54
200	1.67	1.61	1.55	1.50	1.45	1.41	1.38	1.35	1.32	1.29	1.27	1.18	1.12	1.08
300	2.50	2.41	2.32	2.25	2.18	2.12	2.07	2.02	1.98	1.94	1.90	1.77	1.68	1.61
400	3.34	3.21	3.09	2.99	2.90	2.82	2.75	2.69	2.63	2.58	2.53	2.35	2.23	2.15
500	4.17	4.01	3.87	3.74	3.63	3.53	3.44	3.36	3.29	3.22	3.17	2.94	2.79	2.69
600	5.00	4.81	4.64	4.49	4.35	4.23	4.13	4.03	3.95	3.87	3.80	3.53	3.35	3.22
700	5.84	5.61	5.41	5.23	5.08	4.94	4.82	4.70	4.60	4.51	4.43	4.11	3.90	3.76
800	6.67	6.41	6.18	5.98	5.80	5.64	5.50	5.38	5.26	5.16	5.06	4.70	4.46	4.30
900	7.50	7.21	6.95	6.73	6.53	6.35	6.19	6.05	5.92	5.80	5.69	5.29	5.02	4.83
1000	8.34	8.01	7.73	7.47	7.25	7.05	6.88	6.72	6.57	6.44	6.33	5.87	5.57	5.37
2000	16.67	16.02	15.45	14.94	14.50	14.10	13.75	13.43	13.14	12.88	12.65	11.74	11.14	10.73
3000	25.00	24.02	23.17	22.41	21.75	21.15	20.62	20.14	19.71	19.32	18.97	17.61	16.71	16.10
4000	33.33	32.03	30.89	29.88	28.99	28.20	27.49	26.86	26.28	25.76	25.29	23.48	22.28	21.46
5000	41.66	40.03	38.61	37.35	36.24	35.25	34.37	33.57	32.85	32.20	31.61	29.34	27.85	26.82
6000	49.99	48.04	46.33	44.82	43.49	42.30	41.24	40.28	39.42	38.64	37.93	35.21	33.41	32.19
7000	58.32	56.04	54.05	52.29	50.74	49.35	48.11	47.00	45.99	45.08	44.25	41.08	38.98	37.55
8000	66.65	64.05	61.77	59.76	57.98	56.40	54.98	53.71	52.56	51.52	50.58	46.95	44.55	42.91
9000	74.98	72.05	69.49	67.23	65.23	63.45	61.86	60.42	59.13	57.96	56.90	52.81	50.12	48.28
10000	83.31	80.06	77.21	74.70	72.48	70.50	68.73	67.14	65.70	64.40	63.22	58.68	55.69	53.64
11000	91.64	88.06	84.93	82.17	79.73	77.55	75.60	73.85	72.27	70.84	69.54	64.55	61.26	59.00
12000	99.98	96.07	92.65	89.64	86.97	84.60	82.47	80.56	78.84	77.28	75.86	70.42	66.82	64.37
13000	108.31	104.07	100.37	97.11	94.22	91.65	89.34	87.27	85.41	83.72	82.18	76.28	72.39	69.73
14000	116.64	112.08	108.09	104.58	101.47	98.70	96.22	93.99	91.98	90.16	88.50	82.15	77.96	75.09
15000	124.97	120.08	115.81	112.05	108.72	105.75	103.09	100.70	98.55	96.60	94.82	88.02	83.53	80.46
16000	133.30	128.09	123.53	119.52	115.96	112.80	109.96	107.41	105.12	103.04	101.15	93.89	89.10	85.82
17000	141.63	136.09	131.25	126.99	123.21	119.84	116.83	114.13	111.69	109.47	107.47	99.75	94.66	91.18
18000	149.96	144.10	138.97	134.46	130.46	126.89	123.71	120.84	118.25	115.91	113.79	105.62	100.23	96.55
19000	158.29	152.10	146.69	141.93	137.70	133.94	130.58	127.55	124.82	122.35	120.11	111.49	105.80	101.91
20000	166.62	160.11	154.41	149.40	144.95	140.99	137.45	134.27	131.39	128.79	126.43	117.36	111.37	107.27
21000	174.95	168.11	162.13	156.07	152.20	148.04	144.32	140.98	137.96	135.23	132.75	123.22	116.94	112.64
22000	183.28	176.12	169.85	164.34	159.45	155.09	151.19	147.69	144.53	141.67	139.07	129.09	122.51	118.00
23000	191.62	184.13	177.57	171.81	166.69	162.14	158.07	154.41	151.10	148.11	145.40	134.96	128.07	123.36
24000	199.95	192.13	185.29	179.27	173.94	169.19	164.94	161.12	157.67	154.55	151.72	140.83	133.64	128.73
25000	208.28	200.14	193.02	186.74	181.19	176.24	171.81	167.83	164.24	160.99	158.04	146.69	139.21	134.09
26000	216.61	208.14	200.74	194.21	188.44	183.29	178.68	174.54	170.81	167.43	164.36	152.56	144.78	139.45
27000	224.94	216.15	208.46	201.68	195.68	190.34	185.56	181.26	177.38	173.87	170.68	158.43	150.35	144.82
28000	233.27	224.15	216.18	209.15	202.93	197.39	192.43	187.97	183.95	180.31	177.00	164.30	155.92	150.18
29000	241.60	232.16	223.90	216.62	210.18	204.44	199.30	194.68	190.52	186.75	183.32	170.16	161.48	155.54
30000	249.93	240.16	231.62	224.09	217.43	211.49	206.17	201.40	197.09	193.19	189.64	176.03	167.05	160.91
31000	258.26	248.17	239.34	231.56	224.67	218.54	213.05	208.11	203.66	199.63	195.97	181.90	172.62	166.27
32000	266.59	256.17	247.06	239.03	231.92	225.59	219.92	214.82	210.23	206.07	202.29	187.77	178.19	171.63
33000	274.92	264.18	254.78	246.50	239.17	232.64	226.79	221.54	216.80	212.51	208.61	193.63	183.76	177.00
34000	283.26	272.18	262.50	253.97	246.41	239.68	233.66	228.25	223.37	218.94	214.93	199.50	189.32	182.36
35000	291.59	280.19	270.22	261.44	253.66	246.73	240.53	234.96	229.94	225.38	221.25	205.37	194.89	187.72
36000	299.92	288.19	277.94	268.91	260.91	253.78	247.41	241.68	236.50	231.82	227.57	211.24	200.46	193.09
37000	308.25	296.20	285.66	276.38	268.16	260.83	254.28	248.39	243.07	238.26	233.89	217.10	206.03	198.45
38000	316.58	304.20	293.38	283.85	275.40	267.88	261.15	255.10	249.64	244.70	240.21	222.97	211.60	203.81
39000	324.91	312.21	301.10	291.32	282.65	274.93	268.02	261.81	256.21	251.14	246.54	228.84	217.17	209.18
40000	333.24	320.21	308.82	298.79	289.90	281.98	274.90	268.53	262.78	257.58	252.86	234.71	222.73	214.54
41000	341.57	328.22	316.54	306.26	297.15	289.03	281.77	275.24	269.35	264.02	259.18	240.57	228.30	219.90
42000	349.90	336.22	324.26	313.73	304.39	296.08	288.64	281.95	275.92	270.46	265.50	246.44	233.87	225.27
43000	358.23	344.23	331.98	321.20	311.64	303.13	295.51	288.67	282.49	276.90	271.82	252.31	239.44	230.63
44000	366.56	352.24	339.70	328.67	318.89	310.18	302.38	295.38	289.06	283.34	278.14	258.18	245.01	235.99
45000	374.90	360.24	347.42	336.14	326.14	317.23	309.26	302.09	295.63	289.78	284.46	264.04	250.58	241.36
46000	383.23	368.25	355.14	343.61	333.38	324.28	316.13	308.81	302.20	296.22	290.79	269.91	256.14	246.72
47000	391.56	376.25	362.86	351.07	340.63	331.33	323.00	315.52	308.77	302.66	297.11	275.78	261.71	252.08
48000	399.89	384.26	370.58	358.54	347.88	338.38	329.87	322.23	315.34	309.10	303.43	281.65	267.28	257.45
49000	408.22	392.26	378.30	366.01	355.12	345.43	336.75	328.95	321.91	315.54	309.75	287.51	272.85	262.81
50000	416.55	400.27	386.03	373.48	362.37	352.48	343.62	335.66	328.48	321.98	316.07	293.38	278.42	268.17
55000	458.20	440.29	424.63	410.83	398.61	387.72	377.98	369.22	361.32	354.17	347.68	322.72	306.26	294.99
60000	499.86	480.32	463.23	448.18	434.85	422.97	412.34	402.79	394.17	386.37	379.28	352.06	334.10	321.81
65000	541.51	520.35	501.83	485.53	471.08	458.22	446.70	436.35	427.02	418.57	410.89	381.39	361.94	348.62
70000	583.17	560.37	540.43	522.87	507.32	493.46	481.06	469.92	459.87	450.76	442.50	410.73	389.78	375.44
75000	624.82	600.40	579.04	560.22	543.56	528.71	515.43	503.48	492.71	482.96	474.10	440.07	417.62	402.26
80000	666.48	640.42	617.64	597.57	579.79	563.96	549.79	537.05	525.56	515.16	505.71	469.41	445.46	429.07
85000	708.13	680.45	656.24	634.92	616.03	599.20	584.15	570.62	558.41	547.35	537.32	498.75	473.30	455.89
90000	749.79	720.48	694.84	672.27	652.27	634.45	618.51	604.18	591.25	579.55	568.92	528.08	501.15	482.71
95000	791.44	760.50	733.44	709.61	688.50	669.70	652.87	637.75	624.10	611.75	600.53	557.42	528.99	509.52
100000	833.09	800.53	772.05	746.96	724.74	704.95	687.23	671.31	656.95	643.95	632.14	586.76	556.83	536.34

MONTHLY PAYMENT
REQUIRED TO AMORTIZE A LOAN

TERM AMOUNT	1 Year	2 Years	3 Years	4 Years	5 Years	6 Years	7 Years	8 Years	9 Years	10 Years	11 Years	12 Years	13 Years	14 Years
5	.44	.23	.16	.12	.10	.09	.08	.07	.06	.06	.06	.05	.05	.05
10	.87	.45	.31	.24	.20	.17	.15	.14	.12	.12	.11	.10	.10	.09
15	1.30	.67	.46	.36	.29	.25	.22	.20	.18	.17	.16	.15	.14	.14
25	2.16	1.11	.76	.59	.49	.42	.37	.33	.30	.28	.26	.25	.23	.22
50	4.31	2.22	1.52	1.18	.97	.83	.73	.66	.60	.56	.52	.49	.46	.44
75	6.46	3.32	2.28	1.76	1.45	1.24	1.10	.99	.90	.83	.78	.73	.69	.66
100	8.61	4.43	3.04	2.35	1.93	1.66	1.46	1.31	1.20	1.11	1.04	.97	.92	.88
200	17.21	8.86	6.08	4.69	3.86	3.31	2.91	2.62	2.39	2.21	2.07	1.94	1.84	1.75
300	25.81	13.29	9.11	7.03	5.79	4.96	4.37	3.93	3.59	3.32	3.10	2.91	2.76	2.63
400	34.41	17.71	12.15	9.38	7.71	6.61	5.82	5.24	4.78	4.42	4.13	3.88	3.68	3.50
500	43.01	22.14	15.19	11.72	9.64	8.26	7.28	6.55	5.98	5.52	5.16	4.85	4.60	4.38
600	51.61	26.56	18.22	14.06	11.57	9.91	8.73	7.85	7.17	6.63	6.19	5.82	5.51	5.25
700	60.21	30.99	21.26	16.40	13.50	11.56	10.19	9.16	8.37	7.73	7.22	6.79	6.43	6.13
800	68.81	35.42	24.30	18.75	15.42	13.22	11.64	10.47	9.56	8.84	8.25	7.76	7.35	7.00
900	77.41	39.84	27.33	21.09	17.35	14.87	13.10	11.78	10.75	9.94	9.28	8.73	8.27	7.88
1000	86.01	44.27	30.37	23.43	19.28	16.52	14.55	13.09	11.95	11.04	10.31	9.70	9.19	8.75
2000	172.02	88.53	60.74	46.86	38.55	33.03	29.10	26.17	23.89	22.08	20.61	19.39	18.37	17.50
3000	258.03	132.80	91.10	70.29	57.83	49.55	43.65	39.25	35.84	33.12	30.92	29.09	27.55	26.24
4000	344.04	177.06	121.47	93.72	77.10	66.06	58.20	52.33	47.78	44.16	41.22	38.78	36.73	34.99
5000	430.05	221.33	151.83	117.14	96.38	82.57	72.75	65.41	59.73	55.20	51.52	48.47	45.91	43.73
6000	516.06	265.59	182.20	140.57	115.65	99.09	87.30	78.49	71.67	66.24	61.83	58.17	55.10	52.48
7000	602.07	309.86	212.56	164.00	134.93	115.60	101.85	91.57	83.61	77.28	72.13	67.86	64.28	61.23
8000	688.08	354.12	242.93	187.43	154.20	132.12	116.39	104.65	95.56	88.32	82.43	77.56	73.46	69.97
9000	774.09	398.38	273.29	210.85	173.48	148.63	130.94	117.73	107.50	99.36	92.74	87.25	82.64	78.72
10000	860.09	442.65	303.66	234.28	192.75	165.14	145.49	130.81	119.45	110.40	103.04	96.94	91.82	87.46
11000	946.10	486.91	334.02	257.71	212.03	181.66	160.04	143.89	131.39	121.44	113.34	106.64	101.00	96.21
12000	1032.11	531.18	364.39	281.14	231.30	198.17	174.59	156.97	143.33	132.48	123.65	116.33	110.19	104.96
13000	1118.12	575.44	394.75	304.57	250.58	214.69	189.14	170.05	155.28	143.52	133.95	126.03	119.37	113.70
14000	1204.13	619.71	425.12	327.99	269.85	231.20	203.69	183.13	167.22	154.56	144.25	135.72	128.55	122.45
15000	1290.14	663.97	455.48	351.42	289.13	247.71	218.24	196.21	179.17	165.60	154.56	145.41	137.73	131.19
16000	1376.15	708.23	485.85	374.85	308.40	264.23	232.78	209.30	191.11	176.64	164.86	155.11	146.91	139.94
17000	1462.16	752.50	516.22	398.28	327.68	280.74	247.33	222.38	203.05	187.67	175.16	164.80	156.09	148.69
18000	1548.17	796.76	546.58	421.70	346.95	297.26	261.88	235.46	215.00	198.71	185.47	174.50	165.28	157.43
19000	1634.18	841.03	576.95	445.13	366.22	313.77	276.43	248.54	226.94	209.75	195.77	184.19	174.46	166.18
20000	1720.18	885.29	607.31	468.56	385.50	330.28	290.98	261.62	238.89	220.79	206.07	193.88	183.64	174.92
21000	1806.19	929.56	637.68	491.99	404.77	346.80	305.53	274.70	250.83	231.83	216.38	203.58	192.82	183.67
22000	1892.20	973.82	668.04	515.42	424.05	363.31	320.08	287.78	262.77	242.87	226.68	213.27	202.00	192.42
23000	1978.21	1018.08	698.41	538.84	443.32	379.83	334.63	300.86	274.72	253.91	236.98	222.97	211.18	201.16
24000	2064.22	1062.35	728.77	562.27	462.60	396.34	349.17	313.94	286.66	264.95	247.29	232.66	220.37	209.91
25000	2150.23	1106.61	759.14	585.70	481.87	412.85	363.72	327.02	298.61	275.99	257.59	242.35	229.55	218.65
26000	2236.24	1150.88	789.50	609.13	501.15	429.37	378.27	340.10	310.55	287.03	267.89	252.05	238.73	227.40
27000	2322.25	1195.14	819.87	632.55	520.42	445.88	392.82	353.18	322.49	298.07	278.20	261.74	247.91	236.14
28000	2408.26	1239.41	850.23	655.98	539.70	462.40	407.37	366.26	334.44	309.11	288.50	271.44	257.09	244.89
29000	2494.27	1283.67	880.60	679.41	558.97	478.91	421.92	379.34	346.38	320.15	298.80	281.13	266.28	253.64
30000	2580.27	1327.93	910.96	702.84	578.25	495.42	436.47	392.42	358.33	331.19	309.11	290.82	275.46	262.38
31000	2666.28	1372.20	941.33	726.27	597.52	511.94	451.01	405.51	370.27	342.23	319.41	300.52	284.64	271.13
32000	2752.29	1416.46	971.70	749.69	616.80	528.45	465.56	418.59	382.21	353.27	329.71	310.21	293.82	279.87
33000	2838.30	1460.73	1002.06	773.12	636.07	544.97	480.11	431.67	394.16	364.30	340.02	319.90	303.00	288.62
34000	2924.31	1504.99	1032.43	796.55	655.35	561.48	494.66	444.75	406.10	375.34	350.32	329.60	312.18	297.37
35000	3010.32	1549.26	1062.79	819.98	674.62	577.99	509.21	457.83	418.05	386.38	360.62	339.29	321.37	306.11
36000	3096.33	1593.52	1093.16	843.40	693.90	594.51	523.76	470.91	429.99	397.42	370.93	348.99	330.55	314.86
37000	3182.34	1637.78	1123.52	866.83	713.17	611.02	538.31	483.99	441.93	408.46	381.23	358.68	339.73	323.60
38000	3268.35	1682.05	1153.89	890.26	732.44	627.53	552.86	497.07	453.88	419.50	391.53	368.37	348.91	332.35
39000	3354.36	1726.31	1184.25	913.69	751.72	644.05	567.40	510.15	465.82	430.54	401.84	378.07	358.09	341.10
40000	3440.36	1770.58	1214.62	937.12	770.99	660.56	581.95	523.23	477.77	441.58	412.14	387.76	367.27	349.84
41000	3526.37	1814.84	1244.98	960.54	790.27	677.08	596.50	536.31	489.71	452.62	422.45	397.46	376.46	358.59
42000	3612.38	1859.11	1275.35	983.97	809.54	693.59	611.05	549.39	501.65	463.66	432.75	407.15	385.64	367.33
43000	3698.39	1903.37	1305.71	1007.40	828.82	710.10	625.60	562.47	513.60	474.70	443.05	416.84	394.82	376.08
44000	3784.40	1947.63	1336.08	1030.83	848.09	726.62	640.15	575.55	525.54	485.74	453.36	426.54	404.00	384.83
45000	3870.41	1991.90	1366.44	1054.25	867.37	743.13	654.70	588.63	537.49	496.78	463.66	436.23	413.18	393.57
46000	3956.42	2036.16	1396.81	1077.68	886.64	759.65	669.25	601.71	549.43	507.82	473.96	445.93	422.36	402.32
47000	4042.43	2080.43	1427.18	1101.11	905.92	776.16	683.79	614.80	561.37	518.86	484.27	455.62	431.55	411.06
48000	4128.44	2124.69	1457.54	1124.54	925.19	792.67	698.34	627.88	573.32	529.90	494.57	465.31	440.73	419.81
49000	4214.45	2168.96	1487.91	1147.97	944.47	809.19	712.89	640.96	585.26	540.93	504.87	475.01	449.91	428.55
50000	4300.45	2213.22	1518.27	1171.39	963.74	825.70	727.44	654.04	597.21	551.97	515.18	484.70	459.09	437.30
55000	4730.50	2434.54	1670.10	1288.53	1060.12	908.27	800.18	719.44	656.93	607.17	566.69	533.17	505.00	481.03
60000	5160.54	2655.86	1821.92	1405.67	1156.49	990.84	872.93	784.84	716.65	662.37	618.21	581.64	550.91	524.76
65000	5590.59	2877.19	1973.75	1522.81	1252.86	1073.41	945.67	850.25	776.37	717.56	669.73	630.11	596.82	568.49
70000	6020.63	3098.51	2125.58	1639.95	1349.24	1155.98	1018.41	915.65	836.09	772.76	721.24	678.58	642.73	612.22
75000	6450.68	3319.83	2277.40	1757.09	1445.61	1238.55	1091.16	981.05	895.81	827.96	772.76	727.05	688.63	655.95
80000	6880.72	3541.15	2429.23	1874.23	1541.98	1321.12	1163.90	1046.46	955.53	883.16	824.28	775.52	734.54	699.68
85000	7310.77	3762.47	2581.06	1991.36	1638.35	1403.69	1236.64	1111.86	1015.25	938.35	875.80	823.99	780.45	743.41
90000	7740.81	3983.79	2732.88	2108.50	1734.73	1486.26	1309.39	1177.26	1074.97	993.55	927.31	872.46	826.36	787.14
95000	8170.86	4205.11	2884.71	2225.64	1831.10	1568.83	1382.13	1242.67	1134.69	1048.75	978.83	920.93	872.27	830.87
100000	8600.90	4426.44	3036.54	2342.78	1927.48	1651.40	1454.88	1308.07	1194.41	1103.94	1030.35	969.40	918.18	874.60

TERM AMOUNT	15 Years	16 Years	17 Years	18 Years	19 Years	20 Years	21 Years	22 Years	23 Years	24 Years	25 Years	30 Years	35 Years	40 Years
5	.05	.05	.04	.04	.04	.04	.04	.04	.04	.04	.04	.03	.03	.03
10	.09	.09	.08	.08	.08	.08	.07	.07	.07	.07	.07	.06	.06	.06
15	.13	.13	.12	.12	.11	.11	.11	.11	.10	.10	.10	.09	.09	.09
25	.21	.21	.20	.19	.19	.18	.18	.17	.17	.17	.16	.15	.15	.14
50	.42	.41	.39	.38	.37	.36	.35	.34	.34	.33	.32	.30	.29	.28
75	.63	.61	.59	.57	.55	.54	.52	.51	.50	.49	.48	.45	.43	.41
100	.84	.81	.78	.76	.73	.71	.70	.68	.67	.65	.64	.60	.57	.55
200	1.68	1.61	1.56	1.51	1.46	1.42	1.39	1.36	1.33	1.30	1.28	1.19	1.13	1.09
300	2.52	2.42	2.33	2.26	2.19	2.13	2.08	2.03	1.99	1.95	1.92	1.78	1.69	1.63
400	3.35	3.22	3.11	3.01	2.92	2.84	2.77	2.71	2.65	2.60	2.55	2.37	2.25	2.17
500	4.19	4.03	3.89	3.76	3.65	3.55	3.46	3.38	3.31	3.25	3.19	2.96	2.81	2.71
600	5.03	4.83	4.66	4.51	4.38	4.26	4.15	4.06	3.97	3.90	3.83	3.55	3.38	3.25
700	5.86	5.64	5.44	5.26	5.11	4.97	4.85	4.73	4.63	4.54	4.46	4.15	3.94	3.80
800	6.70	6.44	6.21	6.01	5.84	5.68	5.54	5.41	5.30	5.19	5.10	4.74	4.50	4.34
900	7.54	7.25	6.99	6.77	6.57	6.39	6.23	6.09	5.96	5.84	5.74	5.33	5.06	4.88
1000	8.38	8.05	7.77	7.52	7.29	7.10	6.92	6.76	6.62	6.49	6.37	5.92	5.62	5.42
2000	16.75	16.10	15.53	15.03	14.58	14.19	13.84	13.52	13.23	12.97	12.74	11.84	11.24	10.84
3000	25.12	24.14	23.29	22.54	21.87	21.28	20.75	20.28	19.85	19.46	19.11	17.75	16.86	16.25
4000	33.49	32.19	31.05	30.05	29.16	28.37	27.67	27.03	26.46	25.94	25.47	23.67	22.48	21.67
5000	41.86	40.24	38.81	37.56	36.45	35.47	34.58	33.79	33.07	32.43	31.84	29.58	28.10	27.08
6000	50.23	48.28	46.58	45.07	43.74	42.56	41.50	40.55	39.69	38.91	38.21	35.50	33.71	32.50
7000	58.60	56.33	54.34	52.59	51.03	49.65	48.42	47.30	46.30	45.40	44.57	41.41	39.33	37.91
8000	66.97	64.37	62.10	60.10	58.32	56.74	55.33	54.06	52.92	51.88	50.94	47.33	44.95	43.33
9000	75.35	72.42	69.86	67.61	65.61	63.84	62.25	60.82	59.53	58.36	57.31	53.24	50.57	48.74
10000	83.72	80.47	77.62	75.12	72.90	70.93	69.16	67.58	66.14	64.85	63.67	59.16	56.19	54.16
11000	92.09	88.51	85.38	82.63	80.19	78.02	76.08	74.33	72.76	71.33	70.04	65.07	61.81	59.57
12000	100.46	96.56	93.15	90.14	87.48	85.11	82.99	81.09	79.37	77.82	76.41	70.99	67.42	64.99
13000	108.83	104.60	100.91	97.65	94.77	92.21	89.91	87.85	85.99	84.30	82.77	76.90	73.04	70.40
14000	117.20	112.65	108.67	105.17	102.06	99.30	96.83	94.60	92.60	90.79	89.14	82.82	78.66	75.82
15000	125.57	120.70	116.43	112.68	109.35	106.39	103.74	101.36	99.21	97.27	95.51	88.74	84.28	81.23
16000	133.94	128.74	124.19	120.19	116.64	113.48	110.66	108.12	105.83	103.76	101.87	94.65	89.90	86.65
17000	142.32	136.79	131.96	127.70	123.93	120.58	117.57	114.88	112.44	110.24	108.24	100.57	95.51	92.06
18000	150.69	144.83	139.72	135.21	131.22	127.67	124.49	121.63	119.06	116.72	114.61	106.48	101.13	97.48
19000	159.06	152.88	147.48	142.72	138.51	134.76	131.40	128.39	125.67	123.21	120.97	112.40	106.75	102.89
20000	167.43	160.93	155.24	150.23	145.80	141.85	138.32	135.15	132.28	129.69	127.34	118.31	112.37	108.31
21000	175.80	168.97	163.00	157.75	153.09	148.95	145.24	141.90	138.90	136.18	133.71	124.23	117.99	113.73
22000	184.17	177.02	170.76	165.26	160.38	156.04	152.15	148.66	145.51	142.66	140.08	130.14	123.61	119.14
23000	192.54	185.06	178.53	172.77	167.67	163.13	159.07	155.42	152.13	149.15	146.44	136.06	129.22	124.56
24000	200.91	193.11	186.29	180.28	174.96	170.22	165.98	162.17	158.74	155.63	152.81	141.97	134.84	129.97
25000	209.28	201.16	194.05	187.79	182.25	177.31	172.90	168.93	165.35	162.12	159.18	147.89	140.46	135.39
26000	217.66	209.20	201.81	195.30	189.54	184.41	179.81	175.69	171.97	168.60	165.54	153.80	146.08	140.80
27000	226.03	217.25	209.57	202.82	196.83	191.50	186.73	182.45	178.58	175.08	171.91	159.72	151.70	146.22
28000	234.40	225.29	217.33	210.33	204.12	198.59	193.65	189.20	185.20	181.57	178.28	165.64	157.31	151.63
29000	242.77	233.34	225.10	217.84	211.41	205.68	200.56	195.96	191.81	188.05	184.64	171.55	162.93	157.05
30000	251.14	241.39	232.86	225.35	218.70	212.78	207.48	202.72	198.42	194.54	191.01	177.47	168.55	162.46
31000	259.51	249.43	240.62	232.86	225.99	219.87	214.39	209.47	205.04	201.02	197.38	183.38	174.17	167.88
32000	267.88	257.48	248.38	240.37	233.28	226.96	221.31	216.23	211.65	207.51	203.74	189.30	179.79	173.29
33000	276.25	265.53	256.14	247.88	240.57	234.05	228.23	222.99	218.27	213.99	210.11	195.21	185.41	178.71
34000	284.63	273.57	263.91	255.40	247.86	241.15	235.14	229.75	224.88	220.48	216.48	201.13	191.02	184.12
35000	293.00	281.62	271.67	262.91	255.15	248.24	242.06	236.50	231.49	226.96	222.84	207.04	196.64	189.54
36000	301.37	289.66	279.43	270.42	262.44	255.33	248.97	243.26	238.11	233.44	229.21	212.96	202.26	194.95
37000	309.74	297.71	287.19	277.93	269.73	262.42	255.89	250.02	244.72	239.93	235.58	218.87	207.88	200.37
38000	318.11	305.76	294.95	285.44	277.02	269.52	262.80	256.77	251.34	246.41	241.94	224.79	213.50	205.78
39000	326.48	313.80	302.71	292.95	284.31	276.61	269.72	263.53	257.95	252.90	248.31	230.70	219.11	211.20
40000	334.85	321.85	310.48	300.46	291.60	283.70	276.64	270.29	264.56	259.38	254.68	236.62	224.73	216.62
41000	343.22	329.89	318.24	307.98	298.89	290.79	283.55	277.05	271.18	265.87	261.04	242.54	230.35	222.03
42000	351.59	337.94	326.00	315.49	306.18	297.89	290.47	283.80	277.79	272.35	267.41	248.45	235.97	227.45
43000	359.97	345.99	333.76	323.00	313.47	304.98	297.38	290.56	284.40	278.83	273.78	254.37	241.59	232.86
44000	368.34	354.03	341.52	330.51	320.76	312.07	304.30	297.32	291.02	285.32	280.15	260.28	247.21	238.28
45000	376.71	362.08	349.29	336.02	328.05	319.16	311.21	304.07	297.63	291.80	286.51	266.20	252.82	243.69
46000	385.08	370.12	357.05	345.53	335.34	326.25	318.13	310.83	304.25	298.29	292.88	272.11	258.44	249.11
47000	393.45	378.17	364.81	353.04	342.63	333.35	325.05	317.59	310.86	304.77	299.25	278.03	264.06	254.52
48000	401.82	386.22	372.57	360.56	349.92	340.44	331.96	324.34	317.47	311.26	305.61	283.94	269.68	259.94
49000	410.19	394.26	380.33	368.07	357.20	347.53	338.88	331.10	324.09	317.74	311.98	289.86	275.30	265.35
50000	418.56	402.31	388.09	375.58	364.49	354.62	345.79	337.86	330.70	324.23	318.35	295.77	280.92	270.77
55000	460.42	442.54	426.90	413.14	400.94	390.09	380.37	371.64	363.77	356.65	350.18	325.35	309.01	297.84
60000	502.28	482.77	465.71	450.69	437.39	425.55	414.95	405.43	396.84	389.07	382.01	354.93	337.10	324.92
65000	544.13	523.00	504.52	488.25	473.84	461.01	449.53	439.21	429.91	421.49	413.85	384.50	365.19	352.00
70000	585.99	563.23	543.33	525.81	510.29	496.47	484.11	473.00	462.98	453.91	445.68	414.08	393.28	379.07
75000	627.84	603.46	582.14	563.37	546.74	531.93	518.69	506.79	496.05	486.34	477.52	443.66	421.37	406.15
80000	669.70	643.69	620.95	600.92	583.19	567.40	553.27	540.57	529.12	518.76	509.35	473.24	449.46	433.23
85000	711.56	683.92	659.76	638.48	619.64	602.86	587.85	574.36	562.19	551.18	541.18	502.81	477.55	460.30
90000	753.41	724.15	698.57	676.04	656.09	638.32	622.42	608.14	595.26	583.60	573.02	532.39	505.64	487.38
95000	795.27	764.38	737.37	713.60	692.54	673.78	657.00	641.93	628.33	616.02	604.85	561.97	533.73	514.45
100000	837.12	804.61	776.18	751.15	728.98	709.24	691.58	675.71	661.40	648.45	636.69	591.54	561.83	541.53

MONTHLY PAYMENT
REQUIRED TO AMORTIZE A LOAN

5.900%

TERM AMOUNT	1 Year	2 Years	3 Years	4 Years	5 Years	6 Years	7 Years	8 Years	9 Years	10 Years	11 Years	12 Years	13 Years	14 Years
5	.44	.23	.16	.12	.10	.09	.08	.07	.06	.06	.06	.05	.05	.05
10	.87	.45	.31	.24	.20	.17	.15	.14	.12	.12	.11	.10	.10	.09
15	1.30	.67	.46	.36	.29	.25	.22	.20	.18	.17	.16	.15	.14	.14
25	2.16	1.11	.76	.59	.49	.42	.37	.33	.30	.28	.26	.25	.23	.22
50	4.31	2.22	1.52	1.18	.97	.83	.73	.66	.60	.56	.52	.49	.46	.44
75	6.46	3.33	2.28	1.76	1.45	1.24	1.10	.99	.90	.83	.78	.73	.69	.66
100	8.61	4.43	3.04	2.35	1.93	1.66	1.46	1.31	1.20	1.11	1.04	.98	.92	.88
200	17.21	8.86	6.08	4.69	3.86	3.31	2.92	2.62	2.40	2.22	2.07	1.96	1.84	1.76
300	25.81	13.29	9.12	7.04	5.79	4.96	4.37	3.93	3.59	3.32	3.10	2.92	2.76	2.63
400	34.41	17.72	12.16	9.38	7.72	6.62	5.83	5.24	4.79	4.43	4.13	3.89	3.68	3.51
500	43.02	22.14	15.19	11.72	9.65	8.27	7.29	6.55	5.98	5.53	5.16	4.86	4.60	4.38
600	51.62	26.57	18.23	14.07	11.58	9.92	8.74	7.86	7.18	6.64	6.19	5.83	5.52	5.26
700	60.22	31.00	21.27	16.41	13.51	11.57	10.20	9.17	8.37	7.74	7.23	6.80	6.44	6.14
800	68.82	35.43	24.31	18.76	15.43	13.23	11.65	10.48	9.57	8.85	8.26	7.77	7.36	7.01
900	77.42	39.85	27.34	21.10	17.36	14.88	13.11	11.79	10.77	9.95	9.29	8.74	8.28	7.89
1000	86.03	44.28	30.38	23.44	19.29	16.53	14.57	13.10	11.96	11.06	10.32	9.71	9.20	8.76
2000	172.05	88.56	60.76	46.88	38.58	33.06	29.13	26.19	23.92	22.11	20.64	19.42	18.39	17.52
3000	258.07	132.83	91.13	70.32	57.86	49.58	43.69	39.28	35.87	33.16	30.95	29.13	27.59	26.28
4000	344.09	177.11	121.51	93.76	77.15	66.11	58.25	52.38	47.83	44.21	41.27	38.83	36.78	35.04
5000	430.11	221.38	151.89	117.20	96.44	82.63	72.81	65.47	59.79	55.26	51.59	48.54	45.98	43.80
6000	516.13	265.66	182.26	140.64	115.72	99.16	87.37	78.56	71.74	66.32	61.90	58.25	55.17	52.56
7000	602.15	309.93	212.64	164.08	135.01	115.69	101.93	91.65	83.70	77.37	72.22	67.95	64.37	61.32
8000	688.17	354.21	243.02	187.52	154.30	132.21	116.49	104.75	95.66	88.42	82.53	77.66	73.56	70.08
9000	774.19	398.49	273.39	210.96	173.58	148.74	131.05	117.84	107.61	99.47	92.85	87.37	82.76	78.84
10000	860.21	442.76	303.77	234.40	192.87	165.26	145.61	130.93	119.57	110.52	103.17	97.07	91.95	87.60
11000	946.23	487.04	334.15	257.84	212.15	181.79	160.17	144.03	131.52	121.58	113.48	106.78	101.15	96.36
12000	1032.25	531.31	364.52	281.28	231.44	198.31	174.73	157.12	143.48	132.63	123.80	116.49	110.34	105.12
13000	1118.27	575.59	394.90	304.71	250.73	214.84	189.29	170.21	155.44	143.68	134.11	126.19	119.54	113.87
14000	1204.29	619.86	425.28	328.15	270.01	231.37	203.85	183.30	167.39	154.73	144.43	135.90	128.73	122.63
15000	1290.31	664.14	455.65	351.59	289.30	247.89	218.41	196.40	179.35	165.78	154.75	145.61	137.93	131.39
16000	1376.33	708.41	486.03	375.03	308.59	264.42	232.98	209.49	191.31	176.84	165.06	155.31	147.12	140.15
17000	1462.35	752.69	516.41	398.47	327.87	280.94	247.54	222.58	203.26	187.89	175.38	165.02	156.32	148.91
18000	1548.37	796.97	546.78	421.91	347.16	297.47	262.10	235.68	215.22	198.94	185.70	174.73	165.51	157.67
19000	1634.39	841.24	577.16	445.35	366.45	313.99	276.66	248.77	227.18	209.99	196.01	184.43	174.71	166.43
20000	1720.41	885.52	607.54	468.79	385.73	330.52	291.22	261.86	239.13	221.04	206.33	194.14	183.90	175.19
21000	1806.43	929.79	637.91	492.23	405.02	347.05	305.78	274.95	251.09	232.09	216.64	203.85	193.10	183.95
22000	1892.46	974.07	668.29	515.67	424.30	363.57	320.34	288.05	263.04	243.15	226.96	213.56	202.29	192.71
23000	1978.48	1018.34	698.67	539.11	443.59	380.10	334.90	301.14	275.00	254.20	237.28	223.26	211.49	201.47
24000	2064.50	1062.62	729.04	562.55	462.88	396.62	349.46	314.23	286.96	265.25	247.59	232.97	220.68	210.23
25000	2150.52	1106.89	759.42	585.99	482.16	413.15	364.02	327.32	298.91	276.30	257.91	242.68	229.88	218.98
26000	2236.54	1151.17	789.80	609.42	501.45	429.67	378.58	340.42	310.87	287.35	268.22	252.38	239.07	227.74
27000	2322.56	1195.45	820.17	632.86	520.74	446.20	393.14	353.51	322.83	298.41	278.54	262.09	248.26	236.50
28000	2408.58	1239.72	850.55	656.30	540.02	462.73	407.70	366.60	334.78	309.46	288.86	271.80	257.46	245.26
29000	2494.60	1284.00	880.93	679.74	559.31	479.25	422.26	379.70	346.74	320.51	299.17	281.50	266.65	254.02
30000	2580.62	1328.27	911.30	703.18	578.60	495.78	436.82	392.79	358.70	331.56	309.49	291.21	275.85	262.78
31000	2666.64	1372.55	941.68	726.62	597.88	512.30	451.39	405.88	370.65	342.61	319.80	300.92	285.04	271.54
32000	2752.66	1416.82	972.06	750.06	617.17	528.83	465.95	418.97	382.61	353.67	330.12	310.62	294.24	280.30
33000	2838.68	1461.10	1002.43	773.50	636.45	545.35	480.51	432.07	394.56	364.72	340.44	320.33	303.43	289.06
34000	2924.70	1505.37	1032.81	796.94	655.74	561.88	495.07	445.16	406.52	375.77	350.75	330.04	312.63	297.82
35000	3010.72	1549.65	1063.19	820.38	675.03	578.41	509.63	458.25	418.48	386.82	361.07	339.74	321.82	306.58
36000	3096.74	1593.93	1093.56	843.82	694.31	594.93	524.19	471.35	430.43	397.87	371.39	349.45	331.02	315.34
37000	3182.76	1638.20	1123.94	867.26	713.60	611.46	538.75	484.44	442.39	408.93	381.70	359.16	340.21	324.09
38000	3268.78	1682.48	1154.32	890.69	732.89	627.98	553.31	497.53	454.35	419.98	392.02	368.86	349.41	332.85
39000	3354.80	1726.75	1184.69	914.13	752.17	644.51	567.87	510.62	466.30	431.03	402.33	378.57	358.60	341.61
40000	3440.82	1771.03	1215.07	937.57	771.46	661.03	582.43	523.72	478.26	442.08	412.65	388.28	367.80	350.37
41000	3526.84	1815.30	1245.45	961.01	790.74	677.56	596.99	536.81	490.22	453.13	422.97	397.99	376.99	359.13
42000	3612.86	1859.58	1275.82	984.45	810.03	694.09	611.55	549.90	502.17	464.18	433.28	407.69	386.19	367.89
43000	3698.89	1903.85	1306.20	1007.89	829.32	710.61	626.11	563.00	514.13	475.24	443.60	417.40	395.38	376.65
44000	3784.91	1948.13	1336.58	1031.33	848.60	727.14	640.67	576.09	526.08	486.29	453.91	427.11	404.58	385.41
45000	3870.93	1992.41	1366.95	1054.77	867.89	743.66	655.23	589.18	538.04	497.34	464.23	436.81	413.77	394.17
46000	3956.95	2036.68	1397.33	1078.21	887.18	760.19	669.80	602.27	550.00	508.39	474.55	446.52	422.97	402.93
47000	4042.97	2080.96	1427.71	1101.65	906.46	776.71	684.36	615.37	561.95	519.44	484.86	456.23	432.16	411.69
48000	4128.99	2125.23	1458.08	1125.09	925.75	793.24	698.92	628.46	573.91	530.50	495.18	465.93	441.36	420.45
49000	4215.01	2169.51	1488.46	1148.53	945.04	809.77	713.48	641.55	585.87	541.55	505.50	475.64	450.55	429.20
50000	4301.03	2213.78	1518.84	1171.97	964.32	826.29	728.04	654.64	597.82	552.60	515.81	485.35	459.75	437.96
55000	4731.13	2435.16	1670.72	1289.16	1060.75	908.92	800.84	720.11	657.60	607.86	567.39	533.88	505.72	481.76
60000	5161.23	2656.54	1822.60	1406.36	1157.19	991.55	873.64	785.57	717.39	663.12	618.97	582.41	551.69	525.56
65000	5591.34	2877.92	1974.49	1523.55	1253.62	1074.18	946.45	851.04	777.17	718.38	670.55	630.95	597.67	569.35
70000	6021.44	3099.29	2126.37	1640.75	1350.05	1156.81	1019.25	916.50	836.95	773.64	722.13	679.48	643.64	613.15
75000	6451.54	3320.67	2278.25	1757.95	1446.48	1239.43	1092.05	981.96	896.73	828.90	773.71	728.02	689.62	656.94
80000	6881.64	3542.05	2430.14	1875.14	1542.91	1322.06	1164.86	1047.43	956.51	884.16	825.29	776.55	735.59	700.74
85000	7311.75	3763.43	2582.02	1992.34	1639.34	1404.69	1237.66	1112.89	1016.30	939.42	876.88	825.09	781.56	744.54
90000	7741.85	3984.81	2733.90	2109.53	1735.78	1487.32	1310.46	1178.36	1076.08	994.68	928.46	873.62	827.54	788.33
95000	8171.95	4206.18	2885.79	2226.73	1832.21	1569.95	1383.27	1243.82	1135.86	1049.94	980.04	922.15	873.51	832.13
100000	8602.05	4427.56	3037.67	2343.93	1928.64	1652.58	1456.07	1309.28	1195.64	1105.19	1031.62	970.69	919.49	875.92

TERM	15 Years	16 Years	17 Years	18 Years	19 Years	20 Years	21 Years	22 Years	23 Years	24 Years	25 Years	30 Years	35 Years	40 Years
AMOUNT														
5	.05	.05	.04	.04	.04	.04	.04	.04	.04	.04	.04	.03	.03	.03
10	.09	.09	.08	.08	.08	.08	.07	.07	.07	.07	.07	.06	.06	.06
15	.13	.13	.12	.12	.11	.11	.11	.11	.10	.10	.10	.09	.09	.09
25	.21	.21	.20	.19	.19	.18	.18	.17	.17	.17	.16	.15	.15	.14
50	.42	.41	.39	.38	.37	.36	.35	.34	.34	.33	.32	.30	.29	.28
75	.63	.61	.59	.57	.55	.54	.52	.51	.50	.49	.48	.45	.43	.41
100	.84	.81	.78	.76	.74	.72	.70	.68	.67	.65	.64	.60	.57	.55
200	1.68	1.62	1.56	1.51	1.47	1.43	1.39	1.36	1.33	1.30	1.28	1.19	1.13	1.09
300	2.52	2.42	2.34	2.26	2.20	2.14	2.08	2.04	1.99	1.95	1.92	1.78	1.70	1.63
400	3.36	3.23	3.12	3.02	2.93	2.85	2.78	2.71	2.66	2.60	2.56	2.38	2.26	2.18
500	4.20	4.03	3.89	3.77	3.66	3.56	3.47	3.39	3.32	3.25	3.20	2.97	2.82	2.72
600	5.04	4.84	4.67	4.52	4.39	4.27	4.16	4.07	3.98	3.90	3.83	3.56	3.39	3.26
700	5.87	5.65	5.45	5.27	5.12	4.98	4.86	4.75	4.65	4.55	4.47	4.16	3.95	3.81
800	6.71	6.45	6.23	6.03	5.85	5.69	5.55	5.42	5.31	5.20	5.11	4.75	4.51	4.35
900	7.55	7.26	7.00	6.78	6.58	6.40	6.24	6.10	5.97	5.85	5.75	5.34	5.08	4.89
1000	8.39	8.06	7.78	7.53	7.31	7.11	6.94	6.78	6.63	6.50	6.39	5.94	5.64	5.44
2000	16.77	16.12	15.56	15.06	14.61	14.22	13.87	13.55	13.26	13.00	12.77	11.87	11.27	10.87
3000	25.16	24.18	23.33	22.58	21.92	21.33	20.80	20.32	19.89	19.50	19.15	17.80	16.91	16.30
4000	33.54	32.24	31.11	30.11	29.22	28.43	27.73	27.09	26.52	26.00	25.53	23.73	22.54	21.74
5000	41.93	40.30	38.88	37.63	36.52	35.54	34.66	33.86	33.15	32.50	31.92	29.66	28.18	27.17
6000	50.31	48.36	46.66	45.16	43.83	42.65	41.59	40.64	39.78	39.00	38.30	35.59	33.81	32.60
7000	58.70	56.42	54.43	52.68	51.13	49.75	48.52	47.41	46.41	45.50	44.68	41.52	39.45	38.03
8000	67.08	64.48	62.21	60.21	58.44	56.86	55.45	54.18	53.04	52.00	51.06	47.46	45.08	43.47
9000	75.47	72.54	69.99	67.73	65.74	63.97	62.38	60.95	59.66	58.50	57.44	53.39	50.72	48.90
10000	83.85	80.60	77.76	75.26	73.04	71.07	69.31	67.72	66.29	65.00	63.83	59.32	56.35	54.33
11000	92.24	88.66	85.54	82.79	80.35	78.18	76.24	74.49	72.92	71.50	70.21	65.25	61.99	59.76
12000	100.62	96.72	93.31	90.31	87.65	85.29	83.17	81.27	79.55	78.00	76.59	71.18	67.62	65.20
13000	109.01	104.70	101.09	97.84	94.96	92.39	90.10	88.04	86.18	84.50	82.97	77.11	73.26	70.63
14000	117.39	112.84	108.86	105.36	102.26	99.50	97.03	94.81	92.81	91.00	89.35	83.04	78.89	76.06
15000	125.77	120.90	116.64	112.89	109.56	106.61	103.96	101.58	99.44	97.50	95.74	88.98	84.53	81.49
16000	134.16	128.96	124.41	120.41	116.87	113.71	110.89	108.35	106.07	104.00	102.12	94.91	90.16	86.93
17000	142.54	137.02	132.19	127.94	124.17	120.82	117.82	115.13	112.69	110.50	108.50	100.84	95.80	92.36
18000	150.93	145.08	139.97	135.46	131.48	127.93	124.75	121.90	119.32	117.00	114.88	106.77	101.43	97.79
19000	159.31	153.14	147.74	142.99	138.78	135.03	131.68	128.67	125.95	123.49	121.26	112.70	107.07	103.22
20000	167.70	161.20	155.52	150.51	146.08	142.14	138.61	135.44	132.58	129.99	127.65	118.63	112.70	108.66
21000	176.08	169.26	163.29	158.04	153.39	149.25	145.54	142.21	139.21	136.49	134.03	124.56	118.34	114.09
22000	184.47	177.32	171.07	165.57	160.69	156.35	152.47	148.98	145.84	142.99	140.41	130.50	123.97	119.52
23000	192.05	185.30	178.84	173.09	168.00	163.46	159.40	155.76	152.47	149.49	146.79	136.43	129.61	124.95
24000	201.24	193.44	186.62	180.62	175.30	170.57	166.33	162.53	159.10	155.99	153.17	142.36	135.24	130.39
25000	209.62	201.50	194.39	188.14	182.60	177.67	173.26	169.30	165.73	162.49	159.56	148.29	140.88	135.82
26000	218.01	209.56	202.17	195.67	189.91	184.78	180.19	176.07	172.35	168.99	165.94	154.22	146.51	141.25
27000	226.39	217.62	209.95	203.19	197.21	191.89	187.12	182.84	178.98	175.49	172.32	160.15	152.15	146.68
28000	234.77	225.68	217.72	210.72	204.52	198.99	194.05	189.61	185.61	181.99	178.70	166.08	157.78	152.12
29000	243.16	233.74	225.50	218.24	211.82	206.10	200.98	196.39	192.24	188.49	185.08	172.01	163.42	157.55
30000	251.54	241.80	233.27	225.77	219.12	213.21	207.91	203.16	198.87	194.99	191.47	177.95	169.05	162.98
31000	259.93	249.86	241.05	233.30	226.43	220.31	214.84	209.93	205.50	201.49	197.85	183.88	174.69	168.42
32000	268.31	257.92	248.82	240.82	233.73	227.42	221.77	216.70	212.13	207.99	204.23	189.81	180.32	173.85
33000	276.70	265.98	256.60	248.35	241.04	234.53	228.70	223.47	218.76	214.49	210.61	195.74	185.96	179.28
34000	285.08	274.03	264.38	255.87	248.34	241.63	235.64	230.25	225.38	220.99	216.99	201.67	191.59	184.71
35000	293.47	282.09	272.15	263.40	255.64	248.74	242.57	237.02	232.01	227.49	223.38	207.60	197.23	190.15
36000	301.85	290.15	279.93	270.92	262.95	255.85	249.50	243.79	238.64	233.99	229.76	213.53	202.86	195.58
37000	310.24	298.21	287.70	278.45	270.25	262.95	256.43	250.56	245.27	240.48	236.14	219.47	208.50	201.01
38000	318.62	306.27	295.48	285.97	277.56	270.06	263.36	257.33	251.90	246.98	242.52	225.40	214.13	206.44
39000	327.01	314.33	303.25	293.50	284.86	277.17	270.29	264.10	258.53	253.48	248.90	231.33	219.77	211.88
40000	335.39	322.39	311.03	301.02	292.16	284.27	277.22	270.88	265.16	259.98	255.29	237.26	225.40	217.31
41000	343.78	330.45	318.80	308.55	299.47	291.38	284.15	277.65	271.79	266.48	261.67	243.19	231.04	222.74
42000	352.16	338.51	326.58	316.08	306.77	298.49	291.08	284.42	278.42	272.98	268.05	249.12	236.67	228.17
43000	360.54	346.57	334.36	323.60	314.08	305.59	298.01	291.19	285.04	279.48	274.43	255.05	242.31	233.61
44000	368.93	354.63	342.13	331.13	321.38	312.70	304.94	297.96	291.67	285.98	280.81	260.99	247.94	239.04
45000	377.31	362.69	349.91	338.65	328.68	319.81	311.87	304.73	298.30	292.48	287.20	266.92	253.58	244.47
46000	385.70	370.75	357.68	346.18	335.99	326.92	318.80	311.51	304.93	298.98	293.58	272.85	259.21	249.90
47000	394.08	378.81	365.46	353.70	343.29	334.02	325.73	318.28	311.56	305.48	299.96	278.78	264.85	255.34
48000	402.47	386.87	373.23	361.23	350.60	341.13	332.66	325.05	318.19	311.98	306.34	284.71	270.48	260.77
49000	410.85	394.93	381.01	368.75	357.90	348.24	339.59	331.82	324.82	318.48	312.72	290.64	276.12	266.20
50000	419.24	402.99	388.78	376.28	365.20	355.34	346.52	338.59	331.45	324.98	319.11	296.57	281.75	271.63
55000	461.16	443.29	427.66	413.91	401.72	390.88	381.17	372.45	364.59	357.48	351.02	326.23	309.92	298.80
60000	503.08	483.59	466.54	451.53	438.24	426.41	415.82	406.31	397.73	389.97	382.93	355.89	338.10	325.96
65000	545.01	523.89	505.42	489.16	474.76	461.94	450.47	440.17	430.88	422.47	414.84	385.54	366.27	353.12
70000	586.93	564.18	544.30	526.79	511.28	497.48	485.13	474.03	464.02	454.97	446.75	415.20	394.45	380.29
75000	628.85	604.48	583.17	564.42	547.80	533.01	519.78	507.89	497.17	487.46	478.66	444.86	422.62	407.45
80000	670.78	644.78	622.05	602.04	584.32	568.54	554.43	541.75	530.31	519.96	510.57	474.51	450.80	434.61
85000	712.70	685.08	660.93	639.67	620.84	604.08	589.08	575.61	563.45	552.46	542.48	504.17	478.97	461.77
90000	754.62	725.38	699.81	677.30	657.36	639.61	623.73	609.46	596.60	584.96	574.39	533.83	507.15	488.94
95000	796.55	765.68	738.69	714.93	693.88	675.15	658.38	643.32	629.74	617.45	606.30	563.48	535.32	516.10
100000	838.47	805.98	777.56	752.55	730.40	710.68	693.03	677.18	662.89	649.95	638.21	593.14	563.50	543.26

MONTHLY PAYMENT
REQUIRED TO AMORTIZE A LOAN

TERM AMOUNT	1 Year	2 Years	3 Years	4 Years	5 Years	6 Years	7 Years	8 Years	9 Years	10 Years	11 Years	12 Years	13 Years	14 Years
5	.44	.23	.16	.12	.10	.09	.08	.07	.07	.06	.06	.05	.05	.05
10	.87	.45	.31	.24	.20	.17	.15	.14	.13	.12	.11	.10	.10	.09
15	1.30	.67	.46	.36	.29	.25	.22	.20	.19	.17	.16	.15	.14	.14
25	2.16	1.11	.77	.59	.49	.42	.37	.33	.31	.28	.26	.25	.24	.23
50	4.31	2.22	1.53	1.18	.97	.83	.74	.66	.61	.56	.52	.49	.47	.45
75	6.46	3.33	2.29	1.77	1.45	1.25	1.10	.99	.91	.84	.78	.74	.70	.67
100	8.61	4.44	3.05	2.35	1.94	1.66	1.47	1.32	1.21	1.12	1.04	.98	.93	.89
200	17.22	8.87	6.09	4.70	3.87	3.32	2.93	2.63	2.41	2.23	2.08	1.96	1.85	1.77
300	25.82	13.30	9.13	7.05	5.80	4.98	4.39	3.95	3.61	3.34	3.12	2.93	2.78	2.65
400	34.43	17.73	12.17	9.40	7.74	6.63	5.85	5.26	4.81	4.45	4.15	3.91	3.70	3.53
500	43.04	22.17	15.22	11.75	9.67	8.29	7.31	6.58	6.01	5.56	5.19	4.88	4.63	4.41
600	51.64	26.60	18.26	14.10	11.60	9.95	8.77	7.89	7.21	6.67	6.23	5.86	5.55	5.29
700	60.25	31.03	21.30	16.44	13.54	11.61	10.23	9.20	8.41	7.78	7.26	6.84	6.48	6.17
800	68.86	35.46	24.34	18.79	15.47	13.26	11.69	10.52	9.61	8.89	8.30	7.81	7.40	7.05
900	77.46	39.89	27.38	21.14	17.40	14.92	13.15	11.83	10.81	10.00	9.34	8.79	8.33	7.94
1000	86.07	44.33	30.43	23.49	19.34	16.58	14.61	13.15	12.01	11.11	10.37	9.76	9.25	8.82
2000	172.14	88.65	60.85	46.98	38.67	33.15	29.22	26.29	24.02	22.21	20.74	19.52	18.50	17.63
3000	258.20	132.97	91.27	70.46	58.00	49.72	43.83	39.43	36.02	33.31	31.11	29.28	27.75	26.44
4000	344.27	177.29	121.69	93.95	77.34	66.30	58.44	52.57	48.03	44.41	41.47	39.04	36.99	35.25
5000	430.34	221.61	152.11	117.43	96.67	82.87	73.05	65.71	60.03	55.52	51.84	48.80	46.24	44.07
6000	516.40	265.93	182.54	140.92	116.00	99.44	87.66	78.85	72.04	66.62	62.21	58.56	55.49	52.88
7000	602.47	310.25	212.96	164.40	135.34	116.02	102.26	92.00	84.05	77.72	72.57	68.31	64.74	61.69
8000	688.54	354.57	243.38	187.89	154.67	132.59	116.87	105.14	96.05	88.82	82.94	78.07	73.98	70.50
9000	774.60	398.89	273.80	211.37	174.00	149.16	131.48	118.28	108.06	99.92	93.31	87.83	83.23	79.32
10000	860.67	443.21	304.22	234.86	193.33	165.73	146.09	131.42	120.06	111.03	103.68	97.59	92.48	88.13
11000	946.74	487.53	334.65	258.34	212.67	182.31	160.70	144.56	132.07	122.13	114.04	107.35	101.72	96.94
12000	1032.80	531.85	365.07	281.83	232.00	198.88	175.31	157.70	144.07	133.23	124.41	117.11	110.97	105.75
13000	1118.87	576.17	395.49	305.31	251.33	215.45	189.92	170.84	156.08	144.33	134.78	126.87	120.22	114.57
14000	1204.94	620.49	425.91	328.80	270.66	232.03	204.52	183.99	168.09	155.43	145.14	136.62	129.47	123.38
15000	1291.00	664.81	456.33	352.28	290.00	248.60	219.13	197.13	180.09	166.54	155.51	146.38	138.71	132.19
16000	1377.07	709.13	486.76	375.77	309.33	265.17	233.74	210.27	192.10	177.66	165.88	156.14	147.96	141.00
17000	1463.13	753.46	517.18	399.25	328.66	281.74	248.35	223.41	204.10	188.74	176.24	165.90	157.21	149.82
18000	1549.20	797.78	547.60	422.74	348.00	298.32	262.96	236.55	216.11	199.84	186.61	175.66	166.46	158.63
19000	1635.27	842.10	578.02	446.22	367.33	314.89	277.57	249.69	228.11	210.94	196.98	185.42	175.70	167.44
20000	1721.33	886.42	608.44	469.71	386.66	331.46	292.18	262.83	240.12	222.05	207.35	195.18	184.95	176.25
21000	1807.40	930.74	638.87	493.19	405.99	348.04	306.78	275.98	252.13	233.15	217.71	204.93	194.20	185.06
22000	1893.47	975.06	669.29	516.68	425.33	364.61	321.39	289.12	264.13	244.25	228.08	214.69	203.44	193.88
23000	1979.53	1019.38	699.71	540.16	444.66	381.18	336.00	302.26	276.14	255.35	238.45	224.45	212.69	202.69
24000	2065.60	1063.70	730.13	563.65	463.99	397.75	350.61	315.40	288.14	266.45	248.81	234.21	221.94	211.50
25000	2151.67	1108.02	760.55	587.13	483.33	414.33	365.22	328.54	300.15	277.56	259.18	243.97	231.19	220.31
26000	2237.73	1152.34	790.98	610.62	502.66	430.90	379.83	341.68	312.15	288.66	269.55	253.73	240.43	229.13
27000	2323.80	1196.66	821.40	634.10	521.99	447.47	394.44	354.82	324.16	299.76	279.91	263.48	249.68	237.94
28000	2409.87	1240.98	851.82	657.59	541.32	464.05	409.04	367.97	336.17	310.86	290.28	273.24	258.93	246.75
29000	2495.93	1285.30	882.24	681.07	560.66	480.62	423.65	381.11	348.17	321.96	300.65	283.00	268.17	255.56
30000	2582.00	1329.62	912.66	704.56	579.99	497.19	438.26	394.25	360.18	333.07	311.02	292.76	277.42	264.38
31000	2668.06	1373.94	943.09	728.04	599.32	513.76	452.87	407.39	372.18	344.17	321.38	302.52	286.67	273.19
32000	2754.13	1418.26	973.51	751.53	618.65	530.34	467.48	420.53	384.19	355.27	331.75	312.28	295.92	282.00
33000	2840.20	1462.59	1003.93	775.01	637.99	546.91	482.09	433.67	396.19	366.37	342.12	322.04	305.16	290.81
34000	2926.26	1506.91	1034.35	798.50	657.32	563.48	496.70	446.81	408.20	377.47	352.48	331.79	314.41	299.63
35000	3012.33	1551.23	1064.77	821.98	676.65	580.06	511.30	459.96	420.21	388.58	362.85	341.55	323.66	308.44
36000	3098.40	1595.55	1095.19	845.47	695.99	596.63	525.91	473.10	432.21	399.68	373.22	351.31	332.91	317.25
37000	3184.46	1639.87	1125.62	868.95	715.32	613.20	540.52	486.24	444.22	410.78	383.59	361.07	342.15	326.06
38000	3270.53	1684.19	1156.04	892.44	734.65	629.77	555.13	499.38	456.22	421.88	393.95	370.83	351.40	334.87
39000	3356.60	1728.51	1186.46	915.92	753.98	646.35	569.74	512.52	468.23	432.98	404.32	380.59	360.65	343.69
40000	3442.66	1772.83	1216.88	939.41	773.32	662.92	584.35	525.66	480.23	444.09	414.69	390.35	369.89	352.50
41000	3528.73	1817.15	1247.30	962.89	792.65	679.49	598.96	538.80	492.24	455.19	425.05	400.10	379.14	361.31
42000	3614.80	1861.47	1277.73	986.38	811.98	696.07	613.56	551.95	504.25	466.29	435.42	409.86	388.39	370.12
43000	3700.86	1905.79	1308.15	1009.86	831.32	712.64	628.17	565.09	516.25	477.39	445.79	419.62	397.64	378.94
44000	3786.93	1950.11	1338.57	1033.35	850.65	729.21	642.78	578.23	528.26	488.50	456.15	429.38	406.88	387.75
45000	3872.99	1994.43	1368.99	1056.83	869.98	745.78	657.39	591.37	540.26	499.60	466.52	439.14	416.13	396.56
46000	3959.06	2038.75	1399.41	1080.32	889.31	762.36	672.00	604.51	552.27	510.70	476.89	448.90	425.38	405.37
47000	4045.13	2083.07	1429.84	1103.80	908.65	778.93	686.61	617.65	564.28	521.80	487.26	458.65	434.63	414.19
48000	4131.19	2127.39	1460.26	1127.29	927.98	795.50	701.22	630.79	576.28	532.90	497.62	468.41	443.87	423.00
49000	4217.26	2171.71	1490.68	1150.77	947.31	812.08	715.82	643.94	588.29	544.01	507.99	478.17	453.12	431.81
50000	4303.33	2216.04	1521.10	1174.26	966.65	828.65	730.43	657.08	600.29	555.11	518.36	487.93	462.37	440.62
55000	4733.66	2437.64	1673.21	1291.68	1063.31	911.51	803.48	722.78	660.32	610.62	570.19	536.72	508.60	484.68
60000	5163.99	2659.24	1825.32	1409.11	1159.97	994.38	876.52	788.49	720.35	666.13	622.03	585.52	554.84	528.75
65000	5594.32	2880.84	1977.43	1526.53	1256.64	1077.24	949.56	854.20	780.38	721.64	673.86	634.31	601.08	572.81
70000	6024.65	3102.45	2129.54	1643.96	1353.30	1160.11	1022.60	919.91	840.41	777.15	725.70	683.10	647.31	616.87
75000	6454.99	3324.05	2281.65	1761.38	1449.97	1242.97	1095.65	985.61	900.44	832.66	777.53	731.89	693.55	660.93
80000	6885.32	3545.65	2433.76	1878.81	1546.63	1325.84	1168.69	1051.32	960.46	888.17	829.37	780.69	739.78	704.99
85000	7315.65	3767.26	2585.87	1996.23	1643.29	1408.70	1241.73	1117.03	1020.49	943.68	881.20	829.48	786.02	749.06
90000	7745.98	3988.86	2737.98	2113.66	1739.96	1491.56	1314.77	1182.73	1080.52	999.19	933.04	878.27	832.26	793.12
95000	8176.32	4210.46	2890.09	2231.08	1836.62	1574.43	1387.82	1248.44	1140.55	1054.70	984.87	927.06	878.49	837.18
100000	8606.65	4432.07	3042.20	2348.51	1933.29	1657.29	1460.86	1314.15	1200.58	1110.21	1036.71	975.86	924.73	881.24

TERM	15 Years	16 Years	17 Years	18 Years	19 Years	20 Years	21 Years	22 Years	23 Years	24 Years	25 Years	30 Years	35 Years	40 Years
AMOUNT														
5	.05	.05	.04	.04	.04	.04	.04	.04	.04	.04	.04	.03	.03	.03
10	.09	.09	.08	.08	.08	.08	.07	.07	.07	.07	.07	.06	.06	.06
15	.13	.13	.12	.12	.12	.11	.11	.11	.11	.10	.10	.09	.09	.09
25	.22	.21	.20	.19	.19	.18	.18	.18	.17	.17	.17	.15	.15	.14
50	.43	.41	.40	.38	.37	.36	.35	.35	.34	.33	.33	.30	.29	.28
75	.64	.61	.59	.57	.56	.54	.53	.52	.51	.50	.49	.45	.43	.42
100	.85	.82	.79	.76	.74	.72	.70	.69	.67	.66	.65	.60	.58	.56
200	1.69	1.63	1.57	1.52	1.48	1.44	1.40	1.37	1.34	1.32	1.29	1.20	1.15	1.11
300	2.54	2.44	2.35	2.28	2.21	2.15	2.10	2.05	2.01	1.97	1.94	1.80	1.72	1.66
400	3.38	3.25	3.14	3.04	2.95	2.87	2.80	2.74	2.68	2.63	2.58	2.40	2.29	2.21
500	4.22	4.06	3.92	3.80	3.69	3.59	3.50	3.42	3.35	3.28	3.23	3.00	2.86	2.76
600	5.07	4.87	4.70	4.55	4.42	4.30	4.20	4.10	4.02	3.94	3.87	3.60	3.43	3.31
700	5.91	5.69	5.49	5.31	5.16	5.02	4.90	4.79	4.69	4.60	4.52	4.20	4.00	3.86
800	6.76	6.50	6.27	6.07	5.89	5.74	5.60	5.47	5.36	5.25	5.16	4.80	4.57	4.41
900	7.60	7.31	7.05	6.83	6.63	6.45	6.29	6.15	6.02	5.91	5.80	5.40	5.14	4.96
1000	8.44	8.12	7.84	7.59	7.37	7.17	6.99	6.84	6.69	6.56	6.45	6.00	5.71	5.51
2000	16.88	16.23	15.67	15.17	14.73	14.33	13.98	13.67	13.38	13.12	12.89	12.00	11.41	11.01
3000	25.32	24.35	23.50	22.75	22.09	21.50	20.97	20.50	20.07	19.68	19.33	17.99	17.11	16.51
4000	33.76	32.46	31.33	30.33	29.45	28.66	27.96	27.33	26.76	26.24	25.78	23.99	22.81	22.01
5000	42.20	40.58	39.16	37.91	36.81	35.83	34.95	34.16	33.45	32.80	32.22	29.98	28.51	27.52
6000	50.64	48.69	46.99	45.49	44.17	42.99	41.94	40.99	40.14	39.36	38.66	35.98	34.22	33.02
7000	59.07	56.81	54.82	53.08	51.53	50.16	48.92	47.82	46.82	45.92	45.11	41.97	39.92	38.52
8000	67.51	64.92	62.65	60.66	58.89	57.32	55.91	54.65	53.51	52.48	51.55	47.97	45.62	44.02
9000	75.95	73.03	70.48	68.24	66.25	64.48	62.90	61.48	60.20	59.04	57.99	53.96	51.32	49.52
10000	84.39	81.15	78.32	75.82	73.61	71.65	69.89	68.31	66.89	65.60	64.44	59.96	57.02	55.03
11000	92.83	89.26	86.15	83.40	80.97	78.81	76.88	75.14	73.58	72.16	70.88	65.96	62.73	60.53
12000	101.27	97.38	93.98	90.98	88.33	85.98	83.87	81.97	80.27	78.72	77.32	71.95	68.43	66.03
13000	109.71	105.49	101.81	98.57	95.70	93.14	90.86	88.80	86.96	85.28	83.76	77.95	74.13	71.53
14000	118.14	113.61	109.64	106.15	103.06	100.31	97.84	95.64	93.64	91.84	90.21	83.94	79.83	77.03
15000	126.58	121.72	117.47	113.73	110.42	107.47	104.83	102.47	100.33	98.40	96.65	89.94	85.53	82.54
16000	135.02	129.84	125.30	121.31	117.78	114.63	111.82	109.30	107.02	104.96	103.09	95.93	91.24	88.04
17000	143.46	137.95	133.13	128.89	125.14	121.80	118.81	116.13	113.71	111.52	109.54	101.93	96.94	93.54
18000	151.90	146.06	140.96	136.47	132.50	128.96	125.80	122.96	120.40	118.08	115.98	107.92	102.64	99.04
19000	160.34	154.18	148.79	144.06	139.86	136.13	132.79	129.79	127.09	124.64	122.42	113.92	108.34	104.55
20000	168.78	162.29	156.63	151.64	147.22	143.29	139.78	136.62	133.77	131.20	128.87	119.92	114.04	110.05
21000	177.21	170.41	164.46	159.22	154.58	150.46	146.76	143.45	140.46	137.76	135.31	125.91	119.74	115.55
22000	185.65	178.52	172.29	166.80	161.94	157.62	153.75	150.28	147.15	144.32	141.75	131.91	125.45	121.05
23000	194.09	186.64	180.12	174.38	169.30	164.78	160.74	157.11	153.84	150.88	148.19	137.90	131.15	126.55
24000	202.53	194.75	187.95	181.96	176.66	171.95	167.73	163.94	160.53	157.44	154.64	143.90	136.85	132.06
25000	210.97	202.86	195.78	189.55	184.03	179.11	174.72	170.77	167.22	164.00	161.08	149.89	142.55	137.56
26000	219.41	210.98	203.61	197.13	191.39	186.28	181.71	177.60	173.91	170.56	167.52	155.89	148.25	143.06
27000	227.85	219.09	211.44	204.71	198.75	193.44	188.70	184.44	180.59	177.12	173.97	161.88	153.96	148.56
28000	236.28	227.21	219.27	212.29	206.11	200.61	195.68	191.27	187.28	183.68	180.41	167.88	159.66	154.06
29000	244.72	235.32	227.10	219.87	213.47	207.77	202.67	198.10	193.97	190.24	186.85	173.87	165.36	159.57
30000	253.16	243.44	234.94	227.45	220.83	214.93	209.66	204.93	200.66	196.80	193.30	179.87	171.06	165.07
31000	261.60	251.55	242.77	235.04	228.19	222.10	216.65	211.76	207.35	203.36	199.74	185.87	176.76	170.57
32000	270.04	259.67	250.60	242.62	235.55	229.26	223.64	218.59	214.04	209.92	206.18	191.86	182.47	176.07
33000	278.48	267.78	258.43	250.20	242.91	236.43	230.63	225.42	220.72	216.48	212.62	197.86	188.17	181.58
34000	286.92	275.89	266.26	257.78	250.27	243.59	237.62	232.25	227.41	223.04	219.07	203.85	193.87	187.08
35000	295.35	284.01	274.09	265.36	257.63	250.76	244.60	239.08	234.10	229.60	225.51	209.85	199.57	192.58
36000	303.79	292.12	281.92	272.94	264.99	257.92	251.59	245.91	240.79	236.16	231.95	215.84	205.27	198.08
37000	312.23	300.24	289.75	280.53	272.36	265.08	258.58	252.74	247.48	242.72	238.40	221.84	210.98	203.58
38000	320.67	308.35	297.58	288.11	279.72	272.25	265.57	259.57	254.17	249.28	244.84	227.83	216.68	209.09
39000	329.11	316.47	305.41	295.69	287.08	279.41	272.56	266.40	260.86	255.84	251.28	233.83	222.38	214.59
40000	337.55	324.58	313.25	303.27	294.44	286.58	279.55	273.23	267.54	262.40	257.73	239.83	228.08	220.09
41000	345.99	332.69	321.08	310.85	301.80	293.74	286.54	280.07	274.23	268.96	264.17	245.82	233.78	225.59
42000	354.42	340.81	328.91	318.43	309.16	300.91	293.52	286.90	280.92	275.52	270.61	251.82	239.48	231.09
43000	362.86	348.92	336.74	326.01	316.52	308.07	300.51	293.73	287.61	282.08	277.05	257.81	245.19	236.60
44000	371.30	357.04	344.57	333.60	323.88	315.23	307.50	300.56	294.30	288.64	283.50	263.81	250.89	242.10
45000	379.74	365.15	352.40	341.18	331.24	322.40	314.49	307.39	300.99	295.20	289.94	269.80	256.59	247.60
46000	388.18	373.27	360.23	348.76	338.60	329.56	321.48	314.22	307.67	301.75	296.38	275.80	262.29	253.10
47000	396.62	381.38	368.06	356.34	345.96	336.73	328.47	321.05	314.36	308.31	302.83	281.79	267.99	258.61
48000	405.06	389.50	375.89	363.92	353.32	343.89	335.46	327.88	321.05	314.87	309.27	287.79	273.70	264.11
49000	413.49	397.61	383.72	371.50	360.69	351.06	342.44	334.71	327.74	321.43	315.71	293.78	279.40	269.61
50000	421.93	405.72	391.56	379.09	368.05	358.22	349.43	341.54	334.43	327.99	322.16	299.78	285.10	275.11
55000	464.13	446.30	430.71	416.99	404.85	394.04	384.38	375.70	367.87	360.79	354.37	329.76	313.61	302.62
60000	506.32	486.87	469.87	454.90	441.65	429.86	419.32	409.85	401.31	393.59	386.59	359.74	342.12	330.13
65000	548.51	527.44	509.02	492.81	478.46	465.69	454.26	444.00	434.76	426.39	418.80	389.71	370.63	357.64
70000	590.70	568.01	548.18	530.72	515.26	501.51	489.20	478.16	468.20	459.19	451.02	419.69	399.14	385.15
75000	632.90	608.58	587.33	568.63	552.07	537.33	524.15	512.31	501.64	491.99	483.23	449.67	427.65	412.67
80000	675.09	649.16	626.49	606.53	588.87	573.15	559.09	546.46	535.08	524.79	515.45	479.65	456.16	440.18
85000	717.28	689.73	665.64	644.44	625.68	608.97	594.03	580.62	568.53	557.59	547.66	509.62	484.67	467.69
90000	759.48	730.30	704.80	682.35	662.48	644.79	628.98	614.77	601.97	590.39	579.88	539.60	513.18	495.20
95000	801.67	770.87	743.95	720.26	699.28	680.61	663.92	648.93	635.41	623.18	612.09	569.58	541.69	522.71
100000	843.86	811.44	783.11	758.17	736.09	716.44	698.86	683.08	668.85	655.98	644.31	599.56	570.19	550.22

MONTHLY PAYMENT
REQUIRED TO AMORTIZE A LOAN

TERM / AMOUNT	1 Year	2 Years	3 Years	4 Years	5 Years	6 Years	7 Years	8 Years	9 Years	10 Years	11 Years	12 Years	13 Years	14 Years
5	.44	.23	.16	.12	.10	.09	.08	.07	.07	.06	.06	.05	.05	.05
10	.87	.45	.31	.24	.20	.17	.15	.14	.13	.12	.11	.10	.10	.09
15	1.30	.67	.46	.36	.30	.25	.22	.20	.19	.17	.16	.15	.14	.14
25	2.16	1.11	.77	.59	.49	.42	.37	.33	.31	.28	.27	.25	.24	.23
50	4.31	2.22	1.53	1.18	.97	.84	.74	.66	.61	.56	.53	.50	.47	.45
75	6.46	3.33	2.29	1.77	1.46	1.25	1.10	.99	.91	.84	.79	.74	.70	.67
100	8.62	4.44	3.05	2.36	1.94	1.67	1.47	1.32	1.21	1.12	1.05	.99	.93	.89
200	17.23	8.88	6.10	4.71	3.88	3.33	2.94	2.64	2.42	2.24	2.09	1.97	1.86	1.78
300	25.84	13.31	9.15	7.06	5.82	4.99	4.40	3.96	3.62	3.35	3.13	2.95	2.79	2.66
400	34.45	17.75	12.19	9.42	7.76	6.66	5.88	5.28	4.83	4.47	4.17	3.93	3.72	3.55
500	43.06	22.19	15.24	11.77	9.69	8.32	7.33	6.60	6.03	5.58	5.21	4.91	4.65	4.44
600	51.67	26.62	18.29	14.12	11.63	9.98	8.80	7.92	7.24	6.70	6.26	5.89	5.58	5.32
700	60.28	31.06	21.33	16.48	13.57	11.64	10.26	9.24	8.44	7.81	7.30	6.87	6.51	6.21
800	68.89	35.50	24.38	18.83	15.51	13.30	11.73	10.56	9.65	8.93	8.34	7.85	7.44	7.10
900	77.51	39.93	27.43	21.18	17.45	14.96	13.20	11.88	10.85	10.04	9.38	8.83	8.37	7.98
1000	86.12	44.37	30.47	23.54	19.38	16.63	14.66	13.20	12.06	11.16	10.42	9.82	9.30	8.87
2000	172.23	88.74	60.94	47.07	38.76	33.25	29.32	26.39	24.12	22.31	20.84	19.63	18.60	17.74
3000	258.34	133.10	91.41	70.60	58.14	49.87	43.97	39.58	36.17	33.46	31.26	29.44	27.90	26.60
4000	344.45	177.47	121.87	94.13	77.52	66.49	58.63	52.77	48.23	44.61	41.68	39.25	37.20	35.47
5000	430.57	221.83	152.34	117.66	96.90	83.11	73.29	65.96	60.28	55.77	52.10	49.06	46.50	44.33
6000	516.68	266.20	182.81	141.19	116.28	99.73	87.94	79.15	72.34	66.92	62.51	58.87	55.80	53.20
7000	602.79	310.56	213.28	164.72	135.66	116.35	102.60	92.34	84.39	78.07	72.93	68.68	65.10	62.07
8000	688.90	354.93	243.74	188.25	155.04	132.97	117.26	105.53	96.45	89.22	83.35	78.49	74.40	70.93
9000	775.02	399.30	274.21	211.78	174.42	149.59	131.91	118.72	108.50	100.38	93.77	88.30	83.70	79.80
10000	861.13	443.66	304.68	235.31	193.80	166.21	146.57	131.91	120.56	111.53	104.19	98.11	93.00	88.66
11000	947.24	488.03	335.14	258.84	213.18	182.83	161.23	145.10	132.61	122.68	114.60	107.92	102.30	97.53
12000	1033.35	532.39	365.61	282.38	232.56	199.45	175.88	158.29	144.67	133.83	125.02	117.73	111.60	106.39
13000	1119.47	576.76	396.08	305.91	251.94	216.07	190.54	171.48	156.72	144.99	135.44	127.54	120.90	115.26
14000	1205.58	621.12	426.55	329.44	271.32	232.69	205.20	184.67	168.78	156.14	145.86	137.35	130.20	124.13
15000	1291.69	665.49	457.01	352.97	290.70	249.31	219.85	197.86	180.83	167.29	156.28	147.16	139.50	132.99
16000	1377.80	709.86	487.48	376.50	310.07	265.93	234.51	211.05	192.89	178.44	166.69	156.97	148.80	141.86
17000	1463.92	754.22	517.95	400.03	329.45	282.55	249.17	224.24	204.94	189.59	177.11	166.78	158.10	150.72
18000	1550.03	798.59	548.42	423.56	348.83	299.17	263.82	237.43	217.00	200.75	187.53	176.59	167.40	159.59
19000	1636.14	842.95	578.88	447.09	368.21	315.79	278.48	250.62	229.05	211.90	197.95	186.40	176.70	168.45
20000	1722.25	887.32	609.35	470.62	387.59	332.41	293.14	263.81	241.11	223.05	208.37	196.21	186.00	177.32
21000	1808.37	931.68	639.82	494.15	406.97	349.03	307.79	277.00	253.17	234.20	218.78	206.02	195.30	186.19
22000	1894.48	976.05	670.28	517.68	426.35	365.65	322.45	290.19	265.22	245.36	229.20	215.83	204.60	195.05
23000	1980.59	1020.42	700.75	541.22	445.73	382.27	337.11	303.38	277.28	256.51	239.62	225.64	213.90	203.92
24000	2066.70	1064.78	731.22	564.75	465.11	398.89	351.76	316.57	289.33	267.66	250.04	235.45	223.20	212.78
25000	2152.82	1109.15	761.69	588.28	484.49	415.51	366.42	329.76	301.39	278.81	260.46	245.26	232.50	221.65
26000	2238.93	1153.51	792.15	611.81	503.87	432.13	381.08	342.95	313.44	289.97	270.88	255.07	241.80	230.51
27000	2325.04	1197.88	822.62	635.34	523.25	448.75	395.73	356.14	325.50	301.12	281.29	264.88	251.10	239.38
28000	2411.15	1242.24	853.09	658.87	542.63	465.37	410.39	369.33	337.55	312.27	291.71	274.69	260.40	248.25
29000	2497.26	1286.61	883.56	682.40	562.01	481.99	425.04	382.52	349.61	323.42	302.13	284.50	269.70	257.11
30000	2583.38	1330.98	914.02	705.94	581.39	498.61	439.70	395.71	361.66	334.58	312.55	294.31	279.00	265.98
31000	2669.49	1375.34	944.49	729.46	600.76	515.23	454.36	408.90	373.72	345.73	322.97	304.13	288.30	274.84
32000	2755.60	1419.71	974.96	752.99	620.14	531.85	469.01	422.09	385.77	356.88	333.38	313.94	297.60	283.71
33000	2841.71	1464.07	1005.42	776.52	639.52	548.47	483.67	435.28	397.83	368.03	343.80	323.75	306.90	292.57
34000	2927.83	1508.44	1035.89	800.06	658.90	565.09	498.33	448.47	409.88	379.18	354.22	333.56	316.20	301.44
35000	3013.94	1552.80	1066.36	623.59	678.28	581.71	512.98	461.66	421.94	390.34	364.64	343.37	325.50	310.31
36000	3100.05	1597.17	1096.83	847.12	697.66	598.33	527.64	474.85	433.99	401.49	375.06	353.18	334.80	319.17
37000	3186.16	1641.54	1127.29	870.65	717.04	614.95	542.30	488.04	446.05	412.64	385.47	362.99	344.10	328.04
38000	3272.28	1685.90	1157.76	894.18	736.42	631.57	556.95	501.23	458.10	423.79	395.89	372.80	353.40	336.90
39000	3358.39	1730.27	1188.23	917.71	755.80	648.19	571.61	514.42	470.16	434.95	406.31	382.61	362.70	345.77
40000	3444.50	1774.63	1218.70	941.24	775.18	664.81	586.27	527.61	482.22	446.10	416.73	392.42	372.00	354.63
41000	3530.61	1819.00	1249.16	964.77	794.56	681.43	600.92	540.80	494.27	457.25	427.15	402.23	381.30	363.50
42000	3616.73	1863.36	1279.63	988.30	813.94	698.05	615.58	553.99	506.33	468.40	437.56	412.04	390.60	372.37
43000	3702.84	1907.73	1310.10	1011.83	833.32	714.67	630.24	567.18	518.38	479.56	447.98	421.85	399.90	381.23
44000	3788.95	1952.10	1340.56	1035.37	852.70	731.29	644.89	580.37	530.44	490.71	458.40	431.66	409.20	390.10
45000	3875.06	1996.46	1371.03	1058.90	872.08	747.91	659.55	593.56	542.49	501.86	468.82	441.47	418.50	398.96
46000	3961.18	2040.83	1401.50	1082.43	891.45	764.53	674.21	606.75	554.55	513.01	479.24	451.28	427.80	407.83
47000	4047.29	2085.19	1431.97	1105.96	910.83	781.15	688.86	619.94	566.60	524.16	489.66	461.09	437.10	416.69
48000	4133.40	2129.56	1462.43	1129.49	930.21	797.77	703.52	633.13	578.66	535.32	500.07	470.90	446.40	425.56
49000	4219.51	2173.92	1492.90	1153.02	949.59	814.39	718.18	646.32	590.71	546.47	510.49	480.71	455.70	434.43
50000	4305.62	2218.29	1523.37	1176.55	968.97	831.01	732.83	659.51	602.77	557.62	520.91	490.52	465.00	443.29
55000	4736.19	2440.12	1675.70	1294.20	1065.87	914.11	806.11	725.46	663.04	613.38	573.00	539.57	511.50	487.62
60000	5166.75	2661.95	1828.04	1411.86	1162.77	997.21	879.40	791.42	723.32	669.15	625.09	588.62	557.99	531.95
65000	5597.31	2883.77	1980.38	1529.51	1259.66	1080.31	952.68	857.37	783.60	724.91	677.18	637.68	604.49	576.28
70000	6027.87	3105.60	2132.71	1647.17	1356.56	1163.41	1025.96	923.32	843.87	780.67	729.27	686.73	650.99	620.61
75000	6458.43	3327.43	2285.05	1764.82	1453.46	1246.52	1099.25	989.27	904.15	836.43	781.36	735.78	697.49	664.93
80000	6889.00	3549.26	2437.39	1882.48	1550.35	1329.62	1172.53	1055.22	964.43	892.19	833.45	784.83	743.99	709.26
85000	7319.56	3771.09	2589.72	2000.13	1647.25	1412.72	1245.81	1121.17	1024.70	947.95	885.54	833.88	790.49	753.59
90000	7750.12	3992.92	2742.06	2117.79	1744.15	1495.82	1319.09	1187.12	1084.98	1003.72	937.63	882.93	836.99	797.92
95000	8180.68	4214.74	2894.40	2235.44	1841.04	1578.92	1392.38	1253.07	1145.25	1059.48	989.72	931.99	883.49	842.25
100000	8611.25	4436.57	3046.73	2353.10	1937.94	1662.02	1465.66	1319.02	1205.53	1115.24	1041.81	981.04	929.99	886.58

MONTHLY PAYMENT
REQUIRED TO AMORTIZE A LOAN — 6.100%

TERM AMOUNT	15 Years	16 Years	17 Years	18 Years	19 Years	20 Years	21 Years	22 Years	23 Years	24 Years	25 Years	30 Years	35 Years	40 Years
5	.05	.05	.04	.04	.04	.04	.04	.04	.04	.04	.04	.04	.03	.03
10	.09	.09	.08	.08	.08	.08	.08	.07	.07	.07	.07	.07	.06	.06
15	.13	.13	.12	.12	.12	.11	.11	.11	.11	.10	.10	.10	.09	.09
25	.22	.21	.20	.20	.19	.19	.18	.18	.17	.17	.17	.16	.15	.14
50	.43	.41	.40	.39	.38	.37	.36	.35	.34	.34	.33	.31	.29	.28
75	.64	.62	.60	.58	.56	.55	.53	.52	.51	.50	.49	.46	.44	.42
100	.85	.82	.79	.77	.75	.73	.71	.69	.68	.67	.66	.61	.58	.56
200	1.70	1.64	1.58	1.53	1.49	1.45	1.41	1.38	1.35	1.33	1.31	1.22	1.16	1.12
300	2.55	2.46	2.37	2.30	2.23	2.17	2.12	2.07	2.03	1.99	1.96	1.82	1.74	1.68
400	3.40	3.27	3.16	3.06	2.97	2.89	2.82	2.76	2.70	2.65	2.61	2.43	2.31	2.23
500	4.25	4.09	3.95	3.82	3.71	3.62	3.53	3.45	3.38	3.32	3.26	3.03	2.89	2.79
600	5.10	4.91	4.74	4.59	4.46	4.34	4.23	4.14	4.05	3.98	3.91	3.64	3.47	3.35
700	5.95	5.72	5.53	5.35	5.20	5.06	4.94	4.83	4.73	4.64	4.56	4.25	4.04	3.91
800	6.80	6.54	6.31	6.12	5.94	5.78	5.64	5.52	5.40	5.30	5.21	4.85	4.62	4.46
900	7.65	7.36	7.10	6.88	6.68	6.50	6.35	6.21	6.08	5.96	5.86	5.46	5.20	5.02
1000	8.50	8.17	7.89	7.64	7.42	7.23	7.05	6.89	6.75	6.63	6.51	6.06	5.77	5.58
2000	16.99	16.34	15.78	15.28	14.84	14.45	14.10	13.78	13.50	13.25	13.01	12.12	11.54	11.15
3000	25.48	24.51	23.66	22.92	22.26	21.67	21.15	20.67	20.25	19.87	19.52	18.18	17.31	16.72
4000	33.98	32.68	31.55	30.56	29.68	28.89	28.19	27.56	27.00	26.49	26.02	24.24	23.08	22.29
5000	42.47	40.85	39.44	38.19	37.09	36.12	35.24	34.45	33.75	33.11	32.53	30.30	28.85	27.87
6000	50.96	49.02	47.32	45.83	44.51	43.34	42.29	41.34	40.50	39.73	39.03	36.36	34.62	33.44
7000	59.45	57.19	55.21	53.47	51.93	50.56	49.33	48.23	47.24	46.35	45.53	42.42	40.39	39.01
8000	67.95	65.36	63.10	61.11	59.35	57.78	56.38	55.12	53.99	52.97	52.04	48.48	46.16	44.58
9000	76.44	73.53	70.98	68.75	66.77	65.00	63.43	62.01	60.74	59.59	58.54	54.54	51.93	50.15
10000	84.93	81.70	78.87	76.38	74.18	72.23	70.48	68.90	67.49	66.21	65.05	60.60	57.70	55.73
11000	93.42	89.87	86.76	84.02	81.60	79.45	77.52	75.79	74.24	72.83	71.55	66.66	63.47	61.30
12000	101.92	98.04	94.64	91.66	89.02	86.67	84.57	82.68	80.99	79.45	78.06	72.72	69.24	66.87
13000	110.41	106.21	102.53	99.30	96.44	93.89	91.62	89.57	87.73	86.07	84.56	78.78	75.00	72.44
14000	118.90	114.37	110.42	106.94	103.86	101.11	98.66	96.46	94.48	92.69	91.06	84.84	80.77	78.01
15000	127.40	122.54	118.30	114.57	111.27	108.34	105.71	103.35	101.23	99.31	97.57	90.90	86.54	83.59
16000	135.89	130.71	126.19	122.21	118.69	115.56	112.76	110.24	107.98	105.93	104.07	96.96	92.31	89.16
17000	144.38	138.88	134.08	129.85	126.11	122.78	119.81	117.13	114.73	112.55	110.58	103.02	98.08	94.73
18000	152.87	147.05	141.96	137.49	133.53	130.00	126.85	124.02	121.48	119.17	117.08	109.08	103.85	100.30
19000	161.37	155.22	149.85	145.13	140.95	137.23	133.90	130.91	128.22	125.79	123.59	115.14	109.62	105.87
20000	169.86	163.39	157.74	152.76	148.36	144.45	140.95	137.80	134.97	132.41	130.09	121.20	115.39	111.45
21000	178.35	171.56	165.62	160.40	155.78	151.67	147.99	144.69	141.72	139.03	136.59	127.26	121.16	117.02
22000	186.84	179.73	173.51	168.04	163.20	158.89	155.04	151.58	148.47	145.65	143.10	133.32	126.93	122.59
23000	195.34	187.90	181.40	175.68	170.62	166.11	162.09	158.47	155.22	152.27	149.60	139.38	132.70	128.16
24000	203.83	196.07	189.28	183.32	178.04	173.34	169.14	165.36	161.97	158.89	156.11	145.44	138.47	133.73
25000	212.32	204.24	197.17	190.95	185.45	180.56	176.18	172.25	168.71	165.51	162.61	151.50	144.24	139.31
26000	220.81	212.41	205.06	198.59	192.87	187.78	183.23	179.14	175.46	172.13	169.12	157.56	150.00	144.88
27000	229.31	220.57	212.94	206.23	200.29	195.00	190.28	186.03	182.21	178.76	175.62	163.62	155.77	150.45
28000	237.80	228.74	220.83	213.87	207.71	202.22	197.32	192.92	188.96	185.38	182.12	169.68	161.54	156.02
29000	246.29	236.91	228.72	221.51	215.12	209.45	204.37	199.81	195.71	192.00	188.63	175.74	167.31	161.59
30000	254.79	245.08	236.60	229.14	222.54	216.67	211.42	206.70	202.46	198.62	195.13	181.80	173.08	167.17
31000	263.28	253.25	244.49	236.78	229.96	223.89	218.46	213.59	209.21	205.24	201.64	187.86	178.85	172.74
32000	271.77	261.42	252.38	244.42	237.38	231.11	225.51	220.48	215.95	211.86	208.14	193.92	184.62	178.31
33000	280.26	269.59	260.26	252.06	244.80	238.33	232.56	227.37	222.70	218.48	214.65	199.98	190.39	183.88
34000	288.76	277.76	268.15	259.70	252.21	245.56	239.61	234.26	229.45	225.10	221.15	206.04	196.16	189.45
35000	297.25	285.93	276.04	267.33	259.63	252.78	246.65	241.15	236.20	231.72	227.65	212.10	201.93	195.03
36000	305.74	294.10	283.92	274.97	267.05	260.00	253.70	248.04	242.95	238.34	234.16	218.16	207.70	200.60
37000	314.23	302.27	291.81	282.61	274.47	267.22	260.75	254.93	249.70	244.96	240.66	224.22	213.47	206.17
38000	322.73	310.44	299.70	290.25	281.89	274.45	267.79	261.82	256.44	251.58	247.17	230.28	219.24	211.74
39000	331.22	318.61	307.58	297.89	289.30	281.67	274.84	268.71	263.19	258.20	253.67	236.34	225.00	217.31
40000	339.71	326.78	315.47	305.52	296.72	288.89	281.89	275.60	269.94	264.82	260.18	242.40	230.77	222.89
41000	348.21	334.94	323.36	313.16	304.14	296.11	288.94	282.49	276.69	271.44	266.68	248.46	236.54	228.46
42000	356.70	343.11	331.24	320.80	311.56	303.33	295.98	289.38	283.44	278.06	273.18	254.52	242.31	234.03
43000	365.19	351.28	339.13	328.44	318.98	310.56	303.03	296.27	290.19	284.68	279.69	260.58	248.08	239.60
44000	373.68	359.45	347.02	336.08	326.39	317.78	310.08	303.16	296.93	291.30	286.19	266.64	253.85	245.17
45000	382.18	367.62	354.90	343.71	333.81	325.00	317.12	310.05	303.68	297.92	292.70	272.70	259.62	250.75
46000	390.67	375.79	362.79	351.35	341.23	332.22	324.17	316.94	310.43	304.54	299.20	278.76	265.39	256.32
47000	399.16	383.96	370.68	358.99	348.65	339.44	331.22	323.83	317.18	311.16	305.71	284.82	271.16	261.89
48000	407.65	392.13	378.56	366.63	356.07	346.67	338.27	330.72	323.93	317.78	312.21	290.88	276.93	267.46
49000	416.15	400.30	386.45	374.27	363.48	353.89	345.31	337.61	330.68	324.40	318.71	296.94	282.70	273.03
50000	424.64	408.47	394.34	381.90	370.90	361.11	352.36	344.50	337.42	331.02	325.22	303.00	288.47	278.61
55000	467.10	449.31	433.77	420.09	407.99	397.22	387.60	378.95	371.17	364.13	357.74	333.30	317.31	306.47
60000	509.57	490.16	473.20	458.28	445.08	433.33	422.83	413.40	404.91	397.23	390.26	363.60	346.16	334.33
65000	552.03	531.01	512.64	496.47	482.17	469.44	458.07	447.85	438.65	430.33	422.78	393.90	375.00	362.19
70000	594.49	571.85	552.07	534.66	519.26	505.55	493.30	482.30	472.39	463.43	455.30	424.20	403.85	390.05
75000	636.96	612.70	591.50	572.85	556.35	541.66	528.54	516.75	506.13	496.53	487.83	454.50	432.70	417.91
80000	679.42	653.55	630.94	611.04	593.44	577.77	563.77	551.20	539.88	529.64	520.35	484.80	461.54	445.77
85000	721.88	694.39	670.37	649.23	630.53	613.89	599.01	585.65	573.62	562.74	552.87	515.10	490.39	473.63
90000	764.35	735.24	709.80	687.42	667.62	650.00	634.24	620.10	607.36	595.84	585.39	545.40	519.23	501.49
95000	806.81	776.08	749.23	725.61	704.71	686.11	669.48	654.55	641.10	628.94	617.91	575.70	548.08	529.35
100000	849.27	816.93	788.67	763.80	741.80	722.22	704.71	689.00	674.84	662.04	650.43	606.00	576.93	557.21

MONTHLY PAYMENT
REQUIRED TO AMORTIZE A LOAN

TERM AMOUNT	1 Year	2 Years	3 Years	4 Years	5 Years	6 Years	7 Years	8 Years	9 Years	10 Years	11 Years	12 Years	13 Years	14 Years
5	.44	.23	.16	.12	.10	.09	.08	.07	.07	.06	.06	.05	.05	.05
10	.87	.45	.31	.24	.20	.17	.15	.14	.13	.12	.11	.10	.10	.09
15	1.30	.67	.46	.36	.30	.25	.23	.20	.19	.17	.16	.15	.14	.14
25	2.16	1.11	.77	.59	.49	.42	.37	.34	.31	.28	.27	.25	.24	.23
50	4.31	2.22	1.53	1.18	.97	.84	.74	.67	.61	.56	.53	.50	.47	.45
75	6.46	3.33	2.29	1.77	1.46	1.25	1.11	1.00	.91	.84	.79	.74	.70	.67
100	8.62	4.44	3.05	2.36	1.94	1.67	1.47	1.33	1.21	1.12	1.05	.99	.94	.89
200	17.23	8.88	6.10	4.71	3.88	3.33	2.94	2.65	2.42	2.24	2.09	1.97	1.87	1.78
300	25.84	13.32	9.15	7.07	5.82	4.99	4.41	3.97	3.63	3.35	3.13	2.95	2.80	2.67
400	34.45	17.76	12.20	9.42	7.76	6.66	5.87	5.29	4.83	4.47	4.18	3.93	3.73	3.56
500	43.07	22.19	15.24	11.78	9.70	8.32	7.34	6.61	6.04	5.59	5.22	4.92	4.66	4.44
600	51.68	26.63	18.29	14.13	11.64	9.98	8.81	7.93	7.25	6.70	6.26	5.90	5.59	5.33
700	60.29	31.07	21.34	16.48	13.58	11.65	10.27	9.25	8.45	7.82	7.31	6.88	6.52	6.22
800	68.90	35.51	24.39	18.84	15.52	13.31	11.74	10.57	9.66	8.94	8.35	7.86	7.46	7.11
900	77.52	39.94	27.44	21.19	17.46	14.97	13.21	11.89	10.87	10.05	9.39	8.85	8.39	8.00
1000	86.13	44.38	30.48	23.55	19.40	16.64	14.67	13.21	12.07	11.17	10.44	9.83	9.32	8.88
2000	172.25	88.76	60.96	47.09	38.79	33.27	29.34	26.41	24.14	22.33	20.87	19.65	18.63	17.76
3000	258.38	133.14	91.44	70.63	58.18	49.90	44.01	39.61	36.21	33.50	31.30	29.47	27.94	26.64
4000	344.50	177.51	121.92	94.17	77.57	66.53	58.68	52.81	48.28	44.66	41.73	39.30	37.26	35.52
5000	430.62	221.89	152.40	117.72	96.96	83.16	73.35	66.02	60.34	55.83	52.16	49.12	46.57	44.40
6000	516.75	266.27	182.88	141.26	116.35	99.80	88.02	79.22	72.41	66.99	62.59	58.94	55.88	53.28
7000	602.87	310.64	213.36	164.80	135.74	116.43	102.68	92.42	84.48	78.16	73.02	68.77	65.20	62.16
8000	689.00	355.02	243.83	188.34	155.13	133.06	117.35	105.62	96.55	89.32	83.45	78.59	74.51	71.04
9000	775.12	399.40	274.31	211.89	174.52	149.69	132.02	118.83	108.61	100.49	93.88	88.41	83.82	79.92
10000	861.24	443.77	304.79	235.43	193.91	166.32	146.69	132.03	120.68	111.65	104.31	98.24	93.14	88.80
11000	947.37	488.15	335.27	258.97	213.31	182.96	161.36	145.23	132.75	122.82	114.74	108.06	102.45	97.67
12000	1033.49	532.53	365.75	282.51	232.70	199.59	176.03	158.43	144.82	133.98	125.18	117.88	111.76	106.55
13000	1119.62	576.91	396.23	306.06	252.09	216.22	190.70	171.64	156.88	145.15	135.61	127.71	121.07	115.43
14000	1205.74	621.28	426.71	329.60	271.48	232.85	205.36	184.84	168.95	156.31	146.04	137.53	130.39	124.31
15000	1291.86	665.66	457.18	353.14	290.87	249.48	220.03	198.04	181.02	167.48	156.47	147.35	139.70	133.19
16000	1377.99	710.04	487.66	376.68	310.26	266.12	234.70	211.24	193.09	178.64	166.90	157.18	149.01	142.07
17000	1464.11	754.41	518.14	400.23	329.65	282.75	249.37	224.45	205.16	189.81	177.33	167.00	158.33	150.95
18000	1550.24	798.79	548.62	423.77	349.04	299.38	264.04	237.65	217.22	200.97	187.76	176.82	167.64	159.83
19000	1636.36	843.17	579.10	447.31	368.43	316.01	278.71	250.85	229.29	212.14	198.19	186.65	176.95	168.71
20000	1722.48	887.54	609.58	470.85	387.82	332.64	293.38	264.05	241.36	223.30	208.62	196.47	186.27	177.59
21000	1808.61	931.92	640.06	494.40	407.22	349.28	308.04	277.25	253.43	234.47	219.05	206.29	195.58	186.47
22000	1894.73	976.30	670.53	517.94	426.61	365.91	322.71	290.46	265.49	245.63	229.48	216.12	204.89	195.34
23000	1980.85	1020.67	701.01	541.48	446.00	382.54	337.38	303.66	277.56	256.80	239.92	225.94	214.20	204.22
24000	2066.98	1065.05	731.49	565.02	465.39	399.17	352.05	316.86	289.63	267.96	250.35	235.76	223.52	213.10
25000	2153.10	1109.43	761.97	588.56	484.78	415.80	366.72	330.06	301.70	279.13	260.78	245.59	232.83	221.98
26000	2239.23	1153.81	792.45	612.11	504.17	432.44	381.39	343.27	313.76	290.29	271.21	255.41	242.14	230.86
27000	2325.35	1198.18	822.93	635.65	523.56	449.07	396.06	356.47	325.83	301.46	281.64	265.23	251.46	239.74
28000	2411.47	1242.56	853.41	659.19	542.95	465.70	410.72	369.67	337.90	312.62	292.07	275.06	260.77	248.62
29000	2497.60	1286.94	883.88	682.73	562.34	482.33	425.39	382.87	349.97	323.79	302.50	284.88	270.08	257.50
30000	2583.72	1331.31	914.36	706.28	581.73	498.96	440.06	396.08	362.03	334.95	312.93	294.70	279.40	266.38
31000	2669.85	1375.69	944.84	729.82	601.13	515.60	454.73	409.28	374.10	346.12	323.36	304.53	288.71	275.26
32000	2755.97	1420.07	975.32	753.36	620.52	532.23	469.40	422.48	386.17	357.28	333.79	314.35	298.02	284.14
33000	2842.09	1464.44	1005.80	776.90	639.91	548.86	484.07	435.68	398.24	368.45	344.22	324.17	307.33	293.01
34000	2928.22	1508.82	1036.28	800.45	659.30	565.49	498.74	448.89	410.31	379.61	354.65	334.00	316.65	301.89
35000	3014.34	1553.20	1066.76	823.99	678.69	582.12	513.40	462.09	422.37	390.78	365.09	343.82	325.96	310.77
36000	3100.47	1597.58	1097.23	847.53	698.08	598.76	528.07	475.29	434.44	401.94	375.52	353.64	335.27	319.65
37000	3186.59	1641.95	1127.71	871.07	717.47	615.39	542.74	488.49	446.51	413.11	385.95	363.47	344.59	328.53
38000	3272.71	1686.33	1158.19	894.62	736.86	632.02	557.41	501.70	458.58	424.27	396.38	373.29	353.90	337.41
39000	3358.84	1730.71	1188.67	918.16	756.25	648.65	572.08	514.90	470.64	435.44	406.81	383.11	363.21	346.29
40000	3444.96	1775.08	1219.15	941.70	775.64	665.28	586.75	528.10	482.71	446.60	417.24	392.94	372.53	355.17
41000	3531.08	1819.46	1249.63	965.24	795.04	681.92	601.42	541.30	494.78	457.77	427.67	402.76	381.84	364.05
42000	3617.21	1863.84	1280.11	988.79	814.43	698.55	616.08	554.50	506.85	468.93	438.10	412.58	391.15	372.93
43000	3703.33	1908.21	1310.59	1012.33	833.82	715.18	630.75	567.71	518.91	480.10	448.53	422.41	400.46	381.81
44000	3789.46	1952.59	1341.06	1035.87	853.21	731.81	645.42	580.91	530.98	491.26	458.96	432.23	409.78	390.68
45000	3875.58	1996.97	1371.54	1059.41	872.60	748.44	660.09	594.11	543.05	502.43	469.39	442.05	419.09	399.56
46000	3961.70	2041.35	1402.02	1082.95	891.99	765.08	674.76	607.31	555.12	513.59	479.83	451.88	428.40	408.44
47000	4047.83	2085.72	1432.50	1106.50	911.38	781.71	689.43	620.52	567.18	524.76	490.26	461.70	437.72	417.32
48000	4133.95	2130.10	1462.98	1130.04	930.77	798.34	704.10	633.72	579.25	535.92	500.69	471.52	447.03	426.20
49000	4220.08	2174.48	1493.46	1153.58	950.16	814.97	718.76	646.92	591.32	547.09	511.12	481.35	456.34	435.08
50000	4306.20	2218.85	1523.94	1177.12	969.55	831.60	733.43	660.12	603.39	558.25	521.55	491.17	465.66	443.96
55000	4736.82	2440.74	1676.33	1294.84	1066.51	914.76	806.78	726.14	663.73	614.08	573.70	540.29	512.22	488.35
60000	5167.44	2662.62	1828.72	1412.55	1163.46	997.92	880.12	792.15	724.06	669.90	625.86	589.40	558.79	532.75
65000	5598.06	2884.51	1981.11	1530.26	1260.42	1081.08	953.46	858.16	784.40	725.73	678.01	638.52	605.35	577.15
70000	6028.68	3106.39	2133.51	1647.97	1357.37	1164.24	1026.80	924.17	844.74	781.55	730.17	687.64	651.92	621.54
75000	6459.30	3328.28	2285.90	1765.68	1454.33	1247.40	1100.15	990.18	905.08	837.37	782.32	736.75	698.48	665.94
80000	6889.92	3550.16	2438.29	1883.40	1551.28	1330.56	1173.49	1056.20	965.42	893.20	834.48	785.87	745.05	710.33
85000	7320.54	3772.05	2590.69	2001.11	1648.24	1413.72	1246.83	1122.21	1025.76	949.02	886.63	834.99	791.61	754.73
90000	7751.16	3993.93	2743.08	2118.82	1745.19	1496.88	1320.17	1188.22	1086.09	1004.85	938.78	884.10	838.18	799.12
95000	8181.78	4215.82	2895.47	2236.53	1842.15	1580.04	1393.52	1254.23	1146.43	1060.67	990.94	933.22	884.74	843.52
100000	8612.39	4437.70	3047.87	2354.24	1939.10	1663.20	1466.86	1320.24	1206.77	1116.50	1043.09	982.34	931.31	887.91

TERM AMOUNT	15 Years	16 Years	17 Years	18 Years	19 Years	20 Years	21 Years	22 Years	23 Years	24 Years	25 Years	30 Years	35 Years	40 Years
5	.05	.05	.04	.04	.04	.04	.04	.04	.04	.04	.04	.04	.03	.03
10	.09	.09	.08	.08	.08	.08	.08	.07	.07	.07	.07	.07	.06	.06
15	.13	.13	.12	.12	.12	.11	.11	.11	.11	.10	.10	.10	.09	.09
25	.22	.21	.20	.20	.19	.19	.18	.18	.17	.17	.17	.16	.15	.14
50	.43	.41	.40	.39	.38	.37	.36	.35	.34	.34	.33	.31	.29	.28
75	.64	.62	.60	.58	.56	.55	.53	.52	.51	.50	.49	.46	.44	.42
100	.86	.82	.80	.77	.75	.73	.71	.70	.68	.67	.66	.61	.58	.56
200	1.71	1.64	1.59	1.54	1.49	1.45	1.42	1.39	1.36	1.33	1.31	1.22	1.16	1.12
300	2.56	2.46	2.38	2.30	2.23	2.18	2.12	2.08	2.03	2.00	1.96	1.83	1.74	1.68
400	3.41	3.28	3.17	3.07	2.98	2.90	2.83	2.77	2.71	2.66	2.61	2.44	2.32	2.24
500	4.26	4.10	3.96	3.83	3.72	3.62	3.54	3.46	3.39	3.32	3.26	3.04	2.90	2.80
600	5.11	4.91	4.75	4.60	4.46	4.35	4.24	4.15	4.06	3.99	3.92	3.65	3.48	3.36
700	5.96	5.73	5.54	5.36	5.21	5.07	4.95	4.84	4.74	4.65	4.57	4.26	4.06	3.92
800	6.81	6.55	6.33	6.13	5.95	5.79	5.65	5.53	5.42	5.31	5.22	4.87	4.63	4.48
900	7.66	7.37	7.12	6.89	6.69	6.52	6.36	6.22	6.09	5.98	5.87	5.47	5.21	5.04
1000	8.51	8.19	7.91	7.66	7.44	7.24	7.07	6.91	6.77	6.64	6.52	6.08	5.79	5.59
2000	17.02	16.37	15.81	15.31	14.87	14.48	14.13	13.81	13.53	13.28	13.04	12.16	11.58	11.18
3000	25.52	24.55	23.71	22.96	22.30	21.71	21.19	20.72	20.30	19.91	19.56	18.23	17.36	16.77
4000	34.03	32.74	31.61	30.61	29.73	28.95	28.25	27.62	27.06	26.55	26.08	24.31	23.15	22.36
5000	42.54	40.92	39.51	38.27	37.17	36.19	35.31	34.53	33.82	33.18	32.60	30.39	28.94	27.95
6000	51.04	49.10	47.41	45.92	44.60	43.42	42.38	41.43	40.59	39.82	39.12	36.46	34.72	33.54
7000	59.55	57.29	55.31	53.57	52.03	50.66	49.44	48.34	47.35	46.45	45.64	42.54	40.51	39.13
8000	68.05	65.47	63.21	61.22	59.46	57.90	56.50	55.24	54.11	53.09	52.16	48.61	46.29	44.72
9000	76.56	73.65	71.11	68.87	66.90	65.13	63.56	62.15	60.88	59.73	58.68	54.69	52.08	50.31
10000	85.07	81.84	79.01	76.53	74.33	72.37	70.62	69.05	67.64	66.36	65.20	60.77	57.87	55.90
11000	93.57	90.02	86.91	84.18	81.76	79.61	77.68	75.96	74.40	73.00	71.72	66.84	63.65	61.49
12000	102.08	98.20	94.81	91.83	89.19	86.84	84.75	82.86	81.17	79.63	78.24	72.92	69.44	67.08
13000	110.59	106.38	102.71	99.48	96.62	94.08	91.81	89.77	87.93	86.27	84.76	78.99	75.22	72.67
14000	119.09	114.57	110.61	107.13	104.06	101.32	98.87	96.67	94.69	92.90	91.28	85.07	81.01	78.26
15000	127.60	122.75	118.51	114.79	111.49	108.55	105.93	103.58	101.46	99.54	97.80	91.15	86.80	83.85
16000	136.11	130.93	126.41	122.44	118.92	115.79	112.99	110.48	108.22	106.17	104.32	97.22	92.58	89.44
17000	144.61	139.12	134.31	130.09	126.35	123.03	120.05	117.39	114.98	112.81	110.84	103.30	98.37	95.03
18000	153.12	147.30	142.22	137.74	133.79	130.26	127.12	124.29	121.75	119.45	117.36	109.37	104.15	100.62
19000	161.62	155.48	150.12	145.40	141.22	137.50	134.18	131.20	128.51	126.08	123.88	115.45	109.94	106.21
20000	170.13	163.67	158.02	153.05	148.65	144.74	141.24	138.10	135.27	132.72	130.40	121.53	115.73	111.80
21000	178.64	171.85	165.92	160.70	156.09	151.97	148.30	145.01	142.04	139.35	136.92	127.60	121.51	117.38
22000	187.14	180.03	173.82	168.35	163.51	159.21	155.36	151.91	148.80	145.99	143.44	133.68	127.30	122.97
23000	195.65	188.21	181.72	176.00	170.95	166.45	162.43	158.82	155.56	152.62	149.96	139.76	133.09	128.56
24000	204.15	196.40	189.62	183.66	178.38	173.68	169.49	165.72	162.33	159.26	156.48	145.83	138.87	134.15
25000	212.66	204.58	197.52	191.31	185.81	180.92	176.55	172.63	169.09	165.89	163.00	151.91	144.66	139.74
26000	221.17	212.76	205.42	198.96	193.24	188.16	183.61	179.53	175.85	172.53	169.52	157.98	150.44	145.33
27000	229.67	220.95	213.32	206.61	200.68	195.39	190.67	186.43	182.62	179.17	176.04	164.06	156.23	150.92
28000	238.18	229.13	221.22	214.26	208.11	202.63	197.73	193.34	189.38	185.80	182.55	170.14	162.02	156.51
29000	246.69	237.31	229.12	221.92	215.54	209.87	204.80	200.24	196.14	192.44	189.07	176.21	167.80	162.10
30000	255.19	245.50	237.02	229.57	222.97	217.10	211.86	207.15	202.91	199.07	195.59	182.29	173.59	167.69
31000	263.70	253.68	244.92	237.22	230.40	224.34	218.92	214.05	209.67	205.71	202.11	188.36	179.37	173.28
32000	272.20	261.86	252.82	244.87	237.84	231.58	225.98	220.96	216.43	212.34	208.63	194.44	185.16	178.87
33000	280.71	270.04	260.72	252.52	245.27	238.81	233.04	227.86	223.20	218.98	215.15	200.52	190.95	184.46
34000	289.22	278.23	268.62	260.18	252.70	246.05	240.10	234.77	229.96	225.61	221.67	206.59	196.73	190.05
35000	297.72	286.41	276.52	267.83	260.13	253.29	247.17	241.67	236.72	232.25	228.19	212.67	202.52	195.64
36000	306.23	294.59	284.43	275.48	267.57	260.52	254.23	248.58	243.49	238.89	234.71	218.74	208.30	201.23
37000	314.74	302.78	292.33	283.13	275.00	267.76	261.29	255.48	250.25	245.52	241.23	224.82	214.09	206.82
38000	323.24	310.96	300.23	290.79	282.43	275.00	268.35	262.39	257.01	252.16	247.75	230.90	219.88	212.41
39000	331.75	319.14	308.13	298.44	289.86	282.23	275.41	269.29	263.78	258.79	254.27	236.97	225.66	218.00
40000	340.25	327.33	316.03	306.09	297.29	289.47	282.48	276.20	270.54	265.43	260.79	243.05	231.45	223.59
41000	348.76	335.51	323.93	313.74	304.73	296.71	289.54	283.10	277.30	272.06	267.31	249.13	237.23	229.18
42000	357.27	343.69	331.83	321.39	312.16	303.94	296.60	290.01	284.07	278.70	273.83	255.20	243.02	234.76
43000	365.77	351.87	339.73	329.05	319.59	311.18	303.66	296.91	290.83	285.33	280.35	261.28	248.81	240.35
44000	374.28	360.06	347.63	336.70	327.02	318.42	310.72	303.82	297.59	291.97	286.87	267.35	254.59	245.94
45000	382.79	368.24	355.53	344.35	334.46	325.65	317.78	310.72	304.36	298.61	293.39	273.43	260.38	251.53
46000	391.29	376.42	363.43	352.00	341.89	332.89	324.85	317.63	311.12	305.24	299.91	279.51	266.17	257.12
47000	399.80	384.61	371.33	359.65	349.32	340.13	331.91	324.53	317.89	311.88	306.43	285.58	271.95	262.71
48000	408.30	392.79	379.23	367.31	356.75	347.36	338.97	331.44	324.65	318.51	312.95	291.66	277.74	268.30
49000	416.81	400.97	387.13	374.96	364.18	354.60	346.03	338.34	331.41	325.15	319.47	297.73	283.52	273.89
50000	425.32	409.16	395.03	382.61	371.62	361.84	353.09	345.25	338.18	331.78	325.99	303.81	289.31	279.48
55000	467.85	450.07	434.54	420.87	408.78	398.02	388.40	379.77	371.99	364.96	358.59	334.19	318.24	307.43
60000	510.38	490.99	474.04	459.13	445.94	434.20	423.71	414.29	405.81	398.14	391.18	364.57	347.17	335.38
65000	552.91	531.90	513.54	497.39	483.10	470.38	459.02	448.82	439.63	431.32	423.78	394.95	376.10	363.32
70000	595.44	572.82	553.04	535.65	520.26	506.57	494.33	483.34	473.44	464.49	456.38	425.33	405.03	391.27
75000	637.97	613.73	592.55	573.91	557.42	542.75	529.64	517.87	507.26	497.67	488.98	455.71	433.96	419.22
80000	680.50	654.65	632.05	612.17	594.58	578.93	564.95	552.39	541.08	530.85	521.58	486.09	462.89	447.17
85000	723.04	695.56	671.55	650.43	631.74	615.12	600.25	586.91	574.89	564.03	554.17	516.47	491.82	475.11
90000	765.57	736.48	711.06	688.69	668.91	651.30	635.56	621.44	608.71	597.21	586.77	546.85	520.75	503.06
95000	808.10	777.39	750.56	726.96	706.07	687.48	670.87	655.96	642.53	630.38	619.37	577.24	549.68	531.01
100000	850.63	818.31	790.06	765.22	743.23	723.67	706.18	690.49	676.35	663.56	651.97	607.62	578.61	558.96

MONTHLY PAYMENT
REQUIRED TO AMORTIZE A LOAN

TERM / AMOUNT	1 Year	2 Years	3 Years	4 Years	5 Years	6 Years	7 Years	8 Years	9 Years	10 Years	11 Years	12 Years	13 Years	14 Years
5	.44	.23	.16	.12	.10	.09	.08	.07	.07	.06	.06	.05	.05	.05
10	.87	.45	.31	.24	.20	.17	.15	.14	.13	.12	.11	.10	.10	.09
15	1.30	.67	.46	.36	.30	.26	.23	.20	.19	.17	.16	.15	.15	.14
25	2.16	1.12	.77	.59	.49	.42	.37	.34	.31	.29	.27	.25	.24	.23
50	4.31	2.23	1.53	1.18	.98	.84	.74	.67	.61	.57	.53	.50	.47	.45
75	6.47	3.34	2.29	1.77	1.46	1.26	1.11	1.00	.91	.85	.79	.74	.71	.67
100	8.62	4.45	3.06	2.36	1.95	1.67	1.48	1.33	1.22	1.13	1.05	.99	.94	.90
200	17.24	8.89	6.11	4.72	3.89	3.34	2.95	2.65	2.43	2.25	2.10	1.98	1.88	1.79
300	25.85	13.33	9.16	7.08	5.83	5.01	4.42	3.98	3.64	3.37	3.15	2.96	2.81	2.68
400	34.47	17.77	12.21	9.44	7.78	6.67	5.89	5.30	4.85	4.49	4.19	3.93	3.75	3.57
500	43.08	22.21	15.26	11.79	9.72	8.34	7.36	6.62	6.06	5.61	5.24	4.94	4.68	4.46
600	51.70	26.65	18.31	14.15	11.66	10.01	8.83	7.95	7.27	6.73	6.29	5.92	5.62	5.36
700	60.32	31.09	21.36	16.51	13.60	11.67	10.30	9.27	8.48	7.85	7.33	6.91	6.55	6.25
800	68.93	35.53	24.42	18.87	15.55	13.34	11.77	10.60	9.69	8.97	8.38	7.89	7.49	7.14
900	77.55	39.97	27.47	21.22	17.49	15.01	13.24	11.92	10.90	10.09	9.43	8.88	8.42	8.03
1000	86.16	44.42	30.52	23.58	19.43	16.67	14.71	13.24	12.11	11.21	10.47	9.87	9.36	8.92
2000	172.32	88.83	61.03	47.16	38.86	33.34	29.41	26.48	24.21	22.41	20.94	19.73	18.71	17.84
3000	258.48	133.24	91.54	70.74	58.28	50.01	44.12	39.72	36.32	33.61	31.41	29.59	28.06	26.76
4000	344.64	177.65	122.06	94.31	77.71	66.67	58.82	52.96	48.42	44.82	41.88	39.45	37.42	35.68
5000	430.80	222.06	152.57	117.89	97.13	83.34	73.53	66.20	60.53	56.02	52.35	49.32	46.77	44.60
6000	516.96	266.47	183.08	141.47	116.56	100.01	88.23	79.44	72.63	67.22	62.82	59.18	56.12	53.52
7000	603.11	310.88	213.59	165.04	135.99	116.68	102.94	92.68	84.74	78.42	73.29	69.04	65.47	62.44
8000	689.27	355.29	244.11	188.62	155.41	133.34	117.64	105.92	96.84	89.63	83.76	78.90	74.83	71.36
9000	775.43	399.70	274.62	212.20	174.84	150.01	132.35	119.16	108.95	100.83	94.23	88.77	84.18	80.28
10000	861.59	444.11	305.13	235.77	194.26	166.68	147.05	132.40	121.05	112.03	104.70	98.63	93.53	89.20
11000	947.75	488.52	335.64	259.35	213.69	183.35	161.76	145.63	133.16	123.24	115.17	108.49	102.88	98.12
12000	1033.91	532.93	366.16	282.93	233.12	200.01	176.46	158.87	145.26	134.44	125.64	118.35	112.24	107.04
13000	1120.06	577.35	396.67	306.50	252.54	216.68	191.17	172.11	157.37	145.64	136.11	128.22	121.59	115.96
14000	1206.22	621.76	427.18	330.08	271.97	233.35	205.87	185.35	169.47	156.84	146.58	138.08	130.94	124.87
15000	1292.38	666.17	457.69	353.66	291.39	250.02	220.57	198.59	181.58	168.05	157.04	147.94	140.29	133.79
16000	1378.54	710.58	488.21	377.23	310.82	266.68	235.28	211.83	193.68	179.25	167.51	157.80	149.65	142.71
17000	1464.70	754.99	518.72	400.81	330.25	283.35	249.98	225.07	205.79	190.45	177.98	167.66	159.00	151.63
18000	1550.86	799.40	549.23	424.39	349.67	300.02	264.69	238.31	217.89	201.65	188.45	177.53	168.35	160.55
19000	1637.01	843.81	579.75	447.96	369.10	316.69	279.39	251.55	230.00	212.86	198.92	187.39	177.70	169.47
20000	1723.17	888.22	610.26	471.54	388.52	333.35	294.10	264.79	242.10	224.06	209.39	197.25	187.06	178.39
21000	1809.33	932.63	640.77	495.12	407.95	350.02	308.80	278.02	254.21	235.26	219.86	207.11	196.41	187.31
22000	1895.49	977.04	671.28	518.70	427.38	366.69	323.51	291.26	266.31	246.47	230.33	216.98	205.76	196.23
23000	1981.65	1021.45	701.80	542.27	446.80	383.36	338.21	304.50	278.42	257.67	240.60	226.84	215.11	205.15
24000	2067.81	1065.86	732.31	565.85	466.23	400.02	352.92	317.74	290.52	268.87	251.27	236.70	224.47	214.07
25000	2153.96	1110.27	762.82	589.43	485.65	416.69	367.62	330.98	302.63	280.07	261.74	246.56	233.82	222.99
26000	2240.12	1154.69	793.33	613.00	505.08	433.36	382.33	344.22	314.73	291.28	272.21	256.43	243.17	231.91
27000	2326.28	1199.10	823.85	636.58	524.51	450.03	397.03	357.46	326.84	302.48	282.68	266.29	252.53	240.83
28000	2412.44	1243.51	854.36	660.16	543.93	466.69	411.73	370.70	338.94	313.68	293.15	276.15	261.88	249.74
29000	2498.60	1287.92	884.87	683.73	563.36	483.36	426.44	383.94	351.05	324.88	303.61	286.01	271.23	258.66
30000	2584.76	1332.33	915.38	707.31	582.78	500.03	441.14	397.18	363.15	336.09	314.08	295.87	280.58	267.58
31000	2670.91	1376.74	945.90	730.89	602.21	516.70	455.85	410.41	375.26	347.29	324.55	305.74	289.94	276.50
32000	2757.07	1421.15	976.41	754.46	621.63	533.36	470.55	423.65	387.36	358.49	335.02	315.60	299.29	285.42
33000	2843.23	1465.56	1006.92	778.04	641.06	550.03	485.26	436.89	399.47	369.70	345.49	325.46	308.64	294.34
34000	2929.39	1509.97	1037.43	801.62	660.49	566.70	499.96	450.13	411.57	380.90	355.96	335.32	317.99	303.26
35000	3015.55	1554.38	1067.95	825.19	679.91	583.37	514.67	463.37	423.68	392.10	366.43	345.19	327.35	312.18
36000	3101.71	1598.79	1098.46	848.77	699.34	600.03	529.37	476.61	435.78	403.30	376.90	355.05	336.70	321.10
37000	3187.87	1643.20	1128.97	872.35	718.76	616.70	544.08	489.85	447.89	414.51	387.37	364.91	346.05	330.02
38000	3274.02	1687.61	1159.49	895.92	738.19	633.37	558.78	503.09	459.99	425.71	397.84	374.77	355.40	338.94
39000	3360.18	1732.03	1190.00	919.50	757.62	650.04	573.49	516.33	472.10	436.91	408.31	384.64	364.76	347.86
40000	3446.34	1776.44	1220.51	943.08	777.04	666.70	588.19	529.57	484.20	448.12	418.78	394.50	374.11	356.78
41000	3532.50	1820.85	1251.02	966.66	796.47	683.37	602.89	542.81	496.31	459.32	429.25	404.36	383.46	365.69
42000	3618.66	1865.26	1281.54	990.23	815.89	700.04	617.60	556.04	508.41	470.52	439.72	414.22	392.81	374.61
43000	3704.82	1909.67	1312.05	1013.81	835.32	716.71	632.30	569.28	520.52	481.72	450.18	424.08	402.17	383.53
44000	3790.97	1954.08	1342.56	1037.39	854.75	733.37	647.01	582.52	532.62	492.93	460.65	433.95	411.52	392.45
45000	3877.13	1998.49	1373.07	1060.96	874.17	750.04	661.71	595.76	544.73	504.13	471.12	443.81	420.87	401.37
46000	3963.29	2042.90	1403.59	1084.54	893.60	766.71	676.42	609.00	556.83	515.33	481.59	453.67	430.22	410.29
47000	4049.45	2087.31	1434.10	1108.12	913.02	783.38	691.12	622.24	568.94	526.53	492.06	463.53	439.58	419.21
48000	4135.61	2131.72	1464.61	1131.69	932.45	800.04	705.83	635.48	581.04	537.74	502.53	473.40	448.93	428.13
49000	4221.77	2176.13	1495.12	1155.27	951.88	816.71	720.53	648.72	593.14	548.94	513.00	483.26	458.28	437.05
50000	4307.92	2220.54	1525.64	1178.85	971.30	833.38	735.24	661.96	605.25	560.14	523.47	493.12	467.63	445.97
55000	4738.72	2442.60	1678.20	1296.73	1068.43	916.72	808.76	728.15	665.77	616.16	575.82	542.43	514.40	490.56
60000	5169.51	2664.65	1830.76	1414.62	1165.56	1000.05	882.28	794.35	726.30	672.17	628.16	591.74	561.16	535.16
65000	5600.30	2886.71	1983.33	1532.50	1262.69	1083.39	955.81	860.54	786.82	728.18	680.51	641.06	607.92	579.76
70000	6031.09	3108.76	2135.89	1650.38	1359.82	1166.73	1029.33	926.74	847.35	784.20	732.86	690.37	654.69	624.35
75000	6461.88	3330.81	2288.45	1768.27	1456.95	1250.06	1102.85	992.93	907.87	840.21	785.20	739.68	701.45	668.95
80000	6892.68	3552.87	2441.02	1886.15	1554.08	1333.40	1176.37	1059.13	968.40	896.23	837.55	788.99	748.21	713.55
85000	7323.47	3774.92	2593.58	2004.04	1651.21	1416.74	1249.90	1125.32	1028.92	952.24	889.89	838.30	794.98	758.14
90000	7754.26	3996.98	2746.14	2121.92	1748.34	1500.08	1323.42	1191.52	1089.45	1008.25	942.24	887.61	841.74	802.74
95000	8185.05	4219.03	2898.71	2239.80	1845.47	1583.41	1396.94	1257.71	1149.97	1064.27	994.59	936.93	888.50	847.33
100000	8615.84	4441.08	3051.27	2357.69	1942.60	1666.75	1470.47	1323.91	1210.49	1120.28	1046.93	986.24	935.26	891.93

TERM / AMOUNT	15 Years	16 Years	17 Years	18 Years	19 Years	20 Years	21 Years	22 Years	23 Years	24 Years	25 Years	30 Years	35 Years	40 Years
5	.05	.05	.04	.04	.04	.04	.04	.04	.04	.04	.04	.04	.03	.03
10	.09	.09	.08	.08	.08	.08	.08	.07	.07	.07	.07	.07	.06	.06
15	.13	.13	.12	.12	.12	.11	.11	.11	.11	.11	.10	.10	.09	.09
25	.22	.21	.20	.20	.19	.19	.18	.18	.18	.17	.17	.16	.15	.15
50	.43	.42	.40	.39	.38	.37	.36	.35	.35	.34	.33	.31	.30	.29
75	.65	.62	.60	.58	.57	.55	.54	.53	.52	.51	.50	.46	.44	.43
100	.86	.83	.80	.77	.75	.73	.72	.70	.69	.67	.66	.62	.59	.57
200	1.71	1.65	1.59	1.54	1.50	1.46	1.43	1.39	1.37	1.34	1.32	1.23	1.17	1.13
300	2.57	2.47	2.39	2.31	2.25	2.19	2.14	2.09	2.05	2.01	1.97	1.84	1.76	1.70
400	3.42	3.29	3.18	3.08	3.00	2.92	2.85	2.78	2.73	2.68	2.63	2.45	2.34	2.26
500	4.28	4.12	3.98	3.85	3.74	3.65	3.56	3.48	3.41	3.35	3.29	3.07	2.92	2.83
600	5.13	4.94	4.77	4.62	4.49	4.37	4.27	4.17	4.09	4.01	3.94	3.68	3.51	3.39
700	5.99	5.76	5.56	5.39	5.24	5.10	4.98	4.87	4.77	4.68	4.60	4.29	4.09	3.95
800	6.84	6.58	6.36	6.16	5.99	5.83	5.69	5.56	5.45	5.35	5.26	4.90	4.67	4.52
900	7.70	7.41	7.15	6.93	6.73	6.56	6.40	6.26	6.13	6.02	5.91	5.52	5.26	5.08
1000	8.55	8.23	7.95	7.70	7.48	7.29	7.11	6.95	6.81	6.69	6.57	6.13	5.84	5.65
2000	17.10	16.45	15.89	15.39	14.96	14.57	14.22	13.90	13.62	13.37	13.14	12.25	11.68	11.29
3000	25.65	24.68	23.83	23.09	22.43	21.85	21.32	20.85	20.43	20.05	19.70	18.38	17.52	16.93
4000	34.19	32.90	31.77	30.78	29.91	29.13	28.43	27.80	27.24	26.73	26.27	24.50	23.35	22.57
5000	42.74	41.13	39.72	38.48	37.38	36.41	35.53	34.75	34.05	33.41	32.83	30.63	29.19	28.22
6000	51.29	49.35	47.66	46.17	44.86	43.69	42.64	41.70	40.86	40.09	39.40	36.75	35.03	33.86
7000	59.83	57.58	55.60	53.87	52.33	50.97	49.75	48.65	47.66	46.77	45.97	42.88	40.86	39.50
8000	68.38	65.80	63.54	61.56	59.81	58.25	56.85	55.60	54.47	53.45	52.53	49.00	46.70	45.14
9000	76.93	74.02	71.49	69.26	67.28	65.53	63.96	62.55	61.28	60.14	59.10	55.13	52.54	50.78
10000	85.48	82.25	79.43	76.95	74.76	72.81	71.06	69.50	68.09	66.82	65.66	61.25	58.37	56.43
11000	94.02	90.47	87.37	84.65	82.23	80.09	78.17	76.45	74.90	73.50	72.23	67.38	64.21	62.07
12000	102.57	98.70	95.31	92.34	89.71	87.37	85.28	83.40	81.71	80.18	78.79	73.50	70.05	67.71
13000	111.12	106.92	103.26	100.03	97.18	94.65	92.38	90.35	88.52	86.86	85.36	79.63	75.88	73.35
14000	119.66	115.15	111.20	107.73	104.66	101.93	99.49	97.30	95.32	93.54	91.93	85.75	81.72	79.00
15000	128.21	123.37	119.14	115.42	112.13	109.21	106.59	104.25	102.13	100.22	98.49	91.88	87.56	84.64
16000	136.76	131.59	127.08	123.12	119.61	116.49	113.70	111.20	108.94	106.90	105.06	98.00	93.39	90.28
17000	145.30	139.82	135.03	130.81	127.08	123.77	120.80	118.15	115.75	113.59	111.62	104.12	99.23	95.92
18000	153.85	148.04	142.97	138.51	134.56	131.05	127.91	125.10	122.56	120.27	118.19	110.25	105.07	101.56
19000	162.40	156.27	150.91	146.20	142.03	138.33	135.02	132.04	129.37	126.95	124.76	116.37	110.90	107.21
20000	170.95	164.49	158.85	153.90	149.51	145.61	142.12	138.99	136.18	133.63	131.32	122.50	116.74	112.85
21000	179.49	172.72	166.80	161.59	156.98	152.89	149.23	145.94	142.98	140.31	137.89	128.62	122.58	118.49
22000	188.04	180.94	174.74	169.29	164.46	160.17	156.33	152.89	149.79	146.99	144.45	134.75	128.42	124.13
23000	196.59	189.16	182.68	176.98	171.94	167.45	163.44	159.84	156.60	153.67	151.02	140.87	134.25	129.78
24000	205.13	197.39	190.62	184.67	179.41	174.73	170.55	166.79	163.41	160.35	157.58	147.00	140.09	135.42
25000	213.68	205.61	198.57	192.37	186.89	182.01	177.65	173.74	170.22	167.04	164.15	153.12	145.93	141.06
26000	222.23	213.84	206.51	200.06	194.36	189.29	184.76	180.69	177.03	173.72	170.72	159.25	151.76	146.70
27000	230.77	222.06	214.45	207.76	201.84	196.57	191.86	187.64	183.84	180.40	177.28	165.37	157.60	152.34
28000	239.32	230.29	222.39	215.45	209.31	203.85	198.97	194.59	190.64	187.08	183.85	171.50	163.44	157.99
29000	247.87	238.51	230.34	223.15	216.79	211.13	206.07	201.54	197.45	193.76	190.41	177.62	169.27	163.63
30000	256.42	246.73	238.28	230.84	224.26	218.41	213.18	208.49	204.26	200.44	196.98	183.75	175.11	169.27
31000	264.96	254.96	246.22	238.54	231.74	225.69	220.29	215.44	211.07	207.12	203.55	189.87	180.95	174.91
32000	273.51	263.18	254.16	246.23	239.21	232.97	227.39	222.39	217.88	213.80	210.11	196.00	186.78	180.56
33000	282.06	271.41	262.11	253.93	246.69	240.25	234.50	229.34	224.69	220.49	216.68	202.12	192.62	186.20
34000	290.60	279.63	270.05	261.62	254.16	247.53	241.60	236.29	231.50	227.17	223.24	208.24	198.46	191.84
35000	299.15	287.86	277.99	269.31	261.64	254.81	248.71	243.24	238.30	233.85	229.81	214.37	204.29	197.48
36000	307.70	296.08	285.93	277.01	269.11	262.09	255.82	250.19	245.11	240.53	236.37	220.49	210.13	203.12
37000	316.24	304.31	293.88	284.70	276.59	269.37	262.92	257.13	251.92	247.21	242.94	226.62	215.97	208.77
38000	324.79	312.53	301.82	292.40	284.06	276.65	270.03	264.08	258.73	253.89	249.51	232.74	221.80	214.41
39000	333.34	320.75	309.76	300.09	291.54	283.93	277.13	271.03	265.54	260.57	256.07	238.87	227.64	220.05
40000	341.89	328.98	317.70	307.79	299.01	291.21	284.24	277.98	272.35	267.25	262.64	244.99	233.48	225.69
41000	350.43	337.20	325.65	315.48	306.49	298.49	291.35	284.93	279.16	273.94	269.20	251.12	239.32	231.33
42000	358.98	345.43	333.59	323.18	313.96	305.77	298.45	291.88	285.96	280.62	275.77	257.24	245.15	236.98
43000	367.53	353.65	341.53	330.87	321.44	313.05	305.56	298.83	292.77	287.30	282.34	263.37	250.99	242.62
44000	376.07	361.88	349.47	338.57	328.92	320.33	312.66	305.78	299.58	293.98	288.90	269.49	256.83	248.26
45000	384.62	370.10	357.42	346.26	336.39	327.61	319.77	312.73	306.39	300.66	295.47	275.62	262.66	253.90
46000	393.17	378.32	365.36	353.95	343.87	334.89	326.87	319.68	313.20	307.34	302.03	281.74	268.50	259.55
47000	401.71	386.55	373.30	361.65	351.34	342.17	333.98	326.63	320.01	314.02	308.60	287.87	274.34	265.19
48000	410.26	394.77	381.24	369.34	358.82	349.45	341.09	333.58	326.82	320.70	315.16	293.99	280.17	270.83
49000	418.81	403.00	389.19	377.04	366.29	356.73	348.19	340.53	333.62	327.39	321.73	300.11	286.01	276.47
50000	427.36	411.22	397.13	384.73	373.77	364.01	355.30	347.48	340.43	334.07	328.30	306.24	291.85	282.11
55000	470.09	452.34	436.84	423.21	411.14	400.41	390.83	382.22	374.48	367.47	361.13	336.86	321.03	310.33
60000	512.83	493.46	476.55	461.68	448.52	436.82	426.36	416.97	408.52	400.88	393.95	367.49	350.22	338.54
65000	555.56	534.59	516.26	500.15	485.90	473.22	461.89	451.72	442.56	434.29	426.78	398.11	379.40	366.75
70000	598.30	575.71	555.98	538.62	523.27	509.62	497.42	486.47	476.60	467.69	459.61	428.73	408.58	394.96
75000	641.03	616.83	595.69	577.10	560.65	546.02	532.94	521.21	510.65	501.10	492.44	459.36	437.77	423.17
80000	683.77	657.95	635.40	615.57	598.02	582.42	568.47	555.96	544.69	534.50	525.27	489.98	466.95	451.38
85000	726.50	699.07	675.11	654.04	635.40	618.82	604.00	590.71	578.73	567.91	558.10	520.60	496.14	479.59
90000	769.24	740.19	714.83	692.52	672.78	655.22	639.53	625.46	612.78	601.32	590.93	551.23	525.32	507.80
95000	811.97	781.32	754.54	730.99	710.15	691.62	675.06	660.20	646.82	634.72	623.76	581.85	554.50	536.01
100000	854.71	822.44	794.25	769.46	747.53	728.02	710.59	694.95	680.86	668.13	656.59	612.47	583.69	564.22

MONTHLY PAYMENT
REQUIRED TO AMORTIZE A LOAN

TERM AMOUNT	1 Year	2 Years	3 Years	4 Years	5 Years	6 Years	7 Years	8 Years	9 Years	10 Years	11 Years	12 Years	13 Years	14 Years
5	.44	.23	.16	.12	.10	.09	.08	.07	.07	.06	.06	.05	.05	.05
10	.87	.45	.31	.24	.20	.17	.15	.14	.13	.12	.11	.10	.10	.09
15	1.30	.67	.46	.36	.30	.26	.23	.20	.19	.17	.16	.15	.15	.14
25	2.16	1.12	.77	.59	.49	.42	.37	.34	.31	.29	.27	.25	.24	.23
50	4.31	2.23	1.53	1.18	.98	.84	.74	.67	.61	.57	.53	.50	.47	.45
75	6.47	3.34	2.30	1.77	1.46	1.26	1.11	1.00	.91	.85	.79	.75	.71	.68
100	8.62	4.45	3.06	2.36	1.95	1.67	1.48	1.33	1.22	1.13	1.05	.99	.94	.90
200	17.24	8.89	6.11	4.72	3.89	3.34	2.95	2.66	2.43	2.25	2.10	1.98	1.88	1.79
300	25.86	13.34	9.17	7.08	5.84	5.01	4.42	3.98	3.64	3.37	3.15	2.97	2.82	2.69
400	34.48	17.78	12.22	9.44	7.78	6.68	5.90	5.31	4.86	4.50	4.20	3.96	3.76	3.58
500	43.10	22.22	15.27	11.80	9.73	8.35	7.37	6.64	6.07	5.62	5.25	4.95	4.69	4.48
600	51.71	26.67	18.33	14.16	11.67	10.02	8.84	7.96	7.28	6.74	6.30	5.94	5.63	5.37
700	60.33	31.11	21.38	16.52	13.62	11.69	10.32	9.29	8.50	7.86	7.35	6.93	6.57	6.27
800	68.95	35.55	24.43	18.88	15.56	13.36	11.79	10.62	9.71	8.99	8.40	7.92	7.51	7.16
900	77.57	40.00	27.49	21.24	17.51	15.03	13.26	11.94	10.92	10.11	9.45	8.90	8.45	8.06
1000	86.19	44.44	30.54	23.60	19.45	16.70	14.73	13.27	12.13	11.23	10.50	9.89	9.38	8.95
2000	172.37	88.87	61.08	47.20	38.90	33.39	29.46	26.53	24.26	22.46	20.99	19.78	18.76	17.90
3000	258.55	133.31	91.61	70.80	58.35	50.08	44.19	39.80	36.39	33.69	31.49	29.67	28.14	26.84
4000	344.73	177.74	122.15	94.40	77.80	66.77	58.92	53.06	48.52	44.92	41.98	39.56	37.52	35.79
5000	430.91	222.17	152.68	118.00	97.25	83.46	73.65	66.32	60.65	56.15	52.48	49.45	46.90	44.74
6000	517.09	266.61	183.22	141.60	116.70	100.15	88.38	79.59	72.78	67.37	62.97	59.34	56.28	53.68
7000	603.27	311.04	213.75	165.20	136.15	116.84	103.11	92.85	84.91	78.60	73.47	69.22	65.66	62.63
8000	689.46	355.47	244.29	188.80	155.60	133.53	117.83	106.11	97.04	89.83	83.96	79.11	75.04	71.57
9000	775.64	399.91	274.82	212.40	175.05	150.23	132.56	119.38	109.17	101.06	94.46	89.00	84.42	80.52
10000	861.82	444.34	305.36	236.00	194.50	166.92	147.29	132.64	121.30	112.29	104.95	98.89	93.80	89.47
11000	948.00	488.77	335.89	259.60	213.95	183.61	162.02	145.90	133.43	123.51	115.45	108.78	103.17	98.41
12000	1034.18	533.21	366.43	283.20	233.40	200.30	176.75	159.17	145.56	134.74	125.94	118.67	112.55	107.36
13000	1120.36	577.64	396.96	306.80	252.85	216.99	191.48	172.43	157.69	145.97	136.44	128.55	121.93	116.30
14000	1206.54	622.07	427.50	330.40	272.29	233.68	206.21	185.69	169.82	157.20	146.93	138.44	131.31	125.25
15000	1292.73	666.51	458.04	354.00	291.74	250.37	220.94	198.96	181.95	168.43	157.43	148.33	140.69	134.20
16000	1378.91	710.94	488.57	377.60	311.19	267.06	235.66	212.22	194.08	179.65	167.92	158.22	150.07	143.14
17000	1465.09	755.37	519.11	401.20	330.64	283.75	250.39	225.48	206.21	190.88	178.42	168.11	159.45	152.09
18000	1551.27	799.81	549.64	424.80	350.09	300.45	265.12	238.75	218.34	202.11	188.91	178.00	168.83	161.03
19000	1637.45	844.24	580.18	448.40	369.54	317.14	279.85	252.01	230.47	213.34	199.41	187.88	178.21	169.98
20000	1723.63	888.67	610.71	472.00	388.99	333.83	294.58	265.27	242.60	224.57	209.90	197.77	187.59	178.93
21000	1809.81	933.11	641.25	495.60	408.44	350.52	309.31	278.54	254.73	235.79	220.40	207.66	196.96	187.87
22000	1896.00	977.54	671.78	519.20	427.89	367.21	324.04	291.80	266.86	247.02	230.89	217.55	206.34	196.82
23000	1982.18	1021.97	702.32	542.80	447.34	383.90	338.77	305.07	278.99	258.25	241.39	227.44	215.72	205.77
24000	2068.36	1066.41	732.85	566.40	466.79	400.59	353.49	318.33	291.12	269.48	251.88	237.33	225.10	214.71
25000	2154.54	1110.84	763.39	590.00	486.24	417.28	368.22	331.59	303.25	280.71	262.38	247.21	234.48	223.66
26000	2240.72	1155.27	793.92	613.60	505.69	433.98	382.95	344.86	315.38	291.93	272.87	257.10	243.86	232.60
27000	2326.90	1199.71	824.46	637.20	525.14	450.67	397.68	358.12	327.51	303.16	283.37	266.99	253.24	241.55
28000	2413.08	1244.14	854.99	660.80	544.58	467.36	412.41	371.38	339.64	314.39	293.86	276.88	262.62	250.50
29000	2499.27	1288.57	885.53	684.40	564.03	484.05	427.14	384.65	351.77	325.62	304.36	286.77	272.00	259.44
30000	2585.45	1333.01	916.07	708.00	583.48	500.74	441.87	397.91	363.90	336.85	314.85	296.66	281.38	268.39
31000	2671.63	1377.44	946.60	731.60	602.93	517.43	456.59	411.17	376.03	348.07	325.35	306.54	290.76	277.33
32000	2757.81	1421.87	977.14	755.20	622.38	534.12	471.32	424.44	388.16	359.30	335.84	316.43	300.13	286.28
33000	2843.99	1466.31	1007.67	778.80	641.83	550.81	486.05	437.70	400.29	370.53	346.34	326.32	309.51	295.23
34000	2930.17	1510.74	1038.21	802.40	661.28	567.50	500.78	450.96	412.42	381.76	356.83	336.21	318.89	304.17
35000	3016.35	1555.17	1068.74	826.00	680.73	584.20	515.51	464.23	424.55	392.99	367.33	346.10	328.27	313.12
36000	3102.53	1599.61	1099.28	849.60	700.18	600.89	530.24	477.49	436.68	404.21	377.82	355.99	337.65	322.06
37000	3188.72	1644.04	1129.81	873.20	719.63	617.58	544.97	490.75	448.81	415.44	388.32	365.87	347.03	331.01
38000	3274.90	1688.47	1160.35	896.80	739.08	634.27	559.70	504.02	460.94	426.67	398.81	375.76	356.41	339.96
39000	3361.08	1732.91	1190.88	920.40	758.53	650.96	574.42	517.28	473.07	437.90	409.31	385.65	365.79	348.90
40000	3447.26	1777.34	1221.42	944.00	777.98	667.65	589.15	530.54	485.20	449.13	419.80	395.54	375.17	357.85
41000	3533.44	1821.77	1251.95	967.60	797.42	684.34	603.88	543.81	497.33	460.35	430.30	405.43	384.55	366.80
42000	3619.62	1866.21	1282.49	991.20	816.87	701.03	618.61	557.07	509.45	471.58	440.79	415.32	393.92	375.74
43000	3705.80	1910.64	1313.02	1014.80	836.32	717.72	633.34	570.34	521.58	482.81	451.29	425.20	403.30	384.69
44000	3791.99	1955.07	1343.56	1038.40	855.77	734.42	648.07	583.60	533.71	494.04	461.78	435.09	412.68	393.63
45000	3878.17	1999.51	1374.10	1062.00	875.22	751.11	662.80	596.86	545.84	505.27	472.28	444.98	422.06	402.58
46000	3964.35	2043.94	1404.63	1085.60	894.67	767.80	677.53	610.13	557.97	516.49	482.77	454.87	431.44	411.53
47000	4050.53	2088.37	1435.17	1109.20	914.12	784.49	692.25	623.39	570.10	527.72	493.27	464.76	440.82	420.47
48000	4136.71	2132.81	1465.70	1132.80	933.57	801.18	706.98	636.65	582.23	538.95	503.76	474.65	450.20	429.42
49000	4222.89	2177.24	1496.24	1156.40	953.02	817.87	721.71	649.92	594.36	550.18	514.26	484.54	459.58	438.36
50000	4309.07	2221.67	1526.77	1180.00	972.47	834.56	736.44	663.18	606.49	561.41	524.75	494.42	468.96	447.31
55000	4739.98	2443.84	1679.45	1298.00	1069.71	918.02	810.08	729.50	667.14	617.55	577.23	543.87	515.85	492.04
60000	5170.89	2666.01	1832.13	1415.99	1166.96	1001.47	883.73	795.81	727.79	673.69	629.70	593.31	562.75	536.77
65000	5601.79	2888.17	1984.80	1533.99	1264.21	1084.93	957.37	862.13	788.44	729.83	682.18	642.75	609.64	581.50
70000	6032.70	3110.34	2137.48	1651.99	1361.45	1168.39	1031.01	928.45	849.09	785.97	734.65	692.19	656.54	626.23
75000	6463.61	3332.51	2290.16	1769.99	1458.70	1251.84	1104.66	994.77	909.74	842.11	787.13	741.63	703.43	670.96
80000	6894.52	3554.67	2442.83	1887.99	1555.95	1335.30	1178.30	1061.08	970.39	898.25	839.60	791.07	750.33	715.69
85000	7325.42	3776.84	2595.51	2005.99	1653.19	1418.75	1251.94	1127.40	1031.03	954.39	892.08	840.52	797.22	760.42
90000	7756.33	3999.01	2748.19	2123.99	1750.44	1502.21	1325.59	1193.72	1091.68	1010.53	944.55	889.96	844.12	805.15
95000	8187.24	4221.17	2900.86	2241.99	1847.68	1585.66	1399.23	1260.04	1152.33	1066.67	997.03	939.40	891.01	849.88
100000	8618.14	4443.34	3053.54	2359.99	1944.93	1669.12	1472.88	1326.35	1212.98	1122.81	1049.50	988.84	937.91	894.62

MONTHLY PAYMENT
REQUIRED TO AMORTIZE A LOAN

6.250%

TERM	15 Years	16 Years	17 Years	18 Years	19 Years	20 Years	21 Years	22 Years	23 Years	24 Years	25 Years	30 Years	35 Years	40 Years
AMOUNT														
5	.05	.05	.04	.04	.04	.04	.04	.04	.04	.04	.04	.04	.03	.03
10	.09	.09	.08	.08	.08	.08	.08	.07	.07	.07	.07	.07	.06	.06
15	.13	.13	.12	.12	.12	.11	.11	.11	.11	.11	.10	.10	.09	.09
25	.22	.21	.20	.20	.19	.19	.18	.18	.18	.17	.17	.16	.15	.15
50	.43	.42	.40	.39	.38	.37	.36	.35	.35	.34	.33	.31	.30	.29
75	.65	.62	.60	.58	.57	.55	.54	.53	.52	.51	.50	.47	.45	.43
100	.86	.83	.80	.78	.76	.74	.72	.70	.69	.68	.66	.62	.59	.57
200	1.72	1.66	1.60	1.55	1.51	1.47	1.43	1.40	1.37	1.35	1.32	1.24	1.18	1.14
300	2.58	2.48	2.40	2.32	2.26	2.20	2.15	2.10	2.06	2.02	1.98	1.85	1.77	1.71
400	3.43	3.31	3.19	3.09	3.01	2.93	2.86	2.80	2.74	2.69	2.64	2.47	2.35	2.28
500	4.29	4.13	3.99	3.87	3.76	3.66	3.57	3.49	3.42	3.36	3.30	3.08	2.94	2.84
600	5.15	4.96	4.79	4.64	4.51	4.39	4.29	4.19	4.11	4.03	3.96	3.70	3.53	3.41
700	6.01	5.78	5.58	5.41	5.26	5.12	5.00	4.89	4.79	4.70	4.62	4.32	4.11	3.98
800	6.86	6.61	6.38	6.18	6.01	5.85	5.71	5.59	5.48	5.37	5.28	4.93	4.70	4.55
900	7.72	7.43	7.18	6.96	6.76	6.58	6.43	6.29	6.16	6.05	5.94	5.55	5.29	5.11
1000	8.58	8.26	7.98	7.73	7.51	7.31	7.14	6.98	6.84	6.72	6.60	6.16	5.88	5.68
2000	17.15	16.51	15.95	15.45	15.01	14.62	14.28	13.96	13.68	13.43	13.20	12.32	11.75	11.36
3000	25.73	24.76	23.92	23.17	22.52	21.93	21.41	20.94	20.52	20.14	19.80	18.48	17.62	17.04
4000	34.30	33.01	31.89	30.90	30.02	29.24	28.55	27.92	27.36	26.85	26.39	24.63	23.49	22.71
5000	42.88	41.26	39.86	38.62	37.52	36.55	35.68	34.90	34.20	33.56	32.99	30.79	29.36	28.39
6000	51.45	49.52	47.83	46.34	45.03	43.86	42.82	41.88	41.04	40.28	39.59	36.95	35.23	34.07
7000	60.02	57.77	55.80	54.07	52.53	51.17	49.95	48.86	47.88	46.99	46.18	43.11	41.10	39.75
8000	68.60	66.02	63.77	61.79	60.04	58.48	57.09	55.84	54.71	53.70	52.78	49.26	46.97	45.42
9000	77.17	74.27	71.74	69.51	67.54	65.79	64.22	62.82	61.55	60.41	59.38	55.42	52.84	51.10
10000	85.75	82.52	79.71	77.23	75.04	73.10	71.36	69.80	68.39	67.12	65.97	61.58	58.71	56.78
11000	94.32	90.78	87.68	84.96	82.55	80.41	78.49	76.78	75.23	73.83	72.57	67.73	64.58	62.46
12000	102.90	99.03	95.65	92.68	90.05	87.72	85.63	83.76	82.07	80.55	79.17	73.89	70.45	68.13
13000	111.47	107.28	103.62	100.40	97.56	95.03	92.76	90.74	88.91	87.26	85.76	80.05	76.32	73.81
14000	120.04	115.53	111.59	108.13	105.06	102.33	99.90	97.71	95.75	93.97	92.36	86.21	82.20	79.49
15000	128.62	123.78	119.56	115.85	112.56	109.64	107.04	104.69	102.59	100.68	98.96	92.36	88.07	85.17
16000	137.19	132.04	127.53	123.57	120.07	116.95	114.17	111.67	109.42	107.39	105.55	98.52	93.94	90.84
17000	145.77	140.29	135.50	131.29	127.57	124.26	121.31	118.65	116.26	114.11	112.15	104.68	99.81	96.52
18000	154.34	148.54	143.47	139.02	135.08	131.57	128.44	125.63	123.10	120.82	118.75	110.83	105.68	102.20
19000	162.92	156.79	151.44	146.74	142.58	138.88	135.58	132.61	129.94	127.53	125.34	116.99	111.55	107.88
20000	171.49	165.04	159.41	154.46	150.08	146.19	142.71	139.59	136.78	134.24	131.94	123.15	117.42	113.55
21000	180.06	173.30	167.38	162.19	157.59	153.50	149.85	146.57	143.62	140.95	138.54	129.31	123.29	119.23
22000	188.64	181.55	175.35	169.91	165.09	160.81	156.98	153.55	150.46	147.66	145.13	135.46	129.16	124.91
23000	197.21	189.80	183.33	177.63	172.60	168.12	164.12	160.53	157.30	154.38	151.73	141.62	135.03	130.59
24000	205.79	198.05	191.30	185.36	180.10	175.43	171.25	167.51	164.13	161.09	158.33	147.78	140.90	136.26
25000	214.36	206.30	199.27	193.08	187.60	182.74	178.39	174.49	170.97	167.80	164.92	153.93	146.77	141.94
26000	222.93	214.56	207.24	200.80	195.11	190.05	185.52	181.47	177.81	174.51	171.52	160.09	152.64	147.62
27000	231.51	222.81	215.21	208.52	202.61	197.36	192.66	188.45	184.65	181.22	178.12	166.25	158.52	153.29
28000	240.08	231.06	223.18	216.25	210.12	204.66	199.79	195.42	191.49	187.93	184.71	172.41	164.39	158.97
29000	248.66	239.31	231.15	223.97	217.62	211.97	206.93	202.40	198.33	194.65	191.31	178.56	170.26	164.65
30000	257.23	247.56	239.12	231.69	225.12	219.28	214.07	209.38	205.17	201.36	197.91	184.72	176.13	170.33
31000	265.81	255.82	247.09	239.42	232.63	226.59	221.20	216.36	212.01	208.07	204.50	190.88	182.00	176.00
32000	274.38	264.07	255.06	247.14	240.13	233.90	228.34	223.34	218.84	214.78	211.10	197.03	187.87	181.68
33000	282.95	272.32	263.03	254.86	247.64	241.21	235.47	230.32	225.68	221.49	217.70	203.19	193.74	187.36
34000	291.53	280.57	271.00	262.58	255.14	248.52	242.61	237.30	232.52	228.21	224.29	209.35	199.61	193.04
35000	300.10	288.82	278.97	270.31	262.64	255.83	249.74	244.28	239.36	234.92	230.89	215.51	205.48	198.71
36000	308.68	297.07	286.94	278.03	270.15	263.14	256.88	251.26	246.20	241.63	237.49	221.66	211.35	204.39
37000	317.25	305.33	294.91	285.75	277.65	270.45	264.01	258.24	253.04	248.34	244.08	227.82	217.22	210.07
38000	325.83	313.58	302.88	293.48	285.16	277.76	271.15	265.22	259.88	255.05	250.68	233.98	223.09	215.75
39000	334.40	321.83	310.85	301.20	292.66	285.07	278.28	272.20	266.72	261.76	257.28	240.13	228.96	221.42
40000	342.97	330.08	318.82	308.92	300.16	292.38	285.42	279.18	273.55	268.48	263.87	246.29	234.84	227.10
41000	351.55	338.33	326.79	316.65	307.67	299.69	292.55	286.16	280.39	275.19	270.47	252.45	240.71	232.78
42000	360.12	346.59	334.76	324.37	315.17	306.99	299.69	293.13	287.23	281.90	277.07	258.61	246.58	238.46
43000	368.70	354.84	342.73	332.09	322.68	314.30	306.82	300.11	294.07	288.61	283.66	264.76	252.45	244.13
44000	377.27	363.09	350.70	339.81	330.18	321.61	313.96	307.09	300.91	295.32	290.26	270.92	258.32	249.81
45000	385.85	371.34	358.68	347.54	337.68	328.92	321.10	314.07	307.75	302.03	296.86	277.08	264.19	255.49
46000	394.42	379.59	366.65	355.26	345.19	336.23	328.23	321.05	314.59	308.75	303.45	283.23	270.06	261.17
47000	402.99	387.85	374.62	362.98	352.69	343.54	335.37	328.03	321.43	315.46	310.05	289.39	275.93	266.84
48000	411.57	396.10	382.59	370.71	360.20	350.85	342.50	335.01	328.26	322.17	316.65	295.55	281.80	272.52
49000	420.14	404.35	390.56	378.43	367.70	358.16	349.64	341.99	335.10	328.88	323.24	301.71	287.67	278.20
50000	428.72	412.60	398.53	386.15	375.20	365.47	356.77	348.97	341.94	335.59	329.84	307.86	293.54	283.87
55000	471.59	453.86	438.38	424.77	412.72	402.02	392.45	383.87	376.14	369.15	362.82	338.65	322.90	312.26
60000	514.46	495.12	478.23	463.38	450.24	438.56	428.13	418.76	410.33	402.71	395.81	369.44	352.25	340.65
65000	557.33	536.38	518.08	502.00	487.76	475.11	463.80	453.66	444.52	436.27	428.79	400.22	381.60	369.04
70000	600.20	577.64	557.94	540.61	525.28	511.65	499.48	488.55	478.72	469.83	461.77	431.01	410.96	397.42
75000	643.07	618.90	597.79	579.23	562.80	548.20	535.16	523.45	512.91	503.39	494.76	461.79	440.31	425.81
80000	685.94	660.16	637.64	617.84	600.32	584.75	570.83	558.35	547.10	536.95	527.74	492.58	469.67	454.20
85000	728.81	701.42	677.49	656.45	637.84	621.29	606.51	593.24	581.30	570.51	560.72	523.36	499.02	482.58
90000	771.69	742.68	717.35	695.07	675.36	657.84	642.19	628.14	615.49	604.06	593.71	554.15	528.37	510.97
95000	814.56	783.94	757.20	733.68	712.88	694.39	677.86	663.04	649.69	637.62	626.69	584.94	557.73	539.36
100000	857.43	825.20	797.05	772.30	750.40	730.93	713.54	697.93	683.88	671.18	659.67	615.72	587.08	567.74

43

MONTHLY PAYMENT
REQUIRED TO AMORTIZE A LOAN

TERM	1 Year	2 Years	3 Years	4 Years	5 Years	6 Years	7 Years	8 Years	9 Years	10 Years	11 Years	12 Years	13 Years	14 Years
AMOUNT														
5	.44	.23	.16	.12	.10	.09	.08	.07	.07	.06	.06	.05	.05	.05
10	.87	.45	.31	.24	.20	.17	.15	.14	.13	.12	.11	.10	.10	.09
15	1.30	.67	.46	.36	.30	.26	.23	.20	.19	.17	.16	.15	.15	.14
25	2.16	1.12	.77	.60	.49	.42	.37	.34	.31	.29	.27	.25	.24	.23
50	4.32	2.23	1.53	1.19	.98	.84	.74	.67	.61	.57	.53	.50	.48	.45
75	6.47	3.34	2.30	1.78	1.47	1.26	1.11	1.00	.92	.85	.79	.75	.71	.68
100	8.63	4.45	3.06	2.37	1.95	1.68	1.48	1.33	1.22	1.13	1.06	1.00	.95	.90
200	17.25	8.90	6.12	4.73	3.90	3.35	2.96	2.66	2.44	2.26	2.11	1.99	1.89	1.80
300	25.87	13.34	9.17	7.09	5.85	5.03	4.43	3.99	3.65	3.38	3.16	2.98	2.83	2.70
400	34.49	17.79	12.23	9.45	7.79	6.69	5.91	5.32	4.87	4.51	4.21	3.97	3.77	3.59
500	43.11	22.23	15.28	11.82	9.74	8.36	7.38	6.65	6.08	5.63	5.27	4.96	4.71	4.49
600	51.73	26.68	18.34	14.18	11.69	10.03	8.86	7.98	7.30	6.76	6.32	5.95	5.65	5.39
700	60.35	31.12	21.40	16.54	13.64	11.71	10.33	9.31	8.51	7.88	7.37	6.95	6.59	6.29
800	68.97	35.57	24.45	18.90	15.58	13.38	11.81	10.64	9.73	9.01	8.42	7.94	7.53	7.18
900	77.59	40.02	27.51	21.27	17.53	15.05	13.28	11.96	10.94	10.13	9.47	8.93	8.47	8.08
1000	86.21	44.46	30.56	23.63	19.48	16.72	14.76	13.29	12.16	11.26	10.53	9.92	9.41	8.98
2000	172.41	88.92	61.12	47.25	38.95	33.43	29.51	26.58	24.31	22.51	21.05	19.83	18.82	17.95
3000	258.62	133.37	91.68	70.87	58.42	50.15	44.26	39.87	36.47	33.76	31.57	29.75	28.22	26.92
4000	344.82	177.83	122.24	94.50	77.90	66.86	59.02	53.16	48.62	45.02	42.09	39.66	37.63	35.90
5000	431.03	222.28	152.80	118.12	97.37	83.58	73.77	66.44	60.78	56.27	52.61	49.58	47.03	44.87
6000	517.23	266.74	183.35	141.74	116.84	100.29	88.52	79.73	72.93	67.52	63.13	59.49	56.44	53.84
7000	603.44	311.20	213.91	165.36	136.31	117.01	103.27	93.02	85.09	78.78	73.65	69.41	65.84	62.82
8000	689.64	355.65	244.47	188.99	155.79	133.72	118.03	106.31	97.24	90.03	84.17	79.32	75.25	71.79
9000	775.84	400.11	275.03	212.61	175.26	150.44	132.78	119.60	109.40	101.28	94.69	89.24	84.65	80.76
10000	862.05	444.56	305.59	236.23	194.73	167.15	147.53	132.88	121.55	112.54	105.21	99.15	94.06	89.73
11000	948.25	489.02	336.14	259.86	214.20	183.87	162.29	146.17	133.71	123.79	115.73	109.06	103.47	98.71
12000	1034.46	533.48	366.70	283.48	233.68	200.58	177.04	159.46	145.86	135.04	126.25	118.98	112.87	107.68
13000	1120.66	577.93	397.26	307.10	253.15	217.30	191.79	172.75	158.02	146.30	136.77	128.89	122.28	116.65
14000	1206.87	622.39	427.82	330.72	272.62	234.01	206.54	186.04	170.17	157.55	147.29	138.81	131.68	125.63
15000	1293.07	666.84	458.38	354.35	292.09	250.73	221.30	199.32	182.32	168.80	157.81	148.72	141.09	134.60
16000	1379.28	711.30	488.93	377.97	311.57	267.44	236.05	212.61	194.48	180.06	168.34	158.64	150.49	143.57
17000	1465.48	755.76	519.49	401.59	331.04	284.16	250.80	225.90	206.63	191.31	178.86	168.55	159.90	152.55
18000	1551.68	800.21	550.05	425.22	350.51	300.87	265.56	239.19	218.79	202.56	189.38	178.47	169.30	161.52
19000	1637.89	844.67	580.61	448.84	369.98	317.59	280.31	252.48	230.94	213.82	199.90	188.38	178.71	170.49
20000	1724.09	889.12	611.17	472.46	389.46	334.30	295.06	265.76	243.10	225.07	210.42	198.29	188.12	179.46
21000	1810.30	933.58	641.72	496.08	408.93	351.02	309.81	279.05	255.25	236.32	220.94	208.21	197.52	188.44
22000	1896.50	978.04	672.28	519.71	428.40	367.73	324.57	292.34	267.41	247.58	231.46	218.12	206.93	197.41
23000	1982.71	1022.49	702.84	543.33	447.87	384.45	339.32	305.63	279.56	258.83	241.98	228.04	216.33	206.38
24000	2068.91	1066.95	733.40	566.95	467.35	401.16	354.07	318.92	291.72	270.08	252.50	237.95	225.74	215.36
25000	2155.11	1111.40	763.96	590.58	486.82	417.88	368.82	332.20	303.87	281.34	263.02	247.87	235.14	224.33
26000	2241.32	1155.86	794.51	614.20	506.29	434.59	383.58	345.49	316.03	292.59	273.54	257.78	244.55	233.30
27000	2327.52	1200.31	825.07	637.82	525.77	451.31	398.33	358.78	328.18	303.84	284.06	267.70	253.95	242.28
28000	2413.73	1244.77	855.63	661.44	545.24	468.02	413.08	372.07	340.34	315.10	294.58	277.61	263.36	251.25
29000	2499.93	1289.23	886.19	685.07	564.71	484.74	427.84	385.36	352.49	326.35	305.10	287.52	272.77	260.22
30000	2586.14	1333.68	916.75	708.69	584.18	501.45	442.59	398.64	364.64	337.60	315.62	297.44	282.17	269.19
31000	2672.34	1378.14	947.30	732.31	603.66	518.17	457.34	411.93	376.80	348.86	326.14	307.35	291.58	278.17
32000	2758.55	1422.59	977.86	755.94	623.13	534.88	472.09	425.22	388.95	360.11	336.67	317.27	300.98	287.14
33000	2844.75	1467.05	1008.42	779.56	642.60	551.60	486.85	438.51	401.11	371.36	347.19	327.18	310.39	296.11
34000	2930.95	1511.51	1038.98	803.18	662.07	568.31	501.60	451.80	413.26	382.62	357.71	337.10	319.79	305.09
35000	3017.16	1555.96	1069.54	826.80	681.55	585.03	516.35	465.08	425.42	393.87	368.23	347.01	329.20	314.06
36000	3103.36	1600.42	1100.09	850.43	701.02	601.74	531.11	478.37	437.57	405.12	378.75	356.93	338.60	323.03
37000	3189.57	1644.87	1130.65	874.05	720.49	618.46	545.86	491.66	449.73	416.38	389.27	366.84	348.01	332.01
38000	3275.77	1689.33	1161.21	897.67	739.96	635.17	560.61	504.95	461.88	427.63	399.79	376.75	357.42	340.98
39000	3361.98	1733.79	1191.77	921.29	759.44	651.88	575.36	518.24	474.04	438.88	410.31	386.67	366.82	349.95
40000	3448.18	1778.24	1222.33	944.92	778.91	668.60	590.12	531.52	486.19	450.14	420.83	396.58	376.23	358.92
41000	3534.38	1822.70	1252.89	968.54	798.38	685.31	604.87	544.81	498.35	461.39	431.35	406.50	385.63	367.90
42000	3620.59	1867.15	1283.44	992.16	817.85	702.03	619.62	558.10	510.50	472.64	441.87	416.41	395.04	376.87
43000	3706.79	1911.61	1314.00	1015.79	837.33	718.74	634.38	571.39	522.65	483.90	452.39	426.33	404.44	385.84
44000	3793.00	1956.07	1344.56	1039.41	856.80	735.46	649.13	584.68	534.81	495.15	462.91	436.24	413.85	394.82
45000	3879.20	2000.52	1375.12	1063.03	876.27	752.17	663.88	597.96	546.96	506.40	473.43	446.16	423.25	403.79
46000	3965.41	2044.98	1405.68	1086.65	895.74	768.89	678.63	611.25	559.12	517.66	483.95	456.07	432.66	412.76
47000	4051.61	2089.43	1436.23	1110.28	915.22	785.60	693.39	624.54	571.27	528.91	494.48	465.98	442.06	421.74
48000	4137.82	2133.89	1466.79	1133.90	934.69	802.32	708.14	637.83	583.43	540.16	505.00	475.90	451.47	430.71
49000	4224.02	2178.34	1497.35	1157.52	954.16	819.03	722.89	651.12	595.58	551.42	515.52	485.81	460.88	439.68
50000	4310.22	2222.80	1527.91	1181.15	973.64	835.75	737.64	664.40	607.74	562.67	526.04	495.73	470.28	448.65
55000	4741.25	2445.08	1680.70	1299.26	1071.00	919.32	811.41	730.84	668.51	618.94	578.64	545.30	517.31	493.52
60000	5172.27	2667.36	1833.49	1417.37	1168.36	1002.90	885.17	797.28	729.28	675.20	631.24	594.87	564.34	538.38
65000	5603.29	2889.64	1986.28	1535.49	1265.72	1086.47	958.94	863.72	790.06	731.47	683.85	644.44	611.36	583.25
70000	6034.31	3111.92	2139.07	1653.60	1363.09	1170.05	1032.70	930.16	850.83	787.74	736.45	694.02	658.39	628.11
75000	6465.33	3334.20	2291.86	1771.72	1460.45	1253.62	1106.47	996.60	911.60	844.00	789.05	743.59	705.42	672.98
80000	6896.36	3556.48	2444.65	1889.83	1557.81	1337.19	1180.23	1063.04	972.38	900.27	841.66	793.16	752.45	717.84
85000	7327.38	3778.76	2597.44	2007.94	1655.18	1420.77	1253.99	1129.48	1033.15	956.54	894.26	842.73	799.48	762.71
90000	7758.40	4001.04	2750.23	2126.06	1752.54	1504.34	1327.76	1195.92	1093.92	1012.80	946.86	892.31	846.50	807.57
95000	8189.42	4223.32	2903.02	2244.17	1849.90	1587.92	1401.52	1262.36	1154.70	1069.07	999.47	941.88	893.53	852.44
100000	8620.44	4445.60	3055.81	2362.29	1947.27	1671.49	1475.29	1328.80	1215.47	1125.34	1052.07	991.45	940.56	897.30

TERM	15 Years	16 Years	17 Years	18 Years	19 Years	20 Years	21 Years	22 Years	23 Years	24 Years	25 Years	30 Years	35 Years	40 Years
AMOUNT														
5	.05	.05	.04	.04	.04	.04	.04	.04	.04	.04	.04	.04	.03	.03
10	.09	.09	.08	.08	.08	.08	.08	.08	.07	.07	.07	.07	.06	.06
15	.13	.13	.12	.12	.12	.12	.11	.11	.11	.11	.10	.10	.09	.09
25	.22	.21	.20	.20	.19	.19	.18	.18	.18	.17	.17	.16	.15	.15
50	.44	.42	.40	.39	.38	.37	.36	.36	.35	.34	.34	.31	.30	.29
75	.65	.63	.60	.59	.57	.56	.54	.53	.52	.51	.50	.47	.45	.43
100	.87	.83	.80	.78	.76	.74	.72	.71	.69	.68	.67	.62	.60	.58
200	1.73	1.66	1.60	1.56	1.51	1.47	1.44	1.41	1.38	1.35	1.33	1.24	1.19	1.15
300	2.59	2.49	2.40	2.33	2.26	2.21	2.15	2.11	2.07	2.03	1.99	1.86	1.78	1.72
400	3.45	3.32	3.20	3.11	3.02	2.94	2.87	2.81	2.75	2.70	2.66	2.48	2.37	2.29
500	4.31	4.14	4.00	3.88	3.77	3.67	3.59	3.51	3.44	3.38	3.32	3.10	2.96	2.86
600	5.17	4.97	4.80	4.66	4.52	4.41	4.30	4.21	4.13	4.05	3.98	3.72	3.55	3.43
700	6.03	5.80	5.60	5.43	5.28	5.14	5.02	4.91	4.81	4.72	4.64	4.34	4.14	4.00
800	6.89	6.63	6.40	6.21	6.03	5.88	5.74	5.61	5.50	5.40	5.31	4.96	4.73	4.58
900	7.75	7.46	7.20	6.98	6.78	6.61	6.46	6.31	6.19	6.07	5.97	5.58	5.32	5.15
1000	8.61	8.28	8.00	7.76	7.54	7.34	7.17	7.01	6.87	6.75	6.63	6.19	5.91	5.72
2000	17.21	16.56	16.00	15.51	15.07	14.68	14.33	14.02	13.74	13.49	13.26	12.38	11.81	11.43
3000	25.81	24.84	24.00	23.26	22.60	22.02	21.50	21.03	20.61	20.23	19.89	18.57	17.72	17.14
4000	34.41	33.12	32.00	31.01	30.14	29.36	28.66	28.04	27.48	26.97	26.52	24.76	23.62	22.86
5000	43.01	41.40	40.00	38.76	37.67	36.70	35.83	35.05	34.35	33.72	33.14	30.95	29.53	28.57
6000	51.61	49.68	48.00	46.51	45.20	44.04	42.99	42.06	41.22	40.46	39.77	37.14	35.43	34.28
7000	60.22	57.96	55.99	54.26	52.73	51.37	50.16	49.07	48.09	47.20	46.40	43.33	41.34	39.99
8000	68.82	66.24	63.99	62.02	60.27	58.71	57.32	56.08	54.96	53.94	53.03	49.52	47.24	45.71
9000	77.42	74.52	71.99	69.77	67.80	66.05	64.49	63.09	61.83	60.69	59.65	55.71	53.15	51.42
10000	86.02	82.80	79.99	77.52	75.33	73.39	71.65	70.10	68.70	67.43	66.28	61.90	59.05	57.13
11000	94.62	91.08	87.99	85.27	82.87	80.73	78.82	77.11	75.56	74.17	72.91	68.09	64.96	62.84
12000	103.22	99.36	95.99	93.02	90.40	88.07	85.98	84.12	82.43	80.91	79.54	74.28	70.86	68.56
13000	111.82	107.64	103.99	100.77	97.93	95.40	93.15	91.12	89.30	87.66	86.16	80.47	76.77	74.27
14000	120.43	115.92	111.98	108.52	105.46	102.74	100.31	98.13	96.17	94.40	92.79	86.66	82.67	79.98
15000	129.03	124.20	119.98	116.28	113.00	110.08	107.48	105.14	103.04	101.14	99.42	92.85	88.58	85.70
16000	137.63	132.48	127.98	124.03	120.53	117.42	114.64	112.15	109.91	107.88	106.05	99.04	94.48	91.41
17000	146.23	140.76	135.98	131.78	128.06	124.76	121.81	119.16	116.78	114.63	112.67	105.23	100.39	97.12
18000	154.83	149.04	143.98	139.53	135.60	132.10	128.97	126.17	123.65	121.37	119.30	111.42	106.29	102.83
19000	163.43	157.32	151.98	147.28	143.13	139.44	136.14	133.18	130.52	128.11	125.93	117.61	112.20	108.55
20000	172.04	165.60	159.98	155.03	150.66	146.77	143.30	140.19	137.39	134.85	132.56	123.80	118.10	114.26
21000	180.64	173.88	167.97	162.78	158.19	154.11	150.47	147.20	144.25	141.59	139.19	129.99	124.01	119.97
22000	189.24	182.16	175.97	170.53	165.73	161.45	157.63	154.21	151.12	148.34	145.81	136.18	129.91	125.68
23000	197.84	190.44	183.97	178.29	173.26	168.79	164.80	161.22	157.99	155.08	152.44	142.37	135.81	131.40
24000	206.44	198.72	191.97	186.04	180.79	176.13	171.96	168.23	164.86	161.82	159.07	148.56	141.72	137.11
25000	215.04	207.00	199.97	193.79	188.32	183.47	179.13	175.23	171.73	168.56	165.70	154.75	147.62	142.82
26000	223.64	215.27	207.97	201.54	195.86	190.80	186.29	182.24	178.60	175.31	172.32	160.94	153.53	148.53
27000	232.25	223.55	215.96	209.29	203.39	198.14	193.46	189.25	185.47	182.05	178.95	167.13	159.43	154.25
28000	240.85	231.83	223.96	217.04	210.92	205.48	200.62	196.26	192.34	188.79	185.58	173.32	165.34	159.96
29000	249.45	240.11	231.96	224.79	218.46	212.82	207.79	203.27	199.21	195.53	192.21	179.51	171.24	165.67
30000	258.05	248.39	239.96	232.55	225.99	220.16	214.95	210.28	206.08	202.28	198.83	185.70	177.15	171.39
31000	266.65	256.67	247.96	240.30	233.52	227.50	222.12	217.29	212.94	209.02	205.46	191.89	183.05	177.10
32000	275.25	264.95	255.96	248.05	241.05	234.84	229.28	224.30	219.81	215.76	212.09	198.08	188.96	182.81
33000	283.85	273.23	263.96	255.80	248.59	242.17	236.45	231.31	226.68	222.50	218.72	204.27	194.86	188.52
34000	292.46	281.51	271.95	263.55	256.12	249.51	243.61	238.32	233.55	229.25	225.34	210.46	200.77	194.24
35000	301.06	289.79	279.95	271.30	263.65	256.85	250.78	245.33	240.42	235.99	231.97	216.65	206.67	199.95
36000	309.66	298.07	287.95	279.05	271.19	264.19	257.94	252.34	247.29	242.73	238.60	222.84	212.58	205.66
37000	318.26	306.35	295.95	286.81	278.72	271.53	265.11	259.34	254.16	249.47	245.23	229.02	218.48	211.37
38000	326.86	314.63	303.95	294.56	286.25	278.87	272.27	266.35	261.03	256.22	251.86	235.21	224.39	217.09
39000	335.46	322.91	311.95	302.31	293.78	286.20	279.44	273.36	267.90	262.96	258.48	241.40	230.29	222.80
40000	344.07	331.19	319.95	310.06	301.32	293.54	286.60	280.37	274.77	269.70	265.11	247.59	236.20	228.51
41000	352.67	339.47	327.94	317.81	308.85	300.88	293.76	287.38	281.63	276.44	271.74	253.78	242.10	234.22
42000	361.27	347.75	335.94	325.56	316.38	308.22	300.93	294.39	288.50	283.18	278.37	259.97	248.01	239.94
43000	369.87	356.03	343.94	333.31	323.91	315.56	308.09	301.40	295.37	289.93	284.99	266.16	253.91	245.65
44000	378.47	364.31	351.94	341.06	331.45	322.90	315.26	308.41	302.24	296.67	291.62	272.35	259.81	251.36
45000	387.07	372.59	359.94	348.82	338.98	330.24	322.42	315.42	309.11	303.41	298.25	278.54	265.72	257.08
46000	395.67	380.87	367.94	356.57	346.51	337.57	329.59	322.43	315.98	310.15	304.88	284.73	271.62	262.79
47000	404.28	389.15	375.93	364.32	354.05	344.91	336.75	329.44	322.85	316.90	311.50	290.92	277.53	268.50
48000	412.88	397.43	383.93	372.07	361.58	352.25	343.92	336.45	329.72	323.64	318.13	297.11	283.43	274.21
49000	421.48	405.71	391.93	379.82	369.11	359.59	351.08	343.45	336.59	330.38	324.76	303.30	289.34	279.93
50000	430.08	413.99	399.93	387.57	376.64	366.93	358.25	350.46	343.46	337.12	331.39	309.49	295.24	285.64
55000	473.09	455.38	439.92	426.33	414.31	403.62	394.07	385.51	377.80	370.84	364.52	340.44	324.77	314.20
60000	516.10	496.78	479.92	465.09	451.97	440.31	429.90	420.56	412.15	404.55	397.66	371.39	354.29	342.77
65000	559.10	538.18	519.91	503.84	489.64	477.00	465.72	455.60	446.49	438.26	430.80	402.34	383.82	371.33
70000	602.11	579.58	559.90	542.60	527.30	513.70	501.55	490.65	480.84	471.97	463.94	433.29	413.34	399.89
75000	645.12	620.98	599.89	581.36	564.96	550.39	537.37	525.69	515.18	505.68	497.08	464.23	442.86	428.46
80000	688.13	662.37	639.89	620.11	602.63	587.08	573.19	560.74	549.53	539.39	530.22	495.18	472.39	457.02
85000	731.13	703.77	679.88	658.87	640.29	623.77	609.02	595.79	583.87	573.11	563.35	526.13	501.91	485.58
90000	774.14	745.17	719.87	697.63	677.96	660.47	644.84	630.83	618.22	606.82	596.49	557.08	531.43	514.15
95000	817.15	786.57	759.86	736.38	715.62	697.16	680.67	665.88	652.56	640.53	629.63	588.03	560.96	542.71
100000	860.16	827.97	799.86	775.14	753.28	733.85	716.49	700.92	686.91	674.24	662.77	618.98	590.48	571.27

MONTHLY PAYMENT
REQUIRED TO AMORTIZE A LOAN

TERM	1 Year	2 Years	3 Years	4 Years	5 Years	6 Years	7 Years	8 Years	9 Years	10 Years	11 Years	12 Years	13 Years	14 Years
AMOUNT														
5	.44	.23	.16	.12	.10	.09	.08	.07	.07	.06	.06	.05	.05	.05
10	.87	.45	.31	.24	.20	.17	.15	.14	.13	.12	.11	.10	.10	.10
15	1.30	.67	.46	.36	.30	.26	.23	.20	.19	.17	.16	.15	.15	.14
25	2.16	1.12	.77	.60	.49	.42	.37	.34	.31	.29	.27	.25	.24	.23
50	4.32	2.23	1.53	1.19	.98	.84	.74	.67	.61	.57	.53	.50	.48	.46
75	6.47	3.34	2.30	1.78	1.47	1.26	1.11	1.00	.92	.85	.80	.75	.71	.68
100	8.63	4.45	3.06	2.37	1.96	1.68	1.48	1.34	1.22	1.13	1.06	1.00	.95	.91
200	17.25	8.90	6.12	4.74	3.91	3.36	2.96	2.67	2.44	2.26	2.12	2.00	1.89	1.81
300	25.88	13.35	9.18	7.10	5.86	5.03	4.44	4.00	3.66	3.39	3.17	2.99	2.84	2.71
400	34.50	17.80	12.24	9.47	7.81	6.71	5.92	5.33	4.88	4.52	4.23	3.99	3.78	3.61
500	43.12	22.25	15.30	11.83	9.76	8.38	7.40	6.67	6.10	5.65	5.28	4.98	4.73	4.51
600	51.75	26.70	18.36	14.20	11.71	10.06	8.88	8.00	7.32	6.78	6.34	5.98	5.67	5.41
700	60.37	31.15	21.42	16.57	13.66	11.73	10.36	9.33	8.54	7.91	7.40	6.97	6.62	6.31
800	69.00	35.60	24.48	18.93	15.61	13.41	11.84	10.66	9.76	9.04	8.45	7.97	7.56	7.22
900	77.62	40.05	27.54	21.30	17.56	15.08	13.32	12.00	10.98	10.17	9.51	8.96	8.51	8.12
1000	86.24	44.49	30.60	23.66	19.51	16.76	14.79	13.33	12.20	11.30	10.56	9.96	9.45	9.02
2000	172.48	88.98	61.19	47.32	39.02	33.51	29.58	26.65	24.39	22.59	21.12	19.91	18.90	18.03
3000	258.72	133.47	91.78	70.98	58.53	50.26	44.37	39.98	36.58	33.88	31.68	29.87	28.34	27.05
4000	344.96	177.96	122.37	94.63	78.04	67.01	59.16	53.30	48.77	45.17	42.24	39.82	37.79	36.06
5000	431.20	222.45	152.97	118.29	97.54	83.76	73.95	66.63	60.97	56.46	52.80	49.77	47.23	45.07
6000	517.44	266.94	183.56	141.95	117.05	100.51	88.74	79.95	73.16	67.75	63.36	59.73	56.68	54.09
7000	603.68	311.43	214.15	165.61	136.56	117.26	103.53	93.28	85.35	79.04	73.92	69.68	66.12	63.10
8000	689.92	355.92	244.74	189.26	156.07	134.01	118.32	106.60	97.54	90.34	84.48	79.63	75.57	72.11
9000	776.15	400.41	275.33	212.92	175.57	150.76	133.11	119.93	109.73	101.63	95.04	89.59	85.01	81.13
10000	862.39	444.90	305.93	236.58	195.08	167.51	147.89	133.25	121.93	112.92	105.60	99.54	94.46	90.14
11000	948.63	489.39	336.52	260.24	214.59	184.26	162.68	146.58	134.12	124.21	116.16	109.50	103.90	99.15
12000	1034.87	533.88	367.11	283.89	234.10	201.01	177.47	159.90	146.31	135.50	126.72	119.45	113.35	108.17
13000	1121.11	578.37	397.70	307.55	253.60	217.76	192.26	173.23	158.50	146.79	137.28	129.40	122.79	117.18
14000	1207.35	622.86	428.29	331.21	273.11	234.51	207.05	186.55	170.69	158.08	147.83	139.36	132.24	126.19
15000	1293.59	667.35	458.89	354.87	292.62	251.26	221.84	199.88	182.89	169.37	158.39	149.31	141.69	135.21
16000	1379.83	711.84	489.48	378.52	312.13	268.01	236.63	213.20	195.08	180.67	168.95	159.26	151.13	144.22
17000	1466.07	756.33	520.07	402.18	331.64	284.76	251.42	226.53	207.27	191.96	179.51	169.22	160.58	153.23
18000	1552.31	800.82	550.66	425.84	351.14	301.51	266.21	239.85	219.46	203.25	190.07	179.17	170.02	162.25
19000	1638.54	845.31	581.26	449.49	370.65	318.26	281.00	253.18	231.65	214.54	200.63	189.12	179.47	171.26
20000	1724.78	889.80	611.85	473.15	390.16	335.01	295.78	266.50	243.85	225.83	211.19	199.08	188.91	180.27
21000	1811.02	934.29	642.44	496.81	409.67	351.77	310.57	279.83	256.04	237.12	221.75	209.03	198.36	189.29
22000	1897.26	978.78	673.03	520.47	429.17	368.52	325.36	293.15	268.23	248.41	232.31	218.99	207.80	198.30
23000	1983.50	1023.27	703.62	544.12	448.68	385.27	340.15	306.47	280.42	259.70	242.87	228.94	217.25	207.31
24000	2069.74	1067.76	734.22	567.78	468.19	402.02	354.94	319.80	292.61	271.00	253.43	238.89	226.69	216.33
25000	2155.98	1112.25	764.81	591.44	487.70	418.77	369.73	333.12	304.81	282.29	263.99	248.85	236.14	225.34
26000	2242.22	1156.74	795.40	615.10	507.20	435.52	384.52	346.45	317.00	293.58	274.55	258.80	245.58	234.35
27000	2328.46	1201.23	825.99	638.75	526.71	452.27	399.31	359.77	329.19	304.87	285.10	268.75	255.03	243.37
28000	2414.69	1245.72	856.58	662.41	546.22	469.02	414.10	373.10	341.38	316.16	295.66	278.71	264.47	252.38
29000	2500.93	1290.21	887.18	686.07	565.73	485.77	428.89	386.42	353.57	327.45	306.22	288.66	273.92	261.39
30000	2587.17	1334.70	917.77	709.73	585.23	502.52	443.67	399.75	365.77	338.74	316.78	298.62	283.37	270.41
31000	2673.41	1379.19	948.36	733.38	604.74	519.27	458.46	413.07	377.96	350.04	327.34	308.57	292.81	279.42
32000	2759.65	1423.68	978.95	757.04	624.25	536.02	473.25	426.40	390.15	361.33	337.90	318.52	302.26	288.43
33000	2845.89	1468.17	1009.55	780.70	643.76	552.77	488.04	439.72	402.34	372.62	348.46	328.48	311.70	297.45
34000	2932.13	1512.66	1040.14	804.35	663.27	569.52	502.83	453.05	414.53	383.91	359.02	338.43	321.15	306.46
35000	3018.37	1557.15	1070.73	828.01	682.77	586.27	517.62	466.37	426.73	395.20	369.58	348.38	330.59	315.47
36000	3104.60	1601.64	1101.32	851.67	702.28	603.02	532.41	479.70	438.92	406.49	380.14	358.34	340.04	324.49
37000	3190.84	1646.13	1131.91	875.33	721.79	619.77	547.20	493.02	451.11	417.78	390.70	368.29	349.48	333.50
38000	3277.08	1690.62	1162.51	898.98	741.30	636.52	561.99	506.35	463.30	429.07	401.26	378.24	358.93	342.51
39000	3363.32	1735.11	1193.10	922.64	760.80	653.27	576.78	519.67	475.49	440.37	411.82	388.20	368.37	351.53
40000	3449.56	1779.60	1223.69	946.30	780.31	670.02	591.56	533.00	487.69	451.66	422.37	398.15	377.82	360.54
41000	3535.80	1824.09	1254.28	969.96	799.82	686.77	606.35	546.32	499.88	462.95	432.93	408.11	387.26	369.55
42000	3622.04	1868.58	1284.87	993.61	819.33	703.53	621.14	559.65	512.07	474.24	443.49	418.06	396.71	378.57
43000	3708.28	1913.07	1315.47	1017.27	838.83	720.28	635.93	572.97	524.26	485.53	454.05	428.01	406.15	387.58
44000	3794.52	1957.56	1346.06	1040.93	858.34	737.03	650.72	586.30	536.46	496.82	464.61	437.97	415.60	396.59
45000	3880.75	2002.05	1376.65	1064.59	877.85	753.78	665.51	599.62	548.65	508.11	475.17	447.92	425.05	405.61
46000	3966.99	2046.53	1407.24	1088.24	897.36	770.53	680.30	612.94	560.84	519.40	485.73	457.87	434.49	414.62
47000	4053.23	2091.02	1437.84	1111.90	916.86	787.28	695.09	626.27	573.03	530.70	496.29	467.83	443.94	423.63
48000	4139.47	2135.51	1468.43	1135.56	936.37	804.03	709.88	639.59	585.22	541.99	506.85	477.78	453.38	432.65
49000	4225.71	2180.00	1499.02	1159.21	955.88	820.78	724.67	652.92	597.42	553.28	517.41	487.73	462.83	441.66
50000	4311.95	2224.49	1529.61	1182.87	975.39	837.53	739.45	666.24	609.61	564.57	527.97	497.69	472.27	450.67
55000	4743.14	2446.94	1682.57	1301.16	1072.91	921.28	813.40	732.87	670.57	621.03	580.76	547.46	519.50	495.74
60000	5174.34	2669.39	1835.53	1419.45	1170.46	1005.03	887.34	799.49	731.53	677.48	633.56	597.23	566.73	540.81
65000	5605.53	2891.84	1988.49	1537.73	1268.00	1088.79	961.29	866.12	792.49	733.94	686.36	646.99	613.95	585.88
70000	6036.73	3114.29	2141.45	1656.02	1365.54	1172.54	1035.23	932.74	853.45	790.40	739.15	696.76	661.18	630.94
75000	6467.92	3336.74	2294.42	1774.31	1463.08	1256.29	1109.18	999.36	914.41	846.85	791.95	746.53	708.41	676.01
80000	6899.12	3559.19	2447.38	1892.59	1560.62	1340.04	1183.12	1065.99	975.37	903.31	844.74	796.30	755.63	721.08
85000	7330.31	3781.64	2600.34	2010.88	1658.16	1423.80	1257.07	1132.61	1036.33	959.77	897.54	846.07	802.86	766.14
90000	7761.50	4004.08	2753.30	2129.17	1755.69	1507.55	1331.01	1199.24	1097.29	1016.22	950.34	895.84	850.09	811.21
95000	8192.70	4226.53	2906.26	2247.45	1853.23	1591.30	1404.96	1265.86	1158.25	1072.68	1003.13	945.60	897.31	856.28
100000	8623.89	4448.98	3059.22	2365.74	1950.77	1675.05	1478.90	1332.48	1219.21	1129.14	1055.93	995.37	944.54	901.34

MONTHLY PAYMENT
REQUIRED TO AMORTIZE A LOAN   6.375%

TERM	15 Years	16 Years	17 Years	18 Years	19 Years	20 Years	21 Years	22 Years	23 Years	24 Years	25 Years	30 Years	35 Years	40 Years
AMOUNT														
5	.05	.05	.05	.04	.04	.04	.04	.04	.04	.04	.04	.04	.03	.03
10	.09	.09	.09	.08	.08	.08	.08	.08	.07	.07	.07	.07	.06	.06
15	.13	.13	.13	.12	.12	.12	.11	.11	.11	.11	.11	.10	.09	.09
25	.22	.21	.21	.20	.19	.19	.19	.18	.18	.17	.17	.16	.15	.15
50	.44	.42	.41	.39	.38	.37	.37	.36	.35	.34	.34	.32	.30	.29
75	.65	.63	.61	.59	.57	.56	.55	.53	.52	.51	.51	.47	.45	.44
100	.87	.84	.81	.78	.76	.74	.73	.71	.70	.68	.67	.63	.60	.58
200	1.73	1.67	1.61	1.56	1.52	1.48	1.45	1.42	1.39	1.36	1.34	1.25	1.20	1.16
300	2.60	2.50	2.42	2.34	2.28	2.22	2.17	2.12	2.08	2.04	2.01	1.88	1.79	1.73
400	3.46	3.33	3.22	3.12	3.04	2.96	2.89	2.83	2.77	2.72	2.67	2.50	2.39	2.31
500	4.33	4.17	4.03	3.90	3.79	3.70	3.61	3.53	3.46	3.40	3.34	3.12	2.98	2.89
600	5.19	5.00	4.83	4.68	4.55	4.43	4.33	4.24	4.15	4.08	4.01	3.75	3.58	3.46
700	6.05	5.83	5.63	5.46	5.31	5.17	5.05	4.94	4.85	4.76	4.68	4.37	4.17	4.04
800	6.92	6.66	6.44	6.24	6.07	5.91	5.77	5.65	5.54	5.44	5.34	5.00	4.77	4.62
900	7.78	7.49	7.24	7.02	6.82	6.65	6.49	6.35	6.23	6.11	6.01	5.62	5.37	5.19
1000	8.65	8.33	8.05	7.80	7.58	7.39	7.21	7.06	6.92	6.79	6.68	6.24	5.96	5.77
2000	17.29	16.65	16.09	15.59	15.16	14.77	14.42	14.11	13.83	13.58	13.35	12.48	11.92	11.54
3000	25.93	24.97	24.13	23.39	22.73	22.15	21.63	21.17	20.75	20.37	20.03	18.72	17.87	17.30
4000	34.58	33.29	32.17	31.18	30.31	29.53	28.84	28.22	27.66	27.16	26.70	24.96	23.83	23.07
5000	43.22	41.61	40.21	38.98	37.89	36.92	36.05	35.28	34.58	33.95	33.38	31.20	29.78	28.83
6000	51.86	49.93	48.25	46.77	45.46	44.30	43.26	42.33	41.49	40.74	40.05	37.44	35.74	34.60
7000	60.50	58.25	56.29	54.56	53.04	51.68	50.47	49.38	48.41	47.52	46.72	43.68	41.70	40.37
8000	69.15	66.57	64.33	62.36	60.61	59.06	57.68	56.44	55.32	54.31	53.40	49.91	47.65	46.13
9000	77.79	74.90	72.37	70.15	68.19	66.45	64.89	63.49	62.24	61.10	60.07	56.15	53.61	51.90
10000	86.43	83.22	80.41	77.95	75.77	73.83	72.10	70.55	69.15	67.89	66.75	62.39	59.56	57.66
11000	95.07	91.54	88.45	85.74	83.34	81.21	79.31	77.60	76.06	74.68	73.42	68.63	65.52	63.43
12000	103.72	99.86	96.49	93.53	90.92	88.59	86.52	84.65	82.98	81.47	80.10	74.87	71.48	69.19
13000	112.36	108.18	104.53	101.33	98.49	95.98	93.73	91.71	89.89	88.25	86.77	81.11	77.43	74.96
14000	121.00	116.50	112.57	109.12	106.07	103.36	100.94	98.76	96.81	95.04	93.44	87.35	83.39	80.73
15000	129.64	124.82	120.62	116.92	113.65	110.74	108.14	105.82	103.72	101.83	100.12	93.59	89.34	86.49
16000	138.29	133.14	128.66	124.71	121.22	118.12	115.35	112.87	110.64	108.62	106.79	99.82	95.30	92.26
17000	146.93	141.47	136.70	132.50	128.80	125.50	122.56	119.93	117.55	115.41	113.47	106.06	101.26	98.02
18000	155.57	149.79	144.74	140.30	136.37	132.89	129.77	126.98	124.47	122.20	120.14	112.30	107.21	103.79
19000	164.21	158.11	152.78	148.09	143.95	140.27	136.98	134.03	131.38	128.98	126.81	118.54	113.17	109.55
20000	172.86	166.43	160.82	155.89	151.53	147.65	144.19	141.09	138.29	135.77	133.49	124.78	119.12	115.32
21000	181.50	174.75	168.86	163.68	159.10	155.03	151.40	148.14	145.21	142.56	140.16	131.02	125.08	121.09
22000	190.14	183.07	176.90	171.48	166.68	162.42	158.61	155.20	152.12	149.35	146.84	137.26	131.04	126.85
23000	198.78	191.39	184.94	179.27	174.26	169.80	165.82	162.25	159.04	156.14	153.51	143.50	136.99	132.62
24000	207.43	199.71	192.98	187.06	181.83	177.18	173.03	169.30	165.95	162.93	160.19	149.73	142.95	138.38
25000	216.07	208.03	201.02	194.86	189.41	184.56	180.24	176.36	172.87	169.71	166.86	155.97	148.90	144.15
26000	224.71	216.36	209.06	202.65	196.98	191.95	187.45	183.41	179.78	176.50	173.53	162.21	154.86	149.91
27000	233.35	224.68	217.10	210.45	204.56	199.33	194.66	190.47	186.70	183.29	180.21	168.45	160.81	155.68
28000	242.00	233.00	225.14	218.24	212.14	206.71	201.87	197.52	193.61	190.08	186.88	174.69	166.77	161.45
29000	250.64	241.32	233.18	226.03	219.71	214.09	209.07	204.58	200.53	196.87	193.56	180.93	172.73	167.21
30000	259.28	249.64	241.23	233.83	227.29	221.47	216.28	211.63	207.44	203.66	200.23	187.17	178.68	172.98
31000	267.92	257.96	249.27	241.62	234.86	228.86	223.49	218.68	214.35	210.45	206.90	193.40	184.64	178.74
32000	276.57	266.28	257.31	249.42	242.44	236.24	230.70	225.74	221.27	217.23	213.58	199.64	190.59	184.51
33000	285.21	274.60	265.35	257.21	250.02	243.62	237.91	232.79	228.18	224.02	220.25	205.88	196.55	190.27
34000	293.85	282.93	273.39	265.00	257.59	251.00	245.12	239.85	235.10	230.81	226.93	212.12	202.51	196.04
35000	302.49	291.25	281.43	272.80	265.17	258.39	252.33	246.90	242.01	237.60	233.60	218.36	208.46	201.81
36000	311.14	299.57	289.47	280.59	272.74	265.77	259.54	253.95	248.93	244.39	240.28	224.60	214.42	207.57
37000	319.78	307.89	297.51	288.39	280.32	273.15	266.75	261.01	255.84	251.18	246.95	230.84	220.37	213.34
38000	328.42	316.21	305.55	296.18	287.90	280.53	273.96	268.06	262.76	257.96	253.62	237.08	226.33	219.10
39000	337.06	324.53	313.59	303.98	295.47	287.92	281.17	275.12	269.67	264.75	260.30	243.31	232.29	224.87
40000	345.71	332.85	321.63	311.77	303.05	295.30	288.38	282.17	276.58	271.54	266.97	249.55	238.24	230.63
41000	354.35	341.17	329.67	319.56	310.62	302.68	295.59	289.22	283.50	278.33	273.65	255.79	244.20	236.40
42000	362.99	349.50	337.71	327.36	318.20	310.06	302.80	296.28	290.41	285.12	280.32	262.03	250.15	242.17
43000	371.63	357.82	345.75	335.15	325.78	317.44	310.00	303.33	297.33	291.91	286.99	268.27	256.11	247.93
44000	380.28	366.14	353.79	342.95	333.35	324.83	317.21	310.39	304.24	298.69	293.67	274.51	262.07	253.70
45000	388.92	374.46	361.84	350.74	340.93	332.21	324.42	317.44	311.16	305.48	300.34	280.75	268.02	259.46
46000	397.56	382.78	369.88	358.53	348.51	339.59	331.63	324.50	318.07	312.27	307.02	286.99	273.98	265.23
47000	406.20	391.10	377.92	366.33	356.08	346.97	338.84	331.55	324.99	319.06	313.69	293.22	279.93	271.00
48000	414.85	399.42	385.96	374.12	363.66	354.36	346.05	338.60	331.90	325.85	320.37	299.46	285.89	276.76
49000	423.49	407.74	394.00	381.92	371.23	361.74	353.26	345.66	338.82	332.64	327.04	305.70	291.85	282.53
50000	432.13	416.06	402.04	389.71	378.81	369.12	360.47	352.71	345.73	339.42	333.71	311.94	297.80	288.29
55000	475.34	457.67	442.25	428.68	416.69	406.03	396.52	387.98	380.30	373.37	367.08	343.13	327.58	317.12
60000	518.56	499.28	482.45	467.65	454.57	442.94	432.56	423.25	414.87	407.31	400.46	374.33	357.36	345.95
65000	561.77	540.88	522.65	506.62	492.45	479.86	468.61	458.52	449.45	441.25	433.83	405.52	387.14	374.78
70000	604.98	582.49	562.85	545.59	530.33	516.77	504.66	493.79	484.02	475.19	467.20	436.71	416.92	403.61
75000	648.19	624.09	603.06	584.56	568.21	553.68	540.70	529.07	518.59	509.13	500.57	467.91	446.70	432.44
80000	691.41	665.70	643.26	623.53	606.09	590.59	576.75	564.34	553.16	543.08	533.94	499.10	476.48	461.26
85000	734.62	707.31	683.46	662.50	643.97	627.50	612.79	599.61	587.74	577.02	567.31	530.29	506.26	490.09
90000	777.83	748.91	723.67	701.47	681.85	664.41	648.84	634.88	622.31	610.96	600.68	561.49	536.04	518.92
95000	821.04	790.52	763.87	740.44	719.73	701.33	684.89	670.15	656.88	644.90	634.05	592.68	565.82	547.75
100000	864.26	832.12	804.07	779.42	757.61	738.24	720.93	705.42	691.45	678.84	667.42	623.87	595.60	576.58

47

MONTHLY PAYMENT
REQUIRED TO AMORTIZE A LOAN

TERM AMOUNT	1 Year	2 Years	3 Years	4 Years	5 Years	6 Years	7 Years	8 Years	9 Years	10 Years	11 Years	12 Years	13 Years	14 Years
5	.44	.23	.16	.12	.10	.09	.08	.07	.07	.06	.06	.05	.05	.05
10	.87	.45	.31	.24	.20	.17	.15	.14	.13	.12	.11	.10	.10	.10
15	1.30	.67	.46	.36	.30	.26	.23	.21	.19	.17	.16	.15	.15	.14
25	2.16	1.12	.77	.60	.49	.42	.38	.34	.31	.29	.27	.25	.24	.23
50	4.32	2.23	1.54	1.19	.98	.84	.75	.67	.62	.57	.53	.50	.48	.46
75	6.47	3.34	2.30	1.78	1.47	1.26	1.12	1.01	.92	.85	.80	.75	.71	.68
100	8.63	4.46	3.07	2.37	1.96	1.68	1.49	1.34	1.23	1.14	1.06	1.00	.95	.91
200	17.26	8.91	6.13	4.74	3.91	3.36	2.97	2.67	2.45	2.27	2.12	2.00	1.90	1.81
300	25.88	13.36	9.19	7.11	5.86	5.03	4.45	4.01	3.67	3.40	3.18	3.00	2.84	2.71
400	34.51	17.81	12.25	9.47	7.81	6.71	5.93	5.34	4.89	4.53	4.23	3.99	3.79	3.62
500	43.13	22.26	15.31	11.84	9.76	8.39	7.41	6.67	6.11	5.66	5.29	4.99	4.73	4.52
600	51.76	26.71	18.37	14.21	11.72	10.06	8.89	8.01	7.33	6.79	6.35	5.99	5.68	5.42
700	60.38	31.16	21.43	16.57	13.67	11.74	10.37	9.34	8.55	7.92	7.41	6.98	6.63	6.32
800	69.01	35.61	24.49	18.94	15.62	13.41	11.85	10.67	9.77	9.05	8.46	7.98	7.57	7.23
900	77.63	40.06	27.55	21.31	17.57	15.09	13.33	12.01	10.99	10.18	9.52	8.98	8.52	8.13
1000	86.26	44.51	30.61	23.67	19.52	16.77	14.81	13.34	12.21	11.31	10.58	9.97	9.46	9.03
2000	172.51	89.01	61.21	47.34	39.04	33.53	29.61	26.68	24.41	22.61	21.15	19.94	18.92	18.06
3000	258.76	133.51	91.82	71.00	58.56	50.29	44.41	40.02	36.62	33.92	31.72	29.91	28.38	27.09
4000	345.01	178.01	122.42	94.68	78.08	67.05	59.21	53.35	48.82	45.22	42.29	39.87	37.84	36.11
5000	431.26	222.51	153.02	118.35	97.60	83.82	74.01	66.69	61.03	56.52	52.87	49.84	47.30	45.14
6000	517.51	267.01	183.63	142.02	117.12	100.58	88.81	80.03	73.23	67.83	63.44	59.81	56.76	54.17
7000	603.76	311.51	214.23	165.69	136.64	117.34	103.61	93.36	85.44	79.13	74.01	69.77	66.22	63.19
8000	690.01	356.01	244.83	189.36	156.16	134.10	118.41	106.70	97.64	90.44	84.58	79.74	75.67	72.22
9000	776.26	400.51	275.44	213.02	175.68	150.87	133.21	120.04	109.85	101.74	95.15	89.71	85.13	81.25
10000	862.51	445.02	306.04	236.69	195.20	167.63	148.02	133.38	122.05	113.04	105.73	99.67	94.59	90.27
11000	948.76	489.52	336.64	260.36	214.72	184.39	162.82	146.71	134.25	124.35	116.30	109.64	104.05	99.30
12000	1035.01	534.02	367.25	284.03	234.24	201.15	177.62	160.05	146.46	135.65	126.87	119.61	113.51	108.33
13000	1121.26	578.52	397.85	307.70	253.76	217.92	192.42	173.39	158.66	146.96	137.44	129.57	122.97	117.35
14000	1207.51	623.02	428.45	331.37	273.28	234.68	207.22	186.72	170.87	158.26	148.01	139.54	132.43	126.38
15000	1293.76	667.52	459.06	355.04	292.80	251.44	222.02	200.06	183.07	169.56	158.59	149.51	141.88	135.41
16000	1380.01	712.02	489.66	378.71	312.31	268.20	236.82	213.40	195.28	180.87	169.16	159.47	151.34	144.44
17000	1466.26	756.52	520.26	402.38	331.83	284.97	251.62	226.73	207.48	192.17	179.73	169.44	160.80	153.46
18000	1552.51	801.02	550.87	426.04	351.35	301.73	266.42	240.07	219.69	203.48	190.30	179.41	170.26	162.49
19000	1638.76	845.53	581.47	449.71	370.87	318.49	281.23	253.41	231.89	214.78	200.88	189.37	179.72	171.52
20000	1725.01	890.03	612.08	473.38	390.39	335.25	296.03	266.75	244.10	226.08	211.45	199.34	189.18	180.54
21000	1811.26	934.53	642.68	497.05	409.91	352.01	310.83	280.08	256.30	237.39	222.02	209.31	198.64	189.57
22000	1897.51	979.03	673.28	520.72	429.43	368.78	325.63	293.42	268.50	248.69	232.59	219.27	208.09	198.60
23000	1983.76	1023.53	703.89	544.39	448.95	385.54	340.43	306.76	280.71	260.00	243.16	229.24	217.55	207.62
24000	2070.01	1068.03	734.49	568.06	468.47	402.30	355.23	320.09	292.91	271.30	253.74	239.21	227.01	216.65
25000	2156.26	1112.53	765.09	591.73	487.99	419.06	370.03	333.43	305.12	282.60	264.31	249.17	236.47	225.68
26000	2242.52	1157.03	795.70	615.40	507.51	435.83	384.83	346.77	317.32	293.91	274.88	259.14	245.93	234.70
27000	2328.77	1201.53	826.30	639.06	527.03	452.59	399.63	360.11	329.53	305.21	285.45	269.11	255.39	243.73
28000	2415.02	1246.03	856.90	662.73	546.55	469.35	414.43	373.44	341.73	316.52	296.02	279.07	264.85	252.76
29000	2501.27	1290.54	887.51	686.40	566.07	486.11	429.24	386.78	353.94	327.82	306.60	289.04	274.31	261.78
30000	2587.52	1335.04	918.11	710.07	585.59	502.88	444.04	400.12	366.14	339.12	317.17	299.01	283.76	270.81
31000	2673.77	1379.54	948.71	733.74	605.10	519.64	458.84	413.45	378.35	350.43	327.74	308.97	293.22	279.84
32000	2760.02	1424.04	979.32	757.41	624.62	536.40	473.64	426.79	390.55	361.73	338.31	318.94	302.68	288.87
33000	2846.27	1468.54	1009.92	781.08	644.14	553.16	488.44	440.13	402.75	373.04	348.89	328.91	312.14	297.89
34000	2932.52	1513.04	1040.52	804.75	663.66	569.93	503.24	453.46	414.96	384.34	359.46	338.87	321.60	306.92
35000	3018.77	1557.54	1071.13	828.42	683.18	586.69	518.04	466.80	427.16	395.64	370.03	348.84	331.06	315.95
36000	3105.02	1602.04	1101.73	852.08	702.70	603.45	532.84	480.14	439.37	406.95	380.60	358.81	340.52	324.97
37000	3191.27	1646.54	1132.33	875.75	722.22	620.21	547.64	493.48	451.57	418.25	391.17	368.77	349.97	334.00
38000	3277.52	1691.05	1162.94	899.42	741.74	636.97	562.45	506.81	463.78	429.56	401.75	378.74	359.43	343.03
39000	3363.77	1735.55	1193.54	923.09	761.26	653.74	577.25	520.15	475.98	440.86	412.32	388.71	368.89	352.05
40000	3450.02	1780.05	1224.15	946.76	780.78	670.50	592.05	533.49	488.19	452.16	422.89	398.68	378.35	361.08
41000	3536.27	1824.55	1254.75	970.43	800.30	687.26	606.85	546.82	500.39	463.47	433.46	408.64	387.81	370.11
42000	3622.52	1869.05	1285.35	994.10	819.82	704.02	621.65	560.16	512.59	474.77	444.03	418.61	397.27	379.13
43000	3708.77	1913.55	1315.96	1017.77	839.34	720.79	636.45	573.50	524.80	486.08	454.61	428.58	406.73	388.16
44000	3795.02	1958.05	1346.56	1041.43	858.86	737.55	651.25	586.84	537.00	497.38	465.18	438.54	416.18	397.19
45000	3881.27	2002.55	1377.16	1065.10	878.38	754.31	666.05	600.17	549.21	508.68	475.75	448.51	425.64	406.21
46000	3967.52	2047.05	1407.77	1088.77	897.89	771.07	680.85	613.51	561.41	519.99	486.32	458.48	435.10	415.24
47000	4053.77	2091.56	1438.37	1112.44	917.41	787.84	695.66	626.85	573.62	531.29	496.90	468.44	444.56	424.27
48000	4140.02	2136.06	1468.97	1136.11	936.93	804.60	710.46	640.18	585.82	542.60	507.47	478.41	454.02	433.30
49000	4226.27	2180.56	1499.58	1159.78	956.45	821.36	725.26	653.52	598.03	553.90	518.04	488.38	463.48	442.32
50000	4312.52	2225.06	1530.18	1183.45	975.97	838.12	740.06	666.86	610.23	565.20	528.61	498.34	472.94	451.35
55000	4743.78	2447.56	1683.20	1301.79	1073.57	921.93	814.06	733.54	671.25	621.72	581.47	548.18	520.23	496.48
60000	5175.03	2670.07	1836.22	1420.14	1171.17	1005.75	888.07	800.23	732.28	678.24	634.33	598.01	567.52	541.62
65000	5606.28	2892.57	1989.23	1538.48	1268.76	1089.56	962.07	866.91	793.30	734.76	687.19	647.84	614.82	586.75
70000	6037.53	3115.08	2142.25	1656.83	1366.36	1173.37	1036.08	933.60	854.32	791.28	740.05	697.68	662.11	631.89
75000	6468.78	3337.59	2295.27	1775.17	1463.96	1257.18	1110.09	1000.28	915.34	847.80	792.91	747.51	709.40	677.02
80000	6900.04	3560.09	2448.29	1893.51	1561.55	1340.99	1184.09	1066.97	976.37	904.32	845.78	797.35	756.70	722.16
85000	7331.29	3782.60	2601.30	2011.86	1659.15	1424.81	1258.10	1133.65	1037.39	960.84	898.64	847.18	803.99	767.29
90000	7762.54	4005.10	2754.32	2130.20	1756.75	1508.62	1332.10	1200.34	1098.41	1017.36	951.50	897.01	851.28	812.42
95000	8193.79	4227.61	2907.34	2248.55	1854.34	1592.43	1406.11	1267.03	1159.43	1073.88	1004.36	946.85	898.58	857.56
100000	8625.04	4450.11	3060.36	2366.89	1951.94	1676.24	1480.11	1333.71	1220.46	1130.40	1057.22	996.68	945.87	902.69

TERM	15 Years	16 Years	17 Years	18 Years	19 Years	20 Years	21 Years	22 Years	23 Years	24 Years	25 Years	30 Years	35 Years	40 Years
AMOUNT														
5	.05	.05	.05	.04	.04	.04	.04	.04	.04	.04	.04	.04	.03	.03
10	.09	.09	.09	.08	.08	.08	.08	.08	.07	.07	.07	.07	.06	.06
15	.13	.13	.13	.12	.12	.12	.11	.11	.11	.11	.11	.10	.09	.09
25	.22	.21	.21	.20	.19	.19	.19	.18	.18	.18	.17	.16	.15	.15
50	.44	.42	.41	.40	.38	.37	.37	.36	.35	.35	.34	.32	.30	.29
75	.65	.63	.61	.59	.57	.56	.55	.54	.52	.52	.51	.47	.45	.44
100	.87	.84	.81	.79	.76	.74	.73	.71	.70	.69	.67	.63	.60	.58
200	1.74	1.67	1.62	1.57	1.52	1.48	1.45	1.42	1.39	1.37	1.34	1.26	1.20	1.16
300	2.60	2.51	2.42	2.35	2.28	2.22	2.17	2.13	2.08	2.05	2.01	1.88	1.80	1.74
400	3.47	3.34	3.23	3.13	3.04	2.96	2.89	2.83	2.78	2.73	2.68	2.51	2.39	2.32
500	4.33	4.17	4.03	3.91	3.80	3.70	3.62	3.54	3.47	3.41	3.35	3.13	2.99	2.90
600	5.20	5.01	4.84	4.69	4.56	4.44	4.34	4.25	4.16	4.09	4.02	3.76	3.59	3.48
700	6.06	5.84	5.64	5.47	5.32	5.18	5.06	4.95	4.86	4.77	4.69	4.38	4.19	4.05
800	6.93	6.67	6.45	6.25	6.08	5.92	5.78	5.66	5.55	5.45	5.36	5.01	4.78	4.63
900	7.80	7.51	7.25	7.03	6.84	6.66	6.51	6.37	6.24	6.13	6.03	5.63	5.38	5.21
1000	8.66	8.34	8.06	7.81	7.60	7.40	7.23	7.07	6.93	6.81	6.69	6.26	5.98	5.79
2000	17.32	16.68	16.11	15.62	15.19	14.80	14.45	14.14	13.86	13.61	13.38	12.52	11.95	11.57
3000	25.97	25.01	24.17	23.43	22.78	22.20	21.68	21.21	20.79	20.42	20.07	18.77	17.92	17.36
4000	34.63	33.35	32.22	31.24	30.37	29.59	28.90	28.28	27.72	27.22	26.76	25.03	23.90	23.14
5000	43.29	41.68	40.28	39.05	37.96	36.99	36.13	35.35	34.65	34.02	33.45	31.28	29.87	28.92
6000	51.94	50.02	48.33	46.86	45.55	44.39	43.35	42.42	41.58	40.83	40.14	37.54	35.84	34.71
7000	60.60	58.35	56.39	54.66	53.14	51.78	50.57	49.49	48.51	47.63	46.83	43.79	41.82	40.49
8000	69.25	66.69	64.44	62.47	60.73	59.18	57.80	56.56	55.44	54.44	53.52	50.05	47.79	46.27
9000	77.91	75.02	72.50	70.28	68.32	66.58	65.02	63.63	62.37	61.24	60.21	56.30	53.76	52.06
10000	86.57	83.36	80.55	78.09	75.91	73.97	72.25	70.70	69.30	68.04	66.90	62.56	59.74	57.84
11000	95.22	91.69	88.61	85.90	83.50	81.37	79.47	77.77	76.23	74.85	73.59	68.81	65.71	63.62
12000	103.88	100.03	96.66	93.71	91.09	88.77	86.69	84.83	83.16	81.65	80.28	75.07	71.68	69.41
13000	112.54	108.36	104.72	101.51	98.68	96.17	93.92	91.90	90.09	88.45	86.97	81.32	77.65	75.19
14000	121.19	116.70	112.77	109.32	106.27	103.56	101.14	98.97	97.02	95.26	93.66	87.58	83.63	80.97
15000	129.85	125.03	120.83	117.13	113.86	110.96	108.37	106.04	103.95	102.06	100.35	93.83	89.60	86.76
16000	138.50	133.37	128.88	124.94	121.45	118.36	115.59	113.11	110.88	108.87	107.04	100.09	95.57	92.54
17000	147.16	141.70	136.94	132.75	129.04	125.75	122.82	120.18	117.81	115.67	113.73	106.34	101.55	98.32
18000	155.82	150.04	144.99	140.56	136.64	133.15	130.04	127.25	124.74	122.47	120.42	112.60	107.52	104.11
19000	164.47	158.37	153.05	148.36	144.23	140.55	137.26	134.32	131.67	129.28	127.11	118.85	113.49	109.89
20000	173.13	166.71	161.10	156.17	151.82	147.94	144.49	141.39	138.60	136.08	133.80	125.11	119.47	115.67
21000	181.79	175.04	169.15	163.98	159.41	155.34	151.71	148.46	145.53	142.88	140.49	131.36	125.44	121.46
22000	190.44	183.38	177.21	171.79	167.00	162.74	158.94	155.53	152.46	149.69	147.18	137.62	131.41	127.24
23000	199.10	191.71	185.26	179.60	174.59	170.14	166.16	162.60	159.39	156.49	153.87	143.87	137.38	133.02
24000	207.75	200.05	193.32	187.41	182.18	177.53	173.38	169.66	166.32	163.30	160.56	150.13	143.36	138.81
25000	216.41	208.38	201.37	195.21	189.77	184.93	180.61	176.73	173.25	170.10	167.25	156.38	149.33	144.59
26000	225.07	216.72	209.43	203.02	197.36	192.33	187.83	183.80	180.18	176.90	173.94	162.64	155.30	150.38
27000	233.72	225.05	217.48	210.83	204.95	199.72	195.06	190.87	187.11	183.71	180.63	168.89	161.28	156.16
28000	242.38	233.39	225.54	218.64	212.54	207.12	202.28	197.94	194.04	190.51	187.32	175.15	167.25	161.94
29000	251.03	241.72	233.59	226.45	220.13	214.52	209.50	205.01	200.97	197.31	194.01	181.40	173.22	167.73
30000	259.69	250.06	241.65	234.26	227.72	221.91	216.73	212.08	207.90	204.12	200.70	187.66	179.20	173.51
31000	268.35	258.39	249.70	242.06	235.31	229.31	223.95	219.15	214.83	210.92	207.39	193.91	185.17	179.29
32000	277.00	266.73	257.76	249.87	242.90	236.71	231.18	226.22	221.76	217.73	214.08	200.17	191.14	185.08
33000	285.66	275.06	265.81	257.68	250.49	244.11	238.40	233.29	228.68	224.53	220.77	206.42	197.11	190.86
34000	294.32	283.40	273.87	265.49	258.08	251.50	245.63	240.36	235.61	231.33	227.46	212.68	203.09	196.64
35000	302.97	291.73	281.92	273.30	265.67	258.90	252.85	247.43	242.54	238.14	234.15	218.93	209.06	202.43
36000	311.63	300.07	289.98	281.11	273.27	266.30	260.07	254.49	249.47	244.94	240.83	225.19	215.03	208.21
37000	320.28	308.40	298.03	288.91	280.86	273.69	267.30	261.56	256.40	251.74	247.52	231.44	221.01	213.99
38000	328.94	316.74	306.09	296.72	288.45	281.09	274.52	268.63	263.33	258.55	254.21	237.70	226.98	219.78
39000	337.60	325.07	314.14	304.53	296.04	288.49	281.75	275.70	270.26	265.35	260.90	243.95	232.95	225.56
40000	346.25	333.41	322.20	312.34	303.63	295.88	288.97	282.77	277.19	272.16	267.59	250.21	238.93	231.34
41000	354.91	341.74	330.25	320.15	311.22	303.28	296.19	289.84	284.12	278.96	274.28	256.46	244.90	237.13
42000	363.57	350.08	338.30	327.96	318.81	310.68	303.42	296.91	291.05	285.76	280.97	262.72	250.87	242.91
43000	372.22	358.41	346.36	335.77	326.40	318.07	310.64	303.98	297.98	292.57	287.66	268.97	256.84	248.69
44000	380.88	366.75	354.41	343.57	333.99	325.47	317.87	311.05	304.91	299.37	294.35	275.23	262.82	254.48
45000	389.53	375.08	362.47	351.38	341.58	332.87	325.09	318.12	311.84	306.17	301.04	281.48	268.79	260.26
46000	398.19	383.42	370.52	359.19	349.17	340.27	332.31	325.19	318.77	312.98	307.73	287.74	274.76	266.04
47000	406.85	391.75	378.58	367.00	356.76	347.66	339.54	332.26	325.70	319.78	314.42	293.99	280.74	271.83
48000	415.50	400.09	386.63	374.81	364.35	355.06	346.76	339.32	332.63	326.59	321.11	300.25	286.71	277.61
49000	424.16	408.42	394.69	382.62	371.94	362.46	353.99	346.39	339.56	333.39	327.80	306.50	292.68	283.40
50000	432.81	416.76	402.74	390.42	379.53	369.85	361.21	353.46	346.49	340.19	334.49	312.76	298.66	289.18
55000	476.10	458.43	443.02	429.47	417.49	406.84	397.33	388.81	381.14	374.21	367.94	344.03	328.52	318.10
60000	519.38	500.11	483.29	468.51	455.43	443.82	433.45	424.15	415.79	408.23	401.39	375.31	358.39	347.01
65000	562.66	541.79	523.56	507.55	493.39	480.81	469.57	459.50	450.44	442.25	434.84	406.58	388.25	375.93
70000	605.94	583.46	563.84	546.59	531.34	517.79	505.69	494.85	485.08	476.27	468.29	437.86	418.12	404.85
75000	649.22	625.14	604.11	585.63	569.30	554.78	541.81	530.19	519.73	510.29	501.73	469.13	447.98	433.77
80000	692.50	666.81	644.39	624.68	607.25	591.76	577.94	565.54	554.38	544.31	535.18	500.41	477.85	462.68
85000	735.78	708.49	684.66	663.72	645.20	628.75	614.06	600.88	589.03	578.33	568.63	531.69	507.71	491.60
90000	779.06	750.16	724.93	702.76	683.16	665.73	650.18	636.23	623.68	612.34	602.08	562.96	537.58	520.52
95000	822.34	791.84	765.21	741.80	721.11	702.72	686.30	671.58	658.33	646.36	635.53	594.24	567.44	549.44
100000	865.62	833.51	805.48	780.84	759.06	739.70	722.42	706.92	692.97	680.38	668.98	625.51	597.31	578.35

6.500%

TERM	1 Year	2 Years	3 Years	4 Years	5 Years	6 Years	7 Years	8 Years	9 Years	10 Years	11 Years	12 Years	13 Years	14 Years
AMOUNT														
5	.44	.23	.16	.12	.10	.09	.08	.07	.07	.06	.06	.06	.05	.05
10	.87	.45	.31	.24	.20	.17	.15	.14	.13	.12	.11	.11	.10	.10
15	1.30	.67	.46	.36	.30	.26	.23	.21	.19	.18	.16	.16	.15	.14
25	2.16	1.12	.77	.60	.49	.43	.38	.34	.31	.29	.27	.26	.24	.23
50	4.32	2.23	1.54	1.19	.98	.85	.75	.67	.62	.57	.54	.51	.48	.46
75	6.48	3.35	2.30	1.78	1.47	1.27	1.12	1.01	.92	.86	.80	.76	.72	.69
100	8.63	4.46	3.07	2.38	1.96	1.69	1.49	1.34	1.23	1.14	1.07	1.01	.96	.91
200	17.26	8.91	6.13	4.75	3.92	3.37	2.97	2.68	2.46	2.28	2.13	2.01	1.91	1.82
300	25.89	13.37	9.20	7.13	5.87	5.05	4.46	4.02	3.68	3.41	3.19	3.01	2.86	2.73
400	34.52	17.82	12.26	9.49	7.83	6.73	5.94	5.36	4.91	4.55	4.25	4.01	3.81	3.64
500	43.15	22.28	15.33	11.86	9.79	8.41	7.43	6.70	6.13	5.68	5.32	5.01	4.76	4.55
600	51.78	26.73	18.39	14.23	11.74	10.09	8.91	8.04	7.36	6.82	6.38	6.02	5.71	5.45
700	60.41	31.19	21.46	16.61	13.70	11.77	10.40	9.38	8.58	7.95	7.44	7.02	6.66	6.36
800	69.04	35.64	24.52	18.98	15.66	13.45	11.88	10.71	9.81	9.09	8.50	8.02	7.61	7.27
900	77.67	40.10	27.59	21.35	17.61	15.13	13.37	12.05	11.03	10.22	9.57	9.02	8.57	8.18
1000	86.30	44.55	30.65	23.72	19.57	16.81	14.85	13.39	12.26	11.36	10.63	10.02	9.52	9.09
2000	172.60	89.10	61.30	47.43	39.14	33.62	29.70	26.78	24.51	22.71	21.25	20.04	19.03	18.17
3000	258.89	133.64	91.95	71.15	58.70	50.43	44.55	40.16	36.77	34.07	31.88	30.06	28.54	27.25
4000	345.19	178.19	122.60	94.86	78.27	67.24	59.40	53.55	49.02	45.42	42.50	40.08	38.05	36.33
5000	431.49	222.74	153.25	118.58	97.84	84.05	74.25	66.94	61.28	56.78	53.12	50.10	47.56	45.41
6000	517.78	267.28	183.90	142.29	117.40	100.86	89.10	80.32	73.53	68.13	63.75	60.12	57.08	54.49
7000	604.08	311.83	214.55	166.01	136.97	117.67	103.95	93.71	85.79	79.49	74.37	70.14	66.59	63.57
8000	690.38	356.38	245.20	189.72	156.53	134.48	118.80	107.09	98.04	90.84	85.00	80.16	76.10	72.65
9000	776.67	400.92	275.85	213.44	176.10	151.29	133.65	120.48	110.30	102.20	95.62	90.18	85.61	81.73
10000	862.97	445.47	306.50	237.15	195.67	168.10	148.50	133.87	122.55	113.55	106.24	100.20	95.12	90.81
11000	949.27	490.01	337.14	260.87	215.23	184.91	163.35	147.25	134.80	124.91	116.87	110.22	104.64	99.90
12000	1035.56	534.56	367.79	284.58	234.80	201.72	178.20	160.64	147.06	136.26	127.49	120.24	114.15	108.98
13000	1121.86	579.11	398.44	308.30	254.36	218.53	193.05	174.03	159.31	147.62	138.11	130.25	123.66	118.06
14000	1208.15	623.65	429.09	332.01	273.93	235.34	207.90	187.41	171.57	158.97	148.74	140.27	133.17	127.14
15000	1294.45	668.20	459.74	355.73	293.50	252.15	222.75	200.80	183.82	170.33	159.36	150.29	142.68	136.22
16000	1380.75	712.75	490.39	379.44	313.06	268.96	237.60	214.18	196.08	181.68	169.99	160.31	152.20	145.30
17000	1467.04	757.29	521.04	403.16	332.63	285.77	252.45	227.57	208.33	193.04	180.61	170.33	161.71	154.38
18000	1553.34	801.84	551.69	426.87	352.20	302.58	267.29	240.96	220.59	204.39	191.23	180.35	171.22	163.46
19000	1639.64	846.38	582.34	450.59	371.76	319.39	282.14	254.34	232.84	215.75	201.86	190.37	180.73	172.54
20000	1725.93	890.93	612.99	474.30	391.33	336.20	296.99	267.73	245.10	227.10	212.48	200.39	190.24	181.62
21000	1812.23	935.48	643.63	498.02	410.89	353.01	311.84	281.12	257.35	238.46	223.10	210.41	199.75	190.71
22000	1898.53	980.02	674.28	521.73	430.46	369.82	326.69	294.50	269.60	249.81	233.73	220.43	209.27	199.79
23000	1984.82	1024.57	704.93	545.45	450.03	386.63	341.54	307.89	281.86	261.17	244.35	230.45	218.78	208.87
24000	2071.12	1069.12	735.58	569.16	469.59	403.44	356.39	321.27	294.11	272.52	254.98	240.47	228.29	217.95
25000	2157.42	1113.66	766.23	592.88	489.16	420.25	371.24	334.66	306.37	283.87	265.60	250.49	237.80	227.03
26000	2243.71	1158.21	796.88	616.59	508.72	437.06	386.09	348.05	318.62	295.23	276.22	260.50	247.31	236.11
27000	2330.01	1202.75	827.53	640.31	528.29	453.87	400.94	361.43	330.88	306.58	286.85	270.52	256.83	245.19
28000	2416.30	1247.30	858.18	664.02	547.86	470.68	415.79	374.82	343.13	317.94	297.47	280.54	266.34	254.27
29000	2502.60	1291.85	888.83	687.74	567.42	487.49	430.64	388.21	355.39	329.29	308.09	290.56	275.85	263.35
30000	2588.90	1336.39	919.48	711.45	586.99	504.30	445.49	401.59	367.64	340.65	318.72	300.58	285.36	272.43
31000	2675.19	1380.94	950.12	735.17	606.56	521.11	460.34	414.98	379.89	352.00	329.34	310.60	294.87	281.51
32000	2761.49	1425.49	980.77	758.88	626.12	537.92	475.19	428.36	392.15	363.36	339.97	320.62	304.39	290.60
33000	2847.79	1470.03	1011.42	782.60	645.69	554.73	490.04	441.75	404.40	374.71	350.59	330.64	313.90	299.68
34000	2934.08	1514.58	1042.07	806.31	665.25	571.54	504.89	455.14	416.66	386.07	361.21	340.66	323.41	308.76
35000	3020.38	1559.12	1072.72	830.03	684.82	588.35	519.74	468.52	428.91	397.42	371.84	350.68	332.92	317.84
36000	3106.68	1603.67	1103.37	853.74	704.39	605.16	534.58	481.91	441.17	408.78	382.46	360.70	342.43	326.92
37000	3192.97	1648.22	1134.02	877.46	723.95	621.97	549.43	495.30	453.42	420.13	393.08	370.72	351.95	336.00
38000	3279.27	1692.76	1164.67	901.17	743.52	638.78	564.28	508.68	465.68	431.49	403.71	380.74	361.46	345.08
39000	3365.57	1737.31	1195.32	924.89	763.08	655.59	579.13	522.07	477.93	442.84	414.33	390.75	370.97	354.16
40000	3451.86	1781.86	1225.97	948.60	782.65	672.40	593.98	535.45	490.19	454.20	424.96	400.77	380.48	363.24
41000	3538.16	1826.40	1256.61	972.32	802.22	689.21	608.83	548.84	502.44	465.55	435.58	410.79	389.99	372.32
42000	3624.45	1870.95	1287.26	996.03	821.78	706.02	623.68	562.23	514.69	476.91	446.20	420.81	399.50	381.41
43000	3710.75	1915.49	1317.91	1019.75	841.35	722.83	638.53	575.61	526.95	488.26	456.83	430.83	409.02	390.49
44000	3797.05	1960.04	1348.56	1043.46	860.92	739.64	653.38	589.00	539.20	499.62	467.45	440.85	418.53	399.57
45000	3883.34	2004.59	1379.21	1067.18	880.48	756.45	668.23	602.39	551.46	510.97	478.07	450.87	428.04	408.65
46000	3969.64	2049.13	1409.86	1090.89	900.05	773.26	683.08	615.77	563.71	522.33	488.70	460.89	437.55	417.73
47000	4055.94	2093.68	1440.51	1114.61	919.61	790.07	697.93	629.16	575.97	533.68	499.32	470.91	447.06	426.81
48000	4142.23	2138.23	1471.16	1138.32	939.18	806.88	712.78	642.54	588.22	545.04	509.95	480.93	456.58	435.89
49000	4228.53	2182.77	1501.81	1162.04	958.75	823.69	727.63	655.93	600.48	556.39	520.57	490.95	466.09	444.97
50000	4314.83	2227.32	1532.46	1185.75	978.31	840.50	742.48	669.32	612.73	567.74	531.19	500.97	475.60	454.05
55000	4746.31	2450.05	1685.70	1304.33	1076.14	924.55	816.72	736.25	674.00	624.52	584.31	551.06	523.16	499.46
60000	5177.79	2672.78	1838.95	1422.90	1173.97	1008.60	890.97	803.18	735.28	681.29	637.43	601.16	570.72	544.86
65000	5609.27	2895.51	1992.19	1541.48	1271.80	1092.65	965.22	870.11	796.55	738.07	690.55	651.25	618.28	590.27
70000	6040.75	3118.24	2145.44	1660.05	1369.64	1176.70	1039.47	937.04	857.82	794.84	743.67	701.35	665.84	635.67
75000	6472.24	3340.97	2298.68	1778.63	1467.47	1260.75	1113.71	1003.97	919.09	851.61	796.79	751.45	713.40	681.08
80000	6903.72	3563.71	2451.93	1897.20	1565.30	1344.80	1187.96	1070.90	980.37	908.39	849.91	801.54	760.96	726.48
85000	7335.20	3786.44	2605.17	2015.78	1663.13	1428.85	1262.21	1137.83	1041.64	965.16	903.03	851.64	808.52	771.89
90000	7766.68	4009.17	2758.42	2134.35	1760.96	1512.90	1336.45	1204.77	1102.91	1021.94	956.14	901.73	856.08	817.29
95000	8198.17	4231.90	2911.66	2252.93	1858.79	1596.95	1410.70	1271.70	1164.18	1078.71	1009.26	951.83	903.64	862.70
100000	8629.65	4454.63	3064.91	2371.50	1956.62	1681.00	1484.95	1338.63	1225.46	1135.48	1062.38	1001.93	951.20	908.10

TERM	15 Years	16 Years	17 Years	18 Years	19 Years	20 Years	21 Years	22 Years	23 Years	24 Years	25 Years	30 Years	35 Years	40 Years
AMOUNT														
5	.05	.05	.05	.04	.04	.04	.04	.04	.04	.04	.04	.04	.04	.03
10	.09	.09	.09	.08	.08	.08	.08	.08	.07	.07	.07	.07	.07	.06
15	.14	.13	.13	.12	.12	.12	.11	.11	.11	.11	.11	.10	.10	.09
25	.22	.21	.21	.20	.20	.19	.19	.18	.18	.18	.17	.16	.16	.15
50	.44	.42	.41	.40	.39	.38	.37	.36	.35	.35	.34	.32	.31	.30
75	.66	.63	.61	.59	.58	.56	.55	.54	.53	.52	.51	.48	.46	.44
100	.88	.84	.82	.79	.77	.75	.73	.72	.70	.69	.68	.64	.61	.59
200	1.75	1.68	1.63	1.58	1.53	1.50	1.46	1.43	1.40	1.38	1.36	1.27	1.21	1.18
300	2.62	2.52	2.44	2.36	2.30	2.24	2.19	2.14	2.10	2.06	2.03	1.90	1.82	1.76
400	3.49	3.36	3.25	3.15	3.06	2.99	2.92	2.86	2.80	2.75	2.71	2.53	2.42	2.35
500	4.36	4.20	4.06	3.94	3.83	3.73	3.65	3.57	3.50	3.44	3.38	3.17	3.03	2.93
600	5.23	5.04	4.87	4.72	4.59	4.48	4.38	4.28	4.20	4.12	4.06	3.80	3.63	3.52
700	6.10	5.88	5.68	5.51	5.36	5.22	5.10	5.00	4.90	4.81	4.73	4.43	4.23	4.10
800	6.97	6.72	6.49	6.30	6.12	5.97	5.83	5.71	5.60	5.50	5.41	5.06	4.84	4.69
900	7.84	7.56	7.31	7.08	6.89	6.72	6.56	6.42	6.30	6.18	6.08	5.69	5.44	5.27
1000	8.72	8.40	8.12	7.87	7.65	7.46	7.29	7.13	7.00	6.87	6.76	6.33	6.05	5.86
2000	17.43	16.79	16.23	15.74	15.30	14.92	14.57	14.26	13.99	13.74	13.51	12.65	12.09	11.71
3000	26.14	25.18	24.34	23.60	22.95	22.37	21.86	21.39	20.98	20.60	20.26	18.97	18.13	17.57
4000	34.85	33.57	32.45	31.47	30.60	29.83	29.14	28.52	27.97	27.47	27.01	25.29	24.17	23.42
5000	43.56	41.96	40.56	39.33	38.25	37.28	36.42	35.65	34.96	34.33	33.77	31.61	30.21	29.28
6000	52.27	50.35	48.67	47.20	45.90	44.74	43.71	42.78	41.95	41.20	40.52	37.93	36.25	35.13
7000	60.98	58.74	56.78	55.06	53.54	52.20	50.99	49.91	48.94	48.06	47.27	44.25	42.30	40.99
8000	69.69	67.13	64.89	62.93	61.19	59.65	58.27	57.04	55.93	54.93	54.02	50.57	48.34	46.84
9000	78.40	75.52	73.01	70.80	68.84	67.11	65.56	64.17	62.92	61.79	60.77	56.89	54.38	52.70
10000	87.12	83.91	81.12	78.66	76.49	74.56	72.84	71.30	69.91	68.66	67.53	63.21	60.42	58.55
11000	95.83	92.30	89.23	86.53	84.14	82.02	80.12	78.43	76.90	75.52	74.28	69.53	66.46	64.41
12000	104.54	100.69	97.34	94.39	91.79	89.47	87.41	85.56	83.89	82.39	81.03	75.85	72.50	70.26
13000	113.25	109.08	105.45	102.26	99.44	96.93	94.69	92.69	90.88	89.26	87.78	82.17	78.55	76.11
14000	121.96	117.48	113.56	110.12	107.08	104.39	101.98	99.82	97.87	96.12	94.53	88.49	84.59	81.97
15000	130.67	125.87	121.67	117.99	114.73	111.84	109.26	106.95	104.86	102.99	101.29	94.82	90.63	87.82
16000	139.38	134.26	129.78	125.85	122.38	119.30	116.54	114.08	111.86	109.85	108.04	101.14	96.67	93.68
17000	148.09	142.65	137.90	133.72	130.03	126.75	123.83	121.20	110.05	116.72	114.79	107.46	102.71	99.53
18000	156.80	151.04	146.01	141.59	137.68	134.21	131.11	128.33	125.84	123.58	121.54	113.78	108.75	105.39
19000	165.52	159.43	154.12	149.45	145.33	141.66	138.39	135.46	132.83	130.45	128.29	120.10	114.79	111.24
20000	174.23	167.82	162.23	157.32	152.98	149.12	145.68	142.59	139.82	137.31	135.05	126.42	120.84	117.10
21000	182.94	176.21	170.34	165.18	160.62	156.58	152.96	149.72	146.81	144.18	141.80	132.74	126.88	122.95
22000	191.65	184.60	178.45	173.05	168.27	164.03	160.24	156.85	153.80	151.04	148.55	139.06	132.92	128.81
23000	200.36	192.99	186.56	180.91	175.92	171.49	167.53	163.98	160.79	157.91	155.30	145.38	138.96	134.66
24000	209.07	201.38	194.67	188.78	183.57	178.94	174.81	171.11	167.78	164.78	162.05	151.70	145.00	140.51
25000	217.78	209.77	202.79	196.65	191.22	186.40	182.10	178.24	174.77	171.64	168.81	158.02	151.04	146.37
26000	226.49	218.16	210.90	204.51	198.87	193.85	189.38	185.37	181.76	178.51	175.56	164.34	157.09	152.22
27000	235.20	226.56	219.01	212.38	206.52	201.31	196.66	192.50	188.75	185.37	182.31	170.66	163.13	158.08
28000	243.92	234.95	227.12	220.24	214.16	208.77	203.95	199.63	195.74	192.24	189.06	176.98	169.17	163.93
29000	252.63	243.34	235.23	228.11	221.81	216.22	211.23	206.76	202.73	199.10	195.82	183.30	175.21	169.79
30000	261.34	251.73	243.34	235.97	229.46	223.68	218.51	213.89	209.72	205.97	202.57	189.63	181.25	175.64
31000	270.05	260.12	251.45	243.84	237.11	231.13	225.80	221.02	216.72	212.83	209.32	195.95	187.29	181.50
32000	278.76	268.51	259.56	251.70	244.76	238.59	233.08	228.15	223.71	219.70	216.07	202.27	193.33	187.35
33000	287.47	276.90	267.67	259.57	252.41	246.04	240.36	235.27	230.70	226.56	222.82	208.59	199.38	193.21
34000	296.18	285.29	275.79	267.44	260.06	253.50	247.65	242.40	237.69	233.43	229.58	214.91	205.42	199.06
35000	304.89	293.68	283.90	275.30	267.70	260.96	254.93	249.53	244.68	240.29	236.33	221.23	211.46	204.91
36000	313.60	302.07	292.01	283.17	275.35	268.41	262.22	256.66	251.67	247.16	243.08	227.55	217.50	210.77
37000	322.31	310.46	300.12	291.03	283.00	275.87	269.50	263.79	258.66	254.03	249.83	233.87	223.54	216.62
38000	331.03	318.85	308.23	298.90	290.65	283.32	276.78	270.92	265.65	260.89	256.58	240.19	229.58	222.48
39000	339.74	327.24	316.34	306.76	298.30	290.78	284.07	278.05	272.64	267.76	263.34	246.51	235.63	228.33
40000	348.45	335.64	324.45	314.63	305.95	298.23	291.35	285.18	279.63	274.62	270.09	252.83	241.67	234.19
41000	357.16	344.03	332.56	322.50	313.60	305.69	298.63	292.31	286.62	281.49	276.84	259.15	247.71	240.04
42000	365.87	352.42	340.68	330.36	321.24	313.15	305.92	299.44	293.61	288.35	283.59	265.47	253.75	245.90
43000	374.58	360.81	348.79	338.23	328.89	320.60	313.20	306.57	300.60	295.22	290.34	271.79	259.79	251.75
44000	383.29	369.20	356.90	346.09	336.54	328.06	320.48	313.70	307.59	302.08	297.10	278.11	265.83	257.61
45000	392.00	377.59	365.01	353.96	344.19	335.51	327.77	320.83	314.58	308.95	303.85	284.44	271.87	263.46
46000	400.71	385.98	373.12	361.82	351.84	342.97	335.05	327.96	321.57	315.81	310.60	290.76	277.92	269.32
47000	409.43	394.37	381.23	369.69	359.49	350.42	342.34	335.09	328.57	322.68	317.35	297.08	283.96	275.17
48000	418.14	402.76	389.34	377.55	367.14	357.88	349.62	342.22	335.56	329.55	324.10	303.40	290.00	281.02
49000	426.85	411.15	397.45	385.42	374.78	365.34	356.90	349.35	342.55	336.41	330.86	309.72	296.04	286.88
50000	435.56	419.54	405.57	393.29	382.43	372.79	364.19	356.47	349.54	343.28	337.61	316.04	302.08	292.73
55000	479.11	461.50	446.12	432.61	420.68	410.07	400.60	392.12	384.49	377.60	371.37	347.64	332.29	322.01
60000	522.67	503.45	486.68	471.94	458.92	447.35	437.02	427.77	419.44	411.93	405.13	379.25	362.50	351.28
65000	566.22	545.40	527.23	511.27	497.16	484.63	473.44	463.42	454.40	446.26	438.89	410.85	392.71	380.55
70000	609.78	587.36	567.79	550.60	535.40	521.91	509.86	499.06	489.35	480.58	472.65	442.45	422.91	409.82
75000	653.34	629.31	608.35	589.93	573.65	559.18	546.28	534.71	524.30	514.91	506.41	474.06	453.12	439.10
80000	696.89	671.27	648.90	629.25	611.89	596.46	582.70	570.36	559.26	549.24	540.17	505.66	483.33	468.37
85000	740.45	713.22	689.46	668.58	650.13	633.74	619.11	606.00	594.21	583.57	573.93	537.26	513.54	497.64
90000	784.00	755.17	730.01	707.91	688.38	671.02	655.53	641.65	629.16	617.89	607.69	568.87	543.74	526.92
95000	827.56	797.13	770.57	747.24	726.62	708.30	691.95	677.30	664.12	652.22	641.45	600.47	573.95	556.19
100000	871.11	839.08	811.13	786.57	764.86	745.58	728.37	712.94	699.07	686.55	675.21	632.07	604.16	585.46

MONTHLY PAYMENT
REQUIRED TO AMORTIZE A LOAN

TERM AMOUNT	1 Year	2 Years	3 Years	4 Years	5 Years	6 Years	7 Years	8 Years	9 Years	10 Years	11 Years	12 Years	13 Years	14 Years
5	.44	.23	.16	.12	.10	.09	.08	.07	.07	.06	.06	.06	.05	.05
10	.87	.45	.31	.24	.20	.17	.15	.14	.13	.12	.11	.11	.10	.10
15	1.30	.67	.47	.36	.30	.26	.23	.21	.19	.18	.17	.16	.15	.14
25	2.16	1.12	.77	.60	.50	.43	.38	.34	.31	.29	.27	.26	.24	.23
50	4.32	2.23	1.54	1.19	.99	.85	.75	.68	.62	.58	.54	.51	.48	.46
75	6.48	3.35	2.31	1.79	1.48	1.27	1.12	1.01	.93	.86	.81	.76	.72	.69
100	8.64	4.46	3.07	2.38	1.97	1.69	1.49	1.35	1.24	1.15	1.07	1.01	.96	.92
200	17.27	8.92	6.14	4.76	3.93	3.38	2.98	2.69	2.47	2.29	2.14	2.02	1.92	1.83
300	25.91	13.38	9.21	7.13	5.89	5.06	4.47	4.04	3.70	3.43	3.21	3.03	2.87	2.75
400	34.54	17.84	12.28	9.51	7.85	6.75	5.96	5.38	4.93	4.57	4.28	4.03	3.83	3.66
500	43.18	22.30	15.35	11.89	9.81	8.43	7.45	6.72	6.16	5.71	5.34	5.04	4.79	4.57
600	51.81	26.76	18.42	14.26	11.77	10.12	8.94	8.07	7.39	6.85	6.41	6.05	5.74	5.49
700	60.44	31.22	21.49	16.64	13.73	11.81	10.43	9.41	8.62	7.99	7.48	7.06	6.70	6.40
800	69.08	35.68	24.56	19.01	15.70	13.49	11.92	10.75	9.85	9.13	8.55	8.06	7.66	7.31
900	77.71	40.14	27.63	21.39	17.66	15.18	13.41	12.10	11.08	10.27	9.61	9.07	8.61	8.23
1000	86.35	44.60	30.70	23.77	19.62	16.86	14.90	13.44	12.31	11.41	10.68	10.08	9.57	9.14
2000	172.69	89.19	61.39	47.53	39.23	33.72	29.80	26.88	24.61	22.82	21.36	20.15	19.14	18.28
3000	259.03	133.78	92.09	71.29	58.84	50.58	44.70	40.31	36.92	34.22	32.03	30.22	28.70	27.41
4000	345.37	178.37	122.78	95.05	78.46	67.44	59.60	53.75	49.22	45.63	42.71	40.29	38.27	36.55
5000	431.72	222.96	153.48	118.81	98.07	84.29	74.49	67.18	61.53	57.03	53.38	50.36	47.83	45.68
6000	518.06	267.55	184.17	142.57	117.68	101.15	89.39	80.62	73.83	68.44	64.06	60.44	57.40	54.82
7000	604.40	312.15	214.87	166.33	137.30	118.01	104.29	94.05	86.14	79.85	74.73	70.51	66.96	63.95
8000	690.74	356.74	245.56	190.09	156.91	134.87	119.19	107.49	98.44	91.25	85.41	80.58	76.53	73.09
9000	777.09	401.33	276.26	213.85	176.52	151.72	134.09	120.92	110.75	102.66	96.08	90.65	86.09	82.22
10000	863.43	445.92	306.95	237.62	196.14	168.58	148.98	134.36	123.05	114.06	106.76	100.72	95.66	91.36
11000	949.77	490.51	337.64	261.38	215.75	185.44	163.88	147.80	135.36	125.47	117.44	110.80	105.22	100.49
12000	1036.11	535.10	368.34	285.14	235.36	202.30	178.78	161.23	147.66	136.87	128.11	120.87	114.79	109.63
13000	1122.46	579.69	399.03	308.90	254.97	219.15	193.68	174.67	159.97	148.28	138.79	130.94	124.35	118.76
14000	1208.80	624.29	429.73	332.66	274.59	236.01	208.58	188.10	172.27	159.69	149.46	141.01	133.92	127.90
15000	1295.14	668.88	460.42	356.42	294.20	252.87	223.47	201.54	184.57	171.09	160.14	151.08	143.49	137.03
16000	1381.48	713.47	491.12	380.18	313.81	269.73	238.37	214.97	196.88	182.50	170.81	161.15	153.05	146.17
17000	1467.83	758.06	521.81	403.94	333.43	286.58	253.27	228.41	209.18	193.90	181.49	171.23	162.62	155.30
18000	1554.17	802.65	552.51	427.70	353.04	303.44	268.17	241.84	221.49	205.31	192.16	181.30	172.18	164.44
19000	1640.51	847.24	583.20	451.47	372.65	320.30	283.07	255.28	233.79	216.71	202.84	191.37	181.75	173.57
20000	1726.85	891.83	613.90	475.23	392.27	337.16	297.96	268.72	246.10	228.12	213.52	201.44	191.31	182.71
21000	1813.20	936.43	644.59	498.99	411.88	354.01	312.86	282.15	258.40	239.53	224.19	211.51	200.88	191.84
22000	1899.54	981.02	675.28	522.75	431.49	370.87	327.76	295.59	270.71	250.93	234.87	221.59	210.44	200.98
23000	1985.88	1025.61	705.98	546.51	451.10	387.73	342.66	309.02	283.01	262.34	245.54	231.66	220.01	210.11
24000	2072.22	1070.20	736.67	570.27	470.72	404.59	357.55	322.46	295.32	273.74	256.22	241.73	229.57	219.25
25000	2158.57	1114.79	767.37	594.03	490.33	421.44	372.45	335.89	307.62	285.15	266.89	251.80	239.14	228.39
26000	2244.91	1159.38	798.06	617.79	509.94	438.30	387.35	349.33	319.93	296.55	277.57	261.87	248.70	237.52
27000	2331.25	1203.97	828.76	641.55	529.56	455.16	402.25	362.76	332.23	307.96	288.24	271.94	258.27	246.66
28000	2417.59	1248.57	859.45	665.32	549.17	472.02	417.15	376.20	344.53	319.37	298.92	282.02	267.83	255.79
29000	2503.94	1293.16	890.15	689.08	568.78	488.87	432.04	389.63	356.84	330.77	309.60	292.09	277.40	264.93
30000	2590.28	1337.75	920.84	712.84	588.40	505.73	446.94	403.07	369.14	342.18	320.27	302.16	286.97	274.06
31000	2676.62	1382.34	951.54	736.60	608.01	522.59	461.84	416.51	381.45	353.58	330.95	312.23	296.53	283.20
32000	2762.96	1426.93	982.23	760.36	627.62	539.45	476.74	429.94	393.75	364.99	341.62	322.30	306.10	292.33
33000	2849.31	1471.52	1012.92	784.12	647.23	556.31	491.64	443.38	406.06	376.39	352.30	332.38	315.66	301.47
34000	2935.65	1516.11	1043.62	807.88	666.85	573.16	506.53	456.81	418.36	387.80	362.97	342.45	325.23	310.60
35000	3021.99	1560.71	1074.31	831.64	686.46	590.02	521.43	470.25	430.67	399.21	373.65	352.52	334.79	319.74
36000	3108.33	1605.30	1105.01	855.40	706.07	606.88	536.33	483.68	442.97	410.61	384.32	362.59	344.36	328.87
37000	3194.68	1649.89	1135.70	879.17	725.69	623.74	551.23	497.12	455.28	422.02	395.00	372.66	353.92	338.01
38000	3281.02	1694.48	1166.40	902.93	745.30	640.59	566.13	510.55	467.58	433.42	405.68	382.73	363.49	347.14
39000	3367.36	1739.07	1197.09	926.69	764.91	657.45	581.02	523.99	479.89	444.83	416.35	392.81	373.05	356.28
40000	3453.70	1783.66	1227.79	950.45	784.53	674.31	595.92	537.43	492.19	456.23	427.03	402.88	382.62	365.41
41000	3540.05	1828.25	1258.48	974.21	804.14	691.17	610.82	550.86	504.49	467.64	437.70	412.95	392.18	374.55
42000	3626.39	1872.85	1289.18	997.97	823.75	708.02	625.72	564.30	516.80	479.05	448.38	423.02	401.75	383.68
43000	3712.73	1917.44	1319.87	1021.73	843.36	724.88	640.61	577.73	529.10	490.45	459.05	433.09	411.31	392.82
44000	3799.07	1962.03	1350.56	1045.49	862.98	741.74	655.51	591.17	541.41	501.86	469.73	443.17	420.88	401.95
45000	3885.42	2006.62	1381.26	1069.25	882.59	758.60	670.41	604.60	553.71	513.26	480.40	453.24	430.45	411.09
46000	3971.76	2051.21	1411.95	1093.02	902.20	775.45	685.31	618.04	566.02	524.67	491.08	463.31	440.01	420.22
47000	4058.10	2095.80	1442.65	1116.78	921.82	792.31	700.21	631.47	578.32	536.07	501.76	473.38	449.58	429.36
48000	4144.44	2140.40	1473.34	1140.54	941.43	809.17	715.10	644.91	590.63	547.48	512.43	483.45	459.14	438.50
49000	4230.79	2184.99	1504.04	1164.30	961.04	826.03	730.00	658.35	602.93	558.89	523.11	493.52	468.71	447.63
50000	4317.13	2229.58	1534.73	1188.06	980.66	842.88	744.90	671.78	615.24	570.29	533.78	503.60	478.27	456.77
55000	4748.84	2452.54	1688.20	1306.87	1078.72	927.17	819.39	738.96	676.76	627.32	587.16	553.96	526.10	502.44
60000	5180.55	2675.49	1841.68	1425.67	1176.79	1011.46	893.88	806.14	738.28	684.35	640.54	604.31	573.93	548.12
65000	5612.26	2898.45	1995.15	1544.48	1274.85	1095.75	968.37	873.31	799.81	741.38	693.92	654.67	621.75	593.79
70000	6043.98	3121.41	2148.62	1663.28	1372.92	1180.04	1042.86	940.49	861.33	798.41	747.29	705.03	669.58	639.47
75000	6475.69	3344.36	2302.10	1782.09	1470.98	1264.32	1117.35	1007.67	922.85	855.44	800.67	755.39	717.41	685.15
80000	6907.40	3567.32	2455.57	1900.89	1569.05	1348.61	1191.84	1074.85	984.38	912.46	854.05	805.75	765.23	730.82
85000	7339.11	3790.28	2609.04	2019.70	1667.11	1432.90	1266.33	1142.02	1045.90	969.49	907.43	856.11	813.06	776.50
90000	7770.83	4013.24	2762.51	2138.50	1765.18	1517.19	1340.82	1209.20	1107.42	1026.52	960.80	906.47	860.89	822.17
95000	8202.54	4236.19	2915.99	2257.31	1863.24	1601.48	1415.31	1276.38	1168.94	1083.55	1014.18	956.83	908.71	867.85
100000	8634.25	4459.15	3069.46	2376.12	1961.31	1685.76	1489.79	1343.56	1230.47	1140.58	1067.56	1007.19	956.54	913.53

TERM AMOUNT	15 Years	16 Years	17 Years	18 Years	19 Years	20 Years	21 Years	22 Years	23 Years	24 Years	25 Years	30 Years	35 Years	40 Years
5	.05	.05	.05	.04	.04	.04	.04	.04	.04	.04	.04	.04	.04	.03
10	.09	.09	.09	.08	.08	.08	.08	.08	.08	.07	.07	.07	.07	.06
15	.14	.13	.13	.12	.12	.12	.12	.11	.11	.11	.11	.10	.10	.09
25	.22	.22	.21	.20	.20	.19	.19	.18	.18	.18	.18	.16	.16	.15
50	.44	.43	.41	.40	.39	.38	.37	.36	.36	.35	.35	.32	.31	.30
75	.66	.64	.62	.60	.58	.57	.56	.54	.53	.52	.52	.48	.46	.45
100	.88	.85	.82	.80	.78	.76	.74	.72	.71	.70	.69	.64	.62	.60
200	1.76	1.69	1.64	1.59	1.55	1.51	1.47	1.44	1.42	1.39	1.37	1.28	1.23	1.19
300	2.63	2.54	2.46	2.38	2.32	2.26	2.21	2.16	2.12	2.08	2.05	1.92	1.84	1.78
400	3.51	3.38	3.27	3.17	3.09	3.01	2.94	2.88	2.83	2.78	2.73	2.56	2.45	2.38
500	4.39	4.23	4.09	3.97	3.86	3.76	3.68	3.60	3.53	3.47	3.41	3.20	3.06	2.97
600	5.26	5.07	4.91	4.76	4.63	4.51	4.41	4.32	4.24	4.16	4.09	3.84	3.67	3.56
700	6.14	5.92	5.72	5.55	5.40	5.27	5.15	5.04	4.94	4.85	4.78	4.48	4.28	4.15
800	7.02	6.76	6.54	6.34	6.17	6.02	5.88	5.76	5.65	5.55	5.46	5.11	4.89	4.75
900	7.89	7.61	7.36	7.14	6.94	6.77	6.61	6.48	6.35	6.24	6.14	5.75	5.50	5.34
1000	8.77	8.45	8.17	7.93	7.71	7.52	7.35	7.19	7.06	6.93	6.82	6.39	6.12	5.93
2000	17.54	16.90	16.34	15.85	15.42	15.03	14.69	14.38	14.11	13.86	13.63	12.78	12.23	11.86
3000	26.30	25.34	24.51	23.77	23.13	22.55	22.04	21.57	21.16	20.79	20.45	19.16	18.34	17.78
4000	35.07	33.79	32.68	31.70	30.83	30.06	29.38	28.76	28.21	27.71	27.26	25.55	24.45	23.71
5000	43.84	42.24	40.84	39.62	38.54	37.58	36.72	35.95	35.26	34.64	34.08	31.94	30.56	29.63
6000	52.60	50.68	49.01	47.54	46.25	45.09	44.07	43.14	42.32	41.57	40.89	38.32	36.67	35.56
7000	61.37	59.13	57.18	55.47	53.95	52.61	51.41	50.33	49.37	48.50	47.71	44.71	42.78	41.49
8000	70.13	67.58	65.35	63.39	61.66	60.12	58.75	57.52	56.42	55.42	54.52	51.10	48.89	47.41
9000	78.90	76.02	73.52	71.31	69.37	67.64	66.10	64.71	63.47	62.35	61.34	57.48	55.00	53.34
10000	87.67	84.47	81.68	79.24	77.07	75.15	73.44	71.90	70.52	69.28	68.15	63.87	61.11	59.26
11000	96.43	92.92	89.85	87.16	84.78	82.67	80.78	79.09	77.58	76.21	74.97	70.26	67.22	65.19
12000	105.20	101.36	98.02	95.08	92.49	90.18	88.13	86.28	84.63	83.13	81.78	76.64	73.33	71.12
13000	113.96	109.81	106.19	103.00	100.19	97.70	95.47	93.47	91.68	90.06	88.60	83.03	79.44	77.04
14000	122.73	118.26	114.36	110.93	107.90	105.21	102.81	100.66	98.73	96.99	95.41	89.42	85.55	82.97
15000	131.50	126.70	122.52	118.85	115.61	112.73	110.16	107.85	105.78	103.92	102.23	95.80	91.66	88.89
16000	140.26	135.15	130.69	126.77	123.31	120.24	117.50	115.04	112.83	110.84	109.04	102.19	97.77	94.82
17000	149.03	143.60	138.86	134.70	131.02	127.76	124.84	122.23	119.89	117.77	115.85	108.58	103.88	100.75
18000	157.80	152.04	147.03	142.62	138.73	135.27	132.19	129.42	126.94	124.70	122.67	114.96	109.99	106.67
19000	166.56	160.49	155.19	150.54	146.43	142.78	139.53	136.61	133.99	131.62	129.48	121.35	116.10	112.60
20000	175.33	168.94	163.36	158.47	154.14	150.30	146.87	143.80	141.04	138.55	136.30	127.74	122.21	118.52
21000	184.09	177.38	171.53	166.39	161.85	157.81	154.22	150.99	148.09	145.48	143.11	134.12	128.32	124.45
22000	192.86	185.83	179.70	174.31	169.55	165.33	161.56	158.18	155.15	152.41	149.93	140.51	134.43	130.38
23000	201.63	194.28	187.87	182.24	177.26	172.84	168.90	165.37	162.20	159.33	156.74	146.90	140.54	136.30
24000	210.39	202.72	196.03	190.16	184.97	180.36	176.25	172.56	169.25	166.26	163.56	153.28	146.65	142.23
25000	219.16	211.17	204.20	198.08	192.67	187.87	183.59	179.75	176.30	173.19	170.37	159.67	152.76	148.15
26000	227.92	219.62	212.37	206.00	200.38	195.39	190.93	186.94	183.35	180.12	177.19	166.06	158.87	154.08
27000	236.69	228.06	220.54	213.93	208.09	202.90	198.28	194.13	190.41	187.04	184.00	172.44	164.99	160.01
28000	245.46	236.51	228.71	221.85	215.80	210.42	205.62	201.32	197.46	193.97	190.82	178.83	171.10	165.93
29000	254.22	244.96	236.87	229.77	223.50	217.93	212.96	208.51	204.51	200.90	197.63	185.22	177.21	171.86
30000	262.99	253.40	245.04	237.70	231.21	225.45	220.31	215.70	211.56	207.83	204.45	191.60	183.32	177.78
31000	271.76	261.85	253.21	245.62	238.92	232.96	227.65	222.89	218.61	214.75	211.26	197.99	189.43	183.71
32000	280.52	270.30	261.38	253.54	246.62	240.48	234.99	230.08	225.66	221.68	218.08	204.38	195.54	189.64
33000	289.29	278.74	269.54	261.47	254.33	247.99	242.34	237.27	232.72	228.61	224.89	210.76	201.65	195.56
34000	298.05	287.19	277.71	269.39	262.04	255.51	249.68	244.46	239.77	235.53	231.70	217.15	207.76	201.49
35000	306.82	295.64	285.88	277.31	269.74	263.02	257.02	251.65	246.82	242.46	238.52	223.54	213.87	207.41
36000	315.59	304.08	294.05	285.24	277.45	270.53	264.37	258.84	253.87	249.39	245.33	229.92	219.98	213.34
37000	324.35	312.53	302.22	293.16	285.16	278.05	271.71	266.03	260.92	256.32	252.15	236.31	226.09	219.27
38000	333.12	320.98	310.38	301.08	292.86	285.56	279.05	273.22	267.98	263.24	258.96	242.70	232.20	225.19
39000	341.88	329.42	318.55	309.00	300.57	293.08	286.40	280.41	275.03	270.17	265.78	249.08	238.31	231.12
40000	350.65	337.87	326.72	316.93	308.28	300.59	293.74	287.60	282.08	277.10	272.59	255.47	244.42	237.04
41000	359.42	346.32	334.89	324.85	315.98	308.11	301.08	294.79	289.13	284.03	279.41	261.86	250.53	242.97
42000	368.18	354.76	343.06	332.77	323.69	315.62	308.43	301.98	296.18	290.95	286.22	268.24	256.64	248.90
43000	376.95	363.21	351.22	340.70	331.40	323.14	315.77	309.17	303.23	297.88	293.04	274.63	262.75	254.82
44000	385.72	371.66	359.39	348.62	339.10	330.65	323.11	316.36	310.29	304.81	299.85	281.01	268.86	260.75
45000	394.48	380.10	367.56	356.54	346.81	338.17	330.46	323.55	317.34	311.74	306.67	287.40	274.97	266.67
46000	403.25	388.55	375.73	364.47	354.52	345.68	337.80	330.74	324.39	318.66	313.48	293.79	281.08	272.60
47000	412.01	397.00	383.90	372.39	362.22	353.20	345.14	337.93	331.44	325.59	320.30	300.17	287.19	278.52
48000	420.78	405.44	392.06	380.31	369.93	360.71	352.49	345.12	338.49	332.52	327.11	306.56	293.30	284.45
49000	429.55	413.89	400.23	388.24	377.64	368.23	359.83	352.31	345.55	339.44	333.92	312.95	299.41	290.38
50000	438.31	422.34	408.40	396.16	385.34	375.74	367.17	359.50	352.60	346.37	340.74	319.33	305.52	296.30
55000	482.14	464.57	449.24	435.77	423.88	413.31	403.89	395.45	387.86	381.01	374.81	351.27	336.08	325.93
60000	525.97	506.80	490.08	475.39	462.41	450.89	440.61	431.40	423.12	415.65	408.89	383.20	366.63	355.56
65000	569.80	549.04	530.92	515.00	500.95	488.46	477.32	467.35	458.38	450.28	442.96	415.13	397.18	385.19
70000	613.63	591.27	571.76	554.62	539.48	526.04	514.04	503.30	493.63	484.92	477.03	447.07	427.73	414.82
75000	657.47	633.50	612.60	594.23	578.01	563.61	550.76	539.25	528.89	519.56	511.11	479.00	458.28	444.45
80000	701.30	675.73	653.44	633.85	616.55	601.18	587.47	575.19	564.15	554.19	545.18	510.93	488.83	474.08
85000	745.13	717.97	694.27	673.47	655.08	638.76	624.19	611.14	599.41	588.83	579.25	542.86	519.39	503.71
90000	788.96	760.20	735.11	713.08	693.62	676.33	660.91	647.09	634.67	623.47	613.33	574.80	549.94	533.34
95000	832.79	802.43	775.95	752.70	732.15	713.90	697.63	683.04	669.93	658.10	647.40	606.73	580.49	562.97
100000	876.62	844.67	816.79	792.31	770.68	751.48	734.34	718.99	705.19	692.74	681.47	638.66	611.04	592.60

MONTHLY PAYMENT
REQUIRED TO AMORTIZE A LOAN

TERM	1 Year	2 Years	3 Years	4 Years	5 Years	6 Years	7 Years	8 Years	9 Years	10 Years	11 Years	12 Years	13 Years	14 Years
AMOUNT														
5	.44	.23	.16	.12	.10	.09	.08	.07	.07	.06	.06	.06	.05	.05
10	.87	.45	.31	.24	.20	.17	.15	.14	.13	.12	.11	.11	.10	.10
15	1.30	.67	.47	.36	.30	.26	.23	.21	.19	.18	.17	.16	.15	.14
25	2.16	1.12	.77	.60	.50	.43	.38	.34	.31	.29	.27	.26	.24	.23
50	4.32	2.24	1.54	1.19	.99	.85	.75	.68	.62	.58	.54	.51	.48	.46
75	6.48	3.35	2.31	1.79	1.48	1.27	1.12	1.01	.93	.86	.81	.76	.72	.69
100	8.64	4.47	3.08	2.38	1.97	1.69	1.50	1.35	1.24	1.15	1.07	1.01	.96	.92
200	17.28	8.93	6.15	4.76	3.93	3.38	2.99	2.69	2.47	2.29	2.14	2.02	1.92	1.83
300	25.91	13.39	9.22	7.14	5.89	5.07	4.48	4.04	3.70	3.43	3.21	3.03	2.88	2.75
400	34.55	17.85	12.29	9.51	7.85	6.75	5.97	5.38	4.93	4.57	4.28	4.04	3.84	3.66
500	43.18	22.31	15.36	11.89	9.82	8.44	7.46	6.73	6.16	5.71	5.35	5.05	4.79	4.58
600	51.82	26.77	18.43	14.27	11.78	10.13	8.95	8.07	7.40	6.86	6.42	6.06	5.75	5.49
700	60.45	31.23	21.50	16.65	13.74	11.81	10.44	9.42	8.63	8.00	7.49	7.06	6.71	6.41
800	69.09	35.69	24.57	19.02	15.70	13.50	11.93	10.76	9.86	9.14	8.56	8.07	7.67	7.32
900	77.72	40.15	27.64	21.40	17.67	15.19	13.42	12.11	11.09	10.28	9.62	9.08	8.63	8.24
1000	86.36	44.61	30.71	23.78	19.63	16.87	14.92	13.45	12.32	11.42	10.69	10.09	9.58	9.15
2000	172.71	89.21	61.42	47.55	39.25	33.74	29.83	26.90	24.64	22.84	21.38	20.17	19.16	18.30
3000	259.07	133.81	92.12	71.32	58.88	50.61	44.74	40.35	36.96	34.26	32.07	30.26	28.74	27.45
4000	345.42	178.42	122.83	95.10	78.50	67.48	59.65	53.80	49.27	45.68	42.76	40.34	38.32	36.60
5000	431.77	223.02	153.53	118.87	98.13	84.35	74.56	67.24	61.59	57.10	53.45	50.43	47.90	45.75
6000	518.13	267.62	184.24	142.64	117.75	101.22	89.47	80.69	73.91	68.52	64.14	60.51	57.48	54.90
7000	604.48	312.22	214.95	166.41	137.38	118.09	104.38	94.14	86.23	79.93	74.82	70.60	67.06	64.05
8000	690.84	356.83	245.65	190.19	157.00	134.96	119.29	107.59	98.54	91.35	85.51	80.68	76.63	73.20
9000	777.19	401.43	276.36	213.96	176.63	151.83	134.20	121.04	110.86	102.77	96.20	90.77	86.21	82.34
10000	863.54	446.03	307.06	237.73	196.25	168.70	149.11	134.48	123.18	114.19	106.89	100.85	95.79	91.49
11000	949.90	490.64	337.77	261.50	215.88	185.57	164.02	147.93	135.49	125.61	117.58	110.94	105.37	100.64
12000	1036.25	535.24	368.48	285.28	235.50	202.44	178.93	161.38	147.81	137.03	128.27	121.02	114.95	109.79
13000	1122.61	579.84	399.18	309.05	255.13	219.31	193.84	174.83	160.13	148.45	138.96	131.11	124.53	118.94
14000	1208.96	624.44	429.89	332.82	274.75	236.18	208.75	188.27	172.45	159.86	149.64	141.19	134.11	128.09
15000	1295.31	669.05	460.59	356.59	294.38	253.05	223.66	201.72	184.76	171.28	160.33	151.28	143.69	137.24
16000	1381.67	713.65	491.30	380.37	314.00	269.92	238.57	215.17	197.08	182.70	171.02	161.36	153.26	146.39
17000	1468.02	758.25	522.01	404.14	333.63	286.79	253.48	228.62	209.40	194.12	181.71	171.45	162.84	155.53
18000	1554.38	802.85	552.71	427.91	353.25	303.66	268.39	242.07	221.71	205.54	192.40	181.53	172.42	164.68
19000	1640.73	847.46	583.42	451.69	372.88	320.53	283.30	255.51	234.03	216.96	203.09	191.62	182.00	173.83
20000	1727.08	892.06	614.12	475.46	392.50	337.40	298.21	268.96	246.35	228.38	213.78	201.70	191.58	182.98
21000	1813.44	936.66	644.83	499.23	412.12	354.26	313.12	282.41	258.67	239.79	224.46	211.79	201.16	192.13
22000	1899.79	981.27	675.54	523.00	431.75	371.13	328.03	295.86	270.98	251.21	235.15	221.87	210.74	201.28
23000	1986.15	1025.87	706.24	546.78	451.37	388.00	342.94	309.31	283.30	262.63	245.84	231.96	220.32	210.43
24000	2072.50	1070.47	736.95	570.55	471.00	404.87	357.85	322.75	295.62	274.05	256.53	242.04	229.89	219.58
25000	2158.85	1115.07	767.65	594.32	490.62	421.74	372.76	336.20	307.93	285.47	267.22	252.13	239.47	228.73
26000	2245.21	1159.68	798.36	618.09	510.25	438.61	387.67	349.65	320.25	296.89	277.91	262.21	249.05	237.87
27000	2331.56	1204.28	829.07	641.87	529.87	455.48	402.58	363.10	332.57	308.30	288.59	272.30	258.63	247.02
28000	2417.92	1248.88	859.77	665.64	549.50	472.35	417.49	376.54	344.89	319.72	299.28	282.38	268.21	256.17
29000	2504.27	1293.49	890.48	669.41	569.12	489.22	432.40	389.99	357.20	331.14	309.97	292.47	277.79	265.32
30000	2590.62	1338.09	921.18	713.18	588.75	506.09	447.31	403.44	369.52	342.56	320.66	302.55	287.37	274.47
31000	2676.98	1382.69	951.89	736.96	608.37	522.96	462.22	416.89	381.84	353.98	331.35	312.64	296.95	283.62
32000	2763.33	1427.29	982.59	760.73	628.00	539.83	477.13	430.34	394.15	365.40	342.04	322.72	306.52	292.77
33000	2849.69	1471.90	1013.30	784.50	647.62	556.70	492.04	443.78	406.47	376.82	352.73	332.81	316.10	301.92
34000	2936.04	1516.50	1044.01	808.28	667.25	573.57	506.95	457.23	418.79	388.23	363.41	342.89	325.68	311.06
35000	3022.39	1561.10	1074.71	832.05	686.87	590.44	521.86	470.68	431.11	399.65	374.10	352.98	335.26	320.21
36000	3108.75	1605.70	1105.42	855.82	706.50	607.31	536.77	484.13	443.42	411.07	384.79	363.06	344.84	329.36
37000	3195.10	1650.31	1136.12	879.59	726.12	624.18	551.68	497.58	455.74	422.49	395.48	373.15	354.42	338.51
38000	3281.46	1694.91	1166.83	903.37	745.75	641.05	566.59	511.02	468.06	433.91	406.17	383.23	364.00	347.66
39000	3367.81	1739.51	1197.54	927.14	765.37	657.92	581.50	524.47	480.37	445.33	416.86	393.32	373.58	356.81
40000	3454.16	1784.12	1228.24	950.91	785.00	674.79	596.41	537.92	492.69	456.75	427.55	403.40	383.15	365.96
41000	3540.52	1828.72	1258.95	974.68	804.62	691.65	611.32	551.37	505.01	468.16	438.23	413.49	392.73	375.11
42000	3626.87	1873.32	1289.65	998.46	824.24	708.52	626.23	564.81	517.33	479.58	448.92	423.57	402.31	384.25
43000	3713.23	1917.92	1320.36	1022.23	843.87	725.39	641.14	578.26	529.64	491.00	459.61	433.66	411.89	393.40
44000	3799.58	1962.53	1351.07	1046.00	863.49	742.26	656.05	591.71	541.96	502.42	470.30	443.74	421.47	402.55
45000	3885.93	2007.13	1381.77	1069.77	883.12	759.13	670.96	605.16	554.28	513.84	480.99	453.83	431.05	411.70
46000	3972.29	2051.73	1412.48	1093.55	902.74	776.00	685.87	618.61	566.60	525.26	491.68	463.91	440.63	420.85
47000	4058.64	2096.34	1443.18	1117.32	922.37	792.87	700.78	632.05	578.91	536.67	502.37	474.00	450.20	430.00
48000	4145.00	2140.94	1473.89	1141.09	941.99	809.74	715.69	645.50	591.23	548.09	513.05	484.08	459.78	439.15
49000	4231.35	2185.54	1504.60	1164.86	961.62	826.61	730.60	658.95	603.55	559.51	523.74	494.17	469.36	448.30
50000	4317.70	2230.14	1535.30	1188.64	981.24	843.48	745.51	672.40	615.86	570.93	534.43	504.25	478.94	457.45
55000	4749.47	2453.16	1688.83	1307.50	1079.37	927.83	820.06	739.64	677.45	628.02	587.87	554.68	526.83	503.19
60000	5181.24	2676.17	1842.36	1426.36	1177.49	1012.18	894.61	806.88	739.04	685.12	641.32	605.10	574.73	548.93
65000	5613.01	2899.19	1995.89	1545.23	1275.61	1096.52	969.16	874.12	800.62	742.21	694.76	655.53	622.62	594.68
70000	6044.78	3122.20	2149.42	1664.09	1373.74	1180.87	1043.71	941.35	862.21	799.30	748.20	705.95	670.52	640.42
75000	6476.55	3345.21	2302.95	1782.95	1471.86	1265.22	1118.26	1008.59	923.79	856.39	801.64	756.38	718.41	686.17
80000	6908.32	3568.23	2456.48	1901.82	1569.99	1349.57	1192.81	1075.83	985.38	913.49	855.09	806.80	766.30	731.91
85000	7340.09	3791.24	2610.01	2020.68	1668.11	1433.91	1267.36	1143.07	1046.96	970.58	908.53	857.23	814.20	777.65
90000	7771.86	4014.25	2763.54	2139.54	1766.23	1518.26	1341.91	1210.31	1108.55	1027.67	961.97	907.65	862.09	823.40
95000	8203.63	4237.27	2917.07	2258.41	1864.36	1602.61	1416.46	1277.55	1170.14	1084.76	1015.41	958.08	909.98	869.14
100000	8635.40	4460.28	3070.60	2377.27	1962.48	1686.96	1491.01	1344.79	1231.72	1141.86	1068.86	1008.50	957.88	914.89

TERM AMOUNT	15 Years	16 Years	17 Years	18 Years	19 Years	20 Years	21 Years	22 Years	23 Years	24 Years	25 Years	30 Years	35 Years	40 Years
5	.05	.05	.05	.04	.04	.04	.04	.04	.04	.04	.04	.04	.04	.03
10	.09	.09	.09	.08	.08	.08	.08	.08	.08	.07	.07	.07	.07	.06
15	.14	.13	.13	.12	.12	.12	.12	.11	.11	.11	.11	.10	.10	.09
25	.22	.22	.21	.20	.20	.19	.19	.19	.18	.18	.18	.17	.16	.15
50	.44	.43	.41	.40	.39	.38	.37	.37	.36	.35	.35	.33	.31	.30
75	.66	.64	.62	.60	.58	.57	.56	.55	.54	.53	.52	.49	.46	.45
100	.88	.85	.82	.80	.78	.76	.74	.73	.71	.70	.69	.65	.62	.60
200	1.76	1.70	1.64	1.59	1.55	1.51	1.48	1.45	1.42	1.39	1.37	1.29	1.23	1.19
300	2.64	2.54	2.46	2.39	2.32	2.26	2.21	2.17	2.13	2.09	2.05	1.93	1.84	1.79
400	3.52	3.39	3.28	3.18	3.09	3.02	2.95	2.89	2.83	2.78	2.74	2.57	2.46	2.38
500	4.39	4.24	4.10	3.97	3.87	3.77	3.68	3.61	3.54	3.48	3.42	3.21	3.07	2.98
600	5.27	5.08	4.91	4.77	4.64	4.52	4.42	4.33	4.25	4.17	4.10	3.85	3.68	3.57
700	6.15	5.93	5.73	5.56	5.41	5.28	5.16	5.05	4.95	4.87	4.79	4.49	4.29	4.17
800	7.03	6.77	6.55	6.35	6.18	6.03	5.89	5.77	5.66	5.56	5.47	5.13	4.91	4.76
900	7.91	7.62	7.37	7.15	6.95	6.78	6.63	6.49	6.37	6.25	6.15	5.77	5.52	5.35
1000	8.78	8.47	8.19	7.94	7.73	7.53	7.36	7.21	7.07	6.95	6.84	6.41	6.13	5.95
2000	17.56	16.93	16.37	15.88	15.45	15.06	14.72	14.42	14.14	13.89	13.67	12.81	12.26	11.89
3000	26.34	25.39	24.55	23.82	23.17	22.59	22.08	21.62	21.21	20.83	20.50	19.21	18.39	17.84
4000	35.12	33.85	32.73	31.75	30.89	30.12	29.44	28.83	28.27	27.78	27.33	25.62	24.52	23.78
5000	43.90	42.31	40.92	39.69	38.61	37.65	36.80	36.03	35.34	34.72	34.16	32.02	30.64	29.72
6000	52.68	50.77	49.10	47.63	46.33	45.18	44.16	43.24	42.41	41.66	40.99	38.42	36.77	35.67
7000	61.46	59.23	57.28	55.57	54.05	52.71	51.51	50.44	49.48	48.61	47.82	44.83	42.90	41.61
8000	70.24	67.69	65.46	63.50	61.78	60.24	58.87	57.65	56.54	55.55	54.65	51.23	49.03	47.56
9000	79.02	76.15	73.64	71.44	69.50	67.77	66.23	64.85	63.61	62.49	61.48	57.63	55.15	53.50
10000	87.80	84.61	81.83	79.38	77.22	75.30	73.59	72.06	70.68	69.43	68.31	64.04	61.28	59.44
11000	96.58	93.07	90.01	87.32	84.94	82.83	80.95	79.26	77.74	76.38	75.14	70.44	67.41	65.39
12000	105.36	101.53	98.19	95.25	92.66	90.36	88.31	86.47	84.81	83.32	81.97	76.84	73.54	71.33
13000	114.14	109.99	106.37	103.19	100.38	97.89	95.66	93.67	91.88	90.26	88.80	83.25	79.66	77.27
14000	122.92	118.45	114.55	111.13	108.10	105.42	103.02	100.88	98.95	97.21	95.63	89.65	85.79	83.22
15000	131.70	126.91	122.74	119.07	115.83	112.95	110.38	108.08	106.01	104.15	102.46	96.05	91.92	89.16
16000	140.48	135.37	130.92	127.00	123.55	120.48	117.74	115.29	113.08	111.09	109.29	102.45	98.05	95.11
17000	149.26	143.84	139.10	134.94	131.27	128.01	125.10	122.49	120.15	118.03	116.12	108.86	104.17	101.05
18000	158.04	152.30	147.28	142.88	138.99	135.54	132.46	129.70	127.21	124.90	122.95	115.26	110.30	106.99
19000	166.82	160.76	155.46	150.82	146.71	143.07	139.81	136.90	134.28	131.92	129.78	121.66	116.43	112.94
20000	175.60	169.22	163.65	158.75	154.43	150.60	147.17	144.11	141.35	138.86	136.61	120.07	122.56	118.88
21000	184.38	177.68	171.83	166.69	162.15	158.12	154.53	151.31	148.42	145.81	143.44	134.47	128.69	124.83
22000	193.16	186.14	180.01	174.63	169.88	165.65	161.89	158.52	155.48	152.75	150.27	140.87	134.81	130.77
23000	201.94	194.60	188.19	182.57	177.60	173.18	169.25	165.72	162.55	159.69	157.10	147.28	140.94	136.71
24000	210.72	203.06	196.37	190.50	185.32	180.71	176.61	172.93	169.62	166.63	163.93	153.68	147.07	142.66
25000	219.50	211.52	204.56	198.44	193.04	188.24	183.96	180.13	176.68	173.58	170.76	160.08	153.20	148.60
26000	228.28	219.98	212.74	206.38	200.76	195.77	191.32	187.34	183.75	180.52	177.60	166.49	159.32	154.54
27000	237.06	228.44	220.92	214.32	208.48	203.30	198.68	194.54	190.82	187.46	184.43	172.89	165.45	160.49
28000	245.84	236.90	229.10	222.25	216.20	210.83	206.04	201.75	197.89	194.41	191.26	179.29	171.58	166.43
29000	254.62	245.36	237.29	230.19	223.92	218.36	213.40	208.95	204.95	201.35	198.09	185.70	177.71	172.38
30000	263.40	253.82	245.47	238.13	231.65	225.89	220.76	216.16	212.02	208.29	204.92	192.10	183.83	178.32
31000	272.18	262.28	253.65	246.07	239.37	233.42	228.11	223.36	219.09	215.23	211.75	198.50	189.96	184.26
32000	280.96	270.74	261.83	254.00	247.09	240.95	235.47	230.57	226.16	222.18	218.58	204.90	196.09	190.21
33000	289.74	279.21	270.01	261.94	254.81	248.48	242.83	237.77	233.22	229.12	225.41	211.31	202.22	196.15
34000	298.52	287.67	278.20	269.88	262.53	256.01	250.19	244.98	240.29	236.06	232.24	217.71	208.34	202.10
35000	307.30	296.13	286.38	277.82	270.25	263.54	257.55	252.18	247.36	243.01	239.07	224.11	214.47	208.04
36000	316.08	304.59	294.56	285.75	277.97	271.07	264.91	259.39	254.42	249.95	245.90	230.52	220.60	213.98
37000	324.86	313.05	302.74	293.69	285.70	278.60	272.26	266.59	261.49	256.89	252.73	236.92	226.73	219.93
38000	333.64	321.51	310.92	301.63	293.42	286.13	279.62	273.80	268.56	263.83	259.56	243.32	232.85	225.87
39000	342.42	329.97	319.11	309.57	301.14	293.66	286.98	281.00	275.63	270.78	266.39	249.73	238.98	231.81
40000	351.20	338.43	327.29	317.50	308.86	301.19	294.34	288.21	282.69	277.72	273.22	256.13	245.11	237.76
41000	359.98	346.89	335.47	325.44	316.58	308.71	301.70	295.41	289.76	284.66	280.05	262.53	251.24	243.70
42000	368.76	355.35	343.65	333.38	324.30	316.24	309.06	302.62	296.83	291.61	286.88	268.94	257.37	249.65
43000	377.54	363.81	351.83	341.32	332.02	323.77	316.41	309.82	303.89	298.55	293.71	275.34	263.49	255.59
44000	386.32	372.27	360.02	349.25	339.75	331.30	323.77	317.03	310.96	305.49	300.54	281.74	269.62	261.53
45000	395.10	380.73	368.20	357.19	347.47	338.83	331.13	324.23	318.03	312.43	307.37	288.14	275.75	267.48
46000	403.88	389.19	376.38	365.13	355.19	346.36	338.49	331.44	325.10	319.38	314.20	294.55	281.88	273.42
47000	412.66	397.65	384.56	373.07	362.91	353.89	345.85	338.64	332.16	326.32	321.03	300.95	288.00	279.37
48000	421.44	406.11	392.74	381.00	370.63	361.42	353.21	345.85	339.23	333.26	327.86	307.35	294.13	285.31
49000	430.22	414.58	400.93	388.94	378.35	368.95	360.56	353.05	346.30	340.21	334.69	313.76	300.26	291.25
50000	439.00	423.04	409.11	396.88	386.07	376.48	367.92	360.26	353.36	347.15	341.52	320.16	306.39	297.20
55000	482.90	465.34	450.02	436.57	424.68	414.13	404.71	396.28	388.70	381.86	375.68	352.18	337.02	326.92
60000	526.80	507.64	490.93	476.25	463.29	451.78	441.51	432.31	424.04	416.58	409.83	384.19	367.66	356.64
65000	570.70	549.95	531.84	515.94	501.89	489.42	478.30	468.33	459.37	451.29	443.98	416.21	398.30	386.35
70000	614.60	592.25	572.75	555.63	540.50	527.07	515.09	504.36	494.71	486.01	478.13	448.22	428.94	416.07
75000	658.50	634.55	613.66	595.31	579.11	564.72	551.88	540.38	530.04	520.72	512.28	480.24	459.58	445.79
80000	702.40	676.85	654.57	635.00	617.72	602.37	588.67	576.41	565.38	555.43	546.44	512.25	490.22	475.51
85000	746.30	719.16	695.48	674.69	656.32	640.01	625.46	612.43	600.72	590.15	580.59	544.27	520.85	505.23
90000	790.20	761.46	736.39	714.38	694.93	677.66	662.26	648.46	636.05	624.86	614.74	576.28	551.49	534.95
95000	834.10	803.76	777.30	754.06	733.54	715.31	699.05	684.48	671.39	659.58	648.89	608.30	582.13	564.67
100000	878.00	846.07	818.21	793.75	772.14	752.96	735.84	720.51	706.72	694.29	683.04	640.32	612.77	594.39

MONTHLY PAYMENT
REQUIRED TO AMORTIZE A LOAN

TERM	1 Year	2 Years	3 Years	4 Years	5 Years	6 Years	7 Years	8 Years	9 Years	10 Years	11 Years	12 Years	13 Years	14 Years
AMOUNT														
5	.44	.23	.16	.12	.10	.09	.08	.07	.07	.06	.06	.06	.05	.05
10	.87	.45	.31	.24	.20	.17	.15	.14	.13	.12	.11	.11	.10	.10
15	1.30	.67	.47	.36	.30	.26	.23	.21	.19	.18	.17	.16	.15	.14
25	2.16	1.12	.77	.60	.50	.43	.38	.34	.31	.29	.27	.26	.25	.23
50	4.32	2.24	1.54	1.20	.99	.85	.75	.68	.62	.58	.54	.51	.49	.46
75	6.48	3.35	2.31	1.79	1.48	1.27	1.13	1.02	.93	.86	.81	.76	.73	.69
100	8.64	4.47	3.08	2.39	1.97	1.70	1.50	1.35	1.24	1.15	1.08	1.02	.97	.92
200	17.28	8.93	6.15	4.77	3.94	3.39	2.99	2.70	2.48	2.30	2.15	2.03	1.93	1.84
300	25.92	13.40	9.23	7.15	5.90	5.08	4.49	4.05	3.71	3.44	3.22	3.04	2.89	2.76
400	34.56	17.86	12.30	9.53	7.87	6.77	5.98	5.40	4.95	4.59	4.30	4.05	3.85	3.68
500	43.20	22.32	15.38	11.91	9.83	8.46	7.48	6.75	6.18	5.73	5.37	5.07	4.81	4.60
600	51.84	26.79	18.45	14.29	11.80	10.15	8.97	8.10	7.42	6.88	6.44	6.08	5.78	5.52
700	60.48	31.25	21.52	16.67	13.77	11.84	10.47	9.44	8.65	8.02	7.51	7.09	6.74	6.44
800	69.12	35.71	24.60	19.05	15.73	13.53	11.96	10.79	9.89	9.17	8.59	8.10	7.70	7.36
900	77.75	40.18	27.67	21.43	17.70	15.22	13.46	12.14	11.12	10.32	9.66	9.12	8.66	8.28
1000	86.39	44.64	30.75	23.81	19.66	16.91	14.95	13.49	12.36	11.46	10.73	10.13	9.62	9.19
2000	172.78	89.28	61.49	47.62	39.32	33.82	29.90	26.97	24.71	22.92	21.46	20.25	19.24	18.38
3000	259.17	133.92	92.23	71.43	58.98	50.72	44.84	40.46	37.07	34.38	32.19	30.38	28.86	27.57
4000	345.56	178.55	122.97	95.23	78.64	67.63	59.79	53.94	49.42	45.83	42.91	40.50	38.48	36.76
5000	431.95	223.19	153.71	119.04	98.30	84.53	74.74	67.43	61.78	57.29	53.64	50.63	48.10	45.95
6000	518.34	267.83	184.45	142.85	117.96	101.44	89.68	80.91	74.13	68.75	64.37	60.75	57.72	55.14
7000	604.72	312.46	215.19	166.66	137.62	118.34	104.63	94.40	86.49	80.20	75.10	70.88	67.34	64.33
8000	691.11	357.10	245.93	190.46	157.28	135.25	119.58	107.88	98.84	91.66	85.82	81.00	76.96	73.52
9000	777.50	401.74	276.67	214.27	176.94	152.15	134.52	121.37	111.20	103.12	96.55	91.13	86.58	82.71
10000	863.89	446.37	307.41	238.08	196.60	169.06	149.47	134.85	123.55	114.57	107.28	101.25	96.19	91.90
11000	950.28	491.01	338.15	261.89	216.26	185.96	164.42	148.34	135.91	126.03	118.01	111.38	105.81	101.09
12000	1036.67	535.65	368.89	285.69	235.92	202.87	179.36	161.82	148.26	137.49	128.73	121.50	115.43	110.28
13000	1123.06	580.28	399.63	309.50	255.58	219.77	194.31	175.31	160.62	148.94	139.46	131.62	125.05	119.47
14000	1209.44	624.92	430.37	333.31	275.24	236.68	209.26	188.79	172.97	160.40	150.19	141.75	134.67	128.66
15000	1295.83	669.56	461.11	357.11	294.90	253.58	224.20	202.28	185.33	171.86	160.92	151.87	144.29	137.85
16000	1382.22	714.19	491.85	380.92	314.56	270.49	239.15	215.76	197.68	183.31	171.64	162.00	153.91	147.04
17000	1468.61	758.83	522.59	404.73	334.22	287.40	254.09	229.25	210.04	194.77	182.37	172.12	163.53	156.23
18000	1555.00	803.47	553.33	428.54	353.88	304.30	269.04	242.73	222.39	206.23	193.10	182.25	173.15	165.42
19000	1641.39	848.10	584.07	452.34	373.54	321.21	283.99	256.22	234.75	217.68	203.83	192.37	182.76	174.61
20000	1727.78	892.74	614.81	476.15	393.20	338.11	298.93	269.70	247.10	229.14	214.55	202.50	192.38	183.80
21000	1814.16	937.38	645.55	499.96	412.86	355.02	313.88	283.19	259.46	240.60	225.28	212.62	202.00	192.99
22000	1900.55	982.01	676.29	523.77	432.52	371.92	328.83	296.67	271.81	252.06	236.01	222.75	211.62	202.18
23000	1986.94	1026.65	707.03	547.57	452.18	388.83	343.77	310.16	284.17	263.51	246.74	232.87	221.24	211.37
24000	2073.33	1071.29	737.77	571.38	471.84	405.73	358.72	323.64	296.52	274.97	257.46	243.00	230.86	220.56
25000	2159.72	1115.92	768.51	595.19	491.50	422.64	373.67	337.13	308.88	286.43	268.19	253.12	240.48	229.75
26000	2246.11	1160.56	799.25	618.99	511.16	439.54	388.61	350.61	321.23	297.88	278.92	263.24	250.10	238.94
27000	2332.49	1205.20	829.99	642.80	530.82	456.45	403.56	364.10	333.59	309.34	289.65	273.37	259.72	248.13
28000	2418.88	1249.83	860.73	666.61	550.48	473.35	418.51	377.58	345.94	320.80	300.37	283.49	269.34	257.32
29000	2505.27	1294.47	891.47	690.42	570.14	490.26	433.45	391.07	358.30	332.25	311.10	293.62	278.95	266.50
30000	2591.66	1339.11	922.21	714.22	589.80	507.16	448.40	404.55	370.65	343.71	321.83	303.74	288.57	275.69
31000	2678.05	1383.74	952.95	738.03	609.46	524.07	463.34	418.04	383.01	355.17	332.56	313.87	298.19	284.88
32000	2764.44	1428.38	983.69	761.84	629.12	540.98	478.29	431.52	395.36	366.62	343.28	323.99	307.81	294.07
33000	2850.83	1473.02	1014.43	785.65	648.78	557.88	493.24	445.01	407.72	378.08	354.01	334.12	317.43	303.26
34000	2937.21	1517.65	1045.17	809.45	668.44	574.79	508.18	458.49	420.07	389.54	364.74	344.24	327.05	312.45
35000	3023.60	1562.29	1075.91	833.26	688.10	591.69	523.13	471.98	432.43	400.99	375.47	354.37	336.67	321.64
36000	3109.99	1606.93	1106.65	857.07	707.76	608.60	538.08	485.46	444.78	412.45	386.19	364.49	346.29	330.83
37000	3196.38	1651.56	1137.39	880.88	727.42	625.50	553.02	498.95	457.13	423.91	396.92	374.61	355.91	340.02
38000	3282.77	1696.20	1168.13	904.68	747.08	642.41	567.97	512.43	469.49	435.36	407.65	384.74	365.52	349.21
39000	3369.16	1740.84	1198.87	928.49	766.74	659.31	582.92	525.92	481.84	446.82	418.38	394.86	375.14	358.40
40000	3455.55	1785.47	1229.61	952.30	786.40	676.22	597.86	539.40	494.20	458.28	429.10	404.99	384.76	367.59
41000	3541.93	1830.11	1260.35	976.10	806.06	693.12	612.81	552.89	506.55	469.73	439.83	415.11	394.38	376.78
42000	3628.32	1874.75	1291.09	999.91	825.72	710.03	627.76	566.37	518.91	481.19	450.56	425.24	404.00	385.97
43000	3714.71	1919.38	1321.83	1023.72	845.38	726.93	642.70	579.86	531.26	492.65	461.29	435.36	413.62	395.16
44000	3801.10	1964.02	1352.57	1047.53	865.04	743.84	657.65	593.34	543.62	504.11	472.01	445.49	423.24	404.35
45000	3887.49	2008.66	1383.31	1071.33	884.70	760.74	672.60	606.83	555.97	515.56	482.74	455.61	432.86	413.54
46000	3973.88	2053.29	1414.05	1095.14	904.36	777.65	687.54	620.31	568.33	527.02	493.47	465.74	442.48	422.73
47000	4060.26	2097.93	1444.79	1118.95	924.02	794.55	702.49	633.80	580.68	538.48	504.20	475.86	452.10	431.92
48000	4146.65	2142.57	1475.53	1142.76	943.68	811.46	717.43	647.28	593.04	549.93	514.92	485.99	461.71	441.11
49000	4233.04	2187.20	1506.27	1166.56	963.34	828.37	732.38	660.77	605.39	561.39	525.65	496.11	471.33	450.30
50000	4319.43	2231.84	1537.01	1190.37	983.00	845.27	747.33	674.25	617.75	572.85	536.38	506.23	480.95	459.49
55000	4751.37	2455.02	1690.71	1309.41	1081.30	929.80	822.06	741.67	679.52	630.13	590.02	556.86	529.05	505.44
60000	5183.32	2678.21	1844.41	1428.44	1179.60	1014.32	896.79	809.10	741.30	687.41	643.65	607.48	577.14	551.38
65000	5615.26	2901.39	1998.11	1547.48	1277.90	1098.85	971.52	876.52	803.07	744.70	697.29	658.10	625.24	597.33
70000	6047.20	3124.57	2151.81	1666.52	1376.20	1183.38	1046.26	943.95	864.85	801.98	750.93	708.73	673.33	643.28
75000	6479.14	3347.76	2305.51	1785.55	1474.50	1267.90	1120.99	1011.37	926.62	859.27	804.57	759.35	721.43	689.23
80000	6911.09	3570.94	2459.21	1904.59	1572.80	1352.43	1195.72	1078.80	988.39	916.55	858.20	809.97	769.52	735.18
85000	7343.03	3794.12	2612.91	2023.63	1671.10	1436.96	1270.45	1146.22	1050.17	973.83	911.84	860.59	817.61	781.13
90000	7774.97	4017.31	2766.62	2142.66	1769.40	1521.48	1345.19	1213.65	1111.94	1031.12	965.48	911.22	865.71	827.07
95000	8206.91	4240.49	2920.32	2261.70	1867.70	1606.01	1419.92	1281.07	1173.72	1088.40	1019.11	961.84	913.80	873.02
100000	8638.86	4463.68	3074.02	2380.74	1966.00	1690.54	1494.65	1348.50	1235.49	1145.69	1072.75	1012.46	961.90	918.97

MONTHLY PAYMENT
REQUIRED TO AMORTIZE A LOAN

6.700%

TERM / AMOUNT	15 Years	16 Years	17 Years	18 Years	19 Years	20 Years	21 Years	22 Years	23 Years	24 Years	25 Years	30 Years	35 Years	40 Years
5	.05	.05	.05	.04	.04	.04	.04	.04	.04	.04	.04	.04	.04	.03
10	.09	.09	.09	.08	.08	.08	.08	.08	.08	.07	.07	.07	.07	.06
15	.14	.13	.13	.12	.12	.12	.12	.11	.11	.11	.11	.10	.10	.09
25	.23	.22	.21	.21	.20	.19	.19	.19	.18	.18	.18	.17	.16	.15
50	.45	.43	.42	.40	.39	.38	.38	.37	.36	.35	.35	.33	.31	.30
75	.67	.64	.62	.60	.59	.57	.56	.55	.54	.53	.52	.49	.47	.45
100	.89	.86	.83	.80	.78	.76	.75	.73	.72	.70	.69	.65	.62	.60
200	1.77	1.71	1.65	1.60	1.56	1.52	1.49	1.46	1.43	1.40	1.38	1.30	1.24	1.20
300	2.65	2.56	2.47	2.40	2.33	2.28	2.23	2.18	2.14	2.10	2.07	1.94	1.86	1.80
400	3.53	3.41	3.29	3.20	3.11	3.03	2.97	2.91	2.85	2.80	2.76	2.59	2.48	2.40
500	4.42	4.26	4.12	4.00	3.89	3.79	3.71	3.63	3.56	3.50	3.44	3.23	3.09	3.00
600	5.30	5.11	4.94	4.79	4.66	4.55	4.45	4.36	4.27	4.20	4.13	3.88	3.71	3.60
700	6.18	5.96	5.76	5.59	5.44	5.31	5.19	5.08	4.98	4.90	4.82	4.52	4.33	4.20
800	7.06	6.81	6.58	6.39	6.22	6.06	5.93	5.81	5.70	5.60	5.51	5.17	4.95	4.80
900	7.94	7.66	7.41	7.19	6.99	6.82	6.67	6.53	6.41	6.30	6.19	5.81	5.57	5.40
1000	8.83	8.51	8.23	7.99	7.77	7.58	7.41	7.26	7.12	6.99	6.88	6.46	6.18	6.00
2000	17.65	17.01	16.45	15.97	15.54	15.15	14.81	14.51	14.23	13.98	13.76	12.91	12.36	12.00
3000	26.47	25.51	24.68	23.95	23.30	22.73	22.22	21.76	21.34	20.97	20.64	19.36	18.54	18.00
4000	35.29	34.02	32.90	31.93	31.07	30.30	29.62	29.01	28.46	27.96	27.52	25.82	24.72	24.00
5000	44.11	42.52	41.13	39.91	38.83	37.87	37.02	36.26	35.57	34.95	34.39	32.27	30.90	29.99
6000	52.93	51.02	49.35	47.89	46.60	45.45	44.43	43.51	42.68	41.94	41.27	38.72	37.08	35.99
7000	61.75	59.52	57.58	55.87	54.36	53.02	51.83	50.76	49.80	48.93	48.15	45.17	43.26	41.99
8000	70.58	68.03	65.80	63.85	62.13	60.60	59.23	58.01	56.91	55.92	55.03	51.63	49.44	47.99
9000	79.40	76.53	74.03	71.83	69.89	68.17	66.64	65.26	64.02	62.91	61.90	58.08	55.62	53.98
10000	88.22	85.03	82.25	79.81	77.66	75.74	74.04	72.51	71.14	69.90	68.78	64.53	61.80	59.98
11000	97.04	93.53	90.48	87.79	85.42	83.32	81.44	79.76	78.25	76.89	75.66	70.99	67.98	65.98
12000	105.86	102.04	98.70	95.77	93.19	90.89	88.85	87.01	85.36	83.88	82.54	77.44	74.16	71.98
13000	114.68	110.54	106.93	103.75	100.95	98.47	96.25	94.26	92.48	90.87	89.41	83.89	80.34	77.97
14000	123.50	119.04	115.15	111.74	108.72	106.04	103.65	101.51	99.59	97.86	96.29	90.34	86.52	83.97
15000	132.33	127.55	123.38	119.72	116.48	113.61	111.06	108.76	106.70	104.85	103.17	96.80	92.70	89.97
16000	141.15	136.05	131.60	127.70	124.25	121.19	118.46	116.01	113.82	111.84	110.05	103.25	98.88	95.97
17000	149.97	144.55	139.83	135.68	132.01	128.76	125.86	123.27	120.93	118.83	116.92	109.70	105.06	101.96
18000	158.79	153.05	148.05	143.66	139.78	136.34	133.27	130.52	128.04	125.82	123.80	116.16	111.24	107.96
19000	167.61	161.56	156.28	151.64	147.54	143.91	140.67	137.77	135.16	132.81	130.68	122.61	117.42	113.96
20000	176.43	170.06	164.50	159.62	155.31	151.48	148.07	145.02	142.27	139.80	137.56	129.06	123.59	119.96
21000	185.25	178.56	172.72	167.60	163.07	159.06	155.48	152.27	149.38	146.79	144.43	135.51	129.77	125.96
22000	194.08	187.06	180.95	175.58	170.84	166.63	162.88	159.52	156.50	153.77	151.31	141.97	135.95	131.95
23000	202.90	195.57	189.17	183.56	178.61	174.21	170.28	166.77	163.61	160.76	158.19	148.42	142.13	137.95
24000	211.72	204.07	197.40	191.54	186.37	181.78	177.69	174.02	170.72	167.75	165.07	154.87	148.31	143.95
25000	220.54	212.57	205.62	199.52	194.14	189.35	185.09	181.27	177.84	174.74	171.94	161.32	154.49	149.95
26000	229.36	221.08	213.85	207.50	201.90	196.93	192.49	188.52	184.95	181.73	178.82	167.78	160.67	155.94
27000	238.18	229.58	222.07	215.48	209.67	204.50	199.90	195.77	192.06	188.72	185.70	174.23	166.85	161.94
28000	247.00	238.08	230.30	223.47	217.43	212.08	207.30	203.02	199.18	195.71	192.58	180.68	173.03	167.94
29000	255.83	246.58	238.52	231.45	225.20	219.65	214.70	210.27	206.29	202.70	199.45	187.14	179.21	173.94
30000	264.65	255.09	246.75	239.43	232.96	227.22	222.11	217.52	213.40	209.69	206.33	193.59	185.39	179.93
31000	273.47	263.59	254.97	247.41	240.73	234.80	229.51	224.77	220.52	216.68	213.21	200.04	191.57	185.93
32000	282.29	272.09	263.20	255.39	248.49	242.37	236.91	232.02	227.63	223.67	220.09	206.49	197.75	191.93
33000	291.11	280.59	271.42	263.37	256.26	249.95	244.32	239.27	234.74	230.66	226.96	212.95	203.93	197.93
34000	299.93	289.10	279.65	271.35	264.02	257.52	251.72	246.53	241.86	237.65	233.84	219.40	210.11	203.92
35000	308.75	297.60	287.87	279.33	271.79	265.09	259.12	253.78	248.97	244.64	240.72	225.85	216.29	209.92
36000	317.58	306.10	296.10	287.31	279.55	272.67	266.53	261.03	256.08	251.63	247.60	232.31	222.47	215.92
37000	326.40	314.60	304.32	295.29	287.32	280.24	273.93	268.28	263.20	258.62	254.48	238.76	228.65	221.92
38000	335.22	323.11	312.55	303.27	295.08	287.81	281.33	275.53	270.31	265.61	261.35	245.21	234.83	227.91
39000	344.04	331.61	320.77	311.25	302.85	295.39	288.74	282.78	277.42	272.60	268.23	251.66	241.01	233.91
40000	352.86	340.11	329.00	319.23	310.61	302.96	296.14	290.03	284.54	279.59	275.11	258.12	247.18	239.91
41000	361.68	348.62	337.22	327.22	318.38	310.54	303.54	297.28	291.65	286.58	281.99	264.57	253.36	245.91
42000	370.50	357.12	345.44	335.20	326.14	318.11	310.95	304.53	298.76	293.57	288.86	271.02	259.54	251.91
43000	379.33	365.62	353.67	343.18	333.91	325.68	318.35	311.78	305.88	300.55	295.74	277.47	265.72	257.90
44000	388.15	374.12	361.89	351.16	341.68	333.26	325.75	319.03	312.99	307.54	302.62	283.93	271.90	263.90
45000	396.97	382.63	370.12	359.14	349.44	340.83	333.16	326.28	320.10	314.53	309.50	290.38	278.08	269.90
46000	405.79	391.13	378.34	367.12	357.21	348.41	340.56	333.53	327.22	321.52	316.37	296.83	284.26	275.90
47000	414.61	399.63	386.57	375.10	364.97	355.98	347.96	340.78	334.33	328.51	323.25	303.29	290.44	281.89
48000	423.43	408.13	394.79	383.08	372.74	363.55	355.37	348.03	341.44	335.50	330.13	309.74	296.62	287.89
49000	432.25	416.64	403.02	391.06	380.50	371.13	362.77	355.28	348.56	342.49	337.01	316.19	302.80	293.89
50000	441.07	425.14	411.24	399.04	388.27	378.70	370.17	362.53	355.67	349.48	343.88	322.64	308.98	299.89
55000	485.18	467.65	452.37	438.95	427.09	416.57	407.19	398.79	391.24	384.43	378.27	354.91	339.88	329.87
60000	529.29	510.17	493.49	478.85	465.92	454.44	444.21	435.04	426.80	419.38	412.66	387.17	370.77	359.86
65000	573.40	552.68	534.61	518.75	504.75	492.31	481.22	471.29	462.37	454.32	447.05	419.44	401.67	389.85
70000	617.50	595.19	575.74	558.66	543.57	530.18	518.24	507.55	497.94	489.27	481.44	451.70	432.57	419.84
75000	661.61	637.71	616.86	598.56	582.40	568.05	555.26	543.80	533.50	524.22	515.82	483.96	463.47	449.83
80000	705.72	680.22	657.99	638.46	621.22	605.92	592.27	580.05	569.07	559.17	550.21	516.23	494.36	479.82
85000	749.82	722.73	699.11	678.37	660.05	643.79	629.29	616.31	604.64	594.11	584.60	548.49	525.26	509.80
90000	793.93	765.25	740.23	718.27	698.88	681.66	666.31	652.56	640.20	629.06	618.99	580.76	556.16	539.79
95000	838.04	807.76	781.36	758.17	737.70	719.53	703.32	688.81	675.77	664.01	653.37	613.02	587.06	569.78
100000	882.14	850.27	822.48	798.08	776.53	757.40	740.34	725.06	711.34	698.96	687.76	645.28	617.95	599.77

MONTHLY PAYMENT
REQUIRED TO AMORTIZE A LOAN

TERM AMOUNT	1 Year	2 Years	3 Years	4 Years	5 Years	6 Years	7 Years	8 Years	9 Years	10 Years	11 Years	12 Years	13 Years	14 Years
5	.44	.23	.16	.12	.10	.09	.08	.07	.07	.06	.06	.06	.05	.05
10	.87	.45	.31	.24	.20	.17	.15	.14	.13	.12	.11	.11	.10	.10
15	1.30	.67	.47	.36	.30	.26	.23	.21	.19	.18	.17	.16	.15	.14
25	2.17	1.12	.77	.60	.50	.43	.38	.34	.31	.29	.27	.26	.25	.24
50	4.33	2.24	1.54	1.20	.99	.85	.75	.68	.62	.58	.54	.51	.49	.47
75	6.49	3.35	2.31	1.79	1.48	1.27	1.13	1.02	.93	.87	.81	.77	.73	.70
100	8.65	4.47	3.08	2.39	1.97	1.70	1.50	1.36	1.24	1.15	1.08	1.02	.97	.93
200	17.29	8.94	6.16	4.77	3.94	3.39	3.00	2.71	2.48	2.30	2.16	2.04	1.93	1.85
300	25.93	13.40	9.23	7.15	5.91	5.08	4.50	4.06	3.72	3.45	3.23	3.05	2.90	2.77
400	34.57	17.87	12.31	9.54	7.88	6.78	5.99	5.41	4.96	4.60	4.31	4.07	3.86	3.69
500	43.21	22.33	15.39	11.92	9.85	8.47	7.49	6.76	6.20	5.75	5.38	5.08	4.83	4.61
600	51.85	26.80	18.46	14.30	11.82	10.16	8.99	8.11	7.43	6.89	6.46	6.10	5.79	5.54
700	60.49	31.27	21.54	16.69	13.78	11.86	10.48	9.46	8.67	8.04	7.53	7.11	6.76	6.46
800	69.13	35.73	24.62	19.07	15.75	13.55	11.98	10.81	9.91	9.19	8.61	8.13	7.72	7.38
900	77.78	40.20	27.69	21.45	17.72	15.24	13.48	12.16	11.15	10.34	9.68	9.14	8.69	8.30
1000	86.42	44.66	30.77	23.84	19.69	16.93	14.98	13.51	12.39	11.49	10.76	10.16	9.65	9.22
2000	172.83	89.32	61.53	47.67	39.37	33.86	29.95	27.02	24.77	22.97	21.51	20.31	19.30	18.44
3000	259.24	133.98	92.29	71.50	59.06	50.79	44.92	40.53	37.15	34.45	32.27	30.46	28.94	27.66
4000	345.65	178.64	123.06	95.33	78.74	67.72	59.89	54.04	49.53	45.93	43.02	40.61	38.59	36.87
5000	432.06	223.30	153.82	119.16	98.42	84.65	74.86	67.55	61.91	57.42	53.77	50.76	48.23	46.09
6000	518.47	267.96	184.58	142.99	118.11	101.58	89.83	81.06	74.29	68.90	64.53	60.91	57.88	55.31
7000	604.89	312.62	215.35	166.82	137.79	118.51	104.80	94.57	86.67	80.38	75.28	71.06	67.53	64.52
8000	691.30	357.28	246.11	190.65	157.47	135.44	119.77	108.08	99.05	91.86	86.03	81.21	77.17	73.74
9000	777.71	401.94	276.87	214.48	177.16	152.37	134.74	121.59	111.43	103.35	96.79	91.36	86.82	82.96
10000	864.12	446.60	307.63	238.31	196.84	169.30	149.71	135.10	123.81	114.83	107.54	101.52	96.46	92.17
11000	950.53	491.26	338.40	262.14	216.52	186.23	164.68	148.61	136.19	126.31	118.29	111.67	106.11	101.39
12000	1036.94	535.92	369.16	285.97	236.21	203.16	179.65	162.12	148.57	137.79	129.05	121.82	115.75	110.61
13000	1123.36	580.58	399.92	309.80	255.89	220.08	194.62	175.63	160.95	149.28	139.80	131.97	125.40	119.83
14000	1209.77	625.24	430.69	333.63	275.57	237.01	209.60	189.14	173.33	160.76	150.55	142.12	135.05	129.04
15000	1296.18	669.89	461.45	357.46	295.26	253.94	224.57	202.65	185.71	172.24	161.31	152.27	144.69	138.26
16000	1382.59	714.55	492.21	381.29	314.94	270.87	239.54	216.16	198.09	183.72	172.06	162.42	154.34	147.48
17000	1469.00	759.21	522.97	405.12	334.62	287.80	254.51	229.67	210.47	195.21	182.81	172.57	163.98	156.69
18000	1555.41	803.87	553.74	428.95	354.31	304.73	269.48	243.18	222.85	206.69	193.57	182.72	173.63	165.91
19000	1641.82	848.53	584.50	452.78	373.99	321.66	284.45	256.69	235.23	218.17	204.32	192.87	183.28	175.13
20000	1728.24	893.19	615.26	476.61	393.67	338.59	299.42	270.20	247.61	229.65	215.07	203.03	192.92	184.34
21000	1814.65	937.85	646.03	500.44	413.36	355.52	314.39	283.71	259.99	241.14	225.83	213.18	202.57	193.56
22000	1901.06	982.51	676.79	524.27	433.04	372.45	329.36	297.22	272.37	252.62	236.58	223.33	212.21	202.78
23000	1987.47	1027.17	707.55	548.10	452.72	389.38	344.33	310.73	284.75	264.10	247.34	233.48	221.86	211.99
24000	2073.88	1071.83	738.32	571.94	472.41	406.31	359.30	324.24	297.13	275.58	258.09	243.63	231.50	221.21
25000	2160.29	1116.49	769.08	595.77	492.09	423.24	374.27	337.75	309.51	287.07	268.84	253.78	241.15	230.43
26000	2246.71	1161.15	799.84	619.60	511.77	440.16	389.24	351.26	321.89	298.55	279.60	263.93	250.80	239.65
27000	2333.12	1205.81	830.60	643.43	531.46	457.09	404.22	364.77	334.27	310.03	290.35	274.08	260.44	248.86
28000	2419.53	1250.47	861.37	667.26	551.14	474.02	419.19	378.27	346.65	321.51	301.10	284.23	270.09	258.08
29000	2505.94	1295.13	892.13	691.09	570.83	490.95	434.16	391.78	359.03	332.99	311.86	294.38	279.73	267.30
30000	2592.35	1339.78	922.89	714.92	590.51	507.88	449.13	405.29	371.41	344.48	322.61	304.54	289.38	276.51
31000	2678.76	1384.44	953.66	738.75	610.19	524.81	464.10	418.80	383.79	355.96	333.36	314.69	299.02	285.73
32000	2765.17	1429.10	984.42	762.58	629.88	541.74	479.07	432.31	396.17	367.44	344.12	324.84	308.67	294.95
33000	2851.59	1473.76	1015.18	786.41	649.56	558.67	494.04	445.82	408.55	378.92	354.87	334.99	318.32	304.16
34000	2938.00	1518.42	1045.94	810.24	669.24	575.60	509.01	459.33	420.93	390.41	365.62	345.14	327.96	313.38
35000	3024.41	1563.08	1076.71	834.07	688.93	592.53	523.98	472.84	433.31	401.89	376.38	355.29	337.61	322.60
36000	3110.82	1607.74	1107.47	857.90	708.61	609.46	538.95	486.35	445.69	413.37	387.13	365.44	347.25	331.81
37000	3197.23	1652.40	1138.23	881.73	728.29	626.39	553.92	499.86	458.07	424.85	397.88	375.59	356.90	341.03
38000	3283.64	1697.06	1169.00	905.56	747.98	643.32	568.89	513.37	470.45	436.34	408.64	385.74	366.55	350.25
39000	3370.06	1741.72	1199.76	929.39	767.66	660.24	583.86	526.88	482.83	447.82	419.39	395.90	376.19	359.47
40000	3456.47	1786.38	1230.52	953.22	787.34	677.17	598.84	540.39	495.21	459.30	430.14	406.05	385.84	368.68
41000	3542.88	1831.04	1261.28	977.05	807.03	694.10	613.81	553.90	507.59	470.78	440.90	416.20	395.48	377.90
42000	3629.29	1875.70	1292.05	1000.88	826.71	711.03	628.78	567.41	519.97	482.27	451.65	426.35	405.13	387.12
43000	3715.70	1920.36	1322.81	1024.71	846.39	727.96	643.75	580.92	532.35	493.75	462.40	436.50	414.77	396.33
44000	3802.11	1965.02	1353.57	1048.54	866.08	744.89	658.72	594.43	544.73	505.23	473.16	446.65	424.42	405.55
45000	3888.52	2009.67	1384.34	1072.37	885.76	761.82	673.69	607.94	557.11	516.71	483.91	456.80	434.07	414.77
46000	3974.94	2054.33	1415.10	1096.20	905.44	778.75	688.66	621.45	569.49	528.20	494.67	466.95	443.71	423.98
47000	4061.35	2098.99	1445.86	1120.04	925.13	795.68	703.63	634.96	581.87	539.68	505.42	477.10	453.36	433.20
48000	4147.76	2143.65	1476.63	1143.87	944.81	812.61	718.60	648.47	594.25	551.16	516.17	487.25	463.00	442.42
49000	4234.17	2188.31	1507.39	1167.70	964.49	829.54	733.57	661.98	606.63	562.64	526.93	497.41	472.65	451.63
50000	4320.58	2232.97	1538.15	1191.53	984.18	846.47	748.54	675.49	619.01	574.13	537.68	507.56	482.30	460.85
55000	4752.64	2456.27	1691.97	1310.68	1082.60	931.11	823.40	743.04	680.91	631.54	591.45	558.31	530.52	506.94
60000	5184.70	2679.56	1845.78	1429.83	1181.01	1015.76	898.25	810.58	742.81	688.95	645.21	609.07	578.75	553.02
65000	5616.76	2902.86	1999.59	1548.98	1279.43	1100.40	973.10	878.13	804.71	746.36	698.98	659.82	626.98	599.11
70000	6048.81	3126.16	2153.41	1668.13	1377.85	1185.05	1047.96	945.68	866.61	803.77	752.75	710.58	675.21	645.19
75000	6480.87	3349.45	2307.22	1787.29	1476.26	1269.70	1122.81	1013.23	928.51	861.19	806.52	761.33	723.44	691.27
80000	6912.93	3572.75	2461.04	1906.44	1574.68	1354.34	1197.67	1080.78	990.41	918.60	860.28	812.09	771.67	737.36
85000	7344.99	3796.05	2614.85	2025.59	1673.10	1438.99	1272.52	1148.32	1052.31	976.01	914.05	862.84	819.90	783.44
90000	7777.04	4019.34	2768.67	2144.74	1771.52	1523.63	1347.37	1215.87	1114.21	1033.42	967.82	913.60	868.13	829.53
95000	8209.10	4242.64	2922.48	2263.90	1869.93	1608.28	1422.23	1283.42	1176.11	1090.83	1021.59	964.35	916.36	875.61
100000	8641.16	4465.94	3076.30	2383.05	1968.35	1692.93	1497.08	1350.97	1238.01	1148.25	1075.35	1015.11	964.59	921.70

TERM	15 Years	16 Years	17 Years	18 Years	19 Years	20 Years	21 Years	22 Years	23 Years	24 Years	25 Years	30 Years	35 Years	40 Years
AMOUNT														
5	.05	.05	.05	.05	.04	.04	.04	.04	.04	.04	.04	.04	.04	.04
10	.09	.09	.09	.09	.08	.08	.08	.08	.08	.08	.07	.07	.07	.07
15	.14	.13	.13	.13	.12	.12	.12	.11	.11	.11	.11	.10	.10	.10
25	.23	.22	.21	.21	.20	.20	.19	.19	.18	.18	.18	.17	.16	.16
50	.45	.43	.42	.41	.39	.39	.38	.37	.36	.36	.35	.33	.32	.31
75	.67	.64	.62	.61	.59	.58	.56	.55	.54	.53	.52	.49	.47	.46
100	.89	.86	.83	.81	.78	.77	.75	.73	.72	.71	.70	.65	.63	.61
200	1.77	1.71	1.66	1.61	1.56	1.53	1.49	1.46	1.43	1.41	1.39	1.30	1.25	1.21
300	2.66	2.56	2.48	2.41	2.34	2.29	2.24	2.19	2.15	2.11	2.08	1.95	1.87	1.82
400	3.54	3.42	3.31	3.21	3.12	3.05	2.98	2.92	2.86	2.81	2.77	2.60	2.49	2.42
500	4.43	4.27	4.13	4.01	3.90	3.81	3.72	3.65	3.58	3.52	3.46	3.25	3.11	3.02
600	5.31	5.12	4.96	4.81	4.68	4.57	4.47	4.37	4.29	4.22	4.15	3.90	3.73	3.63
700	6.20	5.98	5.78	5.61	5.46	5.33	5.21	5.10	5.01	4.92	4.84	4.55	4.35	4.23
800	7.08	6.83	6.61	6.41	6.24	6.09	5.95	5.83	5.72	5.62	5.53	5.19	4.98	4.83
900	7.97	7.68	7.43	7.21	7.02	6.85	6.70	6.56	6.43	6.32	6.22	5.84	5.60	5.44
1000	8.85	8.54	8.26	8.01	7.80	7.61	7.44	7.29	7.15	7.03	6.91	6.49	6.22	6.04
2000	17.70	17.07	16.51	16.02	15.59	15.21	14.87	14.57	14.29	14.05	13.82	12.98	12.43	12.07
3000	26.55	25.60	24.76	24.03	23.39	22.82	22.31	21.85	21.44	21.07	20.73	19.46	18.65	18.11
4000	35.40	34.13	33.02	32.04	31.18	30.42	29.74	29.13	28.58	28.09	27.64	25.95	24.86	24.14
5000	44.25	42.66	41.27	40.05	38.98	38.02	37.17	36.41	35.73	35.11	34.55	32.43	31.08	30.17
6000	53.10	51.19	49.52	48.06	46.77	45.63	44.61	43.69	42.87	42.13	41.46	38.92	37.29	36.21
7000	61.95	59.72	57.78	56.07	54.57	53.23	52.04	50.97	50.01	49.15	48.37	45.41	43.50	42.24
8000	70.80	68.25	66.03	64.08	62.36	60.83	59.47	58.25	57.16	56.17	55.28	51.89	49.72	48.27
9000	79.65	76.78	74.28	72.09	70.16	68.44	66.91	65.53	64.30	63.19	62.19	58.38	55.93	54.31
10000	88.50	85.31	82.54	80.10	77.95	76.04	74.34	72.82	71.45	70.21	69.10	64.86	62.15	60.34
11000	97.35	93.84	90.79	88.11	85.75	83.65	81.77	80.10	78.59	77.23	76.01	71.35	68.36	66.37
12000	106.19	102.37	99.04	96.12	93.54	91.25	89.21	87.38	85.73	84.25	82.91	77.84	74.57	72.41
13000	115.04	110.91	107.30	104.13	101.33	98.85	96.64	94.66	92.88	91.27	89.82	84.32	80.79	78.44
14000	123.89	119.44	115.55	112.14	109.13	106.46	104.07	101.94	100.02	98.29	96.73	90.81	87.00	84.47
15000	132.74	127.97	123.80	120.15	116.92	114.06	111.51	109.22	107.17	105.32	103.64	97.29	93.22	90.51
16000	141.59	136.50	132.06	128.16	124.72	121.66	118.94	116.50	114.31	112.34	110.55	103.78	99.43	96.54
17000	150.44	145.03	140.31	136.17	132.51	129.27	126.37	123.78	121.46	119.36	117.46	110.27	105.65	102.58
18000	159.29	153.56	148.56	144.18	140.31	136.87	133.81	131.06	128.60	126.38	124.37	116.75	111.86	108.61
19000	168.14	162.09	156.82	152.19	148.10	144.47	141.24	138.34	135.74	133.40	131.28	123.24	118.07	114.64
20000	176.99	170.62	165.07	160.20	155.90	152.08	148.67	145.63	142.89	140.42	138.19	129.72	124.29	120.68
21000	185.84	179.15	173.32	168.21	163.69	159.68	156.11	152.91	150.03	147.44	145.10	136.21	130.50	126.71
22000	194.69	187.68	181.58	176.22	171.49	167.29	163.54	160.19	157.18	154.46	152.01	142.70	136.72	132.74
23000	203.53	196.21	189.83	184.23	179.28	174.89	170.97	167.47	164.32	161.48	158.91	149.18	142.93	138.78
24000	212.38	204.74	198.08	192.24	187.07	182.49	178.41	174.75	171.46	168.50	165.82	155.67	149.14	144.81
25000	221.23	213.28	206.34	200.25	194.87	190.10	185.84	182.03	178.61	175.52	172.73	162.15	155.36	150.84
26000	230.08	221.81	214.59	208.26	202.66	197.70	193.27	189.31	185.75	182.54	179.64	168.64	161.57	156.88
27000	238.93	230.34	222.84	216.27	210.46	205.30	200.71	196.59	192.90	189.56	186.55	175.13	167.79	162.91
28000	247.78	238.87	231.10	224.28	218.25	212.91	208.14	203.87	200.04	196.58	193.46	181.61	174.00	168.94
29000	256.63	247.40	239.35	232.28	226.05	220.51	215.57	211.16	207.18	203.61	200.37	188.10	180.22	174.98
30000	265.48	255.93	247.60	240.29	233.84	228.11	223.01	218.44	214.33	210.63	207.28	194.58	186.43	181.01
31000	274.33	264.46	255.86	248.30	241.64	235.72	230.44	225.72	221.47	217.65	214.19	201.07	192.64	187.05
32000	283.18	272.99	264.11	256.31	249.43	243.32	237.87	233.00	228.62	224.67	221.10	207.56	198.86	193.08
33000	292.03	281.52	272.36	264.32	257.23	250.93	245.31	240.28	235.76	231.69	228.01	214.04	205.07	199.11
34000	300.87	290.05	280.62	272.33	265.02	258.53	252.74	247.56	242.91	238.71	234.91	220.53	211.29	205.15
35000	309.72	298.58	288.87	280.34	272.81	266.13	260.18	254.84	250.05	245.73	241.82	227.01	217.50	211.18
36000	318.57	307.11	297.12	288.35	280.61	273.74	267.61	262.12	257.19	252.75	248.73	233.50	223.71	217.21
37000	327.42	315.64	305.38	296.36	288.40	281.34	275.04	269.40	264.34	259.77	255.64	239.99	229.93	223.25
38000	336.27	324.18	313.63	304.37	296.20	288.94	282.48	276.68	271.48	266.79	262.55	246.47	236.14	229.28
39000	345.12	332.71	321.88	312.38	303.99	296.55	289.91	283.97	278.63	273.81	269.46	252.96	242.36	235.31
40000	353.97	341.24	330.14	320.39	311.79	304.15	297.34	291.25	285.77	280.83	276.37	259.44	248.57	241.35
41000	362.82	349.77	338.39	328.40	319.58	311.75	304.78	298.53	292.91	287.85	283.28	265.93	254.79	247.38
42000	371.67	358.30	346.64	336.41	327.38	319.36	312.21	305.81	300.06	294.87	290.19	272.42	261.00	253.41
43000	380.52	366.83	354.90	344.42	335.17	326.96	319.64	313.09	307.20	301.90	297.10	278.90	267.21	259.45
44000	389.37	375.36	363.15	352.43	342.97	334.57	327.08	320.37	314.35	308.92	304.01	285.39	273.43	265.48
45000	398.21	383.89	371.40	360.44	350.76	342.17	334.51	327.65	321.49	315.94	310.92	291.87	279.64	271.52
46000	407.06	392.42	379.66	368.45	358.55	349.77	341.94	334.93	328.64	322.96	317.82	298.36	285.86	277.55
47000	415.91	400.95	387.91	376.46	366.35	357.38	349.38	342.21	335.78	329.98	324.73	304.85	292.07	283.58
48000	424.76	409.48	396.16	384.47	374.14	364.98	356.81	349.50	342.92	337.00	331.64	311.33	298.28	289.62
49000	433.61	418.01	404.42	392.48	381.94	372.58	364.24	356.78	350.07	344.02	338.55	317.82	304.50	295.65
50000	442.46	426.55	412.67	400.49	389.73	380.19	371.68	364.06	357.21	351.04	345.46	324.30	310.71	301.68
55000	486.71	469.20	453.93	440.54	428.71	418.21	408.84	400.46	392.93	386.14	380.01	356.73	341.78	331.85
60000	530.95	511.85	495.20	480.58	467.68	456.22	446.01	436.87	428.65	421.25	414.55	389.16	372.85	362.02
65000	575.20	554.51	536.47	520.63	506.65	494.24	483.18	473.27	464.37	456.35	449.10	421.59	403.93	392.19
70000	619.44	597.16	577.73	560.68	545.62	532.26	520.35	509.68	500.09	491.45	483.64	454.02	435.00	422.35
75000	663.69	639.82	619.00	600.73	584.60	570.28	557.51	546.08	535.82	526.56	518.19	486.45	466.07	452.52
80000	707.93	682.47	660.27	640.78	623.57	608.30	594.68	582.49	571.54	561.66	552.73	518.88	497.14	482.69
85000	752.18	725.12	701.53	680.83	662.54	646.31	631.85	618.89	607.26	596.77	587.28	551.31	528.21	512.86
90000	796.42	767.78	742.80	720.87	701.51	684.33	669.01	655.30	642.98	631.87	621.83	583.74	559.28	543.03
95000	840.67	810.43	784.07	760.92	740.49	722.35	706.18	691.70	678.70	666.97	656.37	616.17	590.35	573.19
100000	884.91	853.09	825.33	800.97	779.46	760.37	743.35	728.11	714.42	702.08	690.92	648.60	621.42	603.36

MONTHLY PAYMENT
REQUIRED TO AMORTIZE A LOAN

TERM	1 Year	2 Years	3 Years	4 Years	5 Years	6 Years	7 Years	8 Years	9 Years	10 Years	11 Years	12 Years	13 Years	14 Years
AMOUNT														
5	.44	.23	.16	.12	.10	.09	.08	.07	.07	.06	.06	.06	.05	.05
10	.87	.45	.31	.24	.20	.17	.15	.14	.13	.12	.11	.11	.10	.10
15	1.30	.68	.47	.36	.30	.26	.23	.21	.19	.18	.17	.16	.15	.14
25	2.17	1.12	.77	.60	.50	.43	.38	.34	.32	.29	.27	.26	.25	.24
50	4.33	2.24	1.54	1.20	.99	.85	.75	.68	.63	.58	.54	.51	.49	.47
75	6.49	3.36	2.31	1.79	1.48	1.28	1.13	1.02	.94	.87	.81	.77	.73	.70
100	8.65	4.47	3.08	2.39	1.98	1.70	1.50	1.36	1.25	1.16	1.08	1.02	.97	.93
200	17.29	8.94	6.16	4.78	3.95	3.40	3.00	2.71	2.49	2.31	2.16	2.04	1.94	1.85
300	25.94	15.41	9.24	7.16	5.92	5.09	4.50	4.07	3.73	3.46	3.24	3.06	2.91	2.78
400	34.58	17.88	12.32	9.55	7.89	6.79	6.00	5.42	4.97	4.61	4.32	4.08	3.87	3.70
500	43.22	22.35	15.40	11.93	9.86	8.48	7.50	6.77	6.21	5.76	5.39	5.09	4.84	4.63
600	51.87	26.81	18.48	14.32	11.83	10.18	9.00	8.13	7.45	6.91	6.47	6.11	5.81	5.55
700	60.51	31.28	21.56	16.70	13.80	11.87	10.50	9.48	8.69	8.06	7.55	7.13	6.78	6.48
800	69.15	35.75	24.63	19.09	15.77	13.57	12.00	10.83	9.93	9.21	8.63	8.15	7.74	7.40
900	77.80	40.22	27.71	21.47	17.74	15.26	13.50	12.19	11.17	10.36	9.71	9.16	8.71	8.32
1000	86.44	44.69	30.79	23.86	19.71	16.96	15.00	13.54	12.41	11.51	10.78	10.18	9.68	9.25
2000	172.87	89.37	61.58	47.71	39.42	33.91	30.00	27.07	24.82	23.02	21.56	20.36	19.35	18.49
3000	259.31	134.05	92.36	71.57	59.13	50.86	44.99	40.61	37.22	34.53	32.34	30.54	29.02	27.74
4000	345.74	178.73	123.15	95.42	78.83	67.82	59.99	54.14	49.63	46.04	43.12	40.72	38.70	36.98
5000	432.18	223.41	153.93	119.27	98.54	84.77	74.98	67.68	62.03	57.55	53.90	50.89	48.37	46.23
6000	518.61	268.10	184.72	143.13	118.25	101.72	89.98	81.21	74.44	69.05	64.68	61.07	58.04	55.47
7000	605.05	312.78	215.51	166.98	137.95	118.68	104.97	94.75	86.84	80.56	75.46	71.25	67.71	64.71
8000	691.48	357.46	246.29	190.83	157.66	135.63	119.97	108.28	99.25	92.07	86.24	81.43	77.39	73.96
9000	777.92	402.14	277.08	214.69	177.37	152.58	134.96	121.81	111.65	103.58	97.02	91.60	87.06	83.20
10000	864.35	446.82	307.86	238.54	197.07	169.54	149.96	135.35	124.06	115.09	107.80	101.78	96.73	92.45
11000	950.79	491.51	338.65	262.39	216.78	186.49	164.95	148.88	136.46	126.59	118.58	111.96	106.40	101.69
12000	1037.22	536.19	369.43	286.25	236.49	203.44	179.95	162.42	148.87	138.10	129.36	122.14	116.08	110.94
13000	1123.65	580.87	400.22	310.10	256.20	220.40	194.94	175.95	161.27	149.61	140.14	132.31	125.75	120.18
14000	1210.09	625.55	431.01	333.95	275.90	237.35	209.94	189.49	173.68	161.12	150.92	142.49	135.42	129.42
15000	1296.52	670.23	461.79	357.81	295.61	254.30	224.93	203.02	186.08	172.63	161.70	152.67	145.10	138.67
16000	1382.96	714.92	492.58	381.66	315.32	271.26	239.93	216.56	198.49	184.13	172.48	162.85	154.77	147.91
17000	1469.39	759.60	523.36	405.52	335.02	288.21	254.92	230.09	210.89	195.64	183.26	173.02	164.44	157.16
18000	1555.83	804.28	554.15	429.37	354.73	305.16	269.92	243.62	223.30	207.15	194.04	183.20	174.11	166.40
19000	1642.26	848.96	584.93	453.22	374.44	322.11	284.91	257.16	235.70	218.66	204.82	193.38	183.79	175.65
20000	1728.70	893.64	615.72	477.08	394.14	339.07	299.91	270.69	248.11	230.17	215.60	203.56	193.46	184.89
21000	1815.13	938.33	646.51	500.93	413.85	356.02	314.90	284.23	260.51	241.67	226.38	213.73	203.13	194.13
22000	1901.57	983.01	677.29	524.78	433.56	372.97	329.90	297.76	272.92	253.18	237.15	223.91	212.80	203.38
23000	1988.00	1027.69	708.08	548.64	453.27	389.93	344.89	311.30	285.32	264.69	247.93	234.09	222.48	212.62
24000	2074.43	1072.37	738.86	572.49	472.97	406.88	359.89	324.83	297.73	276.20	258.71	244.27	232.15	221.87
25000	2160.87	1117.05	769.65	596.34	492.68	423.83	374.88	338.37	310.14	287.71	269.49	254.44	241.82	231.11
26000	2247.30	1161.74	800.43	620.20	512.39	440.79	389.88	351.90	322.54	299.21	280.27	264.62	251.50	240.36
27000	2333.74	1206.42	831.22	644.05	532.09	457.74	404.87	365.43	334.95	310.72	291.05	274.80	261.17	249.60
28000	2420.17	1251.10	862.01	667.90	551.80	474.69	419.87	378.97	347.35	322.23	301.83	284.98	270.84	258.84
29000	2506.61	1295.78	892.79	691.76	571.51	491.65	434.86	392.50	359.76	333.74	312.61	295.15	280.51	268.09
30000	2593.04	1340.46	923.58	715.61	591.21	508.60	449.86	406.04	372.16	345.25	323.39	305.33	290.19	277.33
31000	2679.48	1385.15	954.36	739.47	610.92	525.55	464.85	419.57	384.57	356.75	334.17	315.51	299.86	286.58
32000	2765.91	1429.83	985.15	763.32	630.63	542.51	479.85	433.11	396.97	368.26	344.95	325.69	309.53	295.82
33000	2852.35	1474.51	1015.93	787.17	650.34	559.46	494.84	446.64	409.38	379.77	355.73	335.86	319.20	305.07
34000	2938.78	1519.19	1046.72	811.03	670.04	576.41	509.84	460.17	421.78	391.28	366.51	346.04	328.88	314.31
35000	3025.22	1563.87	1077.51	834.88	689.75	593.36	524.83	473.71	434.19	402.79	377.29	356.22	338.55	323.55
36000	3111.65	1608.56	1108.29	858.73	709.46	610.32	539.83	487.24	446.59	414.29	388.07	366.40	348.22	332.80
37000	3198.08	1653.24	1139.08	882.59	729.16	627.27	554.82	500.78	459.00	425.80	398.85	376.57	357.90	342.04
38000	3284.52	1697.92	1169.86	906.44	748.87	644.22	569.82	514.31	471.40	437.31	409.63	386.75	367.57	351.29
39000	3370.95	1742.60	1200.65	930.29	768.58	661.18	584.81	527.85	483.81	448.82	420.41	396.93	377.24	360.53
40000	3457.39	1787.28	1231.43	954.15	788.28	678.13	599.81	541.38	496.21	460.33	431.19	407.11	386.91	369.78
41000	3543.82	1831.97	1262.22	978.00	807.99	695.08	614.80	554.92	508.62	471.83	441.97	417.28	396.59	379.02
42000	3630.26	1876.65	1293.01	1001.85	827.70	712.04	629.80	568.45	521.02	483.34	452.75	427.46	406.26	388.26
43000	3716.69	1921.33	1323.79	1025.71	847.40	728.99	644.79	581.98	533.43	494.85	463.53	437.64	415.93	397.51
44000	3803.13	1966.01	1354.58	1049.56	867.11	745.94	659.79	595.52	545.83	506.36	474.30	447.82	425.60	406.75
45000	3889.56	2010.69	1385.36	1073.41	886.82	762.90	674.78	609.05	558.24	517.87	485.08	457.99	435.28	416.00
46000	3976.00	2055.38	1416.15	1097.27	906.53	779.85	689.78	622.59	570.64	529.37	495.86	468.17	444.95	425.24
47000	4062.43	2100.06	1446.93	1121.12	926.23	796.80	704.77	636.12	583.05	540.88	506.64	478.35	454.62	434.49
48000	4148.86	2144.74	1477.72	1144.98	945.94	813.76	719.77	649.66	595.46	552.39	517.42	488.53	464.29	443.73
49000	4235.30	2189.42	1508.51	1168.83	965.65	830.71	734.76	663.19	607.86	563.90	528.20	498.70	473.97	452.97
50000	4321.73	2234.10	1539.29	1192.68	985.35	847.66	749.76	676.73	620.27	575.41	538.98	508.88	483.64	462.22
55000	4753.91	2457.51	1693.22	1311.95	1083.89	932.43	824.74	744.40	682.29	632.95	592.88	559.77	532.00	508.44
60000	5186.08	2680.92	1847.15	1431.22	1182.42	1017.19	899.71	812.07	744.32	690.49	646.78	610.66	580.37	554.66
65000	5618.25	2904.33	2001.08	1550.49	1280.96	1101.96	974.69	879.74	806.34	748.03	700.67	661.54	628.73	600.88
70000	6050.43	3127.74	2155.01	1669.76	1379.49	1186.72	1049.66	947.41	868.37	805.57	754.57	712.43	677.09	647.10
75000	6482.60	3351.15	2308.94	1789.02	1478.03	1271.49	1124.64	1015.09	930.40	863.11	808.47	763.32	725.46	693.32
80000	6914.77	3574.56	2462.86	1908.29	1576.56	1356.26	1199.61	1082.76	992.42	920.65	862.37	814.21	773.82	739.55
85000	7346.94	3797.97	2616.79	2027.56	1675.10	1441.02	1274.59	1150.43	1054.45	978.19	916.27	865.09	822.19	785.77
90000	7779.12	4021.38	2770.72	2146.83	1773.63	1525.79	1349.56	1218.10	1116.47	1035.73	970.16	915.98	870.55	831.99
95000	8211.29	4244.79	2924.65	2266.09	1872.17	1610.55	1424.54	1285.77	1178.50	1093.27	1024.06	966.87	918.91	878.21
100000	8643.46	4468.20	3078.58	2385.36	1970.70	1695.32	1499.52	1353.45	1240.53	1150.81	1077.96	1017.76	967.28	924.43

TERM	15 Years	16 Years	17 Years	18 Years	19 Years	20 Years	21 Years	22 Years	23 Years	24 Years	25 Years	30 Years	35 Years	40 Years
AMOUNT														
5	.05	.05	.05	.05	.04	.04	.04	.04	.04	.04	.04	.04	.04	.04
10	.09	.09	.09	.09	.08	.08	.08	.08	.08	.08	.07	.07	.07	.07
15	.14	.13	.13	.13	.12	.12	.12	.11	.11	.11	.11	.10	.10	.10
25	.23	.22	.21	.21	.20	.20	.19	.19	.18	.18	.18	.17	.16	.16
50	.45	.43	.42	.41	.40	.39	.38	.37	.36	.36	.35	.33	.32	.31
75	.67	.65	.63	.61	.59	.58	.56	.55	.54	.53	.53	.49	.47	.46
100	.89	.86	.83	.81	.79	.77	.75	.74	.72	.71	.70	.66	.63	.61
200	1.78	1.72	1.66	1.61	1.57	1.53	1.50	1.47	1.44	1.42	1.39	1.31	1.25	1.22
300	2.67	2.57	2.49	2.42	2.35	2.30	2.24	2.20	2.16	2.12	2.09	1.96	1.88	1.83
400	3.56	3.43	3.32	3.22	3.13	3.06	2.99	2.93	2.88	2.83	2.78	2.61	2.50	2.43
500	4.44	4.28	4.15	4.02	3.92	3.82	3.74	3.66	3.59	3.53	3.48	3.26	3.13	3.04
600	5.33	5.14	4.97	4.83	4.70	4.59	4.48	4.39	4.31	4.24	4.17	3.92	3.75	3.65
700	6.22	6.00	5.80	5.63	5.48	5.35	5.23	5.12	5.03	4.94	4.86	4.57	4.38	4.25
800	7.11	6.85	6.63	6.44	6.26	6.11	5.98	5.85	5.75	5.65	5.56	5.22	5.00	4.86
900	7.99	7.71	7.46	7.24	7.05	6.88	6.72	6.59	6.46	6.35	6.25	5.87	5.63	5.47
1000	8.88	8.56	8.29	8.04	7.83	7.64	7.47	7.32	7.18	7.06	6.95	6.52	6.25	6.07
2000	17.76	17.12	16.57	16.08	15.65	15.27	14.93	14.63	14.36	14.11	13.89	13.04	12.50	12.14
3000	26.64	25.68	24.85	24.12	23.48	22.91	22.40	21.94	21.53	21.16	20.83	19.56	18.75	18.21
4000	35.51	34.24	33.13	32.16	31.30	30.54	29.86	29.25	28.71	28.21	27.77	26.08	25.00	24.28
5000	44.39	42.80	41.41	40.20	39.12	38.17	37.32	36.56	35.88	35.26	34.71	32.60	31.25	30.35
6000	53.27	51.36	49.70	48.24	46.95	45.81	44.79	43.87	43.06	42.32	41.65	39.12	37.50	36.42
7000	62.14	59.92	57.98	56.28	54.77	53.44	52.25	51.19	50.23	49.37	48.59	45.64	43.75	42.49
8000	71.02	68.48	66.26	64.31	62.60	61.07	59.71	58.50	57.41	56.42	55.53	52.16	50.00	48.56
9000	79.90	77.04	74.54	72.35	70.42	68.71	67.18	65.81	64.58	63.47	62.47	58.68	56.25	54.63
10000	88.77	85.59	82.82	80.39	78.24	76.34	74.64	73.12	71.76	70.52	69.41	65.20	62.49	60.70
11000	97.65	94.15	91.11	88.43	86.07	83.97	82.10	80.43	78.93	77.58	76.35	71.72	68.74	66.77
12000	106.53	102.71	99.39	96.47	93.89	91.61	89.57	87.74	86.11	84.63	83.29	78.24	74.99	72.84
13000	115.40	111.27	107.67	104.51	101.72	99.24	97.03	95.06	93.28	91.68	90.23	84.76	81.24	78.91
14000	124.28	119.83	115.95	112.55	109.54	106.87	104.49	102.37	100.46	98.73	97.18	91.27	87.49	84.98
15000	133.16	128.39	124.23	120.58	117.36	114.51	111.96	109.68	107.63	105.78	104.12	97.79	93.74	91.05
16000	142.03	136.95	132.51	128.62	125.19	122.14	119.42	116.99	114.81	112.84	111.06	104.31	99.99	97.12
17000	150.91	145.51	140.80	136.66	133.01	129.77	126.89	124.30	121.98	119.89	118.00	110.83	106.24	103.19
18000	159.79	154.07	149.08	144.70	140.84	137.41	134.35	131.61	129.16	126.94	124.94	117.35	112.49	109.26
19000	168.66	162.63	157.36	152.74	148.66	145.04	141.81	138.92	136.33	133.99	131.88	123.87	118.73	115.33
20000	177.54	171.18	165.64	160.78	156.48	152.67	149.28	146.24	143.51	141.04	138.82	130.39	124.98	121.40
21000	186.42	179.74	173.92	168.82	164.31	160.31	156.74	153.55	150.68	148.10	145.76	136.91	131.23	127.47
22000	195.30	188.30	182.21	176.85	172.13	167.94	164.20	160.86	157.86	155.15	152.70	143.43	137.48	133.54
23000	204.17	196.86	190.49	184.89	179.95	175.57	171.67	168.17	165.03	162.20	159.64	149.95	143.73	139.61
24000	213.05	205.42	198.77	192.93	187.78	183.21	179.13	175.48	172.21	169.25	166.58	156.47	149.98	145.67
25000	221.93	213.98	207.05	200.97	195.60	190.84	186.59	182.79	179.38	176.30	173.52	162.99	156.23	151.74
26000	230.80	222.54	215.33	209.01	203.43	198.47	194.06	190.11	186.56	183.36	180.46	169.51	162.48	157.81
27000	239.68	231.10	223.61	217.05	211.25	206.11	201.52	197.42	193.73	190.41	187.40	176.02	168.73	163.88
28000	248.56	239.66	231.90	225.09	219.07	213.74	208.98	204.73	200.91	197.46	194.35	182.54	174.97	169.95
29000	257.43	248.21	240.18	233.12	226.90	221.37	216.45	212.04	208.08	204.51	201.29	189.06	181.22	176.02
30000	266.31	256.77	248.46	241.16	234.72	229.01	223.91	219.35	215.26	211.56	208.23	195.58	187.47	182.09
31000	275.19	265.33	256.74	249.20	242.55	236.64	231.38	226.66	222.43	218.62	215.17	202.10	193.72	188.16
32000	284.06	273.89	265.02	257.24	250.37	244.27	238.84	233.98	229.61	225.67	222.11	208.62	199.97	194.23
33000	292.94	282.45	273.31	265.28	258.19	251.91	246.30	241.29	236.78	232.72	229.05	215.14	206.22	200.30
34000	301.82	291.01	281.59	273.32	266.02	259.54	253.77	248.60	243.96	239.77	235.99	221.66	212.47	206.37
35000	310.69	299.57	289.87	281.36	273.84	267.17	261.23	255.91	251.13	246.82	242.93	228.18	218.72	212.44
36000	319.57	308.13	298.15	289.40	281.67	274.81	268.69	263.22	258.31	253.88	249.87	234.70	224.97	218.51
37000	328.45	316.69	306.43	297.43	289.49	282.44	276.16	270.53	265.48	260.93	256.81	241.22	231.21	224.58
38000	337.32	325.25	314.71	305.47	297.31	290.07	283.62	277.84	272.66	267.98	263.75	247.74	237.46	230.65
39000	346.20	333.80	323.00	313.51	305.14	297.71	291.08	285.16	279.83	275.03	270.69	254.26	243.71	236.72
40000	355.08	342.36	331.28	321.55	312.96	305.34	298.55	292.47	287.01	282.08	277.63	260.78	249.96	242.79
41000	363.96	350.92	339.56	329.59	320.79	312.97	306.01	299.78	294.18	289.14	284.57	267.29	256.21	248.86
42000	372.83	359.48	347.84	337.63	328.61	320.61	313.47	307.09	301.36	296.19	291.52	273.81	262.46	254.93
43000	381.71	368.04	356.12	345.67	336.43	328.24	320.94	314.40	308.53	303.24	298.46	280.33	268.71	261.00
44000	390.59	376.60	364.41	353.70	344.26	335.87	328.40	321.71	315.71	310.29	305.40	286.85	274.96	267.07
45000	399.46	385.16	372.69	361.74	352.08	343.51	335.87	329.03	322.88	317.34	312.34	293.37	281.21	273.14
46000	408.34	393.72	380.97	369.78	359.90	351.14	343.33	336.34	330.06	324.40	319.28	299.89	287.45	279.21
47000	417.22	402.28	389.25	377.82	367.73	358.77	350.79	343.65	337.23	331.45	326.22	306.41	293.70	285.28
48000	426.09	410.84	397.53	385.86	375.55	366.41	358.26	350.96	344.41	338.50	333.16	312.93	299.95	291.34
49000	434.97	419.39	405.81	393.90	383.38	374.04	365.72	358.27	351.58	345.55	340.10	319.45	306.20	297.41
50000	443.85	427.95	414.10	401.94	391.20	381.67	373.18	365.58	358.76	352.60	347.04	325.97	312.45	303.48
55000	488.23	470.75	455.51	442.13	430.32	419.84	410.50	402.14	394.63	387.86	381.74	358.56	343.69	333.83
60000	532.62	513.54	496.91	482.32	469.44	458.01	447.82	438.70	430.51	423.12	416.45	391.16	374.94	364.18
65000	577.00	556.34	538.32	522.51	508.56	496.18	485.14	475.26	466.38	458.38	451.15	423.76	406.18	394.53
70000	621.38	599.13	579.73	562.71	547.68	534.34	522.45	511.81	502.26	493.64	485.86	456.35	437.43	424.88
75000	665.77	641.93	621.14	602.90	586.80	572.51	559.77	548.37	538.13	528.90	520.56	488.95	468.67	455.22
80000	710.15	684.72	662.55	643.09	625.92	610.68	597.09	584.93	574.01	564.16	555.26	521.55	499.92	485.57
85000	754.54	727.52	703.96	683.29	665.04	648.84	634.41	621.49	609.88	599.42	589.97	554.14	531.16	515.92
90000	798.92	770.31	745.37	723.48	704.16	687.01	671.73	658.05	645.76	634.68	624.67	586.74	562.41	546.27
95000	843.30	813.11	786.78	763.67	743.28	725.18	709.04	694.60	681.63	669.94	659.37	619.33	593.65	576.62
100000	887.69	855.90	828.19	803.87	782.40	763.34	746.36	731.16	717.51	705.20	694.08	651.93	624.90	606.96

MONTHLY PAYMENT
REQUIRED TO AMORTIZE A LOAN

TERM / AMOUNT	1 Year	2 Years	3 Years	4 Years	5 Years	6 Years	7 Years	8 Years	9 Years	10 Years	11 Years	12 Years	13 Years	14 Years
5	.44	.23	.16	.12	.10	.09	.08	.07	.07	.06	.06	.06	.05	.05
10	.87	.45	.31	.24	.20	.17	.16	.14	.13	.12	.11	.11	.10	.10
15	1.30	.68	.47	.36	.30	.26	.23	.21	.19	.18	.17	.16	.15	.14
25	2.17	1.12	.78	.60	.50	.43	.38	.34	.32	.29	.28	.26	.25	.24
50	4.33	2.24	1.55	1.20	.99	.85	.76	.68	.63	.58	.55	.52	.49	.47
75	6.49	3.36	2.32	1.80	1.49	1.28	1.13	1.02	.94	.87	.82	.77	.73	.70
100	8.65	4.48	3.09	2.39	1.98	1.70	1.51	1.36	1.25	1.16	1.09	1.03	.98	.93
200	17.30	8.95	6.17	4.78	3.95	3.40	3.01	2.72	2.49	2.31	2.17	2.05	1.95	1.86
300	25.95	13.42	9.25	7.17	5.93	5.10	4.51	4.08	3.74	3.47	3.25	3.07	2.92	2.79
400	34.59	17.89	12.33	9.56	7.90	6.80	6.02	5.43	4.98	4.62	4.33	4.09	3.89	3.72
500	43.24	22.36	15.41	11.95	9.88	8.50	7.52	6.79	6.23	5.78	5.41	5.11	4.86	4.65
600	51.89	26.83	18.50	14.34	11.85	10.20	9.02	8.15	7.47	6.93	6.50	6.14	5.83	5.58
700	60.53	31.31	21.58	16.73	13.82	11.90	10.53	9.51	8.72	8.09	7.58	7.16	6.80	6.50
800	69.18	35.78	24.66	19.12	15.80	13.60	12.03	10.86	9.96	9.24	8.66	8.18	7.78	7.43
900	77.83	40.25	27.74	21.50	17.77	15.30	13.53	12.22	11.20	10.40	9.74	9.20	8.75	8.36
1000	86.47	44.72	30.82	23.89	19.75	16.99	15.04	13.58	12.45	11.55	10.82	10.22	9.72	9.29
2000	172.94	89.44	61.64	47.78	39.49	33.98	30.07	27.15	24.89	23.10	21.64	20.44	19.43	18.58
3000	259.41	134.15	92.46	71.67	59.23	50.97	45.10	40.72	37.33	34.64	32.46	30.66	29.14	27.86
4000	345.88	178.87	123.28	95.56	78.97	67.96	60.13	54.29	49.78	46.19	43.28	40.87	38.86	37.15
5000	432.35	223.58	154.10	119.45	98.72	84.95	75.16	67.86	62.22	57.74	54.10	51.09	48.57	46.43
6000	518.82	268.30	184.92	143.33	118.46	101.94	90.19	81.43	74.66	69.28	64.92	61.31	58.28	55.72
7000	605.29	313.02	215.74	167.22	138.20	118.93	105.23	95.01	87.11	80.83	75.74	71.53	68.00	65.00
8000	691.76	357.73	246.56	191.11	157.94	135.92	120.26	108.58	99.55	92.38	86.55	81.74	77.71	74.29
9000	778.23	402.45	277.38	215.00	177.69	152.91	135.29	122.15	111.99	103.92	97.37	91.96	87.42	83.57
10000	864.70	447.16	308.20	238.89	197.43	169.90	150.32	135.72	124.44	115.47	108.19	102.18	97.14	92.86
11000	951.17	491.88	339.02	262.78	217.17	186.88	165.35	149.29	136.88	127.02	119.01	112.40	106.85	102.14
12000	1037.63	536.60	369.84	286.66	236.91	203.87	180.38	162.86	149.32	138.56	129.83	122.61	116.56	111.43
13000	1124.10	581.31	400.66	310.55	256.65	220.86	195.42	176.44	161.76	150.11	140.65	132.83	126.28	120.71
14000	1210.57	626.03	431.48	334.44	276.40	237.85	210.45	190.01	174.21	161.66	151.47	143.05	135.99	130.00
15000	1297.04	670.74	462.30	358.33	296.14	254.84	225.48	203.58	186.65	173.20	162.29	153.26	145.70	139.28
16000	1383.51	715.46	493.12	382.22	315.88	271.83	240.51	217.15	199.09	184.75	173.10	163.48	155.42	148.57
17000	1469.98	760.18	523.94	406.11	335.62	288.82	255.54	230.72	211.54	196.30	183.92	173.70	165.13	157.86
18000	1556.45	804.89	554.76	429.99	355.37	305.81	270.57	244.29	223.98	207.84	194.74	183.92	174.84	167.14
19000	1642.92	849.61	585.58	453.88	375.11	322.80	285.61	257.87	236.42	219.39	205.56	194.13	184.55	176.43
20000	1729.39	894.32	616.40	477.77	394.85	339.79	300.64	271.44	248.87	230.94	216.38	204.35	194.27	185.71
21000	1815.86	939.04	647.22	501.66	414.59	356.77	315.67	285.01	261.31	242.48	227.20	214.57	203.98	195.00
22000	1902.33	983.76	678.04	525.55	434.34	373.76	330.70	298.58	273.75	254.03	238.02	224.79	213.69	204.28
23000	1988.80	1028.47	708.86	549.44	454.08	390.75	345.73	312.15	286.20	265.58	248.83	235.00	223.41	213.57
24000	2075.26	1073.19	739.68	573.32	473.82	407.74	360.76	325.72	298.64	277.12	259.65	245.22	233.12	222.85
25000	2161.73	1117.90	770.50	597.21	493.56	424.73	375.80	339.29	311.08	288.67	270.47	255.44	242.83	232.14
26000	2248.20	1162.62	801.32	621.10	513.30	441.72	390.83	352.87	323.52	300.21	281.29	265.65	252.55	241.42
27000	2334.67	1207.34	832.14	644.99	533.05	458.71	405.86	366.44	335.97	311.76	292.11	275.87	262.26	250.71
28000	2421.14	1252.05	862.96	668.88	552.79	475.70	420.89	380.01	348.41	323.31	302.93	286.09	271.97	259.99
29000	2507.61	1296.77	893.78	692.77	572.53	492.69	435.92	393.58	360.85	334.85	313.75	296.31	281.69	269.28
30000	2594.08	1341.48	924.60	716.65	592.27	509.68	450.95	407.15	373.30	346.40	324.57	306.52	291.40	278.56
31000	2680.55	1386.20	955.42	740.54	612.02	526.67	465.99	420.72	385.74	357.95	335.38	316.74	301.11	287.85
32000	2767.02	1430.91	986.24	764.43	631.76	543.65	481.02	434.30	398.18	369.49	346.20	326.96	310.83	297.14
33000	2853.49	1475.63	1017.06	788.32	651.50	560.64	496.05	447.87	410.63	381.04	357.02	337.18	320.54	306.42
34000	2939.96	1520.35	1047.88	812.21	671.24	577.63	511.08	461.44	423.07	392.59	367.84	347.39	330.25	315.71
35000	3026.42	1565.06	1078.70	836.10	690.98	594.62	526.11	475.01	435.51	404.13	378.66	357.61	339.97	324.99
36000	3112.89	1609.78	1109.52	859.98	710.73	611.61	541.14	488.58	447.96	415.68	389.48	367.83	349.68	334.28
37000	3199.36	1654.49	1140.34	883.87	730.47	628.60	556.18	502.15	460.40	427.23	400.30	378.05	359.39	343.56
38000	3285.83	1699.21	1171.16	907.76	750.21	645.59	571.21	515.73	472.84	438.77	411.11	388.26	369.10	352.85
39000	3372.30	1743.93	1201.98	931.65	769.95	662.58	586.24	529.30	485.28	450.32	421.93	398.48	378.82	362.13
40000	3458.77	1788.64	1232.80	955.54	789.70	679.57	601.27	542.87	497.73	461.87	432.75	408.70	388.53	371.42
41000	3545.24	1833.36	1263.62	979.43	809.44	696.56	616.30	556.44	510.17	473.41	443.57	418.91	398.24	380.70
42000	3631.71	1878.07	1294.44	1003.31	829.18	713.54	631.33	570.01	522.61	484.96	454.39	429.13	407.96	389.99
43000	3718.18	1922.79	1325.26	1027.20	848.92	730.53	646.37	583.58	535.06	496.51	465.21	439.35	417.67	399.27
44000	3804.65	1967.51	1356.08	1051.09	868.67	747.52	661.40	597.16	547.50	508.05	476.03	449.57	427.38	408.56
45000	3891.12	2012.22	1386.90	1074.98	888.41	764.51	676.43	610.73	559.94	519.60	486.85	459.78	437.10	417.84
46000	3977.59	2056.94	1417.72	1098.87	908.15	781.50	691.46	624.30	572.39	531.15	497.66	470.00	446.81	427.13
47000	4064.05	2101.65	1448.54	1122.75	927.89	798.49	706.49	637.87	584.83	542.69	508.48	480.22	456.52	436.42
48000	4150.52	2146.37	1479.36	1146.64	947.63	815.48	721.52	651.44	597.27	554.24	519.30	490.44	466.24	445.70
49000	4236.99	2191.09	1510.18	1170.53	967.38	832.47	736.56	665.01	609.71	565.78	530.12	500.65	475.95	454.99
50000	4323.46	2235.80	1541.00	1194.42	987.12	849.46	751.59	678.58	622.16	577.33	540.94	510.87	485.66	464.27
55000	4755.81	2459.38	1695.10	1313.86	1085.83	934.40	826.75	746.44	684.37	635.06	595.03	561.96	534.23	510.70
60000	5188.15	2682.96	1849.20	1433.30	1184.54	1019.35	901.90	814.30	746.59	692.80	649.13	613.04	582.79	557.12
65000	5620.50	2906.54	2003.30	1552.74	1283.25	1104.29	977.06	882.16	808.80	750.53	703.22	664.13	631.36	603.55
70000	6052.84	3130.12	2157.40	1672.19	1381.96	1189.24	1052.22	950.02	871.02	808.26	757.31	715.22	679.93	649.98
75000	6485.19	3353.70	2311.50	1791.63	1480.68	1274.18	1127.38	1017.87	933.23	865.99	811.41	766.30	728.49	696.40
80000	6917.54	3577.28	2465.60	1911.07	1579.39	1359.13	1202.54	1085.73	995.45	923.73	865.50	817.39	777.06	742.83
85000	7349.88	3800.86	2619.70	2030.51	1678.10	1444.07	1277.70	1153.59	1057.66	981.46	919.59	868.48	825.62	789.26
90000	7782.23	4024.44	2773.80	2149.95	1776.81	1529.02	1352.85	1221.45	1119.88	1039.19	973.69	919.56	874.19	835.68
95000	8214.57	4248.02	2927.90	2269.39	1875.52	1613.96	1428.01	1289.31	1182.10	1096.93	1027.78	970.65	922.75	882.11
100000	8646.92	4471.60	3082.00	2388.83	1974.23	1698.91	1503.17	1357.16	1244.31	1154.66	1081.87	1021.73	971.32	928.54

TERM	15 Years	16 Years	17 Years	18 Years	19 Years	20 Years	21 Years	22 Years	23 Years	24 Years	25 Years	30 Years	35 Years	40 Years
AMOUNT														
5	.05	.05	.05	.05	.04	.04	.04	.04	.04	.04	.04	.04	.04	.04
10	.09	.09	.09	.09	.08	.08	.08	.08	.08	.08	.07	.07	.07	.07
15	.14	.13	.13	.13	.12	.12	.12	.12	.11	.11	.11	.10	.10	.10
25	.23	.22	.21	.21	.20	.20	.19	.19	.19	.18	.18	.17	.16	.16
50	.45	.44	.42	.41	.40	.39	.38	.37	.37	.36	.35	.33	.32	.31
75	.67	.65	.63	.61	.60	.58	.57	.56	.55	.54	.53	.50	.48	.46
100	.90	.87	.84	.81	.79	.77	.76	.74	.73	.71	.70	.66	.64	.62
200	1.79	1.73	1.67	1.62	1.58	1.54	1.51	1.48	1.45	1.42	1.40	1.32	1.27	1.23
300	2.68	2.59	2.50	2.43	2.37	2.31	2.26	2.21	2.17	2.13	2.10	1.98	1.90	1.84
400	3.57	3.45	3.33	3.24	3.15	3.08	3.01	2.95	2.89	2.84	2.80	2.63	2.53	2.45
500	4.46	4.31	4.17	4.05	3.94	3.84	3.76	3.68	3.62	3.55	3.50	3.29	3.16	3.07
600	5.36	5.17	5.00	4.85	4.73	4.61	4.51	4.42	4.34	4.26	4.20	3.95	3.79	3.68
700	6.25	6.03	5.83	5.66	5.51	5.38	5.26	5.16	5.06	4.97	4.90	4.60	4.42	4.29
800	7.14	6.89	6.66	6.47	6.30	6.15	6.01	5.89	5.78	5.68	5.60	5.26	5.05	4.90
900	8.03	7.75	7.50	7.28	7.09	6.92	6.76	6.63	6.50	6.39	6.29	5.92	5.68	5.52
1000	8.92	8.61	8.33	8.09	7.87	7.68	7.51	7.36	7.23	7.10	6.99	6.57	6.31	6.13
2000	17.84	17.21	16.65	16.17	15.74	15.36	15.02	14.72	14.45	14.20	13.98	13.14	12.61	12.25
3000	26.76	25.81	24.98	24.25	23.61	23.04	22.53	22.08	21.67	21.30	20.97	19.71	18.91	18.38
4000	35.68	34.41	33.30	32.33	31.48	30.72	30.04	29.43	28.89	28.40	27.96	26.28	25.21	24.50
5000	44.60	43.01	41.63	40.42	39.35	38.40	37.55	36.79	36.11	35.50	34.95	32.85	31.51	30.62
6000	53.52	51.61	49.95	48.50	47.21	46.07	45.06	44.15	43.33	42.60	41.93	39.42	37.81	36.75
7000	62.43	60.21	58.28	56.58	55.08	53.75	52.57	51.51	50.56	49.70	48.92	45.99	44.11	42.87
8000	71.35	68.82	66.60	64.66	62.95	61.43	60.08	58.86	57.78	56.80	55.91	52.56	50.41	48.99
9000	80.27	77.42	74.93	72.74	70.82	69.11	67.59	66.22	65.00	63.90	62.90	59.13	56.72	55.12
10000	89.19	86.02	83.25	80.83	78.69	76.79	75.09	73.58	72.22	70.99	69.89	65.70	63.02	61.24
11000	98.11	94.62	91.58	88.91	86.55	84.46	82.60	80.94	79.44	78.09	76.88	72.27	69.32	67.37
12000	107.03	103.22	99.90	96.99	94.42	92.14	90.11	88.29	86.66	85.19	83.86	78.84	75.62	73.49
13000	115.95	111.82	108.23	105.07	102.29	99.82	97.62	95.65	93.88	92.29	90.85	85.41	81.92	79.61
14000	124.86	120.42	116.55	113.16	110.16	107.50	105.13	103.01	101.11	99.39	97.84	91.98	88.22	85.74
15000	133.78	129.02	124.88	121.24	118.03	115.18	112.64	110.37	108.33	106.49	104.83	98.54	94.52	91.86
16000	142.70	137.63	133.20	129.32	125.89	122.86	120.15	117.72	115.55	113.59	111.82	105.11	100.82	97.98
17000	151.62	146.23	141.53	137.40	133.76	130.53	127.66	125.08	122.77	120.69	110.01	111.68	107.12	104.11
18000	160.54	154.83	149.05	145.48	141.63	138.21	135.17	132.44	129.99	127.79	125.79	118.25	113.43	110.23
19000	169.46	163.43	158.18	153.57	149.50	145.89	142.67	139.80	137.21	134.89	132.78	124.82	119.73	116.36
20000	178.38	172.03	166.50	161.65	157.37	153.57	150.18	147.15	144.43	141.98	139.77	131.39	126.03	122.48
21000	187.29	180.63	174.83	169.73	165.23	161.25	157.69	154.51	151.66	149.08	146.76	137.96	132.33	128.60
22000	196.21	189.23	183.15	177.81	173.10	168.92	165.20	161.87	158.88	156.18	153.75	144.53	138.63	134.73
23000	205.13	197.83	191.47	185.89	180.97	176.60	172.71	169.23	166.10	163.28	160.73	151.10	144.93	140.85
24000	214.05	206.44	199.80	193.98	188.84	184.28	180.22	176.58	173.32	170.38	167.72	157.67	151.23	146.97
25000	222.97	215.04	208.12	202.06	196.71	191.96	187.73	183.94	180.54	177.48	174.71	164.24	157.53	153.10
26000	231.89	223.64	216.45	210.14	204.57	199.64	195.24	191.30	187.76	184.58	181.70	170.81	163.83	159.22
27000	240.81	232.24	224.77	218.22	212.44	207.31	202.75	198.66	194.98	191.68	188.69	177.38	170.14	165.35
28000	249.72	240.84	233.10	226.31	220.31	214.99	210.25	206.02	202.21	198.78	195.68	183.95	176.44	171.47
29000	258.64	249.44	241.42	234.39	228.18	222.67	217.76	213.37	209.43	205.87	202.66	190.51	182.74	177.59
30000	267.56	258.04	249.75	242.47	236.05	230.35	225.27	220.73	216.65	212.97	209.65	197.08	189.04	183.72
31000	276.48	266.64	258.07	250.55	243.91	238.03	232.78	228.09	223.87	220.07	216.64	203.65	195.34	189.84
32000	285.40	275.25	266.40	258.63	251.78	245.71	240.29	235.44	231.09	227.17	223.63	210.22	201.64	195.96
33000	294.32	283.85	274.72	266.72	259.65	253.38	247.80	242.80	238.31	234.27	230.62	216.79	207.94	202.09
34000	303.24	292.45	283.05	274.80	267.52	261.06	255.31	250.16	245.53	241.37	237.61	223.36	214.24	208.21
35000	312.15	301.05	291.37	282.88	275.39	268.74	262.82	257.52	252.76	248.47	244.59	229.93	220.55	214.34
36000	321.07	309.65	299.70	290.96	283.26	276.42	270.33	264.87	259.98	255.57	251.58	236.50	226.85	220.46
37000	329.99	318.25	308.02	299.05	291.12	284.10	277.83	272.23	267.20	262.67	258.57	243.07	233.15	226.58
38000	338.91	326.85	316.35	307.13	298.99	291.77	285.34	279.59	274.42	269.77	265.56	249.64	239.45	232.71
39000	347.83	335.46	324.67	315.21	306.86	299.45	292.85	286.95	281.64	276.86	272.55	256.21	245.75	238.83
40000	356.75	344.06	333.00	323.29	314.73	307.13	300.36	294.30	288.86	283.96	279.54	262.78	252.05	244.95
41000	365.67	352.66	341.32	331.37	322.60	314.81	307.87	301.66	296.09	291.06	286.52	269.35	258.35	251.08
42000	374.58	361.26	349.65	339.46	330.46	322.49	315.38	309.02	303.31	298.16	293.51	275.92	264.65	257.20
43000	383.50	369.86	357.97	347.54	338.33	330.16	322.89	316.38	310.53	305.26	300.50	282.48	270.95	263.33
44000	392.42	378.46	366.30	355.62	346.20	337.84	330.40	323.73	317.75	312.36	307.49	289.05	277.26	269.45
45000	401.34	387.06	374.62	363.70	354.07	345.52	337.91	331.09	324.97	319.46	314.48	295.62	283.56	275.57
46000	410.26	395.66	382.94	371.78	361.94	353.20	345.41	338.45	332.19	326.56	321.46	302.19	289.86	281.70
47000	419.18	404.27	391.27	379.87	369.80	360.88	352.92	345.81	339.41	333.66	328.45	308.76	296.16	287.82
48000	428.10	412.87	399.59	387.95	377.67	368.56	360.43	353.16	346.64	340.75	335.44	315.33	302.46	293.94
49000	437.01	421.47	407.92	396.03	385.54	376.23	367.94	360.52	353.86	347.85	342.43	321.90	308.76	300.07
50000	445.93	430.07	416.24	404.11	393.41	383.91	375.45	367.88	361.08	354.95	349.42	328.47	315.06	306.19
55000	490.52	473.08	457.87	444.52	432.75	422.30	412.99	404.67	397.19	390.45	384.36	361.32	346.57	336.81
60000	535.12	516.08	499.49	484.94	472.09	460.69	450.54	441.45	433.29	425.94	419.30	394.16	378.07	367.43
65000	579.71	559.09	541.12	525.35	511.43	499.08	488.08	478.24	469.40	461.44	454.24	427.01	409.58	398.05
70000	624.30	602.10	582.74	565.76	550.77	537.47	525.63	515.03	505.51	496.93	489.18	459.86	441.09	428.67
75000	668.90	645.10	624.36	606.17	590.11	575.87	563.17	551.81	541.62	532.43	524.12	492.70	472.59	459.28
80000	713.49	688.11	665.99	646.58	629.45	614.26	600.72	588.60	577.72	567.92	559.07	525.55	504.10	489.90
85000	758.08	731.11	707.61	686.99	668.79	652.65	638.26	625.39	613.83	603.42	594.01	558.39	535.60	520.52
90000	802.67	774.12	749.23	727.40	708.13	691.04	675.80	662.18	649.94	638.91	628.95	591.24	567.11	551.14
95000	847.27	817.13	790.86	767.81	747.47	729.43	713.35	698.96	686.04	674.41	663.89	624.09	598.61	581.76
100000	891.86	860.13	832.48	808.22	786.81	767.82	750.89	735.75	722.15	709.90	698.83	656.93	630.12	612.38

MONTHLY PAYMENT
REQUIRED TO AMORTIZE A LOAN

TERM AMOUNT	1 Year	2 Years	3 Years	4 Years	5 Years	6 Years	7 Years	8 Years	9 Years	10 Years	11 Years	12 Years	13 Years	14 Years
5	.44	.23	.16	.12	.10	.09	.08	.07	.07	.06	.06	.06	.05	.05
10	.87	.45	.31	.24	.20	.18	.16	.14	.13	.12	.11	.11	.10	.10
15	1.30	.68	.47	.36	.30	.26	.23	.21	.19	.18	.17	.16	.15	.14
25	2.17	1.12	.78	.60	.50	.43	.38	.34	.32	.29	.28	.26	.25	.24
50	4.33	2.24	1.55	1.20	.99	.86	.76	.68	.63	.58	.55	.52	.49	.47
75	6.49	3.36	2.32	1.80	1.49	1.28	1.13	1.02	.94	.87	.82	.77	.73	.70
100	8.65	4.48	3.09	2.39	1.98	1.71	1.51	1.36	1.25	1.16	1.09	1.03	.98	.93
200	17.30	8.95	6.17	4.78	3.96	3.41	3.01	2.72	2.50	2.32	2.17	2.05	1.95	1.86
300	25.95	13.42	9.25	7.17	5.93	5.11	4.52	4.08	3.74	3.47	3.25	3.07	2.92	2.79
400	34.60	17.90	12.34	9.56	7.91	6.81	6.02	5.44	4.99	4.63	4.34	4.10	3.90	3.72
500	43.25	22.37	15.42	11.95	9.88	8.51	7.53	6.80	6.23	5.78	5.42	5.12	4.87	4.65
600	51.89	26.84	18.50	14.34	11.86	10.21	9.03	8.16	7.48	6.94	6.50	6.14	5.84	5.58
700	60.54	31.31	21.59	16.73	13.83	11.91	10.54	9.51	8.72	8.10	7.59	7.17	6.81	6.51
800	69.19	35.79	24.67	19.12	15.81	13.61	12.04	10.87	9.97	9.25	8.67	8.19	7.79	7.44
900	77.84	40.26	27.75	21.51	17.78	15.31	13.54	12.23	11.22	10.41	9.75	9.21	8.76	8.37
1000	86.49	44.73	30.84	23.90	19.76	17.01	15.05	13.59	12.46	11.56	10.84	10.24	9.73	9.30
2000	172.97	89.46	61.67	47.80	39.51	34.01	30.09	27.17	24.92	23.12	21.67	20.47	19.46	18.60
3000	259.45	134.19	92.50	71.70	59.27	51.01	45.14	40.76	37.37	34.68	32.50	30.70	29.18	27.90
4000	345.93	178.91	123.33	95.60	79.02	68.01	60.18	54.34	49.83	46.24	43.33	40.93	38.91	37.20
5000	432.41	223.64	154.16	119.50	98.78	85.01	75.22	67.93	62.28	57.80	54.16	51.16	48.64	46.50
6000	518.89	268.37	184.99	143.40	118.53	102.01	90.27	81.51	74.74	69.36	65.00	61.39	58.36	55.80
7000	605.37	313.10	215.82	167.30	138.28	119.01	105.31	95.09	87.19	80.92	75.83	71.62	68.09	65.10
8000	691.85	357.82	246.66	191.20	158.04	136.01	120.36	108.68	99.65	92.48	86.66	81.85	77.82	74.40
9000	778.33	402.55	277.49	215.10	177.79	153.01	135.40	122.26	112.11	104.04	97.49	92.08	87.54	83.70
10000	864.81	447.28	308.32	239.00	197.55	170.02	150.44	135.85	124.56	115.60	108.32	102.31	97.27	93.00
11000	951.29	492.00	339.15	262.90	217.30	187.02	165.49	149.43	137.02	127.16	119.15	112.54	107.00	102.29
12000	1037.77	536.73	369.98	286.80	237.05	204.02	180.53	163.01	149.47	138.72	129.99	122.77	116.72	111.59
13000	1124.25	581.46	400.81	310.70	256.81	221.02	195.57	176.60	161.93	150.28	140.82	133.00	126.45	120.89
14000	1210.73	626.19	431.64	334.60	276.56	238.02	210.62	190.18	174.38	161.84	151.65	143.23	136.18	130.19
15000	1297.21	670.91	462.48	358.50	296.32	255.02	225.66	203.77	186.84	173.40	162.48	153.46	145.90	139.49
16000	1383.70	715.64	493.31	382.40	316.07	272.02	240.71	217.35	199.30	184.96	173.31	163.69	155.63	148.79
17000	1470.18	760.37	524.14	406.30	335.82	289.02	255.75	230.93	211.75	196.51	184.14	173.92	165.36	158.09
18000	1556.66	805.10	554.97	430.20	355.58	306.02	270.79	244.52	224.21	208.07	194.98	184.16	175.08	167.39
19000	1643.14	849.82	585.80	454.10	375.33	323.02	285.84	258.10	236.66	219.63	205.81	194.39	184.81	176.69
20000	1729.62	894.55	616.63	478.00	395.09	340.03	300.88	271.69	249.12	231.19	216.64	204.62	194.54	185.99
21000	1816.10	939.28	647.46	501.90	414.84	357.03	315.93	285.27	261.57	242.75	227.47	214.85	204.26	195.28
22000	1902.58	984.00	678.30	525.80	434.59	374.03	330.97	298.85	274.03	254.31	238.30	225.08	213.99	204.58
23000	1989.06	1028.73	709.13	549.70	454.35	391.03	346.01	312.44	286.49	265.87	249.14	235.31	223.72	213.88
24000	2075.54	1073.46	739.96	573.60	474.10	408.03	361.06	326.02	298.94	277.43	259.97	245.54	233.44	223.18
25000	2162.02	1118.19	770.79	597.50	493.86	425.03	376.10	339.61	311.40	288.99	270.80	255.77	243.17	232.48
26000	2248.50	1162.91	801.62	621.40	513.61	442.03	391.14	353.19	323.85	300.55	281.63	266.00	252.90	241.78
27000	2334.98	1207.64	832.45	645.30	533.36	459.03	406.19	366.77	336.31	312.11	292.46	276.23	262.62	251.08
28000	2421.46	1252.37	863.28	669.20	553.12	476.03	421.23	380.36	348.76	323.67	303.29	286.46	272.35	260.38
29000	2507.94	1297.10	894.12	693.10	572.87	493.03	436.28	393.94	361.22	335.23	314.13	296.69	282.08	269.68
30000	2594.42	1341.82	924.95	717.00	592.63	510.04	451.32	407.53	373.68	346.79	324.96	306.92	291.80	278.98
31000	2680.91	1386.55	955.78	740.90	612.38	527.04	466.36	421.11	386.13	358.35	335.79	317.15	301.53	288.28
32000	2767.39	1431.28	986.61	764.80	632.13	544.04	481.41	434.69	398.59	369.90	346.62	327.38	311.26	297.57
33000	2853.87	1476.00	1017.44	788.70	651.89	561.04	496.45	448.28	411.04	381.46	357.45	337.61	320.98	306.87
34000	2940.35	1520.73	1048.27	812.60	671.64	578.04	511.50	461.86	423.50	393.02	368.28	347.84	330.71	316.17
35000	3026.83	1565.46	1079.10	836.50	691.40	595.04	526.54	475.45	435.95	404.58	379.12	358.08	340.44	325.47
36000	3113.31	1610.19	1109.94	860.40	711.15	612.04	541.58	489.03	448.41	416.14	389.95	368.31	350.16	334.77
37000	3199.79	1654.91	1140.77	884.30	730.90	629.04	556.63	502.61	460.87	427.70	400.78	378.54	359.89	344.07
38000	3286.27	1699.64	1171.60	908.20	750.66	646.04	571.67	516.20	473.32	439.26	411.61	388.77	369.62	353.37
39000	3372.75	1744.37	1202.43	932.10	770.41	663.05	586.71	529.78	485.78	450.82	422.44	399.00	379.34	362.67
40000	3459.23	1789.10	1233.26	956.00	790.17	680.05	601.76	543.37	498.23	462.38	433.27	409.23	389.07	371.97
41000	3545.71	1833.82	1264.09	979.90	809.92	697.05	616.80	556.95	510.69	473.94	444.11	419.46	398.80	381.27
42000	3632.19	1878.55	1294.92	1003.80	829.68	714.05	631.85	570.53	523.14	485.50	454.94	429.69	408.52	390.56
43000	3718.67	1923.28	1325.76	1027.70	849.43	731.05	646.89	584.12	535.60	497.06	465.77	439.92	418.25	399.86
44000	3805.15	1968.00	1356.59	1051.60	869.18	748.05	661.93	597.70	548.06	508.62	476.60	450.15	427.98	409.16
45000	3891.63	2012.73	1387.42	1075.50	888.94	765.05	676.98	611.29	560.51	520.18	487.43	460.38	437.70	418.46
46000	3978.12	2057.46	1418.25	1099.40	908.69	782.05	692.02	624.87	572.97	531.74	498.27	470.61	447.43	427.76
47000	4064.60	2102.19	1449.08	1123.30	928.45	799.05	707.07	638.45	585.42	543.30	509.10	480.84	457.16	437.06
48000	4151.08	2146.91	1479.91	1147.20	948.20	816.05	722.11	652.04	597.88	554.85	519.93	491.07	466.88	446.36
49000	4237.56	2191.64	1510.74	1171.10	967.95	833.06	737.15	665.62	610.33	566.41	530.76	501.30	476.61	455.66
50000	4324.04	2236.37	1541.57	1195.00	987.71	850.06	752.20	679.21	622.79	577.97	541.59	511.53	486.34	464.96
55000	4756.44	2460.00	1695.73	1314.50	1086.48	935.06	827.42	747.13	685.07	635.77	595.75	562.69	534.97	511.45
60000	5188.84	2683.64	1849.89	1434.00	1185.25	1020.07	902.64	815.05	747.35	693.57	649.91	613.84	583.60	557.95
65000	5621.25	2907.28	2004.05	1553.50	1284.02	1105.07	977.85	882.97	809.62	751.36	704.07	664.99	632.24	604.44
70000	6053.65	3130.91	2158.20	1673.00	1382.79	1190.08	1053.07	950.89	871.90	809.16	758.23	716.15	680.87	650.94
75000	6486.05	3354.55	2312.36	1792.50	1481.56	1275.08	1128.29	1018.81	934.18	866.96	812.39	767.30	729.50	697.43
80000	6918.46	3578.19	2466.52	1912.00	1580.33	1360.09	1203.51	1086.73	996.46	924.75	866.54	818.45	778.14	743.93
85000	7350.86	3801.82	2620.67	2031.49	1679.10	1445.09	1278.73	1154.65	1058.74	982.55	920.70	869.60	826.77	790.42
90000	7783.26	4025.46	2774.83	2150.99	1777.87	1530.10	1353.95	1222.57	1121.02	1040.35	974.86	920.76	875.40	836.92
95000	8215.67	4249.09	2928.99	2270.49	1876.64	1615.10	1429.17	1290.49	1183.30	1098.15	1029.02	971.91	924.04	883.41
100000	8648.07	4472.73	3083.14	2389.99	1975.41	1700.11	1504.39	1358.41	1245.57	1155.94	1083.18	1023.06	972.67	929.91

TERM	15 Years	16 Years	17 Years	18 Years	19 Years	20 Years	21 Years	22 Years	23 Years	24 Years	25 Years	30 Years	35 Years	40 Years
AMOUNT														
5	.05	.05	.05	.05	.04	.04	.04	.04	.04	.04	.04	.04	.04	.04
10	.09	.09	.09	.09	.08	.08	.08	.08	.08	.08	.08	.07	.07	.07
15	.14	.13	.13	.13	.12	.12	.12	.12	.11	.11	.11	.10	.10	.10
25	.23	.22	.21	.21	.20	.20	.19	.19	.19	.18	.18	.17	.16	.16
50	.45	.44	.42	.41	.40	.39	.38	.37	.37	.36	.36	.33	.32	.31
75	.67	.65	.63	.61	.60	.58	.57	.56	.55	.54	.53	.50	.48	.47
100	.90	.87	.84	.81	.79	.77	.76	.74	.73	.72	.71	.66	.64	.62
200	1.79	1.73	1.67	1.62	1.58	1.54	1.51	1.48	1.45	1.43	1.41	1.32	1.27	1.23
300	2.68	2.59	2.51	2.43	2.37	2.31	2.26	2.22	2.18	2.14	2.11	1.98	1.90	1.85
400	3.58	3.45	3.34	3.24	3.16	3.08	3.01	2.95	2.90	2.85	2.81	2.64	2.53	2.46
500	4.47	4.31	4.17	4.05	3.95	3.85	3.77	3.69	3.62	3.56	3.51	3.30	3.16	3.08
600	5.36	5.17	5.01	4.86	4.73	4.62	4.52	4.43	4.35	4.27	4.21	3.96	3.80	3.69
700	6.26	6.04	5.84	5.67	5.52	5.39	5.27	5.17	5.07	4.99	4.91	4.62	4.43	4.30
800	7.15	6.90	6.68	6.48	6.31	6.16	6.02	5.90	5.79	5.70	5.61	5.27	5.06	4.92
900	8.04	7.76	7.51	7.29	7.10	6.93	6.78	6.64	6.52	6.41	6.31	5.93	5.69	5.53
1000	8.94	8.62	8.34	8.10	7.89	7.70	7.53	7.38	7.24	7.12	7.01	6.59	6.32	6.15
2000	17.87	17.24	16.68	16.20	15.77	15.39	15.05	14.75	14.48	14.23	14.01	13.18	12.64	12.29
3000	26.80	25.85	25.02	24.30	23.65	23.08	22.58	22.12	21.72	21.35	21.02	19.76	18.96	18.43
4000	35.73	34.47	33.36	32.39	31.54	30.78	30.10	29.50	28.95	28.46	28.02	26.35	25.28	24.57
5000	44.67	43.08	41.70	40.49	39.42	38.47	37.63	36.87	36.19	35.58	35.03	32.94	31.60	30.71
6000	53.60	51.70	50.04	48.59	47.30	46.16	45.15	44.24	43.43	42.69	42.03	39.52	37.92	36.86
7000	62.53	60.31	58.38	56.68	55.18	53.86	52.67	51.61	50.66	49.81	49.03	46.11	44.24	43.00
8000	71.46	68.93	66.72	64.78	63.07	61.55	60.20	58.99	57.90	56.92	56.04	52.69	50.55	49.14
9000	80.40	77.54	75.06	72.88	70.95	69.24	67.72	66.36	65.14	64.04	63.04	59.28	56.87	55.28
10000	89.33	86.16	83.40	80.97	78.83	76.94	75.25	73.73	72.37	71.15	70.05	65.87	63.19	61.42
11000	98.26	94.77	91.74	89.07	86.72	84.63	82.77	81.11	79.61	78.27	77.05	72.45	69.51	67.56
12000	107.19	103.39	100.07	97.17	94.60	92.32	90.29	88.48	86.85	85.38	84.05	79.04	75.83	73.71
13000	116.13	112.01	108.41	105.26	102.48	100.02	97.82	95.85	94.09	92.50	91.06	85.62	82.15	79.85
14000	125.06	120.62	116.75	113.36	110.36	107.71	105.34	103.22	101.32	99.61	98.06	92.21	88.47	85.99
15000	133.99	129.24	125.09	121.46	118.25	115.40	112.87	110.60	108.56	106.72	105.07	98.80	94.78	92.13
16000	142.92	137.85	133.43	129.55	126.13	123.09	120.39	117.97	115.80	113.84	112.07	105.38	101.10	98.27
17000	151.86	146.47	141.77	137.65	134.01	130.79	127.91	125.34	123.03	120.95	119.08	111.97	107.42	104.42
18000	160.79	155.08	150.11	145.75	141.90	138.48	135.44	132.72	130.27	128.07	126.08	118.55	113.74	110.56
19000	169.72	163.70	158.45	153.84	149.78	146.17	142.96	140.09	137.51	135.18	133.08	125.14	120.06	116.70
20000	178.65	172.31	166.79	161.94	157.66	153.87	150.49	147.46	144.74	142.30	140.09	131.73	126.38	122.84
21000	187.59	180.93	175.13	170.04	165.54	161.56	158.01	154.83	151.98	149.41	147.09	138.31	132.70	128.98
22000	196.52	189.54	183.47	178.13	173.43	169.25	165.53	162.21	159.22	156.53	154.10	144.90	139.01	135.12
23000	205.45	198.16	191.80	186.23	181.31	176.95	173.06	169.58	166.46	163.64	161.10	151.48	145.33	141.27
24000	214.38	206.78	200.14	194.33	189.19	184.64	180.58	176.95	173.69	170.76	168.10	158.07	151.65	147.41
25000	223.32	215.39	208.48	202.42	197.08	192.33	188.11	184.32	180.93	177.87	175.11	164.66	157.97	153.55
26000	232.25	224.01	216.82	210.52	204.96	200.03	195.63	191.70	188.17	184.99	182.11	171.24	164.29	159.69
27000	241.18	232.62	225.16	218.62	212.84	207.72	203.15	199.07	195.40	192.10	189.12	177.83	170.61	165.83
28000	250.11	241.24	233.49	226.71	220.72	215.41	210.68	206.44	202.64	199.22	196.12	184.41	176.93	171.98
29000	259.05	249.85	241.84	234.81	228.61	223.10	218.20	213.82	209.88	206.33	203.12	191.00	183.24	178.12
30000	267.98	258.47	250.18	242.91	236.49	230.80	225.73	221.19	217.11	213.44	210.13	197.59	189.56	184.26
31000	276.91	267.08	258.52	251.00	244.37	238.49	233.25	228.56	224.35	220.56	217.13	204.17	195.88	190.40
32000	285.84	275.70	266.86	259.10	252.25	246.18	240.77	235.93	231.59	227.67	224.14	210.76	202.20	196.54
33000	294.78	284.31	275.20	267.20	260.14	253.88	248.30	243.31	238.83	234.79	231.14	217.34	208.52	202.68
34000	303.71	292.93	283.53	275.29	268.02	261.57	255.82	250.68	246.06	241.90	238.15	223.93	214.84	208.83
35000	312.64	301.54	291.87	283.39	275.90	269.26	263.35	258.05	253.30	249.02	245.15	230.52	221.16	214.97
36000	321.57	310.16	300.21	291.49	283.79	276.96	270.87	265.43	260.54	256.13	252.15	237.10	227.47	221.11
37000	330.51	318.78	308.55	299.58	291.67	284.65	278.39	272.80	267.77	263.25	259.16	243.69	233.79	227.25
38000	339.44	327.39	316.89	307.68	299.55	292.34	285.92	280.17	275.01	270.36	266.16	250.27	240.11	233.39
39000	348.37	336.01	325.23	315.78	307.43	300.04	293.44	287.54	282.25	277.48	273.17	256.86	246.43	239.54
40000	357.30	344.62	333.57	323.87	315.32	307.73	300.97	294.92	289.48	284.59	280.17	263.45	252.75	245.68
41000	366.24	353.24	341.91	331.97	323.20	315.42	308.49	302.29	296.72	291.71	287.17	270.03	259.07	251.82
42000	375.17	361.85	350.25	340.07	331.08	323.11	316.01	309.66	303.96	298.82	294.18	276.62	265.39	257.96
43000	384.10	370.47	358.59	348.16	338.97	330.81	323.54	317.03	311.20	305.94	301.18	283.20	271.70	264.10
44000	393.03	379.08	366.93	356.26	346.85	338.50	331.06	324.41	318.43	313.05	308.19	289.79	278.02	270.24
45000	401.97	387.70	375.27	364.36	354.73	346.19	338.59	331.78	325.67	320.16	315.19	296.38	284.34	276.39
46000	410.90	396.31	383.60	372.45	362.61	353.89	346.11	339.15	332.91	327.28	322.19	302.96	290.66	282.53
47000	419.83	404.93	391.94	380.55	370.50	361.58	353.63	346.53	340.14	334.39	329.20	309.55	296.98	288.67
48000	428.76	413.55	400.28	388.65	378.38	369.27	361.16	353.90	347.38	341.51	336.20	316.13	303.30	294.81
49000	437.70	422.16	408.62	396.74	386.26	376.97	368.68	361.27	354.62	348.62	343.21	322.72	309.62	300.95
50000	446.63	430.78	416.96	404.84	394.15	384.66	376.21	368.64	361.85	355.74	350.21	329.31	315.93	307.10
55000	491.29	473.85	458.66	445.32	433.56	423.12	413.83	405.51	398.04	391.31	385.23	362.24	347.53	337.80
60000	535.95	516.93	500.35	485.81	472.97	461.59	451.45	442.37	434.22	426.88	420.25	395.17	379.12	368.51
65000	580.62	560.01	542.05	526.29	512.39	500.06	489.07	479.24	470.41	462.46	455.27	428.10	410.71	399.22
70000	625.28	603.08	583.74	566.77	551.80	538.52	526.69	516.10	506.59	498.03	490.29	461.03	442.31	429.93
75000	669.94	646.16	625.44	607.26	591.22	576.99	564.31	552.96	542.78	533.60	525.31	493.96	473.90	460.64
80000	714.60	689.24	667.13	647.74	630.63	615.45	601.93	589.83	578.96	569.18	560.34	526.89	505.49	491.35
85000	759.26	732.32	708.83	688.23	670.04	653.92	639.55	626.69	615.15	604.75	595.36	559.82	537.09	522.06
90000	803.93	775.39	750.53	728.71	709.46	692.38	677.17	663.56	651.33	640.32	630.38	592.75	568.68	552.77
95000	848.59	818.47	792.22	769.19	748.87	730.85	714.79	700.42	687.52	675.90	665.40	625.68	600.27	583.48
100000	893.25	861.55	833.92	809.68	788.29	769.31	752.41	737.28	723.70	711.47	700.42	658.61	631.86	614.19

MONTHLY PAYMENT
REQUIRED TO AMORTIZE A LOAN

TERM	1 Year	2 Years	3 Years	4 Years	5 Years	6 Years	7 Years	8 Years	9 Years	10 Years	11 Years	12 Years	13 Years	14 Years
AMOUNT														
5	.44	.23	.16	.12	.10	.09	.08	.07	.07	.06	.06	.06	.05	.05
10	.87	.45	.31	.24	.20	.18	.16	.14	.13	.12	.11	.11	.10	.10
15	1.30	.68	.47	.36	.30	.26	.23	.21	.19	.18	.17	.16	.15	.15
25	2.17	1.12	.78	.60	.50	.43	.38	.35	.32	.30	.28	.26	.25	.24
50	4.33	2.24	1.55	1.20	1.00	.86	.76	.69	.63	.59	.55	.52	.49	.47
75	6.49	3.36	2.32	1.80	1.49	1.28	1.14	1.03	.94	.88	.82	.78	.74	.71
100	8.66	4.48	3.09	2.40	1.99	1.71	1.51	1.37	1.26	1.17	1.09	1.03	.98	.94
200	17.31	8.96	6.18	4.79	3.97	3.41	3.02	2.73	2.51	2.33	2.18	2.06	1.96	1.88
300	25.96	13.44	9.27	7.19	5.95	5.12	4.53	4.10	3.76	3.49	3.27	3.09	2.94	2.81
400	34.62	17.91	12.36	9.58	7.93	6.82	6.04	5.46	5.01	4.65	4.36	4.12	3.92	3.75
500	43.27	22.39	15.44	11.98	9.91	8.53	7.55	6.82	6.26	5.81	5.45	5.15	4.90	4.68
600	51.92	26.87	18.53	14.37	11.89	10.23	9.06	8.19	7.51	6.97	6.54	6.18	5.87	5.62
700	60.57	31.35	21.62	16.77	13.87	11.94	10.57	9.55	8.76	8.13	7.62	7.20	6.85	6.55
800	69.23	35.82	24.71	19.16	15.85	13.64	12.08	10.91	10.01	9.29	8.71	8.23	7.83	7.49
900	77.88	40.30	27.79	21.56	17.83	15.35	13.59	12.28	11.26	10.45	9.80	9.26	8.81	8.42
1000	86.53	44.78	30.88	23.95	19.81	17.05	15.10	13.64	12.51	11.62	10.89	10.29	9.79	9.36
2000	173.06	89.55	61.76	47.90	39.61	34.10	30.19	27.27	25.02	23.23	21.77	20.57	19.57	18.71
3000	259.59	134.32	92.64	71.84	59.41	51.15	45.28	40.91	37.52	34.84	32.66	30.86	29.35	28.07
4000	346.11	179.10	123.51	95.79	79.21	68.20	60.38	54.54	50.03	46.45	43.54	41.14	39.13	37.42
5000	432.64	223.87	154.39	119.74	99.01	85.25	75.47	68.17	62.54	58.06	54.43	51.42	48.91	46.78
6000	519.17	268.64	185.27	143.68	118.81	102.30	90.56	81.81	75.04	69.67	65.31	61.71	58.69	56.13
7000	605.69	313.41	216.14	167.63	138.61	119.35	105.65	95.44	87.55	81.28	76.19	71.99	68.47	65.48
8000	692.22	358.19	247.02	191.57	158.41	136.40	120.75	109.07	100.06	92.89	87.08	82.28	78.25	74.84
9000	778.75	402.96	277.90	215.52	178.22	153.45	135.84	122.71	112.56	104.50	97.96	92.56	88.03	84.19
10000	865.27	447.73	308.78	239.47	198.02	170.50	150.93	136.34	125.07	116.11	108.85	102.84	97.81	93.55
11000	951.80	492.50	339.65	263.41	217.82	187.54	166.02	149.98	137.57	127.72	119.73	113.13	107.59	102.90
12000	1038.33	537.28	370.53	287.36	237.62	204.59	181.12	163.61	150.08	139.34	130.61	123.41	117.37	112.25
13000	1124.85	582.05	401.41	311.31	257.42	221.64	196.21	177.24	162.59	150.95	141.50	133.69	127.15	121.61
14000	1211.38	626.82	432.28	335.25	277.22	238.69	211.30	190.88	175.09	162.56	152.38	143.98	136.94	130.96
15000	1297.91	671.59	463.16	359.20	297.02	255.74	226.40	204.51	187.60	174.17	163.27	154.26	146.72	140.32
16000	1384.43	716.37	494.04	383.14	316.82	272.79	241.49	218.14	200.11	185.78	174.15	164.55	156.50	149.67
17000	1470.96	761.14	524.92	407.09	336.63	289.84	256.58	231.78	212.61	197.39	185.03	174.83	166.28	159.02
18000	1557.49	805.91	555.79	431.04	356.43	306.89	271.67	245.41	225.12	209.00	195.92	185.11	176.06	168.38
19000	1644.01	850.68	586.67	454.98	376.23	323.94	286.77	259.05	237.62	220.61	206.80	195.40	185.84	177.73
20000	1730.54	895.46	617.55	478.93	396.03	340.99	301.86	272.68	250.13	232.22	217.69	205.68	195.62	187.09
21000	1817.07	940.23	648.42	502.88	415.83	358.03	316.95	286.31	262.64	243.83	228.57	215.97	205.40	196.44
22000	1903.59	985.00	679.30	526.82	435.63	375.08	332.04	299.95	275.14	255.44	239.46	226.25	215.18	205.79
23000	1990.12	1029.77	710.18	550.77	455.43	392.13	347.14	313.58	287.65	267.05	250.34	236.53	224.96	215.15
24000	2076.65	1074.55	741.06	574.71	475.23	409.18	362.23	327.21	300.16	278.67	261.22	246.82	234.74	224.50
25000	2163.17	1119.32	771.93	598.66	495.03	426.23	377.32	340.85	312.66	290.28	272.11	257.10	244.52	233.86
26000	2249.70	1164.09	802.81	622.61	514.84	443.28	392.41	354.48	325.17	301.89	282.99	267.38	254.30	243.21
27000	2336.23	1208.86	833.69	646.55	534.64	460.33	407.51	368.12	337.67	313.50	293.88	277.67	264.09	252.56
28000	2422.75	1253.64	864.56	670.50	554.44	477.38	422.60	381.75	350.18	325.11	304.76	287.95	273.87	261.92
29000	2509.28	1298.41	895.44	694.45	574.24	494.43	437.69	395.38	362.69	336.72	315.64	298.24	283.65	271.27
30000	2595.81	1343.18	926.32	718.39	594.04	511.48	452.79	409.02	375.19	348.33	326.53	308.52	293.43	280.63
31000	2682.33	1387.95	957.20	742.34	613.84	528.52	467.88	422.65	387.70	359.94	337.41	318.80	303.21	289.98
32000	2768.86	1432.73	988.07	766.28	633.64	545.57	482.97	436.28	400.21	371.55	348.30	329.09	312.99	299.33
33000	2855.39	1477.50	1018.95	790.23	653.44	562.62	498.06	449.92	412.71	383.16	359.18	339.37	322.77	308.69
34000	2941.91	1522.27	1049.83	814.18	673.25	579.67	513.16	463.55	425.22	394.77	370.06	349.65	332.55	318.04
35000	3028.44	1567.05	1080.70	838.12	693.05	596.72	528.25	477.19	437.72	406.38	380.95	359.94	342.33	327.40
36000	3114.97	1611.82	1111.58	862.07	712.85	613.77	543.34	490.82	450.23	418.00	391.83	370.22	352.11	336.75
37000	3201.49	1656.59	1142.46	886.02	732.65	630.82	558.43	504.45	462.74	429.61	402.72	380.51	361.89	346.10
38000	3288.02	1701.36	1173.33	909.96	752.45	647.87	573.53	518.09	475.24	441.22	413.60	390.79	371.67	355.46
39000	3374.55	1746.14	1204.21	933.91	772.25	664.92	588.62	531.72	487.75	452.83	424.48	401.07	381.45	364.81
40000	3461.07	1790.91	1235.09	957.85	792.05	681.97	603.71	545.35	500.26	464.44	435.37	411.36	391.23	374.17
41000	3547.60	1835.68	1265.97	981.80	811.85	699.01	618.80	558.99	512.76	476.05	446.25	421.64	401.02	383.52
42000	3634.13	1880.45	1296.84	1005.75	831.66	716.06	633.90	572.62	525.27	487.66	457.14	431.93	410.80	392.87
43000	3720.66	1925.23	1327.72	1029.69	851.46	733.11	648.99	586.25	537.77	499.27	468.02	442.21	420.58	402.23
44000	3807.18	1970.00	1358.60	1053.64	871.26	750.16	664.08	599.89	550.28	510.88	478.91	452.49	430.36	411.58
45000	3893.71	2014.77	1389.47	1077.59	891.06	767.21	679.18	613.52	562.79	522.49	489.79	462.78	440.14	420.94
46000	3980.24	2059.54	1420.35	1101.53	910.86	784.26	694.27	627.16	575.29	534.10	500.67	473.06	449.92	430.29
47000	4066.76	2104.32	1451.23	1125.48	930.66	801.31	709.36	640.79	587.80	545.71	511.56	483.34	459.70	439.64
48000	4153.29	2149.09	1482.11	1149.42	950.46	818.36	724.45	654.42	600.31	557.33	522.44	493.63	469.48	449.00
49000	4239.82	2193.86	1512.98	1173.37	970.26	835.41	739.55	668.06	612.81	568.94	533.33	503.91	479.26	458.35
50000	4326.34	2238.63	1543.86	1197.32	990.06	852.46	754.64	681.69	625.32	580.55	544.21	514.20	489.04	467.71
55000	4758.98	2462.50	1698.25	1317.05	1089.07	937.70	830.10	749.86	687.85	638.60	598.63	565.61	537.95	514.48
60000	5191.61	2686.36	1852.63	1436.78	1188.08	1022.95	905.57	818.03	750.38	696.66	653.05	617.03	586.85	561.25
65000	5624.24	2910.22	2007.02	1556.51	1287.08	1108.19	981.03	886.20	812.91	754.71	707.47	668.45	635.75	608.02
70000	6056.88	3134.09	2161.40	1676.24	1386.09	1193.44	1056.49	954.37	875.44	812.76	761.89	719.87	684.66	654.79
75000	6489.51	3357.95	2315.79	1795.97	1485.09	1278.68	1131.96	1022.53	937.98	870.82	816.31	771.29	733.56	701.56
80000	6922.14	3581.81	2470.17	1915.70	1584.10	1363.93	1207.42	1090.70	1000.51	928.87	870.73	822.71	782.46	748.33
85000	7354.78	3805.67	2624.56	2035.44	1683.11	1449.17	1282.88	1158.87	1063.04	986.93	925.15	874.13	831.37	795.10
90000	7787.41	4029.54	2778.94	2155.17	1782.11	1534.42	1358.35	1227.04	1125.57	1044.98	979.57	925.55	880.27	841.87
95000	8220.05	4253.40	2933.33	2274.90	1881.12	1619.66	1433.81	1295.21	1188.10	1103.04	1033.99	976.97	929.18	888.64
100000	8652.68	4477.26	3087.71	2394.63	1980.12	1704.91	1509.27	1363.38	1250.63	1161.09	1088.42	1028.39	978.08	935.41

TERM	15 Years	16 Years	17 Years	18 Years	19 Years	20 Years	21 Years	22 Years	23 Years	24 Years	25 Years	30 Years	35 Years	40 Years
AMOUNT														
5	.05	.05	.05	.05	.04	.04	.04	.04	.04	.04	.04	.04	.04	.04
10	.09	.09	.09	.09	.08	.08	.08	.08	.08	.08	.08	.07	.07	.07
15	.14	.14	.13	.13	.12	.12	.12	.12	.11	.11	.11	.10	.10	.10
25	.23	.22	.21	.21	.20	.20	.19	.19	.19	.18	.18	.17	.16	.16
50	.45	.44	.42	.41	.40	.39	.38	.38	.37	.36	.36	.34	.32	.32
75	.68	.66	.63	.62	.60	.59	.57	.56	.55	.54	.54	.50	.48	.47
100	.90	.87	.84	.82	.80	.78	.76	.75	.73	.72	.71	.67	.64	.63
200	1.80	1.74	1.68	1.64	1.59	1.56	1.52	1.49	1.46	1.44	1.42	1.34	1.28	1.25
300	2.70	2.61	2.52	2.45	2.39	2.33	2.28	2.24	2.19	2.16	2.13	2.00	1.92	1.87
400	3.60	3.47	3.36	3.27	3.18	3.11	3.04	2.98	2.92	2.88	2.83	2.67	2.56	2.49
500	4.50	4.34	4.20	4.08	3.98	3.88	3.80	3.72	3.65	3.59	3.54	3.33	3.20	3.11
600	5.40	5.21	5.04	4.90	4.77	4.66	4.56	4.47	4.38	4.31	4.25	4.00	3.84	3.73
700	6.30	6.08	5.88	5.71	5.56	5.43	5.31	5.21	5.11	5.03	4.95	4.66	4.48	4.36
800	7.20	6.94	6.72	6.53	6.36	6.21	6.07	5.95	5.84	5.75	5.66	5.33	5.12	4.98
900	8.09	7.81	7.56	7.34	7.15	6.98	6.83	6.70	6.57	6.46	6.37	5.99	5.75	5.60
1000	8.99	8.68	8.40	8.16	7.95	7.76	7.59	7.44	7.30	7.18	7.07	6.66	6.39	6.22
2000	17.98	17.35	16.80	16.32	15.89	15.51	15.17	14.87	14.60	14.36	14.14	13.31	12.78	12.43
3000	26.97	26.02	25.19	24.47	23.83	23.26	22.76	22.31	21.90	21.54	21.21	19.96	19.17	18.65
4000	35.96	34.69	33.59	32.63	31.77	31.02	30.34	29.74	29.20	28.72	28.28	26.62	25.56	24.86
5000	44.95	43.37	41.99	40.78	39.71	38.77	37.93	37.18	36.50	35.89	35.34	33.27	31.95	31.08
6000	53.93	52.04	50.38	48.94	47.66	46.52	45.51	44.61	43.80	43.07	42.41	39.92	38.34	37.29
7000	62.92	60.71	58.78	57.09	55.60	54.28	53.10	52.04	51.10	50.25	49.48	46.58	44.72	43.51
8000	71.91	69.38	67.18	65.25	63.54	62.03	60.68	59.48	58.40	57.43	56.55	53.23	51.11	49.72
9000	80.90	78.05	75.57	73.40	71.48	69.78	68.27	66.91	65.70	64.60	63.62	59.88	57.50	55.93
10000	89.89	86.73	83.97	81.56	79.42	77.53	75.85	74.35	73.00	71.78	70.68	66.54	63.89	62.15
11000	98.88	95.40	92.37	89.71	87.37	85.29	83.44	81.78	80.30	78.96	77.75	73.19	70.28	68.36
12000	107.86	104.07	100.76	97.87	95.31	93.04	91.02	89.22	87.60	86.14	84.82	79.84	76.67	74.58
13000	116.85	112.74	109.16	106.02	103.25	100.79	98.61	96.65	94.89	93.31	91.89	86.49	83.06	80.79
14000	125.84	121.41	117.56	114.18	111.19	108.55	106.19	104.08	102.19	100.49	98.95	93.15	89.44	87.01
15000	134.83	130.09	125.95	122.33	119.13	116.30	113.78	111.52	109.49	107.67	106.02	99.80	95.83	93.22
16000	143.82	138.76	134.35	130.49	127.08	124.05	121.36	118.95	116.79	114.85	113.09	106.45	102.22	99.43
17000	152.81	147.43	142.75	138.64	135.02	131.81	128.95	126.39	124.09	122.02	120.16	113.11	108.61	105.65
18000	161.79	156.10	151.14	146.80	142.96	139.56	136.53	133.82	131.39	129.20	127.23	119.76	115.00	111.86
19000	170.78	164.77	159.54	154.95	150.90	147.31	144.11	141.26	138.69	136.38	134.29	126.41	121.39	118.08
20000	179.77	173.45	167.94	163.11	158.84	155.06	151.70	148.69	145.99	143.56	141.36	133.07	127.78	124.29
21000	188.76	182.12	176.33	171.26	166.79	162.82	159.28	156.12	153.29	150.73	148.43	139.72	134.16	130.51
22000	197.75	190.79	184.73	179.42	174.73	170.57	166.87	163.56	160.59	157.91	155.50	146.37	140.55	136.72
23000	206.74	199.46	193.13	187.57	182.67	170.32	174.45	170.99	167.89	165.09	162.56	153.02	146.94	142.93
24000	215.72	208.13	201.52	195.73	190.61	186.08	182.04	178.43	175.19	172.27	169.63	159.68	153.33	149.15
25000	224.71	216.81	209.92	203.88	198.55	193.83	189.62	185.86	182.40	179.44	176.70	166.33	159.72	155.36
26000	233.70	225.48	218.32	212.04	206.50	201.58	197.21	193.30	189.78	186.62	183.77	172.98	166.11	161.58
27000	242.69	234.15	226.71	220.19	214.44	209.34	204.79	200.73	197.08	193.80	190.84	179.64	172.50	167.79
28000	251.68	242.82	235.11	228.35	222.38	217.09	212.38	208.16	204.38	200.98	197.90	186.29	178.88	174.01
29000	260.67	251.50	243.51	236.50	230.32	224.84	219.96	215.60	211.68	208.16	204.97	192.94	185.27	180.22
30000	269.65	260.17	251.90	244.66	238.26	232.59	227.55	223.03	218.98	215.33	212.04	199.60	191.66	186.43
31000	278.64	268.84	260.30	252.81	246.20	240.35	235.13	230.47	226.28	222.51	219.11	206.25	198.05	192.65
32000	287.63	277.51	268.70	260.97	254.15	248.10	242.72	237.90	233.58	229.69	226.17	212.90	204.44	198.86
33000	296.62	286.18	277.09	269.12	262.09	255.85	250.30	245.33	240.88	236.87	233.24	219.55	210.83	205.08
34000	305.61	294.86	285.49	277.28	270.03	263.61	257.89	252.77	248.18	244.04	240.31	226.21	217.22	211.29
35000	314.59	303.53	293.89	285.43	277.97	271.36	265.47	260.20	255.48	251.22	247.38	232.86	223.60	217.51
36000	323.58	312.20	302.28	293.59	285.91	279.11	273.05	267.64	262.78	258.40	254.45	239.51	229.99	223.72
37000	332.57	320.87	310.68	301.74	293.86	286.87	280.64	275.07	270.08	265.58	261.51	246.17	236.38	229.93
38000	341.56	329.54	319.08	309.90	301.80	294.62	288.22	282.51	277.37	272.75	268.58	252.82	242.77	236.15
39000	350.55	338.22	327.47	318.05	309.74	302.37	295.81	289.94	284.67	279.93	275.65	259.47	249.16	242.36
40000	359.54	346.89	335.87	326.21	317.68	310.12	303.39	297.37	291.97	287.11	282.72	266.13	255.55	248.58
41000	368.52	355.56	344.27	334.36	325.62	317.88	310.98	304.81	299.27	294.29	289.78	272.78	261.94	254.79
42000	377.51	364.23	352.66	342.52	333.57	325.63	318.56	312.24	306.57	301.46	296.85	279.43	268.32	261.01
43000	386.50	372.90	361.06	350.67	341.51	333.38	326.15	319.68	313.87	308.64	303.92	286.09	274.71	267.22
44000	395.49	381.58	369.46	358.83	349.45	341.14	333.73	327.11	321.17	315.82	310.99	292.74	281.10	273.43
45000	404.48	390.25	377.85	366.98	357.39	348.89	341.32	334.55	328.47	323.00	318.06	299.39	287.49	279.65
46000	413.47	398.92	386.25	375.14	365.33	356.64	348.90	341.98	335.77	330.17	325.12	306.04	293.88	285.86
47000	422.45	407.59	394.65	383.29	373.28	364.40	356.49	349.41	343.07	337.35	332.19	312.70	300.27	292.08
48000	431.44	416.26	403.04	391.45	381.22	372.15	364.07	356.85	350.37	344.53	339.26	319.35	306.66	298.29
49000	440.43	424.94	411.44	399.60	389.16	379.90	371.66	364.28	357.67	351.71	346.33	326.00	313.04	304.51
50000	449.42	433.61	419.84	407.76	397.10	387.65	379.24	371.72	364.96	358.88	353.39	332.66	319.43	310.72
55000	494.36	476.97	461.82	448.53	436.81	426.42	417.16	408.89	401.46	394.77	388.73	365.92	351.38	341.79
60000	539.30	520.33	503.80	489.31	476.52	465.18	455.09	446.06	437.96	430.66	424.07	399.19	383.32	372.86
65000	584.24	563.69	545.78	530.08	516.23	503.95	493.01	483.23	474.45	466.55	459.41	432.45	415.26	403.94
70000	629.18	607.05	587.77	570.86	555.94	542.71	530.94	520.40	510.95	502.44	494.75	465.72	447.20	435.01
75000	674.13	650.41	629.75	611.63	595.65	581.48	568.86	557.57	547.44	538.32	530.09	498.98	479.15	466.08
80000	719.07	693.77	671.73	652.41	635.36	620.24	606.78	594.74	583.94	574.21	565.43	532.25	511.09	497.15
85000	764.01	737.13	713.72	693.18	675.07	659.01	644.71	631.92	620.44	610.10	600.77	565.51	543.03	528.22
90000	808.95	780.49	755.70	733.96	714.78	697.77	682.63	669.09	656.93	645.99	636.11	598.78	574.98	559.29
95000	853.89	823.85	797.68	774.73	754.49	736.54	720.55	706.26	693.43	681.88	671.45	632.04	606.92	590.36
100000	898.83	867.21	839.67	815.51	794.20	775.30	758.48	743.43	729.92	717.76	706.78	665.31	638.86	621.44

MONTHLY PAYMENT
REQUIRED TO AMORTIZE A LOAN

TERM	1 Year	2 Years	3 Years	4 Years	5 Years	6 Years	7 Years	8 Years	9 Years	10 Years	11 Years	12 Years	13 Years	14 Years
AMOUNT														
5	.44	.23	.16	.12	.10	.09	.08	.07	.07	.06	.06	.06	.05	.05
10	.87	.45	.31	.24	.20	.18	.16	.14	.13	.12	.11	.11	.10	.10
15	1.30	.68	.47	.36	.30	.26	.23	.21	.19	.18	.17	.16	.15	.15
25	2.17	1.13	.78	.60	.50	.43	.38	.35	.32	.30	.28	.26	.25	.24
50	4.33	2.25	1.55	1.20	1.00	.86	.76	.69	.63	.59	.55	.52	.50	.48
75	6.50	3.37	2.32	1.80	1.49	1.29	1.14	1.03	.95	.88	.83	.78	.74	.71
100	8.66	4.49	3.10	2.40	1.99	1.71	1.52	1.37	1.26	1.17	1.10	1.04	.99	.95
200	17.32	8.97	6.19	4.80	3.97	3.42	3.03	2.74	2.52	2.34	2.19	2.07	1.97	1.89
300	25.98	13.45	9.28	7.20	5.96	5.13	4.55	4.11	3.77	3.50	3.29	3.11	2.96	2.83
400	34.63	17.93	12.37	9.60	7.94	6.84	6.06	5.48	5.03	4.67	4.38	4.14	3.94	3.77
500	43.29	22.41	15.47	12.00	9.93	8.55	7.58	6.85	6.28	5.84	5.47	5.17	4.92	4.71
600	51.95	26.90	18.56	14.40	11.91	10.26	9.09	8.22	7.54	7.00	6.57	6.21	5.91	5.65
700	60.61	31.38	21.65	16.80	13.90	11.97	10.60	9.58	8.79	8.17	7.66	7.24	6.89	6.59
800	69.26	35.86	24.74	19.20	15.88	13.68	12.12	10.95	10.05	9.33	8.75	8.27	7.87	7.53
900	77.92	40.34	27.84	21.60	17.87	15.39	13.63	12.32	11.31	10.50	9.85	9.31	8.86	8.47
1000	86.58	44.82	30.93	24.00	19.85	17.10	15.15	13.69	12.56	11.67	10.94	10.34	9.84	9.41
2000	173.15	89.64	61.85	47.99	39.70	34.20	30.29	27.37	25.12	23.33	21.88	20.68	19.68	18.82
3000	259.72	134.46	92.77	71.98	59.55	51.30	45.43	41.06	37.68	34.99	32.81	31.02	29.51	28.23
4000	346.30	179.28	123.70	95.98	79.40	68.39	60.57	54.74	50.23	46.65	43.75	41.35	39.35	37.64
5000	432.87	224.09	154.62	119.97	99.25	85.49	75.71	68.42	62.79	58.32	54.69	51.69	49.18	47.05
6000	519.44	268.91	185.54	143.96	119.10	102.59	90.85	82.11	75.35	69.98	65.62	62.03	59.02	56.46
7000	606.01	313.73	216.46	167.95	138.94	119.68	106.00	95.79	87.90	81.64	76.56	72.37	68.85	65.87
8000	692.59	358.55	247.39	191.95	158.79	136.78	121.14	109.47	100.46	93.30	87.50	82.70	78.69	75.28
9000	779.16	403.37	278.31	215.94	178.64	153.88	136.28	123.16	113.02	104.97	98.43	93.04	88.52	84.69
10000	865.73	448.18	309.23	239.93	198.49	170.98	151.42	136.84	125.57	116.63	109.37	103.38	98.36	94.10
11000	952.31	493.00	340.16	263.92	218.34	188.07	166.56	150.52	138.13	128.29	120.31	113.71	108.19	103.51
12000	1038.88	537.82	371.08	287.92	238.19	205.17	181.70	164.21	150.69	139.95	131.24	124.05	118.03	112.91
13000	1125.45	582.64	402.00	311.91	258.03	222.27	196.85	177.89	163.25	151.62	142.18	134.39	127.86	122.32
14000	1212.02	627.46	432.92	335.90	277.88	239.36	211.99	191.57	175.80	163.28	153.12	144.73	137.70	131.73
15000	1298.60	672.27	463.85	359.90	297.73	256.46	227.13	205.26	188.36	174.94	164.05	155.06	147.53	141.14
16000	1385.17	717.09	494.77	383.89	317.58	273.56	242.27	218.94	200.92	186.60	174.99	165.40	157.37	150.55
17000	1471.74	761.91	525.69	407.88	337.43	290.66	257.41	232.63	213.47	198.27	185.93	175.74	167.20	159.96
18000	1558.32	806.73	556.62	431.87	357.28	307.75	272.55	246.31	226.03	209.93	196.86	186.07	177.04	169.37
19000	1644.89	851.55	587.54	455.87	377.12	324.85	287.70	259.99	238.59	221.59	207.80	196.41	186.87	178.78
20000	1731.46	896.36	618.46	479.86	396.97	341.95	302.84	273.68	251.14	233.25	218.74	206.75	196.71	188.19
21000	1818.03	941.18	649.38	503.85	416.82	359.04	317.98	287.36	263.70	244.92	229.67	217.09	206.54	197.60
22000	1904.61	986.00	680.31	527.84	436.67	376.14	333.12	301.04	276.26	256.58	240.61	227.42	216.38	207.01
23000	1991.18	1030.82	711.23	551.84	456.52	393.24	348.26	314.73	288.82	268.24	251.55	237.76	226.21	216.42
24000	2077.75	1075.64	742.15	575.83	476.37	410.33	363.40	328.41	301.37	279.90	262.48	248.10	236.05	225.82
25000	2164.33	1120.45	773.08	599.82	496.22	427.43	378.55	342.09	313.93	291.57	273.42	258.43	245.88	235.23
26000	2250.90	1165.27	804.00	623.81	516.06	444.53	393.69	355.78	326.49	303.23	284.36	268.77	255.72	244.64
27000	2337.47	1210.09	834.92	647.80	535.91	461.63	408.83	369.46	339.04	314.89	295.29	279.11	265.55	254.05
28000	2424.04	1254.91	865.84	671.80	555.76	478.72	423.97	383.14	351.60	326.55	306.23	289.45	275.39	263.46
29000	2510.62	1299.72	896.77	695.79	575.61	495.82	439.11	396.83	364.16	338.22	317.17	299.78	285.22	272.87
30000	2597.19	1344.54	927.69	719.79	595.46	512.92	454.25	410.51	376.71	349.88	328.10	310.12	295.06	282.28
31000	2683.76	1389.36	958.61	743.78	615.31	530.01	469.39	424.19	389.27	361.54	339.04	320.46	304.89	291.69
32000	2770.34	1434.18	989.54	767.77	635.15	547.11	484.54	437.88	401.83	373.20	349.98	330.80	314.73	301.10
33000	2856.91	1479.00	1020.46	791.76	655.00	564.21	499.68	451.56	414.39	384.87	360.91	341.13	324.56	310.51
34000	2943.48	1523.81	1051.38	815.76	674.85	581.31	514.82	465.25	426.94	396.53	371.85	351.47	334.40	319.92
35000	3030.05	1568.63	1082.30	839.75	694.70	598.40	529.96	478.93	439.50	408.19	382.79	361.81	344.23	329.32
36000	3116.63	1613.45	1113.23	863.74	714.55	615.50	545.10	492.61	452.06	419.85	393.72	372.14	354.07	338.73
37000	3203.20	1658.27	1144.15	887.73	734.40	632.60	560.24	506.30	464.61	431.52	404.66	382.48	363.90	348.14
38000	3289.77	1703.09	1175.07	911.73	754.24	649.69	575.39	519.98	477.17	443.18	415.60	392.82	373.74	357.55
39000	3376.35	1747.90	1206.00	935.72	774.09	666.79	590.53	533.66	489.73	454.84	426.53	403.16	383.57	366.96
40000	3462.92	1792.72	1236.92	959.71	793.94	683.89	605.67	547.35	502.28	466.50	437.47	413.49	393.41	376.37
41000	3549.49	1837.54	1267.84	983.70	813.79	700.98	620.81	561.03	514.84	478.17	448.41	423.83	403.24	385.78
42000	3636.06	1882.36	1298.76	1007.70	833.64	718.08	635.95	574.71	527.40	489.83	459.34	434.17	413.08	395.19
43000	3722.64	1927.18	1329.69	1031.69	853.49	735.18	651.09	588.40	539.96	501.49	470.28	444.50	422.91	404.60
44000	3809.21	1971.99	1360.61	1055.68	873.34	752.28	666.24	602.08	552.51	513.15	481.22	454.84	432.75	414.01
45000	3895.78	2016.81	1391.53	1079.68	893.18	769.37	681.38	615.76	565.07	524.82	492.15	465.18	442.58	423.42
46000	3982.36	2061.63	1422.46	1103.67	913.03	786.47	696.52	629.45	577.63	536.48	503.09	475.52	452.42	432.83
47000	4068.93	2106.45	1453.38	1127.66	932.88	803.57	711.66	643.13	590.18	548.14	514.03	485.85	462.25	442.23
48000	4155.50	2151.27	1484.30	1151.65	952.73	820.66	726.80	656.81	602.74	559.80	524.96	496.19	472.09	451.64
49000	4242.07	2196.08	1515.22	1175.65	972.58	837.76	741.94	670.50	615.30	571.47	535.90	506.53	481.92	461.05
50000	4328.65	2240.90	1546.15	1199.64	992.43	854.86	757.09	684.18	627.85	583.13	546.83	516.86	491.76	470.46
55000	4761.51	2464.99	1700.76	1319.60	1091.67	940.34	832.79	752.60	690.64	641.44	601.52	568.55	540.93	517.51
60000	5194.38	2689.08	1855.38	1439.57	1190.91	1025.83	908.50	821.02	753.42	699.75	656.20	620.24	590.11	564.55
65000	5627.24	2913.17	2009.99	1559.53	1290.15	1111.31	984.21	889.43	816.21	758.06	710.88	671.92	639.28	611.60
70000	6060.10	3137.26	2164.60	1679.49	1389.39	1196.80	1059.92	957.85	878.99	816.38	765.57	723.61	688.46	658.64
75000	6492.97	3361.35	2319.22	1799.46	1488.64	1282.28	1135.63	1026.27	941.78	874.69	820.25	775.29	737.63	705.69
80000	6925.83	3585.44	2473.83	1919.42	1587.88	1367.77	1211.33	1094.69	1004.56	933.00	874.93	826.98	786.81	752.74
85000	7358.70	3809.53	2628.45	2039.38	1687.12	1453.26	1287.04	1163.11	1067.35	991.31	929.62	878.67	835.98	799.78
90000	7791.56	4033.62	2783.06	2159.35	1786.36	1538.74	1362.75	1231.52	1130.13	1049.63	984.30	930.35	885.16	846.83
95000	8224.43	4257.71	2937.67	2279.31	1885.60	1624.23	1438.46	1299.94	1192.92	1107.94	1038.98	982.04	934.33	893.87
100000	8657.29	4481.80	3092.29	2399.27	1984.85	1709.71	1514.17	1368.36	1255.70	1166.25	1093.66	1033.72	983.51	940.92

MONTHLY PAYMENT
REQUIRED TO AMORTIZE A LOAN

7.100%

TERM	15 Years	16 Years	17 Years	18 Years	19 Years	20 Years	21 Years	22 Years	23 Years	24 Years	25 Years	30 Years	35 Years	40 Years
AMOUNT														
5	.05	.05	.05	.05	.05	.04	.04	.04	.04	.04	.04	.04	.04	.04
10	.10	.09	.09	.09	.09	.08	.08	.08	.08	.08	.08	.07	.07	.07
15	.14	.14	.13	.13	.13	.12	.12	.12	.12	.11	.11	.11	.10	.10
25	.23	.22	.22	.21	.21	.20	.20	.19	.19	.19	.18	.17	.17	.16
50	.46	.44	.43	.42	.41	.40	.39	.38	.37	.37	.36	.34	.33	.32
75	.68	.66	.64	.62	.61	.59	.58	.57	.56	.55	.54	.51	.49	.48
100	.91	.88	.85	.83	.81	.79	.77	.75	.74	.73	.72	.68	.65	.63
200	1.81	1.75	1.70	1.65	1.61	1.57	1.53	1.50	1.48	1.45	1.43	1.35	1.30	1.26
300	2.72	2.62	2.54	2.47	2.41	2.35	2.30	2.25	2.21	2.18	2.14	2.02	1.94	1.89
400	3.62	3.50	3.39	3.29	3.21	3.13	3.06	3.00	2.95	2.90	2.86	2.69	2.59	2.52
500	4.53	4.37	4.23	4.11	4.01	3.91	3.83	3.75	3.69	3.63	3.57	3.37	3.23	3.15
600	5.43	5.24	5.08	4.93	4.81	4.69	4.59	4.50	4.42	4.35	4.28	4.04	3.88	3.78
700	6.34	6.12	5.92	5.75	5.61	5.47	5.36	5.25	5.16	5.07	5.00	4.71	4.53	4.41
800	7.24	6.99	6.77	6.58	6.41	6.26	6.12	6.00	5.89	5.80	5.71	5.38	5.17	5.03
900	8.14	7.86	7.61	7.40	7.21	7.04	6.89	6.75	6.63	6.52	6.42	6.05	5.82	5.66
1000	9.05	8.73	8.46	8.22	8.01	7.82	7.65	7.50	7.37	7.25	7.14	6.73	6.46	6.29
2000	18.09	17.46	16.91	16.43	16.01	15.63	15.30	15.00	14.73	14.49	14.27	13.45	12.92	12.58
3000	27.14	26.19	25.37	24.65	24.01	23.44	22.94	22.49	22.09	21.73	21.40	20.17	19.38	18.87
4000	36.18	34.92	33.82	32.86	32.01	31.26	30.59	29.99	29.45	28.97	28.53	26.89	25.84	25.15
5000	45.23	43.65	42.28	41.07	40.01	39.07	38.23	37.48	36.81	36.21	35.66	33.61	32.30	31.44
6000	54.27	52.38	50.73	49.29	48.01	46.88	45.88	44.98	44.17	43.45	42.80	40.33	38.76	37.73
7000	63.31	61.11	59.19	57.50	56.01	54.70	53.52	52.48	51.54	50.69	49.93	47.05	45.22	44.01
8000	72.36	69.84	67.64	65.71	64.02	62.51	61.17	59.97	58.90	57.93	57.06	53.77	51.68	50.30
9000	81.40	78.57	76.09	73.93	72.02	70.32	68.82	67.47	66.26	65.17	64.19	60.49	58.13	56.59
10000	90.45	87.29	84.55	82.14	80.02	78.14	76.46	74.96	73.62	72.41	71.32	67.21	64.59	62.88
11000	99.49	96.02	93.00	90.35	88.02	85.95	84.11	82.46	80.98	79.65	78.45	73.93	71.05	69.16
12000	108.54	104.75	101.46	98.57	96.02	93.76	91.75	89.96	88.34	86.89	85.59	80.65	77.51	75.45
13000	117.58	113.48	109.91	106.78	104.02	101.58	99.40	97.45	95.71	94.14	92.72	87.37	83.97	81.74
14000	126.62	122.21	118.37	114.99	112.02	109.39	107.04	104.95	103.07	101.38	99.85	94.09	90.43	88.02
15000	135.67	130.94	126.82	123.21	120.02	117.20	114.69	112.44	110.43	108.62	106.98	100.81	96.89	94.31
16000	144.71	139.67	135.27	131.42	128.03	125.02	122.34	119.94	117.79	115.86	114.11	107.53	103.35	100.60
17000	153.76	148.40	143.73	139.64	136.03	132.83	129.98	127.44	125.15	123.10	121.24	114.25	109.80	106.89
18000	162.80	157.13	152.18	147.85	144.03	140.64	137.63	134.93	132.51	130.34	128.38	120.97	116.26	113.17
19000	171.05	165.85	160.64	156.06	152.03	148.45	145.27	142.43	139.88	137.58	135.51	127.69	122.72	119.46
20000	180.89	174.58	169.09	164.28	160.03	156.27	152.92	149.92	147.24	144.82	142.64	134.41	129.18	125.75
21000	189.93	183.31	177.55	172.49	168.03	164.08	160.56	157.42	154.60	152.06	149.77	141.13	135.64	132.03
22000	198.98	192.04	186.00	180.70	176.03	171.89	168.21	164.92	161.96	159.30	156.90	147.85	142.10	138.32
23000	208.02	200.77	194.45	188.92	184.03	179.71	175.85	172.41	169.32	166.54	164.03	154.57	148.56	144.61
24000	217.07	209.50	202.91	197.13	192.04	187.52	183.50	179.91	176.68	173.78	171.17	161.29	155.02	150.89
25000	226.11	218.23	211.36	205.34	200.04	195.33	191.15	187.40	184.05	181.02	178.30	168.01	161.48	157.18
26000	235.16	226.96	219.82	213.56	208.04	203.15	198.79	194.90	191.41	188.27	185.43	174.73	167.93	163.47
27000	244.20	235.69	228.27	221.77	216.04	210.96	206.44	202.40	198.77	195.51	192.56	181.45	174.39	169.76
28000	253.24	244.42	236.73	229.98	224.04	218.77	214.08	209.89	206.13	202.75	199.69	188.17	180.85	176.04
29000	262.29	253.14	245.18	238.20	232.04	226.59	221.73	217.39	213.49	209.99	206.82	194.89	187.31	182.33
30000	271.33	261.87	253.63	246.41	240.04	234.40	229.37	224.88	220.85	217.23	213.96	201.61	193.77	188.62
31000	280.38	270.60	262.09	254.62	248.04	242.21	237.02	232.38	228.22	224.47	221.09	208.33	200.23	194.90
32000	289.42	279.33	270.54	262.84	256.05	250.03	244.67	239.88	235.58	231.71	228.22	215.06	206.69	201.19
33000	298.47	288.06	279.00	271.05	264.05	257.84	252.31	247.37	242.94	238.95	235.35	221.78	213.15	207.48
34000	307.51	296.79	287.45	279.27	272.05	265.65	259.96	254.87	250.30	246.19	242.48	228.50	219.60	213.77
35000	316.55	305.52	295.91	287.48	280.05	273.46	267.60	262.36	257.66	253.43	249.61	235.22	226.06	220.05
36000	325.60	314.25	304.36	295.69	288.05	281.28	275.25	269.86	265.02	260.67	256.75	241.94	232.52	226.34
37000	334.64	322.98	312.81	303.91	296.05	289.09	282.89	277.35	272.39	267.91	263.88	248.66	238.98	232.63
38000	343.69	331.70	321.27	312.12	304.05	296.90	290.54	284.85	279.75	275.16	271.01	255.38	245.44	238.91
39000	352.73	340.43	329.72	320.33	312.05	304.72	298.19	292.35	287.11	282.40	278.14	262.10	251.90	245.20
40000	361.78	349.16	338.18	328.55	320.06	312.53	305.83	299.84	294.47	289.64	285.27	268.82	258.36	251.49
41000	370.82	357.89	346.63	336.76	328.06	320.34	313.48	307.34	301.83	296.88	292.41	275.54	264.82	257.78
42000	379.86	366.62	355.09	344.97	336.06	328.16	321.12	314.83	309.19	304.12	299.54	282.26	271.27	264.06
43000	388.91	375.35	363.54	353.19	344.06	335.97	328.77	322.33	316.56	311.36	306.67	288.98	277.73	270.35
44000	397.95	384.08	371.99	361.40	352.06	343.78	336.41	329.83	323.92	318.60	313.80	295.70	284.19	276.64
45000	407.00	392.81	380.45	369.61	360.06	351.60	344.06	337.32	331.28	325.84	320.93	302.42	290.65	282.92
46000	416.04	401.54	388.90	377.83	368.06	359.41	351.70	344.82	338.64	333.08	328.06	309.14	297.11	289.21
47000	425.09	410.26	397.36	386.04	376.06	367.22	359.35	352.31	346.00	340.32	335.20	315.86	303.57	295.50
48000	434.13	418.99	405.81	394.26	384.07	375.04	367.00	359.81	353.36	347.56	342.33	322.58	310.03	301.78
49000	443.17	427.72	414.27	402.47	392.07	382.85	374.64	367.31	360.73	354.80	349.46	329.30	316.49	308.07
50000	452.22	436.45	422.72	410.68	400.07	390.66	382.29	374.80	368.09	362.04	356.59	336.02	322.95	314.36
55000	497.44	480.10	464.99	451.75	440.07	429.73	420.52	412.28	404.90	398.25	392.25	369.62	355.24	345.79
60000	542.66	523.74	507.26	492.82	480.08	468.79	458.75	449.76	441.70	434.45	427.91	403.22	387.53	377.23
65000	587.88	567.39	549.53	533.89	520.09	507.86	496.97	487.24	478.51	470.66	463.57	436.83	419.83	408.67
70000	633.10	611.03	591.81	574.95	560.09	546.92	535.20	524.72	515.32	506.86	499.22	470.43	452.12	440.10
75000	678.33	654.67	634.08	616.02	600.10	585.99	573.43	562.20	552.13	543.06	534.88	504.03	484.42	471.54
80000	723.55	698.32	676.35	657.09	640.11	625.06	611.66	599.68	588.94	579.27	570.54	537.63	516.71	502.97
85000	768.77	741.96	718.62	698.16	680.11	664.12	649.88	637.16	625.74	615.47	606.20	571.23	549.00	534.41
90000	813.99	785.61	760.89	739.22	720.12	703.19	688.11	674.64	662.55	651.68	641.86	604.83	581.30	565.84
95000	859.21	829.25	803.16	780.29	760.12	742.25	726.34	712.12	699.36	687.88	677.52	638.44	613.59	597.28
100000	904.43	872.90	845.43	821.36	800.13	781.32	764.57	749.60	736.17	724.08	713.18	672.04	645.89	628.71

MONTHLY PAYMENT
REQUIRED TO AMORTIZE A LOAN

TERM AMOUNT	1 Year	2 Years	3 Years	4 Years	5 Years	6 Years	7 Years	8 Years	9 Years	10 Years	11 Years	12 Years	13 Years	14 Years
5	.44	.23	.16	.13	.10	.09	.08	.07	.07	.06	.06	.06	.05	.05
10	.87	.45	.31	.25	.20	.18	.16	.14	.13	.12	.11	.11	.10	.10
15	1.30	.68	.47	.37	.30	.26	.23	.21	.19	.18	.17	.16	.15	.15
25	2.17	1.13	.78	.61	.50	.43	.38	.35	.32	.30	.28	.26	.25	.24
50	4.33	2.25	1.55	1.21	1.00	.86	.76	.69	.63	.59	.55	.52	.50	.48
75	6.50	3.37	2.33	1.81	1.49	1.29	1.14	1.03	.95	.88	.83	.78	.74	.71
100	8.66	4.49	3.10	2.41	1.99	1.72	1.52	1.37	1.26	1.17	1.10	1.04	.99	.95
200	17.32	8.97	6.19	4.81	3.98	3.43	3.04	2.74	2.52	2.34	2.19	2.08	1.97	1.89
300	25.98	13.45	9.29	7.21	5.96	5.14	4.55	4.11	3.78	3.51	3.29	3.11	2.96	2.83
400	34.64	17.94	12.38	9.61	7.95	6.85	6.07	5.48	5.03	4.68	4.38	4.15	3.94	3.77
500	43.30	22.42	15.47	12.01	9.94	8.56	7.58	6.85	6.29	5.84	5.48	5.18	4.93	4.72
600	51.96	26.90	18.57	14.41	11.92	10.27	9.10	8.22	7.55	7.01	6.57	6.22	5.91	5.66
700	60.61	31.39	21.66	16.81	13.91	11.98	10.61	9.59	8.80	8.18	7.67	7.25	6.90	6.60
800	69.27	35.87	24.75	19.21	15.89	13.69	12.13	10.96	10.06	9.35	8.76	8.29	7.88	7.54
900	77.93	40.35	27.85	21.61	17.88	15.40	13.64	12.33	11.32	10.51	9.86	9.32	8.87	8.49
1000	86.59	44.83	30.94	24.01	19.87	17.11	15.16	13.70	12.57	11.68	10.95	10.36	9.85	9.43
2000	173.17	89.66	61.87	48.01	39.73	34.22	30.31	27.40	25.14	23.36	21.90	20.71	19.70	18.85
3000	259.76	134.49	92.81	72.02	59.59	51.33	45.47	41.09	37.71	35.03	32.85	31.06	29.55	28.27
4000	346.34	179.32	123.74	96.02	79.45	68.44	60.62	54.79	50.28	46.71	43.80	41.41	39.40	37.70
5000	432.93	224.15	154.68	120.03	99.31	85.55	75.77	68.49	62.85	58.38	54.75	51.76	49.25	47.12
6000	519.51	268.98	185.61	144.03	119.17	102.66	90.93	82.18	75.42	70.06	65.70	62.11	59.10	56.54
7000	606.10	313.81	216.54	168.03	139.03	119.77	106.08	95.88	87.99	81.73	76.65	72.46	68.95	65.97
8000	692.68	358.64	247.48	192.04	158.89	136.88	121.24	109.57	100.56	93.41	87.60	82.81	78.79	75.39
9000	779.26	403.47	278.41	216.04	178.75	153.99	136.39	123.27	113.13	105.08	98.55	93.16	88.64	84.81
10000	865.85	448.30	309.35	240.05	198.61	171.10	151.54	136.97	125.70	116.76	109.50	103.51	98.49	94.23
11000	952.43	493.13	340.28	264.05	218.47	188.21	166.70	150.66	138.27	128.43	120.45	113.86	108.34	103.66
12000	1039.02	537.96	371.22	288.06	238.33	205.31	181.85	164.36	150.84	140.11	131.40	124.21	118.19	113.08
13000	1125.60	582.79	402.15	312.06	258.19	222.42	197.01	178.05	163.41	151.78	142.35	134.56	128.04	122.50
14000	1212.19	627.61	433.08	336.06	278.05	239.53	212.16	191.75	175.98	163.46	153.30	144.91	137.89	131.93
15000	1298.77	672.44	464.02	360.07	297.91	256.64	227.31	205.45	188.55	175.14	164.25	155.26	147.73	141.35
16000	1385.36	717.27	494.95	384.07	317.77	273.75	242.47	219.14	201.12	186.81	175.20	165.61	157.58	150.77
17000	1471.94	762.10	525.89	408.08	337.63	290.86	257.62	232.84	213.69	198.49	186.15	175.96	167.43	160.20
18000	1558.52	806.93	556.82	432.08	357.49	307.97	272.77	246.53	226.26	210.16	197.10	186.32	177.28	169.62
19000	1645.11	851.76	587.76	456.08	377.35	325.08	287.93	260.23	238.83	221.84	208.05	196.67	187.13	179.04
20000	1731.69	896.59	618.69	480.09	397.21	342.19	303.08	273.93	251.40	233.51	219.00	207.02	196.98	188.46
21000	1818.28	941.42	649.62	504.09	417.07	359.30	318.24	287.62	263.97	245.19	229.95	217.37	206.83	197.89
22000	1904.86	986.25	680.56	528.10	436.93	376.41	333.39	301.32	276.54	256.86	240.90	227.72	216.67	207.31
23000	1991.45	1031.08	711.49	552.10	456.79	393.51	348.54	315.01	289.11	268.54	251.85	238.07	226.52	216.73
24000	2078.03	1075.91	742.43	576.11	476.65	410.62	363.70	328.71	301.68	280.21	262.80	248.42	236.37	226.16
25000	2164.61	1120.74	773.36	600.11	496.51	427.73	378.85	342.41	314.25	291.89	273.75	258.77	246.22	235.58
26000	2251.20	1165.57	804.30	624.12	516.37	444.84	394.01	356.10	326.82	303.56	284.70	269.12	256.07	245.00
27000	2337.78	1210.40	835.23	648.12	536.23	461.95	409.16	369.80	339.39	315.24	295.65	279.47	265.92	254.42
28000	2424.37	1255.22	866.16	672.12	556.09	479.06	424.31	383.49	351.96	326.92	306.60	289.82	275.77	263.85
29000	2510.95	1300.05	897.10	696.13	575.95	496.17	439.47	397.19	364.53	338.59	317.55	300.17	285.61	273.27
30000	2597.54	1344.88	928.03	720.13	595.81	513.28	454.62	410.89	377.10	350.27	328.50	310.52	295.46	282.69
31000	2684.12	1389.71	958.97	744.14	615.67	530.39	469.77	424.58	389.67	361.94	339.45	320.87	305.31	292.12
32000	2770.71	1434.54	989.90	768.14	635.53	547.50	484.93	438.28	402.23	373.62	350.40	331.22	315.16	301.54
33000	2857.29	1479.37	1020.84	792.15	655.39	564.61	500.08	451.97	414.80	385.29	361.35	341.57	325.01	310.96
34000	2943.87	1524.20	1051.77	816.15	675.25	581.71	515.24	465.67	427.37	396.97	372.30	351.92	334.86	320.39
35000	3030.46	1569.03	1082.70	840.15	695.11	598.82	530.39	479.37	439.94	408.64	383.25	362.27	344.71	329.81
36000	3117.04	1613.86	1113.64	864.16	714.97	615.93	545.54	493.06	452.51	420.32	394.20	372.63	354.55	339.23
37000	3203.63	1658.69	1144.57	888.16	734.83	633.04	560.70	506.76	465.08	431.99	405.15	382.98	364.40	348.65
38000	3290.21	1703.52	1175.51	912.17	754.69	650.15	575.85	520.45	477.65	443.67	416.10	393.33	374.25	358.08
39000	3376.80	1748.35	1206.44	936.17	774.55	667.26	591.01	534.15	490.22	455.34	427.04	403.68	384.10	367.50
40000	3463.38	1793.18	1237.38	960.18	794.41	684.37	606.16	547.85	502.79	467.02	437.99	414.03	393.95	376.92
41000	3549.96	1838.01	1268.31	984.18	814.27	701.48	621.31	561.54	515.35	478.70	448.94	424.38	403.80	386.35
42000	3636.55	1882.83	1299.24	1008.18	834.13	718.59	636.47	575.24	527.93	490.37	459.89	434.73	413.65	395.77
43000	3723.13	1927.66	1330.18	1032.19	853.99	735.70	651.62	588.93	540.50	502.05	470.84	445.08	423.49	405.19
44000	3809.72	1972.49	1361.11	1056.19	873.85	752.81	666.77	602.63	553.07	513.72	481.79	455.43	433.34	414.61
45000	3896.30	2017.32	1392.05	1080.20	893.72	769.91	681.93	616.33	565.64	525.40	492.74	465.78	443.19	424.04
46000	3982.89	2062.15	1422.98	1104.20	913.58	787.02	697.08	630.02	578.21	537.07	503.69	476.13	453.04	433.46
47000	4069.47	2106.98	1453.92	1128.21	933.44	804.13	712.24	643.72	590.78	548.75	514.64	486.48	462.89	442.88
48000	4156.06	2151.81	1484.85	1152.21	953.30	821.24	727.39	657.41	603.35	560.42	525.59	496.83	472.74	452.31
49000	4242.64	2196.64	1515.78	1176.21	973.16	838.35	742.54	671.11	615.92	572.10	536.54	507.18	482.59	461.73
50000	4329.22	2241.47	1546.72	1200.22	993.02	855.46	757.70	684.81	628.49	583.77	547.49	517.53	492.43	471.15
55000	4762.15	2465.61	1701.39	1320.24	1092.32	941.01	833.47	753.29	691.34	642.15	602.24	569.29	541.68	518.27
60000	5195.07	2689.76	1856.06	1440.26	1191.62	1026.55	909.24	821.77	754.19	700.53	656.99	621.04	590.92	565.38
65000	5627.99	2913.91	2010.73	1560.28	1290.92	1112.10	985.01	890.25	817.03	758.90	711.74	672.79	640.16	612.50
70000	6060.91	3138.05	2165.40	1680.30	1390.22	1197.64	1060.78	958.73	879.88	817.28	766.49	724.54	689.41	659.61
75000	6493.83	3362.20	2320.08	1800.33	1489.52	1283.19	1136.54	1027.21	942.73	875.66	821.24	776.30	738.65	706.73
80000	6926.76	3586.35	2474.75	1920.35	1588.82	1368.73	1212.31	1095.69	1005.58	934.03	875.98	828.05	787.89	753.84
85000	7359.68	3810.49	2629.42	2040.37	1688.12	1454.28	1288.08	1164.17	1068.43	992.41	930.73	879.80	837.14	800.96
90000	7792.60	4034.64	2784.09	2160.39	1787.43	1539.82	1363.85	1232.65	1131.28	1050.79	985.48	931.56	886.38	848.07
95000	8225.52	4258.79	2938.76	2280.41	1886.73	1625.37	1439.62	1301.13	1194.12	1109.17	1040.23	983.31	935.62	895.19
100000	8658.44	4482.93	3093.43	2400.43	1986.03	1710.91	1515.39	1369.61	1256.97	1167.54	1094.98	1035.06	984.86	942.30

TERM	15 Years	16 Years	17 Years	18 Years	19 Years	20 Years	21 Years	22 Years	23 Years	24 Years	25 Years	30 Years	35 Years	40 Years
AMOUNT														
5	.05	.05	.05	.05	.05	.04	.04	.04	.04	.04	.04	.04	.04	.04
10	.10	.09	.09	.09	.09	.08	.08	.08	.08	.08	.08	.07	.07	.07
15	.14	.14	.13	.13	.13	.12	.12	.12	.12	.11	.11	.11	.10	.10
25	.23	.22	.22	.21	.21	.20	.20	.19	.19	.19	.18	.17	.17	.16
50	.46	.44	.43	.42	.41	.40	.39	.38	.37	.37	.36	.34	.33	.32
75	.68	.66	.64	.62	.61	.59	.58	.57	.56	.55	.54	.51	.49	.48
100	.91	.88	.85	.83	.81	.79	.77	.76	.74	.73	.72	.68	.65	.64
200	1.82	1.75	1.70	1.65	1.61	1.57	1.54	1.51	1.48	1.46	1.43	1.35	1.30	1.27
300	2.72	2.63	2.55	2.47	2.41	2.35	2.30	2.26	2.22	2.18	2.15	2.03	1.95	1.90
400	3.63	3.50	3.39	3.30	3.21	3.14	3.07	3.01	2.96	2.91	2.86	2.70	2.60	2.53
500	4.53	4.38	4.24	4.12	4.01	3.92	3.84	3.76	3.69	3.63	3.58	3.37	3.24	3.16
600	5.44	5.25	5.09	4.94	4.81	4.70	4.60	4.51	4.43	4.36	4.29	4.05	3.89	3.79
700	6.35	6.13	5.93	5.76	5.62	5.48	5.37	5.26	5.17	5.08	5.01	4.72	4.54	4.42
800	7.25	7.00	6.78	6.59	6.42	6.27	6.13	6.01	5.91	5.81	5.72	5.39	5.19	5.05
900	8.16	7.87	7.63	7.41	7.22	7.05	6.90	6.77	6.64	6.54	6.44	6.07	5.83	5.68
1000	9.06	8.75	8.47	8.23	8.02	7.83	7.67	7.52	7.38	7.26	7.15	6.74	6.48	6.31
2000	18.12	17.49	16.94	16.46	16.04	15.66	15.33	15.03	14.76	14.52	14.30	13.48	12.96	12.62
3000	27.18	26.23	25.41	24.69	24.05	23.49	22.99	22.54	22.14	21.77	21.45	20.22	19.43	18.92
4000	36.24	34.98	33.88	32.92	32.07	31.32	30.65	30.05	29.51	29.03	28.60	26.95	25.91	25.23
5000	45.30	43.72	42.35	41.15	40.09	39.15	38.31	37.56	36.89	36.29	35.74	33.69	32.39	31.53
6000	54.35	52.46	50.82	49.37	48.10	46.97	45.97	45.07	44.27	43.54	42.89	40.43	38.86	37.84
7000	63.41	61.21	59.29	57.60	56.12	54.80	53.63	52.58	51.65	50.80	50.04	47.17	45.34	44.14
8000	72.47	69.95	67.76	65.83	64.13	62.63	61.29	60.10	59.02	58.06	57.19	53.90	51.82	50.45
9000	81.53	78.69	76.22	74.06	72.15	70.46	68.95	67.61	66.40	65.31	64.33	60.64	58.29	56.75
10000	90.59	87.44	84.69	82.29	80.17	78.29	76.61	75.12	73.78	72.57	71.48	67.38	64.77	63.06
11000	99.65	96.18	93.16	90.52	88.18	86.12	84.28	82.63	81.16	79.83	78.63	74.11	71.25	69.36
12000	108.70	104.92	101.63	98.74	96.20	93.94	91.94	90.14	88.53	87.08	85.78	80.85	77.72	75.67
13000	117.76	113.67	110.10	106.97	104.21	101.77	99.60	97.65	95.91	94.34	92.93	87.59	84.20	81.97
14000	126.82	122.41	118.57	115.20	112.23	109.60	107.26	105.16	103.29	101.60	100.07	94.33	90.67	88.28
15000	135.88	131.15	127.04	123.43	120.25	117.43	114.92	112.68	110.66	108.85	107.22	101.06	97.15	94.58
16000	144.94	139.90	135.51	131.66	128.26	125.26	122.58	120.19	118.04	116.11	114.37	107.80	103.63	100.89
17000	154.00	148.64	143.97	139.88	136.28	133.08	130.24	127.70	125.42	123.37	121.52	114.54	110.10	107.20
18000	163.05	157.38	152.44	148.11	144.30	140.91	137.90	135.21	132.80	130.62	128.66	121.27	116.58	113.50
19000	172.11	166.13	160.91	156.34	152.31	148.74	145.56	142.72	140.17	137.88	135.81	128.01	123.06	119.81
20000	181.17	174.87	169.38	164.57	160.33	156.57	153.22	150.23	147.55	145.14	142.96	134.75	129.53	126.11
21000	190.23	183.61	177.85	172.80	168.34	164.40	160.88	157.74	154.93	152.39	150.11	141.49	136.01	132.42
22000	199.29	192.35	186.32	181.03	176.36	172.23	168.55	165.26	162.31	159.65	157.26	148.22	142.49	138.72
23000	208.35	201.10	194.79	189.25	184.38	180.05	176.21	172.77	169.68	166.91	164.40	154.96	140.96	145.03
24000	217.40	209.84	203.26	197.48	192.39	187.88	183.87	180.28	177.06	174.16	171.55	161.70	155.44	151.33
25000	226.46	218.58	211.72	205.71	200.41	195.71	191.53	187.79	184.44	181.42	178.70	168.43	161.92	157.64
26000	235.52	227.33	220.19	213.94	208.42	203.54	199.19	195.30	191.81	188.68	185.85	175.17	168.39	163.94
27000	244.58	236.07	228.66	222.17	216.44	211.37	206.85	202.81	199.19	195.93	192.99	181.91	174.87	170.25
28000	253.64	244.81	237.13	230.39	224.46	219.19	214.51	210.32	206.57	203.19	200.14	188.65	181.34	176.55
29000	262.70	253.56	245.60	238.62	232.47	227.02	222.17	217.84	213.95	210.45	207.29	195.38	187.82	182.86
30000	271.75	262.30	254.07	246.85	240.49	234.85	229.83	225.35	221.32	217.70	214.44	202.12	194.30	189.16
31000	280.81	271.04	262.54	255.08	248.51	242.68	237.49	232.86	228.70	224.96	221.58	208.86	200.77	195.47
32000	289.87	279.79	271.01	263.31	256.52	250.51	245.15	240.37	236.08	232.22	228.73	215.59	207.25	201.78
33000	298.93	288.53	279.47	271.54	264.54	258.34	252.82	247.88	243.46	239.47	235.88	222.33	213.73	208.08
34000	307.99	297.27	287.94	279.76	272.55	266.16	260.48	255.39	250.83	246.73	243.03	229.07	220.20	214.39
35000	317.05	306.02	296.41	287.99	280.57	273.99	268.14	262.90	258.21	253.99	250.18	235.81	226.68	220.69
36000	326.10	314.76	304.88	296.22	288.59	281.82	275.80	270.42	265.59	261.24	257.32	242.54	233.16	227.00
37000	335.16	323.50	313.35	304.45	296.60	289.65	283.46	277.93	272.97	268.50	264.47	249.28	239.63	233.30
38000	344.22	332.25	321.82	312.68	304.62	297.48	291.12	285.44	280.34	275.76	271.62	256.02	246.11	239.61
39000	353.28	340.99	330.29	320.91	312.63	305.30	298.78	292.95	287.72	283.01	278.77	262.76	252.58	245.91
40000	362.34	349.73	338.76	329.13	320.65	313.13	306.44	300.46	295.10	290.27	285.91	269.49	259.06	252.22
41000	371.40	358.48	347.22	337.36	328.67	320.96	314.10	307.97	302.47	297.53	293.06	276.23	265.54	258.52
42000	380.45	367.22	355.69	345.59	336.68	328.79	321.76	315.48	309.85	304.78	300.21	282.97	272.01	264.83
43000	389.51	375.96	364.16	353.82	344.70	336.62	329.42	323.00	317.23	312.04	307.36	289.70	278.49	271.13
44000	398.57	384.70	372.63	362.05	352.71	344.45	337.09	330.51	324.61	319.30	314.51	296.44	284.97	277.44
45000	407.63	393.45	381.10	370.27	360.73	352.27	344.75	338.02	331.98	326.55	321.65	303.18	291.44	283.74
46000	416.69	402.19	389.57	378.50	368.75	360.10	352.41	345.53	339.36	333.81	328.80	309.92	297.92	290.05
47000	425.75	410.93	398.04	386.73	376.76	367.93	360.07	353.04	346.74	341.07	335.95	316.65	304.40	296.35
48000	434.80	419.68	406.51	394.96	384.78	375.76	367.73	360.55	354.12	348.32	343.10	323.39	310.87	302.66
49000	443.86	428.42	414.97	403.19	392.80	383.59	375.39	368.06	361.49	355.58	350.24	330.13	317.35	308.97
50000	452.92	437.16	423.44	411.42	400.81	391.41	383.05	375.58	368.87	362.84	357.39	336.86	323.83	315.27
55000	498.21	480.88	465.79	452.56	440.89	430.56	421.36	413.15	405.76	399.12	393.13	370.55	356.21	346.80
60000	543.50	524.60	508.13	493.70	480.97	469.70	459.66	450.69	442.64	435.40	428.87	404.24	388.59	378.32
65000	588.60	568.31	550.47	534.84	521.05	508.84	497.96	488.25	479.53	471.69	464.61	437.92	420.97	409.85
70000	634.09	612.03	592.82	575.98	561.13	547.98	536.27	525.80	516.42	507.97	500.35	471.61	453.35	441.38
75000	679.38	655.74	635.16	617.12	601.21	587.12	574.57	563.36	553.30	544.25	536.08	505.29	485.74	472.90
80000	724.67	699.46	677.51	658.26	641.30	626.26	612.88	600.92	590.19	580.54	571.82	538.98	518.12	504.43
85000	769.96	743.17	719.85	699.40	681.38	665.40	651.18	638.47	627.08	616.82	607.56	572.67	550.50	535.96
90000	815.25	786.89	762.19	740.54	721.46	704.54	689.49	676.03	663.96	653.10	643.30	606.35	582.88	567.48
95000	860.54	830.61	804.54	781.68	761.54	743.68	727.79	713.59	700.85	689.38	679.04	640.04	615.26	599.01
100000	905.84	874.32	846.88	822.83	801.62	782.82	766.10	751.15	737.73	725.67	714.78	673.72	647.65	630.54

7.200%

MONTHLY PAYMENT
REQUIRED TO AMORTIZE A LOAN

TERM AMOUNT	1 Year	2 Years	3 Years	4 Years	5 Years	6 Years	7 Years	8 Years	9 Years	10 Years	11 Years	12 Years	13 Years	14 Years
5	.11	.00	.10	.13	.10	.09	.08	.07	.07	.06	.06	.06	.05	.05
10	.87	.45	.31	.25	.20	.18	.16	.14	.13	.12	.11	.11	.10	.10
15	1.30	.68	.47	.37	.30	.26	.23	.21	.19	.18	.17	.16	.15	.15
25	2.17	1.13	.78	.61	.50	.43	.38	.35	.32	.30	.28	.26	.25	.24
50	4.34	2.25	1.55	1.21	1.00	.86	.76	.69	.64	.59	.55	.52	.50	.48
75	6.50	3.37	2.33	1.81	1.50	1.29	1.14	1.04	.95	.88	.83	.78	.75	.71
100	8.67	4.49	3.10	2.41	1.99	1.72	1.52	1.38	1.27	1.18	1.10	1.04	.99	.95
200	17.33	8.98	6.20	4.81	3.98	3.43	3.04	2.75	2.53	2.35	2.20	2.08	1.98	1.90
300	25.99	13.46	9.30	7.22	5.97	5.15	4.56	4.13	3.79	3.52	3.30	3.12	2.97	2.84
400	34.65	17.95	12.39	9.62	7.96	6.86	6.08	5.50	5.05	4.69	4.40	4.16	3.96	3.79
500	43.31	22.44	15.49	12.02	9.95	8.58	7.60	6.87	6.31	5.86	5.50	5.20	4.95	4.74
600	51.98	26.92	18.59	14.43	11.94	10.29	9.12	8.25	7.57	7.03	6.60	6.24	5.94	5.68
700	60.64	31.41	21.68	16.83	13.93	12.01	10.64	9.62	8.83	8.20	7.70	7.28	6.93	6.63
800	69.30	35.90	24.78	19.24	15.92	13.72	12.16	10.99	10.09	9.38	8.80	8.32	7.92	7.58
900	77.96	40.38	27.88	21.64	17.91	15.44	13.68	12.37	11.35	10.55	9.90	9.36	8.91	8.52
1000	86.62	44.87	30.97	24.04	19.90	17.15	15.20	13.74	12.61	11.72	10.99	10.40	9.89	9.47
2000	173.24	89.73	61.94	48.08	39.80	34.30	30.39	27.47	25.22	23.43	21.98	20.79	19.78	18.93
3000	259.86	134.59	92.91	72.12	59.69	51.44	45.58	41.21	37.83	35.15	32.97	31.18	29.67	28.40
4000	346.48	179.46	123.88	96.16	79.59	68.59	60.77	54.94	50.44	46.86	43.96	41.57	39.56	37.86
5000	433.10	224.32	154.85	120.20	99.48	85.73	75.96	68.67	63.04	58.58	54.95	51.96	49.45	47.33
6000	519.72	269.18	185.82	144.24	119.38	102.88	91.15	82.41	75.65	70.29	65.94	62.35	59.34	56.79
7000	606.34	314.05	216.79	168.28	139.27	120.02	106.34	96.14	88.26	82.00	76.93	72.74	69.23	66.26
8000	692.96	358.91	247.75	192.32	159.17	137.17	121.53	109.87	100.87	93.72	87.92	83.13	79.12	75.72
9000	779.58	403.77	278.72	216.36	179.07	154.31	136.72	123.61	113.48	105.43	98.91	93.52	89.01	85.19
10000	866.19	448.64	309.69	240.40	198.96	171.46	151.91	137.34	126.08	117.15	109.90	103.91	98.90	94.65
11000	952.81	493.50	340.66	264.44	218.86	188.60	167.10	151.07	138.69	128.86	120.89	114.30	108.79	104.11
12000	1039.43	538.36	371.63	288.47	238.75	205.75	182.29	164.81	151.30	140.58	131.88	124.69	118.68	113.58
13000	1126.05	583.23	402.60	312.51	258.65	222.89	197.48	178.54	163.91	152.29	142.87	135.08	128.57	123.04
14000	1212.67	628.09	433.57	336.55	278.54	240.04	212.67	192.27	176.51	164.00	153.85	145.48	138.46	132.51
15000	1299.29	672.95	464.53	360.59	298.44	257.18	227.86	206.01	189.12	175.72	164.84	155.87	148.35	141.97
16000	1385.91	717.82	495.50	384.63	318.34	274.33	243.06	219.74	201.73	187.43	175.83	166.26	158.24	151.44
17000	1472.53	762.68	526.47	408.67	338.23	291.47	258.25	233.47	214.34	199.15	186.82	176.65	168.13	160.90
18000	1559.15	807.54	557.44	432.71	358.13	308.62	273.44	247.21	226.95	210.86	197.81	187.04	178.01	170.37
19000	1645.77	852.41	588.41	456.75	378.02	325.76	288.63	260.94	239.55	222.57	208.80	197.43	187.90	179.83
20000	1732.38	897.27	619.38	480.79	397.92	342.91	303.82	274.67	252.16	234.29	219.79	207.82	197.79	189.29
21000	1819.00	942.13	650.35	504.83	417.81	360.05	319.01	288.41	264.77	246.00	230.78	218.21	207.68	198.76
22000	1905.62	987.00	681.31	528.87	437.71	377.20	334.20	302.14	277.38	257.72	241.77	228.60	217.57	208.22
23000	1992.24	1031.86	712.28	552.91	457.61	394.34	349.39	315.87	289.98	269.43	252.76	238.99	227.46	217.69
24000	2078.86	1076.72	743.25	576.94	477.50	411.49	364.58	329.61	302.59	281.15	263.75	249.38	237.35	227.15
25000	2165.48	1121.59	774.22	600.98	497.40	428.64	379.77	343.34	315.20	292.86	274.74	259.77	247.24	236.62
26000	2252.10	1166.45	805.19	625.02	517.29	445.78	394.96	357.07	327.81	304.57	285.73	270.16	257.13	246.08
27000	2338.72	1211.31	836.16	649.06	537.19	462.93	410.15	370.81	340.42	316.29	296.71	280.55	267.02	255.55
28000	2425.34	1256.18	867.13	673.10	557.08	480.07	425.34	384.54	353.02	328.00	307.70	290.95	276.91	265.01
29000	2511.96	1301.04	898.10	697.14	576.98	497.22	440.53	398.28	365.63	339.72	318.69	301.34	286.80	274.47
30000	2598.57	1345.90	929.06	721.18	596.88	514.36	455.72	412.01	378.24	351.43	329.68	311.73	296.69	283.94
31000	2685.19	1390.77	960.03	745.22	616.77	531.51	470.91	425.74	390.85	363.14	340.67	322.12	306.58	293.40
32000	2771.81	1435.63	991.00	769.26	636.67	548.65	486.11	439.48	403.46	374.86	351.66	332.51	316.47	302.87
33000	2858.43	1480.49	1021.97	793.30	656.56	565.80	501.30	453.21	416.06	386.57	362.65	342.90	326.36	312.33
34000	2945.05	1525.36	1052.94	817.34	676.46	582.94	516.49	466.94	428.67	398.29	373.64	353.29	336.25	321.80
35000	3031.67	1570.22	1083.91	841.38	696.35	600.09	531.68	480.68	441.28	410.00	384.63	363.68	346.14	331.26
36000	3118.29	1615.08	1114.88	865.41	716.25	617.23	546.87	494.41	453.89	421.72	395.62	374.07	356.02	340.73
37000	3204.91	1659.95	1145.84	889.45	736.15	634.38	562.06	508.14	466.49	433.43	406.61	384.46	365.91	350.19
38000	3291.53	1704.81	1176.81	913.49	756.04	651.52	577.25	521.88	479.10	445.14	417.60	394.85	375.80	359.65
39000	3378.15	1749.67	1207.78	937.53	775.94	668.67	592.44	535.61	491.71	456.86	428.59	405.24	385.69	369.12
40000	3464.77	1794.54	1238.75	961.57	795.83	685.81	607.63	549.34	504.32	468.57	439.57	415.63	395.58	378.58
41000	3551.38	1839.40	1269.72	985.61	815.73	702.96	622.82	563.08	516.93	480.29	450.56	426.03	405.47	388.05
42000	3638.00	1884.26	1300.69	1009.65	835.62	720.10	638.01	576.81	529.53	492.00	461.55	436.42	415.36	397.51
43000	3724.62	1929.13	1331.66	1033.69	855.52	737.25	653.20	590.54	542.14	503.72	472.54	446.81	425.25	406.98
44000	3811.24	1973.99	1362.62	1057.73	875.42	754.39	668.39	604.28	554.75	515.43	483.53	457.20	435.14	416.44
45000	3897.86	2018.85	1393.59	1081.77	895.31	771.54	683.58	618.01	567.36	527.14	494.52	467.59	445.03	425.91
46000	3984.48	2063.72	1424.56	1105.81	915.21	788.68	698.77	631.74	579.96	538.86	505.51	477.98	454.92	435.37
47000	4071.10	2108.58	1455.53	1129.84	935.10	805.83	713.96	645.48	592.57	550.57	516.50	488.37	464.81	444.83
48000	4157.72	2153.44	1486.50	1153.88	955.00	822.97	729.16	659.21	605.18	562.29	527.49	498.76	474.70	454.30
49000	4244.33	2198.31	1517.47	1177.92	974.89	840.12	744.35	672.94	617.79	574.00	538.48	509.15	484.59	463.76
50000	4330.95	2243.17	1548.44	1201.96	994.79	857.27	759.54	686.68	630.40	585.71	549.47	519.54	494.48	473.23
55000	4764.05	2467.49	1703.28	1322.16	1094.27	942.99	835.49	755.35	693.43	644.29	604.41	571.50	543.92	520.55
60000	5197.14	2691.80	1858.12	1442.35	1193.75	1028.72	911.44	824.01	756.47	702.86	659.36	623.45	593.37	567.87
65000	5630.24	2916.12	2012.97	1562.55	1293.23	1114.44	987.40	892.68	819.51	761.43	714.31	675.40	642.82	615.19
70000	6063.33	3140.44	2167.81	1682.75	1392.70	1200.17	1063.35	961.35	882.55	820.00	769.25	727.36	692.27	662.52
75000	6496.43	3364.75	2322.65	1802.94	1492.18	1285.90	1139.30	1030.01	945.59	878.57	824.20	779.31	741.71	709.84
80000	6929.52	3589.07	2477.49	1923.14	1591.66	1371.62	1215.26	1098.68	1008.63	937.14	879.14	831.26	791.16	757.16
85000	7362.62	3813.39	2632.34	2043.33	1691.14	1457.35	1291.21	1167.35	1071.67	995.71	934.09	883.22	840.61	804.48
90000	7795.71	4037.70	2787.18	2163.53	1790.62	1543.07	1367.16	1236.02	1134.71	1054.28	989.04	935.17	890.05	851.81
95000	8228.81	4262.02	2942.02	2283.72	1890.10	1628.80	1443.12	1304.68	1197.75	1112.85	1043.98	987.12	939.50	899.13
100000	8661.90	4486.34	3096.87	2403.92	1989.57	1714.53	1519.07	1373.35	1260.79	1171.42	1098.93	1039.08	988.95	946.45

TERM	15 Years	16 Years	17 Years	18 Years	19 Years	20 Years	21 Years	22 Years	23 Years	24 Years	25 Years	30 Years	35 Years	40 Years
AMOUNT														
5	.05	.05	.05	.05	.05	.04	.04	.04	.04	.04	.04	.04	.04	.04
10	.10	.09	.09	.09	.09	.08	.08	.08	.08	.08	.08	.07	.07	.07
15	.14	.14	.13	.13	.13	.12	.12	.12	.12	.11	.11	.11	.10	.10
25	.23	.22	.22	.21	.21	.20	.20	.19	.19	.19	.18	.17	.17	.16
50	.46	.44	.43	.42	.41	.40	.39	.38	.38	.37	.36	.34	.33	.32
75	.69	.66	.64	.63	.61	.60	.58	.57	.56	.55	.54	.51	.49	.48
100	.92	.88	.86	.83	.81	.79	.78	.76	.75	.74	.72	.68	.66	.64
200	1.83	1.76	1.71	1.66	1.62	1.58	1.55	1.52	1.49	1.47	1.44	1.36	1.31	1.28
300	2.74	2.64	2.56	2.49	2.42	2.37	2.32	2.27	2.23	2.20	2.16	2.04	1.96	1.91
400	3.65	3.52	3.41	3.31	3.23	3.15	3.09	3.03	2.97	2.93	2.88	2.72	2.62	2.55
500	4.56	4.40	4.26	4.14	4.04	3.94	3.86	3.78	3.72	3.66	3.60	3.40	3.27	3.19
600	5.47	5.28	5.11	4.97	4.84	4.73	4.63	4.54	4.46	4.39	4.32	4.08	3.92	3.82
700	6.38	6.16	5.96	5.80	5.65	5.52	5.40	5.30	5.20	5.12	5.04	4.76	4.58	4.46
800	7.29	7.03	6.81	6.62	6.45	6.30	6.17	6.05	5.94	5.85	5.76	5.44	5.23	5.09
900	8.20	7.91	7.67	7.45	7.26	7.09	6.94	6.81	6.69	6.58	6.48	6.11	5.88	5.73
1000	9.11	8.79	8.52	8.28	8.07	7.88	7.71	7.56	7.43	7.31	7.20	6.79	6.53	6.37
2000	18.21	17.58	17.03	16.55	16.13	15.75	15.42	15.12	14.85	14.61	14.40	13.58	13.06	12.73
3000	27.31	26.36	25.54	24.82	24.19	23.63	23.13	22.68	22.28	21.92	21.59	20.37	19.59	19.09
4000	36.41	35.15	34.05	33.09	32.25	31.50	30.83	30.24	29.70	29.22	28.79	27.16	26.12	25.45
5000	45.51	43.93	42.57	41.37	40.31	39.37	38.54	37.79	37.13	36.53	35.98	33.94	32.65	31.81
6000	54.61	52.72	51.08	49.64	48.37	47.25	46.25	45.35	44.55	43.83	43.18	40.73	39.18	38.17
7000	63.71	61.51	59.59	57.91	56.43	55.12	53.95	52.91	51.98	51.13	50.38	47.52	45.71	44.53
8000	72.81	70.29	68.10	66.18	64.49	62.99	61.66	60.47	59.40	58.44	57.57	54.31	52.24	50.89
9000	81.91	79.08	76.61	74.46	72.55	70.87	69.37	68.03	66.82	65.74	64.77	61.10	58.77	57.25
10000	91.01	87.86	85.13	82.73	80.61	78.74	77.07	75.58	74.25	73.05	71.96	67.88	65.30	63.61
11000	100.11	96.65	93.64	91.00	88.67	86.61	84.78	83.14	81.67	80.35	79.16	74.67	71.83	69.97
12000	109.21	105.44	102.15	99.27	96.73	94.49	92.49	90.70	89.10	87.66	86.36	81.46	78.36	76.33
13000	118.31	114.22	110.66	107.54	104.80	102.36	100.19	98.26	96.52	94.96	93.55	88.25	84.89	82.69
14000	127.41	123.01	119.18	115.82	112.86	110.23	107.90	105.82	103.95	102.26	100.75	95.04	91.42	89.05
15000	136.51	131.79	127.69	124.09	120.92	118.11	115.61	113.37	111.37	109.57	107.94	101.82	97.94	95.41
16000	145.61	140.58	136.20	132.36	128.98	125.98	123.31	120.93	118.79	116.87	115.14	108.61	104.47	101.77
17000	154.71	149.37	144.71	140.63	137.04	133.85	131.02	128.49	126.22	124.18	122.34	115.40	111.00	108.13
18000	163.81	158.15	153.22	148.91	145.10	141.73	138.73	136.05	133.64	131.48	129.53	122.19	117.53	114.49
19000	172.91	166.94	161.74	157.18	153.16	149.60	146.43	143.60	141.07	138.79	136.73	128.97	124.06	120.85
20000	182.01	175.72	170.25	165.45	161.22	157.47	154.14	151.16	148.49	146.09	143.92	135.76	130.59	127.21
21000	191.11	184.51	178.76	173.72	169.28	165.35	161.85	158.72	155.92	153.39	151.12	142.55	137.12	133.57
22000	200.22	193.30	187.27	182.00	177.34	173.22	169.55	166.28	163.34	160.70	158.31	149.34	143.65	139.93
23000	209.32	202.08	195.79	190.27	185.40	181.10	177.26	173.84	170.76	168.00	165.51	156.13	150.18	146.29
24000	218.42	210.87	204.30	198.54	193.46	188.97	184.97	181.39	178.19	175.31	172.71	162.91	156.71	152.65
25000	227.52	219.65	212.81	206.81	201.53	196.84	192.68	188.95	185.61	182.61	179.90	169.70	163.24	159.01
26000	236.62	228.44	221.32	215.08	209.59	204.72	200.38	196.51	193.04	189.92	187.10	176.49	169.77	165.37
27000	245.72	237.23	229.83	223.36	217.65	212.59	208.09	204.07	200.46	197.22	194.29	183.28	176.30	171.73
28000	254.82	246.01	238.35	231.63	225.71	220.46	215.80	211.63	207.89	204.52	201.49	190.07	182.83	178.09
29000	263.92	254.80	246.86	239.90	233.77	228.34	223.50	219.18	215.31	211.83	208.69	196.85	189.36	184.45
30000	273.02	263.58	255.37	248.17	241.83	236.21	231.21	226.74	222.74	219.13	215.88	203.64	195.88	190.81
31000	282.12	272.37	263.88	256.45	249.89	244.08	238.92	234.30	230.16	226.44	223.08	210.43	202.41	197.17
32000	291.22	281.16	272.40	264.72	257.95	251.96	246.62	241.86	237.58	233.74	230.27	217.22	208.94	203.53
33000	300.32	289.94	280.91	272.99	266.01	259.83	254.33	249.41	245.01	241.04	237.47	224.01	215.47	209.89
34000	309.42	298.73	289.42	281.26	274.07	267.70	262.04	256.97	252.43	248.35	244.67	230.79	222.00	216.25
35000	318.52	307.51	297.93	289.53	282.13	275.58	269.74	264.53	259.86	255.65	251.86	237.58	228.53	222.61
36000	327.62	316.30	306.44	297.81	290.19	283.45	277.45	272.09	267.28	262.96	259.06	244.37	235.06	228.97
37000	336.72	325.09	314.96	306.08	298.26	291.32	285.16	279.65	274.71	270.26	266.25	251.16	241.59	235.33
38000	345.82	333.87	323.47	314.35	306.32	299.20	292.86	287.20	282.13	277.57	273.45	257.94	248.12	241.69
39000	354.92	342.66	331.98	322.62	314.38	307.07	300.57	294.76	289.55	284.87	280.64	264.73	254.65	248.05
40000	364.02	351.44	340.49	330.90	322.44	314.94	308.28	302.32	296.98	292.17	287.84	271.52	261.18	254.41
41000	373.12	360.23	349.01	339.17	330.50	322.82	315.98	309.88	304.40	299.48	295.04	278.31	267.71	260.77
42000	382.22	369.02	357.52	347.44	338.56	330.69	323.69	317.44	311.83	306.78	302.23	285.10	274.24	267.13
43000	391.33	377.80	366.03	355.71	346.62	338.57	331.40	324.99	319.25	314.09	309.43	291.88	280.77	273.49
44000	400.43	386.59	374.54	363.99	354.68	346.44	339.10	332.55	326.68	321.39	316.62	298.67	287.29	279.85
45000	409.53	395.37	383.05	372.26	362.74	354.31	346.81	340.11	334.10	328.70	323.82	305.46	293.82	286.21
46000	418.63	404.16	391.57	380.53	370.80	362.19	354.52	347.67	341.52	336.00	331.02	312.25	300.35	292.57
47000	427.73	412.95	400.08	388.80	378.86	370.06	362.22	355.23	348.95	343.30	338.21	319.04	306.88	298.93
48000	436.83	421.73	408.59	397.07	386.92	377.93	369.93	362.78	356.37	350.61	345.41	325.82	313.41	305.29
49000	445.93	430.52	417.10	405.35	394.99	385.81	377.64	370.34	363.80	357.91	352.60	332.61	319.94	311.65
50000	455.03	439.30	425.61	413.62	403.05	393.68	385.35	377.90	371.22	365.22	359.80	339.40	326.47	318.01
55000	500.53	483.23	468.18	454.98	443.35	433.05	423.88	415.69	408.34	401.74	395.78	373.34	359.12	349.81
60000	546.03	527.16	510.74	496.34	483.65	472.41	462.41	453.48	445.47	438.26	431.76	407.28	391.76	381.61
65000	591.54	571.09	553.30	537.70	523.96	511.78	500.95	491.27	482.59	474.78	467.74	441.22	424.41	413.41
70000	637.04	615.02	595.86	579.06	564.26	551.15	539.48	529.06	519.71	511.30	503.72	475.16	457.06	445.21
75000	682.54	658.95	638.42	620.43	604.57	590.52	578.02	566.85	556.83	547.82	539.70	509.10	489.70	477.01
80000	728.04	702.88	680.98	661.79	644.87	629.88	616.55	604.64	593.95	584.34	575.68	543.04	522.35	508.81
85000	773.54	746.81	723.54	703.15	685.17	669.25	655.08	642.42	631.07	620.87	611.66	576.97	555.00	540.61
90000	819.05	790.74	766.10	744.51	725.48	708.62	693.62	680.21	668.20	657.39	647.63	610.91	587.64	572.41
95000	864.55	834.67	808.66	785.87	765.78	747.99	732.15	718.00	705.32	693.91	683.61	644.85	620.29	604.22
100000	910.05	878.60	851.22	827.23	806.09	787.35	770.69	755.79	742.44	730.43	719.59	678.79	652.94	636.02

TERM AMOUNT	1 Year	2 Years	3 Years	4 Years	5 Years	6 Years	7 Years	8 Years	9 Years	10 Years	11 Years	12 Years	13 Years	14 Years
5	.44	.23	.16	.13	.10	.09	.08	.07	.07	.06	.06	.06	.05	.05
10	.87	.45	.31	.25	.20	.18	.16	.14	.13	.12	.12	.11	.10	.10
15	1.30	.68	.47	.37	.30	.26	.23	.21	.19	.18	.17	.16	.15	.15
25	2.17	1.13	.78	.61	.50	.43	.39	.35	.32	.30	.28	.27	.25	.24
50	4.34	2.25	1.55	1.21	1.00	.86	.77	.69	.64	.59	.56	.53	.50	.48
75	6.50	3.37	2.33	1.81	1.50	1.29	1.15	1.04	.95	.89	.83	.79	.75	.72
100	8.67	4.49	3.10	2.41	2.00	1.72	1.53	1.38	1.27	1.18	1.11	1.05	1.00	.95
200	17.33	8.98	6.20	4.82	3.99	3.44	3.05	2.76	2.53	2.35	2.21	2.09	1.99	1.90
300	26.00	13.47	9.30	7.22	5.98	5.16	4.57	4.13	3.79	3.53	3.31	3.13	2.98	2.85
400	34.66	17.96	12.40	9.63	7.97	6.87	6.09	5.51	5.06	4.70	4.41	4.17	3.97	3.80
500	43.33	22.45	15.50	12.04	9.96	8.59	7.61	6.88	6.32	5.88	5.51	5.21	4.96	4.75
600	51.99	26.94	18.60	14.44	11.96	10.31	9.13	8.26	7.58	7.05	6.61	6.26	5.96	5.70
700	60.65	31.43	21.70	16.85	13.95	12.02	10.66	9.64	8.85	8.22	7.72	7.30	6.95	6.65
800	69.32	35.91	24.80	19.25	15.94	13.74	12.18	11.01	10.11	9.40	8.82	8.34	7.94	7.60
900	77.98	40.40	27.90	21.66	17.93	15.46	13.70	12.39	11.37	10.57	9.92	9.38	8.93	8.55
1000	86.65	44.89	31.00	24.07	19.92	17.17	15.22	13.76	12.64	11.75	11.02	10.42	9.92	9.50
2000	173.29	89.78	61.99	48.13	39.84	34.34	30.44	27.52	25.27	23.49	22.04	20.84	19.84	18.99
3000	259.93	134.66	92.98	72.19	59.76	51.51	45.65	41.28	37.90	35.23	33.05	31.26	29.76	28.48
4000	346.57	179.55	123.97	96.25	79.68	68.68	60.87	55.04	50.54	46.97	44.07	41.68	39.67	37.97
5000	433.22	224.44	154.96	120.32	99.60	85.85	76.08	68.80	63.17	58.71	55.08	52.09	49.59	47.47
6000	519.86	269.32	185.95	144.38	119.52	103.02	91.30	82.56	75.80	70.45	66.10	62.51	59.51	56.96
7000	606.50	314.21	216.95	168.44	139.44	120.19	106.51	96.31	88.44	82.19	77.11	72.93	69.42	66.45
8000	693.14	359.09	247.94	192.50	159.36	137.36	121.73	110.07	101.07	93.93	88.13	83.35	79.34	75.94
9000	779.78	403.98	278.93	216.57	179.28	154.53	136.94	123.83	113.70	105.67	99.15	93.76	89.26	85.43
10000	866.43	448.87	309.92	240.63	199.20	171.70	152.16	137.59	126.34	117.41	110.16	104.18	99.17	94.93
11000	953.07	493.75	340.91	264.69	219.12	188.87	167.37	151.35	138.97	129.15	121.18	114.60	109.09	104.42
12000	1039.71	538.64	371.90	288.75	239.04	206.04	182.59	165.11	151.60	140.89	132.19	125.02	119.01	113.91
13000	1126.35	583.52	402.89	312.82	258.96	223.21	197.80	178.86	164.24	152.63	143.21	135.43	128.92	123.40
14000	1212.99	628.41	433.89	336.88	278.88	240.38	213.02	192.62	176.87	164.37	154.22	145.85	138.84	132.90
15000	1299.64	673.30	464.88	360.94	298.80	257.54	228.23	206.38	189.50	176.11	165.24	156.27	148.76	142.39
16000	1386.28	718.18	495.87	385.00	318.71	274.71	243.45	220.14	202.14	187.85	176.25	166.69	158.67	151.88
17000	1472.92	763.07	526.86	409.07	338.63	291.88	258.66	233.90	214.77	199.59	187.27	177.10	168.59	161.37
18000	1559.56	807.95	557.85	433.13	358.55	309.05	273.88	247.66	227.40	211.33	198.29	187.52	178.51	170.86
19000	1646.20	852.84	588.84	457.19	378.47	326.22	289.09	261.42	240.04	223.07	209.30	197.94	188.42	180.36
20000	1732.85	897.73	619.84	481.25	398.39	343.39	304.31	275.17	252.67	234.81	220.32	208.36	198.34	189.85
21000	1819.49	942.61	650.83	505.32	418.31	360.56	319.52	288.93	265.30	246.55	231.33	218.77	208.26	199.34
22000	1906.13	987.50	681.82	529.38	438.23	377.73	334.74	302.69	277.94	258.29	242.35	229.19	218.17	208.83
23000	1992.77	1032.38	712.81	553.44	458.15	394.90	349.95	316.45	290.57	270.03	253.36	239.61	228.09	218.33
24000	2079.41	1077.27	743.80	577.50	478.07	412.07	365.17	330.21	303.20	281.77	264.38	250.03	238.01	227.82
25000	2166.06	1122.16	774.79	601.57	497.99	429.24	380.38	343.97	315.84	293.51	275.40	260.44	247.92	237.31
26000	2252.70	1167.04	805.78	625.63	517.91	446.41	395.60	357.72	328.47	305.25	286.41	270.86	257.84	246.80
27000	2339.34	1211.93	836.78	649.69	537.83	463.58	410.81	371.48	341.10	316.99	297.43	281.28	267.76	256.29
28000	2425.98	1256.81	867.77	673.75	557.75	480.75	426.03	385.24	353.74	328.73	308.44	291.70	277.67	265.79
29000	2512.62	1301.70	898.76	697.81	577.67	497.91	441.25	399.00	366.37	340.47	319.46	302.11	287.59	275.28
30000	2599.27	1346.59	929.75	721.88	597.59	515.08	456.46	412.76	379.00	352.21	330.47	312.53	297.51	284.77
31000	2685.91	1391.47	960.74	745.94	617.51	532.25	471.68	426.52	391.64	363.95	341.49	322.95	307.42	294.26
32000	2772.55	1436.36	991.73	770.00	637.42	549.42	486.89	440.28	404.27	375.69	352.50	333.37	317.34	303.75
33000	2859.19	1481.24	1022.73	794.06	657.34	566.59	502.11	454.03	416.90	387.43	363.52	343.78	327.26	313.25
34000	2945.83	1526.13	1053.72	818.13	677.26	583.76	517.32	467.79	429.54	399.17	374.54	354.20	337.17	322.74
35000	3032.48	1571.02	1084.71	842.19	697.18	600.93	532.54	481.55	442.17	410.91	385.55	364.62	347.09	332.23
36000	3119.12	1615.90	1115.70	866.25	717.10	618.10	547.75	495.31	454.80	422.65	396.57	375.04	357.01	341.72
37000	3205.76	1660.79	1146.69	890.31	737.02	635.27	562.97	509.07	467.44	434.39	407.58	385.45	366.92	351.22
38000	3292.40	1705.67	1177.68	914.38	756.94	652.44	578.18	522.83	480.07	446.13	418.60	395.87	376.84	360.71
39000	3379.04	1750.56	1208.67	938.44	776.86	669.61	593.40	536.58	492.70	457.87	429.61	406.29	386.76	370.20
40000	3465.69	1795.45	1239.67	962.50	796.78	686.78	608.61	550.34	505.34	469.61	440.63	416.71	396.67	379.69
41000	3552.33	1840.33	1270.66	986.56	816.70	703.95	623.83	564.10	517.97	481.35	451.64	427.12	406.59	389.18
42000	3638.97	1885.22	1301.65	1010.63	836.62	721.12	639.04	577.86	530.60	493.09	462.66	437.54	416.51	398.68
43000	3725.61	1930.10	1332.64	1034.69	856.54	738.29	654.26	591.62	543.24	504.83	473.68	447.96	426.42	408.17
44000	3812.25	1974.99	1363.63	1058.75	876.46	755.45	669.47	605.38	555.87	516.57	484.69	458.38	436.34	417.66
45000	3898.90	2019.88	1394.62	1082.81	896.38	772.62	684.69	619.14	568.50	528.31	495.71	468.80	446.26	427.15
46000	3985.54	2064.76	1425.62	1106.88	916.30	789.79	699.90	632.89	581.14	540.05	506.72	479.21	456.17	436.65
47000	4072.18	2109.65	1456.61	1130.94	936.21	806.96	715.12	646.65	593.77	551.79	517.74	489.63	466.09	446.14
48000	4158.82	2154.53	1487.60	1155.00	956.13	824.13	730.33	660.41	606.40	563.53	528.75	500.05	476.01	455.63
49000	4245.46	2199.42	1518.59	1179.06	976.05	841.30	745.55	674.17	619.04	575.27	539.77	510.47	485.92	465.12
50000	4332.11	2244.31	1549.58	1203.13	995.97	858.47	760.76	687.93	631.67	587.01	550.79	520.88	495.84	474.61
55000	4765.32	2468.74	1704.54	1323.44	1095.57	944.32	836.84	756.72	694.84	645.71	605.86	572.97	545.42	522.07
60000	5198.53	2693.17	1859.50	1443.75	1195.17	1030.16	912.92	825.51	758.00	704.41	660.94	625.06	595.01	569.54
65000	5631.74	2917.60	2014.45	1564.06	1294.76	1116.01	988.99	894.30	821.17	763.11	716.02	677.15	644.59	617.00
70000	6064.95	3142.03	2169.41	1684.37	1394.36	1201.86	1065.07	963.10	884.33	821.81	771.10	729.23	694.17	664.46
75000	6498.16	3366.46	2324.37	1804.69	1493.96	1287.70	1141.14	1031.89	947.50	880.51	826.18	781.32	743.76	711.92
80000	6931.37	3590.89	2479.33	1925.00	1593.55	1373.55	1217.22	1100.68	1010.67	939.21	881.25	833.41	793.34	759.38
85000	7364.58	3815.32	2634.29	2045.31	1693.15	1459.40	1293.30	1169.47	1073.83	997.91	936.33	885.50	842.93	806.84
90000	7797.79	4039.75	2789.24	2165.63	1792.75	1545.24	1369.37	1238.27	1137.00	1056.61	991.41	937.59	892.51	854.30
95000	8231.00	4264.18	2944.20	2285.93	1892.34	1631.09	1445.45	1307.06	1200.17	1115.31	1046.49	989.67	942.09	901.76
100000	8664.21	4488.61	3099.16	2406.25	1991.94	1716.94	1521.52	1375.85	1263.33	1174.02	1101.57	1041.76	991.68	949.22

TERM AMOUNT	15 Years	16 Years	17 Years	18 Years	19 Years	20 Years	21 Years	22 Years	23 Years	24 Years	25 Years	30 Years	35 Years	40 Years
5	.05	.05	.05	.05	.05	.04	.04	.04	.04	.04	.04	.04	.04	.04
10	.10	.09	.09	.09	.09	.08	.08	.08	.08	.08	.08	.07	.07	.07
15	.14	.14	.13	.13	.13	.12	.12	.12	.12	.12	.11	.11	.10	.10
25	.23	.23	.22	.21	.21	.20	.20	.19	.19	.19	.19	.18	.17	.16
50	.46	.45	.43	.42	.41	.40	.39	.38	.38	.37	.37	.35	.33	.32
75	.69	.67	.65	.63	.61	.60	.59	.57	.56	.56	.55	.52	.50	.48
100	.92	.89	.86	.84	.81	.80	.78	.76	.75	.74	.73	.69	.66	.64
200	1.83	1.77	1.71	1.67	1.62	1.59	1.55	1.52	1.50	1.47	1.45	1.37	1.32	1.28
300	2.74	2.65	2.57	2.50	2.43	2.38	2.33	2.28	2.24	2.21	2.17	2.05	1.97	1.92
400	3.66	3.53	3.42	3.33	3.24	3.17	3.10	3.04	2.99	2.94	2.90	2.73	2.63	2.56
500	4.57	4.41	4.28	4.16	4.05	3.96	3.87	3.80	3.73	3.67	3.62	3.42	3.29	3.20
600	5.48	5.29	5.13	4.99	4.86	4.75	4.65	4.56	4.48	4.41	4.34	4.10	3.94	3.84
700	6.40	6.18	5.98	5.82	5.67	5.54	5.42	5.32	5.22	5.14	5.06	4.78	4.60	4.48
800	7.31	7.06	6.84	6.65	6.48	6.33	6.19	6.08	5.97	5.87	5.79	5.46	5.26	5.12
900	8.22	7.94	7.69	7.48	7.29	7.12	6.97	6.84	6.72	6.61	6.51	6.14	5.91	5.76
1000	9.13	8.82	8.55	8.31	8.10	7.91	7.74	7.59	7.46	7.34	7.23	6.83	6.57	6.40
2000	18.26	17.63	17.09	16.61	16.19	15.81	15.48	15.18	14.92	14.68	14.46	13.65	13.13	12.80
3000	27.39	26.45	25.63	24.91	24.28	23.72	23.22	22.77	22.37	22.01	21.69	20.47	19.70	19.20
4000	36.52	35.26	34.17	33.21	32.37	31.62	30.95	30.36	29.83	29.35	28.92	27.29	26.26	25.59
5000	45.65	44.08	42.71	41.51	40.46	39.52	38.69	37.95	37.28	36.69	36.15	34.11	32.83	31.99
6000	54.78	52.89	51.25	49.82	48.55	47.43	46.43	45.54	44.74	44.02	43.37	40.94	39.39	38.39
7000	63.91	61.71	59.79	58.12	56.64	55.33	54.17	53.13	52.20	51.36	50.60	47.76	45.96	44.78
8000	73.03	70.52	68.33	66.42	64.73	63.24	61.90	60.72	59.65	58.69	57.83	54.58	52.52	51.18
9000	82.16	79.34	76.88	74.72	72.82	71.14	69.64	68.31	67.11	66.03	65.06	61.40	59.09	57.58
10000	91.29	88.15	85.42	83.02	80.91	79.04	77.38	75.89	74.56	73.37	72.29	68.22	65.65	63.97
11000	100.42	96.97	93.96	91.32	89.00	86.95	85.12	83.48	82.02	80.70	79.51	75.04	72.22	70.37
12000	109.55	105.78	102.50	99.63	97.09	94.85	92.85	91.07	89.47	88.04	86.74	81.87	78.78	76.77
13000	118.68	114.59	111.04	107.93	105.18	102.75	100.59	98.66	96.93	95.37	93.97	88.69	85.35	83.16
14000	127.81	123.41	119.58	116.23	113.27	110.66	108.33	106.25	104.39	102.71	101.20	95.51	91.91	89.56
15000	136.93	132.22	128.12	124.53	121.37	118.56	116.07	113.84	111.84	110.05	108.43	102.33	98.48	95.96
16000	146.06	141.04	136.66	132.83	129.46	126.47	123.80	121.43	119.30	117.38	115.65	109.15	105.04	102.35
17000	155.19	149.85	145.21	141.13	137.55	134.37	131.54	129.02	126.75	124.72	122.88	115.97	111.60	108.75
18000	164.32	158.67	153.75	149.44	145.64	142.27	139.28	136.61	134.21	132.05	130.11	122.80	118.17	115.15
19000	173.45	167.48	162.29	157.74	153.73	150.18	147.02	144.19	141.66	139.39	137.34	129.62	124.73	121.54
20000	182.58	176.30	170.83	166.04	161.82	158.08	154.75	151.78	149.12	146.73	144.57	136.44	131.30	127.94
21000	191.71	185.11	179.37	174.34	169.91	165.98	162.49	159.37	156.58	154.06	151.79	143.26	137.86	134.34
22000	200.83	193.93	187.91	182.64	178.00	173.89	170.23	166.96	164.03	161.40	159.02	150.08	144.43	140.73
23000	209.96	202.74	196.45	190.94	186.09	181.79	177.97	174.55	171.49	168.73	166.25	156.91	150.99	147.13
24000	219.09	211.55	204.99	199.25	194.18	189.70	185.70	182.14	178.94	176.07	173.48	163.73	157.56	153.53
25000	228.22	220.37	213.54	207.55	202.27	197.60	193.44	189.73	186.40	183.41	180.71	170.55	164.12	159.92
26000	237.35	229.18	222.08	215.85	210.36	205.50	201.18	197.32	193.86	190.74	187.93	177.37	170.69	166.32
27000	246.48	238.00	230.62	224.15	218.45	213.41	208.92	204.91	201.31	198.08	195.16	184.19	177.25	172.72
28000	255.61	246.81	239.16	232.45	226.54	221.31	216.65	212.50	208.77	205.41	202.39	191.01	183.82	179.11
29000	264.74	255.63	247.70	240.75	234.63	229.21	224.39	220.08	216.22	212.75	209.62	197.84	190.38	185.51
30000	273.86	264.44	256.24	249.06	242.73	237.12	232.13	227.67	223.68	220.09	216.85	204.66	196.95	191.91
31000	282.99	273.26	264.78	257.36	250.82	245.02	239.87	235.26	231.13	227.42	224.08	211.48	203.51	198.30
32000	292.12	282.07	273.32	265.66	258.91	252.93	247.60	242.85	238.59	234.76	231.30	218.30	210.07	204.70
33000	301.25	290.89	281.87	273.96	267.00	260.83	255.34	250.44	246.05	242.09	238.53	225.12	216.64	211.10
34000	310.38	299.70	290.41	282.26	275.09	268.73	263.08	258.03	253.50	249.43	245.76	231.94	223.20	217.49
35000	319.51	308.52	298.95	290.57	283.18	276.64	270.82	265.62	260.96	256.77	252.99	238.77	229.77	223.89
36000	328.64	317.33	307.49	298.87	291.27	284.54	278.55	273.21	268.41	264.10	260.22	245.59	236.33	230.29
37000	337.76	326.14	316.03	307.17	299.36	292.44	286.29	280.80	275.87	271.44	267.44	252.41	242.90	236.68
38000	346.89	334.96	324.57	315.47	307.45	300.35	294.03	288.38	283.32	278.77	274.67	259.23	249.46	243.08
39000	356.02	343.77	333.11	323.77	315.54	308.25	301.77	295.97	290.78	286.11	281.90	266.05	256.03	249.48
40000	365.15	352.59	341.65	332.07	323.63	316.16	309.50	303.56	298.24	293.45	289.13	272.88	262.59	255.87
41000	374.28	361.40	350.20	340.38	331.72	324.06	317.24	311.15	305.69	300.78	296.36	279.70	269.16	262.27
42000	383.41	370.22	358.74	348.68	339.81	331.96	324.98	318.74	313.15	308.12	303.58	286.52	275.72	268.67
43000	392.54	379.03	367.28	356.98	347.90	339.87	332.72	326.33	320.60	315.46	310.81	293.34	282.29	275.06
44000	401.66	387.85	375.82	365.28	355.99	347.77	340.45	333.92	328.06	322.79	318.04	300.16	288.85	281.46
45000	410.79	396.66	384.36	373.58	364.09	355.67	348.19	341.51	335.52	330.13	325.27	306.98	295.42	287.86
46000	419.92	405.48	392.90	381.88	372.18	363.58	355.93	349.10	342.97	337.46	332.50	313.81	301.98	294.25
47000	429.05	414.29	401.44	390.19	380.27	371.48	363.67	356.68	350.43	344.80	339.72	320.63	308.54	300.65
48000	438.18	423.10	409.98	398.49	388.36	379.39	371.40	364.27	357.88	352.14	346.95	327.45	315.11	307.05
49000	447.31	431.92	418.52	406.79	396.45	387.29	379.14	371.86	365.34	359.47	354.18	334.27	321.67	313.44
50000	456.44	440.73	427.07	415.09	404.54	395.19	386.88	379.45	372.79	366.81	361.41	341.09	328.24	319.84
55000	502.08	484.81	469.77	456.60	444.99	434.71	425.57	417.40	410.07	403.49	397.55	375.20	361.06	351.82
60000	547.72	528.88	512.48	498.11	485.45	474.23	464.25	455.34	447.35	440.17	433.69	409.31	393.89	383.81
65000	593.37	572.95	555.18	539.62	525.90	513.75	502.94	493.29	484.63	476.85	469.83	443.42	426.71	415.79
70000	639.01	617.03	597.89	581.13	566.35	553.27	541.63	531.23	521.91	513.53	505.97	477.53	459.53	447.78
75000	684.65	661.10	640.60	622.63	606.81	592.79	580.32	569.18	559.19	550.21	542.11	511.64	492.36	479.76
80000	730.30	705.17	683.30	664.14	647.26	632.31	619.00	607.12	596.47	586.89	578.25	545.75	525.18	511.74
85000	775.94	749.24	726.01	705.65	687.71	671.82	657.69	645.06	633.75	623.57	614.39	579.85	558.00	543.73
90000	821.58	793.32	768.71	747.16	728.17	711.34	696.38	683.01	671.03	660.25	650.53	613.96	590.83	575.71
95000	867.22	837.39	811.42	788.67	768.62	750.86	735.06	720.95	708.30	696.93	686.67	648.07	623.65	607.69
100000	912.87	881.46	854.13	830.18	809.07	790.38	773.75	758.90	745.58	733.61	722.81	682.18	656.47	639.68

MONTHLY PAYMENT
REQUIRED TO AMORTIZE A LOAN

TERM / AMOUNT	1 Year	2 Years	3 Years	4 Years	5 Years	6 Years	7 Years	8 Years	9 Years	10 Years	11 Years	12 Years	13 Years	14 Years
5	.44	.23	.16	.13	.10	.09	.08	.07	.07	.06	.06	.06	.05	.05
10	.87	.45	.32	.25	.20	.18	.16	.14	.13	.12	.12	.11	.10	.10
15	1.30	.68	.47	.37	.30	.26	.23	.21	.19	.18	.17	.16	.15	.15
25	2.17	1.13	.78	.61	.50	.43	.39	.35	.32	.30	.28	.27	.25	.24
50	4.34	2.25	1.56	1.21	1.00	.86	.77	.69	.64	.59	.56	.53	.50	.48
75	6.50	3.37	2.33	1.81	1.50	1.29	1.15	1.04	.95	.89	.83	.79	.75	.72
100	8.67	4.50	3.11	2.41	2.00	1.72	1.53	1.38	1.27	1.18	1.11	1.05	1.00	.96
200	17.34	8.99	6.21	4.82	3.99	3.44	3.05	2.76	2.54	2.36	2.21	2.09	1.99	1.91
300	26.00	13.48	9.31	7.23	5.99	5.16	4.58	4.14	3.80	3.53	3.32	3.14	2.99	2.86
400	34.67	17.97	12.41	9.64	7.98	6.88	6.10	5.52	5.07	4.71	4.42	4.18	3.98	3.81
500	43.34	22.46	15.51	12.05	9.98	8.60	7.62	6.90	6.33	5.89	5.53	5.23	4.98	4.76
600	52.00	26.95	18.61	14.46	11.97	10.32	9.15	8.28	7.60	7.06	6.63	6.27	5.97	5.72
700	60.67	31.44	21.72	16.86	13.97	12.04	10.67	9.65	8.87	8.24	7.73	7.32	6.97	6.67
800	69.34	35.93	24.82	19.27	15.96	13.76	12.20	11.03	10.13	9.42	8.84	8.36	7.96	7.62
900	78.00	40.42	27.92	21.68	17.95	15.48	13.72	12.41	11.40	10.59	9.94	9.40	8.95	8.57
1000	86.67	44.91	31.02	24.09	19.95	17.20	15.24	13.79	12.66	11.77	11.05	10.45	9.95	9.52
2000	173.34	89.82	62.03	48.18	39.89	34.39	30.48	27.57	25.32	23.54	22.09	20.89	19.89	19.04
3000	260.00	134.73	93.05	72.26	59.83	51.59	45.72	41.36	37.98	35.30	33.13	31.34	29.84	28.56
4000	346.67	179.64	124.06	96.35	79.78	68.78	60.96	55.14	50.64	47.07	44.17	41.78	39.78	38.08
5000	433.33	224.55	155.C8	120.43	99.72	85.97	76.20	68.92	63.30	58.84	55.22	52.23	49.73	47.60
6000	520.00	269.46	186.09	144.52	119.66	103.17	91.44	82.71	75.96	70.60	66.26	62.67	59.67	57.12
7000	606.66	314.37	217.11	168.60	139.61	120.36	106.68	96.49	88.62	82.37	77.30	73.12	69.61	66.64
8000	693.33	359.27	248.12	192.69	159.55	137.55	121.92	110.27	101.28	94.13	88.34	83.56	79.56	76.16
9000	779.99	404.18	279.14	216.78	179.49	154.75	137.16	124.06	113.93	105.90	99.38	94.00	89.50	85.68
10000	866.66	449.09	310.15	240.86	199.44	171.94	152.40	137.84	126.59	117.67	110.43	104.45	99.45	95.20
11000	953.32	494.00	341.16	264.95	219.38	189.13	167.64	151.62	139.25	129.43	121.47	114.89	109.39	104.72
12000	1039.99	538.91	372.18	289.03	239.32	206.33	182.88	165.41	151.91	141.20	132.51	125.34	119.33	114.24
13000	1126.65	583.82	403.19	313.12	259.26	223.52	198.12	179.19	164.57	152.96	143.55	135.78	129.28	123.76
14000	1213.32	628.73	434.21	337.20	279.21	240.71	213.36	192.97	177.23	164.73	154.59	146.23	139.22	133.28
15000	1299.98	673.64	465.22	361.29	299.15	257.91	228.60	206.76	189.89	176.50	165.64	156.67	149.17	142.80
16000	1386.65	718.54	496.24	385.38	319.09	275.10	243.84	220.54	202.55	188.26	176.68	167.12	159.11	152.32
17000	1473.31	763.45	527.25	409.46	339.04	292.29	259.08	234.32	215.20	200.03	187.72	177.56	169.05	161.84
18000	1559.98	808.36	558.27	433.55	358.98	309.49	274.32	248.11	227.86	211.79	198.76	188.00	179.00	171.36
19000	1646.64	853.27	589.28	457.63	378.92	326.68	289.56	261.89	240.52	223.56	209.80	198.45	188.94	180.88
20000	1733.31	898.18	620.29	481.72	398.87	343.87	304.80	275.67	253.18	235.33	220.85	208.89	198.89	190.40
21000	1819.97	943.09	651.31	505.80	418.81	361.07	320.04	289.46	265.84	247.09	231.89	219.34	208.83	199.92
22000	1906.64	988.00	682.32	529.89	438.75	378.26	335.28	303.24	278.50	258.86	242.93	229.78	218.77	209.44
23000	1993.30	1032.91	713.34	553.98	458.70	395.45	350.52	317.03	291.16	270.62	253.97	240.23	228.72	218.96
24000	2079.97	1077.81	744.35	578.06	478.64	412.65	365.76	330.81	303.82	282.39	265.01	250.67	238.66	228.48
25000	2166.63	1122.72	775.37	602.15	498.58	429.84	381.00	344.59	316.47	294.16	276.06	261.12	248.61	238.00
26000	2253.30	1167.63	806.38	626.23	518.52	447.03	396.24	358.38	329.13	305.92	287.10	271.56	258.55	247.52
27000	2339.96	1212.54	837.40	650.32	538.47	464.23	411.48	372.16	341.79	317.69	298.14	282.00	268.49	257.04
28000	2426.63	1257.45	868.41	674.40	558.41	481.42	426.72	385.94	354.45	329.45	309.18	292.45	278.44	266.56
29000	2513.29	1302.36	899.42	698.49	578.35	498.61	441.96	399.73	367.11	341.22	320.22	302.89	288.38	276.08
30000	2599.96	1347.27	930.44	722.58	598.30	515.81	457.20	413.51	379.77	352.99	331.27	313.34	298.33	285.60
31000	2686.62	1392.17	961.45	746.66	618.24	533.00	472.44	427.29	392.43	364.75	342.31	323.78	308.27	295.12
32000	2773.29	1437.08	992.47	770.75	638.18	550.19	487.68	441.08	405.09	376.52	353.35	334.23	318.21	304.64
33000	2859.95	1481.99	1023.48	794.83	658.13	567.39	502.92	454.86	417.74	388.28	364.39	344.67	328.16	314.16
34000	2946.62	1526.90	1054.50	818.92	678.07	584.58	518.16	468.64	430.40	400.05	375.43	355.12	338.10	323.68
35000	3033.28	1571.81	1085.51	843.00	698.01	601.77	533.40	482.43	443.06	411.82	386.48	365.56	348.05	333.20
36000	3119.95	1616.72	1116.53	867.09	717.95	618.97	548.64	496.21	455.72	423.58	397.52	376.00	357.99	342.72
37000	3206.61	1661.63	1147.54	891.17	737.90	636.16	563.88	509.99	468.38	435.35	408.56	386.45	367.93	352.24
38000	3293.28	1706.54	1178.55	915.26	757.84	653.36	579.12	523.78	481.04	447.12	419.60	396.89	377.88	361.76
39000	3379.94	1751.44	1209.57	939.35	777.78	670.55	594.36	537.56	493.70	458.88	430.64	407.34	387.82	371.28
40000	3466.61	1796.35	1240.58	963.43	797.73	687.74	609.60	551.34	506.36	470.65	441.69	417.78	397.77	380.80
41000	3553.27	1841.26	1271.60	987.52	817.67	704.94	624.83	565.13	519.01	482.41	452.73	428.23	407.71	390.32
42000	3639.94	1886.17	1302.61	1011.60	837.61	722.13	640.07	578.91	531.67	494.18	463.77	438.67	417.65	399.84
43000	3726.60	1931.08	1333.63	1035.69	857.56	739.32	655.31	592.70	544.33	505.95	474.81	449.12	427.60	409.36
44000	3813.27	1975.99	1364.64	1059.77	877.50	756.52	670.55	606.48	556.99	517.71	485.85	459.56	437.54	418.88
45000	3899.93	2020.90	1395.66	1083.86	897.44	773.71	685.79	620.26	569.65	529.48	496.90	470.00	447.49	428.40
46000	3986.60	2065.81	1426.67	1107.95	917.39	790.90	701.03	634.05	582.31	541.24	507.94	480.45	457.43	437.92
47000	4073.27	2110.71	1457.68	1132.03	937.33	808.10	716.27	647.83	594.97	553.01	518.98	490.89	467.37	447.44
48000	4159.93	2155.62	1488.7C	1156.12	957.27	825.29	731.51	661.61	607.63	564.78	530.02	501.34	477.32	456.96
49000	4246.60	2200.53	1519.71	1180.20	977.21	842.48	746.75	675.40	620.28	576.54	541.06	511.78	487.26	466.48
50000	4333.26	2245.44	1550.73	1204.29	997.16	859.68	761.99	689.18	632.94	588.31	552.11	522.23	497.21	476.00
55000	4766.59	2469.98	1705.80	1324.72	1096.87	945.64	838.19	758.10	696.24	647.14	607.32	574.45	546.93	523.60
60000	5199.91	2694.53	1860.87	1445.15	1196.59	1031.61	914.39	827.01	759.53	705.97	662.53	626.67	596.65	571.20
65000	5633.24	2919.07	2015.94	1565.57	1296.30	1117.58	990.59	895.93	822.82	764.80	717.74	678.89	646.37	618.80
70000	6066.56	3143.61	2171.02	1686.00	1396.02	1203.54	1066.79	964.85	886.12	823.63	772.95	731.11	696.09	666.40
75000	6499.89	3368.16	2326.09	1806.43	1495.73	1289.51	1142.99	1033.77	949.41	882.46	828.16	783.34	745.81	714.00
80000	6933.21	3592.70	2481.16	1926.86	1595.45	1375.48	1219.19	1102.68	1012.71	941.29	883.37	835.56	795.53	761.60
85000	7366.54	3817.24	2636.23	2047.29	1695.16	1461.45	1295.38	1171.60	1076.00	1000.12	938.58	887.78	845.25	809.20
90000	7799.86	4041.79	2791.31	2167.72	1794.88	1547.41	1371.58	1240.52	1139.29	1058.95	993.79	940.00	894.97	856.80
95000	8233.19	4266.33	2946.38	2288.14	1894.59	1633.38	1447.78	1309.44	1202.59	1117.78	1049.00	992.23	944.69	904.40
100000	8666.52	4490.88	3101.45	2408.57	1994.31	1719.35	1523.98	1378.35	1265.88	1176.61	1104.21	1044.45	994.41	952.00

MONTHLY PAYMENT
REQUIRED TO AMORTIZE A LOAN

7.300%

TERM	15 Years	16 Years	17 Years	18 Years	19 Years	20 Years	21 Years	22 Years	23 Years	24 Years	25 Years	30 Years	35 Years	40 Years
AMOUNT														
5	.05	.05	.05	.05	.05	.04	.04	.04	.04	.04	.04	.04	.04	.04
10	.10	.09	.09	.09	.09	.08	.08	.08	.08	.08	.08	.07	.07	.07
15	.14	.14	.13	.13	.13	.12	.12	.12	.12	.12	.11	.11	.10	.10
25	.23	.23	.22	.21	.21	.20	.20	.20	.19	.19	.19	.18	.17	.17
50	.46	.45	.43	.42	.41	.40	.39	.39	.38	.37	.37	.35	.34	.33
75	.69	.67	.65	.63	.61	.60	.59	.58	.57	.56	.55	.52	.50	.49
100	.92	.89	.86	.84	.82	.80	.78	.77	.75	.74	.73	.69	.67	.65
200	1.84	1.77	1.72	1.67	1.63	1.59	1.56	1.53	1.50	1.48	1.46	1.38	1.33	1.29
300	2.75	2.66	2.58	2.50	2.44	2.39	2.34	2.29	2.25	2.22	2.18	2.06	1.99	1.94
400	3.67	3.54	3.43	3.34	3.25	3.18	3.11	3.05	3.00	2.95	2.91	2.75	2.65	2.58
500	4.58	4.43	4.29	4.17	4.07	3.97	3.89	3.82	3.75	3.69	3.64	3.43	3.31	3.22
600	5.50	5.31	5.15	5.00	4.88	4.77	4.67	4.58	4.50	4.43	4.36	4.12	3.97	3.87
700	6.41	6.20	6.00	5.84	5.69	5.56	5.44	5.34	5.25	5.16	5.09	4.80	4.63	4.51
800	7.33	7.08	6.86	6.67	6.50	6.35	6.22	6.10	5.99	5.90	5.81	5.49	5.29	5.15
900	8.25	7.96	7.72	7.50	7.31	7.15	7.00	6.86	6.74	6.64	6.54	6.18	5.95	5.80
1000	9.16	8.85	8.58	8.34	8.13	7.94	7.77	7.63	7.49	7.37	7.27	6.86	6.61	6.44
2000	18.32	17.69	17.15	16.67	16.25	15.87	15.54	15.25	14.98	14.74	14.53	13.72	13.21	12.87
3000	27.48	26.53	25.72	25.00	24.37	23.81	23.31	22.87	22.47	22.11	21.79	20.57	19.81	19.31
4000	36.63	35.38	34.29	33.33	32.49	31.74	31.08	30.49	29.95	29.48	29.05	27.43	26.41	25.74
5000	45.79	44.22	42.86	41.66	40.61	39.68	38.85	38.11	37.44	36.84	36.31	34.28	33.01	32.17
6000	54.95	53.06	51.43	49.99	48.73	47.61	46.61	45.73	44.93	44.21	43.57	41.14	39.61	38.61
7000	64.10	61.91	60.00	58.32	56.85	55.54	54.38	53.35	52.42	51.58	50.83	47.99	46.21	45.04
8000	73.26	70.75	68.57	66.65	64.97	63.48	62.15	60.97	59.90	58.95	58.09	54.85	52.81	51.47
9000	82.42	79.59	77.14	74.99	73.09	71.41	69.92	68.59	67.39	66.32	65.35	61.71	59.41	57.91
10000	91.57	88.44	85.71	83.32	81.21	79.35	77.69	76.21	74.88	73.68	72.61	68.56	66.01	64.34
11000	100.73	97.28	94.28	91.65	89.33	87.28	85.46	83.83	82.37	81.05	79.87	75.42	72.61	70.77
12000	109.89	106.12	102.85	99.98	97.45	95.21	93.22	91.45	89.85	88.42	87.13	82.27	79.21	77.21
13000	119.04	114.97	111.42	108.31	105.57	103.15	100.99	99.07	97.34	95.79	94.39	89.13	85.81	83.64
14000	128.20	123.81	119.99	116.64	113.69	111.08	108.76	106.69	104.83	103.16	101.65	95.98	92.41	90.07
15000	137.36	132.65	128.56	124.97	121.81	119.02	116.53	114.31	112.31	110.52	108.91	102.84	99.01	96.51
16000	146.51	141.50	137.13	133.30	129.93	126.95	124.30	121.93	119.80	117.89	116.17	109.70	105.61	102.94
17000	155.67	150.34	145.70	141.64	138.06	134.88	132.06	129.55	127.29	125.26	123.43	116.55	112.21	109.37
18000	164.83	159.18	154.27	149.97	146.18	142.82	139.83	137.17	134.78	132.63	130.69	123.41	118.81	115.81
19000	173.98	168.03	162.84	158.30	154.30	150.75	147.60	144.79	142.26	140.00	137.95	130.26	125.41	122.24
20000	183.14	176.87	171.41	166.63	162.42	158.69	155.37	152.41	149.75	147.36	145.21	137.12	132.01	128.67
21000	192.30	185.71	179.98	174.96	170.54	166.62	163.14	160.03	157.24	154.73	152.47	143.97	138.61	135.11
22000	201.46	194.56	188.55	183.29	178.66	174.55	170.91	167.65	164.73	162.10	159.73	150.83	145.21	141.54
23000	210.61	203.40	197.12	191.62	186.78	182.49	178.67	175.27	172.21	169.47	166.99	157.69	151.81	147.97
24000	219.77	212.24	205.69	199.95	194.90	190.42	186.44	182.89	179.70	176.84	174.25	164.54	158.41	154.41
25000	228.93	221.09	214.26	208.29	203.02	198.36	194.21	190.51	187.19	184.20	181.51	171.40	165.01	160.84
26000	238.08	229.93	222.83	216.62	211.14	206.29	201.98	198.13	194.67	191.57	188.77	178.25	171.61	167.27
27000	247.24	238.77	231.40	224.95	219.26	214.23	209.75	205.75	202.16	198.94	196.03	185.11	178.21	173.71
28000	256.40	247.62	239.97	233.28	227.38	222.16	217.51	213.37	209.65	206.31	203.29	191.96	184.81	180.14
29000	265.55	256.46	248.54	241.61	235.50	230.09	225.28	220.99	217.14	213.67	210.55	198.82	191.41	186.57
30000	274.71	265.30	257.11	249.94	243.62	238.03	233.05	228.61	224.62	221.04	217.81	205.68	198.01	193.01
31000	283.87	274.14	265.68	258.27	251.74	245.96	240.82	236.23	232.11	228.41	225.07	212.53	204.61	199.44
32000	293.02	282.99	274.25	266.60	259.86	253.90	248.59	243.85	239.60	235.78	232.34	219.39	211.21	205.87
33000	302.18	291.83	282.82	274.94	267.98	261.83	256.36	251.47	247.09	243.15	239.60	226.24	217.81	212.31
34000	311.34	300.67	291.40	283.27	276.11	269.76	264.12	259.09	254.57	250.51	246.86	233.10	224.41	218.74
35000	320.49	309.52	299.97	291.60	284.23	277.70	271.89	266.71	262.06	257.88	254.12	239.95	231.01	225.17
36000	329.65	318.36	308.54	299.93	292.35	285.63	279.66	274.33	269.55	265.25	261.38	246.81	237.61	231.61
37000	338.81	327.20	317.11	308.26	300.47	293.57	287.43	281.95	277.03	272.62	268.64	253.67	244.21	238.04
38000	347.96	336.05	325.68	316.59	308.59	301.50	295.20	289.57	284.52	279.99	275.90	260.52	250.81	244.47
39000	357.12	344.89	334.25	324.92	316.71	309.43	302.96	297.19	292.01	287.35	283.16	267.38	257.41	250.91
40000	366.28	353.73	342.82	333.25	324.83	317.37	310.73	304.81	299.50	294.72	290.42	274.23	264.01	257.34
41000	375.44	362.58	351.39	341.59	332.95	325.30	318.50	312.43	306.98	302.09	297.68	281.09	270.61	263.77
42000	384.59	371.42	359.96	349.92	341.07	333.24	326.27	320.05	314.47	309.46	304.94	287.94	277.21	270.21
43000	393.75	380.26	368.53	358.25	349.19	341.17	334.04	327.67	321.96	316.83	312.20	294.80	283.81	276.64
44000	402.91	389.11	377.10	366.58	357.31	349.10	341.81	335.29	329.45	324.19	319.46	301.66	290.41	283.07
45000	412.06	397.95	385.67	374.91	365.43	357.04	349.57	342.91	336.93	331.56	326.72	308.51	297.01	289.51
46000	421.22	406.79	394.24	383.24	373.55	364.97	357.34	350.53	344.42	338.93	333.98	315.37	303.61	295.94
47000	430.38	415.64	402.81	391.57	381.67	372.91	365.11	358.15	351.91	346.30	341.24	322.22	310.21	302.37
48000	439.53	424.48	411.38	399.90	389.79	380.84	372.88	365.77	359.39	353.67	348.50	329.08	316.81	308.81
49000	448.69	433.32	419.95	408.23	397.91	388.78	380.65	373.39	366.88	361.03	355.76	335.93	323.41	315.24
50000	457.85	442.17	428.52	416.57	406.03	396.71	388.41	381.01	374.37	368.40	363.02	342.79	330.01	321.67
55000	503.63	486.38	471.37	458.22	446.64	436.38	427.26	419.11	411.81	405.24	399.32	377.07	363.01	353.84
60000	549.42	530.60	514.22	499.88	487.24	476.05	466.10	457.21	449.24	442.08	435.62	411.35	396.01	386.01
65000	595.20	574.81	557.07	541.53	527.84	515.72	504.94	495.31	486.68	478.92	471.93	445.63	429.01	418.18
70000	640.98	619.03	599.93	583.19	568.45	555.39	543.78	533.41	524.12	515.76	508.23	479.90	462.01	450.34
75000	686.77	663.25	642.78	624.85	609.05	595.06	582.62	571.51	561.55	552.60	544.53	514.18	495.01	482.51
80000	732.55	707.46	685.63	666.50	649.65	634.73	621.46	609.61	598.99	589.44	580.83	548.46	528.01	514.68
85000	778.34	751.68	728.48	708.16	690.26	674.40	660.30	647.71	636.42	626.28	617.13	582.74	561.01	546.84
90000	824.12	795.89	771.33	749.81	730.86	714.07	699.14	685.81	673.86	663.12	653.43	617.02	594.01	579.01
95000	869.90	840.11	814.18	791.47	771.46	753.74	737.98	723.91	711.30	699.96	689.73	651.30	627.01	611.18
100000	915.69	884.33	857.03	833.13	812.06	793.41	776.82	762.01	748.73	736.80	726.04	685.58	660.01	643.34

MONTHLY PAYMENT
REQUIRED TO AMORTIZE A LOAN

TERM AMOUNT	1 Year	2 Years	3 Years	4 Years	5 Years	6 Years	7 Years	8 Years	9 Years	10 Years	11 Years	12 Years	13 Years	14 Years
5	.44	.23	.16	.13	.10	.09	.08	.07	.07	.06	.06	.06	.05	.05
10	.87	.45	.32	.25	.20	.18	.16	.14	.13	.12	.12	.11	.10	.10
15	1.31	.68	.47	.37	.30	.26	.23	.21	.20	.18	.17	.16	.15	.15
25	2.17	1.13	.78	.61	.50	.44	.39	.35	.32	.30	.28	.27	.25	.24
50	4.34	2.25	1.56	1.21	1.00	.87	.77	.70	.64	.60	.56	.53	.50	.48
75	6.51	3.38	2.33	1.81	1.50	1.30	1.15	1.04	.96	.89	.84	.79	.75	.72
100	8.67	4.50	3.11	2.42	2.00	1.73	1.53	1.39	1.27	1.19	1.11	1.05	1.00	.96
200	17.34	8.99	6.21	4.83	4.00	3.45	3.06	2.77	2.54	2.37	2.22	2.10	2.00	1.92
300	26.01	13.49	9.32	7.24	6.00	5.17	4.59	4.15	3.81	3.55	3.33	3.15	3.00	2.87
400	34.68	17.98	12.42	9.65	8.00	6.90	6.12	5.53	5.08	4.73	4.44	4.20	4.00	3.83
500	43.35	22.48	15.53	12.07	9.99	8.62	7.64	6.92	6.35	5.91	5.55	5.25	5.00	4.79
600	52.02	26.97	18.63	14.48	11.99	10.34	9.17	8.30	7.62	7.09	6.65	6.30	6.00	5.74
700	60.69	31.46	21.74	16.89	13.99	12.07	10.70	9.68	8.89	8.27	7.76	7.34	6.99	6.70
800	69.36	35.96	24.84	19.30	15.99	13.79	12.23	11.06	10.16	9.45	8.87	8.39	7.99	7.65
900	78.03	40.45	27.95	21.71	17.99	15.51	13.75	12.44	11.43	10.63	9.98	9.44	8.99	8.61
1000	86.70	44.95	31.05	24.13	19.98	17.23	15.28	13.83	12.70	11.81	11.09	10.49	9.99	9.57
2000	173.40	89.89	62.10	48.25	39.96	34.46	30.56	27.65	25.40	23.62	22.17	20.97	19.98	19.13
3000	260.10	134.83	93.15	72.37	59.94	51.69	45.83	41.47	38.10	35.42	33.25	31.46	29.96	28.69
4000	346.80	179.78	124.20	96.49	79.92	68.92	61.11	55.29	50.79	47.23	44.33	41.94	39.95	38.25
5000	433.50	224.72	155.25	120.61	99.90	86.15	76.39	69.11	63.49	59.03	55.41	52.43	49.93	47.81
6000	520.20	269.66	186.30	144.73	119.88	103.38	91.66	82.93	76.19	70.84	66.50	62.91	59.92	57.38
7000	606.90	314.60	217.35	168.85	139.86	120.61	106.94	96.75	88.88	82.64	77.58	73.40	69.90	66.94
8000	693.60	359.55	248.40	192.97	159.83	137.84	122.22	110.57	101.58	94.45	88.66	83.88	79.89	76.50
9000	780.30	404.49	279.44	217.09	179.81	155.07	137.49	124.39	114.28	106.25	99.74	94.37	89.87	86.06
10000	867.00	449.43	310.49	241.21	199.79	172.30	152.77	138.22	126.98	118.06	110.82	104.85	99.86	95.62
11000	953.70	494.38	341.54	265.33	219.77	189.53	168.05	152.04	139.67	129.86	121.90	115.34	109.84	105.18
12000	1040.40	539.32	372.59	289.45	239.75	206.76	183.32	165.86	152.37	141.67	132.99	125.82	119.83	114.75
13000	1127.10	584.26	403.64	313.57	259.73	223.99	198.60	179.68	165.07	153.47	144.07	136.31	129.81	124.31
14000	1213.80	629.20	434.69	337.69	279.71	241.22	213.88	193.50	177.76	165.28	155.15	146.79	139.80	133.87
15000	1300.50	674.15	465.74	361.81	299.68	258.45	229.15	207.32	190.46	177.08	166.23	157.28	149.78	143.43
16000	1387.20	719.09	496.79	385.93	319.66	275.68	244.43	221.14	203.16	188.89	177.31	167.76	159.77	152.99
17000	1473.90	764.03	527.84	410.06	339.64	292.91	259.71	234.96	215.85	200.69	188.39	178.25	169.75	162.55
18000	1560.60	808.97	558.88	434.18	359.62	310.14	274.98	248.78	228.55	212.50	199.48	188.73	179.74	172.12
19000	1647.30	853.92	589.93	458.30	379.60	327.37	290.26	262.61	241.25	224.30	210.56	199.22	189.72	181.68
20000	1734.00	898.86	620.98	482.42	399.58	344.60	305.54	276.43	253.95	236.11	221.64	209.70	199.71	191.24
21000	1820.70	943.80	652.03	506.54	419.56	361.83	320.81	290.25	266.64	247.91	232.72	220.19	209.69	200.80
22000	1907.40	988.75	683.08	530.66	439.53	379.06	336.09	304.07	279.34	259.72	243.80	230.67	219.68	210.36
23000	1994.10	1033.69	714.13	554.78	459.51	396.29	351.37	317.89	292.04	271.52	254.88	241.16	229.66	219.92
24000	2080.80	1078.63	745.18	578.90	479.49	413.52	366.64	331.71	304.73	283.33	265.97	251.64	239.65	229.49
25000	2167.50	1123.57	776.23	603.02	499.47	430.75	381.92	345.53	317.43	295.13	277.05	262.12	249.63	239.05
26000	2254.20	1168.52	807.27	627.14	519.45	447.98	397.20	359.35	330.13	306.94	288.13	272.61	259.62	248.61
27000	2340.90	1213.46	838.32	651.26	539.43	465.21	412.47	373.17	342.83	318.74	299.21	283.09	269.60	258.17
28000	2427.60	1258.40	869.37	675.38	559.41	482.44	427.75	387.00	355.52	330.55	310.29	293.58	279.59	267.73
29000	2514.30	1303.35	900.42	699.50	579.38	499.66	443.03	400.82	368.22	342.35	321.37	304.06	289.57	277.29
30000	2601.00	1348.29	931.47	723.62	599.36	516.89	458.30	414.64	380.92	354.16	332.46	314.55	299.56	286.86
31000	2687.70	1393.23	962.52	747.74	619.34	534.12	473.58	428.46	393.61	365.96	343.54	325.03	309.54	296.42
32000	2774.40	1438.17	993.57	771.86	639.32	551.35	488.86	442.28	406.31	377.77	354.62	335.52	319.53	305.98
33000	2861.10	1483.12	1024.62	795.99	659.30	568.58	504.13	456.10	419.01	389.57	365.70	346.00	329.51	315.54
34000	2947.80	1528.06	1055.67	820.11	679.28	585.81	519.41	469.92	431.70	401.38	376.78	356.49	339.50	325.10
35000	3034.50	1573.00	1086.71	844.23	699.26	603.04	534.69	483.74	444.40	413.18	387.86	366.97	349.48	334.66
36000	3121.19	1617.94	1117.76	868.35	719.23	620.27	549.96	497.56	457.10	424.99	398.95	377.46	359.47	344.23
37000	3207.89	1662.89	1148.81	892.47	739.21	637.50	565.24	511.39	469.80	436.79	410.03	387.94	369.45	353.79
38000	3294.59	1707.83	1179.86	916.59	759.19	654.73	580.52	525.21	482.49	448.60	421.11	398.43	379.44	363.35
39000	3381.29	1752.77	1210.91	940.71	779.17	671.96	595.79	539.03	495.19	460.40	432.19	408.91	389.42	372.91
40000	3467.99	1797.72	1241.96	964.83	799.15	689.19	611.07	552.85	507.89	472.21	443.27	419.40	399.41	382.47
41000	3554.69	1842.66	1273.01	988.95	819.13	706.42	626.35	566.67	520.58	484.01	454.35	429.88	409.39	392.03
42000	3641.39	1887.60	1304.06	1013.07	839.11	723.65	641.62	580.49	533.28	495.82	465.44	440.37	419.38	401.60
43000	3728.09	1932.54	1335.11	1037.19	859.08	740.88	656.90	594.31	545.98	507.62	476.52	450.85	429.36	411.16
44000	3814.79	1977.49	1366.15	1061.31	879.06	758.11	672.18	608.13	558.68	519.43	487.60	461.34	439.35	420.72
45000	3901.49	2022.43	1397.20	1085.43	899.04	775.34	687.45	621.95	571.37	531.23	498.68	471.82	449.33	430.28
46000	3988.19	2067.37	1428.25	1109.55	919.02	792.57	702.73	635.77	584.07	543.04	509.76	482.31	459.32	439.84
47000	4074.90	2112.32	1459.30	1133.67	939.00	809.80	718.01	649.60	596.77	554.84	520.84	492.79	469.30	449.40
48000	4161.59	2157.26	1490.35	1157.79	958.98	827.03	733.28	663.42	609.46	566.65	531.93	503.27	479.29	458.97
49000	4248.29	2202.20	1521.40	1181.91	978.96	844.26	748.56	677.24	622.16	578.45	543.01	513.76	489.27	468.53
50000	4334.99	2247.14	1552.45	1206.04	998.94	861.49	763.84	691.06	634.86	590.26	554.09	524.24	499.26	478.09
55000	4768.49	2471.86	1707.69	1326.64	1098.83	947.64	840.22	760.16	698.34	649.28	609.50	576.67	549.18	525.90
60000	5201.99	2696.57	1862.94	1447.24	1198.72	1033.78	916.60	829.27	761.83	708.31	664.91	629.09	599.11	573.71
65000	5635.49	2921.29	2018.18	1567.84	1298.61	1119.93	992.99	898.38	825.31	767.33	720.32	681.52	649.04	621.51
70000	6068.99	3146.00	2173.42	1688.45	1398.51	1206.08	1069.37	967.48	888.80	826.36	775.72	733.94	698.96	669.32
75000	6502.48	3370.71	2328.67	1809.05	1498.40	1292.23	1145.75	1036.59	952.28	885.38	831.13	786.36	748.89	717.13
80000	6935.98	3595.43	2483.91	1929.65	1598.29	1378.38	1222.14	1105.69	1015.77	944.41	886.54	838.79	798.81	764.94
85000	7369.48	3820.14	2639.16	2050.26	1698.19	1464.52	1298.52	1174.80	1079.25	1003.43	941.95	891.21	848.74	812.75
90000	7802.98	4044.85	2794.40	2170.86	1798.08	1550.67	1374.90	1243.90	1142.74	1062.46	997.36	943.64	898.66	860.56
95000	8236.48	4269.57	2949.64	2291.46	1897.97	1636.82	1451.29	1313.01	1206.23	1121.48	1052.77	996.06	948.59	908.36
100000	8669.98	4494.28	3104.89	2412.07	1997.87	1722.97	1527.67	1382.11	1269.71	1180.51	1108.17	1048.48	998.51	956.17

MONTHLY PAYMENT
REQUIRED TO AMORTIZE A LOAN

7.375%

TERM AMOUNT	15 Years	16 Years	17 Years	18 Years	19 Years	20 Years	21 Years	22 Years	23 Years	24 Years	25 Years	30 Years	35 Years	40 Years
5	.05	.05	.05	.05	.05	.04	.04	.04	.04	.04	.04	.04	.04	.04
10	.10	.09	.09	.09	.09	.08	.08	.08	.08	.08	.08	.07	.07	.07
15	.14	.14	.13	.13	.13	.12	.12	.12	.12	.12	.11	.11	.10	.10
25	.23	.23	.22	.21	.21	.20	.20	.20	.19	.19	.19	.18	.17	.17
50	.46	.45	.44	.42	.41	.40	.40	.39	.38	.38	.37	.35	.34	.33
75	.69	.67	.65	.63	.62	.60	.59	.58	.57	.56	.55	.52	.50	.49
100	.92	.89	.87	.84	.82	.80	.79	.77	.76	.75	.74	.70	.67	.65
200	1.84	1.78	1.73	1.68	1.64	1.60	1.57	1.54	1.51	1.49	1.47	1.39	1.34	1.30
300	2.76	2.67	2.59	2.52	2.45	2.40	2.35	2.31	2.27	2.23	2.20	2.08	2.00	1.95
400	3.68	3.56	3.45	3.36	3.27	3.20	3.13	3.07	3.02	2.97	2.93	2.77	2.67	2.60
500	4.60	4.45	4.31	4.19	4.09	3.99	3.91	3.84	3.77	3.71	3.66	3.46	3.33	3.25
600	5.52	5.34	5.17	5.03	4.90	4.79	4.69	4.61	4.53	4.45	4.39	4.15	4.00	3.90
700	6.44	6.23	6.03	5.87	5.72	5.59	5.48	5.37	5.28	5.20	5.12	4.84	4.66	4.55
800	7.36	7.11	6.90	6.71	6.54	6.39	6.26	6.14	6.03	5.94	5.85	5.53	5.33	5.20
900	8.28	8.00	7.76	7.54	7.35	7.19	7.04	6.91	6.79	6.68	6.58	6.22	5.99	5.84
1000	9.20	8.89	8.62	8.38	8.17	7.98	7.82	7.67	7.54	7.42	7.31	6.91	6.66	6.49
2000	18.40	17.78	17.23	16.76	16.34	15.96	15.63	15.34	15.07	14.84	14.62	13.82	13.31	12.98
3000	27.60	26.66	25.85	25.13	24.50	23.94	23.45	23.01	22.61	22.25	21.93	20.73	19.97	19.47
4000	36.80	35.55	34.46	33.51	32.67	31.92	31.26	30.67	30.14	29.67	29.24	27.63	26.62	25.96
5000	46.00	44.44	43.08	41.88	40.83	39.90	39.08	38.34	37.68	37.08	36.55	34.54	33.27	32.45
6000	55.20	53.32	51.69	50.26	49.00	47.88	46.89	46.01	45.21	44.50	43.86	41.45	39.93	38.94
7000	64.40	62.21	60.30	58.63	57.16	55.86	54.71	53.67	52.75	51.92	51.17	48.35	46.58	45.42
8000	73.60	71.10	68.92	67.01	65.33	63.84	62.52	61.34	60.28	59.33	58.48	55.26	53.23	51.91
9000	82.80	79.98	77.53	75.39	73.50	71.82	70.33	69.01	67.82	66.75	65.78	62.17	59.89	58.40
10000	92.00	88.87	86.15	83.76	81.66	79.80	78.15	76.67	75.35	74.16	73.09	69.07	66.54	64.89
11000	101.20	97.75	94.76	92.14	89.83	87.78	85.96	84.34	82.89	81.58	80.40	75.98	73.19	71.38
12000	110.40	106.64	103.37	100.51	97.99	95.76	93.78	92.01	90.42	89.00	87.71	82.89	79.85	77.87
13000	119.60	115.53	111.99	108.89	106.16	103.74	101.59	99.67	97.96	96.41	95.02	89.79	86.50	84.36
14000	128.79	124.41	120.60	117.26	114.32	111.72	109.41	107.34	105.49	103.83	102.33	96.70	93.15	90.84
15000	137.99	133.30	129.22	125.64	122.49	119.70	117.22	115.01	113.02	111.24	109.64	103.61	99.81	97.33
16000	147.19	142.19	137.83	134.01	130.65	127.68	125.04	122.67	120.56	118.66	116.95	110.51	106.46	103.82
17000	156.39	151.07	146.44	142.39	138.82	135.66	132.85	130.34	128.09	126.07	124.25	117.42	113.11	110.31
18000	165.59	159.96	155.06	150.77	146.99	143.64	140.66	138.01	135.63	133.49	131.56	124.33	119.77	116.80
19000	174.79	168.84	163.67	159.14	155.15	151.62	148.48	145.67	143.16	140.91	138.87	131.23	126.42	123.29
20000	183.99	177.73	172.29	167.52	163.32	159.60	156.29	153.34	150.70	148.32	146.18	138.14	133.07	129.78
21000	193.19	186.62	180.90	175.89	171.48	167.58	164.11	161.01	158.23	155.74	153.49	145.05	139.73	136.26
22000	202.39	195.50	189.51	184.27	179.65	175.56	171.92	168.68	165.77	163.15	160.80	151.95	146.38	142.75
23000	211.59	204.39	198.13	192.64	187.81	183.54	179.74	176.34	173.30	170.57	168.11	158.86	153.03	149.24
24000	220.79	213.28	206.74	201.02	195.98	191.52	187.55	184.01	180.84	177.99	175.42	165.77	159.69	155.73
25000	229.99	222.16	215.36	209.39	204.14	199.50	195.36	191.68	188.37	185.40	182.72	172.67	166.34	162.22
26000	239.19	231.05	223.97	217.77	212.31	207.48	203.18	199.34	195.91	192.82	190.03	179.58	172.99	168.71
27000	248.38	239.93	232.58	226.15	220.48	215.46	210.99	207.01	203.44	200.23	197.34	186.49	179.65	175.20
28000	257.58	248.82	241.20	234.52	228.64	223.44	218.81	214.68	210.98	207.65	204.65	193.39	186.30	181.68
29000	266.78	257.71	249.81	242.90	236.81	231.42	226.62	222.34	218.51	215.06	211.96	200.30	192.95	188.17
30000	275.98	266.59	258.43	251.27	244.97	239.40	234.44	230.01	226.04	222.48	219.27	207.21	199.61	194.66
31000	285.18	275.48	267.04	259.65	253.14	247.37	242.25	237.68	233.58	229.90	226.58	214.11	206.26	201.15
32000	294.38	284.37	275.65	268.02	261.30	255.35	250.07	245.34	241.11	237.31	233.89	221.02	212.91	207.64
33000	303.58	293.25	284.27	276.40	269.47	263.33	257.88	253.01	248.65	244.73	241.20	227.93	219.57	214.13
34000	312.78	302.14	292.88	284.77	277.63	271.31	265.69	260.68	256.18	252.14	248.50	234.83	226.22	220.61
35000	321.98	311.02	301.50	293.15	285.80	279.29	273.51	268.34	263.72	259.56	255.81	241.74	232.87	227.10
36000	331.18	319.91	310.11	301.53	293.97	287.27	281.32	276.01	271.25	266.98	263.12	248.65	239.53	233.59
37000	340.38	328.80	318.72	309.90	302.13	295.25	289.14	283.68	278.79	274.39	270.43	255.55	246.18	240.08
38000	349.58	337.68	327.34	318.28	310.30	303.23	296.95	291.34	286.32	281.81	277.74	262.46	252.83	246.57
39000	358.78	346.57	335.95	326.65	318.46	311.21	304.77	299.01	293.86	289.22	285.05	269.37	259.49	253.06
40000	367.97	355.46	344.57	335.03	326.63	319.19	312.58	306.68	301.39	296.64	292.36	276.28	266.14	259.55
41000	377.17	364.34	353.18	343.40	334.79	327.17	320.39	314.35	308.93	304.06	299.67	283.18	272.79	266.03
42000	386.37	373.23	361.79	351.78	342.96	335.15	328.21	322.01	316.46	311.47	306.97	290.09	279.45	272.52
43000	395.57	382.11	370.41	360.15	351.12	343.13	336.02	329.68	324.00	318.89	314.28	297.00	286.10	279.01
44000	404.77	391.00	379.02	368.53	359.29	351.11	343.84	337.35	331.53	326.30	321.59	303.90	292.75	285.50
45000	413.97	399.89	387.64	376.91	367.46	359.09	351.65	345.01	339.06	333.72	328.90	310.81	299.41	291.99
46000	423.17	408.77	396.25	385.28	375.62	367.07	359.47	352.68	346.60	341.13	336.21	317.72	306.06	298.48
47000	432.37	417.66	404.86	393.66	383.79	375.05	367.28	360.35	354.13	348.55	343.52	324.62	312.71	304.97
48000	441.57	426.55	413.48	402.03	391.95	383.03	375.10	368.01	361.67	355.97	350.83	331.53	319.37	311.45
49000	450.77	435.43	422.09	410.41	400.12	391.01	382.91	375.68	369.20	363.38	358.14	338.44	326.02	317.94
50000	459.97	444.32	430.71	418.78	408.28	398.99	390.72	383.35	376.74	370.80	365.44	345.34	332.67	324.43
55000	505.96	488.75	473.78	460.66	449.11	438.89	429.80	421.68	414.41	407.88	401.99	379.88	365.94	356.87
60000	551.96	533.18	516.85	502.54	489.94	478.79	468.87	460.02	452.08	444.96	438.53	414.41	399.21	389.32
65000	597.96	577.61	559.92	544.42	530.77	518.68	507.94	498.35	489.76	482.04	475.08	448.94	432.47	421.76
70000	643.95	622.04	602.99	586.29	571.59	558.58	547.01	536.68	527.43	519.12	511.62	483.48	465.74	454.20
75000	689.95	666.48	646.06	628.17	612.42	598.48	586.08	575.02	565.10	556.19	548.16	518.01	499.01	486.64
80000	735.94	710.91	689.13	670.05	653.25	638.38	625.16	613.35	602.78	593.27	584.71	552.55	532.27	519.09
85000	781.94	755.34	732.20	711.93	694.08	678.28	664.23	651.69	640.45	630.35	621.25	587.08	565.54	551.53
90000	827.94	799.77	775.27	753.81	734.91	718.18	703.30	690.02	678.12	667.43	657.80	621.61	598.81	583.97
95000	873.93	844.20	818.34	795.68	775.73	758.07	742.37	728.35	715.80	704.51	694.34	656.15	632.07	616.41
100000	919.93	888.63	861.41	837.56	816.56	797.97	781.44	766.69	753.47	741.59	730.88	690.68	665.34	648.86

MONTHLY PAYMENT
REQUIRED TO AMORTIZE A LOAN

TERM / AMOUNT	1 Year	2 Years	3 Years	4 Years	5 Years	6 Years	7 Years	8 Years	9 Years	10 Years	11 Years	12 Years	13 Years	14 Years
5	.44	.23	.16	.13	.10	.09	.08	.07	.07	.06	.06	.06	.05	.05
10	.87	.45	.32	.25	.20	.18	.16	.14	.13	.12	.12	.11	.10	.10
15	1.31	.68	.47	.37	.30	.26	.23	.21	.20	.18	.17	.16	.15	.15
25	2.17	1.13	.78	.61	.50	.44	.39	.35	.32	.30	.28	.27	.25	.24
50	4.34	2.25	1.56	1.21	1.00	.87	.77	.70	.64	.60	.56	.53	.50	.48
75	6.51	3.38	2.33	1.81	1.50	1.30	1.15	1.04	.96	.89	.84	.79	.75	.72
100	8.68	4.50	3.11	2.42	2.00	1.73	1.53	1.39	1.28	1.19	1.11	1.05	1.00	.96
200	17.35	9.00	6.22	4.83	4.00	3.45	3.06	2.77	2.55	2.37	2.22	2.10	2.00	1.92
300	26.02	13.49	9.32	7.24	6.00	5.18	4.59	4.16	3.82	3.55	3.33	3.15	3.00	2.88
400	34.69	17.99	12.43	9.66	8.00	6.90	6.12	5.54	5.09	4.73	4.44	4.20	4.00	3.84
500	43.36	22.48	15.54	12.07	10.00	8.63	7.65	6.92	6.36	5.91	5.55	5.25	5.00	4.79
600	52.03	26.98	18.64	14.48	12.00	10.35	9.18	8.31	7.63	7.10	6.66	6.30	6.00	5.75
700	60.70	31.47	21.75	16.90	14.00	12.07	10.71	9.69	8.90	8.28	7.77	7.35	7.00	6.71
800	69.37	35.97	24.85	19.31	16.00	13.80	12.24	11.07	10.17	9.46	8.88	8.40	8.00	7.67
900	78.05	40.46	27.96	21.72	18.00	15.52	13.77	12.46	11.44	10.64	9.99	9.45	9.00	8.62
1000	86.72	44.96	31.07	24.14	20.00	17.25	15.29	13.84	12.71	11.82	11.10	10.50	10.00	9.58
2000	173.43	89.91	62.13	48.27	39.99	34.49	30.58	27.67	25.42	23.64	22.19	21.00	20.00	19.16
3000	260.14	134.87	93.19	72.40	59.98	51.73	45.87	41.51	38.13	35.46	33.29	31.50	30.00	28.73
4000	346.85	179.82	124.25	96.53	79.97	68.97	61.16	55.34	50.84	47.28	44.38	42.00	40.00	38.31
5000	433.56	224.78	155.31	120.67	99.96	86.21	76.45	69.17	63.55	59.10	55.48	52.50	50.00	47.88
6000	520.27	269.73	186.37	144.80	119.95	103.46	91.74	83.01	76.26	70.91	66.57	62.99	60.00	57.46
7000	606.98	314.68	217.43	168.93	139.94	120.70	107.03	96.84	88.97	82.73	77.67	73.49	70.00	67.03
8000	693.70	359.64	248.49	193.06	159.93	137.94	122.32	110.67	101.68	94.55	88.76	83.99	80.00	76.61
9000	780.41	404.59	279.55	217.20	179.92	155.18	137.61	124.51	114.39	106.37	99.86	94.49	89.99	86.19
10000	867.12	449.55	310.61	241.33	199.91	172.42	152.89	138.34	127.10	118.19	110.95	104.99	99.99	95.76
11000	953.83	494.50	341.67	265.46	219.90	189.66	168.18	152.17	139.81	130.00	122.05	115.49	109.99	105.34
12000	1040.54	539.45	372.73	289.59	239.89	206.91	183.47	166.01	152.52	141.82	133.14	125.98	119.99	114.91
13000	1127.25	584.41	403.79	313.72	259.88	224.15	198.76	179.84	165.23	153.64	144.24	136.48	129.99	124.49
14000	1213.96	629.36	434.85	337.86	279.87	241.39	214.05	193.68	177.94	165.46	155.33	146.98	139.99	134.06
15000	1300.67	674.32	465.91	361.99	299.86	258.63	229.34	207.51	190.65	177.28	166.43	157.48	149.99	143.64
16000	1387.39	719.27	496.97	386.12	319.85	275.87	244.63	221.34	203.36	189.09	177.52	167.98	159.99	153.21
17000	1474.10	764.23	528.03	410.25	339.84	293.11	259.92	235.18	216.07	200.91	188.62	178.48	169.98	162.79
18000	1560.81	809.18	559.09	434.39	359.83	310.36	275.21	249.01	228.78	212.73	199.71	188.97	179.98	172.37
19000	1647.52	854.13	590.15	458.52	379.82	327.60	290.50	262.84	241.49	224.55	210.81	199.47	189.98	181.94
20000	1734.23	899.09	621.21	482.65	399.81	344.84	305.78	276.68	254.20	236.37	221.90	209.97	199.98	191.52
21000	1820.94	944.04	652.27	506.78	419.80	362.08	321.07	290.51	266.91	248.18	233.00	220.47	209.98	201.09
22000	1907.65	989.00	683.33	530.91	439.80	379.32	336.36	304.34	279.62	260.00	244.09	230.97	219.98	210.67
23000	1994.36	1033.95	714.39	555.05	459.79	396.56	351.65	318.18	292.33	271.82	255.19	241.47	229.98	220.24
24000	2081.08	1078.90	745.45	579.18	479.78	413.81	366.94	332.01	305.04	283.64	266.28	251.96	239.98	229.82
25000	2167.79	1123.86	776.51	603.31	499.77	431.05	382.23	345.85	317.75	295.46	277.38	262.46	249.97	239.40
26000	2254.50	1168.81	807.57	627.44	519.76	448.29	397.52	359.68	330.46	307.27	288.47	272.96	259.97	248.97
27000	2341.21	1213.77	838.63	651.58	539.75	465.53	412.81	373.51	343.17	319.09	299.57	283.46	269.97	258.55
28000	2427.92	1258.72	869.69	675.71	559.74	482.77	428.10	387.35	355.88	330.91	310.66	293.96	279.97	268.12
29000	2514.63	1303.67	900.75	699.84	579.73	500.02	443.39	401.18	368.59	342.73	321.76	304.45	289.97	277.70
30000	2601.34	1348.63	931.81	723.97	599.72	517.26	458.67	415.01	381.30	354.55	332.85	314.95	299.97	287.27
31000	2688.05	1393.58	962.87	748.11	619.71	534.50	473.96	428.85	394.01	366.36	343.95	325.45	309.97	296.85
32000	2774.77	1438.54	993.93	772.24	639.70	551.74	489.25	442.68	406.72	378.18	355.04	335.95	319.97	306.42
33000	2861.48	1483.49	1025.00	796.37	659.69	568.98	504.54	456.51	419.43	390.00	366.14	346.45	329.96	316.00
34000	2948.19	1528.45	1056.06	820.50	679.68	586.22	519.83	470.35	432.14	401.82	377.23	356.95	339.96	325.58
35000	3034.90	1573.40	1087.12	844.63	699.67	603.47	535.12	484.18	444.85	413.64	388.33	367.44	349.96	335.15
36000	3121.61	1618.35	1118.18	868.77	719.66	620.71	550.41	498.02	457.56	425.45	399.42	377.94	359.96	344.73
37000	3208.32	1663.31	1149.24	892.90	739.65	637.95	565.70	511.85	470.27	437.27	410.52	388.44	369.96	354.30
38000	3295.03	1708.26	1180.30	917.03	759.64	655.19	580.99	525.68	482.98	449.09	421.61	398.94	379.96	363.88
39000	3381.74	1753.22	1211.36	941.16	779.63	672.43	596.27	539.52	495.69	460.91	432.71	409.44	389.96	373.45
40000	3468.46	1798.17	1242.42	965.30	799.62	689.67	611.56	553.35	508.40	472.73	443.80	419.94	399.96	383.03
41000	3555.17	1843.13	1273.48	989.43	819.61	706.92	626.85	567.18	521.11	484.55	454.90	430.43	409.96	392.60
42000	3641.88	1888.08	1304.54	1013.56	839.60	724.16	642.14	581.02	533.82	496.36	465.99	440.93	419.95	402.18
43000	3728.59	1933.03	1335.60	1037.69	859.59	741.40	657.43	594.85	546.53	508.18	477.09	451.43	429.95	411.76
44000	3815.30	1977.99	1366.66	1061.82	879.59	758.64	672.72	608.68	559.24	520.00	488.18	461.93	439.95	421.33
45000	3902.01	2022.94	1397.72	1085.96	899.58	775.88	688.01	622.52	571.95	531.82	499.28	472.43	449.95	430.91
46000	3988.72	2067.90	1428.78	1110.09	919.57	793.12	703.30	636.35	584.66	543.64	510.37	482.93	459.95	440.48
47000	4075.43	2112.85	1459.84	1134.22	939.56	810.37	718.59	650.19	597.37	555.45	521.47	493.42	469.95	450.06
48000	4162.15	2157.80	1490.90	1158.35	959.55	827.61	733.88	664.02	610.08	567.27	532.56	503.92	479.95	459.63
49000	4248.86	2202.76	1521.96	1182.49	979.54	844.85	749.16	677.85	622.79	579.09	543.66	514.42	489.95	469.21
50000	4335.57	2247.71	1553.02	1206.62	999.53	862.09	764.45	691.69	635.50	590.91	554.75	524.92	499.94	478.79
55000	4769.12	2472.48	1708.32	1327.28	1099.48	948.30	840.90	760.85	699.05	650.00	610.23	577.41	549.94	526.66
60000	5202.68	2697.25	1863.62	1447.94	1199.43	1034.51	917.34	830.02	762.59	709.09	665.70	629.90	599.93	574.54
65000	5636.24	2922.02	2018.93	1568.60	1299.39	1120.72	993.79	899.19	826.14	768.18	721.18	682.39	649.93	622.42
70000	6069.79	3146.79	2174.23	1689.26	1399.34	1206.93	1070.23	968.36	889.69	827.27	776.65	734.88	699.92	670.30
75000	6503.35	3371.56	2329.53	1809.92	1499.29	1293.13	1146.68	1037.53	953.24	886.36	832.13	787.37	749.91	718.18
80000	6936.91	3596.34	2484.83	1930.59	1599.24	1379.34	1223.12	1106.70	1016.79	945.45	887.60	839.87	799.91	766.05
85000	7370.46	3821.11	2640.13	2051.25	1699.19	1465.55	1299.57	1175.86	1080.34	1004.54	943.07	892.36	849.90	813.93
90000	7804.02	4045.88	2795.43	2171.91	1799.15	1551.76	1376.01	1245.03	1143.89	1063.63	998.55	944.85	899.90	861.81
95000	8237.57	4270.65	2950.73	2292.57	1899.10	1637.97	1452.46	1314.20	1207.44	1122.72	1054.02	997.34	949.89	909.69
100000	8671.13	4495.42	3106.04	2413.23	1999.05	1724.18	1528.90	1383.37	1270.99	1181.81	1109.50	1049.83	999.88	957.57

TERM AMOUNT	15 Years	16 Years	17 Years	18 Years	19 Years	20 Years	21 Years	22 Years	23 Years	24 Years	25 Years	30 Years	35 Years	40 Years
5	.05	.05	.05	.05	.05	.04	.04	.04	.04	.04	.04	.04	.04	.04
10	.10	.09	.09	.09	.09	.08	.08	.08	.08	.08	.08	.07	.07	.07
15	.14	.14	.13	.13	.13	.12	.12	.12	.12	.12	.11	.11	.11	.10
25	.24	.23	.22	.21	.21	.20	.20	.20	.19	.19	.19	.18	.17	.17
50	.47	.45	.44	.42	.41	.40	.40	.39	.38	.38	.37	.35	.34	.33
75	.70	.67	.65	.63	.62	.60	.59	.58	.57	.56	.55	.52	.51	.49
100	.93	.90	.87	.84	.82	.80	.79	.77	.76	.75	.74	.70	.67	.66
200	1.85	1.79	1.73	1.68	1.64	1.60	1.57	1.54	1.52	1.49	1.47	1.39	1.34	1.31
300	2.77	2.68	2.59	2.52	2.46	2.40	2.35	2.31	2.27	2.23	2.20	2.08	2.01	1.96
400	3.69	3.57	3.46	3.36	3.28	3.20	3.14	3.08	3.03	2.98	2.93	2.77	2.67	2.61
500	4.61	4.46	4.32	4.20	4.10	4.00	3.92	3.85	3.78	3.72	3.67	3.47	3.34	3.26
600	5.53	5.35	5.18	5.04	4.91	4.80	4.70	4.61	4.54	4.46	4.40	4.16	4.01	3.91
700	6.45	6.24	6.05	5.88	5.73	5.60	5.49	5.38	5.29	5.21	5.13	4.85	4.67	4.56
800	7.38	7.13	6.91	6.72	6.55	6.40	6.27	6.15	6.05	5.95	5.86	5.54	5.34	5.21
900	8.30	8.02	7.77	7.56	7.37	7.20	7.05	6.92	6.80	6.69	6.60	6.24	6.01	5.86
1000	9.22	8.91	8.63	8.40	8.19	8.00	7.83	7.69	7.56	7.44	7.33	6.93	6.68	6.51
2000	18.43	17.81	17.26	16.79	16.37	15.99	15.66	15.37	15.11	14.87	14.65	13.85	13.35	13.02
3000	27.65	26.71	25.89	25.18	24.55	23.99	23.49	23.05	22.66	22.30	21.98	20.78	20.02	19.53
4000	36.86	35.61	34.52	33.57	32.73	31.98	31.32	30.73	30.21	29.73	29.30	27.70	26.69	26.03
5000	46.07	44.51	43.15	41.96	40.91	39.98	39.15	38.42	37.76	37.16	36.63	34.62	33.36	32.54
6000	55.29	53.41	51.78	50.35	49.09	47.97	46.98	46.10	45.31	44.60	43.95	41.55	40.03	39.05
7000	64.50	62.31	60.41	58.74	57.27	55.97	54.81	53.78	52.86	52.03	51.28	48.47	46.70	45.55
8000	73.71	71.21	69.03	67.13	65.45	63.96	62.64	61.46	60.41	59.46	58.60	55.40	53.37	52.06
9000	82.93	80.11	77.66	75.52	73.63	71.96	70.47	69.15	67.96	66.89	65.93	62.32	60.05	58.57
10000	92.14	89.01	86.29	83.91	81.81	79.95	78.30	76.83	75.51	74.32	73.25	69.24	66.72	65.07
11000	101.35	97.91	94.92	92.30	89.99	87.95	86.13	84.51	83.06	81.76	80.58	76.17	73.39	71.58
12000	110.57	106.81	103.55	100.69	98.17	95.94	93.96	92.19	90.61	89.19	87.90	83.09	80.06	78.09
13000	119.78	115.71	112.18	109.08	106.35	103.94	101.79	99.88	98.16	96.62	95.23	90.01	86.73	84.60
14000	128.99	124.61	120.81	117.47	114.53	111.93	109.62	107.56	105.71	104.05	102.55	96.94	93.40	91.10
15000	138.21	133.51	129.43	125.86	122.71	119.93	117.45	115.24	113.26	111.48	109.88	103.86	100.07	97.61
16000	147.42	142.42	138.06	134.25	130.89	127.92	125.28	122.92	120.81	118.91	117.20	110.79	106.74	104.12
17000	156.63	151.32	146.69	142.64	139.07	135.92	133.11	130.61	128.36	126.35	124.53	117.71	113.41	110.62
18000	165.85	160.22	155.32	151.03	147.26	143.91	140.94	138.29	135.91	133.78	131.85	124.63	120.09	117.13
19000	175.06	169.12	163.95	159.42	155.44	151.91	148.77	145.97	143.46	141.21	139.18	131.56	126.76	123.64
20000	184.27	178.02	172.58	167.81	163.62	159.90	156.60	153.65	151.01	148.64	146.50	138.48	133.43	130.14
21000	193.49	186.92	181.21	176.20	171.80	167.90	164.43	161.34	158.56	156.07	153.83	145.40	140.10	136.65
22000	202.70	195.82	189.83	184.59	179.98	175.89	172.26	169.02	166.12	163.51	161.15	152.33	146.77	143.16
23000	211.91	204.72	198.46	192.98	188.16	183.89	180.09	176.70	173.67	170.94	168.48	159.25	153.44	149.66
24000	221.13	213.62	207.09	201.37	196.34	191.88	187.92	184.38	181.22	178.37	175.80	166.18	160.11	156.17
25000	230.34	222.52	215.72	209.76	204.52	199.88	195.75	192.07	188.77	185.80	183.13	173.10	166.78	162.68
26000	239.55	231.42	224.35	218.15	212.70	207.87	203.58	199.75	196.32	193.23	190.45	180.02	173.45	169.19
27000	248.77	240.32	232.98	226.55	220.88	215.87	211.41	207.43	203.87	200.67	197.78	186.95	180.13	175.69
28000	257.98	249.22	241.61	234.94	229.06	223.86	219.24	215.11	211.42	208.10	205.10	193.87	186.80	182.20
29000	267.19	258.12	250.23	243.33	237.24	231.86	227.07	222.80	218.97	215.53	212.43	200.80	193.47	188.71
30000	276.41	267.02	258.86	251.72	245.42	239.85	234.90	230.48	226.52	222.96	219.75	207.72	200.14	195.21
31000	285.62	275.93	267.49	260.11	253.60	247.85	242.73	238.16	234.07	230.39	227.08	214.64	206.81	201.72
32000	294.83	284.83	276.12	268.50	261.78	255.84	250.56	245.84	241.62	237.82	234.40	221.57	213.48	208.23
33000	304.05	293.73	284.75	276.89	269.96	263.84	258.39	253.53	249.17	245.26	241.73	228.49	220.15	214.73
34000	313.26	302.63	293.38	285.28	278.14	271.83	266.22	261.21	256.72	252.69	249.05	235.41	226.82	221.24
35000	322.47	311.53	302.01	293.67	286.33	279.83	274.05	268.89	264.27	260.12	256.38	242.34	233.49	227.75
36000	331.69	320.43	310.63	302.06	294.51	287.82	281.88	276.57	271.82	267.55	263.70	249.26	240.17	234.25
37000	340.90	329.33	319.26	310.45	302.69	295.82	289.71	284.26	279.37	274.98	271.03	256.19	246.84	240.76
38000	350.11	338.23	327.89	318.84	310.87	303.81	297.54	291.94	286.92	282.42	278.35	263.11	253.51	247.27
39000	359.33	347.13	336.52	327.23	319.05	311.81	305.37	299.62	294.47	289.85	285.68	270.03	260.18	253.78
40000	368.54	356.03	345.15	335.62	327.23	319.80	313.20	307.30	302.02	297.28	293.00	276.96	266.85	260.28
41000	377.75	364.93	353.78	344.01	335.41	327.80	321.03	314.99	309.57	304.71	300.33	283.88	273.52	266.79
42000	386.97	373.83	362.41	352.40	343.59	335.79	328.86	322.67	317.12	312.14	307.65	290.80	280.19	273.30
43000	396.18	382.73	371.03	360.79	351.77	343.79	336.69	330.35	324.68	319.58	314.98	297.73	286.86	279.80
44000	405.39	391.63	379.66	369.18	359.95	351.78	344.52	338.03	332.23	327.01	322.30	304.65	293.53	286.31
45000	414.61	400.53	388.29	377.57	368.13	359.78	352.35	345.72	339.78	334.44	329.63	311.58	300.21	292.82
46000	423.82	409.43	396.92	385.96	376.31	367.77	360.18	353.40	347.33	341.87	336.95	318.50	306.88	299.32
47000	433.03	418.34	405.55	394.35	384.49	375.77	368.01	361.08	354.88	349.30	344.28	325.42	313.55	305.83
48000	442.25	427.24	414.18	402.74	392.67	383.76	375.84	368.76	362.43	356.73	351.60	332.35	320.22	312.34
49000	451.46	436.14	422.81	411.13	400.85	391.75	383.67	376.45	369.98	364.17	358.93	339.27	326.89	318.84
50000	460.67	445.04	431.43	419.52	409.03	399.75	391.50	384.13	377.53	371.60	366.25	346.19	333.56	325.35
55000	506.74	489.54	474.58	461.48	449.94	439.72	430.66	422.54	415.28	408.76	402.88	380.81	366.92	357.89
60000	552.81	534.04	517.72	503.43	490.84	479.70	469.79	460.95	453.03	445.92	439.50	415.43	400.27	390.42
65000	598.88	578.55	560.86	545.38	531.74	519.67	508.94	499.36	490.79	483.08	476.13	450.05	433.63	422.96
70000	644.94	623.05	604.01	587.33	572.65	559.65	548.09	537.78	528.54	520.24	512.75	484.67	466.98	455.49
75000	691.01	667.55	647.15	629.28	613.55	599.62	587.24	576.19	566.29	557.40	549.38	519.29	500.34	488.02
80000	737.08	712.06	690.29	671.23	654.45	639.60	626.39	614.60	604.04	594.55	586.00	553.91	533.70	520.56
85000	783.15	756.56	733.44	713.19	695.35	679.57	665.54	653.01	641.80	631.71	622.63	588.53	567.05	553.09
90000	829.21	801.06	776.58	755.14	736.26	719.55	704.69	691.43	679.55	668.87	659.25	623.15	600.41	585.63
95000	875.28	845.57	819.72	797.09	777.16	759.52	743.84	729.84	717.30	706.03	695.88	657.77	633.76	618.16
100000	921.34	890.07	862.86	839.04	818.06	799.49	782.99	768.25	755.05	743.19	732.50	692.38	667.12	650.70

MONTHLY PAYMENT
REQUIRED TO AMORTIZE A LOAN

TERM AMOUNT	1 Year	2 Years	3 Years	4 Years	5 Years	6 Years	7 Years	8 Years	9 Years	10 Years	11 Years	12 Years	13 Years	14 Years
5	.44	.23	.16	.13	.11	.09	.08	.07	.07	.06	.06	.06	.06	.05
10	.87	.45	.32	.25	.21	.18	.16	.14	.13	.12	.12	.11	.11	.10
15	1.31	.68	.47	.37	.31	.26	.24	.21	.20	.18	.17	.16	.16	.15
25	2.17	1.13	.78	.61	.51	.44	.39	.35	.32	.30	.28	.27	.26	.25
50	4.34	2.25	1.56	1.21	1.01	.87	.77	.70	.64	.60	.56	.53	.51	.49
75	6.51	3.38	2.34	1.82	1.51	1.30	1.16	1.05	.96	.90	.84	.80	.76	.73
100	8.68	4.50	3.12	2.42	2.01	1.73	1.54	1.39	1.28	1.19	1.12	1.06	1.01	.97
200	17.36	9.00	6.23	4.84	4.01	3.46	3.07	2.78	2.56	2.38	2.23	2.12	2.02	1.93
300	26.03	13.50	9.34	7.26	6.02	5.19	4.61	4.17	3.83	3.57	3.35	3.17	3.02	2.89
400	34.71	18.00	12.45	9.68	8.02	6.92	6.14	5.56	5.11	4.75	4.46	4.23	4.03	3.86
500	43.38	22.50	15.56	12.09	10.02	8.65	7.67	6.95	6.39	5.94	5.58	5.28	5.03	4.82
600	52.06	27.00	18.67	14.51	12.03	10.38	9.21	8.34	7.66	7.13	6.69	6.34	6.04	5.78
700	60.74	31.50	21.78	16.93	14.03	12.11	10.74	9.72	8.94	8.31	7.81	7.39	7.04	6.75
800	69.41	36.00	24.89	19.35	16.04	13.84	12.28	11.11	10.21	9.50	8.92	8.45	8.05	7.71
900	78.09	40.50	28.00	21.77	18.04	15.57	13.81	12.50	11.49	10.69	10.04	9.50	9.05	8.67
1000	86.76	45.00	31.11	24.18	20.04	17.30	15.34	13.89	12.77	11.88	11.15	10.56	10.06	9.64
2000	173.52	90.00	62.22	48.36	40.08	34.59	30.68	27.77	25.53	23.75	22.30	21.11	20.11	19.27
3000	260.28	135.00	93.32	72.54	60.12	51.88	46.02	41.66	38.29	35.62	33.45	31.66	30.17	28.90
4000	347.03	180.00	124.43	96.72	80.16	69.17	61.36	55.54	51.05	47.49	44.60	42.21	40.22	38.53
5000	433.79	225.00	155.54	120.90	100.19	86.46	76.70	69.42	63.81	59.36	55.75	52.77	50.27	48.16
6000	520.55	270.00	186.64	145.08	120.23	103.75	92.03	83.31	76.57	71.23	66.89	63.32	60.33	57.79
7000	607.31	315.00	217.75	169.26	140.27	121.04	107.37	97.19	89.33	83.10	78.04	73.87	70.38	67.43
8000	694.06	360.00	248.85	193.44	160.31	138.33	122.71	111.08	102.09	94.97	89.19	84.42	80.43	77.06
9000	780.82	405.00	279.96	217.62	180.35	155.62	138.05	124.96	114.85	106.84	100.34	94.98	90.49	86.69
10000	867.58	450.00	311.07	241.79	200.38	172.91	153.39	138.84	127.62	118.71	111.49	105.53	100.54	96.32
11000	954.34	495.00	342.17	265.97	220.42	190.20	168.73	152.73	140.38	130.58	122.63	116.08	110.60	105.95
12000	1041.09	540.00	373.28	290.15	240.46	207.49	184.06	166.61	153.14	142.45	133.78	126.63	120.65	115.58
13000	1127.85	585.00	404.39	314.33	260.50	224.78	199.40	180.50	165.90	154.32	144.93	137.18	130.70	125.21
14000	1214.61	630.00	435.49	338.51	280.54	242.07	214.74	194.38	178.66	166.19	156.08	147.74	140.76	134.85
15000	1301.37	675.00	466.60	362.69	300.57	259.36	230.08	208.26	191.42	178.06	167.23	158.29	150.81	144.48
16000	1388.12	720.00	497.70	386.87	320.61	276.65	245.42	222.15	204.18	189.93	178.37	168.84	160.86	154.11
17000	1474.88	765.00	528.81	411.05	340.65	293.94	260.76	236.03	216.94	201.80	189.52	179.39	170.92	163.74
18000	1561.64	810.00	559.92	435.23	360.69	311.23	276.09	249.91	229.70	213.67	200.67	189.95	180.97	173.37
19000	1648.40	855.00	591.02	459.40	380.73	328.52	291.43	263.80	242.46	225.54	211.82	200.50	191.03	183.00
20000	1735.15	900.00	622.13	483.58	400.76	345.81	306.77	277.68	255.23	237.41	222.97	211.05	201.08	192.63
21000	1821.91	945.00	653.24	507.76	420.80	363.10	322.11	291.57	267.99	249.28	234.11	221.60	211.13	202.27
22000	1908.67	990.00	684.34	531.94	440.84	380.39	337.45	305.45	280.75	261.15	245.26	232.15	221.19	211.90
23000	1995.43	1035.00	715.45	556.12	460.88	397.68	352.79	319.33	293.51	273.02	256.41	242.71	231.24	221.53
24000	2082.18	1080.00	746.55	580.30	480.92	414.97	368.12	333.22	306.27	284.89	267.56	253.26	241.29	231.16
25000	2168.94	1124.99	777.66	604.48	500.95	432.26	383.46	347.10	319.03	296.76	278.71	263.81	251.35	240.79
26000	2255.70	1169.99	808.77	628.66	520.99	449.55	398.80	360.99	331.79	308.63	289.85	274.36	261.40	250.42
27000	2342.46	1214.99	839.87	652.84	541.03	466.84	414.14	374.87	344.55	320.50	301.00	284.92	271.46	260.05
28000	2429.21	1259.99	870.98	677.01	561.07	484.13	429.48	388.75	357.31	332.37	312.15	295.47	281.51	269.69
29000	2515.97	1304.99	902.09	701.19	581.11	501.42	444.82	402.64	370.07	344.24	323.30	306.02	291.56	279.32
30000	2602.73	1349.99	933.19	725.37	601.14	518.71	460.15	416.52	382.84	356.11	334.45	316.57	301.62	288.95
31000	2689.48	1394.99	964.30	749.55	621.18	536.00	475.49	430.40	395.60	367.98	345.59	327.13	311.67	298.58
32000	2776.24	1439.99	995.40	773.73	641.22	553.29	490.83	444.29	408.36	379.85	356.74	337.68	321.72	308.21
33000	2863.00	1484.99	1026.51	797.91	661.26	570.58	506.17	458.17	421.12	391.72	367.89	348.23	331.78	317.84
34000	2949.76	1529.99	1057.62	822.09	681.30	587.87	521.51	472.06	433.88	403.59	379.04	358.78	341.83	327.47
35000	3036.51	1574.99	1088.72	846.27	701.33	605.16	536.84	485.94	446.64	415.46	390.19	369.33	351.88	337.11
36000	3123.27	1619.99	1119.83	870.45	721.37	622.45	552.18	499.82	459.40	427.33	401.33	379.89	361.94	346.74
37000	3210.03	1664.99	1150.94	894.62	741.41	639.74	567.52	513.71	472.16	439.20	412.48	390.44	371.99	356.37
38000	3296.79	1709.99	1182.04	918.80	761.45	657.03	582.86	527.59	484.92	451.07	423.63	400.99	382.05	366.00
39000	3383.54	1754.99	1213.15	942.98	781.48	674.32	598.20	541.48	497.68	462.94	434.78	411.54	392.10	375.63
40000	3470.30	1799.99	1244.25	967.16	801.52	691.61	613.54	555.36	510.45	474.81	445.93	422.10	402.15	385.26
41000	3557.06	1844.99	1275.36	991.34	821.56	708.90	628.87	569.24	523.21	486.68	457.07	432.65	412.21	394.89
42000	3643.82	1889.99	1306.47	1015.52	841.60	726.19	644.21	583.13	535.97	498.55	468.22	443.20	422.26	404.53
43000	3730.57	1934.99	1337.57	1039.70	861.64	743.48	659.55	597.01	548.73	510.42	479.37	453.75	432.31	414.16
44000	3817.33	1979.99	1368.68	1063.88	881.67	760.77	674.89	610.90	561.49	522.29	490.52	464.30	442.37	423.79
45000	3904.09	2024.99	1399.78	1088.06	901.71	778.06	690.23	624.78	574.25	534.16	501.67	474.86	452.42	433.42
46000	3990.85	2069.99	1430.89	1112.23	921.75	795.35	705.57	638.66	587.01	546.03	512.81	485.41	462.48	443.05
47000	4077.60	2114.99	1462.00	1136.41	941.79	812.64	720.90	652.55	599.77	557.90	523.96	495.96	472.53	452.68
48000	4164.36	2159.99	1493.10	1160.59	961.83	829.93	736.24	666.43	612.53	569.77	535.11	506.51	482.58	462.31
49000	4251.12	2204.99	1524.21	1184.77	981.86	847.22	751.58	680.31	625.29	581.64	546.26	517.07	492.64	471.95
50000	4337.88	2249.98	1555.32	1208.95	1001.90	864.51	766.92	694.20	638.06	593.51	557.41	527.62	502.69	481.58
55000	4771.66	2474.98	1710.85	1329.84	1102.09	950.96	843.61	763.62	701.86	652.86	613.15	580.38	552.96	529.73
60000	5205.45	2699.98	1866.38	1450.74	1202.28	1037.41	920.30	833.04	765.67	712.22	668.89	633.14	603.23	577.89
65000	5639.24	2924.98	2021.91	1571.63	1302.47	1123.86	996.99	902.46	829.47	771.57	724.63	685.90	653.50	626.05
70000	6073.02	3149.98	2177.44	1692.53	1402.66	1210.31	1073.68	971.88	893.28	830.92	780.37	738.66	703.76	674.21
75000	6506.81	3374.98	2332.97	1813.42	1502.85	1296.76	1150.38	1041.30	957.08	890.27	836.11	791.42	754.03	722.36
80000	6940.60	3599.97	2488.50	1934.32	1603.04	1383.21	1227.07	1110.71	1020.89	949.62	891.85	844.19	804.30	770.52
85000	7374.39	3824.97	2644.03	2055.21	1703.23	1469.66	1303.76	1180.13	1084.69	1008.97	947.59	896.95	854.57	818.68
90000	7808.17	4049.97	2799.56	2176.11	1803.42	1556.12	1380.45	1249.55	1148.50	1068.32	1003.33	949.71	904.84	866.83
95000	8241.96	4274.97	2955.10	2297.00	1903.61	1642.57	1457.14	1318.97	1212.30	1127.67	1059.07	1002.47	955.11	914.99
100000	8675.75	4499.96	3110.63	2417.90	2003.80	1729.02	1533.83	1388.39	1276.11	1187.02	1114.81	1055.23	1005.38	963.15

TERM	15 Years	16 Years	17 Years	18 Years	19 Years	20 Years	21 Years	22 Years	23 Years	24 Years	25 Years	30 Years	35 Years	40 Years
AMOUNT														
5	.05	.05	.05	.05	.05	.05	.04	.04	.04	.04	.04	.04	.04	.04
10	.10	.09	.09	.09	.09	.09	.08	.08	.08	.08	.08	.07	.07	.07
15	.14	.14	.14	.13	.13	.13	.12	.12	.12	.12	.12	.11	.11	.10
25	.24	.23	.22	.22	.21	.21	.20	.20	.20	.19	.19	.18	.17	.17
50	.47	.45	.44	.43	.42	.41	.40	.39	.39	.38	.37	.35	.34	.33
75	.70	.68	.66	.64	.62	.61	.60	.59	.58	.57	.56	.53	.51	.50
100	.93	.90	.87	.85	.83	.81	.79	.78	.77	.75	.74	.70	.68	.66
200	1.86	1.80	1.74	1.69	1.65	1.62	1.58	1.55	1.53	1.50	1.48	1.40	1.35	1.32
300	2.79	2.69	2.61	2.54	2.48	2.42	2.37	2.33	2.29	2.25	2.22	2.10	2.03	1.98
400	3.71	3.59	3.48	3.38	3.30	3.23	3.16	3.10	3.05	3.00	2.96	2.80	2.70	2.64
500	4.64	4.48	4.35	4.23	4.13	4.03	3.95	3.88	3.81	3.75	3.70	3.50	3.38	3.30
600	5.57	5.38	5.22	5.07	4.95	4.84	4.74	4.65	4.57	4.50	4.44	4.20	4.05	3.95
700	6.49	6.28	6.09	5.92	5.77	5.64	5.53	5.43	5.33	5.25	5.18	4.90	4.72	4.61
800	7.42	7.17	6.95	6.76	6.60	6.45	6.32	6.20	6.10	6.00	5.92	5.60	5.40	5.27
900	8.35	8.07	7.82	7.61	7.42	7.26	7.11	6.98	6.86	6.75	6.66	6.30	6.07	5.93
1000	9.28	8.96	8.69	8.45	8.25	8.06	7.90	7.75	7.62	7.50	7.39	7.00	6.75	6.59
2000	18.55	17.92	17.38	16.90	16.49	16.12	15.79	15.50	15.23	15.00	14.78	13.99	13.49	13.17
3000	27.82	26.88	26.07	25.35	24.73	24.17	23.68	23.24	22.85	22.49	22.17	20.98	20.23	19.75
4000	37.09	35.84	34.75	33.80	32.97	32.23	31.57	30.99	30.46	29.99	29.56	27.97	26.97	26.33
5000	46.36	44.80	43.44	42.25	41.21	40.28	39.46	38.73	38.07	37.49	36.95	34.97	33.72	32.91
6000	55.63	53.75	52.13	50.70	49.45	48.34	47.35	46.48	45.69	44.98	44.34	41.96	40.46	39.49
7000	64.90	62.71	60.81	59.15	57.69	56.40	55.25	54.22	53.30	52.48	51.73	48.95	47.20	46.07
8000	74.17	71.67	69.50	67.60	65.93	64.45	63.14	61.97	60.92	59.97	59.12	55.94	53.94	52.65
9000	83.44	80.63	78.19	76.05	74.17	72.51	71.03	69.71	68.53	67.47	66.51	62.93	60.69	59.23
10000	92.71	89.59	86.88	84.50	82.41	80.56	78.92	77.46	76.14	74.97	73.90	69.93	67.43	65.81
11000	101.98	98.55	95.56	92.95	90.65	88.62	86.81	85.20	83.76	82.46	81.29	76.92	74.17	72.39
12000	111.25	107.50	104.25	101.40	98.89	96.68	94.70	92.95	91.37	89.96	88.60	83.91	80.91	78.97
13000	120.52	116.46	112.94	109.85	107.14	104.73	102.60	100.69	98.99	97.45	96.07	90.90	87.66	85.55
14000	129.79	125.42	121.62	118.30	115.38	112.79	110.49	108.44	106.60	104.95	103.46	97.90	94.40	92.13
15000	139.06	134.38	130.31	126.75	123.62	120.84	118.38	116.18	114.21	112.45	110.85	104.89	101.14	98.72
16000	148.33	143.34	139.00	135.20	131.86	128.90	126.27	123.93	121.83	119.94	118.24	111.88	107.88	105.30
17000	157.60	152.30	147.69	143.65	140.10	136.96	134.16	131.67	129.44	127.44	125.63	118.87	114.63	111.88
18000	166.87	161.25	156.37	152.10	148.34	145.01	142.05	139.42	137.06	134.93	133.02	125.86	121.37	118.46
19000	176.14	170.21	165.06	160.55	156.58	153.07	149.95	147.16	144.67	142.43	140.41	132.86	128.11	125.04
20000	185.41	179.17	173.75	169.00	164.82	161.12	157.84	154.91	152.28	149.93	147.80	139.85	134.85	131.62
21000	194.68	188.13	182.43	177.45	173.06	169.18	165.73	162.65	159.90	157.42	155.19	146.84	141.60	138.20
22000	203.95	197.09	191.12	185.90	181.30	177.24	173.62	170.40	167.51	164.92	162.58	153.83	148.34	144.78
23000	213.22	206.05	199.81	194.35	189.54	185.29	181.51	178.14	175.12	172.41	169.97	160.82	155.08	151.36
24000	222.49	215.00	208.50	202.80	197.78	193.35	189.40	185.89	182.74	179.91	177.36	167.82	161.82	157.94
25000	231.76	223.96	217.18	211.25	206.02	201.40	197.30	193.63	190.35	187.41	184.75	174.81	168.57	164.52
26000	241.03	232.92	225.87	219.70	214.27	209.46	205.19	201.38	197.97	194.90	192.14	181.80	175.31	171.10
27000	250.30	241.88	234.56	228.15	222.51	217.52	213.08	209.12	205.58	202.40	199.53	188.79	182.05	177.68
28000	259.57	250.84	243.24	236.60	230.75	225.57	220.97	216.87	213.19	209.89	206.92	195.79	188.79	184.26
29000	268.84	259.80	251.93	245.05	238.99	233.63	228.86	224.61	220.81	217.39	214.31	202.78	195.54	190.85
30000	278.11	268.75	260.62	253.50	247.23	241.68	236.75	232.36	228.42	224.89	221.70	209.77	202.28	197.43
31000	287.38	277.71	269.30	261.95	255.47	249.74	244.65	240.10	236.04	232.38	229.09	216.76	209.02	204.01
32000	296.65	286.67	277.99	270.40	263.71	257.79	252.54	247.85	243.65	239.88	236.48	223.75	215.76	210.59
33000	305.92	295.63	286.68	278.85	271.95	265.85	260.43	255.59	251.26	247.37	243.87	230.75	222.51	217.17
34000	315.19	304.59	295.37	287.30	280.19	273.91	268.32	263.34	258.88	254.87	251.26	237.74	229.25	223.75
35000	324.46	313.54	304.05	295.75	288.43	281.96	276.21	271.08	266.49	262.37	258.65	244.73	235.99	230.33
36000	333.73	322.50	312.74	304.20	296.67	290.02	284.10	278.83	274.11	269.86	266.04	251.72	242.73	236.91
37000	343.00	331.46	321.43	312.65	304.91	298.07	292.00	286.57	281.72	277.36	273.43	258.71	249.47	243.49
38000	352.27	340.42	330.11	321.09	313.15	306.13	299.89	294.32	289.33	284.85	280.82	265.71	256.22	250.07
39000	361.54	349.38	338.80	329.54	321.40	314.19	307.78	302.06	296.95	292.35	288.21	272.70	262.96	256.65
40000	370.81	358.34	347.49	337.99	329.64	322.24	315.67	309.81	304.56	299.85	295.60	279.69	269.70	263.23
41000	380.08	367.29	356.18	346.44	337.88	330.30	323.56	317.55	312.17	307.34	302.99	286.68	276.44	269.81
42000	389.35	376.25	364.86	354.89	346.12	338.35	331.45	325.30	319.79	314.84	310.38	293.68	283.19	276.39
43000	398.62	385.21	373.55	363.34	354.36	346.41	339.35	333.04	327.40	322.34	317.77	300.67	289.93	282.98
44000	407.89	394.17	382.24	371.79	362.60	354.47	347.24	340.79	335.02	329.83	325.16	307.66	296.67	289.56
45000	417.16	403.13	390.92	380.24	370.84	362.52	355.13	348.53	342.63	337.33	332.55	314.65	303.41	296.14
46000	426.43	412.09	399.61	388.69	379.08	370.58	363.02	356.28	350.24	344.82	339.94	321.64	310.16	302.72
47000	435.70	421.04	408.30	397.14	387.32	378.63	370.91	364.02	357.86	352.32	347.33	328.64	316.90	309.30
48000	444.97	430.00	416.99	405.59	395.56	386.69	378.80	371.77	365.47	359.82	354.72	335.63	323.64	315.88
49000	454.24	438.96	425.67	414.04	403.80	394.75	386.70	379.52	373.09	367.31	362.11	342.62	330.38	322.46
50000	463.51	447.92	434.36	422.49	412.04	402.80	394.59	387.26	380.70	374.81	369.50	349.61	337.13	329.04
55000	509.86	492.71	477.80	464.74	453.25	443.08	434.05	425.99	418.77	412.29	406.45	384.57	370.84	361.94
60000	556.21	537.50	521.23	506.99	494.45	483.36	473.50	464.71	456.84	449.77	443.40	419.53	404.55	394.85
65000	602.56	582.29	564.67	549.24	535.66	523.64	512.96	503.44	494.91	487.25	480.35	454.49	438.26	427.75
70000	648.91	627.08	608.10	591.49	576.86	563.92	552.42	542.16	532.98	524.73	517.30	489.46	471.97	460.65
75000	695.26	671.88	651.54	633.73	618.06	604.20	591.88	580.89	571.05	562.21	554.25	524.42	505.69	493.56
80000	741.61	716.67	694.97	675.98	659.27	644.48	631.34	619.61	609.12	599.69	591.20	559.38	539.40	526.46
85000	787.97	761.46	738.41	718.23	700.47	684.76	670.80	658.34	647.19	637.17	628.15	594.34	573.11	559.37
90000	834.32	806.25	781.84	760.48	741.68	725.04	710.25	697.06	685.26	674.65	665.10	629.30	606.82	592.27
95000	880.67	851.04	825.28	802.73	782.88	765.32	749.71	735.79	723.32	712.13	702.05	664.26	640.54	625.17
100000	927.02	895.83	868.71	844.98	824.08	805.60	789.17	774.52	761.39	749.61	739.00	699.22	674.25	658.08

MONTHLY PAYMENT
REQUIRED TO AMORTIZE A LOAN

TERM AMOUNT	1 Year	2 Years	3 Years	4 Years	5 Years	6 Years	7 Years	8 Years	9 Years	10 Years	11 Years	12 Years	13 Years	14 Years
5	.44	.23	.16	.13	.11	.09	.08	.07	.07	.06	.06	.06	.06	.05
10	.87	.46	.32	.25	.21	.18	.16	.14	.13	.12	.12	.11	.11	.10
15	1.31	.68	.47	.37	.31	.27	.24	.21	.20	.18	.17	.16	.16	.15
25	2.18	1.13	.78	.61	.51	.44	.39	.35	.33	.30	.29	.27	.26	.25
50	4.35	2.26	1.56	1.22	1.01	.87	.77	.70	.65	.60	.57	.54	.51	.49
75	6.52	3.38	2.34	1.82	1.51	1.31	1.16	1.05	.97	.90	.85	.80	.76	.73
100	8.69	4.51	3.12	2.43	2.01	1.74	1.54	1.40	1.29	1.20	1.13	1.07	1.02	.97
200	17.37	9.01	6.24	4.85	4.02	3.47	3.08	2.79	2.57	2.39	2.25	2.13	2.03	1.94
300	26.05	13.52	9.35	7.27	6.03	5.21	4.62	4.19	3.85	3.58	3.37	3.19	3.04	2.91
400	34.73	18.02	12.47	9.70	8.04	6.94	6.16	5.58	5.13	4.77	4.49	4.25	4.05	3.88
500	43.41	22.53	15.58	12.12	10.05	8.67	7.70	6.97	6.41	5.97	5.61	5.31	5.06	4.85
600	52.09	27.03	18.70	14.54	12.06	10.41	9.24	8.37	7.69	7.16	6.73	6.37	6.07	5.82
700	60.77	31.54	21.81	16.96	14.06	12.14	10.78	9.76	8.97	8.35	7.85	7.43	7.08	6.79
800	69.45	36.04	24.93	19.39	16.07	13.88	12.32	11.15	10.25	9.54	8.97	8.49	8.09	7.75
900	78.13	40.55	28.04	21.81	18.08	15.61	13.85	12.55	11.54	10.74	10.09	9.55	9.10	8.72
1000	86.81	45.05	31.16	24.23	20.09	17.34	15.39	13.94	12.82	11.93	11.21	10.61	10.11	9.69
2000	173.61	90.10	62.31	48.46	40.18	34.68	30.78	27.87	25.63	23.85	22.41	21.22	20.22	19.38
3000	260.42	135.14	93.46	72.68	60.26	52.02	46.17	41.81	38.44	35.77	33.61	31.82	30.33	29.07
4000	347.22	180.19	124.61	96.91	80.35	69.36	61.56	55.74	51.25	47.69	44.81	42.43	40.44	38.75
5000	434.02	225.23	155.77	121.13	100.43	86.70	76.94	69.68	64.07	59.62	56.01	53.04	50.55	48.44
6000	520.83	270.28	186.92	145.36	120.52	104.04	92.33	83.61	76.88	71.54	67.21	63.64	60.66	58.13
7000	607.63	315.32	218.07	169.58	140.60	121.38	107.72	97.54	89.69	83.46	78.41	74.25	70.77	67.82
8000	694.43	360.37	249.22	193.81	160.69	138.71	123.11	111.48	102.50	95.38	89.61	84.86	80.88	77.50
9000	781.24	405.41	280.37	218.04	180.77	156.05	138.49	125.41	115.32	107.31	100.82	95.46	90.98	87.19
10000	868.04	450.46	311.53	242.26	200.86	173.39	153.88	139.35	128.13	119.23	112.02	106.07	101.09	96.88
11000	954.84	495.50	342.68	266.49	220.95	190.73	169.27	153.28	140.94	131.15	123.22	116.68	111.20	106.57
12000	1041.65	540.55	373.83	290.71	241.03	208.07	184.66	167.22	153.75	143.07	134.42	127.28	121.31	116.25
13000	1128.45	585.59	404.98	314.94	261.12	225.41	200.04	181.15	166.57	155.00	145.62	137.89	131.42	125.94
14000	1215.26	630.64	436.14	339.16	281.20	242.75	215.43	195.08	179.38	166.92	156.82	148.49	141.53	135.63
15000	1302.06	675.68	467.29	363.39	301.29	260.08	230.82	209.02	192.19	178.84	168.02	159.10	151.64	145.32
16000	1388.86	720.73	498.44	387.61	321.37	277.42	246.21	222.95	205.00	190.76	179.22	169.71	161.75	155.00
17000	1475.67	765.77	529.59	411.84	341.46	294.76	261.60	236.89	217.81	202.69	190.43	180.31	171.85	164.69
18000	1562.47	810.82	560.74	436.07	361.54	312.10	276.98	250.82	230.63	214.61	201.63	190.92	181.96	174.38
19000	1649.27	855.86	591.90	460.29	381.63	329.44	292.37	264.76	243.44	226.53	212.83	201.53	192.07	184.07
20000	1736.08	900.91	623.05	484.52	401.72	346.78	307.76	278.69	256.25	238.45	224.03	212.13	202.18	193.75
21000	1822.88	945.95	654.20	508.74	421.80	364.12	323.15	292.62	269.06	250.38	235.23	222.74	212.29	203.44
22000	1909.68	991.00	685.35	532.97	441.89	381.45	338.53	306.56	281.88	262.30	246.43	233.35	222.40	213.13
23000	1996.49	1036.04	716.50	557.19	461.97	398.79	353.92	320.49	294.69	274.22	257.63	243.95	232.51	222.82
24000	2083.29	1081.09	747.66	581.42	482.06	416.13	369.31	334.43	307.50	286.14	268.83	254.56	242.62	232.50
25000	2170.09	1126.13	778.81	605.64	502.14	433.47	384.70	348.36	320.31	298.07	280.04	265.17	252.72	242.19
26000	2256.90	1171.18	809.96	629.87	522.23	450.81	400.08	362.29	333.13	309.99	291.24	275.77	262.83	251.88
27000	2343.70	1216.22	841.11	654.10	542.31	468.15	415.47	376.23	345.94	321.91	302.44	286.38	272.94	261.57
28000	2430.51	1261.27	872.27	678.32	562.40	485.49	430.86	390.16	358.75	333.83	313.64	296.98	283.05	271.25
29000	2517.31	1306.31	903.42	702.55	582.48	502.82	446.25	404.10	371.56	345.76	324.84	307.59	293.16	280.94
30000	2604.11	1351.36	934.57	726.77	602.57	520.16	461.64	418.03	384.37	357.68	336.04	318.20	303.27	290.63
31000	2690.92	1396.40	965.72	751.00	622.66	537.50	477.02	431.97	397.19	369.60	347.24	328.80	313.38	300.32
32000	2777.72	1441.45	996.87	775.22	642.74	554.84	492.41	445.90	410.00	381.52	358.44	339.41	323.49	310.00
33000	2864.52	1486.49	1028.03	799.45	662.83	572.18	507.80	459.83	422.81	393.45	369.64	350.02	333.59	319.69
34000	2951.33	1531.54	1059.18	823.68	682.91	589.52	523.19	473.77	435.62	405.37	380.85	360.62	343.70	329.38
35000	3038.13	1576.58	1090.33	847.90	703.00	606.86	538.57	487.70	448.44	417.29	392.05	371.23	353.81	339.07
36000	3124.93	1621.63	1121.48	872.13	723.08	624.19	553.96	501.64	461.25	429.21	403.25	381.84	363.92	348.75
37000	3211.74	1666.67	1152.64	896.35	743.17	641.53	569.35	515.57	474.06	441.14	414.45	392.44	374.03	358.44
38000	3298.54	1711.72	1183.79	920.58	763.25	658.87	584.74	529.51	486.87	453.06	425.65	403.05	384.14	368.13
39000	3385.35	1756.76	1214.94	944.80	783.34	676.21	600.12	543.44	499.69	464.98	436.85	413.66	394.25	377.82
40000	3472.15	1801.81	1246.09	969.03	803.43	693.55	615.51	557.37	512.50	476.90	448.05	424.26	404.36	387.50
41000	3558.95	1846.85	1277.24	993.25	823.51	710.89	630.90	571.31	525.31	488.82	459.25	434.87	414.47	397.19
42000	3645.76	1891.90	1308.40	1017.48	843.60	728.23	646.29	585.24	538.12	500.75	470.46	445.47	424.57	406.88
43000	3732.56	1936.94	1339.55	1041.71	863.68	745.56	661.68	599.18	550.93	512.67	481.66	456.08	434.68	416.56
44000	3819.36	1981.99	1370.70	1065.93	883.77	762.90	677.06	613.11	563.75	524.59	492.86	466.69	444.79	426.25
45000	3906.17	2027.03	1401.85	1090.16	903.85	780.24	692.45	627.04	576.56	536.51	504.06	477.29	454.90	435.94
46000	3992.97	2072.08	1433.00	1114.38	923.94	797.58	707.84	640.98	589.37	548.44	515.26	487.90	465.01	445.63
47000	4079.77	2117.12	1464.16	1138.61	944.02	814.92	723.23	654.91	602.18	560.36	526.46	498.51	475.12	455.31
48000	4166.58	2162.17	1495.31	1162.83	964.11	832.26	738.61	668.85	615.00	572.28	537.66	509.11	485.23	465.00
49000	4253.38	2207.21	1526.46	1187.06	984.19	849.60	754.00	682.78	627.81	584.20	548.86	519.72	495.34	474.69
50000	4340.18	2252.26	1557.61	1211.28	1004.28	866.93	769.39	696.72	640.62	596.13	560.07	530.33	505.44	484.38
55000	4774.20	2477.48	1713.37	1332.41	1104.71	953.63	846.33	766.39	704.68	655.74	616.07	583.36	555.99	532.81
60000	5208.22	2702.71	1869.13	1453.54	1205.14	1040.32	923.27	836.06	768.74	715.35	672.08	636.39	606.53	581.25
65000	5642.24	2927.94	2024.90	1574.67	1305.56	1127.01	1000.20	905.73	832.81	774.96	728.08	689.42	657.08	629.69
70000	6076.26	3153.16	2180.66	1695.80	1405.99	1213.71	1077.14	975.40	896.87	834.58	784.09	742.45	707.62	678.13
75000	6510.27	3378.39	2336.42	1816.92	1506.42	1300.40	1154.08	1045.07	960.93	894.19	840.10	795.49	758.16	726.56
80000	6944.29	3603.61	2492.18	1938.05	1606.85	1387.09	1231.02	1114.74	1024.99	953.80	896.10	848.52	808.71	775.00
85000	7378.31	3828.84	2647.94	2059.18	1707.27	1473.78	1307.96	1184.41	1089.05	1013.41	952.11	901.55	859.25	823.44
90000	7812.33	4054.06	2803.70	2180.31	1807.70	1560.48	1384.90	1254.08	1153.11	1073.02	1008.11	954.58	909.80	871.87
95000	8246.35	4279.29	2959.46	2301.44	1908.13	1647.17	1461.83	1323.76	1217.18	1132.64	1064.12	1007.61	960.34	920.31
100000	8680.36	4504.51	3115.22	2422.56	2008.56	1733.86	1538.77	1393.43	1281.24	1192.25	1120.13	1060.65	1010.88	968.75

TERM	15 Years	16 Years	17 Years	18 Years	19 Years	20 Years	21 Years	22 Years	23 Years	24 Years	25 Years	30 Years	35 Years	40 Years
AMOUNT														
5	.05	.05	.05	.05	.05	.05	.04	.04	.04	.04	.04	.04	.04	.04
10	.10	.10	.09	.09	.09	.09	.08	.08	.08	.08	.08	.08	.07	.07
15	.14	.14	.14	.13	.13	.13	.12	.12	.12	.12	.12	.11	.11	.10
25	.24	.23	.22	.22	.21	.21	.20	.20	.20	.19	.19	.18	.18	.17
50	.47	.46	.44	.43	.42	.41	.40	.40	.39	.38	.38	.36	.35	.34
75	.70	.68	.66	.64	.63	.61	.60	.59	.58	.57	.56	.53	.52	.50
100	.94	.91	.88	.86	.84	.82	.80	.79	.77	.76	.75	.71	.69	.67
200	1.87	1.81	1.75	1.71	1.67	1.63	1.60	1.57	1.54	1.52	1.50	1.42	1.37	1.34
300	2.80	2.71	2.63	2.56	2.50	2.44	2.39	2.35	2.31	2.27	2.24	2.12	2.05	2.00
400	3.74	3.61	3.50	3.41	3.33	3.25	3.19	3.13	3.08	3.03	2.99	2.83	2.73	2.67
500	4.67	4.51	4.38	4.26	4.16	4.06	3.98	3.91	3.84	3.79	3.73	3.54	3.41	3.33
600	5.60	5.41	5.25	5.11	4.99	4.88	4.78	4.69	4.61	4.54	4.48	4.24	4.09	4.00
700	6.53	6.32	6.13	5.96	5.82	5.69	5.57	5.47	5.38	5.30	5.22	4.95	4.77	4.66
800	7.47	7.22	7.00	6.81	6.65	6.50	6.37	6.25	6.15	6.05	5.97	5.65	5.45	5.33
900	8.40	8.12	7.88	7.66	7.48	7.31	7.16	7.03	6.91	6.81	6.71	6.36	6.14	5.99
1000	9.33	9.02	8.75	8.51	8.31	8.12	7.96	7.81	7.68	7.57	7.46	7.07	6.82	6.66
2000	18.66	18.04	17.50	17.02	16.61	16.24	15.91	15.62	15.36	15.13	14.92	14.13	13.63	13.31
3000	27.99	27.05	26.24	25.53	24.91	24.36	23.87	23.43	23.04	22.69	22.37	21.19	20.45	19.97
4000	37.31	36.07	34.99	34.04	33.21	32.47	31.82	31.24	30.72	30.25	29.83	28.25	27.26	26.62
5000	46.64	45.09	43.73	42.55	41.51	40.59	39.77	39.04	38.39	37.81	37.28	35.31	34.07	33.28
6000	55.97	54.10	52.48	51.06	49.81	48.71	47.73	46.85	46.07	45.37	44.74	42.37	40.89	39.93
7000	65.29	63.12	61.23	59.57	58.11	56.83	55.68	54.66	53.75	52.93	52.19	49.43	47.70	46.59
8000	74.62	72.13	69.97	68.08	66.41	64.94	63.63	62.47	61.43	60.49	59.65	56.49	54.52	53.24
9000	83.95	81.15	78.72	76.59	74.72	73.06	71.59	70.28	69.10	68.05	67.10	63.55	61.33	59.90
10000	93.28	90.17	87.46	85.10	83.02	81.18	79.54	78.08	76.78	75.61	74.56	70.61	68.14	66.55
11000	102.60	99.18	96.21	93.61	91.32	89.29	87.50	85.89	84.46	83.17	82.01	77.67	74.96	73.21
12000	111.93	108.20	104.95	102.12	99.62	97.41	95.45	93.70	92.14	90.73	89.47	84.73	81.77	79.86
13000	121.26	117.21	113.70	110.63	107.92	105.53	103.40	101.51	99.81	98.29	96.92	91.79	88.59	86.52
14000	130.58	126.23	122.45	119.14	116.22	113.65	111.36	109.32	107.49	105.85	104.38	98.86	95.40	93.17
15000	139.91	135.25	131.19	127.64	124.52	121.76	119.31	117.12	115.17	113.41	111.83	105.92	102.21	99.83
16000	149.24	144.26	139.94	136.15	132.82	129.88	127.26	124.93	122.05	120.97	119.29	112.98	109.03	106.48
17000	158.56	153.28	148.68	144.66	141.13	138.00	135.22	132.74	130.52	128.53	126.74	120.04	115.84	113.14
18000	167.89	162.29	157.43	153.17	149.43	146.11	143.17	140.55	138.20	136.09	134.20	127.10	122.66	119.79
19000	177.22	171.31	166.18	161.68	157.73	154.23	151.13	148.36	145.88	143.65	141.65	134.16	129.47	126.44
20000	186.55	180.33	174.92	170.19	166.03	162.35	159.08	156.16	153.56	151.21	149.11	141.22	136.28	133.10
21000	195.87	189.34	183.67	178.70	174.33	170.47	167.03	163.97	161.23	158.77	156.56	148.28	143.10	139.75
22000	205.20	198.36	192.41	187.21	182.63	178.58	174.99	171.78	168.91	166.34	164.02	155.34	149.91	146.41
23000	214.53	207.38	201.16	195.72	190.93	186.70	182.94	179.59	176.59	173.90	171.47	162.40	156.73	153.06
24000	223.85	216.39	209.90	204.23	199.23	194.82	190.89	187.40	184.27	181.46	178.93	169.46	163.54	159.72
25000	233.18	225.41	218.65	212.74	207.54	202.93	198.85	195.20	191.94	189.02	186.38	176.52	170.35	166.37
26000	242.51	234.42	227.40	221.25	215.84	211.05	206.80	203.01	199.62	196.58	193.84	183.58	177.17	173.03
27000	251.84	243.44	236.14	229.76	224.14	219.17	214.76	210.82	207.30	204.14	201.29	190.65	183.98	179.68
28000	261.16	252.46	244.89	238.27	232.44	227.29	222.71	218.63	214.98	211.70	208.75	197.71	190.80	186.34
29000	270.49	261.47	253.63	246.77	240.74	235.40	230.66	226.44	222.65	219.26	216.20	204.77	197.61	192.99
30000	279.82	270.49	262.38	255.28	249.04	243.52	238.62	234.24	230.33	226.82	223.66	211.83	204.42	199.65
31000	289.14	279.50	271.12	263.79	257.34	251.64	246.57	242.05	238.01	234.38	231.11	218.89	211.24	206.30
32000	298.47	288.52	279.87	272.30	265.64	259.76	254.52	249.86	245.69	241.94	238.57	225.95	218.05	212.96
33000	307.80	297.54	288.62	280.81	273.94	267.87	262.48	257.67	253.36	249.50	246.02	233.01	224.87	219.61
34000	317.12	306.55	297.36	289.32	282.25	275.99	270.43	265.48	261.04	257.06	253.48	240.07	231.68	226.27
35000	326.45	315.57	306.11	297.83	290.55	284.11	278.39	273.28	268.72	264.62	260.93	247.13	238.49	232.92
36000	335.78	324.58	314.85	306.34	298.85	292.22	286.34	281.09	276.40	272.18	268.39	254.19	245.31	239.58
37000	345.11	333.60	323.60	314.85	307.15	300.34	294.29	288.90	284.07	279.74	275.84	261.25	252.12	246.23
38000	354.43	342.62	332.35	323.36	315.45	308.46	302.25	296.71	291.75	287.30	283.30	268.31	258.94	252.88
39000	363.76	351.63	341.09	331.87	323.75	316.58	310.20	304.52	299.43	294.86	290.75	275.37	265.75	259.54
40000	373.09	360.65	349.84	340.38	332.05	324.69	318.15	312.32	307.11	302.42	298.21	282.43	272.56	266.19
41000	382.41	369.66	358.58	348.89	340.35	332.81	326.11	320.13	314.78	309.98	305.66	289.50	279.38	272.85
42000	391.74	378.68	367.33	357.40	348.66	340.93	334.06	327.94	322.46	317.54	313.12	296.56	286.19	279.50
43000	401.07	387.70	376.07	365.90	356.96	349.04	342.02	335.75	330.14	325.11	320.57	303.62	293.01	286.16
44000	410.39	396.71	384.82	374.41	365.26	357.16	349.97	343.56	337.82	332.67	328.03	310.68	299.82	292.81
45000	419.72	405.73	393.57	382.92	373.56	365.28	357.92	351.36	345.49	340.23	335.48	317.74	306.63	299.47
46000	429.05	414.75	402.31	391.43	381.86	373.40	365.88	359.17	353.17	347.79	342.94	324.80	313.45	306.12
47000	438.38	423.76	411.06	399.94	390.16	381.51	373.83	366.98	360.85	355.35	350.39	331.86	320.26	312.78
48000	447.70	432.78	419.80	408.45	398.46	389.63	381.78	374.79	368.53	362.91	357.85	338.92	327.08	319.43
49000	457.03	441.79	428.55	416.96	406.76	397.75	389.74	382.60	376.21	370.47	365.30	345.98	333.89	326.09
50000	466.36	450.81	437.29	425.47	415.07	405.86	397.69	390.40	383.88	378.03	372.76	353.04	340.70	332.74
55000	512.99	495.89	481.02	468.02	456.57	446.45	437.46	429.44	422.27	415.83	410.03	388.35	374.77	366.02
60000	559.63	540.97	524.75	510.56	498.08	487.04	477.23	468.48	460.66	453.63	447.31	423.65	408.84	399.29
65000	606.26	586.05	568.48	553.11	539.58	527.62	517.00	507.52	499.05	491.44	484.59	458.95	442.91	432.56
70000	652.90	631.13	612.21	595.66	581.09	568.21	556.77	546.56	537.43	529.24	521.86	494.26	476.98	465.84
75000	699.53	676.21	655.94	638.20	622.60	608.79	596.54	585.60	575.82	567.04	559.14	529.56	511.05	499.11
80000	746.17	721.29	699.67	680.75	664.10	649.38	636.30	624.64	614.21	604.84	596.41	564.86	545.12	532.38
85000	792.80	766.37	743.40	723.30	705.61	689.97	676.07	663.68	652.60	642.65	633.69	600.17	579.19	565.66
90000	839.44	811.45	787.13	765.84	747.11	730.55	715.84	702.72	690.98	680.45	670.96	635.47	613.26	598.93
95000	886.07	856.53	830.86	808.39	788.62	771.14	755.61	741.76	729.37	718.25	708.24	670.78	647.33	632.20
100000	932.71	901.61	874.58	850.94	830.13	811.72	795.38	780.80	767.76	756.05	745.51	706.08	681.40	665.48

MONTHLY PAYMENT
REQUIRED TO AMORTIZE A LOAN

TERM	1 Year	2 Years	3 Years	4 Years	5 Years	6 Years	7 Years	8 Years	9 Years	10 Years	11 Years	12 Years	13 Years	14 Years
AMOUNT														
5	.44	.23	.16	.13	.11	.09	.08	.07	.07	.06	.06	.06	.06	.05
10	.87	.46	.32	.25	.21	.18	.16	.14	.13	.12	.12	.11	.11	.10
15	1.31	.68	.47	.37	.31	.27	.24	.21	.20	.18	.17	.16	.16	.15
25	2.18	1.13	.78	.61	.51	.44	.39	.35	.33	.30	.29	.27	.26	.25
50	4.35	2.26	1.56	1.22	1.01	.87	.78	.70	.65	.60	.57	.54	.51	.49
75	6.52	3.38	2.34	1.82	1.51	1.31	1.16	1.05	.97	.90	.85	.80	.76	.73
100	8.69	4.51	3.12	2.43	2.01	1.74	1.55	1.40	1.29	1.20	1.13	1.07	1.02	.98
200	17.37	9.02	6.24	4.85	4.02	3.48	3.09	2.79	2.57	2.39	2.25	2.13	2.03	1.95
300	26.05	13.52	9.35	7.20	6.03	5.21	4.63	4.19	3.85	3.59	3.37	3.19	3.04	2.92
400	34.73	18.03	12.47	9.70	8.04	6.95	6.17	5.58	5.14	4.78	4.49	4.25	4.05	3.89
500	43.41	22.53	15.59	12.12	10.05	8.68	7.71	6.98	6.42	5.97	5.61	5.31	5.07	4.86
600	52.09	27.04	18.70	14.55	12.06	10.42	9.25	8.37	7.70	7.17	6.73	6.38	6.08	5.83
700	60.78	31.54	21.82	16.97	14.07	12.15	10.79	9.77	8.98	8.36	7.86	7.44	7.09	6.80
800	69.46	36.05	24.94	19.39	16.08	13.89	12.33	11.16	10.27	9.55	8.98	8.50	8.10	7.77
900	78.14	40.56	28.05	21.82	18.09	15.62	13.87	12.56	11.55	10.75	10.10	9.56	9.12	8.74
1000	86.82	45.06	31.17	24.24	20.10	17.36	15.41	13.95	12.83	11.94	11.22	10.62	10.13	9.71
2000	173.64	90.12	62.33	48.48	40.20	34.71	30.81	27.90	25.66	23.88	22.43	21.24	20.25	19.41
3000	260.45	135.17	93.50	72.72	60.30	52.06	46.21	41.85	38.48	35.81	33.65	31.86	30.37	29.11
4000	347.27	180.23	124.66	96.95	80.39	69.41	61.61	55.79	51.31	47.75	44.86	42.48	40.50	38.81
5000	434.08	225.29	155.82	121.19	100.49	86.76	77.01	69.74	64.13	59.68	56.08	53.10	50.62	48.51
6000	520.90	270.34	186.99	145.43	120.59	104.11	92.41	83.69	76.96	71.62	67.29	63.72	60.74	58.21
7000	607.71	315.40	218.15	169.67	140.69	121.46	107.81	97.63	89.78	83.55	78.51	74.34	70.86	67.92
8000	694.53	360.46	249.31	193.90	160.78	138.81	123.21	111.58	102.61	95.49	89.72	84.96	80.99	77.62
9000	781.34	405.51	280.48	218.14	180.88	156.16	138.61	125.53	115.43	107.42	100.94	95.58	91.11	87.32
10000	868.16	450.57	311.64	242.38	200.98	173.51	154.01	139.47	128.26	119.36	112.15	106.20	101.23	97.02
11000	954.97	495.63	342.81	266.62	221.08	190.86	169.41	153.42	141.08	131.30	123.36	116.82	111.35	106.72
12000	1041.79	540.68	373.97	290.85	241.17	208.21	184.81	167.37	153.91	143.23	134.58	127.44	121.48	116.42
13000	1128.60	585.74	405.13	315.09	261.27	225.56	200.21	181.31	166.73	155.17	145.79	138.06	131.60	126.12
14000	1215.42	630.80	436.30	339.33	281.37	242.91	215.61	195.26	179.56	167.10	157.01	148.68	141.72	135.83
15000	1302.23	675.85	467.46	363.56	301.47	260.27	231.01	209.21	192.38	179.04	168.22	159.30	151.84	145.53
16000	1389.05	720.91	498.62	387.80	321.56	277.62	246.41	223.15	205.21	190.97	179.44	169.92	161.97	155.23
17000	1475.86	765.96	529.79	412.04	341.66	294.97	261.81	237.10	218.03	202.91	190.65	180.54	172.09	164.93
18000	1562.68	811.02	560.95	436.28	361.76	312.32	277.21	251.05	230.86	214.84	201.87	191.16	182.21	174.63
19000	1649.49	856.08	592.11	460.51	381.86	329.67	292.61	264.99	243.68	226.78	213.08	201.78	192.33	184.33
20000	1736.31	901.13	623.28	484.75	401.95	347.02	308.01	278.94	256.51	238.72	224.30	212.40	202.46	194.03
21000	1823.12	946.19	654.44	508.99	422.05	364.37	323.41	292.89	269.33	250.65	235.51	223.02	212.58	203.74
22000	1909.94	991.25	685.61	533.23	442.15	381.72	338.81	306.84	282.16	262.59	246.72	233.64	222.70	213.44
23000	1996.75	1036.30	716.77	557.46	462.25	399.07	354.21	320.78	294.98	274.52	257.94	244.26	232.82	223.14
24000	2083.57	1081.36	747.93	581.70	482.34	416.42	369.61	334.73	307.81	286.46	269.15	254.88	242.95	232.84
25000	2170.38	1126.42	779.10	605.94	502.44	433.77	385.01	348.68	320.63	298.39	280.37	265.50	253.07	242.54
26000	2257.20	1171.47	810.26	630.17	522.54	451.12	400.41	362.62	333.46	310.33	291.58	276.12	263.19	252.24
27000	2344.01	1216.53	841.42	654.41	542.63	468.47	415.81	376.57	346.28	322.26	302.80	286.74	273.31	261.94
28000	2430.83	1261.59	872.59	678.65	562.73	485.82	431.21	390.52	359.11	334.20	314.01	297.36	283.44	271.65
29000	2517.64	1306.64	903.75	702.89	582.83	503.18	446.61	404.46	371.93	346.14	325.23	307.98	293.56	281.35
30000	2604.46	1351.70	934.91	727.12	602.93	520.53	462.01	418.41	384.76	358.07	336.44	318.60	303.68	291.05
31000	2691.27	1396.76	966.08	751.36	623.02	537.88	477.41	432.36	397.59	370.01	347.66	329.22	313.81	300.75
32000	2778.09	1441.81	997.24	775.60	643.12	555.23	492.81	446.30	410.41	381.94	358.87	339.84	323.93	310.45
33000	2864.90	1486.87	1028.41	799.84	663.22	572.58	508.21	460.25	423.24	393.88	370.08	350.46	334.05	320.15
34000	2951.72	1531.92	1059.57	824.07	683.32	589.93	523.61	474.20	436.06	405.81	381.30	361.08	344.17	329.85
35000	3038.53	1576.98	1090.73	848.31	703.41	607.28	539.01	488.14	448.89	417.75	392.51	371.70	354.30	339.56
36000	3125.35	1622.04	1121.90	872.55	723.51	624.63	554.41	502.09	461.71	429.68	403.73	382.32	364.42	349.26
37000	3212.17	1667.09	1153.06	896.78	743.61	641.98	569.81	516.04	474.54	441.62	414.94	392.94	374.54	358.96
38000	3298.98	1712.15	1184.22	921.02	763.71	659.33	585.21	529.98	487.36	453.55	426.16	403.56	384.66	368.66
39000	3385.80	1757.21	1215.39	945.26	783.80	676.68	600.61	543.93	500.19	465.49	437.37	414.18	394.79	378.36
40000	3472.61	1802.26	1246.55	969.50	803.90	694.03	616.01	557.88	513.01	477.43	448.59	424.80	404.91	388.06
41000	3559.43	1847.32	1277.72	993.73	824.00	711.38	631.41	571.82	525.84	489.36	459.80	435.42	415.03	397.77
42000	3646.24	1892.38	1308.88	1017.97	844.10	728.73	646.81	585.77	538.66	501.30	471.02	446.04	425.15	407.47
43000	3733.06	1937.43	1340.04	1042.21	864.19	746.09	662.21	599.72	551.49	513.23	482.23	456.66	435.28	417.17
44000	3819.87	1982.49	1371.21	1066.45	884.29	763.44	677.61	613.67	564.31	525.17	493.44	467.28	445.40	426.87
45000	3906.69	2027.55	1402.37	1090.68	904.39	780.79	693.01	627.61	577.14	537.10	504.66	477.90	455.52	436.57
46000	3993.50	2072.60	1433.53	1114.92	924.49	798.14	708.41	641.56	589.96	549.04	515.87	488.52	465.64	446.27
47000	4080.32	2117.66	1464.70	1139.16	944.58	815.49	723.81	655.51	602.79	560.97	527.09	499.14	475.77	455.97
48000	4167.13	2162.71	1495.86	1163.39	964.68	832.84	739.21	669.45	615.61	572.91	538.30	509.76	485.89	465.68
49000	4253.95	2207.77	1527.02	1187.63	984.78	850.19	754.61	683.40	628.44	584.85	549.52	520.38	496.01	475.38
50000	4340.76	2252.83	1558.19	1211.87	1004.88	867.54	770.01	697.35	641.26	596.78	560.73	531.00	506.13	485.08
55000	4774.84	2478.11	1714.01	1333.06	1105.36	954.29	847.01	767.08	705.39	656.46	616.80	584.10	556.75	533.59
60000	5208.91	2703.39	1869.82	1454.24	1205.85	1041.05	924.01	836.81	769.51	716.14	672.88	637.20	607.36	582.09
65000	5642.99	2928.67	2025.64	1575.43	1306.34	1127.80	1001.01	906.55	833.64	775.81	728.95	690.30	657.97	630.60
70000	6077.06	3153.96	2181.46	1696.61	1406.82	1214.55	1078.01	976.28	897.77	835.49	785.02	743.40	708.59	679.11
75000	6511.14	3379.24	2337.28	1817.80	1507.31	1301.31	1155.01	1046.02	961.89	895.17	841.10	796.50	759.20	727.62
80000	6945.22	3604.52	2493.10	1938.99	1607.80	1388.06	1232.01	1115.75	1026.02	954.85	897.17	849.60	809.81	776.12
85000	7379.29	3829.80	2648.92	2060.17	1708.28	1474.81	1309.01	1185.49	1090.14	1014.52	953.24	902.70	860.42	824.63
90000	7813.37	4055.09	2804.73	2181.36	1808.77	1561.57	1386.01	1255.22	1154.27	1074.20	1009.31	955.80	911.04	873.14
95000	8247.44	4280.37	2960.55	2302.55	1909.26	1648.32	1463.01	1324.95	1218.40	1133.88	1065.39	1008.90	961.65	921.64
100000	8681.52	4505.65	3116.37	2423.73	2009.75	1735.08	1540.01	1394.69	1282.52	1193.56	1121.46	1062.00	1012.26	970.15

TERM	15 Years	16 Years	17 Years	18 Years	19 Years	20 Years	21 Years	22 Years	23 Years	24 Years	25 Years	30 Years	35 Years	40 Years
AMOUNT														
5	.05	.05	.05	.05	.05	.05	.04	.04	.04	.04	.04	.04	.04	.04
10	.10	.10	.09	.09	.09	.09	.08	.08	.08	.08	.08	.08	.07	.07
15	.15	.14	.14	.13	.13	.13	.12	.12	.12	.12	.12	.11	.11	.11
25	.24	.23	.22	.22	.21	.21	.20	.20	.20	.19	.19	.18	.18	.17
50	.47	.46	.44	.43	.42	.41	.40	.40	.39	.38	.38	.36	.35	.34
75	.71	.68	.66	.64	.63	.61	.60	.59	.58	.57	.57	.54	.52	.51
100	.94	.91	.88	.86	.84	.82	.80	.79	.77	.76	.75	.71	.69	.67
200	1.87	1.81	1.76	1.71	1.67	1.63	1.60	1.57	1.54	1.52	1.50	1.42	1.37	1.34
300	2.81	2.71	2.63	2.56	2.50	2.44	2.40	2.35	2.31	2.28	2.25	2.13	2.05	2.01
400	3.74	3.62	3.51	3.41	3.33	3.26	3.19	3.13	3.08	3.04	2.99	2.84	2.74	2.67
500	4.68	4.52	4.39	4.27	4.16	4.07	3.99	3.92	3.85	3.79	3.74	3.54	3.42	3.34
600	5.61	5.42	5.26	5.12	4.99	4.88	4.79	4.70	4.62	4.55	4.49	4.25	4.10	4.01
700	6.54	6.33	6.14	5.97	5.83	5.70	5.58	5.48	5.39	5.31	5.23	4.96	4.79	4.68
800	7.48	7.23	7.01	6.82	6.66	6.51	6.38	6.26	6.16	6.07	5.98	5.67	5.47	5.34
900	8.41	8.13	7.89	7.68	7.49	7.32	7.18	7.05	6.93	6.82	6.73	6.38	6.15	6.01
1000	9.35	9.04	8.77	8.53	8.32	8.14	7.97	7.83	7.70	7.58	7.48	7.08	6.84	6.68
2000	18.69	18.07	17.53	17.05	16.64	16.27	15.94	15.65	15.39	15.16	14.95	14.16	13.67	13.35
3000	28.03	27.10	26.29	25.58	24.95	24.40	23.91	23.48	23.09	22.73	22.42	21.24	20.50	20.02
4000	37.37	36.13	35.05	34.10	33.27	32.54	31.88	31.30	30.78	30.31	29.89	28.32	27.33	26.70
5000	46.71	45.16	43.81	42.63	41.59	40.67	39.85	39.12	38.47	37.89	37.36	35.39	34.16	33.37
6000	56.05	54.19	52.57	51.15	49.90	48.80	47.82	46.95	46.17	45.46	44.83	42.47	41.00	40.04
7000	65.39	63.22	61.33	59.67	58.22	56.93	55.79	54.77	53.86	53.04	52.30	49.55	47.83	46.72
8000	74.74	72.25	70.09	68.20	66.54	65.07	63.76	62.59	61.55	60.62	59.78	56.63	54.66	53.39
9000	84.08	81.28	78.85	76.72	74.85	73.20	71.73	70.42	69.25	68.19	67.25	63.71	61.49	60.06
10000	93.42	90.31	87.61	85.25	83.17	81.33	79.70	78.24	76.94	75.77	74.72	70.78	68.32	66.74
11000	102.76	99.34	96.37	93.77	91.48	89.46	87.67	86.07	84.63	83.35	82.19	77.86	75.16	73.41
12000	112.10	108.37	105.13	102.30	99.80	97.60	95.64	93.89	92.33	90.92	89.66	84.94	81.99	80.08
13000	121.44	117.40	113.89	110.82	108.12	105.73	103.61	101.71	100.02	98.50	97.13	92.02	88.82	86.76
14000	130.70	126.43	122.65	119.34	116.43	113.86	111.58	109.54	107.71	106.08	104.60	99.10	95.65	93.43
15000	140.12	135.46	131.41	127.87	124.75	121.99	119.54	117.36	115.41	113.65	112.08	106.17	102.48	100.10
16000	149.47	144.49	140.17	136.39	133.07	130.13	127.51	125.18	123.10	121.23	119.55	113.25	109.32	106.78
17000	158.81	153.52	148.93	144.92	141.38	138.26	135.48	133.01	130.79	128.81	127.02	120.33	116.15	113.45
18000	168.15	162.56	157.69	153.44	149.70	146.39	143.45	140.83	138.49	136.38	134.49	127.41	122.98	120.12
19000	177.49	171.59	166.45	161.97	158.02	154.52	151.42	148.66	146.18	143.96	141.96	134.49	129.81	126.80
20000	186.83	180.62	175.21	170.49	166.33	162.66	159.39	156.48	153.88	151.54	149.43	141.56	136.64	133.47
21000	196.17	189.65	183.98	179.01	174.65	170.79	167.36	164.30	161.57	159.11	156.90	148.64	143.47	140.14
22000	205.51	198.68	192.74	187.54	182.96	178.92	175.33	172.13	169.26	166.69	164.38	155.72	150.31	146.82
23000	214.85	207.71	201.50	196.06	191.28	187.05	183.30	179.95	176.96	174.27	171.85	162.80	157.14	153.49
24000	224.20	216.74	210.26	204.59	199.60	195.19	191.27	187.77	184.65	181.84	179.32	169.88	163.97	160.16
25000	233.54	225.77	219.02	213.11	207.91	203.32	199.24	195.60	192.34	189.42	186.79	176.95	170.80	166.84
26000	242.88	234.80	227.78	221.63	216.23	211.45	207.21	203.42	200.04	197.00	194.26	184.03	177.63	173.51
27000	252.22	243.83	236.54	230.16	224.55	219.58	215.18	211.25	207.73	204.57	201.73	191.11	184.47	180.18
28000	261.56	252.86	245.30	238.68	232.86	227.72	223.15	219.07	215.42	212.15	209.20	198.19	191.30	186.86
29000	270.90	261.89	254.06	247.21	241.18	235.85	231.11	226.89	223.12	219.73	216.68	205.27	198.13	193.53
30000	280.24	270.92	262.82	255.73	249.50	243.98	239.08	234.72	230.81	227.30	224.15	212.34	204.96	200.20
31000	289.59	279.95	271.58	264.26	257.81	252.11	247.05	242.54	238.50	234.88	231.62	219.42	211.79	206.88
32000	298.93	288.98	280.34	272.78	266.13	260.25	255.02	250.36	246.20	242.46	239.09	226.50	218.63	213.55
33000	308.27	298.01	289.10	281.30	274.44	268.38	262.99	258.19	253.89	250.03	246.56	233.58	225.46	220.22
34000	317.61	307.04	297.86	289.83	282.76	276.51	270.96	266.01	261.58	257.61	254.03	240.65	232.29	226.90
35000	326.95	316.08	306.62	298.35	291.08	284.64	278.93	273.84	269.28	265.19	261.50	247.73	239.12	233.57
36000	336.29	325.11	315.38	306.88	299.39	292.78	286.90	281.66	276.97	272.76	268.98	254.81	245.95	240.24
37000	345.63	334.14	324.14	315.40	307.71	300.91	294.87	289.48	284.66	280.34	276.45	261.89	252.79	246.92
38000	354.97	343.17	332.90	323.93	316.03	309.04	302.84	297.31	292.36	287.92	283.92	268.97	259.62	253.59
39000	364.32	352.20	341.66	332.45	324.34	317.17	310.81	305.13	300.05	295.49	291.39	276.04	266.45	260.26
40000	373.66	361.23	350.42	340.97	332.66	325.31	318.78	312.95	307.75	303.07	298.86	283.12	273.28	266.94
41000	383.00	370.26	359.19	349.50	340.98	333.44	326.75	320.78	315.44	310.65	306.33	290.20	280.11	273.61
42000	392.34	379.29	367.95	358.02	349.29	341.57	334.72	328.60	323.13	318.22	313.80	297.28	286.94	280.28
43000	401.68	388.32	376.71	366.55	357.61	349.70	342.68	336.43	330.83	325.80	321.28	304.36	293.78	286.96
44000	411.02	397.35	385.47	375.07	365.92	357.84	350.65	344.25	338.52	333.38	328.75	311.43	300.61	293.63
45000	420.36	406.38	394.23	383.60	374.24	365.97	358.62	352.07	346.21	340.95	336.22	318.51	307.44	300.30
46000	429.70	415.41	402.99	392.12	382.56	374.10	366.59	359.90	353.91	348.53	343.69	325.59	314.27	306.98
47000	439.05	424.44	411.75	400.64	390.87	382.23	374.56	367.72	361.60	356.11	351.16	332.67	321.10	313.65
48000	448.39	433.47	420.51	409.17	399.19	390.37	382.53	375.54	369.29	363.68	358.63	339.75	327.94	320.32
49000	457.73	442.50	429.27	417.69	407.51	398.50	390.50	383.37	376.99	371.26	366.10	346.82	334.77	327.00
50000	467.07	451.53	438.03	426.22	415.82	406.63	398.47	391.19	384.68	378.84	373.58	353.90	341.60	333.67
55000	513.78	496.69	481.83	468.84	457.40	447.29	438.32	430.31	423.15	416.72	410.93	389.29	375.76	367.03
60000	560.48	541.84	525.63	511.46	498.99	487.96	478.16	469.43	461.62	454.60	448.29	424.68	409.92	400.40
65000	607.19	586.99	569.44	554.08	540.57	528.62	518.01	508.55	500.08	492.49	485.65	460.07	444.08	433.77
70000	653.90	632.15	613.24	596.70	582.15	569.28	557.86	547.67	538.55	530.37	523.00	495.46	478.24	467.13
75000	700.60	677.30	657.04	639.32	623.73	609.95	597.70	586.79	577.02	568.25	560.36	530.85	512.40	500.50
80000	747.31	722.45	700.84	681.94	665.31	650.61	637.55	625.90	615.49	606.13	597.72	566.24	546.56	533.87
85000	794.02	767.60	744.65	724.56	706.89	691.27	677.39	665.02	653.95	644.02	635.07	601.63	580.72	567.23
90000	840.72	812.76	788.45	767.19	748.48	731.93	717.24	704.14	692.42	681.90	672.43	637.02	614.88	600.60
95000	887.43	857.91	832.25	809.81	790.06	772.60	757.09	743.26	730.89	719.78	709.79	672.41	649.04	633.97
100000	934.13	903.06	876.05	852.43	831.64	813.26	796.93	782.38	769.36	757.67	747.15	707.80	683.19	667.33

MONTHLY PAYMENT
REQUIRED TO AMORTIZE A LOAN

TERM / AMOUNT	1 Year	2 Years	3 Years	4 Years	5 Years	6 Years	7 Years	8 Years	9 Years	10 Years	11 Years	12 Years	13 Years	14 Years
5	.44	.23	.16	.13	.11	.09	.08	.07	.07	.06	.06	.06	.06	.05
10	.87	.46	.32	.25	.21	.18	.16	.14	.13	.12	.12	.11	.11	.10
15	1.31	.68	.47	.37	.31	.27	.24	.21	.20	.18	.17	.16	.16	.15
25	2.18	1.13	.78	.61	.51	.44	.39	.35	.33	.30	.29	.27	.26	.25
50	4.35	2.26	1.56	1.22	1.01	.87	.78	.70	.65	.60	.57	.54	.51	.49
75	6.52	3.39	2.34	1.83	1.51	1.31	1.16	1.05	.97	.90	.85	.80	.77	.74
100	8.69	4.51	3.12	2.43	2.02	1.74	1.55	1.40	1.29	1.20	1.13	1.07	1.02	.98
200	17.37	9.02	6.24	4.86	4.03	3.48	3.09	2.80	2.58	2.40	2.26	2.14	2.04	1.95
300	26.06	13.53	9.36	7.29	6.04	5.22	4.64	4.20	3.86	3.60	3.38	3.20	3.05	2.93
400	34.74	18.04	12.48	9.71	8.06	6.96	6.18	5.60	5.15	4.79	4.51	4.27	4.07	3.90
500	43.43	22.55	15.60	12.14	10.07	8.70	7.72	7.00	6.44	5.99	5.63	5.34	5.09	4.88
600	52.11	27.06	18.72	14.57	12.08	10.44	9.27	8.40	7.72	7.19	6.76	6.40	6.10	5.85
700	60.80	31.57	21.84	17.00	14.10	12.18	10.81	9.79	9.01	8.39	7.88	7.47	7.12	6.83
800	69.48	36.08	24.96	19.42	16.11	13.91	12.35	11.19	10.30	9.58	9.01	8.53	8.14	7.80
900	78.17	40.59	28.08	21.85	18.12	15.65	13.90	12.59	11.58	10.78	10.13	9.60	9.15	8.77
1000	86.85	45.10	31.20	24.28	20.14	17.39	15.44	13.99	12.87	11.98	11.26	10.67	10.17	9.75
2000	173.70	90.19	62.40	48.55	40.27	34.78	30.88	27.97	25.73	23.95	22.51	21.33	20.33	19.49
3000	260.55	135.28	93.60	72.82	60.40	52.17	46.32	41.96	38.60	35.93	33.77	31.99	30.50	29.24
4000	347.40	180.37	124.80	97.09	80.54	69.55	61.75	55.94	51.46	47.90	45.02	42.65	40.66	38.98
5000	434.25	225.46	156.00	121.37	100.67	86.94	77.19	69.93	64.32	59.88	56.28	53.31	50.83	48.72
6000	521.10	270.55	187.19	145.64	120.80	104.33	92.63	83.91	77.19	71.85	67.53	63.97	60.99	58.47
7000	607.95	315.64	218.39	169.91	140.94	121.71	108.07	97.90	90.05	83.83	78.79	74.63	71.15	68.21
8000	694.80	360.73	249.59	194.18	161.07	139.10	123.50	111.88	102.91	95.80	90.04	85.29	81.32	77.95
9000	781.65	405.82	280.79	218.46	181.20	156.49	138.94	125.87	115.78	107.78	101.30	95.95	91.48	87.70
10000	868.50	450.91	311.99	242.73	201.34	173.88	154.38	139.85	128.64	119.75	112.55	106.61	101.65	97.44
11000	955.35	496.00	343.18	267.00	221.47	191.26	169.81	153.84	141.51	131.73	123.81	117.27	111.81	107.18
12000	1042.20	541.09	374.38	291.27	241.60	208.65	185.25	167.82	154.37	143.70	135.06	127.93	121.97	116.93
13000	1129.05	586.18	405.58	315.55	261.74	226.04	200.69	181.81	167.23	155.68	146.31	138.59	132.14	126.67
14000	1215.90	631.27	436.78	339.82	281.87	243.42	216.13	195.79	180.10	167.65	157.57	149.25	142.30	136.42
15000	1302.75	676.36	467.98	364.09	302.00	260.81	231.56	209.78	192.96	179.63	168.82	159.92	152.47	146.16
16000	1389.60	721.45	499.18	388.36	322.13	278.20	247.00	223.76	205.82	191.60	180.08	170.58	162.63	155.90
17000	1476.45	766.55	530.37	412.63	342.27	295.59	262.44	237.74	218.69	203.58	191.33	181.24	172.79	165.65
18000	1563.30	811.64	561.57	436.91	362.40	312.97	277.87	251.73	231.55	215.55	202.59	191.90	182.96	175.39
19000	1650.15	856.73	592.77	461.18	382.53	330.36	293.31	265.71	244.42	227.53	213.84	202.56	193.12	185.13
20000	1737.00	901.82	623.97	485.45	402.67	347.75	308.75	279.70	257.28	239.50	225.10	213.22	203.29	194.88
21000	1823.85	946.91	655.17	509.72	422.80	365.13	324.19	293.68	270.14	251.48	236.35	223.88	213.45	204.62
22000	1910.70	992.00	686.36	534.00	442.93	382.52	339.62	307.67	283.01	263.45	247.61	234.54	223.61	214.36
23000	1997.55	1037.09	717.56	558.27	463.07	399.91	355.06	321.65	295.87	275.43	258.86	245.20	233.78	224.11
24000	2084.40	1082.18	748.76	582.54	483.20	417.30	370.50	335.64	308.73	287.40	270.11	255.86	243.94	233.85
25000	2171.25	1127.27	779.96	606.81	503.33	434.68	365.93	349.62	321.60	299.38	281.37	266.52	254.11	243.60
26000	2258.10	1172.36	811.16	631.09	523.47	452.07	401.37	363.61	334.46	311.35	292.62	277.18	264.27	253.34
27000	2344.95	1217.45	842.36	655.36	543.60	469.46	416.81	377.59	347.33	323.33	303.88	287.84	274.43	263.08
28000	2431.80	1262.54	873.55	679.63	563.73	486.84	432.25	391.58	360.19	335.30	315.13	298.50	284.60	272.83
29000	2518.65	1307.63	904.75	703.90	583.87	504.23	447.68	405.56	373.05	347.27	326.39	309.17	294.76	282.57
30000	2605.50	1352.72	935.95	728.18	604.00	521.62	463.12	419.55	385.92	359.25	337.64	319.83	304.93	292.31
31000	2692.35	1397.81	967.15	752.45	624.13	539.01	478.56	433.53	398.78	371.22	348.90	330.49	315.09	302.06
32000	2779.20	1442.90	998.35	776.72	644.26	556.39	493.99	447.51	411.64	383.20	360.15	341.15	325.25	311.80
33000	2866.05	1487.99	1029.54	800.99	664.40	573.78	509.43	461.50	424.51	395.17	371.41	351.81	335.42	321.54
34000	2952.90	1533.09	1060.74	825.26	684.53	591.17	524.87	475.48	437.37	407.15	382.66	362.47	345.58	331.29
35000	3039.75	1578.18	1091.94	849.54	704.66	608.55	540.31	489.47	450.24	419.12	393.91	373.13	355.75	341.03
36000	3126.60	1623.27	1123.14	873.81	724.80	625.94	555.74	503.45	463.10	431.10	405.17	383.79	365.91	350.78
37000	3213.45	1668.36	1154.34	898.08	744.93	643.33	571.18	517.44	475.96	443.07	416.42	394.45	376.07	360.52
38000	3300.30	1713.45	1185.53	922.35	765.06	660.72	586.62	531.42	488.83	455.05	427.68	405.11	386.24	370.26
39000	3387.15	1758.54	1216.73	946.63	785.20	678.10	602.05	545.41	501.69	467.02	438.93	415.77	396.40	380.01
40000	3474.00	1803.63	1247.93	970.90	805.33	695.49	617.49	559.39	514.55	479.00	450.19	426.43	406.57	389.75
41000	3560.85	1848.72	1279.13	995.17	825.46	712.88	632.93	573.38	527.42	490.97	461.44	437.09	416.73	399.49
42000	3647.70	1893.81	1310.33	1019.44	845.60	730.26	648.37	587.36	540.28	502.95	472.70	447.75	426.89	409.24
43000	3734.55	1938.90	1341.53	1043.72	865.73	747.65	663.80	601.35	553.15	514.92	483.95	458.42	437.06	418.98
44000	3821.40	1983.99	1372.72	1067.99	885.86	765.04	679.24	615.33	566.01	526.90	495.21	469.08	447.22	428.72
45000	3908.25	2029.08	1403.92	1092.26	906.00	782.43	694.68	629.32	578.87	538.87	506.46	479.74	457.39	438.47
46000	3995.09	2074.17	1435.12	1116.53	926.13	799.81	710.11	643.30	591.74	550.85	517.71	490.40	467.55	448.21
47000	4081.94	2119.26	1466.32	1140.81	946.26	817.20	725.55	657.28	604.60	562.82	528.97	501.06	477.71	457.96
48000	4168.79	2164.35	1497.52	1165.08	966.39	834.59	740.99	671.27	617.46	574.80	540.22	511.72	487.88	467.70
49000	4255.64	2209.44	1528.71	1189.35	986.53	851.97	756.43	685.25	630.33	586.77	551.48	522.38	498.04	477.44
50000	4342.49	2254.53	1559.91	1213.62	1006.66	869.36	771.86	699.24	643.19	598.75	562.73	533.04	508.21	487.19
55000	4776.74	2479.99	1715.90	1334.98	1107.33	956.30	849.05	769.16	707.51	658.62	619.01	586.34	559.03	535.90
60000	5210.99	2705.44	1871.89	1456.35	1207.99	1043.23	926.24	839.09	771.83	718.49	675.28	639.65	609.85	584.62
65000	5645.24	2930.89	2027.89	1577.71	1308.66	1130.17	1003.42	909.01	836.15	778.37	731.55	692.95	660.67	633.34
70000	6079.49	3156.35	2183.88	1699.07	1409.32	1217.10	1080.61	978.93	900.47	838.24	787.82	746.25	711.49	682.06
75000	6513.74	3381.80	2339.87	1820.43	1509.99	1304.04	1157.79	1048.86	964.79	898.12	844.10	799.56	762.31	730.78
80000	6947.99	3607.25	2495.86	1941.79	1610.65	1390.97	1234.98	1118.78	1029.10	957.99	900.37	852.86	813.13	779.49
85000	7382.24	3832.71	2651.85	2063.15	1711.32	1477.91	1312.16	1188.70	1093.42	1017.86	956.64	906.17	863.95	828.21
90000	7816.49	4058.16	2807.84	2184.52	1811.99	1564.85	1389.35	1258.63	1157.74	1077.74	1012.92	959.47	914.77	876.93
95000	8250.73	4283.61	2963.83	2305.88	1912.65	1651.78	1466.54	1328.55	1222.06	1137.61	1069.19	1012.77	965.59	925.65
100000	8684.98	4509.06	3119.82	2427.24	2013.32	1738.72	1543.72	1398.47	1286.38	1197.49	1125.46	1066.08	1016.41	974.37

TERM	15 Years	16 Years	17 Years	18 Years	19 Years	20 Years	21 Years	22 Years	23 Years	24 Years	25 Years	30 Years	35 Years	40 Years
AMOUNT														
5	.05	.05	.05	.05	.05	.05	.05	.04	.04	.04	.04	.04	.04	.04
10	.10	.10	.09	.09	.09	.09	.09	.08	.08	.08	.08	.08	.07	.07
15	.15	.14	.14	.13	.13	.13	.13	.12	.12	.12	.12	.11	.11	.11
25	.24	.23	.23	.22	.21	.21	.21	.20	.20	.20	.19	.18	.18	.17
50	.47	.46	.45	.43	.42	.41	.41	.40	.39	.39	.38	.36	.35	.34
75	.71	.69	.67	.65	.63	.62	.61	.60	.59	.58	.57	.54	.52	.51
100	.94	.91	.89	.86	.84	.82	.81	.79	.78	.77	.76	.72	.69	.68
200	1.88	1.82	1.77	1.72	1.68	1.64	1.61	1.58	1.55	1.53	1.51	1.43	1.38	1.35
300	2.82	2.73	2.65	2.58	2.51	2.46	2.41	2.37	2.33	2.29	2.26	2.14	2.07	2.02
400	3.76	3.63	3.53	3.43	3.35	3.28	3.21	3.15	3.10	3.06	3.01	2.86	2.76	2.70
500	4.70	4.54	4.41	4.29	4.19	4.09	4.01	3.94	3.88	3.82	3.77	3.57	3.45	3.37
600	5.64	5.45	5.29	5.15	5.02	4.91	4.81	4.73	4.65	4.58	4.52	4.28	4.14	4.04
700	6.57	6.36	6.17	6.00	5.86	5.73	5.62	5.51	5.42	5.34	5.27	5.00	4.83	4.72
800	7.51	7.26	7.05	6.86	6.69	6.55	6.42	6.30	6.20	6.11	6.02	5.71	5.51	5.39
900	8.45	8.17	7.93	7.72	7.53	7.37	7.22	7.09	6.97	6.87	6.77	6.42	6.20	6.06
1000	9.39	9.08	8.81	8.57	8.37	8.18	8.02	7.88	7.75	7.63	7.53	7.13	6.89	6.73
2000	18.77	18.15	17.61	17.14	16.73	16.36	16.04	15.75	15.49	15.26	15.05	14.26	13.78	13.46
3000	28.16	27.23	26.42	25.71	25.09	24.54	24.05	23.62	23.23	22.88	22.57	21.39	20.66	20.19
4000	37.54	36.30	35.22	34.28	33.45	32.72	32.07	31.49	30.97	30.51	30.09	28.52	27.55	26.92
5000	46.93	45.38	44.03	42.85	41.81	40.90	40.09	39.36	38.71	38.13	37.61	35.65	34.43	33.65
6000	56.31	54.45	52.83	51.42	50.18	49.08	48.10	47.23	46.45	45.76	45.13	42.78	41.32	40.38
7000	65.69	63.52	61.64	59.99	58.54	57.26	56.12	55.10	54.20	53.38	52.65	49.91	48.21	47.11
8000	75.08	72.60	70.44	68.56	66.90	65.43	64.13	62.97	61.94	61.01	60.17	57.04	55.09	53.84
9000	84.46	81.67	79.25	77.13	75.26	73.61	72.15	70.84	69.68	68.63	67.69	64.17	61.98	60.57
10000	93.85	90.75	88.05	85.70	83.62	81.79	80.17	78.72	77.42	76.26	75.21	71.30	68.86	67.29
11000	103.23	99.82	96.86	94.26	91.99	89.97	88.18	86.59	85.16	83.88	82.73	78.43	75.75	74.02
12000	112.61	108.89	105.66	102.83	100.35	98.15	96.20	94.46	92.90	91.51	90.25	85.56	82.63	80.75
13000	122.00	117.97	114.47	111.40	108.71	106.33	104.21	102.33	100.64	99.13	97.77	92.69	89.52	87.48
14000	131.38	127.04	123.27	119.97	117.07	114.51	112.23	110.20	108.39	106.76	105.29	99.82	96.41	94.21
15000	140.77	136.12	132.08	128.54	125.43	122.68	120.25	118.07	116.13	114.38	112.81	106.95	103.29	100.94
16000	150.15	145.19	140.88	137.11	133.79	130.86	128.26	125.94	123.87	122.01	120.33	114.08	110.18	107.67
17000	159.54	154.26	149.68	145.68	142.16	139.04	136.28	133.81	131.61	129.63	127.85	121.21	117.06	114.40
18000	168.92	163.34	158.49	154.25	150.52	147.22	144.29	141.68	139.35	137.26	135.37	128.34	123.95	121.13
19000	178.30	172.41	167.29	162.82	158.88	155.40	152.31	149.56	147.09	144.88	142.89	135.47	130.83	127.86
20000	187.69	181.49	176.10	171.39	167.24	163.58	160.33	157.43	154.83	152.51	150.41	142.60	137.72	134.58
21000	197.07	190.56	184.90	179.96	175.60	171.76	168.34	165.30	162.58	160.13	157.94	149.73	144.61	141.31
22000	206.46	199.64	193.71	188.52	183.97	179.94	176.36	173.17	170.32	167.76	165.46	156.86	151.49	140.04
23000	215.84	208.71	202.51	197.09	192.33	188.11	184.37	181.04	178.06	175.38	172.98	163.99	158.38	154.77
24000	225.22	217.78	211.32	205.66	200.69	196.29	192.39	188.91	185.80	183.01	180.50	171.12	165.26	161.50
25000	234.61	226.86	220.12	214.23	209.05	204.47	200.41	196.78	193.54	190.63	188.02	178.25	172.15	168.23
26000	243.99	235.93	228.93	222.80	217.41	212.65	208.42	204.65	201.28	198.26	195.54	185.37	179.04	174.96
27000	253.38	245.01	237.73	231.37	225.77	220.83	216.44	212.52	209.02	205.88	203.06	192.50	185.92	181.69
28000	262.76	254.08	246.54	239.94	234.14	229.01	224.45	220.40	216.77	213.51	210.58	199.63	192.81	188.42
29000	272.15	263.15	255.34	248.51	242.50	237.19	232.47	228.27	224.51	221.13	218.10	206.76	199.69	195.15
30000	281.53	272.23	264.15	257.08	250.86	245.36	240.49	236.14	232.25	228.76	225.62	213.89	206.58	201.87
31000	290.91	281.30	272.95	265.65	259.22	253.54	248.50	244.01	239.99	236.38	233.14	221.02	213.46	208.60
32000	300.30	290.38	281.76	274.22	267.58	261.72	256.52	251.88	247.73	244.01	240.66	228.15	220.35	215.33
33000	309.68	299.45	290.56	282.78	275.95	269.90	264.53	259.75	255.47	251.63	248.18	235.28	227.24	222.06
34000	319.07	308.52	299.36	291.35	284.31	278.08	272.55	267.62	263.21	259.26	255.70	242.41	234.12	228.79
35000	328.45	317.60	308.17	299.92	292.67	286.26	280.57	275.49	270.96	266.88	263.22	249.54	241.01	235.52
36000	337.83	326.67	316.97	308.49	301.03	294.44	288.58	283.36	278.70	274.51	270.74	256.67	247.89	242.25
37000	347.22	335.75	325.78	317.06	309.39	302.62	296.60	291.24	286.44	282.14	278.26	263.80	254.78	248.98
38000	356.60	344.82	334.58	325.63	317.76	310.79	304.61	299.11	294.18	289.76	205.78	270.93	261.66	255.71
39000	365.99	353.89	343.39	334.20	326.12	318.97	312.63	306.98	301.92	297.39	293.30	278.06	268.55	262.44
40000	375.37	362.97	352.19	342.77	334.48	327.15	320.65	314.85	309.66	305.01	300.82	285.19	275.44	269.16
41000	384.75	372.04	361.00	351.34	342.84	335.33	328.66	322.72	317.40	312.64	308.35	292.32	282.32	275.89
42000	394.14	381.12	369.80	359.91	351.20	343.51	336.68	330.59	325.15	320.26	315.87	299.45	289.21	282.62
43000	403.52	390.19	378.61	368.48	359.56	351.69	344.69	338.46	332.89	327.89	323.39	306.58	296.09	289.35
44000	412.91	399.27	387.41	377.00	367.93	359.87	352.71	346.33	340.63	335.51	330.91	313.71	302.98	296.08
45000	422.29	408.34	396.22	385.61	376.29	368.04	360.73	354.20	348.37	343.14	338.43	320.84	309.86	302.81
46000	431.68	417.41	405.02	394.18	384.65	376.22	368.74	362.08	356.11	350.76	345.95	327.97	316.75	309.54
47000	441.06	426.49	413.83	402.75	393.01	384.40	376.76	369.95	363.85	358.39	353.47	335.10	323.64	316.27
48000	450.44	435.56	422.63	411.32	401.37	392.58	384.77	377.82	371.59	366.01	360.99	342.23	330.52	323.00
49000	459.83	444.64	431.43	419.89	409.74	400.76	392.79	385.69	379.34	373.64	368.51	349.36	337.41	329.73
50000	469.21	453.71	440.24	428.46	418.10	408.94	400.81	393.56	387.08	381.26	376.03	356.49	344.29	336.45
55000	516.13	499.08	484.26	471.30	459.91	449.83	440.89	432.91	425.78	419.39	413.63	392.13	378.72	370.10
60000	563.05	544.45	528.29	514.15	501.72	490.72	480.97	472.27	464.49	457.51	451.23	427.78	413.15	403.74
65000	609.97	589.82	572.31	556.99	543.52	531.62	521.05	511.63	503.20	495.64	488.84	463.43	447.58	437.39
70000	656.89	635.19	616.33	599.84	585.33	572.51	561.13	550.98	541.91	533.76	526.44	499.08	482.01	471.03
75000	703.82	680.56	660.36	642.69	627.14	613.40	601.21	590.34	580.61	571.89	564.04	534.73	516.44	504.68
80000	750.74	725.93	704.38	685.53	668.95	654.30	641.29	629.69	619.32	610.02	601.64	570.37	550.87	538.32
85000	797.66	771.30	748.40	728.38	710.76	695.19	681.37	669.05	658.03	648.14	639.25	606.02	585.30	571.97
90000	844.58	816.67	792.43	771.22	752.57	736.08	721.45	708.40	696.74	686.27	676.85	641.67	619.72	605.61
95000	891.50	862.04	836.45	814.07	794.38	776.98	761.53	747.76	735.44	724.39	714.45	677.32	654.15	639.26
100000	938.42	907.41	880.47	856.91	836.19	817.87	801.61	787.11	774.15	762.52	752.05	712.97	688.58	672.90

MONTHLY PAYMENT
REQUIRED TO AMORTIZE A LOAN

TERM	1 Year	2 Years	3 Years	4 Years	5 Years	6 Years	7 Years	8 Years	9 Years	10 Years	11 Years	12 Years	13 Years	14 Years
AMOUNT														
5	.44	.23	.16	.13	.11	.09	.08	.08	.07	.07	.06	.06	.06	.06
10	.87	.46	.32	.25	.21	.18	.16	.15	.13	.13	.12	.11	.11	.10
15	1.31	.68	.47	.37	.31	.27	.24	.22	.20	.19	.17	.17	.16	.15
25	2.18	1.13	.79	.61	.51	.44	.39	.36	.33	.31	.29	.27	.26	.25
50	4.35	2.26	1.57	1.22	1.01	.88	.78	.71	.65	.61	.57	.54	.51	.49
75	6.52	3.39	2.35	1.83	1.52	1.31	1.16	1.06	.97	.91	.85	.81	.77	.74
100	8.69	4.52	3.13	2.43	2.02	1.75	1.55	1.41	1.29	1.21	1.13	1.07	1.02	.98
200	17.38	9.03	6.25	4.86	4.04	3.49	3.10	2.81	2.58	2.41	2.26	2.14	2.04	1.96
300	26.07	13.54	9.37	7.29	6.05	5.23	4.64	4.21	3.87	3.61	3.39	3.21	3.06	2.94
400	34.75	18.05	12.49	9.72	8.07	6.97	6.19	5.61	5.16	4.81	4.52	4.28	4.08	3.91
500	43.44	22.56	15.62	12.15	10.08	8.71	7.74	7.01	6.45	6.01	5.65	5.35	5.10	4.89
600	52.13	27.07	18.74	14.58	12.10	10.45	9.28	8.41	7.74	7.21	6.77	6.42	6.12	5.87
700	60.82	31.58	21.86	17.01	14.11	12.19	10.83	9.81	9.03	8.41	7.90	7.49	7.14	6.85
800	69.50	36.10	24.98	19.44	16.13	13.93	12.37	11.21	10.32	9.61	9.03	8.56	8.16	7.82
900	78.19	40.61	28.10	21.87	18.15	15.68	13.92	12.61	11.61	10.81	10.16	9.62	9.18	8.80
1000	86.88	45.12	31.23	24.30	20.16	17.42	15.47	14.01	12.89	12.01	11.29	10.69	10.20	9.78
2000	173.75	90.23	62.45	48.60	40.32	34.83	30.93	28.02	25.78	24.01	22.57	21.38	20.39	19.55
3000	260.62	135.35	93.67	72.89	60.48	52.24	46.39	42.03	38.67	36.01	33.85	32.07	30.58	29.32
4000	347.50	180.46	124.89	97.19	80.63	69.65	61.85	56.04	51.56	48.01	45.13	42.76	40.77	39.09
5000	434.37	225.57	156.11	121.48	100.79	87.06	77.31	70.05	64.45	60.01	56.41	53.44	50.96	48.86
6000	521.24	270.69	187.33	145.78	120.95	104.47	92.78	84.06	77.34	72.01	67.69	64.13	61.16	58.64
7000	608.12	315.80	218.55	170.08	141.10	121.88	108.24	98.07	90.23	84.01	78.97	74.82	71.35	68.41
8000	694.99	360.91	249.77	194.37	161.26	139.30	123.70	112.08	103.12	96.01	90.26	85.51	81.54	78.18
9000	781.86	406.03	281.00	218.67	181.42	156.71	139.16	126.09	116.01	108.01	101.54	96.20	91.73	87.95
10000	868.73	451.14	312.22	242.96	201.57	174.12	154.62	140.10	128.90	120.02	112.82	106.88	101.92	97.72
11000	955.61	496.25	343.44	267.26	221.73	191.53	170.09	154.11	141.79	132.02	124.10	117.57	112.11	107.49
12000	1042.48	541.37	374.66	291.55	241.89	208.94	185.55	168.12	154.68	144.02	135.38	128.26	122.31	117.27
13000	1129.35	586.48	405.88	315.85	262.05	226.35	201.01	182.13	167.57	156.02	146.66	138.95	132.50	127.04
14000	1216.23	631.59	437.10	340.15	282.20	243.76	216.47	196.14	180.46	168.02	157.94	149.64	142.69	136.81
15000	1303.10	676.71	468.32	364.44	302.36	261.18	231.93	210.15	193.35	180.02	169.22	160.32	152.88	146.58
16000	1389.97	721.82	499.54	388.74	322.52	278.59	247.40	224.16	206.24	192.02	180.51	171.01	163.07	156.35
17000	1476.84	766.93	530.76	413.03	342.67	296.00	262.86	238.17	219.13	204.02	191.79	181.70	173.26	166.13
18000	1563.72	812.05	561.99	437.33	362.83	313.41	278.32	252.18	232.02	216.02	203.07	192.39	183.46	175.90
19000	1650.59	857.16	593.21	461.62	382.99	330.82	293.78	266.19	244.91	228.03	214.35	203.08	193.65	185.67
20000	1737.46	902.27	624.43	485.92	403.14	348.23	309.24	280.20	257.79	240.03	225.63	213.76	203.84	195.44
21000	1824.34	947.39	655.65	510.22	423.30	365.64	324.71	294.21	270.68	252.03	236.91	224.45	214.03	205.21
22000	1911.21	992.50	686.87	534.51	443.46	383.06	340.17	308.22	283.57	264.03	248.19	235.14	224.22	214.98
23000	1998.08	1037.61	718.09	558.81	463.62	400.47	355.63	322.23	296.46	276.03	259.47	245.83	234.41	224.76
24000	2084.95	1082.73	749.31	583.10	483.77	417.88	371.09	336.24	309.35	288.03	270.76	256.52	244.61	234.53
25000	2171.83	1127.84	780.53	607.40	503.93	435.29	386.55	350.25	322.24	300.03	282.04	267.20	254.80	244.30
26000	2258.70	1172.95	811.76	631.69	524.09	452.70	402.02	364.26	335.13	312.03	293.32	277.89	264.99	254.07
27000	2345.57	1218.07	842.98	655.99	544.24	470.11	417.48	378.27	348.02	324.03	304.60	288.58	275.18	263.84
28000	2432.45	1263.18	874.20	680.29	564.40	487.52	432.94	392.28	360.91	336.03	315.88	299.27	285.37	273.61
29000	2519.32	1308.29	905.42	704.58	584.56	504.94	448.40	406.29	373.80	348.04	327.16	309.95	295.56	283.39
30000	2606.19	1353.41	936.64	728.83	604.71	522.35	463.86	420.30	386.69	360.04	338.44	320.64	305.76	293.16
31000	2693.06	1398.52	967.86	753.17	624.87	539.76	479.33	434.31	399.58	372.04	349.72	331.33	315.95	302.93
32000	2779.94	1443.63	999.08	777.47	645.03	557.17	494.79	448.32	412.47	384.04	361.01	342.02	326.14	312.70
33000	2866.81	1488.75	1030.30	801.76	665.18	574.58	510.25	462.33	425.36	396.04	372.29	352.71	336.33	322.47
34000	2953.68	1533.86	1061.52	826.06	685.34	591.99	525.71	476.34	438.25	408.04	383.57	363.39	346.52	332.25
35000	3040.56	1578.97	1092.75	850.36	705.50	609.40	541.17	490.35	451.14	420.04	394.85	374.08	356.72	342.02
36000	3127.43	1624.09	1123.97	874.65	725.66	626.82	556.64	504.36	464.03	432.04	406.13	384.77	366.91	351.79
37000	3214.30	1669.20	1155.19	898.95	745.81	644.23	572.10	518.37	476.92	444.04	417.41	395.46	377.10	361.56
38000	3301.17	1714.31	1186.41	923.24	765.97	661.64	587.56	532.38	489.81	456.05	428.69	406.15	387.29	371.33
39000	3388.05	1759.43	1217.63	947.54	786.13	679.05	603.02	546.39	502.70	468.05	439.98	416.83	397.48	381.10
40000	3474.92	1804.54	1248.85	971.83	806.28	696.46	618.48	560.40	515.58	480.05	451.26	427.52	407.67	390.88
41000	3561.79	1849.65	1280.07	996.13	826.44	713.87	633.95	574.41	528.47	492.05	462.54	438.21	417.87	400.65
42000	3648.67	1894.77	1311.29	1020.43	846.60	731.28	649.41	588.42	541.36	504.05	473.82	448.90	428.06	410.42
43000	3735.54	1939.88	1342.52	1044.72	866.75	748.70	664.87	602.43	554.25	516.05	485.10	459.59	438.25	420.19
44000	3822.41	1984.99	1373.74	1069.02	886.91	766.11	680.33	616.44	567.14	528.05	496.38	470.27	448.44	429.96
45000	3909.28	2030.11	1404.96	1093.31	907.07	783.52	695.79	630.45	580.03	540.05	507.66	480.96	458.63	439.73
46000	3996.16	2075.22	1436.18	1117.61	927.23	800.93	711.25	644.46	592.92	552.05	518.94	491.65	468.82	449.51
47000	4083.03	2120.33	1467.40	1141.90	947.38	818.34	726.72	658.47	605.81	564.05	530.23	502.34	479.02	459.28
48000	4169.90	2165.45	1498.62	1166.20	967.54	835.75	742.18	672.48	618.70	576.06	541.51	513.03	489.21	469.05
49000	4256.78	2210.56	1529.84	1190.50	987.70	853.16	757.64	686.49	631.59	588.06	552.79	523.71	499.40	478.82
50000	4343.65	2255.67	1561.06	1214.79	1007.85	870.58	773.10	700.50	644.48	600.06	564.07	534.40	509.59	488.59
55000	4778.01	2481.24	1717.17	1336.27	1108.64	957.63	850.41	770.55	708.93	660.06	620.48	587.84	560.55	537.45
60000	5212.38	2706.81	1873.27	1457.75	1209.42	1044.69	927.72	840.60	773.37	720.07	676.88	641.28	611.51	586.31
65000	5646.74	2932.37	2029.38	1579.23	1310.21	1131.75	1005.03	910.65	837.82	780.07	733.29	694.72	662.47	635.17
70000	6081.11	3157.94	2185.49	1700.71	1410.99	1218.80	1082.34	980.70	902.27	840.08	789.70	748.16	713.43	684.03
75000	6515.47	3383.51	2341.59	1822.19	1511.78	1305.86	1159.65	1050.75	966.72	900.08	846.10	801.60	764.38	732.89
80000	6949.84	3609.07	2497.70	1943.66	1612.56	1392.92	1236.96	1120.80	1031.16	960.09	902.51	855.04	815.34	781.75
85000	7384.20	3834.64	2653.80	2065.14	1713.35	1479.98	1314.27	1190.85	1095.61	1020.10	958.91	908.48	866.30	830.61
90000	7818.56	4060.21	2809.91	2186.62	1814.13	1567.03	1391.58	1260.90	1160.06	1080.10	1015.32	961.92	917.26	879.46
95000	8252.93	4285.77	2966.02	2308.10	1914.92	1654.09	1468.89	1330.95	1224.51	1140.11	1071.73	1015.36	968.22	928.32
100000	8687.29	4511.34	3122.12	2429.58	2015.70	1741.15	1546.20	1401.00	1288.95	1200.11	1128.13	1068.80	1019.18	977.18

TERM	15 Years	16 Years	17 Years	18 Years	19 Years	20 Years	21 Years	22 Years	23 Years	24 Years	25 Years	30 Years	35 Years	40 Years
AMOUNT														
5	.05	.05	.05	.05	.05	.05	.05	.04	.04	.04	.04	.04	.04	.04
10	.10	.10	.09	.09	.09	.09	.09	.08	.08	.08	.08	.08	.07	.07
15	.15	.14	.14	.13	.13	.13	.13	.12	.12	.12	.12	.11	.11	.11
25	.24	.23	.23	.22	.21	.21	.21	.20	.20	.20	.19	.18	.18	.17
50	.48	.46	.45	.43	.42	.42	.41	.40	.39	.39	.38	.36	.35	.34
75	.71	.69	.67	.65	.63	.62	.61	.60	.59	.58	.57	.54	.52	.51
100	.95	.92	.89	.86	.84	.83	.81	.80	.78	.77	.76	.72	.70	.68
200	1.89	1.83	1.77	1.72	1.68	1.65	1.61	1.59	1.56	1.54	1.52	1.44	1.39	1.36
300	2.83	2.74	2.66	2.58	2.52	2.47	2.42	2.38	2.34	2.30	2.27	2.15	2.08	2.03
400	3.77	3.65	3.54	3.44	3.36	3.29	3.22	3.17	3.11	3.07	3.03	2.87	2.77	2.71
500	4.71	4.56	4.42	4.30	4.20	4.11	4.03	3.96	3.89	3.83	3.78	3.59	3.47	3.39
600	5.65	5.47	5.31	5.16	5.04	4.93	4.83	4.75	4.67	4.60	4.54	4.30	4.16	4.06
700	6.59	6.38	6.19	6.02	5.88	5.75	5.64	5.54	5.45	5.37	5.29	5.02	4.85	4.74
800	7.54	7.29	7.07	6.88	6.72	6.57	6.44	6.33	6.22	6.13	6.05	5.74	5.54	5.42
900	8.48	8.20	7.96	7.74	7.56	7.39	7.25	7.12	7.00	6.90	6.80	6.45	6.23	6.09
1000	9.42	9.11	8.84	8.60	8.40	8.21	8.05	7.91	7.78	7.66	7.56	7.17	6.93	6.77
2000	18.83	18.21	17.67	17.20	16.79	16.42	16.10	15.81	15.55	15.32	15.11	14.33	13.85	13.54
3000	28.24	27.31	26.51	25.80	25.18	24.63	24.15	23.71	23.33	22.98	22.66	21.50	20.77	20.30
4000	37.66	36.42	35.34	34.40	33.57	32.84	32.19	31.62	31.10	30.64	30.22	28.66	27.69	27.07
5000	47.07	45.52	44.18	43.00	41.97	41.05	40.24	39.52	38.87	38.29	37.77	35.83	34.61	33.84
6000	56.48	54.62	53.01	51.60	50.36	49.26	48.29	47.42	46.65	45.95	45.32	42.99	41.54	40.60
7000	65.89	63.73	61.84	60.20	58.75	57.47	56.34	55.32	54.42	53.61	52.88	50.15	48.46	47.37
8000	75.31	72.83	70.68	68.80	67.14	65.68	64.38	63.23	62.19	61.27	60.43	57.32	55.38	54.13
9000	84.72	81.93	79.51	77.40	75.54	73.89	72.43	71.13	69.97	68.92	67.98	64.48	62.30	60.90
10000	94.13	91.04	88.35	86.00	83.93	82.10	80.48	79.03	77.74	76.58	75.54	71.65	69.22	67.67
11000	103.55	100.14	97.18	94.59	92.32	90.31	88.52	86.94	85.51	84.24	83.09	78.81	76.14	74.43
12000	112.96	109.24	106.02	103.19	100.71	98.52	96.57	94.84	93.29	91.90	90.64	85.97	83.07	81.20
13000	122.37	118.35	114.85	111.79	109.10	106.73	104.62	102.74	101.06	99.55	98.20	93.14	89.99	87.97
14000	131.78	127.45	123.68	120.39	117.50	114.94	112.67	110.64	108.83	107.21	105.75	100.30	96.91	94.73
15000	141.20	136.55	132.52	128.99	125.89	123.15	120.71	118.55	116.61	114.87	113.30	107.47	103.83	101.50
16000	150.61	145.66	141.35	137.59	134.28	131.36	126.45	126.45	124.38	122.53	120.86	114.63	110.75	108.26
17000	160.02	154.76	150.19	146.19	142.67	139.57	136.81	134.35	132.15	130.18	128.41	121.80	117.67	115.03
18000	169.43	163.86	159.02	154.79	151.07	147.78	144.86	142.25	139.93	137.84	135.96	128.96	124.60	121.80
19000	178.85	172.97	167.86	163.39	159.46	155.99	152.90	150.16	147.70	145.50	143.52	136.12	131.52	128.56
20000	188.26	182.07	176.69	171.99	167.85	164.19	160.95	158.06	155.47	153.16	151.07	143.29	138.44	135.33
21000	197.67	191.17	185.52	180.58	176.24	172.40	169.00	165.96	163.25	160.81	158.62	150.45	145.36	142.10
22000	207.09	200.27	194.36	189.18	184.63	180.61	177.04	173.87	171.02	168.47	166.18	157.62	152.28	148.86
23000	216.50	209.38	203.19	197.78	193.03	188.82	185.09	181.77	170.80	176.13	173.73	164.78	159.21	155.63
24000	225.91	218.48	212.03	206.38	201.42	197.03	193.14	189.67	186.57	183.79	181.28	171.94	166.13	162.39
25000	235.32	227.58	220.86	214.98	209.81	205.24	201.19	197.57	194.34	191.44	188.84	179.11	173.05	169.16
26000	244.74	236.69	229.69	223.58	218.20	213.45	209.23	205.48	202.12	199.10	196.39	186.27	179.97	175.93
27000	254.15	245.79	238.53	232.18	226.60	221.66	217.28	213.38	209.89	206.76	203.94	193.44	186.89	182.69
28000	263.56	254.89	247.36	240.78	234.99	229.87	225.33	221.28	217.66	214.42	211.50	200.60	193.81	189.46
29000	272.97	264.00	256.20	249.38	243.38	238.08	233.38	229.18	225.44	222.07	219.05	207.76	200.74	196.22
30000	282.39	273.10	265.03	257.98	251.77	246.29	241.42	237.09	233.21	229.73	226.60	214.93	207.66	202.99
31000	291.80	282.20	273.87	266.58	260.16	254.50	249.47	244.99	240.98	237.39	234.16	222.09	214.58	209.76
32000	301.21	291.31	282.70	275.17	268.56	262.71	257.52	252.89	248.76	245.05	241.71	229.26	221.50	216.52
33000	310.63	300.41	291.53	283.77	276.95	270.92	265.56	260.80	256.53	252.70	249.26	236.42	228.42	223.29
34000	320.04	309.51	300.37	292.37	285.34	279.13	273.61	268.70	264.30	260.36	256.82	243.59	235.34	230.06
35000	329.45	318.62	309.20	300.97	293.73	287.34	281.66	276.60	272.08	268.02	264.37	250.75	242.27	236.82
36000	338.86	327.72	318.04	309.57	302.13	295.55	289.71	284.50	279.85	275.68	271.92	257.91	249.19	243.59
37000	348.28	336.82	326.87	318.17	310.52	303.76	297.75	292.41	287.62	283.33	279.48	265.08	256.11	250.35
38000	357.69	345.93	335.71	326.77	318.91	311.97	305.80	300.31	295.40	290.99	287.03	272.24	263.03	257.12
39000	367.10	355.03	344.54	335.37	327.30	320.17	313.85	308.21	303.17	298.65	294.58	279.41	269.95	263.89
40000	376.52	364.13	353.37	343.97	335.69	328.38	321.90	316.11	310.94	306.31	302.14	286.57	276.88	270.65
41000	385.93	373.24	362.21	352.57	344.09	336.59	329.94	324.02	318.72	313.96	309.69	293.73	283.80	277.42
42000	395.34	382.34	371.04	361.16	352.48	344.80	337.99	331.92	326.49	321.62	317.24	300.90	290.72	284.19
43000	404.75	391.44	379.88	369.76	360.87	353.01	346.04	339.82	334.26	329.28	324.80	308.06	297.64	290.95
44000	414.17	400.54	388.71	378.36	369.26	361.22	354.08	347.73	342.04	336.94	332.35	315.23	304.56	297.72
45000	423.58	409.65	397.54	386.96	377.66	369.43	362.13	355.63	349.81	344.60	339.90	322.39	311.48	304.48
46000	432.99	418.75	406.38	395.56	386.05	377.64	370.18	363.53	357.59	352.25	347.46	329.55	318.41	311.25
47000	442.40	427.85	415.21	404.16	394.44	385.85	378.23	371.43	365.36	359.91	355.01	336.72	325.33	318.02
48000	451.82	436.96	424.05	412.76	402.83	394.06	386.27	379.34	373.13	367.57	362.56	343.88	332.25	324.78
49000	461.23	446.06	432.88	421.36	411.22	402.27	394.32	387.24	380.91	375.23	370.12	351.05	339.17	331.55
50000	470.64	455.16	441.72	429.96	419.62	410.48	402.37	395.14	388.68	382.88	377.67	358.21	346.09	338.31
55000	517.71	500.68	485.89	472.95	461.58	451.53	442.60	434.66	427.55	421.17	415.44	394.03	380.70	372.15
60000	564.77	546.20	530.06	515.95	503.54	492.57	482.84	474.17	466.41	459.46	453.20	429.85	415.31	405.98
65000	611.83	591.71	574.23	558.94	545.50	533.62	523.08	513.68	505.28	497.75	490.97	465.67	449.92	439.81
70000	658.90	637.23	618.40	601.94	587.46	574.67	563.31	553.20	544.15	536.03	528.74	501.49	484.53	473.64
75000	705.96	682.74	662.57	644.93	629.42	615.72	603.55	592.71	583.02	574.32	566.50	537.31	519.14	507.47
80000	753.03	728.26	706.74	687.93	671.38	656.76	643.79	632.22	621.88	612.61	604.27	573.13	553.75	541.30
85000	800.09	773.77	750.91	730.92	713.35	697.81	684.02	671.74	660.75	650.90	642.03	608.96	588.35	575.13
90000	847.15	819.29	795.08	773.92	755.31	738.86	724.26	711.25	699.62	689.19	679.80	644.78	622.96	608.96
95000	894.22	864.81	839.26	816.91	797.27	779.91	764.50	750.76	738.49	727.47	717.57	680.60	657.57	642.79
100000	941.28	910.32	883.43	859.91	839.23	820.95	804.73	790.28	777.35	765.76	755.33	716.42	692.18	676.62

MONTHLY PAYMENT
REQUIRED TO AMORTIZE A LOAN

TERM AMOUNT	1 Year	2 Years	3 Years	4 Years	5 Years	6 Years	7 Years	8 Years	9 Years	10 Years	11 Years	12 Years	13 Years	14 Years
5	.44	.23	.16	.13	.11	.09	.08	.08	.07	.07	.06	.06	.06	.05
10	.87	.46	.32	.25	.21	.18	.16	.15	.13	.13	.12	.11	.11	.10
15	1.31	.68	.47	.37	.31	.27	.24	.22	.20	.19	.17	.17	.16	.15
25	2.18	1.13	.79	.61	.51	.44	.39	.36	.33	.31	.29	.27	.26	.25
50	4.35	2.26	1.57	1.22	1.01	.88	.78	.71	.65	.61	.57	.54	.52	.49
75	6.52	3.39	2.35	1.83	1.52	1.31	1.17	1.06	.97	.91	.85	.81	.77	.74
100	8.69	4.52	3.13	2.44	2.02	1.75	1.55	1.41	1.30	1.21	1.14	1.08	1.03	.98
200	17.38	9.03	6.25	4.87	4.04	3.49	3.10	2.81	2.59	2.41	2.27	2.15	2.05	1.96
300	26.07	13.55	9.38	7.30	6.06	5.24	4.65	4.22	3.88	3.61	3.40	3.22	3.07	2.94
400	34.76	18.06	12.50	9.73	8.08	6.98	6.20	5.62	5.17	4.82	4.53	4.29	4.09	3.92
500	43.45	22.57	15.63	12.16	10.10	8.72	7.75	7.02	6.46	6.02	5.66	5.36	5.11	4.90
600	52.14	27.09	18.75	14.60	12.11	10.47	9.30	8.43	7.75	7.22	6.79	6.43	6.14	5.88
700	60.83	31.60	21.88	17.03	14.13	12.21	10.85	9.83	9.05	8.42	7.92	7.51	7.16	6.86
800	69.52	36.11	25.00	19.46	16.15	13.95	12.39	11.23	10.34	9.63	9.05	8.58	8.18	7.84
900	78.21	40.63	28.12	21.89	18.17	15.70	13.94	12.64	11.63	10.83	10.18	9.65	9.20	8.82
1000	86.90	45.14	31.25	24.32	20.19	17.44	15.49	14.04	12.92	12.03	11.31	10.72	10.22	9.80
2000	173.80	90.28	62.49	48.64	40.37	34.88	30.98	28.08	25.84	24.06	22.62	21.44	20.44	19.60
3000	260.69	135.41	93.74	72.96	60.55	52.31	46.47	42.11	38.75	36.09	33.93	32.15	30.66	29.40
4000	347.59	180.55	124.98	97.28	80.73	69.75	61.95	56.15	51.67	48.11	45.24	42.87	40.88	39.20
5000	434.48	225.69	156.23	121.60	100.91	87.18	77.44	70.18	64.58	60.14	56.55	53.58	51.10	49.00
6000	521.38	270.82	187.47	145.92	121.09	104.62	92.93	84.22	77.50	72.17	67.85	64.30	61.32	58.80
7000	608.28	315.96	218.71	170.24	141.27	122.06	108.41	98.25	90.41	84.20	79.16	75.01	71.54	68.60
8000	695.17	361.09	249.96	194.56	161.45	139.49	123.90	112.29	103.33	96.22	90.47	85.73	81.76	78.40
9000	782.07	406.23	281.20	218.88	181.63	156.93	139.39	126.32	116.24	108.25	101.78	96.44	91.98	88.20
10000	868.96	451.37	312.45	243.20	201.81	174.36	154.87	140.36	129.16	120.28	113.09	107.16	102.20	98.00
11000	955.86	496.50	343.69	267.52	221.99	191.80	170.36	154.39	142.07	132.31	124.39	117.87	112.42	107.80
12000	1042.76	541.64	374.94	291.83	242.17	209.23	185.85	168.43	154.99	144.33	135.70	128.59	122.64	117.60
13000	1129.65	586.77	406.18	316.15	262.36	226.67	201.33	182.46	167.90	156.36	147.01	139.30	132.86	127.40
14000	1216.55	631.91	437.42	340.47	282.54	244.11	216.82	196.50	180.82	168.39	158.32	150.02	143.08	137.20
15000	1303.44	677.05	468.67	364.79	302.72	261.54	232.31	210.53	193.73	180.42	169.63	160.73	153.30	147.00
16000	1390.34	722.18	499.91	389.11	322.90	278.98	247.79	224.57	206.65	192.44	180.93	171.45	163.52	156.80
17000	1477.24	767.32	531.16	413.43	343.08	296.41	263.28	238.60	219.56	204.47	192.24	182.16	173.74	166.60
18000	1564.13	812.46	562.40	437.75	363.26	313.85	278.77	252.64	232.48	216.50	203.55	192.88	183.95	176.40
19000	1651.03	857.59	593.64	462.07	383.44	331.28	294.25	266.67	245.40	228.52	214.86	203.59	194.17	186.20
20000	1737.92	902.73	624.89	486.39	403.62	348.72	309.74	280.71	258.31	240.55	226.17	214.31	204.39	196.00
21000	1824.82	947.86	656.13	510.71	423.80	366.16	325.23	294.75	271.23	252.58	237.47	225.02	214.61	205.80
22000	1911.72	993.00	687.38	535.03	443.98	383.59	340.71	308.78	284.14	264.61	248.78	235.74	224.83	215.60
23000	1998.61	1038.14	718.62	559.35	464.16	401.03	356.20	322.82	297.06	276.63	260.09	246.45	235.05	225.40
24000	2085.51	1083.27	749.87	583.66	484.34	418.46	371.69	336.85	309.97	288.66	271.40	257.17	245.27	235.20
25000	2172.40	1128.41	781.11	607.98	504.53	435.90	387.17	350.89	322.89	300.69	282.71	267.88	255.49	245.00
26000	2259.30	1173.54	812.35	632.30	524.71	453.33	402.66	364.92	335.80	312.72	294.01	278.60	265.71	254.80
27000	2346.20	1218.68	843.60	656.62	544.89	470.77	418.15	378.96	348.72	324.74	305.32	289.31	275.93	264.60
28000	2433.09	1263.82	874.84	680.94	565.07	488.21	433.63	392.99	361.63	336.77	316.63	300.03	286.15	274.40
29000	2519.99	1308.95	906.09	705.26	585.25	505.64	449.12	407.03	374.55	348.80	327.94	310.74	296.37	284.20
30000	2606.88	1354.09	937.33	729.58	605.43	523.08	464.61	421.06	387.46	360.83	339.25	321.46	306.59	294.00
31000	2693.78	1399.23	968.57	753.90	625.61	540.51	480.09	435.10	400.38	372.85	350.55	332.18	316.81	303.80
32000	2780.68	1444.36	999.82	778.22	645.79	557.95	495.58	449.13	413.29	384.88	361.86	342.89	327.03	313.60
33000	2867.57	1489.50	1031.06	802.54	665.97	575.38	511.07	463.17	426.21	396.91	373.17	353.61	337.25	323.40
34000	2954.47	1534.63	1062.31	826.86	686.15	592.82	526.55	477.20	439.12	408.93	384.48	364.32	347.47	333.20
35000	3041.36	1579.77	1093.55	851.18	706.33	610.26	542.04	491.24	452.04	420.96	395.79	375.04	357.69	343.00
36000	3128.26	1624.91	1124.80	875.49	726.51	627.69	557.53	505.27	464.96	432.99	407.09	385.75	367.90	352.80
37000	3215.16	1670.04	1156.04	899.81	746.70	645.13	573.02	519.31	477.87	445.02	418.40	396.47	378.12	362.60
38000	3302.05	1715.18	1187.28	924.13	766.88	662.56	588.50	533.34	490.79	457.04	429.71	407.18	388.34	372.40
39000	3388.95	1760.31	1218.53	948.45	787.06	680.00	603.99	547.38	503.70	469.07	441.02	417.90	398.56	382.20
40000	3475.84	1805.45	1249.77	972.77	807.24	697.43	619.48	561.41	516.62	481.10	452.33	428.61	408.78	392.00
41000	3562.74	1850.59	1281.02	997.09	827.42	714.87	634.96	575.45	529.53	493.13	463.63	439.33	419.00	401.80
42000	3649.64	1895.72	1312.26	1021.41	847.60	732.31	650.45	589.48	542.45	505.15	474.94	450.04	429.22	411.60
43000	3736.53	1940.86	1343.50	1045.73	867.78	749.74	665.94	603.52	555.36	517.18	486.25	460.76	439.44	421.40
44000	3823.43	1985.99	1374.75	1070.05	887.96	767.18	681.42	617.56	568.28	529.21	497.56	471.47	449.66	431.20
45000	3910.32	2031.13	1405.99	1094.37	908.14	784.61	696.91	631.59	581.19	541.24	508.87	482.19	459.88	441.00
46000	3997.22	2076.27	1437.24	1118.69	928.32	802.05	712.40	645.63	594.11	553.26	520.18	492.90	470.10	450.80
47000	4084.12	2121.40	1468.48	1143.01	948.50	819.49	727.88	659.66	607.02	565.29	531.48	503.62	480.32	460.60
48000	4171.01	2166.54	1499.73	1167.32	968.68	836.92	743.37	673.70	619.94	577.32	542.79	514.33	490.54	470.40
49000	4257.91	2211.68	1530.97	1191.64	988.86	854.36	758.86	687.73	632.85	589.34	554.10	525.05	500.76	480.20
50000	4344.80	2256.81	1562.21	1215.96	1009.05	871.79	774.34	701.77	645.77	601.37	565.41	535.76	510.98	490.00
55000	4779.28	2482.49	1718.44	1337.56	1109.95	958.97	851.78	771.94	710.35	661.51	621.95	589.34	562.07	539.00
60000	5213.76	2708.17	1874.66	1459.15	1210.85	1046.15	929.21	842.12	774.92	721.65	678.49	642.91	613.17	588.00
65000	5648.24	2933.85	2030.88	1580.75	1311.76	1133.33	1006.64	912.30	839.50	781.78	735.03	696.49	664.27	637.00
70000	6082.72	3159.53	2187.10	1702.35	1412.66	1220.51	1084.08	982.47	904.07	841.92	791.57	750.07	715.37	686.00
75000	6517.20	3385.21	2343.32	1823.94	1513.57	1307.69	1161.51	1052.65	968.65	902.06	848.11	803.64	766.46	735.00
80000	6951.68	3610.90	2499.54	1945.54	1614.47	1394.86	1238.95	1122.82	1033.23	962.19	904.65	857.22	817.56	784.00
85000	7386.16	3836.58	2655.76	2067.13	1715.37	1482.04	1316.38	1193.00	1097.80	1022.33	961.19	910.79	868.66	833.00
90000	7820.64	4062.26	2811.98	2188.73	1816.28	1569.22	1393.81	1263.18	1162.38	1082.47	1017.73	964.37	919.75	882.00
95000	8255.12	4287.94	2968.20	2310.32	1917.18	1656.40	1471.25	1333.35	1226.96	1142.60	1074.27	1017.95	970.85	931.00
100000	8689.60	4513.62	3124.42	2431.92	2018.09	1743.58	1548.68	1403.53	1291.53	1202.74	1130.81	1071.52	1021.95	980.00

TERM	15 Years	16 Years	17 Years	18 Years	19 Years	20 Years	21 Years	22 Years	23 Years	24 Years	25 Years	30 Years	35 Years	40 Years
AMOUNT														
5	.05	.05	.05	.05	.05	.05	.05	.04	.04	.04	.04	.04	.04	.04
10	.10	.10	.09	.09	.09	.09	.09	.08	.08	.08	.08	.08	.07	.07
15	.15	.14	.14	.13	.13	.13	.13	.12	.12	.12	.12	.11	.11	.11
25	.24	.23	.23	.22	.22	.21	.21	.20	.20	.20	.19	.18	.18	.18
50	.48	.46	.45	.44	.43	.42	.41	.40	.40	.39	.38	.36	.35	.35
75	.71	.69	.67	.65	.64	.62	.61	.60	.59	.58	.57	.54	.53	.52
100	.95	.92	.89	.87	.85	.83	.81	.80	.79	.77	.76	.72	.70	.69
200	1.89	1.83	1.78	1.73	1.69	1.65	1.62	1.59	1.57	1.54	1.52	1.44	1.40	1.37
300	2.84	2.74	2.66	2.59	2.53	2.48	2.43	2.39	2.35	2.31	2.28	2.16	2.09	2.05
400	3.78	3.66	3.55	3.46	3.37	3.30	3.24	3.18	3.13	3.08	3.04	2.88	2.79	2.73
500	4.73	4.57	4.44	4.32	4.22	4.13	4.04	3.97	3.91	3.85	3.80	3.60	3.48	3.41
600	5.67	5.48	5.32	5.18	5.06	4.95	4.85	4.77	4.69	4.62	4.56	4.32	4.18	4.09
700	6.61	6.40	6.21	6.05	5.90	5.77	5.66	5.56	5.47	5.39	5.32	5.04	4.88	4.77
800	7.56	7.31	7.10	6.91	6.74	6.60	6.47	6.35	6.25	6.16	6.07	5.76	5.57	5.45
900	8.50	8.22	7.98	7.77	7.59	7.42	7.28	7.15	7.03	6.93	6.83	6.48	6.27	6.13
1000	9.45	9.14	8.87	8.63	8.43	8.25	8.08	7.94	7.81	7.70	7.59	7.20	6.96	6.81
2000	18.89	18.27	17.73	17.26	16.85	16.49	16.16	15.87	15.62	15.39	15.18	14.40	13.92	13.61
3000	28.33	27.40	26.60	25.89	25.27	24.73	24.24	23.81	23.42	23.08	22.76	21.60	20.88	20.42
4000	37.77	36.53	35.46	34.52	33.70	32.97	32.32	31.74	31.23	30.77	30.35	28.80	27.84	27.22
5000	47.21	45.67	44.32	43.15	42.12	41.21	40.40	39.68	39.03	38.46	37.94	36.00	34.79	34.02
6000	56.65	54.80	53.19	51.78	50.54	49.45	48.48	47.61	46.84	46.15	45.52	43.20	41.75	40.83
7000	66.09	63.93	62.05	60.41	58.96	57.69	56.55	55.55	54.64	53.84	53.11	50.40	48.71	47.63
8000	75.54	73.06	70.92	69.04	67.39	65.93	64.63	63.48	62.45	61.53	60.69	57.59	55.67	54.43
9000	84.98	82.20	79.78	77.67	75.81	74.17	72.71	71.41	70.26	69.22	68.28	64.79	62.63	61.24
10000	94.42	91.33	88.64	86.30	84.23	82.41	80.79	79.35	78.06	76.91	75.87	71.99	69.58	68.04
11000	103.86	100.46	97.51	94.92	92.65	90.65	88.87	87.28	85.87	84.60	83.45	79.19	76.54	74.84
12000	113.30	109.59	106.37	103.55	101.08	98.89	96.95	95.22	93.67	92.29	91.04	86.39	83.50	81.65
13000	122.74	118.72	115.23	112.18	109.50	107.13	105.03	103.15	101.48	99.98	98.62	93.59	90.46	88.45
14000	132.18	127.86	124.10	120.81	117.92	115.37	113.10	111.09	109.28	107.67	106.21	100.79	97.41	95.25
15000	141.63	136.99	132.96	129.44	126.35	123.61	121.18	119.02	117.09	115.36	113.80	107.99	104.37	102.06
16000	151.07	146.12	141.83	138.07	134.77	131.85	129.26	126.96	124.89	123.05	121.38	115.18	111.33	108.86
17000	160.51	155.25	150.69	146.70	143.19	140.09	137.34	134.89	132.70	130.74	128.97	122.38	118.29	115.66
18000	169.95	164.39	159.55	155.33	151.61	148.33	145.42	142.82	140.51	138.43	136.56	129.58	125.25	122.47
19000	179.39	173.52	168.42	163.96	160.04	156.57	153.50	150.76	148.31	146.12	144.14	136.78	132.20	129.27
20000	188.83	182.65	177.28	172.59	168.46	164.81	161.58	158.69	156.12	153.81	151.73	143.98	139.16	136.07
21000	198.27	191.78	186.14	181.22	176.88	173.05	169.65	166.63	163.92	161.50	159.31	151.18	146.12	142.88
22000	207.72	200.92	195.01	189.04	185.30	181.29	177.73	174.56	171.73	169.19	166.90	158.38	153.08	149.68
23000	217.16	210.05	203.87	198.47	193.73	189.53	185.81	182.50	179.53	176.88	174.49	165.58	160.03	156.48
24000	226.60	219.18	212.74	207.10	202.15	197.77	193.89	190.43	187.34	184.57	182.07	172.77	166.99	163.29
25000	236.04	228.31	221.60	215.73	210.57	206.01	201.97	198.37	195.14	192.26	189.66	179.97	173.95	170.09
26000	245.48	237.44	230.46	224.36	218.99	214.25	210.05	206.30	202.95	199.95	197.24	187.17	180.91	176.90
27000	254.92	246.58	239.33	232.99	227.42	222.49	218.13	214.23	210.76	207.64	204.83	194.37	187.87	183.70
28000	264.36	255.71	248.19	241.62	235.84	230.74	226.20	222.17	218.56	215.33	212.42	201.57	194.82	190.50
29000	273.81	264.84	257.05	250.25	244.26	238.98	234.28	230.10	226.37	223.02	220.00	208.77	201.78	197.31
30000	283.25	273.97	265.92	258.88	252.69	247.22	242.36	238.04	234.17	230.71	227.59	215.97	208.74	204.11
31000	292.69	283.11	274.78	267.51	261.11	255.46	250.44	245.97	241.98	238.40	235.18	223.16	215.70	210.91
32000	302.13	292.24	283.65	276.13	269.53	263.70	258.52	253.91	249.78	246.09	242.76	230.36	222.65	217.72
33000	311.57	301.37	292.51	284.76	277.95	271.94	266.60	261.84	257.59	253.78	250.35	237.56	229.61	224.52
34000	321.01	310.50	301.37	293.39	286.38	280.18	274.68	269.78	265.39	261.47	257.93	244.76	236.57	231.32
35000	330.45	319.64	310.24	302.02	294.80	288.42	282.75	277.71	273.20	269.16	265.52	251.96	243.53	238.13
36000	339.90	328.77	319.10	310.65	303.22	296.66	290.83	285.64	281.01	276.85	273.11	259.16	250.49	244.93
37000	349.34	337.90	327.97	319.28	311.64	304.90	298.91	293.58	288.81	284.54	280.69	266.36	257.44	251.73
38000	358.78	347.03	336.83	327.91	320.07	313.14	306.99	301.51	296.62	292.23	288.28	273.56	264.40	258.54
39000	368.22	356.16	345.69	336.54	328.49	321.38	315.07	309.45	304.42	299.92	295.86	280.75	271.36	265.34
40000	377.66	365.30	354.56	345.17	336.91	329.62	323.15	317.38	312.23	307.61	303.45	287.95	278.32	272.14
41000	387.10	374.43	363.42	353.80	345.34	337.86	331.23	325.32	320.03	315.30	311.04	295.15	285.28	278.95
42000	396.54	383.56	372.28	362.43	353.76	346.10	339.30	333.25	327.84	322.99	318.62	302.35	292.23	285.75
43000	405.99	392.69	381.15	371.05	362.18	354.34	347.38	341.19	335.64	330.68	326.21	309.55	299.19	292.55
44000	415.43	401.83	390.01	379.68	370.60	362.58	355.46	349.12	343.45	338.37	333.80	316.75	306.15	299.36
45000	424.87	410.96	398.88	388.31	379.03	370.82	363.54	357.05	351.26	346.06	341.38	323.95	313.11	306.16
46000	434.31	420.09	407.74	396.94	387.45	379.06	371.62	364.99	359.06	353.75	348.97	331.15	320.06	312.96
47000	443.75	429.22	416.60	405.57	395.87	387.30	379.70	372.92	366.87	361.44	356.55	338.34	327.02	319.77
48000	453.19	438.36	425.47	414.20	404.29	395.54	387.78	380.86	374.67	369.13	364.14	345.54	333.98	326.57
49000	462.63	447.49	434.33	422.83	412.72	403.78	395.85	388.79	382.48	376.82	371.73	352.74	340.94	333.38
50000	472.08	456.62	443.19	431.46	421.14	412.02	403.93	396.73	390.28	384.51	379.31	359.94	347.90	340.18
55000	519.28	502.28	487.51	474.60	463.25	453.22	444.33	436.40	429.31	422.96	417.24	395.93	382.68	374.20
60000	566.49	547.94	531.83	517.75	505.37	494.43	484.72	476.07	468.34	461.41	455.17	431.93	417.47	408.21
65000	613.70	593.60	576.15	560.89	547.48	535.63	525.11	515.74	507.37	499.86	493.10	467.92	452.26	442.23
70000	660.90	639.27	620.47	604.04	589.59	576.83	565.50	555.41	546.40	538.31	531.04	503.91	487.05	476.25
75000	708.11	684.93	664.79	647.18	631.71	618.03	605.90	595.09	585.42	576.76	568.97	539.91	521.84	510.27
80000	755.32	730.59	709.11	690.33	673.82	659.23	646.29	634.76	624.45	615.21	606.90	575.90	556.63	544.28
85000	802.53	776.25	753.43	733.47	715.93	700.44	686.68	674.43	663.48	653.66	644.83	611.89	591.42	578.30
90000	849.73	821.91	797.75	776.62	758.05	741.64	727.08	714.10	702.51	692.11	682.76	647.89	626.21	612.32
95000	896.94	867.57	842.06	819.77	800.16	782.84	767.47	753.78	741.53	730.56	720.69	683.88	661.00	646.33
100000	944.15	913.23	886.38	862.91	842.27	824.04	807.86	793.45	780.56	769.01	758.62	719.88	695.79	680.35

TERM AMOUNT	1 Year	2 Years	3 Years	4 Years	5 Years	6 Years	7 Years	8 Years	9 Years	10 Years	11 Years	12 Years	13 Years	14 Years
5	.44	.23	.16	.13	.11	.09	.08	.08	.07	.07	.06	.06	.06	.05
10	.87	.46	.32	.25	.21	.18	.16	.15	.13	.13	.12	.11	.11	.10
15	1.31	.68	.47	.37	.31	.27	.24	.22	.20	.19	.18	.17	.16	.15
25	2.18	1.13	.79	.61	.51	.44	.39	.36	.33	.31	.29	.27	.26	.25
50	4.35	2.26	1.57	1.22	1.02	.88	.78	.71	.65	.61	.57	.54	.52	.50
75	6.52	3.39	2.35	1.83	1.52	1.32	1.17	1.06	.98	.91	.86	.81	.77	.74
100	8.70	4.52	3.13	2.44	2.03	1.75	1.56	1.41	1.30	1.21	1.14	1.08	1.03	.99
200	17.39	9.04	6.26	4.88	4.05	3.50	3.11	2.82	2.60	2.42	2.27	2.16	2.06	1.97
300	26.08	13.56	9.39	7.31	6.07	5.25	4.66	4.23	3.89	3.63	3.41	3.23	3.08	2.96
400	34.78	18.07	12.52	9.75	8.09	6.99	6.21	5.63	5.19	4.83	4.54	4.31	4.11	3.94
500	43.47	22.59	15.64	12.18	10.11	8.74	7.77	7.04	6.48	6.04	5.68	5.38	5.14	4.93
600	52.16	27.11	18.77	14.62	12.13	10.49	9.32	8.45	7.78	7.25	6.81	6.46	6.16	5.91
700	60.86	31.62	21.90	17.05	14.16	12.24	10.87	9.86	9.07	8.45	7.95	7.53	7.19	6.89
800	69.55	36.14	25.03	19.49	16.18	13.98	12.42	11.26	10.37	9.66	9.08	8.61	8.21	7.88
900	78.24	40.66	28.16	21.92	18.20	15.73	13.98	12.67	11.66	10.87	10.22	9.69	9.24	8.86
1000	86.94	45.18	31.28	24.36	20.22	17.48	15.53	14.08	12.96	12.07	11.35	10.76	10.27	9.85
2000	173.87	90.35	62.56	48.71	40.44	34.95	31.05	28.15	25.91	24.14	22.70	21.52	20.53	19.69
3000	260.80	135.52	93.84	73.07	60.65	52.42	46.58	42.22	38.87	36.21	34.05	32.27	30.79	29.53
4000	347.73	180.69	125.12	97.42	80.87	69.89	62.10	56.30	51.82	48.27	45.40	43.03	41.05	39.37
5000	434.66	225.86	156.40	121.78	101.09	87.37	77.63	70.37	64.78	60.34	56.75	53.79	51.31	49.22
6000	521.59	271.03	187.68	146.13	121.30	104.84	93.15	84.44	77.73	72.41	68.09	64.54	61.57	59.06
7000	608.52	316.20	218.96	170.49	141.52	122.31	108.67	98.52	90.68	84.47	79.44	75.30	71.83	68.90
8000	695.45	361.37	250.23	194.84	161.74	139.78	124.20	112.59	103.64	96.54	90.79	86.05	82.09	78.74
9000	782.38	406.54	281.51	219.19	181.95	157.26	139.72	126.66	116.59	108.61	102.14	96.81	92.35	88.59
10000	869.31	451.71	312.79	243.55	202.17	174.73	155.25	140.74	129.55	120.67	113.49	107.57	102.62	98.43
11000	956.24	496.88	344.07	267.90	222.39	192.20	170.77	154.81	142.50	132.74	124.84	118.32	112.88	108.27
12000	1043.17	542.05	375.35	292.26	242.60	209.67	186.29	168.88	155.45	144.81	136.18	129.08	123.14	118.11
13000	1130.10	587.22	406.63	316.61	262.82	227.14	201.82	182.96	168.41	156.87	147.53	139.83	133.40	127.96
14000	1217.03	632.39	437.91	340.97	283.04	244.62	217.34	197.03	181.36	168.94	158.88	150.59	143.66	137.80
15000	1303.96	677.56	469.19	365.32	303.25	262.09	232.87	211.10	194.32	181.01	170.23	161.35	153.92	147.64
16000	1390.90	722.73	500.46	389.67	323.47	279.56	248.39	225.18	207.27	193.07	181.58	172.10	164.18	157.48
17000	1477.83	767.90	531.74	414.03	343.69	297.03	263.91	239.25	220.22	205.14	192.93	182.86	174.44	167.32
18000	1564.76	813.07	563.02	438.38	363.90	314.51	279.44	253.32	233.18	217.21	204.27	193.61	184.70	177.17
19000	1651.69	858.24	594.30	462.74	384.12	331.98	294.96	267.40	246.13	229.27	215.62	204.37	194.97	187.01
20000	1738.62	903.41	625.58	487.09	404.34	349.45	310.49	281.47	259.09	241.34	226.97	215.13	205.23	196.85
21000	1825.55	948.58	656.86	511.45	424.55	366.92	326.01	295.54	272.04	253.41	238.32	225.88	215.49	206.69
22000	1912.48	993.75	688.14	535.80	444.77	384.39	341.53	309.62	284.99	265.47	249.67	236.64	225.75	216.54
23000	1999.41	1038.92	719.42	560.15	464.99	401.87	357.06	323.69	297.95	277.54	261.01	247.40	236.01	226.38
24000	2086.34	1084.09	750.69	584.51	485.20	419.34	372.58	337.76	310.90	289.61	272.36	258.15	246.27	236.22
25000	2173.27	1129.26	781.97	608.86	505.42	436.81	388.11	351.84	323.86	301.68	283.71	268.91	256.53	246.06
26000	2260.20	1174.43	813.25	633.22	525.64	454.28	403.63	365.91	336.81	313.74	295.06	279.66	266.79	255.91
27000	2347.13	1219.60	844.53	657.57	545.85	471.76	419.15	379.98	349.76	325.81	306.41	290.42	277.05	265.75
28000	2434.06	1264.77	875.81	681.93	566.07	489.23	434.68	394.06	362.72	337.88	317.76	301.18	287.32	275.59
29000	2520.99	1309.94	907.09	706.28	586.29	506.70	450.20	408.13	375.67	349.94	329.10	311.93	297.58	285.43
30000	2607.92	1355.11	938.37	730.63	606.50	524.17	465.73	422.20	388.63	362.01	340.45	322.69	307.84	295.28
31000	2694.85	1400.28	969.65	754.99	626.72	541.65	481.25	436.28	401.58	374.08	351.80	333.44	318.10	305.12
32000	2781.79	1445.45	1000.92	779.34	646.94	559.12	496.77	450.35	414.53	386.14	363.15	344.20	328.36	314.96
33000	2868.72	1490.63	1032.20	803.70	667.15	576.59	512.30	464.42	427.49	398.21	374.50	354.96	338.62	324.80
34000	2955.65	1535.80	1063.48	828.05	687.37	594.06	527.82	478.49	440.44	410.28	385.85	365.71	348.88	334.64
35000	3042.58	1580.97	1094.76	852.41	707.59	611.53	543.35	492.57	453.40	422.34	397.19	376.47	359.14	344.49
36000	3129.51	1626.14	1126.04	876.76	727.80	629.01	558.87	506.64	466.35	434.41	408.54	387.22	369.40	354.33
37000	3216.44	1671.31	1157.32	901.11	748.02	646.48	574.39	520.71	479.30	446.48	419.89	397.98	379.67	364.17
38000	3303.37	1716.48	1188.60	925.47	768.24	663.95	589.92	534.79	492.26	458.54	431.24	408.74	389.93	374.01
39000	3390.30	1761.65	1219.88	949.82	788.45	681.42	605.44	548.86	505.21	470.61	442.59	419.49	400.19	383.86
40000	3477.23	1806.82	1251.15	974.18	808.67	698.90	620.97	562.93	518.17	482.68	453.94	430.25	410.45	393.70
41000	3564.16	1851.99	1282.43	998.53	828.89	716.37	636.49	577.01	531.12	494.74	465.28	441.01	420.71	403.54
42000	3651.09	1897.16	1313.71	1022.89	849.10	733.84	652.01	591.08	544.07	506.81	476.63	451.76	430.97	413.38
43000	3738.02	1942.33	1344.99	1047.24	869.32	751.31	667.54	605.15	557.03	518.88	487.98	462.52	441.23	423.23
44000	3824.95	1987.50	1376.27	1071.59	889.54	768.78	683.06	619.23	569.98	530.94	499.33	473.27	451.49	433.07
45000	3911.88	2032.67	1407.55	1095.95	909.75	786.26	698.59	633.30	582.94	543.01	510.68	484.03	461.75	442.91
46000	3998.81	2077.84	1438.83	1120.30	929.97	803.73	714.11	647.37	595.89	555.08	522.02	494.79	472.02	452.75
47000	4085.75	2123.01	1470.11	1144.66	950.19	821.20	729.63	661.45	608.84	567.15	533.37	505.54	482.28	462.60
48000	4172.68	2168.18	1501.38	1169.01	970.40	838.67	745.16	675.52	621.80	579.21	544.72	516.30	492.54	472.44
49000	4259.61	2213.35	1532.66	1193.37	990.62	856.15	760.68	689.59	634.75	591.28	556.07	527.05	502.80	482.28
50000	4346.54	2258.52	1563.94	1217.72	1010.84	873.62	776.21	703.67	647.71	603.35	567.42	537.81	513.06	492.12
55000	4781.19	2484.37	1720.34	1339.49	1111.92	960.98	853.83	774.03	712.48	663.68	624.16	591.59	564.37	541.33
60000	5215.84	2710.22	1876.73	1461.26	1213.00	1048.34	931.45	844.40	777.25	724.01	680.90	645.37	615.67	590.55
65000	5650.50	2936.07	2033.12	1583.03	1314.09	1135.70	1009.07	914.76	842.02	784.35	737.64	699.15	666.98	639.76
70000	6085.15	3161.93	2189.52	1704.81	1415.17	1223.06	1086.69	985.13	906.79	844.68	794.38	752.93	718.28	688.97
75000	6519.80	3387.78	2345.91	1826.58	1516.25	1310.43	1164.31	1055.50	971.56	905.02	851.12	806.71	769.59	738.18
80000	6954.46	3613.63	2502.30	1948.35	1617.33	1397.79	1241.93	1125.86	1036.33	965.35	907.87	860.49	820.89	787.39
85000	7389.11	3839.48	2658.70	2070.12	1718.42	1485.15	1319.55	1196.23	1101.10	1025.68	964.61	914.27	872.20	836.60
90000	7823.76	4065.33	2815.09	2191.89	1819.50	1572.51	1397.17	1266.60	1165.87	1086.02	1021.35	968.05	923.50	885.82
95000	8258.42	4291.18	2971.48	2313.66	1920.58	1659.87	1474.79	1336.96	1230.64	1146.35	1078.09	1021.83	974.81	935.03
100000	8693.07	4517.04	3127.88	2435.43	2021.67	1747.23	1552.41	1407.33	1295.41	1206.69	1134.83	1075.62	1026.12	984.24

TERM AMOUNT	15 Years	16 Years	17 Years	18 Years	19 Years	20 Years	21 Years	22 Years	23 Years	24 Years	25 Years	30 Years	35 Years	40 Years
5	.05	.05	.05	.05	.05	.05	.05	.04	.04	.04	.04	.04	.04	.04
10	.10	.10	.09	.09	.09	.09	.09	.08	.08	.08	.08	.08	.08	.07
15	.15	.14	.14	.14	.13	.13	.13	.12	.12	.12	.12	.11	.11	.11
25	.24	.23	.23	.22	.22	.21	.21	.20	.20	.20	.20	.19	.18	.18
50	.48	.46	.45	.44	.43	.42	.41	.40	.40	.39	.39	.37	.36	.35
75	.72	.69	.67	.66	.64	.63	.61	.60	.59	.59	.58	.55	.53	.52
100	.95	.92	.90	.87	.85	.83	.82	.80	.79	.78	.77	.73	.71	.69
200	1.90	1.84	1.79	1.74	1.70	1.66	1.63	1.60	1.58	1.55	1.53	1.46	1.41	1.38
300	2.85	2.76	2.68	2.61	2.55	2.49	2.44	2.40	2.36	2.33	2.30	2.18	2.11	2.06
400	3.80	3.68	3.57	3.47	3.39	3.32	3.26	3.20	3.15	3.10	3.06	2.91	2.81	2.75
500	4.75	4.59	4.46	4.34	4.24	4.15	4.07	4.00	3.93	3.87	3.82	3.63	3.51	3.43
600	5.70	5.51	5.35	5.21	5.09	4.98	4.88	4.79	4.72	4.65	4.59	4.36	4.21	4.12
700	6.64	6.43	6.24	6.08	5.93	5.81	5.69	5.59	5.50	5.42	5.35	5.08	4.91	4.81
800	7.59	7.35	7.13	6.94	6.78	6.63	6.51	6.39	6.29	6.20	6.11	5.81	5.61	5.49
900	8.54	8.26	8.02	7.81	7.63	7.46	7.32	7.19	7.07	6.97	6.88	6.53	6.32	6.18
1000	9.49	9.18	8.91	8.68	8.47	8.29	8.13	7.99	7.86	7.74	7.64	7.26	7.02	6.86
2000	18.97	18.36	17.82	17.35	16.94	16.58	16.26	15.97	15.71	15.48	15.28	14.51	14.03	13.72
3000	28.46	27.53	26.73	26.03	25.41	24.87	24.38	23.95	23.57	23.22	22.91	21.76	21.04	20.58
4000	37.94	36.71	35.64	34.70	33.88	33.15	32.51	31.93	31.42	30.96	30.55	29.01	28.05	27.44
5000	47.43	45.89	44.55	43.38	42.35	41.44	40.63	39.92	39.27	38.70	38.18	36.26	35.06	34.30
6000	56.91	55.06	53.45	52.05	50.82	49.73	48.76	47.90	47.13	46.44	45.82	43.51	42.08	41.16
7000	66.40	64.24	62.36	60.72	59.28	58.01	56.88	55.88	54.98	54.18	53.45	50.76	49.09	48.02
8000	75.88	73.41	71.27	69.40	67.75	66.30	65.01	63.86	62.84	61.92	61.09	58.01	56.10	54.88
9000	85.37	82.59	80.18	78.07	76.22	74.59	73.14	71.84	70.69	69.65	68.72	65.26	63.11	61.74
10000	94.85	91.77	89.09	86.75	84.69	82.87	81.26	79.83	78.54	77.39	76.36	72.51	70.12	68.60
11000	104.33	100.94	98.00	95.42	93.16	91.16	89.39	87.81	86.40	85.13	84.00	79.76	77.14	75.46
12000	113.82	110.12	106.90	104.10	101.63	99.45	97.51	95.79	94.25	92.87	91.63	87.01	84.15	82.32
13000	123.30	119.29	115.81	112.77	110.10	107.73	105.64	103.77	102.10	100.61	99.27	94.26	91.16	89.18
14000	132.79	128.47	124.72	121.44	118.56	116.02	113.76	111.75	109.96	108.35	106.90	101.51	98.17	96.04
15000	142.27	137.65	133.63	130.12	127.03	124.31	121.89	119.74	117.81	116.09	114.54	108.77	105.18	102.90
16000	151.76	146.82	142.54	138.79	135.50	132.59	130.01	127.72	125.67	123.83	122.17	116.02	112.20	109.76
17000	161.24	156.00	151.45	147.47	143.97	140.88	138.14	135.70	133.52	131.57	129.81	123.27	119.21	116.62
18000	170.73	165.17	160.35	156.14	152.44	149.17	146.27	143.68	141.37	139.30	137.44	130.52	126.22	123.48
19000	180.21	174.35	169.26	164.81	160.91	157.45	154.39	151.66	149.23	147.04	145.08	137.77	133.23	130.34
20000	189.69	183.53	178.17	173.49	169.37	165.74	162.52	159.65	157.08	154.78	152.72	145.02	140.24	137.19
21000	199.18	192.70	187.08	182.16	177.84	174.03	170.64	167.63	164.94	162.52	160.35	152.27	147.26	144.05
22000	208.66	201.88	195.99	190.84	186.31	182.31	178.77	175.61	172.79	170.26	167.99	159.52	154.27	150.91
23000	218.15	211.05	204.89	199.51	194.78	190.60	186.89	183.59	180.64	178.00	175.62	166.77	161.28	157.77
24000	227.63	220.23	213.80	208.19	203.25	198.89	195.02	191.57	188.50	185.74	183.26	174.02	168.29	164.63
25000	237.12	229.41	222.71	216.86	211.72	207.17	203.15	199.56	196.35	193.48	190.89	181.27	175.30	171.49
26000	246.60	238.58	231.62	225.53	220.19	215.46	211.27	207.54	204.20	201.22	198.53	188.52	182.32	178.35
27000	256.09	247.76	240.53	234.21	228.65	223.75	219.40	215.52	212.06	208.95	206.16	195.77	189.33	185.21
28000	265.57	256.93	249.44	242.88	237.12	232.03	227.52	223.50	219.91	216.69	213.80	203.02	196.34	192.07
29000	275.06	266.11	258.34	251.56	245.59	240.32	235.65	231.49	227.77	224.43	221.44	210.28	203.35	198.93
30000	284.54	275.29	267.25	260.23	254.06	248.61	243.77	239.47	235.62	232.17	229.07	217.53	210.36	205.79
31000	294.02	284.46	276.16	268.90	262.53	256.90	251.90	247.45	243.47	239.91	236.71	224.78	217.38	212.65
32000	303.51	293.64	285.07	277.58	271.00	265.18	260.02	255.43	251.33	247.65	244.34	232.03	224.39	219.51
33000	312.99	302.82	293.98	286.25	279.46	273.47	268.15	263.41	259.18	255.39	251.98	239.28	231.40	226.37
34000	322.48	311.99	302.89	294.93	287.93	281.76	276.27	271.40	267.04	263.13	259.61	246.53	238.41	233.23
35000	331.96	321.17	311.79	303.60	296.40	290.04	284.40	279.38	274.89	270.87	267.25	253.78	245.42	240.09
36000	341.45	330.34	320.70	312.28	304.87	298.33	292.53	287.36	282.74	278.60	274.88	261.03	252.44	246.95
37000	350.93	339.52	329.61	320.95	313.34	306.62	300.65	295.34	290.60	286.34	282.52	268.28	259.45	253.81
38000	360.42	348.70	338.52	329.62	321.81	314.90	308.78	303.32	298.45	294.08	290.16	275.53	266.46	260.67
39000	369.90	357.87	347.43	338.30	330.28	323.19	316.90	311.31	306.30	301.82	297.79	282.78	273.47	267.52
40000	379.38	367.05	356.33	346.97	338.74	331.48	325.03	319.29	314.16	309.56	305.43	290.03	280.48	274.38
41000	388.87	376.22	365.24	355.65	347.21	339.76	333.15	327.27	322.01	317.30	313.06	297.28	287.50	281.24
42000	398.35	385.40	374.15	364.32	355.68	348.05	341.28	335.25	329.87	325.04	320.70	304.53	294.51	288.10
43000	407.84	394.58	383.06	372.99	364.15	356.34	349.41	343.23	337.72	332.78	328.33	311.78	301.52	294.96
44000	417.32	403.75	391.97	381.67	372.62	364.62	357.53	351.22	345.57	340.52	335.97	319.04	308.53	301.82
45000	426.81	412.93	400.88	390.34	381.09	372.91	365.66	359.20	353.43	348.25	343.60	326.29	315.54	308.68
46000	436.29	422.10	409.78	399.02	389.55	381.20	373.78	367.18	361.28	355.99	351.24	333.54	322.56	315.54
47000	445.78	431.28	418.69	407.69	398.02	389.48	381.91	375.16	369.13	363.73	358.88	340.79	329.57	322.40
48000	455.26	440.46	427.60	416.37	406.49	397.77	390.03	383.14	376.99	371.47	366.51	348.04	336.58	329.26
49000	464.75	449.63	436.51	425.04	414.96	406.06	398.16	391.13	384.84	379.21	374.15	355.29	343.59	336.12
50000	474.23	458.81	445.42	433.71	423.43	414.34	406.29	399.11	392.70	386.95	381.78	362.54	350.60	342.98
55000	521.65	504.69	489.96	477.08	465.77	455.78	446.91	439.02	431.97	425.64	419.96	398.79	385.66	377.28
60000	569.07	550.57	534.50	520.46	508.11	497.21	487.54	478.93	471.23	464.34	458.14	435.05	420.72	411.57
65000	616.50	596.45	579.04	563.83	550.46	538.65	528.17	518.84	510.50	503.03	496.32	471.30	455.78	445.87
70000	663.92	642.33	623.58	607.20	592.80	580.08	568.80	558.75	549.77	541.73	534.49	507.55	490.84	480.17
75000	711.34	688.21	668.12	650.57	635.14	621.51	609.43	598.66	589.04	580.42	572.67	543.81	525.90	514.47
80000	758.76	734.09	712.66	693.94	677.48	662.95	650.05	638.57	628.31	619.11	610.85	580.06	560.96	548.76
85000	806.19	779.97	757.21	737.31	719.82	704.38	690.68	678.48	667.58	657.81	649.03	616.31	596.02	583.06
90000	853.61	825.85	801.75	780.68	762.17	745.81	731.31	718.39	706.85	696.50	687.20	652.57	631.08	617.36
95000	901.03	871.73	846.29	824.05	804.51	787.25	771.94	758.30	746.12	735.20	725.38	688.82	666.14	651.66
100000	948.45	917.61	890.83	867.42	846.85	828.68	812.57	798.21	785.39	773.89	763.56	725.07	701.20	685.95

MONTHLY PAYMENT
REQUIRED TO AMORTIZE A LOAN

TERM	1 Year	2 Years	3 Years	4 Years	5 Years	6 Years	7 Years	8 Years	9 Years	10 Years	11 Years	12 Years	13 Years	14 Years
AMOUNT														
5	.44	.23	.16	.13	.11	.09	.08	.08	.07	.07	.06	.06	.06	.05
10	.87	.46	.32	.25	.21	.18	.16	.15	.13	.13	.12	.11	.11	.10
15	1.31	.68	.47	.37	.31	.27	.24	.22	.20	.19	.18	.17	.16	.15
25	2.18	1.13	.79	.61	.51	.44	.39	.36	.33	.31	.29	.27	.26	.25
50	4.35	2.26	1.57	1.22	1.02	.88	.78	.71	.65	.61	.57	.54	.52	.50
75	6.53	3.39	2.35	1.83	1.52	1.32	1.17	1.06	.98	.91	.86	.81	.78	.74
100	8.70	4.52	3.13	2.44	2.03	1.75	1.56	1.41	1.30	1.21	1.14	1.08	1.03	.99
200	17.39	9.04	6.26	4.88	4.05	3.50	3.11	2.82	2.60	2.42	2.28	2.16	2.06	1.98
300	26.09	13.56	9.39	7.31	6.07	5.25	4.67	4.23	3.90	3.63	3.41	3.24	3.09	2.96
400	34.78	18.08	12.52	9.75	8.10	7.00	6.22	5.64	5.19	4.84	4.55	4.31	4.12	3.95
500	43.48	22.60	15.65	12.19	10.12	8.75	7.77	7.05	6.49	6.04	5.69	5.39	5.14	4.93
600	52.17	27.11	18.78	14.62	12.14	10.50	9.33	8.46	7.79	7.25	6.82	6.47	6.17	5.92
700	60.86	31.63	21.91	17.06	14.16	12.24	10.88	9.87	9.08	8.46	7.96	7.54	7.20	6.90
800	69.56	36.15	25.04	19.50	16.19	13.99	12.43	11.27	10.38	9.67	9.09	8.62	8.23	7.89
900	78.25	40.67	28.17	21.93	18.21	15.74	13.99	12.68	11.68	10.88	10.23	9.70	9.25	8.88
1000	86.95	45.19	31.30	24.37	20.23	17.49	15.54	14.09	12.97	12.08	11.37	10.77	10.28	9.86
2000	173.89	90.37	62.59	48.74	40.46	34.97	31.08	28.18	25.94	24.16	22.73	21.54	20.56	19.72
3000	260.83	135.55	93.88	73.10	60.69	52.46	46.61	42.26	38.91	36.24	34.09	32.31	30.83	29.57
4000	347.77	180.73	125.17	97.47	80.92	69.94	62.15	56.35	51.87	48.32	45.45	43.08	41.11	39.43
5000	434.72	225.91	156.46	121.84	101.15	87.43	77.69	70.43	64.84	60.40	56.81	53.85	51.38	49.29
6000	521.66	271.10	187.75	146.20	121.38	104.91	93.22	84.52	77.81	72.48	68.18	64.62	61.66	59.14
7000	608.60	316.28	219.04	170.57	141.60	122.40	108.76	98.61	90.77	84.56	79.54	75.39	71.93	69.00
8000	695.54	361.46	250.33	194.93	161.83	139.88	124.30	112.69	103.74	96.64	90.90	86.16	82.21	78.86
9000	782.48	406.64	281.62	219.30	182.06	157.37	139.83	126.78	116.71	108.72	102.26	96.93	92.48	88.71
10000	869.43	451.82	312.91	243.67	202.29	174.85	155.37	140.86	129.67	120.80	113.62	107.70	102.76	98.57
11000	956.37	497.00	344.20	268.03	222.52	192.33	170.91	154.95	142.64	132.88	124.98	118.47	113.03	108.43
12000	1043.31	542.19	375.49	292.40	242.75	209.82	186.44	169.04	155.61	144.96	136.35	129.24	123.31	118.28
13000	1130.25	587.37	406.78	316.76	262.98	227.30	201.98	183.12	168.58	157.04	147.71	140.01	133.58	128.14
14000	1217.20	632.55	438.07	341.13	283.20	244.79	217.52	197.21	181.54	169.12	159.07	150.78	143.86	138.00
15000	1304.14	677.73	469.36	365.50	303.43	262.27	233.05	211.29	194.51	181.20	170.43	161.55	154.13	147.85
16000	1391.08	722.91	500.65	389.86	323.66	279.76	248.59	225.38	207.48	193.28	181.79	172.32	164.41	157.71
17000	1478.02	768.09	531.94	414.23	343.89	297.24	264.12	239.47	220.44	205.36	193.15	183.09	174.68	167.57
18000	1564.96	813.28	563.23	438.59	364.12	314.73	279.66	253.55	233.41	217.44	204.52	193.86	184.96	177.42
19000	1651.91	858.46	594.52	462.96	384.35	332.21	295.20	267.64	246.38	229.52	215.88	204.63	195.23	187.28
20000	1738.85	903.64	625.81	487.33	404.58	349.69	310.73	281.72	259.34	241.60	227.24	215.40	205.51	197.13
21000	1825.79	948.82	657.10	511.69	424.80	367.18	326.27	295.81	272.31	253.68	238.60	226.17	215.78	206.99
22000	1912.73	994.00	688.39	536.06	445.03	384.66	341.81	309.89	285.28	265.76	249.96	236.94	226.06	216.85
23000	1999.68	1039.18	719.68	560.42	465.26	402.15	357.34	323.98	298.24	277.84	261.32	247.71	236.33	226.70
24000	2086.62	1084.37	750.97	584.79	485.49	419.63	372.88	338.07	311.21	289.92	272.69	258.48	246.61	236.56
25000	2173.56	1129.55	782.26	609.16	505.72	437.12	388.42	352.15	324.18	302.00	284.05	269.25	256.88	246.42
26000	2260.50	1174.73	813.55	633.52	525.95	454.60	403.95	366.24	337.15	314.08	295.41	280.02	267.16	256.27
27000	2347.44	1219.91	844.84	657.89	546.18	472.09	419.49	380.32	350.11	326.16	306.77	290.79	277.43	266.13
28000	2434.39	1265.09	876.13	682.25	566.40	489.57	435.03	394.41	363.08	338.24	318.13	301.56	287.71	275.99
29000	2521.33	1310.27	907.42	706.62	586.63	507.05	450.56	408.50	376.05	350.32	329.49	312.33	297.98	285.84
30000	2608.27	1355.46	938.71	730.99	606.86	524.54	466.10	422.58	389.01	362.40	340.86	323.10	308.26	295.70
31000	2695.21	1400.64	970.00	755.35	627.09	542.02	481.63	436.67	401.98	374.48	352.22	333.87	318.53	305.56
32000	2782.16	1445.82	1001.29	779.72	647.32	559.51	497.17	450.75	414.95	386.56	363.58	344.64	328.81	315.41
33000	2869.10	1491.00	1032.58	804.08	667.55	576.99	512.71	464.84	427.91	398.64	374.94	355.41	339.08	325.27
34000	2956.04	1536.18	1063.87	828.45	687.78	594.48	528.24	478.93	440.88	410.72	386.30	366.18	349.36	335.13
35000	3042.98	1581.36	1095.16	852.82	708.00	611.96	543.78	493.01	453.85	422.80	397.66	376.95	359.63	344.98
36000	3129.92	1626.55	1126.45	877.18	728.23	629.45	559.32	507.10	466.81	434.88	409.03	387.72	369.91	354.84
37000	3216.87	1671.73	1157.74	901.55	748.46	646.93	574.85	521.18	479.78	446.96	420.39	398.49	380.18	364.70
38000	3303.81	1716.91	1189.03	925.91	768.69	664.41	590.39	535.27	492.75	459.04	431.75	409.26	390.46	374.55
39000	3390.75	1762.09	1220.32	950.28	788.92	681.90	605.93	549.36	505.72	471.12	443.11	420.03	400.73	384.41
40000	3477.69	1807.27	1251.62	974.65	809.15	699.38	621.46	563.44	518.68	483.20	454.47	430.80	411.01	394.26
41000	3564.64	1852.45	1282.91	999.01	829.38	716.87	637.00	577.53	531.65	495.28	465.83	441.57	421.28	404.12
42000	3651.58	1897.64	1314.20	1023.38	849.60	734.35	652.54	591.61	544.62	507.36	477.20	452.34	431.56	413.98
43000	3738.52	1942.82	1345.49	1047.74	869.83	751.84	668.07	605.70	557.58	519.44	488.56	463.11	441.83	423.83
44000	3825.46	1988.00	1376.78	1072.11	890.06	769.32	683.61	619.78	570.55	531.52	499.92	473.87	452.11	433.69
45000	3912.41	2033.18	1408.07	1096.48	910.29	786.81	699.14	633.87	583.52	543.60	511.28	484.64	462.38	443.55
46000	3999.35	2078.36	1439.36	1120.84	930.52	804.29	714.68	647.96	596.48	555.68	522.64	495.41	472.66	453.40
47000	4086.29	2123.54	1470.65	1145.21	950.75	821.77	730.22	662.04	609.45	567.76	534.00	506.18	482.93	463.26
48000	4173.23	2168.73	1501.94	1169.57	970.98	839.26	745.75	676.13	622.42	579.84	545.37	516.95	493.21	473.12
49000	4260.17	2213.91	1533.23	1193.94	991.20	856.74	761.29	690.21	635.39	591.92	556.73	527.72	503.48	482.97
50000	4347.11	2259.09	1564.52	1218.31	1011.43	874.23	776.83	704.30	648.35	604.00	568.09	538.49	513.76	492.83
55000	4781.83	2485.00	1720.97	1340.14	1112.58	961.65	854.51	774.73	713.19	664.40	624.90	592.34	565.13	542.11
60000	5216.54	2710.91	1877.42	1461.97	1213.72	1049.07	932.19	845.16	778.02	724.80	681.71	646.19	616.51	591.39
65000	5651.25	2936.82	2033.87	1583.80	1314.86	1136.49	1009.87	915.59	842.86	785.20	738.51	700.04	667.88	640.68
70000	6085.96	3162.72	2190.32	1705.63	1416.00	1223.92	1087.56	986.02	907.69	845.60	795.32	753.89	719.26	689.96
75000	6520.67	3388.63	2346.77	1827.46	1517.15	1311.34	1165.24	1056.45	972.53	906.00	852.13	807.74	770.63	739.24
80000	6955.38	3614.54	2503.23	1949.29	1618.29	1398.76	1242.92	1126.88	1037.36	966.40	908.94	861.59	822.01	788.52
85000	7390.09	3840.45	2659.68	2071.12	1719.43	1486.18	1320.60	1197.31	1102.19	1026.80	965.75	915.44	873.38	837.81
90000	7824.80	4066.36	2816.13	2192.95	1820.58	1573.61	1398.28	1267.74	1167.03	1087.20	1022.56	969.28	924.76	887.09
95000	8259.51	4292.27	2972.58	2314.78	1921.72	1661.03	1475.97	1338.17	1231.86	1147.60	1079.36	1023.13	976.13	936.37
100000	8694.23	4518.17	3129.03	2436.61	2022.86	1748.45	1553.65	1408.60	1296.70	1208.00	1136.17	1076.98	1027.51	985.65

TERM AMOUNT	15 Years	16 Years	17 Years	18 Years	19 Years	20 Years	21 Years	22 Years	23 Years	24 Years	25 Years	30 Years	35 Years	40 Years
5	.05	.05	.05	.05	.05	.05	.05	.04	.04	.04	.04	.04	.04	.04
10	.10	.10	.09	.09	.09	.09	.09	.08	.08	.08	.08	.08	.08	.07
15	.15	.14	.14	.14	.13	.13	.13	.12	.12	.12	.12	.11	.11	.11
25	.24	.23	.23	.22	.22	.21	.21	.20	.20	.20	.20	.19	.18	.18
50	.48	.46	.45	.44	.43	.42	.41	.40	.40	.39	.39	.37	.36	.35
75	.72	.69	.67	.66	.64	.63	.62	.60	.60	.59	.58	.55	.53	.52
100	.95	.92	.90	.87	.85	.84	.82	.80	.79	.78	.77	.73	.71	.69
200	1.90	1.84	1.79	1.74	1.70	1.67	1.63	1.60	1.58	1.56	1.54	1.46	1.41	1.38
300	2.85	2.76	2.68	2.61	2.55	2.50	2.45	2.40	2.37	2.33	2.30	2.19	2.11	2.07
400	3.80	3.68	3.57	3.48	3.40	3.33	3.26	3.20	3.15	3.11	3.07	2.91	2.82	2.76
500	4.75	4.60	4.47	4.35	4.25	4.16	4.08	4.00	3.94	3.88	3.83	3.64	3.52	3.44
600	5.70	5.52	5.36	5.22	5.10	4.99	4.89	4.80	4.73	4.66	4.60	4.37	4.22	4.13
700	6.65	6.44	6.25	6.09	5.94	5.82	5.70	5.60	5.51	5.43	5.36	5.09	4.93	4.82
800	7.60	7.36	7.14	6.96	6.79	6.65	6.52	6.40	6.30	6.21	6.13	5.82	5.63	5.51
900	8.55	8.28	8.04	7.83	7.64	7.48	7.33	7.20	7.09	6.98	6.89	6.55	6.33	6.20
1000	9.50	9.20	8.93	8.69	8.49	8.31	8.15	8.00	7.87	7.76	7.66	7.27	7.04	6.88
2000	19.00	18.39	17.85	17.38	16.97	16.61	16.29	16.00	15.74	15.52	15.31	14.54	14.07	13.76
3000	28.50	27.58	26.77	26.07	25.46	24.91	24.43	24.00	23.61	23.27	22.96	21.81	21.10	20.64
4000	38.00	36.77	35.70	34.76	33.94	33.21	32.57	32.00	31.48	31.03	30.61	29.08	28.13	27.52
5000	47.50	45.96	44.62	43.45	42.42	41.52	40.71	39.99	39.35	38.78	38.27	36.35	35.16	34.40
6000	57.00	55.15	53.54	52.14	50.91	49.82	48.85	47.99	47.22	46.54	45.92	43.61	42.19	41.27
7000	66.50	64.34	62.47	60.83	59.39	58.12	56.99	55.99	55.09	54.29	53.57	50.88	49.22	48.15
8000	76.00	73.53	71.39	69.52	67.87	66.42	65.14	63.99	62.96	62.05	61.22	58.15	56.25	55.03
9000	85.49	82.72	80.31	78.21	76.36	74.73	73.28	71.99	70.83	69.80	68.87	65.42	63.28	61.91
10000	94.99	91.91	89.24	86.90	84.84	83.03	81.42	79.98	78.70	77.56	76.53	72.69	70.31	68.79
11000	104.49	101.10	98.16	95.59	93.33	91.33	89.56	87.98	86.57	85.31	84.18	79.95	77.34	75.67
12000	113.99	110.29	107.08	104.28	101.81	99.63	97.70	95.98	94.44	93.07	91.83	87.22	84.37	82.54
13000	123.49	119.48	116.01	112.97	110.29	107.93	105.84	103.98	102.31	100.82	99.48	94.49	91.40	89.42
14000	132.99	128.67	124.93	121.65	118.78	116.24	113.98	111.98	110.18	108.58	107.13	101.76	98.43	96.30
15000	142.49	137.87	133.85	130.34	127.26	124.54	122.12	119.97	118.05	116.33	114.79	109.03	105.46	103.18
16000	151.99	147.06	142.77	139.03	135.74	132.84	130.27	127.97	125.92	124.09	122.44	116.29	112.49	110.06
17000	161.49	156.25	151.70	147.72	144.23	141.14	138.41	135.97	133.79	131.84	130.09	123.56	119.52	116.93
18000	170.98	165.44	160.62	156.41	152.71	149.45	146.55	143.97	141.66	139.60	137.74	130.83	126.55	123.81
19000	180.48	174.63	169.54	165.10	161.20	157.75	154.69	151.97	149.53	147.35	145.39	138.10	133.58	130.69
20000	189.98	183.82	178.47	173.79	169.68	166.05	162.83	159.96	157.40	155.11	153.05	145.37	140.61	137.57
21000	199.48	193.01	187.39	182.48	178.16	174.35	170.97	167.96	165.27	162.86	160.70	152.63	147.64	144.45
22000	208.98	202.20	196.31	191.17	186.65	182.66	179.11	175.96	173.14	170.62	168.35	159.90	154.67	151.33
23000	218.48	211.39	205.24	199.86	195.13	190.96	187.26	183.96	181.01	178.37	176.00	167.17	161.70	158.20
24000	227.98	220.58	214.16	208.55	203.61	199.26	195.40	191.96	188.88	186.13	183.65	174.44	168.73	165.08
25000	237.48	229.77	223.08	217.24	212.10	207.56	203.54	199.95	196.75	193.88	191.31	181.71	175.76	171.96
26000	246.98	238.96	232.01	225.93	220.58	215.86	211.68	207.95	204.62	201.64	198.96	188.97	182.79	178.84
27000	256.47	248.15	240.93	234.61	229.07	224.17	219.82	215.95	212.49	209.39	206.61	196.24	189.82	185.72
28000	265.97	257.34	249.85	243.30	237.55	232.47	227.96	223.95	220.36	217.15	214.26	203.51	196.85	192.59
29000	275.47	266.53	258.77	251.99	246.03	240.77	236.10	231.95	228.23	224.90	221.91	210.78	203.88	199.47
30000	284.97	275.73	267.70	260.68	254.52	249.07	244.24	239.94	236.10	232.66	229.57	218.05	210.91	206.35
31000	294.47	284.92	276.62	269.37	263.00	257.38	252.39	247.94	243.97	240.42	237.22	225.31	217.94	213.23
32000	303.97	294.11	285.54	278.06	271.48	265.68	260.53	255.94	251.84	248.17	244.87	232.58	224.97	220.11
33000	313.47	303.30	294.47	286.75	279.97	273.98	268.67	263.94	259.71	255.93	252.52	239.85	232.00	226.99
34000	322.97	312.49	303.39	295.44	288.45	282.28	276.81	271.94	267.58	263.68	260.17	247.12	239.03	233.86
35000	332.47	321.68	312.31	304.13	296.94	290.58	284.95	279.93	275.45	271.44	267.83	254.39	246.06	240.74
36000	341.96	330.87	321.24	312.82	305.42	298.89	293.09	287.93	283.32	279.19	275.48	261.65	253.09	247.62
37000	351.46	340.06	330.16	321.51	313.90	307.19	301.23	295.93	291.19	286.95	283.13	268.92	260.12	254.50
38000	360.96	349.25	339.08	330.20	322.39	315.49	309.37	303.93	299.06	294.70	290.78	276.19	267.15	261.38
39000	370.46	358.44	348.01	338.89	330.87	323.79	317.52	311.93	306.93	302.46	298.43	283.46	274.18	268.25
40000	379.96	367.63	356.93	347.57	339.35	332.10	325.66	319.92	314.80	310.21	306.09	290.73	281.21	275.13
41000	389.46	376.82	365.85	356.26	347.84	340.40	333.80	327.92	322.67	317.97	313.74	298.00	288.24	282.01
42000	398.96	386.01	374.77	364.95	356.32	348.70	341.94	335.92	330.54	325.72	321.39	305.26	295.27	288.89
43000	408.46	395.20	383.70	373.64	364.81	357.00	350.08	343.92	338.41	333.48	329.04	312.53	302.30	295.77
44000	417.96	404.39	392.62	382.33	373.29	365.30	358.22	351.92	346.28	341.23	336.69	319.80	309.33	302.65
45000	427.45	413.59	401.54	391.02	381.77	373.61	366.36	359.91	354.15	348.99	344.35	327.07	316.36	309.52
46000	436.95	422.78	410.47	399.71	390.26	381.91	374.51	367.91	362.02	356.74	352.00	334.34	323.39	316.40
47000	446.45	431.97	419.39	408.40	398.74	390.21	382.65	375.91	369.89	364.50	359.65	341.60	330.42	323.28
48000	455.95	441.16	428.31	417.09	407.22	398.51	390.79	383.91	377.76	372.25	367.30	348.87	337.45	330.16
49000	465.45	450.35	437.24	425.78	415.71	406.82	398.93	391.91	385.63	380.01	374.95	356.14	344.48	337.04
50000	474.95	459.54	446.16	434.47	424.19	415.12	407.07	399.90	393.50	387.76	382.61	363.41	351.51	343.91
55000	522.44	505.49	490.77	477.91	466.61	456.63	447.78	439.89	432.85	426.54	420.87	399.75	386.66	378.31
60000	569.94	551.45	535.39	521.36	509.03	498.14	488.48	479.88	472.20	465.32	459.13	436.09	421.81	412.70
65000	617.43	597.40	580.01	564.81	551.45	539.65	529.19	519.87	511.55	504.09	497.39	472.43	456.96	447.09
70000	664.93	643.35	624.62	608.25	593.87	581.16	569.90	559.86	550.90	542.87	535.65	508.77	492.11	481.48
75000	712.42	689.31	669.24	651.70	636.29	622.68	610.60	599.85	590.25	581.64	573.91	545.11	527.26	515.87
80000	759.92	735.26	713.85	695.14	678.70	664.19	651.31	639.84	629.60	620.42	612.17	581.45	562.41	550.26
85000	807.41	781.21	758.47	738.59	721.12	705.70	692.02	679.83	668.95	659.19	650.43	617.79	597.56	584.65
90000	854.90	827.17	803.08	782.04	763.54	747.21	732.72	719.82	708.30	697.97	688.69	654.13	632.71	619.04
95000	902.40	873.12	847.70	825.48	805.96	788.72	773.43	759.81	747.65	736.75	726.95	690.47	667.86	653.43
100000	949.89	919.07	892.31	868.93	848.38	830.23	814.14	799.80	787.00	775.52	765.21	726.81	703.01	687.82

MONTHLY PAYMENT
REQUIRED TO AMORTIZE A LOAN

TERM	1 Year	2 Years	3 Years	4 Years	5 Years	6 Years	7 Years	8 Years	9 Years	10 Years	11 Years	12 Years	13 Years	14 Years
AMOUNT														
5	.44	.23	.16	.13	.11	.09	.08	.08	.07	.07	.06	.06	.06	.05
10	.87	.46	.32	.25	.21	.18	.16	.15	.14	.13	.12	.11	.11	.10
15	1.31	.68	.48	.37	.31	.27	.24	.22	.20	.19	.18	.17	.16	.15
25	2.18	1.14	.79	.62	.51	.44	.39	.36	.33	.31	.29	.28	.26	.25
50	4.35	2.27	1.57	1.23	1.02	.88	.78	.71	.66	.61	.58	.55	.52	.50
75	6.53	3.40	2.36	1.84	1.53	1.32	1.17	1.07	.98	.91	.86	.82	.78	.75
100	8.70	4.53	3.14	2.45	2.03	1.76	1.56	1.42	1.31	1.22	1.15	1.09	1.04	1.00
200	17.40	9.05	6.27	4.89	4.06	3.51	3.12	2.83	2.61	2.43	2.29	2.17	2.07	1.99
300	26.10	13.57	9.41	7.33	6.09	5.26	4.68	4.25	3.91	3.64	3.43	3.25	3.10	2.98
400	34.80	18.10	12.54	9.77	8.12	7.02	6.24	5.66	5.21	4.86	4.57	4.33	4.14	3.97
500	43.50	22.62	15.67	12.21	10.14	8.77	7.80	7.07	6.51	6.07	5.71	5.42	5.17	4.96
600	52.20	27.14	18.81	14.65	12.17	10.52	9.36	8.49	7.82	7.28	6.85	6.50	6.20	5.95
700	60.90	31.66	21.94	17.09	14.20	12.28	10.92	9.90	9.12	8.50	8.00	7.58	7.24	6.94
800	69.60	36.19	25.07	19.54	16.23	14.03	12.47	11.31	10.42	9.71	9.14	8.66	8.27	7.94
900	78.29	40.71	28.21	21.98	18.25	15.78	14.03	12.73	11.72	10.92	10.28	9.75	9.30	8.93
1000	86.99	45.23	31.34	24.42	20.28	17.54	15.59	14.14	13.02	12.14	11.42	10.83	10.34	9.92
2000	173.98	90.46	62.68	48.83	40.56	35.07	31.18	28.28	26.04	24.27	22.84	21.65	20.67	19.83
3000	260.97	135.69	94.01	73.24	60.83	52.60	46.76	42.42	39.06	36.40	34.25	32.48	31.00	29.74
4000	347.96	180.91	125.35	97.66	81.11	70.14	62.35	56.55	52.08	48.54	45.67	43.30	41.33	39.66
5000	434.95	226.14	156.69	122.07	101.39	87.67	77.94	70.69	65.10	60.67	57.08	54.13	51.66	49.57
6000	521.94	271.37	188.02	146.48	121.66	105.20	93.52	84.83	78.12	72.80	68.50	64.95	61.99	59.48
7000	608.92	316.60	219.36	170.90	141.94	122.74	109.11	98.96	91.14	84.93	79.91	75.78	72.32	69.40
8000	695.91	361.82	250.70	195.31	162.22	140.27	124.69	113.10	104.15	97.07	91.33	86.60	82.65	79.31
9000	782.90	407.05	282.03	219.72	182.49	157.80	140.28	127.24	117.17	109.20	102.74	97.43	92.98	89.22
10000	869.89	452.28	313.37	244.13	202.77	175.34	155.87	141.37	130.19	121.33	114.16	108.25	103.31	99.14
11000	956.88	497.51	344.71	268.55	223.05	192.87	171.45	155.51	143.21	133.47	125.57	119.07	113.64	109.05
12000	1043.87	542.73	376.04	292.96	243.32	210.40	187.04	169.65	156.23	145.60	136.99	129.90	123.97	118.96
13000	1130.85	587.96	407.38	317.37	263.60	227.94	202.63	183.78	169.25	157.73	148.41	140.72	134.30	128.88
14000	1217.84	633.19	438.71	341.79	283.87	245.47	218.21	197.92	182.27	169.86	159.82	151.55	144.64	138.79
15000	1304.83	678.41	470.05	366.20	304.15	263.00	233.80	212.06	195.29	182.00	171.24	162.37	154.97	148.70
16000	1391.82	723.64	501.39	390.61	324.43	280.54	249.38	226.19	208.30	194.13	182.65	173.20	165.30	158.62
17000	1478.81	768.87	532.72	415.02	344.70	298.07	264.97	240.33	221.32	206.26	194.07	184.02	175.63	168.53
18000	1565.80	814.10	564.06	439.44	364.98	315.60	280.56	254.47	234.34	218.39	205.48	194.85	185.96	178.44
19000	1652.79	859.32	595.40	463.85	385.26	333.14	296.14	268.60	247.36	230.53	216.90	205.67	196.29	188.36
20000	1739.77	904.55	626.73	488.26	405.53	350.67	311.73	282.74	260.38	242.66	228.31	216.50	206.62	198.27
21000	1826.76	949.78	658.07	512.68	425.81	368.20	327.32	296.88	273.40	254.79	239.73	227.32	216.95	208.18
22000	1913.75	995.01	689.41	537.09	446.09	385.74	342.90	311.01	286.42	266.93	251.14	238.14	227.28	218.10
23000	2000.74	1040.23	720.74	561.50	466.36	403.27	358.49	325.15	299.44	279.06	262.56	248.97	237.61	228.01
24000	2087.73	1085.46	752.08	585.92	486.64	420.80	374.07	339.29	312.45	291.19	273.98	259.79	247.94	237.92
25000	2174.72	1130.69	783.41	610.33	506.91	438.34	389.66	353.42	325.47	303.32	285.39	270.62	258.27	247.83
26000	2261.70	1175.91	814.75	634.74	527.19	455.87	405.25	367.56	338.49	315.46	296.81	281.44	268.60	257.75
27000	2348.69	1221.14	846.09	659.15	547.47	473.40	420.83	381.70	351.51	327.59	308.22	292.27	278.93	267.66
28000	2435.68	1266.37	877.42	683.57	567.74	490.94	436.42	395.83	364.53	339.72	319.64	303.09	289.27	277.57
29000	2522.67	1311.60	908.76	707.98	588.02	508.47	452.01	409.97	377.55	351.86	331.05	313.92	299.60	287.49
30000	2609.66	1356.82	940.10	732.39	608.30	526.00	467.59	424.11	390.57	363.99	342.47	324.74	309.93	297.40
31000	2696.65	1402.05	971.43	756.81	628.57	543.54	483.18	438.24	403.59	376.12	353.88	335.57	320.26	307.31
32000	2783.63	1447.28	1002.77	781.22	648.85	561.07	498.76	452.38	416.60	388.25	365.30	346.39	330.59	317.23
33000	2870.62	1492.51	1034.11	805.63	669.13	578.60	514.35	466.52	429.62	400.39	376.71	357.21	340.92	327.14
34000	2957.61	1537.73	1065.44	830.04	689.40	596.14	529.94	480.65	442.64	412.52	388.13	368.04	351.25	337.05
35000	3044.60	1582.96	1096.78	854.46	709.68	613.67	545.52	494.79	455.66	424.65	399.55	378.86	361.58	346.97
36000	3131.59	1628.19	1128.11	878.87	729.96	631.20	561.11	508.93	468.68	436.78	410.96	389.69	371.91	356.88
37000	3218.58	1673.41	1159.45	903.28	750.23	648.73	576.69	523.06	481.70	448.92	422.38	400.51	382.24	366.79
38000	3305.57	1718.64	1190.79	927.70	770.51	666.27	592.28	537.20	494.72	461.05	433.79	411.34	392.57	376.71
39000	3392.55	1763.87	1222.12	952.11	790.78	683.80	607.87	551.34	507.73	473.18	445.21	422.16	402.90	386.62
40000	3479.54	1809.10	1253.46	976.52	811.06	701.33	623.45	565.47	520.75	485.32	456.62	432.99	413.23	396.53
41000	3566.53	1854.32	1284.80	1000.93	831.34	718.87	639.04	579.61	533.77	497.45	468.04	443.81	423.57	406.45
42000	3653.52	1899.55	1316.13	1025.35	851.61	736.40	654.63	593.75	546.79	509.58	479.45	454.64	433.90	416.36
43000	3740.51	1944.78	1347.47	1049.76	871.89	753.93	670.21	607.88	559.81	521.71	490.87	465.46	444.23	426.27
44000	3827.50	1990.01	1378.81	1074.17	892.17	771.47	685.80	622.02	572.83	533.85	502.28	476.28	454.56	436.19
45000	3914.48	2035.23	1410.14	1098.59	912.44	789.00	701.38	636.16	585.85	545.98	513.70	487.11	464.89	446.10
46000	4001.47	2080.46	1441.48	1123.00	932.72	806.53	716.97	650.29	598.87	558.11	525.12	497.93	475.22	456.01
47000	4088.46	2125.69	1472.81	1147.41	953.00	824.07	732.56	664.43	611.88	570.24	536.53	508.76	485.55	465.92
48000	4175.45	2170.92	1504.15	1171.83	973.27	841.60	748.14	678.57	624.90	582.38	547.95	519.58	495.88	475.84
49000	4262.44	2216.14	1535.49	1196.24	993.55	859.13	763.73	692.70	637.92	594.51	559.36	530.41	506.21	485.75
50000	4349.43	2261.37	1566.82	1220.65	1013.82	876.67	779.32	706.84	650.94	606.64	570.78	541.23	516.54	495.66
55000	4784.37	2487.51	1723.51	1342.72	1115.21	964.33	857.25	777.52	716.03	667.31	627.85	595.35	568.20	545.23
60000	5219.31	2713.64	1880.19	1464.78	1216.59	1052.00	935.18	848.21	781.13	727.97	684.93	649.48	619.85	594.80
65000	5654.25	2939.78	2036.87	1586.84	1317.97	1139.67	1013.11	918.89	846.22	788.63	742.01	703.60	671.50	644.36
70000	6089.20	3165.92	2193.55	1708.91	1419.35	1227.33	1091.04	989.57	911.32	849.30	799.09	757.72	723.16	693.93
75000	6524.14	3392.05	2350.23	1830.97	1520.73	1315.00	1168.97	1060.26	976.41	909.96	856.16	811.84	774.81	743.49
80000	6959.08	3618.19	2506.91	1953.04	1622.12	1402.66	1246.90	1130.94	1041.50	970.63	913.24	865.97	826.46	793.06
85000	7394.02	3844.32	2663.60	2075.10	1723.50	1490.33	1324.83	1201.62	1106.60	1031.29	970.32	920.09	878.12	842.63
90000	7828.96	4070.46	2820.28	2197.17	1824.88	1577.99	1402.76	1272.31	1171.69	1091.95	1027.40	974.21	929.77	892.19
95000	8263.91	4296.60	2976.96	2319.23	1926.26	1665.66	1480.70	1342.99	1236.78	1152.62	1084.47	1028.33	981.43	941.76
100000	8698.85	4522.73	3133.64	2441.30	2027.64	1753.33	1558.63	1413.67	1301.88	1213.28	1141.55	1082.46	1033.08	991.32

TERM	15 Years	16 Years	17 Years	18 Years	19 Years	20 Years	21 Years	22 Years	23 Years	24 Years	25 Years	30 Years	35 Years	40 Years
AMOUNT														
5	.05	.05	.05	.05	.05	.05	.05	.05	.04	.04	.04	.04	.04	.04
10	.10	.10	.09	.09	.09	.09	.09	.09	.08	.08	.08	.08	.08	.07
15	.15	.14	.14	.14	.13	.13	.13	.13	.12	.12	.12	.12	.11	.11
25	.24	.24	.23	.22	.22	.21	.21	.21	.20	.20	.20	.19	.18	.18
50	.48	.47	.45	.44	.43	.42	.42	.41	.40	.40	.39	.37	.36	.35
75	.72	.70	.68	.66	.65	.63	.62	.61	.60	.59	.58	.56	.54	.53
100	.96	.93	.90	.88	.86	.84	.83	.81	.80	.79	.78	.74	.72	.70
200	1.92	1.85	1.80	1.75	1.71	1.68	1.65	1.62	1.59	1.57	1.55	1.47	1.43	1.40
300	2.87	2.78	2.70	2.63	2.57	2.51	2.47	2.42	2.39	2.35	2.32	2.21	2.14	2.09
400	3.83	3.70	3.60	3.50	3.42	3.35	3.29	3.23	3.18	3.13	3.09	2.94	2.85	2.79
500	4.78	4.63	4.50	4.38	4.28	4.19	4.11	4.04	3.97	3.92	3.86	3.67	3.56	3.48
600	5.74	5.55	5.39	5.25	5.13	5.02	4.93	4.84	4.77	4.70	4.64	4.41	4.27	4.18
700	6.69	6.48	6.29	6.13	5.99	5.86	5.75	5.65	5.56	5.48	5.41	5.14	4.98	4.87
800	7.65	7.40	7.19	7.00	6.84	6.70	6.57	6.45	6.35	6.26	6.18	5.88	5.69	5.57
900	8.61	8.33	8.09	7.88	7.70	7.53	7.39	7.26	7.15	7.04	6.95	6.61	6.40	6.26
1000	9.56	9.25	8.99	8.75	8.55	8.37	8.21	8.07	7.94	7.83	7.72	7.34	7.11	6.96
2000	19.12	18.50	17.97	17.50	17.10	16.73	16.41	16.13	15.87	15.65	15.44	14.68	14.21	13.91
3000	28.67	27.75	26.95	26.25	25.64	25.10	24.62	24.19	23.81	23.47	23.16	22.02	21.31	20.86
4000	38.23	37.00	35.94	35.00	34.19	33.46	32.82	32.25	31.74	31.29	30.88	29.36	28.42	27.82
5000	47.79	46.25	44.92	43.75	42.73	41.83	41.03	40.31	39.68	39.11	38.60	36.69	35.52	34.77
6000	57.34	55.50	53.90	52.50	51.28	50.19	49.23	48.38	47.61	46.93	46.31	44.03	42.62	41.72
7000	66.90	64.75	62.88	61.25	59.82	58.56	57.43	56.44	55.55	54.75	54.03	51.37	49.72	48.68
8000	76.46	74.00	71.87	70.00	68.37	66.92	65.64	64.50	63.48	62.57	61.75	58.71	56.83	55.63
9000	86.01	83.25	80.85	78.75	76.91	75.28	73.84	72.56	71.42	70.39	69.47	66.04	63.93	62.58
10000	95.57	92.50	89.83	87.50	85.46	83.65	82.05	80.62	79.35	78.21	77.19	73.38	71.03	69.54
11000	105.13	101.75	98.81	96.25	94.00	92.01	90.25	88.68	87.28	86.03	84.90	80.72	78.13	76.49
12000	114.68	111.00	107.80	105.00	102.55	100.38	98.46	96.75	95.22	93.85	92.62	88.06	85.24	83.44
13000	124.24	120.25	116.78	113.75	111.09	108.74	106.66	104.81	103.15	101.67	100.34	95.39	92.34	90.40
14000	133.80	129.49	125.76	122.50	119.64	117.11	114.86	112.87	111.09	109.49	108.06	102.73	99.44	97.35
15000	143.35	138.74	134.74	131.25	128.18	125.47	123.07	120.93	119.02	117.31	115.78	110.07	106.54	104.30
16000	152.91	147.99	143.73	140.00	136.73	133.84	131.27	128.99	126.96	125.13	123.50	117.41	113.65	111.25
17000	162.47	157.24	152.71	148.75	145.27	142.20	139.48	137.06	134.89	132.95	131.21	124.74	120.75	118.21
18000	172.02	166.49	161.69	157.50	153.82	150.56	147.68	145.12	142.83	140.77	138.93	132.08	127.85	125.16
19000	181.58	175.74	170.67	166.25	162.36	158.93	155.89	153.18	150.76	148.60	146.65	139.42	134.95	132.11
20000	191.14	184.99	179.66	175.00	170.91	167.29	164.09	161.24	158.70	156.42	154.37	146.76	142.06	139.07
21000	200.69	194.24	188.64	183.75	179.45	175.66	172.29	169.30	166.63	164.24	162.09	154.10	149.16	146.02
22000	210.25	203.49	197.62	192.50	188.00	184.02	180.50	177.36	174.56	172.06	169.80	161.43	156.26	152.97
23000	219.80	212.74	206.60	201.25	196.54	192.39	188.70	185.43	182.50	179.88	177.52	168.77	163.37	159.93
24000	229.36	221.99	215.59	210.00	205.09	200.75	196.91	193.49	190.43	187.70	185.24	176.11	170.47	166.88
25000	238.92	231.24	224.57	218.75	213.63	209.12	205.11	201.55	198.37	195.52	192.96	183.45	177.57	173.83
26000	248.47	240.49	233.55	227.50	222.18	217.48	213.32	209.61	206.30	203.34	200.68	190.78	184.67	180.79
27000	258.03	249.73	242.53	236.24	230.72	225.84	221.52	217.67	214.24	211.16	208.40	198.12	191.78	187.74
28000	267.59	258.98	251.52	244.99	239.27	234.21	229.72	225.73	222.17	218.98	216.11	205.46	198.88	194.69
29000	277.14	268.23	260.50	253.74	247.81	242.57	237.93	233.80	230.11	226.80	223.83	212.80	205.98	201.65
30000	286.70	277.48	269.48	262.49	256.36	250.94	246.13	241.86	238.04	234.62	231.55	220.13	213.08	208.60
31000	296.26	286.73	278.46	271.24	264.90	259.30	254.34	249.92	245.98	242.44	239.27	227.47	220.19	215.55
32000	305.81	295.98	287.45	279.99	273.45	267.67	262.54	257.98	253.91	250.26	246.99	234.81	227.29	222.50
33000	315.37	305.23	296.43	288.74	281.99	276.03	270.75	266.04	261.84	258.08	254.70	242.15	234.39	229.46
34000	324.93	314.48	305.41	297.49	290.54	284.39	278.95	274.11	269.78	265.90	262.42	249.48	241.49	236.41
35000	334.48	323.73	314.39	306.24	299.08	292.76	287.15	282.17	277.71	273.72	270.14	256.82	248.60	243.36
36000	344.04	332.98	323.38	314.99	307.63	301.12	295.36	290.23	285.65	281.54	277.86	264.16	255.70	250.32
37000	353.60	342.23	332.36	323.74	316.17	309.49	303.56	298.29	293.58	289.37	285.58	271.50	262.80	257.27
38000	363.15	351.48	341.34	332.49	324.72	317.85	311.77	306.35	301.52	297.19	293.30	278.84	269.90	264.22
39000	372.71	360.73	350.33	341.24	333.26	326.22	319.97	314.41	309.45	305.01	301.01	286.17	277.01	271.18
40000	382.27	369.98	359.31	349.99	341.81	334.58	328.18	322.48	317.39	312.83	308.73	293.51	284.11	278.13
41000	391.82	379.22	368.29	358.74	350.35	342.95	336.38	330.54	325.32	320.65	316.45	300.85	291.21	285.08
42000	401.38	388.47	377.27	367.49	358.90	351.31	344.58	338.60	333.26	328.47	324.17	308.19	298.31	292.04
43000	410.94	397.72	386.26	376.24	367.44	359.67	352.79	346.66	341.19	336.29	331.89	315.52	305.42	298.99
44000	420.49	406.97	395.24	384.99	375.99	368.04	360.99	354.72	349.12	344.11	339.60	322.86	312.52	305.94
45000	430.05	416.22	404.22	393.74	384.53	376.40	369.20	362.79	357.06	351.93	347.32	330.20	319.62	312.90
46000	439.60	425.47	413.20	402.49	393.08	384.77	377.40	370.85	364.99	359.75	355.04	337.54	326.73	319.85
47000	449.16	434.72	422.19	411.24	401.62	393.13	385.61	378.91	372.93	367.57	362.76	344.87	333.83	326.80
48000	458.72	443.97	431.17	419.99	410.17	401.50	393.81	386.97	380.86	375.39	370.48	352.21	340.93	333.75
49000	468.27	453.22	440.15	428.74	418.71	409.86	402.01	395.03	388.80	383.21	378.19	359.55	348.03	340.71
50000	477.83	462.47	449.13	437.49	427.26	418.23	410.22	403.09	396.73	391.03	385.91	366.89	355.14	347.66
55000	525.61	508.71	494.05	481.23	469.98	460.05	451.24	443.40	436.40	430.13	424.50	403.58	390.65	382.43
60000	573.40	554.96	538.96	524.98	512.71	501.87	492.26	483.71	476.08	469.24	463.09	440.26	426.16	417.19
65000	621.18	601.21	583.87	568.73	555.43	543.69	533.28	524.02	515.75	508.34	501.69	476.95	461.67	451.96
70000	668.96	647.45	628.78	612.48	598.16	585.51	574.30	564.33	555.42	547.44	540.28	513.64	497.19	486.72
75000	716.74	693.70	673.70	656.23	640.88	627.34	615.33	604.64	595.09	586.55	578.87	550.33	532.70	521.49
80000	764.53	739.95	718.61	699.98	683.61	669.16	656.35	644.95	634.77	625.65	617.46	587.02	568.21	556.25
85000	812.31	786.19	763.52	743.72	726.33	710.98	697.37	685.26	674.44	664.75	656.05	623.70	603.73	591.02
90000	860.09	832.44	808.44	787.47	769.06	752.80	738.39	725.57	714.11	703.85	694.64	660.39	639.24	625.79
95000	907.87	878.68	853.35	831.22	811.78	794.62	779.41	765.87	753.78	742.96	733.23	697.08	674.75	660.55
100000	955.66	924.93	898.26	874.97	854.51	836.45	820.43	806.18	793.46	782.06	771.82	733.77	710.27	695.32

MONTHLY PAYMENT
REQUIRED TO AMORTIZE A LOAN

TERM AMOUNT	1 Year	2 Years	3 Years	4 Years	5 Years	6 Years	7 Years	8 Years	9 Years	10 Years	11 Years	12 Years	13 Years	14 Years
5	.44	.23	.16	.13	.11	.09	.08	.08	.07	.07	.06	.06	.06	.05
10	.88	.46	.32	.25	.21	.18	.16	.15	.14	.13	.12	.11	.11	.10
15	1.31	.68	.48	.37	.31	.27	.24	.22	.20	.19	.18	.17	.16	.15
25	2.18	1.14	.79	.62	.51	.44	.40	.36	.33	.31	.29	.28	.26	.25
50	4.36	2.27	1.57	1.23	1.02	.88	.79	.71	.66	.61	.58	.55	.52	.50
75	6.53	3.40	2.36	1.84	1.53	1.32	1.18	1.07	.99	.92	.87	.82	.78	.75
100	8.71	4.53	3.14	2.45	2.04	1.76	1.57	1.42	1.31	1.22	1.15	1.09	1.04	1.00
200	17.41	9.06	6.28	4.90	4.07	3.52	3.13	2.84	2.62	2.44	2.30	2.18	2.08	2.00
300	26.12	13.59	9.42	7.34	6.10	5.28	4.70	4.26	3.93	3.66	3.45	3.27	3.12	3.00
400	34.82	18.11	12.56	9.79	8.13	7.04	6.26	5.68	5.23	4.88	4.59	4.36	4.16	3.99
500	43.52	22.64	15.70	12.23	10.17	8.80	7.82	7.10	6.54	6.10	5.74	5.44	5.20	4.99
600	52.23	27.17	18.83	14.68	12.20	10.55	9.39	8.52	7.85	7.32	6.89	6.53	6.24	5.99
700	60.93	31.70	21.97	17.13	14.23	12.31	10.95	9.94	9.15	8.53	8.03	7.62	7.28	6.98
800	69.63	36.22	25.11	19.57	16.26	14.07	12.51	11.36	10.46	9.75	9.18	8.71	8.31	7.98
900	78.34	40.75	28.25	22.02	18.30	15.83	14.08	12.77	11.77	10.97	10.33	9.80	9.35	8.98
1000	87.04	45.28	31.39	24.46	20.33	17.59	15.64	14.19	13.08	12.19	11.47	10.88	10.39	9.98
2000	174.07	90.55	62.77	48.92	40.65	35.17	31.28	28.38	26.15	24.38	22.94	21.76	20.78	19.95
3000	261.11	135.82	94.15	73.38	60.98	52.75	46.91	42.57	39.22	36.56	34.41	32.64	31.16	29.92
4000	348.14	181.10	125.54	97.84	81.30	70.33	62.55	56.76	52.29	48.75	45.88	43.52	41.55	39.89
5000	435.18	226.37	156.92	122.30	101.63	87.92	78.19	70.94	65.36	60.93	57.35	54.40	51.94	49.86
6000	522.21	271.64	188.30	146.76	121.95	105.50	93.82	85.13	78.43	73.12	68.82	65.28	62.32	59.83
7000	609.25	316.92	219.68	171.22	142.28	123.08	109.46	99.32	91.50	85.30	80.29	76.16	72.71	69.80
8000	696.28	362.19	251.07	195.68	162.60	140.66	125.09	113.51	104.57	97.49	91.76	87.04	83.10	79.77
9000	783.32	407.46	282.45	220.14	182.92	158.24	140.73	127.69	117.64	109.68	103.23	97.92	93.48	89.74
10000	870.35	452.73	313.83	244.60	203.25	175.83	156.37	141.88	130.71	121.86	114.70	108.80	103.87	99.71
11000	957.39	498.01	345.21	269.06	223.57	193.41	172.00	156.07	143.78	134.05	126.17	119.68	114.26	109.68
12000	1044.42	543.28	376.60	293.52	243.90	210.99	187.64	170.26	156.85	146.23	137.64	130.56	124.64	119.65
13000	1131.46	588.55	407.98	317.98	264.22	228.57	203.27	184.44	169.92	158.42	149.11	141.44	135.03	129.62
14000	1218.49	633.83	439.36	342.44	284.55	246.15	218.91	198.63	182.99	170.60	160.58	152.32	145.42	139.59
15000	1305.53	679.10	470.74	366.90	304.87	263.74	234.55	212.82	196.06	182.79	172.05	163.20	155.80	149.56
16000	1392.56	724.37	502.13	391.36	325.19	281.32	250.18	227.01	209.13	194.98	183.51	174.08	166.19	159.53
17000	1479.59	769.64	533.51	415.82	345.52	298.90	265.82	241.19	222.21	207.16	194.98	184.96	176.58	169.50
18000	1566.63	814.92	564.89	440.28	365.84	316.48	281.45	255.38	235.28	219.35	206.45	195.83	186.96	179.47
19000	1653.66	860.19	596.27	464.74	386.17	334.07	297.09	269.57	248.35	231.53	217.92	206.71	197.35	189.44
20000	1740.70	905.46	627.66	489.20	406.49	351.65	312.73	283.76	261.42	243.72	229.39	217.59	207.74	199.41
21000	1827.73	950.74	659.04	513.66	426.82	369.23	328.36	297.94	274.49	255.90	240.86	228.47	218.12	209.38
22000	1914.77	996.01	690.42	538.12	447.14	386.81	344.00	312.13	287.56	268.09	252.33	239.35	228.51	219.35
23000	2001.80	1041.28	721.80	562.58	467.46	404.39	359.63	326.32	300.63	280.28	263.80	250.23	238.90	229.32
24000	2088.84	1086.55	753.19	587.04	487.79	421.98	375.27	340.51	313.70	292.46	275.27	261.11	249.28	239.29
25000	2175.87	1131.83	784.57	611.50	508.11	439.56	390.91	354.69	326.77	304.65	286.74	271.99	259.67	249.26
26000	2262.91	1177.10	815.95	635.96	528.44	457.14	406.54	368.88	339.84	316.83	298.21	282.87	270.06	259.23
27000	2349.94	1222.37	847.33	660.42	548.76	474.72	422.18	383.07	352.91	329.02	309.68	293.75	280.44	269.20
28000	2436.98	1267.65	878.72	684.88	569.09	492.30	437.82	397.26	365.98	341.20	321.15	304.63	290.83	279.17
29000	2524.01	1312.92	910.10	709.34	589.41	509.89	453.45	411.44	379.05	353.39	332.62	315.51	301.22	289.14
30000	2611.05	1358.19	941.48	733.80	609.73	527.47	469.09	425.63	392.12	365.57	344.09	326.39	311.60	299.11
31000	2698.08	1403.47	972.86	758.26	630.06	545.05	484.72	439.82	405.19	377.76	355.56	337.27	321.99	309.08
32000	2785.11	1448.74	1004.25	782.72	650.38	562.63	500.36	454.01	418.26	389.95	367.02	348.15	332.38	319.05
33000	2872.15	1494.01	1035.63	807.18	670.71	580.21	516.00	468.19	431.34	402.13	378.49	359.03	342.76	329.02
34000	2959.18	1539.28	1067.01	831.64	691.03	597.80	531.63	482.38	444.41	414.32	389.96	369.91	353.15	338.99
35000	3046.22	1584.56	1098.39	856.10	711.36	615.38	547.27	496.57	457.48	426.50	401.43	380.79	363.54	348.96
36000	3133.25	1629.83	1129.78	880.56	731.68	632.96	562.90	510.76	470.55	438.69	412.90	391.66	373.92	358.93
37000	3220.29	1675.10	1161.16	905.02	752.00	650.54	578.54	524.94	483.62	450.87	424.37	402.54	384.31	368.90
38000	3307.32	1720.38	1192.54	929.48	772.33	668.13	594.18	539.13	496.69	463.06	435.84	413.42	394.70	378.87
39000	3394.36	1765.65	1223.92	953.94	792.65	685.71	609.81	553.32	509.76	475.25	447.31	424.30	405.08	388.84
40000	3481.39	1810.92	1255.31	978.40	812.98	703.29	625.45	567.51	522.83	487.43	458.78	435.18	415.47	398.81
41000	3568.43	1856.19	1286.69	1002.86	833.30	720.87	641.08	581.69	535.90	499.62	470.25	446.06	425.86	408.78
42000	3655.46	1901.47	1318.07	1027.32	853.63	738.45	656.72	595.88	548.97	511.80	481.72	456.94	436.24	418.75
43000	3742.50	1946.74	1349.45	1051.78	873.95	756.04	672.36	610.07	562.04	523.99	493.19	467.82	446.63	428.72
44000	3829.53	1992.01	1380.84	1076.24	894.27	773.62	687.99	624.26	575.11	536.17	504.66	478.70	457.02	438.69
45000	3916.57	2037.29	1412.22	1100.70	914.60	791.20	703.63	638.45	588.18	548.36	516.13	489.58	467.40	448.66
46000	4003.60	2082.56	1443.60	1125.16	934.92	808.78	719.26	652.63	601.25	560.55	527.60	500.46	477.79	458.63
47000	4090.63	2127.83	1474.98	1149.62	955.25	826.36	734.90	666.82	614.32	572.73	539.06	511.34	488.18	468.60
48000	4177.67	2173.10	1506.37	1174.08	975.57	843.95	750.54	681.01	627.39	584.92	550.53	522.22	498.56	478.57
49000	4264.70	2218.38	1537.75	1198.54	995.90	861.53	766.17	695.20	640.46	597.10	562.00	533.10	508.95	488.54
50000	4351.74	2263.65	1569.13	1223.00	1016.22	879.11	781.81	709.38	653.54	609.29	573.47	543.98	519.34	498.51
55000	4786.91	2490.02	1726.04	1345.30	1117.84	967.02	859.99	780.32	718.89	670.22	630.82	598.37	571.27	548.36
60000	5222.09	2716.38	1882.96	1467.60	1219.46	1054.93	938.17	851.26	784.24	731.14	688.17	652.77	623.20	598.21
65000	5657.26	2942.74	2039.87	1589.90	1321.08	1142.84	1016.35	922.20	849.59	792.07	745.51	707.17	675.14	648.06
70000	6092.43	3169.11	2196.78	1712.20	1422.71	1230.75	1094.53	993.13	914.95	853.00	802.86	761.57	727.07	697.91
75000	6527.61	3395.47	2353.69	1834.50	1524.33	1318.66	1172.71	1064.07	980.30	913.93	860.21	815.96	779.00	747.76
80000	6962.78	3621.84	2510.61	1956.80	1625.95	1406.57	1250.89	1135.01	1045.65	974.86	917.55	870.36	830.94	797.61
85000	7397.95	3848.20	2667.52	2079.10	1727.57	1494.48	1329.07	1205.95	1111.01	1035.79	974.90	924.76	882.87	847.46
90000	7833.13	4074.57	2824.43	2201.40	1829.19	1582.39	1407.25	1276.89	1176.36	1096.71	1032.25	979.15	934.80	897.31
95000	8268.30	4300.93	2981.34	2323.69	1930.81	1670.31	1485.43	1347.82	1241.71	1157.64	1089.59	1033.55	986.73	947.16
100000	8703.47	4527.30	3138.26	2445.99	2032.43	1758.22	1563.61	1418.76	1307.07	1218.57	1146.94	1087.95	1038.67	997.01

TERM	15 Years	16 Years	17 Years	18 Years	19 Years	20 Years	21 Years	22 Years	23 Years	24 Years	25 Years	30 Years	35 Years	40 Years
AMOUNT														
5	.05	.05	.05	.05	.05	.05	.05	.05	.04	.04	.04	.04	.04	.04
10	.10	.10	.10	.09	.09	.09	.09	.09	.08	.08	.08	.08	.08	.08
15	.15	.14	.14	.14	.13	.13	.13	.13	.12	.12	.12	.12	.11	.11
25	.25	.24	.23	.23	.22	.22	.21	.21	.20	.20	.20	.19	.18	.18
50	.49	.47	.46	.45	.44	.43	.42	.41	.40	.40	.39	.38	.36	.36
75	.73	.70	.68	.67	.65	.64	.63	.61	.60	.60	.59	.56	.54	.53
100	.97	.94	.91	.89	.87	.85	.83	.82	.80	.79	.78	.75	.72	.71
200	1.93	1.87	1.81	1.77	1.73	1.69	1.66	1.63	1.60	1.58	1.56	1.49	1.44	1.41
300	2.89	2.80	2.72	2.65	2.59	2.53	2.49	2.44	2.40	2.37	2.34	2.23	2.16	2.11
400	3.85	3.73	3.62	3.53	3.45	3.38	3.31	3.26	3.20	3.16	3.12	2.97	2.88	2.82
500	4.81	4.66	4.53	4.41	4.31	4.22	4.14	4.07	4.00	3.95	3.90	3.71	3.59	3.52
600	5.77	5.59	5.43	5.29	5.17	5.06	4.97	4.88	4.80	4.74	4.68	4.45	4.31	4.22
700	6.74	6.52	6.33	6.17	6.03	5.90	5.79	5.69	5.60	5.53	5.45	5.19	5.03	4.92
800	7.70	7.45	7.24	7.05	6.89	6.75	6.62	6.51	6.40	6.31	6.23	5.93	5.75	5.63
900	8.66	8.38	8.14	7.93	7.75	7.59	7.45	7.32	7.20	7.10	7.01	6.67	6.46	6.33
1000	9.62	9.31	9.05	8.82	8.61	8.43	8.27	8.13	8.00	7.89	7.79	7.41	7.18	7.03
2000	19.23	18.62	18.09	17.63	17.22	16.86	16.54	16.26	16.00	15.78	15.57	14.82	14.36	14.06
3000	28.85	27.93	27.13	26.44	25.82	25.29	24.81	24.38	24.00	23.66	23.36	22.23	21.53	21.09
4000	38.46	37.24	36.17	35.25	34.43	33.71	33.07	32.51	32.00	31.55	31.14	29.63	28.71	28.12
5000	48.08	46.55	45.22	44.06	43.04	42.14	41.34	40.63	40.00	39.44	38.93	37.04	35.88	35.15
6000	57.69	55.85	54.26	52.87	51.64	50.57	49.61	48.76	48.00	47.32	46.71	44.45	43.06	42.17
7000	67.31	65.16	63.30	61.68	60.25	58.99	57.88	56.89	56.00	55.21	54.50	51.86	50.23	49.20
8000	76.92	74.47	72.34	70.49	68.86	67.42	66.14	65.01	64.00	63.09	62.28	59.26	57.41	56.23
9000	86.53	83.78	81.39	79.30	77.46	75.85	74.41	73.14	72.00	70.98	70.07	66.67	64.58	63.26
10000	96.15	93.09	90.43	88.11	86.07	84.27	82.68	81.26	80.00	78.87	77.85	74.08	71.76	70.29
11000	105.76	102.39	99.47	96.92	94.68	92.70	90.95	89.39	88.00	86.75	85.63	81.49	78.93	77.32
12000	115.38	111.70	108.51	105.73	103.28	101.13	99.21	97.51	96.00	94.64	93.42	88.89	86.11	84.34
13000	124.99	121.01	117.55	114.54	111.89	109.55	107.48	105.64	104.00	102.52	101.20	96.30	93.28	91.37
14000	134.61	130.32	126.60	123.35	120.50	117.98	115.75	113.77	112.00	110.41	108.99	103.71	100.46	98.40
15000	144.22	139.63	135.64	132.16	129.10	126.41	124.02	121.89	120.00	118.30	116.77	111.12	107.64	105.43
16000	153.83	148.93	144.68	140.97	137.71	134.83	132.28	130.02	127.99	126.18	124.56	118.52	114.81	112.46
17000	163.45	158.24	153.72	149.78	146.32	143.26	140.55	138.14	135.99	134.07	132.34	125.93	121.99	119.49
18000	173.06	167.55	162.77	158.59	154.92	151.69	148.82	146.27	143.99	141.96	140.13	133.34	129.16	126.51
19000	182.68	176.86	171.81	167.40	163.53	160.11	157.09	154.40	151.99	149.84	147.91	140.75	136.34	133.54
20000	192.29	186.17	180.85	176.21	172.13	168.54	165.35	162.52	159.99	157.73	155.70	148.15	143.51	140.57
21000	201.91	195.47	189.89	185.02	180.74	176.97	173.62	170.65	167.99	165.61	163.48	155.56	150.69	147.60
22000	211.52	204.78	198.93	193.83	189.35	185.39	181.89	178.77	175.99	173.50	171.26	162.97	157.86	154.63
23000	221.13	214.09	207.98	202.64	197.95	193.82	190.16	186.90	183.99	181.39	179.05	170.38	165.04	161.66
24000	230.75	223.40	217.02	211.45	206.56	202.25	198.42	195.02	191.99	189.27	186.83	177.78	172.21	168.68
25000	240.36	232.71	226.06	220.26	215.17	210.67	206.69	203.15	199.99	197.16	194.62	185.19	179.39	175.71
26000	249.98	242.01	235.10	229.07	223.77	219.10	214.96	211.28	207.99	205.04	202.40	192.60	186.56	182.74
27000	259.59	251.32	244.15	237.88	232.38	227.53	223.23	219.40	215.99	212.93	210.19	200.01	193.74	189.77
28000	269.21	260.63	253.19	246.69	240.99	235.95	231.49	227.53	223.99	220.82	217.97	207.41	200.92	196.80
29000	278.82	269.94	262.23	255.50	249.59	244.38	239.76	235.65	231.99	228.70	225.76	214.82	208.09	203.82
30000	288.44	279.25	271.27	264.31	258.20	252.81	248.03	243.78	239.99	236.59	233.54	222.23	215.27	210.85
31000	298.05	288.55	280.31	273.12	266.81	261.23	256.30	251.90	247.98	244.48	241.33	229.64	222.44	217.88
32000	307.66	297.86	289.36	281.93	275.41	269.66	264.56	260.03	255.98	252.36	249.11	237.04	229.62	224.91
33000	317.28	307.17	298.40	290.74	284.02	278.09	272.83	268.16	263.98	260.25	256.89	244.45	236.79	231.94
34000	326.89	316.48	307.44	299.55	292.63	286.51	281.10	276.28	271.98	268.13	264.68	251.86	243.97	238.97
35000	336.51	325.79	316.48	308.36	301.23	294.94	289.37	284.41	279.98	276.02	272.46	259.27	251.14	245.99
36000	346.12	335.09	325.53	317.17	309.84	303.37	297.63	292.53	287.98	283.91	280.25	266.67	258.32	253.02
37000	355.74	344.40	334.57	325.98	318.45	311.79	305.90	300.66	295.98	291.79	288.03	274.08	265.49	260.05
38000	365.35	353.71	343.61	334.79	327.05	320.22	314.17	308.79	303.98	299.68	295.82	281.49	272.67	267.08
39000	374.96	363.02	352.65	343.60	335.66	328.65	322.44	316.91	311.98	307.56	303.60	288.90	279.84	274.11
40000	384.58	372.33	361.70	352.41	344.26	337.07	330.70	325.04	319.98	315.45	311.39	296.30	287.02	281.14
41000	394.19	381.63	370.74	361.22	352.87	345.50	338.97	333.16	327.98	323.34	319.17	303.71	294.19	288.16
42000	403.81	390.94	379.78	370.03	361.48	353.93	347.24	341.29	335.98	331.22	326.96	311.12	301.37	295.19
43000	413.42	400.25	388.82	378.84	370.08	362.35	355.51	349.41	343.98	339.11	334.74	318.53	308.55	302.22
44000	423.04	409.56	397.86	387.65	378.69	370.78	363.77	357.54	351.98	347.00	342.52	325.93	315.72	309.25
45000	432.65	418.87	406.91	396.46	387.30	379.21	372.04	365.67	359.98	354.88	350.31	333.34	322.90	316.28
46000	442.26	428.17	415.95	405.27	395.90	387.64	380.31	373.79	367.97	362.77	358.09	340.75	330.07	323.31
47000	451.88	437.48	424.99	414.09	404.51	396.06	388.58	381.92	375.97	370.65	365.88	348.16	337.25	330.33
48000	461.49	446.79	434.03	422.90	413.12	404.49	396.84	390.04	383.97	378.54	373.66	355.56	344.42	337.36
49000	471.11	456.10	443.08	431.71	421.72	412.92	405.11	398.17	391.97	386.43	381.45	362.97	351.60	344.39
50000	480.72	465.41	452.12	440.52	430.33	421.34	413.38	406.29	399.97	394.31	389.23	370.38	358.77	351.42
55000	528.79	511.95	497.33	484.57	473.36	463.48	454.72	446.92	439.97	433.74	428.15	407.42	394.65	386.56
60000	576.87	558.49	542.54	528.62	516.39	505.61	496.05	487.55	479.97	473.17	467.08	444.45	430.53	421.70
65000	624.94	605.03	587.75	572.67	559.43	547.74	537.39	528.18	519.96	512.60	506.00	481.49	466.40	456.84
70000	673.01	651.57	632.96	616.72	602.46	589.88	578.73	568.81	559.96	552.03	544.92	518.53	502.28	491.98
75000	721.08	698.11	678.17	660.77	645.49	632.01	620.07	609.44	599.96	591.47	583.84	555.57	538.16	527.13
80000	769.15	744.65	723.39	704.82	688.52	674.14	661.40	650.07	639.95	630.90	622.77	592.60	574.03	562.27
85000	817.22	791.19	768.60	748.87	731.56	716.28	702.74	690.70	679.95	670.33	661.69	629.64	609.91	597.41
90000	865.30	837.73	813.81	792.92	774.59	758.41	744.08	731.33	719.95	709.76	700.61	666.68	645.79	632.55
95000	913.37	884.27	859.02	836.98	817.62	800.55	785.41	771.96	759.94	749.19	739.53	703.72	681.66	667.69
100000	961.44	930.81	904.23	881.03	860.65	842.68	826.75	812.58	799.94	788.62	778.46	740.75	717.54	702.83

MONTHLY PAYMENT
REQUIRED TO AMORTIZE A LOAN

TERM	1 Year	2 Years	3 Years	4 Years	5 Years	6 Years	7 Years	8 Years	9 Years	10 Years	11 Years	12 Years	13 Years	14 Years
AMOUNT														
5	.44	.23	.18	.13	.11	.09	.08	.08	.07	.07	.06	.06	.06	.05
10	.88	.46	.32	.25	.21	.18	.16	.15	.14	.13	.12	.11	.11	.10
15	1.31	.68	.48	.37	.31	.27	.24	.22	.20	.19	.18	.17	.16	.15
25	2.18	1.14	.79	.62	.51	.44	.40	.36	.33	.31	.29	.28	.27	.25
50	4.36	2.27	1.57	1.23	1.02	.88	.79	.72	.66	.61	.58	.55	.53	.50
75	6.53	3.40	2.36	1.84	1.53	1.32	1.18	1.07	.99	.92	.87	.82	.79	.75
100	8.71	4.53	3.14	2.45	2.04	1.76	1.57	1.43	1.31	1.22	1.15	1.09	1.05	1.00
200	17.41	9.06	6.28	4.90	4.07	3.52	3.13	2.85	2.62	2.44	2.30	2.18	2.09	2.00
300	26.12	13.59	9.42	7.35	6.11	5.28	4.70	4.27	3.93	3.66	3.45	3.27	3.13	3.00
400	34.82	18.12	12.56	9.79	8.14	7.04	6.26	5.69	5.24	4.88	4.60	4.36	4.17	4.00
500	43.53	22.65	15.70	12.24	10.17	8.80	7.83	7.11	6.55	6.10	5.75	5.45	5.21	5.00
600	52.23	27.18	18.84	14.69	12.21	10.56	9.39	8.53	7.86	7.32	6.89	6.54	6.25	6.00
700	60.94	31.70	21.98	17.14	14.24	12.32	10.96	9.95	9.16	8.54	8.04	7.63	7.29	6.99
800	69.64	36.23	25.12	19.58	16.27	14.08	12.52	11.37	10.47	9.76	9.19	8.72	8.33	7.99
900	78.35	40.76	28.26	22.03	18.31	15.84	14.09	12.79	11.78	10.98	10.34	9.81	9.37	8.99
1000	87.05	45.29	31.40	24.48	20.34	17.60	15.65	14.21	13.09	12.20	11.49	10.90	10.41	9.99
2000	174.10	90.57	62.79	48.95	40.68	35.19	31.30	28.41	26.17	24.40	22.97	21.79	20.81	19.97
3000	261.14	135.86	94.19	73.42	61.01	52.79	46.95	42.61	39.26	36.60	34.45	32.68	31.21	29.96
4000	348.19	181.14	125.58	97.89	81.35	70.38	62.60	56.81	52.34	48.80	45.94	43.58	41.61	39.94
5000	435.24	226.43	156.98	122.36	101.69	87.98	78.25	71.01	65.42	61.00	57.42	54.47	52.01	49.93
6000	522.28	271.71	188.37	146.83	122.02	105.57	93.90	85.21	78.51	73.20	68.90	65.36	62.41	59.91
7000	609.33	317.00	219.76	171.31	142.36	123.17	109.54	99.41	91.59	85.40	80.38	76.26	72.81	69.90
8000	696.37	362.28	251.16	195.78	162.70	140.76	125.19	113.61	104.67	97.60	91.87	87.15	83.21	79.88
9000	783.42	407.56	282.55	220.25	183.03	158.35	140.84	127.81	117.76	109.80	103.35	98.04	93.61	89.86
10000	870.47	452.85	313.95	244.72	203.37	175.95	156.49	142.01	130.84	121.99	114.83	108.94	104.01	99.85
11000	957.51	498.13	345.34	269.19	223.70	193.54	172.14	156.21	143.92	134.19	126.32	119.83	114.41	109.83
12000	1044.56	543.42	376.73	293.66	244.04	211.14	187.79	170.41	157.01	146.39	137.80	130.72	124.81	119.82
13000	1131.61	588.70	408.13	318.14	264.38	228.73	203.44	184.61	170.09	158.59	149.28	141.62	135.21	129.80
14000	1218.65	633.99	439.52	342.61	284.71	246.33	219.08	198.81	183.18	170.79	160.76	152.51	145.61	139.79
15000	1305.70	679.27	470.92	367.08	305.05	263.92	234.73	213.01	196.26	182.99	172.25	163.40	156.01	149.77
16000	1392.74	724.55	502.31	391.55	325.39	281.51	250.38	227.21	209.34	195.19	183.73	174.30	166.42	159.75
17000	1479.79	769.84	533.70	416.02	345.72	299.11	266.03	241.41	222.43	207.39	195.21	185.19	176.82	169.74
18000	1566.84	815.12	565.10	440.49	366.06	316.70	281.68	255.61	235.51	219.59	206.70	196.08	187.22	179.72
19000	1653.88	860.41	596.49	464.97	386.39	334.30	297.33	269.81	248.59	231.78	218.18	206.98	197.62	189.71
20000	1740.93	905.69	627.89	489.44	406.73	351.89	312.98	284.01	261.68	243.98	229.66	217.87	208.02	199.69
21000	1827.98	950.98	659.28	513.91	427.07	369.49	328.62	298.21	274.76	256.18	241.14	228.76	218.42	209.68
22000	1915.02	996.26	690.67	538.38	447.40	387.08	344.27	312.41	287.84	268.38	252.63	239.66	228.82	219.66
23000	2002.07	1041.54	722.07	562.85	467.74	404.67	359.92	326.61	300.93	280.58	264.11	250.55	239.22	229.64
24000	2089.11	1086.83	753.46	587.32	488.08	422.27	375.57	340.81	314.01	292.78	275.59	261.44	249.62	239.63
25000	2176.16	1132.11	784.86	611.80	508.41	439.86	391.22	355.01	327.09	304.98	287.08	272.33	260.02	249.61
26000	2263.21	1177.40	816.25	636.27	528.75	457.46	406.87	369.21	340.18	317.18	298.56	283.23	270.42	259.60
27000	2350.25	1222.68	847.64	660.74	549.08	475.05	422.52	383.41	353.26	329.38	310.04	294.12	280.82	269.58
28000	2437.30	1267.97	879.04	685.21	569.42	492.65	438.16	397.61	366.35	341.57	321.52	305.01	291.22	279.57
29000	2524.35	1313.25	910.43	709.68	589.76	510.24	453.81	411.81	379.43	353.77	333.01	315.91	301.62	289.55
30000	2611.39	1358.53	941.83	734.15	610.09	527.84	469.46	426.01	392.51	365.97	344.49	326.80	312.02	299.53
31000	2698.44	1403.82	973.22	758.63	630.43	545.43	485.11	440.21	405.60	378.17	355.97	337.69	322.42	309.52
32000	2785.48	1449.10	1004.62	783.10	650.77	563.02	500.76	454.41	418.68	390.37	367.46	348.59	332.83	319.50
33000	2872.53	1494.39	1036.01	807.57	671.10	580.62	516.41	468.61	431.76	402.57	378.94	359.48	343.23	329.49
34000	2959.58	1539.67	1067.40	832.04	691.44	598.21	532.06	482.82	444.85	414.77	390.42	370.37	353.63	339.47
35000	3046.62	1584.96	1098.80	856.51	711.77	615.81	547.70	497.02	457.93	426.97	401.90	381.27	364.03	349.46
36000	3133.67	1630.24	1130.19	880.98	732.11	633.40	563.35	511.22	471.01	439.17	413.39	392.16	374.43	359.44
37000	3220.72	1675.52	1161.59	905.46	752.45	651.00	579.00	525.42	484.10	451.36	424.87	403.05	384.83	369.42
38000	3307.76	1720.81	1192.98	929.93	772.78	668.59	594.65	539.62	497.18	463.56	436.35	413.95	395.23	379.41
39000	3394.81	1766.09	1224.37	954.40	793.12	686.18	610.30	553.82	510.27	475.76	447.84	424.84	405.63	389.39
40000	3481.85	1811.38	1255.77	978.87	813.46	703.78	625.95	568.02	523.35	487.96	459.32	435.73	416.03	399.38
41000	3568.90	1856.66	1287.16	1003.34	833.79	721.37	641.60	582.22	536.43	500.16	470.80	446.63	426.43	409.36
42000	3655.95	1901.95	1318.56	1027.81	854.13	738.97	657.24	596.42	549.52	512.36	482.28	457.52	436.83	419.35
43000	3742.99	1947.23	1349.95	1052.29	874.46	756.56	672.89	610.62	562.60	524.56	493.77	468.41	447.23	429.33
44000	3830.04	1992.52	1381.34	1076.76	894.80	774.16	688.54	624.82	575.68	536.76	505.25	479.31	457.63	439.31
45000	3917.09	2037.80	1412.74	1101.23	915.14	791.75	704.19	639.02	588.77	548.96	516.73	490.20	468.03	449.30
46000	4004.13	2083.08	1444.13	1125.70	935.47	809.34	719.84	653.22	601.85	561.15	528.22	501.09	478.43	459.28
47000	4091.18	2128.37	1475.53	1150.17	955.81	826.94	735.49	667.42	614.93	573.35	539.70	511.98	488.83	469.27
48000	4178.22	2173.65	1506.92	1174.64	976.15	844.53	751.14	681.62	628.02	585.55	551.18	522.88	499.24	479.25
49000	4265.27	2218.94	1538.31	1199.12	996.48	862.13	766.78	695.82	641.10	597.75	562.66	533.77	509.64	489.24
50000	4352.32	2264.22	1569.71	1223.59	1016.82	879.72	782.43	710.02	654.18	609.95	574.15	544.66	520.04	499.22
55000	4787.55	2490.64	1726.68	1345.95	1118.50	967.69	860.68	781.02	719.60	670.95	631.56	599.13	572.04	549.14
60000	5222.78	2717.06	1883.65	1468.30	1220.18	1055.67	938.92	852.02	785.02	731.94	688.98	653.60	624.04	599.06
65000	5658.01	2943.49	2040.62	1590.66	1321.86	1143.64	1017.16	923.02	850.44	792.93	746.39	708.06	676.05	648.98
70000	6093.24	3169.91	2197.59	1713.02	1423.54	1231.61	1095.40	994.03	915.86	853.93	803.80	762.53	728.05	698.91
75000	6528.47	3396.33	2354.56	1835.38	1525.23	1319.58	1173.65	1065.03	981.27	914.92	861.22	816.99	780.05	748.83
80000	6963.70	3622.75	2511.53	1957.74	1626.91	1407.55	1251.89	1136.03	1046.69	975.92	918.63	871.46	832.06	798.75
85000	7398.94	3849.17	2668.50	2080.09	1728.59	1495.52	1330.13	1207.03	1112.11	1036.91	976.05	925.93	884.06	848.67
90000	7834.17	4075.59	2825.47	2202.45	1830.27	1583.50	1408.38	1278.03	1177.53	1097.91	1033.46	980.39	936.06	898.59
95000	8269.40	4302.02	2982.44	2324.81	1931.95	1671.47	1486.62	1349.03	1242.95	1158.90	1090.88	1034.86	988.06	948.51
100000	8704.63	4528.44	3139.41	2447.17	2033.63	1759.44	1564.86	1420.03	1308.37	1219.90	1148.29	1089.32	1040.07	998.43

TERM	15 Years	16 Years	17 Years	18 Years	19 Years	20 Years	21 Years	22 Years	23 Years	24 Years	25 Years	30 Years	35 Years	40 Years
AMOUNT														
5	.05	.05	.05	.05	.05	.05	.05	.05	.05	.04	.04	.04	.04	.04
10	.10	.10	.10	.09	.09	.09	.09	.09	.09	.08	.08	.08	.08	.08
15	.15	.14	.14	.14	.13	.13	.13	.13	.13	.12	.12	.12	.11	.11
25	.25	.24	.23	.23	.22	.22	.21	.21	.21	.20	.20	.19	.18	.18
50	.49	.47	.46	.45	.44	.43	.42	.41	.41	.40	.40	.38	.36	.36
75	.73	.70	.68	.67	.65	.64	.63	.62	.61	.60	.59	.56	.54	.53
100	.97	.94	.91	.89	.87	.85	.83	.82	.81	.80	.79	.75	.72	.71
200	1.93	1.87	1.82	1.77	1.73	1.69	1.66	1.63	1.61	1.59	1.57	1.49	1.44	1.41
300	2.89	2.80	2.72	2.65	2.59	2.54	2.49	2.45	2.41	2.38	2.35	2.23	2.16	2.12
400	3.86	3.73	3.63	3.54	3.45	3.38	3.32	3.26	3.21	3.17	3.13	2.97	2.88	2.82
500	4.82	4.67	4.53	4.42	4.32	4.23	4.15	4.08	4.01	3.96	3.91	3.72	3.60	3.53
600	5.78	5.60	5.44	5.30	5.18	5.07	4.97	4.89	4.81	4.75	4.69	4.46	4.32	4.23
700	6.75	6.53	6.35	6.18	6.04	5.91	5.80	5.70	5.62	5.54	5.47	5.20	5.04	4.94
800	7.71	7.46	7.25	7.07	6.90	6.76	6.63	6.52	6.42	6.33	6.25	5.94	5.76	5.64
900	8.67	8.40	8.16	7.95	7.76	7.60	7.46	7.33	7.22	7.12	7.03	6.69	6.48	6.35
1000	9.63	9.33	9.06	8.83	8.63	8.45	8.29	8.15	8.02	7.91	7.81	7.43	7.20	7.05
2000	19.26	18.65	18.12	17.66	17.25	16.89	16.57	16.29	16.04	15.81	15.61	14.85	14.39	14.10
3000	28.89	27.97	27.18	26.48	25.87	25.33	24.85	24.43	24.05	23.71	23.41	22.28	21.59	21.15
4000	38.52	37.30	36.23	35.31	34.49	33.77	33.14	32.57	32.07	31.62	31.21	29.70	28.78	28.19
5000	48.15	46.62	45.29	44.13	43.11	42.22	41.42	40.71	40.08	39.52	39.01	37.13	35.97	35.24
6000	57.78	55.94	54.35	52.96	51.74	50.66	49.70	48.86	48.10	47.42	46.81	44.55	43.17	42.29
7000	67.41	65.26	63.41	61.78	60.36	59.10	57.99	57.00	56.11	55.32	54.61	51.98	50.36	49.33
8000	77.04	74.59	72.46	70.61	68.98	67.54	66.27	65.14	64.13	63.23	62.41	59.40	57.55	56.38
9000	86.66	83.91	81.52	79.43	77.60	75.99	74.55	73.28	72.15	71.13	70.22	66.83	64.75	63.43
10000	96.29	93.23	90.58	88.26	86.22	84.43	82.84	81.42	80.16	79.03	78.02	74.25	71.94	70.48
11000	105.92	102.56	99.63	97.08	94.85	92.87	91.12	89.57	88.18	86.93	85.82	81.68	79.13	77.52
12000	115.55	111.88	108.69	105.91	103.47	101.31	99.40	97.71	96.19	94.84	93.62	89.10	86.33	84.57
13000	125.18	121.20	117.75	114.74	112.09	109.76	107.69	105.85	104.21	102.74	101.42	96.53	93.52	91.62
14000	134.81	130.52	126.81	123.56	120.71	118.20	115.97	113.99	112.22	110.64	109.22	103.95	100.72	98.66
15000	144.44	139.85	135.86	132.39	129.33	126.64	124.25	122.13	120.24	118.54	117.02	111.38	107.91	105.71
16000	154.07	149.17	144.92	141.21	137.96	135.08	132.54	130.27	128.25	126.45	124.82	118.80	115.10	112.76
17000	163.69	158.49	153.98	150.04	146.58	143.53	140.82	138.42	136.27	134.35	132.62	126.23	122.30	119.01
18000	173.32	167.81	163.03	158.86	155.20	151.97	149.10	146.56	144.29	142.25	140.43	133.65	129.49	126.85
19000	182.95	177.14	172.09	167.69	163.82	160.41	157.39	154.70	152.30	150.15	148.23	141.08	136.68	133.90
20000	192.58	186.46	181.15	176.51	172.44	168.85	165.67	162.84	160.32	158.06	156.03	148.50	143.88	140.95
21000	202.21	195.78	190.21	185.34	181.06	177.29	173.95	170.98	168.33	165.96	163.83	155.93	151.07	147.99
22000	211.84	205.11	199.26	194.16	189.69	185.74	182.24	179.13	176.35	173.86	171.63	163.35	158.26	155.04
23000	221.47	214.43	208.32	202.99	198.31	194.10	190.52	187.27	184.36	181.76	179.43	170.78	165.46	162.09
24000	231.10	223.75	217.38	211.81	206.93	202.62	198.80	195.41	192.38	189.67	187.23	178.20	172.65	169.14
25000	240.73	233.07	226.44	220.64	215.55	211.06	207.09	203.55	200.39	197.57	195.03	185.63	179.84	176.18
26000	250.35	242.40	235.49	229.47	224.17	219.51	215.37	211.69	208.41	205.47	202.83	193.05	187.04	183.23
27000	259.98	251.72	244.55	238.29	232.80	227.95	223.65	219.83	216.43	213.37	210.63	200.48	194.23	190.28
28000	269.61	261.04	253.61	247.12	241.42	236.39	231.94	227.98	224.44	221.28	218.44	207.90	201.43	197.32
29000	279.24	270.36	262.66	255.94	250.04	244.83	240.22	236.12	232.46	229.18	226.24	215.33	208.62	204.37
30000	288.87	279.69	271.72	264.77	258.66	253.28	248.50	244.26	240.47	237.08	234.04	222.75	215.81	211.42
31000	298.50	289.01	280.78	273.59	267.28	261.72	256.79	252.40	248.49	244.98	241.84	230.18	223.01	218.46
32000	308.13	298.33	289.84	282.42	275.91	270.16	265.07	260.54	256.50	252.89	249.64	237.60	230.20	225.51
33000	317.76	307.66	298.89	291.24	284.53	278.60	273.35	268.69	264.52	260.79	257.44	245.03	237.39	232.56
34000	327.38	316.98	307.95	300.07	293.15	287.05	281.64	276.83	272.53	268.69	265.24	252.45	244.59	239.61
35000	337.01	326.30	317.01	308.89	301.77	295.49	289.92	284.97	280.55	276.60	273.05	259.88	251.78	246.65
36000	346.64	335.62	326.06	317.72	310.39	303.93	298.20	293.11	288.57	284.50	280.85	267.30	258.97	253.70
37000	356.27	344.95	335.12	326.54	319.01	312.37	306.49	301.25	296.58	292.40	288.65	274.73	266.17	260.75
38000	365.90	354.27	344.18	335.37	327.64	320.81	314.77	309.39	304.60	300.30	296.45	282.15	273.36	267.79
39000	375.53	363.59	353.24	344.20	336.26	329.26	323.05	317.54	312.61	308.21	304.25	289.58	280.55	274.84
40000	385.16	372.91	362.29	353.02	344.88	337.70	331.34	325.68	320.63	316.11	312.05	297.00	287.75	281.89
41000	394.79	382.24	371.35	361.85	353.50	346.14	339.62	333.82	328.64	324.01	319.85	304.43	294.94	288.94
42000	404.42	391.56	380.41	370.67	362.12	354.58	347.90	341.96	336.66	331.91	327.65	311.85	302.14	295.98
43000	414.04	400.88	389.46	379.50	370.75	363.03	356.19	350.10	344.68	339.82	335.45	319.28	309.33	303.03
44000	423.67	410.21	398.52	388.32	379.37	371.47	364.47	358.25	352.69	347.72	343.26	326.70	316.52	310.08
45000	433.30	419.53	407.58	397.15	387.99	379.91	372.75	366.39	360.71	355.62	351.06	334.13	323.72	317.12
46000	442.93	428.85	416.64	405.97	396.61	388.35	381.04	374.53	368.72	363.52	358.86	341.55	330.91	324.17
47000	452.56	438.17	425.69	414.80	405.23	396.80	389.32	382.67	376.74	371.43	366.66	348.98	338.10	331.22
48000	462.19	447.50	434.75	423.62	413.86	405.24	397.60	390.81	384.75	379.33	374.46	356.40	345.30	338.27
49000	471.82	456.82	443.81	432.45	422.48	413.68	405.89	398.95	392.77	387.23	382.26	363.83	352.49	345.31
50000	481.45	466.14	452.87	441.27	431.10	422.12	414.17	407.10	400.78	395.13	390.06	371.25	359.68	352.36
55000	529.59	512.76	498.15	485.40	474.21	464.33	455.59	447.81	440.86	434.65	429.07	408.38	395.65	387.59
60000	577.73	559.37	543.44	529.53	517.32	506.55	497.00	488.51	480.94	474.16	468.07	445.50	431.62	422.83
65000	625.88	605.98	588.72	573.66	560.43	548.76	538.42	529.22	521.02	513.67	507.08	482.63	467.59	458.07
70000	674.02	652.60	634.01	617.78	603.54	590.97	579.84	569.93	561.10	553.19	546.09	519.75	503.56	493.30
75000	722.17	699.21	679.30	661.91	646.65	633.18	621.25	610.64	601.17	592.70	585.09	556.88	539.52	528.54
80000	770.31	745.82	724.58	706.04	689.76	675.39	662.67	651.35	641.25	632.21	624.10	594.00	575.49	563.77
85000	818.45	792.44	769.87	750.16	732.87	717.61	704.09	692.06	681.33	671.72	663.10	631.13	611.46	599.01
90000	866.60	839.05	815.15	794.29	775.98	759.82	745.50	732.77	721.41	711.24	702.11	668.25	647.43	634.24
95000	914.74	885.66	860.44	838.42	819.08	802.03	786.92	773.48	761.49	750.75	741.11	705.38	683.40	669.48
100000	962.89	932.28	905.73	882.54	862.19	844.24	828.33	814.19	801.56	790.26	780.12	742.50	719.36	704.71

8.200%

MONTHLY PAYMENT
REQUIRED TO AMORTIZE A LOAN

TERM AMOUNT	1 Year	2 Years	3 Years	4 Years	5 Years	6 Years	7 Years	8 Years	9 Years	10 Years	11 Years	12 Years	13 Years	14 Years
5	.44	.23	.16	.13	.11	.09	.08	.08	.07	.07	.06	.06	.06	.06
10	.88	.46	.32	.25	.21	.18	.16	.15	.14	.13	.12	.11	.11	.11
15	1.31	.68	.48	.37	.31	.27	.24	.22	.20	.19	.18	.17	.16	.16
25	2.18	1.14	.79	.62	.51	.45	.40	.36	.33	.31	.29	.28	.27	.26
50	4.36	2.27	1.58	1.23	1.02	.89	.79	.72	.66	.62	.58	.55	.53	.51
75	6.54	3.40	2.36	1.84	1.53	1.33	1.18	1.07	.99	.92	.87	.83	.79	.76
100	8.71	4.54	3.15	2.46	2.04	1.77	1.57	1.43	1.32	1.23	1.16	1.10	1.05	1.01
200	17.42	9.07	6.29	4.91	4.08	3.53	3.14	2.85	2.63	2.45	2.31	2.19	2.09	2.01
300	26.13	13.60	9.43	7.36	6.12	5.29	4.71	4.28	3.94	3.68	3.46	3.29	3.14	3.01
400	34.84	18.13	12.58	9.81	8.15	7.06	6.28	5.70	5.25	4.90	4.61	4.38	4.18	4.02
500	43.55	22.66	15.72	12.26	10.19	8.82	7.85	7.12	6.57	6.12	5.77	5.47	5.23	5.02
600	52.25	27.20	18.86	14.71	12.23	10.58	9.42	8.55	7.88	7.35	6.92	6.57	6.27	6.02
700	60.96	31.73	22.01	17.16	14.27	12.35	10.99	9.97	9.19	8.57	8.07	7.66	7.31	7.02
800	69.67	36.26	25.15	19.61	16.30	14.11	12.55	11.40	10.50	9.80	9.22	8.75	8.36	8.03
900	78.38	40.79	28.29	22.06	18.34	15.87	14.12	12.82	11.82	11.02	10.38	9.85	9.40	9.03
1000	87.09	45.32	31.43	24.51	20.38	17.64	15.69	14.24	13.13	12.24	11.53	10.94	10.45	10.03
2000	174.17	90.64	62.86	49.02	40.75	35.27	31.38	28.48	26.25	24.48	23.05	21.87	20.89	20.06
3000	261.25	135.96	94.29	73.53	61.12	52.90	47.06	42.72	39.37	36.72	34.58	32.81	31.33	30.09
4000	348.33	181.28	125.72	98.03	81.49	70.53	62.75	56.96	52.50	48.96	46.10	43.74	41.78	40.11
5000	435.41	226.60	157.15	122.54	101.87	88.16	78.44	71.20	65.62	61.20	57.62	54.68	52.22	50.14
6000	522.49	271.92	188.58	147.05	122.24	105.79	94.12	85.44	78.74	73.44	69.15	65.61	62.66	60.17
7000	609.57	317.23	220.01	171.55	142.61	123.42	109.81	99.67	91.86	85.68	80.67	76.55	73.10	70.19
8000	696.65	362.55	251.43	196.06	162.98	141.05	125.49	113.91	104.99	97.91	92.19	87.48	83.55	80.22
9000	783.73	407.87	282.86	220.57	183.36	158.68	141.18	128.15	118.11	110.15	103.72	98.42	93.99	90.25
10000	870.81	453.19	314.29	245.07	203.73	176.32	156.87	142.39	131.23	122.39	115.24	109.35	104.43	100.28
11000	957.90	498.51	345.72	269.58	224.10	193.95	172.55	156.63	144.35	134.63	126.76	120.28	114.87	110.30
12000	1044.98	543.83	377.15	294.09	244.47	211.58	188.24	170.87	157.48	146.87	138.29	131.22	125.32	120.33
13000	1132.06	589.15	408.58	318.59	264.84	229.21	203.92	185.11	170.60	159.11	149.81	142.15	135.76	130.36
14000	1219.14	634.46	440.01	343.10	285.22	246.84	219.61	199.34	183.72	171.35	161.33	153.09	146.20	140.38
15000	1306.22	679.78	471.44	367.61	305.59	264.47	235.30	213.58	196.84	183.59	172.86	164.02	156.65	150.41
16000	1393.30	725.10	502.86	392.12	325.96	282.10	250.98	227.82	209.97	195.82	184.38	174.96	167.09	160.44
17000	1480.38	770.42	534.29	416.62	346.33	299.73	266.67	242.06	223.09	208.06	195.90	185.89	177.53	170.47
18000	1567.46	815.74	565.72	441.13	366.71	317.36	282.35	256.30	236.21	220.30	207.43	196.83	187.97	180.49
19000	1654.54	861.06	597.15	465.64	387.08	335.00	298.04	270.54	249.33	232.54	218.95	207.76	198.42	190.52
20000	1741.62	906.38	628.58	490.14	407.45	352.63	313.73	284.78	262.46	244.78	230.47	218.69	208.86	200.55
21000	1828.70	951.69	660.01	514.65	427.82	370.26	329.41	299.01	275.58	257.02	242.00	229.63	219.30	210.57
22000	1915.79	997.01	691.44	539.16	448.19	387.89	345.10	313.25	288.70	269.26	253.52	240.56	229.74	220.60
23000	2002.87	1042.33	722.87	563.66	468.57	405.52	360.78	327.49	301.83	281.50	265.04	251.50	240.19	230.63
24000	2089.95	1087.65	754.29	588.17	488.94	423.15	376.47	341.73	314.95	293.73	276.57	262.43	250.63	240.65
25000	2177.03	1132.97	785.72	612.68	509.31	440.78	392.16	355.97	328.07	305.97	288.09	273.37	261.07	250.68
26000	2264.11	1178.29	817.15	637.18	529.68	458.41	407.84	370.21	341.19	318.21	299.61	284.30	271.51	260.71
27000	2351.19	1223.61	848.58	661.69	550.06	476.04	423.53	384.45	354.32	330.45	311.14	295.24	281.96	270.74
28000	2438.27	1268.92	880.01	686.20	570.43	493.67	439.21	398.68	367.44	342.69	322.66	306.17	292.40	280.76
29000	2525.35	1314.24	911.44	710.71	590.80	511.31	454.90	412.92	380.56	354.93	334.18	317.11	302.84	290.79
30000	2612.43	1359.56	942.87	735.21	611.17	528.94	470.59	427.16	393.68	367.17	345.71	328.04	313.29	300.82
31000	2699.51	1404.88	974.30	759.72	631.54	546.57	486.27	441.40	406.81	379.40	357.23	338.97	323.73	310.84
32000	2786.59	1450.20	1005.72	784.23	651.92	564.20	501.96	455.64	419.93	391.64	368.75	349.91	334.17	320.87
33000	2873.68	1495.52	1037.15	808.73	672.29	581.83	517.64	469.88	433.05	403.88	380.28	360.84	344.61	330.90
34000	2960.76	1540.84	1068.58	833.24	692.66	599.46	533.33	484.12	446.17	416.12	391.80	371.78	355.06	340.93
35000	3047.84	1586.15	1100.01	857.75	713.03	617.09	549.02	498.35	459.30	428.36	403.32	382.71	365.50	350.95
36000	3134.92	1631.47	1131.44	882.25	733.41	634.72	564.70	512.59	472.42	440.60	414.85	393.65	375.94	360.98
37000	3222.00	1676.79	1162.87	906.76	753.78	652.35	580.39	526.83	485.54	452.84	426.37	404.58	386.38	371.01
38000	3309.08	1722.11	1194.30	931.27	774.15	669.99	596.07	541.07	498.66	465.08	437.89	415.52	396.83	381.03
39000	3396.16	1767.43	1225.72	955.77	794.52	687.62	611.76	555.31	511.79	477.31	449.42	426.45	407.27	391.06
40000	3483.24	1812.75	1257.15	980.28	814.89	705.25	627.45	569.55	524.91	489.55	460.94	437.38	417.71	401.09
41000	3570.32	1858.07	1288.58	1004.79	835.27	722.88	643.13	583.79	538.03	501.79	472.46	448.32	428.15	411.12
42000	3657.40	1903.38	1320.01	1029.30	855.64	740.51	658.82	598.02	551.15	514.03	483.99	459.25	438.60	421.14
43000	3744.49	1948.70	1351.44	1053.80	876.01	758.14	674.50	612.26	564.28	526.27	495.51	470.19	449.04	431.17
44000	3831.57	1994.02	1382.87	1078.31	896.38	775.77	690.19	626.50	577.40	538.51	507.03	481.12	459.48	441.20
45000	3918.65	2039.34	1414.30	1102.82	916.76	793.40	705.88	640.74	590.52	550.75	518.56	492.06	469.93	451.22
46000	4005.73	2084.66	1445.73	1127.32	937.13	811.03	721.56	654.98	603.65	562.99	530.08	502.99	480.37	461.25
47000	4092.81	2129.98	1477.15	1151.83	957.50	828.66	737.25	669.22	616.77	575.22	541.61	513.93	490.81	471.28
48000	4179.89	2175.30	1508.58	1176.34	977.87	846.30	752.94	683.46	629.89	587.46	553.13	524.86	501.25	481.30
49000	4266.97	2220.61	1540.01	1200.84	998.25	863.93	768.62	697.69	643.01	599.70	564.65	535.79	511.70	491.33
50000	4354.05	2265.93	1571.44	1225.35	1018.62	881.56	784.31	711.93	656.14	611.94	576.18	546.73	522.14	501.36
55000	4789.46	2492.53	1728.58	1347.89	1120.48	969.71	862.74	783.12	721.75	673.13	633.79	601.40	574.35	551.49
60000	5224.86	2719.12	1885.73	1470.42	1222.34	1057.87	941.17	854.32	787.36	734.33	691.41	656.07	626.57	601.63
65000	5660.27	2945.71	2042.87	1592.95	1324.20	1146.02	1019.60	925.51	852.98	795.52	749.03	710.75	678.78	651.76
70000	6095.67	3172.30	2200.01	1715.49	1426.06	1234.18	1098.03	996.70	918.59	856.71	806.64	765.42	730.99	701.90
75000	6531.07	3398.90	2357.16	1838.02	1527.92	1322.33	1176.46	1067.90	984.20	917.91	864.26	820.09	783.21	752.04
80000	6966.48	3625.49	2514.30	1960.56	1629.78	1410.49	1254.89	1139.09	1049.81	979.10	921.88	874.76	835.42	802.17
85000	7401.88	3852.08	2671.45	2083.09	1731.65	1498.64	1333.32	1210.28	1115.43	1040.29	979.49	929.44	887.63	852.31
90000	7837.29	4078.68	2828.59	2205.63	1833.51	1586.80	1411.75	1281.47	1181.04	1101.49	1037.11	984.11	939.85	902.44
95000	8272.69	4305.27	2985.73	2328.16	1935.37	1674.96	1490.18	1352.67	1246.65	1162.68	1094.73	1038.78	992.06	952.58
100000	8708.10	4531.86	3142.88	2450.70	2037.23	1763.11	1568.61	1423.86	1312.27	1223.87	1152.35	1093.45	1044.27	1002.71

TERM	15 Years	16 Years	17 Years	18 Years	19 Years	20 Years	21 Years	22 Years	23 Years	24 Years	25 Years	30 Years	35 Years	40 Years
AMOUNT														
5	.05	.05	.05	.05	.05	.05	.05	.05	.05	.04	.04	.04	.04	.04
10	.10	.10	.10	.09	.09	.09	.09	.09	.09	.08	.08	.08	.08	.08
15	.15	.15	.14	.14	.14	.13	.13	.13	.13	.12	.12	.12	.11	.11
25	.25	.24	.23	.23	.22	.22	.21	.21	.21	.20	.20	.19	.19	.18
50	.49	.47	.46	.45	.44	.43	.42	.41	.41	.40	.40	.38	.37	.36
75	.73	.71	.69	.67	.66	.64	.63	.62	.61	.60	.59	.57	.55	.54
100	.97	.94	.92	.89	.87	.85	.84	.82	.81	.80	.79	.75	.73	.72
200	1.94	1.88	1.83	1.78	1.74	1.70	1.67	1.64	1.62	1.60	1.58	1.50	1.45	1.43
300	2.91	2.82	2.74	2.67	2.61	2.55	2.50	2.46	2.42	2.39	2.36	2.25	2.18	2.14
400	3.87	3.75	3.65	3.55	3.47	3.40	3.34	3.28	3.23	3.19	3.15	3.00	2.90	2.85
500	4.84	4.69	4.56	4.44	4.34	4.25	4.17	4.10	4.04	3.98	3.93	3.74	3.63	3.56
600	5.81	5.63	5.47	5.33	5.21	5.10	5.00	4.92	4.84	4.78	4.72	4.49	4.35	4.27
700	6.78	6.56	6.38	6.21	6.07	5.95	5.84	5.74	5.65	5.57	5.50	5.24	5.08	4.98
800	7.74	7.50	7.29	7.10	6.94	6.80	6.67	6.56	6.46	6.37	6.29	5.99	5.80	5.69
900	8.71	8.44	8.20	7.99	7.81	7.65	7.50	7.38	7.26	7.16	7.07	6.73	6.53	6.40
1000	9.68	9.37	9.11	8.88	8.67	8.49	8.34	8.20	8.07	7.96	7.86	7.48	7.25	7.11
2000	19.35	18.74	18.21	17.75	17.34	16.98	16.67	16.39	16.13	15.91	15.71	14.96	14.50	14.21
3000	29.02	28.11	27.31	26.62	26.01	25.47	25.00	24.58	24.20	23.86	23.56	22.44	21.75	21.32
4000	38.69	37.47	36.41	35.49	34.68	33.96	33.33	32.77	32.26	31.81	31.41	29.92	29.00	28.42
5000	48.37	46.84	45.52	44.36	43.35	42.45	41.66	40.96	40.33	39.76	39.26	37.39	36.25	35.52
6000	58.04	56.21	54.62	53.23	52.01	50.94	49.99	49.15	48.39	47.72	47.11	44.87	43.50	42.63
7000	67.71	65.57	63.72	62.10	60.68	59.43	58.32	57.34	56.46	55.67	54.96	52.35	50.74	49.73
8000	77.38	74.94	72.82	70.97	69.35	67.92	66.65	65.53	64.52	63.62	62.81	59.83	57.99	56.83
9000	87.06	84.31	81.92	79.84	78.02	76.41	74.98	73.72	72.58	71.57	70.67	67.30	65.24	63.94
10000	96.73	93.67	91.03	88.72	86.69	84.90	83.31	81.91	80.65	79.52	78.52	74.78	72.49	71.04
11000	106.40	103.04	100.13	97.59	95.35	93.39	91.64	90.10	88.71	87.48	86.37	82.26	79.74	78.14
12000	116.07	112.41	109.23	106.46	104.02	101.88	99.98	98.29	96.78	95.43	94.22	89.74	86.99	85.25
13000	125.75	121.78	118.33	115.33	112.69	110.37	108.31	106.48	104.84	103.38	102.07	97.21	94.23	92.35
14000	135.42	131.14	127.43	124.20	121.36	118.86	116.64	114.67	112.91	111.33	109.92	104.69	101.48	99.46
15000	145.09	140.51	136.54	133.07	130.03	127.34	124.97	122.86	120.97	119.28	117.77	112.17	108.73	106.56
16000	154.76	149.88	145.64	141.94	138.70	135.83	133.30	131.05	129.04	127.24	125.62	119.65	115.98	113.66
17000	164.43	159.24	154.74	150.81	147.36	144.32	141.63	139.24	137.10	135.19	133.47	127.12	123.23	120.77
18000	174.11	168.61	163.84	159.68	156.03	152.81	149.96	147.43	145.16	143.14	141.33	134.60	130.48	127.87
19000	183.78	177.98	172.95	168.55	164.70	161.30	158.29	155.62	153.23	151.09	149.18	142.08	137.72	134.97
20000	193.45	187.34	182.05	177.43	173.37	169.79	166.62	163.81	161.29	159.04	157.03	149.56	144.97	142.08
21000	203.12	196.71	191.15	186.30	182.04	178.28	174.95	172.00	169.36	167.00	164.88	157.03	152.22	149.18
22000	212.80	206.08	200.25	195.17	190.70	186.77	183.28	180.19	177.42	174.95	172.73	164.51	159.47	156.28
23000	222.47	215.45	209.35	204.04	199.37	195.26	191.62	188.38	185.49	182.90	180.58	171.99	166.72	163.39
24000	232.14	224.81	218.46	212.91	208.04	203.75	199.95	196.57	193.55	190.85	188.43	179.47	173.97	170.49
25000	241.81	234.18	227.56	221.78	216.71	212.24	208.28	204.76	201.61	198.80	196.28	186.94	181.21	177.60
26000	251.49	243.55	236.66	230.65	225.38	220.73	216.61	212.95	209.68	206.76	204.13	194.42	188.46	184.70
27000	261.16	252.91	245.76	239.52	234.05	229.22	224.94	221.14	217.74	214.71	211.99	201.90	195.71	191.80
28000	270.83	262.28	254.86	248.39	242.71	237.71	233.27	229.33	225.81	222.66	219.84	209.38	202.96	198.91
29000	280.50	271.65	263.97	257.26	251.38	246.19	241.60	237.52	233.87	230.61	227.69	216.85	210.21	206.01
30000	290.18	281.01	273.07	266.14	260.05	254.68	249.93	245.71	241.94	238.56	235.54	224.33	217.46	213.11
31000	299.85	290.38	282.17	275.01	268.72	263.17	258.26	253.90	250.00	246.52	243.39	231.81	224.70	220.22
32000	309.52	299.75	291.27	283.88	277.39	271.66	266.59	262.09	258.07	254.47	251.24	239.29	231.95	227.32
33000	319.19	309.11	300.38	292.75	286.05	280.15	274.92	270.28	266.13	262.42	259.09	246.76	239.20	234.42
34000	328.86	318.48	309.48	301.62	294.72	288.64	283.25	278.47	274.19	270.37	266.94	254.24	246.45	241.53
35000	338.54	327.85	318.58	310.49	303.39	297.13	291.59	286.66	282.26	278.32	274.79	261.72	253.70	248.63
36000	348.21	337.22	327.68	319.36	312.06	305.62	299.92	294.85	290.32	286.28	282.65	269.20	260.95	255.74
37000	357.88	346.58	336.78	328.23	320.73	314.11	308.25	303.04	298.39	294.23	290.50	276.67	268.19	262.84
38000	367.55	355.95	345.89	337.10	329.40	322.60	316.58	311.23	306.45	302.18	298.35	284.15	275.44	269.94
39000	377.23	365.32	354.99	345.97	338.06	331.09	324.91	319.42	314.52	310.13	306.20	291.63	282.69	277.05
40000	386.90	374.68	364.09	354.85	346.73	339.58	333.24	327.61	322.58	318.08	314.05	299.11	289.94	284.15
41000	396.57	384.05	373.19	363.72	355.40	348.07	341.57	335.80	330.64	326.04	321.90	306.58	297.19	291.25
42000	406.24	393.42	382.29	372.59	364.07	356.56	349.90	343.99	338.71	333.99	329.75	314.06	304.44	298.36
43000	415.92	402.78	391.40	381.46	372.74	365.04	358.23	352.18	346.77	341.94	337.60	321.54	311.68	305.46
44000	425.59	412.15	400.50	390.33	381.40	373.53	366.56	360.37	354.84	349.89	345.45	329.02	318.93	312.56
45000	435.26	421.52	409.60	399.20	390.07	382.02	374.89	368.56	362.90	357.84	353.31	336.49	326.18	319.67
46000	444.93	430.89	418.70	408.07	398.74	390.51	383.23	376.75	370.97	365.80	361.16	343.97	333.43	326.77
47000	454.60	440.25	427.81	416.94	407.41	399.00	391.56	384.94	379.03	373.75	369.01	351.45	340.68	333.88
48000	464.28	449.62	436.91	425.81	416.08	407.49	399.89	393.13	387.10	381.70	376.86	358.93	347.93	340.98
49000	473.95	458.99	446.01	434.68	424.75	415.98	408.22	401.32	395.16	389.65	384.71	366.40	355.17	348.08
50000	483.62	468.35	455.11	443.56	433.41	424.47	416.55	409.51	403.22	397.60	392.56	373.88	362.42	355.19
55000	531.98	515.19	500.62	487.91	476.75	466.92	458.20	450.46	443.55	437.36	431.82	411.27	398.66	390.70
60000	580.35	562.02	546.13	532.27	520.10	509.36	499.86	491.41	483.87	477.12	471.07	448.66	434.91	426.22
65000	628.71	608.86	591.64	576.62	563.44	551.81	541.51	532.36	524.19	516.88	510.33	486.05	471.15	461.74
70000	677.07	655.69	637.15	620.98	606.78	594.26	583.17	573.31	564.51	556.64	549.58	523.43	507.39	497.26
75000	725.43	702.53	682.66	665.33	650.12	636.70	624.82	614.26	604.83	596.40	588.84	560.82	543.63	532.78
80000	773.79	749.36	728.18	709.69	693.46	679.15	666.48	655.21	645.16	636.16	628.09	598.21	579.87	568.30
85000	822.15	796.20	773.69	754.04	736.80	721.60	708.13	696.16	685.48	675.92	667.35	635.60	616.11	603.81
90000	870.52	843.03	819.20	798.40	780.14	764.04	749.78	737.11	725.80	715.68	706.61	672.98	652.36	639.33
95000	918.88	889.87	864.71	842.75	823.48	806.49	791.44	778.06	766.12	755.44	745.86	710.37	688.60	674.85
100000	967.24	936.70	910.22	887.11	866.82	848.93	833.09	819.01	806.44	795.20	785.12	747.76	724.84	710.37

8.250%

TERM	1 Year	2 Years	3 Years	4 Years	5 Years	6 Years	7 Years	8 Years	9 Years	10 Years	11 Years	12 Years	13 Years	14 Years
AMOUNT														
5	.44	.23	.16	.13	.11	.09	.08	.08	.07	.07	.06	.06	.06	.06
10	.88	.46	.32	.25	.21	.18	.16	.15	.14	.13	.12	.11	.11	.11
15	1.31	.69	.48	.37	.31	.27	.24	.22	.20	.19	.18	.17	.16	.16
25	2.18	1.14	.79	.62	.51	.45	.40	.36	.33	.31	.29	.28	.27	.26
50	4.36	2.27	1.58	1.23	1.02	.89	.79	.72	.66	.62	.58	.55	.53	.51
75	6.54	3.41	2.36	1.84	1.53	1.33	1.18	1.07	.99	.92	.87	.83	.79	.76
100	8.72	4.54	3.15	2.46	2.04	1.77	1.58	1.43	1.32	1.23	1.16	1.10	1.05	1.01
200	17.43	9.07	6.30	4.91	4.08	3.54	3.15	2.86	2.63	2.46	2.32	2.20	2.10	2.02
300	26.14	13.61	9.44	7.36	5.30	4.72	4.28	3.95	3.68	3.47	3.29	3.15	3.02
400	34.85	18.14	12.59	9.82	8.16	7.07	6.29	5.71	5.26	4.91	4.63	4.39	4.19	4.03
500	43.56	22.68	15.73	12.27	10.20	8.83	7.86	7.14	6.58	6.14	5.78	5.49	5.24	5.03
600	52.27	27.21	18.88	14.72	12.24	10.60	9.43	8.56	7.89	7.36	6.94	6.58	6.29	6.04
700	60.98	31.74	22.02	17.18	14.28	12.36	11.00	9.99	9.21	8.59	8.09	7.68	7.33	7.04
800	69.69	36.28	25.17	19.63	16.32	14.13	12.57	11.42	10.52	9.82	9.25	8.77	8.38	8.05
900	78.40	40.81	28.31	22.08	18.36	15.90	14.14	12.84	11.84	11.04	10.40	9.87	9.43	9.06
1000	87.11	45.35	31.46	24.54	20.40	17.66	15.72	14.27	13.15	12.27	11.56	10.97	10.48	10.06
2000	174.21	90.69	62.91	49.07	40.80	35.32	31.43	28.53	26.30	24.54	23.11	21.93	20.95	20.12
3000	261.32	136.03	94.36	73.60	61.19	52.97	47.14	42.80	39.45	36.80	34.66	32.89	31.42	30.17
4000	348.42	181.37	125.81	98.13	81.59	70.63	62.85	57.06	52.60	49.07	46.21	43.85	41.89	40.23
5000	435.53	226.71	157.26	122.66	101.99	88.28	78.56	71.33	65.75	61.33	57.76	54.82	52.36	50.28
6000	522.63	272.05	188.72	147.19	122.38	105.94	94.27	85.59	78.90	73.60	69.31	65.78	62.83	60.34
7000	609.73	317.39	220.17	171.72	142.78	123.59	109.98	99.85	92.05	85.86	80.86	76.74	73.30	70.39
8000	696.84	362.74	251.62	196.25	163.18	141.25	125.69	114.12	105.19	98.13	92.41	87.70	83.77	80.45
9000	783.94	408.08	283.07	220.78	183.57	158.91	141.40	128.38	118.34	110.39	103.96	98.66	94.24	90.51
10000	871.05	453.42	314.52	245.31	203.97	176.56	157.12	142.65	131.49	122.66	115.51	109.63	104.71	100.56
11000	958.15	498.76	345.98	269.84	224.36	194.22	172.83	156.91	144.64	134.92	127.06	120.59	115.18	110.62
12000	1045.25	544.10	377.43	294.37	244.76	211.87	188.54	171.17	157.79	147.19	138.61	131.55	125.65	120.67
13000	1132.36	589.44	408.88	318.90	265.16	229.53	204.25	185.44	170.94	159.45	150.16	142.51	136.12	130.73
14000	1219.46	634.78	440.33	343.43	285.55	247.18	219.96	199.70	184.09	171.72	161.71	153.47	146.60	140.78
15000	1306.57	680.13	471.78	367.96	305.95	264.84	235.67	213.97	197.24	183.98	173.26	164.44	157.07	150.84
16000	1393.67	725.47	503.23	392.49	326.35	282.49	251.38	228.23	210.38	196.25	184.81	175.40	167.54	160.90
17000	1480.77	770.81	534.69	417.02	346.74	300.15	267.09	242.49	223.53	208.51	196.36	186.36	178.01	170.95
18000	1567.88	816.15	566.14	441.55	367.14	317.81	282.80	256.76	236.68	220.78	207.91	197.32	188.48	181.01
19000	1654.98	861.49	597.59	466.08	387.53	335.46	298.52	271.02	249.83	233.04	219.46	208.28	198.95	191.06
20000	1742.09	906.83	629.04	490.61	407.93	353.12	314.23	285.29	262.98	245.31	231.01	219.25	209.42	201.12
21000	1829.19	952.17	660.49	515.14	428.33	370.77	329.94	299.55	276.13	257.58	242.57	230.21	219.89	211.17
22000	1916.29	997.52	691.95	539.67	448.72	388.43	345.65	313.81	289.28	269.84	254.12	241.17	230.36	221.23
23000	2003.40	1042.86	723.40	564.21	469.12	406.08	361.36	328.08	302.42	282.11	265.67	252.13	240.83	231.29
24000	2090.50	1088.20	754.85	588.74	489.52	423.74	377.07	342.34	315.57	294.37	277.22	263.09	251.30	241.34
25000	2177.61	1133.54	786.30	613.27	509.91	441.39	392.78	356.61	328.72	306.64	288.77	274.06	261.77	251.40
26000	2264.71	1178.88	817.75	637.80	530.31	459.05	408.49	370.87	341.87	318.90	300.32	285.02	272.24	261.45
27000	2351.81	1224.22	849.20	662.33	550.70	476.71	424.20	385.14	355.02	331.17	311.87	295.98	282.72	271.51
28000	2438.92	1269.56	880.66	686.86	571.10	494.36	439.91	399.40	368.17	343.43	323.42	306.94	293.19	281.56
29000	2526.02	1314.91	912.11	711.39	591.50	512.02	455.63	413.66	381.32	355.70	334.97	317.91	303.66	291.62
30000	2613.13	1360.25	943.56	735.92	611.89	529.67	471.34	427.93	394.47	367.96	346.52	328.87	314.13	301.67
31000	2700.23	1405.59	975.01	760.45	632.29	547.33	487.05	442.19	407.61	380.23	358.07	339.83	324.60	311.73
32000	2787.34	1450.93	1006.46	784.98	652.69	564.98	502.76	456.46	420.76	392.49	369.62	350.79	335.07	321.79
33000	2874.44	1496.27	1037.92	809.51	673.08	582.64	518.47	470.72	433.91	404.76	381.17	361.75	345.54	331.84
34000	2961.54	1541.61	1069.37	834.04	693.48	600.29	534.18	484.98	447.06	417.02	392.72	372.72	356.01	341.90
35000	3048.65	1586.95	1100.82	858.57	713.87	617.95	549.89	499.25	460.21	429.29	404.27	383.68	366.48	351.95
36000	3135.75	1632.30	1132.27	883.10	734.27	635.61	565.60	513.51	473.36	441.55	415.82	394.64	376.95	362.01
37000	3222.86	1677.64	1163.72	907.63	754.67	653.26	581.31	527.78	486.51	453.82	427.37	405.60	387.42	372.06
38000	3309.96	1722.98	1195.17	932.16	775.06	670.92	597.03	542.04	499.65	466.08	438.92	416.56	397.89	382.12
39000	3397.06	1768.32	1226.63	956.69	795.46	688.57	612.74	556.30	512.80	478.35	450.47	427.53	408.36	392.18
40000	3484.17	1813.66	1258.08	981.22	815.86	706.23	628.45	570.57	525.95	490.62	462.02	438.49	418.84	402.23
41000	3571.27	1859.00	1289.53	1005.75	836.25	723.88	644.16	584.83	539.10	502.88	473.57	449.45	429.31	412.29
42000	3658.38	1904.34	1320.98	1030.28	856.65	741.54	659.87	599.10	552.25	515.15	485.13	460.41	439.78	422.34
43000	3745.48	1949.69	1352.43	1054.81	877.04	759.19	675.58	613.36	565.40	527.41	496.68	471.37	450.25	432.40
44000	3832.58	1995.03	1383.89	1079.34	897.44	776.85	691.29	627.62	578.55	539.68	508.23	482.34	460.72	442.45
45000	3919.69	2040.37	1415.34	1103.87	917.84	794.51	707.00	641.89	591.70	551.94	519.78	493.30	471.19	452.51
46000	4006.79	2085.71	1446.79	1128.41	938.23	812.16	722.71	656.15	604.84	564.21	531.33	504.26	481.66	462.57
47000	4093.90	2131.05	1478.24	1152.94	958.63	829.82	738.42	670.42	617.99	576.47	542.88	515.22	492.13	472.62
48000	4181.00	2176.39	1509.69	1177.47	979.03	847.47	754.14	684.68	631.14	588.74	554.43	526.18	502.60	482.68
49000	4268.10	2221.73	1541.14	1202.00	999.42	865.13	769.85	698.94	644.29	601.00	565.98	537.15	513.07	492.73
50000	4355.21	2267.07	1572.60	1226.53	1019.82	882.78	785.56	713.21	657.44	613.27	577.53	548.11	523.54	502.79
55000	4790.73	2493.78	1729.86	1349.18	1121.80	971.06	864.11	784.53	723.18	674.59	635.28	602.92	575.90	553.07
60000	5226.25	2720.49	1887.11	1471.83	1223.78	1059.34	942.67	855.85	788.93	735.92	693.03	657.73	628.25	603.34
65000	5661.77	2947.20	2044.37	1594.48	1325.76	1147.62	1021.22	927.17	854.67	797.25	750.79	712.54	680.60	653.62
70000	6097.29	3173.90	2201.63	1717.14	1427.74	1235.89	1099.78	998.49	920.41	858.57	808.54	767.35	732.96	703.90
75000	6532.81	3400.61	2358.89	1839.79	1529.72	1324.17	1178.33	1069.81	986.16	919.90	866.29	822.16	785.31	754.18
80000	6968.33	3627.32	2516.15	1962.44	1631.71	1412.45	1256.89	1141.13	1051.90	981.23	924.04	876.97	837.67	804.46
85000	7403.85	3854.02	2673.41	2085.09	1733.69	1500.73	1335.45	1212.45	1117.64	1042.55	981.80	931.78	890.02	854.74
90000	7839.37	4080.73	2830.67	2207.74	1835.67	1589.01	1414.00	1283.77	1183.39	1103.88	1039.55	986.59	942.37	905.01
95000	8274.89	4307.44	2987.93	2330.40	1937.65	1677.28	1492.56	1355.09	1249.13	1165.20	1097.30	1041.40	994.73	955.29
100000	8710.41	4534.14	3145.19	2453.05	2039.63	1765.56	1571.11	1426.41	1314.87	1226.53	1155.05	1096.21	1047.08	1005.57

TERM AMOUNT	15 Years	16 Years	17 Years	18 Years	19 Years	20 Years	21 Years	22 Years	23 Years	24 Years	25 Years	30 Years	35 Years	40 Years
5	.05	.05	.05	.05	.05	.05	.05	.05	.05	.04	.04	.04	.04	.04
10	.10	.10	.10	.09	.09	.09	.09	.09	.09	.08	.08	.08	.08	.08
15	.15	.15	.14	.14	.14	.13	.13	.13	.13	.12	.12	.12	.11	.11
25	.25	.24	.23	.23	.22	.22	.21	.21	.21	.20	.20	.19	.19	.18
50	.49	.47	.46	.45	.44	.43	.42	.42	.41	.40	.40	.38	.37	.36
75	.73	.71	.69	.67	.66	.64	.63	.62	.61	.60	.60	.57	.55	.54
100	.98	.94	.92	.90	.87	.86	.84	.83	.81	.80	.79	.76	.73	.72
200	1.95	1.88	1.83	1.79	1.74	1.71	1.68	1.65	1.62	1.60	1.58	1.51	1.46	1.43
300	2.92	2.82	2.74	2.68	2.61	2.56	2.51	2.47	2.43	2.40	2.37	2.26	2.19	2.15
400	3.89	3.76	3.66	3.57	3.48	3.41	3.35	3.29	3.24	3.20	3.16	3.01	2.92	2.86
500	4.86	4.70	4.57	4.46	4.35	4.27	4.19	4.12	4.05	4.00	3.95	3.76	3.65	3.58
600	5.83	5.64	5.48	5.35	5.22	5.12	5.02	4.94	4.86	4.80	4.74	4.51	4.38	4.29
700	6.80	6.58	6.40	6.24	6.09	5.97	5.86	5.76	5.67	5.59	5.52	5.26	5.10	5.00
800	7.77	7.52	7.31	7.13	6.96	6.82	6.70	6.58	6.48	6.39	6.31	6.02	5.83	5.72
900	8.74	8.46	8.22	8.02	7.83	7.67	7.53	7.41	7.29	7.19	7.10	6.77	6.56	6.43
1000	9.71	9.40	9.14	8.91	8.70	8.53	8.37	8.23	8.10	7.99	7.89	7.52	7.29	7.15
2000	19.41	18.80	18.27	17.81	17.40	17.05	16.73	16.45	16.20	15.97	15.77	15.03	14.57	14.29
3000	29.11	28.19	27.40	26.71	26.10	25.57	25.09	24.67	24.30	23.96	23.66	22.54	21.86	21.43
4000	38.81	37.59	36.53	35.61	34.80	34.09	33.46	32.89	32.39	31.94	31.54	30.06	29.14	28.57
5000	48.51	46.99	45.67	44.51	43.50	42.61	41.82	41.12	40.49	39.93	39.43	37.57	36.43	35.71
6000	58.21	56.38	54.80	53.41	52.20	51.13	50.18	49.34	48.59	47.91	47.31	45.08	43.71	42.85
7000	67.91	65.78	63.93	62.32	60.90	59.65	58.54	57.56	56.68	55.90	55.20	52.59	51.00	49.99
8000	77.62	75.18	73.06	71.22	69.60	68.17	66.91	65.78	64.78	63.88	63.08	60.11	58.28	57.14
9000	87.32	84.57	82.19	80.12	78.30	76.69	75.27	74.01	72.88	71.87	70.97	67.62	65.57	64.28
10000	97.02	93.97	91.33	89.02	87.00	85.21	83.63	82.23	80.97	79.85	78.85	75.13	72.85	71.42
11000	106.72	103.37	100.46	97.92	95.70	93.73	91.99	90.45	89.07	87.84	86.73	82.64	80.14	78.56
12000	116.42	112.76	109.59	106.82	104.39	102.25	100.36	98.67	97.17	95.82	94.62	90.16	87.42	85.70
13000	126.12	122.16	118.72	115.72	113.09	110.77	108.72	106.89	105.27	103.81	102.50	97.67	94.71	92.84
14000	135.82	131.56	127.85	124.63	121.79	119.29	117.08	115.12	113.36	111.79	110.39	105.18	101.99	99.98
15000	145.53	140.95	136.99	133.53	130.49	127.81	125.44	123.34	121.46	119.78	118.27	112.69	109.28	107.13
16000	155.23	150.35	146.12	142.43	139.19	136.34	133.81	131.56	129.56	127.76	126.16	120.21	116.56	114.27
17000	164.93	159.75	155.25	151.33	147.89	144.86	142.17	139.78	137.65	135.75	134.04	127.72	123.85	121.41
18000	174.63	169.14	164.38	160.23	156.59	153.38	150.53	148.01	145.75	143.73	141.93	135.23	131.13	128.55
19000	184.33	178.54	173.52	169.13	165.29	161.90	158.90	156.23	153.85	151.72	149.81	142.75	138.42	135.69
20000	194.03	187.94	182.65	178.03	173.99	170.42	167.26	164.45	161.94	159.70	157.70	150.26	145.70	142.83
21000	203.73	197.33	191.78	186.94	182.69	178.94	175.62	172.67	170.04	167.69	165.58	157.77	152.99	149.97
22000	213.44	206.73	200.91	195.84	191.39	187.46	183.98	180.89	178.14	175.67	173.46	165.28	160.27	157.12
23000	223.14	216.12	210.04	204.74	200.08	195.98	192.35	189.12	186.24	183.66	181.35	172.80	167.56	164.26
24000	232.84	225.52	219.18	213.64	208.78	204.50	200.71	197.34	194.33	191.64	189.23	180.31	174.84	171.40
25000	242.54	234.92	228.31	222.54	217.48	213.02	209.07	205.56	202.43	199.63	197.12	187.82	182.13	178.54
26000	252.24	244.31	237.44	231.44	226.18	221.54	217.43	213.78	210.53	207.61	205.00	195.33	189.41	185.68
27000	261.94	253.71	246.57	240.34	234.88	230.06	225.80	222.01	218.62	215.60	212.89	202.85	196.70	192.82
28000	271.64	263.11	255.70	249.25	243.58	238.58	234.16	230.23	226.72	223.58	220.77	210.36	203.98	199.96
29000	281.35	272.50	264.84	258.15	252.28	247.10	242.52	238.45	234.82	231.57	228.66	217.87	211.27	207.11
30000	291.05	281.90	273.97	267.05	260.98	255.62	250.88	246.67	242.91	239.55	236.54	225.38	218.55	214.25
31000	300.75	291.30	283.10	275.95	269.68	264.15	259.25	254.89	251.01	247.54	244.42	232.90	225.84	221.39
32000	310.45	300.69	292.23	284.85	278.38	272.67	267.61	263.12	259.11	255.52	252.31	240.41	233.12	228.53
33000	320.15	310.09	301.37	293.75	287.08	281.19	275.97	271.34	267.21	263.51	260.19	247.92	240.41	235.67
34000	329.85	319.49	310.50	302.66	295.77	289.71	284.34	279.56	275.30	271.49	268.08	255.44	247.69	242.81
35000	339.55	328.88	319.63	311.56	304.47	298.23	292.70	287.78	283.40	279.48	275.96	262.95	254.98	249.95
36000	349.26	338.28	328.76	320.46	313.17	306.75	301.06	296.01	291.50	287.46	283.85	270.46	262.26	257.09
37000	358.96	347.68	337.89	329.36	321.87	315.27	309.42	304.23	299.59	295.45	291.73	277.97	269.55	264.24
38000	368.66	357.07	347.03	338.26	330.57	323.79	317.79	312.45	307.69	303.43	299.62	285.49	276.83	271.38
39000	378.36	366.47	356.16	347.16	339.27	332.31	326.15	320.67	315.79	311.42	307.50	293.00	284.12	278.52
40000	388.06	375.87	365.29	356.06	347.97	340.83	334.51	328.89	323.88	319.40	315.39	300.51	291.40	285.66
41000	397.76	385.26	374.42	364.97	356.67	349.35	342.87	337.12	331.98	327.39	323.27	308.02	298.69	292.80
42000	407.46	394.66	383.55	373.87	365.37	357.87	351.24	345.34	340.08	335.37	331.15	315.54	305.97	299.94
43000	417.17	404.05	392.69	382.77	374.07	366.39	359.60	353.56	348.18	343.36	339.04	323.05	313.26	307.08
44000	426.87	413.45	401.82	391.67	382.77	374.91	367.96	361.78	356.27	351.34	346.92	330.56	320.54	314.23
45000	436.57	422.85	410.95	400.57	391.46	383.43	376.32	370.01	364.37	359.33	354.81	338.07	327.83	321.37
46000	446.27	432.24	420.08	409.47	400.16	391.96	384.69	378.23	372.47	367.31	362.69	345.59	335.11	328.51
47000	455.97	441.64	429.22	418.37	408.86	400.48	393.05	386.45	380.56	375.30	370.58	353.10	342.40	335.65
48000	465.67	451.04	438.35	427.28	417.56	409.00	401.41	394.67	388.66	383.28	378.46	360.61	349.68	342.79
49000	475.37	460.43	447.48	436.18	426.26	417.52	409.78	402.89	396.76	391.27	386.35	368.13	356.97	349.93
50000	485.08	469.83	456.61	445.08	434.96	426.04	418.14	411.12	404.85	399.25	394.23	375.64	364.25	357.07
55000	533.58	516.81	502.27	489.59	478.46	468.64	459.95	452.23	445.34	439.18	433.65	413.20	400.68	392.78
60000	582.09	563.80	547.93	534.09	521.95	511.24	501.76	493.34	485.82	479.10	473.08	450.76	437.10	428.49
65000	630.60	610.78	593.59	578.60	565.45	553.85	543.58	534.45	526.31	519.03	512.50	488.33	473.52	464.20
70000	679.10	657.76	639.25	623.11	608.94	596.45	585.39	575.56	566.79	558.95	551.92	525.89	509.95	499.90
75000	727.61	704.74	684.92	667.62	652.44	639.05	627.20	616.67	607.28	598.88	591.34	563.45	546.37	535.61
80000	776.12	751.73	730.58	712.12	695.93	681.66	669.02	657.78	647.76	638.80	630.77	601.02	582.80	571.32
85000	824.62	798.71	776.24	756.63	739.43	724.26	710.83	698.89	688.25	678.73	670.19	638.58	619.22	607.02
90000	873.13	845.69	821.90	801.14	782.92	766.86	752.64	740.01	728.73	718.65	709.61	676.14	655.65	642.73
95000	921.64	892.67	867.56	845.65	826.42	809.47	794.46	781.12	769.22	758.58	749.03	713.71	692.07	678.44
100000	970.15	939.66	913.22	890.15	869.91	852.07	836.27	822.23	809.70	798.50	788.46	751.27	728.50	714.14

MONTHLY PAYMENT
REQUIRED TO AMORTIZE A LOAN

TERM AMOUNT	1 Year	2 Years	3 Years	4 Years	5 Years	6 Years	7 Years	8 Years	9 Years	10 Years	11 Years	12 Years	13 Years	14 Years
5	.44	.23	.16	.13	.11	.09	.08	.08	.07	.07	.06	.06	.06	.06
10	.88	.46	.32	.25	.21	.18	.16	.15	.14	.13	.12	.11	.11	.11
15	1.31	.69	.48	.37	.31	.27	.24	.22	.20	.19	.18	.17	.16	.16
25	2.18	1.14	.79	.62	.52	.45	.40	.36	.33	.31	.29	.28	.27	.26
50	4.36	2.27	1.58	1.23	1.03	.89	.79	.72	.66	.62	.58	.55	.53	.51
75	6.54	3.41	2.37	1.85	1.54	1.33	1.19	1.08	.99	.93	.87	.83	.79	.76
100	8.72	4.54	3.15	2.46	2.05	1.77	1.58	1.43	1.32	1.23	1.16	1.10	1.05	1.01
200	17.43	9.08	6.30	4.92	4.09	3.54	3.15	2.86	2.64	2.46	2.32	2.20	2.10	2.02
300	26.14	13.61	9.45	7.37	6.13	5.31	4.73	4.29	3.96	3.69	3.48	3.30	3.15	3.03
400	34.86	18.15	12.59	9.83	8.17	7.08	6.30	5.72	5.27	4.92	4.64	4.40	4.20	4.04
500	43.57	22.69	15.74	12.28	10.22	8.85	7.87	7.15	6.59	6.15	5.79	5.50	5.25	5.05
600	52.28	27.22	18.89	14.74	12.26	10.61	9.45	8.58	7.91	7.38	6.95	6.60	6.30	6.06
700	60.99	31.76	22.04	17.19	14.30	12.38	11.02	10.01	9.23	8.61	8.11	7.70	7.35	7.06
800	69.71	36.30	25.18	19.65	16.34	14.15	12.59	11.44	10.54	9.84	9.27	8.80	8.40	8.07
900	78.42	40.83	28.33	22.10	18.38	15.92	14.17	12.87	11.86	11.07	10.42	9.90	9.45	9.08
1000	87.13	45.37	31.48	24.56	20.43	17.69	15.74	14.29	13.18	12.30	11.58	10.99	10.50	10.09
2000	174.26	90.73	62.95	49.11	40.85	35.37	31.48	28.58	26.35	24.59	23.16	21.98	21.00	20.17
3000	261.39	136.10	94.43	73.67	61.27	53.05	47.21	42.87	39.53	36.88	34.74	32.97	31.50	30.26
4000	348.51	181.46	125.90	98.22	81.69	70.73	62.95	57.16	52.70	49.17	46.32	43.96	42.00	40.34
5000	435.64	226.83	157.38	122.77	102.11	88.41	78.69	71.45	65.88	61.46	57.89	54.95	52.50	50.43
6000	522.77	272.19	188.85	147.33	122.53	106.09	94.42	85.74	79.05	73.76	69.47	65.94	63.00	60.51
7000	609.90	317.55	220.33	171.88	142.95	123.77	110.16	100.03	92.23	86.05	81.05	76.93	73.50	70.59
8000	697.02	362.92	251.80	196.44	163.37	141.45	125.89	114.32	105.40	98.34	92.63	87.92	84.00	80.68
9000	784.15	408.28	283.28	220.99	183.79	159.13	141.63	128.61	118.58	110.63	104.20	98.91	94.50	90.76
10000	871.28	453.65	314.75	245.54	204.21	176.81	157.37	142.90	131.75	122.92	115.78	109.90	104.99	100.85
11000	958.40	499.01	346.23	270.10	224.63	194.49	173.10	157.19	144.93	135.22	127.36	120.89	115.49	110.93
12000	1045.53	544.38	377.70	294.65	245.05	212.17	188.84	171.48	158.10	147.51	138.94	131.88	125.99	121.02
13000	1132.66	589.74	409.18	319.21	265.47	229.85	204.57	185.77	171.28	159.80	150.51	142.87	136.49	131.10
14000	1219.79	635.10	440.65	343.76	285.89	247.53	220.31	200.06	184.45	172.09	162.09	153.86	146.99	141.18
15000	1306.91	680.47	472.13	368.31	306.31	265.21	236.05	214.35	197.63	184.38	173.67	164.85	157.49	151.27
16000	1394.04	725.83	503.60	392.87	326.73	282.89	251.78	228.64	210.80	196.67	185.25	175.84	167.99	161.35
17000	1481.17	771.20	535.08	417.42	347.15	300.57	267.52	242.93	223.98	208.97	196.82	186.83	178.49	171.44
18000	1568.29	816.56	566.55	441.98	367.57	318.25	283.25	257.22	237.15	221.26	208.40	197.82	188.99	181.52
19000	1655.42	861.93	598.03	466.53	387.99	335.93	298.99	271.51	250.33	233.55	219.98	208.81	199.48	191.61
20000	1742.55	907.29	629.50	491.08	408.41	353.61	314.73	285.80	263.50	245.84	231.56	219.80	209.98	201.69
21000	1829.68	952.65	660.98	515.64	428.83	371.29	330.46	300.09	276.67	258.13	243.13	230.79	220.48	211.77
22000	1916.80	998.02	692.45	540.19	449.25	388.97	346.20	314.38	289.85	270.43	254.71	241.78	230.98	221.86
23000	2003.93	1043.38	723.93	564.75	469.67	406.65	361.94	328.67	303.02	282.72	266.29	252.77	241.48	231.94
24000	2091.06	1088.75	755.40	589.30	490.09	424.33	377.67	342.96	316.20	295.01	277.87	263.76	251.98	242.03
25000	2178.19	1134.11	786.88	613.85	510.51	442.01	393.41	357.25	329.37	307.30	289.44	274.75	262.48	252.11
26000	2265.31	1179.48	818.35	638.41	530.93	459.69	409.14	371.54	342.55	319.59	301.02	285.74	272.98	262.20
27000	2352.44	1224.84	849.83	662.96	551.35	477.37	424.88	385.83	355.72	331.89	312.60	296.73	283.48	272.28
28000	2439.57	1270.20	881.30	687.52	571.77	495.05	440.62	400.11	368.90	344.18	324.18	307.72	293.97	282.36
29000	2526.69	1315.57	912.78	712.07	592.19	512.73	456.35	414.40	382.07	356.47	335.76	318.71	304.47	292.45
30000	2613.82	1360.93	944.25	736.62	612.61	530.41	472.09	428.69	395.25	368.76	347.33	329.70	314.97	302.53
31000	2700.95	1406.30	975.73	761.18	633.03	548.09	487.82	442.98	408.42	381.05	358.91	340.69	325.47	312.62
32000	2788.08	1451.66	1007.20	785.73	653.45	565.77	503.56	457.27	421.60	393.34	370.49	351.68	335.97	322.70
33000	2875.20	1497.02	1038.68	810.29	673.87	583.45	519.30	471.56	434.77	405.64	382.07	362.66	346.47	332.79
34000	2962.33	1542.39	1070.15	834.84	694.29	601.13	535.03	485.85	447.95	417.93	393.64	373.65	356.97	342.87
35000	3049.46	1587.75	1101.63	859.39	714.71	618.81	550.77	500.14	461.12	430.22	405.22	384.64	367.47	352.95
36000	3136.58	1633.12	1133.10	883.95	735.13	636.49	566.50	514.43	474.30	442.51	416.80	395.63	377.97	363.04
37000	3223.71	1678.48	1164.58	908.50	755.56	654.17	582.24	528.72	487.47	454.80	428.38	406.62	388.46	373.12
38000	3310.84	1723.85	1196.05	933.06	775.98	671.85	597.98	543.01	500.65	467.10	439.95	417.61	398.96	383.21
39000	3397.97	1769.21	1227.53	957.61	796.40	689.53	613.71	557.30	513.82	479.39	451.53	428.60	409.46	393.29
40000	3485.09	1814.57	1259.00	982.16	816.82	707.21	629.45	571.59	526.99	491.68	463.11	439.59	419.96	403.38
41000	3572.22	1859.94	1290.48	1006.72	837.24	724.89	645.19	585.88	540.17	503.97	474.69	450.58	430.46	413.46
42000	3659.35	1905.30	1321.95	1031.27	857.66	742.57	660.92	600.17	553.34	516.26	486.26	461.57	440.96	423.54
43000	3746.47	1950.67	1353.43	1055.83	878.08	760.25	676.66	614.46	566.52	528.55	497.84	472.56	451.46	433.63
44000	3833.60	1996.03	1384.90	1080.38	898.50	777.93	692.39	628.75	579.69	540.85	509.42	483.55	461.96	443.71
45000	3920.73	2041.40	1416.38	1104.93	918.92	795.61	708.13	643.04	592.87	553.14	521.00	494.54	472.46	453.80
46000	4007.86	2086.76	1447.85	1129.49	939.34	813.29	723.87	657.33	606.04	565.43	532.57	505.53	482.95	463.88
47000	4094.98	2132.12	1479.33	1154.04	959.76	830.97	739.60	671.62	619.22	577.72	544.15	516.52	493.45	473.97
48000	4182.11	2177.49	1510.80	1178.60	980.18	848.65	755.34	685.91	632.39	590.01	555.73	527.51	503.95	484.05
49000	4269.24	2222.85	1542.28	1203.15	1000.60	866.33	771.07	700.20	645.57	602.31	567.31	538.50	514.45	494.13
50000	4356.37	2268.22	1573.75	1227.70	1021.02	884.01	786.81	714.49	658.74	614.60	578.88	549.49	524.95	504.22
55000	4792.00	2495.04	1731.13	1350.47	1123.12	972.41	865.49	785.93	724.62	676.06	636.77	604.44	577.44	554.64
60000	5227.64	2721.86	1888.50	1473.24	1225.22	1060.81	944.17	857.38	790.49	737.52	694.66	659.39	629.94	605.06
65000	5663.27	2948.68	2045.88	1596.01	1327.32	1149.21	1022.85	928.83	856.36	798.98	752.55	714.34	682.43	655.48
70000	6098.91	3175.50	2203.25	1718.78	1429.42	1237.61	1101.53	1000.28	922.24	860.44	810.44	769.28	734.93	705.90
75000	6534.55	3402.32	2360.63	1841.55	1531.53	1326.01	1180.21	1071.73	988.11	921.89	868.32	824.23	787.42	756.33
80000	6970.18	3629.14	2518.00	1964.32	1633.63	1414.41	1258.89	1143.18	1053.98	983.35	926.21	879.18	839.92	806.75
85000	7405.82	3855.97	2675.38	2087.09	1735.73	1502.81	1337.57	1214.62	1119.86	1044.81	984.10	934.13	892.41	857.17
90000	7841.45	4082.79	2832.75	2209.86	1837.83	1591.21	1416.25	1286.07	1185.73	1106.27	1041.99	989.08	944.91	907.59
95000	8277.09	4309.61	2990.12	2332.63	1939.93	1679.61	1494.93	1357.52	1251.61	1167.73	1099.88	1044.03	997.40	958.01
100000	8712.73	4536.43	3147.50	2455.40	2042.03	1768.01	1573.61	1428.97	1317.48	1229.19	1157.76	1098.97	1049.89	1008.43

TERM	15 Years	16 Years	17 Years	18 Years	19 Years	20 Years	21 Years	22 Years	23 Years	24 Years	25 Years	30 Years	35 Years	40 Years
AMOUNT														
5	.05	.05	.05	.05	.05	.05	.05	.05	.05	.05	.04	.04	.04	.04
10	.10	.10	.10	.09	.09	.09	.09	.09	.09	.09	.08	.08	.08	.08
15	.15	.15	.14	.14	.14	.13	.13	.13	.13	.13	.12	.12	.11	.11
25	.25	.24	.23	.23	.22	.22	.21	.21	.21	.21	.20	.19	.19	.18
50	.49	.48	.46	.45	.44	.43	.42	.42	.41	.41	.40	.38	.37	.36
75	.73	.71	.69	.67	.66	.65	.63	.62	.61	.61	.60	.57	.55	.54
100	.98	.95	.92	.90	.88	.86	.84	.83	.82	.81	.80	.76	.74	.72
200	1.95	1.89	1.84	1.79	1.75	1.72	1.68	1.66	1.63	1.61	1.59	1.51	1.47	1.44
300	2.92	2.83	2.75	2.68	2.62	2.57	2.52	2.48	2.44	2.41	2.38	2.27	2.20	2.16
400	3.90	3.78	3.67	3.58	3.50	3.43	3.36	3.31	3.26	3.21	3.17	3.02	2.93	2.88
500	4.87	4.72	4.59	4.47	4.37	4.28	4.20	4.13	4.07	4.01	3.96	3.78	3.67	3.59
600	5.84	5.66	5.50	5.36	5.24	5.14	5.04	4.96	4.88	4.82	4.76	4.53	4.40	4.31
700	6.82	6.60	6.42	6.26	6.12	5.99	5.88	5.78	5.70	5.62	5.55	5.29	5.13	5.03
800	7.79	7.55	7.33	7.15	6.99	6.85	6.72	6.61	6.51	6.42	6.34	6.04	5.86	5.75
900	8.76	8.49	8.25	8.04	7.86	7.70	7.56	7.43	7.32	7.22	7.13	6.80	6.59	6.47
1000	9.74	9.43	9.17	8.94	8.74	8.56	8.40	8.26	8.13	8.02	7.92	7.55	7.33	7.18
2000	19.47	18.86	18.33	17.87	17.47	17.11	16.79	16.51	16.26	16.04	15.84	15.10	14.65	14.36
3000	29.20	28.28	27.49	26.80	26.20	25.66	25.19	24.77	24.39	24.06	23.76	22.65	21.97	21.54
4000	38.93	37.71	36.65	35.73	34.93	34.21	33.58	33.02	32.52	32.08	31.68	30.20	29.29	28.72
5000	48.66	47.14	45.82	44.66	43.66	42.77	41.98	41.28	40.65	40.10	39.59	37.74	36.61	35.90
6000	58.39	56.56	54.98	53.60	52.39	51.32	50.37	49.53	48.78	48.11	47.51	45.29	43.93	43.08
7000	68.12	65.99	64.14	62.53	61.12	59.87	58.77	57.79	56.91	56.13	55.43	52.84	51.26	50.26
8000	77.85	75.41	73.30	71.46	69.85	68.42	67.16	66.04	65.04	64.15	63.35	60.39	58.58	57.44
9000	87.58	84.84	82.46	80.39	78.58	76.97	75.56	74.30	73.17	72.17	71.27	67.94	65.90	64.62
10000	97.31	94.27	91.63	89.32	87.31	85.53	83.95	82.55	81.30	80.19	79.18	75.48	73.22	71.80
11000	107.04	103.69	100.79	98.26	96.04	94.08	92.34	90.80	89.43	88.20	87.10	83.03	80.54	78.98
12000	116.77	113.12	109.95	107.19	104.77	102.63	100.74	99.06	97.56	96.22	95.02	90.58	87.86	86.16
13000	126.50	122.54	119.11	116.12	113.50	111.18	109.13	107.31	105.69	104.24	102.94	98.13	95.19	93.33
14000	136.23	131.97	128.28	125.05	122.23	119.73	117.53	115.57	113.82	112.26	110.86	105.67	102.51	100.51
15000	145.96	141.40	137.44	133.98	130.96	128.29	125.92	123.82	121.95	120.28	118.77	113.22	109.83	107.69
16000	155.69	150.82	146.60	142.92	139.69	136.84	134.32	132.08	130.08	128.29	126.69	120.77	117.15	114.87
17000	165.42	160.25	155.76	151.85	148.42	145.39	142.71	140.33	138.21	136.31	134.61	128.32	124.47	122.05
18000	175.15	169.67	164.92	160.78	157.15	153.94	151.11	148.59	146.34	144.33	142.53	135.87	131.79	129.23
19000	184.88	179.10	174.09	169.71	165.88	162.49	159.50	156.84	154.47	152.35	150.45	143.41	139.11	136.41
20000	194.62	188.53	183.25	178.64	174.61	171.05	167.89	165.09	162.60	160.37	158.36	150.96	146.44	143.59
21000	204.35	197.95	192.41	187.58	183.34	179.60	176.29	173.35	170.73	168.38	166.28	158.51	153.76	150.77
22000	214.08	207.38	201.57	196.51	192.07	188.15	184.68	181.60	178.86	176.40	174.20	166.06	161.08	157.95
23000	223.81	216.81	210.74	205.44	200.80	196.70	193.08	189.86	186.99	184.42	182.12	173.61	168.40	165.13
24000	233.54	226.23	219.90	214.37	209.53	205.25	201.47	198.11	195.12	192.44	190.04	181.15	175.72	172.31
25000	243.27	235.66	229.06	223.30	218.26	213.81	209.87	206.37	203.25	200.46	197.95	188.70	183.04	179.48
26000	253.00	245.08	238.22	232.24	226.99	222.36	218.26	214.62	211.38	208.47	205.87	196.25	190.37	186.66
27000	262.73	254.51	247.38	241.17	235.72	230.91	226.66	222.88	219.51	216.49	213.79	203.80	197.69	193.84
28000	272.46	263.94	256.55	250.10	244.45	239.46	235.05	231.13	227.64	224.51	221.71	211.34	205.01	201.02
29000	282.19	273.36	265.71	259.03	253.18	248.01	243.45	239.39	235.77	232.53	229.63	218.89	212.33	208.20
30000	291.92	282.79	274.87	267.96	261.91	256.57	251.84	247.64	243.89	240.55	237.54	226.44	219.65	215.38
31000	301.65	292.21	284.03	276.90	270.64	265.12	260.23	255.89	252.02	248.56	245.46	233.99	226.97	222.56
32000	311.38	301.64	293.20	285.83	279.37	273.67	268.63	264.15	260.15	256.58	253.38	241.54	234.29	229.74
33000	321.11	311.07	302.36	294.76	288.10	282.22	277.02	272.40	268.28	264.60	261.30	249.08	241.62	236.92
34000	330.84	320.49	311.52	303.69	296.83	290.78	285.42	280.66	276.41	272.62	269.22	256.63	248.94	244.10
35000	340.57	329.92	320.68	312.62	305.56	299.33	293.81	288.91	284.54	280.64	277.13	264.18	256.26	251.28
36000	350.30	339.34	329.84	321.56	314.29	307.88	302.21	297.17	292.67	288.65	285.05	271.73	263.58	258.46
37000	360.03	348.77	339.01	330.49	323.02	316.43	310.60	305.42	300.80	296.67	292.97	279.28	270.90	265.64
38000	369.76	358.20	348.17	339.42	331.75	324.98	319.00	313.68	308.93	304.69	300.89	286.82	278.22	272.81
39000	379.50	367.62	357.33	348.35	340.48	333.54	327.39	321.93	317.06	312.71	308.80	294.37	285.55	279.99
40000	389.23	377.05	366.49	357.28	349.21	342.09	335.78	330.18	325.19	320.73	316.72	301.92	292.87	287.17
41000	398.96	386.47	375.66	366.22	357.94	350.64	344.18	338.44	333.32	328.74	324.64	309.47	300.19	294.35
42000	408.69	395.90	384.82	375.15	366.67	359.19	352.57	346.69	341.45	336.76	332.56	317.01	307.51	301.53
43000	418.42	405.33	393.98	384.08	375.40	367.74	360.97	354.95	349.58	344.78	340.48	324.56	314.83	308.71
44000	428.15	414.75	403.14	393.01	384.13	376.30	369.36	363.20	357.71	352.80	348.39	332.11	322.15	315.89
45000	437.88	424.18	412.30	401.94	392.86	384.85	377.76	371.46	365.84	360.82	356.31	339.66	329.47	323.07
46000	447.61	433.61	421.47	410.88	401.59	393.40	386.15	379.71	373.97	368.83	364.23	347.21	336.80	330.25
47000	457.34	443.03	430.63	419.81	410.32	401.95	394.55	387.97	382.10	376.85	372.15	354.75	344.12	337.43
48000	467.07	452.46	439.79	428.74	419.05	410.50	402.94	396.22	390.23	384.87	380.07	362.30	351.44	344.61
49000	476.80	461.88	448.95	437.67	427.78	419.06	411.34	404.47	398.36	392.89	387.98	369.85	358.76	351.79
50000	486.53	471.31	458.12	446.60	436.51	427.61	419.73	412.73	406.49	400.91	395.90	377.40	366.08	358.96
55000	535.18	518.44	503.93	491.26	480.16	470.37	461.70	454.00	447.14	441.00	435.49	415.14	402.69	394.86
60000	583.84	565.57	549.74	535.92	523.81	513.13	503.67	495.27	487.78	481.09	475.08	452.88	439.30	430.76
65000	632.49	612.70	595.55	580.58	567.46	555.89	545.65	536.55	528.43	521.18	514.67	490.61	475.91	466.65
70000	681.14	659.83	641.36	625.24	611.11	598.65	587.62	577.82	569.08	561.27	554.26	528.35	512.51	502.55
75000	729.79	706.96	687.17	669.90	654.76	641.41	629.59	619.09	609.73	601.36	593.85	566.09	549.12	538.44
80000	778.45	754.09	732.98	714.56	698.41	684.17	671.56	660.36	650.38	641.45	633.44	603.83	585.73	574.34
85000	827.10	801.22	778.79	759.22	742.06	726.93	713.54	701.64	691.03	681.54	673.03	641.57	622.34	610.24
90000	875.75	848.35	824.60	803.88	785.71	769.69	755.51	742.91	731.67	721.63	712.62	679.31	658.96	646.13
95000	924.40	895.48	870.41	848.54	829.36	812.45	797.48	784.18	772.32	761.72	752.21	717.05	695.55	682.03
100000	973.06	942.61	916.23	893.20	873.01	855.21	839.45	825.45	812.97	801.81	791.80	754.79	732.16	717.92

8.375%

TERM AMOUNT	1 Year	2 Years	3 Years	4 Years	5 Years	6 Years	7 Years	8 Years	9 Years	10 Years	11 Years	12 Years	13 Years	14 Years
5	.44	.23	.16	.13	.11	.09	.08	.08	.07	.07	.06	.06	.06	.06
10	.88	.46	.32	.25	.21	.18	.16	.15	.14	.13	.12	.12	.11	.11
15	1.31	.69	.48	.37	.31	.27	.24	.22	.20	.19	.18	.17	.16	.16
25	2.18	1.14	.79	.62	.52	.45	.40	.36	.34	.31	.30	.28	.27	.26
50	4.36	2.27	1.58	1.23	1.03	.89	.79	.72	.67	.62	.59	.56	.53	.51
75	6.54	3.41	2.37	1.85	1.54	1.33	1.19	1.08	1.00	.93	.88	.83	.80	.76
100	8.72	4.54	3.16	2.46	2.05	1.78	1.58	1.44	1.33	1.24	1.17	1.11	1.06	1.02
200	17.44	9.08	6.31	4.92	4.10	3.55	3.16	2.87	2.65	2.47	2.33	2.21	2.11	2.03
300	26.15	13.62	9.46	7.38	6.14	5.32	4.74	4.30	3.97	3.70	3.49	3.31	3.17	3.04
400	34.87	18.16	12.61	9.84	8.19	7.09	6.31	5.74	5.29	4.94	4.65	4.42	4.22	4.06
500	43.59	22.70	15.76	12.30	10.23	8.86	7.89	7.17	6.61	6.17	5.81	5.52	5.28	5.07
600	52.30	27.24	18.91	14.76	12.28	10.64	9.47	8.60	7.93	7.40	6.98	6.62	6.33	6.08
700	61.02	31.78	22.06	17.22	14.32	12.41	11.05	10.03	9.25	8.64	8.14	7.73	7.38	7.09
800	69.73	36.32	25.21	19.68	16.37	14.18	12.62	11.47	10.58	9.87	9.30	8.83	8.44	8.11
900	78.45	40.86	28.36	22.14	18.42	15.95	14.20	12.90	11.90	11.10	10.46	9.93	9.49	9.12
1000	87.17	45.40	31.51	24.59	20.46	17.72	15.78	14.33	13.22	12.34	11.62	11.04	10.55	10.13
2000	174.33	90.80	63.02	49.18	40.92	35.44	31.55	28.66	26.43	24.67	23.24	22.07	21.09	20.26
3000	261.49	136.20	94.53	73.77	61.37	53.16	47.33	42.99	39.65	37.00	34.86	33.10	31.63	30.39
4000	348.65	181.60	126.04	98.36	81.83	70.87	63.10	57.32	52.86	49.33	46.48	44.13	42.17	40.51
5000	435.81	227.00	157.55	122.95	102.29	88.59	78.87	71.65	66.07	61.66	58.10	55.16	52.71	50.64
6000	522.98	272.40	189.06	147.54	122.74	106.31	94.65	85.97	79.29	74.00	69.71	66.19	63.25	60.77
7000	610.14	317.79	220.57	172.13	143.20	124.02	110.42	100.30	92.50	86.33	81.33	77.22	73.79	70.90
8000	697.30	363.19	252.08	196.72	163.66	141.74	126.19	114.63	105.72	98.66	92.95	88.25	84.33	81.02
9000	784.46	408.59	283.59	221.31	184.11	159.46	141.97	128.96	118.93	110.99	104.57	99.29	94.88	91.15
10000	871.62	453.99	315.10	245.90	204.57	177.17	157.74	143.29	132.14	123.32	116.19	110.32	105.42	101.28
11000	958.79	499.39	346.61	270.49	225.02	194.89	173.52	157.61	145.36	135.65	127.81	121.35	115.96	111.41
12000	1045.95	544.79	378.12	295.08	245.48	212.61	189.29	171.94	158.57	147.99	139.42	132.38	126.50	121.53
13000	1133.11	590.19	409.63	319.67	265.94	230.32	205.06	186.27	171.79	160.32	151.04	143.41	137.04	131.66
14000	1220.27	635.58	441.14	344.26	286.39	248.04	220.84	200.60	185.00	172.65	162.66	154.44	147.58	141.79
15000	1307.43	680.98	472.65	368.84	306.85	265.76	236.61	214.93	198.21	184.98	174.28	165.47	158.12	151.91
16000	1394.60	726.38	504.16	393.43	327.31	283.48	252.38	229.25	211.43	197.31	185.90	176.50	168.66	162.04
17000	1481.76	771.78	535.67	418.02	347.76	301.19	268.16	243.58	224.64	209.65	197.52	187.54	179.20	172.17
18000	1568.92	817.18	567.18	442.61	368.22	318.91	283.93	257.91	237.86	221.98	209.13	198.57	189.75	182.30
19000	1656.08	862.58	598.69	467.20	388.68	336.63	299.71	272.24	251.07	234.31	220.75	209.60	200.29	192.42
20000	1743.24	907.98	630.20	491.79	409.13	354.34	315.48	286.57	264.28	246.64	232.37	220.63	210.83	202.55
21000	1830.41	953.37	661.71	516.38	429.59	372.06	331.25	300.89	277.50	258.97	243.99	231.66	221.37	212.68
22000	1917.57	998.77	693.22	540.97	450.04	389.78	347.03	315.22	290.71	271.30	255.61	242.69	231.91	222.81
23000	2004.73	1044.17	724.73	565.56	470.50	407.49	362.80	329.55	303.93	283.64	267.23	253.72	242.45	232.93
24000	2091.89	1089.57	756.24	590.15	490.96	425.21	378.57	343.88	317.14	295.97	278.84	264.75	252.99	243.06
25000	2179.05	1134.97	787.75	614.74	511.41	442.93	394.35	358.21	330.35	308.30	290.46	275.78	263.53	253.19
26000	2266.21	1180.37	819.26	639.33	531.87	460.64	410.12	372.53	343.57	320.63	302.08	286.82	274.08	263.31
27000	2353.38	1225.76	850.77	663.92	552.33	478.36	425.89	386.86	356.78	332.96	313.70	297.85	284.62	273.44
28000	2440.54	1271.16	882.28	688.51	572.78	496.08	441.67	401.19	369.99	345.30	325.32	308.88	295.16	283.57
29000	2527.70	1316.56	913.78	713.10	593.24	513.80	457.44	415.52	383.21	357.63	336.94	319.91	305.70	293.70
30000	2614.86	1361.96	945.29	737.68	613.70	531.51	473.22	429.85	396.42	369.96	348.55	330.94	316.24	303.82
31000	2702.02	1407.36	976.80	762.27	634.15	549.23	488.99	444.17	409.64	382.29	360.17	341.97	326.78	313.95
32000	2789.19	1452.76	1008.31	786.86	654.61	566.95	504.76	458.50	422.85	394.62	371.79	353.00	337.32	324.08
33000	2876.35	1498.16	1039.82	811.45	675.06	584.66	520.54	472.83	436.06	406.95	383.41	364.03	347.86	334.21
34000	2963.51	1543.55	1071.33	836.04	695.52	602.38	536.31	487.16	449.28	419.29	395.03	375.07	358.40	344.33
35000	3050.67	1588.95	1102.84	860.63	715.98	620.10	552.08	501.49	462.49	431.62	406.65	386.10	368.95	354.46
36000	3137.83	1634.35	1134.35	885.22	736.43	637.81	567.86	515.81	475.71	443.95	418.26	397.13	379.49	364.59
37000	3225.00	1679.75	1165.86	909.81	756.89	655.53	583.63	530.14	488.92	456.28	429.88	408.16	390.03	374.71
38000	3312.16	1725.15	1197.37	934.40	777.35	673.25	599.41	544.47	502.13	468.61	441.50	419.19	400.57	384.84
39000	3399.32	1770.55	1228.88	958.99	797.80	690.96	615.18	558.80	515.35	480.95	453.12	430.22	411.11	394.97
40000	3486.48	1815.95	1260.39	983.58	818.26	708.68	630.95	573.13	528.56	493.28	464.74	441.25	421.65	405.10
41000	3573.64	1861.34	1291.90	1008.17	838.71	726.40	646.73	587.45	541.78	505.61	476.36	452.28	432.19	415.22
42000	3660.81	1906.74	1323.41	1032.76	859.17	744.12	662.50	601.78	554.99	517.94	487.97	463.32	442.73	425.35
43000	3747.97	1952.14	1354.92	1057.35	879.63	761.83	678.27	616.11	568.20	530.27	499.59	474.35	453.27	435.48
44000	3835.13	1997.54	1386.43	1081.94	900.08	779.55	694.05	630.44	581.42	542.60	511.21	485.38	463.82	445.61
45000	3922.29	2042.94	1417.94	1106.52	920.54	797.27	709.82	644.77	594.63	554.94	522.83	496.41	474.36	455.73
46000	4009.45	2088.34	1449.45	1131.11	941.00	814.98	725.60	659.09	607.85	567.27	534.45	507.44	484.90	465.86
47000	4096.61	2133.74	1480.96	1155.70	961.45	832.70	741.37	673.42	621.06	579.60	546.07	518.47	495.44	475.99
48000	4183.78	2179.13	1512.47	1180.29	981.91	850.42	757.14	687.75	634.27	591.93	557.68	529.50	505.98	486.11
49000	4270.94	2224.53	1543.98	1204.88	1002.37	868.13	772.92	702.08	647.49	604.26	569.30	540.53	516.52	496.24
50000	4358.10	2269.93	1575.49	1229.47	1022.82	885.85	788.69	716.41	660.70	616.60	580.92	551.56	527.06	506.37
55000	4793.91	2496.92	1733.04	1352.42	1125.10	974.44	867.56	788.05	726.77	678.25	639.01	606.72	579.77	557.01
60000	5229.72	2723.92	1890.58	1475.36	1227.39	1063.02	946.43	859.69	792.84	739.91	697.10	661.88	632.47	607.64
65000	5665.53	2950.91	2048.13	1598.31	1329.67	1151.60	1025.30	931.33	858.91	801.57	755.20	717.03	685.18	658.28
70000	6101.34	3177.90	2205.68	1721.26	1431.95	1240.19	1104.16	1002.97	924.98	863.23	813.29	772.19	737.89	708.92
75000	6537.15	3404.89	2363.23	1844.20	1534.23	1328.77	1183.03	1074.61	991.05	924.89	871.38	827.34	790.59	759.55
80000	6972.96	3631.89	2520.78	1967.15	1636.51	1417.36	1261.90	1146.25	1057.12	986.55	929.47	882.50	843.30	810.19
85000	7408.77	3858.88	2678.33	2090.10	1738.79	1505.94	1340.77	1217.89	1123.19	1048.21	987.56	937.66	896.00	860.82
90000	7844.58	4085.87	2835.87	2213.04	1841.08	1594.53	1419.64	1289.53	1189.26	1109.87	1045.65	992.81	948.71	911.46
95000	8280.39	4312.86	2993.42	2335.99	1943.36	1683.11	1498.51	1361.17	1255.33	1171.53	1103.75	1047.97	1001.41	962.10
100000	8716.20	4539.86	3150.97	2458.94	2045.64	1771.70	1577.38	1432.81	1321.40	1233.19	1161.84	1103.12	1054.12	1012.73

TERM	15 Years	16 Years	17 Years	18 Years	19 Years	20 Years	21 Years	22 Years	23 Years	24 Years	25 Years	30 Years	35 Years	40 Years
AMOUNT														
5	.05	.05	.05	.05	.05	.05	.05	.05	.05	.05	.04	.04	.04	.04
10	.10	.10	.10	.09	.09	.09	.09	.09	.09	.09	.08	.08	.08	.08
15	.15	.15	.14	.14	.14	.13	.13	.13	.13	.13	.12	.12	.12	.11
25	.25	.24	.24	.23	.22	.22	.22	.21	.21	.21	.20	.20	.19	.19
50	.49	.48	.47	.45	.44	.43	.43	.42	.41	.41	.40	.39	.37	.37
75	.74	.72	.70	.68	.66	.65	.64	.63	.62	.61	.60	.58	.56	.55
100	.98	.95	.93	.90	.88	.86	.85	.84	.82	.81	.80	.77	.74	.73
200	1.96	1.90	1.85	1.80	1.76	1.72	1.69	1.67	1.64	1.62	1.60	1.53	1.48	1.45
300	2.94	2.85	2.77	2.70	2.64	2.58	2.54	2.50	2.46	2.43	2.40	2.29	2.22	2.18
400	3.91	3.79	3.69	3.60	3.52	3.44	3.38	3.33	3.28	3.23	3.19	3.05	2.96	2.90
500	4.89	4.74	4.61	4.49	4.39	4.30	4.23	4.16	4.09	4.04	3.99	3.81	3.69	3.62
600	5.87	5.69	5.53	5.39	5.27	5.16	5.07	4.99	4.91	4.85	4.79	4.57	4.43	4.35
700	6.85	6.63	6.45	6.29	6.15	6.02	5.91	5.82	5.73	5.65	5.58	5.33	5.17	5.07
800	7.82	7.58	7.37	7.19	7.03	6.88	6.76	6.65	6.55	6.46	6.38	6.09	5.91	5.79
900	8.80	8.53	8.29	8.09	7.90	7.74	7.60	7.48	7.37	7.27	7.18	6.85	6.64	6.52
1000	9.78	9.48	9.21	8.98	8.78	8.60	8.45	8.31	8.18	8.07	7.97	7.61	7.38	7.24
2000	19.55	18.95	18.42	17.96	17.56	17.20	16.89	16.61	16.36	16.14	15.94	15.21	14.76	14.48
3000	29.33	28.42	27.63	26.94	26.33	25.80	25.33	24.91	24.54	24.21	23.91	22.81	22.13	21.71
4000	39.10	37.89	36.83	35.92	35.11	34.40	33.77	33.22	32.72	32.28	31.88	30.41	29.51	28.95
5000	48.88	47.36	46.04	44.89	43.89	43.00	42.22	41.52	40.90	40.34	39.85	38.01	36.89	36.19
6000	58.65	56.83	55.25	53.87	52.66	51.60	50.66	49.82	49.08	48.41	47.81	45.61	44.26	43.42
7000	68.42	66.30	64.46	62.85	61.44	60.20	59.10	58.13	57.26	56.48	55.78	53.21	51.64	50.66
8000	78.20	75.77	73.66	71.83	70.22	68.80	67.54	66.43	65.44	64.55	63.75	60.81	59.02	57.89
9000	87.97	85.24	82.87	80.81	78.99	77.40	75.99	74.73	73.61	72.61	71.72	68.41	66.39	65.13
10000	97.75	94.71	92.08	89.78	87.77	86.00	84.43	83.03	81.79	80.68	79.69	76.01	73.77	72.37
11000	107.52	104.18	101.29	98.76	96.55	94.60	92.87	91.34	89.97	88.75	87.66	83.61	81.15	79.60
12000	117.30	113.65	110.49	107.74	105.32	103.20	101.31	99.64	90.15	96.82	95.63	91.21	88.52	86.84
13000	127.07	123.12	119.70	116.72	114.10	111.80	109.76	107.94	106.33	104.89	103.59	98.81	95.90	94.07
14000	136.84	132.59	128.91	125.70	122.88	120.39	118.20	116.25	114.51	112.95	111.56	106.42	103.28	101.31
15000	146.62	142.06	138.12	134.67	131.65	128.99	126.64	124.55	122.69	121.02	119.53	114.02	110.65	108.55
16000	156.39	151.53	147.32	143.65	140.43	137.59	135.08	132.85	130.87	129.09	127.50	121.62	118.03	115.78
17000	166.17	161.00	156.53	152.63	149.21	146.19	143.53	141.16	139.04	137.16	135.46	129.22	125.41	123.02
18000	175.94	170.48	165.74	161.61	157.98	154.79	151.97	149.46	147.22	145.22	143.43	136.82	132.78	130.25
19000	185.72	179.95	174.95	170.58	166.76	163.39	160.41	157.76	155.40	153.29	151.40	144.42	140.16	137.49
20000	195.49	189.42	184.15	179.56	175.54	171.99	168.85	166.06	163.58	161.36	159.37	152.02	147.54	144.73
21000	205.26	198.89	193.36	188.54	184.31	180.59	177.29	174.37	171.76	169.43	167.34	159.62	154.91	151.96
22000	215.04	208.36	202.57	197.52	193.09	189.19	185.74	182.67	179.94	177.49	175.31	167.22	162.29	159.20
23000	224.81	217.83	211.77	206.50	201.87	197.79	194.18	190.97	188.12	185.56	183.27	174.82	169.67	166.43
24000	234.59	227.30	220.98	215.47	210.64	206.39	202.62	199.28	196.30	193.63	191.24	182.42	177.04	173.67
25000	244.36	236.77	230.19	224.45	219.42	214.99	211.06	207.58	204.47	201.70	199.21	190.02	184.42	180.91
26000	254.14	246.24	239.40	233.43	228.20	223.59	219.51	215.88	212.65	209.77	207.18	197.62	191.80	188.14
27000	263.91	255.71	248.60	242.41	236.97	232.19	227.95	224.19	220.83	217.83	215.15	205.22	199.17	195.38
28000	273.68	265.18	257.81	251.39	245.75	240.78	236.39	232.49	229.01	225.90	223.11	212.83	206.55	202.61
29000	283.46	274.65	267.02	260.36	254.53	249.38	244.83	240.79	237.19	233.97	231.08	220.43	213.93	209.85
30000	293.23	284.12	276.23	269.34	263.30	257.98	253.28	249.09	245.37	242.04	239.05	228.03	221.30	217.09
31000	303.01	293.59	285.43	278.32	272.08	266.58	261.72	257.40	253.55	250.10	247.02	235.63	228.68	224.32
32000	312.78	303.06	294.64	287.30	280.86	275.18	270.16	265.70	261.73	258.17	254.99	243.23	236.06	231.56
33000	322.56	312.53	303.85	296.27	289.63	283.78	278.60	274.00	269.90	266.24	262.96	250.83	243.43	238.79
34000	332.33	322.00	313.06	305.25	298.41	292.38	287.05	282.31	278.08	274.31	270.92	258.43	250.81	246.03
35000	342.10	331.47	322.26	314.23	307.19	300.98	295.49	290.61	286.26	282.38	278.89	266.03	258.19	253.27
36000	351.88	340.95	331.47	323.21	315.96	309.58	303.93	298.91	294.44	290.44	286.86	273.63	265.56	260.50
37000	361.65	350.42	340.68	332.19	324.74	318.18	312.37	307.22	302.62	298.51	294.83	281.23	272.94	267.74
38000	371.43	359.89	349.89	341.16	333.52	326.78	320.81	315.52	310.80	306.58	302.80	288.83	280.32	274.97
39000	381.20	369.36	359.09	350.14	342.29	335.38	329.26	323.82	318.98	314.65	310.77	296.43	287.69	282.21
40000	390.98	378.83	368.30	359.12	351.07	343.98	337.70	332.12	327.16	322.71	318.73	304.03	295.07	289.45
41000	400.75	388.30	377.51	368.10	359.85	352.58	346.14	340.43	335.33	330.78	326.70	311.63	302.45	296.68
42000	410.52	397.77	386.72	377.08	368.62	361.17	354.58	348.73	343.51	338.85	334.67	319.24	309.82	303.92
43000	420.30	407.24	395.92	386.05	377.40	369.77	363.03	357.03	351.69	346.92	342.64	326.84	317.20	311.15
44000	430.07	416.71	405.13	395.03	386.18	378.37	371.47	365.34	359.87	354.98	350.61	334.44	324.57	318.39
45000	439.85	426.18	414.34	404.01	394.95	386.97	379.91	373.64	368.05	363.05	358.57	342.04	331.95	325.63
46000	449.62	435.65	423.54	412.99	403.73	395.57	388.35	381.94	376.23	371.12	366.54	349.64	339.33	332.86
47000	459.40	445.12	432.75	421.96	412.51	404.17	396.80	390.24	384.41	379.19	374.51	357.24	346.70	340.10
48000	469.17	454.59	441.96	430.94	421.28	412.77	405.24	398.55	392.59	387.26	382.48	364.84	354.08	347.33
49000	478.94	464.06	451.17	439.92	430.06	421.37	413.68	406.85	400.76	395.32	390.45	372.44	361.46	354.57
50000	488.72	473.53	460.37	448.90	438.84	429.97	422.12	415.15	408.94	403.39	398.42	380.04	368.83	361.81
55000	537.59	520.89	506.41	493.79	482.72	472.97	464.33	456.67	449.84	443.73	438.26	418.04	405.72	397.99
60000	586.46	568.24	552.45	538.68	526.60	515.96	506.55	498.18	490.73	484.07	478.10	456.05	442.60	434.17
65000	635.33	615.59	598.48	583.57	570.48	558.96	548.76	539.70	531.62	524.41	517.94	494.05	479.48	470.35
70000	684.20	662.94	644.52	628.46	614.37	601.95	590.97	581.21	572.52	564.75	557.78	532.06	516.37	506.53
75000	733.07	710.30	690.56	673.35	658.25	644.95	633.18	622.73	613.41	605.08	597.62	570.06	553.25	542.71
80000	781.95	757.65	736.60	718.23	702.13	687.95	675.39	664.24	654.31	645.42	637.46	608.06	590.13	578.89
85000	830.82	805.00	782.63	763.12	746.02	730.94	717.61	705.76	695.20	685.76	677.30	646.07	627.02	615.07
90000	879.69	852.36	828.67	808.01	789.90	773.94	759.82	747.27	736.09	726.10	717.14	684.07	663.90	651.25
95000	928.56	899.71	874.71	852.90	833.78	816.94	802.03	788.79	776.99	766.44	756.98	722.07	700.78	687.43
100000	977.43	947.06	920.74	897.79	877.67	859.93	844.24	830.30	817.88	806.78	796.83	760.08	737.66	723.61

TERM AMOUNT	1 Year	2 Years	3 Years	4 Years	5 Years	6 Years	7 Years	8 Years	9 Years	10 Years	11 Years	12 Years	13 Years	14 Years
5	.44	.23	.16	.13	.11	.09	.08	.08	.07	.07	.06	.06	.06	.06
10	.88	.46	.32	.25	.21	.18	.16	.15	.14	.13	.12	.12	.11	.11
15	1.31	.69	.48	.37	.31	.27	.24	.22	.20	.19	.18	.17	.16	.16
25	2.18	1.14	.79	.62	.52	.45	.40	.36	.34	.31	.30	.28	.27	.26
50	4.36	2.28	1.58	1.24	1.03	.89	.79	.72	.67	.62	.59	.56	.53	.51
75	6.54	3.41	2.37	1.85	1.54	1.33	1.19	1.08	1.00	.93	.88	.83	.80	.77
100	8.72	4.55	3.16	2.47	2.05	1.78	1.58	1.44	1.33	1.24	1.17	1.11	1.06	1.02
200	17.44	9.09	6.31	4.93	4.10	3.55	3.16	2.87	2.65	2.47	2.33	2.21	2.12	2.03
300	26.16	13.63	9.46	7.39	6.15	5.32	4.74	4.31	3.97	3.71	3.49	3.32	3.17	3.05
400	34.87	18.17	12.61	9.85	8.19	7.10	6.32	5.74	5.30	4.94	4.66	4.42	4.23	4.06
500	43.59	22.71	15.77	12.31	10.24	8.87	7.90	7.18	6.62	6.18	5.82	5.53	5.28	5.08
600	52.31	27.25	18.92	14.77	12.29	10.64	9.48	8.61	7.94	7.41	6.98	6.63	6.34	6.09
700	61.03	31.79	22.07	17.23	14.33	12.42	11.06	10.04	9.26	8.65	8.15	7.74	7.39	7.10
800	69.74	36.33	25.22	19.69	16.38	14.19	12.63	11.48	10.59	9.88	9.31	8.84	8.45	8.12
900	78.46	40.87	28.37	22.15	18.43	15.96	14.21	12.91	11.91	11.12	10.47	9.95	9.50	9.13
1000	87.18	45.41	31.53	24.61	20.47	17.73	15.79	14.35	13.23	12.35	11.64	11.05	10.56	10.15
2000	174.35	90.82	63.05	49.21	40.94	35.46	31.58	28.69	26.46	24.70	23.27	22.10	21.12	20.29
3000	261.53	136.23	94.57	73.81	61.41	53.19	47.36	43.03	39.69	37.04	34.90	33.14	31.67	30.43
4000	348.70	181.64	126.09	98.41	81.88	70.92	63.15	57.37	52.91	49.39	46.53	44.19	42.23	40.57
5000	435.87	227.05	157.61	123.01	102.35	88.65	78.94	71.71	66.14	61.73	58.16	55.23	52.78	50.71
6000	523.05	272.46	189.13	147.61	122.82	106.38	94.72	86.05	79.37	74.08	69.80	66.28	63.34	60.85
7000	610.22	317.87	220.65	172.21	143.28	124.11	110.51	100.39	92.59	86.42	81.43	77.32	73.89	71.00
8000	697.39	363.28	252.17	196.81	163.75	141.84	126.29	114.73	105.82	98.77	93.06	88.37	84.45	81.14
9000	784.57	408.69	283.70	221.42	184.22	159.57	142.08	129.07	119.05	111.11	104.69	99.41	95.00	91.28
10000	871.74	454.10	315.22	246.02	204.69	177.30	157.87	143.41	132.27	123.46	116.32	110.46	105.56	101.42
11000	958.91	499.51	346.74	270.62	225.16	195.03	173.65	157.75	145.50	135.80	127.96	121.50	116.11	111.56
12000	1046.09	544.92	378.26	295.22	245.63	212.76	189.44	172.09	158.73	148.15	139.59	132.55	126.67	121.70
13000	1133.26	590.33	409.78	319.82	266.09	230.48	205.23	186.44	171.96	160.49	151.22	143.59	137.22	131.85
14000	1220.43	635.74	441.30	344.42	286.56	248.21	221.01	200.78	185.18	172.84	162.85	154.64	147.78	141.99
15000	1307.61	681.15	472.82	369.02	307.03	265.94	236.80	215.12	198.41	185.18	174.48	165.68	158.33	152.13
16000	1394.78	726.56	504.34	393.62	327.50	283.67	252.58	229.46	211.64	197.53	186.12	176.73	168.89	162.27
17000	1481.95	771.97	535.87	418.22	347.97	301.40	268.37	243.80	224.86	209.87	197.75	187.77	179.44	172.41
18000	1569.13	817.38	567.39	442.83	368.44	319.13	284.16	258.14	238.09	222.22	209.38	198.82	190.00	182.55
19000	1656.30	862.79	598.91	467.43	388.90	336.86	299.94	272.48	251.32	234.56	221.01	209.86	200.55	192.70
20000	1743.47	908.20	630.43	492.03	409.37	354.59	315.73	286.82	264.54	246.91	232.64	220.91	211.11	202.84
21000	1830.65	953.61	661.95	516.63	429.84	372.32	331.52	301.16	277.77	259.25	244.28	231.95	221.67	212.98
22000	1917.82	999.02	693.47	541.23	450.31	390.05	347.30	315.50	291.00	271.60	255.91	243.00	232.22	223.12
23000	2005.00	1044.43	724.99	565.83	470.78	407.78	363.09	329.84	304.23	283.94	267.54	254.04	242.78	233.26
24000	2092.17	1089.84	756.51	590.43	491.25	425.51	378.87	344.18	317.45	296.29	279.17	265.09	253.33	243.40
25000	2179.34	1135.25	788.04	615.03	511.71	443.23	394.66	358.53	330.68	308.63	290.80	276.13	263.89	253.55
26000	2266.52	1180.66	819.56	639.63	532.18	460.96	410.45	372.87	343.91	320.98	302.44	287.18	274.44	263.69
27000	2353.69	1226.07	851.08	664.24	552.65	478.69	426.23	387.21	357.13	333.32	314.07	298.22	285.00	273.83
28000	2440.86	1271.48	882.60	688.84	573.12	496.42	442.02	401.55	370.36	345.67	325.70	309.27	295.55	283.97
29000	2528.04	1316.89	914.12	713.44	593.59	514.15	457.81	415.89	383.59	358.01	337.33	320.31	306.11	294.11
30000	2615.21	1362.30	945.64	738.04	614.06	531.88	473.59	430.23	396.81	370.36	348.96	331.36	316.66	304.25
31000	2702.38	1407.71	977.16	762.64	634.52	549.61	489.38	444.57	410.04	382.70	360.59	342.40	327.22	314.40
32000	2789.56	1453.12	1008.68	787.24	654.99	567.34	505.16	458.91	423.27	395.05	372.23	353.45	337.77	324.54
33000	2876.73	1498.53	1040.21	811.84	675.46	585.07	520.95	473.25	436.50	407.39	383.86	364.49	348.33	334.68
34000	2963.90	1543.94	1071.73	836.44	695.93	602.80	536.74	487.59	449.72	419.74	395.49	375.54	358.88	344.82
35000	3051.08	1589.35	1103.25	861.04	716.40	620.53	552.52	501.93	462.95	432.09	407.12	386.58	369.44	354.96
36000	3138.25	1634.76	1134.77	885.65	736.87	638.26	568.31	516.27	476.18	444.43	418.75	397.63	379.99	365.10
37000	3225.42	1680.17	1166.29	910.25	757.33	655.99	584.10	530.62	489.40	456.78	430.39	408.67	390.55	375.25
38000	3312.60	1725.58	1197.81	934.85	777.80	673.71	599.88	544.96	502.63	469.12	442.02	419.72	401.10	385.39
39000	3399.77	1770.99	1229.33	959.45	798.27	691.44	615.67	559.30	515.86	481.47	453.65	430.76	411.66	395.53
40000	3486.94	1816.40	1260.85	984.05	818.74	709.17	631.45	573.64	529.08	493.81	465.28	441.81	422.22	405.67
41000	3574.12	1861.81	1292.38	1008.65	839.21	726.90	647.24	587.98	542.31	506.16	476.91	452.85	432.77	415.81
42000	3661.29	1907.22	1323.90	1033.25	859.68	744.63	663.03	602.32	555.54	518.50	488.55	463.90	443.33	425.95
43000	3748.46	1952.63	1355.42	1057.85	880.14	762.36	678.81	616.66	568.77	530.85	500.18	474.94	453.88	436.10
44000	3835.64	1998.04	1386.94	1082.45	900.61	780.09	694.60	631.00	581.99	543.19	511.81	485.99	464.44	446.24
45000	3922.81	2043.45	1418.46	1107.06	921.08	797.82	710.39	645.34	595.22	555.54	523.44	497.03	474.99	456.38
46000	4009.99	2088.86	1449.98	1131.66	941.55	815.55	726.17	659.68	608.45	567.88	535.07	508.08	485.55	466.52
47000	4097.16	2134.27	1481.50	1156.26	962.02	833.28	741.96	674.02	621.67	580.23	546.71	519.12	496.10	476.66
48000	4184.33	2179.68	1513.02	1180.86	982.49	851.01	757.74	688.36	634.90	592.57	558.34	530.17	506.66	486.80
49000	4271.51	2225.09	1544.54	1205.46	1002.96	868.74	773.53	702.71	648.13	604.92	569.97	541.21	517.21	496.95
50000	4358.68	2270.50	1576.07	1230.06	1023.42	886.46	789.32	717.05	661.35	617.26	581.60	552.26	527.77	507.09
55000	4794.55	2497.55	1733.67	1353.07	1125.77	975.11	868.25	788.75	727.49	678.99	639.76	607.48	580.54	557.80
60000	5230.41	2724.60	1891.28	1476.07	1228.11	1063.76	947.18	860.45	793.62	740.71	697.92	662.71	633.32	608.50
65000	5666.28	2951.65	2048.88	1599.08	1330.45	1152.40	1026.11	932.16	859.76	802.44	756.08	717.93	686.10	659.21
70000	6102.15	3178.70	2206.49	1722.08	1432.79	1241.05	1105.04	1003.86	925.89	864.17	814.24	773.16	738.87	709.92
75000	6538.02	3405.75	2364.10	1535.13	1535.13	1329.69	1183.97	1075.57	992.03	925.89	872.40	828.38	791.65	760.63
80000	6973.88	3632.80	2521.70	1968.09	1637.45	1418.34	1262.90	1147.27	1058.16	987.62	930.56	883.61	844.43	811.34
85000	7409.75	3859.85	2679.31	2091.10	1739.82	1506.99	1341.84	1218.98	1124.30	1049.34	988.72	938.83	897.20	862.05
90000	7845.62	4086.90	2836.91	2214.11	1842.16	1595.63	1420.77	1290.68	1190.43	1111.07	1046.88	994.06	949.98	912.75
95000	8281.49	4313.95	2994.52	2337.11	1944.50	1684.28	1499.70	1362.38	1256.57	1172.79	1105.04	1049.28	1002.75	963.46
100000	8717.35	4541.00	3152.13	2460.12	2046.84	1772.92	1578.63	1434.09	1322.70	1234.52	1163.20	1104.51	1055.53	1014.17

TERM	15 Years	16 Years	17 Years	18 Years	19 Years	20 Years	21 Years	22 Years	23 Years	24 Years	25 Years	30 Years	35 Years	40 Years
AMOUNT														
5	.05	.05	.05	.05	.05	.05	.05	.05	.05	.05	.04	.04	.04	.04
10	.10	.10	.10	.09	.09	.09	.09	.09	.09	.09	.08	.08	.08	.08
15	.15	.15	.14	.14	.14	.13	.13	.13	.13	.13	.12	.12	.12	.11
25	.25	.24	.24	.23	.22	.22	.22	.21	.21	.21	.20	.20	.19	.19
50	.49	.48	.47	.45	.44	.44	.43	.42	.41	.41	.40	.39	.37	.37
75	.74	.72	.70	.68	.66	.65	.64	.63	.62	.61	.60	.58	.56	.55
100	.98	.95	.93	.90	.87	.87	.85	.84	.82	.81	.80	.77	.74	.73
200	1.96	1.90	1.85	1.80	1.76	1.73	1.70	1.67	1.64	1.62	1.60	1.53	1.48	1.46
300	2.94	2.85	2.77	2.70	2.64	2.59	2.54	2.50	2.46	2.43	2.40	2.29	2.22	2.18
400	3.92	3.80	3.69	3.60	3.52	3.45	3.39	3.33	3.28	3.24	3.20	3.05	2.96	2.91
500	4.90	4.75	4.62	4.50	4.40	4.31	4.23	4.16	4.10	4.05	4.00	3.81	3.70	3.63
600	5.88	5.70	5.54	5.40	5.28	5.17	5.08	5.00	4.92	4.86	4.80	4.58	4.44	4.36
700	6.86	6.64	6.46	6.30	6.16	6.04	5.93	5.83	5.74	5.66	5.59	5.34	5.18	5.08
800	7.84	7.59	7.38	7.20	7.04	6.90	6.77	6.66	6.56	6.47	6.39	6.10	5.92	5.81
900	8.81	8.54	8.31	8.10	7.92	7.76	7.62	7.49	7.38	7.28	7.19	6.86	6.66	6.53
1000	9.79	9.49	9.23	9.00	8.80	8.62	8.46	8.32	8.20	8.09	7.99	7.62	7.40	7.26
2000	19.58	18.98	18.45	17.99	17.59	17.24	16.92	16.64	16.40	16.17	15.97	15.24	14.79	14.51
3000	29.37	28.46	27.67	26.98	26.38	25.85	25.38	24.96	24.59	24.26	23.96	22.86	22.19	21.77
4000	39.16	37.95	36.89	35.98	35.17	34.47	33.84	33.28	32.79	32.34	31.94	30.48	29.58	29.02
5000	48.95	47.43	46.12	44.97	43.97	43.08	42.30	41.60	40.98	40.43	39.93	38.10	36.98	36.28
6000	58.74	56.92	55.34	53.96	52.76	51.70	50.76	49.92	49.18	48.51	47.91	45.72	44.37	43.53
7000	68.53	66.40	64.56	62.96	61.55	60.31	59.21	58.24	57.37	56.60	55.90	53.33	51.77	50.79
8000	78.32	75.89	73.78	71.95	70.34	68.93	67.67	66.56	65.57	64.68	63.88	60.95	59.16	58.04
9000	88.10	85.37	83.01	80.94	79.13	77.54	76.13	74.88	73.76	72.76	71.87	68.57	66.56	65.30
10000	97.89	94.86	92.23	89.94	87.93	86.16	84.59	83.20	81.96	80.85	79.85	76.19	73.95	72.55
11000	107.68	104.34	101.45	98.93	96.72	94.77	93.05	91.52	90.15	88.93	87.84	83.81	81.35	79.81
12000	117.47	113.83	110.67	107.92	105.51	103.39	101.51	99.83	98.35	97.02	95.82	91.43	88.74	87.06
13000	127.26	123.32	119.90	116.92	114.30	112.00	109.96	108.15	106.54	105.10	103.81	99.04	96.14	94.32
14000	137.05	132.80	129.12	125.91	123.10	120.62	118.42	116.47	114.74	113.19	111.79	106.66	103.53	101.57
15000	146.84	142.29	138.34	134.90	131.89	129.23	126.88	124.79	122.93	121.27	119.78	114.28	110.93	108.83
16000	156.63	151.77	147.56	143.90	140.68	137.85	135.34	133.11	131.13	129.35	127.76	121.90	118.32	116.08
17000	166.42	161.26	156.79	152.09	149.47	146.46	143.80	141.43	139.32	137.44	135.75	129.52	125.72	123.34
18000	176.20	170.74	166.01	161.88	158.26	155.08	152.26	149.75	147.52	145.52	143.73	137.14	133.11	130.59
19000	185.99	180.23	175.23	170.88	167.06	163.69	160.71	158.07	155.71	153.61	151.72	144.75	140.51	137.85
20000	195.78	189.71	184.45	179.87	175.85	172.31	169.17	166.39	163.91	161.69	159.70	152.37	147.90	145.10
21000	205.57	199.20	193.68	188.86	184.64	180.92	177.63	174.71	172.10	169.78	167.69	159.99	155.30	152.36
22000	215.36	208.68	202.90	197.86	193.43	189.54	186.09	183.03	180.30	177.86	175.67	167.61	162.69	159.61
23000	225.15	218.17	212.12	206.85	202.22	198.15	194.55	191.35	188.49	185.94	183.66	175.23	170.09	166.87
24000	234.94	227.65	221.34	215.84	211.02	206.77	203.01	199.66	196.69	194.03	191.64	182.85	177.48	174.12
25000	244.73	237.14	230.57	224.83	219.81	215.38	211.46	207.98	204.88	202.11	199.63	190.46	184.88	181.30
26000	254.52	246.63	239.79	233.83	228.60	224.00	219.92	216.30	213.08	210.20	207.61	198.08	192.27	188.63
27000	264.30	256.11	249.01	242.82	237.39	232.61	228.38	224.62	221.27	218.28	215.60	205.70	199.67	195.89
28000	274.09	265.60	258.23	251.81	246.19	241.23	236.84	232.94	229.47	226.37	223.58	213.32	207.06	203.14
29000	283.88	275.08	267.46	260.81	254.98	249.84	245.30	241.26	237.66	234.45	231.57	220.94	214.46	210.40
30000	293.67	284.57	276.68	269.80	263.77	258.46	253.76	249.58	245.86	242.53	239.55	228.56	221.85	217.65
31000	303.46	294.05	285.90	278.79	272.56	267.07	262.21	257.90	254.05	250.62	247.54	236.17	229.25	224.91
32000	313.25	303.54	295.12	287.79	281.35	275.69	270.67	266.22	262.25	258.70	255.52	243.79	236.64	232.16
33000	323.04	313.02	304.35	296.78	290.15	284.30	279.13	274.54	270.45	266.79	263.51	251.41	244.04	239.42
34000	332.83	322.51	313.57	305.77	298.94	292.92	287.59	282.86	278.64	274.87	271.49	259.03	251.43	246.67
35000	342.62	331.99	322.79	314.77	307.73	301.53	296.05	291.18	286.84	282.96	279.48	266.65	258.83	253.93
36000	352.40	341.48	332.01	323.76	316.52	310.15	304.51	299.49	295.03	291.04	287.46	274.27	266.22	261.18
37000	362.19	350.97	341.24	332.76	325.31	318.76	312.96	307.81	303.23	299.12	295.45	281.88	273.62	268.44
38000	371.98	360.45	350.46	341.75	334.11	327.38	321.42	316.13	311.42	307.21	303.43	289.50	281.01	275.69
39000	381.77	369.94	359.68	350.74	342.90	335.99	329.88	324.45	319.62	315.29	311.42	297.12	288.41	282.95
40000	391.56	379.42	368.90	359.73	351.69	344.61	338.34	332.77	327.81	323.38	319.40	304.74	295.80	290.20
41000	401.35	388.91	378.13	368.73	360.48	353.22	346.80	341.09	336.01	331.46	327.39	312.36	303.20	297.46
42000	411.14	398.39	387.35	377.72	369.28	361.84	355.26	349.41	344.20	339.55	335.37	319.98	310.59	304.71
43000	420.93	407.88	396.57	386.71	378.07	370.45	363.71	357.73	352.40	347.63	343.36	327.60	317.99	311.97
44000	430.72	417.36	405.79	395.71	386.86	379.07	372.17	366.05	360.59	355.71	351.34	335.21	325.38	319.22
45000	440.50	426.85	415.02	404.70	395.65	387.68	380.63	374.37	368.79	363.80	359.33	342.83	332.78	326.48
46000	450.29	436.33	424.24	413.69	404.44	396.30	389.09	382.69	376.98	371.88	367.31	350.45	340.17	333.73
47000	460.08	445.82	433.46	422.68	413.24	404.91	397.55	391.01	385.18	379.97	375.30	358.07	347.57	340.99
48000	469.87	455.30	442.68	431.68	422.03	413.53	406.01	399.32	393.37	388.05	383.28	365.69	354.96	348.24
49000	479.66	464.79	451.91	440.67	430.82	422.14	414.46	407.64	401.57	396.14	391.27	373.31	362.36	355.50
50000	489.45	474.28	461.13	449.66	439.61	430.76	422.92	415.96	409.76	404.22	399.25	380.92	369.75	362.75
55000	538.39	521.70	507.24	494.63	483.57	473.83	465.21	457.56	450.74	444.64	439.18	419.02	406.73	399.03
60000	587.34	569.13	553.35	539.60	527.53	516.91	507.51	499.15	491.71	485.06	479.10	457.11	443.70	435.30
65000	636.28	616.56	599.47	584.56	571.50	559.98	549.80	540.75	532.69	525.49	519.03	495.20	480.68	471.58
70000	685.23	663.98	645.58	629.53	615.46	603.06	592.09	582.35	573.67	565.91	558.95	533.29	517.65	507.85
75000	734.17	711.41	691.69	674.49	659.42	646.13	634.38	623.94	614.64	606.33	598.88	571.38	554.63	544.13
80000	783.11	758.84	737.80	719.46	703.38	689.21	676.67	665.54	655.62	646.75	638.80	609.48	591.60	580.40
85000	832.06	806.26	783.91	764.43	747.34	732.28	718.96	707.13	696.59	687.17	678.73	647.57	628.58	616.68
90000	881.00	853.69	830.03	809.39	791.30	775.36	761.26	748.73	737.57	727.59	718.65	685.66	665.55	652.95
95000	929.95	901.12	876.14	854.36	835.26	818.43	803.55	790.33	778.54	768.01	758.58	723.75	702.53	689.23
100000	978.89	948.55	922.25	899.32	879.22	861.51	845.84	831.92	819.52	808.44	798.50	761.84	739.50	725.50

MONTHLY PAYMENT
REQUIRED TO AMORTIZE A LOAN

TERM	1 Year	2 Years	3 Years	4 Years	5 Years	6 Years	7 Years	8 Years	9 Years	10 Years	11 Years	12 Years	13 Years	14 Years
AMOUNT														
5	.44	.23	.16	.13	.11	.09	.08	.08	.07	.07	.06	.06	.06	.06
10	.88	.46	.32	.25	.21	.18	.16	.15	.14	.13	.12	.12	.11	.11
15	1.31	.69	.48	.37	.31	.27	.24	.22	.20	.19	.18	.17	.16	.16
25	2.19	1.14	.79	.62	.52	.45	.40	.36	.34	.31	.30	.28	.27	.26
50	4.37	2.28	1.58	1.24	1.03	.89	.80	.72	.67	.62	.59	.56	.54	.51
75	6.55	3.41	2.37	1.85	1.54	1.34	1.19	1.08	1.00	.93	.88	.84	.80	.77
100	8.73	4.55	3.16	2.47	2.06	1.78	1.59	1.44	1.33	1.24	1.17	1.12	1.07	1.02
200	17.45	9.10	6.32	4.93	4.11	3.56	3.17	2.88	2.66	2.48	2.34	2.23	2.13	2.04
300	26.17	13.64	9.48	7.40	6.16	5.34	4.76	4.32	3.99	3.72	3.51	3.34	3.19	3.06
400	34.89	18.19	12.63	9.86	8.21	7.12	6.34	5.76	5.32	4.96	4.68	4.45	4.25	4.08
500	43.61	22.73	15.79	12.33	10.26	8.89	7.92	7.20	6.64	6.20	5.85	5.56	5.31	5.10
600	52.34	27.28	18.95	14.79	12.31	10.67	9.51	8.64	7.97	7.44	7.02	6.67	6.37	6.12
700	61.06	31.82	22.10	17.26	14.37	12.45	11.09	10.08	9.30	8.68	8.19	7.78	7.43	7.14
800	69.78	36.37	25.26	19.72	16.42	14.23	12.67	11.52	10.63	9.92	9.35	8.89	8.49	8.16
900	78.50	40.92	28.42	22.19	18.47	16.01	14.26	12.96	11.96	11.16	10.52	10.00	9.56	9.18
1000	87.22	45.46	31.57	24.65	20.52	17.78	15.84	14.40	13.28	12.40	11.69	11.11	10.62	10.20
2000	174.44	90.92	63.14	49.30	41.04	35.56	31.68	28.79	26.56	24.80	23.38	22.21	21.23	20.40
3000	261.66	136.37	94.71	73.95	61.55	53.34	47.51	43.18	39.84	37.20	35.06	33.31	31.84	30.60
4000	348.88	181.83	126.28	98.60	82.07	71.12	63.35	57.57	53.12	49.60	46.75	44.41	42.45	40.80
5000	436.10	227.28	157.84	123.25	102.59	88.90	79.19	71.97	66.40	62.00	58.44	55.51	53.06	51.00
6000	523.32	272.74	189.41	147.89	123.10	106.68	95.02	86.36	79.68	74.40	70.12	66.61	63.68	61.20
7000	610.54	318.19	220.98	172.54	143.62	124.45	110.86	100.75	92.96	86.79	81.81	77.71	74.29	71.40
8000	697.76	363.65	252.55	197.19	164.14	142.23	126.70	115.14	106.24	99.19	93.50	88.81	84.90	81.60
9000	784.98	409.11	284.11	221.84	184.65	160.01	142.53	129.53	119.52	111.59	105.18	99.91	95.51	91.80
10000	872.20	454.56	315.68	246.49	205.17	177.79	158.37	143.93	132.80	123.99	116.87	111.01	106.12	102.00
11000	959.42	500.02	347.25	271.14	225.69	195.57	174.21	158.32	146.08	136.39	128.56	122.11	116.73	112.20
12000	1046.64	545.47	378.82	295.78	246.20	213.35	190.04	172.71	159.36	148.79	140.24	133.21	127.35	122.40
13000	1133.86	590.93	410.38	320.43	266.72	231.12	205.88	187.10	172.64	161.19	151.93	144.31	137.96	132.59
14000	1221.08	636.38	441.95	345.08	287.24	248.90	221.72	201.49	185.92	173.58	163.61	155.41	148.57	142.79
15000	1308.30	681.84	473.52	369.73	307.75	266.68	237.55	215.89	199.20	185.98	175.30	166.51	159.18	152.99
16000	1395.52	727.30	505.09	394.38	328.27	284.46	253.39	230.28	212.47	198.38	186.99	177.61	169.79	163.19
17000	1482.74	772.75	536.65	419.03	348.79	302.24	269.23	244.67	225.75	210.78	198.67	188.71	180.41	173.39
18000	1569.96	818.21	568.22	443.67	369.30	320.02	285.06	259.06	239.03	223.18	210.36	199.82	191.02	183.59
19000	1657.18	863.66	599.79	468.32	389.82	337.79	300.90	273.46	252.31	235.58	222.05	210.92	201.63	193.79
20000	1744.40	909.12	631.36	492.97	410.34	355.57	316.73	287.85	265.59	247.98	233.73	222.02	212.24	203.99
21000	1831.62	954.57	662.92	517.62	430.85	373.35	332.57	302.24	278.87	260.37	245.42	233.12	222.85	214.19
22000	1918.84	1000.03	694.49	542.27	451.37	391.13	348.41	316.63	292.15	272.77	257.11	244.22	233.46	224.39
23000	2006.06	1045.49	726.06	566.92	471.89	408.91	364.24	331.02	305.43	285.17	268.79	255.32	244.08	234.59
24000	2093.28	1090.94	757.63	591.56	492.40	426.69	380.08	345.42	318.71	297.57	280.48	266.42	254.69	244.79
25000	2180.50	1136.40	789.19	616.21	512.92	444.46	395.92	359.81	331.99	309.97	292.16	277.52	265.30	254.98
26000	2267.72	1181.85	820.76	640.86	533.43	462.24	411.75	374.20	345.27	322.37	303.85	288.62	275.91	265.18
27000	2354.94	1227.31	852.33	665.51	553.95	480.02	427.59	388.59	358.55	334.77	315.54	299.72	286.52	275.38
28000	2442.16	1272.76	883.90	690.16	574.47	497.80	443.43	402.98	371.83	347.16	327.22	310.82	297.14	285.58
29000	2529.38	1318.22	915.46	714.81	594.98	515.58	459.26	417.38	385.11	359.56	338.91	321.92	307.75	295.78
30000	2616.60	1363.68	947.03	739.45	615.50	533.36	475.10	431.77	398.39	371.96	350.60	333.02	318.36	305.98
31000	2703.82	1409.13	978.60	764.10	636.02	551.13	490.94	446.16	411.66	384.36	362.28	344.12	328.97	316.18
32000	2791.04	1454.59	1010.17	788.75	656.53	568.91	506.77	460.55	424.94	396.76	373.97	355.22	339.58	326.38
33000	2878.26	1500.04	1041.73	813.40	677.05	586.69	522.61	474.95	438.22	409.16	385.66	366.32	350.19	336.58
34000	2965.48	1545.50	1073.30	838.05	697.57	604.47	538.45	489.34	451.50	421.56	397.34	377.42	360.81	346.78
35000	3052.70	1590.95	1104.87	862.70	718.08	622.25	554.28	503.73	464.78	433.95	409.03	388.52	371.42	356.98
36000	3139.92	1636.41	1136.44	887.34	738.60	640.03	570.12	518.12	478.06	446.35	420.72	399.63	382.03	367.18
37000	3227.14	1681.87	1168.00	911.99	759.12	657.81	585.95	532.51	491.34	458.75	432.40	410.73	392.64	377.37
38000	3314.36	1727.32	1199.57	936.64	779.63	675.58	601.79	546.91	504.62	471.15	444.09	421.83	403.25	387.57
39000	3401.58	1772.78	1231.14	961.29	800.15	693.36	617.63	561.30	517.90	483.55	455.77	432.93	413.86	397.77
40000	3488.80	1818.23	1262.71	985.94	820.67	711.14	633.46	575.69	531.18	495.95	467.46	444.03	424.48	407.97
41000	3576.02	1863.69	1294.27	1010.59	841.18	728.92	649.30	590.08	544.46	508.35	479.15	455.13	435.09	418.17
42000	3663.24	1909.14	1325.84	1035.23	861.70	746.70	665.14	604.47	557.74	520.74	490.83	466.23	445.70	428.37
43000	3750.46	1954.60	1357.41	1059.88	882.22	764.48	680.97	618.87	571.02	533.14	502.52	477.33	456.31	438.57
44000	3837.68	2000.05	1388.98	1084.53	902.73	782.25	696.81	633.26	584.30	545.54	514.21	488.43	466.92	448.77
45000	3924.90	2045.51	1420.54	1109.18	923.25	800.03	712.65	647.65	597.58	557.94	525.89	499.53	477.54	458.97
46000	4012.12	2090.97	1452.11	1133.83	943.77	817.81	728.49	662.04	610.86	570.34	537.58	510.63	488.15	469.17
47000	4099.33	2136.42	1483.68	1158.48	964.28	835.59	744.32	676.44	624.13	582.74	549.27	521.73	498.76	479.37
48000	4186.55	2181.88	1515.25	1183.12	984.80	853.37	760.16	690.83	637.41	595.14	560.95	532.83	509.37	489.57
49000	4273.77	2227.33	1546.81	1207.77	1005.32	871.15	775.99	705.22	650.69	607.53	572.64	543.93	519.98	499.77
50000	4360.99	2272.79	1578.38	1232.42	1025.83	888.92	791.83	719.61	663.97	619.93	584.32	555.03	530.59	509.96
55000	4797.09	2500.07	1736.22	1355.66	1128.41	977.82	871.01	791.57	730.37	681.93	642.76	610.54	583.65	560.96
60000	5233.19	2727.35	1894.06	1478.90	1231.00	1066.71	950.19	863.53	796.77	743.92	701.19	666.04	636.71	611.96
65000	5669.29	2954.62	2051.89	1602.14	1333.58	1155.60	1029.38	935.49	863.16	805.91	759.62	721.54	689.77	662.95
70000	6105.39	3181.90	2209.73	1725.39	1436.16	1244.49	1108.56	1007.45	929.56	867.90	818.05	777.04	742.83	713.95
75000	6541.49	3409.18	2367.57	1848.63	1538.74	1333.38	1187.74	1079.41	995.96	929.90	876.48	832.55	795.89	764.94
80000	6977.59	3636.46	2525.41	1971.87	1641.33	1422.28	1266.92	1151.38	1062.35	991.89	934.92	888.05	848.95	815.94
85000	7413.69	3863.74	2683.25	2095.11	1743.91	1511.17	1346.11	1223.34	1128.75	1053.88	993.35	943.55	902.01	866.94
90000	7849.79	4091.02	2841.08	2218.35	1846.49	1600.06	1425.29	1295.30	1195.15	1115.88	1051.78	999.05	955.07	917.93
95000	8285.88	4318.29	2998.92	2341.59	1949.08	1688.95	1504.47	1367.26	1261.54	1177.87	1110.21	1054.56	1008.13	968.93
100000	8721.98	4545.57	3156.76	2464.84	2051.66	1777.84	1583.65	1439.22	1327.94	1239.86	1168.64	1110.06	1061.18	1019.92

TERM AMOUNT	15 Years	16 Years	17 Years	18 Years	19 Years	20 Years	21 Years	22 Years	23 Years	24 Years	25 Years	30 Years	35 Years	40 Years
5	.05	.05	.05	.05	.05	.05	.05	.05	.05	.05	.05	.04	.04	.04
10	.10	.10	.10	.10	.09	.09	.09	.09	.09	.09	.09	.08	.08	.08
15	.15	.15	.14	.14	.14	.14	.13	.13	.13	.13	.13	.12	.12	.11
25	.25	.24	.24	.23	.23	.22	.22	.21	.21	.21	.21	.20	.19	.19
50	.50	.48	.47	.46	.45	.44	.43	.42	.42	.41	.41	.39	.38	.37
75	.74	.72	.70	.68	.67	.66	.64	.63	.62	.62	.61	.58	.57	.55
100	.99	.96	.93	.91	.89	.87	.86	.84	.83	.82	.81	.77	.75	.74
200	1.97	1.91	1.86	1.82	1.78	1.74	1.71	1.68	1.66	1.64	1.62	1.54	1.50	1.47
300	2.96	2.87	2.79	2.72	2.66	2.61	2.56	2.52	2.48	2.45	2.42	2.31	2.25	2.20
400	3.94	3.82	3.72	3.63	3.55	3.48	3.41	3.36	3.31	3.27	3.23	3.08	2.99	2.94
500	4.93	4.78	4.65	4.53	4.43	4.34	4.27	4.20	4.14	4.08	4.03	3.85	3.74	3.67
600	5.91	5.73	5.57	5.44	5.32	5.21	5.12	5.04	4.96	4.90	4.84	4.62	4.49	4.40
700	6.90	6.69	6.50	6.34	6.20	6.08	5.97	5.87	5.79	5.71	5.64	5.39	5.23	5.14
800	7.88	7.64	7.43	7.25	7.09	6.95	6.82	6.71	6.61	6.53	6.45	6.16	5.98	5.87
900	8.87	8.60	8.36	8.15	7.97	7.82	7.68	7.55	7.44	7.34	7.25	6.93	6.73	6.60
1000	9.85	9.55	9.29	9.06	8.86	8.68	8.53	8.39	8.27	8.16	8.06	7.69	7.47	7.34
2000	19.70	19.09	18.57	18.11	17.71	17.36	17.05	16.77	16.53	16.31	16.11	15.38	14.94	14.67
3000	29.55	28.64	27.85	27.17	26.57	26.04	25.57	25.16	24.79	24.46	24.16	23.07	22.41	22.00
4000	39.39	38.18	37.14	36.22	35.42	34.72	34.09	33.54	33.05	32.61	32.21	30.76	29.88	29.33
5000	49.24	47.73	46.42	45.28	44.28	43.40	42.62	41.93	41.31	40.76	40.27	38.45	37.35	36.66
6000	59.09	57.27	55.70	54.33	53.13	52.07	51.14	50.31	49.57	48.91	48.32	46.14	44.82	43.99
7000	68.94	66.82	64.99	63.39	61.99	60.75	59.66	58.69	57.83	57.06	56.37	53.83	52.29	51.32
8000	78.78	76.36	74.27	72.44	70.84	69.43	68.18	67.08	66.09	65.21	64.42	61.52	59.75	58.65
9000	88.63	85.91	83.55	81.50	79.70	78.11	76.71	75.46	74.35	73.36	72.48	69.21	67.22	65.98
10000	98.48	95.45	92.83	90.55	88.55	86.79	85.23	83.85	82.61	81.51	80.53	76.90	74.69	73.31
11000	108.33	105.00	102.12	99.61	97.40	95.47	93.75	92.23	90.87	89.66	88.58	84.59	82.16	80.65
12000	118.17	114.54	111.40	108.66	106.26	104.14	102.27	100.61	99.14	97.81	96.63	92.27	89.63	87.98
13000	128.02	124.09	120.68	117.71	115.11	112.82	110.80	109.00	107.40	105.97	104.68	99.96	97.10	95.31
14000	137.87	133.63	129.97	126.77	123.97	121.50	119.32	117.38	115.66	114.12	112.74	107.65	104.57	102.64
15000	147.72	143.18	139.25	135.82	132.82	130.18	127.84	125.77	123.92	122.27	120.79	115.34	112.03	109.97
16000	157.56	152.72	148.53	144.00	141.60	138.86	136.36	134.15	132.18	130.42	128.84	123.03	119.50	117.30
17000	167.41	162.27	157.81	153.93	150.53	147.53	144.89	142.53	140.44	138.57	136.89	130.72	126.97	124.63
18000	177.26	171.81	167.10	162.99	159.39	156.21	153.41	150.92	140.70	146.72	144.95	138.41	134.44	131.96
19000	187.11	181.36	176.38	172.04	168.24	164.89	161.93	159.30	156.96	154.87	153.00	146.10	141.91	139.29
20000	196.95	190.90	185.66	181.10	177.09	173.57	170.45	167.69	165.22	163.02	161.05	153.79	149.38	146.62
21000	206.80	200.45	194.95	190.15	185.95	182.25	178.98	176.07	173.48	171.17	169.10	161.48	156.85	153.95
22000	216.65	209.99	204.23	199.21	194.80	190.93	187.50	184.45	181.74	179.32	177.15	169.17	164.31	161.29
23000	226.50	219.54	213.51	208.26	203.66	199.60	196.02	192.84	190.00	187.47	185.21	176.86	171.78	168.62
24000	236.34	229.08	222.80	217.31	212.51	208.28	204.54	201.22	198.27	195.62	193.26	184.54	179.25	175.95
25000	246.19	238.63	232.08	226.37	221.37	216.96	213.06	209.61	206.53	203.78	201.31	192.23	186.72	183.28
26000	256.04	248.17	241.36	235.42	230.22	225.64	221.59	217.99	214.79	211.93	209.36	199.92	194.19	190.61
27000	265.88	257.72	250.64	244.48	239.08	234.32	230.11	226.37	223.05	220.08	217.42	207.61	201.66	197.94
28000	275.73	267.26	259.93	253.53	247.93	243.00	238.63	234.76	231.31	228.23	225.47	215.30	209.13	205.27
29000	285.58	276.81	269.21	262.59	256.78	251.67	247.15	243.14	239.57	236.38	233.52	222.99	216.59	212.60
30000	295.43	286.35	278.49	271.64	265.64	260.35	255.68	251.53	247.83	244.53	241.57	230.68	224.06	219.93
31000	305.27	295.90	287.78	280.70	274.49	269.03	264.20	259.91	256.09	252.68	249.63	238.37	231.53	227.26
32000	315.12	305.44	297.06	289.75	283.35	277.71	272.72	268.29	264.35	260.83	257.68	246.06	239.00	234.60
33000	324.97	314.99	306.34	298.81	292.20	286.39	281.24	276.68	272.61	268.98	265.73	253.75	246.47	241.93
34000	334.82	324.53	315.62	307.86	301.06	295.06	289.77	285.06	280.87	277.13	273.78	261.44	253.94	249.26
35000	344.66	334.08	324.91	316.92	309.91	303.74	298.29	293.45	289.14	285.28	281.83	269.12	261.41	256.59
36000	354.51	343.62	334.19	325.97	318.77	312.42	306.81	301.83	297.40	293.43	289.89	276.81	268.87	263.92
37000	364.36	353.17	343.47	335.02	327.62	321.10	315.33	310.22	305.66	301.59	297.94	284.50	276.34	271.25
38000	374.21	362.71	352.76	344.08	336.47	329.78	323.86	318.60	313.92	309.74	305.99	292.19	283.81	278.58
39000	384.05	372.26	362.04	353.13	345.33	338.46	332.38	326.98	322.18	317.89	314.04	299.88	291.28	285.91
40000	393.90	381.80	371.32	362.19	354.18	347.13	340.90	335.37	330.44	326.04	322.10	307.57	298.75	293.24
41000	403.75	391.35	380.60	371.24	363.04	355.81	349.42	343.75	338.70	334.19	330.15	315.26	306.22	300.57
42000	413.60	400.89	389.89	380.30	371.89	364.49	357.95	352.14	346.96	342.34	338.20	322.95	313.69	307.90
43000	423.44	410.44	399.17	389.35	380.75	373.17	366.47	360.52	355.22	350.49	346.25	330.64	321.16	315.24
44000	433.29	419.98	408.45	398.41	389.60	381.85	374.99	368.90	363.48	358.64	354.30	338.33	328.62	322.57
45000	443.14	429.53	417.74	407.46	398.46	390.53	383.51	377.29	371.74	366.79	362.36	346.02	336.09	329.90
46000	452.99	439.07	427.02	416.52	407.31	399.20	392.04	385.67	380.00	374.94	370.41	353.71	343.56	337.23
47000	462.83	448.62	436.30	425.57	416.16	407.88	400.56	394.06	388.27	383.09	378.46	361.39	351.03	344.56
48000	472.68	458.16	445.59	434.62	425.02	416.56	409.08	402.44	396.53	391.24	386.51	369.08	358.50	351.89
49000	482.53	467.71	454.87	443.68	433.87	425.24	417.60	410.82	404.79	399.40	394.57	376.77	365.97	359.22
50000	492.37	477.25	464.15	452.73	442.73	433.92	426.12	419.21	413.05	407.55	402.62	384.46	373.44	366.55
55000	541.61	524.98	510.57	498.01	487.00	477.31	468.74	461.13	454.35	448.30	442.88	422.91	410.78	403.21
60000	590.85	572.70	556.98	543.28	531.27	520.70	511.35	503.05	495.66	489.05	483.14	461.35	448.12	439.86
65000	640.09	620.42	603.39	588.55	575.54	564.09	553.96	544.97	536.96	529.81	523.40	499.80	485.46	476.52
70000	689.32	668.15	649.81	633.83	619.82	607.48	596.57	586.89	578.27	570.56	563.66	538.24	522.81	513.17
75000	738.56	715.87	696.22	679.10	664.09	650.87	639.18	628.81	619.57	611.32	603.93	576.69	560.15	549.83
80000	787.80	763.60	742.64	724.37	708.36	694.26	681.80	670.73	660.87	652.07	644.19	615.14	597.49	586.48
85000	837.03	811.32	789.05	769.64	752.63	737.65	724.41	712.65	702.18	692.82	684.45	653.58	634.84	623.13
90000	886.27	859.05	835.47	814.92	796.91	781.05	767.02	754.57	743.48	733.58	724.71	692.03	672.18	659.79
95000	935.51	906.77	881.88	860.19	841.18	824.44	809.63	796.49	784.79	774.33	764.97	730.47	709.52	696.44
100000	984.74	954.50	928.30	905.46	885.45	867.83	852.24	838.41	826.09	815.09	805.23	768.92	746.87	733.10

8.600%

MONTHLY PAYMENT
REQUIRED TO AMORTIZE A LOAN

TERM AMOUNT	1 Year	2 Years	3 Years	4 Years	5 Years	6 Years	7 Years	8 Years	9 Years	10 Years	11 Years	12 Years	13 Years	14 Years
5	.44	.23	.16	.13	.11	.09	.08	.08	.07	.07	.06	.06	.06	.06
10	.88	.46	.32	.25	.21	.18	.16	.15	.14	.13	.12	.12	.11	.11
15	1.31	.69	.48	.38	.31	.27	.24	.22	.20	.19	.18	.17	.17	.16
25	2.19	1.14	.80	.62	.52	.45	.40	.37	.34	.32	.30	.28	.27	.26
50	4.37	2.28	1.59	1.24	1.03	.90	.80	.73	.67	.63	.59	.56	.54	.52
75	6.55	3.42	2.38	1.86	1.55	1.34	1.20	1.09	1.00	.94	.89	.84	.81	.77
100	8.73	4.56	3.17	2.47	2.06	1.79	1.59	1.45	1.34	1.25	1.18	1.12	1.07	1.03
200	17.46	9.11	6.33	4.94	4.12	3.57	3.18	2.89	2.67	2.50	2.35	2.24	2.14	2.06
300	26.18	13.66	9.49	7.41	6.17	5.35	4.77	4.34	4.00	3.74	3.53	3.35	3.21	3.08
400	34.91	18.21	12.65	9.88	8.23	7.14	6.36	5.78	5.34	4.99	4.70	4.47	4.27	4.11
500	43.64	22.76	15.81	12.35	10.29	8.92	7.95	7.23	6.67	6.23	5.88	5.58	5.34	5.13
600	52.36	27.31	18.97	14.82	12.34	10.70	9.54	8.67	8.00	7.48	7.05	6.70	6.41	6.16
700	61.09	31.86	22.13	17.29	14.40	12.48	11.13	10.12	9.34	8.72	8.22	7.81	7.47	7.18
800	69.82	36.41	25.30	19.76	16.46	14.27	12.71	11.56	10.67	9.97	9.40	8.93	8.54	8.21
900	78.54	40.96	28.46	22.23	18.51	16.05	14.30	13.00	12.00	11.21	10.57	10.05	9.61	9.24
1000	87.27	45.51	31.62	24.70	20.57	17.83	15.89	14.45	13.34	12.46	11.75	11.16	10.67	10.26
2000	174.54	91.01	63.23	49.40	41.13	35.66	31.78	28.89	26.67	24.91	23.49	22.32	21.34	20.52
3000	261.80	136.51	94.85	74.09	61.70	53.49	47.67	43.34	40.00	37.36	35.23	33.47	32.01	30.78
4000	349.07	182.01	126.46	98.79	82.26	71.32	63.55	57.78	53.33	49.81	46.97	44.63	42.68	41.03
5000	436.34	227.51	158.07	123.48	102.83	89.14	79.44	72.22	66.66	62.27	58.71	55.79	53.35	51.29
6000	523.60	273.01	189.69	148.18	123.39	106.97	95.33	86.67	80.00	74.72	70.45	66.94	64.02	61.55
7000	610.87	318.52	221.30	172.87	143.96	124.80	111.21	101.11	93.33	87.17	82.19	78.10	74.68	71.80
8000	698.13	364.02	252.92	197.57	164.52	142.63	127.10	115.55	106.66	99.62	93.93	89.25	85.35	82.06
9000	785.40	409.52	284.53	222.26	185.09	160.45	142.99	130.00	119.99	112.07	105.67	100.41	96.02	92.32
10000	872.67	455.02	316.14	246.96	205.65	178.28	158.87	144.44	133.32	124.53	117.41	111.57	106.69	102.57
11000	959.93	500.52	347.76	271.66	226.22	196.11	174.76	158.88	146.66	136.98	129.16	122.72	117.36	112.83
12000	1047.20	546.02	379.37	296.35	246.78	213.94	190.65	173.33	159.99	149.43	140.90	133.88	128.03	123.09
13000	1134.46	591.52	410.99	321.05	267.35	231.76	206.53	187.77	173.32	161.88	152.64	145.04	138.70	133.34
14000	1221.73	637.03	442.60	345.74	287.91	249.59	222.42	202.21	186.65	174.33	164.38	156.19	149.36	143.60
15000	1309.00	682.53	474.21	370.44	308.48	267.42	238.31	216.66	199.98	186.79	176.12	167.35	160.03	153.86
16000	1396.26	728.03	505.83	395.13	329.04	285.25	254.19	231.10	213.31	199.24	187.86	178.50	170.70	164.12
17000	1483.53	773.53	537.44	419.83	349.61	303.08	270.08	245.55	226.65	211.69	199.60	189.66	181.37	174.37
18000	1570.79	819.03	569.06	444.52	370.17	320.90	285.97	259.99	239.98	224.14	211.34	200.82	192.04	184.63
19000	1658.06	864.53	600.67	469.22	390.74	338.73	301.85	274.43	253.31	236.60	223.08	211.97	202.71	194.89
20000	1745.33	910.03	632.28	493.92	411.30	356.56	317.74	288.88	266.64	249.05	234.82	223.13	213.37	205.14
21000	1832.59	955.54	663.90	518.61	431.86	374.39	333.63	303.32	279.97	261.50	246.57	234.29	224.04	215.40
22000	1919.86	1001.04	695.51	543.31	452.43	392.21	349.52	317.76	293.31	273.95	258.31	245.44	234.71	225.66
23000	2007.13	1046.54	727.12	568.00	472.99	410.04	365.40	332.21	306.64	286.40	270.05	256.60	245.38	235.91
24000	2094.39	1092.04	758.74	592.70	493.56	427.87	381.29	346.65	319.97	298.86	281.79	267.75	256.05	246.17
25000	2181.66	1137.54	790.35	617.39	514.12	445.70	397.18	361.09	333.30	311.31	293.53	278.91	266.72	256.43
26000	2268.92	1183.04	821.97	642.09	534.69	463.52	413.06	375.54	346.63	323.76	305.27	290.07	277.39	266.68
27000	2356.19	1228.54	853.58	666.78	555.25	481.35	428.95	389.98	359.96	336.21	317.01	301.22	288.05	276.94
28000	2443.46	1274.05	885.19	691.48	575.82	499.18	444.84	404.42	373.30	348.66	328.75	312.38	298.72	287.20
29000	2530.72	1319.55	916.81	716.18	596.38	517.01	460.72	418.87	386.63	361.12	340.49	323.54	309.39	297.45
30000	2617.99	1365.05	948.42	740.87	616.95	534.83	476.61	433.31	399.96	373.57	352.23	334.69	320.06	307.71
31000	2705.25	1410.55	980.04	765.57	637.51	552.66	492.50	447.75	413.29	386.02	363.98	345.85	330.73	317.97
32000	2792.52	1456.05	1011.65	790.26	658.08	570.49	508.38	462.20	426.62	398.47	375.72	357.00	341.40	328.23
33000	2879.79	1501.55	1043.26	814.96	678.64	588.32	524.27	476.64	439.96	410.92	387.46	368.16	352.06	338.48
34000	2967.05	1547.05	1074.88	839.65	699.21	606.15	540.16	491.09	453.29	423.38	399.20	379.32	362.73	348.74
35000	3054.32	1592.56	1106.49	864.35	719.77	623.97	556.04	505.53	466.62	435.83	410.94	390.47	373.40	359.00
36000	3141.58	1638.06	1138.11	889.04	740.34	641.80	571.93	519.97	479.95	448.28	422.68	401.63	384.07	369.25
37000	3228.85	1683.56	1169.72	913.74	760.90	659.63	587.82	534.42	493.28	460.73	434.42	412.78	394.74	379.51
38000	3316.12	1729.06	1201.33	938.44	781.47	677.46	603.70	548.86	506.61	473.19	446.16	423.94	405.41	389.77
39000	3403.38	1774.56	1232.95	963.13	802.03	695.28	619.59	563.30	519.95	485.64	457.90	435.10	416.08	400.02
40000	3490.65	1820.06	1264.56	987.83	822.60	713.11	635.48	577.75	533.28	498.09	469.64	446.25	426.74	410.28
41000	3577.91	1865.56	1296.17	1012.52	843.16	730.94	651.36	592.19	546.61	510.54	481.39	457.41	437.41	420.54
42000	3665.18	1911.07	1327.79	1037.22	863.72	748.77	667.25	606.63	559.94	522.99	493.13	468.57	448.08	430.79
43000	3752.45	1956.57	1359.40	1061.91	884.29	766.59	683.14	621.08	573.27	535.45	504.87	479.72	458.75	441.05
44000	3839.71	2002.07	1391.02	1086.61	904.85	784.42	699.03	635.52	586.61	547.90	516.61	490.88	469.42	451.31
45000	3926.98	2047.57	1422.63	1111.30	925.42	802.25	714.91	649.96	599.94	560.35	528.35	502.03	480.09	461.57
46000	4014.25	2093.07	1454.24	1136.00	945.98	820.08	730.80	664.41	613.27	572.80	540.09	513.19	490.76	471.82
47000	4101.51	2138.57	1485.86	1160.70	966.55	837.90	746.69	678.85	626.60	585.25	551.83	524.35	501.42	482.08
48000	4188.78	2184.07	1517.47	1185.39	987.11	855.73	762.57	693.29	639.93	597.71	563.57	535.50	512.09	492.34
49000	4276.04	2229.58	1549.09	1210.09	1007.68	873.56	778.46	707.74	653.26	610.16	575.31	546.66	522.76	502.59
50000	4363.31	2275.08	1580.70	1234.78	1028.24	891.39	794.35	722.18	666.60	622.61	587.05	557.82	533.43	512.85
55000	4799.64	2502.58	1738.77	1358.26	1131.07	980.53	873.78	794.40	733.26	684.87	645.76	613.60	586.77	564.13
60000	5235.97	2730.09	1896.84	1481.74	1233.89	1069.66	953.21	866.62	799.91	747.13	704.46	669.38	640.11	615.42
65000	5672.30	2957.60	2054.91	1605.22	1336.71	1158.80	1032.65	938.83	866.57	809.39	763.17	725.16	693.46	666.70
70000	6108.63	3185.11	2212.98	1728.69	1439.54	1247.94	1112.08	1011.05	933.23	871.65	821.87	780.94	746.80	717.99
75000	6544.96	3412.61	2371.05	1852.17	1542.36	1337.08	1191.52	1083.27	999.89	933.91	880.58	836.72	800.14	769.27
80000	6981.29	3640.12	2529.12	1975.65	1645.19	1426.22	1270.95	1155.49	1066.55	996.17	939.28	892.50	853.48	820.56
85000	7417.62	3867.63	2687.19	2099.13	1748.01	1515.36	1350.38	1227.71	1133.21	1058.43	997.99	948.28	906.83	871.84
90000	7853.95	4095.13	2845.26	2222.60	1850.83	1604.49	1429.82	1299.92	1199.87	1120.70	1056.69	1004.06	960.17	923.13
95000	8290.28	4322.64	3003.33	2346.08	1953.66	1693.63	1509.25	1372.14	1266.53	1182.96	1115.40	1059.84	1013.51	974.41
100000	8726.61	4550.15	3161.39	2469.56	2056.48	1782.77	1588.69	1444.36	1333.19	1245.22	1174.10	1115.63	1066.85	1025.69

TERM	15 Years	16 Years	17 Years	18 Years	19 Years	20 Years	21 Years	22 Years	23 Years	24 Years	25 Years	30 Years	35 Years	40 Years
AMOUNT														
5	.05	.05	.05	.05	.05	.05	.05	.05	.05	.05	.05	.04	.04	.04
10	.10	.10	.10	.10	.09	.09	.09	.09	.09	.09	.09	.08	.08	.08
15	.15	.15	.15	.14	.14	.14	.13	.13	.13	.13	.13	.12	.12	.12
25	.25	.25	.24	.23	.23	.22	.22	.22	.21	.21	.21	.20	.19	.19
50	.50	.49	.47	.46	.45	.44	.43	.43	.42	.42	.41	.39	.38	.38
75	.75	.73	.71	.69	.67	.66	.65	.64	.63	.62	.61	.59	.57	.56
100	1.00	.97	.94	.92	.90	.88	.86	.85	.84	.83	.82	.78	.76	.75
200	1.99	1.93	1.87	1.83	1.79	1.75	1.72	1.69	1.67	1.65	1.63	1.56	1.51	1.49
300	2.98	2.89	2.81	2.74	2.68	2.63	2.58	2.54	2.50	2.47	2.44	2.33	2.27	2.23
400	3.97	3.85	3.74	3.65	3.57	3.50	3.44	3.38	3.34	3.29	3.25	3.11	3.02	2.97
500	4.96	4.81	4.68	4.56	4.46	4.38	4.30	4.23	4.17	4.11	4.06	3.89	3.78	3.71
600	5.95	5.77	5.61	5.47	5.36	5.25	5.16	5.07	5.00	4.94	4.88	4.66	4.53	4.45
700	6.94	6.73	6.55	6.39	6.25	6.12	6.02	5.92	5.83	5.76	5.69	5.44	5.28	5.19
800	7.93	7.69	7.48	7.30	7.14	7.00	6.87	6.76	6.67	6.58	6.50	6.21	6.04	5.93
900	8.92	8.65	8.41	8.21	8.03	7.87	7.73	7.61	7.50	7.40	7.31	6.99	6.79	6.67
1000	9.91	9.61	9.35	9.12	8.92	8.75	8.59	8.45	8.33	8.22	8.12	7.77	7.55	7.41
2000	19.82	19.21	18.69	18.24	17.84	17.49	17.18	16.90	16.66	16.44	16.24	15.53	15.09	14.82
3000	29.72	28.82	28.04	27.35	26.76	26.23	25.76	25.35	24.99	24.66	24.36	23.29	22.63	22.23
4000	39.63	38.42	37.38	36.47	35.67	34.97	34.35	33.80	33.31	32.88	32.48	31.05	30.17	29.63
5000	49.54	48.03	46.72	45.59	44.59	43.71	42.94	42.25	41.64	41.09	40.60	38.81	37.72	37.04
6000	59.44	57.63	56.07	54.70	53.51	52.45	51.52	50.70	49.97	49.31	48.72	46.57	45.26	44.45
7000	69.35	67.24	65.41	63.82	62.42	61.20	60.11	59.15	58.29	57.53	56.84	54.33	52.80	51.85
8000	79.25	76.84	74.75	72.93	71.34	69.94	68.70	67.60	66.62	65.75	64.96	62.09	60.34	59.26
9000	89.16	86.45	84.10	82.05	80.26	78.68	77.28	76.05	74.95	73.96	73.08	69.85	67.89	66.67
10000	99.07	96.05	93.44	91.17	89.17	87.42	85.87	84.50	83.27	82.18	81.20	77.61	75.43	74.08
11000	108.97	105.66	102.78	100.28	98.09	96.16	94.46	92.95	91.60	90.40	89.32	85.37	82.97	81.48
12000	118.88	115.26	112.13	109.40	107.01	104.90	103.04	101.40	99.93	98.62	97.44	93.13	90.51	88.89
13000	128.78	124.86	121.47	118.52	115.93	113.65	111.63	109.84	108.25	106.83	105.56	100.89	98.06	96.30
14000	138.69	134.47	130.81	127.63	124.84	122.39	120.22	118.29	116.58	115.05	113.68	108.65	105.60	103.70
15000	148.60	144.07	140.16	136.75	133.76	131.13	128.80	126.74	124.91	123.27	121.80	116.41	113.14	111.11
16000	150.50	153.68	149.50	145.86	142.68	139.87	137.39	135.19	133.23	131.49	129.92	124.17	120.68	118.52
17000	168.41	163.28	158.85	154.98	151.59	148.61	145.98	143.64	141.56	139.70	138.04	131.93	128.23	125.93
18000	178.31	172.89	168.19	164.10	160.51	157.35	154.56	152.09	149.89	147.92	146.16	139.69	135.77	133.33
19000	188.22	182.49	177.53	173.21	169.43	166.10	163.15	160.54	158.21	156.14	154.28	147.45	143.31	140.74
20000	198.13	192.10	186.88	182.33	178.34	174.84	171.74	168.99	166.54	164.36	162.40	155.21	150.85	148.15
21000	208.03	201.70	196.22	191.44	187.26	183.58	180.32	177.44	174.87	172.57	170.52	162.97	158.40	155.55
22000	217.94	211.31	205.56	200.56	196.18	192.32	188.91	185.89	183.19	180.79	178.64	170.73	165.94	162.96
23000	227.85	220.91	214.91	209.68	205.10	201.06	197.50	194.34	191.52	189.01	186.76	178.49	173.48	170.37
24000	237.75	230.52	224.25	218.79	214.01	209.80	206.08	202.79	199.85	197.23	194.88	186.25	181.02	177.78
25000	247.66	240.12	233.59	227.91	222.93	218.55	214.67	211.23	208.17	205.44	203.00	194.01	188.57	185.18
26000	257.56	249.72	242.94	237.03	231.85	227.29	223.26	219.68	216.50	213.66	211.12	201.77	196.11	192.59
27000	267.47	259.33	252.28	246.14	240.76	236.03	231.84	228.13	224.83	221.88	219.24	209.53	203.65	200.00
28000	277.38	268.93	261.62	255.26	249.68	244.77	240.43	236.58	233.16	230.10	227.36	217.29	211.19	207.40
29000	287.28	278.54	270.97	264.37	258.60	253.51	249.02	245.03	241.48	238.31	235.48	225.05	218.74	214.81
30000	297.19	288.14	280.31	273.49	267.51	262.25	257.60	253.48	249.81	246.53	243.60	232.81	226.28	222.22
31000	307.09	297.75	289.66	282.61	276.43	271.00	266.19	261.93	258.14	254.75	251.72	240.57	233.82	229.63
32000	317.00	307.35	299.00	291.72	285.35	279.74	274.78	270.38	266.46	262.97	259.84	248.33	241.36	237.03
33000	326.91	316.96	308.34	300.84	294.26	288.48	283.36	278.83	274.79	271.18	267.96	256.09	248.91	244.44
34000	336.81	326.56	317.69	309.95	303.18	297.22	291.95	287.28	283.12	279.40	276.08	263.85	256.45	251.85
35000	346.72	336.17	327.03	319.07	312.10	305.96	300.54	295.73	291.44	287.62	284.20	271.61	263.99	259.25
36000	356.62	345.77	336.37	328.19	321.02	314.70	309.12	304.18	299.77	295.84	292.32	279.37	271.53	266.66
37000	366.53	355.38	345.72	337.30	329.93	323.45	317.71	312.62	308.10	304.05	300.44	287.13	279.08	274.07
38000	376.44	364.98	355.06	346.42	338.85	332.19	326.30	321.07	316.42	312.27	308.56	294.89	286.62	281.47
39000	386.34	374.58	364.40	355.54	347.77	340.93	334.88	329.52	324.75	320.49	316.68	302.65	294.16	288.88
40000	396.25	384.19	373.75	364.65	356.68	349.67	343.47	337.97	333.08	328.71	324.80	310.41	301.70	296.29
41000	406.16	393.79	383.09	373.77	365.60	358.41	352.06	346.42	341.40	336.92	332.92	318.17	309.25	303.70
42000	416.06	403.40	392.43	382.88	374.52	367.15	360.64	354.87	349.73	345.14	341.04	325.93	316.79	311.10
43000	425.97	413.00	401.78	392.00	383.43	375.89	369.23	363.32	358.06	353.36	349.16	333.69	324.33	318.51
44000	435.87	422.61	411.12	401.12	392.35	384.64	377.82	371.77	366.38	361.58	357.27	341.45	331.87	325.92
45000	445.78	432.21	420.47	410.23	401.27	393.38	386.40	380.22	374.71	369.79	365.39	349.21	339.42	333.32
46000	455.69	441.82	429.81	419.35	410.19	402.12	394.99	388.67	383.04	378.01	373.51	356.97	346.96	340.73
47000	465.59	451.42	439.15	428.46	419.10	410.86	403.58	397.12	391.36	386.23	381.63	364.73	354.50	348.14
48000	475.50	461.03	448.50	437.58	428.02	419.60	412.16	405.57	399.69	394.45	389.75	372.49	362.04	355.55
49000	485.40	470.63	457.84	446.70	436.94	428.34	420.75	414.01	408.02	402.67	397.87	380.25	369.59	362.95
50000	495.31	480.23	467.18	455.81	445.85	437.09	429.34	422.46	416.34	410.88	405.99	388.01	377.13	370.36
55000	544.84	528.26	513.90	501.39	490.44	480.79	472.27	464.71	457.98	451.97	446.59	426.81	414.84	407.40
60000	594.37	576.28	560.62	546.97	535.02	524.50	515.20	506.96	499.61	493.06	487.19	465.61	452.55	444.43
65000	643.90	624.30	607.34	592.56	579.61	568.21	558.14	549.20	541.25	534.15	527.79	504.41	490.26	481.47
70000	693.43	672.33	654.05	638.14	624.19	611.92	601.07	591.45	582.88	575.23	568.39	543.21	527.98	518.50
75000	742.96	720.35	700.77	683.72	668.78	655.63	644.00	633.69	624.51	616.32	608.99	582.01	565.69	555.54
80000	792.49	768.37	747.49	729.30	713.36	699.34	686.94	675.94	666.15	657.41	649.59	620.81	603.40	592.57
85000	842.02	816.40	794.21	774.88	757.95	743.04	729.87	718.18	707.78	698.50	690.19	659.61	641.11	629.61
90000	891.55	864.42	840.93	820.46	802.53	786.75	772.80	760.43	749.42	739.58	730.78	698.42	678.83	666.64
95000	941.08	912.44	887.64	866.04	847.12	830.46	815.74	802.68	791.05	780.67	771.38	737.22	716.54	703.68
100000	990.62	960.46	934.36	911.62	891.70	874.17	858.67	844.92	832.68	821.76	811.98	776.02	754.25	740.72

MONTHLY PAYMENT
REQUIRED TO AMORTIZE A LOAN

TERM AMOUNT	1 Year	2 Years	3 Years	4 Years	5 Years	6 Years	7 Years	8 Years	9 Years	10 Years	11 Years	12 Years	13 Years	14 Years
5	.44	.23	.16	.13	.11	.09	.08	.08	.07	.07	.06	.06	.06	.06
10	.88	.46	.32	.25	.21	.18	.16	.15	.14	.13	.12	.12	.11	.11
15	1.31	.69	.48	.38	.31	.27	.24	.22	.21	.19	.18	.17	.17	.16
25	2.19	1.14	.80	.62	.52	.45	.40	.37	.34	.32	.30	.28	.27	.26
50	4.37	2.28	1.59	1.24	1.03	.90	.80	.73	.67	.63	.59	.56	.54	.52
75	6.55	3.42	2.38	1.86	1.55	1.34	1.20	1.09	1.01	.94	.89	.84	.81	.78
100	8.73	4.56	3.17	2.48	2.06	1.79	1.59	1.45	1.34	1.25	1.18	1.12	1.07	1.03
200	17.46	9.11	6.33	4.95	4.12	3.57	3.18	2.90	2.67	2.50	2.36	2.24	2.14	2.06
300	26.19	13.66	9.49	7.42	6.18	5.36	4.77	4.34	4.01	3.74	3.53	3.36	3.21	3.09
400	34.92	18.21	12.66	9.89	8.24	7.14	6.36	5.79	5.34	4.99	4.71	4.47	4.28	4.11
500	43.64	22.76	15.82	12.36	10.29	8.92	7.95	7.23	6.68	6.24	5.88	5.59	5.35	5.14
600	52.37	27.31	18.98	14.83	12.35	10.71	9.54	8.68	8.01	7.48	7.06	6.71	6.41	6.17
700	61.10	31.86	22.14	17.30	14.41	12.49	11.13	10.12	9.35	8.73	8.23	7.82	7.48	7.19
800	69.83	36.42	25.31	19.77	16.47	14.28	12.72	11.57	10.68	9.98	9.41	8.94	8.55	8.22
900	78.55	40.97	28.47	22.24	18.52	16.06	14.31	13.02	12.02	11.22	10.58	10.06	9.62	9.25
1000	87.28	45.52	31.63	24.71	20.58	17.84	15.90	14.46	13.35	12.47	11.76	11.18	10.69	10.28
2000	174.56	91.03	63.26	49.42	41.16	35.68	31.80	28.92	26.69	24.94	23.51	22.35	21.37	20.55
3000	261.84	136.54	94.88	74.13	61.74	53.52	47.70	43.37	40.04	37.40	35.27	33.52	32.05	30.82
4000	349.12	182.06	126.51	98.83	82.31	71.36	63.60	57.83	53.38	49.87	47.02	44.69	42.74	41.09
5000	436.39	227.57	158.13	123.54	102.89	89.20	79.50	72.29	66.73	62.33	58.78	55.86	53.42	51.36
6000	523.67	273.08	189.76	148.25	123.47	107.04	95.40	86.74	80.07	74.80	70.53	67.03	64.10	61.63
7000	610.95	318.60	221.38	172.96	144.04	124.88	111.30	101.20	93.42	87.26	82.29	78.20	74.78	71.90
8000	698.23	364.11	253.01	197.66	164.62	142.72	127.20	115.66	106.76	99.73	94.04	89.37	85.47	82.18
9000	785.50	409.62	284.63	222.37	185.20	160.56	143.10	130.11	120.11	112.19	105.80	100.54	96.15	92.45
10000	872.78	455.13	316.26	247.08	205.77	178.40	159.00	144.57	133.45	124.66	117.55	111.71	106.83	102.72
11000	960.06	500.65	347.89	271.79	226.35	196.24	174.90	159.03	146.80	137.13	129.31	122.88	117.51	112.99
12000	1047.34	546.16	379.51	296.49	246.93	214.08	190.80	173.48	160.14	149.59	141.06	134.05	128.20	123.26
13000	1134.61	591.67	411.14	321.20	267.50	231.92	206.70	187.94	173.49	162.06	152.82	145.22	138.88	133.53
14000	1221.89	637.19	442.76	345.91	288.08	249.76	222.60	202.39	186.83	174.52	164.57	156.39	149.56	143.80
15000	1309.17	682.70	474.39	370.62	308.66	267.60	238.50	216.85	200.18	186.99	176.33	167.56	160.25	154.08
16000	1396.45	728.21	506.01	395.32	329.23	285.44	254.40	231.31	213.52	199.45	188.08	178.73	170.93	164.35
17000	1483.73	773.72	537.64	420.03	349.81	303.28	270.30	245.76	226.87	211.92	199.83	189.90	181.61	174.62
18000	1571.00	819.24	569.26	444.74	370.39	321.12	286.19	260.22	240.21	224.38	211.59	201.07	192.29	184.89
19000	1658.28	864.75	600.89	469.44	390.96	338.96	302.09	274.68	253.56	236.85	223.34	212.24	202.98	195.16
20000	1745.56	910.26	632.51	494.15	411.54	356.80	317.99	289.13	266.90	249.32	235.10	223.41	213.66	205.43
21000	1832.84	955.78	664.14	518.86	432.12	374.64	333.89	303.59	280.25	261.78	246.85	234.58	224.34	215.70
22000	1920.11	1001.29	695.77	543.57	452.70	392.48	349.79	318.05	293.59	274.25	258.61	245.75	235.02	225.97
23000	2007.39	1046.80	727.39	568.27	473.27	410.32	365.69	332.50	306.94	286.71	270.36	256.92	245.71	236.25
24000	2094.67	1092.31	759.02	592.98	493.85	428.16	381.59	346.96	320.28	299.18	282.12	268.09	256.39	246.52
25000	2181.95	1137.83	790.64	617.69	514.43	446.00	397.49	361.42	333.63	311.64	293.87	279.26	267.07	256.79
26000	2269.22	1183.34	822.27	642.40	535.00	463.84	413.39	375.87	346.97	324.11	305.63	290.43	277.75	267.06
27000	2356.50	1228.85	853.89	667.10	555.58	481.68	429.29	390.33	360.32	336.57	317.38	301.60	288.44	277.33
28000	2443.78	1274.37	885.52	691.81	576.16	499.52	445.19	404.78	373.66	349.04	329.14	312.77	299.12	287.60
29000	2531.06	1319.88	917.14	716.52	596.73	517.36	461.09	419.24	387.01	361.51	340.89	323.94	309.80	297.87
30000	2618.34	1365.39	948.77	741.23	617.31	535.20	476.99	433.70	400.35	373.97	352.65	335.11	320.49	308.15
31000	2705.61	1410.90	980.40	765.93	637.89	553.04	492.89	448.15	413.70	386.44	364.40	346.28	331.17	318.42
32000	2792.89	1456.42	1012.02	790.64	658.46	570.88	508.79	462.61	427.04	398.90	376.15	357.45	341.85	328.69
33000	2880.17	1501.93	1043.65	815.35	679.04	588.72	524.69	477.07	440.39	411.37	387.91	368.62	352.53	338.96
34000	2967.45	1547.44	1075.27	840.06	699.62	606.56	540.59	491.52	453.73	423.83	399.66	379.79	363.22	349.23
35000	3054.72	1592.96	1106.90	864.76	720.19	624.40	556.48	505.98	467.08	436.30	411.42	390.96	373.90	359.50
36000	3142.00	1638.47	1138.52	889.47	740.77	642.24	572.38	520.44	480.42	448.76	423.17	402.13	384.58	369.77
37000	3229.28	1683.98	1170.15	914.18	761.35	660.08	588.28	534.89	493.77	461.23	434.93	413.30	395.26	380.04
38000	3316.56	1729.49	1201.77	938.88	781.92	677.92	604.18	549.35	507.11	473.69	446.68	424.47	405.95	390.32
39000	3403.83	1775.01	1233.40	963.59	802.50	695.76	620.08	563.80	520.46	486.16	458.44	435.64	416.63	400.59
40000	3491.11	1820.52	1265.02	988.30	823.08	713.60	635.98	578.26	533.80	498.63	470.19	446.81	427.31	410.86
41000	3578.39	1866.03	1296.65	1013.01	843.66	731.44	651.88	592.72	547.15	511.09	481.95	457.98	437.99	421.13
42000	3665.67	1911.55	1328.28	1037.71	864.23	749.28	667.78	607.17	560.49	523.56	493.70	469.15	448.68	431.40
43000	3752.95	1957.06	1359.90	1062.42	884.81	767.12	683.68	621.63	573.84	536.02	505.46	480.32	459.36	441.67
44000	3840.22	2002.57	1391.53	1087.13	905.39	784.96	699.58	636.09	587.18	548.49	517.21	491.49	470.04	451.94
45000	3927.50	2048.08	1423.15	1111.84	925.96	802.80	715.48	650.54	600.53	560.95	528.97	502.66	480.73	462.22
46000	4014.78	2093.60	1454.78	1136.54	946.54	820.64	731.38	665.00	613.87	573.42	540.72	513.83	491.41	472.49
47000	4102.06	2139.11	1486.40	1161.25	967.12	838.48	747.28	679.46	627.22	585.88	552.47	525.00	502.09	482.76
48000	4189.33	2184.62	1518.03	1185.96	987.69	856.32	763.18	693.91	640.56	598.35	564.23	536.17	512.77	493.03
49000	4276.61	2230.14	1549.65	1210.67	1008.27	874.16	779.08	708.37	653.91	610.82	575.98	547.34	523.46	503.30
50000	4363.89	2275.65	1581.28	1235.37	1028.85	892.00	794.98	722.83	667.25	623.28	587.74	558.51	534.14	513.57
55000	4800.28	2503.21	1739.41	1358.91	1131.73	981.20	874.47	795.11	733.98	685.61	646.51	614.36	587.55	564.93
60000	5236.67	2730.78	1897.53	1482.45	1234.61	1070.40	953.97	867.39	800.70	747.94	705.29	670.21	640.97	616.29
65000	5673.05	2958.34	2055.66	1605.98	1337.50	1159.60	1033.47	939.67	867.43	810.26	764.06	726.06	694.38	667.64
70000	6109.44	3185.91	2213.79	1729.52	1440.38	1248.80	1112.96	1011.95	934.15	872.59	822.83	781.92	747.79	719.00
75000	6545.83	3413.47	2371.92	1853.06	1543.27	1338.00	1192.46	1084.24	1000.88	934.92	881.61	837.77	801.21	770.36
80000	6982.22	3641.04	2530.04	1976.59	1646.15	1427.20	1271.96	1156.52	1067.60	997.25	940.38	893.62	854.62	821.71
85000	7418.61	3868.60	2688.17	2100.13	1749.04	1516.40	1351.46	1228.80	1134.33	1059.57	999.15	949.47	908.03	873.07
90000	7855.00	4096.16	2846.30	2223.67	1851.92	1605.60	1430.95	1301.08	1201.05	1121.90	1057.93	1005.32	961.45	924.43
95000	8291.38	4323.73	3004.43	2347.20	1954.80	1694.80	1510.45	1373.36	1267.78	1184.23	1116.70	1061.17	1014.86	975.78
100000	8727.77	4551.29	3162.55	2470.74	2057.69	1784.00	1589.95	1445.65	1334.50	1246.56	1175.47	1117.02	1068.27	1027.14

TERM / AMOUNT	15 Years	16 Years	17 Years	18 Years	19 Years	20 Years	21 Years	22 Years	23 Years	24 Years	25 Years	30 Years	35 Years	40 Years
5	.05	.05	.05	.05	.05	.05	.05	.05	.05	.05	.05	.04	.04	.04
10	.10	.10	.10	.10	.09	.09	.09	.09	.09	.09	.09	.08	.08	.08
15	.15	.15	.15	.14	.14	.14	.13	.13	.13	.13	.13	.12	.12	.12
25	.25	.25	.24	.23	.23	.22	.22	.22	.21	.21	.21	.20	.19	.19
50	.50	.49	.47	.46	.45	.44	.44	.43	.42	.42	.41	.39	.38	.38
75	.75	.73	.71	.69	.67	.66	.65	.64	.63	.62	.62	.59	.57	.56
100	1.00	.97	.94	.92	.90	.88	.87	.85	.84	.83	.82	.78	.76	.75
200	1.99	1.93	1.88	1.83	1.79	1.76	1.73	1.70	1.67	1.65	1.63	1.56	1.52	1.49
300	2.98	2.89	2.81	2.74	2.68	2.63	2.59	2.54	2.51	2.48	2.45	2.34	2.27	2.23
400	3.97	3.85	3.75	3.66	3.58	3.51	3.45	3.39	3.34	3.30	3.26	3.12	3.03	2.98
500	4.97	4.81	4.68	4.57	4.47	4.38	4.31	4.24	4.18	4.12	4.07	3.89	3.79	3.72
600	5.96	5.78	5.62	5.48	5.36	5.26	5.17	5.08	5.01	4.95	4.89	4.67	4.54	4.46
700	6.95	6.74	6.56	6.40	6.26	6.14	6.03	5.93	5.85	5.77	5.70	5.45	5.30	5.20
800	7.94	7.70	7.49	7.31	7.15	7.01	6.89	6.78	6.68	6.59	6.51	6.23	6.05	5.95
900	8.93	8.66	8.43	8.22	8.04	7.89	7.75	7.62	7.51	7.42	7.33	7.01	6.81	6.69
1000	9.93	9.62	9.36	9.14	8.94	8.76	8.61	8.47	8.35	8.24	8.14	7.78	7.57	7.43
2000	19.85	19.24	18.72	18.27	17.87	17.52	17.21	16.94	16.69	16.47	16.28	15.56	15.13	14.86
3000	29.77	28.86	28.08	27.40	26.80	26.28	25.81	25.40	25.03	24.71	24.42	23.34	22.69	22.28
4000	39.69	38.48	37.44	36.53	35.74	35.04	34.42	33.87	33.38	32.94	32.55	31.12	30.25	29.71
5000	49.61	48.10	46.80	45.66	44.67	43.79	43.02	42.33	41.72	41.18	40.69	38.89	37.81	37.14
6000	59.53	57.72	56.16	54.79	53.60	52.55	51.62	50.80	50.06	49.41	48.83	46.67	45.37	44.56
7000	69.45	67.34	65.52	63.93	62.53	61.31	60.22	59.26	58.41	57.64	56.96	54.45	52.93	51.99
8000	79.37	76.96	74.88	73.06	71.47	70.07	68.83	67.73	66.75	65.88	65.10	62.23	60.49	59.41
9000	89.29	86.58	84.23	82.19	80.40	78.82	77.43	76.19	75.09	74.11	73.24	70.01	68.05	66.84
10000	99.21	96.20	93.59	91.32	89.33	87.58	86.03	84.66	83.44	82.35	81.37	77.78	75.61	74.27
11000	109.13	105.82	102.95	100.45	98.26	96.34	94.64	93.13	91.78	90.58	89.51	85.56	83.18	81.69
12000	119.05	115.44	112.31	109.58	107.20	105.10	103.24	101.59	100.12	98.82	97.65	93.34	90.74	89.12
13000	128.98	125.06	121.67	118.72	116.13	113.85	111.84	110.06	108.47	107.05	105.78	101.12	98.30	96.55
14000	138.90	134.68	131.03	127.85	125.06	122.61	120.44	118.52	116.81	115.28	113.92	108.90	105.86	103.97
15000	148.82	144.30	140.39	136.98	133.99	131.37	129.05	126.99	125.15	123.52	122.06	116.67	113.42	111.40
16000	158.74	153.92	149.75	146.11	142.93	140.12	137.65	135.45	133.50	131.75	130.19	124.45	120.98	118.82
17000	168.66	163.54	159.10	155.24	151.86	148.88	146.25	143.92	141.84	139.99	138.33	132.23	128.54	126.25
18000	178.58	173.16	168.46	164.37	160.79	157.64	154.85	152.38	150.18	148.22	146.47	140.01	136.10	133.68
19000	188.50	182.78	177.82	173.51	169.72	166.40	163.46	160.85	158.53	156.46	154.60	147.79	143.66	141.10
20000	198.42	192.40	187.18	182.64	178.66	175.16	172.06	169.31	166.87	164.69	162.74	155.56	151.22	148.53
21000	208.34	202.02	196.54	191.77	187.59	183.91	180.66	177.78	175.21	172.92	170.88	163.34	158.79	155.95
22000	218.26	211.64	205.90	200.90	196.52	192.67	189.27	186.25	183.56	181.16	179.01	171.12	166.35	163.38
23000	228.18	221.25	215.26	210.03	205.46	201.43	197.87	194.71	191.90	189.39	187.15	178.90	173.91	170.81
24000	238.10	230.87	224.62	219.16	214.39	210.19	206.47	203.18	200.24	197.63	195.29	186.67	181.47	178.23
25000	248.03	240.49	233.97	228.29	223.32	218.94	215.07	211.64	208.59	205.86	203.42	194.45	189.03	185.66
26000	257.95	250.11	243.33	237.43	232.25	227.70	223.68	220.11	216.93	214.10	211.56	202.23	196.59	193.09
27000	267.87	259.73	252.69	246.56	241.19	236.46	232.28	228.57	225.27	222.33	219.70	210.01	204.15	200.51
28000	277.79	269.35	262.05	255.69	250.12	245.22	240.88	237.04	233.62	230.56	227.83	217.79	211.71	207.94
29000	287.71	278.97	271.41	264.82	259.05	253.97	249.48	245.50	241.96	238.80	235.97	225.56	219.27	215.36
30000	297.63	288.59	280.77	273.95	267.98	262.73	258.09	253.97	250.30	247.03	244.11	233.34	226.83	222.79
31000	307.55	298.21	290.13	283.08	276.92	271.49	266.69	262.44	258.65	255.27	252.24	241.12	234.39	230.22
32000	317.47	307.83	299.49	292.22	285.85	280.25	275.29	270.90	266.99	263.50	260.38	248.90	241.96	237.64
33000	327.39	317.45	308.84	301.35	294.78	289.00	283.90	279.37	275.33	271.74	268.52	256.68	249.52	245.07
34000	337.31	327.07	318.20	310.48	303.71	297.76	292.50	287.83	283.68	279.97	276.65	264.45	257.08	252.49
35000	347.23	336.69	327.56	319.61	312.65	306.52	301.10	296.30	292.02	288.20	284.79	272.23	264.64	259.92
36000	357.15	346.31	336.92	328.74	321.58	315.28	309.70	304.76	300.36	296.44	292.93	280.01	272.20	267.35
37000	367.07	355.93	346.28	337.87	330.51	324.03	318.31	313.23	308.71	304.67	301.06	287.79	279.76	274.77
38000	377.00	365.55	355.64	347.01	339.44	332.79	326.91	321.69	317.05	312.91	309.20	295.57	287.32	282.20
39000	386.92	375.17	365.00	356.14	348.38	341.55	335.51	330.16	325.39	321.14	317.34	303.34	294.88	289.63
40000	396.84	384.79	374.36	365.27	357.31	350.31	344.12	338.62	333.74	329.38	325.47	311.12	302.44	297.05
41000	406.76	394.41	383.71	374.40	366.24	359.06	352.72	347.09	342.08	337.61	333.61	318.90	310.00	304.48
42000	416.68	404.03	393.07	383.53	375.17	367.82	361.32	355.56	350.42	345.84	341.75	326.68	317.57	311.90
43000	426.60	413.65	402.43	392.66	384.11	376.58	369.92	364.02	358.77	354.08	349.88	334.45	325.13	319.33
44000	436.52	423.27	411.79	401.79	393.04	385.34	378.53	372.49	367.11	362.31	358.02	342.23	332.69	326.76
45000	446.44	432.88	421.15	410.93	401.97	394.09	387.13	380.95	375.45	370.55	366.16	350.01	340.25	334.18
46000	456.36	442.50	430.51	420.06	410.91	402.85	395.73	389.42	383.80	378.78	374.29	357.79	347.81	341.61
47000	466.28	452.12	439.87	429.19	419.84	411.61	404.33	397.88	392.14	387.02	382.43	365.57	355.37	349.04
48000	476.20	461.74	449.23	438.32	428.77	420.37	412.94	406.35	400.48	395.25	390.57	373.34	362.93	356.46
49000	486.12	471.36	458.58	447.45	437.70	429.12	421.54	414.81	408.83	403.48	398.70	381.12	370.49	363.89
50000	496.05	480.98	467.94	456.58	446.64	437.88	430.14	423.28	417.17	411.72	406.84	388.90	378.05	371.31
55000	545.65	529.08	514.74	502.24	491.30	481.67	473.16	465.61	458.89	452.89	447.52	427.79	415.86	408.44
60000	595.25	577.18	561.53	547.90	535.96	525.46	516.17	507.93	500.60	494.06	488.21	466.68	453.66	445.58
65000	644.86	625.28	608.32	593.56	580.62	569.24	559.18	550.26	542.32	535.23	528.89	505.57	491.47	482.71
70000	694.46	673.37	655.12	639.22	625.29	613.03	602.20	592.59	584.04	576.40	569.57	544.46	529.27	519.84
75000	744.07	721.47	701.91	684.87	669.95	656.82	645.21	634.92	625.75	617.58	610.26	583.35	567.08	556.97
80000	793.67	769.57	748.71	730.53	714.61	700.61	688.23	677.24	667.47	658.75	650.94	622.24	604.88	594.10
85000	843.27	817.67	795.50	776.19	759.28	744.39	731.24	719.57	709.19	699.92	691.62	661.13	642.69	631.23
90000	892.88	865.76	842.29	821.85	803.94	788.18	774.25	761.90	750.90	741.09	732.31	700.02	680.49	668.36
95000	942.48	913.86	889.09	867.51	848.60	831.97	817.27	804.23	792.62	782.26	772.99	738.91	718.30	705.49
100000	992.09	961.96	935.88	913.16	893.27	875.76	860.28	846.55	834.34	823.43	813.67	777.79	756.10	742.62

MONTHLY PAYMENT
REQUIRED TO AMORTIZE A LOAN

TERM AMOUNT	1 Year	2 Years	3 Years	4 Years	5 Years	6 Years	7 Years	8 Years	9 Years	10 Years	11 Years	12 Years	13 Years	14 Years
5	.44	.23	.16	.13	.11	.09	.08	.08	.07	.07	.06	.06	.06	.06
10	.88	.46	.32	.25	.21	.18	.16	.15	.14	.13	.12	.12	.11	.11
15	1.31	.69	.48	.38	.31	.27	.24	.22	.21	.19	.18	.17	.17	.16
25	2.19	1.14	.80	.62	.52	.45	.40	.37	.34	.32	.30	.29	.27	.26
50	4.37	2.28	1.59	1.24	1.04	.90	.80	.73	.67	.63	.59	.57	.54	.52
75	6.55	3.42	2.38	1.86	1.55	1.35	1.20	1.09	1.01	.94	.89	.85	.81	.78
100	8.74	4.56	3.17	2.48	2.07	1.79	1.60	1.45	1.34	1.26	1.18	1.13	1.08	1.04
200	17.47	9.11	6.34	4.95	4.13	3.58	3.19	2.90	2.68	2.51	2.36	2.25	2.15	2.07
300	26.20	13.67	9.50	7.43	6.19	5.37	4.79	4.35	4.02	3.76	3.54	3.37	3.22	3.10
400	34.93	18.22	12.67	9.90	8.25	7.16	6.38	5.80	5.36	5.01	4.72	4.49	4.30	4.13
500	43.66	22.78	15.84	12.38	10.31	8.94	7.97	7.25	6.70	6.26	5.90	5.61	5.37	5.16
600	52.39	27.33	19.00	14.85	12.37	10.73	9.57	8.70	8.04	7.51	7.08	6.73	6.44	6.19
700	61.12	31.89	22.17	17.32	14.43	12.52	11.16	10.15	9.37	8.76	8.26	7.85	7.51	7.23
800	69.85	36.44	25.33	19.80	16.50	14.31	12.75	11.60	10.71	10.01	9.44	8.97	8.59	8.26
900	78.59	41.00	28.50	22.27	18.56	16.09	14.35	13.05	12.05	11.26	10.62	10.10	9.66	9.29
1000	87.32	45.55	31.67	24.75	20.62	17.88	15.94	14.50	13.39	12.51	11.80	11.22	10.73	10.32
2000	174.63	91.10	63.33	49.49	41.23	35.76	31.88	29.00	26.77	25.02	23.60	22.43	21.46	20.63
3000	261.94	136.65	94.99	74.23	61.84	53.64	47.82	43.49	40.16	37.52	35.39	33.64	32.18	30.95
4000	349.25	182.19	126.65	98.98	82.46	71.51	63.75	57.99	53.54	50.03	47.19	44.85	42.91	41.26
5000	436.57	227.74	158.31	123.72	103.07	89.39	79.69	72.48	66.93	62.53	58.98	56.07	53.63	51.58
6000	523.88	273.29	189.97	148.46	123.68	107.27	95.63	86.98	80.31	75.04	70.78	67.28	64.36	61.89
7000	611.19	318.84	221.63	173.20	144.30	125.14	111.57	101.47	93.70	87.55	82.58	78.49	75.08	72.21
8000	698.50	364.38	253.29	197.95	164.91	143.02	127.50	115.97	107.08	100.05	94.37	89.70	85.81	82.52
9000	785.82	409.93	284.95	222.69	185.52	160.90	143.44	130.46	120.46	112.56	106.17	100.91	96.53	92.84
10000	873.13	455.48	316.61	247.43	206.14	178.78	159.38	144.96	133.85	125.06	117.96	112.13	107.26	103.15
11000	960.44	501.02	348.27	272.18	226.75	196.65	175.31	159.45	147.23	137.57	129.76	123.34	117.98	113.47
12000	1047.75	546.57	379.93	296.92	247.36	214.53	191.25	173.95	160.62	150.07	141.55	134.55	128.71	123.78
13000	1135.07	592.12	411.59	321.66	267.97	232.41	207.19	188.44	174.00	162.58	153.35	145.76	139.43	134.10
14000	1222.38	637.67	443.25	346.40	288.59	250.28	223.13	202.94	187.39	175.09	165.15	156.97	150.16	144.41
15000	1309.69	683.21	474.91	371.15	309.20	268.16	239.06	217.43	200.77	187.59	176.94	168.19	160.88	154.73
16000	1397.00	728.76	506.57	395.89	329.81	286.04	255.00	231.93	214.16	200.10	188.74	179.40	171.61	165.04
17000	1484.32	774.31	538.23	420.63	350.43	303.91	270.94	246.42	227.54	212.60	200.53	190.61	182.34	175.36
18000	1571.63	819.85	569.89	445.38	371.04	321.79	286.88	260.92	240.92	225.11	212.33	201.82	193.06	185.67
19000	1658.94	865.40	601.55	470.12	391.65	339.67	302.81	275.41	254.31	237.62	224.12	213.03	203.79	195.99
20000	1746.25	910.95	633.21	494.86	412.27	357.55	318.75	289.91	267.69	250.12	235.92	224.25	214.51	206.30
21000	1833.57	956.50	664.87	519.60	432.88	375.42	334.69	304.40	281.08	262.63	247.72	235.46	225.24	216.62
22000	1920.88	1002.04	696.53	544.35	453.49	393.30	350.62	318.90	294.46	275.13	259.51	246.67	235.96	226.93
23000	2008.19	1047.59	728.19	569.09	474.11	411.18	366.56	333.39	307.85	287.64	271.31	257.88	246.69	237.24
24000	2095.50	1093.14	759.85	593.83	494.72	429.05	382.50	347.89	321.23	300.14	283.10	269.09	257.41	247.56
25000	2182.82	1138.69	791.51	618.58	515.33	446.93	398.44	362.38	334.62	312.65	294.90	280.31	268.14	257.87
26000	2270.13	1184.23	823.17	643.32	535.94	464.81	414.37	376.88	348.00	325.16	306.69	291.52	278.86	268.19
27000	2357.44	1229.78	854.83	668.06	556.56	482.68	430.31	391.37	361.38	337.66	318.49	302.73	289.59	278.50
28000	2444.75	1275.33	886.49	692.80	577.17	500.56	446.25	405.87	374.77	350.17	330.29	313.94	300.31	288.82
29000	2532.07	1320.88	918.15	717.55	597.78	518.44	462.19	420.36	388.15	362.67	342.08	325.15	311.04	299.13
30000	2619.38	1366.42	949.81	742.29	618.40	536.32	478.12	434.86	401.54	375.18	353.88	336.37	321.76	309.45
31000	2706.69	1411.97	981.47	767.03	639.01	554.19	494.06	449.35	414.92	387.68	365.67	347.58	332.49	319.76
32000	2794.00	1457.52	1013.13	791.78	659.62	572.07	510.00	463.85	428.31	400.19	377.47	358.79	343.22	330.08
33000	2881.31	1503.06	1044.79	816.52	680.24	589.95	525.93	478.34	441.69	412.70	389.26	370.00	353.94	340.39
34000	2968.63	1548.61	1076.45	841.26	700.85	607.82	541.87	492.84	455.08	425.20	401.06	381.21	364.67	350.71
35000	3055.94	1594.16	1108.12	866.00	721.46	625.70	557.81	507.33	468.46	437.71	412.86	392.43	375.39	361.02
36000	3143.25	1639.70	1139.78	890.75	742.08	643.58	573.75	521.83	481.84	450.21	424.65	403.64	386.12	371.34
37000	3230.56	1685.25	1171.44	915.49	762.69	661.45	589.68	536.32	495.23	462.72	436.45	414.85	396.84	381.65
38000	3317.88	1730.80	1203.10	940.23	783.30	679.33	605.62	550.82	508.61	475.23	448.24	426.06	407.57	391.97
39000	3405.19	1776.35	1234.76	964.98	803.91	697.21	621.56	565.31	522.00	487.73	460.04	437.27	418.29	402.28
40000	3492.50	1821.89	1266.42	989.72	824.53	715.09	637.49	579.81	535.38	500.24	471.83	448.49	429.02	412.60
41000	3579.81	1867.44	1298.08	1014.46	845.14	732.96	653.43	594.30	548.77	512.74	483.63	459.70	439.74	422.91
42000	3667.13	1912.99	1329.74	1039.20	865.75	750.84	669.37	608.80	562.15	525.25	495.43	470.91	450.47	433.23
43000	3754.44	1958.54	1361.40	1063.95	886.37	768.72	685.31	623.29	575.54	537.75	507.22	482.12	461.19	443.54
44000	3841.75	2004.08	1393.06	1088.69	906.98	786.59	701.24	637.79	588.92	550.26	519.02	493.33	471.92	453.85
45000	3929.06	2049.63	1424.72	1113.43	927.59	804.47	717.18	652.28	602.30	562.77	530.81	504.55	482.64	464.17
46000	4016.38	2095.18	1456.38	1138.18	948.21	822.35	733.12	666.78	615.69	575.27	542.61	515.76	493.37	474.48
47000	4103.69	2140.72	1488.04	1162.92	968.82	840.22	749.06	681.27	629.07	587.78	554.40	526.97	504.10	484.80
48000	4191.00	2186.27	1519.70	1187.66	989.43	858.10	764.99	695.77	642.46	600.28	566.20	538.18	514.82	495.11
49000	4278.31	2231.82	1551.36	1212.40	1010.04	875.98	780.93	710.26	655.84	612.79	578.00	549.39	525.55	505.43
50000	4365.63	2277.37	1583.02	1237.15	1030.66	893.86	796.87	724.76	669.23	625.29	589.79	560.61	536.27	515.74
55000	4802.19	2505.10	1741.32	1360.86	1133.72	983.24	876.55	797.23	736.15	687.82	648.77	616.67	589.90	567.32
60000	5238.75	2732.84	1899.62	1484.58	1236.79	1072.63	956.24	869.71	803.07	750.35	707.75	672.73	643.52	618.89
65000	5675.31	2960.57	2057.92	1608.29	1339.85	1162.01	1035.93	942.18	869.99	812.88	766.73	728.79	697.15	670.46
70000	6111.87	3188.31	2216.23	1732.00	1442.92	1251.40	1115.61	1014.66	936.91	875.41	825.71	784.85	750.78	722.04
75000	6548.44	3416.05	2374.53	1855.72	1545.98	1340.78	1195.30	1087.13	1003.84	937.94	884.69	840.91	804.40	773.61
80000	6985.00	3643.78	2532.83	1979.43	1649.05	1430.17	1274.98	1159.61	1070.76	1000.47	943.66	896.97	858.03	825.19
85000	7421.56	3871.52	2691.13	2103.15	1752.12	1519.55	1354.67	1232.08	1137.68	1063.00	1002.64	953.03	911.66	876.76
90000	7858.12	4099.25	2849.43	2226.86	1855.18	1608.94	1434.36	1304.56	1204.60	1125.53	1061.62	1009.09	965.28	928.33
95000	8294.69	4326.99	3007.73	2350.57	1958.25	1698.32	1514.04	1377.03	1271.53	1188.06	1120.60	1065.15	1018.91	979.91
100000	8731.25	4554.73	3166.03	2474.29	2061.31	1787.71	1593.73	1449.51	1338.45	1250.58	1179.58	1121.21	1072.54	1031.48

TERM AMOUNT	15 Years	16 Years	17 Years	18 Years	19 Years	20 Years	21 Years	22 Years	23 Years	24 Years	25 Years	30 Years	35 Years	40 Years
5	.05	.05	.05	.05	.05	.05	.05	.05	.05	.05	.05	.04	.04	.04
10	.10	.10	.10	.10	.09	.09	.09	.09	.09	.09	.09	.08	.08	.08
15	.15	.15	.15	.14	.14	.14	.13	.13	.13	.13	.13	.12	.12	.12
25	.25	.25	.24	.23	.23	.23	.22	.22	.21	.21	.21	.20	.20	.19
50	.50	.49	.48	.46	.45	.45	.44	.43	.42	.42	.41	.40	.39	.38
75	.75	.73	.71	.69	.68	.67	.65	.64	.63	.63	.62	.59	.58	.57
100	1.00	.97	.95	.92	.90	.89	.87	.86	.84	.83	.82	.79	.77	.75
200	2.00	1.94	1.89	1.84	1.80	1.77	1.74	1.71	1.68	1.66	1.64	1.57	1.53	1.50
300	2.99	2.90	2.83	2.76	2.70	2.65	2.60	2.56	2.52	2.49	2.46	2.35	2.29	2.25
400	3.99	3.87	3.77	3.68	3.60	3.53	3.47	3.41	3.36	3.32	3.28	3.14	3.05	3.00
500	4.99	4.84	4.71	4.59	4.49	4.41	4.33	4.26	4.20	4.15	4.10	3.92	3.81	3.75
600	5.98	5.80	5.65	5.51	5.39	5.29	5.20	5.11	5.04	4.98	4.92	4.70	4.57	4.50
700	6.98	6.77	6.59	6.43	6.29	6.17	6.06	5.97	5.88	5.80	5.74	5.49	5.34	5.24
800	7.98	7.74	7.53	7.35	7.19	7.05	6.93	6.82	6.72	6.63	6.55	6.27	6.10	5.99
900	8.97	8.70	8.47	8.27	8.09	7.93	7.79	7.67	7.56	7.46	7.37	7.05	6.86	6.74
1000	9.97	9.67	9.41	9.18	8.98	8.81	8.66	8.52	8.40	8.29	8.19	7.84	7.62	7.49
2000	19.93	19.33	18.81	18.36	17.96	17.62	17.31	17.03	16.79	16.57	16.38	15.67	15.24	14.97
3000	29.90	29.00	28.22	27.54	26.94	26.42	25.96	25.55	25.18	24.86	24.57	23.50	22.85	22.46
4000	39.86	38.66	37.62	36.72	35.92	35.23	34.61	34.06	33.58	33.14	32.75	31.33	30.47	29.94
5000	49.83	48.33	47.03	45.89	44.90	44.03	43.26	42.58	41.97	41.43	40.94	39.16	38.09	37.42
6000	59.79	57.99	56.43	55.07	53.88	52.84	51.91	51.09	50.36	49.71	49.13	46.99	45.70	44.91
7000	69.76	67.66	65.84	64.25	62.86	61.64	60.56	59.61	58.76	58.00	57.32	54.82	53.32	52.39
8000	79.72	77.32	75.24	73.43	71.84	70.45	69.21	68.12	67.15	66.28	65.50	62.66	60.94	59.87
9000	89.69	86.99	84.64	82.61	80.82	79.25	77.87	76.64	75.54	74.57	73.69	70.49	68.55	67.36
10000	99.65	96.65	94.05	91.78	89.80	88.06	86.52	85.15	83.93	82.85	81.88	78.32	76.17	74.84
11000	109.62	106.31	103.45	100.96	98.78	96.86	95.17	93.66	92.33	91.13	90.07	86.15	83.79	82.32
12000	119.58	115.98	112.86	110.14	107.76	105.67	103.82	102.18	100.72	99.42	98.25	93.98	91.40	89.81
13000	129.55	125.64	122.26	119.32	116.74	114.47	112.47	110.69	109.11	107.70	106.44	101.81	99.02	97.29
14000	139.51	135.31	131.67	128.50	125.72	123.28	121.12	119.21	117.51	115.99	114.63	109.64	106.64	104.77
15000	149.48	144.97	141.07	137.67	134.70	132.08	129.77	127.72	125.90	124.27	122.82	117.47	114.25	112.26
16000	159.44	154.64	150.48	146.85	143.68	140.89	138.42	136.24	134.29	132.56	131.00	125.31	121.87	119.74
17000	169.41	164.30	159.88	156.03	152.66	149.69	147.07	144.75	142.69	140.84	139.19	133.14	129.49	127.22
18000	179.37	173.97	169.28	165.21	161.64	158.50	155.73	153.27	151.08	149.13	147.38	140.97	137.10	134.71
19000	189.34	183.63	178.69	174.39	170.62	167.30	164.38	161.78	159.47	157.41	155.57	148.80	144.72	142.19
20000	199.30	193.29	188.09	183.56	179.60	176.11	173.03	170.29	167.86	165.70	163.75	156.63	152.34	149.67
21000	209.27	202.96	197.50	192.74	188.58	184.91	181.68	178.81	176.26	173.98	171.94	164.46	159.95	157.16
22000	219.23	212.62	206.90	201.92	197.56	193.72	190.33	187.32	184.65	182.26	180.13	172.29	167.57	164.64
23000	229.20	222.29	216.31	211.10	206.54	202.53	198.98	195.84	193.04	190.55	188.32	180.13	175.19	172.12
24000	239.16	231.95	225.71	220.28	215.52	211.33	207.63	204.35	201.44	198.83	196.50	187.96	182.80	179.61
25000	249.13	241.62	235.12	229.45	224.50	220.14	216.28	212.87	209.83	207.12	204.69	195.79	190.42	187.09
26000	259.09	251.28	244.52	238.63	233.48	228.94	224.93	221.38	218.22	215.40	212.88	203.62	198.03	194.57
27000	269.06	260.95	253.92	247.81	242.46	237.75	233.59	229.90	226.61	223.69	221.07	211.45	205.65	202.06
28000	279.02	270.61	263.33	256.99	251.44	246.55	242.24	238.41	235.01	231.97	229.25	219.28	213.27	209.54
29000	288.99	280.27	272.73	266.17	260.42	255.36	250.89	246.93	243.40	240.26	237.44	227.11	220.88	217.03
30000	298.95	289.94	282.14	275.34	269.39	264.16	259.54	255.44	251.79	248.54	245.63	234.94	228.50	224.51
31000	308.92	299.60	291.54	284.52	278.37	272.97	268.19	263.95	260.19	256.82	253.82	242.78	236.12	231.99
32000	318.88	309.27	300.95	293.70	287.35	281.77	276.84	272.47	268.58	265.11	262.00	250.61	243.73	239.48
33000	328.85	318.93	310.35	302.88	296.33	290.58	285.49	280.98	276.97	273.39	270.19	258.44	251.35	246.96
34000	338.81	328.60	319.75	312.05	305.31	299.38	294.14	289.50	285.37	281.68	278.38	266.27	258.97	254.44
35000	348.78	338.26	329.16	321.23	314.29	308.19	302.79	298.01	293.76	289.96	286.57	274.10	266.58	261.93
36000	358.74	347.93	338.56	330.41	323.27	316.99	311.45	306.53	302.15	298.25	294.75	281.93	274.20	269.41
37000	368.71	357.59	347.97	339.59	332.25	325.80	320.10	315.04	310.54	306.53	302.94	289.76	281.82	276.89
38000	378.67	367.25	357.37	348.77	341.23	334.60	328.75	323.56	318.94	314.82	311.13	297.60	289.43	284.38
39000	388.64	376.92	366.78	357.94	350.21	343.41	337.40	332.07	327.33	323.10	319.32	305.43	297.05	291.86
40000	398.60	386.58	376.18	367.12	359.19	352.21	346.05	340.58	335.72	331.39	327.50	313.26	304.67	299.34
41000	408.57	396.25	385.59	376.30	368.17	361.02	354.70	349.10	344.12	339.67	335.69	321.09	312.28	306.83
42000	418.53	405.91	394.99	385.48	377.15	369.82	363.35	357.61	352.51	347.95	343.88	328.92	319.90	314.31
43000	428.50	415.58	404.39	394.66	386.13	378.63	372.00	366.13	360.90	356.24	352.07	336.75	327.52	321.79
44000	438.46	425.24	413.80	403.83	395.11	387.44	380.65	374.64	369.29	364.52	360.25	344.58	335.13	329.28
45000	448.43	434.91	423.20	413.01	404.09	396.24	389.31	383.16	377.69	372.81	368.44	352.41	342.75	336.76
46000	458.39	444.57	432.61	422.19	413.07	405.05	397.96	391.67	386.08	381.09	376.63	360.25	350.37	344.24
47000	468.36	454.23	442.01	431.37	422.05	413.85	406.61	400.19	394.47	389.38	384.82	368.08	357.98	351.73
48000	478.32	463.90	451.42	440.55	431.03	422.66	415.26	408.70	402.87	397.66	393.00	375.91	365.60	359.21
49000	488.29	473.56	460.82	449.72	440.01	431.46	423.91	417.22	411.26	405.95	401.19	383.74	373.21	366.69
50000	498.25	483.23	470.23	458.90	448.99	440.27	432.56	425.73	419.65	414.23	409.38	391.57	380.83	374.18
55000	548.08	531.55	517.25	504.79	493.89	484.29	475.82	468.30	461.62	455.65	450.32	430.73	418.91	411.60
60000	597.90	579.87	564.27	550.68	538.78	528.32	519.07	510.87	503.58	497.08	491.25	469.88	457.00	449.01
65000	647.73	628.20	611.29	596.57	583.68	572.34	562.33	553.45	545.55	538.50	532.19	509.04	495.08	486.43
70000	697.55	676.52	658.31	642.46	628.58	616.37	605.58	596.02	587.51	579.92	573.13	548.20	533.16	523.85
75000	747.38	724.84	705.34	688.35	673.48	660.40	648.84	638.59	629.48	621.34	614.07	587.35	571.24	561.26
80000	797.20	773.16	752.36	734.24	718.38	704.42	692.10	681.16	671.44	662.77	655.00	626.51	609.33	598.68
85000	847.03	821.48	799.38	780.13	763.28	748.45	735.35	723.74	713.41	704.19	695.94	665.67	647.41	636.10
90000	896.85	869.81	846.40	826.02	808.17	792.48	778.61	766.31	755.37	745.61	736.88	704.82	685.49	673.52
95000	946.68	918.13	893.42	871.91	853.07	836.50	821.86	808.88	797.34	787.03	777.82	743.98	723.57	710.93
100000	996.50	966.45	940.45	917.80	897.97	880.53	865.12	851.45	839.30	828.46	818.75	783.14	761.66	748.35

MONTHLY PAYMENT
REQUIRED TO AMORTIZE A LOAN

TERM AMOUNT	1 Year	2 Years	3 Years	4 Years	5 Years	6 Years	7 Years	8 Years	9 Years	10 Years	11 Years	12 Years	13 Years	14 Years
5	.44	.23	.16	.13	.11	.09	.08	.08	.07	.07	.06	.06	.06	.06
10	.88	.46	.32	.25	.21	.18	.16	.15	.14	.13	.12	.12	.11	.11
15	1.32	.69	.48	.38	.31	.27	.24	.22	.21	.19	.18	.17	.17	.16
25	2.19	1.14	.80	.62	.52	.45	.40	.37	.34	.32	.30	.29	.27	.26
50	4.37	2.28	1.59	1.24	1.04	.90	.80	.73	.68	.63	.60	.57	.54	.52
75	6.56	3.42	2.38	1.86	1.55	1.35	1.20	1.09	1.01	.94	.89	.85	.81	.78
100	8.74	4.56	3.17	2.48	2.07	1.80	1.60	1.46	1.35	1.26	1.19	1.13	1.08	1.04
200	17.47	9.12	6.34	4.96	4.13	3.59	3.20	2.91	2.69	2.51	2.37	2.25	2.16	2.07
300	26.21	13.68	9.51	7.43	6.20	5.38	4.79	4.36	4.03	3.76	3.55	3.38	3.23	3.11
400	34.94	18.23	12.68	9.91	8.26	7.17	6.39	5.81	5.37	5.02	4.73	4.50	4.31	4.14
500	43.67	22.79	15.85	12.39	10.32	8.96	7.99	7.27	6.71	6.27	5.92	5.62	5.38	5.18
600	52.41	27.35	19.02	14.86	12.39	10.75	9.58	8.72	8.05	7.52	7.10	6.75	6.46	6.21
700	61.14	31.90	22.18	17.34	14.45	12.54	11.18	10.17	9.39	8.78	8.28	7.87	7.53	7.25
800	69.87	36.46	25.35	19.82	16.51	14.33	12.77	11.62	10.73	10.03	9.46	9.00	8.61	8.28
900	78.61	41.02	28.52	22.29	18.58	16.12	14.37	13.07	12.07	11.28	10.65	10.12	9.68	9.31
1000	87.34	45.58	31.69	24.77	20.64	17.91	15.97	14.53	13.42	12.54	11.83	11.24	10.76	10.35
2000	174.68	91.15	63.37	49.54	41.28	35.81	31.93	29.05	26.83	25.07	23.65	22.48	21.51	20.69
3000	262.01	136.72	95.06	74.30	61.92	53.71	47.89	43.57	40.24	37.60	35.47	33.72	32.27	31.04
4000	349.35	182.29	126.74	99.07	82.55	71.61	63.85	58.09	53.65	50.14	47.30	44.96	43.02	41.38
5000	436.68	227.86	158.42	123.84	103.19	89.51	79.82	72.61	67.06	62.67	59.12	56.20	53.77	51.72
6000	524.02	273.43	190.11	148.60	123.83	107.42	95.78	87.13	80.47	75.20	70.94	67.44	64.53	62.07
7000	611.35	319.00	221.79	173.37	144.47	125.32	111.74	101.65	93.88	87.73	82.77	78.68	75.28	72.41
8000	698.69	364.57	253.47	198.14	165.10	143.22	127.70	116.17	107.29	100.27	94.59	89.92	86.04	82.76
9000	786.03	410.14	285.16	222.90	185.74	161.12	143.67	130.69	120.70	112.80	106.41	101.16	96.79	93.10
10000	873.36	455.71	316.84	247.67	206.38	179.02	159.63	145.21	134.11	125.33	118.24	112.40	107.54	103.44
11000	960.70	501.28	348.52	272.44	227.01	196.92	175.59	159.73	147.52	137.86	130.06	123.64	118.30	113.79
12000	1048.03	546.85	380.21	297.20	247.65	214.83	191.55	174.26	160.93	150.40	141.88	134.88	129.05	124.13
13000	1135.37	592.42	411.89	321.97	268.29	232.73	207.52	188.78	174.34	162.93	153.71	146.12	139.80	134.47
14000	1222.70	637.99	443.57	346.74	288.93	250.63	223.48	203.30	187.76	175.46	165.53	157.36	150.56	144.82
15000	1310.04	683.56	475.26	371.50	309.56	268.53	239.44	217.82	201.17	188.00	177.35	168.60	161.31	155.16
16000	1397.37	729.13	506.94	396.27	330.20	286.43	255.40	232.34	214.58	200.53	189.18	179.84	172.07	165.51
17000	1484.71	774.70	538.62	421.04	350.84	304.33	271.37	246.86	227.99	213.06	201.00	191.08	182.82	175.85
18000	1572.05	820.27	570.31	445.80	371.48	322.24	287.33	261.38	241.40	225.59	212.82	202.32	193.57	186.19
19000	1659.38	865.84	601.99	470.57	392.11	340.14	303.29	275.90	254.81	238.13	224.65	213.56	204.33	196.54
20000	1746.72	911.41	633.68	495.34	412.75	358.04	319.25	290.42	268.22	250.66	236.47	224.80	215.08	206.88
21000	1834.05	956.98	665.36	520.10	433.39	375.94	335.22	304.94	281.63	263.19	248.29	236.04	225.83	217.22
22000	1921.39	1002.55	697.04	544.87	454.02	393.84	351.18	319.46	295.04	275.72	260.11	247.28	236.59	227.57
23000	2008.72	1048.12	728.73	569.63	474.66	411.74	367.14	333.98	308.45	288.26	271.94	258.52	247.34	237.91
24000	2096.06	1093.69	760.41	594.40	495.30	429.65	383.10	348.51	321.86	300.79	283.76	269.76	258.10	248.26
25000	2183.39	1139.26	792.09	619.17	515.94	447.55	399.07	363.03	335.27	313.32	295.58	281.00	268.85	258.60
26000	2270.73	1184.83	823.78	643.93	536.57	465.45	415.03	377.55	348.68	325.85	307.41	292.24	279.60	268.94
27000	2358.07	1230.40	855.46	668.70	557.21	483.35	430.99	392.07	362.10	338.39	319.23	303.48	290.36	279.29
28000	2445.40	1275.97	887.14	693.47	577.85	501.25	446.95	406.59	375.51	350.92	331.05	314.72	301.11	289.63
29000	2532.74	1321.54	918.83	718.23	598.48	519.15	462.92	421.11	388.92	363.45	342.88	325.96	311.87	299.97
30000	2620.07	1367.11	950.51	743.00	619.12	537.06	478.88	435.63	402.33	375.99	354.70	337.20	322.62	310.32
31000	2707.41	1412.68	982.19	767.77	639.76	554.96	494.84	450.15	415.74	388.52	366.52	348.44	333.37	320.66
32000	2794.74	1458.25	1013.88	792.53	660.40	572.86	510.80	464.67	429.15	401.05	378.35	359.68	344.13	331.01
33000	2882.08	1503.82	1045.56	817.30	681.03	590.76	526.77	479.19	442.56	413.58	390.17	370.92	354.88	341.35
34000	2969.41	1549.39	1077.24	842.07	701.67	608.66	542.73	493.71	455.97	426.12	401.99	382.16	365.63	351.69
35000	3056.75	1594.96	1108.93	866.83	722.31	626.56	558.69	508.23	469.38	438.65	413.82	393.40	376.39	362.04
36000	3144.09	1640.53	1140.61	891.60	742.95	644.47	574.65	522.76	482.79	451.18	425.64	404.64	387.14	372.38
37000	3231.42	1686.10	1172.29	916.37	763.58	662.37	590.62	537.28	496.20	463.71	437.46	415.88	397.90	382.72
38000	3318.76	1731.67	1203.98	941.13	784.22	680.27	606.58	551.80	509.61	476.25	449.29	427.12	408.65	393.07
39000	3406.09	1777.24	1235.66	965.90	804.86	698.17	622.54	566.32	523.02	488.78	461.11	438.36	419.40	403.41
40000	3493.43	1822.81	1267.35	990.67	825.49	716.07	638.50	580.84	536.44	501.31	472.93	449.60	430.16	413.76
41000	3580.76	1868.38	1299.03	1015.43	846.13	733.98	654.47	595.36	549.85	513.84	484.75	460.84	440.91	424.10
42000	3668.10	1913.95	1330.71	1040.20	866.77	751.88	670.43	609.88	563.26	526.38	496.58	472.08	451.66	434.44
43000	3755.44	1959.52	1362.40	1064.96	887.41	769.78	686.39	624.40	576.67	538.91	508.40	483.32	462.42	444.79
44000	3842.77	2005.09	1394.08	1089.73	908.04	787.68	702.35	638.92	590.08	551.44	520.22	494.56	473.17	455.13
45000	3930.11	2050.66	1425.76	1114.50	928.68	805.58	718.32	653.44	603.49	563.98	532.05	505.80	483.93	465.47
46000	4017.44	2096.23	1457.45	1139.26	949.32	823.48	734.28	667.96	616.90	576.51	543.87	517.04	494.68	475.82
47000	4104.78	2141.80	1489.13	1164.03	969.95	841.39	750.24	682.48	630.31	589.04	555.69	528.28	505.43	486.16
48000	4192.11	2187.37	1520.81	1188.80	990.59	859.29	766.20	697.01	643.72	601.57	567.52	539.52	516.19	496.51
49000	4279.45	2232.94	1552.50	1213.56	1011.23	877.19	782.17	711.53	657.13	614.11	579.34	550.76	526.94	506.85
50000	4366.78	2278.51	1584.18	1238.33	1031.87	895.09	798.13	726.05	670.54	626.64	591.16	562.00	537.70	517.19
55000	4803.46	2506.36	1742.60	1362.16	1135.05	984.60	877.94	798.65	737.60	689.30	650.28	618.20	591.46	568.91
60000	5240.14	2734.21	1901.02	1486.00	1238.24	1074.11	957.75	871.26	804.65	751.97	709.40	674.40	645.23	620.63
65000	5676.82	2962.06	2059.43	1609.83	1341.43	1163.62	1037.57	943.86	871.70	814.63	768.51	730.60	699.00	672.35
70000	6113.50	3189.91	2217.85	1733.66	1444.61	1253.12	1117.38	1016.46	938.76	877.29	827.63	786.80	752.77	724.07
75000	6550.17	3417.76	2376.27	1857.49	1547.80	1342.63	1197.19	1089.07	1005.81	939.96	886.74	843.00	806.54	775.79
80000	6986.85	3645.61	2534.69	1981.33	1650.98	1432.14	1277.00	1161.67	1072.87	1002.62	945.86	899.20	860.31	827.51
85000	7423.53	3873.47	2693.10	2105.16	1754.17	1521.65	1356.82	1234.28	1139.92	1065.28	1004.97	955.40	914.08	879.22
90000	7860.21	4101.32	2851.52	2228.99	1857.36	1611.16	1436.63	1306.88	1206.97	1127.95	1064.09	1011.60	967.85	930.94
95000	8296.89	4329.17	3009.94	2352.82	1960.54	1700.67	1516.44	1379.48	1274.03	1190.61	1123.21	1067.80	1021.62	982.66
100000	8733.56	4557.02	3168.36	2476.66	2063.73	1790.18	1596.25	1452.09	1341.08	1253.27	1182.32	1124.00	1075.39	1034.38

TERM	15 Years	16 Years	17 Years	18 Years	19 Years	20 Years	21 Years	22 Years	23 Years	24 Years	25 Years	30 Years	35 Years	40 Years
AMOUNT														
5	.05	.05	.05	.05	.05	.05	.05	.05	.05	.05	.05	.04	.04	.04
10	.10	.10	.10	.10	.10	.09	.09	.09	.09	.09	.09	.08	.08	.08
15	.15	.15	.15	.14	.14	.14	.14	.13	.13	.13	.13	.12	.12	.12
25	.25	.25	.24	.24	.23	.23	.22	.22	.22	.21	.21	.20	.20	.19
50	.50	.49	.48	.47	.46	.45	.44	.43	.43	.42	.42	.40	.39	.38
75	.75	.73	.71	.70	.68	.67	.66	.65	.64	.63	.62	.60	.58	.57
100	1.00	.97	.95	.93	.91	.89	.87	.86	.85	.84	.83	.79	.77	.76
200	2.00	1.94	1.89	1.85	1.81	1.77	1.74	1.71	1.69	1.67	1.65	1.58	1.54	1.51
300	3.00	2.91	2.84	2.77	2.71	2.66	2.61	2.57	2.53	2.50	2.47	2.37	2.30	2.26
400	4.00	3.88	3.78	3.69	3.61	3.54	3.48	3.42	3.38	3.33	3.29	3.15	3.07	3.01
500	5.00	4.85	4.72	4.61	4.51	4.42	4.35	4.28	4.22	4.16	4.12	3.94	3.83	3.77
600	6.00	5.82	5.67	5.53	5.41	5.31	5.22	5.13	5.06	5.00	4.94	4.73	4.60	4.52
700	7.00	6.79	6.61	6.45	6.31	6.19	6.08	5.99	5.90	5.83	5.76	5.51	5.36	5.27
800	8.00	7.76	7.55	7.37	7.21	7.07	6.95	6.84	6.75	6.66	6.58	6.30	6.13	6.02
900	9.00	8.73	8.50	8.29	8.11	7.96	7.82	7.70	7.59	7.49	7.40	7.09	6.89	6.77
1000	10.00	9.70	9.44	9.21	9.02	8.84	8.69	8.55	8.43	8.32	8.23	7.87	7.66	7.53
2000	19.99	19.39	18.87	18.42	18.03	17.68	17.37	17.10	16.86	16.64	16.45	15.74	15.31	15.05
3000	29.99	29.09	28.31	27.63	27.04	26.52	26.06	25.65	25.28	24.96	24.67	23.61	22.97	22.57
4000	39.98	38.78	37.74	36.84	36.05	35.35	34.74	34.19	33.71	33.28	32.89	31.47	30.62	30.09
5000	49.98	48.48	47.18	46.05	45.06	44.19	43.42	42.74	42.14	41.60	41.11	39.34	38.27	37.61
6000	59.97	58.17	56.61	55.26	54.07	53.03	52.11	51.29	50.56	49.91	49.33	47.21	45.93	45.14
7000	69.97	67.87	66.05	64.47	63.08	61.86	60.79	59.84	58.99	58.23	57.56	55.07	53.58	52.66
8000	79.96	77.56	75.48	73.68	72.09	70.70	69.47	68.38	67.41	66.55	65.78	62.94	61.23	60.18
9000	89.96	87.26	84.92	82.89	81.10	79.54	78.16	76.93	75.84	74.87	74.00	70.81	68.89	67.70
10000	99.95	96.95	94.35	92.09	90.12	88.38	86.84	85.48	84.27	83.19	82.22	78.68	76.54	75.22
11000	109.94	106.64	103.79	101.30	99.13	97.21	95.52	94.02	92.69	91.50	90.44	86.54	84.19	82.74
12000	119.94	116.34	113.22	110.51	108.14	106.05	104.21	102.57	101.12	99.82	98.66	94.41	91.85	90.27
13000	129.93	126.03	122.66	119.72	117.15	114.89	112.89	111.12	109.54	108.14	106.88	102.28	99.50	97.79
14000	139.93	135.73	132.09	128.93	126.16	123.72	121.57	119.67	117.97	116.46	115.11	110.14	107.16	105.31
15000	149.92	145.42	141.53	138.14	135.17	132.56	130.26	128.21	126.40	124.78	123.33	118.01	114.81	112.83
16000	159.92	155.12	150.96	147.35	144.18	141.40	138.94	136.76	134.82	133.09	131.55	125.88	122.46	120.35
17000	169.91	164.81	160.40	156.56	153.19	150.24	147.62	145.31	143.25	141.41	139.77	133.74	130.12	127.87
18000	179.91	174.51	169.83	165.77	162.20	159.07	156.31	153.86	151.67	149.73	147.99	141.61	137.77	135.40
19000	189.90	184.20	179.27	174.97	171.22	167.91	164.99	162.40	160.10	158.05	156.21	149.48	145.42	142.92
20000	199.89	193.89	188.70	184.18	180.23	176.75	173.67	170.95	168.53	166.37	164.43	157.35	153.08	150.44
21000	209.89	203.59	198.14	193.39	189.24	185.58	182.36	179.50	176.95	174.68	172.66	165.21	160.73	157.96
22000	219.88	213.28	207.57	202.60	198.25	194.42	191.04	188.04	185.38	183.00	180.88	173.00	168.38	165.48
23000	229.88	222.98	217.01	211.81	207.26	203.26	199.72	196.59	193.81	191.32	189.10	180.95	176.04	173.00
24000	239.87	232.67	226.44	221.02	216.27	212.10	208.41	205.14	202.23	199.64	197.32	188.81	183.69	180.53
25000	249.87	242.37	235.88	230.23	225.28	220.93	217.09	213.69	210.66	207.96	205.54	196.68	191.35	188.05
26000	259.86	252.06	245.31	239.44	234.29	229.77	225.77	222.23	219.08	216.27	213.76	204.55	199.00	195.57
27000	269.86	261.76	254.75	248.65	243.30	238.61	234.46	230.78	227.51	224.59	221.98	212.41	206.65	203.09
28000	279.85	271.45	264.18	257.85	252.32	247.44	243.14	239.33	235.94	232.91	230.21	220.28	214.31	210.61
29000	289.85	281.14	273.62	267.06	261.33	256.28	251.83	247.87	244.36	241.23	238.43	228.15	221.96	218.13
30000	299.84	290.84	283.05	276.27	270.34	265.12	260.51	256.42	252.79	249.55	246.65	236.02	229.61	225.66
31000	309.83	300.53	292.49	285.48	279.35	273.96	269.19	264.97	261.21	257.86	254.87	243.88	237.27	233.18
32000	319.83	310.23	301.92	294.69	288.36	282.79	277.88	273.52	269.64	266.18	263.09	251.75	244.92	240.70
33000	329.82	319.92	311.36	303.90	297.37	291.63	286.56	282.06	278.07	274.50	271.31	259.62	252.57	248.22
34000	339.82	329.62	320.79	313.11	306.38	300.47	295.24	290.61	286.49	282.82	279.53	267.48	260.23	255.74
35000	349.81	339.31	330.23	322.32	315.39	309.30	303.93	299.16	294.92	291.14	287.76	275.35	267.88	263.26
36000	359.81	349.01	339.66	331.53	324.40	318.14	312.61	307.71	303.34	299.46	295.98	283.22	275.54	270.79
37000	369.80	358.70	349.10	340.73	333.42	326.98	321.29	316.25	311.77	307.77	304.20	291.08	283.19	278.31
38000	379.80	368.39	358.53	349.94	342.43	335.82	329.98	324.80	320.20	316.09	312.42	298.95	290.84	285.83
39000	389.79	378.09	367.97	359.15	351.44	344.65	338.66	333.35	328.62	324.41	320.64	306.82	298.50	293.35
40000	399.78	387.78	377.40	368.36	360.45	353.49	347.34	341.89	337.05	332.73	328.86	314.69	306.15	300.87
41000	409.78	397.48	386.84	377.57	369.46	362.33	356.03	350.44	345.48	341.05	337.08	322.55	313.80	308.39
42000	419.77	407.17	396.27	386.78	378.47	371.16	364.71	358.99	353.90	349.36	345.31	330.42	321.46	315.92
43000	429.77	416.87	405.71	395.99	387.48	380.00	373.39	367.54	362.33	357.68	353.53	338.29	329.11	323.44
44000	439.76	426.56	415.14	405.20	396.49	388.84	382.08	376.08	370.75	366.00	361.75	346.15	336.76	330.96
45000	449.76	436.26	424.58	414.41	405.50	397.67	390.76	384.63	379.18	374.32	369.97	354.02	344.42	338.48
46000	459.75	445.95	434.01	423.61	414.52	406.51	399.44	393.18	387.61	382.64	378.19	361.89	352.07	346.00
47000	469.75	455.64	443.44	432.82	423.53	415.35	408.13	401.73	396.03	390.95	386.41	369.75	359.73	353.53
48000	479.74	465.34	452.88	442.03	432.54	424.19	416.81	410.27	404.46	399.27	394.63	377.62	367.38	361.05
49000	489.73	475.03	462.31	451.24	441.55	433.02	425.49	418.82	412.88	407.59	402.86	385.49	375.03	368.57
50000	499.73	484.73	471.75	460.45	450.56	441.86	434.18	427.37	421.31	415.91	411.08	393.36	382.69	376.09
55000	549.70	533.20	518.92	506.49	495.61	486.05	477.59	470.10	463.44	457.50	452.18	432.69	420.95	413.70
60000	599.67	581.67	566.10	552.54	540.67	530.23	521.01	512.84	505.57	499.09	493.29	472.03	459.22	451.31
65000	649.65	630.15	613.27	598.58	585.73	574.42	564.43	555.58	547.70	540.68	534.40	511.36	497.49	488.92
70000	699.62	678.62	660.45	644.63	630.78	618.60	607.85	598.31	589.83	582.27	575.51	550.70	535.76	526.52
75000	749.59	727.09	707.62	690.67	675.84	662.79	651.26	641.05	631.96	623.86	616.61	590.03	574.03	564.13
80000	799.56	775.56	754.80	736.72	720.89	706.97	694.68	683.78	674.09	665.45	657.72	629.37	612.30	601.74
85000	849.54	824.03	801.97	782.76	765.95	751.16	738.10	726.52	716.22	707.04	698.83	668.70	650.56	639.35
90000	899.51	872.51	849.15	828.81	811.00	795.34	781.52	769.26	758.35	748.63	739.93	708.04	688.83	676.96
95000	949.48	920.98	896.32	874.85	856.06	839.53	824.93	811.99	800.48	790.22	781.04	747.37	727.10	714.57
100000	999.45	969.45	943.49	920.90	901.11	883.72	868.35	854.73	842.62	831.81	822.15	786.71	765.37	752.18

MONTHLY PAYMENT
REQUIRED TO AMORTIZE A LOAN

TERM AMOUNT	1 Year	2 Years	3 Years	4 Years	5 Years	6 Years	7 Years	8 Years	9 Years	10 Years	11 Years	12 Years	13 Years	14 Years
5	.44	.23	.16	.13	.11	.09	.08	.08	.07	.07	.06	.06	.06	.06
10	.88	.46	.32	.25	.21	.18	.16	.15	.14	.13	.12	.12	.11	.11
15	1.32	.69	.48	.38	.31	.27	.24	.22	.21	.19	.18	.17	.17	.16
25	2.19	1.14	.80	.62	.52	.45	.40	.37	.34	.32	.30	.29	.27	.26
50	4.37	2.28	1.59	1.24	1.04	.90	.80	.73	.68	.63	.60	.57	.54	.52
75	6.56	3.42	2.38	1.86	1.55	1.35	1.20	1.10	1.01	.95	.89	.85	.81	.78
100	8.74	4.56	3.18	2.48	2.07	1.80	1.60	1.46	1.35	1.26	1.19	1.13	1.08	1.04
200	17.48	9.12	6.35	4.96	4.14	3.59	3.20	2.91	2.69	2.52	2.38	2.26	2.16	2.08
300	26.21	13.68	9.52	7.44	6.20	5.38	4.80	4.37	4.04	3.77	3.56	3.39	3.24	3.12
400	34.95	18.24	12.69	9.92	8.21	7.18	6.40	5.82	5.38	5.03	4.75	4.51	4.32	4.15
500	43.68	22.80	15.86	12.40	10.34	8.97	8.00	7.28	6.72	6.28	5.93	5.64	5.40	5.19
600	52.42	27.36	19.03	14.88	12.40	10.76	9.60	8.73	8.07	7.54	7.12	6.77	6.47	6.23
700	61.16	31.92	22.20	17.36	14.47	12.55	11.20	10.19	9.41	8.80	8.30	7.89	7.55	7.27
800	69.89	36.48	25.37	19.84	16.53	14.35	12.80	11.64	10.75	10.05	9.49	9.02	8.63	8.30
900	78.63	41.04	28.54	22.32	18.60	16.14	14.39	13.10	12.10	11.31	10.67	10.15	9.71	9.34
1000	87.36	45.60	31.71	24.80	20.67	17.93	15.99	14.55	13.44	12.56	11.86	11.27	10.79	10.38
2000	174.72	91.19	63.42	49.59	41.33	35.86	31.99	29.10	26.88	25.12	23.71	22.54	21.57	20.75
3000	262.08	136.78	95.13	74.38	61.99	53.78	47.97	43.64	40.32	37.68	35.56	33.81	32.35	31.12
4000	349.44	182.38	126.83	99.17	82.65	71.71	63.96	58.19	53.75	50.24	47.41	45.08	43.13	41.50
5000	436.80	227.97	158.54	123.96	103.31	89.64	79.94	72.74	67.19	62.80	59.26	56.34	53.92	51.87
6000	524.16	273.56	190.25	148.75	123.97	107.56	95.93	87.28	80.63	75.36	71.11	67.61	64.70	62.24
7000	611.52	319.16	221.95	173.54	144.63	125.49	111.92	101.83	94.06	87.92	82.96	78.88	75.48	72.61
8000	698.88	364.75	253.66	198.33	165.30	143.42	127.91	116.38	107.50	100.48	94.81	90.15	86.26	82.99
9000	786.23	410.34	285.37	223.12	185.96	161.34	143.89	130.92	120.94	113.04	106.66	101.42	97.05	93.36
10000	873.59	455.94	317.07	247.91	206.62	179.27	159.88	145.47	134.38	125.60	118.51	112.68	107.83	103.73
11000	960.95	501.53	348.78	272.70	227.28	197.20	175.87	160.02	147.81	138.16	130.36	123.95	118.61	114.11
12000	1048.31	547.12	380.49	297.49	247.94	215.12	191.86	174.56	161.25	150.72	142.21	135.22	129.39	124.48
13000	1135.67	592.71	412.19	322.28	268.60	233.05	207.85	189.11	174.69	163.28	154.06	146.49	140.18	134.85
14000	1223.03	638.31	443.90	347.07	289.26	250.98	223.83	203.66	188.12	175.84	165.91	157.76	150.96	145.22
15000	1310.39	683.90	475.61	371.86	309.93	268.90	239.82	218.20	201.56	188.40	177.76	169.02	161.74	155.60
16000	1397.75	729.49	507.31	396.65	330.59	286.83	255.81	232.75	215.00	200.96	189.62	180.29	172.52	165.97
17000	1485.10	775.09	539.02	421.44	351.25	304.75	271.80	247.30	228.44	213.52	201.47	191.56	183.30	176.34
18000	1572.46	820.68	570.73	446.23	371.91	322.68	287.78	261.84	241.87	226.08	213.32	202.83	194.09	186.72
19000	1659.82	866.27	602.43	471.02	392.57	340.61	303.77	276.39	255.31	238.64	225.17	214.10	204.87	197.09
20000	1747.18	911.87	634.14	495.81	413.23	358.53	319.76	290.94	268.75	251.20	237.02	225.36	215.65	207.46
21000	1834.54	957.46	665.85	520.60	433.89	376.46	335.75	305.48	282.18	263.76	248.87	236.63	226.43	217.83
22000	1921.90	1003.05	697.55	545.39	454.56	394.39	351.74	320.03	295.62	276.32	260.72	247.90	237.22	228.21
23000	2009.26	1048.64	729.26	570.18	475.22	412.31	367.72	334.58	309.06	288.88	272.57	259.17	248.00	238.58
24000	2096.62	1094.24	760.97	594.97	495.88	430.24	383.71	349.12	322.50	301.44	284.42	270.44	258.78	248.95
25000	2183.97	1139.83	792.67	619.76	516.54	448.17	399.70	363.67	335.93	313.99	296.27	281.70	269.56	259.33
26000	2271.33	1185.42	824.38	644.55	537.20	466.09	415.69	378.22	349.37	326.55	308.12	292.97	280.35	269.70
27000	2358.69	1231.02	856.09	669.34	557.86	484.02	431.67	392.76	362.81	339.11	319.97	304.24	291.13	280.07
28000	2446.05	1276.61	887.79	694.13	578.52	501.95	447.66	407.31	376.24	351.67	331.82	315.51	301.91	290.44
29000	2533.41	1322.20	919.50	718.92	599.19	519.87	463.65	421.86	389.68	364.23	343.67	326.78	312.69	300.82
30000	2620.77	1367.80	951.21	743.71	619.85	537.80	479.64	436.40	403.12	376.79	355.52	338.04	323.47	311.19
31000	2708.13	1413.39	982.91	768.50	640.51	555.72	495.63	450.95	416.56	389.35	367.37	349.31	334.26	321.56
32000	2795.49	1458.98	1014.62	793.29	661.17	573.65	511.61	465.50	429.99	401.91	379.23	360.58	345.04	331.93
33000	2882.84	1504.58	1046.33	818.08	681.83	591.58	527.60	480.04	443.43	414.47	391.08	371.85	355.82	342.31
34000	2970.20	1550.17	1078.03	842.87	702.49	609.50	543.59	494.59	456.87	427.03	402.93	383.12	366.60	352.68
35000	3057.56	1595.76	1109.74	867.66	723.15	627.43	559.58	509.14	470.30	439.59	414.78	394.38	377.39	363.05
36000	3144.92	1641.35	1141.45	892.45	743.82	645.36	575.56	523.68	483.74	452.15	426.63	405.65	388.17	373.43
37000	3232.28	1686.95	1173.15	917.24	764.48	663.28	591.55	538.23	497.18	464.71	438.48	416.92	398.95	383.80
38000	3319.64	1732.54	1204.86	942.03	785.14	681.21	607.54	552.78	510.62	477.27	450.33	428.19	409.73	394.17
39000	3407.00	1778.13	1236.57	966.82	805.80	699.14	623.53	567.32	524.05	489.83	462.18	439.46	420.52	404.54
40000	3494.36	1823.73	1268.27	991.61	826.46	717.06	639.52	581.87	537.49	502.39	474.03	450.72	431.30	414.92
41000	3581.71	1869.32	1299.98	1016.40	847.12	734.99	655.50	596.42	550.93	514.95	485.88	461.99	442.08	425.29
42000	3669.07	1914.91	1331.69	1041.19	867.78	752.92	671.49	610.96	564.36	527.51	497.73	473.26	452.86	435.66
43000	3756.43	1960.51	1363.39	1065.98	888.45	770.84	687.48	625.51	577.80	540.07	509.58	484.53	463.65	446.04
44000	3843.79	2006.10	1395.10	1090.77	909.11	788.77	703.47	640.06	591.24	552.63	521.43	495.80	474.43	456.41
45000	3931.15	2051.69	1426.81	1115.56	929.77	806.69	719.45	654.60	604.68	565.19	533.28	507.06	485.21	466.78
46000	4018.51	2097.28	1458.51	1140.35	950.43	824.62	735.44	669.15	618.11	577.75	545.13	518.33	495.99	477.15
47000	4105.87	2142.88	1490.22	1165.14	971.09	842.55	751.43	683.70	631.55	590.31	556.98	529.60	506.77	487.53
48000	4193.23	2188.47	1521.93	1189.93	991.75	860.47	767.42	698.24	644.99	602.87	568.84	540.87	517.56	497.90
49000	4280.58	2234.06	1553.63	1214.72	1012.41	878.40	783.41	712.79	658.42	615.43	580.69	552.14	528.34	508.27
50000	4367.94	2279.66	1585.34	1239.51	1033.08	896.33	799.39	727.34	671.86	627.98	592.54	563.40	539.12	518.65
55000	4804.74	2507.62	1743.88	1363.47	1136.38	985.96	879.33	800.07	739.05	690.78	651.79	619.74	593.03	570.51
60000	5241.53	2735.59	1902.41	1487.42	1239.69	1075.59	959.27	872.80	806.23	753.58	711.04	676.08	646.94	622.37
65000	5678.32	2963.55	2060.94	1611.37	1343.00	1165.22	1039.21	945.54	873.42	816.38	770.30	732.42	700.86	674.24
70000	6115.12	3191.52	2219.48	1735.32	1446.30	1254.86	1119.15	1018.27	940.60	879.18	829.55	788.76	754.77	726.10
75000	6551.91	3419.48	2378.01	1859.27	1549.61	1344.49	1199.09	1091.00	1007.79	941.97	888.80	845.10	808.68	777.97
80000	6988.71	3647.45	2536.54	1983.22	1652.92	1434.12	1279.03	1163.74	1074.98	1004.77	948.06	901.44	862.59	829.83
85000	7425.50	3875.41	2695.08	2107.17	1756.23	1523.75	1358.96	1236.47	1142.16	1067.57	1007.31	957.78	916.50	881.69
90000	7862.29	4103.38	2853.61	2231.12	1859.53	1613.38	1438.90	1309.35	1209.35	1130.37	1066.56	1014.12	970.41	933.56
95000	8299.09	4331.34	3012.14	2355.07	1962.84	1703.02	1518.84	1381.94	1276.53	1193.17	1125.81	1070.46	1024.33	985.42
100000	8735.88	4559.31	3170.68	2479.02	2066.15	1792.65	1598.78	1454.67	1343.72	1255.96	1185.07	1126.80	1078.24	1037.29

TERM AMOUNT	15 Years	16 Years	17 Years	18 Years	19 Years	20 Years	21 Years	22 Years	23 Years	24 Years	25 Years	30 Years	35 Years	40 Years
5	.06	.05	.05	.05	.05	.05	.05	.05	.05	.05	.05	.04	.04	.04
10	.11	.10	.10	.10	.10	.09	.09	.09	.09	.09	.09	.08	.08	.08
15	.16	.15	.15	.14	.14	.14	.14	.13	.13	.13	.13	.12	.12	.12
25	.26	.25	.24	.24	.23	.23	.22	.22	.22	.21	.21	.20	.20	.19
50	.51	.49	.48	.47	.46	.45	.44	.43	.43	.42	.42	.40	.39	.38
75	.76	.73	.71	.70	.68	.67	.66	.65	.64	.63	.62	.60	.58	.57
100	1.01	.98	.95	.93	.91	.89	.88	.86	.85	.84	.83	.80	.77	.76
200	2.01	1.95	1.90	1.85	1.81	1.78	1.75	1.72	1.70	1.68	1.66	1.59	1.54	1.52
300	3.01	2.92	2.84	2.78	2.72	2.67	2.62	2.58	2.54	2.51	2.48	2.38	2.31	2.27
400	4.01	3.89	3.79	3.70	3.62	3.55	3.49	3.44	3.39	3.35	3.31	3.17	3.08	3.03
500	5.02	4.87	4.74	4.62	4.53	4.44	4.36	4.30	4.23	4.18	4.13	3.96	3.85	3.78
600	6.02	5.84	5.68	5.55	5.43	5.33	5.23	5.15	5.08	5.02	4.96	4.75	4.62	4.54
700	7.02	6.81	6.63	6.47	6.33	6.21	6.11	6.01	5.93	5.85	5.78	5.54	5.39	5.30
800	8.02	7.78	7.58	7.40	7.24	7.10	6.98	6.87	6.77	6.69	6.61	6.33	6.16	6.05
900	9.03	8.76	8.52	8.32	8.14	7.99	7.85	7.73	7.62	7.52	7.43	7.12	6.93	6.81
1000	10.03	9.73	9.47	9.24	9.05	8.87	8.72	8.59	8.46	8.36	8.26	7.91	7.70	7.56
2000	20.05	19.45	18.94	18.48	18.09	17.74	17.44	17.17	16.92	16.71	16.52	15.81	15.39	15.12
3000	30.08	29.18	28.40	27.72	27.13	26.61	26.15	25.75	25.38	25.06	24.77	23.71	23.08	22.68
4000	40.10	38.90	37.87	36.96	36.18	35.48	34.87	34.33	33.84	33.41	33.03	31.62	30.77	30.24
5000	50.13	48.63	47.33	46.20	45.22	44.35	43.58	42.91	42.30	41.76	41.28	39.52	38.46	37.80
6000	60.15	58.35	56.80	55.44	54.26	53.22	52.30	51.49	50.76	50.12	49.54	47.42	46.15	45.36
7000	70.17	68.08	66.26	64.68	63.30	62.09	61.02	60.07	59.22	58.47	57.79	55.32	53.84	52.92
8000	80.20	77.80	75.73	73.92	72.35	70.96	69.73	68.65	67.68	66.82	66.05	63.23	61.53	60.48
9000	90.22	87.53	85.19	83.16	81.39	79.83	78.45	77.23	76.14	75.17	74.30	71.13	69.22	68.04
10000	100.25	97.25	94.66	92.40	90.43	88.70	87.16	85.81	84.60	83.52	82.56	79.03	76.91	75.60
11000	110.27	106.97	104.12	101.64	99.47	97.56	95.88	94.39	93.06	91.87	90.81	86.94	84.60	83.16
12000	120.29	116.70	113.59	110.88	108.52	106.43	104.59	102.97	101.52	100.23	99.07	94.84	92.29	90.72
13000	130.32	126.42	123.06	120.12	117.56	115.30	113.31	111.55	109.98	108.58	107.33	102.74	99.99	98.28
14000	140.34	136.15	132.52	129.36	126.60	124.17	122.03	120.13	118.44	116.93	115.58	110.64	107.68	105.84
15000	150.37	145.87	141.99	138.60	135.64	133.04	130.74	128.71	126.89	125.28	123.84	118.55	115.37	113.40
16000	160.39	155.60	151.45	147.84	144.69	141.91	139.46	137.29	135.35	133.63	132.09	126.45	123.06	120.96
17000	170.41	165.32	160.92	157.08	153.73	150.78	148.17	145.87	143.81	141.98	140.35	134.35	130.75	128.52
18000	180.44	175.05	170.38	166.32	162.77	159.65	156.89	154.45	152.27	150.34	148.60	142.25	138.44	136.08
19000	190.46	184.77	179.85	175.56	171.81	168.52	165.61	163.03	160.73	158.69	156.86	150.16	146.13	143.64
20000	200.49	194.50	189.31	184.80	180.86	177.39	174.32	171.61	169.19	167.04	165.11	158.06	153.82	151.20
21000	210.51	204.22	198.78	194.04	189.90	186.25	183.04	180.19	177.65	175.39	173.37	165.96	161.51	158.76
22000	220.53	213.94	208.24	203.28	198.94	195.12	191.75	188.77	186.11	183.74	181.62	173.87	169.20	166.32
23000	230.56	223.67	217.71	212.52	207.98	203.99	200.47	197.35	194.57	192.09	189.88	181.77	176.89	173.88
24000	240.58	233.39	227.18	221.76	217.03	212.86	209.18	205.93	203.03	200.45	198.14	189.67	184.58	181.44
25000	250.61	243.12	236.64	231.00	226.07	221.73	217.90	214.51	211.49	208.80	206.39	197.57	192.27	189.00
26000	260.63	252.84	246.11	240.24	235.11	230.60	226.62	223.09	219.95	217.15	214.65	205.48	199.97	196.56
27000	270.65	262.57	255.57	249.48	244.15	239.47	235.33	231.67	228.41	225.50	222.90	213.38	207.66	204.12
28000	280.68	272.29	265.04	258.72	253.20	248.34	244.05	240.25	236.87	233.85	231.16	221.28	215.35	211.68
29000	290.70	282.02	274.50	267.96	262.24	257.21	252.76	248.83	245.33	242.20	239.41	229.18	223.04	219.24
30000	300.73	291.74	283.97	277.20	271.28	266.08	261.48	257.41	253.78	250.56	247.67	237.09	230.73	226.80
31000	310.75	301.46	293.43	286.44	280.32	274.95	270.20	265.99	262.24	258.91	255.92	244.99	238.42	234.36
32000	320.77	311.19	302.90	295.68	289.37	283.81	278.91	274.57	270.70	267.26	264.18	252.89	246.11	241.92
33000	330.80	320.91	312.36	304.92	298.41	292.68	287.63	283.15	279.16	275.61	272.43	260.80	253.80	249.48
34000	340.82	330.64	321.83	314.16	307.45	301.55	296.34	291.73	287.62	283.96	280.69	268.70	261.49	257.04
35000	350.85	340.36	331.29	323.40	316.49	310.42	305.06	300.31	296.08	292.31	288.95	276.60	269.18	264.60
36000	360.87	350.09	340.76	332.64	325.54	319.29	313.77	308.89	304.54	300.67	297.20	284.50	276.87	272.16
37000	370.89	359.81	350.23	341.88	334.58	328.16	322.49	317.47	313.00	309.02	305.46	292.41	284.56	279.72
38000	380.92	369.54	359.69	351.12	343.62	337.03	331.21	326.05	321.46	317.37	313.71	300.31	292.26	287.28
39000	390.94	379.26	369.16	360.36	352.67	345.90	339.92	334.63	329.92	325.72	321.97	308.21	299.95	294.84
40000	400.97	388.99	378.62	369.60	361.71	354.77	348.64	343.21	338.38	334.07	330.22	316.11	307.64	302.40
41000	410.99	398.71	388.09	378.84	370.75	363.64	357.35	351.79	346.84	342.42	338.48	324.02	315.33	309.96
42000	421.01	408.43	397.55	388.08	379.79	372.50	366.07	360.37	355.30	350.78	346.73	331.92	323.02	317.52
43000	431.04	418.16	407.02	397.32	388.84	381.37	374.79	368.95	363.76	359.13	354.99	339.82	330.71	325.08
44000	441.06	427.88	416.48	406.56	397.88	390.24	383.50	377.53	372.21	367.48	363.24	347.73	338.40	332.64
45000	451.09	437.61	425.95	415.80	406.92	399.11	392.22	386.11	380.67	375.83	371.50	355.63	346.09	340.20
46000	461.11	447.33	435.41	425.04	415.96	407.98	400.93	394.69	389.13	384.18	379.75	363.53	353.78	347.76
47000	471.13	457.06	444.88	434.28	425.01	416.85	409.65	403.27	397.59	392.53	388.01	371.43	361.47	355.32
48000	481.16	466.78	454.35	443.52	434.05	425.72	418.36	411.85	406.05	400.89	396.27	379.34	369.16	362.88
49000	491.18	476.51	463.81	452.76	443.09	434.59	427.08	420.43	414.51	409.24	404.52	387.24	376.85	370.44
50000	501.21	486.23	473.28	462.00	452.13	443.46	435.80	429.01	422.97	417.59	412.78	395.14	384.54	378.00
55000	551.33	534.85	520.60	508.20	497.35	487.80	479.38	471.91	465.27	459.35	454.05	434.66	423.00	415.80
60000	601.45	583.48	567.93	554.40	542.56	532.15	522.95	514.81	507.56	501.11	495.33	474.17	461.45	453.60
65000	651.57	632.10	615.26	600.60	587.77	576.49	566.53	557.71	549.86	542.86	536.61	513.68	499.91	491.40
70000	701.69	680.72	662.58	646.80	632.98	620.84	610.11	600.61	592.16	584.62	577.89	553.20	538.36	529.20
75000	751.81	729.34	709.91	693.00	678.20	665.18	653.69	643.51	634.45	626.38	619.16	592.71	576.81	567.00
80000	801.93	777.97	757.24	739.20	723.41	709.53	697.27	686.41	676.75	668.14	660.44	632.22	615.27	604.80
85000	852.05	826.59	804.57	785.40	768.62	753.87	740.85	729.31	719.05	709.90	701.72	671.74	653.72	642.60
90000	902.17	875.21	851.89	831.60	813.84	798.22	784.43	772.21	761.34	751.66	742.99	711.25	692.18	680.40
95000	952.29	923.83	899.22	877.80	859.05	842.56	828.01	815.11	803.64	793.41	784.27	750.77	730.63	718.20
100000	1002.41	972.46	946.55	924.00	904.26	886.91	871.59	858.01	845.94	835.17	825.55	790.28	769.08	756.00

MONTHLY PAYMENT
REQUIRED TO AMORTIZE A LOAN

TERM AMOUNT	1 Year	2 Years	3 Years	4 Years	5 Years	6 Years	7 Years	8 Years	9 Years	10 Years	11 Years	12 Years	13 Years	14 Years
5	.44	.23	.16	.13	.11	.09	.09	.08	.07	.07	.06	.06	.06	.06
10	.88	.46	.32	.25	.21	.18	.17	.15	.14	.13	.12	.12	.11	.11
15	1.32	.69	.48	.38	.32	.27	.25	.22	.21	.19	.18	.17	.17	.16
25	2.19	1.15	.80	.63	.52	.45	.41	.37	.34	.32	.30	.29	.28	.27
50	4.37	2.29	1.59	1.25	1.04	.90	.81	.73	.68	.64	.60	.57	.55	.53
75	6.56	3.43	2.39	1.87	1.56	1.35	1.21	1.10	1.02	.95	.90	.85	.82	.79
100	8.74	4.57	3.18	2.49	2.07	1.80	1.61	1.46	1.35	1.27	1.19	1.14	1.09	1.05
200	17.48	9.13	6.35	4.97	4.14	3.60	3.21	2.92	2.70	2.53	2.38	2.27	2.17	2.09
300	26.22	13.69	9.53	7.45	6.21	5.39	4.81	4.38	4.05	3.79	3.57	3.40	3.25	3.13
400	34.96	18.26	12.70	9.94	8.28	7.19	6.42	5.84	5.40	5.05	4.76	4.53	4.34	4.17
500	43.70	22.82	15.88	12.42	10.35	8.99	8.02	7.30	6.74	6.31	5.95	5.66	5.42	5.21
600	52.44	27.38	19.05	14.90	12.42	10.78	9.62	8.76	8.09	7.57	7.14	6.79	6.50	6.25
700	61.18	31.94	22.22	17.38	14.49	12.58	11.22	10.21	9.44	8.83	8.33	7.92	7.58	7.30
800	69.92	36.51	25.40	19.87	16.56	14.38	12.83	11.67	10.79	10.09	9.52	9.05	8.67	8.34
900	78.66	41.07	28.57	22.35	18.63	16.17	14.43	13.13	12.13	11.35	10.71	10.18	9.75	9.38
1000	87.40	45.63	31.75	24.83	20.70	17.97	16.03	14.59	13.48	12.61	11.90	11.32	10.83	10.42
2000	174.79	91.26	63.49	49.66	41.40	35.93	32.06	29.18	26.96	25.21	23.79	22.63	21.66	20.84
3000	262.19	136.89	95.23	74.48	62.10	53.90	48.08	43.76	40.44	37.81	35.68	33.94	32.48	31.25
4000	349.58	182.51	126.97	99.31	82.80	71.86	64.11	58.35	53.91	50.41	47.57	45.25	43.31	41.67
5000	436.97	228.14	158.71	124.13	103.49	89.82	80.13	72.93	67.39	63.01	59.46	56.56	54.13	52.09
6000	524.37	273.77	190.45	148.96	124.19	107.79	96.16	87.52	80.87	75.61	71.36	67.87	64.96	62.50
7000	611.76	319.40	222.20	173.79	144.89	125.75	112.18	102.10	94.34	88.21	83.25	79.18	75.78	72.92
8000	699.15	365.02	253.94	198.61	165.59	143.71	128.21	116.69	107.82	100.81	95.14	90.49	86.61	83.34
9000	786.55	410.65	285.68	223.44	186.28	161.68	144.24	131.27	121.30	113.41	107.03	101.80	97.43	93.75
10000	873.94	456.28	317.42	248.26	206.98	179.64	160.26	145.86	134.77	126.01	118.92	113.11	108.26	104.17
11000	961.33	501.91	349.16	273.09	227.68	197.60	176.29	160.44	148.25	138.61	130.82	124.42	119.08	114.59
12000	1048.73	547.53	380.90	297.91	248.38	215.57	192.31	175.03	161.73	151.21	142.71	135.73	129.91	125.00
13000	1136.12	593.16	412.65	322.74	269.08	233.53	208.34	189.62	175.20	163.81	154.60	147.04	140.73	135.42
14000	1223.51	638.79	444.39	347.57	289.77	251.49	224.36	204.20	188.68	176.41	166.49	158.35	151.56	145.84
15000	1310.91	684.42	476.13	372.39	310.47	269.46	240.39	218.79	202.16	189.01	178.38	169.66	162.38	156.25
16000	1398.30	730.04	507.87	397.22	331.17	287.42	256.42	233.37	215.63	201.61	190.28	180.97	173.21	166.67
17000	1485.69	775.67	539.61	422.04	351.87	305.39	272.44	247.96	229.11	214.21	202.17	192.28	184.03	177.08
18000	1573.09	821.30	571.35	446.87	372.56	323.35	288.47	262.54	242.59	226.81	214.06	203.59	194.86	187.50
19000	1660.48	866.93	603.10	471.69	393.26	341.31	304.49	277.13	256.06	239.41	225.95	214.90	205.68	197.92
20000	1747.88	912.55	634.84	496.52	413.96	359.28	320.52	291.71	269.54	252.01	237.84	226.21	216.51	208.33
21000	1835.27	958.18	666.58	521.35	434.66	377.24	336.54	306.30	283.02	264.61	249.73	237.52	227.33	218.75
22000	1922.66	1003.81	698.32	546.17	455.36	395.20	352.57	320.88	296.49	277.21	261.63	248.83	238.16	229.17
23000	2010.06	1049.44	730.06	571.00	476.05	413.17	368.60	335.47	309.97	289.81	273.52	260.14	248.98	239.58
24000	2097.45	1095.06	761.80	595.82	496.75	431.13	384.62	350.06	323.45	302.41	285.41	271.45	259.81	250.00
25000	2184.84	1140.69	793.54	620.65	517.45	449.09	400.65	364.64	336.92	315.01	297.30	282.76	270.63	260.42
26000	2272.24	1186.32	825.29	645.47	538.15	467.06	416.67	379.23	350.40	327.61	309.19	294.07	281.46	270.83
27000	2359.63	1231.95	857.03	670.30	558.84	485.02	432.70	393.81	363.88	340.21	321.09	305.38	292.28	281.25
28000	2447.02	1277.57	888.77	695.13	579.54	502.98	448.72	408.40	377.35	352.81	332.98	316.69	303.11	291.67
29000	2534.42	1323.20	920.51	719.95	600.24	520.95	464.75	422.98	390.83	365.41	344.87	328.00	313.94	302.08
30000	2621.81	1368.83	952.25	744.78	620.94	538.91	480.78	437.57	404.31	378.01	356.76	339.31	324.76	312.50
31000	2709.20	1414.45	983.99	769.60	641.63	556.88	496.80	452.15	417.78	390.61	368.65	350.62	335.59	322.91
32000	2796.60	1460.08	1015.74	794.43	662.33	574.84	512.83	466.74	431.26	403.21	380.55	361.93	346.41	333.33
33000	2883.99	1505.71	1047.48	819.25	683.03	592.80	528.85	481.32	444.74	415.81	392.44	373.24	357.24	343.75
34000	2971.38	1551.34	1079.22	844.08	703.73	610.77	544.88	495.91	458.21	428.41	404.33	384.55	368.06	354.16
35000	3058.78	1596.96	1110.96	868.91	724.43	628.73	560.90	510.50	471.69	441.01	416.22	395.86	378.89	364.58
36000	3146.17	1642.59	1142.70	893.73	745.12	646.69	576.93	525.08	485.17	453.61	428.11	407.17	389.71	375.00
37000	3233.57	1688.22	1174.44	918.56	765.82	664.66	592.96	539.67	498.64	466.21	440.00	418.48	400.54	385.41
38000	3320.96	1733.85	1206.19	943.38	786.52	682.62	608.98	554.25	512.12	478.81	451.90	429.79	411.36	395.83
39000	3408.35	1779.47	1237.93	968.21	807.22	700.58	625.01	568.84	525.60	491.41	463.79	441.10	422.19	406.25
40000	3495.75	1825.10	1269.67	993.03	827.91	718.55	641.03	583.42	539.07	504.01	475.68	452.41	433.01	416.66
41000	3583.14	1870.73	1301.41	1017.86	848.61	736.51	657.06	598.01	552.55	516.61	487.57	463.72	443.84	427.08
42000	3670.53	1916.36	1333.15	1042.69	869.31	754.47	673.08	612.59	566.03	529.21	499.46	475.03	454.66	437.50
43000	3757.93	1961.98	1364.89	1067.51	890.01	772.44	689.11	627.18	579.51	541.81	511.36	486.34	465.49	447.91
44000	3845.32	2007.61	1396.63	1092.34	910.71	790.40	705.14	641.76	592.98	554.41	523.25	497.65	476.31	458.33
45000	3932.71	2053.24	1428.38	1117.16	931.40	808.37	721.16	656.35	606.46	567.01	535.14	508.96	487.14	468.74
46000	4020.11	2098.87	1460.12	1141.99	952.10	826.33	737.19	670.94	619.94	579.61	547.03	520.27	497.96	479.16
47000	4107.50	2144.49	1491.86	1166.81	972.80	844.29	753.21	685.52	633.41	592.21	558.92	531.58	508.79	489.58
48000	4194.89	2190.12	1523.60	1191.64	993.50	862.26	769.24	700.11	646.89	604.81	570.82	542.89	519.61	499.99
49000	4282.29	2235.75	1555.34	1216.47	1014.19	880.22	785.26	714.69	660.37	617.41	582.71	554.20	530.44	510.41
50000	4369.68	2281.38	1587.08	1241.29	1034.89	898.18	801.29	729.28	673.84	630.01	594.60	565.51	541.26	520.83
55000	4806.65	2509.51	1745.79	1365.42	1138.38	988.00	881.42	802.20	741.23	693.01	654.06	622.06	595.39	572.91
60000	5243.62	2737.65	1904.50	1489.55	1241.87	1077.82	961.55	875.13	808.61	756.01	713.52	678.61	649.52	624.99
65000	5680.58	2965.79	2063.21	1613.68	1345.36	1167.64	1041.68	948.06	875.99	819.01	772.98	735.16	703.64	677.07
70000	6117.55	3193.92	2221.92	1737.81	1448.85	1257.45	1121.80	1020.99	943.38	882.01	832.44	791.71	757.77	729.16
75000	6554.52	3422.06	2380.62	1861.93	1552.34	1347.27	1201.93	1093.91	1010.76	945.01	891.90	848.26	811.89	781.24
80000	6991.49	3650.20	2539.33	1986.06	1655.82	1437.09	1282.06	1166.84	1078.14	1008.01	951.36	904.81	866.02	833.32
85000	7428.45	3878.34	2698.04	2110.19	1759.31	1526.91	1362.19	1239.77	1145.53	1071.01	1010.81	961.36	920.15	885.40
90000	7865.42	4106.47	2856.75	2234.32	1862.80	1616.73	1442.32	1312.69	1212.91	1134.01	1070.27	1017.91	974.27	937.48
95000	8302.39	4334.61	3015.46	2358.45	1966.29	1706.54	1522.45	1385.62	1280.30	1197.01	1129.73	1074.46	1028.40	989.57
100000	8739.36	4562.75	3174.16	2482.58	2069.78	1796.36	1602.58	1458.55	1347.68	1260.01	1189.19	1131.01	1082.52	1041.65

TERM	15 Years	16 Years	17 Years	18 Years	19 Years	20 Years	21 Years	22 Years	23 Years	24 Years	25 Years	30 Years	35 Years	40 Years
AMOUNT														
5	.06	.05	.05	.05	.05	.05	.05	.05	.05	.05	.05	.04	.04	.04
10	.11	.10	.10	.10	.10	.09	.09	.09	.09	.09	.09	.08	.08	.08
15	.16	.15	.15	.14	.14	.14	.14	.13	.13	.13	.13	.12	.12	.12
25	.26	.25	.24	.24	.23	.23	.22	.22	.22	.22	.21	.20	.20	.20
50	.51	.49	.48	.47	.46	.45	.44	.44	.43	.43	.42	.40	.39	.39
75	.76	.74	.72	.70	.69	.67	.66	.65	.64	.64	.63	.60	.59	.58
100	1.01	.98	.96	.93	.91	.90	.88	.87	.86	.85	.84	.80	.78	.77
200	2.02	1.96	1.91	1.86	1.82	1.79	1.76	1.73	1.71	1.69	1.67	1.60	1.55	1.53
300	3.03	2.94	2.86	2.79	2.73	2.68	2.63	2.59	2.56	2.53	2.50	2.39	2.33	2.29
400	4.03	3.91	3.81	3.72	3.64	3.57	3.51	3.46	3.41	3.37	3.33	3.19	3.10	3.05
500	5.04	4.89	4.76	4.65	4.55	4.46	4.39	4.32	4.26	4.21	4.16	3.98	3.88	3.81
600	6.05	5.87	5.71	5.58	5.46	5.36	5.26	5.18	5.11	5.05	4.99	4.78	4.65	4.58
700	7.05	6.84	6.66	6.51	6.37	6.25	6.14	6.05	5.96	5.89	5.82	5.57	5.43	5.34
800	8.06	7.82	7.61	7.43	7.28	7.14	7.02	6.91	6.81	6.73	6.65	6.37	6.20	6.10
900	9.07	8.80	8.57	8.36	8.19	8.03	7.89	7.77	7.66	7.57	7.48	7.17	6.98	6.86
1000	10.07	9.77	9.52	9.29	9.09	8.92	8.77	8.63	8.51	8.41	8.31	7.96	7.75	7.62
2000	20.14	19.54	19.03	18.58	18.18	17.84	17.53	17.26	17.02	16.81	16.62	15.92	15.50	15.24
3000	30.21	29.31	28.54	27.86	27.27	26.76	26.30	25.89	25.53	25.21	24.92	23.87	23.24	22.86
4000	40.28	39.08	38.05	37.15	36.36	35.67	35.06	34.52	34.04	33.61	33.23	31.83	30.99	30.48
5000	50.35	48.85	47.56	46.44	45.45	44.59	43.83	43.15	42.55	42.02	41.54	39.79	38.74	38.09
6000	60.42	58.62	57.07	55.72	54.54	53.51	52.59	51.78	51.06	50.42	49.84	47.74	46.48	45.71
7000	70.48	68.39	66.58	65.01	63.63	62.42	61.36	60.41	59.57	58.82	58.15	55.70	54.23	53.33
8000	80.55	78.16	76.10	74.30	72.72	71.34	70.12	69.04	68.08	67.22	66.46	63.66	61.98	60.95
9000	90.62	87.93	85.61	83.58	81.81	80.26	78.89	77.67	76.59	75.62	74.76	71.61	69.72	68.56
10000	100.69	97.70	95.12	92.87	90.90	89.18	87.65	86.30	85.10	84.03	83.07	79.57	77.47	76.18
11000	110.76	107.47	104.63	102.16	99.99	98.09	96.41	94.93	93.61	92.43	91.38	87.53	85.22	83.80
12000	120.83	117.24	114.14	111.44	109.08	107.01	105.18	103.56	102.12	100.83	99.68	95.48	92.96	91.42
13000	130.89	127.01	123.65	120.73	118.17	115.93	113.94	112.19	110.62	109.23	107.99	103.44	100.71	99.03
14000	140.96	136.78	133.16	130.02	127.26	124.84	122.71	120.82	119.13	117.64	116.30	111.40	108.46	106.65
15000	151.03	146.55	142.67	139.30	136.35	133.76	131.47	129.44	127.64	126.04	124.60	119.35	116.20	114.27
16000	161.10	156.32	152.19	148.59	145.44	142.68	140.24	138.07	136.15	134.44	132.91	127.31	123.95	121.89
17000	171.17	166.09	161.70	157.88	154.53	151.59	149.00	146.70	144.66	142.84	141.22	135.26	131.70	129.50
18000	181.24	175.86	171.21	167.16	163.62	160.51	157.77	155.33	153.17	151.24	149.52	143.22	139.44	137.12
19000	191.31	185.63	180.72	176.45	172.71	169.43	166.53	163.96	161.68	159.65	157.83	151.18	147.19	144.74
20000	201.37	195.40	190.23	185.74	181.80	178.35	175.29	172.59	170.19	168.05	166.14	159.13	154.94	152.36
21000	211.44	205.17	199.74	195.02	190.89	187.26	184.06	181.22	178.70	176.45	174.44	167.09	162.68	159.97
22000	221.51	214.94	209.25	204.31	199.98	196.18	192.82	189.85	187.21	184.85	182.75	175.05	170.43	167.59
23000	231.58	224.71	218.77	213.60	209.07	205.10	201.59	198.48	195.72	193.26	191.06	183.00	178.18	175.21
24000	241.65	234.48	228.28	222.88	218.16	214.01	210.35	207.11	204.23	201.66	199.36	190.96	185.92	182.83
25000	251.72	244.25	237.79	232.17	227.25	222.93	219.12	215.74	212.74	210.06	207.67	198.92	193.67	190.44
26000	261.78	254.02	247.30	241.45	236.34	231.85	227.88	224.37	221.24	218.46	215.97	206.87	201.42	198.06
27000	271.85	263.79	256.81	250.74	245.43	240.76	236.65	233.00	229.75	226.86	224.28	214.83	209.16	205.68
28000	281.92	273.56	266.32	260.03	254.52	249.68	245.41	241.63	238.26	235.27	232.59	222.79	216.91	213.30
29000	291.99	283.33	275.83	269.31	263.61	258.60	254.17	250.26	246.77	243.67	240.89	230.74	224.66	220.91
30000	302.06	293.10	285.34	278.60	272.70	267.52	262.94	258.88	255.28	252.07	249.20	238.70	232.40	228.53
31000	312.13	302.86	294.86	287.89	281.79	276.43	271.70	267.51	263.79	260.47	257.51	246.65	240.15	236.15
32000	322.20	312.63	304.37	297.17	290.88	285.35	280.47	276.14	272.30	268.87	265.81	254.61	247.90	243.77
33000	332.26	322.40	313.88	306.46	299.97	294.27	289.23	284.77	280.81	277.28	274.12	262.57	255.64	251.38
34000	342.33	332.17	323.39	315.75	309.06	303.18	298.00	293.40	289.32	285.68	282.43	270.52	263.39	259.00
35000	352.40	341.94	332.90	325.03	318.15	312.10	306.76	302.03	297.83	294.08	290.73	278.48	271.14	266.62
36000	362.47	351.71	342.41	334.32	327.24	321.02	315.53	310.66	306.34	302.48	299.04	286.44	278.88	274.24
37000	372.54	361.48	351.92	343.61	336.33	329.93	324.29	319.29	314.85	310.89	307.35	294.39	286.63	281.85
38000	382.61	371.25	361.44	352.89	345.42	338.85	333.05	327.92	323.36	319.29	315.65	302.35	294.38	289.47
39000	392.67	381.02	370.95	362.18	354.51	347.77	341.82	336.55	331.86	327.69	323.96	310.31	302.12	297.09
40000	402.74	390.79	380.46	371.47	363.60	356.69	350.58	345.18	340.37	336.09	332.27	318.26	309.87	304.71
41000	412.81	400.56	389.97	380.75	372.69	365.60	359.35	353.81	348.88	344.49	340.57	326.22	317.62	312.32
42000	422.88	410.33	399.48	390.04	381.78	374.52	368.11	362.44	357.39	352.90	348.88	334.18	325.36	319.94
43000	432.95	420.10	408.99	399.33	390.87	383.44	376.88	371.07	365.90	361.30	357.19	342.13	333.11	327.56
44000	443.02	429.87	418.50	408.61	399.96	392.35	385.64	379.70	374.41	369.70	365.49	350.09	340.86	335.18
45000	453.08	439.64	428.01	417.90	409.05	401.27	394.41	388.32	382.92	378.10	373.80	358.05	348.60	342.79
46000	463.15	449.41	437.53	427.19	418.14	410.19	403.17	396.95	391.43	386.51	382.11	366.00	356.35	350.41
47000	473.22	459.18	447.04	436.47	427.23	419.11	411.94	405.58	399.94	394.91	390.41	373.96	364.10	358.03
48000	483.29	468.95	456.55	445.76	436.32	428.02	420.70	414.21	408.45	403.31	398.72	381.91	371.84	365.65
49000	493.36	478.72	466.06	455.04	445.41	436.94	429.46	422.84	416.96	411.71	407.03	389.87	379.59	373.26
50000	503.43	488.49	475.57	464.33	454.50	445.86	438.23	431.47	425.47	420.11	415.33	397.83	387.34	380.88
55000	553.77	537.34	523.13	510.76	499.95	490.44	482.05	474.62	468.01	462.13	456.86	437.61	426.07	418.97
60000	604.11	586.19	570.68	557.20	545.40	535.03	525.87	517.76	510.56	504.14	498.40	477.39	464.80	457.06
65000	654.45	635.03	618.24	603.63	590.85	579.61	569.70	560.91	553.10	546.15	539.93	517.17	503.54	495.14
70000	704.80	683.88	665.80	650.06	636.30	624.20	613.52	604.06	595.65	588.16	581.46	556.96	542.27	533.23
75000	755.14	732.73	713.35	696.49	681.75	668.78	657.34	647.20	638.20	630.17	622.99	596.74	581.00	571.32
80000	805.48	781.58	760.91	742.93	727.19	713.37	701.16	690.35	680.74	672.18	664.53	636.52	619.74	609.41
85000	855.82	830.43	808.47	789.36	772.64	757.95	744.98	733.50	723.29	714.19	706.06	676.30	658.47	647.49
90000	906.16	879.28	856.02	835.79	818.09	802.54	788.81	776.64	765.84	756.20	747.59	716.09	697.20	685.58
95000	956.51	928.12	903.58	882.22	863.54	847.12	832.63	819.79	808.38	798.21	789.13	755.87	735.93	723.67
100000	1006.85	976.97	951.14	928.66	908.99	891.71	876.45	862.94	850.93	840.22	830.66	795.65	774.67	761.76

8.900%

MONTHLY PAYMENT
REQUIRED TO AMORTIZE A LOAN

TERM	1 Year	2 Years	3 Years	4 Years	5 Years	6 Years	7 Years	8 Years	9 Years	10 Years	11 Years	12 Years	13 Years	14 Years
AMOUNT														
5	.44	.23	.16	.13	.11	.09	.09	.08	.07	.07	.06	.06	.06	.06
10	.88	.46	.32	.25	.21	.18	.17	.15	.14	.13	.12	.12	.11	.11
15	1.32	.69	.48	.38	.32	.27	.25	.22	.21	.19	.18	.17	.17	.16
25	2.19	1.15	.80	.63	.52	.45	.41	.37	.34	.32	.30	.29	.28	.27
50	4.38	2.29	1.59	1.25	1.04	.90	.81	.73	.68	.64	.60	.57	.55	.53
75	6.56	3.43	2.39	1.87	1.56	1.35	1.21	1.10	1.02	.95	.90	.85	.82	.79
100	8.75	4.57	3.18	2.49	2.08	1.80	1.61	1.46	1.35	1.27	1.20	1.14	1.09	1.05
200	17.49	9.13	6.36	4.97	4.15	3.60	3.21	2.92	2.70	2.53	2.39	2.27	2.17	2.09
300	26.23	13.70	9.53	7.46	6.22	5.40	4.82	4.38	4.05	3.79	3.58	3.40	3.26	3.13
400	34.97	18.26	12.71	9.94	8.29	7.20	6.42	5.84	5.40	5.05	4.77	4.53	4.34	4.18
500	43.71	22.82	15.88	12.42	10.36	8.99	8.02	7.30	6.75	6.31	5.96	5.67	5.42	5.22
600	52.45	27.39	19.06	14.91	12.43	10.79	9.63	8.76	8.10	7.57	7.15	6.80	6.51	6.26
700	61.19	31.95	22.23	17.39	14.50	12.59	11.23	10.22	9.45	8.83	8.34	7.93	7.59	7.31
800	69.93	36.52	25.41	19.88	16.57	14.39	12.84	11.68	10.80	10.10	9.53	9.06	8.68	8.35
900	78.67	41.08	28.58	22.36	18.64	16.18	14.44	13.14	12.15	11.36	10.72	10.20	9.76	9.39
1000	87.41	45.64	31.76	24.84	20.71	17.98	16.04	14.60	13.49	12.62	11.91	11.33	10.84	10.44
2000	174.82	91.28	63.51	49.68	41.42	35.96	32.08	29.20	26.98	25.23	23.82	22.65	21.68	20.87
3000	262.22	136.92	95.26	74.52	62.13	53.93	48.12	43.80	40.47	37.85	35.72	33.98	32.52	31.30
4000	349.63	182.56	127.02	99.36	82.84	71.91	64.16	58.40	53.96	50.46	47.63	45.30	43.36	41.73
5000	437.03	228.20	158.77	124.19	103.55	89.88	80.20	73.00	67.45	63.07	59.53	56.63	54.20	52.16
6000	524.44	273.84	190.52	149.03	124.26	107.86	96.24	87.60	80.94	75.69	71.44	67.95	65.04	62.59
7000	611.84	319.48	222.28	173.87	144.97	125.84	112.27	102.19	94.43	88.30	83.34	79.27	75.88	73.02
8000	699.25	365.12	254.03	198.71	165.68	143.81	128.31	116.79	107.92	100.91	95.25	90.60	86.72	83.45
9000	786.65	410.75	285.78	223.54	186.39	161.79	144.35	131.39	121.41	113.53	107.16	101.92	97.56	93.88
10000	874.06	456.39	317.54	248.38	207.10	179.76	160.39	145.99	134.90	126.14	119.06	113.25	108.40	104.32
11000	961.46	502.03	349.29	273.22	227.81	197.74	176.43	160.59	148.39	138.75	130.97	124.57	119.24	114.75
12000	1048.87	547.67	381.04	298.06	248.52	215.72	192.47	175.19	161.88	151.37	142.87	135.89	130.08	125.18
13000	1136.27	593.31	412.80	322.89	269.23	233.69	208.50	189.78	175.37	163.98	154.78	147.22	140.92	135.61
14000	1223.68	638.95	444.55	347.73	289.94	251.67	224.54	204.38	188.86	176.59	166.68	158.54	151.76	146.04
15000	1311.08	684.59	476.30	372.57	310.65	269.64	240.58	218.98	202.35	189.21	178.59	169.87	162.60	156.47
16000	1398.49	730.23	508.06	397.41	331.36	287.62	256.62	233.58	215.84	201.82	190.50	181.19	173.44	166.90
17000	1485.89	775.87	539.81	422.24	352.07	305.60	272.66	248.18	229.33	214.43	202.40	192.51	184.28	177.33
18000	1573.30	821.50	571.56	447.08	372.78	323.57	288.70	262.78	242.82	227.05	214.31	203.84	195.12	187.76
19000	1660.70	867.14	603.32	471.92	393.49	341.55	304.73	277.37	256.31	239.66	226.21	215.16	205.96	198.19
20000	1748.11	912.78	635.07	496.76	414.20	359.52	320.77	291.97	269.80	252.28	238.12	226.49	216.79	208.63
21000	1835.51	958.42	666.82	521.59	434.91	377.50	336.81	306.57	283.29	264.89	250.02	237.81	227.63	219.06
22000	1922.92	1004.06	698.58	546.43	455.62	395.48	352.85	321.17	296.78	277.50	261.93	249.13	238.47	229.49
23000	2010.32	1049.70	730.33	571.27	476.33	413.45	368.89	335.77	310.27	290.12	273.83	260.46	249.31	239.92
24000	2097.73	1095.34	762.08	596.11	497.04	431.43	384.93	350.37	323.76	302.73	285.74	271.78	260.15	250.35
25000	2185.13	1140.98	793.84	620.94	517.75	449.40	400.96	364.96	337.25	315.34	297.65	283.11	270.99	260.78
26000	2272.54	1186.62	825.59	645.78	538.46	467.38	417.00	379.56	350.74	327.96	309.55	294.43	281.83	271.21
27000	2359.94	1232.25	857.34	670.62	559.17	485.36	433.04	394.16	364.23	340.57	321.46	305.75	292.67	281.64
28000	2447.35	1277.89	889.09	695.46	579.88	503.33	449.08	408.76	377.72	353.18	333.36	317.08	303.51	292.07
29000	2534.75	1323.53	920.85	720.29	600.59	521.31	465.12	423.36	391.21	365.80	345.27	328.40	314.35	302.50
30000	2622.16	1369.17	952.60	745.13	621.30	539.28	481.16	437.96	404.70	378.41	357.17	339.73	325.19	312.94
31000	2709.56	1414.81	984.35	769.97	642.01	557.26	497.19	452.55	418.19	391.02	369.08	351.05	336.03	323.37
32000	2796.97	1460.45	1016.11	794.81	662.72	575.24	513.23	467.15	431.68	403.64	380.99	362.37	346.87	333.80
33000	2884.37	1506.09	1047.86	819.65	683.43	593.21	529.27	481.75	445.17	416.25	392.89	373.70	357.71	344.23
34000	2971.78	1551.73	1079.61	844.48	704.14	611.19	545.31	496.35	458.66	428.86	404.80	385.02	368.55	354.66
35000	3059.18	1597.37	1111.37	869.32	724.85	629.16	561.35	510.95	472.15	441.48	416.70	396.35	379.39	365.09
36000	3146.59	1643.00	1143.12	894.16	745.56	647.14	577.39	525.55	485.64	454.09	428.61	407.67	390.23	375.52
37000	3233.99	1688.64	1174.87	919.00	766.27	665.12	593.42	540.15	499.13	466.71	440.51	419.00	401.07	385.95
38000	3321.40	1734.28	1206.63	943.83	786.98	683.09	609.46	554.74	512.62	479.32	452.42	430.32	411.91	396.38
39000	3408.80	1779.92	1238.38	968.67	807.69	701.07	625.50	569.34	526.11	491.93	464.33	441.64	422.75	406.81
40000	3496.21	1825.56	1270.13	993.51	828.40	719.04	641.54	583.94	539.60	504.55	476.23	452.97	433.58	417.25
41000	3583.61	1871.20	1301.89	1018.35	849.11	737.02	657.58	598.54	553.09	517.16	488.14	464.29	444.42	427.68
42000	3671.02	1916.84	1333.64	1043.18	869.82	754.99	673.62	613.14	566.58	529.77	500.04	475.62	455.26	438.11
43000	3758.42	1962.48	1365.39	1068.02	890.53	772.97	689.66	627.74	580.07	542.39	511.95	486.94	466.10	448.54
44000	3845.83	2008.12	1397.15	1092.86	911.24	790.95	705.69	642.33	593.56	555.00	523.85	498.26	476.94	458.97
45000	3933.24	2053.75	1428.90	1117.70	931.95	808.92	721.73	656.93	607.05	567.61	535.76	509.59	487.78	469.40
46000	4020.64	2099.39	1460.65	1142.53	952.66	826.90	737.77	671.53	620.54	580.23	547.66	520.91	498.62	479.83
47000	4108.05	2145.03	1492.41	1167.37	973.37	844.87	753.81	686.13	634.03	592.84	559.57	532.24	509.46	490.26
48000	4195.45	2190.67	1524.16	1192.21	994.08	862.85	769.85	700.73	647.52	605.45	571.48	543.56	520.30	500.69
49000	4282.86	2236.31	1555.91	1217.05	1014.79	880.83	785.89	715.33	661.01	618.07	583.38	554.88	531.14	511.12
50000	4370.26	2281.95	1587.67	1241.88	1035.50	898.80	801.92	729.92	674.50	630.68	595.29	566.21	541.98	521.56
55000	4807.29	2510.14	1746.43	1366.07	1139.05	988.68	882.12	802.92	741.95	693.75	654.82	622.83	596.18	573.71
60000	5244.31	2738.34	1905.20	1490.26	1242.60	1078.56	962.31	875.91	809.40	756.82	714.34	679.45	650.37	625.87
65000	5681.34	2966.53	2063.96	1614.45	1346.15	1168.44	1042.50	948.90	876.85	819.88	773.87	736.07	704.57	678.02
70000	6118.36	3194.73	2222.73	1738.64	1449.69	1258.32	1122.69	1021.89	944.30	882.95	833.40	792.69	758.77	730.18
75000	6555.39	3422.92	2381.50	1862.82	1553.24	1348.20	1202.88	1094.88	1011.75	946.02	892.93	849.31	812.97	782.33
80000	6992.41	3651.11	2540.26	1987.01	1656.79	1438.08	1283.08	1167.88	1079.20	1009.09	952.46	905.93	867.16	834.49
85000	7429.44	3879.31	2699.03	2111.20	1760.34	1527.96	1363.27	1240.87	1146.65	1072.15	1011.98	962.55	921.36	886.64
90000	7866.46	4107.50	2857.79	2235.39	1863.89	1617.84	1443.46	1313.86	1214.10	1135.22	1071.51	1019.17	975.56	938.80
95000	8303.49	4335.70	3016.56	2359.58	1967.44	1707.72	1523.65	1386.85	1281.55	1198.29	1131.04	1075.79	1029.76	990.95
100000	8740.52	4563.89	3175.33	2483.76	2070.99	1797.60	1603.84	1459.84	1349.00	1261.36	1190.57	1132.41	1083.95	1043.11

TERM	15 Years	16 Years	17 Years	18 Years	19 Years	20 Years	21 Years	22 Years	23 Years	24 Years	25 Years	30 Years	35 Years	40 Years
AMOUNT														
5	.06	.05	.05	.05	.05	.05	.05	.05	.05	.05	.05	.04	.04	.04
10	.11	.10	.10	.10	.10	.09	.09	.09	.09	.09	.09	.08	.08	.08
15	.16	.15	.15	.14	.14	.14	.14	.13	.13	.13	.13	.12	.12	.12
25	.26	.25	.24	.24	.23	.23	.22	.22	.22	.22	.21	.20	.20	.20
50	.51	.49	.48	.47	.46	.45	.44	.44	.43	.43	.42	.40	.39	.39
75	.76	.74	.72	.70	.69	.67	.66	.65	.64	.64	.63	.60	.59	.58
100	1.01	.98	.96	.94	.92	.90	.88	.87	.86	.85	.84	.80	.78	.77
200	2.02	1.96	1.91	1.87	1.83	1.79	1.76	1.73	1.71	1.69	1.67	1.60	1.56	1.53
300	3.03	2.94	2.86	2.80	2.74	2.68	2.64	2.60	2.56	2.53	2.50	2.40	2.33	2.30
400	4.04	3.92	3.82	3.73	3.65	3.58	3.52	3.46	3.42	3.37	3.33	3.19	3.11	3.06
500	5.05	4.90	4.77	4.66	4.56	4.47	4.40	4.33	4.27	4.21	4.17	3.99	3.89	3.82
600	6.05	5.88	5.72	5.59	5.47	5.36	5.27	5.19	5.12	5.06	5.00	4.79	4.66	4.59
700	7.06	6.85	6.67	6.52	6.38	6.26	6.15	6.06	5.97	5.90	5.83	5.59	5.44	5.35
800	8.07	7.83	7.63	7.45	7.29	7.15	7.03	6.92	6.83	6.74	6.66	6.38	6.22	6.11
900	9.08	8.81	8.58	8.38	8.20	8.04	7.91	7.79	7.68	7.58	7.50	7.18	6.99	6.88
1000	10.09	9.79	9.53	9.31	9.11	8.94	8.79	8.65	8.53	8.42	8.33	7.98	7.77	7.64
2000	20.17	19.57	19.06	18.61	18.22	17.87	17.57	17.30	17.06	16.84	16.65	15.95	15.54	15.28
3000	30.25	29.36	28.58	27.91	27.32	26.80	26.35	25.94	25.58	25.26	24.98	23.93	23.30	22.92
4000	40.34	39.14	38.11	37.21	36.43	35.74	35.13	34.59	34.11	33.68	33.30	31.90	31.07	30.55
5000	50.42	48.93	47.64	46.52	45.53	44.67	43.91	43.23	42.63	42.10	41.62	39.88	38.83	38.19
6000	60.50	58.71	57.16	55.82	54.64	53.60	52.69	51.88	51.16	50.52	49.95	47.85	46.60	45.83
7000	70.59	68.50	66.69	65.12	63.74	62.54	61.47	60.53	59.69	58.94	58.27	55.83	54.36	53.46
8000	80.67	78.28	76.22	74.42	72.85	71.47	70.25	69.17	68.21	67.36	66.59	63.80	62.13	61.10
9000	90.75	88.07	85.74	83.72	81.96	80.40	79.03	77.82	76.74	75.78	74.92	71.77	69.89	68.74
10000	100.84	97.85	95.27	93.03	91.06	89.34	87.81	86.46	85.26	84.20	83.24	79.75	77.66	76.37
11000	110.92	107.64	104.80	102.33	100.17	98.27	96.59	95.11	93.79	92.61	91.56	87.72	85.42	84.01
12000	121.00	117.42	114.32	111.63	109.27	107.20	105.37	103.75	102.32	101.03	99.89	95.70	93.19	91.65
13000	131.09	127.21	123.85	120.93	118.38	116.13	114.15	112.40	110.84	109.45	108.21	103.67	100.95	99.28
14000	141.17	136.99	133.38	130.23	127.48	125.07	122.93	121.05	119.37	117.87	116.54	111.65	108.72	106.92
15000	151.25	146.78	142.90	139.54	136.59	134.00	131.72	129.69	127.89	126.29	124.86	119.62	116.48	114.56
16000	161.34	156.56	152.43	148.84	145.70	142.93	140.50	138.34	136.42	134.71	133.18	127.60	124.25	122.19
17000	171.42	166.35	161.96	158.14	154.80	151.87	149.28	146.98	144.95	143.13	141.51	135.57	132.01	129.83
18000	181.50	176.13	171.48	167.44	163.91	160.80	158.06	155.63	153.47	151.55	149.83	143.54	139.78	137.47
19000	191.59	185.92	181.01	176.74	173.01	169.73	166.84	164.27	162.00	159.97	158.15	151.52	147.54	145.10
20000	201.67	195.70	190.54	186.05	182.12	178.67	175.62	172.92	170.52	168.39	166.48	159.49	155.31	152.74
21000	211.75	205.48	200.06	195.35	191.22	187.60	184.40	181.57	179.05	176.81	174.80	167.47	163.08	160.38
22000	221.84	215.27	209.59	204.65	200.33	196.53	193.18	190.21	187.57	185.22	183.12	175.44	170.84	168.01
23000	231.92	225.05	219.12	213.95	209.44	205.47	201.96	198.86	196.10	193.64	191.45	183.42	178.61	175.65
24000	242.00	234.84	228.64	223.26	218.54	214.40	210.74	207.50	204.63	202.06	199.77	191.39	186.37	183.29
25000	252.09	244.62	238.17	232.56	227.65	223.33	219.52	216.15	213.15	210.48	208.09	199.36	194.14	190.92
26000	262.17	254.41	247.70	241.86	236.75	232.26	228.30	224.80	221.68	218.90	216.42	207.34	201.90	198.56
27000	272.25	264.19	257.22	251.16	245.86	241.20	237.08	233.44	230.20	227.32	224.74	215.31	209.67	206.20
28000	282.34	273.98	266.75	260.46	254.96	250.13	245.86	242.09	238.73	235.74	233.07	223.29	217.43	213.83
29000	292.42	283.76	276.28	269.77	264.07	259.06	254.65	250.73	247.26	244.16	241.39	231.26	225.20	221.47
30000	302.50	293.55	285.80	279.07	273.18	268.00	263.43	259.38	255.78	252.58	249.71	239.24	232.96	229.11
31000	312.59	303.33	295.33	288.37	282.28	276.93	272.21	268.02	264.31	261.00	258.04	247.21	240.73	236.74
32000	322.67	313.12	304.86	297.67	291.39	285.86	280.99	276.67	272.83	269.41	266.36	255.19	248.49	244.38
33000	332.75	322.90	314.38	306.97	300.49	294.80	289.77	285.32	281.36	277.83	274.68	263.16	256.26	252.02
34000	342.84	332.69	323.91	316.28	309.60	303.73	298.55	293.96	289.89	286.25	283.01	271.13	264.02	259.65
35000	352.92	342.47	333.44	325.58	318.70	312.66	307.33	302.61	298.41	294.67	291.33	279.11	271.79	267.29
36000	363.00	352.26	342.96	334.88	327.81	321.59	316.11	311.25	306.94	303.09	299.65	287.08	279.55	274.93
37000	373.09	362.04	352.49	344.18	336.91	330.53	324.89	319.90	315.46	311.51	307.98	295.06	287.32	282.56
38000	383.17	371.83	362.02	353.48	346.02	339.46	333.67	328.54	323.99	319.93	316.30	303.03	295.08	290.20
39000	393.25	381.61	371.54	362.79	355.13	348.39	342.45	337.19	332.51	328.35	324.63	311.01	302.85	297.84
40000	403.34	391.39	381.07	372.09	364.23	357.33	351.23	345.84	341.04	336.77	332.95	318.98	310.62	305.47
41000	413.42	401.18	390.60	381.39	373.34	366.26	360.01	354.48	349.57	345.19	341.27	326.95	318.38	313.11
42000	423.50	410.96	400.12	390.69	382.44	375.19	368.79	363.13	358.09	353.61	349.60	334.93	326.15	320.75
43000	433.59	420.75	409.65	399.99	391.55	384.13	377.58	371.77	366.62	362.02	357.92	342.90	333.91	328.38
44000	443.67	430.53	419.18	409.30	400.65	393.06	386.36	380.42	375.14	370.44	366.24	350.88	341.68	336.02
45000	453.75	440.32	428.70	418.60	409.76	401.99	395.14	389.07	383.67	378.86	374.57	358.85	349.44	343.66
46000	463.84	450.10	438.23	427.90	418.87	410.93	403.92	397.71	392.20	387.28	382.89	366.83	357.21	351.29
47000	473.92	459.89	447.76	437.20	427.97	419.86	412.70	406.36	400.72	395.70	391.21	374.80	364.97	358.93
48000	484.00	469.67	457.28	446.51	437.08	428.79	421.48	415.00	409.25	404.12	399.54	382.78	372.74	366.57
49000	494.08	479.46	466.81	455.81	446.18	437.72	430.26	423.65	417.77	412.54	407.86	390.75	380.50	374.20
50000	504.17	489.24	476.34	465.11	455.29	446.66	439.04	432.29	426.30	420.96	416.18	398.72	388.27	381.84
55000	554.58	538.17	523.97	511.62	500.82	491.32	482.94	475.52	468.93	463.05	457.80	438.60	427.09	420.02
60000	605.00	587.09	571.60	558.13	546.35	535.99	526.85	518.75	511.56	505.15	499.42	478.47	465.92	458.21
65000	655.42	636.01	619.24	604.64	591.87	580.65	570.75	561.98	554.19	547.24	541.04	518.34	504.75	496.39
70000	705.83	684.94	666.87	651.15	637.40	625.32	614.65	605.21	596.82	589.34	582.66	558.21	543.57	534.58
75000	756.25	733.86	714.50	697.66	682.93	669.98	658.55	648.44	639.45	631.43	624.27	598.08	582.40	572.76
80000	806.67	782.78	762.14	744.17	728.46	714.65	702.46	691.67	682.08	673.53	665.89	637.96	621.23	610.94
85000	857.08	831.71	809.77	790.68	773.99	759.31	746.37	734.90	724.71	715.62	707.51	677.83	660.05	649.13
90000	907.50	880.63	857.40	837.19	819.52	803.98	790.27	778.13	767.34	757.72	749.13	717.70	698.88	687.31
95000	957.92	929.56	905.04	883.70	865.04	848.64	834.17	821.35	809.96	799.81	790.75	757.57	737.70	725.49
100000	1008.33	978.48	952.67	930.21	910.57	893.31	878.08	864.58	852.59	841.91	832.36	797.44	776.53	763.68

MONTHLY PAYMENT
REQUIRED TO AMORTIZE A LOAN

TERM	1 Year	2 Years	3 Years	4 Years	5 Years	6 Years	7 Years	8 Years	9 Years	10 Years	11 Years	12 Years	13 Years	14 Years
AMOUNT														
5	.44	.23	.16	.13	.11	.10	.09	.08	.07	.07	.06	.06	.06	.06
10	.88	.46	.32	.25	.21	.19	.17	.15	.14	.13	.12	.12	.11	.11
15	1.32	.69	.48	.38	.32	.28	.25	.22	.21	.20	.18	.18	.17	.16
25	2.19	1.15	.80	.63	.52	.46	.41	.37	.34	.32	.30	.29	.28	.27
50	4.38	2.29	1.59	1.25	1.04	.91	.81	.74	.68	.64	.60	.57	.55	.53
75	6.56	3.43	2.39	1.87	1.56	1.36	1.21	1.10	1.02	.96	.90	.86	.82	.79
100	8.75	4.57	3.18	2.49	2.08	1.81	1.61	1.47	1.36	1.27	1.20	1.14	1.09	1.05
200	17.50	9.14	6.36	4.98	4.16	3.61	3.22	2.94	2.71	2.54	2.40	2.28	2.18	2.10
300	26.24	13.71	9.54	7.47	6.23	5.41	4.83	4.40	4.07	3.81	3.59	3.42	3.27	3.15
400	34.99	18.28	12.72	9.96	8.31	7.22	6.44	5.87	5.42	5.07	4.79	4.56	4.36	4.20
500	43.73	22.85	15.90	12.45	10.38	9.02	8.05	7.33	6.78	6.34	5.99	5.70	5.45	5.25
600	52.48	27.42	19.08	14.94	12.46	10.82	9.66	8.80	8.13	7.61	7.18	6.83	6.54	6.30
700	61.22	31.98	22.26	17.42	14.54	12.62	11.27	10.26	9.49	8.87	8.38	7.97	7.63	7.35
800	69.97	36.55	25.44	19.91	16.61	14.43	12.88	11.73	10.84	10.14	9.57	9.11	8.72	8.40
900	78.71	41.12	28.62	22.40	18.69	16.23	14.49	13.19	12.19	11.41	10.77	10.25	9.81	9.45
1000	87.46	45.69	31.80	24.89	20.76	18.03	16.09	14.66	13.55	12.67	11.97	11.39	10.90	10.49
2000	174.91	91.37	63.60	49.78	41.52	36.06	32.18	29.31	27.09	25.34	23.93	22.77	21.80	20.98
3000	262.36	137.06	95.40	74.66	62.28	54.08	48.27	43.96	40.63	38.01	35.89	34.15	32.70	31.47
4000	349.81	182.74	127.20	99.55	83.04	72.11	64.36	58.61	54.18	50.68	47.85	45.53	43.59	41.96
5000	437.26	228.43	159.00	124.43	103.80	90.13	80.45	73.26	67.72	63.34	59.81	56.91	54.49	52.45
6000	524.71	274.11	190.80	149.32	124.56	108.16	96.54	87.91	81.26	76.01	71.77	68.29	65.39	62.94
7000	612.17	319.80	222.60	174.20	145.31	126.18	112.63	102.56	94.81	88.68	83.73	79.67	76.28	73.43
8000	699.62	365.48	254.40	199.09	166.07	144.21	128.72	117.21	108.35	101.35	95.69	91.05	87.18	83.92
9000	787.07	411.17	286.20	223.97	186.83	162.23	144.81	131.86	121.89	114.01	107.65	102.43	98.08	94.41
10000	874.52	456.85	318.00	248.86	207.59	180.26	160.90	146.51	135.43	126.68	119.61	113.81	108.97	104.90
11000	961.97	502.54	349.80	273.74	228.35	198.29	176.98	161.16	148.98	139.35	131.57	125.19	119.87	115.39
12000	1049.42	548.22	381.60	298.63	249.11	216.31	193.07	175.81	162.52	152.02	143.53	136.57	130.77	125.88
13000	1136.87	593.91	413.40	323.51	269.86	234.34	209.16	190.46	176.06	164.68	155.50	147.95	141.66	136.37
14000	1224.33	639.59	445.20	348.40	290.62	252.36	225.25	205.11	189.61	177.35	167.46	159.33	152.56	146.86
15000	1311.78	685.28	477.00	373.28	311.38	270.39	241.34	219.76	203.15	190.02	179.42	170.71	163.46	157.35
16000	1399.23	730.96	508.80	398.17	332.14	288.41	257.43	234.41	216.69	202.69	191.38	182.09	174.35	167.84
17000	1486.68	776.65	540.60	423.05	352.90	306.44	273.52	249.06	230.23	215.35	203.34	193.47	185.25	178.32
18000	1574.13	822.33	572.40	447.94	373.66	324.46	289.61	263.71	243.78	228.02	215.30	204.85	196.15	188.81
19000	1661.58	868.02	604.20	472.82	394.41	342.49	305.70	278.36	257.32	240.69	227.26	216.23	207.04	199.30
20000	1749.03	913.70	636.00	497.71	415.17	360.52	321.79	293.01	270.86	253.36	239.22	227.61	217.94	209.79
21000	1836.49	959.38	667.80	522.59	435.93	378.54	337.88	307.66	284.41	266.02	251.18	238.99	228.84	220.28
22000	1923.94	1005.07	699.60	547.48	456.69	396.57	353.96	322.31	297.95	278.69	263.14	250.37	239.73	230.77
23000	2011.39	1050.75	731.40	572.36	477.45	414.59	370.05	336.96	311.49	291.36	275.10	261.75	250.63	241.26
24000	2098.84	1096.44	763.20	597.25	498.21	432.62	386.14	351.61	325.03	304.03	287.06	273.13	261.53	251.75
25000	2186.29	1142.12	795.00	622.13	518.96	450.64	402.23	366.26	338.58	316.69	299.03	284.51	272.43	262.24
26000	2273.74	1187.81	826.80	647.02	539.72	468.67	418.32	380.91	352.12	329.36	310.99	295.89	283.32	272.73
27000	2361.19	1233.49	858.60	671.90	560.48	486.69	434.41	395.56	365.66	342.03	322.95	307.27	294.22	283.22
28000	2448.65	1279.18	890.40	696.79	581.24	504.72	450.50	410.21	379.21	354.70	334.91	318.65	305.12	293.71
29000	2536.10	1324.86	922.20	721.67	602.00	522.75	466.59	424.86	392.75	367.36	346.87	330.03	316.01	304.20
30000	2623.55	1370.55	954.00	746.56	622.76	540.77	482.68	439.51	406.29	380.03	358.83	341.41	326.91	314.69
31000	2711.00	1416.23	985.80	771.44	643.51	558.80	498.77	454.16	419.84	392.70	370.79	352.79	337.81	325.18
32000	2798.45	1461.92	1017.60	796.33	664.27	576.82	514.86	468.81	433.38	405.37	382.75	364.17	348.70	335.67
33000	2885.90	1507.60	1049.40	821.21	685.03	594.85	530.94	483.46	446.92	418.04	394.71	375.56	359.60	346.15
34000	2973.36	1553.29	1081.20	846.10	705.79	612.87	547.03	498.11	460.46	430.70	406.67	386.94	370.50	356.64
35000	3060.81	1598.97	1113.00	870.98	726.55	630.90	563.12	512.76	474.01	443.37	418.63	398.32	381.39	367.13
36000	3148.26	1644.66	1144.80	895.87	747.31	648.92	579.21	527.41	487.55	456.04	430.59	409.70	392.29	377.62
37000	3235.71	1690.34	1176.60	920.75	768.06	666.95	595.30	542.06	501.09	468.71	442.55	421.08	403.19	388.11
38000	3323.16	1736.03	1208.39	945.64	788.82	684.98	611.39	556.71	514.64	481.37	454.52	432.46	414.08	398.60
39000	3410.61	1781.71	1240.19	970.52	809.58	703.00	627.48	571.36	528.18	494.04	466.48	443.84	424.98	409.09
40000	3498.06	1827.39	1271.99	995.41	830.34	721.03	643.57	586.01	541.72	506.71	478.44	455.22	435.88	419.58
41000	3585.52	1873.08	1303.79	1020.29	851.10	739.05	659.66	600.66	555.26	519.38	490.40	466.60	446.77	430.07
42000	3672.97	1918.76	1335.59	1045.18	871.86	757.08	675.75	615.31	568.81	532.04	502.36	477.98	457.67	440.56
43000	3760.42	1964.45	1367.39	1070.06	892.61	775.10	691.84	629.96	582.35	544.71	514.32	489.36	468.57	451.05
44000	3847.87	2010.13	1399.19	1094.95	913.37	793.13	707.92	644.61	595.89	557.38	526.28	500.74	479.46	461.54
45000	3935.32	2055.82	1430.99	1119.83	934.13	811.15	724.01	659.26	609.44	570.05	538.24	512.12	490.36	472.03
46000	4022.77	2101.50	1462.79	1144.72	954.89	829.18	740.10	673.91	622.98	582.71	550.20	523.50	501.26	482.52
47000	4110.22	2147.19	1494.59	1169.60	975.65	847.21	756.19	688.56	636.52	595.38	562.16	534.88	512.15	493.01
48000	4197.68	2192.87	1526.39	1194.49	996.41	865.23	772.28	703.21	650.06	608.05	574.12	546.26	523.05	503.50
49000	4285.13	2238.56	1558.19	1219.37	1017.16	883.26	788.37	717.86	663.61	620.72	586.08	557.64	533.95	513.98
50000	4372.58	2284.24	1589.99	1244.26	1037.92	901.28	804.46	732.52	677.15	633.38	598.05	569.02	544.85	524.47
55000	4809.84	2512.67	1748.99	1368.68	1141.71	991.41	884.90	805.77	744.86	696.72	657.85	625.92	599.33	576.92
60000	5247.09	2741.09	1907.99	1493.11	1245.51	1081.54	965.35	879.02	812.58	760.06	717.65	682.82	653.81	629.37
65000	5684.35	2969.51	2066.99	1617.53	1349.30	1171.66	1045.80	952.27	880.29	823.40	777.46	739.72	708.30	681.81
70000	6121.61	3197.94	2225.99	1741.96	1453.09	1261.79	1126.24	1025.52	948.01	886.74	837.26	796.63	762.78	734.26
75000	6558.87	3426.36	2384.98	1866.38	1556.88	1351.92	1206.69	1098.77	1015.72	950.07	897.07	853.53	817.27	786.71
80000	6996.12	3654.78	2543.98	1990.81	1660.67	1442.05	1287.13	1172.02	1083.44	1013.41	956.87	910.43	871.75	839.16
85000	7433.38	3883.21	2702.98	2115.23	1764.47	1532.18	1367.58	1245.27	1151.15	1076.75	1016.67	967.33	926.23	891.60
90000	7870.64	4111.63	2861.98	2239.66	1868.26	1622.30	1448.02	1318.52	1218.87	1140.09	1076.48	1024.23	980.72	944.05
95000	8307.90	4340.06	3020.98	2364.08	1972.05	1712.43	1528.47	1391.77	1286.58	1203.42	1136.28	1081.13	1035.20	996.50
100000	8745.15	4568.48	3179.98	2488.51	2075.84	1802.56	1608.91	1465.03	1354.30	1266.76	1196.09	1138.04	1089.69	1048.94

9%

TERM / AMOUNT	15 Years	16 Years	17 Years	18 Years	19 Years	20 Years	21 Years	22 Years	23 Years	24 Years	25 Years	30 Years	35 Years	40 Years
5	.06	.05	.05	.05	.05	.05	.05	.05	.05	.05	.05	.05	.04	.04
10	.11	.10	.10	.10	.10	.09	.09	.09	.09	.09	.09	.09	.08	.08
15	.16	.15	.15	.15	.14	.14	.14	.14	.13	.13	.13	.13	.12	.12
25	.26	.25	.24	.24	.23	.23	.23	.22	.22	.22	.21	.21	.20	.20
50	.51	.50	.48	.47	.46	.45	.45	.44	.43	.43	.42	.41	.40	.39
75	.77	.74	.72	.71	.69	.68	.67	.66	.65	.64	.63	.61	.59	.58
100	1.02	.99	.96	.94	.92	.90	.89	.88	.86	.85	.84	.81	.79	.78
200	2.03	1.97	1.92	1.88	1.84	1.80	1.77	1.75	1.72	1.70	1.68	1.61	1.57	1.55
300	3.05	2.96	2.88	2.81	2.76	2.70	2.66	2.62	2.58	2.55	2.52	2.42	2.36	2.32
400	4.06	3.94	3.84	3.75	3.67	3.60	3.54	3.49	3.44	3.40	3.36	3.22	3.14	3.09
500	5.08	4.93	4.80	4.69	4.59	4.50	4.43	4.36	4.30	4.25	4.20	4.03	3.92	3.86
600	6.09	5.91	5.76	5.62	5.51	5.40	5.31	5.23	5.16	5.10	5.04	4.83	4.71	4.63
700	7.10	6.90	6.72	6.56	6.42	6.30	6.20	6.10	6.02	5.95	5.88	5.64	5.49	5.40
800	8.12	7.88	7.68	7.50	7.34	7.20	7.08	6.97	6.88	6.79	6.72	6.44	6.28	6.18
900	9.13	8.87	8.63	8.43	8.26	8.10	7.97	7.85	7.74	7.64	7.56	7.25	7.06	6.95
1000	10.15	9.85	9.59	9.37	9.17	9.00	8.85	8.72	8.60	8.49	8.40	8.05	7.84	7.72
2000	20.29	19.70	19.18	18.73	18.34	18.00	17.70	17.43	17.19	16.98	16.79	16.10	15.68	15.43
3000	30.43	29.54	28.77	28.10	27.51	27.00	26.54	26.14	25.78	25.46	25.18	24.14	23.52	23.15
4000	40.58	39.39	38.36	37.46	36.68	35.99	35.39	34.85	34.38	33.95	33.57	32.19	31.36	30.86
5000	50.72	49.23	47.95	46.83	45.85	44.99	44.23	43.56	42.97	42.44	41.96	40.24	39.20	38.57
6000	60.86	59.08	57.53	56.19	55.02	53.99	53.08	52.28	51.56	50.92	50.36	48.28	47.04	46.29
7000	71.00	68.92	67.12	65.56	64.19	62.99	61.93	60.99	60.15	59.41	58.75	56.33	54.88	54.00
8000	81.15	78.77	76.71	74.92	73.36	71.98	70.77	69.70	68.75	67.90	67.14	64.37	62.72	61.71
9000	91.29	88.61	86.30	84.29	82.53	80.98	79.62	78.41	77.34	76.38	75.53	72.42	70.56	69.43
10000	101.43	98.46	95.89	93.65	91.69	89.98	88.46	87.12	85.93	84.87	83.92	80.47	78.40	77.14
11000	111.57	108.30	105.47	103.01	100.86	98.97	97.31	95.83	94.52	93.36	92.32	88.51	86.24	84.85
12000	121.72	118.15	115.06	112.38	110.03	107.97	106.15	104.55	103.12	101.84	100.71	96.56	94.08	92.57
13000	131.86	127.99	124.65	121.74	119.20	116.97	115.00	113.26	111.71	110.33	109.10	104.61	101.92	100.28
14000	142.00	137.84	134.24	131.11	128.37	125.97	123.85	121.97	120.30	118.82	117.49	112.65	109.76	108.00
15000	152.14	147.68	143.83	140.47	137.54	134.96	132.69	130.68	128.90	127.30	125.88	120.70	117.60	115.71
16000	162.29	157.53	153.41	149.84	146.71	143.96	141.54	139.39	137.49	135.79	134.28	128.74	125.44	123.42
17000	172.43	167.37	163.00	159.20	155.88	152.96	150.38	148.10	146.08	144.28	142.67	136.79	133.28	131.14
18000	182.57	177.22	172.59	168.57	165.05	161.96	159.23	156.82	154.67	152.76	151.06	144.84	141.12	138.85
19000	192.72	187.06	182.18	177.93	174.22	170.95	168.08	165.53	163.27	161.25	159.45	152.88	148.96	146.56
20000	202.86	196.91	191.77	187.29	183.38	179.95	176.92	174.24	171.86	169.74	167.84	160.93	156.80	154.28
21000	213.00	206.75	201.35	196.66	192.55	188.95	185.77	182.95	180.45	178.22	176.24	168.98	164.64	161.99
22000	223.14	216.60	210.94	206.02	201.72	197.94	194.61	191.66	189.04	186.71	184.63	177.02	172.48	169.70
23000	233.29	226.44	220.53	215.39	210.90	206.94	203.46	200.38	197.64	195.20	193.02	185.07	180.32	177.42
24000	243.43	236.29	230.12	224.75	220.06	215.94	212.30	209.09	206.23	203.68	201.41	193.11	188.16	185.13
25000	253.57	246.13	239.71	234.12	229.23	224.94	221.15	217.80	214.82	212.17	209.80	201.16	196.00	192.85
26000	263.71	255.98	249.29	243.48	238.40	233.93	230.00	226.51	223.41	220.66	218.20	209.21	203.84	200.56
27000	273.86	265.82	258.88	252.85	247.57	242.93	238.84	235.22	232.01	229.14	226.59	217.25	211.68	208.27
28000	284.00	275.67	268.47	262.21	256.74	251.93	247.69	243.93	240.60	237.63	234.98	225.30	219.52	215.99
29000	294.14	285.51	278.06	271.57	265.91	260.93	256.53	252.65	249.19	246.12	243.37	233.35	227.36	223.70
30000	304.28	295.36	287.65	280.94	275.07	269.92	265.38	261.36	257.79	254.60	251.76	241.39	235.20	231.41
31000	314.43	305.20	297.23	290.30	284.24	278.92	274.23	270.07	266.38	263.09	260.16	249.44	243.04	239.13
32000	324.57	315.05	306.82	299.67	293.41	287.92	283.07	278.78	274.97	271.58	268.55	257.48	250.88	246.84
33000	334.71	324.90	316.41	309.03	302.58	296.91	291.92	287.49	283.56	280.06	276.94	265.53	258.72	254.55
34000	344.86	334.74	326.00	318.40	311.75	305.91	300.76	296.20	292.16	288.55	285.33	273.58	266.56	262.27
35000	355.00	344.59	335.59	327.76	320.92	314.91	309.61	304.92	300.75	297.04	293.72	281.62	274.40	269.98
36000	365.14	354.43	345.17	337.13	330.09	323.91	318.45	313.63	309.34	305.52	302.12	289.67	282.24	277.70
37000	375.28	364.28	354.76	346.49	339.26	332.90	327.30	322.34	317.93	314.01	310.51	297.72	290.08	285.41
38000	385.43	374.12	364.35	355.85	348.43	341.90	336.15	331.05	326.53	322.50	318.90	305.76	297.92	293.12
39000	395.57	383.97	373.94	365.22	357.59	350.90	344.99	339.76	335.12	330.98	327.29	313.81	305.76	300.04
40000	405.71	393.81	383.53	374.58	366.76	359.90	353.84	348.47	343.71	339.47	335.68	321.85	313.60	308.55
41000	415.85	403.66	393.11	383.95	375.93	368.89	362.68	357.19	352.30	347.96	344.08	329.90	321.44	316.26
42000	426.00	413.50	402.70	393.31	385.10	377.89	371.53	365.90	360.90	356.44	352.47	337.95	329.28	323.98
43000	436.14	423.35	412.29	402.68	394.27	386.89	380.37	374.61	369.49	364.93	360.86	345.99	337.12	331.69
44000	446.28	433.19	421.88	412.04	403.44	395.88	389.22	383.32	378.08	373.42	369.25	354.04	344.96	339.40
45000	456.42	443.04	431.47	421.41	412.61	404.88	398.07	392.03	386.68	381.90	377.64	362.09	352.80	347.12
46000	466.57	452.88	441.05	430.77	421.78	413.88	406.91	400.75	395.27	390.39	386.04	370.13	360.64	354.83
47000	476.71	462.73	450.64	440.13	430.95	422.88	415.76	409.46	403.86	398.88	394.43	378.18	368.48	362.54
48000	486.85	472.57	460.23	449.50	440.12	431.87	424.60	418.17	412.45	407.36	402.82	386.22	376.32	370.26
49000	497.00	482.42	469.82	458.86	449.28	440.87	433.45	426.88	421.05	415.85	411.21	394.27	384.16	377.97
50000	507.14	492.26	479.41	468.23	458.45	449.87	442.30	435.59	429.64	424.34	419.60	402.32	392.00	385.69
55000	557.85	541.49	527.35	515.05	504.30	494.85	486.52	479.15	472.60	466.77	461.56	442.55	431.20	424.25
60000	608.56	590.71	575.29	561.87	550.14	539.84	530.75	522.71	515.57	509.20	503.52	482.78	470.40	462.82
65000	659.28	639.94	623.23	608.69	595.99	584.83	574.98	566.27	558.53	551.64	545.48	523.01	509.60	501.39
70000	709.99	689.17	671.17	655.52	641.83	629.81	619.21	609.83	601.49	594.07	587.44	563.24	548.80	539.96
75000	760.70	738.39	719.11	702.34	687.68	674.80	663.44	653.39	644.46	636.50	629.40	603.47	588.00	578.53
80000	811.42	787.62	767.05	749.16	733.52	719.79	707.67	696.96	687.42	678.94	671.36	643.70	627.20	617.09
85000	862.13	836.84	814.99	795.98	779.37	764.77	751.90	740.50	730.38	721.37	713.32	683.93	666.40	655.66
90000	912.84	886.07	862.93	842.81	825.21	809.76	796.13	784.06	773.35	763.80	755.28	724.17	705.60	694.23
95000	963.56	935.30	910.87	889.63	871.06	854.74	840.36	827.62	816.31	806.24	797.24	764.40	744.80	732.80
100000	1014.27	984.52	958.81	936.45	916.90	899.73	884.59	871.18	859.27	848.67	839.20	804.63	784.00	771.37

MONTHLY PAYMENT
REQUIRED TO AMORTIZE A LOAN

TERM	1 Year	2 Years	3 Years	4 Years	5 Years	6 Years	7 Years	8 Years	9 Years	10 Years	11 Years	12 Years	13 Years	14 Years
AMOUNT														
5	.44	.23	.16	.13	.11	.10	.09	.08	.07	.07	.07	.06	.06	.06
10	.88	.46	.32	.25	.21	.19	.17	.15	.14	.13	.13	.12	.11	.11
15	1.32	.69	.48	.38	.32	.28	.25	.23	.21	.20	.19	.18	.17	.16
25	2.19	1.15	.80	.63	.53	.46	.41	.37	.34	.32	.31	.29	.28	.27
50	4.38	2.29	1.60	1.25	1.05	.91	.81	.74	.68	.64	.61	.58	.55	.53
75	6.57	3.43	2.39	1.87	1.57	1.36	1.22	1.11	1.02	.96	.91	.86	.83	.80
100	8.75	4.58	3.19	2.50	2.09	1.81	1.62	1.48	1.36	1.28	1.21	1.15	1.10	1.06
200	17.50	9.15	6.37	4.99	4.17	3.62	3.23	2.95	2.72	2.55	2.41	2.29	2.20	2.11
300	26.25	13.72	9.56	7.48	6.25	5.43	4.85	4.42	4.08	3.82	3.61	3.44	3.29	3.17
400	35.00	18.30	12.74	9.98	8.33	7.24	6.46	5.89	5.44	5.09	4.81	4.58	4.39	4.22
500	43.75	22.87	15.93	12.47	10.41	9.04	8.07	7.36	6.80	6.37	6.01	5.72	5.48	5.28
600	52.50	27.44	19.11	14.96	12.49	10.85	9.69	8.83	8.16	7.64	7.21	6.87	6.58	6.33
700	61.25	32.02	22.30	17.46	14.57	12.66	11.30	10.30	9.52	8.91	8.42	8.01	7.67	7.39
800	70.00	36.59	25.48	19.95	16.65	14.47	12.92	11.77	10.88	10.18	9.62	9.15	8.77	8.44
900	78.75	41.16	28.67	22.44	18.73	16.27	14.53	13.24	12.24	11.45	10.82	10.30	9.86	9.50
1000	87.50	45.74	31.85	24.94	20.81	18.08	16.14	14.71	13.60	12.73	12.02	11.44	10.96	10.55
2000	175.00	91.47	63.70	49.87	41.62	36.16	32.28	29.41	27.20	25.45	24.04	22.88	21.91	21.10
3000	262.50	137.20	95.54	74.80	62.43	54.23	48.42	44.11	40.79	38.17	36.05	34.32	32.87	31.65
4000	350.00	182.93	127.39	99.74	83.23	72.31	64.56	58.81	54.39	50.89	48.07	45.75	43.82	42.20
5000	437.49	228.66	159.24	124.67	104.04	90.38	80.70	73.52	67.98	63.61	60.09	57.19	54.78	52.74
6000	524.99	274.39	191.08	149.60	124.85	108.46	96.84	88.22	81.58	76.34	72.10	68.63	65.73	63.29
7000	612.49	320.12	222.93	174.53	145.65	126.53	112.98	102.92	95.18	89.06	84.12	80.06	76.68	73.84
8000	699.99	365.85	254.78	199.47	166.46	144.61	129.12	117.62	108.77	101.78	96.13	91.50	87.64	84.39
9000	787.49	411.58	286.62	224.40	187.27	162.68	145.26	132.32	122.37	114.50	108.15	102.94	98.59	94.94
10000	874.98	457.31	318.47	249.33	208.07	180.76	161.40	147.03	135.96	127.22	120.17	114.37	109.55	105.48
11000	962.48	503.04	350.31	274.26	228.88	198.83	177.54	161.73	149.56	139.94	132.18	125.81	120.50	116.03
12000	1049.98	548.77	382.16	299.20	249.69	216.91	193.68	176.43	163.16	152.67	144.20	137.25	131.46	126.58
13000	1137.48	594.50	414.01	324.13	270.49	234.98	209.82	191.13	176.75	165.39	156.21	148.68	142.41	137.13
14000	1224.98	640.23	445.85	349.06	291.30	253.06	225.96	205.83	190.35	178.11	168.23	160.12	153.36	147.68
15000	1312.47	685.96	477.70	373.99	312.11	271.13	242.10	220.54	203.94	190.83	180.25	171.56	164.32	158.22
16000	1399.97	731.70	509.55	398.93	332.92	289.21	258.24	235.24	217.54	203.55	192.26	182.99	175.27	168.77
17000	1487.47	777.43	541.39	423.86	353.72	307.28	274.38	249.94	231.14	216.27	204.28	194.43	186.23	179.32
18000	1574.97	823.16	573.24	448.79	374.53	325.36	290.52	264.64	244.73	229.00	216.29	205.87	197.18	189.87
19000	1662.46	868.89	605.08	473.72	395.34	343.43	306.66	279.35	258.33	241.72	228.31	217.30	208.14	200.42
20000	1749.96	914.62	636.93	498.66	416.14	361.51	322.80	294.05	271.92	254.44	240.33	228.74	219.09	210.96
21000	1837.46	960.35	668.78	523.59	436.95	379.58	338.94	308.75	285.52	267.16	252.34	240.18	230.04	221.51
22000	1924.96	1006.08	700.62	548.52	457.76	397.66	355.08	323.45	299.12	279.88	264.36	251.61	241.00	232.06
23000	2012.46	1051.81	732.47	573.45	478.56	415.73	371.22	338.15	312.71	292.61	276.38	263.05	251.95	242.61
24000	2099.95	1097.54	764.32	598.39	499.37	433.81	387.36	352.86	326.31	305.33	288.39	274.49	262.91	253.15
25000	2187.45	1143.27	796.16	623.32	520.18	451.89	403.50	367.56	339.90	318.05	300.41	285.92	273.86	263.70
26000	2274.95	1189.00	828.01	648.25	540.98	469.96	419.64	382.26	353.50	330.77	312.42	297.36	284.82	274.25
27000	2362.45	1234.73	859.85	673.18	561.79	488.04	435.78	396.96	367.10	343.49	324.44	308.80	295.77	284.80
28000	2449.95	1280.46	891.70	698.12	582.60	506.11	451.92	411.66	380.69	356.21	336.46	320.23	306.72	295.35
29000	2537.44	1326.19	923.55	723.05	603.41	524.19	468.06	426.37	394.29	368.94	348.47	331.67	317.68	305.89
30000	2624.94	1371.92	955.39	747.98	624.21	542.26	484.20	441.07	407.88	381.66	360.49	343.11	328.63	316.44
31000	2712.44	1417.65	987.24	772.91	645.02	560.34	500.34	455.77	421.48	394.38	372.50	354.54	339.59	326.99
32000	2799.94	1463.39	1019.09	797.85	665.83	578.41	516.48	470.47	435.08	407.10	384.52	365.98	350.54	337.54
33000	2887.43	1509.12	1050.93	822.78	686.63	596.49	532.62	485.18	448.67	419.82	396.54	377.42	361.50	348.09
34000	2974.93	1554.85	1082.78	847.71	707.44	614.56	548.76	499.88	462.27	432.54	408.55	388.85	372.45	358.63
35000	3062.43	1600.58	1114.63	872.64	728.25	632.64	564.90	514.58	475.86	445.27	420.57	400.29	383.40	369.18
36000	3149.93	1646.31	1146.47	897.58	749.05	650.71	581.04	529.28	489.46	457.99	432.58	411.73	394.36	379.73
37000	3237.43	1692.04	1178.32	922.51	769.86	668.79	597.18	543.98	503.06	470.71	444.60	423.16	405.31	390.28
38000	3324.92	1737.77	1210.16	947.44	790.67	686.86	613.32	558.69	516.65	483.43	456.62	434.60	416.27	400.83
39000	3412.42	1783.50	1242.01	972.37	811.47	704.94	629.46	573.39	530.25	496.15	468.63	446.04	427.22	411.37
40000	3499.92	1829.23	1273.86	997.31	832.28	723.01	645.60	588.09	543.84	508.88	480.65	457.47	438.18	421.92
41000	3587.42	1874.96	1305.70	1022.24	853.09	741.09	661.74	602.79	557.44	521.60	492.67	468.91	449.13	432.47
42000	3674.91	1920.69	1337.55	1047.17	873.90	759.16	677.88	617.49	571.04	534.32	504.68	480.35	460.08	443.02
43000	3762.41	1966.42	1369.40	1072.10	894.70	777.24	694.02	632.20	584.63	547.04	516.70	491.78	471.04	453.57
44000	3849.91	2012.15	1401.24	1097.04	915.51	795.31	710.16	646.90	598.23	559.76	528.71	503.22	481.99	464.11
45000	3937.41	2057.88	1433.09	1121.97	936.32	813.39	726.30	661.60	611.82	572.48	540.73	514.66	492.95	474.66
46000	4024.91	2103.61	1464.93	1146.90	957.12	831.46	742.44	676.30	625.42	585.21	552.75	526.09	503.90	485.21
47000	4112.40	2149.35	1496.78	1171.84	977.93	849.54	758.58	691.01	639.02	597.93	564.76	537.53	514.86	495.76
48000	4199.90	2195.08	1528.63	1196.77	998.74	867.61	774.72	705.71	652.61	610.65	576.78	548.97	525.81	506.30
49000	4287.40	2240.81	1560.47	1221.70	1019.54	885.69	790.86	720.41	666.21	623.37	588.79	560.40	536.76	516.85
50000	4374.90	2286.54	1592.32	1246.63	1040.35	903.77	807.00	735.11	679.80	636.09	600.81	571.84	547.72	527.40
55000	4812.39	2515.19	1751.55	1371.30	1144.39	994.14	887.70	808.62	747.78	699.70	660.89	629.02	602.49	580.14
60000	5249.88	2743.84	1910.78	1495.96	1248.42	1084.52	968.40	882.13	815.76	763.31	720.97	686.21	657.26	632.88
65000	5687.37	2972.50	2070.01	1620.62	1352.45	1174.89	1049.10	955.64	883.74	826.92	781.05	743.39	712.03	685.62
70000	6124.85	3201.15	2229.25	1745.28	1456.49	1265.27	1129.80	1029.15	951.72	890.53	841.13	800.57	766.80	738.36
75000	6562.34	3429.80	2388.48	1869.95	1560.52	1355.65	1210.50	1102.66	1019.70	954.14	901.21	857.76	821.58	791.10
80000	6999.83	3658.46	2547.71	1994.61	1664.56	1446.02	1291.19	1176.16	1087.68	1017.75	961.29	914.94	876.35	843.84
85000	7437.32	3887.11	2706.94	2119.27	1768.59	1536.40	1371.89	1249.69	1155.66	1081.35	1021.37	972.12	931.12	896.58
90000	7874.81	4115.76	2866.17	2243.93	1872.63	1626.77	1452.59	1323.20	1223.64	1144.96	1081.45	1029.31	985.89	949.32
95000	8312.30	4344.42	3025.40	2368.60	1976.66	1717.15	1533.29	1396.71	1291.62	1208.57	1141.53	1086.49	1040.66	1002.06
100000	8749.79	4573.07	3184.63	2493.26	2080.70	1807.53	1613.99	1470.22	1359.60	1272.18	1201.61	1143.68	1095.43	1054.80

TERM	15 Years	16 Years	17 Years	18 Years	19 Years	20 Years	21 Years	22 Years	23 Years	24 Years	25 Years	30 Years	35 Years	40 Years
AMOUNT														
5	.06	.05	.05	.05	.05	.05	.05	.05	.05	.05	.05	.05	.04	.04
10	.11	.10	.10	.10	.10	.10	.09	.09	.09	.09	.09	.09	.08	.08
15	.16	.15	.15	.15	.14	.14	.14	.14	.13	.13	.13	.13	.12	.12
25	.26	.25	.25	.24	.24	.23	.23	.22	.22	.22	.22	.21	.20	.20
50	.52	.50	.49	.48	.47	.46	.45	.44	.44	.43	.43	.41	.40	.39
75	.77	.75	.73	.71	.70	.68	.67	.66	.65	.65	.64	.61	.60	.59
100	1.03	1.00	.97	.95	.93	.91	.90	.88	.87	.86	.85	.82	.80	.78
200	2.05	1.99	1.93	1.89	1.85	1.82	1.79	1.76	1.74	1.72	1.70	1.63	1.59	1.56
300	3.07	2.98	2.90	2.83	2.77	2.72	2.68	2.64	2.60	2.57	2.54	2.44	2.38	2.34
400	4.09	3.97	3.86	3.78	3.70	3.63	3.57	3.52	3.47	3.43	3.39	3.25	3.17	3.12
500	5.11	4.96	4.83	4.72	4.62	4.54	4.46	4.39	4.33	4.28	4.24	4.06	3.96	3.90
600	6.13	5.95	5.79	5.66	5.54	5.44	5.35	5.27	5.20	5.14	5.08	4.88	4.75	4.68
700	7.15	6.94	6.76	6.60	6.47	6.35	6.24	6.15	6.07	5.99	5.93	5.69	5.55	5.46
800	8.17	7.93	7.72	7.55	7.39	7.25	7.13	7.03	6.93	6.85	6.77	6.50	6.34	6.24
900	9.19	8.92	8.69	8.49	8.31	8.16	8.03	7.91	7.80	7.70	7.62	7.31	7.13	7.02
1000	10.21	9.91	9.65	9.43	9.24	9.07	8.92	8.78	8.66	8.56	8.47	8.12	7.92	7.80
2000	20.41	19.82	19.30	18.86	18.47	18.13	17.83	17.56	17.32	17.11	16.93	16.24	15.83	15.59
3000	30.61	29.72	28.95	28.29	27.70	27.19	26.74	26.34	25.98	25.67	25.39	24.36	23.75	23.38
4000	40.81	39.63	38.60	37.71	36.93	36.25	35.65	35.12	34.64	34.22	33.85	32.48	31.66	31.17
5000	51.02	49.53	48.25	47.14	46.17	45.31	44.56	43.89	43.30	42.78	42.31	40.60	39.58	38.96
6000	61.22	59.44	57.90	56.57	55.40	54.38	53.47	52.67	51.96	51.33	50.77	48.71	47.49	46.75
7000	71.42	69.35	67.55	65.99	64.63	63.44	62.38	61.45	60.62	59.89	59.23	56.83	55.41	54.54
8000	81.62	79.25	77.20	75.42	73.86	72.50	71.29	70.23	69.28	68.44	67.69	64.95	63.32	62.33
9000	91.83	89.16	86.85	84.85	83.10	81.56	80.21	79.01	77.94	77.00	76.15	73.07	71.24	70.12
10000	102.03	99.06	96.50	94.28	92.33	90.62	89.12	87.78	86.60	85.55	84.61	81.19	79.15	77.91
11000	112.23	108.97	106.15	103.70	101.56	99.68	98.03	96.56	95.26	94.10	93.07	89.31	87.07	85.70
12000	122.43	118.87	115.80	113.13	110.79	108.75	106.94	105.34	103.92	102.66	101.53	97.42	94.98	93.49
13000	132.63	128.78	125.45	122.56	120.03	117.81	115.85	114.12	112.58	111.21	109.99	105.54	102.90	101.20
14000	142.84	138.69	135.10	131.98	129.26	126.87	124.76	122.90	121.24	119.77	118.45	113.66	110.81	109.07
15000	153.04	148.59	144.75	141.41	138.49	135.93	133.67	131.67	129.90	128.32	126.91	121.78	118.73	116.87
16000	163.24	158.50	154.40	150.84	147.72	144.99	142.58	140.45	138.56	136.88	135.37	129.90	126.64	124.66
17000	173.44	168.40	164.05	160.26	156.96	154.05	151.49	149.23	147.22	145.43	143.83	138.02	134.56	132.45
18000	183.65	178.31	173.70	169.69	166.19	163.12	160.41	158.01	155.88	153.99	152.29	146.13	142.47	140.24
19000	193.85	188.21	183.35	179.12	175.42	172.18	169.32	166.79	164.54	162.54	160.76	154.25	150.39	148.03
20000	204.05	198.12	193.00	188.55	184.65	181.24	178.23	175.56	173.20	171.09	169.22	162.37	158.30	155.82
21000	214.25	208.03	202.65	197.97	193.89	190.30	187.14	184.34	181.86	179.65	177.68	170.49	166.22	163.61
22000	224.45	217.93	212.30	207.40	203.12	199.36	196.05	193.12	190.52	188.20	186.14	178.61	174.13	171.40
23000	234.66	227.84	221.95	216.83	212.35	208.42	204.96	201.90	199.18	196.76	194.60	186.73	182.05	179.19
24000	244.86	237.74	231.60	226.25	221.58	217.49	213.87	210.67	207.84	205.31	203.06	194.84	189.96	186.98
25000	255.06	247.65	241.25	235.68	230.82	226.55	222.78	219.45	216.50	213.87	211.52	202.96	197.87	194.77
26000	265.26	257.55	250.90	245.11	240.05	235.61	231.69	228.23	225.16	222.42	219.98	211.08	205.79	202.56
27000	275.47	267.46	260.54	254.53	249.28	244.67	240.61	237.01	233.82	230.98	228.44	219.20	213.70	210.35
28000	285.67	277.37	270.19	263.96	258.51	253.73	249.52	245.79	242.48	239.53	236.90	227.32	221.62	218.14
29000	295.87	287.27	279.84	273.39	267.75	262.79	258.43	254.56	251.14	248.08	245.36	235.44	229.53	225.93
30000	306.07	297.18	289.49	282.82	276.98	271.86	267.34	263.34	259.80	256.64	253.82	243.55	237.45	233.73
31000	316.27	307.08	299.14	292.24	286.21	280.92	276.25	272.12	268.46	265.19	262.28	251.67	245.36	241.52
32000	326.48	316.99	308.79	301.67	295.44	289.98	285.16	280.90	277.11	273.75	270.74	259.79	253.28	249.31
33000	336.68	326.89	318.44	311.10	304.68	299.04	294.07	289.68	285.77	282.30	279.20	267.91	261.19	257.10
34000	346.88	336.80	328.09	320.52	313.91	308.10	302.98	298.45	294.43	290.86	287.66	276.03	269.11	264.89
35000	357.08	346.71	337.74	329.95	323.14	317.16	311.89	307.23	303.09	299.41	296.12	284.14	277.02	272.68
36000	367.29	356.61	347.39	339.38	332.37	326.23	320.81	316.01	311.75	307.97	304.58	292.26	284.94	280.47
37000	377.49	366.52	357.04	348.80	341.61	335.29	329.72	324.79	320.41	316.52	313.05	300.38	292.85	288.26
38000	387.69	376.42	366.69	358.23	350.84	344.35	338.63	333.57	329.07	325.07	321.51	308.50	300.77	296.05
39000	397.89	386.33	376.34	367.66	360.07	353.41	347.54	342.34	337.73	333.63	329.97	316.62	308.68	303.84
40000	408.09	396.24	385.99	377.09	369.30	362.47	356.45	351.12	346.39	342.18	338.43	324.74	316.60	311.63
41000	418.30	406.14	395.64	386.51	378.54	371.53	365.36	359.90	355.05	350.74	346.89	332.85	324.51	319.42
42000	428.50	416.05	405.29	395.94	387.77	380.60	374.27	368.68	363.71	359.29	355.35	340.97	332.43	327.21
43000	438.70	425.95	414.94	405.37	397.00	389.66	383.18	377.46	372.37	367.85	363.81	349.09	340.34	335.00
44000	448.90	435.86	424.59	414.79	406.23	398.72	392.09	386.23	381.03	376.40	372.27	357.21	348.26	342.80
45000	459.11	445.76	434.24	424.22	415.47	407.78	401.01	395.01	389.69	384.96	380.73	365.33	356.17	350.59
46000	469.31	455.67	443.89	433.65	424.70	416.84	409.92	403.79	398.35	393.51	389.19	373.45	364.09	358.38
47000	479.51	465.58	453.54	443.07	433.93	425.90	418.83	412.57	407.01	402.06	397.65	381.56	372.00	366.17
48000	489.71	475.48	463.19	452.50	443.16	434.97	427.74	421.34	415.67	410.62	406.11	389.68	379.92	373.96
49000	499.91	485.39	472.84	461.93	452.40	444.03	436.65	430.12	424.33	419.17	414.57	397.80	387.83	381.75
50000	510.12	495.29	482.49	471.36	461.63	453.09	445.56	438.90	432.99	427.73	423.03	405.92	395.74	389.54
55000	561.13	544.82	530.73	518.49	507.79	498.40	490.12	482.79	476.29	470.50	465.34	446.51	435.32	428.49
60000	612.14	594.35	578.98	565.63	553.95	543.71	534.67	526.68	519.59	513.27	507.64	487.10	474.89	467.45
65000	663.15	643.88	627.23	612.76	600.12	589.01	579.23	570.57	562.88	556.04	549.94	527.69	514.47	506.40
70000	714.16	693.41	675.48	659.90	646.28	634.32	623.78	614.46	606.18	598.82	592.24	568.28	554.04	545.35
75000	765.17	742.94	723.73	707.03	692.44	679.63	668.34	658.35	649.48	641.59	634.55	608.88	593.61	584.31
80000	816.18	792.47	771.97	754.17	738.60	724.94	712.89	702.24	692.78	684.36	676.85	649.47	633.19	623.26
85000	867.20	841.99	820.22	801.30	784.76	770.25	757.45	746.13	736.08	727.13	719.15	690.06	672.76	662.21
90000	918.21	891.52	868.47	848.44	830.93	815.56	802.01	790.02	779.38	769.91	761.45	730.65	712.34	701.17
95000	969.22	941.05	916.72	895.57	877.09	860.86	846.56	833.91	822.67	812.68	803.76	771.24	751.91	740.12
100000	1020.23	990.58	964.97	942.71	923.25	906.17	891.12	877.80	865.97	855.45	846.06	811.83	791.48	779.07

MONTHLY PAYMENT
REQUIRED TO AMORTIZE A LOAN

TERM AMOUNT	1 Year	2 Years	3 Years	4 Years	5 Years	6 Years	7 Years	8 Years	9 Years	10 Years	11 Years	12 Years	13 Years	14 Years
5	.44	.23	.16	.13	.11	.10	.09	.08	.07	.07	.07	.06	.06	.06
10	.88	.46	.32	.25	.21	.19	.17	.15	.14	.13	.13	.12	.11	.11
15	1.32	.69	.48	.38	.32	.28	.25	.23	.21	.20	.19	.18	.17	.16
25	2.19	1.15	.80	.63	.53	.46	.41	.37	.35	.32	.31	.29	.28	.27
50	4.38	2.29	1.60	1.25	1.05	.91	.81	.74	.69	.64	.61	.58	.55	.53
75	6.57	3.44	2.39	1.88	1.57	1.36	1.22	1.11	1.03	.96	.91	.86	.83	.80
100	8.76	4.58	3.19	2.50	2.09	1.81	1.62	1.48	1.37	1.28	1.21	1.15	1.10	1.06
200	17.51	9.15	6.38	4.99	4.17	3.62	3.24	2.95	2.73	2.55	2.41	2.30	2.20	2.12
300	26.26	13.73	9.56	7.49	6.25	5.43	4.85	4.42	4.09	3.83	3.61	3.44	3.30	3.17
400	35.01	18.30	12.75	9.98	8.33	7.24	6.47	5.89	5.45	5.10	4.82	4.59	4.39	4.23
500	43.76	22.88	15.93	12.48	10.41	9.05	8.08	7.36	6.81	6.37	6.02	5.73	5.49	5.29
600	52.51	27.45	19.12	14.97	12.50	10.86	9.70	8.83	8.17	7.65	7.22	6.88	6.59	6.34
700	61.26	32.02	22.31	17.47	14.58	12.67	11.31	10.31	9.53	8.92	8.43	8.02	7.68	7.40
800	70.01	36.60	25.49	19.96	16.66	14.48	12.93	11.78	10.89	10.19	9.63	9.17	8.78	8.46
900	78.76	41.17	28.68	22.45	18.74	16.28	14.54	13.25	12.25	11.47	10.83	10.31	9.88	9.51
1000	87.51	45.75	31.86	24.95	20.82	18.09	16.16	14.72	13.61	12.74	12.03	11.46	10.97	10.57
2000	175.02	91.49	63.72	49.89	41.64	36.18	32.31	29.44	27.22	25.48	24.06	22.91	21.94	21.13
3000	262.53	137.23	95.58	74.84	62.46	54.27	48.46	44.15	40.83	38.21	36.09	34.36	32.91	31.69
4000	350.04	182.97	127.44	99.78	83.28	72.36	64.62	58.87	54.44	50.95	48.12	45.81	43.88	42.26
5000	437.55	228.72	159.29	124.73	104.10	90.44	80.77	73.58	68.05	63.68	60.15	57.26	54.85	52.82
6000	525.06	274.46	191.15	149.67	124.92	108.53	96.92	88.30	81.66	76.42	72.18	68.71	65.82	63.38
7000	612.57	320.20	223.01	174.62	145.74	126.62	113.07	103.01	95.27	89.15	84.21	80.16	76.79	73.94
8000	700.08	365.94	254.87	199.56	166.56	144.71	129.23	117.73	108.88	101.89	96.24	91.61	87.75	84.51
9000	787.59	411.68	286.73	224.50	187.38	162.79	145.38	132.44	122.49	114.62	108.27	103.06	98.72	95.07
10000	875.10	457.43	318.58	249.45	208.20	180.88	161.53	147.16	136.10	127.36	120.30	114.51	109.69	105.63
11000	962.61	503.17	350.44	274.39	229.01	198.97	177.68	161.87	149.71	140.09	132.33	125.96	120.66	116.19
12000	1050.12	548.91	382.30	299.34	249.83	217.06	193.84	176.59	163.32	152.83	144.36	137.41	131.63	126.76
13000	1137.63	594.65	414.16	324.28	270.65	235.14	209.99	191.30	176.93	165.56	156.39	148.87	142.60	137.32
14000	1225.14	640.39	446.02	349.23	291.47	253.23	226.14	206.02	190.53	178.30	168.42	160.32	153.57	147.88
15000	1312.65	686.14	477.87	374.17	312.29	271.32	242.29	220.73	204.14	191.03	180.45	171.77	164.54	158.44
16000	1400.16	731.88	509.73	399.12	333.11	289.41	258.45	235.45	217.75	203.77	192.48	183.22	175.50	169.01
17000	1487.67	777.62	541.59	424.06	353.93	307.49	274.60	250.16	231.36	216.51	204.51	194.67	186.47	179.57
18000	1575.18	823.36	573.45	449.00	374.75	325.58	290.75	264.88	244.97	229.24	216.54	206.12	197.44	190.13
19000	1662.68	869.11	605.31	473.95	395.57	343.67	306.90	279.59	258.58	241.98	228.57	217.57	208.41	200.69
20000	1750.19	914.85	637.16	498.89	416.39	361.76	323.06	294.31	272.19	254.71	240.60	229.02	219.38	211.26
21000	1837.70	960.59	669.02	523.84	437.21	379.85	339.21	309.02	285.80	267.45	252.63	240.47	230.35	221.82
22000	1925.21	1006.33	700.88	548.78	458.02	397.93	355.36	323.74	299.41	280.18	264.66	251.92	241.32	232.38
23000	2012.72	1052.07	732.74	573.73	478.84	416.02	371.51	338.45	313.02	292.92	276.69	263.37	252.28	242.94
24000	2100.23	1097.82	764.60	598.67	499.66	434.11	387.67	353.17	326.63	305.65	288.72	274.82	263.25	253.51
25000	2187.74	1143.56	796.45	623.62	520.48	452.20	403.82	367.88	340.24	318.39	300.75	286.28	274.22	264.07
26000	2275.25	1189.30	828.31	648.56	541.30	470.28	419.97	382.60	353.85	331.12	312.78	297.73	285.19	274.63
27000	2362.76	1235.04	860.17	673.50	562.12	488.37	436.12	397.31	367.45	343.86	324.81	309.18	296.16	285.19
28000	2450.27	1280.78	892.03	698.45	582.94	506.46	452.28	412.03	381.06	356.59	336.84	320.63	307.13	295.76
29000	2537.78	1326.53	923.89	723.39	603.76	524.55	468.43	426.74	394.67	369.33	348.87	332.08	318.10	306.32
30000	2625.28	1372.27	955.74	748.34	624.58	542.63	484.58	441.46	408.28	382.06	360.90	343.53	329.07	316.88
31000	2712.80	1418.01	987.60	773.28	645.40	560.72	500.74	456.17	421.89	394.80	372.93	354.98	340.03	327.44
32000	2800.31	1463.75	1019.46	798.23	666.22	578.81	516.89	470.89	435.50	407.54	384.96	366.43	351.00	338.01
33000	2887.82	1509.49	1051.32	823.17	687.03	596.90	533.04	485.60	449.11	420.27	396.99	377.88	361.97	348.57
34000	2975.33	1555.24	1083.18	848.12	707.85	614.98	549.19	500.32	462.72	433.01	409.02	389.33	372.94	359.13
35000	3062.84	1600.98	1115.03	873.06	728.67	633.07	565.35	515.03	476.33	445.74	421.05	400.78	383.91	369.69
36000	3150.35	1646.72	1146.89	898.00	749.49	651.16	581.50	529.75	489.94	458.48	433.08	412.23	394.88	380.26
37000	3237.85	1692.46	1178.75	922.95	770.31	669.25	597.65	544.46	503.55	471.21	445.11	423.69	405.85	390.82
38000	3325.36	1738.21	1210.61	947.89	791.13	687.34	613.80	559.18	517.16	483.95	457.14	435.14	416.81	401.38
39000	3412.87	1783.95	1242.46	972.84	811.95	705.42	629.96	573.90	530.77	496.68	469.17	446.59	427.78	411.95
40000	3500.38	1829.69	1274.32	997.78	832.77	723.51	646.11	588.61	544.38	509.42	481.20	458.04	438.75	422.51
41000	3587.89	1875.43	1306.18	1022.73	853.59	741.60	662.26	603.33	557.98	522.15	493.23	469.49	449.72	433.07
42000	3675.40	1921.17	1338.04	1047.67	874.41	759.69	678.41	618.04	571.59	534.89	505.26	480.94	460.69	443.63
43000	3762.91	1966.92	1369.90	1072.62	895.23	777.77	694.57	632.76	585.20	547.62	517.29	492.39	471.66	454.20
44000	3850.42	2012.66	1401.75	1097.56	916.04	795.86	710.72	647.47	598.81	560.36	529.32	503.84	482.63	464.76
45000	3937.93	2058.40	1433.61	1122.50	936.86	813.95	726.87	662.19	612.42	573.09	541.35	515.29	493.60	475.32
46000	4025.44	2104.14	1465.47	1147.45	957.68	832.04	743.02	676.90	626.03	585.83	553.38	526.74	504.56	485.88
47000	4112.95	2149.88	1497.33	1172.39	978.50	850.12	759.18	691.62	639.64	598.57	565.41	538.19	515.53	496.45
48000	4200.46	2195.63	1529.19	1197.34	999.32	868.21	775.33	706.33	653.25	611.30	577.44	549.64	526.50	507.01
49000	4287.97	2241.37	1561.04	1222.28	1020.14	886.30	791.48	721.05	666.86	624.04	589.47	561.10	537.47	517.57
50000	4375.48	2287.11	1592.90	1247.23	1040.96	904.39	807.63	735.76	680.47	636.77	601.50	572.55	548.44	528.13
55000	4813.02	2515.82	1752.19	1371.95	1145.05	994.83	888.40	809.34	748.51	700.45	661.65	629.80	603.28	580.95
60000	5250.57	2744.53	1911.48	1496.67	1249.15	1085.26	969.16	882.91	816.56	764.12	721.80	687.05	658.13	633.76
65000	5688.12	2973.24	2070.77	1621.39	1353.24	1175.70	1049.92	956.49	884.61	827.80	781.95	744.31	712.97	686.57
70000	6125.67	3201.95	2230.06	1746.12	1457.34	1266.14	1130.69	1030.06	952.65	891.48	842.10	801.56	767.81	739.38
75000	6563.21	3430.66	2389.35	1870.84	1561.44	1356.58	1211.45	1103.64	1020.70	955.15	902.25	858.82	822.66	792.20
80000	7000.76	3659.37	2548.64	1995.56	1665.53	1447.02	1292.21	1177.22	1088.75	1018.83	962.40	916.07	877.50	845.01
85000	7438.31	3888.08	2707.93	2120.28	1769.63	1537.45	1372.98	1250.79	1156.79	1082.51	1022.55	973.32	932.34	897.82
90000	7875.86	4116.80	2867.22	2245.00	1873.72	1627.89	1453.74	1324.37	1224.84	1146.18	1082.70	1030.58	987.19	950.64
95000	8313.40	4345.51	3026.51	2369.73	1977.82	1718.33	1534.50	1397.94	1292.88	1209.86	1142.85	1087.83	1042.03	1003.45
100000	8750.95	4574.22	3185.80	2494.45	2081.91	1808.77	1615.26	1471.52	1360.93	1273.54	1203.00	1145.09	1096.87	1056.26

TERM AMOUNT	15 Years	16 Years	17 Years	18 Years	19 Years	20 Years	21 Years	22 Years	23 Years	24 Years	25 Years	30 Years	35 Years	40 Years
5	.06	.05	.05	.05	.05	.05	.05	.05	.05	.05	.05	.05	.04	.04
10	.11	.10	.10	.10	.10	.10	.09	.09	.09	.09	.09	.09	.08	.08
15	.16	.15	.15	.15	.14	.14	.14	.14	.14	.13	.13	.13	.12	.12
25	.26	.25	.25	.24	.24	.23	.23	.22	.22	.22	.22	.21	.20	.20
50	.52	.50	.49	.48	.47	.46	.45	.44	.44	.43	.43	.41	.40	.40
75	.77	.75	.73	.71	.70	.69	.67	.66	.66	.65	.64	.62	.60	.59
100	1.03	1.00	.97	.95	.93	.91	.90	.88	.87	.86	.85	.82	.80	.79
200	2.05	1.99	1.94	1.89	1.85	1.82	1.79	1.76	1.74	1.72	1.70	1.63	1.59	1.57
300	3.07	2.98	2.90	2.84	2.78	2.73	2.68	2.64	2.61	2.58	2.55	2.45	2.39	2.35
400	4.09	3.97	3.87	3.78	3.70	3.64	3.58	3.52	3.48	3.43	3.40	3.26	3.18	3.13
500	5.11	4.97	4.84	4.73	4.63	4.54	4.47	4.40	4.34	4.29	4.24	4.07	3.97	3.91
600	6.14	5.96	5.80	5.67	5.55	5.45	5.36	5.28	5.21	5.15	5.09	4.89	4.77	4.69
700	7.16	6.95	6.77	6.61	6.48	6.36	6.25	6.16	6.08	6.01	5.94	5.70	5.56	5.47
800	8.18	7.94	7.74	7.56	7.40	7.27	7.15	7.04	6.95	6.86	6.79	6.51	6.35	6.25
900	9.20	8.93	8.70	8.50	8.33	8.18	8.04	7.92	7.81	7.72	7.63	7.33	7.15	7.03
1000	10.22	9.93	9.67	9.45	9.25	9.08	8.93	8.80	8.68	8.58	8.48	8.14	7.94	7.81
2000	20.44	19.85	19.34	18.89	18.50	18.16	17.86	17.59	17.36	17.15	16.96	16.28	15.87	15.62
3000	30.66	29.77	29.00	28.33	27.75	27.24	26.79	26.39	26.03	25.72	25.44	24.41	23.81	23.43
4000	40.87	39.69	38.67	37.78	37.00	36.32	35.71	35.18	34.71	34.29	33.92	32.55	31.74	31.24
5000	51.09	49.61	48.33	47.22	46.25	45.39	44.64	43.98	43.39	42.86	42.39	40.69	39.67	39.05
6000	61.31	59.53	58.00	56.66	55.50	54.47	53.57	52.77	52.06	51.43	50.87	48.82	47.61	46.86
7000	71.53	69.45	67.66	66.10	64.74	63.55	62.50	61.57	60.74	60.01	59.35	56.96	55.54	54.67
8000	81.74	79.37	77.33	75.55	73.99	72.63	71.42	70.36	69.42	68.58	67.83	65.10	63.47	62.48
9000	91.96	89.29	86.99	84.99	83.24	81.71	80.35	79.16	78.09	77.15	76.30	73.23	71.41	70.29
10000	102.18	99.21	96.66	94.43	92.49	90.78	89.28	87.95	86.77	85.72	84.78	81.37	79.34	78.10
11000	112.39	109.14	106.32	103.87	101.74	99.86	98.21	96.74	95.45	94.29	93.26	89.50	87.27	85.91
12000	122.61	119.06	115.99	113.32	110.99	108.94	107.13	105.54	104.12	102.86	101.74	97.64	95.21	93.72
13000	132.83	128.98	125.65	122.76	120.23	118.02	116.06	114.33	112.80	111.43	110.22	105.78	103.14	101.53
14000	143.05	138.90	135.32	132.20	129.48	127.09	124.99	123.13	121.48	120.01	118.69	113.91	111.07	109.34
15000	153.26	148.82	144.98	141.65	138.73	136.17	133.92	131.92	130.15	128.58	127.17	122.05	119.01	117.15
16000	163.48	158.74	154.65	151.09	147.98	145.25	142.84	140.72	138.83	137.15	135.65	130.19	126.94	124.96
17000	173.70	168.66	164.31	160.53	157.23	154.33	151.77	149.51	147.50	145.72	144.13	130.32	134.88	132.77
18000	183.91	178.58	173.98	169.97	166.48	163.41	160.70	158.31	156.18	154.29	152.60	146.46	142.81	140.58
19000	194.13	188.50	183.64	179.42	175.72	172.48	169.63	167.10	164.86	162.86	161.08	154.60	150.74	140.39
20000	204.35	198.42	193.31	188.86	184.97	181.56	178.55	175.89	173.53	171.43	169.56	162.73	158.68	156.20
21000	214.57	208.34	202.97	198.30	194.22	190.64	187.48	184.69	182.21	180.01	178.04	170.87	166.61	164.01
22000	224.78	218.27	212.64	207.74	203.47	199.72	196.41	193.48	190.89	188.58	186.52	179.00	174.54	171.82
23000	235.00	228.19	222.30	217.19	212.72	208.79	205.34	202.28	199.56	197.15	194.99	187.14	182.48	179.63
24000	245.22	230.11	231.97	226.63	221.97	217.87	214.26	211.07	208.24	205.72	203.47	195.28	190.41	187.44
25000	255.43	248.03	241.63	236.07	231.21	226.95	223.19	219.87	216.92	214.29	211.95	203.41	198.34	195.25
26000	265.65	257.95	251.30	245.51	240.46	236.03	232.12	228.66	225.59	222.86	220.43	211.55	206.28	203.06
27000	275.87	267.87	260.96	254.96	249.71	245.11	241.05	237.46	234.27	231.43	228.90	219.69	214.21	210.87
28000	286.09	277.79	270.63	264.40	258.96	254.18	249.97	246.25	242.95	240.01	237.38	227.82	222.14	218.68
29000	296.30	287.71	280.29	273.84	268.21	263.26	258.90	255.04	251.62	248.58	245.86	235.96	230.08	226.49
30000	306.52	297.63	289.96	283.29	277.46	272.34	267.83	263.84	260.30	257.15	254.34	244.09	238.01	234.30
31000	316.74	307.55	299.62	292.73	286.70	281.42	276.76	272.63	268.98	265.72	262.81	252.23	245.94	242.11
32000	326.95	317.47	309.29	302.17	295.95	290.49	285.68	281.43	277.65	274.29	271.29	260.37	253.88	249.92
33000	337.17	327.40	318.95	311.61	305.20	299.57	294.61	290.22	286.33	282.86	279.77	268.50	261.81	257.73
34000	347.39	337.32	328.62	321.06	314.45	308.65	303.54	299.02	295.00	291.43	288.25	276.64	269.75	265.54
35000	357.61	347.24	338.28	330.50	323.70	317.73	312.47	307.81	303.68	300.01	296.73	284.78	277.68	273.35
36000	367.82	357.16	347.95	339.94	332.95	326.81	321.39	316.61	312.36	308.58	305.20	292.91	285.61	281.16
37000	378.04	367.08	357.61	349.38	342.19	335.88	330.32	325.40	321.03	317.15	313.68	301.05	293.55	288.97
38000	388.26	377.00	367.28	358.83	351.44	344.96	339.25	334.20	329.71	325.72	322.16	309.19	301.48	296.78
39000	398.47	386.92	376.94	368.27	360.69	354.04	348.18	342.99	338.39	334.29	330.64	317.32	309.41	304.59
40000	408.69	396.84	386.61	377.71	369.94	363.12	357.10	351.78	347.06	342.86	339.11	325.46	317.35	312.40
41000	418.91	406.76	396.27	387.15	379.19	372.20	366.03	360.58	355.74	351.43	347.59	333.59	325.28	320.21
42000	429.13	416.68	405.94	396.60	388.44	381.27	374.96	369.37	364.42	360.01	356.07	341.73	333.21	328.02
43000	439.34	426.60	415.60	406.04	397.68	390.35	383.89	378.17	373.09	368.58	364.55	349.87	341.15	335.83
44000	449.56	436.53	425.27	415.48	406.93	399.43	392.81	386.96	381.77	377.15	373.03	358.00	349.08	343.64
45000	459.78	446.45	434.93	424.93	416.18	408.51	401.74	395.76	390.45	385.72	381.50	366.14	357.01	351.45
46000	469.99	456.37	444.60	434.37	425.43	417.58	410.67	404.55	399.12	394.29	389.98	374.28	364.95	359.26
47000	480.21	466.29	454.26	443.81	434.68	426.66	419.60	413.35	407.80	402.86	398.46	382.41	372.88	367.07
48000	490.43	476.21	463.93	453.25	443.93	435.74	428.52	422.14	416.48	411.43	406.94	390.55	380.81	374.88
49000	500.65	486.13	473.59	462.70	453.18	444.82	437.45	430.93	425.15	420.01	415.41	398.69	388.75	382.69
50000	510.86	496.05	483.26	472.14	462.42	453.90	446.38	439.73	433.83	428.58	423.89	406.82	396.68	390.50
55000	561.95	545.66	531.58	519.35	508.67	499.28	491.02	483.70	477.21	471.43	466.28	447.50	436.35	429.55
60000	613.03	595.26	579.91	566.57	554.91	544.67	535.65	527.67	520.59	514.29	508.67	488.18	476.02	468.60
65000	664.12	644.87	628.23	613.78	601.15	590.06	580.29	571.65	563.98	557.15	551.06	528.87	515.68	507.65
70000	715.21	694.47	676.56	660.99	647.39	635.45	624.93	615.62	607.36	600.01	593.45	569.55	555.35	546.70
75000	766.29	744.07	724.88	708.21	693.63	680.84	669.57	659.59	650.74	642.86	635.83	610.23	595.02	585.75
80000	817.38	793.68	773.21	755.42	739.87	726.23	714.20	703.56	694.12	685.72	678.22	650.91	634.69	624.80
85000	868.46	843.28	821.53	802.63	786.12	771.62	758.84	747.54	737.50	728.58	720.61	691.59	674.36	663.85
90000	919.55	892.89	869.86	849.85	832.36	817.01	803.48	791.51	780.89	771.43	763.00	732.27	714.02	702.90
95000	970.64	942.49	918.18	897.06	878.60	862.40	848.11	835.48	824.27	814.29	805.39	772.96	753.69	741.95
100000	1021.72	992.10	966.51	944.27	924.84	907.79	892.75	879.45	867.65	857.15	847.78	813.64	793.36	781.00

MONTHLY PAYMENT
REQUIRED TO AMORTIZE A LOAN

TERM	1 Year	2 Years	3 Years	4 Years	5 Years	6 Years	7 Years	8 Years	9 Years	10 Years	11 Years	12 Years	13 Years	14 Years
AMOUNT														
5	.44	.23	.18	.13	.11	.10	.09	.08	.07	.07	.07	.06	.06	.06
10	.88	.46	.32	.25	.21	.19	.17	.15	.14	.13	.13	.12	.12	.11
15	1.32	.69	.48	.38	.32	.28	.25	.23	.21	.20	.19	.18	.17	.16
25	2.19	1.15	.80	.63	.53	.46	.41	.37	.35	.32	.31	.29	.28	.27
50	4.38	2.29	1.60	1.25	1.05	.91	.81	.74	.69	.64	.61	.58	.56	.54
75	6.57	3.44	2.40	1.88	1.57	1.36	1.22	1.11	1.03	.96	.91	.87	.83	.80
100	8.76	4.58	3.19	2.50	2.09	1.82	1.62	1.48	1.37	1.28	1.21	1.15	1.11	1.07
200	17.51	9.16	6.38	5.00	4.18	3.63	3.24	2.96	2.73	2.56	2.42	2.30	2.21	2.13
300	26.27	13.74	9.57	7.50	6.26	5.44	4.86	4.43	4.10	3.84	3.63	3.45	3.31	3.19
400	35.02	18.32	12.76	10.00	8.35	7.25	6.48	5.91	5.46	5.12	4.83	4.60	4.41	4.25
500	43.78	22.89	15.95	12.50	10.43	9.07	8.10	7.38	6.83	6.39	6.04	5.75	5.51	5.31
600	52.53	27.47	19.14	14.99	12.52	10.88	9.72	8.86	8.19	7.67	7.25	6.90	6.61	6.37
700	61.29	32.05	22.33	17.49	14.60	12.69	11.34	10.33	9.56	8.95	8.46	8.05	7.71	7.43
800	70.04	36.63	25.52	19.99	16.69	14.50	12.96	11.81	10.92	10.23	9.66	9.20	8.81	8.49
900	78.79	41.20	28.71	22.49	18.78	16.32	14.58	13.28	12.29	11.50	10.87	10.35	9.92	9.55
1000	87.55	45.78	31.90	24.99	20.86	18.13	16.20	14.76	13.65	12.78	12.08	11.50	11.02	10.61
2000	175.09	91.56	63.79	49.97	41.72	36.25	32.39	29.51	27.30	25.56	24.15	22.99	22.03	21.22
3000	262.64	137.33	95.68	74.95	62.57	54.38	48.58	44.27	40.95	38.33	36.22	34.48	33.04	31.82
4000	350.18	183.11	127.58	99.93	83.43	72.50	64.77	59.02	54.60	51.11	48.29	45.98	44.05	42.43
5000	437.73	228.89	159.47	124.91	104.28	90.63	80.96	73.78	68.25	63.89	60.36	57.47	55.06	53.04
6000	525.27	274.66	191.36	149.89	125.14	108.75	97.15	88.53	81.90	76.66	72.43	68.96	66.08	63.64
7000	612.81	320.44	223.26	174.87	145.99	126.88	113.34	103.28	95.55	89.44	84.51	80.46	77.09	74.25
8000	700.36	366.22	255.15	199.85	166.85	145.00	129.53	118.04	109.20	102.21	96.58	91.95	88.10	84.86
9000	787.90	411.99	287.04	224.83	187.71	163.13	145.72	132.79	122.85	114.99	108.65	103.44	99.11	95.46
10000	875.45	457.77	318.93	249.81	208.56	181.25	161.91	147.55	136.50	127.77	120.72	114.94	110.12	106.07
11000	962.99	503.55	350.83	274.79	229.42	199.38	178.10	162.30	150.15	140.54	132.79	126.43	121.14	116.68
12000	1050.54	549.32	382.72	299.77	250.27	217.50	194.29	177.05	163.79	153.32	144.86	137.92	132.15	127.28
13000	1138.08	595.10	414.61	324.75	271.13	235.63	210.48	191.81	177.44	166.09	156.93	149.42	143.16	137.89
14000	1225.62	640.88	446.51	349.73	291.98	253.75	226.68	206.56	191.09	178.87	169.01	160.91	154.17	148.50
15000	1313.17	686.65	478.40	374.71	312.84	271.88	242.87	221.32	204.74	191.65	181.08	172.40	165.18	159.10
16000	1400.71	732.43	510.29	399.69	333.69	290.00	259.06	236.07	218.39	204.42	193.15	183.90	176.20	169.71
17000	1488.26	778.21	542.18	424.67	354.55	308.13	275.25	250.83	232.04	217.20	205.22	195.39	187.21	180.32
18000	1575.80	823.98	574.08	449.65	375.41	326.25	291.44	265.58	245.69	229.97	217.29	206.88	198.22	190.92
19000	1663.35	869.76	605.97	474.63	396.26	344.38	307.63	280.33	259.34	242.75	229.36	218.38	209.23	201.53
20000	1750.89	915.54	637.86	499.61	417.12	362.50	323.82	295.09	272.99	255.53	241.44	229.87	220.24	212.14
21000	1838.43	961.31	669.76	524.59	437.97	380.63	340.01	309.84	286.64	268.30	253.51	241.36	231.26	222.74
22000	1925.98	1007.09	701.65	549.57	458.83	398.75	356.20	324.60	300.29	281.08	265.58	252.86	242.27	233.35
23000	2013.52	1052.87	733.54	574.55	479.68	416.88	372.39	339.35	313.94	293.85	277.65	264.35	253.28	243.96
24000	2101.07	1098.64	765.43	599.53	500.54	435.00	388.58	354.10	327.58	306.63	289.72	275.84	264.29	254.56
25000	2188.61	1144.42	797.33	624.51	521.39	453.13	404.77	368.86	341.23	319.41	301.79	287.34	275.30	265.17
26000	2276.16	1190.20	829.22	649.49	542.25	471.25	420.96	383.61	354.88	332.18	313.86	298.83	286.31	275.78
27000	2363.70	1235.97	861.11	674.47	563.11	489.38	437.16	398.37	368.53	344.96	325.94	310.32	297.33	286.38
28000	2451.24	1281.75	893.01	699.45	583.96	507.50	453.35	413.12	382.18	357.73	338.01	321.82	308.34	296.99
29000	2538.79	1327.53	924.90	724.43	604.82	525.63	469.54	427.88	395.83	370.51	350.08	333.31	319.35	307.60
30000	2626.33	1373.30	956.79	749.41	625.67	543.75	485.73	442.63	409.48	383.29	362.15	344.80	330.36	318.20
31000	2713.88	1419.08	988.68	774.39	646.53	561.88	501.92	457.38	423.13	396.06	374.22	356.30	341.37	328.81
32000	2801.42	1464.85	1020.58	799.37	667.38	580.00	518.11	472.14	436.78	408.84	386.29	367.79	352.39	339.42
33000	2888.97	1510.63	1052.47	824.35	688.24	598.13	534.30	486.89	450.43	421.62	398.37	379.28	363.40	350.02
34000	2976.51	1556.41	1084.36	849.33	709.09	616.25	550.49	501.65	464.08	434.39	410.44	390.78	374.41	360.63
35000	3064.05	1602.18	1116.26	874.31	729.95	634.38	566.68	516.40	477.73	447.17	422.51	402.27	385.42	371.24
36000	3151.60	1647.96	1148.15	899.29	750.81	652.50	582.87	531.15	491.37	459.94	434.58	413.76	396.43	381.84
37000	3239.14	1693.74	1180.04	924.27	771.66	670.63	599.06	545.91	505.02	472.72	446.65	425.25	407.45	392.45
38000	3326.69	1739.51	1211.94	949.25	792.52	688.75	615.25	560.66	518.67	485.50	458.72	436.75	418.46	403.06
39000	3414.23	1785.29	1243.83	974.23	813.37	706.88	631.44	575.42	532.32	498.27	470.79	448.24	429.47	413.66
40000	3501.78	1831.07	1275.72	999.21	834.23	725.00	647.64	590.17	545.97	511.05	482.87	459.73	440.48	424.27
41000	3589.32	1876.84	1307.61	1024.19	855.08	743.13	663.83	604.93	559.62	523.82	494.94	471.23	451.49	434.88
42000	3676.86	1922.62	1339.51	1049.17	875.94	761.25	680.02	619.68	573.27	536.60	507.01	482.72	462.51	445.48
43000	3764.41	1968.40	1371.40	1074.15	896.79	779.38	696.21	634.43	586.92	549.38	519.08	494.21	473.52	456.09
44000	3851.95	2014.17	1403.29	1099.13	917.65	797.50	712.40	649.19	600.57	562.15	531.15	505.71	484.53	466.70
45000	3939.50	2059.95	1435.19	1124.11	938.51	815.63	728.59	663.94	614.22	574.93	543.22	517.20	495.54	477.30
46000	4027.04	2105.73	1467.08	1149.09	959.36	833.75	744.78	678.70	627.87	587.70	555.30	528.69	506.55	487.91
47000	4114.58	2151.50	1498.97	1174.07	980.22	851.88	760.97	693.45	641.51	600.48	567.37	540.19	517.56	498.52
48000	4202.13	2197.28	1530.86	1199.05	1001.07	870.00	777.16	708.20	655.16	613.26	579.44	551.68	528.58	509.12
49000	4289.67	2243.06	1562.76	1224.03	1021.93	888.13	793.35	722.96	668.81	626.03	591.51	563.17	539.59	519.73
50000	4377.22	2288.83	1594.65	1249.01	1042.78	906.25	809.54	737.71	682.46	638.81	603.58	574.67	550.60	530.34
55000	4814.94	2517.72	1754.11	1373.91	1147.06	996.88	890.50	811.48	750.71	702.69	663.94	632.13	605.66	583.37
60000	5252.66	2746.60	1913.58	1498.81	1251.34	1087.50	971.45	885.25	818.95	766.57	724.30	689.60	660.72	636.40
65000	5690.38	2975.48	2073.04	1623.71	1355.62	1178.13	1052.40	959.03	887.20	830.45	784.65	747.07	715.78	689.43
70000	6128.10	3204.36	2232.51	1748.61	1459.89	1268.75	1133.36	1032.80	955.45	894.33	845.01	804.53	770.84	742.47
75000	6565.82	3433.25	2391.97	1873.51	1564.17	1359.38	1214.31	1106.57	1023.69	958.21	905.37	862.00	825.90	795.50
80000	7003.55	3662.13	2551.44	1998.41	1668.45	1450.00	1295.27	1180.34	1091.94	1022.09	965.73	919.46	880.96	848.53
85000	7441.27	3891.01	2710.90	2123.32	1772.73	1540.63	1376.22	1254.11	1160.18	1085.97	1026.09	976.93	936.02	901.57
90000	7878.99	4119.90	2870.37	2248.22	1877.01	1631.25	1457.17	1327.88	1228.43	1149.85	1086.44	1034.40	991.08	954.60
95000	8316.71	4348.78	3029.83	2373.12	1981.28	1721.88	1538.13	1401.65	1296.67	1213.73	1146.80	1091.86	1046.14	1007.63
100000	8754.43	4577.66	3189.29	2498.02	2085.56	1812.50	1619.08	1475.42	1364.92	1277.61	1207.16	1149.33	1101.20	1060.67

TERM	15 Years	16 Years	17 Years	18 Years	19 Years	20 Years	21 Years	22 Years	23 Years	24 Years	25 Years	30 Years	35 Years	40 Years
AMOUNT														
5	.06	.05	.05	.05	.05	.05	.05	.05	.05	.05	.05	.05	.04	.04
10	.11	.10	.10	.10	.10	.10	.09	.09	.09	.09	.09	.09	.08	.08
15	.16	.15	.15	.15	.14	.14	.14	.14	.14	.13	.13	.13	.12	.12
25	.26	.25	.25	.24	.24	.23	.23	.23	.22	.22	.22	.21	.20	.20
50	.52	.50	.49	.48	.47	.46	.45	.45	.44	.44	.43	.41	.40	.40
75	.77	.75	.73	.72	.70	.69	.68	.67	.66	.65	.64	.62	.60	.60
100	1.03	1.00	.98	.95	.93	.92	.90	.89	.88	.87	.86	.82	.80	.79
200	2.06	2.00	1.95	1.90	1.86	1.83	1.80	1.77	1.75	1.73	1.71	1.64	1.60	1.58
300	3.08	2.99	2.92	2.85	2.79	2.74	2.70	2.66	2.62	2.59	2.56	2.46	2.40	2.37
400	4.11	3.99	3.89	3.80	3.72	3.66	3.60	3.54	3.50	3.45	3.42	3.28	3.20	3.15
500	5.14	4.99	4.86	4.75	4.65	4.57	4.49	4.43	4.37	4.32	4.27	4.10	4.00	3.94
600	6.16	5.98	5.83	5.70	5.58	5.48	5.39	5.31	5.24	5.18	5.12	4.92	4.80	4.73
700	7.19	6.98	6.80	6.65	6.51	6.39	6.29	6.20	6.11	6.04	5.98	5.74	5.60	5.51
800	8.21	7.98	7.77	7.60	7.44	7.31	7.19	7.08	6.99	6.90	6.83	6.56	6.40	6.30
900	9.24	8.97	8.75	8.55	8.37	8.22	8.08	7.96	7.86	7.77	7.68	7.38	7.20	7.09
1000	10.27	9.97	9.72	9.49	9.30	9.13	8.98	8.85	8.73	8.63	8.53	8.20	7.99	7.87
2000	20.53	19.94	19.43	18.98	18.60	18.26	17.96	17.69	17.46	17.25	17.06	16.39	15.98	15.74
3000	30.79	29.90	29.14	28.47	27.89	27.38	26.93	26.54	26.19	25.87	25.59	24.58	23.97	23.61
4000	41.05	39.87	38.85	37.96	37.19	36.51	35.91	35.38	34.91	34.49	34.12	32.77	31.96	31.48
5000	51.31	49.84	48.56	47.45	46.49	45.64	44.89	44.23	43.64	43.12	42.65	40.96	39.95	39.34
6000	61.58	59.80	58.27	56.94	55.78	54.76	53.86	53.07	52.37	51.74	51.18	49.15	47.94	47.21
7000	71.84	69.77	67.98	66.43	65.08	63.89	62.84	61.91	61.09	60.36	59.71	57.34	55.93	55.08
8000	82.10	79.74	77.70	75.92	74.37	73.02	71.82	70.76	69.82	68.98	68.24	65.53	63.92	62.95
9000	92.36	89.70	87.41	85.41	83.67	82.14	80.79	79.60	78.55	77.61	76.77	73.72	71.91	70.82
10000	102.62	99.67	97.12	94.90	92.97	91.27	89.77	88.45	87.27	86.23	85.30	81.91	79.90	78.68
11000	112.89	109.64	106.83	104.39	102.26	100.39	98.75	97.29	96.00	94.85	93.83	90.10	87.89	86.55
12000	123.15	119.60	116.54	113.88	111.56	109.52	107.72	106.14	104.73	103.47	102.36	98.29	95.88	94.42
13000	133.41	129.57	126.25	123.37	120.86	118.65	116.70	114.98	113.45	112.10	110.89	106.48	103.87	102.29
14000	143.67	139.54	135.96	132.86	130.15	127.77	125.68	123.82	122.18	120.72	119.42	114.67	111.86	110.16
15000	153.93	149.50	145.68	142.35	139.45	136.90	134.65	132.67	130.91	129.34	127.95	122.86	119.85	118.02
16000	164.20	159.47	155.39	151.84	148.74	146.03	143.63	141.51	139.64	137.96	136.47	131.05	127.84	125.89
17000	174.46	169.44	165.10	161.33	158.04	155.15	152.61	150.36	148.36	146.59	145.00	139.24	135.83	133.76
18000	184.72	179.40	174.81	170.82	167.34	164.28	161.58	159.20	157.09	155.21	153.53	147.43	143.82	141.63
19000	194.98	189.37	184.52	180.31	176.63	173.40	170.56	168.05	165.82	163.83	162.06	155.63	151.81	149.50
20000	205.24	199.34	194.23	189.80	185.93	182.53	179.54	176.89	174.54	172.45	170.59	163.82	159.80	157.36
21000	215.51	209.30	203.94	199.29	195.22	191.66	188.51	185.73	183.27	181.08	179.12	172.01	167.79	165.23
22000	225.77	219.27	213.66	208.78	204.52	200.78	197.49	194.58	192.00	189.70	187.65	180.20	175.78	173.10
23000	236.03	229.23	223.37	218.27	213.82	209.91	206.47	203.42	200.72	198.32	196.18	188.39	103.77	180.97
24000	246.29	239.20	233.08	227.76	223.11	219.04	215.44	212.27	209.45	206.94	204.71	196.58	191.76	188.84
25000	256.55	249.17	242.79	237.25	232.41	228.16	224.42	221.11	218.18	215.57	213.24	204.77	199.75	196.70
26000	266.82	259.13	252.50	246.74	241.71	237.29	233.40	229.96	226.90	224.19	221.77	212.96	207.74	204.57
27000	277.08	269.10	262.21	256.23	251.00	246.41	242.37	238.80	235.63	232.81	230.30	221.15	215.73	212.44
28000	287.34	279.07	271.92	265.72	260.30	255.54	251.35	247.64	244.36	241.43	238.83	229.34	223.72	220.31
29000	297.60	289.03	281.64	275.21	269.59	264.67	260.33	256.49	253.08	250.06	247.36	237.53	231.71	228.17
30000	307.86	299.00	291.35	284.70	278.89	273.79	269.30	265.33	261.81	258.68	255.89	245.72	239.70	236.04
31000	318.13	308.97	301.06	294.19	288.19	282.92	278.28	274.18	270.54	267.30	264.41	253.91	247.69	243.91
32000	328.39	318.93	310.77	303.68	297.48	292.05	287.26	283.02	279.27	275.92	272.94	262.10	255.68	251.78
33000	338.65	328.90	320.48	313.17	306.78	301.17	296.23	291.87	287.99	284.55	281.47	270.29	263.67	259.65
34000	348.91	338.87	330.19	322.66	316.07	310.30	305.21	300.71	296.72	293.17	290.00	278.48	271.66	267.51
35000	359.17	348.83	339.90	332.15	325.37	319.43	314.19	309.55	305.45	301.79	298.53	286.67	279.65	275.38
36000	369.44	358.80	349.62	341.64	334.67	328.55	323.16	318.40	314.17	310.41	307.06	294.86	287.64	283.25
37000	379.70	368.77	359.33	351.13	343.96	337.68	332.14	327.24	322.90	319.04	315.59	303.06	295.63	291.12
38000	389.96	378.73	369.04	360.62	353.26	346.80	341.12	336.09	331.63	327.66	324.12	311.25	303.62	298.99
39000	400.22	388.70	378.75	370.11	362.56	355.93	350.09	344.93	340.35	336.28	332.65	319.44	311.61	306.85
40000	410.48	398.67	388.46	379.59	371.85	365.06	359.07	353.78	349.08	344.90	341.18	327.63	319.60	314.72
41000	420.75	408.63	398.17	389.08	381.15	374.18	368.05	362.62	357.81	353.53	349.71	335.82	327.59	322.59
42000	431.01	418.60	407.88	398.57	390.44	383.31	377.02	371.46	366.53	362.15	358.24	344.01	335.58	330.46
43000	441.27	428.57	417.59	408.06	399.74	392.44	386.00	380.31	375.26	370.77	366.77	352.20	343.57	338.33
44000	451.53	438.53	427.31	417.55	409.04	401.56	394.98	389.15	383.99	379.39	375.30	360.39	351.56	346.19
45000	461.79	448.50	437.02	427.04	418.33	410.69	403.95	398.00	392.72	388.02	383.83	368.58	359.55	354.06
46000	472.06	458.46	446.73	436.53	427.63	419.81	412.93	406.84	401.44	396.64	392.35	376.77	367.54	361.93
47000	482.32	468.43	456.44	446.02	436.92	428.94	421.91	415.69	410.17	405.26	400.88	384.96	375.53	369.80
48000	492.58	478.40	466.15	455.51	446.22	438.07	430.88	424.53	418.90	413.88	409.41	393.15	383.52	377.67
49000	502.84	488.36	475.86	465.00	455.52	447.19	439.86	433.37	427.62	422.51	417.94	401.34	391.51	385.53
50000	513.10	498.33	485.57	474.49	464.81	456.32	448.84	442.22	436.35	431.13	426.47	409.53	399.50	393.40
55000	564.41	548.16	534.13	521.94	511.29	501.95	493.72	486.44	479.98	474.24	469.12	450.49	439.45	432.74
60000	615.72	598.00	582.69	569.39	557.77	547.58	538.60	530.66	523.62	517.35	511.77	491.44	479.40	472.08
65000	667.03	647.83	631.25	616.84	604.26	593.21	583.49	574.88	567.25	560.47	554.41	532.39	519.34	511.42
70000	718.34	697.66	679.80	664.29	650.74	638.85	628.37	619.10	610.89	603.58	597.06	573.34	559.29	550.76
75000	769.65	747.49	728.36	711.74	697.22	684.48	673.25	663.33	654.52	646.69	639.71	614.30	599.24	590.10
80000	820.96	797.33	776.92	759.18	743.70	730.11	718.13	707.55	698.16	689.80	682.35	655.25	639.19	629.44
85000	872.27	847.16	825.47	806.63	790.18	775.74	763.02	751.77	741.79	732.91	725.00	696.20	679.14	668.78
90000	923.58	896.99	874.03	854.08	836.66	821.37	807.90	795.99	785.43	776.03	767.65	737.15	719.09	708.12
95000	974.89	946.82	922.59	901.53	883.14	867.00	852.78	840.21	829.06	819.14	810.29	778.11	759.04	747.46
100000	1026.20	996.66	971.14	948.98	929.62	912.63	897.67	884.43	872.69	862.25	852.94	819.06	798.99	786.80

MONTHLY PAYMENT
REQUIRED TO AMORTIZE A LOAN

TERM AMOUNT	1 Year	2 Years	3 Years	4 Years	5 Years	6 Years	7 Years	8 Years	9 Years	10 Years	11 Years	12 Years	13 Years	14 Years
5	.44	.23	.16	.13	.11	.10	.09	.08	.07	.07	.07	.06	.06	.06
10	.88	.46	.32	.26	.21	.19	.17	.15	.14	.13	.13	.12	.12	.11
15	1.32	.69	.48	.38	.32	.28	.25	.23	.21	.20	.19	.18	.17	.16
25	2.19	1.15	.80	.63	.53	.46	.41	.37	.35	.33	.31	.29	.28	.27
50	4.38	2.29	1.60	1.26	1.05	.91	.82	.74	.69	.65	.61	.58	.56	.54
75	6.57	3.44	2.40	1.88	1.57	1.37	1.22	1.11	1.03	.97	.91	.87	.83	.80
100	8.76	4.58	3.20	2.51	2.09	1.82	1.63	1.48	1.37	1.29	1.21	1.16	1.11	1.07
200	17.52	9.16	6.39	5.01	4.18	3.63	3.25	2.96	2.74	2.57	2.42	2.31	2.21	2.13
300	26.28	13.74	9.58	7.51	6.27	5.45	4.87	4.44	4.11	3.85	3.63	3.46	3.32	3.20
400	35.03	18.32	12.77	10.01	8.36	7.26	6.49	5.92	5.48	5.13	4.84	4.61	4.42	4.26
500	43.79	22.90	15.96	12.51	10.44	9.08	8.11	7.40	6.84	6.41	6.05	5.77	5.53	5.32
600	52.55	27.48	19.15	15.01	12.53	10.89	9.73	8.87	8.21	7.69	7.26	6.92	6.63	6.39
700	61.30	32.06	22.35	17.51	14.62	12.71	11.36	10.35	9.58	8.97	8.47	8.07	7.73	7.45
800	70.06	36.64	25.54	20.01	16.71	14.52	12.98	11.83	10.95	10.25	9.68	9.22	8.84	8.51
900	78.82	41.22	28.73	22.51	18.80	16.34	14.60	13.31	12.31	11.53	10.89	10.37	9.94	9.58
1000	87.57	45.80	31.92	25.01	20.88	18.15	16.22	14.79	13.68	12.81	12.10	11.53	11.05	10.64
2000	175.14	91.60	63.84	50.01	41.76	36.30	32.44	29.57	27.36	25.61	24.20	23.05	22.09	21.28
3000	262.71	137.40	95.75	75.02	62.64	54.45	48.65	44.35	41.03	38.41	36.30	34.57	33.13	31.91
4000	350.27	183.20	127.67	100.02	83.52	72.60	64.87	59.13	54.71	51.22	48.40	46.09	44.17	42.55
5000	437.84	229.00	159.59	125.02	104.40	90.75	81.09	73.91	68.38	64.02	60.50	57.61	55.21	53.19
6000	525.41	274.80	191.50	150.03	125.28	108.90	97.30	88.69	82.06	76.82	72.60	69.13	66.25	63.82
7000	612.98	320.60	223.42	175.03	146.16	127.05	113.52	103.47	95.74	89.63	84.70	80.66	77.29	74.46
8000	700.54	366.40	255.33	200.04	167.04	145.20	129.73	118.25	109.41	102.43	96.80	92.18	88.33	85.09
9000	788.11	412.20	287.25	225.04	187.92	163.35	145.95	133.03	123.09	115.23	108.90	103.70	99.37	95.73
10000	875.68	458.00	319.17	250.04	208.80	181.50	162.17	147.81	136.76	128.04	121.00	115.22	110.41	106.37
11000	963.25	503.80	351.08	275.05	229.68	199.65	178.38	162.59	150.44	140.84	133.10	126.74	121.45	117.00
12000	1050.81	549.60	383.00	300.05	250.56	217.80	194.60	177.37	164.11	153.64	145.20	138.26	132.49	127.64
13000	1138.38	595.40	414.92	325.05	271.44	235.95	210.82	192.15	177.79	166.45	157.30	149.79	143.54	138.27
14000	1225.95	641.20	446.83	350.06	292.32	254.10	227.03	206.93	191.47	179.25	169.40	161.31	154.58	148.91
15000	1313.52	687.00	478.75	375.06	313.20	272.25	243.25	221.71	205.14	192.05	181.49	172.83	165.62	159.55
16000	1401.08	732.80	510.66	400.07	334.08	290.40	259.46	236.49	218.82	204.86	193.59	184.35	176.66	170.18
17000	1488.65	778.60	542.58	425.07	354.96	308.55	275.68	251.27	232.49	217.66	205.69	195.87	187.70	180.82
18000	1576.22	824.40	574.50	450.08	375.84	326.70	291.90	266.05	246.17	230.46	217.79	207.39	198.74	191.45
19000	1663.79	870.20	606.41	475.08	396.72	344.85	308.11	280.83	259.84	243.27	229.89	218.91	209.78	202.09
20000	1751.35	916.00	638.33	500.08	417.60	363.00	324.33	295.61	273.52	256.07	241.99	230.44	220.82	212.73
21000	1838.92	961.80	670.25	525.09	438.48	381.15	340.55	310.39	287.20	268.87	254.09	241.96	231.86	223.36
22000	1926.49	1007.59	702.16	550.09	459.36	399.30	356.76	325.17	300.87	281.68	266.19	253.48	242.90	234.00
23000	2014.06	1053.39	734.08	575.10	480.24	417.45	372.98	339.95	314.55	294.48	278.29	265.00	253.94	244.63
24000	2101.62	1099.19	765.99	600.10	501.12	435.60	389.19	354.73	328.22	307.28	290.39	276.52	264.98	255.27
25000	2189.19	1144.99	797.91	625.10	522.00	453.75	405.41	369.51	341.90	320.09	302.49	288.04	276.02	265.91
26000	2276.76	1190.79	829.83	650.11	542.88	471.90	421.63	384.29	355.58	332.89	314.59	299.57	287.07	276.54
27000	2364.33	1236.59	861.74	675.11	563.76	490.05	437.84	399.07	369.25	345.69	326.69	311.09	298.11	287.18
28000	2451.89	1282.39	893.66	700.11	584.64	508.20	454.06	413.85	382.93	358.50	338.79	322.61	309.15	297.81
29000	2539.46	1328.19	925.58	725.12	605.52	526.35	470.28	428.63	396.60	371.30	350.88	334.13	320.19	308.45
30000	2627.03	1373.99	957.49	750.12	626.40	544.50	486.49	443.41	410.28	384.10	362.98	345.65	331.23	319.09
31000	2714.60	1419.79	989.41	775.13	647.28	562.65	502.71	458.19	423.95	396.91	375.08	357.17	342.27	329.72
32000	2802.16	1465.59	1021.32	800.13	668.16	580.80	518.92	472.97	437.63	409.71	387.18	368.70	353.31	340.36
33000	2889.73	1511.39	1053.24	825.13	689.04	598.95	535.14	487.75	451.31	422.51	399.28	380.22	364.35	350.99
34000	2977.30	1557.19	1085.16	850.14	709.92	617.10	551.36	502.53	464.98	435.32	411.38	391.74	375.39	361.63
35000	3064.87	1602.99	1117.07	875.14	730.80	635.25	567.57	517.31	478.66	448.12	423.48	403.26	386.43	372.27
36000	3152.43	1648.79	1148.99	900.15	751.68	653.40	583.79	532.09	492.33	460.92	435.58	414.78	397.47	382.90
37000	3240.00	1694.59	1180.90	925.15	772.56	671.55	600.01	546.87	506.01	473.73	447.68	426.30	408.51	393.54
38000	3327.57	1740.39	1212.82	950.15	793.44	689.70	616.22	561.65	519.68	486.53	459.78	437.82	419.55	404.17
39000	3415.14	1786.19	1244.74	975.16	814.32	707.85	632.44	576.43	533.36	499.33	471.88	449.35	430.60	414.81
40000	3502.70	1831.99	1276.65	1000.16	835.20	726.00	648.65	591.21	547.04	512.14	483.98	460.87	441.64	425.45
41000	3590.27	1877.79	1308.57	1025.17	856.08	744.15	664.87	605.99	560.71	524.94	496.08	472.39	452.68	436.08
42000	3677.84	1923.59	1340.49	1050.17	876.96	762.30	681.09	620.77	574.39	537.74	508.18	483.91	463.72	446.72
43000	3765.41	1969.38	1372.40	1075.17	897.84	780.45	697.30	635.55	588.06	550.55	520.27	495.43	474.76	457.35
44000	3852.97	2015.18	1404.32	1100.18	918.72	798.60	713.52	650.33	601.74	563.35	532.37	506.95	485.80	467.99
45000	3940.54	2060.98	1436.23	1125.18	939.60	816.75	729.74	665.11	615.41	576.15	544.47	518.48	496.84	478.63
46000	4028.11	2106.78	1468.15	1150.19	960.48	834.90	745.95	679.90	629.09	588.96	556.57	530.00	507.88	489.26
47000	4115.68	2152.58	1500.07	1175.19	981.36	853.05	762.17	694.68	642.77	601.76	568.67	541.52	518.92	499.90
48000	4203.24	2198.38	1531.98	1200.19	1002.24	871.20	778.38	709.46	656.44	614.56	580.77	553.04	529.96	510.53
49000	4290.81	2244.18	1563.90	1225.20	1023.12	889.35	794.60	724.24	670.12	627.37	592.87	564.56	541.00	521.17
50000	4378.38	2289.98	1595.82	1250.20	1044.00	907.50	810.82	739.02	683.79	640.17	604.97	576.08	552.04	531.81
55000	4816.21	2518.98	1755.40	1375.22	1148.40	998.25	891.90	812.92	752.17	704.18	665.47	633.69	607.25	584.99
60000	5254.05	2747.98	1914.98	1500.24	1252.80	1089.00	972.98	886.82	820.55	768.20	725.96	691.30	662.45	638.17
65000	5691.89	2976.97	2074.56	1625.26	1357.20	1179.75	1054.06	960.72	888.93	832.22	786.46	748.91	717.66	691.35
70000	6129.73	3205.97	2234.14	1750.28	1461.60	1270.50	1135.14	1034.62	957.31	896.23	846.96	806.51	772.86	744.53
75000	6567.56	3434.97	2393.72	1875.30	1566.00	1361.24	1216.22	1108.52	1025.69	960.25	907.45	864.12	828.06	797.71
80000	7005.40	3663.97	2553.30	2000.32	1670.40	1451.99	1297.30	1182.42	1094.07	1024.27	967.95	921.73	883.27	850.89
85000	7443.24	3892.97	2712.88	2125.34	1774.80	1542.74	1378.39	1256.32	1162.45	1088.28	1028.45	979.34	938.47	904.07
90000	7881.08	4121.96	2872.46	2250.36	1879.20	1633.49	1459.47	1330.22	1230.82	1152.30	1088.94	1036.95	993.68	957.25
95000	8318.91	4350.96	3032.05	2375.38	1983.60	1724.24	1540.55	1404.13	1299.20	1216.32	1149.44	1094.55	1048.88	1010.43
100000	8756.75	4579.96	3191.63	2500.40	2087.99	1814.99	1621.63	1478.03	1367.58	1280.33	1209.93	1152.16	1104.08	1063.61

MONTHLY PAYMENT
REQUIRED TO AMORTIZE A LOAN

9.250%

TERM AMOUNT	15 Years	16 Years	17 Years	18 Years	19 Years	20 Years	21 Years	22 Years	23 Years	24 Years	25 Years	30 Years	35 Years	40 Years
5	.06	.05	.05	.05	.05	.05	.05	.05	.05	.05	.05	.05	.05	.04
10	.11	.10	.10	.10	.10	.10	.10	.09	.09	.09	.09	.09	.09	.08
15	.16	.15	.15	.15	.14	.14	.14	.14	.14	.13	.13	.13	.13	.12
25	.26	.25	.25	.24	.24	.23	.23	.23	.22	.22	.22	.21	.21	.20
50	.52	.50	.49	.48	.47	.46	.46	.45	.44	.44	.43	.42	.41	.40
75	.78	.75	.74	.72	.70	.69	.68	.67	.66	.65	.65	.62	.61	.60
100	1.03	1.00	.98	.96	.94	.92	.91	.89	.88	.87	.86	.83	.81	.80
200	2.06	2.00	1.95	1.91	1.87	1.84	1.81	1.78	1.76	1.74	1.72	1.65	1.61	1.59
300	3.09	3.00	2.93	2.86	2.80	2.75	2.71	2.67	2.63	2.60	2.57	2.47	2.41	2.38
400	4.12	4.00	3.90	3.81	3.74	3.67	3.61	3.56	3.51	3.47	3.43	3.30	3.22	3.17
500	5.15	5.00	4.88	4.77	4.67	4.58	4.51	4.44	4.39	4.33	4.29	4.12	4.02	3.96
600	6.18	6.00	5.85	5.72	5.60	5.50	5.41	5.33	5.26	5.20	5.14	4.94	4.82	4.75
700	7.21	7.00	6.82	6.67	6.53	6.42	6.31	6.22	6.14	6.06	6.00	5.76	5.62	5.54
800	8.24	8.00	7.80	7.62	7.47	7.33	7.21	7.11	7.01	6.93	6.86	6.59	6.43	6.33
900	9.27	9.00	8.77	8.57	8.40	8.25	8.11	7.99	7.89	7.80	7.71	7.41	7.23	7.12
1000	10.30	10.00	9.75	9.53	9.33	9.16	9.01	8.88	8.77	8.66	8.57	8.23	8.03	7.91
2000	20.59	20.00	19.49	19.05	18.66	18.32	18.02	17.76	17.53	17.32	17.13	16.46	16.06	15.82
3000	30.88	30.00	29.23	28.57	27.99	27.48	27.03	26.64	26.29	25.97	25.70	24.69	24.09	23.72
4000	41.17	39.99	38.97	38.09	37.32	36.64	36.04	35.52	35.05	34.63	34.26	32.91	32.11	31.63
5000	51.46	49.99	48.72	47.61	46.65	45.80	45.05	44.39	43.81	43.29	42.82	41.14	40.14	39.54
6000	61.76	59.99	58.46	57.13	55.97	54.96	54.06	53.27	52.57	51.94	51.39	49.37	48.17	47.44
7000	72.05	69.98	68.20	66.65	65.30	64.12	63.07	62.15	61.33	60.60	59.95	57.59	56.20	55.35
8000	82.34	79.98	77.94	76.17	74.63	73.27	72.08	71.03	70.09	69.26	68.52	65.82	64.22	63.26
9000	92.63	89.98	87.69	85.70	83.96	82.43	81.09	79.90	78.85	77.91	77.08	74.05	72.25	71.16
10000	102.92	99.97	97.43	95.22	93.29	91.59	90.10	88.78	87.61	86.57	85.64	82.27	80.28	79.07
11000	113.22	109.97	107.17	104.74	102.61	100.75	99.11	97.66	96.37	95.23	94.21	90.50	88.31	86.98
12000	123.51	119.97	116.91	114.26	111.94	109.91	108.12	106.54	105.13	103.88	102.77	98.73	96.33	94.88
13000	133.80	129.97	126.66	123.78	121.27	119.07	117.13	115.41	113.89	112.54	111.33	106.95	104.36	102.79
14000	144.09	139.96	136.40	133.30	130.60	128.23	126.14	124.29	122.65	121.20	119.90	115.18	112.39	110.70
15000	154.38	149.96	146.14	142.82	139.93	137.39	135.15	133.17	131.41	129.85	128.46	123.41	120.42	118.60
16000	164.68	159.96	155.88	152.34	149.25	146.54	144.16	142.05	140.17	138.51	137.03	131.63	128.44	126.51
17000	174.97	169.95	165.62	161.87	158.58	155.70	153.17	150.92	148.93	147.17	145.59	139.86	136.47	134.42
18000	185.26	179.95	175.37	171.39	167.91	164.86	162.18	159.80	157.70	155.82	154.15	148.09	144.50	142.32
19000	195.55	189.95	185.11	180.91	177.24	174.02	171.18	168.68	166.46	164.48	162.72	156.31	152.53	150.23
20000	205.84	199.94	194.85	190.43	186.57	183.18	180.19	177.56	175.22	173.14	171.28	164.54	160.55	158.14
21000	216.14	209.94	204.59	199.95	195.89	192.34	189.20	186.43	183.98	181.79	179.85	172.77	168.58	166.04
22000	226.43	219.94	214.34	209.47	205.22	201.50	198.21	195.31	192.74	190.45	188.41	180.99	176.61	173.95
23000	236.72	229.94	224.08	218.99	214.55	210.65	207.22	204.19	201.50	199.11	196.97	189.22	184.64	181.86
24000	247.01	239.93	233.82	228.51	223.88	219.81	216.23	213.07	210.26	207.76	205.54	197.45	192.66	189.76
25000	257.30	249.93	243.56	238.03	233.21	228.97	225.24	221.94	219.02	216.42	214.10	205.67	200.69	197.67
26000	267.59	259.93	253.31	247.56	242.54	238.13	234.25	230.82	227.78	225.08	222.66	213.90	208.72	205.58
27000	277.89	269.92	263.05	257.08	251.86	247.29	243.26	239.70	236.54	233.73	231.23	222.13	216.75	213.48
28000	288.18	279.92	272.79	266.60	261.19	256.45	252.27	248.58	245.30	242.39	239.79	230.35	224.77	221.39
29000	298.47	289.92	282.53	276.12	270.52	265.61	261.28	257.45	254.06	251.04	248.36	238.58	232.80	229.30
30000	308.76	299.91	292.28	285.64	279.85	274.77	270.29	266.33	262.82	259.70	256.92	246.81	240.83	237.20
31000	319.05	309.91	302.02	295.16	289.18	283.92	279.30	275.21	271.58	268.36	265.48	255.03	248.86	245.11
32000	329.35	319.91	311.76	304.68	298.50	293.08	288.31	284.09	280.34	277.01	274.05	263.26	256.88	253.02
33000	339.64	329.91	321.50	314.20	307.83	302.24	297.32	292.96	289.10	285.67	282.61	271.49	264.91	260.92
34000	349.93	339.90	331.24	323.73	317.16	311.40	306.33	301.84	297.86	294.33	291.17	279.71	272.94	268.83
35000	360.22	349.90	340.99	333.25	326.49	320.56	315.34	310.72	306.62	302.98	299.74	287.94	280.97	276.74
36000	370.51	359.90	350.73	342.77	335.82	329.72	324.35	319.60	315.39	311.64	308.30	296.17	288.99	284.64
37000	380.81	369.89	360.47	352.29	345.14	338.88	333.35	328.47	324.15	320.30	316.87	304.39	297.02	292.55
38000	391.10	379.89	370.21	361.81	354.47	348.03	342.36	337.35	332.91	328.95	325.43	312.62	305.05	300.46
39000	401.39	389.89	379.96	371.33	363.80	357.19	351.37	346.23	341.67	337.61	333.99	320.85	313.08	308.36
40000	411.68	399.88	389.70	380.85	373.13	366.35	360.38	355.11	350.43	346.27	342.56	329.08	321.10	316.27
41000	421.97	409.88	399.44	390.37	382.46	375.51	369.39	363.98	359.19	354.92	351.12	337.30	329.13	324.18
42000	432.27	419.88	409.18	399.90	391.78	384.67	378.40	372.86	367.95	363.58	359.69	345.53	337.16	332.08
43000	442.56	429.87	418.93	409.42	401.11	393.83	387.41	381.74	376.71	372.24	368.25	353.76	345.19	339.99
44000	452.85	439.87	428.67	418.94	410.44	402.99	396.42	390.62	385.47	380.89	376.81	361.98	353.21	347.90
45000	463.14	449.87	438.41	428.46	419.77	412.15	405.43	399.49	394.23	389.55	385.38	370.21	361.24	355.80
46000	473.43	459.87	448.15	437.98	429.10	421.30	414.44	408.37	402.99	398.21	393.94	378.44	369.27	363.71
47000	483.73	469.86	457.90	447.50	438.42	430.46	423.45	417.25	411.75	406.86	402.50	386.66	377.29	371.62
48000	494.02	479.86	467.64	457.02	447.75	439.62	432.46	426.13	420.51	415.52	411.07	394.89	385.32	379.52
49000	504.31	489.86	477.38	466.54	457.08	448.78	441.47	435.00	429.27	424.18	419.63	403.12	393.35	387.43
50000	514.60	499.85	487.12	476.06	466.41	457.94	450.48	443.88	438.03	432.83	428.20	411.34	401.38	395.34
55000	566.06	549.84	535.83	523.67	513.05	503.73	495.52	488.27	481.84	476.12	471.02	452.48	441.51	434.87
60000	617.52	599.82	584.55	571.28	559.69	549.53	540.57	532.66	525.64	519.40	513.83	493.61	481.65	474.40
65000	668.98	649.81	633.26	618.88	606.33	595.32	585.62	577.05	569.44	562.68	556.65	534.74	521.79	513.93
70000	720.44	699.79	681.97	666.49	652.97	641.11	630.67	621.43	613.24	605.96	599.47	575.88	561.93	553.47
75000	771.90	749.78	730.68	714.09	699.61	686.91	675.71	665.82	657.05	649.25	642.29	617.01	602.06	593.00
80000	823.36	799.76	779.39	761.70	746.25	732.70	720.76	710.21	700.85	692.53	685.11	658.15	642.20	632.53
85000	874.82	849.75	828.10	809.31	792.89	778.49	765.81	754.60	744.65	735.81	727.93	699.28	682.34	672.07
90000	926.28	899.73	876.82	856.91	839.53	824.29	810.86	798.98	788.46	779.09	770.75	740.41	722.47	711.60
95000	977.74	949.72	925.53	904.52	886.17	870.08	855.90	843.37	832.26	822.38	813.57	781.55	762.61	751.13
100000	1029.20	999.70	974.24	952.12	932.81	915.87	900.95	887.76	876.06	865.66	856.39	822.68	802.75	790.67

MONTHLY PAYMENT
REQUIRED TO AMORTIZE A LOAN

TERM AMOUNT	1 Year	2 Years	3 Years	4 Years	5 Years	6 Years	7 Years	8 Years	9 Years	10 Years	11 Years	12 Years	13 Years	14 Years
5	.44	.23	.16	.13	.11	.10	.09	.08	.07	.07	.07	.06	.06	.06
10	.88	.46	.32	.26	.21	.19	.17	.15	.14	.13	.13	.12	.12	.11
15	1.32	.69	.48	.38	.32	.28	.25	.23	.21	.20	.19	.18	.17	.16
25	2.19	1.15	.80	.63	.53	.46	.41	.38	.35	.33	.31	.29	.28	.27
50	4.38	2.30	1.60	1.26	1.05	.91	.82	.75	.69	.65	.61	.58	.56	.54
75	6.57	3.44	2.40	1.88	1.57	1.37	1.22	1.12	1.03	.97	.91	.87	.84	.80
100	8.76	4.59	3.20	2.51	2.10	1.82	1.63	1.49	1.38	1.29	1.22	1.16	1.11	1.07
200	17.52	9.17	6.39	5.01	4.19	3.64	3.25	2.97	2.75	2.57	2.43	2.31	2.22	2.14
300	26.28	13.75	9.59	7.51	6.28	5.46	4.88	4.45	4.12	3.85	3.64	3.47	3.33	3.20
400	35.04	18.33	12.78	10.02	8.37	7.27	6.50	5.93	5.49	5.14	4.86	4.62	4.43	4.27
500	43.80	22.92	15.97	12.52	10.46	9.09	8.13	7.41	6.86	6.42	6.07	5.78	5.54	5.34
600	52.56	27.50	19.17	15.02	12.55	10.91	9.75	8.89	8.23	7.70	7.28	6.93	6.65	6.40
700	61.32	32.08	22.36	17.52	14.64	12.73	11.37	10.37	9.60	8.99	8.49	8.09	7.75	7.47
800	70.08	36.66	25.56	20.03	16.73	14.54	13.00	11.85	10.97	10.27	9.71	9.24	8.86	8.54
900	78.84	41.25	28.75	22.53	18.82	16.36	14.62	13.33	12.34	11.55	10.92	10.40	9.97	9.60
1000	87.60	45.83	31.94	25.03	20.91	18.18	16.25	14.81	13.71	12.84	12.13	11.55	11.07	10.67
2000	175.19	91.65	63.88	50.06	41.81	36.35	32.49	29.62	27.41	25.67	24.26	23.10	22.14	21.34
3000	262.78	137.47	95.82	75.09	62.72	54.53	48.73	44.42	41.11	38.50	36.39	34.65	33.21	32.00
4000	350.37	183.30	127.76	100.12	83.62	72.70	64.97	59.23	54.81	51.33	48.51	46.20	44.28	42.67
5000	437.96	229.12	159.70	125.14	104.53	90.88	81.21	74.04	68.52	64.16	60.64	57.75	55.35	53.33
6000	525.55	274.94	191.64	150.17	125.43	109.05	97.46	88.84	82.22	76.99	72.77	69.30	66.42	64.00
7000	613.14	320.76	223.58	175.20	146.33	127.23	113.70	103.65	95.92	89.82	84.89	80.85	77.49	74.66
8000	700.73	366.59	255.52	200.23	167.24	145.40	129.94	118.46	109.62	102.65	97.02	92.40	88.56	85.33
9000	788.32	412.41	287.46	225.25	188.14	163.58	146.18	133.26	123.33	115.48	109.15	103.95	99.63	95.99
10000	875.91	458.23	319.40	250.28	209.05	181.75	162.42	148.07	137.03	128.31	121.28	115.50	110.70	106.66
11000	963.50	504.05	351.34	275.31	229.95	199.93	178.66	162.87	150.73	141.14	133.40	127.05	121.77	117.33
12000	1051.09	549.88	383.28	300.34	250.86	218.10	194.91	177.68	164.43	153.97	145.53	138.60	132.84	127.99
13000	1138.68	595.70	415.22	325.37	271.76	236.28	211.15	192.49	178.14	166.80	157.66	150.15	143.91	138.66
14000	1226.27	641.52	447.16	350.39	292.66	254.45	227.39	207.29	191.84	179.63	169.78	161.70	154.98	149.32
15000	1313.86	687.34	479.10	375.42	313.57	272.63	243.63	222.10	205.54	192.46	181.91	173.25	166.05	159.99
16000	1401.46	733.17	511.04	400.45	334.47	290.80	259.87	236.91	219.24	205.29	194.04	184.80	177.12	170.65
17000	1489.05	778.99	542.98	425.48	355.38	308.98	276.11	251.71	232.95	218.12	206.17	196.35	188.19	181.32
18000	1576.64	824.81	574.92	450.50	376.28	327.15	292.36	266.52	246.65	230.95	218.29	207.90	199.26	191.98
19000	1664.23	870.63	606.86	475.53	397.19	345.33	308.60	281.32	260.35	243.78	230.42	219.45	210.33	202.65
20000	1751.82	916.46	638.80	500.56	418.09	363.50	324.84	296.13	274.05	256.62	242.55	231.00	221.40	213.31
21000	1839.41	962.28	670.74	525.59	438.99	381.68	341.08	310.94	287.76	269.45	254.67	242.55	232.47	223.98
22000	1927.00	1008.10	702.67	550.62	459.90	399.85	357.32	325.74	301.46	282.28	266.80	254.10	243.54	234.65
23000	2014.59	1053.92	734.61	575.64	480.80	418.03	373.57	340.55	315.16	295.11	278.93	265.65	254.61	245.31
24000	2102.18	1099.75	766.55	600.67	501.71	436.20	389.81	355.36	328.86	307.94	291.06	277.20	265.68	255.98
25000	2189.77	1145.57	798.49	625.70	522.61	454.37	406.05	370.16	342.57	320.77	303.18	288.75	276.75	266.64
26000	2277.36	1191.39	830.43	650.73	543.52	472.55	422.29	384.97	356.27	333.60	315.31	300.30	287.82	277.31
27000	2364.95	1237.21	862.37	675.75	564.42	490.72	438.53	399.78	369.97	346.43	327.44	311.85	298.89	287.97
28000	2452.54	1283.04	894.31	700.78	585.32	508.90	454.77	414.58	383.67	359.26	339.56	323.40	309.96	298.64
29000	2540.13	1328.86	926.25	725.81	606.23	527.07	471.02	429.39	397.38	372.09	351.69	334.95	321.03	309.30
30000	2627.72	1374.68	958.19	750.84	627.13	545.25	487.26	444.19	411.08	384.92	363.82	346.50	332.10	319.97
31000	2715.32	1420.50	990.13	775.86	648.04	563.42	503.50	459.00	424.78	397.75	375.95	358.05	343.17	330.63
32000	2802.91	1466.33	1022.07	800.89	668.94	581.60	519.74	473.81	438.48	410.58	388.07	369.60	354.24	341.30
33000	2890.50	1512.15	1054.01	825.92	689.85	599.77	535.98	488.61	452.19	423.41	400.20	381.15	365.30	351.97
34000	2978.09	1557.97	1085.95	850.95	710.75	617.95	552.22	503.42	465.89	436.24	412.33	392.70	376.37	362.63
35000	3065.68	1603.79	1117.89	875.98	731.65	636.12	568.47	518.23	479.59	449.07	424.45	404.25	387.44	373.30
36000	3153.27	1649.62	1149.83	901.00	752.56	654.30	584.71	533.03	493.29	461.90	436.58	415.80	398.51	383.96
37000	3240.86	1695.44	1181.77	926.03	773.46	672.47	600.95	547.84	507.00	474.73	448.71	427.35	409.58	394.63
38000	3328.45	1741.26	1213.71	951.06	794.37	690.65	617.19	562.64	520.70	487.56	460.83	438.90	420.65	405.29
39000	3416.04	1787.08	1245.65	976.09	815.27	708.82	633.43	577.45	534.40	500.39	472.96	450.45	431.72	415.96
40000	3503.63	1832.91	1277.59	1001.11	836.18	727.00	649.67	592.26	548.10	513.23	485.09	462.00	442.79	426.62
41000	3591.22	1878.73	1309.53	1026.14	857.08	745.17	665.92	607.06	561.80	526.06	497.22	473.55	453.86	437.29
42000	3678.81	1924.55	1341.47	1051.17	877.98	763.35	682.16	621.87	575.51	538.89	509.34	485.10	464.93	447.95
43000	3766.40	1970.37	1373.41	1076.20	898.89	781.52	698.40	636.68	589.21	551.72	521.47	496.65	476.00	458.62
44000	3853.99	2016.20	1405.34	1101.23	919.79	799.70	714.64	651.48	602.91	564.55	533.60	508.20	487.07	469.29
45000	3941.58	2062.02	1437.28	1126.25	940.70	817.87	730.88	666.29	616.61	577.38	545.72	519.75	498.14	479.95
46000	4029.18	2107.84	1469.22	1151.28	961.60	836.05	747.13	681.09	630.32	590.21	557.85	531.30	509.21	490.62
47000	4116.77	2153.66	1501.16	1176.31	982.51	854.22	763.37	695.90	644.02	603.04	569.98	542.85	520.28	501.28
48000	4204.36	2199.49	1533.10	1201.34	1003.41	872.39	779.61	710.71	657.72	615.87	582.11	554.40	531.35	511.95
49000	4291.95	2245.31	1565.04	1226.36	1024.31	890.57	795.85	725.51	671.42	628.70	594.23	565.95	542.42	522.61
50000	4379.54	2291.13	1596.98	1251.39	1045.22	908.74	812.09	740.32	685.13	641.53	606.36	577.50	553.49	533.28
55000	4817.49	2520.24	1756.68	1376.53	1149.74	999.62	893.30	814.35	753.64	705.68	667.00	635.25	608.84	586.61
60000	5255.44	2749.36	1916.38	1501.67	1254.26	1090.49	974.51	888.38	822.15	769.84	727.63	693.00	664.19	639.93
65000	5693.40	2978.47	2076.08	1626.81	1358.78	1181.37	1055.72	962.41	890.66	833.99	788.27	750.75	719.53	693.26
70000	6131.35	3207.58	2235.77	1751.95	1463.30	1272.24	1136.93	1036.45	959.18	898.14	848.90	808.50	774.88	746.59
75000	6569.30	3436.69	2395.47	1877.09	1567.82	1363.11	1218.14	1110.48	1027.69	962.29	909.54	866.25	830.23	799.92
80000	7007.26	3665.81	2555.17	2002.22	1672.35	1453.99	1299.34	1184.51	1096.20	1026.45	970.17	924.00	885.58	853.24
85000	7445.21	3894.92	2714.87	2127.36	1776.87	1544.86	1380.55	1258.54	1164.71	1090.60	1030.81	981.75	940.93	906.57
90000	7883.16	4124.03	2874.56	2252.50	1881.39	1635.74	1461.76	1332.57	1233.22	1154.75	1091.44	1039.50	996.28	959.90
95000	8321.12	4353.14	3034.26	2377.64	1985.91	1726.61	1542.97	1406.60	1301.74	1218.90	1152.08	1097.25	1051.63	1013.22
100000	8759.07	4582.26	3193.96	2502.78	2090.43	1817.48	1624.18	1480.64	1370.25	1283.06	1212.72	1155.00	1106.97	1066.55

MONTHLY PAYMENT
REQUIRED TO AMORTIZE A LOAN

9.300%

TERM	15 Years	16 Years	17 Years	18 Years	19 Years	20 Years	21 Years	22 Years	23 Years	24 Years	25 Years	30 Years	35 Years	40 Years
AMOUNT														
5	.06	.06	.05	.05	.05	.05	.05	.05	.05	.05	.05	.05	.05	.04
10	.11	.11	.10	.10	.10	.10	.10	.09	.09	.09	.09	.09	.09	.08
15	.16	.16	.15	.15	.15	.14	.14	.14	.14	.14	.13	.13	.13	.12
25	.26	.26	.25	.24	.24	.23	.23	.23	.22	.22	.22	.21	.21	.20
50	.52	.51	.49	.48	.47	.46	.46	.45	.44	.44	.43	.42	.41	.40
75	.78	.76	.74	.72	.71	.69	.68	.67	.66	.66	.65	.62	.61	.60
100	1.04	1.01	.98	.96	.94	.92	.91	.90	.88	.87	.86	.83	.81	.80
200	2.07	2.01	1.96	1.92	1.88	1.84	1.81	1.79	1.76	1.74	1.72	1.66	1.62	1.59
300	3.10	3.01	2.94	2.87	2.81	2.76	2.72	2.68	2.64	2.61	2.58	2.48	2.42	2.39
400	4.13	4.02	3.91	3.83	3.75	3.68	3.62	3.57	3.52	3.48	3.44	3.31	3.23	3.18
500	5.17	5.02	4.89	4.78	4.69	4.60	4.53	4.46	4.40	4.35	4.30	4.14	4.04	3.98
600	6.20	6.02	5.87	5.74	5.62	5.52	5.43	5.35	5.28	5.22	5.16	4.96	4.84	4.77
700	7.23	7.02	6.85	6.69	6.56	6.44	6.33	6.24	6.16	6.09	6.02	5.79	5.65	5.57
800	8.26	8.03	7.82	7.65	7.49	7.36	7.24	7.13	7.04	6.96	6.88	6.62	6.46	6.36
900	9.29	9.03	8.80	8.60	8.43	8.28	8.14	8.02	7.92	7.83	7.74	7.44	7.26	7.16
1000	10.33	10.03	9.78	9.56	9.37	9.20	9.05	8.92	8.80	8.70	8.60	8.27	8.07	7.95
2000	20.65	20.06	19.55	19.11	18.73	18.39	18.09	17.83	17.59	17.39	17.20	16.53	16.14	15.90
3000	30.97	30.09	29.33	28.66	28.09	27.58	27.13	26.74	26.39	26.08	25.80	24.79	24.20	23.84
4000	41.29	40.11	39.10	38.22	37.45	36.77	36.17	35.65	35.18	34.77	34.40	33.06	32.27	31.79
5000	51.61	50.14	48.87	47.77	46.81	45.96	45.22	44.56	43.98	43.46	43.00	41.32	40.33	39.73
6000	61.94	60.17	58.65	57.32	56.17	55.15	54.26	53.47	52.77	52.15	51.60	49.58	48.40	47.68
7000	72.26	70.20	68.42	66.87	65.53	64.34	63.30	62.38	61.57	60.84	60.19	57.85	56.46	55.62
8000	82.58	80.22	78.19	76.43	74.89	73.53	72.34	71.29	70.36	69.53	68.79	66.11	64.53	63.57
9000	92.90	90.25	87.97	85.98	84.25	82.72	81.39	80.20	79.15	78.22	77.39	74.37	72.59	71.51
10000	103.22	100.28	97.74	95.53	93.61	91.92	90.43	89.11	87.95	86.91	85.99	82.64	80.66	79.46
11000	113.55	110.31	107.51	105.08	102.97	101.11	99.47	98.02	96.74	95.60	94.59	90.90	88.72	87.40
12000	123.87	120.33	117.29	114.64	112.33	110.30	108.51	106.94	105.54	104.29	103.19	99.16	96.79	95.35
13000	134.19	130.36	127.06	124.19	121.69	119.49	117.56	115.85	114.33	112.98	111.78	107.42	104.85	103.29
14000	144.51	140.39	136.83	133.74	131.05	128.68	126.60	124.76	123.13	121.67	120.38	115.69	112.92	111.24
15000	154.83	150.42	146.61	143.30	140.41	137.87	135.64	133.67	131.92	130.37	128.98	123.95	120.98	119.18
16000	165.16	160.44	156.38	152.85	149.77	147.06	144.68	142.58	140.71	139.06	137.58	132.21	129.05	127.13
17000	175.48	170.47	166.15	162.40	159.13	156.25	153.72	151.49	149.51	147.75	146.18	140.48	137.11	135.08
18000	185.80	180.50	175.93	171.95	168.49	165.44	162.77	160.40	158.30	156.44	154.78	148.74	145.18	143.02
19000	196.12	190.53	185.70	181.51	177.85	174.64	171.81	169.31	167.10	165.13	163.37	157.00	153.24	150.97
20000	206.44	200.55	195.47	191.06	187.21	183.83	180.85	178.22	175.89	173.82	171.97	165.27	161.31	158.91
21000	216.76	210.58	205.25	200.61	196.57	193.02	189.89	187.13	184.69	182.51	180.57	173.53	169.37	166.86
22000	227.09	220.61	215.02	210.16	205.93	202.21	198.94	196.04	193.48	191.20	189.17	181.79	177.44	174.80
23000	237.41	230.64	224.79	219.72	215.29	211.40	207.98	204.95	202.27	199.89	197.77	190.05	185.50	182.75
24000	247.73	240.66	234.57	229.27	224.65	220.59	217.02	213.87	211.07	208.58	206.37	198.32	193.57	190.69
25000	258.05	250.69	244.34	238.82	234.01	229.78	226.06	222.78	219.86	217.27	214.96	206.58	201.63	198.64
26000	268.37	260.72	254.11	248.37	243.37	238.97	235.11	231.69	228.66	225.96	223.56	214.84	209.70	206.58
27000	278.70	270.75	263.89	257.93	252.73	248.16	244.15	240.60	237.45	234.65	232.16	223.11	217.76	214.53
28000	289.02	280.77	273.66	267.48	262.09	257.36	253.19	249.51	246.25	243.34	240.76	231.37	225.83	222.47
29000	299.34	290.80	283.43	277.03	271.45	266.55	262.23	258.42	255.04	252.03	249.36	239.63	233.89	230.42
30000	309.66	300.83	293.21	286.59	280.81	275.74	271.27	267.33	263.83	260.73	257.96	247.90	241.96	238.36
31000	319.98	310.86	302.98	296.14	290.17	284.93	280.32	276.24	272.63	269.42	266.55	256.16	250.02	246.31
32000	330.31	320.88	312.75	305.69	299.53	294.12	289.36	285.15	281.42	278.11	275.15	264.42	258.09	254.26
33000	340.63	330.91	322.53	315.24	308.89	303.31	298.40	294.06	290.22	286.80	283.75	272.68	266.15	262.20
34000	350.95	340.94	332.30	324.80	318.25	312.50	307.44	302.97	299.01	295.49	292.35	280.95	274.22	270.15
35000	361.27	350.97	342.07	334.35	327.61	321.69	316.49	311.88	307.81	304.18	300.95	289.21	282.28	278.09
36000	371.59	360.99	351.85	343.90	336.97	330.88	325.53	320.80	316.60	312.87	309.55	297.47	290.35	286.04
37000	381.92	371.02	361.62	353.45	346.33	340.08	334.57	329.71	325.39	321.56	318.14	305.74	298.41	293.98
38000	392.24	381.05	371.39	363.01	355.69	349.27	343.61	338.62	334.19	330.25	326.74	314.00	306.48	301.93
39000	402.56	391.08	381.17	372.56	365.05	358.46	352.66	347.53	342.98	338.94	335.34	322.26	314.54	309.87
40000	412.88	401.10	390.94	382.11	374.41	367.65	361.70	356.44	351.78	347.63	343.94	330.53	322.61	317.82
41000	423.20	411.13	400.71	391.66	383.77	376.84	370.74	365.35	360.57	356.32	352.54	338.79	330.67	325.76
42000	433.52	421.16	410.49	401.22	393.13	386.03	379.78	374.26	369.37	365.01	361.14	347.05	338.74	333.71
43000	443.85	431.19	420.26	410.77	402.49	395.22	388.83	383.17	378.16	373.70	369.73	355.31	346.80	341.65
44000	454.17	441.21	430.03	420.32	411.85	404.41	397.87	392.08	386.95	382.40	378.33	363.58	354.87	349.60
45000	464.49	451.24	439.81	429.88	421.21	413.60	406.91	400.99	395.75	391.09	386.93	371.84	362.93	357.54
46000	474.81	461.27	449.58	439.43	430.57	422.80	415.95	409.90	404.54	399.78	395.53	380.10	371.00	365.49
47000	485.13	471.30	459.35	448.98	439.93	431.99	424.99	418.82	413.34	408.47	404.13	388.37	379.06	373.44
48000	495.46	481.32	469.13	458.53	449.29	441.18	434.04	427.73	422.13	417.16	412.73	396.63	387.13	381.38
49000	505.78	491.35	478.90	468.09	458.65	450.37	443.08	436.64	430.93	425.85	421.32	404.89	395.19	389.33
50000	516.10	501.38	488.67	477.64	468.01	459.56	452.12	445.55	439.72	434.54	429.92	413.16	403.26	397.27
55000	567.71	551.52	537.54	525.40	514.81	505.52	497.33	490.10	483.69	477.99	472.91	454.47	443.58	437.00
60000	619.32	601.65	586.41	573.17	561.61	551.47	542.54	534.66	527.66	521.45	515.91	495.79	483.91	476.72
65000	670.93	651.79	635.27	620.93	608.41	597.43	587.76	579.21	571.63	564.90	558.90	537.10	524.24	516.45
70000	722.54	701.93	684.14	668.69	655.21	643.38	632.97	623.76	615.61	608.35	601.89	578.42	564.56	556.18
75000	774.15	752.07	733.01	716.46	702.01	689.34	678.18	668.32	659.58	651.81	644.88	619.73	604.89	595.90
80000	825.76	802.20	781.87	764.22	748.81	735.29	723.39	712.87	703.55	695.26	687.87	661.05	645.21	635.63
85000	877.37	852.34	830.74	811.98	795.61	781.25	768.60	757.43	747.52	738.71	730.86	702.36	685.54	675.36
90000	928.98	902.48	879.61	859.75	842.41	827.20	813.81	801.98	791.49	782.17	773.86	743.68	725.86	715.08
95000	980.59	952.61	928.47	907.51	889.21	873.16	859.03	846.54	835.46	825.62	816.85	784.99	766.19	754.81
100000	1032.20	1002.75	977.34	955.27	936.01	919.11	904.24	891.09	879.44	869.07	859.84	826.31	806.51	794.54

9.375%

TERM	1 Year	2 Years	3 Years	4 Years	5 Years	6 Years	7 Years	8 Years	9 Years	10 Years	11 Years	12 Years	13 Years	14 Years
AMOUNT														
5	.44	.23	.16	.13	.11	.10	.09	.08	.07	.07	.07	.06	.06	.06
10	.88	.46	.32	.26	.21	.19	.17	.15	.14	.13	.13	.12	.12	.11
15	1.32	.69	.48	.36	.32	.28	.25	.23	.21	.20	.19	.18	.17	.17
25	2.20	1.15	.80	.63	.53	.46	.41	.38	.35	.33	.31	.29	.28	.27
50	4.39	2.30	1.60	1.26	1.05	.92	.82	.75	.69	.65	.61	.58	.56	.54
75	6.58	3.44	2.40	1.88	1.58	1.37	1.23	1.12	1.04	.97	.92	.87	.84	.81
100	8.77	4.59	3.20	2.51	2.10	1.83	1.63	1.49	1.38	1.29	1.22	1.16	1.12	1.08
200	17.53	9.18	6.40	5.02	4.19	3.65	3.26	2.97	2.75	2.58	2.44	2.32	2.23	2.15
300	26.29	13.76	9.60	7.52	6.29	5.47	4.89	4.46	4.13	3.87	3.66	3.48	3.34	3.22
400	35.06	18.35	12.79	10.03	8.38	7.29	6.52	5.94	5.50	5.15	4.87	4.64	4.45	4.29
500	43.82	22.93	15.99	12.54	10.48	9.11	8.15	7.43	6.88	6.44	6.09	5.80	5.56	5.36
600	52.58	27.52	19.19	15.04	12.57	10.93	9.77	8.91	8.25	7.73	7.31	6.96	6.67	6.43
700	61.34	32.10	22.39	17.55	14.66	12.75	11.40	10.40	9.62	9.01	8.52	8.12	7.78	7.50
800	70.11	36.69	25.58	20.06	16.76	14.57	13.03	11.88	11.00	10.30	9.74	9.28	8.90	8.57
900	78.87	41.28	28.78	22.56	18.85	16.40	14.66	13.37	12.37	11.59	10.96	10.44	10.01	9.64
1000	87.63	45.86	31.98	25.07	20.95	18.22	16.29	14.85	13.75	12.88	12.17	11.60	11.12	10.71
2000	175.26	91.72	63.95	50.13	41.89	36.43	32.57	29.70	27.49	25.75	24.34	23.19	22.23	21.42
3000	262.88	137.58	95.93	75.20	62.83	54.64	48.85	44.54	41.23	38.62	36.51	34.78	33.34	32.13
4000	350.51	183.43	127.90	100.26	83.77	72.85	65.13	59.39	54.97	51.49	48.68	46.38	44.46	42.84
5000	438.13	229.29	159.88	125.32	104.71	91.07	81.41	74.23	68.72	64.36	60.85	57.97	55.57	53.55
6000	525.76	275.15	191.85	150.39	125.65	109.28	97.69	89.08	82.46	77.23	73.02	69.56	66.68	64.26
7000	613.38	321.00	223.83	175.45	146.59	127.49	113.97	103.92	96.20	90.10	85.19	81.15	77.80	74.97
8000	701.01	366.86	255.80	200.51	167.53	145.70	130.25	118.77	109.94	102.98	97.36	92.75	88.91	85.68
9000	788.63	412.72	287.78	225.58	188.47	163.91	146.53	133.61	123.69	115.85	109.52	104.34	100.02	96.39
10000	876.26	458.57	319.75	250.64	209.41	182.13	162.81	148.46	137.43	128.72	121.69	115.93	111.14	107.10
11000	963.89	504.43	351.73	275.70	230.35	200.34	179.09	163.31	151.17	141.59	133.86	127.52	122.25	117.81
12000	1051.51	550.29	383.70	300.77	251.29	218.55	195.37	178.15	164.91	154.46	146.03	139.12	133.36	128.52
13000	1139.14	596.15	415.67	325.83	272.24	236.76	211.65	193.00	178.66	167.33	158.20	150.71	144.48	139.23
14000	1226.76	642.00	447.65	350.89	293.18	254.98	227.93	207.84	192.40	180.20	170.37	162.30	155.59	149.94
15000	1314.39	687.86	479.62	375.96	314.12	273.19	244.21	222.69	206.14	193.08	182.54	173.89	166.70	160.65
16000	1402.01	733.72	511.60	401.02	335.06	291.40	260.49	237.53	219.88	205.95	194.71	185.49	177.82	171.36
17000	1489.64	779.57	543.57	426.08	356.00	309.61	276.77	252.38	233.63	218.82	206.88	197.08	188.93	182.07
18000	1577.26	825.43	575.55	451.15	376.94	327.82	293.05	267.22	247.37	231.69	219.04	2C8.67	200.04	192.78
19000	1664.89	871.29	607.52	476.21	397.88	346.04	309.33	282.07	261.11	244.56	231.21	220.26	211.15	203.49
20000	1752.51	917.14	639.50	501.27	418.82	364.25	325.61	296.91	274.85	257.43	243.38	231.86	222.27	214.20
21000	1840.14	963.00	671.47	526.34	439.76	382.46	341.89	311.76	288.60	270.30	255.55	243.45	233.38	224.91
22000	1927.77	1008.86	703.45	551.40	460.70	400.67	358.17	326.61	302.34	283.18	267.72	255.04	244.49	235.62
23000	2015.39	1054.72	735.42	576.47	481.64	418.89	374.45	341.45	316.08	296.05	279.89	266.63	255.61	246.33
24000	2103.02	1100.57	767.39	601.53	502.58	437.10	390.73	356.30	329.82	308.92	292.06	278.23	266.72	257.04
25000	2190.64	1146.43	799.37	626.59	523.53	455.31	407.01	371.14	343.57	321.79	304.23	289.82	277.83	267.75
26000	2278.27	1192.29	831.34	651.66	544.47	473.52	423.29	385.99	357.31	334.66	316.40	301.41	288.95	278.46
27000	2365.89	1238.14	863.32	676.72	565.41	491.73	439.57	400.83	371.05	347.53	328.56	313.00	300.06	289.17
28000	2453.52	1284.00	895.29	701.78	586.35	509.95	455.85	415.68	384.79	360.40	340.73	324.60	311.17	299.88
29000	2541.14	1329.86	927.27	726.85	607.29	528.16	472.13	430.52	398.54	373.28	352.90	336.19	322.29	310.59
30000	2628.77	1375.71	959.24	751.91	628.23	546.37	488.41	445.37	412.28	386.15	365.07	347.78	333.40	321.30
31000	2716.39	1421.57	991.22	776.97	649.17	564.58	504.69	460.21	426.02	399.02	377.24	359.37	344.51	332.01
32000	2804.02	1467.43	1023.19	802.04	670.11	582.80	520.97	475.06	439.76	411.89	389.41	370.97	355.63	342.72
33000	2891.65	1513.29	1055.17	827.10	691.05	601.01	537.25	489.91	453.51	424.76	401.58	382.56	366.74	353.43
34000	2979.27	1559.14	1087.14	852.16	711.99	619.22	553.53	504.75	467.25	437.63	413.75	394.15	377.85	364.14
35000	3066.90	1605.00	1119.11	877.23	732.93	637.43	569.81	519.60	480.99	450.50	425.92	405.74	388.96	374.85
36000	3154.52	1650.86	1151.09	902.29	753.87	655.64	586.09	534.44	494.73	463.38	438.08	417.34	400.08	385.55
37000	3242.15	1696.71	1183.06	927.35	774.82	673.86	602.37	549.29	508.48	476.25	450.25	428.93	411.19	396.26
38000	3329.77	1742.57	1215.04	952.42	795.76	692.07	618.65	564.13	522.22	489.12	462.42	440.52	422.30	406.97
39000	3417.40	1788.43	1247.01	977.48	816.70	710.28	634.93	578.98	535.96	501.99	474.59	452.11	433.42	417.68
40000	3505.02	1834.28	1278.99	1002.54	837.64	728.49	651.21	593.82	549.70	514.86	486.76	463.71	444.53	428.39
41000	3592.65	1880.14	1310.96	1027.61	858.58	746.71	667.49	608.67	563.45	527.73	498.93	475.30	455.64	439.10
42000	3680.27	1926.00	1342.94	1052.67	879.52	764.92	683.77	623.51	577.19	540.60	511.10	486.89	466.76	449.81
43000	3767.90	1971.86	1374.91	1077.73	900.46	783.13	700.05	638.36	590.93	553.48	523.27	498.48	477.87	460.52
44000	3855.53	2017.71	1406.89	1102.80	921.40	801.34	716.33	653.21	604.67	566.35	535.44	510.08	488.98	471.23
45000	3943.15	2063.57	1438.86	1127.86	942.34	819.55	732.61	668.05	618.42	579.22	547.60	521.67	500.10	481.94
46000	4030.78	2109.43	1470.83	1152.93	963.28	837.77	748.89	682.90	632.16	592.09	559.77	533.26	511.21	492.65
47000	4118.40	2155.28	1502.81	1177.99	984.22	855.98	765.17	697.74	645.90	604.96	571.94	544.85	522.32	503.36
48000	4206.03	2201.14	1534.78	1203.05	1005.16	874.19	781.45	712.59	659.64	617.83	584.11	556.45	533.44	514.07
49000	4293.65	2247.00	1566.76	1228.12	1026.11	892.40	797.73	727.43	673.39	630.70	596.28	568.04	544.55	524.78
50000	4381.28	2292.85	1598.73	1253.18	1047.05	910.62	814.01	742.28	687.13	643.58	608.45	579.63	555.66	535.49
55000	4819.41	2522.14	1758.61	1378.50	1151.75	1001.68	895.41	816.51	755.84	707.93	669.29	637.59	611.23	589.04
60000	5257.53	2751.42	1918.48	1503.81	1256.45	1092.74	976.81	890.73	824.55	772.29	730.14	695.56	666.79	642.59
65000	5695.66	2980.71	2078.35	1629.13	1361.16	1183.80	1058.21	964.96	893.27	836.65	790.98	753.52	722.36	696.14
70000	6133.79	3209.99	2238.22	1754.45	1465.86	1274.86	1139.61	1039.19	961.98	901.00	851.83	811.48	777.92	749.69
75000	6571.92	3439.28	2398.10	1879.77	1570.57	1365.92	1221.01	1113.42	1030.69	965.36	912.67	869.45	833.49	803.23
80000	7010.04	3668.56	2557.97	2005.08	1675.27	1456.98	1302.41	1187.64	1099.40	1029.72	973.51	927.41	889.06	856.78
85000	7448.17	3897.85	2717.84	2130.40	1779.98	1548.04	1383.81	1261.87	1168.12	1094.08	1034.36	985.37	944.62	910.33
90000	7886.30	4127.13	2877.71	2255.72	1884.68	1639.10	1465.21	1336.10	1236.83	1158.43	1095.20	1043.33	1000.19	963.88
95000	8324.43	4356.42	3037.59	2381.04	1989.38	1730.17	1546.61	1410.32	1305.54	1222.79	1156.05	1101.30	1055.75	1017.43
100000	8762.55	4585.70	3197.46	2506.35	2094.09	1821.23	1628.01	1484.55	1374.25	1287.15	1216.89	1159.26	1111.32	1070.98

MONTHLY PAYMENT
REQUIRED TO AMORTIZE A LOAN

9.375%

TERM AMOUNT	15 Years	16 Years	17 Years	18 Years	19 Years	20 Years	21 Years	22 Years	23 Years	24 Years	25 Years	30 Years	35 Years	40 Years
5	.06	.06	.05	.05	.05	.05	.05	.05	.05	.05	.05	.05	.05	.05
10	.11	.11	.10	.10	.10	.10	.10	.09	.09	.09	.09	.09	.09	.09
15	.16	.16	.15	.15	.15	.14	.14	.14	.14	.14	.13	.13	.13	.13
25	.26	.26	.25	.25	.24	.24	.23	.23	.23	.22	.22	.21	.21	.21
50	.52	.51	.50	.49	.48	.47	.46	.45	.45	.44	.44	.42	.41	.41
75	.78	.76	.74	.73	.71	.70	.69	.68	.67	.66	.65	.63	.61	.61
100	1.04	1.01	.99	.97	.95	.93	.91	.90	.89	.88	.87	.84	.82	.81
200	2.08	2.02	1.97	1.93	1.89	1.85	1.82	1.80	1.77	1.75	1.74	1.67	1.63	1.61
300	3.12	3.03	2.95	2.89	2.83	2.78	2.73	2.69	2.66	2.63	2.60	2.50	2.44	2.41
400	4.15	4.03	3.93	3.85	3.77	3.70	3.64	3.59	3.54	3.50	3.47	3.33	3.25	3.21
500	5.19	5.04	4.91	4.81	4.71	4.62	4.55	4.49	4.43	4.38	4.33	4.16	4.07	4.01
600	6.23	6.05	5.90	5.77	5.65	5.55	5.46	5.38	5.31	5.25	5.20	5.00	4.88	4.81
700	7.26	7.06	6.88	6.73	6.59	6.47	6.37	6.28	6.20	6.12	6.06	5.83	5.69	5.61
800	8.30	8.06	7.86	7.69	7.53	7.40	7.28	7.17	7.08	7.00	6.93	6.66	6.50	6.41
900	9.34	9.07	8.84	8.65	8.47	8.32	8.19	8.07	7.97	7.87	7.79	7.49	7.31	7.21
1000	10.37	10.08	9.82	9.61	9.41	9.24	9.10	8.97	8.85	8.75	8.66	8.32	8.13	8.01
2000	20.74	20.15	19.64	19.21	18.82	18.48	18.19	17.93	17.69	17.49	17.31	16.64	16.25	16.01
3000	31.11	30.22	29.46	28.81	28.23	27.72	27.28	26.89	26.54	26.23	25.96	24.96	24.37	24.02
4000	41.47	40.30	39.28	38.41	37.64	36.96	36.37	35.85	35.38	34.97	34.61	33.27	32.49	32.02
5000	51.84	50.37	49.10	48.01	47.05	46.20	45.46	44.81	44.23	43.71	43.26	41.59	40.61	40.02
6000	62.21	60.44	58.92	57.61	56.45	55.44	54.56	53.77	53.07	52.46	51.91	49.91	48.73	48.03
7000	72.57	70.52	68.74	67.21	65.86	64.68	63.65	62.73	61.92	61.20	60.56	58.23	56.86	56.03
8000	82.94	80.59	78.56	76.81	75.27	73.92	72.74	71.69	70.76	69.94	69.21	66.54	64.98	64.03
9000	93.31	90.66	88.38	86.41	84.68	83.16	81.83	80.65	79.61	78.68	77.86	74.86	73.10	72.04
10000	103.67	100.74	98.20	96.01	94.09	92.40	90.92	89.61	88.45	87.42	86.51	83.18	81.22	80.04
11000	114.04	110.81	108.02	105.61	103.49	101.64	100.01	98.58	97.30	96.17	95.16	91.50	89.34	88.04
12000	124.41	120.88	117.84	115.21	112.90	110.00	109.11	107.54	106.14	104.91	103.81	99.81	97.46	96.05
13000	134.78	130.96	127.66	124.81	122.31	120.12	118.20	116.50	114.99	113.65	112.46	108.13	105.59	104.05
14000	145.14	141.03	137.48	134.41	131.72	129.36	127.29	125.46	123.83	122.39	121.11	116.45	113.71	112.05
15000	155.51	151.10	147.30	144.01	141.13	138.60	136.38	134.42	132.68	131.13	129.76	124.77	121.83	120.06
16000	165.88	161.18	157.12	153.61	150.53	147.84	145.47	143.38	141.52	139.88	138.41	133.08	129.95	128.06
17000	176.24	171.25	166.94	163.21	159.94	157.08	154.56	152.34	150.37	148.62	147.06	141.40	138.07	136.06
18000	186.61	181.32	176.76	172.81	169.35	166.32	163.66	161.30	159.21	157.36	155.71	149.72	146.19	144.07
19000	196.98	191.40	186.58	182.41	178.76	175.56	172.75	170.26	168.06	166.10	164.36	158.04	154.32	152.07
20000	207.34	201.47	196.40	192.01	188.17	184.80	181.84	179.22	176.90	174.84	173.01	166.35	162.44	160.07
21000	217.71	211.54	206.22	201.61	197.57	194.04	190.93	188.18	185.75	183.59	181.66	174.67	170.56	168.08
22000	228.08	221.62	216.04	211.21	206.98	203.28	200.02	197.15	194.59	192.33	190.31	182.99	178.68	176.08
23000	238.44	231.69	225.86	220.81	216.39	212.52	209.12	206.11	203.44	201.07	198.96	191.31	186.80	184.09
24000	248.81	241.76	235.68	230.41	225.80	221.76	218.21	215.07	212.28	209.81	207.61	199.62	194.92	192.09
25000	259.18	251.84	245.50	240.01	235.21	231.00	227.30	224.03	221.13	218.55	216.26	207.94	203.05	200.09
26000	269.55	261.91	255.32	249.61	244.62	240.24	236.39	232.99	229.97	227.30	224.91	216.26	211.17	208.10
27000	279.91	271.98	265.14	259.21	254.02	249.48	245.48	241.95	238.82	236.04	233.56	224.58	219.29	216.10
28000	290.28	282.06	274.96	268.81	263.43	258.72	254.57	250.91	247.66	244.78	242.21	232.89	227.41	224.10
29000	300.65	292.13	284.78	278.41	272.84	267.96	263.67	259.87	256.51	253.52	250.86	241.21	235.53	232.11
30000	311.01	302.20	294.60	288.01	282.25	277.20	272.76	268.83	265.35	262.26	259.51	249.53	243.65	240.11
31000	321.38	312.28	304.42	297.61	291.66	286.44	281.85	277.79	274.20	271.01	268.16	257.85	251.78	248.11
32000	331.75	322.35	314.24	307.21	301.06	295.68	290.94	286.75	283.04	279.75	276.81	266.16	259.90	256.12
33000	342.11	332.42	324.06	316.81	310.47	304.92	300.03	295.72	291.89	288.49	285.46	274.48	268.02	264.12
34000	352.48	342.50	333.88	326.41	319.88	314.16	309.12	304.68	300.73	297.23	294.11	282.80	276.14	272.12
35000	362.85	352.57	343.70	336.01	329.29	323.40	318.22	313.64	309.58	305.97	302.76	291.12	284.26	280.13
36000	373.22	362.64	353.52	345.61	338.70	332.64	327.31	322.60	318.42	314.72	311.41	299.43	292.38	288.13
37000	383.58	372.72	363.34	355.21	348.10	341.88	336.40	331.56	327.27	323.46	320.06	307.75	300.51	296.13
38000	393.95	382.79	373.16	364.81	357.51	351.12	345.49	340.52	336.11	332.20	328.71	316.07	308.63	304.14
39000	404.32	392.86	382.98	374.41	366.92	360.36	354.58	349.48	344.96	340.94	337.36	324.39	316.75	312.14
40000	414.68	402.94	392.80	384.01	376.33	369.60	363.67	358.44	353.80	349.68	346.01	332.70	324.87	320.14
41000	425.05	413.01	402.62	393.61	385.74	378.84	372.77	367.40	362.65	358.43	354.66	341.02	332.99	328.15
42000	435.42	423.08	412.44	403.21	395.14	388.08	381.86	376.36	371.49	367.17	363.31	349.34	341.11	336.15
43000	445.78	433.16	422.26	412.81	404.55	397.32	390.95	385.32	380.34	375.91	371.97	357.66	349.24	344.15
44000	456.15	443.23	432.08	422.41	413.96	406.56	400.04	394.29	389.18	384.65	380.62	365.97	357.36	352.16
45000	466.52	453.30	441.90	432.01	423.37	415.80	409.13	403.25	398.03	393.39	389.27	374.29	365.48	360.16
46000	476.88	463.38	451.72	441.61	432.78	425.04	418.23	412.21	406.87	402.14	397.92	382.61	373.60	368.17
47000	487.25	473.45	461.54	451.21	442.19	434.28	427.32	421.17	415.72	410.88	406.57	390.93	381.72	376.17
48000	497.62	483.52	471.36	460.81	451.59	443.52	436.41	430.13	424.56	419.62	415.22	399.24	389.84	384.17
49000	507.99	493.60	481.18	470.41	461.00	452.76	445.50	439.09	433.41	428.36	423.87	407.56	397.97	392.18
50000	518.35	503.67	491.00	480.01	470.41	462.00	454.59	448.05	442.25	437.10	432.52	415.88	406.09	400.18
55000	570.19	554.04	540.10	528.01	517.45	508.20	500.05	492.86	486.48	480.81	475.77	457.47	446.70	440.20
60000	622.02	604.40	589.20	576.01	564.49	554.40	545.51	537.66	530.70	524.52	519.02	499.05	487.30	480.21
65000	673.86	654.77	638.30	624.01	611.53	600.59	590.97	582.46	574.93	568.23	562.27	540.64	527.91	520.23
70000	725.69	705.14	687.40	672.01	658.57	646.79	636.43	627.27	619.15	611.94	605.52	582.23	568.52	560.25
75000	777.53	755.50	736.50	720.01	705.61	692.99	681.89	672.07	663.38	655.65	648.77	623.82	609.13	600.27
80000	829.36	805.87	785.60	768.01	752.65	739.19	727.34	716.88	707.60	699.36	692.02	665.40	649.74	640.28
85000	881.20	856.24	834.70	816.01	799.69	785.39	772.80	761.68	751.83	743.07	735.27	706.99	690.34	680.30
90000	933.03	906.60	883.80	864.01	846.73	831.59	818.26	806.49	796.05	786.78	778.53	748.58	730.95	720.32
95000	984.87	956.97	932.90	912.01	893.77	877.79	863.72	851.29	840.28	830.49	821.78	790.17	771.56	760.34
100000	1036.70	1007.33	982.00	960.01	940.81	923.99	909.18	896.10	884.50	874.20	865.03	831.75	812.17	800.35

9.400%

TERM AMOUNT	1 Year	2 Years	3 Years	4 Years	5 Years	6 Years	7 Years	8 Years	9 Years	10 Years	11 Years	12 Years	13 Years	14 Years
5	.44	.23	.16	.13	.11	.10	.09	.08	.07	.07	.07	.06	.06	.06
10	.88	.46	.32	.26	.21	.19	.17	.15	.14	.13	.13	.12	.12	.11
15	1.32	.69	.48	.38	.32	.28	.25	.23	.21	.20	.19	.18	.17	.17
25	2.20	1.15	.80	.63	.53	.46	.41	.38	.35	.33	.31	.30	.28	.27
50	4.39	2.30	1.60	1.26	1.05	.92	.82	.75	.69	.65	.61	.59	.56	.54
75	6.58	3.45	2.40	1.89	1.58	1.37	1.23	1.12	1.04	.97	.92	.88	.84	.81
100	8.77	4.59	3.20	2.51	2.10	1.83	1.63	1.49	1.38	1.29	1.22	1.17	1.12	1.08
200	17.53	9.18	6.40	5.02	4.20	3.65	3.26	2.98	2.76	2.58	2.44	2.33	2.23	2.15
300	26.30	13.77	9.60	7.53	6.29	5.47	4.89	4.46	4.13	3.87	3.66	3.49	3.34	3.22
400	35.06	18.35	12.80	10.04	8.39	7.29	6.52	5.95	5.51	5.16	4.88	4.65	4.46	4.29
500	43.82	22.94	16.00	12.54	10.48	9.12	8.15	7.43	6.88	6.45	6.10	5.81	5.57	5.37
600	52.59	27.53	19.20	15.05	12.58	10.94	9.78	8.92	8.26	7.74	7.31	6.97	6.68	6.44
700	61.35	32.11	22.40	17.56	14.67	12.76	11.41	10.41	9.63	9.02	8.53	8.13	7.79	7.51
800	70.11	36.70	25.59	20.07	16.77	14.58	13.04	11.89	11.01	10.31	9.75	9.29	8.91	8.58
900	78.88	41.29	28.79	22.57	18.86	16.41	14.67	13.38	12.39	11.60	10.97	10.45	10.02	9.66
1000	87.64	45.87	31.99	25.08	20.96	18.23	16.30	14.86	13.76	12.89	12.19	11.61	11.13	10.73
2000	175.28	91.74	63.98	50.16	41.91	36.45	32.59	29.72	27.52	25.78	24.37	23.22	22.26	21.45
3000	262.92	137.61	95.96	75.23	62.86	54.68	48.88	44.58	41.27	38.66	36.55	34.83	33.39	32.18
4000	350.55	183.48	127.95	100.31	83.82	72.90	65.18	59.44	55.03	51.55	48.74	46.43	44.52	42.90
5000	438.19	229.35	159.94	125.38	104.77	91.13	81.47	74.30	68.78	64.43	60.92	58.04	55.64	53.63
6000	525.83	275.22	191.92	150.46	125.72	109.35	97.76	89.16	82.54	77.32	73.10	69.65	66.77	64.35
7000	613.46	321.08	223.91	175.53	146.68	127.58	114.05	104.01	96.30	90.20	85.28	81.25	77.90	75.08
8000	701.10	366.95	255.89	200.61	167.63	145.80	130.35	118.87	110.05	103.09	97.47	92.86	89.03	85.80
9000	788.74	412.82	287.88	225.68	188.58	164.03	146.64	133.73	123.81	115.97	109.65	104.47	100.15	96.53
10000	876.38	458.69	319.87	250.76	209.54	182.25	162.93	148.59	137.56	128.86	121.83	116.07	111.28	107.25
11000	964.01	504.56	351.85	275.83	230.49	200.48	179.23	163.45	151.32	141.74	134.02	127.68	122.41	117.97
12000	1051.65	550.43	383.84	300.91	251.44	218.70	195.52	178.31	165.08	154.63	146.20	139.29	133.54	128.70
13000	1139.29	596.30	415.83	325.99	272.39	236.93	211.81	193.17	178.83	167.51	158.38	150.89	144.66	139.42
14000	1226.92	642.16	447.81	351.06	293.35	255.15	228.10	208.02	192.59	180.40	170.56	162.50	155.79	150.15
15000	1314.56	688.03	479.80	376.14	314.30	273.38	244.40	222.88	206.34	193.28	182.75	174.11	166.92	160.87
16000	1402.20	733.90	511.78	401.21	335.25	291.60	260.69	237.74	220.10	206.17	194.93	185.71	178.05	171.60
17000	1489.84	779.77	543.77	426.29	356.21	309.82	276.98	252.60	233.85	219.05	207.11	197.32	189.17	182.32
18000	1577.47	825.64	575.76	451.36	377.16	328.05	293.28	267.46	247.61	231.94	219.30	208.93	200.30	193.05
19000	1665.11	871.51	607.74	476.44	398.11	346.27	309.57	282.32	261.37	244.82	231.48	220.53	211.43	203.77
20000	1752.75	917.37	639.73	501.51	419.07	364.50	325.86	297.18	275.12	257.71	243.66	232.14	222.56	214.49
21000	1840.38	963.24	671.72	526.59	440.02	382.72	342.15	312.03	288.88	270.59	255.84	243.75	233.69	225.22
22000	1928.02	1009.11	703.70	551.66	460.97	400.95	358.45	326.89	302.63	283.48	268.03	255.35	244.81	235.94
23000	2015.66	1054.98	735.69	576.74	481.92	419.17	374.74	341.75	316.39	296.36	280.21	266.96	255.94	246.67
24000	2103.29	1100.85	767.67	601.81	502.88	437.40	391.03	356.61	330.15	309.25	292.39	278.57	267.07	257.39
25000	2190.93	1146.72	799.66	626.89	523.83	455.62	407.33	371.47	343.90	322.13	304.58	290.17	278.20	268.12
26000	2278.57	1192.59	831.65	651.97	544.78	473.85	423.62	386.33	357.66	335.02	316.76	301.78	289.32	278.84
27000	2366.21	1238.45	863.63	677.04	565.74	492.07	439.91	401.19	371.41	347.90	328.94	313.39	300.45	289.57
28000	2453.84	1284.32	895.62	702.12	586.69	510.30	456.20	416.04	385.17	360.79	341.12	324.99	311.58	300.29
29000	2541.48	1330.19	927.61	727.19	607.64	528.52	472.50	430.90	398.92	373.67	353.31	336.60	322.71	311.02
30000	2629.12	1376.06	959.59	752.27	628.60	546.75	488.79	445.76	412.68	386.56	365.49	348.21	333.83	321.74
31000	2716.75	1421.93	991.58	777.34	649.55	564.97	505.08	460.62	426.44	399.44	377.67	359.81	344.96	332.46
32000	2804.39	1467.80	1023.56	802.42	670.50	583.20	521.38	475.48	440.19	412.33	389.85	371.42	356.09	343.19
33000	2892.03	1513.67	1055.55	827.49	691.45	601.42	537.67	490.34	453.95	425.21	402.04	383.03	367.22	353.91
34000	2979.67	1559.53	1087.54	852.57	712.41	619.64	553.96	505.20	467.70	438.10	414.22	394.63	378.34	364.64
35000	3067.30	1605.40	1119.52	877.64	733.36	637.87	570.25	520.05	481.46	450.98	426.40	406.24	389.47	375.36
36000	3154.94	1651.27	1151.51	902.72	754.31	656.09	586.55	534.91	495.22	463.87	438.59	417.85	400.60	386.09
37000	3242.58	1697.14	1183.50	927.80	775.27	674.32	602.84	549.77	508.97	476.75	450.77	429.45	411.73	396.81
38000	3330.21	1743.01	1215.48	952.87	796.22	692.54	619.13	564.63	522.73	489.64	462.95	441.06	422.85	407.54
39000	3417.85	1788.88	1247.47	977.95	817.17	710.77	635.42	579.49	536.48	502.52	475.13	452.67	433.98	418.26
40000	3505.49	1834.74	1279.45	1003.02	838.13	728.99	651.72	594.35	550.24	515.41	487.32	464.28	445.11	428.98
41000	3593.13	1880.61	1311.44	1028.10	859.08	747.22	668.01	609.21	563.99	528.29	499.50	475.88	456.24	439.71
42000	3680.76	1926.48	1343.43	1053.17	880.03	765.44	684.30	624.06	577.75	541.18	511.68	487.49	467.37	450.43
43000	3768.40	1972.35	1375.41	1078.25	900.99	783.67	700.60	638.92	591.51	554.06	523.87	499.10	478.49	461.16
44000	3856.04	2018.22	1407.40	1103.32	921.94	801.89	716.89	653.78	605.26	566.95	536.05	510.70	489.62	471.88
45000	3943.67	2064.09	1439.39	1128.40	942.89	820.12	733.18	668.64	619.02	579.83	548.23	522.31	500.75	482.61
46000	4031.31	2109.96	1471.37	1153.47	963.84	838.34	749.47	683.50	632.77	592.72	560.41	533.92	511.88	493.33
47000	4118.95	2155.82	1503.36	1178.55	984.80	856.57	765.77	698.36	646.53	605.60	572.60	545.52	523.00	504.06
48000	4206.58	2201.69	1535.34	1203.62	1005.75	874.79	782.06	713.22	660.29	618.49	584.78	557.13	534.13	514.78
49000	4294.22	2247.56	1567.33	1228.70	1026.70	893.02	798.35	728.07	674.04	631.37	596.96	568.74	545.26	525.51
50000	4381.86	2293.43	1599.32	1253.78	1047.66	911.24	814.65	742.93	687.80	644.26	609.15	580.34	556.39	536.23
55000	4820.04	2522.77	1759.25	1379.15	1152.42	1002.36	896.11	817.22	756.58	708.68	670.06	638.38	612.02	589.85
60000	5258.23	2752.11	1919.18	1504.53	1257.19	1093.49	977.57	891.52	825.36	773.11	730.97	696.41	667.66	643.47
65000	5696.42	2981.46	2079.11	1629.91	1361.95	1184.61	1059.04	965.81	894.13	837.53	791.89	754.44	723.30	697.10
70000	6134.60	3210.80	2239.04	1755.28	1466.72	1275.73	1140.50	1040.10	962.91	901.96	852.80	812.48	778.94	750.72
75000	6572.79	3440.14	2398.97	1880.66	1571.48	1366.86	1221.97	1114.40	1031.69	966.39	913.72	870.51	834.58	804.34
80000	7010.97	3669.48	2558.90	2006.04	1676.25	1457.98	1303.43	1188.69	1100.47	1030.81	974.63	928.55	890.22	857.96
85000	7449.16	3898.83	2718.83	2131.41	1781.01	1549.10	1384.89	1262.98	1169.25	1095.24	1035.54	986.58	945.85	911.59
90000	7887.34	4128.17	2878.77	2256.79	1885.78	1640.23	1466.36	1337.27	1238.03	1159.66	1096.46	1044.61	1001.49	965.21
95000	8325.53	4357.51	3038.70	2382.17	1990.54	1731.35	1547.82	1411.57	1306.81	1224.09	1157.37	1102.65	1057.13	1018.83
100000	8763.71	4586.85	3198.63	2507.55	2095.31	1822.48	1629.29	1485.86	1375.59	1288.51	1218.29	1160.68	1112.77	1072.45

TERM	15 Years	16 Years	17 Years	18 Years	19 Years	20 Years	21 Years	22 Years	23 Years	24 Years	25 Years	30 Years	35 Years	40 Years
AMOUNT														
5	.06	.06	.05	.05	.05	.05	.05	.05	.05	.05	.05	.05	.05	.05
10	.11	.11	.10	.10	.10	.10	.10	.09	.09	.09	.09	.09	.09	.09
15	.16	.16	.15	.15	.15	.14	.14	.14	.14	.14	.14	.13	.13	.13
25	.26	.26	.25	.25	.24	.24	.23	.23	.23	.22	.22	.21	.21	.21
50	.52	.51	.50	.49	.48	.47	.46	.45	.45	.44	.44	.42	.41	.41
75	.78	.76	.74	.73	.71	.70	.69	.68	.67	.66	.66	.63	.62	.61
100	1.04	1.01	.99	.97	.95	.93	.92	.90	.89	.88	.87	.84	.82	.81
200	2.08	2.02	1.97	1.93	1.89	1.86	1.83	1.80	1.78	1.76	1.74	1.67	1.63	1.61
300	3.12	3.03	2.96	2.89	2.83	2.78	2.74	2.70	2.66	2.63	2.61	2.51	2.45	2.41
400	4.16	4.04	3.94	3.85	3.77	3.71	3.65	3.60	3.55	3.51	3.47	3.34	3.26	3.21
500	5.20	5.05	4.92	4.81	4.72	4.63	4.56	4.49	4.44	4.38	4.34	4.17	4.08	4.02
600	6.23	6.06	5.91	5.77	5.66	5.56	5.47	5.39	5.32	5.26	5.21	5.01	4.89	4.82
700	7.27	7.07	6.89	6.74	6.60	6.48	6.38	6.29	6.21	6.14	6.07	5.84	5.70	5.62
800	8.31	8.08	7.87	7.70	7.54	7.41	7.29	7.19	7.09	7.01	6.94	6.67	6.52	6.42
900	9.35	9.08	8.86	8.66	8.49	8.34	8.20	8.08	7.98	7.89	7.81	7.51	7.33	7.23
1000	10.39	10.09	9.84	9.62	9.43	9.26	9.11	8.98	8.87	8.76	8.67	8.34	8.15	8.03
2000	20.77	20.18	19.68	19.24	18.85	18.52	18.22	17.96	17.73	17.52	17.34	16.68	16.29	16.05
3000	31.15	30.27	29.51	28.85	28.28	27.77	27.33	26.94	26.59	26.28	26.01	25.01	24.43	24.07
4000	41.53	40.36	39.35	38.47	37.70	37.03	36.44	35.92	35.45	35.04	34.68	33.35	32.57	32.10
5000	51.91	50.45	49.18	48.06	47.13	46.29	45.55	44.89	44.31	43.80	43.34	41.68	40.71	40.12
6000	62.30	60.54	59.02	57.70	56.55	55.54	54.65	53.87	53.18	52.56	52.01	50.02	48.85	48.14
7000	72.68	70.63	68.85	67.32	65.97	64.80	63.76	62.85	62.04	61.32	60.68	58.35	56.99	56.17
8000	83.06	80.71	78.69	76.93	75.40	74.05	72.87	71.83	70.90	70.08	69.35	66.69	65.13	64.19
9000	93.44	90.80	88.52	86.55	84.82	83.31	81.98	80.80	79.76	78.84	78.01	75.03	73.27	72.21
10000	103.82	100.89	98.36	96.16	94.25	92.57	91.09	89.78	88.62	87.60	86.68	83.36	81.41	80.23
11000	114.21	110.98	108.20	105.78	103.67	101.82	100.20	98.76	97.49	96.36	95.35	91.70	89.55	88.26
12000	124.59	121.07	118.03	115.39	113.09	111.08	109.30	107.74	106.35	105.11	104.02	100.03	97.69	96.28
13000	134.97	131.16	127.87	125.01	122.52	120.33	118.41	116.71	115.21	113.87	112.68	108.37	105.83	104.30
14000	145.35	141.25	137.70	134.63	131.94	129.59	127.52	125.69	124.07	122.63	121.35	116.70	113.97	112.33
15000	155.73	151.33	147.54	144.24	141.37	138.85	136.63	134.67	132.93	131.39	130.02	125.04	122.11	120.35
16000	166.12	161.42	157.37	153.86	150.79	148.10	145.74	143.65	141.80	140.15	138.69	133.38	130.25	128.37
17000	176.50	171.51	167.21	163.47	160.22	157.36	154.85	152.62	150.66	148.91	147.35	141.71	138.39	136.39
18000	186.88	181.60	177.04	173.09	169.64	166.61	163.95	161.60	159.52	157.67	156.02	150.05	146.53	144.42
19000	197.26	191.69	186.88	182.71	179.06	175.87	173.06	170.58	168.38	166.43	164.69	158.38	154.67	152.44
20000	207.64	201.78	196.71	192.32	188.49	185.13	182.17	179.56	177.24	175.19	173.36	166.72	162.82	160.46
21000	218.03	211.87	206.55	201.94	197.91	194.38	191.28	188.54	186.11	183.95	182.02	175.05	170.96	168.49
22000	228.41	221.95	216.39	211.55	207.34	203.64	200.39	197.51	194.97	192.71	190.69	183.39	179.10	176.51
23000	238.79	232.04	226.22	221.17	216.76	212.90	209.49	206.49	203.83	201.46	199.36	191.73	187.24	184.53
24000	249.17	242.13	236.06	230.78	226.18	222.15	218.60	215.47	212.69	210.22	208.03	200.06	195.38	192.55
25000	259.55	252.22	245.89	240.40	235.61	231.41	227.71	224.45	221.55	218.98	216.69	208.40	203.52	200.58
26000	269.94	262.31	255.73	250.02	245.03	240.66	236.82	233.42	230.41	227.74	225.36	216.73	211.66	208.60
27000	280.32	272.40	265.56	259.63	254.46	249.92	245.93	242.40	239.28	236.50	234.03	225.07	219.80	216.62
28000	290.70	282.49	275.40	269.25	263.88	259.18	255.04	251.38	248.14	245.26	242.70	233.40	227.94	224.65
29000	301.08	292.57	285.23	278.86	273.30	268.43	264.14	260.36	257.00	254.02	251.36	241.74	236.08	232.67
30000	311.46	302.66	295.07	288.48	282.73	277.69	273.25	269.33	265.86	262.78	260.03	250.08	244.22	240.69
31000	321.85	312.75	304.91	298.09	292.15	286.94	282.36	278.31	274.72	271.54	268.70	258.41	252.36	248.71
32000	332.23	322.84	314.74	307.71	301.58	296.20	291.47	287.29	283.59	280.30	277.37	266.75	260.50	256.74
33000	342.61	332.93	324.58	317.33	311.00	305.46	300.58	296.27	292.45	289.06	286.03	275.08	268.64	264.76
34000	352.99	343.02	334.41	326.94	320.43	314.71	309.69	305.24	301.31	297.81	294.70	283.42	276.78	272.78
35000	363.37	353.11	344.25	336.56	329.85	323.97	318.79	314.22	310.17	306.57	303.37	291.75	284.92	280.81
36000	373.76	363.19	354.08	346.17	339.27	333.22	327.90	323.20	319.03	315.33	312.04	300.09	293.06	288.83
37000	384.14	373.28	363.92	355.79	348.70	342.48	337.01	332.18	327.90	324.09	320.70	308.43	301.20	296.85
38000	394.52	383.37	373.75	365.41	358.12	351.74	346.12	341.16	336.76	332.85	329.37	316.76	309.34	304.87
39000	404.90	393.46	383.59	375.02	367.55	360.99	355.23	350.13	345.62	341.61	338.04	325.10	317.48	312.90
40000	415.28	403.55	393.42	384.64	376.97	370.25	364.33	359.11	354.48	350.37	346.71	333.43	325.63	320.92
41000	425.67	413.64	403.26	394.25	386.39	379.51	373.44	368.09	363.34	359.13	355.37	341.77	333.77	328.94
42000	436.05	423.73	413.10	403.87	395.82	388.76	382.55	377.07	372.21	367.89	364.04	350.10	341.91	336.97
43000	446.43	433.81	422.93	413.48	405.24	398.02	391.66	386.04	381.07	376.65	372.71	358.44	350.05	344.99
44000	456.81	443.90	432.77	423.10	414.67	407.27	400.77	395.02	389.93	385.41	381.38	366.77	358.19	353.01
45000	467.19	453.99	442.60	432.72	424.09	416.53	409.88	404.00	398.79	394.17	390.04	375.11	366.33	361.04
46000	477.58	464.08	452.44	442.33	433.51	425.79	418.98	412.98	407.65	402.92	398.71	383.45	374.47	369.06
47000	487.96	474.17	462.27	451.95	442.94	435.04	428.09	421.95	416.52	411.68	407.38	391.78	382.61	377.08
48000	498.34	484.26	472.11	461.56	452.36	444.30	437.20	430.93	425.38	420.44	416.05	400.12	390.75	385.10
49000	508.72	494.35	481.94	471.18	461.79	453.55	446.31	439.91	434.24	429.20	424.72	408.45	398.89	393.13
50000	519.10	504.43	491.78	480.80	471.21	462.81	455.42	448.89	443.10	437.96	433.38	416.79	407.03	401.15
55000	571.01	554.88	540.96	528.87	518.33	509.09	500.96	493.77	487.41	481.76	476.72	458.47	447.73	441.26
60000	622.92	605.32	590.13	576.95	565.45	555.37	546.50	538.66	531.72	525.55	520.06	500.15	488.44	481.38
65000	674.83	655.76	639.31	625.03	612.57	601.65	592.04	583.55	576.03	569.35	563.40	541.82	529.14	521.49
70000	726.74	706.21	688.49	673.11	659.69	647.93	637.58	628.44	620.34	613.14	606.73	583.50	569.84	561.61
75000	778.65	756.65	737.67	721.19	706.81	694.21	683.12	673.33	664.65	656.94	650.07	625.18	610.54	601.72
80000	830.56	807.09	786.84	769.27	753.93	740.49	728.66	718.22	708.96	700.73	693.41	666.86	651.25	641.84
85000	882.47	857.54	836.02	817.35	801.06	786.77	774.21	763.10	753.27	744.53	736.75	708.54	691.95	681.95
90000	934.38	907.98	885.20	865.43	848.18	833.05	819.75	807.99	797.58	788.33	780.08	750.22	732.65	722.07
95000	986.29	958.42	934.38	913.51	895.30	879.34	865.29	852.88	841.89	832.12	823.42	791.89	773.35	762.18
100000	1038.20	1008.86	983.55	961.59	942.42	925.62	910.83	897.77	886.20	875.92	866.76	833.57	814.06	802.29

MONTHLY PAYMENT
REQUIRED TO AMORTIZE A LOAN

TERM AMOUNT	1 Year	2 Years	3 Years	4 Years	5 Years	6 Years	7 Years	8 Years	9 Years	10 Years	11 Years	12 Years	13 Years	14 Years
5	.44	.23	.17	.13	.11	.10	.09	.08	.07	.07	.07	.06	.06	.06
10	.88	.46	.33	.26	.22	.19	.17	.15	.14	.13	.13	.12	.12	.11
15	1.32	.69	.49	.38	.32	.28	.25	.23	.21	.20	.19	.18	.17	.17
25	2.20	1.15	.81	.63	.53	.46	.41	.38	.35	.33	.31	.30	.28	.27
50	4.39	2.30	1.61	1.26	1.06	.92	.82	.75	.70	.65	.62	.59	.56	.54
75	6.58	3.45	2.41	1.89	1.58	1.38	1.23	1.12	1.04	.98	.92	.88	.84	.81
100	8.77	4.60	3.21	2.52	2.11	1.83	1.64	1.50	1.39	1.30	1.23	1.17	1.12	1.08
200	17.54	9.19	6.41	5.03	4.21	3.66	3.27	2.99	2.77	2.59	2.45	2.34	2.24	2.16
300	26.31	13.78	9.61	7.54	6.31	5.49	4.91	4.48	4.15	3.89	3.68	3.50	3.36	3.24
400	35.08	18.37	12.82	10.05	8.41	7.31	6.54	5.97	5.55	5.10	4.90	4.67	4.48	4.32
500	43.85	22.96	16.02	12.57	10.51	9.14	8.18	7.46	6.91	6.47	6.12	5.84	5.60	5.40
600	52.62	27.55	19.22	15.08	12.61	10.97	9.81	8.95	8.29	7.77	7.35	7.00	6.72	6.48
700	61.38	32.15	22.43	17.59	14.71	12.80	11.45	10.44	9.67	9.06	8.57	8.17	7.84	7.55
800	70.15	36.74	25.63	20.10	16.81	14.62	13.08	11.93	11.05	10.36	9.80	9.34	8.95	8.63
900	78.92	41.33	28.83	22.62	18.91	16.45	14.71	13.42	12.43	11.65	11.02	10.50	10.07	9.71
1000	87.69	45.92	32.04	25.13	21.01	18.28	16.35	14.92	13.81	12.94	12.24	11.67	11.19	10.79
2000	175.37	91.83	64.07	50.25	42.01	36.55	32.69	29.83	27.62	25.88	24.48	23.33	22.38	21.57
3000	263.06	137.75	96.10	75.37	63.01	54.83	49.04	44.74	41.43	38.82	36.72	35.00	33.56	32.36
4000	350.74	183.66	128.14	100.50	84.01	73.10	65.38	59.65	55.24	51.76	48.96	46.66	44.75	43.14
5000	438.42	229.58	160.17	125.62	105.01	91.38	81.72	74.56	69.05	64.70	61.20	58.32	55.93	53.92
6000	526.11	275.49	192.20	150.74	126.02	109.65	98.07	89.47	82.86	77.64	73.44	69.99	67.12	64.71
7000	613.79	321.41	224.24	175.87	147.02	127.93	114.41	104.38	96.67	90.58	85.68	81.65	78.31	75.49
8000	701.47	367.32	256.27	200.99	168.02	146.20	130.76	119.29	110.48	103.52	97.91	93.31	89.49	86.27
9000	789.16	413.24	288.30	226.11	189.02	164.48	147.10	134.20	124.29	116.46	110.15	104.98	100.68	97.06
10000	876.84	459.15	320.33	251.24	210.02	182.75	163.44	149.11	138.10	129.40	122.39	116.64	111.86	107.84
11000	964.52	505.06	352.37	276.36	231.03	201.03	179.79	164.02	151.91	142.34	134.63	128.31	123.05	118.63
12000	1052.21	550.98	384.40	301.48	252.03	219.30	196.13	178.94	165.72	155.28	146.87	139.97	134.23	129.41
13000	1139.89	596.89	416.43	326.61	273.03	237.58	212.48	193.85	179.53	168.22	159.11	151.63	145.42	140.19
14000	1227.57	642.81	448.47	351.73	294.03	255.85	228.82	208.76	193.34	181.16	171.35	163.30	156.61	150.98
15000	1315.26	688.72	480.50	376.85	315.03	274.13	245.16	223.67	207.15	194.10	183.58	174.96	167.79	161.76
16000	1402.94	734.64	512.53	401.98	336.03	292.40	261.51	238.58	220.95	207.04	195.82	186.62	178.98	172.54
17000	1490.62	780.55	544.57	427.10	357.04	310.67	277.85	253.49	234.76	219.98	208.06	198.29	190.16	183.33
18000	1578.31	826.47	576.60	452.22	378.04	328.95	294.20	268.40	248.57	232.92	220.30	209.95	201.35	194.11
19000	1665.99	872.38	608.63	477.34	399.04	347.22	310.54	283.31	262.38	245.86	232.54	221.62	212.53	204.89
20000	1753.68	918.29	640.66	502.47	420.04	365.50	326.88	298.22	276.19	258.80	244.78	233.28	223.72	215.68
21000	1841.36	964.21	672.70	527.59	441.04	383.77	343.23	313.13	290.00	271.74	257.02	244.94	234.91	226.46
22000	1929.04	1010.12	704.73	552.71	462.05	402.05	359.57	328.04	303.81	284.68	269.26	256.61	246.09	237.25
23000	2016.73	1056.04	736.76	577.84	483.05	420.32	375.92	342.96	317.62	297.62	281.49	268.27	257.28	248.03
24000	2104.41	1101.95	768.80	602.96	504.05	438.60	392.26	357.87	331.43	310.56	293.73	279.93	268.46	258.81
25000	2192.09	1147.87	800.83	628.08	525.05	456.87	408.60	372.78	345.24	323.50	305.97	291.60	279.65	269.60
26000	2279.78	1193.78	832.86	653.21	546.05	475.15	424.95	387.69	359.05	336.44	318.21	303.26	290.83	280.38
27000	2367.46	1239.70	864.89	678.33	567.06	493.42	441.29	402.60	372.86	349.38	330.45	314.93	302.02	291.16
28000	2455.14	1285.61	896.93	703.45	588.06	511.70	457.64	417.51	386.67	362.32	342.69	326.59	313.21	301.95
29000	2542.83	1331.53	928.96	728.58	609.06	529.97	473.98	432.42	400.48	375.26	354.93	338.25	324.39	312.73
30000	2630.51	1377.44	960.99	753.70	630.06	548.25	490.32	447.33	414.29	388.20	367.16	349.92	335.58	323.52
31000	2718.19	1423.35	993.03	778.82	651.06	566.52	506.67	462.24	428.10	401.14	379.40	361.58	346.76	334.30
32000	2805.88	1469.27	1025.06	803.95	672.06	584.80	523.01	477.15	441.90	414.08	391.64	373.24	357.95	345.08
33000	2893.56	1515.18	1057.09	829.07	693.07	603.07	539.36	492.06	455.71	427.02	403.88	384.91	369.13	355.87
34000	2981.24	1561.10	1089.13	854.19	714.07	621.34	555.70	506.98	469.52	439.96	416.12	396.57	380.32	366.65
35000	3068.93	1607.01	1121.16	879.31	735.07	639.62	572.04	521.89	483.33	452.90	428.36	408.24	391.51	377.43
36000	3156.61	1652.93	1153.19	904.44	756.07	657.89	588.39	536.80	497.14	465.84	440.60	419.90	402.69	388.22
37000	3244.29	1698.84	1185.22	929.56	777.07	676.17	604.73	551.71	510.95	478.78	452.83	431.56	413.88	399.00
38000	3331.98	1744.76	1217.26	954.68	798.08	694.44	621.08	566.62	524.76	491.72	465.07	443.23	425.06	409.78
39000	3419.66	1790.67	1249.29	979.81	819.08	712.72	637.42	581.53	538.57	504.66	477.31	454.89	436.25	420.57
40000	3507.35	1836.58	1281.32	1004.93	840.08	730.99	653.76	596.44	552.38	517.60	489.55	466.55	447.43	431.35
41000	3595.03	1882.50	1313.36	1030.05	861.08	749.27	670.11	611.35	566.19	530.53	501.79	478.22	458.62	442.14
42000	3682.71	1928.41	1345.39	1055.18	882.08	767.54	686.45	626.26	580.00	543.47	514.03	489.88	469.81	452.92
43000	3770.40	1974.33	1377.42	1080.30	903.09	785.82	702.80	641.17	593.81	556.41	526.27	501.55	480.99	463.70
44000	3858.08	2020.24	1409.45	1105.42	924.09	804.09	719.14	656.08	607.62	569.35	538.51	513.21	492.18	474.49
45000	3945.76	2066.16	1441.49	1130.55	945.09	822.37	735.48	670.99	621.43	582.29	550.74	524.87	503.36	485.27
46000	4033.45	2112.07	1473.52	1155.67	966.09	840.64	751.83	685.91	635.24	595.23	562.98	536.54	514.55	496.05
47000	4121.13	2157.99	1505.55	1180.79	987.09	858.92	768.17	700.82	649.04	608.17	575.22	548.20	525.73	506.84
48000	4208.81	2203.90	1537.59	1205.92	1008.09	877.19	784.52	715.73	662.85	621.11	587.46	559.86	536.92	517.62
49000	4296.50	2249.82	1569.62	1231.04	1029.10	895.46	800.86	730.64	676.66	634.05	599.70	571.53	548.11	528.41
50000	4384.18	2295.73	1601.65	1256.16	1050.10	913.74	817.20	745.55	690.47	646.99	611.94	583.19	559.29	539.19
55000	4822.60	2525.30	1761.82	1381.78	1155.11	1005.11	898.92	820.10	759.52	711.69	673.13	641.51	615.22	593.11
60000	5261.02	2754.87	1921.98	1507.39	1260.12	1096.49	980.64	894.66	828.57	776.39	734.32	699.83	671.15	647.03
65000	5699.43	2984.45	2082.15	1633.01	1365.13	1187.86	1062.36	969.21	897.61	841.09	795.52	758.15	727.08	700.94
70000	6137.85	3214.02	2242.31	1758.62	1470.14	1279.23	1144.08	1043.77	966.66	905.79	856.71	816.47	783.01	754.86
75000	6576.27	3443.59	2402.48	1884.24	1575.14	1370.61	1225.80	1118.32	1035.71	970.49	917.90	874.78	838.93	808.78
80000	7014.69	3673.16	2562.64	2009.86	1680.15	1461.98	1307.52	1192.88	1104.75	1035.19	979.10	933.10	894.86	862.70
85000	7453.10	3902.74	2722.81	2135.47	1785.16	1553.35	1389.24	1267.43	1173.80	1099.88	1040.29	991.42	950.79	916.62
90000	7891.52	4132.31	2882.97	2261.09	1890.17	1644.73	1470.96	1341.98	1242.85	1164.58	1101.48	1049.74	1006.72	970.54
95000	8329.94	4361.88	3043.14	2386.70	1995.18	1736.10	1552.68	1416.54	1311.89	1229.28	1162.68	1108.06	1062.65	1024.45
100000	8768.36	4591.45	3203.30	2512.32	2100.19	1827.47	1634.40	1491.09	1380.94	1293.98	1223.87	1166.38	1118.58	1078.37

TERM AMOUNT	15 Years	16 Years	17 Years	18 Years	19 Years	20 Years	21 Years	22 Years	23 Years	24 Years	25 Years	30 Years	35 Years	40 Years
5	.06	.06	.05	.05	.05	.05	.05	.05	.05	.05	.05	.05	.05	.05
10	.11	.11	.10	.10	.10	.10	.10	.10	.09	.09	.09	.09	.09	.09
15	.16	.16	.15	.15	.15	.14	.14	.14	.14	.14	.14	.13	.13	.13
25	.27	.26	.25	.25	.24	.24	.23	.23	.23	.23	.22	.22	.21	.21
50	.53	.51	.50	.49	.48	.47	.46	.46	.45	.45	.44	.43	.42	.41
75	.79	.77	.75	.73	.72	.70	.69	.68	.67	.67	.66	.64	.62	.61
100	1.05	1.02	.99	.97	.95	.94	.92	.91	.90	.89	.88	.85	.83	.82
200	2.09	2.03	1.98	1.94	1.90	1.87	1.84	1.81	1.79	1.77	1.75	1.69	1.65	1.63
300	3.14	3.05	2.97	2.91	2.85	2.80	2.76	2.72	2.68	2.65	2.63	2.53	2.47	2.44
400	4.18	4.06	3.96	3.88	3.80	3.73	3.67	3.62	3.58	3.54	3.50	3.37	3.29	3.25
500	5.23	5.08	4.95	4.84	4.75	4.67	4.59	4.53	4.47	4.42	4.37	4.21	4.11	4.06
600	6.27	6.09	5.94	5.81	5.70	5.60	5.51	5.43	5.36	5.30	5.25	5.05	4.93	4.87
700	7.31	7.11	6.93	6.78	6.65	6.53	6.43	6.34	6.26	6.18	6.12	5.89	5.76	5.68
800	8.36	8.12	7.92	7.75	7.60	7.46	7.34	7.24	7.15	7.07	6.99	6.73	6.58	6.49
900	9.40	9.14	8.91	8.72	8.54	8.39	8.26	8.15	8.04	7.95	7.87	7.57	7.40	7.30
1000	10.45	10.15	9.90	9.68	9.49	9.33	9.18	9.05	8.93	8.83	8.74	8.41	8.22	8.11
2000	20.89	20.30	19.80	19.36	18.98	18.65	18.35	18.09	17.86	17.66	17.48	16.82	16.44	16.21
3000	31.33	30.45	29.70	29.04	28.47	27.97	27.53	27.14	26.79	26.49	26.22	25.23	24.65	24.31
4000	41.77	40.60	39.60	38.72	37.96	37.29	36.70	36.18	35.72	35.32	34.95	33.64	32.87	32.41
5000	52.22	50.75	49.49	48.40	47.45	46.61	45.88	45.23	44.65	44.14	43.69	42.05	41.09	40.51
6000	62.66	60.90	59.39	58.08	56.94	55.93	55.05	54.27	53.58	52.97	52.43	50.46	49.30	48.61
7000	73.10	71.05	69.29	67.76	66.42	65.25	64.23	63.32	62.51	61.80	61.16	58.86	57.52	56.71
8000	83.54	81.20	79.19	77.44	75.91	74.58	73.40	72.36	71.44	70.63	69.90	67.27	65.73	64.81
9000	93.99	91.35	89.09	87.12	85.40	83.90	82.57	81.41	80.37	79.45	78.64	75.68	73.95	72.91
10000	104.43	101.50	98.98	96.80	94.89	93.22	91.75	90.45	89.30	88.28	87.37	84.09	82.17	81.01
11000	114.87	111.65	108.88	106.40	104.38	102.54	100.92	99.50	98.23	97.11	96.11	92.50	90.38	89.11
12000	125.31	121.80	118.78	116.15	113.87	111.86	110.10	108.54	107.16	105.94	104.85	100.91	98.60	97.21
13000	135.75	131.95	128.68	125.83	123.35	121.18	119.27	117.58	116.09	114.77	113.59	109.32	106.81	105.31
14000	146.20	142.10	138.57	135.51	132.84	130.50	128.45	126.63	125.02	123.59	122.32	117.72	115.03	113.41
15000	156.64	152.25	148.47	145.19	142.33	139.82	137.62	135.67	133.95	132.42	131.06	126.13	123.25	121.51
16000	167.08	162.40	158.37	154.87	151.82	149.15	146.79	144.72	142.88	141.25	139.80	134.54	131.46	129.61
17000	177.52	172.55	168.27	164.55	161.31	158.47	155.97	153.76	151.81	150.08	148.53	142.95	139.68	137.72
18000	187.97	182.70	178.17	174.23	170.80	167.79	165.14	162.81	160.74	158.90	157.27	151.36	147.90	145.82
19000	198.41	192.85	188.06	183.91	180.28	177.11	174.32	171.85	169.67	167.73	166.01	159.77	156.11	153.92
20000	208.85	203.00	197.96	193.59	189.77	186.43	183.49	180.90	178.60	176.56	174.74	168.18	164.33	162.02
21000	219.29	213.15	207.86	203.27	199.26	195.75	192.67	189.94	187.53	185.39	183.48	176.58	172.54	170.12
22000	229.73	223.30	217.76	212.95	208.75	205.07	201.84	198.99	196.46	194.22	192.22	184.99	180.76	178.22
23000	240.18	233.45	227.65	222.62	218.24	214.40	211.01	208.03	205.39	203.04	200.96	193.40	188.98	186.32
24000	250.62	243.60	237.55	232.30	227.73	223.72	220.19	217.08	214.32	211.87	209.69	201.81	197.19	194.42
25000	261.06	253.75	247.45	241.98	237.21	233.04	229.36	226.12	223.25	220.70	218.43	210.22	205.41	202.52
26000	271.50	263.90	257.35	251.66	246.70	242.36	238.54	235.16	232.18	229.53	227.17	218.63	213.62	210.62
27000	281.95	274.05	267.25	261.34	256.19	251.68	247.71	244.21	241.11	238.35	235.90	227.04	221.84	218.72
28000	292.39	284.20	277.14	271.02	265.68	261.00	256.89	253.25	250.04	247.18	244.64	235.44	230.06	226.82
29000	302.83	294.35	287.04	280.70	275.17	270.32	266.06	262.30	258.97	256.01	253.38	243.85	238.27	234.92
30000	313.27	304.50	296.94	290.38	284.66	279.64	275.24	271.34	267.90	264.84	262.11	252.26	246.49	243.02
31000	323.71	314.65	306.84	300.06	294.15	288.97	284.41	280.39	276.83	273.67	270.85	260.67	254.70	251.12
32000	334.16	324.80	316.73	309.74	303.63	298.29	293.58	289.43	285.76	282.49	279.59	269.08	262.92	259.22
33000	344.60	334.95	326.63	319.42	313.12	307.61	302.76	298.48	294.69	291.32	288.32	277.49	271.14	267.33
34000	355.04	345.10	336.53	329.09	322.61	316.93	311.93	307.52	303.62	300.15	297.06	285.90	279.35	275.43
35000	365.48	355.25	346.43	338.77	332.10	326.25	321.11	316.57	312.55	308.98	305.80	294.30	287.57	283.53
36000	375.93	365.40	356.33	348.45	341.59	335.57	330.28	325.61	321.48	317.80	314.54	302.71	295.79	291.63
37000	386.37	375.55	366.22	358.13	351.08	344.89	339.46	334.66	330.41	326.63	323.27	311.12	304.00	299.73
38000	396.81	385.70	376.12	367.81	360.56	354.21	348.63	343.70	339.34	335.46	332.01	319.53	312.22	307.83
39000	407.25	395.85	386.02	377.49	370.05	363.54	357.80	352.74	348.26	344.29	340.75	327.94	320.43	315.93
40000	417.69	406.00	395.92	387.17	379.54	372.86	366.98	361.79	357.19	353.11	349.48	336.35	328.65	324.03
41000	428.14	416.15	405.82	396.85	389.03	382.18	376.15	370.83	366.12	361.94	358.22	344.76	336.87	332.13
42000	438.58	426.30	415.71	406.53	398.52	391.50	385.33	379.88	375.05	370.77	366.96	353.16	345.08	340.23
43000	449.02	436.45	425.61	416.21	408.01	400.82	394.50	388.92	383.98	379.60	375.69	361.57	353.30	348.33
44000	459.46	446.60	435.51	425.89	417.49	410.14	403.68	397.97	392.91	388.43	384.43	369.98	361.51	356.43
45000	469.91	456.75	445.41	435.57	426.98	419.46	412.85	407.01	401.84	397.25	393.17	378.39	369.73	364.53
46000	480.35	466.90	455.30	445.24	436.47	428.79	422.02	416.06	410.77	406.08	401.91	386.80	377.95	372.63
47000	490.79	477.05	465.20	454.92	445.96	438.11	431.20	425.10	419.70	414.91	410.64	395.21	386.16	380.73
48000	501.23	487.20	475.10	464.60	455.45	447.43	440.37	434.15	428.63	423.74	419.38	403.62	394.38	388.83
49000	511.68	497.35	485.00	474.28	464.94	456.75	449.55	443.19	437.56	432.56	428.12	412.02	402.59	396.94
50000	522.12	507.50	494.90	483.96	474.42	466.07	458.72	452.24	446.49	441.39	436.85	420.43	410.81	405.04
55000	574.33	558.25	544.38	532.36	521.87	512.68	504.59	497.46	491.14	485.53	480.54	462.47	451.89	445.54
60000	626.54	609.00	593.87	580.75	569.31	559.28	550.47	542.68	535.79	529.67	524.22	504.52	492.97	486.04
65000	678.75	659.75	643.36	629.15	616.75	605.89	596.34	587.90	580.44	573.81	567.91	546.56	534.05	526.55
70000	730.96	710.50	692.85	677.54	664.19	652.50	642.21	633.13	625.09	617.95	611.59	588.60	575.13	567.05
75000	783.17	761.25	742.34	725.94	711.63	699.10	688.08	678.35	669.74	662.09	655.28	630.65	616.21	607.55
80000	835.38	812.00	791.83	774.33	759.08	745.71	733.95	723.57	714.38	706.22	698.96	672.69	657.29	648.05
85000	887.60	862.75	841.32	822.73	806.52	792.32	779.82	768.80	759.03	750.36	742.65	714.73	698.37	688.56
90000	939.81	913.50	890.81	871.13	853.96	838.92	825.70	814.02	803.68	794.50	786.33	756.77	739.46	729.06
95000	992.02	964.25	940.30	919.52	901.40	885.53	871.57	859.24	848.33	838.64	830.02	798.82	780.54	769.56
100000	1044.23	1014.99	989.79	967.92	948.84	932.14	917.44	904.47	892.98	882.78	873.70	840.86	821.62	810.07

MONTHLY PAYMENT
REQUIRED TO AMORTIZE A LOAN

TERM AMOUNT	1 Year	2 Years	3 Years	4 Years	5 Years	6 Years	7 Years	8 Years	9 Years	10 Years	11 Years	12 Years	13 Years	14 Years
5	.44	.23	.17	.13	.11	.10	.09	.08	.07	.07	.07	.06	.06	.06
10	.88	.46	.33	.26	.22	.19	.17	.15	.14	.13	.13	.12	.12	.11
15	1.32	.69	.49	.38	.32	.28	.25	.23	.21	.20	.19	.18	.17	.17
25	2.20	1.15	.81	.63	.53	.46	.41	.38	.35	.33	.31	.30	.29	.28
50	4.39	2.30	1.61	1.26	1.06	.92	.82	.75	.70	.65	.62	.59	.57	.55
75	6.58	3.45	2.41	1.89	1.58	1.38	1.23	1.13	1.04	.98	.93	.88	.85	.82
100	8.78	4.60	3.21	2.52	2.11	1.84	1.64	1.50	1.39	1.30	1.23	1.18	1.13	1.09
200	17.55	9.20	6.42	5.04	4.22	3.67	3.28	3.00	2.78	2.60	2.46	2.35	2.25	2.17
300	26.32	13.79	9.63	7.56	6.32	5.50	4.92	4.49	4.16	3.90	3.69	3.52	3.38	3.26
400	35.10	18.39	12.84	10.07	8.43	7.33	6.56	5.99	5.55	5.20	4.92	4.69	4.50	4.34
500	43.87	22.99	16.04	12.59	10.53	9.17	8.20	7.49	6.94	6.50	6.15	5.87	5.63	5.43
600	52.64	27.58	19.25	15.11	12.64	11.00	9.84	8.98	8.32	7.80	7.38	7.04	6.75	6.51
700	61.42	32.18	22.46	17.62	14.74	12.83	11.48	10.48	9.71	9.10	8.61	8.21	7.88	7.60
800	70.19	36.77	25.67	20.14	16.85	14.66	13.12	11.98	11.10	10.40	9.84	9.38	9.00	8.68
900	78.96	41.37	28.88	22.66	18.95	16.50	14.76	13.47	12.48	11.70	11.07	10.55	10.12	9.76
1000	87.73	45.97	32.08	25.18	21.06	18.33	16.40	14.97	13.87	13.00	12.30	11.73	11.25	10.85
2000	175.46	91.93	64.16	50.35	42.11	36.65	32.80	29.93	27.73	25.99	24.59	23.45	22.49	21.69
3000	263.19	137.89	96.24	75.52	63.16	54.98	49.19	44.90	41.59	38.99	36.89	35.17	33.74	32.53
4000	350.92	183.85	128.32	100.69	84.21	73.30	65.59	59.86	55.46	51.98	49.18	46.89	44.98	43.38
5000	438.65	229.81	160.40	125.86	105.26	91.63	81.98	74.82	69.32	64.98	61.48	58.61	56.22	54.22
6000	526.38	275.77	192.48	151.03	126.31	109.95	98.38	89.79	83.18	77.97	73.77	70.33	67.47	65.06
7000	614.11	321.73	224.56	176.20	147.36	128.28	114.77	104.75	97.05	90.97	86.07	82.05	78.71	75.91
8000	701.84	367.69	256.64	201.37	168.41	146.60	131.17	119.71	110.91	103.96	98.36	93.77	89.96	86.75
9000	789.57	413.65	288.72	226.54	189.46	164.93	147.56	134.68	124.77	116.96	110.66	105.49	101.20	97.59
10000	877.30	459.61	320.80	251.71	210.51	183.25	163.96	149.64	138.63	129.95	122.95	117.21	112.44	108.44
11000	965.03	505.57	352.88	276.89	231.56	201.58	180.35	164.60	152.50	142.95	135.25	128.93	123.69	119.28
12000	1052.76	551.53	384.96	302.06	252.61	219.90	196.75	179.57	166.36	155.94	147.54	140.66	134.93	130.12
13000	1140.49	597.49	417.04	327.23	273.66	238.23	213.14	194.53	180.22	168.93	159.84	152.38	146.18	140.96
14000	1228.22	643.45	449.12	352.40	294.72	256.55	229.54	209.49	194.09	181.93	172.13	164.10	157.42	151.81
15000	1315.95	689.41	481.20	377.57	315.77	274.88	245.93	224.46	207.95	194.92	184.42	175.82	168.66	162.65
16000	1403.68	735.37	513.28	402.74	336.82	293.20	262.33	239.42	221.81	207.92	196.72	187.54	179.91	173.49
17000	1491.41	781.33	545.36	427.91	357.87	311.53	278.72	254.38	235.68	220.91	209.01	199.26	191.15	184.34
18000	1579.14	827.29	577.44	453.08	378.92	329.85	295.12	269.35	249.54	233.91	221.31	210.98	202.40	195.18
19000	1666.87	873.25	609.52	478.25	399.97	348.18	311.51	284.31	263.40	246.90	233.60	222.70	213.64	206.02
20000	1754.60	919.22	641.60	503.42	421.02	366.50	327.91	299.27	277.26	259.90	245.90	234.42	224.88	216.87
21000	1842.33	965.18	673.68	528.59	442.07	384.82	344.31	314.24	291.13	272.89	258.19	246.14	236.13	227.71
22000	1930.06	1011.14	705.76	553.77	463.12	403.15	360.70	329.20	304.99	285.89	270.49	257.86	247.37	238.55
23000	2017.79	1057.10	737.84	578.94	484.17	421.47	377.10	344.16	318.85	298.88	282.78	269.58	258.62	249.39
24000	2105.52	1103.06	769.92	604.11	505.22	439.80	393.49	359.13	332.72	311.88	295.08	281.31	269.86	260.24
25000	2193.25	1149.02	802.00	629.28	526.27	458.12	409.89	374.09	346.58	324.87	307.37	293.03	281.10	271.08
26000	2280.98	1194.98	834.08	654.45	547.32	476.45	426.28	389.05	360.44	337.86	319.67	304.75	292.35	281.92
27000	2368.71	1240.94	866.16	679.62	568.38	494.77	442.68	404.02	374.31	350.86	331.96	316.47	303.59	292.77
28000	2456.44	1286.90	898.24	704.79	589.43	513.10	459.07	418.98	388.17	363.85	344.25	328.19	314.84	303.61
29000	2544.17	1332.86	930.32	729.96	610.48	531.42	475.47	433.94	402.03	376.85	356.55	339.91	326.08	314.45
30000	2631.90	1378.82	962.40	755.13	631.53	549.75	491.86	448.91	415.89	389.84	368.84	351.63	337.32	325.30
31000	2719.63	1424.78	994.48	780.30	652.58	568.07	508.26	463.87	429.76	402.84	381.14	363.35	348.57	336.14
32000	2807.36	1470.74	1026.56	805.47	673.63	586.40	524.65	478.83	443.62	415.83	393.43	375.07	359.81	346.98
33000	2895.09	1516.70	1058.64	830.65	694.68	604.72	541.05	493.80	457.48	428.83	405.73	386.79	371.06	357.82
34000	2982.82	1562.66	1090.72	855.82	715.73	623.05	557.44	508.76	471.35	441.82	418.02	398.51	382.30	368.67
35000	3070.55	1608.62	1122.80	880.99	736.78	641.37	573.84	523.72	485.21	454.81	430.32	410.23	393.54	379.51
36000	3158.28	1654.58	1154.87	906.16	757.83	659.70	590.23	538.69	499.07	467.81	442.61	421.96	404.79	390.35
37000	3246.01	1700.54	1186.95	931.33	778.88	678.02	606.63	553.65	512.94	480.80	454.91	433.68	416.03	401.20
38000	3333.74	1746.50	1219.03	956.50	799.93	696.35	623.02	568.61	526.80	493.80	467.20	445.40	427.28	412.04
39000	3421.47	1792.47	1251.11	981.67	820.98	714.67	639.42	583.58	540.66	506.79	479.50	457.12	438.52	422.88
40000	3509.20	1838.43	1283.19	1006.84	842.04	733.00	655.81	598.54	554.52	519.79	491.79	468.84	449.76	433.73
41000	3596.93	1884.39	1315.27	1032.01	863.09	751.32	672.21	613.50	568.39	532.78	504.08	480.56	461.01	444.57
42000	3684.66	1930.35	1347.35	1057.18	884.14	769.64	688.61	628.47	582.25	545.78	516.38	492.28	472.25	455.41
43000	3772.39	1976.31	1379.43	1082.35	905.19	787.97	705.00	643.43	596.11	558.77	528.67	504.00	483.50	466.26
44000	3860.12	2022.27	1411.51	1107.53	926.24	806.29	721.40	658.39	609.98	571.77	540.97	515.72	494.74	477.10
45000	3947.85	2068.23	1443.59	1132.70	947.29	824.62	737.79	673.36	623.84	584.76	553.26	527.44	505.98	487.94
46000	4035.58	2114.19	1475.67	1157.87	968.34	842.94	754.19	688.32	637.70	597.76	565.56	539.16	517.23	498.78
47000	4123.31	2160.15	1507.75	1183.04	989.39	861.27	770.58	703.28	651.57	610.75	577.85	550.89	528.47	509.63
48000	4211.04	2206.11	1539.83	1208.21	1010.44	879.59	786.98	718.25	665.43	623.74	590.15	562.61	539.72	520.47
49000	4298.77	2252.07	1571.91	1233.38	1031.49	897.92	803.37	733.21	679.29	636.74	602.44	574.33	550.96	531.31
50000	4386.50	2298.03	1603.99	1258.55	1052.54	916.24	819.77	748.17	693.15	649.73	614.74	586.05	562.20	542.16
55000	4825.15	2527.83	1764.39	1384.41	1157.80	1007.87	901.74	822.99	762.47	714.71	676.21	644.65	618.42	596.37
60000	5263.80	2757.64	1924.79	1510.26	1263.05	1099.49	983.72	897.81	831.78	779.68	737.68	703.26	674.64	650.59
65000	5702.45	2987.44	2085.19	1636.11	1368.30	1191.11	1065.70	972.62	901.10	844.65	799.16	761.86	730.86	704.80
70000	6141.10	3217.24	2245.59	1761.97	1473.56	1282.74	1147.67	1047.44	970.41	909.62	860.63	820.46	787.08	759.02
75000	6579.75	3447.04	2405.98	1887.82	1578.81	1374.36	1229.65	1122.26	1039.73	974.60	922.10	879.07	843.30	813.23
80000	7018.40	3676.85	2566.38	2013.68	1684.07	1465.99	1311.62	1197.07	1109.04	1039.57	983.57	937.67	899.52	867.45
85000	7457.05	3906.65	2726.78	2139.53	1789.32	1557.61	1393.60	1271.89	1178.36	1104.54	1045.05	996.28	955.74	921.66
90000	7895.70	4136.45	2887.18	2265.39	1894.57	1649.23	1475.58	1346.71	1247.67	1169.52	1106.52	1054.88	1011.96	975.88
95000	8334.35	4366.25	3047.58	2391.24	1999.83	1740.86	1557.55	1421.52	1316.99	1234.49	1167.99	1113.49	1068.18	1030.09
100000	8773.00	4596.06	3207.98	2517.10	2105.08	1832.48	1639.53	1496.34	1386.30	1299.46	1229.47	1172.09	1124.40	1084.31

TERM AMOUNT	15 Years	16 Years	17 Years	18 Years	19 Years	20 Years	21 Years	22 Years	23 Years	24 Years	25 Years	30 Years	35 Years	40 Years
5	.06	.06	.05	.05	.05	.05	.05	.05	.05	.05	.05	.05	.05	.05
10	.11	.11	.10	.10	.10	.10	.10	.10	.09	.09	.09	.09	.09	.09
15	.16	.16	.15	.15	.15	.15	.14	.14	.14	.14	.14	.13	.13	.13
25	.27	.26	.25	.25	.24	.24	.24	.23	.23	.23	.23	.22	.21	.21
50	.53	.52	.50	.49	.48	.47	.47	.46	.45	.45	.45	.43	.42	.41
75	.79	.77	.75	.74	.72	.71	.70	.69	.68	.67	.67	.64	.63	.62
100	1.06	1.03	1.00	.98	.96	.94	.93	.92	.90	.89	.89	.85	.83	.82
200	2.11	2.05	2.00	1.95	1.92	1.88	1.85	1.83	1.80	1.78	1.77	1.70	1.66	1.64
300	3.16	3.07	2.99	2.93	2.87	2.82	2.78	2.74	2.70	2.67	2.65	2.55	2.49	2.46
400	4.21	4.09	3.99	3.90	3.83	3.76	3.70	3.65	3.60	3.56	3.53	3.40	3.32	3.28
500	5.26	5.11	4.99	4.88	4.78	4.70	4.63	4.56	4.50	4.45	4.41	4.25	4.15	4.09
600	6.31	6.13	5.98	5.85	5.74	5.64	5.55	5.47	5.40	5.34	5.29	5.09	4.98	4.91
700	7.36	7.15	6.98	6.82	6.69	6.58	6.47	6.38	6.30	6.23	6.17	5.94	5.81	5.73
800	8.41	8.17	7.97	7.80	7.65	7.51	7.40	7.29	7.20	7.12	7.05	6.79	6.64	6.55
900	9.46	9.20	8.97	8.77	8.60	8.45	8.32	8.21	8.10	8.01	7.93	7.64	7.47	7.37
1000	10.51	10.22	9.97	9.75	9.56	9.39	9.25	9.12	9.00	8.90	8.81	8.49	8.30	8.18
2000	21.01	20.43	19.93	19.49	19.11	18.78	18.49	18.23	18.00	17.80	17.62	16.97	16.59	16.36
3000	31.51	30.64	29.89	29.23	28.66	28.17	27.73	27.34	27.00	26.69	26.42	25.45	24.88	24.54
4000	42.02	40.85	39.85	38.98	38.22	37.55	36.97	36.45	36.00	35.59	35.23	33.93	33.17	32.72
5000	52.52	51.06	49.81	48.72	47.77	46.94	46.21	45.56	44.99	44.49	44.04	42.41	41.46	40.90
6000	63.02	61.27	59.77	58.46	57.32	56.33	55.45	54.68	53.99	53.38	52.84	50.89	49.76	49.08
7000	73.52	71.48	69.73	68.20	66.88	65.71	64.69	63.79	62.99	62.28	61.65	59.38	58.05	57.25
8000	84.03	81.70	79.69	77.95	76.43	75.10	73.93	72.90	71.99	71.18	70.46	67.86	66.34	65.43
9000	94.53	91.91	89.65	87.69	85.98	84.49	83.17	82.01	80.98	80.07	79.26	76.34	74.63	73.61
10000	105.03	102.12	99.61	97.43	95.53	93.87	92.41	91.12	89.98	88.97	88.07	84.82	82.92	81.79
11000	115.53	112.33	109.57	107.17	105.09	103.26	101.65	100.23	98.98	97.87	96.88	93.30	91.22	89.97
12000	126.04	122.54	119.53	116.92	114.64	112.65	110.89	109.35	107.98	106.76	105.68	101.78	99.51	98.15
13000	136.54	132.75	129.49	126.66	124.19	122.03	120.13	118.46	116.98	115.66	114.49	110.27	107.80	106.33
14000	147.04	142.96	139.45	136.40	133.75	131.42	129.37	127.57	125.97	124.56	123.30	118.75	116.09	114.50
15000	157.55	153.18	149.41	146.14	143.30	140.81	138.61	136.68	134.97	133.45	132.10	127.23	124.38	122.68
16000	168.05	163.39	159.37	155.89	152.85	150.19	147.86	145.79	143.97	142.35	140.91	135.71	132.68	130.86
17000	178.55	173.60	169.33	165.63	162.40	159.58	157.10	154.91	152.97	151.25	149.72	144.19	140.97	139.04
18000	189.05	183.81	179.29	175.37	171.96	168.97	166.34	164.02	161.96	160.14	158.52	152.67	149.26	147.22
19000	199.56	194.02	189.25	185.11	181.51	178.35	175.58	173.13	170.96	169.04	167.33	161.16	157.55	155.40
20000	210.06	204.23	199.21	194.86	191.06	187.74	184.82	182.24	179.96	177.94	176.14	169.64	165.84	163.57
21000	220.56	214.44	209.17	204.60	200.62	197.13	194.06	191.35	188.96	186.83	184.94	178.12	174.13	171.75
22000	231.06	224.66	219.13	214.34	210.17	206.51	203.30	200.46	197.96	195.73	193.75	186.60	182.43	179.93
23000	241.57	234.87	229.09	224.09	219.72	215.90	212.54	209.58	206.95	204.63	202.56	195.08	190.72	188.11
24000	252.07	245.08	239.05	233.83	229.27	225.29	221.78	218.69	215.95	213.52	211.36	203.56	199.01	196.29
25000	262.57	255.29	249.01	243.57	238.83	234.67	231.02	227.80	224.95	222.42	220.17	212.04	207.30	204.47
26000	273.07	265.50	258.97	253.31	248.38	244.06	240.26	236.91	233.95	231.32	228.98	220.53	215.59	212.65
27000	283.58	275.71	268.93	263.06	257.93	253.45	249.50	246.02	242.94	240.21	237.78	229.01	223.89	220.82
28000	294.08	285.92	278.89	272.80	267.49	262.83	258.74	255.14	251.94	249.11	246.59	237.49	232.18	229.00
29000	304.58	296.13	288.85	282.54	277.04	272.22	267.98	264.25	260.94	258.01	255.40	245.97	240.47	237.18
30000	315.09	306.35	298.81	292.28	286.59	281.61	277.22	273.36	269.94	266.90	264.20	254.45	248.76	245.36
31000	325.59	316.56	308.77	302.03	296.14	290.99	286.47	282.47	278.94	275.80	273.01	262.93	257.05	253.54
32000	336.09	326.77	318.73	311.77	305.70	300.38	295.71	291.58	287.93	284.70	281.82	271.42	265.35	261.72
33000	346.59	336.98	328.70	321.51	315.25	309.77	304.95	300.69	296.93	293.59	290.62	279.90	273.64	269.90
34000	357.10	347.19	338.66	331.25	324.80	319.15	314.19	309.81	305.93	302.49	299.43	288.38	281.93	278.07
35000	367.60	357.40	348.62	341.00	334.36	328.54	323.43	318.92	314.93	311.39	308.24	296.86	290.22	286.25
36000	378.10	367.61	358.58	350.74	343.91	337.93	332.67	328.03	323.92	320.28	317.04	305.34	298.51	294.43
37000	388.60	377.83	368.54	360.48	353.46	347.31	341.91	337.14	332.92	329.18	325.85	313.82	306.81	302.61
38000	399.11	388.04	378.50	370.22	363.01	356.70	351.15	346.25	341.92	338.08	334.66	322.31	315.10	310.79
39000	409.61	398.25	388.46	379.97	372.57	366.09	360.39	355.36	350.92	346.97	343.46	330.79	323.39	318.97
40000	420.11	408.46	398.42	389.71	382.12	375.47	369.63	364.48	359.92	355.87	352.27	339.27	331.68	327.14
41000	430.61	418.67	408.38	399.45	391.67	384.86	378.87	373.59	368.91	364.76	361.07	347.75	339.97	335.32
42000	441.12	428.88	418.34	409.19	401.23	394.25	388.11	382.70	377.91	373.66	369.88	356.23	348.26	343.50
43000	451.62	439.09	428.30	418.94	410.78	403.63	397.35	391.81	386.91	382.56	378.69	364.71	356.56	351.68
44000	462.12	449.31	438.26	428.68	420.33	413.02	406.59	400.92	395.91	391.45	387.49	373.20	364.85	359.86
45000	472.63	459.52	448.22	438.42	429.88	422.41	415.83	410.04	404.90	400.35	396.30	381.68	373.14	368.04
46000	483.13	469.73	458.18	448.17	439.44	431.79	425.07	419.15	413.90	409.25	405.11	390.16	381.43	376.22
47000	493.63	479.94	468.14	457.91	448.99	441.18	434.32	428.26	422.90	418.14	413.91	398.64	389.72	384.39
48000	504.13	490.15	478.10	467.65	458.54	450.57	443.56	437.37	431.90	427.04	422.72	407.12	398.02	392.57
49000	514.64	500.36	488.06	477.39	468.10	459.95	452.80	446.48	440.90	435.94	431.53	415.60	406.31	400.75
50000	525.14	510.57	498.02	487.14	477.65	469.34	462.04	455.59	449.89	444.83	440.33	424.08	414.60	408.93
55000	577.65	561.63	547.82	535.85	525.41	516.27	508.24	501.15	494.88	489.32	484.37	466.49	456.06	449.82
60000	630.17	612.69	597.62	584.56	573.18	563.21	554.44	546.71	539.87	533.80	528.40	508.90	497.52	490.71
65000	682.68	663.74	647.42	633.27	620.94	610.14	600.65	592.27	584.86	578.28	572.43	551.31	538.98	531.61
70000	735.19	714.80	697.23	681.99	668.71	657.07	646.85	637.83	629.85	622.77	616.47	593.72	580.44	572.50
75000	787.71	765.86	747.03	730.70	716.47	704.01	693.05	683.39	674.84	667.25	660.50	636.12	621.90	613.39
80000	840.22	816.91	796.83	779.41	764.23	750.94	739.26	728.95	719.83	711.73	704.53	678.53	663.36	654.28
85000	892.73	867.97	846.63	828.13	812.00	797.88	785.46	774.51	764.81	756.21	748.56	720.94	704.82	695.18
90000	945.25	919.03	896.43	876.84	859.76	844.81	831.66	820.07	809.80	800.70	792.60	763.35	746.28	736.07
95000	997.76	970.09	946.23	925.55	907.53	891.74	877.87	865.63	854.79	845.18	836.63	805.76	787.74	776.96
100000	1050.27	1021.14	996.04	974.27	955.29	938.68	924.07	911.18	899.78	889.66	880.66	848.16	829.19	817.85

MONTHLY PAYMENT
REQUIRED TO AMORTIZE A LOAN

TERM	1 Year	2 Years	3 Years	4 Years	5 Years	6 Years	7 Years	8 Years	9 Years	10 Years	11 Years	12 Years	13 Years	14 Years
AMOUNT														
5	.44	.23	.17	.13	.11	.10	.09	.08	.07	.07	.07	.06	.06	.06
10	.88	.46	.33	.26	.22	.19	.17	.15	.14	.14	.13	.12	.12	.11
15	1.32	.69	.49	.38	.32	.28	.25	.23	.21	.20	.19	.18	.17	.17
25	2.20	1.15	.81	.63	.53	.46	.42	.38	.35	.33	.31	.30	.29	.28
50	4.39	2.30	1.61	1.26	1.06	.92	.83	.75	.70	.66	.62	.59	.57	.55
75	6.59	3.45	2.41	1.89	1.58	1.38	1.24	1.13	1.05	.98	.93	.89	.85	.82
100	8.78	4.60	3.21	2.52	2.11	1.84	1.65	1.50	1.39	1.31	1.24	1.18	1.13	1.09
200	17.55	9.20	6.42	5.04	4.22	3.67	3.29	3.00	2.78	2.61	2.47	2.35	2.26	2.18
300	26.33	13.80	9.63	7.56	6.32	5.51	4.93	4.50	4.17	3.91	3.70	3.53	3.38	3.26
400	35.10	18.39	12.84	10.08	8.43	7.34	6.57	6.00	5.56	5.21	4.93	4.70	4.51	4.35
500	43.88	22.99	16.05	12.60	10.54	9.17	8.21	7.49	6.94	6.51	6.16	5.87	5.63	5.43
600	52.65	27.59	19.26	15.11	12.64	11.01	9.85	8.99	8.33	7.81	7.39	7.05	6.76	6.52
700	61.42	32.19	22.47	17.63	14.75	12.84	11.49	10.49	9.72	9.11	8.62	8.22	7.89	7.61
800	70.20	36.78	25.68	20.15	16.86	14.67	13.13	11.99	11.11	10.41	9.85	9.39	9.01	8.69
900	78.97	41.38	28.89	22.67	18.96	16.51	14.77	13.48	12.49	11.71	11.08	10.57	10.14	9.78
1000	87.75	45.98	32.10	25.19	21.07	18.34	16.41	14.98	13.88	13.01	12.31	11.74	11.26	10.86
2000	175.49	91.95	64.19	50.37	42.13	36.68	32.82	29.96	27.76	26.02	24.62	23.48	22.52	21.72
3000	263.23	137.92	96.28	75.55	63.19	55.02	49.23	44.93	41.63	39.03	36.93	35.21	33.78	32.58
4000	350.97	183.89	128.37	100.74	84.26	73.35	65.64	59.91	55.51	52.04	49.24	46.95	45.04	43.44
5000	438.71	229.87	160.46	125.92	105.32	91.69	82.05	74.89	69.39	65.05	61.55	58.68	56.30	54.29
6000	526.45	275.84	192.55	151.10	126.38	110.03	98.45	89.86	83.26	78.05	73.86	70.42	67.56	65.15
7000	614.20	321.81	224.64	176.29	147.45	128.37	114.86	104.84	97.14	91.06	86.17	82.15	78.81	76.01
8000	701.94	367.78	256.74	201.47	168.51	146.70	131.27	119.82	111.02	104.07	98.47	93.89	90.07	86.87
9000	789.68	413.75	288.83	226.65	189.57	165.04	147.68	134.79	124.89	117.08	110.78	105.62	101.33	97.73
10000	877.42	459.73	320.92	251.83	210.64	183.38	164.09	149.77	138.77	130.09	123.09	117.36	112.59	108.58
11000	965.16	505.70	353.01	277.02	231.70	201.72	180.49	164.75	152.65	143.10	135.40	129.09	123.85	119.44
12000	1052.90	551.67	385.10	302.20	252.76	220.05	196.90	179.72	166.52	156.10	147.71	140.83	135.11	130.30
13000	1140.65	597.64	417.19	327.38	273.82	238.39	213.31	194.70	180.40	169.11	160.02	152.56	146.37	141.16
14000	1228.39	643.61	449.28	352.57	294.89	256.73	229.72	209.68	194.27	182.12	172.33	164.30	157.62	152.02
15000	1316.13	689.59	481.38	377.75	315.95	275.06	246.13	224.65	208.15	195.13	184.63	176.03	168.88	162.87
16000	1403.87	735.56	513.47	402.93	337.01	293.40	262.53	239.63	222.03	208.14	196.94	187.77	180.14	173.73
17000	1491.61	781.53	545.56	428.11	358.08	311.74	278.94	254.60	235.90	221.15	209.25	199.50	191.40	184.59
18000	1579.35	827.50	577.65	453.30	379.14	330.08	295.35	269.58	249.78	234.15	221.56	211.24	202.66	195.45
19000	1667.09	873.47	609.74	478.48	400.20	348.41	311.76	284.56	263.66	247.16	233.87	222.97	213.92	206.30
20000	1754.84	919.45	641.83	503.66	421.27	366.75	328.17	299.53	277.53	260.17	246.18	234.71	225.18	217.16
21000	1842.58	965.42	673.92	528.85	442.33	385.09	344.57	314.51	291.41	273.18	258.49	246.44	236.43	228.02
22000	1930.32	1011.39	706.02	554.03	463.39	403.43	360.98	329.49	305.29	286.19	270.80	258.18	247.69	238.88
23000	2018.06	1057.36	738.11	579.21	484.45	421.76	377.39	344.46	319.16	299.20	283.10	269.91	258.95	249.74
24000	2105.80	1103.33	770.20	604.39	505.52	440.10	393.80	359.44	333.04	312.20	295.41	281.65	270.21	260.59
25000	2193.54	1149.31	802.29	629.58	526.58	458.44	410.21	374.42	346.92	325.21	307.72	293.38	281.47	271.45
26000	2281.29	1195.28	834.38	654.76	547.64	476.77	426.61	389.39	360.79	338.22	320.03	305.12	292.73	282.31
27000	2369.03	1241.25	866.47	679.94	568.71	495.11	443.02	404.37	374.67	351.23	332.34	316.85	303.99	293.17
28000	2456.77	1287.22	898.56	705.13	589.77	513.45	459.43	419.35	388.54	364.24	344.65	328.59	315.24	304.03
29000	2544.51	1333.19	930.66	730.31	610.83	531.79	475.84	434.32	402.42	377.25	356.96	340.32	326.50	314.88
30000	2632.25	1379.17	962.75	755.49	631.90	550.12	492.25	449.30	416.30	390.25	369.26	352.06	337.76	325.74
31000	2719.99	1425.14	994.84	780.67	652.96	568.46	508.66	464.28	430.17	403.26	381.57	363.79	349.02	336.60
32000	2807.74	1471.11	1026.93	805.86	674.02	586.80	525.06	479.25	444.05	416.27	393.88	375.53	360.28	347.46
33000	2895.48	1517.08	1059.02	831.04	695.08	605.14	541.47	494.23	457.93	429.28	406.19	387.27	371.54	358.32
34000	2983.22	1563.05	1091.11	856.22	716.15	623.47	557.88	509.20	471.80	442.29	418.50	399.00	382.80	369.17
35000	3070.96	1609.03	1123.20	881.41	737.21	641.81	574.29	524.18	485.68	455.30	430.81	410.74	394.05	380.03
36000	3158.70	1655.00	1155.30	906.59	758.27	660.15	590.70	539.16	499.56	468.30	443.12	422.47	405.31	390.89
37000	3246.44	1700.97	1187.39	931.77	779.34	678.48	607.10	554.13	513.43	481.31	455.42	434.21	416.57	401.75
38000	3334.18	1746.94	1219.48	956.95	800.40	696.82	623.51	569.11	527.31	494.32	467.73	445.94	427.83	412.60
39000	3421.93	1792.91	1251.57	982.14	821.46	715.16	639.92	584.09	541.19	507.33	480.04	457.68	439.09	423.46
40000	3509.67	1838.89	1283.66	1007.32	842.53	733.50	656.33	599.06	555.06	520.34	492.35	469.41	450.35	434.32
41000	3597.41	1884.86	1315.75	1032.50	863.59	751.83	672.74	614.04	568.94	533.34	504.66	481.15	461.61	445.18
42000	3685.15	1930.83	1347.84	1057.69	884.65	770.17	689.14	629.02	582.81	546.35	516.97	492.88	472.86	456.04
43000	3772.89	1976.80	1379.94	1082.87	905.71	788.51	705.55	643.99	596.69	559.36	529.28	504.62	484.12	466.89
44000	3860.63	2022.77	1412.03	1108.05	926.78	806.85	721.96	658.97	610.57	572.37	541.59	516.35	495.38	477.75
45000	3948.38	2068.75	1444.12	1133.23	947.84	825.18	738.37	673.95	624.44	585.38	553.89	528.09	506.64	488.61
46000	4036.12	2114.72	1476.21	1158.42	968.90	843.52	754.78	688.92	638.32	598.39	566.20	539.82	517.90	499.47
47000	4123.86	2160.69	1508.30	1183.60	989.97	861.86	771.18	703.90	652.20	611.39	578.51	551.56	529.16	510.33
48000	4211.60	2206.66	1540.39	1208.78	1011.03	880.19	787.59	718.88	666.07	624.40	590.82	563.29	540.42	521.18
49000	4299.34	2252.63	1572.48	1233.97	1032.09	898.53	804.00	733.85	679.95	637.41	603.13	575.03	551.67	532.04
50000	4387.08	2298.61	1604.58	1259.15	1053.16	916.87	820.41	748.83	693.83	650.42	615.44	586.76	562.93	542.90
55000	4825.79	2528.47	1765.03	1385.06	1158.47	1008.56	902.45	823.71	763.21	715.46	676.98	645.44	619.23	597.19
60000	5264.50	2758.33	1925.49	1510.98	1263.79	1100.24	984.49	898.59	832.59	780.50	738.52	704.11	675.52	651.48
65000	5703.21	2988.19	2085.95	1636.89	1369.10	1191.93	1066.53	973.48	901.97	845.54	800.07	762.79	731.81	705.77
70000	6141.92	3218.05	2246.40	1762.81	1474.42	1283.62	1148.57	1048.36	971.35	910.59	861.61	821.47	788.10	760.06
75000	6580.62	3447.91	2406.86	1888.73	1579.73	1375.30	1230.61	1123.24	1040.74	975.63	923.15	880.14	844.40	814.35
80000	7019.33	3677.77	2567.32	2014.63	1685.05	1466.99	1312.65	1198.12	1110.12	1040.67	984.70	938.82	900.69	868.64
85000	7458.04	3907.63	2727.78	2140.55	1790.36	1558.67	1394.69	1273.00	1179.50	1105.71	1046.24	997.49	956.98	922.93
90000	7896.75	4137.49	2888.23	2266.46	1895.68	1650.36	1476.73	1347.89	1248.88	1170.75	1107.78	1056.17	1013.27	977.22
95000	8335.45	4367.35	3048.69	2392.38	2000.99	1742.05	1558.77	1422.77	1318.27	1235.79	1169.33	1114.84	1069.57	1031.50
100000	8774.16	4597.21	3209.15	2518.29	2106.31	1833.73	1640.81	1497.65	1387.65	1300.83	1230.87	1173.52	1125.86	1085.79

TERM AMOUNT	15 Years	16 Years	17 Years	18 Years	19 Years	20 Years	21 Years	22 Years	23 Years	24 Years	25 Years	30 Years	35 Years	40 Years
5	.06	.06	.05	.05	.05	.05	.05	.05	.05	.05	.05	.05	.05	.05
10	.11	.11	.10	.10	.10	.10	.10	.10	.10	.09	.09	.09	.09	.09
15	.16	.16	.15	.15	.15	.15	.14	.14	.14	.14	.14	.13	.13	.13
25	.27	.26	.25	.25	.24	.24	.24	.23	.23	.23	.23	.22	.21	.21
50	.53	.52	.50	.49	.48	.48	.47	.46	.46	.45	.45	.43	.42	.41
75	.79	.77	.75	.74	.72	.71	.70	.69	.68	.67	.67	.64	.63	.62
100	1.06	1.03	1.00	.98	.96	.95	.93	.92	.91	.90	.89	.85	.84	.82
200	2.11	2.05	2.00	1.96	1.92	1.89	1.86	1.83	1.81	1.79	1.77	1.70	1.67	1.64
300	3.16	3.07	3.00	2.93	2.88	2.83	2.78	2.74	2.71	2.68	2.65	2.55	2.50	2.46
400	4.21	4.10	4.00	3.91	3.83	3.77	3.71	3.66	3.61	3.57	3.53	3.40	3.33	3.28
500	5.26	5.12	4.99	4.88	4.79	4.71	4.63	4.57	4.51	4.46	4.42	4.25	4.16	4.10
600	6.32	6.14	5.99	5.86	5.75	5.65	5.56	5.48	5.41	5.35	5.30	5.10	4.99	4.92
700	7.37	7.16	6.99	6.84	6.70	6.59	6.49	6.40	6.32	6.24	6.18	5.95	5.82	5.74
800	8.42	8.19	7.99	7.81	7.66	7.53	7.41	7.31	7.22	7.14	7.06	6.80	6.65	6.56
900	9.47	9.21	8.98	8.79	8.62	8.47	8.34	8.22	8.12	8.03	7.95	7.65	7.48	7.38
1000	10.52	10.23	9.98	9.76	9.57	9.41	9.26	9.13	9.02	8.92	8.83	8.50	8.32	8.20
2000	21.04	20.46	19.96	19.52	19.14	18.81	18.52	18.26	18.03	17.83	17.65	17.00	16.63	16.40
3000	31.56	30.69	29.93	29.28	28.71	28.21	27.78	27.39	27.05	26.75	26.48	25.50	24.94	24.60
4000	42.08	40.91	39.91	39.04	38.28	37.62	37.03	36.52	36.06	35.66	35.30	34.00	33.25	32.80
5000	52.59	51.14	49.88	48.80	47.85	47.02	46.29	45.65	45.08	44.57	44.13	42.50	41.56	40.99
6000	63.11	61.37	59.86	58.56	57.42	56.42	55.55	54.78	54.09	53.49	52.95	51.00	49.87	49.19
7000	73.63	71.59	69.84	68.31	66.99	65.83	64.81	63.91	63.11	62.40	61.77	59.50	58.18	57.39
8000	84.15	81.82	79.81	78.07	76.56	75.23	74.06	73.03	72.12	71.32	70.60	68.00	66.49	65.59
9000	94.67	92.05	89.79	87.83	86.13	84.63	83.32	82.16	81.14	80.23	79.42	76.50	74.80	73.79
10000	105.18	102.27	99.76	97.59	95.70	94.04	92.58	91.29	90.15	89.14	88.25	85.00	83.11	81.98
11000	115.70	112.50	109.74	107.35	105.26	103.44	101.83	100.42	99.17	98.06	97.07	93.50	91.42	90.18
12000	126.22	122.73	119.72	117.11	114.83	112.84	111.09	109.55	108.18	106.97	105.89	102.00	99.74	98.38
13000	136.74	132.95	129.69	126.87	124.40	122.25	120.35	118.68	117.20	115.88	114.72	110.50	108.05	106.58
14000	147.25	143.18	139.67	136.62	133.97	131.65	129.61	127.81	126.21	124.80	123.54	119.00	116.36	114.78
15000	157.77	153.41	149.64	146.38	143.54	141.05	138.86	136.93	135.23	133.71	132.37	127.50	124.67	122.97
16000	168.29	163.63	159.62	156.14	153.11	150.45	148.12	146.06	144.24	142.63	141.19	136.00	132.98	131.17
17000	178.81	173.86	169.60	165.90	162.68	159.86	157.38	155.19	153.26	151.54	150.01	144.50	141.29	139.37
18000	189.33	184.09	179.57	175.66	172.25	169.26	166.64	164.32	162.27	160.45	158.84	153.00	149.60	147.57
19000	199.84	194.31	189.55	185.42	181.82	178.66	175.89	173.45	171.29	169.37	167.66	161.50	157.91	155.77
20000	210.36	204.54	199.52	195.18	191.39	188.07	185.15	182.58	180.30	178.28	176.49	170.00	166.22	163.96
21000	220.88	214.77	209.50	204.93	200.95	197.47	194.41	191.71	189.32	187.20	185.31	178.50	174.53	172.16
22000	231.40	224.99	219.48	214.69	210.52	206.87	203.66	200.83	198.33	196.11	194.13	187.00	182.84	180.36
23000	241.91	235.22	229.45	224.45	220.09	216.28	212.92	209.96	207.35	205.02	202.96	195.50	191.16	188.56
24000	252.43	245.45	239.43	234.21	229.66	225.68	222.18	219.09	216.36	213.94	211.78	204.00	199.47	196.76
25000	262.95	255.67	249.40	243.97	239.23	235.08	231.44	228.22	225.38	222.85	220.61	212.50	207.78	204.95
26000	273.47	265.90	259.38	253.73	248.80	244.49	240.69	237.35	234.39	231.76	229.43	221.00	216.09	213.15
27000	283.99	276.13	269.36	263.48	258.37	253.89	249.95	246.48	243.40	240.68	238.25	229.50	224.40	221.35
28000	294.50	286.35	279.33	273.24	267.94	263.29	259.21	255.61	252.42	249.59	247.08	238.00	232.71	229.55
29000	305.02	296.58	289.31	283.00	277.51	272.69	268.47	264.73	261.43	258.51	255.90	246.50	241.02	237.75
30000	315.54	306.81	299.28	292.76	287.08	282.10	277.72	273.86	270.45	267.42	264.73	255.00	249.33	245.94
31000	326.06	317.03	309.26	302.52	296.64	291.50	286.98	282.99	279.46	276.33	273.55	263.50	257.64	254.14
32000	336.57	327.26	319.24	312.28	306.21	300.90	296.24	292.12	288.48	285.25	282.37	272.00	265.95	262.34
33000	347.09	337.49	329.21	322.04	315.78	310.31	305.49	301.25	297.49	294.16	291.20	280.50	274.26	270.54
34000	357.61	347.72	339.19	331.79	325.35	319.71	314.75	310.38	306.51	303.07	300.02	289.00	282.57	278.74
35000	368.13	357.94	349.16	341.55	334.92	329.11	324.01	319.51	315.52	311.99	308.85	297.50	290.89	286.93
36000	378.65	368.17	359.14	351.31	344.49	338.52	333.27	328.64	324.54	320.90	317.67	306.00	299.20	295.13
37000	389.16	378.40	369.12	361.07	354.06	347.92	342.52	337.76	333.55	329.82	326.49	314.50	307.51	303.33
38000	399.68	388.62	379.09	370.83	363.63	357.32	351.78	346.89	342.57	338.73	335.32	323.00	315.82	311.53
39000	410.20	398.85	389.07	380.59	373.20	366.73	361.04	356.02	351.58	347.64	344.14	331.50	324.13	319.73
40000	420.72	409.08	399.04	390.35	382.77	376.13	370.30	365.15	360.60	356.56	352.97	340.00	332.44	327.92
41000	431.24	419.30	409.02	400.10	392.33	385.53	379.55	374.28	369.61	365.47	361.79	348.50	340.75	336.12
42000	441.75	429.53	419.00	409.86	401.90	394.93	388.81	383.41	378.63	374.39	370.61	357.00	349.06	344.32
43000	452.27	439.76	428.97	419.62	411.47	404.34	398.07	392.54	387.64	383.30	379.44	365.50	357.37	352.52
44000	462.79	449.98	438.95	429.38	421.04	413.74	407.32	401.66	396.66	392.21	388.26	374.00	365.68	360.72
45000	473.31	460.21	448.92	439.14	430.61	423.14	416.58	410.79	405.67	401.13	397.09	382.50	373.99	368.91
46000	483.82	470.44	458.90	448.90	440.18	432.55	425.84	419.92	414.69	410.04	405.91	391.00	382.31	377.11
47000	494.34	480.66	468.88	458.66	449.75	441.95	435.10	429.05	423.70	418.95	414.73	399.50	390.62	385.31
48000	504.86	490.89	478.85	468.41	459.32	451.35	444.35	438.18	432.72	427.87	423.56	408.00	398.93	393.51
49000	515.38	501.12	488.83	478.17	468.89	460.76	453.61	447.31	441.73	436.78	432.38	416.50	407.24	401.71
50000	525.90	511.34	498.80	487.93	478.46	470.16	462.87	456.44	450.75	445.70	441.21	425.00	415.55	409.90
55000	578.48	562.48	548.68	536.72	526.30	517.17	509.15	502.08	495.82	490.27	485.33	467.50	457.10	450.89
60000	631.07	613.61	598.56	585.52	574.15	564.19	555.44	547.72	540.89	534.83	529.45	510.00	498.66	491.88
65000	683.66	664.75	648.44	634.31	621.99	611.21	601.73	593.37	585.97	579.40	573.57	552.50	540.21	532.87
70000	736.25	715.88	698.32	683.10	669.84	658.22	648.01	639.01	631.04	623.97	617.69	595.00	581.77	573.86
75000	788.84	767.01	748.20	731.89	717.68	705.24	694.30	684.65	676.12	668.54	661.81	637.50	623.32	614.85
80000	841.43	818.15	798.08	780.69	765.53	752.25	740.59	730.29	721.19	713.11	705.93	680.00	664.87	655.84
85000	894.02	869.28	847.96	829.48	813.37	799.27	786.87	775.94	766.26	757.68	750.05	722.50	706.43	696.83
90000	946.61	920.41	897.84	878.27	861.22	846.28	833.16	821.58	811.34	802.25	794.17	765.00	747.98	737.82
95000	999.20	971.55	947.72	927.06	909.06	893.30	879.44	867.22	856.41	846.82	838.29	807.49	789.54	778.81
100000	1051.79	1022.68	997.60	975.86	956.91	940.31	925.73	912.87	901.49	891.39	882.41	849.99	831.09	819.80

MONTHLY PAYMENT
REQUIRED TO AMORTIZE A LOAN

TERM	1 Year	2 Years	3 Years	4 Years	5 Years	6 Years	7 Years	8 Years	9 Years	10 Years	11 Years	12 Years	13 Years	14 Years
AMOUNT														
5	.44	.24	.17	.13	.11	.10	.09	.08	.07	.07	.07	.06	.06	.06
10	.88	.47	.33	.26	.22	.19	.17	.16	.14	.14	.13	.12	.12	.11
15	1.32	.70	.49	.38	.32	.28	.25	.23	.21	.20	.19	.18	.17	.17
25	2.20	1.16	.81	.64	.46	.46	.42	.38	.35	.33	.31	.30	.29	.28
50	4.39	2.31	1.61	1.27	1.06	.92	.83	.76	.70	.66	.62	.59	.57	.55
75	6.59	3.46	2.41	1.90	1.59	1.38	1.24	1.13	1.05	.98	.93	.89	.85	.82
100	8.78	4.61	3.22	2.53	2.11	1.84	1.65	1.51	1.40	1.31	1.24	1.18	1.14	1.10
200	17.56	9.21	6.43	5.05	4.22	3.68	3.29	3.01	2.79	2.61	2.48	2.36	2.27	2.19
300	26.34	13.81	9.64	7.57	6.33	5.52	4.94	4.51	4.18	3.92	3.71	3.54	3.40	3.28
400	35.12	18.41	12.86	10.09	8.44	7.35	6.58	6.01	5.57	5.22	4.95	4.72	4.53	4.37
500	43.89	23.01	16.07	12.61	10.55	9.19	8.23	7.51	6.96	6.53	6.18	5.89	5.66	5.46
600	52.67	27.61	19.28	15.14	12.66	11.03	9.87	9.01	8.36	7.83	7.42	7.07	6.79	6.55
700	61.45	32.21	22.49	17.66	14.77	12.87	11.52	10.52	9.75	9.14	8.65	8.25	7.92	7.64
800	70.23	36.81	25.71	20.18	16.88	14.70	13.16	12.02	11.14	10.44	9.89	9.43	9.05	8.73
900	79.00	41.41	28.92	22.70	18.99	16.54	14.81	13.52	12.53	11.75	11.12	10.61	10.18	9.82
1000	87.78	46.01	32.13	25.22	21.10	18.38	16.45	15.02	13.92	13.05	12.36	11.78	11.31	10.91
2000	175.56	92.02	64.26	50.44	42.20	36.75	32.90	30.04	27.84	26.10	24.71	23.56	22.61	21.81
3000	263.33	138.02	96.38	75.66	63.30	55.13	49.34	45.05	41.76	39.15	37.06	35.34	33.91	32.71
4000	351.11	184.03	128.51	100.88	84.40	73.50	65.79	60.07	55.67	52.20	49.41	47.12	45.21	43.62
5000	438.89	230.04	160.64	126.10	105.50	91.88	82.24	75.08	69.59	65.25	61.76	58.90	56.52	54.52
6000	526.66	276.04	192.76	151.32	126.60	110.25	98.68	90.10	83.51	78.30	74.11	70.67	67.82	65.42
7000	614.44	322.05	224.89	176.54	147.70	128.63	115.13	105.12	97.42	91.35	86.46	82.45	79.12	76.32
8000	702.22	368.06	257.02	201.76	168.80	147.00	131.58	120.13	111.34	104.40	98.81	94.23	90.42	87.23
9000	789.99	414.06	289.14	226.97	189.90	165.38	148.02	135.15	125.26	117.45	111.16	106.01	101.73	98.13
10000	877.77	460.07	321.27	252.19	211.00	183.75	164.47	150.16	139.17	130.50	123.51	117.79	113.03	109.03
11000	965.55	506.08	353.40	277.41	232.10	202.13	180.92	165.18	153.09	143.55	135.86	129.56	124.33	119.93
12000	1053.32	552.08	385.52	302.63	253.20	220.50	197.36	180.20	167.01	156.60	148.21	141.34	135.63	130.84
13000	1141.10	598.09	417.65	327.85	274.30	238.88	213.81	195.21	180.92	169.65	160.56	153.12	146.94	141.74
14000	1228.87	644.10	449.78	353.07	295.40	257.25	230.26	210.23	194.84	182.70	172.92	164.90	158.24	152.64
15000	1316.65	690.10	481.90	378.29	316.50	275.63	246.70	225.24	208.76	195.75	185.27	176.68	169.54	163.54
16000	1404.43	736.11	514.03	403.51	337.60	294.00	263.15	240.26	222.67	208.80	197.62	188.45	180.84	174.45
17000	1492.20	782.12	546.16	428.72	358.70	312.38	279.60	255.28	236.59	221.85	209.97	200.23	192.15	185.35
18000	1579.98	828.12	578.28	453.94	379.80	330.75	296.04	270.29	250.51	234.90	222.32	212.01	203.45	196.25
19000	1667.76	874.13	610.41	479.16	400.90	349.13	312.49	285.31	264.42	247.95	234.67	223.79	214.75	207.15
20000	1755.53	920.14	642.54	504.38	422.00	367.50	328.94	300.32	278.34	261.00	247.02	235.57	226.05	218.06
21000	1843.31	966.14	674.66	529.60	443.10	385.88	345.38	315.34	292.26	274.04	259.37	247.35	237.35	228.96
22000	1931.09	1012.15	706.79	554.82	464.20	404.25	361.83	330.35	306.17	287.09	271.72	259.12	248.66	239.86
23000	2018.86	1058.16	738.92	580.04	485.30	422.63	378.28	345.37	320.09	300.14	284.07	270.90	259.96	250.76
24000	2106.64	1104.16	771.04	605.26	506.40	441.00	394.72	360.39	334.01	313.19	296.42	282.68	271.26	261.67
25000	2194.42	1150.17	803.17	630.47	527.50	459.38	411.17	375.40	347.92	326.24	308.77	294.46	282.56	272.57
26000	2282.19	1196.18	835.29	655.69	548.60	477.75	427.62	390.42	361.84	339.29	321.12	306.24	293.87	283.47
27000	2369.97	1242.18	867.42	680.91	569.70	496.13	444.06	405.43	375.76	352.34	333.47	318.01	305.17	294.37
28000	2457.74	1288.19	899.55	706.13	590.80	514.50	460.51	420.45	389.67	365.39	345.83	329.79	316.47	305.28
29000	2545.52	1334.20	931.67	731.35	611.90	532.88	476.96	435.47	403.59	378.44	358.18	341.57	327.77	316.18
30000	2633.30	1380.20	963.80	756.57	633.00	551.25	493.40	450.48	417.51	391.49	370.53	353.35	339.08	327.08
31000	2721.07	1426.21	995.93	781.79	654.10	569.63	509.85	465.50	431.42	404.54	382.88	365.13	350.38	337.98
32000	2808.85	1472.22	1028.05	807.01	675.20	588.00	526.30	480.51	445.34	417.59	395.23	376.90	361.68	348.89
33000	2896.63	1518.22	1060.18	832.22	696.30	606.38	542.74	495.53	459.26	430.64	407.58	388.68	372.98	359.79
34000	2984.40	1564.23	1092.31	857.44	717.40	624.75	559.19	510.55	473.17	443.69	419.93	400.46	384.29	370.69
35000	3072.18	1610.24	1124.43	882.66	738.50	643.13	575.64	525.56	487.09	456.74	432.28	412.24	395.59	381.59
36000	3159.96	1656.24	1156.56	907.88	759.60	661.50	592.08	540.58	501.01	469.79	444.63	424.02	406.89	392.50
37000	3247.73	1702.25	1188.69	933.10	780.70	679.88	608.53	555.59	514.92	482.84	456.98	435.80	418.19	403.40
38000	3335.51	1748.26	1220.81	958.32	801.79	698.25	624.98	570.61	528.84	495.89	469.33	447.57	429.49	414.30
39000	3423.29	1794.26	1252.94	983.54	822.89	716.63	641.42	585.62	542.76	508.94	481.68	459.35	440.80	425.20
40000	3511.06	1840.27	1285.07	1008.76	843.99	735.00	657.87	600.64	556.67	521.99	494.03	471.13	452.10	436.11
41000	3598.84	1886.27	1317.19	1033.97	865.09	753.38	674.32	615.66	570.59	535.03	506.39	482.91	463.40	447.01
42000	3686.61	1932.28	1349.32	1059.19	886.19	771.75	690.76	630.67	584.51	548.08	518.74	494.69	474.70	457.91
43000	3774.39	1978.29	1381.45	1084.41	907.29	790.13	707.21	645.69	598.43	561.13	531.09	506.46	486.01	468.81
44000	3862.17	2024.29	1413.57	1109.63	928.39	808.50	723.65	660.70	612.34	574.18	543.44	518.24	497.31	479.72
45000	3949.94	2070.30	1445.70	1134.85	949.49	826.88	740.10	675.72	626.26	587.23	555.79	530.02	508.61	490.62
46000	4037.72	2116.31	1477.83	1160.07	970.59	845.25	756.55	690.74	640.18	600.28	568.14	541.80	519.91	501.52
47000	4125.50	2162.31	1509.95	1185.29	991.69	863.63	772.99	705.75	654.09	613.33	580.49	553.58	531.22	512.42
48000	4213.27	2208.32	1542.08	1210.51	1012.79	882.00	789.44	720.77	668.01	626.38	592.84	565.35	542.52	523.33
49000	4301.05	2254.33	1574.20	1235.72	1033.89	900.38	805.89	735.78	681.93	639.43	605.19	577.13	553.82	534.23
50000	4388.83	2300.33	1606.33	1260.94	1054.99	918.75	822.33	750.80	695.84	652.48	617.54	588.91	565.12	545.13
55000	4827.71	2530.37	1766.96	1387.04	1160.49	1010.63	904.57	825.88	765.43	717.73	679.30	647.80	621.64	599.64
60000	5266.59	2760.40	1927.60	1513.13	1265.99	1102.50	986.80	900.96	835.01	782.98	741.05	706.69	678.15	654.16
65000	5705.47	2990.43	2088.23	1639.22	1371.49	1194.37	1069.03	976.04	904.59	848.22	802.80	765.58	734.66	708.67
70000	6144.35	3220.47	2248.86	1765.32	1476.99	1286.25	1151.27	1051.12	974.18	913.47	864.56	824.47	791.17	763.18
75000	6583.24	3450.50	2409.49	1891.41	1582.49	1378.12	1233.50	1126.20	1043.76	978.72	926.31	883.36	847.68	817.70
80000	7022.12	3680.53	2570.13	2017.51	1687.98	1470.00	1315.73	1201.28	1113.34	1043.97	988.06	942.25	904.19	872.21
85000	7461.00	3910.56	2730.76	2143.60	1793.48	1561.87	1397.96	1276.36	1182.93	1109.21	1049.82	1001.15	960.71	926.72
90000	7899.88	4140.60	2891.39	2269.69	1898.98	1653.75	1480.20	1351.43	1252.51	1174.46	1111.57	1060.04	1017.22	981.23
95000	8338.77	4370.63	3052.02	2395.79	2004.48	1745.62	1562.43	1426.51	1322.10	1239.71	1173.32	1118.93	1073.73	1035.75
100000	8777.65	4600.66	3212.66	2521.88	2109.98	1837.50	1644.66	1501.59	1391.68	1304.96	1235.08	1177.82	1130.24	1090.26

TERM	15 Years	16 Years	17 Years	18 Years	19 Years	20 Years	21 Years	22 Years	23 Years	24 Years	25 Years	30 Years	35 Years	40 Years
AMOUNT														
5	.06	.06	.06	.05	.05	.05	.05	.05	.05	.05	.05	.05	.05	.05
10	.11	.11	.11	.10	.10	.10	.10	.10	.10	.09	.09	.09	.09	.09
15	.16	.16	.16	.15	.15	.15	.14	.14	.14	.14	.14	.13	.13	.13
25	.27	.26	.26	.25	.25	.24	.24	.23	.23	.23	.23	.22	.21	.21
50	.53	.52	.51	.50	.49	.48	.47	.46	.46	.45	.45	.43	.42	.42
75	.80	.78	.76	.74	.73	.71	.70	.69	.68	.68	.67	.65	.63	.62
100	1.06	1.03	1.01	.99	.97	.95	.94	.92	.91	.90	.89	.86	.84	.83
200	2.12	2.06	2.01	1.97	1.93	1.90	1.87	1.84	1.82	1.80	1.78	1.72	1.68	1.66
300	3.17	3.09	3.01	2.95	2.89	2.84	2.80	2.76	2.72	2.69	2.67	2.57	2.52	2.48
400	4.23	4.11	4.01	3.93	3.85	3.79	3.73	3.68	3.63	3.59	3.56	3.43	3.35	3.31
500	5.29	5.14	5.02	4.91	4.81	4.73	4.66	4.59	4.54	4.49	4.44	4.28	4.19	4.13
600	6.34	6.17	6.02	5.89	5.78	5.68	5.59	5.51	5.44	5.38	5.33	5.14	5.03	4.96
700	7.40	7.20	7.02	6.87	6.74	6.62	6.52	6.43	6.35	6.28	6.22	5.99	5.86	5.78
800	8.46	8.22	8.02	7.85	7.70	7.57	7.45	7.35	7.26	7.18	7.11	6.85	6.70	6.61
900	9.51	9.25	9.03	8.83	8.66	8.51	8.38	8.27	8.16	8.07	7.99	7.70	7.54	7.44
1000	10.57	10.28	10.03	9.81	9.62	9.46	9.31	9.18	9.07	8.97	8.88	8.56	8.37	8.26
2000	21.13	20.55	20.05	19.62	19.24	18.91	18.62	18.36	18.14	17.94	17.76	17.11	16.74	16.52
3000	31.69	30.82	30.07	29.42	28.86	28.36	27.93	27.54	27.20	26.90	26.63	25.67	25.11	24.77
4000	42.26	41.10	40.10	39.23	38.48	37.81	37.23	36.72	36.27	35.87	35.51	34.22	33.48	33.03
5000	52.82	51.37	50.12	49.04	48.09	47.27	46.54	45.90	45.33	44.83	44.39	42.78	41.84	41.29
6000	63.38	61.64	60.14	58.84	57.71	56.72	55.85	55.08	54.40	53.80	53.26	51.33	50.21	49.54
7000	73.95	71.92	70.17	68.65	67.33	66.17	65.16	64.26	63.47	62.76	62.14	59.89	58.58	57.80
8000	84.51	82.19	80.19	78.46	76.95	75.62	74.46	73.44	72.53	71.73	71.02	68.44	66.95	66.06
9000	95.07	92.46	90.21	88.26	86.56	85.08	83.77	82.62	81.60	80.70	79.89	77.00	75.32	74.31
10000	105.64	102.74	100.23	98.07	96.18	94.53	93.08	91.80	90.66	89.66	88.77	85.55	83.68	82.57
11000	116.20	113.01	110.26	107.87	105.80	103.98	102.38	100.98	99.73	98.63	97.65	94.11	92.05	90.83
12000	126.76	123.28	120.28	117.68	115.42	113.43	111.69	110.16	108.80	107.59	106.52	102.66	100.42	99.08
13000	137.33	133.55	130.30	127.49	125.03	122.88	121.00	119.33	117.86	116.56	115.40	111.22	108.79	107.34
14000	147.89	143.83	140.33	137.29	134.65	132.34	130.31	128.51	126.93	125.52	124.27	119.77	117.15	115.60
15000	158.45	154.10	150.35	147.10	144.27	141.79	139.61	137.69	135.99	134.49	133.15	128.33	125.52	123.85
16000	169.02	164.37	160.37	156.91	153.89	151.24	148.92	146.87	145.06	143.45	142.03	136.88	133.89	132.11
17000	179.58	174.65	170.40	166.71	163.50	160.69	158.23	156.05	154.13	152.42	150.90	145.44	142.26	140.37
18000	190.14	184.92	180.42	176.52	173.12	170.15	167.53	165.23	163.19	161.39	159.78	153.99	150.63	148.62
19000	200.71	195.19	190.44	186.32	182.74	179.60	176.84	174.41	172.26	170.35	168.66	162.55	158.99	156.88
20000	211.27	205.47	200.46	196.13	192.36	189.05	186.15	183.59	181.32	179.32	177.53	171.10	167.36	165.14
21000	221.83	215.74	210.49	205.94	201.97	198.50	195.46	192.77	190.39	188.28	186.41	179.66	175.73	173.39
22000	232.40	226.01	220.51	215.74	211.59	207.96	204.76	201.95	199.46	197.25	195.29	188.21	184.10	181.65
23000	242.96	236.28	230.53	225.55	221.21	217.41	214.07	211.13	208.52	206.21	204.16	196.77	192.47	189.90
24000	253.52	246.56	240.56	235.36	230.83	226.86	223.38	220.31	217.59	215.18	213.04	205.32	200.83	198.16
25000	264.09	256.83	250.58	245.16	240.44	236.31	232.68	229.48	226.65	224.15	221.91	213.88	209.20	206.42
26000	274.65	267.10	260.60	254.97	250.06	245.76	241.99	238.66	235.72	233.11	230.79	222.43	217.57	214.67
27000	285.21	277.38	270.63	264.77	259.68	255.22	251.30	247.84	244.79	242.08	239.67	230.99	225.94	222.93
28000	295.78	287.65	280.65	274.58	269.30	264.67	260.61	257.02	253.85	251.04	248.54	239.54	234.30	231.19
29000	306.34	297.92	290.67	284.39	278.91	274.12	269.91	266.20	262.92	260.01	257.42	248.10	242.67	239.44
30000	316.90	308.20	300.69	294.19	288.53	283.57	279.22	275.38	271.98	268.97	266.30	256.65	251.04	247.70
31000	327.47	318.47	310.72	304.00	298.15	293.03	288.53	284.56	281.05	277.94	275.17	265.21	259.41	255.96
32000	338.03	328.74	320.74	313.81	307.77	302.48	297.83	293.74	290.12	286.90	284.05	273.76	267.78	264.21
33000	348.59	339.01	330.76	323.61	317.38	311.93	307.14	302.92	299.18	295.87	292.93	282.32	276.14	272.47
34000	359.16	349.29	340.79	333.42	327.00	321.38	316.45	312.10	308.25	304.84	301.80	290.87	284.51	280.73
35000	369.72	359.56	350.81	343.23	336.62	330.84	325.76	321.28	317.31	313.80	310.68	299.42	292.88	288.98
36000	380.28	369.83	360.83	353.03	346.24	340.29	335.06	330.46	326.38	322.77	319.56	307.98	301.25	297.24
37000	390.85	380.11	370.86	362.84	355.85	349.74	344.37	339.63	335.45	331.73	328.43	316.53	309.62	305.50
38000	401.41	390.38	380.88	372.64	365.47	359.19	353.68	348.81	344.51	340.70	337.31	325.09	317.98	313.75
39000	411.97	400.65	390.90	382.45	375.09	368.64	362.98	357.99	353.58	349.66	346.18	333.64	326.35	322.01
40000	422.54	410.93	400.92	392.26	384.71	378.10	372.29	367.17	362.64	358.63	355.06	342.20	334.72	330.27
41000	433.10	421.20	410.95	402.06	394.32	387.55	381.60	376.35	371.71	367.60	363.94	350.75	343.09	338.52
42000	443.66	431.47	420.97	411.87	403.94	397.00	390.91	385.53	380.78	376.56	372.81	359.31	351.45	346.78
43000	454.23	441.75	430.99	421.68	413.56	406.45	400.21	394.71	389.84	385.53	381.69	367.86	359.82	355.04
44000	464.79	452.02	441.02	431.48	423.18	415.91	409.52	403.89	398.91	394.49	390.57	376.42	368.19	363.29
45000	475.35	462.29	451.04	441.29	432.79	425.36	418.83	413.07	407.97	403.46	399.44	384.97	376.56	371.55
46000	485.92	472.56	461.06	451.09	442.41	434.81	428.13	422.25	417.04	412.42	408.32	393.53	384.93	379.80
47000	496.48	482.84	471.09	460.90	452.03	444.26	437.44	431.43	426.11	421.39	417.20	402.08	393.29	388.06
48000	507.04	493.11	481.11	470.71	461.65	453.72	446.75	440.61	435.17	430.35	426.07	410.64	401.66	396.32
49000	517.61	503.38	491.13	480.51	471.26	463.17	456.06	449.78	444.24	439.32	434.95	419.19	410.03	404.57
50000	528.17	513.66	501.15	490.32	480.88	472.62	465.36	458.96	453.30	448.29	443.82	427.75	418.40	412.83
55000	580.98	565.02	551.27	539.35	528.97	519.88	511.90	504.86	498.63	493.11	488.21	470.52	460.24	454.11
60000	633.80	616.39	601.38	588.38	577.06	567.14	558.43	550.76	543.96	537.94	532.59	513.30	502.08	495.40
65000	686.62	667.75	651.50	637.41	625.14	614.40	604.97	596.65	589.29	582.77	576.97	556.07	543.92	536.68
70000	739.43	719.12	701.61	686.45	673.23	661.67	651.51	642.55	634.62	627.60	621.35	598.84	585.75	577.96
75000	792.25	770.48	751.73	735.48	721.32	708.93	698.04	688.44	679.95	672.43	665.73	641.62	627.59	619.24
80000	845.07	821.85	801.84	784.51	769.41	756.19	744.58	734.34	725.28	717.25	710.12	684.39	669.43	660.53
85000	897.88	873.21	851.96	833.54	817.49	803.45	791.11	780.23	770.61	762.08	754.50	727.17	711.27	701.81
90000	950.70	924.58	902.07	882.57	865.58	850.71	837.65	826.13	815.94	806.91	798.88	769.94	753.11	743.09
95000	1003.52	975.94	952.19	931.60	913.67	897.97	884.18	872.03	861.27	851.74	843.26	812.72	794.95	784.37
100000	1056.33	1027.31	1002.30	980.63	961.76	945.24	930.72	917.92	906.60	896.57	887.64	855.49	836.79	825.66

MONTHLY PAYMENT
REQUIRED TO AMORTIZE A LOAN

TERM AMOUNT	1 Year	2 Years	3 Years	4 Years	5 Years	6 Years	7 Years	8 Years	9 Years	10 Years	11 Years	12 Years	13 Years	14 Years
5	.44	.24	.17	.13	.11	.10	.09	.08	.07	.07	.07	.06	.06	.06
10	.88	.47	.33	.26	.22	.19	.17	.16	.14	.14	.13	.12	.12	.11
15	1.32	.70	.49	.38	.32	.28	.25	.23	.21	.20	.19	.18	.17	.17
25	2.20	1.16	.81	.64	.53	.47	.42	.38	.35	.33	.31	.30	.29	.28
50	4.39	2.31	1.61	1.27	1.06	.93	.83	.76	.70	.66	.62	.60	.57	.55
75	6.59	3.46	2.42	1.90	1.59	1.39	1.24	1.13	1.05	.99	.93	.89	.85	.82
100	8.78	4.61	3.22	2.53	2.12	1.85	1.65	1.51	1.40	1.31	1.24	1.19	1.14	1.10
200	17.56	9.21	6.43	5.05	4.23	3.69	3.30	3.01	2.79	2.62	2.48	2.37	2.27	2.19
300	26.34	13.81	9.65	7.58	6.34	5.53	4.95	4.52	4.19	3.93	3.72	3.55	3.40	3.28
400	35.12	18.42	12.86	10.10	8.45	7.37	6.59	6.02	5.58	5.24	4.96	4.73	4.54	4.38
500	43.90	23.02	16.08	12.63	10.57	9.21	8.24	7.53	6.98	6.54	6.19	5.91	5.67	5.47
600	52.68	27.62	19.29	15.15	12.68	11.05	9.89	9.03	8.37	7.85	7.43	7.09	6.80	6.56
700	61.46	32.23	22.51	17.67	14.79	12.89	11.54	10.53	9.77	9.16	8.67	8.27	7.94	7.66
800	70.24	36.83	25.72	20.20	16.90	14.73	13.18	12.04	11.16	10.47	9.91	9.45	9.07	8.75
900	79.02	41.43	28.94	22.72	19.02	16.57	14.83	13.54	12.55	11.77	11.15	10.63	10.20	9.84
1000	87.80	46.03	32.15	25.25	21.13	18.41	16.48	15.05	13.95	13.08	12.38	11.81	11.34	10.94
2000	175.60	92.06	64.30	50.49	42.25	36.81	32.95	30.09	27.89	26.16	24.76	23.62	22.67	21.87
3000	263.40	138.09	96.45	75.73	63.38	55.21	49.42	45.13	41.84	39.24	37.14	35.43	34.00	32.80
4000	351.20	184.12	128.60	100.98	84.50	73.61	65.89	60.17	55.78	52.31	49.52	47.23	45.33	43.73
5000	439.00	230.15	160.75	126.22	105.63	92.01	82.37	75.22	69.72	65.39	61.90	59.04	56.66	54.67
6000	526.80	276.18	192.90	151.46	126.75	110.41	98.84	90.26	83.67	78.47	74.28	70.85	67.99	65.60
7000	614.60	322.21	225.05	176.70	147.87	128.81	115.31	105.30	97.61	91.54	86.66	82.65	79.33	76.53
8000	702.40	368.24	257.20	201.95	169.00	147.21	131.78	120.34	111.55	104.62	99.04	94.46	90.66	87.46
9000	790.20	414.27	289.35	227.19	190.12	165.61	148.26	135.38	125.50	117.70	111.41	106.27	101.99	98.40
10000	878.00	460.30	321.50	252.43	211.25	184.01	164.73	150.43	139.44	130.78	123.79	118.07	113.32	109.33
11000	965.80	506.33	353.65	277.67	232.37	202.41	181.20	165.47	153.39	143.85	136.17	129.88	124.65	120.26
12000	1053.60	552.36	385.80	302.92	253.50	220.81	197.67	180.51	167.33	156.93	148.55	141.69	135.98	131.19
13000	1141.40	598.39	417.95	328.16	274.62	239.21	214.14	195.55	181.27	170.01	160.93	153.49	147.32	142.13
14000	1229.20	644.42	450.10	353.40	295.74	257.61	230.62	210.60	195.22	183.08	173.31	165.30	158.65	153.06
15000	1317.00	690.45	482.25	378.65	316.87	276.01	247.09	225.64	209.16	196.16	185.69	177.11	169.98	163.99
16000	1404.80	736.48	514.40	403.89	337.99	294.41	263.56	240.68	223.10	209.24	198.07	188.91	181.31	174.92
17000	1492.60	782.51	546.55	429.13	359.12	312.81	280.03	255.72	237.05	222.31	210.45	200.72	192.64	185.86
18000	1580.40	828.54	578.70	454.37	380.24	331.21	296.51	270.76	250.99	235.39	222.82	212.53	203.97	196.79
19000	1668.20	874.57	610.85	479.62	401.37	349.61	312.98	285.81	264.93	248.47	235.20	224.33	215.31	207.72
20000	1756.00	920.60	643.00	504.86	422.49	368.01	329.45	300.85	278.88	261.55	247.58	236.14	226.64	218.65
21000	1843.80	966.63	675.15	530.10	443.61	386.41	345.92	315.89	292.82	274.62	259.96	247.95	237.97	229.58
22000	1931.60	1012.66	707.30	555.34	464.74	404.81	362.40	330.93	306.77	287.70	272.34	259.75	249.30	240.52
23000	2019.40	1058.69	739.45	580.59	485.86	423.21	378.87	345.98	320.71	300.78	284.72	271.56	260.63	251.45
24000	2107.20	1104.72	771.60	605.83	506.99	441.61	395.34	361.02	334.65	313.85	297.10	283.37	271.96	262.38
25000	2195.00	1150.75	803.75	631.07	528.11	460.01	411.81	376.06	348.60	326.93	309.48	295.18	283.30	273.31
26000	2282.80	1196.78	835.90	656.31	549.24	478.41	428.28	391.10	362.54	340.01	321.85	306.98	294.63	284.25
27000	2370.60	1242.80	868.05	681.56	570.36	496.81	444.76	406.14	376.48	353.08	334.23	318.79	305.96	295.18
28000	2458.40	1288.83	900.20	706.80	591.48	515.21	461.23	421.19	390.43	366.16	346.61	330.60	317.29	306.11
29000	2546.20	1334.86	932.35	732.04	612.61	533.61	477.70	436.23	404.37	379.24	358.99	342.40	328.62	317.04
30000	2633.99	1380.89	964.50	757.29	633.73	552.01	494.17	451.27	418.31	392.32	371.37	354.21	339.95	327.98
31000	2721.79	1426.92	996.65	782.53	654.86	570.41	510.65	466.31	432.26	405.39	383.75	366.02	351.29	338.91
32000	2809.59	1472.95	1028.80	807.77	675.98	588.81	527.12	481.36	446.20	418.47	396.13	377.82	362.62	349.84
33000	2897.39	1518.98	1060.95	833.01	697.11	607.21	543.59	496.40	460.15	431.55	408.51	389.63	373.95	360.77
34000	2985.19	1565.01	1093.10	858.26	718.23	625.61	560.06	511.44	474.09	444.62	420.89	401.44	385.28	371.70
35000	3072.99	1611.04	1125.25	883.50	739.35	644.01	576.54	526.48	488.03	457.70	433.26	413.24	396.61	382.64
36000	3160.79	1657.07	1157.40	908.74	760.48	662.41	593.01	541.52	501.98	470.78	445.64	425.05	407.94	393.57
37000	3248.59	1703.10	1189.55	933.98	781.60	680.81	609.48	556.57	515.92	483.85	458.02	436.86	419.28	404.50
38000	3336.39	1749.13	1221.70	959.23	802.73	699.21	625.95	571.61	529.86	496.93	470.40	448.66	430.61	415.43
39000	3424.19	1795.16	1253.85	984.47	823.85	717.61	642.42	586.65	543.81	510.01	482.78	460.47	441.94	426.37
40000	3511.99	1841.19	1286.00	1009.71	844.97	736.01	658.90	601.69	557.75	523.09	495.16	472.28	453.27	437.30
41000	3599.79	1887.22	1318.15	1034.96	866.10	754.41	675.37	616.74	571.70	536.16	507.54	484.08	464.60	448.23
42000	3687.59	1933.25	1350.30	1060.20	887.22	772.81	691.84	631.78	585.64	549.24	519.92	495.89	475.93	459.16
43000	3775.39	1979.28	1382.45	1085.44	908.35	791.21	708.31	646.82	599.58	562.32	532.30	507.70	487.26	470.10
44000	3863.19	2025.31	1414.60	1110.68	929.47	809.61	724.79	661.86	613.53	575.39	544.67	519.50	498.60	481.03
45000	3950.99	2071.34	1446.75	1135.93	950.60	828.01	741.26	676.90	627.47	588.47	557.05	531.31	509.93	491.96
46000	4038.79	2117.37	1478.90	1161.17	971.72	846.41	757.73	691.95	641.41	601.55	569.43	543.12	521.26	502.89
47000	4126.59	2163.40	1511.05	1186.41	992.84	864.81	774.20	706.99	655.36	614.63	581.81	554.92	532.59	513.83
48000	4214.39	2209.43	1543.20	1211.65	1013.97	883.21	790.68	722.03	669.30	627.70	594.19	566.73	543.92	524.76
49000	4302.19	2255.46	1575.35	1236.90	1035.09	901.61	807.15	737.07	683.24	640.78	606.57	578.54	555.25	535.69
50000	4389.99	2301.49	1607.50	1262.14	1056.22	920.01	823.62	752.12	697.19	653.86	618.95	590.35	566.59	546.62
55000	4828.99	2531.63	1768.25	1388.35	1161.84	1012.01	905.98	827.33	766.91	719.24	680.84	649.38	623.24	601.28
60000	5267.98	2761.78	1929.00	1514.57	1267.46	1104.01	988.34	902.54	836.62	784.63	742.74	708.41	679.90	655.95
65000	5706.98	2991.93	2089.75	1640.78	1373.08	1196.01	1070.70	977.75	906.34	850.01	804.63	767.45	736.56	710.61
70000	6145.98	3222.08	2250.50	1766.99	1478.70	1288.01	1153.07	1052.96	976.06	915.40	866.52	826.48	793.22	765.27
75000	6584.98	3452.23	2411.25	1893.21	1584.32	1380.01	1235.43	1128.17	1045.78	980.78	928.42	885.52	849.88	819.93
80000	7023.98	3682.37	2572.00	2019.42	1689.94	1472.01	1317.79	1203.38	1115.50	1046.17	990.31	944.55	906.54	874.59
85000	7462.98	3912.52	2732.75	2145.63	1795.57	1564.01	1400.15	1278.59	1185.22	1111.55	1052.21	1003.58	963.19	929.25
90000	7901.97	4142.67	2893.50	2271.85	1901.19	1656.01	1482.51	1353.80	1254.93	1176.94	1114.10	1062.62	1019.85	983.92
95000	8340.97	4372.82	3054.25	2398.06	2006.81	1748.01	1564.87	1429.01	1324.65	1242.32	1175.99	1121.65	1076.51	1038.58
100000	8779.97	4602.97	3215.00	2524.27	2112.43	1840.01	1647.23	1504.23	1394.37	1307.71	1237.89	1180.69	1133.17	1093.24

MONTHLY PAYMENT
REQUIRED TO AMORTIZE A LOAN

9.750%

TERM AMOUNT	15 Years	16 Years	17 Years	18 Years	19 Years	20 Years	21 Years	22 Years	23 Years	24 Years	25 Years	30 Years	35 Years	40 Years
5	.06	.06	.06	.05	.05	.05	.05	.05	.05	.05	.05	.05	.05	.05
10	.11	.11	.11	.10	.10	.10	.10	.10	.10	.10	.09	.09	.09	.09
15	.16	.16	.16	.15	.15	.15	.15	.14	.14	.14	.13	.13	.13	.13
25	.27	.26	.26	.25	.25	.24	.24	.24	.23	.23	.23	.22	.22	.21
50	.53	.52	.51	.50	.49	.48	.47	.47	.46	.46	.45	.43	.43	.42
75	.80	.78	.76	.74	.73	.72	.71	.70	.69	.68	.67	.65	.64	.63
100	1.06	1.04	1.01	.99	.97	.95	.94	.93	.92	.91	.90	.86	.85	.83
200	2.12	2.07	2.02	1.97	1.93	1.90	1.87	1.85	1.83	1.81	1.79	1.72	1.69	1.66
300	3.18	3.10	3.02	2.96	2.90	2.85	2.81	2.77	2.74	2.71	2.68	2.58	2.53	2.49
400	4.24	4.13	4.03	3.94	3.86	3.80	3.74	3.69	3.65	3.61	3.57	3.44	3.37	3.32
500	5.30	5.16	5.03	4.92	4.83	4.75	4.68	4.61	4.56	4.51	4.46	4.30	4.21	4.15
600	6.36	6.19	6.04	5.91	5.79	5.70	5.61	5.53	5.47	5.41	5.35	5.16	5.05	4.98
700	7.42	7.22	7.04	6.89	6.76	6.64	6.54	6.45	6.38	6.31	6.24	6.02	5.89	5.81
800	8.48	8.25	8.05	7.88	7.72	7.59	7.48	7.38	7.29	7.21	7.13	6.88	6.73	6.64
900	9.54	9.28	9.05	8.86	8.69	8.54	8.41	8.30	8.20	8.11	8.03	7.74	7.57	7.47
1000	10.60	10.31	10.06	9.84	9.65	9.49	9.35	9.22	9.11	9.01	8.92	8.60	8.41	8.30
2000	21.19	20.61	20.11	19.68	19.30	18.98	18.69	18.43	18.21	18.01	17.83	17.19	16.82	16.60
3000	31.79	30.92	30.17	29.52	28.95	28.46	28.03	27.64	27.31	27.01	26.74	25.78	25.22	24.89
4000	42.38	41.22	40.22	39.36	38.60	37.95	37.37	36.86	36.41	36.01	35.65	34.37	33.63	33.19
5000	52.97	51.52	50.28	49.20	48.25	47.43	46.71	46.07	45.51	45.01	44.56	42.96	42.03	41.48
6000	63.57	61.83	60.33	59.03	57.90	56.92	56.05	55.28	54.61	54.01	53.47	51.55	50.44	49.78
7000	74.16	72.13	70.39	68.87	67.55	66.40	65.39	64.50	63.71	63.01	62.38	60.15	58.85	58.07
8000	84.75	82.44	80.44	78.71	77.20	75.89	74.73	73.71	72.81	72.01	71.30	68.74	67.25	66.37
9000	95.35	92.74	90.49	88.55	86.85	85.37	84.07	82.92	81.91	81.01	80.21	77.33	75.66	74.67
10000	105.94	103.04	100.55	98.39	96.50	94.86	93.41	92.13	91.01	90.01	89.12	85.92	84.06	82.96
11000	116.53	113.35	110.60	108.23	106.15	104.34	102.75	101.35	100.11	99.01	98.03	94.51	92.47	91.26
12000	127.13	123.65	120.66	118.06	115.80	113.83	112.09	110.56	109.21	108.01	106.94	103.10	100.88	99.55
13000	137.72	133.96	130.71	127.90	125.45	123.31	121.43	119.77	118.31	117.01	115.85	111.70	109.28	107.85
14000	148.32	144.26	140.77	137.74	135.10	132.80	130.77	128.99	127.41	126.01	124.76	120.29	117.69	116.14
15000	158.91	154.56	150.82	147.58	144.75	142.28	140.11	138.20	136.51	135.01	133.68	128.88	126.09	124.44
16000	169.50	164.87	160.88	157.42	154.40	151.77	149.45	147.41	145.61	144.01	142.59	137.47	134.50	132.73
17000	180.10	175.17	170.93	167.25	164.05	161.25	158.79	156.62	154.71	153.01	151.50	146.06	142.91	141.03
18000	190.69	185.48	180.98	177.09	173.70	170.74	168.13	165.84	163.81	162.01	160.41	154.65	151.31	149.33
19000	201.28	195.78	191.04	186.93	183.35	180.22	177.47	175.05	172.91	171.01	169.32	163.24	159.72	157.62
20000	211.88	206.08	201.09	196.77	193.00	189.71	186.81	184.26	182.01	180.01	178.23	171.84	168.12	165.92
21000	222.47	216.39	211.15	206.61	202.65	199.19	196.15	193.48	191.11	189.01	187.14	180.43	176.53	174.21
22000	233.06	226.69	221.20	216.45	212.30	208.68	205.50	202.69	200.21	198.01	196.06	189.02	184.93	182.51
23000	243.66	237.00	231.26	226.28	221.95	218.16	214.84	211.90	209.31	207.01	204.97	197.61	193.34	190.80
24000	254.25	247.30	241.31	236.12	231.60	227.65	224.18	221.12	218.41	216.01	213.88	206.20	201.75	199.10
25000	264.85	257.60	251.36	245.96	241.25	237.13	233.52	230.33	227.51	225.01	222.79	214.79	210.15	207.39
26000	275.44	267.91	261.42	255.80	250.90	246.62	242.86	239.54	236.61	234.01	231.70	223.39	218.56	215.69
27000	286.03	278.21	271.47	265.64	260.55	256.10	252.20	248.75	245.71	243.01	240.61	231.98	226.96	223.99
28000	296.63	288.51	281.53	275.47	270.20	265.59	261.54	257.97	254.81	252.01	249.52	240.57	235.37	232.28
29000	307.22	298.82	291.58	285.31	279.85	275.07	270.88	267.18	263.91	261.01	258.43	249.16	243.78	240.58
30000	317.81	309.12	301.64	295.15	289.50	284.56	280.22	276.39	273.01	270.01	267.35	257.75	252.18	248.87
31000	328.41	319.43	311.69	304.99	299.15	294.05	289.56	285.61	282.11	279.01	276.26	266.34	260.59	257.17
32000	339.00	329.73	321.75	314.83	308.80	303.53	298.90	294.82	291.21	288.01	285.17	274.93	268.99	265.46
33000	349.59	340.03	331.80	324.67	318.45	313.02	308.24	304.03	300.31	297.01	294.08	283.53	277.40	273.76
34000	360.19	350.34	341.85	334.50	328.10	322.50	317.58	313.24	309.41	306.01	302.99	292.12	285.81	282.05
35000	370.78	360.64	351.91	344.34	337.75	331.99	326.92	322.46	318.51	315.01	311.90	300.71	294.21	290.35
36000	381.38	370.95	361.96	354.18	347.40	341.47	336.26	331.67	327.61	324.01	320.81	309.30	302.62	298.65
37000	391.97	381.25	372.02	364.02	357.05	350.96	345.60	340.88	336.71	333.01	329.73	317.89	311.02	306.94
38000	402.56	391.55	382.07	373.86	366.70	360.44	354.94	350.10	345.81	342.01	338.64	326.48	319.43	315.24
39000	413.16	401.86	392.13	383.69	376.35	369.93	364.28	359.31	354.91	351.01	347.55	335.08	327.83	323.53
40000	423.75	412.16	402.18	393.53	386.00	379.41	373.62	368.52	364.01	360.01	356.46	343.67	336.24	331.83
41000	434.34	422.47	412.24	403.37	395.65	388.90	382.96	377.74	373.11	369.01	365.37	352.26	344.65	340.12
42000	444.94	432.77	422.29	413.21	405.30	398.38	392.30	386.95	382.21	378.01	374.28	360.85	353.05	348.42
43000	455.53	443.07	432.34	423.05	414.95	407.87	401.65	396.16	391.31	387.01	383.19	369.44	361.46	356.72
44000	466.12	453.38	442.40	432.89	424.60	417.35	410.99	405.37	400.41	396.01	392.11	378.03	369.86	365.01
45000	476.72	463.68	452.45	442.72	434.25	426.84	420.33	414.59	409.51	405.01	401.02	386.62	378.27	373.31
46000	487.31	473.99	462.51	452.56	443.90	436.32	429.67	423.80	418.61	414.01	409.93	395.22	386.68	381.60
47000	497.91	484.29	472.56	462.40	453.55	445.81	439.01	433.01	427.71	423.01	418.84	403.81	395.08	389.90
48000	508.50	494.59	482.62	472.24	463.20	455.29	448.35	442.23	436.81	432.01	427.75	412.40	403.49	398.19
49000	519.09	504.90	492.67	482.08	472.85	464.78	457.69	451.44	445.91	441.02	436.66	420.99	411.89	406.49
50000	529.69	515.20	502.72	491.92	482.50	474.26	467.03	460.65	455.01	450.02	445.57	429.58	420.30	414.78
55000	582.65	566.72	553.00	541.11	530.75	521.69	513.73	506.72	500.51	495.02	490.13	472.54	462.33	456.26
60000	635.62	618.24	603.27	590.30	579.00	569.12	560.43	552.78	546.02	540.02	534.69	515.50	504.36	497.74
65000	688.59	669.76	653.54	639.49	627.25	616.54	607.14	598.85	591.52	585.02	579.24	558.46	546.39	539.22
70000	741.56	721.28	703.81	688.68	675.50	663.97	653.84	644.91	637.02	630.02	623.80	601.41	588.42	580.70
75000	794.53	772.80	754.08	737.87	723.75	711.39	700.54	690.97	682.52	675.02	668.36	644.37	630.45	622.17
80000	847.50	824.32	804.36	787.06	772.00	758.82	747.24	737.04	728.02	720.02	712.91	687.33	672.48	663.65
85000	900.46	875.84	854.63	836.25	820.25	806.24	793.94	783.10	773.52	765.02	757.47	730.29	714.51	705.13
90000	953.43	927.36	904.90	885.44	868.50	853.67	840.65	829.17	819.02	810.02	802.03	773.24	756.54	746.61
95000	1006.40	978.88	955.17	934.63	916.75	901.10	887.35	875.23	864.52	855.02	846.59	816.20	798.56	788.09
100000	1059.37	1030.40	1005.44	983.83	965.00	948.52	934.05	921.30	910.02	900.03	891.14	859.16	840.59	829.56

MONTHLY PAYMENT
REQUIRED TO AMORTIZE A LOAN

TERM AMOUNT	1 Year	2 Years	3 Years	4 Years	5 Years	6 Years	7 Years	8 Years	9 Years	10 Years	11 Years	12 Years	13 Years	14 Years
5	.44	.24	.17	.13	.11	.10	.09	.08	.07	.07	.07	.06	.06	.06
10	.88	.47	.33	.26	.22	.19	.17	.16	.14	.14	.13	.12	.12	.11
15	1.32	.70	.49	.38	.32	.28	.25	.23	.21	.20	.19	.18	.18	.17
25	2.20	1.16	.81	.64	.53	.47	.42	.38	.35	.33	.32	.30	.29	.28
50	4.40	2.31	1.61	1.27	1.06	.93	.83	.76	.70	.66	.63	.60	.57	.55
75	6.59	3.46	2.42	1.90	1.59	1.39	1.24	1.14	1.05	.99	.94	.89	.86	.83
100	8.79	4.61	3.22	2.53	2.12	1.85	1.65	1.51	1.40	1.32	1.25	1.19	1.14	1.10
200	17.57	9.22	6.44	5.06	4.23	3.69	3.30	3.02	2.80	2.63	2.49	2.37	2.28	2.20
300	26.35	13.82	9.66	7.58	6.35	5.53	4.95	4.53	4.20	3.94	3.73	3.56	3.41	3.29
400	35.13	18.43	12.87	10.11	8.46	7.38	6.60	6.03	5.59	5.25	4.97	4.74	4.55	4.39
500	43.92	23.03	16.09	12.64	10.58	9.22	8.25	7.54	6.99	6.56	6.21	5.92	5.69	5.49
600	52.70	27.64	19.31	15.16	12.69	11.06	9.90	9.05	8.39	7.87	7.45	7.11	6.82	6.58
700	61.48	32.24	22.53	17.69	14.81	12.90	11.55	10.55	9.78	9.18	8.69	8.29	7.96	7.68
800	70.26	36.85	25.74	20.22	16.92	14.75	13.20	12.06	11.18	10.49	9.93	9.47	9.09	8.77
900	79.05	41.45	28.96	22.74	19.04	16.59	14.85	13.57	12.58	11.80	11.17	10.66	10.23	9.87
1000	87.83	46.06	32.18	25.27	21.15	18.43	16.50	15.07	13.98	13.11	12.41	11.84	11.37	10.97
2000	175.65	92.11	64.35	50.54	42.30	36.86	33.00	30.14	27.95	26.21	24.82	23.68	22.73	21.93
3000	263.47	138.16	96.53	75.80	63.45	55.28	49.50	45.21	41.92	39.32	37.23	35.51	34.09	32.89
4000	351.30	184.22	128.70	101.07	84.60	73.71	66.00	60.28	55.89	52.42	49.63	47.35	45.45	43.85
5000	439.12	230.27	160.87	126.34	105.75	92.13	82.50	75.35	69.86	65.53	62.04	59.18	56.81	54.82
6000	526.94	276.32	193.05	151.60	126.90	110.56	98.99	90.42	83.83	78.63	74.45	71.02	68.17	65.78
7000	614.77	322.37	225.22	176.87	148.05	128.98	115.49	105.48	97.80	91.74	86.85	82.85	79.53	76.74
8000	702.59	368.43	257.39	202.14	169.20	147.41	131.99	120.55	111.77	104.84	99.26	94.69	90.89	87.70
9000	790.41	414.48	289.57	227.40	190.34	165.83	148.49	135.62	125.74	117.95	111.67	106.52	102.25	98.66
10000	878.23	460.53	321.74	252.67	211.49	184.26	164.99	150.69	139.71	131.05	124.07	118.36	113.61	109.63
11000	966.06	506.58	353.91	277.94	232.64	202.68	181.48	165.76	153.68	144.16	136.48	130.20	124.98	120.59
12000	1053.88	552.64	386.09	303.20	253.79	221.11	197.98	180.83	167.65	157.26	148.89	142.03	136.34	131.55
13000	1141.70	598.69	418.26	328.47	274.94	239.53	214.48	195.90	181.62	170.36	161.30	153.87	147.70	142.51
14000	1229.53	644.74	450.43	353.74	296.09	257.96	230.98	210.96	195.59	183.47	173.70	165.70	159.06	153.48
15000	1317.35	690.80	482.61	379.00	317.24	276.38	247.48	226.03	209.56	196.57	186.11	177.54	170.42	164.44
16000	1405.17	736.85	514.78	404.27	338.39	294.81	263.97	241.10	223.53	209.68	198.52	189.37	181.78	175.40
17000	1492.99	782.90	546.95	429.54	359.53	313.23	280.47	256.17	237.51	222.78	210.92	201.21	193.14	186.36
18000	1580.82	828.95	579.13	454.80	380.68	331.66	296.97	271.24	251.48	235.89	223.33	213.04	204.50	197.32
19000	1668.64	875.01	611.30	480.07	401.83	350.08	313.47	286.31	265.45	248.99	235.74	224.88	215.86	208.29
20000	1756.46	921.06	643.47	505.34	422.98	368.51	329.97	301.38	279.42	262.10	248.14	236.72	227.22	219.25
21000	1844.29	967.11	675.65	530.60	444.13	386.93	346.46	316.44	293.39	275.20	260.55	248.55	238.58	230.21
22000	1932.11	1013.16	707.82	555.87	465.28	405.36	362.96	331.51	307.36	288.31	272.96	260.39	249.95	241.17
23000	2019.93	1059.22	739.99	581.14	486.43	423.78	379.46	346.58	321.33	301.41	285.37	272.22	261.31	252.14
24000	2107.75	1105.27	772.17	606.40	507.58	442.21	395.96	361.65	335.30	314.51	297.77	284.06	272.67	263.10
25000	2195.58	1151.32	804.34	631.67	528.72	460.63	412.46	376.72	349.27	327.62	310.18	295.89	284.03	274.06
26000	2283.40	1197.37	836.51	656.94	549.87	479.06	428.95	391.79	363.24	340.72	322.59	307.73	295.39	285.02
27000	2371.22	1243.43	868.69	682.20	571.02	497.48	445.45	406.86	377.21	353.83	334.99	319.56	306.75	295.98
28000	2459.05	1289.48	900.86	707.47	592.17	515.91	461.95	421.92	391.18	366.93	347.40	331.40	318.11	306.95
29000	2546.87	1335.53	933.03	732.74	613.32	534.33	478.45	436.99	405.15	380.04	359.81	343.24	329.47	317.91
30000	2634.69	1381.59	965.21	758.00	634.47	552.76	494.95	452.06	419.12	393.14	372.21	355.07	340.83	328.87
31000	2722.51	1427.64	997.38	783.27	655.62	571.18	511.44	467.13	433.09	406.25	384.62	366.91	352.19	339.83
32000	2810.34	1473.69	1029.55	808.54	676.77	589.61	527.94	482.20	447.06	419.35	397.03	378.74	363.55	350.80
33000	2898.16	1519.74	1061.73	833.80	697.91	608.03	544.44	497.27	461.04	432.46	409.44	390.58	374.92	361.76
34000	2985.98	1565.80	1093.90	859.07	719.06	626.46	560.94	512.34	475.01	445.56	421.84	402.41	386.28	372.72
35000	3073.81	1611.85	1126.07	884.34	740.21	644.88	577.44	527.40	488.98	458.67	434.25	414.25	397.64	383.68
36000	3161.63	1657.90	1158.25	909.60	761.36	663.31	593.93	542.47	502.95	471.77	446.66	426.08	409.00	394.64
37000	3249.45	1703.95	1190.42	934.87	782.51	681.74	610.43	557.54	516.92	484.87	459.06	437.92	420.36	405.61
38000	3337.28	1750.01	1222.59	960.14	803.66	700.16	626.93	572.61	530.89	497.98	471.47	449.76	431.72	416.57
39000	3425.10	1796.06	1254.77	985.40	824.81	718.59	643.43	587.68	544.86	511.08	483.88	461.59	443.08	427.53
40000	3512.92	1842.11	1286.94	1010.67	845.96	737.01	659.93	602.75	558.83	524.19	496.28	473.43	454.44	438.49
41000	3600.74	1888.16	1319.11	1035.94	867.10	755.44	676.42	617.82	572.80	537.29	508.69	485.26	465.80	449.46
42000	3688.57	1934.22	1351.29	1061.20	888.25	773.86	692.92	632.88	586.77	550.40	521.10	497.10	477.16	460.42
43000	3776.39	1980.27	1383.46	1086.47	909.40	792.29	709.42	647.95	600.74	563.50	533.51	508.93	488.52	471.38
44000	3864.21	2026.32	1415.63	1111.74	930.55	810.71	725.92	663.02	614.71	576.61	545.91	520.77	499.89	482.34
45000	3952.04	2072.38	1447.81	1137.00	951.70	829.14	742.42	678.09	628.68	589.71	558.32	532.60	511.25	493.30
46000	4039.86	2118.43	1479.98	1162.27	972.85	847.56	758.91	693.16	642.65	602.82	570.73	544.44	522.61	504.27
47000	4127.68	2164.48	1512.15	1187.54	994.00	865.99	775.41	708.23	656.62	615.92	583.13	556.27	533.97	515.23
48000	4215.50	2210.53	1544.33	1212.80	1015.15	884.41	791.91	723.30	670.59	629.02	595.54	568.11	545.33	526.19
49000	4303.33	2256.59	1576.50	1238.07	1036.29	902.84	808.41	738.36	684.57	642.13	607.95	579.95	556.69	537.15
50000	4391.15	2302.64	1608.67	1263.34	1057.44	921.26	824.91	753.43	698.54	655.23	620.35	591.78	568.05	548.12
55000	4830.26	2532.90	1769.54	1389.67	1163.19	1013.39	907.40	828.77	768.39	720.76	682.39	650.96	624.86	602.93
60000	5269.38	2763.17	1930.41	1516.00	1268.93	1105.51	989.89	904.12	838.24	786.28	744.42	710.14	681.66	657.74
65000	5708.49	2993.43	2091.27	1642.34	1374.68	1197.64	1072.38	979.46	908.09	851.80	806.46	769.31	738.46	712.55
70000	6147.61	3223.69	2252.14	1768.67	1480.42	1289.76	1154.87	1054.80	977.95	917.33	868.49	828.49	795.27	767.36
75000	6586.72	3453.96	2413.01	1895.00	1586.16	1381.89	1237.36	1130.15	1047.80	982.85	930.53	887.67	852.07	822.17
80000	7025.84	3684.22	2573.87	2021.34	1691.91	1474.02	1319.85	1205.49	1117.65	1048.37	992.56	946.85	908.88	876.98
85000	7464.95	3914.48	2734.74	2147.67	1797.65	1566.14	1402.34	1280.83	1187.51	1113.89	1054.60	1006.03	965.68	931.79
90000	7904.07	4144.75	2895.61	2274.00	1903.39	1658.27	1484.83	1356.17	1257.36	1179.42	1116.63	1065.20	1022.49	986.60
95000	8343.18	4375.01	3056.48	2400.34	2009.14	1750.39	1567.32	1431.52	1327.21	1244.94	1178.67	1124.38	1079.29	1041.41
100000	8782.30	4605.27	3217.34	2526.67	2114.88	1842.52	1649.81	1506.86	1397.07	1310.46	1240.70	1183.56	1136.10	1096.23

TERM AMOUNT	15 Years	16 Years	17 Years	18 Years	19 Years	20 Years	21 Years	22 Years	23 Years	24 Years	25 Years	30 Years	35 Years	40 Years
5	.06	.06	.06	.05	.05	.05	.05	.05	.05	.05	.05	.05	.05	.05
10	.11	.11	.11	.10	.10	.10	.10	.10	.10	.10	.10	.09	.09	.09
15	.16	.16	.16	.15	.15	.15	.15	.14	.14	.14	.14	.13	.13	.13
25	.27	.26	.26	.25	.25	.24	.24	.24	.23	.23	.23	.22	.22	.21
50	.54	.52	.51	.50	.49	.48	.47	.47	.46	.46	.45	.44	.43	.42
75	.80	.78	.76	.75	.73	.72	.71	.70	.69	.68	.68	.65	.64	.63
100	1.07	1.04	1.01	.99	.97	.96	.94	.93	.92	.91	.90	.87	.85	.84
200	2.13	2.07	2.02	1.98	1.94	1.91	1.88	1.85	1.83	1.81	1.79	1.73	1.69	1.67
300	3.19	3.11	3.03	2.97	2.91	2.86	2.82	2.78	2.75	2.72	2.69	2.59	2.54	2.51
400	4.25	4.14	4.04	3.95	3.88	3.81	3.75	3.70	3.66	3.62	3.58	3.46	3.38	3.34
500	5.32	5.17	5.05	4.94	4.85	4.76	4.69	4.63	4.57	4.52	4.48	4.32	4.23	4.17
600	6.38	6.21	6.06	5.93	5.81	5.72	5.63	5.55	5.49	5.43	5.37	5.18	5.07	5.01
700	7.44	7.24	7.07	6.91	6.78	6.67	6.57	6.48	6.40	6.33	6.27	6.04	5.92	5.84
800	8.50	8.27	8.07	7.90	7.75	7.62	7.50	7.40	7.31	7.23	7.16	6.91	6.76	6.67
900	9.57	9.31	9.08	8.89	8.72	8.57	8.44	8.33	8.23	8.14	8.06	7.77	7.60	7.51
1000	10.63	10.34	10.09	9.88	9.69	9.52	9.30	9.25	9.14	9.04	8.95	8.63	8.45	8.34
2000	21.25	20.67	20.18	19.75	19.37	19.04	18.75	18.50	18.27	18.07	17.90	17.26	16.89	16.67
3000	31.88	31.01	30.26	29.62	29.05	28.56	28.13	27.75	27.41	27.11	26.84	25.89	25.34	25.01
4000	42.50	41.34	40.35	39.49	38.73	38.08	37.50	36.99	36.54	36.14	35.79	34.52	33.78	33.34
5000	53.13	51.68	50.43	49.36	48.42	47.60	46.87	46.24	45.68	45.18	44.74	43.15	42.22	41.68
6000	63.75	62.01	60.52	59.23	58.10	57.11	56.25	55.49	54.81	54.21	53.68	51.77	50.67	50.01
7000	74.37	72.35	70.61	69.10	67.78	66.63	65.62	64.73	63.95	63.25	62.63	60.40	59.11	58.35
8000	85.00	82.68	80.69	78.97	77.46	76.15	75.00	73.98	73.08	72.28	71.58	69.03	67.56	66.68
9000	95.62	93.02	90.78	88.84	87.15	85.67	84.37	83.23	82.21	81.32	80.52	77.66	76.00	75.02
10000	106.25	103.35	100.86	98.71	96.83	95.19	93.74	92.47	91.35	90.35	89.47	86.29	84.44	83.35
11000	116.87	113.69	110.95	108.58	106.51	104.70	103.12	101.72	100.48	99.39	98.42	94.92	92.89	91.69
12000	127.49	124.02	121.04	118.45	116.19	114.22	112.49	110.97	109.62	108.42	107.36	103.54	101.33	100.02
13000	138.12	134.36	131.12	128.32	125.88	123.74	121.86	120.21	118.75	117.46	116.31	112.17	109.78	108.36
14000	148.74	144.69	141.21	138.19	135.56	133.26	131.24	129.46	127.89	126.49	125.25	120.80	118.22	116.69
15000	159.37	155.03	151.29	148.06	145.24	142.78	140.61	138.71	137.02	135.53	134.20	129.43	126.66	125.03
16000	169.99	165.36	161.38	157.93	154.92	152.29	149.99	147.95	146.16	144.56	143.15	138.06	135.11	133.36
17000	180.61	175.70	171.46	167.80	164.60	161.81	159.36	157.20	155.29	153.60	152.09	146.69	143.55	141.69
18000	191.24	186.03	181.55	177.67	174.29	171.33	168.73	166.45	164.42	162.63	161.04	155.31	152.00	150.03
19000	201.86	196.37	191.64	187.54	183.97	180.85	178.11	175.69	173.56	171.67	169.99	163.94	160.44	158.36
20000	212.49	206.70	201.72	197.41	193.65	190.37	187.48	184.94	182.69	180.70	178.93	172.57	168.88	166.70
21000	223.11	217.04	211.81	207.28	203.33	199.88	196.86	194.19	191.83	189.74	187.88	181.20	177.33	175.03
22000	233.73	227.37	221.89	217.15	213.02	209.40	206.23	203.43	200.96	198.77	196.83	189.83	185.77	183.37
23000	244.36	237.71	231.98	227.02	222.70	218.92	215.60	212.68	210.10	207.81	205.77	198.46	194.22	191.70
24000	254.98	248.04	242.07	236.89	232.38	228.44	224.98	221.93	219.23	216.84	214.72	207.08	202.66	200.04
25000	265.61	258.38	252.15	246.76	242.06	237.96	234.35	231.17	228.37	225.88	223.67	215.71	211.10	208.37
26000	276.23	268.71	262.24	256.63	251.75	247.48	243.72	240.42	237.50	234.91	232.61	224.34	219.55	216.71
27000	286.85	279.05	272.32	266.50	261.43	256.99	253.10	249.67	246.63	243.95	241.56	232.97	227.99	225.04
28000	297.48	289.38	282.41	276.37	271.11	266.51	262.47	258.91	255.77	252.98	250.50	241.60	236.44	233.38
29000	308.10	299.72	292.49	286.24	280.79	276.03	271.85	268.16	264.90	262.02	259.45	250.23	244.88	241.71
30000	318.73	310.05	302.58	296.11	290.48	285.55	281.22	277.41	274.04	271.05	268.40	258.85	253.32	250.05
31000	329.35	320.39	312.67	305.98	300.16	295.07	290.59	286.65	283.17	280.09	277.34	267.48	261.77	258.38
32000	339.97	330.72	322.75	315.85	309.84	304.58	299.97	295.90	292.31	289.12	286.29	276.11	270.21	266.72
33000	350.60	341.06	332.84	325.72	319.52	314.10	309.34	305.15	301.44	298.15	295.24	284.74	278.66	275.05
34000	361.22	351.39	342.92	335.59	329.20	323.62	318.72	314.39	310.57	307.19	304.18	293.37	287.10	283.38
35000	371.85	361.72	353.01	345.46	338.89	333.14	328.09	323.64	319.71	316.22	313.13	302.00	295.54	291.72
36000	382.47	372.06	363.10	355.33	348.57	342.66	337.46	332.89	328.84	325.26	322.08	310.62	303.99	300.05
37000	393.09	382.39	373.18	365.20	358.25	352.17	346.84	342.13	337.98	334.29	331.02	319.25	312.43	308.39
38000	403.72	392.73	383.27	375.07	367.93	361.69	356.21	351.38	347.11	343.33	339.97	327.88	320.88	316.72
39000	414.34	403.06	393.35	384.94	377.62	371.21	365.58	360.63	356.25	352.36	348.91	336.51	329.32	325.06
40000	424.97	413.40	403.44	394.81	387.30	380.73	374.96	369.87	365.38	361.40	357.86	345.14	337.76	333.39
41000	435.59	423.73	413.52	404.68	396.98	390.25	384.33	379.12	374.52	370.43	366.81	353.76	346.21	341.73
42000	446.21	434.07	423.61	414.55	406.66	399.76	393.71	388.37	383.65	379.47	375.75	362.39	354.65	350.06
43000	456.84	444.40	433.70	424.42	416.35	409.28	403.08	397.61	392.78	388.50	384.70	371.02	363.10	358.40
44000	467.46	454.74	443.78	434.29	426.03	418.80	412.45	406.86	401.92	397.54	393.65	379.65	371.54	366.73
45000	478.09	465.07	453.87	444.16	435.71	428.32	421.83	416.11	411.05	406.57	402.59	388.28	379.98	375.07
46000	488.71	475.41	463.95	454.03	445.39	437.84	431.20	425.35	420.19	415.61	411.54	396.91	388.43	383.40
47000	499.33	485.74	474.04	463.90	455.08	447.35	440.58	434.60	429.32	424.64	420.49	405.53	396.87	391.74
48000	509.96	496.08	484.13	473.77	464.76	456.87	449.95	443.85	438.46	433.68	429.43	414.16	405.32	400.07
49000	520.58	506.41	494.21	483.64	474.44	466.39	459.32	453.10	447.59	442.71	438.38	422.79	413.76	408.40
50000	531.21	516.75	504.30	493.51	484.12	475.91	468.70	462.34	456.73	451.75	447.33	431.42	422.20	416.74
55000	584.33	568.42	554.73	542.86	532.53	523.50	515.57	508.58	502.40	496.92	492.06	474.56	464.42	458.41
60000	637.45	620.10	605.16	592.21	580.95	571.09	562.44	554.81	548.07	542.10	536.79	517.70	506.64	500.09
65000	690.57	671.77	655.59	641.57	629.36	618.68	609.30	601.04	593.74	587.27	581.52	560.84	548.86	541.76
70000	743.69	723.44	706.01	690.92	677.77	666.27	656.17	647.28	639.41	632.44	626.25	603.99	591.08	583.43
75000	796.81	775.12	756.44	740.27	726.18	713.86	703.04	693.51	685.09	677.62	670.99	647.13	633.30	625.11
80000	849.93	826.79	806.87	789.62	774.59	761.45	749.91	739.74	730.76	722.79	715.72	690.27	675.52	666.78
85000	903.05	878.47	857.30	838.97	823.00	809.04	796.78	785.98	776.43	767.97	760.45	733.41	717.74	708.45
90000	956.17	930.14	907.73	888.32	871.42	856.63	843.65	832.21	822.10	813.14	805.18	776.55	759.96	750.13
95000	1009.29	981.82	958.16	937.67	919.83	904.22	890.52	878.45	867.77	858.32	849.91	819.69	802.18	791.80
100000	1062.41	1033.49	1008.59	987.02	968.24	951.81	937.39	924.68	913.45	903.49	894.65	862.83	844.40	833.47

MONTHLY PAYMENT
REQUIRED TO AMORTIZE A LOAN

TERM AMOUNT	1 Year	2 Years	3 Years	4 Years	5 Years	6 Years	7 Years	8 Years	9 Years	10 Years	11 Years	12 Years	13 Years	14 Years
5	.44	.24	.17	.13	.11	.10	.09	.08	.08	.07	.07	.06	.06	.06
10	.88	.47	.33	.26	.22	.19	.17	.16	.15	.14	.13	.12	.12	.12
15	1.32	.70	.49	.38	.32	.28	.25	.23	.22	.20	.19	.18	.18	.17
25	2.20	1.16	.81	.64	.53	.47	.42	.38	.36	.33	.32	.30	.29	.28
50	4.40	2.31	1.62	1.27	1.06	.93	.83	.76	.71	.66	.63	.60	.58	.56
75	6.59	3.46	2.42	1.90	1.59	1.39	1.25	1.14	1.06	.99	.94	.90	.86	.83
100	8.79	4.61	3.23	2.54	2.12	1.85	1.66	1.52	1.41	1.32	1.25	1.19	1.15	1.11
200	17.58	9.22	6.45	5.07	4.24	3.70	3.31	3.03	2.81	2.63	2.49	2.38	2.29	2.21
300	26.36	13.83	9.67	7.60	6.36	5.54	4.97	4.54	4.21	3.95	3.74	3.57	3.43	3.31
400	35.15	18.44	12.89	10.13	8.48	7.39	6.62	6.05	5.61	5.26	4.98	4.76	4.57	4.41
500	43.93	23.05	16.11	12.66	10.60	9.24	8.27	7.56	7.01	6.58	6.23	5.94	5.71	5.51
600	52.72	27.66	19.33	15.19	12.72	11.08	9.93	9.07	8.41	7.89	7.47	7.13	6.85	6.61
700	61.51	32.27	22.55	17.72	14.83	12.93	11.58	10.58	9.81	9.21	8.72	8.32	7.99	7.71
800	70.29	36.87	25.77	20.25	16.95	14.78	13.23	12.09	11.21	10.52	9.96	9.51	9.13	8.81
900	79.08	41.48	28.99	22.78	19.07	16.62	14.89	13.60	12.61	11.84	11.21	10.70	10.27	9.91
1000	87.86	46.09	32.21	25.31	21.19	18.47	16.54	15.11	14.02	13.15	12.45	11.88	11.41	11.01
2000	175.72	92.18	64.42	50.61	42.38	36.93	33.08	30.22	28.03	26.30	24.90	23.76	22.81	22.02
3000	263.58	138.27	96.63	75.91	63.56	55.39	49.62	45.33	42.04	39.44	37.35	35.64	34.22	33.03
4000	351.44	184.35	128.84	101.22	84.75	73.86	66.15	60.44	56.05	52.59	49.80	47.52	45.62	44.03
5000	439.29	230.44	161.05	126.52	105.93	92.32	82.69	75.55	70.06	65.73	62.25	59.40	57.03	55.04
6000	527.15	276.53	193.26	151.82	127.12	110.78	99.23	90.65	84.07	78.88	74.70	71.28	68.43	66.05
7000	615.01	322.62	225.46	177.12	148.30	129.25	115.76	105.76	98.08	92.03	87.15	83.16	79.84	77.05
8000	702.87	368.70	257.67	202.43	169.49	147.71	132.30	120.87	112.09	105.17	99.60	95.03	91.24	88.06
9000	790.72	414.79	289.88	227.73	190.68	166.17	148.84	135.98	126.10	118.32	112.05	106.91	102.65	99.07
10000	878.58	460.88	322.09	253.03	211.86	184.63	165.37	151.09	140.12	131.46	124.50	118.79	114.05	110.08
11000	966.44	506.96	354.30	278.33	233.05	203.10	181.91	166.19	154.13	144.61	136.95	130.67	125.46	121.08
12000	1054.30	553.05	386.51	303.64	254.23	221.56	198.45	181.30	168.14	157.76	149.40	142.55	136.86	132.09
13000	1142.16	599.14	418.72	328.94	275.42	240.02	214.98	196.41	182.15	170.90	161.85	154.43	148.27	143.10
14000	1230.01	645.23	450.92	354.24	296.60	258.49	231.52	211.52	196.16	184.05	174.29	166.31	159.67	154.10
15000	1317.87	691.31	483.13	379.54	317.79	276.95	248.06	226.63	210.17	197.19	186.74	178.19	171.08	165.11
16000	1405.73	737.40	515.34	404.85	338.97	295.41	264.59	241.73	224.18	210.34	159.19	190.06	182.48	176.12
17000	1493.59	783.49	547.55	430.15	360.16	313.87	281.13	256.84	238.19	223.49	211.64	201.94	193.89	187.13
18000	1581.44	829.58	579.76	455.45	381.35	332.34	297.67	271.95	252.20	236.63	224.09	213.82	205.29	198.13
19000	1669.30	875.66	611.97	480.75	402.53	350.80	314.20	287.06	266.22	249.78	236.54	225.70	216.70	209.14
20000	1757.16	921.75	644.18	506.06	423.72	369.26	330.74	302.17	280.23	262.92	248.99	237.58	228.10	220.15
21000	1845.02	967.84	676.38	531.36	444.90	387.73	347.28	317.28	294.24	276.07	261.44	249.46	239.51	231.15
22000	1932.88	1013.92	708.59	556.66	466.09	406.19	363.81	332.38	308.25	289.22	273.89	261.34	250.91	242.16
23000	2020.73	1060.01	740.80	581.96	487.27	424.65	380.35	347.49	322.26	302.36	286.34	273.21	262.32	253.17
24000	2108.59	1106.10	773.01	607.27	508.46	443.11	396.89	362.60	336.27	315.51	298.79	285.09	273.72	264.17
25000	2196.45	1152.19	805.22	632.57	529.64	461.58	413.42	377.71	350.28	328.65	311.24	296.97	285.13	275.18
26000	2284.31	1198.27	837.43	657.87	550.83	480.04	429.96	392.82	364.29	341.80	323.69	308.85	296.53	286.19
27000	2372.16	1244.36	869.64	683.18	572.02	498.50	446.50	407.92	378.30	354.95	336.13	320.73	307.94	297.20
28000	2460.02	1290.45	901.84	708.48	593.20	516.97	463.03	423.03	392.32	368.09	348.58	332.61	319.34	308.20
29000	2547.88	1336.54	934.05	733.78	614.39	535.43	479.57	438.14	406.33	381.24	361.03	344.49	330.75	319.21
30000	2635.74	1382.62	966.26	759.08	635.57	553.89	496.11	453.25	420.34	394.38	373.48	356.37	342.15	330.22
31000	2723.60	1428.71	998.47	784.39	656.76	572.35	512.64	468.36	434.35	407.53	385.93	368.24	353.56	341.22
32000	2811.45	1474.80	1030.68	809.69	677.94	590.82	529.18	483.46	448.36	420.68	398.38	380.12	364.96	352.23
33000	2899.31	1520.88	1062.89	834.99	699.13	609.28	545.72	498.57	462.37	433.82	410.83	392.00	376.37	363.24
34000	2987.17	1566.97	1095.10	860.29	720.32	627.74	562.25	513.68	476.38	446.97	423.28	403.88	387.77	374.25
35000	3075.03	1613.06	1127.30	885.60	741.50	646.21	578.79	528.79	490.39	460.11	435.73	415.76	399.18	385.25
36000	3162.88	1659.15	1159.51	910.90	762.69	664.67	595.33	543.90	504.40	473.26	448.18	427.64	410.58	396.26
37000	3250.74	1705.23	1191.72	936.20	783.87	683.13	611.86	559.00	518.42	486.41	460.63	439.52	421.99	407.27
38000	3338.60	1751.32	1223.93	961.50	805.06	701.59	628.40	574.11	532.43	499.55	473.08	451.39	433.39	418.27
39000	3426.46	1797.41	1256.14	986.81	826.24	720.06	644.94	589.22	546.44	512.70	485.53	463.27	444.80	429.28
40000	3514.32	1843.50	1288.35	1012.11	847.43	738.52	661.47	604.33	560.45	525.84	497.98	475.15	456.20	440.29
41000	3602.17	1889.58	1320.55	1037.41	868.61	756.98	678.01	619.44	574.46	538.99	510.42	487.03	467.61	451.29
42000	3690.03	1935.67	1352.76	1062.71	889.80	775.45	694.55	634.55	588.47	552.13	522.87	498.91	479.01	462.30
43000	3777.89	1981.76	1384.97	1088.02	910.99	793.91	711.08	649.65	602.48	565.28	535.32	510.79	490.42	473.31
44000	3865.75	2027.84	1417.18	1113.32	932.17	812.37	727.62	664.76	616.49	578.43	547.77	522.67	501.82	484.32
45000	3953.60	2073.93	1449.39	1138.62	953.36	830.83	744.16	679.87	630.50	591.57	560.22	534.55	513.23	495.32
46000	4041.46	2120.02	1481.60	1163.92	974.54	849.30	760.69	694.98	644.51	604.72	572.67	546.42	524.63	506.33
47000	4129.32	2166.11	1513.81	1189.23	995.73	867.76	777.23	710.09	658.53	617.86	585.12	558.30	536.04	517.34
48000	4217.18	2212.19	1546.01	1214.53	1016.91	886.22	793.77	725.19	672.54	631.01	597.57	570.18	547.44	528.34
49000	4305.04	2258.28	1578.22	1239.83	1038.10	904.69	810.30	740.30	686.55	644.16	610.02	582.06	558.85	539.35
50000	4392.89	2304.37	1610.43	1265.13	1059.28	923.15	826.84	755.41	700.56	657.30	622.47	593.94	570.25	550.36
55000	4832.18	2534.80	1771.47	1391.65	1165.21	1015.46	909.52	830.95	770.61	723.03	684.71	653.33	627.28	605.39
60000	5271.47	2765.24	1932.52	1518.16	1271.14	1107.78	992.21	906.49	840.67	788.76	746.96	712.73	684.30	660.43
65000	5710.76	2995.68	2093.56	1644.67	1377.07	1200.09	1074.89	982.03	910.73	854.49	809.21	772.12	741.33	715.46
70000	6150.05	3226.11	2254.60	1771.19	1483.00	1292.41	1157.57	1057.57	980.78	920.22	871.45	831.51	798.35	770.50
75000	6589.34	3456.55	2415.64	1897.70	1588.92	1384.72	1240.26	1133.11	1050.84	985.95	933.70	890.91	855.38	825.53
80000	7028.63	3686.99	2576.69	2024.21	1694.85	1477.03	1322.94	1208.65	1120.89	1051.68	995.95	950.30	912.40	880.57
85000	7467.91	3917.42	2737.73	2150.73	1800.78	1569.35	1405.62	1284.19	1190.95	1117.41	1058.19	1009.69	969.42	935.61
90000	7907.20	4147.86	2898.77	2277.24	1906.71	1661.66	1488.31	1359.73	1261.00	1183.14	1120.44	1069.09	1026.45	990.64
95000	8346.49	4378.29	3059.82	2403.75	2012.64	1753.98	1570.99	1435.27	1331.06	1248.87	1182.68	1128.48	1083.47	1045.68
100000	8785.78	4608.73	3220.86	2530.26	2118.56	1846.29	1653.67	1510.82	1401.11	1314.60	1244.93	1187.87	1140.50	1100.71

TERM AMOUNT	15 Years	16 Years	17 Years	18 Years	19 Years	20 Years	21 Years	22 Years	23 Years	24 Years	25 Years	30 Years	35 Years	40 Years
5	.06	.06	.06	.05	.05	.05	.05	.05	.05	.05	.05	.05	.05	.05
10	.11	.11	.11	.10	.10	.10	.10	.10	.10	.10	.09	.09	.09	.09
15	.17	.16	.16	.15	.15	.15	.15	.14	.14	.14	.14	.14	.13	.13
25	.27	.26	.26	.25	.25	.24	.24	.24	.23	.23	.23	.22	.22	.21
50	.54	.52	.51	.50	.49	.48	.48	.47	.46	.46	.45	.44	.43	.42
75	.81	.78	.76	.75	.73	.72	.71	.70	.69	.69	.68	.66	.64	.63
100	1.07	1.04	1.02	1.00	.98	.96	.95	.93	.92	.91	.90	.87	.86	.84
200	2.14	2.08	2.03	1.99	1.95	1.92	1.89	1.86	1.84	1.82	1.80	1.74	1.71	1.68
300	3.21	3.12	3.04	2.98	2.92	2.88	2.83	2.79	2.76	2.73	2.70	2.61	2.56	2.52
400	4.27	4.16	4.06	3.97	3.90	3.83	3.77	3.72	3.68	3.64	3.60	3.48	3.41	3.36
500	5.34	5.20	5.07	4.96	4.87	4.79	4.72	4.65	4.60	4.55	4.50	4.35	4.26	4.20
600	6.41	6.23	6.08	5.96	5.84	5.75	5.66	5.58	5.52	5.46	5.40	5.22	5.11	5.04
700	7.47	7.27	7.10	6.95	6.82	6.70	6.60	6.51	6.44	6.37	6.30	6.08	5.96	5.88
800	8.54	8.31	8.11	7.94	7.79	7.66	7.54	7.44	7.35	7.27	7.20	6.95	6.81	6.72
900	9.61	9.35	9.12	8.93	8.76	8.62	8.49	8.37	8.27	8.18	8.10	7.82	7.66	7.56
1000	10.67	10.39	10.14	9.92	9.74	9.57	9.43	9.30	9.19	9.09	9.00	8.69	8.51	8.40
2000	21.34	20.77	20.27	19.84	19.47	19.14	18.85	18.60	18.38	18.18	18.00	17.37	17.01	16.79
3000	32.01	31.15	30.40	29.76	29.20	28.71	28.28	27.90	27.56	27.27	27.00	26.06	25.51	25.19
4000	42.68	41.53	40.54	39.68	38.93	38.28	37.70	37.20	36.75	36.35	36.00	34.74	34.01	33.58
5000	53.35	51.91	50.67	49.60	48.66	47.84	47.12	46.49	45.93	45.44	45.00	43.42	42.51	41.97
6000	64.02	62.29	60.80	59.51	58.39	57.41	56.55	55.79	55.12	54.53	54.00	52.11	51.01	50.37
7000	74.69	72.67	70.94	69.43	68.12	66.98	65.97	65.09	64.31	63.61	63.00	60.79	59.51	58.76
8000	85.36	83.06	81.07	79.35	77.85	76.55	75.40	74.39	73.49	72.70	72.00	69.47	68.01	67.15
9000	96.03	93.44	91.20	89.27	87.58	86.11	84.82	83.68	82.68	81.79	81.00	78.16	76.52	75.55
10000	106.70	103.82	101.34	99.19	97.32	95.68	94.24	92.98	91.86	90.87	90.00	86.84	85.02	83.94
11000	117.37	114.20	111.47	109.10	107.05	105.25	103.67	102.28	101.05	99.96	98.99	95.52	93.52	92.33
12000	128.04	124.58	121.60	119.02	116.78	114.82	113.09	111.58	110.24	109.05	107.99	104.21	102.02	100.73
13000	138.71	134.96	131.74	128.94	126.51	124.38	122.52	120.87	119.42	118.13	116.99	112.89	110.52	109.12
14000	149.38	145.34	141.87	138.86	136.24	133.95	131.94	130.17	128.61	127.22	125.99	121.57	119.02	117.51
15000	160.05	155.72	152.00	148.78	145.97	143.52	141.36	139.47	137.79	136.31	134.99	130.26	127.52	125.91
16000	170.72	166.11	162.13	158.70	155.70	153.09	150.79	148.77	146.98	145.40	143.99	138.94	136.02	134.30
17000	181.39	176.49	172.27	168.61	165.45	162.65	160.21	158.06	156.16	154.48	152.99	147.62	144.53	142.69
18000	192.06	186.87	182.40	178.53	175.16	172.22	169.64	167.36	165.35	163.57	161.99	156.31	153.03	151.09
19000	202.73	197.25	192.53	188.45	184.90	181.79	179.06	176.66	174.54	172.66	170.99	164.99	161.53	159.48
20000	213.40	207.63	202.67	198.37	194.63	191.36	188.48	185.96	183.72	181.74	179.99	173.67	170.03	167.87
21000	224.07	218.01	212.80	208.29	204.36	200.92	197.91	195.25	192.91	190.83	188.98	182.36	178.53	176.27
22000	234.74	228.39	222.93	218.20	214.09	210.49	207.33	204.55	202.09	199.92	197.98	191.04	187.03	184.66
23000	245.41	238.78	233.07	228.12	223.82	220.06	216.76	213.85	211.28	209.00	206.98	199.73	195.53	193.05
24000	256.08	249.16	243.20	238.04	233.55	229.63	226.18	223.15	220.47	218.09	215.98	208.41	204.03	201.45
25000	266.75	259.54	253.33	247.96	243.28	239.19	235.60	232.44	229.65	227.18	224.98	217.09	212.53	209.84
26000	277.42	269.92	263.47	257.88	253.01	248.76	245.03	241.74	238.84	236.26	233.98	225.78	221.04	218.23
27000	288.09	280.30	273.60	267.80	262.74	258.33	254.45	251.04	248.02	245.35	242.98	234.46	229.54	226.63
28000	298.76	290.68	283.73	277.71	272.48	267.90	263.88	260.34	257.21	254.44	251.98	243.14	238.04	235.02
29000	309.43	301.06	293.87	287.63	282.21	277.46	273.30	269.63	266.39	263.52	260.98	251.83	246.54	243.41
30000	320.10	311.44	304.00	297.55	291.94	287.03	282.72	278.93	275.58	272.61	269.98	260.51	255.04	251.81
31000	330.77	321.83	314.13	307.47	301.67	296.60	292.15	288.23	284.77	281.70	278.98	269.19	263.54	260.20
32000	341.44	332.21	324.26	317.39	311.40	306.17	301.57	297.53	293.95	290.79	287.97	277.88	272.04	268.59
33000	352.11	342.59	334.40	327.30	321.13	315.73	311.00	306.82	303.14	299.87	296.97	286.56	280.54	276.99
34000	362.78	352.97	344.53	337.22	330.86	325.30	320.42	316.12	312.32	308.96	305.97	295.24	289.05	285.38
35000	373.44	363.35	354.66	347.14	340.59	334.87	329.84	325.42	321.51	318.05	314.97	303.93	297.55	293.77
36000	384.11	373.73	364.80	357.06	350.32	344.44	339.27	334.72	330.70	327.13	323.97	312.61	306.05	302.17
37000	394.78	384.11	374.93	366.98	360.06	354.00	348.69	344.01	339.88	336.22	332.97	321.29	314.55	310.56
38000	405.45	394.50	385.06	376.90	369.79	363.57	358.12	353.31	349.07	345.31	341.97	329.98	323.05	318.95
39000	416.12	404.88	395.20	386.81	379.52	373.14	367.54	362.61	358.25	354.39	350.97	338.66	331.55	327.35
40000	426.79	415.26	405.33	396.73	389.25	382.71	376.96	371.91	367.44	363.48	359.97	347.34	340.05	335.74
41000	437.46	425.64	415.46	406.65	398.98	392.27	386.39	381.20	376.62	372.57	368.97	356.03	348.55	344.13
42000	448.13	436.02	425.60	416.57	408.71	401.84	395.81	390.50	385.81	381.65	377.96	364.71	357.05	352.53
43000	458.80	446.40	435.73	426.49	418.44	411.41	405.24	399.80	395.00	390.74	386.96	373.39	365.56	360.92
44000	469.47	456.78	445.86	436.40	428.17	420.98	414.66	409.10	404.18	399.83	395.96	382.08	374.06	369.32
45000	480.14	467.16	456.00	446.32	437.90	430.54	424.08	418.39	413.37	408.92	404.96	390.76	382.56	377.71
46000	490.81	477.55	466.13	456.24	447.64	440.11	433.51	427.69	422.55	418.00	413.96	399.45	391.06	386.10
47000	501.48	487.93	476.26	466.16	457.37	449.68	442.93	436.99	431.74	427.09	422.96	408.13	399.56	394.50
48000	512.15	498.31	486.39	476.08	467.10	459.25	452.36	446.29	440.93	436.18	431.96	416.81	408.06	402.89
49000	522.82	508.69	496.53	486.00	476.83	468.81	461.78	455.58	450.11	445.26	440.96	425.50	416.56	411.28
50000	533.49	519.07	506.66	495.91	486.56	478.38	471.20	464.88	459.30	454.35	449.96	434.18	425.06	419.68
55000	586.84	570.98	557.33	545.50	535.22	526.22	518.32	511.37	505.23	499.78	494.95	477.60	467.57	461.64
60000	640.19	622.88	607.99	595.10	583.87	574.06	565.44	557.86	551.16	545.22	539.95	521.01	510.08	503.61
65000	693.54	674.79	658.66	644.69	632.53	621.90	612.56	604.35	597.08	590.65	584.94	564.43	552.58	545.58
70000	746.88	726.70	709.32	694.28	681.18	669.73	659.68	650.83	643.01	636.09	629.94	607.85	595.09	587.54
75000	800.23	778.60	759.99	743.87	729.84	717.57	706.80	697.32	688.94	681.52	674.93	651.27	637.59	629.51
80000	853.58	830.51	810.65	793.46	778.49	765.41	753.92	743.81	734.87	726.96	719.93	694.68	680.10	671.48
85000	906.93	882.42	861.32	843.05	827.15	813.25	801.04	790.30	780.80	772.39	764.92	738.10	722.61	713.45
90000	960.28	934.32	911.99	892.64	875.80	861.08	848.16	836.78	826.73	817.83	809.92	781.52	765.11	755.41
95000	1013.63	986.23	962.65	942.23	924.46	908.92	895.28	883.27	872.66	863.26	854.91	824.94	807.62	797.38
100000	1066.98	1038.14	1013.32	991.82	973.12	956.76	942.40	929.76	918.59	908.69	899.91	868.35	850.12	839.35

9.900%

TERM	1 Year	2 Years	3 Years	4 Years	5 Years	6 Years	7 Years	8 Years	9 Years	10 Years	11 Years	12 Years	13 Years	14 Years
AMOUNT														
5	.44	.24	.17	.13	.11	.10	.09	.08	.08	.07	.07	.06	.06	.06
10	.88	.47	.33	.26	.22	.19	.17	.16	.15	.14	.13	.12	.12	.12
15	1.32	.70	.49	.38	.32	.28	.25	.23	.22	.20	.19	.18	.18	.17
25	2.20	1.16	.81	.64	.53	.47	.42	.38	.36	.33	.32	.30	.29	.28
50	4.40	2.31	1.62	1.27	1.06	.93	.83	.76	.71	.66	.63	.60	.58	.56
75	6.60	3.46	2.42	1.90	1.59	1.39	1.25	1.14	1.06	.99	.94	.90	.86	.83
100	8.79	4.61	3.23	2.54	2.12	1.85	1.66	1.52	1.41	1.32	1.25	1.19	1.15	1.11
200	17.58	9.22	6.45	5.07	4.24	3.70	3.31	3.03	2.81	2.64	2.50	2.38	2.29	2.21
300	26.37	13.83	9.67	7.60	6.36	5.55	4.97	4.54	4.21	3.95	3.74	3.57	3.43	3.31
400	35.15	18.44	12.89	10.13	8.48	7.40	6.62	6.05	5.61	5.27	4.99	4.76	4.57	4.41
500	43.94	23.05	16.12	12.66	10.60	9.24	8.28	7.57	7.02	6.58	6.24	5.95	5.71	5.52
600	52.73	27.66	19.34	15.19	12.72	11.09	9.93	9.08	8.42	7.90	7.48	7.14	6.86	6.62
700	61.51	32.27	22.56	17.73	14.84	12.94	11.59	10.59	9.82	9.22	8.73	8.33	8.00	7.72
800	70.30	36.88	25.78	20.26	16.96	14.79	13.24	12.10	11.22	10.53	9.98	9.52	9.14	8.82
900	79.09	41.49	29.00	22.79	19.08	16.63	14.90	13.61	12.63	11.85	11.22	10.71	10.28	9.92
1000	87.87	46.10	32.23	25.32	21.20	18.48	16.55	15.13	14.03	13.16	12.47	11.90	11.42	11.03
2000	175.74	92.20	64.45	50.63	42.40	36.96	33.10	30.25	28.05	26.32	24.93	23.79	22.84	22.05
3000	263.61	138.30	96.67	75.95	63.60	55.43	49.65	45.37	42.08	39.48	37.40	35.68	34.26	33.07
4000	351.48	184.40	128.89	101.26	84.80	73.91	66.20	60.49	56.10	52.64	49.86	47.58	45.68	44.09
5000	439.35	230.50	161.11	126.58	105.99	92.38	82.75	75.61	70.13	65.80	62.32	59.47	57.10	55.12
6000	527.22	276.60	193.33	151.89	127.19	110.86	99.30	90.73	84.15	78.96	74.79	71.36	68.52	66.14
7000	615.09	322.70	225.55	177.21	148.39	129.33	115.85	105.85	98.18	92.12	87.25	83.26	79.94	77.16
8000	702.96	368.80	257.77	202.52	169.59	147.81	132.40	120.98	112.20	105.28	99.71	95.15	91.36	88.18
9000	790.83	414.89	289.99	227.84	190.79	166.28	148.95	136.10	126.23	118.44	112.18	107.04	102.78	99.20
10000	878.70	460.99	322.21	253.15	211.98	184.76	165.50	151.22	140.25	131.60	124.64	118.94	114.20	110.23
11000	966.57	507.09	354.43	278.47	233.18	203.23	182.05	166.34	154.28	144.76	137.10	130.83	125.62	121.25
12000	1054.44	553.19	386.65	303.78	254.38	221.71	198.60	181.46	168.30	157.92	149.57	142.72	137.04	132.27
13000	1142.31	599.29	418.87	329.09	275.58	240.19	215.15	196.58	182.32	171.08	162.03	154.62	148.46	143.29
14000	1230.18	645.39	451.09	354.41	296.78	258.66	231.70	211.70	196.35	184.24	174.49	166.51	159.88	154.31
15000	1318.05	691.49	483.31	379.72	317.97	277.14	248.25	226.82	210.37	197.40	186.96	178.40	171.30	165.34
16000	1405.92	737.59	515.53	405.04	339.17	295.61	264.80	241.95	224.40	210.56	199.42	190.29	182.72	176.36
17000	1493.78	783.68	547.75	430.35	360.37	314.09	281.35	257.07	238.42	223.72	211.88	202.19	194.14	187.38
18000	1581.65	829.78	579.97	455.67	381.57	332.56	297.90	272.19	252.45	236.88	224.35	214.08	205.56	198.40
19000	1669.52	875.88	612.19	480.98	402.76	351.04	314.45	287.31	266.47	250.04	236.81	225.97	216.98	209.42
20000	1757.39	921.98	644.41	506.30	423.96	369.51	331.00	302.43	280.50	263.20	249.27	237.87	228.40	220.45
21000	1845.26	968.08	676.63	531.61	445.16	387.99	347.55	317.55	294.52	276.36	261.74	249.76	239.82	231.47
22000	1933.13	1014.18	708.85	556.93	466.36	406.46	364.10	332.67	308.55	289.52	274.20	261.65	251.24	242.49
23000	2021.00	1060.28	741.07	582.24	487.56	424.94	380.64	347.79	322.57	302.68	286.66	273.55	262.66	253.51
24000	2108.87	1106.38	773.29	607.56	508.75	443.42	397.19	362.92	336.60	315.84	299.13	285.44	274.08	264.53
25000	2196.74	1152.47	805.51	632.87	529.95	461.89	413.74	378.04	350.62	329.00	311.59	297.33	285.50	275.56
26000	2284.61	1198.57	837.73	658.18	551.15	480.37	430.29	393.16	364.64	342.16	324.05	309.23	296.92	286.58
27000	2372.48	1244.67	869.95	683.50	572.35	498.84	446.84	408.28	378.67	355.32	336.52	321.12	308.33	297.60
28000	2460.35	1290.77	902.17	708.81	593.55	517.32	463.39	423.40	392.69	368.48	348.98	333.01	319.75	308.62
29000	2548.22	1336.87	934.39	734.13	614.74	535.79	479.94	438.52	406.72	381.64	361.44	344.90	331.17	319.64
30000	2636.09	1382.97	966.61	759.44	635.94	554.27	496.49	453.64	420.74	394.80	373.91	356.80	342.59	330.67
31000	2723.96	1429.07	998.83	784.76	657.14	572.74	513.04	468.77	434.77	407.96	386.37	368.69	354.01	341.69
32000	2811.83	1475.17	1031.05	810.07	678.34	591.22	529.59	483.89	448.79	421.12	398.83	380.58	365.43	352.71
33000	2899.69	1521.26	1063.27	835.39	699.53	609.69	546.14	499.01	462.82	434.29	411.30	392.48	376.85	363.73
34000	2987.56	1567.36	1095.49	860.70	720.73	628.17	562.69	514.13	476.84	447.44	423.76	404.37	388.27	374.75
35000	3075.43	1613.46	1127.71	886.02	741.93	646.65	579.24	529.25	490.87	460.60	436.22	416.26	399.69	385.78
36000	3163.30	1659.56	1159.93	911.33	763.13	665.12	595.79	544.37	504.89	473.76	448.69	428.16	411.11	396.80
37000	3251.17	1705.66	1192.15	936.64	784.33	683.60	612.34	559.49	518.91	486.92	461.15	440.05	422.53	407.82
38000	3339.04	1751.76	1224.37	961.96	805.52	702.07	628.89	574.61	532.94	500.08	473.61	451.94	433.95	418.84
39000	3426.91	1797.86	1256.60	987.27	826.72	720.55	645.44	589.74	546.96	513.24	486.08	463.84	445.37	429.86
40000	3514.78	1843.96	1288.82	1012.59	847.92	739.02	661.99	604.86	560.99	526.40	498.54	475.73	456.79	440.89
41000	3602.65	1890.06	1321.04	1037.90	869.12	757.50	678.54	619.98	575.01	539.56	511.00	487.62	468.21	451.91
42000	3690.52	1936.15	1353.26	1063.22	890.32	775.97	695.09	635.10	589.04	552.71	523.47	499.51	479.63	462.93
43000	3778.39	1982.25	1385.48	1088.53	911.51	794.45	711.64	650.22	603.06	565.87	535.93	511.41	491.05	473.95
44000	3866.26	2028.35	1417.70	1113.85	932.71	812.92	728.19	665.34	617.09	579.03	548.39	523.30	502.47	484.97
45000	3954.13	2074.45	1449.92	1139.16	953.91	831.40	744.74	680.46	631.11	592.19	560.86	535.19	513.89	496.00
46000	4042.00	2120.55	1482.14	1164.48	975.11	849.88	761.28	695.58	645.14	605.35	573.32	547.09	525.31	507.02
47000	4129.87	2166.65	1514.36	1189.79	996.31	868.35	777.83	710.71	659.16	618.51	585.78	558.98	536.73	518.04
48000	4217.74	2212.75	1546.58	1215.11	1017.50	886.83	794.38	725.83	673.19	631.67	598.25	570.87	548.15	529.06
49000	4305.60	2258.85	1578.80	1240.42	1038.70	905.30	810.93	740.95	687.21	644.83	610.71	582.77	559.57	540.08
50000	4393.47	2304.94	1611.02	1265.73	1059.90	923.78	827.48	756.07	701.23	657.99	623.17	594.66	570.99	551.11
55000	4832.82	2535.44	1772.12	1392.31	1165.89	1016.15	910.23	831.68	771.36	723.79	685.49	654.12	628.08	606.22
60000	5272.17	2765.93	1933.22	1518.88	1271.88	1108.53	992.98	907.28	841.48	789.59	747.81	713.59	685.18	661.33
65000	5711.52	2996.43	2094.32	1645.45	1377.87	1200.91	1075.73	982.89	911.60	855.39	810.12	773.06	742.28	716.44
70000	6150.86	3226.92	2255.42	1772.03	1483.86	1293.29	1158.47	1058.50	981.73	921.19	872.44	832.52	799.38	771.55
75000	6590.21	3457.41	2416.52	1898.60	1589.85	1385.66	1241.22	1134.10	1051.85	986.99	934.76	891.99	856.48	826.66
80000	7029.56	3687.91	2577.63	2025.17	1695.83	1478.04	1323.97	1209.71	1121.97	1052.79	997.07	951.45	913.57	881.77
85000	7468.90	3918.40	2738.73	2151.74	1801.82	1570.42	1406.72	1285.32	1192.10	1118.58	1059.39	1010.92	970.67	936.88
90000	7908.25	4148.90	2899.83	2278.32	1907.81	1662.80	1489.47	1360.92	1262.22	1184.38	1121.71	1070.38	1027.77	991.99
95000	8347.60	4379.39	3060.93	2404.89	2013.80	1755.17	1572.21	1436.53	1332.34	1250.18	1184.02	1129.85	1084.87	1047.10
100000	8786.94	4609.88	3222.03	2531.46	2119.79	1847.55	1654.96	1512.14	1402.46	1315.98	1246.34	1189.31	1141.97	1102.21

MONTHLY PAYMENT
REQUIRED TO AMORTIZE A LOAN

9.900%

TERM AMOUNT	15 Years	16 Years	17 Years	18 Years	19 Years	20 Years	21 Years	22 Years	23 Years	24 Years	25 Years	30 Years	35 Years	40 Years
5	.06	.06	.06	.05	.05	.05	.05	.05	.05	.05	.05	.05	.05	.05
10	.11	.11	.11	.10	.10	.10	.10	.10	.10	.10	.10	.09	.09	.09
15	.17	.16	.16	.15	.15	.15	.15	.14	.14	.14	.14	.14	.13	.13
25	.27	.26	.26	.25	.25	.24	.24	.24	.24	.23	.23	.22	.22	.22
50	.54	.52	.51	.50	.49	.48	.48	.47	.47	.46	.46	.44	.43	.43
75	.81	.78	.77	.75	.74	.72	.71	.70	.70	.69	.68	.66	.64	.64
100	1.07	1.04	1.02	1.00	.98	.96	.95	.94	.93	.92	.91	.88	.86	.85
200	2.14	2.08	2.03	1.99	1.95	1.92	1.89	1.87	1.85	1.83	1.81	1.75	1.71	1.69
300	3.21	3.12	3.05	2.99	2.93	2.88	2.84	2.80	2.77	2.74	2.71	2.62	2.56	2.53
400	4.28	4.16	4.06	3.98	3.90	3.84	3.78	3.73	3.69	3.65	3.61	3.49	3.41	3.37
500	5.35	5.20	5.08	4.97	4.88	4.80	4.73	4.66	4.61	4.56	4.51	4.36	4.27	4.21
600	6.42	6.24	6.09	5.97	5.85	5.76	5.67	5.59	5.53	5.47	5.41	5.23	5.12	5.05
700	7.48	7.28	7.11	6.96	6.83	6.71	6.61	6.53	6.45	6.38	6.32	6.10	5.97	5.89
800	8.55	8.32	8.12	7.95	7.80	7.67	7.56	7.46	7.37	7.29	7.22	6.97	6.82	6.74
900	9.62	9.36	9.14	8.95	8.78	8.63	8.50	8.39	8.29	8.20	8.12	7.84	7.67	7.58
1000	10.69	10.40	10.15	9.94	9.75	9.59	9.45	9.32	9.21	9.11	9.02	8.71	8.53	8.42
2000	21.37	20.80	20.30	19.87	19.50	19.17	18.89	18.63	18.41	18.21	18.04	17.41	17.05	16.83
3000	32.06	31.20	30.45	29.81	29.25	28.76	28.33	27.95	27.61	27.32	27.05	26.11	25.57	25.24
4000	42.74	41.59	40.60	39.74	38.99	38.34	37.77	37.26	36.82	36.42	36.07	34.81	34.09	33.66
5000	53.43	51.99	50.75	49.68	48.74	47.93	47.21	46.58	46.02	45.53	45.09	43.51	42.61	42.07
6000	64.11	62.39	60.90	59.61	58.49	57.51	56.65	55.89	55.22	54.63	54.10	52.22	51.13	50.48
7000	74.80	72.78	71.05	69.54	68.24	67.09	66.09	65.21	64.43	63.73	63.12	60.92	59.65	58.90
8000	85.48	83.18	81.20	79.48	77.98	76.68	75.53	74.52	73.63	72.84	72.14	69.62	68.17	67.31
9000	96.17	93.58	91.34	89.41	87.73	86.26	84.97	83.84	82.83	81.94	81.15	78.32	76.69	75.72
10000	106.85	103.97	101.49	99.35	97.48	95.85	94.41	93.15	92.04	91.05	90.17	87.02	85.21	84.14
11000	117.54	114.37	111.64	109.28	107.23	105.43	103.85	102.46	101.24	100.15	99.19	95.73	93.73	92.55
12000	128.22	124.77	121.79	119.22	116.97	115.01	113.29	111.78	110.44	109.26	108.20	104.43	102.25	100.96
13000	138.91	135.16	131.94	129.15	126.72	124.60	122.73	121.09	119.64	118.36	117.22	113.13	110.77	109.37
14000	149.59	145.56	142.09	139.08	136.47	134.18	132.18	130.41	128.85	127.46	126.24	121.83	119.29	117.79
15000	160.28	155.96	152.24	149.02	146.22	143.77	141.62	139.72	138.05	136.57	135.25	130.53	127.81	126.20
16000	170.96	166.35	162.39	158.95	155.96	153.35	151.06	149.04	147.25	145.67	144.27	139.24	136.33	134.61
17000	181.65	176.75	172.54	168.89	165.71	162.93	160.50	158.35	156.46	154.78	153.29	147.94	144.85	143.03
18000	192.33	187.15	182.68	178.82	175.46	172.52	169.94	167.67	165.66	163.88	162.30	156.64	153.37	151.44
19000	203.02	197.55	192.83	188.75	185.21	182.10	179.38	176.98	174.86	172.99	171.32	165.34	161.89	159.85
20000	213.70	207.94	202.98	198.69	194.95	191.69	188.82	186.30	184.07	182.09	180.34	174.04	170.41	168.27
21000	224.39	218.34	213.13	208.62	204.70	201.27	198.26	195.61	193.27	191.19	189.35	182.75	178.93	176.68
22000	235.07	228.74	223.28	218.56	214.45	210.85	207.70	204.92	202.47	200.30	198.37	191.45	187.45	185.09
23000	245.76	239.13	233.43	228.49	224.19	220.44	217.14	214.24	211.67	209.40	207.39	200.15	195.97	193.50
24000	256.44	249.53	243.58	238.43	233.94	230.02	226.58	223.55	220.88	218.51	216.40	208.85	204.49	201.92
25000	267.13	259.93	253.73	248.36	243.69	239.61	236.02	232.87	230.08	227.61	225.42	217.55	213.01	210.33
26000	277.81	270.32	263.88	258.29	253.44	249.19	245.46	242.18	239.28	236.72	234.44	226.25	221.53	218.74
27000	288.50	280.72	274.02	268.23	263.18	258.77	254.90	251.50	248.49	245.82	243.45	234.96	230.05	227.16
28000	299.18	291.12	284.17	278.16	272.93	268.36	264.35	260.81	257.69	254.92	252.47	243.66	238.57	235.57
29000	309.87	301.51	294.32	288.10	282.68	277.94	273.79	270.13	266.89	264.03	261.49	252.36	247.09	243.98
30000	320.55	311.91	304.47	298.03	292.43	287.53	283.23	279.44	276.10	273.13	270.50	261.06	255.61	252.40
31000	331.24	322.31	314.62	307.97	302.17	297.11	292.67	288.75	285.30	282.24	279.52	269.76	264.13	260.81
32000	341.92	332.70	324.77	317.90	311.92	306.69	302.11	298.07	294.50	291.34	288.54	278.47	272.65	269.22
33000	352.61	343.10	334.92	327.83	321.67	316.28	311.55	307.38	303.70	300.45	297.55	287.17	281.17	277.63
34000	363.29	353.50	345.07	337.77	331.42	325.86	320.99	316.70	312.91	309.55	306.57	295.87	289.69	286.05
35000	373.98	363.89	355.22	347.70	341.16	335.45	330.43	326.01	322.11	318.65	315.59	304.57	298.21	294.46
36000	384.66	374.29	365.36	357.64	350.91	345.03	339.87	335.33	331.31	327.76	324.60	313.27	306.73	302.87
37000	395.35	384.69	375.51	367.57	360.66	354.62	349.31	344.64	340.52	336.86	333.62	321.98	315.25	311.29
38000	406.03	395.09	385.66	377.50	370.41	364.20	358.75	353.96	349.72	345.97	342.64	330.68	323.78	319.70
39000	416.72	405.48	395.81	387.44	380.15	373.78	368.19	363.27	358.92	355.07	351.65	339.38	332.30	328.11
40000	427.40	415.88	405.96	397.37	389.90	383.37	377.63	372.59	368.13	364.18	360.67	348.08	340.82	336.53
41000	438.09	426.28	416.11	407.31	399.65	392.95	387.07	381.90	377.33	373.28	369.69	356.78	349.34	344.94
42000	448.77	436.67	426.26	417.24	409.39	402.54	396.52	391.21	386.53	382.38	378.70	365.49	357.86	353.35
43000	459.46	447.07	436.41	427.18	419.14	412.12	405.96	400.53	395.73	391.49	387.72	374.19	366.38	361.76
44000	470.14	457.47	446.56	437.11	428.89	421.70	415.40	409.84	404.94	400.59	396.74	382.89	374.90	370.18
45000	480.83	467.86	456.70	447.04	438.64	431.29	424.84	419.16	414.14	409.70	405.75	391.59	383.42	378.59
46000	491.51	478.26	466.85	456.98	448.38	440.87	434.28	428.47	423.34	418.80	414.77	400.29	391.94	387.00
47000	502.20	488.66	477.00	466.91	458.13	450.46	443.72	437.79	432.55	427.91	423.79	408.99	400.46	395.42
48000	512.88	499.05	487.15	476.85	467.88	460.04	453.16	447.10	441.75	437.01	432.80	417.70	408.98	403.83
49000	523.57	509.45	497.30	486.78	477.63	469.62	462.60	456.42	450.95	446.11	441.82	426.40	417.50	412.24
50000	534.25	519.85	507.45	496.72	487.37	479.21	472.04	465.73	460.16	455.22	450.84	435.10	426.02	420.66
55000	587.68	571.83	558.19	546.39	536.11	527.13	519.24	512.30	506.17	500.74	495.92	478.61	468.62	462.72
60000	641.10	623.82	608.94	596.06	584.85	575.05	566.45	558.88	552.19	546.26	541.00	522.12	511.22	504.79
65000	694.53	675.80	659.68	645.73	633.58	622.97	613.65	605.45	598.20	591.78	586.08	565.63	553.82	546.85
70000	747.95	727.78	710.43	695.40	682.32	670.89	660.86	652.02	644.22	637.30	631.17	609.14	596.42	588.92
75000	801.38	779.77	761.17	745.07	731.06	718.81	708.06	698.59	690.23	682.83	676.25	652.65	639.03	630.98
80000	854.80	831.75	811.92	794.74	779.80	766.73	755.26	745.17	736.25	728.35	721.33	696.16	681.63	673.05
85000	908.23	883.74	862.66	844.41	828.53	814.65	802.47	791.74	782.26	773.87	766.42	739.67	724.23	715.11
90000	961.65	935.72	913.40	894.08	877.27	862.57	849.67	838.31	828.28	819.39	811.50	783.18	766.83	757.18
95000	1015.08	987.71	964.15	943.75	926.01	910.49	896.87	884.88	874.29	864.91	856.58	826.69	809.43	799.24
100000	1068.50	1039.69	1014.89	993.43	974.74	958.41	944.08	931.46	920.31	910.43	901.67	870.20	852.03	841.31

MONTHLY PAYMENT
REQUIRED TO AMORTIZE A LOAN

TERM	1 Year	2 Years	3 Years	4 Years	5 Years	6 Years	7 Years	8 Years	9 Years	10 Years	11 Years	12 Years	13 Years	14 Years
AMOUNT														
5	.44	.24	.17	.13	.11	.10	.09	.08	.08	.07	.07	.06	.06	.06
10	.88	.47	.33	.26	.22	.19	.17	.16	.15	.14	.13	.12	.12	.12
15	1.32	.70	.49	.39	.32	.28	.25	.23	.22	.20	.19	.18	.18	.17
25	2.20	1.16	.81	.64	.54	.47	.42	.38	.36	.34	.32	.30	.29	.28
50	4.40	2.31	1.62	1.27	1.07	.93	.84	.76	.71	.67	.63	.60	.58	.56
75	6.60	3.47	2.43	1.91	1.60	1.39	1.25	1.14	1.06	1.00	.94	.90	.87	.84
100	8.80	4.62	3.23	2.54	2.13	1.86	1.67	1.52	1.41	1.33	1.26	1.20	1.15	1.11
200	17.59	9.23	6.46	5.08	4.25	3.71	3.33	3.04	2.82	2.65	2.51	2.40	2.30	2.22
300	26.38	13.85	9.69	7.61	6.38	5.56	4.99	4.56	4.23	3.97	3.76	3.59	3.45	3.33
400	35.17	18.46	12.91	10.15	8.50	7.42	6.65	6.07	5.64	5.29	5.01	4.79	4.60	4.44
500	43.96	23.08	16.14	12.69	10.63	9.27	8.31	7.59	7.04	6.61	6.26	5.98	5.74	5.55
600	52.75	27.69	19.37	15.22	12.75	11.12	9.97	9.11	8.45	7.93	7.52	7.18	6.89	6.65
700	61.55	32.31	22.59	17.76	14.88	12.97	11.63	10.63	9.86	9.26	8.77	8.37	8.04	7.76
800	70.34	36.92	25.82	20.30	17.00	14.83	13.29	12.14	11.27	10.58	10.02	9.57	9.19	8.87
900	79.13	41.54	29.05	22.83	19.13	16.68	14.95	13.66	12.68	11.90	11.27	10.76	10.34	9.98
1000	87.92	46.15	32.27	25.37	21.25	18.53	16.61	15.18	14.08	13.22	12.52	11.96	11.48	11.09
2000	175.84	92.29	64.54	50.73	42.50	37.06	33.21	30.35	28.16	26.44	25.04	23.91	22.96	22.17
3000	263.75	138.44	96.81	76.09	63.75	55.58	49.81	45.53	42.24	39.65	37.56	35.86	34.44	33.25
4000	351.67	184.58	129.07	101.46	84.99	74.11	66.41	60.70	56.32	52.87	50.08	47.81	45.92	44.33
5000	439.58	230.73	161.34	126.82	106.24	92.63	83.01	75.88	70.40	66.08	62.60	59.76	57.40	55.42
6000	527.50	276.87	193.61	152.18	127.49	111.16	99.61	91.05	84.48	79.30	75.12	71.71	68.88	66.50
7000	615.42	323.02	225.88	177.54	148.73	129.69	116.21	106.22	98.56	92.51	87.64	83.66	80.35	77.58
8000	703.33	369.16	258.14	202.91	169.98	148.21	132.81	121.40	112.63	105.73	100.16	95.61	91.83	88.66
9000	791.25	415.31	290.41	228.27	191.23	166.74	149.42	136.57	126.71	118.94	112.68	107.56	103.31	99.74
10000	879.16	461.45	322.68	253.63	212.48	185.26	166.02	151.75	140.79	132.16	125.20	119.51	114.79	110.83
11000	967.08	507.60	354.94	278.99	233.72	203.79	182.62	166.92	154.87	145.37	137.72	131.46	126.27	121.91
12000	1055.00	553.74	387.21	304.36	254.97	222.32	199.22	182.09	168.95	158.59	150.24	143.41	137.75	132.99
13000	1142.91	599.89	419.48	329.72	276.22	240.84	215.82	197.27	183.03	171.80	162.76	155.37	149.23	144.07
14000	1230.83	646.03	451.75	355.08	297.46	259.37	232.42	212.44	197.11	185.02	175.28	167.32	160.70	155.15
15000	1318.74	692.18	484.01	380.44	318.71	277.89	249.02	227.62	211.19	198.23	187.80	179.27	172.18	166.24
16000	1406.66	738.32	516.28	405.81	339.96	296.42	265.62	242.79	225.26	211.45	200.32	191.22	183.66	177.32
17000	1494.58	784.47	548.55	431.17	361.20	314.94	282.23	257.97	239.34	224.66	212.84	203.17	195.14	188.40
18000	1582.49	830.61	580.81	456.53	382.45	333.47	298.83	273.14	253.42	237.88	225.36	215.12	206.62	199.48
19000	1670.41	876.76	613.08	481.89	403.70	352.00	315.43	288.31	267.50	251.09	237.88	227.07	218.10	210.56
20000	1758.32	922.90	645.35	507.26	424.95	370.52	332.03	303.49	281.58	264.31	250.40	239.02	229.57	221.65
21000	1846.24	969.05	677.62	532.62	446.19	389.05	348.63	318.66	295.66	277.52	262.92	250.97	241.05	232.73
22000	1934.15	1015.19	709.88	557.98	467.44	407.57	365.23	333.84	309.74	290.74	275.44	262.92	252.53	243.81
23000	2022.07	1061.34	742.15	583.34	488.69	426.10	381.83	349.01	323.81	303.95	287.96	274.87	264.01	254.89
24000	2109.99	1107.48	774.42	608.71	509.93	444.63	398.43	364.18	337.89	317.17	300.48	286.82	275.49	265.97
25000	2197.90	1153.63	806.68	634.07	531.18	463.15	415.03	379.36	351.97	330.38	313.00	298.77	286.97	277.06
26000	2285.82	1199.77	838.95	659.43	552.43	481.68	431.64	394.53	366.05	343.60	325.52	310.73	298.45	288.14
27000	2373.73	1245.92	871.22	684.79	573.68	500.20	448.24	409.71	380.13	356.81	338.04	322.68	309.92	299.22
28000	2461.65	1292.06	903.49	710.16	594.92	518.73	464.84	424.88	394.21	370.03	350.56	334.63	321.40	310.30
29000	2549.57	1338.21	935.75	735.52	616.17	537.25	481.44	440.06	408.29	383.24	363.08	346.58	332.88	321.38
30000	2637.48	1384.35	968.02	760.88	637.42	555.78	498.04	455.23	422.37	396.46	375.60	358.53	344.36	332.47
31000	2725.40	1430.50	1000.29	786.25	658.66	574.31	514.64	470.40	436.44	409.67	388.12	370.48	355.84	343.55
32000	2813.31	1476.64	1032.56	811.61	679.91	592.83	531.24	485.58	450.52	422.89	400.64	382.43	367.32	354.63
33000	2901.23	1522.79	1064.82	836.97	701.16	611.36	547.84	500.75	464.60	436.10	413.16	394.38	378.79	365.71
34000	2989.15	1568.93	1097.09	862.33	722.40	629.88	564.45	515.93	478.68	449.32	425.68	406.33	390.27	376.79
35000	3077.06	1615.08	1129.36	887.70	743.65	648.41	581.05	531.10	492.76	462.53	438.20	418.28	401.75	387.88
36000	3164.98	1661.22	1161.62	913.06	764.90	666.94	597.65	546.27	506.84	475.75	450.72	430.23	413.23	398.96
37000	3252.89	1707.37	1193.89	938.42	786.15	685.46	614.25	561.45	520.92	488.96	463.24	442.18	424.71	410.04
38000	3340.81	1753.51	1226.16	963.78	807.39	703.99	630.85	576.62	535.00	502.18	475.76	454.13	436.19	421.12
39000	3428.72	1799.66	1258.43	989.15	828.64	722.51	647.45	591.80	549.07	515.39	488.28	466.09	447.67	432.20
40000	3516.64	1845.80	1290.69	1014.51	849.89	741.04	664.05	606.97	563.15	528.61	500.80	478.04	459.14	443.29
41000	3604.56	1891.95	1322.96	1039.87	871.13	759.56	680.65	622.15	577.23	541.82	513.32	489.99	470.62	454.37
42000	3692.47	1938.09	1355.23	1065.23	892.38	778.09	697.25	637.32	591.31	555.04	525.84	501.94	482.10	465.45
43000	3780.39	1984.24	1387.49	1090.60	913.63	796.62	713.86	652.49	605.39	568.25	538.36	513.89	493.58	476.53
44000	3868.30	2030.38	1419.76	1115.96	934.87	815.14	730.46	667.67	619.47	581.47	550.88	525.84	505.06	487.61
45000	3956.22	2076.53	1452.03	1141.32	956.12	833.67	747.06	682.84	633.55	594.68	563.40	537.79	516.54	498.70
46000	4044.14	2122.67	1484.30	1166.68	977.37	852.19	763.66	698.02	647.62	607.90	575.92	549.74	528.02	509.78
47000	4132.05	2168.82	1516.56	1192.05	998.62	870.72	780.26	713.19	661.70	621.11	588.44	561.69	539.49	520.86
48000	4219.97	2214.96	1548.83	1217.41	1019.86	889.25	796.86	728.36	675.78	634.33	600.96	573.64	550.97	531.94
49000	4307.88	2261.11	1581.10	1242.77	1041.11	907.77	813.46	743.54	689.86	647.54	613.48	585.59	562.45	543.02
50000	4395.80	2307.25	1613.36	1268.13	1062.36	926.30	830.06	758.71	703.94	660.76	626.00	597.54	573.93	554.11
55000	4835.38	2537.98	1774.70	1394.95	1168.59	1018.93	913.07	834.58	774.33	726.83	688.60	657.30	631.32	609.52
60000	5274.96	2768.70	1936.04	1521.76	1274.83	1111.56	996.08	910.45	844.73	792.91	751.20	717.05	688.71	664.93
65000	5714.54	2999.43	2097.37	1648.57	1381.06	1204.18	1079.08	986.33	915.12	858.98	813.80	776.81	746.11	720.34
70000	6154.12	3230.15	2258.71	1775.39	1487.30	1296.81	1162.09	1062.20	985.51	925.06	876.40	836.56	803.50	775.75
75000	6593.70	3460.87	2420.04	1902.20	1593.53	1389.44	1245.09	1138.07	1055.91	991.14	939.00	896.31	860.89	831.16
80000	7033.28	3691.60	2581.38	2029.01	1699.77	1482.07	1328.10	1213.94	1126.30	1057.21	1001.60	956.07	918.28	886.57
85000	7472.86	3922.32	2742.72	2155.82	1806.00	1574.70	1411.11	1289.81	1196.69	1123.29	1064.19	1015.82	975.68	941.98
90000	7912.43	4153.05	2904.05	2282.64	1912.24	1667.33	1494.11	1365.68	1267.09	1189.36	1126.79	1075.58	1033.07	997.39
95000	8352.01	4383.77	3065.39	2409.45	2018.47	1759.96	1577.12	1441.55	1337.48	1255.44	1189.39	1135.33	1090.46	1052.80
100000	8791.59	4614.50	3226.72	2536.26	2124.71	1852.59	1660.12	1517.42	1407.87	1321.51	1251.99	1195.08	1147.85	1108.21

TERM AMOUNT	15 Years	16 Years	17 Years	18 Years	19 Years	20 Years	21 Years	22 Years	23 Years	24 Years	25 Years	30 Years	35 Years	40 Years
5	.06	.06	.06	.05	.05	.05	.05	.05	.05	.05	.05	.05	.05	.05
10	.11	.11	.11	.10	.10	.10	.10	.10	.10	.10	.10	.09	.09	.09
15	.17	.16	.16	.15	.15	.15	.15	.15	.14	.14	.14	.14	.13	.13
25	.27	.27	.26	.25	.25	.25	.24	.24	.24	.23	.23	.22	.22	.22
50	.54	.53	.52	.50	.50	.49	.48	.47	.47	.46	.46	.44	.43	.43
75	.81	.79	.77	.75	.74	.73	.72	.71	.70	.69	.69	.66	.65	.64
100	1.08	1.05	1.03	1.00	.99	.97	.96	.94	.93	.92	.91	.88	.86	.85
200	2.15	2.10	2.05	2.00	1.97	1.94	1.91	1.88	1.86	1.84	1.82	1.76	1.72	1.70
300	3.23	3.14	3.07	3.00	2.95	2.90	2.86	2.82	2.79	2.76	2.73	2.64	2.58	2.55
400	4.30	4.19	4.09	4.00	3.93	3.87	3.81	3.76	3.71	3.67	3.64	3.52	3.44	3.40
500	5.38	5.23	5.11	5.00	4.91	4.83	4.76	4.70	4.64	4.59	4.55	4.39	4.30	4.25
600	6.45	6.28	6.13	6.00	5.89	5.80	5.71	5.63	5.57	5.51	5.46	5.27	5.16	5.10
700	7.53	7.33	7.15	7.00	6.87	6.76	6.66	6.57	6.50	6.43	6.37	6.15	6.02	5.95
800	8.60	8.37	8.17	8.00	7.86	7.73	7.61	7.51	7.42	7.34	7.27	7.03	6.88	6.80
900	9.68	9.42	9.20	9.00	8.84	8.69	8.56	8.45	8.35	8.26	8.18	7.90	7.74	7.65
1000	10.75	10.46	10.22	10.00	9.82	9.66	9.51	9.39	9.28	9.18	9.09	8.78	8.60	8.50
2000	21.50	20.92	20.43	20.00	19.63	19.31	19.02	18.77	18.55	18.35	18.18	17.56	17.20	16.99
3000	32.24	31.38	30.64	30.00	29.44	28.96	28.53	28.15	27.82	27.53	27.27	26.33	25.80	25.48
4000	42.99	41.84	40.85	40.00	39.26	38.61	38.04	37.53	37.09	36.70	36.35	35.11	34.39	33.97
5000	53.74	52.30	51.07	50.00	49.07	48.26	47.54	46.92	46.36	45.87	45.44	43.88	42.99	42.46
6000	64.48	62.76	61.28	60.00	58.88	57.91	57.05	56.30	55.64	55.05	54.53	52.66	51.59	50.95
7000	75.23	73.22	71.49	69.99	68.69	67.56	66.56	65.68	64.91	64.22	63.61	61.44	60.18	59.45
8000	85.97	83.68	81.70	79.99	78.51	77.21	76.07	75.06	74.18	73.40	72.70	70.21	68.78	67.94
9000	96.72	94.14	91.91	89.99	88.32	86.86	85.58	84.45	83.45	82.57	81.79	78.99	77.38	76.43
10000	107.47	104.60	102.13	99.99	98.13	96.51	95.08	93.83	92.72	91.74	90.88	87.76	85.97	84.92
11000	118.21	115.05	112.34	109.99	107.94	106.16	104.59	103.21	101.99	100.92	99.96	96.54	94.57	93.41
12000	128.96	125.51	122.55	119.99	117.76	115.81	114.10	112.59	111.27	110.09	109.05	105.31	103.17	101.90
13000	139.70	135.97	132.76	129.98	127.57	125.46	123.61	121.98	120.54	119.27	118.14	114.09	111.76	110.39
14000	150.45	146.43	142.97	139.98	137.38	135.11	133.11	131.36	129.81	128.44	127.22	122.87	120.36	118.89
15000	161.20	156.89	153.19	149.98	147.19	144.76	142.62	140.74	139.08	137.61	136.31	131.64	128.96	127.38
16000	171.94	167.35	163.40	159.98	157.01	154.41	152.13	150.12	148.35	146.79	145.40	140.42	137.55	135.87
17000	182.69	177.81	173.61	169.98	166.82	164.06	161.64	159.51	157.63	155.96	154.48	149.19	146.15	144.36
18000	193.43	188.27	183.82	179.98	176.63	173.71	171.15	168.89	166.90	165.13	163.57	157.97	154.75	152.85
19000	204.18	198.73	194.03	189.98	186.44	183.36	180.65	178.27	176.17	174.31	172.66	166.74	163.34	161.34
20000	214.93	209.19	204.25	199.97	196.26	193.01	190.16	187.65	185.44	183.48	181.75	175.52	171.94	169.83
21000	225.67	219.64	214.46	209.97	206.07	202.66	199.67	197.04	194.71	192.66	190.83	184.30	180.54	178.33
22000	236.42	230.10	224.67	219.97	215.88	212.31	209.18	206.42	203.98	201.83	199.92	193.07	189.13	186.82
23000	247.16	240.56	234.88	229.97	225.69	221.96	218.68	215.80	213.26	211.00	209.01	201.85	197.73	195.31
24000	257.91	251.02	245.10	239.97	235.51	231.61	228.19	225.18	222.53	220.18	218.09	210.62	206.33	203.80
25000	268.66	261.48	255.31	249.97	245.32	241.26	237.70	234.57	231.80	229.35	227.18	219.40	214.92	212.29
26000	279.40	271.94	265.52	259.96	255.13	250.91	247.21	243.95	241.07	238.53	236.27	228.17	223.52	220.78
27000	290.15	282.40	275.73	269.96	264.94	260.56	256.72	253.33	250.34	247.70	245.35	236.95	232.12	229.27
28000	300.89	292.86	285.94	279.96	274.76	270.21	266.22	262.71	259.62	256.87	254.44	245.73	240.71	237.77
29000	311.64	303.32	296.16	289.96	284.57	279.86	275.73	272.10	268.89	266.05	263.53	254.50	249.31	246.26
30000	322.39	313.78	306.37	299.96	294.38	289.51	285.24	281.48	278.16	275.22	272.62	263.28	257.91	254.75
31000	333.13	324.23	316.58	309.96	304.20	299.16	294.75	290.86	287.43	284.40	281.70	272.05	266.50	263.24
32000	343.88	334.69	326.79	319.95	314.01	308.81	304.25	300.24	296.70	293.57	290.79	280.83	275.10	271.73
33000	354.62	345.15	337.00	329.95	323.82	318.46	313.76	309.63	305.97	302.74	299.88	289.60	283.70	280.22
34000	365.37	355.61	347.22	339.95	333.63	328.11	323.27	319.01	315.25	311.92	308.96	298.38	292.29	288.71
35000	376.12	366.07	357.43	349.95	343.45	337.76	332.78	328.39	324.52	321.09	318.05	307.16	300.89	297.21
36000	386.86	376.53	367.64	359.95	353.26	347.41	342.29	337.77	333.79	330.26	327.14	315.93	309.49	305.70
37000	397.61	386.99	377.85	369.95	363.07	357.06	351.79	347.16	343.06	339.44	336.22	324.71	318.08	314.19
38000	408.35	397.45	388.06	379.95	372.88	366.71	361.30	356.54	352.33	348.61	345.31	333.48	326.68	322.68
39000	419.10	407.91	398.28	389.94	382.70	376.36	370.81	365.92	361.61	357.79	354.40	342.26	335.28	331.17
40000	429.85	418.37	408.49	399.94	392.51	386.01	380.32	375.30	370.88	366.96	363.49	351.03	343.87	339.66
41000	440.59	428.82	418.70	409.94	402.32	395.66	389.82	384.69	380.15	376.13	372.57	359.81	352.47	348.15
42000	451.34	439.28	428.91	419.94	412.13	405.31	399.33	394.07	389.42	385.31	381.66	368.59	361.07	356.65
43000	462.09	449.74	439.13	429.94	421.95	414.96	408.84	403.45	398.69	394.48	390.75	377.36	369.66	365.14
44000	472.83	460.20	449.34	439.94	431.76	424.61	418.35	412.83	407.96	403.66	399.83	386.14	378.26	373.63
45000	483.58	470.66	459.55	449.93	441.57	434.26	427.86	422.22	417.24	412.83	408.92	394.91	386.86	382.12
46000	494.32	481.12	469.76	459.93	451.38	443.91	437.36	431.60	426.51	422.00	418.01	403.69	395.45	390.61
47000	505.07	491.58	479.97	469.93	461.20	453.57	446.87	440.98	435.78	431.18	427.09	412.46	404.05	399.10
48000	515.82	502.04	490.19	479.93	471.01	463.22	456.38	450.36	445.05	440.35	436.18	421.24	412.65	407.60
49000	526.56	512.50	500.40	489.93	480.82	472.87	465.89	459.75	454.32	449.53	445.27	430.02	421.24	416.09
50000	537.31	522.96	510.61	499.93	490.63	482.52	475.40	469.13	463.60	458.70	454.36	438.79	429.84	424.58
55000	591.04	575.25	561.67	549.92	539.70	530.77	522.93	516.04	509.95	504.57	499.79	482.67	472.82	467.04
60000	644.77	627.55	612.73	599.91	588.76	579.02	570.47	562.95	556.31	550.44	545.23	526.55	515.81	509.49
65000	698.50	679.84	663.79	649.90	637.82	627.27	618.01	609.86	602.67	596.31	590.66	570.43	558.79	551.95
70000	752.23	732.14	714.85	699.90	686.89	675.52	665.55	656.78	649.03	642.18	636.10	614.31	601.78	594.41
75000	805.96	784.43	765.91	749.89	735.95	723.77	713.09	703.69	695.39	688.05	681.53	658.18	644.76	636.86
80000	859.69	836.73	816.97	799.88	785.01	772.02	760.63	750.60	741.75	733.92	726.97	702.06	687.74	679.32
85000	913.42	889.02	868.03	849.87	834.08	820.27	808.17	797.51	788.11	779.79	772.40	745.94	730.73	721.78
90000	967.15	941.32	919.09	899.86	883.14	868.52	855.71	844.43	834.47	825.65	817.84	789.82	773.71	764.24
95000	1020.88	993.61	970.15	949.86	932.20	916.78	903.25	891.34	880.83	871.52	863.27	833.70	816.69	806.69
100000	1074.61	1045.91	1021.22	999.85	981.26	965.03	950.79	938.25	927.19	917.39	908.71	877.58	859.68	849.15

10%

10.100%

TERM / AMOUNT	1 Year	2 Years	3 Years	4 Years	5 Years	6 Years	7 Years	8 Years	9 Years	10 Years	11 Years	12 Years	13 Years	14 Years
5	.44	.24	.17	.13	.11	.10	.09	.08	.08	.07	.07	.07	.06	.06
10	.88	.47	.33	.26	.22	.19	.17	.16	.15	.14	.13	.13	.12	.12
15	1.32	.70	.49	.39	.32	.28	.25	.23	.22	.20	.19	.19	.18	.17
25	2.20	1.16	.81	.64	.54	.47	.42	.39	.36	.34	.32	.31	.29	.28
50	4.40	2.31	1.62	1.28	1.07	.93	.84	.77	.71	.67	.63	.61	.58	.56
75	6.60	3.47	2.43	1.91	1.60	1.40	1.25	1.15	1.06	1.00	.95	.91	.87	.84
100	8.80	4.62	3.24	2.55	2.13	1.86	1.67	1.53	1.42	1.33	1.26	1.21	1.16	1.12
200	17.60	9.24	6.47	5.09	4.26	3.72	3.34	3.05	2.83	2.66	2.52	2.41	2.31	2.23
300	26.39	13.86	9.70	7.63	6.39	5.58	5.00	4.57	4.24	3.99	3.78	3.61	3.47	3.35
400	35.19	18.49	12.93	10.17	8.52	7.44	6.67	6.10	5.66	5.31	5.04	4.81	4.62	4.46
500	43.99	23.10	16.16	12.71	10.65	9.29	8.33	7.62	7.07	6.64	6.29	6.01	5.77	5.58
600	52.78	27.72	19.39	15.25	12.78	11.15	10.00	9.14	8.48	7.97	7.55	7.21	6.93	6.69
700	61.58	32.34	22.62	17.79	14.91	13.01	11.66	10.66	9.90	9.29	8.81	8.41	8.08	7.80
800	70.37	36.96	25.86	20.33	17.04	14.87	13.33	12.19	11.31	10.62	10.07	9.61	9.23	8.92
900	79.17	41.58	29.09	22.87	19.17	16.72	14.99	13.71	12.72	11.95	11.32	10.81	10.39	10.03
1000	87.97	46.20	32.32	25.42	21.30	18.58	16.66	15.23	14.14	13.28	12.58	12.01	11.54	11.15
2000	175.93	92.39	64.63	50.83	42.60	37.16	33.31	30.46	28.27	26.55	25.16	24.02	23.08	22.29
3000	263.89	138.58	96.95	76.24	63.89	55.73	49.96	45.69	42.40	39.82	37.73	36.03	34.62	33.43
4000	351.85	184.77	129.26	101.65	85.19	74.31	66.62	60.91	56.54	53.09	50.31	48.04	46.15	44.57
5000	439.82	230.96	161.58	127.06	106.49	92.89	83.27	76.14	70.67	66.36	62.89	60.05	57.69	55.72
6000	527.78	277.15	193.89	152.47	127.78	111.46	99.92	91.37	84.80	79.63	75.46	72.06	69.23	66.86
7000	615.74	323.34	226.20	177.88	149.08	130.04	116.58	106.59	98.94	92.90	88.04	84.07	80.77	78.00
8000	703.70	369.53	258.52	203.29	170.38	148.62	133.23	121.82	113.07	106.17	100.62	96.07	92.30	89.14
9000	791.67	415.72	290.83	228.70	191.67	167.19	149.88	137.05	127.20	119.44	113.19	108.08	103.84	100.28
10000	879.63	461.92	323.15	254.11	212.97	185.77	166.53	152.28	141.33	132.71	125.77	120.09	115.38	111.43
11000	967.59	508.11	355.46	279.52	234.26	204.34	183.19	167.50	155.47	145.98	138.35	132.10	126.92	122.57
12000	1055.55	554.30	387.77	304.93	255.56	222.92	199.84	182.73	169.60	159.25	150.92	144.11	138.45	133.71
13000	1143.52	600.49	420.09	330.34	276.86	241.50	216.49	197.96	183.73	172.52	163.50	156.12	149.99	144.85
14000	1231.48	646.68	452.40	355.75	298.15	260.07	233.15	213.18	197.87	185.79	176.08	168.13	161.53	156.00
15000	1319.44	692.87	484.72	381.16	319.45	278.65	249.80	228.41	212.00	199.06	188.65	180.13	173.07	167.14
16000	1407.40	739.06	517.03	406.58	340.75	297.23	266.45	243.64	226.13	212.33	201.23	192.14	184.60	178.28
17000	1495.37	785.25	549.35	431.99	362.04	315.80	283.10	258.87	240.26	225.60	213.81	204.15	196.14	189.42
18000	1583.33	831.44	581.66	457.40	383.34	334.38	299.76	274.09	254.40	238.87	226.38	216.16	207.68	200.56
19000	1671.29	877.64	613.97	482.81	404.63	352.95	316.41	289.32	268.53	252.14	238.96	228.17	219.22	211.71
20000	1759.25	923.83	646.29	508.22	425.93	371.53	333.06	304.55	282.66	265.42	251.54	240.18	230.75	222.85
21000	1847.22	970.02	678.60	533.63	447.23	390.11	349.72	319.77	296.80	278.69	264.11	252.19	242.29	233.99
22000	1935.18	1016.21	710.92	559.04	468.52	408.68	366.37	335.00	310.93	291.96	276.69	264.19	253.83	245.13
23000	2023.14	1062.40	743.23	584.45	489.82	427.26	383.02	350.23	325.06	305.23	289.27	276.20	265.37	256.28
24000	2111.10	1108.59	775.54	609.86	511.12	445.84	399.67	365.46	339.19	318.50	301.84	288.21	276.90	267.42
25000	2199.07	1154.78	807.86	635.27	532.41	464.41	416.33	380.68	353.33	331.77	314.42	300.22	288.44	278.56
26000	2287.03	1200.97	840.17	660.68	553.71	482.99	432.98	395.91	367.46	345.04	326.99	312.23	299.98	289.70
27000	2374.99	1247.16	872.45	686.09	575.00	501.57	449.63	411.14	381.59	358.31	339.57	324.24	311.52	300.84
28000	2462.95	1293.36	904.80	711.50	596.30	520.14	466.29	426.36	395.73	371.58	352.15	336.25	323.05	311.99
29000	2550.91	1339.55	937.12	736.91	617.60	538.72	482.94	441.59	409.86	384.85	364.72	348.26	334.59	323.13
30000	2638.88	1385.74	969.43	762.32	638.89	557.29	499.59	456.82	423.99	398.12	377.30	360.26	346.13	334.27
31000	2726.84	1431.93	1001.74	787.73	660.19	575.87	516.24	472.05	438.12	411.39	389.88	372.27	357.67	345.41
32000	2814.80	1478.12	1034.06	813.15	681.49	594.45	532.90	487.27	452.26	424.66	402.45	384.28	369.20	356.55
33000	2902.76	1524.31	1066.37	838.56	702.78	613.02	549.55	502.50	466.39	437.93	415.03	396.29	380.74	367.70
34000	2990.73	1570.50	1098.69	863.97	724.08	631.60	566.20	517.73	480.52	451.20	427.61	408.30	392.28	378.84
35000	3078.69	1616.69	1131.00	889.38	745.37	650.18	582.86	532.95	494.66	464.47	440.18	420.31	403.82	389.98
36000	3166.65	1662.88	1163.31	914.79	766.67	668.75	599.51	548.18	508.79	477.74	452.76	432.32	415.35	401.12
37000	3254.61	1709.08	1195.63	940.20	787.97	687.33	616.16	563.41	522.92	491.01	465.34	444.32	426.89	412.27
38000	3342.58	1755.27	1227.94	965.61	809.26	705.90	632.82	578.64	537.05	504.28	477.91	456.33	438.43	423.41
39000	3430.54	1801.46	1260.26	991.02	830.56	724.48	649.47	593.86	551.19	517.55	490.49	468.34	449.97	434.55
40000	3518.50	1847.65	1292.57	1016.43	851.86	743.06	666.12	609.09	565.32	530.83	503.07	480.35	461.50	445.69
41000	3606.46	1893.84	1324.89	1041.84	873.15	761.63	682.77	624.32	579.45	544.10	515.64	492.36	473.04	456.83
42000	3694.43	1940.03	1357.20	1067.25	894.45	780.21	699.43	639.54	593.59	557.37	528.22	504.37	484.58	467.98
43000	3782.39	1986.22	1389.51	1092.66	915.75	798.79	716.08	654.77	607.72	570.64	540.80	516.38	496.12	479.12
44000	3870.35	2032.41	1421.83	1118.07	937.04	817.36	732.73	670.00	621.85	583.91	553.37	528.38	507.65	490.26
45000	3958.31	2078.60	1454.14	1143.48	958.34	835.94	749.39	685.23	635.99	597.18	565.95	540.39	519.19	501.40
46000	4046.28	2124.80	1486.46	1168.89	979.63	854.52	766.04	700.45	650.12	610.45	578.53	552.40	530.73	512.55
47000	4134.24	2170.99	1518.77	1194.30	1000.93	873.09	782.69	715.68	664.25	623.72	591.10	564.41	542.27	523.69
48000	4222.20	2217.18	1551.08	1219.72	1022.23	891.67	799.34	730.91	678.38	636.99	603.68	576.42	553.80	534.83
49000	4310.16	2263.37	1583.40	1245.13	1043.52	910.24	816.00	746.13	692.52	650.26	616.25	588.43	565.34	545.97
50000	4398.13	2309.56	1615.71	1270.54	1064.82	928.82	832.65	761.36	706.65	663.53	628.83	600.44	576.88	557.11
55000	4837.94	2540.52	1777.28	1397.59	1171.30	1021.70	915.91	837.50	777.31	729.88	691.71	660.48	634.57	612.82
60000	5277.75	2771.47	1938.85	1524.64	1277.78	1114.58	999.18	913.63	847.98	796.24	754.60	720.52	692.25	668.54
65000	5717.56	3002.43	2100.43	1651.70	1384.26	1207.46	1082.44	989.77	918.64	862.59	817.48	780.57	749.94	724.25
70000	6157.37	3233.38	2262.00	1778.75	1490.74	1300.35	1165.71	1065.90	989.31	928.94	880.36	840.61	807.63	779.96
75000	6597.19	3464.34	2423.57	1905.80	1597.23	1393.23	1248.97	1142.04	1059.97	995.29	943.24	900.65	865.32	835.67
80000	7037.00	3695.29	2585.14	2032.86	1703.71	1486.11	1332.24	1218.18	1130.64	1061.65	1006.13	960.69	923.00	891.38
85000	7476.81	3926.24	2746.71	2159.91	1810.19	1578.99	1415.50	1294.31	1201.30	1128.00	1069.01	1020.74	980.69	947.09
90000	7916.62	4157.20	2908.28	2286.96	1916.67	1671.87	1498.77	1370.45	1271.97	1194.35	1131.89	1080.78	1038.63	1002.80
95000	8356.43	4388.16	3069.85	2414.02	2023.15	1764.75	1582.03	1446.58	1342.63	1260.70	1194.78	1140.82	1096.07	1058.51
100000	8796.25	4619.11	3231.42	2541.07	2129.63	1857.64	1665.29	1522.72	1413.29	1327.06	1257.66	1200.87	1153.75	1114.22

TERM AMOUNT	15 Years	16 Years	17 Years	18 Years	19 Years	20 Years	21 Years	22 Years	23 Years	24 Years	25 Years	30 Years	35 Years	40 Years
5	.06	.06	.06	.06	.05	.05	.05	.05	.05	.05	.05	.05	.05	.05
10	.11	.11	.11	.11	.10	.10	.10	.10	.10	.10	.10	.09	.09	.09
15	.17	.16	.16	.16	.15	.15	.15	.15	.15	.14	.14	.14	.14	.13
25	.28	.27	.26	.26	.25	.25	.24	.24	.24	.24	.23	.23	.22	.22
50	.55	.53	.52	.51	.50	.49	.48	.48	.47	.47	.46	.45	.44	.43
75	.82	.79	.78	.76	.75	.73	.72	.71	.71	.70	.69	.67	.66	.65
100	1.09	1.06	1.03	1.01	.99	.98	.96	.95	.94	.93	.92	.89	.87	.86
200	2.17	2.11	2.06	2.02	1.98	1.95	1.92	1.90	1.87	1.85	1.84	1.77	1.74	1.72
300	3.25	3.16	3.09	3.02	2.97	2.92	2.88	2.84	2.81	2.78	2.75	2.66	2.61	2.58
400	4.33	4.21	4.12	4.03	3.96	3.89	3.84	3.79	3.74	3.70	3.67	3.54	3.47	3.43
500	5.41	5.27	5.14	5.04	4.94	4.86	4.79	4.73	4.68	4.63	4.58	4.43	4.34	4.29
600	6.49	6.32	6.17	6.04	5.93	5.83	5.75	5.68	5.61	5.55	5.50	5.31	5.21	5.15
700	7.57	7.37	7.20	7.05	6.92	6.81	6.71	6.62	6.54	6.48	6.42	6.20	6.08	6.00
800	8.65	8.42	8.23	8.06	7.91	7.78	7.67	7.57	7.48	7.40	7.33	7.08	6.94	6.86
900	9.73	9.47	9.25	9.06	8.90	8.75	8.62	8.51	8.41	8.32	8.25	7.97	7.81	7.72
1000	10.81	10.53	10.28	10.07	9.88	9.72	9.58	9.46	9.35	9.25	9.16	8.85	8.68	8.58
2000	21.62	21.05	20.56	20.13	19.76	19.44	19.16	18.91	18.69	18.49	18.32	17.70	17.35	17.15
3000	32.43	31.57	30.83	30.19	29.64	29.15	28.73	28.36	28.03	27.74	27.48	26.55	26.03	25.72
4000	43.23	42.09	41.11	40.26	39.52	38.87	38.31	37.81	37.37	36.98	36.64	35.40	34.70	34.29
5000	54.04	52.61	51.38	50.32	49.39	48.59	47.88	47.26	46.71	46.22	45.79	44.25	43.37	42.86
6000	64.85	63.13	61.66	60.38	59.27	58.30	57.46	56.71	56.05	55.47	54.95	53.10	52.05	51.43
7000	75.66	73.65	71.93	70.44	69.15	68.02	67.03	66.16	65.39	64.71	64.11	61.95	60.72	60.00
8000	86.46	84.18	82.21	80.51	79.03	77.74	76.61	75.61	74.73	73.95	73.27	70.80	69.39	68.57
9000	97.27	94.70	92.48	90.57	88.91	87.45	86.18	85.06	84.07	83.20	82.42	79.65	78.07	77.14
10000	108.08	105.22	102.76	100.63	98.78	97.17	95.76	94.51	93.41	92.44	91.58	88.50	86.74	85.71
11000	118.89	115.74	113.04	110.70	108.66	106.89	105.33	103.96	102.75	101.69	100.74	97.35	95.41	94.28
12000	129.69	126.26	123.31	120.76	118.54	116.60	114.91	113.41	112.09	110.93	109.90	106.20	104.09	102.85
13000	140.50	136.78	133.59	130.82	128.42	126.32	124.48	122.86	121.44	120.17	119.05	115.05	112.76	111.42
14000	151.31	147.30	143.86	140.88	138.30	136.04	134.06	132.31	130.78	129.42	128.21	123.90	121.43	119.99
15000	162.11	157.83	154.14	150.95	148.17	145.75	143.63	141.76	140.12	138.66	137.37	132.75	130.11	128.56
16000	172.92	168.35	164.41	161.01	158.05	155.47	153.21	151.21	149.46	147.90	146.53	141.60	138.78	137.13
17000	183.73	178.87	174.69	171.07	167.93	165.19	162.78	160.67	158.80	157.15	155.68	150.45	147.45	145.70
18000	194.54	189.39	184.96	181.14	177.81	174.90	172.36	170.12	168.14	166.39	164.84	159.30	156.13	154.27
19000	205.34	199.91	195.24	191.20	187.69	184.62	181.93	179.57	177.48	175.64	174.00	168.15	164.80	162.84
20000	216.15	210.43	205.51	201.26	197.56	194.34	191.51	189.02	186.82	184.88	183.16	177.00	173.47	171.41
21000	226.96	220.95	215.79	211.32	207.44	204.05	201.08	198.47	196.16	194.12	192.31	185.85	182.15	179.98
22000	237.77	231.47	226.07	221.39	217.32	213.77	210.66	207.92	205.50	203.37	201.47	194.70	190.82	188.55
23000	248.57	242.00	236.34	231.45	227.20	223.49	220.23	217.37	214.84	212.61	210.63	203.55	199.49	197.12
24000	259.38	252.52	246.62	241.51	237.08	233.20	229.81	226.82	224.18	221.85	219.79	212.40	208.17	205.69
25000	270.19	263.04	256.89	251.58	246.95	242.92	239.38	236.27	233.53	231.10	228.94	221.25	216.84	214.26
26000	281.00	273.56	267.17	261.64	256.83	252.64	248.96	245.72	242.87	240.34	238.10	230.10	225.51	222.83
27000	291.80	284.08	277.44	271.70	266.71	262.35	258.53	255.17	252.21	249.58	247.26	238.95	234.19	231.40
28000	302.61	294.60	287.72	281.76	276.59	272.07	268.11	264.62	261.55	258.83	256.42	247.80	242.86	239.97
29000	313.42	305.12	297.99	291.83	286.47	281.79	277.68	274.07	270.89	268.07	265.58	256.65	251.53	248.54
30000	324.22	315.65	308.27	301.89	296.34	291.50	287.26	283.52	280.23	277.32	274.73	265.50	260.21	257.11
31000	335.03	326.17	318.55	311.95	306.22	301.22	296.83	292.97	289.57	286.56	283.89	274.35	268.88	265.68
32000	345.84	336.69	328.82	322.02	316.10	310.94	306.41	302.42	298.91	295.80	293.05	283.20	277.55	274.25
33000	356.65	347.21	339.10	332.08	325.98	320.65	315.98	311.88	308.25	305.05	302.21	292.05	286.23	282.82
34000	367.45	357.73	349.37	342.14	335.86	330.37	325.56	321.33	317.59	314.29	311.36	300.89	294.90	291.39
35000	378.26	368.25	359.65	352.20	345.73	340.08	335.13	330.78	326.93	323.53	320.52	309.74	303.57	299.96
36000	389.07	378.77	369.92	362.27	355.61	349.80	344.71	340.23	336.27	332.78	329.68	318.59	312.25	308.53
37000	399.88	389.30	380.20	372.33	365.49	359.52	354.28	349.68	345.62	342.02	338.84	327.44	320.92	317.10
38000	410.68	399.82	390.47	382.39	375.37	369.23	363.86	359.13	354.96	351.27	347.99	336.29	329.59	325.67
39000	421.49	410.34	400.75	392.46	385.25	378.95	373.43	368.58	364.30	360.51	357.15	345.14	338.27	334.24
40000	432.30	420.86	411.02	402.52	395.12	388.67	383.01	378.03	373.64	369.75	366.31	353.99	346.94	342.81
41000	443.10	431.38	421.30	412.58	405.00	398.38	392.58	387.48	382.98	379.00	375.47	362.84	355.61	351.38
42000	453.91	441.90	431.58	422.64	414.88	408.10	402.16	396.93	392.32	388.24	384.62	371.69	364.29	359.95
43000	464.72	452.42	441.85	432.71	424.76	417.82	411.73	406.38	401.66	397.48	393.78	380.54	372.96	368.52
44000	475.53	462.94	452.13	442.77	434.64	427.53	421.31	415.83	411.00	406.73	402.94	389.39	381.63	377.09
45000	486.33	473.47	462.40	452.83	444.51	437.25	430.88	425.28	420.34	415.97	412.10	398.24	390.31	385.66
46000	497.14	483.99	472.68	462.90	454.39	446.97	440.46	434.73	429.68	425.22	421.25	407.09	398.98	394.23
47000	507.95	494.51	482.95	472.96	464.27	456.68	450.03	444.18	439.02	434.46	430.41	415.94	407.65	402.80
48000	518.76	505.03	493.23	483.02	474.15	466.40	459.61	453.63	448.36	443.70	439.57	424.79	416.33	411.37
49000	529.56	515.55	503.50	493.08	484.03	476.12	469.18	463.08	457.70	452.95	448.73	433.64	425.00	419.94
50000	540.37	526.07	513.78	503.15	493.90	485.83	478.76	472.54	467.05	462.19	457.88	442.49	433.67	428.51
55000	594.41	578.68	565.16	553.46	543.29	534.42	526.63	519.79	513.75	508.41	503.67	486.74	477.04	471.36
60000	648.44	631.29	616.53	603.78	592.68	583.00	574.51	567.04	560.45	554.63	549.46	530.99	520.41	514.21
65000	702.48	683.89	667.91	654.09	642.07	631.58	622.38	614.29	607.16	600.85	595.25	575.24	563.77	557.06
70000	756.52	736.50	719.29	704.40	691.46	680.16	670.26	661.55	653.86	647.06	641.04	619.48	607.14	599.91
75000	810.55	789.11	770.67	754.72	740.85	728.75	718.13	708.80	700.57	693.28	686.82	663.73	650.51	642.76
80000	864.59	841.71	822.04	805.03	790.24	777.33	766.01	756.05	747.27	739.50	732.61	707.98	693.87	685.61
85000	918.63	894.32	873.42	855.35	839.63	825.91	813.89	803.31	793.97	785.72	778.40	752.23	737.24	728.46
90000	972.66	946.93	924.80	905.66	889.02	874.50	861.76	850.56	840.68	831.94	824.19	796.48	780.61	771.31
95000	1026.70	999.53	976.18	955.98	938.41	923.08	909.64	897.81	887.38	878.16	869.98	840.73	823.97	814.16
100000	1080.74	1052.14	1027.55	1006.29	987.80	971.66	957.51	945.07	934.09	924.37	915.76	884.98	867.34	857.01

MONTHLY PAYMENT
REQUIRED TO AMORTIZE A LOAN

10.125%

TERM AMOUNT	1 Year	2 Years	3 Years	4 Years	5 Years	6 Years	7 Years	8 Years	9 Years	10 Years	11 Years	12 Years	13 Years	14 Years
5	.44	.24	.17	.13	.11	.10	.09	.08	.08	.07	.07	.07	.06	.06
10	.88	.47	.33	.26	.22	.19	.17	.16	.15	.14	.13	.13	.12	.12
15	1.32	.70	.49	.39	.32	.28	.25	.23	.22	.20	.19	.19	.18	.17
25	2.20	1.16	.81	.64	.54	.47	.42	.39	.36	.34	.32	.31	.29	.28
50	4.40	2.32	1.62	1.28	1.07	.93	.84	.77	.71	.67	.63	.61	.58	.56
75	6.60	3.47	2.43	1.91	1.60	1.40	1.25	1.15	1.07	1.00	.95	.91	.87	.84
100	8.80	4.63	3.24	2.55	2.14	1.86	1.67	1.53	1.42	1.33	1.26	1.21	1.16	1.12
200	17.60	9.25	6.47	5.09	4.27	3.72	3.34	3.05	2.83	2.66	2.52	2.41	2.32	2.24
300	26.40	13.87	9.70	7.63	6.40	5.58	5.00	4.58	4.25	3.99	3.78	3.61	3.47	3.35
600	35.19	18.49	12.94	10.17	8.53	7.44	6.67	6.10	5.66	5.32	5.04	4.81	4.63	4.47
500	43.99	23.11	16.17	12.72	10.66	9.30	8.34	7.63	7.08	6.65	6.30	6.02	5.78	5.58
600	52.79	27.73	19.40	15.26	12.79	11.16	10.00	9.15	8.49	7.98	7.56	7.22	6.94	6.70
700	61.59	32.35	22.63	17.80	14.92	13.02	11.67	10.67	9.91	9.30	8.82	8.42	8.09	7.82
800	70.38	36.97	25.87	20.34	17.05	14.88	13.34	12.20	11.32	10.63	10.08	9.62	9.25	8.93
900	79.18	41.59	29.10	22.89	19.18	16.74	15.00	13.72	12.74	11.96	11.34	10.83	10.40	10.05
1000	87.98	46.21	32.33	25.43	21.31	18.59	16.67	15.25	14.15	13.29	12.60	12.03	11.56	11.16
2000	175.95	92.41	64.66	50.85	42.62	37.18	33.34	30.49	28.30	26.57	25.19	24.05	23.11	22.32
3000	263.93	138.61	96.98	76.27	63.93	55.77	50.00	45.73	42.44	39.86	37.78	36.07	34.66	33.48
4000	351.90	184.82	129.31	101.70	85.24	74.36	66.67	60.97	56.59	53.14	50.37	48.10	46.21	44.63
5000	439.88	231.02	161.63	127.12	106.55	92.95	83.33	76.21	70.74	66.43	62.96	60.12	57.77	55.79
6000	527.85	277.22	193.96	152.54	127.86	111.54	100.00	91.45	84.88	79.71	75.55	72.14	69.32	66.95
7000	615.82	323.42	226.29	177.96	149.17	130.13	116.67	106.69	99.03	93.00	88.14	84.17	80.87	78.11
8000	703.80	369.63	258.61	203.39	170.47	148.72	133.33	121.93	113.18	106.28	100.73	96.19	92.42	89.26
9000	791.77	415.83	290.94	228.81	191.78	167.31	150.00	137.17	127.32	119.56	113.32	108.21	103.98	100.42
10000	879.75	462.03	323.26	254.23	213.09	185.89	166.66	152.41	141.47	132.85	125.91	120.24	115.53	111.58
11000	967.72	508.23	355.59	279.65	234.40	204.48	183.33	167.65	155.62	146.13	138.50	132.26	127.08	122.73
12000	1055.69	554.44	387.92	305.08	255.71	223.07	200.00	182.89	169.76	159.42	151.09	144.28	138.63	133.89
13000	1143.67	600.64	420.24	330.50	277.02	241.66	216.66	198.13	183.91	172.70	163.68	156.31	150.18	145.05
14000	1231.64	646.84	452.57	355.92	298.33	260.25	233.33	213.37	198.06	185.99	176.27	168.33	161.74	156.21
15000	1319.62	693.04	484.89	381.34	319.63	278.84	249.99	228.61	212.20	199.27	188.87	180.35	173.29	167.36
16000	1407.59	739.25	517.22	406.77	340.94	297.43	266.66	243.85	226.35	212.56	201.46	192.37	184.84	178.52
17000	1495.56	785.45	549.55	432.19	362.25	316.02	283.32	259.09	240.49	225.84	214.05	204.40	196.39	189.68
18000	1583.54	831.65	581.87	457.61	383.56	334.61	299.99	274.33	254.64	239.12	226.64	216.42	207.95	200.84
19000	1671.51	877.86	614.20	483.04	404.87	353.19	316.66	289.57	268.79	252.41	239.23	228.44	219.50	211.99
20000	1759.49	924.06	646.52	508.46	426.18	371.78	333.32	304.81	282.93	265.69	251.82	240.47	231.05	223.15
21000	1847.46	970.26	678.85	533.88	447.49	390.37	349.99	320.05	297.08	278.98	264.41	252.49	242.60	234.31
22000	1935.43	1016.46	711.17	559.30	468.79	408.96	366.65	335.29	311.23	292.26	277.00	264.51	254.15	245.46
23000	2023.41	1062.67	743.50	584.73	490.10	427.55	383.32	350.53	325.37	305.55	289.59	276.54	265.71	256.62
24000	2111.38	1108.87	775.83	610.15	511.41	446.14	399.99	365.77	339.52	318.83	302.18	288.56	277.26	267.78
25000	2199.36	1155.07	808.15	635.57	532.72	464.73	416.65	381.01	353.67	332.11	314.77	300.58	288.81	278.94
26000	2287.33	1201.27	840.48	660.99	554.03	483.32	433.32	396.26	367.81	345.40	327.36	312.61	300.36	290.09
27000	2375.30	1247.48	872.80	686.42	575.34	501.91	449.98	411.50	381.96	358.68	339.95	324.63	311.92	301.25
28000	2463.28	1293.68	905.13	711.84	596.65	520.50	466.65	426.74	396.11	371.97	352.54	336.65	323.47	312.41
29000	2551.25	1339.88	937.46	737.26	617.95	539.08	483.31	441.98	410.25	385.25	365.14	348.68	335.02	323.56
30000	2639.23	1386.08	969.78	762.68	639.26	557.67	499.98	457.22	424.40	398.54	377.73	360.70	346.57	334.72
31000	2727.20	1432.29	1002.11	788.11	660.57	576.26	516.65	472.46	438.55	411.82	390.32	372.72	358.13	345.88
32000	2815.17	1478.49	1034.43	813.53	681.88	594.85	533.31	487.70	452.69	425.11	402.91	384.74	369.68	357.04
33000	2903.15	1524.69	1066.76	838.95	703.19	613.44	549.98	502.94	466.84	438.39	415.50	396.77	381.23	368.19
34000	2991.12	1570.89	1099.09	864.38	724.50	632.03	566.64	518.18	480.98	451.67	428.09	408.79	392.78	379.35
35000	3079.10	1617.10	1131.41	889.80	745.81	650.62	583.31	533.42	495.13	464.96	440.68	420.81	404.33	390.51
36000	3167.07	1663.30	1163.74	915.22	767.11	669.21	599.98	548.66	509.28	478.24	453.27	432.84	415.89	401.67
37000	3255.04	1709.50	1196.06	940.64	788.42	687.80	616.64	563.90	523.42	491.53	465.86	444.86	427.44	412.82
38000	3343.02	1755.71	1228.39	966.07	809.73	706.38	633.31	579.14	537.57	504.81	478.45	456.88	438.99	423.98
39000	3430.99	1801.91	1260.72	991.49	831.04	724.97	649.97	594.38	551.72	518.10	491.04	468.91	450.54	435.14
40000	3518.97	1848.11	1293.04	1016.91	852.35	743.56	666.64	609.62	565.86	531.38	503.63	480.93	462.10	446.29
41000	3606.94	1894.31	1325.37	1042.33	873.66	762.15	683.30	624.86	580.01	544.66	516.22	492.95	473.65	457.45
42000	3694.91	1940.52	1357.69	1067.76	894.97	780.74	699.97	640.10	594.16	557.95	528.81	504.98	485.20	468.61
43000	3782.89	1986.72	1390.02	1093.18	916.27	799.33	716.64	655.34	608.30	571.23	541.41	517.00	496.75	479.77
44000	3870.86	2032.92	1422.34	1118.60	937.58	817.92	733.30	670.58	622.45	584.52	554.00	529.02	508.30	490.92
45000	3958.84	2079.12	1454.67	1144.02	958.89	836.51	749.97	685.82	636.60	597.80	566.59	541.04	519.86	502.08
46000	4046.81	2125.33	1487.00	1169.45	980.20	855.10	766.63	701.06	650.74	611.09	579.18	553.07	531.41	513.24
47000	4134.78	2171.53	1519.32	1194.87	1001.51	873.68	783.30	716.30	664.89	624.37	591.77	565.09	542.96	524.40
48000	4222.76	2217.73	1551.65	1220.29	1022.82	892.27	799.97	731.54	679.04	637.66	604.36	577.11	554.51	535.55
49000	4310.73	2263.93	1583.97	1245.72	1044.13	910.86	816.63	746.78	693.18	650.94	616.95	589.14	566.07	546.71
50000	4398.71	2310.14	1616.30	1271.14	1065.44	929.45	833.30	762.02	707.33	664.22	629.54	601.16	577.62	557.87
55000	4838.58	2541.15	1777.93	1398.25	1171.98	1022.40	916.63	838.23	778.06	730.65	692.49	661.28	635.38	613.65
60000	5278.45	2772.16	1939.56	1525.36	1278.52	1115.34	999.96	914.43	848.79	797.07	755.45	721.39	693.14	669.44
65000	5718.32	3003.18	2101.19	1652.48	1385.06	1208.29	1083.28	990.63	919.53	863.49	818.40	781.51	750.90	725.23
70000	6158.19	3234.19	2262.82	1779.59	1491.61	1301.23	1166.61	1066.83	990.26	929.91	881.35	841.62	808.66	781.01
75000	6598.06	3465.20	2424.45	1906.70	1598.15	1394.18	1249.94	1143.03	1060.99	996.33	944.31	901.74	866.42	836.80
80000	7037.93	3696.22	2586.08	2033.82	1704.69	1487.12	1333.27	1219.24	1131.72	1062.76	1007.26	961.85	924.19	892.58
85000	7477.80	3927.23	2747.71	2160.93	1811.24	1580.06	1416.60	1295.44	1202.45	1129.18	1070.22	1021.97	981.95	948.37
90000	7917.67	4158.24	2909.34	2288.04	1917.78	1673.01	1499.93	1371.64	1273.19	1195.60	1133.17	1082.08	1039.71	1004.16
95000	8357.54	4389.26	3070.97	2415.16	2024.32	1765.95	1583.26	1447.84	1343.92	1262.02	1196.12	1142.20	1097.47	1059.94
100000	8797.41	4620.27	3232.60	2542.27	2130.87	1858.90	1666.59	1524.04	1414.65	1328.44	1259.08	1202.32	1155.23	1115.73

TERM	15 Years	16 Years	17 Years	18 Years	19 Years	20 Years	21 Years	22 Years	23 Years	24 Years	25 Years	30 Years	35 Years	40 Years
AMOUNT
5	.06	.06	.06	.06	.05	.05	.05	.05	.05	.05	.05	.05	.05	.05
10	.11	.11	.11	.11	.10	.10	.10	.10	.10	.10	.10	.09	.09	.09
15	.17	.16	.16	.16	.15	.15	.15	.15	.15	.14	.14	.14	.14	.13
25	.28	.27	.26	.26	.25	.25	.24	.24	.24	.24	.23	.23	.22	.22
50	.55	.53	.52	.51	.50	.49	.48	.48	.47	.47	.46	.45	.44	.43
75	.82	.80	.78	.76	.75	.73	.72	.72	.71	.70	.69	.67	.66	.65
100	1.09	1.06	1.03	1.01	.99	.98	.96	.95	.94	.93	.92	.89	.87	.86
200	2.17	2.11	2.06	2.02	1.98	1.95	1.92	1.90	1.88	1.86	1.84	1.78	1.74	1.72
300	3.25	3.17	3.09	3.03	2.97	2.92	2.88	2.85	2.81	2.78	2.76	2.67	2.61	2.58
400	4.33	4.22	4.12	4.04	3.96	3.90	3.84	3.79	3.75	3.71	3.68	3.55	3.48	3.44
500	5.42	5.27	5.15	5.04	4.95	4.87	4.80	4.74	4.68	4.64	4.59	4.44	4.35	4.30
600	6.50	6.33	6.18	6.05	5.94	5.84	5.76	5.69	5.62	5.56	5.51	5.33	5.22	5.16
700	7.58	7.38	7.21	7.06	6.93	6.82	6.72	6.63	6.56	6.49	6.43	6.21	6.09	6.02
800	8.66	8.43	8.24	8.07	7.92	7.79	7.68	7.58	7.49	7.41	7.35	7.10	6.96	6.88
900	9.75	9.49	9.27	9.08	8.91	8.76	8.64	8.53	8.43	8.34	8.26	7.99	7.83	7.74
1000	10.83	10.54	10.30	10.08	9.90	9.74	9.60	9.47	9.36	9.27	9.18	8.87	8.70	8.59
2000	21.65	21.08	20.59	20.16	19.79	19.47	19.19	18.94	18.72	18.53	18.36	17.74	17.39	17.18
3000	32.47	31.62	30.88	30.24	29.69	29.20	28.78	28.41	28.08	27.79	27.53	26.61	26.08	25.77
4000	43.30	42.15	41.17	40.32	39.58	38.94	38.37	37.88	37.44	37.05	36.71	35.48	34.78	34.36
5000	54.12	52.69	51.46	50.40	49.48	48.67	47.96	47.34	46.80	46.31	45.88	44.35	43.47	42.95
6000	64.94	63.23	61.75	60.48	59.37	58.40	57.56	56.81	56.15	55.57	55.06	53.21	52.16	51.54
7000	75.76	73.76	72.04	70.56	69.27	68.14	67.15	66.28	65.51	64.83	64.23	62.08	60.85	60.13
8000	86.59	84.30	82.34	80.64	79.16	77.87	76.74	75.75	74.87	74.09	73.41	70.95	69.55	68.72
9000	97.41	94.84	92.63	90.72	89.05	87.60	86.33	85.21	84.23	83.36	82.58	79.82	78.24	77.31
10000	108.23	105.37	102.92	100.79	98.95	97.34	95.92	94.68	93.59	92.62	91.76	88.69	86.93	85.90
11000	119.05	115.91	113.21	110.87	108.84	107.07	105.52	104.15	102.94	101.88	100.93	97.56	95.62	94.49
12000	129.88	126.45	123.50	120.95	118.74	116.80	115.11	113.62	112.30	111.14	110.11	106.42	104.32	103.08
13000	140.70	136.99	133.79	131.03	128.63	126.54	124.70	123.08	121.66	120.40	119.20	115.29	113.01	111.67
14000	151.52	147.52	144.08	141.11	138.53	136.27	134.29	132.55	131.02	129.66	128.46	124.16	121.70	120.26
15000	162.34	158.06	154.38	151.19	148.42	146.00	143.88	142.02	140.38	138.92	137.63	133.03	130.39	128.85
16000	173.17	168.60	164.67	161.27	158.31	155.74	153.48	151.49	149.73	148.18	146.81	141.90	139.09	137.44
17000	183.99	179.13	174.96	171.35	168.21	165.47	163.07	160.96	159.09	157.45	155.98	150.76	147.70	146.03
18000	194.81	189.67	185.25	181.43	178.10	175.20	172.66	170.42	168.45	166.71	165.16	159.63	156.47	154.62
19000	205.64	200.21	195.54	191.51	188.00	184.94	182.25	179.89	177.81	175.97	174.34	168.50	165.16	163.21
20000	216.46	210.74	205.83	201.58	197.89	194.67	191.84	189.36	187.17	185.23	183.51	177.37	173.86	171.80
21000	227.28	221.28	216.12	211.66	207.79	204.40	201.44	198.83	196.52	194.49	192.69	186.24	182.55	180.39
22000	238.10	231.82	226.42	221.74	217.68	214.13	211.03	208.29	205.88	203.75	201.86	195.11	191.24	188.98
23000	248.93	242.36	236.71	231.82	227.58	223.87	220.62	217.76	215.24	213.01	211.04	203.97	199.93	197.57
24000	259.75	252.89	247.00	241.90	237.47	233.60	230.21	227.23	224.60	222.27	220.21	212.84	208.63	206.16
25000	270.57	263.43	257.29	251.98	247.36	243.33	239.80	236.70	233.96	231.53	229.39	221.71	217.32	214.75
26000	281.39	273.97	267.58	262.06	257.26	253.07	249.39	246.16	243.32	240.80	238.56	230.58	226.01	223.34
27000	292.22	284.50	277.87	272.14	267.15	262.80	258.99	255.63	252.67	250.06	247.74	239.45	234.70	231.93
28000	303.04	295.04	288.16	282.22	277.05	272.53	268.58	265.10	262.03	259.32	256.91	248.32	243.40	240.52
29000	313.86	305.58	298.45	292.30	286.94	282.27	278.17	274.57	271.39	268.58	266.09	257.18	252.09	249.11
30000	324.68	316.11	308.75	302.37	296.84	292.00	287.76	284.04	280.75	277.84	275.26	266.05	260.78	257.70
31000	335.51	326.65	319.04	312.45	306.73	301.73	297.35	293.50	290.11	287.10	284.44	274.92	269.47	266.29
32000	346.33	337.19	329.33	322.53	316.62	311.47	306.95	302.97	299.46	296.36	293.61	283.79	278.17	274.88
33000	357.15	347.73	339.62	332.61	326.52	321.20	316.54	312.44	308.82	305.62	302.79	292.66	286.86	283.47
34000	367.98	358.26	349.91	342.69	336.41	330.93	326.13	321.91	318.18	314.89	311.96	301.52	295.55	292.06
35000	378.80	368.80	360.20	352.77	346.31	340.67	335.72	331.37	327.54	324.15	321.14	310.39	304.24	300.65
36000	389.62	379.34	370.49	362.85	356.20	350.40	345.31	340.84	336.90	333.41	330.31	319.26	312.94	309.23
37000	400.44	389.87	380.79	372.93	366.10	360.13	354.91	350.31	346.25	342.67	339.49	328.13	321.63	317.82
38000	411.27	400.41	391.08	383.01	375.99	369.87	364.50	359.78	355.61	351.93	348.67	337.00	330.32	326.41
39000	422.09	410.95	401.37	393.09	385.89	379.60	374.09	369.24	364.97	361.19	357.84	345.87	339.01	335.00
40000	432.91	421.48	411.66	403.16	395.78	389.33	383.68	378.71	374.33	370.45	367.02	354.73	347.71	343.59
41000	443.73	432.02	421.95	413.24	405.67	399.07	393.27	388.18	383.69	379.71	376.19	363.60	356.40	352.18
42000	454.56	442.56	432.24	423.32	415.57	408.80	402.87	397.65	393.04	388.97	385.37	372.47	365.09	360.77
43000	465.38	453.09	442.53	433.40	425.46	418.53	412.46	407.11	402.40	398.24	394.54	381.34	373.78	369.36
44000	476.20	463.63	452.83	443.48	435.36	428.26	422.05	416.58	411.76	407.50	403.72	390.21	382.48	377.95
45000	487.02	474.17	463.12	453.56	445.25	438.00	431.64	426.05	421.12	416.76	412.89	399.08	391.17	386.54
46000	497.85	484.71	473.41	463.64	455.15	447.73	441.23	435.52	430.48	426.02	422.07	407.94	399.86	395.13
47000	508.67	495.24	483.70	473.72	465.04	457.46	450.82	444.99	439.84	435.28	431.24	416.81	408.55	403.72
48000	519.49	505.78	493.99	483.80	474.93	467.20	460.42	454.45	449.19	444.54	440.42	425.68	417.25	412.31
49000	530.31	516.32	504.28	493.87	484.83	476.93	470.01	463.92	458.55	453.80	449.59	434.55	425.94	420.90
50000	541.14	526.85	514.57	503.95	494.72	486.66	479.60	473.39	467.91	463.06	458.77	443.42	434.63	429.49
55000	595.25	579.54	566.03	554.35	544.19	535.33	527.56	520.73	514.70	509.37	504.65	487.76	478.09	472.44
60000	649.36	632.22	617.49	604.74	593.67	584.00	575.52	568.07	561.49	555.68	550.52	532.10	521.56	515.39
65000	703.48	684.91	668.94	655.14	643.14	632.66	623.48	615.40	608.28	601.98	596.40	576.44	565.02	558.34
70000	757.59	737.59	720.40	705.53	692.61	681.33	671.44	662.74	655.07	648.29	642.27	620.78	608.48	601.29
75000	811.70	790.28	771.86	755.93	742.08	729.99	719.40	710.08	701.86	694.59	688.15	665.12	651.94	644.23
80000	865.82	842.96	823.31	806.32	791.55	778.66	767.36	757.42	748.65	740.90	734.03	709.46	695.41	687.18
85000	919.93	895.65	874.77	856.72	841.03	827.33	815.32	804.76	795.44	787.21	779.90	753.80	738.87	730.13
90000	974.04	948.33	926.23	907.11	890.50	875.99	863.28	852.10	842.23	833.51	825.78	798.15	782.33	773.08
95000	1028.16	1001.02	977.69	957.51	939.97	924.66	911.24	899.43	889.02	879.82	871.66	842.49	825.79	816.03
100000	1082.27	1053.70	1029.14	1007.90	989.44	973.32	959.20	946.77	935.81	926.12	917.53	886.83	869.26	858.98

MONTHLY PAYMENT
REQUIRED TO AMORTIZE A LOAN

TERM / AMOUNT	1 Year	2 Years	3 Years	4 Years	5 Years	6 Years	7 Years	8 Years	9 Years	10 Years	11 Years	12 Years	13 Years	14 Years
5	.45	.24	.17	.13	.11	.10	.09	.08	.08	.07	.07	.07	.06	.06
10	.89	.47	.33	.26	.22	.19	.17	.16	.15	.14	.13	.13	.12	.12
15	1.33	.70	.49	.39	.33	.28	.26	.23	.22	.20	.19	.19	.18	.17
25	2.21	1.16	.81	.64	.54	.47	.42	.39	.36	.34	.32	.31	.29	.29
50	4.41	2.32	1.62	1.28	1.07	.94	.84	.77	.71	.67	.64	.61	.58	.57
75	6.61	3.47	2.43	1.91	1.61	1.40	1.26	1.15	1.07	1.00	.95	.91	.87	.85
100	8.81	4.63	3.24	2.55	2.14	1.87	1.68	1.53	1.42	1.34	1.27	1.21	1.16	1.13
200	17.61	9.25	6.48	5.10	4.27	3.73	3.35	3.06	2.84	2.67	2.53	2.42	2.32	2.25
300	26.41	13.88	9.71	7.64	6.41	5.59	5.02	4.59	4.26	4.00	3.79	3.62	3.48	3.37
400	35.21	18.50	12.95	10.19	8.54	7.46	6.69	6.12	5.68	5.34	5.06	4.83	4.64	4.49
500	44.01	23.12	16.19	12.73	10.68	9.32	8.36	7.65	7.10	6.67	6.32	6.04	5.80	5.61
600	52.81	27.75	19.42	15.28	12.81	11.18	10.03	9.17	8.52	8.00	7.58	7.24	6.96	6.73
700	61.61	32.37	22.66	17.83	14.95	13.04	11.70	10.70	9.94	9.33	8.85	8.45	8.12	7.85
800	70.41	36.99	25.89	20.37	17.08	14.91	13.37	12.23	11.35	10.67	10.11	9.66	9.28	8.97
900	79.21	41.62	29.13	22.92	19.22	16.77	15.04	13.76	12.77	12.00	11.37	10.86	10.44	10.09
1000	88.01	46.24	32.37	25.46	21.35	18.63	16.71	15.29	14.19	13.33	12.64	12.07	11.60	11.21
2000	176.02	92.48	64.73	50.92	42.70	37.26	33.41	30.57	28.38	26.66	25.27	24.14	23.20	22.41
3000	264.03	138.72	97.09	76.38	64.04	55.89	50.12	45.85	42.57	39.98	37.90	36.20	34.79	33.61
4000	352.04	184.95	129.45	101.84	85.39	74.51	66.82	61.13	56.75	53.31	50.54	48.27	46.39	44.81
5000	440.05	231.19	161.81	127.30	106.73	93.14	83.53	76.41	70.94	66.64	63.17	60.34	57.99	56.02
6000	528.06	277.43	194.17	152.76	128.08	111.77	100.23	91.69	85.13	79.96	75.80	72.40	69.58	67.22
7000	616.07	323.67	226.53	178.22	149.42	130.39	116.94	106.97	99.32	93.29	88.44	84.47	81.18	78.42
8000	704.08	369.90	258.89	203.67	170.77	149.02	133.64	122.25	113.50	106.61	101.07	96.54	92.78	89.62
9000	792.09	416.14	291.26	229.13	192.12	167.65	150.35	137.53	127.69	119.94	113.70	108.60	104.37	100.83
10000	880.09	462.38	323.62	254.59	213.46	186.27	167.05	152.81	141.88	133.27	126.34	120.67	115.97	112.03
11000	968.10	508.62	355.98	280.05	234.81	204.90	183.76	168.09	156.06	146.59	138.97	132.74	127.57	123.23
12000	1056.11	554.85	388.34	305.51	256.15	223.53	200.46	183.37	170.25	159.92	151.60	144.80	139.16	134.43
13000	1144.12	601.09	420.70	330.97	277.50	242.15	217.17	198.65	184.44	173.24	164.24	156.87	150.76	145.64
14000	1232.13	647.33	453.06	356.43	298.84	260.78	233.87	213.93	198.63	186.57	176.87	168.94	162.36	156.84
15000	1320.14	693.56	485.42	381.89	320.19	279.41	250.58	229.21	212.81	199.90	189.50	181.00	173.95	168.04
16000	1408.15	739.80	517.78	407.34	341.53	298.03	267.28	244.49	227.00	213.22	202.14	193.07	185.55	179.24
17000	1496.16	786.04	550.14	432.80	362.88	316.66	283.99	259.77	241.19	226.55	214.77	205.14	197.15	190.45
18000	1584.17	832.28	582.51	458.26	384.23	335.29	300.69	275.05	255.37	239.87	227.40	217.20	208.74	201.65
19000	1672.17	878.51	614.87	483.72	405.57	353.92	317.39	290.33	269.56	253.20	240.04	229.27	220.34	212.85
20000	1760.18	924.75	647.23	509.18	426.92	372.54	334.10	305.61	283.75	266.53	252.67	241.34	231.94	224.05
21000	1848.19	970.99	679.59	534.64	448.26	391.17	350.80	320.89	297.94	279.85	265.30	253.40	243.53	235.26
22000	1936.20	1017.23	711.95	560.10	469.61	409.80	367.51	336.17	312.12	293.18	277.94	265.47	255.13	246.46
23000	2024.21	1063.46	744.31	585.56	490.95	428.42	384.21	351.45	326.31	306.50	290.57	277.54	266.73	257.66
24000	2112.22	1109.70	776.67	611.01	512.30	447.05	400.92	366.73	340.50	319.83	303.20	289.60	278.32	268.86
25000	2200.23	1155.94	809.03	636.47	533.64	465.68	417.62	382.01	354.69	333.16	315.84	301.67	289.92	280.07
26000	2288.24	1202.17	841.40	661.93	554.99	484.30	434.33	397.29	368.87	346.48	328.47	313.74	301.52	291.27
27000	2376.25	1248.41	873.76	687.39	576.34	502.93	451.03	412.57	383.06	359.81	341.10	325.80	313.11	302.47
28000	2464.26	1294.65	906.12	712.85	597.68	521.56	467.74	427.85	397.25	373.14	353.74	337.87	324.71	313.67
29000	2552.26	1340.89	938.48	738.31	619.03	540.18	484.44	443.13	411.43	386.46	366.37	349.94	336.31	324.88
30000	2640.27	1387.12	970.84	763.77	640.37	558.81	501.15	458.41	425.62	399.79	379.00	362.00	347.90	336.08
31000	2728.28	1433.36	1003.20	789.23	661.72	577.44	517.85	473.69	439.81	413.11	391.64	374.07	359.50	347.28
32000	2816.29	1479.60	1035.56	814.68	683.06	596.06	534.56	488.97	454.00	426.44	404.27	386.14	371.10	358.48
33000	2904.30	1525.84	1067.92	840.14	704.41	614.69	551.26	504.25	468.18	439.77	416.90	398.20	382.69	369.69
34000	2992.31	1572.07	1100.28	865.60	725.75	633.32	567.97	519.53	482.37	453.09	429.54	410.27	394.29	380.89
35000	3080.32	1618.31	1132.65	891.06	747.10	651.94	584.67	534.81	496.56	466.42	442.17	422.34	405.89	392.09
36000	3168.33	1664.55	1165.01	916.52	768.45	670.57	601.37	550.09	510.74	479.74	454.80	434.40	417.48	403.29
37000	3256.34	1710.78	1197.37	941.98	789.79	689.20	618.08	565.37	524.93	493.07	467.44	446.47	429.08	414.50
38000	3344.34	1757.02	1229.73	967.44	811.14	707.83	634.78	580.65	539.12	506.40	480.07	458.54	440.68	425.70
39000	3432.35	1803.26	1262.09	992.90	832.48	726.45	651.49	595.93	553.31	519.72	492.70	470.60	452.27	436.90
40000	3520.36	1849.50	1294.45	1018.35	853.83	745.08	668.19	611.21	567.49	533.05	505.34	482.67	463.87	448.10
41000	3608.37	1895.73	1326.81	1043.81	875.17	763.71	684.90	626.49	581.68	546.37	517.97	494.74	475.47	459.31
42000	3696.38	1941.97	1359.17	1069.27	896.52	782.33	701.60	641.77	595.87	559.70	530.60	506.80	487.06	470.51
43000	3784.39	1988.21	1391.54	1094.73	917.87	800.96	718.31	657.05	610.06	573.03	543.24	518.87	498.66	481.71
44000	3872.40	2034.45	1423.90	1120.19	939.21	819.59	735.01	672.33	624.24	586.35	555.87	530.94	510.26	492.91
45000	3960.41	2080.68	1456.26	1145.65	960.56	838.21	751.72	687.61	638.43	599.68	568.50	543.00	521.85	504.12
46000	4048.42	2126.92	1488.62	1171.11	981.90	856.84	768.42	702.89	652.62	613.00	581.14	555.07	533.45	515.32
47000	4136.42	2173.16	1520.98	1196.57	1003.25	875.47	785.13	718.17	666.80	626.33	593.77	567.14	545.05	526.52
48000	4224.43	2219.39	1553.34	1222.02	1024.59	894.09	801.83	733.45	680.99	639.66	606.40	579.20	556.64	537.72
49000	4312.44	2265.63	1585.70	1247.48	1045.94	912.72	818.54	748.73	695.18	652.98	619.04	591.27	568.24	548.93
50000	4400.45	2311.87	1618.06	1272.94	1067.28	931.35	835.24	764.01	709.37	666.31	631.67	603.34	579.84	560.13
55000	4840.50	2543.06	1779.87	1400.24	1174.01	1024.48	918.76	840.42	780.30	732.94	694.84	663.67	637.82	616.14
60000	5280.54	2774.24	1941.68	1527.53	1280.74	1117.62	1002.29	916.82	851.24	799.57	758.00	724.00	695.80	672.15
65000	5720.59	3005.43	2103.48	1654.82	1387.47	1210.75	1085.81	993.22	922.17	866.20	821.17	784.33	753.79	728.17
70000	6160.63	3236.62	2265.29	1782.12	1494.20	1303.88	1169.33	1069.62	993.11	932.83	884.34	844.67	811.77	784.18
75000	6600.67	3467.80	2427.09	1909.41	1600.92	1397.02	1252.86	1146.02	1064.05	999.46	947.50	905.00	869.75	840.19
80000	7040.72	3698.99	2588.90	2036.70	1707.65	1490.15	1336.38	1222.42	1134.98	1066.09	1010.67	965.33	927.74	896.20
85000	7480.76	3930.17	2750.70	2164.00	1814.38	1583.29	1419.91	1298.82	1205.92	1132.72	1073.84	1025.67	985.72	952.22
90000	7920.81	4161.36	2912.51	2291.29	1921.11	1676.42	1503.43	1375.22	1276.85	1199.35	1137.00	1086.00	1043.70	1008.23
95000	8360.85	4392.55	3074.32	2418.59	2027.84	1769.56	1586.95	1451.62	1347.79	1265.98	1200.17	1146.33	1101.69	1064.24
100000	8800.90	4623.73	3236.12	2545.88	2134.56	1862.69	1670.48	1528.02	1418.73	1332.61	1263.34	1206.67	1159.67	1120.25

TERM	15 Years	16 Years	17 Years	18 Years	19 Years	20 Years	21 Years	22 Years	23 Years	24 Years	25 Years	30 Years	35 Years	40 Years
AMOUNT														
5	.06	.06	.06	.06	.05	.05	.05	.05	.05	.05	.05	.05	.05	.05
10	.11	.11	.11	.11	.10	.10	.10	.10	.10	.10	.10	.09	.09	.09
15	.17	.16	.16	.16	.15	.15	.15	.15	.15	.14	.14	.14	.14	.13
25	.28	.27	.26	.26	.25	.25	.25	.24	.24	.24	.24	.23	.22	.22
50	.55	.53	.52	.51	.50	.49	.49	.48	.48	.47	.47	.45	.44	.44
75	.82	.80	.78	.76	.75	.74	.73	.72	.71	.70	.70	.67	.66	.65
100	1.09	1.06	1.04	1.02	1.00	.98	.97	.96	.95	.94	.93	.90	.88	.87
200	2.18	2.12	2.07	2.03	1.99	1.96	1.93	1.91	1.89	1.87	1.85	1.79	1.76	1.73
300	3.27	3.18	3.11	3.04	2.99	2.94	2.90	2.86	2.83	2.80	2.77	2.68	2.63	2.60
400	4.35	4.24	4.14	4.06	3.98	3.92	3.86	3.81	3.77	3.73	3.70	3.57	3.51	3.46
500	5.44	5.30	5.17	5.07	4.98	4.90	4.83	4.76	4.71	4.66	4.62	4.47	4.38	4.33
600	6.53	6.36	6.21	6.08	5.97	5.87	5.79	5.72	5.65	5.59	5.54	5.36	5.26	5.19
700	7.61	7.41	7.24	7.09	6.97	6.85	6.75	6.67	6.59	6.52	6.46	6.25	6.13	6.06
800	8.70	8.47	8.28	8.11	7.96	7.83	7.72	7.62	7.53	7.46	7.39	7.14	7.01	6.92
900	9.79	9.53	9.31	9.12	8.95	8.81	8.68	8.57	8.47	8.39	8.31	8.04	7.88	7.79
1000	10.87	10.59	10.34	10.13	9.95	9.79	9.65	9.52	9.41	9.32	9.23	8.93	8.76	8.65
2000	21.74	21.17	20.68	20.26	19.89	19.57	19.29	19.04	18.82	18.63	18.46	17.85	17.51	17.30
3000	32.61	31.76	31.02	30.39	29.84	29.35	28.93	28.56	28.23	27.95	27.69	26.78	26.26	25.95
4000	43.48	42.34	41.36	40.51	39.78	39.14	38.58	38.08	37.64	37.26	36.92	35.70	35.01	34.60
5000	54.35	52.92	51.70	50.64	49.72	48.92	48.22	47.60	47.05	46.57	46.15	44.62	43.76	43.25
6000	65.22	63.51	62.04	60.77	59.67	58.70	57.86	57.12	56.46	55.89	55.38	53.55	52.51	51.90
7000	76.09	74.09	72.38	70.90	69.61	68.49	67.50	66.64	65.87	65.20	64.60	62.47	61.26	60.55
8000	86.95	84.68	82.72	81.02	79.55	78.27	77.15	76.16	75.28	74.51	73.83	71.40	70.01	69.20
9000	97.82	95.26	93.06	91.15	89.50	88.05	86.79	85.68	84.69	83.83	83.06	80.32	78.76	77.84
10000	108.69	105.84	103.40	101.28	99.44	97.84	96.43	95.19	94.10	93.14	92.29	89.24	87.51	86.49
11000	119.56	116.43	113.73	111.41	109.38	107.62	106.07	104.71	103.51	102.46	101.52	98.17	96.26	95.14
12000	130.43	127.01	124.07	121.53	119.33	117.40	115.72	114.23	112.92	111.77	110.75	107.09	105.01	103.79
13000	141.30	137.60	134.41	131.66	129.27	127.19	125.36	123.75	122.33	121.08	119.97	116.02	113.76	112.44
14000	152.17	148.18	144.75	141.79	139.21	136.97	135.00	133.27	131.74	130.40	129.20	124.94	122.51	121.09
15000	163.04	158.76	155.09	151.92	149.16	146.75	144.64	142.79	141.15	139.71	138.43	133.86	131.26	129.74
16000	173.90	169.35	165.43	162.04	159.10	156.53	154.29	152.31	150.56	149.02	147.66	142.79	140.01	138.39
17000	184.77	179.93	175.77	172.17	169.05	166.32	163.93	161.83	159.97	158.34	156.89	151.71	140.76	147.03
18000	195.64	190.51	186.11	182.30	178.99	176.10	173.57	171.35	169.38	167.65	166.12	160.63	157.51	155.68
19000	206.51	201.10	196.45	192.43	188.93	185.88	183.21	180.86	178.79	176.97	175.34	169.56	166.26	164.33
20000	217.38	211.68	206.79	202.55	198.88	195.67	192.86	190.38	188.20	186.28	184.57	178.48	175.01	172.98
21000	228.25	222.27	217.13	212.68	208.82	205.45	202.50	199.90	197.61	195.59	193.80	187.41	183.76	181.63
22000	239.12	232.85	227.46	222.81	218.76	215.23	212.14	209.42	207.02	204.91	203.03	196.33	192.51	190.28
23000	249.99	243.43	237.80	232.94	228.71	225.02	221.78	218.94	216.43	214.22	212.26	205.25	201.26	198.93
24000	260.85	254.02	248.14	243.06	238.65	234.80	231.43	228.46	225.84	223.53	221.49	214.18	210.01	207.58
25000	271.72	264.60	258.48	253.19	248.59	244.58	241.07	237.98	235.25	232.85	230.71	223.10	218.76	216.22
26000	282.59	275.19	268.82	263.32	258.54	254.37	250.71	247.50	244.66	242.16	239.94	232.03	227.51	224.87
27000	293.46	285.77	279.16	273.45	268.48	264.15	260.35	257.02	254.07	251.47	249.17	240.95	236.26	233.52
28000	304.33	296.35	289.50	283.57	278.42	273.93	270.00	266.54	263.48	260.79	258.40	249.87	245.01	242.17
29000	315.20	306.94	299.84	293.70	288.37	283.71	279.64	276.05	272.89	270.10	267.63	258.80	253.76	250.82
30000	326.07	317.52	310.18	303.83	298.31	293.50	289.28	285.57	282.30	279.42	276.86	267.72	262.51	259.47
31000	336.94	328.11	320.52	313.96	308.26	303.28	298.92	295.09	291.71	288.73	286.08	276.64	271.26	268.12
32000	347.80	338.69	330.86	324.08	318.20	313.06	308.57	304.61	301.12	298.04	295.31	285.57	280.01	276.77
33000	358.67	349.27	341.19	334.21	328.14	322.85	318.21	314.13	310.53	307.36	304.54	294.49	288.76	285.41
34000	369.54	359.86	351.53	344.34	338.09	332.63	327.85	323.65	319.94	316.67	313.77	303.42	297.51	294.06
35000	380.41	370.44	361.87	354.47	348.03	342.41	337.49	333.17	329.35	325.98	323.00	312.34	306.26	302.71
36000	391.28	381.02	372.21	364.59	357.97	352.20	347.14	342.69	338.76	335.30	332.23	321.26	315.01	311.36
37000	402.15	391.61	382.55	374.72	367.92	361.98	356.78	352.21	348.17	344.61	341.45	330.19	323.76	320.01
38000	413.02	402.19	392.89	384.85	377.86	371.76	366.42	361.72	357.58	353.93	350.68	339.11	332.51	328.66
39000	423.09	412.70	403.23	394.98	387.80	381.55	376.06	371.24	366.99	363.24	359.91	348.04	341.26	337.31
40000	434.75	423.36	413.57	405.10	397.75	391.33	385.71	380.76	376.40	372.55	369.14	356.96	350.01	345.96
41000	445.62	433.94	423.91	415.23	407.69	401.11	395.35	390.28	385.81	381.87	378.37	365.88	358.76	354.60
42000	456.49	444.53	434.25	425.36	417.63	410.90	404.99	399.80	395.22	391.18	387.60	374.81	367.51	363.25
43000	467.36	455.11	444.58	435.48	427.58	420.68	414.63	409.32	404.63	400.49	396.83	383.73	376.26	371.90
44000	478.23	465.70	454.92	445.61	437.52	430.46	424.28	418.84	414.04	409.81	406.05	392.66	385.01	380.55
45000	489.10	476.28	465.26	455.74	447.47	440.24	433.92	428.36	423.45	419.12	415.28	401.58	393.76	389.20
46000	499.97	486.86	475.60	465.87	457.41	450.03	443.56	437.88	432.86	428.44	424.51	410.50	402.51	397.85
47000	510.84	497.45	485.94	475.99	467.35	459.81	453.20	447.40	442.27	437.75	433.74	419.43	411.26	406.50
48000	521.70	508.03	496.28	486.12	477.30	469.59	462.85	456.91	451.68	447.06	442.97	428.35	420.01	415.15
49000	532.57	518.61	506.62	496.25	487.24	479.38	472.49	466.43	461.09	456.38	452.20	437.27	428.76	423.79
50000	543.44	529.20	516.96	506.38	497.18	489.16	482.13	475.95	470.50	465.69	461.42	446.20	437.51	432.44
55000	597.79	582.12	568.65	557.01	546.90	538.08	530.34	523.55	517.55	512.26	507.57	490.82	481.26	475.69
60000	652.13	635.04	620.35	607.65	596.62	586.99	578.56	571.14	564.60	558.83	553.71	535.44	525.01	518.93
65000	706.47	687.96	672.04	658.29	646.34	635.91	626.77	618.74	611.65	605.40	599.85	580.06	568.76	562.18
70000	760.82	740.88	723.74	708.93	696.05	684.82	674.98	666.33	658.70	651.96	645.99	624.68	612.51	605.42
75000	815.16	793.80	775.43	759.56	745.77	733.74	723.19	713.93	705.75	698.53	692.13	669.29	656.26	648.66
80000	869.50	846.71	827.13	810.20	795.49	782.65	771.41	761.52	752.80	745.10	738.27	713.91	700.01	691.91
85000	923.85	899.63	878.83	860.84	845.21	831.57	819.62	809.12	799.85	791.67	784.42	758.53	743.76	735.15
90000	978.19	952.55	930.52	911.47	894.93	880.48	867.83	856.71	846.90	838.24	830.56	803.15	787.52	778.39
95000	1032.53	1005.47	982.22	962.11	944.64	929.40	916.04	904.30	893.95	884.81	876.70	847.77	831.27	821.64
100000	1086.88	1058.39	1033.91	1012.75	994.36	978.31	964.26	951.90	941.00	931.37	922.84	892.39	875.02	864.88

MONTHLY PAYMENT
REQUIRED TO AMORTIZE A LOAN

TERM	1 Year	2 Years	3 Years	4 Years	5 Years	6 Years	7 Years	8 Years	9 Years	10 Years	11 Years	12 Years	13 Years	14 Years
AMOUNT														
5	.45	.24	.17	.13	.11	.10	.09	.08	.08	.07	.07	.07	.06	.06
10	.89	.47	.33	.26	.22	.19	.17	.16	.15	.14	.13	.13	.12	.12
15	1.33	.70	.49	.39	.33	.28	.26	.23	.22	.21	.19	.19	.18	.17
25	2.21	1.16	.81	.64	.54	.47	.42	.39	.36	.34	.32	.31	.30	.29
50	4.41	2.32	1.62	1.28	1.07	.94	.84	.77	.72	.67	.64	.61	.59	.57
75	6.61	3.47	2.43	1.92	1.61	1.40	1.26	1.15	1.07	1.01	.95	.91	.88	.85
100	8.81	4.63	3.24	2.55	2.14	1.87	1.68	1.54	1.43	1.34	1.27	1.21	1.17	1.13
200	17.61	9.26	6.48	5.10	4.28	3.74	3.35	3.07	2.85	2.68	2.54	2.42	2.33	2.25
300	26.41	13.88	9.72	7.65	6.42	5.60	5.02	4.60	4.27	4.01	3.80	3.63	3.49	3.37
400	35.22	18.51	12.96	10.20	8.55	7.47	6.70	6.13	5.69	5.35	5.07	4.84	4.66	4.50
500	44.02	23.14	16.20	12.75	10.69	9.33	8.37	7.66	7.11	6.68	6.34	6.05	5.82	5.62
600	52.82	27.76	19.44	15.29	12.83	11.20	10.04	9.19	8.53	8.02	7.60	7.26	6.98	6.74
700	61.63	32.39	22.67	17.84	14.96	13.06	11.72	10.72	9.96	9.35	8.87	8.47	8.14	7.87
800	70.43	37.01	25.91	20.39	17.10	14.93	13.39	12.25	11.38	10.69	10.13	9.68	9.31	8.99
900	79.23	41.64	29.15	22.94	19.24	16.79	15.06	13.78	12.80	12.02	11.40	10.89	10.47	10.11
1000	88.04	46.27	32.39	25.49	21.38	18.66	16.74	15.31	14.22	13.36	12.67	12.10	11.63	11.24
2000	176.07	92.53	64.77	50.97	42.75	37.31	33.47	30.62	28.43	26.71	25.33	24.20	23.26	22.47
3000	264.10	138.79	97.16	76.45	64.12	55.96	50.20	45.93	42.65	40.07	37.99	36.29	34.88	33.70
4000	352.13	185.05	129.54	101.94	85.49	74.61	66.93	61.23	56.86	53.42	50.65	48.39	46.51	44.94
5000	440.17	231.31	161.93	127.42	106.86	93.27	83.66	76.54	71.08	66.77	63.31	60.48	58.14	56.17
6000	528.20	277.57	194.31	152.90	128.23	111.92	100.39	91.85	85.29	80.13	75.98	72.58	69.76	67.40
7000	616.23	323.83	226.70	178.38	149.60	130.57	117.12	107.15	99.51	93.48	88.64	84.67	81.39	78.63
8000	704.26	370.09	259.08	203.87	170.97	149.22	133.85	122.46	113.72	106.84	101.30	96.77	93.02	89.87
9000	792.29	416.35	291.47	229.35	192.34	167.87	150.58	137.77	127.93	120.19	113.96	108.87	104.64	101.10
10000	880.33	462.61	323.85	254.83	213.71	186.53	167.31	153.07	142.15	133.54	126.62	120.96	116.27	112.33
11000	968.36	508.87	356.24	280.32	235.08	205.18	184.04	168.38	156.36	146.90	139.28	133.06	127.89	123.56
12000	1056.39	555.13	388.62	305.80	256.45	223.83	200.77	183.69	170.58	160.25	151.95	145.15	139.52	134.80
13000	1144.42	601.39	421.01	331.28	277.82	242.48	217.50	198.99	184.79	173.61	164.61	157.25	151.15	146.03
14000	1232.46	647.65	453.39	356.76	299.19	261.14	234.23	214.30	199.01	186.96	177.27	169.34	162.77	157.26
15000	1320.49	693.91	485.78	382.25	320.56	279.79	250.96	229.61	213.22	200.31	189.93	181.44	174.40	168.50
16000	1408.52	740.17	518.16	407.73	341.93	298.44	267.70	244.91	227.44	213.67	202.59	193.54	186.03	179.73
17000	1496.55	786.43	550.54	433.21	363.30	317.09	284.43	260.22	241.65	227.02	215.25	205.63	197.65	190.96
18000	1584.58	832.69	582.93	458.70	384.67	335.74	301.16	275.53	255.86	240.38	227.92	217.73	209.28	202.19
19000	1672.62	878.95	615.31	484.18	406.04	354.40	317.89	290.83	270.08	253.73	240.58	229.82	220.90	213.43
20000	1760.65	925.21	647.70	509.66	427.41	373.05	334.62	306.14	284.29	267.08	253.24	241.92	232.53	224.66
21000	1848.68	971.47	680.08	535.14	448.78	391.70	351.35	321.45	298.51	280.44	265.90	254.01	244.16	235.89
22000	1936.71	1017.73	712.47	560.63	470.15	410.35	368.08	336.75	312.72	293.79	278.56	266.11	255.78	247.12
23000	2024.75	1063.99	744.85	586.11	491.52	429.00	384.81	352.06	326.94	307.14	291.23	278.20	267.41	258.36
24000	2112.78	1110.25	777.24	611.59	512.89	447.66	401.54	367.37	341.15	320.50	303.89	290.30	279.04	269.59
25000	2200.81	1156.52	809.62	637.08	534.26	466.31	418.27	382.67	355.37	333.85	316.55	302.40	290.66	280.82
26000	2288.84	1202.78	842.01	662.56	555.63	484.96	435.00	397.98	369.58	347.21	329.21	314.49	302.29	292.06
27000	2376.87	1249.04	874.39	688.04	577.00	503.61	451.73	413.29	383.79	360.56	341.87	326.59	313.91	303.29
28000	2464.91	1295.30	906.78	713.52	598.37	522.27	468.46	428.59	398.01	373.91	354.53	338.68	325.54	314.52
29000	2552.94	1341.56	939.16	739.01	619.74	540.92	485.19	443.90	412.22	387.27	367.20	350.78	337.17	325.75
30000	2640.97	1387.82	971.55	764.49	641.11	559.57	501.92	459.21	426.44	400.62	379.86	362.87	348.79	336.99
31000	2729.00	1434.08	1003.93	789.97	662.48	578.22	518.65	474.51	440.65	413.98	392.52	374.97	360.42	348.22
32000	2817.04	1480.34	1036.32	815.46	683.85	596.87	535.39	489.82	454.87	427.33	405.18	387.07	372.05	359.45
33000	2905.07	1526.60	1068.70	840.94	705.22	615.53	552.12	505.13	469.08	440.69	417.84	399.16	383.67	370.68
34000	2993.10	1572.86	1101.08	866.42	726.59	634.18	568.85	520.44	483.30	454.04	430.50	411.26	395.30	381.92
35000	3081.13	1619.12	1133.47	891.90	747.96	652.83	585.58	535.74	497.51	467.39	443.17	423.35	406.92	393.15
36000	3169.16	1665.38	1165.85	917.39	769.33	671.48	602.31	551.05	511.72	480.75	455.83	435.45	418.55	404.38
37000	3257.20	1711.64	1198.24	942.87	790.70	690.13	619.04	566.36	525.94	494.10	468.49	447.54	430.18	415.61
38000	3345.23	1757.90	1230.62	968.35	812.08	708.79	635.77	581.66	540.15	507.45	481.15	459.64	441.80	426.85
39000	3433.26	1804.16	1263.01	993.83	833.45	727.44	652.50	596.97	554.37	520.81	493.81	471.74	453.43	438.08
40000	3521.29	1850.42	1295.39	1019.32	854.82	746.09	669.23	612.28	568.58	534.16	506.48	483.83	465.06	449.31
41000	3609.33	1896.68	1327.78	1044.80	876.19	764.74	685.96	627.58	582.80	547.51	519.14	495.93	476.68	460.55
42000	3697.36	1942.94	1360.16	1070.28	897.56	783.40	702.69	642.89	597.01	560.87	531.80	508.02	488.31	471.78
43000	3785.39	1989.20	1392.55	1095.77	918.93	802.05	719.42	658.20	611.23	574.22	544.46	520.12	499.94	483.01
44000	3873.42	2035.46	1424.93	1121.25	940.30	820.70	736.15	673.50	625.44	587.58	557.12	532.21	511.56	494.24
45000	3961.45	2081.72	1457.32	1146.73	961.67	839.35	752.88	688.81	639.65	600.93	569.78	544.31	523.19	505.48
46000	4049.49	2127.98	1489.70	1172.21	983.04	858.00	769.61	704.12	653.87	614.28	582.45	556.40	534.81	516.71
47000	4137.52	2174.24	1522.09	1197.70	1004.41	876.66	786.35	719.42	668.08	627.64	595.11	568.50	546.44	527.94
48000	4225.55	2220.50	1554.47	1223.18	1025.78	895.31	803.08	734.73	682.30	640.99	607.77	580.60	558.07	539.17
49000	4313.58	2266.76	1586.85	1248.66	1047.15	913.96	819.81	750.04	696.51	654.35	620.43	592.69	569.69	550.41
50000	4401.62	2313.02	1619.24	1274.15	1068.52	932.61	836.54	765.34	710.73	667.70	633.09	604.79	581.32	561.64
55000	4841.78	2544.33	1781.16	1401.56	1175.37	1025.87	920.19	841.88	781.80	734.47	696.40	665.27	639.45	617.80
60000	5281.94	2775.63	1943.09	1528.97	1282.22	1119.13	1003.84	918.41	852.87	801.24	759.71	725.74	697.58	673.97
65000	5722.10	3006.93	2105.01	1656.39	1389.07	1212.40	1087.50	994.95	923.94	868.01	823.02	786.22	755.71	730.13
70000	6162.26	3238.23	2266.93	1783.80	1495.92	1305.66	1171.15	1071.48	995.01	934.78	886.33	846.70	813.84	786.29
75000	6602.42	3469.53	2428.86	1911.22	1602.77	1398.92	1254.80	1148.01	1066.09	1001.55	949.64	907.18	871.98	842.46
80000	7042.58	3700.84	2590.78	2038.63	1709.63	1492.18	1338.46	1224.55	1137.16	1068.32	1012.95	967.66	930.11	898.62
85000	7482.74	3932.14	2752.70	2166.04	1816.48	1585.44	1422.11	1301.08	1208.23	1135.09	1076.25	1028.14	988.24	954.78
90000	7922.90	4163.44	2914.63	2293.46	1923.33	1678.70	1505.76	1377.61	1279.30	1201.86	1139.56	1088.61	1046.37	1010.95
95000	8363.06	4394.74	3076.55	2420.87	2030.18	1771.96	1589.42	1454.15	1350.37	1268.63	1202.87	1149.09	1104.50	1067.11
100000	8803.23	4626.04	3238.47	2548.29	2137.03	1865.22	1673.07	1530.68	1421.45	1335.40	1266.18	1209.57	1162.63	1123.27

TERM	15 Years	16 Years	17 Years	18 Years	19 Years	20 Years	21 Years	22 Years	23 Years	24 Years	25 Years	30 Years	35 Years	40 Years
AMOUNT														
5	.06	.06	.06	.06	.05	.05	.05	.05	.05	.05	.05	.05	.05	.05
10	.11	.11	.11	.11	.10	.10	.10	.10	.10	.10	.10	.09	.09	.09
15	.17	.16	.16	.16	.15	.15	.15	.15	.15	.15	.14	.14	.14	.14
25	.28	.27	.26	.26	.25	.25	.25	.24	.24	.24	.24	.23	.22	.22
50	.55	.54	.52	.51	.50	.50	.49	.48	.48	.47	.47	.45	.44	.44
75	.82	.80	.78	.77	.75	.74	.73	.72	.71	.71	.70	.68	.66	.66
100	1.09	1.07	1.04	1.02	1.00	.99	.97	.96	.95	.94	.93	.90	.88	.87
200	2.18	2.13	2.08	2.04	2.00	1.97	1.94	1.92	1.89	1.87	1.86	1.80	1.76	1.74
300	3.27	3.19	3.12	3.05	3.00	2.95	2.91	2.87	2.84	2.81	2.78	2.69	2.64	2.61
400	4.36	4.25	4.15	4.07	4.00	3.93	3.88	3.83	3.78	3.74	3.71	3.59	3.52	3.48
500	5.45	5.31	5.19	5.08	4.99	4.91	4.84	4.78	4.73	4.68	4.64	4.49	4.40	4.35
600	6.54	6.37	6.23	6.10	5.99	5.89	5.81	5.74	5.67	5.61	5.56	5.38	5.28	5.22
700	7.63	7.44	7.26	7.12	6.99	6.88	6.78	6.69	6.62	6.55	6.49	6.28	6.16	6.09
800	8.72	8.50	8.30	8.13	7.99	7.86	7.75	7.65	7.56	7.48	7.42	7.17	7.04	6.96
900	9.81	9.56	9.34	9.15	8.98	8.84	8.71	8.60	8.51	8.42	8.34	8.07	7.91	7.82
1000	10.90	10.62	10.38	10.16	9.98	9.82	9.68	9.56	9.45	9.35	9.27	8.97	8.79	8.69
2000	21.80	21.24	20.75	20.32	19.96	19.64	19.36	19.11	18.89	18.70	18.53	17.93	17.58	17.38
3000	32.70	31.85	31.12	30.48	29.93	29.45	29.03	28.66	28.34	28.05	27.80	26.89	26.37	26.07
4000	43.60	42.47	41.49	40.64	39.91	39.27	38.71	38.22	37.78	37.40	37.06	35.85	35.16	34.76
5000	54.50	53.08	51.86	50.80	49.89	49.09	48.39	47.77	47.23	46.75	46.32	44.81	43.95	43.45
6000	65.40	63.70	62.23	60.96	59.86	58.90	58.06	57.32	56.67	56.10	55.59	53.77	52.74	52.13
7000	76.30	74.31	72.60	71.12	69.84	68.72	67.74	66.88	66.12	65.45	64.85	62.73	61.52	60.82
8000	87.20	84.93	82.97	81.28	79.82	78.54	77.42	76.43	75.56	74.80	74.12	71.69	70.31	69.51
9000	98.10	95.54	93.34	91.44	89.79	88.35	87.09	85.98	85.01	84.14	83.38	80.65	79.10	78.20
10000	109.00	106.16	103.71	101.60	99.77	98.17	96.77	95.54	94.45	93.49	92.64	89.62	87.89	86.89
11000	119.90	116.77	114.09	111.76	109.75	107.99	106.44	105.09	103.90	102.84	101.91	98.58	96.68	95.58
12000	130.80	127.39	124.46	121.92	119.72	117.80	116.12	114.64	113.34	112.19	111.17	107.54	105.47	104.26
13000	141.70	138.00	134.83	132.08	129.70	127.62	125.80	124.20	122.79	121.54	120.43	116.50	114.26	112.95
14000	152.60	148.62	145.20	142.24	139.67	137.44	135.47	133.75	132.23	130.89	129.70	125.46	123.04	121.64
15000	163.50	159.23	155.57	152.40	149.65	147.25	145.15	143.30	141.67	140.24	138.96	134.42	131.83	130.33
16000	174.40	169.85	165.94	162.56	159.63	157.07	154.83	152.86	151.12	149.59	148.23	143.38	140.62	139.02
17000	185.30	180.46	176.31	172.72	169.60	166.88	164.50	162.41	160.56	158.93	157.49	152.34	149.41	147.70
18000	196.20	191.08	186.68	182.88	179.58	176.70	174.18	171.96	170.01	168.28	166.75	161.30	158.20	156.39
19000	207.10	201.69	197.05	193.04	189.56	186.52	183.85	181.52	179.45	177.63	176.02	170.26	166.99	165.08
20000	218.00	212.31	207.42	203.20	199.53	196.33	193.53	191.07	188.90	186.98	185.28	179.23	175.78	173.77
21000	228.89	222.92	217.79	213.36	209.51	206.15	203.21	200.62	198.34	196.33	194.55	188.19	184.56	182.46
22000	239.79	233.54	228.17	223.52	219.49	215.97	212.88	210.18	207.79	205.68	203.81	197.15	193.35	191.15
23000	250.69	244.15	238.54	233.60	229.46	225.70	222.56	219.73	217.23	215.03	213.07	206.11	202.14	199.83
24000	261.59	254.77	248.91	243.84	239.44	235.60	232.24	229.28	226.68	224.38	222.34	215.07	210.93	208.52
25000	272.49	265.38	259.28	254.00	249.42	245.42	241.91	238.83	236.12	233.72	231.60	224.03	219.72	217.21
26000	283.39	276.00	269.65	264.16	259.39	255.23	251.59	248.39	245.57	243.07	240.86	232.99	228.51	225.90
27000	294.29	286.62	280.02	274.32	269.37	265.05	261.27	257.94	255.01	252.42	250.13	241.95	237.30	234.59
28000	305.19	297.23	290.39	284.48	279.34	274.87	270.94	267.49	264.46	261.77	259.39	250.91	246.08	243.27
29000	316.09	307.85	300.76	294.64	289.32	284.68	280.62	277.05	273.90	271.12	268.66	259.87	254.87	251.96
30000	326.99	318.46	311.13	304.80	299.30	294.50	290.29	286.60	283.34	280.47	277.92	268.84	263.66	260.65
31000	337.89	329.08	321.50	314.96	309.27	304.31	299.97	296.15	292.79	289.82	287.18	277.80	272.45	269.34
32000	348.79	339.69	331.87	325.12	319.25	314.13	309.65	305.71	302.23	299.17	296.45	286.76	281.24	278.03
33000	359.69	350.31	342.25	335.28	329.23	323.95	319.32	315.26	311.68	308.51	305.71	295.72	290.03	286.72
34000	370.59	360.92	352.62	345.44	339.20	333.76	329.00	324.81	321.12	317.86	314.98	304.68	298.82	295.40
35000	381.49	371.54	362.99	355.60	349.18	343.58	338.68	334.37	330.57	327.21	324.24	313.64	307.60	304.09
36000	392.39	382.15	373.36	365.76	359.16	353.40	348.35	343.92	340.01	336.56	333.50	322.60	316.39	312.78
37000	403.29	392.77	383.73	375.92	369.13	363.21	358.03	353.47	349.46	345.91	342.77	331.56	325.18	321.47
38000	414.19	403.38	394.10	386.08	379.11	373.03	367.70	363.03	358.90	355.26	352.03	340.52	333.97	330.16
39000	425.09	414.00	404.47	396.24	389.09	382.85	377.38	372.58	368.35	364.61	361.29	349.48	342.76	338.84
40000	435.99	424.61	414.84	406.40	399.06	392.66	387.06	382.13	377.79	373.96	370.56	358.45	351.55	347.53
41000	446.88	435.23	425.21	416.56	409.04	402.48	396.73	391.69	387.24	383.30	379.82	367.41	360.34	356.22
42000	457.78	445.84	435.58	426.72	419.01	412.30	406.41	401.24	396.68	392.65	389.09	376.37	369.12	364.91
43000	468.68	456.46	445.95	436.88	428.99	422.11	416.09	410.79	406.13	402.00	398.35	385.33	377.91	373.60
44000	479.58	467.07	456.33	447.04	438.97	431.93	425.76	420.35	415.57	411.35	407.61	394.29	386.70	382.29
45000	490.48	477.69	466.70	457.20	448.94	441.74	435.44	429.90	425.01	420.70	416.88	403.25	395.49	390.97
46000	501.38	488.30	477.07	467.36	458.92	451.56	445.12	439.45	434.46	430.05	426.14	412.21	404.28	399.66
47000	512.28	498.92	487.44	477.52	468.90	461.38	454.79	449.00	443.90	439.40	435.41	421.17	413.07	408.35
48000	523.18	509.53	497.81	487.68	478.87	471.19	464.47	458.56	453.35	448.75	444.67	430.13	421.86	417.04
49000	534.08	520.15	508.18	497.84	488.85	481.01	474.14	468.11	462.79	458.09	453.93	439.09	430.64	425.73
50000	544.98	530.76	518.55	508.00	498.83	490.83	483.82	477.66	472.24	467.44	463.20	448.06	439.43	434.41
55000	599.48	583.84	570.41	558.79	548.71	539.91	532.20	525.43	519.46	514.19	509.52	492.86	483.38	477.86
60000	653.98	636.92	622.26	609.59	598.59	588.99	580.58	573.20	566.68	560.93	555.83	537.67	527.32	521.30
65000	708.47	689.99	674.11	660.39	648.47	638.07	628.97	620.96	613.91	607.67	602.15	582.47	571.26	564.74
70000	762.97	743.07	725.97	711.19	698.35	687.16	677.35	668.73	661.13	654.42	648.47	627.28	615.20	608.18
75000	817.47	796.14	777.82	761.99	748.24	736.24	725.73	716.49	708.35	701.16	694.79	672.08	659.15	651.62
80000	871.97	849.22	829.68	812.79	798.12	785.32	774.11	764.26	755.58	747.91	741.11	716.89	703.09	695.06
85000	926.46	902.30	881.53	863.59	848.00	834.40	822.49	812.03	802.80	794.65	787.43	761.69	747.03	738.50
90000	980.96	955.37	933.39	914.39	897.88	883.48	870.87	859.79	850.02	841.39	833.75	806.50	790.98	781.94
95000	1035.46	1008.45	985.24	965.19	947.77	932.57	919.25	907.56	897.25	888.14	880.07	851.30	834.92	825.38
100000	1089.96	1061.52	1037.10	1015.99	997.65	981.65	967.64	955.32	944.47	934.88	926.39	896.11	878.86	868.82

MONTHLY PAYMENT
REQUIRED TO AMORTIZE A LOAN

TERM AMOUNT	1 Year	2 Years	3 Years	4 Years	5 Years	6 Years	7 Years	8 Years	9 Years	10 Years	11 Years	12 Years	13 Years	14 Years
5	.45	.24	.17	.13	.11	.10	.09	.08	.08	.07	.07	.07	.06	.06
10	.89	.47	.33	.26	.22	.19	.17	.16	.15	.14	.13	.13	.12	.12
15	1.33	.70	.49	.39	.33	.29	.26	.24	.22	.21	.20	.19	.18	.17
25	2.21	1.16	.82	.64	.54	.47	.42	.39	.36	.34	.32	.31	.30	.29
50	4.41	2.32	1.63	1.28	1.07	.94	.84	.77	.72	.67	.64	.61	.59	.57
75	6.61	3.48	2.44	1.92	1.61	1.41	1.26	1.16	1.07	1.01	.96	.91	.88	.85
100	8.81	4.63	3.25	2.56	2.14	1.87	1.68	1.54	1.43	1.34	1.27	1.22	1.17	1.13
200	17.62	9.26	6.49	5.11	4.28	3.74	3.36	3.07	2.85	2.68	2.54	2.43	2.34	2.26
300	26.42	13.89	9.73	7.66	6.42	5.61	5.03	4.61	4.28	4.02	3.81	3.64	3.50	3.38
400	35.23	18.52	12.97	10.21	8.56	7.48	6.71	6.14	5.70	5.36	5.08	4.85	4.67	4.51
500	44.03	23.15	16.21	12.76	10.70	9.34	8.38	7.67	7.13	6.70	6.35	6.07	5.83	5.64
600	52.84	27.78	19.45	15.31	12.84	11.21	10.06	9.21	8.55	8.03	7.62	7.28	7.00	6.76
700	61.64	32.40	22.69	17.86	14.98	13.08	11.73	10.74	9.97	9.37	8.89	8.49	8.16	7.89
800	70.45	37.03	25.93	20.41	17.12	14.95	13.41	12.27	11.40	10.71	10.16	9.70	9.33	9.02
900	79.25	41.66	29.17	22.96	19.26	16.81	15.09	13.81	12.82	12.05	11.43	10.92	10.50	10.14
1000	88.06	46.29	32.41	25.51	21.40	18.68	16.76	15.34	14.25	13.39	12.70	12.13	11.66	11.27
2000	176.12	92.57	64.82	51.02	42.79	37.36	33.52	30.67	28.49	26.77	25.39	24.25	23.32	22.53
3000	264.17	138.86	97.23	76.53	64.19	56.04	50.27	46.01	42.73	40.15	38.08	36.38	34.97	33.79
4000	352.23	185.14	129.64	102.03	85.58	74.71	67.03	61.34	56.97	53.53	50.77	48.50	46.63	45.06
5000	440.28	231.42	162.05	127.54	106.98	93.39	83.79	76.67	71.21	66.91	63.46	60.63	58.28	56.32
6000	528.34	277.71	194.45	153.05	128.37	112.07	100.54	92.01	85.45	80.30	76.15	72.75	69.94	67.58
7000	616.39	323.99	226.86	178.55	149.77	130.75	117.30	107.34	99.70	93.68	88.84	84.88	81.60	78.85
8000	704.45	370.27	259.27	204.06	171.16	149.42	134.06	122.67	113.94	107.06	101.53	97.00	93.25	90.11
9000	792.50	416.56	291.68	229.57	192.56	168.10	150.81	138.01	128.18	120.44	114.22	109.13	104.91	101.37
10000	880.56	462.84	324.09	255.07	213.95	186.78	167.57	153.34	142.42	133.82	126.91	121.25	116.56	112.63
11000	968.62	509.12	356.50	280.58	235.35	205.46	184.33	168.67	156.66	147.20	139.60	133.38	128.22	123.90
12000	1056.67	555.41	388.90	306.09	256.74	224.13	201.08	184.01	170.90	160.59	152.29	145.50	139.88	135.16
13000	1144.73	601.69	421.31	331.59	278.14	242.81	217.84	199.34	185.15	173.97	164.98	157.63	151.53	146.42
14000	1232.78	647.97	453.72	357.10	299.53	261.49	234.60	214.67	199.39	187.35	177.67	169.75	163.19	157.69
15000	1320.84	694.26	486.13	382.61	320.93	280.17	251.35	230.01	213.63	200.73	190.36	181.88	174.84	168.95
16000	1408.89	740.54	518.54	408.12	342.32	298.84	268.11	245.34	227.87	214.11	203.05	194.00	186.50	180.21
17000	1496.95	786.82	550.94	433.62	363.72	317.52	284.87	260.67	242.11	227.49	215.74	206.13	198.16	191.48
18000	1585.00	833.11	583.35	459.13	385.11	336.20	301.62	276.01	256.35	240.88	228.43	218.25	209.81	202.74
19000	1673.06	879.39	615.76	484.64	406.51	354.88	318.38	291.34	270.60	254.26	241.12	230.37	221.47	214.00
20000	1761.11	925.68	648.17	510.14	427.90	373.55	335.14	306.67	284.84	267.64	253.81	242.50	233.12	225.26
21000	1849.17	971.96	680.58	535.65	449.30	392.23	351.89	322.01	299.08	281.02	266.50	254.62	244.78	236.53
22000	1937.23	1018.24	712.99	561.16	470.69	410.91	368.65	337.34	313.32	294.40	279.19	266.75	256.44	247.79
23000	2025.28	1064.53	745.39	586.66	492.09	429.59	385.41	352.67	327.56	307.79	291.88	278.87	268.09	259.05
24000	2113.34	1110.81	777.80	612.17	513.48	448.26	402.16	368.01	341.80	321.17	304.57	291.00	279.75	270.32
25000	2201.39	1157.09	810.21	637.68	534.88	466.94	418.92	383.34	356.05	334.55	317.26	303.12	291.40	281.58
26000	2289.45	1203.38	842.62	663.18	556.27	485.62	435.68	398.67	370.29	347.93	329.95	315.25	303.06	292.84
27000	2377.50	1249.66	875.03	688.69	577.67	504.30	452.43	414.01	384.53	361.31	342.64	327.37	314.72	304.10
28000	2465.56	1295.94	907.44	714.20	599.06	522.97	469.19	429.34	398.77	374.69	355.33	339.50	326.37	315.37
29000	2553.61	1342.23	939.84	739.71	620.46	541.65	485.95	444.67	413.01	388.08	368.02	351.62	338.03	326.63
30000	2641.67	1388.51	972.25	765.21	641.85	560.33	502.70	460.01	427.25	401.46	380.71	363.75	349.68	337.89
31000	2729.72	1434.79	1004.66	790.72	663.25	579.01	519.46	475.34	441.50	414.84	393.40	375.87	361.34	349.16
32000	2817.78	1481.08	1037.07	816.23	684.64	597.68	536.22	490.67	455.74	428.22	406.09	388.00	373.00	360.42
33000	2905.84	1527.36	1069.48	841.73	706.04	616.36	552.97	506.01	469.98	441.60	418.78	400.12	384.65	371.68
34000	2993.89	1573.64	1101.88	867.24	727.43	635.04	569.73	521.34	484.22	454.98	431.47	412.25	396.31	382.95
35000	3081.95	1619.93	1134.29	892.75	748.83	653.72	586.49	536.67	498.46	468.37	444.16	424.37	407.96	394.21
36000	3170.00	1666.21	1166.70	918.25	770.22	672.39	603.24	552.01	512.70	481.75	456.85	436.50	419.62	405.47
37000	3258.06	1712.50	1199.11	943.76	791.62	691.07	620.00	567.34	526.95	495.13	469.54	448.62	431.28	416.73
38000	3346.11	1758.78	1231.52	969.27	813.01	709.75	636.76	582.67	541.19	508.51	482.23	460.74	442.93	428.00
39000	3434.17	1805.06	1263.93	994.77	834.41	728.43	653.51	598.01	555.43	521.89	494.92	472.87	454.59	439.26
40000	3522.22	1851.35	1296.33	1020.28	855.80	747.10	670.27	613.34	569.67	535.28	507.61	484.99	466.24	450.52
41000	3610.28	1897.63	1328.74	1045.79	877.20	765.78	687.03	628.67	583.91	548.66	520.30	497.12	477.90	461.79
42000	3698.34	1943.91	1361.15	1071.29	898.59	784.46	703.78	644.01	598.15	562.04	532.99	509.24	489.56	473.05
43000	3786.39	1990.20	1393.56	1096.80	919.99	803.14	720.54	659.34	612.40	575.42	545.68	521.37	501.21	484.31
44000	3874.45	2036.48	1425.97	1122.31	941.38	821.81	737.30	674.67	626.64	588.80	558.37	533.49	512.87	495.57
45000	3962.50	2082.76	1458.37	1147.82	962.78	840.49	754.05	690.01	640.88	602.18	571.07	545.62	524.52	506.84
46000	4050.56	2129.05	1490.78	1173.32	984.17	859.17	770.81	705.34	655.12	615.57	583.76	557.74	536.18	518.10
47000	4138.61	2175.33	1523.19	1198.83	1005.57	877.85	787.57	720.67	669.36	628.95	596.45	569.87	547.83	529.36
48000	4226.67	2221.61	1555.60	1224.34	1026.96	896.52	804.32	736.01	683.60	642.33	609.14	581.99	559.49	540.63
49000	4314.72	2267.90	1588.01	1249.84	1048.36	915.20	821.08	751.34	697.85	655.71	621.83	594.12	571.15	551.89
50000	4402.78	2314.18	1620.42	1275.35	1069.75	933.88	837.84	766.67	712.09	669.09	634.52	606.24	582.80	563.15
55000	4843.06	2545.60	1782.46	1402.88	1176.73	1027.27	921.62	843.34	783.30	736.00	697.97	666.87	641.08	619.47
60000	5283.33	2777.02	1944.50	1530.42	1283.70	1120.65	1005.40	920.01	854.50	802.91	761.42	727.49	699.36	675.78
65000	5723.61	3008.43	2106.54	1657.95	1390.68	1214.04	1089.18	996.67	925.71	869.82	824.87	788.11	757.64	732.10
70000	6163.89	3239.85	2268.58	1785.49	1497.65	1307.43	1172.97	1073.34	996.92	936.73	888.32	848.74	815.92	788.41
75000	6604.17	3471.27	2430.62	1913.02	1604.63	1400.82	1256.75	1150.01	1068.13	1003.64	951.77	909.36	874.20	844.73
80000	7044.45	3702.69	2592.66	2040.56	1711.60	1494.20	1340.53	1226.67	1139.34	1070.55	1015.22	969.98	932.48	901.04
85000	7484.72	3934.10	2754.70	2168.09	1818.58	1587.59	1424.32	1303.34	1210.55	1137.45	1078.67	1030.61	990.76	957.36
90000	7925.00	4165.52	2916.74	2295.63	1925.55	1680.98	1508.10	1380.01	1281.75	1204.36	1142.13	1091.23	1049.04	1013.67
95000	8365.28	4396.94	3078.79	2423.16	2032.53	1774.37	1591.88	1456.67	1352.96	1271.27	1205.58	1151.85	1107.32	1069.98
100000	8805.55	4628.36	3240.83	2550.69	2139.50	1867.75	1675.67	1533.34	1424.17	1338.18	1269.03	1212.48	1165.60	1126.30

TERM	15 Years	16 Years	17 Years	18 Years	19 Years	20 Years	21 Years	22 Years	23 Years	24 Years	25 Years	30 Years	35 Years	40 Years
AMOUNT														
5	.06	.06	.06	.06	.06	.05	.05	.05	.05	.05	.05	.05	.05	.05
10	.11	.11	.11	.11	.11	.10	.10	.10	.10	.10	.10	.09	.09	.09
15	.17	.16	.16	.16	.16	.15	.15	.15	.15	.15	.14	.14	.14	.14
25	.28	.27	.27	.26	.26	.25	.25	.24	.24	.24	.24	.23	.23	.22
50	.55	.54	.53	.51	.51	.50	.49	.48	.48	.47	.47	.45	.45	.44
75	.82	.80	.79	.77	.76	.74	.73	.72	.72	.71	.70	.68	.67	.66
100	1.10	1.07	1.05	1.02	1.01	.99	.98	.96	.95	.94	.93	.90	.89	.88
200	2.19	2.13	2.09	2.04	2.01	1.97	1.95	1.92	1.90	1.88	1.86	1.80	1.77	1.75
300	3.28	3.20	3.13	3.06	3.01	2.96	2.92	2.88	2.85	2.82	2.79	2.70	2.65	2.62
400	4.38	4.26	4.17	4.08	4.01	3.94	3.89	3.84	3.80	3.76	3.72	3.60	3.54	3.50
500	5.47	5.33	5.21	5.10	5.01	4.93	4.86	4.80	4.74	4.70	4.65	4.50	4.42	4.37
600	6.56	6.39	6.25	6.12	6.01	5.91	5.83	5.76	5.69	5.64	5.58	5.40	5.30	5.24
700	7.66	7.46	7.29	7.14	7.01	6.90	6.80	6.72	6.64	6.57	6.51	6.30	6.18	6.11
800	8.75	8.52	8.33	8.16	8.01	7.88	7.77	7.67	7.59	7.51	7.44	7.20	7.07	6.99
900	9.84	9.59	9.37	9.18	9.01	8.87	8.74	8.63	8.54	8.45	8.37	8.10	7.95	7.86
1000	10.94	10.65	10.41	10.20	10.01	9.85	9.72	9.59	9.48	9.39	9.30	9.00	8.83	8.73
2000	21.87	21.30	20.81	20.39	20.02	19.70	19.43	19.18	18.96	18.77	18.60	18.00	17.66	17.46
3000	32.80	31.94	31.21	30.58	30.03	29.55	29.14	28.77	28.44	28.16	27.90	27.00	26.49	26.19
4000	43.73	42.59	41.62	40.77	40.04	39.40	38.85	38.35	37.92	37.54	37.20	36.00	35.31	34.92
5000	54.66	53.24	52.02	50.97	50.05	49.25	48.56	47.94	47.40	46.92	46.50	45.00	44.14	43.64
6000	65.59	63.88	62.42	61.16	60.06	59.10	58.27	57.53	56.88	56.31	55.80	53.99	52.97	52.37
7000	76.52	74.53	72.82	71.35	70.07	68.95	67.98	67.12	66.36	65.69	65.10	62.99	61.79	61.10
8000	87.45	85.18	83.23	81.54	80.08	78.80	77.69	76.70	75.84	75.08	74.40	71.99	70.62	69.83
9000	98.38	95.82	93.63	91.73	90.09	88.65	87.40	86.29	85.32	84.46	83.70	80.99	79.45	78.55
10000	109.31	106.47	104.03	101.93	100.10	98.50	97.11	95.88	94.80	93.84	93.00	89.99	88.28	87.28
11000	120.24	117.12	114.44	112.12	110.11	108.35	106.82	105.47	104.28	103.23	102.30	98.99	97.10	96.01
12000	131.17	127.76	124.84	122.31	120.12	118.20	116.53	115.05	113.76	112.61	111.60	107.98	105.93	104.74
13000	142.10	138.41	135.24	132.50	130.13	128.05	126.24	124.64	123.24	122.00	120.90	116.90	114.76	113.46
14000	153.03	149.06	145.64	142.70	140.14	137.90	135.95	134.23	132.72	131.38	130.20	125.98	123.58	122.19
15000	163.96	159.70	156.05	152.89	150.14	147.75	145.66	143.82	142.20	140.76	139.50	134.98	132.41	130.92
16000	174.89	170.35	166.45	163.08	160.15	157.60	155.37	153.40	151.67	150.15	148.79	143.98	141.24	139.65
17000	185.82	181.00	176.85	173.27	170.16	167.45	165.08	162.99	161.15	159.53	158.09	152.97	150.06	148.37
18000	196.75	191.64	187.26	183.46	180.17	177.30	174.79	172.58	170.63	168.91	167.39	161.97	158.89	157.10
19000	207.68	202.29	197.66	193.66	190.18	187.15	184.50	182.17	180.11	178.30	176.69	170.97	167.72	165.83
20000	218.61	212.94	208.06	203.85	200.19	197.00	194.21	191.75	189.59	187.68	185.99	179.97	176.55	174.56
21000	229.54	223.58	218.46	214.04	210.20	206.85	203.92	201.34	199.07	197.07	195.29	188.97	185.37	183.29
22000	240.47	234.23	228.87	224.23	220.21	216.70	213.63	210.93	208.55	206.45	204.59	197.97	194.20	192.01
23000	251.40	244.88	239.27	234.43	230.22	226.55	223.34	220.52	218.03	215.83	213.89	206.96	203.03	200.74
24000	262.33	255.52	249.67	244.62	240.23	236.40	233.05	230.10	227.51	225.22	223.19	215.96	211.85	209.47
25000	273.26	266.17	260.08	254.81	250.24	246.25	242.76	239.69	236.99	234.60	232.49	224.96	220.68	218.20
26000	284.19	276.02	270.48	265.00	260.25	256.10	252.47	249.28	246.47	243.99	241.79	233.96	229.51	226.92
27000	295.12	287.46	280.88	275.19	270.26	265.95	262.18	258.87	255.95	253.37	251.09	242.96	238.34	235.65
28000	306.05	298.11	291.28	285.39	280.27	275.80	271.89	268.45	265.43	262.75	260.39	251.95	247.16	244.38
29000	316.98	308.76	301.69	295.58	290.28	285.65	281.60	278.04	274.91	272.14	269.69	260.95	255.99	253.11
30000	327.91	319.40	312.09	305.77	300.28	295.50	291.31	287.63	284.39	281.52	278.99	269.95	264.82	261.83
31000	338.85	330.05	322.49	315.96	310.29	305.35	301.02	297.22	293.87	290.91	288.28	278.95	273.64	270.56
32000	349.78	340.69	332.89	326.16	320.30	315.20	310.73	306.80	303.34	300.29	297.58	287.95	282.47	279.29
33000	360.71	351.34	343.30	336.35	330.31	325.05	320.44	316.39	312.82	309.67	306.88	296.95	291.30	288.02
34000	371.64	361.99	353.70	346.54	340.32	334.90	330.15	325.98	322.30	319.06	316.18	305.94	300.12	296.74
35000	382.57	372.63	364.10	356.73	350.33	344.75	339.86	335.57	331.78	328.44	325.48	314.94	308.95	305.47
36000	393.50	383.28	374.51	366.92	360.34	354.60	349.57	345.15	341.26	337.82	334.78	323.94	317.78	314.20
37000	404.43	393.93	384.91	377.12	370.35	364.45	359.28	354.74	350.74	347.21	344.08	332.94	326.61	322.93
38000	415.36	404.57	395.31	387.31	380.36	374.30	368.99	364.33	360.22	356.59	353.38	341.94	335.43	331.65
39000	426.29	415.22	405.71	397.50	390.37	384.15	378.70	373.92	369.70	365.98	362.68	350.93	344.26	340.38
40000	437.22	425.87	416.12	407.69	400.38	394.00	388.41	383.50	379.18	375.36	371.98	359.93	353.09	349.11
41000	448.15	436.51	426.52	417.89	410.39	403.85	398.12	393.09	388.66	384.74	381.28	368.93	361.91	357.84
42000	459.08	447.16	436.92	428.08	420.40	413.70	407.83	402.68	398.14	394.13	390.58	377.93	370.74	366.57
43000	470.01	457.81	447.33	438.27	430.41	423.55	417.54	412.27	407.62	403.51	399.88	386.93	379.57	375.29
44000	480.94	468.45	457.73	448.46	440.42	433.40	427.25	421.85	417.10	412.90	409.18	395.93	388.39	384.02
45000	491.87	479.10	468.13	458.65	450.42	443.25	436.96	431.44	426.58	422.28	418.48	404.92	397.22	392.75
46000	502.80	489.75	478.53	468.85	460.43	453.10	446.67	441.03	436.06	431.66	427.77	413.92	406.05	401.48
47000	513.73	500.39	488.94	479.04	470.44	462.95	456.38	450.62	445.54	441.05	437.07	422.92	414.88	410.20
48000	524.66	511.04	499.34	489.23	480.45	472.80	466.09	460.20	455.01	450.43	446.37	431.92	423.70	418.93
49000	535.59	521.69	509.74	499.42	490.46	482.65	475.80	469.79	464.49	459.82	455.67	440.92	432.53	427.66
50000	546.52	532.33	520.15	509.62	500.47	492.50	485.51	479.38	473.97	469.20	464.97	449.92	441.36	436.39
55000	601.17	585.57	572.16	560.58	550.52	541.74	534.06	527.32	521.37	516.12	511.47	494.91	485.49	480.02
60000	655.82	638.80	624.17	611.54	600.56	590.99	582.61	575.25	568.77	563.04	557.97	539.90	529.63	523.66
65000	710.48	692.03	676.19	662.50	650.61	640.24	631.17	623.19	616.16	609.96	604.46	584.89	573.76	567.30
70000	765.13	745.26	728.20	713.46	700.66	689.49	679.72	671.13	663.56	656.88	650.96	629.88	617.90	610.94
75000	819.78	798.50	780.22	764.42	750.70	738.74	728.27	719.07	710.96	703.80	697.46	674.87	662.03	654.58
80000	874.43	851.73	832.23	815.38	800.75	787.99	776.82	766.70	758.35	750.72	743.95	719.86	706.17	698.21
85000	929.08	904.96	884.24	866.34	850.80	837.24	825.37	814.94	805.75	797.63	790.45	764.85	750.30	741.85
90000	983.73	958.19	936.26	917.30	900.84	886.49	873.92	862.88	853.15	844.55	836.95	809.84	794.44	785.49
95000	1038.39	1011.43	988.27	968.26	950.89	935.74	922.47	910.81	900.55	891.47	883.44	854.83	838.57	829.13
100000	1093.04	1064.66	1040.29	1019.23	1000.94	984.99	971.02	958.75	947.94	938.39	929.94	899.83	882.71	872.77

10.375%

MONTHLY PAYMENT
REQUIRED TO AMORTIZE A LOAN

TERM	1 Year	2 Years	3 Years	4 Years	5 Years	6 Years	7 Years	8 Years	9 Years	10 Years	11 Years	12 Years	13 Years	14 Years
AMOUNT														
5	.45	.24	.17	.13	.11	.10	.09	.08	.08	.07	.07	.07	.06	.06
10	.89	.47	.33	.26	.22	.19	.17	.16	.15	.14	.13	.13	.12	.12
15	1.33	.70	.49	.39	.33	.29	.26	.24	.22	.21	.20	.19	.18	.17
25	2.21	1.16	.82	.64	.54	.47	.42	.39	.36	.34	.32	.31	.30	.29
50	4.41	2.32	1.63	1.28	1.08	.94	.84	.77	.72	.68	.64	.61	.59	.57
75	6.61	3.48	2.44	1.92	1.61	1.41	1.26	1.16	1.08	1.01	.96	.92	.88	.85
100	8.81	4.64	3.25	2.56	2.15	1.88	1.54	1.43	1.35	1.28	1.22	1.18	1.14	
200	17.62	9.27	6.49	5.11	4.29	3.75	3.36	3.08	2.86	2.69	2.55	2.44	2.35	2.27
300	26.43	13.90	9.74	7.67	6.43	5.62	5.04	4.62	4.29	4.03	3.82	3.66	3.52	3.40
400	35.24	18.53	12.98	10.22	8.58	7.49	6.72	6.15	5.72	5.37	5.10	4.87	4.69	4.53
500	44.05	23.16	16.23	12.78	10.72	9.36	8.40	7.69	7.15	6.72	6.37	6.09	5.86	5.66
600	52.86	27.80	19.47	15.33	12.86	11.23	10.08	9.23	8.57	8.06	7.64	7.31	7.03	6.79
700	61.67	32.43	22.72	17.89	15.01	13.11	11.76	10.77	10.00	9.40	8.92	8.52	8.20	7.92
800	70.48	37.06	25.96	20.44	17.15	14.98	13.44	12.30	11.43	10.74	10.19	9.74	9.37	9.05
900	79.29	41.69	29.20	22.99	19.29	16.85	15.12	13.84	12.86	12.09	11.46	10.96	10.54	10.18
1000	88.10	46.32	32.45	25.55	21.44	18.72	16.80	15.38	14.29	13.43	12.74	12.17	11.71	11.31
2000	176.19	92.64	64.89	51.09	42.87	37.44	33.60	30.75	28.57	26.85	25.47	24.34	23.41	22.62
3000	264.28	138.96	97.34	76.63	64.30	56.15	50.39	46.12	42.85	40.28	38.20	36.51	35.11	33.93
4000	352.37	185.28	129.78	102.18	85.73	74.87	67.19	61.50	57.14	53.70	50.94	48.68	46.81	45.24
5000	440.46	231.60	162.22	127.72	107.17	93.58	83.98	76.87	71.42	67.12	63.67	60.85	58.51	56.55
6000	528.55	277.91	194.67	153.26	128.60	112.30	100.78	92.24	85.70	80.55	76.40	73.02	70.21	67.86
7000	616.64	324.23	227.11	178.81	150.03	131.01	117.57	107.62	99.98	93.97	89.14	85.18	81.91	79.16
8000	704.73	370.55	259.55	204.35	171.46	149.73	134.37	122.99	114.27	107.39	101.87	97.35	93.61	90.47
9000	792.82	416.87	292.00	229.89	192.89	168.44	151.17	138.36	128.55	120.82	114.60	109.52	105.31	101.78
10000	880.91	463.19	324.44	255.44	214.33	187.16	167.96	153.74	142.83	134.24	127.34	121.69	117.01	113.09
11000	969.00	509.51	356.88	280.98	235.76	205.88	184.76	169.11	157.11	147.66	140.07	133.86	128.71	124.40
12000	1057.09	555.82	389.33	306.52	257.19	224.59	201.55	184.48	171.40	161.09	152.80	146.03	140.41	135.71
13000	1145.18	602.14	421.77	332.06	278.62	243.31	218.35	199.86	185.68	174.51	165.53	158.19	152.11	147.01
14000	1233.27	648.46	454.21	357.61	300.05	262.02	235.14	215.23	199.96	187.94	178.27	170.36	163.81	158.32
15000	1321.36	694.78	486.66	383.15	321.49	280.74	251.94	230.60	214.24	201.36	191.00	182.53	175.51	169.63
16000	1409.45	741.10	519.10	408.69	342.92	299.45	268.73	245.98	228.53	214.78	203.73	194.70	187.21	180.94
17000	1497.54	787.41	551.55	434.24	364.35	318.17	285.53	261.35	242.81	228.21	216.47	206.87	198.91	192.25
18000	1585.63	833.73	583.99	459.78	385.78	336.88	302.33	276.72	257.09	241.63	229.20	219.04	210.61	203.56
19000	1673.72	880.05	616.43	485.32	407.21	355.60	319.12	292.10	271.37	255.05	241.93	231.20	222.32	214.86
20000	1761.81	926.37	648.88	510.87	428.65	374.32	335.92	307.47	285.66	268.48	254.67	243.37	234.02	226.17
21000	1849.90	972.69	681.32	536.41	450.08	393.03	352.71	322.84	299.94	281.90	267.40	255.54	245.72	237.48
22000	1937.99	1019.01	713.76	561.95	471.51	411.75	369.51	338.22	314.22	295.32	280.13	267.71	257.42	248.79
23000	2026.08	1065.32	746.21	587.50	492.94	430.46	386.30	353.59	328.50	308.75	292.86	279.88	269.12	260.10
24000	2114.17	1111.64	778.65	613.04	514.37	449.18	403.10	368.96	342.79	322.17	305.60	292.05	280.82	271.41
25000	2202.26	1157.96	811.09	638.58	535.81	467.89	419.89	384.34	357.07	335.60	318.33	304.22	292.52	282.71
26000	2290.36	1204.28	843.54	664.12	557.24	486.61	436.69	399.71	371.35	349.02	331.06	316.38	304.22	294.02
27000	2378.45	1250.60	875.98	689.67	578.67	505.32	453.49	415.08	385.63	362.44	343.80	328.55	315.92	305.33
28000	2466.54	1296.91	908.42	715.21	600.10	524.04	470.28	430.46	399.92	375.87	356.53	340.72	327.62	316.64
29000	2554.63	1343.23	940.87	740.75	621.53	542.75	487.08	445.83	414.20	389.29	369.26	352.89	339.32	327.95
30000	2642.72	1389.55	973.31	766.30	642.97	561.47	503.87	461.20	428.48	402.71	382.00	365.06	351.02	339.26
31000	2730.81	1435.87	1005.75	791.84	664.40	580.19	520.67	476.58	442.76	416.14	394.73	377.23	362.72	350.57
32000	2818.90	1482.19	1038.20	817.38	685.83	598.90	537.46	491.95	457.05	429.56	407.46	389.39	374.42	361.87
33000	2906.99	1528.51	1070.64	842.93	707.26	617.62	554.26	507.32	471.33	442.98	420.19	401.56	386.12	373.18
34000	2995.08	1574.82	1103.09	868.47	728.69	636.33	571.05	522.70	485.61	456.41	432.93	413.73	397.82	384.49
35000	3083.17	1621.14	1135.53	894.01	750.13	655.05	587.85	538.07	499.89	469.83	445.66	425.90	409.52	395.80
36000	3171.26	1667.46	1167.97	919.55	771.56	673.76	604.65	553.44	514.18	483.25	458.39	438.07	421.22	407.11
37000	3259.35	1713.78	1200.42	945.10	792.99	692.48	621.44	568.82	528.46	496.68	471.13	450.24	432.92	418.42
38000	3347.44	1760.10	1232.86	970.64	814.42	711.19	638.24	584.19	542.74	510.10	483.86	462.40	444.63	429.72
39000	3435.53	1806.41	1265.30	996.18	835.85	729.91	655.03	599.56	557.02	523.53	496.59	474.57	456.33	441.03
40000	3523.62	1852.73	1297.75	1021.73	857.29	748.63	671.83	614.94	571.31	536.95	509.33	486.74	468.03	452.34
41000	3611.71	1899.05	1330.19	1047.27	878.72	767.34	688.62	630.31	585.59	550.37	522.06	498.91	479.73	463.65
42000	3699.80	1945.37	1362.63	1072.81	900.15	786.06	705.42	645.68	599.87	563.80	534.79	511.08	491.43	474.96
43000	3787.89	1991.69	1395.08	1098.36	921.58	804.77	722.22	661.06	614.15	577.22	547.52	523.25	503.13	486.27
44000	3875.98	2038.01	1427.52	1123.90	943.01	823.49	739.01	676.43	628.44	590.64	560.26	535.42	514.83	497.57
45000	3964.07	2084.32	1459.96	1149.44	964.45	842.20	755.81	691.80	642.72	604.07	572.99	547.58	526.53	508.88
46000	4052.16	2130.64	1492.41	1174.99	985.88	860.92	772.60	707.18	657.00	617.49	585.72	559.75	538.23	520.19
47000	4140.25	2176.96	1524.85	1200.53	1007.31	879.63	789.40	722.55	671.28	630.91	598.46	571.92	549.93	531.50
48000	4228.34	2223.28	1557.29	1226.07	1028.74	898.35	806.19	737.92	685.57	644.34	611.19	584.09	561.63	542.81
49000	4316.43	2269.60	1589.74	1251.61	1050.17	917.06	822.99	753.30	699.85	657.76	623.92	596.26	573.33	554.12
50000	4404.52	2315.91	1622.18	1277.16	1071.61	935.78	839.78	768.67	714.13	671.19	636.66	608.43	585.03	565.42
55000	4844.98	2547.51	1784.40	1404.87	1178.77	1029.36	923.76	845.54	785.55	738.30	700.32	669.27	643.53	621.97
60000	5285.43	2779.10	1946.62	1532.59	1285.93	1122.94	1007.74	922.40	856.96	805.42	763.99	730.11	702.04	678.51
65000	5725.88	3010.69	2108.83	1660.30	1393.09	1216.51	1091.72	999.27	928.37	872.54	827.65	790.95	760.54	735.05
70000	6166.33	3242.28	2271.05	1788.02	1500.25	1310.09	1175.70	1076.14	999.78	939.66	891.32	851.79	819.04	791.59
75000	6606.78	3473.87	2433.27	1915.73	1607.41	1403.67	1259.67	1153.00	1071.20	1006.78	954.98	912.64	877.55	848.13
80000	7047.24	3705.46	2595.49	2043.45	1714.57	1497.25	1343.65	1229.87	1142.61	1073.89	1018.65	973.48	936.05	904.68
85000	7487.69	3937.05	2757.71	2171.16	1821.73	1590.82	1427.63	1306.74	1214.02	1141.01	1082.31	1034.32	994.55	961.22
90000	7928.14	4168.64	2919.92	2298.88	1928.89	1684.40	1511.61	1383.60	1285.43	1208.13	1145.98	1095.16	1053.05	1017.76
95000	8368.59	4400.23	3082.14	2426.60	2036.05	1777.98	1595.59	1460.47	1356.85	1275.25	1209.64	1156.00	1111.56	1074.30
100000	8809.04	4631.82	3244.36	2554.31	2143.21	1871.56	1679.56	1537.34	1428.26	1342.37	1273.31	1216.85	1170.06	1130.84

TERM AMOUNT	15 Years	16 Years	17 Years	18 Years	19 Years	20 Years	21 Years	22 Years	23 Years	24 Years	25 Years	30 Years	35 Years	40 Years
5	.06	.06	.06	.06	.06	.05	.05	.05	.05	.05	.05	.05	.05	.05
10	.11	.11	.11	.11	.11	.10	.10	.10	.10	.10	.10	.10	.09	.09
15	.17	.17	.16	.16	.16	.15	.15	.15	.15	.15	.15	.14	.14	.14
25	.28	.27	.27	.26	.26	.25	.25	.25	.24	.24	.24	.23	.23	.22
50	.55	.54	.53	.52	.51	.50	.49	.49	.48	.48	.47	.46	.45	.44
75	.83	.81	.79	.77	.76	.75	.74	.73	.72	.71	.71	.68	.67	.66
100	1.10	1.07	1.05	1.03	1.01	.99	.98	.97	.96	.95	.94	.91	.89	.88
200	2.20	2.14	2.10	2.05	2.02	1.98	1.96	1.93	1.91	1.89	1.88	1.82	1.78	1.76
300	3.30	3.21	3.14	3.08	3.02	2.97	2.93	2.90	2.86	2.84	2.81	2.72	2.67	2.64
400	4.40	4.28	4.19	4.10	4.03	3.96	3.91	3.86	3.82	3.78	3.75	3.63	3.56	3.52
500	5.49	5.35	5.23	5.13	5.03	4.95	4.89	4.82	4.77	4.72	4.68	4.53	4.45	4.40
600	6.59	6.42	6.28	6.15	6.04	5.94	5.86	5.79	5.72	5.67	5.62	5.44	5.34	5.28
700	7.69	7.49	7.32	7.17	7.05	6.93	6.84	6.75	6.68	6.61	6.55	6.34	6.22	6.16
800	8.79	8.56	8.37	8.20	8.05	7.92	7.81	7.72	7.63	7.55	7.49	7.25	7.11	7.03
900	9.88	9.63	9.41	9.22	9.06	8.91	8.79	8.68	8.58	8.50	8.42	8.15	8.00	7.91
1000	10.98	10.70	10.46	10.25	10.06	9.90	9.77	9.64	9.54	9.44	9.36	9.06	8.89	8.79
2000	21.96	21.39	20.91	20.49	20.12	19.80	19.53	19.28	19.07	18.88	18.71	18.11	17.77	17.58
3000	32.93	32.09	31.36	30.73	30.18	29.70	29.29	28.92	28.60	28.31	28.06	27.17	26.66	26.37
4000	43.91	42.78	41.81	40.97	40.24	39.60	39.05	38.56	38.13	37.75	37.42	36.22	35.54	35.15
5000	54.89	53.47	52.26	51.21	50.30	49.50	48.81	48.20	47.66	47.19	46.77	45.28	44.43	43.94
6000	65.86	64.17	62.71	61.45	60.36	59.40	58.57	57.84	57.19	56.62	56.12	54.33	53.31	52.73
7000	76.84	74.86	73.16	71.69	70.42	69.30	68.33	67.48	66.73	66.06	65.47	63.38	62.20	61.51
8000	87.82	85.55	83.61	81.93	80.48	79.20	78.09	77.12	76.26	75.50	74.83	72.44	71.08	70.30
9000	98.79	96.25	94.06	92.17	90.53	89.10	87.85	86.76	85.79	84.93	84.18	81.49	79.97	79.09
10000	109.77	106.94	104.51	102.41	100.59	99.00	97.62	96.39	95.32	94.37	93.53	90.55	88.85	87.87
11000	120.75	117.64	114.96	112.65	110.65	108.90	107.38	106.03	104.85	103.81	102.88	99.60	97.74	96.66
12000	131.72	128.33	125.41	122.90	120.71	118.80	117.14	115.67	114.38	113.24	112.24	108.65	106.62	105.45
13000	142.70	139.02	135.86	133.14	130.77	128.70	126.90	125.31	123.91	122.68	121.59	117.71	115.51	114.23
14000	153.68	149.72	146.32	143.38	140.83	138.60	136.66	134.95	133.45	132.12	130.94	126.76	124.39	123.02
15000	164.65	160.41	156.77	153.62	150.89	148.50	146.42	144.59	142.98	141.55	140.30	135.82	133.28	131.81
16000	175.63	171.10	167.22	163.86	160.95	158.40	156.18	154.23	152.51	150.99	149.65	144.87	142.16	140.59
17000	186.61	181.80	177.67	174.10	171.00	168.30	165.94	163.87	162.04	160.43	159.00	153.92	151.05	149.38
18000	197.58	192.49	188.12	184.34	181.06	178.20	175.70	173.51	171.57	169.86	168.35	162.98	159.93	158.17
19000	208.56	203.18	198.57	194.58	191.12	188.10	185.46	183.15	181.10	179.30	177.71	172.03	168.82	166.96
20000	219.54	213.88	209.02	204.82	201.18	198.00	195.23	192.78	190.64	188.74	187.06	181.09	177.70	175.74
21000	230.51	224.57	219.47	215.06	211.24	207.90	204.99	202.42	200.17	198.17	196.41	190.14	186.59	184.53
22000	241.49	235.27	229.92	225.30	221.30	217.80	214.75	212.06	209.70	207.61	205.76	199.19	195.47	193.32
23000	252.47	245.96	240.37	235.55	231.36	227.70	224.51	221.70	219.23	217.05	215.12	208.25	204.36	202.10
24000	263.44	256.65	250.82	245.79	241.42	237.60	234.27	231.34	228.76	226.48	224.47	217.30	213.24	210.89
25000	274.42	267.35	261.27	256.03	251.47	247.50	244.03	240.98	238.29	235.92	233.82	226.36	222.13	219.68
26000	285.40	278.04	271.72	266.27	261.53	257.40	253.79	250.62	247.82	245.36	243.17	235.40	231.01	228.46
27000	296.37	288.73	282.17	276.51	271.59	267.30	263.55	260.26	257.36	254.79	252.53	244.46	239.90	237.25
28000	307.35	299.43	292.63	286.75	281.65	277.20	273.31	269.90	266.89	264.23	261.88	253.52	248.78	246.04
29000	318.33	310.12	303.08	296.99	291.71	287.10	283.07	279.54	276.42	273.67	271.23	262.57	257.67	254.82
30000	329.30	320.82	313.53	307.23	301.77	297.00	292.84	289.17	285.95	283.10	280.59	271.63	266.55	263.61
31000	340.28	331.51	323.98	317.47	311.83	306.90	302.60	298.81	295.48	292.54	289.94	280.68	275.43	272.40
32000	351.26	342.20	334.43	327.71	321.89	316.80	312.36	308.45	305.01	301.98	299.29	289.74	284.32	281.18
33000	362.23	352.90	344.88	337.95	331.94	326.70	322.12	318.09	314.55	311.41	308.64	298.79	293.20	289.97
34000	373.21	363.59	355.33	348.20	342.00	336.60	331.88	327.73	324.08	320.85	318.00	307.84	302.09	298.76
35000	384.19	374.28	365.78	358.44	352.06	346.50	341.64	337.37	333.61	330.29	327.35	316.90	310.97	307.54
36000	395.16	384.98	376.23	368.68	362.12	356.40	351.40	347.01	343.14	339.72	336.70	325.95	319.86	316.33
37000	406.14	395.67	386.68	378.92	372.18	366.30	361.16	356.65	352.67	349.16	346.05	335.01	328.74	325.12
38000	417.12	406.36	397.13	389.16	382.24	376.20	370.92	366.29	362.20	358.60	355.41	344.06	337.63	333.91
39000	428.09	417.06	407.58	399.40	392.30	386.10	380.68	375.93	371.73	368.03	364.76	353.11	346.51	342.69
40000	439.07	427.75	418.03	409.64	402.36	396.00	390.45	385.56	381.27	377.47	374.11	362.17	355.40	351.48
41000	450.05	438.45	428.48	419.88	412.41	405.90	400.21	395.20	390.80	386.91	383.46	371.22	364.28	360.27
42000	461.02	449.14	438.94	430.12	422.47	415.80	409.97	404.84	400.33	396.34	392.82	380.28	373.17	369.05
43000	472.00	459.83	449.39	440.36	432.53	425.70	419.73	414.48	409.86	405.78	402.17	389.33	382.05	377.84
44000	482.98	470.53	459.84	450.60	442.59	435.60	429.49	424.12	419.39	415.22	411.52	398.38	390.94	386.63
45000	493.95	481.22	470.29	460.85	452.65	445.50	439.25	433.76	428.92	424.65	420.88	407.44	399.82	395.41
46000	504.93	491.91	480.74	471.09	462.71	455.40	449.01	443.40	438.46	434.09	430.23	416.49	408.71	404.20
47000	515.91	502.61	491.19	481.33	472.77	465.30	458.77	453.04	447.99	443.53	439.58	425.55	417.59	412.99
48000	526.88	513.30	501.64	491.57	482.83	475.20	468.53	462.68	457.52	452.96	448.93	434.60	426.48	421.77
49000	537.86	524.00	512.09	501.81	492.88	485.10	478.29	472.32	467.05	462.40	458.29	443.65	435.36	430.56
50000	548.84	534.69	522.54	512.05	502.94	495.00	488.06	481.95	476.58	471.84	467.64	452.71	444.25	439.35
55000	603.72	588.16	574.80	563.25	553.24	544.50	536.86	530.15	524.24	519.02	514.40	497.98	488.67	483.28
60000	658.60	641.63	627.05	614.46	603.53	594.00	585.67	578.34	571.90	566.20	561.17	543.25	533.09	527.22
65000	713.49	695.09	679.30	665.66	653.82	643.50	634.47	626.54	619.55	613.39	607.93	588.52	577.52	571.15
70000	768.37	748.56	731.56	716.87	704.12	693.00	683.28	674.73	667.21	660.57	654.69	633.79	621.94	615.08
75000	823.25	802.03	783.81	768.07	754.41	742.50	732.08	722.93	714.87	707.75	701.46	679.06	666.37	659.02
80000	878.13	855.50	836.06	819.28	804.71	792.00	780.89	771.12	762.53	754.94	748.22	724.33	710.79	702.95
85000	933.02	908.97	888.32	870.48	855.00	841.50	829.69	819.32	810.18	802.12	794.98	769.60	755.22	746.89
90000	987.90	962.44	940.57	921.69	905.29	891.00	878.50	867.51	857.84	849.30	841.75	814.87	799.64	790.82
95000	1042.78	1015.90	992.82	972.89	955.59	940.50	927.30	915.71	905.50	896.49	888.51	860.14	844.06	834.76
100000	1097.67	1069.37	1045.08	1024.10	1005.88	990.00	976.11	963.90	953.16	943.67	935.27	905.41	888.49	878.69

MONTHLY PAYMENT
REQUIRED TO AMORTIZE A LOAN

TERM	1 Year	2 Years	3 Years	4 Years	5 Years	6 Years	7 Years	8 Years	9 Years	10 Years	11 Years	12 Years	13 Years	14 Years
AMOUNT														
5	.45	.24	.17	.13	.11	.10	.09	.08	.08	.07	.07	.07	.06	.06
10	.89	.47	.33	.26	.22	.19	.17	.16	.15	.14	.13	.13	.12	.12
15	1.33	.70	.49	.39	.33	.29	.26	.24	.22	.21	.20	.19	.18	.17
25	2.21	1.16	.82	.64	.54	.47	.43	.39	.36	.34	.32	.31	.30	.29
50	4.41	2.32	1.63	1.28	1.08	.94	.85	.77	.72	.68	.64	.61	.59	.57
75	6.61	3.48	2.44	1.92	1.61	1.41	1.27	1.16	1.08	1.01	.96	.92	.88	.85
100	8.82	4.64	3.25	2.56	2.15	1.88	1.69	1.54	1.43	1.35	1.28	1.22	1.18	1.14
200	17.63	9.27	6.50	5.12	4.29	3.75	3.37	3.08	2.86	2.69	2.55	2.44	2.35	2.27
300	26.44	13.90	9.74	7.67	6.44	5.62	5.05	4.62	4.29	4.04	3.83	3.66	3.52	3.40
400	35.25	18.54	12.99	10.23	8.58	7.50	6.73	6.16	5.72	5.38	5.10	4.88	4.69	4.53
500	44.06	23.17	16.23	12.78	10.73	9.37	8.41	7.70	7.15	6.72	6.38	6.10	5.86	5.67
600	52.87	27.80	19.48	15.34	12.87	11.24	10.09	9.24	8.58	8.07	7.65	7.31	7.03	6.80
700	61.68	32.44	22.72	17.89	15.02	13.11	11.77	10.78	10.01	9.41	8.93	8.53	8.21	7.93
800	70.49	37.07	25.97	20.45	17.16	14.99	13.45	12.31	11.44	10.76	10.20	9.75	9.38	9.06
900	79.30	41.70	29.21	23.00	19.30	16.86	15.13	13.85	12.87	12.10	11.48	10.97	10.55	10.20
1000	88.11	46.33	32.46	25.56	21.45	18.73	16.81	15.39	14.30	13.44	12.75	12.19	11.72	11.33
2000	176.21	92.66	64.92	51.12	42.89	37.46	33.62	30.78	28.60	26.88	25.50	24.37	23.44	22.65
3000	264.31	138.99	97.37	76.67	64.34	56.19	50.43	46.16	42.89	40.32	38.25	36.55	35.15	33.98
4000	352.41	185.32	129.83	102.23	85.78	74.92	67.24	61.55	57.19	53.76	50.99	48.74	46.87	45.30
5000	440.52	231.65	162.28	127.78	107.23	93.65	84.05	76.94	71.49	67.19	63.74	60.92	58.58	56.62
6000	528.62	277.98	194.74	153.34	128.67	112.37	100.86	92.32	85.78	80.63	76.49	73.10	70.30	67.95
7000	616.72	324.31	227.19	178.89	150.12	131.10	117.67	107.71	100.08	94.07	89.24	85.29	82.01	79.27
8000	704.82	370.64	259.65	204.45	171.56	149.83	134.47	123.10	114.37	107.51	101.98	97.47	93.73	90.59
9000	792.92	416.97	292.10	230.00	193.00	168.56	151.28	138.48	128.67	120.94	114.73	109.65	105.44	101.92
10000	881.03	463.30	324.56	255.56	214.45	187.29	168.09	153.87	142.97	134.38	127.48	121.83	117.16	113.24
11000	969.13	509.63	357.01	281.11	235.89	206.02	184.90	169.26	157.26	147.82	140.23	134.02	128.87	124.56
12000	1057.23	555.96	389.47	306.67	257.34	224.74	201.71	184.64	171.56	161.26	152.97	146.20	140.59	135.89
13000	1145.33	602.29	421.92	332.22	278.78	243.47	218.52	200.03	185.86	174.69	165.72	158.38	152.31	147.21
14000	1233.43	648.62	454.38	357.78	300.23	262.20	235.33	215.42	200.15	188.13	178.47	170.57	164.02	158.53
15000	1321.54	694.95	486.83	383.33	321.67	280.93	252.13	230.80	214.45	201.57	191.21	182.75	175.74	169.86
16000	1409.64	741.28	519.29	408.89	343.12	299.66	268.94	246.19	228.74	215.01	203.96	194.93	187.45	181.18
17000	1497.74	787.61	551.75	434.44	364.56	318.38	285.75	261.58	243.04	228.44	216.71	207.12	199.17	192.51
18000	1585.84	833.94	584.20	460.00	386.00	337.11	302.56	276.96	257.34	241.88	229.46	219.30	210.88	203.83
19000	1673.94	880.27	616.66	485.55	407.45	355.84	319.37	292.35	271.63	255.32	242.20	231.48	222.60	215.15
20000	1762.05	926.60	649.11	511.11	428.89	374.57	336.18	307.74	285.93	268.76	254.95	243.66	234.31	226.48
21000	1850.15	972.93	681.57	536.66	450.34	393.30	352.99	323.12	300.23	282.19	267.70	255.85	246.03	237.80
22000	1938.25	1019.26	714.02	562.22	471.78	412.03	369.79	338.51	314.52	295.63	280.45	268.03	257.74	249.12
23000	2026.35	1065.59	746.48	587.77	493.23	430.75	386.60	353.90	328.82	309.07	293.19	280.21	269.46	260.45
24000	2114.45	1111.92	778.93	613.33	514.67	449.48	403.41	369.28	343.11	322.51	305.94	292.40	281.17	271.77
25000	2202.56	1158.25	811.39	638.88	536.11	468.21	420.22	384.67	357.41	335.94	318.69	304.58	292.89	283.09
26000	2290.66	1204.58	843.84	664.44	557.56	486.94	437.03	400.06	371.71	349.38	331.43	316.76	304.61	294.42
27000	2378.76	1250.91	876.30	689.99	579.00	505.67	453.84	415.44	386.00	362.82	344.18	328.95	316.32	305.74
28000	2466.86	1297.24	908.75	715.55	600.45	524.39	470.65	430.83	400.30	376.26	356.93	341.13	328.04	317.06
29000	2554.96	1343.57	941.21	741.10	621.89	543.12	487.45	446.22	414.59	389.69	369.68	353.31	339.75	328.39
30000	2643.07	1389.90	973.66	766.66	643.34	561.85	504.26	461.60	428.89	403.13	382.42	365.49	351.47	339.71
31000	2731.17	1436.23	1006.12	792.21	664.78	580.58	521.07	476.99	443.19	416.57	395.17	377.68	363.18	351.04
32000	2819.27	1482.56	1038.57	817.77	686.23	599.31	537.88	492.38	457.48	430.01	407.92	389.86	374.90	362.36
33000	2907.37	1528.89	1071.03	843.32	707.67	618.04	554.69	507.76	471.78	443.44	420.67	402.04	386.61	373.68
34000	2995.47	1575.22	1103.49	868.88	729.11	636.76	571.50	523.15	486.08	456.88	433.41	414.23	398.33	385.01
35000	3083.58	1621.55	1135.94	894.43	750.56	655.49	588.31	538.54	500.37	470.32	446.16	426.41	410.04	396.33
36000	3171.68	1667.88	1168.40	919.99	772.00	674.22	605.11	553.92	514.67	483.76	458.91	438.59	421.76	407.65
37000	3259.78	1714.21	1200.85	945.54	793.45	692.95	621.92	569.31	528.96	497.19	471.65	450.78	433.48	418.98
38000	3347.88	1760.54	1233.31	971.10	814.89	711.68	638.73	584.70	543.26	510.63	484.40	462.96	445.19	430.30
39000	3435.98	1806.87	1265.76	996.65	836.34	730.40	655.54	600.08	557.56	524.07	497.15	475.14	456.91	441.62
40000	3524.09	1853.20	1298.22	1022.21	857.78	749.13	672.35	615.47	571.85	537.51	509.90	487.32	468.62	452.95
41000	3612.19	1899.53	1330.67	1047.76	879.23	767.86	689.16	630.86	586.15	550.95	522.64	499.51	480.34	464.27
42000	3700.29	1945.86	1363.13	1073.32	900.67	786.59	705.97	646.24	600.45	564.38	535.39	511.69	492.05	475.59
43000	3788.39	1992.18	1395.58	1098.87	922.11	805.32	722.77	661.63	614.74	577.82	548.14	523.87	503.77	486.92
44000	3876.49	2038.51	1428.04	1124.43	943.56	824.05	739.58	677.02	629.04	591.26	560.89	536.06	515.48	498.24
45000	3964.60	2084.84	1460.49	1149.99	965.00	842.77	756.39	692.40	643.33	604.70	573.63	548.24	527.20	509.57
46000	4052.70	2131.17	1492.95	1175.54	986.45	861.50	773.20	707.79	657.63	618.13	586.38	560.42	538.91	520.89
47000	4140.80	2177.50	1525.40	1201.10	1007.89	880.23	790.01	723.18	671.93	631.57	599.13	572.61	550.63	532.21
48000	4228.90	2223.83	1557.86	1226.65	1029.34	898.96	806.82	738.56	686.22	645.01	611.87	584.79	562.34	543.54
49000	4317.00	2270.16	1590.32	1252.21	1050.78	917.69	823.63	753.95	700.52	658.45	624.62	596.97	574.06	554.86
50000	4405.11	2316.49	1622.77	1277.76	1072.22	936.41	840.43	769.34	714.81	671.88	637.37	609.15	585.78	566.18
55000	4845.62	2548.14	1785.05	1405.54	1179.45	1030.06	924.48	846.27	786.30	739.07	701.11	670.07	644.35	622.80
60000	5286.13	2779.79	1947.32	1533.31	1286.67	1123.70	1008.52	923.20	857.78	806.26	764.84	730.98	702.93	679.42
65000	5726.64	3011.44	2109.60	1661.09	1393.89	1217.34	1092.56	1000.14	929.26	873.45	828.58	791.90	761.51	736.04
70000	6167.15	3243.09	2271.88	1788.86	1501.11	1310.98	1176.61	1077.07	1000.74	940.63	892.31	852.81	820.08	792.65
75000	6607.66	3474.74	2434.15	1916.64	1608.33	1404.62	1260.65	1154.00	1072.22	1007.82	956.05	913.73	878.66	849.27
80000	7048.17	3706.39	2596.43	2044.41	1715.56	1498.26	1344.69	1230.94	1143.70	1075.01	1019.79	974.64	937.24	905.89
85000	7488.68	3938.03	2758.71	2172.19	1822.78	1591.90	1428.74	1307.87	1215.18	1142.20	1083.52	1035.56	995.82	962.51
90000	7929.19	4169.68	2920.98	2299.97	1930.00	1685.54	1512.78	1384.80	1286.66	1209.39	1147.26	1096.47	1054.39	1019.13
95000	8369.70	4401.33	3083.26	2427.74	2037.22	1779.18	1596.82	1461.74	1358.14	1276.57	1211.00	1157.39	1112.97	1075.74
100000	8810.21	4632.98	3245.54	2555.52	2144.44	1872.82	1680.86	1538.67	1429.62	1343.76	1274.73	1218.30	1171.55	1132.36

TERM AMOUNT	15 Years	16 Years	17 Years	18 Years	19 Years	20 Years	21 Years	22 Years	23 Years	24 Years	25 Years	30 Years	35 Years	40 Years
5	.06	.06	.06	.06	.06	.05	.05	.05	.05	.05	.05	.05	.05	.05
10	.11	.11	.11	.11	.11	.10	.10	.10	.10	.10	.10	.10	.09	.09
15	.17	.17	.16	.16	.16	.15	.15	.15	.15	.15	.15	.14	.14	.14
25	.28	.27	.27	.26	.26	.25	.25	.25	.24	.24	.24	.23	.23	.23
50	.55	.54	.53	.52	.51	.50	.49	.49	.48	.48	.47	.46	.45	.45
75	.83	.81	.79	.77	.76	.75	.74	.73	.72	.71	.71	.69	.67	.67
100	1.10	1.08	1.05	1.03	1.01	1.00	.98	.97	.96	.95	.94	.91	.90	.89
200	2.20	2.15	2.10	2.06	2.02	1.99	1.96	1.94	1.91	1.90	1.88	1.82	1.79	1.77
300	3.30	3.22	3.15	3.08	3.03	2.98	2.94	2.90	2.87	2.84	2.82	2.73	2.68	2.65
400	4.40	4.29	4.19	4.11	4.04	3.97	3.92	3.87	3.82	3.79	3.75	3.63	3.57	3.53
500	5.50	5.36	5.24	5.13	5.04	4.96	4.89	4.83	4.78	4.73	4.69	4.54	4.46	4.41
600	6.60	6.43	6.29	6.16	6.05	5.96	5.87	5.80	5.73	5.68	5.63	5.45	5.35	5.29
700	7.70	7.50	7.33	7.19	7.06	6.95	6.85	6.76	6.69	6.62	6.56	6.36	6.24	6.17
800	8.80	8.57	8.38	8.21	8.07	7.94	7.83	7.73	7.64	7.57	7.50	7.26	7.13	7.05
900	9.90	9.64	9.43	9.24	9.07	8.93	8.81	8.70	8.60	8.51	8.44	8.17	8.02	7.93
1000	11.00	10.71	10.47	10.26	10.08	9.92	9.78	9.66	9.55	9.46	9.38	9.08	8.91	8.81
2000	21.99	21.42	20.94	20.52	20.16	19.84	19.56	19.32	19.10	18.91	18.75	18.15	17.81	17.62
3000	32.98	32.13	31.41	30.78	30.23	29.76	29.34	28.97	28.65	28.37	28.12	27.22	26.72	26.42
4000	43.97	42.84	41.87	41.03	40.31	39.67	39.12	38.63	38.20	37.82	37.49	36.30	35.62	35.23
5000	54.97	53.55	52.34	51.29	50.38	49.59	48.89	48.29	47.75	47.28	46.86	45.37	44.53	44.04
6000	65.96	64.26	62.81	61.55	60.46	59.51	58.67	57.94	57.30	56.73	56.23	54.44	53.43	52.84
7000	76.95	74.97	73.27	71.81	70.53	69.42	68.45	67.60	66.85	66.18	65.60	63.51	62.33	61.65
8000	87.94	85.68	83.74	82.06	80.61	79.34	78.23	77.25	76.40	75.64	74.97	72.59	71.24	70.46
9000	98.93	96.39	94.21	92.32	90.68	89.26	88.01	86.91	85.95	85.09	84.34	81.66	80.14	79.26
10000	109.93	107.10	104.67	102.58	100.76	99.17	97.78	96.57	95.49	94.55	93.71	90.73	89.05	88.07
11000	120.92	117.81	115.14	112.83	110.83	109.09	107.56	106.22	105.04	104.00	103.08	99.80	97.95	96.88
12000	131.91	128.52	125.61	123.09	120.91	119.01	117.34	115.88	114.59	113.46	112.45	108.88	106.85	105.68
13000	142.90	139.23	136.07	133.35	130.98	128.92	127.12	125.54	124.14	122.91	121.82	117.95	115.76	114.49
14000	153.89	149.94	146.54	143.61	141.06	138.84	136.90	135.19	133.69	132.36	131.19	127.02	124.66	123.30
15000	164.89	160.65	157.01	153.86	151.13	148.76	146.67	144.85	143.24	141.82	140.56	136.10	133.57	132.10
16000	175.88	171.36	167.47	164.12	161.21	158.67	156.45	154.50	152.79	151.27	149.93	145.17	142.47	140.91
17000	186.87	182.06	177.94	174.38	171.28	168.59	166.23	164.16	162.34	160.73	159.30	154.24	151.37	149.72
18000	197.86	192.77	188.41	184.63	181.36	178.51	176.01	173.82	171.89	170.18	168.67	163.31	160.28	158.52
19000	208.85	203.48	198.87	194.89	191.44	188.42	185.79	183.47	181.43	179.64	178.04	172.39	169.18	167.33
20000	219.85	214.19	209.34	205.15	201.51	198.34	195.56	193.13	190.98	189.09	187.41	181.46	178.09	176.14
21000	230.84	224.90	219.81	215.41	211.59	208.26	205.34	202.78	200.53	198.54	196.79	190.53	186.99	184.94
22000	241.83	235.61	230.27	225.66	221.66	218.17	215.12	212.44	210.08	208.00	206.16	199.60	195.90	193.75
23000	252.82	246.32	240.74	235.92	231.74	228.09	224.90	222.10	219.63	217.45	215.53	208.68	204.80	202.56
24000	263.81	257.03	251.21	246.18	241.81	238.01	234.68	231.75	229.18	226.91	224.90	217.75	213.70	211.36
25000	274.81	267.74	261.67	256.43	251.89	247.92	244.45	241.41	230.73	236.36	234.27	226.82	222.61	220.17
26000	285.80	278.45	272.14	266.69	261.96	257.84	254.23	251.07	248.28	245.82	243.64	235.90	231.51	228.98
27000	296.79	289.16	282.61	276.95	272.04	267.76	264.01	260.72	257.83	255.27	253.01	244.97	240.42	237.78
28000	307.78	299.87	293.07	287.21	282.11	277.67	273.79	270.38	267.38	264.72	262.38	254.04	249.32	246.59
29000	318.78	310.58	303.54	297.46	292.19	287.59	283.57	280.03	276.92	274.18	271.75	263.11	258.22	255.40
30000	329.77	321.29	314.01	307.72	302.26	297.51	293.34	289.69	286.47	283.63	281.12	272.19	267.13	264.20
31000	340.76	332.00	324.47	317.98	312.34	307.42	303.12	299.35	296.02	293.09	290.49	281.26	276.03	273.01
32000	351.75	342.71	334.94	328.23	322.41	317.34	312.90	309.00	305.57	302.54	299.86	290.33	284.94	281.82
33000	362.74	353.42	345.41	338.49	332.49	327.26	322.68	318.66	315.12	312.00	309.23	299.40	293.84	290.62
34000	373.74	364.12	355.87	348.75	342.56	337.17	332.46	328.32	324.67	321.45	318.60	308.48	302.74	299.43
35000	384.73	374.83	366.34	359.01	352.64	347.09	342.23	337.97	334.22	330.90	327.97	317.55	311.65	308.24
36000	395.72	385.54	376.81	369.26	362.71	357.01	352.01	347.63	343.77	340.36	337.34	326.62	320.55	317.04
37000	406.71	396.25	387.27	379.52	372.79	366.92	361.79	357.28	353.32	349.81	346.71	335.70	329.46	325.85
38000	417.70	406.96	397.74	389.78	382.87	376.84	371.57	366.94	362.86	359.27	356.08	344.77	338.36	334.66
39000	428.70	417.67	408.21	400.03	392.94	386.76	381.35	376.60	372.41	368.72	365.45	353.84	347.27	343.46
40000	439.69	428.38	418.67	410.29	403.02	396.67	391.12	386.25	381.96	378.18	374.82	362.91	356.17	352.27
41000	450.68	439.09	429.14	420.55	413.09	406.59	400.90	395.91	391.51	387.63	384.19	371.99	365.07	361.08
42000	461.67	449.80	439.61	430.81	423.17	416.51	410.68	405.56	401.06	397.08	393.57	381.06	373.98	369.88
43000	472.66	460.51	450.07	441.06	433.24	426.42	420.46	415.22	410.61	406.54	402.94	390.13	382.88	378.69
44000	483.66	471.22	460.54	451.32	443.32	436.34	430.24	424.88	420.16	415.99	412.31	399.20	391.79	387.50
45000	494.65	481.93	471.01	461.58	453.39	446.26	440.01	434.53	429.71	425.45	421.68	408.28	400.69	396.30
46000	505.64	492.64	481.47	471.83	463.47	456.17	449.79	444.19	439.26	434.90	431.05	417.35	409.59	405.11
47000	516.63	503.35	491.94	482.09	473.54	466.09	459.57	453.85	448.80	444.35	440.42	426.42	418.50	413.92
48000	527.62	514.06	502.41	492.35	483.62	476.01	469.35	463.50	458.35	453.81	449.79	435.50	427.40	422.72
49000	538.62	524.77	512.87	502.61	493.69	485.92	479.13	473.16	467.90	463.26	459.16	444.57	436.31	431.53
50000	549.61	535.48	523.34	512.86	503.77	495.84	488.90	482.81	477.45	472.72	468.53	453.64	445.21	440.34
55000	604.57	589.02	575.67	564.15	554.14	545.42	537.79	531.09	525.20	519.99	515.38	499.00	489.73	484.37
60000	659.53	642.57	628.01	615.43	604.52	595.01	586.68	579.38	572.94	567.26	562.23	544.37	534.25	528.40
65000	714.49	696.12	680.34	666.72	654.90	644.59	635.57	627.66	620.69	614.53	609.09	589.73	578.77	572.43
70000	769.45	749.66	732.68	718.01	705.27	694.18	684.46	675.94	668.43	661.80	655.94	635.09	623.29	616.47
75000	824.41	803.21	785.01	769.29	755.65	743.76	733.35	724.22	716.17	709.07	702.79	680.46	667.81	660.50
80000	879.37	856.76	837.34	820.58	806.03	793.34	782.24	772.50	763.92	756.35	749.64	725.82	712.33	704.53
85000	934.33	910.30	889.68	871.86	856.40	842.93	831.13	820.78	811.66	803.62	796.50	771.19	756.85	748.57
90000	989.29	963.85	942.01	923.15	906.78	892.51	880.02	869.06	859.41	850.89	843.35	816.55	801.38	792.60
95000	1044.25	1017.40	994.34	974.43	957.16	942.09	928.91	917.34	907.15	898.16	890.20	861.91	845.90	836.63
100000	1099.21	1070.95	1046.68	1025.72	1007.53	991.68	977.80	965.62	954.90	945.43	937.05	907.28	890.42	880.67

MONTHLY PAYMENT
REQUIRED TO AMORTIZE A LOAN

TERM	1 Year	2 Years	3 Years	4 Years	5 Years	6 Years	7 Years	8 Years	9 Years	10 Years	11 Years	12 Years	13 Years	14 Years
AMOUNT														
5	.45	.24	.17	.13	.11	.10	.09	.08	.08	.07	.07	.07	.06	.06
10	.89	.47	.33	.26	.22	.19	.17	.16	.15	.14	.13	.13	.12	.12
15	1.33	.70	.49	.39	.33	.29	.26	.24	.22	.21	.20	.19	.18	.18
25	2.21	1.16	.82	.65	.54	.47	.43	.39	.36	.34	.33	.31	.30	.29
50	4.41	2.32	1.63	1.29	1.08	.94	.85	.78	.72	.68	.65	.62	.59	.57
75	6.62	3.48	2.44	1.93	1.62	1.41	1.27	1.16	1.08	1.02	.97	.92	.89	.86
100	8.82	4.64	3.26	2.57	2.15	1.88	1.69	1.55	1.44	1.35	1.29	1.23	1.18	1.14
200	17.63	9.28	6.51	5.13	4.30	3.76	3.38	3.09	2.88	2.70	2.57	2.45	2.36	2.28
300	26.45	13.92	9.76	7.69	6.45	5.64	5.06	4.64	4.31	4.05	3.85	3.68	3.54	3.42
400	35.26	18.56	13.01	10.25	8.60	7.52	6.75	6.18	5.75	5.40	5.13	4.90	4.72	4.56
500	44.08	23.19	16.26	12.81	10.75	9.39	8.44	7.73	7.18	6.75	6.41	6.13	5.89	5.70
600	52.89	27.83	19.51	15.37	12.90	11.27	10.12	9.27	8.62	8.10	7.69	7.35	7.07	6.84
700	61.71	32.47	22.76	17.93	15.05	13.15	11.81	10.81	10.05	9.45	8.97	8.57	8.25	7.97
800	70.52	37.11	26.01	20.49	17.20	15.03	13.49	12.36	11.49	10.80	10.25	9.80	9.43	9.11
900	79.34	41.74	29.26	23.05	19.35	16.91	15.18	13.90	12.92	12.15	11.53	11.02	10.60	10.25
1000	88.15	46.38	32.51	25.61	21.50	18.78	16.87	15.45	14.36	13.50	12.81	12.25	11.78	11.39
2000	176.30	92.76	65.01	51.21	42.99	37.56	33.73	30.89	28.71	26.99	25.61	24.49	23.56	22.77
3000	264.45	139.13	97.51	76.82	64.49	56.34	50.59	46.33	43.06	40.49	38.42	36.73	35.33	34.16
4000	352.60	185.51	130.01	102.42	85.98	75.12	67.45	61.77	57.41	53.98	51.22	48.97	47.11	45.54
5000	440.75	231.89	162.52	128.02	107.47	93.90	84.31	77.21	71.76	67.47	64.03	61.21	58.88	56.93
6000	528.90	278.26	195.02	153.63	128.97	112.68	101.17	92.65	86.11	80.97	76.83	73.45	70.66	68.31
7000	617.05	324.64	227.52	179.23	150.46	131.46	118.03	108.09	100.46	94.46	89.64	85.69	82.43	79.70
8000	705.19	371.01	260.02	204.83	171.96	150.24	134.89	123.53	114.81	107.95	102.44	97.94	94.21	91.08
9000	793.34	417.39	292.53	230.44	193.45	169.02	151.75	138.97	129.16	121.45	115.25	110.18	105.98	102.46
10000	881.49	463.77	325.03	256.04	214.94	187.79	168.61	154.41	143.51	134.94	128.05	122.42	117.76	113.85
11000	969.64	510.14	357.53	281.64	236.44	206.57	185.47	169.85	157.86	148.43	140.85	134.66	129.53	125.23
12000	1057.79	556.52	390.03	307.25	257.93	225.35	202.33	185.29	172.22	161.93	153.66	146.90	141.31	136.62
13000	1145.94	602.89	422.54	332.85	279.43	244.13	219.19	200.73	186.57	175.42	166.46	159.14	153.08	148.00
14000	1234.09	649.27	455.04	358.45	300.92	262.91	236.05	216.17	200.92	188.91	179.27	171.38	164.86	159.39
15000	1322.23	695.65	487.54	384.06	322.41	281.69	252.92	231.61	215.27	202.41	192.07	183.63	176.63	170.77
16000	1410.38	742.02	520.04	409.66	343.91	300.47	269.78	247.05	229.62	215.90	204.88	195.87	188.41	182.15
17000	1498.53	788.40	552.55	435.26	365.40	319.25	286.64	262.49	243.97	229.39	217.68	208.11	200.18	193.54
18000	1586.68	834.77	585.05	460.87	386.90	338.03	303.50	277.93	258.32	242.89	230.49	220.35	211.96	204.92
19000	1674.83	881.15	617.55	486.47	408.39	356.81	320.36	293.37	272.67	256.38	243.29	232.59	223.73	216.31
20000	1762.98	927.53	650.05	512.07	429.88	375.58	337.22	308.81	287.02	269.87	256.09	244.83	235.51	227.69
21000	1851.13	973.90	682.56	537.68	451.38	394.36	354.08	324.25	301.37	283.37	268.90	257.07	247.28	239.08
22000	1939.27	1020.28	715.06	563.28	472.87	413.14	370.94	339.69	315.72	296.86	281.70	269.32	259.06	250.46
23000	2027.42	1066.65	747.56	588.88	494.36	431.92	387.80	355.13	330.07	310.36	294.51	281.56	270.83	261.84
24000	2115.57	1113.03	780.06	614.49	515.86	450.70	404.66	370.57	344.43	323.85	307.31	293.80	282.61	273.23
25000	2203.72	1159.41	812.57	640.09	537.35	469.48	421.52	386.01	358.78	337.34	320.12	306.04	294.38	284.61
26000	2291.87	1205.78	845.07	665.69	558.85	488.26	438.38	401.45	373.13	350.84	332.92	318.28	306.16	296.00
27000	2380.02	1252.16	877.57	691.30	580.34	507.04	455.24	416.89	387.48	364.33	345.73	330.52	317.93	307.38
28000	2468.17	1298.53	910.07	716.90	601.83	525.82	472.10	432.33	401.83	377.82	358.53	342.76	329.71	318.77
29000	2556.31	1344.91	942.58	742.50	623.33	544.60	488.96	447.77	416.18	391.32	371.33	355.01	341.48	330.15
30000	2644.46	1391.29	975.08	768.11	644.82	563.37	505.83	463.21	430.53	404.81	384.14	367.25	353.26	341.54
31000	2732.61	1437.66	1007.58	793.71	666.32	582.15	522.69	478.65	444.88	418.30	396.94	379.49	365.03	352.92
32000	2820.76	1484.04	1040.08	819.31	687.81	600.93	539.55	494.09	459.23	431.80	409.75	391.73	376.81	364.30
33000	2908.91	1530.41	1072.59	844.92	709.30	619.71	556.41	509.53	473.58	445.29	422.55	403.97	388.58	375.69
34000	2997.06	1576.79	1105.09	870.52	730.80	638.49	573.27	524.97	487.93	458.78	435.36	416.21	400.36	387.07
35000	3085.21	1623.17	1137.59	896.12	752.29	657.27	590.13	540.41	502.29	472.28	448.16	428.45	412.13	398.46
36000	3173.35	1669.54	1170.09	921.73	773.79	676.05	606.99	555.85	516.64	485.77	460.97	440.70	423.91	409.84
37000	3261.50	1715.92	1202.60	947.33	795.28	694.83	623.85	571.29	530.99	499.26	473.77	452.94	435.68	421.23
38000	3349.65	1762.29	1235.10	972.93	816.77	713.61	640.71	586.73	545.34	512.76	486.57	465.18	447.46	432.61
39000	3437.80	1808.67	1267.60	998.54	838.27	732.38	657.57	602.17	559.69	526.25	499.38	477.42	459.23	443.99
40000	3525.95	1855.05	1300.10	1024.14	859.76	751.16	674.43	617.61	574.04	539.74	512.18	489.66	471.01	455.38
41000	3614.10	1901.42	1332.61	1049.74	881.25	769.94	691.29	633.05	588.39	553.24	524.99	501.90	482.78	466.76
42000	3702.25	1947.80	1365.11	1075.35	902.75	788.72	708.15	648.49	602.74	566.73	537.79	514.14	494.56	478.15
43000	3790.39	1994.17	1397.61	1100.95	924.24	807.50	725.01	663.93	617.09	580.23	550.60	526.39	506.33	489.53
44000	3878.54	2040.55	1430.11	1126.55	945.74	826.28	741.87	679.37	631.44	593.72	563.40	538.63	518.11	500.92
45000	3966.69	2086.93	1462.61	1152.16	967.23	845.06	758.74	694.81	645.79	607.21	576.21	550.87	529.88	512.30
46000	4054.84	2133.30	1495.12	1177.76	988.72	863.84	775.60	710.25	660.14	620.71	589.01	563.11	541.66	523.68
47000	4142.99	2179.68	1527.62	1203.36	1010.22	882.62	792.46	725.69	674.50	634.20	601.81	575.35	553.43	535.07
48000	4231.14	2226.06	1560.12	1228.97	1031.71	901.40	809.32	741.13	688.85	647.69	614.62	587.59	565.21	546.45
49000	4319.29	2272.43	1592.62	1254.57	1053.21	920.17	826.18	756.57	703.20	661.19	627.42	599.83	576.98	557.84
50000	4407.44	2318.81	1625.13	1280.17	1074.70	938.95	843.04	772.01	717.55	674.68	640.23	612.08	588.76	569.22
55000	4848.18	2550.69	1787.64	1408.19	1182.17	1032.85	927.34	849.21	789.30	742.15	704.25	673.28	647.63	626.14
60000	5288.92	2782.57	1950.15	1536.21	1289.64	1126.74	1011.65	926.41	861.06	809.61	768.27	734.49	706.51	683.07
65000	5729.66	3014.45	2112.66	1664.22	1397.11	1220.64	1095.95	1003.61	932.81	877.08	832.29	795.70	765.38	739.99
70000	6170.41	3246.33	2275.18	1792.24	1504.58	1314.53	1180.25	1080.81	1004.57	944.55	896.32	856.90	824.26	796.91
75000	6611.15	3478.21	2437.69	1920.26	1612.05	1408.43	1264.56	1158.01	1076.32	1012.02	960.34	918.11	883.13	853.83
80000	7051.89	3710.09	2600.20	2048.28	1719.52	1502.32	1348.86	1235.21	1148.07	1079.49	1024.36	979.32	942.01	910.75
85000	7492.64	3941.97	2762.71	2176.29	1826.99	1596.22	1433.16	1312.41	1219.83	1146.95	1088.38	1040.52	1000.88	967.67
90000	7933.38	4173.85	2925.22	2304.31	1934.46	1690.11	1517.47	1389.61	1291.58	1214.42	1152.41	1101.73	1059.76	1024.60
95000	8374.12	4405.73	3087.74	2432.33	2041.93	1784.01	1601.77	1466.81	1363.34	1281.89	1216.43	1162.94	1118.63	1081.52
100000	8814.87	4637.61	3250.25	2560.34	2149.40	1877.90	1686.07	1544.01	1435.09	1349.36	1280.45	1224.15	1177.51	1138.44

TERM AMOUNT	15 Years	16 Years	17 Years	18 Years	19 Years	20 Years	21 Years	22 Years	23 Years	24 Years	25 Years	30 Years	35 Years	40 Years
5	.06	.06	.06	.06	.06	.05	.05	.05	.05	.05	.05	.05	.05	.05
10	.12	.11	.11	.11	.11	.10	.10	.10	.10	.10	.10	.10	.09	.09
15	.17	.17	.16	.16	.16	.15	.15	.15	.15	.15	.15	.14	.14	.14
25	.28	.27	.27	.26	.26	.25	.25	.25	.25	.24	.24	.23	.23	.23
50	.56	.54	.53	.52	.51	.50	.50	.49	.49	.48	.48	.46	.45	.45
75	.83	.81	.79	.78	.77	.75	.74	.73	.73	.72	.71	.69	.68	.67
100	1.11	1.08	1.06	1.04	1.02	1.00	.99	.98	.97	.96	.95	.92	.90	.89
200	2.22	2.16	2.11	2.07	2.03	2.00	1.97	1.95	1.93	1.91	1.89	1.83	1.80	1.78
300	3.32	3.24	3.16	3.10	3.05	3.00	2.96	2.92	2.89	2.86	2.84	2.75	2.70	2.67
400	4.43	4.31	4.22	4.13	4.06	4.00	3.94	3.90	3.85	3.81	3.78	3.66	3.60	3.56
500	5.53	5.39	5.27	5.17	5.08	5.00	4.93	4.87	4.81	4.77	4.73	4.58	4.50	4.45
600	6.64	6.47	6.32	6.20	6.09	6.00	5.91	5.84	5.78	5.72	5.67	5.49	5.39	5.34
700	7.74	7.55	7.38	7.23	7.10	6.99	6.90	6.81	6.74	6.67	6.61	6.41	6.29	6.22
800	8.85	8.62	8.43	8.26	8.12	7.99	7.88	7.79	7.70	7.62	7.56	7.32	7.19	7.11
900	9.95	9.70	9.48	9.30	9.13	8.99	8.87	8.76	8.66	8.58	8.50	8.24	8.09	8.00
1000	11.06	10.78	10.54	10.33	10.15	9.99	9.85	9.73	9.62	9.53	9.45	9.15	8.99	8.89
2000	22.11	21.55	21.07	20.65	20.29	19.97	19.70	19.46	19.24	19.05	18.89	18.30	17.97	17.78
3000	33.17	32.32	31.60	30.97	30.43	29.96	29.54	29.18	28.86	28.58	28.33	27.45	26.95	26.66
4000	44.22	43.09	42.13	41.29	40.57	39.94	39.39	38.91	38.48	38.10	37.77	36.59	35.93	35.55
5000	55.27	53.87	52.66	51.62	50.71	49.92	49.23	48.63	48.10	47.63	47.21	45.74	44.91	44.43
6000	66.33	64.64	63.19	61.94	60.85	59.91	59.08	58.36	57.72	57.15	56.66	54.89	53.89	53.32
7000	77.38	75.41	73.72	72.26	70.99	69.89	68.93	68.08	67.34	66.68	66.10	64.04	62.87	62.20
8000	88.44	86.18	84.25	82.58	81.14	79.88	78.77	77.81	76.95	76.20	75.54	73.18	71.86	71.09
9000	99.49	96.96	94.78	92.91	91.28	89.86	88.62	87.53	86.57	85.73	84.98	82.33	80.84	79.98
10000	110.54	107.73	105.31	103.23	101.42	99.84	98.46	97.26	96.19	95.25	94.42	91.48	89.82	88.86
11000	121.60	118.50	115.84	113.55	111.56	109.83	108.31	106.98	105.81	104.78	103.86	100.63	98.80	97.75
12000	132.65	129.27	126.37	123.87	121.70	119.81	118.16	116.71	115.43	114.30	113.31	109.77	107.78	106.63
13000	143.71	140.05	136.91	134.19	131.84	129.79	128.00	126.43	125.05	123.83	122.75	118.92	116.76	115.52
14000	154.76	150.82	147.44	144.52	141.98	139.78	137.85	136.16	134.67	133.35	132.19	128.07	125.74	124.40
15000	165.81	161.59	157.97	154.84	152.13	149.76	147.69	145.88	144.29	142.88	141.63	137.22	134.73	133.29
16000	176.87	172.36	168.50	165.16	162.27	159.75	157.54	155.61	153.90	152.40	151.07	146.36	143.71	142.18
17000	187.92	183.14	179.03	175.48	172.41	169.73	167.39	165.33	163.52	161.93	160.52	155.51	152.69	151.06
18000	198.98	193.91	189.56	185.81	182.55	179.71	177.23	175.06	173.14	171.45	169.96	164.66	161.67	159.95
19000	210.03	204.68	200.09	196.13	192.69	189.70	187.08	184.78	182.76	180.98	179.40	173.81	170.65	168.83
20000	221.08	215.45	210.62	206.45	202.83	199.68	196.92	194.51	192.38	190.50	188.84	182.95	179.63	177.72
21000	232.14	226.23	221.15	216.77	212.97	209.66	206.77	204.23	202.00	200.03	198.28	192.10	188.61	186.60
22000	243.19	237.00	231.68	227.10	223.12	219.65	216.62	213.96	211.62	209.55	207.72	201.25	197.59	195.49
23000	254.25	247.77	242.21	237.42	233.26	229.63	226.46	223.68	221.23	219.08	217.17	210.40	206.58	204.38
24000	265.30	258.54	252.74	247.74	243.40	239.62	236.31	233.41	230.85	228.60	226.61	219.54	215.56	213.26
25000	276.35	269.32	263.28	258.06	253.54	249.60	246.15	243.13	240.47	238.13	236.05	228.69	224.54	222.15
26000	287.41	280.09	273.81	268.38	263.68	259.58	256.00	252.86	250.09	247.65	245.49	237.84	233.52	231.03
27000	298.46	290.86	284.34	278.71	273.82	269.57	265.85	262.58	259.71	257.17	254.93	246.98	242.50	239.92
28000	309.52	301.63	294.87	289.03	283.96	279.55	275.69	272.31	269.33	266.70	264.38	256.13	251.48	248.80
29000	320.57	312.41	305.40	299.35	294.11	289.54	285.54	282.03	278.95	276.22	273.82	265.28	260.46	257.69
30000	331.62	323.18	315.93	309.67	304.25	299.52	295.38	291.76	288.57	285.75	283.26	274.43	269.45	266.58
31000	342.68	333.95	326.46	320.00	314.39	309.50	305.23	301.48	298.18	295.27	292.70	283.57	278.43	275.46
32000	353.73	344.72	336.99	330.32	324.53	319.49	315.08	311.21	307.80	304.80	302.14	292.72	287.41	284.35
33000	364.79	355.50	347.52	340.64	334.67	329.47	324.92	320.93	317.42	314.32	311.58	301.87	296.39	293.23
34000	375.84	366.27	358.05	350.96	344.81	339.45	334.77	330.66	327.04	323.85	321.03	311.02	305.37	302.12
35000	386.89	377.04	368.58	361.28	354.95	349.44	344.61	340.38	336.66	333.37	330.47	320.16	314.35	311.00
36000	397.95	387.81	379.11	371.61	365.10	359.42	354.46	350.11	346.28	342.90	339.91	329.31	323.33	319.89
37000	409.00	398.58	389.65	381.93	375.24	369.41	364.31	359.83	355.90	352.42	349.35	338.46	332.31	328.78
38000	420.06	409.36	400.18	392.25	385.38	379.39	374.15	369.56	365.51	361.95	358.79	347.61	341.30	337.66
39000	431.11	420.13	410.71	402.57	395.52	389.37	384.00	379.28	375.13	371.47	368.24	356.75	350.28	346.55
40000	442.16	430.90	421.24	412.90	405.66	399.36	393.84	389.01	384.75	381.00	377.68	365.90	359.26	355.43
41000	453.22	441.67	431.77	423.22	415.80	409.34	403.69	398.73	394.37	390.52	387.12	375.05	368.24	364.32
42000	464.27	452.45	442.30	433.54	425.94	419.32	413.54	408.46	403.99	400.05	396.56	384.20	377.22	373.20
43000	475.33	463.22	452.83	443.86	436.08	429.31	423.38	418.18	413.61	409.57	406.00	393.34	386.20	382.09
44000	486.38	473.99	463.36	454.19	446.23	439.29	433.23	427.91	423.23	419.10	415.44	402.49	395.18	390.98
45000	497.43	484.76	473.89	464.51	456.37	449.28	443.07	437.63	432.85	428.62	424.89	411.64	404.17	399.86
46000	508.49	495.54	484.42	474.83	466.51	459.26	452.92	447.36	442.46	438.15	434.33	420.79	413.15	408.75
47000	519.54	506.31	494.95	485.15	476.65	469.24	462.77	457.08	452.08	447.67	443.77	429.93	422.13	417.63
48000	530.60	517.08	505.48	495.47	486.79	479.23	472.61	466.81	461.70	457.20	453.21	439.08	431.11	426.52
49000	541.65	527.85	516.01	505.80	496.93	489.21	482.46	476.53	471.32	466.72	462.65	448.23	440.09	435.40
50000	552.70	538.63	526.55	516.12	507.07	499.19	492.30	486.26	480.94	476.25	472.10	457.37	449.07	444.29
55000	607.97	592.49	579.20	567.73	557.78	549.11	541.53	534.88	529.03	523.87	519.30	503.11	493.98	488.72
60000	663.24	646.35	631.85	619.34	608.49	599.03	590.76	583.51	577.13	571.49	566.51	548.85	538.89	533.15
65000	718.51	700.21	684.51	670.95	659.20	648.95	639.99	632.13	625.22	619.12	613.72	594.59	583.79	577.58
70000	773.78	754.07	737.16	722.56	709.90	698.87	689.22	680.76	673.31	666.74	660.93	640.32	628.70	622.00
75000	829.05	807.94	789.82	774.18	760.61	748.79	738.45	729.39	721.41	714.37	708.14	686.06	673.61	666.43
80000	884.32	861.80	842.47	825.79	811.32	798.71	787.68	778.01	769.50	761.99	755.35	731.80	718.51	710.86
85000	939.59	915.66	895.12	877.40	862.02	848.63	836.91	826.64	817.59	809.61	802.56	777.53	763.42	755.29
90000	994.86	969.52	947.78	929.01	912.73	898.55	886.14	875.26	865.69	857.24	849.77	823.27	808.33	799.72
95000	1050.13	1023.39	1000.43	980.62	963.44	948.47	935.37	923.89	913.78	904.86	896.98	869.01	853.23	844.15
100000	1105.40	1077.25	1053.09	1032.23	1014.14	998.38	984.60	972.51	961.87	952.49	944.19	914.74	898.14	888.58

MONTHLY PAYMENT
REQUIRED TO AMORTIZE A LOAN

TERM	1 Year	2 Years	3 Years	4 Years	5 Years	6 Years	7 Years	8 Years	9 Years	10 Years	11 Years	12 Years	13 Years	14 Years
AMOUNT														
5	.45	.24	.17	.13	.11	.10	.09	.08	.08	.07	.07	.07	.06	.06
10	.89	.47	.33	.26	.22	.19	.17	.16	.15	.14	.13	.13	.12	.12
15	1.33	.70	.49	.39	.33	.29	.26	.24	.22	.21	.20	.19	.18	.18
25	2.21	1.17	.82	.65	.54	.48	.43	.39	.37	.34	.33	.31	.30	.29
50	4.41	2.33	1.63	1.29	1.08	.95	.85	.78	.73	.68	.65	.62	.60	.58
75	6.62	3.49	2.45	1.93	1.62	1.42	1.27	1.17	1.09	1.02	.97	.93	.89	.86
100	8.82	4.65	3.26	2.57	2.16	1.89	1.70	1.55	1.45	1.36	1.29	1.23	1.19	1.15
200	17.64	9.29	6.51	5.14	4.31	3.77	3.39	3.10	2.89	2.71	2.58	2.46	2.37	2.29
300	26.46	13.93	9.77	7.70	6.47	5.65	5.08	4.65	4.33	4.07	3.86	3.69	3.56	3.44
400	35.28	18.57	13.02	10.27	8.62	7.54	6.77	6.20	5.77	5.42	5.15	4.92	4.74	4.58
500	44.10	23.22	16.28	12.83	10.78	9.42	8.46	7.75	7.21	6.78	6.44	6.15	5.92	5.73
600	52.92	27.86	19.53	15.40	12.93	11.30	10.15	9.30	8.65	8.13	7.72	7.38	7.11	6.87
700	61.74	32.50	22.79	17.96	15.09	13.19	11.84	10.85	10.09	9.49	9.01	8.61	8.29	8.02
800	70.56	37.14	26.04	20.53	17.24	15.07	13.54	12.40	11.53	10.84	10.29	9.84	9.47	9.16
900	79.38	41.79	29.30	23.09	19.39	16.95	15.23	13.95	12.97	12.20	11.58	11.07	10.66	10.31
1000	88.20	46.43	32.55	25.66	21.55	18.83	16.92	15.50	14.41	13.55	12.87	12.30	11.84	11.45
2000	176.40	92.85	65.10	51.31	43.09	37.66	33.83	30.99	28.82	27.10	25.73	24.60	23.67	22.90
3000	264.59	139.27	97.65	76.96	64.64	56.49	50.74	46.49	43.22	40.65	38.59	36.90	35.51	34.34
4000	352.79	185.69	130.20	102.61	86.18	75.32	67.66	61.98	57.63	54.20	51.45	49.20	47.34	45.79
5000	440.98	232.12	162.75	128.26	107.72	94.15	84.57	77.47	72.03	67.75	64.31	61.50	59.18	57.23
6000	529.18	278.54	195.30	153.92	129.27	112.98	101.48	92.97	86.44	81.30	77.18	73.80	71.01	68.68
7000	617.37	324.96	227.85	179.57	150.81	131.81	118.39	108.46	100.84	94.85	90.04	86.10	82.85	80.12
8000	705.57	371.38	260.40	205.22	172.35	150.64	135.31	123.95	115.25	108.40	102.90	98.40	94.68	91.57
9000	793.76	417.81	292.95	230.87	193.90	169.47	152.22	139.45	129.66	121.95	115.76	110.70	106.52	103.01
10000	881.96	464.23	325.50	256.52	215.44	188.30	169.13	154.94	144.06	135.50	128.62	123.00	118.35	114.46
11000	970.15	510.65	358.05	282.17	236.98	207.13	186.05	170.43	158.47	149.05	141.48	135.30	130.19	125.90
12000	1058.35	557.07	390.60	307.83	258.53	225.96	202.96	185.93	172.87	162.60	154.35	147.60	142.02	137.35
13000	1146.54	603.50	423.15	333.48	280.07	244.79	219.87	201.42	187.28	176.15	167.21	159.90	153.86	148.79
14000	1234.74	649.92	455.70	359.13	301.61	263.62	236.78	216.91	201.68	189.70	180.07	172.20	165.69	160.24
15000	1322.93	696.34	488.25	384.78	323.16	282.45	253.70	232.41	216.09	203.25	192.93	184.50	177.53	171.68
16000	1411.13	742.76	520.80	410.43	344.70	301.28	270.61	247.90	230.50	216.80	205.79	196.80	189.36	183.13
17000	1499.32	789.18	553.35	436.08	366.24	320.11	287.52	263.39	244.90	230.35	218.66	209.10	201.20	194.57
18000	1587.52	835.61	585.90	461.74	387.79	338.94	304.44	278.89	259.31	243.90	231.52	221.40	213.03	206.02
19000	1675.71	882.03	618.45	487.39	409.33	357.77	321.35	294.38	273.71	257.45	244.38	233.70	224.87	217.47
20000	1763.91	928.45	651.00	513.04	430.87	376.60	338.26	309.87	288.12	271.00	257.24	246.00	236.70	228.91
21000	1852.10	974.87	683.55	538.69	452.42	395.43	355.17	325.37	302.52	284.55	270.10	258.30	248.54	240.36
22000	1940.30	1021.30	716.10	564.34	473.96	414.26	372.09	340.86	316.93	298.10	282.96	270.60	260.37	251.80
23000	2028.49	1067.72	748.65	589.99	495.50	433.09	389.00	356.36	331.33	311.64	295.83	282.90	272.20	263.25
24000	2116.69	1114.14	781.20	615.65	517.05	451.92	405.91	371.85	345.74	325.19	308.69	295.20	284.04	274.69
25000	2204.88	1160.56	813.75	641.30	538.59	470.75	422.83	387.34	360.15	338.74	321.55	307.50	295.87	286.14
26000	2293.08	1206.99	846.30	666.95	560.14	489.58	439.74	402.84	374.55	352.29	334.41	319.80	307.71	297.58
27000	2381.28	1253.41	878.84	692.60	581.68	508.41	456.65	418.33	388.96	365.84	347.27	332.10	319.54	309.03
28000	2469.47	1299.83	911.39	718.25	603.22	527.24	473.56	433.82	403.36	379.39	360.13	344.40	331.38	320.47
29000	2557.67	1346.25	943.94	743.90	624.77	546.07	490.48	449.32	417.77	392.94	373.00	356.70	343.21	331.92
30000	2645.86	1392.68	976.49	769.56	646.31	564.90	507.39	464.81	432.17	406.49	385.86	369.00	355.05	343.36
31000	2734.06	1439.10	1009.04	795.21	667.85	583.73	524.30	480.30	446.58	420.04	398.72	381.30	366.88	354.81
32000	2822.25	1485.52	1041.59	820.86	689.40	602.56	541.22	495.80	460.99	433.59	411.58	393.60	378.72	366.25
33000	2910.45	1531.94	1074.14	846.51	710.94	621.39	558.13	511.29	475.39	447.14	424.44	405.90	390.55	377.70
34000	2998.64	1578.36	1106.69	872.16	732.48	640.22	575.04	526.78	489.80	460.69	437.31	418.20	402.39	389.14
35000	3086.84	1624.79	1139.24	897.81	754.03	659.05	591.95	542.28	504.20	474.24	450.17	430.50	414.22	400.59
36000	3175.03	1671.21	1171.79	923.47	775.57	677.88	608.87	557.77	518.61	487.79	463.03	442.80	426.06	412.03
37000	3263.23	1717.63	1204.34	949.12	797.11	696.71	625.78	573.26	533.01	501.34	475.89	455.10	437.89	423.48
38000	3351.42	1764.05	1236.89	974.77	818.66	715.54	642.69	588.76	547.42	514.89	488.75	467.40	449.73	434.93
39000	3439.62	1810.48	1269.44	1000.42	840.20	734.37	659.60	604.25	561.82	528.44	501.61	479.70	461.56	446.37
40000	3527.81	1856.90	1301.99	1026.07	861.74	753.20	676.52	619.74	576.23	541.99	514.48	492.00	473.40	457.82
41000	3616.01	1903.32	1334.54	1051.72	883.29	772.03	693.43	635.24	590.64	555.54	527.34	504.30	485.23	469.26
42000	3704.20	1949.74	1367.09	1077.38	904.83	790.86	710.34	650.73	605.04	569.09	540.20	516.60	497.07	480.71
43000	3792.40	1996.17	1399.64	1103.03	926.37	809.69	727.26	666.23	619.45	582.64	553.06	528.90	508.90	492.15
44000	3880.59	2042.59	1432.19	1128.68	947.92	828.52	744.17	681.72	633.85	596.19	565.92	541.20	520.74	503.60
45000	3968.79	2089.01	1464.74	1154.33	969.46	847.35	761.08	697.21	648.26	609.73	578.78	553.50	532.57	515.04
46000	4056.98	2135.43	1497.29	1179.98	991.00	866.18	778.00	712.71	662.66	623.28	591.65	565.80	544.40	526.49
47000	4145.18	2181.86	1529.84	1205.63	1012.55	885.01	794.91	728.20	677.07	636.83	604.51	578.10	556.24	537.93
48000	4233.37	2228.28	1562.39	1231.29	1034.09	903.84	811.82	743.69	691.48	650.38	617.37	590.40	568.07	549.38
49000	4321.57	2274.70	1594.94	1256.94	1055.64	922.67	828.73	759.19	705.88	663.93	630.23	602.70	579.91	560.82
50000	4409.76	2321.12	1627.49	1282.59	1077.18	941.50	845.65	774.68	720.29	677.48	643.09	615.00	591.74	572.27
55000	4850.74	2553.23	1790.23	1410.85	1184.90	1035.65	930.21	852.15	792.31	745.23	707.40	676.50	650.92	629.49
60000	5291.72	2785.35	1952.98	1539.11	1292.61	1129.80	1014.78	929.61	864.34	812.98	771.71	738.00	710.09	686.72
65000	5732.69	3017.46	2115.73	1667.37	1400.33	1223.94	1099.34	1007.08	936.37	880.73	836.02	799.50	769.27	743.95
70000	6173.67	3249.57	2278.48	1795.62	1508.05	1318.09	1183.90	1084.55	1008.40	948.47	900.33	861.00	828.44	801.17
75000	6614.64	3481.68	2441.23	1923.88	1615.77	1412.24	1268.47	1162.02	1080.40	1016.22	964.64	922.50	887.61	858.40
80000	7055.62	3713.79	2603.97	2052.14	1723.48	1506.39	1353.03	1239.48	1152.46	1083.97	1028.95	984.00	946.79	915.63
85000	7496.60	3945.90	2766.72	2180.40	1831.20	1600.54	1437.60	1316.95	1224.48	1151.72	1093.26	1045.50	1005.96	972.85
90000	7937.57	4178.02	2929.47	2308.66	1938.92	1694.69	1522.16	1394.42	1296.51	1219.46	1157.56	1107.00	1065.13	1030.08
95000	8378.55	4410.13	3092.22	2436.92	2046.63	1788.84	1606.73	1471.89	1368.54	1287.21	1221.87	1168.50	1124.31	1087.31
100000	8819.52	4642.24	3254.97	2565.18	2154.35	1882.99	1691.29	1549.35	1440.57	1354.96	1286.18	1230.00	1183.48	1144.53

TERM AMOUNT	15 Years	16 Years	17 Years	18 Years	19 Years	20 Years	21 Years	22 Years	23 Years	24 Years	25 Years	30 Years	35 Years	40 Years
5	.06	.06	.06	.06	.06	.06	.05	.05	.05	.05	.05	.05	.05	.05
10	.12	.11	.11	.11	.11	.11	.10	.10	.10	.10	.10	.10	.10	.09
15	.17	.17	.16	.16	.16	.16	.15	.15	.15	.15	.15	.14	.14	.14
25	.28	.28	.27	.26	.26	.26	.25	.25	.25	.24	.24	.24	.23	.23
50	.56	.55	.53	.52	.52	.51	.50	.49	.49	.48	.48	.47	.46	.45
75	.84	.82	.80	.78	.77	.76	.75	.74	.73	.72	.72	.70	.68	.68
100	1.12	1.09	1.06	1.04	1.03	1.01	1.00	.98	.97	.96	.96	.93	.91	.90
200	2.23	2.17	2.12	2.08	2.05	2.02	1.99	1.96	1.94	1.92	1.91	1.85	1.82	1.80
300	3.34	3.26	3.18	3.12	3.07	3.02	2.98	2.94	2.91	2.88	2.86	2.77	2.72	2.69
400	4.45	4.34	4.24	4.16	4.09	4.03	3.97	3.92	3.88	3.84	3.81	3.69	3.63	3.59
500	5.56	5.42	5.30	5.20	5.11	5.03	4.96	4.90	4.85	4.80	4.76	4.62	4.53	4.49
600	6.67	6.51	6.36	6.24	6.13	6.04	5.95	5.88	5.82	5.76	5.71	5.54	5.44	5.38
700	7.79	7.59	7.42	7.28	7.15	7.04	6.94	6.86	6.79	6.72	6.66	6.46	6.35	6.28
800	8.90	8.67	8.48	8.32	8.17	8.05	7.94	7.84	7.76	7.68	7.62	7.38	7.25	7.18
900	10.01	9.76	9.54	9.35	9.19	9.05	8.93	8.82	8.72	8.64	8.57	8.31	8.16	8.07
1000	11.12	10.84	10.60	10.39	10.21	10.06	9.92	9.80	9.69	9.60	9.52	9.23	9.06	8.97
2000	22.24	21.68	21.20	20.78	20.42	20.11	19.83	19.59	19.38	19.20	19.03	18.45	18.12	17.93
3000	33.35	32.51	31.79	31.17	30.63	30.16	29.75	29.39	29.07	28.79	28.54	27.67	27.18	26.90
4000	44.47	43.35	42.39	41.56	40.84	40.21	39.66	39.18	38.76	38.39	38.06	36.89	36.24	35.86
5000	55.59	54.18	52.98	51.94	51.04	50.26	49.58	48.98	48.45	47.98	47.57	46.12	45.30	44.83
6000	66.70	65.02	63.58	62.33	61.25	60.31	59.49	58.77	58.14	57.58	57.08	55.34	54.36	53.79
7000	77.82	75.85	74.17	72.72	71.46	70.36	69.40	68.56	67.83	67.17	66.60	64.56	63.42	62.76
8000	88.93	86.69	84.77	83.11	81.67	80.41	79.32	78.36	77.51	76.77	76.11	73.78	72.47	71.72
9000	100.05	97.53	95.36	93.49	91.87	90.46	89.23	88.15	87.20	86.36	85.62	83.01	81.53	80.69
10000	111.17	108.36	105.96	103.88	102.08	100.52	99.15	97.95	96.89	95.96	95.14	92.23	90.59	89.65
11000	122.28	119.20	116.55	114.27	112.29	110.57	109.06	107.74	106.58	105.56	104.65	101.45	99.65	98.62
12000	133.40	130.03	127.15	124.66	122.50	120.62	118.98	117.53	116.27	115.15	114.16	110.67	108.71	107.58
13000	144.51	140.87	137.74	135.04	132.70	130.67	128.89	127.33	125.96	124.75	123.68	119.89	117.77	116.55
14000	155.63	151.70	148.34	145.43	142.91	140.72	138.80	137.12	135.65	134.34	133.19	129.12	126.83	125.51
15000	166.75	162.54	158.93	155.82	153.12	150.77	148.72	146.92	145.33	143.94	142.70	138.34	135.89	134.48
16000	177.86	173.37	169.53	166.21	163.33	160.82	158.63	156.71	155.02	153.53	152.22	147.56	144.94	143.44
17000	188.98	184.21	180.12	176.59	173.54	170.87	168.55	166.51	164.71	163.13	161.73	156.78	154.00	152.41
18000	200.09	195.05	190.72	186.98	183.74	180.92	178.46	176.30	174.40	172.72	171.24	166.01	163.06	161.37
19000	211.21	205.88	201.31	197.37	193.95	190.98	188.37	186.09	184.09	182.32	180.76	175.23	172.12	170.34
20000	222.33	216.72	211.91	207.76	204.16	201.03	198.29	195.89	193.78	191.92	190.27	184.45	181.18	179.30
21000	233.44	227.55	222.50	218.14	214.37	211.08	208.20	205.68	203.47	201.51	199.78	193.67	190.24	188.27
22000	244.56	238.39	233.10	228.53	224.57	221.13	218.12	215.48	213.15	211.11	209.30	202.89	199.30	197.23
23000	255.67	249.22	243.69	238.92	234.78	231.18	228.03	225.27	222.84	220.70	218.81	212.12	208.36	206.20
24000	266.79	260.06	254.29	249.31	244.99	241.23	237.95	235.06	232.53	230.30	228.32	221.34	217.41	215.16
25000	277.91	270.90	264.88	259.69	255.20	251.28	247.86	244.86	242.22	239.89	237.84	230.56	226.47	224.13
26000	289.02	281.73	275.48	270.08	265.40	261.33	257.77	254.65	251.91	249.49	247.35	239.78	235.53	233.09
27000	300.14	292.57	286.07	280.47	275.61	271.38	267.69	264.45	261.60	259.08	256.86	249.01	244.59	242.06
28000	311.25	303.40	296.67	290.86	285.82	281.43	277.60	274.24	271.29	268.68	266.38	258.23	253.65	251.02
29000	322.37	314.24	307.26	301.24	296.03	291.49	287.52	284.04	280.97	278.28	275.89	267.45	262.71	259.99
30000	333.49	325.07	317.86	311.63	306.24	301.54	297.43	293.83	290.66	287.87	285.40	276.67	271.77	268.95
31000	344.60	335.91	328.45	322.02	316.44	311.59	307.34	303.62	300.35	297.47	294.92	285.89	280.83	277.92
32000	355.72	346.74	339.05	332.41	326.65	321.64	317.26	313.42	310.04	307.06	304.43	295.12	289.88	286.88
33000	366.84	357.58	349.64	342.79	336.86	331.69	327.17	323.21	319.73	316.66	313.94	304.34	298.94	295.85
34000	377.95	368.42	360.24	353.18	347.07	341.74	337.09	333.01	329.42	326.25	323.46	313.56	308.00	304.81
35000	389.07	379.25	370.83	363.57	357.27	351.79	347.00	342.80	339.11	335.85	332.97	322.78	317.06	313.78
36000	400.18	390.09	381.43	373.96	367.48	361.84	356.92	352.59	348.79	345.44	342.48	332.01	326.12	322.74
37000	411.30	400.92	392.02	384.35	377.69	371.89	366.83	362.39	358.48	355.04	352.00	341.23	335.18	331.71
38000	422.42	411.76	402.62	394.73	387.90	381.95	376.74	372.18	368.17	364.64	361.51	350.45	344.24	340.67
39000	433.53	422.59	413.21	405.12	398.10	392.00	386.66	381.98	377.86	374.23	371.02	359.67	353.29	349.64
40000	444.65	433.43	423.81	415.51	408.31	402.05	396.57	391.77	387.55	383.83	380.54	368.89	362.35	358.60
41000	455.76	444.27	434.40	425.90	418.52	412.10	406.49	401.56	397.24	393.42	390.05	378.12	371.41	367.57
42000	466.88	455.10	445.00	436.28	428.73	422.15	416.40	411.36	406.93	403.02	399.56	387.34	380.47	376.53
43000	478.00	465.94	455.59	446.67	438.94	432.20	426.31	421.15	416.61	412.61	409.08	396.56	389.53	385.50
44000	489.11	476.77	466.19	457.06	449.14	442.25	436.23	430.95	426.30	422.21	418.59	405.78	398.59	394.46
45000	500.23	487.61	476.78	467.45	459.35	452.30	446.14	440.74	435.99	431.80	428.10	415.01	407.65	403.43
46000	511.34	498.44	487.38	477.83	469.56	462.35	456.06	450.54	445.68	441.40	437.62	424.23	416.71	412.39
47000	522.46	509.28	497.97	488.22	479.77	472.40	465.97	460.33	455.37	451.00	447.13	433.45	425.76	421.36
48000	533.58	520.11	508.57	498.61	489.97	482.46	475.89	470.12	465.06	460.59	456.64	442.67	434.82	430.32
49000	544.69	530.95	519.16	509.00	500.18	492.51	485.80	479.92	474.75	470.19	466.16	451.89	443.88	439.29
50000	555.81	541.79	529.76	519.38	510.39	502.56	495.71	489.71	484.43	479.78	475.67	461.12	452.94	448.25
55000	611.39	595.96	582.73	571.32	561.43	552.81	545.28	538.68	532.88	527.76	523.24	507.23	498.23	493.08
60000	666.97	650.14	635.71	623.26	612.47	603.07	594.86	587.65	581.32	575.74	570.80	553.34	543.53	537.90
65000	722.55	704.32	688.68	675.20	663.50	653.32	644.43	636.62	629.76	623.72	618.37	599.45	588.82	582.73
70000	778.13	758.50	741.66	727.14	714.54	703.58	694.00	685.60	678.21	671.69	665.94	645.56	634.11	627.55
75000	833.71	812.68	794.64	779.07	765.58	753.83	743.57	734.57	726.65	719.67	713.50	691.67	679.41	672.37
80000	889.29	866.85	847.61	831.01	816.62	804.09	793.14	783.54	775.09	767.65	761.07	737.78	724.70	717.20
85000	944.87	921.03	900.59	882.95	867.66	854.35	842.71	832.51	823.54	815.63	808.64	783.90	770.00	762.02
90000	1000.45	975.21	953.56	934.89	918.70	904.60	892.28	881.48	871.98	863.60	856.20	830.01	815.29	806.85
95000	1056.03	1029.39	1006.54	986.82	969.74	954.86	941.85	930.45	920.42	911.58	903.77	876.12	860.58	851.67
100000	1111.61	1083.57	1059.51	1038.76	1020.77	1005.11	991.42	979.42	968.86	959.56	951.34	922.23	905.88	896.50

10.625%

TERM	1 Year	2 Years	3 Years	4 Years	5 Years	6 Years	7 Years	8 Years	9 Years	10 Years	11 Years	12 Years	13 Years	14 Years
AMOUNT														
5	.45	.24	.17	.13	.11	.10	.09	.08	.08	.07	.07	.07	.06	.06
10	.89	.47	.33	.26	.22	.19	.17	.16	.15	.14	.13	.13	.12	.12
15	1.33	.70	.49	.39	.33	.29	.26	.24	.22	.21	.20	.19	.18	.18
25	2.21	1.17	.82	.65	.54	.48	.43	.39	.37	.34	.33	.31	.30	.29
50	4.42	2.33	1.63	1.29	1.08	.95	.85	.78	.73	.68	.65	.62	.60	.58
75	6.62	3.49	2.45	1.93	1.62	1.42	1.27	1.17	1.09	1.02	.97	.93	.89	.86
100	8.83	4.65	3.26	2.57	2.16	1.89	1.70	1.56	1.45	1.36	1.29	1.24	1.19	1.15
200	17.65	9.29	6.52	5.14	4.32	3.77	3.39	3.11	2.89	2.72	2.58	2.47	2.37	2.30
300	26.47	13.94	9.77	7.70	6.47	5.66	5.08	4.66	4.33	4.07	3.87	3.70	3.56	3.44
400	35.29	18.58	13.03	10.27	8.63	7.54	6.70	6.21	5.77	5.43	5.16	4.93	4.74	4.59
500	44.11	23.22	16.29	12.84	10.78	9.43	8.47	7.76	7.21	6.79	6.44	6.16	5.93	5.74
600	52.93	27.87	19.54	15.40	12.94	11.31	10.16	9.31	8.66	8.14	7.73	7.39	7.11	6.88
700	61.75	32.51	22.80	17.97	15.09	13.19	11.85	10.86	10.10	9.50	9.02	8.63	8.30	8.03
800	70.57	37.15	26.05	20.54	17.25	15.08	13.55	12.41	11.54	10.86	10.31	9.86	9.48	9.17
900	79.39	41.80	29.31	23.10	19.41	16.96	15.24	13.96	12.98	12.21	11.59	11.09	10.67	10.32
1000	88.21	46.44	32.57	25.67	21.56	18.85	16.93	15.51	14.42	13.57	12.88	12.32	11.85	11.47
2000	176.42	92.87	65.13	51.33	43.12	37.69	33.86	31.02	28.84	27.13	25.76	24.63	23.70	22.93
3000	264.63	139.31	97.69	77.00	64.67	56.53	50.78	46.53	43.26	40.70	38.63	36.95	35.55	34.39
4000	352.83	185.74	130.25	102.66	86.23	75.38	67.71	62.03	57.68	54.26	51.51	49.26	47.40	45.85
5000	441.04	232.17	162.81	128.32	107.78	94.22	84.63	77.54	72.10	67.82	64.39	61.58	59.25	57.31
6000	529.25	278.61	195.37	153.99	129.34	113.06	101.56	93.05	86.52	81.39	77.26	73.89	71.10	68.77
7000	617.45	325.04	227.93	179.65	150.90	131.90	118.49	108.55	100.94	94.95	90.14	86.21	82.95	80.23
8000	705.66	371.48	260.50	205.32	172.45	150.75	135.41	124.06	115.36	108.51	103.01	98.52	94.80	91.69
9000	793.87	417.91	293.06	230.98	194.01	169.59	152.34	139.57	129.78	122.08	115.89	110.84	106.65	103.15
10000	882.07	464.34	325.62	256.64	215.56	188.43	169.26	155.07	144.20	135.64	128.77	123.15	118.50	114.61
11000	970.28	510.78	358.18	282.31	237.12	207.27	186.19	170.58	158.62	149.20	141.64	135.47	130.35	126.07
12000	1058.49	557.21	390.74	307.97	258.68	226.12	203.12	186.09	173.04	162.77	154.52	147.78	142.20	137.53
13000	1146.69	603.65	423.30	333.63	280.23	244.96	220.04	201.59	187.46	176.33	167.39	160.10	154.05	148.99
14000	1234.90	650.08	455.86	359.30	301.79	263.80	236.97	217.10	201.88	189.90	180.27	172.41	165.90	160.45
15000	1323.11	696.51	488.43	384.96	323.34	282.64	253.89	232.61	216.30	203.46	193.15	184.72	177.75	171.91
16000	1411.31	742.95	520.99	410.63	344.90	301.49	270.82	248.12	230.71	217.02	206.02	197.04	189.60	183.37
17000	1499.52	789.38	553.55	436.29	366.45	320.33	287.75	263.62	245.13	230.59	218.90	209.35	201.45	194.83
18000	1587.73	835.82	586.11	461.95	388.01	339.17	304.67	279.13	259.55	244.15	231.78	221.67	213.30	206.29
19000	1675.93	882.25	618.67	487.62	409.57	358.01	321.60	294.64	273.97	257.71	244.65	233.98	225.15	217.76
20000	1764.14	928.68	651.23	513.28	431.12	376.86	338.52	310.14	288.39	271.28	257.53	246.30	237.00	229.22
21000	1852.35	975.12	683.79	538.94	452.68	395.70	355.45	325.65	302.81	284.84	270.40	258.61	248.85	240.68
22000	1940.56	1021.55	716.36	564.61	474.23	414.54	372.37	341.16	317.23	298.40	283.28	270.93	260.70	252.14
23000	2028.76	1067.99	748.92	590.27	495.79	433.38	389.30	356.66	331.65	311.97	296.16	283.24	272.55	263.60
24000	2116.97	1114.42	781.48	615.94	517.35	452.23	406.23	372.17	346.07	325.53	309.03	295.56	284.40	275.06
25000	2205.18	1160.85	814.04	641.60	538.90	471.07	423.15	387.68	360.49	339.09	321.91	307.87	296.25	286.52
26000	2293.38	1207.29	846.60	667.26	560.46	489.91	440.08	403.18	374.91	352.66	334.78	320.18	308.10	297.98
27000	2381.59	1253.72	879.16	692.93	582.01	508.75	457.00	418.69	389.33	366.22	347.66	332.50	319.95	309.44
28000	2469.80	1300.16	911.72	718.59	603.57	527.60	473.93	434.20	403.75	379.79	360.54	344.81	331.80	320.90
29000	2558.00	1346.59	944.29	744.25	625.13	546.44	490.86	449.70	418.17	393.35	373.41	357.13	343.65	332.36
30000	2646.21	1393.02	976.85	769.92	646.68	565.28	507.78	465.21	432.59	406.91	386.29	369.44	355.50	343.82
31000	2734.42	1439.46	1009.41	795.58	668.24	584.12	524.71	480.72	447.00	420.48	399.16	381.76	367.35	355.28
32000	2822.62	1485.89	1041.97	821.25	689.79	602.97	541.63	496.23	461.42	434.04	412.04	394.07	379.20	366.74
33000	2910.83	1532.32	1074.53	846.91	711.35	621.81	558.56	511.73	475.84	447.60	424.92	406.39	391.05	378.20
34000	2999.04	1578.76	1107.09	872.57	732.90	640.65	575.49	527.24	490.26	461.17	437.79	418.70	402.90	389.66
35000	3087.24	1625.19	1139.65	898.24	754.46	659.49	592.41	542.75	504.68	474.73	450.67	431.02	414.75	401.12
36000	3175.45	1671.63	1172.22	923.90	776.02	678.34	609.34	558.25	519.10	488.29	463.55	443.33	426.60	412.58
37000	3263.66	1718.06	1204.78	949.57	797.57	697.18	626.26	573.76	533.52	501.86	476.42	455.65	438.45	424.04
38000	3351.86	1764.49	1237.34	975.23	819.13	716.02	643.19	589.27	547.94	515.42	489.30	467.96	450.30	435.51
39000	3440.07	1810.93	1269.90	1000.89	840.68	734.86	660.12	604.77	562.36	528.98	502.17	480.27	462.14	446.97
40000	3528.28	1857.36	1302.46	1026.56	862.24	753.71	677.04	620.28	576.78	542.55	515.05	492.59	473.99	458.43
41000	3616.49	1903.80	1335.02	1052.22	883.80	772.55	693.97	635.79	591.20	556.11	527.93	504.90	485.84	469.89
42000	3704.69	1950.23	1367.58	1077.88	905.35	791.39	710.89	651.29	605.62	569.68	540.80	517.22	497.69	481.35
43000	3792.90	1996.66	1400.15	1103.55	926.91	810.24	727.82	666.80	620.04	583.24	553.68	529.53	509.54	492.81
44000	3881.11	2043.10	1432.71	1129.21	948.46	829.08	744.74	682.31	634.46	596.80	566.55	541.85	521.39	504.27
45000	3969.31	2089.53	1465.27	1154.88	970.02	847.92	761.67	697.81	648.88	610.37	579.43	554.16	533.24	515.73
46000	4057.52	2135.97	1497.83	1180.54	991.58	866.76	778.60	713.32	663.29	623.93	592.31	566.48	545.09	527.19
47000	4145.73	2182.40	1530.39	1206.20	1013.13	885.61	795.52	728.83	677.71	637.49	605.18	578.79	556.94	538.65
48000	4233.93	2228.83	1562.95	1231.87	1034.69	904.45	812.45	744.34	692.13	651.06	618.06	591.11	568.79	550.11
49000	4322.14	2275.27	1595.51	1257.53	1056.24	923.29	829.37	759.84	706.55	664.62	630.94	603.42	580.64	561.57
50000	4410.35	2321.70	1628.08	1283.19	1077.80	942.13	846.30	775.35	720.97	678.18	643.81	615.74	592.49	573.03
55000	4851.38	2553.87	1790.88	1411.51	1185.58	1036.35	930.93	852.88	793.07	746.00	708.19	677.31	651.74	630.33
60000	5292.42	2786.04	1953.69	1539.83	1293.36	1130.56	1015.56	930.42	865.17	813.82	772.57	738.88	710.99	687.64
65000	5733.45	3018.21	2116.50	1668.15	1401.14	1224.77	1100.19	1007.95	937.26	881.64	836.95	800.45	770.24	744.94
70000	6174.48	3250.38	2279.30	1796.47	1508.92	1318.98	1184.82	1085.49	1009.36	949.46	901.33	862.03	829.49	802.24
75000	6615.52	3482.55	2442.11	1924.79	1616.70	1413.20	1269.45	1163.02	1081.46	1017.27	965.71	923.60	888.74	859.54
80000	7056.55	3714.72	2604.92	2053.11	1724.48	1507.41	1354.08	1240.56	1153.55	1085.09	1030.09	985.17	947.98	916.85
85000	7497.59	3946.89	2767.73	2181.43	1832.25	1601.62	1438.71	1318.09	1225.65	1152.91	1094.48	1046.75	1007.23	974.15
90000	7938.62	4179.06	2930.53	2309.75	1940.03	1695.84	1523.34	1395.62	1297.75	1220.73	1158.86	1108.32	1066.48	1031.45
95000	8379.65	4411.23	3093.34	2438.07	2047.81	1790.05	1607.97	1473.16	1369.84	1288.55	1223.24	1169.89	1125.73	1088.76
100000	8820.69	4643.40	3256.15	2566.38	2155.59	1884.26	1692.60	1550.69	1441.94	1356.36	1287.62	1231.47	1184.98	1146.06

TERM	15 Years	16 Years	17 Years	18 Years	19 Years	20 Years	21 Years	22 Years	23 Years	24 Years	25 Years	30 Years	35 Years	40 Years
AMOUNT														
5	.06	.06	.06	.06	.06	.06	.05	.05	.05	.05	.05	.05	.05	.05
10	.12	.11	.11	.11	.11	.11	.10	.10	.10	.10	.10	.10	.10	.09
15	.17	.17	.16	.16	.16	.16	.15	.15	.15	.15	.15	.14	.14	.14
25	.28	.28	.27	.27	.26	.26	.25	.25	.25	.25	.24	.24	.23	.23
50	.56	.55	.54	.53	.52	.51	.50	.50	.49	.49	.48	.47	.46	.45
75	.84	.82	.80	.79	.77	.76	.75	.74	.73	.73	.72	.70	.69	.68
100	1.12	1.09	1.07	1.05	1.03	1.01	1.00	.99	.98	.97	.96	.93	.91	.90
200	2.23	2.18	2.13	2.09	2.05	2.02	1.99	1.97	1.95	1.93	1.91	1.85	1.82	1.80
300	3.34	3.26	3.19	3.13	3.07	3.03	2.98	2.95	2.92	2.89	2.86	2.78	2.73	2.70
400	4.46	4.35	4.25	4.17	4.09	4.03	3.98	3.93	3.89	3.85	3.82	3.70	3.64	3.60
500	5.57	5.43	5.31	5.21	5.12	5.04	4.97	4.91	4.86	4.81	4.77	4.63	4.54	4.50
600	6.68	6.52	6.37	6.25	6.14	6.05	5.96	5.89	5.83	5.77	5.72	5.55	5.45	5.40
700	7.80	7.60	7.43	7.29	7.16	7.05	6.96	6.87	6.80	6.73	6.68	6.47	6.36	6.29
800	8.91	8.69	8.49	8.33	8.18	8.06	7.95	7.85	7.77	7.70	7.63	7.40	7.27	7.19
900	10.02	9.77	9.56	9.37	9.21	9.07	8.94	8.84	8.74	8.66	8.58	8.32	8.18	8.09
1000	11.14	10.86	10.62	10.41	10.23	10.07	9.94	9.82	9.71	9.62	9.54	9.25	9.08	8.99
2000	22.27	21.71	21.23	20.81	20.45	20.14	19.87	19.63	19.42	19.23	19.07	18.49	18.16	17.97
3000	33.40	32.56	31.84	31.22	30.68	30.21	29.80	29.44	29.12	28.84	28.60	27.73	27.24	26.96
4000	44.53	43.41	42.45	41.62	40.90	40.28	39.73	39.25	38.83	38.46	38.13	36.97	36.32	35.94
5000	55.66	54.26	53.06	52.02	51.13	50.34	49.66	49.06	48.54	48.07	47.66	46.21	45.40	44.93
6000	66.79	65.11	63.67	62.43	61.35	60.41	59.59	58.87	58.24	57.68	57.19	55.45	54.47	53.91
7000	77.93	75.97	74.28	72.83	71.58	70.48	69.52	68.69	67.95	67.30	66.72	64.69	63.55	62.90
8000	89.06	86.82	84.89	83.24	81.80	80.55	79.45	78.50	77.65	76.91	76.25	73.93	72.63	71.88
9000	100.19	97.67	95.51	93.64	92.02	90.62	89.39	88.31	87.36	86.52	85.79	83.17	81.71	80.87
10000	111.32	108.52	106.12	104.04	102.25	100.68	99.32	98.12	97.07	96.14	95.32	92.41	90.79	89.85
11000	122.45	119.37	116.73	114.45	112.47	110.75	109.25	107.93	106.77	105.75	104.85	101.66	99.86	98.84
12000	133.58	130.22	127.34	124.85	122.70	120.82	119.18	117.74	116.48	115.36	114.38	110.90	108.94	107.82
13000	144.72	141.07	137.95	135.26	132.92	130.89	129.11	127.55	126.18	124.98	123.91	120.14	118.02	116.81
14000	155.85	151.93	148.56	145.66	143.15	140.96	139.04	137.37	135.89	134.59	133.44	129.38	127.10	125.79
15000	166.98	162.78	159.17	156.06	153.37	151.02	148.97	147.18	145.60	144.20	142.97	138.62	136.18	134.78
16000	178.11	173.63	169.78	166.47	163.59	161.09	158.90	156.99	155.30	153.82	152.50	147.86	145.25	143.76
17000	189.24	184.48	180.39	176.87	173.82	171.16	168.84	166.80	165.01	163.43	162.04	157.10	154.33	152.75
18000	200.37	195.33	191.01	187.28	184.04	181.23	178.77	176.61	174.71	173.04	171.57	166.34	163.41	161.73
19000	211.51	206.18	201.62	197.68	194.27	191.30	188.70	186.42	184.42	182.66	181.10	175.58	172.49	170.72
20000	222.64	217.03	212.23	208.08	204.49	201.36	198.63	196.23	194.13	192.27	190.63	184.82	181.57	179.70
21000	233.77	227.89	222.84	218.49	214.72	211.43	208.56	206.05	203.83	201.88	200.16	194.07	190.64	188.68
22000	244.90	238.74	233.45	228.89	224.94	221.50	218.49	215.86	213.54	211.50	209.69	203.31	199.72	197.67
23000	256.03	249.59	244.06	239.30	235.16	231.57	228.42	225.67	223.25	221.11	219.22	212.55	208.80	206.65
24000	267.16	260.44	254.67	249.70	245.39	241.63	238.35	235.48	232.95	230.72	228.75	221.79	217.88	215.64
25000	278.30	271.29	265.28	260.10	255.61	251.70	248.29	245.29	242.66	240.34	238.29	231.03	226.96	224.62
26000	289.43	282.14	275.90	270.51	265.84	261.77	258.22	255.10	252.36	249.95	247.82	240.27	236.03	233.61
27000	300.56	292.99	286.51	280.91	276.06	271.84	268.15	264.91	262.07	259.56	257.35	249.51	245.11	242.59
28000	311.69	303.85	297.12	291.31	286.29	281.91	278.08	274.73	271.78	269.18	266.88	258.75	254.19	251.58
29000	322.82	314.70	307.73	301.72	296.51	291.97	288.01	284.54	281.48	278.79	276.41	267.99	263.27	260.56
30000	333.95	325.55	318.34	312.12	306.74	302.04	297.94	294.35	291.19	288.40	285.94	277.23	272.35	269.55
31000	345.08	336.40	328.95	322.53	316.96	312.11	307.87	304.16	300.89	298.02	295.47	286.48	281.43	278.53
32000	356.22	347.25	339.56	332.93	327.18	322.18	317.80	313.97	310.60	307.63	305.00	295.72	290.50	287.52
33000	367.35	358.10	350.17	343.33	337.41	332.25	327.74	323.78	320.31	317.24	314.54	304.96	299.58	296.50
34000	378.48	368.95	360.78	353.74	347.63	342.31	337.67	333.59	330.01	326.86	324.07	314.20	308.66	305.49
35000	389.61	379.81	371.40	364.14	357.86	352.38	347.60	343.41	339.72	336.47	333.60	323.44	317.74	314.47
36000	400.74	390.66	382.01	374.55	368.08	362.45	357.53	353.22	349.42	346.08	343.13	332.68	326.82	323.46
37000	411.87	401.51	392.62	384.95	378.30	372.52	367.46	363.03	359.13	355.70	352.66	341.92	335.89	332.44
38000	423.01	412.36	403.23	395.35	388.53	382.59	377.39	372.84	368.84	365.31	362.19	351.16	344.97	341.43
39000	434.14	423.21	413.84	405.76	398.75	392.65	387.32	382.65	378.54	374.92	371.72	360.40	354.05	350.41
40000	445.27	434.06	424.45	416.16	408.98	402.72	397.25	392.46	388.25	384.54	381.25	369.64	363.13	359.39
41000	456.40	444.91	435.06	426.57	419.20	412.79	407.19	402.27	397.96	394.15	390.79	378.89	372.21	368.38
42000	467.53	455.77	445.67	436.97	429.43	422.86	417.12	412.09	407.66	403.76	400.32	388.13	381.28	377.36
43000	478.66	466.62	456.29	447.37	439.65	432.92	427.05	421.90	417.37	413.38	409.85	397.37	390.36	386.35
44000	489.80	477.47	466.90	457.78	449.87	442.99	436.98	431.71	427.07	422.99	419.38	406.61	399.44	395.33
45000	500.93	488.32	477.51	468.18	460.10	453.06	446.91	441.52	436.78	432.60	428.91	415.85	408.52	404.32
46000	512.06	499.17	488.12	478.59	470.32	463.13	456.84	451.33	446.49	442.21	438.44	425.09	417.60	413.30
47000	523.19	510.02	498.73	488.99	480.55	473.20	466.77	461.14	456.19	451.83	447.97	434.33	426.67	422.29
48000	534.32	520.87	509.34	499.39	490.77	483.26	476.70	470.95	465.90	461.44	457.50	443.57	435.75	431.27
49000	545.45	531.73	519.95	509.80	501.00	493.33	486.64	480.77	475.60	471.05	467.04	452.81	444.83	440.26
50000	556.59	542.58	530.56	520.20	511.22	503.40	496.57	490.58	485.31	480.67	476.57	462.05	453.91	449.24
55000	612.24	596.83	583.62	572.22	562.34	553.74	546.22	539.63	533.84	528.73	524.22	508.26	499.30	494.17
60000	667.90	651.09	636.67	624.24	613.46	604.08	595.88	588.69	582.37	576.80	571.88	554.46	544.69	539.09
65000	723.56	705.35	689.73	676.26	664.59	654.42	645.54	637.75	630.90	624.87	619.54	600.67	590.08	584.01
70000	779.22	759.61	742.79	728.28	715.71	704.76	695.19	686.81	679.43	672.93	667.19	646.87	635.47	628.94
75000	834.88	813.86	795.84	780.30	766.83	755.10	744.85	735.86	727.96	721.00	714.85	693.08	680.86	673.86
80000	890.53	868.12	848.90	832.32	817.95	805.44	794.50	784.92	776.49	769.07	762.50	739.28	726.25	718.78
85000	946.19	922.38	901.95	884.34	869.07	855.78	844.16	833.98	825.02	817.13	810.16	785.49	771.64	763.71
90000	1001.85	976.63	955.01	936.36	920.19	906.12	893.82	883.03	873.55	865.20	857.82	831.69	817.03	808.63
95000	1057.51	1030.89	1008.07	988.38	971.31	956.46	943.47	932.09	922.09	913.26	905.47	877.90	862.42	853.56
100000	1113.17	1085.15	1061.12	1040.40	1022.43	1006.80	993.13	981.15	970.62	961.33	953.13	924.10	907.81	898.48

10.700%

TERM	1 Year	2 Years	3 Years	4 Years	5 Years	6 Years	7 Years	8 Years	9 Years	10 Years	11 Years	12 Years	13 Years	14 Years
AMOUNT														
5	.45	.24	.17	.13	.11	.10	.09	.08	.08	.07	.07	.07	.06	.06
10	.89	.47	.33	.26	.22	.19	.17	.16	.15	.14	.13	.13	.12	.12
15	1.33	.70	.49	.39	.33	.29	.26	.24	.22	.21	.20	.19	.18	.18
25	2.21	1.17	.82	.65	.54	.48	.43	.39	.37	.35	.33	.31	.30	.29
50	4.42	2.33	1.63	1.29	1.08	.95	.85	.78	.73	.69	.65	.62	.60	.58
75	6.62	3.49	2.45	1.93	1.62	1.42	1.28	1.17	1.09	1.03	.97	.93	.90	.87
100	8.83	4.65	3.26	2.58	2.16	1.89	1.70	1.56	1.45	1.37	1.30	1.24	1.19	1.16
200	17.65	9.30	6.52	5.15	4.32	3.78	3.40	3.11	2.90	2.73	2.59	2.48	2.38	2.31
300	26.48	13.95	9.78	7.72	6.48	5.67	5.09	4.67	4.34	4.09	3.88	3.71	3.57	3.46
400	35.30	18.59	13.04	10.29	8.64	7.56	6.79	6.22	5.79	5.45	5.17	4.95	4.76	4.61
500	44.13	23.24	16.30	12.86	10.80	9.45	8.49	7.78	7.24	6.81	6.46	6.18	5.95	5.76
600	52.95	27.89	19.56	15.43	12.96	11.33	10.18	9.33	8.68	8.17	7.76	7.42	7.14	6.91
700	61.77	32.53	22.82	18.00	15.12	13.22	11.88	10.89	10.13	9.53	9.05	8.66	8.33	8.06
800	70.60	37.18	26.08	20.57	17.28	15.11	13.58	12.44	11.57	10.89	10.34	9.89	9.52	9.21
900	79.42	41.83	29.34	23.14	19.44	17.00	15.27	14.00	13.02	12.25	11.63	11.13	10.71	10.36
1000	88.25	46.47	32.60	25.71	21.60	18.89	16.97	15.55	14.47	13.61	12.92	12.36	11.90	11.51
2000	176.49	92.94	65.20	51.41	43.19	37.77	33.94	31.10	28.93	27.22	25.84	24.72	23.79	23.02
3000	264.73	139.41	97.80	77.11	64.78	56.65	50.90	46.65	43.39	40.82	38.76	37.08	35.69	34.52
4000	352.97	185.88	130.39	102.81	86.38	75.53	67.87	62.19	57.85	54.43	51.68	49.44	47.58	46.03
5000	441.21	232.35	162.99	128.51	107.97	94.41	84.83	77.74	72.31	68.03	64.60	61.80	59.48	57.54
6000	529.46	278.82	195.59	154.21	129.56	113.29	101.80	93.29	86.77	81.64	77.52	74.16	71.37	69.04
7000	617.70	325.29	228.18	179.91	151.16	132.17	118.76	108.83	101.23	95.25	90.44	86.52	83.27	80.55
8000	705.94	371.75	260.78	205.61	172.75	151.05	135.73	124.38	115.69	108.85	103.36	98.87	95.16	92.06
9000	794.18	418.22	293.38	231.31	194.34	169.93	152.69	139.93	130.15	122.46	116.28	111.23	107.06	103.56
10000	882.42	464.69	325.97	257.01	215.94	188.81	169.66	155.48	144.61	136.06	129.20	123.59	118.95	115.07
11000	970.66	511.16	358.57	282.71	237.53	207.69	186.62	171.02	159.07	149.67	142.12	135.95	130.85	126.57
12000	1058.91	557.63	391.17	308.41	259.12	226.57	203.59	186.57	173.53	163.27	155.04	148.31	142.74	138.08
13000	1147.15	604.10	423.76	334.11	280.72	245.46	220.55	202.12	187.99	176.88	167.95	160.67	154.64	149.59
14000	1235.39	650.57	456.36	359.81	302.31	264.34	237.52	217.66	202.45	190.49	180.87	173.03	166.53	161.09
15000	1323.63	697.04	488.96	385.51	323.90	283.22	254.48	233.21	216.91	204.09	193.79	185.38	178.43	172.60
16000	1411.87	743.50	521.55	411.21	345.49	302.10	271.45	248.76	231.37	217.70	206.71	197.74	190.32	184.11
17000	1500.12	789.97	554.15	436.91	367.09	320.98	288.41	264.31	245.83	231.30	219.63	210.10	202.21	195.61
18000	1588.36	836.44	586.75	462.61	388.68	339.86	305.38	279.85	260.29	244.91	232.55	222.46	214.11	207.12
19000	1676.60	882.91	619.34	488.31	410.27	358.74	322.34	295.40	274.75	258.51	245.47	234.82	226.00	218.63
20000	1764.84	929.38	651.94	514.01	431.87	377.62	339.31	310.95	289.22	272.12	258.39	247.18	237.90	230.13
21000	1853.08	975.85	684.54	539.71	453.46	396.50	356.27	326.49	303.68	285.73	271.31	259.54	249.79	241.64
22000	1941.32	1022.32	717.14	565.41	475.05	415.38	373.24	342.04	318.14	299.33	284.23	271.90	261.69	253.14
23000	2029.57	1068.78	749.73	591.11	496.65	434.26	390.20	357.59	332.60	312.94	297.15	284.27	273.58	264.65
24000	2117.81	1115.25	782.33	616.81	518.24	453.14	407.17	373.13	347.06	326.54	310.07	296.61	285.48	276.16
25000	2206.05	1161.72	814.93	642.51	539.83	472.02	424.13	388.68	361.52	340.15	322.99	308.97	297.37	287.66
26000	2294.29	1208.19	847.52	668.21	561.43	490.91	441.10	404.23	375.98	353.75	335.90	321.33	309.27	299.17
27000	2382.53	1254.66	880.12	693.91	583.02	509.79	458.06	419.78	390.44	367.36	348.82	333.69	321.16	310.68
28000	2470.77	1301.13	912.72	719.61	604.61	528.67	475.03	435.32	404.90	380.97	361.74	346.05	333.06	322.18
29000	2559.02	1347.60	945.31	745.31	626.21	547.55	491.99	450.87	419.36	394.57	374.66	358.41	344.95	333.69
30000	2647.26	1394.07	977.91	771.01	647.80	566.43	508.96	466.42	433.82	408.18	387.58	370.76	356.85	345.20
31000	2735.50	1440.53	1010.51	796.71	669.39	585.31	525.92	481.96	448.28	421.78	400.50	383.12	368.74	356.70
32000	2823.74	1487.00	1043.10	822.41	690.98	604.19	542.89	497.51	462.74	435.39	413.42	395.48	380.63	368.21
33000	2911.98	1533.47	1075.70	848.11	712.58	623.07	559.85	513.06	477.20	448.99	426.34	407.84	392.53	379.71
34000	3000.23	1579.94	1108.30	873.81	734.17	641.95	576.82	528.61	491.66	462.60	439.26	420.20	404.42	391.22
35000	3088.47	1626.41	1140.89	899.51	755.76	660.83	593.78	544.15	506.12	476.21	452.18	432.56	416.32	402.73
36000	3176.71	1672.88	1173.49	925.21	777.36	679.71	610.75	559.70	520.58	489.81	465.10	444.92	428.21	414.23
37000	3264.95	1719.35	1206.09	950.91	798.95	698.59	627.71	575.25	535.04	503.42	478.02	457.27	440.11	425.74
38000	3353.19	1765.81	1238.68	976.61	820.54	717.47	644.68	590.79	549.50	517.02	490.94	469.63	452.00	437.25
39000	3441.43	1812.28	1271.28	1002.31	842.14	736.36	661.64	606.34	563.97	530.63	503.85	481.99	463.90	448.75
40000	3529.68	1858.75	1303.88	1028.01	863.73	755.24	678.61	621.89	578.43	544.23	516.77	494.35	475.79	460.26
41000	3617.92	1905.22	1336.48	1053.71	885.32	774.12	695.57	637.44	592.89	557.84	529.69	506.71	487.69	471.77
42000	3706.16	1951.69	1369.07	1079.41	906.92	793.00	712.54	652.98	607.35	571.45	542.61	519.07	499.58	483.27
43000	3794.40	1998.16	1401.67	1105.11	928.51	811.88	729.50	668.53	621.81	585.05	555.53	531.43	511.48	494.78
44000	3882.64	2044.63	1434.27	1130.81	950.10	830.76	746.47	684.08	636.27	598.66	568.45	543.79	523.37	506.28
45000	3970.89	2091.10	1466.86	1156.51	971.69	849.64	763.43	699.62	650.73	612.26	581.37	556.14	535.27	517.79
46000	4059.13	2137.56	1499.46	1182.21	993.29	868.52	780.40	715.17	665.19	625.87	594.29	568.50	547.16	529.30
47000	4147.37	2184.03	1532.06	1207.91	1014.88	887.40	797.36	730.72	679.65	639.47	607.21	580.86	559.05	540.80
48000	4235.61	2230.50	1564.65	1233.61	1036.47	906.28	814.33	746.26	694.11	653.08	620.13	593.22	570.95	552.31
49000	4323.85	2276.97	1597.25	1259.31	1058.07	925.16	831.30	761.81	708.57	666.69	633.05	605.58	582.84	563.82
50000	4412.09	2323.44	1629.85	1285.01	1079.66	944.04	848.26	777.36	723.03	680.29	645.97	617.94	594.74	575.32
55000	4853.30	2555.78	1792.83	1413.51	1187.63	1038.45	933.09	855.09	795.33	748.32	710.56	679.73	654.21	632.85
60000	5294.51	2788.13	1955.81	1542.01	1295.59	1132.85	1017.91	932.83	867.64	816.35	775.16	741.52	713.69	690.39
65000	5735.72	3020.47	2118.80	1670.51	1403.56	1227.26	1102.74	1010.56	939.94	884.38	839.75	803.32	773.16	747.92
70000	6176.93	3252.81	2281.78	1799.01	1511.52	1321.66	1187.56	1088.30	1012.24	952.41	904.35	865.11	832.63	805.45
75000	6618.14	3485.16	2444.77	1927.51	1619.49	1416.06	1272.39	1166.04	1084.54	1020.43	968.95	926.90	892.11	862.98
80000	7059.35	3717.50	2607.75	2056.01	1727.45	1510.47	1357.21	1243.77	1156.85	1088.46	1033.54	988.70	951.58	920.51
85000	7500.56	3949.84	2770.74	2184.51	1835.42	1604.87	1442.04	1321.51	1229.15	1156.49	1098.14	1050.49	1011.05	978.05
90000	7941.77	4182.19	2933.72	2313.01	1943.38	1699.27	1526.86	1399.24	1301.45	1224.52	1162.73	1112.28	1070.53	1035.58
95000	8382.97	4414.53	3096.70	2441.51	2051.35	1793.68	1611.69	1476.98	1373.75	1292.55	1227.33	1174.08	1130.00	1093.11
100000	8824.18	4646.87	3259.69	2570.01	2159.32	1888.08	1696.52	1554.71	1446.06	1360.58	1291.93	1235.87	1189.47	1150.64

TERM / AMOUNT	15 Years	16 Years	17 Years	18 Years	19 Years	20 Years	21 Years	22 Years	23 Years	24 Years	25 Years	30 Years	35 Years	40 Years
5	.06	.06	.06	.06	.06	.06	.05	.05	.05	.05	.05	.05	.05	.05
10	.12	.11	.11	.11	.11	.11	.10	.10	.10	.10	.10	.10	.10	.10
15	.17	.17	.16	.16	.16	.16	.15	.15	.15	.15	.15	.14	.14	.14
25	.28	.28	.27	.27	.26	.26	.25	.25	.25	.25	.24	.24	.23	.23
50	.56	.55	.54	.53	.52	.51	.50	.50	.49	.49	.48	.47	.46	.46
75	.84	.82	.8C	.79	.78	.76	.75	.74	.74	.73	.72	.7C	.69	.68
100	1.12	1.09	1.07	1.05	1.03	1.02	1.00	.99	.98	.97	.96	.93	.92	.91
200	2.24	2.18	2.14	2.10	2.06	2.03	2.00	1.98	1.96	1.94	1.92	1.86	1.83	1.81
300	3.36	3.27	3.20	3.14	3.09	3.04	3.00	2.96	2.93	2.90	2.88	2.79	2.75	2.72
400	4.48	4.36	4.27	4.19	4.11	4.05	4.00	3.95	3.91	3.87	3.84	3.72	3.66	3.62
500	5.59	5.45	5.33	5.23	5.14	5.06	5.00	4.94	4.88	4.84	4.80	4.65	4.57	4.53
600	6.71	6.54	6.40	6.28	6.17	6.08	5.99	5.92	5.86	5.80	5.76	5.58	5.49	5.43
700	7.83	7.63	7.47	7.32	7.20	7.09	6.99	6.91	6.84	6.77	6.71	6.51	6.40	6.34
800	8.95	8.72	8.53	8.37	8.22	8.10	7.99	7.90	7.81	7.74	7.67	7.44	7.31	7.24
900	10.07	9.81	9.60	9.41	9.25	9.11	8.99	8.88	8.79	8.70	8.63	8.37	8.23	8.14
1000	11.18	10.90	10.66	10.46	10.28	10.12	9.99	9.87	9.76	9.67	9.59	9.30	9.14	9.05
2000	22.36	21.80	21.32	20.91	20.55	20.24	19.97	19.73	19.52	19.34	19.18	18.60	18.28	18.09
3000	33.54	32.70	31.98	31.36	30.83	30.36	29.95	29.60	29.28	29.00	28.76	27.90	27.41	27.14
4000	44.72	43.60	42.64	41.82	41.10	40.48	39.94	39.46	39.04	38.67	38.35	37.19	36.55	36.18
5000	55.90	54.50	53.30	52.27	51.38	50.60	49.92	49.32	48.80	48.34	47.93	46.49	45.69	45.23
6000	67.07	65.40	63.96	62.72	61.65	60.72	59.90	59.19	58.56	58.00	57.52	55.79	54.82	54.27
7000	78.25	76.30	74.62	73.18	71.92	70.83	69.88	69.05	68.32	67.67	67.10	65.09	63.96	63.31
8000	89.43	87.20	85.28	83.63	82.20	80.95	79.87	78.91	78.07	77.34	76.69	74.38	73.09	72.36
9000	100.61	98.10	95.94	94.08	92.47	91.07	89.85	88.78	87.83	87.00	86.27	83.68	82.23	81.40
10000	111.79	108.99	106.60	104.54	102.75	101.19	99.83	98.64	97.59	96.67	95.86	92.98	91.37	90.45
11000	122.97	119.89	117.26	114.99	113.02	111.31	109.81	108.50	107.35	106.34	105.44	102.27	100.50	99.49
12000	134.14	130.79	127.92	125.44	123.29	121.43	119.80	118.37	117.11	116.00	115.03	111.57	109.64	108.54
13000	145.32	141.69	138.58	135.89	133.57	131.55	129.78	128.23	126.87	125.67	124.61	120.87	118.78	117.58
14000	156.50	152.59	149.24	146.35	143.84	141.66	139.76	138.09	136.63	135.34	134.20	130.17	127.91	126.62
15000	167.68	163.49	159.90	156.80	154.12	151.78	149.74	147.96	146.39	145.00	143.78	139.46	137.05	135.67
16000	178.86	174.39	170.56	167.25	164.39	161.90	159.73	157.82	156.14	154.67	153.37	148.76	146.18	144.71
17000	190.04	185.29	181.22	177.71	174.67	172.02	169.71	167.68	165.90	164.33	162.95	158.06	155.32	153.76
18000	201.21	196.19	191.88	188.16	184.94	182.14	179.69	177.55	175.66	174.00	172.54	167.36	164.46	162.80
19000	212.39	207.09	202.54	198.61	195.21	192.26	189.67	187.41	185.42	183.67	182.12	176.65	173.59	171.85
20000	223.57	217.98	213.20	209.07	205.49	202.38	199.66	197.27	195.18	193.33	191.71	185.95	182.73	180.89
21000	234.75	228.88	223.85	219.52	215.76	212.49	209.64	207.14	204.94	203.00	201.29	195.25	191.87	189.93
22000	245.93	239.78	234.51	229.97	226.04	222.61	219.62	217.00	214.70	212.67	210.88	204.54	201.00	198.98
23000	257.11	250.68	245.17	240.43	236.31	232.73	229.60	226.86	224.46	222.33	220.46	213.84	210.14	208.02
24000	268.28	261.58	255.83	250.88	246.58	242.85	239.58	236.73	234.21	232.00	230.05	223.14	219.27	217.07
25000	279.46	272.48	266.49	261.33	256.86	252.97	249.57	246.59	243.97	241.67	239.63	232.44	228.41	226.11
26000	290.64	283.38	277.15	271.78	267.13	263.09	259.55	256.45	253.73	251.33	249.22	241.73	237.55	235.16
27000	301.82	294.28	287.81	282.24	277.41	273.20	269.53	266.32	263.49	261.00	258.80	251.03	246.68	244.20
28000	313.00	305.18	298.47	292.69	287.68	283.32	279.52	276.18	273.25	270.67	268.39	260.33	255.82	253.24
29000	324.18	316.07	309.13	303.14	297.96	293.44	289.50	286.04	283.01	280.33	277.97	269.63	264.96	262.29
30000	335.35	326.97	319.79	313.60	308.23	303.56	299.48	295.91	292.77	290.00	287.56	278.92	274.09	271.33
31000	346.53	337.87	330.45	324.05	318.50	313.68	309.46	305.77	302.52	299.67	297.14	288.22	283.23	280.38
32000	357.71	348.77	341.11	334.50	328.78	323.80	319.45	315.63	312.28	309.33	306.73	297.52	292.36	289.42
33000	368.89	359.67	351.77	344.96	339.05	333.92	329.50	325.50	322.04	319.00	316.31	306.81	301.50	298.47
34000	380.07	370.57	362.43	355.41	349.33	344.03	339.41	335.36	331.80	328.66	325.90	316.11	310.64	307.51
35000	391.25	381.47	373.09	365.86	359.60	354.15	349.39	345.22	341.56	338.33	335.48	325.41	319.77	316.55
36000	402.42	392.37	383.75	376.31	369.87	364.27	359.38	355.09	351.32	348.00	345.07	334.71	328.91	325.60
37000	413.60	403.27	394.41	386.77	380.15	374.39	369.36	364.95	361.08	357.66	354.65	344.00	338.05	334.64
38000	424.78	414.17	405.07	397.22	390.42	384.51	379.34	374.81	370.84	367.33	364.24	353.30	347.18	343.69
39000	435.96	425.06	415.73	407.67	400.70	394.63	389.32	384.68	380.59	377.00	373.82	362.60	356.32	352.73
40000	447.14	435.96	426.39	418.13	410.97	404.75	399.31	394.54	390.35	386.66	383.41	371.89	365.45	361.78
41000	458.32	446.86	437.04	428.58	421.25	414.86	409.29	404.40	400.11	396.33	392.99	381.19	374.59	370.82
42000	469.49	457.76	447.70	439.03	431.52	424.98	419.27	414.27	409.87	406.00	402.58	390.49	383.73	379.86
43000	480.67	468.66	458.36	449.49	441.79	435.10	429.25	424.13	419.63	415.66	412.16	399.79	392.86	388.91
44000	491.85	479.56	469.02	459.94	452.07	445.22	439.24	433.99	429.39	425.33	421.75	409.08	402.00	397.95
45000	503.03	490.46	479.68	470.39	462.34	455.34	449.22	443.86	439.15	435.00	431.33	418.38	411.13	407.00
46000	514.21	501.36	490.34	480.85	472.62	465.46	459.20	453.72	448.91	444.66	440.92	427.68	420.27	416.04
47000	525.39	512.26	501.00	491.30	482.89	475.57	469.18	463.58	458.66	454.33	450.50	436.98	429.41	425.09
48000	536.56	523.16	511.66	501.75	493.16	485.69	479.17	473.45	468.42	464.00	460.09	446.27	438.54	434.13
49000	547.74	534.05	522.32	512.20	503.44	495.81	489.15	483.31	478.18	473.66	469.67	455.57	447.68	443.17
50000	558.92	544.95	532.98	522.66	513.71	505.93	499.13	493.18	487.94	483.33	479.26	464.87	456.82	452.22
55000	614.81	599.45	586.28	574.92	565.08	556.52	549.04	542.49	536.73	531.66	527.18	511.35	502.50	497.44
60000	670.70	653.94	639.58	627.19	616.45	607.12	598.96	591.81	585.53	579.99	575.11	557.84	548.18	542.66
65000	726.59	708.44	692.87	679.45	667.83	657.71	648.87	641.13	634.32	628.32	623.03	604.33	593.86	587.88
70000	782.49	762.93	746.17	731.72	719.20	708.30	698.78	690.44	683.11	676.66	670.96	650.81	639.54	633.10
75000	838.38	817.43	799.47	783.98	770.57	758.89	748.70	739.76	731.91	724.99	718.88	697.30	685.22	678.32
80000	894.27	871.92	852.77	836.25	821.94	809.49	798.61	789.08	780.70	773.32	766.81	743.78	730.90	723.55
85000	950.16	926.42	906.06	888.51	873.31	860.08	848.52	838.39	829.49	821.65	814.73	790.27	776.58	768.77
90000	1006.05	980.91	959.36	940.78	924.68	910.67	898.43	887.71	878.29	869.99	862.66	836.76	822.26	813.99
95000	1061.94	1035.41	1012.66	993.04	976.05	961.26	948.35	937.03	927.08	918.32	910.58	883.24	867.95	859.21
100000	1117.84	1089.90	1065.96	1045.31	1027.42	1011.86	998.26	986.35	975.88	966.65	958.51	929.73	913.63	904.43

MONTHLY PAYMENT
REQUIRED TO AMORTIZE A LOAN

TERM AMOUNT	1 Year	2 Years	3 Years	4 Years	5 Years	6 Years	7 Years	8 Years	9 Years	10 Years	11 Years	12 Years	13 Years	14 Years
5	.45	.24	.17	.13	.11	.10	.09	.08	.08	.07	.07	.07	.06	.06
10	.89	.47	.33	.26	.22	.19	.17	.16	.15	.14	.13	.13	.12	.12
15	1.33	.70	.49	.39	.33	.29	.26	.24	.22	.21	.20	.19	.18	.18
25	2.21	1.17	.82	.65	.55	.48	.43	.39	.37	.35	.33	.31	.30	.29
50	4.42	2.33	1.64	1.29	1.09	.95	.85	.78	.73	.69	.65	.62	.60	.58
75	6.62	3.49	2.45	1.93	1.63	1.42	1.28	1.17	1.09	1.03	.98	.93	.90	.87
100	8.83	4.65	3.27	2.58	2.17	1.90	1.70	1.56	1.45	1.37	1.30	1.24	1.20	1.16
200	17.66	9.30	6.53	5.15	4.33	3.79	3.40	3.12	2.90	2.73	2.59	2.48	2.39	2.31
300	26.48	13.95	9.79	7.72	6.49	5.68	5.10	4.68	4.35	4.10	3.89	3.72	3.58	3.47
400	35.31	18.60	13.05	10.29	8.65	7.57	6.80	6.23	5.80	5.46	5.18	4.96	4.77	4.62
500	44.14	23.25	16.32	12.87	10.81	9.46	8.50	7.79	7.25	6.82	6.48	6.20	5.97	5.77
600	52.96	27.90	19.58	15.44	12.98	11.35	10.20	9.35	8.70	8.19	7.77	7.44	7.16	6.93
700	61.79	32.55	22.84	18.01	15.14	13.24	11.90	10.91	10.15	9.55	9.07	8.68	8.35	8.08
800	70.62	37.20	26.10	20.58	17.30	15.13	13.60	12.46	11.60	10.91	10.36	9.92	9.54	9.23
900	79.44	41.85	29.36	23.16	19.46	17.02	15.30	14.02	13.04	12.28	11.66	11.15	10.74	10.39
1000	88.27	46.50	32.63	25.73	21.62	18.91	17.00	15.58	14.49	13.64	12.95	12.39	11.93	11.54
2000	176.54	92.99	65.25	51.45	43.24	37.82	33.99	31.15	28.98	27.27	25.90	24.78	23.85	23.08
3000	264.80	139.48	97.87	77.18	64.86	56.72	50.98	46.73	43.47	40.91	38.85	37.17	35.78	34.62
4000	353.07	185.97	130.49	102.90	86.48	75.63	67.97	62.30	57.96	54.54	51.80	49.56	47.70	46.15
5000	441.33	232.46	163.11	128.63	108.09	94.54	84.96	77.87	72.45	68.17	64.74	61.95	59.63	57.69
6000	529.60	278.96	195.73	154.35	129.71	113.44	101.95	93.45	86.93	81.81	77.69	74.33	71.55	69.23
7000	617.86	325.45	228.35	180.07	151.33	132.35	118.94	109.02	101.42	95.44	90.64	86.72	83.48	80.76
8000	706.13	371.94	260.97	205.80	172.95	151.26	135.94	124.60	115.91	109.08	103.59	99.11	95.40	92.30
9000	794.39	418.43	293.59	231.52	194.57	170.16	152.93	140.17	130.40	122.71	116.54	111.50	107.33	103.84
10000	882.66	464.92	326.21	257.25	216.18	189.07	169.92	155.74	144.89	136.34	129.48	123.89	119.25	115.37
11000	970.92	511.42	358.83	282.97	237.80	207.97	186.91	171.32	159.37	149.98	142.43	136.27	131.18	126.91
12000	1059.19	557.91	391.45	308.70	259.42	226.88	203.90	186.89	173.86	163.61	155.38	148.66	143.10	138.45
13000	1147.45	604.40	424.07	334.42	281.04	245.79	220.89	202.47	188.35	177.25	168.33	161.05	155.03	149.99
14000	1235.72	650.89	456.69	360.14	302.66	264.69	237.88	218.04	202.84	190.88	181.28	173.44	166.95	161.52
15000	1323.98	697.38	489.31	385.87	324.27	283.60	254.87	233.61	217.33	204.51	194.22	185.83	178.88	173.06
16000	1412.25	743.87	521.93	411.59	345.89	302.51	271.87	249.19	231.81	218.15	207.17	198.21	190.80	184.60
17000	1500.51	790.37	554.55	437.32	367.51	321.41	288.86	264.76	246.30	231.78	220.12	210.60	202.72	196.13
18000	1588.78	836.86	587.17	463.04	389.13	340.32	305.85	280.34	260.79	245.41	233.07	222.99	214.65	207.67
19000	1677.04	883.35	619.79	488.77	410.75	359.22	322.84	295.91	275.28	259.05	246.02	235.38	226.57	219.21
20000	1765.31	929.84	652.41	514.49	432.36	378.13	339.83	311.48	289.77	272.68	258.96	247.77	238.50	230.74
21000	1853.57	976.33	685.03	540.21	453.98	397.04	356.82	327.06	304.25	286.32	271.91	260.15	250.42	242.28
22000	1941.84	1022.83	717.65	565.94	475.60	415.94	373.81	342.63	318.74	299.95	284.86	272.54	262.35	253.82
23000	2030.10	1069.32	750.28	591.66	497.22	434.85	390.80	358.20	333.23	313.58	297.81	284.93	274.27	265.36
24000	2118.37	1115.81	782.90	617.39	518.84	453.76	407.80	373.78	347.72	327.22	310.76	297.32	286.20	276.89
25000	2206.63	1162.30	815.52	643.11	540.45	472.66	424.79	389.35	362.21	340.85	323.70	309.71	298.12	288.43
26000	2294.90	1208.79	848.14	668.84	562.07	491.57	441.78	404.93	376.69	354.49	336.65	322.09	310.05	299.97
27000	2383.16	1255.29	880.76	694.56	583.69	510.47	458.77	420.50	391.18	368.12	349.60	334.48	321.97	311.50
28000	2471.43	1301.78	913.38	720.28	605.31	529.38	475.76	436.07	405.67	381.75	362.55	346.87	333.90	323.04
29000	2559.69	1348.27	946.00	746.01	626.93	548.29	492.75	451.65	420.16	395.39	375.50	359.26	345.82	334.58
30000	2647.96	1394.76	978.62	771.73	648.54	567.19	509.74	467.22	434.65	409.02	388.44	371.65	357.75	346.11
31000	2736.22	1441.25	1011.24	797.46	670.16	586.10	526.73	482.80	449.13	422.65	401.39	384.03	369.67	357.65
32000	2824.49	1487.74	1043.86	823.18	691.78	605.01	543.73	498.37	463.62	436.29	414.34	396.42	381.59	369.19
33000	2912.75	1534.24	1076.48	848.91	713.40	623.91	560.72	513.94	478.11	449.92	427.29	408.81	393.52	380.72
34000	3001.02	1580.73	1109.10	874.63	735.02	642.82	577.71	529.52	492.60	463.56	440.24	421.20	405.44	392.26
35000	3089.28	1627.22	1141.72	900.35	756.63	661.72	594.70	545.09	507.09	477.19	453.18	433.59	417.37	403.80
36000	3177.55	1673.71	1174.34	926.08	778.25	680.63	611.69	560.67	521.57	490.82	466.13	445.97	429.29	415.34
37000	3265.81	1720.20	1206.96	951.80	799.87	699.54	628.68	576.24	536.06	504.46	479.08	458.36	441.22	426.87
38000	3354.08	1766.70	1239.58	977.53	821.49	718.44	645.67	591.81	550.55	518.09	492.03	470.75	453.14	438.41
39000	3442.34	1813.19	1272.20	1003.25	843.11	737.35	662.66	607.39	565.04	531.73	504.98	483.14	465.07	449.95
40000	3530.61	1859.68	1304.82	1028.98	864.72	756.26	679.66	622.96	579.53	545.36	517.92	495.53	476.99	461.48
41000	3618.87	1906.17	1337.44	1054.70	886.34	775.16	696.65	638.54	594.01	558.99	530.87	507.91	488.92	473.02
42000	3707.14	1952.66	1370.06	1080.42	907.96	794.07	713.64	654.11	608.50	572.63	543.82	520.30	500.84	484.56
43000	3795.40	1999.15	1402.68	1106.15	929.58	812.97	730.63	669.68	622.99	586.26	556.77	532.69	512.77	496.09
44000	3883.67	2045.65	1435.30	1131.87	951.19	831.88	747.62	685.26	637.48	599.90	569.72	545.08	524.69	507.63
45000	3971.93	2092.14	1467.93	1157.60	972.81	850.79	764.61	700.83	651.97	613.53	582.66	557.47	536.62	519.17
46000	4060.20	2138.63	1500.55	1183.32	994.43	869.69	781.60	716.40	666.45	627.16	595.61	569.85	548.54	530.71
47000	4148.46	2185.12	1533.17	1209.05	1016.05	888.60	798.59	731.98	680.94	640.80	608.56	582.24	560.47	542.24
48000	4236.73	2231.61	1565.79	1234.77	1037.67	907.51	815.59	747.55	695.43	654.43	621.51	594.63	572.39	553.78
49000	4324.99	2278.11	1598.41	1260.49	1059.28	926.41	832.58	763.13	709.92	668.06	634.46	607.02	584.31	565.32
50000	4413.26	2324.60	1631.03	1286.22	1080.90	945.32	849.57	778.70	724.41	681.70	647.40	619.41	596.24	576.85
55000	4854.58	2557.06	1794.13	1414.84	1188.99	1039.85	934.52	856.57	796.85	749.87	712.14	681.35	655.86	634.54
60000	5295.91	2789.52	1957.23	1543.46	1297.08	1134.38	1019.48	934.44	869.29	818.04	776.88	743.29	715.49	692.22
65000	5737.24	3021.98	2120.33	1672.08	1405.17	1228.91	1104.44	1012.31	941.73	886.21	841.62	805.23	775.11	749.91
70000	6178.56	3254.43	2283.44	1800.70	1513.26	1323.44	1189.39	1090.18	1014.17	954.38	906.36	867.17	834.73	807.59
75000	6619.89	3486.89	2446.54	1929.33	1621.35	1417.98	1274.35	1168.05	1086.61	1022.55	971.10	929.11	894.36	865.28
80000	7061.21	3719.35	2609.64	2057.95	1729.44	1512.51	1359.31	1245.92	1159.05	1090.71	1035.84	991.05	953.98	922.96
85000	7502.54	3951.81	2772.74	2186.57	1837.53	1607.04	1444.26	1323.79	1231.49	1158.88	1100.58	1052.99	1013.60	980.65
90000	7943.86	4184.27	2935.85	2315.19	1945.62	1701.57	1529.22	1401.66	1303.93	1227.05	1165.32	1114.93	1073.23	1038.33
95000	8385.19	4416.73	3098.95	2443.81	2053.71	1796.10	1614.18	1479.53	1376.37	1295.22	1230.06	1176.87	1132.85	1096.02
100000	8826.51	4649.19	3262.05	2572.43	2161.80	1890.63	1699.13	1557.40	1448.81	1363.39	1294.80	1238.81	1192.47	1153.70

TERM AMOUNT	15 Years	16 Years	17 Years	18 Years	19 Years	20 Years	21 Years	22 Years	23 Years	24 Years	25 Years	30 Years	35 Years	40 Years
5	.06	.06	.06	.06	.06	.06	.06	.05	.05	.05	.05	.05	.05	.05
10	.12	.11	.11	.11	.11	.11	.11	.10	.10	.10	.10	.10	.10	.10
15	.17	.17	.17	.16	.16	.16	.16	.15	.15	.15	.15	.15	.14	.14
25	.29	.28	.27	.27	.26	.26	.26	.25	.25	.25	.25	.24	.23	.23
50	.57	.55	.54	.53	.52	.51	.51	.50	.49	.49	.49	.47	.46	.46
75	.85	.82	.81	.79	.78	.77	.76	.75	.74	.73	.73	.71	.69	.69
100	1.13	1.10	1.07	1.05	1.04	1.02	1.01	.99	.98	.98	.97	.94	.92	.91
200	2.25	2.19	2.14	2.10	2.07	2.04	2.01	1.98	1.96	1.95	1.93	1.87	1.84	1.82
300	3.37	3.28	3.21	3.15	3.10	3.05	3.01	2.97	2.94	2.92	2.89	2.81	2.76	2.73
400	4.49	4.38	4.28	4.20	4.13	4.07	4.01	3.96	3.92	3.89	3.85	3.74	3.68	3.64
500	5.61	5.47	5.35	5.25	5.16	5.08	5.01	4.95	4.90	4.86	4.82	4.67	4.59	4.55
600	6.73	6.56	6.42	6.30	6.19	6.10	6.02	5.94	5.88	5.83	5.78	5.61	5.51	5.46
700	7.85	7.66	7.49	7.35	7.22	7.11	7.02	6.93	6.86	6.80	6.74	6.54	6.43	6.36
800	8.97	8.75	8.56	8.39	8.25	8.13	8.02	7.92	7.84	7.77	7.70	7.47	7.35	7.27
900	10.09	9.84	9.63	9.44	9.28	9.14	9.02	8.91	8.82	8.74	8.66	8.41	8.26	8.18
1000	11.21	10.94	10.70	10.49	10.31	10.16	10.02	9.90	9.80	9.71	9.63	9.34	9.18	9.09
2000	22.42	21.87	21.39	20.98	20.62	20.31	20.04	19.80	19.59	19.41	19.25	18.67	18.36	18.17
3000	33.63	32.80	32.08	31.46	30.93	30.46	30.06	29.70	29.39	29.11	28.87	28.01	27.53	27.26
4000	44.84	43.73	42.77	41.95	41.23	40.61	40.07	39.60	39.18	38.81	38.49	37.34	36.71	36.34
5000	56.05	54.66	53.46	52.43	51.54	50.77	50.09	49.50	48.97	48.51	48.11	46.68	45.88	45.42
6000	67.26	65.59	64.16	62.92	61.85	60.92	60.11	59.39	58.77	58.22	57.73	56.01	55.06	54.51
7000	78.47	76.52	74.85	73.41	72.16	71.07	70.12	69.29	68.56	67.92	67.35	65.35	64.23	63.59
8000	89.68	87.45	85.54	83.89	82.46	81.22	80.14	79.19	78.36	77.62	76.97	74.68	73.41	72.68
9000	100.89	98.38	96.23	94.38	92.77	91.38	90.16	89.09	88.15	87.32	86.59	84.02	82.58	81.76
10000	112.10	109.31	106.92	104.86	103.08	101.53	100.17	98.99	97.94	97.02	96.21	93.35	91.76	90.84
11000	123.31	120.24	117.61	115.35	113.39	111.68	110.19	108.88	107.74	106.73	105.84	102.69	100.93	99.93
12000	134.52	131.17	128.31	125.84	123.69	121.83	120.21	118.78	117.53	116.43	115.46	112.02	110.11	109.01
13000	145.73	142.10	139.00	136.32	134.00	131.98	130.22	128.68	127.32	126.13	125.08	121.36	119.28	118.10
14000	156.94	153.03	149.69	146.81	144.31	142.14	140.24	138.58	137.12	135.83	134.70	130.69	128.46	127.18
15000	168.15	163.97	160.38	157.29	154.62	152.29	150.26	148.48	146.91	145.53	144.32	140.03	137.63	136.26
16000	179.36	174.90	171.07	167.78	164.92	162.44	160.27	158.37	156.71	155.24	153.94	149.36	146.81	145.35
17000	190.57	185.83	181.77	178.26	175.23	172.59	170.29	168.27	166.50	164.94	163.56	158.70	155.98	154.43
18000	201.78	196.76	192.46	188.75	185.54	182.75	180.31	178.17	176.29	174.64	173.18	168.03	165.16	163.52
19000	212.99	207.69	203.15	199.24	195.85	192.90	190.32	188.07	186.09	184.34	182.80	177.37	174.33	172.60
20000	224.19	218.62	213.84	209.72	206.15	203.05	200.34	197.97	195.88	194.04	192.42	186.70	183.51	181.68
21000	235.40	229.55	224.53	220.21	216.46	213.20	210.36	207.87	205.68	203.75	202.04	196.04	192.68	190.77
22000	246.61	240.48	235.22	230.69	226.77	223.36	220.37	217.76	215.47	213.45	211.67	205.37	201.06	199.85
23000	257.82	251.41	245.92	241.18	237.08	233.51	230.39	227.66	225.26	223.15	221.29	214.71	211.03	208.94
24000	269.03	262.34	256.61	251.67	247.38	243.66	240.41	237.56	235.06	232.85	230.91	224.04	211.03	218.02
25000	280.24	273.27	267.30	262.15	257.69	253.81	250.42	247.46	244.85	242.55	240.53	233.38	229.38	227.10
26000	291.45	284.20	277.99	272.64	268.00	263.96	260.44	257.36	254.64	252.26	250.15	242.71	238.56	236.19
27000	302.66	295.13	288.68	283.12	278.31	274.12	270.46	267.25	264.44	261.96	259.77	252.04	247.73	245.27
28000	313.87	306.06	299.37	293.61	288.61	284.27	280.48	277.15	274.23	271.66	269.39	261.38	256.91	254.36
29000	325.08	317.00	310.07	304.09	298.92	294.42	290.49	287.05	284.03	281.36	279.01	270.71	266.08	263.44
30000	336.29	327.93	320.76	314.58	309.23	304.57	300.51	296.95	293.82	291.06	288.63	280.05	275.26	272.52
31000	347.50	338.86	331.45	325.07	319.54	314.73	310.53	306.85	303.61	300.77	298.25	289.38	284.43	281.61
32000	358.71	349.79	342.14	335.55	329.84	324.88	320.54	316.74	313.41	310.47	307.87	298.72	293.61	290.69
33000	369.92	360.72	352.83	346.04	340.15	335.03	330.56	326.64	323.20	320.17	317.50	308.05	302.78	299.78
34000	381.13	371.65	363.53	356.52	350.46	345.18	340.58	336.54	332.99	329.87	327.12	317.39	311.96	308.86
35000	392.34	382.58	374.22	367.01	360.77	355.34	350.59	346.44	342.79	339.57	336.74	326.72	321.13	317.94
36000	403.55	393.51	384.91	377.50	371.07	365.49	360.61	356.34	352.58	349.28	346.36	336.06	330.31	327.03
37000	414.76	404.44	395.60	387.98	381.38	375.64	370.63	366.23	362.38	358.98	355.98	345.39	339.48	336.11
38000	425.97	415.37	406.29	398.47	391.69	385.79	380.64	376.13	372.17	368.68	365.60	354.73	348.66	345.20
39000	437.17	426.30	416.98	408.95	402.00	395.94	390.66	386.03	381.96	378.38	375.22	364.06	357.83	354.28
40000	448.38	437.23	427.68	419.44	412.30	406.10	400.68	395.93	391.76	388.08	384.84	373.40	367.01	363.36
41000	459.59	448.16	438.37	429.92	422.61	416.25	410.69	405.83	401.55	397.79	394.46	382.73	376.18	372.45
42000	470.80	459.09	449.06	440.41	432.92	426.40	420.71	415.73	411.35	407.49	404.08	392.07	385.36	381.53
43000	482.01	470.03	459.75	450.90	443.23	436.55	430.73	425.62	421.14	417.19	413.70	401.40	394.53	390.62
44000	493.22	480.96	470.44	461.38	453.53	446.71	440.74	435.52	430.93	426.89	423.33	410.74	403.71	399.70
45000	504.43	491.89	481.14	471.87	463.84	456.86	450.76	445.42	440.73	436.59	432.95	420.07	412.88	408.78
46000	515.64	502.82	491.83	482.35	474.15	467.01	460.78	455.32	450.52	446.30	442.57	429.41	422.06	417.87
47000	526.85	513.75	502.52	492.84	484.46	477.16	470.79	465.22	460.31	456.00	452.19	438.74	431.23	426.95
48000	538.06	524.68	513.21	503.33	494.76	487.31	480.81	475.11	470.11	465.70	461.81	448.08	440.41	436.04
49000	549.27	535.61	523.90	513.81	505.07	497.47	490.83	485.01	479.90	475.40	471.43	457.41	449.58	445.12
50000	560.48	546.54	534.59	524.30	515.38	507.62	500.84	494.91	489.70	485.10	481.05	466.75	458.76	454.20
55000	616.53	601.19	588.05	576.73	566.92	558.38	550.93	544.40	538.67	533.61	529.16	513.42	504.63	499.62
60000	672.57	655.85	641.51	629.16	618.45	609.14	601.01	593.89	587.63	582.12	577.26	560.09	550.51	545.04
65000	728.62	710.50	694.97	681.59	669.99	659.90	651.10	643.38	636.60	630.63	625.37	606.77	596.38	590.46
70000	784.67	765.15	748.43	734.01	721.53	710.67	701.18	692.87	685.57	679.14	673.47	653.44	642.26	635.88
75000	840.72	819.81	801.89	786.44	773.07	761.43	751.26	742.36	734.54	727.65	721.57	700.12	688.13	681.30
80000	896.76	874.46	855.35	838.87	824.60	812.19	801.35	791.85	783.51	776.16	769.68	746.79	734.01	726.72
85000	952.81	929.11	908.81	891.30	876.14	862.95	851.43	841.34	832.48	824.67	817.78	793.46	779.88	772.14
90000	1008.86	983.77	962.27	943.73	927.68	913.71	901.52	890.83	881.45	873.18	865.89	840.14	825.76	817.56
95000	1064.91	1038.42	1015.72	996.16	979.21	964.47	951.60	940.32	930.42	921.69	913.99	886.81	871.63	862.98
100000	1120.95	1093.07	1069.18	1048.59	1030.75	1015.23	1001.68	989.81	979.39	970.20	962.10	933.49	917.51	908.40

10.800%

TERM AMOUNT	1 Year	2 Years	3 Years	4 Years	5 Years	6 Years	7 Years	8 Years	9 Years	10 Years	11 Years	12 Years	13 Years	14 Years
5	.45	.24	.17	.13	.11	.10	.09	.08	.08	.07	.07	.07	.06	.06
10	.89	.47	.33	.26	.22	.19	.18	.16	.15	.14	.13	.13	.12	.12
15	1.33	.70	.49	.39	.33	.29	.26	.24	.22	.21	.20	.19	.18	.18
25	2.21	1.17	.82	.65	.55	.48	.43	.40	.37	.35	.33	.32	.30	.29
50	4.42	2.33	1.64	1.29	1.09	.95	.86	.79	.73	.69	.65	.63	.60	.58
75	6.63	3.49	2.45	1.94	1.63	1.42	1.28	1.18	1.09	1.03	.98	.94	.90	.87
100	8.83	4.66	3.27	2.58	2.17	1.90	1.71	1.57	1.46	1.37	1.30	1.25	1.20	1.16
200	17.66	9.31	6.53	5.15	4.33	3.79	3.41	3.13	2.91	2.74	2.60	2.49	2.40	2.32
300	26.49	13.96	9.80	7.73	6.50	5.68	5.11	4.69	4.36	4.10	3.90	3.73	3.59	3.48
400	35.32	18.61	13.06	10.30	8.66	7.58	6.81	6.25	5.81	5.47	5.20	4.97	4.79	4.63
500	44.15	23.26	16.33	12.88	10.83	9.47	8.51	7.81	7.26	6.84	6.49	6.21	5.98	5.79
600	52.98	27.91	19.59	15.45	12.99	11.36	10.22	9.37	8.71	8.20	7.79	7.46	7.18	6.95
700	61.81	32.57	22.86	18.03	15.15	13.26	11.92	10.93	10.17	9.57	9.09	8.70	8.37	8.10
800	70.64	37.22	26.12	20.60	17.32	15.15	13.62	12.49	11.62	10.93	10.39	9.94	9.57	9.26
900	79.46	41.87	29.38	23.18	19.48	17.04	15.32	14.05	13.07	12.30	11.68	11.18	10.76	10.42
1000	88.29	46.52	32.65	25.75	21.65	18.94	17.02	15.61	14.52	13.67	12.98	12.42	11.96	11.57
2000	176.58	93.04	65.29	51.50	43.29	37.87	34.04	31.21	29.04	27.33	25.96	24.84	23.91	23.14
3000	264.87	139.55	97.94	77.25	64.93	56.80	51.06	46.81	43.55	40.99	38.94	37.26	35.87	34.71
4000	353.16	186.07	130.58	103.00	86.58	75.73	68.07	62.41	58.07	54.65	51.91	49.67	47.82	46.28
5000	441.45	232.58	163.23	128.75	108.22	94.66	85.09	78.01	72.58	68.32	64.89	62.09	59.78	57.84
6000	529.74	279.10	195.87	154.50	129.86	113.60	102.11	93.61	87.10	81.98	77.87	74.51	71.73	69.41
7000	618.02	325.61	228.51	180.24	151.50	132.53	119.13	109.21	101.61	95.64	90.84	86.93	83.69	80.98
8000	706.31	372.13	261.16	205.99	173.15	151.46	136.14	124.81	116.13	109.30	103.82	99.34	95.64	92.55
9000	794.60	418.64	293.80	231.74	194.79	170.39	153.16	140.41	130.64	122.96	116.80	111.76	107.60	104.11
10000	882.89	465.16	326.45	257.49	216.43	189.32	170.18	156.01	145.16	136.63	129.77	124.18	119.55	115.68
11000	971.18	511.67	359.09	283.24	238.08	208.25	187.20	171.61	159.68	150.29	142.75	136.60	131.51	127.25
12000	1059.47	558.19	391.73	308.99	259.72	227.19	204.21	187.21	174.19	163.95	155.73	149.01	143.46	138.82
13000	1147.75	604.70	424.38	334.74	281.36	246.12	221.23	202.81	188.71	177.61	168.70	161.43	155.42	150.38
14000	1236.04	651.22	457.02	360.48	303.00	265.05	238.25	218.42	203.22	191.27	181.68	173.85	167.37	161.95
15000	1324.33	697.73	489.67	386.23	324.65	283.98	255.27	234.02	217.74	204.94	194.66	186.27	179.33	173.52
16000	1412.62	744.25	522.31	411.98	346.29	302.91	272.28	249.62	232.25	218.60	207.63	198.68	191.28	185.09
17000	1500.91	790.76	554.95	437.73	367.93	321.85	289.30	265.22	246.77	232.26	220.61	211.10	203.24	196.65
18000	1589.20	837.28	587.60	463.48	389.58	340.78	306.32	280.82	261.28	245.92	233.59	223.52	215.19	208.22
19000	1677.48	883.79	620.24	489.23	411.22	359.71	323.34	296.42	275.80	259.58	246.56	235.94	227.14	219.79
20000	1765.77	930.31	652.89	514.98	432.86	378.64	340.35	312.02	290.32	273.25	259.54	248.35	239.10	231.36
21000	1854.06	976.82	685.53	540.72	454.50	397.57	357.37	327.62	304.83	286.91	272.52	260.77	251.05	242.92
22000	1942.35	1023.34	718.17	566.47	476.15	416.50	374.39	343.22	319.35	300.57	285.49	273.19	263.01	254.49
23000	2030.64	1069.85	750.82	592.22	497.79	435.44	391.41	358.82	333.86	314.23	298.47	285.61	274.96	266.06
24000	2118.93	1116.37	783.46	617.97	519.43	454.37	408.42	374.42	348.38	327.89	311.45	298.02	286.92	277.63
25000	2207.21	1162.88	816.11	643.72	541.08	473.30	425.44	390.02	362.89	341.56	324.42	310.44	298.87	289.19
26000	2295.50	1209.40	848.75	669.47	562.72	492.23	442.46	405.62	377.41	355.22	337.40	322.86	310.83	300.76
27000	2383.79	1255.91	881.40	695.21	584.36	511.16	459.48	421.23	391.92	368.88	350.38	335.28	322.78	312.33
28000	2472.08	1302.43	914.04	720.96	606.00	530.10	476.49	436.83	406.44	382.54	363.36	347.69	334.74	323.90
29000	2560.37	1348.94	946.68	746.71	627.65	549.03	493.51	452.43	420.96	396.20	376.33	360.11	346.69	335.47
30000	2648.66	1395.46	979.33	772.46	649.29	567.96	510.53	468.03	435.47	409.87	389.31	372.53	358.65	347.03
31000	2736.95	1441.97	1011.97	798.21	670.93	586.89	527.55	483.63	449.99	423.53	402.29	384.95	370.60	358.60
32000	2825.23	1488.49	1044.62	823.96	692.58	605.82	544.56	499.23	464.50	437.19	415.26	397.36	382.56	370.17
33000	2913.52	1535.00	1077.26	849.71	714.22	624.75	561.58	514.83	479.02	450.85	428.24	409.78	394.51	381.74
34000	3001.81	1581.52	1109.90	875.45	735.86	643.69	578.60	530.43	493.53	464.51	441.22	422.20	406.47	393.30
35000	3090.10	1628.03	1142.55	901.20	757.50	662.62	595.62	546.03	508.05	478.18	454.19	434.62	418.42	404.87
36000	3178.39	1674.55	1175.19	926.95	779.15	681.55	612.63	561.63	522.56	491.84	467.17	447.03	430.38	416.44
37000	3266.68	1721.06	1207.84	952.70	800.79	700.48	629.65	577.23	537.08	505.50	480.15	459.45	442.33	428.01
38000	3354.96	1767.58	1240.48	978.45	822.43	719.41	646.67	592.83	551.59	519.16	493.12	471.87	454.28	439.57
39000	3443.25	1814.09	1273.12	1004.20	844.07	738.35	663.69	608.43	566.11	532.82	506.10	484.29	466.24	451.14
40000	3531.54	1860.61	1305.77	1029.95	865.72	757.28	680.70	624.04	580.63	546.49	519.08	496.70	478.19	462.71
41000	3619.83	1907.12	1338.41	1055.69	887.36	776.21	697.72	639.64	595.14	560.15	532.05	509.12	490.15	474.28
42000	3708.12	1953.64	1371.06	1081.44	909.00	795.14	714.74	655.24	609.66	573.81	545.03	521.54	502.10	485.84
43000	3796.41	2000.15	1403.70	1107.19	930.65	814.07	731.76	670.84	624.17	587.47	558.01	533.96	514.06	497.41
44000	3884.69	2046.67	1436.34	1132.94	952.29	833.00	748.77	686.44	638.69	601.13	570.98	546.37	526.01	508.98
45000	3972.98	2093.18	1468.99	1158.69	973.93	851.94	765.79	702.04	653.20	614.80	583.96	558.79	537.97	520.55
46000	4061.27	2139.70	1501.63	1184.44	995.57	870.87	782.81	717.64	667.72	628.46	596.94	571.21	549.92	532.11
47000	4149.56	2186.21	1534.28	1210.18	1017.22	889.80	799.83	733.24	682.23	642.12	609.91	583.63	561.88	543.68
48000	4237.85	2232.73	1566.92	1235.93	1038.86	908.73	816.84	748.84	696.75	655.78	622.89	596.04	573.83	555.25
49000	4326.14	2279.24	1599.57	1261.68	1060.50	927.66	833.86	764.44	711.27	669.44	635.87	608.46	585.79	566.82
50000	4414.42	2325.76	1632.21	1287.43	1082.15	946.59	850.88	780.04	725.78	683.11	648.84	620.88	597.74	578.38
55000	4855.87	2558.33	1795.43	1416.17	1190.36	1041.25	935.97	858.05	798.36	751.42	713.73	682.97	657.52	636.22
60000	5297.31	2790.91	1958.65	1544.92	1298.57	1135.91	1021.05	936.05	870.94	819.73	778.61	745.05	717.29	694.06
65000	5738.75	3023.48	2121.87	1673.66	1406.79	1230.57	1106.14	1014.05	943.51	888.04	843.50	807.14	777.06	751.90
70000	6180.19	3256.06	2285.09	1802.40	1515.00	1325.23	1191.23	1092.06	1016.09	956.35	908.38	869.23	836.84	809.74
75000	6621.63	3488.63	2448.31	1931.14	1623.22	1419.89	1276.31	1170.06	1088.67	1024.66	973.26	931.32	896.61	867.57
80000	7063.08	3721.21	2611.53	2059.89	1731.43	1514.55	1361.40	1248.07	1161.25	1092.97	1038.15	993.40	956.38	925.41
85000	7504.52	3953.78	2774.75	2188.63	1839.64	1609.21	1446.49	1326.07	1233.82	1161.28	1103.03	1055.49	1016.16	983.25
90000	7945.96	4186.36	2937.97	2317.37	1947.86	1703.87	1531.58	1404.07	1306.40	1229.59	1167.92	1117.58	1075.93	1041.09
95000	8387.40	4418.93	3101.19	2446.11	2056.07	1798.53	1616.66	1482.08	1378.98	1297.90	1232.80	1179.67	1135.70	1098.93
100000	8828.84	4651.51	3264.41	2574.86	2164.29	1893.18	1701.75	1560.08	1451.56	1366.21	1297.68	1241.75	1195.48	1156.77

TERM	15 Years	16 Years	17 Years	18 Years	19 Years	20 Years	21 Years	22 Years	23 Years	24 Years	25 Years	30 Years	35 Years	40 Years
AMOUNT														
5	.06	.06	.06	.06	.06	.06	.06	.05	.05	.05	.05	.05	.05	.05
10	.12	.11	.11	.11	.11	.11	.11	.10	.10	.10	.10	.10	.10	.10
15	.17	.17	.17	.16	.16	.16	.16	.15	.15	.15	.15	.15	.14	.14
25	.29	.28	.27	.27	.26	.26	.26	.25	.25	.25	.25	.24	.24	.23
50	.57	.55	.54	.53	.52	.51	.51	.50	.50	.49	.49	.47	.47	.46
75	.85	.83	.81	.79	.78	.77	.76	.75	.74	.74	.73	.71	.70	.69
100	1.13	1.10	1.08	1.06	1.04	1.02	1.01	1.00	.99	.98	.97	.94	.93	.92
200	2.25	2.20	2.15	2.11	2.07	2.04	2.02	1.99	1.97	1.95	1.94	1.88	1.85	1.83
300	3.38	3.29	3.22	3.16	3.11	3.06	3.02	2.98	2.95	2.93	2.90	2.82	2.77	2.74
400	4.50	4.39	4.29	4.21	4.14	4.08	4.03	3.98	3.94	3.90	3.87	3.75	3.69	3.65
500	5.63	5.49	5.37	5.26	5.18	5.10	5.03	4.97	4.92	4.87	4.83	4.69	4.61	4.57
600	6.75	6.58	6.44	6.32	6.21	6.12	6.04	5.96	5.90	5.85	5.80	5.63	5.53	5.48
700	7.87	7.68	7.51	7.37	7.24	7.14	7.04	6.96	6.89	6.82	6.76	6.57	6.45	6.39
800	9.00	8.77	8.58	8.42	8.28	8.15	8.05	7.95	7.87	7.80	7.73	7.50	7.38	7.30
900	10.12	9.87	9.66	9.47	9.31	9.17	9.05	8.94	8.85	8.77	8.70	8.44	8.30	8.22
1000	11.25	10.97	10.73	10.52	10.35	10.19	10.06	9.94	9.83	9.74	9.66	9.38	9.22	9.13
2000	22.49	21.93	21.45	21.04	20.69	20.38	20.11	19.87	19.66	19.48	19.32	18.75	18.43	18.25
3000	33.73	32.89	32.18	31.56	31.03	30.56	30.16	29.80	29.49	29.22	28.98	28.12	27.65	27.38
4000	44.97	43.85	42.90	42.08	41.37	40.75	40.21	39.74	39.32	38.96	38.63	37.49	36.86	36.50
5000	56.21	54.82	53.63	52.60	51.71	50.94	50.26	49.67	49.15	48.69	48.29	46.87	46.07	45.62
6000	67.45	65.78	64.35	63.12	62.05	61.12	60.31	59.60	58.98	58.43	57.95	56.24	55.29	54.75
7000	78.69	76.74	75.07	73.64	72.39	71.31	70.36	69.53	68.81	68.17	67.60	65.61	64.50	63.87
8000	89.93	87.70	85.80	84.15	82.73	81.49	80.41	79.47	78.64	77.91	77.26	74.98	73.72	72.99
9000	101.17	98.67	96.52	94.67	93.07	91.68	90.46	89.40	88.47	87.64	86.92	84.36	82.93	82.12
10000	112.41	109.63	107.25	105.19	103.41	101.87	100.52	99.33	98.29	97.38	96.57	93.73	92.14	91.24
11000	123.65	120.59	117.97	115.71	113.75	112.05	110.57	109.27	108.12	107.12	106.23	103.10	101.36	100.37
12000	134.89	131.55	128.69	126.23	124.09	122.24	120.62	119.20	117.95	116.86	115.89	112.47	110.57	109.49
13000	146.13	142.52	139.42	136.75	134.44	132.42	130.67	129.13	127.78	126.59	125.54	121.85	119.79	118.61
14000	157.37	153.48	150.14	147.27	144.78	142.61	140.72	139.06	137.61	136.33	135.20	131.22	129.00	127.74
15000	168.62	164.44	160.87	157.79	155.12	152.80	150.77	149.00	147.44	146.07	144.86	140.59	138.21	136.86
16000	179.86	175.40	171.59	168.30	165.46	162.98	160.82	158.93	157.27	155.81	154.52	149.96	147.43	145.98
17000	191.10	186.37	182.31	178.82	175.80	173.17	170.87	168.87	167.10	165.54	164.17	159.34	156.64	155.11
18000	202.34	197.33	193.04	189.34	186.14	183.36	180.92	178.80	176.93	175.28	173.83	168.71	165.85	164.23
19000	213.58	208.29	203.76	199.86	196.48	193.54	190.98	188.73	186.76	185.02	183.49	178.08	175.07	173.36
20000	224.82	219.25	214.49	210.38	206.82	203.73	201.03	198.66	196.58	194.76	193.14	187.45	184.28	182.48
21000	236.06	230.22	225.21	220.90	217.16	213.91	211.08	208.59	206.41	204.49	202.80	196.83	193.50	191.60
22000	247.30	241.18	235.94	231.42	227.50	224.10	221.13	218.53	216.24	214.23	212.46	206.20	202.71	200.73
23000	258.54	252.14	246.66	241.93	237.84	234.29	231.18	228.46	226.07	223.97	222.11	215.57	211.92	209.85
24000	269.78	263.10	257.38	252.45	248.18	244.47	241.23	238.39	235.90	233.71	231.77	224.94	221.14	218.97
25000	281.02	274.07	268.11	262.97	258.53	254.66	251.28	248.33	245.73	243.44	241.43	234.32	230.35	228.10
26000	292.26	285.03	278.83	273.49	268.87	264.84	261.33	258.26	255.56	253.18	251.08	243.69	239.57	237.22
27000	303.50	295.99	289.56	284.01	279.21	275.03	271.38	268.19	265.39	262.92	260.74	253.06	248.78	246.35
28000	314.74	306.95	300.28	294.53	289.55	285.22	281.44	278.12	275.22	272.66	270.40	262.43	257.99	255.47
29000	325.99	317.92	311.00	305.05	299.89	295.40	291.49	288.06	285.05	282.39	280.05	271.81	267.21	264.59
30000	337.23	328.88	321.73	315.57	310.23	305.59	301.54	297.99	294.87	292.13	289.71	281.18	276.42	273.72
31000	348.47	339.84	332.45	326.08	320.57	315.77	311.59	307.92	304.70	301.87	299.37	290.55	285.64	282.84
32000	359.71	350.80	343.18	336.60	330.91	325.96	321.64	317.86	314.53	311.61	309.03	299.92	294.85	291.96
33000	370.95	361.77	353.90	347.12	341.25	336.15	331.69	327.79	324.36	321.34	318.68	309.29	304.06	301.09
34000	382.19	372.73	364.62	357.64	351.59	346.33	341.74	337.72	334.19	331.08	328.34	318.67	313.28	310.21
35000	393.43	383.69	375.35	368.16	361.93	356.52	351.79	347.65	344.02	340.82	338.00	328.04	322.49	319.33
36000	404.67	394.65	386.07	378.68	372.27	366.71	361.84	357.59	353.85	350.56	347.65	337.41	331.70	328.46
37000	415.91	405.62	396.80	389.20	382.62	376.89	371.90	367.52	363.68	360.29	357.31	346.78	340.92	337.58
38000	427.15	416.58	407.52	399.72	392.96	387.08	381.95	377.45	373.51	370.03	366.97	356.16	350.13	346.71
39000	438.39	427.54	418.24	410.23	403.30	397.26	392.00	387.39	383.34	379.77	376.62	365.53	359.35	355.83
40000	449.63	438.50	428.97	420.75	413.64	407.45	402.05	397.32	393.16	389.51	386.28	374.90	368.56	364.95
41000	460.87	449.47	439.69	431.27	423.98	417.64	412.10	407.25	402.99	399.24	395.94	384.27	377.77	374.08
42000	472.11	460.43	450.42	441.79	434.32	427.82	422.15	417.18	412.82	408.98	405.59	393.65	386.99	383.20
43000	483.36	471.39	461.14	452.31	444.66	438.01	432.20	427.12	422.65	418.72	415.25	403.02	396.20	392.32
44000	494.60	482.35	471.87	462.83	455.00	448.19	442.25	437.05	432.48	428.46	424.91	412.39	405.42	401.45
45000	505.84	493.32	482.59	473.35	465.34	458.38	452.30	446.98	442.31	438.19	434.56	421.76	414.63	410.57
46000	517.08	504.28	493.31	483.86	475.68	468.57	462.36	456.92	452.14	447.93	444.22	431.14	423.84	419.70
47000	528.32	515.24	504.04	494.38	486.02	478.75	472.41	466.85	461.97	457.67	453.88	440.51	433.06	428.82
48000	539.56	526.20	514.76	504.90	496.36	488.94	482.46	476.78	471.80	467.41	463.54	449.88	442.27	437.94
49000	550.80	537.17	525.49	515.42	506.70	499.12	492.51	486.71	481.63	477.15	473.19	459.25	451.48	447.07
50000	562.04	548.13	536.21	525.94	517.05	509.31	502.56	496.65	491.45	486.88	482.85	468.63	460.70	456.19
55000	618.24	602.94	589.83	578.53	568.75	560.24	552.81	546.31	540.60	535.57	531.13	515.49	506.77	501.81
60000	674.45	657.75	643.45	631.13	620.45	611.17	603.07	595.98	589.74	584.26	579.42	562.35	552.84	547.43
65000	730.65	712.57	697.07	683.72	672.16	662.10	653.33	645.64	638.89	632.95	627.70	609.21	598.91	593.05
70000	786.85	767.38	750.69	736.31	723.86	713.03	703.58	695.30	688.03	681.63	675.99	656.07	644.98	638.66
75000	843.06	822.19	804.31	788.91	775.57	763.96	753.84	744.97	737.18	730.32	724.27	702.94	691.05	684.28
80000	899.26	877.00	857.93	841.50	827.27	814.89	804.09	794.63	786.32	779.00	772.56	749.80	737.11	729.90
85000	955.46	931.82	911.55	894.09	878.97	865.83	854.35	844.30	835.47	827.70	820.84	796.66	783.18	775.52
90000	1011.67	986.63	965.17	946.69	930.68	916.76	904.60	893.96	884.61	876.38	869.12	843.52	829.25	821.14
95000	1067.87	1041.44	1018.79	999.28	982.38	967.69	954.86	943.62	933.76	925.07	917.41	890.38	875.32	866.76
100000	1124.07	1096.25	1072.42	1051.87	1034.09	1018.62	1005.11	993.29	982.90	973.76	965.69	937.25	921.39	912.38

MONTHLY PAYMENT
REQUIRED TO AMORTIZE A LOAN

TERM	1 Year	2 Years	3 Years	4 Years	5 Years	6 Years	7 Years	8 Years	9 Years	10 Years	11 Years	12 Years	13 Years	14 Years
AMOUNT														
5	.45	.24	.17	.13	.11	.10	.09	.08	.08	.07	.07	.07	.06	.06
10	.89	.47	.33	.26	.22	.19	.18	.16	.15	.14	.14	.13	.12	.12
15	1.33	.70	.50	.39	.33	.29	.26	.24	.22	.21	.20	.19	.18	.18
25	2.21	1.17	.82	.65	.55	.48	.43	.40	.37	.35	.33	.32	.30	.30
50	4.42	2.33	1.64	1.29	1.09	.95	.86	.79	.73	.69	.66	.63	.60	.59
75	6.63	3.50	2.46	1.94	1.63	1.43	1.28	1.18	1.10	1.03	.98	.94	.90	.88
100	8.84	4.66	3.27	2.58	2.17	1.90	1.71	1.57	1.46	1.38	1.31	1.25	1.20	1.17
200	17.67	9.31	6.54	5.16	4.34	3.80	3.42	3.13	2.92	2.75	2.61	2.50	2.40	2.33
300	26.50	13.97	9.81	7.74	6.51	5.70	5.12	4.70	4.37	4.12	3.91	3.74	3.60	3.49
400	35.33	18.62	13.08	10.32	8.68	7.59	6.83	6.26	5.83	5.49	5.21	4.99	4.80	4.65
500	44.17	23.28	16.34	12.90	10.85	9.49	8.53	7.83	7.28	6.86	6.52	6.24	6.00	5.81
600	53.00	27.93	19.61	15.48	13.01	11.39	10.24	9.39	8.74	8.23	7.82	7.48	7.20	6.97
700	61.83	32.59	22.88	18.05	15.18	13.28	11.94	10.95	10.19	9.60	9.12	8.73	8.40	8.13
800	70.66	37.24	26.15	20.63	17.35	15.18	13.65	12.52	11.65	10.97	10.42	9.97	9.60	9.30
900	79.50	41.90	29.42	23.21	19.52	17.08	15.36	14.08	13.11	12.34	11.72	11.22	10.80	10.46
1000	88.33	46.55	32.68	25.79	21.69	18.98	17.06	15.65	14.56	13.71	13.03	12.47	12.00	11.62
2000	176.65	93.10	65.36	51.57	43.37	37.95	34.12	31.29	29.12	27.41	26.05	24.93	24.00	23.23
3000	264.98	139.65	98.04	77.36	65.05	56.92	51.18	46.93	43.68	41.12	39.07	37.39	36.00	34.85
4000	353.30	186.20	130.72	103.14	86.73	75.89	68.23	62.57	58.23	54.82	52.09	49.85	48.00	46.46
5000	441.62	232.75	163.40	128.93	108.41	94.86	85.29	78.21	72.79	68.53	65.11	62.31	60.00	58.07
6000	529.95	279.30	196.08	154.71	130.09	113.83	102.35	93.85	87.35	82.23	78.13	74.78	72.00	69.69
7000	618.27	325.85	228.76	180.50	151.77	132.80	119.40	109.49	101.90	95.94	91.15	87.24	84.00	81.30
8000	706.59	372.40	261.44	206.28	173.45	151.77	136.46	125.13	116.46	109.64	104.17	99.70	96.00	92.91
9000	794.92	418.95	294.12	232.07	195.13	170.74	153.52	140.77	131.02	123.34	117.19	112.16	108.00	104.53
10000	883.24	465.50	326.80	257.85	216.81	189.71	170.57	156.42	145.57	137.05	130.21	124.62	120.00	116.14
11000	971.56	512.05	359.48	283.64	238.49	208.68	187.63	172.06	160.13	150.75	143.23	137.08	132.00	127.75
12000	1059.89	558.60	392.16	309.42	260.17	227.65	204.69	187.70	174.69	164.46	156.25	149.55	144.00	139.37
13000	1148.21	605.15	424.84	335.21	281.85	246.62	221.74	203.34	189.24	178.16	169.27	162.01	156.00	150.98
14000	1236.53	651.70	457.52	360.99	303.53	265.59	238.80	218.98	203.80	191.87	182.29	174.47	168.00	162.60
15000	1324.86	698.25	490.20	386.78	325.21	284.56	255.86	234.62	218.36	205.57	195.31	186.93	180.00	174.21
16000	1413.18	744.80	522.88	412.56	346.89	303.53	272.91	250.26	232.91	219.27	208.33	199.39	192.00	185.82
17000	1501.50	791.35	555.56	438.35	368.57	322.50	289.97	265.90	247.47	232.98	221.35	211.85	204.00	197.44
18000	1589.83	837.90	588.24	464.13	390.25	341.47	307.03	281.54	262.03	246.68	234.37	224.32	216.00	209.05
19000	1678.15	884.45	620.92	489.92	411.93	360.44	324.08	297.19	276.59	260.39	247.39	236.78	228.00	220.66
20000	1766.50	931.00	653.60	515.70	433.61	379.41	341.14	312.83	291.14	274.09	260.41	249.24	240.00	232.28
21000	1854.80	977.55	686.28	541.49	455.29	398.38	358.20	328.47	305.70	287.80	273.43	261.70	252.00	243.89
22000	1943.12	1024.10	718.96	567.27	476.97	417.35	375.25	344.11	320.26	301.50	286.45	274.16	264.00	255.50
23000	2031.44	1070.65	751.63	593.06	498.65	436.32	392.31	359.75	334.81	315.20	299.47	286.62	276.00	267.12
24000	2119.77	1117.20	784.31	618.84	520.33	455.29	409.37	375.39	349.37	328.91	312.49	299.09	288.00	278.73
25000	2208.09	1163.75	816.99	644.63	542.01	474.26	426.42	391.03	363.93	342.61	325.51	311.55	300.00	290.35
26000	2296.41	1210.30	849.67	670.41	563.69	493.23	443.48	406.67	378.48	356.32	338.53	324.01	312.00	301.96
27000	2384.74	1256.85	882.35	696.20	585.37	512.20	460.54	422.31	393.04	370.02	351.55	336.47	324.00	313.57
28000	2473.06	1303.40	915.03	721.98	607.05	531.17	477.59	437.95	407.60	383.73	364.57	348.93	336.00	325.19
29000	2561.38	1349.95	947.71	747.77	628.73	550.14	494.65	453.60	422.15	397.43	377.59	361.39	348.00	336.80
30000	2649.71	1396.50	980.39	773.55	650.41	569.11	511.71	469.24	436.71	411.14	390.61	373.86	360.00	348.41
31000	2738.03	1443.05	1013.07	799.34	672.09	588.08	528.77	484.88	451.27	424.84	403.63	386.32	372.00	360.03
32000	2826.35	1489.60	1045.75	825.12	693.77	607.05	545.82	500.52	465.82	438.54	416.65	398.78	384.00	371.64
33000	2914.68	1536.15	1078.43	850.91	715.45	626.02	562.88	516.16	480.38	452.25	429.67	411.24	396.00	383.25
34000	3003.00	1582.70	1111.11	876.69	737.13	644.99	579.94	531.80	494.94	465.95	442.69	423.70	408.00	394.87
35000	3091.32	1629.25	1143.79	902.48	758.81	663.96	596.99	547.44	509.49	479.66	455.71	436.16	420.00	406.48
36000	3179.65	1675.80	1176.47	928.26	780.49	682.93	614.05	563.08	524.05	493.36	468.73	448.63	432.00	418.10
37000	3267.97	1722.35	1209.15	954.04	802.17	701.90	631.11	578.73	538.61	507.07	481.75	461.09	444.00	429.71
38000	3356.29	1768.90	1241.83	979.83	823.85	720.87	648.16	594.37	553.17	520.77	494.77	473.55	456.00	441.32
39000	3444.62	1815.45	1274.51	1005.61	845.53	739.84	665.22	610.01	567.72	534.47	507.79	486.01	468.00	452.94
40000	3532.94	1862.00	1307.19	1031.40	867.21	758.81	682.28	625.65	582.28	548.18	520.81	498.47	480.00	464.55
41000	3621.26	1908.55	1339.87	1057.18	888.89	777.78	699.33	641.29	596.84	561.88	533.83	510.93	492.00	476.16
42000	3709.59	1955.10	1372.55	1082.97	910.57	796.75	716.39	656.93	611.39	575.59	546.85	523.40	504.00	487.78
43000	3797.91	2001.65	1405.23	1108.75	932.25	815.72	733.45	672.57	625.95	589.29	559.87	535.86	516.00	499.39
44000	3886.23	2048.20	1437.91	1134.54	953.93	834.69	750.50	688.21	640.51	603.00	572.89	548.32	528.00	511.00
45000	3974.56	2094.75	1470.58	1160.32	975.61	853.66	767.56	703.85	655.06	616.70	585.91	560.78	540.00	522.62
46000	4062.88	2141.30	1503.26	1186.11	997.29	872.63	784.62	719.49	669.62	630.40	598.93	573.24	552.00	534.23
47000	4151.20	2187.85	1535.94	1211.89	1018.97	891.60	801.67	735.14	684.18	644.11	611.95	585.70	564.00	545.85
48000	4239.53	2234.40	1568.62	1237.68	1040.65	910.57	818.73	750.78	698.73	657.81	624.97	598.17	576.00	557.46
49000	4327.85	2280.95	1601.30	1263.46	1062.33	929.54	835.79	766.42	713.29	671.52	637.99	610.63	588.00	569.07
50000	4416.17	2327.50	1633.98	1289.25	1084.01	948.51	852.84	782.06	727.85	685.22	651.01	623.09	600.00	580.69
55000	4857.79	2560.25	1797.38	1418.17	1192.41	1043.36	938.13	860.26	800.63	753.74	716.11	685.40	660.00	638.75
60000	5299.41	2792.99	1960.78	1547.10	1300.81	1138.21	1023.41	938.47	873.42	822.27	781.21	747.71	720.00	696.82
65000	5741.02	3025.74	2124.18	1676.02	1409.21	1233.06	1108.70	1016.68	946.20	890.79	846.31	810.01	780.00	754.89
70000	6182.64	3258.49	2287.57	1804.95	1517.61	1327.91	1193.98	1094.88	1018.99	959.31	911.41	872.32	840.00	812.96
75000	6624.26	3491.24	2450.97	1933.87	1626.02	1422.76	1279.26	1173.09	1091.77	1027.83	976.51	934.63	899.99	871.03
80000	7065.87	3723.99	2614.37	2062.79	1734.42	1517.61	1364.55	1251.29	1164.55	1096.35	1041.61	996.94	959.99	929.10
85000	7507.49	3956.74	2777.77	2191.72	1842.82	1612.46	1449.83	1329.50	1237.34	1164.87	1106.71	1059.25	1019.99	987.16
90000	7949.11	4189.49	2941.16	2320.64	1951.22	1707.32	1535.12	1407.70	1310.12	1233.40	1171.81	1121.56	1079.99	1045.23
95000	8390.72	4422.24	3104.56	2449.57	2059.62	1802.17	1620.40	1485.91	1382.91	1301.92	1236.91	1183.87	1139.99	1103.30
100000	8832.34	4654.99	3267.96	2578.49	2168.02	1897.02	1705.68	1564.11	1455.69	1370.44	1302.01	1246.17	1199.99	1161.37

TERM AMOUNT	15 Years	16 Years	17 Years	18 Years	19 Years	20 Years	21 Years	22 Years	23 Years	24 Years	25 Years	30 Years	35 Years	40 Years
5	.06	.06	.06	.06	.06	.06	.06	.05	.05	.05	.05	.05	.05	.05
10	.12	.12	.11	.11	.11	.11	.11	.10	.10	.10	.10	.10	.10	.10
15	.17	.17	.17	.16	.16	.16	.16	.15	.15	.15	.15	.15	.14	.14
25	.29	.28	.27	.27	.26	.26	.26	.25	.25	.25	.25	.24	.24	.23
50	.57	.56	.54	.53	.52	.52	.51	.50	.50	.49	.49	.48	.47	.46
75	.85	.83	.81	.80	.78	.77	.76	.75	.75	.74	.73	.71	.70	.69
100	1.13	1.11	1.08	1.06	1.04	1.03	1.02	1.00	.99	.98	.98	.95	.93	.92
200	2.26	2.21	2.16	2.12	2.08	2.05	2.03	2.00	1.98	1.96	1.95	1.89	1.86	1.84
300	3.39	3.31	3.24	3.18	3.12	3.08	3.04	3.00	2.97	2.94	2.92	2.83	2.79	2.76
400	4.52	4.41	4.31	4.23	4.16	4.10	4.05	4.00	3.96	3.92	3.89	3.78	3.71	3.68
500	5.65	5.51	5.39	5.29	5.20	5.12	5.06	5.00	4.95	4.90	4.86	4.72	4.64	4.60
600	6.78	6.61	6.47	6.35	6.24	6.15	6.07	6.00	5.93	5.88	5.83	5.66	5.57	5.52
700	7.91	7.71	7.55	7.40	7.28	7.17	7.08	6.99	6.92	6.86	6.80	6.61	6.50	6.43
800	9.04	8.81	8.62	8.46	8.32	8.19	8.09	7.99	7.91	7.84	7.77	7.55	7.42	7.35
900	10.16	9.91	9.70	9.52	9.36	9.22	9.10	8.99	8.90	8.82	8.74	8.49	8.35	8.27
1000	11.29	11.02	10.78	10.57	10.40	10.24	10.11	9.99	9.89	9.80	9.72	9.43	9.28	9.19
2000	22.58	22.03	21.55	21.14	20.79	20.48	20.21	19.98	19.77	19.59	19.43	18.86	18.55	18.37
3000	33.87	33.04	32.32	31.71	31.18	30.72	30.31	29.96	29.65	29.38	29.14	28.29	27.82	27.56
4000	45.16	44.05	43.10	42.28	41.57	40.95	40.42	39.95	39.53	39.17	38.85	37.72	37.09	36.74
5000	56.44	55.06	53.87	52.85	51.96	51.19	50.52	49.93	49.41	48.96	48.56	47.15	46.37	45.92
6000	67.73	66.07	64.64	63.41	62.35	61.43	60.62	59.92	59.30	58.75	58.27	56.58	55.64	55.11
7000	79.02	77.08	75.41	73.98	72.74	71.66	70.72	69.90	69.18	68.54	67.98	66.01	64.91	64.29
8000	90.31	88.09	86.19	84.55	83.13	81.90	80.83	79.89	79.06	78.33	77.69	75.44	74.18	73.47
9000	101.59	99.10	96.96	95.12	93.52	92.14	90.93	89.87	88.94	88.12	87.40	84.87	83.45	82.66
10000	112.88	110.11	107.73	105.69	103.91	102.37	101.03	99.86	98.82	97.91	97.11	94.29	92.73	91.84
11000	124.17	121.12	118.50	116.25	114.31	112.61	111.13	109.84	108.70	107.71	106.82	103.72	102.00	101.02
12000	135.46	132.13	129.28	126.82	124.70	122.85	121.24	119.83	118.59	117.50	116.54	113.15	111.27	110.21
13000	146.74	143.14	140.05	137.39	135.09	133.09	131.34	129.81	128.47	127.29	126.25	122.58	120.54	119.39
14000	158.03	154.15	150.82	147.96	145.48	143.32	141.44	139.80	138.35	137.08	135.96	132.01	129.82	128.57
15000	169.32	165.16	161.59	158.53	155.87	153.56	151.54	149.78	148.23	146.87	145.67	141.44	139.09	137.76
16000	180.61	176.17	172.37	169.09	166.26	163.80	161.65	159.77	158.11	156.66	155.38	150.87	148.36	146.94
17000	191.89	187.10	183.14	179.66	176.65	174.03	171.75	169.75	168.00	166.45	165.09	160.30	157.63	156.12
18000	203.18	198.19	193.91	190.23	187.04	184.27	181.85	179.74	177.88	176.24	174.80	169.73	166.90	165.31
19000	214.47	209.20	204.69	200.80	197.43	194.51	191.95	189.72	187.76	186.03	184.51	179.15	176.18	174.49
20000	225.76	220.21	215.46	211.37	207.82	204.74	202.06	199.71	197.64	195.82	194.22	188.58	185.45	183.67
21000	237.04	231.22	226.23	221.93	218.21	214.98	212.16	209.69	207.52	205.62	203.93	198.01	194.72	192.86
22000	248.33	242.23	237.00	232.50	228.61	225.22	222.26	219.68	217.40	215.41	213.64	207.44	203.99	202.04
23000	259.62	253.24	247.78	243.07	239.00	235.45	232.37	229.66	227.29	225.20	223.36	216.87	213.27	211.22
24000	270.91	264.25	258.55	253.64	249.39	245.69	242.47	239.65	237.17	234.99	233.07	226.30	222.54	220.41
25000	282.20	275.26	269.32	264.21	259.78	255.93	252.57	249.63	247.05	244.78	242.78	235.73	231.81	229.59
26000	293.48	286.27	280.09	274.77	270.17	266.17	262.67	259.62	256.93	254.57	252.49	245.16	241.08	238.77
27000	304.77	297.28	290.87	285.34	280.56	276.40	272.78	269.60	266.81	264.36	262.20	254.59	250.35	247.96
28000	316.06	308.29	301.64	295.91	290.95	286.64	282.88	279.59	276.70	274.15	271.91	264.01	259.63	257.14
29000	327.35	319.30	312.41	306.48	301.34	296.88	292.98	289.57	286.58	283.94	281.62	273.44	268.90	266.32
30000	338.63	330.31	323.18	317.05	311.73	307.11	303.08	299.56	296.46	293.73	291.33	282.87	278.17	275.51
31000	349.92	341.32	333.96	327.61	322.12	317.35	313.19	309.54	306.34	303.53	301.04	292.30	287.44	284.69
32000	361.21	352.33	344.73	338.18	332.51	327.59	323.29	319.53	316.22	313.32	310.75	301.73	296.72	293.87
33000	372.50	363.34	355.50	348.75	342.91	337.82	333.39	329.51	326.10	323.11	320.46	311.16	305.99	303.06
34000	383.78	374.35	366.28	359.32	353.30	348.06	343.49	339.50	335.99	332.90	330.18	320.59	315.26	312.24
35000	395.07	385.36	377.05	369.89	363.69	358.30	353.60	349.48	345.87	342.69	339.89	330.02	324.53	321.42
36000	406.36	396.37	387.82	380.45	374.08	368.54	363.70	359.47	355.75	352.48	349.60	339.45	333.80	330.61
37000	417.65	407.38	398.59	391.02	384.47	378.77	373.80	369.45	365.63	362.27	359.31	348.87	343.08	339.79
38000	428.93	418.39	409.37	401.59	394.86	389.01	383.90	379.44	375.51	372.06	369.02	358.30	352.35	348.97
39000	440.22	429.40	420.14	412.16	405.25	399.25	394.01	389.42	385.40	381.85	378.73	367.73	361.62	358.16
40000	451.51	440.41	430.91	422.73	415.64	409.48	404.11	399.41	395.28	391.64	388.44	377.16	370.89	367.34
41000	462.80	451.42	441.68	433.29	426.03	419.72	414.21	409.39	405.16	401.44	398.15	386.59	380.17	376.52
42000	474.08	462.43	452.46	443.86	436.42	429.96	424.31	419.38	415.04	411.23	407.86	396.02	389.44	385.71
43000	485.37	473.44	463.23	454.43	446.81	440.19	434.42	429.36	424.92	421.02	417.57	405.45	398.71	394.89
44000	496.66	484.45	474.00	465.00	457.21	450.43	444.52	439.35	434.80	430.81	427.28	414.88	407.98	404.07
45000	507.95	495.47	484.77	475.57	467.60	460.67	454.62	449.33	444.69	440.60	437.00	424.31	417.25	413.26
46000	519.23	506.48	495.55	486.13	477.99	470.90	464.73	459.32	454.57	450.39	446.71	433.73	426.53	422.44
47000	530.52	517.49	506.32	496.70	488.38	481.14	474.83	469.30	464.45	460.18	456.42	443.16	435.80	431.62
48000	541.81	528.50	517.09	507.27	498.77	491.38	484.93	479.29	474.33	469.97	466.13	452.59	445.07	440.81
49000	553.10	539.51	527.87	517.84	509.16	501.62	495.03	489.27	484.21	479.76	475.84	462.02	454.34	449.99
50000	564.39	550.52	538.64	528.41	519.55	511.85	505.14	499.26	494.10	489.55	485.55	471.45	463.61	459.17
55000	620.82	605.57	592.50	581.25	571.51	563.04	555.65	549.18	543.50	538.51	534.10	518.59	509.98	505.09
60000	677.26	660.62	646.36	634.09	623.46	614.22	606.16	599.11	592.91	587.46	582.66	565.74	556.34	551.01
65000	733.70	715.67	700.23	686.93	675.41	665.41	656.67	649.03	642.32	636.42	631.21	612.88	602.70	596.92
70000	790.14	770.72	754.09	739.77	727.37	716.59	707.19	698.96	691.73	685.37	679.77	660.03	649.06	642.84
75000	846.58	825.77	807.95	792.61	779.32	767.78	757.70	748.88	741.14	734.33	728.32	707.17	695.42	688.76
80000	903.01	880.82	861.82	845.45	831.28	818.96	808.21	798.81	790.55	783.28	776.88	754.32	741.78	734.67
85000	959.45	935.87	915.68	898.29	883.23	870.15	858.73	848.73	839.96	832.24	825.43	801.46	788.14	780.59
90000	1015.89	990.93	969.54	951.13	935.19	921.33	909.24	898.66	889.37	881.19	873.99	848.61	834.50	826.51
95000	1072.33	1045.98	1023.41	1003.97	987.14	972.52	959.75	948.58	938.78	930.15	922.54	895.75	880.86	872.43
100000	1128.77	1101.03	1077.27	1056.81	1039.10	1023.70	1010.27	998.51	988.19	979.10	971.09	942.90	927.22	918.34

MONTHLY PAYMENT
REQUIRED TO AMORTIZE A LOAN

TERM AMOUNT	1 Year	2 Years	3 Years	4 Years	5 Years	6 Years	7 Years	8 Years	9 Years	10 Years	11 Years	12 Years	13 Years	14 Years
5	.45	.24	.17	.13	.11	.10	.09	.08	.08	.07	.07	.07	.07	.06
10	.89	.47	.33	.26	.22	.19	.18	.16	.15	.14	.14	.13	.13	.12
15	1.33	.70	.50	.39	.33	.29	.26	.24	.22	.21	.20	.19	.19	.18
25	2.21	1.17	.82	.65	.55	.48	.43	.40	.37	.35	.33	.32	.31	.30
50	4.42	2.33	1.64	1.29	1.09	.95	.86	.79	.73	.69	.66	.63	.61	.59
75	6.63	3.50	2.46	1.94	1.63	1.43	1.29	1.18	1.10	1.03	.98	.94	.91	.88
100	8.84	4.66	3.27	2.58	2.17	1.90	1.71	1.57	1.46	1.38	1.31	1.25	1.21	1.17
200	17.67	9.32	6.54	5.16	4.34	3.80	3.42	3.14	2.92	2.75	2.61	2.50	2.41	2.33
300	26.51	13.97	9.81	7.74	6.51	5.70	5.13	4.70	4.38	4.12	3.92	3.75	3.61	3.49
400	35.34	18.63	13.08	10.32	8.68	7.60	6.83	6.27	5.83	5.49	5.22	5.00	4.81	4.66
500	44.17	23.29	16.35	12.90	10.85	9.50	8.54	7.83	7.29	6.86	6.52	6.24	6.01	5.82
600	53.01	27.94	19.62	15.48	13.02	11.39	10.25	9.40	8.75	8.24	7.83	7.49	7.21	6.98
700	61.84	32.60	22.89	18.06	15.19	13.29	11.95	10.96	10.20	9.61	9.13	8.74	8.42	8.15
800	70.67	37.25	26.16	20.64	17.36	15.19	13.66	12.53	11.66	10.98	10.43	9.99	9.62	9.31
900	79.51	41.91	29.43	23.22	19.53	17.09	15.37	14.09	13.12	12.35	11.74	11.23	10.82	10.47
1000	88.34	46.57	32.70	25.80	21.70	18.99	17.07	15.66	14.58	13.72	13.04	12.48	12.02	11.63
2000	176.68	93.13	65.39	51.60	43.39	37.97	34.14	31.31	29.15	27.44	26.07	24.96	24.03	23.26
3000	265.01	139.69	98.08	77.40	65.08	56.95	51.21	46.97	43.72	41.16	39.11	37.43	36.05	34.89
4000	353.35	186.25	130.77	103.19	86.78	75.94	68.28	62.62	58.29	54.88	52.14	49.91	48.06	46.52
5000	441.68	232.81	163.46	128.99	108.47	94.92	85.35	78.28	72.86	68.60	65.18	62.39	60.08	58.15
6000	530.02	279.37	196.15	154.79	130.16	113.90	102.42	93.93	87.43	82.32	78.21	74.86	72.09	69.78
7000	618.35	325.93	228.84	180.58	151.85	132.89	119.49	109.59	102.00	96.03	91.25	87.34	84.11	81.41
8000	706.69	372.50	261.54	206.38	173.55	151.87	136.56	125.24	116.57	109.75	104.28	99.82	96.12	93.04
9000	795.02	419.06	294.23	232.18	195.24	170.85	153.63	140.90	131.14	123.47	117.32	112.29	108.14	104.67
10000	883.36	465.62	326.92	257.97	216.93	189.83	170.70	156.55	145.71	137.19	130.35	124.77	120.15	116.29
11000	971.69	512.18	359.61	283.77	238.62	208.82	187.77	172.20	160.28	150.91	143.38	137.25	132.17	127.92
12000	1060.03	558.74	392.30	309.57	260.32	227.80	204.84	187.86	174.85	164.63	156.42	149.72	144.18	139.55
13000	1148.36	605.30	424.99	335.37	282.01	246.78	221.91	203.51	189.42	178.34	169.45	162.20	156.20	151.18
14000	1236.70	651.86	457.68	361.16	303.70	265.77	238.98	219.17	203.99	192.06	182.49	174.68	168.21	162.81
15000	1325.03	698.43	490.38	386.96	325.39	284.75	256.05	234.82	218.56	205.78	195.52	187.15	180.23	174.44
16000	1413.37	744.99	523.07	412.76	347.09	303.73	273.12	250.48	233.14	219.50	208.56	199.63	192.24	186.07
17000	1501.70	791.55	555.76	438.55	368.78	322.71	290.19	266.13	247.71	233.22	221.59	212.10	204.26	197.70
18000	1590.04	838.11	588.45	464.35	390.47	341.70	307.26	281.79	262.28	246.94	234.63	224.58	216.27	209.33
19000	1678.37	884.67	621.14	490.15	412.16	360.68	324.33	297.44	276.85	260.66	247.66	237.06	228.29	220.96
20000	1766.71	931.23	653.83	515.94	433.86	379.66	341.40	313.10	291.42	274.37	260.70	249.53	240.30	232.58
21000	1855.04	977.79	686.52	541.74	455.55	398.65	358.47	328.75	305.99	288.09	273.73	262.01	252.32	244.21
22000	1943.38	1024.36	719.22	567.54	477.24	417.63	375.54	344.40	320.56	301.81	286.76	274.49	264.33	255.84
23000	2031.71	1070.92	751.91	593.34	498.93	436.61	392.61	360.06	335.13	315.53	299.80	286.96	276.35	267.47
24000	2120.05	1117.48	784.60	619.13	520.63	455.59	409.68	375.71	349.70	329.25	312.83	299.44	288.36	279.10
25000	2208.38	1164.04	817.29	644.93	542.32	474.58	426.75	391.37	364.27	342.97	325.87	311.92	300.38	290.73
26000	2296.72	1210.60	849.98	670.73	564.01	493.56	443.82	407.02	378.84	356.68	338.90	324.39	312.39	302.36
27000	2385.05	1257.16	882.67	696.52	585.70	512.54	460.89	422.68	393.41	370.40	351.94	336.87	324.41	313.99
28000	2473.39	1303.72	915.36	722.32	607.40	531.53	477.96	438.33	407.98	384.12	364.97	349.35	336.42	325.62
29000	2561.72	1350.29	948.06	748.12	629.09	550.51	495.03	453.99	422.55	397.84	378.01	361.82	348.44	337.25
30000	2650.06	1396.85	980.75	773.91	650.78	569.49	512.10	469.64	437.12	411.56	391.04	374.30	360.45	348.87
31000	2738.39	1443.41	1013.44	799.71	672.48	588.47	529.17	485.30	451.69	425.28	404.07	386.77	372.47	360.50
32000	2826.73	1489.97	1046.13	825.51	694.17	607.46	546.24	500.95	466.27	439.00	417.11	399.25	384.48	372.13
33000	2915.06	1536.53	1078.82	851.31	715.86	626.44	563.31	516.60	480.84	452.71	430.14	411.73	396.50	383.76
34000	3003.40	1583.09	1111.51	877.10	737.55	645.42	580.38	532.26	495.41	466.43	443.18	424.20	408.51	395.39
35000	3091.73	1629.65	1144.20	902.90	759.25	664.41	597.45	547.91	509.98	480.15	456.21	436.68	420.53	407.02
36000	3180.07	1676.22	1176.89	928.70	780.94	683.39	614.52	563.57	524.55	493.87	469.25	449.16	432.54	418.65
37000	3268.40	1722.78	1209.59	954.49	802.63	702.37	631.59	579.22	539.12	507.59	482.28	461.63	444.56	430.28
38000	3356.74	1769.34	1242.28	980.29	824.32	721.36	648.66	594.88	553.69	521.31	495.32	474.11	456.57	441.91
39000	3445.07	1815.90	1274.97	1006.09	846.02	740.34	665.73	610.53	568.26	535.02	508.35	486.59	468.59	453.54
40000	3533.41	1862.46	1307.66	1031.88	867.71	759.32	682.80	626.19	582.83	548.74	521.39	499.06	480.60	465.16
41000	3621.74	1909.02	1340.35	1057.68	889.40	778.30	699.87	641.84	597.40	562.46	534.42	511.54	492.62	476.79
42000	3710.08	1955.58	1373.04	1083.48	911.09	797.29	716.94	657.50	611.97	576.18	547.45	524.02	504.63	488.42
43000	3798.41	2002.15	1405.73	1109.28	932.79	816.27	734.01	673.15	626.54	589.90	560.49	536.49	516.65	500.05
44000	3886.75	2048.71	1438.43	1135.07	954.48	835.25	751.08	688.80	641.11	603.62	573.52	548.97	528.66	511.68
45000	3975.08	2095.27	1471.12	1160.87	976.17	854.24	768.15	704.46	655.68	617.34	586.56	561.44	540.68	523.31
46000	4063.42	2141.83	1503.81	1186.67	997.86	873.22	785.22	720.11	670.25	631.05	599.59	573.92	552.69	534.94
47000	4151.75	2188.39	1536.50	1212.46	1019.56	892.20	802.29	735.77	684.82	644.77	612.63	586.40	564.71	546.57
48000	4240.09	2234.95	1569.19	1238.26	1041.25	911.18	819.36	751.42	699.40	658.49	625.66	598.87	576.72	558.20
49000	4328.42	2281.51	1601.88	1264.06	1062.94	930.17	836.43	767.08	713.97	672.21	638.70	611.35	588.74	569.83
50000	4416.76	2328.08	1634.57	1289.85	1084.63	949.15	853.50	782.73	728.54	685.93	651.73	623.83	600.75	581.45
55000	4858.43	2560.88	1798.03	1418.84	1193.10	1044.06	938.85	861.00	801.39	754.52	716.90	686.21	660.83	639.60
60000	5300.11	2793.69	1961.49	1547.82	1301.56	1138.98	1024.20	939.28	874.24	823.11	782.08	748.59	720.90	697.74
65000	5741.78	3026.50	2124.94	1676.81	1410.02	1233.89	1109.55	1017.55	947.10	891.70	847.25	810.97	780.98	755.89
70000	6183.46	3259.30	2288.40	1805.79	1518.49	1328.81	1194.90	1095.82	1019.95	960.30	912.42	873.36	841.05	814.03
75000	6625.13	3492.11	2451.86	1934.78	1626.95	1423.72	1280.25	1174.10	1092.80	1028.89	977.59	935.74	901.12	872.18
80000	7066.81	3724.92	2615.32	2063.76	1735.41	1518.64	1365.60	1252.37	1165.66	1097.48	1042.77	998.12	961.20	930.32
85000	7508.48	3957.73	2778.77	2192.75	1843.87	1613.55	1450.95	1330.64	1238.51	1166.07	1107.94	1060.50	1021.27	988.47
90000	7950.16	4190.53	2942.23	2321.73	1952.34	1708.47	1536.30	1408.91	1311.36	1234.67	1173.11	1122.89	1081.35	1046.61
95000	8391.83	4423.34	3105.69	2450.72	2060.80	1803.38	1621.65	1487.19	1384.22	1303.26	1238.28	1185.27	1141.42	1104.76
100000	8833.51	4656.15	3269.14	2579.70	2169.26	1898.29	1707.00	1565.46	1457.07	1371.85	1303.46	1247.65	1201.50	1162.90

TERM / AMOUNT	15 Years	16 Years	17 Years	18 Years	19 Years	20 Years	21 Years	22 Years	23 Years	24 Years	25 Years	30 Years	35 Years	40 Years
5	.06	.06	.06	.06	.06	.06	.06	.06	.05	.05	.05	.05	.05	.05
10	.12	.12	.11	.11	.11	.11	.11	.11	.10	.10	.10	.10	.10	.10
15	.17	.17	.17	.16	.16	.16	.16	.16	.15	.15	.15	.15	.14	.14
25	.29	.28	.27	.27	.27	.26	.26	.26	.25	.25	.25	.24	.24	.24
50	.57	.56	.54	.53	.53	.52	.51	.51	.50	.50	.49	.48	.47	.47
75	.85	.83	.81	.80	.79	.77	.76	.76	.75	.74	.73	.71	.70	.70
100	1.14	1.11	1.08	1.06	1.05	1.03	1.02	1.01	.99	.99	.98	.95	.93	.93
200	2.27	2.21	2.16	2.12	2.09	2.06	2.03	2.01	1.98	1.97	1.95	1.89	1.86	1.85
300	3.40	3.31	3.24	3.18	3.13	3.08	3.04	3.01	2.97	2.95	2.92	2.84	2.79	2.77
400	4.53	4.42	4.32	4.24	4.17	4.11	4.05	4.01	3.96	3.93	3.90	3.78	3.72	3.69
500	5.66	5.52	5.40	5.30	5.21	5.13	5.06	5.01	4.95	4.91	4.87	4.73	4.65	4.61
600	6.79	6.62	6.48	6.36	6.25	6.16	6.08	6.01	5.94	5.89	5.84	5.67	5.58	5.53
700	7.92	7.72	7.56	7.41	7.29	7.18	7.09	7.01	6.93	6.87	6.82	6.62	6.51	6.45
800	9.05	8.83	8.64	8.47	8.33	8.21	8.10	8.01	7.92	7.85	7.79	7.56	7.44	7.37
900	10.18	9.93	9.71	9.53	9.37	9.23	9.11	9.01	8.91	8.83	8.76	8.51	8.37	8.29
1000	11.31	11.03	10.79	10.59	10.41	10.26	10.12	10.01	9.90	9.81	9.73	9.45	9.30	9.21
2000	22.61	22.06	21.58	21.17	20.82	20.51	20.24	20.01	19.80	19.62	19.46	18.90	18.59	18.41
3000	33.91	33.08	32.37	31.76	31.23	30.77	30.36	30.01	29.70	29.43	29.19	28.35	27.88	27.61
4000	45.22	44.11	43.16	42.34	41.64	41.02	40.48	40.01	39.60	39.24	38.92	37.80	37.17	36.82
5000	56.52	55.14	53.95	52.93	52.04	51.27	50.60	50.02	49.50	49.05	48.65	47.24	46.46	46.02
6000	67.82	66.16	64.74	63.51	62.45	61.53	60.72	60.02	59.40	58.86	58.38	56.69	55.75	55.22
7000	79.13	77.19	75.53	74.10	72.86	71.78	70.84	70.02	69.30	68.67	68.11	66.14	65.05	64.43
8000	90.43	88.21	86.32	84.68	83.27	82.04	80.96	80.02	79.20	78.48	77.84	75.59	74.34	73.63
9000	101.73	99.24	97.10	95.27	93.67	92.29	91.08	90.03	89.10	88.28	87.57	85.03	83.63	82.83
10000	113.04	110.27	107.89	105.85	104.08	102.54	101.20	100.03	99.00	98.09	97.29	94.48	92.92	92.04
11000	124.34	121.29	118.68	116.43	114.49	112.80	111.32	110.03	108.90	107.90	107.02	103.93	102.21	101.24
12000	135.64	132.32	129.47	127.02	124.90	123.05	121.44	120.03	118.80	117.71	116.75	113.38	111.50	110.44
13000	146.95	143.35	140.26	137.60	135.30	133.31	131.56	130.04	128.70	127.52	126.48	122.83	120.80	119.65
14000	158.25	154.37	151.05	148.19	145.71	143.56	141.68	140.04	138.60	137.33	136.21	132.27	130.09	128.85
15000	169.55	165.40	161.84	158.77	156.12	153.81	151.80	150.04	148.50	147.14	145.94	141.72	139.38	138.05
16000	180.86	176.42	172.63	169.36	166.53	164.07	161.92	160.04	158.40	156.95	155.67	151.17	148.67	147.26
17000	192.16	187.45	183.42	179.94	176.93	174.32	172.04	170.05	168.30	166.75	165.40	160.62	157.96	156.46
18000	203.46	198.48	194.20	190.53	187.34	184.58	182.16	180.05	178.20	176.56	175.13	170.06	167.25	165.66
19000	214.77	209.50	204.99	201.11	197.75	194.83	192.28	190.05	188.09	186.37	184.85	179.51	176.55	174.87
20000	226.07	220.53	215.78	211.70	208.16	205.08	202.40	200.05	197.99	196.18	194.58	188.96	185.84	184.07
21000	237.37	231.55	226.57	222.28	218.57	215.34	212.52	210.06	207.89	205.99	204.31	198.41	195.13	193.27
22000	248.68	242.58	237.36	232.86	228.97	225.59	222.64	220.06	217.79	215.80	214.04	207.86	204.42	202.48
23000	259.98	253.61	248.15	243.45	239.38	235.85	232.76	230.06	227.69	225.61	223.77	217.30	213.71	211.68
24000	271.28	264.63	258.94	254.03	249.79	246.10	242.88	240.06	237.59	235.42	233.50	226.75	223.00	220.08
25000	282.59	275.66	269.73	264.62	260.20	256.35	253.00	250.07	247.49	245.23	243.23	236.20	232.30	230.09
26000	293.89	286.69	280.52	275.20	270.60	266.61	263.12	260.07	257.39	255.03	252.96	245.65	241.59	239.29
27000	305.19	297.71	291.30	285.79	281.01	276.86	273.24	270.07	267.29	264.84	262.69	255.09	250.88	248.49
28000	316.50	308.74	302.09	296.37	291.42	287.11	283.36	280.07	277.19	274.65	272.41	264.54	260.17	257.70
29000	327.80	319.76	312.88	306.96	301.83	297.37	293.48	290.08	287.09	284.46	282.14	273.99	269.46	266.90
30000	339.10	330.79	323.67	317.54	312.23	307.62	303.60	300.08	296.99	294.27	291.87	283.44	278.75	276.10
31000	350.41	341.82	334.46	328.12	322.64	317.88	313.72	310.08	306.89	304.08	301.60	292.89	288.05	285.31
32000	361.71	352.84	345.25	338.71	333.05	328.13	323.84	320.08	316.79	313.89	311.33	302.33	297.34	294.51
33000	373.01	363.87	356.04	349.29	343.46	338.38	333.96	330.09	326.69	323.70	321.06	311.78	306.63	303.71
34000	384.32	374.89	366.83	359.88	353.86	348.64	344.08	340.09	336.59	333.50	330.79	321.23	315.92	312.92
35000	395.62	385.92	377.62	370.46	364.27	358.89	354.20	350.09	346.49	343.31	340.52	330.68	325.21	322.12
36000	406.92	396.95	388.40	381.05	374.68	369.15	364.32	360.09	356.39	353.12	350.25	340.12	334.50	331.32
37000	418.23	407.97	399.19	391.63	385.09	379.40	374.44	370.10	366.28	362.93	359.98	349.57	343.80	340.53
38000	429.53	419.00	409.98	402.22	395.50	389.65	384.56	380.10	376.18	372.74	369.70	359.02	353.09	349.73
39000	440.83	430.03	420.77	412.80	405.90	399.91	394.68	390.10	386.08	382.55	379.43	368.47	362.38	358.93
40000	452.14	441.05	431.56	423.39	416.31	410.16	404.80	400.10	395.98	392.36	389.16	377.91	371.67	368.14
41000	463.44	452.08	442.35	433.97	426.72	420.42	414.92	410.11	405.88	402.17	398.89	387.36	380.96	377.34
42000	474.74	463.10	453.14	444.55	437.13	430.67	425.04	420.11	415.78	411.98	408.62	396.81	390.25	386.54
43000	486.04	474.13	463.93	455.14	447.53	440.92	435.16	430.11	425.68	421.78	418.35	406.26	399.55	395.75
44000	497.35	485.16	474.72	465.72	457.94	451.18	445.28	440.11	435.58	431.59	428.08	415.71	408.84	404.95
45000	508.65	496.18	485.50	476.31	468.35	461.43	455.40	450.12	445.48	441.40	437.81	425.15	418.13	414.15
46000	519.95	507.21	496.29	486.89	478.76	471.69	465.52	460.12	455.38	451.21	447.54	434.60	427.42	423.36
47000	531.26	518.23	507.08	497.48	489.16	481.94	475.64	470.12	465.28	461.02	457.26	444.05	436.71	432.56
48000	542.56	529.26	517.87	508.06	499.57	492.19	485.76	480.12	475.18	470.83	466.99	453.50	446.00	441.76
49000	553.86	540.29	528.66	518.65	509.98	502.45	495.88	490.12	485.08	480.64	476.72	462.94	455.30	450.97
50000	565.17	551.31	539.45	529.23	520.39	512.70	506.00	500.13	494.98	490.45	486.45	472.39	464.59	460.17
55000	621.68	606.44	593.39	582.15	572.43	563.97	556.59	550.14	544.47	539.49	535.10	519.63	511.05	506.19
60000	678.20	661.57	647.34	635.08	624.46	615.24	607.19	600.15	593.97	588.53	583.74	566.87	557.50	552.20
65000	734.72	716.71	701.28	688.00	676.50	666.51	657.79	650.16	643.47	637.58	632.38	614.11	603.96	598.22
70000	791.23	771.84	755.23	740.92	728.54	717.78	708.39	700.18	692.97	686.62	681.03	661.35	650.42	644.23
75000	847.75	826.97	809.17	793.84	780.58	769.05	758.99	750.19	742.46	735.67	729.67	708.59	696.88	690.25
80000	904.27	882.10	863.11	846.77	832.62	820.32	809.59	800.20	791.96	784.71	778.32	755.82	743.34	736.27
85000	960.78	937.23	917.06	899.69	884.65	871.59	860.19	850.21	841.46	833.75	826.96	803.06	789.80	782.28
90000	1017.30	992.36	971.00	952.61	936.69	922.86	910.79	900.23	890.96	882.80	875.61	850.30	836.25	828.30
95000	1073.81	1047.49	1024.95	1005.53	988.73	974.13	961.39	950.24	940.45	931.84	924.25	897.54	882.71	874.32
100000	1130.33	1102.62	1078.89	1058.46	1040.77	1025.40	1011.99	1000.25	989.95	980.89	972.90	944.78	929.17	920.33

11.000%

MONTHLY PAYMENT
REQUIRED TO AMORTIZE A LOAN

TERM AMOUNT	1 Year	2 Years	3 Years	4 Years	5 Years	6 Years	7 Years	8 Years	9 Years	10 Years	11 Years	12 Years	13 Years	14 Years
5	.45	.24	.17	.13	.11	.10	.09	.08	.08	.07	.07	.07	.07	.06
10	.89	.47	.33	.26	.22	.20	.18	.16	.15	.14	.14	.13	.13	.12
15	1.33	.70	.50	.39	.33	.29	.26	.24	.22	.21	.20	.19	.19	.18
25	2.21	1.17	.82	.65	.55	.48	.43	.40	.37	.35	.33	.32	.31	.30
50	4.42	2.34	1.64	1.30	1.09	.96	.86	.79	.74	.69	.66	.63	.61	.59
75	6.63	3.50	2.46	1.94	1.64	1.43	1.29	1.18	1.10	1.04	.99	.95	.91	.88
100	8.84	4.67	3.28	2.59	2.18	1.91	1.72	1.58	1.47	1.38	1.31	1.26	1.21	1.17
200	17.68	9.33	6.55	5.17	4.35	3.81	3.43	3.15	2.93	2.76	2.62	2.51	2.42	2.34
300	26.52	13.99	9.83	7.76	6.53	5.72	5.14	4.72	4.39	4.14	3.93	3.77	3.63	3.51
400	35.36	18.65	13.10	10.34	8.70	7.62	6.86	6.29	5.86	5.52	5.24	5.02	4.84	4.68
500	44.20	23.31	16.37	12.93	10.88	9.52	8.57	7.86	7.32	6.89	6.55	6.27	6.04	5.85
600	53.03	27.97	19.65	15.51	13.05	11.43	10.28	9.43	8.78	8.27	7.86	7.53	7.25	7.02
700	61.87	32.63	22.92	18.10	15.22	13.33	11.99	11.00	10.24	9.65	9.17	8.78	8.46	8.19
800	70.71	37.29	26.20	20.68	17.40	15.23	13.70	12.57	11.71	11.03	10.48	10.03	9.67	9.36
900	79.55	41.95	29.47	23.27	19.57	17.14	15.42	14.14	13.17	12.40	11.79	11.29	10.87	10.53
1000	88.39	46.61	32.74	25.85	21.75	19.04	17.13	15.71	14.63	13.78	13.10	12.54	12.08	11.70
2000	176.77	93.22	65.48	51.70	43.49	38.07	34.25	31.42	29.26	27.56	26.19	25.08	24.16	23.39
3000	265.15	139.83	98.22	77.54	65.23	57.11	51.37	47.13	43.88	41.33	39.28	37.61	36.23	35.08
4000	353.53	186.44	130.96	103.39	86.97	76.14	68.49	62.84	58.51	55.11	52.37	50.15	48.31	46.77
5000	441.91	233.04	163.70	129.23	108.72	95.18	85.62	78.55	73.13	68.88	65.47	62.68	60.38	58.46
6000	530.29	279.65	196.44	155.08	130.46	114.21	102.74	94.26	87.76	82.66	78.56	75.22	72.46	70.15
7000	618.68	326.26	229.18	180.92	152.20	133.24	119.86	109.96	102.39	96.43	91.65	87.75	84.53	81.84
8000	707.06	372.87	261.91	206.77	173.94	152.28	136.98	125.67	117.01	110.21	104.74	100.29	96.61	93.53
9000	795.44	419.48	294.65	232.61	195.69	171.31	154.11	141.38	131.64	123.98	117.84	112.82	108.68	105.22
10000	883.82	466.08	327.39	258.46	217.43	190.35	171.23	157.09	146.26	137.76	130.93	125.36	120.76	116.91
11000	972.20	512.69	360.13	284.31	239.17	209.38	188.35	172.80	160.89	151.53	144.02	137.90	132.83	128.60
12000	1060.58	559.30	392.87	310.15	260.91	228.41	205.47	188.51	175.52	165.31	157.11	150.43	144.91	140.29
13000	1148.97	605.91	425.61	336.00	282.66	247.45	222.60	204.21	190.14	179.08	170.21	162.97	156.98	151.98
14000	1237.35	652.51	458.35	361.84	304.40	266.48	239.72	219.92	204.77	192.86	183.30	175.50	169.06	163.67
15000	1325.73	699.12	491.09	387.69	326.14	285.52	256.84	235.63	219.39	206.63	196.39	188.04	181.13	175.36
16000	1414.11	745.73	523.82	413.53	347.88	304.55	273.96	251.34	234.02	220.41	209.48	200.57	193.21	187.05
17000	1502.49	792.34	556.56	439.38	369.63	323.58	291.09	267.05	248.64	234.18	222.57	213.11	205.28	198.74
18000	1590.87	838.95	589.30	465.22	391.37	342.62	308.21	282.76	263.27	247.96	235.67	225.64	217.36	210.43
19000	1679.26	885.55	622.04	491.07	413.11	361.65	325.33	298.47	277.90	261.73	248.76	238.18	229.44	222.13
20000	1767.64	932.16	654.78	516.92	434.85	380.69	342.45	314.17	292.52	275.51	261.85	250.72	241.51	233.82
21000	1856.02	978.77	687.52	542.76	456.60	399.72	359.58	329.88	307.15	289.28	274.94	263.25	253.59	245.51
22000	1944.40	1025.38	720.26	568.61	478.34	418.75	376.70	345.59	321.77	303.06	288.04	275.79	265.66	257.20
23000	2032.78	1071.99	753.00	594.45	500.08	437.79	393.82	361.30	336.40	316.83	301.13	288.32	277.74	268.89
24000	2121.16	1118.59	785.73	620.30	521.82	456.82	410.94	377.01	351.03	330.61	314.22	300.86	289.81	280.58
25000	2209.55	1165.20	818.47	646.14	543.57	475.86	428.07	392.72	365.65	344.38	327.31	313.39	301.89	292.27
26000	2297.93	1211.81	851.21	671.99	565.31	494.89	445.19	408.42	380.28	358.16	340.41	325.93	313.96	303.96
27000	2386.31	1258.42	883.95	697.83	587.05	513.93	462.31	424.13	394.90	371.93	353.50	338.46	326.04	315.65
28000	2474.69	1305.02	916.69	723.68	608.79	532.96	479.43	439.84	409.53	385.71	366.59	351.00	338.11	327.34
29000	2563.07	1351.63	949.43	749.53	630.54	551.99	496.56	455.55	424.15	399.48	379.68	363.54	350.19	339.03
30000	2651.45	1398.24	982.17	775.37	652.28	571.03	513.68	471.26	438.78	413.26	392.78	376.07	362.26	350.72
31000	2739.84	1444.85	1014.91	801.22	674.02	590.06	530.80	486.97	453.41	427.03	405.87	388.61	374.34	362.41
32000	2828.22	1491.46	1047.64	827.06	695.76	609.10	547.92	502.67	468.03	440.81	418.96	401.14	386.41	374.10
33000	2916.60	1538.06	1080.38	852.91	717.50	628.13	565.05	518.38	482.66	454.58	432.05	413.68	398.49	385.79
34000	3004.98	1584.67	1113.12	878.75	739.25	647.16	582.17	534.09	497.28	468.36	445.14	426.21	410.56	397.48
35000	3093.36	1631.28	1145.86	904.60	760.99	666.20	599.29	549.80	511.91	482.13	458.24	438.75	422.64	409.17
36000	3181.74	1677.89	1178.60	930.44	782.73	685.23	616.41	565.51	526.54	495.91	471.33	451.28	434.71	420.86
37000	3270.13	1724.50	1211.34	956.29	804.47	704.27	633.54	581.22	541.16	509.68	484.42	463.82	446.79	432.56
38000	3358.51	1771.10	1244.08	982.13	826.22	723.30	650.66	596.93	555.79	523.46	497.51	476.36	458.87	444.25
39000	3446.89	1817.71	1276.82	1007.98	847.96	742.33	667.78	612.63	570.41	537.23	510.61	488.89	470.94	455.94
40000	3535.27	1864.32	1309.55	1033.83	869.70	761.37	684.90	628.34	585.04	551.01	523.70	501.43	483.02	467.63
41000	3623.65	1910.93	1342.29	1059.67	891.44	780.40	702.02	644.05	599.67	564.78	536.79	513.96	495.09	479.32
42000	3712.03	1957.53	1375.03	1085.52	913.19	799.44	719.15	659.76	614.29	578.56	549.88	526.50	507.17	491.01
43000	3800.42	2004.14	1407.77	1111.36	934.93	818.47	736.27	675.47	628.92	592.33	562.98	539.03	519.24	502.70
44000	3888.80	2050.75	1440.51	1137.21	956.67	837.50	753.39	691.18	643.54	606.11	576.07	551.57	531.32	514.39
45000	3977.18	2097.36	1473.25	1163.05	978.41	856.54	770.51	706.88	658.17	619.88	589.16	564.10	543.39	526.08
46000	4065.56	2143.97	1505.99	1188.90	1000.16	875.57	787.64	722.59	672.79	633.66	602.25	576.64	555.47	537.77
47000	4153.94	2190.57	1538.72	1214.74	1021.90	894.61	804.76	738.30	687.42	647.43	615.35	589.18	567.54	549.46
48000	4242.32	2237.18	1571.46	1240.59	1043.64	913.64	821.88	754.01	702.05	661.21	628.44	601.71	579.62	561.15
49000	4330.71	2283.79	1604.20	1266.44	1065.38	932.67	839.00	769.72	716.67	674.98	641.53	614.25	591.69	572.84
50000	4419.09	2330.40	1636.94	1292.28	1087.13	951.71	856.13	785.43	731.30	688.76	654.62	626.78	603.77	584.53
55000	4861.00	2563.44	1800.63	1421.51	1195.84	1046.88	941.74	863.97	804.43	757.63	720.08	689.46	664.15	642.98
60000	5302.90	2796.48	1964.33	1550.74	1304.55	1142.05	1027.35	942.51	877.56	826.51	785.55	752.14	724.52	701.44
65000	5744.81	3029.51	2128.02	1679.96	1413.26	1237.22	1112.96	1021.05	950.69	895.38	851.01	814.82	784.90	759.89
70000	6186.72	3262.55	2291.72	1809.19	1521.97	1332.39	1198.58	1099.59	1023.82	964.26	916.47	877.49	845.27	818.34
75000	6628.63	3495.59	2455.41	1938.42	1630.69	1427.56	1284.19	1178.14	1096.94	1033.13	981.93	940.17	905.65	876.80
80000	7070.54	3728.63	2619.10	2067.65	1739.40	1522.73	1369.80	1256.68	1170.07	1102.01	1047.39	1002.85	966.03	935.25
85000	7512.45	3961.67	2782.80	2196.87	1848.11	1617.90	1455.41	1335.22	1243.20	1170.88	1112.85	1065.53	1026.40	993.70
90000	7954.35	4194.71	2946.49	2326.10	1956.82	1713.07	1541.02	1413.76	1316.33	1239.76	1178.32	1128.20	1086.78	1052.15
95000	8396.26	4427.75	3110.18	2455.33	2065.54	1808.24	1626.64	1492.31	1389.46	1308.63	1243.78	1190.88	1147.16	1110.61
100000	8838.17	4660.79	3273.88	2584.56	2174.25	1903.41	1712.25	1570.85	1462.59	1377.51	1309.24	1253.56	1207.53	1169.06

11%

TERM	15 Years	16 Years	17 Years	18 Years	19 Years	20 Years	21 Years	22 Years	23 Years	24 Years	25 Years	30 Years	35 Years	40 Years
AMOUNT														
5	.06	.06	.06	.06	.06	.06	.06	.06	.05	.05	.05	.05	.05	.05
10	.12	.12	.11	.11	.11	.11	.11	.11	.10	.10	.10	.10	.10	.10
15	.18	.17	.17	.16	.16	.16	.16	.16	.15	.15	.15	.15	.15	.14
25	.29	.28	.28	.27	.27	.26	.26	.26	.25	.25	.25	.24	.24	.24
50	.57	.56	.55	.54	.53	.52	.51	.51	.50	.50	.50	.48	.47	.47
75	.86	.84	.82	.80	.79	.78	.77	.76	.75	.75	.74	.72	.71	.70
100	1.14	1.11	1.09	1.07	1.05	1.04	1.02	1.01	1.00	.99	.99	.96	.94	.93
200	2.28	2.22	2.18	2.14	2.10	2.07	2.04	2.02	2.00	1.98	1.97	1.91	1.88	1.86
300	3.41	3.33	3.26	3.20	3.15	3.10	3.06	3.03	3.00	2.97	2.95	2.86	2.82	2.79
400	4.55	4.44	4.35	4.27	4.19	4.13	4.08	4.03	3.99	3.96	3.93	3.81	3.75	3.72
500	5.69	5.55	5.43	5.33	5.24	5.17	5.10	5.04	4.99	4.95	4.91	4.77	4.69	4.65
600	6.82	6.66	6.52	6.40	6.29	6.20	6.12	6.05	5.99	5.93	5.89	5.72	5.63	5.57
700	7.96	7.77	7.60	7.46	7.34	7.23	7.14	7.06	6.98	6.92	6.87	6.67	6.56	6.50
800	9.10	8.88	8.69	8.53	8.38	8.26	8.16	8.06	7.98	7.91	7.85	7.62	7.50	7.43
900	10.23	9.99	9.77	9.59	9.43	9.29	9.17	9.07	8.98	8.90	8.83	8.58	8.44	8.36
1000	11.37	11.10	10.86	10.66	10.48	10.33	10.19	10.08	9.98	9.89	9.81	9.53	9.37	9.29
2000	22.74	22.19	21.71	21.31	20.95	20.65	20.38	20.15	19.95	19.77	19.61	19.05	18.74	18.57
3000	34.10	33.28	32.57	31.96	31.43	30.97	30.57	30.22	29.92	29.65	29.41	28.57	28.11	27.85
4000	45.47	44.37	43.42	42.61	41.90	41.29	40.76	40.29	39.89	39.53	39.21	38.10	37.48	37.14
5000	56.83	55.46	54.27	53.26	52.38	51.61	50.95	50.37	49.86	49.41	49.01	47.62	46.85	46.42
6000	68.20	66.55	65.13	63.91	62.85	61.94	61.14	60.44	59.83	59.29	58.81	57.14	56.22	55.70
7000	79.57	77.64	75.98	74.56	73.33	72.26	71.33	70.51	69.80	69.17	68.61	66.67	65.59	64.99
8000	90.93	88.73	86.84	85.21	83.80	82.58	81.51	80.58	79.77	79.05	78.41	76.19	74.96	74.27
9000	102.30	99.82	97.69	95.86	94.28	92.90	91.70	90.65	89.74	88.93	88.22	85.71	84.33	83.55
10000	113.66	110.91	108.54	106.51	104.75	103.22	101.89	100.73	99.71	98.81	98.02	95.24	93.70	92.83
11000	125.03	122.00	119.40	117.16	115.23	113.55	112.08	110.80	109.68	108.69	107.82	104.76	103.07	102.12
12000	136.40	133.09	130.25	127.81	125.70	123.87	122.27	120.87	119.65	118.57	117.62	114.28	112.44	111.40
13000	147.76	144.18	141.10	138.46	136.18	134.19	132.46	130.94	129.62	128.45	127.42	123.81	121.81	120.60
14000	159.13	155.27	151.96	149.11	146.65	144.51	142.65	141.02	139.59	138.33	137.22	133.33	131.18	129.97
15000	170.49	166.36	162.81	159.76	157.12	154.83	152.84	151.09	149.56	148.21	147.02	142.85	140.55	139.25
16000	181.86	177.45	173.67	170.41	167.60	165.16	163.02	161.16	159.53	158.09	156.82	152.38	149.92	148.53
17000	193.23	188.54	184.52	181.06	178.07	175.48	173.21	171.23	169.50	167.97	166.62	161.90	159.29	157.82
18000	204.59	199.63	195.37	191.71	188.55	185.80	183.40	181.31	179.47	177.85	176.43	171.42	168.66	167.10
19000	215.96	210.72	206.23	202.36	199.02	196.12	193.59	191.38	189.44	187.73	186.23	180.95	178.03	176.38
20000	227.32	221.81	217.08	213.01	209.50	206.44	203.78	201.45	199.41	197.61	196.03	190.47	187.40	185.66
21000	238.69	232.90	227.93	223.67	219.97	216.76	213.97	211.52	209.38	207.49	205.83	199.99	196.77	194.95
22000	250.06	243.99	238.79	234.32	230.45	227.09	224.16	221.59	219.35	217.37	215.63	209.52	206.14	204.23
23000	261.42	255.08	249.64	244.97	240.92	237.41	234.35	231.67	229.32	227.25	225.43	219.04	215.51	213.51
24000	272.79	266.17	260.50	255.62	251.40	247.73	244.53	241.74	239.29	237.13	235.23	228.56	224.87	222.80
25000	284.15	277.26	271.35	266.27	261.87	258.05	254.72	251.81	249.26	247.01	245.03	238.09	234.24	232.08
26000	295.52	288.35	282.20	276.92	272.35	268.37	264.91	261.88	259.23	256.89	254.83	247.61	243.61	241.36
27000	306.89	299.44	293.06	287.57	282.82	278.70	275.10	271.96	269.20	266.77	264.64	257.13	252.98	250.64
28000	318.25	310.53	303.91	298.22	293.29	289.02	285.29	282.03	279.17	276.65	274.44	266.66	262.35	259.93
29000	329.62	321.62	314.77	308.87	303.77	299.34	295.48	292.10	289.14	286.53	284.24	276.18	271.72	269.21
30000	340.98	332.71	325.62	319.52	314.24	309.66	305.67	302.17	299.11	296.41	294.04	285.70	281.09	278.49
31000	352.35	343.80	336.47	330.17	324.72	319.98	315.85	312.24	309.08	306.29	303.84	295.23	290.46	287.78
32000	363.72	354.89	347.33	340.82	335.19	330.31	326.04	322.32	319.05	316.17	313.64	304.75	299.83	297.06
33000	375.08	365.98	358.18	351.47	345.67	340.63	336.23	332.39	329.02	326.05	323.44	314.27	309.20	306.34
34000	386.45	377.07	369.03	362.12	356.14	350.95	346.42	342.46	338.99	335.93	333.24	323.79	318.57	315.63
35000	397.81	388.16	379.89	372.77	366.62	361.27	356.61	352.53	348.96	345.81	343.04	333.32	327.94	324.91
36000	409.18	399.25	390.74	383.42	377.09	371.59	366.80	362.61	358.93	355.69	352.85	342.84	337.31	334.19
37000	420.55	410.34	401.60	394.07	387.57	381.91	376.99	372.68	368.90	365.57	362.65	352.36	346.68	343.47
38000	431.91	421.43	412.45	404.72	398.04	392.24	387.18	382.75	378.87	375.46	372.45	361.89	356.05	352.76
39000	443.28	432.52	423.30	415.37	408.52	402.56	397.36	392.82	388.84	385.34	382.25	371.41	365.42	362.04
40000	454.64	443.61	434.16	426.02	418.99	412.88	407.55	402.89	398.81	395.22	392.05	380.93	374.79	371.32
41000	466.01	454.70	445.01	436.68	429.47	423.20	417.74	412.97	408.78	405.10	401.85	390.46	384.16	380.61
42000	477.38	465.79	455.86	447.33	439.94	433.52	427.93	423.04	418.75	414.98	411.65	399.98	393.53	389.89
43000	488.74	476.88	466.72	457.98	450.41	443.85	438.12	433.11	428.72	424.86	421.45	409.50	402.90	399.17
44000	500.11	487.97	477.57	468.63	460.89	454.17	448.31	443.18	438.69	434.74	431.25	419.03	412.27	408.45
45000	511.47	499.05	488.43	479.28	471.36	464.49	458.50	453.26	448.66	444.62	441.06	428.55	421.64	417.74
46000	522.84	510.15	499.28	489.93	481.84	474.81	468.69	463.33	458.63	454.50	450.86	438.07	431.01	427.02
47000	534.21	521.24	510.13	500.58	492.31	485.13	478.87	473.40	468.60	464.38	460.66	447.60	440.38	436.30
48000	545.57	532.33	520.99	511.23	502.79	495.46	489.06	483.47	478.57	474.26	470.46	457.12	449.74	445.59
49000	556.94	543.42	531.84	521.88	513.26	505.78	499.25	493.54	488.54	484.14	480.26	466.64	459.11	454.87
50000	568.30	554.51	542.70	532.53	523.74	516.10	509.44	503.62	498.51	494.02	490.06	476.17	468.48	464.15
55000	625.13	609.96	596.96	585.78	576.11	567.71	560.38	553.98	548.36	543.42	539.07	523.78	515.33	510.57
60000	681.96	665.41	651.23	639.03	628.48	619.32	611.33	604.34	598.21	592.82	588.07	571.40	562.18	556.98
65000	738.79	720.86	705.50	692.29	680.86	670.93	662.27	654.70	648.06	642.22	637.08	619.02	609.03	603.40
70000	795.62	776.31	759.77	745.54	733.23	722.54	713.21	705.06	697.91	691.62	686.08	666.63	655.88	649.81
75000	852.45	831.76	814.04	798.79	785.60	774.15	764.16	755.42	747.76	741.02	735.09	714.25	702.72	696.23
80000	909.28	887.21	868.31	852.04	837.98	825.76	815.10	805.78	797.61	790.43	784.10	761.86	749.57	742.64
85000	966.11	942.66	922.58	905.30	890.35	877.37	866.05	856.14	847.46	839.83	833.10	809.48	796.42	789.06
90000	1022.94	998.11	976.85	958.55	942.72	928.97	916.99	906.51	897.31	889.23	882.11	857.10	843.27	835.47
95000	1079.77	1053.56	1031.12	1011.80	995.10	980.58	967.93	956.87	947.16	938.63	931.11	904.71	890.11	881.88
100000	1136.60	1109.01	1085.39	1065.05	1047.47	1032.19	1018.88	1007.23	997.01	988.03	980.12	952.33	936.96	928.30

MONTHLY PAYMENT
REQUIRED TO AMORTIZE A LOAN

TERM	1 Year	2 Years	3 Years	4 Years	5 Years	6 Years	7 Years	8 Years	9 Years	10 Years	11 Years	12 Years	13 Years	14 Years
AMOUNT														
5	.45	.24	.17	.13	.11	.10	.09	.08	.08	.07	.07	.07	.07	.06
10	.89	.47	.33	.26	.22	.20	.18	.16	.15	.14	.14	.13	.13	.12
15	1.33	.70	.50	.39	.33	.29	.26	.24	.23	.21	.20	.19	.19	.18
25	2.22	1.17	.82	.65	.55	.48	.43	.40	.37	.35	.33	.32	.31	.30
50	4.43	2.34	1.64	1.30	1.09	.96	.86	.79	.74	.70	.66	.63	.61	.59
75	6.64	3.50	2.46	1.95	1.64	1.44	1.29	1.19	1.11	1.04	.99	.95	.92	.89
100	8.85	4.67	3.28	2.59	2.18	1.91	1.72	1.58	1.47	1.39	1.32	1.26	1.22	1.18
200	17.69	9.34	6.56	5.18	4.36	3.82	3.44	3.16	2.94	2.77	2.64	2.52	2.43	2.36
300	26.53	14.00	9.84	7.77	6.54	5.73	5.16	4.73	4.41	4.15	3.95	3.78	3.65	3.53
400	35.38	18.67	13.12	10.36	8.72	7.64	6.88	6.31	5.88	5.54	5.27	5.04	4.86	4.71
500	44.22	23.33	16.40	12.95	10.90	9.55	8.59	7.89	7.35	6.92	6.58	6.30	6.07	5.88
600	53.06	28.00	19.68	15.54	13.08	11.46	10.31	9.46	8.81	8.30	7.90	7.56	7.29	7.06
700	61.90	32.66	22.96	18.13	15.26	13.36	12.03	11.04	10.28	9.69	9.21	8.82	8.50	8.23
800	70.75	37.33	26.23	20.72	17.44	15.27	13.75	12.61	11.75	11.07	10.53	10.08	9.71	9.41
900	79.59	41.99	29.51	23.31	19.62	17.18	15.46	14.19	13.22	12.45	11.84	11.34	10.93	10.58
1000	88.43	46.66	32.79	25.90	21.80	19.09	17.18	15.77	14.69	13.84	13.16	12.60	12.14	11.76
2000	176.86	93.31	65.58	51.79	43.59	38.18	34.36	31.53	29.37	27.67	26.31	25.19	24.28	23.51
3000	265.29	139.97	98.36	77.69	65.38	57.26	51.53	47.29	44.05	41.50	39.46	37.79	36.41	35.26
4000	353.72	186.62	131.15	103.58	87.17	76.35	68.71	63.05	58.73	55.33	52.61	50.38	48.55	47.01
5000	442.15	233.28	163.94	129.48	108.97	95.43	85.88	78.82	73.41	69.16	65.76	62.98	60.68	58.77
6000	530.57	279.93	196.72	155.37	130.76	114.52	103.06	94.58	88.09	83.00	78.91	75.57	72.82	70.52
7000	619.00	326.58	229.51	181.26	152.55	133.60	120.23	110.34	102.77	96.83	92.06	88.17	84.96	82.27
8000	707.43	373.24	262.29	207.16	174.34	152.69	137.41	126.10	117.45	110.66	105.21	100.76	97.09	94.02
9000	795.86	419.89	295.08	233.05	196.14	171.77	154.58	141.87	132.14	124.49	118.36	113.36	109.23	105.78
10000	884.29	466.55	327.87	258.95	217.93	190.86	171.76	157.63	146.82	138.32	131.51	125.95	121.36	117.53
11000	972.72	513.20	360.65	284.84	239.72	209.94	188.93	173.39	161.50	152.15	144.66	138.55	133.50	129.28
12000	1061.14	559.86	393.44	310.73	261.51	229.03	206.11	189.15	176.18	165.99	157.81	151.14	145.63	141.03
13000	1149.57	606.51	426.22	336.63	283.31	248.11	223.28	204.92	190.86	179.82	170.96	163.74	157.77	152.78
14000	1238.00	653.16	459.01	362.52	305.10	267.20	240.46	220.68	205.54	193.65	184.11	176.33	169.91	164.54
15000	1326.43	699.82	491.80	388.42	326.89	286.29	257.63	236.44	220.22	207.48	197.26	188.93	182.04	176.29
16000	1414.86	746.47	524.58	414.31	348.68	305.37	274.81	252.20	234.90	221.31	210.41	201.52	194.18	188.04
17000	1503.29	793.13	557.37	440.20	370.47	324.46	291.98	267.97	249.59	235.14	223.56	214.12	206.31	199.79
18000	1591.71	839.78	590.15	466.10	392.27	343.54	309.16	283.73	264.27	248.98	236.71	226.71	218.45	211.55
19000	1680.14	886.44	622.94	491.99	414.06	362.63	326.33	299.49	278.95	262.81	249.86	239.31	230.58	223.30
20000	1768.57	933.09	655.73	517.89	435.85	381.71	343.51	315.25	293.63	276.64	263.01	251.90	242.72	235.05
21000	1857.00	979.74	688.51	543.78	457.64	400.80	360.68	331.02	308.31	290.47	276.16	264.50	254.86	246.80
22000	1945.43	1026.40	721.30	569.68	479.44	419.88	377.86	346.78	322.99	304.30	289.31	277.09	266.99	258.55
23000	2033.86	1073.05	754.09	595.57	501.23	438.97	395.03	362.54	337.67	318.13	302.46	289.69	279.13	270.31
24000	2122.28	1119.71	786.87	621.46	523.02	458.05	412.21	378.30	352.35	331.97	315.61	302.28	291.26	282.06
25000	2210.71	1166.36	819.66	647.36	544.81	477.14	429.38	394.07	367.03	345.80	328.76	314.87	303.40	293.81
26000	2299.14	1213.02	852.44	673.25	566.61	496.22	446.56	409.83	381.72	359.63	341.91	327.47	315.53	305.56
27000	2387.57	1259.67	885.23	699.15	588.40	515.31	463.73	425.59	396.40	373.46	355.06	340.06	327.67	317.32
28000	2476.00	1306.32	918.02	725.04	610.19	534.39	480.91	441.35	411.08	387.29	368.21	352.66	339.81	329.07
29000	2564.43	1352.98	950.80	750.93	631.98	553.48	498.08	457.11	425.76	401.12	381.36	365.25	351.94	340.82
30000	2652.85	1399.63	983.59	776.83	653.77	572.57	515.26	472.88	440.44	414.96	394.51	377.85	364.08	352.57
31000	2741.28	1446.29	1016.37	802.72	675.57	591.65	532.43	488.64	455.12	428.79	407.66	390.44	376.21	364.32
32000	2829.71	1492.94	1049.16	828.62	697.36	610.74	549.61	504.40	469.80	442.62	420.82	403.04	388.35	376.08
33000	2918.14	1539.60	1081.95	854.51	719.15	629.82	566.78	520.16	484.48	456.45	433.97	415.63	400.49	387.83
34000	3006.57	1586.25	1114.73	880.40	740.94	648.91	583.96	535.93	499.17	470.28	447.12	428.23	412.62	399.58
35000	3095.00	1632.90	1147.52	906.30	762.74	667.99	601.13	551.69	513.85	484.11	460.27	440.82	424.76	411.33
36000	3183.42	1679.56	1180.30	932.19	784.53	687.08	618.31	567.45	528.53	497.95	473.42	453.42	436.89	423.09
37000	3271.85	1726.21	1213.09	958.09	806.32	706.16	635.48	583.21	543.21	511.78	486.57	466.01	449.03	434.84
38000	3360.28	1772.87	1245.88	983.98	828.11	725.25	652.66	598.98	557.89	525.61	499.72	478.61	461.16	446.59
39000	3448.71	1819.52	1278.66	1009.88	849.91	744.33	669.83	614.74	572.57	539.44	512.87	491.20	473.30	458.34
40000	3537.14	1866.18	1311.45	1035.77	871.70	763.42	687.01	630.50	587.25	553.27	526.02	503.80	485.44	470.09
41000	3625.57	1912.83	1344.23	1061.66	893.49	782.50	704.18	646.26	601.93	567.10	539.17	516.39	497.57	481.85
42000	3713.99	1959.48	1377.02	1087.56	915.28	801.59	721.36	662.03	616.62	580.94	552.32	528.99	509.71	493.60
43000	3802.42	2006.14	1409.81	1113.45	937.08	820.67	738.53	677.79	631.30	594.77	565.47	541.58	521.84	505.35
44000	3890.85	2052.79	1442.59	1139.35	958.87	839.76	755.71	693.55	645.98	608.60	578.62	554.18	533.98	517.10
45000	3979.28	2099.45	1475.38	1165.24	980.66	858.85	772.88	709.31	660.66	622.43	591.77	566.77	546.11	528.86
46000	4067.71	2146.10	1508.17	1191.13	1002.45	877.93	790.06	725.08	675.34	636.26	604.92	579.37	558.25	540.61
47000	4156.14	2192.76	1540.95	1217.03	1024.24	897.02	807.23	740.84	690.02	650.09	618.07	591.96	570.39	552.36
48000	4244.56	2239.41	1573.74	1242.92	1046.04	916.10	824.41	756.60	704.70	663.93	631.22	604.56	582.52	564.11
49000	4332.99	2286.06	1606.52	1268.82	1067.83	935.19	841.58	772.36	719.38	677.76	644.37	617.15	594.66	575.86
50000	4421.42	2332.72	1639.31	1294.71	1089.62	954.27	858.76	788.13	734.06	691.59	657.52	629.74	606.79	587.62
55000	4863.56	2565.99	1803.24	1424.18	1198.58	1049.70	944.63	866.94	807.47	760.75	723.27	692.72	667.47	646.38
60000	5305.70	2799.26	1967.17	1553.65	1307.54	1145.13	1030.51	945.75	880.88	829.91	789.02	755.69	728.15	705.14
65000	5747.85	3032.53	2131.10	1683.12	1416.51	1240.55	1116.38	1024.56	954.28	899.06	854.78	818.67	788.83	763.90
70000	6189.99	3265.80	2295.03	1812.59	1525.47	1335.98	1202.26	1103.37	1027.69	968.22	920.53	881.64	849.51	822.66
75000	6632.13	3499.08	2458.96	1942.06	1634.43	1431.41	1288.13	1182.19	1101.09	1037.38	986.28	944.61	910.19	881.42
80000	7074.27	3732.35	2622.89	2071.53	1743.39	1526.83	1374.01	1261.00	1174.50	1106.54	1052.03	1007.59	970.87	940.18
85000	7516.41	3965.62	2786.82	2201.00	1852.35	1622.26	1459.89	1339.81	1247.91	1175.70	1117.78	1070.56	1031.55	998.95
90000	7958.55	4198.89	2950.75	2330.48	1961.31	1717.69	1545.76	1418.62	1321.31	1244.86	1183.53	1133.54	1092.22	1057.71
95000	8400.69	4432.16	3114.68	2459.95	2070.28	1813.11	1631.64	1497.43	1394.72	1314.01	1249.29	1196.51	1152.90	1116.47
100000	8842.84	4665.43	3278.61	2589.42	2179.24	1908.54	1717.51	1576.25	1468.12	1383.17	1315.04	1259.49	1213.58	1175.23

TERM	15 Years	16 Years	17 Years	18 Years	19 Years	20 Years	21 Years	22 Years	23 Years	24 Years	25 Years	30 Years	35 Years	40 Years
AMOUNT														
5	.06	.06	.06	.06	.06	.06	.06	.06	.06	.05	.05	.05	.05	.05
10	.12	.12	.11	.11	.11	.11	.11	.11	.11	.10	.10	.10	.10	.10
15	.18	.17	.17	.17	.16	.16	.16	.16	.16	.15	.15	.15	.15	.15
25	.29	.28	.28	.27	.27	.26	.26	.26	.26	.25	.25	.24	.24	.24
50	.58	.56	.55	.54	.53	.52	.52	.51	.51	.50	.50	.48	.48	.47
75	.86	.84	.82	.81	.80	.78	.77	.77	.76	.75	.75	.72	.71	.71
100	1.15	1.12	1.10	1.08	1.06	1.04	1.03	1.02	1.01	1.00	.99	.96	.95	.94
200	2.29	2.24	2.19	2.15	2.11	2.08	2.06	2.03	2.01	2.00	1.98	1.92	1.89	1.88
300	3.43	3.35	3.28	3.22	3.17	3.12	3.08	3.05	3.02	2.99	2.97	2.88	2.84	2.81
400	4.58	4.47	4.37	4.29	4.22	4.16	4.11	4.06	4.02	3.99	3.95	3.84	3.78	3.75
500	5.72	5.58	5.46	5.36	5.28	5.20	5.13	5.08	5.03	4.98	4.94	4.80	4.73	4.69
600	6.86	6.70	6.56	6.43	6.33	6.24	6.16	6.09	6.03	5.98	5.93	5.76	5.67	5.62
700	8.01	7.81	7.65	7.51	7.38	7.28	7.19	7.10	7.03	6.97	6.92	6.72	6.62	6.56
800	9.15	8.93	8.74	8.58	8.44	8.32	8.21	8.12	8.04	7.97	7.90	7.68	7.56	7.50
900	10.29	10.04	9.83	9.65	9.49	9.36	9.24	9.13	9.04	8.96	8.89	8.64	8.51	8.43
1000	11.43	11.16	10.92	10.72	10.55	10.40	10.26	10.15	10.05	9.96	9.88	9.60	9.45	9.37
2000	22.86	22.31	21.84	21.44	21.09	20.79	20.52	20.29	20.09	19.91	19.75	19.20	18.90	18.73
3000	34.29	33.47	32.76	32.15	31.63	31.18	30.78	30.43	30.13	29.86	29.63	28.80	28.35	28.09
4000	45.72	44.62	43.68	42.87	42.17	41.57	41.04	40.57	40.17	39.81	39.50	38.40	37.80	37.46
5000	57.15	55.78	54.60	53.59	52.71	51.96	51.29	50.72	50.21	49.76	49.37	48.00	47.24	46.82
6000	68.58	66.93	65.52	64.30	63.26	62.35	61.55	60.86	60.25	59.72	59.25	57.60	56.69	56.18
7000	80.01	78.08	76.44	75.02	73.80	72.74	71.81	71.00	70.29	69.67	69.12	67.20	66.14	65.54
8000	91.44	89.24	87.36	85.74	84.34	83.13	82.07	81.14	80.33	79.62	78.99	76.80	75.59	74.91
9000	102.86	100.39	98.28	96.45	94.88	93.52	92.33	91.28	90.37	89.57	88.87	86.39	85.03	84.27
10000	114.29	111.55	109.19	107.17	105.42	103.91	102.58	101.43	100.41	99.52	98.74	95.99	94.48	93.63
11000	125.72	122.70	120.11	117.89	115.96	114.30	112.84	111.57	110.45	109.48	108.61	105.59	103.93	102.99
12000	137.15	133.85	131.03	128.60	126.51	124.69	123.10	121.71	120.50	119.43	118.49	115.19	113.38	112.36
13000	148.58	145.01	141.95	139.32	137.05	135.08	133.36	131.85	130.54	129.38	128.36	124.79	122.82	121.72
14000	160.01	156.16	152.87	150.04	147.59	145.47	143.61	142.00	140.58	139.33	138.23	134.39	132.27	131.08
15000	171.44	167.32	163.79	160.75	158.13	155.86	153.87	152.14	150.62	149.28	148.11	143.99	141.72	140.45
16000	182.87	178.47	174.71	171.47	168.67	166.25	164.13	162.28	160.66	159.24	157.98	153.59	151.17	149.81
17000	194.30	189.62	185.63	182.19	179.22	176.64	174.39	172.42	170.70	169.19	167.85	163.19	160.61	159.17
18000	205.72	200.78	196.55	192.90	189.76	187.03	184.65	182.56	180.74	179.14	177.73	172.78	170.06	168.53
19000	217.15	211.93	207.46	203.62	200.30	197.42	194.90	192.71	190.78	189.09	187.60	182.38	179.51	177.90
20000	228.58	223.09	218.38	214.34	210.84	207.81	205.16	202.85	200.82	199.04	197.48	191.98	188.96	187.26
21000	240.01	234.24	229.30	225.05	221.38	218.20	215.42	212.99	210.86	208.99	207.35	201.58	198.41	196.62
22000	251.44	245.39	240.22	235.77	231.92	228.59	225.68	223.13	220.90	218.95	217.22	211.18	207.85	205.98
23000	262.87	256.55	251.14	246.49	242.47	238.98	235.93	233.28	230.95	228.90	227.10	220.78	217.30	215.35
24000	274.30	267.70	262.06	257.20	253.01	249.37	246.19	243.42	240.99	238.85	236.97	230.38	226.75	224.71
25000	285.73	278.86	272.98	267.92	263.55	259.76	256.45	253.56	251.03	248.80	246.84	239.98	236.20	234.07
26000	297.15	290.01	283.90	278.64	274.09	270.15	266.71	263.70	261.07	258.75	256.72	249.58	245.64	243.44
27000	308.58	301.16	294.82	289.35	284.63	280.54	276.97	273.84	271.11	268.71	266.59	259.17	255.09	252.80
28000	320.01	312.32	305.73	300.07	295.18	290.93	287.22	283.99	281.15	278.66	276.46	268.77	264.54	262.16
29000	331.44	323.47	316.65	310.79	305.72	301.32	297.48	294.13	291.19	288.61	286.34	278.37	273.99	271.52
30000	342.87	334.63	327.57	321.50	316.26	311.71	307.74	304.27	301.23	298.56	296.21	287.97	283.43	280.89
31000	354.30	345.78	338.49	332.22	326.80	322.10	318.00	314.41	311.27	308.51	306.08	297.57	292.88	290.25
32000	365.73	356.93	349.41	342.94	337.34	332.49	328.25	324.56	321.31	318.47	315.96	307.17	302.33	299.61
33000	377.16	368.09	360.33	353.65	347.88	342.88	338.51	334.70	331.35	328.42	325.83	316.77	311.78	308.97
34000	388.59	379.24	371.25	364.37	358.43	353.27	348.77	344.84	341.40	338.37	335.70	326.37	321.22	318.34
35000	400.01	390.40	382.17	375.09	368.97	363.66	359.03	354.98	351.44	348.32	345.58	335.97	330.67	327.70
36000	411.44	401.55	393.09	385.80	379.51	374.05	369.29	365.12	361.48	358.27	355.45	345.56	340.12	337.06
37000	422.87	412.70	404.00	396.52	390.05	384.44	379.54	375.27	371.52	368.22	365.32	355.16	349.57	346.43
38000	434.30	423.86	414.92	407.24	400.59	394.83	389.80	385.41	381.56	378.18	375.20	364.76	359.01	355.79
39000	445.73	435.01	425.84	417.95	411.14	405.22	400.06	395.55	391.60	388.13	385.07	374.36	368.46	365.15
40000	457.16	446.17	436.76	428.67	421.68	415.61	410.32	405.69	401.64	398.08	394.95	383.96	377.91	374.51
41000	468.59	457.32	447.68	439.39	432.22	426.00	420.57	415.84	411.68	408.03	404.82	393.56	387.36	383.88
42000	480.02	468.47	458.60	450.10	442.76	436.39	430.83	425.98	421.72	417.98	414.69	403.16	396.81	393.24
43000	491.45	479.63	469.52	460.82	453.30	446.78	441.09	436.12	431.76	427.94	424.57	412.76	406.25	402.60
44000	502.87	490.78	480.44	471.54	463.84	457.17	451.35	446.26	441.80	437.89	434.44	422.36	415.70	411.96
45000	514.30	501.94	491.36	482.25	474.39	467.56	461.61	456.40	451.84	447.84	444.31	431.95	425.15	421.33
46000	525.73	513.09	502.27	492.97	484.93	477.95	471.86	466.55	461.89	457.79	454.19	441.55	434.60	430.69
47000	537.16	524.24	513.19	503.69	495.47	488.34	482.12	476.69	471.93	467.74	464.06	451.15	444.04	440.05
48000	548.59	535.40	524.11	514.40	506.01	498.73	492.38	486.83	481.97	477.70	473.93	460.75	453.49	449.42
49000	560.02	546.55	535.03	525.12	516.55	509.12	502.64	496.97	492.01	487.65	483.81	470.35	462.94	458.78
50000	571.45	557.71	545.95	535.84	527.10	519.51	512.89	507.11	502.05	497.60	493.68	479.95	472.39	468.14
55000	628.59	613.48	600.54	589.42	579.80	571.46	564.18	557.83	552.25	547.36	543.05	527.94	519.62	514.95
60000	685.74	669.25	655.14	643.00	632.51	623.41	615.47	608.54	602.46	597.12	592.42	575.94	566.86	561.77
65000	742.88	725.02	709.73	696.59	685.22	675.36	666.76	659.25	652.66	646.88	641.78	623.93	614.10	608.58
70000	800.02	780.79	764.33	750.17	737.93	727.31	718.05	710.96	702.87	696.64	691.15	671.93	661.34	655.40
75000	857.17	836.56	818.92	803.75	790.64	779.26	769.34	760.67	753.07	746.40	740.52	719.92	708.58	702.21
80000	914.31	892.33	873.52	857.34	843.35	831.21	820.63	811.38	803.28	796.16	789.89	767.91	755.82	749.02
85000	971.46	948.10	928.11	910.92	896.06	883.16	871.92	862.09	853.48	845.91	839.25	815.91	803.05	795.84
90000	1028.60	1003.87	982.71	964.50	948.77	935.11	923.21	912.80	903.68	895.67	888.62	863.90	850.29	842.65
95000	1085.75	1059.64	1037.30	1018.09	1001.48	987.06	974.49	963.51	953.89	945.43	937.99	911.90	897.53	889.46
100000	1142.89	1115.41	1091.90	1071.67	1054.19	1039.01	1025.78	1014.22	1004.09	995.19	987.36	959.89	944.77	936.28

MONTHLY PAYMENT
REQUIRED TO AMORTIZE A LOAN

TERM / AMOUNT	1 Year	2 Years	3 Years	4 Years	5 Years	6 Years	7 Years	8 Years	9 Years	10 Years	11 Years	12 Years	13 Years	14 Years
5	.45	.24	.17	.13	.11	.10	.09	.08	.08	.07	.07	.07	.07	.06
10	.89	.47	.33	.26	.22	.20	.18	.16	.15	.14	.14	.13	.13	.12
15	1.33	.70	.50	.39	.33	.29	.26	.24	.23	.21	.20	.19	.19	.18
25	2.22	1.17	.82	.65	.55	.48	.43	.40	.37	.35	.33	.32	.31	.30
50	4.43	2.34	1.64	1.30	1.10	.96	.86	.79	.74	.70	.66	.64	.61	.59
75	6.64	3.50	2.46	1.95	1.64	1.44	1.29	1.19	1.11	1.04	.99	.95	.92	.89
100	8.85	4.67	3.28	2.60	2.19	1.91	1.72	1.58	1.47	1.39	1.32	1.27	1.22	1.18
200	17.69	9.34	6.56	5.19	4.37	3.82	3.44	3.16	2.94	2.77	2.64	2.53	2.44	2.36
300	26.54	14.00	9.84	7.78	6.55	5.73	5.16	4.74	4.41	4.16	3.95	3.79	3.65	3.54
400	35.38	18.67	13.12	10.37	8.73	7.64	6.88	6.32	5.88	5.54	5.27	5.05	4.87	4.71
500	44.22	23.34	16.40	12.96	10.91	9.55	8.60	7.89	7.35	6.93	6.59	6.31	6.08	5.89
600	53.07	28.00	19.68	15.55	13.09	11.46	10.32	9.47	8.82	8.31	7.90	7.57	7.30	7.07
700	61.91	32.67	22.96	18.14	15.27	13.37	12.04	11.05	10.29	9.70	9.22	8.83	8.51	8.24
800	70.76	37.34	26.24	20.73	17.45	15.28	13.76	12.63	11.76	11.08	10.54	10.09	9.73	9.42
900	79.60	42.00	29.52	23.32	19.63	17.19	15.47	14.20	13.23	12.47	11.85	11.35	10.94	10.60
1000	88.44	46.67	32.80	25.91	21.81	19.10	17.19	15.78	14.70	13.85	13.17	12.61	12.16	11.77
2000	176.88	93.34	65.60	51.82	43.61	38.20	34.38	31.56	29.40	27.70	26.33	25.22	24.31	23.54
3000	265.32	140.00	98.40	77.72	65.42	57.30	51.57	47.33	44.09	41.54	39.50	37.83	36.46	35.31
4000	353.76	186.67	131.20	103.63	87.22	76.40	68.76	63.11	58.79	55.39	52.66	50.44	48.61	47.08
5000	442.20	233.33	163.99	129.54	109.03	95.50	85.95	78.88	73.48	69.23	65.83	63.05	60.76	58.84
6000	530.64	280.00	196.79	155.44	130.83	114.59	103.13	94.66	88.18	83.08	78.99	75.66	72.91	70.61
7000	619.08	326.67	229.59	181.35	152.64	133.69	120.32	110.44	102.87	96.93	92.16	88.27	85.06	82.38
8000	707.52	373.33	262.39	207.26	174.44	152.79	137.51	126.21	117.57	110.77	105.32	100.88	97.21	94.15
9000	795.96	420.00	295.19	233.16	196.25	171.89	154.70	141.99	132.26	124.62	118.49	113.49	109.36	105.91
10000	884.40	466.66	327.98	259.07	218.05	190.99	171.89	157.76	146.96	138.46	131.65	126.10	121.51	117.68
11000	972.84	513.33	360.78	284.97	239.86	210.08	189.08	173.54	161.65	152.31	144.82	138.71	133.67	129.45
12000	1061.28	560.00	393.58	310.88	261.66	229.18	206.26	189.32	176.35	166.16	157.98	151.32	145.82	141.22
13000	1149.72	606.66	426.38	336.79	283.47	248.28	223.45	205.09	191.04	180.00	171.15	163.93	157.97	152.98
14000	1238.16	653.33	459.18	362.69	305.27	267.38	240.64	220.87	205.74	193.85	184.31	176.54	170.12	164.75
15000	1326.60	699.99	491.97	388.60	327.08	286.48	257.83	236.64	220.43	207.69	197.48	189.15	182.27	176.52
16000	1415.04	746.66	524.77	414.51	348.88	305.58	275.02	252.42	235.13	221.54	210.64	201.76	194.42	188.29
17000	1503.48	793.33	557.57	440.41	370.69	324.67	292.20	268.20	249.82	235.38	223.81	214.37	206.57	200.06
18000	1591.92	839.99	590.37	466.32	392.49	343.77	309.39	283.97	264.52	249.23	236.97	226.98	218.72	211.82
19000	1680.36	886.66	623.17	492.22	414.30	362.87	326.58	299.75	279.21	263.08	250.14	239.59	230.87	223.59
20000	1768.80	933.32	655.96	518.13	436.10	381.97	343.77	315.52	293.91	276.92	263.30	252.20	243.02	235.36
21000	1857.24	979.99	688.76	544.04	457.91	401.07	360.96	331.30	308.60	290.77	276.47	264.81	255.17	247.13
22000	1945.68	1026.65	721.56	569.94	479.71	420.16	378.15	347.08	323.30	304.61	289.63	277.42	267.33	258.89
23000	2034.12	1073.32	754.36	595.85	501.52	439.26	395.33	362.85	337.99	318.46	302.80	290.03	279.48	270.66
24000	2122.56	1119.99	787.16	621.76	523.32	458.36	412.52	378.63	352.69	332.31	315.96	302.64	291.63	282.43
25000	2211.00	1166.65	819.95	647.66	545.13	477.46	429.71	394.40	367.38	346.15	329.13	315.25	303.78	294.20
26000	2299.44	1213.32	852.75	673.57	566.93	496.56	446.90	410.18	382.08	360.00	342.29	327.86	315.93	305.96
27000	2387.88	1259.98	885.55	699.47	588.73	515.66	464.09	425.95	396.77	373.84	355.46	340.47	328.08	317.73
28000	2476.32	1306.65	918.35	725.38	610.54	534.75	481.28	441.73	411.47	387.69	368.62	353.07	340.23	329.50
29000	2564.76	1353.32	951.15	751.29	632.34	553.85	498.46	457.51	426.16	401.53	381.79	365.68	352.38	341.27
30000	2653.20	1399.98	983.94	777.19	654.15	572.95	515.65	473.28	440.86	415.38	394.95	378.29	364.53	353.04
31000	2741.64	1446.65	1016.74	803.10	675.95	592.05	532.84	489.06	455.55	429.23	408.11	390.90	376.68	364.80
32000	2830.08	1493.31	1049.54	829.01	697.76	611.15	550.03	504.83	470.25	443.07	421.28	403.51	388.83	376.57
33000	2918.52	1539.98	1082.34	854.91	719.56	630.24	567.22	520.61	484.94	456.92	434.44	416.12	400.99	388.34
34000	3006.96	1586.65	1115.14	880.82	741.37	649.34	584.40	536.39	499.64	470.76	447.61	428.73	413.14	400.11
35000	3095.40	1633.31	1147.93	906.72	763.17	668.44	601.59	552.16	514.33	484.61	460.77	441.34	425.29	411.87
36000	3183.84	1679.98	1180.73	932.63	784.98	687.54	618.78	567.94	529.03	498.46	473.94	453.95	437.44	423.64
37000	3272.28	1726.64	1213.53	958.54	806.78	706.64	635.97	583.71	543.72	512.30	487.10	466.56	449.59	435.41
38000	3360.72	1773.31	1246.33	984.44	828.59	725.74	653.16	599.49	558.42	526.15	500.27	479.17	461.74	447.18
39000	3449.16	1819.97	1279.12	1010.35	850.39	744.83	670.35	615.27	573.11	539.99	513.43	491.78	473.89	458.94
40000	3537.60	1866.64	1311.92	1036.26	872.20	763.93	687.53	631.04	587.81	553.84	526.60	504.39	486.04	470.71
41000	3626.04	1913.31	1344.72	1062.16	894.00	783.03	704.72	646.82	602.50	567.68	539.76	517.00	498.19	482.48
42000	3714.48	1959.97	1377.52	1088.07	915.81	802.13	721.91	662.59	617.20	581.53	552.93	529.61	510.34	494.25
43000	3802.92	2006.64	1410.32	1113.97	937.61	821.23	739.10	678.37	631.89	595.38	566.09	542.22	522.49	506.02
44000	3891.36	2053.30	1443.11	1139.88	959.42	840.32	756.29	694.15	646.59	609.22	579.26	554.83	534.65	517.78
45000	3979.80	2099.97	1475.91	1165.79	981.22	859.42	773.48	709.92	661.28	623.07	592.42	567.44	546.80	529.55
46000	4068.24	2146.64	1508.71	1191.69	1003.03	878.52	790.66	725.70	675.98	636.91	605.59	580.05	558.95	541.32
47000	4156.68	2193.30	1541.51	1217.60	1024.83	897.62	807.85	741.47	690.67	650.76	618.75	592.66	571.10	553.09
48000	4245.12	2239.97	1574.31	1243.51	1046.64	916.72	825.04	757.25	705.37	664.61	631.92	605.27	583.25	564.85
49000	4333.56	2286.63	1607.10	1269.41	1068.44	935.82	842.23	773.03	720.06	678.45	645.08	617.88	595.40	576.62
50000	4422.00	2333.30	1639.90	1295.32	1090.25	954.91	859.42	788.80	734.76	692.30	658.25	630.49	607.55	588.39
55000	4864.20	2566.63	1803.89	1424.85	1199.27	1050.40	945.36	867.68	808.23	761.53	724.07	693.53	668.31	647.23
60000	5306.40	2799.96	1967.88	1554.38	1308.29	1145.89	1031.30	946.56	881.71	830.76	789.90	756.58	729.06	706.07
65000	5748.60	3033.29	2131.87	1683.91	1417.32	1241.39	1117.24	1025.44	955.18	899.99	855.72	819.63	789.81	764.90
70000	6190.80	3266.62	2295.86	1813.44	1526.34	1336.88	1203.18	1104.32	1028.66	969.21	921.54	882.68	850.57	823.74
75000	6633.00	3499.95	2459.85	1942.98	1635.37	1432.37	1289.12	1183.20	1102.13	1038.44	987.37	945.73	911.32	882.58
80000	7075.20	3733.28	2623.84	2072.51	1744.39	1527.86	1375.06	1262.08	1175.61	1107.67	1053.19	1008.78	972.08	941.42
85000	7517.40	3966.61	2787.83	2202.04	1853.41	1623.35	1461.00	1340.96	1249.08	1176.90	1119.02	1071.82	1032.83	1000.26
90000	7959.60	4199.94	2951.82	2331.57	1962.44	1718.84	1546.95	1419.84	1322.56	1246.13	1184.84	1134.87	1093.59	1059.10
95000	8401.80	4433.26	3115.81	2461.10	2071.46	1814.33	1632.89	1498.72	1396.03	1315.36	1250.66	1197.92	1154.34	1117.94
100000	8844.00	4666.59	3279.80	2590.63	2180.49	1909.82	1718.83	1577.60	1469.51	1384.59	1316.49	1260.97	1215.10	1176.77

TERM	15 Years	16 Years	17 Years	18 Years	19 Years	20 Years	21 Years	22 Years	23 Years	24 Years	25 Years	30 Years	35 Years	40 Years
AMOUNT														
5	.06	.06	.06	.06	.06	.06	.06	.06	.06	.05	.05	.05	.05	.05
10	.12	.12	.11	.11	.11	.11	.11	.11	.11	.10	.10	.10	.10	.10
15	.18	.17	.17	.17	.16	.16	.16	.16	.16	.15	.15	.15	.15	.15
25	.29	.28	.28	.27	.27	.27	.26	.26	.26	.25	.25	.25	.24	.24
50	.58	.56	.55	.54	.53	.53	.52	.51	.51	.50	.50	.49	.48	.47
75	.86	.84	.83	.81	.80	.79	.78	.77	.76	.75	.75	.73	.72	.71
100	1.15	1.12	1.10	1.08	1.06	1.05	1.03	1.02	1.01	1.00	.99	.95	.95	.94
200	2.29	2.24	2.19	2.15	2.12	2.09	2.06	2.04	2.02	2.00	1.98	1.93	1.90	1.88
300	3.44	3.36	3.29	3.22	3.17	3.13	3.09	3.05	3.02	3.00	2.97	2.89	2.85	2.82
400	4.58	4.47	4.38	4.30	4.23	4.17	4.12	4.07	4.03	3.99	3.96	3.85	3.79	3.76
500	5.73	5.59	5.47	5.37	5.28	5.21	5.14	5.08	5.03	4.99	4.95	4.81	4.74	4.70
600	6.87	6.71	6.57	6.44	6.34	6.25	6.17	6.10	6.04	5.99	5.94	5.78	5.69	5.63
700	8.02	7.82	7.66	7.52	7.40	7.29	7.20	7.12	7.05	6.98	6.93	6.74	6.63	6.57
800	9.16	8.94	8.75	8.59	8.45	8.33	8.23	8.13	8.05	7.98	7.92	7.70	7.58	7.51
900	10.31	10.06	9.85	9.66	9.51	9.37	9.25	9.15	9.06	8.98	8.91	8.66	8.53	8.45
1000	11.45	11.18	10.94	10.74	10.56	10.41	10.28	10.16	10.06	9.97	9.90	9.62	9.47	9.39
2000	22.89	22.35	21.88	21.47	21.12	20.82	20.56	20.32	20.12	19.94	19.79	19.24	18.94	18.77
3000	34.34	33.52	32.81	32.20	31.68	31.23	30.83	30.48	30.18	29.91	29.68	28.86	28.41	28.15
4000	45.78	44.69	43.75	42.94	42.24	41.63	41.11	40.64	40.24	39.88	39.57	38.48	37.87	37.54
5000	57.23	55.86	54.68	53.67	52.80	52.04	51.38	50.80	50.30	49.85	49.46	48.09	47.34	46.92
6000	68.67	67.03	65.62	64.40	63.36	62.45	61.66	60.96	60.36	59.82	59.35	57.71	56.81	56.30
7000	80.12	78.20	76.55	75.14	73.92	72.85	71.93	71.12	70.42	69.79	69.25	67.33	66.28	65.68
8000	91.56	89.37	87.49	85.87	84.47	83.26	82.21	81.28	80.47	79.76	79.14	76.95	75.74	75.07
9000	103.01	100.54	98.42	96.60	95.03	93.67	92.48	91.44	90.53	89.73	89.03	86.57	85.21	84.45
10000	114.45	111.71	109.36	107.34	105.59	104.08	102.76	101.60	100.59	99.70	98.92	96.18	94.68	93.83
11000	125.90	122.88	120.29	118.07	116.15	114.48	113.03	111.76	110.65	109.67	108.81	105.80	104.14	103.21
12000	137.34	134.05	131.23	128.80	126.71	124.89	123.31	121.92	120.71	119.64	118.70	115.42	113.61	112.60
13000	148.78	145.22	142.16	139.54	137.27	135.30	133.58	132.08	130.77	129.61	128.60	125.04	123.08	121.98
14000	160.23	156.39	153.10	150.27	147.83	145.70	143.86	142.24	140.83	139.58	138.49	134.65	132.55	131.36
15000	171.67	167.56	164.03	161.00	158.38	156.11	154.13	152.40	150.88	149.55	148.38	144.27	142.01	140.75
16000	183.12	178.73	174.97	171.74	168.94	166.52	164.41	162.56	160.94	159.52	158.27	153.89	151.48	150.13
17000	194.56	189.90	185.90	182.47	179.50	176.93	174.60	172.72	171.00	169.49	168.16	163.51	160.95	159.51
18000	206.01	201.07	196.84	193.20	190.06	187.33	184.96	182.88	181.06	179.46	178.05	173.13	170.41	168.89
19000	217.45	212.24	207.77	203.94	200.62	197.74	195.23	193.04	191.12	189.43	187.95	182.74	179.88	178.28
20000	228.90	223.41	218.71	214.67	211.18	208.15	205.51	203.20	201.18	199.40	197.84	192.36	189.35	187.66
21000	240.34	234.58	229.64	225.40	221.74	218.55	215.78	213.36	211.24	209.37	207.73	201.98	198.82	197.04
22000	251.79	245.75	240.58	236.14	232.29	228.96	226.06	223.52	221.29	219.34	217.62	211.60	208.28	206.42
23000	263.23	256.92	251.51	246.87	242.85	239.37	236.33	233.68	231.35	229.31	227.51	221.21	217.75	215.81
24000	274.68	268.09	262.45	257.60	253.41	249.78	246.61	243.84	241.41	239.28	237.40	230.83	227.22	225.19
25000	286.12	279.26	273.39	268.34	263.97	260.18	256.88	254.00	251.47	249.25	247.30	240.45	236.68	234.57
26000	297.56	290.43	284.32	279.07	274.53	270.59	267.16	264.16	261.53	259.22	257.19	250.07	246.15	243.95
27000	309.01	301.60	295.26	289.80	285.09	281.00	277.43	274.32	271.59	269.19	267.08	259.69	255.62	253.34
28000	320.45	312.77	306.19	300.54	295.65	291.40	287.71	284.48	281.65	279.16	276.97	269.30	265.09	262.72
29000	331.90	323.94	317.13	311.27	306.21	301.81	297.98	294.64	291.70	289.13	286.86	278.92	274.55	272.10
30000	343.34	335.11	328.06	322.00	316.76	312.22	308.26	304.80	301.76	299.10	296.75	288.54	284.02	281.49
31000	354.79	346.28	339.00	332.73	327.32	322.62	318.53	314.96	311.82	309.07	306.65	298.16	293.49	290.87
32000	366.23	357.45	349.93	343.47	337.88	333.03	328.81	325.12	321.88	319.04	316.54	307.77	302.95	300.25
33000	377.68	368.62	360.87	354.20	348.44	343.44	339.08	335.28	331.94	329.01	326.43	317.39	312.42	309.63
34000	389.12	379.79	371.80	364.93	359.00	353.85	349.36	345.44	342.00	338.98	336.32	327.01	321.89	319.02
35000	400.57	390.96	382.74	375.67	369.56	364.25	359.63	355.59	352.06	348.95	346.21	336.63	331.36	328.40
36000	412.01	402.13	393.67	386.40	380.12	374.66	369.91	365.75	362.12	358.92	356.10	346.25	340.82	337.78
37000	423.45	413.30	404.61	397.13	390.67	385.07	380.18	375.91	372.17	368.89	366.00	355.86	350.29	347.16
38000	434.90	424.47	415.54	407.87	401.23	395.47	390.46	386.07	382.23	378.86	375.89	365.48	359.76	356.55
39000	446.34	435.64	426.48	418.60	411.79	405.88	400.73	396.23	392.29	388.83	385.78	375.10	369.22	365.93
40000	457.79	446.81	437.41	429.33	422.35	416.29	411.01	406.39	402.35	398.80	395.67	384.72	378.69	375.31
41000	469.23	457.98	448.35	440.07	432.91	426.70	421.28	416.55	412.41	408.77	405.56	394.34	388.16	384.69
42000	480.68	469.15	459.28	450.80	443.47	437.10	431.56	426.71	422.47	418.74	415.45	403.95	397.63	394.08
43000	492.12	480.32	470.22	461.53	454.03	447.51	441.83	436.87	432.53	428.71	425.35	413.57	407.09	403.46
44000	503.57	491.49	481.15	472.27	464.58	457.92	452.11	447.03	442.58	438.68	435.24	423.19	416.56	412.84
45000	515.01	502.66	492.09	483.00	475.14	468.32	462.38	457.19	452.64	448.65	445.13	432.81	426.03	422.23
46000	526.46	513.83	503.02	493.73	485.70	478.73	472.66	467.35	462.70	458.62	455.02	442.42	435.49	431.61
47000	537.90	525.00	513.96	504.47	496.26	489.14	482.93	477.51	472.76	468.59	464.91	452.04	444.96	440.99
48000	549.35	536.17	524.90	515.20	506.82	499.55	493.21	487.67	482.82	478.56	474.80	461.66	454.43	450.37
49000	560.79	547.34	535.83	525.93	517.38	509.95	503.48	497.83	492.88	488.53	484.69	471.28	463.90	459.76
50000	572.23	558.51	546.77	536.67	527.94	520.36	513.76	507.99	502.94	498.50	494.59	480.90	473.36	469.14
55000	629.46	614.36	601.44	590.33	580.73	572.39	565.13	558.79	553.23	548.34	544.04	528.98	520.70	516.05
60000	686.68	670.21	656.12	644.00	633.52	624.43	616.51	609.59	603.52	598.19	593.50	577.07	568.03	562.97
65000	743.90	726.06	710.79	697.66	686.32	676.47	667.88	660.39	653.82	648.04	642.96	625.16	615.37	609.88
70000	801.13	781.91	765.47	751.33	739.11	728.50	719.26	711.18	704.11	697.89	692.42	673.25	662.71	656.79
75000	858.35	837.76	820.15	805.00	791.90	780.54	770.64	761.98	754.40	747.74	741.88	721.34	710.04	703.71
80000	915.57	893.61	874.82	858.66	844.70	832.57	822.01	812.78	804.69	797.59	791.34	769.43	757.38	750.62
85000	972.79	949.46	929.50	912.33	897.49	884.61	873.39	863.58	854.99	847.44	840.79	817.52	804.71	797.53
90000	1030.02	1005.31	984.17	965.99	950.28	936.64	924.76	914.38	905.28	897.29	890.25	865.61	852.05	844.45
95000	1087.24	1061.16	1038.85	1019.66	1003.07	988.68	976.14	965.18	955.57	947.14	939.71	913.70	899.39	891.36
100000	1144.46	1117.01	1093.53	1073.33	1055.87	1040.71	1027.51	1015.98	1005.87	996.99	989.17	961.79	946.72	938.27

MONTHLY PAYMENT
REQUIRED TO AMORTIZE A LOAN

TERM AMOUNT	1 Year	2 Years	3 Years	4 Years	5 Years	6 Years	7 Years	8 Years	9 Years	10 Years	11 Years	12 Years	13 Years	14 Years
5	.45	.24	.17	.13	.11	.10	.09	.08	.08	.07	.07	.07	.07	.06
10	.89	.47	.33	.26	.22	.20	.18	.16	.15	.14	.14	.13	.13	.12
15	1.33	.71	.50	.39	.33	.29	.26	.24	.23	.21	.20	.19	.19	.18
25	2.22	1.17	.83	.65	.55	.48	.44	.40	.37	.35	.34	.32	.31	.30
50	4.43	2.34	1.65	1.30	1.10	.96	.87	.80	.74	.70	.67	.64	.61	.60
75	6.64	3.51	2.47	1.95	1.64	1.44	1.30	1.19	1.11	1.05	1.00	.95	.92	.89
100	8.85	4.68	3.29	2.60	2.19	1.92	1.73	1.59	1.48	1.39	1.33	1.27	1.22	1.19
200	17.70	9.35	6.57	5.19	4.37	3.83	3.45	3.17	2.95	2.78	2.65	2.54	2.44	2.37
300	26.55	14.02	9.86	7.79	6.56	5.75	5.17	4.75	4.43	4.17	3.97	3.80	3.66	3.55
400	35.39	18.69	13.14	10.38	8.74	7.66	6.90	6.33	5.90	5.56	5.29	5.07	4.88	4.73
500	44.24	23.36	16.42	12.98	10.93	9.57	8.62	7.91	7.37	6.95	6.61	6.33	6.10	5.91
600	53.09	28.03	19.71	15.57	13.11	11.49	10.34	9.49	8.85	8.34	7.93	7.60	7.32	7.09
700	61.94	32.70	22.99	18.16	15.29	13.40	12.06	11.08	10.32	9.73	9.25	8.86	8.54	8.27
800	70.78	37.37	26.27	20.76	17.48	15.31	13.79	12.66	11.79	11.12	10.57	10.13	9.76	9.46
900	79.63	42.04	29.56	23.35	19.66	17.23	15.51	14.24	13.27	12.50	11.89	11.39	10.98	10.64
1000	88.48	46.71	32.84	25.95	21.85	19.14	17.23	15.82	14.74	13.89	13.21	12.66	12.20	11.82
2000	176.95	93.41	65.67	51.89	43.69	38.28	34.46	31.64	29.48	27.78	26.42	25.31	24.40	23.63
3000	265.43	140.11	98.51	77.83	65.53	57.42	51.69	47.45	44.21	41.67	39.63	37.97	36.59	35.45
4000	353.90	186.81	131.34	103.78	87.37	76.55	68.92	63.27	58.95	55.56	52.84	50.62	48.79	47.26
5000	442.38	233.51	164.17	129.72	109.22	95.69	86.14	79.09	73.69	69.45	66.05	63.28	60.99	59.08
6000	530.85	280.21	197.01	155.66	131.06	114.83	103.37	94.90	88.42	83.34	79.26	75.93	73.18	70.89
7000	619.33	326.91	229.84	181.60	152.90	133.96	120.60	110.72	103.16	97.22	92.46	88.58	85.38	82.70
8000	707.80	373.61	262.67	207.55	174.74	153.10	137.83	126.54	117.90	111.11	105.67	101.24	97.58	94.52
9000	796.28	420.31	295.51	233.49	196.59	172.24	155.05	142.35	132.63	125.00	118.88	113.89	109.77	106.33
10000	884.75	467.01	328.34	259.43	218.43	191.37	172.28	158.17	147.37	138.89	132.09	126.55	121.97	118.15
11000	973.23	513.71	361.17	285.38	240.27	210.51	189.51	173.99	162.11	152.78	145.30	139.20	134.17	129.96
12000	1061.70	560.41	394.01	311.32	262.11	229.65	206.74	189.80	176.84	166.67	158.51	151.86	146.36	141.77
13000	1150.18	607.11	426.84	337.26	283.95	248.78	223.97	205.62	191.58	180.55	171.71	164.51	156.56	153.59
14000	1238.65	653.82	459.67	363.20	305.80	267.92	241.19	221.44	206.32	194.44	184.92	177.16	170.75	165.40
15000	1327.13	700.52	492.51	389.15	327.64	287.06	258.42	237.25	221.05	208.33	198.13	189.82	182.95	177.22
16000	1415.60	747.22	525.34	415.09	349.48	306.19	275.65	253.07	235.79	222.22	211.34	202.47	195.15	189.03
17000	1504.08	793.92	558.17	441.03	371.32	325.33	292.88	268.89	250.53	236.11	224.55	215.13	207.34	200.84
18000	1592.55	840.62	591.01	466.97	393.17	344.47	310.10	284.70	265.26	250.00	237.76	227.78	219.54	212.66
19000	1681.03	887.32	623.84	492.92	415.01	363.60	327.33	300.52	280.00	263.89	250.97	240.43	231.74	224.47
20000	1769.50	934.02	656.68	518.86	436.85	382.74	344.56	316.34	294.74	277.77	264.17	253.09	243.93	236.29
21000	1857.98	980.72	689.51	544.80	458.69	401.88	361.79	332.15	309.47	291.66	277.38	265.74	256.13	248.10
22000	1946.45	1027.42	722.34	570.75	480.54	421.01	379.02	347.97	324.21	305.55	290.59	278.40	268.33	259.92
23000	2034.93	1074.12	755.18	596.69	502.38	440.15	396.24	363.78	338.95	319.44	303.80	291.05	280.52	271.73
24000	2123.40	1120.82	788.01	622.63	524.22	459.29	413.47	379.60	353.68	333.33	317.01	303.71	292.72	283.54
25000	2211.88	1167.52	820.84	648.57	546.06	478.42	430.70	395.42	368.42	347.22	330.22	316.36	304.92	295.36
26000	2300.35	1214.22	853.68	674.52	567.90	497.56	447.93	411.23	383.16	361.10	343.42	329.01	317.11	307.17
27000	2388.83	1260.93	886.51	700.46	589.75	516.70	465.15	427.05	397.89	374.99	356.63	341.67	329.31	318.99
28000	2477.30	1307.63	919.34	726.40	611.59	535.83	482.38	442.87	412.63	388.88	369.84	354.32	341.50	330.80
29000	2565.78	1354.33	952.18	752.34	633.43	554.97	499.61	458.68	427.37	402.77	383.05	366.98	353.70	342.61
30000	2654.25	1401.03	985.01	778.29	655.27	574.11	516.84	474.50	442.10	416.66	396.26	379.63	365.90	354.43
31000	2742.73	1447.73	1017.84	804.23	677.12	593.24	534.07	490.32	456.84	430.55	409.47	392.28	378.09	366.24
32000	2831.20	1494.43	1050.68	830.17	698.96	612.38	551.29	506.13	471.58	444.44	422.67	404.94	390.29	378.06
33000	2919.68	1541.13	1083.51	856.12	720.80	631.52	568.52	521.95	486.31	458.32	435.88	417.59	402.49	389.87
34000	3008.15	1587.83	1116.34	882.06	742.64	650.65	585.75	537.77	501.05	472.21	449.09	430.25	414.68	401.68
35000	3096.63	1634.53	1149.18	908.00	764.49	669.79	602.98	553.58	515.79	486.10	462.30	442.90	426.88	413.50
36000	3185.10	1681.23	1182.01	933.94	786.33	688.93	620.20	569.40	530.52	499.99	475.51	455.56	439.08	425.31
37000	3273.58	1727.93	1214.84	959.89	808.17	708.06	637.43	585.22	545.26	513.88	488.72	468.21	451.27	437.13
38000	3362.05	1774.63	1247.68	985.83	830.01	727.20	654.66	601.03	560.00	527.77	501.93	480.86	463.47	448.94
39000	3450.53	1821.33	1280.51	1011.77	851.85	746.34	671.89	616.85	574.73	541.65	515.13	493.52	475.66	460.75
40000	3539.00	1868.03	1313.35	1037.72	873.70	765.47	689.12	632.67	589.47	555.54	528.34	506.17	487.86	472.57
41000	3627.48	1914.74	1346.18	1063.66	895.54	784.61	706.34	648.48	604.21	569.43	541.55	518.83	500.06	484.38
42000	3715.95	1961.44	1379.01	1089.60	917.38	803.75	723.57	664.30	618.94	583.32	554.76	531.48	512.25	496.20
43000	3804.43	2008.14	1411.85	1115.54	939.22	822.88	740.80	680.11	633.68	597.21	567.97	544.13	524.45	508.01
44000	3892.90	2054.84	1444.68	1141.49	961.07	842.02	758.03	695.93	648.42	611.10	581.18	556.79	536.65	519.83
45000	3981.38	2101.54	1477.51	1167.43	982.91	861.16	775.25	711.75	663.15	624.99	594.38	569.44	548.84	531.64
46000	4069.85	2148.24	1510.35	1193.37	1004.75	880.29	792.48	727.56	677.89	638.87	607.59	582.10	561.04	543.45
47000	4158.33	2194.94	1543.18	1219.31	1026.59	899.43	809.71	743.38	692.63	652.76	620.80	594.75	573.24	555.27
48000	4246.80	2241.64	1576.01	1245.26	1048.44	918.57	826.94	759.20	707.36	666.65	634.01	607.41	585.43	567.08
49000	4335.28	2288.34	1608.85	1271.20	1070.28	937.70	844.17	775.01	722.10	680.54	647.22	620.06	597.63	578.90
50000	4423.75	2335.04	1641.68	1297.14	1092.12	956.84	861.39	790.83	736.84	694.43	660.43	632.71	609.83	590.71
55000	4866.13	2568.55	1805.85	1426.86	1201.33	1052.52	947.53	869.91	810.52	763.87	726.47	695.99	670.81	649.78
60000	5308.50	2802.05	1970.02	1556.57	1310.54	1148.21	1033.67	949.00	884.20	833.31	792.51	759.26	731.79	708.85
65000	5750.88	3035.55	2134.18	1686.28	1419.75	1243.89	1119.81	1028.08	957.89	902.75	858.55	822.53	792.77	767.92
70000	6193.25	3269.06	2298.35	1816.00	1528.97	1339.57	1205.95	1107.16	1031.57	972.20	924.59	885.80	853.75	826.99
75000	6635.63	3502.56	2462.52	1945.71	1638.18	1435.26	1292.09	1186.24	1105.25	1041.64	990.64	949.07	914.74	886.06
80000	7078.00	3736.06	2626.69	2075.43	1747.39	1530.94	1378.23	1265.33	1178.94	1111.08	1056.68	1012.34	975.72	945.13
85000	7520.38	3969.57	2790.85	2205.14	1856.60	1626.62	1464.37	1344.41	1252.62	1180.52	1122.72	1075.61	1036.70	1004.20
90000	7962.75	4203.07	2955.02	2334.85	1965.81	1722.31	1550.50	1423.49	1326.30	1249.97	1188.76	1138.88	1097.68	1063.27
95000	8405.13	4436.58	3119.19	2464.57	2075.02	1817.99	1636.64	1502.57	1399.99	1319.41	1254.81	1202.15	1158.66	1122.34
100000	8847.50	4670.08	3283.36	2594.28	2184.23	1913.67	1722.78	1581.66	1473.67	1388.85	1320.85	1265.42	1219.65	1181.41

TERM	15 Years	16 Years	17 Years	18 Years	19 Years	20 Years	21 Years	22 Years	23 Years	24 Years	25 Years	30 Years	35 Years	40 Years
AMOUNT														
5	.06	.06	.06	.06	.06	.06	.06	.06	.06	.06	.05	.05	.05	.05
10	.12	.12	.11	.11	.11	.11	.11	.11	.11	.11	.10	.10	.10	.10
15	.18	.17	.17	.17	.16	.16	.16	.16	.16	.16	.15	.15	.15	.15
25	.29	.29	.28	.27	.27	.27	.26	.26	.26	.26	.25	.25	.24	.24
50	.58	.57	.55	.54	.54	.53	.52	.52	.51	.51	.50	.49	.48	.48
75	.87	.85	.83	.81	.80	.79	.78	.77	.76	.76	.75	.73	.72	.71
100	1.15	1.13	1.10	1.08	1.07	1.05	1.04	1.03	1.02	1.01	1.00	.97	.96	.95
200	2.30	2.25	2.20	2.16	2.13	2.10	2.07	2.05	2.03	2.01	1.99	1.94	1.91	1.89
300	3.45	3.37	3.30	3.24	3.19	3.14	3.10	3.07	3.04	3.01	2.99	2.91	2.86	2.84
400	4.60	4.49	4.40	4.32	4.25	4.19	4.14	4.09	4.05	4.01	3.98	3.87	3.82	3.78
500	5.75	5.61	5.50	5.40	5.31	5.23	5.17	5.11	5.06	5.02	4.98	4.84	4.77	4.73
600	6.90	6.74	6.60	6.47	6.37	6.28	6.20	6.13	6.07	6.02	5.97	5.81	5.72	5.67
700	8.05	7.86	7.69	7.55	7.43	7.33	7.23	7.15	7.08	7.02	6.97	6.78	6.67	6.61
800	9.20	8.98	8.79	8.63	8.49	8.37	8.27	8.17	8.09	8.02	7.96	7.74	7.63	7.56
900	10.35	10.10	9.89	9.71	9.55	9.42	9.30	9.20	9.11	9.03	8.96	8.71	8.58	8.50
1000	11.50	11.22	10.99	10.79	10.61	10.46	10.33	10.22	10.12	10.03	9.95	9.68	9.53	9.45
2000	22.99	22.44	21.97	21.57	21.22	20.92	20.66	20.43	20.23	20.05	19.90	19.35	19.06	18.89
3000	34.48	33.66	32.96	32.35	31.83	31.38	30.99	30.64	30.34	30.08	29.84	29.03	28.58	28.33
4000	45.97	44.88	43.94	43.14	42.44	41.84	41.31	40.85	40.45	40.10	39.79	38.70	38.11	37.78
5000	57.46	56.10	54.93	53.92	53.05	52.30	51.64	51.07	50.56	50.12	49.74	48.38	47.63	47.22
6000	68.96	67.31	65.91	64.70	63.66	62.76	61.97	61.28	60.68	60.15	59.68	58.05	57.16	56.66
7000	80.45	78.53	76.89	75.49	74.27	73.21	72.29	71.49	70.79	70.17	69.63	67.73	66.69	66.10
8000	91.94	89.75	87.88	86.27	84.88	83.67	82.62	81.70	80.90	80.19	79.57	77.40	76.21	75.55
9000	103.43	100.97	98.86	97.05	95.49	94.13	92.95	91.92	91.01	90.22	89.52	87.08	85.74	84.99
10000	114.92	112.19	109.85	107.83	106.10	104.59	103.28	102.13	101.12	100.24	99.47	96.75	95.26	94.43
11000	126.42	123.40	120.83	118.62	116.71	115.05	113.60	112.34	111.24	110.27	109.41	106.43	104.79	103.87
12000	137.91	134.62	131.82	129.40	127.31	125.51	123.93	122.55	121.35	120.29	119.36	116.10	114.31	113.32
13000	149.40	145.84	142.80	140.18	137.92	135.96	134.26	132.77	131.46	130.31	129.30	125.78	123.84	122.76
14000	160.89	157.06	153.78	150.97	148.53	146.42	144.58	142.98	141.57	140.34	139.25	135.45	133.37	132.20
15000	172.38	168.28	164.77	161.75	159.14	156.88	154.91	153.19	151.68	150.36	149.20	145.12	142.89	141.64
16000	183.87	179.50	175.75	172.53	169.75	167.34	165.24	163.40	161.79	160.38	159.14	154.80	152.42	151.09
17000	195.37	190.71	186.74	183.32	180.36	177.80	175.56	173.61	171.91	170.41	169.09	164.47	161.94	160.53
18000	206.86	201.93	197.72	194.10	190.97	188.26	185.89	183.83	182.02	180.43	179.03	174.15	171.47	169.97
19000	218.35	213.15	208.70	204.88	201.58	198.71	196.22	194.04	192.13	190.45	188.98	183.82	181.00	179.41
20000	229.84	224.37	219.69	215.66	212.19	209.17	206.55	204.25	202.24	200.48	198.93	193.50	190.52	188.86
21000	241.33	235.59	230.67	226.45	222.80	219.63	216.87	214.46	212.35	210.50	208.87	203.17	200.05	198.30
22000	252.83	246.80	241.66	237.23	233.41	230.09	227.20	224.68	222.47	220.53	218.82	212.85	209.57	207.74
23000	264.32	258.02	252.64	248.01	244.02	240.55	237.53	234.89	232.50	230.55	228.76	222.52	219.10	217.18
24000	275.81	269.24	263.63	258.80	254.62	251.01	247.85	245.10	242.69	240.57	238.71	232.20	228.62	226.63
25000	287.30	280.46	274.61	269.58	265.23	261.46	258.18	255.31	252.80	250.60	248.66	241.87	238.15	236.07
26000	298.79	291.68	285.59	280.36	275.84	271.92	268.51	265.53	262.91	260.62	258.60	251.55	247.68	245.51
27000	310.29	302.90	296.58	291.15	286.45	282.38	278.83	275.74	273.03	270.64	268.55	261.22	257.20	254.96
28000	321.78	314.11	307.56	301.93	297.06	292.84	289.16	285.95	283.14	280.67	278.49	270.90	266.73	264.40
29000	333.27	325.33	318.55	312.71	307.67	303.30	299.49	296.16	293.25	290.69	288.44	280.57	276.25	273.84
30000	344.76	336.55	329.53	323.49	318.28	313.76	309.82	306.37	303.36	300.71	298.39	290.24	285.78	283.28
31000	356.25	347.77	340.51	334.28	328.89	324.21	320.14	316.59	313.47	310.74	308.33	299.92	295.30	292.73
32000	367.74	358.99	351.50	345.06	339.50	334.67	330.47	326.80	323.58	320.76	318.28	309.59	304.83	302.17
33000	379.24	370.20	362.48	355.84	350.11	345.13	340.80	337.01	333.70	330.79	328.22	319.27	314.36	311.61
34000	390.73	381.42	373.47	366.63	360.72	355.59	351.12	347.22	343.81	340.81	338.17	328.94	323.88	321.05
35000	402.22	392.64	384.45	377.41	371.33	366.05	361.45	357.44	353.92	350.83	348.12	338.62	333.41	330.50
36000	413.71	403.86	395.44	388.19	381.93	376.51	371.78	367.65	364.03	360.86	358.06	348.29	342.93	339.94
37000	425.20	415.08	406.42	398.98	392.54	386.96	382.10	377.86	374.14	370.88	368.01	357.97	352.46	349.38
38000	436.70	426.30	417.40	409.76	403.15	397.42	392.43	388.07	384.26	380.90	377.96	367.64	361.99	358.82
39000	448.19	437.51	428.39	420.54	413.76	407.88	402.76	398.29	394.37	390.93	387.90	377.32	371.51	368.27
40000	459.68	448.73	439.37	431.32	424.37	418.34	413.09	408.50	404.48	400.95	397.85	386.99	381.04	377.71
41000	471.17	459.95	450.36	442.11	434.98	428.80	423.41	418.71	414.59	410.98	407.79	396.67	390.56	387.15
42000	482.66	471.17	461.34	452.89	445.59	439.26	433.74	428.92	424.70	421.00	417.74	406.34	400.09	396.59
43000	494.16	482.39	472.32	463.67	456.20	449.71	444.07	439.14	434.82	431.02	427.69	416.02	409.61	406.04
44000	505.65	493.60	483.31	474.46	466.81	460.17	454.39	449.35	444.93	441.05	437.63	425.69	419.14	415.48
45000	517.14	504.82	494.29	485.24	477.42	470.63	464.72	459.56	455.04	451.07	447.58	435.36	428.67	424.92
46000	528.63	516.04	505.28	496.02	488.03	481.09	475.05	469.77	465.15	461.09	457.52	445.04	438.19	434.36
47000	540.12	527.26	516.26	506.80	498.64	491.55	485.38	479.98	475.26	471.12	467.47	454.71	447.72	443.81
48000	551.61	538.48	527.25	517.59	509.24	502.01	495.70	490.20	485.37	481.14	477.42	464.39	457.24	453.25
49000	563.11	549.70	538.23	528.37	519.85	512.46	506.03	500.41	495.49	491.16	487.36	474.06	466.77	462.69
50000	574.60	560.91	549.21	539.15	530.46	522.92	516.36	510.62	505.60	501.19	497.31	483.74	476.30	472.13
55000	632.06	617.00	604.13	593.07	583.51	575.21	567.99	561.68	556.16	551.31	547.04	532.11	523.92	519.35
60000	689.52	673.10	659.06	646.98	636.55	627.51	619.63	612.74	606.72	601.42	596.77	580.48	571.55	566.56
65000	746.98	729.19	713.98	700.90	689.60	679.80	671.26	663.81	657.28	651.54	646.50	628.86	619.18	613.77
70000	804.44	785.28	768.90	754.81	742.65	732.09	722.90	714.87	707.84	701.66	696.23	677.23	666.81	660.99
75000	861.90	841.37	823.82	808.73	795.69	784.38	774.53	765.93	758.40	751.78	745.96	725.60	714.44	708.20
80000	919.35	897.46	878.74	862.64	848.74	836.67	826.17	816.99	808.95	801.90	795.69	773.98	762.07	755.41
85000	976.81	953.55	933.66	916.56	901.78	888.96	877.80	868.05	859.51	852.02	845.42	822.35	809.70	802.63
90000	1034.27	1009.64	988.58	970.47	954.83	941.26	929.45	919.11	910.07	902.13	895.15	870.72	857.33	849.84
95000	1091.73	1065.73	1043.50	1024.39	1007.87	993.55	981.07	970.18	960.63	952.25	944.88	919.10	904.96	897.05
100000	1149.19	1121.82	1098.42	1078.30	1060.92	1045.84	1032.71	1021.24	1011.19	1002.37	994.61	967.47	952.59	944.26

MONTHLY PAYMENT
REQUIRED TO AMORTIZE A LOAN

TERM	1 Year	2 Years	3 Years	4 Years	5 Years	6 Years	7 Years	8 Years	9 Years	10 Years	11 Years	12 Years	13 Years	14 Years
AMOUNT														
5	.45	.24	.17	.15	.11	.10	.09	.09	.08	.07	.07	.07	.07	.06
10	.89	.47	.33	.26	.22	.20	.18	.16	.15	.14	.14	.13	.13	.12
15	1.33	.71	.50	.39	.33	.29	.26	.24	.23	.21	.20	.20	.19	.18
25	2.22	1.17	.83	.65	.55	.48	.44	.40	.37	.35	.34	.32	.31	.30
50	4.43	2.34	1.65	1.30	1.10	.96	.87	.80	.74	.70	.67	.64	.62	.60
75	6.64	3.51	2.47	1.95	1.65	1.44	1.30	1.19	1.11	1.05	1.00	.96	.92	.89
100	8.85	4.68	3.29	2.60	2.19	1.92	1.73	1.59	1.48	1.40	1.33	1.27	1.23	1.19
200	17.70	9.35	6.58	5.20	4.38	3.84	3.46	3.17	2.96	2.79	2.65	2.54	2.45	2.37
300	26.55	14.02	9.86	7.80	6.57	5.75	5.18	4.76	4.43	4.18	3.98	3.81	3.67	3.56
400	35.40	18.69	13.15	10.39	8.75	7.67	6.91	6.34	5.91	5.57	5.30	5.08	4.90	4.74
500	44.25	23.37	16.43	12.99	10.94	9.59	8.63	7.93	7.39	6.96	6.62	6.35	6.12	5.93
600	53.10	28.04	19.72	15.59	13.13	11.50	10.36	9.51	8.86	8.36	7.95	7.62	7.34	7.11
700	61.95	32.71	23.01	18.18	15.31	13.42	12.08	11.10	10.34	9.75	9.27	8.88	8.56	8.30
800	70.80	37.38	26.29	20.78	17.50	15.33	13.81	12.68	11.82	11.14	10.60	10.15	9.79	9.48
900	79.65	42.06	29.58	23.38	19.69	17.25	15.53	14.26	13.29	12.53	11.92	11.42	11.01	10.67
1000	88.50	46.73	32.86	25.97	21.87	19.17	17.26	15.85	14.77	13.92	13.24	12.69	12.23	11.85
2000	177.00	93.45	65.72	51.94	43.74	38.33	34.51	31.69	29.53	27.84	26.48	25.37	24.46	23.70
3000	265.50	140.18	98.58	77.91	65.61	57.49	51.77	47.54	44.30	41.76	39.72	38.06	36.69	35.54
4000	354.00	186.90	131.43	103.87	87.47	76.65	69.02	63.38	59.06	55.67	52.96	50.74	48.91	47.39
5000	442.50	233.62	164.29	129.84	109.34	95.82	86.28	79.22	73.83	69.59	66.19	63.42	61.14	59.23
6000	530.99	280.35	197.15	155.81	131.21	114.98	103.53	95.07	88.59	83.51	79.43	76.11	73.37	71.08
7000	619.49	327.07	230.01	181.77	153.08	134.14	120.78	110.91	103.36	97.42	92.67	88.79	85.59	82.92
8000	707.99	373.80	262.86	207.74	174.94	153.30	138.04	126.75	118.12	111.34	105.91	101.48	97.82	94.77
9000	796.49	420.52	295.72	233.71	196.81	172.47	155.29	142.60	132.88	125.26	119.14	114.16	110.05	106.61
10000	884.99	467.24	328.58	259.68	218.68	191.63	172.55	158.44	147.65	139.17	132.38	126.84	122.27	118.46
11000	973.49	513.97	361.43	285.64	240.55	210.79	189.80	174.28	162.41	153.09	145.62	139.53	134.50	130.30
12000	1061.98	560.69	394.29	311.61	262.41	229.95	207.06	190.13	177.18	167.01	158.86	152.21	146.73	142.15
13000	1150.48	607.42	427.15	337.58	284.28	249.12	224.31	205.97	191.94	180.92	172.09	164.90	158.95	153.99
14000	1238.98	654.14	460.01	363.54	306.15	268.28	241.56	221.82	206.71	194.84	185.33	177.58	171.18	165.84
15000	1327.48	700.86	492.86	389.51	328.01	287.44	258.82	237.66	221.47	208.76	198.57	190.26	183.41	177.68
16000	1415.98	747.59	525.72	415.48	349.88	306.60	276.07	253.50	236.24	222.68	211.81	202.95	195.63	189.53
17000	1504.48	794.31	558.58	441.45	371.75	325.77	293.33	269.35	251.00	236.59	225.04	215.63	207.86	201.37
18000	1592.97	841.04	591.44	467.41	393.62	344.93	310.58	285.19	265.76	250.51	238.28	228.32	220.09	213.22
19000	1681.47	887.76	624.29	493.38	415.48	364.09	327.83	301.03	280.53	264.43	251.52	241.00	232.31	225.06
20000	1769.97	934.48	657.15	519.35	437.35	383.25	345.09	316.88	295.29	278.34	264.76	253.68	244.54	236.91
21000	1858.47	981.21	690.01	545.31	459.22	402.41	362.34	332.72	310.06	292.26	277.99	266.37	256.77	248.75
22000	1946.97	1027.93	722.86	571.28	481.09	421.58	379.60	348.56	324.82	306.18	291.23	279.05	268.99	260.60
23000	2035.47	1074.66	755.72	597.25	502.95	440.74	396.85	364.41	339.59	320.09	304.47	291.74	281.22	272.44
24000	2123.96	1121.38	788.58	623.22	524.82	459.90	414.11	380.25	354.35	334.01	317.71	304.42	293.44	284.29
25000	2212.46	1168.10	821.44	649.18	546.69	479.06	431.36	396.09	369.12	347.93	330.94	317.10	305.67	296.13
26000	2300.96	1214.83	854.29	675.15	568.56	498.23	448.61	411.94	383.88	361.84	344.18	329.79	317.90	307.98
27000	2389.46	1261.55	887.15	701.12	590.42	517.39	465.87	427.78	398.64	375.76	357.42	342.47	330.13	319.82
28000	2477.96	1308.28	920.01	727.08	612.29	536.55	483.12	443.63	413.41	389.68	370.66	355.16	342.35	331.67
29000	2566.46	1355.00	952.86	753.05	634.16	555.71	500.38	459.47	428.17	403.59	383.89	367.84	354.58	343.51
30000	2654.95	1401.72	985.72	779.02	656.02	574.88	517.63	475.31	442.94	417.51	397.13	380.52	366.81	355.36
31000	2743.45	1448.45	1018.58	804.99	677.89	594.04	534.88	491.16	457.70	431.43	410.37	393.21	379.03	367.20
32000	2831.95	1495.17	1051.44	830.95	699.76	613.20	552.14	507.00	472.47	445.35	423.61	405.89	391.26	379.05
33000	2920.45	1541.90	1084.29	856.92	721.63	632.36	569.39	522.84	487.23	459.26	436.84	418.57	403.49	390.89
34000	3008.95	1588.62	1117.15	882.89	743.49	651.53	586.65	538.69	502.00	473.18	450.08	431.26	415.72	402.74
35000	3097.45	1635.34	1150.01	908.85	765.36	670.69	603.90	554.53	516.76	487.10	463.32	443.94	427.94	414.58
36000	3185.94	1682.07	1182.87	934.82	787.23	689.85	621.16	570.37	531.52	501.01	476.56	456.63	440.17	426.43
37000	3274.44	1728.79	1215.72	960.79	809.10	709.01	638.41	586.22	546.29	514.93	489.79	469.31	452.40	438.27
38000	3362.94	1775.52	1248.58	986.76	830.96	728.18	655.66	602.06	561.05	528.85	503.03	481.99	464.62	450.12
39000	3451.44	1822.24	1281.44	1012.72	852.83	747.34	672.92	617.90	575.82	542.76	516.27	494.68	476.85	461.96
40000	3539.94	1868.96	1314.29	1038.69	874.70	766.50	690.17	633.75	590.58	556.68	529.51	507.36	489.08	473.81
41000	3628.44	1915.69	1347.15	1064.66	896.56	785.66	707.43	649.59	605.35	570.60	542.74	520.05	501.30	485.65
42000	3716.93	1962.41	1380.01	1090.62	918.43	804.82	724.68	665.44	620.11	584.51	555.98	532.73	513.53	497.50
43000	3805.43	2009.14	1412.87	1116.59	940.30	823.99	741.93	681.28	634.87	598.43	569.22	545.41	525.76	509.34
44000	3893.93	2055.86	1445.72	1142.56	962.17	843.15	759.19	697.12	649.64	612.35	582.46	558.10	537.98	521.19
45000	3982.43	2102.58	1478.58	1168.52	984.03	862.31	776.44	712.97	664.40	626.27	595.69	570.78	550.21	533.03
46000	4070.93	2149.31	1511.44	1194.49	1005.90	881.47	793.70	728.81	679.17	640.18	608.93	583.47	562.44	544.88
47000	4159.43	2196.03	1544.30	1220.46	1027.77	900.64	810.95	744.65	693.93	654.10	622.17	596.15	574.66	556.72
48000	4247.92	2242.76	1577.15	1246.43	1049.64	919.80	828.21	760.50	708.70	668.02	635.41	608.83	586.89	568.57
49000	4336.42	2289.48	1610.01	1272.39	1071.50	938.96	845.46	776.34	723.46	681.93	648.64	621.52	599.12	580.41
50000	4424.92	2336.20	1642.87	1298.36	1093.37	958.12	862.71	792.18	738.23	695.85	661.88	634.20	611.34	592.26
55000	4867.41	2569.82	1807.15	1428.20	1202.71	1053.94	948.98	871.40	812.05	765.43	728.07	697.62	672.48	651.48
60000	5309.90	2803.44	1971.44	1558.03	1312.04	1149.75	1035.26	950.62	885.87	835.02	794.26	761.04	733.61	710.71
65000	5752.40	3037.06	2135.73	1687.87	1421.38	1245.56	1121.53	1029.84	959.69	904.60	860.44	824.46	794.75	769.94
70000	6194.89	3270.68	2300.01	1817.70	1530.72	1341.37	1207.80	1109.06	1033.51	974.19	926.63	887.88	855.88	829.16
75000	6637.38	3504.30	2464.30	1947.54	1640.05	1437.18	1294.07	1188.27	1107.34	1043.77	992.82	951.30	917.01	888.39
80000	7079.87	3737.92	2628.58	2077.37	1749.39	1532.99	1380.34	1267.49	1181.16	1113.36	1059.01	1014.72	978.15	947.61
85000	7522.36	3971.54	2792.87	2207.21	1858.73	1628.81	1466.61	1346.71	1254.98	1182.94	1125.19	1078.14	1039.28	1006.84
90000	7964.85	4205.16	2957.16	2337.04	1968.06	1724.62	1552.88	1425.93	1328.80	1252.53	1191.38	1141.56	1100.41	1066.06
95000	8407.35	4438.78	3121.44	2466.88	2077.40	1820.43	1639.15	1505.15	1402.62	1322.11	1257.57	1204.98	1161.55	1125.29
100000	8849.84	4672.40	3285.73	2596.71	2186.74	1916.24	1725.42	1584.36	1476.45	1391.69	1323.76	1268.40	1222.68	1184.51

TERM	15 Years	16 Years	17 Years	18 Years	19 Years	20 Years	21 Years	22 Years	23 Years	24 Years	25 Years	30 Years	35 Years	40 Years
AMOUNT														
5	.06	.06	.06	.06	.06	.06	.06	.06	.06	.06	.05	.05	.05	.05
10	.12	.12	.12	.11	.11	.11	.11	.11	.11	.11	.10	.10	.10	.10
15	.18	.17	.17	.17	.16	.16	.16	.16	.16	.16	.15	.15	.15	.15
25	.29	.29	.28	.28	.27	.27	.26	.26	.26	.26	.25	.25	.24	.24
50	.58	.57	.56	.55	.54	.53	.52	.52	.51	.51	.50	.49	.48	.48
75	.87	.85	.83	.82	.80	.79	.78	.77	.77	.76	.75	.73	.72	.72
100	1.16	1.13	1.11	1.09	1.07	1.05	1.04	1.03	1.02	1.01	1.00	.98	.96	.95
200	2.31	2.26	2.21	2.17	2.13	2.10	2.08	2.05	2.03	2.02	2.00	1.95	1.92	1.90
300	3.46	3.38	3.31	3.25	3.20	3.15	3.11	3.08	3.05	3.02	3.00	2.92	2.87	2.85
400	4.61	4.51	4.41	4.33	4.26	4.20	4.15	4.10	4.06	4.03	4.00	3.89	3.83	3.80
500	5.77	5.63	5.51	5.41	5.33	5.25	5.19	5.13	5.08	5.03	5.00	4.86	4.79	4.75
600	6.92	6.76	6.62	6.49	6.39	6.30	6.22	6.15	6.09	6.04	5.99	5.83	5.74	5.69
700	8.07	7.88	7.72	7.58	7.46	7.35	7.26	7.18	7.11	7.05	6.99	6.80	6.70	6.64
800	9.22	9.01	8.82	8.66	8.52	8.40	8.29	8.20	8.12	8.05	7.99	7.78	7.66	7.59
900	10.38	10.13	9.92	9.74	9.58	9.45	9.33	9.23	9.14	9.06	8.99	8.75	8.61	8.54
1000	11.53	11.26	11.02	10.82	10.65	10.50	10.37	10.25	10.15	10.06	9.99	9.72	9.57	9.49
2000	23.05	22.51	22.04	21.64	21.29	20.99	20.73	20.50	20.30	20.12	19.97	19.43	19.13	18.97
3000	34.58	33.76	33.06	32.45	31.93	31.48	31.09	30.75	30.45	30.18	29.95	29.14	28.70	28.45
4000	46.10	45.01	44.07	43.27	42.58	41.98	41.45	40.99	40.59	40.24	39.93	38.86	38.26	37.94
5000	57.62	56.26	55.09	54.09	53.22	52.47	51.81	51.24	50.74	50.30	49.92	48.57	47.83	47.42
6000	69.15	67.51	66.11	64.90	63.86	62.96	62.18	61.49	60.89	60.36	59.90	58.28	57.39	56.90
7000	80.67	78.76	77.12	75.72	74.51	73.45	72.54	71.74	71.04	70.42	69.88	67.99	66.96	66.38
8000	92.19	90.01	88.14	86.53	85.15	83.95	82.90	81.98	81.18	80.48	79.86	77.71	76.52	75.87
9000	103.72	101.26	99.16	97.35	95.79	94.44	93.26	92.23	91.33	90.54	89.85	87.42	86.09	85.35
10000	115.24	112.51	110.17	108.17	106.43	104.93	103.62	102.48	101.48	100.60	99.83	97.13	95.65	94.83
11000	126.76	123.76	121.19	118.98	117.08	115.42	113.98	112.73	111.63	110.66	109.81	106.84	105.22	104.31
12000	138.29	135.01	132.21	129.80	127.72	125.92	124.35	122.97	121.77	120.72	119.79	116.56	114.78	113.80
13000	149.81	146.26	143.22	140.62	138.36	136.41	134.71	133.22	131.92	130.70	129.70	126.27	124.35	123.28
14000	161.33	157.51	154.24	151.43	149.01	146.90	145.07	143.47	142.07	140.84	139.76	135.98	133.91	132.76
15000	172.86	168.76	165.26	162.25	159.65	157.39	155.43	153.72	152.22	150.90	149.74	145.69	143.48	142.24
16000	184.38	180.01	176.27	173.06	170.29	167.89	165.79	163.96	162.36	160.96	159.72	155.41	153.04	151.73
17000	195.90	191.26	187.29	183.88	180.93	178.38	176.15	174.21	172.51	171.02	169.71	165.12	162.61	161.21
18000	207.43	202.51	198.31	194.70	191.58	188.87	186.52	184.46	182.66	181.08	179.69	174.83	172.17	170.69
19000	218.95	213.76	209.33	205.51	202.22	199.36	196.88	194.71	192.81	191.14	189.67	184.54	181.74	180.17
20000	230.47	225.01	220.34	216.33	212.86	209.86	207.24	204.95	202.95	201.20	199.65	194.26	191.30	189.66
21000	242.00	236.26	231.36	227.15	223.51	220.35	217.60	215.20	213.10	211.26	209.64	203.97	200.87	199.14
22000	253.52	247.51	242.38	237.96	234.15	230.84	227.96	225.45	223.25	221.32	219.62	213.68	210.43	208.62
23000	265.04	258.76	253.39	248.78	244.79	241.33	238.32	235.70	233.40	231.30	229.60	223.40	220.00	218.10
24000	276.57	270.01	264.41	259.59	255.43	251.83	248.69	245.94	243.54	241.44	239.58	233.11	229.56	227.59
25000	288.09	281.26	275.43	270.41	266.08	262.32	259.05	256.19	253.69	251.50	249.56	242.82	239.13	237.07
26000	299.61	292.51	286.44	281.23	276.72	272.81	269.41	266.44	263.84	261.56	259.55	252.53	248.69	246.55
27000	311.14	303.76	297.46	292.04	287.36	283.30	279.77	276.69	273.99	271.61	269.53	262.25	258.26	256.03
28000	322.66	315.01	308.48	302.86	298.01	293.80	290.13	286.93	284.13	281.67	279.51	271.96	267.82	265.52
29000	334.18	326.26	319.49	313.67	308.65	304.29	300.49	297.18	294.28	291.73	289.49	281.67	277.39	275.00
30000	345.71	337.51	330.51	324.49	319.29	314.78	310.86	307.43	304.43	301.79	299.48	291.38	286.95	284.48
31000	357.23	348.76	341.53	335.31	329.93	325.27	321.22	317.68	314.58	311.85	309.46	301.10	296.52	293.96
32000	368.76	360.02	352.54	346.12	340.58	335.77	331.58	327.92	324.72	321.91	319.44	310.81	306.08	303.45
33000	380.28	371.27	363.56	356.94	351.22	346.26	341.94	338.17	334.87	331.97	329.42	320.52	315.65	312.93
34000	391.80	382.52	374.58	367.76	361.86	356.75	352.30	348.42	345.02	342.03	339.41	330.23	325.21	322.41
35000	403.33	393.77	385.60	378.57	372.51	367.24	362.66	358.67	355.16	352.09	349.39	339.95	334.78	331.90
36000	414.85	405.02	396.61	389.39	383.15	377.74	373.03	368.91	365.31	362.15	359.37	349.66	344.34	341.38
37000	426.37	416.27	407.63	400.20	393.79	388.23	383.39	379.16	375.46	372.21	369.35	359.37	353.91	350.86
38000	437.90	427.52	418.65	411.02	404.43	398.72	393.75	389.41	385.61	382.27	379.34	369.08	363.47	360.34
39000	449.42	438.77	429.66	421.84	415.08	409.21	404.11	399.66	395.75	392.33	389.32	378.80	373.04	369.83
40000	460.94	450.02	440.68	432.65	425.72	419.71	414.47	409.90	405.90	402.39	399.30	388.51	382.60	379.31
41000	472.47	461.27	451.70	443.47	436.36	430.20	424.84	420.15	416.05	412.45	409.28	398.22	392.17	388.79
42000	483.99	472.52	462.71	454.29	447.01	440.69	435.20	430.40	426.20	422.51	419.27	407.93	401.73	398.27
43000	495.51	483.77	473.73	465.10	457.65	451.19	445.56	440.65	436.34	432.57	429.25	417.65	411.30	407.76
44000	507.04	495.02	484.75	475.92	468.29	461.68	455.92	450.89	446.49	442.63	439.23	427.36	420.86	417.24
45000	518.56	506.27	495.76	486.73	478.93	472.17	466.28	461.14	456.64	452.69	449.21	437.07	430.43	426.72
46000	530.08	517.52	506.78	497.55	489.58	482.66	476.64	471.39	466.79	462.75	459.20	446.79	439.99	436.20
47000	541.61	528.77	517.80	508.37	500.22	493.16	487.01	481.64	476.93	472.81	469.18	456.50	449.56	445.69
48000	553.13	540.02	528.81	519.18	510.86	503.65	497.37	491.88	487.08	482.87	479.16	466.21	459.12	455.17
49000	564.65	551.27	539.83	530.00	521.51	514.14	507.73	502.13	497.23	492.93	489.14	475.92	468.69	464.65
50000	576.18	562.52	550.85	540.82	532.15	524.63	518.09	512.38	507.38	502.99	499.12	485.64	478.25	474.13
55000	633.79	618.77	605.93	594.90	585.36	577.10	569.90	563.62	558.11	553.28	549.04	534.20	526.08	521.55
60000	691.41	675.02	661.02	648.98	638.58	629.56	621.71	614.85	608.85	603.58	598.95	582.76	573.90	568.96
65000	749.03	731.28	716.10	703.06	691.79	682.02	673.52	666.09	659.59	653.88	648.86	631.32	621.73	616.37
70000	806.65	787.53	771.19	757.14	745.01	734.48	725.32	717.33	710.32	704.18	698.77	679.89	669.55	663.79
75000	864.26	843.78	826.27	811.22	798.22	786.95	777.13	768.56	761.06	754.48	748.68	728.45	717.38	711.20
80000	921.88	900.03	881.35	865.30	851.44	839.41	828.94	819.80	811.80	804.77	798.60	777.01	765.20	758.61
85000	979.50	956.28	936.44	919.38	904.65	891.87	880.75	871.04	862.54	855.07	848.51	825.58	813.02	806.02
90000	1037.12	1012.53	991.52	973.46	957.86	944.34	932.56	922.28	913.27	905.37	898.42	874.14	860.85	853.44
95000	1094.73	1068.79	1046.61	1027.54	1011.08	996.80	984.37	973.51	964.01	955.67	948.33	922.70	908.67	900.85
100000	1152.35	1125.04	1101.69	1081.63	1064.29	1049.26	1036.18	1024.75	1014.75	1005.97	998.24	971.27	956.50	948.26

11.300%

TERM AMOUNT	1 Year	2 Years	3 Years	4 Years	5 Years	6 Years	7 Years	8 Years	9 Years	10 Years	11 Years	12 Years	13 Years	14 Years
5	.45	.24	.17	.13	.11	.10	.09	.08	.08	.07	.07	.07	.07	.06
10	.89	.47	.33	.26	.22	.20	.18	.16	.15	.14	.14	.13	.13	.12
15	1.33	.71	.50	.39	.33	.29	.26	.24	.23	.21	.20	.20	.19	.18
25	2.22	1.17	.83	.65	.55	.48	.44	.40	.37	.35	.34	.32	.31	.30
50	4.43	2.34	1.65	1.30	1.10	.96	.87	.80	.74	.70	.67	.64	.62	.60
75	6.64	3.51	2.47	1.95	1.65	1.44	1.30	1.20	1.11	1.05	1.00	.96	.92	.90
100	8.86	4.68	3.29	2.60	2.19	1.92	1.73	1.59	1.48	1.40	1.33	1.28	1.23	1.19
200	17.71	9.35	6.58	5.20	4.38	3.84	3.46	3.18	2.96	2.79	2.66	2.55	2.46	2.38
300	26.56	14.03	9.87	7.80	6.57	5.76	5.19	4.77	4.44	4.19	3.98	3.82	3.68	3.57
400	35.41	18.70	13.16	10.40	8.76	7.68	6.92	6.35	5.92	5.58	5.31	5.09	4.91	4.76
500	44.27	23.38	16.45	13.00	10.95	9.60	8.65	7.94	7.40	6.98	6.64	6.36	6.13	5.94
600	53.12	28.05	19.73	15.60	13.14	11.52	10.37	9.53	8.88	8.37	7.96	7.63	7.36	7.13
700	61.97	32.73	23.02	18.20	15.33	13.44	12.10	11.11	10.36	9.77	9.29	8.90	8.59	8.32
800	70.82	37.40	26.31	20.80	17.52	15.36	13.83	12.70	11.84	11.16	10.62	10.18	9.81	9.51
900	79.67	42.08	29.60	23.40	19.71	17.27	15.56	14.29	13.32	12.56	11.94	11.45	11.04	10.69
1000	88.53	46.75	32.89	26.00	21.90	19.19	17.29	15.88	14.80	13.95	13.27	12.72	12.26	11.88
2000	177.05	93.50	65.77	51.99	43.79	38.38	34.57	31.75	29.59	27.90	26.54	25.43	24.52	23.76
3000	265.57	140.25	98.65	77.98	65.68	57.57	51.85	47.62	44.38	41.84	39.80	38.15	36.78	35.63
4000	354.09	186.99	131.53	103.97	87.57	76.76	69.13	63.49	59.17	55.79	53.07	50.86	49.03	47.51
5000	442.61	233.74	164.41	129.96	109.47	95.95	86.41	79.36	73.97	69.73	66.34	63.57	61.29	59.39
6000	531.13	280.49	197.29	155.95	131.36	115.13	103.69	95.23	88.76	83.68	79.60	76.29	73.55	71.26
7000	619.66	327.24	230.17	181.95	153.25	134.32	120.97	111.10	103.55	97.62	92.87	89.00	85.81	83.14
8000	708.18	373.98	263.05	207.94	175.14	153.51	138.25	126.97	118.34	111.57	106.14	101.71	98.06	95.01
9000	796.70	420.73	295.93	233.93	197.04	172.70	155.53	142.84	133.13	125.51	119.40	114.43	110.32	106.89
10000	885.22	467.48	328.81	259.92	218.93	191.89	172.81	158.71	147.93	139.46	132.67	127.14	122.58	118.77
11000	973.74	514.22	361.70	285.91	240.82	211.07	190.09	174.58	162.72	153.40	145.94	139.86	134.83	130.64
12000	1062.26	560.97	394.58	311.90	262.71	230.26	207.37	190.45	177.51	167.35	159.20	152.57	147.09	142.52
13000	1150.79	607.72	427.46	337.89	284.61	249.45	224.65	206.32	192.30	181.29	172.47	165.28	159.35	154.39
14000	1239.31	654.47	460.34	363.89	306.50	268.64	241.93	222.19	207.10	195.24	185.74	178.00	171.61	166.27
15000	1327.83	701.21	493.22	389.88	328.39	287.83	259.21	238.07	221.89	209.19	199.00	190.71	183.86	178.15
16000	1416.35	747.96	526.10	415.87	350.28	307.01	276.49	253.94	236.68	223.13	212.27	203.42	196.12	190.02
17000	1504.87	794.71	558.98	441.86	372.17	326.20	293.77	269.81	251.47	237.08	225.54	216.14	208.38	201.90
18000	1593.39	841.46	591.86	467.85	394.07	345.39	311.06	285.68	266.26	251.02	238.80	228.85	220.63	213.77
19000	1681.92	888.20	624.74	493.84	415.96	364.58	328.34	301.55	281.06	264.97	252.07	241.57	232.89	225.65
20000	1770.44	934.95	657.62	519.83	437.85	383.77	345.62	317.42	295.85	278.91	265.34	254.28	245.15	237.53
21000	1858.96	981.70	690.51	545.83	459.74	402.95	362.90	333.29	310.64	292.86	278.60	266.99	257.41	249.40
22000	1947.48	1028.44	723.39	571.82	481.64	422.14	380.18	349.16	325.43	306.80	291.87	279.71	269.66	261.28
23000	2036.00	1075.19	756.27	597.81	503.53	441.33	397.46	365.03	340.23	320.75	305.14	292.42	281.92	273.16
24000	2124.52	1121.94	789.15	623.80	525.42	460.52	414.74	380.90	355.02	334.69	318.40	305.13	294.18	285.03
25000	2213.05	1168.69	822.03	649.79	547.31	479.71	432.02	396.77	369.81	348.64	331.67	317.85	306.43	296.91
26000	2301.57	1215.43	854.91	675.78	569.21	498.90	449.30	412.64	384.60	362.58	344.94	330.56	318.69	308.78
27000	2390.09	1262.18	887.79	701.77	591.10	518.08	466.58	428.51	399.39	376.53	358.20	343.28	330.95	320.66
28000	2478.61	1308.93	920.67	727.77	612.99	537.27	483.86	444.38	414.19	390.48	371.47	355.99	343.21	332.54
29000	2567.13	1355.68	953.55	753.76	634.88	556.46	501.14	460.26	428.98	404.42	384.74	368.70	355.46	344.41
30000	2655.65	1402.42	986.43	779.75	656.78	575.65	518.42	476.13	443.77	418.37	398.00	381.42	367.72	356.29
31000	2744.18	1449.17	1019.32	805.74	678.67	594.84	535.70	492.00	458.56	432.31	411.27	394.13	379.98	368.16
32000	2832.70	1495.92	1052.20	831.73	700.56	614.02	552.98	507.87	473.36	446.26	424.54	406.84	392.23	380.04
33000	2921.22	1542.66	1085.08	857.72	722.45	633.21	570.26	523.74	488.15	460.20	437.80	419.56	404.49	391.92
34000	3009.74	1589.41	1117.96	883.71	744.34	652.40	587.54	539.61	502.94	474.15	451.07	432.27	416.75	403.79
35000	3098.26	1636.16	1150.84	909.71	766.24	671.59	604.83	555.48	517.73	488.09	464.34	444.98	429.01	415.67
36000	3186.78	1682.91	1183.72	935.70	788.13	690.78	622.11	571.35	532.52	502.04	477.60	457.70	441.26	427.54
37000	3275.31	1729.65	1216.60	961.69	810.02	709.96	639.39	587.22	547.32	515.98	490.87	470.41	453.52	439.42
38000	3363.83	1776.40	1249.48	987.68	831.91	729.15	656.67	603.09	562.11	529.93	504.14	483.13	465.78	451.30
39000	3452.35	1823.15	1282.36	1013.67	853.81	748.34	673.95	618.96	576.90	543.87	517.40	495.84	478.04	463.17
40000	3540.87	1869.89	1315.24	1039.66	875.70	767.53	691.23	634.83	591.69	557.82	530.67	508.55	490.29	475.05
41000	3629.39	1916.64	1348.12	1065.65	897.59	786.72	708.51	650.70	606.49	571.76	543.94	521.27	502.55	486.92
42000	3717.91	1963.39	1381.01	1091.65	919.48	805.90	725.79	666.57	621.28	585.71	557.20	533.98	514.81	498.80
43000	3806.44	2010.14	1413.89	1117.64	941.38	825.09	743.07	682.44	636.07	599.66	570.47	546.69	527.06	510.68
44000	3894.96	2056.88	1446.77	1143.63	963.27	844.28	760.35	698.32	650.86	613.60	583.74	559.41	539.32	522.55
45000	3983.48	2103.63	1479.65	1169.62	985.16	863.47	777.63	714.19	665.65	627.55	597.00	572.12	551.58	534.43
46000	4072.00	2150.38	1512.53	1195.61	1007.05	882.66	794.91	730.06	680.45	641.49	610.27	584.84	563.84	546.31
47000	4160.52	2197.13	1545.41	1221.61	1028.94	901.85	812.19	745.93	695.24	655.44	623.54	597.55	576.09	558.18
48000	4249.04	2243.87	1578.29	1247.59	1050.84	921.03	829.47	761.80	710.03	669.38	636.80	610.26	588.35	570.06
49000	4337.57	2290.62	1611.17	1273.59	1072.73	940.22	846.75	777.67	724.82	683.33	650.07	622.98	600.61	581.93
50000	4426.09	2337.37	1644.05	1299.58	1094.62	959.41	864.03	793.54	739.62	697.27	663.34	635.69	612.86	593.81
55000	4868.70	2571.10	1808.46	1429.53	1204.08	1055.35	950.44	872.89	813.58	767.00	729.67	699.26	674.15	653.19
60000	5311.30	2804.84	1972.86	1559.49	1313.55	1151.29	1036.84	952.25	887.54	836.73	796.00	762.83	735.44	712.57
65000	5753.91	3038.58	2137.27	1689.44	1423.01	1247.23	1123.24	1031.60	961.50	906.45	862.34	826.40	796.72	771.95
70000	6196.52	3272.31	2301.67	1819.41	1532.47	1343.17	1209.65	1110.95	1035.46	976.18	928.67	889.96	858.01	831.33
75000	6639.13	3506.05	2466.08	1949.36	1641.93	1439.11	1296.05	1190.31	1109.42	1045.91	995.00	953.53	919.29	890.71
80000	7081.74	3739.78	2630.48	2079.32	1751.39	1535.05	1382.45	1269.66	1183.38	1115.63	1061.34	1017.10	980.58	950.09
85000	7524.35	3973.52	2794.89	2209.28	1860.85	1630.99	1468.85	1349.01	1257.34	1185.36	1127.67	1080.67	1041.87	1009.47
90000	7966.95	4207.26	2959.29	2339.24	1970.32	1726.93	1555.26	1428.37	1331.30	1255.09	1194.00	1144.24	1103.15	1068.85
95000	8409.56	4440.99	3123.70	2469.19	2079.78	1822.87	1641.66	1507.72	1405.26	1324.81	1260.34	1207.81	1164.44	1128.23
100000	8852.17	4674.73	3288.10	2599.15	2189.24	1918.81	1728.06	1587.07	1479.23	1394.54	1326.67	1271.38	1225.72	1187.61

TERM AMOUNT	15 Years	16 Years	17 Years	18 Years	19 Years	20 Years	21 Years	22 Years	23 Years	24 Years	25 Years	30 Years	35 Years	40 Years
5	.06	.06	.06	.06	.06	.06	.06	.06	.06	.06	.06	.05	.05	.05
10	.12	.12	.12	.11	.11	.11	.11	.11	.11	.11	.11	.10	.10	.10
15	.18	.17	.17	.17	.17	.16	.16	.16	.16	.16	.16	.15	.15	.15
25	.29	.29	.28	.28	.27	.27	.26	.26	.26	.26	.26	.25	.25	.24
50	.58	.57	.56	.55	.54	.53	.52	.52	.51	.51	.51	.49	.49	.48
75	.87	.85	.83	.82	.81	.79	.78	.78	.77	.76	.76	.74	.73	.72
100	1.16	1.13	1.11	1.09	1.07	1.06	1.04	1.03	1.02	1.01	1.01	.98	.97	.96
200	2.32	2.26	2.21	2.17	2.14	2.11	2.08	2.06	2.04	2.02	2.01	1.96	1.93	1.91
300	3.47	3.39	3.32	3.26	3.21	3.16	3.12	3.09	3.06	3.03	3.01	2.93	2.89	2.86
400	4.63	4.52	4.42	4.34	4.28	4.22	4.16	4.12	4.08	4.04	4.01	3.91	3.85	3.81
500	5.78	5.65	5.53	5.43	5.34	5.27	5.20	5.15	5.10	5.05	5.01	4.88	4.81	4.77
600	6.94	6.77	6.63	6.51	6.41	6.32	6.24	6.17	6.11	6.06	6.02	5.86	5.77	5.72
700	8.09	7.90	7.74	7.60	7.48	7.37	7.28	7.20	7.13	7.07	7.02	6.83	6.73	6.67
800	9.25	9.03	8.84	8.68	8.55	8.43	8.32	8.23	8.15	8.08	8.02	7.81	7.69	7.62
900	10.40	10.16	9.95	9.77	9.61	9.48	9.36	9.26	9.17	9.09	9.02	8.78	8.65	8.58
1000	11.56	11.29	11.05	10.85	10.68	10.53	10.40	10.29	10.19	10.10	10.02	9.76	9.61	9.53
2000	23.12	22.57	22.10	21.70	21.36	21.06	20.80	20.57	20.37	20.20	20.04	19.51	19.21	19.05
3000	34.67	33.85	33.15	32.55	32.03	31.59	31.19	30.85	30.55	30.29	30.06	29.26	28.82	28.57
4000	46.23	45.14	44.20	43.40	42.71	42.11	41.59	41.14	40.74	40.39	40.08	39.01	38.42	38.10
5000	57.78	56.42	55.25	54.25	53.39	52.64	51.99	51.42	50.92	50.48	50.10	48.76	48.03	47.62
6000	69.34	67.70	66.30	65.10	64.06	63.17	62.38	61.70	61.10	60.58	60.12	58.51	57.63	57.14
7000	80.89	78.98	77.35	75.95	74.74	73.69	72.78	71.98	71.29	70.67	70.14	68.26	67.23	66.66
8000	92.45	90.27	88.40	86.80	85.42	84.22	83.18	82.27	81.47	80.77	80.16	78.01	76.84	76.19
9000	104.00	101.55	99.45	97.65	96.09	94.75	93.57	92.55	91.65	90.87	90.17	87.76	86.44	85.71
10000	115.56	112.83	110.50	108.50	106.77	105.27	103.97	102.83	101.84	100.96	100.19	97.51	96.05	95.23
11000	127.11	124.11	121.55	119.35	117.45	115.80	114.37	113.11	112.02	111.06	110.21	107.26	105.65	104.75
12000	138.67	135.40	132.60	130.20	128.12	126.33	124.76	123.40	122.20	121.15	120.23	117.01	115.25	114.28
13000	150.22	146.68	143.65	141.05	138.80	136.85	135.16	133.68	132.38	131.25	130.25	126.76	124.86	123.80
14000	161.78	157.96	154.70	151.90	149.48	147.38	145.56	143.96	142.57	141.34	140.27	136.51	134.46	133.32
15000	173.33	169.24	165.75	162.75	160.15	157.91	155.95	154.24	152.75	151.44	150.29	146.26	144.07	142.84
16000	184.89	180.53	176.80	173.60	170.83	168.43	166.35	164.53	162.93	161.53	160.31	156.01	153.67	152.37
17000	196.44	191.81	187.85	184.45	181.51	178.96	176.74	174.81	173.12	171.63	170.32	165.77	163.27	161.89
18000	208.00	203.09	198.90	195.30	192.10	189.49	187.14	185.09	183.30	181.73	180.34	175.52	172.88	171.41
19000	219.55	214.37	209.95	206.14	202.86	200.01	197.54	195.37	193.48	191.82	190.36	185.27	182.48	180.93
20000	231.11	225.66	221.00	216.99	213.54	210.54	207.93	205.66	203.67	201.92	200.38	195.02	192.09	190.46
21000	242.66	236.94	232.05	227.84	224.21	221.07	218.33	215.94	213.85	212.01	210.40	204.77	201.69	199.98
22000	254.22	248.22	243.10	238.69	234.89	231.60	228.73	226.22	224.03	222.11	220.42	214.52	211.30	209.50
23000	265.77	259.50	254.15	249.54	245.57	242.12	239.12	236.51	234.21	232.20	230.44	224.27	220.90	219.02
24000	277.33	270.79	265.20	260.39	256.24	252.65	249.52	246.79	244.40	242.30	240.46	234.02	230.50	228.55
25000	288.88	282.07	276.25	271.24	266.92	263.18	259.92	257.07	254.58	252.40	250.47	243.77	240.11	238.07
26000	300.44	293.35	287.29	282.09	277.60	273.70	270.31	267.35	264.76	262.49	260.49	253.52	249.71	247.59
27000	311.99	304.63	298.34	292.94	288.27	284.23	280.71	277.64	274.95	272.59	270.51	263.27	259.32	257.11
28000	323.55	315.92	309.39	303.79	298.95	294.76	291.11	287.92	285.13	282.68	280.53	273.02	268.92	266.64
29000	335.10	327.20	320.44	314.64	309.63	305.28	301.50	298.20	295.31	292.78	290.55	282.77	278.52	276.16
30000	346.66	338.48	331.49	325.49	320.30	315.81	311.90	308.48	305.50	302.87	300.57	292.52	288.13	285.68
31000	358.21	349.76	342.54	336.34	330.98	326.34	322.29	318.77	315.68	312.97	310.59	302.27	297.73	295.20
32000	369.77	361.05	353.59	347.19	341.66	336.86	332.69	329.05	325.86	323.06	320.61	312.02	307.33	304.73
33000	381.32	372.33	364.64	358.04	352.33	347.39	343.09	339.33	336.04	333.16	330.62	321.77	316.94	314.25
34000	392.88	383.61	375.69	368.89	363.01	357.92	353.48	349.61	346.23	343.26	340.64	331.53	326.54	323.77
35000	404.43	394.89	386.74	379.74	373.69	368.44	363.88	359.90	356.41	353.35	350.66	341.28	336.15	333.30
36000	415.99	406.18	397.79	390.59	384.36	378.97	374.28	370.18	366.59	363.45	360.68	351.03	345.75	342.82
37000	427.54	417.46	408.84	401.44	395.04	389.50	384.67	380.46	376.78	373.54	370.70	360.78	355.36	352.34
38000	439.10	428.74	419.89	412.28	405.72	400.02	395.07	390.74	386.96	383.64	380.72	370.53	364.96	361.86
39000	450.65	440.02	430.94	423.13	416.39	410.55	405.47	401.03	397.14	393.73	390.74	380.28	374.57	371.39
40000	462.21	451.31	441.99	433.98	427.07	421.08	415.86	411.31	407.33	403.83	400.76	390.03	384.17	380.91
41000	473.76	462.59	453.04	444.83	437.75	431.60	426.26	421.59	417.51	413.93	410.77	399.78	393.77	390.43
42000	485.32	473.87	464.09	455.68	448.42	442.13	436.66	431.88	427.69	424.02	420.79	409.53	403.38	399.95
43000	496.87	485.15	475.14	466.53	459.10	452.66	447.05	442.16	437.87	434.12	430.81	419.28	412.98	409.48
44000	508.43	496.44	486.19	477.38	469.78	463.19	457.45	452.44	448.06	444.22	440.83	429.03	422.59	419.00
45000	519.98	507.72	497.24	488.23	480.45	473.71	467.84	462.72	458.24	454.31	450.85	438.78	432.19	428.52
46000	531.54	519.00	508.29	499.08	491.13	484.24	478.24	473.01	468.42	464.40	460.87	448.53	441.79	438.04
47000	543.09	530.28	519.34	509.93	501.81	494.77	488.64	483.29	478.61	474.50	470.89	458.28	451.40	447.57
48000	554.65	541.57	530.39	520.78	512.48	505.29	499.03	493.57	488.79	484.59	480.91	468.03	461.00	457.09
49000	566.20	552.85	541.44	531.63	523.16	515.82	509.43	503.85	498.97	494.69	490.92	477.78	470.61	466.61
50000	577.76	564.13	552.49	542.48	533.84	526.35	519.83	514.14	509.16	504.79	500.94	487.54	480.21	476.13
55000	635.53	620.54	607.73	596.73	587.22	578.98	571.81	565.55	560.07	555.26	551.04	536.29	528.23	523.75
60000	693.31	676.96	662.98	650.97	640.60	631.61	623.79	616.96	610.99	605.74	601.13	585.04	576.25	571.36
65000	751.08	733.37	718.23	705.22	693.99	684.25	675.77	668.38	661.90	656.22	651.23	633.79	624.27	618.97
70000	808.86	789.78	773.48	759.47	747.37	736.88	727.76	719.79	712.82	706.70	701.32	682.55	672.29	666.59
75000	866.63	846.19	828.73	813.72	800.75	789.52	779.74	771.20	763.73	757.18	751.41	731.30	720.31	714.20
80000	924.41	902.61	883.97	867.96	854.14	842.15	831.72	822.62	814.65	807.65	801.51	780.05	768.33	761.81
85000	982.19	959.02	939.22	922.21	907.52	894.78	883.70	874.03	865.56	858.13	851.60	828.81	816.35	809.42
90000	1039.96	1015.43	994.47	976.46	960.90	947.42	935.68	925.44	916.48	908.61	901.69	877.56	864.37	857.04
95000	1097.74	1071.84	1049.72	1030.70	1014.29	1000.05	987.67	976.85	967.39	959.09	951.79	926.31	912.40	904.65
100000	1155.51	1128.26	1104.97	1084.95	1067.67	1052.69	1039.65	1028.27	1018.31	1009.57	1001.88	975.07	960.42	952.26

11.375%

TERM AMOUNT	1 Year	2 Years	3 Years	4 Years	5 Years	6 Years	7 Years	8 Years	9 Years	10 Years	11 Years	12 Years	13 Years	14 Years
5	.65	.24	.17	.14	.11	.10	.09	.08	.08	.07	.07	.07	.07	.06
10	.89	.47	.33	.27	.22	.20	.18	.16	.15	.14	.14	.13	.13	.12
15	1.33	.71	.50	.40	.33	.29	.26	.24	.23	.21	.20	.20	.19	.18
25	2.22	1.17	.83	.66	.55	.49	.44	.40	.38	.35	.34	.32	.31	.30
50	4.43	2.34	1.65	1.31	1.10	.97	.87	.80	.75	.70	.67	.64	.62	.60
75	6.65	3.51	2.47	1.96	1.65	1.45	1.30	1.20	1.12	1.05	1.00	.96	.93	.90
100	8.86	4.68	3.30	2.61	2.20	1.93	1.74	1.60	1.49	1.40	1.34	1.28	1.24	1.20
200	17.72	9.36	6.59	5.21	4.39	3.85	3.47	3.19	2.97	2.80	2.67	2.56	2.47	2.39
300	26.57	14.04	9.88	7.81	6.58	5.77	5.20	4.78	4.46	4.20	4.00	3.83	3.70	3.58
400	35.43	18.72	13.17	10.42	8.78	7.70	6.93	6.37	5.94	5.60	5.33	5.11	4.93	4.77
500	44.28	23.40	16.46	13.02	10.97	9.62	8.67	7.96	7.42	7.00	6.66	6.38	6.16	5.97
600	53.14	28.07	19.75	15.62	13.16	11.54	10.40	9.55	8.91	8.40	7.99	7.66	7.39	7.16
700	61.99	32.75	23.05	18.22	15.36	13.46	12.13	11.14	10.39	9.80	9.32	8.94	8.62	8.35
800	70.85	37.43	26.34	20.83	17.55	15.39	13.86	12.73	11.87	11.20	10.65	10.21	9.85	9.54
900	79.71	42.11	29.63	23.43	19.74	17.31	15.59	14.33	13.36	12.59	11.98	11.49	11.08	10.74
1000	88.56	46.79	32.92	26.03	21.93	19.23	17.33	15.92	14.84	13.99	13.32	12.76	12.31	11.93
2000	177.12	93.57	65.84	52.06	43.86	38.46	34.65	31.83	29.67	27.98	26.63	25.52	24.61	23.85
3000	265.68	140.35	98.75	78.09	65.79	57.69	51.97	47.74	44.51	41.97	39.94	38.28	36.91	35.77
4000	354.23	187.13	131.67	104.12	87.72	76.91	69.29	63.65	59.34	55.96	53.25	51.04	49.22	47.70
5000	442.79	233.92	164.59	130.15	109.65	96.14	86.61	79.56	74.17	69.95	66.56	63.80	61.52	59.62
6000	531.35	280.70	197.50	156.17	131.58	115.37	103.93	95.47	89.01	83.93	79.87	76.56	73.82	71.54
7000	619.90	327.48	230.42	182.20	153.51	134.59	121.25	111.38	103.84	97.92	93.18	89.31	86.13	83.46
8000	708.46	374.26	263.34	208.23	175.44	153.82	138.57	127.30	118.68	111.91	106.49	102.07	98.43	95.39
9000	797.02	421.04	296.25	234.26	197.37	173.05	155.89	143.21	133.51	125.90	119.80	114.83	110.73	107.31
10000	885.57	467.83	329.17	260.29	219.30	192.27	173.21	159.12	148.34	139.89	133.11	127.59	123.03	119.23
11000	974.13	514.61	362.09	286.31	241.23	211.50	190.53	175.03	163.18	153.87	146.42	140.35	135.34	131.15
12000	1062.69	561.39	395.00	312.34	263.16	230.73	207.85	190.94	178.01	167.86	159.73	153.11	147.64	143.08
13000	1151.24	608.17	427.92	338.37	285.09	249.95	225.17	206.85	192.85	181.85	173.04	165.86	159.94	155.00
14000	1239.80	654.95	460.84	364.40	307.02	269.18	242.49	222.76	207.68	195.84	186.35	178.62	172.25	166.92
15000	1328.36	701.74	493.75	390.43	328.95	288.41	259.81	238.68	222.51	209.83	199.66	191.38	184.55	178.85
16000	1416.91	748.52	526.67	416.45	350.88	307.63	277.13	254.59	237.35	223.82	212.97	204.14	196.85	190.77
17000	1505.47	795.30	559.59	442.48	372.81	326.86	294.45	270.50	252.18	237.80	226.28	216.90	209.15	202.69
18000	1594.03	842.08	592.50	468.51	394.74	346.09	311.77	286.41	267.02	251.79	239.59	229.66	221.46	214.61
19000	1682.58	888.87	625.42	494.54	416.67	365.31	329.09	302.32	281.85	265.78	252.90	242.42	233.76	226.54
20000	1771.14	935.65	658.34	520.57	438.60	384.54	346.41	318.23	296.68	279.77	266.21	255.17	246.06	238.46
21000	1859.70	982.43	691.25	546.59	460.53	403.77	363.73	334.14	311.52	293.76	279.52	267.93	258.37	250.38
22000	1948.25	1029.21	724.17	572.62	482.46	422.99	381.05	350.06	326.35	307.74	292.83	280.69	270.67	262.30
23000	2036.81	1075.99	757.09	598.65	504.39	442.22	398.37	365.97	341.19	321.73	306.14	293.45	282.97	274.23
24000	2125.37	1122.78	790.00	624.68	526.32	461.45	415.69	381.88	356.02	335.72	319.45	306.21	295.27	286.15
25000	2213.92	1169.56	822.92	650.71	548.25	480.67	433.01	397.79	370.85	349.71	332.77	318.97	307.58	298.07
26000	2302.48	1216.34	855.84	676.73	570.18	499.90	450.33	413.70	385.69	363.70	346.08	331.72	319.88	310.00
27000	2391.04	1263.12	888.75	702.76	592.11	519.13	467.65	429.61	400.52	377.68	359.39	344.48	332.18	321.92
28000	2479.59	1309.90	921.67	728.79	614.04	538.35	484.97	445.52	415.36	391.67	372.70	357.24	344.49	333.84
29000	2568.15	1356.69	954.59	754.82	635.97	557.58	502.29	461.44	430.19	405.66	386.01	370.00	356.79	345.76
30000	2656.71	1403.47	987.50	780.85	657.90	576.81	519.61	477.35	445.02	419.65	399.32	382.76	369.09	357.69
31000	2745.26	1450.25	1020.42	806.87	679.83	596.03	536.93	493.26	459.86	433.64	412.63	395.52	381.39	369.61
32000	2833.82	1497.03	1053.34	832.90	701.76	615.26	554.25	509.17	474.69	447.63	425.94	408.28	393.70	381.53
33000	2922.38	1543.82	1086.25	858.93	723.69	634.49	571.57	525.08	489.53	461.61	439.25	421.03	406.00	393.45
34000	3010.93	1590.60	1119.17	884.96	745.62	653.71	588.89	540.99	504.36	475.60	452.56	433.79	418.30	405.38
35000	3099.49	1637.38	1152.09	910.99	767.55	672.94	606.21	556.90	519.19	489.59	465.87	446.55	430.61	417.30
36000	3188.05	1684.16	1185.00	937.01	789.48	692.17	623.53	572.82	534.03	503.58	479.18	459.31	442.91	429.22
37000	3276.60	1730.94	1217.92	963.04	811.41	711.39	640.85	588.73	548.86	517.57	492.49	472.07	455.21	441.14
38000	3365.16	1777.73	1250.84	989.07	833.34	730.62	658.17	604.64	563.70	531.55	505.80	484.83	467.51	453.07
39000	3453.72	1824.51	1283.75	1015.10	855.27	749.85	675.49	620.55	578.53	545.54	519.11	497.58	479.82	464.99
40000	3542.27	1871.29	1316.67	1041.13	877.20	769.07	692.81	636.46	593.36	559.53	532.42	510.34	492.12	476.91
41000	3630.83	1918.07	1349.59	1067.15	899.13	788.30	710.13	652.37	608.20	573.52	545.73	523.10	504.42	488.84
42000	3719.39	1964.85	1382.50	1093.18	921.06	807.53	727.46	668.28	623.03	587.51	559.04	535.86	516.73	500.76
43000	3807.94	2011.64	1415.42	1119.21	942.99	826.75	744.78	684.20	637.86	601.49	572.35	548.62	529.03	512.68
44000	3896.50	2058.42	1448.33	1145.24	964.92	845.98	762.10	700.11	652.70	615.48	585.66	561.38	541.33	524.60
45000	3985.06	2105.20	1481.25	1171.27	986.85	865.21	779.42	716.02	667.53	629.47	598.97	574.13	553.63	536.53
46000	4073.61	2151.98	1514.17	1197.29	1008.78	884.43	796.74	731.93	682.37	643.46	612.28	586.89	565.94	548.45
47000	4162.17	2198.77	1547.08	1223.32	1030.71	903.66	814.06	747.84	697.20	657.45	625.59	599.65	578.24	560.37
48000	4250.73	2245.55	1580.00	1249.35	1052.64	922.89	831.38	763.75	712.03	671.44	638.90	612.41	590.54	572.29
49000	4339.28	2292.33	1612.92	1275.38	1074.57	942.11	848.70	779.66	726.87	685.42	652.22	625.17	602.85	584.22
50000	4427.84	2339.11	1645.83	1301.41	1096.50	961.34	866.02	795.57	741.70	699.41	665.53	637.93	615.15	596.14
55000	4870.62	2573.02	1810.42	1431.55	1206.15	1057.47	952.62	875.13	815.87	769.35	732.08	701.72	676.66	655.75
60000	5313.41	2806.93	1975.00	1561.69	1315.80	1153.61	1039.22	954.69	890.04	839.29	798.63	765.51	738.18	715.37
65000	5756.19	3040.84	2139.58	1691.83	1425.45	1249.74	1125.82	1034.25	964.21	909.23	865.18	829.30	799.69	774.98
70000	6198.97	3274.75	2304.17	1821.97	1535.10	1345.87	1212.42	1113.80	1038.38	979.17	931.73	893.10	861.21	834.59
75000	6641.76	3508.66	2468.75	1952.11	1644.75	1442.01	1299.02	1193.36	1112.55	1049.11	998.29	956.89	922.72	894.21
80000	7084.54	3742.58	2633.33	2082.25	1754.40	1538.14	1385.62	1272.92	1186.72	1119.06	1064.84	1020.68	984.23	953.82
85000	7527.32	3976.49	2797.92	2212.39	1864.05	1634.27	1472.23	1352.47	1260.89	1189.00	1131.39	1084.47	1045.75	1013.43
90000	7970.11	4210.40	2962.50	2342.53	1973.70	1730.41	1558.83	1432.03	1335.06	1258.94	1197.94	1148.26	1107.26	1073.05
95000	8412.89	4444.31	3127.08	2472.67	2083.35	1826.54	1645.43	1511.59	1409.23	1328.88	1264.49	1212.06	1168.78	1132.66
100000	8855.67	4678.22	3291.66	2602.81	2193.00	1922.68	1732.03	1591.15	1483.40	1398.82	1331.05	1275.85	1230.29	1192.27

MONTHLY PAYMENT
REQUIRED TO AMORTIZE A LOAN

11.375%

TERM	15 Years	16 Years	17 Years	18 Years	19 Years	20 Years	21 Years	22 Years	23 Years	24 Years	25 Years	30 Years	35 Years	40 Years
AMOUNT														
5	.06	.06	.06	.06	.06	.06	.06	.06	.06	.06	.06	.05	.05	.05
10	.12	.12	.12	.11	.11	.11	.11	.11	.11	.11	.11	.10	.10	.10
15	.18	.17	.17	.17	.17	.16	.16	.16	.16	.16	.16	.15	.15	.15
25	.30	.29	.28	.28	.27	.27	.27	.26	.26	.26	.26	.25	.25	.24
50	.59	.57	.56	.55	.54	.53	.53	.52	.52	.51	.51	.50	.49	.48
75	.88	.85	.84	.82	.81	.80	.79	.78	.77	.77	.76	.74	.73	.72
100	1.17	1.14	1.11	1.09	1.08	1.06	1.05	1.04	1.03	1.02	1.01	.99	.97	.96
200	2.33	2.27	2.22	2.18	2.15	2.12	2.09	2.07	2.05	2.03	2.02	1.97	1.94	1.92
300	3.49	3.40	3.33	3.27	3.22	3.18	3.14	3.11	3.08	3.05	3.03	2.95	2.90	2.88
400	4.65	4.54	4.44	4.36	4.30	4.24	4.18	4.14	4.10	4.06	4.03	3.93	3.87	3.84
500	5.81	5.67	5.55	5.45	5.37	5.29	5.23	5.17	5.12	5.08	5.04	4.91	4.84	4.80
600	6.97	6.80	6.66	6.54	6.44	6.35	6.27	6.21	6.15	6.09	6.05	5.89	5.80	5.75
700	8.13	7.94	7.77	7.63	7.51	7.41	7.32	7.24	7.17	7.11	7.06	6.87	6.77	6.71
800	9.29	9.07	8.88	8.72	8.59	8.47	8.36	8.27	8.19	8.12	8.06	7.85	7.74	7.67
900	10.45	10.20	9.99	9.81	9.66	9.53	9.41	9.31	9.22	9.14	9.07	8.83	8.70	8.63
1000	11.61	11.34	11.10	10.90	10.73	10.58	10.45	10.34	10.24	10.15	10.08	9.81	9.67	9.59
2000	23.21	22.67	22.20	21.80	21.46	21.16	20.90	20.68	20.48	20.30	20.15	19.62	19.33	19.17
3000	34.81	34.00	33.30	32.70	32.19	31.74	31.35	31.01	30.71	30.45	30.23	29.43	28.99	28.75
4000	46.42	45.33	44.40	43.60	42.91	42.32	41.80	41.35	40.95	40.60	40.30	39.24	38.66	38.34
5000	58.02	56.66	55.50	54.50	53.64	52.90	52.25	51.68	51.19	50.75	50.37	49.04	48.32	47.92
6000	69.62	67.99	66.60	65.40	64.37	63.47	62.70	62.02	61.42	60.90	60.45	58.85	57.98	57.50
7000	81.22	79.32	77.70	76.30	75.10	74.05	73.15	72.35	71.66	71.05	70.52	68.66	67.65	67.08
8000	92.83	90.65	88.80	87.20	85.82	84.63	83.59	82.69	81.90	81.20	80.59	78.47	77.31	76.67
9000	104.43	101.98	99.89	98.10	96.55	95.21	94.04	93.02	92.13	91.35	90.67	88.27	86.97	86.25
10000	116.03	113.31	110.99	109.00	107.28	105.79	104.49	103.36	102.37	101.50	100.74	98.08	96.63	95.83
11000	127.63	124.64	122.09	119.90	118.01	116.37	114.94	113.70	112.61	111.65	110.81	107.89	106.30	105.41
12000	139.24	135.98	133.19	130.80	128.73	126.94	125.39	124.03	122.84	121.80	120.89	117.70	115.96	115.00
13000	150.84	147.31	144.29	141.70	139.46	137.52	135.84	134.37	133.00	131.95	130.96	127.50	125.62	124.58
14000	162.44	158.64	155.39	152.60	150.19	148.10	146.29	144.70	143.32	142.10	141.03	137.31	135.29	134.16
15000	174.04	169.97	166.49	163.50	160.92	158.68	156.73	155.04	153.55	152.25	151.11	147.12	144.95	143.74
16000	185.65	181.30	177.59	174.40	171.64	169.26	167.18	165.37	163.79	162.40	161.18	156.93	154.61	153.33
17000	197.25	192.63	188.68	185.30	182.37	179.84	177.63	175.71	174.03	172.55	171.25	166.74	164.27	162.91
18000	208.85	203.96	199.78	196.20	193.10	190.41	188.08	186.04	184.26	182.70	181.33	176.54	173.94	172.49
19000	220.45	215.29	210.88	207.09	203.83	200.99	198.53	196.38	194.50	192.85	191.40	186.35	183.60	182.07
20000	232.06	226.62	221.98	217.99	214.55	211.57	208.98	206.71	204.73	203.00	201.47	196.16	193.26	191.66
21000	243.66	237.95	233.08	228.89	225.28	222.15	219.43	217.05	214.97	213.15	211.55	205.97	202.93	201.24
22000	255.26	249.28	244.18	239.79	236.01	232.73	229.87	227.39	225.21	223.30	221.62	215.77	212.59	210.82
23000	266.86	260.61	255.28	250.69	246.74	243.31	240.32	237.72	235.44	233.45	231.69	225.58	222.25	220.41
24000	278.47	271.95	266.38	261.59	257.46	253.88	250.77	248.06	245.68	243.60	241.77	235.39	231.91	229.99
25000	290.07	283.28	277.47	272.49	268.19	264.46	261.22	258.39	255.92	253.75	251.84	245.20	241.58	239.57
26000	301.67	294.61	288.57	283.39	278.92	275.04	271.67	268.73	266.15	263.90	261.91	255.00	251.24	249.15
27000	313.27	305.94	299.67	294.29	289.64	285.62	282.12	279.06	276.39	274.05	271.99	264.81	260.90	258.74
28000	324.88	317.27	310.77	305.19	300.37	296.20	292.57	289.40	286.63	284.20	282.06	274.62	270.57	268.32
29000	336.48	328.60	321.87	316.09	311.10	306.78	303.01	299.73	296.86	294.35	292.13	284.43	280.23	277.90
30000	348.08	339.93	332.97	326.99	321.83	317.35	313.46	310.07	307.10	304.50	302.21	294.23	289.89	287.48
31000	359.68	351.26	344.07	337.89	332.55	327.93	323.91	320.40	317.34	314.65	312.28	304.04	299.56	297.07
32000	371.29	362.59	355.17	348.79	343.28	338.51	334.36	330.74	327.57	324.80	322.35	313.85	309.22	306.65
33000	382.89	373.92	366.27	359.69	354.01	349.09	344.81	341.08	337.81	334.94	332.43	323.66	318.88	316.23
34000	394.49	385.25	377.36	370.59	364.74	359.67	355.26	351.41	348.05	345.09	342.50	333.47	328.54	325.81
35000	406.09	396.59	388.46	381.49	375.46	370.25	365.71	361.75	358.28	355.24	352.57	343.27	338.21	335.40
36000	417.70	407.92	399.56	392.39	386.19	380.82	376.16	372.08	368.52	365.39	362.65	353.08	347.87	344.98
37000	429.30	419.25	410.66	403.28	396.92	391.40	386.60	382.42	378.76	375.54	372.72	362.89	357.53	354.56
38000	440.90	430.58	421.76	414.18	407.65	401.98	397.05	392.75	388.99	385.69	382.79	372.70	367.20	364.14
39000	452.50	441.91	432.86	425.08	418.37	412.56	407.50	403.09	399.23	395.84	392.87	382.50	376.86	373.73
40000	464.11	453.24	443.96	435.98	429.10	423.14	417.95	413.42	409.46	405.99	402.94	392.31	386.52	383.31
41000	475.71	464.57	455.06	446.88	439.83	433.72	428.40	423.76	419.70	416.14	413.02	402.12	396.18	392.89
42000	487.31	475.90	466.15	457.78	450.56	444.29	438.85	434.09	429.94	426.29	423.09	411.93	405.85	402.48
43000	498.91	487.23	477.25	468.68	461.28	454.87	449.30	444.43	440.17	436.44	433.16	421.73	415.51	412.06
44000	510.52	498.56	488.35	479.58	472.01	465.45	459.74	454.77	450.41	446.59	443.24	431.54	425.17	421.64
45000	522.12	509.89	499.45	490.48	482.74	476.03	470.19	465.10	460.65	456.74	453.31	441.35	434.84	431.22
46000	533.72	521.22	510.55	501.38	493.47	486.61	480.64	475.44	470.88	466.89	463.38	451.16	444.50	440.81
47000	545.32	532.56	521.65	512.28	504.19	497.18	491.09	485.77	481.12	477.04	473.46	460.96	454.16	450.39
48000	556.93	543.89	532.75	523.18	514.92	507.76	501.54	496.11	491.36	487.19	483.53	470.77	463.82	459.97
49000	568.53	555.22	543.85	534.08	525.65	518.34	511.99	506.44	501.59	497.34	493.60	480.58	473.49	469.55
50000	580.13	566.55	554.94	544.98	536.38	528.92	522.44	516.78	511.83	507.49	503.68	490.39	483.15	479.14
55000	638.15	623.20	610.44	599.47	590.01	581.81	574.68	568.46	563.01	558.24	554.04	539.43	531.47	527.05
60000	696.16	679.86	665.93	653.97	643.65	634.70	626.92	620.13	614.19	608.99	604.41	588.46	579.78	574.96
65000	754.17	736.51	721.43	708.47	697.29	687.59	679.16	671.81	665.38	659.73	654.78	637.50	628.09	622.88
70000	812.18	793.17	776.92	762.97	750.92	740.49	731.41	723.49	716.56	710.48	705.14	686.54	676.41	670.79
75000	870.20	849.82	832.41	817.46	804.56	793.38	783.65	775.17	767.74	761.23	755.51	735.58	724.72	718.70
80000	928.21	906.47	887.91	871.96	858.20	846.27	835.89	826.84	818.92	811.98	805.88	784.62	773.04	766.61
85000	986.22	963.13	943.40	926.46	911.83	899.16	888.14	878.52	870.11	862.73	856.25	833.66	821.35	814.53
90000	1044.23	1019.78	998.90	980.96	965.47	952.05	940.38	930.20	921.29	913.48	906.61	882.69	869.67	862.44
95000	1102.25	1076.44	1054.39	1035.45	1019.11	1004.94	992.62	981.87	972.47	964.23	956.98	931.73	917.98	910.35
100000	1160.26	1133.09	1109.88	1089.95	1072.75	1057.83	1044.87	1033.55	1023.65	1014.97	1007.35	980.77	966.30	958.27

11.400%

TERM	1 Year	2 Years	3 Years	4 Years	5 Years	6 Years	7 Years	8 Years	9 Years	10 Years	11 Years	12 Years	13 Years	14 Years
AMOUNT														
5	.45	.24	.17	.14	.11	.10	.09	.08	.08	.08	.07	.07	.07	.06
10	.89	.47	.33	.27	.22	.20	.18	.16	.15	.15	.14	.13	.13	.12
15	1.33	.71	.50	.40	.33	.29	.27	.24	.23	.22	.20	.20	.19	.18
25	2.22	1.17	.83	.66	.55	.49	.44	.40	.38	.36	.34	.32	.31	.30
50	4.43	2.34	1.65	1.31	1.10	.97	.87	.80	.75	.71	.67	.64	.62	.60
75	6.65	3.51	2.47	1.96	1.65	1.45	1.31	1.20	1.12	1.06	1.00	.96	.93	.90
100	8.86	4.68	3.30	2.61	2.20	1.93	1.74	1.60	1.49	1.41	1.34	1.28	1.24	1.20
200	17.72	9.36	6.59	5.21	4.39	3.85	3.47	3.19	2.97	2.81	2.67	2.56	2.47	2.39
300	26.58	14.04	9.88	7.82	6.59	5.78	5.21	4.78	4.46	4.21	4.00	3.84	3.70	3.59
400	35.43	18.72	13.10	10.42	8.78	7.70	6.94	6.37	5.94	5.61	5.34	5.11	4.93	4.78
500	44.29	23.40	16.47	13.03	10.98	9.62	8.67	7.97	7.43	7.01	6.67	6.39	6.16	5.97
600	53.15	28.08	19.76	15.63	13.17	11.55	10.41	9.56	8.91	8.41	8.00	7.67	7.40	7.17
700	62.00	32.76	23.05	18.23	13.47	12.14	12.14	11.15	10.40	9.81	9.33	8.95	8.63	8.36
800	70.86	37.44	26.35	20.84	17.56	15.40	13.87	12.74	11.88	11.21	10.67	10.22	9.86	9.56
900	79.72	42.12	29.64	23.44	19.75	17.32	15.61	14.34	13.37	12.61	12.00	11.50	11.09	10.75
1000	88.57	46.80	32.93	26.05	21.95	19.24	17.34	15.93	14.85	14.01	13.33	12.78	12.32	11.94
2000	177.14	93.59	65.86	52.09	43.89	38.48	34.67	31.85	29.70	28.01	26.66	25.55	24.64	23.88
3000	265.71	140.39	98.79	78.13	65.83	57.72	52.01	47.78	44.55	42.01	39.98	38.33	36.96	35.82
4000	354.28	187.18	131.72	104.17	87.77	76.96	69.34	63.70	59.40	56.01	53.31	51.10	49.28	47.76
5000	442.85	233.97	164.65	130.21	109.72	96.20	86.67	79.63	74.24	70.02	66.63	63.87	61.60	59.70
6000	531.42	280.77	197.58	156.25	131.66	115.44	104.01	95.55	89.09	84.02	79.96	76.65	73.91	71.63
7000	619.98	327.56	230.50	182.29	153.60	134.68	121.34	111.48	103.94	98.02	93.28	89.42	86.23	83.57
8000	708.55	374.36	263.43	208.33	175.54	153.92	138.67	127.40	118.79	112.02	106.61	102.19	98.55	95.51
9000	797.12	421.15	296.36	234.37	197.49	173.16	156.01	143.33	133.64	126.03	119.93	114.97	110.87	107.45
10000	885.69	467.94	329.29	260.41	219.43	192.40	173.34	159.25	148.48	140.03	133.26	127.74	123.19	119.39
11000	974.26	514.74	362.22	286.45	241.37	211.64	190.67	175.18	163.33	154.03	146.58	140.51	135.50	131.33
12000	1062.83	561.53	395.15	312.49	263.31	230.88	208.01	191.10	178.18	168.03	159.91	153.29	147.82	143.26
13000	1151.39	608.32	428.08	338.53	285.26	250.12	225.34	207.03	193.03	182.04	173.23	166.06	160.14	155.20
14000	1239.96	655.12	461.00	364.57	307.20	269.36	242.67	222.95	207.88	196.04	186.56	178.83	172.46	167.14
15000	1328.53	701.91	493.93	390.61	329.14	288.60	260.01	238.88	222.72	210.04	199.88	191.61	184.78	179.08
16000	1417.10	748.71	526.86	416.65	351.08	307.84	277.34	254.80	237.57	224.04	213.21	204.38	197.09	191.02
17000	1505.67	795.50	559.79	442.69	373.03	327.08	294.67	270.73	252.42	238.05	226.53	217.15	209.41	202.96
18000	1594.24	842.29	592.72	468.73	394.97	346.32	312.01	286.65	267.27	252.05	239.86	229.93	221.73	214.89
19000	1682.80	889.09	625.65	494.77	416.91	365.56	329.34	302.58	282.11	266.05	253.18	242.70	234.05	226.83
20000	1771.37	935.88	658.57	520.81	438.85	384.80	346.67	318.50	296.96	280.05	266.51	255.47	246.37	238.77
21000	1859.94	982.67	691.50	546.85	460.80	404.04	364.01	334.43	311.81	294.06	279.83	268.25	258.69	250.71
22000	1948.51	1029.47	724.43	572.89	482.74	423.28	381.34	350.35	326.66	308.06	293.16	281.02	271.00	262.65
23000	2037.08	1076.26	757.36	598.93	504.68	442.52	398.67	366.28	341.51	322.06	306.48	293.79	283.32	274.58
24000	2125.65	1123.06	790.29	624.97	526.62	461.76	416.01	382.20	356.35	336.06	319.81	306.57	295.64	286.52
25000	2214.21	1169.85	823.22	651.01	548.57	480.99	433.34	398.13	371.20	350.06	333.13	319.34	307.96	298.46
26000	2302.78	1216.64	856.15	677.05	570.51	500.23	450.68	414.05	386.05	364.07	346.46	332.11	320.28	310.40
27000	2391.35	1263.44	889.07	703.09	592.45	519.47	468.01	429.98	400.90	378.07	359.78	344.89	332.59	322.34
28000	2479.92	1310.23	922.00	729.13	614.39	538.71	485.34	445.90	415.75	392.07	373.11	357.66	344.91	334.28
29000	2568.49	1357.02	954.93	755.17	636.34	557.95	502.68	461.83	430.59	406.07	386.43	370.43	357.23	346.21
30000	2657.06	1403.82	987.86	781.21	658.28	577.19	520.01	477.75	445.44	420.08	399.76	383.21	369.55	358.15
31000	2745.62	1450.61	1020.79	807.25	680.22	596.43	537.34	493.68	460.29	434.08	413.08	395.98	381.87	370.09
32000	2834.19	1497.41	1053.72	833.29	702.16	615.67	554.68	509.60	475.14	448.08	426.41	408.75	394.18	382.03
33000	2922.76	1544.20	1086.64	859.33	724.11	634.91	572.01	525.53	489.98	462.08	439.73	421.53	406.50	393.97
34000	3011.33	1590.99	1119.57	885.37	746.05	654.15	589.34	541.45	504.83	476.09	453.06	434.30	418.82	405.91
35000	3099.90	1637.79	1152.50	911.41	767.99	673.39	606.68	557.38	519.68	490.09	466.38	447.07	431.14	417.84
36000	3188.47	1684.58	1185.43	937.45	789.93	692.63	624.01	573.30	534.53	504.09	479.71	459.85	443.46	429.78
37000	3277.03	1731.37	1218.36	963.49	811.88	711.87	641.34	589.23	549.38	518.09	493.03	472.62	455.77	441.72
38000	3365.60	1778.17	1251.29	989.53	833.82	731.11	658.68	605.15	564.22	532.10	506.36	485.39	468.09	453.66
39000	3454.17	1824.96	1284.22	1015.57	855.76	750.35	676.01	621.08	579.07	546.10	519.68	498.17	480.41	465.60
40000	3542.74	1871.76	1317.14	1041.61	877.70	769.59	693.34	637.00	593.92	560.10	533.01	510.94	492.73	477.54
41000	3631.31	1918.55	1350.07	1067.65	899.64	788.83	710.68	652.93	608.77	574.10	546.33	523.71	505.05	489.47
42000	3719.88	1965.34	1383.00	1093.69	921.59	808.07	728.01	668.85	623.62	588.11	559.66	536.49	517.37	501.41
43000	3808.44	2012.14	1415.93	1119.73	943.53	827.31	745.34	684.78	638.46	602.11	572.98	549.26	529.68	513.35
44000	3897.01	2058.93	1448.86	1145.77	965.47	846.55	762.68	700.70	653.31	616.11	586.31	562.03	542.00	525.29
45000	3985.58	2105.72	1481.79	1171.81	987.41	865.79	780.01	716.63	668.16	630.11	599.63	574.81	554.32	537.23
46000	4074.15	2152.52	1514.71	1197.85	1009.36	885.03	797.34	732.55	683.01	644.12	612.96	587.58	566.64	549.16
47000	4162.72	2199.31	1547.64	1223.89	1031.30	904.27	814.68	748.48	697.86	658.12	626.28	600.35	578.96	561.10
48000	4251.29	2246.11	1580.57	1249.93	1053.24	923.51	832.01	764.40	712.70	672.12	639.61	613.13	591.27	573.04
49000	4339.85	2292.90	1613.50	1275.98	1075.18	942.74	849.35	780.33	727.55	686.12	652.93	625.90	603.59	584.98
50000	4428.42	2339.69	1646.43	1302.02	1097.13	961.98	866.68	796.25	742.40	700.12	666.26	638.67	615.91	596.92
55000	4871.26	2573.66	1811.07	1432.22	1206.84	1058.18	953.35	875.88	816.64	770.14	732.88	702.54	677.50	656.61
60000	5314.11	2807.63	1975.71	1562.42	1316.55	1154.38	1040.01	955.50	890.88	840.15	799.51	766.41	739.09	716.30
65000	5756.95	3041.60	2140.36	1692.62	1426.26	1250.58	1126.68	1035.13	965.12	910.16	866.13	830.27	800.68	775.99
70000	6199.79	3275.57	2305.00	1822.82	1535.98	1346.78	1213.35	1114.75	1039.36	980.17	932.76	894.14	862.27	835.68
75000	6642.63	3509.54	2469.64	1953.02	1645.69	1442.97	1300.02	1194.38	1113.60	1050.18	999.38	958.01	923.86	895.37
80000	7085.47	3743.51	2634.28	2083.22	1755.40	1539.17	1386.68	1274.00	1187.84	1120.20	1066.01	1021.87	985.45	955.07
85000	7528.31	3977.48	2798.92	2213.42	1865.11	1635.37	1473.35	1353.63	1262.07	1190.21	1132.63	1085.74	1047.04	1014.76
90000	7971.16	4211.44	2963.57	2343.62	1974.82	1731.57	1560.02	1433.25	1336.31	1260.22	1199.26	1149.61	1108.63	1074.45
95000	8414.00	4445.41	3128.21	2473.82	2084.54	1827.77	1646.69	1512.88	1410.55	1330.23	1265.88	1213.48	1170.23	1134.14
100000	8856.84	4679.38	3292.85	2604.03	2194.25	1923.96	1733.35	1592.50	1484.79	1400.24	1332.51	1277.34	1231.82	1193.83

TERM AMOUNT	15 Years	16 Years	17 Years	18 Years	19 Years	20 Years	21 Years	22 Years	23 Years	24 Years	25 Years	30 Years	35 Years	40 Years
5	.06	.06	.06	.06	.06	.06	.06	.06	.06	.06	.06	.05	.05	.05
10	.12	.12	.12	.11	.11	.11	.11	.11	.11	.11	.11	.10	.10	.10
15	.18	.18	.17	.17	.17	.16	.16	.16	.16	.16	.16	.15	.15	.15
25	.30	.29	.28	.28	.27	.27	.27	.26	.26	.26	.26	.25	.25	.25
50	.59	.57	.56	.55	.54	.53	.53	.52	.52	.52	.51	.50	.49	.49
75	.88	.86	.84	.82	.81	.80	.79	.78	.77	.77	.76	.74	.73	.73
100	1.17	1.14	1.12	1.10	1.08	1.06	1.05	1.04	1.03	1.02	1.01	.99	.97	.97
200	2.33	2.27	2.23	2.19	2.15	2.12	2.10	2.08	2.06	2.04	2.02	1.97	1.94	1.93
300	3.49	3.41	3.34	3.28	3.23	3.18	3.14	3.11	3.08	3.06	3.03	2.95	2.91	2.89
400	4.65	4.54	4.45	4.37	4.30	4.24	4.19	4.15	4.11	4.07	4.04	3.94	3.88	3.85
500	5.81	5.68	5.56	5.46	5.38	5.30	5.24	5.18	5.13	5.09	5.05	4.92	4.85	4.81
600	6.98	6.81	6.67	6.55	6.45	6.36	6.28	6.22	6.16	6.11	6.06	5.90	5.81	5.77
700	8.14	7.95	7.79	7.65	7.53	7.42	7.33	7.25	7.18	7.12	7.07	6.88	6.78	6.73
800	9.30	9.08	8.90	8.74	8.60	8.48	8.38	8.29	8.21	8.14	8.08	7.87	7.75	7.69
900	10.46	10.22	10.01	9.83	9.67	9.54	9.42	9.32	9.23	9.16	9.09	8.85	8.72	8.65
1000	11.62	11.35	11.12	10.92	10.75	10.60	10.47	10.36	10.26	10.17	10.10	9.83	9.69	9.61
2000	23.24	22.70	22.24	21.84	21.49	21.20	20.94	20.71	20.51	20.34	20.19	19.66	19.37	19.21
3000	34.86	34.05	33.35	32.75	32.24	31.79	31.40	31.06	30.77	30.51	30.28	29.49	29.05	28.81
4000	46.48	45.39	44.47	43.67	42.98	42.39	41.87	41.42	41.02	40.68	40.37	39.31	38.74	38.42
5000	58.10	56.74	55.58	54.59	53.73	52.98	52.34	51.77	51.28	50.84	50.46	49.14	48.42	48.02
6000	69.72	68.09	66.70	65.50	64.47	63.58	62.80	62.12	61.53	61.01	60.55	58.97	58.10	57.62
7000	81.33	79.43	77.81	76.42	75.22	74.17	73.27	72.48	71.79	71.18	70.65	68.79	67.78	67.22
8000	92.95	90.78	88.93	87.33	85.96	84.77	83.73	82.83	82.04	81.35	80.74	78.62	77.47	76.83
9000	104.57	102.13	100.04	98.25	96.70	95.36	94.20	93.18	92.29	91.51	90.83	88.45	87.15	86.43
10000	116.19	113.48	111.16	109.17	107.45	105.96	104.67	103.54	102.55	101.68	100.92	98.27	96.83	96.03
11000	127.81	124.82	122.27	120.08	118.19	116.56	115.13	113.89	112.80	111.85	111.01	108.10	106.51	105.63
12000	139.43	136.17	133.39	131.00	128.94	127.15	125.60	124.24	123.06	122.02	121.10	117.93	116.20	115.24
13000	151.04	147.52	144.50	141.91	139.68	137.75	136.06	134.60	133.31	132.19	131.20	127.75	125.88	124.84
14000	162.66	158.86	155.62	152.83	150.43	148.34	146.53	144.95	143.57	142.35	141.29	137.58	135.56	134.44
15000	174.28	170.21	166.73	163.75	161.17	158.94	157.00	155.30	153.82	152.52	151.38	147.41	145.24	144.04
16000	185.90	181.56	177.85	174.66	171.91	169.53	167.46	165.65	164.07	162.69	161.47	157.23	154.93	153.65
17000	197.52	192.90	188.96	185.58	182.66	180.13	177.93	176.01	174.33	172.86	171.56	167.06	164.61	163.25
18000	209.14	204.25	200.08	196.50	193.40	190.72	188.39	186.36	184.58	183.02	181.65	176.89	174.29	172.85
19000	220.75	215.60	211.19	207.41	204.15	201.32	198.86	196.71	194.84	193.19	191.75	186.71	183.97	182.46
20000	232.37	226.95	222.31	218.33	214.89	211.91	209.33	207.07	205.09	203.36	201.84	196.54	193.66	192.06
21000	243.99	238.29	233.42	229.24	225.64	222.51	219.79	217.42	215.35	213.53	211.93	206.37	203.34	201.66
22000	255.61	249.64	244.54	240.16	236.38	233.11	230.26	227.77	225.60	223.70	222.02	216.19	213.02	211.26
23000	267.23	260.99	255.65	251.08	247.12	243.70	240.72	238.13	235.85	233.86	232.11	226.02	222.70	220.87
24000	278.85	272.33	266.77	261.99	257.87	254.30	251.19	248.48	246.11	244.03	242.20	235.85	232.39	230.47
25000	290.47	283.68	277.89	272.91	268.61	264.89	261.66	258.83	256.36	254.20	252.30	245.67	242.07	240.07
26000	302.08	295.03	289.00	283.82	279.36	275.49	272.12	269.19	266.62	264.37	262.39	255.50	251.75	249.67
27000	313.70	306.37	300.12	294.74	290.10	286.08	282.59	279.54	276.87	274.53	272.48	265.33	261.43	259.28
28000	325.32	317.72	311.23	305.66	300.85	296.68	293.05	289.89	287.13	284.70	282.57	275.15	271.12	268.88
29000	336.94	329.07	322.35	316.57	311.59	307.27	303.52	300.24	297.38	294.87	292.66	284.98	280.80	278.48
30000	348.56	340.42	333.46	327.49	322.34	317.87	313.99	310.60	307.63	305.04	302.75	294.81	290.48	288.08
31000	360.18	351.76	344.58	338.41	333.08	328.46	324.45	320.95	317.89	315.20	312.85	304.63	300.16	297.69
32000	371.79	363.11	355.69	349.32	343.82	339.06	334.92	331.30	328.14	325.37	322.94	314.46	309.85	307.29
33000	383.41	374.46	366.81	360.24	354.57	349.66	345.38	341.66	338.40	335.54	333.03	324.29	319.53	316.89
34000	395.03	385.80	377.92	371.15	365.31	360.25	355.85	352.01	348.65	345.71	343.12	334.11	329.21	326.50
35000	406.65	397.15	389.04	382.07	376.06	370.85	366.32	362.36	358.91	355.88	353.21	343.94	338.89	336.10
36000	418.27	408.50	400.15	392.99	386.80	381.44	376.78	372.72	369.16	366.04	363.30	353.77	348.58	345.70
37000	429.89	419.84	411.27	403.90	397.55	392.04	387.25	383.07	379.42	376.21	373.40	363.59	358.26	355.30
38000	441.50	431.19	422.38	414.82	408.29	402.63	397.71	393.42	389.67	386.38	383.49	373.42	367.94	364.91
39000	453.12	442.54	433.50	425.73	419.03	413.23	408.18	403.78	399.92	396.55	393.58	383.25	377.62	374.51
40000	464.74	453.89	444.61	436.65	429.78	423.82	418.65	414.13	410.18	406.71	403.67	393.07	387.31	384.11
41000	476.36	465.23	455.73	447.57	440.52	434.42	429.11	424.48	420.43	416.88	413.76	402.90	396.99	393.71
42000	487.98	476.58	466.84	458.48	451.27	445.01	439.58	434.84	430.69	427.05	423.85	412.73	406.67	403.32
43000	499.60	487.93	477.96	469.40	462.01	455.61	450.04	445.19	440.94	437.22	433.95	422.55	416.35	412.92
44000	511.21	499.27	489.07	480.31	472.76	466.21	460.51	455.54	451.20	447.39	444.04	432.38	426.04	422.52
45000	522.83	510.62	500.19	491.23	483.50	476.80	470.98	465.89	461.45	457.55	454.13	442.21	435.72	432.12
46000	534.45	521.97	511.30	502.15	494.24	487.40	481.44	476.25	471.70	467.72	464.22	452.03	445.40	441.73
47000	546.07	533.31	522.42	513.06	504.99	497.99	491.91	486.60	481.96	477.89	474.31	461.86	455.08	451.33
48000	557.69	544.66	533.53	523.98	515.73	508.59	502.37	496.95	492.21	488.06	484.40	471.69	464.77	460.93
49000	569.31	556.01	544.65	534.90	526.48	519.18	512.84	507.31	502.47	498.22	494.50	481.51	474.45	470.53
50000	580.93	567.36	555.77	545.81	537.22	529.78	523.31	517.66	512.72	508.39	504.59	491.34	484.13	480.14
55000	639.02	624.09	611.34	600.39	590.94	582.76	575.64	569.43	563.99	559.23	555.05	540.47	532.54	528.15
60000	697.11	680.83	666.92	654.97	644.67	635.73	627.97	621.19	615.26	610.07	605.50	589.61	580.96	576.16
65000	755.20	737.56	722.49	709.55	698.39	688.71	680.30	672.96	666.54	660.91	655.96	638.74	629.37	624.18
70000	813.29	794.30	778.07	764.13	752.11	741.69	732.63	724.72	717.81	711.75	706.42	687.87	677.78	672.19
75000	871.39	851.03	833.65	818.71	805.83	794.67	784.96	776.49	769.08	762.58	756.88	737.01	726.19	720.20
80000	929.48	907.77	889.22	873.30	859.55	847.64	837.29	828.25	820.35	813.42	807.34	786.14	774.61	768.22
85000	987.57	964.50	944.80	927.88	913.27	900.62	889.62	880.02	871.62	864.26	857.80	835.27	823.02	816.23
90000	1045.66	1021.24	1000.37	982.46	967.00	953.60	941.95	931.78	922.89	915.10	908.25	884.41	871.43	864.24
95000	1103.75	1077.97	1055.95	1037.04	1020.72	1006.58	994.28	983.55	974.17	965.94	958.71	933.54	919.85	912.26
100000	1161.85	1134.71	1111.53	1091.62	1074.44	1059.55	1046.61	1035.32	1025.44	1016.78	1009.17	982.67	968.26	960.27

MONTHLY PAYMENT
REQUIRED TO AMORTIZE A LOAN

TERM AMOUNT	1 Year	2 Years	3 Years	4 Years	5 Years	6 Years	7 Years	8 Years	9 Years	10 Years	11 Years	12 Years	13 Years	14 Years
5	.45	.24	.17	.14	.11	.10	.09	.08	.08	.08	.07	.07	.07	.07
10	.89	.47	.33	.27	.22	.20	.18	.16	.15	.15	.14	.13	.13	.13
15	1.33	.71	.50	.40	.33	.29	.27	.24	.23	.22	.21	.20	.19	.19
25	2.22	1.18	.83	.66	.55	.49	.44	.40	.38	.36	.34	.33	.31	.31
50	4.44	2.35	1.65	1.31	1.10	.97	.87	.80	.75	.71	.67	.65	.62	.61
75	6.65	3.52	2.48	1.96	1.65	1.45	1.31	1.20	1.12	1.06	1.01	.97	.93	.91
100	8.87	4.69	3.30	2.61	2.20	1.93	1.74	1.60	1.50	1.41	1.34	1.29	1.24	1.21
200	17.73	9.37	6.60	5.22	4.40	3.86	3.48	3.20	2.99	2.82	2.68	2.57	2.48	2.41
300	26.59	14.06	9.90	7.83	6.60	5.79	5.22	4.80	4.48	4.22	4.02	3.85	3.72	3.61
400	35.45	18.74	13.20	10.44	8.80	7.72	6.96	6.40	5.97	5.63	5.36	5.14	4.96	4.81
500	44.31	23.43	16.49	13.05	11.00	9.65	8.70	7.99	7.46	7.03	6.70	6.42	6.19	6.01
600	53.17	28.11	19.79	15.66	13.20	11.58	10.44	9.59	8.95	8.44	8.04	7.70	7.43	7.21
700	62.04	32.79	23.09	18.27	15.40	13.51	12.18	11.19	10.44	9.85	9.37	8.99	8.67	8.41
800	70.90	37.48	26.39	20.88	17.60	15.44	13.91	12.79	11.93	11.25	10.71	10.27	9.91	9.61
900	79.76	42.16	29.68	23.49	19.80	17.37	15.65	14.39	13.42	12.66	12.05	11.55	11.15	10.81
1000	88.62	46.85	32.98	26.09	22.00	19.30	17.39	15.98	14.91	14.06	13.39	12.84	12.38	12.01
2000	177.24	93.69	65.96	52.18	43.99	38.59	34.78	31.96	29.81	28.12	26.77	25.67	24.76	24.01
3000	265.85	140.53	98.93	78.27	65.98	57.88	52.16	47.94	44.72	42.18	40.16	38.50	37.14	36.01
4000	354.47	187.37	131.91	104.36	87.98	77.17	69.55	63.92	59.62	56.24	53.54	51.34	49.52	48.01
5000	443.08	234.21	164.89	130.45	109.97	96.46	86.94	79.90	74.52	70.30	66.92	64.17	61.90	60.01
6000	531.70	281.05	197.86	156.54	131.96	115.75	104.32	95.88	89.43	84.36	80.31	77.00	74.28	72.01
7000	620.31	327.89	230.84	182.63	153.95	135.04	121.71	111.86	104.33	98.42	93.69	89.84	86.66	84.01
8000	708.93	374.73	263.81	208.72	175.95	154.33	139.10	127.84	119.23	112.48	107.07	102.67	99.04	96.01
9000	797.54	421.57	296.79	234.81	197.94	173.63	156.48	143.82	134.14	126.54	120.46	115.50	111.42	108.01
10000	886.16	468.41	329.77	260.90	219.93	192.92	173.87	159.80	149.04	140.60	133.84	128.34	123.80	120.01
11000	974.77	515.25	362.74	286.98	241.92	212.21	191.26	175.78	163.95	154.66	147.22	141.17	136.18	132.01
12000	1063.39	562.09	395.72	313.07	263.92	231.50	208.64	191.76	178.85	168.72	160.61	154.00	148.56	144.01
13000	1152.00	608.93	428.69	339.16	285.91	250.79	226.03	207.74	193.75	182.78	173.99	166.84	160.93	156.01
14000	1240.62	655.77	461.67	365.25	307.90	270.08	243.42	223.72	208.66	196.84	187.37	179.67	173.31	168.01
15000	1329.23	702.61	494.65	391.34	329.89	289.37	260.80	239.70	223.56	210.90	200.76	192.50	185.69	180.01
16000	1417.85	749.45	527.62	417.43	351.89	308.66	278.19	255.67	238.46	224.96	214.14	205.34	198.07	192.01
17000	1506.46	796.29	560.60	443.52	373.88	327.95	295.57	271.65	253.37	239.02	227.52	218.17	210.45	204.01
18000	1595.08	843.13	593.57	469.61	395.87	347.25	312.96	287.63	268.27	253.08	240.91	231.00	222.83	216.01
19000	1683.69	889.97	626.55	495.70	417.86	366.54	330.35	303.61	283.17	267.14	254.29	243.84	235.21	228.02
20000	1772.31	936.81	659.53	521.79	439.86	385.83	347.73	319.59	298.08	281.20	267.68	256.67	247.59	240.02
21000	1860.92	983.65	692.50	547.87	461.85	405.12	365.12	335.57	312.98	295.26	281.06	269.50	259.97	252.02
22000	1949.54	1030.49	725.48	573.96	483.84	424.41	382.51	351.55	327.89	309.31	294.44	282.33	272.35	264.02
23000	2038.15	1077.33	758.45	600.05	505.83	443.70	399.89	367.53	342.79	323.37	307.83	295.17	284.73	276.02
24000	2126.77	1124.17	791.43	626.14	527.83	462.99	417.28	383.51	357.69	337.43	321.21	308.00	297.11	288.02
25000	2215.38	1171.01	824.41	652.23	549.82	482.28	434.67	399.49	372.60	351.49	334.59	320.83	309.48	300.02
26000	2304.00	1217.85	857.38	678.32	571.81	501.58	452.05	415.47	387.50	365.55	347.98	333.67	321.86	312.02
27000	2392.61	1264.69	890.36	704.41	593.81	520.87	469.44	431.45	402.40	379.61	361.36	346.50	334.24	324.02
28000	2481.23	1311.53	923.33	730.50	615.80	540.16	486.83	447.43	417.31	393.67	374.74	359.33	346.62	336.02
29000	2569.84	1358.37	956.31	756.59	637.79	559.45	504.21	463.41	432.21	407.73	388.13	372.17	359.00	348.02
30000	2658.46	1405.21	989.29	782.68	659.78	578.74	521.60	479.39	447.11	421.79	401.51	385.00	371.38	360.02
31000	2747.07	1452.05	1022.26	808.76	681.78	598.03	538.99	495.37	462.02	435.85	414.89	397.83	383.76	372.02
32000	2835.69	1498.90	1055.24	834.85	703.77	617.32	556.37	511.34	476.92	449.91	428.28	410.67	396.14	384.02
33000	2924.30	1545.74	1088.21	860.94	725.76	636.61	573.76	527.32	491.83	463.97	441.66	423.50	408.52	396.02
34000	3012.92	1592.58	1121.19	887.03	747.75	655.90	591.14	543.30	506.73	478.03	455.04	436.33	420.90	408.02
35000	3101.53	1639.42	1154.17	913.12	769.75	675.20	608.53	559.28	521.63	492.09	468.43	449.17	433.28	420.02
36000	3190.15	1686.26	1187.14	939.21	791.74	694.49	625.92	575.26	536.54	506.15	481.81	462.00	445.66	432.02
37000	3278.76	1733.10	1220.12	965.30	813.73	713.78	643.30	591.24	551.44	520.21	495.19	474.83	458.03	444.03
38000	3367.38	1779.94	1253.09	991.39	835.72	733.07	660.69	607.22	566.34	534.27	508.58	487.67	470.41	456.03
39000	3455.99	1826.78	1286.07	1017.48	857.72	752.36	678.08	623.20	581.25	548.33	521.96	500.50	482.79	468.03
40000	3544.61	1873.62	1319.05	1043.57	879.71	771.65	695.46	639.18	596.15	562.39	535.35	513.33	495.17	480.03
41000	3633.22	1920.46	1352.02	1069.65	901.70	790.94	712.85	655.16	611.06	576.45	548.73	526.16	507.55	492.03
42000	3721.84	1967.30	1385.00	1095.74	923.69	810.23	730.24	671.14	625.96	590.51	562.11	539.00	519.93	504.03
43000	3810.45	2014.14	1417.97	1121.83	945.69	829.52	747.62	687.12	640.86	604.57	575.50	551.83	532.31	516.03
44000	3899.07	2060.98	1450.95	1147.92	967.68	848.82	765.01	703.10	655.77	618.62	588.88	564.66	544.69	528.03
45000	3987.68	2107.82	1483.93	1174.01	989.67	868.11	782.40	719.08	670.67	632.68	602.26	577.50	557.07	540.03
46000	4076.30	2154.66	1516.90	1200.10	1011.66	887.40	799.78	735.06	685.57	646.74	615.65	590.33	569.45	552.03
47000	4164.91	2201.50	1549.88	1226.19	1033.66	906.69	817.17	751.04	700.48	660.80	629.03	603.16	581.83	564.03
48000	4253.53	2248.34	1582.85	1252.28	1055.65	925.98	834.56	767.01	715.38	674.86	642.41	616.00	594.21	576.03
49000	4342.14	2295.18	1615.83	1278.37	1077.64	945.27	851.94	782.99	730.28	688.92	655.80	628.83	606.58	588.03
50000	4430.76	2342.02	1648.81	1304.46	1099.64	964.56	869.33	798.97	745.19	702.98	669.18	641.66	618.96	600.03
55000	4873.83	2576.22	1813.69	1434.90	1209.60	1061.02	956.26	878.87	819.71	773.28	736.10	705.83	680.86	660.04
60000	5316.91	2810.42	1978.57	1565.35	1319.56	1157.47	1043.19	958.77	894.22	843.58	803.02	769.99	742.76	720.04
65000	5759.98	3044.63	2143.45	1695.79	1429.52	1253.93	1130.12	1038.66	968.74	913.88	869.93	834.16	804.65	780.04
70000	6203.06	3278.83	2308.33	1826.24	1539.49	1350.39	1217.06	1118.56	1043.26	984.17	936.85	898.33	866.55	840.04
75000	6646.13	3513.03	2473.21	1956.68	1649.45	1446.84	1303.99	1198.46	1117.78	1054.47	1003.77	962.49	928.44	900.05
80000	7089.21	3747.23	2638.09	2087.13	1759.41	1543.30	1390.92	1278.35	1192.30	1124.77	1070.69	1026.66	990.34	960.05
85000	7532.28	3981.43	2802.97	2217.57	1869.38	1639.75	1477.85	1358.25	1266.82	1195.07	1137.60	1090.82	1052.24	1020.05
90000	7975.36	4215.63	2967.85	2348.02	1979.34	1736.21	1564.79	1438.15	1341.33	1265.36	1204.52	1154.99	1114.13	1080.05
95000	8418.44	4449.83	3132.73	2478.46	2089.30	1832.66	1651.72	1518.05	1415.85	1335.66	1271.44	1219.16	1176.03	1140.06
100000	8861.51	4684.04	3297.61	2608.91	2199.27	1929.12	1738.65	1597.94	1490.37	1405.96	1338.36	1283.32	1237.92	1200.06

TERM	15 Years	16 Years	17 Years	18 Years	19 Years	20 Years	21 Years	22 Years	23 Years	24 Years	25 Years	30 Years	35 Years	40 Years
AMOUNT														
5	.06	.06	.06	.06	.06	.06	.06	.06	.06	.06	.06	.05	.05	.05
10	.12	.12	.12	.11	.11	.11	.11	.11	.11	.11	.11	.10	.10	.10
15	.18	.18	.17	.17	.17	.16	.16	.16	.16	.16	.16	.15	.15	.15
25	.30	.29	.28	.28	.28	.27	.27	.27	.26	.26	.26	.25	.25	.25
50	.59	.58	.56	.55	.55	.54	.53	.53	.52	.52	.51	.50	.49	.49
75	.88	.86	.84	.83	.82	.80	.80	.79	.78	.77	.77	.75	.74	.73
100	1.17	1.15	1.12	1.10	1.09	1.07	1.06	1.05	1.04	1.03	1.02	1.00	.98	.97
200	2.34	2.29	2.24	2.20	2.17	2.14	2.11	2.09	2.07	2.05	2.04	1.99	1.96	1.94
300	3.51	3.43	3.36	3.30	3.25	3.20	3.17	3.13	3.10	3.08	3.05	2.98	2.93	2.91
400	4.68	4.57	4.48	4.40	4.33	4.27	4.22	4.17	4.14	4.10	4.07	3.97	3.91	3.88
500	5.85	5.71	5.60	5.50	5.41	5.34	5.27	5.22	5.17	5.13	5.09	4.96	4.89	4.85
600	7.01	6.85	6.71	6.59	6.49	6.40	6.33	6.26	6.20	6.15	6.10	5.95	5.86	5.81
700	8.18	7.99	7.83	7.69	7.57	7.47	7.38	7.30	7.23	7.17	7.12	6.94	6.84	6.78
800	9.35	9.13	8.95	8.79	8.65	8.54	8.43	8.34	8.27	8.20	8.14	7.93	7.81	7.75
900	10.52	10.28	10.07	9.89	9.74	9.60	9.49	9.39	9.30	9.22	9.15	8.92	8.79	8.72
1000	11.69	11.42	11.19	10.99	10.82	10.67	10.54	10.43	10.33	10.25	10.17	9.91	9.77	9.69
2000	23.37	22.83	22.37	21.97	21.63	21.33	21.08	20.85	20.66	20.49	20.33	19.81	19.53	19.37
3000	35.05	34.24	33.55	32.95	32.44	32.00	31.61	31.28	30.98	30.73	30.50	29.71	29.29	29.05
4000	46.73	45.65	44.73	43.94	43.25	42.66	42.15	41.70	41.31	40.97	40.66	39.62	39.05	38.74
5000	58.41	57.06	55.91	54.92	54.07	53.33	52.68	52.12	51.63	51.21	50.83	49.52	48.81	48.42
6000	70.10	68.47	67.09	65.90	64.88	63.99	63.22	62.55	61.96	61.45	60.99	59.42	58.57	58.10
7000	81.78	79.89	78.27	76.89	75.69	74.66	73.76	72.97	72.29	71.69	71.16	69.33	68.33	67.78
8000	93.46	91.30	89.45	87.87	86.50	85.32	84.29	83.39	82.61	81.93	81.32	79.23	78.09	77.47
9000	105.14	102.71	100.63	98.85	97.31	95.98	94.83	93.82	92.94	92.17	91.49	89.13	87.85	87.15
10000	116.82	114.12	111.81	109.83	108.13	106.65	105.36	104.24	103.26	102.41	101.65	99.03	97.62	96.83
11000	128.51	125.53	123.00	120.82	118.94	117.31	115.90	114.67	113.59	112.65	111.82	108.94	107.38	106.52
12000	140.19	136.94	134.18	131.80	129.75	127.98	126.43	125.09	123.91	122.89	121.98	118.84	117.14	116.20
13000	151.87	148.36	145.36	142.78	140.56	138.64	136.97	135.51	134.24	133.13	132.15	128.74	126.90	125.88
14000	163.55	159.77	156.54	153.77	151.38	149.31	147.51	145.94	144.57	143.37	142.31	138.65	136.66	135.56
15000	175.23	171.18	167.72	164.75	162.19	159.97	158.04	156.36	154.89	153.61	152.48	148.55	146.42	145.25
16000	186.92	182.59	178.90	175.73	173.00	170.63	168.58	166.78	165.22	163.85	162.64	158.45	156.18	154.93
17000	198.60	194.00	190.08	186.72	183.81	181.30	179.11	177.21	175.54	174.09	172.80	168.35	165.94	164.61
18000	210.28	205.41	201.26	197.70	194.62	191.96	189.65	187.63	185.87	184.33	182.97	178.26	175.70	174.30
19000	221.96	216.83	212.44	208.68	205.44	202.63	200.18	198.06	196.20	194.57	193.13	188.16	185.47	183.98
20000	233.64	228.24	223.62	219.66	216.25	213.29	210.72	208.48	206.52	204.81	203.30	198.06	195.23	193.66
21000	245.32	239.65	234.81	230.65	227.06	223.96	221.26	218.90	216.85	215.05	213.46	207.97	204.99	203.34
22000	257.01	251.06	245.99	241.63	237.87	234.62	231.79	229.33	227.17	225.29	223.63	217.87	214.75	213.03
23000	268.69	262.47	257.17	252.61	248.69	245.28	242.33	239.75	237.50	235.53	233.79	227.77	224.51	222.71
24000	280.37	273.88	268.35	263.60	259.50	255.95	252.86	250.17	247.82	245.77	243.96	237.67	234.27	232.39
25000	292.05	285.30	279.53	274.58	270.31	266.61	263.40	260.60	258.15	256.01	254.12	247.58	244.03	242.08
26000	303.73	296.71	290.71	285.56	281.12	277.28	273.94	271.02	268.48	266.25	264.29	257.48	253.79	251.76
27000	315.42	308.12	301.89	296.54	291.93	287.94	284.47	281.45	278.80	276.49	274.45	267.38	263.55	261.44
28000	327.10	319.53	313.07	307.53	302.75	298.61	295.01	291.87	289.13	286.73	284.62	277.29	273.32	271.12
29000	338.78	330.94	324.25	318.51	313.56	309.27	305.54	302.29	299.45	296.97	294.78	287.19	283.08	280.81
30000	350.46	342.35	335.43	329.49	324.37	319.93	316.08	312.72	309.78	307.21	304.95	297.09	292.84	290.49
31000	362.14	353.77	346.61	340.48	335.18	330.60	326.61	323.14	320.11	317.45	315.11	307.00	302.60	300.17
32000	373.83	365.18	357.80	351.46	345.99	341.26	337.15	333.56	330.43	327.69	325.28	316.90	312.36	309.86
33000	385.51	376.59	368.98	362.44	356.81	351.93	347.69	343.99	340.76	337.93	335.44	326.80	322.12	319.54
34000	397.19	388.00	380.16	373.43	367.62	362.59	358.22	354.41	351.08	348.17	345.60	336.70	331.88	329.22
35000	408.87	399.41	391.34	384.41	378.43	373.26	368.76	364.84	361.41	358.41	355.77	346.61	341.64	338.90
36000	420.55	410.82	402.52	395.39	389.24	383.92	379.29	375.26	371.73	368.65	365.93	356.51	351.40	348.59
37000	432.24	422.24	413.70	406.37	400.06	394.58	389.83	385.68	382.06	378.89	376.10	366.41	361.16	358.27
38000	443.92	433.65	424.88	417.36	410.87	405.25	400.36	396.11	392.39	389.13	386.26	376.32	370.93	367.95
39000	455.60	445.06	436.06	428.34	421.68	415.91	410.90	406.53	402.71	399.37	396.43	386.22	380.69	377.63
40000	467.28	456.47	447.24	439.32	432.49	426.58	421.44	416.95	413.04	409.61	406.59	396.12	390.45	387.32
41000	478.96	467.88	458.42	450.31	443.30	437.24	431.97	427.38	423.36	419.85	416.76	406.02	400.21	397.00
42000	490.64	479.29	469.61	461.29	454.12	447.91	442.51	437.80	433.69	430.09	426.92	415.93	409.97	406.68
43000	502.33	490.71	480.79	472.27	464.93	458.57	453.04	448.23	444.01	440.33	437.09	425.83	419.73	416.37
44000	514.01	502.12	491.97	483.25	475.74	469.23	463.58	458.65	454.34	450.57	447.25	435.73	429.49	426.05
45000	525.69	513.53	503.15	494.24	486.55	479.90	474.11	469.07	464.67	460.81	457.42	445.64	439.25	435.73
46000	537.37	524.94	514.33	505.22	497.37	490.56	484.65	479.50	474.99	471.05	467.58	455.54	449.01	445.41
47000	549.05	536.35	525.51	516.20	508.18	501.23	495.19	489.92	485.32	481.29	477.75	465.44	458.78	455.10
48000	560.74	547.76	536.69	527.19	518.99	511.89	505.72	500.34	495.64	491.53	487.91	475.34	468.54	464.78
49000	572.42	559.18	547.87	538.17	529.80	522.56	516.26	510.77	505.97	501.77	498.07	485.25	478.30	474.46
50000	584.10	570.59	559.05	549.15	540.61	533.22	526.79	521.19	516.30	512.01	508.24	495.15	488.06	484.15
55000	642.51	627.65	614.96	604.07	594.67	586.54	579.47	573.31	567.92	563.21	559.06	544.67	536.86	532.56
60000	700.92	684.70	670.86	658.98	648.74	639.86	632.15	625.43	619.55	614.41	609.89	594.18	585.67	580.97
65000	759.33	741.76	726.77	713.90	702.80	693.18	684.83	677.55	671.18	665.61	660.71	643.69	634.47	629.39
70000	817.74	798.82	782.67	768.81	756.86	746.51	737.51	729.67	722.81	716.81	711.53	693.21	683.28	677.80
75000	876.15	855.88	838.58	823.73	810.92	799.83	790.19	781.79	774.44	768.01	762.36	742.72	732.09	726.22
80000	934.56	912.94	894.48	878.64	864.98	853.15	842.87	833.90	826.07	819.21	813.18	792.24	780.89	774.63
85000	992.97	970.00	950.39	933.56	919.04	906.47	895.55	886.02	877.70	870.41	864.00	841.75	829.70	823.04
90000	1051.38	1027.05	1006.29	988.47	973.10	959.79	948.22	938.14	929.33	921.61	914.83	891.27	878.50	871.46
95000	1109.79	1084.11	1062.20	1043.39	1027.16	1013.11	1000.90	990.26	980.96	972.81	965.65	940.78	927.31	919.87
100000	1168.19	1141.17	1118.10	1098.30	1081.22	1066.43	1053.58	1042.38	1032.59	1024.01	1016.47	990.30	976.11	968.29

MONTHLY PAYMENT
REQUIRED TO AMORTIZE A LOAN

TERM AMOUNT	1 Year	2 Years	3 Years	4 Years	5 Years	6 Years	7 Years	8 Years	9 Years	10 Years	11 Years	12 Years	13 Years	14 Years
5	.45	.24	.17	.14	.12	.10	.09	.09	.08	.08	.07	.07	.07	.07
10	.89	.47	.34	.27	.23	.20	.18	.17	.15	.15	.14	.13	.13	.13
15	1.33	.71	.50	.40	.34	.30	.27	.25	.23	.22	.21	.20	.19	.19
25	2.22	1.18	.83	.66	.56	.49	.44	.41	.38	.36	.34	.33	.32	.31
50	4.44	2.35	1.66	1.31	1.11	.97	.88	.81	.75	.71	.68	.65	.63	.61
75	6.65	3.52	2.48	1.97	1.66	1.46	1.31	1.21	1.13	1.06	1.01	.97	.94	.91
100	8.87	4.69	3.31	2.62	2.21	1.94	1.75	1.61	1.50	1.42	1.35	1.29	1.25	1.21
200	17.74	9.38	6.61	5.23	4.41	3.87	3.49	3.21	3.00	2.83	2.69	2.58	2.49	2.42
300	26.60	14.07	9.91	7.85	6.62	5.81	5.24	4.82	4.49	4.24	4.04	3.87	3.74	3.62
400	35.47	18.76	13.21	10.46	8.82	7.74	6.98	6.42	5.99	5.65	5.38	5.16	4.98	4.83
500	44.34	23.45	16.52	13.07	11.03	9.68	8.72	8.02	7.48	7.06	6.73	6.45	6.23	6.04
600	53.20	28.14	19.82	15.69	13.23	11.61	10.47	9.63	8.98	8.48	8.07	7.74	7.47	7.24
700	62.07	32.83	23.12	18.30	15.43	13.54	12.21	11.23	10.48	9.89	9.41	9.03	8.71	8.45
800	70.93	37.51	26.42	20.92	17.64	15.48	13.96	12.83	11.97	11.30	10.76	10.32	9.96	9.66
900	79.80	42.20	29.73	23.53	19.84	17.41	15.70	14.44	13.47	12.71	12.10	11.61	11.20	10.86
1000	88.67	46.89	33.03	26.14	22.05	19.35	17.44	16.04	14.96	14.12	13.45	12.90	12.45	12.07
2000	177.33	93.78	66.05	52.28	44.09	38.69	34.88	32.07	29.92	28.24	26.89	25.79	24.89	24.13
3000	265.99	140.67	99.08	78.42	66.13	58.03	52.32	48.11	44.88	42.36	40.33	38.68	37.33	36.19
4000	354.65	187.55	132.10	104.56	88.18	77.38	69.76	64.14	59.84	56.47	53.77	51.58	49.77	48.26
5000	443.31	234.44	165.12	130.69	110.22	96.72	87.20	80.17	74.80	70.59	67.22	64.47	62.21	60.32
6000	531.98	281.33	198.15	156.83	132.26	116.06	104.64	96.21	89.76	84.71	80.66	77.36	74.65	72.38
7000	620.64	328.21	231.17	182.97	154.30	135.40	122.08	112.24	104.72	98.82	94.10	90.26	87.09	84.45
8000	709.30	375.10	264.19	209.11	176.35	154.75	139.52	128.28	119.68	112.94	107.54	103.15	99.53	96.51
9000	797.96	421.99	297.22	235.25	198.39	174.09	156.96	144.31	134.64	127.06	120.98	116.04	111.97	108.57
10000	886.62	468.87	330.24	261.38	220.43	193.43	174.40	160.34	149.60	141.17	134.43	128.94	124.41	120.64
11000	975.28	515.76	363.26	287.52	242.48	212.78	191.84	176.38	164.56	155.29	147.87	141.83	136.85	132.70
12000	1063.95	562.65	396.29	313.66	264.52	232.12	209.28	192.41	179.52	169.41	161.31	154.72	149.29	144.76
13000	1152.61	609.53	429.31	339.80	286.56	251.46	226.72	208.45	194.48	183.52	174.75	167.62	161.73	156.82
14000	1241.27	656.42	462.34	365.94	308.60	270.80	244.16	224.48	209.44	197.64	188.19	180.51	174.17	168.89
15000	1329.93	703.31	495.36	392.07	330.65	290.15	261.60	240.51	224.40	211.76	201.64	193.40	186.61	180.95
16000	1418.59	750.20	528.38	418.21	352.69	309.49	279.04	256.55	239.36	225.87	215.08	206.29	199.05	193.01
17000	1507.26	797.08	561.41	444.35	374.73	328.83	296.48	272.58	254.32	239.99	228.52	219.19	211.49	205.08
18000	1595.92	843.97	594.43	470.49	396.78	348.18	313.92	288.61	269.28	254.11	241.96	232.08	223.93	217.14
19000	1684.58	890.86	627.45	496.62	418.82	367.52	331.36	304.65	284.24	268.22	255.41	244.97	236.37	229.20
20000	1773.24	937.74	660.48	522.76	440.86	386.86	348.80	320.68	299.20	282.34	268.85	257.87	248.81	241.27
21000	1861.90	984.63	693.50	548.90	462.90	406.20	366.24	336.72	314.16	296.46	282.29	270.76	261.25	253.33
22000	1950.56	1031.52	726.52	575.04	484.95	425.55	383.67	352.75	329.12	310.57	295.73	283.65	273.69	265.39
23000	2039.23	1078.40	759.55	601.18	506.99	444.89	401.11	368.78	344.07	324.69	309.17	296.55	286.13	277.45
24000	2127.89	1125.29	792.57	627.31	529.03	464.23	418.55	384.82	359.03	338.81	322.62	309.44	298.57	289.52
25000	2216.55	1172.18	825.59	653.45	551.08	483.58	435.99	400.85	373.99	352.93	336.06	322.33	311.01	301.58
26000	2305.21	1219.06	858.62	679.59	573.12	502.92	453.43	416.89	388.95	367.04	349.50	335.23	323.46	313.64
27000	2393.87	1265.95	891.64	705.73	595.16	522.26	470.87	432.92	403.91	381.16	362.94	348.12	335.90	325.71
28000	2482.53	1312.84	924.67	731.87	617.20	541.60	488.31	448.95	418.87	395.28	376.38	361.01	348.34	337.77
29000	2571.20	1359.72	957.69	758.00	639.25	560.95	505.75	464.99	433.83	409.39	389.83	373.90	360.78	349.83
30000	2659.86	1406.61	990.71	784.14	661.29	580.29	523.19	481.02	448.79	423.51	403.27	386.80	373.22	361.90
31000	2748.52	1453.50	1023.74	810.28	683.33	599.63	540.63	497.05	463.75	437.63	416.71	399.69	385.66	373.96
32000	2837.18	1500.39	1056.76	836.42	705.38	618.97	558.07	513.09	478.71	451.74	430.15	412.58	398.10	386.02
33000	2925.84	1547.27	1089.78	862.55	727.42	638.32	575.51	529.12	493.67	465.86	443.60	425.48	410.54	398.08
34000	3014.51	1594.16	1122.81	888.69	749.46	657.66	592.95	545.16	508.63	479.98	457.04	438.37	422.98	410.15
35000	3103.17	1641.05	1155.83	914.83	771.50	677.00	610.39	561.19	523.59	494.09	470.48	451.26	435.42	422.21
36000	3191.83	1687.93	1188.85	940.97	793.55	696.35	627.83	577.22	538.55	508.21	483.92	464.16	447.86	434.27
37000	3280.49	1734.82	1221.88	967.11	815.59	715.69	645.27	593.26	553.51	522.33	497.36	477.05	460.30	446.34
38000	3369.15	1781.71	1254.90	993.24	837.63	735.03	662.71	609.29	568.47	536.44	510.81	489.94	472.74	458.40
39000	3457.81	1828.59	1287.92	1019.38	859.68	754.37	680.15	625.33	583.43	550.56	524.25	502.84	485.18	470.46
40000	3546.48	1875.48	1320.95	1045.52	881.72	773.72	697.59	641.36	598.39	564.68	537.69	515.73	497.62	482.53
41000	3635.14	1922.37	1353.97	1071.66	903.76	793.06	715.03	657.39	613.35	578.79	551.13	528.62	510.06	494.59
42000	3723.80	1969.25	1387.00	1097.80	925.80	812.40	732.47	673.43	628.31	592.91	564.57	541.52	522.50	506.65
43000	3812.46	2016.14	1420.02	1123.93	947.85	831.75	749.91	689.46	643.27	607.03	578.02	554.41	534.94	518.71
44000	3901.12	2063.03	1453.04	1150.07	969.89	851.09	767.34	705.50	658.23	621.14	591.46	567.30	547.38	530.78
45000	3989.78	2109.92	1486.07	1176.21	991.93	870.43	784.78	721.53	673.18	635.26	604.90	580.19	559.82	542.84
46000	4078.45	2156.80	1519.09	1202.35	1013.98	889.77	802.22	737.56	688.14	649.38	618.34	593.09	572.26	554.90
47000	4167.11	2203.69	1552.11	1228.48	1036.02	909.12	819.66	753.60	703.10	663.50	631.78	605.98	584.70	566.97
48000	4255.77	2250.58	1585.14	1254.62	1058.06	928.46	837.10	769.63	718.06	677.61	645.23	618.87	597.14	579.03
49000	4344.43	2297.46	1618.16	1280.76	1080.10	947.80	854.54	785.66	733.02	691.73	658.67	631.77	609.58	591.09
50000	4433.09	2344.35	1651.18	1306.90	1102.15	967.15	871.98	801.70	747.98	705.85	672.11	644.66	622.02	603.16
55000	4876.40	2578.78	1816.30	1437.59	1212.36	1063.86	959.18	881.87	822.78	776.43	739.32	709.13	684.23	663.47
60000	5319.71	2813.22	1981.42	1568.28	1322.58	1160.57	1046.38	962.04	897.58	847.01	806.53	773.59	746.43	723.79
65000	5763.02	3047.65	2146.54	1698.97	1432.79	1257.29	1133.57	1042.21	972.38	917.60	873.74	838.06	808.63	784.10
70000	6206.33	3282.09	2311.66	1829.66	1543.00	1354.00	1220.77	1122.38	1047.17	988.18	940.95	902.52	870.83	844.42
75000	6649.64	3516.52	2476.77	1960.35	1653.22	1450.72	1307.97	1202.55	1121.97	1058.77	1008.16	966.99	933.03	904.73
80000	7092.95	3750.96	2641.89	2091.03	1763.43	1547.43	1395.17	1282.71	1196.77	1129.35	1075.37	1031.45	995.24	965.05
85000	7536.26	3985.39	2807.01	2221.72	1873.65	1644.14	1482.37	1362.88	1271.57	1199.93	1142.59	1095.92	1057.44	1025.36
90000	7979.56	4219.83	2972.13	2352.41	1983.86	1740.86	1569.56	1443.05	1346.36	1270.52	1209.80	1160.38	1119.64	1085.68
95000	8422.87	4454.26	3137.25	2483.10	2094.08	1837.57	1656.76	1523.22	1421.16	1341.10	1277.01	1224.85	1181.84	1145.99
100000	8866.18	4688.69	3302.36	2613.79	2204.29	1934.29	1743.96	1603.39	1495.96	1411.69	1344.22	1289.32	1244.04	1206.31

TERM AMOUNT	15 Years	16 Years	17 Years	18 Years	19 Years	20 Years	21 Years	22 Years	23 Years	24 Years	25 Years	30 Years	35 Years	40 Years
5	.06	.06	.06	.06	.06	.06	.06	.06	.06	.06	.06	.05	.05	.05
10	.12	.12	.12	.12	.11	.11	.11	.11	.11	.11	.11	.10	.10	.10
15	.18	.18	.17	.17	.17	.17	.16	.16	.16	.16	.16	.15	.15	.15
25	.30	.29	.29	.28	.28	.27	.27	.27	.26	.26	.26	.25	.25	.25
50	.59	.58	.57	.56	.55	.54	.54	.53	.52	.52	.52	.50	.50	.49
75	.89	.87	.85	.83	.82	.81	.80	.79	.78	.78	.77	.75	.74	.74
100	1.18	1.15	1.13	1.11	1.09	1.08	1.07	1.05	1.04	1.04	1.03	1.00	.99	.98
200	2.35	2.30	2.25	2.21	2.18	2.15	2.13	2.10	2.08	2.07	2.05	2.00	1.97	1.96
300	3.53	3.45	3.38	3.32	3.27	3.22	3.19	3.15	3.12	3.10	3.08	3.00	2.96	2.93
400	4.70	4.60	4.50	4.42	4.36	4.30	4.25	4.20	4.16	4.13	4.10	4.00	3.94	3.91
500	5.88	5.74	5.63	5.53	5.45	5.37	5.31	5.25	5.20	5.16	5.12	4.99	4.92	4.89
600	7.05	6.89	6.75	6.63	6.53	6.44	6.37	6.30	6.24	6.19	6.15	5.99	5.91	5.86
700	8.23	8.04	7.88	7.74	7.62	7.52	7.43	7.35	7.28	7.22	7.17	6.99	6.89	6.84
800	9.40	9.19	9.00	8.84	8.71	8.59	8.49	8.40	8.32	8.25	8.20	7.99	7.88	7.82
900	10.58	10.33	10.13	9.95	9.80	9.66	9.55	9.45	9.36	9.29	9.22	8.99	8.86	8.79
1000	11.75	11.48	11.25	11.05	10.89	10.74	10.61	10.50	10.40	10.32	10.24	9.98	9.84	9.77
2000	23.50	22.96	22.50	22.10	21.77	21.47	21.22	20.99	20.80	20.63	20.48	19.96	19.68	19.53
3000	35.24	34.43	33.75	33.15	32.65	32.20	31.82	31.49	31.20	30.94	30.72	29.94	29.52	29.29
4000	46.99	45.91	44.99	44.20	43.53	42.94	42.43	41.98	41.59	41.25	40.96	39.92	39.36	39.06
5000	58.73	57.39	56.24	55.25	54.41	53.67	53.03	52.48	51.99	51.57	51.19	49.90	49.20	48.82
6000	70.48	68.86	67.49	66.30	65.29	64.40	63.64	62.97	62.39	61.88	61.43	59.88	59.04	58.58
7000	82.22	80.34	78.73	77.35	76.17	75.14	74.24	73.47	72.79	72.19	71.67	69.86	68.88	68.35
8000	93.97	91.82	89.98	88.40	87.05	85.87	84.85	83.96	83.18	82.50	81.91	79.84	78.72	78.11
9000	105.71	103.29	101.23	99.45	97.93	96.60	95.46	94.46	93.58	92.82	92.15	89.82	88.56	87.87
10000	117.46	114.77	112.47	110.50	108.81	107.34	106.06	104.95	103.98	103.13	102.38	99.80	98.40	97.64
11000	129.21	126.25	123.72	121.55	119.69	118.07	116.67	115.44	114.38	113.44	112.62	109.78	108.24	107.40
12000	140.95	137.72	134.97	132.60	130.57	128.80	127.27	125.94	124.77	123.75	122.86	119.76	118.08	117.16
13000	152.70	149.20	146.21	143.65	141.45	139.54	137.88	136.43	135.17	134.07	133.10	129.74	127.92	126.93
14000	164.44	160.68	157.46	154.70	152.33	150.27	148.48	146.93	145.57	144.38	143.34	139.71	137.76	136.69
15000	176.19	172.15	168.71	165.75	163.21	161.00	159.09	157.42	155.97	154.69	153.57	149.69	147.60	146.45
16000	187.93	183.63	179.96	176.80	174.09	171.74	169.70	167.92	166.36	165.00	163.81	159.67	157.44	156.21
17000	199.68	195.10	191.20	187.85	184.97	182.47	180.30	178.41	176.76	175.32	174.05	169.65	167.28	165.98
18000	211.42	206.58	202.45	198.90	195.85	193.20	190.91	188.91	187.16	185.63	184.29	179.63	177.12	175.74
19000	223.17	218.06	213.70	209.95	206.73	203.94	201.51	199.40	197.56	195.94	194.52	189.61	186.96	185.50
20000	234.92	229.53	224.94	221.00	217.61	214.67	212.12	209.90	207.95	206.25	204.76	199.59	196.80	195.27
21000	246.66	241.01	236.19	232.05	228.49	225.40	222.72	220.39	218.35	216.57	215.00	209.57	206.64	205.03
22000	258.41	252.49	247.44	243.10	239.37	236.14	233.33	230.89	228.75	226.88	225.24	219.55	216.48	214.79
23000	270.15	263.96	258.68	254.15	250.25	246.87	243.94	241.38	239.15	237.19	235.48	229.53	226.32	224.56
24000	281.90	275.44	269.93	265.20	261.13	257.60	254.54	251.87	249.54	247.50	245.71	239.51	236.16	234.32
25000	293.64	286.92	281.18	276.25	272.01	268.34	265.15	262.37	259.94	257.82	255.95	249.49	246.00	244.08
26000	305.39	298.39	292.42	287.30	282.89	279.07	275.75	272.86	270.34	268.13	266.19	259.47	255.84	253.85
27000	317.13	309.87	303.67	298.35	293.77	289.80	286.36	283.36	280.74	278.44	276.43	269.45	265.68	263.61
28000	328.88	321.35	314.92	309.40	304.65	300.54	296.96	293.85	291.13	288.75	286.67	279.42	275.52	273.37
29000	340.63	332.82	326.16	320.45	315.53	311.27	307.57	304.35	301.53	299.07	296.90	289.40	285.36	283.13
30000	352.37	344.30	337.41	331.50	326.41	322.00	318.18	314.84	311.93	309.38	307.14	299.38	295.20	292.90
31000	364.12	355.78	348.66	342.55	337.29	332.74	328.78	325.34	322.33	319.69	317.38	309.36	305.04	302.66
32000	375.86	367.25	359.91	353.60	348.17	343.47	339.39	335.83	332.72	330.00	327.62	319.34	314.88	312.42
33000	387.61	378.73	371.15	364.65	359.05	354.20	349.99	346.33	343.12	340.32	337.86	329.32	324.72	322.19
34000	399.35	390.20	382.40	375.70	369.93	364.94	360.60	356.82	353.52	350.63	348.09	339.30	334.56	331.95
35000	411.10	401.68	393.65	386.75	380.81	375.67	371.20	367.31	363.92	360.94	358.33	349.28	344.40	341.71
36000	422.84	413.16	404.89	397.80	391.69	386.40	381.81	377.81	374.31	371.25	368.57	359.26	354.24	351.48
37000	434.59	424.63	416.14	408.85	402.57	397.14	392.42	388.30	384.71	381.57	378.81	369.24	364.08	361.24
38000	446.34	436.11	427.39	419.90	413.45	407.87	403.02	398.80	395.11	391.88	389.04	379.22	373.91	371.00
39000	458.08	447.59	438.63	430.95	424.33	418.60	413.63	409.29	405.51	402.19	399.28	389.20	383.75	380.77
40000	469.83	459.06	449.88	442.00	435.21	429.34	424.23	419.79	415.90	412.50	409.52	399.18	393.59	390.53
41000	481.57	470.54	461.13	453.05	446.09	440.07	434.84	430.28	426.30	422.82	419.76	409.16	403.43	400.29
42000	493.32	482.02	472.37	464.10	456.97	450.80	445.44	440.78	436.70	433.13	430.00	419.13	413.27	410.05
43000	505.06	493.49	483.62	475.15	467.85	461.54	456.05	451.27	447.10	443.44	440.23	429.11	423.11	419.82
44000	516.81	504.97	494.87	486.20	478.73	472.27	466.66	461.77	457.49	453.75	450.47	439.09	432.95	429.58
45000	528.55	516.45	506.11	497.25	489.61	483.00	477.26	472.26	467.89	464.07	460.71	449.07	442.79	439.34
46000	540.30	527.92	517.36	508.30	500.49	493.74	487.87	482.75	478.29	474.38	470.95	459.05	452.63	449.11
47000	552.05	539.40	528.61	519.35	511.37	504.47	498.47	493.25	488.69	484.69	481.19	469.03	462.47	458.87
48000	563.79	550.87	539.86	530.40	522.25	515.20	509.08	503.74	499.08	495.00	491.42	479.01	472.31	468.63
49000	575.54	562.35	551.10	541.45	533.13	525.94	519.68	514.24	509.48	505.32	501.66	488.99	482.15	478.40
50000	587.28	573.83	562.35	552.50	544.01	536.67	530.29	524.73	519.88	515.63	511.90	498.97	491.99	488.16
55000	646.01	631.21	618.58	607.75	598.42	590.34	583.32	577.20	571.87	567.19	563.09	548.87	541.19	536.97
60000	704.74	688.59	674.82	663.00	652.82	644.00	636.35	629.68	623.85	618.75	614.28	598.76	590.39	585.79
65000	763.47	745.97	731.05	718.25	707.22	697.67	689.38	682.15	675.84	670.31	665.47	648.66	639.59	634.61
70000	822.19	803.36	787.29	773.50	761.62	751.33	742.40	734.62	727.83	721.88	716.66	698.55	688.79	683.42
75000	880.92	860.74	843.52	828.75	816.02	805.00	795.43	787.10	779.81	773.44	767.85	748.45	737.99	732.24
80000	939.65	918.12	899.76	884.00	870.42	858.67	848.46	839.57	831.80	825.00	819.04	798.35	787.18	781.05
85000	998.38	975.50	955.99	939.25	924.82	912.33	901.49	892.04	883.79	876.56	870.23	848.24	836.38	829.87
90000	1057.10	1032.89	1012.22	994.50	979.22	966.00	954.52	944.51	935.78	928.13	921.41	898.14	885.58	878.68
95000	1115.83	1090.27	1068.46	1049.75	1033.62	1019.67	1007.55	996.99	987.76	979.69	972.60	948.04	934.78	927.50
100000	1174.56	1147.65	1124.69	1105.00	1088.02	1073.33	1060.57	1049.46	1039.75	1031.25	1023.79	997.93	983.98	976.31

MONTHLY PAYMENT
REQUIRED TO AMORTIZE A LOAN

TERM AMOUNT	1 Year	2 Years	3 Years	4 Years	5 Years	6 Years	7 Years	8 Years	9 Years	10 Years	11 Years	12 Years	13 Years	14 Years
5	.45	.24	.17	.14	.12	.10	.09	.09	.08	.08	.07	.07	.07	.07
10	.89	.47	.34	.27	.23	.20	.18	.17	.15	.15	.14	.13	.13	.13
15	1.34	.71	.50	.40	.34	.30	.27	.25	.23	.22	.21	.20	.19	.19
25	2.22	1.18	.83	.66	.56	.49	.44	.41	.38	.36	.34	.33	.32	.31
50	4.44	2.35	1.66	1.31	1.11	.97	.88	.81	.75	.71	.68	.65	.63	.61
75	6.66	3.52	2.48	1.97	1.66	1.46	1.31	1.21	1.13	1.06	1.01	.97	.94	.91
100	8.87	4.69	3.31	2.62	2.21	1.94	1.75	1.61	1.50	1.42	1.35	1.30	1.25	1.21
200	17.74	9.38	6.61	5.24	4.42	3.88	3.50	3.21	3.00	2.83	2.70	2.59	2.50	2.42
300	26.61	14.07	9.92	7.85	6.62	5.81	5.24	4.82	4.50	4.24	4.04	3.88	3.74	3.63
400	35.47	18.76	13.22	10.47	8.83	7.75	6.99	6.42	5.99	5.66	5.39	5.17	4.99	4.84
500	44.34	23.45	16.52	13.08	11.03	9.68	8.73	8.03	7.49	7.07	6.73	6.46	6.23	6.04
600	53.21	28.14	19.83	15.70	13.24	11.62	10.48	9.63	8.99	8.48	8.08	7.75	7.48	7.25
700	62.08	32.83	23.13	18.31	15.44	13.55	12.22	11.24	10.49	9.90	9.42	9.04	8.72	8.46
800	70.94	37.52	26.43	20.93	17.65	15.49	13.97	12.84	11.98	11.31	10.77	10.33	9.97	9.67
900	79.81	42.21	29.74	23.54	19.85	17.43	15.71	14.45	13.48	12.72	12.12	11.62	11.22	10.88
1000	88.68	46.90	33.04	26.16	22.06	19.36	17.46	16.05	14.98	14.14	13.46	12.91	12.46	12.08
2000	177.35	93.80	66.08	52.31	44.12	38.72	34.91	32.10	29.95	28.27	26.92	25.82	24.92	24.16
3000	266.03	140.70	99.11	78.46	66.17	58.07	52.36	48.15	44.93	42.40	40.38	38.73	37.37	36.24
4000	354.70	187.60	132.15	104.61	88.23	77.43	69.82	64.20	59.90	56.53	53.83	51.64	49.83	48.32
5000	443.37	234.50	165.18	130.76	110.28	96.78	87.27	80.24	74.87	70.66	67.29	64.55	62.28	60.40
6000	532.05	281.40	198.22	156.91	132.34	116.14	104.72	96.29	89.85	84.79	80.75	77.45	74.74	72.48
7000	620.72	328.29	231.25	183.06	154.39	135.50	122.17	112.34	104.82	98.92	94.20	90.36	87.20	84.56
8000	709.39	375.19	264.29	209.21	176.45	154.85	139.63	128.39	119.79	113.05	107.66	103.27	99.65	96.63
9000	798.07	422.09	297.32	235.36	198.50	174.21	157.08	144.43	134.77	127.19	121.12	116.18	112.11	108.71
10000	886.74	468.99	330.36	261.51	220.56	193.56	174.53	160.48	149.74	141.32	134.57	129.09	124.56	120.79
11000	975.41	515.89	363.40	287.66	242.61	212.92	191.99	176.53	164.71	155.45	148.03	141.99	137.02	132.87
12000	1064.09	562.79	396.43	313.81	264.67	232.27	209.44	192.58	179.69	169.58	161.49	154.90	149.47	144.95
13000	1152.76	609.69	429.47	339.96	286.73	251.63	226.89	208.62	194.66	183.71	174.94	167.81	161.93	157.03
14000	1241.43	656.58	462.50	366.11	308.78	270.99	244.34	224.67	209.63	197.84	188.40	180.72	174.39	169.11
15000	1330.11	703.48	495.54	392.26	330.84	290.34	261.80	240.72	224.61	211.97	201.86	193.63	186.84	181.18
16000	1418.78	750.38	528.57	418.41	352.89	309.70	279.25	256.77	239.58	226.10	215.31	206.53	199.30	193.26
17000	1507.45	797.28	561.61	444.56	374.95	329.05	296.70	272.81	254.56	240.23	228.77	219.44	211.75	205.34
18000	1596.13	844.18	594.64	470.71	397.00	348.41	314.16	288.86	269.53	254.37	242.23	232.35	224.21	217.42
19000	1684.80	891.08	627.68	496.86	419.06	367.76	331.61	304.91	284.50	268.50	255.68	245.26	236.66	229.50
20000	1773.47	937.98	660.71	523.01	441.11	387.12	349.06	320.96	299.48	282.63	269.14	258.17	249.12	241.58
21000	1862.15	984.87	693.75	549.16	463.17	406.48	366.51	337.00	314.45	296.76	282.60	271.08	261.58	253.66
22000	1950.82	1031.77	726.79	575.31	485.22	425.83	383.97	353.05	329.42	310.89	296.05	283.98	274.03	265.74
23000	2039.49	1078.67	759.82	601.46	507.28	445.19	401.42	369.10	344.40	325.02	309.51	296.89	286.49	277.81
24000	2128.17	1125.57	792.86	627.61	529.33	464.54	418.87	385.15	359.37	339.15	322.97	309.80	298.94	289.89
25000	2216.84	1172.47	825.89	653.76	551.39	483.90	436.33	401.19	374.34	353.28	336.42	322.71	311.40	301.97
26000	2305.51	1219.37	858.93	679.91	573.45	503.25	453.78	417.24	389.32	367.41	349.88	335.62	323.85	314.05
27000	2394.19	1266.27	891.96	706.06	595.50	522.61	471.23	433.29	404.29	381.55	363.34	348.52	336.31	326.13
28000	2482.86	1313.16	925.00	732.21	617.56	541.97	488.68	449.34	419.26	395.68	376.80	361.43	348.77	338.21
29000	2571.54	1360.06	958.03	758.36	639.61	561.32	506.14	465.38	434.24	409.81	390.25	374.34	361.22	350.29
30000	2660.21	1406.96	991.07	784.51	661.67	580.68	523.59	481.43	449.21	423.94	403.71	387.25	373.68	362.36
31000	2748.88	1453.86	1024.11	810.66	683.72	600.03	541.04	497.48	464.18	438.07	417.17	400.16	386.13	374.44
32000	2837.56	1500.76	1057.14	836.81	705.78	619.39	558.50	513.53	479.16	452.20	430.62	413.06	398.59	386.52
33000	2926.23	1547.66	1090.18	862.96	727.83	638.74	575.95	529.57	494.13	466.33	444.08	425.97	411.04	398.60
34000	3014.90	1594.56	1123.21	889.11	749.89	658.10	593.40	545.62	509.11	480.46	457.54	438.88	423.50	410.68
35000	3103.58	1641.45	1156.25	915.26	771.94	677.46	610.85	561.67	524.08	494.60	470.99	451.79	435.96	422.76
36000	3192.25	1688.35	1189.28	941.41	794.00	696.81	628.31	577.72	539.05	508.73	484.45	464.70	448.41	434.84
37000	3280.92	1735.25	1222.32	967.56	816.06	716.17	645.76	593.76	554.03	522.86	497.91	477.60	460.87	446.91
38000	3369.60	1782.15	1255.35	993.71	838.11	735.52	663.21	609.81	569.00	536.99	511.36	490.51	473.32	458.99
39000	3458.27	1829.05	1288.39	1019.86	860.17	754.88	680.66	625.86	583.97	551.12	524.82	503.42	485.78	471.07
40000	3546.94	1875.95	1321.42	1046.01	882.22	774.23	698.12	641.91	598.95	565.25	538.28	516.33	498.23	483.15
41000	3635.62	1922.85	1354.46	1072.16	904.28	793.59	715.57	657.95	613.92	579.38	551.73	529.24	510.69	495.23
42000	3724.29	1969.74	1387.50	1098.31	926.33	812.95	733.02	674.00	628.89	593.51	565.19	542.15	523.15	507.31
43000	3812.96	2016.64	1420.53	1124.46	948.39	832.30	750.48	690.05	643.87	607.64	578.65	555.05	535.60	519.39
44000	3901.64	2063.54	1453.57	1150.61	970.44	851.66	767.93	706.10	658.84	621.78	592.10	567.96	548.06	531.47
45000	3990.31	2110.44	1486.60	1176.76	992.50	871.01	785.38	722.14	673.81	635.91	605.56	580.87	560.51	543.54
46000	4078.98	2157.34	1519.64	1202.91	1014.55	890.37	802.83	738.19	688.79	650.04	619.02	593.78	572.97	555.62
47000	4167.66	2204.24	1552.67	1229.06	1036.61	909.72	820.29	754.24	703.76	664.17	632.47	606.69	585.42	567.70
48000	4256.33	2251.13	1585.71	1255.21	1058.66	929.08	837.74	770.29	718.74	678.30	645.93	619.59	597.88	579.78
49000	4345.00	2298.03	1618.74	1281.36	1080.72	948.44	855.19	786.33	733.71	692.43	659.39	632.50	610.34	591.86
50000	4433.68	2344.93	1651.78	1307.51	1102.78	967.79	872.65	802.38	748.68	706.56	672.84	645.41	622.79	603.94
55000	4877.05	2579.42	1816.96	1438.26	1213.05	1064.57	959.91	882.62	823.55	777.22	740.13	709.95	685.07	664.33
60000	5320.41	2813.92	1982.13	1569.01	1323.33	1161.35	1047.17	962.86	898.42	847.87	807.41	774.49	747.35	724.72
65000	5763.78	3048.41	2147.31	1699.76	1433.61	1258.13	1134.44	1043.09	973.29	918.53	874.70	839.03	809.63	785.12
70000	6207.15	3282.90	2312.49	1830.51	1543.88	1354.91	1221.70	1123.33	1048.15	989.19	941.98	903.57	871.91	845.51
75000	6650.51	3517.40	2477.67	1961.26	1654.16	1451.68	1308.97	1203.57	1123.02	1059.84	1009.26	968.11	934.18	905.90
80000	7093.88	3751.89	2642.84	2092.01	1764.44	1548.46	1396.23	1283.81	1197.89	1130.50	1076.55	1032.65	996.46	966.30
85000	7537.25	3986.38	2808.02	2222.76	1874.72	1645.24	1483.49	1364.04	1272.76	1201.15	1143.83	1097.19	1058.74	1026.69
90000	7980.62	4220.87	2973.20	2353.51	1984.99	1742.02	1570.76	1444.28	1347.62	1271.81	1211.12	1161.73	1121.02	1087.08
95000	8423.98	4455.37	3138.38	2484.26	2095.27	1838.80	1658.02	1524.52	1422.49	1342.46	1278.40	1226.27	1183.30	1147.48
100000	8867.35	4689.86	3303.55	2615.01	2205.55	1935.58	1745.29	1604.76	1497.36	1413.12	1345.68	1290.82	1245.58	1207.87

TERM	15 Years	16 Years	17 Years	18 Years	19 Years	20 Years	21 Years	22 Years	23 Years	24 Years	25 Years	30 Years	35 Years	40 Years
AMOUNT														
5	.06	.06	.06	.06	.06	.06	.06	.06	.06	.06	.06	.05	.05	.05
10	.12	.12	.12	.12	.11	.11	.11	.11	.11	.11	.11	.10	.10	.10
15	.18	.18	.17	.17	.17	.17	.16	.16	.16	.16	.16	.15	.15	.15
25	.30	.29	.29	.28	.28	.27	.27	.27	.27	.26	.26	.25	.25	.25
50	.59	.58	.57	.56	.55	.54	.54	.53	.53	.52	.52	.50	.50	.49
75	.89	.87	.85	.84	.82	.81	.80	.79	.79	.78	.77	.75	.74	.74
100	1.18	1.15	1.13	1.11	1.09	1.08	1.07	1.06	1.05	1.04	1.03	1.00	.99	.98
200	2.36	2.30	2.26	2.22	2.18	2.16	2.13	2.11	2.09	2.07	2.06	2.00	1.98	1.96
300	3.53	3.45	3.38	3.33	3.27	3.23	3.19	3.16	3.13	3.10	3.08	3.00	2.96	2.94
400	4.71	4.60	4.51	4.43	4.36	4.31	4.25	4.21	4.17	4.14	4.11	4.00	3.95	3.92
500	5.89	5.75	5.64	5.54	5.45	5.38	5.32	5.26	5.21	5.17	5.13	5.00	4.93	4.90
600	7.06	6.90	6.76	6.65	6.54	6.46	6.38	6.31	6.25	6.20	6.16	6.00	5.92	5.87
700	8.24	8.05	7.89	7.75	7.63	7.53	7.44	7.36	7.30	7.24	7.18	7.00	6.91	6.85
800	9.41	9.20	9.02	8.86	8.72	8.61	8.50	8.41	8.34	8.27	8.21	8.00	7.89	7.83
900	10.59	10.35	10.14	9.97	9.81	9.68	9.57	9.47	9.38	9.30	9.24	9.00	8.88	8.81
1000	11.77	11.50	11.27	11.07	10.90	10.76	10.63	10.52	10.42	10.34	10.26	10.00	9.86	9.79
2000	23.53	22.99	22.53	22.14	21.80	21.51	21.25	21.03	20.84	20.67	20.52	20.00	19.72	19.57
3000	35.29	34.48	33.80	33.21	32.70	32.26	31.87	31.54	31.25	31.00	30.77	30.00	29.58	29.35
4000	47.05	45.98	45.06	44.27	43.59	43.01	42.50	42.05	41.67	41.33	41.03	40.00	39.44	39.14
5000	58.81	57.47	56.32	55.34	54.49	53.76	53.12	52.57	52.08	51.66	51.29	50.00	49.30	48.92
6000	70.57	68.96	67.59	66.41	65.39	64.51	63.74	63.08	62.50	61.99	61.54	60.00	59.16	58.70
7000	82.34	80.45	78.85	77.47	76.29	75.26	74.37	73.59	72.91	72.32	71.80	69.99	69.02	68.49
8000	94.10	91.95	90.11	88.54	87.18	86.01	84.99	84.10	83.33	82.65	82.05	79.99	78.88	78.27
9000	105.86	103.44	101.38	99.61	98.08	96.76	95.61	94.62	93.74	92.98	92.31	89.99	88.74	88.05
10000	117.62	114.93	112.64	110.67	108.98	107.51	106.24	105.13	104.16	103.31	102.57	99.99	98.60	97.84
11000	129.38	126.42	123.90	121.74	119.87	118.26	116.86	115.64	114.57	113.64	112.82	109.99	108.46	107.62
12000	141.14	137.92	135.17	132.81	130.77	129.01	127.48	126.15	124.99	123.97	123.08	119.99	118.32	117.40
13000	152.90	149.41	146.43	143.87	141.67	139.76	138.11	136.66	135.41	134.30	133.34	129.98	128.18	127.19
14000	164.67	160.90	157.69	154.94	152.57	150.51	148.73	147.18	145.82	144.63	143.59	139.98	138.04	136.97
15000	176.43	172.40	168.96	166.01	163.46	161.26	159.35	157.69	156.24	154.96	153.85	149.98	147.90	146.75
16000	188.19	183.89	180.22	177.07	174.36	172.01	169.98	168.20	166.65	165.29	164.10	159.98	157.76	156.54
17000	199.95	195.38	191.48	188.14	185.26	182.76	180.60	178.71	177.07	175.63	174.36	169.98	167.62	166.32
18000	211.71	206.87	202.75	199.21	196.15	193.51	191.22	189.23	187.48	185.96	184.62	179.98	177.47	176.10
19000	223.47	218.37	214.01	210.27	207.05	204.27	201.85	199.74	197.90	196.29	194.87	189.97	187.33	185.89
20000	235.23	229.86	225.27	221.34	217.95	215.02	212.47	210.25	208.31	206.62	205.13	199.97	197.19	195.67
21000	247.00	241.35	236.54	232.41	228.85	225.77	223.09	220.76	218.73	216.95	215.39	209.97	207.05	205.45
22000	258.76	252.84	247.80	243.47	239.74	236.52	233.72	231.27	229.14	227.28	225.64	219.97	216.91	215.23
23000	270.52	264.34	259.06	254.54	250.64	247.27	244.34	241.79	239.56	237.61	235.90	229.97	226.77	225.02
24000	282.28	275.83	270.33	265.61	261.54	258.02	254.96	252.30	249.97	247.94	246.15	239.97	236.63	234.80
25000	294.04	287.32	281.59	276.67	272.44	268.77	265.58	262.01	260.39	258.27	256.41	249.96	246.49	244.58
26000	305.80	298.81	292.85	287.74	283.33	279.52	276.21	273.32	270.81	268.60	266.67	259.96	256.35	254.37
27000	317.57	310.31	304.12	298.81	294.23	290.27	286.83	283.84	281.22	278.93	276.92	269.96	266.21	264.15
28000	329.33	321.80	315.38	309.87	305.13	301.02	297.45	294.35	291.64	289.26	287.18	279.96	276.07	273.93
29000	341.09	333.29	326.64	320.94	316.02	311.77	308.08	304.86	302.05	299.59	297.44	289.96	285.93	283.72
30000	352.85	344.79	337.91	332.01	326.92	322.52	318.70	315.37	312.47	309.92	307.69	299.96	295.79	293.50
31000	364.61	356.28	349.17	343.07	337.82	333.27	329.32	325.89	322.88	320.25	317.95	309.96	305.65	303.28
32000	376.37	367.77	360.43	354.14	348.72	344.02	339.95	336.40	333.30	330.58	328.20	319.95	315.51	313.07
33000	388.13	379.26	371.70	365.21	359.61	354.77	350.57	346.91	343.71	340.91	338.46	329.95	325.37	322.85
34000	399.90	390.76	382.96	376.27	370.51	365.52	361.19	357.42	354.13	351.25	348.72	339.95	335.23	332.63
35000	411.66	402.25	394.22	387.34	381.41	376.27	371.82	367.93	364.54	361.58	358.97	349.95	345.08	342.42
36000	423.42	413.74	405.49	398.41	392.30	387.02	382.44	378.45	374.96	371.91	369.23	359.95	354.94	352.20
37000	435.18	425.23	416.75	409.47	403.20	397.78	393.06	388.96	385.37	382.24	379.48	369.95	364.80	361.98
38000	446.94	436.73	428.01	420.54	414.10	408.53	403.69	399.47	395.79	392.57	389.74	379.94	374.66	371.77
39000	458.70	448.22	439.28	431.61	425.00	419.28	414.31	409.98	406.21	402.90	400.00	389.94	384.52	381.55
40000	470.46	459.71	450.54	442.67	435.89	430.03	424.93	420.50	416.62	413.23	410.25	399.94	394.38	391.33
41000	482.23	471.21	461.80	453.74	446.79	440.78	435.56	431.01	427.04	423.56	420.51	409.94	404.24	401.11
42000	493.99	482.70	473.07	464.81	457.69	451.53	446.18	441.52	437.45	433.89	430.77	419.94	414.10	410.90
43000	505.75	494.19	484.33	475.87	468.59	462.28	456.80	452.03	447.87	444.22	441.02	429.94	423.96	420.68
44000	517.51	505.68	495.59	486.94	479.48	473.03	467.43	462.54	458.28	454.55	451.28	439.93	433.82	430.46
45000	529.27	517.18	506.86	498.01	490.38	483.78	478.05	473.06	468.70	464.88	461.53	449.93	443.68	440.25
46000	541.03	528.67	518.12	509.07	501.28	494.53	488.67	483.57	479.11	475.21	471.79	459.93	453.54	450.03
47000	552.79	540.16	529.38	520.14	512.17	505.28	499.30	494.08	489.53	485.54	482.05	469.93	463.40	459.81
48000	564.56	551.65	540.65	531.21	523.07	516.03	509.92	504.59	499.94	495.87	492.30	479.93	473.26	469.60
49000	576.32	563.15	551.91	542.27	533.97	526.78	520.54	515.11	510.36	506.20	502.56	489.93	483.12	479.38
50000	588.08	574.64	563.17	553.34	544.87	537.53	531.16	525.62	520.77	516.53	512.82	499.92	492.98	489.16
55000	646.89	632.10	619.49	608.67	599.35	591.29	584.28	578.18	572.85	568.19	564.10	549.92	542.27	538.08
60000	705.69	689.57	675.81	664.01	653.84	645.04	637.40	630.74	624.93	619.84	615.38	599.91	591.57	586.99
65000	764.50	747.03	732.13	719.34	708.32	698.79	690.51	683.30	677.01	671.49	666.66	649.90	640.87	635.91
70000	823.31	804.49	788.44	774.67	762.81	752.54	743.63	735.86	729.08	723.15	717.94	699.89	690.16	684.83
75000	882.12	861.96	844.76	830.01	817.30	806.30	796.74	788.43	781.16	774.80	769.22	749.88	739.46	733.74
80000	940.92	919.42	901.08	885.34	871.78	860.05	849.86	840.99	833.24	826.45	820.50	799.88	788.76	782.66
85000	999.73	976.88	957.39	940.68	926.27	913.80	902.98	893.55	885.31	878.11	871.78	849.87	838.06	831.57
90000	1058.54	1034.35	1013.71	996.01	980.75	967.55	956.09	946.11	937.39	929.76	923.06	899.86	887.35	880.49
95000	1117.35	1091.81	1070.03	1051.34	1035.24	1021.31	1009.21	998.67	989.47	981.41	974.35	949.85	936.65	929.41
100000	1176.15	1149.27	1126.34	1106.68	1089.73	1075.06	1062.33	1051.23	1041.54	1033.06	1025.63	999.84	985.95	978.32

MONTHLY PAYMENT
REQUIRED TO AMORTIZE A LOAN

TERM AMOUNT	1 Year	2 Years	3 Years	4 Years	5 Years	6 Years	7 Years	8 Years	9 Years	10 Years	11 Years	12 Years	13 Years	14 Years
5	.45	.24	.17	.14	.12	.10	.09	.09	.08	.08	.07	.07	.07	.07
10	.89	.47	.34	.27	.23	.20	.18	.17	.16	.15	.14	.13	.13	.13
15	1.34	.71	.50	.40	.34	.30	.27	.25	.23	.22	.21	.20	.19	.19
25	2.22	1.18	.83	.66	.56	.49	.44	.41	.38	.36	.34	.33	.32	.31
50	4.44	2.35	1.66	1.31	1.11	.97	.88	.81	.76	.71	.68	.65	.63	.61
75	6.66	3.53	2.49	1.97	1.66	1.46	1.32	1.21	1.13	1.07	1.02	.98	.94	.91
100	8.88	4.70	3.31	2.62	2.21	1.94	1.75	1.61	1.51	1.42	1.36	1.30	1.26	1.22
200	17.75	9.39	6.62	5.24	4.42	3.88	3.50	3.22	3.01	2.84	2.71	2.60	2.51	2.43
300	26.62	14.09	9.93	7.86	6.63	5.82	5.25	4.83	4.51	4.26	4.06	3.89	3.76	3.64
400	35.49	18.78	13.23	10.48	8.84	7.76	7.00	6.44	6.01	5.67	5.41	5.19	5.01	4.86
500	44.36	23.47	16.54	13.10	11.05	9.70	8.75	8.05	7.51	7.09	6.76	6.48	6.26	6.07
600	53.23	28.17	19.85	15.72	13.26	11.64	10.50	9.66	9.01	8.51	8.11	7.78	7.51	7.28
700	62.10	32.86	23.15	18.34	15.47	13.58	12.25	11.27	10.52	9.93	9.46	9.07	8.76	8.49
800	70.97	37.55	26.46	20.95	17.68	15.52	14.00	12.88	12.02	11.34	10.81	10.37	10.01	9.71
900	79.84	42.25	29.77	23.57	19.89	17.46	15.75	14.48	13.52	12.76	12.16	11.66	11.26	10.92
1000	88.71	46.94	33.08	26.19	22.10	19.40	17.50	16.09	15.02	14.18	13.51	12.96	12.51	12.13
2000	177.42	93.87	66.15	52.38	44.19	38.79	34.99	32.18	30.04	28.35	27.01	25.91	25.01	24.26
3000	266.13	140.81	99.22	78.57	66.28	58.19	52.48	48.27	45.05	42.53	40.51	38.86	37.51	36.38
4000	354.84	187.74	132.29	104.75	88.38	77.58	69.98	64.36	60.07	56.70	54.01	51.82	50.01	48.51
5000	443.55	234.67	165.36	130.94	110.47	96.98	87.47	80.45	75.08	70.88	67.51	64.77	62.51	60.63
6000	532.26	281.61	198.43	157.13	132.56	116.37	104.96	96.54	90.10	85.05	81.01	77.72	75.02	72.76
7000	620.96	328.54	231.50	183.31	154.66	135.77	122.45	112.62	105.11	99.22	94.51	90.68	87.52	84.88
8000	709.67	375.47	264.57	209.50	176.75	155.16	139.95	128.71	120.13	113.40	108.01	103.63	100.02	97.01
9000	798.38	422.41	297.65	235.69	198.84	174.56	157.44	144.80	135.15	127.57	121.51	116.58	112.52	109.14
10000	887.09	469.34	330.72	261.87	220.94	193.95	174.93	160.89	150.16	141.75	135.01	129.54	125.02	121.26
11000	975.80	516.27	363.79	288.06	243.03	213.34	192.42	176.98	165.18	155.92	148.51	142.49	137.52	133.39
12000	1064.51	563.21	396.86	314.25	265.12	232.74	209.92	193.07	180.19	170.10	162.02	155.44	150.03	145.51
13000	1153.22	610.14	429.93	340.43	287.22	252.13	227.41	209.15	195.21	184.27	175.52	168.40	162.53	157.64
14000	1241.92	657.07	463.00	366.62	309.31	271.53	244.90	225.24	210.22	198.44	189.02	181.35	175.03	169.76
15000	1330.63	704.01	496.07	392.81	331.40	290.92	262.40	241.33	225.24	212.62	202.52	194.30	187.53	181.89
16000	1419.34	750.94	529.14	418.99	353.50	310.32	279.89	257.42	240.25	226.79	216.02	207.26	200.03	194.01
17000	1508.05	797.87	562.22	445.18	375.59	329.71	297.38	273.51	255.27	240.97	229.52	220.21	212.53	206.14
18000	1596.76	844.81	595.29	471.37	397.68	349.11	314.87	289.60	270.29	255.14	243.02	233.16	225.04	218.27
19000	1685.47	891.74	628.36	497.55	419.77	368.50	332.37	305.69	285.30	269.31	256.52	246.12	237.54	230.39
20000	1774.18	938.67	661.43	523.74	441.87	387.90	349.86	321.77	300.32	283.49	270.02	259.07	250.04	242.52
21000	1862.88	985.61	694.50	549.93	463.96	407.29	367.35	337.86	315.33	297.66	283.52	272.02	262.54	254.64
22000	1951.59	1032.54	727.57	576.11	486.05	426.68	384.84	353.95	330.35	311.84	297.02	284.97	275.04	266.77
23000	2040.30	1079.48	760.64	602.30	508.15	446.08	402.34	370.04	345.36	326.01	310.53	297.93	287.55	278.89
24000	2129.01	1126.41	793.71	628.49	530.24	465.47	419.83	386.13	360.38	340.19	324.03	310.88	300.05	291.02
25000	2217.72	1173.34	826.79	654.67	552.33	484.87	437.32	402.22	375.39	354.36	337.53	323.83	312.55	303.15
26000	2306.43	1220.28	859.86	680.86	574.43	504.26	454.82	418.30	390.41	368.53	351.03	336.79	325.05	315.27
27000	2395.13	1267.21	892.93	707.05	596.52	523.66	472.31	434.39	405.43	382.71	364.53	349.74	337.55	327.40
28000	2483.84	1314.14	926.00	733.23	618.61	543.05	489.80	450.48	420.44	396.88	378.03	362.69	350.05	339.52
29000	2572.55	1361.08	959.07	759.42	640.71	562.45	507.29	466.57	435.46	411.06	391.53	375.65	362.56	351.65
30000	2661.26	1408.01	992.14	785.61	662.80	581.84	524.79	482.66	450.47	425.23	405.03	388.60	375.06	363.77
31000	2749.97	1454.94	1025.21	811.80	684.89	601.24	542.28	498.75	465.49	439.41	418.53	401.55	387.56	375.90
32000	2838.68	1501.88	1058.28	837.98	706.99	620.63	559.77	514.84	480.50	453.58	432.03	414.51	400.06	388.02
33000	2927.39	1548.81	1091.35	864.17	729.08	640.02	577.26	530.92	495.52	467.75	445.53	427.46	412.56	400.15
34000	3016.09	1595.74	1124.43	890.36	751.17	659.42	594.76	547.01	510.53	481.93	459.03	440.41	425.06	412.28
35000	3104.80	1642.68	1157.50	916.54	773.27	678.81	612.25	563.10	525.55	496.10	472.54	453.37	437.57	424.40
36000	3193.51	1689.61	1190.57	942.73	795.36	698.21	629.74	579.19	540.57	510.28	486.04	466.32	450.07	436.53
37000	3282.22	1736.54	1223.64	968.92	817.45	717.60	647.23	595.28	555.58	524.45	499.54	479.27	462.57	448.65
38000	3370.93	1783.48	1256.71	995.10	839.54	737.00	664.73	611.37	570.60	538.62	513.04	492.23	475.07	460.78
39000	3459.64	1830.41	1289.78	1021.29	861.64	756.39	682.22	627.45	585.61	552.80	526.54	505.18	487.57	472.90
40000	3548.35	1877.34	1322.85	1047.48	883.73	775.79	699.71	643.54	600.63	566.97	540.04	518.13	500.07	485.03
41000	3637.05	1924.28	1355.92	1073.66	905.82	795.18	717.21	659.63	615.64	581.15	553.54	531.08	512.58	497.15
42000	3725.76	1971.21	1389.00	1099.85	927.92	814.58	734.70	675.72	630.66	595.32	567.04	544.04	525.08	509.28
43000	3814.47	2018.15	1422.07	1126.04	950.01	833.97	752.19	691.81	645.67	609.50	580.54	556.99	537.58	521.41
44000	3903.18	2065.08	1455.14	1152.22	972.10	853.36	769.68	707.90	660.69	623.67	594.04	569.94	550.08	533.53
45000	3991.89	2112.01	1488.21	1178.41	994.20	872.76	787.18	723.99	675.71	637.84	607.54	582.90	562.58	545.66
46000	4080.60	2158.95	1521.28	1204.60	1016.29	892.15	804.67	740.07	690.72	652.02	621.05	595.85	575.09	557.78
47000	4169.30	2205.88	1554.35	1230.78	1038.38	911.55	822.16	756.16	705.74	666.19	634.55	608.80	587.59	569.91
48000	4258.01	2252.81	1587.42	1256.97	1060.48	930.94	839.65	772.25	720.75	680.37	648.05	621.76	600.09	582.03
49000	4346.72	2299.75	1620.49	1283.16	1082.57	950.34	857.15	788.34	735.77	694.54	661.55	634.71	612.59	594.16
50000	4435.43	2346.68	1653.57	1309.34	1104.66	969.73	874.64	804.43	750.78	708.72	675.05	647.66	625.09	606.29
55000	4878.97	2581.35	1818.92	1440.28	1215.13	1066.70	962.10	884.87	825.86	779.59	742.55	712.43	687.60	666.91
60000	5322.52	2816.01	1984.28	1571.21	1325.59	1163.68	1049.57	965.31	900.94	850.46	810.06	777.20	750.11	727.54
65000	5766.06	3050.68	2149.63	1702.15	1436.06	1260.65	1137.03	1045.75	976.02	921.33	877.56	841.96	812.62	788.17
70000	6209.60	3285.35	2314.99	1833.08	1546.53	1357.62	1224.49	1126.20	1051.09	992.20	945.07	906.73	875.13	848.80
75000	6653.14	3520.02	2480.35	1964.01	1656.99	1454.60	1311.96	1206.64	1126.17	1063.07	1012.57	971.49	937.64	909.43
80000	7096.69	3754.68	2645.70	2094.95	1767.46	1551.57	1399.42	1287.08	1201.25	1133.94	1080.07	1036.26	1000.14	970.05
85000	7540.23	3989.35	2811.06	2225.88	1877.92	1648.54	1486.88	1367.52	1276.33	1204.81	1147.58	1101.02	1062.65	1030.68
90000	7983.77	4224.02	2976.41	2356.82	1988.39	1745.51	1574.35	1447.97	1351.41	1275.68	1215.08	1165.79	1125.16	1091.31
95000	8427.31	4458.69	3141.77	2487.75	2098.85	1842.49	1661.81	1528.41	1426.48	1346.55	1282.59	1230.56	1187.67	1151.94
100000	8870.86	4693.35	3307.13	2618.68	2209.32	1939.46	1749.28	1608.85	1501.56	1417.43	1350.09	1295.32	1250.18	1212.57

TERM	15 Years	16 Years	17 Years	18 Years	19 Years	20 Years	21 Years	22 Years	23 Years	24 Years	25 Years	30 Years	35 Years	40 Years
AMOUNT														
5	.06	.06	.06	.06	.06	.06	.06	.06	.06	.06	.06	.06	.05	.05
10	.12	.12	.12	.12	.11	.11	.11	.11	.11	.11	.11	.11	.10	.10
15	.18	.18	.17	.17	.17	.17	.17	.16	.16	.16	.16	.16	.15	.15
25	.30	.29	.29	.28	.28	.28	.27	.27	.27	.26	.26	.26	.25	.25
50	.60	.58	.57	.56	.55	.55	.54	.53	.53	.52	.52	.51	.50	.50
75	.89	.87	.85	.84	.83	.82	.81	.80	.79	.78	.78	.76	.75	.74
100	1.19	1.16	1.14	1.12	1.10	1.09	1.07	1.06	1.05	1.04	1.04	1.01	1.00	.99
200	2.37	2.31	2.27	2.23	2.19	2.17	2.14	2.12	2.10	2.08	2.07	2.02	1.99	1.97
300	3.55	3.47	3.40	3.34	3.29	3.25	3.21	3.17	3.15	3.12	3.10	3.02	2.98	2.96
400	4.73	4.62	4.53	4.45	4.38	4.33	4.28	4.23	4.19	4.16	4.13	4.03	3.97	3.94
500	5.91	5.78	5.66	5.56	5.48	5.41	5.34	5.29	5.24	5.20	5.16	5.03	4.96	4.93
600	7.09	6.93	6.79	6.68	6.57	6.49	6.41	6.34	6.29	6.24	6.19	6.04	5.96	5.91
700	8.27	8.08	7.92	7.79	7.67	7.57	7.48	7.40	7.33	7.27	7.22	7.04	6.95	6.90
800	9.45	9.24	9.06	8.90	8.76	8.65	8.55	8.46	8.38	8.31	8.25	8.05	7.94	7.88
900	10.63	10.39	10.19	10.01	9.86	9.73	9.61	9.51	9.43	9.35	9.29	9.06	8.93	8.86
1000	11.81	11.55	11.32	11.12	10.95	10.81	10.68	10.57	10.47	10.39	10.32	10.06	9.92	9.85
2000	23.62	23.09	22.63	22.24	21.90	21.61	21.36	21.14	20.94	20.78	20.63	20.12	19.84	19.69
3000	35.43	34.63	33.94	33.36	32.85	32.41	32.03	31.70	31.41	31.16	30.94	30.17	29.76	29.54
4000	47.24	46.17	45.26	44.47	43.80	43.21	42.71	42.27	41.88	41.55	41.25	40.23	39.68	39.38
5000	59.05	57.71	56.57	55.59	54.75	54.02	53.38	52.83	52.35	51.93	51.56	50.28	49.60	49.22
6000	70.86	69.25	67.88	66.71	65.70	64.82	64.06	63.40	62.82	62.32	61.87	60.34	59.52	59.07
7000	82.67	80.79	79.20	77.82	76.64	75.62	74.74	73.96	73.29	72.70	72.18	70.40	69.43	68.91
8000	94.48	92.34	90.51	88.94	87.59	86.42	85.41	84.53	83.76	83.09	82.49	80.45	79.35	78.75
9000	106.29	103.88	101.82	100.06	98.54	97.23	96.09	95.09	94.23	93.47	92.81	90.51	89.27	88.60
10000	118.10	115.42	113.13	111.18	109.49	108.03	106.76	105.66	104.70	103.86	103.12	100.56	99.19	98.44
11000	129.91	126.96	124.45	122.29	120.44	118.83	117.44	116.23	115.17	114.24	113.43	110.62	109.11	108.28
12000	141.72	138.50	135.76	133.41	131.39	129.63	128.11	126.79	125.64	124.63	123.74	120.67	119.03	118.13
13000	153.53	150.04	147.07	144.53	142.33	140.44	138.79	137.36	136.11	135.01	134.05	130.73	128.95	127.97
14000	165.34	161.58	158.39	155.64	153.28	151.24	149.47	147.92	146.57	145.40	144.36	140.79	138.86	137.81
15000	177.15	173.13	169.70	166.76	164.23	162.04	160.14	158.49	157.04	155.78	154.67	150.84	148.78	147.66
16000	188.95	184.67	181.01	177.88	175.18	172.84	170.82	169.05	167.51	166.17	164.98	160.90	158.70	157.50
17000	200.76	196.21	192.33	189.00	186.13	183.65	181.49	179.62	177.98	176.55	175.30	170.95	168.62	167.34
18000	212.57	207.75	203.64	200.11	197.08	194.45	192.17	190.18	188.45	186.94	185.61	181.01	178.54	177.19
19000	224.38	219.29	214.95	211.23	208.02	205.25	202.84	200.75	198.92	197.32	195.92	191.07	188.46	187.03
20000	236.19	230.83	226.26	222.35	218.97	216.05	213.52	211.32	209.39	207.71	206.23	201.12	198.38	196.87
21000	248.00	242.37	237.58	233.46	229.92	226.86	224.20	221.88	219.86	218.09	216.54	211.18	208.29	206.72
22000	259.81	253.92	248.89	244.58	240.87	237.66	234.87	232.45	230.33	228.48	226.85	221.23	218.21	216.56
23000	271.62	265.46	260.20	255.70	251.82	248.46	245.55	243.01	240.80	238.86	237.16	231.29	228.13	226.40
24000	283.43	277.00	271.52	266.82	262.77	259.26	256.22	253.58	251.27	249.25	247.47	241.34	238.05	236.25
25000	295.24	288.54	282.83	277.93	273.71	270.07	266.90	264.14	261.74	259.63	257.79	251.40	247.97	246.09
26000	307.05	300.08	294.14	289.05	284.66	280.87	277.58	274.71	272.21	270.02	268.10	261.46	257.89	255.93
27000	318.86	311.62	305.45	300.17	295.61	291.67	288.25	285.27	282.68	280.40	278.41	271.51	267.80	265.78
28000	330.67	323.16	316.77	311.28	306.56	302.47	298.93	295.84	293.14	290.79	288.72	281.57	277.72	275.62
29000	342.48	334.71	328.08	322.40	317.51	313.28	309.60	306.40	303.61	301.17	299.03	291.62	287.64	285.46
30000	354.29	346.25	339.39	333.52	328.46	324.08	320.28	316.97	314.08	311.56	309.34	301.68	297.56	295.31
31000	366.09	357.79	350.71	344.63	339.40	334.88	330.95	327.54	324.55	321.94	319.65	311.73	307.48	305.15
32000	377.90	369.33	362.02	355.75	350.35	345.68	335.00	338.10	335.03	332.33	329.96	321.79	317.40	314.99
33000	389.71	380.87	373.33	366.87	361.30	356.49	352.31	348.67	345.49	342.71	340.28	331.85	327.32	324.84
34000	401.52	392.41	384.65	377.99	372.25	367.29	362.98	359.23	355.96	353.10	350.59	341.90	337.23	334.68
35000	413.33	403.95	395.96	389.10	383.20	378.09	373.66	369.80	366.43	363.48	360.90	351.96	347.15	344.53
36000	425.14	415.50	407.27	400.22	394.15	388.89	384.33	380.36	376.90	373.87	371.21	362.01	357.07	354.37
37000	436.95	427.04	418.58	411.34	405.09	399.70	395.01	390.93	387.37	384.25	381.52	372.07	366.99	364.21
38000	448.76	438.58	429.90	422.45	416.04	410.50	405.68	401.49	397.84	394.64	391.83	382.13	376.91	374.06
39000	460.57	450.12	441.21	433.57	426.99	421.30	416.36	412.06	408.31	405.02	402.14	392.18	386.83	383.90
40000	472.38	461.66	452.52	444.69	437.94	432.10	427.04	422.63	418.78	415.41	412.45	402.24	396.75	393.74
41000	484.19	473.20	463.84	455.81	448.89	442.90	437.71	433.19	429.24	425.79	422.77	412.29	406.66	403.59
42000	496.00	484.74	475.15	466.92	459.84	453.71	448.39	443.76	439.71	436.18	433.08	422.35	416.58	413.43
43000	507.81	496.29	486.46	478.04	470.78	464.51	459.06	454.32	450.18	446.56	443.39	432.40	426.50	423.27
44000	519.62	507.83	497.78	489.16	481.73	475.31	469.74	464.89	460.65	456.95	453.70	442.46	436.42	433.12
45000	531.43	519.37	509.09	500.27	492.68	486.11	480.41	475.45	471.12	467.33	464.01	452.52	446.34	442.96
46000	543.24	530.91	520.40	511.39	503.63	496.92	491.09	486.02	481.59	477.72	474.32	462.57	456.26	452.80
47000	555.04	542.45	531.71	522.51	514.58	507.72	501.77	496.58	492.06	488.10	484.63	472.63	466.17	462.65
48000	566.85	553.99	543.03	533.63	525.53	518.52	512.44	507.15	502.53	498.49	494.94	482.68	476.09	472.49
49000	578.66	565.53	554.34	544.74	536.47	529.32	523.12	517.72	513.00	508.87	505.26	492.74	486.01	482.33
50000	590.47	577.08	565.65	555.86	547.42	540.13	533.79	528.28	523.47	519.26	515.57	502.79	495.93	492.18
55000	649.52	634.78	622.22	611.44	602.17	594.14	587.17	581.11	575.81	571.18	567.12	553.07	545.52	541.39
60000	708.57	692.49	678.78	667.03	656.91	648.15	640.55	633.94	628.16	623.11	618.68	603.35	595.12	590.61
65000	767.61	750.20	735.35	722.62	711.65	702.16	693.93	686.76	680.51	675.03	670.24	653.63	644.71	639.83
70000	826.66	807.90	791.91	778.20	766.39	756.18	747.31	739.59	732.85	726.96	721.79	703.91	694.30	689.05
75000	885.71	865.61	848.48	833.79	821.13	810.19	800.69	792.42	785.20	778.88	773.35	754.19	743.89	738.26
80000	944.75	923.32	905.04	889.37	875.87	864.20	854.07	845.25	837.55	830.81	824.90	804.47	793.49	787.48
85000	1003.80	981.03	961.61	944.96	930.62	918.21	907.45	898.07	889.89	882.74	876.46	854.75	843.08	836.70
90000	1062.85	1038.73	1018.17	1000.54	985.36	972.22	960.82	950.90	942.24	934.66	928.02	905.03	892.67	885.91
95000	1121.89	1096.44	1074.74	1056.13	1040.10	1026.24	1014.20	1003.73	994.59	986.59	979.57	955.31	942.26	935.13
100000	1180.94	1154.15	1131.30	1111.71	1094.84	1080.25	1067.58	1056.56	1046.93	1038.51	1031.13	1005.58	991.86	984.35

MONTHLY PAYMENT
REQUIRED TO AMORTIZE A LOAN

TERM AMOUNT	1 Year	2 Years	3 Years	4 Years	5 Years	6 Years	7 Years	8 Years	9 Years	10 Years	11 Years	12 Years	13 Years	14 Years
5	.45	.24	.17	.14	.12	.10	.09	.09	.08	.08	.07	.07	.07	.07
10	.89	.47	.34	.27	.23	.20	.18	.17	.16	.15	.14	.13	.13	.13
15	1.34	.71	.50	.40	.34	.30	.27	.25	.23	.22	.21	.20	.19	.19
25	2.22	1.18	.83	.66	.56	.49	.44	.41	.38	.36	.34	.33	.32	.31
50	4.44	2.35	1.66	1.32	1.11	.98	.88	.81	.76	.72	.68	.65	.63	.61
75	6.66	3.53	2.49	1.97	1.66	1.46	1.32	1.21	1.13	1.07	1.02	.98	.94	.92
100	8.88	4.70	3.31	2.63	2.22	1.95	1.76	1.62	1.51	1.43	1.36	1.30	1.26	1.22
200	17.75	9.40	6.62	5.25	4.43	3.89	3.51	3.23	3.01	2.85	2.71	2.60	2.51	2.44
300	26.62	14.09	9.93	7.87	6.64	5.83	5.26	4.84	4.52	4.27	4.06	3.90	3.76	3.65
400	35.50	18.79	13.24	10.49	8.85	7.77	7.01	6.45	6.02	5.69	5.42	5.20	5.02	4.87
500	44.37	23.48	16.55	13.11	11.06	9.72	8.76	8.06	7.53	7.11	6.77	6.50	6.27	6.08
600	53.24	28.18	19.86	15.73	13.28	11.66	10.52	9.67	9.03	8.53	8.12	7.79	7.52	7.30
700	62.12	32.87	23.17	18.35	15.49	13.60	12.27	11.29	10.54	9.95	9.48	9.09	8.78	8.51
800	70.99	37.57	26.48	20.97	17.70	15.54	14.02	12.90	12.04	11.37	10.83	10.39	10.03	9.73
900	79.86	42.27	29.79	23.60	19.91	17.48	15.77	14.51	13.54	12.79	12.18	11.69	11.28	10.95
1000	88.74	46.96	33.10	26.22	22.12	19.43	17.52	16.12	15.05	14.21	13.54	12.99	12.54	12.16
2000	177.47	93.92	66.20	52.43	44.24	38.85	35.04	32.24	30.09	28.41	27.07	25.97	25.07	24.32
3000	266.20	140.88	99.29	78.64	66.36	58.27	52.56	48.35	45.14	42.61	40.60	38.95	37.60	36.48
4000	354.93	187.83	132.39	104.85	88.48	77.69	70.08	64.47	60.18	56.82	54.13	51.94	50.13	48.63
5000	443.66	234.79	165.48	131.06	110.60	97.11	87.60	80.58	75.22	71.02	67.66	64.92	62.67	60.79
6000	532.40	281.75	198.58	157.27	132.71	116.53	105.12	96.70	90.27	85.22	81.19	77.90	75.20	72.95
7000	621.13	328.70	231.67	183.48	154.83	135.95	122.64	112.82	105.31	99.43	94.72	90.89	87.73	85.10
8000	709.86	375.66	264.77	209.70	176.95	155.37	140.16	128.93	120.35	113.63	108.25	103.87	100.26	97.26
9000	798.59	422.62	297.86	235.91	199.07	174.79	157.68	145.05	135.40	127.83	121.78	116.85	112.80	109.42
10000	887.32	469.57	330.96	262.12	221.19	194.21	175.20	161.16	150.44	142.03	135.31	129.84	125.33	121.57
11000	976.06	516.53	364.05	288.33	243.31	213.63	192.72	177.28	165.48	156.24	148.84	142.82	137.86	133.73
12000	1064.79	563.49	397.15	314.54	265.42	233.05	210.24	193.39	180.53	170.44	162.37	155.80	150.39	145.89
13000	1153.52	610.44	430.24	340.75	287.54	252.47	227.76	209.51	195.57	184.64	175.90	168.79	162.93	158.05
14000	1242.25	657.40	463.34	366.96	309.66	271.89	245.28	225.63	210.62	198.85	189.43	181.77	175.46	170.20
15000	1330.98	704.36	496.43	393.17	331.78	291.31	262.79	241.74	225.66	213.05	202.96	194.75	187.99	182.36
16000	1419.72	751.31	529.53	419.39	353.90	310.73	280.31	257.86	240.70	227.25	216.49	207.74	200.52	194.52
17000	1508.45	798.27	562.62	445.60	376.02	330.15	297.83	273.97	255.75	241.46	230.02	220.72	213.06	206.67
18000	1597.18	845.23	595.72	471.81	398.13	349.57	315.35	290.09	270.79	255.66	243.55	233.70	225.59	218.83
19000	1685.91	892.18	628.81	498.02	420.25	368.99	332.87	306.21	285.83	269.86	257.08	246.69	238.12	230.99
20000	1774.64	939.14	661.91	524.23	442.37	388.41	350.39	322.32	300.88	284.06	270.61	259.67	250.65	243.14
21000	1863.37	986.10	695.00	550.44	464.49	407.83	367.91	338.44	315.92	298.27	284.14	272.65	263.19	255.30
22000	1952.11	1033.05	728.10	576.65	486.61	427.25	385.43	354.55	330.96	312.47	297.67	285.64	275.72	267.46
23000	2040.84	1080.01	761.19	602.86	508.73	446.67	402.95	370.67	346.01	326.67	311.20	298.62	288.25	279.62
24000	2129.57	1126.97	794.29	629.08	530.84	466.10	420.47	386.78	361.05	340.88	324.73	311.60	300.78	291.77
25000	2218.30	1173.93	827.38	655.29	552.96	485.52	437.99	402.90	376.10	355.08	338.26	324.59	313.32	303.93
26000	2307.03	1220.88	860.48	681.50	575.08	504.94	455.51	419.02	391.14	369.28	351.79	337.57	325.85	316.09
27000	2395.77	1267.84	893.57	707.71	597.20	524.36	473.03	435.13	406.18	383.48	365.32	350.55	338.38	328.24
28000	2484.50	1314.80	926.67	733.92	619.32	543.78	490.55	451.25	421.23	397.69	378.85	363.54	350.91	340.40
29000	2573.23	1361.75	959.76	760.13	641.44	563.20	508.07	467.36	436.27	411.89	392.38	376.52	363.45	352.56
30000	2661.96	1408.71	992.86	786.34	663.55	582.62	525.58	483.48	451.31	426.09	405.91	389.50	375.98	364.71
31000	2750.69	1455.67	1025.95	812.55	685.67	602.04	543.10	499.59	466.36	440.30	419.44	402.49	388.51	376.87
32000	2839.43	1502.62	1059.05	838.77	707.79	621.46	560.62	515.71	481.40	454.50	432.97	415.47	401.04	389.03
33000	2928.16	1549.58	1092.14	864.98	729.91	640.88	578.14	531.83	496.44	468.70	446.50	428.45	413.58	401.18
34000	3016.89	1596.54	1125.24	891.19	752.03	660.30	595.66	547.94	511.49	482.91	460.03	441.44	426.11	413.34
35000	3105.62	1643.49	1158.33	917.40	774.15	679.72	613.18	564.06	526.53	497.11	473.57	454.42	438.64	425.50
36000	3194.35	1690.45	1191.43	943.61	796.26	699.14	630.70	580.17	541.57	511.31	487.10	467.40	451.17	437.66
37000	3283.08	1737.41	1224.52	969.82	818.38	718.56	648.22	596.29	556.62	525.51	500.63	480.39	463.71	449.81
38000	3371.82	1784.36	1257.62	996.03	840.50	737.98	665.74	612.41	571.66	539.72	514.16	493.37	476.24	461.97
39000	3460.55	1831.32	1290.71	1022.24	862.62	757.40	683.26	628.52	586.71	553.92	527.69	506.35	488.77	474.13
40000	3549.28	1878.28	1323.81	1048.46	884.74	776.82	700.78	644.64	601.75	568.12	541.22	519.34	501.30	486.28
41000	3638.01	1925.23	1356.90	1074.67	906.86	796.24	718.30	660.75	616.79	582.33	554.75	532.32	513.84	498.44
42000	3726.74	1972.19	1390.00	1100.88	928.97	815.66	735.82	676.87	631.84	596.53	568.28	545.30	526.37	510.60
43000	3815.48	2019.15	1423.09	1127.09	951.09	835.08	753.34	692.98	646.88	610.73	581.81	558.28	538.90	522.75
44000	3904.21	2066.10	1456.19	1153.30	973.21	854.50	770.85	709.10	661.92	624.93	595.34	571.27	551.43	534.91
45000	3992.94	2113.06	1489.28	1179.51	995.33	873.92	788.37	725.22	676.97	639.14	608.87	584.25	563.97	547.07
46000	4081.67	2160.02	1522.38	1205.72	1017.45	893.34	805.89	741.33	692.01	653.34	622.40	597.23	576.50	559.23
47000	4170.40	2206.98	1555.47	1231.93	1039.57	912.77	823.41	757.45	707.05	667.54	635.93	610.22	589.03	571.38
48000	4259.14	2253.93	1588.57	1258.15	1061.68	932.19	840.93	773.56	722.10	681.75	649.46	623.20	601.56	583.54
49000	4347.87	2300.89	1621.66	1284.36	1083.80	951.61	858.45	789.68	737.14	695.95	662.99	636.18	614.10	595.70
50000	4436.60	2347.85	1654.76	1310.57	1105.92	971.03	875.97	805.79	752.19	710.15	676.52	649.17	626.63	607.85
55000	4880.26	2582.63	1820.23	1441.62	1216.51	1068.13	963.57	886.37	827.40	781.17	744.17	714.08	689.29	668.64
60000	5323.92	2817.41	1985.71	1572.68	1327.10	1165.23	1051.16	966.95	902.62	852.18	811.82	779.00	751.95	729.42
65000	5767.58	3052.20	2151.18	1703.74	1437.70	1262.33	1138.76	1047.53	977.84	923.20	879.47	843.92	814.62	790.21
70000	6211.24	3286.98	2316.66	1834.79	1548.29	1359.44	1226.36	1128.11	1053.06	994.21	947.13	908.83	877.28	850.99
75000	6654.90	3521.77	2482.13	1965.85	1658.88	1456.54	1313.95	1208.69	1128.28	1065.23	1014.78	973.75	939.94	911.78
80000	7098.56	3756.55	2647.61	2096.91	1769.47	1553.64	1401.55	1289.27	1203.49	1136.24	1082.43	1038.67	1002.60	972.56
85000	7542.21	3991.33	2813.08	2227.96	1880.06	1650.74	1489.15	1369.85	1278.71	1207.26	1150.08	1103.58	1065.27	1033.35
90000	7985.87	4226.12	2978.56	2359.02	1990.65	1747.84	1576.74	1450.43	1353.93	1278.27	1217.73	1168.50	1127.93	1094.13
95000	8429.53	4460.90	3144.03	2490.07	2101.25	1844.95	1664.34	1531.01	1429.15	1349.28	1285.38	1233.41	1190.59	1154.92
100000	8873.19	4695.69	3309.51	2621.13	2211.84	1942.05	1751.94	1611.58	1504.37	1420.30	1353.03	1298.33	1253.25	1215.70

MONTHLY PAYMENT
REQUIRED TO AMORTIZE A LOAN

11.750%

TERM AMOUNT	15 Years	16 Years	17 Years	18 Years	19 Years	20 Years	21 Years	22 Years	23 Years	24 Years	25 Years	30 Years	35 Years	40 Years
5	.06	.06	.06	.06	.06	.06	.06	.06	.06	.06	.06	.06	.05	.05
10	.12	.12	.12	.12	.11	.11	.11	.11	.11	.11	.11	.11	.10	.10
15	.18	.18	.18	.17	.17	.17	.17	.16	.16	.16	.16	.16	.15	.15
25	.30	.29	.29	.28	.28	.28	.27	.27	.27	.27	.26	.26	.25	.25
50	.60	.58	.57	.56	.55	.55	.54	.54	.53	.53	.52	.51	.50	.50
75	.89	.87	.86	.84	.83	.82	.81	.80	.79	.79	.78	.76	.75	.75
100	1.19	1.16	1.14	1.12	1.10	1.09	1.08	1.07	1.06	1.05	1.04	1.01	1.00	.99
200	2.37	2.32	2.27	2.24	2.20	2.17	2.15	2.13	2.11	2.09	2.07	2.02	2.00	1.98
300	3.56	3.48	3.41	3.35	3.30	3.26	3.22	3.19	3.16	3.13	3.11	3.03	2.99	2.97
400	4.74	4.63	4.54	4.47	4.40	4.34	4.29	4.25	4.21	4.17	4.14	4.04	3.99	3.96
500	5.93	5.79	5.68	5.58	5.50	5.42	5.36	5.31	5.26	5.22	5.18	5.05	4.98	4.95
600	7.11	6.95	6.81	6.70	6.59	6.51	6.43	6.37	6.31	6.26	6.21	6.06	5.98	5.94
700	8.29	8.11	7.95	7.81	7.69	7.59	7.50	7.43	7.36	7.30	7.25	7.07	6.98	6.92
800	9.48	9.26	9.08	8.93	8.79	8.67	8.57	8.49	8.41	8.34	8.28	8.08	7.97	7.91
900	10.66	10.42	10.22	10.04	9.89	9.76	9.64	9.55	9.46	9.38	9.32	9.09	8.97	8.90
1000	11.85	11.58	11.35	11.16	10.99	10.84	10.72	10.61	10.51	10.43	10.35	10.10	9.96	9.89
2000	23.69	23.15	22.70	22.31	21.97	21.68	21.43	21.21	21.02	20.85	20.70	20.19	19.92	19.77
3000	35.53	34.73	34.04	33.46	32.95	32.52	32.14	31.81	31.52	31.27	31.05	30.29	29.88	29.66
4000	47.37	46.30	45.39	44.61	43.94	43.35	42.85	42.41	42.03	41.69	41.40	40.38	39.84	39.54
5000	59.21	57.87	56.74	55.76	54.92	54.19	53.56	53.01	52.53	52.11	51.74	50.48	49.79	49.42
6000	71.05	69.45	68.08	66.91	65.90	65.03	64.27	63.61	63.04	62.53	62.09	60.57	59.75	59.31
7000	82.89	81.02	79.43	78.06	76.88	75.86	74.98	74.21	73.54	72.95	72.44	70.66	69.71	69.19
8000	94.74	92.60	90.77	89.21	87.87	86.70	85.69	84.81	84.05	83.38	82.79	80.76	79.67	79.07
9000	106.58	104.17	102.12	100.36	98.85	97.54	96.40	95.41	94.55	93.80	93.14	90.85	89.63	88.96
10000	118.42	115.74	113.47	111.51	109.83	108.38	107.11	106.02	105.06	104.22	103.48	100.95	99.58	98.84
11000	130.26	127.32	124.81	122.66	120.81	119.21	117.82	116.62	115.56	114.64	113.83	111.04	109.54	108.73
12000	142.10	138.89	136.16	133.81	131.80	130.05	128.54	127.22	126.07	125.06	124.18	121.13	119.50	110.61
13000	153.94	150.47	147.50	144.96	142.78	140.89	139.25	137.82	136.57	135.48	134.53	131.23	129.46	128.49
14000	165.78	162.04	158.85	156.12	153.76	151.72	149.96	148.42	147.08	145.90	144.88	141.32	139.42	138.38
15000	177.62	173.61	170.20	167.27	164.74	162.56	160.67	159.02	157.58	156.33	155.22	151.42	149.37	148.26
16000	189.47	185.19	181.54	178.42	175.73	173.40	171.38	169.62	168.09	166.75	165.57	161.51	159.33	158.14
17000	201.31	196.76	192.89	189.57	186.71	184.24	182.09	180.22	178.59	177.17	175.92	171.60	169.29	168.03
18000	213.15	208.34	204.23	200.72	197.69	195.07	192.80	190.82	189.10	187.59	186.27	181.70	179.25	177.91
19000	224.99	219.91	215.58	211.87	208.67	205.91	203.51	201.43	199.60	198.01	196.62	191.79	189.21	187.79
20000	236.83	231.48	226.93	223.02	219.66	216.75	214.22	212.03	210.11	208.43	206.96	201.89	199.16	197.68
21000	248.67	243.06	238.27	234.17	230.64	227.58	224.93	222.63	220.61	218.85	217.31	211.98	209.12	207.56
22000	260.51	254.63	249.62	245.32	241.62	238.42	235.64	233.23	231.12	229.28	227.66	222.00	219.08	217.45
23000	272.36	266.21	260.96	256.47	252.60	249.26	246.36	243.83	241.63	239.70	238.01	232.17	229.04	227.33
24000	284.20	277.78	272.31	267.62	263.59	260.09	257.07	254.43	252.13	250.12	248.36	242.26	239.00	237.21
25000	296.04	289.35	283.66	278.77	274.57	270.93	267.78	265.03	262.64	260.54	258.70	252.36	248.95	247.10
26000	307.88	300.93	295.00	289.92	285.55	281.77	278.49	275.63	273.14	270.96	269.05	262.45	258.91	256.98
27000	319.72	312.50	306.35	301.07	296.53	292.61	289.20	286.23	283.65	281.38	279.40	272.55	268.87	266.86
28000	331.56	324.08	317.69	312.23	307.52	303.44	299.91	296.83	294.15	291.80	289.75	282.64	278.83	276.75
29000	343.40	335.65	329.04	323.38	318.50	314.28	310.62	307.44	304.66	302.23	300.10	292.73	288.79	286.63
30000	355.24	347.22	340.39	334.53	329.48	325.12	321.33	318.04	315.16	312.65	310.44	302.83	298.74	296.51
31000	367.09	358.80	351.73	345.68	340.46	335.95	332.04	328.64	325.67	323.07	320.79	312.92	308.70	306.40
32000	378.93	370.37	363.08	356.83	351.45	346.79	342.75	339.24	336.17	333.49	331.14	323.02	318.66	316.28
33000	390.77	381.95	374.43	367.98	362.43	357.63	353.46	349.84	346.68	343.91	341.49	333.11	328.62	326.17
34000	402.61	393.52	385.77	379.13	373.41	368.47	364.17	360.44	357.18	354.33	351.84	343.20	338.57	336.05
35000	414.45	405.09	397.12	390.28	384.39	379.30	374.89	371.04	367.69	364.75	362.18	353.30	348.53	345.93
36000	426.29	416.67	408.46	401.43	395.38	390.14	385.60	381.64	378.19	375.18	372.53	363.39	358.49	355.82
37000	438.13	428.24	419.81	412.58	406.36	400.98	396.31	392.24	388.70	385.60	382.88	373.49	368.45	365.70
38000	449.97	439.82	431.16	423.73	417.34	411.81	407.02	402.85	399.20	396.02	393.23	383.58	378.41	375.58
39000	461.82	451.39	442.50	434.88	428.32	422.65	417.73	413.45	409.71	406.44	403.58	393.67	388.36	385.47
40000	473.66	462.96	453.85	446.03	439.31	433.49	428.44	424.05	420.21	416.86	413.92	403.77	398.32	395.35
41000	485.50	474.54	465.19	457.18	450.29	444.32	439.15	434.65	430.72	427.28	424.27	413.86	408.28	405.23
42000	497.34	486.11	476.54	468.34	461.27	455.16	449.86	445.25	441.22	437.70	434.62	423.96	418.24	415.12
43000	509.18	497.69	487.89	479.49	472.25	466.00	460.57	455.85	451.73	448.13	444.97	434.05	428.20	425.00
44000	521.02	509.26	499.23	490.64	483.24	476.84	471.28	466.45	462.24	458.55	455.32	444.15	438.15	434.89
45000	532.86	520.83	510.58	501.79	494.22	487.67	481.99	477.05	472.74	468.97	465.66	454.24	448.11	444.77
46000	544.71	532.41	521.92	512.94	505.20	498.51	492.71	487.65	483.25	479.39	476.01	464.33	458.07	454.65
47000	556.55	543.98	533.27	524.09	516.18	509.35	503.42	498.25	493.75	489.81	486.36	474.43	468.03	464.54
48000	568.39	555.56	544.62	535.24	527.17	520.18	514.13	508.86	504.26	500.23	496.71	484.52	477.99	474.42
49000	580.23	567.13	555.96	546.39	538.15	531.02	524.84	519.46	514.76	510.65	507.06	494.62	487.94	484.30
50000	592.07	578.70	567.31	557.54	549.13	541.86	535.55	530.06	525.27	521.08	517.40	504.71	497.90	494.19
55000	651.28	636.57	624.04	613.29	604.04	596.04	589.10	583.06	577.79	573.18	569.14	555.18	547.69	543.61
60000	710.48	694.44	680.77	669.05	658.96	650.23	642.66	636.07	630.32	625.29	620.88	605.65	597.48	593.02
65000	769.69	752.31	737.50	724.80	713.87	704.41	696.21	689.07	682.85	677.40	672.62	656.12	647.27	642.44
70000	828.90	810.18	794.23	780.56	768.78	758.60	749.77	742.08	735.37	729.50	724.36	706.59	697.06	691.86
75000	888.10	868.05	850.96	836.31	823.69	812.79	803.32	795.08	787.90	781.61	776.10	757.06	746.85	741.28
80000	947.31	925.92	907.69	892.06	878.61	866.97	856.88	848.09	840.42	833.72	827.84	807.53	796.64	790.70
85000	1006.52	983.79	964.42	947.82	933.52	921.16	910.43	901.09	892.95	885.83	879.58	858.00	846.43	840.11
90000	1065.72	1041.66	1021.15	1003.57	988.43	975.34	963.98	954.10	945.48	937.93	931.32	908.47	896.22	889.53
95000	1124.93	1099.53	1077.88	1059.32	1043.34	1029.53	1017.54	1007.11	998.00	990.04	983.06	958.94	946.01	938.95
100000	1184.14	1157.40	1134.61	1115.08	1098.26	1083.71	1071.09	1060.11	1050.53	1042.15	1034.80	1009.41	995.80	988.37

MONTHLY PAYMENT
REQUIRED TO AMORTIZE A LOAN

TERM	1 Year	2 Years	3 Years	4 Years	5 Years	6 Years	7 Years	8 Years	9 Years	10 Years	11 Years	12 Years	13 Years	14 Years
AMOUNT														
5	.45	.24	.17	.14	.12	.10	.09	.09	.08	.08	.07	.07	.07	.07
10	.89	.47	.34	.27	.23	.20	.18	.17	.16	.15	.14	.14	.13	.13
15	1.34	.71	.50	.40	.34	.30	.27	.25	.23	.22	.21	.20	.19	.19
25	2.22	1.18	.83	.66	.56	.49	.44	.41	.38	.36	.34	.33	.32	.31
50	4.44	2.35	1.66	1.32	1.11	.98	.88	.81	.76	.72	.68	.66	.63	.61
75	6.66	3.53	2.49	1.97	1.67	1.46	1.32	1.22	1.14	1.07	1.02	.98	.95	.92
100	8.88	4.70	3.32	2.63	2.22	1.95	1.76	1.62	1.51	1.43	1.36	1.31	1.26	1.22
200	17.76	9.40	6.63	5.25	4.43	3.89	3.51	3.23	3.02	2.85	2.72	2.61	2.52	2.44
300	26.63	14.10	9.94	7.88	6.65	5.84	5.27	4.85	4.53	4.27	4.07	3.91	3.77	3.66
400	35.51	18.80	13.25	10.50	8.88	7.78	7.02	6.46	6.00	5.70	5.43	5.21	5.03	4.88
500	44.38	23.50	16.56	13.12	11.08	9.73	8.78	8.08	7.54	7.12	6.78	6.51	6.29	6.10
600	53.26	28.19	19.88	15.75	13.29	11.67	10.53	9.69	9.05	8.54	8.14	7.81	7.54	7.32
700	62.13	32.89	23.19	18.37	15.51	13.62	12.29	11.31	10.56	9.97	9.50	9.11	8.80	8.54
800	71.01	37.59	26.50	20.99	17.72	15.56	14.04	12.92	12.06	11.39	10.85	10.42	10.06	9.76
900	79.88	42.29	29.81	23.62	19.93	17.51	15.80	14.53	13.57	12.81	12.21	11.72	11.31	10.97
1000	88.76	46.99	33.12	26.24	22.15	19.45	17.55	16.15	15.08	14.24	13.56	13.02	12.57	12.19
2000	177.52	93.97	66.24	52.48	44.29	38.90	35.10	32.29	30.15	28.47	27.12	26.03	25.13	24.38
3000	266.27	140.95	99.36	78.71	66.44	58.34	52.64	48.43	45.22	42.70	40.68	39.05	37.69	36.57
4000	355.03	187.93	132.48	104.95	88.58	77.79	70.19	64.58	60.29	56.93	54.24	52.06	50.26	48.76
5000	443.78	234.91	165.60	131.18	110.72	97.24	87.73	80.72	75.36	71.16	67.80	65.07	62.82	60.95
6000	532.54	281.89	198.72	157.42	132.87	116.68	105.28	96.86	90.44	85.40	81.36	78.09	75.38	73.14
7000	621.29	328.87	231.84	183.66	155.01	136.13	122.83	113.01	105.51	99.63	94.92	91.10	87.95	85.32
8000	710.05	375.85	264.96	209.89	177.15	155.58	140.37	129.15	120.58	113.86	108.48	104.11	100.51	97.51
9000	798.80	422.83	298.07	236.13	199.30	175.02	157.92	145.29	135.65	128.09	122.04	117.13	113.07	109.70
10000	887.56	469.81	331.19	262.36	221.44	194.47	175.46	161.44	150.72	142.32	135.60	130.14	125.64	121.89
11000	976.31	516.79	364.31	288.60	243.58	213.91	193.01	177.58	165.79	156.55	149.16	143.15	138.20	134.08
12000	1065.07	563.77	397.43	314.83	265.73	233.36	210.56	193.72	180.87	170.79	162.72	156.17	150.76	146.27
13000	1153.82	610.75	430.55	341.07	287.87	252.81	228.10	209.87	195.94	185.02	176.28	169.18	163.33	158.45
14000	1242.58	657.73	463.67	367.31	310.01	272.25	245.65	226.01	211.01	199.25	189.84	182.19	175.89	170.64
15000	1331.33	704.71	496.79	393.54	332.16	291.70	263.19	242.15	226.08	213.48	203.40	195.21	188.45	182.83
16000	1420.09	751.69	529.91	419.78	354.30	311.15	280.74	258.30	241.15	227.71	216.96	208.22	201.02	195.02
17000	1508.84	798.67	563.03	446.01	376.44	330.59	298.29	274.44	256.22	241.94	230.52	221.23	213.58	207.21
18000	1597.60	845.65	596.14	472.25	398.59	350.04	315.83	290.58	271.30	256.18	244.08	234.25	226.14	219.40
19000	1686.35	892.63	629.26	498.48	420.73	369.49	333.38	306.72	286.37	270.41	257.64	247.26	238.71	231.58
20000	1775.11	939.61	662.38	524.72	442.88	388.93	350.92	322.87	301.44	284.64	271.20	260.27	251.27	243.77
21000	1863.87	986.59	695.50	550.96	465.02	408.38	368.47	339.01	316.51	298.87	284.76	273.29	263.83	255.96
22000	1952.62	1033.57	728.62	577.19	487.16	427.82	386.02	355.15	331.58	313.10	298.32	286.30	276.40	268.15
23000	2041.38	1080.55	761.74	603.43	509.31	447.27	403.56	371.30	346.65	327.33	311.88	299.31	288.96	280.34
24000	2130.13	1127.53	794.86	629.66	531.45	466.72	421.11	387.44	361.73	341.57	325.44	312.33	301.52	292.53
25000	2218.89	1174.51	827.98	655.90	553.59	486.16	438.65	403.58	376.80	355.80	339.00	325.34	314.09	304.71
26000	2307.64	1221.49	861.10	682.13	575.74	505.61	456.20	419.73	391.87	370.03	352.56	338.35	326.65	316.90
27000	2396.40	1268.47	894.21	708.37	597.88	525.06	473.75	435.87	406.94	384.26	366.12	351.37	339.21	329.09
28000	2485.15	1315.45	927.33	734.61	620.02	544.50	491.29	452.01	422.01	398.49	379.68	364.38	351.78	341.28
29000	2573.91	1362.43	960.45	760.84	642.17	563.95	508.84	468.16	437.08	412.72	393.24	377.39	364.34	353.47
30000	2662.66	1409.40	993.57	787.08	664.31	583.40	526.38	484.30	452.16	426.96	406.80	390.41	376.90	365.66
31000	2751.42	1456.39	1026.69	813.31	686.45	602.84	543.93	500.44	467.23	441.19	420.36	403.42	389.47	377.84
32000	2840.17	1503.37	1059.81	839.55	708.60	622.29	561.48	516.59	482.30	455.42	433.92	416.43	402.03	390.03
33000	2928.93	1550.35	1092.93	865.78	730.74	641.73	579.02	532.73	497.37	469.65	447.48	429.45	414.59	402.22
34000	3017.68	1597.33	1126.05	892.02	752.88	661.18	596.57	548.87	512.44	483.88	461.04	442.46	427.16	414.41
35000	3106.44	1644.31	1159.17	918.26	775.03	680.63	614.11	565.02	527.51	498.12	474.60	455.47	439.72	426.60
36000	3195.19	1691.29	1192.28	944.49	797.17	700.07	631.66	581.16	542.59	512.35	488.16	468.49	452.28	438.79
37000	3283.95	1738.27	1225.40	970.73	819.31	719.52	649.21	597.30	557.66	526.58	501.72	481.50	464.84	450.97
38000	3372.70	1785.25	1258.52	996.96	841.46	738.97	666.75	613.44	572.73	540.81	515.28	494.51	477.41	463.16
39000	3461.46	1832.23	1291.64	1023.20	863.60	758.41	684.30	629.59	587.80	555.04	528.84	507.53	489.97	475.35
40000	3550.22	1879.21	1324.76	1049.43	885.75	777.86	701.84	645.73	602.87	569.27	542.39	520.54	502.53	487.54
41000	3638.97	1926.19	1357.88	1075.67	907.89	797.31	719.39	661.87	617.94	583.51	555.95	533.55	515.10	499.73
42000	3727.73	1973.17	1391.00	1101.91	930.03	816.75	736.94	678.02	633.02	597.74	569.51	546.57	527.66	511.92
43000	3816.48	2020.15	1424.12	1128.14	952.18	836.20	754.48	694.16	648.09	611.97	583.07	559.58	540.22	524.10
44000	3905.24	2067.13	1457.24	1154.38	974.32	855.64	772.03	710.30	663.16	626.20	596.63	572.59	552.79	536.29
45000	3993.99	2114.11	1490.35	1180.61	996.46	875.09	789.57	726.45	678.23	640.43	610.19	585.61	565.35	548.48
46000	4082.75	2161.09	1523.47	1206.85	1018.61	894.54	807.12	742.59	693.30	654.66	623.75	598.62	577.91	560.67
47000	4171.50	2208.07	1556.59	1233.09	1040.75	913.98	824.66	758.73	708.37	668.90	637.31	611.63	590.48	572.86
48000	4260.26	2255.05	1589.71	1259.32	1062.89	933.43	842.21	774.88	723.45	683.13	650.87	624.65	603.04	585.05
49000	4349.01	2302.03	1622.83	1285.56	1085.04	952.88	859.76	791.02	738.52	697.36	664.43	637.66	615.60	597.23
50000	4437.77	2349.01	1655.95	1311.79	1107.18	972.32	877.30	807.16	753.59	711.59	677.99	650.67	628.17	609.42
55000	4881.54	2583.91	1821.54	1442.97	1217.90	1069.55	965.03	887.88	828.95	782.75	745.79	715.74	690.98	670.36
60000	5325.32	2818.81	1987.14	1574.15	1328.62	1166.79	1052.76	968.59	904.31	853.91	813.59	780.81	753.80	731.31
65000	5769.10	3053.71	2152.73	1705.33	1439.33	1264.02	1140.49	1049.31	979.66	925.07	881.39	845.87	816.62	792.25
70000	6212.87	3288.61	2318.33	1836.51	1550.05	1361.25	1228.22	1130.03	1055.02	996.23	949.19	910.94	879.43	853.19
75000	6656.65	3523.51	2483.92	1967.69	1660.77	1458.48	1315.95	1210.74	1130.38	1067.38	1016.99	976.01	942.25	914.13
80000	7100.43	3758.42	2649.51	2098.86	1771.49	1555.71	1403.68	1291.46	1205.74	1138.54	1084.78	1041.08	1005.06	975.07
85000	7544.20	3993.32	2815.11	2230.04	1882.20	1652.94	1491.41	1372.17	1281.10	1209.70	1152.58	1106.14	1067.88	1036.02
90000	7987.98	4228.22	2980.70	2361.22	1992.92	1750.18	1579.14	1452.89	1356.46	1280.86	1220.38	1171.21	1130.70	1096.96
95000	8431.75	4463.12	3146.30	2492.40	2103.64	1847.41	1666.87	1533.60	1431.81	1352.02	1288.18	1236.28	1193.51	1157.90
100000	8875.53	4698.02	3311.89	2623.58	2214.36	1944.64	1754.60	1614.32	1507.17	1423.18	1355.98	1301.34	1256.33	1218.84

TERM	15 Years	16 Years	17 Years	18 Years	19 Years	20 Years	21 Years	22 Years	23 Years	24 Years	25 Years	30 Years	35 Years	40 Years
AMOUNT														
5	.06	.06	.06	.06	.06	.06	.06	.06	.06	.06	.06	.06	.05	.05
10	.12	.12	.12	.12	.12	.11	.11	.11	.11	.11	.11	.11	.10	.10
15	.18	.18	.18	.17	.17	.17	.17	.16	.16	.16	.16	.16	.15	.15
25	.30	.30	.29	.28	.28	.28	.27	.27	.27	.27	.26	.26	.25	.25
50	.60	.59	.57	.56	.56	.55	.54	.54	.53	.53	.52	.51	.50	.50
75	.90	.88	.86	.84	.83	.82	.81	.80	.80	.79	.78	.76	.75	.75
100	1.19	1.17	1.14	1.12	1.11	1.09	1.08	1.07	1.06	1.05	1.04	1.02	1.00	1.00
200	2.38	2.33	2.28	2.24	2.21	2.18	2.15	2.13	2.11	2.10	2.08	2.03	2.00	1.99
300	3.57	3.49	3.42	3.36	3.31	3.27	3.23	3.20	3.17	3.14	3.12	3.04	3.00	2.98
400	4.75	4.65	4.56	4.48	4.41	4.35	4.30	4.26	4.22	4.19	4.16	4.06	4.00	3.97
500	5.94	5.81	5.69	5.60	5.51	5.44	5.38	5.32	5.28	5.23	5.20	5.07	5.00	4.97
600	7.13	6.97	6.83	6.72	6.62	6.53	6.45	6.39	6.33	6.28	6.24	6.08	6.00	5.96
700	8.32	8.13	7.97	7.83	7.72	7.62	7.53	7.45	7.38	7.33	7.27	7.10	7.00	6.95
800	9.50	9.29	9.11	8.95	8.82	8.70	8.60	8.51	8.44	8.37	8.31	8.11	8.00	7.94
900	10.69	10.45	10.25	10.07	9.92	9.79	9.68	9.58	9.49	9.42	9.35	9.12	9.00	8.94
1000	11.88	11.61	11.38	11.19	11.02	10.88	10.75	10.64	10.55	10.46	10.39	10.14	10.00	9.93
2000	23.75	23.22	22.76	22.37	22.04	21.75	21.50	21.28	21.09	20.92	20.77	20.27	20.00	19.85
3000	35.62	34.82	34.14	33.56	33.06	32.62	32.24	31.91	31.63	31.38	31.16	30.40	30.00	29.78
4000	47.50	46.43	45.52	44.74	44.07	43.49	42.99	42.55	42.17	41.84	41.54	40.53	39.99	39.70
5000	59.37	58.04	56.90	55.93	55.09	54.36	53.74	53.19	52.71	52.29	51.93	50.67	49.99	49.62
6000	71.24	69.64	68.28	67.11	66.11	65.24	64.48	63.82	63.25	62.75	62.31	60.80	59.99	59.55
7000	83.12	81.25	79.66	78.30	77.12	76.11	75.23	74.46	73.79	73.21	72.70	70.93	69.99	69.47
8000	94.99	92.86	91.04	89.48	88.14	86.98	85.97	85.10	84.33	83.67	83.08	81.06	79.98	79.40
9000	106.86	104.46	102.42	100.66	99.16	97.85	96.72	95.73	94.88	94.13	93.47	91.20	89.98	89.32
10000	118.74	116.07	113.80	111.85	110.17	108.72	107.47	106.37	105.42	104.58	103.85	101.33	99.98	99.24
11000	130.61	127.68	125.18	123.03	121.19	119.59	118.21	117.01	115.96	115.04	114.24	111.46	109.98	109.17
12000	142.48	139.28	136.56	134.22	132.21	130.47	128.96	127.64	126.50	125.50	124.62	121.59	119.97	119.09
13000	154.36	150.89	147.93	145.40	143.22	141.34	139.70	138.28	137.04	135.96	135.01	131.73	129.97	129.02
14000	166.23	162.50	159.31	156.59	154.24	152.21	150.45	148.92	147.58	146.41	145.39	141.86	139.97	138.94
15000	178.10	174.10	170.69	167.77	165.26	163.08	161.20	159.55	158.12	156.87	155.78	151.99	149.97	148.86
16000	189.98	185.71	182.07	178.96	176.27	173.95	171.94	170.19	168.66	167.33	166.16	162.12	159.96	158.79
17000	201.85	197.32	193.45	190.14	187.29	184.82	182.69	180.83	179.21	177.79	176.55	172.26	169.96	168.71
18000	213.72	208.92	204.83	201.32	198.31	195.70	193.43	191.46	189.75	188.25	186.93	182.39	179.96	178.63
19000	225.60	220.53	216.21	212.51	209.32	206.57	204.18	202.10	200.29	198.70	197.32	192.52	189.96	188.56
20000	237.47	232.14	227.59	223.69	220.34	217.44	214.93	212.74	210.83	209.16	207.70	202.65	199.95	198.48
21000	249.34	243.74	238.97	234.88	231.36	228.31	225.67	223.37	221.37	219.62	218.08	212.79	209.95	208.41
22000	261.22	255.35	250.35	246.06	242.37	239.18	236.42	234.01	231.91	230.08	228.47	222.92	219.95	218.33
23000	273.09	266.96	261.73	257.25	253.39	250.06	247.16	244.65	242.45	240.53	238.85	233.05	229.95	228.25
24000	284.96	278.56	273.11	268.43	264.41	260.93	257.91	255.28	252.99	250.99	249.24	243.18	239.94	238.18
25000	296.84	290.17	284.49	279.62	275.42	271.80	268.66	265.92	263.54	261.45	259.62	253.32	249.94	248.10
26000	308.71	301.78	295.86	290.80	286.44	282.67	279.40	276.56	274.08	271.91	270.01	263.45	259.94	258.03
27000	320.58	313.38	307.24	301.98	297.46	293.54	290.15	287.19	284.62	282.37	280.39	273.58	269.93	267.95
28000	332.46	324.99	318.62	313.17	308.47	304.41	300.89	297.83	295.16	292.82	290.78	283.71	279.93	277.87
29000	344.33	336.59	330.00	324.35	319.49	315.29	311.64	308.47	305.70	303.28	301.16	293.85	289.93	287.80
30000	356.20	348.20	341.38	335.54	330.51	326.16	322.39	319.10	316.24	313.74	311.55	303.98	299.93	297.72
31000	368.08	359.81	352.76	346.72	341.52	337.03	333.13	329.74	326.78	324.20	321.93	314.11	309.92	307.64
32000	379.95	371.41	364.14	357.91	352.54	347.90	343.88	340.38	337.32	334.66	332.32	324.24	319.92	317.57
33000	391.82	383.02	375.52	369.09	363.56	358.77	354.62	351.01	347.87	345.11	342.70	334.38	329.92	327.49
34000	403.70	394.63	386.90	380.27	374.57	369.64	365.37	361.65	358.41	355.57	353.09	344.51	339.92	337.42
35000	415.57	406.23	398.28	391.46	385.59	380.52	376.12	372.29	368.95	366.03	363.47	354.64	349.91	347.34
36000	427.44	417.84	409.66	402.64	396.61	391.39	386.86	382.92	379.49	376.49	373.86	364.77	359.91	357.26
37000	439.32	429.45	421.04	413.83	407.62	402.26	397.61	393.56	390.03	386.94	384.24	374.91	369.91	367.19
38000	451.19	441.05	432.41	425.01	418.64	413.13	408.35	404.20	400.57	397.40	394.63	385.04	379.91	377.11
39000	463.06	452.66	443.79	436.20	429.66	424.00	419.10	414.83	411.11	407.86	405.01	395.17	389.90	387.04
40000	474.94	464.27	455.17	447.38	440.67	434.87	429.85	425.47	421.65	418.32	415.40	405.30	399.90	396.96
41000	486.81	475.87	466.55	458.57	451.69	445.75	436.11	432.20	428.78	425.78	415.43	409.90	406.88	
42000	498.68	487.48	477.93	469.75	462.71	456.62	451.34	446.74	442.74	439.23	436.16	425.57	419.90	416.81
43000	510.56	499.09	489.31	480.93	473.72	467.49	462.08	457.38	453.28	449.69	446.55	435.70	429.89	426.73
44000	522.43	510.69	500.69	492.12	484.74	478.36	472.83	468.02	463.82	460.15	456.93	445.83	439.89	436.66
45000	534.30	522.30	512.07	503.30	495.76	489.23	483.58	478.65	474.36	470.61	467.32	455.96	449.89	446.58
46000	546.18	533.91	523.45	514.49	506.77	500.11	494.32	489.29	484.90	481.06	477.70	466.10	459.89	456.50
47000	558.05	545.51	534.83	525.67	517.79	510.98	505.07	499.93	495.44	491.52	488.09	476.23	469.88	466.43
48000	569.92	557.12	546.21	536.86	528.81	521.85	515.81	510.56	505.98	501.98	498.47	486.36	479.88	476.35
49000	581.80	568.73	557.59	548.04	539.82	532.72	526.56	521.20	516.53	512.44	508.86	456.49	489.88	486.27
50000	593.67	580.33	568.97	559.23	550.84	543.59	537.31	531.84	527.07	522.90	519.24	506.63	499.87	496.20
55000	653.04	638.36	625.86	615.15	605.92	597.95	591.04	585.02	579.77	575.19	571.17	557.29	549.86	545.82
60000	712.40	696.40	682.76	671.07	661.01	652.31	644.77	638.20	632.48	627.47	623.09	607.95	599.85	595.44
65000	771.77	754.43	739.65	726.99	716.09	706.67	698.50	691.39	685.19	679.76	675.01	658.61	649.84	645.06
70000	831.14	812.46	796.55	782.91	771.17	761.03	752.23	744.57	737.89	732.05	726.94	709.28	699.82	694.68
75000	890.50	870.50	853.45	838.84	826.26	815.39	805.96	797.75	790.60	784.34	778.86	759.94	749.81	744.30
80000	949.87	928.53	910.34	894.76	881.34	869.74	859.69	850.94	843.30	836.63	830.79	810.60	799.80	793.91
85000	1009.24	986.56	967.24	950.68	936.42	924.10	913.42	904.12	896.01	888.92	882.71	861.26	849.78	843.53
90000	1068.60	1044.59	1024.13	1006.60	991.51	978.46	967.15	957.30	948.72	941.21	934.63	911.92	899.77	893.15
95000	1127.97	1102.63	1081.03	1062.52	1046.59	1032.82	1020.88	1010.49	1001.42	993.50	986.56	962.59	949.76	942.77
100000	1187.34	1160.66	1137.93	1118.45	1101.68	1087.18	1074.61	1063.67	1054.13	1045.79	1038.48	1013.25	999.74	992.39

MONTHLY PAYMENT
REQUIRED TO AMORTIZE A LOAN

TERM	1 Year	2 Years	3 Years	4 Years	5 Years	6 Years	7 Years	8 Years	9 Years	10 Years	11 Years	12 Years	13 Years	14 Years
AMOUNT														
5	.45	.24	.17	.14	.12	.10	.09	.09	.08	.08	.07	.07	.07	.07
10	.89	.48	.34	.27	.23	.20	.18	.17	.16	.15	.14	.14	.13	.13
15	1.34	.71	.50	.40	.34	.30	.27	.25	.23	.22	.21	.20	.19	.19
25	2.22	1.18	.83	.66	.56	.49	.44	.41	.38	.36	.35	.33	.32	.31
50	4.44	2.36	1.66	1.32	1.11	.98	.88	.81	.76	.72	.69	.66	.64	.62
75	6.66	3.53	2.49	1.98	1.67	1.47	1.32	1.22	1.14	1.08	1.03	.98	.95	.92
100	8.88	4.71	3.32	2.63	2.22	1.95	1.76	1.62	1.52	1.43	1.37	1.31	1.27	1.23
200	17.76	9.41	6.64	5.26	4.44	3.90	3.52	3.24	3.03	2.86	2.73	2.62	2.53	2.45
300	26.64	16.11	9.95	7.89	6.66	5.85	5.28	4.86	4.54	4.29	4.09	3.92	3.79	3.68
400	35.52	18.81	13.27	10.51	8.88	7.80	7.04	6.48	6.05	5.71	5.45	5.23	5.05	4.90
500	44.40	23.51	16.58	13.14	11.10	9.75	8.80	8.10	7.56	7.14	6.81	6.53	6.31	6.12
600	53.28	28.21	19.90	15.77	13.31	11.70	10.56	9.72	9.07	8.57	8.17	7.84	7.57	7.35
700	62.16	32.92	23.21	18.40	15.53	13.64	12.32	11.33	10.58	10.00	9.53	9.15	8.83	8.57
800	71.04	37.62	26.53	21.02	17.75	15.59	14.07	12.95	12.10	11.42	10.89	10.45	10.09	9.79
900	79.92	42.32	29.84	23.65	19.97	17.54	15.83	14.57	13.61	12.85	12.25	11.76	11.35	11.02
1000	88.80	47.02	33.16	26.28	22.19	19.49	17.59	16.19	15.12	14.28	13.61	13.06	12.61	12.24
2000	177.59	94.04	66.31	52.55	44.37	38.98	35.18	32.37	30.23	28.55	27.21	26.12	25.22	24.48
3000	266.38	141.05	99.47	78.82	66.55	58.46	52.76	48.56	45.35	42.83	40.82	39.18	37.83	36.71
4000	355.17	188.07	132.62	105.10	88.73	77.95	70.35	64.74	60.46	57.10	54.42	52.24	50.44	48.95
5000	443.96	235.08	165.78	131.37	110.91	97.43	87.93	80.93	75.57	71.38	68.02	65.30	63.05	61.18
6000	532.75	282.10	198.93	157.64	133.09	116.92	105.52	97.11	90.69	85.65	81.63	78.36	75.66	73.42
7000	621.54	329.11	232.09	183.91	155.27	136.40	123.11	113.29	105.80	99.93	95.23	91.42	88.27	85.65
8000	710.33	376.13	265.24	210.19	177.46	155.89	140.69	129.48	120.92	114.20	108.84	104.47	100.88	97.89
9000	799.12	423.14	298.40	236.46	199.64	175.37	158.28	145.66	136.03	128.48	122.44	117.53	113.49	110.12
10000	887.91	470.16	331.55	262.73	221.82	194.86	175.86	161.85	151.14	142.75	136.04	130.59	126.10	122.36
11000	976.70	517.17	364.71	289.00	244.00	214.34	193.45	178.03	166.26	157.03	149.65	143.65	138.71	134.60
12000	1065.49	564.19	397.86	315.28	266.18	233.83	211.04	194.22	181.37	171.30	163.25	156.71	151.32	146.83
13000	1154.28	611.20	431.02	341.55	288.36	253.31	228.62	210.40	196.48	185.58	176.86	169.77	163.93	159.07
14000	1243.07	658.22	464.17	367.82	310.54	272.80	246.21	226.58	211.60	199.85	190.46	182.83	176.54	171.30
15000	1331.86	705.23	497.32	394.09	332.72	292.28	263.79	242.77	226.71	214.13	204.06	195.88	189.15	183.54
16000	1420.65	752.25	530.48	420.37	354.91	311.77	281.38	258.95	241.83	228.40	217.67	208.94	201.76	195.77
17000	1509.44	799.26	563.63	446.64	377.09	331.25	298.97	275.14	256.94	242.68	231.27	222.00	214.37	208.01
18000	1598.23	846.28	596.79	472.91	399.27	350.74	316.55	291.32	272.05	256.95	244.88	235.06	226.98	220.24
19000	1687.02	893.29	629.94	499.18	421.45	370.22	334.14	307.51	287.17	271.23	258.48	248.12	239.58	232.48
20000	1775.81	940.31	663.10	525.46	443.63	389.71	351.72	323.69	302.28	285.50	272.08	261.18	252.19	244.72
21000	1864.60	987.32	696.25	551.73	465.81	409.20	369.31	339.87	317.40	299.78	285.69	274.24	264.80	256.95
22000	1953.39	1034.34	729.41	578.00	487.99	428.68	386.90	356.06	332.51	314.05	299.29	287.29	277.41	269.19
23000	2042.18	1081.35	762.56	604.27	510.18	448.17	404.48	372.24	347.62	328.33	312.90	300.35	290.02	281.42
24000	2130.97	1128.37	795.72	630.55	532.36	467.65	422.07	388.43	362.74	342.60	326.50	313.41	302.63	293.66
25000	2219.76	1175.38	828.87	656.82	554.54	487.14	439.65	404.61	377.85	356.88	340.10	326.47	315.24	305.89
26000	2308.55	1222.40	862.03	683.09	576.72	506.62	457.24	420.80	392.96	371.15	353.71	339.53	327.85	318.13
27000	2397.34	1269.41	895.18	709.36	598.90	526.11	474.83	436.98	408.08	385.43	367.31	352.59	340.46	330.36
28000	2486.13	1316.43	928.33	735.64	621.08	545.59	492.41	453.16	423.19	399.70	380.92	365.65	353.07	342.60
29000	2574.92	1363.44	961.49	761.91	643.26	565.08	510.00	469.35	438.31	413.98	394.52	378.70	365.68	354.83
30000	2663.71	1410.46	994.64	788.18	665.44	584.56	527.58	485.53	453.42	428.25	408.12	391.76	378.29	367.07
31000	2752.51	1457.47	1027.80	814.45	687.63	604.05	545.17	501.72	468.53	442.53	421.73	404.82	390.90	379.31
32000	2841.30	1504.49	1060.95	840.73	709.81	623.53	562.76	517.90	483.65	456.80	435.33	417.88	403.51	391.54
33000	2930.09	1551.50	1094.11	867.00	731.99	643.02	580.34	534.08	498.76	471.08	448.94	430.94	416.12	403.78
34000	3018.88	1598.52	1127.26	893.27	754.17	662.50	597.93	550.27	513.88	485.35	462.54	444.00	428.73	416.01
35000	3107.67	1645.53	1160.42	919.54	776.35	681.99	615.51	566.45	528.99	499.63	476.14	457.06	441.34	428.25
36000	3196.46	1692.55	1193.57	945.82	798.53	701.47	633.10	582.64	544.10	513.90	489.75	470.12	453.95	440.48
37000	3285.25	1739.56	1226.73	972.09	820.71	720.96	650.69	598.82	559.22	528.18	503.35	483.17	466.55	452.72
38000	3374.04	1786.58	1259.88	998.36	842.90	740.44	668.27	615.01	574.33	542.45	516.96	496.23	479.16	464.95
39000	3462.83	1833.59	1293.04	1024.63	865.08	759.93	685.86	631.19	589.44	556.73	530.56	509.29	491.77	477.19
40000	3551.62	1880.61	1326.19	1050.91	887.26	779.42	703.44	647.37	604.56	571.00	544.16	522.35	504.38	489.43
41000	3640.41	1927.62	1359.35	1077.18	909.44	798.90	721.03	663.56	619.67	585.28	557.77	535.41	516.99	501.66
42000	3729.20	1974.64	1392.50	1103.45	931.62	818.39	738.62	679.74	634.79	599.55	571.37	548.47	529.60	513.90
43000	3817.99	2021.66	1425.65	1129.72	953.80	837.87	756.20	695.93	649.90	613.83	584.98	561.53	542.21	526.13
44000	3906.78	2068.67	1458.81	1156.00	975.98	857.36	773.79	712.11	665.01	628.10	598.58	574.58	554.82	538.37
45000	3995.57	2115.69	1491.96	1182.27	998.16	876.84	791.37	728.30	680.13	642.38	612.18	587.64	567.43	550.60
46000	4084.36	2162.70	1525.12	1208.54	1020.35	896.33	808.96	744.48	695.24	656.65	625.79	600.70	580.04	562.84
47000	4173.15	2209.72	1558.27	1234.81	1042.53	915.81	826.54	760.66	710.36	670.93	639.39	613.76	592.65	575.07
48000	4261.94	2256.73	1591.43	1261.09	1064.71	935.30	844.13	776.85	725.47	685.20	653.00	626.82	605.26	587.31
49000	4350.73	2303.75	1624.58	1287.36	1086.89	954.78	861.72	793.03	740.58	699.48	666.60	639.88	617.87	599.55
50000	4439.52	2350.76	1657.74	1313.63	1109.07	974.27	879.30	809.22	755.70	713.75	680.20	652.94	630.48	611.78
55000	4883.47	2585.84	1823.51	1444.99	1219.98	1071.69	967.23	890.14	831.27	785.13	748.22	718.23	693.53	672.96
60000	5327.42	2820.91	1989.28	1576.36	1330.88	1169.12	1055.16	971.06	906.83	856.50	816.24	783.52	756.57	734.14
65000	5771.38	3055.99	2155.06	1707.72	1441.79	1266.55	1143.09	1051.98	982.40	927.88	884.26	848.82	819.62	795.31
70000	6215.33	3291.06	2320.83	1839.08	1552.70	1363.97	1231.02	1132.90	1057.97	999.25	952.28	914.11	882.67	856.49
75000	6659.28	3526.14	2486.60	1970.44	1663.60	1461.40	1318.95	1213.82	1133.54	1070.62	1020.30	979.40	945.71	917.67
80000	7103.23	3761.21	2652.38	2101.81	1774.51	1558.83	1406.88	1294.74	1209.11	1142.00	1088.32	1044.69	1008.76	978.85
85000	7547.18	3996.29	2818.15	2233.17	1885.42	1656.25	1494.81	1375.67	1284.68	1213.37	1156.34	1109.99	1071.81	1040.02
90000	7991.13	4231.37	2983.92	2364.53	1753.68	1582.74	1456.59	1360.25	1284.75	1224.36	1175.28	1134.86	1101.20	
95000	8435.09	4466.44	3149.70	2495.89	2107.23	1851.10	1670.67	1537.51	1435.82	1356.12	1292.38	1240.57	1197.90	1162.38
100000	8879.04	4701.52	3315.47	2627.26	2218.14	1948.53	1758.60	1618.43	1511.39	1427.50	1360.40	1305.87	1260.95	1223.56

TERM	15 Years	16 Years	17 Years	18 Years	19 Years	20 Years	21 Years	22 Years	23 Years	24 Years	25 Years	30 Years	35 Years	40 Years
AMOUNT														
5	.06	.06	.06	.06	.06	.06	.06	.06	.06	.06	.06	.06	.06	.05
10	.12	.12	.12	.12	.12	.11	.11	.11	.11	.11	.11	.11	.11	.10
15	.18	.18	.18	.17	.17	.17	.17	.17	.16	.16	.16	.16	.16	.15
25	.30	.30	.29	.29	.28	.28	.27	.27	.27	.27	.27	.26	.26	.25
50	.60	.59	.58	.57	.56	.55	.54	.54	.53	.53	.53	.51	.51	.50
75	.90	.88	.86	.85	.84	.82	.81	.81	.80	.79	.79	.77	.76	.75
100	1.20	1.17	1.15	1.13	1.11	1.10	1.08	1.07	1.06	1.06	1.05	1.02	1.01	1.00
200	2.39	2.34	2.29	2.25	2.22	2.19	2.16	2.14	2.12	2.11	2.09	2.04	2.02	2.00
300	3.58	3.50	3.43	3.38	3.33	3.28	3.24	3.21	3.18	3.16	3.14	3.06	3.02	3.00
400	4.77	4.67	4.58	4.50	4.43	4.37	4.32	4.28	4.24	4.21	4.18	4.08	4.03	4.00
500	5.97	5.83	5.72	5.62	5.54	5.47	5.40	5.35	5.30	5.26	5.22	5.10	5.03	5.00
600	7.16	7.00	6.86	6.75	6.65	6.56	6.48	6.42	6.36	6.31	6.27	6.12	6.04	6.00
700	8.35	8.16	8.01	7.87	7.75	7.65	7.56	7.49	7.42	7.36	7.31	7.14	7.04	6.99
800	9.54	9.33	9.15	8.99	8.86	8.74	8.64	8.56	8.48	8.42	8.36	8.16	8.05	7.99
900	10.73	10.49	10.29	10.12	9.97	9.84	9.72	9.63	9.54	9.47	9.40	9.18	9.06	8.99
1000	11.93	11.66	11.43	11.24	11.07	10.93	10.80	10.70	10.60	10.52	10.44	10.20	10.06	9.99
2000	23.85	23.32	22.86	22.47	22.14	21.85	21.60	21.39	21.20	21.03	20.88	20.39	20.12	19.97
3000	35.77	34.97	34.29	33.71	33.21	32.78	32.40	32.08	31.79	31.54	31.32	30.58	30.17	29.96
4000	47.69	46.63	45.72	44.94	44.28	43.70	43.20	42.77	42.39	42.06	41.76	40.77	40.23	39.94
5000	59.61	58.28	57.15	56.18	55.35	54.62	54.00	53.46	52.98	52.57	52.20	50.96	50.29	49.93
6000	71.53	69.94	68.58	67.41	66.41	65.55	64.80	64.15	63.58	63.08	62.64	61.15	60.34	59.91
7000	83.45	81.59	80.01	78.65	77.48	76.47	75.60	74.84	74.17	73.59	73.08	71.34	70.40	69.89
8000	95.38	93.25	91.44	89.88	88.55	87.40	86.40	85.53	84.77	84.11	83.52	81.53	80.46	79.88
9000	107.30	104.90	102.87	101.12	99.62	98.32	97.19	96.22	95.36	94.62	93.96	91.72	90.51	89.86
10000	119.22	116.56	114.29	112.35	110.69	109.24	107.99	106.91	105.96	105.13	104.40	101.91	100.57	99.85
11000	131.14	128.22	125.72	123.59	121.75	120.17	118.79	117.60	116.55	115.64	114.84	112.10	110.63	109.83
12000	143.06	139.87	137.15	134.82	132.82	131.09	129.59	128.29	127.15	126.16	125.28	122.29	120.68	119.82
13000	154.98	151.53	148.58	146.06	143.89	142.01	140.39	138.98	137.74	136.67	135.72	132.48	130.74	129.80
14000	166.90	163.18	160.01	157.29	154.96	152.94	151.19	149.67	148.34	147.18	146.16	142.67	140.80	139.78
15000	178.83	174.84	171.44	168.53	166.03	163.86	161.99	160.36	158.93	157.69	156.60	152.86	150.85	149.77
16000	190.75	186.49	182.87	179.76	177.09	174.79	172.79	171.05	169.53	168.21	167.04	163.05	160.91	159.75
17000	202.67	198.15	194.30	191.00	188.16	185.71	183.58	181.74	180.13	170.72	177.48	173.24	170.97	169.74
18000	214.59	209.80	205.73	202.23	199.23	196.63	194.38	192.43	190.72	189.23	187.92	183.43	181.02	179.72
19000	226.51	221.46	217.16	213.47	210.30	207.56	205.18	203.12	201.32	199.74	198.36	193.62	191.08	189.71
20000	238.43	233.11	228.58	224.70	221.37	218.48	215.98	213.81	211.91	210.26	208.80	203.81	201.14	199.69
21000	250.35	244.77	240.01	235.94	232.43	229.41	226.78	224.50	222.51	220.77	219.24	214.00	211.19	209.67
22000	262.28	256.43	251.44	247.17	243.50	240.33	237.58	235.19	233.10	231.28	229.68	224.19	221.25	219.66
23000	274.20	268.08	262.87	258.41	254.57	251.25	248.38	245.88	243.70	241.79	240.12	234.38	231.31	229.64
24000	286.12	279.74	274.30	269.64	265.64	262.18	259.18	256.57	254.29	252.31	250.56	244.57	241.36	239.63
25000	298.04	291.39	285.73	280.88	276.71	273.10	269.98	267.26	264.89	262.82	261.00	254.76	251.42	249.61
26000	309.96	303.05	297.16	292.11	287.77	284.02	280.77	277.95	275.48	273.33	271.44	264.95	261.48	259.60
27000	321.88	314.70	308.59	303.35	298.84	294.95	291.57	288.64	286.08	283.84	281.88	275.14	271.53	269.58
28000	333.80	326.36	320.02	314.58	309.91	305.87	302.37	299.33	296.67	294.36	292.32	285.33	281.59	279.56
29000	345.72	338.01	331.45	325.82	320.98	316.80	313.17	310.02	307.27	304.87	302.76	295.52	291.65	289.55
30000	357.65	349.67	342.87	337.05	332.05	327.72	323.97	320.71	317.86	315.38	313.20	305.71	301.70	299.53
31000	369.57	361.33	354.30	348.29	343.11	338.64	334.77	331.40	328.46	325.89	323.64	315.90	311.76	309.52
32000	381.49	372.98	365.73	359.52	354.18	349.57	345.57	342.09	339.06	336.41	334.08	326.09	321.82	319.50
33000	393.41	384.64	377.16	370.76	365.25	360.49	356.37	352.78	349.65	346.92	344.52	336.28	331.87	329.49
34000	405.33	396.29	388.59	381.99	376.32	371.42	367.16	363.47	360.25	357.43	354.96	346.47	341.93	339.47
35000	417.25	407.95	400.02	393.23	387.39	382.34	377.96	374.16	370.84	367.94	365.40	356.66	351.99	349.45
36000	429.17	419.60	411.45	404.46	398.46	393.26	388.76	384.85	381.44	378.46	375.84	366.85	362.04	359.44
37000	441.10	431.26	422.88	415.70	409.52	404.19	399.56	395.54	392.03	388.97	386.28	377.04	372.10	369.42
38000	453.02	442.91	434.31	426.93	420.59	415.11	410.36	406.23	402.63	399.48	396.72	387.23	382.16	379.41
39000	464.94	454.57	445.74	438.17	431.66	426.03	421.16	416.92	413.22	409.99	407.16	397.42	392.21	389.39
40000	476.86	466.22	457.16	449.40	442.73	436.96	431.96	427.61	423.82	420.51	417.60	407.61	402.27	399.38
41000	488.78	477.88	468.59	460.64	453.80	447.88	442.76	438.30	434.41	431.02	428.04	417.80	412.33	409.36
42000	500.70	489.54	480.02	471.87	464.86	458.81	453.56	448.99	445.01	441.53	438.48	427.99	422.38	419.34
43000	512.62	501.19	491.45	483.11	475.93	469.73	464.35	459.68	455.60	452.04	448.92	438.18	432.44	429.33
44000	524.55	512.85	502.88	494.34	487.00	480.65	475.15	470.37	466.20	462.56	459.36	448.37	442.50	439.31
45000	536.47	524.50	514.31	505.58	498.07	491.58	485.95	481.06	476.79	473.07	469.80	458.56	452.55	449.30
46000	548.39	536.16	525.74	516.81	509.14	502.50	496.75	491.75	487.39	483.58	480.24	468.75	462.61	459.28
47000	560.31	547.81	537.17	528.05	520.20	513.43	507.55	502.44	497.98	494.09	490.68	478.94	472.67	469.26
48000	572.23	559.47	548.60	539.28	531.27	524.35	518.35	513.13	508.58	504.61	501.12	489.13	482.72	479.25
49000	584.15	571.12	560.03	550.52	542.34	535.27	529.15	523.82	519.18	515.12	511.56	499.32	492.78	489.23
50000	596.07	582.78	571.45	561.75	553.41	546.20	539.95	534.51	529.77	525.63	522.00	509.51	502.84	499.22
55000	655.68	641.06	628.60	617.93	608.75	600.82	593.94	587.96	582.75	578.19	574.20	560.46	553.12	549.14
60000	715.29	699.33	685.74	674.10	664.09	655.44	647.93	641.41	635.72	630.76	626.40	611.41	603.40	599.06
65000	774.89	757.61	742.89	730.28	719.43	710.05	701.93	694.86	688.70	683.32	678.60	662.36	653.69	648.98
70000	834.50	815.89	800.03	786.45	774.77	764.67	755.92	748.31	741.68	735.88	730.80	713.31	703.97	698.90
75000	894.11	874.17	857.18	842.63	830.11	819.29	809.92	801.76	794.65	788.44	783.00	764.26	754.25	748.82
80000	953.72	932.44	914.32	898.80	885.45	873.91	863.91	855.21	847.63	841.01	835.20	815.21	804.54	798.75
85000	1013.32	990.72	971.47	954.98	940.79	928.53	917.90	908.66	900.61	893.57	887.40	866.16	854.82	848.67
90000	1072.93	1049.00	1028.61	1011.15	996.13	983.15	971.90	962.11	953.58	946.13	939.60	917.11	905.10	898.59
95000	1132.54	1107.28	1085.76	1067.33	1051.47	1037.77	1025.89	1015.56	1006.56	998.69	991.80	968.06	955.39	948.51
100000	1192.14	1165.55	1142.90	1123.50	1106.81	1092.39	1079.89	1069.01	1059.54	1051.26	1044.00	1019.01	1005.67	998.43

MONTHLY PAYMENT
REQUIRED TO AMORTIZE A LOAN

TERM	1 Year	2 Years	3 Years	4 Years	5 Years	6 Years	7 Years	8 Years	9 Years	10 Years	11 Years	12 Years	13 Years	14 Years
AMOUNT														
5	.45	.24	.17	.14	.12	.10	.09	.09	.08	.00	.07	.07	.07	.07
10	.89	.48	.34	.27	.23	.20	.18	.17	.16	.15	.14	.14	.13	.13
15	1.34	.71	.50	.40	.34	.30	.27	.25	.23	.22	.21	.20	.19	.19
25	2.23	1.18	.83	.66	.56	.49	.44	.41	.38	.36	.35	.33	.32	.31
50	4.45	2.36	1.66	1.32	1.11	.98	.88	.81	.76	.72	.69	.66	.64	.62
75	6.67	3.53	2.49	1.98	1.67	1.47	1.32	1.22	1.14	1.08	1.03	.99	.95	.92
100	8.89	4.71	3.32	2.63	2.22	1.95	1.76	1.62	1.52	1.43	1.37	1.31	1.27	1.23
200	17.77	9.41	6.64	5.26	4.44	3.90	3.52	3.24	3.03	2.86	2.73	2.62	2.53	2.46
300	26.65	14.11	9.95	7.89	6.66	5.85	5.28	4.86	4.54	4.29	4.09	3.93	3.79	3.68
400	35.53	18.82	13.27	10.52	8.88	7.80	7.04	6.48	6.06	5.72	5.45	5.23	5.05	4.91
500	44.41	23.52	16.59	13.15	11.10	9.75	8.80	8.10	7.57	7.15	6.81	6.54	6.32	6.13
600	53.29	28.22	19.90	15.78	13.32	11.70	10.56	9.72	9.08	8.58	8.18	7.85	7.58	7.36
700	62.17	32.92	23.22	18.40	15.54	13.65	12.32	11.34	10.59	10.01	9.54	9.16	8.84	8.58
800	71.05	37.63	26.54	21.03	17.76	15.60	14.08	12.96	12.11	11.44	10.90	10.46	10.10	9.81
900	79.93	42.33	29.85	23.66	19.98	17.55	15.84	14.58	13.62	12.87	12.26	11.77	11.37	11.03
1000	88.81	47.03	33.17	26.29	22.20	19.50	17.60	16.20	15.13	14.29	13.62	13.08	12.63	12.26
2000	177.61	94.06	66.34	52.57	44.39	39.00	35.20	32.40	30.26	28.58	27.24	26.15	25.25	24.51
3000	266.41	141.09	99.50	78.86	66.59	58.50	52.80	48.60	45.39	42.87	40.86	39.23	37.88	36.76
4000	355.21	188.11	132.67	105.14	88.78	78.00	70.40	64.80	60.52	57.16	54.48	52.30	50.50	49.01
5000	444.02	235.14	165.84	131.43	110.97	97.50	88.00	80.99	75.64	71.45	68.10	65.37	63.13	61.26
6000	532.82	282.17	199.00	157.71	133.17	116.99	105.60	97.19	90.77	85.74	81.72	78.45	75.75	73.51
7000	621.62	329.19	232.17	184.00	155.36	136.49	123.20	113.39	105.90	100.03	95.34	91.52	88.38	85.76
8000	710.42	376.22	265.34	210.28	177.56	155.99	140.80	129.59	121.03	114.32	108.95	104.59	101.00	98.02
9000	799.22	423.25	298.50	236.57	199.75	175.49	158.40	145.79	136.16	128.61	122.57	117.67	113.63	110.27
10000	888.03	470.27	331.67	262.85	221.94	194.99	176.00	161.98	151.28	142.90	136.19	130.74	126.25	122.52
11000	976.83	517.30	364.84	289.14	244.14	214.49	193.60	178.18	166.41	157.19	149.81	143.82	138.88	134.77
12000	1065.63	564.33	398.00	315.42	266.33	233.98	211.20	194.38	181.54	171.48	163.43	156.89	151.50	147.02
13000	1154.03	611.35	431.17	341.71	288.53	253.48	228.80	210.58	196.67	185.77	177.05	169.96	164.13	159.27
14000	1243.23	658.38	464.34	367.99	310.72	272.98	246.40	226.78	211.80	200.06	190.67	183.04	176.75	171.52
15000	1332.04	705.41	497.50	394.28	332.91	292.48	263.99	242.97	226.92	214.35	204.29	196.11	189.38	183.77
16000	1420.84	752.43	530.67	420.56	355.11	311.98	281.59	259.17	242.05	228.63	217.90	209.18	202.00	196.03
17000	1509.64	799.46	563.84	446.85	377.30	331.47	299.19	275.37	257.18	242.92	231.52	222.26	214.63	208.28
18000	1598.44	846.49	597.00	473.13	399.50	350.97	316.79	291.57	272.31	257.21	245.14	235.33	227.25	220.53
19000	1687.24	893.51	630.17	499.42	421.69	370.47	334.39	307.77	287.44	271.50	258.76	248.41	239.88	232.78
20000	1776.05	940.54	663.34	525.70	443.88	389.97	351.99	323.96	302.56	285.79	272.38	261.48	252.50	245.03
21000	1864.85	987.57	696.50	551.99	466.08	409.47	369.59	340.16	317.69	300.08	286.00	274.55	265.13	257.28
22000	1953.65	1034.59	729.67	578.27	488.27	428.97	387.19	356.36	332.82	314.37	299.62	287.63	277.75	269.53
23000	2042.45	1081.62	762.84	604.55	510.47	448.46	404.79	372.56	347.95	328.66	313.24	300.70	290.38	281.78
24000	2131.25	1128.65	796.00	630.84	532.66	467.96	422.39	388.76	363.07	342.95	326.85	313.77	303.00	294.04
25000	2220.06	1175.67	829.17	657.12	554.85	487.46	439.99	404.95	378.20	357.24	340.47	326.85	315.63	306.29
26000	2308.86	1222.70	862.34	683.41	577.05	506.96	457.59	421.15	393.33	371.53	354.09	339.92	328.25	318.54
27000	2397.66	1269.73	895.50	709.69	599.24	526.46	475.19	437.35	408.46	385.82	367.71	353.00	340.88	330.79
28000	2486.46	1316.76	928.67	735.98	621.44	545.96	492.79	453.55	423.59	400.11	381.33	366.07	353.50	343.04
29000	2575.26	1363.78	961.84	762.26	643.63	565.45	510.38	469.75	438.71	414.40	394.95	379.14	366.13	355.29
30000	2664.07	1410.81	995.00	788.55	665.82	584.95	527.98	485.94	453.84	428.69	408.57	392.22	378.75	367.54
31000	2752.87	1457.84	1028.17	814.83	688.02	604.45	545.58	502.14	468.97	442.97	422.19	405.29	391.38	379.79
32000	2841.67	1504.86	1061.34	841.12	710.21	623.95	563.18	518.34	484.10	457.26	435.80	418.36	404.00	392.05
33000	2930.47	1551.89	1094.50	867.40	732.41	643.45	580.78	534.54	499.23	471.55	449.42	431.44	416.63	404.30
34000	3019.27	1598.92	1127.67	893.69	754.60	662.94	598.38	550.74	514.35	485.84	463.04	444.51	429.25	416.55
35000	3108.08	1645.94	1160.83	919.97	776.79	682.44	615.98	566.93	529.48	500.13	476.66	457.59	441.88	428.80
36000	3196.88	1692.97	1194.00	946.26	798.99	701.94	633.58	583.13	544.61	514.42	490.28	470.66	454.50	441.05
37000	3285.68	1740.00	1227.17	972.54	821.18	721.44	651.18	599.33	559.74	528.71	503.90	483.73	467.13	453.30
38000	3374.48	1787.02	1260.33	998.83	843.38	740.94	668.78	615.53	574.87	543.00	517.52	496.81	479.75	465.55
39000	3463.28	1834.05	1293.50	1025.11	865.57	760.44	686.38	631.72	589.99	557.29	531.14	509.88	492.38	477.80
40000	3552.09	1881.08	1326.67	1051.40	887.76	779.93	703.98	647.92	605.12	571.58	544.75	522.95	505.00	490.06
41000	3640.89	1928.10	1359.83	1077.68	909.96	799.43	721.58	664.12	620.25	585.87	558.37	536.03	517.63	502.31
42000	3729.69	1975.13	1393.00	1103.97	932.15	818.93	739.18	680.32	635.38	600.16	571.99	549.10	530.25	514.56
43000	3818.49	2022.16	1426.17	1130.25	954.34	838.43	756.77	696.52	650.50	614.45	585.61	562.17	542.87	526.81
44000	3907.29	2069.18	1459.33	1156.53	976.54	857.93	774.37	712.71	665.63	628.74	599.23	575.25	555.50	539.06
45000	3996.10	2116.21	1492.50	1182.82	998.73	877.43	791.97	728.91	680.76	643.03	612.85	588.32	568.12	551.31
46000	4084.90	2163.24	1525.67	1209.10	1020.93	896.92	809.57	745.11	695.89	657.31	626.47	601.40	580.75	563.56
47000	4173.70	2210.26	1558.83	1235.39	1043.12	916.42	827.17	761.31	711.02	671.60	640.09	614.47	593.37	575.81
48000	4262.50	2257.29	1592.00	1261.67	1065.31	935.92	844.77	777.51	726.14	685.89	653.70	627.54	606.00	588.07
49000	4351.30	2304.32	1625.17	1287.96	1087.51	955.42	862.37	793.70	741.27	700.18	667.32	640.62	618.62	600.32
50000	4440.11	2351.34	1658.33	1314.24	1109.70	974.92	879.97	809.90	756.40	714.47	680.94	653.69	631.25	612.57
55000	4884.12	2586.48	1824.17	1445.67	1220.67	1072.41	967.97	890.89	832.04	785.92	749.04	719.06	694.37	673.82
60000	5328.13	2821.61	1990.00	1577.09	1331.64	1169.90	1055.96	971.88	907.68	857.37	817.13	784.43	757.50	735.08
65000	5772.14	3056.75	2155.83	1708.51	1442.61	1267.39	1143.96	1052.87	983.32	928.81	885.22	849.80	820.62	796.34
70000	6216.15	3291.88	2321.66	1839.94	1553.58	1364.88	1231.96	1133.86	1058.96	1000.26	953.32	915.17	883.75	857.59
75000	6660.16	3527.01	2487.50	1971.36	1664.55	1462.37	1319.95	1214.85	1134.60	1071.71	1021.41	980.53	946.87	918.85
80000	7104.17	3762.15	2653.33	2102.79	1775.52	1559.86	1407.95	1295.84	1210.24	1143.15	1089.50	1045.90	1010.00	980.11
85000	7548.18	3997.28	2819.16	2234.21	1886.49	1657.35	1495.95	1376.83	1285.88	1214.60	1157.60	1111.27	1073.12	1041.36
90000	7992.19	4232.42	2985.00	2365.63	1997.46	1754.85	1583.94	1457.82	1361.52	1286.05	1225.69	1176.64	1136.24	1102.62
95000	8436.20	4467.55	3150.83	2497.06	2108.43	1852.34	1671.94	1538.81	1437.16	1357.49	1293.79	1242.01	1199.37	1163.87
100000	8880.21	4702.68	3316.66	2628.48	2219.40	1949.83	1759.93	1619.80	1512.79	1428.94	1361.88	1307.38	1262.49	1225.13

TERM AMOUNT	15 Years	16 Years	17 Years	18 Years	19 Years	20 Years	21 Years	22 Years	23 Years	24 Years	25 Years	30 Years	35 Years	40 Years
5	.06	.06	.06	.06	.06	.06	.06	.06	.06	.06	.06	.06	.06	.06
10	.12	.12	.12	.12	.12	.11	.11	.11	.11	.11	.11	.11	.11	.11
15	.18	.18	.18	.17	.17	.17	.17	.17	.16	.16	.16	.16	.16	.16
25	.30	.30	.29	.29	.28	.28	.28	.27	.27	.27	.27	.26	.26	.26
50	.60	.59	.58	.57	.56	.55	.55	.54	.54	.53	.53	.52	.51	.51
75	.90	.88	.86	.85	.84	.83	.82	.81	.80	.79	.79	.77	.76	.76
100	1.20	1.17	1.15	1.13	1.11	1.10	1.09	1.08	1.07	1.06	1.05	1.03	1.01	1.01
200	2.39	2.34	2.29	2.26	2.22	2.19	2.17	2.15	2.13	2.11	2.10	2.05	2.02	2.01
300	3.59	3.51	3.44	3.38	3.33	3.29	3.25	3.22	3.19	3.16	3.14	3.07	3.03	3.01
400	4.78	4.67	4.58	4.51	4.44	4.38	4.33	4.29	4.25	4.22	4.19	4.09	4.04	4.01
500	5.97	5.84	5.73	5.63	5.55	5.48	5.41	5.36	5.31	5.27	5.23	5.11	5.04	5.01
600	7.17	7.01	6.87	6.76	6.66	6.57	6.49	6.43	6.37	6.32	6.28	6.13	6.05	6.01
700	8.36	8.18	8.02	7.88	7.76	7.66	7.58	7.50	7.43	7.38	7.33	7.15	7.06	7.01
800	9.55	9.34	9.16	9.01	8.87	8.76	8.66	8.57	8.50	8.43	8.37	8.17	8.07	8.01
900	10.75	10.51	10.31	10.13	9.98	9.85	9.74	9.64	9.56	9.48	9.42	9.19	9.07	9.01
1000	11.94	11.68	11.45	11.26	11.09	10.95	10.82	10.71	10.62	10.54	10.46	10.21	10.08	10.01
2000	23.88	23.35	22.90	22.51	22.18	21.89	21.64	21.42	21.23	21.07	20.92	20.42	20.16	20.01
3000	35.82	35.02	34.34	33.76	33.26	32.83	32.45	32.13	31.85	31.60	31.38	30.63	30.23	30.02
4000	47.75	46.69	45.79	45.01	44.35	43.77	43.27	42.84	42.46	42.13	41.84	40.84	40.31	40.02
5000	59.69	58.36	57.23	56.26	55.43	54.71	54.09	53.54	53.07	52.66	52.30	51.05	50.39	50.03
6000	71.63	70.04	68.68	67.52	66.52	65.65	64.90	64.25	63.69	63.19	62.76	61.26	60.46	60.03
7000	83.57	81.71	80.12	78.77	77.60	76.59	75.72	74.96	74.30	73.72	73.21	71.47	70.54	70.04
8000	95.50	93.38	91.57	90.02	88.69	87.53	86.54	85.67	84.91	84.25	83.67	81.68	80.62	80.04
9000	107.44	105.05	103.02	101.27	99.77	98.48	97.35	96.38	95.53	94.78	94.13	91.89	90.69	90.04
10000	119.38	116.72	114.46	112.52	110.86	109.42	108.17	107.08	106.14	105.31	104.59	102.10	100.77	100.05
11000	131.32	128.40	125.91	123.78	121.94	120.36	118.99	117.79	116.75	115.84	115.05	112.31	110.85	110.05
12000	143.25	140.07	137.35	135.03	133.03	131.30	129.00	120.50	127.37	126.37	125.51	122.52	120.92	120.06
13000	155.19	151.74	148.80	146.28	144.11	142.24	140.62	139.21	137.98	136.90	135.96	132.72	131.00	130.06
14000	167.13	163.41	160.24	157.53	155.20	153.18	151.44	149.92	148.59	147.44	146.42	142.93	141.07	140.07
15000	179.07	175.08	171.69	168.78	166.28	164.12	162.25	160.62	159.21	157.97	156.88	153.14	151.15	150.07
16000	191.00	186.75	183.13	180.03	177.37	175.06	173.07	171.33	169.82	168.50	167.34	163.35	161.23	160.08
17000	202.94	198.43	194.58	191.29	188.45	186.01	183.88	182.04	180.43	179.03	177.80	173.56	171.30	170.08
18000	214.88	210.10	206.03	202.54	199.54	196.95	194.70	192.75	191.05	189.56	188.26	183.77	181.38	180.00
19000	226.82	221.77	217.47	213.79	210.62	207.89	205.52	203.46	201.66	200.09	198.72	193.98	191.46	190.09
20000	238.75	233.44	228.92	225.04	221.71	218.83	216.33	214.16	212.27	210.62	209.17	204.19	201.53	200.09
21000	250.69	245.11	240.36	236.29	232.79	229.77	227.15	224.87	222.89	221.15	219.63	214.40	211.61	210.10
22000	262.63	256.79	251.81	247.55	243.88	240.71	237.97	235.50	233.50	231.68	230.09	224.61	221.69	220.10
23000	274.57	268.46	263.25	258.80	254.96	251.65	248.78	246.29	244.11	242.21	240.55	234.82	231.76	230.11
24000	286.50	280.13	274.70	270.05	266.05	262.59	259.60	257.00	254.73	252.74	251.01	245.03	241.84	240.11
25000	298.44	291.80	286.15	281.30	277.13	273.54	270.42	267.70	265.34	263.27	261.47	255.24	251.91	250.11
26000	310.38	303.47	297.59	292.55	288.22	284.48	281.23	278.41	275.95	273.80	271.92	265.44	261.99	260.12
27000	322.32	315.14	309.04	303.81	299.31	295.42	292.05	289.12	286.57	284.34	282.38	275.65	272.07	270.12
28000	334.25	326.82	320.48	315.06	310.39	306.36	302.87	299.83	297.18	294.87	292.84	285.86	282.14	280.13
29000	346.19	338.49	331.93	326.31	321.48	317.30	313.68	310.54	307.79	305.40	303.30	296.07	292.22	290.13
30000	358.13	350.16	343.37	337.56	332.56	328.24	324.50	321.24	318.41	315.93	313.76	306.28	302.30	300.14
31000	370.07	361.83	354.82	348.81	343.65	339.18	335.31	331.95	329.02	326.46	324.22	316.49	312.37	310.14
32000	382.00	373.50	366.26	360.06	354.73	350.12	346.13	342.66	339.63	336.99	334.67	326.70	322.45	320.15
33000	393.94	385.18	377.71	371.32	365.82	361.07	356.95	353.37	350.25	347.52	345.13	336.91	332.53	330.15
34000	405.88	396.85	389.16	382.57	376.90	372.01	367.76	364.07	360.86	358.05	355.59	347.12	342.60	340.15
35000	417.81	408.52	400.60	393.82	387.99	382.95	378.58	374.78	371.47	368.58	366.05	357.33	352.68	350.16
36000	429.75	420.19	412.05	405.07	399.07	393.89	389.40	385.49	382.09	379.11	376.51	367.54	362.76	360.16
37000	441.69	431.86	423.49	416.32	410.16	404.83	400.21	396.20	392.70	389.64	386.97	377.75	372.83	370.17
38000	453.63	443.53	434.94	427.58	421.24	415.77	411.03	406.91	403.31	400.17	397.43	387.96	382.91	380.17
39000	465.56	455.21	446.38	438.83	432.33	426.71	421.85	417.61	413.93	410.70	407.88	398.16	392.98	390.18
40000	477.50	466.88	457.83	450.08	443.41	437.65	432.66	428.32	424.54	421.23	418.34	408.37	403.06	400.18
41000	489.44	478.55	469.27	461.33	454.50	448.60	443.48	439.03	435.15	431.77	428.80	418.58	413.14	410.19
42000	501.38	490.22	480.72	472.58	465.58	459.54	454.30	449.74	445.77	442.30	439.26	428.79	423.21	420.19
43000	513.31	501.89	492.17	483.84	476.67	470.48	465.11	460.45	456.38	452.83	449.72	439.00	433.29	430.19
44000	525.25	513.57	503.61	495.09	487.75	481.42	475.93	471.15	466.99	463.36	460.18	449.21	443.37	440.20
45000	537.19	525.24	515.06	506.34	498.84	492.36	486.74	481.86	477.61	473.89	470.63	459.42	453.44	450.20
46000	549.13	536.91	526.50	517.59	509.92	503.30	497.56	492.57	488.22	484.42	481.09	469.63	463.52	460.21
47000	561.06	548.58	537.95	528.84	521.01	514.24	508.38	503.28	498.83	494.95	491.55	479.84	473.60	470.21
48000	573.00	560.25	549.39	540.09	532.09	525.18	519.19	513.99	509.45	505.48	502.01	490.05	483.67	480.22
49000	584.94	571.92	560.84	551.35	543.18	536.12	530.01	524.69	520.06	516.01	512.47	500.26	493.75	490.22
50000	596.88	583.60	572.28	562.60	554.26	547.07	540.83	535.40	530.67	526.54	522.93	510.47	503.82	500.22
55000	656.56	641.96	629.51	618.86	609.69	601.77	594.91	588.94	583.74	579.20	575.22	561.51	554.21	550.25
60000	716.25	700.31	686.74	675.12	665.12	656.48	648.99	642.48	636.81	631.85	627.51	612.56	604.59	600.27
65000	775.94	758.67	743.97	731.38	720.54	711.18	703.07	696.02	689.87	684.50	679.80	663.60	654.97	650.29
70000	835.62	817.03	801.20	787.64	775.97	765.89	757.16	749.56	742.94	737.16	732.09	714.65	705.35	700.31
75000	895.31	875.39	858.42	843.90	831.39	820.60	811.24	803.10	796.01	789.81	784.39	765.70	755.73	750.33
80000	955.00	933.75	915.65	900.15	886.82	875.30	865.32	856.64	849.07	842.46	836.68	816.74	806.12	800.36
85000	1014.69	992.11	972.88	956.41	942.25	930.01	919.40	910.18	902.14	895.12	888.97	867.79	856.50	850.38
90000	1074.37	1050.47	1030.11	1012.67	997.67	984.72	973.48	963.72	955.21	947.77	941.26	918.83	906.88	900.40
95000	1134.06	1108.83	1087.34	1068.93	1053.10	1039.42	1027.57	1017.26	1008.27	1000.43	993.56	969.88	957.26	950.42
100000	1193.75	1167.19	1144.57	1125.19	1108.52	1094.13	1081.65	1070.80	1061.34	1053.08	1045.85	1020.93	1007.64	1000.44

12.000%

TERM	1 Year	2 Years	3 Years	4 Years	5 Years	6 Years	7 Years	8 Years	9 Years	10 Years	11 Years	12 Years	13 Years	14 Years
AMOUNT														
5	.45	.24	.17	.14	.12	.10	.09	.09	.08	.08	.07	.07	.07	.07
10	.89	.48	.34	.27	.23	.20	.18	.17	.16	.15	.14	.14	.13	.13
15	1.34	.71	.50	.40	.34	.30	.27	.25	.23	.22	.21	.20	.20	.19
25	2.23	1.18	.84	.66	.56	.49	.45	.41	.38	.36	.35	.33	.32	.31
50	4.45	2.36	1.67	1.32	1.12	.98	.89	.82	.76	.72	.69	.66	.64	.62
75	6.67	3.54	2.50	1.98	1.67	1.47	1.33	1.22	1.14	1.08	1.03	.99	.96	.93
100	8.89	4.71	3.33	2.64	2.23	1.96	1.77	1.63	1.52	1.44	1.37	1.32	1.27	1.24
200	17.77	9.42	6.65	5.27	4.45	3.92	3.54	3.26	3.04	2.87	2.74	2.63	2.54	2.47
300	26.66	14.13	9.97	7.91	6.68	5.87	5.30	4.88	4.56	4.31	4.11	3.95	3.81	3.70
400	35.54	18.83	13.29	10.54	8.90	7.83	7.07	6.51	6.08	5.74	5.48	5.26	5.08	4.93
500	44.43	23.54	16.61	13.17	11.13	9.78	8.83	8.13	7.60	7.18	6.84	6.57	6.35	6.16
600	53.31	28.25	19.93	15.81	13.35	11.74	10.60	9.76	9.12	8.61	8.21	7.89	7.62	7.39
700	62.20	32.96	23.26	18.44	15.58	13.69	12.36	11.38	10.63	10.05	9.58	9.20	8.89	8.63
800	71.08	37.66	26.58	21.07	17.80	15.65	14.13	13.01	12.15	11.48	10.95	10.51	10.15	9.86
900	79.97	42.37	29.90	23.71	20.03	17.60	15.89	14.63	13.67	12.92	12.32	11.83	11.42	11.09
1000	88.85	47.08	33.22	26.34	22.25	19.56	17.66	16.26	15.19	14.35	13.68	13.14	12.69	12.32
2000	177.70	94.15	66.43	52.67	44.49	39.11	35.31	32.51	30.37	28.70	27.36	26.27	25.38	24.63
3000	266.55	141.23	99.65	79.01	66.74	58.66	52.96	48.76	45.56	43.05	41.04	39.41	38.06	36.95
4000	355.40	188.30	132.86	105.34	88.98	78.21	70.62	65.02	60.74	57.39	54.72	52.54	50.75	49.26
5000	444.25	235.37	166.08	131.67	111.23	97.76	88.27	81.27	75.93	71.74	68.39	65.68	63.44	61.58
6000	533.10	282.45	199.29	158.01	133.47	117.31	105.92	97.52	91.11	86.09	82.07	78.81	76.12	73.89
7000	621.95	329.52	232.51	184.34	155.72	136.86	123.57	113.77	106.29	100.43	95.75	91.94	88.81	86.21
8000	710.80	376.59	265.72	210.68	177.96	156.41	141.23	130.03	121.48	114.78	109.43	105.08	101.50	98.52
9000	799.64	423.67	298.93	237.01	200.21	175.96	158.88	146.28	136.66	129.13	123.11	118.21	114.18	110.83
10000	888.49	470.74	332.15	263.34	222.45	195.51	176.53	162.53	151.85	143.48	136.78	131.35	126.87	123.15
11000	977.34	517.81	365.36	289.68	244.69	215.06	194.19	178.79	167.03	157.82	150.46	144.48	139.56	135.46
12000	1066.19	564.89	398.58	316.01	266.94	234.61	211.84	195.04	182.22	172.17	164.14	157.62	152.24	147.78
13000	1155.04	611.96	431.79	342.34	289.18	254.16	229.49	211.29	197.40	186.52	177.82	170.75	164.93	160.09
14000	1243.89	659.03	465.01	368.68	311.43	273.71	247.14	227.54	212.58	200.86	191.50	183.88	177.62	172.41
15000	1332.74	706.11	498.22	395.01	333.67	293.26	264.80	243.80	227.77	215.21	205.17	197.02	190.30	184.72
16000	1421.59	753.18	531.43	421.35	355.92	312.81	282.45	260.05	242.95	229.56	218.85	210.15	202.99	197.03
17000	1510.43	800.25	564.65	447.68	378.16	332.36	300.10	276.30	258.14	243.91	232.53	223.29	215.68	209.35
18000	1599.28	847.33	597.86	474.01	400.41	351.91	317.75	292.56	273.32	258.25	246.21	236.42	228.36	221.66
19000	1688.13	894.40	631.08	500.35	422.65	371.46	335.41	308.81	288.51	272.60	259.88	249.55	241.05	233.98
20000	1776.98	941.47	664.29	526.68	444.89	391.01	353.06	325.06	303.69	286.95	273.56	262.69	253.74	246.29
21000	1865.83	988.55	697.51	553.02	467.14	410.56	370.71	341.31	318.87	301.29	287.24	275.82	266.42	258.61
22000	1954.68	1035.62	730.72	579.35	489.38	430.11	388.37	357.57	334.06	315.64	300.92	288.96	279.11	270.92
23000	2043.53	1082.69	763.93	605.68	511.63	449.66	406.02	373.82	349.24	329.99	314.60	302.09	291.80	283.23
24000	2132.38	1129.77	797.15	632.02	533.87	469.21	423.67	390.07	364.43	344.34	328.27	315.23	304.48	295.55
25000	2221.22	1176.84	830.36	658.35	556.12	488.76	441.32	406.33	379.61	358.68	341.95	328.36	317.17	307.86
26000	2310.07	1223.92	863.58	684.68	578.36	508.31	458.98	422.58	394.80	373.03	355.63	341.49	329.86	320.18
27000	2398.92	1270.99	896.79	711.02	600.61	527.86	476.63	438.83	409.98	387.38	369.31	354.63	342.54	332.49
28000	2487.77	1318.06	930.01	737.35	622.85	547.41	494.28	455.08	425.16	401.72	382.99	367.76	355.23	344.81
29000	2576.62	1365.14	963.22	763.69	645.09	566.96	511.93	471.34	440.35	416.07	396.66	380.90	367.92	357.12
30000	2665.47	1412.21	996.43	790.02	667.34	586.51	529.59	487.59	455.53	430.42	410.34	394.03	380.60	369.43
31000	2754.32	1459.28	1029.65	816.35	689.58	606.06	547.24	503.84	470.72	444.76	424.02	407.16	393.29	381.75
32000	2843.17	1506.36	1062.86	842.69	711.83	625.61	564.89	520.10	485.90	459.11	437.70	420.30	405.98	394.06
33000	2932.02	1553.43	1096.08	869.02	734.07	645.16	582.55	536.35	501.08	473.46	451.38	433.43	418.66	406.38
34000	3020.86	1600.50	1129.29	895.36	756.32	664.71	600.20	552.60	516.27	487.81	465.05	446.57	431.35	418.69
35000	3109.71	1647.58	1162.51	921.69	778.56	684.26	617.85	568.85	531.45	502.15	478.73	459.70	444.04	431.01
36000	3198.56	1694.65	1195.72	948.02	800.81	703.81	635.50	585.11	546.64	516.50	492.41	472.84	456.72	443.32
37000	3287.41	1741.72	1228.93	974.36	823.05	723.36	653.16	601.36	561.82	530.85	506.09	485.97	469.41	455.63
38000	3376.26	1788.80	1262.15	1000.69	845.29	742.91	670.81	617.61	577.01	545.19	519.76	499.10	482.10	467.95
39000	3465.11	1835.87	1295.36	1027.02	867.54	762.46	688.46	633.87	592.19	559.54	533.44	512.24	494.78	480.26
40000	3553.96	1882.94	1328.58	1053.36	889.78	782.01	706.11	650.12	607.37	573.89	547.12	525.37	507.47	492.58
41000	3642.81	1930.02	1361.79	1079.69	912.03	801.56	723.77	666.37	622.56	588.24	560.80	538.51	520.16	504.89
42000	3731.65	1977.09	1395.01	1106.03	934.27	821.11	741.42	682.62	637.74	602.58	574.48	551.64	532.84	517.21
43000	3820.50	2024.16	1428.22	1132.36	956.52	840.66	759.07	698.88	652.93	616.93	588.15	564.78	545.53	529.52
44000	3909.35	2071.24	1461.43	1158.69	978.76	860.21	776.73	715.13	668.11	631.28	601.83	577.91	558.22	541.83
45000	3998.20	2118.31	1494.65	1185.03	1001.01	879.76	794.38	731.38	683.30	645.62	615.51	591.04	570.90	554.15
46000	4087.05	2165.38	1527.86	1211.36	1023.25	899.31	812.03	747.64	698.48	659.97	629.19	604.18	583.59	566.46
47000	4175.90	2212.46	1561.08	1237.70	1045.49	918.86	829.68	763.89	713.66	674.32	642.87	617.31	596.28	578.78
48000	4264.75	2259.53	1594.29	1264.03	1067.74	938.41	847.34	780.14	728.85	688.67	656.54	630.45	608.96	591.09
49000	4353.60	2306.61	1627.51	1290.36	1089.98	957.96	864.99	796.39	744.03	703.01	670.22	643.58	621.65	603.41
50000	4442.44	2353.68	1660.72	1316.70	1112.23	977.51	882.64	812.65	759.22	717.36	683.90	656.71	634.34	615.72
55000	4886.69	2589.05	1826.79	1448.37	1223.45	1075.27	970.91	893.91	835.14	789.10	752.29	722.39	697.77	677.29
60000	5330.93	2824.41	1992.86	1580.04	1334.67	1173.02	1059.17	975.18	911.06	860.83	820.68	788.06	761.20	738.86
65000	5775.18	3059.78	2158.94	1711.70	1445.89	1270.77	1147.43	1056.44	986.98	932.57	889.07	853.73	824.64	800.43
70000	6219.42	3295.15	2325.01	1843.37	1557.12	1368.52	1235.70	1137.70	1062.90	1004.30	957.46	919.40	888.07	862.01
75000	6663.66	3530.52	2491.08	1975.04	1668.34	1466.27	1323.96	1218.97	1138.82	1076.04	1025.85	985.07	951.50	923.58
80000	7107.91	3765.88	2657.15	2106.71	1779.56	1564.02	1412.22	1300.23	1214.74	1147.77	1094.24	1050.74	1014.94	985.15
85000	7552.15	4001.25	2823.22	2238.38	1890.78	1661.77	1500.49	1381.50	1290.66	1219.51	1162.62	1116.41	1078.37	1046.72
90000	7996.40	4236.62	2989.29	2370.05	2002.01	1759.52	1588.75	1462.76	1366.59	1291.24	1231.01	1182.08	1141.80	1108.29
95000	8440.64	4471.98	3155.36	2501.72	2113.23	1857.27	1677.01	1544.02	1442.51	1362.98	1299.40	1247.75	1205.24	1169.86
100000	8884.88	4707.35	3321.44	2633.39	2224.45	1955.02	1765.28	1625.29	1518.43	1434.71	1367.79	1313.42	1268.67	1231.43

12%

TERM / AMOUNT	15 Years	16 Years	17 Years	18 Years	19 Years	20 Years	21 Years	22 Years	23 Years	24 Years	25 Years	30 Years	35 Years	40 Years
5	.07	.06	.06	.06	.06	.06	.06	.06	.06	.06	.06	.06	.06	.06
10	.13	.12	.12	.12	.12	.12	.11	.11	.11	.11	.11	.11	.11	.11
15	.19	.18	.18	.17	.17	.17	.17	.17	.17	.16	.16	.16	.16	.16
25	.31	.30	.29	.29	.28	.28	.28	.27	.27	.27	.27	.26	.26	.26
50	.61	.59	.58	.57	.56	.56	.55	.54	.54	.54	.53	.52	.51	.51
75	.91	.89	.87	.85	.84	.83	.82	.81	.81	.80	.79	.78	.77	.76
100	1.21	1.18	1.16	1.14	1.12	1.11	1.09	1.08	1.07	1.07	1.06	1.03	1.02	1.01
200	2.41	2.35	2.31	2.27	2.24	2.21	2.18	2.16	2.14	2.13	2.11	2.06	2.04	2.02
300	3.61	3.53	3.46	3.40	3.35	3.31	3.27	3.24	3.21	3.19	3.16	3.09	3.05	3.03
400	4.81	4.70	4.61	4.53	4.47	4.41	4.36	4.32	4.28	4.25	4.22	4.12	4.07	4.04
500	6.01	5.87	5.76	5.66	5.58	5.51	5.45	5.39	5.35	5.31	5.27	5.15	5.08	5.05
600	7.21	7.05	6.91	6.80	6.70	6.61	6.54	6.47	6.42	6.37	6.32	6.18	6.10	6.06
700	8.41	8.22	8.06	7.93	7.81	7.71	7.63	7.55	7.48	7.43	7.38	7.21	7.11	7.06
800	9.61	9.39	9.21	9.06	8.93	8.81	8.71	8.63	8.55	8.49	8.43	8.23	8.13	8.07
900	10.81	10.57	10.37	10.19	10.04	9.91	9.80	9.71	9.62	9.55	9.48	9.26	9.14	9.08
1000	12.01	11.74	11.52	11.32	11.16	11.02	10.89	10.78	10.69	10.61	10.54	10.29	10.16	10.09
2000	24.01	23.48	23.03	22.64	22.31	22.03	21.78	21.56	21.38	21.21	21.07	20.58	20.32	20.17
3000	36.01	35.22	34.54	33.96	33.47	33.04	32.67	32.34	32.06	31.82	31.60	30.86	30.47	30.26
4000	48.01	46.95	46.05	45.28	44.62	44.05	43.55	43.12	42.75	42.42	42.13	41.15	40.63	40.34
5000	60.01	58.69	57.57	56.60	55.77	55.06	54.44	53.90	53.43	53.02	52.67	51.44	50.78	50.43
6000	72.02	70.43	69.08	67.92	66.93	66.07	65.33	64.68	64.12	63.63	63.20	61.72	60.94	60.51
7000	84.02	82.17	80.59	79.24	78.08	77.08	76.21	75.46	74.80	74.23	73.73	72.01	71.09	70.60
8000	96.02	93.90	92.10	90.56	89.24	88.09	87.10	86.24	85.49	84.84	84.26	82.29	81.25	80.68
9000	108.02	105.64	103.61	101.88	100.39	99.10	97.99	97.02	96.18	95.44	94.80	92.58	91.40	90.77
10000	120.02	117.38	115.13	113.20	111.54	110.11	108.87	107.80	106.86	106.04	105.33	102.87	101.56	100.85
11000	132.02	129.11	126.64	124.52	122.70	121.12	119.76	118.58	117.55	116.65	115.86	113.15	111.72	110.94
12000	144.03	140.85	138.15	135.84	133.85	132.14	130.65	129.36	128.23	127.25	126.39	123.44	121.87	121.02
13000	156.03	152.59	149.66	147.16	145.01	143.15	141.54	140.14	138.92	137.85	136.92	133.72	132.03	131.11
14000	168.03	164.33	161.18	158.48	156.16	154.16	152.42	150.92	149.60	148.46	147.46	144.01	142.18	141.19
15000	180.03	176.06	172.69	169.80	167.31	165.17	163.31	161.70	160.29	159.06	157.99	154.30	152.34	151.28
16000	192.03	187.80	184.20	181.12	178.47	176.18	174.20	172.48	170.98	169.67	168.52	164.58	162.49	161.36
17000	204.03	199.54	195.71	192.44	189.62	187.19	185.08	183.25	181.66	180.27	179.05	174.87	172.65	171.45
18000	216.04	211.28	207.22	203.76	200.77	198.20	195.97	194.03	192.35	190.87	189.59	185.16	182.80	181.53
19000	228.04	223.01	218.74	215.08	211.93	209.21	206.86	204.81	203.03	201.48	200.12	195.44	192.96	191.62
20000	240.04	234.75	230.25	226.40	223.08	220.22	217.74	215.59	213.72	212.08	210.65	205.73	203.11	201.70
21000	252.04	246.49	241.76	237.71	234.24	231.23	228.63	226.37	224.40	222.69	221.18	216.01	213.27	211.79
22000	264.04	258.22	253.27	249.03	245.39	242.24	239.52	237.15	235.09	233.29	231.71	226.30	223.43	221.87
23000	276.04	269.96	264.78	260.35	256.54	253.25	250.41	247.93	245.77	243.89	242.25	236.59	233.58	231.96
24000	288.05	281.70	276.30	271.67	267.70	264.27	261.29	258.71	256.46	254.50	252.78	246.87	243.74	242.04
25000	300.05	293.44	287.81	282.99	278.85	275.28	272.18	269.49	267.15	265.10	263.31	257.16	253.89	252.13
26000	312.05	305.17	299.32	294.31	290.01	286.29	283.07	280.27	277.83	275.70	273.84	267.44	264.05	262.21
27000	324.05	316.91	310.83	305.63	301.16	297.30	293.95	291.05	288.52	286.31	284.38	277.73	274.20	272.30
28000	336.05	328.65	322.35	316.95	312.31	308.31	304.84	301.83	299.20	296.91	294.91	288.02	284.36	282.38
29000	348.05	340.39	333.86	328.27	323.47	319.32	315.73	312.61	309.89	307.52	305.44	298.30	294.51	292.47
30000	360.06	352.12	345.37	339.59	334.62	330.33	326.61	323.39	320.57	318.12	315.97	308.59	304.67	302.55
31000	372.06	363.86	356.88	350.91	345.77	341.34	337.50	334.17	331.26	328.72	326.50	318.87	314.83	312.64
32000	384.06	375.60	368.39	362.23	356.93	352.35	348.39	344.95	341.95	339.33	337.04	329.16	324.98	322.72
33000	396.06	387.33	379.91	373.55	368.08	363.36	359.28	355.72	352.63	349.93	347.57	339.45	335.14	332.81
34000	408.06	399.07	391.42	384.87	379.24	374.37	370.16	366.50	363.32	360.53	358.10	349.73	345.29	342.89
35000	420.06	410.81	402.93	396.19	390.39	385.39	381.05	377.28	374.00	371.14	368.63	360.02	355.45	352.98
36000	432.07	422.55	414.44	407.51	401.54	396.40	391.94	388.06	384.69	381.74	379.17	370.31	365.60	363.06
37000	444.07	434.28	425.95	418.83	412.70	407.41	402.82	398.84	395.37	392.35	389.70	380.59	375.76	373.15
38000	456.07	446.02	437.47	430.15	423.85	418.42	413.71	409.62	406.06	402.95	400.23	390.88	385.91	383.23
39000	468.07	457.76	448.98	441.47	435.01	429.43	424.60	420.40	416.75	413.55	410.76	401.16	396.07	393.32
40000	480.07	469.50	460.49	452.79	446.16	440.44	435.48	431.18	427.43	424.16	421.29	411.45	406.22	403.40
41000	492.07	481.23	472.00	464.10	457.31	451.45	446.37	441.96	438.12	434.76	431.83	421.74	416.38	413.49
42000	504.08	492.97	483.52	475.42	468.47	462.46	457.26	452.74	448.80	445.37	442.36	432.02	426.54	423.57
43000	516.08	504.71	495.03	486.74	479.62	473.47	468.15	463.52	459.49	455.97	452.89	442.31	436.69	433.66
44000	528.08	516.44	506.54	498.06	490.77	484.48	479.03	474.30	470.17	466.57	463.42	452.59	446.85	443.74
45000	540.08	528.18	518.05	509.38	501.93	495.49	489.92	485.08	480.86	477.18	473.96	462.88	457.00	453.83
46000	552.08	539.92	529.56	520.70	513.08	506.50	500.81	495.86	491.54	487.78	484.49	473.17	467.16	463.91
47000	564.08	551.66	541.08	532.02	524.24	517.52	511.69	506.64	502.23	498.38	495.02	483.45	477.31	474.00
48000	576.09	563.39	552.59	543.34	535.39	528.53	522.58	517.42	512.92	508.99	505.55	493.74	487.47	484.08
49000	588.09	575.13	564.10	554.66	546.54	539.54	533.47	528.19	523.60	519.59	516.08	504.03	497.62	494.17
50000	600.09	586.87	575.61	565.98	557.70	550.55	544.35	538.97	534.29	530.20	526.62	514.31	507.78	504.25
55000	660.10	645.55	633.17	622.58	613.47	605.60	598.79	592.87	587.72	583.22	579.28	565.74	558.56	554.68
60000	720.11	704.24	690.73	679.18	669.24	660.66	653.22	646.77	641.14	636.23	631.94	617.17	609.33	605.10
65000	780.11	762.93	748.30	735.77	725.01	715.71	707.66	700.66	694.57	689.25	684.60	668.60	660.11	655.53
70000	840.12	821.61	805.86	792.37	780.77	770.77	762.09	754.56	748.00	742.27	737.26	720.03	710.89	705.95
75000	900.13	880.30	863.42	848.97	836.54	825.82	816.53	808.46	801.43	795.29	789.92	771.46	761.67	756.38
80000	960.14	938.99	920.98	905.57	892.31	880.87	870.96	862.36	854.86	848.31	842.58	822.90	812.44	806.80
85000	1020.15	997.67	978.54	962.16	948.08	935.93	925.40	916.25	908.29	901.33	895.25	874.33	863.22	857.23
90000	1080.16	1056.36	1036.10	1018.76	1003.85	990.98	979.83	970.15	961.71	954.35	947.91	925.76	914.00	907.65
95000	1140.16	1115.04	1093.66	1075.36	1059.62	1046.04	1034.27	1024.05	1015.14	1007.37	1000.57	977.19	964.78	958.08
100000	1200.17	1173.73	1151.22	1131.96	1115.39	1101.09	1088.70	1077.94	1068.57	1060.39	1053.23	1028.62	1015.55	1008.50

MONTHLY PAYMENT
REQUIRED TO AMORTIZE A LOAN

TERM AMOUNT	1 Year	2 Years	3 Years	4 Years	5 Years	6 Years	7 Years	8 Years	9 Years	10 Years	11 Years	12 Years	13 Years	14 Years
5	.45	.24	.17	.14	.12	.10	.09	.09	.08	.08	.07	.07	.07	.07
10	.89	.48	.34	.27	.23	.20	.18	.17	.16	.15	.14	.14	.13	.13
15	1.34	.71	.50	.40	.34	.30	.27	.25	.23	.22	.21	.20	.20	.19
25	2.23	1.18	.84	.66	.56	.50	.45	.41	.39	.37	.35	.33	.32	.31
50	4.45	2.36	1.67	1.32	1.12	.99	.89	.82	.77	.73	.69	.66	.64	.62
75	6.67	3.54	2.50	1.98	1.68	1.48	1.33	1.23	1.15	1.09	1.04	.99	.96	.93
100	8.89	4.72	3.33	2.64	2.23	1.97	1.78	1.64	1.53	1.45	1.38	1.32	1.28	1.24
200	17.78	9.43	6.66	5.28	4.46	3.93	3.55	3.27	3.05	2.89	2.75	2.64	2.55	2.48
300	26.67	14.14	9.98	7.92	6.69	5.89	5.32	4.90	4.58	4.33	4.13	3.96	3.83	3.72
400	35.56	18.85	13.31	10.56	8.92	7.85	7.09	6.53	6.10	5.77	5.50	5.28	5.10	4.96
500	44.45	23.57	16.64	13.20	11.15	9.81	8.86	8.16	7.63	7.21	6.87	6.60	6.38	6.19
600	53.34	28.28	19.96	15.83	13.38	11.77	10.63	9.79	9.15	8.65	8.25	7.92	7.65	7.43
700	62.23	32.99	23.29	18.47	15.61	13.73	12.40	11.42	10.67	10.09	9.62	9.24	8.93	8.67
800	71.12	37.70	26.61	21.11	17.84	15.69	14.17	13.05	12.20	11.53	10.99	10.56	10.20	9.91
900	80.01	42.41	29.94	23.75	20.07	17.65	15.94	14.68	13.72	12.97	12.37	11.88	11.48	11.14
1000	88.90	47.13	33.27	26.39	22.30	19.61	17.71	16.31	15.25	14.41	13.74	13.20	12.75	12.38
2000	177.80	94.25	66.53	52.77	44.60	39.21	35.42	32.62	30.49	28.81	27.48	26.39	25.50	24.76
3000	266.69	141.37	99.79	79.15	66.89	58.81	53.12	48.93	45.73	43.22	41.22	39.59	38.25	37.14
4000	355.59	188.49	133.05	105.54	89.19	78.41	70.83	65.24	60.97	57.62	54.95	52.78	51.00	49.51
5000	444.48	235.61	166.32	131.92	111.48	98.02	88.54	81.54	76.21	72.03	68.69	65.98	63.75	61.89
6000	533.38	282.73	199.58	158.30	133.78	117.62	106.24	97.85	91.45	86.43	82.43	79.17	76.50	74.27
7000	622.27	329.85	232.84	184.69	156.07	137.22	123.95	114.16	106.69	100.84	96.16	92.37	89.25	86.65
8000	711.17	376.97	266.10	211.07	178.37	156.82	141.66	130.47	121.93	115.24	109.90	105.56	101.99	99.02
9000	800.07	424.09	299.36	237.45	200.66	176.43	159.36	146.78	137.17	129.65	123.64	118.76	114.74	111.40
10000	888.96	471.21	332.63	263.83	222.96	196.03	177.07	163.08	152.41	144.05	137.38	131.95	127.49	123.78
11000	977.86	518.33	365.89	290.22	245.25	215.63	194.77	179.39	167.65	158.46	151.11	145.15	140.24	136.16
12000	1066.75	565.45	399.15	316.60	267.55	235.23	212.48	195.70	182.89	172.86	164.85	158.34	152.99	148.53
13000	1155.65	612.57	432.41	342.98	289.84	254.83	230.19	212.01	198.13	187.27	178.59	171.54	165.74	160.91
14000	1244.54	659.69	465.67	369.37	312.14	274.44	247.89	228.31	213.37	201.67	192.32	184.73	178.49	173.29
15000	1333.44	706.81	498.94	395.75	334.43	294.04	265.60	244.62	228.62	216.08	206.06	197.93	191.23	185.67
16000	1422.33	753.93	532.20	422.13	356.73	313.64	283.31	260.93	243.86	230.48	219.80	211.12	203.98	198.04
17000	1511.23	801.05	565.46	448.52	379.02	333.24	301.01	277.24	259.10	244.89	233.54	224.32	216.73	210.42
18000	1600.13	848.17	598.72	474.90	401.32	352.85	318.72	293.55	274.34	259.29	247.27	237.51	229.48	222.80
19000	1689.02	895.29	631.98	501.28	423.61	372.45	336.42	309.85	289.58	273.70	261.01	250.71	242.23	235.18
20000	1777.92	942.41	665.25	527.66	445.91	392.05	354.13	326.16	304.82	288.10	274.75	263.90	254.98	247.55
21000	1866.81	989.53	698.51	554.05	468.20	411.65	371.84	342.47	320.06	302.51	288.48	277.10	267.73	259.93
22000	1955.71	1036.65	731.77	580.43	490.50	431.25	389.54	358.78	335.30	316.91	302.22	290.29	280.47	272.31
23000	2044.60	1083.77	765.03	606.81	512.79	450.86	407.25	375.09	350.54	331.32	315.96	303.49	293.22	284.69
24000	2133.50	1130.89	798.30	633.20	535.09	470.46	424.96	391.39	365.78	345.72	329.70	316.68	305.97	297.06
25000	2222.39	1178.01	831.56	659.58	557.38	490.06	442.66	407.70	381.02	360.13	343.43	329.88	318.72	309.44
26000	2311.29	1225.13	864.82	685.96	579.68	509.66	460.37	424.01	396.26	374.53	357.17	343.07	331.47	321.82
27000	2400.19	1272.25	898.08	712.34	601.97	529.27	478.07	440.32	411.50	388.94	370.91	356.26	344.22	334.20
28000	2489.08	1319.37	931.34	738.73	624.27	548.87	495.78	456.62	426.74	403.34	384.64	369.46	356.97	346.57
29000	2577.98	1366.49	964.61	765.11	646.56	568.47	513.49	472.93	441.98	417.75	398.38	382.65	369.71	358.95
30000	2666.87	1413.61	997.87	791.49	668.86	588.07	531.19	489.24	457.23	432.15	412.12	395.85	382.46	371.33
31000	2755.77	1460.73	1031.13	817.88	691.15	607.67	548.90	505.55	472.47	446.56	425.86	409.04	395.21	383.71
32000	2844.66	1507.85	1064.39	844.26	713.45	627.28	566.61	521.86	487.71	460.96	439.59	422.24	407.96	396.08
33000	2933.56	1554.97	1097.65	870.64	735.74	646.88	584.31	538.16	502.95	475.37	453.33	435.43	420.71	408.46
34000	3022.45	1602.09	1130.92	897.03	758.04	666.48	602.02	554.47	518.19	489.77	467.07	448.63	433.46	420.84
35000	3111.35	1649.21	1164.18	923.41	780.33	686.08	619.72	570.78	533.43	504.18	480.80	461.82	446.21	433.22
36000	3200.25	1696.33	1197.44	949.79	802.63	705.69	637.43	587.09	548.67	518.58	494.54	475.02	458.95	445.59
37000	3289.14	1743.45	1230.70	976.17	824.92	725.29	655.14	603.39	563.91	532.99	508.28	488.21	471.70	457.97
38000	3378.04	1790.57	1263.96	1002.56	847.22	744.89	672.84	619.70	579.15	547.39	522.02	501.41	484.45	470.35
39000	3466.93	1837.69	1297.23	1028.94	869.51	764.49	690.55	636.01	594.39	561.80	535.75	514.60	497.20	482.73
40000	3555.83	1884.81	1330.49	1055.32	891.81	784.09	708.26	652.32	609.63	576.20	549.49	527.80	509.95	495.10
41000	3644.72	1931.93	1363.75	1081.71	914.10	803.70	725.96	668.63	624.87	590.61	563.23	540.99	522.70	507.48
42000	3733.62	1979.05	1397.01	1108.09	936.40	823.30	743.67	684.93	640.11	605.01	576.96	554.19	535.45	519.86
43000	3822.51	2026.17	1430.27	1134.47	958.69	842.90	761.37	701.24	655.35	619.42	590.70	567.38	548.19	532.24
44000	3911.41	2073.29	1463.54	1160.86	980.99	862.50	779.08	717.55	670.59	633.82	604.44	580.58	560.94	544.61
45000	4000.31	2120.41	1496.80	1187.24	1003.28	882.11	796.79	733.86	685.84	648.23	618.18	593.77	573.69	556.99
46000	4089.20	2167.53	1530.06	1213.62	1025.58	901.71	814.49	750.17	701.08	662.63	631.91	606.97	586.44	569.37
47000	4178.10	2214.65	1563.32	1240.00	1047.87	921.31	832.20	766.47	716.32	677.04	645.65	620.16	599.19	581.75
48000	4266.99	2261.77	1596.59	1266.39	1070.17	940.91	849.91	782.78	731.56	691.44	659.39	633.36	611.94	594.12
49000	4355.89	2308.89	1629.85	1292.77	1092.46	960.51	867.61	799.09	746.80	705.85	673.12	646.55	624.69	606.50
50000	4444.78	2356.01	1663.11	1319.15	1114.76	980.12	885.32	815.40	762.04	720.25	686.86	659.75	637.43	618.88
55000	4889.26	2591.62	1829.42	1451.07	1226.23	1078.13	973.85	896.94	838.24	792.28	755.55	725.72	701.18	680.77
60000	5333.74	2827.22	1995.73	1582.98	1337.71	1176.14	1062.38	978.48	914.45	864.30	824.23	791.69	764.92	742.65
65000	5778.22	3062.82	2162.04	1714.90	1449.18	1274.15	1150.91	1060.01	990.65	936.33	892.92	857.67	828.66	804.54
70000	6222.70	3298.42	2328.35	1846.81	1560.66	1372.16	1239.44	1141.55	1066.85	1008.35	961.60	923.64	892.41	866.43
75000	6667.17	3534.02	2494.66	1978.73	1672.13	1470.17	1327.97	1223.09	1143.06	1080.38	1030.29	989.62	956.15	928.32
80000	7111.65	3769.62	2660.97	2110.64	1783.61	1568.18	1416.51	1304.63	1219.26	1152.40	1098.98	1055.59	1019.89	990.20
85000	7556.13	4005.22	2827.28	2242.56	1895.08	1666.19	1505.04	1386.17	1295.46	1224.43	1167.66	1121.56	1083.63	1052.09
90000	8000.61	4240.82	2993.59	2374.47	2006.56	1764.21	1593.57	1467.71	1371.67	1296.45	1236.35	1187.54	1147.38	1113.98
95000	8445.09	4476.42	3159.90	2506.39	2118.03	1862.22	1682.10	1549.25	1447.87	1368.48	1305.03	1253.51	1211.12	1175.87
100000	8889.56	4712.02	3326.21	2638.30	2229.51	1960.23	1770.63	1630.79	1524.07	1440.50	1373.72	1319.49	1274.86	1237.75

TERM AMOUNT	15 Years	16 Years	17 Years	18 Years	19 Years	20 Years	21 Years	22 Years	23 Years	24 Years	25 Years	30 Years	35 Years	40 Years
5	.07	.06	.06	.06	.06	.06	.06	.06	.06	.06	.06	.06	.06	.06
10	.13	.12	.12	.12	.12	.12	.11	.11	.11	.11	.11	.11	.11	.11
15	.19	.18	.18	.18	.17	.17	.17	.17	.17	.17	.16	.16	.16	.16
25	.31	.30	.29	.29	.29	.28	.28	.28	.27	.27	.27	.26	.26	.26
50	.61	.60	.58	.57	.57	.56	.55	.55	.54	.54	.54	.52	.52	.51
75	.91	.89	.87	.86	.85	.84	.83	.82	.81	.81	.80	.78	.77	.77
100	1.21	1.19	1.16	1.14	1.13	1.11	1.10	1.09	1.08	1.07	1.07	1.04	1.03	1.02
200	2.42	2.37	2.32	2.28	2.25	2.22	2.20	2.18	2.16	2.14	2.13	2.08	2.05	2.04
300	3.62	3.55	3.48	3.42	3.37	3.33	3.29	3.26	3.23	3.21	3.19	3.11	3.08	3.05
400	4.83	4.73	4.64	4.56	4.49	4.44	4.39	4.35	4.31	4.28	4.25	4.15	4.10	4.07
500	6.04	5.91	5.79	5.70	5.62	5.55	5.48	5.43	5.38	5.34	5.31	5.19	5.12	5.09
600	7.24	7.09	6.95	6.84	6.74	6.65	6.58	6.52	6.46	6.41	6.37	6.22	6.15	6.10
700	8.45	8.27	8.11	7.98	7.86	7.76	7.68	7.60	7.54	7.48	7.43	7.26	7.17	7.12
800	9.66	9.45	9.27	9.11	8.98	8.87	8.77	8.69	8.61	8.55	8.49	8.30	8.19	8.14
900	10.86	10.63	10.43	10.25	10.11	9.98	9.87	9.77	9.69	9.61	9.55	9.33	9.22	9.15
1000	12.07	11.81	11.58	11.39	11.23	11.09	10.96	10.86	10.76	10.68	10.61	10.37	10.24	10.17
2000	24.14	23.61	23.16	22.78	22.45	22.17	21.92	21.71	21.52	21.36	21.22	20.73	20.47	20.34
3000	36.20	35.41	34.74	34.17	33.67	33.25	32.88	32.56	32.28	32.04	31.82	31.09	30.71	30.50
4000	48.27	47.22	46.32	45.55	44.90	44.33	43.84	43.41	43.04	42.71	42.43	41.46	40.94	40.67
5000	60.34	59.02	57.90	56.94	56.12	55.41	54.79	54.26	53.80	53.39	53.04	51.82	51.18	50.83
6000	72.40	70.82	69.48	68.33	67.34	66.49	65.75	65.11	64.55	64.07	63.64	62.18	61.41	61.00
7000	84.47	82.62	81.06	79.72	78.56	77.57	76.71	75.96	75.31	74.74	74.25	72.55	71.65	71.16
8000	96.53	94.43	92.64	91.10	89.79	88.65	87.67	86.81	86.07	85.42	84.85	82.91	81.88	81.33
9000	108.60	106.23	104.21	102.49	101.01	99.73	98.62	97.66	96.83	96.10	95.46	93.27	92.12	91.50
10000	120.67	118.03	115.79	113.88	112.23	110.81	109.58	108.51	107.59	106.78	106.07	103.64	102.35	101.66
11000	132.73	129.84	127.37	125.27	123.45	121.89	120.54	119.37	118.34	117.45	116.67	114.00	112.59	111.83
12000	144.80	141.64	138.95	136.65	134.68	132.97	131.50	130.22	129.10	128.13	127.28	124.36	122.82	121.99
13000	156.86	153.44	150.53	148.04	145.90	144.05	142.46	141.07	139.86	130.01	137.09	134.73	133.06	132.16
14000	168.93	165.24	162.11	159.43	157.12	155.13	153.41	151.92	150.62	149.48	148.49	145.09	143.29	142.32
15000	181.00	177.05	173.69	170.81	168.35	166.21	164.37	162.77	161.38	160.16	159.10	155.45	153.53	152.49
16000	193.06	188.85	185.27	182.20	179.57	177.30	175.33	173.62	172.13	170.84	169.70	165.82	163.76	162.66
17000	205.13	200.65	196.85	193.59	190.79	188.38	186.29	184.47	182.89	181.51	180.31	176.18	174.00	172.82
18000	217.19	212.46	208.42	204.98	202.01	199.46	197.24	195.32	193.65	192.19	190.92	186.54	184.23	182.99
19000	229.26	224.26	220.00	216.36	213.24	210.54	208.20	206.17	204.41	202.87	201.52	196.91	194.46	193.15
20000	241.33	236.06	231.58	227.75	224.46	221.62	219.16	217.02	215.17	213.55	212.13	207.27	204.70	203.32
21000	253.39	247.86	243.16	239.14	235.68	232.70	230.12	227.88	225.92	224.22	222.74	217.63	214.93	213.48
22000	265.46	259.67	254.74	250.53	246.90	243.78	241.07	238.73	236.68	234.90	233.34	227.99	225.17	223.65
23000	277.53	271.47	266.32	261.91	258.13	254.86	252.03	249.58	247.44	245.58	243.95	238.36	235.40	233.82
24000	289.59	283.27	277.90	273.30	269.35	265.94	262.99	260.43	258.20	256.25	254.55	248.72	245.64	243.98
25000	301.66	295.08	289.48	284.69	280.57	277.02	273.95	271.20	268.96	266.93	265.16	259.08	255.87	254.15
26000	313.72	306.88	301.06	296.07	291.79	288.10	284.91	282.13	279.72	277.61	275.77	269.45	266.11	264.31
27000	325.79	318.68	312.63	307.46	303.02	299.18	295.86	292.98	290.47	288.29	286.37	279.81	276.34	274.48
28000	337.86	330.48	324.21	318.85	314.24	310.26	306.82	303.83	301.23	298.96	296.98	290.17	286.58	284.64
29000	349.92	342.29	335.79	330.24	325.46	321.34	317.78	314.68	311.99	309.64	307.59	300.54	296.81	294.81
30000	361.99	354.09	347.37	341.62	336.69	332.42	328.74	325.53	322.75	320.32	318.19	310.90	307.05	304.98
31000	374.05	365.89	358.95	353.01	347.91	343.51	339.69	336.39	333.51	330.99	328.80	321.26	317.28	315.14
32000	386.12	377.70	370.53	364.40	359.13	354.59	350.65	347.24	344.26	341.67	339.40	331.63	327.52	325.31
33000	398.19	389.50	382.11	375.79	370.35	365.67	361.61	358.09	355.02	352.35	350.01	341.99	337.75	335.47
34000	410.25	401.30	393.69	387.17	381.58	376.75	372.57	368.94	365.78	363.02	360.62	352.35	347.99	345.64
35000	422.32	413.10	405.27	398.56	392.80	387.83	383.53	379.79	376.54	373.70	371.22	362.72	358.22	355.80
36000	434.38	424.91	416.84	409.95	404.02	398.91	394.48	390.64	387.30	384.38	381.83	373.08	368.45	365.97
37000	446.45	436.71	428.42	421.33	415.24	409.99	405.44	401.49	398.05	395.06	392.43	383.44	378.69	376.14
38000	458.52	448.51	440.00	432.72	426.47	421.07	416.40	412.34	408.81	405.73	403.04	393.81	388.92	386.30
39000	470.58	460.32	451.58	444.11	437.69	432.15	427.36	423.19	419.57	416.41	413.65	404.17	399.16	396.47
40000	482.65	472.12	463.16	455.50	448.91	443.23	438.31	434.04	430.33	427.09	424.25	414.53	409.39	406.63
41000	494.71	483.92	474.74	466.88	460.13	454.31	449.27	444.90	441.09	437.76	434.86	424.89	419.63	416.80
42000	506.78	495.72	486.32	478.27	471.36	465.39	460.23	455.75	451.84	448.44	445.47	435.26	429.86	426.96
43000	518.85	507.53	497.90	489.66	482.58	476.47	471.19	466.60	462.60	459.12	456.07	445.62	440.10	437.13
44000	530.91	519.33	509.48	501.05	493.80	487.55	482.14	477.45	473.36	469.80	466.68	455.98	450.33	447.30
45000	542.98	531.13	521.05	512.43	505.03	498.63	493.10	488.30	484.12	480.47	477.28	466.35	460.57	457.46
46000	555.05	542.94	532.63	523.82	516.25	509.72	504.06	499.15	494.88	491.15	487.89	476.71	470.80	467.63
47000	567.11	554.74	544.21	535.21	527.47	520.80	515.02	510.00	505.64	501.83	498.50	487.07	481.04	477.79
48000	579.18	566.54	555.79	546.60	538.69	531.88	525.98	520.85	516.39	512.50	509.10	497.44	491.27	487.96
49000	591.24	578.34	567.37	557.98	549.92	542.96	536.93	531.70	527.15	523.18	519.71	507.80	501.51	498.12
50000	603.31	590.15	578.95	569.37	561.14	554.04	547.89	542.55	537.91	533.86	530.32	518.16	511.74	508.29
55000	663.64	649.16	636.84	626.31	617.25	609.44	602.68	596.81	591.70	587.24	583.35	569.98	562.91	559.12
60000	723.97	708.18	694.74	683.24	673.37	664.84	657.47	651.06	645.49	640.63	636.38	621.79	614.09	609.95
65000	784.30	767.19	752.63	740.18	729.48	720.25	712.26	705.32	699.28	694.01	689.41	673.61	665.26	660.77
70000	844.63	826.20	810.53	797.12	785.59	775.65	767.05	759.57	753.07	747.40	742.44	725.43	716.43	711.60
75000	904.96	885.22	868.42	854.05	841.71	831.05	821.83	813.83	806.86	800.78	795.47	777.24	767.61	762.43
80000	965.29	944.23	926.31	910.99	897.82	886.46	876.62	868.08	860.65	854.17	848.50	829.06	818.78	813.26
85000	1025.62	1003.25	984.21	967.92	953.93	941.86	931.41	922.34	914.44	907.55	901.53	880.87	869.96	864.09
90000	1085.95	1062.26	1042.10	1024.86	1010.05	997.26	986.20	976.59	968.23	960.94	954.56	932.69	921.13	914.92
95000	1146.28	1121.27	1100.00	1081.80	1066.16	1052.67	1040.99	1030.85	1022.02	1014.32	1007.59	984.51	972.30	965.75
100000	1206.61	1180.29	1157.89	1138.73	1122.27	1108.07	1095.78	1085.10	1075.81	1067.71	1060.63	1036.32	1023.48	1016.57

MONTHLY PAYMENT
REQUIRED TO AMORTIZE A LOAN

TERM / AMOUNT	1 Year	2 Years	3 Years	4 Years	5 Years	6 Years	7 Years	8 Years	9 Years	10 Years	11 Years	12 Years	13 Years	14 Years
5	.15	.04	.17	.16	.12	.10	.09	.09	.08	.08	.07	.07	.07	.07
10	.89	.48	.34	.27	.23	.20	.18	.17	.16	.15	.14	.14	.13	.13
15	1.34	.71	.50	.40	.34	.30	.27	.25	.23	.22	.21	.20	.20	.19
25	2.23	1.18	.84	.66	.56	.50	.45	.41	.39	.37	.35	.34	.32	.31
50	4.45	2.36	1.67	1.32	1.12	.99	.89	.82	.77	.73	.69	.67	.64	.62
75	6.67	3.54	2.50	1.98	1.68	1.48	1.33	1.23	1.15	1.09	1.04	1.00	.96	.93
100	8.90	4.72	3.33	2.64	2.24	1.97	1.78	1.64	1.53	1.45	1.38	1.33	1.28	1.24
200	17.79	9.43	6.66	5.28	4.47	3.93	3.55	3.27	3.06	2.89	2.76	2.65	2.56	2.48
300	26.68	14.14	9.99	7.92	6.70	5.89	5.32	4.90	4.58	4.33	4.13	3.97	3.83	3.72
400	35.57	18.86	13.31	10.56	8.93	7.85	7.09	6.53	6.11	5.77	5.51	5.29	5.11	4.96
500	44.46	23.57	16.64	13.20	11.16	9.81	8.86	8.17	7.63	7.21	6.88	6.61	6.39	6.20
600	53.35	28.28	19.97	15.84	13.39	11.77	10.64	9.80	9.16	8.66	8.26	7.93	7.66	7.44
700	62.24	33.00	23.30	18.48	15.62	13.74	12.41	11.43	10.68	10.10	9.63	9.25	8.94	8.68
800	71.13	37.71	26.62	21.12	17.85	15.70	14.18	13.06	12.21	11.54	11.01	10.57	10.22	9.92
900	80.02	42.42	29.95	23.76	20.08	17.66	15.95	14.69	13.73	12.98	12.38	11.89	11.49	11.16
1000	88.91	47.14	33.28	26.40	22.31	19.62	17.72	16.33	15.26	14.42	13.76	13.21	12.77	12.40
2000	177.82	94.27	66.55	52.80	44.62	39.24	35.44	32.65	30.51	28.84	27.51	26.42	25.53	24.79
3000	266.73	141.40	99.83	79.19	66.93	58.85	53.16	48.97	45.77	43.26	41.26	39.63	38.30	37.18
4000	355.63	188.53	133.10	105.59	89.24	78.47	70.88	65.29	61.02	57.68	55.01	52.84	51.06	49.58
5000	444.54	235.66	166.38	131.98	111.54	98.08	88.60	81.61	76.28	72.10	68.76	66.05	63.83	61.97
6000	533.45	282.80	199.65	158.38	133.85	117.70	106.32	97.93	91.53	86.52	82.52	79.26	76.59	74.36
7000	622.36	329.93	232.92	184.77	156.16	137.31	124.04	114.26	106.79	100.94	96.27	92.47	89.35	86.76
8000	711.26	377.06	266.20	211.17	178.47	156.93	141.76	130.58	122.04	115.36	110.02	105.68	102.12	99.15
9000	800.17	424.19	299.47	237.56	200.77	176.54	159.48	146.90	137.30	129.78	123.77	118.89	114.88	111.54
10000	889.08	471.32	332.75	263.96	223.08	196.16	177.20	163.22	152.55	144.20	137.52	132.10	127.65	123.94
11000	977.99	518.46	366.02	290.35	245.39	215.77	194.92	179.54	167.81	158.62	151.28	145.31	140.41	136.33
12000	1066.89	565.59	399.29	316.75	267.70	235.39	212.64	195.86	183.06	173.04	165.03	158.52	153.17	148.72
13000	1155.80	612.72	432.57	343.14	290.00	255.00	230.36	212.19	198.32	187.46	178.78	171.73	165.94	161.12
14000	1244.71	659.85	465.84	369.54	312.31	274.62	248.08	228.51	213.57	201.88	192.53	184.94	178.70	173.51
15000	1333.61	706.98	499.12	395.93	334.62	294.23	265.80	244.83	228.83	216.30	206.28	198.15	191.47	185.90
16000	1422.52	754.11	532.39	422.33	356.93	313.85	283.52	261.15	244.08	230.72	220.04	211.36	204.23	198.30
17000	1511.43	801.25	565.66	448.72	379.24	333.46	301.24	277.47	259.34	245.14	233.79	224.57	216.99	210.69
18000	1600.34	848.38	598.94	475.12	401.54	353.08	318.96	293.79	274.59	259.56	247.54	237.78	229.76	223.08
19000	1689.24	895.51	632.21	501.51	423.85	372.69	336.68	310.12	289.85	273.97	261.29	250.99	242.52	235.48
20000	1778.15	942.64	665.49	527.91	446.16	392.31	354.40	326.44	305.10	288.39	275.04	264.20	255.29	247.87
21000	1867.06	989.77	698.76	554.31	468.47	411.93	372.12	342.76	320.36	302.81	288.80	277.41	268.05	260.26
22000	1955.97	1036.91	732.03	580.70	490.77	431.54	389.84	359.08	335.61	317.23	302.55	290.62	280.81	272.66
23000	2044.87	1084.04	765.31	607.10	513.08	451.16	407.56	375.40	350.87	331.65	316.30	303.83	293.58	285.05
24000	2133.78	1131.17	798.58	633.49	535.39	470.77	425.28	391.72	366.12	346.07	330.05	317.04	306.34	297.44
25000	2222.69	1178.30	831.86	659.89	557.70	490.39	443.00	408.04	381.38	360.49	343.80	330.25	319.11	309.84
26000	2311.59	1225.43	865.13	686.28	580.00	510.00	460.72	424.37	396.63	374.91	357.56	343.46	331.87	322.23
27000	2400.50	1272.57	898.40	712.68	602.31	529.62	478.44	440.69	411.88	389.33	371.31	356.67	344.64	334.62
28000	2489.41	1319.70	931.68	739.07	624.62	549.23	496.16	457.01	427.14	403.75	385.06	369.88	357.40	347.02
29000	2578.32	1366.83	964.95	765.47	646.93	568.85	513.87	473.33	442.39	418.17	398.81	383.09	370.16	359.41
30000	2667.22	1413.96	998.23	791.86	669.23	588.46	531.59	489.65	457.65	432.59	412.56	396.30	382.93	371.80
31000	2756.13	1461.09	1031.50	818.26	691.54	608.08	549.31	505.97	472.90	447.01	426.32	409.51	395.69	384.20
32000	2845.04	1508.22	1064.77	844.65	713.85	627.69	567.03	522.30	488.16	461.43	440.07	422.72	408.46	396.59
33000	2933.95	1555.36	1098.05	871.05	736.16	647.31	584.75	538.62	503.41	475.85	453.82	435.93	421.22	408.98
34000	3022.85	1602.49	1131.32	897.44	758.47	666.92	602.47	554.94	518.67	490.27	467.57	449.14	433.98	421.38
35000	3111.76	1649.62	1164.60	923.84	780.77	686.54	620.19	571.26	533.92	504.69	481.32	462.35	446.75	433.77
36000	3200.67	1696.75	1197.87	950.23	803.08	706.15	637.91	587.58	549.18	519.11	495.08	475.56	459.51	446.16
37000	3289.57	1743.88	1231.14	976.63	825.39	725.77	655.63	603.90	564.43	533.52	508.83	488.77	472.28	458.56
38000	3378.48	1791.02	1264.42	1003.02	847.70	745.38	673.35	620.23	579.69	547.94	522.58	501.98	485.04	470.95
39000	3467.39	1838.15	1297.69	1029.42	870.00	765.00	691.07	636.55	594.94	562.36	536.33	515.19	497.80	483.34
40000	3556.30	1885.28	1330.97	1055.82	892.31	784.62	708.79	652.87	610.20	576.78	550.08	528.40	510.57	495.74
41000	3645.20	1932.41	1364.24	1082.21	914.62	804.23	726.51	669.19	625.45	591.20	563.84	541.61	523.33	508.13
42000	3734.11	1979.54	1397.51	1108.61	936.93	823.85	744.23	685.51	640.71	605.62	577.59	554.82	536.10	520.52
43000	3823.02	2026.68	1430.79	1135.00	959.23	843.46	761.95	701.83	655.96	620.04	591.34	568.03	548.86	532.92
44000	3911.93	2073.81	1464.06	1161.40	981.54	863.08	779.67	718.16	671.22	634.46	605.09	581.24	561.62	545.31
45000	4000.83	2120.94	1497.34	1187.79	1003.85	882.69	797.39	734.48	686.47	648.88	618.84	594.45	574.39	557.70
46000	4089.74	2168.07	1530.61	1214.19	1026.16	902.31	815.11	750.80	701.73	663.30	632.60	607.66	587.15	570.10
47000	4178.65	2215.20	1563.89	1240.58	1048.47	921.92	832.83	767.12	716.98	677.72	646.35	620.87	599.92	582.49
48000	4267.55	2262.33	1597.16	1266.98	1070.77	941.54	850.55	783.44	732.24	692.14	660.10	634.08	612.68	594.88
49000	4356.46	2309.47	1630.43	1293.37	1093.08	961.15	868.27	799.76	747.49	706.56	673.85	647.29	625.45	607.28
50000	4445.37	2356.60	1663.71	1319.77	1115.39	980.77	885.99	816.08	762.75	720.98	687.60	660.50	638.21	619.67
55000	4889.91	2592.26	1830.08	1451.74	1226.93	1078.84	974.59	897.69	839.02	793.07	756.36	726.55	702.03	681.64
60000	5334.44	2827.92	1996.45	1583.72	1338.46	1176.92	1063.18	979.30	915.29	865.17	825.12	792.60	765.85	743.60
65000	5778.98	3063.58	2162.82	1715.70	1450.00	1275.00	1151.78	1060.91	991.57	937.27	893.88	858.65	829.67	805.57
70000	6223.51	3299.24	2329.19	1847.67	1561.54	1373.07	1240.38	1142.52	1067.84	1009.37	962.64	924.70	893.49	867.54
75000	6668.05	3534.90	2495.56	1979.65	1673.08	1471.15	1328.98	1224.13	1144.12	1081.46	1031.40	990.75	957.31	929.50
80000	7112.59	3770.55	2661.93	2111.63	1784.62	1569.23	1417.58	1305.73	1220.39	1153.56	1100.16	1056.80	1021.13	991.47
85000	7557.12	4006.21	2828.30	2243.60	1896.16	1667.30	1506.18	1387.34	1296.66	1225.66	1168.92	1122.85	1084.95	1053.44
90000	8001.66	4241.87	2994.67	2375.58	2007.69	1765.38	1594.77	1468.95	1372.94	1297.76	1237.68	1188.90	1148.77	1115.40
95000	8446.20	4477.53	3161.04	2507.55	2119.23	1863.45	1683.37	1550.56	1449.21	1369.85	1306.44	1254.95	1212.59	1177.37
100000	8890.73	4713.19	3327.41	2639.53	2230.77	1961.53	1771.97	1632.17	1525.49	1441.95	1375.20	1321.00	1276.41	1239.34

TERM	15 Years	16 Years	17 Years	18 Years	19 Years	20 Years	21 Years	22 Years	23 Years	24 Years	25 Years	30 Years	35 Years	40 Years
AMOUNT														
5	.07	.06	.06	.06	.06	.06	.06	.06	.06	.06	.06	.06	.06	.06
10	.13	.12	.12	.12	.12	.12	.11	.11	.11	.11	.11	.11	.11	.11
15	.19	.18	.18	.18	.17	.17	.17	.17	.17	.17	.16	.16	.16	.16
25	.31	.30	.29	.29	.29	.28	.28	.28	.27	.27	.27	.26	.26	.26
50	.61	.60	.58	.58	.57	.56	.55	.55	.54	.54	.54	.52	.52	.51
75	.91	.89	.87	.86	.85	.84	.83	.82	.81	.81	.80	.78	.77	.77
100	1.21	1.19	1.16	1.15	1.13	1.11	1.10	1.09	1.08	1.07	1.07	1.04	1.03	1.02
200	2.42	2.37	2.32	2.29	2.25	2.22	2.20	2.18	2.16	2.14	2.13	2.08	2.06	2.04
300	3.63	3.55	3.48	3.43	3.38	3.33	3.30	3.27	3.24	3.21	3.19	3.12	3.08	3.06
400	4.84	4.73	4.64	4.57	4.50	4.44	4.40	4.35	4.32	4.28	4.25	4.16	4.11	4.08
500	6.05	5.91	5.80	5.71	5.62	5.55	5.49	5.44	5.39	5.35	5.32	5.20	5.13	5.10
600	7.25	7.10	6.96	6.85	6.75	6.66	6.59	6.53	6.47	6.42	6.38	6.23	6.16	6.12
700	8.46	8.28	8.12	7.99	7.87	7.77	7.69	7.61	7.55	7.49	7.44	7.27	7.18	7.14
800	9.67	9.46	9.28	9.13	9.00	8.88	8.79	8.70	8.63	8.56	8.50	8.31	8.21	8.15
900	10.88	10.64	10.44	10.27	10.12	9.99	9.88	9.79	9.70	9.63	9.57	9.35	9.23	9.17
1000	12.09	11.82	11.60	11.41	11.24	11.10	10.98	10.87	10.78	10.70	10.63	10.39	10.26	10.19
2000	24.17	23.64	23.20	22.81	22.48	22.20	21.96	21.74	21.56	21.40	21.25	20.77	20.51	20.38
3000	36.25	35.46	34.79	34.22	33.72	33.30	32.93	32.61	32.33	32.09	31.88	31.15	30.77	30.56
4000	48.33	47.28	46.39	45.62	44.96	44.40	43.91	43.48	43.11	42.79	42.50	41.53	41.02	40.75
5000	60.42	59.10	57.98	57.03	56.20	55.50	54.88	54.35	53.89	53.48	53.13	51.92	51.28	50.93
6000	72.50	70.92	69.58	68.43	67.44	66.59	65.86	65.22	64.66	64.18	63.75	62.30	61.53	61.12
7000	84.58	82.74	81.17	79.83	78.68	77.69	76.83	76.09	75.44	74.87	74.38	72.68	71.79	71.31
8000	96.66	94.56	92.77	91.24	89.92	88.79	87.81	86.96	86.21	85.57	85.00	83.06	82.04	81.49
9000	108.74	106.38	104.37	102.64	101.16	99.89	98.78	97.83	96.99	96.26	95.63	93.45	92.30	91.68
10000	120.83	118.20	115.96	114.05	112.40	110.99	109.76	108.69	107.77	106.96	106.25	103.83	102.55	101.86
11000	132.91	130.02	127.56	125.45	123.64	122.08	120.73	119.56	118.54	117.65	116.88	114.21	112.80	112.05
12000	144.99	141.84	139.15	136.86	134.88	133.18	131.71	130.43	129.32	128.35	127.50	124.59	123.06	122.24
13000	157.07	153.66	150.75	148.26	146.12	144.28	142.69	141.30	140.10	139.04	138.13	134.98	133.31	132.42
14000	169.16	165.47	162.34	159.66	157.36	155.38	153.66	152.17	150.87	149.74	148.75	145.36	143.57	142.61
15000	181.24	177.29	173.94	171.07	168.60	166.48	164.64	163.04	161.65	160.44	159.38	155.74	153.82	152.79
16000	193.32	189.11	185.53	182.47	179.84	177.58	175.61	173.91	172.42	171.13	170.00	166.12	164.08	162.98
17000	205.40	200.93	197.13	193.88	191.08	188.67	186.59	184.78	183.20	181.83	180.63	176.51	174.33	173.16
18000	217.48	212.75	208.73	205.28	202.32	199.77	197.56	195.65	193.98	192.52	191.25	186.89	184.59	183.35
19000	229.57	224.57	220.32	216.69	213.56	210.87	208.54	206.51	204.75	203.22	201.87	197.27	194.84	193.54
20000	241.65	236.39	231.92	228.09	224.80	221.97	219.51	217.38	215.53	213.91	212.50	207.65	205.10	203.72
21000	253.73	248.21	243.51	239.49	236.04	233.07	230.49	228.25	226.31	224.61	223.12	218.04	215.35	213.91
22000	265.81	260.03	255.11	250.90	247.28	244.16	241.46	239.12	237.08	235.30	233.75	228.42	225.60	224.09
23000	277.90	271.85	266.70	262.30	258.52	255.26	252.44	249.99	247.86	246.00	244.37	238.80	235.86	234.28
24000	289.98	283.67	278.30	273.71	269.76	266.36	263.42	260.86	258.63	256.69	255.00	249.18	246.11	244.47
25000	302.06	295.49	289.89	285.11	281.00	277.46	274.39	271.73	269.41	267.39	265.62	259.57	256.37	254.65
26000	314.14	307.31	301.49	296.52	292.24	288.56	285.37	282.60	280.19	278.08	276.25	269.95	266.62	264.84
27000	326.22	319.12	313.09	307.92	303.48	299.65	296.34	293.47	290.96	288.78	286.87	280.33	276.88	275.02
28000	338.31	330.94	324.68	319.32	314.72	310.75	307.32	304.33	301.74	299.48	297.50	290.71	287.13	285.21
29000	350.39	342.76	336.28	330.73	325.96	321.85	318.29	315.20	312.52	310.17	308.12	301.10	297.39	295.40
30000	362.47	354.58	347.87	342.13	337.20	332.95	329.27	326.07	323.29	320.87	318.75	311.48	307.64	305.58
31000	374.55	366.40	359.47	353.54	348.44	344.05	340.24	336.94	334.07	331.56	329.37	321.86	317.90	315.77
32000	386.64	378.22	371.06	364.94	359.68	355.15	351.22	347.81	344.84	342.26	340.00	332.24	328.15	325.95
33000	398.72	390.04	382.66	376.35	370.92	366.24	362.19	358.68	355.62	352.95	350.62	342.63	338.40	336.14
34000	410.80	401.86	394.25	387.75	382.16	377.34	373.17	369.55	366.40	363.65	361.25	353.01	348.66	346.32
35000	422.88	413.68	405.85	399.15	393.40	388.44	384.14	380.42	377.17	374.34	371.87	363.39	358.91	356.51
36000	434.96	425.50	417.45	410.56	404.64	399.54	395.12	391.29	387.95	385.04	382.50	373.77	369.17	366.70
37000	447.05	437.32	429.04	421.96	415.88	410.64	406.10	402.15	398.73	395.73	393.12	384.16	379.42	376.88
38000	459.13	449.14	440.64	433.37	427.12	421.73	417.07	413.02	409.50	406.43	403.74	394.54	389.68	387.07
39000	471.21	460.96	452.23	444.77	438.36	432.83	428.05	423.89	420.28	417.12	414.37	404.92	399.93	397.25
40000	483.29	472.78	463.83	456.18	449.60	443.93	439.02	434.76	431.05	427.82	424.99	415.30	410.19	407.44
41000	495.38	484.59	475.42	467.58	460.84	455.03	450.00	445.63	441.83	438.52	435.62	425.69	420.44	417.63
42000	507.46	496.41	487.02	478.98	472.08	466.13	460.97	456.50	452.61	449.21	446.24	436.07	430.70	427.81
43000	519.54	508.23	498.61	490.39	483.32	477.22	471.95	467.37	463.38	459.91	456.87	446.45	440.95	438.00
44000	531.62	520.05	510.21	501.79	494.56	488.32	482.92	478.24	474.16	470.60	467.49	456.83	451.20	448.18
45000	543.70	531.87	521.81	513.20	505.80	499.42	493.90	489.11	484.94	481.30	478.12	467.22	461.46	458.37
46000	555.79	543.69	533.40	524.60	517.04	510.52	504.87	499.98	495.71	491.99	488.74	477.60	471.71	468.56
47000	567.87	555.51	545.00	536.01	528.28	521.62	515.85	510.84	506.49	502.69	499.37	487.98	481.97	478.74
48000	579.95	567.33	556.59	547.41	539.52	532.72	526.83	521.71	517.26	513.38	509.99	498.36	492.22	488.93
49000	592.03	579.15	568.19	558.81	550.76	543.81	537.80	532.58	528.04	524.08	520.62	508.74	502.48	499.11
50000	604.12	590.97	579.78	570.22	562.00	554.91	548.78	543.45	538.82	534.77	531.24	519.13	512.73	509.30
55000	664.53	650.06	637.76	627.24	618.20	610.40	603.65	597.80	592.70	588.25	584.36	571.04	564.00	560.23
60000	724.94	709.16	695.74	684.26	674.40	665.89	658.53	652.14	646.58	641.73	637.49	622.95	615.28	611.16
65000	785.35	768.26	753.72	741.28	730.60	721.38	713.41	706.48	700.46	695.20	690.61	674.86	666.55	662.09
70000	845.76	827.35	811.69	798.30	786.80	776.87	768.28	760.83	754.34	748.68	743.74	726.78	717.82	713.02
75000	906.17	886.45	869.67	855.32	843.00	832.36	823.16	815.17	808.22	802.16	796.86	778.69	769.09	763.95
80000	966.58	945.55	927.65	912.35	899.20	887.86	878.04	869.52	862.10	855.64	849.98	830.60	820.37	814.87
85000	1026.99	1004.64	985.63	969.37	955.40	943.35	932.92	923.86	915.98	909.11	903.11	882.51	871.64	865.80
90000	1087.40	1063.74	1043.61	1026.39	1011.60	998.84	987.79	978.21	969.87	962.59	956.23	934.43	922.91	916.73
95000	1147.82	1122.83	1101.58	1083.41	1067.80	1054.33	1042.67	1032.55	1023.75	1016.07	1009.35	986.34	974.18	967.66
100000	1208.23	1181.93	1159.56	1140.43	1124.00	1109.82	1097.55	1086.90	1077.63	1069.54	1062.48	1038.25	1025.46	1018.59

MONTHLY PAYMENT
REQUIRED TO AMORTIZE A LOAN

TERM	1 Year	2 Years	3 Years	4 Years	5 Years	6 Years	7 Years	8 Years	9 Years	10 Years	11 Years	12 Years	13 Years	14 Years
AMOUNT														
5	.45	.24	.17	.14	.12	.10	.09	.09	.08	.08	.07	.07	.07	.07
10	.89	.48	.34	.27	.23	.20	.18	.17	.16	.15	.14	.14	.13	.13
15	1.34	.71	.50	.40	.34	.30	.27	.25	.23	.22	.21	.20	.20	.19
25	2.23	1.18	.84	.67	.56	.50	.45	.41	.39	.37	.35	.34	.33	.32
50	4.45	2.36	1.67	1.33	1.12	.99	.89	.82	.77	.73	.69	.67	.65	.63
75	6.68	3.54	2.50	1.99	1.68	1.48	1.34	1.23	1.15	1.09	1.04	1.00	.97	.94
100	8.90	4.72	3.34	2.65	2.24	1.97	1.78	1.64	1.53	1.45	1.38	1.33	1.29	1.25
200	17.79	9.44	6.67	5.29	4.47	3.94	3.56	3.28	3.06	2.90	2.76	2.66	2.57	2.49
300	26.69	14.16	10.00	7.93	6.71	5.90	5.33	4.91	4.59	4.34	4.14	3.98	3.85	3.74
400	35.58	18.87	13.33	10.58	8.94	7.87	7.11	6.55	6.12	5.79	5.52	5.31	5.13	4.98
500	44.48	23.59	16.66	13.22	11.18	9.83	8.88	8.19	7.65	7.24	6.90	6.63	6.41	6.23
600	53.37	28.31	19.99	15.86	13.41	11.80	10.66	9.82	9.18	8.68	8.28	7.96	7.69	7.47
700	62.26	33.02	23.32	18.51	15.65	13.76	12.44	11.46	10.71	10.13	9.66	9.28	8.97	8.71
800	71.16	37.74	26.65	21.15	17.88	15.73	14.21	13.10	12.24	11.58	11.04	10.61	10.25	9.96
900	80.05	42.46	29.98	23.79	20.12	17.69	15.99	14.73	13.77	13.02	12.42	11.93	11.53	11.20
1000	88.95	47.17	33.31	26.44	22.35	19.66	17.76	16.37	15.30	14.47	13.80	13.26	12.82	12.45
2000	177.89	94.34	66.62	52.87	44.70	39.31	35.52	32.73	30.60	28.93	27.60	26.52	25.63	24.89
3000	266.83	141.51	99.93	79.30	67.04	58.97	53.28	49.09	45.90	43.39	41.39	39.77	38.44	37.33
4000	355.77	188.67	133.24	105.73	89.39	78.62	71.04	65.46	61.19	57.86	55.19	53.03	51.25	49.77
5000	444.72	235.84	166.55	132.17	111.73	98.28	88.80	81.82	76.49	72.32	68.99	66.28	64.06	62.21
6000	533.66	283.01	199.86	158.60	134.08	117.93	106.56	98.18	91.79	86.78	82.78	79.54	76.87	74.65
7000	622.60	330.17	233.17	185.03	156.42	137.59	124.32	114.55	107.09	101.25	96.58	92.79	89.68	87.09
8000	711.54	377.34	266.48	211.46	178.77	157.24	142.08	130.91	122.38	115.71	110.38	106.05	102.49	99.53
9000	800.49	424.51	299.79	237.89	201.12	176.89	159.84	147.27	137.68	130.17	124.17	119.30	115.30	111.97
10000	889.43	471.67	333.10	264.33	223.46	196.55	177.60	163.63	152.98	144.63	137.97	132.56	128.11	124.41
11000	978.37	518.84	366.41	290.76	245.81	216.20	195.36	180.00	168.27	159.10	151.77	145.82	140.92	136.85
12000	1067.31	566.01	399.72	317.19	268.15	235.86	213.12	196.36	183.57	173.56	165.56	159.07	153.73	149.29
13000	1156.26	613.18	433.03	343.62	290.50	255.51	230.88	212.72	198.87	188.02	179.36	172.33	166.54	161.74
14000	1245.20	660.34	466.34	370.05	312.84	275.17	248.64	229.09	214.17	202.49	193.16	185.58	179.35	174.18
15000	1334.14	707.51	499.65	396.49	335.19	294.82	266.40	245.45	229.46	216.95	206.95	198.84	192.16	186.62
16000	1423.08	754.68	532.96	422.92	357.54	314.47	284.16	261.81	244.76	231.41	220.75	212.09	204.98	199.06
17000	1512.03	801.84	566.27	449.35	379.88	334.13	301.92	278.17	260.06	245.88	234.55	225.35	217.79	211.50
18000	1600.97	849.01	599.58	475.78	402.23	353.78	319.68	294.54	275.36	260.34	248.34	238.60	230.60	223.94
19000	1689.91	896.18	632.89	502.22	424.57	373.44	337.44	310.90	290.65	274.80	262.14	251.86	243.41	236.38
20000	1778.85	943.34	666.20	528.65	446.92	393.09	355.20	327.26	305.95	289.26	275.94	265.12	256.22	248.82
21000	1867.79	990.51	699.51	555.08	469.26	412.75	372.96	343.63	321.25	303.73	289.73	278.37	269.03	261.26
22000	1956.74	1037.68	732.82	581.51	491.61	432.40	390.72	359.99	336.54	318.19	303.53	291.63	281.84	273.70
23000	2045.68	1084.84	766.13	607.94	513.95	452.06	408.48	376.35	351.84	332.65	317.32	304.88	294.65	286.14
24000	2134.62	1132.01	799.44	634.38	536.30	471.71	426.24	392.72	367.14	347.12	331.12	318.14	307.46	298.58
25000	2223.56	1179.18	832.75	660.81	558.65	491.36	444.00	409.08	382.44	361.58	344.92	331.39	320.27	311.03
26000	2312.51	1226.35	866.06	687.24	580.99	511.02	461.76	425.44	397.73	376.04	358.71	344.65	333.08	323.47
27000	2401.45	1273.51	899.37	713.67	603.34	530.67	479.52	441.80	413.03	390.50	372.51	357.90	345.89	335.91
28000	2490.39	1320.68	932.68	740.10	625.68	550.33	497.28	458.17	428.33	404.97	386.31	371.16	358.70	348.35
29000	2579.33	1367.85	965.99	766.54	648.03	569.98	515.04	474.53	443.62	419.43	400.10	384.42	371.51	360.79
30000	2668.28	1415.01	999.30	792.97	670.37	589.64	532.80	490.89	458.92	433.89	413.90	397.67	384.32	373.23
31000	2757.22	1462.18	1032.61	819.40	692.72	609.29	550.56	507.26	474.22	448.36	427.70	410.93	397.13	385.67
32000	2846.16	1509.35	1065.92	845.83	715.07	628.94	568.32	523.62	489.52	462.82	441.49	424.18	409.95	398.11
33000	2935.10	1556.51	1099.23	872.27	737.41	648.60	586.08	539.98	504.81	477.28	455.29	437.44	422.76	410.55
34000	3024.05	1603.68	1132.54	898.70	759.76	668.25	603.84	556.34	520.11	491.75	469.09	450.69	435.57	422.99
35000	3112.99	1650.85	1165.85	925.13	782.10	687.91	621.60	572.71	535.41	506.21	482.88	463.95	448.38	435.43
36000	3201.93	1698.01	1199.16	951.56	804.45	707.56	639.36	589.07	550.71	520.67	496.68	477.20	461.19	447.87
37000	3290.87	1745.18	1232.47	977.99	826.79	727.22	657.12	605.43	566.00	535.13	510.48	490.46	474.00	460.32
38000	3379.82	1792.35	1265.78	1004.43	849.14	746.87	674.88	621.80	581.30	549.60	524.27	503.72	486.81	472.76
39000	3468.76	1839.52	1299.09	1030.86	871.49	766.52	692.64	638.16	596.60	564.06	538.07	516.97	499.62	485.20
40000	3557.70	1886.68	1332.40	1057.29	893.83	786.18	710.40	654.52	611.89	578.52	551.87	530.23	512.43	497.64
41000	3646.64	1933.85	1365.71	1083.72	916.18	805.83	728.16	670.89	627.19	592.99	565.66	543.48	525.24	510.08
42000	3735.58	1981.02	1399.02	1110.15	938.52	825.49	745.92	687.25	642.49	607.45	579.46	556.74	538.05	522.52
43000	3824.53	2028.18	1432.33	1136.59	960.87	845.14	763.68	703.61	657.79	621.91	593.26	569.99	550.86	534.96
44000	3913.47	2075.35	1465.64	1163.02	983.21	864.80	781.44	719.97	673.08	636.37	607.05	583.25	563.67	547.40
45000	4002.41	2122.52	1498.95	1189.45	1005.56	884.45	799.20	736.34	688.38	650.84	620.85	596.50	576.48	559.84
46000	4091.35	2169.68	1532.26	1215.88	1027.90	904.11	816.96	752.70	703.68	665.30	634.64	609.76	589.29	572.28
47000	4180.30	2216.85	1565.57	1242.32	1050.25	923.76	834.72	769.06	718.97	679.76	648.44	623.02	602.11	584.72
48000	4269.24	2264.02	1598.88	1268.75	1072.60	943.41	852.48	785.43	734.27	694.23	662.24	636.27	614.92	597.16
49000	4358.18	2311.18	1632.19	1295.18	1094.94	963.07	870.24	801.79	749.57	708.69	676.03	649.53	627.73	609.61
50000	4447.12	2358.35	1665.50	1321.61	1117.29	982.72	888.00	818.15	764.87	723.15	689.83	662.78	640.54	622.05
55000	4891.84	2594.19	1832.05	1453.77	1229.02	1080.99	976.80	899.97	841.35	795.47	758.81	729.06	704.59	684.25
60000	5336.55	2830.02	1998.60	1585.93	1340.74	1179.27	1065.60	981.78	917.84	867.78	827.80	795.34	768.64	746.45
65000	5781.26	3065.86	2165.15	1718.09	1452.47	1277.54	1154.40	1063.60	994.33	940.10	896.78	861.62	832.70	808.66
70000	6225.97	3301.69	2331.70	1850.25	1564.20	1375.81	1243.20	1145.41	1070.81	1012.41	965.76	927.89	896.75	870.86
75000	6670.68	3537.52	2498.25	1982.42	1675.93	1474.08	1332.00	1227.22	1147.30	1084.73	1034.74	994.17	960.80	933.07
80000	7115.40	3773.36	2664.80	2114.58	1787.66	1572.35	1420.79	1309.04	1223.78	1157.04	1103.73	1060.45	1024.86	995.27
85000	7560.11	4009.19	2831.35	2246.74	1899.38	1670.63	1509.59	1390.85	1300.27	1229.36	1172.71	1126.73	1088.91	1057.47
90000	8004.82	4245.03	2997.90	2378.90	2011.11	1768.90	1598.39	1472.67	1376.76	1301.67	1241.69	1193.00	1152.96	1119.68
95000	8449.53	4480.86	3164.45	2511.06	2122.84	1867.17	1687.19	1554.48	1453.24	1373.99	1310.67	1259.28	1217.02	1181.88
100000	8894.24	4716.70	3331.00	2643.22	2234.57	1965.44	1775.99	1636.30	1529.73	1446.30	1379.66	1325.56	1281.07	1244.09

MONTHLY PAYMENT
REQUIRED TO AMORTIZE A LOAN

12.200%

TERM AMOUNT	15 Years	16 Years	17 Years	18 Years	19 Years	20 Years	21 Years	22 Years	23 Years	24 Years	25 Years	30 Years	35 Years	40 Years
5	.07	.06	.06	.06	.06	.06	.06	.06	.06	.06	.06	.06	.06	.06
10	.13	.12	.12	.12	.12	.12	.12	.11	.11	.11	.11	.11	.11	.11
15	.19	.18	.18	.18	.17	.17	.17	.17	.17	.17	.17	.16	.16	.16
25	.31	.30	.30	.29	.29	.28	.28	.28	.28	.27	.27	.27	.26	.26
50	.61	.60	.59	.58	.57	.56	.56	.55	.55	.54	.54	.53	.52	.52
75	.91	.90	.88	.86	.85	.84	.83	.82	.82	.81	.81	.79	.78	.77
100	1.22	1.19	1.17	1.15	1.13	1.12	1.11	1.10	1.09	1.08	1.07	1.05	1.04	1.03
200	2.43	2.38	2.33	2.30	2.26	2.24	2.21	2.19	2.17	2.16	2.14	2.09	2.07	2.05
300	3.64	3.57	3.50	3.44	3.39	3.35	3.31	3.28	3.25	3.23	3.21	3.14	3.10	3.08
400	4.86	4.75	4.66	4.59	4.52	4.47	4.42	4.37	4.34	4.31	4.28	4.18	4.13	4.10
500	6.07	5.94	5.83	5.73	5.65	5.58	5.52	5.47	5.42	5.38	5.35	5.23	5.16	5.13
600	7.28	7.13	6.99	6.88	6.78	6.70	6.62	6.56	6.50	6.46	6.41	6.27	6.19	6.15
700	8.50	8.31	8.16	8.02	7.91	7.81	7.73	7.65	7.59	7.53	7.48	7.31	7.22	7.18
800	9.71	9.50	9.32	9.17	9.04	8.93	8.83	8.74	8.67	8.61	8.55	8.36	8.26	8.20
900	10.92	10.69	10.49	10.31	10.17	10.04	9.93	9.84	9.75	9.68	9.62	9.40	9.29	9.23
1000	12.14	11.87	11.65	11.46	11.30	11.16	11.03	10.93	10.84	10.76	10.69	10.45	10.32	10.25
2000	24.27	23.74	23.30	22.92	22.59	22.31	22.06	21.85	21.67	21.51	21.37	20.89	20.63	20.50
3000	36.40	35.61	34.94	34.37	33.88	33.46	33.09	32.77	32.50	32.26	32.05	31.33	30.95	30.74
4000	48.53	47.48	46.59	45.83	45.17	44.61	44.12	43.70	43.33	43.01	42.73	41.77	41.26	40.99
5000	60.66	59.35	58.23	57.28	56.46	55.76	55.15	54.62	54.16	53.76	53.41	52.21	51.58	51.24
6000	72.79	71.22	69.88	68.74	67.75	66.91	66.18	65.54	64.99	64.51	64.09	62.65	61.89	61.48
7000	84.92	83.09	81.53	80.19	79.05	78.06	77.21	76.46	75.82	75.26	74.77	73.09	72.20	71.73
8000	97.05	94.95	93.17	91.65	90.34	89.21	88.23	87.39	86.65	86.01	85.45	83.53	82.52	81.98
9000	109.18	106.82	104.82	103.10	101.63	100.36	99.26	98.31	97.48	96.76	96.13	93.97	92.83	92.22
10000	121.31	118.69	116.46	114.56	112.92	111.51	110.29	109.23	108.31	107.51	106.81	104.41	103.15	102.47
11000	133.44	130.56	128.11	126.01	124.21	122.66	121.32	120.16	119.14	118.26	117.49	114.85	113.46	112.72
12000	145.57	142.43	139.75	137.47	135.50	133.81	132.35	131.08	129.97	129.01	128.17	125.29	123.77	122.96
13000	157.70	154.30	151.40	148.92	146.80	144.96	143.38	142.00	140.80	139.76	138.85	135.73	134.09	133.21
14000	169.83	166.17	163.05	160.38	158.09	156.11	154.41	152.92	151.63	150.51	149.53	146.17	144.40	143.46
15000	181.96	178.03	174.69	171.83	169.38	167.26	165.43	163.85	162.47	161.26	160.21	156.61	154.72	153.70
16000	194.10	189.90	186.34	183.29	180.67	178.41	176.46	174.77	173.30	172.01	170.89	167.05	165.03	163.95
17000	206.23	201.77	197.98	194.74	191.96	189.57	187.49	185.69	184.13	182.76	181.57	177.49	175.34	174.19
18000	218.36	213.64	209.63	206.20	203.25	200.72	198.52	196.61	194.96	193.51	192.25	187.93	185.66	184.44
19000	230.49	225.51	221.27	217.65	214.55	211.87	209.55	207.54	205.79	204.26	202.93	198.37	195.97	194.69
20000	242.62	237.38	232.92	229.11	225.84	223.02	220.58	218.46	216.62	215.01	213.61	208.81	206.29	204.93
21000	254.75	249.25	244.57	240.57	237.13	234.17	231.61	229.38	227.45	225.76	224.29	219.25	216.60	215.18
22000	266.88	261.11	256.21	252.02	248.42	245.32	242.63	240.31	238.28	236.51	234.97	229.69	226.91	225.43
23000	279.01	272.98	267.86	263.48	259.71	256.47	253.66	251.23	249.11	247.26	245.65	240.13	237.23	235.67
24000	291.14	284.85	279.50	274.93	271.00	267.62	264.69	262.15	259.94	258.02	256.33	250.57	247.54	245.92
25000	303.27	296.72	291.15	286.39	282.30	278.77	275.72	273.07	270.77	268.77	267.01	261.01	257.86	256.17
26000	315.40	308.59	302.79	297.84	293.59	289.92	286.75	284.00	281.60	279.52	277.69	271.45	268.17	266.41
27000	327.53	320.46	314.44	309.30	304.88	301.07	297.78	294.92	292.43	290.27	288.37	281.89	278.48	276.66
28000	339.66	332.33	326.09	320.75	316.17	312.22	308.81	305.84	303.26	301.02	299.05	292.33	288.80	286.91
29000	351.79	344.19	337.73	332.21	327.46	323.37	319.83	316.76	314.09	311.77	309.73	302.77	299.11	297.15
30000	363.92	356.06	349.38	343.66	338.75	334.52	330.86	327.69	324.93	322.52	320.41	313.22	309.43	307.40
31000	376.06	367.93	361.02	355.12	350.05	345.67	341.89	338.61	335.76	333.27	331.10	323.66	319.74	317.64
32000	388.19	379.80	372.67	366.57	361.34	356.82	352.92	349.53	346.59	344.02	341.78	334.10	330.05	327.89
33000	400.32	391.67	384.31	378.03	372.63	367.98	363.95	360.46	357.42	354.77	352.46	344.54	340.37	338.14
34000	412.45	403.54	395.96	389.48	383.92	379.13	374.98	371.38	368.25	365.52	363.14	354.98	350.68	348.38
35000	424.58	415.41	407.61	400.94	395.21	390.28	386.01	382.30	379.08	376.27	373.82	365.42	361.00	358.63
36000	436.71	427.27	419.25	412.39	406.50	401.43	397.03	393.22	389.91	387.02	384.50	375.86	371.31	368.88
37000	448.84	439.14	430.90	423.85	417.80	412.58	408.06	404.15	400.74	397.77	395.18	386.30	381.62	379.12
38000	460.97	451.01	442.54	435.30	429.09	423.73	419.09	415.07	411.57	408.52	405.86	396.74	391.94	389.37
39000	473.10	462.88	454.19	446.76	440.38	434.88	430.12	425.99	422.40	419.27	416.54	407.18	402.25	399.62
40000	485.23	474.75	465.83	458.21	451.67	446.03	441.15	436.92	433.23	430.02	427.22	417.62	412.57	409.86
41000	497.36	486.62	477.48	469.67	462.96	457.18	452.18	447.84	444.06	440.77	437.90	428.06	422.88	420.11
42000	509.49	498.49	489.13	481.13	474.25	468.33	463.21	458.76	454.89	451.52	448.58	438.50	433.19	430.36
43000	521.62	510.35	500.77	492.58	485.55	479.48	474.24	469.68	465.72	462.27	459.26	448.94	443.51	440.60
44000	533.75	522.22	512.42	504.04	496.84	490.63	485.26	480.61	476.56	473.02	469.94	459.38	453.82	450.85
45000	545.88	534.09	524.06	515.49	508.13	501.78	496.29	491.53	487.39	483.77	480.62	469.82	464.14	461.10
46000	558.01	545.96	535.71	526.95	519.42	512.93	507.32	502.45	498.22	494.52	491.30	480.26	474.45	471.34
47000	570.15	557.83	547.35	538.40	530.71	524.08	518.35	513.37	509.05	505.27	501.98	490.70	484.76	481.59
48000	582.28	569.70	559.00	549.86	542.00	535.23	529.38	524.30	519.88	516.03	512.66	501.14	495.08	491.83
49000	594.41	581.57	570.65	561.31	553.30	546.38	540.41	535.22	530.71	526.78	523.34	511.58	505.39	502.08
50000	606.54	593.43	582.29	572.77	564.59	557.54	551.44	546.14	541.54	537.53	534.02	522.02	515.71	512.33
55000	667.19	652.78	640.52	630.04	621.05	613.29	606.58	600.76	595.69	591.28	587.42	574.22	567.28	563.56
60000	727.84	712.12	698.75	687.32	677.50	669.04	661.72	655.37	649.85	645.03	640.82	626.43	618.85	614.79
65000	788.50	771.46	756.98	744.60	733.96	724.79	716.86	709.98	704.00	698.78	694.23	678.63	670.42	666.02
70000	849.15	830.81	815.21	801.87	790.42	780.55	772.01	764.60	758.15	752.53	747.63	730.83	721.99	717.26
75000	909.80	890.15	873.44	859.15	846.88	836.30	827.15	819.21	812.31	806.29	801.03	783.03	773.56	768.49
80000	970.46	949.49	931.66	916.42	903.34	892.05	882.29	873.83	866.46	860.04	854.43	835.23	825.13	819.72
85000	1031.11	1008.83	989.89	973.70	959.80	947.81	937.44	928.44	920.61	913.79	907.83	887.43	876.70	870.95
90000	1091.76	1068.18	1048.12	1030.98	1016.25	1003.56	992.58	983.05	974.77	967.54	961.23	939.64	928.27	922.19
95000	1152.42	1127.52	1106.35	1088.25	1072.71	1059.31	1047.72	1037.67	1028.92	1021.30	1014.64	991.84	979.84	973.42
100000	1213.07	1186.86	1164.58	1145.53	1129.17	1115.07	1102.87	1092.28	1083.07	1075.05	1068.04	1044.04	1031.41	1024.65

MONTHLY PAYMENT
REQUIRED TO AMORTIZE A LOAN

TERM AMOUNT	1 Year	2 Years	3 Years	4 Years	5 Years	6 Years	7 Years	8 Years	9 Years	10 Years	11 Years	12 Years	13 Years	14 Years
5	.45	.24	.17	.14	.12	.10	.09	.09	.08	.08	.07	.07	.07	.07
10	.89	.48	.34	.27	.23	.20	.18	.17	.16	.15	.14	.14	.13	.13
15	1.34	.71	.51	.40	.34	.30	.27	.25	.23	.22	.21	.20	.20	.19
25	2.23	1.18	.84	.67	.56	.50	.45	.41	.39	.37	.35	.34	.33	.32
50	4.45	2.36	1.67	1.33	1.12	.99	.89	.82	.77	.73	.70	.67	.65	.63
75	6.68	3.54	2.51	1.99	1.68	1.48	1.34	1.23	1.15	1.09	1.04	1.00	.97	.94
100	8.90	4.72	3.34	2.65	2.24	1.97	1.78	1.64	1.54	1.45	1.39	1.33	1.29	1.25
200	17.80	9.44	6.67	5.30	4.48	3.94	3.56	3.28	3.07	2.90	2.77	2.66	2.57	2.50
300	26.69	14.16	10.01	7.94	6.72	5.91	5.34	4.92	4.60	4.35	4.15	3.99	3.86	3.75
400	35.59	18.88	13.34	10.59	8.95	7.88	7.12	6.56	6.14	5.80	5.54	5.32	5.14	4.99
500	44.49	23.60	16.67	13.23	11.19	9.85	8.90	8.20	7.67	7.25	6.92	6.65	6.43	6.24
600	53.38	28.32	20.01	15.88	13.43	11.81	10.68	9.84	9.20	8.70	8.30	7.98	7.71	7.49
700	62.28	33.04	23.34	18.52	15.66	13.78	12.46	11.48	10.73	10.15	9.68	9.31	8.99	8.74
800	71.18	37.76	26.67	21.17	17.90	15.75	14.23	13.12	12.27	11.60	11.07	10.63	10.28	9.98
900	80.07	42.48	30.01	23.82	20.14	17.72	16.01	14.76	13.80	13.05	12.45	11.96	11.56	11.23
1000	88.97	47.20	33.34	26.46	22.38	19.69	17.79	16.40	15.33	14.50	13.83	13.29	12.85	12.48
2000	177.94	94.39	66.67	52.92	44.75	39.37	35.58	32.79	30.66	28.99	27.66	26.58	25.69	24.95
3000	266.90	141.58	100.01	79.38	67.12	59.05	53.37	49.18	45.98	43.48	41.48	39.86	38.53	37.42
4000	355.87	188.77	133.34	105.83	89.49	78.73	71.15	65.57	61.31	57.97	55.31	53.15	51.37	49.90
5000	444.83	235.96	166.67	132.29	111.86	98.41	88.94	81.96	76.63	72.46	69.14	66.43	64.21	62.37
6000	533.80	283.15	200.01	158.75	134.23	118.09	106.73	98.35	91.96	86.96	82.96	79.72	77.06	74.84
7000	622.77	330.34	233.34	185.20	156.60	137.77	124.51	114.74	107.28	101.45	96.79	93.01	89.90	87.31
8000	711.73	377.53	266.68	211.66	178.97	157.45	142.30	131.13	122.61	115.94	110.62	106.29	102.74	99.79
9000	800.70	424.72	300.01	238.12	201.34	177.13	160.09	147.52	137.93	130.43	124.44	119.58	115.58	112.26
10000	889.66	471.91	333.34	264.57	223.71	196.81	177.87	163.91	153.26	144.92	138.27	132.86	128.42	124.73
11000	978.63	519.10	366.68	291.03	246.09	216.49	195.66	180.30	168.59	159.42	152.09	146.15	141.26	137.20
12000	1067.59	566.29	400.01	317.49	268.46	236.17	213.45	196.69	183.91	173.91	165.92	159.44	154.11	149.68
13000	1156.56	613.48	433.34	343.94	290.83	255.85	231.23	213.08	199.24	188.40	179.75	172.72	166.95	162.15
14000	1245.53	660.67	466.68	370.40	313.20	275.53	249.02	229.47	214.56	202.89	193.57	186.01	179.79	174.62
15000	1334.49	707.86	500.01	396.86	335.57	295.21	266.81	245.86	229.89	217.38	207.40	199.29	192.63	187.09
16000	1423.46	755.05	533.35	423.31	357.94	314.89	284.59	262.25	245.21	231.88	221.23	212.58	205.47	199.57
17000	1512.42	802.24	566.68	449.77	380.31	334.57	302.38	278.64	260.54	246.37	235.05	225.87	218.31	212.04
18000	1601.39	849.43	600.01	476.23	402.68	354.25	320.17	295.03	275.86	260.86	248.88	239.15	231.16	224.51
19000	1690.35	896.62	633.35	502.68	425.05	373.93	337.95	311.42	291.19	275.35	262.70	252.44	244.00	236.98
20000	1779.32	943.81	666.68	529.14	447.42	393.61	355.74	327.82	306.52	289.84	276.53	265.72	256.84	249.46
21000	1868.29	991.00	700.02	555.60	469.80	413.29	373.53	344.21	321.84	304.34	290.36	279.01	269.68	261.93
22000	1957.25	1038.19	733.35	582.05	492.17	432.97	391.31	360.60	337.17	318.83	304.18	292.30	282.52	274.40
23000	2046.22	1085.38	766.68	608.51	514.54	452.66	409.10	376.99	352.49	333.32	318.01	305.58	295.36	286.87
24000	2135.18	1132.57	800.02	634.97	536.91	472.34	426.89	393.38	367.82	347.81	331.84	318.87	308.21	299.35
25000	2224.15	1179.76	833.35	661.42	559.28	492.02	444.67	409.77	383.14	362.30	345.66	332.15	321.05	311.82
26000	2313.12	1226.95	866.68	687.88	581.65	511.70	462.46	426.16	398.47	376.80	359.49	345.44	333.89	324.29
27000	2402.08	1274.14	900.02	714.34	604.02	531.38	480.25	442.55	413.79	391.29	373.31	358.73	346.73	336.76
28000	2491.05	1321.33	933.35	740.79	626.39	551.06	498.03	458.94	429.12	405.78	387.14	372.01	359.57	349.24
29000	2580.01	1368.52	966.69	767.25	648.76	570.74	515.82	475.33	444.45	420.27	400.97	385.30	372.42	361.71
30000	2668.98	1415.71	1000.02	793.71	671.13	590.42	533.61	491.72	459.77	434.76	414.79	398.58	385.26	374.18
31000	2757.94	1462.90	1033.35	820.16	693.51	610.10	551.39	508.11	475.10	449.26	428.62	411.87	398.10	386.65
32000	2846.91	1510.09	1066.69	846.62	715.88	629.78	569.18	524.50	490.42	463.75	442.45	425.16	410.94	399.13
33000	2935.88	1557.29	1100.02	873.08	738.25	649.46	586.97	540.89	505.75	478.24	456.27	438.44	423.78	411.60
34000	3024.84	1604.48	1133.36	899.53	760.62	669.14	604.75	557.28	521.07	492.73	470.10	451.73	436.62	424.07
35000	3113.81	1651.67	1166.69	925.99	782.99	688.82	622.54	573.67	536.40	507.22	483.92	465.01	449.47	436.54
36000	3202.77	1698.86	1200.02	952.45	805.36	708.50	640.33	590.06	551.72	521.72	497.75	478.30	462.31	449.02
37000	3291.74	1746.05	1233.36	978.90	827.73	728.18	658.11	606.45	567.05	536.21	511.58	491.59	475.15	461.49
38000	3380.70	1793.24	1266.69	1005.36	850.10	747.86	675.90	622.84	582.38	550.70	525.40	504.87	487.99	473.96
39000	3469.67	1840.43	1300.00	1031.82	872.47	767.54	693.69	639.24	597.70	565.19	539.23	518.16	500.83	486.43
40000	3558.64	1887.62	1333.36	1058.28	894.84	787.22	711.47	655.63	613.03	579.68	553.06	531.44	513.67	498.91
41000	3647.60	1934.81	1366.69	1084.73	917.22	806.90	729.26	672.02	628.35	594.18	566.88	544.73	526.52	511.38
42000	3736.57	1982.00	1400.03	1111.19	939.59	826.58	747.05	688.41	643.68	608.67	580.71	558.02	539.36	523.85
43000	3825.53	2029.19	1433.36	1137.65	961.96	846.26	764.83	704.80	659.00	623.16	594.53	571.30	552.20	536.32
44000	3914.50	2076.38	1466.69	1164.10	984.33	865.94	782.62	721.19	674.33	637.65	608.36	584.59	565.04	548.80
45000	4003.47	2123.57	1500.03	1190.56	1006.70	885.62	800.41	737.58	689.65	652.14	622.19	597.87	577.88	561.27
46000	4092.43	2170.76	1533.36	1217.02	1029.07	905.31	818.19	753.97	704.98	666.64	636.01	611.16	590.72	573.74
47000	4181.40	2217.95	1566.70	1243.47	1051.44	924.99	835.98	770.36	720.31	681.13	649.84	624.45	603.57	586.21
48000	4270.36	2265.14	1600.03	1269.93	1073.81	944.67	853.77	786.75	735.63	695.62	663.67	637.73	616.41	598.69
49000	4359.33	2312.33	1633.36	1296.39	1096.18	964.35	871.55	803.14	750.96	710.11	677.49	651.02	629.25	611.16
50000	4448.29	2359.52	1666.70	1322.84	1118.55	984.03	889.34	819.53	766.28	724.60	691.32	664.30	642.09	623.63
55000	4893.12	2595.47	1833.37	1455.13	1230.41	1082.43	978.27	901.48	842.91	797.06	760.45	730.73	706.30	685.99
60000	5337.95	2831.42	2000.04	1587.41	1342.26	1180.83	1067.21	983.44	919.54	869.52	829.58	797.16	770.51	748.36
65000	5782.78	3067.37	2166.70	1719.69	1454.12	1279.23	1156.14	1065.39	996.17	941.98	898.71	863.59	834.72	810.72
70000	6227.61	3303.33	2333.37	1851.98	1565.97	1377.64	1245.07	1147.34	1072.79	1014.44	967.84	930.02	898.93	873.08
75000	6672.44	3539.28	2500.04	1984.26	1677.83	1476.04	1334.01	1229.29	1149.42	1086.90	1036.97	996.45	963.13	935.45
80000	7117.27	3775.23	2666.71	2116.55	1789.68	1574.44	1422.94	1311.25	1226.05	1159.36	1106.11	1062.88	1027.34	997.81
85000	7562.10	4011.18	2833.38	2248.83	1901.54	1672.84	1511.88	1393.20	1302.68	1231.82	1175.24	1129.31	1091.55	1060.17
90000	8006.93	4247.13	3000.05	2381.11	2013.39	1771.24	1600.81	1475.15	1379.30	1304.28	1244.37	1195.74	1155.76	1122.53
95000	8451.75	4483.08	3166.72	2513.40	2125.25	1869.65	1689.74	1557.10	1455.93	1376.74	1313.50	1262.17	1219.97	1184.90
100000	8896.58	4719.04	3333.39	2645.68	2237.10	1968.05	1778.68	1639.06	1532.56	1449.20	1382.63	1328.60	1284.18	1247.26

TERM	15 Years	16 Years	17 Years	18 Years	19 Years	20 Years	21 Years	22 Years	23 Years	24 Years	25 Years	30 Years	35 Years	40 Years
AMOUNT														
5	.07	.06	.06	.06	.06	.06	.06	.06	.06	.06	.06	.06	.06	.06
10	.13	.12	.12	.12	.12	.12	.12	.11	.11	.11	.11	.11	.11	.11
15	.19	.18	.18	.18	.17	.17	.17	.17	.17	.17	.17	.16	.16	.16
25	.31	.30	.30	.29	.29	.28	.28	.28	.28	.27	.27	.27	.26	.26
50	.61	.60	.59	.58	.57	.56	.56	.55	.55	.54	.54	.53	.52	.52
75	.92	.90	.88	.87	.85	.84	.83	.83	.82	.81	.81	.79	.78	.78
100	1.22	1.20	1.17	1.15	1.14	1.12	1.11	1.10	1.09	1.08	1.08	1.05	1.04	1.03
200	2.44	2.39	2.34	2.30	2.27	2.24	2.22	2.20	2.18	2.16	2.15	2.10	2.08	2.06
300	3.65	3.58	3.51	3.45	3.40	3.36	3.32	3.29	3.27	3.24	3.22	3.15	3.11	3.09
400	4.87	4.77	4.68	4.60	4.54	4.48	4.43	4.39	4.35	4.32	4.29	4.20	4.15	4.12
500	6.09	5.96	5.84	5.75	5.67	5.60	5.54	5.48	5.44	5.40	5.36	5.24	5.18	5.15
600	7.30	7.15	7.01	6.90	6.80	6.72	6.64	6.58	6.53	6.48	6.44	6.29	6.22	6.18
700	8.52	8.34	8.18	8.05	7.93	7.83	7.75	7.68	7.61	7.56	7.51	7.34	7.25	7.21
800	9.74	9.53	9.35	9.20	9.07	8.95	8.86	8.77	8.70	8.63	8.58	8.39	8.29	8.23
900	10.95	10.72	10.52	10.35	10.20	10.07	9.96	9.87	9.79	9.71	9.65	9.44	9.32	9.26
1000	12.17	11.91	11.68	11.49	11.33	11.19	11.07	10.96	10.87	10.79	10.72	10.48	10.36	10.29
2000	24.33	23.81	23.36	22.98	22.66	22.38	22.13	21.92	21.74	21.58	21.44	20.96	20.71	20.58
3000	36.49	35.71	35.04	34.47	33.98	33.56	33.20	32.88	32.61	32.37	32.16	31.44	31.07	30.87
4000	48.66	47.61	46.72	45.96	45.31	44.75	44.26	43.84	43.47	43.15	42.87	41.92	41.42	41.15
5000	60.82	59.51	58.40	57.45	56.64	55.93	55.33	54.80	54.34	53.94	53.59	52.40	51.77	51.44
6000	72.98	71.41	70.08	68.94	67.96	67.12	66.39	65.76	65.21	64.73	64.31	62.88	62.13	61.73
7000	85.15	83.32	81.76	80.43	79.29	78.30	77.45	76.72	76.07	75.52	75.03	73.36	72.48	72.01
8000	97.31	95.22	93.44	91.92	90.61	89.49	88.52	87.67	86.94	86.30	85.74	83.84	82.83	82.30
9000	109.47	107.12	105.12	103.41	101.94	100.68	99.58	98.63	97.81	97.09	96.46	94.32	93.19	92.59
10000	121.63	119.02	116.80	114.90	113.27	111.86	110.65	109.59	108.68	107.88	107.18	104.79	103.54	102.87
11000	133.80	130.92	128.48	126.39	124.59	123.05	121.71	120.55	119.54	118.66	117.90	115.27	113.90	113.16
12000	145.96	142.82	140.16	137.88	135.92	134.23	132.77	131.51	130.41	129.45	128.61	125.75	124.25	123.45
13000	158.12	154.72	151.83	149.37	147.25	145.42	143.84	142.47	141.28	140.24	139.33	136.23	134.60	133.73
14000	170.29	166.63	163.51	160.85	158.57	156.60	154.90	153.43	152.14	151.03	150.05	146.71	144.96	144.02
15000	182.45	178.53	175.19	172.34	169.90	167.79	165.97	164.39	163.01	161.81	160.77	157.19	155.31	154.31
16000	194.61	190.43	186.87	183.83	181.22	178.98	177.03	175.34	173.88	172.60	171.48	167.67	165.66	164.59
17000	206.78	202.33	198.55	195.32	192.55	190.16	188.09	186.30	184.74	183.39	182.20	178.15	176.02	174.88
18000	218.94	214.23	210.23	206.81	203.88	201.35	199.16	197.26	195.61	194.17	192.92	188.63	186.37	185.17
19000	231.10	226.13	221.91	218.30	215.20	212.53	210.22	208.22	206.48	204.96	203.64	199.11	196.73	195.46
20000	243.26	238.04	233.59	229.79	226.53	223.72	221.29	219.18	217.35	215.75	214.35	209.58	207.08	205.74
21000	255.43	249.94	245.27	241.28	237.86	234.90	232.35	230.14	228.21	226.54	225.07	220.06	217.43	216.03
22000	267.59	261.84	256.95	252.77	249.18	246.09	243.42	241.10	239.08	237.32	235.79	230.54	227.79	226.32
23000	279.75	273.74	268.63	264.26	260.51	257.27	254.48	252.05	249.95	248.11	246.51	241.02	238.14	236.60
24000	291.92	285.64	280.31	275.75	271.83	268.46	265.54	263.01	260.81	258.90	257.22	251.50	248.49	246.89
25000	304.00	297.54	291.99	287.24	283.16	279.65	276.61	273.97	271.68	269.68	267.94	261.98	258.85	257.18
26000	316.24	309.44	303.66	298.73	294.49	290.83	287.67	284.93	282.55	280.47	278.66	272.46	269.20	267.46
27000	328.41	321.35	315.34	310.22	305.81	302.02	298.74	295.89	293.41	291.26	289.38	282.94	279.56	277.75
28000	340.57	333.25	327.02	321.70	317.14	313.20	309.80	306.85	304.28	302.05	300.09	293.42	289.91	288.04
29000	352.73	345.15	338.70	333.19	328.46	324.39	320.86	317.81	315.15	312.83	310.81	303.89	300.26	298.32
30000	364.89	357.05	350.38	344.68	339.79	335.57	331.93	328.77	326.02	323.62	321.53	314.37	310.62	308.61
31000	377.06	368.95	362.06	356.17	351.12	346.76	342.99	339.72	336.88	334.41	332.25	324.85	320.97	318.90
32000	389.22	380.85	373.74	367.66	362.44	357.95	354.06	350.68	347.75	345.19	342.96	335.33	331.32	329.18
33000	401.38	392.75	385.42	379.15	373.77	369.13	365.12	361.64	358.62	355.98	353.68	345.81	341.68	339.47
34000	413.55	404.66	397.10	390.64	385.10	380.32	376.18	372.60	369.48	366.77	364.40	356.29	352.03	349.76
35000	425.71	416.56	408.78	402.13	396.42	391.50	387.25	383.56	380.35	377.56	375.12	366.77	362.38	360.05
36000	437.87	428.46	420.46	413.62	407.75	402.69	398.31	394.52	391.22	388.34	385.83	377.25	372.74	370.33
37000	450.04	440.36	432.14	425.11	419.07	413.87	409.38	405.48	402.09	399.13	396.55	387.73	383.09	380.62
38000	462.20	452.26	443.82	436.60	430.40	425.06	420.44	416.44	412.95	409.92	407.27	398.21	393.45	390.91
39000	474.36	464.16	455.49	448.09	441.73	436.25	431.51	427.39	423.82	420.70	417.99	408.68	403.80	401.19
40000	486.52	476.07	467.17	459.58	453.05	447.43	442.57	438.35	434.69	431.49	428.70	419.16	414.15	411.48
41000	498.69	487.97	478.85	471.07	464.38	458.62	453.63	449.31	445.55	442.28	439.42	429.64	424.51	421.77
42000	510.85	499.87	490.53	482.55	475.71	469.80	464.70	460.27	456.42	453.07	450.14	440.12	434.86	432.05
43000	523.01	511.77	502.21	494.04	487.03	480.99	475.76	471.23	467.29	463.85	460.85	450.60	445.21	442.34
44000	535.18	523.67	513.89	505.53	498.36	492.17	486.82	482.19	478.15	474.64	471.57	461.08	455.57	452.63
45000	547.34	535.57	525.57	517.02	509.68	503.36	497.89	493.15	489.02	485.43	482.29	471.56	465.92	462.91
46000	559.50	547.47	537.25	528.51	521.01	514.54	508.95	504.10	499.89	496.21	493.01	482.04	476.28	473.20
47000	571.67	559.38	548.93	540.00	532.34	525.73	520.02	515.06	510.76	507.00	503.72	492.52	486.63	483.49
48000	583.83	571.28	560.61	551.49	543.66	536.92	531.08	526.02	521.62	517.79	514.44	503.00	496.98	493.77
49000	595.99	583.18	572.29	562.98	554.99	548.10	542.15	536.98	532.49	528.58	525.16	513.47	507.34	504.06
50000	608.15	595.08	583.97	574.47	566.31	559.29	553.21	547.94	543.36	539.36	535.88	523.95	517.69	514.35
55000	668.97	654.59	642.36	631.91	622.95	615.22	608.53	602.73	597.69	593.30	589.46	576.35	569.46	565.78
60000	729.78	714.10	700.76	689.36	679.58	671.14	663.85	657.53	652.03	647.24	643.05	628.74	621.23	617.22
65000	790.60	773.60	759.15	746.81	736.21	727.07	719.17	712.32	706.36	701.17	696.64	681.14	673.00	668.65
70000	851.41	833.11	817.55	804.25	792.84	783.00	774.49	767.11	760.70	755.11	750.23	733.53	724.76	720.09
75000	912.23	892.62	875.95	861.70	849.47	838.93	829.81	821.91	815.03	809.04	803.81	785.93	776.53	771.52
80000	973.04	952.13	934.34	919.15	906.10	894.86	885.13	876.70	869.37	862.98	857.40	838.32	828.30	822.95
85000	1033.86	1011.63	992.74	976.59	962.73	950.78	940.45	931.49	923.70	916.91	910.99	890.72	880.07	874.39
90000	1094.67	1071.14	1051.14	1034.04	1019.36	1006.71	995.77	986.29	978.03	970.85	964.57	943.11	931.84	925.82
95000	1155.49	1130.65	1109.53	1091.49	1075.99	1062.64	1051.09	1041.08	1032.37	1024.79	1018.16	995.51	983.61	977.26
100000	1216.30	1190.16	1167.93	1148.93	1132.62	1118.57	1106.42	1095.87	1086.71	1078.72	1071.75	1047.90	1035.38	1028.69

MONTHLY PAYMENT
REQUIRED TO AMORTIZE A LOAN

TERM	1 Year	2 Years	3 Years	4 Years	5 Years	6 Years	7 Years	8 Years	9 Years	10 Years	11 Years	12 Years	13 Years	14 Years
AMOUNT														
5	.45	.24	.17	.14	.12	.10	.09	.09	.08	.08	.07	.07	.07	.07
10	.89	.48	.34	.27	.23	.20	.18	.17	.16	.15	.14	.14	.13	.13
15	1.34	.71	.51	.40	.34	.30	.27	.25	.24	.22	.21	.20	.20	.19
25	2.23	1.19	.84	.67	.56	.50	.45	.42	.39	.37	.35	.34	.33	.32
50	4.45	2.37	1.67	1.33	1.12	.99	.90	.83	.77	.73	.70	.67	.65	.63
75	6.68	3.55	2.51	1.99	1.68	1.48	1.34	1.24	1.16	1.09	1.04	1.00	.97	.94
100	8.90	4.73	3.34	2.65	2.24	1.98	1.79	1.65	1.54	1.46	1.39	1.34	1.29	1.26
200	17.80	9.45	6.68	5.30	4.48	3.95	3.57	3.29	3.08	2.91	2.78	2.67	2.58	2.51
300	26.70	14.17	10.01	7.95	6.72	5.92	5.35	4.93	4.61	4.36	4.16	4.00	3.87	3.76
400	35.60	18.89	13.35	10.60	8.96	7.89	7.13	6.57	6.15	5.81	5.55	5.33	5.15	5.01
500	44.50	23.61	16.68	13.25	11.20	9.86	8.91	8.21	7.68	7.27	6.93	6.66	6.44	6.26
600	53.40	28.33	20.02	15.89	13.44	11.83	10.69	9.86	9.22	8.72	8.32	7.99	7.73	7.51
700	62.30	33.05	23.36	18.54	15.68	13.80	12.47	11.50	10.75	10.17	9.70	9.33	9.02	8.76
800	71.20	37.78	26.69	21.19	17.92	15.77	14.26	13.14	12.29	11.62	11.09	10.66	10.30	10.01
900	80.10	42.50	30.03	23.84	20.16	17.74	16.04	14.78	13.82	13.07	12.48	11.99	11.59	11.26
1000	88.99	47.22	33.36	26.49	22.40	19.71	17.82	16.42	15.36	14.53	13.86	13.32	12.88	12.51
2000	177.98	94.43	66.72	52.97	44.80	39.42	35.63	32.84	30.71	29.05	27.72	26.64	25.75	25.01
3000	266.97	141.65	100.08	79.45	67.19	59.12	53.45	49.26	46.07	43.57	41.57	39.95	38.62	37.52
4000	355.96	188.86	133.44	105.93	89.59	78.83	71.26	65.68	61.42	58.09	55.43	53.27	51.50	50.02
5000	444.95	236.07	166.79	132.41	111.99	98.54	89.07	82.10	76.77	72.61	69.29	66.59	64.37	62.53
6000	533.94	283.29	200.15	158.89	134.38	118.24	106.89	98.51	92.13	87.13	83.14	79.90	77.24	75.03
7000	622.93	330.50	233.51	185.37	156.78	137.95	124.70	114.93	107.48	101.65	97.00	93.22	90.11	87.54
8000	711.92	377.71	266.87	211.86	179.18	157.66	142.51	131.35	122.84	116.17	110.85	106.54	102.99	100.04
9000	800.91	424.93	300.23	238.34	201.57	177.36	160.33	147.77	138.19	130.69	124.71	119.85	115.86	112.54
10000	889.90	472.14	333.58	264.82	223.97	197.07	178.14	164.19	153.54	145.22	138.57	133.17	128.73	125.05
11000	978.89	519.36	366.94	291.30	246.36	216.78	195.95	180.60	168.90	159.74	152.42	146.49	141.61	137.55
12000	1067.88	566.57	400.30	317.78	268.76	236.48	213.77	197.02	184.25	174.26	166.28	159.80	154.48	150.06
13000	1156.86	613.78	433.66	344.26	291.16	256.19	231.58	213.44	199.61	188.78	180.13	173.12	167.35	162.56
14000	1245.85	661.00	467.01	370.74	313.55	275.90	249.39	229.86	214.96	203.30	193.99	186.43	180.22	175.07
15000	1334.84	708.21	500.37	397.23	335.95	295.60	267.21	246.28	230.31	217.82	207.85	199.75	193.10	187.57
16000	1423.83	755.42	533.73	423.71	358.35	315.31	285.02	262.69	245.67	232.34	221.70	213.07	205.97	200.07
17000	1512.82	802.64	567.09	450.19	380.74	335.02	302.84	279.11	261.02	246.86	235.56	226.38	218.84	212.58
18000	1601.81	849.85	600.45	476.67	403.14	354.72	320.65	295.53	276.38	261.38	249.41	239.70	231.72	225.08
19000	1690.80	897.07	633.80	503.15	425.54	374.43	338.46	311.95	291.73	275.91	263.27	253.02	244.59	237.59
20000	1779.79	944.28	667.16	529.63	447.93	394.14	356.28	328.37	307.08	290.43	277.13	266.33	257.46	250.09
21000	1868.78	991.49	700.52	556.11	470.33	413.84	374.09	344.79	322.44	304.95	290.98	279.65	270.33	262.60
22000	1957.77	1038.71	733.88	582.60	492.72	433.55	391.90	361.20	337.79	319.47	304.84	292.97	283.21	275.10
23000	2046.76	1085.92	767.23	609.08	515.12	453.26	409.72	377.62	353.14	333.99	318.69	306.28	296.08	287.60
24000	2135.75	1133.13	800.59	635.56	537.52	472.96	427.53	394.04	368.50	348.51	332.55	319.60	308.95	300.11
25000	2224.73	1180.35	833.95	662.04	559.91	492.67	445.34	410.46	383.85	363.03	346.41	332.92	321.83	312.61
26000	2313.72	1227.56	867.31	688.52	582.31	512.38	463.16	426.88	399.21	377.55	360.26	346.23	334.70	325.12
27000	2402.71	1274.77	900.67	715.00	604.71	532.08	480.97	443.29	414.56	392.07	374.12	359.55	347.57	337.62
28000	2491.70	1321.99	934.02	741.48	627.10	551.79	498.78	459.71	429.91	406.59	387.97	372.86	360.44	350.13
29000	2580.69	1369.20	967.38	767.96	649.50	571.49	516.60	476.13	445.27	421.12	401.83	386.18	373.32	362.63
30000	2669.68	1416.42	1000.74	794.45	671.90	591.20	534.41	492.55	460.62	435.64	415.69	399.50	386.19	375.13
31000	2758.67	1463.63	1034.10	820.93	694.29	610.91	552.23	508.97	475.98	450.16	429.54	412.81	399.06	387.64
32000	2847.66	1510.84	1067.45	847.41	716.69	630.61	570.04	525.38	491.33	464.68	443.40	426.13	411.94	400.14
33000	2936.65	1558.06	1100.81	873.89	739.08	650.32	587.85	541.80	506.68	479.20	457.25	439.45	424.81	412.65
34000	3025.64	1605.27	1134.17	900.37	761.48	670.03	605.67	558.22	522.04	493.72	471.11	452.76	437.68	425.15
35000	3114.63	1652.48	1167.53	926.85	783.88	689.73	623.48	574.64	537.39	508.24	484.97	466.08	450.55	437.66
36000	3203.62	1699.70	1200.89	953.33	806.27	709.44	641.29	591.06	552.75	522.76	498.82	479.40	463.43	450.16
37000	3292.61	1746.91	1234.24	979.82	828.67	729.15	659.11	607.48	568.10	537.28	512.68	492.71	476.30	462.66
38000	3381.59	1794.13	1267.60	1006.30	851.07	748.85	676.92	623.89	583.45	551.81	526.53	506.03	489.17	475.17
39000	3470.58	1841.34	1300.96	1032.78	873.46	768.56	694.73	640.31	598.81	566.33	540.39	519.35	502.05	487.67
40000	3559.57	1888.55	1334.32	1059.26	895.86	788.27	712.55	656.73	614.16	580.85	554.25	532.66	514.92	500.18
41000	3648.56	1935.77	1367.67	1085.74	918.26	807.97	730.36	673.15	629.51	595.37	568.10	545.98	527.79	512.68
42000	3737.55	1982.98	1401.03	1112.22	940.65	827.68	748.17	689.57	644.87	609.89	581.96	559.29	540.66	525.19
43000	3826.54	2030.19	1434.39	1138.70	963.05	847.39	765.99	705.98	660.22	624.41	595.81	572.61	553.54	537.69
44000	3915.53	2077.41	1467.75	1165.19	985.44	867.09	783.80	722.40	675.58	638.93	609.67	585.93	566.41	550.19
45000	4004.52	2124.62	1501.11	1191.67	1007.84	886.80	801.62	738.82	690.93	653.45	623.53	599.24	579.28	562.70
46000	4093.51	2171.83	1534.46	1218.15	1030.24	906.51	819.43	755.24	706.28	667.97	637.38	612.56	592.16	575.20
47000	4182.50	2219.05	1567.82	1244.63	1052.63	926.21	837.24	771.66	721.64	682.49	651.24	625.88	605.03	587.71
48000	4271.49	2266.26	1601.18	1271.11	1075.03	945.92	855.06	788.07	736.99	697.02	665.09	639.19	617.90	600.21
49000	4360.48	2313.48	1634.54	1297.59	1097.43	965.63	872.87	804.49	752.35	711.54	678.95	652.51	630.77	612.72
50000	4449.46	2360.69	1667.89	1324.07	1119.82	985.33	890.68	820.91	767.70	726.06	692.81	665.83	643.65	625.22
55000	4894.41	2596.76	1834.68	1456.48	1231.80	1083.87	979.75	903.00	844.47	798.66	762.09	732.41	708.01	687.74
60000	5339.36	2832.83	2001.47	1588.89	1343.79	1182.40	1068.82	985.09	921.24	871.27	831.37	798.99	772.38	750.26
65000	5784.30	3068.90	2168.26	1721.29	1455.77	1280.93	1157.89	1067.18	998.01	943.87	900.65	865.57	836.74	812.78
70000	6229.25	3304.96	2335.05	1853.70	1567.75	1379.46	1246.95	1149.27	1074.78	1016.48	969.93	932.15	901.10	875.31
75000	6674.19	3541.03	2501.84	1986.11	1679.73	1478.00	1336.02	1231.36	1151.55	1089.08	1039.21	998.74	965.47	937.83
80000	7119.14	3777.10	2668.63	2118.51	1791.71	1576.53	1425.09	1313.45	1228.32	1161.69	1108.49	1065.32	1029.83	1000.35
85000	7564.09	4013.17	2835.42	2250.92	1903.69	1675.06	1514.16	1395.55	1305.09	1234.29	1177.77	1131.90	1094.20	1062.87
90000	8009.03	4249.24	3002.21	2383.33	2015.68	1773.59	1603.23	1477.64	1381.86	1306.90	1247.05	1198.48	1158.56	1125.39
95000	8453.98	4485.31	3168.99	2515.74	2127.66	1872.13	1692.29	1559.73	1458.63	1379.51	1316.33	1265.07	1222.93	1187.91
100000	8898.92	4721.37	3335.78	2648.14	2239.64	1970.66	1781.36	1641.82	1535.39	1452.11	1385.61	1331.65	1287.29	1250.43

TERM	15 Years	16 Years	17 Years	18 Years	19 Years	20 Years	21 Years	22 Years	23 Years	24 Years	25 Years	30 Years	35 Years	40 Years
AMOUNT														
5	.07	.06	.06	.06	.06	.06	.06	.06	.06	.06	.06	.06	.06	.06
10	.13	.12	.12	.12	.12	.12	.12	.11	.11	.11	.11	.11	.11	.11
15	.19	.18	.18	.18	.18	.17	.17	.17	.17	.17	.17	.16	.16	.16
25	.31	.30	.30	.29	.29	.29	.28	.28	.28	.28	.27	.27	.26	.26
50	.61	.60	.59	.58	.57	.57	.56	.55	.55	.55	.54	.53	.52	.52
75	.92	.90	.88	.87	.86	.85	.84	.83	.82	.82	.81	.79	.78	.78
100	1.22	1.20	1.18	1.16	1.14	1.13	1.11	1.10	1.10	1.09	1.08	1.06	1.04	1.04
200	2.44	2.39	2.35	2.31	2.28	2.25	2.22	2.20	2.19	2.17	2.16	2.11	2.08	2.07
300	3.66	3.59	3.52	3.46	3.41	3.37	3.33	3.30	3.28	3.25	3.23	3.16	3.12	3.10
400	4.88	4.78	4.69	4.61	4.55	4.49	4.44	4.40	4.37	4.33	4.31	4.21	4.16	4.14
500	6.10	5.97	5.86	5.77	5.69	5.62	5.55	5.50	5.46	5.42	5.38	5.26	5.20	5.17
600	7.32	7.17	7.03	6.92	6.82	6.74	6.66	6.60	6.55	6.50	6.46	6.32	6.24	6.20
700	8.54	8.36	8.20	8.07	7.96	7.86	7.77	7.70	7.64	7.58	7.53	7.37	7.28	7.23
800	9.76	9.55	9.38	9.22	9.09	8.98	8.88	8.80	8.73	8.66	8.61	8.42	8.32	8.27
900	10.98	10.75	10.55	10.38	10.23	10.10	9.99	9.90	9.82	9.75	9.68	9.47	9.36	9.30
1000	12.20	11.94	11.72	11.53	11.37	11.23	11.10	11.00	10.91	10.83	10.76	10.52	10.40	10.33
2000	24.40	23.87	23.43	23.05	22.73	22.45	22.20	21.99	21.81	21.65	21.51	21.04	20.79	20.66
3000	36.59	35.81	35.14	34.58	34.09	33.67	33.30	32.99	32.72	32.48	32.27	31.56	31.19	30.99
4000	48.79	47.74	46.86	46.10	45.45	44.89	44.40	43.98	43.62	43.30	43.02	42.08	41.58	41.31
5000	60.98	59.68	58.57	57.62	56.81	56.11	55.50	54.98	54.52	54.12	53.78	52.59	51.97	51.64
6000	73.18	71.61	70.28	69.15	68.17	67.33	66.60	65.97	65.43	64.95	64.53	63.11	62.37	61.97
7000	85.37	83.55	81.99	80.67	79.53	78.55	77.70	76.97	76.33	75.77	75.29	73.63	72.76	72.30
8000	97.57	95.48	93.71	92.19	90.89	89.77	88.80	87.96	87.23	86.60	86.04	84.15	83.15	82.62
9000	109.76	107.42	105.42	103.72	102.25	100.99	99.90	98.96	98.14	97.42	96.80	94.66	93.55	92.95
10000	121.96	119.35	117.13	115.24	113.61	112.21	111.00	109.95	109.04	108.24	107.55	105.18	103.94	103.28
11000	134.15	131.28	128.85	126.76	124.97	123.43	122.10	120.95	119.94	119.07	118.31	115.70	114.33	113.61
12000	146.35	143.22	140.56	138.29	136.33	134.65	133.20	131.94	130.85	129.89	129.06	126.22	124.73	123.93
13000	158.54	155.15	152.27	149.81	147.70	145.87	144.30	142.94	141.75	140.72	139.81	136.73	135.12	134.26
14000	170.74	167.09	163.98	161.33	159.06	157.10	155.40	153.93	152.65	151.54	150.57	147.25	145.51	144.59
15000	182.94	179.02	175.70	172.86	170.42	168.32	166.50	164.93	163.56	162.36	161.32	157.77	155.91	154.91
16000	195.13	190.96	187.41	184.38	181.78	179.54	177.60	175.92	174.46	173.19	172.08	168.29	166.30	165.24
17000	207.33	202.89	199.12	195.90	193.14	190.76	188.70	186.91	185.36	184.01	182.83	178.80	176.69	175.57
18000	219.52	214.83	210.83	207.43	204.50	201.98	199.80	197.91	196.27	194.84	193.59	189.32	187.09	185.90
19000	231.72	226.76	222.55	218.95	215.86	213.20	210.90	208.90	207.17	205.66	204.34	199.84	197.48	196.22
20000	243.91	238.69	234.26	230.47	227.22	224.42	222.00	219.90	218.07	216.48	215.10	210.36	207.87	206.55
21000	256.11	250.63	245.97	242.00	238.58	235.64	233.10	230.89	228.98	227.31	225.85	220.88	218.27	216.88
22000	268.30	262.56	257.69	253.52	249.94	246.86	244.20	241.89	239.88	238.13	236.61	231.39	228.66	227.21
23000	280.50	274.50	269.40	265.04	261.30	258.08	255.30	252.88	250.78	248.96	247.36	241.91	239.05	237.53
24000	292.69	286.43	281.11	276.57	272.66	269.30	266.40	263.88	261.69	259.78	258.12	252.43	249.45	247.86
25000	304.89	298.37	292.82	288.09	284.02	280.52	277.50	274.87	272.59	270.60	268.87	262.95	259.84	258.19
26000	317.08	310.30	304.54	299.61	295.39	291.74	288.60	285.87	283.49	281.43	279.62	273.46	270.23	268.51
27000	329.28	322.24	316.25	311.14	306.75	302.96	299.70	296.86	294.40	292.25	290.38	283.98	280.63	278.84
28000	341.48	334.17	327.96	322.66	318.11	314.19	310.80	307.86	305.30	303.08	301.13	294.50	291.02	289.17
29000	353.67	346.10	339.67	334.18	329.47	325.41	321.89	318.85	316.20	313.90	311.89	305.02	301.41	299.50
30000	365.87	358.04	351.39	345.71	340.83	336.63	332.99	329.85	327.11	324.72	322.64	315.53	311.81	309.82
31000	378.06	369.97	363.10	357.23	352.19	347.85	344.09	340.84	338.01	335.55	333.40	326.05	322.20	320.15
32000	390.26	381.91	374.81	368.75	363.55	359.07	355.19	351.83	348.91	346.37	344.15	336.57	332.59	330.48
33000	402.45	393.84	386.53	380.28	374.91	370.29	366.29	362.83	359.82	357.20	354.91	347.09	342.99	340.81
34000	414.65	405.78	398.24	391.80	386.27	381.51	377.39	373.82	370.72	368.02	365.66	357.60	353.38	351.13
35000	426.84	417.71	409.95	403.32	397.63	392.73	388.49	384.82	381.62	378.84	376.42	368.12	363.78	361.46
36000	439.04	429.65	421.66	414.85	408.99	403.95	399.59	395.81	392.53	389.67	387.17	378.64	374.17	371.79
37000	451.23	441.58	433.38	426.37	420.35	415.17	410.69	406.81	403.43	400.49	397.92	389.16	384.56	382.11
38000	463.43	453.51	445.09	437.89	431.71	426.39	421.79	417.80	414.34	411.32	408.68	399.67	394.96	392.44
39000	475.62	465.45	456.80	449.42	443.08	437.61	432.89	428.80	425.24	422.14	419.43	410.19	405.35	402.77
40000	487.82	477.38	468.52	460.94	454.44	448.83	443.99	439.79	436.14	432.96	430.19	420.71	415.74	413.10
41000	500.01	489.32	480.23	472.46	465.80	460.05	455.09	450.79	447.05	443.79	440.94	431.23	426.14	423.42
42000	512.21	501.25	491.94	483.99	477.16	471.28	466.19	461.78	457.95	454.61	451.70	441.75	436.53	433.75
43000	524.41	513.19	503.65	495.51	488.52	482.50	477.29	472.78	468.85	465.43	462.45	452.26	446.92	444.08
44000	536.60	525.12	515.37	507.03	499.88	493.72	488.39	483.77	479.76	476.26	473.21	462.78	457.32	454.41
45000	548.80	537.06	527.08	518.56	511.24	504.94	499.49	494.77	490.66	487.08	483.96	473.30	467.71	464.73
46000	560.99	548.99	538.79	530.08	522.60	516.16	510.59	505.76	501.56	497.91	494.72	483.82	478.10	475.06
47000	573.19	560.92	550.50	541.60	533.96	527.38	521.69	516.75	512.47	508.73	505.47	494.33	488.50	485.39
48000	585.38	572.86	562.22	553.13	545.32	538.60	532.79	527.75	523.37	519.55	516.23	504.85	498.89	495.72
49000	597.58	584.79	573.93	564.65	556.68	549.82	543.89	538.74	534.27	530.38	526.98	515.37	509.28	506.04
50000	609.77	596.73	585.64	576.17	568.04	561.04	554.99	549.74	545.18	541.20	537.73	525.89	519.68	516.37
55000	670.75	656.40	644.21	633.79	624.85	617.14	610.49	604.71	599.69	595.32	591.51	578.47	571.64	568.01
60000	731.73	716.07	702.77	691.41	681.65	673.25	665.98	659.69	654.21	649.44	645.28	631.06	623.61	619.64
65000	792.70	775.75	761.33	749.02	738.46	729.35	721.48	714.66	708.73	703.56	699.05	683.65	675.58	671.28
70000	853.68	835.42	819.90	806.64	795.26	785.46	776.98	769.63	763.24	757.68	752.83	736.24	727.55	722.92
75000	914.66	895.09	878.46	864.26	852.06	841.56	832.48	824.61	817.76	811.80	806.60	788.83	779.51	774.55
80000	975.63	954.76	937.03	921.87	908.87	897.66	887.98	879.58	872.28	865.92	860.37	841.42	831.48	826.19
85000	1036.61	1014.43	995.59	979.49	965.67	953.77	943.47	934.55	926.80	920.04	914.14	894.00	883.45	877.82
90000	1097.59	1074.11	1054.15	1037.11	1022.48	1009.87	998.97	989.53	981.31	974.16	967.92	946.59	935.41	929.46
95000	1158.56	1133.78	1112.72	1094.72	1079.28	1065.97	1054.47	1044.50	1035.83	1028.28	1021.69	999.18	987.38	981.10
100000	1219.54	1193.45	1171.28	1152.34	1136.08	1122.08	1109.97	1099.47	1090.35	1082.40	1075.46	1051.77	1039.35	1032.73

MONTHLY PAYMENT
REQUIRED TO AMORTIZE A LOAN

TERM / AMOUNT	1 Year	2 Years	3 Years	4 Years	5 Years	6 Years	7 Years	8 Years	9 Years	10 Years	11 Years	12 Years	13 Years	14 Years
5	.45	.24	.17	.14	.12	.10	.09	.09	.08	.08	.07	.07	.07	.07
10	.90	.48	.34	.27	.23	.20	.18	.17	.16	.15	.14	.14	.13	.13
15	1.34	.71	.51	.40	.34	.30	.27	.25	.24	.22	.21	.21	.20	.19
25	2.23	1.19	.84	.67	.57	.50	.45	.42	.39	.37	.35	.34	.33	.32
50	4.46	2.37	1.67	1.33	1.13	.99	.90	.83	.77	.73	.70	.67	.65	.63
75	6.68	3.55	2.51	1.99	1.69	1.49	1.34	1.24	1.16	1.10	1.05	1.01	.97	.95
100	8.91	4.73	3.34	2.66	2.25	1.98	1.79	1.65	1.54	1.46	1.40	1.34	1.30	1.26
200	17.81	9.45	6.68	5.31	4.49	3.95	3.58	3.30	3.08	2.92	2.79	2.68	2.59	2.52
300	26.71	14.18	10.02	7.96	6.74	5.93	5.36	4.94	4.62	4.37	4.18	4.01	3.88	3.77
400	35.61	18.90	13.36	10.61	8.98	7.90	7.15	6.59	6.16	5.83	5.57	5.35	5.17	5.03
500	44.52	23.63	16.70	13.26	11.22	9.88	8.93	8.23	7.70	7.29	6.96	6.69	6.46	6.28
600	53.42	28.35	20.04	15.92	13.47	11.85	10.72	9.88	9.24	8.74	8.35	8.02	7.76	7.54
700	62.32	33.08	23.38	18.57	15.71	13.83	12.50	11.53	10.78	10.20	9.74	9.36	9.05	8.79
800	71.22	37.80	26.72	21.22	17.95	15.80	14.29	13.17	12.32	11.66	11.13	10.69	10.34	10.05
900	80.13	42.53	30.06	23.87	20.20	17.78	16.07	14.82	13.86	13.11	12.52	12.03	11.63	11.30
1000	89.03	47.25	33.40	26.52	22.44	19.75	17.86	16.46	15.40	14.57	13.91	13.37	12.92	12.56
2000	178.05	94.50	66.79	53.04	44.87	39.50	35.71	32.92	30.80	29.13	27.81	26.73	25.84	25.11
3000	267.08	141.75	100.19	79.56	67.31	59.24	53.57	49.38	46.19	43.70	41.71	40.09	38.76	37.66
4000	356.10	189.00	133.58	106.08	89.74	78.99	71.42	65.84	61.59	58.26	55.61	53.45	51.68	50.21
5000	445.13	236.25	166.97	132.60	112.18	98.73	89.27	82.30	76.99	72.83	69.51	66.82	64.60	62.76
6000	534.15	283.50	200.37	159.12	134.61	118.48	107.13	98.76	92.38	87.39	83.41	80.18	77.52	75.32
7000	623.18	330.75	233.76	185.63	157.05	138.23	124.98	115.22	107.78	101.96	97.31	93.54	90.44	87.87
8000	712.20	378.00	267.15	212.15	179.48	157.97	142.84	131.68	123.18	116.52	111.21	106.90	103.36	100.42
9000	801.22	425.24	300.55	238.67	201.91	177.72	160.69	148.14	138.57	131.09	125.11	120.26	116.28	112.97
10000	890.25	472.49	333.94	265.19	224.35	197.46	178.54	164.60	153.97	145.65	139.01	133.63	129.20	125.52
11000	979.27	519.74	367.34	291.71	246.78	217.21	196.40	181.06	169.37	160.22	152.91	146.99	142.12	138.08
12000	1068.30	566.99	400.73	318.22	269.22	236.95	214.25	197.52	184.76	174.78	166.81	160.35	155.04	150.63
13000	1157.32	614.24	434.12	344.74	291.65	256.70	232.11	213.98	200.16	189.35	180.71	173.71	167.96	163.18
14000	1246.35	661.49	467.52	371.26	314.09	276.45	249.96	230.44	215.56	203.91	194.62	187.08	180.88	175.73
15000	1335.37	708.74	500.91	397.78	336.52	296.19	267.81	246.90	230.95	218.48	208.52	200.44	193.80	188.28
16000	1424.39	755.99	534.30	424.30	358.96	315.94	285.67	263.36	246.35	233.04	222.42	213.80	206.72	200.84
17000	1513.42	803.23	567.70	450.82	381.39	335.68	303.52	279.82	261.74	247.61	236.32	227.16	219.64	213.39
18000	1602.44	850.48	601.09	477.33	403.82	355.43	321.38	296.28	277.14	262.17	250.22	240.52	232.56	225.94
19000	1691.47	897.73	634.49	503.85	426.26	375.17	339.23	312.74	292.54	276.73	264.12	253.89	245.48	238.49
20000	1780.49	944.98	667.88	530.37	448.69	394.92	357.08	329.20	307.93	291.30	278.02	267.25	258.40	251.04
21000	1869.52	992.23	701.27	556.89	471.13	414.67	374.94	345.66	323.33	305.86	291.92	280.61	271.32	263.60
22000	1958.54	1039.48	734.67	583.41	493.56	434.41	392.79	362.12	338.73	320.43	305.82	293.97	284.24	276.15
23000	2047.56	1086.73	768.06	609.93	454.16	410.64	378.58	354.12	334.99	319.72	307.33	297.16	288.70	288.70
24000	2136.59	1133.98	801.45	636.44	538.43	473.90	428.50	395.04	369.52	349.56	333.62	320.70	310.08	301.25
25000	2225.61	1181.22	834.85	662.96	560.87	493.65	446.35	411.49	384.92	364.12	347.52	334.06	322.99	313.80
26000	2314.64	1228.47	868.24	689.48	583.30	513.39	464.21	427.95	400.31	378.69	361.42	347.42	335.91	326.36
27000	2403.66	1275.72	901.63	716.00	605.73	533.14	482.06	444.41	415.71	393.25	375.33	360.78	348.83	338.91
28000	2492.69	1322.97	935.03	742.52	628.17	552.89	499.91	460.87	431.11	407.82	389.23	374.15	361.75	351.46
29000	2581.71	1370.22	968.42	769.04	650.60	572.63	517.77	477.33	446.50	422.38	403.13	387.51	374.67	364.01
30000	2670.73	1417.47	1001.82	795.55	673.04	592.38	535.62	493.79	461.90	436.95	417.03	400.87	387.59	376.56
31000	2759.76	1464.72	1035.21	822.07	695.47	612.12	553.48	510.25	477.30	451.51	430.93	414.23	400.51	389.12
32000	2848.78	1511.97	1068.60	848.59	717.91	631.87	571.33	526.71	492.69	466.08	444.83	427.59	413.43	401.67
33000	2937.81	1559.21	1102.00	875.11	740.34	651.61	589.18	543.17	508.09	480.64	458.73	440.96	426.35	414.22
34000	3026.83	1606.46	1135.39	901.63	762.77	671.36	607.04	559.63	523.48	495.21	472.63	454.32	439.27	426.77
35000	3115.86	1653.71	1168.78	928.15	785.21	691.11	624.89	576.09	538.88	509.77	486.53	467.68	452.19	439.32
36000	3204.88	1700.96	1202.18	954.66	807.64	710.85	642.75	592.55	554.28	524.33	500.43	481.04	465.11	451.88
37000	3293.90	1748.21	1235.57	981.18	830.08	730.60	660.60	609.01	569.67	538.90	514.33	494.41	478.03	464.43
38000	3382.93	1795.46	1268.97	1007.70	852.51	750.34	678.45	625.47	585.07	553.46	528.23	507.77	490.95	476.98
39000	3471.95	1842.71	1302.36	1034.22	874.95	770.09	696.31	641.93	600.47	568.03	542.13	521.13	503.87	489.53
40000	3560.98	1889.96	1335.75	1060.74	897.38	789.83	714.16	658.39	615.86	582.59	556.03	534.49	516.79	502.08
41000	3650.00	1937.21	1369.15	1087.26	919.82	809.58	732.02	674.85	631.26	597.16	569.94	547.85	529.71	514.64
42000	3739.03	1984.45	1402.54	1113.78	942.25	829.33	749.87	691.31	646.66	611.72	583.84	561.22	542.63	527.19
43000	3828.05	2031.70	1435.93	1140.29	964.68	849.07	767.72	707.77	662.05	626.29	597.74	574.58	555.55	539.74
44000	3917.07	2078.95	1469.33	1166.81	987.12	868.82	785.58	724.23	677.45	640.85	611.64	587.94	568.47	552.29
45000	4006.10	2126.20	1502.72	1193.33	1009.55	888.56	803.43	740.69	692.85	655.42	625.54	601.30	581.39	564.84
46000	4095.12	2173.45	1536.12	1219.85	1031.99	908.31	821.28	757.15	708.24	669.98	639.44	614.66	594.31	577.40
47000	4184.15	2220.70	1569.51	1246.37	1054.42	928.06	839.14	773.61	723.64	684.55	653.34	628.03	607.23	589.95
48000	4273.17	2267.95	1602.90	1272.89	1076.86	947.80	856.99	790.07	739.04	699.11	667.24	641.39	620.15	602.50
49000	4362.20	2315.20	1636.30	1299.40	1099.29	967.55	874.85	806.52	754.43	713.68	681.14	654.75	633.06	615.05
50000	4451.22	2362.44	1669.69	1325.92	1121.73	987.29	892.70	822.98	769.83	728.24	695.04	668.11	645.98	627.60
55000	4896.34	2598.69	1836.66	1458.51	1233.90	1086.02	981.97	905.28	846.81	801.06	764.55	734.92	710.58	690.36
60000	5341.46	2834.93	2003.63	1591.11	1346.07	1184.75	1071.24	987.58	923.79	873.89	834.05	801.73	775.18	753.12
65000	5786.59	3071.18	2170.60	1723.70	1458.24	1283.48	1160.51	1069.88	1000.78	946.71	903.55	868.55	839.78	815.88
70000	6231.71	3307.42	2337.56	1856.29	1570.41	1382.21	1249.78	1152.18	1077.76	1019.53	973.06	935.36	904.38	878.64
75000	6676.83	3543.66	2504.53	1988.88	1682.59	1480.94	1339.05	1234.47	1154.74	1092.36	1042.56	1002.17	968.97	941.40
80000	7121.95	3779.91	2671.50	2121.47	1794.76	1579.67	1428.32	1316.77	1231.72	1165.18	1112.06	1068.98	1033.57	1004.16
85000	7567.07	4016.15	2838.47	2254.06	1906.93	1678.39	1517.59	1399.07	1308.70	1238.01	1181.57	1135.79	1098.17	1066.92
90000	8012.19	4252.40	3005.44	2386.65	2019.10	1777.12	1606.86	1481.37	1385.69	1310.83	1251.07	1202.60	1162.77	1129.68
95000	8457.32	4488.64	3172.41	2519.25	2131.27	1875.85	1696.13	1563.67	1462.67	1383.65	1320.58	1269.41	1227.37	1192.44
100000	8902.44	4724.88	3339.38	2651.84	2243.45	1974.58	1785.40	1645.96	1539.65	1456.48	1390.08	1336.22	1291.96	1255.20

MONTHLY PAYMENT
REQUIRED TO AMORTIZE A LOAN

12.375%

TERM	15 Years	16 Years	17 Years	18 Years	19 Years	20 Years	21 Years	22 Years	23 Years	24 Years	25 Years	30 Years	35 Years	40 Years
AMOUNT														
5	.07	.06	.06	.06	.06	.06	.06	.06	.06	.06	.06	.06	.06	.06
10	.13	.12	.12	.12	.12	.12	.12	.12	.11	.11	.11	.11	.11	.11
15	.19	.18	.18	.18	.18	.17	.17	.17	.17	.17	.17	.16	.16	.16
25	.31	.30	.30	.29	.29	.29	.28	.28	.28	.28	.28	.27	.27	.26
50	.62	.60	.59	.58	.58	.57	.56	.56	.55	.55	.55	.53	.53	.52
75	.92	.90	.89	.87	.86	.85	.84	.83	.83	.82	.82	.80	.79	.78
100	1.23	1.20	1.18	1.16	1.15	1.13	1.12	1.11	1.10	1.09	1.09	1.06	1.05	1.04
200	2.45	2.40	2.36	2.32	2.29	2.26	2.24	2.21	2.20	2.18	2.17	2.12	2.10	2.08
300	3.68	3.60	3.53	3.48	3.43	3.39	3.35	3.32	3.29	3.27	3.25	3.18	3.14	3.12
400	4.90	4.80	4.71	4.63	4.57	4.51	4.47	4.42	4.39	4.36	4.33	4.24	4.19	4.16
500	6.13	6.00	5.89	5.79	5.71	5.64	5.58	5.53	5.48	5.44	5.41	5.29	5.23	5.20
600	7.35	7.20	7.06	6.95	6.85	6.77	6.70	6.63	6.58	6.53	6.49	6.35	6.28	6.24
700	8.58	8.39	8.24	8.11	7.99	7.90	7.81	7.74	7.68	7.62	7.57	7.41	7.32	7.28
800	9.80	9.59	9.42	9.26	9.14	9.02	8.93	8.84	8.77	8.71	8.65	8.47	8.37	8.32
900	11.02	10.79	10.59	10.42	10.28	10.15	10.04	9.95	9.87	9.80	9.73	9.52	9.41	9.35
1000	12.25	11.99	11.77	11.58	11.42	11.28	11.16	11.05	10.96	10.88	10.82	10.58	10.46	10.39
2000	24.49	23.97	23.53	23.15	22.83	22.55	22.31	22.10	21.92	21.76	21.63	21.16	20.91	20.78
3000	36.74	35.96	35.29	34.73	34.24	33.83	33.46	33.15	32.88	32.64	32.44	31.73	31.36	31.17
4000	48.98	47.94	47.06	46.30	45.66	45.10	44.62	44.20	43.84	43.52	43.25	42.31	41.82	41.56
5000	61.22	59.92	58.82	57.88	57.07	56.37	55.77	55.25	54.80	54.40	54.06	52.88	52.27	51.94
6000	73.47	71.91	70.58	69.45	68.48	67.65	66.92	66.30	65.75	65.28	64.87	63.46	62.72	62.33
7000	85.71	83.89	82.35	81.03	79.89	78.92	78.08	77.35	76.71	76.16	75.68	74.03	73.18	72.72
8000	97.96	95.88	94.11	92.60	91.31	90.19	89.23	88.39	87.67	87.04	86.49	84.61	83.63	83.11
9000	110.20	107.86	105.87	104.18	102.72	101.47	100.38	99.44	98.63	97.92	97.30	95.19	94.08	93.50
10000	122.44	119.84	117.64	115.75	114.13	112.74	111.54	110.49	109.59	108.80	108.11	105.76	104.54	103.88
11000	134.69	131.83	129.40	127.32	125.55	124.01	122.69	121.54	120.54	119.68	118.92	116.34	114.99	114.27
12000	146.93	143.81	141.16	138.90	136.96	135.29	133.84	132.59	131.50	130.56	129.73	126.91	125.44	124.66
13000	159.18	155.80	152.93	150.47	148.37	146.56	144.99	143.64	142.46	141.43	140.54	137.49	135.89	135.05
14000	171.42	167.78	164.69	162.05	159.78	157.83	156.15	154.69	153.42	152.31	151.35	148.06	146.35	145.44
15000	183.66	179.76	176.45	173.62	171.20	169.11	167.30	165.74	164.38	163.19	162.16	158.64	156.80	155.82
16000	195.91	191.75	188.21	185.20	182.61	180.38	178.45	176.78	175.33	174.07	172.97	169.22	167.25	166.21
17000	208.15	203.73	199.98	196.77	194.02	191.65	189.61	187.83	186.29	184.95	183.78	179.79	177.71	176.60
18000	220.40	215.72	211.74	208.35	205.43	202.93	200.76	198.88	197.25	195.83	194.59	190.37	188.16	186.99
19000	232.64	227.70	223.50	219.92	216.85	214.20	211.91	209.93	208.21	206.71	205.40	200.94	198.61	197.38
20000	244.88	239.68	235.27	231.50	228.26	225.47	223.07	220.98	219.17	217.59	216.21	211.52	209.07	207.76
21000	257.13	251.67	247.03	243.07	239.67	236.75	234.22	232.03	230.12	228.47	227.02	222.09	219.52	218.15
22000	269.37	263.65	258.79	254.64	251.09	248.02	245.37	243.08	241.08	239.35	237.83	232.67	229.97	228.54
23000	281.62	275.64	270.56	266.22	262.50	259.29	256.52	254.13	252.04	250.23	248.64	243.25	240.43	238.93
24000	293.86	287.62	282.32	277.79	273.91	270.57	267.68	265.17	263.00	261.11	259.45	253.82	250.88	249.32
25000	306.10	299.60	294.08	289.37	285.32	281.84	278.83	276.22	273.96	271.98	270.26	264.40	261.33	259.70
26000	318.35	311.59	305.85	300.94	296.74	293.11	289.98	287.27	284.92	282.86	281.07	274.97	271.78	270.09
27000	330.59	323.57	317.61	312.52	308.15	304.39	301.14	298.32	295.87	293.74	291.89	285.55	282.24	280.48
28000	342.84	335.56	329.37	324.09	319.56	315.66	312.29	309.37	306.83	304.62	302.70	296.12	292.69	290.87
29000	355.08	347.54	341.14	335.67	330.97	326.93	323.44	320.42	317.79	315.50	313.51	306.70	303.14	301.26
30000	367.32	359.52	352.90	347.24	342.39	338.21	334.60	331.47	328.75	326.38	324.32	317.28	313.60	311.64
31000	379.57	371.51	364.66	358.82	353.80	349.48	345.75	342.51	339.71	337.26	335.13	327.85	324.05	322.03
32000	391.81	383.49	376.42	370.39	365.21	360.75	356.90	353.56	350.66	348.14	345.94	338.43	334.50	332.42
33000	404.06	395.48	388.19	381.96	376.63	372.03	368.05	364.61	361.62	359.02	356.75	349.00	344.96	342.81
34000	416.30	407.46	399.95	393.54	388.04	383.30	379.21	375.66	372.58	369.90	367.56	359.58	355.41	353.20
35000	428.54	419.44	411.71	405.11	399.45	394.57	390.36	386.71	383.54	380.78	378.37	370.15	365.86	363.58
36000	440.79	431.43	423.48	416.69	410.86	405.85	401.51	397.76	394.50	391.66	389.18	380.73	376.31	373.97
37000	453.03	443.41	435.24	428.26	422.28	417.12	412.67	408.81	405.45	402.54	399.99	391.31	386.77	384.36
38000	465.28	455.40	447.00	439.84	433.69	428.39	423.82	419.06	416.41	413.41	410.80	401.88	397.22	394.75
39000	477.52	467.38	458.77	451.41	445.10	439.67	434.97	430.90	427.37	424.29	421.61	412.46	407.67	405.14
40000	489.76	479.36	470.53	462.99	456.51	450.94	446.13	441.95	438.33	435.17	432.42	423.03	418.13	415.52
41000	502.01	491.35	482.29	474.56	467.93	462.21	457.28	453.00	449.29	446.05	443.23	433.61	428.58	425.91
42000	514.25	503.33	494.06	486.13	479.34	473.49	468.43	464.05	460.24	456.93	454.04	444.18	439.03	436.30
43000	526.50	515.32	505.82	497.71	490.75	484.76	479.58	475.10	471.20	467.81	464.85	454.76	449.49	446.69
44000	538.74	527.30	517.58	509.28	502.17	496.03	490.74	486.15	482.16	478.69	475.66	465.33	459.94	457.08
45000	550.98	539.28	529.35	520.86	513.58	507.31	501.89	497.20	493.12	489.57	486.47	475.91	470.39	467.46
46000	563.23	551.27	541.11	532.43	524.99	518.58	513.04	508.25	504.08	500.45	497.28	486.49	480.85	477.85
47000	575.47	563.25	552.87	544.01	536.40	529.86	524.20	519.29	515.04	511.33	508.09	497.06	491.30	488.24
48000	587.72	575.24	564.63	555.58	547.82	541.13	535.35	530.34	525.99	522.21	518.90	507.64	501.75	498.63
49000	599.96	587.22	576.40	567.16	559.23	552.40	546.50	541.39	536.95	533.09	529.71	518.21	512.20	509.02
50000	612.20	599.20	588.16	578.73	570.64	563.68	557.66	552.44	547.91	543.96	540.52	528.79	522.66	519.40
55000	673.42	659.12	646.98	636.60	627.71	620.04	613.42	607.68	602.70	598.36	594.58	581.67	574.92	571.34
60000	734.64	719.04	705.79	694.48	684.77	676.41	669.19	662.93	657.49	652.76	648.63	634.55	627.19	623.28
65000	795.86	778.96	764.61	752.35	741.83	732.78	724.95	718.17	712.28	707.15	702.68	687.42	679.45	675.22
70000	857.08	838.88	823.42	810.22	798.90	789.14	780.72	773.41	767.07	761.55	756.73	740.30	731.72	727.16
75000	918.30	898.80	882.24	868.09	855.96	845.51	836.48	828.66	821.86	815.94	810.78	793.18	783.98	779.10
80000	979.52	958.72	941.05	925.97	913.02	901.88	892.25	883.90	876.65	870.34	864.84	846.06	836.25	831.04
85000	1040.74	1018.64	999.87	983.84	970.09	958.24	948.01	939.15	931.44	924.74	918.89	898.94	888.51	882.98
90000	1101.96	1078.56	1058.69	1041.71	1027.15	1014.61	1003.78	994.39	986.23	979.13	972.94	951.82	940.78	934.92
95000	1163.18	1138.48	1117.50	1099.58	1084.21	1070.98	1059.54	1049.63	1041.02	1033.53	1026.99	1004.69	993.04	986.86
100000	1224.40	1198.40	1176.32	1157.46	1141.28	1127.35	1115.31	1104.88	1095.81	1087.92	1081.04	1057.57	1045.31	1038.80

MONTHLY PAYMENT
REQUIRED TO AMORTIZE A LOAN

TERM AMOUNT	1 Year	2 Years	3 Years	4 Years	5 Years	6 Years	7 Years	8 Years	9 Years	10 Years	11 Years	12 Years	13 Years	14 Years
5	.45	.24	.17	.14	.12	.10	.09	.09	.08	.08	.07	.07	.07	.07
10	.90	.48	.34	.27	.23	.20	.18	.17	.16	.15	.14	.14	.13	.13
15	1.34	.71	.51	.40	.34	.30	.27	.25	.24	.22	.21	.21	.20	.19
25	2.23	1.19	.84	.67	.57	.50	.45	.42	.39	.37	.35	.34	.33	.32
50	4.46	2.37	1.68	1.33	1.13	.99	.90	.83	.78	.73	.70	.67	.65	.63
75	6.68	3.55	2.51	1.99	1.69	1.49	1.35	1.24	1.16	1.10	1.05	1.01	.98	.95
100	8.91	4.73	3.35	2.66	2.25	1.98	1.79	1.65	1.55	1.46	1.40	1.34	1.30	1.26
200	17.81	9.46	6.69	5.31	4.49	3.96	3.58	3.30	3.09	2.92	2.79	2.68	2.59	2.52
300	26.72	14.19	10.03	7.96	6.74	5.93	5.37	4.95	4.63	4.38	4.18	4.02	3.89	3.78
400	35.62	18.91	13.37	10.62	8.98	7.91	7.15	6.59	6.17	5.84	5.57	5.36	5.18	5.03
500	44.52	23.64	16.71	13.27	11.23	9.88	8.94	8.24	7.71	7.29	6.96	6.69	6.47	6.29
600	53.43	28.36	20.05	15.92	13.47	11.86	10.73	9.89	9.25	8.75	8.35	8.03	7.77	7.55
700	62.33	33.09	23.39	18.58	15.72	13.84	12.51	11.54	10.79	10.21	9.75	9.37	9.06	8.80
800	71.23	37.81	26.73	21.23	17.96	15.81	14.30	13.18	12.33	11.67	11.14	10.71	10.35	10.06
900	80.14	42.54	30.07	23.88	20.21	17.79	16.09	14.83	13.87	13.13	12.53	12.04	11.65	11.32
1000	89.04	47.27	33.41	26.54	22.45	19.76	17.87	16.48	15.42	14.58	13.92	13.38	12.94	12.57
2000	178.08	94.53	66.82	53.07	44.90	39.52	35.74	32.95	30.83	29.16	27.84	26.76	25.88	25.14
3000	267.11	141.79	100.22	79.60	67.35	59.28	53.61	49.43	46.24	43.74	41.75	40.14	38.81	37.71
4000	356.15	189.05	133.63	106.13	89.79	79.04	71.47	65.90	61.65	58.32	55.67	53.51	51.75	50.28
5000	445.19	236.31	167.03	132.66	112.24	98.80	89.34	82.37	77.06	72.90	69.58	66.89	64.68	62.84
6000	534.22	283.57	200.44	159.19	134.69	118.56	107.21	98.85	92.47	87.48	83.50	80.27	77.62	75.41
7000	623.26	330.83	233.84	185.72	157.13	138.32	125.08	115.32	107.88	102.06	97.41	93.65	90.55	87.98
8000	712.29	378.09	267.25	212.25	179.58	158.08	142.94	131.79	123.29	116.64	111.33	107.02	103.49	100.55
9000	801.33	425.35	300.66	238.78	202.03	177.83	160.81	148.27	138.70	131.22	125.25	120.40	116.42	113.12
10000	890.37	472.61	334.06	265.31	224.48	197.59	178.68	164.74	154.11	145.80	139.16	133.78	129.36	125.68
11000	979.40	519.87	367.47	291.84	246.92	217.35	196.55	181.21	169.52	160.38	153.08	147.16	142.29	138.25
12000	1068.44	567.13	400.87	318.37	269.37	237.11	214.41	197.69	184.93	174.96	166.99	160.53	155.23	150.82
13000	1157.47	614.39	434.28	344.90	291.82	256.87	232.28	214.16	200.34	189.54	180.91	173.91	168.16	163.39
14000	1246.51	661.65	467.68	371.43	314.26	276.63	250.15	230.63	215.75	204.11	194.82	187.29	181.10	175.96
15000	1335.55	708.91	501.09	397.96	336.71	296.39	268.02	247.11	231.17	218.69	208.74	200.67	194.03	188.52
16000	1424.58	756.17	534.50	424.50	359.16	316.15	285.88	263.58	246.58	233.27	222.66	214.04	206.97	201.09
17000	1513.62	803.43	567.90	451.03	381.61	335.91	303.75	280.05	261.99	247.85	236.57	227.42	219.90	213.66
18000	1602.65	850.69	601.31	477.56	404.05	355.66	321.62	296.53	277.40	262.43	250.49	240.80	232.84	226.23
19000	1691.69	897.95	634.71	504.09	426.50	375.42	339.48	313.00	292.81	277.01	264.40	254.18	245.77	238.80
20000	1780.73	945.21	668.12	530.62	448.95	395.18	357.35	329.47	308.22	291.59	278.32	267.55	258.71	251.36
21000	1869.76	992.48	701.52	557.15	471.39	414.94	375.22	345.95	323.63	306.17	292.23	280.93	271.64	263.93
22000	1958.80	1039.74	734.93	583.68	493.84	434.70	393.09	362.42	339.04	320.75	306.15	294.31	284.58	276.50
23000	2047.83	1087.00	768.34	610.21	516.29	454.46	410.95	378.89	354.45	335.33	320.07	307.69	297.51	289.07
24000	2136.87	1134.26	801.74	636.74	538.74	474.22	428.82	395.37	369.86	349.91	333.98	321.06	310.45	301.64
25000	2225.91	1181.52	835.15	663.27	561.18	493.98	446.69	411.84	385.27	364.49	347.90	334.44	323.38	314.20
26000	2314.94	1228.78	868.55	689.80	583.63	513.73	464.56	428.31	400.68	379.07	361.81	347.82	336.32	326.77
27000	2403.98	1276.04	901.96	716.33	606.08	533.49	482.42	444.79	416.09	393.65	375.73	361.20	349.25	339.34
28000	2493.01	1323.30	935.36	742.86	628.52	553.25	500.29	461.26	431.50	408.22	389.64	374.57	362.19	351.91
29000	2582.05	1370.56	968.77	769.39	650.97	573.01	518.16	477.73	446.91	422.80	403.56	387.95	375.13	364.47
30000	2671.09	1417.82	1002.18	795.92	673.42	592.77	536.03	494.21	462.33	437.38	417.48	401.33	388.06	377.04
31000	2760.12	1465.08	1035.58	822.46	695.87	612.53	553.89	510.68	477.74	451.96	431.39	414.71	401.00	389.61
32000	2849.16	1512.34	1068.99	848.99	718.31	632.29	571.76	527.15	493.15	466.54	445.31	428.08	413.93	402.18
33000	2938.19	1559.60	1102.39	875.52	740.76	652.05	589.63	543.63	508.56	481.12	459.22	441.46	426.87	414.75
34000	3027.23	1606.86	1135.80	902.05	763.21	671.81	607.50	560.10	523.97	495.70	473.14	454.84	439.80	427.31
35000	3116.27	1654.12	1169.20	928.58	785.65	691.56	625.36	576.57	539.38	510.28	487.05	468.22	452.74	439.88
36000	3205.30	1701.38	1202.61	955.11	808.10	711.32	643.23	593.05	554.79	524.86	500.97	481.59	465.67	452.45
37000	3294.34	1748.64	1236.02	981.64	830.55	731.08	661.10	609.52	570.20	539.44	514.88	494.97	478.61	465.02
38000	3383.37	1795.90	1269.42	1008.17	853.00	750.84	678.96	625.99	585.61	554.02	528.80	508.35	491.54	477.59
39000	3472.41	1843.16	1302.83	1034.70	875.44	770.60	696.83	642.47	601.02	568.60	542.72	521.72	504.48	490.15
40000	3561.45	1890.42	1336.23	1061.23	897.89	790.36	714.70	658.94	616.43	583.18	556.63	535.10	517.41	502.72
41000	3650.48	1937.69	1369.64	1087.76	920.34	810.12	732.57	675.42	631.84	597.76	570.55	548.48	530.35	515.29
42000	3739.52	1984.95	1403.04	1114.29	942.78	829.88	750.43	691.89	647.25	612.33	584.46	561.86	543.28	527.86
43000	3828.55	2032.21	1436.45	1140.82	965.23	849.63	768.30	708.36	662.66	626.91	598.38	575.23	556.22	540.43
44000	3917.59	2079.47	1469.86	1167.35	987.68	869.39	786.17	724.84	678.07	641.49	612.29	588.61	569.15	552.99
45000	4006.63	2126.73	1503.26	1193.88	1010.12	889.15	804.04	741.31	693.49	656.07	626.21	601.99	582.09	565.56
46000	4095.66	2173.99	1536.67	1220.42	1032.57	908.91	821.90	757.78	708.90	670.65	640.13	615.37	595.02	578.13
47000	4184.70	2221.25	1570.07	1246.95	1055.02	928.67	839.77	774.26	724.31	685.23	654.04	628.74	607.96	590.70
48000	4273.73	2268.51	1603.48	1273.48	1077.47	948.43	857.64	790.73	739.72	699.81	667.96	642.12	620.89	603.27
49000	4362.77	2315.77	1636.88	1300.01	1099.91	968.19	875.51	807.20	755.13	714.39	681.87	655.50	633.83	615.83
50000	4451.81	2363.03	1670.29	1326.54	1122.36	987.95	893.37	823.68	770.54	728.97	695.79	668.88	646.76	628.40
55000	4896.99	2599.33	1837.32	1459.19	1234.60	1086.74	982.71	906.04	847.59	801.87	765.37	735.76	711.44	691.24
60000	5342.17	2835.63	2004.35	1591.84	1346.83	1185.53	1072.05	988.41	924.65	874.76	834.95	802.65	776.12	754.08
65000	5787.35	3071.94	2171.37	1724.50	1459.07	1284.33	1161.38	1070.78	1001.70	947.66	904.52	869.54	840.79	816.92
70000	6232.53	3308.24	2338.40	1857.15	1571.30	1383.12	1250.72	1153.14	1078.75	1020.55	974.10	936.43	905.47	879.76
75000	6677.71	3544.54	2505.43	1989.80	1683.54	1481.92	1340.06	1235.51	1155.81	1093.45	1043.68	1003.31	970.14	942.60
80000	7122.89	3780.84	2672.46	2122.46	1795.77	1580.71	1429.39	1317.88	1232.86	1166.35	1113.26	1070.20	1034.82	1005.44
85000	7568.07	4017.15	2839.49	2255.11	1908.01	1679.51	1518.73	1400.25	1309.91	1239.24	1182.84	1137.09	1099.50	1068.28
90000	8013.25	4253.45	3006.52	2387.76	2020.24	1778.30	1608.07	1482.61	1386.97	1312.14	1252.42	1203.97	1164.17	1131.12
95000	8458.43	4489.75	3173.54	2520.42	2132.48	1877.09	1697.41	1564.98	1464.02	1385.04	1321.99	1270.86	1228.85	1193.96
100000	8903.61	4726.05	3340.57	2653.07	2244.72	1975.89	1786.74	1647.35	1541.07	1457.93	1391.57	1337.75	1293.52	1256.80

MONTHLY PAYMENT
REQUIRED TO AMORTIZE A LOAN

12.400%

TERM	15 Years	16 Years	17 Years	18 Years	19 Years	20 Years	21 Years	22 Years	23 Years	24 Years	25 Years	30 Years	35 Years	40 Years
AMOUNT														
5	.07	.07	.06	.06	.06	.06	.06	.06	.06	.06	.06	.06	.06	.06
10	.13	.13	.12	.12	.12	.12	.12	.12	.11	.11	.11	.11	.11	.11
15	.19	.19	.18	.18	.18	.17	.17	.17	.17	.17	.17	.16	.16	.16
25	.31	.31	.30	.29	.29	.29	.28	.28	.28	.28	.28	.27	.27	.27
50	.62	.61	.59	.58	.58	.57	.56	.56	.55	.55	.55	.53	.53	.53
75	.92	.91	.89	.87	.86	.85	.84	.84	.83	.82	.82	.80	.79	.79
100	1.23	1.21	1.18	1.16	1.15	1.13	1.12	1.11	1.10	1.09	1.09	1.06	1.05	1.05
200	2.46	2.41	2.36	2.32	2.29	2.26	2.24	2.22	2.20	2.18	2.17	2.12	2.10	2.09
300	3.68	3.61	3.54	3.48	3.43	3.39	3.36	3.33	3.30	3.27	3.25	3.18	3.15	3.13
400	4.91	4.81	4.72	4.64	4.58	4.52	4.47	4.43	4.40	4.36	4.34	4.24	4.19	4.17
500	6.14	6.01	5.89	5.80	5.72	5.65	5.59	5.54	5.49	5.45	5.42	5.30	5.24	5.21
600	7.36	7.21	7.07	6.96	6.86	6.78	6.71	6.65	6.59	6.54	6.50	6.36	6.29	6.25
700	8.59	8.41	8.25	8.12	8.01	7.91	7.82	7.75	7.69	7.63	7.59	7.42	7.34	7.29
800	9.81	9.61	9.43	9.28	9.15	9.04	8.94	8.86	8.79	8.72	8.67	8.48	8.38	8.33
900	11.04	10.81	10.61	10.44	10.29	10.17	10.06	9.97	9.88	9.81	9.75	9.54	9.43	9.37
1000	12.27	12.01	11.78	11.60	11.44	11.30	11.18	11.07	10.98	10.90	10.83	10.60	10.48	10.41
2000	24.53	24.01	23.56	23.19	22.87	22.59	22.35	22.14	21.96	21.80	21.66	21.20	20.95	20.82
3000	36.79	36.01	35.34	34.78	34.30	33.88	33.52	33.21	32.93	32.70	32.49	31.79	31.42	31.23
4000	49.05	48.01	47.12	46.37	45.73	45.17	44.69	44.27	43.91	43.60	43.32	42.39	41.90	41.64
5000	61.31	60.01	58.90	57.96	57.16	56.46	55.86	55.34	54.89	54.49	54.15	52.98	52.37	52.05
6000	73.57	72.01	70.68	69.55	68.59	67.75	67.03	66.41	65.86	65.39	64.98	63.58	62.84	62.45
7000	85.83	84.01	82.46	81.15	80.02	79.04	78.20	77.47	76.84	76.29	75.81	74.17	73.32	72.86
8000	98.09	96.01	94.24	92.74	91.45	90.33	89.37	88.54	87.82	87.19	86.64	84.77	83.79	83.27
9000	110.35	108.01	106.02	104.33	102.88	101.62	100.54	99.61	98.79	98.08	97.47	95.36	94.26	93.68
10000	122.61	120.01	117.80	115.92	114.31	112.91	111.71	110.67	109.77	108.98	108.29	105.96	104.73	104.09
11000	134.87	132.01	129.58	127.51	125.74	124.21	122.88	121.74	120.74	119.88	119.12	116.55	115.21	114.50
12000	147.13	144.01	141.36	139.10	137.17	135.50	134.06	132.81	131.72	130.78	129.95	127.15	125.68	124.90
13000	159.39	156.01	153.14	150.70	148.60	146.79	145.23	143.87	142.70	141.67	140.78	137.74	136.15	135.31
14000	171.65	168.01	164.92	162.29	160.03	158.08	156.40	154.94	153.67	152.57	151.61	148.34	146.63	145.72
15000	183.91	180.01	176.70	173.88	171.46	169.37	167.57	166.01	164.65	163.47	162.44	158.93	157.10	156.13
16000	196.17	192.01	188.48	185.47	182.89	180.66	178.74	177.07	175.63	174.37	173.27	169.53	167.57	166.54
17000	208.43	204.01	200.26	197.06	194.32	191.95	189.91	188.14	186.60	185.26	184.10	180.12	178.04	176.94
18000	220.69	216.01	212.04	208.65	205.75	203.24	201.08	199.21	197.58	196.16	194.93	190.72	188.52	187.35
19000	232.95	228.01	223.82	220.25	217.18	214.53	212.25	210.27	208.56	207.06	205.76	201.31	198.99	197.76
20000	245.21	240.02	235.60	231.84	228.61	225.82	223.42	221.34	219.53	217.96	216.58	211.91	209.46	208.17
21000	257.47	252.02	247.38	243.43	240.04	237.12	234.59	232.41	230.51	228.86	227.41	222.50	219.94	218.58
22000	269.73	264.02	259.16	255.02	251.47	248.41	245.76	243.47	241.48	239.75	238.24	233.10	230.41	228.99
23000	281.99	276.02	270.94	266.61	262.90	259.70	256.93	254.54	252.46	250.65	249.07	243.69	240.88	239.39
24000	294.25	288.02	282.72	278.20	274.33	270.99	268.11	265.61	263.44	261.55	259.90	254.29	251.36	249.80
25000	306.51	300.02	294.50	289.79	285.76	282.28	279.28	276.67	274.41	272.45	270.73	264.88	261.83	260.21
26000	318.77	312.02	306.28	301.39	297.19	293.57	290.45	287.74	285.39	283.34	281.56	275.48	272.30	270.62
27000	331.03	324.02	318.06	312.98	308.62	304.86	301.62	298.81	296.37	294.24	292.39	286.07	282.77	281.03
28000	343.29	336.02	329.84	324.57	320.05	316.15	312.79	309.87	307.34	305.14	303.22	296.67	293.25	291.43
29000	355.55	348.02	341.62	336.16	331.48	327.44	323.96	320.94	318.32	316.04	314.05	307.26	303.72	301.84
30000	367.81	360.02	353.40	347.75	342.91	338.73	335.13	332.01	329.29	326.93	324.87	317.86	314.19	312.25
31000	380.07	372.02	365.18	359.34	354.34	350.03	346.30	343.07	340.27	337.83	335.70	328.45	324.67	322.66
32000	392.33	384.02	376.96	370.94	365.77	361.32	357.47	354.14	351.25	348.73	346.53	339.05	335.14	333.07
33000	404.59	396.02	388.74	382.53	377.20	372.61	368.64	365.21	362.22	359.63	357.36	349.64	345.61	343.48
34000	416.85	408.02	400.52	394.12	388.63	383.90	379.81	376.27	373.20	370.52	368.19	360.24	356.08	353.88
35000	429.11	420.02	412.30	405.71	400.06	395.19	390.98	387.34	384.18	381.42	379.02	370.83	366.56	364.29
36000	441.37	432.02	424.08	417.30	411.49	406.48	402.16	398.41	395.15	392.32	389.85	381.43	377.03	374.70
37000	453.63	444.02	435.86	428.89	422.92	417.77	413.33	409.47	406.13	403.22	400.68	392.02	387.50	385.11
38000	465.89	456.02	447.64	440.49	434.35	429.06	424.50	420.54	417.11	414.11	411.51	402.62	397.98	395.52
39000	478.15	468.02	459.42	452.08	445.78	440.35	435.67	431.61	428.08	425.01	422.34	413.21	408.45	405.93
40000	490.41	480.03	471.20	463.67	457.21	451.64	446.84	442.67	439.06	435.91	433.16	423.81	418.92	416.33
41000	502.67	492.03	482.98	475.26	468.64	462.94	458.01	453.74	450.03	446.81	443.99	434.40	429.40	426.74
42000	514.93	504.03	494.76	486.85	480.07	474.23	469.18	464.81	461.01	457.71	454.82	445.00	439.87	437.15
43000	527.19	516.03	506.54	498.44	491.50	485.52	480.35	475.87	471.99	468.60	465.65	455.59	450.34	447.56
44000	539.45	528.03	518.32	510.04	502.93	496.81	491.52	486.94	482.96	479.50	476.48	466.19	460.81	457.97
45000	551.71	540.03	530.10	521.63	514.36	508.10	502.69	498.01	493.94	490.40	487.31	476.78	471.29	468.37
46000	563.97	552.03	541.88	533.22	525.79	519.39	513.86	509.07	504.92	501.30	498.14	487.38	481.76	478.78
47000	576.24	564.03	553.66	544.81	537.22	530.68	525.03	520.14	515.89	512.19	508.97	497.97	492.23	489.19
48000	588.50	576.03	565.44	556.40	548.65	541.97	536.21	531.21	526.87	523.09	519.80	508.57	502.71	499.60
49000	600.76	588.03	577.22	567.99	560.08	553.26	547.38	542.28	537.84	533.99	530.63	519.16	513.18	510.01
50000	613.02	600.03	589.00	579.58	571.51	564.55	558.55	553.34	548.82	544.89	541.45	529.76	523.65	520.42
55000	674.32	660.04	647.90	637.54	628.66	621.01	614.40	608.68	603.70	599.37	595.60	582.73	576.02	572.46
60000	735.62	720.04	706.80	695.50	685.81	677.46	670.26	664.01	658.58	653.86	649.74	635.71	628.38	624.50
65000	796.92	780.04	765.70	753.46	742.96	733.92	726.11	719.34	713.47	708.35	703.89	688.68	680.75	676.54
70000	858.22	840.04	824.60	811.42	800.11	790.37	781.96	774.68	768.35	762.84	758.03	741.66	733.11	728.58
75000	919.52	900.04	883.50	869.37	857.26	846.83	837.82	830.01	823.23	817.33	812.18	794.63	785.48	780.62
80000	980.82	960.05	942.40	927.33	914.41	903.28	893.67	885.34	878.11	871.81	866.32	847.61	837.84	832.66
85000	1042.12	1020.05	1001.30	985.29	971.56	959.74	949.53	940.68	932.99	926.30	920.47	900.58	890.20	884.70
90000	1103.42	1080.05	1060.20	1043.25	1028.71	1016.19	1005.38	996.01	987.87	980.79	974.61	953.56	942.57	936.74
95000	1164.73	1140.05	1119.10	1101.21	1085.86	1072.65	1061.23	1051.35	1042.76	1035.28	1028.76	1006.53	994.93	988.78
100000	1226.03	1200.06	1178.00	1159.16	1143.01	1129.10	1117.09	1106.68	1097.64	1089.77	1082.90	1059.51	1047.30	1040.83

MONTHLY PAYMENT
REQUIRED TO AMORTIZE A LOAN

TERM	1 Year	2 Years	3 Years	4 Years	5 Years	6 Years	7 Years	8 Years	9 Years	10 Years	11 Years	12 Years	13 Years	14 Years
AMOUNT														
5	.45	.24	.17	.14	.12	.10	.09	.09	.08	.08	.07	.07	.07	.07
10	.90	.48	.34	.27	.23	.20	.18	.17	.16	.15	.14	.14	.13	.13
15	1.34	.71	.51	.40	.34	.30	.27	.25	.24	.22	.21	.21	.20	.19
25	2.23	1.19	.84	.67	.57	.50	.45	.42	.39	.37	.35	.34	.33	.32
50	4.46	2.37	1.68	1.33	1.13	1.00	.90	.83	.78	.74	.70	.68	.65	.64
75	6.69	3.55	2.51	2.00	1.69	1.49	1.35	1.24	1.17	1.10	1.05	1.01	.98	.95
100	8.91	4.74	3.35	2.66	2.25	1.99	1.80	1.66	1.55	1.47	1.40	1.35	1.30	1.27
200	17.82	9.47	6.70	5.32	4.50	3.97	3.59	3.31	3.10	2.93	2.80	2.69	2.60	2.53
300	26.73	14.20	10.04	7.98	6.75	5.95	5.38	4.96	4.65	4.40	4.20	4.04	3.90	3.79
400	35.64	18.93	13.39	10.64	9.00	7.93	7.17	6.62	6.19	5.86	5.60	5.38	5.20	5.06
500	44.55	23.66	16.73	13.29	11.25	9.91	8.97	8.27	7.74	7.32	6.99	6.72	6.50	6.32
600	53.45	28.39	20.08	15.95	13.50	11.89	10.76	9.92	9.29	8.79	8.39	8.07	7.80	7.58
700	62.36	33.12	23.42	18.61	15.75	13.87	12.55	11.58	10.83	10.25	9.79	9.41	9.10	8.85
800	71.27	37.85	26.77	21.27	18.00	15.85	14.34	13.23	12.38	11.72	11.19	10.76	10.40	10.11
900	80.18	42.58	30.11	23.93	20.25	17.84	16.13	14.88	13.93	13.18	12.58	12.10	11.70	11.37
1000	89.09	47.31	33.46	26.58	22.50	19.82	17.93	16.53	15.47	14.64	13.98	13.44	13.00	12.64
2000	178.17	94.62	66.91	53.16	45.00	39.63	35.85	33.06	30.94	29.28	27.96	26.88	26.00	25.27
3000	267.25	141.93	100.37	79.74	67.50	59.44	53.77	49.59	46.41	43.92	41.93	40.32	39.00	37.90
4000	356.34	189.23	133.82	106.32	90.00	79.25	71.69	66.12	61.88	58.56	55.91	53.76	52.00	50.53
5000	445.42	236.54	167.27	132.90	112.49	99.06	89.61	82.65	77.34	73.19	69.88	67.20	64.99	63.16
6000	534.50	283.85	200.73	159.48	134.99	118.87	107.53	99.18	92.81	87.83	83.86	80.64	77.99	75.80
7000	623.59	331.16	234.18	186.06	157.49	138.68	125.45	115.71	108.28	102.47	97.83	94.08	90.99	88.43
8000	712.67	378.46	267.63	212.64	179.99	158.49	143.37	132.24	123.75	117.11	111.81	107.51	103.99	101.06
9000	801.75	425.77	301.09	239.22	202.49	178.31	161.30	148.76	139.21	131.74	125.78	120.95	116.98	113.69
10000	890.83	473.08	334.54	265.80	224.98	198.12	179.22	165.29	154.68	146.38	139.76	134.39	129.98	126.32
11000	979.92	520.39	367.99	292.38	247.48	217.93	197.14	181.82	170.15	161.02	153.73	147.83	142.98	138.95
12000	1069.00	567.69	401.45	318.96	269.98	237.74	215.06	198.35	185.62	175.66	167.71	161.27	155.98	151.59
13000	1158.08	615.00	434.90	345.54	292.48	257.55	232.98	214.88	201.08	190.29	181.69	174.71	168.97	164.22
14000	1247.17	662.31	468.36	372.12	314.98	277.36	250.90	231.41	216.55	204.93	195.66	188.15	181.97	176.85
15000	1336.25	709.61	501.81	398.70	337.47	297.17	268.82	247.94	232.02	219.57	209.64	201.58	194.97	189.48
16000	1425.33	756.92	535.26	425.28	359.97	316.98	286.74	264.47	247.49	234.21	223.61	215.02	207.97	202.11
17000	1514.41	804.23	568.72	451.86	382.47	336.80	304.67	280.99	262.95	248.84	237.59	228.46	220.97	214.74
18000	1603.50	851.54	602.17	478.44	404.97	356.61	322.59	297.52	278.42	263.48	251.56	241.90	233.96	227.38
19000	1692.58	898.84	635.62	505.02	427.47	376.42	340.51	314.05	293.89	278.12	265.54	255.34	246.96	240.01
20000	1781.66	946.15	669.08	531.60	449.96	396.23	358.43	330.58	309.36	292.76	279.51	268.78	259.96	252.64
21000	1870.75	993.46	702.53	558.18	472.46	416.04	376.35	347.11	324.82	307.39	293.49	282.22	272.96	265.27
22000	1959.83	1040.77	735.98	584.76	494.96	435.85	394.27	363.64	340.29	322.03	307.46	295.65	285.95	277.90
23000	2048.91	1088.07	769.44	611.34	517.46	455.66	412.19	380.17	355.76	336.67	321.44	309.09	298.95	290.53
24000	2137.99	1135.38	802.89	637.92	539.96	475.47	430.11	396.70	371.23	351.31	335.42	322.53	311.95	303.17
25000	2227.08	1182.69	836.35	664.50	562.45	495.28	448.04	413.23	386.69	365.95	349.39	335.97	324.95	315.80
26000	2316.16	1230.00	869.80	691.08	584.95	515.10	465.96	429.75	402.16	380.58	363.37	349.41	337.94	328.43
27000	2405.24	1277.30	903.25	717.66	607.45	534.91	483.88	446.28	417.63	395.22	377.34	362.85	350.94	341.06
28000	2494.33	1324.61	936.71	744.24	629.95	554.72	501.80	462.81	433.10	409.86	391.32	376.29	363.94	353.69
29000	2583.41	1371.92	970.16	770.82	652.45	574.53	519.72	479.34	448.56	424.50	405.29	389.72	376.94	366.32
30000	2672.49	1419.22	1003.61	797.40	674.94	594.34	537.64	495.87	464.03	439.13	419.27	403.16	389.93	378.96
31000	2761.57	1466.53	1037.07	823.98	697.44	614.15	555.56	512.40	479.50	453.77	433.24	416.60	402.93	391.59
32000	2850.66	1513.84	1070.52	850.56	719.94	633.96	573.48	528.93	494.97	468.41	447.22	430.04	415.93	404.22
33000	2939.74	1561.15	1103.97	877.14	742.44	653.77	591.41	545.46	510.43	483.05	461.19	443.48	428.93	416.85
34000	3028.82	1608.45	1137.43	903.72	764.93	673.59	609.33	561.98	525.90	497.68	475.17	456.92	441.93	429.48
35000	3117.91	1655.76	1170.88	930.30	787.43	693.40	627.25	578.51	541.37	512.32	489.15	470.36	454.92	442.11
36000	3206.99	1703.07	1204.34	956.88	809.93	713.21	645.17	595.04	556.84	526.96	503.12	483.79	467.92	454.75
37000	3296.07	1750.38	1237.79	983.46	832.43	733.02	663.09	611.57	572.30	541.60	517.10	497.23	480.92	467.38
38000	3385.15	1797.68	1271.24	1010.04	854.93	752.83	681.01	628.10	587.77	556.23	531.07	510.67	493.92	480.01
39000	3474.24	1844.99	1304.70	1036.63	877.42	772.64	698.93	644.63	603.24	570.87	545.05	524.11	506.91	492.64
40000	3563.32	1892.30	1338.15	1063.20	899.92	792.45	716.85	661.16	618.71	585.51	559.02	537.55	519.91	505.27
41000	3652.40	1939.60	1371.60	1089.78	922.42	812.26	734.78	677.69	634.17	600.15	573.00	550.99	532.91	517.90
42000	3741.49	1986.91	1405.06	1116.36	944.92	832.07	752.70	694.21	649.64	614.78	586.97	564.43	545.91	530.54
43000	3830.57	2034.22	1438.51	1142.94	967.42	851.89	770.62	710.74	665.11	629.42	600.95	577.86	558.90	543.17
44000	3919.65	2081.53	1471.96	1169.52	989.91	871.70	788.54	727.27	680.58	644.06	614.92	591.30	571.90	555.80
45000	4008.73	2128.83	1505.42	1196.10	1012.41	891.51	806.46	743.80	696.04	658.70	628.90	604.74	584.90	568.43
46000	4097.82	2176.14	1538.87	1222.68	1034.91	911.32	824.38	760.33	711.51	673.34	642.87	618.18	597.90	581.06
47000	4186.90	2223.45	1572.33	1249.26	1057.41	931.13	842.30	776.86	726.98	687.97	656.85	631.62	610.90	593.69
48000	4275.98	2270.76	1605.78	1275.84	1079.91	950.94	860.22	793.39	742.45	702.61	670.83	645.06	623.89	606.33
49000	4365.07	2318.06	1639.23	1302.42	1102.40	970.75	878.15	809.92	757.91	717.25	684.80	658.50	636.89	618.96
50000	4454.15	2365.37	1672.69	1329.00	1124.90	990.56	896.07	826.45	773.38	731.89	698.78	671.93	649.89	631.59
55000	4899.56	2601.91	1839.95	1461.90	1237.39	1089.62	985.67	909.09	850.72	805.07	768.65	739.13	714.88	694.75
60000	5344.98	2838.44	2007.22	1594.80	1349.88	1188.68	1075.28	991.73	928.06	878.26	838.53	806.32	779.86	757.91
65000	5790.39	3074.98	2174.49	1727.70	1462.37	1287.73	1164.89	1074.38	1005.40	951.45	908.41	873.51	844.85	821.06
70000	6235.81	3311.52	2341.76	1860.60	1574.86	1386.79	1254.49	1157.02	1082.73	1024.64	978.29	940.71	909.84	884.22
75000	6681.22	3548.05	2509.03	1993.50	1687.35	1485.84	1344.10	1239.67	1160.07	1097.83	1048.16	1007.90	974.83	947.38
80000	7126.63	3784.59	2676.30	2126.40	1799.84	1584.90	1433.70	1322.31	1237.41	1171.01	1118.04	1075.09	1039.82	1010.54
85000	7572.05	4021.13	2843.56	2259.30	1912.33	1683.96	1523.31	1404.95	1314.75	1244.20	1187.92	1142.28	1104.81	1073.70
90000	8017.46	4257.66	3010.83	2392.20	2024.82	1783.01	1612.92	1487.60	1392.08	1317.39	1257.79	1209.48	1169.79	1136.86
95000	8462.88	4494.20	3178.10	2525.10	2137.31	1882.07	1702.52	1570.24	1469.42	1390.58	1327.67	1276.67	1234.78	1200.01
100000	8908.29	4730.74	3345.37	2658.00	2249.80	1981.12	1792.13	1652.89	1546.76	1463.77	1397.55	1343.86	1299.77	1263.17

TERM	15 Years	16 Years	17 Years	18 Years	19 Years	20 Years	21 Years	22 Years	23 Years	24 Years	25 Years	30 Years	35 Years	40 Years
AMOUNT														
5	.07	.07	.06	.06	.06	.06	.06	.06	.06	.06	.06	.06	.06	.06
10	.13	.13	.12	.12	.12	.12	.12	.12	.12	.11	.11	.11	.11	.11
15	.19	.19	.18	.18	.18	.18	.17	.17	.17	.17	.17	.17	.16	.16
25	.31	.31	.30	.30	.29	.29	.29	.28	.28	.28	.28	.27	.27	.27
50	.62	.61	.60	.59	.58	.57	.57	.56	.56	.55	.55	.54	.53	.53
75	.93	.91	.89	.88	.87	.86	.85	.84	.83	.83	.82	.81	.80	.79
100	1.24	1.21	1.19	1.17	1.15	1.14	1.13	1.12	1.11	1.10	1.10	1.07	1.06	1.05
200	2.47	2.42	2.37	2.34	2.30	2.28	2.25	2.23	2.21	2.20	2.19	2.14	2.12	2.10
300	3.70	3.63	3.56	3.50	3.45	3.41	3.38	3.35	3.32	3.30	3.28	3.21	3.17	3.15
400	4.94	4.83	4.74	4.67	4.60	4.55	4.50	4.46	4.42	4.39	4.37	4.27	4.23	4.20
500	6.17	6.04	5.93	5.84	5.75	5.69	5.63	5.57	5.53	5.49	5.46	5.34	5.28	5.25
600	7.40	7.25	7.11	7.00	6.90	6.82	6.75	6.69	6.63	6.59	6.55	6.41	6.34	6.30
700	8.63	8.45	8.30	8.17	8.05	7.96	7.87	7.80	7.74	7.69	7.64	7.48	7.39	7.35
800	9.87	9.66	9.48	9.33	9.20	9.09	9.00	8.92	8.84	8.78	8.73	8.54	8.45	8.40
900	11.10	10.87	10.67	10.50	10.35	10.23	10.12	10.03	9.95	9.88	9.82	9.61	9.50	9.45
1000	12.33	12.07	11.85	11.67	11.50	11.37	11.25	11.14	11.05	10.98	10.91	10.68	10.56	10.49
2000	24.66	24.14	23.70	23.33	23.00	22.73	22.49	22.28	22.10	21.95	21.81	21.35	21.11	20.98
3000	36.98	36.21	35.55	34.99	34.50	34.09	33.73	33.42	33.15	32.92	32.72	32.02	31.66	31.47
4000	49.31	48.27	47.39	46.65	46.00	45.45	44.97	44.56	44.20	43.89	43.62	42.70	42.22	41.96
5000	61.63	60.34	59.24	58.31	57.50	56.81	56.22	55.70	55.25	54.86	54.52	53.37	52.77	52.45
6000	73.96	72.41	71.09	69.97	69.00	68.17	67.46	66.84	66.30	65.83	65.43	64.04	63.32	62.94
7000	86.28	84.47	82.94	81.63	80.50	79.53	78.70	77.98	77.35	76.81	76.33	74.71	73.87	73.43
8000	98.61	96.54	94.78	93.29	92.00	90.90	89.94	89.12	88.40	87.78	87.23	85.39	84.43	83.92
9000	110.93	108.61	106.63	104.95	103.50	102.26	101.18	100.26	99.45	98.75	98.14	96.06	94.98	94.41
10000	123.26	120.67	118.48	116.61	115.00	113.62	112.43	111.39	110.50	109.72	109.04	106.73	105.53	104.90
11000	135.58	132.74	130.32	128.27	126.50	124.98	123.67	122.53	121.55	120.69	119.94	117.40	116.08	115.39
12000	147.91	144.81	142.17	139.93	138.00	136.34	134.91	133.67	132.60	131.66	130.85	120.00	126.64	125.88
13000	160.23	156.87	154.02	151.59	149.50	147.70	146.15	144.81	143.65	142.63	141.75	138.75	137.19	136.36
14000	172.56	168.94	165.87	163.25	161.00	159.06	157.40	155.95	154.70	153.61	152.65	149.42	147.74	146.85
15000	184.88	181.01	177.71	174.91	172.50	170.43	168.64	167.09	165.75	164.58	163.56	160.09	158.29	157.34
16000	197.21	193.07	189.56	186.57	184.00	181.79	179.88	178.23	176.79	175.55	174.46	170.77	168.85	167.83
17000	209.53	205.14	201.41	198.23	195.50	193.15	191.12	189.37	187.84	186.52	185.37	181.44	179.40	178.32
18000	221.86	217.21	213.26	209.89	207.00	204.51	202.36	200.51	198.89	197.49	196.27	192.11	189.95	188.81
19000	234.18	229.27	225.10	221.55	218.50	215.87	213.61	211.65	209.94	208.46	207.17	202.78	200.50	199.30
20000	246.51	241.34	236.95	233.21	230.00	227.23	224.85	222.78	220.99	219.43	218.08	213.46	211.06	209.79
21000	258.83	253.41	248.80	244.87	241.49	238.59	236.09	233.92	232.04	230.41	228.98	224.13	221.61	220.28
22000	271.16	265.47	260.64	256.53	252.99	249.96	247.33	245.06	243.09	241.38	239.88	234.80	232.16	230.77
23000	283.49	277.54	272.49	268.19	264.49	261.32	258.58	256.20	254.14	252.35	250.79	245.47	242.71	241.26
24000	295.01	289.61	284.34	279.85	275.99	272.68	269.82	267.34	265.19	263.32	261.69	256.15	253.27	251.75
25000	308.14	301.67	296.19	291.51	287.49	284.04	281.06	278.48	276.24	274.29	272.59	266.82	263.82	262.23
26000	320.46	313.74	308.03	303.17	298.99	295.40	292.30	289.62	287.29	285.26	283.50	277.49	274.37	272.72
27000	332.79	325.81	319.88	314.83	310.49	306.76	303.54	300.76	298.34	296.23	294.40	288.16	284.92	283.21
28000	345.11	337.87	331.73	326.49	321.99	318.12	314.79	311.90	309.39	307.21	305.30	298.84	295.48	293.70
29000	357.44	349.94	343.58	338.15	333.49	329.49	326.03	323.03	320.44	318.18	316.21	309.51	306.03	304.19
30000	369.76	362.01	355.42	349.81	344.99	340.85	337.27	334.17	331.49	329.15	327.11	320.18	316.58	314.68
31000	382.09	374.07	367.27	361.47	356.49	352.21	348.51	345.31	342.54	340.12	338.01	330.85	327.13	325.17
32000	394.41	386.14	379.12	373.13	367.99	363.57	359.75	356.45	353.58	351.09	348.92	341.53	337.69	335.66
33000	406.74	398.21	390.96	384.79	379.49	374.93	371.00	367.59	364.63	362.06	359.82	352.20	348.24	346.15
34000	419.06	410.27	402.81	396.45	390.99	386.29	382.24	378.73	375.68	373.03	370.73	362.87	358.79	356.64
35000	431.39	422.34	414.66	408.11	402.49	397.65	393.48	389.87	386.73	384.01	381.63	373.55	369.34	367.13
36000	443.71	434.41	426.51	419.77	413.99	409.02	404.72	401.01	397.78	394.98	392.53	384.22	379.90	377.62
37000	456.04	446.47	438.35	431.43	425.49	420.38	415.97	412.15	408.83	405.95	403.44	394.89	390.45	388.11
38000	468.36	458.54	450.20	443.09	436.99	431.74	427.21	423.29	419.88	416.92	414.34	405.56	401.00	398.59
39000	480.69	470.61	462.05	454.75	448.49	443.10	438.45	434.42	430.93	427.89	425.24	416.24	411.55	409.08
40000	493.01	482.67	473.90	466.41	459.99	454.46	449.69	445.56	441.98	438.86	436.15	426.91	422.11	419.57
41000	505.34	494.74	485.74	478.07	471.48	465.82	460.93	456.70	453.03	449.83	447.05	437.58	432.66	430.06
42000	517.66	506.81	497.59	489.73	482.98	477.18	472.18	467.84	464.08	460.81	457.95	448.25	443.21	440.55
43000	529.99	518.87	509.44	501.39	494.48	488.55	483.42	478.98	475.13	471.78	468.86	458.93	453.76	451.04
44000	542.31	530.94	521.28	513.05	505.98	499.91	494.66	490.12	486.18	482.75	479.76	469.60	464.32	461.53
45000	554.64	543.01	533.13	524.71	517.48	511.27	505.90	501.26	497.23	493.72	490.66	480.27	474.87	472.02
46000	566.97	555.07	544.98	536.37	528.98	522.63	517.15	512.40	508.28	504.69	501.57	490.94	485.42	482.51
47000	579.29	567.14	556.83	548.03	540.48	533.99	528.39	523.54	519.33	515.66	512.47	501.62	495.97	493.00
48000	591.62	579.21	568.67	559.69	551.98	545.35	539.63	534.67	530.37	526.63	523.37	512.29	506.53	503.49
49000	603.94	591.27	580.52	571.35	563.48	556.71	550.87	545.81	541.42	537.61	534.28	522.96	517.08	513.98
50000	616.27	603.34	592.37	583.01	574.98	568.08	562.11	556.95	552.47	548.58	545.18	533.63	527.63	524.46
55000	677.89	663.67	651.60	641.31	632.48	624.88	618.32	612.65	607.72	603.43	599.70	587.00	580.39	576.91
60000	739.52	724.01	710.84	699.61	689.98	681.69	674.54	668.34	662.97	658.29	654.22	640.36	633.16	629.36
65000	801.14	784.34	770.08	757.91	747.47	738.50	730.75	724.04	718.21	713.15	708.74	693.72	685.92	681.80
70000	862.77	844.67	829.31	816.21	804.97	795.30	786.96	779.73	773.46	768.01	763.25	747.09	738.68	734.25
75000	924.40	905.01	888.55	874.51	862.47	852.11	843.17	835.43	828.71	822.86	817.77	800.45	791.45	786.69
80000	986.02	965.34	947.79	932.81	919.97	908.92	899.38	891.12	883.95	877.72	872.29	853.81	844.21	839.14
85000	1047.65	1025.67	1007.02	991.11	977.46	965.72	955.59	946.82	939.20	932.58	926.81	907.17	896.97	891.59
90000	1109.27	1086.01	1066.26	1049.41	1034.96	1022.53	1011.80	1002.51	994.45	987.44	981.32	960.54	949.73	944.03
95000	1170.90	1146.34	1125.49	1107.71	1092.46	1079.34	1068.01	1058.21	1049.70	1042.29	1035.84	1013.90	1002.50	996.48
100000	1232.53	1206.67	1184.73	1166.01	1149.96	1136.15	1124.22	1113.90	1104.94	1097.15	1090.36	1067.26	1055.26	1048.92

MONTHLY PAYMENT
REQUIRED TO AMORTIZE A LOAN

TERM AMOUNT	1 Year	2 Years	3 Years	4 Years	5 Years	6 Years	7 Years	8 Years	9 Years	10 Years	11 Years	12 Years	13 Years	14 Years
5	.45	.24	.17	.14	.12	.10	.09	.09	.08	.08	.08	.07	.07	.07
10	.90	.48	.34	.27	.23	.20	.18	.17	.16	.15	.15	.14	.14	.13
15	1.34	.72	.51	.40	.34	.30	.27	.25	.24	.23	.22	.21	.20	.20
25	2.23	1.19	.84	.67	.57	.50	.45	.42	.39	.37	.36	.34	.33	.32
50	4.46	2.37	1.68	1.34	1.13	1.00	.90	.83	.78	.74	.71	.68	.66	.64
75	6.69	3.56	2.52	2.00	1.70	1.49	1.35	1.25	1.17	1.11	1.06	1.02	.98	.96
100	8.92	4.74	3.36	2.67	2.26	1.99	1.80	1.66	1.56	1.47	1.41	1.35	1.31	1.27
200	17.83	9.48	6.71	5.33	4.51	3.98	3.60	3.32	3.11	2.94	2.81	2.70	2.62	2.54
300	26.74	14.21	10.06	7.99	6.77	5.96	5.40	4.98	4.66	4.41	4.22	4.05	3.92	3.81
400	35.66	18.95	13.41	10.66	9.02	7.95	7.20	6.64	6.21	5.88	5.62	5.40	5.23	5.08
500	44.57	23.68	16.76	13.32	11.28	9.94	8.99	8.30	7.77	7.35	7.02	6.75	6.54	6.35
600	53.48	28.42	20.11	15.98	13.53	11.92	10.79	9.96	9.32	8.82	8.43	8.10	7.84	7.62
700	62.40	33.15	23.46	18.65	15.79	13.91	12.59	11.61	10.87	10.29	9.83	9.45	9.15	8.89
800	71.31	37.89	26.81	21.31	18.04	15.90	14.39	13.27	12.42	11.76	11.23	10.80	10.45	10.16
900	80.22	42.62	30.16	23.97	20.30	17.88	16.18	14.93	13.98	13.23	12.64	12.15	11.76	11.43
1000	89.13	47.36	33.51	26.63	22.55	19.87	17.98	16.59	15.53	14.70	14.04	13.50	13.07	12.70
2000	178.26	94.71	67.01	53.26	45.10	39.73	35.96	33.17	31.05	29.40	28.08	27.00	26.13	25.40
3000	267.39	142.07	100.51	79.89	67.65	59.60	53.93	49.76	46.58	44.09	42.11	40.50	39.19	38.09
4000	356.52	189.42	134.01	106.52	90.20	79.46	71.91	66.34	62.10	58.79	56.15	54.00	52.25	50.79
5000	445.65	236.78	167.51	133.15	112.75	99.32	89.88	82.93	77.63	73.49	70.18	67.50	65.31	63.48
6000	534.78	284.13	201.01	159.78	135.30	119.19	107.86	99.51	93.15	88.18	84.22	81.00	78.37	76.18
7000	623.91	331.48	234.52	186.41	157.85	139.05	125.83	116.10	108.68	102.88	98.25	94.50	91.43	88.87
8000	713.04	378.84	268.02	213.04	180.40	158.91	143.81	132.68	124.20	117.57	112.29	108.00	104.49	101.57
9000	802.17	426.19	301.52	239.67	202.94	178.78	161.78	149.26	139.73	132.27	126.32	121.50	117.55	114.27
10000	891.30	473.55	335.02	266.30	225.49	198.64	179.76	165.85	155.25	146.97	140.36	135.00	130.61	126.96
11000	980.43	520.90	368.52	292.93	248.04	218.50	197.73	182.43	170.77	161.66	154.39	148.50	143.67	139.66
12000	1069.56	568.25	402.02	319.56	270.59	238.37	215.71	199.02	186.30	176.36	168.43	162.00	156.73	152.35
13000	1158.69	615.61	435.53	346.19	293.14	258.23	233.68	215.60	201.82	191.05	182.46	175.50	169.79	165.05
14000	1247.82	662.96	469.03	372.82	315.69	278.10	251.66	232.19	217.35	205.75	196.50	189.00	182.85	177.74
15000	1336.95	710.32	502.53	399.45	338.24	297.96	269.63	248.77	232.87	220.45	210.53	202.50	195.91	190.44
16000	1426.08	757.67	536.03	426.08	360.79	317.82	287.61	265.35	248.40	235.14	224.57	216.00	208.97	203.13
17000	1515.21	805.03	569.53	452.70	383.34	337.69	305.58	281.94	263.92	249.84	238.61	229.50	222.03	215.83
18000	1604.34	852.38	603.03	479.33	405.88	357.55	323.56	298.52	279.45	264.53	252.64	243.00	235.09	228.53
19000	1693.47	899.73	636.54	505.96	428.43	377.41	341.53	315.11	294.97	279.23	266.68	256.50	248.15	241.22
20000	1782.60	947.09	670.04	532.59	450.98	397.28	359.51	331.69	310.50	293.93	280.71	270.00	261.21	253.92
21000	1871.73	994.44	703.54	559.22	473.53	417.14	377.48	348.28	326.02	308.62	294.75	283.50	274.27	266.61
22000	1960.86	1041.80	737.04	585.85	496.08	437.00	395.46	364.86	341.54	323.32	308.78	297.00	287.33	279.31
23000	2049.99	1089.15	770.54	612.48	518.63	456.87	413.43	381.44	357.07	338.01	322.82	310.50	300.39	292.00
24000	2139.12	1136.50	804.04	639.11	541.18	476.73	431.41	398.03	372.59	352.71	336.85	324.00	313.45	304.70
25000	2228.25	1183.86	837.55	665.74	563.73	496.60	449.39	414.61	388.12	367.41	350.89	337.50	326.51	317.39
26000	2317.38	1231.21	871.05	692.37	586.27	516.46	467.36	431.20	403.64	382.10	364.92	351.00	339.57	330.09
27000	2406.51	1278.57	904.55	719.00	608.82	536.32	485.34	447.78	419.17	396.80	378.96	364.50	352.63	342.79
28000	2495.64	1325.92	938.05	745.63	631.37	556.19	503.31	464.37	434.69	411.50	392.99	378.00	365.69	355.48
29000	2584.77	1373.28	971.55	772.26	653.92	576.05	521.29	480.95	450.22	426.19	407.03	391.50	378.75	368.18
30000	2673.90	1420.63	1005.05	798.89	676.47	595.91	539.26	497.53	465.74	440.89	421.06	405.00	391.81	380.87
31000	2763.03	1467.98	1038.55	825.52	699.02	615.78	557.24	514.12	481.27	455.58	435.10	418.50	404.87	393.57
32000	2852.16	1515.34	1072.06	852.15	721.57	635.64	575.21	530.70	496.79	470.28	449.14	432.00	417.93	406.26
33000	2941.29	1562.69	1105.56	878.77	744.12	655.50	593.19	547.29	512.31	484.98	463.17	445.50	430.99	418.96
34000	3030.42	1610.05	1139.06	905.40	766.67	675.37	611.16	563.87	527.84	499.67	477.21	459.00	444.05	431.66
35000	3119.55	1657.40	1172.56	932.03	789.21	695.23	629.14	580.46	543.36	514.37	491.24	472.50	457.11	444.35
36000	3208.67	1704.75	1206.06	958.66	811.76	715.09	647.11	597.04	558.89	529.06	505.28	486.00	470.17	457.05
37000	3297.80	1752.11	1239.56	985.29	834.31	734.96	665.09	613.62	574.41	543.76	519.31	499.50	483.24	469.74
38000	3386.93	1799.46	1273.07	1011.92	856.86	754.82	683.06	630.21	589.94	558.46	533.35	513.00	496.30	482.44
39000	3476.06	1846.82	1306.57	1038.55	879.41	774.69	701.04	646.79	605.46	573.15	547.38	526.50	509.36	495.13
40000	3565.19	1894.17	1340.07	1065.18	901.96	794.55	719.01	663.38	620.99	587.85	561.42	540.00	522.42	507.83
41000	3654.32	1941.53	1373.57	1091.81	924.51	814.41	736.99	679.96	636.51	602.54	575.45	553.50	535.48	520.52
42000	3743.45	1988.88	1407.07	1118.44	947.06	834.28	754.96	696.55	652.04	617.24	589.49	567.00	548.54	533.22
43000	3832.58	2036.23	1440.57	1145.07	969.60	854.14	772.94	713.13	667.56	631.94	603.52	580.50	561.60	545.92
44000	3921.71	2083.59	1474.08	1171.70	992.15	874.00	790.91	729.71	683.08	646.63	617.56	594.00	574.66	558.61
45000	4010.84	2130.94	1507.58	1198.33	1014.70	893.87	808.89	746.30	698.61	661.33	631.59	607.50	587.72	571.31
46000	4099.97	2178.30	1541.08	1224.96	1037.25	913.73	826.86	762.88	714.13	676.02	645.63	621.00	600.78	584.00
47000	4189.10	2225.65	1574.58	1251.59	1059.80	933.59	844.84	779.47	729.66	690.72	659.66	634.50	613.84	596.70
48000	4278.23	2273.00	1608.08	1278.22	1082.35	953.46	862.81	796.05	745.18	705.42	673.70	648.00	626.90	609.39
49000	4367.36	2320.36	1641.58	1304.85	1104.90	973.32	880.79	812.64	760.71	720.11	687.74	661.50	639.96	622.09
50000	4456.49	2367.71	1675.09	1331.47	1127.45	993.19	898.77	829.22	776.23	734.81	701.77	675.00	653.02	634.78
55000	4902.14	2604.48	1842.59	1464.62	1240.19	1092.50	988.64	912.14	853.85	808.29	771.95	742.50	718.32	698.26
60000	5347.79	2841.25	2010.10	1597.77	1352.94	1191.82	1078.52	995.06	931.48	881.77	842.12	810.00	783.62	761.74
65000	5793.44	3078.03	2177.61	1730.92	1465.68	1291.14	1168.39	1077.98	1009.10	955.25	912.30	877.50	848.92	825.22
70000	6239.09	3314.80	2345.12	1864.06	1578.42	1390.46	1258.27	1160.91	1086.72	1028.73	982.48	944.99	914.22	888.70
75000	6684.73	3551.57	2512.63	1997.21	1691.17	1489.78	1348.15	1243.83	1164.35	1102.21	1052.65	1012.49	979.53	952.17
80000	7130.38	3788.34	2680.13	2130.36	1803.91	1589.09	1438.02	1326.75	1241.97	1175.69	1122.83	1079.99	1044.83	1015.65
85000	7576.03	4025.11	2847.64	2263.50	1916.66	1688.41	1527.90	1409.67	1319.59	1249.17	1193.01	1147.49	1110.13	1079.13
90000	8021.68	4261.88	3015.15	2396.65	2029.40	1787.73	1617.77	1492.59	1397.21	1322.65	1263.18	1214.99	1175.43	1142.61
95000	8467.33	4498.65	3182.66	2529.80	2142.14	1887.05	1707.65	1575.51	1474.84	1396.13	1333.36	1282.49	1240.73	1206.09
100000	8912.98	4735.42	3350.17	2662.94	2254.89	1986.37	1797.53	1658.44	1552.46	1469.61	1403.54	1349.99	1306.03	1269.56

TERM	15 Years	16 Years	17 Years	18 Years	19 Years	20 Years	21 Years	22 Years	23 Years	24 Years	25 Years	30 Years	35 Years	40 Years
AMOUNT														
5	.07	.07	.06	.06	.06	.06	.06	.06	.06	.06	.06	.06	.06	.06
10	.13	.13	.12	.12	.12	.12	.12	.12	.12	.12	.11	.11	.11	.11
15	.19	.19	.18	.18	.18	.18	.17	.17	.17	.17	.17	.17	.16	.16
25	.31	.31	.30	.30	.29	.29	.29	.29	.28	.28	.28	.27	.27	.27
50	.62	.61	.60	.59	.58	.58	.57	.57	.56	.56	.55	.54	.54	.53
75	.93	.91	.90	.88	.87	.86	.85	.85	.84	.83	.83	.81	.80	.80
100	1.24	1.22	1.20	1.18	1.16	1.15	1.14	1.13	1.12	1.11	1.10	1.08	1.07	1.06
200	2.48	2.43	2.39	2.35	2.32	2.29	2.27	2.25	2.23	2.21	2.20	2.16	2.13	2.12
300	3.72	3.64	3.58	3.52	3.48	3.43	3.40	3.37	3.34	3.32	3.30	3.23	3.19	3.18
400	4.96	4.86	4.77	4.70	4.63	4.58	4.53	4.49	4.45	4.42	4.40	4.31	4.26	4.23
500	6.20	6.07	5.96	5.87	5.79	5.72	5.66	5.61	5.57	5.53	5.49	5.38	5.32	5.29
600	7.44	7.28	7.15	7.04	6.95	6.86	6.79	6.73	6.68	6.63	6.59	6.46	6.38	6.35
700	8.68	8.50	8.35	8.22	8.10	8.01	7.92	7.85	7.79	7.74	7.69	7.53	7.45	7.40
800	9.92	9.71	9.54	9.39	9.26	9.15	9.06	8.97	8.90	8.84	8.79	8.61	8.51	8.46
900	11.16	10.92	10.73	10.56	10.42	10.29	10.19	10.10	10.02	9.95	9.89	9.68	9.57	9.52
1000	12.40	12.14	11.92	11.73	11.57	11.44	11.32	11.22	11.13	11.05	10.98	10.76	10.64	10.58
2000	24.79	24.27	23.83	23.46	23.14	22.87	22.63	22.43	22.25	22.10	21.96	21.51	21.27	21.15
3000	37.18	36.40	35.75	35.19	34.71	34.30	33.95	33.64	33.37	33.14	32.94	32.26	31.90	31.72
4000	49.57	48.54	47.66	46.92	46.28	45.73	45.26	44.85	44.50	44.19	43.92	43.01	42.53	42.29
5000	61.96	60.67	59.58	58.65	57.85	57.16	56.57	56.06	55.62	55.23	54.90	53.76	53.17	52.86
6000	74.35	72.80	71.49	70.38	69.42	68.60	67.89	67.27	66.74	66.28	65.87	64.51	63.80	63.43
7000	86.74	84.94	83.41	82.11	80.99	80.03	79.20	78.48	77.86	77.32	76.85	75.26	74.43	74.00
8000	99.13	97.07	95.32	93.83	92.56	91.46	90.51	89.70	88.99	88.37	87.83	86.01	85.06	84.57
9000	111.52	109.20	107.24	105.56	104.13	102.89	101.83	100.91	100.11	99.41	98.81	96.76	95.70	95.14
10000	123.91	121.34	119.15	117.29	115.70	114.32	113.14	112.12	111.23	110.46	109.79	107.51	106.33	105.71
11000	136.30	133.47	131.07	129.02	127.27	125.76	124.46	123.33	122.35	121.50	120.77	118.26	116.96	116.28
12000	148.69	145.60	142.98	140.75	138.83	137.19	135.77	134.54	133.48	132.55	131.74	129.01	127.59	126.85
13000	161.08	157.73	154.90	152.48	150.40	148.62	147.08	145.75	144.60	143.60	142.72	139.76	138.22	137.42
14000	173.47	169.87	166.81	164.21	161.97	160.05	158.40	156.96	155.72	154.64	153.70	150.51	148.86	147.99
15000	185.86	182.00	178.73	175.93	173.54	171.48	169.71	168.17	166.84	165.69	164.68	161.26	159.49	158.56
16000	198.25	194.13	190.64	187.66	185.11	182.92	181.02	179.39	177.97	176.73	175.66	172.01	170.12	169.13
17000	210.64	206.27	202.56	199.39	196.68	194.35	192.34	190.60	189.09	187.78	186.63	182.76	180.75	179.70
18000	223.03	218.40	214.47	211.12	208.25	205.78	203.65	201.81	200.21	198.82	197.61	193.51	191.39	190.27
19000	235.42	230.53	226.39	222.85	219.82	217.21	214.96	213.02	211.33	209.87	208.59	204.26	202.02	200.84
20000	247.81	242.67	238.30	234.58	231.39	228.64	226.28	224.23	222.46	220.91	219.57	215.01	212.65	211.41
21000	260.20	254.80	250.21	246.31	242.96	240.08	237.59	235.44	233.58	231.96	230.55	225.76	223.28	221.98
22000	272.59	266.93	262.13	258.03	254.53	251.51	248.91	246.65	244.70	243.00	241.53	236.51	233.91	232.55
23000	284.98	279.06	274.04	269.76	266.09	262.94	260.22	257.87	255.82	254.05	252.50	247.26	244.55	243.12
24000	297.37	291.20	285.96	281.49	277.66	274.37	271.53	269.08	266.95	265.09	263.48	258.01	255.18	253.69
25000	309.76	303.33	297.87	293.22	289.23	285.80	282.85	280.29	278.07	276.14	274.46	268.76	265.81	264.26
26000	322.15	315.46	309.79	304.95	300.80	297.24	294.16	291.50	289.19	287.19	285.44	279.51	276.44	274.83
27000	334.55	327.60	321.70	316.68	312.37	308.67	305.47	302.71	300.31	298.23	296.42	290.26	287.08	285.40
28000	346.94	339.73	333.62	328.41	323.94	320.10	316.79	313.92	311.44	309.28	307.40	301.01	297.71	295.97
29000	359.33	351.86	345.53	340.13	335.51	331.53	328.10	325.13	322.56	320.32	318.37	311.76	308.34	306.54
30000	371.72	364.00	357.45	351.86	347.08	342.96	339.42	336.34	333.68	331.37	329.35	322.51	318.97	317.11
31000	384.11	376.13	369.36	363.59	358.65	354.40	350.73	347.56	344.80	342.41	340.33	333.26	329.60	327.68
32000	396.50	388.26	381.28	375.32	370.22	365.83	362.04	358.77	355.93	353.46	351.31	344.01	340.24	338.25
33000	408.89	400.40	393.19	387.05	381.79	377.26	373.36	369.98	367.05	364.50	362.29	354.76	350.87	348.82
34000	421.28	412.53	405.11	398.78	393.35	388.69	384.67	381.19	378.17	375.55	373.26	365.51	361.50	359.39
35000	433.67	424.66	417.02	410.51	404.92	400.12	395.98	392.40	389.29	386.59	384.24	376.26	372.13	369.96
36000	446.06	436.79	428.94	422.23	416.49	411.56	407.30	403.61	400.42	397.64	395.22	387.01	382.77	380.53
37000	458.45	448.93	440.85	433.96	428.06	422.99	418.61	414.82	411.54	408.69	406.20	397.76	393.40	391.10
38000	470.84	461.06	452.76	445.69	439.63	434.42	429.92	426.04	422.66	419.73	417.18	408.51	404.03	401.67
39000	483.23	473.19	464.68	457.42	451.20	445.85	441.24	437.25	433.78	430.78	428.16	419.26	414.66	412.24
40000	495.62	485.33	476.59	469.15	462.77	457.28	452.55	448.46	444.91	441.82	439.13	430.01	425.29	422.82
41000	508.01	497.46	488.51	480.88	474.34	468.72	463.87	459.67	456.03	452.87	450.11	440.76	435.93	433.39
42000	520.40	509.59	500.42	492.61	485.91	480.15	475.18	470.88	467.15	463.91	461.09	451.51	446.56	443.96
43000	532.79	521.73	512.34	504.33	497.48	491.58	486.49	482.09	478.28	474.96	472.07	462.26	457.19	454.53
44000	545.18	533.86	524.25	516.06	509.05	503.01	497.81	493.30	489.40	486.00	483.05	473.02	467.82	465.10
45000	557.57	545.99	536.17	527.79	520.61	514.44	509.12	504.51	500.52	497.05	494.03	483.77	478.46	475.67
46000	569.96	558.12	548.08	539.52	532.18	525.88	520.43	515.73	511.64	508.09	505.00	494.52	489.09	486.24
47000	582.35	570.26	560.00	551.25	543.75	537.31	531.75	526.94	522.77	519.14	515.98	505.27	499.72	496.81
48000	594.74	582.39	571.91	562.98	555.32	548.74	543.06	538.15	533.89	530.18	526.96	516.02	510.35	507.38
49000	607.13	594.52	583.83	574.71	566.89	560.17	554.38	549.36	545.01	541.23	537.94	526.77	520.98	517.95
50000	619.52	606.66	595.74	586.43	578.46	571.60	565.69	560.57	556.13	552.28	548.92	537.52	531.62	528.52
55000	681.48	667.32	655.32	645.08	636.31	628.76	622.26	616.63	611.75	607.50	603.81	591.27	584.78	581.37
60000	743.43	727.99	714.89	703.72	694.15	685.92	678.83	672.68	667.36	662.73	658.70	645.02	637.94	634.22
65000	805.38	788.65	774.46	762.36	752.00	743.08	735.39	728.74	722.97	717.96	713.59	698.77	691.10	687.07
70000	867.33	849.32	834.04	821.01	809.84	800.24	791.96	784.80	778.58	773.18	768.48	752.52	744.26	739.92
75000	929.28	909.98	893.61	879.65	867.69	857.40	848.53	840.85	834.20	828.41	823.37	806.27	797.42	792.77
80000	991.23	970.65	953.18	938.29	925.53	914.56	905.10	896.91	889.81	883.64	878.26	860.02	850.58	845.63
85000	1053.19	1031.31	1012.76	996.93	983.38	971.72	961.67	952.97	945.42	938.86	933.15	913.77	903.75	898.48
90000	1115.14	1091.98	1072.33	1055.58	1041.22	1028.88	1018.24	1009.02	1001.04	994.09	988.05	967.53	956.91	951.33
95000	1177.09	1152.64	1131.91	1114.22	1099.07	1086.04	1074.80	1065.08	1056.65	1049.32	1042.94	1021.28	1010.07	1004.18
100000	1239.04	1213.31	1191.48	1172.86	1156.92	1143.20	1131.37	1121.14	1112.26	1104.55	1097.83	1075.03	1063.23	1057.03

MONTHLY PAYMENT
REQUIRED TO AMORTIZE A LOAN

TERM AMOUNT	1 Year	2 Years	3 Years	4 Years	5 Years	6 Years	7 Years	8 Years	9 Years	10 Years	11 Years	12 Years	13 Years	14 Years
5	.45	.24	.17	.14	.12	.10	.09	.09	.08	.08	.08	.07	.07	.07
10	.90	.48	.34	.27	.23	.20	.18	.17	.16	.15	.15	.14	.14	.13
15	1.34	.72	.51	.40	.34	.30	.27	.25	.24	.23	.22	.21	.20	.20
25	2.23	1.19	.84	.67	.57	.50	.45	.42	.39	.37	.36	.34	.33	.32
50	4.46	2.37	1.68	1.34	1.13	1.00	.90	.83	.78	.74	.71	.68	.66	.64
75	6.69	3.56	2.52	2.00	1.70	1.50	1.35	1.25	1.17	1.11	1.06	1.02	.99	.96
100	8.92	4.74	3.36	2.67	2.26	1.99	1.80	1.66	1.56	1.48	1.41	1.36	1.31	1.28
200	17.83	9.48	6.71	5.33	4.52	3.98	3.60	3.32	3.11	2.95	2.82	2.71	2.62	2.55
300	26.75	14.21	10.06	8.00	6.77	5.97	5.40	4.98	4.67	4.42	4.22	4.06	3.93	3.82
400	35.66	18.95	13.41	10.66	9.03	7.96	7.20	6.64	6.22	5.89	5.63	5.41	5.24	5.09
500	44.58	23.69	16.76	13.33	11.29	9.94	9.00	8.30	7.77	7.36	7.03	6.76	6.54	6.36
600	53.49	28.42	20.11	15.99	13.54	11.93	10.80	9.96	9.33	8.83	8.44	8.11	7.85	7.63
700	62.40	33.16	23.46	18.65	15.80	13.92	12.60	11.62	10.88	10.30	9.84	9.47	9.16	8.90
800	71.32	37.90	26.82	21.32	18.05	15.91	14.40	13.28	12.44	11.77	11.25	10.82	10.47	10.17
900	80.23	42.63	30.17	23.98	20.31	17.89	16.19	14.94	13.99	13.24	12.65	12.17	11.77	11.45
1000	89.15	47.37	33.52	26.65	22.57	19.88	17.99	16.60	15.54	14.72	14.06	13.52	13.08	12.72
2000	178.29	94.74	67.03	53.29	45.13	39.76	35.98	33.20	31.08	29.43	28.11	27.04	26.16	25.43
3000	267.43	142.10	100.55	79.93	67.69	59.64	53.97	49.80	46.62	44.14	42.16	40.55	39.23	38.14
4000	356.57	189.47	134.06	106.57	90.25	79.51	71.96	66.40	62.16	58.85	56.21	54.07	52.31	50.85
5000	445.71	236.83	167.57	133.21	112.81	99.39	89.95	83.00	77.70	73.56	70.26	67.58	65.38	63.56
6000	534.85	284.20	201.09	159.86	135.37	119.27	107.94	99.59	93.24	88.27	84.31	81.10	78.46	76.27
7000	624.00	331.57	234.60	186.50	157.94	139.14	125.93	116.19	108.78	102.98	98.36	94.61	91.54	88.99
8000	713.14	378.93	268.11	213.14	180.50	159.02	143.91	132.79	124.32	117.69	112.41	108.13	104.61	101.70
9000	802.28	426.30	301.63	239.78	203.06	178.90	161.90	149.39	139.85	132.40	126.46	121.64	117.69	114.41
10000	891.42	473.66	335.14	266.42	225.62	198.77	179.89	165.99	155.39	147.11	140.51	135.16	130.76	127.12
11000	980.56	521.03	368.65	293.06	248.18	218.65	197.88	182.59	170.93	161.82	154.56	148.67	143.84	139.83
12000	1069.70	568.40	402.17	319.71	270.74	238.53	215.87	199.18	186.47	176.53	168.61	162.19	156.92	152.54
13000	1158.84	615.76	435.68	346.35	293.31	258.40	233.86	215.78	202.01	191.24	182.66	175.70	169.99	165.26
14000	1247.99	663.13	469.20	372.99	315.87	278.28	251.85	232.38	217.55	205.95	196.71	189.22	183.07	177.97
15000	1337.13	710.49	502.71	399.63	338.43	298.16	269.84	248.98	233.09	220.67	210.76	202.73	196.14	190.68
16000	1426.27	757.86	536.22	426.27	360.99	318.03	287.82	265.58	248.63	235.38	224.81	216.25	209.22	203.39
17000	1515.41	805.22	569.74	452.91	383.55	337.91	305.81	282.17	264.16	250.09	238.86	229.76	222.30	216.10
18000	1604.55	852.59	603.25	479.56	406.11	357.79	323.80	298.77	279.70	264.80	252.91	243.28	235.37	228.81
19000	1693.69	899.96	636.76	506.20	428.67	377.66	341.79	315.37	295.24	279.51	266.96	256.79	248.45	241.53
20000	1782.83	947.32	670.28	532.84	451.24	397.54	359.78	331.97	310.78	294.22	281.01	270.31	261.52	254.24
21000	1871.98	994.69	703.79	559.48	473.80	417.42	377.77	348.57	326.32	308.93	295.06	283.82	274.60	266.95
22000	1961.12	1042.05	737.30	586.12	496.36	437.29	395.76	365.17	341.86	323.64	309.11	297.34	287.68	279.66
23000	2050.26	1089.42	770.82	612.77	518.92	457.17	413.75	381.76	357.40	338.35	323.16	310.85	300.75	292.37
24000	2139.40	1136.79	804.33	639.41	541.49	477.05	431.73	398.36	372.94	353.06	337.21	324.37	313.83	305.08
25000	2228.54	1184.15	837.85	666.05	564.04	496.92	449.72	414.96	388.48	367.77	351.26	337.88	326.90	317.79
26000	2317.68	1231.52	871.36	692.69	586.61	516.80	467.71	431.56	404.01	382.48	365.31	351.40	339.98	330.51
27000	2406.82	1278.88	904.87	719.33	609.17	536.68	485.70	448.16	419.55	397.19	379.36	364.92	353.06	343.22
28000	2495.97	1326.25	938.39	745.97	631.73	556.55	503.69	464.75	435.09	411.90	393.41	378.43	366.13	355.93
29000	2585.11	1373.62	971.90	772.62	654.29	576.43	521.68	481.35	450.63	426.62	407.46	391.95	379.21	368.64
30000	2674.25	1420.98	1005.41	799.26	676.85	596.31	539.67	497.95	466.17	441.33	421.51	405.46	392.28	381.35
31000	2763.39	1468.35	1038.93	825.90	699.41	616.18	557.66	514.55	481.71	456.04	435.56	418.98	405.36	394.06
32000	2852.53	1515.71	1072.44	852.54	721.98	636.06	575.64	531.15	497.25	470.75	449.61	432.49	418.44	406.78
33000	2941.67	1563.08	1105.95	879.18	744.54	655.94	593.63	547.75	512.79	485.46	463.67	446.01	431.51	419.49
34000	3030.81	1610.44	1139.47	905.82	767.10	675.81	611.62	564.34	528.32	500.17	477.72	459.52	444.59	432.20
35000	3119.96	1657.81	1172.98	932.47	789.66	695.69	629.61	580.94	543.86	514.88	491.77	473.04	457.66	444.91
36000	3209.10	1705.18	1206.50	959.11	812.22	715.57	647.60	597.54	559.40	529.59	505.82	486.55	470.74	457.62
37000	3298.24	1752.54	1240.01	985.75	834.78	735.44	665.59	614.14	574.94	544.30	519.87	500.07	483.82	470.33
38000	3387.38	1799.91	1273.52	1012.39	857.34	755.32	683.58	630.74	590.48	559.01	533.92	513.58	496.89	483.05
39000	3476.52	1847.27	1307.04	1039.03	879.91	775.20	701.56	647.33	606.02	573.72	547.97	527.10	509.97	495.76
40000	3565.66	1894.64	1340.55	1065.67	902.47	795.07	719.55	663.93	621.56	588.43	562.02	540.61	523.04	508.47
41000	3654.80	1942.01	1374.06	1092.32	925.03	814.95	737.54	680.53	637.10	603.14	576.07	554.13	536.12	521.18
42000	3743.95	1989.37	1407.58	1118.96	947.59	834.83	755.53	697.13	652.63	617.85	590.12	567.64	549.19	533.89
43000	3833.09	2036.74	1441.09	1145.60	970.15	854.70	773.52	713.73	668.17	632.57	604.17	581.16	562.27	546.60
44000	3922.23	2084.10	1474.60	1172.24	992.71	874.58	791.51	730.33	683.71	647.28	618.22	594.67	575.35	559.31
45000	4011.37	2131.47	1508.12	1198.88	1015.28	894.46	809.50	746.92	699.25	661.99	632.27	608.19	588.42	572.03
46000	4100.51	2178.84	1541.63	1225.53	1037.84	914.33	827.49	763.52	714.79	676.70	646.32	621.70	601.50	584.74
47000	4189.65	2226.20	1575.14	1252.17	1060.40	934.21	845.47	780.12	730.33	691.41	660.37	635.22	614.57	597.45
48000	4278.79	2273.57	1608.66	1278.81	1082.96	954.09	863.46	796.72	745.87	706.12	674.42	648.73	627.65	610.16
49000	4367.94	2320.93	1642.17	1305.45	1105.52	973.96	881.45	813.32	761.41	720.83	688.47	662.25	640.73	622.87
50000	4457.08	2368.30	1675.69	1332.09	1128.08	993.84	899.44	829.91	776.95	735.54	702.52	675.76	653.80	635.58
55000	4902.78	2605.13	1843.25	1465.30	1240.89	1093.23	989.38	912.91	854.64	809.09	772.77	743.34	719.18	699.14
60000	5348.49	2841.96	2010.82	1598.51	1353.70	1192.61	1079.33	995.90	932.33	882.65	843.02	810.92	784.56	762.70
65000	5794.20	3078.79	2178.39	1731.72	1466.51	1291.99	1169.27	1078.89	1010.03	956.20	913.27	878.49	849.94	826.26
70000	6239.91	3315.62	2345.96	1864.93	1579.31	1391.38	1259.21	1161.88	1087.72	1029.75	983.53	946.07	915.32	889.82
75000	6685.61	3552.45	2513.53	1998.14	1692.12	1490.76	1349.16	1244.87	1165.42	1103.31	1053.78	1013.64	980.70	953.37
80000	7131.32	3789.27	2681.09	2131.34	1804.93	1590.14	1439.10	1327.86	1243.11	1176.86	1124.03	1081.22	1046.08	1016.93
85000	7577.03	4026.10	2848.66	2264.55	1917.74	1689.53	1529.05	1410.85	1320.80	1250.42	1194.28	1148.80	1111.46	1080.49
90000	8022.73	4262.93	3016.23	2397.76	2030.55	1788.91	1618.99	1493.84	1398.50	1323.97	1264.53	1216.37	1176.84	1144.05
95000	8468.44	4499.76	3183.80	2530.97	2143.35	1888.29	1708.93	1576.83	1476.19	1397.52	1334.78	1283.95	1242.22	1207.61
100000	8914.15	4736.59	3351.37	2664.18	2256.16	1987.68	1798.88	1659.82	1553.89	1471.08	1405.04	1351.52	1307.60	1271.16

TERM	15 Years	16 Years	17 Years	18 Years	19 Years	20 Years	21 Years	22 Years	23 Years	24 Years	25 Years	30 Years	35 Years	40 Years
AMOUNT														
5	.07	.07	.06	.06	.06	.06	.06	.06	.06	.06	.06	.06	.06	.06
10	.13	.13	.12	.12	.12	.12	.12	.12	.12	.12	.11	.11	.11	.11
15	.19	.19	.18	.18	.18	.18	.17	.17	.17	.17	.17	.17	.16	.16
25	.32	.31	.30	.30	.29	.29	.29	.29	.28	.28	.28	.27	.27	.27
50	.63	.61	.60	.59	.58	.58	.57	.57	.56	.56	.55	.54	.54	.53
75	.94	.92	.90	.89	.87	.86	.85	.85	.84	.83	.83	.81	.80	.80
100	1.25	1.22	1.20	1.18	1.16	1.15	1.14	1.13	1.12	1.11	1.10	1.08	1.07	1.06
200	2.49	2.43	2.39	2.35	2.32	2.29	2.27	2.25	2.23	2.22	2.20	2.16	2.14	2.12
300	3.73	3.65	3.58	3.53	3.48	3.44	3.40	3.37	3.35	3.32	3.30	3.24	3.20	3.18
400	4.97	4.86	4.78	4.70	4.64	4.58	4.54	4.50	4.46	4.43	4.40	4.31	4.27	4.24
500	6.21	6.08	5.97	5.88	5.80	5.73	5.67	5.62	5.58	5.54	5.50	5.39	5.33	5.30
600	7.45	7.29	7.16	7.05	6.96	6.87	6.80	6.74	6.69	6.64	6.60	6.47	6.40	6.36
700	8.69	8.51	8.36	8.23	8.12	8.02	7.94	7.87	7.80	7.75	7.70	7.54	7.46	7.42
800	9.93	9.72	9.55	9.40	9.27	9.16	9.07	8.99	8.92	8.86	8.80	8.62	8.53	8.48
900	11.17	10.94	10.74	10.58	10.43	10.31	10.20	10.11	10.03	9.96	9.90	9.70	9.59	9.54
1000	12.41	12.15	11.94	11.75	11.59	11.45	11.34	11.23	11.15	11.07	11.00	10.77	10.66	10.60
2000	24.82	24.30	23.87	23.50	23.18	22.90	22.67	22.46	22.29	22.13	22.00	21.54	21.31	21.19
3000	37.23	36.45	35.80	35.24	34.76	34.35	34.00	33.69	33.43	33.20	33.00	32.31	31.96	31.78
4000	49.63	48.60	47.73	46.99	46.35	45.80	45.33	44.92	44.57	44.26	43.99	43.08	42.61	42.37
5000	62.04	60.75	59.66	58.73	57.94	57.25	56.66	56.15	55.71	55.32	54.99	53.85	53.27	52.96
6000	74.45	72.90	71.59	70.48	69.52	68.70	67.99	67.38	66.85	66.39	65.99	64.62	63.92	63.55
7000	86.85	85.05	83.53	82.23	81.11	80.15	79.33	78.61	77.99	77.45	76.98	75.39	74.57	74.14
8000	99.26	97.20	95.46	93.97	92.70	91.60	90.66	89.84	89.13	88.52	87.98	86.16	85.22	84.73
9000	111.67	109.35	107.39	105.72	104.28	103.05	101.99	101.07	100.27	99.58	98.98	96.93	95.87	95.32
10000	124.07	121.50	119.32	117.46	115.87	114.50	113.32	112.30	111.41	110.64	109.97	107.70	106.53	105.91
11000	136.48	133.65	131.25	129.21	127.46	125.95	124.65	123.53	122.55	121.71	120.97	118.47	117.18	116.50
12000	148.89	145.80	143.18	140.95	139.04	137.40	135.98	134.76	133.70	132.77	131.97	129.24	127.83	127.09
13000	161.29	157.95	155.12	152.70	150.63	148.85	147.32	145.99	144.84	143.84	142.97	140.01	138.48	137.68
14000	173.70	170.10	167.05	164.45	162.22	160.30	158.65	157.22	155.98	154.90	153.96	150.78	149.14	148.27
15000	186.11	182.25	178.98	176.19	173.80	171.75	169.98	168.45	167.12	165.96	164.96	161.55	159.79	158.86
16000	198.51	194.40	190.91	187.94	185.39	183.20	181.31	179.68	178.26	177.03	175.96	172.32	170.44	169.45
17000	210.92	206.55	202.84	199.68	196.98	194.65	192.64	190.91	189.40	188.09	186.95	183.09	181.09	180.04
18000	223.33	218.70	214.77	211.43	208.56	206.10	203.97	202.13	200.54	199.16	197.95	193.86	191.74	190.63
19000	235.73	230.85	226.71	223.17	220.15	217.55	215.30	213.36	211.68	210.22	208.95	204.63	202.40	201.22
20000	248.14	243.00	238.64	234.92	231.74	229.00	226.64	224.59	222.82	221.28	219.94	215.40	213.05	211.82
21000	260.55	255.15	250.57	246.67	243.32	240.45	237.97	235.82	233.96	232.35	230.94	226.17	223.70	222.41
22000	272.95	267.30	262.50	258.41	254.91	251.90	249.30	247.05	245.10	243.41	241.94	236.94	234.35	233.00
23000	285.36	279.45	274.43	270.16	266.50	263.35	260.63	258.28	256.25	254.48	252.93	247.71	245.01	243.59
24000	297.77	291.60	286.36	281.90	278.08	274.80	271.96	269.51	267.39	265.54	263.93	258.48	255.66	254.18
25000	310.17	303.75	298.30	293.65	289.67	286.25	283.29	280.74	278.53	276.60	274.93	269.25	266.31	264.77
26000	322.58	315.90	310.23	305.39	301.25	297.70	294.63	291.97	289.67	287.67	285.93	280.02	276.96	275.36
27000	334.99	328.05	322.16	317.14	312.84	309.15	305.96	303.20	300.81	298.73	296.92	290.79	287.61	285.95
28000	347.39	340.20	334.09	328.89	324.43	320.60	317.29	314.43	311.95	309.79	307.92	301.56	298.27	296.54
29000	359.80	352.34	346.02	340.63	336.01	332.04	328.62	325.66	323.09	320.86	318.92	312.33	308.92	307.13
30000	372.21	364.49	357.95	352.38	347.60	343.49	339.95	336.89	334.23	331.92	329.91	323.09	319.57	317.72
31000	384.61	376.64	369.89	364.12	359.19	354.94	351.28	348.12	345.37	342.99	340.91	333.86	330.22	328.31
32000	397.02	388.79	381.82	375.87	370.77	366.39	362.62	359.35	356.51	354.05	351.91	344.63	340.87	338.90
33000	409.43	400.94	393.75	387.61	382.36	377.84	373.95	370.58	367.65	365.11	362.90	355.40	351.53	349.49
34000	421.83	413.09	405.68	399.36	393.95	389.29	385.28	381.81	378.79	376.18	373.90	366.17	362.18	360.08
35000	434.24	425.24	417.61	411.11	405.53	400.74	396.61	393.04	389.94	387.24	384.90	376.94	372.83	370.67
36000	446.65	437.39	429.54	422.85	417.12	412.19	407.94	404.26	401.08	398.31	395.89	387.71	383.48	381.26
37000	459.05	449.54	441.48	434.60	428.71	423.64	419.27	415.49	412.22	409.37	406.89	398.48	394.14	391.85
38000	471.46	461.69	453.41	446.34	440.29	435.09	430.60	426.72	423.36	420.43	417.89	409.25	404.79	402.44
39000	483.87	473.84	465.34	458.09	451.88	446.54	441.94	437.95	434.50	431.50	428.89	420.02	415.44	413.04
40000	496.27	485.99	477.27	469.83	463.47	457.99	453.27	449.18	445.64	442.56	439.88	430.79	426.09	423.63
41000	508.68	498.14	489.20	481.58	475.05	469.44	464.60	460.41	456.78	453.63	450.88	441.56	436.74	434.22
42000	521.09	510.29	501.13	493.33	486.64	480.89	475.93	471.64	467.92	464.69	461.88	452.33	447.40	444.81
43000	533.49	522.44	513.07	505.07	498.23	492.34	487.26	482.87	479.06	475.75	472.87	463.10	458.05	455.40
44000	545.90	534.59	525.00	516.82	509.81	503.79	498.59	494.10	490.20	486.82	483.87	473.87	468.70	465.99
45000	558.31	546.74	536.93	528.56	521.40	515.24	509.93	505.33	501.34	497.88	494.87	484.64	479.35	476.58
46000	570.71	558.89	548.86	540.31	532.99	526.69	521.26	516.56	512.49	508.95	505.86	495.41	490.01	487.17
47000	583.12	571.04	560.79	552.05	544.57	538.14	532.59	527.79	523.63	520.01	516.86	506.18	500.66	497.76
48000	595.53	583.19	572.72	563.80	556.16	549.59	543.92	539.02	534.77	531.07	527.86	516.95	511.31	508.35
49000	607.93	595.34	584.65	575.55	567.74	561.04	555.25	550.25	545.91	542.14	538.85	527.72	521.96	518.94
50000	620.34	607.49	596.59	587.29	579.33	572.49	566.58	561.48	557.05	553.20	549.85	538.49	532.61	529.53
55000	682.37	668.24	656.24	646.02	637.26	629.74	623.24	617.62	612.75	608.52	604.84	592.34	585.87	582.48
60000	744.41	728.98	715.90	704.75	695.20	686.98	679.90	673.77	668.46	663.84	659.82	646.18	639.14	635.44
65000	806.44	789.73	775.56	763.48	753.13	744.23	736.56	729.92	724.16	719.16	714.81	700.03	692.40	688.39
70000	868.47	850.48	835.22	822.21	811.06	801.48	793.22	786.07	779.87	774.48	769.79	753.88	745.66	741.34
75000	930.51	911.23	894.88	880.94	868.99	858.73	849.87	842.21	835.57	829.80	824.77	807.73	798.92	794.29
80000	992.54	971.98	954.54	939.66	926.93	915.98	906.53	898.36	891.28	885.12	879.76	861.58	852.18	847.25
85000	1054.57	1032.73	1014.19	998.39	984.86	973.22	963.19	954.51	946.98	940.44	934.74	915.43	905.44	900.20
90000	1116.61	1093.47	1073.85	1057.12	1042.79	1030.47	1019.85	1010.65	1002.68	995.76	989.73	969.27	958.70	953.15
95000	1178.64	1154.22	1133.51	1115.85	1100.72	1087.72	1076.50	1066.80	1058.39	1051.08	1044.71	1023.12	1011.96	1006.10
100000	1240.67	1214.97	1193.17	1174.58	1158.66	1144.97	1133.16	1122.95	1114.09	1106.40	1099.70	1076.97	1065.22	1059.06

MONTHLY PAYMENT
REQUIRED TO AMORTIZE A LOAN

TERM / AMOUNT	1 Year	2 Years	3 Years	4 Years	5 Years	6 Years	7 Years	8 Years	9 Years	10 Years	11 Years	12 Years	13 Years	14 Years
5	.45	.24	.17	.14	.12	.10	.10	.09	.08	.08	.08	.07	.07	.07
10	.90	.48	.34	.27	.23	.20	.19	.17	.16	.15	.15	.14	.14	.13
15	1.34	.72	.51	.41	.34	.30	.28	.25	.24	.23	.22	.21	.20	.20
25	2.23	1.19	.84	.67	.57	.50	.46	.42	.39	.37	.36	.34	.33	.32
50	4.46	2.38	1.68	1.34	1.13	1.00	.91	.84	.78	.74	.71	.68	.66	.64
75	6.69	3.56	2.52	2.01	1.70	1.50	1.36	1.25	1.17	1.11	1.06	1.02	.99	.96
100	8.92	4.75	3.36	2.67	2.26	2.00	1.81	1.67	1.56	1.48	1.41	1.36	1.32	1.28
200	17.84	9.49	6.71	5.34	4.52	3.99	3.61	3.33	3.12	2.96	2.82	2.72	2.63	2.56
300	26.76	14.23	10.07	8.01	6.78	5.99	5.41	5.00	4.68	4.43	4.23	4.07	3.94	3.83
400	35.68	18.97	13.42	10.68	9.04	7.97	7.22	6.66	6.24	5.91	5.64	5.43	5.25	5.11
500	44.59	23.71	16.78	13.34	11.30	9.96	9.02	8.32	7.80	7.38	7.05	6.79	6.57	6.38
600	53.51	28.45	20.13	16.01	13.56	11.95	10.82	9.99	9.35	8.86	8.46	8.14	7.88	7.66
700	62.43	33.19	23.49	18.68	15.82	13.95	12.63	11.65	10.91	10.33	9.87	9.50	9.19	8.94
800	71.35	37.93	26.84	21.35	18.08	15.94	14.43	13.32	12.47	11.81	11.28	10.85	10.50	10.21
900	80.26	42.67	30.20	24.02	20.34	17.93	16.23	14.98	14.03	13.28	12.69	12.21	11.82	11.49
1000	89.18	47.41	33.55	26.68	22.60	19.92	18.03	16.64	15.59	14.76	14.10	13.57	13.13	12.76
2000	178.36	94.81	67.10	53.36	45.20	39.84	36.06	33.28	31.17	29.51	28.20	27.13	26.25	25.52
3000	267.53	142.21	100.65	80.04	67.80	59.75	54.09	49.92	46.75	44.27	42.29	40.69	39.37	38.28
4000	356.71	189.61	134.20	106.72	90.40	79.67	72.12	66.56	62.33	59.02	56.39	54.25	52.50	51.04
5000	445.89	237.01	167.75	133.40	113.00	99.59	90.15	83.20	77.91	73.78	70.48	67.81	65.62	63.80
6000	535.06	284.41	201.30	160.08	135.60	119.50	108.18	99.84	93.49	88.53	84.58	81.37	78.74	76.56
7000	624.24	331.81	234.85	186.76	158.20	139.42	126.21	116.48	109.08	103.29	98.67	94.93	91.87	89.32
8000	713.42	379.21	268.40	213.44	180.80	159.33	144.24	133.12	124.66	118.04	112.77	108.50	104.99	102.08
9000	802.59	426.61	301.95	240.11	203.40	179.25	162.27	149.76	140.24	132.80	126.86	122.06	118.11	114.84
10000	891.77	474.02	335.50	266.79	226.00	199.17	180.30	166.40	155.82	147.55	140.96	135.62	131.24	127.60
11000	980.95	521.42	369.05	293.47	248.60	219.08	198.33	183.04	171.40	162.31	155.05	149.18	144.36	140.36
12000	1070.12	568.82	402.60	320.15	271.20	239.00	216.36	199.68	186.98	177.06	169.15	162.74	157.48	153.12
13000	1159.30	616.22	436.15	346.83	293.80	258.91	234.39	216.32	202.57	191.82	183.24	176.30	170.60	165.88
14000	1248.48	663.62	469.70	373.51	316.40	278.83	252.41	232.96	218.15	206.57	197.34	189.86	183.73	178.64
15000	1337.65	711.02	503.25	400.19	339.00	298.75	270.44	249.60	233.73	221.32	211.43	203.42	196.85	191.40
16000	1426.83	758.42	536.80	426.87	361.60	318.66	288.47	266.24	249.31	236.08	225.53	216.99	209.97	204.16
17000	1516.01	805.82	570.35	453.55	384.20	338.58	306.50	282.88	264.89	250.83	239.63	230.55	223.10	216.92
18000	1605.18	853.22	603.90	480.22	406.80	358.50	324.53	299.52	280.47	265.59	253.72	244.11	236.22	229.68
19000	1694.36	900.62	637.45	506.90	429.40	378.41	342.56	316.16	296.06	280.34	267.82	257.67	249.34	242.44
20000	1783.54	948.03	671.00	533.58	452.00	398.33	360.59	332.80	311.64	295.10	281.91	271.23	262.47	255.20
21000	1872.71	995.43	704.55	560.26	474.60	418.24	378.62	349.44	327.22	309.85	296.01	284.79	275.59	267.96
22000	1961.89	1042.83	738.10	586.94	497.20	438.16	396.65	366.08	342.80	324.61	310.10	298.35	288.71	280.72
23000	2051.07	1090.23	771.65	613.62	519.80	458.08	414.68	382.72	358.38	339.36	324.20	311.91	301.83	293.48
24000	2140.24	1137.63	805.20	640.30	542.40	477.99	432.71	399.36	373.96	354.12	338.29	325.48	314.96	306.24
25000	2229.42	1185.03	838.75	666.98	565.00	497.91	450.74	416.00	389.55	368.87	352.39	339.04	328.08	319.00
26000	2318.60	1232.43	872.30	693.65	587.60	517.82	468.77	432.64	405.13	383.63	366.48	352.60	341.20	331.76
27000	2407.77	1279.83	905.85	720.33	610.20	537.74	486.80	449.28	420.71	398.38	380.58	366.16	354.33	344.52
28000	2496.95	1327.23	939.39	747.01	632.80	557.66	504.82	465.92	436.29	413.14	394.67	379.72	367.45	357.27
29000	2586.13	1374.63	972.94	773.69	655.40	577.57	522.85	482.56	451.87	427.89	408.77	393.28	380.57	370.03
30000	2675.30	1422.04	1006.49	800.37	678.00	597.49	540.88	499.20	467.45	442.64	422.86	406.84	393.70	382.79
31000	2764.48	1469.44	1040.04	827.05	700.60	617.40	558.91	515.84	483.04	457.40	436.96	420.40	406.82	395.55
32000	2853.66	1516.84	1073.59	853.73	723.20	637.32	576.94	532.48	498.62	472.15	451.06	433.97	419.94	408.31
33000	2942.83	1564.24	1107.14	880.41	745.80	657.24	594.97	549.12	514.20	486.91	465.15	447.53	433.06	421.07
34000	3032.01	1611.64	1140.69	907.09	768.40	677.15	613.00	565.76	529.78	501.66	479.25	461.09	446.19	433.83
35000	3121.19	1659.04	1174.24	933.76	791.00	697.07	631.03	582.40	545.36	516.42	493.34	474.65	459.31	446.59
36000	3210.36	1706.44	1207.79	960.44	813.60	716.99	649.06	599.04	560.94	531.17	507.44	488.21	472.43	459.35
37000	3299.54	1753.84	1241.34	987.12	836.20	736.90	667.09	615.68	576.53	545.93	521.53	501.77	485.56	472.11
38000	3388.72	1801.24	1274.89	1013.80	858.80	756.82	685.12	632.32	592.11	560.68	535.63	515.33	498.68	484.87
39000	3477.89	1848.65	1308.44	1040.48	881.40	776.73	703.15	648.96	607.69	575.44	549.72	528.89	511.80	497.63
40000	3567.07	1896.05	1341.99	1067.16	904.00	796.65	721.18	665.60	623.27	590.19	563.82	542.46	524.93	510.39
41000	3656.25	1943.45	1375.54	1093.84	926.60	816.57	739.20	682.24	638.85	604.95	577.91	556.02	538.05	523.15
42000	3745.42	1990.85	1409.09	1120.52	949.20	836.48	757.23	698.88	654.43	619.70	592.01	569.58	551.17	535.91
43000	3834.60	2038.25	1442.64	1147.20	971.80	856.40	775.26	715.52	670.02	634.46	606.10	583.14	564.30	548.67
44000	3923.77	2085.65	1476.19	1173.87	994.40	876.31	793.29	732.16	685.60	649.21	620.20	596.70	577.42	561.43
45000	4012.95	2133.05	1509.74	1200.55	1017.00	896.23	811.32	748.80	701.18	663.96	634.29	610.26	590.54	574.19
46000	4102.13	2180.45	1543.29	1227.23	1039.60	916.15	829.35	765.44	716.76	678.72	648.39	623.82	603.66	586.95
47000	4191.30	2227.85	1576.84	1253.91	1062.20	936.06	847.38	782.08	732.34	693.47	662.49	637.38	616.79	599.71
48000	4280.48	2275.25	1610.39	1280.59	1084.80	955.98	865.41	798.72	747.92	708.23	676.58	650.95	629.91	612.47
49000	4369.66	2322.66	1643.94	1307.27	1107.40	975.89	883.44	815.36	763.51	722.98	690.68	664.51	643.03	625.23
50000	4458.83	2370.06	1677.49	1333.95	1129.99	995.81	901.47	832.00	779.09	737.74	704.77	678.07	656.16	637.99
55000	4904.72	2607.06	1845.23	1467.34	1242.99	1095.39	991.61	915.20	857.00	811.51	775.25	745.87	721.77	701.79
60000	5350.60	2844.07	2012.98	1600.74	1355.99	1194.97	1081.76	998.40	934.90	885.28	845.72	813.68	787.39	765.58
65000	5796.48	3081.07	2180.73	1734.13	1468.99	1294.55	1171.91	1081.60	1012.81	959.06	916.20	881.49	853.00	829.38
70000	6242.37	3318.08	2348.48	1867.52	1581.99	1394.13	1262.05	1164.80	1090.72	1032.83	986.68	949.29	918.62	893.18
75000	6688.25	3555.08	2516.23	2000.92	1694.99	1493.71	1352.20	1248.00	1168.63	1106.60	1057.15	1017.10	984.23	956.98
80000	7134.13	3792.09	2683.98	2134.31	1807.99	1593.29	1442.35	1331.20	1246.54	1180.38	1127.63	1084.91	1049.85	1020.78
85000	7580.01	4029.09	2851.72	2267.71	1920.99	1692.87	1532.49	1414.40	1324.44	1254.15	1198.11	1152.71	1115.46	1084.57
90000	8025.90	4266.10	3019.47	2401.10	2033.99	1792.46	1622.64	1497.60	1402.35	1327.92	1268.58	1220.52	1181.08	1148.37
95000	8471.78	4503.10	3187.22	2534.49	2146.99	1892.04	1712.79	1580.79	1480.26	1401.70	1339.06	1288.32	1246.69	1212.17
100000	8917.66	4740.11	3354.97	2667.89	2259.98	1991.62	1802.93	1663.99	1558.17	1475.47	1409.54	1356.13	1312.31	1275.97

TERM	15 Years	16 Years	17 Years	18 Years	19 Years	20 Years	21 Years	22 Years	23 Years	24 Years	25 Years	30 Years	35 Years	40 Years
AMOUNT														
5	.07	.07	.06	.06	.06	.06	.06	.06	.06	.06	.06	.06	.06	.06
10	.13	.13	.12	.12	.12	.12	.12	.12	.12	.12	.12	.11	.11	.11
15	.19	.19	.18	.18	.18	.18	.18	.17	.17	.17	.17	.17	.17	.16
25	.32	.31	.30	.30	.30	.29	.29	.29	.28	.28	.28	.28	.27	.27
50	.63	.61	.60	.59	.59	.58	.57	.57	.56	.56	.56	.55	.54	.54
75	.94	.92	.90	.89	.88	.87	.86	.85	.84	.84	.83	.82	.81	.80
100	1.25	1.22	1.20	1.18	1.17	1.16	1.14	1.13	1.12	1.12	1.11	1.09	1.08	1.07
200	2.50	2.44	2.40	2.36	2.33	2.31	2.28	2.26	2.24	2.23	2.22	2.17	2.15	2.14
300	3.74	3.66	3.60	3.54	3.50	3.46	3.42	3.39	3.36	3.34	3.32	3.25	3.22	3.20
400	4.99	4.88	4.80	4.72	4.66	4.61	4.56	4.52	4.48	4.45	4.43	4.34	4.29	4.27
500	6.23	6.10	6.00	5.90	5.82	5.76	5.70	5.65	5.60	5.56	5.53	5.42	5.36	5.33
600	7.48	7.32	7.19	7.08	6.99	6.91	6.84	6.78	6.72	6.68	6.64	6.50	6.43	6.40
700	8.72	8.54	8.39	8.26	8.15	8.06	7.97	7.90	7.84	7.79	7.74	7.58	7.50	7.46
800	9.97	9.76	9.59	9.44	9.32	9.21	9.11	9.03	8.96	8.90	8.85	8.67	8.57	8.53
900	11.22	10.98	10.79	10.62	10.48	10.36	10.25	10.16	10.08	10.01	9.95	9.75	9.65	9.59
1000	12.46	12.20	11.99	11.80	11.64	11.51	11.39	11.29	11.20	11.12	11.06	10.83	10.72	10.66
2000	24.92	24.40	23.97	23.60	23.28	23.01	22.78	22.57	22.40	22.24	22.11	21.66	21.43	21.31
3000	37.37	36.60	35.95	35.40	34.92	34.51	34.16	33.86	33.59	33.36	33.16	32.49	32.14	31.96
4000	49.83	48.80	47.93	47.19	46.56	46.02	45.55	45.14	44.79	44.48	44.22	43.32	42.85	42.61
5000	62.28	61.00	59.92	58.99	58.20	57.52	56.93	56.42	55.98	55.60	55.27	54.15	53.57	53.26
6000	74.74	73.20	71.90	70.79	69.84	69.02	68.32	67.71	67.18	66.72	66.32	64.97	64.28	63.91
7000	87.19	85.40	83.88	82.59	81.48	80.52	79.70	78.99	78.38	77.84	77.38	75.80	74.99	74.56
8000	99.65	97.60	95.86	94.38	93.12	92.03	91.09	90.28	89.57	88.96	88.43	86.63	85.70	85.22
9000	112.11	109.80	107.85	106.18	104.75	103.53	102.47	101.56	100.77	100.08	99.48	97.46	96.41	95.87
10000	124.56	122.00	119.83	117.98	116.39	115.03	113.86	112.84	111.96	111.20	110.54	108.29	107.13	106.52
11000	137.02	134.20	131.81	129.78	128.03	126.53	125.24	124.13	123.16	122.32	121.59	119.11	117.84	117.17
12000	149.47	146.40	143.79	141.57	139.67	138.04	136.63	135.41	134.36	133.44	132.64	129.94	128.55	127.82
13000	161.93	150.60	155.78	153.37	151.31	149.54	148.01	146.69	145.55	144.56	143.69	140.77	139.26	138.47
14000	174.38	170.80	167.76	165.17	162.95	161.04	159.40	157.98	156.75	155.68	154.75	151.60	149.97	149.12
15000	186.84	183.00	179.74	176.96	174.59	172.55	170.78	169.26	167.94	166.80	165.80	162.43	160.69	159.78
16000	199.30	195.20	191.72	188.76	186.23	184.05	182.17	180.55	179.14	177.92	176.85	173.25	171.40	170.43
17000	211.75	207.40	203.71	200.56	197.87	195.55	193.56	191.83	190.34	189.04	187.91	184.08	182.11	181.08
18000	224.21	219.60	215.69	212.36	209.50	207.05	204.94	203.11	201.53	200.16	198.96	194.91	192.82	191.73
19000	236.66	231.80	227.67	224.15	221.14	218.56	216.33	214.40	212.73	211.28	210.01	205.74	203.53	202.38
20000	249.12	244.00	239.65	235.95	232.78	230.06	227.71	225.68	223.92	222.40	221.07	216.57	214.25	213.03
21000	261.57	256.20	251.63	247.75	244.42	241.56	239.10	236.97	235.12	233.51	232.12	227.39	224.96	223.68
22000	274.03	268.39	263.62	259.55	256.06	253.06	250.48	248.25	246.31	244.63	243.17	238.22	235.67	234.34
23000	286.49	280.59	275.60	271.34	267.70	264.57	261.87	259.53	257.51	255.75	254.23	249.05	246.38	244.99
24000	298.94	292.79	287.58	283.14	279.34	276.07	273.25	270.82	268.71	266.87	265.28	259.88	257.09	255.64
25000	311.40	304.99	299.56	294.94	290.98	287.57	284.64	282.10	279.90	277.99	276.33	270.71	267.81	266.29
26000	323.85	317.19	311.55	306.73	302.62	299.08	296.02	293.38	291.10	289.11	287.38	281.53	278.52	276.94
27000	336.31	329.39	323.53	318.53	314.25	310.58	307.41	304.67	302.29	300.23	298.44	292.36	289.23	287.59
28000	348.76	341.59	335.51	330.33	325.89	322.08	318.79	315.95	313.49	311.35	309.49	303.19	299.94	298.24
29000	361.22	353.79	347.49	342.13	337.53	333.58	330.18	327.24	324.69	322.47	320.54	314.02	310.65	308.89
30000	373.68	365.99	359.48	353.92	349.17	345.09	341.56	338.52	335.88	333.59	331.60	324.85	321.37	319.55
31000	386.13	378.19	371.46	365.72	360.81	356.59	352.95	349.80	347.08	344.71	342.65	335.67	332.08	330.20
32000	398.59	390.39	383.44	377.52	372.45	368.09	364.34	361.09	358.27	355.83	353.70	346.50	342.79	340.85
33000	411.04	402.59	395.42	389.32	384.09	379.59	375.72	372.37	369.47	366.95	364.76	357.33	353.50	351.50
34000	423.50	414.79	407.41	401.11	395.73	391.10	387.11	383.66	380.67	378.07	375.81	368.16	364.21	362.15
35000	435.95	426.99	419.39	412.91	407.36	402.60	398.49	394.94	391.86	389.19	386.86	378.99	374.93	372.80
36000	448.41	439.19	431.37	424.71	419.00	414.10	409.88	406.22	403.06	400.31	397.92	389.81	385.64	383.45
37000	460.86	451.39	443.35	436.50	430.64	425.60	421.26	417.51	414.25	411.43	408.97	400.64	396.35	394.11
38000	473.32	463.59	455.33	448.30	442.28	437.11	432.65	428.79	425.45	422.55	420.02	411.47	407.06	404.76
39000	485.78	475.79	467.32	460.10	453.92	448.61	444.03	440.07	436.64	433.67	431.07	422.30	417.77	415.41
40000	498.23	487.99	479.30	471.90	465.56	460.11	455.42	451.36	447.84	444.79	442.13	433.13	428.49	426.06
41000	510.69	500.19	491.28	483.69	477.20	471.62	466.80	462.64	459.04	455.91	453.18	443.95	439.20	436.71
42000	523.14	512.39	503.26	495.49	488.84	483.12	478.19	473.93	470.23	467.02	464.23	454.78	449.91	447.36
43000	535.60	524.58	515.25	507.29	500.48	494.62	489.57	485.21	481.43	478.14	475.29	465.61	460.62	458.01
44000	548.05	536.78	527.23	519.09	512.11	506.12	500.96	496.49	492.62	489.26	486.34	476.44	471.33	468.67
45000	560.51	548.98	539.21	530.88	523.75	517.63	512.34	507.78	503.82	500.38	497.39	487.27	482.05	479.32
46000	572.97	561.18	551.19	542.68	535.39	529.13	523.73	519.06	515.02	511.50	508.45	498.09	492.76	489.97
47000	585.42	573.38	563.18	554.48	547.03	540.63	535.12	530.35	526.21	522.62	519.50	508.92	503.47	500.62
48000	597.88	585.58	575.16	566.27	558.67	552.13	546.50	541.63	537.41	533.74	530.55	519.75	514.18	511.27
49000	610.33	597.78	587.14	578.07	570.31	563.64	557.89	552.91	548.60	544.86	541.60	530.58	524.89	521.92
50000	622.79	609.98	599.12	589.87	581.95	575.14	569.27	564.20	559.80	555.98	552.66	541.41	535.61	532.57
55000	685.07	670.98	659.04	648.86	640.14	632.65	626.20	620.62	615.78	611.58	607.92	595.55	589.17	585.83
60000	747.35	731.98	718.95	707.84	698.34	690.17	683.12	677.04	671.76	667.18	663.19	649.69	642.73	639.09
65000	809.62	792.97	778.86	766.83	756.53	747.68	740.05	733.45	727.74	722.77	718.45	703.83	696.29	692.34
70000	871.90	853.97	838.77	825.82	814.72	805.19	796.98	789.87	783.72	778.37	773.72	757.97	749.85	745.60
75000	934.18	914.97	898.68	884.80	872.92	862.71	853.90	846.29	839.70	833.97	828.98	812.11	803.41	798.86
80000	996.46	975.97	958.59	943.79	931.11	920.22	910.83	902.71	895.68	889.57	884.25	866.25	856.97	852.12
85000	1058.74	1036.96	1018.51	1002.77	989.31	977.73	967.76	959.13	951.66	945.16	939.51	920.39	910.53	905.37
90000	1121.02	1097.96	1078.42	1061.76	1047.50	1035.25	1024.68	1015.55	1007.64	1000.76	994.78	974.53	964.09	958.63
95000	1183.29	1158.96	1138.33	1120.75	1105.70	1092.76	1081.61	1071.97	1063.62	1056.36	1050.05	1028.67	1017.65	1011.89
100000	1245.57	1219.96	1198.24	1179.73	1163.89	1150.27	1138.54	1128.39	1119.59	1111.96	1105.31	1082.81	1071.21	1065.14

12.750%

MONTHLY PAYMENT
REQUIRED TO AMORTIZE A LOAN

TERM AMOUNT	1 Year	2 Years	3 Years	4 Years	5 Years	6 Years	7 Years	8 Years	9 Years	10 Years	11 Years	12 Years	13 Years	14 Years
5	.45	.24	.17	.14	.12	.10	.10	.09	.08	.08	.08	.07	.07	.07
10	.90	.48	.34	.27	.23	.20	.19	.17	.16	.15	.15	.14	.14	.13
15	1.34	.72	.51	.41	.34	.30	.28	.26	.24	.23	.22	.21	.20	.20
25	2.24	1.19	.84	.67	.57	.50	.46	.42	.40	.37	.36	.34	.33	.32
50	4.47	2.38	1.68	1.34	1.14	1.00	.91	.84	.79	.74	.71	.68	.66	.64
75	6.70	3.56	2.52	2.01	1.70	1.50	1.36	1.26	1.18	1.11	1.06	1.02	.99	.96
100	8.93	4.75	3.36	2.68	2.27	2.00	1.81	1.67	1.57	1.48	1.42	1.36	1.32	1.28
200	17.85	9.49	6.72	5.35	4.53	3.99	3.62	3.34	3.13	2.96	2.83	2.72	2.64	2.56
300	26.77	14.23	10.08	8.02	6.79	5.99	5.42	5.01	4.69	4.44	4.24	4.08	3.95	3.84
400	35.69	18.97	13.43	10.69	9.06	7.98	7.23	6.67	6.25	5.92	5.66	5.44	5.27	5.12
500	44.61	23.72	16.79	13.36	11.32	9.98	9.03	8.34	7.81	7.40	7.07	6.80	6.58	6.40
600	53.53	28.46	20.15	16.03	13.58	11.97	10.84	10.01	9.37	8.88	8.48	8.16	7.90	7.68
700	62.45	33.20	23.51	18.70	15.84	13.96	12.64	11.67	10.93	10.35	9.89	9.52	9.21	8.96
800	71.37	37.94	26.86	21.37	18.11	15.96	14.45	13.34	12.49	11.83	11.31	10.88	10.53	10.24
900	80.29	42.69	30.22	24.04	20.37	17.95	16.26	15.01	14.05	13.31	12.72	12.24	11.84	11.52
1000	89.21	47.43	33.58	26.71	22.63	19.95	18.06	16.67	15.62	14.79	14.13	13.60	13.16	12.80
2000	178.41	94.85	67.15	53.41	45.26	39.89	36.12	33.34	31.23	29.57	28.26	27.19	26.31	25.59
3000	267.61	142.28	100.73	80.12	67.88	59.83	54.17	50.01	46.84	44.36	42.38	40.78	39.47	38.38
4000	356.81	189.70	134.30	106.82	90.51	79.77	72.23	66.68	62.45	59.14	56.51	54.37	52.62	51.17
5000	446.01	237.13	167.87	133.52	113.13	99.72	90.29	83.34	78.06	73.92	70.63	67.97	65.78	63.96
6000	535.21	284.55	201.45	160.23	135.76	119.66	108.34	100.01	93.67	88.71	84.76	81.56	78.93	76.76
7000	624.41	331.98	235.02	186.93	158.38	139.60	126.40	116.68	109.28	103.49	98.88	95.15	92.09	89.55
8000	713.61	379.40	268.59	213.63	181.01	159.54	144.46	133.35	124.89	118.28	113.01	108.74	105.24	102.34
9000	802.81	426.83	302.17	240.34	203.63	179.49	162.51	150.01	140.50	133.06	127.13	122.33	118.40	115.13
10000	892.01	474.25	335.74	267.04	226.26	199.43	180.57	166.68	156.11	147.84	141.26	135.93	131.55	127.92
11000	981.21	521.67	369.32	293.74	248.88	219.37	198.62	183.35	171.72	162.63	155.38	149.52	144.70	140.71
12000	1070.41	569.10	402.89	320.45	271.51	239.31	216.68	200.02	187.33	177.41	169.51	163.11	157.86	153.51
13000	1159.61	616.52	436.46	347.15	294.13	259.26	234.74	216.69	202.94	192.20	183.63	176.70	171.01	166.30
14000	1248.81	663.95	470.04	373.86	316.76	279.20	252.79	233.35	218.55	206.98	197.76	190.29	184.17	179.09
15000	1338.01	711.37	503.61	400.56	339.38	299.14	270.85	250.02	234.16	221.76	211.89	203.89	197.32	191.88
16000	1427.21	758.80	537.18	427.26	362.01	319.08	288.91	266.69	249.77	236.55	226.01	217.48	210.48	204.67
17000	1516.41	806.22	570.76	453.97	384.64	339.03	306.96	283.36	265.38	251.33	240.14	231.07	223.63	217.46
18000	1605.61	853.65	604.33	480.67	407.26	358.97	325.02	300.02	280.99	266.12	254.26	244.66	236.79	230.26
19000	1694.81	901.07	637.90	507.37	429.89	378.91	343.08	316.69	296.60	280.90	268.39	258.25	249.94	243.05
20000	1784.01	948.49	671.48	534.08	452.51	398.85	361.13	333.36	312.21	295.68	282.51	271.85	263.09	255.84
21000	1873.21	995.92	705.05	560.78	475.14	418.80	379.19	350.03	327.82	310.47	296.64	285.44	276.25	268.63
22000	1962.41	1043.34	738.63	587.48	497.76	438.74	397.24	366.69	343.43	325.25	310.76	299.03	289.40	281.42
23000	2051.61	1090.77	772.20	614.19	520.39	458.68	415.30	383.36	359.04	340.04	324.89	312.62	302.56	294.21
24000	2140.81	1138.19	805.77	640.89	543.01	478.62	433.36	400.03	374.65	354.82	339.01	326.21	315.71	307.01
25000	2230.01	1185.62	839.35	667.59	565.64	498.57	451.41	416.70	390.26	369.60	353.14	339.81	328.87	319.80
26000	2319.21	1233.04	872.92	694.30	588.26	518.51	469.47	433.37	405.87	384.39	367.26	353.40	342.02	332.59
27000	2408.41	1280.47	906.49	721.00	610.89	538.45	487.53	450.03	421.48	399.17	381.39	366.99	355.18	345.38
28000	2497.61	1327.89	940.07	747.71	633.51	558.39	505.58	466.70	437.09	413.96	395.52	380.58	368.33	358.17
29000	2586.81	1375.31	973.64	774.41	656.14	578.33	523.64	483.37	452.70	428.74	409.64	394.17	381.48	370.96
30000	2676.01	1422.74	1007.21	801.11	678.76	598.28	541.69	500.04	468.31	443.52	423.77	407.77	394.64	383.76
31000	2765.21	1470.16	1040.79	827.82	701.39	618.22	559.75	516.70	483.92	458.31	437.89	421.36	407.79	396.55
32000	2854.41	1517.59	1074.36	854.52	724.01	638.16	577.81	533.37	499.53	473.09	452.02	434.95	420.95	409.34
33000	2943.61	1565.01	1107.94	881.22	746.64	658.10	595.86	550.04	515.14	487.88	466.14	448.54	434.10	422.13
34000	3032.81	1612.44	1141.51	907.93	769.27	678.05	613.92	566.71	530.75	502.66	480.27	462.13	447.26	434.92
35000	3122.01	1659.86	1175.08	934.63	791.89	697.99	631.98	583.38	546.36	517.44	494.39	475.73	460.41	447.72
36000	3211.21	1707.29	1208.66	961.33	814.52	717.93	650.03	600.04	561.97	532.23	508.52	489.32	473.57	460.51
37000	3300.41	1754.71	1242.23	988.04	837.14	737.87	668.09	616.71	577.58	547.01	522.64	502.91	486.72	473.30
38000	3389.61	1802.14	1275.80	1014.74	859.77	757.82	686.15	633.38	593.19	561.80	536.77	516.50	499.87	486.09
39000	3478.81	1849.56	1309.38	1041.44	882.39	777.76	704.20	650.05	608.80	576.58	550.89	530.09	513.03	498.88
40000	3568.01	1896.99	1342.95	1068.15	905.02	797.70	722.26	666.71	624.41	591.36	565.02	543.69	526.18	511.67
41000	3657.21	1944.41	1376.53	1094.85	927.64	817.64	740.31	683.38	640.02	606.15	579.15	557.28	539.34	524.47
42000	3746.41	1991.83	1410.10	1121.56	950.27	837.59	758.37	700.05	655.63	620.93	593.27	570.87	552.49	537.26
43000	3835.61	2039.26	1443.67	1148.26	972.89	857.53	776.43	716.72	671.24	635.72	607.40	584.46	565.65	550.05
44000	3924.81	2086.68	1477.25	1174.96	995.52	877.47	794.48	733.38	686.86	650.50	621.52	598.05	578.80	562.84
45000	4014.01	2134.11	1510.82	1201.67	1018.14	897.41	812.54	750.05	702.47	665.28	635.65	611.65	591.96	575.63
46000	4103.21	2181.53	1544.39	1228.37	1040.77	917.36	830.60	766.72	718.08	680.07	649.77	625.24	605.11	588.42
47000	4192.41	2228.96	1577.97	1255.07	1063.39	937.30	848.65	783.39	733.69	694.85	663.90	638.83	618.26	601.22
48000	4281.61	2276.38	1611.54	1281.78	1086.02	957.24	866.71	800.06	749.30	709.64	678.02	652.42	631.42	614.01
49000	4370.81	2323.80	1645.11	1308.48	1108.64	977.18	884.76	816.72	764.91	724.42	692.15	666.01	644.57	626.80
50000	4460.01	2371.23	1678.69	1335.18	1131.27	997.13	902.82	833.39	780.52	739.20	706.27	679.61	657.73	639.59
55000	4906.01	2608.35	1846.56	1468.70	1244.40	1096.84	993.10	916.73	858.57	813.12	776.90	747.57	723.50	703.55
60000	5352.01	2845.47	2014.42	1602.22	1357.52	1196.55	1083.38	1000.07	936.62	887.04	847.53	815.53	789.27	767.51
65000	5798.01	3082.60	2182.29	1735.74	1470.65	1296.26	1173.67	1083.41	1014.67	960.96	918.15	883.49	855.04	831.47
70000	6244.01	3319.72	2350.16	1869.26	1583.78	1395.97	1263.95	1166.75	1092.72	1034.88	988.78	951.45	920.82	895.43
75000	6690.01	3556.84	2518.03	2002.77	1696.90	1495.69	1354.23	1250.08	1170.77	1108.80	1059.41	1019.41	986.59	959.38
80000	7136.01	3793.96	2685.90	2136.29	1810.03	1595.40	1444.51	1333.42	1248.82	1182.72	1130.04	1087.37	1052.36	1023.34
85000	7582.01	4031.09	2853.77	2269.81	1923.16	1695.11	1534.79	1416.76	1326.87	1256.64	1200.66	1155.33	1118.13	1087.30
90000	8028.01	4268.21	3021.63	2403.33	2036.28	1794.82	1625.07	1500.10	1404.93	1330.56	1271.29	1223.29	1183.91	1151.26
95000	8474.01	4505.33	3189.50	2536.85	2149.41	1894.53	1715.36	1583.44	1482.98	1404.48	1341.92	1291.25	1249.68	1215.22
100000	8920.01	4742.45	3357.37	2670.36	2262.54	1994.25	1805.64	1666.78	1561.03	1478.40	1412.54	1359.21	1315.45	1279.18

TERM AMOUNT	15 Years	16 Years	17 Years	18 Years	19 Years	20 Years	21 Years	22 Years	23 Years	24 Years	25 Years	30 Years	35 Years	40 Years
5	.07	.07	.07	.06	.06	.06	.06	.06	.06	.06	.06	.06	.06	.06
10	.13	.13	.13	.12	.12	.12	.12	.12	.12	.12	.12	.11	.11	.11
15	.19	.19	.19	.18	.18	.18	.18	.17	.17	.17	.17	.17	.17	.17
25	.32	.31	.31	.30	.30	.29	.29	.29	.29	.28	.28	.28	.27	.27
50	.63	.62	.61	.60	.59	.58	.58	.57	.57	.56	.56	.55	.54	.54
75	.94	.92	.91	.89	.88	.87	.86	.85	.85	.84	.84	.82	.81	.81
100	1.25	1.23	1.21	1.19	1.17	1.16	1.15	1.14	1.13	1.12	1.11	1.09	1.08	1.07
200	2.50	2.45	2.41	2.37	2.34	2.31	2.29	2.27	2.25	2.24	2.22	2.18	2.16	2.14
300	3.75	3.67	3.61	3.55	3.51	3.47	3.43	3.40	3.37	3.35	3.33	3.27	3.23	3.21
400	5.00	4.90	4.81	4.74	4.67	4.62	4.57	4.53	4.50	4.47	4.44	4.35	4.31	4.28
500	6.25	6.12	6.01	5.92	5.84	5.77	5.72	5.67	5.62	5.58	5.55	5.44	5.38	5.35
600	7.50	7.34	7.21	7.10	7.01	6.93	6.86	6.80	6.74	6.70	6.66	6.53	6.46	6.42
700	8.75	8.57	8.42	8.29	8.18	8.08	8.00	7.93	7.87	7.81	7.77	7.61	7.53	7.49
800	10.00	9.79	9.62	9.47	9.34	9.24	9.14	9.06	8.99	8.93	8.88	8.70	8.61	8.56
900	11.24	11.01	10.82	10.65	10.51	10.39	10.28	10.19	10.11	10.05	9.99	9.79	9.68	9.63
1000	12.49	12.24	12.02	11.84	11.68	11.54	11.43	11.33	11.24	11.16	11.10	10.87	10.76	10.70
2000	24.98	24.47	24.04	23.67	23.35	23.08	22.85	22.65	22.47	22.32	22.19	21.74	21.51	21.39
3000	37.47	36.70	36.05	35.50	35.03	34.62	34.27	33.97	33.70	33.47	33.28	32.61	32.26	32.08
4000	49.96	48.94	48.07	47.33	46.70	46.16	45.69	45.29	44.94	44.63	44.37	43.47	43.01	42.77
5000	62.45	61.17	60.09	59.16	58.37	57.70	57.11	56.61	56.17	55.79	55.46	54.34	53.76	53.46
6000	74.94	73.40	72.10	71.00	70.05	69.23	68.53	67.93	67.40	66.94	66.55	65.21	64.52	64.16
7000	87.42	85.63	84.12	82.83	81.72	80.77	79.95	79.25	78.63	78.10	77.64	76.07	75.27	74.85
8000	99.91	97.87	96.13	94.66	93.40	92.31	91.37	90.57	89.87	89.26	88.73	86.94	86.02	85.54
9000	112.40	110.10	108.15	106.49	105.07	103.85	102.80	101.89	101.10	100.41	99.82	97.81	96.77	96.23
10000	124.89	122.33	120.17	118.32	116.74	115.39	114.22	113.21	112.33	111.57	110.91	108.67	107.52	106.92
11000	137.38	134.57	132.18	130.15	128.42	126.92	125.64	124.53	123.56	122.73	122.00	119.54	118.28	117.62
12000	149.87	146.80	144.20	141.99	140.09	138.46	137.06	135.85	134.80	133.90	133.09	130.41	129.03	128.31
13000	162.35	159.03	156.22	153.82	151.76	150.00	148.48	147.17	146.03	145.04	144.18	141.28	139.78	139.00
14000	174.84	171.26	168.23	165.65	163.44	161.54	159.90	158.49	157.26	156.20	155.27	152.14	150.53	149.69
15000	187.33	183.50	180.25	177.48	175.11	173.08	171.32	169.81	168.49	167.35	166.36	163.01	161.28	160.38
16000	199.82	195.73	192.26	189.31	186.79	184.61	182.74	181.13	179.73	178.51	177.45	173.88	172.04	171.08
17000	212.31	207.96	204.28	201.14	198.46	196.15	194.17	192.45	190.96	189.67	188.54	184.74	182.79	181.77
18000	224.80	220.20	216.30	212.98	210.13	207.69	205.59	203.77	202.19	200.82	199.63	195.61	193.54	192.46
19000	237.28	232.43	228.31	224.81	221.81	219.23	217.01	215.09	213.42	211.98	210.72	206.48	204.29	203.15
20000	249.77	244.66	240.33	236.64	233.48	230.77	228.43	226.41	224.66	223.14	221.82	217.34	215.04	213.84
21000	262.26	256.89	252.35	248.47	245.15	242.31	239.85	237.73	235.89	234.29	232.91	228.21	225.80	224.54
22000	274.75	269.13	264.36	260.30	256.83	253.84	251.27	249.05	247.12	245.45	244.00	239.08	236.55	235.23
23000	287.24	281.36	276.38	272.13	268.50	265.38	262.69	260.37	258.36	256.61	255.09	249.94	247.30	245.92
24000	299.73	293.59	288.39	283.97	280.18	276.92	274.11	271.69	269.59	267.76	266.18	260.81	258.05	256.61
25000	312.21	305.83	300.41	295.80	291.85	288.46	285.54	283.01	280.82	278.92	277.27	271.68	268.80	267.30
26000	324.70	318.06	312.43	307.63	303.52	300.00	296.96	294.33	292.05	290.08	288.36	282.55	279.56	278.00
27000	337.19	330.29	324.44	319.46	315.20	311.53	308.38	305.65	303.29	301.23	299.45	293.41	290.31	288.69
28000	349.68	342.52	336.46	331.29	326.87	323.07	319.80	316.97	314.52	312.39	310.54	304.28	301.06	299.38
29000	362.17	354.76	348.48	343.12	338.54	334.61	331.22	328.29	325.75	323.55	321.63	315.15	311.81	310.07
30000	374.66	366.99	360.49	354.96	350.22	346.15	342.64	339.61	336.98	334.70	332.72	326.01	322.56	320.76
31000	387.14	379.22	372.51	366.79	361.89	357.69	354.06	350.93	348.22	345.86	343.81	336.88	333.32	331.46
32000	399.63	391.46	384.52	378.62	373.57	369.22	365.48	362.25	359.45	357.02	354.90	347.75	344.07	342.15
33000	412.12	403.69	396.54	390.45	385.24	380.76	376.90	373.57	370.68	368.17	365.99	358.61	354.82	352.84
34000	424.61	415.92	408.56	402.28	396.91	392.30	388.33	384.89	381.91	379.33	377.08	369.48	365.57	363.53
35000	437.10	428.15	420.57	414.11	408.59	403.84	399.75	396.21	393.15	390.49	388.17	380.35	376.32	374.22
36000	449.59	440.39	432.59	425.95	420.26	415.38	411.17	407.53	404.38	401.64	399.26	391.21	387.08	384.92
37000	462.07	452.62	444.61	437.78	431.93	426.92	422.59	418.85	415.61	412.80	410.35	402.08	397.83	395.61
38000	474.56	464.85	456.62	449.61	443.61	438.45	434.01	430.17	426.84	423.96	421.44	412.95	408.58	406.30
39000	487.05	477.09	468.64	461.44	455.28	449.99	445.43	441.49	438.08	435.11	432.54	423.82	419.33	416.99
40000	499.54	489.32	480.65	473.27	466.96	461.53	456.85	452.81	449.31	446.27	443.63	434.68	430.08	427.68
41000	512.03	501.55	492.67	485.10	478.63	473.07	468.27	464.13	460.54	457.43	454.72	445.55	440.84	438.38
42000	524.52	513.78	504.69	496.94	490.30	484.61	479.70	475.45	471.77	468.58	465.81	456.42	451.59	449.07
43000	537.00	526.02	516.70	508.77	501.98	496.14	491.12	486.77	483.01	479.74	476.90	467.28	462.34	459.76
44000	549.49	538.25	528.72	520.60	513.65	507.68	502.54	498.09	494.24	490.90	487.99	478.15	473.09	470.45
45000	561.98	550.48	540.74	532.43	525.32	519.22	513.96	509.41	505.47	502.05	499.08	489.02	483.84	481.14
46000	574.47	562.72	552.75	544.26	537.00	530.76	525.38	520.73	516.71	513.21	510.17	499.88	494.60	491.84
47000	586.96	574.95	564.77	556.09	548.67	542.30	536.80	532.05	527.94	524.37	521.26	510.75	505.35	502.53
48000	599.45	587.18	576.78	567.93	560.35	553.83	548.22	543.37	539.17	535.52	532.35	521.62	516.10	513.22
49000	611.94	599.41	588.80	579.76	572.02	565.37	559.64	554.69	550.40	546.68	543.44	532.48	526.85	523.91
50000	624.42	611.65	600.82	591.59	583.69	576.91	571.07	566.01	561.64	557.84	554.53	543.35	537.60	534.60
55000	686.87	672.81	660.90	650.75	642.06	634.60	628.17	622.61	617.80	613.62	609.98	597.69	591.36	588.06
60000	749.31	733.97	720.98	709.91	700.43	692.29	685.28	679.21	673.96	669.40	665.44	652.02	645.12	641.52
65000	811.75	795.14	781.06	769.07	758.80	749.98	742.38	735.82	730.13	725.19	720.89	706.36	698.88	694.98
70000	874.19	856.30	841.14	828.22	817.17	807.67	799.49	792.42	786.29	780.97	776.34	760.69	752.64	748.44
75000	936.63	917.47	901.22	887.38	875.54	865.36	856.60	849.02	842.45	836.75	831.79	815.02	806.40	801.90
80000	999.07	978.63	961.30	946.54	933.91	923.05	913.70	905.62	898.61	892.53	887.25	869.36	860.16	855.36
85000	1061.52	1039.80	1021.39	1005.70	992.28	980.74	970.81	962.22	954.78	948.32	942.70	923.69	913.92	908.82
90000	1123.96	1100.96	1081.47	1064.86	1050.64	1038.44	1027.91	1018.82	1010.94	1004.10	998.15	978.03	967.68	962.28
95000	1186.40	1162.12	1141.55	1124.02	1109.01	1096.13	1085.02	1075.42	1067.10	1059.88	1053.60	1032.36	1021.44	1015.74
100000	1248.84	1223.29	1201.63	1183.17	1167.38	1153.82	1142.13	1132.02	1123.27	1115.67	1109.06	1086.70	1075.20	1069.20

MONTHLY PAYMENT
REQUIRED TO AMORTIZE A LOAN

TERM AMOUNT	1 Year	2 Years	3 Years	4 Years	5 Years	6 Years	7 Years	8 Years	9 Years	10 Years	11 Years	12 Years	13 Years	14 Years
5	.45	.24	.17	.14	.12	.10	.10	.09	.08	.00	.08	.07	.07	.07
10	.90	.48	.34	.27	.23	.20	.19	.17	.16	.15	.15	.14	.14	.13
15	1.34	.72	.51	.41	.34	.30	.28	.26	.24	.23	.22	.21	.20	.20
25	2.24	1.19	.84	.67	.57	.50	.46	.42	.40	.38	.36	.35	.33	.33
50	4.47	2.38	1.68	1.34	1.14	1.00	.91	.84	.79	.75	.71	.69	.66	.65
75	6.70	3.56	2.52	2.01	1.70	1.50	1.36	1.26	1.18	1.12	1.07	1.03	.99	.97
100	8.93	4.75	3.36	2.68	2.27	2.00	1.81	1.67	1.57	1.49	1.42	1.37	1.32	1.29
200	17.85	9.49	6.72	5.35	4.54	4.00	3.62	3.34	3.13	2.97	2.84	2.73	2.64	2.57
300	26.77	14.24	10.08	8.02	6.80	6.00	5.43	5.01	4.70	4.45	4.25	4.09	3.96	3.85
400	35.69	18.98	13.44	10.70	9.07	7.99	7.24	6.60	6.24	5.93	5.67	5.45	5.28	5.13
500	44.62	23.73	16.80	13.37	11.33	9.99	9.05	8.35	7.82	7.41	7.08	6.82	6.60	6.42
600	53.54	28.47	20.16	16.04	13.60	11.99	10.86	10.02	9.39	8.89	8.50	8.18	7.92	7.70
700	62.46	33.22	23.52	18.71	15.86	13.98	12.66	11.69	10.95	10.37	9.91	9.54	9.24	8.98
800	71.38	37.96	26.88	21.39	18.13	15.98	14.47	13.36	12.52	11.86	11.33	10.90	10.55	10.26
900	80.31	42.71	30.24	24.06	20.39	17.98	16.28	15.03	14.08	13.34	12.74	12.27	11.87	11.55
1000	89.23	47.45	33.60	26.73	22.66	19.97	18.09	16.70	15.64	14.82	14.16	13.63	13.19	12.83
2000	178.45	94.90	67.20	53.46	45.31	39.94	36.17	33.40	31.28	29.63	28.32	27.25	26.38	25.65
3000	267.68	142.35	100.80	80.19	67.96	59.91	54.26	50.09	46.92	44.45	42.47	40.87	39.56	38.48
4000	356.90	189.80	134.40	106.92	90.61	79.88	72.34	66.79	62.56	59.26	56.63	54.50	52.75	51.30
5000	446.12	237.24	167.99	133.65	113.26	99.85	90.42	83.48	78.20	74.07	70.78	68.12	65.93	64.12
6000	535.35	284.69	201.59	160.38	135.91	119.82	108.51	100.18	93.84	88.89	84.94	81.74	79.12	76.95
7000	624.57	332.14	235.19	187.10	158.56	139.79	126.59	116.87	109.48	103.70	99.09	95.36	92.31	89.77
8000	713.79	379.59	268.79	213.83	181.21	159.75	144.67	133.57	125.12	118.51	113.25	108.99	105.49	102.60
9000	803.02	427.04	302.38	240.56	203.86	179.72	162.76	150.27	140.75	133.33	127.40	122.61	118.68	115.42
10000	892.24	474.48	335.98	267.29	226.51	199.69	180.84	166.96	156.39	148.14	141.56	136.23	131.86	128.24
11000	981.46	521.93	369.58	294.02	249.16	219.66	198.92	183.66	172.03	162.95	155.72	149.86	145.05	141.07
12000	1070.69	569.38	403.18	320.75	271.81	239.63	217.01	200.35	187.67	177.77	169.87	163.48	158.24	153.89
13000	1159.91	616.83	436.78	347.47	294.47	259.60	235.09	217.05	203.31	192.58	184.03	177.10	171.42	166.71
14000	1249.13	664.28	470.37	374.20	317.12	279.57	253.17	233.74	218.95	207.39	198.18	190.72	184.61	179.54
15000	1338.36	711.72	503.97	400.93	339.77	299.54	271.26	250.44	234.59	222.21	212.34	204.35	197.79	192.36
16000	1427.58	759.17	537.57	427.66	362.42	319.50	289.34	267.13	250.23	237.02	226.49	217.97	210.98	205.19
17000	1516.80	806.62	571.17	454.39	385.07	339.47	307.42	283.83	265.87	251.83	240.65	231.59	224.17	218.01
18000	1606.03	854.07	604.76	481.12	407.72	359.44	325.51	300.53	281.50	266.65	254.80	245.22	237.35	230.83
19000	1695.25	901.52	638.36	507.84	430.37	379.41	343.59	317.22	297.14	281.46	268.96	258.84	250.54	243.66
20000	1784.47	948.96	671.96	534.57	453.02	399.38	361.67	333.92	312.78	296.27	283.11	272.46	263.72	256.48
21000	1873.70	996.41	705.56	561.30	475.67	419.35	379.76	350.61	328.42	311.09	297.27	286.08	276.91	269.31
22000	1962.92	1043.86	739.15	588.03	498.32	439.32	397.84	367.31	344.06	325.90	311.43	299.71	290.10	282.13
23000	2052.14	1091.31	772.75	614.76	520.97	459.29	415.92	384.00	359.70	340.71	325.58	313.33	303.28	294.95
24000	2141.37	1138.76	806.35	641.49	543.62	479.25	434.01	400.70	375.34	355.53	339.74	326.95	316.47	307.78
25000	2230.59	1186.20	839.95	668.21	566.28	499.22	452.09	417.39	390.98	370.34	353.89	340.57	329.65	320.60
26000	2319.82	1233.65	873.55	694.94	588.93	519.19	470.17	434.09	406.62	385.15	368.05	354.20	342.84	333.42
27000	2409.04	1281.10	907.14	721.67	611.58	539.16	488.26	450.79	422.25	399.97	382.20	367.82	356.02	346.25
28000	2498.26	1328.55	940.74	748.40	634.23	559.13	506.34	467.48	437.89	414.78	396.36	381.44	369.21	359.07
29000	2587.49	1376.00	974.34	775.13	656.88	579.10	524.42	484.18	453.53	429.59	410.51	395.07	382.40	371.90
30000	2676.71	1423.44	1007.94	801.86	679.53	599.07	542.51	500.87	469.17	444.41	424.67	408.69	395.58	384.72
31000	2765.93	1470.89	1041.53	828.58	702.18	619.03	560.59	517.57	484.81	459.22	438.82	422.31	408.77	397.54
32000	2855.16	1518.34	1075.13	855.31	724.83	639.00	578.67	534.26	500.45	474.03	452.98	435.93	421.95	410.37
33000	2944.38	1565.79	1108.73	882.04	747.48	658.97	596.76	550.96	516.09	488.85	467.14	449.56	435.14	423.19
34000	3033.60	1613.23	1142.33	908.77	770.13	678.94	614.84	567.65	531.73	503.66	481.29	463.18	448.33	436.02
35000	3122.83	1660.68	1175.92	935.50	792.78	698.91	632.92	584.35	547.36	518.47	495.45	476.80	461.51	448.84
36000	3212.05	1708.13	1209.52	962.23	815.43	718.88	651.01	601.05	563.00	533.29	509.60	490.43	474.70	461.66
37000	3301.27	1755.58	1243.12	988.95	838.09	738.85	669.09	617.74	578.64	548.10	523.76	504.05	487.88	474.49
38000	3390.50	1803.03	1276.72	1015.68	860.74	758.82	687.17	634.44	594.28	562.91	537.91	517.67	501.07	487.31
39000	3479.72	1850.47	1310.32	1042.41	883.39	778.78	705.26	651.13	609.92	577.73	552.07	531.29	514.26	500.13
40000	3568.94	1897.92	1343.91	1069.14	906.04	798.75	723.34	667.83	625.56	592.54	566.22	544.92	527.44	512.96
41000	3658.17	1945.37	1377.51	1095.87	928.69	818.72	741.42	684.52	641.20	607.35	580.38	558.54	540.63	525.78
42000	3747.39	1992.82	1411.11	1122.60	951.34	838.69	759.51	701.22	656.84	622.17	594.53	572.16	553.81	538.61
43000	3836.61	2040.27	1444.71	1149.32	973.99	858.66	777.59	717.91	672.48	636.98	608.69	585.78	567.00	551.43
44000	3925.84	2087.71	1478.30	1176.05	996.64	878.63	795.67	734.61	688.11	651.79	622.85	599.41	580.19	564.25
45000	4015.06	2135.16	1511.90	1202.78	1019.29	898.60	813.76	751.31	703.75	666.61	637.00	613.03	593.37	577.08
46000	4104.28	2182.61	1545.50	1229.51	1041.94	918.57	831.84	768.00	719.39	681.42	651.16	626.65	606.56	589.90
47000	4193.51	2230.06	1579.10	1256.24	1064.59	938.53	849.93	784.70	735.03	696.23	665.31	640.28	619.74	602.73
48000	4282.73	2277.51	1612.69	1282.97	1087.24	958.50	868.01	801.39	750.67	711.05	679.47	653.90	632.93	615.55
49000	4371.96	2324.95	1646.29	1309.69	1109.90	978.47	886.09	818.09	766.31	725.86	693.62	667.52	646.11	628.37
50000	4461.18	2372.40	1679.89	1336.42	1132.55	998.44	904.18	834.78	781.95	740.67	707.78	681.14	659.30	641.20
55000	4907.30	2609.64	1847.88	1470.06	1245.80	1098.28	994.59	918.26	860.14	814.74	778.56	749.26	725.23	705.32
60000	5353.41	2846.88	2015.87	1603.71	1359.05	1198.13	1085.01	1001.74	938.34	888.81	849.33	817.37	791.16	769.43
65000	5799.53	3084.12	2183.86	1737.35	1472.31	1297.97	1175.43	1085.22	1016.53	962.87	920.11	885.49	857.09	833.55
70000	6245.65	3321.36	2351.84	1870.99	1585.56	1397.81	1265.84	1168.70	1094.72	1036.94	990.89	953.60	923.02	897.67
75000	6691.77	3558.60	2519.83	2004.63	1698.82	1497.66	1356.26	1252.17	1172.92	1111.01	1061.66	1021.71	988.95	961.79
80000	7137.88	3795.84	2687.82	2138.27	1812.07	1597.50	1446.68	1335.65	1251.11	1185.07	1132.44	1089.83	1054.88	1025.91
85000	7584.00	4033.08	2855.81	2271.91	1925.32	1697.34	1537.09	1419.13	1329.31	1259.14	1203.22	1157.94	1120.81	1090.03
90000	8030.12	4270.32	3023.80	2405.56	2038.58	1797.19	1627.51	1502.61	1407.50	1333.21	1274.00	1226.06	1186.74	1154.15
95000	8476.24	4507.56	3191.79	2539.20	2151.83	1897.03	1717.93	1586.09	1485.70	1407.27	1344.77	1294.17	1252.67	1218.27
100000	8922.35	4744.80	3359.78	2672.84	2265.09	1996.88	1808.35	1669.56	1563.89	1481.34	1415.55	1362.28	1318.60	1282.39

TERM	15 Years	16 Years	17 Years	18 Years	19 Years	20 Years	21 Years	22 Years	23 Years	24 Years	25 Years	30 Years	35 Years	40 Years
AMOUNT														
5	.07	.07	.07	.06	.06	.06	.06	.06	.06	.06	.06	.06	.06	.06
10	.13	.13	.13	.12	.12	.12	.12	.12	.12	.12	.12	.11	.11	.11
15	.19	.19	.19	.18	.18	.18	.18	.18	.17	.17	.17	.17	.17	.17
25	.32	.31	.31	.30	.30	.29	.29	.29	.29	.28	.28	.28	.27	.27
50	.63	.62	.61	.60	.59	.58	.58	.57	.57	.56	.56	.55	.54	.54
75	.94	.92	.91	.89	.88	.87	.86	.86	.85	.84	.84	.82	.81	.81
100	1.26	1.23	1.21	1.19	1.18	1.16	1.15	1.14	1.13	1.12	1.12	1.10	1.08	1.08
200	2.51	2.46	2.42	2.38	2.35	2.32	2.30	2.28	2.26	2.24	2.23	2.19	2.16	2.15
300	3.76	3.68	3.62	3.56	3.52	3.48	3.44	3.41	3.39	3.36	3.34	3.28	3.24	3.22
400	5.01	4.91	4.83	4.75	4.69	4.63	4.59	4.55	4.51	4.48	4.46	4.37	4.32	4.30
500	6.27	6.14	6.03	5.94	5.86	5.79	5.73	5.68	5.64	5.60	5.57	5.46	5.40	5.37
600	7.52	7.36	7.24	7.12	7.03	6.95	6.88	6.82	6.77	6.72	6.68	6.55	6.48	6.44
700	8.77	8.59	8.44	8.31	8.20	8.11	8.02	7.95	7.89	7.84	7.79	7.64	7.56	7.52
800	10.02	9.82	9.65	9.50	9.37	9.26	9.17	9.09	9.02	8.96	8.91	8.73	8.64	8.59
900	11.27	11.04	10.85	10.68	10.54	10.42	10.32	10.23	10.15	10.08	10.02	9.82	9.72	9.66
1000	12.53	12.27	12.06	11.87	11.71	11.58	11.46	11.36	11.27	11.20	11.13	10.91	10.80	10.74
2000	25.05	24.54	24.11	23.74	23.42	23.15	22.92	22.72	22.54	22.39	22.26	21.82	21.59	21.47
3000	37.57	36.80	36.16	35.60	35.13	34.73	34.38	34.07	33.81	33.59	33.39	32.72	32.38	32.20
4000	50.09	49.07	48.21	47.47	46.84	46.30	45.83	45.43	45.08	44.78	44.52	43.63	43.17	42.94
5000	62.61	61.34	60.26	59.34	58.55	57.87	57.29	56.79	56.35	55.97	55.65	54.53	53.96	53.67
6000	75.13	73.60	72.31	71.20	70.26	69.45	68.75	68.14	67.62	67.17	66.77	65.44	64.76	64.40
7000	87.65	85.87	84.36	83.07	81.97	81.02	80.20	79.50	78.89	78.36	77.90	76.35	75.55	75.13
8000	100.17	98.13	96.41	94.93	93.67	92.59	91.66	90.86	90.16	89.56	89.03	87.25	86.34	85.87
9000	112.69	110.40	108.46	106.80	105.38	104.17	103.12	102.21	101.43	100.75	100.16	98.16	97.13	96.60
10000	125.22	122.67	120.51	118.67	117.09	115.74	114.58	113.57	112.70	111.94	111.29	109.06	107.92	107.33
11000	137.74	134.93	132.56	130.53	128.80	127.31	126.03	124.93	123.97	123.14	122.41	119.97	118.72	118.06
12000	150.26	147.20	144.61	142.40	140.51	138.89	137.49	136.28	135.24	134.33	133.54	130.88	129.51	128.80
13000	162.70	159.47	156.66	154.26	152.22	150.46	148.95	147.64	146.51	145.52	144.67	141.78	140.30	139.53
14000	175.30	171.73	168.71	166.13	163.93	162.03	160.40	159.00	157.78	156.72	155.80	152.69	151.09	150.26
15000	187.82	184.00	180.76	178.00	175.64	173.61	171.86	170.35	169.05	167.91	166.93	163.59	161.88	160.99
16000	200.34	196.26	192.81	189.86	187.34	185.18	183.32	181.71	180.32	179.11	178.05	174.50	172.68	171.73
17000	212.86	208.53	204.86	201.73	199.05	196.76	194.78	193.07	191.58	190.30	189.18	185.41	183.47	182.46
18000	225.38	220.80	216.91	213.60	210.76	208.33	206.23	204.42	202.85	201.49	200.31	196.31	194.26	193.19
19000	237.91	233.06	228.96	225.46	222.47	219.90	217.69	215.78	214.12	212.69	211.44	207.22	205.05	203.92
20000	250.43	245.33	241.01	237.33	234.18	231.48	229.15	227.14	225.39	223.88	222.57	218.12	215.84	214.66
21000	262.95	257.59	253.06	249.19	245.89	243.05	240.60	238.49	236.66	235.07	233.69	229.03	226.64	225.39
22000	275.47	269.86	265.11	261.06	257.60	254.62	252.06	249.85	247.93	246.27	244.82	239.93	237.43	236.12
23000	287.99	282.13	277.16	272.93	269.31	266.20	263.52	261.20	259.20	257.46	255.95	250.84	248.22	246.85
24000	300.51	294.39	289.21	284.79	281.01	277.77	274.98	272.56	270.47	268.66	267.08	261.75	259.01	257.59
25000	313.03	306.66	301.26	296.66	292.72	289.34	286.43	283.92	281.74	279.85	278.21	272.65	269.80	268.32
26000	325.55	318.93	313.31	308.52	304.43	300.92	297.89	295.27	293.01	291.04	289.33	283.56	280.59	279.05
27000	338.07	331.19	325.36	320.39	316.14	312.49	309.35	306.63	304.28	302.24	300.46	294.46	291.39	289.78
28000	350.60	343.46	337.41	332.26	327.85	324.06	320.80	317.99	315.55	313.43	311.59	305.37	302.18	300.52
29000	363.12	355.72	349.46	344.12	339.56	335.64	332.26	329.34	326.82	324.62	322.72	316.28	312.97	311.25
30000	375.64	367.99	361.51	355.99	351.27	347.21	343.72	340.70	338.09	335.82	333.85	327.18	323.76	321.98
31000	388.16	380.26	373.56	367.86	362.98	358.79	355.18	352.06	349.36	347.01	344.97	338.09	334.55	332.71
32000	400.68	392.52	385.61	379.72	374.68	370.36	366.63	363.41	360.63	358.21	356.10	348.99	345.35	343.45
33000	413.20	404.79	397.66	391.59	386.39	381.93	378.09	374.77	371.89	369.40	367.23	359.90	356.14	354.18
34000	425.72	417.05	409.71	403.45	398.10	393.51	389.55	386.13	383.16	380.59	378.36	370.81	366.93	364.91
35000	438.24	429.32	421.76	415.32	409.81	405.08	401.00	397.48	394.43	391.79	389.49	381.71	377.72	375.64
36000	450.76	441.59	433.81	427.19	421.52	416.65	412.46	408.84	405.70	402.98	400.61	392.62	388.51	386.38
37000	463.29	453.85	445.86	439.05	433.23	428.23	423.92	420.20	416.97	414.17	411.74	403.52	399.31	397.11
38000	475.81	466.12	457.91	450.92	444.94	439.80	435.38	431.55	428.24	425.37	422.87	414.43	410.10	407.84
39000	488.33	478.39	469.96	462.78	456.65	451.37	446.83	442.91	439.51	436.56	434.00	425.33	420.89	418.58
40000	500.85	490.65	482.01	474.65	468.35	462.95	458.29	454.27	450.78	447.76	445.13	436.24	431.68	429.31
41000	513.37	502.92	494.06	486.52	480.06	474.52	469.75	465.62	462.05	458.95	456.25	447.15	442.47	440.04
42000	525.89	515.18	506.11	498.38	491.77	486.09	481.20	476.98	473.32	470.14	467.38	458.05	453.27	450.77
43000	538.41	527.45	518.16	510.25	503.48	497.67	492.66	488.33	484.59	481.34	478.51	468.96	464.06	461.51
44000	550.93	539.72	530.21	522.12	515.19	509.24	504.12	499.69	495.86	492.53	489.64	479.86	474.85	472.24
45000	563.45	551.98	542.26	533.98	526.90	520.82	515.58	511.05	507.13	503.72	500.77	490.77	485.64	482.97
46000	575.98	564.25	554.31	545.85	538.61	532.39	527.03	522.40	518.40	514.92	511.89	501.68	496.43	493.70
47000	588.50	576.51	566.36	557.71	550.32	543.96	538.49	533.76	529.67	526.11	523.02	512.58	507.22	504.44
48000	601.02	588.78	578.41	569.58	562.02	555.54	549.95	545.12	540.94	537.31	534.15	523.49	518.02	515.17
49000	613.54	601.05	590.46	581.45	573.73	567.11	561.40	556.47	552.20	548.50	545.28	534.39	528.81	525.90
50000	626.06	613.31	602.51	593.31	585.44	578.68	572.86	567.83	563.47	559.69	556.41	545.30	539.60	536.63
55000	688.67	674.64	662.76	652.64	643.99	636.55	630.15	624.61	619.82	615.66	612.05	599.83	593.56	590.30
60000	751.27	735.97	723.01	711.97	702.53	694.42	687.43	681.40	676.17	671.63	667.69	654.36	647.52	643.96
65000	813.88	797.31	783.26	771.30	761.07	752.29	744.72	738.18	732.51	727.60	723.33	708.89	701.48	697.62
70000	876.48	858.64	843.52	830.64	819.62	810.15	802.00	794.96	788.86	783.57	778.97	763.42	755.44	751.28
75000	939.09	919.97	903.77	889.97	878.16	868.02	859.29	851.74	845.21	839.54	834.61	817.95	809.40	804.95
80000	1001.69	981.30	964.02	949.30	936.70	925.89	916.57	908.53	901.56	895.51	890.25	872.48	863.36	858.61
85000	1064.30	1042.63	1024.27	1008.63	995.25	983.76	973.86	965.31	957.90	951.47	945.89	927.01	917.32	912.27
90000	1126.90	1103.96	1084.52	1067.96	1053.79	1041.63	1031.15	1022.09	1014.25	1007.44	1001.53	981.54	971.28	965.94
95000	1189.51	1165.29	1144.77	1127.29	1112.34	1099.49	1088.43	1078.87	1070.60	1063.41	1057.17	1036.06	1025.24	1019.60
100000	1252.12	1226.62	1205.02	1186.62	1170.88	1157.36	1145.72	1135.66	1126.94	1119.38	1112.81	1090.59	1079.20	1073.26

MONTHLY PAYMENT
REQUIRED TO AMORTIZE A LOAN

TERM AMOUNT	1 Year	2 Years	3 Years	4 Years	5 Years	6 Years	7 Years	8 Years	9 Years	10 Years	11 Years	12 Years	13 Years	14 Years
5	.45	.24	.17	.14	.12	.11	.10	.09	.08	.08	.08	.07	.07	.07
10	.90	.48	.34	.27	.23	.21	.19	.17	.16	.15	.15	.14	.14	.13
15	1.34	.72	.51	.41	.35	.31	.28	.26	.24	.23	.22	.21	.20	.20
25	2.24	1.19	.85	.67	.57	.51	.46	.42	.40	.38	.36	.35	.34	.33
50	4.47	2.38	1.69	1.34	1.14	1.01	.91	.84	.79	.75	.72	.69	.67	.65
75	6.70	3.57	2.53	2.01	1.71	1.51	1.36	1.26	1.18	1.12	1.07	1.03	1.00	.97
100	8.93	4.75	3.37	2.68	2.27	2.01	1.82	1.68	1.57	1.49	1.43	1.37	1.33	1.29
200	17.86	9.50	6.73	5.36	4.54	4.01	3.63	3.35	3.14	2.98	2.85	2.74	2.65	2.58
300	26.78	14.25	10.10	8.03	6.81	6.01	5.44	5.03	4.71	4.46	4.27	4.11	3.97	3.87
400	35.71	19.00	13.46	10.71	9.08	8.01	7.25	6.70	6.28	5.95	5.69	5.47	5.30	5.15
500	44.63	23.75	16.82	13.39	11.35	10.01	9.07	8.37	7.85	7.43	7.11	6.84	6.62	6.44
600	53.56	28.49	20.19	16.06	13.62	12.01	10.88	10.05	9.41	8.92	8.53	8.21	7.94	7.73
700	62.49	33.24	23.55	18.74	15.89	14.01	12.69	11.72	10.98	10.41	9.95	9.57	9.27	9.02
800	71.41	37.99	26.91	21.42	18.16	16.01	14.50	13.39	12.55	11.89	11.37	10.94	10.59	10.30
900	80.34	42.74	30.28	24.09	20.43	18.01	16.32	15.07	14.12	13.38	12.79	12.31	11.91	11.59
1000	89.26	47.49	33.64	26.77	22.69	20.01	18.13	16.74	15.69	14.86	14.21	13.67	13.24	12.88
2000	178.52	94.97	67.27	53.54	45.38	40.02	36.25	33.48	31.37	29.72	28.41	27.34	26.47	25.75
3000	267.78	142.45	100.91	80.30	68.07	60.03	54.38	50.22	47.05	44.58	42.61	41.01	39.70	38.62
4000	357.04	189.94	134.54	107.07	90.76	80.04	72.50	66.95	62.73	59.43	56.81	54.68	52.94	51.49
5000	446.30	237.42	168.17	133.83	113.45	100.05	90.63	83.69	78.41	74.29	71.01	68.35	66.17	64.37
6000	535.56	284.90	201.81	160.60	136.14	120.05	108.75	100.43	94.10	89.15	85.21	82.02	79.40	77.24
7000	624.82	332.39	235.44	187.36	158.83	140.06	126.87	117.17	109.78	104.01	99.41	95.69	92.64	90.11
8000	714.07	379.87	269.08	214.13	181.52	160.07	145.00	133.90	125.46	118.86	113.61	109.36	105.87	102.98
9000	803.33	427.35	302.71	240.89	204.21	180.08	163.12	150.64	141.14	133.72	127.81	123.03	119.10	115.85
10000	892.59	474.84	336.34	267.66	226.90	200.09	181.25	167.38	156.82	148.58	142.01	136.70	132.34	128.73
11000	981.85	522.32	369.98	294.43	249.59	220.10	199.37	184.12	172.51	163.44	156.21	150.36	145.57	141.60
12000	1071.11	569.80	403.61	321.19	272.27	240.10	217.49	200.85	188.19	178.29	170.41	164.03	158.80	154.47
13000	1160.37	617.29	437.24	347.96	294.96	260.11	235.62	217.59	203.87	193.15	184.61	177.70	172.04	167.34
14000	1249.63	664.77	470.88	374.72	317.65	280.12	253.74	234.33	219.55	208.01	198.81	191.37	185.27	180.21
15000	1338.88	712.25	504.51	401.49	340.34	300.13	271.87	251.07	235.23	222.87	213.01	205.04	198.50	193.09
16000	1428.14	759.74	538.15	428.25	363.03	320.14	289.99	267.80	250.91	237.72	227.22	218.71	211.74	205.96
17000	1517.40	807.22	571.78	455.02	385.72	340.14	308.11	284.54	266.60	252.58	241.42	232.38	224.97	218.83
18000	1606.66	854.70	605.41	481.78	408.41	360.15	326.24	301.28	282.28	267.44	255.62	246.05	238.20	231.70
19000	1695.92	902.18	639.05	508.55	431.10	380.16	344.36	318.02	297.96	282.30	269.82	259.72	251.44	244.57
20000	1785.18	949.67	672.68	535.31	453.79	400.17	362.49	334.75	313.64	297.15	284.02	273.39	264.67	257.45
21000	1874.44	997.15	706.31	562.08	476.48	420.18	380.61	351.49	329.32	312.01	298.22	287.05	277.90	270.32
22000	1963.70	1044.63	739.95	588.85	499.17	440.19	398.73	368.23	345.01	326.87	312.42	300.72	291.13	283.19
23000	2052.95	1092.12	773.58	615.61	521.86	460.19	416.86	384.97	360.69	341.73	326.62	314.39	304.37	296.06
24000	2142.21	1139.60	807.22	642.38	544.54	480.20	434.98	401.70	376.37	356.58	340.82	328.06	317.60	308.93
25000	2231.47	1187.08	840.85	669.14	567.23	500.21	453.11	418.44	392.05	371.44	355.02	341.73	330.83	321.81
26000	2320.73	1234.57	874.48	695.91	589.92	520.22	471.23	435.18	407.73	386.30	369.22	355.40	344.07	334.68
27000	2409.99	1282.05	908.12	722.67	612.61	540.23	489.36	451.92	423.41	401.16	383.42	369.07	357.30	347.55
28000	2499.25	1329.53	941.75	749.44	635.30	560.23	507.48	468.65	439.10	416.01	397.62	382.74	370.53	360.42
29000	2588.51	1377.02	975.38	776.20	657.99	580.24	525.60	485.39	454.78	430.87	411.82	396.41	383.77	373.29
30000	2677.76	1424.50	1009.02	802.97	680.68	600.25	543.73	502.13	470.46	445.73	426.02	410.08	397.00	386.17
31000	2767.02	1471.98	1042.65	829.74	703.37	620.26	561.85	518.86	486.14	460.59	440.23	423.74	410.23	399.04
32000	2856.28	1519.47	1076.29	856.50	726.06	640.27	579.98	535.60	501.82	475.44	454.43	437.41	423.47	411.91
33000	2945.54	1566.95	1109.92	883.27	748.75	660.28	598.10	552.34	517.51	490.30	468.63	451.08	436.70	424.78
34000	3034.80	1614.43	1143.55	910.03	771.44	680.28	616.22	569.08	533.19	505.16	482.83	464.75	449.93	437.66
35000	3124.06	1661.91	1177.19	936.80	794.12	700.29	634.35	585.81	548.87	520.02	497.03	478.42	463.17	450.53
36000	3213.32	1709.40	1210.82	963.56	816.81	720.30	652.47	602.55	564.55	534.87	511.23	492.09	476.40	463.40
37000	3302.57	1756.88	1244.45	990.33	839.50	740.31	670.60	619.29	580.23	549.73	525.43	505.76	489.63	476.27
38000	3391.83	1804.36	1278.09	1017.09	862.19	760.32	688.72	636.03	595.91	564.59	539.63	519.43	502.87	489.14
39000	3481.09	1851.85	1311.72	1043.86	884.88	780.32	706.84	652.76	611.60	579.45	553.83	533.10	516.10	502.02
40000	3570.35	1899.33	1345.36	1070.62	907.57	800.33	724.97	669.50	627.28	594.30	568.03	546.77	529.33	514.89
41000	3659.61	1946.81	1378.99	1097.39	930.26	820.34	743.09	686.24	642.96	609.16	582.23	560.44	542.57	527.76
42000	3748.87	1994.30	1412.62	1124.16	952.95	840.35	761.22	702.98	658.64	624.02	596.43	574.10	555.80	540.63
43000	3838.13	2041.78	1446.26	1150.92	975.64	860.36	779.34	719.71	674.32	638.87	610.63	587.77	569.03	553.50
44000	3927.39	2089.26	1479.89	1177.69	998.33	880.37	797.46	736.45	690.01	653.73	624.83	601.44	582.26	566.38
45000	4016.64	2136.75	1513.52	1204.45	1021.02	900.37	815.59	753.19	705.69	668.59	639.03	615.11	595.50	579.25
46000	4105.90	2184.23	1547.16	1231.22	1043.71	920.38	833.71	769.93	721.37	683.45	653.23	628.78	608.73	592.12
47000	4195.16	2231.71	1580.79	1257.98	1066.39	940.39	851.84	786.66	737.05	698.30	667.44	642.45	621.96	604.99
48000	4284.42	2279.20	1614.43	1284.75	1089.08	960.40	869.96	803.40	752.73	713.16	681.64	656.12	635.20	617.86
49000	4373.68	2326.68	1648.06	1311.51	1111.77	980.41	888.08	820.14	768.41	728.02	695.84	669.79	648.43	630.74
50000	4462.94	2374.16	1681.69	1338.28	1134.46	1000.41	906.21	836.88	784.10	742.88	710.04	683.46	661.66	643.61
55000	4909.23	2611.58	1849.86	1472.11	1247.91	1100.46	996.83	920.56	862.51	817.16	781.04	751.80	727.83	707.97
60000	5355.52	2848.99	2018.03	1605.93	1361.35	1200.50	1087.45	1004.25	940.91	891.45	852.04	820.15	794.00	772.33
65000	5801.82	3086.41	2186.20	1739.76	1474.80	1300.54	1178.07	1087.94	1019.32	965.74	923.05	888.49	860.16	836.69
70000	6248.11	3323.82	2354.37	1873.59	1588.24	1400.58	1268.69	1171.62	1097.73	1040.03	994.05	956.84	926.33	901.05
75000	6694.40	3561.24	2522.54	2007.42	1701.69	1500.62	1359.31	1255.31	1176.14	1114.31	1065.05	1025.18	992.49	965.41
80000	7140.70	3798.66	2690.71	2141.24	1815.14	1600.66	1449.93	1339.00	1254.55	1188.60	1136.06	1093.53	1058.66	1029.77
85000	7586.99	4036.07	2858.88	2275.07	1928.58	1700.70	1540.55	1422.69	1332.96	1262.89	1207.06	1161.87	1124.82	1094.13
90000	8033.28	4273.49	3027.04	2408.90	2042.03	1800.74	1631.17	1506.37	1411.37	1337.17	1278.06	1230.22	1190.99	1158.49
95000	8479.58	4510.90	3195.21	2542.73	2155.47	1900.78	1721.79	1590.06	1489.78	1411.46	1349.07	1298.56	1257.16	1222.85
100000	8925.87	4748.32	3363.38	2676.55	2268.92	2000.82	1812.41	1673.75	1568.19	1485.75	1420.07	1366.91	1323.32	1287.21

TERM AMOUNT	15 Years	16 Years	17 Years	18 Years	19 Years	20 Years	21 Years	22 Years	23 Years	24 Years	25 Years	30 Years	35 Years	40 Years
5	.07	.07	.07	.06	.06	.06	.06	.06	.06	.06	.06	.06	.06	.06
10	.13	.13	.13	.12	.12	.12	.12	.12	.12	.12	.12	.11	.11	.11
15	.19	.19	.19	.18	.18	.18	.18	.18	.17	.17	.17	.17	.17	.17
25	.32	.31	.31	.30	.30	.30	.29	.29	.29	.29	.28	.28	.28	.27
50	.63	.62	.61	.60	.59	.59	.58	.58	.57	.57	.56	.55	.55	.54
75	.95	.93	.91	.90	.89	.88	.87	.86	.85	.85	.84	.83	.82	.81
100	1.26	1.24	1.22	1.20	1.18	1.17	1.16	1.15	1.14	1.13	1.12	1.10	1.09	1.08
200	2.52	2.47	2.43	2.39	2.36	2.33	2.31	2.29	2.27	2.25	2.24	2.20	2.18	2.16
300	3.78	3.70	3.64	3.58	3.53	3.49	3.46	3.43	3.40	3.38	3.36	3.29	3.26	3.24
400	5.03	4.93	4.85	4.77	4.71	4.66	4.61	4.57	4.53	4.50	4.48	4.39	4.35	4.32
500	6.29	6.16	6.06	5.96	5.89	5.82	5.76	5.71	5.67	5.63	5.60	5.49	5.43	5.40
600	7.55	7.39	7.27	7.16	7.06	6.98	6.91	6.85	6.80	6.75	6.72	6.58	6.52	6.48
700	8.80	8.63	8.48	8.35	8.24	8.14	8.06	7.99	7.93	7.88	7.83	7.68	7.60	7.56
800	10.06	9.86	9.69	9.54	9.41	9.31	9.21	9.13	9.06	9.00	8.95	8.78	8.69	8.64
900	11.32	11.09	10.90	10.73	10.59	10.47	10.36	10.27	10.20	10.13	10.07	9.87	9.77	9.72
1000	12.58	12.32	12.11	11.92	11.77	11.63	11.52	11.42	11.33	11.25	11.19	10.97	10.86	10.80
2000	25.15	24.64	24.21	23.84	23.53	23.26	23.03	22.83	22.65	22.50	22.37	21.93	21.71	21.59
3000	37.72	36.95	36.31	35.76	35.29	34.89	34.54	34.24	33.98	33.75	33.56	32.90	32.56	32.39
4000	50.29	49.27	48.41	47.68	47.05	46.51	46.05	45.65	45.30	45.00	44.74	43.86	43.41	43.18
5000	62.86	61.59	60.51	59.59	58.81	58.14	57.56	57.06	56.63	56.25	55.93	54.83	54.26	53.97
6000	75.43	73.90	72.61	71.51	70.57	69.77	69.07	68.47	67.95	67.50	67.11	65.79	65.12	64.77
7000	88.00	86.22	84.71	83.43	82.33	81.39	80.58	79.88	79.28	78.75	78.30	76.76	75.97	75.56
8000	100.57	98.53	96.81	95.35	94.10	93.02	92.09	91.29	90.60	90.00	89.48	87.72	86.82	86.35
9000	113.14	110.85	108.91	107.27	105.86	104.65	103.60	102.70	101.93	101.25	100.66	98.68	97.67	97.15
10000	125.71	123.17	121.02	119.18	117.62	116.27	115.12	114.12	113.25	112.50	111.85	109.65	108.52	107.94
11000	138.28	135.48	133.12	131.10	129.38	127.90	126.63	125.53	124.58	123.75	123.03	120.61	119.38	118.73
12000	150.85	147.80	145.22	143.02	141.14	139.53	138.14	136.94	135.90	135.00	134.22	131.58	130.23	129.53
13000	163.42	160.12	157.32	154.94	152.90	151.15	149.65	148.35	147.22	146.25	145.40	142.54	141.08	140.32
14000	175.99	172.43	169.42	166.86	164.66	162.78	161.16	159.76	158.55	157.50	156.59	153.51	151.93	151.11
15000	188.56	184.75	181.52	178.77	176.42	174.41	172.67	171.17	169.87	168.75	167.77	164.47	162.78	161.91
16000	201.13	197.06	193.62	190.69	188.19	186.03	184.18	182.58	181.20	180.00	178.95	175.44	173.64	172.70
17000	213.70	209.38	205.72	202.61	199.95	197.66	195.69	193.99	192.52	191.25	190.14	186.40	184.49	183.49
18000	226.27	221.70	217.82	214.53	211.71	209.29	207.20	205.40	203.85	202.50	201.32	197.36	195.34	194.29
19000	238.84	234.01	229.93	226.45	223.47	220.91	218.72	216.82	215.17	213.75	212.51	208.33	206.19	205.08
20000	251.41	246.33	242.03	238.36	235.23	232.54	230.23	228.23	226.50	225.00	223.69	219.29	217.04	215.88
21000	263.98	258.65	254.13	250.28	246.99	244.17	241.74	239.64	237.82	236.25	234.88	230.26	227.89	226.67
22000	276.55	270.96	266.23	262.20	258.75	255.80	253.25	251.05	249.15	247.49	246.06	241.22	238.75	237.46
23000	289.12	283.28	278.33	274.12	270.51	267.42	264.76	262.46	260.47	258.74	257.24	252.19	249.60	248.26
24000	301.69	295.59	290.43	286.03	282.28	279.05	276.27	273.87	271.79	269.99	268.43	263.15	260.45	259.05
25000	314.26	307.91	302.53	297.95	294.04	290.68	287.78	285.28	283.12	281.24	279.61	274.11	271.30	269.84
26000	326.83	320.23	314.63	309.87	305.80	302.30	299.29	296.69	294.44	292.49	290.80	285.08	282.15	280.64
27000	339.40	332.54	326.73	321.79	317.56	313.93	310.80	308.10	305.77	303.74	301.98	296.04	293.01	291.43
28000	351.97	344.86	338.84	333.71	329.32	325.56	322.31	319.52	317.09	314.99	313.17	307.01	303.86	302.22
29000	364.54	357.18	350.94	345.62	341.08	337.18	333.83	330.93	328.42	326.24	324.35	317.97	314.71	313.02
30000	377.11	369.49	363.04	357.54	352.84	348.81	345.34	342.34	339.74	337.49	335.54	328.94	325.56	323.81
31000	389.68	381.81	375.14	369.46	364.60	360.44	356.85	353.75	351.07	348.74	346.72	339.90	336.41	334.60
32000	402.25	394.12	387.24	381.38	376.37	372.06	368.36	365.16	362.39	359.99	357.90	350.87	347.27	345.40
33000	414.82	406.44	399.34	393.30	388.13	383.69	379.87	376.57	373.72	371.24	369.09	361.83	358.12	356.19
34000	427.39	418.76	411.44	405.21	399.89	395.32	391.38	387.98	385.04	382.49	380.27	372.79	368.97	366.98
35000	439.96	431.07	423.54	417.13	411.65	406.94	402.89	399.39	396.37	393.74	391.46	383.76	379.82	377.78
36000	452.54	443.39	435.64	429.05	423.41	418.57	414.40	410.80	407.69	404.99	402.64	394.72	390.67	388.57
37000	465.11	455.71	447.74	440.97	435.17	430.20	425.91	422.22	419.01	416.24	413.83	405.69	401.52	399.36
38000	477.68	468.02	459.85	452.89	446.93	441.82	437.43	433.63	430.34	427.49	425.01	416.65	412.38	410.16
39000	490.25	480.34	471.95	464.80	458.69	453.45	448.94	445.04	441.66	438.74	436.19	427.62	423.23	420.95
40000	502.82	492.65	484.05	476.72	470.46	465.08	460.45	456.45	452.99	449.99	447.38	438.58	434.08	431.75
41000	515.39	504.97	496.15	488.64	482.22	476.70	471.96	467.86	464.31	461.24	458.56	449.54	444.93	442.54
42000	527.96	517.29	508.25	500.56	493.98	488.33	483.47	479.27	475.64	472.49	469.75	460.51	455.78	453.33
43000	540.53	529.60	520.35	512.47	505.74	499.96	494.98	490.68	486.96	483.74	480.93	471.47	466.64	464.13
44000	553.10	541.92	532.45	524.39	517.50	511.59	506.49	502.09	498.29	494.98	492.12	482.44	477.49	474.92
45000	565.67	554.24	544.55	536.31	529.26	523.21	518.00	513.50	509.61	506.23	503.30	493.40	488.34	485.71
46000	578.24	566.55	556.65	548.23	541.02	534.84	529.51	524.92	520.94	517.48	514.48	504.37	499.19	496.51
47000	590.81	578.87	568.76	560.15	552.78	546.47	541.02	536.33	532.26	528.73	525.67	515.33	510.04	507.30
48000	603.38	591.18	580.86	572.06	564.55	558.09	552.54	547.74	543.58	539.98	536.85	526.30	520.90	518.09
49000	615.95	603.50	592.96	583.98	576.31	569.72	564.05	559.15	554.91	551.23	548.04	537.26	531.75	528.89
50000	628.52	615.82	605.06	595.90	588.07	581.35	575.56	570.56	566.23	562.48	559.22	548.22	542.60	539.68
55000	691.37	677.40	665.56	655.49	646.87	639.48	633.11	627.62	622.86	618.73	615.14	603.05	596.86	593.65
60000	754.22	738.98	726.07	715.08	705.68	697.61	690.67	684.67	679.48	674.98	671.07	657.87	651.12	647.62
65000	817.07	800.56	786.57	774.67	764.49	755.75	748.22	741.73	736.10	731.22	726.99	712.69	705.38	701.58
70000	879.92	862.14	847.08	834.26	823.29	813.88	805.78	798.78	792.73	787.47	782.91	767.51	759.64	755.55
75000	942.78	923.72	907.59	893.85	882.10	872.02	863.33	855.84	849.35	843.72	838.83	822.33	813.90	809.52
80000	1005.63	985.30	968.09	953.44	940.91	930.15	920.89	912.89	905.97	899.97	894.75	877.16	868.16	863.49
85000	1068.48	1046.89	1028.60	1013.03	999.71	988.28	978.44	969.95	962.59	956.22	950.67	931.98	922.41	917.45
90000	1131.33	1108.47	1089.10	1072.62	1058.52	1046.42	1036.00	1027.00	1019.22	1012.46	1006.60	986.80	976.67	971.42
95000	1194.18	1170.05	1149.61	1132.21	1117.32	1104.55	1093.56	1084.06	1075.84	1068.71	1062.52	1041.62	1030.93	1025.39
100000	1257.03	1231.63	1210.11	1191.79	1176.13	1162.69	1151.11	1141.11	1132.46	1124.96	1118.44	1096.44	1085.19	1079.36

MONTHLY PAYMENT
REQUIRED TO AMORTIZE A LOAN

TERM / AMOUNT	1 Year	2 Years	3 Years	4 Years	5 Years	6 Years	7 Years	8 Years	9 Years	10 Years	11 Years	12 Years	13 Years	14 Years
5	.45	.24	.17	.14	.12	.11	.10	.09	.08	.08	.08	.07	.07	.07
10	.90	.48	.34	.27	.23	.21	.19	.17	.16	.15	.15	.14	.14	.13
15	1.34	.72	.51	.41	.35	.31	.28	.26	.24	.23	.22	.21	.20	.20
25	2.24	1.19	.85	.67	.57	.51	.46	.42	.40	.38	.36	.35	.34	.33
50	4.47	2.38	1.69	1.34	1.14	1.01	.91	.84	.79	.75	.72	.69	.67	.65
75	6.70	3.57	2.53	2.01	1.71	1.51	1.37	1.26	1.18	1.12	1.07	1.03	1.00	.97
100	8.93	4.75	3.37	2.68	2.28	2.01	1.82	1.68	1.57	1.49	1.43	1.37	1.33	1.29
200	17.86	9.50	6.73	5.36	4.55	4.01	3.63	3.36	3.14	2.98	2.85	2.74	2.65	2.58
300	26.79	14.25	10.10	8.04	6.82	6.01	5.45	5.03	4.71	4.47	4.27	4.11	3.98	3.87
400	35.71	19.00	13.46	10.70	9.09	8.01	7.26	6.71	6.28	5.95	5.69	5.48	5.30	5.16
500	44.64	23.75	16.83	13.39	11.36	10.02	9.07	8.38	7.85	7.44	7.11	6.85	6.63	6.45
600	53.57	28.50	20.19	16.07	13.63	12.02	10.89	10.06	9.42	8.93	8.53	8.22	7.95	7.74
700	62.49	33.25	23.56	18.75	15.90	14.02	12.70	11.73	10.99	10.42	9.96	9.58	9.28	9.03
800	71.42	38.00	26.92	21.43	18.17	16.02	14.52	13.41	12.56	11.90	11.38	10.95	10.60	10.32
900	80.35	42.75	30.29	24.11	20.44	18.02	16.33	15.08	14.13	13.39	12.80	12.32	11.93	11.60
1000	89.28	47.50	33.65	26.78	22.71	20.03	18.14	16.76	15.70	14.88	14.22	13.69	13.25	12.89
2000	178.55	94.99	67.30	53.56	45.41	40.05	36.28	33.51	31.40	29.75	28.44	27.37	26.50	25.78
3000	267.82	142.49	100.94	80.34	68.11	60.07	54.42	50.26	47.09	44.62	42.65	41.06	39.75	38.67
4000	357.09	189.98	134.59	107.12	90.81	80.09	72.56	67.01	62.79	59.49	56.87	54.74	53.00	51.56
5000	446.36	237.48	168.23	133.89	113.51	100.11	90.69	83.76	78.49	74.37	71.08	68.43	66.25	64.45
6000	535.63	284.97	201.88	160.67	136.22	120.13	108.83	100.51	94.18	89.24	85.30	82.11	79.50	77.33
7000	624.90	332.47	235.53	187.45	158.92	140.15	126.97	117.26	109.88	104.11	99.52	95.80	92.75	90.22
8000	714.17	379.96	269.17	214.23	181.62	160.18	145.11	134.02	125.57	118.98	113.73	109.48	106.00	103.11
9000	803.44	427.46	302.82	241.01	204.32	180.20	163.24	150.77	141.27	133.85	127.95	123.17	119.25	116.00
10000	892.71	474.95	336.46	267.78	227.02	200.22	181.38	167.52	156.97	148.73	142.16	136.85	132.49	128.89
11000	981.98	522.45	370.11	294.56	249.73	220.24	199.52	184.27	172.66	163.60	156.38	150.53	145.74	141.77
12000	1071.25	569.94	403.75	321.34	272.43	240.26	217.66	201.02	188.36	178.47	170.59	164.22	158.99	154.66
13000	1160.52	617.44	437.40	348.12	295.13	260.28	235.79	217.77	204.06	193.34	184.81	177.90	172.24	167.55
14000	1249.79	664.93	471.05	374.90	317.83	280.30	253.93	234.52	219.75	208.22	199.03	191.59	185.49	180.44
15000	1339.06	712.43	504.69	401.67	340.53	300.33	272.07	251.28	235.45	223.09	213.24	205.27	198.74	193.33
16000	1428.33	759.92	538.34	428.45	363.24	320.35	290.21	268.03	251.14	237.96	227.46	218.96	211.99	206.22
17000	1517.60	807.42	571.98	455.23	385.94	340.37	308.34	284.78	266.84	252.83	241.67	232.64	225.24	219.10
18000	1606.87	854.91	605.63	482.01	408.64	360.39	326.48	301.53	282.54	267.70	255.89	246.33	238.49	231.99
19000	1696.14	902.41	639.28	508.78	431.34	380.41	344.62	318.28	298.23	282.58	270.10	260.01	251.73	244.88
20000	1785.41	949.90	672.92	535.56	454.04	400.43	362.76	335.03	313.93	297.45	284.32	273.69	264.98	257.77
21000	1874.68	997.40	706.57	562.34	476.75	420.45	380.90	351.78	329.62	312.32	298.54	287.38	278.23	270.66
22000	1963.95	1044.89	740.21	589.12	499.45	440.48	399.03	368.54	345.32	327.19	312.75	301.06	291.48	283.54
23000	2053.22	1092.39	773.86	615.90	522.15	460.50	417.17	385.29	361.02	342.06	326.97	314.75	304.73	296.43
24000	2142.49	1139.88	807.50	642.67	544.85	480.52	435.31	402.04	376.71	356.94	341.18	328.43	317.98	309.32
25000	2231.76	1187.38	841.15	669.45	567.55	500.54	453.45	418.79	392.41	371.81	355.40	342.12	331.23	322.21
26000	2321.03	1234.87	874.80	696.23	590.25	520.56	471.58	435.54	408.11	386.68	369.61	355.80	344.48	335.10
27000	2410.30	1282.37	908.44	723.01	612.96	540.58	489.72	452.29	423.80	401.55	383.83	369.49	357.73	347.99
28000	2499.58	1329.86	942.09	749.79	635.66	560.60	507.86	469.04	439.50	416.43	398.05	383.17	370.98	360.87
29000	2588.85	1377.36	975.73	776.56	658.36	580.62	526.00	485.79	455.19	431.30	412.26	396.85	384.22	373.76
30000	2678.12	1424.85	1009.38	803.34	681.06	600.65	544.13	502.55	470.89	446.17	426.48	410.54	397.47	386.65
31000	2767.39	1472.35	1043.03	830.12	703.76	620.67	562.27	519.30	486.59	461.04	440.69	424.22	410.72	399.54
32000	2856.66	1519.84	1076.67	856.90	726.47	640.69	580.41	536.05	502.28	475.91	454.91	437.91	423.97	412.43
33000	2945.93	1567.34	1110.32	883.68	749.17	660.71	598.55	552.80	517.98	490.79	469.12	451.59	437.22	425.31
34000	3035.20	1614.83	1143.96	910.45	771.87	680.73	616.68	569.55	533.67	505.66	483.34	465.28	450.47	438.20
35000	3124.47	1662.33	1177.61	937.23	794.57	700.75	634.82	586.30	549.37	520.53	497.56	478.96	463.72	451.09
36000	3213.74	1709.82	1211.25	964.01	817.27	720.77	652.96	603.05	565.07	535.40	511.77	492.65	476.97	463.98
37000	3303.01	1757.32	1244.90	990.79	839.98	740.80	671.10	619.81	580.76	550.27	525.99	506.33	490.22	476.87
38000	3392.28	1804.81	1278.55	1017.56	862.68	760.82	689.24	636.56	596.46	565.15	540.20	520.01	503.46	489.76
39000	3481.55	1852.30	1312.19	1044.34	885.38	780.84	707.37	653.31	612.16	580.02	554.42	533.70	516.71	502.64
40000	3570.82	1899.80	1345.84	1071.12	908.08	800.86	725.51	670.06	627.85	594.89	568.63	547.38	529.96	515.53
41000	3660.09	1947.29	1379.48	1097.90	930.78	820.88	743.65	686.81	643.55	609.76	582.85	561.07	543.21	528.42
42000	3749.36	1994.79	1413.13	1124.68	953.49	840.90	761.79	703.56	659.24	624.64	597.07	574.75	556.46	541.31
43000	3838.63	2042.28	1446.77	1151.45	976.19	860.92	779.92	720.31	674.94	639.51	611.28	588.44	569.71	554.20
44000	3927.90	2089.78	1480.42	1178.23	998.89	880.95	798.06	737.07	690.64	654.38	625.50	602.12	582.96	567.08
45000	4017.17	2137.27	1514.07	1205.01	1021.59	900.97	816.20	753.82	706.33	669.25	639.71	615.81	596.21	579.97
46000	4106.44	2184.77	1547.71	1231.79	1044.29	920.99	834.34	770.57	722.03	684.12	653.93	629.49	609.46	592.86
47000	4195.71	2232.26	1581.36	1258.57	1067.00	941.01	852.47	787.32	737.72	699.00	668.14	643.17	622.71	605.75
48000	4284.98	2279.76	1615.00	1285.34	1089.70	961.03	870.61	804.07	753.42	713.87	682.36	656.86	635.95	618.64
49000	4374.25	2327.25	1648.65	1312.12	1112.40	981.05	888.75	820.82	769.12	728.74	696.58	670.54	649.20	631.53
50000	4463.52	2374.75	1682.30	1338.90	1135.10	1001.07	906.89	837.57	784.81	743.61	710.79	684.23	662.45	644.41
55000	4909.88	2612.22	1850.52	1472.79	1248.61	1101.18	997.58	921.33	863.29	817.97	781.87	752.65	728.70	708.85
60000	5356.23	2849.70	2018.75	1606.68	1362.12	1201.29	1088.26	1005.09	941.77	892.33	852.95	821.07	794.94	773.29
65000	5802.58	3087.17	2186.98	1740.57	1475.63	1301.39	1178.95	1088.84	1020.26	966.69	924.03	889.49	861.19	837.74
70000	6248.93	3324.65	2355.21	1874.46	1589.14	1401.50	1269.64	1172.60	1098.74	1041.06	995.11	957.92	927.43	902.18
75000	6695.28	3562.12	2523.44	2008.35	1702.65	1501.61	1360.33	1256.36	1177.22	1115.42	1066.18	1026.34	993.68	966.62
80000	7141.63	3799.59	2691.67	2142.24	1816.16	1601.71	1451.02	1340.11	1255.70	1189.78	1137.26	1094.76	1059.92	1031.06
85000	7587.99	4037.07	2859.90	2276.13	1929.67	1701.82	1541.70	1423.87	1334.18	1264.14	1208.34	1163.18	1126.17	1095.50
90000	8034.34	4274.54	3028.13	2410.02	2043.18	1801.93	1632.39	1507.63	1412.66	1338.50	1279.42	1231.61	1192.41	1159.94
95000	8480.69	4512.02	3196.36	2543.90	2156.69	1902.03	1723.08	1591.39	1491.14	1412.86	1350.50	1300.03	1258.65	1224.38
100000	8927.04	4749.49	3364.59	2677.79	2270.20	2002.14	1813.77	1675.14	1569.62	1487.22	1421.58	1368.45	1324.90	1288.82

MONTHLY PAYMENT
REQUIRED TO AMORTIZE A LOAN

12.900%

TERM	15 Years	16 Years	17 Years	18 Years	19 Years	20 Years	21 Years	22 Years	23 Years	24 Years	25 Years	30 Years	35 Years	40 Years
AMOUNT														
5	.07	.07	.07	.06	.06	.06	.06	.06	.06	.06	.06	.06	.06	.06
10	.13	.13	.13	.12	.12	.12	.12	.12	.12	.12	.12	.11	.11	.11
15	.19	.19	.19	.18	.18	.18	.18	.18	.18	.17	.17	.17	.17	.17
25	.32	.31	.31	.30	.30	.30	.29	.29	.29	.29	.29	.28	.28	.28
50	.63	.62	.61	.60	.59	.59	.58	.58	.57	.57	.57	.55	.55	.55
75	.95	.93	.91	.90	.89	.88	.87	.86	.86	.85	.85	.83	.82	.82
100	1.26	1.24	1.22	1.20	1.18	1.17	1.16	1.15	1.14	1.13	1.13	1.10	1.09	1.09
200	2.52	2.47	2.43	2.39	2.36	2.33	2.31	2.29	2.27	2.26	2.25	2.20	2.18	2.17
300	3.78	3.70	3.64	3.59	3.54	3.50	3.46	3.43	3.41	3.39	3.37	3.30	3.27	3.25
400	5.04	4.94	4.85	4.78	4.72	4.66	4.62	4.58	4.54	4.51	4.49	4.40	4.35	4.33
500	6.30	6.17	6.06	5.97	5.89	5.83	5.77	5.72	5.68	5.64	5.61	5.50	5.44	5.41
600	7.56	7.40	7.28	7.17	7.07	6.99	6.92	6.86	6.81	6.77	6.73	6.60	6.53	6.49
700	8.82	8.64	8.49	8.36	8.25	8.16	8.08	8.01	7.95	7.89	7.85	7.69	7.62	7.57
800	10.07	9.87	9.70	9.55	9.43	9.32	9.23	9.15	9.08	9.02	8.97	8.79	8.70	8.66
900	11.33	11.10	10.91	10.75	10.61	10.49	10.38	10.29	10.21	10.15	10.09	9.89	9.79	9.74
1000	12.59	12.34	12.12	11.94	11.78	11.65	11.53	11.43	11.35	11.27	11.21	10.99	10.88	10.82
2000	25.18	24.67	24.24	23.88	23.56	23.29	23.06	22.86	22.69	22.54	22.41	21.97	21.75	21.63
3000	37.77	37.00	36.36	35.81	35.34	34.94	34.59	34.29	34.03	33.81	33.61	32.96	32.62	32.45
4000	50.35	49.34	48.48	47.75	47.12	46.58	46.12	45.72	45.38	45.08	44.82	43.94	43.49	43.26
5000	62.94	61.67	60.60	59.68	58.90	58.23	57.65	57.15	56.72	56.35	56.02	54.92	54.36	54.07
6000	75.53	74.00	72.71	71.62	70.68	69.87	69.18	68.58	68.06	67.61	67.22	65.91	65.24	64.89
7000	88.11	86.34	84.83	83.55	82.46	81.52	80.71	80.01	79.41	78.88	78.43	76.89	76.11	75.70
8000	100.70	98.67	96.95	95.49	94.24	93.16	92.24	91.44	90.75	90.15	89.63	87.88	86.98	86.52
9000	113.29	111.00	109.07	107.42	106.01	104.81	103.77	102.87	102.09	101.42	100.83	98.86	97.85	97.33
10000	125.87	123.33	121.19	119.36	117.79	116.45	115.30	114.30	113.43	112.69	112.04	109.84	108.72	108.14
11000	138.46	135.67	133.30	131.29	129.57	128.10	126.82	125.73	124.78	123.95	123.24	120.83	119.60	118.96
12000	151.05	148.00	145.42	143.23	141.35	139.74	138.35	137.16	136.12	135.22	134.44	131.81	130.47	129.77
13000	163.63	160.33	157.54	155.16	153.13	151.38	149.88	148.59	147.46	146.49	145.65	142.80	141.34	140.58
14000	176.22	172.67	169.66	167.10	164.91	163.03	161.41	160.02	158.81	157.76	156.85	153.78	152.21	151.40
15000	188.81	185.00	181.78	179.03	176.69	174.67	172.94	171.44	170.15	169.03	168.05	164.76	163.08	162.21
16000	201.39	197.33	193.89	190.97	188.47	186.32	184.47	182.87	181.49	180.30	179.25	175.75	173.95	173.03
17000	213.98	209.67	206.01	202.90	200.24	197.96	196.00	194.30	192.04	191.56	190.46	186.73	184.83	183.84
18000	226.57	222.00	218.13	214.84	212.02	209.61	207.53	205.73	204.18	202.83	201.66	197.71	195.70	194.65
19000	239.15	234.33	230.25	226.77	223.80	221.25	219.06	217.16	215.52	214.10	212.86	208.70	206.57	205.47
20000	251.74	246.66	242.37	238.71	235.58	232.90	230.59	228.59	226.86	225.37	224.07	219.68	217.44	216.28
21000	264.33	259.00	254.48	250.64	247.36	244.54	242.12	240.02	238.21	236.64	235.27	230.67	228.31	227.10
22000	276.91	271.33	266.60	262.58	259.14	256.19	253.66	251.45	249.55	247.90	246.47	241.65	239.19	237.91
23000	289.50	283.66	278.72	274.51	270.92	267.83	265.17	262.88	260.89	259.17	257.68	252.63	250.06	248.72
24000	302.09	296.00	290.84	286.45	282.70	279.48	276.70	274.31	272.24	270.44	268.88	263.62	260.93	259.54
25000	314.67	308.33	302.96	298.38	294.47	291.12	288.23	285.74	283.58	281.71	280.08	274.60	271.80	270.35
26000	327.26	320.66	315.07	310.32	306.25	302.76	299.76	297.17	294.92	292.98	291.29	285.59	282.67	281.16
27000	339.85	332.99	327.19	322.25	318.03	314.41	311.29	308.60	306.27	304.24	302.49	296.57	293.55	291.98
28000	352.43	345.33	339.31	334.19	329.81	326.05	322.82	320.03	317.61	315.51	313.69	307.55	304.42	302.79
29000	365.02	357.66	351.43	346.12	341.59	337.70	334.35	331.46	328.95	326.78	324.90	318.54	315.29	313.61
30000	377.61	369.99	363.55	358.06	353.37	349.34	345.88	342.88	340.29	338.05	336.10	329.52	326.16	324.42
31000	390.19	382.33	375.67	370.00	365.15	360.99	357.41	354.31	351.64	349.32	347.30	340.51	337.03	335.23
32000	402.78	394.66	387.78	381.93	376.93	372.63	368.93	365.74	362.98	360.59	358.50	351.49	347.91	346.05
33000	415.37	406.99	399.90	393.87	388.70	384.28	380.46	377.17	374.32	371.85	369.71	362.47	358.78	356.86
34000	427.95	419.33	412.02	405.80	400.48	395.92	391.99	388.60	385.67	383.12	380.91	373.46	369.65	367.67
35000	440.54	431.66	424.14	417.74	412.26	407.57	403.52	400.03	397.01	394.39	392.11	384.44	380.52	378.49
36000	453.13	443.99	436.26	429.67	424.04	419.21	415.05	411.46	408.35	405.66	403.32	395.42	391.39	389.30
37000	465.71	456.32	448.37	441.61	435.82	430.85	426.58	422.89	419.70	416.93	414.52	406.41	402.26	400.12
38000	478.30	468.66	460.49	453.54	447.60	442.50	438.11	434.32	431.04	428.19	425.72	417.39	413.14	410.93
39000	490.89	480.99	472.61	465.48	459.30	454.14	449.64	445.75	442.38	439.46	436.93	428.38	424.01	421.74
40000	503.47	493.32	484.73	477.41	471.16	465.79	461.17	457.18	453.72	450.73	448.13	439.36	434.88	432.56
41000	516.06	505.65	496.85	489.35	482.94	477.43	472.70	468.61	465.07	462.00	459.33	450.34	445.75	443.37
42000	528.65	517.99	508.96	501.28	494.71	489.08	484.23	480.04	476.41	473.27	470.54	461.33	456.62	454.19
43000	541.23	530.32	521.08	513.22	506.49	500.72	495.75	491.47	487.75	484.54	481.74	472.31	467.50	465.00
44000	553.82	542.65	533.20	525.15	518.27	512.37	507.28	502.89	499.10	495.80	492.94	483.30	478.37	475.81
45000	566.41	554.99	545.32	537.09	530.05	524.01	518.81	514.32	510.44	507.07	504.15	494.28	489.24	486.63
46000	578.99	567.32	557.44	549.02	541.83	535.66	530.34	525.75	521.78	518.34	515.35	505.26	500.11	497.44
47000	591.58	579.65	569.55	560.96	553.61	547.30	541.87	537.18	533.13	529.61	526.55	516.25	510.98	508.25
48000	604.17	591.99	581.67	572.89	565.39	558.95	553.40	548.61	544.47	540.88	537.75	527.23	521.86	519.07
49000	616.75	604.32	593.79	584.83	577.17	570.59	564.93	560.04	555.81	552.14	548.96	538.22	532.73	529.88
50000	629.34	616.65	605.91	596.76	588.94	582.23	576.46	571.47	567.15	563.41	560.16	549.20	543.60	540.70
55000	692.27	678.32	666.50	656.44	647.84	640.46	634.10	628.62	623.87	619.75	616.18	604.12	597.96	594.77
60000	755.21	739.98	727.09	716.11	706.73	698.68	691.75	685.76	680.58	676.09	672.19	659.04	652.32	648.83
65000	818.14	801.65	787.68	775.79	765.63	756.90	749.39	742.91	737.30	732.43	728.21	713.96	706.68	702.90
70000	881.07	863.31	848.27	835.47	824.52	815.13	807.04	800.06	794.01	788.78	784.22	768.88	761.04	756.97
75000	944.01	924.98	908.86	895.14	883.41	873.35	864.68	857.20	850.73	845.12	840.24	823.80	815.40	811.04
80000	1006.94	986.64	969.45	954.82	942.31	931.57	922.33	914.35	907.44	901.46	896.25	878.72	869.76	865.11
85000	1069.87	1048.31	1030.04	1014.49	1001.20	989.80	979.97	971.50	964.16	957.80	952.27	933.64	924.12	919.18
90000	1132.81	1109.97	1090.63	1074.17	1060.10	1048.02	1037.62	1028.64	1020.87	1014.14	1008.29	988.55	978.47	973.25
95000	1195.74	1171.64	1151.22	1133.85	1118.99	1106.24	1095.27	1085.79	1077.59	1070.48	1064.30	1043.47	1032.83	1027.32
100000	1258.67	1233.30	1211.81	1193.52	1177.88	1164.46	1152.91	1142.94	1134.30	1126.82	1120.32	1098.39	1087.19	1081.39

MONTHLY PAYMENT
REQUIRED TO AMORTIZE A LOAN

TERM AMOUNT	1 Year	2 Years	3 Years	4 Years	5 Years	6 Years	7 Years	8 Years	9 Years	10 Years	11 Years	12 Years	13 Years	14 Years
5	.45	.24	.17	.14	.12	.11	.10	.09	.08	.08	.08	.07	.07	.07
10	.90	.48	.34	.27	.23	.21	.19	.17	.16	.15	.15	.14	.14	.13
15	1.34	.72	.51	.41	.35	.31	.28	.26	.24	.23	.22	.21	.20	.20
25	2.24	1.19	.85	.68	.57	.51	.46	.43	.40	.38	.36	.35	.34	.33
50	4.47	2.38	1.69	1.35	1.14	1.01	.91	.85	.79	.75	.72	.69	.67	.65
75	6.70	3.57	2.53	2.02	1.71	1.51	1.37	1.27	1.19	1.12	1.08	1.04	1.00	.98
100	8.94	4.76	3.37	2.69	2.28	2.01	1.82	1.69	1.58	1.50	1.43	1.38	1.34	1.30
200	17.87	9.51	6.74	5.37	4.56	4.02	3.64	3.37	3.16	2.99	2.86	2.75	2.67	2.60
300	26.80	14.27	10.11	8.05	6.83	6.03	5.46	5.05	4.73	4.48	4.29	4.13	4.00	3.89
400	35.73	19.02	13.48	10.74	9.11	8.03	7.28	6.73	6.31	5.98	5.72	5.50	5.33	5.19
500	44.66	23.78	16.85	13.42	11.38	10.04	9.10	8.41	7.88	7.47	7.14	6.88	6.66	6.48
600	53.60	28.53	20.22	16.10	13.66	12.05	10.92	10.09	9.46	8.96	8.57	8.25	7.99	7.78
700	62.53	33.28	23.59	18.78	15.93	14.06	12.74	11.77	11.03	10.46	10.00	9.63	9.32	9.07
800	71.46	38.04	26.96	21.47	18.21	16.06	14.56	13.45	12.61	11.95	11.43	11.00	10.65	10.37
900	80.39	42.79	30.33	24.15	20.48	18.07	16.38	15.13	14.18	13.44	12.85	12.38	11.99	11.66
1000	89.32	47.55	33.70	26.83	22.76	20.08	18.20	16.81	15.76	14.94	14.28	13.75	13.32	12.96
2000	178.64	95.09	67.39	53.66	45.51	40.15	36.39	33.62	31.51	29.87	28.56	27.50	26.63	25.91
3000	267.96	142.63	101.09	80.49	68.26	60.23	54.58	50.43	47.27	44.80	42.83	41.24	39.94	38.86
4000	357.27	190.17	134.78	107.31	91.02	80.30	72.77	67.23	63.02	59.73	57.11	54.99	53.25	51.82
5000	446.59	237.71	168.47	134.14	113.77	100.38	90.96	84.04	78.77	74.66	71.39	68.74	66.57	64.77
6000	535.91	285.26	202.17	160.97	136.52	120.45	109.16	100.85	94.53	89.59	85.66	82.48	79.88	77.72
7000	625.23	332.80	235.86	187.80	159.28	140.52	127.35	117.66	110.28	104.52	99.94	96.23	93.19	90.67
8000	714.54	380.34	269.56	214.62	182.03	160.60	145.54	134.46	126.03	119.45	114.21	109.98	106.50	103.63
9000	803.86	427.88	303.25	241.45	204.78	180.67	163.73	151.27	141.79	134.38	128.49	123.72	119.81	116.58
10000	893.18	475.42	336.94	268.28	227.54	200.75	181.92	168.08	157.54	149.32	142.77	137.47	133.13	129.53
11000	982.50	522.97	370.64	295.11	250.29	220.82	200.12	184.88	173.29	164.25	157.04	151.21	146.44	142.48
12000	1071.81	570.51	404.33	321.93	273.04	240.89	218.31	201.69	189.05	179.18	171.32	164.96	159.75	155.44
13000	1161.13	618.05	438.03	348.76	295.79	260.97	236.50	218.50	204.80	194.11	185.59	178.71	173.06	168.39
14000	1250.45	665.59	471.72	375.59	318.55	281.04	254.69	235.31	220.56	209.04	199.87	192.45	186.37	181.34
15000	1339.76	713.13	505.41	402.42	341.30	301.12	272.88	252.11	236.31	223.97	214.15	206.20	199.69	194.29
16000	1429.08	760.67	539.11	429.24	364.05	321.19	291.08	268.92	252.06	238.90	228.42	219.95	213.00	207.25
17000	1518.40	808.22	572.80	456.07	386.81	341.26	309.27	285.73	267.82	253.83	242.70	233.69	226.31	220.20
18000	1607.72	855.76	606.50	482.90	409.56	361.34	327.46	302.54	283.57	268.76	256.97	247.44	239.62	233.15
19000	1697.03	903.30	640.19	509.73	432.31	381.41	345.65	319.34	299.32	283.70	271.25	261.18	252.93	246.11
20000	1786.35	950.84	673.88	536.55	455.07	401.49	363.84	336.15	315.08	298.63	285.53	274.93	266.25	259.06
21000	1875.67	998.38	707.58	563.38	477.82	421.56	382.04	352.96	330.83	313.56	299.80	288.68	279.56	272.01
22000	1964.99	1045.93	741.27	590.21	500.57	441.64	400.23	369.76	346.58	328.49	314.08	302.42	292.87	284.96
23000	2054.30	1093.47	774.97	617.04	523.33	461.71	418.42	386.57	362.34	343.42	328.36	316.17	306.18	297.92
24000	2143.62	1141.01	808.66	643.86	546.08	481.78	436.61	403.38	378.09	358.35	342.63	329.92	319.50	310.87
25000	2232.94	1188.55	842.35	670.69	568.83	501.86	454.80	420.19	393.84	373.28	356.91	343.66	332.81	323.82
26000	2322.25	1236.09	876.05	697.52	591.58	521.93	473.00	436.99	409.60	388.21	371.18	357.41	346.12	336.77
27000	2411.57	1283.63	909.74	724.35	614.34	542.01	491.19	453.80	425.35	403.14	385.46	371.15	359.43	349.73
28000	2500.89	1331.18	943.44	751.17	637.09	562.08	509.38	470.61	441.11	418.08	399.74	384.90	372.74	362.68
29000	2590.21	1378.72	977.13	778.00	659.84	582.15	527.57	487.42	456.86	433.01	414.01	398.65	386.06	375.63
30000	2679.52	1426.26	1010.82	804.83	682.60	602.23	545.76	504.22	472.61	447.94	428.29	412.39	399.37	388.58
31000	2768.84	1473.80	1044.52	831.66	705.35	622.30	563.96	521.03	488.37	462.87	442.56	426.14	412.68	401.54
32000	2858.16	1521.34	1078.21	858.48	728.10	642.38	582.15	537.84	504.12	477.80	456.84	439.89	425.99	414.49
33000	2947.48	1568.89	1111.91	885.31	750.86	662.45	600.34	554.64	519.87	492.73	471.12	453.63	439.30	427.44
34000	3036.79	1616.43	1145.60	912.14	773.61	682.52	618.53	571.45	535.63	507.66	485.39	467.38	452.62	440.39
35000	3126.11	1663.97	1179.29	938.97	796.36	702.60	636.72	588.26	551.38	522.59	499.67	481.12	465.93	453.35
36000	3215.43	1711.51	1212.99	965.79	819.12	722.67	654.92	605.07	567.13	537.52	513.94	494.87	479.24	466.30
37000	3304.74	1759.05	1246.68	992.62	841.87	742.75	673.11	621.87	582.89	552.45	528.22	508.62	492.55	479.25
38000	3394.06	1806.59	1280.38	1019.45	864.62	762.82	691.30	638.68	598.64	567.39	542.50	522.36	505.86	492.21
39000	3483.38	1854.14	1314.07	1046.28	887.37	782.90	709.49	655.49	614.39	582.32	556.77	536.11	519.18	505.16
40000	3572.70	1901.68	1347.76	1073.10	910.13	802.97	727.68	672.30	630.15	597.25	571.05	549.86	532.49	518.11
41000	3662.01	1949.22	1381.46	1099.93	932.88	823.04	745.88	689.10	645.90	612.18	585.33	563.60	545.80	531.06
42000	3751.33	1996.76	1415.15	1126.76	955.63	843.12	764.07	705.91	661.66	627.11	599.60	577.35	559.11	544.02
43000	3840.65	2044.30	1448.84	1153.59	978.39	863.19	782.26	722.72	677.41	642.04	613.88	591.09	572.43	556.97
44000	3929.97	2091.85	1482.54	1180.41	1001.14	883.27	800.45	739.52	693.16	656.97	628.15	604.84	585.74	569.92
45000	4019.28	2139.39	1516.23	1207.24	1023.89	903.34	818.64	756.33	708.92	671.90	642.43	618.59	599.05	582.87
46000	4108.60	2186.93	1549.93	1234.07	1046.65	923.41	836.84	773.14	724.67	686.83	656.71	632.33	612.36	595.83
47000	4197.92	2234.47	1583.62	1260.90	1069.40	943.49	855.03	789.95	740.42	701.77	670.98	646.08	625.67	608.78
48000	4287.23	2282.01	1617.31	1287.72	1092.15	963.56	873.22	806.75	756.18	716.70	685.26	659.83	638.99	621.73
49000	4376.55	2329.55	1651.01	1314.55	1114.91	983.64	891.41	823.56	771.93	731.63	699.53	673.57	652.30	634.68
50000	4465.87	2377.10	1684.70	1341.38	1137.66	1003.71	909.60	840.37	787.68	746.56	713.81	687.32	665.61	647.64
55000	4912.46	2614.81	1853.17	1475.52	1251.42	1104.08	1000.56	924.40	866.45	821.21	785.19	756.05	732.17	712.40
60000	5359.04	2852.51	2021.64	1609.65	1365.19	1204.45	1091.52	1008.44	945.22	895.87	856.57	824.78	798.73	777.16
65000	5805.63	3090.22	2190.11	1743.79	1478.95	1304.82	1182.48	1092.48	1023.99	970.52	927.95	893.51	865.29	841.93
70000	6252.21	3327.93	2358.58	1877.93	1592.72	1405.19	1273.44	1176.51	1102.76	1045.18	999.33	962.24	931.85	906.69
75000	6698.80	3565.64	2527.05	2012.07	1706.49	1505.56	1364.40	1260.55	1181.52	1119.84	1070.71	1030.97	998.41	971.45
80000	7145.39	3803.35	2695.52	2146.20	1820.25	1605.93	1455.36	1344.59	1260.29	1194.49	1142.09	1099.71	1064.97	1036.22
85000	7591.97	4041.06	2863.99	2280.34	1934.02	1706.30	1546.32	1428.62	1339.06	1269.15	1213.47	1168.44	1131.53	1100.98
90000	8038.56	4278.77	3032.46	2414.48	2047.78	1806.67	1637.28	1512.66	1417.83	1343.80	1284.85	1237.17	1198.09	1165.74
95000	8485.15	4516.48	3200.93	2548.62	2161.55	1907.05	1728.24	1596.69	1496.60	1418.46	1356.24	1305.90	1264.65	1230.51
100000	8931.73	4754.19	3369.40	2682.75	2275.31	2007.42	1819.20	1680.73	1575.36	1493.11	1427.62	1374.63	1331.22	1295.27

MONTHLY PAYMENT
REQUIRED TO AMORTIZE A LOAN

13.000%

TERM	15 Years	16 Years	17 Years	18 Years	19 Years	20 Years	21 Years	22 Years	23 Years	24 Years	25 Years	30 Years	35 Years	40 Years
AMOUNT														
5	.07	.07	.07	.07	.06	.06	.06	.06	.06	.06	.06	.06	.06	.06
10	.13	.13	.13	.13	.12	.12	.12	.12	.12	.12	.12	.12	.11	.11
15	.19	.19	.19	.19	.18	.18	.18	.18	.18	.18	.17	.17	.17	.17
25	.32	.31	.31	.31	.30	.30	.30	.29	.29	.29	.29	.28	.28	.28
50	.64	.62	.61	.61	.60	.59	.59	.58	.58	.57	.57	.56	.55	.55
75	.95	.93	.92	.91	.89	.88	.88	.87	.86	.86	.85	.83	.83	.82
100	1.27	1.24	1.22	1.21	1.19	1.18	1.17	1.16	1.15	1.14	1.13	1.11	1.10	1.09
200	2.54	2.48	2.44	2.41	2.37	2.35	2.33	2.31	2.29	2.27	2.26	2.22	2.20	2.18
300	3.80	3.72	3.66	3.61	3.56	3.52	3.49	3.46	3.43	3.41	3.39	3.32	3.29	3.27
400	5.07	4.96	4.88	4.81	4.74	4.69	4.65	4.61	4.57	4.54	4.52	4.43	4.39	4.36
500	6.33	6.20	6.10	6.01	5.93	5.86	5.81	5.76	5.71	5.68	5.64	5.54	5.48	5.45
600	7.60	7.44	7.32	7.21	7.11	7.03	6.97	6.91	6.86	6.81	6.77	6.64	6.58	6.54
700	8.86	8.68	8.54	8.41	8.30	8.21	8.13	8.06	8.00	7.94	7.90	7.75	7.67	7.63
800	10.13	9.92	9.75	9.61	9.48	9.38	9.29	9.21	9.14	9.08	9.03	8.85	8.77	8.72
900	11.39	11.16	10.97	10.81	10.67	10.55	10.45	10.36	10.28	10.21	10.16	9.96	9.86	9.81
1000	12.66	12.40	12.19	12.01	11.85	11.72	11.61	11.51	11.42	11.35	11.28	11.07	10.96	10.90
2000	25.31	24.80	24.38	24.01	23.70	23.44	23.21	23.01	22.84	22.69	22.56	22.13	21.91	21.80
3000	37.96	37.20	36.56	36.02	35.55	35.15	34.81	34.51	34.26	34.03	33.84	33.19	32.86	32.69
4000	50.61	49.60	48.75	48.02	47.40	46.87	46.41	46.01	45.67	45.38	45.12	44.25	43.81	43.59
5000	63.27	62.00	60.94	60.03	59.25	58.58	58.01	57.52	57.09	56.72	56.40	55.31	54.76	54.48
6000	75.92	74.40	73.12	72.03	71.10	70.30	69.61	69.02	68.51	68.06	67.68	66.38	65.72	65.38
7000	88.57	86.80	85.31	84.04	82.95	82.02	81.21	80.52	79.92	79.40	78.95	77.44	76.67	76.27
8000	101.22	99.20	97.49	96.04	94.80	93.73	92.81	92.02	91.34	90.75	90.23	88.50	87.62	87.17
9000	113.88	111.60	109.68	108.04	106.65	105.45	104.42	103.53	102.76	102.09	101.51	99.56	98.57	98.06
10000	126.53	124.00	121.87	120.05	118.49	117.16	116.02	115.03	114.17	113.43	112.79	110.62	109.52	108.96
11000	139.18	136.40	134.05	132.05	130.34	128.88	127.62	126.53	125.59	124.77	124.07	121.69	120.48	119.85
12000	151.83	148.80	146.24	144.06	142.19	140.59	139.22	138.03	137.01	136.12	135.35	132.75	131.43	130.75
13000	164.49	161.20	158.42	156.06	154.04	152.31	150.82	149.53	148.42	147.46	146.62	143.81	142.38	141.64
14000	177.14	173.60	170.61	168.07	165.89	164.03	162.42	161.04	159.84	158.80	157.90	154.87	153.33	152.54
15000	189.79	186.00	182.80	180.07	177.74	175.74	174.02	172.54	171.26	170.15	169.18	165.93	164.28	163.43
16000	202.44	198.40	194.98	192.07	189.59	187.46	185.62	184.04	182.67	181.49	180.46	177.00	175.24	174.33
17000	215.10	210.80	207.17	204.08	201.44	199.17	197.22	195.54	194.09	192.83	191.74	188.06	186.19	185.22
18000	227.75	223.20	219.36	216.08	213.29	210.89	208.83	207.05	205.51	204.17	203.02	199.12	197.14	196.12
19000	240.40	235.60	231.54	228.09	225.14	222.60	220.43	218.55	216.92	215.52	214.29	210.18	208.09	207.01
20000	253.05	248.00	243.73	240.09	236.98	234.32	232.03	230.05	228.34	226.86	225.57	221.24	219.04	217.91
21000	265.71	260.40	255.91	252.10	248.83	246.04	243.63	241.55	239.76	238.20	236.85	232.31	230.00	228.80
22000	278.36	272.80	268.10	264.10	260.68	257.75	255.23	253.05	251.17	249.54	248.13	243.37	240.95	239.70
23000	291.01	285.20	280.29	276.10	272.53	269.47	266.83	264.56	262.59	260.89	259.41	254.43	251.90	250.59
24000	303.66	297.60	292.47	288.11	284.38	281.18	278.43	276.06	274.01	272.23	270.69	265.49	262.85	261.49
25000	316.32	310.00	304.66	300.11	296.23	292.90	290.03	287.56	285.42	283.57	281.96	276.55	273.80	272.38
26000	328.97	322.40	316.84	312.12	308.08	304.61	301.63	299.06	296.84	294.91	293.24	287.62	284.76	283.28
27000	341.62	334.80	329.03	324.12	319.93	316.33	313.24	310.57	308.26	306.26	304.52	298.68	295.71	294.17
28000	354.27	347.20	341.22	336.13	331.78	328.05	324.84	322.07	319.67	317.60	315.80	309.74	306.66	305.07
29000	366.93	359.60	353.40	348.13	343.63	339.76	336.44	333.57	331.09	328.94	327.08	320.80	317.61	315.96
30000	379.58	372.00	365.59	360.13	355.47	351.48	348.04	345.07	342.51	340.29	338.36	331.86	328.56	326.86
31000	392.23	384.40	377.78	372.14	367.32	363.19	359.64	356.58	353.92	351.63	349.63	342.93	339.51	337.75
32000	404.88	396.80	389.96	384.14	379.17	374.91	371.24	368.08	365.34	362.97	360.91	353.99	350.47	348.65
33000	417.53	409.20	402.15	396.15	391.02	386.62	382.84	379.58	376.76	374.31	372.19	365.05	361.42	359.54
34000	430.19	421.60	414.33	408.15	402.87	398.34	394.44	391.08	388.17	385.66	383.47	376.11	372.37	370.44
35000	442.84	434.00	426.52	420.16	414.72	410.06	406.04	402.58	399.59	397.00	394.75	387.17	383.32	381.33
36000	455.49	446.40	438.71	432.16	426.57	421.77	417.65	414.09	411.01	408.34	406.03	398.24	394.27	392.23
37000	468.14	458.80	450.89	444.17	438.42	433.49	429.25	425.59	422.43	419.68	417.30	409.30	405.23	403.13
38000	480.80	471.20	463.08	456.17	450.27	445.20	437.09	433.84	437.09	431.03	428.58	420.36	416.18	414.02
39000	493.45	483.60	475.26	468.17	462.12	456.92	452.45	448.59	445.26	442.37	439.86	431.42	427.13	424.92
40000	506.10	496.00	487.45	480.18	473.96	468.64	464.05	460.10	456.68	453.71	451.14	442.48	438.08	435.81
41000	518.75	508.40	499.64	492.18	485.81	480.35	475.65	471.60	468.09	465.05	462.42	453.55	449.03	446.71
42000	531.41	520.80	511.82	504.19	497.66	492.07	487.25	483.10	479.51	476.40	473.70	464.61	459.99	457.60
43000	544.06	533.20	524.01	516.19	509.51	503.78	498.85	494.60	490.93	487.74	484.97	475.67	470.94	468.50
44000	556.71	545.60	536.20	528.20	521.36	515.50	510.45	506.10	502.34	499.08	496.25	486.73	481.89	479.39
45000	569.36	558.00	548.38	540.20	533.21	527.21	522.06	517.61	513.76	510.43	507.53	497.79	492.84	490.29
46000	582.02	570.40	560.57	552.20	545.06	538.93	533.66	529.11	525.18	521.77	518.81	508.86	503.79	501.18
47000	594.67	582.80	572.75	564.21	556.91	550.65	545.26	540.61	536.59	533.11	530.09	519.92	514.75	512.08
48000	607.32	595.20	584.94	576.21	568.76	562.36	556.86	552.11	548.01	544.45	541.37	530.98	525.70	522.97
49000	619.97	607.60	597.13	588.22	580.61	574.08	568.46	563.62	559.43	555.80	552.64	542.04	536.65	533.87
50000	632.63	620.00	609.31	600.22	592.45	585.79	580.06	575.12	570.84	567.14	563.92	553.10	547.60	544.76
55000	695.89	682.00	670.24	660.24	651.70	644.37	638.07	632.63	627.93	623.85	620.31	608.41	602.36	599.24
60000	759.15	744.00	731.17	720.26	710.94	702.95	696.07	690.14	685.01	680.57	676.71	663.72	657.12	653.71
65000	822.41	806.00	792.10	780.29	770.19	761.53	754.08	747.65	742.09	737.28	733.10	719.03	711.88	708.19
70000	885.67	868.00	853.04	840.31	829.43	820.11	812.08	805.16	799.18	793.99	789.49	774.34	766.64	762.66
75000	948.94	930.00	913.97	900.33	888.68	878.69	870.09	862.67	856.26	850.71	845.88	829.65	821.40	817.14
80000	1012.20	992.00	974.90	960.35	947.92	937.27	928.09	920.19	913.35	907.42	902.27	884.96	876.16	871.62
85000	1075.46	1053.99	1035.83	1020.37	1007.17	995.84	986.10	977.70	970.43	964.13	958.67	940.27	930.92	926.09
90000	1138.72	1115.99	1096.76	1080.39	1066.41	1054.42	1044.11	1035.21	1027.51	1020.85	1015.06	995.58	985.68	980.57
95000	1201.99	1177.99	1157.69	1140.42	1125.66	1113.00	1102.11	1092.72	1084.60	1077.56	1071.45	1050.89	1040.44	1035.04
100000	1265.25	1239.99	1218.62	1200.44	1184.90	1171.58	1160.12	1150.23	1141.68	1134.27	1127.84	1106.20	1095.20	1089.52

13%

MONTHLY PAYMENT
REQUIRED TO AMORTIZE A LOAN

TERM	1 Year	2 Years	3 Years	4 Years	5 Years	6 Years	7 Years	8 Years	9 Years	10 Years	11 Years	12 Years	13 Years	14 Years
AMOUNT														
5	.45	.24	.17	.14	.12	.11	.10	.09	.08	.08	.08	.07	.07	.07
10	.90	.48	.34	.27	.23	.21	.19	.17	.16	.15	.15	.14	.14	.14
15	1.35	.72	.51	.41	.35	.31	.28	.26	.24	.23	.22	.21	.21	.20
25	2.24	1.19	.85	.68	.58	.51	.46	.43	.40	.38	.36	.35	.34	.33
50	4.47	2.38	1.69	1.35	1.15	1.01	.92	.85	.80	.75	.72	.70	.67	.66
75	6.71	3.57	2.54	2.02	1.72	1.51	1.37	1.27	1.19	1.13	1.08	1.04	1.01	.98
100	8.94	4.76	3.38	2.69	2.29	2.02	1.83	1.69	1.59	1.50	1.44	1.39	1.34	1.31
200	17.88	9.52	6.75	5.38	4.57	4.03	3.65	3.38	3.17	3.00	2.87	2.77	2.68	2.61
300	26.81	14.28	10.13	8.07	6.85	6.04	5.48	5.06	4.75	4.50	4.31	4.15	4.02	3.91
400	35.75	19.04	13.50	10.76	9.13	8.06	7.30	6.75	6.33	6.00	5.74	5.53	5.36	5.21
500	44.69	23.80	16.88	13.44	11.41	10.07	9.13	8.44	7.91	7.50	7.17	6.91	6.69	6.51
600	53.62	28.56	20.25	16.13	13.69	12.08	10.95	10.12	9.49	9.00	8.61	8.29	8.03	7.82
700	62.56	33.32	23.62	18.82	15.97	14.09	12.78	11.81	11.07	10.50	10.04	9.67	9.37	9.12
800	71.50	38.08	27.00	21.51	18.25	16.11	14.60	13.50	12.65	12.00	11.47	11.05	10.71	10.42
900	80.43	42.83	30.37	24.19	20.53	18.12	16.43	15.18	14.24	13.50	12.91	12.43	12.04	11.72
1000	89.37	47.59	33.75	26.88	22.81	20.13	18.25	16.87	15.82	15.00	14.34	13.81	13.38	13.02
2000	178.73	95.18	67.49	53.76	45.61	40.26	36.50	33.73	31.63	29.99	28.68	27.62	26.76	26.04
3000	268.10	142.77	101.23	80.64	68.42	60.39	54.74	50.59	47.44	44.98	43.01	41.43	40.13	39.06
4000	357.46	190.36	134.97	107.51	91.22	80.51	72.99	67.46	63.25	59.97	57.35	55.24	53.51	52.07
5000	446.83	237.95	168.72	134.39	114.03	100.64	91.24	84.32	79.06	74.96	71.69	69.05	66.88	65.09
6000	536.19	285.54	202.46	161.27	136.83	120.77	109.48	101.18	94.87	89.95	86.02	82.85	80.26	78.11
7000	625.55	333.13	236.20	188.15	159.64	140.89	127.73	118.05	110.68	104.94	100.36	96.66	93.63	91.13
8000	714.92	380.72	269.94	215.02	182.44	161.02	145.98	134.91	126.49	119.93	114.70	110.47	107.01	104.14
9000	804.28	428.30	303.68	241.90	205.24	181.15	164.22	151.77	142.31	134.92	129.03	124.28	120.38	117.16
10000	893.65	475.89	337.43	268.78	228.05	201.27	182.47	168.64	158.12	149.91	143.37	138.09	133.76	130.18
11000	983.01	523.48	371.17	295.65	250.85	221.40	200.72	185.50	173.93	164.90	157.71	151.89	147.13	143.19
12000	1072.38	571.07	404.91	322.53	273.66	241.53	218.96	202.36	189.74	179.89	172.04	165.70	160.51	156.21
13000	1161.74	618.66	438.65	349.41	296.46	261.65	237.21	219.23	205.55	194.88	186.38	179.51	173.89	169.23
14000	1251.10	666.25	472.39	376.29	319.27	281.78	255.45	236.09	221.36	209.87	200.72	193.32	187.26	182.25
15000	1340.47	713.84	506.14	403.16	342.07	301.91	273.70	252.95	237.17	224.86	215.05	207.13	200.64	195.26
16000	1429.83	761.43	539.88	430.04	364.87	322.04	291.95	269.82	252.98	239.85	229.39	220.94	214.01	208.28
17000	1519.20	809.01	573.62	456.92	387.68	342.16	310.19	286.68	268.79	254.84	243.73	234.74	227.39	221.30
18000	1608.56	856.60	607.36	483.79	410.48	362.29	328.44	303.54	284.61	269.83	258.06	248.55	240.76	234.32
19000	1697.92	904.19	641.11	510.67	433.29	382.42	346.69	320.41	300.42	284.82	272.40	262.36	254.14	247.33
20000	1787.29	951.78	674.85	537.55	456.09	402.54	364.93	337.27	316.23	299.81	286.74	276.17	267.51	260.35
21000	1876.65	999.37	708.59	564.43	478.90	422.67	383.18	354.13	332.04	314.80	301.07	289.98	280.89	273.37
22000	1966.02	1046.96	742.33	591.30	501.70	442.80	401.43	371.00	347.85	329.79	315.41	303.78	294.26	286.38
23000	2055.38	1094.55	776.07	618.18	524.50	462.92	419.67	387.86	363.66	344.78	329.75	317.59	307.64	299.40
24000	2144.75	1142.14	809.82	645.06	547.31	483.05	437.92	404.72	379.47	359.77	344.08	331.40	321.01	312.42
25000	2234.11	1189.73	843.56	671.93	570.11	503.18	456.16	421.59	395.28	374.76	358.42	345.21	334.39	325.44
26000	2323.47	1237.31	877.30	698.81	592.92	523.30	474.41	438.45	411.09	389.75	372.76	359.02	347.77	338.45
27000	2412.84	1284.90	911.04	725.69	615.72	543.43	492.66	455.31	426.91	404.74	387.09	372.83	361.14	351.47
28000	2502.20	1332.49	944.78	752.57	638.53	563.56	510.90	472.18	442.72	419.73	401.43	386.63	374.52	364.49
29000	2591.57	1380.08	978.53	779.44	661.33	583.69	529.15	489.04	458.53	434.72	415.77	400.44	387.89	377.51
30000	2680.93	1427.67	1012.27	806.32	684.13	603.81	547.40	505.90	474.34	449.71	430.10	414.25	401.27	390.52
31000	2770.30	1475.26	1046.01	833.20	706.94	623.94	565.64	522.77	490.15	464.70	444.44	428.06	414.64	403.54
32000	2859.66	1522.85	1079.75	860.07	729.74	644.07	583.89	539.63	505.96	479.69	458.78	441.87	428.02	416.56
33000	2949.02	1570.44	1113.50	886.95	752.55	664.19	602.14	556.49	521.77	494.68	473.11	455.67	441.39	429.57
34000	3038.39	1618.02	1147.24	913.83	775.35	684.32	620.38	573.36	537.58	509.67	487.45	469.48	454.77	442.59
35000	3127.75	1665.61	1180.98	940.71	798.16	704.45	638.63	590.22	553.39	524.66	501.79	483.29	468.14	455.61
36000	3217.12	1713.20	1214.72	967.58	820.96	724.57	656.87	607.08	569.21	539.65	516.12	497.10	481.52	468.63
37000	3306.48	1760.79	1248.46	994.46	843.76	744.70	675.12	623.94	585.02	554.64	530.46	510.91	494.89	481.64
38000	3395.84	1808.38	1282.21	1021.34	866.57	764.83	693.37	640.81	600.83	569.63	544.80	524.72	508.27	494.66
39000	3485.21	1855.97	1315.95	1048.21	889.37	784.95	711.61	657.67	616.64	584.62	559.13	538.52	521.65	507.68
40000	3574.57	1903.56	1349.69	1075.09	912.18	805.08	729.86	674.53	632.45	599.61	573.47	552.33	535.02	520.69
41000	3663.94	1951.15	1383.43	1101.97	934.98	825.21	748.11	691.40	648.26	614.60	587.81	566.14	548.40	533.71
42000	3753.30	1998.73	1417.17	1128.85	957.79	845.34	766.35	708.26	664.07	629.59	602.14	579.95	561.77	546.73
43000	3842.67	2046.32	1450.92	1155.72	980.59	865.46	784.60	725.12	679.88	644.58	616.48	593.76	575.15	559.75
44000	3932.03	2093.91	1484.66	1182.60	1003.39	885.59	802.85	741.99	695.69	659.57	630.82	607.56	588.52	572.76
45000	4021.39	2141.50	1518.40	1209.48	1026.20	905.72	821.09	758.85	711.51	674.56	645.15	621.37	601.90	585.78
46000	4110.76	2189.09	1552.14	1236.35	1049.00	925.84	839.34	775.71	727.32	689.55	659.49	635.18	615.27	598.80
47000	4200.12	2236.68	1585.89	1263.23	1071.81	945.97	857.58	792.58	743.13	704.54	673.83	648.99	628.65	611.82
48000	4289.49	2284.27	1619.63	1290.11	1094.61	966.10	875.83	809.44	758.94	719.53	688.16	662.80	642.02	624.83
49000	4378.85	2331.86	1653.37	1316.99	1117.42	986.22	894.08	826.30	774.75	734.52	702.50	676.61	655.40	637.85
50000	4468.21	2379.45	1687.11	1343.86	1140.22	1006.35	912.32	843.17	790.56	749.51	716.84	690.41	668.77	650.87
55000	4915.04	2617.39	1855.82	1478.25	1254.24	1106.99	1003.56	927.48	869.62	824.46	788.52	759.45	735.65	715.95
60000	5361.86	2855.33	2024.53	1612.63	1368.26	1207.62	1094.79	1011.80	948.67	899.41	860.20	828.50	802.53	781.04
65000	5808.68	3093.28	2193.24	1747.02	1482.28	1308.26	1186.02	1096.12	1027.73	974.36	931.88	897.54	869.41	846.13
70000	6255.50	3331.22	2361.95	1881.41	1596.31	1408.89	1277.25	1180.43	1106.78	1049.31	1003.57	966.58	936.28	911.21
75000	6702.32	3569.17	2530.67	2015.79	1710.33	1509.52	1368.48	1264.75	1185.84	1124.26	1075.25	1035.62	1003.16	976.30
80000	7149.14	3807.11	2699.38	2150.18	1824.35	1610.16	1459.71	1349.06	1264.89	1199.21	1146.93	1104.66	1070.04	1041.38
85000	7595.96	4045.05	2868.09	2284.56	1938.37	1710.79	1550.95	1433.38	1343.95	1274.16	1218.62	1173.70	1136.91	1106.47
90000	8042.78	4283.00	3036.80	2418.95	2052.39	1811.43	1642.18	1517.70	1423.01	1349.12	1290.30	1242.74	1203.79	1171.56
95000	8489.60	4520.94	3205.51	2553.33	2166.41	1912.06	1733.41	1602.01	1502.06	1424.07	1361.98	1311.78	1270.67	1236.64
100000	8936.43	4758.89	3374.22	2687.72	2280.43	2012.70	1824.64	1686.33	1581.12	1499.02	1433.67	1380.82	1337.54	1301.73

TERM AMOUNT	15 Years	16 Years	17 Years	18 Years	19 Years	20 Years	21 Years	22 Years	23 Years	24 Years	25 Years	30 Years	35 Years	40 Years
5	.07	.07	.07	.07	.06	.06	.06	.06	.06	.06	.06	.06	.06	.06
10	.13	.13	.13	.13	.12	.12	.12	.12	.12	.12	.12	.12	.12	.11
15	.20	.19	.19	.19	.18	.18	.18	.18	.18	.18	.18	.17	.17	.17
25	.32	.32	.31	.31	.30	.30	.30	.29	.29	.29	.29	.28	.28	.28
50	.64	.63	.62	.61	.60	.59	.59	.58	.58	.58	.57	.56	.56	.55
75	.96	.94	.92	.91	.90	.89	.88	.87	.87	.86	.86	.84	.83	.83
100	1.28	1.25	1.23	1.21	1.20	1.18	1.17	1.16	1.15	1.15	1.14	1.12	1.11	1.10
200	2.55	2.50	2.46	2.42	2.39	2.36	2.34	2.32	2.30	2.29	2.28	2.23	2.21	2.20
300	3.82	3.75	3.68	3.63	3.58	3.54	3.51	3.48	3.45	3.43	3.41	3.35	3.31	3.30
400	5.09	4.99	4.91	4.83	4.77	4.72	4.67	4.64	4.60	4.57	4.55	4.46	4.42	4.40
500	6.36	6.24	6.13	6.04	5.96	5.90	5.84	5.79	5.75	5.71	5.68	5.58	5.52	5.49
600	7.64	7.49	7.36	7.25	7.16	7.08	7.01	6.95	6.90	6.86	6.82	6.69	6.62	6.59
700	8.91	8.73	8.58	8.46	8.35	8.26	8.18	8.11	8.05	8.00	7.95	7.80	7.73	7.69
800	10.18	9.98	9.81	9.66	9.54	9.43	9.34	9.27	9.20	9.14	9.09	8.92	8.83	8.79
900	11.45	11.23	11.03	10.87	10.73	10.61	10.51	10.42	10.35	10.28	10.22	10.03	9.93	9.88
1000	12.72	12.47	12.26	12.08	11.92	11.79	11.68	11.58	11.50	11.42	11.36	11.15	11.04	10.98
2000	25.44	24.94	24.51	24.15	23.84	23.58	23.35	23.16	22.99	22.84	22.71	22.29	22.07	21.96
3000	38.16	37.41	36.77	36.23	35.76	35.37	35.03	34.73	34.48	34.26	34.07	33.43	33.10	32.93
4000	50.88	49.87	49.02	48.30	47.68	47.15	46.70	46.31	45.97	45.67	45.42	44.57	44.13	43.91
5000	63.60	62.34	61.28	60.37	59.60	58.94	58.37	57.88	57.46	57.09	56.77	55.71	55.17	54.89
6000	76.31	74.81	73.53	72.45	71.52	70.73	70.05	69.46	68.95	68.51	68.13	66.85	66.20	65.86
7000	89.03	87.27	85.79	84.52	83.44	82.51	81.72	81.03	80.44	79.93	79.48	77.99	77.23	76.84
8000	101.75	99.74	98.04	96.59	95.36	94.30	93.39	92.61	91.93	91.34	90.83	89.13	88.26	87.82
9000	114.47	112.21	110.29	108.67	107.28	106.09	105.07	104.18	103.42	102.76	102.19	100.27	99.29	98.79
10000	127.19	124.67	122.55	120.74	119.20	117.88	116.74	115.76	114.91	114.18	113.54	111.41	110.33	109.77
11000	139.91	137.14	134.80	132.81	131.12	129.66	128.41	127.33	126.40	125.60	124.90	122.55	121.36	120.75
12000	152.62	149.61	147.06	144.89	143.04	141.45	140.09	138.91	137.89	137.01	136.25	133.69	132.39	131.72
13000	165.34	162.08	159.31	156.96	154.96	153.24	151.76	150.48	149.38	148.43	147.60	144.83	143.42	142.70
14000	178.06	174.54	171.57	169.04	166.88	165.02	163.43	162.06	160.87	159.85	158.96	155.97	154.45	153.68
15000	190.78	187.01	183.82	181.11	178.79	176.81	175.11	173.64	172.36	171.26	170.31	167.11	165.49	164.65
16000	203.50	199.48	196.07	193.18	190.71	188.60	186.78	185.21	183.86	182.68	181.66	178.25	176.52	175.63
17000	216.22	211.94	208.33	205.26	202.63	200.39	198.45	196.79	195.35	194.10	193.02	189.39	187.55	186.61
18000	228.93	224.41	220.58	217.33	214.55	212.17	210.13	208.36	206.84	205.52	204.37	200.53	198.58	197.58
19000	241.65	236.88	232.84	229.40	226.47	223.96	221.80	219.94	218.33	216.93	215.73	211.67	209.61	208.56
20000	254.37	249.34	245.09	241.48	238.39	235.75	233.47	231.51	229.82	220.35	227.08	222.81	220.65	219.54
21000	267.09	261.81	257.35	253.55	250.31	247.53	245.15	243.09	241.31	239.77	238.43	233.95	231.68	230.51
22000	279.81	274.28	269.60	265.62	262.23	259.32	256.82	254.66	252.80	251.19	249.79	245.09	242.71	241.49
23000	292.53	286.74	281.86	277.70	274.15	271.11	268.49	266.24	264.29	262.60	261.14	256.23	253.74	252.46
24000	305.24	299.21	294.11	289.77	286.07	282.89	280.17	277.81	275.78	274.02	272.49	267.37	264.77	263.44
25000	317.96	311.68	306.36	301.85	297.99	294.68	291.84	289.39	287.27	285.44	283.85	278.51	275.81	274.42
26000	330.68	324.15	318.62	313.92	309.91	306.47	303.51	300.96	298.76	296.86	295.20	289.65	286.84	285.39
27000	343.40	336.61	330.87	325.99	321.83	318.26	315.19	312.54	310.25	308.27	306.56	300.79	297.87	296.37
28000	356.12	349.08	343.13	338.07	333.75	330.04	326.86	324.11	321.74	319.69	317.91	311.93	308.90	307.35
29000	368.84	361.55	355.38	350.14	345.67	341.83	338.53	335.69	333.23	331.11	329.26	323.07	319.93	318.32
30000	381.55	374.01	367.64	362.21	357.58	353.62	350.21	347.27	344.72	342.52	340.62	334.21	330.97	329.30
31000	394.27	386.48	379.89	374.29	369.50	365.40	361.88	358.84	356.22	353.94	351.97	345.35	342.00	340.28
32000	406.99	398.95	392.14	386.36	381.42	377.19	373.55	370.42	367.71	365.36	363.32	356.49	353.03	351.25
33000	419.71	411.41	404.40	398.43	393.34	388.98	385.23	381.99	379.20	376.78	374.68	367.63	364.06	362.23
34000	432.43	423.88	416.65	410.51	405.26	400.77	396.90	393.57	390.69	388.19	386.03	378.77	375.10	373.21
35000	445.15	436.35	428.91	422.58	417.18	412.55	408.57	405.14	402.18	399.61	397.39	389.91	386.13	384.18
36000	457.86	448.82	441.16	434.66	429.10	424.34	420.25	416.72	413.67	411.03	408.74	401.05	397.16	395.16
37000	470.58	461.28	453.42	446.73	441.02	436.13	431.92	428.29	425.16	422.45	420.09	412.19	408.19	406.14
38000	483.30	473.75	465.67	458.80	452.94	447.91	443.59	439.87	436.65	433.86	431.45	423.33	419.22	417.11
39000	496.02	486.22	477.93	470.88	464.86	459.70	455.27	451.44	448.14	445.28	442.80	434.47	430.26	428.09
40000	508.74	498.68	490.18	482.95	476.78	471.49	466.94	463.02	459.63	456.70	454.15	445.61	441.29	439.07
41000	521.45	511.15	502.43	495.02	488.70	483.27	478.61	474.59	471.12	468.12	465.51	456.75	452.32	450.04
42000	534.17	523.62	514.69	507.10	500.62	495.06	490.29	486.17	482.61	479.53	476.86	467.89	463.35	461.02
43000	546.89	536.08	526.94	519.17	512.54	506.85	501.96	497.75	494.10	490.95	488.21	479.03	474.38	472.00
44000	559.61	548.55	539.20	531.24	524.46	518.64	513.63	509.32	505.59	502.37	499.57	490.17	485.42	482.97
45000	572.33	561.02	551.45	543.32	536.37	530.42	525.31	520.90	517.08	513.78	510.92	501.31	496.45	493.95
46000	585.05	573.48	563.71	555.39	548.29	542.21	536.98	532.47	528.58	525.20	522.28	512.45	507.48	504.92
47000	597.76	585.95	575.96	567.47	560.21	554.00	548.65	544.05	540.07	536.62	533.63	523.59	518.51	515.90
48000	610.48	598.42	588.21	579.54	572.13	565.78	560.33	555.62	551.56	548.04	544.98	534.74	529.54	526.88
49000	623.20	610.89	600.47	591.61	584.05	577.57	572.00	567.20	563.05	559.45	556.34	545.88	540.58	537.85
50000	635.92	623.35	612.72	603.69	595.97	589.36	583.67	578.77	574.54	570.87	567.69	557.02	551.61	548.83
55000	699.51	685.69	674.00	664.05	655.57	648.29	642.04	636.65	631.99	627.96	624.46	612.72	606.77	603.71
60000	763.10	748.02	735.27	724.42	715.16	707.23	700.41	694.53	689.44	685.04	681.23	668.42	661.93	658.60
65000	826.69	810.36	796.54	784.79	774.76	766.16	758.77	752.40	746.90	742.13	738.00	724.12	717.09	713.48
70000	890.29	872.69	857.81	845.16	834.36	825.10	817.14	810.28	804.35	799.22	794.77	779.82	772.25	768.36
75000	953.88	935.03	919.08	905.53	893.95	884.04	875.51	868.16	861.80	856.30	851.53	835.52	827.41	823.24
80000	1017.47	997.36	980.35	965.90	953.55	942.97	933.87	926.03	919.26	913.39	908.30	891.22	882.57	878.13
85000	1081.06	1059.70	1041.63	1026.26	1013.15	1001.91	992.24	983.91	976.71	970.48	965.07	946.92	937.73	933.01
90000	1144.65	1122.03	1102.90	1086.63	1072.74	1060.84	1050.61	1041.79	1034.16	1027.56	1021.84	1002.62	992.89	987.89
95000	1208.24	1184.37	1164.17	1147.00	1132.34	1119.78	1108.98	1099.66	1091.62	1084.65	1078.61	1058.33	1048.05	1042.77
100000	1271.83	1246.70	1225.44	1207.37	1191.94	1178.71	1167.34	1157.54	1149.07	1141.74	1135.38	1114.03	1103.21	1097.66

MONTHLY PAYMENT
REQUIRED TO AMORTIZE A LOAN

TERM AMOUNT	1 Year	2 Years	3 Years	4 Years	5 Years	6 Years	7 Years	8 Years	9 Years	10 Years	11 Years	12 Years	13 Years	14 Years
5	.45	.24	.17	.14	.12	.11	.10	.09	.08	.08	.08	.07	.07	.07
10	.90	.48	.34	.27	.23	.21	.19	.17	.16	.16	.15	.14	.14	.14
15	1.35	.72	.51	.41	.35	.31	.28	.26	.24	.23	.22	.21	.21	.20
25	2.24	1.20	.85	.68	.58	.51	.46	.43	.40	.38	.36	.35	.34	.33
50	4.47	2.39	1.69	1.35	1.15	1.01	.92	.85	.80	.76	.72	.70	.67	.66
75	6.71	3.58	2.54	2.02	1.72	1.52	1.37	1.27	1.19	1.13	1.08	1.04	1.01	.98
100	8.94	4.77	3.38	2.69	2.29	2.02	1.83	1.69	1.59	1.51	1.44	1.39	1.34	1.31
200	17.88	9.53	6.76	5.38	4.57	4.03	3.66	3.38	3.17	3.01	2.88	2.77	2.68	2.61
300	26.82	14.29	10.13	8.07	6.85	6.05	5.48	5.07	4.75	4.51	4.31	4.15	4.02	3.92
400	35.76	19.05	13.51	10.76	9.13	8.06	7.31	6.76	6.34	6.01	5.75	5.53	5.36	5.22
500	44.69	23.81	16.88	13.45	11.41	10.08	9.13	8.44	7.92	7.51	7.18	6.92	6.70	6.52
600	53.63	28.57	20.26	16.14	13.70	12.09	10.96	10.13	9.50	9.01	8.62	8.30	8.04	7.83
700	62.57	33.33	23.63	18.83	15.98	14.10	12.79	11.82	11.08	10.51	10.05	9.68	9.38	9.13
800	71.51	38.09	27.01	21.52	18.26	16.12	14.61	13.51	12.67	12.01	11.49	11.06	10.72	10.43
900	80.44	42.85	30.38	24.21	20.54	18.13	16.44	15.19	14.25	13.51	12.92	12.45	12.06	11.74
1000	89.38	47.61	33.76	26.89	22.82	20.15	18.26	16.88	15.83	15.01	14.36	13.83	13.40	13.04
2000	178.76	95.21	67.51	53.78	45.64	40.29	36.52	33.76	31.66	30.01	28.71	27.65	26.79	26.07
3000	268.13	142.81	101.27	80.67	68.46	60.43	54.78	50.64	47.48	45.02	43.06	41.48	40.18	39.11
4000	357.51	190.41	135.02	107.56	91.27	80.57	73.04	67.51	63.31	60.02	57.41	55.30	53.57	52.14
5000	446.88	238.01	168.78	134.45	114.09	100.71	91.30	84.39	79.13	75.03	71.76	69.12	66.96	65.17
6000	536.26	285.61	202.53	161.34	136.91	120.85	109.56	101.27	94.96	90.03	86.12	82.95	80.35	78.21
7000	625.64	333.21	236.28	188.23	159.72	140.99	127.82	118.15	110.78	105.04	100.47	96.77	93.74	91.24
8000	715.01	380.81	270.04	215.12	182.54	161.13	146.08	135.02	126.61	120.04	114.82	110.59	107.13	104.27
9000	804.39	428.41	303.79	242.01	205.36	181.27	164.34	151.90	142.43	135.05	129.17	124.42	120.53	117.31
10000	893.76	476.01	337.55	268.90	228.18	201.41	182.60	168.78	158.26	150.05	143.52	138.24	133.92	130.34
11000	983.14	523.61	371.30	295.79	250.99	221.55	200.86	185.65	174.09	165.06	157.87	152.07	147.31	143.37
12000	1072.52	571.21	405.06	322.68	273.81	241.69	219.12	202.53	189.91	180.06	172.23	165.89	160.70	156.41
13000	1161.89	618.81	438.81	349.57	296.63	261.83	237.38	219.41	205.74	195.07	186.58	179.71	174.09	169.44
14000	1251.27	666.41	472.56	376.46	319.44	281.97	255.64	236.29	221.56	210.07	200.93	193.54	187.48	182.47
15000	1340.64	714.01	506.32	403.35	342.26	302.11	273.90	253.16	237.39	225.08	215.28	207.36	200.87	195.51
16000	1430.02	761.61	540.07	430.24	365.08	322.25	292.16	270.04	253.21	240.08	229.63	221.18	214.26	208.54
17000	1519.40	809.21	573.83	457.13	387.90	342.39	310.42	286.92	269.04	255.09	243.98	235.01	227.66	221.57
18000	1608.77	856.82	607.58	484.02	410.71	362.53	328.68	303.80	284.86	270.09	258.34	248.83	241.05	234.61
19000	1698.15	904.42	641.33	510.91	433.53	382.67	346.94	320.67	300.69	285.10	272.69	262.65	254.44	247.64
20000	1787.52	952.02	675.09	537.80	456.35	402.81	365.20	337.55	316.52	300.10	287.04	276.48	267.83	260.67
21000	1876.90	999.62	708.84	564.69	479.16	422.95	383.46	354.43	332.34	315.11	301.39	290.30	281.22	273.71
22000	1966.28	1047.22	742.60	591.58	501.98	443.09	401.72	371.30	348.17	330.11	315.74	304.13	294.61	286.74
23000	2055.65	1094.82	776.35	618.47	524.80	463.23	419.98	388.18	363.99	345.12	330.10	317.95	308.00	299.77
24000	2145.03	1142.42	810.11	645.35	547.62	483.37	438.24	405.06	379.82	360.12	344.45	331.77	321.39	312.81
25000	2234.40	1190.02	843.86	672.24	570.43	503.51	456.50	421.94	395.64	375.13	358.80	345.60	334.79	325.84
26000	2323.78	1237.62	877.61	699.13	593.25	523.65	474.76	438.81	411.47	390.13	373.15	359.42	348.18	338.87
27000	2413.16	1285.22	911.37	726.02	616.07	543.79	493.02	455.69	427.29	405.14	387.50	373.24	361.57	351.91
28000	2502.53	1332.82	945.12	752.91	638.88	563.93	511.28	472.57	443.12	420.14	401.85	387.07	374.96	364.94
29000	2591.91	1380.42	978.88	779.80	661.70	584.07	529.54	489.45	458.95	435.15	416.21	400.89	388.35	377.97
30000	2681.28	1428.02	1012.63	806.69	684.52	604.21	547.80	506.32	474.77	450.15	430.56	414.72	401.74	391.01
31000	2770.66	1475.62	1046.38	833.58	707.34	624.35	566.06	523.20	490.60	465.16	444.91	428.54	415.13	404.04
32000	2860.03	1523.22	1080.14	860.47	730.15	644.49	584.32	540.08	506.42	480.16	459.26	442.36	428.52	417.07
33000	2949.41	1570.82	1113.89	887.36	752.97	664.63	602.58	556.95	522.25	495.17	473.61	456.19	441.92	430.11
34000	3038.79	1618.42	1147.65	914.25	775.79	684.77	620.84	573.83	538.07	510.17	487.96	470.01	455.31	443.14
35000	3128.16	1666.02	1181.40	941.14	798.60	704.91	639.10	590.71	553.90	525.18	502.32	483.83	468.70	456.17
36000	3217.54	1713.63	1215.16	968.03	821.42	725.05	657.36	607.59	569.72	540.18	516.67	497.66	482.09	469.21
37000	3306.91	1761.23	1248.91	994.92	844.24	745.19	675.62	624.46	585.55	555.19	531.02	511.48	495.48	482.24
38000	3396.29	1808.83	1282.66	1021.81	867.06	765.33	693.88	641.34	601.37	570.19	545.37	525.30	508.87	495.27
39000	3485.67	1856.43	1316.42	1048.70	889.87	785.47	712.14	658.22	617.20	585.20	559.72	539.13	522.26	508.31
40000	3575.04	1904.03	1350.17	1075.59	912.69	805.61	730.40	675.10	633.03	600.20	574.08	552.95	535.65	521.34
41000	3664.42	1951.63	1383.93	1102.48	935.51	825.75	748.66	691.97	648.85	615.21	588.43	566.78	549.05	534.38
42000	3753.79	1999.23	1417.68	1129.37	958.32	845.89	766.92	708.85	664.68	630.21	602.78	580.60	562.44	547.41
43000	3843.17	2046.83	1451.44	1156.26	981.14	866.03	785.18	725.73	680.50	645.22	617.13	594.42	575.83	560.44
44000	3932.55	2094.43	1485.19	1183.15	1003.96	886.17	803.44	742.60	696.33	660.22	631.48	608.25	589.22	573.48
45000	4021.92	2142.03	1518.94	1210.04	1026.78	906.31	821.70	759.48	712.15	675.23	645.83	622.07	602.61	586.51
46000	4111.30	2189.63	1552.70	1236.93	1049.59	926.45	839.96	776.36	727.98	690.23	660.19	635.89	616.00	599.54
47000	4200.67	2237.23	1586.45	1263.82	1072.41	946.59	858.22	793.24	743.80	705.23	674.54	649.72	629.39	612.58
48000	4290.05	2284.83	1620.21	1290.70	1095.23	966.73	876.48	810.11	759.63	720.24	688.89	663.54	642.78	625.61
49000	4379.43	2332.43	1653.96	1317.59	1118.04	986.87	894.74	826.99	775.46	735.24	703.24	677.37	656.18	638.64
50000	4468.80	2380.03	1687.71	1344.48	1140.86	1007.01	913.00	843.87	791.28	750.25	717.59	691.19	669.57	651.68
55000	4915.68	2618.04	1856.49	1478.93	1254.95	1107.71	1004.30	928.25	870.41	825.27	789.35	760.31	736.52	716.84
60000	5362.56	2856.04	2025.26	1613.38	1369.03	1208.41	1095.60	1012.64	949.54	900.30	861.11	829.43	803.48	782.01
65000	5809.44	3094.04	2194.03	1747.83	1483.12	1309.11	1186.90	1097.03	1028.66	975.32	932.87	898.54	870.44	847.18
70000	6256.32	3332.04	2362.80	1882.28	1597.20	1409.81	1278.20	1181.41	1107.79	1050.35	1004.63	967.66	937.39	912.34
75000	6703.20	3570.05	2531.57	2016.72	1711.29	1510.52	1369.50	1265.80	1186.92	1125.37	1076.39	1036.78	1004.35	977.51
80000	7150.08	3808.05	2700.34	2151.17	1825.37	1611.22	1460.80	1350.19	1266.05	1200.40	1148.15	1105.90	1071.30	1042.68
85000	7596.96	4046.05	2869.11	2285.62	1939.46	1711.92	1552.10	1434.57	1345.17	1275.42	1219.90	1175.02	1138.26	1107.85
90000	8043.84	4284.06	3037.88	2420.07	2053.55	1812.62	1643.40	1518.96	1424.30	1350.45	1291.66	1244.14	1205.22	1173.01
95000	8490.72	4522.06	3206.65	2554.51	2167.63	1913.32	1734.70	1603.34	1503.43	1425.47	1363.42	1313.25	1272.17	1238.18
100000	8937.60	4760.06	3375.42	2688.96	2281.72	2014.02	1826.00	1687.73	1582.56	1500.49	1435.18	1382.37	1339.13	1303.35

TERM	15 Years	16 Years	17 Years	18 Years	19 Years	20 Years	21 Years	22 Years	23 Years	24 Years	25 Years	30 Years	35 Years	40 Years
AMOUNT														
5	.07	.07	.07	.07	.06	.06	.06	.06	.06	.06	.06	.06	.06	.06
10	.13	.13	.13	.13	.12	.12	.12	.12	.12	.12	.12	.12	.12	.11
15	.20	.19	.19	.19	.18	.18	.18	.18	.18	.18	.18	.17	.17	.17
25	.32	.32	.31	.31	.30	.30	.30	.29	.29	.29	.29	.28	.28	.28
50	.64	.63	.62	.61	.60	.60	.59	.58	.58	.58	.57	.56	.56	.55
75	.96	.94	.93	.91	.90	.89	.88	.87	.87	.86	.86	.84	.83	.83
100	1.28	1.25	1.23	1.21	1.20	1.19	1.17	1.16	1.16	1.15	1.14	1.12	1.11	1.10
200	2.55	2.50	2.46	2.42	2.39	2.37	2.34	2.32	2.31	2.29	2.28	2.24	2.22	2.20
300	3.83	3.75	3.69	3.63	3.59	3.55	3.51	3.48	3.46	3.44	3.42	3.35	3.32	3.30
400	5.10	5.00	4.91	4.84	4.78	4.73	4.68	4.64	4.61	4.58	4.55	4.47	4.43	4.40
500	6.37	6.25	6.14	6.05	5.97	5.91	5.85	5.80	5.76	5.72	5.69	5.58	5.53	5.50
600	7.65	7.50	7.37	7.26	7.17	7.09	7.02	6.96	6.91	6.87	6.83	6.70	6.64	6.60
700	8.92	8.74	8.60	8.47	8.36	8.27	8.19	8.12	8.06	8.01	7.97	7.82	7.74	7.70
800	10.19	9.99	9.82	9.68	9.55	9.45	9.36	9.28	9.21	9.15	9.10	8.93	8.85	8.80
900	11.47	11.24	11.05	10.89	10.75	10.63	10.53	10.44	10.36	10.30	10.24	10.05	9.95	9.90
1000	12.74	12.49	12.28	12.10	11.94	11.81	11.70	11.60	11.51	11.44	11.38	11.16	11.06	11.00
2000	25.47	24.97	24.55	24.19	23.88	23.61	23.39	23.19	23.02	22.88	22.75	22.32	22.11	22.00
3000	38.21	37.46	36.82	36.28	35.82	35.42	35.08	34.79	34.53	34.31	34.12	33.48	33.16	33.00
4000	50.94	49.94	49.09	48.37	47.75	47.22	46.77	46.38	46.04	45.75	45.50	44.64	44.21	43.99
5000	63.68	62.42	61.36	60.46	59.69	59.03	58.46	57.97	57.55	57.19	56.87	55.80	55.27	54.99
6000	76.41	74.91	73.63	72.55	71.63	70.83	70.15	69.57	69.06	68.62	68.24	66.96	66.32	65.99
7000	89.15	87.39	85.91	84.64	83.56	82.64	81.85	81.16	80.57	80.06	79.61	78.12	77.37	76.98
8000	101.88	99.87	98.18	96.73	95.50	94.44	93.54	92.75	92.08	91.49	90.99	89.28	88.42	87.98
9000	114.62	112.36	110.45	108.82	107.44	106.25	105.23	104.35	103.59	102.93	102.36	100.44	99.47	98.98
10000	127.35	124.84	122.72	120.91	119.37	118.05	116.92	115.94	115.10	114.37	113.73	111.60	110.53	109.97
11000	140.09	137.33	134.99	133.01	131.31	129.86	128.61	127.54	126.61	125.80	125.10	122.76	121.58	120.97
12000	152.82	149.81	147.26	145.10	143.25	141.66	140.30	139.13	138.11	137.24	136.48	133.92	132.63	131.97
13000	165.56	162.29	159.53	157.19	155.19	153.47	151.99	150.72	149.62	148.67	147.85	145.00	143.68	142.96
14000	178.29	174.78	171.81	169.28	167.12	165.27	163.69	162.32	161.13	160.11	159.22	156.24	154.73	153.96
15000	191.03	187.26	184.08	181.37	179.06	177.08	175.38	173.91	172.64	171.55	170.59	167.40	165.79	164.96
16000	203.76	199.74	196.35	193.46	191.00	188.88	187.07	185.50	184.15	182.98	181.97	178.56	176.84	175.96
17000	216.50	212.23	208.62	205.55	202.93	200.69	198.76	197.10	195.66	194.42	193.34	189.72	187.89	186.95
18000	229.23	224.71	220.89	217.64	214.87	212.49	210.45	208.69	207.17	205.85	204.71	200.88	198.94	197.95
19000	241.97	237.20	233.16	229.73	226.81	224.30	222.14	220.28	218.68	217.29	216.08	212.04	210.00	208.95
20000	254.70	249.68	245.43	241.82	238.74	236.10	233.83	231.88	230.19	228.73	227.46	223.20	221.05	219.94
21000	267.44	262.16	257.71	253.92	250.68	247.91	245.53	243.47	241.70	240.16	238.83	234.36	232.10	230.94
22000	280.17	274.65	269.98	266.01	262.62	259.71	257.22	255.07	253.21	251.60	250.20	245.52	243.15	241.94
23000	292.90	287.13	282.25	278.10	274.55	271.52	268.91	266.66	264.72	263.03	261.57	256.68	254.20	252.93
24000	305.64	299.61	294.52	290.19	286.49	283.32	280.60	278.25	276.22	274.47	272.95	267.84	265.26	263.93
25000	318.37	312.10	306.79	302.28	298.43	295.13	292.29	289.85	287.73	285.91	284.32	279.00	276.31	274.93
26000	331.11	324.58	319.06	314.37	310.37	306.93	303.98	301.44	299.24	297.34	295.69	290.16	287.36	285.92
27000	343.84	337.07	331.33	326.46	322.30	318.74	315.68	313.03	310.75	308.78	307.06	301.32	298.41	296.92
28000	356.58	349.55	343.61	338.55	334.24	330.54	327.37	324.63	322.26	320.21	318.44	312.48	309.46	307.92
29000	369.31	362.03	355.88	350.64	346.18	342.35	339.06	336.22	333.77	331.65	329.81	323.64	320.52	318.91
30000	382.05	374.52	368.15	362.73	358.11	354.15	350.75	347.81	345.28	343.09	341.18	334.80	331.57	329.91
31000	394.78	387.00	380.42	374.83	370.05	365.96	362.44	359.41	356.79	354.52	352.55	345.96	342.62	340.91
32000	407.52	399.48	392.69	386.92	381.99	377.76	374.13	371.00	368.30	365.96	363.93	357.12	353.67	351.90
33000	420.25	411.97	404.96	399.01	393.92	389.57	385.82	382.60	379.81	377.39	375.30	368.28	364.72	362.90
34000	432.99	424.45	417.23	411.10	405.86	401.37	397.51	394.19	391.32	388.83	386.67	379.44	375.78	373.90
35000	445.72	436.94	429.51	423.19	417.80	413.18	409.21	405.78	402.83	400.27	398.05	390.60	386.83	384.90
36000	458.46	449.42	441.78	435.28	429.73	424.98	420.90	417.38	414.33	411.70	409.42	401.76	397.88	395.89
37000	471.19	461.90	454.05	447.37	441.67	436.79	432.59	428.97	425.84	423.14	420.79	412.92	408.93	406.89
38000	483.93	474.39	466.32	459.46	453.61	448.59	444.28	440.56	437.35	434.57	432.16	424.08	419.99	417.89
39000	496.66	486.87	478.59	471.55	465.55	460.40	455.97	452.16	448.86	446.01	443.54	435.24	431.04	428.88
40000	509.40	499.35	490.86	483.64	477.48	472.20	467.66	463.75	460.37	457.45	454.91	446.40	442.09	439.88
41000	522.13	511.84	503.13	495.74	489.42	484.01	479.35	475.34	471.88	468.88	466.28	457.56	453.14	450.88
42000	534.87	524.32	515.41	507.83	501.36	495.81	491.05	486.94	483.39	480.32	477.65	468.72	464.19	461.87
43000	547.60	536.81	527.68	519.92	513.29	507.62	502.74	498.53	494.90	491.75	489.03	479.88	475.25	472.87
44000	560.34	549.29	539.95	532.01	525.23	519.42	514.43	510.13	506.41	503.19	500.40	491.04	486.30	483.87
45000	573.07	561.77	552.22	544.10	537.17	531.23	526.12	521.72	517.92	514.63	511.77	502.20	497.35	494.86
46000	585.80	574.26	564.49	556.19	549.10	543.03	537.81	533.31	529.43	526.06	523.14	513.36	508.40	505.86
47000	598.54	586.74	576.76	568.28	561.04	554.84	549.50	544.91	540.94	537.50	534.52	524.51	519.45	516.86
48000	611.27	599.22	589.03	580.37	572.98	566.64	561.19	556.50	552.44	548.93	545.89	535.67	530.51	527.85
49000	624.01	611.71	601.31	592.46	584.91	578.45	572.89	568.09	563.95	560.37	557.26	546.83	541.56	538.85
50000	636.74	624.19	613.58	604.55	596.85	590.25	584.58	579.69	575.46	571.81	568.63	557.99	552.61	549.85
55000	700.42	686.61	674.93	665.01	656.54	649.28	643.03	637.66	633.01	628.99	625.50	613.79	607.87	604.83
60000	764.09	749.03	736.29	725.46	716.22	708.30	701.49	695.62	690.55	686.17	682.36	669.59	663.13	659.82
65000	827.77	811.45	797.65	785.92	775.91	767.32	759.95	753.59	748.10	743.35	739.22	725.39	718.39	714.80
70000	891.44	873.87	859.01	846.37	835.59	826.35	818.41	811.56	805.65	800.53	796.09	781.19	773.65	769.79
75000	955.11	936.29	920.36	906.83	895.27	885.37	876.86	869.53	863.19	857.71	852.95	836.99	828.91	824.77
80000	1018.79	998.70	981.72	967.28	954.96	944.40	935.32	927.50	920.74	914.89	909.81	892.79	884.17	879.75
85000	1082.46	1061.12	1043.08	1027.74	1014.64	1003.42	993.78	985.47	978.28	972.07	966.67	948.59	939.43	934.74
90000	1146.14	1123.54	1104.43	1088.19	1074.33	1062.45	1052.24	1043.43	1035.83	1029.25	1023.54	1004.39	994.70	989.72
95000	1209.81	1185.96	1165.79	1148.65	1134.01	1121.47	1110.69	1101.40	1093.37	1086.43	1080.40	1060.18	1049.96	1044.71
100000	1273.48	1248.38	1227.15	1209.10	1193.70	1180.50	1169.15	1159.37	1150.92	1143.61	1137.26	1115.98	1105.22	1099.69

MONTHLY PAYMENT
REQUIRED TO AMORTIZE A LOAN

TERM AMOUNT	1 Year	2 Years	3 Years	4 Years	5 Years	6 Years	7 Years	8 Years	9 Years	10 Years	11 Years	12 Years	13 Years	14 Years
5	.45	.24	.17	.14	.12	.11	.10	.09	.08	.08	.08	.07	.07	.07
10	.90	.48	.34	.27	.23	.21	.19	.17	.16	.16	.15	.14	.14	.14
15	1.35	.72	.51	.41	.35	.31	.28	.26	.24	.23	.22	.21	.21	.20
25	2.24	1.20	.85	.68	.58	.51	.46	.43	.40	.38	.36	.35	.34	.33
50	4.48	2.39	1.69	1.35	1.15	1.01	.92	.85	.80	.76	.72	.70	.68	.66
75	6.71	3.58	2.54	2.02	1.72	1.52	1.38	1.27	1.20	1.13	1.08	1.05	1.01	.99
100	8.95	4.77	3.38	2.70	2.29	2.02	1.84	1.70	1.59	1.51	1.44	1.39	1.35	1.31
200	17.89	9.53	6.76	5.39	4.58	4.04	3.67	3.39	3.18	3.01	2.88	2.78	2.69	2.62
300	26.83	14.30	10.14	8.08	6.86	6.06	5.50	5.08	4.77	4.52	4.32	4.17	4.04	3.93
400	35.77	19.06	13.52	10.78	9.15	8.08	7.33	6.77	6.35	6.02	5.76	5.55	5.38	5.24
500	44.71	23.82	16.90	13.47	11.43	10.09	9.16	8.46	7.94	7.53	7.20	6.94	6.72	6.55
600	53.65	28.59	20.28	16.16	13.72	12.11	10.99	10.16	9.53	9.03	8.64	8.33	8.07	7.85
700	62.59	33.35	23.66	18.85	16.00	14.13	12.82	11.85	11.11	10.54	10.08	9.71	9.41	9.16
800	71.53	38.11	27.04	21.55	18.29	16.15	14.65	13.54	12.70	12.04	11.52	11.10	10.75	10.47
900	80.48	42.88	30.42	24.24	20.58	18.17	16.48	15.23	14.29	13.55	12.96	12.49	12.10	11.78
1000	89.42	47.64	33.80	26.93	22.86	20.18	18.31	16.92	15.87	15.05	14.40	13.88	13.44	13.09
2000	178.83	95.28	67.59	53.86	45.72	40.36	36.61	33.84	31.74	30.10	28.80	27.75	26.88	26.17
3000	268.24	142.91	101.38	80.79	68.57	60.54	54.91	50.76	47.61	45.15	43.20	41.62	40.32	39.25
4000	357.65	190.55	135.17	107.71	91.43	80.72	73.21	67.68	63.48	60.20	57.59	55.49	53.76	52.33
5000	447.06	238.18	168.96	134.64	114.28	100.90	91.51	84.60	79.35	75.25	71.99	69.36	67.20	65.41
6000	536.47	285.82	202.75	161.57	137.14	121.08	109.81	101.52	95.22	90.30	86.39	83.23	80.64	78.50
7000	625.88	333.46	236.54	188.49	159.99	141.26	128.11	118.44	111.09	105.35	100.79	97.10	94.08	91.58
8000	715.29	381.09	270.33	215.42	182.85	161.44	146.41	135.36	126.96	120.40	115.18	110.97	107.52	104.66
9000	804.71	428.73	304.12	242.35	205.71	181.62	164.71	152.28	142.82	135.45	129.58	124.84	120.95	117.74
10000	894.12	476.36	337.91	269.27	228.56	201.80	183.01	169.20	158.69	150.50	143.98	138.71	134.39	130.82
11000	983.53	524.00	371.70	296.20	251.42	221.98	201.31	186.12	174.56	165.55	158.37	152.58	147.83	143.91
12000	1072.94	571.63	405.49	323.13	274.27	242.16	219.62	203.04	190.43	180.60	172.77	166.45	161.27	156.99
13000	1162.35	619.27	439.28	350.05	297.13	262.34	237.92	219.96	206.30	195.65	187.17	180.32	174.71	170.07
14000	1251.76	666.91	473.07	376.98	319.98	282.52	256.22	236.88	222.17	210.69	201.57	194.19	188.15	183.15
15000	1341.17	714.54	506.86	403.91	342.84	302.70	274.52	253.79	238.04	225.74	215.96	208.06	201.59	196.23
16000	1430.58	762.18	540.65	430.83	365.69	322.88	292.82	270.71	253.91	240.79	230.36	221.93	215.03	209.32
17000	1519.99	809.81	574.44	457.76	388.55	343.06	311.12	287.63	269.77	255.84	244.76	235.80	228.47	222.40
18000	1609.41	857.45	608.23	484.69	411.41	363.24	329.42	304.55	285.64	270.89	259.16	249.67	241.90	235.48
19000	1698.82	905.09	642.02	511.62	434.26	383.42	347.72	321.47	301.51	285.94	273.55	263.54	255.34	248.56
20000	1788.23	952.72	675.81	538.54	457.12	403.60	366.02	338.39	317.38	300.99	287.95	277.41	268.78	261.64
21000	1877.64	1000.36	709.60	565.47	479.97	423.78	384.32	355.31	333.25	316.04	302.35	291.28	282.22	274.73
22000	1967.05	1047.99	743.39	592.40	502.83	443.96	402.62	372.23	349.12	331.09	316.74	305.15	295.66	287.81
23000	2056.46	1095.63	777.18	619.32	525.68	464.14	420.93	389.15	364.99	346.14	331.14	319.02	309.10	300.89
24000	2145.87	1143.26	810.97	646.25	548.54	484.32	439.23	406.07	380.86	361.19	345.54	332.89	322.54	313.97
25000	2235.28	1190.90	844.76	673.18	571.39	504.50	457.53	422.99	396.72	376.24	359.94	346.76	335.98	327.05
26000	2324.69	1238.54	878.55	700.10	594.25	524.68	475.83	439.91	412.59	391.29	374.33	360.63	349.41	340.14
27000	2414.11	1286.17	912.34	727.03	617.11	544.86	494.13	456.83	428.46	406.34	388.73	374.50	362.85	353.22
28000	2503.52	1333.81	946.14	753.96	639.96	565.04	512.43	473.75	444.33	421.38	403.13	388.37	376.29	366.30
29000	2592.93	1381.44	979.93	780.88	662.82	585.22	530.73	490.67	460.20	436.43	417.53	402.24	389.73	379.38
30000	2682.34	1429.08	1013.72	807.81	685.67	605.40	549.03	507.58	476.07	451.48	431.92	416.11	403.17	392.46
31000	2771.75	1476.72	1047.51	834.74	708.53	625.58	567.33	524.50	491.94	466.53	446.32	429.98	416.61	405.55
32000	2861.16	1524.35	1081.30	861.66	731.38	645.76	585.63	541.42	507.81	481.58	460.72	443.85	430.05	418.63
33000	2950.57	1571.99	1115.09	888.59	754.24	665.94	603.93	558.34	523.67	496.63	475.11	457.72	443.49	431.71
34000	3039.98	1619.62	1148.88	915.52	777.09	686.12	622.23	575.26	539.54	511.68	489.51	471.59	456.93	444.79
35000	3129.39	1667.26	1182.67	942.45	799.95	706.30	640.54	592.18	555.41	526.73	503.91	485.46	470.36	457.87
36000	3218.81	1714.89	1216.46	969.37	822.81	726.48	658.84	609.10	571.28	541.78	518.31	499.33	483.80	470.96
37000	3308.22	1762.53	1250.25	996.30	845.66	746.66	677.14	626.02	587.15	556.83	532.70	513.20	497.24	484.04
38000	3397.63	1810.17	1284.04	1023.23	868.52	766.84	695.44	642.94	603.02	571.88	547.10	527.07	510.68	497.12
39000	3487.04	1857.80	1317.83	1050.15	891.37	787.02	713.74	659.86	618.89	586.93	561.50	540.94	524.12	510.20
40000	3576.45	1905.44	1351.62	1077.08	914.23	807.20	732.04	676.78	634.76	601.98	575.89	554.81	537.56	523.28
41000	3665.86	1953.07	1385.41	1104.01	937.08	827.38	750.34	693.70	650.62	617.03	590.29	568.68	551.00	536.37
42000	3755.27	2000.71	1419.20	1130.93	959.94	847.56	768.64	710.62	666.49	632.07	604.69	582.55	564.44	549.45
43000	3844.68	2048.35	1452.99	1157.86	982.80	867.74	786.94	727.54	682.36	647.12	619.09	596.43	577.87	562.53
44000	3934.10	2095.98	1486.78	1184.79	1005.65	887.92	805.24	744.46	698.23	662.17	633.48	610.30	591.31	575.61
45000	4023.51	2143.62	1520.57	1211.71	1028.51	908.10	823.54	761.37	714.10	677.22	647.88	624.17	604.75	588.69
46000	4112.92	2191.25	1554.36	1238.64	1051.36	928.28	841.85	778.29	729.97	692.27	662.28	638.04	618.19	601.78
47000	4202.33	2238.89	1588.15	1265.57	1074.22	948.46	860.15	795.21	745.84	707.32	676.68	651.91	631.63	614.86
48000	4291.74	2286.52	1621.94	1292.49	1097.07	968.64	878.45	812.13	761.71	722.37	691.07	665.78	645.07	627.94
49000	4381.15	2334.16	1655.73	1319.42	1119.93	988.82	896.75	829.05	777.57	737.42	705.47	679.65	658.51	641.02
50000	4470.56	2381.80	1689.52	1346.35	1142.78	1009.00	915.05	845.97	793.44	752.47	719.87	693.52	671.95	654.10
55000	4917.62	2619.98	1858.48	1480.98	1257.06	1109.89	1006.55	930.57	872.79	827.71	791.85	762.87	739.14	719.51
60000	5364.67	2858.15	2027.43	1615.62	1371.34	1210.79	1098.06	1015.16	952.13	902.96	863.84	832.22	806.33	784.92
65000	5811.73	3096.33	2196.38	1750.25	1485.62	1311.69	1189.56	1099.76	1031.47	978.21	935.83	901.57	873.53	850.33
70000	6258.78	3334.51	2365.33	1884.89	1599.90	1412.59	1281.07	1184.36	1110.82	1053.45	1007.81	970.92	940.72	915.74
75000	6705.84	3572.69	2534.28	2019.52	1714.17	1513.49	1372.57	1268.95	1190.16	1128.70	1079.80	1040.27	1007.92	981.15
80000	7152.90	3810.87	2703.23	2154.15	1828.45	1614.39	1464.07	1353.55	1269.51	1203.95	1151.78	1109.62	1075.11	1046.56
85000	7599.95	4049.05	2872.19	2288.79	1942.73	1715.29	1555.58	1438.15	1348.85	1279.19	1223.77	1178.97	1142.31	1111.97
90000	8047.01	4287.23	3041.14	2423.42	2057.01	1816.19	1647.08	1522.74	1428.19	1354.44	1295.76	1248.33	1209.50	1177.38
95000	8494.06	4525.41	3210.09	2558.06	2171.29	1917.09	1738.59	1607.34	1507.54	1429.69	1367.74	1317.68	1276.69	1242.79
100000	8941.12	4763.59	3379.04	2692.69	2285.56	2017.99	1830.09	1691.94	1586.88	1504.93	1439.73	1387.03	1343.89	1308.20

TERM	15 Years	16 Years	17 Years	18 Years	19 Years	20 Years	21 Years	22 Years	23 Years	24 Years	25 Years	30 Years	35 Years	40 Years
AMOUNT														
5	.07	.07	.07	.07	.06	.06	.06	.06	.06	.06	.06	.06	.06	.06
10	.13	.13	.13	.13	.12	.12	.12	.12	.12	.12	.12	.12	.12	.12
15	.20	.19	.19	.19	.18	.18	.18	.18	.18	.18	.18	.17	.17	.17
25	.32	.32	.31	.31	.30	.30	.30	.30	.29	.29	.29	.29	.28	.28
50	.64	.63	.62	.61	.60	.60	.59	.59	.58	.58	.58	.57	.56	.56
75	.96	.95	.93	.92	.90	.89	.89	.88	.87	.87	.86	.85	.84	.83
100	1.28	1.26	1.24	1.22	1.20	1.19	1.18	1.17	1.16	1.15	1.15	1.13	1.12	1.11
200	2.56	2.51	2.47	2.43	2.40	2.38	2.35	2.33	2.32	2.30	2.29	2.25	2.23	2.22
300	3.84	3.77	3.70	3.65	3.60	3.56	3.53	3.50	3.47	3.45	3.43	3.37	3.34	3.32
400	5.12	5.02	4.93	4.86	4.80	4.75	4.70	4.66	4.63	4.60	4.58	4.49	4.45	4.43
500	6.40	6.27	6.17	6.08	6.00	5.93	5.88	5.83	5.79	5.75	5.72	5.61	5.56	5.53
600	7.68	7.53	7.40	7.29	7.20	7.12	7.05	6.99	6.94	6.90	6.86	6.74	6.67	6.64
700	8.95	8.78	8.63	8.51	8.40	8.31	8.23	8.16	8.10	8.05	8.01	7.86	7.78	7.75
800	10.23	10.03	9.86	9.72	9.60	9.49	9.40	9.32	9.26	9.20	9.15	8.98	8.89	8.85
900	11.51	11.29	11.10	10.93	10.80	10.68	10.58	10.49	10.41	10.35	10.29	10.10	10.01	9.96
1000	12.79	12.54	12.33	12.15	11.99	11.86	11.75	11.65	11.57	11.50	11.43	11.22	11.12	11.06
2000	25.57	25.07	24.65	24.29	23.98	23.72	23.50	23.30	23.13	22.99	22.86	22.44	22.23	22.12
3000	38.36	37.61	36.97	36.43	35.97	35.58	35.24	34.95	34.70	34.48	34.29	33.66	33.34	33.18
4000	51.14	50.14	49.30	48.58	47.96	47.44	46.99	46.60	46.26	45.97	45.72	44.88	44.45	44.24
5000	63.93	62.68	61.62	60.72	59.95	59.30	58.73	58.25	57.83	57.47	57.15	56.10	55.57	55.29
6000	76.71	75.21	73.94	72.86	71.94	71.16	70.48	69.90	69.39	68.96	68.58	67.32	66.68	66.35
7000	89.50	87.74	86.26	85.01	83.93	83.01	82.23	81.55	80.96	80.45	80.01	78.53	77.79	77.41
8000	102.28	100.28	98.59	97.15	95.92	94.87	93.97	93.19	92.52	91.94	91.44	89.75	88.90	88.47
9000	115.06	112.81	110.91	109.29	107.91	106.73	105.72	104.84	104.09	103.43	102.87	100.97	100.02	99.53
10000	127.85	125.35	123.23	121.44	119.90	118.59	117.46	116.49	115.65	114.93	114.30	112.19	111.13	110.50
11000	140.63	137.88	135.56	133.58	131.89	130.45	129.21	128.14	127.22	126.42	125.73	123.41	122.24	121.64
12000	153.42	150.42	147.88	145.72	143.88	142.31	140.95	139.79	138.78	137.91	137.16	134.63	133.35	132.70
13000	166.20	162.95	160.20	157.87	155.87	154.17	152.70	151.44	150.35	149.40	148.58	145.85	144.46	143.76
14000	178.99	175.48	172.52	170.01	167.86	166.02	164.45	163.09	161.91	160.89	160.01	157.06	155.58	154.82
15000	191.77	188.02	184.85	182.15	179.85	177.88	176.19	174.73	173.48	172.39	171.44	168.28	166.69	165.87
16000	204.55	200.55	197.17	194.29	191.84	189.74	187.94	186.38	185.04	183.88	182.87	179.50	177.80	176.93
17000	217.34	213.09	209.49	206.44	203.83	201.60	199.68	198.03	196.60	195.37	194.30	190.72	188.91	187.99
18000	230.12	225.62	221.81	218.58	215.82	213.46	211.43	209.68	208.17	206.86	205.73	201.94	200.03	199.05
19000	242.91	238.15	234.14	230.72	227.81	225.32	223.17	221.33	219.73	218.36	217.16	213.16	211.14	210.11
20000	255.69	250.69	246.46	242.87	239.80	237.18	234.92	232.98	231.30	229.85	228.59	224.38	222.25	221.16
21000	268.48	263.22	258.78	255.01	251.79	249.03	246.67	244.63	242.86	241.34	240.02	235.59	233.36	232.22
22000	281.26	275.76	271.11	267.15	263.78	260.89	258.41	256.27	254.43	252.83	251.45	246.81	244.48	243.28
23000	294.04	288.29	283.43	279.30	275.77	272.75	270.16	267.92	265.99	264.32	262.88	258.03	255.59	254.34
24000	306.83	300.83	295.75	291.44	287.76	284.61	281.90	279.57	277.56	275.82	274.31	269.25	266.70	265.40
25000	319.61	313.36	308.07	303.58	299.75	296.47	293.65	291.22	289.12	287.31	285.74	280.47	277.81	276.45
26000	332.40	325.89	320.40	315.73	311.74	308.33	305.39	302.87	300.69	298.80	297.16	291.69	288.92	287.51
27000	345.18	338.43	332.72	327.87	323.73	320.19	317.14	314.52	312.25	310.29	308.59	302.91	300.04	298.57
28000	357.97	350.96	345.04	340.01	335.72	332.04	328.89	326.17	323.82	321.78	320.02	314.12	311.15	309.63
29000	370.75	363.50	357.36	352.15	347.71	343.90	340.63	337.81	335.38	333.28	331.45	325.34	322.26	320.69
30000	383.53	376.03	369.69	364.30	359.70	355.76	352.38	349.46	346.95	344.77	342.88	336.56	333.37	331.74
31000	396.32	388.56	382.01	376.44	371.69	367.62	364.12	361.11	358.51	356.26	354.31	347.78	344.49	342.80
32000	409.10	401.10	394.33	388.58	383.68	379.48	375.87	372.76	370.08	367.75	365.74	359.00	355.60	353.86
33000	421.89	413.63	406.66	400.73	395.67	391.34	387.61	384.41	381.64	379.24	377.17	370.22	366.71	364.92
34000	434.67	426.17	418.98	412.87	407.66	403.19	399.36	396.06	393.20	390.74	388.60	381.44	377.82	375.98
35000	447.46	438.70	431.30	425.01	419.65	415.05	411.11	407.71	404.77	402.23	400.03	392.65	388.93	387.03
36000	460.24	451.24	443.62	437.16	431.64	426.91	422.85	419.35	416.33	413.72	411.46	403.87	400.05	398.09
37000	473.02	463.77	455.95	449.30	443.63	438.77	434.60	431.00	427.90	425.21	422.89	415.09	411.16	409.15
38000	485.81	476.30	468.27	461.44	455.62	450.63	446.34	442.65	439.46	436.71	434.31	426.31	422.27	420.21
39000	498.59	488.84	480.59	473.59	467.61	462.49	458.09	454.30	451.03	448.20	445.74	437.53	433.38	431.27
40000	511.38	501.37	492.91	485.73	479.60	474.35	469.83	465.95	462.59	459.69	457.17	448.75	444.50	442.32
41000	524.16	513.91	505.24	497.87	491.59	486.20	481.58	477.60	474.16	471.18	468.60	459.96	455.61	453.38
42000	536.95	526.44	517.56	510.01	503.58	498.06	493.33	489.25	485.72	482.67	480.03	471.18	466.72	464.44
43000	549.73	538.97	529.88	522.16	515.57	509.92	505.07	500.89	497.29	494.17	491.46	482.40	477.83	475.50
44000	562.51	551.51	542.21	534.30	527.56	521.78	516.82	512.54	508.85	505.66	502.89	493.62	488.95	486.56
45000	575.30	564.04	554.53	546.44	539.55	533.64	528.56	524.19	520.42	517.15	514.32	504.84	500.06	497.61
46000	588.08	576.58	566.85	558.59	551.54	545.50	540.31	535.84	531.98	528.64	525.75	516.06	511.17	508.67
47000	600.87	589.11	579.17	570.73	563.53	557.36	552.05	547.49	543.55	540.13	537.18	527.28	522.28	519.73
48000	613.65	601.65	591.50	582.87	575.52	569.21	563.80	559.14	555.11	551.63	548.61	538.49	533.39	530.79
49000	626.44	614.18	603.82	595.02	587.51	581.07	575.55	570.79	566.68	563.12	560.04	549.71	544.51	541.84
50000	639.22	626.71	616.14	607.16	599.50	592.93	587.29	582.43	578.24	574.61	571.47	560.93	555.62	552.90
55000	703.14	689.38	677.76	667.87	659.44	652.22	646.02	640.68	636.06	632.07	628.61	617.02	611.18	608.19
60000	767.06	752.06	739.37	728.59	719.39	711.52	704.75	698.92	693.89	689.53	685.76	673.12	666.74	663.48
65000	830.98	814.73	800.98	789.31	779.34	770.81	763.48	757.16	751.71	746.99	742.90	729.21	722.30	718.77
70000	894.91	877.40	862.60	850.02	839.29	830.10	822.21	815.41	809.53	804.45	800.05	785.30	777.86	774.06
75000	958.83	940.07	924.21	910.74	899.24	889.39	880.94	873.65	867.36	861.91	857.20	841.40	833.43	829.35
80000	1022.75	1002.74	985.82	971.45	959.19	948.69	939.66	931.89	925.18	919.37	914.34	897.49	888.99	884.64
85000	1086.67	1065.41	1047.44	1032.17	1019.14	1007.98	998.39	990.13	983.00	976.83	971.49	953.58	944.55	939.93
90000	1150.59	1128.08	1109.05	1092.88	1079.09	1067.27	1057.12	1048.38	1040.83	1034.30	1028.63	1009.67	1000.11	995.22
95000	1214.51	1190.75	1170.66	1153.60	1139.04	1126.56	1115.85	1106.62	1098.65	1091.76	1085.78	1065.77	1055.67	1050.51
100000	1278.44	1253.42	1232.28	1214.31	1198.99	1185.86	1174.58	1164.86	1156.47	1149.22	1142.93	1121.86	1111.23	1105.80

13.250%

TERM	1 Year	2 Years	3 Years	4 Years	5 Years	6 Years	7 Years	8 Years	9 Years	10 Years	11 Years	12 Years	13 Years	14 Years
AMOUNT														
5	.45	.24	.17	.14	.12	.11	.10	.09	.08	.08	.08	.07	.07	.07
10	.90	.48	.34	.27	.23	.21	.19	.17	.16	.16	.15	.14	.14	.14
15	1.35	.72	.51	.41	.35	.31	.28	.26	.24	.23	.22	.21	.21	.20
25	2.24	1.20	.85	.68	.58	.51	.46	.43	.40	.38	.37	.35	.34	.33
50	4.48	2.39	1.70	1.35	1.15	1.02	.92	.85	.80	.76	.73	.70	.68	.66
75	6.71	3.58	2.54	2.03	1.72	1.52	1.38	1.28	1.20	1.14	1.09	1.05	1.02	.99
100	8.95	4.77	3.39	2.70	2.29	2.03	1.84	1.70	1.59	1.51	1.45	1.40	1.35	1.32
200	17.89	9.54	6.77	5.40	4.58	4.05	3.67	3.39	3.18	3.02	2.89	2.79	2.70	2.63
300	26.84	14.30	10.15	8.09	6.87	6.07	5.50	5.09	4.77	4.53	4.33	4.18	4.05	3.94
400	35.78	19.07	13.53	10.79	9.16	8.09	7.34	6.78	6.36	6.04	5.78	5.57	5.39	5.25
500	44.72	23.83	16.91	13.48	11.45	10.11	9.17	8.48	7.95	7.54	7.22	6.96	6.74	6.56
600	53.67	28.60	20.29	16.18	13.73	12.13	11.00	10.17	9.54	9.05	8.66	8.35	8.09	7.87
700	62.61	33.37	23.68	18.87	16.02	14.15	12.83	11.87	11.13	10.56	10.10	9.74	9.43	9.19
800	71.55	38.13	27.06	21.57	18.31	16.17	14.67	13.56	12.72	12.07	11.55	11.13	10.78	10.50
900	80.50	42.90	30.44	24.26	20.60	18.19	16.50	15.26	14.31	13.58	12.99	12.52	12.13	11.81
1000	89.44	47.66	33.82	26.96	22.89	20.21	18.33	16.95	15.90	15.08	14.43	13.91	13.48	13.12
2000	178.87	95.32	67.63	53.91	45.77	40.42	36.66	33.90	31.80	30.16	28.86	27.81	26.95	26.23
3000	268.31	142.98	101.45	80.86	68.65	60.62	54.99	50.85	47.70	45.24	43.29	41.71	40.42	39.35
4000	357.74	190.64	135.26	107.81	91.53	80.83	73.32	67.79	63.60	60.32	57.72	55.61	53.89	52.46
5000	447.18	238.30	169.08	134.76	114.41	101.04	91.65	84.74	79.49	75.40	72.14	69.51	67.36	65.58
6000	536.61	285.96	202.89	161.72	137.29	121.24	109.97	101.69	95.39	90.48	86.57	83.41	80.83	78.69
7000	626.05	333.62	236.71	188.67	160.17	141.45	128.30	118.64	111.29	105.56	101.00	97.31	94.30	91.81
8000	715.48	381.28	270.52	215.62	183.06	161.66	146.63	135.58	127.19	120.64	115.43	111.22	107.77	104.92
9000	804.92	428.94	304.34	242.57	205.94	181.86	164.96	152.53	143.08	135.72	129.85	125.12	121.24	118.03
10000	894.35	476.60	338.15	269.52	228.82	202.07	183.29	169.48	158.98	150.79	144.28	139.02	134.71	131.15
11000	983.79	524.26	371.96	296.47	251.70	222.27	201.61	186.43	174.88	165.87	158.71	152.92	148.18	144.26
12000	1073.22	571.92	405.78	323.43	274.58	242.48	219.94	203.37	190.78	180.95	173.14	166.82	161.65	157.38
13000	1162.65	619.58	439.59	350.38	297.46	262.69	238.27	220.32	206.67	196.03	187.56	180.72	175.12	170.49
14000	1252.09	667.24	473.41	377.33	320.34	282.89	256.60	237.27	222.57	211.11	201.99	194.62	188.59	183.61
15000	1341.52	714.90	507.22	404.28	343.22	303.10	274.93	254.22	238.47	226.19	216.42	208.52	202.06	196.72
16000	1430.96	762.55	541.04	431.23	366.11	323.31	293.26	271.16	254.37	241.27	230.85	222.43	215.53	209.84
17000	1520.39	810.21	574.85	458.18	388.99	343.51	311.58	288.11	270.26	256.35	245.27	236.33	229.01	222.95
18000	1609.83	857.87	608.67	485.14	411.87	363.72	329.91	305.06	286.16	271.43	259.70	250.23	242.48	236.06
19000	1699.26	905.53	642.48	512.09	434.75	383.92	348.24	322.01	302.06	286.50	274.13	264.13	255.95	249.18
20000	1788.70	953.19	676.29	539.04	457.63	404.13	366.57	338.95	317.96	301.58	288.56	278.03	269.42	262.29
21000	1878.13	1000.85	710.11	565.99	480.51	424.34	384.90	355.90	333.85	316.66	302.98	291.93	282.89	275.41
22000	1967.57	1048.51	743.92	592.94	503.39	444.54	403.22	372.85	349.75	331.74	317.41	305.83	296.36	288.52
23000	2057.00	1096.17	777.74	619.90	526.27	464.75	421.55	389.80	365.65	346.82	331.84	319.74	309.83	301.64
24000	2146.44	1143.83	811.55	646.85	549.16	484.96	439.88	406.74	381.55	361.90	346.27	333.64	323.30	314.75
25000	2235.87	1191.49	845.37	673.80	572.04	505.16	458.21	423.69	397.45	376.98	360.70	347.54	336.77	327.87
26000	2325.30	1239.15	879.18	700.75	594.92	525.37	476.54	440.64	413.34	392.06	375.12	361.44	350.24	340.98
27000	2414.74	1286.81	913.00	727.70	617.80	545.57	494.87	457.58	429.24	407.14	389.55	375.34	363.71	354.09
28000	2504.17	1334.47	946.81	754.65	640.68	565.78	513.19	474.53	445.14	422.21	403.98	389.24	377.18	367.21
29000	2593.61	1382.13	980.63	781.61	663.56	585.99	531.52	491.48	461.04	437.29	418.41	403.14	390.65	380.32
30000	2683.04	1429.79	1014.44	808.56	686.44	606.19	549.85	508.43	476.93	452.37	432.83	417.04	404.12	393.44
31000	2772.48	1477.44	1048.25	835.51	709.32	626.40	568.18	525.37	492.83	467.45	447.26	430.95	417.59	406.55
32000	2861.91	1525.10	1082.07	862.46	732.21	646.61	586.51	542.32	508.73	482.53	461.69	444.85	431.06	419.67
33000	2951.35	1572.76	1115.88	889.41	755.09	666.81	604.83	559.27	524.63	497.61	476.12	458.75	444.53	432.78
34000	3040.78	1620.42	1149.70	916.36	777.97	687.02	623.16	576.22	540.52	512.69	490.54	472.65	458.01	445.90
35000	3130.22	1668.08	1183.51	943.32	800.85	707.23	641.49	593.16	556.42	527.77	504.97	486.55	471.48	459.01
36000	3219.65	1715.74	1217.33	970.27	823.73	727.43	659.82	610.11	572.32	542.85	519.40	500.45	484.95	472.12
37000	3309.09	1763.40	1251.14	997.22	846.61	747.64	678.15	627.06	588.22	557.92	533.83	514.35	498.42	485.24
38000	3398.52	1811.06	1284.96	1024.17	869.49	767.84	696.47	644.01	604.11	573.00	548.25	528.25	511.89	498.35
39000	3487.95	1858.72	1318.77	1051.12	892.37	788.05	714.80	660.95	620.01	588.08	562.68	542.16	525.36	511.47
40000	3577.39	1906.38	1352.58	1078.07	915.26	808.26	733.13	677.90	635.91	603.16	577.11	556.06	538.83	524.58
41000	3666.82	1954.04	1386.40	1105.03	938.14	828.46	751.46	694.85	651.81	618.24	591.54	569.96	552.30	537.70
42000	3756.26	2001.70	1420.21	1131.98	961.02	848.67	769.79	711.80	667.70	633.32	605.96	583.86	565.77	550.81
43000	3845.69	2049.36	1454.03	1158.93	983.90	868.88	788.12	728.74	683.60	648.40	620.39	597.76	579.24	563.93
44000	3935.13	2097.02	1487.84	1185.88	1006.78	889.08	806.44	745.69	699.50	663.48	634.82	611.66	592.71	577.04
45000	4024.56	2144.68	1521.66	1212.83	1029.66	909.29	824.77	762.64	715.40	678.56	649.25	625.56	606.18	590.15
46000	4114.00	2192.33	1555.47	1239.79	1052.54	929.49	843.10	779.59	731.30	693.63	663.67	639.47	619.65	603.27
47000	4203.43	2239.99	1589.29	1266.74	1075.42	949.70	861.43	796.53	747.19	708.71	678.10	653.37	633.12	616.38
48000	4292.87	2287.65	1623.10	1293.69	1098.31	969.91	879.76	813.48	763.09	723.79	692.53	667.27	646.59	629.50
49000	4382.30	2335.31	1656.92	1320.64	1121.19	990.11	898.08	830.43	778.99	738.87	706.96	681.17	660.06	642.61
50000	4471.74	2382.97	1690.73	1347.59	1144.07	1010.32	916.41	847.38	794.89	753.95	721.39	695.07	673.53	655.73
55000	4918.91	2621.27	1859.80	1482.35	1258.47	1111.35	1008.05	932.11	874.37	829.34	793.52	764.58	740.89	721.30
60000	5366.08	2859.57	2028.87	1617.11	1372.88	1212.38	1099.69	1016.85	953.86	904.74	865.66	834.08	808.24	786.87
65000	5813.25	3097.86	2197.95	1751.87	1487.29	1313.41	1191.34	1101.59	1033.35	980.13	937.80	903.59	875.59	852.44
70000	6260.43	3336.16	2367.02	1886.63	1601.69	1414.45	1282.98	1186.32	1112.84	1055.53	1009.94	973.10	942.95	918.01
75000	6707.60	3574.46	2536.09	2021.39	1716.10	1515.48	1374.62	1271.06	1192.33	1130.92	1082.08	1042.60	1010.30	983.59
80000	7154.77	3812.75	2705.16	2156.14	1830.51	1616.51	1466.26	1355.80	1271.81	1206.32	1154.21	1112.11	1077.65	1049.16
85000	7601.95	4051.05	2874.24	2290.90	1944.91	1717.54	1557.90	1440.53	1351.30	1281.71	1226.35	1181.62	1145.01	1114.73
90000	8049.12	4289.35	3043.31	2425.66	2059.32	1818.57	1649.54	1525.27	1430.79	1357.11	1298.49	1251.12	1212.36	1180.30
95000	8496.29	4527.64	3212.38	2560.42	2173.72	1919.60	1741.18	1610.01	1510.28	1432.50	1370.63	1320.63	1279.71	1245.88
100000	8943.47	4765.94	3381.45	2695.18	2288.13	2020.63	1832.82	1694.75	1589.77	1507.89	1442.77	1390.14	1347.06	1311.45

TERM	15 Years	16 Years	17 Years	18 Years	19 Years	20 Years	21 Years	22 Years	23 Years	24 Years	25 Years	30 Years	35 Years	40 Years
AMOUNT														
5	.07	.07	.07	.07	.07	.06	.06	.06	.06	.06	.06	.06	.06	.06
10	.13	.13	.13	.13	.13	.12	.12	.12	.12	.12	.12	.12	.12	.12
15	.20	.19	.19	.19	.19	.18	.18	.18	.18	.18	.18	.17	.17	.17
25	.33	.32	.31	.31	.31	.30	.30	.30	.30	.29	.29	.29	.28	.28
50	.65	.63	.62	.61	.61	.60	.59	.59	.59	.58	.58	.57	.56	.56
75	.97	.95	.93	.92	.91	.90	.89	.88	.88	.87	.87	.85	.85	.84
100	1.29	1.26	1.24	1.22	1.21	1.19	1.18	1.17	1.17	1.16	1.15	1.13	1.12	1.11
200	2.57	2.52	2.48	2.44	2.41	2.38	2.36	2.34	2.33	2.31	2.30	2.26	2.24	2.22
300	3.85	3.78	3.71	3.66	3.61	3.57	3.54	3.51	3.49	3.46	3.45	3.38	3.35	3.33
400	5.13	5.03	4.95	4.88	4.82	4.76	4.72	4.68	4.65	4.62	4.59	4.51	4.47	4.44
500	6.41	6.29	6.18	6.09	6.02	5.95	5.90	5.85	5.81	5.77	5.74	5.63	5.58	5.55
600	7.70	7.55	7.42	7.31	7.22	7.14	7.07	7.02	6.97	6.92	6.89	6.76	6.70	6.66
700	8.98	8.80	8.65	8.53	8.42	8.33	8.25	8.18	8.13	8.08	8.03	7.89	7.81	7.77
800	10.26	10.06	9.89	9.75	9.63	9.52	9.43	9.35	9.29	9.23	9.18	9.01	8.93	8.88
900	11.54	11.32	11.13	10.97	10.83	10.71	10.61	10.52	10.45	10.38	10.33	10.14	10.04	9.99
1000	12.82	12.57	12.36	12.18	12.03	11.90	11.79	11.69	11.61	11.53	11.47	11.26	11.16	11.10
2000	25.64	25.14	24.72	24.36	24.06	23.79	23.57	23.38	23.21	23.06	22.94	22.52	22.31	22.20
3000	38.46	37.71	37.08	36.54	36.08	35.69	35.35	35.06	34.81	34.59	34.41	33.78	33.46	33.30
4000	51.27	50.28	49.43	48.72	48.11	47.58	47.13	46.75	46.41	46.12	45.87	45.04	44.61	44.40
5000	64.09	62.84	61.79	60.89	60.13	59.48	58.91	58.43	58.01	57.65	57.34	56.29	55.77	55.50
6000	76.91	75.41	74.15	73.07	72.16	71.37	70.70	70.12	69.62	69.18	68.81	67.55	66.92	66.60
7000	89.73	87.98	86.50	85.25	84.18	83.27	82.48	81.80	81.22	80.71	80.27	78.81	78.07	77.70
8000	102.54	100.55	98.86	97.43	96.21	95.16	94.26	93.49	92.82	92.24	91.74	90.07	89.22	88.79
9000	115.36	113.12	111.22	109.61	108.23	107.05	106.04	105.17	104.42	103.77	103.21	101.32	100.38	99.89
10000	128.18	125.68	123.57	121.78	120.26	118.95	117.82	116.86	116.02	115.30	114.68	112.58	111.53	110.99
11000	141.00	138.25	135.93	133.96	132.28	130.84	129.61	128.54	127.62	126.83	126.14	123.84	122.68	122.09
12000	153.81	150.82	148.29	146.14	144.31	142.74	141.39	140.23	139.23	138.36	137.61	135.10	133.83	133.19
13000	166.63	163.39	160.65	158.32	156.33	154.63	153.17	151.91	150.83	149.89	149.08	146.36	144.99	144.29
14000	179.45	175.95	173.00	170.50	168.36	166.53	164.95	163.60	162.43	161.42	160.54	157.61	156.14	155.39
15000	192.27	188.52	185.36	182.67	180.38	178.42	176.73	175.28	174.03	172.95	172.01	168.87	167.29	166.49
16000	205.08	201.09	197.72	194.85	192.41	190.31	188.52	186.97	185.63	184.48	183.48	180.13	178.44	177.58
17000	217.90	213.66	210.07	207.03	204.43	202.21	200.30	198.65	197.24	196.01	194.94	191.39	189.60	188.68
18000	230.72	226.23	222.43	219.21	216.46	214.10	212.08	210.34	208.84	207.54	206.41	202.64	200.75	199.78
19000	243.53	238.79	234.79	231.38	228.48	226.00	223.86	222.02	220.44	219.07	217.88	213.90	211.90	210.88
20000	256.35	251.36	247.14	243.56	240.51	237.89	235.64	233.71	232.04	230.60	229.35	225.16	223.05	221.98
21000	269.17	263.93	259.50	255.74	252.53	249.79	247.43	245.40	243.64	242.13	240.81	236.42	234.21	233.08
22000	281.99	276.50	271.86	267.92	264.56	261.68	259.21	257.08	255.24	253.66	252.28	247.68	245.36	244.18
23000	294.80	289.07	284.22	280.10	276.58	273.57	270.99	268.77	266.85	265.18	263.75	258.93	256.51	255.28
24000	307.62	301.63	296.57	292.27	288.61	285.47	282.77	280.45	278.45	276.71	275.21	270.19	267.66	266.37
25000	320.44	314.20	308.93	304.45	300.63	297.36	294.55	292.14	290.05	288.24	286.68	281.45	278.82	277.47
26000	333.26	326.77	321.29	316.63	312.66	309.26	306.34	303.82	301.65	299.77	298.15	292.71	289.97	288.57
27000	346.07	339.34	333.64	328.81	324.68	321.15	318.12	315.51	313.25	311.30	309.61	303.96	301.12	299.67
28000	358.89	351.90	346.00	340.99	336.71	333.05	329.90	327.19	324.85	322.83	321.08	315.22	312.27	310.77
29000	371.71	364.47	358.36	353.16	348.73	344.94	341.68	338.88	336.46	334.36	332.55	326.48	323.43	321.87
30000	384.53	377.04	370.71	365.34	360.76	356.83	353.46	350.56	348.06	345.89	344.02	337.74	334.58	332.97
31000	397.34	389.61	383.07	377.52	372.78	368.73	365.25	362.25	359.66	357.42	355.48	348.99	345.73	344.06
32000	410.16	402.18	395.43	389.70	384.81	380.62	377.03	373.93	371.26	368.95	366.95	360.25	356.88	355.16
33000	422.98	414.74	407.78	401.87	396.83	392.52	388.81	385.62	382.86	380.48	378.42	371.51	368.03	366.26
34000	435.80	427.31	420.14	414.05	408.86	404.41	400.59	397.30	394.47	392.01	389.88	382.77	379.19	377.36
35000	448.61	439.88	432.50	426.23	420.88	416.31	412.37	408.99	406.07	403.54	401.35	394.03	390.34	388.46
36000	461.43	452.45	444.86	438.41	432.91	428.20	424.16	420.67	417.67	415.07	412.82	405.28	401.49	399.56
37000	474.25	465.01	457.21	450.59	444.93	440.09	435.94	432.36	429.27	426.60	424.28	416.54	412.64	410.66
38000	487.06	477.58	469.57	462.76	456.96	451.99	447.72	444.04	440.87	438.13	435.75	427.80	423.80	421.76
39000	499.88	490.15	481.93	474.94	468.98	463.88	459.50	455.73	452.47	449.66	447.22	439.06	434.95	432.85
40000	512.70	502.72	494.28	487.12	481.01	475.78	471.28	467.42	464.08	461.19	458.69	450.31	446.10	443.95
41000	525.52	515.29	506.64	499.30	493.03	487.67	483.07	479.10	475.68	472.72	470.15	461.57	457.25	455.05
42000	538.33	527.85	519.00	511.48	505.06	499.57	494.85	490.79	487.28	484.25	481.62	472.83	468.41	466.15
43000	551.15	540.42	531.35	523.65	517.08	511.46	506.63	502.47	498.88	495.78	493.09	484.09	479.56	477.25
44000	563.97	552.99	543.71	535.83	529.11	523.35	518.41	514.16	510.48	507.31	504.55	495.35	490.71	488.35
45000	576.79	565.56	556.07	548.01	541.13	535.25	530.19	525.84	522.08	518.84	516.02	506.60	501.86	499.45
46000	589.60	578.13	568.43	560.19	553.16	547.14	541.98	537.53	533.69	530.36	527.49	517.86	513.02	510.55
47000	602.42	590.69	580.78	572.36	565.18	559.04	553.76	549.21	545.29	541.89	538.95	529.12	524.17	521.64
48000	615.24	603.26	593.14	584.54	577.21	570.93	565.54	560.90	556.89	553.42	550.42	540.38	535.32	532.74
49000	628.06	615.83	605.50	596.72	589.23	582.83	577.32	572.58	568.49	564.95	561.89	551.63	546.47	543.84
50000	640.87	628.40	617.85	608.90	601.26	594.72	589.10	584.27	580.09	576.48	573.36	562.89	557.63	554.94
55000	704.96	691.24	679.64	669.79	661.39	654.19	648.01	642.69	638.10	634.13	630.69	619.18	613.39	610.43
60000	769.05	754.08	741.42	730.68	721.51	713.66	706.92	701.12	696.11	691.78	688.03	675.47	669.15	665.93
65000	833.13	816.91	803.21	791.57	781.64	773.13	765.83	759.55	754.12	749.43	745.36	731.76	724.91	721.42
70000	897.22	879.75	864.99	852.46	841.76	832.61	824.74	817.97	812.13	807.07	802.70	788.05	780.67	776.91
75000	961.31	942.59	926.78	913.35	901.89	892.08	883.65	876.40	870.14	864.72	860.03	844.34	836.44	832.41
80000	1025.39	1005.43	988.57	974.23	962.01	951.55	942.56	934.83	928.15	922.37	917.37	900.62	892.20	887.90
85000	1089.48	1068.27	1050.35	1035.12	1022.14	1011.02	1001.47	993.25	986.16	980.02	974.70	956.91	947.96	943.39
90000	1153.57	1131.11	1112.13	1096.01	1082.26	1070.49	1060.38	1051.68	1044.16	1037.67	1032.04	1013.20	1003.72	998.89
95000	1217.65	1193.95	1173.92	1156.90	1142.39	1129.96	1119.29	1110.10	1102.17	1095.31	1089.37	1069.49	1059.49	1054.38
100000	1281.74	1256.79	1235.70	1217.79	1202.51	1189.44	1178.20	1168.53	1160.18	1152.96	1146.71	1125.78	1115.25	1109.88

TERM	1 Year	2 Years	3 Years	4 Years	5 Years	6 Years	7 Years	8 Years	9 Years	10 Years	11 Years	12 Years	13 Years	14 Years
AMOUNT														
5	.45	.24	.17	.14	.12	.11	.10	.09	.08	.08	.08	.07	.07	.07
10	.90	.48	.34	.27	.23	.21	.19	.17	.16	.16	.15	.14	.14	.14
15	1.35	.72	.51	.41	.35	.31	.28	.26	.24	.23	.22	.21	.21	.20
25	2.24	1.20	.85	.68	.58	.51	.46	.43	.40	.38	.37	.35	.34	.33
50	4.48	2.39	1.70	1.35	1.15	1.02	.92	.85	.80	.76	.73	.70	.68	.66
75	6.71	3.58	2.54	2.03	1.72	1.52	1.38	1.28	1.20	1.14	1.09	1.05	1.02	.99
100	8.95	4.77	3.39	2.70	2.30	2.03	1.84	1.70	1.60	1.52	1.45	1.40	1.36	1.32
200	17.90	9.54	6.77	5.40	4.59	4.05	3.68	3.40	3.19	3.03	2.90	2.79	2.71	2.63
300	26.84	14.31	10.16	8.10	6.88	6.07	5.51	5.10	4.78	4.54	4.34	4.18	4.06	3.95
400	35.79	19.08	13.54	10.80	9.17	8.10	7.35	6.80	6.38	6.05	5.79	5.58	5.41	5.26
500	44.73	23.85	16.92	13.49	11.46	10.12	9.18	8.49	7.97	7.56	7.23	6.97	6.76	6.58
600	53.68	28.61	20.31	16.19	13.75	12.14	11.02	10.19	9.56	9.07	8.68	8.36	8.11	7.89
700	62.63	33.38	23.69	18.89	16.04	14.17	12.85	11.89	11.15	10.58	10.13	9.76	9.46	9.21
800	71.57	38.15	27.08	21.59	18.33	16.19	14.69	13.59	12.75	12.09	11.57	11.15	10.81	10.52
900	80.52	42.92	30.46	24.28	20.62	18.21	16.52	15.28	14.34	13.60	13.02	12.54	12.16	11.84
1000	89.46	47.69	33.84	26.98	22.91	20.24	18.36	16.98	15.93	15.11	14.46	13.94	13.51	13.15
2000	178.92	95.37	67.68	53.96	45.82	40.47	36.72	33.96	31.86	30.22	28.92	27.87	27.01	26.30
3000	268.38	143.05	101.52	80.93	68.73	60.70	55.07	50.93	47.78	45.33	43.38	41.80	40.51	39.45
4000	357.84	190.74	135.36	107.91	91.63	80.94	73.43	67.91	63.71	60.44	57.84	55.73	54.01	52.59
5000	447.30	238.42	169.20	134.89	114.54	101.17	91.78	84.88	79.64	75.55	72.29	69.67	67.52	65.74
6000	536.75	286.10	203.04	161.86	137.45	121.40	110.14	101.86	95.56	90.66	86.75	83.60	81.02	78.89
7000	626.21	333.78	236.88	188.84	160.35	141.63	128.49	118.83	111.49	105.76	101.21	97.53	94.52	92.03
8000	715.67	381.47	270.71	215.82	183.26	161.87	146.85	135.81	127.42	120.87	115.67	111.46	108.02	105.18
9000	805.13	429.15	304.55	242.79	206.17	182.10	165.20	152.78	143.34	135.98	130.13	125.40	121.53	118.33
10000	894.59	476.83	338.39	269.77	229.07	202.33	183.56	169.76	159.27	151.09	144.58	139.33	135.03	131.47
11000	984.04	524.52	372.23	296.75	251.98	222.57	201.92	186.74	175.20	166.20	159.04	153.26	148.53	144.62
12000	1073.50	572.20	406.07	323.72	274.89	242.80	220.27	203.71	191.12	181.31	173.50	167.19	162.03	157.77
13000	1162.96	619.88	439.91	350.70	297.80	263.03	238.63	220.69	207.05	196.42	187.96	181.13	175.54	170.91
14000	1252.42	667.56	473.75	377.68	320.70	283.26	256.98	237.66	222.98	211.52	202.42	195.06	189.04	184.06
15000	1341.88	715.25	507.58	404.65	343.61	303.50	275.34	254.64	238.90	226.63	216.87	208.99	202.54	197.21
16000	1431.33	762.93	541.42	431.63	366.52	323.73	293.69	271.61	254.83	241.74	231.33	222.92	216.04	210.36
17000	1520.79	810.61	575.26	458.61	389.42	343.96	312.05	288.59	270.76	256.85	245.79	236.86	229.55	223.50
18000	1610.25	858.30	609.10	485.58	412.33	364.20	330.40	305.56	286.68	271.96	260.25	250.79	243.05	236.65
19000	1699.71	905.98	642.94	512.56	435.24	384.43	348.76	322.54	302.61	287.07	274.71	264.72	256.55	249.80
20000	1789.17	953.66	676.78	539.54	458.14	404.66	367.11	339.52	318.54	302.18	289.16	278.65	270.05	262.94
21000	1878.62	1001.34	710.62	566.51	481.05	424.89	385.47	356.49	334.46	317.28	303.62	292.59	283.56	276.09
22000	1968.08	1049.03	744.45	593.49	503.96	445.13	403.83	373.47	350.39	332.39	318.08	306.52	297.06	289.24
23000	2057.54	1096.71	778.29	620.47	526.86	465.36	422.18	390.44	366.31	347.50	332.54	320.45	310.56	302.38
24000	2147.00	1144.39	812.13	647.44	549.77	485.59	440.54	407.42	382.24	362.61	347.00	334.38	324.06	315.53
25000	2236.46	1192.08	845.97	674.42	572.68	505.82	458.89	424.39	398.17	377.72	361.45	348.32	337.56	328.68
26000	2325.92	1239.76	879.81	701.40	595.59	526.06	477.25	441.37	414.09	392.83	375.91	362.25	351.07	341.82
27000	2415.37	1287.44	913.65	728.37	618.49	546.29	495.60	458.34	430.02	407.94	390.37	376.18	364.57	354.97
28000	2504.83	1335.13	947.49	755.35	641.40	566.52	513.96	475.32	445.95	423.04	404.83	390.11	378.07	368.12
29000	2594.29	1382.81	981.33	782.33	664.31	586.76	532.31	492.29	461.87	438.15	419.29	404.05	391.57	381.26
30000	2683.75	1430.49	1015.16	809.30	687.21	606.99	550.67	509.27	477.80	453.26	433.74	417.98	405.08	394.41
31000	2773.21	1478.17	1049.00	836.28	710.12	627.22	569.02	526.25	493.73	468.37	448.20	431.91	418.58	407.56
32000	2862.66	1525.86	1082.84	863.26	733.03	647.45	587.38	543.22	509.65	483.48	462.66	445.84	432.08	420.71
33000	2952.12	1573.54	1116.68	890.23	755.93	667.69	605.74	560.20	525.58	498.59	477.12	459.77	445.58	433.85
34000	3041.58	1621.22	1150.52	917.21	778.84	687.92	624.09	577.17	541.51	513.70	491.58	473.71	459.09	447.00
35000	3131.04	1668.91	1184.36	944.19	801.75	708.15	642.45	594.15	557.43	528.80	506.03	487.64	472.59	460.15
36000	3220.50	1716.59	1218.20	971.16	824.65	728.39	660.80	611.12	573.36	543.91	520.49	501.57	486.09	473.29
37000	3309.95	1764.27	1252.03	998.14	847.56	748.62	679.16	628.10	589.29	559.02	534.95	515.50	499.59	486.44
38000	3399.41	1811.95	1285.87	1025.12	870.47	768.85	697.51	645.07	605.21	574.13	549.41	529.44	513.10	499.59
39000	3488.87	1859.64	1319.71	1052.09	893.38	789.08	715.87	662.05	621.14	589.24	563.87	543.37	526.60	512.73
40000	3578.33	1907.32	1353.55	1079.07	916.28	809.32	734.22	679.03	637.07	604.35	578.32	557.30	540.10	525.88
41000	3667.79	1955.00	1387.39	1106.05	939.19	829.55	752.58	696.00	652.99	619.46	592.78	571.23	553.60	539.03
42000	3757.24	2002.69	1421.23	1133.02	962.10	849.78	770.93	712.98	668.92	634.56	607.24	585.17	567.11	552.17
43000	3846.70	2050.37	1455.07	1160.00	985.00	870.01	789.29	729.95	684.84	649.67	621.70	599.10	580.61	565.32
44000	3936.16	2098.05	1488.90	1186.98	1007.91	890.25	807.65	746.93	700.77	664.78	636.16	613.03	594.11	578.47
45000	4025.62	2145.73	1522.74	1213.95	1030.82	910.48	826.00	763.90	716.70	679.89	650.61	626.96	607.61	591.61
46000	4115.08	2193.42	1556.58	1240.93	1053.72	930.71	844.36	780.88	732.62	695.00	665.07	640.90	621.11	604.76
47000	4204.54	2241.10	1590.42	1267.91	1076.63	950.95	862.71	797.85	748.55	710.11	679.53	654.83	634.62	617.91
48000	4293.99	2288.78	1624.26	1294.88	1099.54	971.18	881.07	814.83	764.48	725.22	693.99	668.76	648.12	631.06
49000	4383.45	2336.47	1658.10	1321.86	1122.45	991.41	899.42	831.80	780.40	740.32	708.45	682.69	661.62	644.20
50000	4472.91	2384.15	1691.94	1348.84	1145.35	1011.64	917.78	848.78	796.33	755.43	722.90	696.63	675.12	657.35
55000	4920.20	2622.56	1861.13	1483.72	1259.89	1112.81	1009.56	933.66	875.96	830.97	795.19	766.29	742.64	723.08
60000	5367.49	2860.98	2030.32	1618.60	1374.42	1213.97	1101.33	1018.54	955.60	906.52	867.48	835.95	810.15	788.82
65000	5814.78	3099.39	2199.52	1753.49	1488.96	1315.14	1193.11	1103.41	1035.23	982.06	939.77	905.61	877.66	854.55
70000	6262.07	3337.80	2368.71	1888.37	1603.49	1416.30	1284.89	1188.29	1114.86	1057.60	1012.06	975.27	945.17	920.29
75000	6709.36	3576.22	2537.90	2023.25	1718.03	1517.46	1376.66	1273.17	1194.49	1133.15	1084.35	1044.94	1012.68	986.02
80000	7156.65	3814.63	2707.10	2158.14	1832.56	1618.63	1468.44	1358.05	1274.13	1208.69	1156.64	1114.60	1080.20	1051.76
85000	7603.94	4053.05	2876.29	2293.02	1947.09	1719.79	1560.22	1442.92	1353.76	1284.23	1228.93	1184.26	1147.71	1117.49
90000	8051.23	4291.46	3045.48	2427.90	2061.63	1820.96	1652.00	1527.80	1433.39	1359.77	1301.22	1253.92	1215.22	1183.22
95000	8498.52	4529.88	3214.68	2562.79	2176.16	1922.12	1743.77	1612.68	1513.02	1435.32	1373.51	1323.58	1282.73	1248.96
100000	8945.81	4768.29	3383.87	2697.67	2290.70	2023.28	1835.55	1697.56	1592.66	1510.86	1445.80	1393.25	1350.24	1314.69

TERM	15 Years	16 Years	17 Years	18 Years	19 Years	20 Years	21 Years	22 Years	23 Years	24 Years	25 Years	30 Years	35 Years	40 Years
AMOUNT														
5	.07	.07	.07	.07	.07	.06	.06	.06	.06	.06	.06	.06	.06	.06
10	.13	.13	.13	.13	.13	.12	.12	.12	.12	.12	.12	.12	.12	.12
15	.20	.19	.19	.19	.19	.18	.18	.18	.18	.18	.18	.17	.17	.17
25	.33	.32	.31	.31	.31	.30	.30	.30	.30	.29	.29	.29	.28	.28
50	.65	.64	.62	.62	.61	.60	.60	.59	.59	.58	.58	.57	.56	.56
75	.97	.95	.93	.92	.91	.90	.89	.88	.88	.87	.87	.85	.84	.84
100	1.29	1.27	1.24	1.23	1.21	1.20	1.19	1.18	1.17	1.16	1.16	1.13	1.12	1.12
200	2.58	2.53	2.48	2.45	2.42	2.39	2.37	2.35	2.33	2.32	2.31	2.26	2.24	2.23
300	3.86	3.79	3.72	3.67	3.62	3.58	3.55	3.52	3.50	3.48	3.46	3.39	3.36	3.35
400	5.15	5.05	4.96	4.89	4.83	4.78	4.73	4.69	4.66	4.63	4.61	4.52	4.48	4.46
500	6.43	6.31	6.20	6.11	6.04	5.97	5.91	5.87	5.82	5.79	5.76	5.65	5.60	5.57
600	7.72	7.57	7.44	7.33	7.24	7.16	7.10	7.04	6.99	6.95	6.91	6.78	6.72	6.69
700	9.00	8.83	8.68	8.55	8.45	8.36	8.28	8.21	8.15	8.10	8.06	7.91	7.84	7.80
800	10.29	10.09	9.92	9.78	9.65	9.55	9.46	9.38	9.32	9.26	9.21	9.04	8.96	8.92
900	11.57	11.35	11.16	11.00	10.86	10.74	10.64	10.55	10.48	10.42	10.36	10.17	10.08	10.03
1000	12.86	12.61	12.40	12.22	12.07	11.94	11.82	11.73	11.64	11.57	11.51	11.30	11.20	11.14
2000	25.71	25.21	24.79	24.43	24.13	23.87	23.64	23.45	23.28	23.14	23.01	22.60	22.39	22.28
3000	38.56	37.81	37.18	36.64	36.19	35.80	35.46	35.17	34.92	34.71	34.52	33.90	33.58	33.42
4000	51.41	50.41	49.57	48.86	48.25	47.73	47.28	46.89	46.56	46.27	46.02	45.19	44.78	44.56
5000	64.26	63.01	61.96	61.07	60.31	59.66	59.10	58.61	58.20	57.84	57.53	56.49	55.97	55.70
6000	77.11	75.61	74.35	73.28	72.37	71.59	70.91	70.34	69.84	69.41	69.03	67.79	67.16	66.84
7000	89.96	88.22	86.74	85.49	84.43	83.52	82.73	82.06	81.48	80.97	80.54	79.08	78.35	77.98
8000	102.81	100.82	99.13	97.71	96.49	95.45	94.55	93.78	93.12	92.54	92.04	90.38	89.55	89.12
9000	115.66	113.42	111.53	109.92	108.55	107.38	106.37	105.50	104.75	104.11	103.55	101.68	100.74	100.26
10000	128.51	126.02	123.92	122.13	120.61	119.31	118.19	117.22	116.39	115.68	115.05	112.97	111.93	111.40
11000	141.36	138.62	136.31	134.34	132.67	131.24	130.01	128.95	128.03	127.24	126.56	124.27	123.12	122.54
12000	154.21	151.22	148.70	146.56	144.73	143.17	141.82	140.67	139.67	138.81	138.06	135.57	134.32	133.68
13000	167.06	163.82	161.09	158.77	156.79	155.10	153.64	152.39	151.31	150.38	149.57	146.87	145.51	144.82
14000	179.91	176.43	173.48	170.98	168.85	167.03	165.46	164.11	162.95	161.94	161.07	158.16	156.70	155.96
15000	192.76	189.03	185.87	183.20	180.91	178.96	177.28	175.83	174.59	173.51	172.58	169.46	167.89	167.10
16000	205.61	201.63	198.26	195.41	192.97	190.89	189.10	187.56	186.23	185.08	184.08	180.76	179.09	178.24
17000	218.46	214.23	210.66	207.62	205.03	202.82	200.92	199.28	197.87	196.64	195.59	192.05	190.28	189.38
18000	231.31	226.83	223.05	219.83	217.09	214.75	212.73	211.00	209.50	208.21	207.09	203.35	201.47	200.52
19000	244.16	239.43	235.44	232.05	229.15	226.68	224.55	222.72	221.14	219.78	218.60	214.65	212.66	211.65
20000	257.01	252.04	247.83	244.26	241.21	238.61	236.37	234.44	232.78	231.35	230.10	225.94	223.86	222.79
21000	269.86	264.64	260.22	256.47	253.27	250.54	248.19	246.17	244.42	242.91	241.61	237.24	235.05	233.93
22000	282.72	277.24	272.61	268.68	265.33	262.47	260.01	257.89	256.06	254.48	253.11	248.54	246.24	245.07
23000	295.57	289.84	285.00	280.90	277.39	274.40	271.82	269.61	267.70	266.05	264.62	259.84	257.43	256.21
24000	308.42	302.44	297.39	293.11	289.46	286.33	283.64	281.33	279.34	277.61	276.12	271.13	268.63	267.35
25000	321.27	315.04	309.79	305.32	301.52	298.26	295.46	293.05	290.98	289.18	287.63	282.43	279.82	278.49
26000	334.12	327.64	322.18	317.53	313.58	310.19	307.28	304.78	302.62	300.75	299.13	293.73	291.01	289.63
27000	346.97	340.25	334.57	329.75	325.64	322.12	319.10	316.50	314.25	312.32	310.64	305.02	302.20	300.77
28000	359.82	352.85	346.96	341.96	337.70	334.05	330.92	328.22	325.89	323.88	322.14	316.32	313.40	311.91
29000	372.67	365.45	359.35	354.17	349.76	345.98	342.73	339.94	337.53	335.45	333.65	327.62	324.59	323.05
30000	385.52	378.05	371.74	366.39	361.82	357.91	354.55	351.66	349.17	347.02	345.15	338.91	335.78	334.19
31000	398.37	390.65	384.13	378.60	373.88	369.84	366.37	363.39	360.81	358.58	356.65	350.21	346.98	345.33
32000	411.22	403.25	396.52	390.81	385.94	381.77	378.19	375.11	372.45	370.15	368.16	361.51	358.17	356.47
33000	424.07	415.86	408.92	403.02	398.00	393.70	390.01	386.83	384.09	381.72	379.66	372.80	369.36	367.61
34000	436.92	428.46	421.31	415.24	410.06	405.63	401.83	398.55	395.73	393.28	391.17	384.10	380.55	378.75
35000	449.77	441.06	433.70	427.45	422.12	417.56	413.64	410.27	407.37	404.85	402.67	395.40	391.75	389.89
36000	462.62	453.66	446.09	439.66	434.18	429.49	425.46	422.00	419.00	416.42	414.18	406.70	402.94	401.03
37000	475.47	466.26	458.48	451.87	446.24	441.42	437.28	433.72	430.64	427.99	425.68	417.99	414.13	412.16
38000	488.32	478.86	470.87	464.09	458.30	453.35	449.10	445.44	442.28	439.55	437.19	429.29	425.32	423.30
39000	501.17	491.46	483.26	476.30	470.36	465.28	460.92	457.16	453.92	451.12	448.69	440.59	436.52	434.44
40000	514.02	504.07	495.65	488.51	482.42	477.21	472.74	468.88	465.56	462.69	460.20	451.88	447.71	445.58
41000	526.87	516.67	508.05	500.73	494.48	489.14	484.55	480.61	477.20	474.25	471.70	463.18	458.90	456.72
42000	539.72	529.27	520.44	512.94	506.54	501.07	496.37	492.33	488.84	485.82	483.21	474.48	470.09	467.86
43000	552.57	541.87	532.83	525.15	518.60	513.00	508.19	504.05	500.48	497.39	494.71	485.77	481.29	479.00
44000	565.43	554.47	545.22	537.36	530.66	524.93	520.01	515.77	512.12	508.95	506.22	497.07	492.48	490.14
45000	578.28	567.07	557.61	549.58	542.72	536.86	531.83	527.49	523.75	520.52	517.72	508.37	503.67	501.28
46000	591.13	579.68	570.00	561.79	554.78	548.79	543.64	539.22	535.39	532.09	529.23	519.67	514.86	512.42
47000	603.98	592.28	582.39	574.00	566.85	560.72	555.46	550.94	547.03	543.66	540.73	530.96	526.06	523.56
48000	616.83	604.88	594.78	586.21	578.91	572.65	567.28	562.66	558.67	555.22	552.24	542.26	537.25	534.70
49000	629.68	617.48	607.18	598.43	590.97	584.58	579.10	574.38	570.31	566.79	563.74	553.56	548.44	545.84
50000	642.53	630.08	619.57	610.64	603.03	596.51	590.92	586.10	581.95	578.36	575.25	564.85	559.63	556.98
55000	706.78	693.09	681.52	671.70	663.33	656.16	650.01	644.71	640.14	636.19	632.77	621.34	615.60	612.68
60000	771.03	756.10	743.48	732.77	723.63	715.81	709.10	703.32	698.34	694.03	690.29	677.82	671.56	668.37
65000	835.28	819.10	805.44	793.83	783.93	775.46	768.19	761.93	756.53	751.86	747.82	734.31	727.52	724.07
70000	899.54	882.11	867.39	854.89	844.24	835.11	827.28	820.54	814.73	809.70	805.34	790.79	783.49	779.77
75000	963.79	945.12	929.35	915.96	904.54	894.76	886.37	879.15	872.92	867.53	862.87	847.28	839.45	835.46
80000	1028.04	1008.13	991.30	977.02	964.84	954.42	945.47	937.76	931.11	925.37	920.39	903.76	895.41	891.16
85000	1092.29	1071.14	1053.26	1038.08	1025.14	1014.07	1004.56	996.37	989.31	983.20	977.92	960.25	951.37	946.86
90000	1156.55	1134.14	1115.22	1099.15	1085.44	1073.72	1063.65	1054.98	1047.50	1041.04	1035.44	1016.73	1007.34	1002.56
95000	1220.80	1197.15	1177.17	1160.21	1145.75	1133.37	1122.74	1113.59	1105.70	1098.87	1092.96	1073.22	1063.30	1058.25
100000	1285.05	1260.16	1239.13	1221.27	1206.05	1193.02	1181.83	1172.20	1163.89	1156.71	1150.49	1129.70	1119.26	1113.95

13.375%

MONTHLY PAYMENT
REQUIRED TO AMORTIZE A LOAN

TERM	1 Year	2 Years	3 Years	4 Years	5 Years	6 Years	7 Years	8 Years	9 Years	10 Years	11 Years	12 Years	13 Years	14 Years
AMOUNT														
5	.45	.24	.17	.14	.12	.11	.10	.09	.08	.08	.08	.07	.07	.07
10	.90	.48	.34	.28	.23	.21	.19	.18	.16	.16	.15	.14	.14	.14
15	1.35	.72	.51	.41	.35	.31	.28	.26	.24	.23	.22	.21	.21	.20
25	2.24	1.20	.85	.68	.58	.51	.46	.43	.40	.38	.37	.35	.34	.33
50	4.48	2.39	1.70	1.36	1.15	1.02	.92	.86	.80	.76	.73	.70	.68	.66
75	6.72	3.58	2.55	2.03	1.73	1.53	1.38	1.28	1.20	1.14	1.09	1.05	1.02	.99
100	8.95	4.78	3.39	2.71	2.30	2.03	1.84	1.71	1.60	1.52	1.46	1.40	1.36	1.32
200	17.90	9.55	6.78	5.41	4.59	4.06	3.68	3.41	3.20	3.04	2.91	2.80	2.72	2.64
300	26.85	14.32	10.17	8.11	6.89	6.09	5.52	5.11	4.80	4.55	4.36	4.20	4.07	3.96
400	35.80	19.09	13.55	10.81	9.18	8.11	7.36	6.81	6.39	6.07	5.81	5.60	5.43	5.28
500	44.75	23.86	16.94	13.51	11.48	10.14	9.20	8.51	7.99	7.58	7.26	6.99	6.78	6.60
600	53.70	28.64	20.33	16.21	13.77	12.17	11.04	10.22	9.59	9.10	8.71	8.39	8.14	7.92
700	62.65	33.41	23.72	18.91	16.07	14.20	12.88	11.92	11.18	10.61	10.16	9.79	9.49	9.24
800	71.60	38.18	27.10	21.62	18.36	16.22	14.72	13.62	12.78	12.13	11.61	11.19	10.85	10.56
900	80.55	42.95	30.49	24.32	20.66	18.25	16.56	15.32	14.38	13.64	13.06	12.59	12.20	11.88
1000	89.50	47.72	33.88	27.02	22.95	20.28	18.40	17.02	15.97	15.16	14.51	13.98	13.56	13.20
2000	178.99	95.44	67.75	54.03	45.90	40.55	36.80	34.04	31.94	30.31	29.01	27.96	27.11	26.40
3000	268.48	143.16	101.63	81.05	68.84	60.82	55.19	51.06	47.91	45.46	43.52	41.94	40.66	39.59
4000	357.98	190.88	135.50	108.06	91.79	81.10	73.59	68.08	63.88	60.62	58.02	55.92	54.21	52.79
5000	447.47	238.60	169.38	135.07	114.73	101.37	91.99	85.09	79.85	75.77	72.52	69.90	67.76	65.98
6000	536.96	286.31	203.25	162.09	137.68	121.64	110.38	102.11	95.82	90.92	87.03	83.88	81.31	79.18
7000	626.46	334.03	237.13	189.10	160.62	141.91	128.78	119.13	111.79	106.08	101.53	97.86	94.86	92.37
8000	715.95	381.75	271.00	216.12	183.57	162.19	147.18	136.15	127.76	121.23	116.03	111.84	108.41	105.57
9000	805.44	429.47	304.88	243.13	206.51	182.46	165.57	153.16	143.73	136.38	130.54	125.82	121.96	118.77
10000	894.94	477.19	338.75	270.14	229.46	202.73	183.97	170.18	159.70	151.54	145.04	139.80	135.51	131.96
11000	984.43	524.90	372.63	297.16	252.41	223.00	202.37	187.20	175.67	166.69	159.55	153.78	149.06	145.16
12000	1073.92	572.62	406.50	324.17	275.35	243.28	220.76	204.22	191.64	181.84	174.05	167.75	162.61	158.35
13000	1163.42	620.34	440.38	351.19	298.30	263.55	239.16	221.24	207.61	196.99	188.55	181.73	176.16	171.55
14000	1252.91	668.06	474.25	378.20	321.24	283.82	257.56	238.25	223.58	212.15	203.06	195.71	189.71	184.74
15000	1342.40	715.78	508.13	405.21	344.19	304.09	275.95	255.27	239.55	227.30	217.56	209.69	203.26	197.94
16000	1431.90	763.50	542.00	432.23	367.13	324.37	294.35	272.29	255.52	242.45	232.06	223.67	216.81	211.14
17000	1521.39	811.21	575.88	459.24	390.08	344.64	312.74	289.31	271.49	257.61	246.57	237.65	230.36	224.33
18000	1610.88	858.93	609.75	486.26	413.02	364.91	331.14	306.32	287.46	272.76	261.07	251.63	243.91	237.53
19000	1700.38	906.65	643.63	513.27	435.97	385.18	349.54	323.34	303.43	287.91	275.57	265.61	257.46	250.72
20000	1789.87	954.37	677.50	540.28	458.91	405.46	367.93	340.36	319.40	303.07	290.08	279.59	271.01	263.92
21000	1879.36	1002.09	711.38	567.30	481.86	425.73	386.33	357.38	335.37	318.22	304.58	293.57	284.56	277.11
22000	1968.86	1049.80	745.25	594.31	504.81	446.00	404.73	374.39	351.34	333.37	319.09	307.55	298.11	290.31
23000	2058.35	1097.52	779.13	621.33	527.75	466.27	423.12	391.41	367.31	348.53	333.59	321.53	311.66	303.50
24000	2147.84	1145.24	813.00	648.34	550.70	486.55	441.52	408.43	383.28	363.68	348.09	335.50	325.21	316.70
25000	2237.34	1192.96	846.88	675.35	573.64	506.82	459.92	425.45	399.25	378.83	362.60	349.48	338.76	329.90
26000	2326.83	1240.68	880.75	702.37	596.59	527.09	478.31	442.47	415.22	393.98	377.10	363.46	352.31	343.09
27000	2416.32	1288.40	914.63	729.38	619.53	547.36	496.71	459.48	431.19	409.14	391.60	377.44	365.86	356.29
28000	2505.82	1336.11	948.50	756.40	642.48	567.64	515.11	476.50	447.16	424.29	406.11	391.42	379.41	369.48
29000	2595.31	1383.83	982.38	783.41	665.42	587.91	533.50	493.52	463.13	439.44	420.61	405.40	392.96	382.68
30000	2684.80	1431.55	1016.25	810.42	688.37	608.18	551.90	510.54	479.10	454.60	435.11	419.38	406.51	395.87
31000	2774.30	1479.27	1050.13	837.44	711.32	628.45	570.30	527.55	495.07	469.75	449.62	433.36	420.06	409.07
32000	2863.79	1526.99	1084.00	864.45	734.26	648.73	588.69	544.57	511.04	484.90	464.12	447.34	433.61	422.27
33000	2953.28	1574.70	1117.88	891.47	757.21	669.00	607.09	561.59	527.01	500.06	478.63	461.32	447.16	435.46
34000	3042.78	1622.42	1151.75	918.48	780.15	689.27	625.48	578.61	542.98	515.21	493.13	475.30	460.71	448.66
35000	3132.27	1670.14	1185.63	945.49	803.10	709.54	643.88	595.62	558.95	530.36	507.63	489.27	474.26	461.85
36000	3221.76	1717.86	1219.50	972.51	826.04	729.82	662.28	612.64	574.92	545.52	522.14	503.25	487.81	475.05
37000	3311.26	1765.58	1253.37	999.52	848.99	750.09	680.67	629.66	590.89	560.67	536.64	517.23	501.36	488.24
38000	3400.75	1813.29	1287.25	1026.54	871.93	770.36	699.07	646.68	606.86	575.82	551.14	531.21	514.91	501.44
39000	3490.24	1861.01	1321.12	1053.55	894.88	790.64	717.47	663.70	622.83	590.97	565.65	545.19	528.46	514.63
40000	3579.74	1908.73	1355.00	1080.56	917.82	810.91	735.86	680.71	638.80	606.13	580.15	559.17	542.01	527.83
41000	3669.23	1956.45	1388.87	1107.58	940.77	831.18	754.26	697.73	654.77	621.28	594.65	573.15	555.56	541.03
42000	3758.72	2004.17	1422.75	1134.59	963.72	851.45	772.66	714.75	670.74	636.43	609.16	587.13	569.11	554.22
43000	3848.22	2051.89	1456.62	1161.61	986.66	871.73	791.05	731.77	686.71	651.59	623.66	601.11	582.66	567.42
44000	3937.71	2099.60	1490.50	1188.62	1009.61	892.00	809.45	748.78	702.68	666.74	638.17	615.09	596.21	580.61
45000	4027.20	2147.32	1524.37	1215.63	1032.55	912.27	827.85	765.80	718.65	681.89	652.67	629.07	609.76	593.81
46000	4116.70	2195.04	1558.25	1242.65	1055.50	932.54	846.24	782.82	734.62	697.05	667.17	643.05	623.31	607.00
47000	4206.19	2242.76	1592.12	1269.66	1078.44	952.82	864.64	799.84	750.59	712.20	681.68	657.02	636.86	620.20
48000	4295.68	2290.48	1626.00	1296.68	1101.39	973.09	883.03	816.85	766.56	727.35	696.18	671.00	650.41	633.40
49000	4385.18	2338.19	1659.87	1323.69	1124.33	993.36	901.43	833.87	782.53	742.51	710.68	684.98	663.96	646.59
50000	4474.67	2385.91	1693.75	1350.70	1147.28	1013.63	919.83	850.89	798.50	757.66	725.19	698.96	677.51	659.79
55000	4922.14	2624.50	1863.12	1485.77	1262.01	1115.00	1011.81	935.98	878.35	833.42	797.71	768.86	745.26	725.77
60000	5369.60	2863.09	2032.50	1620.84	1376.74	1216.36	1103.79	1021.07	958.20	909.19	870.22	838.75	813.01	791.74
65000	5817.07	3101.68	2201.87	1755.91	1491.46	1317.72	1195.77	1106.16	1038.05	984.95	942.74	908.65	880.76	857.72
70000	6264.54	3340.28	2371.25	1890.98	1606.19	1419.08	1287.76	1191.24	1117.90	1060.72	1015.26	978.54	948.52	923.70
75000	6712.00	3578.87	2540.62	2026.05	1720.92	1520.45	1379.74	1276.33	1197.75	1136.49	1087.78	1048.44	1016.27	989.68
80000	7159.47	3817.46	2709.99	2161.12	1835.65	1621.81	1471.72	1361.42	1277.60	1212.25	1160.30	1118.34	1084.02	1055.66
85000	7606.94	4056.05	2879.37	2296.19	1950.37	1723.17	1563.70	1446.51	1357.45	1288.02	1232.81	1188.23	1151.77	1121.63
90000	8054.40	4294.64	3048.74	2431.26	2065.10	1824.54	1655.69	1531.60	1437.29	1363.78	1305.33	1258.13	1219.52	1187.61
95000	8501.87	4533.23	3218.12	2566.33	2179.83	1925.90	1747.67	1616.69	1517.14	1439.55	1377.85	1328.02	1287.27	1253.59
100000	8949.34	4771.82	3387.49	2701.40	2294.55	2027.26	1839.65	1701.78	1596.99	1515.31	1450.37	1397.92	1355.02	1319.57

TERM	15 Years	16 Years	17 Years	18 Years	19 Years	20 Years	21 Years	22 Years	23 Years	24 Years	25 Years	30 Years	35 Years	40 Years
AMOUNT														
5	.07	.07	.07	.07	.07	.06	.06	.06	.06	.06	.06	.06	.06	.06
10	.13	.13	.13	.13	.13	.12	.12	.12	.12	.12	.12	.12	.12	.12
15	.20	.19	.19	.19	.19	.18	.18	.18	.18	.18	.18	.18	.17	.17
25	.33	.32	.32	.31	.31	.30	.30	.30	.30	.30	.29	.29	.29	.29
50	.65	.64	.63	.62	.61	.60	.60	.59	.59	.59	.58	.57	.57	.57
75	.97	.95	.94	.92	.91	.90	.90	.89	.88	.88	.87	.86	.85	.85
100	1.30	1.27	1.25	1.23	1.22	1.20	1.19	1.18	1.17	1.17	1.16	1.14	1.13	1.13
200	2.59	2.54	2.49	2.46	2.43	2.40	2.38	2.36	2.34	2.33	2.32	2.28	2.26	2.25
300	3.88	3.80	3.74	3.68	3.64	3.60	3.57	3.54	3.51	3.49	3.47	3.41	3.38	3.37
400	5.17	5.07	4.98	4.91	4.85	4.80	4.75	4.72	4.68	4.65	4.63	4.55	4.51	4.49
500	6.46	6.33	6.23	6.14	6.06	6.00	5.94	5.89	5.85	5.82	5.79	5.68	5.63	5.61
600	7.75	7.60	7.47	7.36	7.27	7.20	7.13	7.07	7.02	6.98	6.94	6.82	6.76	6.73
700	9.04	8.86	8.71	8.59	8.48	8.39	8.32	8.25	8.19	8.14	8.10	7.95	7.88	7.85
800	10.33	10.13	9.96	9.82	9.70	9.59	9.50	9.43	9.36	9.30	9.25	9.09	9.01	8.97
900	11.62	11.39	11.20	11.04	10.91	10.79	10.69	10.60	10.53	10.47	10.41	10.23	10.13	10.09
1000	12.91	12.66	12.45	12.27	12.12	11.99	11.88	11.78	11.70	11.63	11.57	11.36	11.26	11.21
2000	25.81	25.31	24.89	24.53	24.23	23.97	23.75	23.56	23.39	23.25	23.13	22.72	22.51	22.41
3000	38.71	37.96	37.33	36.80	36.35	35.96	35.62	35.34	35.09	34.87	34.69	34.07	33.76	33.61
4000	51.61	50.61	49.78	49.06	48.46	47.94	47.50	47.11	46.78	46.50	46.25	45.43	45.02	44.81
5000	64.51	63.27	62.22	61.33	60.57	59.92	59.37	58.89	58.48	58.12	57.81	56.78	56.27	56.01
6000	77.41	75.92	74.66	73.59	72.69	71.91	71.24	70.67	70.17	69.74	69.37	68.14	67.52	67.21
7000	90.31	88.57	87.10	85.86	84.80	83.89	83.11	82.44	81.87	81.37	80.94	79.50	78.77	78.41
8000	103.21	101.22	99.55	98.12	96.91	95.88	94.99	94.22	93.56	92.99	92.50	90.85	90.03	89.61
9000	116.11	113.87	111.99	110.39	109.03	107.86	106.86	106.00	105.26	104.61	104.06	102.21	101.28	100.81
10000	129.01	126.53	124.43	122.65	121.14	119.84	118.73	117.78	116.95	116.24	115.62	113.56	112.53	112.01
11000	141.91	139.18	136.87	134.92	133.25	131.83	130.61	129.55	128.65	127.86	127.18	124.92	123.79	123.21
12000	154.81	151.83	149.32	147.18	145.37	143.81	142.48	141.33	140.34	139.48	138.74	136.28	135.04	134.41
13000	167.71	164.48	161.76	159.45	157.48	155.80	154.35	153.11	152.03	151.11	150.31	147.63	146.29	145.61
14000	180.61	177.14	174.20	171.71	169.59	167.78	166.22	164.88	163.73	162.73	161.87	158.99	157.54	156.81
15000	193.51	189.79	186.65	183.98	181.71	179.76	178.10	176.66	175.42	174.35	173.43	170.34	168.80	168.01
16000	206.41	202.44	199.09	196.24	193.82	191.75	189.97	188.44	187.12	185.98	184.99	181.70	180.05	179.21
17000	219.31	215.09	211.53	208.51	205.93	203.73	201.84	200.22	198.81	197.60	196.55	193.05	191.30	190.42
18000	232.21	227.74	223.97	220.77	218.05	215.72	213.71	211.99	210.51	209.22	208.11	204.41	202.56	201.62
19000	245.11	240.40	236.42	233.04	230.16	227.70	225.59	223.77	222.20	220.85	219.68	215.77	213.01	212.82
20000	258.01	253.05	248.86	245.30	242.27	239.68	237.46	235.55	233.90	232.47	231.24	227.12	225.06	224.02
21000	270.91	265.70	261.30	257.57	254.39	251.67	249.33	247.32	245.59	244.09	242.80	238.48	236.31	235.22
22000	283.81	278.35	273.74	269.83	266.50	263.65	261.21	259.10	257.29	255.72	254.36	249.83	247.57	246.42
23000	296.71	291.00	286.19	282.10	278.62	275.64	273.08	270.88	268.98	267.34	265.92	261.19	258.82	257.62
24000	309.61	303.66	298.63	294.36	290.73	287.62	284.95	282.65	280.68	278.96	277.48	272.55	270.07	268.82
25000	322.51	316.31	311.07	306.63	302.84	299.60	296.82	294.43	292.37	290.59	289.05	283.90	281.33	280.02
26000	335.41	328.96	323.52	318.89	314.96	311.59	308.70	306.21	304.06	302.21	300.61	295.26	292.58	291.22
27000	348.31	341.61	335.96	331.16	327.07	323.57	320.57	317.99	315.76	313.83	312.17	306.61	303.83	302.42
28000	361.21	354.27	348.40	343.42	339.18	335.55	332.44	329.76	327.45	325.46	323.73	317.97	315.08	313.62
29000	374.11	366.92	360.84	355.69	351.30	347.54	344.31	341.54	339.15	337.08	335.29	329.32	326.34	324.82
30000	387.01	379.57	373.29	367.95	363.41	359.52	356.19	353.32	350.84	348.70	346.85	340.68	337.59	336.02
31000	399.91	392.22	385.73	380.22	375.52	371.51	368.06	365.09	362.54	360.33	358.42	352.04	348.84	347.22
32000	412.81	404.87	398.17	392.48	387.64	383.49	379.93	376.87	374.23	371.95	369.98	363.39	360.10	358.42
33000	425.71	417.53	410.61	404.75	399.75	395.47	391.81	388.65	385.93	383.57	381.54	374.75	371.35	369.63
34000	438.61	430.18	423.06	417.01	411.86	407.46	403.68	400.43	397.62	395.20	393.10	386.10	382.60	380.83
35000	451.51	442.83	435.50	429.28	423.98	419.44	415.55	412.20	409.32	406.82	404.66	397.46	393.85	392.03
36000	464.41	455.48	447.94	441.54	436.09	431.43	427.42	423.98	421.01	418.44	416.22	408.82	405.11	403.23
37000	477.31	468.13	460.39	453.81	448.20	443.41	439.30	435.76	432.70	430.07	427.79	420.17	416.36	414.43
38000	490.21	480.79	472.83	466.07	460.32	455.39	451.17	447.53	444.40	441.69	439.35	431.53	427.61	425.63
39000	503.11	493.44	485.27	478.34	472.43	467.38	463.04	459.31	456.09	453.31	450.91	442.88	438.87	436.83
40000	516.01	506.09	497.71	490.60	484.54	479.36	474.91	471.09	467.79	464.94	462.47	454.24	450.12	448.03
41000	528.91	518.74	510.16	502.87	496.66	491.35	486.79	482.87	479.48	476.56	474.03	465.59	461.37	459.23
42000	541.81	531.40	522.60	515.13	508.77	503.33	498.66	494.64	491.18	488.18	485.59	476.95	472.62	470.43
43000	554.71	544.05	535.04	527.40	520.89	515.31	510.53	506.42	502.87	499.81	497.16	488.31	483.88	481.63
44000	567.61	556.70	547.48	539.66	533.00	527.30	522.41	518.20	514.57	511.43	508.72	499.66	495.13	492.83
45000	580.51	569.35	559.93	551.93	545.11	539.28	534.28	529.97	526.26	523.05	520.28	511.02	506.38	504.03
46000	593.41	582.00	572.37	564.19	557.23	551.27	546.15	541.75	537.96	534.68	531.84	522.37	517.64	515.23
47000	606.31	594.66	584.81	576.46	569.34	563.25	558.02	553.53	549.65	546.30	543.40	533.73	528.89	526.43
48000	619.21	607.31	597.26	588.72	581.45	575.23	569.90	565.30	561.35	557.92	554.96	545.09	540.14	537.63
49000	632.11	619.96	609.70	600.99	593.57	587.22	581.77	577.08	573.04	569.55	566.52	556.44	551.39	548.84
50000	645.01	632.61	622.14	613.25	605.68	599.20	593.64	588.86	584.73	581.17	578.09	567.80	562.65	560.04
55000	709.51	695.87	684.35	674.58	666.25	659.12	653.01	647.74	643.21	639.29	635.89	624.58	618.91	616.04
60000	774.01	759.13	746.57	735.90	726.82	719.04	712.37	706.63	701.68	697.40	693.70	681.36	675.18	672.04
65000	838.52	822.39	808.78	797.23	787.38	778.96	771.73	765.51	760.15	755.52	751.51	738.14	731.44	728.04
70000	903.02	885.66	871.00	858.55	847.95	838.88	831.10	824.40	818.63	813.64	809.32	794.91	787.70	784.05
75000	967.52	948.92	933.21	919.88	908.52	898.80	890.46	883.29	877.10	871.75	867.13	851.69	843.97	840.05
80000	1032.02	1012.18	995.42	981.20	969.08	958.72	949.82	942.17	935.57	929.87	924.94	908.47	900.23	896.05
85000	1096.52	1075.44	1057.64	1042.53	1029.65	1018.64	1009.19	1001.06	994.04	987.99	982.74	965.25	956.50	952.06
90000	1161.02	1138.70	1119.85	1103.85	1090.22	1078.56	1068.55	1059.94	1052.52	1046.10	1040.55	1022.03	1012.76	1008.06
95000	1225.52	1201.96	1182.06	1165.18	1150.79	1138.48	1127.91	1118.83	1110.99	1104.22	1098.36	1078.81	1069.03	1064.06
100000	1290.02	1265.22	1244.28	1226.50	1211.35	1198.40	1187.28	1177.71	1169.46	1162.34	1156.17	1135.59	1125.29	1120.07

MONTHLY PAYMENT
REQUIRED TO AMORTIZE A LOAN

TERM	1 Year	2 Years	3 Years	4 Years	5 Years	6 Years	7 Years	8 Years	9 Years	10 Years	11 Years	12 Years	13 Years	14 Years
AMOUNT														
5	.45	.24	.17	.14	.12	.11	.10	.09	.08	.08	.08	.07	.07	.07
10	.90	.48	.34	.28	.23	.21	.19	.18	.16	.16	.15	.14	.14	.14
15	1.35	.72	.51	.41	.35	.31	.28	.26	.24	.23	.22	.21	.21	.20
25	2.24	1.20	.85	.68	.58	.51	.47	.43	.40	.38	.37	.35	.34	.34
50	4.48	2.39	1.70	1.36	1.15	1.02	.93	.86	.80	.76	.73	.70	.68	.67
75	6.72	3.58	2.55	2.03	1.73	1.53	1.39	1.28	1.20	1.14	1.09	1.05	1.02	1.00
100	8.96	4.78	3.39	2.71	2.30	2.03	1.85	1.71	1.60	1.52	1.46	1.40	1.36	1.33
200	17.91	9.55	6.78	5.41	4.60	4.06	3.69	3.41	3.20	3.04	2.91	2.80	2.72	2.65
300	26.86	14.32	10.17	8.11	6.89	6.09	5.53	5.11	4.80	4.56	4.36	4.20	4.07	3.97
400	35.81	19.10	13.56	10.82	9.19	8.12	7.37	6.82	6.40	6.07	5.81	5.60	5.43	5.29
500	44.76	23.87	16.95	13.52	11.48	10.15	9.21	8.52	8.00	7.59	7.26	7.00	6.79	6.61
600	53.71	28.64	20.34	16.22	13.78	12.18	11.05	10.22	9.60	9.11	8.72	8.40	8.14	7.93
700	62.66	33.42	23.73	18.92	16.08	14.21	12.89	11.93	11.19	10.62	10.17	9.80	9.50	9.25
800	71.61	38.19	27.11	21.63	18.37	16.23	14.73	13.63	12.79	12.14	11.62	11.20	10.86	10.57
900	80.56	42.96	30.50	24.33	20.67	18.26	16.57	15.33	14.39	13.66	13.07	12.60	12.21	11.90
1000	89.51	47.73	33.89	27.03	22.96	20.29	18.42	17.04	15.99	15.17	14.52	14.00	13.57	13.22
2000	179.02	95.46	67.78	54.06	45.92	40.58	36.83	34.07	31.97	30.34	29.04	27.99	27.14	26.43
3000	268.52	143.19	101.67	81.08	68.88	60.86	55.24	51.10	47.96	45.51	43.56	41.99	40.70	39.64
4000	358.03	190.92	135.55	108.11	91.84	81.15	73.65	68.13	63.94	60.68	58.08	55.98	54.27	52.85
5000	447.53	238.65	169.44	135.14	114.80	101.43	92.06	85.16	79.93	75.84	72.60	69.98	67.84	66.06
6000	537.04	286.38	203.33	162.16	137.76	121.72	110.47	102.20	95.91	91.01	87.12	83.97	81.40	79.28
7000	626.54	334.11	237.21	189.19	160.71	142.01	128.88	119.23	111.90	106.18	101.64	97.97	94.97	92.49
8000	716.05	381.84	271.10	216.22	183.67	162.29	147.29	136.26	127.88	121.35	116.16	111.96	108.53	105.70
9000	805.55	429.57	304.99	243.24	206.63	182.58	165.70	153.29	143.86	136.52	130.67	125.96	122.10	118.91
10000	895.06	477.30	338.87	270.27	229.59	202.86	184.11	170.32	159.85	151.68	145.19	139.95	135.67	132.12
11000	984.56	525.03	372.76	297.30	252.55	223.15	202.52	187.35	175.83	166.85	159.71	153.95	149.23	145.34
12000	1074.07	572.76	406.65	324.32	275.51	243.44	220.93	204.39	191.82	182.02	174.23	167.94	162.80	158.55
13000	1163.57	620.49	440.54	351.35	298.46	263.72	239.34	221.42	207.80	197.19	188.75	181.94	176.36	171.76
14000	1253.08	668.22	474.42	378.38	321.42	284.01	257.75	238.45	223.79	212.36	203.27	195.93	189.93	184.97
15000	1342.58	715.95	508.31	405.40	344.38	304.29	276.16	255.48	239.77	227.52	217.79	209.93	203.50	198.18
16000	1432.09	763.68	542.20	432.43	367.34	324.58	294.57	272.51	255.75	242.69	232.31	223.92	217.06	211.40
17000	1521.59	811.41	576.08	459.45	390.30	344.86	312.98	289.55	271.74	257.86	246.83	237.92	230.63	224.61
18000	1611.10	859.14	609.97	486.48	413.26	365.15	331.39	306.58	287.72	273.03	261.34	251.91	244.19	237.82
19000	1700.60	906.87	643.86	513.51	436.21	385.44	349.80	323.61	303.71	288.20	275.86	265.90	257.76	251.03
20000	1790.11	954.60	677.74	540.53	459.17	405.72	368.21	340.64	319.69	303.36	290.38	279.90	271.33	264.24
21000	1879.61	1002.33	711.63	567.56	482.13	426.01	386.62	357.67	335.68	318.53	304.90	293.89	284.89	277.46
22000	1969.12	1050.06	745.52	594.59	505.09	446.29	405.03	374.70	351.66	333.70	319.42	307.89	298.46	290.67
23000	2058.62	1097.79	779.40	621.61	528.05	466.58	423.44	391.74	367.65	348.87	333.94	321.88	312.03	303.88
24000	2148.13	1145.52	813.29	648.64	551.01	486.87	441.85	408.77	383.63	364.04	348.46	335.88	325.59	317.09
25000	2237.63	1193.25	847.18	675.67	573.96	507.15	460.26	425.80	399.61	379.20	362.98	349.87	339.16	330.30
26000	2327.14	1240.98	881.07	702.69	596.92	527.44	478.67	442.83	415.60	394.37	377.50	363.87	352.72	343.51
27000	2416.64	1288.71	914.95	729.72	619.88	547.72	497.08	459.86	431.58	409.54	392.01	377.86	366.29	356.73
28000	2506.15	1336.44	948.84	756.75	642.84	568.01	515.49	476.89	447.57	424.71	406.53	391.86	379.86	369.94
29000	2595.65	1384.17	982.73	783.77	665.80	588.29	533.90	493.93	463.55	439.87	421.05	405.85	393.42	383.15
30000	2685.16	1431.90	1016.61	810.80	688.76	608.58	552.31	510.96	479.54	455.04	435.57	419.85	406.99	396.36
31000	2774.66	1479.63	1050.50	837.82	711.71	628.87	570.72	527.99	495.52	470.21	450.09	433.84	420.55	409.57
32000	2864.17	1527.36	1084.39	864.85	734.67	649.15	589.13	545.02	511.50	485.38	464.61	447.84	434.12	422.79
33000	2953.67	1575.09	1118.27	891.88	757.63	669.44	607.54	562.05	527.49	500.55	479.13	461.83	447.69	436.00
34000	3043.18	1622.82	1152.16	918.90	780.59	689.72	625.95	579.09	543.47	515.71	493.65	475.83	461.25	449.21
35000	3132.68	1670.55	1186.05	945.93	803.55	710.01	644.36	596.12	559.46	530.88	508.17	489.82	474.82	462.42
36000	3222.19	1718.28	1219.93	972.96	826.51	730.30	662.77	613.15	575.44	546.05	522.68	503.82	488.38	475.63
37000	3311.69	1766.01	1253.82	999.98	849.46	750.58	681.18	630.18	591.43	561.22	537.20	517.81	501.95	488.85
38000	3401.20	1813.74	1287.71	1027.01	872.42	770.87	699.59	647.21	607.41	576.39	551.72	531.80	515.52	502.06
39000	3490.70	1861.47	1321.60	1054.04	895.38	791.15	718.00	664.24	623.39	591.55	566.24	545.80	529.08	515.27
40000	3580.21	1909.20	1355.48	1081.06	918.34	811.44	736.41	681.28	639.38	606.72	580.76	559.79	542.65	528.48
41000	3669.71	1956.93	1389.37	1108.09	941.30	831.72	754.82	698.31	655.36	621.89	595.28	573.79	556.21	541.69
42000	3759.22	2004.66	1423.26	1135.12	964.26	852.01	773.23	715.34	671.35	637.06	609.80	587.78	569.78	554.91
43000	3848.72	2052.39	1457.14	1162.14	987.21	872.30	791.64	732.37	687.33	652.23	624.32	601.78	583.35	568.12
44000	3938.23	2100.12	1491.03	1189.17	1010.17	892.58	810.05	749.40	703.32	667.39	638.84	615.77	596.91	581.33
45000	4027.73	2147.85	1524.92	1216.20	1033.13	912.87	828.46	766.44	719.30	682.56	653.35	629.77	610.48	594.54
46000	4117.24	2195.58	1558.80	1243.22	1056.09	933.15	846.87	783.47	735.29	697.73	667.87	643.76	624.05	607.75
47000	4206.74	2243.31	1592.69	1270.25	1079.05	953.44	865.28	800.50	751.27	712.90	682.39	657.76	637.61	620.96
48000	4296.25	2291.04	1626.58	1297.27	1102.01	973.73	883.69	817.53	767.25	728.07	696.91	671.75	651.18	634.18
49000	4385.75	2338.77	1660.47	1324.30	1124.96	994.01	902.10	834.56	783.24	743.23	711.43	685.75	664.74	647.39
50000	4475.26	2386.50	1694.35	1351.33	1147.92	1014.30	920.51	851.59	799.22	758.40	725.95	699.74	678.31	660.60
55000	4922.78	2625.15	1863.79	1486.46	1262.71	1115.73	1012.56	936.75	879.14	834.24	798.54	769.72	746.14	726.66
60000	5370.31	2863.80	2033.22	1621.59	1377.51	1217.16	1104.61	1021.91	959.07	910.08	871.14	839.69	813.97	792.72
65000	5817.83	3102.45	2202.66	1756.72	1492.30	1318.58	1196.66	1107.07	1038.99	985.92	943.73	909.66	881.80	858.78
70000	6265.36	3341.10	2372.09	1891.86	1607.09	1420.01	1288.71	1192.23	1118.91	1061.76	1016.33	979.64	949.63	924.84
75000	6712.88	3579.75	2541.53	2026.99	1721.88	1521.44	1380.76	1277.39	1198.83	1137.60	1088.92	1049.61	1017.46	990.90
80000	7160.41	3818.40	2710.96	2162.12	1836.67	1622.87	1472.82	1362.55	1278.75	1213.44	1161.51	1119.58	1085.29	1056.96
85000	7607.93	4057.05	2880.39	2297.25	1951.47	1724.30	1564.87	1447.71	1358.68	1289.28	1234.11	1189.56	1153.12	1123.02
90000	8055.46	4295.70	3049.83	2432.39	2066.26	1825.73	1656.92	1532.87	1438.60	1365.12	1306.70	1259.53	1220.95	1189.08
95000	8502.99	4534.35	3219.26	2567.52	2181.05	1927.16	1748.97	1618.02	1518.52	1440.96	1379.30	1329.50	1288.78	1255.14
100000	8950.51	4773.00	3388.70	2702.65	2295.84	2028.59	1841.02	1703.18	1598.44	1516.80	1451.89	1399.48	1356.61	1321.20

TERM AMOUNT	15 Years	16 Years	17 Years	18 Years	19 Years	20 Years	21 Years	22 Years	23 Years	24 Years	25 Years	30 Years	35 Years	40 Years
5	.07	.07	.07	.07	.07	.07	.06	.06	.06	.06	.06	.06	.06	.06
10	.13	.13	.13	.13	.13	.13	.12	.12	.12	.12	.12	.12	.12	.12
15	.20	.20	.19	.19	.19	.19	.18	.18	.18	.18	.18	.18	.17	.17
25	.33	.32	.32	.31	.31	.31	.30	.30	.30	.30	.29	.29	.29	.29
50	.65	.64	.63	.62	.61	.61	.60	.59	.59	.59	.58	.57	.57	.57
75	.97	.96	.94	.93	.91	.91	.90	.89	.88	.88	.87	.86	.85	.85
100	1.30	1.27	1.25	1.23	1.22	1.21	1.19	1.18	1.18	1.17	1.16	1.14	1.13	1.13
200	2.59	2.54	2.50	2.46	2.43	2.41	2.38	2.36	2.35	2.33	2.32	2.28	2.26	2.25
300	3.88	3.81	3.74	3.69	3.64	3.61	3.57	3.54	3.52	3.50	3.48	3.42	3.39	3.37
400	5.17	5.07	4.99	4.92	4.86	4.81	4.76	4.72	4.69	4.66	4.64	4.56	4.51	4.49
500	6.46	6.34	6.23	6.15	6.07	6.01	5.95	5.90	5.86	5.83	5.80	5.69	5.64	5.62
600	7.76	7.61	7.48	7.37	7.28	7.21	7.14	7.08	7.03	6.99	6.95	6.83	6.77	6.74
700	9.05	8.87	8.73	8.60	8.50	8.41	8.33	8.26	8.20	8.15	8.11	7.97	7.90	7.86
800	10.34	10.14	9.97	9.83	9.71	9.61	9.52	9.44	9.38	9.32	9.27	9.11	9.02	8.98
900	11.63	11.41	11.22	11.06	10.92	10.81	10.71	10.62	10.55	10.48	10.43	10.24	10.15	10.10
1000	12.92	12.67	12.46	12.29	12.14	12.01	11.90	11.80	11.72	11.65	11.59	11.38	11.28	11.23
2000	25.84	25.34	24.92	24.57	24.27	24.01	23.79	23.60	23.43	23.29	23.17	22.76	22.55	22.45
3000	38.76	38.01	37.38	36.85	36.40	36.01	35.68	35.39	35.14	34.93	34.75	34.13	33.82	33.67
4000	51.67	50.68	49.84	49.13	48.53	48.01	47.57	47.19	46.86	46.57	46.33	45.51	45.10	44.89
5000	64.59	63.35	62.30	61.42	60.66	60.01	59.46	58.98	58.57	58.22	57.91	56.88	56.37	56.11
6000	77.51	76.02	74.76	73.70	72.79	72.02	71.35	70.78	70.28	69.86	69.49	68.26	67.64	67.33
7000	90.42	88.69	87.22	85.98	84.92	84.02	83.24	82.57	82.00	81.50	81.07	79.63	78.92	78.55
8000	103.34	101.36	99.68	98.26	97.05	96.02	95.13	94.37	93.71	93.14	92.65	91.01	90.19	89.77
9000	116.26	114.03	112.14	110.55	109.19	108.02	107.02	106.16	105.42	104.78	104.23	102.38	101.46	100.99
10000	129.17	126.70	124.60	122.83	121.32	120.02	118.91	117.96	117.14	116.43	115.81	113.76	112.73	112.22
11000	142.09	139.36	137.06	135.11	133.45	132.03	130.80	129.76	128.85	128.07	127.39	125.14	124.01	123.44
12000	155.01	152.03	149.52	147.39	145.58	144.03	142.70	141.55	140.56	139.71	138.97	136.51	135.28	134.66
13000	167.92	164.70	161.98	159.68	157.71	156.03	154.59	153.35	152.28	151.35	150.55	147.89	146.55	145.88
14000	180.84	177.37	174.44	171.96	169.84	168.03	166.48	165.14	163.99	162.99	162.13	159.26	157.83	157.10
15000	193.76	190.04	186.90	184.24	181.97	180.03	178.37	176.94	175.70	174.64	173.71	170.64	169.10	168.32
16000	206.67	202.71	199.36	196.52	194.10	192.03	190.26	188.73	187.42	186.28	185.29	182.01	180.37	179.54
17000	219.59	215.38	211.82	208.81	206.24	204.04	202.15	200.53	199.13	197.92	196.87	193.39	191.65	190.76
18000	232.51	228.05	224.28	221.09	218.37	216.04	214.04	212.32	210.84	209.56	208.46	204.76	202.92	201.98
19000	245.42	240.72	236.74	233.37	230.50	228.04	225.93	224.12	222.56	221.20	220.04	216.14	214.19	213.20
20000	258.34	253.39	249.20	245.65	242.63	240.04	237.82	235.91	234.27	232.85	231.62	227.51	225.46	224.43
21000	271.26	266.05	261.66	257.94	254.76	252.04	249.71	247.71	245.98	244.49	243.20	238.89	236.74	235.65
22000	284.17	278.72	274.12	270.22	266.89	264.05	261.60	259.51	257.69	256.13	254.78	250.27	248.01	246.87
23000	297.09	291.39	286.58	282.50	279.02	276.05	273.50	271.30	269.41	267.77	266.36	261.64	259.28	258.09
24000	310.01	304.06	299.04	294.78	291.15	288.05	285.39	283.10	281.12	279.42	277.94	273.02	270.56	269.31
25000	322.92	316.73	311.50	307.07	303.29	300.05	297.28	294.89	292.83	291.06	289.52	284.39	281.83	280.53
26000	335.84	329.40	323.96	319.35	315.42	312.05	309.17	306.69	304.55	302.70	301.10	295.77	293.10	291.75
27000	348.76	342.07	336.42	331.63	327.55	324.06	321.06	318.48	316.26	314.34	312.68	307.14	304.37	302.97
28000	361.67	354.74	348.88	343.91	336.06	332.95	330.28	327.97	325.98	324.26	318.52	315.65	314.19
29000	374.59	367.41	361.34	356.20	351.81	348.06	344.84	342.07	339.69	337.63	335.84	329.89	326.92	325.41
30000	387.51	380.08	373.80	368.48	363.94	360.06	356.73	353.87	351.40	349.27	347.42	341.27	338.19	336.64
31000	400.42	392.75	386.26	380.76	376.07	372.06	368.62	365.66	363.11	360.91	359.00	352.65	349.47	347.86
32000	413.34	405.41	398.72	393.04	388.20	384.06	380.51	377.46	374.83	372.55	370.58	364.02	360.74	359.08
33000	426.26	418.08	411.18	405.33	400.33	396.07	392.40	389.26	386.54	384.19	382.16	375.40	372.01	370.30
34000	439.17	430.75	423.64	417.61	412.47	408.07	404.30	401.05	398.25	395.84	393.74	386.77	383.29	381.52
35000	452.09	443.42	436.10	429.89	424.60	420.07	416.19	412.85	409.97	407.48	405.33	398.15	394.56	392.74
36000	465.01	456.09	448.56	442.17	436.73	432.07	428.08	424.64	421.68	419.12	416.91	409.52	405.83	403.96
37000	477.92	468.76	461.02	454.45	448.86	444.07	439.97	436.44	433.39	430.76	428.49	420.90	417.10	415.18
38000	490.84	481.43	473.48	466.74	460.99	456.08	451.86	448.23	445.11	442.40	440.07	432.27	428.38	426.40
39000	503.76	494.10	485.94	479.02	473.12	468.08	463.75	460.03	456.82	454.05	451.65	443.65	439.65	437.62
40000	516.68	506.77	498.40	491.30	485.25	480.08	475.64	471.82	468.53	465.69	463.23	455.02	450.92	448.85
41000	529.59	519.44	510.86	503.58	497.38	492.08	487.53	483.62	480.25	477.33	474.81	466.40	462.20	460.07
42000	542.51	532.10	523.32	515.87	509.52	504.08	499.42	495.41	491.96	488.97	486.39	477.78	473.47	471.29
43000	555.43	544.77	535.78	528.15	521.65	516.09	511.31	507.21	503.67	500.61	497.97	489.15	484.74	482.51
44000	568.34	557.44	548.24	540.43	533.78	528.09	523.20	519.01	515.38	512.26	509.55	500.53	496.02	493.73
45000	581.26	570.11	560.70	552.71	545.91	540.09	535.10	530.80	527.10	523.90	521.13	511.90	507.29	504.95
46000	594.18	582.85	573.16	565.00	558.04	552.09	546.99	542.60	538.81	535.54	532.71	523.28	518.56	516.17
47000	607.09	595.45	585.62	577.28	570.17	564.09	558.88	554.39	550.52	547.18	544.29	534.65	529.83	527.39
48000	620.01	608.12	598.08	589.56	582.30	576.09	570.77	566.19	562.24	558.83	555.87	546.03	541.11	538.61
49000	632.93	620.79	610.54	601.84	594.43	588.10	582.66	577.98	573.95	570.47	567.45	557.40	552.38	549.83
50000	645.84	633.46	623.00	614.13	606.57	600.10	594.55	589.78	585.66	582.11	579.03	568.78	563.65	561.06
55000	710.43	696.80	685.30	675.54	667.22	660.11	654.00	648.76	644.23	640.32	636.94	625.66	620.02	617.16
60000	775.01	760.15	747.60	736.95	727.88	720.12	713.46	707.73	702.80	698.53	694.84	682.53	676.38	673.27
65000	839.59	823.49	809.90	798.36	788.53	780.13	772.91	766.71	761.36	756.74	752.74	739.41	732.75	729.37
70000	904.18	886.84	872.20	859.77	849.19	840.14	832.37	825.69	819.93	814.95	810.65	796.29	789.11	785.48
75000	968.76	950.18	934.50	921.19	909.85	900.14	891.82	884.66	878.49	873.16	868.55	853.17	845.48	841.58
80000	1033.35	1013.53	996.80	982.60	970.50	960.15	951.28	943.64	937.06	931.37	926.45	910.04	901.84	897.69
85000	1097.93	1076.87	1059.10	1044.01	1031.16	1020.16	1010.73	1002.62	995.62	989.58	984.35	966.92	958.21	953.79
90000	1162.51	1140.22	1121.40	1105.42	1091.81	1080.17	1070.19	1061.60	1054.19	1047.79	1042.26	1023.80	1014.57	1009.90
95000	1227.10	1203.56	1183.69	1166.84	1152.47	1140.18	1129.64	1120.57	1112.76	1106.00	1100.16	1080.68	1070.94	1066.00
100000	1291.68	1266.91	1245.99	1228.25	1213.13	1200.19	1189.10	1179.55	1171.32	1164.21	1158.06	1137.55	1127.30	1122.11

MONTHLY PAYMENT
REQUIRED TO AMORTIZE A LOAN

TERM	1 Year	2 Years	3 Years	4 Years	5 Years	6 Years	7 Years	8 Years	9 Years	10 Years	11 Years	12 Years	13 Years	14 Years
AMOUNT														
5	.45	.24	.17	.14	.12	.11	.10	.09	.09	.08	.08	.08	.07	.07
10	.90	.48	.34	.28	.24	.21	.19	.18	.17	.16	.15	.15	.14	.14
15	1.35	.72	.51	.41	.35	.31	.28	.26	.25	.23	.22	.22	.21	.20
25	2.24	1.20	.85	.68	.58	.51	.47	.43	.41	.39	.37	.36	.35	.34
50	4.48	2.39	1.70	1.36	1.16	1.02	.93	.86	.81	.77	.73	.71	.69	.67
75	6.72	3.59	2.55	2.04	1.73	1.53	1.39	1.29	1.21	1.15	1.10	1.06	1.03	1.00
100	8.96	4.78	3.40	2.71	2.31	2.04	1.85	1.71	1.61	1.53	1.46	1.41	1.37	1.33
200	17.92	9.56	6.79	5.42	4.61	4.07	3.70	3.42	3.21	3.05	2.92	2.82	2.73	2.66
300	26.87	14.34	10.19	8.13	6.91	6.11	5.54	5.13	4.82	4.57	4.38	4.22	4.09	3.99
400	35.83	19.12	13.58	10.84	9.21	8.14	7.39	6.84	6.42	6.10	5.84	5.63	5.46	5.32
500	44.78	23.89	16.97	13.54	11.51	10.17	9.24	8.55	8.03	7.62	7.29	7.03	6.82	6.64
600	53.74	28.67	20.37	16.25	13.81	12.21	11.08	10.26	9.63	9.14	8.75	8.44	8.18	7.97
700	62.69	33.45	23.76	18.96	16.11	14.24	12.93	11.97	11.23	10.66	10.21	9.85	9.55	9.30
800	71.65	38.23	27.15	21.67	18.41	16.28	14.78	13.68	12.84	12.19	11.67	11.25	10.91	10.63
900	80.60	43.00	30.55	24.37	20.71	18.31	16.62	15.38	14.44	13.71	13.13	12.66	12.27	11.95
1000	89.56	47.78	33.94	27.08	23.01	20.34	18.47	17.09	16.05	15.23	14.58	14.06	13.63	13.28
2000	179.11	95.56	67.88	54.16	46.02	40.68	36.93	34.18	32.09	30.46	29.16	28.12	27.26	26.56
3000	268.66	143.34	101.81	81.23	69.03	61.02	55.40	51.27	48.13	45.69	43.74	42.18	40.89	39.84
4000	358.21	191.11	135.75	108.31	92.04	81.36	73.86	68.36	64.17	60.91	58.32	56.23	54.52	53.11
5000	447.77	238.89	169.68	135.39	115.05	101.70	92.33	85.45	80.22	76.14	72.90	70.29	68.15	66.39
6000	537.32	286.67	203.62	162.46	138.06	122.04	110.79	102.53	96.26	91.37	87.48	84.35	81.78	79.67
7000	626.87	334.44	237.55	189.54	161.07	142.38	129.26	119.62	112.30	106.60	102.06	98.41	95.41	92.94
8000	716.42	382.22	271.49	216.62	184.08	162.72	147.72	136.71	128.34	121.82	116.64	112.46	109.04	106.22
9000	805.97	430.00	305.42	243.69	207.09	183.06	166.19	153.80	144.39	137.05	131.22	126.52	122.67	119.50
10000	895.53	477.78	339.36	270.77	230.10	203.39	184.65	170.89	160.43	152.28	145.80	140.58	136.30	132.78
11000	985.08	525.55	373.29	297.84	253.11	223.73	203.12	187.97	176.47	167.51	160.38	154.63	149.93	146.05
12000	1074.63	573.33	407.23	324.92	276.12	244.07	221.58	205.06	192.51	182.73	174.96	168.69	163.56	159.33
13000	1164.18	621.11	441.16	352.00	299.13	264.41	240.05	222.15	208.56	197.96	189.54	182.75	177.19	172.61
14000	1253.73	668.88	475.10	379.07	322.14	284.75	258.51	239.24	224.60	213.19	204.12	196.81	190.82	185.88
15000	1343.29	716.66	509.03	406.15	345.15	305.09	276.98	256.33	240.64	228.42	218.70	210.86	204.45	199.16
16000	1432.84	764.44	542.97	433.23	368.16	325.43	295.44	273.42	256.68	243.64	233.28	224.92	218.08	212.44
17000	1522.39	812.21	576.90	460.30	391.17	345.77	313.91	290.50	272.72	258.87	247.86	238.98	231.71	225.72
18000	1611.94	859.99	610.84	487.38	414.18	366.11	332.37	307.59	288.77	274.10	262.44	253.03	245.34	238.99
19000	1701.49	907.77	644.78	514.46	437.19	386.45	350.84	324.68	304.81	289.33	277.02	267.09	258.97	252.27
20000	1791.05	955.55	678.71	541.53	460.20	406.78	369.30	341.77	320.85	304.55	291.60	281.15	272.60	265.55
21000	1880.60	1003.32	712.65	568.61	483.21	427.12	387.77	358.86	336.89	319.78	306.18	295.21	286.23	278.82
22000	1970.15	1051.10	746.58	595.68	506.22	447.46	406.23	375.94	352.94	335.01	320.76	309.26	299.86	292.10
23000	2059.70	1098.88	780.52	622.76	529.23	467.80	424.70	393.03	368.98	350.24	335.34	323.32	313.49	305.38
24000	2149.25	1146.65	814.45	649.84	552.24	488.14	443.16	410.12	385.02	365.46	349.92	337.38	327.12	318.65
25000	2238.81	1194.43	848.39	676.91	575.25	508.48	461.63	427.21	401.06	380.69	364.50	351.43	340.75	331.93
26000	2328.36	1242.21	882.32	703.99	598.26	528.82	480.09	444.30	417.11	395.92	379.08	365.49	354.38	345.21
27000	2417.91	1289.98	916.26	731.07	621.27	549.16	498.56	461.39	433.15	411.15	393.66	379.55	368.01	358.49
28000	2507.46	1337.76	950.19	758.14	644.28	569.50	517.02	478.47	449.19	426.37	408.24	393.61	381.64	371.76
29000	2597.01	1385.54	984.13	785.22	667.29	589.83	535.49	495.56	465.23	441.60	422.82	407.66	395.27	385.04
30000	2686.57	1433.32	1018.06	812.29	690.30	610.17	553.95	512.65	481.27	456.83	437.40	421.72	408.90	398.32
31000	2776.12	1481.09	1052.00	839.37	713.31	630.51	572.42	529.74	497.32	472.06	451.98	435.78	422.53	411.59
32000	2865.67	1528.87	1085.93	866.45	736.32	650.85	590.88	546.83	513.36	487.28	466.56	449.83	436.16	424.87
33000	2955.22	1576.65	1119.87	893.52	759.33	671.19	609.35	563.91	529.40	502.51	481.14	463.89	449.79	438.15
34000	3044.77	1624.42	1153.80	920.60	782.34	691.53	627.81	581.00	545.44	517.74	495.72	477.95	463.42	451.43
35000	3134.33	1672.20	1187.74	947.68	805.35	711.87	646.28	598.09	561.49	532.97	510.30	492.01	477.05	464.70
36000	3223.88	1719.98	1221.68	974.75	828.36	732.21	664.74	615.18	577.53	548.19	524.88	506.06	490.68	477.98
37000	3313.43	1767.75	1255.61	1001.83	851.37	752.55	683.21	632.27	593.57	563.42	539.46	520.12	504.31	491.26
38000	3402.98	1815.53	1289.55	1028.91	874.38	772.89	701.67	649.36	609.61	578.65	554.04	534.18	517.94	504.53
39000	3492.53	1863.31	1323.48	1055.98	897.39	793.22	720.14	666.44	625.66	593.87	568.62	548.23	531.57	517.81
40000	3582.09	1911.09	1357.42	1083.06	920.40	813.56	738.60	683.53	641.70	609.10	583.20	562.29	545.20	531.09
41000	3671.64	1958.86	1391.35	1110.13	943.41	833.90	757.07	700.62	657.74	624.33	597.78	576.35	558.83	544.36
42000	3761.19	2006.64	1425.29	1137.21	966.42	854.24	775.53	717.71	673.78	639.56	612.36	590.41	572.46	557.64
43000	3850.74	2054.42	1459.22	1164.29	989.43	874.58	794.00	734.80	689.82	654.78	626.94	604.46	586.09	570.92
44000	3940.29	2102.19	1493.16	1191.36	1012.44	894.92	812.46	751.88	705.87	670.01	641.52	618.52	599.72	584.20
45000	4029.85	2149.97	1527.09	1218.44	1035.45	915.26	830.93	768.97	721.91	685.24	656.10	632.58	613.35	597.47
46000	4119.40	2197.75	1561.03	1245.52	1058.46	935.60	849.39	786.06	737.95	700.47	670.68	646.63	626.98	610.75
47000	4208.95	2245.52	1594.96	1272.59	1081.47	955.94	867.85	803.15	753.99	715.69	685.26	660.69	640.61	624.03
48000	4298.50	2293.30	1628.90	1299.67	1104.48	976.28	886.32	820.24	770.04	730.92	699.84	674.75	654.24	637.30
49000	4388.05	2341.08	1662.83	1326.74	1127.49	996.61	904.78	837.32	786.08	746.15	714.42	688.81	667.87	650.58
50000	4477.61	2388.86	1696.77	1353.82	1150.50	1016.95	923.25	854.41	802.12	761.38	729.00	702.86	681.50	663.86
55000	4925.37	2627.74	1866.45	1489.20	1265.55	1118.65	1015.57	939.85	882.33	837.51	801.90	773.15	749.65	730.24
60000	5373.13	2866.63	2036.12	1624.58	1380.60	1220.34	1107.90	1025.29	962.54	913.65	874.80	843.44	817.80	796.63
65000	5820.89	3105.51	2205.80	1759.97	1495.65	1322.04	1200.22	1110.74	1042.76	989.79	947.70	913.72	885.95	863.01
70000	6268.65	3344.40	2375.48	1895.35	1610.69	1423.73	1292.55	1196.18	1122.97	1065.93	1020.60	984.01	954.10	929.40
75000	6716.41	3583.28	2545.15	2030.73	1725.74	1525.43	1384.87	1281.62	1203.18	1142.06	1093.50	1054.29	1022.25	995.78
80000	7164.17	3822.17	2714.83	2166.11	1840.79	1627.12	1477.20	1367.06	1283.39	1218.20	1166.40	1124.58	1090.40	1062.17
85000	7611.93	4061.05	2884.50	2301.49	1955.84	1728.82	1569.52	1452.50	1363.60	1294.34	1239.29	1194.86	1158.55	1128.56
90000	8059.69	4299.94	3054.18	2436.87	2070.89	1830.51	1661.85	1537.94	1443.81	1370.47	1312.19	1265.15	1226.70	1194.94
95000	8507.45	4538.82	3223.86	2572.26	2185.94	1932.21	1754.17	1623.38	1524.02	1446.61	1385.09	1335.44	1294.85	1261.33
100000	8955.21	4777.71	3393.53	2707.64	2300.99	2033.90	1846.49	1708.82	1604.24	1522.75	1457.99	1405.72	1363.00	1327.71

TERM AMOUNT	15 Years	16 Years	17 Years	18 Years	19 Years	20 Years	21 Years	22 Years	23 Years	24 Years	25 Years	30 Years	35 Years	40 Years
5	.07	.07	.07	.07	.07	.07	.06	.06	.06	.06	.06	.06	.06	.06
10	.13	.13	.13	.13	.13	.13	.12	.12	.12	.12	.12	.12	.12	.12
15	.20	.20	.19	.19	.19	.19	.18	.18	.18	.18	.18	.18	.18	.17
25	.33	.32	.32	.31	.31	.31	.30	.30	.30	.30	.30	.29	.29	.29
50	.65	.64	.63	.62	.62	.61	.60	.60	.59	.59	.59	.58	.57	.57
75	.98	.96	.94	.93	.92	.91	.90	.90	.89	.88	.88	.86	.86	.85
100	1.30	1.28	1.26	1.24	1.23	1.21	1.20	1.19	1.18	1.18	1.17	1.15	1.14	1.14
200	2.60	2.55	2.51	2.48	2.45	2.42	2.40	2.38	2.36	2.35	2.34	2.30	2.28	2.27
300	3.90	3.83	3.76	3.71	3.67	3.63	3.59	3.57	3.54	3.52	3.50	3.44	3.41	3.40
400	5.20	5.10	5.02	4.95	4.89	4.83	4.79	4.75	4.72	4.69	4.67	4.59	4.55	4.53
500	6.50	6.37	6.27	6.18	6.11	6.04	5.99	5.94	5.90	5.86	5.83	5.73	5.68	5.66
600	7.79	7.65	7.52	7.42	7.33	7.25	7.18	7.13	7.08	7.04	7.00	6.88	6.82	6.79
700	9.09	8.92	8.78	8.65	8.55	8.46	8.38	8.31	8.26	8.21	8.16	8.02	7.95	7.92
800	10.39	10.19	10.03	9.89	9.77	9.66	9.58	9.50	9.44	9.38	9.33	9.17	9.09	9.05
900	11.69	11.47	11.28	11.12	10.99	10.87	10.77	10.69	10.61	10.55	10.50	10.31	10.22	10.18
1000	12.99	12.74	12.53	12.36	12.21	12.08	11.97	11.87	11.79	11.72	11.66	11.46	11.36	11.31
2000	25.97	25.48	25.06	24.71	24.41	24.15	23.93	23.74	23.58	23.44	23.32	22.91	22.71	22.61
3000	38.95	38.22	37.59	37.06	36.61	36.23	35.90	35.61	35.37	35.16	34.97	34.37	34.07	33.91
4000	51.94	50.95	50.12	49.41	48.81	48.30	47.86	47.48	47.16	46.87	46.63	45.82	45.42	45.22
5000	64.92	63.69	62.65	61.77	61.02	60.37	59.82	59.35	58.94	58.59	58.29	57.28	56.77	56.52
6000	77.90	76.43	75.18	74.12	73.22	72.45	71.79	71.22	70.73	70.31	69.94	68.73	68.13	67.82
7000	90.89	89.16	87.71	86.47	85.42	84.52	83.75	83.09	82.52	82.03	81.60	80.18	79.48	79.12
8000	103.87	101.90	100.23	98.82	97.62	96.59	95.71	94.96	94.31	93.74	93.26	91.64	90.83	90.43
9000	116.85	114.64	112.76	111.18	109.82	108.67	107.68	106.83	106.09	105.46	104.91	103.09	102.19	101.73
10000	129.84	127.37	125.29	123.53	122.03	120.74	119.64	118.70	117.88	117.18	116.57	114.55	113.54	113.03
11000	142.82	140.11	137.82	135.88	134.23	132.82	131.61	130.57	129.67	128.89	128.23	126.00	124.89	124.33
12000	155.80	152.85	150.35	148.23	146.43	144.89	143.57	142.43	141.46	140.61	139.88	137.45	136.25	135.64
13000	168.79	165.58	162.88	160.59	158.63	156.96	155.53	154.30	153.24	152.33	151.54	148.91	147.60	146.94
14000	181.77	178.32	175.41	172.94	170.83	169.04	167.50	166.17	165.03	164.05	163.20	160.36	158.95	158.24
15000	194.75	191.06	187.94	185.29	183.04	181.11	179.46	178.04	176.82	175.76	174.85	171.82	170.31	169.54
16000	207.74	203.79	200.46	197.64	195.24	193.18	191.42	189.91	188.61	187.48	186.51	183.27	181.66	180.85
17000	220.72	216.53	212.99	209.99	207.44	205.26	203.39	201.78	200.39	199.20	198.16	194.73	193.01	192.15
18000	233.70	229.27	225.52	222.35	219.64	217.33	215.35	213.65	212.18	210.92	209.82	206.18	204.37	203.45
19000	246.69	242.00	238.05	234.70	231.85	229.41	227.32	225.52	223.97	222.63	221.48	217.63	215.72	214.75
20000	259.67	254.74	250.58	247.05	244.05	241.48	239.28	237.39	235.76	234.35	233.13	229.09	227.07	226.06
21000	272.65	267.48	263.11	259.40	256.25	253.55	251.24	249.26	247.54	246.07	244.79	240.54	238.43	237.36
22000	285.64	280.21	275.64	271.76	268.45	265.63	263.21	261.13	259.33	257.78	256.45	252.00	249.78	248.66
23000	290.62	292.95	288.16	284.11	280.65	277.70	275.17	272.99	271.12	269.50	268.10	263.45	261.13	259.97
24000	311.60	305.69	300.69	296.46	292.86	289.77	287.13	284.86	282.91	281.22	279.76	274.90	272.49	271.27
25000	324.58	318.42	313.22	308.81	305.06	301.85	299.10	296.73	294.70	292.94	291.42	286.36	283.84	282.57
26000	337.57	331.16	325.75	321.17	317.26	313.92	311.06	308.60	306.48	304.65	303.07	297.81	295.19	293.87
27000	350.55	343.90	338.28	333.52	329.46	326.00	323.02	320.47	318.27	316.37	314.73	309.27	306.55	305.18
28000	363.53	356.63	350.81	345.87	341.66	338.07	334.99	332.34	330.06	328.09	326.39	320.72	317.90	316.48
29000	376.52	369.37	363.34	358.22	353.87	350.14	346.95	344.21	341.85	339.81	338.04	332.17	329.25	327.78
30000	389.50	382.11	375.87	370.57	366.07	362.22	358.92	356.08	353.63	351.52	349.70	343.63	340.61	339.08
31000	402.48	394.84	388.39	382.93	378.27	374.29	370.88	367.95	365.42	363.24	361.35	355.08	351.96	350.39
32000	415.47	407.58	400.92	395.28	390.47	386.36	382.84	379.82	377.21	374.96	373.01	366.54	363.31	361.69
33000	428.45	420.32	413.45	407.63	402.67	398.44	394.81	391.69	389.00	386.67	384.67	377.99	374.67	372.99
34000	441.43	433.05	425.98	419.90	414.88	410.51	406.77	403.55	400.78	398.39	396.32	389.45	386.02	384.29
35000	454.42	445.79	438.51	432.34	427.08	422.59	418.73	415.42	412.57	410.11	407.98	400.90	397.37	395.60
36000	467.40	458.53	451.04	444.69	439.28	434.66	430.70	427.29	424.36	421.83	419.64	412.35	408.73	406.90
37000	480.38	471.26	463.57	457.04	451.48	446.73	442.66	439.16	436.15	433.54	431.29	423.81	420.08	418.20
38000	493.37	484.00	476.10	469.39	463.69	458.81	454.63	451.03	447.93	445.26	442.95	435.26	431.43	429.50
39000	506.35	496.74	488.62	481.75	475.89	470.88	466.59	462.90	459.72	456.98	454.61	446.72	442.79	440.81
40000	519.33	509.47	501.15	494.10	488.09	482.95	478.55	474.77	471.51	468.70	466.26	458.17	454.14	452.11
41000	532.32	522.21	513.68	506.45	500.29	495.03	490.52	486.64	483.30	480.41	477.92	469.62	465.49	463.41
42000	545.30	534.95	526.21	518.80	512.49	507.10	502.48	498.51	495.08	492.13	489.58	481.08	476.85	474.71
43000	558.28	547.68	538.74	531.15	524.70	519.18	514.44	510.38	506.87	503.85	501.23	492.53	488.20	486.02
44000	571.27	560.42	551.27	543.51	536.90	531.25	526.41	522.25	518.66	515.56	512.89	503.99	499.55	497.32
45000	584.25	573.16	563.80	555.86	549.10	543.32	538.37	534.11	530.45	527.28	524.55	515.44	510.91	508.62
46000	597.23	585.89	576.32	568.21	561.30	555.40	550.34	545.98	542.24	539.00	536.20	526.89	522.26	519.93
47000	610.21	598.63	588.85	580.56	573.50	567.47	562.30	557.85	554.02	550.72	547.86	538.35	533.62	531.23
48000	623.20	611.37	601.38	592.92	585.71	579.54	574.26	569.72	565.81	562.43	559.51	549.80	544.97	542.53
49000	636.18	624.10	613.91	605.27	597.91	591.62	586.23	581.59	577.60	574.15	571.17	561.26	556.32	553.83
50000	649.16	636.84	626.44	617.62	610.11	603.69	598.19	593.46	589.39	585.87	582.83	572.71	567.68	565.14
55000	714.08	700.52	689.08	679.38	671.12	664.06	658.01	652.81	648.32	644.45	641.11	629.98	624.44	621.65
60000	779.00	764.21	751.73	741.14	732.13	724.43	717.83	712.15	707.26	703.04	699.39	687.25	681.21	678.16
65000	843.91	827.89	814.37	802.91	793.14	784.80	777.65	771.50	766.20	761.63	757.67	744.52	737.98	734.67
70000	908.83	891.57	877.01	864.67	854.15	845.17	837.46	830.84	825.14	820.21	815.96	801.79	794.74	791.19
75000	973.74	955.26	939.66	926.43	915.16	905.54	897.28	890.19	884.08	878.80	874.24	859.06	851.51	847.70
80000	1038.66	1018.94	1002.30	988.19	976.17	965.90	957.10	949.53	943.01	937.39	932.52	916.33	908.28	904.21
85000	1103.58	1082.62	1064.94	1049.95	1037.18	1026.27	1016.92	1008.88	1001.95	995.97	990.80	973.61	965.04	960.73
90000	1168.49	1146.31	1127.59	1111.71	1098.20	1086.64	1076.74	1068.22	1060.89	1054.56	1049.09	1030.88	1021.81	1017.24
95000	1233.41	1209.99	1190.23	1173.47	1159.21	1147.01	1136.56	1127.57	1119.83	1113.15	1107.37	1088.15	1078.58	1073.75
100000	1298.32	1273.67	1252.87	1235.24	1220.22	1207.38	1196.37	1186.92	1178.77	1171.73	1165.65	1145.42	1135.35	1130.27

MONTHLY PAYMENT
REQUIRED TO AMORTIZE A LOAN

TERM AMOUNT	1 Year	2 Years	3 Years	4 Years	5 Years	6 Years	7 Years	8 Years	9 Years	10 Years	11 Years	12 Years	13 Years	14 Years
5	.45	.24	.17	.14	.12	.11	.10	.09	.09	.08	.08	.08	.07	.07
10	.90	.48	.34	.28	.24	.21	.19	.18	.17	.16	.15	.15	.14	.14
15	1.35	.72	.51	.41	.35	.31	.28	.26	.25	.23	.22	.22	.21	.21
25	2.24	1.20	.85	.68	.58	.51	.47	.43	.41	.39	.37	.36	.35	.34
50	4.48	2.40	1.70	1.36	1.16	1.02	.93	.86	.81	.77	.74	.71	.69	.67
75	6.72	3.59	2.55	2.04	1.73	1.53	1.39	1.29	1.21	1.15	1.10	1.06	1.03	1.01
100	8.96	4.79	3.40	2.72	2.31	2.04	1.86	1.72	1.62	1.53	1.47	1.42	1.37	1.34
200	17.92	9.57	6.80	5.43	4.62	4.08	3.71	3.43	3.23	3.06	2.93	2.83	2.74	2.67
300	26.88	14.35	10.20	8.14	6.92	6.12	5.56	5.15	4.84	4.59	4.40	4.24	4.11	4.01
400	35.84	19.13	13.60	10.86	9.23	8.16	7.41	6.86	6.45	6.12	5.86	5.65	5.48	5.34
500	44.80	23.92	17.00	13.57	11.54	10.20	9.26	8.58	8.06	7.65	7.33	7.06	6.85	6.68
600	53.76	28.70	20.40	16.28	13.84	12.24	11.12	10.29	9.67	9.18	8.79	8.48	8.22	8.01
700	62.72	33.48	23.79	18.99	16.15	14.28	12.97	12.01	11.28	10.71	10.25	9.89	9.59	9.34
800	71.68	38.26	27.19	21.71	18.45	16.32	14.82	13.72	12.89	12.23	11.72	11.30	10.96	10.68
900	80.64	43.05	30.59	24.42	20.76	18.36	16.67	15.44	14.50	13.76	13.18	12.71	12.33	12.01
1000	89.60	47.83	33.99	27.13	23.07	20.40	18.52	17.15	16.11	15.29	14.65	14.12	13.70	13.35
2000	179.20	95.65	67.97	54.26	46.13	40.79	37.04	34.29	32.21	30.58	29.29	28.24	27.39	26.69
3000	268.80	143.48	101.96	81.38	69.19	61.18	55.56	51.44	48.31	45.87	43.93	42.36	41.09	40.03
4000	358.40	191.30	135.94	108.51	92.25	81.57	74.08	68.58	64.41	61.15	58.57	56.48	54.78	53.37
5000	448.00	239.13	169.92	135.64	115.31	101.97	92.60	85.73	80.51	76.44	73.21	70.60	68.47	66.72
6000	537.60	286.95	203.91	162.76	138.37	122.36	111.12	102.87	96.61	91.73	87.85	84.72	82.17	80.06
7000	627.20	334.77	237.89	189.89	161.43	142.75	129.64	120.02	112.71	107.01	102.49	98.84	95.86	93.40
8000	716.80	382.60	271.87	217.01	184.50	163.14	148.16	137.16	128.81	122.30	117.13	112.96	109.56	106.74
9000	806.40	430.42	305.86	244.14	207.56	183.53	166.68	154.31	144.91	137.59	131.77	127.08	123.25	120.09
10000	896.00	478.25	339.84	271.27	230.62	203.93	185.20	171.45	161.01	152.88	146.41	141.20	136.94	133.43
11000	985.59	526.07	373.83	298.39	253.68	224.32	203.72	188.60	177.11	168.16	161.06	155.32	150.64	146.77
12000	1075.19	573.89	407.81	325.52	276.74	244.71	222.24	205.74	193.21	183.45	175.70	169.44	164.33	160.11
13000	1164.79	621.72	441.79	352.65	299.80	265.10	240.76	222.89	209.31	198.74	190.34	183.56	178.03	173.46
14000	1254.39	669.54	475.78	379.77	322.86	285.50	259.28	240.03	225.41	214.02	204.98	197.68	191.72	186.80
15000	1343.99	717.37	509.76	406.90	345.93	305.89	277.80	257.17	241.51	229.31	219.62	211.80	205.41	200.14
16000	1433.59	765.19	543.74	434.02	368.99	326.28	296.32	274.32	257.61	244.60	234.26	225.92	219.11	213.48
17000	1523.19	813.02	577.73	461.15	392.05	346.67	314.84	291.46	273.71	259.88	248.90	240.04	232.80	226.83
18000	1612.79	860.84	611.71	488.28	415.11	367.06	333.36	308.61	289.81	275.17	263.54	254.16	246.49	240.17
19000	1702.39	908.66	645.69	515.40	438.17	387.46	351.88	325.75	305.91	290.46	278.18	268.28	260.19	253.51
20000	1791.99	956.49	679.68	542.53	461.23	407.85	370.40	342.90	322.01	305.75	292.82	282.40	273.88	266.85
21000	1881.58	1004.31	713.66	569.66	484.29	428.24	388.92	360.04	338.11	321.03	307.47	296.52	287.58	280.19
22000	1971.18	1052.14	747.65	596.78	507.36	448.63	407.44	377.19	354.21	336.32	322.11	310.64	301.27	293.54
23000	2060.78	1099.96	781.63	623.91	530.42	469.02	425.96	394.33	370.31	351.61	336.75	324.76	314.96	306.88
24000	2150.38	1147.78	815.61	651.03	553.48	489.42	444.48	411.48	386.41	366.89	351.39	338.88	328.66	320.22
25000	2239.98	1195.61	849.60	678.16	576.54	509.81	463.00	428.62	402.51	382.18	366.03	353.00	342.35	333.56
26000	2329.58	1243.43	883.58	705.29	599.60	530.20	481.52	445.77	418.61	397.47	380.67	367.12	356.05	346.91
27000	2419.18	1291.26	917.56	732.41	622.66	550.59	500.04	462.91	434.72	412.76	395.31	381.24	369.74	360.25
28000	2508.78	1339.08	951.55	759.54	645.72	570.99	518.56	480.05	450.82	428.04	409.95	395.36	383.43	373.59
29000	2598.38	1386.90	985.53	786.67	668.79	591.38	537.08	497.20	466.92	443.33	424.59	409.48	397.13	386.93
30000	2687.98	1434.73	1019.52	813.79	691.85	611.77	555.60	514.34	483.02	458.62	439.23	423.60	410.82	400.28
31000	2777.57	1482.55	1053.50	840.92	714.91	632.16	574.12	531.49	499.12	473.90	453.88	437.72	424.52	413.62
32000	2867.17	1530.38	1087.48	868.04	737.97	652.55	592.64	548.63	515.23	489.19	468.52	451.84	438.21	426.96
33000	2956.77	1578.20	1121.47	895.17	761.03	672.95	611.16	565.78	531.32	504.48	483.16	465.96	451.90	440.30
34000	3046.37	1626.03	1155.45	922.30	784.09	693.34	629.68	582.92	547.42	519.76	497.80	480.08	465.60	453.65
35000	3135.97	1673.85	1189.43	949.42	807.15	713.73	648.20	600.07	563.52	535.05	512.44	494.20	479.29	466.99
36000	3225.57	1721.67	1223.42	976.55	830.22	734.12	666.72	617.21	579.62	550.34	527.08	508.32	492.98	480.33
37000	3315.17	1769.50	1257.40	1003.68	853.28	754.52	685.24	634.36	595.72	565.63	541.72	522.44	506.68	493.67
38000	3404.77	1817.32	1291.38	1030.80	876.34	774.91	703.76	651.50	611.82	580.91	556.36	536.56	520.37	507.01
39000	3494.37	1865.15	1325.37	1057.93	899.40	795.30	722.27	668.65	627.92	596.20	571.00	550.67	534.07	520.36
40000	3583.97	1912.97	1359.35	1085.05	922.46	815.69	740.79	685.79	644.02	611.49	585.64	564.79	547.76	533.70
41000	3673.56	1960.79	1393.34	1112.18	945.52	836.08	759.31	702.93	660.12	626.77	600.29	578.91	561.45	547.04
42000	3763.16	2008.62	1427.32	1139.31	968.58	856.48	777.83	720.08	676.22	642.06	614.93	593.03	575.15	560.38
43000	3852.76	2056.44	1461.30	1166.43	991.65	876.87	796.35	737.22	692.32	657.35	629.57	607.15	588.84	573.73
44000	3942.36	2104.27	1495.29	1193.56	1014.71	897.26	814.87	754.37	708.42	672.63	644.21	621.27	602.54	587.07
45000	4031.96	2152.09	1529.27	1220.69	1037.77	917.65	833.39	771.51	724.52	687.92	658.85	635.39	616.23	600.41
46000	4121.56	2199.92	1563.25	1247.81	1060.83	938.04	851.91	788.66	740.62	703.21	673.49	649.51	629.92	613.75
47000	4211.16	2247.74	1597.24	1274.94	1083.89	958.44	870.43	805.80	756.72	718.50	688.13	663.63	643.62	627.10
48000	4300.76	2295.56	1631.22	1302.06	1106.95	978.83	888.95	822.95	772.82	733.78	702.77	677.75	657.31	640.44
49000	4390.36	2343.39	1665.21	1329.19	1130.01	999.22	907.47	840.09	788.92	749.07	717.41	691.87	671.01	653.78
50000	4479.96	2391.21	1699.19	1356.32	1153.07	1019.61	925.99	857.24	805.02	764.36	732.05	705.99	684.70	667.12
55000	4927.95	2630.33	1869.11	1491.95	1268.38	1121.57	1018.59	942.96	885.53	840.79	805.26	776.59	753.17	733.84
60000	5375.95	2869.45	2039.03	1627.58	1383.69	1223.53	1111.19	1028.68	966.03	917.23	878.46	847.19	821.64	800.55
65000	5823.94	3108.57	2208.94	1763.21	1499.00	1325.50	1203.79	1114.41	1046.53	993.66	951.67	917.79	890.11	867.26
70000	6271.94	3347.69	2378.86	1898.84	1614.30	1427.46	1296.39	1200.13	1127.03	1070.10	1024.87	988.39	958.58	933.97
75000	6719.93	3586.82	2548.78	2034.47	1729.61	1529.42	1388.99	1285.85	1207.53	1146.53	1098.08	1058.99	1027.05	1000.68
80000	7167.93	3825.94	2718.70	2170.10	1844.92	1631.38	1481.58	1371.58	1288.04	1222.97	1171.28	1129.58	1095.52	1067.39
85000	7615.92	4065.06	2888.62	2305.74	1960.22	1733.34	1574.18	1457.30	1368.54	1299.40	1244.49	1200.18	1163.98	1134.11
90000	8063.92	4304.18	3058.54	2441.37	2075.53	1835.30	1666.78	1543.02	1449.04	1375.84	1317.69	1270.78	1232.45	1200.82
95000	8511.91	4543.30	3228.45	2577.00	2190.84	1937.26	1759.38	1628.75	1529.54	1452.27	1390.90	1341.38	1300.92	1267.53
100000	8959.91	4782.42	3398.37	2712.63	2306.14	2039.22	1851.98	1714.47	1610.04	1528.71	1464.10	1411.98	1369.39	1334.24

TERM AMOUNT	15 Years	16 Years	17 Years	18 Years	19 Years	20 Years	21 Years	22 Years	23 Years	24 Years	25 Years	30 Years	35 Years	40 Years
5	.07	.07	.07	.07	.07	.07	.07	.06	.06	.06	.06	.06	.06	.06
10	.14	.13	.13	.13	.13	.13	.13	.12	.12	.12	.12	.12	.12	.12
15	.20	.20	.19	.19	.19	.19	.19	.18	.18	.18	.18	.18	.18	.18
25	.33	.33	.32	.32	.31	.31	.31	.30	.30	.30	.30	.29	.29	.29
50	.66	.65	.63	.63	.62	.61	.61	.60	.60	.59	.59	.58	.58	.57
75	.98	.97	.95	.94	.93	.92	.91	.90	.89	.89	.88	.87	.86	.86
100	1.31	1.29	1.26	1.25	1.23	1.22	1.21	1.20	1.19	1.18	1.18	1.16	1.15	1.14
200	2.61	2.57	2.52	2.49	2.46	2.43	2.41	2.39	2.38	2.36	2.35	2.31	2.29	2.28
300	3.92	3.85	3.78	3.73	3.69	3.65	3.62	3.59	3.56	3.54	3.52	3.46	3.44	3.42
400	5.22	5.13	5.04	4.97	4.91	4.86	4.82	4.78	4.75	4.72	4.70	4.62	4.58	4.56
500	6.53	6.41	6.30	6.22	6.14	6.08	6.02	5.98	5.94	5.90	5.87	5.77	5.72	5.70
600	7.83	7.69	7.56	7.46	7.37	7.29	7.23	7.17	7.12	7.08	7.04	6.92	6.87	6.84
700	9.14	8.97	8.82	8.70	8.60	8.51	8.43	8.37	8.31	8.26	8.22	8.08	8.01	7.97
800	10.44	10.25	10.08	9.94	9.82	9.72	9.63	9.56	9.49	9.44	9.39	9.23	9.15	9.11
900	11.75	11.53	11.34	11.19	11.05	10.94	10.84	10.75	10.68	10.62	10.56	10.38	10.30	10.25
1000	13.05	12.81	12.60	12.43	12.28	12.15	12.04	11.95	11.87	11.80	11.74	11.54	11.44	11.39
2000	26.10	25.61	25.20	24.85	24.55	24.30	24.08	23.89	23.73	23.59	23.47	23.07	22.87	22.77
3000	39.15	38.42	37.80	37.27	36.82	36.44	36.11	35.83	35.59	35.38	35.20	34.60	34.31	34.16
4000	52.20	51.22	50.40	49.69	49.10	48.59	48.15	47.78	47.45	47.18	46.93	46.14	45.74	45.54
5000	65.25	64.03	62.99	62.12	61.37	60.73	60.19	59.72	59.32	58.97	58.67	57.67	57.17	56.93
6000	78.30	76.83	75.59	74.54	73.64	72.88	72.22	71.66	71.18	70.76	70.40	69.20	68.61	68.31
7000	91.35	89.64	88.19	86.96	85.92	85.03	84.26	83.61	83.04	82.55	82.13	80.73	80.04	79.69
8000	104.40	102.44	100.79	99.38	98.19	97.17	96.30	95.55	94.90	94.35	93.86	92.27	91.48	91.08
9000	117.45	115.25	113.38	111.81	110.46	109.32	108.33	107.49	106.76	106.14	105.60	103.80	102.91	102.46
10000	130.50	128.05	125.98	124.23	122.74	121.46	120.37	119.43	118.63	117.93	117.33	115.33	114.34	113.85
11000	143.55	140.85	138.58	136.65	135.01	133.61	132.41	131.38	130.49	129.72	129.06	126.87	125.78	125.23
12000	156.60	153.66	151.18	149.07	147.28	145.75	144.44	143.32	142.35	141.52	140.79	138.40	137.21	136.62
13000	169.65	166.46	163.77	161.50	159.56	157.90	156.48	155.26	154.21	153.31	152.53	149.93	148.65	148.00
14000	182.70	179.27	176.37	173.92	171.83	170.05	168.52	167.21	166.08	165.10	164.26	161.46	160.08	159.38
15000	195.75	192.07	188.97	186.34	184.10	182.19	180.55	179.15	177.94	176.89	175.99	173.00	171.51	170.77
16000	208.80	204.88	201.57	198.76	196.38	194.34	192.59	191.09	189.80	188.69	187.72	184.53	182.95	182.15
17000	221.85	217.68	214.16	211.18	208.65	206.48	204.63	203.03	201.66	200.48	199.46	196.06	194.38	193.54
18000	234.90	230.49	226.76	223.61	220.92	218.63	216.66	214.98	213.52	212.27	211.19	207.60	205.82	204.92
19000	247.95	243.29	239.36	236.03	233.20	230.77	228.70	226.92	225.39	224.06	222.92	219.13	217.25	216.31
20000	261.00	256.09	251.96	248.45	245.47	242.92	240.74	238.86	237.25	235.86	234.65	230.66	228.68	227.69
21000	274.05	268.90	264.56	260.87	257.74	255.07	252.77	250.81	249.11	247.65	246.39	242.19	240.12	239.07
22000	287.10	281.70	277.15	273.30	270.01	267.21	264.81	262.75	260.97	259.44	258.12	253.73	251.56	250.46
23000	300.15	294.51	289.75	285.72	282.29	279.36	276.85	274.69	272.84	271.23	269.85	265.26	262.99	261.84
24000	313.20	307.31	302.35	298.14	294.56	291.50	288.88	286.63	284.70	283.03	281.58	276.79	274.42	273.23
25000	326.25	320.12	314.95	310.56	306.83	303.65	300.92	298.58	296.56	294.82	293.32	288.33	285.85	284.61
26000	339.30	332.92	327.54	322.99	319.11	315.79	312.96	310.52	308.42	306.61	305.05	299.86	297.29	296.00
27000	352.35	345.73	340.14	335.41	331.38	327.94	324.99	322.46	320.28	318.40	316.78	311.39	308.72	307.38
28000	365.40	358.53	352.74	347.83	343.65	340.09	337.03	334.41	332.15	330.20	328.51	322.92	320.16	318.76
29000	378.45	371.33	365.34	360.25	355.93	352.23	349.07	346.35	344.01	341.99	340.25	334.46	331.59	330.15
30000	391.50	384.14	377.93	372.68	368.20	364.38	361.10	358.29	355.87	353.78	351.98	345.99	343.02	341.53
31000	404.55	396.94	390.53	385.10	380.47	376.52	373.14	370.23	367.73	365.57	363.71	357.52	354.46	352.92
32000	417.60	409.75	403.13	397.52	392.75	388.67	385.18	382.18	379.59	377.37	375.44	369.06	365.89	364.30
33000	430.65	422.55	415.73	409.94	405.02	400.82	397.21	394.12	391.46	389.16	387.18	380.59	377.32	375.69
34000	443.70	435.36	428.32	422.36	417.29	412.96	409.25	406.06	403.32	400.95	398.91	392.12	388.76	387.07
35000	456.75	448.16	440.92	434.79	429.57	425.11	421.29	418.01	415.18	412.75	410.64	403.65	400.19	398.45
36000	469.80	460.97	453.52	447.21	441.84	437.25	433.32	429.95	427.04	424.54	422.37	415.19	411.63	409.84
37000	482.85	473.77	466.12	459.63	454.11	449.40	445.36	441.89	438.91	436.33	434.11	426.72	423.06	421.22
38000	495.90	486.57	478.71	472.05	466.39	461.54	457.40	453.83	450.77	448.12	445.84	438.25	434.49	432.61
39000	508.95	499.38	491.31	484.48	478.66	473.69	469.43	465.78	462.63	459.92	457.57	449.79	445.93	443.99
40000	522.00	512.18	503.91	496.90	490.93	485.84	481.47	477.72	474.49	471.71	469.30	461.32	457.36	455.38
41000	535.05	524.99	516.51	509.32	503.20	497.98	493.51	489.66	486.35	483.50	481.04	472.85	468.80	466.76
42000	548.09	537.79	529.11	521.74	515.48	510.13	505.54	501.61	498.22	495.29	492.77	484.38	480.23	478.14
43000	561.14	550.60	541.70	534.17	527.75	522.27	517.58	513.55	510.08	507.09	504.50	495.92	491.66	489.53
44000	574.19	563.40	554.30	546.59	540.02	534.42	529.62	525.49	521.94	518.88	516.23	507.45	503.10	500.91
45000	587.24	576.21	566.90	559.01	552.30	546.56	541.65	537.43	533.80	530.67	527.96	518.98	514.53	512.30
46000	600.29	589.01	579.50	571.43	564.57	558.71	553.69	549.38	545.67	542.46	539.70	530.52	525.97	523.68
47000	613.34	601.81	592.09	583.85	576.84	570.86	565.73	561.32	557.53	554.26	551.43	542.05	537.40	535.07
48000	626.39	614.62	604.69	596.28	589.12	583.00	577.76	573.26	569.39	566.05	563.16	553.58	548.83	546.45
49000	639.44	627.42	617.29	608.70	601.39	595.15	589.80	585.21	581.25	577.84	574.89	565.11	560.27	557.83
50000	652.49	640.23	629.89	621.12	613.66	607.29	601.84	597.15	593.11	589.63	586.63	576.65	571.70	569.22
55000	717.74	704.25	692.87	683.23	675.03	668.02	662.02	656.86	652.43	648.60	645.29	634.31	628.87	626.14
60000	782.99	768.27	755.86	745.35	736.40	728.75	722.20	716.58	711.74	707.56	703.95	691.98	686.04	683.06
65000	848.24	832.30	818.85	807.46	797.76	789.48	782.39	776.29	771.05	766.52	762.61	749.64	743.21	739.98
70000	913.49	896.32	881.84	869.57	859.13	850.21	842.57	836.01	830.36	825.49	821.28	807.30	800.38	796.90
75000	978.74	960.34	944.83	931.68	920.49	910.94	902.75	895.72	889.67	884.45	879.94	864.97	857.55	853.83
80000	1043.99	1024.36	1007.81	993.79	981.86	971.67	962.94	955.44	948.98	943.41	938.60	922.63	914.72	910.75
85000	1109.23	1088.38	1070.80	1055.90	1043.22	1032.40	1023.12	1015.15	1008.29	1002.37	997.26	980.30	971.89	967.67
90000	1174.48	1152.41	1133.79	1118.02	1104.59	1093.12	1083.30	1074.86	1067.60	1061.34	1055.92	1037.96	1029.06	1024.59
95000	1239.73	1216.43	1196.78	1180.13	1165.96	1153.85	1143.48	1134.58	1126.91	1120.30	1114.59	1095.63	1086.23	1081.51
100000	1304.98	1280.45	1259.77	1242.24	1227.32	1214.58	1203.67	1194.29	1186.22	1179.26	1173.25	1153.29	1143.40	1138.43

MONTHLY PAYMENT
REQUIRED TO AMORTIZE A LOAN

13.625%

TERM AMOUNT	1 Year	2 Years	3 Years	4 Years	5 Years	6 Years	7 Years	8 Years	9 Years	10 Years	11 Years	12 Years	13 Years	14 Years
5	.45	.24	.17	.14	.12	.11	.10	.09	.09	.08	.08	.08	.07	.07
10	.90	.48	.34	.28	.24	.21	.19	.18	.17	.16	.15	.15	.14	.14
15	1.35	.72	.51	.41	.35	.31	.28	.26	.25	.23	.22	.22	.21	.21
25	2.25	1.20	.85	.68	.58	.52	.47	.43	.41	.39	.37	.36	.35	.34
50	4.49	2.40	1.70	1.36	1.16	1.03	.93	.86	.81	.77	.74	.71	.69	.67
75	6.73	3.59	2.55	2.04	1.74	1.54	1.40	1.29	1.21	1.15	1.10	1.07	1.03	1.01
100	8.97	4.79	3.40	2.72	2.31	2.05	1.86	1.72	1.62	1.54	1.47	1.42	1.38	1.34
200	17.93	9.57	6.80	5.43	4.62	4.09	3.71	3.44	3.23	3.07	2.94	2.83	2.75	2.68
300	26.99	14.36	10.20	8.15	6.93	6.13	5.57	5.15	4.84	4.60	4.40	4.25	4.12	4.01
400	35.85	19.14	13.60	10.86	9.23	8.17	7.42	6.87	6.45	6.13	5.87	5.66	5.49	5.35
500	44.81	23.92	17.00	13.57	11.54	10.21	9.27	8.58	8.06	7.66	7.33	7.07	6.86	6.68
600	53.77	28.71	20.40	16.29	13.85	12.25	11.13	10.30	9.67	9.19	8.80	8.49	8.23	8.02
700	62.73	33.49	23.80	19.00	16.16	14.29	12.98	12.02	11.29	10.72	10.26	9.90	9.60	9.36
800	71.69	38.27	27.20	21.72	18.46	16.33	14.83	13.73	12.90	12.25	11.73	11.31	10.97	10.69
900	80.65	43.06	30.60	24.43	20.77	18.37	16.69	15.45	14.51	13.78	13.20	12.73	12.34	12.03
1000	89.62	47.84	34.00	27.14	23.08	20.41	18.54	17.16	16.12	15.31	14.66	14.14	13.71	13.36
2000	179.23	95.68	68.00	54.28	46.15	40.82	37.07	34.32	32.23	30.61	29.32	28.28	27.42	26.72
3000	268.84	143.51	101.99	81.42	69.23	61.22	55.61	51.48	48.35	45.91	43.97	42.41	41.13	40.08
4000	358.45	191.35	135.99	108.56	92.30	81.63	74.14	68.64	64.46	61.21	58.63	56.55	54.84	53.44
5000	448.06	239.18	169.98	135.70	115.38	102.03	92.67	85.80	80.58	76.51	73.29	70.68	68.55	66.80
6000	537.67	287.02	203.98	162.84	138.45	122.44	111.21	102.96	96.69	91.82	87.94	84.82	82.26	80.16
7000	627.28	334.86	237.98	189.98	161.53	142.84	129.74	120.12	112.81	107.12	102.60	98.95	95.97	93.52
8000	716.89	382.69	271.97	217.11	184.60	163.25	148.27	137.28	128.92	122.42	117.26	113.09	109.68	106.87
9000	806.50	430.53	305.97	244.25	207.67	183.65	166.81	154.43	145.04	137.72	131.91	127.22	123.39	120.23
10000	896.11	478.36	339.96	271.39	230.75	204.06	185.34	171.59	161.15	153.02	146.57	141.36	137.10	133.59
11000	985.72	526.20	373.96	298.53	253.82	224.47	203.87	188.75	177.27	168.33	161.22	155.49	150.81	146.95
12000	1075.33	574.04	407.95	325.67	276.90	244.87	222.41	205.91	193.38	183.63	175.88	169.63	164.52	160.31
13000	1164.95	621.87	441.95	352.81	299.97	265.28	240.94	223.07	209.50	198.93	190.54	183.77	178.23	173.67
14000	1254.56	669.71	475.95	379.95	323.05	285.68	259.47	240.23	225.61	214.23	205.19	197.90	191.94	187.03
15000	1344.17	717.54	509.94	407.09	346.12	306.09	278.01	257.39	241.73	229.53	219.85	212.04	205.65	200.39
16000	1433.78	765.38	543.94	434.22	369.19	326.49	296.54	274.55	257.84	244.84	234.51	226.17	219.36	213.74
17000	1523.39	813.22	577.93	461.36	392.27	346.90	315.07	291.70	273.96	260.14	249.16	240.31	233.07	227.10
18000	1613.00	861.05	611.93	488.50	415.34	367.30	333.61	308.86	290.07	275.44	263.82	254.44	246.78	240.46
19000	1702.61	908.89	645.92	515.64	438.42	387.71	352.14	326.02	306.19	290.74	278.47	268.58	260.49	253.82
20000	1792.22	956.72	679.92	542.78	461.49	408.11	370.67	343.18	322.30	306.04	293.13	282.71	274.20	267.18
21000	1881.83	1004.56	713.92	569.92	484.57	428.52	389.21	360.34	338.42	321.35	307.79	296.85	287.91	280.54
22000	1971.44	1052.40	747.91	597.06	507.64	448.93	407.74	377.50	354.53	336.65	322.44	310.98	301.62	293.90
23000	2061.05	1100.23	781.91	624.20	530.71	469.33	426.27	394.66	370.65	351.95	337.10	325.12	315.33	307.26
24000	2150.66	1148.07	815.90	651.33	553.79	489.74	444.81	411.82	386.76	367.25	351.76	339.25	329.04	320.61
25000	2240.27	1195.90	849.90	678.47	576.86	510.14	463.34	428.97	402.88	382.55	366.41	353.39	342.75	333.97
26000	2329.88	1243.74	883.90	705.61	599.94	530.55	481.88	446.13	418.99	397.86	381.07	367.53	356.46	347.33
27000	2419.50	1291.57	917.89	732.75	623.01	550.95	500.41	463.29	435.11	413.16	395.72	381.66	370.17	360.69
28000	2509.11	1339.41	951.89	759.89	646.09	571.36	518.94	480.45	451.22	428.46	410.38	395.80	383.88	374.05
29000	2598.72	1387.25	985.88	787.03	669.16	591.76	537.48	497.61	467.34	443.76	425.04	409.93	397.59	387.41
30000	2688.33	1435.08	1019.88	814.17	692.23	612.17	556.01	514.77	483.45	459.06	439.69	424.07	411.30	400.77
31000	2777.94	1482.92	1053.87	841.31	715.31	632.57	574.54	531.93	499.57	474.37	454.35	438.20	425.01	414.13
32000	2867.55	1530.75	1087.87	868.44	738.38	652.98	593.08	549.09	515.68	489.67	469.01	452.34	438.72	427.48
33000	2957.16	1578.59	1121.87	895.58	761.46	673.39	611.61	566.24	531.80	504.97	483.66	466.47	452.43	440.84
34000	3046.77	1626.43	1155.86	922.72	784.53	693.79	630.14	583.40	547.91	520.27	498.32	480.61	466.14	454.20
35000	3136.38	1674.26	1189.86	949.86	807.61	714.20	648.68	600.56	564.03	535.57	512.97	494.74	479.85	467.56
36000	3225.99	1722.10	1223.85	977.00	830.68	734.60	667.21	617.72	580.14	550.88	527.63	508.88	493.56	480.92
37000	3315.60	1769.93	1257.85	1004.14	853.75	755.01	685.74	634.88	596.26	566.18	542.29	523.01	507.27	494.28
38000	3405.21	1817.77	1291.84	1031.28	876.83	775.41	704.28	652.04	612.37	581.48	556.94	537.15	520.98	507.64
39000	3494.83	1865.61	1325.84	1058.42	899.90	795.82	722.81	669.20	628.49	596.78	571.60	551.29	534.69	520.99
40000	3584.44	1913.44	1359.84	1085.55	922.98	816.22	741.34	686.36	644.60	612.08	586.26	565.42	548.40	534.35
41000	3674.05	1961.28	1393.83	1112.69	946.05	836.63	759.88	703.51	660.72	627.39	600.91	579.56	562.11	547.71
42000	3763.66	2009.11	1427.83	1139.83	969.13	857.04	778.41	720.67	676.83	642.69	615.57	593.69	575.82	561.07
43000	3853.27	2056.95	1461.82	1166.97	992.20	877.44	796.94	737.83	692.95	657.99	630.23	607.83	589.53	574.43
44000	3942.88	2104.79	1495.82	1194.11	1015.27	897.85	815.48	754.99	709.06	673.29	644.88	621.96	603.24	587.79
45000	4032.49	2152.62	1529.82	1221.25	1038.35	918.25	834.01	772.15	725.18	688.59	659.54	636.10	616.95	601.15
46000	4122.10	2200.46	1563.81	1248.39	1061.42	938.66	852.54	789.31	741.29	703.90	674.19	650.23	630.66	614.51
47000	4211.71	2248.29	1597.81	1275.53	1084.50	959.06	871.08	806.47	757.41	719.20	688.85	664.37	644.37	627.86
48000	4301.32	2296.13	1631.80	1302.66	1107.57	979.47	889.61	823.63	773.52	734.50	703.51	678.50	658.08	641.22
49000	4390.93	2343.97	1665.80	1329.80	1130.65	999.87	908.14	840.78	789.64	749.80	718.16	692.64	671.79	654.58
50000	4480.54	2391.80	1699.79	1356.94	1153.72	1020.28	926.68	857.94	805.75	765.10	732.82	706.78	685.50	667.94
55000	4928.60	2630.98	1869.77	1492.64	1269.09	1122.31	1019.35	943.74	886.33	841.61	806.10	777.45	754.05	734.73
60000	5376.65	2870.16	2039.75	1628.33	1384.46	1224.33	1112.01	1029.53	966.90	918.12	879.38	848.13	822.60	801.53
65000	5824.70	3109.34	2209.73	1764.02	1499.83	1326.36	1204.68	1115.32	1047.47	994.63	952.66	918.81	891.15	868.32
70000	6272.76	3348.52	2379.71	1899.72	1615.21	1428.39	1297.35	1201.12	1128.05	1071.14	1025.94	989.48	959.70	935.11
75000	6720.81	3587.70	2549.69	2035.41	1730.58	1530.42	1390.02	1286.91	1208.62	1147.65	1099.23	1060.16	1028.25	1001.91
80000	7168.87	3826.88	2719.67	2171.10	1845.95	1632.44	1482.68	1372.71	1289.20	1224.16	1172.51	1130.84	1096.80	1068.70
85000	7616.92	4066.06	2889.65	2306.80	1961.32	1734.47	1575.35	1458.50	1369.77	1300.67	1245.79	1201.51	1165.35	1135.50
90000	8064.97	4305.24	3059.63	2442.49	2076.69	1836.50	1668.02	1544.29	1450.35	1377.18	1319.07	1272.19	1233.90	1202.29
95000	8513.03	4544.42	3229.60	2578.19	2192.06	1938.53	1760.68	1630.09	1530.92	1453.69	1392.35	1342.87	1302.44	1269.08
100000	8961.08	4783.60	3399.58	2713.88	2307.43	2040.55	1853.35	1715.88	1611.50	1530.20	1465.63	1413.55	1370.99	1335.88

TERM	15 Years	16 Years	17 Years	18 Years	19 Years	20 Years	21 Years	22 Years	23 Years	24 Years	25 Years	30 Years	35 Years	40 Years
AMOUNT														
5	.07	.07	.07	.07	.07	.07	.07	.06	.06	.06	.06	.06	.06	.06
10	.14	.13	.13	.13	.13	.13	.13	.12	.12	.12	.12	.12	.12	.12
15	.20	.20	.19	.19	.19	.19	.19	.18	.18	.18	.18	.18	.18	.18
25	.33	.33	.32	.32	.31	.31	.31	.30	.30	.30	.30	.29	.29	.29
50	.66	.65	.64	.63	.62	.61	.61	.60	.60	.60	.59	.58	.58	.58
75	.98	.97	.95	.94	.93	.92	.91	.90	.90	.89	.89	.87	.86	.86
100	1.31	1.29	1.27	1.25	1.23	1.22	1.21	1.20	1.19	1.19	1.18	1.16	1.15	1.15
200	2.62	2.57	2.53	2.49	2.46	2.44	2.42	2.40	2.38	2.37	2.36	2.32	2.30	2.29
300	3.92	3.85	3.79	3.74	3.69	3.65	3.62	3.59	3.57	3.55	3.53	3.47	3.44	3.43
400	5.23	5.13	5.05	4.98	4.92	4.87	4.83	4.79	4.76	4.73	4.71	4.63	4.59	4.57
500	6.54	6.42	6.31	6.22	6.15	6.09	6.03	5.99	5.95	5.91	5.88	5.78	5.73	5.71
600	7.84	7.70	7.57	7.47	7.38	7.30	7.24	7.18	7.13	7.09	7.06	6.94	6.88	6.85
700	9.15	8.98	8.84	8.71	8.61	8.52	8.44	8.38	8.32	8.27	8.23	8.09	8.02	7.99
800	10.46	10.26	10.10	9.96	9.84	9.74	9.65	9.57	9.51	9.45	9.41	9.25	9.17	9.13
900	11.76	11.54	11.36	11.20	11.07	10.95	10.85	10.77	10.70	10.64	10.58	10.40	10.31	10.27
1000	13.07	12.83	12.62	12.44	12.30	12.17	12.06	11.97	11.89	11.82	11.76	11.56	11.46	11.41
2000	26.14	25.65	25.23	24.88	24.59	24.33	24.11	23.93	23.77	23.63	23.51	23.11	22.91	22.81
3000	39.20	38.47	37.85	37.32	36.88	36.50	36.17	35.89	35.65	35.44	35.26	34.66	34.37	34.22
4000	52.27	51.29	50.46	49.76	49.17	48.66	48.22	47.85	47.53	47.25	47.01	46.22	45.82	45.62
5000	65.34	64.11	63.08	62.20	61.46	60.82	60.28	59.81	59.41	59.06	58.76	57.77	57.28	57.03
6000	78.40	76.93	75.69	74.64	73.75	72.99	72.33	71.77	71.29	70.87	70.51	69.32	68.73	68.43
7000	91.47	89.76	88.31	87.08	86.04	85.15	84.39	83.73	83.17	82.68	82.27	80.87	80.18	79.84
8000	104.54	102.58	100.92	99.52	98.33	97.32	96.44	95.70	95.05	94.50	94.02	92.43	91.64	91.24
9000	117.60	115.40	113.54	111.96	110.62	109.48	108.50	107.66	106.93	106.31	105.77	103.98	103.09	102.65
10000	130.67	128.22	126.15	124.40	122.91	121.64	120.55	119.62	118.81	118.12	117.52	115.53	114.55	114.05
11000	143.74	141.04	138.77	136.84	135.21	133.81	132.61	131.58	130.69	129.93	129.27	127.08	126.00	125.46
12000	156.80	153.86	151.38	149.28	147.50	145.97	144.66	143.54	142.58	141.74	141.02	138.64	137.45	136.86
13000	169.87	166.68	164.00	161.72	159.79	158.13	156.72	155.50	154.46	153.55	152.77	150.19	148.91	148.27
14000	182.93	179.51	176.61	174.16	172.08	170.30	168.77	167.46	166.34	165.36	164.53	161.74	160.36	159.67
15000	196.00	192.33	189.23	186.60	184.37	182.46	180.83	179.43	178.22	177.18	176.28	173.29	171.82	171.08
16000	209.07	205.15	201.84	199.04	196.66	194.63	192.88	191.39	190.10	188.99	188.03	184.85	183.27	182.48
17000	222.13	217.97	214.46	211.48	208.95	206.79	204.94	203.35	201.98	200.80	199.78	196.40	194.72	193.88
18000	235.20	230.79	227.07	223.92	221.24	218.95	216.99	215.31	213.86	212.61	211.53	207.95	206.18	205.29
19000	248.27	243.61	239.69	236.36	233.53	231.12	229.05	227.27	225.74	224.42	223.28	219.50	217.63	216.69
20000	261.33	256.43	252.30	248.80	245.82	243.28	241.10	239.23	237.62	236.23	235.03	231.06	229.09	228.10
21000	274.40	269.26	264.92	261.24	258.12	255.44	253.16	251.19	249.50	248.04	246.79	242.61	240.54	239.50
22000	287.47	282.08	277.53	273.68	270.41	267.61	265.21	263.15	261.38	259.86	258.54	254.16	251.99	250.91
23000	300.53	294.90	290.15	286.12	282.70	279.77	277.27	275.12	273.26	271.67	270.29	265.71	263.45	262.31
24000	313.60	307.72	302.76	298.56	294.99	291.94	289.32	287.08	285.15	283.48	282.04	277.27	274.90	273.72
25000	326.67	320.54	315.38	311.00	307.28	304.10	301.38	299.04	297.03	295.29	293.79	288.82	286.36	285.12
26000	339.73	333.36	327.99	323.44	319.57	316.26	313.43	311.00	308.91	307.10	305.54	300.37	297.81	296.53
27000	352.80	346.18	340.61	335.88	331.86	328.43	325.49	322.96	320.79	318.91	317.29	311.92	309.26	307.93
28000	365.86	359.01	353.22	348.32	344.15	340.59	337.54	334.92	332.67	330.72	329.05	323.48	320.72	319.34
29000	378.93	371.83	365.84	360.76	356.44	352.76	349.60	346.88	344.55	342.54	340.80	335.03	332.17	330.74
30000	392.00	384.65	378.45	373.20	368.73	364.92	361.65	358.85	356.43	354.35	352.55	346.58	343.63	342.15
31000	405.06	397.47	391.07	385.64	381.02	377.08	373.71	370.81	368.31	366.16	364.30	358.13	355.08	353.55
32000	418.13	410.29	403.68	398.08	393.32	389.25	385.76	382.77	380.19	377.97	376.05	369.69	366.54	364.96
33000	431.20	423.11	416.30	410.52	405.61	401.41	397.82	394.73	392.07	389.78	387.80	381.24	377.99	376.36
34000	444.26	435.93	428.91	422.96	417.90	413.57	409.87	406.69	403.95	401.59	399.55	392.79	389.44	387.76
35000	457.33	448.76	441.53	435.40	430.19	425.74	421.93	418.65	415.83	413.40	411.31	404.34	400.90	399.17
36000	470.40	461.58	454.14	447.84	442.48	437.90	433.98	430.61	427.72	425.22	423.06	415.90	412.35	410.57
37000	483.46	474.40	466.76	460.28	454.77	450.07	446.04	442.57	439.60	437.03	434.81	427.45	423.81	421.98
38000	496.53	487.22	479.37	472.72	467.06	462.23	458.09	454.54	451.48	448.84	446.56	439.00	435.26	433.38
39000	509.60	500.04	491.99	485.16	479.35	474.39	470.15	466.50	463.36	460.65	458.31	450.55	446.71	444.79
40000	522.66	512.86	504.60	497.60	491.64	486.56	482.20	478.46	475.24	472.46	470.06	462.11	458.17	456.19
41000	535.73	525.68	517.22	510.04	503.93	498.72	494.26	490.42	487.12	484.27	481.81	473.66	469.62	467.60
42000	548.79	538.51	529.83	522.48	516.23	510.88	506.31	502.38	499.00	496.08	493.57	485.21	481.08	479.00
43000	561.86	551.33	542.44	534.92	528.52	523.05	518.36	514.34	510.88	507.90	505.32	496.76	492.53	490.41
44000	574.93	564.15	555.06	547.36	540.81	535.21	530.42	526.30	522.76	519.71	517.07	508.32	503.98	501.81
45000	587.99	576.97	567.67	559.80	553.10	547.38	542.47	538.27	534.64	531.52	528.82	519.87	515.44	513.22
46000	601.06	589.79	580.29	572.24	565.39	559.54	554.53	550.23	546.52	543.33	540.57	531.42	526.89	524.62
47000	614.13	602.61	592.90	584.68	577.68	571.70	566.58	562.19	558.40	555.14	552.32	542.97	538.35	536.03
48000	627.19	615.43	605.52	597.12	589.97	583.87	578.64	574.15	570.29	566.95	564.08	554.53	549.80	547.43
49000	640.26	628.26	618.13	609.56	602.26	596.03	590.69	586.11	582.17	578.76	575.83	566.08	561.25	558.83
50000	653.33	641.08	630.75	622.00	614.55	608.19	602.75	598.07	594.05	590.58	587.58	577.63	572.71	570.24
55000	718.66	705.18	693.82	684.20	676.01	669.01	663.02	657.88	653.45	649.63	646.34	635.40	629.98	627.26
60000	783.99	769.29	756.90	746.40	737.46	729.83	723.30	717.69	712.86	708.69	705.09	693.16	687.25	684.29
65000	849.32	833.40	819.97	808.60	798.92	790.65	783.57	777.49	772.26	767.75	763.85	750.92	744.52	741.31
70000	914.65	897.51	883.05	870.80	860.37	851.47	843.85	837.30	831.66	826.80	822.61	808.68	801.79	798.33
75000	979.99	961.61	946.12	933.00	921.83	912.29	904.12	897.11	891.07	885.86	881.36	866.45	859.06	855.36
80000	1045.32	1025.72	1009.20	995.19	983.28	973.11	964.40	956.91	950.47	944.92	940.12	924.21	916.33	912.38
85000	1110.65	1089.83	1072.27	1057.39	1044.74	1033.93	1024.67	1016.72	1009.88	1003.98	998.88	981.97	973.60	969.40
90000	1175.98	1153.93	1135.34	1119.59	1106.19	1094.75	1084.94	1076.53	1069.28	1063.03	1057.64	1039.73	1030.87	1026.43
95000	1241.32	1218.04	1198.42	1181.79	1167.65	1155.57	1145.22	1136.33	1128.69	1122.09	1116.39	1097.50	1088.14	1083.45
100000	1306.65	1282.15	1261.49	1243.99	1229.10	1216.38	1205.49	1196.14	1188.09	1181.15	1175.15	1155.26	1145.41	1140.47

13.700%

MONTHLY PAYMENT
REQUIRED TO AMORTIZE A LOAN

TERM	1 Year	2 Years	3 Years	4 Years	5 Years	6 Years	7 Years	8 Years	9 Years	10 Years	11 Years	12 Years	13 Years	14 Years
AMOUNT														
5	.45	.24	.18	.14	.12	.11	.10	.09	.09	.08	.08	.08	.07	.07
10	.90	.48	.35	.28	.24	.21	.19	.18	.17	.16	.15	.15	.14	.14
15	1.35	.72	.52	.41	.35	.31	.28	.26	.25	.24	.23	.22	.21	.21
25	2.25	1.20	.86	.68	.58	.52	.47	.44	.41	.39	.37	.36	.35	.34
50	4.49	2.40	1.71	1.36	1.16	1.03	.93	.87	.81	.77	.74	.71	.69	.68
75	6.73	3.60	2.56	2.04	1.74	1.54	1.40	1.30	1.22	1.16	1.11	1.07	1.04	1.01
100	8.97	4.79	3.41	2.72	2.32	2.05	1.86	1.73	1.62	1.54	1.48	1.42	1.38	1.35
200	17.93	9.58	6.81	5.44	4.63	4.09	3.72	3.45	3.24	3.07	2.95	2.84	2.76	2.69
300	26.90	14.37	10.21	8.16	6.94	6.14	5.58	5.17	4.85	4.61	4.42	4.26	4.13	4.03
400	35.86	19.15	13.62	10.88	9.25	8.18	7.43	6.89	6.47	6.14	5.89	5.68	5.51	5.37
500	44.83	23.94	17.02	13.59	11.56	10.23	9.29	8.61	8.08	7.68	7.36	7.10	6.88	6.71
600	53.79	28.73	20.42	16.31	13.87	12.27	11.15	10.33	9.70	9.21	8.83	8.51	8.26	8.05
700	62.76	33.51	23.83	19.03	16.18	14.32	13.01	12.05	11.32	10.75	10.30	9.93	9.64	9.39
800	71.72	38.30	27.23	21.75	18.50	16.36	14.86	13.77	12.93	12.28	11.77	11.35	11.01	10.73
900	80.69	43.09	30.63	24.46	20.81	18.41	16.72	15.49	14.55	13.82	13.24	12.77	12.39	12.07
1000	89.65	47.88	34.04	27.18	23.12	20.45	18.58	17.21	16.16	15.35	14.71	14.19	13.76	13.41
2000	179.30	95.75	68.07	54.36	46.23	40.90	37.15	34.41	32.32	30.70	29.41	28.37	27.52	26.82
3000	268.94	143.62	102.10	81.53	69.34	61.34	55.73	51.61	48.48	46.05	44.11	42.55	41.28	40.23
4000	358.59	191.49	136.13	108.70	92.46	81.79	74.30	68.81	64.64	61.39	58.81	56.73	55.04	53.64
5000	448.24	239.36	170.17	135.89	115.57	102.23	92.88	86.01	80.80	76.74	73.52	70.92	68.79	67.04
6000	537.88	287.23	204.20	163.06	138.68	122.68	111.45	103.21	96.96	92.09	88.22	85.10	82.55	80.45
7000	627.53	335.10	238.23	190.24	161.80	143.12	130.03	120.41	113.11	107.43	102.92	99.28	96.31	93.86
8000	717.17	382.98	272.26	217.41	184.91	163.57	148.60	137.61	129.27	122.78	117.62	113.46	110.07	107.27
9000	806.82	430.85	306.29	244.59	208.02	184.01	167.18	154.82	145.43	138.13	132.33	127.65	123.83	120.68
10000	896.47	478.72	340.33	271.77	231.14	204.46	185.75	172.02	161.59	153.47	147.03	141.83	137.58	134.08
11000	986.11	526.59	374.36	298.94	254.25	224.90	204.33	189.22	177.75	168.82	161.73	156.01	151.34	147.49
12000	1075.76	574.46	408.39	326.12	277.36	245.35	222.90	206.42	193.91	184.17	176.43	170.19	165.10	160.90
13000	1165.40	622.33	442.42	353.30	300.47	265.80	241.48	223.62	210.07	199.51	191.13	184.38	178.86	174.31
14000	1255.05	670.20	476.45	380.47	323.59	286.24	260.05	240.82	226.22	214.86	205.84	198.56	192.62	187.71
15000	1344.70	718.07	510.49	407.65	346.70	306.69	278.63	258.02	242.38	230.21	220.54	212.74	206.37	201.12
16000	1434.34	765.95	544.52	434.82	369.81	327.13	297.20	275.22	258.54	245.55	235.24	226.92	220.13	214.53
17000	1523.99	813.82	578.55	462.00	392.93	347.58	315.77	292.43	274.70	260.90	249.94	241.11	233.89	227.94
18000	1613.63	861.69	612.58	489.18	416.04	368.02	334.35	309.63	290.86	276.25	264.65	255.29	247.65	241.35
19000	1703.28	909.56	646.61	516.35	439.15	388.47	352.92	326.83	307.02	291.59	279.35	269.47	261.41	254.75
20000	1792.93	957.43	680.65	543.53	462.27	408.91	371.50	344.03	323.18	306.94	294.05	283.65	275.16	268.16
21000	1882.57	1005.30	714.68	570.71	485.38	429.36	390.07	361.23	339.33	322.29	308.75	297.84	288.92	281.57
22000	1972.22	1053.17	748.71	597.88	508.49	449.80	408.65	378.43	355.49	337.63	323.45	312.02	302.68	294.98
23000	2061.86	1101.04	782.74	625.06	531.60	470.25	427.22	395.63	371.65	352.98	338.16	326.20	316.44	308.38
24000	2151.51	1148.92	816.78	652.23	554.72	490.70	445.80	412.83	387.81	368.33	352.86	340.38	330.20	321.79
25000	2241.16	1196.79	850.81	679.41	577.83	511.14	464.37	430.04	403.97	383.67	367.56	354.57	343.95	335.20
26000	2330.80	1244.66	884.84	706.59	600.94	531.59	482.95	447.24	420.13	399.02	382.26	368.75	357.71	348.61
27000	2420.45	1292.53	918.87	733.76	624.06	552.03	501.52	464.44	436.29	414.37	396.97	382.93	371.47	362.02
28000	2510.09	1340.40	952.90	760.94	647.17	572.48	520.10	481.64	452.44	429.71	411.67	397.11	385.23	375.42
29000	2599.74	1388.27	986.94	788.12	670.28	592.92	538.67	498.84	468.60	445.06	426.37	411.30	398.99	388.83
30000	2689.39	1436.14	1020.97	815.29	693.40	613.37	557.25	516.04	484.76	460.41	441.07	425.48	412.74	402.24
31000	2779.03	1484.01	1055.00	842.47	716.51	633.81	575.82	533.24	500.92	475.75	455.77	439.66	426.50	415.65
32000	2868.68	1531.89	1089.03	869.64	739.62	654.26	594.39	550.44	517.08	491.10	470.48	453.84	440.26	429.05
33000	2958.32	1579.76	1123.06	896.82	762.73	674.70	612.97	567.64	533.24	506.45	485.18	468.03	454.02	442.46
34000	3047.97	1627.63	1157.10	924.00	785.85	695.15	631.54	584.85	549.40	521.80	499.88	482.21	467.78	455.87
35000	3137.62	1675.50	1191.13	951.17	808.96	715.60	650.12	602.05	565.55	537.14	514.58	496.39	481.53	469.28
36000	3227.26	1723.37	1225.16	978.35	832.07	736.04	668.69	619.25	581.71	552.49	529.29	510.57	495.29	482.69
37000	3316.91	1771.24	1259.19	1005.53	855.19	756.49	687.27	636.45	597.87	567.84	543.99	524.76	509.05	496.09
38000	3406.55	1819.11	1293.22	1032.70	878.30	776.93	705.84	653.65	614.03	583.18	558.69	538.94	522.81	509.50
39000	3496.20	1866.98	1327.26	1059.88	901.41	797.38	724.42	670.85	630.19	598.53	573.39	553.12	536.57	522.91
40000	3585.85	1914.86	1361.29	1087.05	924.53	817.82	742.99	688.05	646.35	613.88	588.09	567.30	550.32	536.32
41000	3675.49	1962.73	1395.32	1114.23	947.64	838.27	761.57	705.25	662.51	629.22	602.80	581.48	564.08	549.72
42000	3765.14	2010.60	1429.35	1141.41	970.75	858.71	780.14	722.46	678.66	644.57	617.50	595.67	577.84	563.13
43000	3854.78	2058.47	1463.39	1168.58	993.86	879.16	798.72	739.66	694.82	659.92	632.20	609.85	591.60	576.54
44000	3944.43	2106.34	1497.42	1195.76	1016.98	899.60	817.29	756.86	710.98	675.26	646.90	624.03	605.36	589.95
45000	4034.08	2154.21	1531.45	1222.94	1040.09	920.05	835.87	774.06	727.14	690.61	661.61	638.21	619.11	603.36
46000	4123.72	2202.08	1565.48	1250.11	1063.20	940.50	854.44	791.26	743.30	705.96	676.31	652.40	632.87	616.76
47000	4213.37	2249.96	1599.51	1277.29	1086.32	960.94	873.01	808.46	759.46	721.30	691.01	666.58	646.63	630.17
48000	4303.01	2297.83	1633.55	1304.46	1109.43	981.39	891.59	825.66	775.62	736.65	705.71	680.76	660.39	643.58
49000	4392.66	2345.70	1667.58	1331.64	1132.54	1001.83	910.16	842.86	791.77	752.00	720.41	694.94	674.15	656.99
50000	4482.31	2393.57	1701.61	1358.82	1155.66	1022.28	928.74	860.07	807.93	767.34	735.12	709.13	687.90	670.39
55000	4930.54	2632.93	1871.77	1494.70	1271.22	1124.50	1021.61	946.07	888.73	844.08	808.63	780.04	756.69	737.43
60000	5378.77	2872.28	2041.93	1630.58	1386.79	1226.73	1114.49	1032.08	969.52	920.81	882.14	850.95	825.48	804.47
65000	5827.00	3111.64	2212.09	1766.46	1502.35	1328.96	1207.36	1118.08	1050.31	997.55	955.65	921.86	894.27	871.51
70000	6275.23	3350.99	2382.25	1902.34	1617.92	1431.19	1300.23	1204.09	1131.10	1074.28	1029.16	992.78	963.06	938.55
75000	6723.46	3590.35	2552.41	2038.22	1733.48	1533.41	1393.11	1290.10	1211.90	1151.01	1102.67	1063.69	1031.85	1005.59
80000	7171.69	3829.71	2722.57	2174.10	1849.05	1635.64	1485.98	1376.10	1292.69	1227.75	1176.18	1134.60	1100.64	1072.63
85000	7619.92	4069.06	2892.73	2309.98	1964.61	1737.87	1578.85	1462.11	1373.48	1304.48	1249.69	1205.51	1169.43	1139.67
90000	8068.15	4308.42	3062.89	2445.87	2080.18	1840.09	1671.73	1548.11	1454.27	1381.21	1323.21	1276.42	1238.22	1206.71
95000	8516.38	4547.78	3233.05	2581.75	2195.74	1942.32	1764.60	1634.12	1535.07	1457.95	1396.72	1347.34	1307.01	1273.75
100000	8964.61	4787.13	3403.22	2717.63	2311.31	2044.55	1857.47	1720.13	1615.86	1534.68	1470.23	1418.25	1375.80	1340.78

TERM AMOUNT	15 Years	16 Years	17 Years	18 Years	19 Years	20 Years	21 Years	22 Years	23 Years	24 Years	25 Years	30 Years	35 Years	40 Years
5	.07	.07	.07	.07	.07	.07	.07	.07	.06	.06	.06	.06	.06	.06
10	.14	.13	.13	.13	.13	.13	.13	.13	.12	.12	.12	.12	.12	.12
15	.20	.20	.20	.19	.19	.19	.19	.19	.18	.18	.18	.18	.18	.18
25	.33	.33	.32	.32	.31	.31	.31	.31	.30	.30	.30	.30	.29	.29
50	.66	.65	.64	.63	.62	.62	.61	.61	.60	.60	.60	.59	.58	.58
75	.99	.97	.96	.94	.93	.92	.91	.91	.90	.90	.89	.88	.87	.86
100	1.32	1.29	1.27	1.25	1.24	1.23	1.22	1.21	1.20	1.19	1.19	1.17	1.16	1.15
200	2.63	2.58	2.54	2.50	2.47	2.45	2.43	2.41	2.39	2.38	2.37	2.33	2.31	2.30
300	3.94	3.87	3.81	3.75	3.71	3.67	3.64	3.61	3.59	3.57	3.55	3.49	3.46	3.44
400	5.25	5.15	5.07	5.00	4.94	4.89	4.85	4.81	4.78	4.75	4.73	4.65	4.61	4.59
500	6.56	6.44	6.34	6.25	6.18	6.11	6.06	6.01	5.97	5.94	5.91	5.81	5.76	5.74
600	7.87	7.73	7.61	7.50	7.41	7.34	7.27	7.22	7.17	7.13	7.09	6.97	6.91	6.88
700	9.19	9.02	8.87	8.75	8.65	8.56	8.48	8.42	8.36	8.31	8.27	8.13	8.07	8.03
800	10.50	10.30	10.14	10.00	9.88	9.78	9.69	9.62	9.55	9.50	9.45	9.29	9.22	9.18
900	11.81	11.59	11.41	11.25	11.11	11.00	10.90	10.82	10.75	10.69	10.63	10.46	10.37	10.32
1000	13.12	12.88	12.67	12.50	12.35	12.22	12.11	12.02	11.94	11.87	11.81	11.62	11.52	11.47
2000	26.24	25.75	25.34	24.99	24.69	24.44	24.22	24.04	23.88	23.74	23.62	23.23	23.03	22.94
3000	39.35	38.62	38.01	37.48	37.04	36.66	36.33	36.06	35.82	35.61	35.43	34.84	34.55	34.40
4000	52.47	51.49	50.67	49.98	49.38	48.88	48.44	48.07	47.75	47.48	47.24	46.45	46.06	45.87
5000	65.59	64.37	63.34	62.47	61.73	61.09	60.55	60.09	59.69	59.35	59.05	58.06	57.58	57.33
6000	78.70	77.24	76.01	74.96	74.07	73.31	72.66	72.11	71.63	71.21	70.86	69.68	69.09	68.80
7000	91.82	90.11	88.67	87.45	86.42	85.53	84.77	84.12	83.56	83.08	82.66	81.29	80.61	80.27
8000	104.94	102.98	101.34	99.95	98.76	97.75	96.88	96.14	95.50	94.95	94.47	92.90	92.12	91.73
9000	118.05	115.86	114.01	112.44	111.10	109.97	108.99	108.16	107.44	106.82	106.28	104.51	103.64	103.20
10000	131.17	128.73	126.67	124.93	123.45	122.18	121.10	120.17	119.37	118.69	118.09	116.12	115.15	114.66
11000	144.29	141.60	139.34	137.42	135.79	134.40	133.21	132.19	131.31	130.55	129.90	127.73	126.66	126.13
12000	157.40	154.47	152.01	149.92	148.14	146.62	145.32	144.21	143.25	142.42	141.71	139.35	138.18	137.60
13000	170.52	167.35	164.67	162.41	160.48	158.84	157.43	156.22	155.18	154.29	153.52	150.96	149.69	149.06
14000	183.64	180.22	177.34	174.90	172.83	171.06	169.54	168.24	167.12	166.16	165.32	162.57	161.21	160.53
15000	196.75	193.09	190.01	187.39	185.17	183.27	181.65	180.26	179.06	178.03	177.13	174.18	172.72	171.99
16000	209.87	205.96	202.67	199.89	197.51	195.49	193.76	192.27	191.00	189.89	188.94	185.79	184.24	183.46
17000	222.98	218.84	215.34	212.30	209.86	207.71	205.87	204.29	202.93	201.76	200.75	197.40	195.75	194.93
18000	236.10	231.71	228.01	224.87	222.20	219.93	217.98	216.31	214.87	213.63	212.56	209.02	207.27	206.39
19000	249.22	244.58	240.67	237.36	234.55	232.15	230.09	228.32	226.81	225.50	224.37	220.63	218.78	217.86
20000	262.33	257.45	253.34	249.86	246.89	244.36	242.20	240.34	238.74	237.37	236.18	232.24	230.30	229.32
21000	275.45	270.33	266.01	262.35	259.24	256.58	254.31	252.36	250.68	249.23	247.98	243.85	241.81	240.79
22000	288.57	283.20	278.67	274.84	271.58	268.80	266.42	264.37	262.62	261.10	259.79	255.46	253.32	252.26
23000	301.68	296.07	291.34	287.33	283.93	281.02	278.53	276.39	274.55	272.97	271.60	267.07	264.84	263.72
24000	314.80	308.94	304.01	299.83	296.27	293.24	290.64	288.41	286.49	284.84	283.41	278.69	276.35	275.19
25000	327.92	321.81	316.67	312.32	308.61	305.45	302.75	300.42	298.43	296.71	295.22	290.30	287.87	286.65
26000	341.03	334.69	329.34	324.81	320.96	317.67	314.86	312.44	310.36	308.57	307.03	301.91	299.38	298.12
27000	354.15	347.56	342.01	337.30	333.30	329.89	326.97	324.46	322.30	320.44	318.84	313.52	310.90	309.59
28000	367.27	360.43	354.67	349.80	345.65	342.11	339.08	336.48	334.24	332.31	330.64	325.13	322.41	321.05
29000	380.38	373.30	367.34	362.29	357.99	354.32	351.19	348.49	346.17	344.18	342.45	336.74	333.93	332.52
30000	393.50	386.18	380.01	374.78	370.34	366.54	363.30	360.51	358.11	356.05	354.26	348.36	345.44	343.98
31000	406.62	399.05	392.67	387.27	382.68	378.76	375.41	372.53	370.05	367.91	366.07	359.97	356.96	355.45
32000	419.73	411.92	405.34	399.77	395.02	390.98	387.52	384.54	381.99	379.78	377.88	371.58	368.47	366.92
33000	432.85	424.79	418.01	412.26	407.37	403.20	399.62	396.56	393.92	391.65	389.69	383.19	379.98	378.38
34000	445.96	437.67	430.67	424.75	419.71	415.41	411.73	408.58	405.86	403.52	401.50	394.80	391.50	389.85
35000	459.08	450.54	443.34	437.24	432.06	427.63	423.84	420.59	417.80	415.39	413.30	406.41	403.01	401.31
36000	472.20	463.41	456.01	449.74	444.40	439.85	435.95	432.61	429.73	427.25	425.11	418.03	414.53	412.78
37000	485.31	476.28	468.67	462.23	456.75	452.07	448.06	444.63	441.67	439.12	436.92	429.64	426.04	424.25
38000	498.43	489.16	481.34	474.72	469.09	464.29	460.17	456.64	453.61	450.99	448.73	441.25	437.56	435.71
39000	511.55	502.03	494.01	487.21	481.44	476.50	472.28	468.66	465.54	462.86	460.54	452.86	449.07	447.18
40000	524.66	514.90	506.67	499.71	493.78	488.72	484.39	480.68	477.48	474.73	472.35	464.47	460.59	458.64
41000	537.78	527.77	519.34	512.20	506.12	500.94	496.50	492.69	489.42	486.59	484.16	476.08	472.10	470.11
42000	550.90	540.65	532.01	524.69	518.47	513.16	508.61	504.71	501.35	498.46	495.96	487.70	483.62	481.58
43000	564.01	553.52	544.67	537.18	530.81	525.38	520.72	516.73	513.29	510.33	507.77	499.31	495.13	493.04
44000	577.13	566.39	557.34	549.68	543.16	537.59	532.83	528.74	525.23	522.20	519.58	510.92	506.64	504.51
45000	590.25	579.26	570.01	562.17	555.50	549.81	544.94	540.76	537.16	534.07	531.39	522.53	518.16	515.97
46000	603.36	592.13	582.67	574.66	567.85	562.03	557.05	552.78	549.10	545.93	543.20	534.14	529.67	527.44
47000	616.48	605.01	595.34	587.15	580.19	574.25	569.16	564.79	561.04	557.80	555.01	545.75	541.19	538.91
48000	629.60	617.88	608.01	599.65	592.53	586.47	581.27	576.81	572.98	569.67	566.82	557.37	552.70	550.37
49000	642.71	630.75	620.67	612.14	604.88	598.68	593.38	588.83	584.91	581.54	578.62	568.98	564.22	561.84
50000	655.83	643.62	633.34	624.63	617.22	610.90	605.49	600.84	596.85	593.41	590.43	580.59	575.73	573.30
55000	721.41	707.99	696.67	687.09	678.94	671.99	666.04	660.93	656.53	652.75	649.48	638.65	633.30	630.63
60000	786.99	772.35	760.01	749.56	740.67	733.08	726.59	721.01	716.22	712.09	708.52	696.71	690.88	687.96
65000	852.58	836.71	823.34	812.02	802.39	794.17	787.13	781.10	775.90	771.43	767.56	754.76	748.45	745.29
70000	918.16	901.07	886.67	874.48	864.11	855.26	847.68	841.18	835.59	830.77	826.60	812.82	806.02	802.62
75000	983.74	965.43	950.01	936.94	925.83	916.35	908.23	901.26	895.27	890.11	885.65	870.88	863.59	859.95
80000	1049.32	1029.80	1013.34	999.41	987.55	977.44	968.78	961.35	954.96	949.45	944.69	928.94	921.17	917.28
85000	1114.90	1094.16	1076.67	1061.87	1049.28	1038.53	1029.33	1021.43	1014.64	1008.79	1003.73	987.00	978.74	974.61
90000	1180.49	1158.52	1140.01	1124.33	1111.00	1099.62	1089.88	1081.52	1074.32	1068.13	1062.78	1045.06	1036.31	1031.94
95000	1246.07	1222.88	1203.34	1186.79	1172.72	1160.71	1150.43	1141.60	1134.01	1127.47	1121.82	1103.11	1093.88	1089.27
100000	1311.65	1287.24	1266.68	1249.26	1234.44	1221.80	1210.97	1201.68	1193.69	1186.81	1180.86	1161.17	1151.46	1146.60

MONTHLY PAYMENT
REQUIRED TO AMORTIZE A LOAN

TERM AMOUNT	1 Year	2 Years	3 Years	4 Years	5 Years	6 Years	7 Years	8 Years	9 Years	10 Years	11 Years	12 Years	13 Years	14 Years
5	.45	.24	.18	.14	.12	.11	.10	.09	.09	.09	.08	.08	.07	.07
10	.90	.48	.35	.28	.24	.21	.19	.18	.17	.16	.15	.15	.14	.14
15	1.35	.72	.52	.41	.35	.31	.28	.26	.25	.24	.23	.22	.21	.21
25	2.25	1.20	.86	.69	.58	.52	.47	.44	.41	.39	.37	.36	.35	.34
50	4.49	2.40	1.71	1.37	1.16	1.03	.94	.87	.81	.77	.74	.72	.69	.68
75	6.73	3.60	2.56	2.05	1.74	1.54	1.40	1.30	1.22	1.16	1.11	1.07	1.04	1.01
100	8.97	4.79	3.41	2.73	2.32	2.05	1.87	1.73	1.62	1.54	1.48	1.43	1.38	1.35
200	17.94	9.58	6.82	5.45	4.63	4.10	3.73	3.45	3.24	3.08	2.95	2.85	2.76	2.69
300	26.91	14.37	10.22	8.17	6.95	6.15	5.59	5.17	4.86	4.62	4.42	4.27	4.14	4.04
400	35.87	19.16	13.63	10.89	9.26	8.19	7.45	6.90	6.48	6.16	5.90	5.69	5.52	5.38
500	44.84	23.95	17.03	13.61	11.57	10.24	9.31	8.62	8.10	7.69	7.37	7.11	6.90	6.73
600	53.81	28.74	20.44	16.33	13.89	12.29	11.17	10.34	9.72	9.23	8.84	8.53	8.28	8.07
700	62.77	33.53	23.84	19.05	16.20	14.34	13.03	12.07	11.34	10.77	10.32	9.95	9.66	9.41
800	71.74	38.32	27.25	21.77	18.52	16.38	14.89	13.79	12.96	12.31	11.79	11.38	11.04	10.76
900	80.71	43.11	30.66	24.49	20.83	18.43	16.75	15.51	14.57	13.84	13.26	12.80	12.42	12.10
1000	89.67	47.90	34.06	27.21	23.14	20.48	18.61	17.23	16.19	15.38	14.74	14.22	13.80	13.45
2000	179.34	95.79	68.12	54.41	46.28	40.95	37.21	34.46	32.38	30.76	29.47	28.43	27.59	26.89
3000	269.01	143.69	102.17	81.61	69.42	61.42	55.81	51.69	48.57	46.14	44.20	42.65	41.38	40.33
4000	358.68	191.58	136.23	108.81	92.56	81.89	74.41	68.92	64.76	61.51	58.94	56.86	55.17	53.77
5000	448.35	239.48	170.29	136.01	115.70	102.37	93.02	86.15	80.94	76.89	73.67	71.07	68.96	67.21
6000	538.02	287.37	204.34	163.21	138.84	122.84	111.62	103.38	97.13	92.27	88.40	85.29	82.75	80.65
7000	627.69	335.27	238.40	190.41	161.98	143.31	130.22	120.61	113.32	107.64	103.14	99.50	96.54	94.09
8000	717.36	383.16	272.46	217.61	185.12	163.78	148.82	137.84	129.51	123.02	117.87	113.72	110.33	107.53
9000	807.03	431.06	306.51	244.82	208.25	184.25	167.42	155.07	145.69	138.40	132.60	127.93	124.12	120.97
10000	896.70	478.95	340.57	272.02	231.39	204.73	186.03	172.30	161.88	153.77	147.33	142.14	137.91	134.41
11000	986.37	526.85	374.62	299.22	254.53	225.20	204.63	189.53	178.07	169.15	162.07	156.36	151.70	147.85
12000	1076.04	574.74	408.68	326.42	277.67	245.67	223.23	206.76	194.26	184.53	176.80	170.57	165.49	161.29
13000	1165.71	622.64	442.74	353.62	300.81	266.14	241.83	223.99	210.44	199.90	191.53	184.78	179.28	174.73
14000	1255.38	670.53	476.79	380.82	323.95	286.61	260.44	241.22	226.63	215.28	206.27	199.00	193.07	188.17
15000	1345.05	718.43	510.85	408.02	347.09	307.09	279.04	258.45	242.82	230.66	221.00	213.21	206.86	201.61
16000	1434.72	766.32	544.91	435.22	370.23	327.56	297.64	275.68	259.01	246.03	235.73	227.43	220.65	215.05
17000	1524.39	814.22	578.96	462.43	393.37	348.03	316.24	292.91	275.20	261.41	250.46	241.64	234.44	228.49
18000	1614.06	862.11	613.02	489.63	416.50	368.50	334.84	310.14	291.38	276.79	265.20	255.85	248.23	241.94
19000	1703.73	910.01	647.08	516.83	439.64	388.98	353.45	327.37	307.57	292.16	279.93	270.07	262.02	255.38
20000	1793.40	957.90	681.13	544.03	462.78	409.45	372.05	344.60	323.76	307.54	294.66	284.28	275.81	268.82
21000	1883.07	1005.80	715.19	571.23	485.92	429.92	390.65	361.83	339.95	322.92	309.40	298.50	289.60	282.26
22000	1972.73	1053.69	749.24	598.43	509.06	450.39	409.25	379.05	356.13	338.29	324.13	312.71	303.39	295.70
23000	2062.40	1101.59	783.30	625.63	532.20	470.86	427.86	396.28	372.32	353.67	338.86	326.92	317.18	309.14
24000	2152.07	1149.48	817.36	652.83	555.34	491.34	446.46	413.51	388.51	369.05	353.59	341.14	330.97	322.58
25000	2241.74	1197.38	851.41	680.04	578.48	511.81	465.06	430.74	404.70	384.42	368.33	355.35	344.76	336.02
26000	2331.41	1245.27	885.47	707.24	601.61	532.28	483.66	447.97	420.88	399.80	383.06	369.56	358.55	349.46
27000	2421.08	1293.17	919.53	734.44	624.75	552.75	502.26	465.20	437.07	415.18	397.79	383.78	372.34	362.90
28000	2510.75	1341.06	953.58	761.64	647.89	573.22	520.87	482.43	453.26	430.55	412.53	397.99	386.13	376.34
29000	2600.42	1388.96	987.64	788.84	671.03	593.70	539.47	499.66	469.45	445.93	427.26	412.21	399.92	389.78
30000	2690.09	1436.85	1021.69	816.04	694.17	614.17	558.07	516.89	485.64	461.31	441.99	426.42	413.71	403.22
31000	2779.76	1484.75	1055.75	843.24	717.31	634.64	576.67	534.12	501.82	476.68	456.72	440.63	427.50	416.66
32000	2869.43	1532.64	1089.81	870.44	740.45	655.11	595.27	551.35	518.01	492.06	471.46	454.85	441.29	430.10
33000	2959.10	1580.54	1123.86	897.65	763.59	675.58	613.88	568.58	534.20	507.44	486.19	469.06	455.08	443.54
34000	3048.77	1628.43	1157.92	924.85	786.73	696.06	632.48	585.81	550.39	522.81	500.92	483.28	468.87	456.98
35000	3138.44	1676.33	1191.98	952.05	809.86	716.53	651.08	603.04	566.57	538.19	515.66	497.49	482.66	470.42
36000	3228.11	1724.22	1226.03	979.25	833.00	737.00	669.68	620.27	582.76	553.57	530.39	511.70	496.45	483.87
37000	3317.78	1772.12	1260.09	1006.45	856.14	757.47	688.29	637.50	598.95	568.94	545.12	525.92	510.24	497.31
38000	3407.45	1820.01	1294.15	1033.65	879.28	777.95	706.89	654.73	615.14	584.32	559.85	540.13	524.03	510.75
39000	3497.12	1867.90	1328.20	1060.85	902.42	798.42	725.49	671.96	631.32	599.70	574.59	554.34	537.82	524.19
40000	3586.79	1915.80	1362.26	1088.05	925.56	818.89	744.09	689.19	647.51	615.07	589.32	568.56	551.61	537.63
41000	3676.46	1963.69	1396.31	1115.26	948.70	839.36	762.69	706.42	663.70	630.45	604.05	582.77	565.40	551.07
42000	3766.13	2011.59	1430.37	1142.46	971.84	859.83	781.30	723.65	679.89	645.83	618.79	596.99	579.19	564.51
43000	3855.79	2059.48	1464.43	1169.66	994.98	880.31	799.90	740.87	696.08	661.20	633.52	611.20	592.98	577.95
44000	3945.46	2107.38	1498.48	1196.86	1018.11	900.78	818.50	758.10	712.26	676.58	648.25	625.41	606.77	591.39
45000	4035.13	2155.27	1532.54	1224.06	1041.25	921.25	837.10	775.33	728.45	691.96	662.98	639.63	620.56	604.83
46000	4124.80	2203.17	1566.60	1251.26	1064.39	941.72	855.71	792.56	744.64	707.33	677.72	653.84	634.35	618.27
47000	4214.47	2251.06	1600.65	1278.46	1087.53	962.19	874.31	809.79	760.83	722.71	692.45	668.05	648.14	631.71
48000	4304.14	2298.96	1634.71	1305.66	1110.67	982.67	892.91	827.02	777.01	738.09	707.18	682.27	661.93	645.15
49000	4393.81	2346.85	1668.77	1332.87	1133.81	1003.14	911.51	844.25	793.20	753.46	721.92	696.48	675.72	658.59
50000	4483.48	2394.75	1702.82	1360.07	1156.95	1023.61	930.11	861.48	809.39	768.84	736.65	710.70	689.51	672.03
55000	4931.83	2634.22	1873.10	1496.07	1272.64	1125.97	1023.12	947.63	890.33	845.72	810.31	781.77	758.46	739.24
60000	5380.18	2873.70	2043.39	1632.08	1388.34	1228.33	1116.14	1033.78	971.27	922.61	883.98	852.83	827.41	806.44
65000	5828.52	3113.17	2213.67	1768.09	1504.03	1330.69	1209.15	1119.92	1052.20	999.49	957.64	923.90	896.36	873.64
70000	6276.87	3352.65	2383.95	1904.09	1619.72	1433.05	1302.16	1206.07	1133.14	1076.37	1031.31	994.97	965.31	940.84
75000	6725.22	3592.12	2554.23	2040.10	1735.42	1535.41	1395.17	1292.22	1214.08	1153.26	1104.97	1066.04	1034.26	1008.05
80000	7173.57	3831.59	2724.51	2176.10	1851.11	1637.77	1488.18	1378.37	1295.02	1230.14	1178.64	1137.11	1103.21	1075.25
85000	7621.92	4071.07	2894.79	2312.11	1966.81	1740.13	1581.19	1464.51	1375.96	1307.02	1252.30	1208.18	1172.16	1142.45
90000	8070.26	4310.54	3065.07	2448.12	2082.50	1842.50	1674.20	1550.66	1456.90	1383.91	1325.97	1279.25	1241.11	1209.66
95000	8518.61	4550.02	3235.36	2584.12	2198.20	1944.86	1767.21	1636.81	1537.83	1460.79	1399.63	1350.32	1310.06	1276.86
100000	8966.96	4789.49	3405.64	2720.13	2313.89	2047.22	1860.22	1722.96	1618.77	1537.67	1473.29	1421.39	1379.01	1344.06

TERM AMOUNT	15 Years	16 Years	17 Years	18 Years	19 Years	20 Years	21 Years	22 Years	23 Years	24 Years	25 Years	30 Years	35 Years	40 Years
5	.07	.07	.07	.07	.07	.07	.07	.07	.06	.06	.06	.06	.06	.06
10	.14	.13	.13	.13	.13	.13	.13	.13	.12	.12	.12	.12	.12	.12
15	.20	.20	.20	.19	.19	.19	.19	.19	.18	.18	.18	.18	.18	.18
25	.33	.33	.32	.32	.31	.31	.31	.31	.30	.30	.30	.30	.29	.29
50	.66	.65	.64	.63	.62	.62	.61	.61	.60	.60	.60	.59	.58	.58
75	.99	.97	.96	.94	.93	.92	.92	.91	.90	.90	.89	.88	.87	.87
100	1.32	1.30	1.28	1.26	1.24	1.23	1.22	1.21	1.20	1.20	1.19	1.17	1.16	1.16
200	2.63	2.59	2.55	2.51	2.48	2.46	2.43	2.42	2.40	2.39	2.37	2.34	2.32	2.31
300	3.95	3.88	3.82	3.76	3.72	3.68	3.65	3.62	3.60	3.58	3.56	3.50	3.47	3.46
400	5.26	5.17	5.09	5.02	4.96	4.91	4.86	4.83	4.79	4.77	4.74	4.67	4.63	4.61
500	6.58	6.46	6.36	6.27	6.20	6.13	6.08	6.03	5.99	5.96	5.93	5.83	5.78	5.76
600	7.89	7.75	7.63	7.52	7.43	7.36	7.29	7.24	7.19	7.15	7.11	7.00	6.94	6.91
700	9.21	9.04	8.90	8.77	8.67	8.58	8.51	8.44	8.39	8.34	8.30	8.16	8.09	8.06
800	10.52	10.33	10.17	10.03	9.91	9.81	9.72	9.65	9.58	9.53	9.48	9.33	9.25	9.21
900	11.84	11.62	11.44	11.28	11.15	11.03	10.94	10.85	10.78	10.72	10.67	10.49	10.40	10.36
1000	13.15	12.91	12.71	12.53	12.39	12.26	12.15	12.06	11.98	11.91	11.85	11.66	11.56	11.51
2000	26.30	25.82	25.41	25.06	24.77	24.51	24.30	24.11	23.95	23.82	23.70	23.31	23.11	23.02
3000	39.45	38.72	38.11	37.59	37.15	36.77	36.44	36.17	35.93	35.72	35.54	34.96	34.67	34.53
4000	52.60	51.63	50.81	50.12	49.53	49.02	48.59	48.22	47.90	47.63	47.39	46.61	46.22	46.03
5000	65.75	64.54	63.51	62.64	61.91	61.28	60.74	60.27	59.88	59.53	59.24	58.26	57.78	57.54
6000	78.90	77.44	76.21	75.17	74.29	73.53	72.88	72.33	71.85	71.44	71.08	69.91	69.33	69.05
7000	92.05	90.35	88.91	87.70	86.67	85.78	85.03	84.38	83.82	83.35	82.93	81.56	80.89	80.55
8000	105.20	103.26	101.62	100.23	99.05	98.04	97.18	96.44	95.80	95.25	94.78	93.21	92.44	92.06
9000	118.35	116.16	114.32	112.75	111.43	110.29	109.32	108.49	107.77	107.16	106.62	104.87	104.00	103.57
10000	131.50	129.07	127.02	125.28	123.81	122.55	121.47	120.54	119.75	119.06	118.47	116.52	115.55	115.07
11000	144.65	141.98	139.72	137.81	136.19	134.80	133.61	132.60	131.72	130.97	130.32	128.17	127.11	126.58
12000	157.80	154.88	152.42	150.34	148.57	147.05	145.76	144.65	143.70	142.87	142.16	139.82	138.66	138.09
13000	170.95	167.79	165.12	162.86	160.95	159.31	157.91	156.70	155.67	154.78	154.01	151.47	150.22	149.59
14000	184.10	180.69	177.82	175.39	173.33	171.56	170.05	168.76	167.64	166.69	165.86	163.12	161.77	161.10
15000	197.25	193.60	190.52	187.92	185.71	183.82	182.20	180.81	179.62	178.59	177.70	174.77	173.33	172.61
16000	210.40	206.51	203.23	200.45	198.09	196.07	194.35	192.87	191.59	190.50	189.55	186.42	184.88	184.11
17000	223.55	219.41	215.93	212.97	210.47	208.32	206.49	204.92	203.57	202.40	201.40	198.07	196.44	195.62
18000	236.70	232.32	228.63	225.50	222.85	220.58	218.64	216.97	215.54	214.31	213.24	209.73	207.99	207.13
19000	249.85	245.23	241.33	238.03	235.23	232.83	230.78	229.03	227.52	226.21	225.09	221.38	219.55	218.64
20000	263.00	258.13	254.03	250.56	247.61	245.09	242.93	241.08	239.49	238.12	236.94	233.03	231.10	230.14
21000	276.15	271.04	266.73	263.09	259.99	257.34	255.08	253.13	251.46	250.03	248.78	244.68	242.66	241.65
22000	289.30	283.95	279.43	275.61	272.37	269.59	267.22	265.19	263.44	261.93	260.63	256.33	254.21	253.16
23000	302.45	296.85	292.13	288.14	284.75	281.85	279.37	277.24	275.41	273.84	272.48	267.98	265.77	264.66
24000	315.60	309.76	304.84	300.67	297.13	294.10	291.52	289.30	287.39	285.74	284.32	279.63	277.32	276.17
25000	328.75	322.67	317.54	313.20	309.51	306.36	303.66	301.35	299.36	297.65	296.17	291.28	288.88	287.68
26000	341.90	335.57	330.24	325.72	321.89	318.61	315.81	313.40	311.34	309.56	308.02	302.93	300.43	299.18
27000	355.05	348.48	342.94	338.25	334.27	330.86	327.95	325.46	323.31	321.46	319.86	314.59	311.99	310.69
28000	368.20	361.38	355.64	350.78	346.65	343.12	340.10	337.51	335.28	333.37	331.71	326.24	323.54	322.20
29000	381.35	374.29	368.34	363.31	359.03	355.37	352.25	349.57	347.26	345.27	343.56	337.89	335.10	333.70
30000	394.50	387.20	381.04	375.83	371.41	367.63	364.39	361.62	359.23	357.18	355.40	349.54	346.65	345.21
31000	407.65	400.10	393.75	388.36	383.79	379.88	376.54	373.67	371.21	369.08	367.25	361.19	358.21	356.72
32000	420.80	413.01	406.45	400.89	396.17	392.13	388.69	385.73	383.18	380.99	379.10	372.84	369.76	368.22
33000	433.95	425.92	419.15	413.42	408.55	404.39	400.83	397.78	395.16	392.90	390.94	384.49	381.32	379.73
34000	447.10	438.82	431.85	425.94	420.93	416.64	412.98	409.83	407.13	404.80	402.79	396.14	392.87	391.24
35000	460.25	451.73	444.55	438.47	433.31	428.90	425.12	421.89	419.10	416.71	414.64	407.79	404.42	402.74
36000	473.40	464.64	457.25	451.00	445.69	441.15	437.27	433.94	431.08	428.61	426.48	419.45	415.98	414.25
37000	486.55	477.54	469.95	463.53	458.07	453.40	449.42	446.00	443.05	440.52	438.33	431.10	427.53	425.76
38000	499.70	490.45	482.65	476.06	470.45	465.66	461.56	458.05	455.03	452.42	450.10	442.75	439.09	437.27
39000	512.85	503.35	495.36	488.58	482.83	477.91	473.71	470.10	467.00	464.33	462.02	454.40	450.64	448.77
40000	526.00	516.26	508.06	501.11	495.21	490.17	485.86	482.16	478.98	476.24	473.87	466.05	462.20	460.28
41000	539.15	529.17	520.76	513.64	507.59	502.42	498.00	494.21	490.95	488.14	485.72	477.70	473.75	471.79
42000	552.30	542.07	533.46	526.17	519.97	514.68	510.15	506.26	502.92	500.05	497.56	489.35	485.31	483.29
43000	565.45	554.98	546.16	538.69	532.35	526.93	522.29	518.32	514.90	511.95	509.41	500.90	496.86	494.80
44000	578.60	567.89	558.86	551.22	544.73	539.18	534.44	530.37	526.87	523.86	521.26	512.65	508.42	506.31
45000	591.75	580.79	571.56	563.75	557.11	551.44	546.59	542.43	538.85	535.76	533.10	524.31	519.97	517.81
46000	604.90	593.70	584.26	576.28	569.49	563.69	558.73	554.48	550.82	547.67	544.95	535.96	531.53	529.32
47000	618.05	606.61	596.97	588.80	581.87	575.95	570.88	566.53	562.80	559.58	556.80	547.61	543.08	540.83
48000	631.20	619.51	609.67	601.33	594.25	588.20	583.03	578.59	574.77	571.48	568.64	559.26	554.64	552.33
49000	644.35	632.42	622.37	613.86	606.63	600.45	595.17	590.64	586.74	583.39	580.49	570.91	566.19	563.84
50000	657.50	645.33	635.07	626.39	619.01	612.71	607.32	602.69	598.72	595.29	592.34	582.56	577.75	575.35
55000	723.25	709.86	698.58	689.03	680.91	673.98	668.05	662.96	658.59	654.82	651.57	640.82	635.52	632.88
60000	789.00	774.39	762.08	751.66	742.81	735.25	728.78	723.23	718.46	714.35	710.80	699.07	693.30	690.42
65000	854.75	838.92	825.59	814.30	804.71	796.52	789.51	783.50	778.33	773.88	770.04	757.33	751.07	747.95
70000	920.50	903.45	889.10	876.94	866.61	857.79	850.24	843.77	838.20	833.41	829.27	815.58	808.84	805.48
75000	986.25	967.99	952.60	939.58	928.51	919.06	910.98	904.04	898.08	892.94	888.50	873.84	866.62	863.02
80000	1051.99	1032.52	1016.11	1002.22	990.41	980.33	971.71	964.31	957.95	952.47	947.74	932.10	924.39	920.55
85000	1117.74	1097.05	1079.61	1064.85	1052.31	1041.60	1032.44	1024.58	1017.82	1012.00	1006.97	990.35	982.17	978.09
90000	1183.49	1161.58	1143.12	1127.49	1114.21	1102.87	1093.17	1084.85	1077.69	1071.52	1066.20	1048.61	1039.94	1035.62
95000	1249.24	1226.11	1206.63	1190.13	1176.11	1164.14	1153.90	1145.12	1137.56	1131.05	1125.44	1106.86	1097.72	1093.16
100000	1314.99	1290.65	1270.13	1252.77	1238.01	1225.41	1214.63	1205.38	1197.43	1190.58	1184.67	1165.12	1155.49	1150.69

13.800%

TERM	1 Year	2 Years	3 Years	4 Years	5 Years	6 Years	7 Years	8 Years	9 Years	10 Years	11 Years	12 Years	13 Years	14 Years
AMOUNT														
5	.45	.24	.18	.14	.12	.11	.10	.09	.09	.08	.08	.08	.07	.07
10	.90	.48	.35	.28	.24	.21	.19	.18	.17	.16	.15	.15	.14	.14
15	1.35	.72	.52	.41	.35	.31	.28	.26	.25	.24	.23	.22	.21	.21
25	2.25	1.20	.86	.69	.58	.52	.47	.44	.41	.39	.37	.36	.35	.34
50	4.49	2.40	1.71	1.37	1.16	1.03	.94	.87	.82	.78	.74	.72	.70	.68
75	6.73	3.60	2.56	2.05	1.74	1.54	1.40	1.30	1.22	1.16	1.11	1.07	1.04	1.02
100	8.97	4.80	3.41	2.73	2.32	2.05	1.87	1.73	1.63	1.55	1.48	1.43	1.39	1.35
200	17.94	9.59	6.82	5.45	4.64	4.10	3.73	3.46	3.25	3.09	2.96	2.85	2.77	2.70
300	26.91	14.38	10.23	8.17	6.95	6.15	5.59	5.18	4.87	4.63	4.43	4.28	4.15	4.05
400	35.88	19.17	13.64	10.90	9.27	8.20	7.46	6.91	6.49	6.17	5.91	5.70	5.53	5.39
500	44.85	23.96	17.05	13.62	11.59	10.25	9.32	8.63	8.11	7.71	7.39	7.13	6.92	6.74
600	53.82	28.76	20.45	16.34	13.90	12.30	11.18	10.36	9.74	9.25	8.86	8.55	8.30	8.09
700	62.79	33.55	23.86	19.06	16.22	14.35	13.05	12.09	11.36	10.79	10.34	9.98	9.68	9.44
800	71.76	38.34	27.27	21.79	18.54	16.40	14.91	13.81	12.98	12.33	11.82	11.40	11.06	10.78
900	80.73	43.13	30.68	24.51	20.85	18.45	16.77	15.54	14.60	13.87	13.29	12.83	12.44	12.13
1000	89.70	47.92	34.09	27.23	23.17	20.50	18.63	17.26	16.22	15.41	14.77	14.25	13.83	13.48
2000	179.39	95.84	68.17	54.46	46.33	41.00	37.26	34.52	32.44	30.82	29.53	28.50	27.65	26.95
3000	269.08	143.76	102.25	81.68	69.50	61.50	55.89	51.78	48.66	46.22	44.30	42.74	41.47	40.43
4000	358.78	191.68	136.33	108.91	92.66	82.00	74.52	69.04	64.87	61.63	59.06	56.99	55.29	53.90
5000	448.47	239.60	170.41	136.14	115.83	102.50	93.15	86.29	81.09	77.04	73.82	71.23	69.12	67.37
6000	538.16	287.52	204.49	163.36	138.99	123.00	111.78	103.55	97.31	92.44	88.59	85.48	82.94	80.85
7000	627.86	335.43	238.57	190.59	162.16	143.50	130.41	120.81	113.52	107.85	103.35	99.72	96.76	94.32
8000	717.55	383.35	272.65	217.82	185.32	164.00	149.04	138.07	129.74	123.26	118.11	113.97	110.58	107.79
9000	807.24	431.27	306.73	245.04	208.49	184.49	167.67	155.33	145.96	138.66	132.88	128.21	124.40	121.27
10000	896.94	479.19	340.81	272.27	231.65	204.99	186.30	172.58	162.17	154.07	147.64	142.46	138.23	134.74
11000	986.63	527.11	374.89	299.49	254.82	225.49	204.93	189.84	178.39	169.48	162.40	156.70	152.05	148.21
12000	1076.32	575.03	408.97	326.72	277.98	245.99	223.56	207.10	194.61	184.88	177.17	170.95	165.87	161.69
13000	1166.01	622.94	443.05	353.95	301.15	266.49	242.19	224.36	210.82	200.29	191.93	185.19	179.69	175.16
14000	1255.71	670.86	477.13	381.17	324.31	286.99	260.82	241.62	227.04	215.70	206.70	199.44	193.52	188.63
15000	1345.40	718.78	511.21	408.40	347.48	307.49	279.45	258.87	243.26	231.10	221.46	213.68	207.34	202.11
16000	1435.09	766.70	545.29	435.63	370.64	327.99	298.08	276.13	259.47	246.51	236.22	227.93	221.16	215.58
17000	1524.79	814.62	579.37	462.85	393.80	348.48	316.71	293.39	275.69	261.92	250.99	242.17	234.98	229.05
18000	1614.48	862.54	613.46	490.08	416.97	368.98	335.34	310.65	291.91	277.32	265.75	256.42	248.80	242.53
19000	1704.17	910.46	647.54	517.30	440.13	389.48	353.97	327.90	308.12	292.73	280.51	270.66	262.63	256.00
20000	1793.87	958.37	681.62	544.53	463.30	409.98	372.60	345.16	324.34	308.14	295.28	284.91	276.45	269.47
21000	1883.56	1006.29	715.70	571.76	486.46	430.48	391.23	362.42	340.56	323.54	310.04	299.16	290.27	282.95
22000	1973.25	1054.21	749.78	598.98	509.63	450.98	409.86	379.68	356.78	338.95	324.80	313.40	304.09	296.42
23000	2062.94	1102.13	783.86	626.21	532.79	471.48	428.49	396.94	372.99	354.36	339.57	327.65	317.92	309.89
24000	2152.64	1150.05	817.94	653.44	555.96	491.98	447.12	414.19	389.21	369.76	354.33	341.89	331.74	323.37
25000	2242.33	1197.97	852.02	680.66	579.12	512.47	465.75	431.45	405.43	385.17	369.09	356.14	345.56	336.84
26000	2332.02	1245.88	886.10	707.89	602.29	532.97	484.38	448.71	421.64	400.58	383.86	370.38	359.38	350.31
27000	2421.72	1293.80	920.18	735.11	625.45	553.47	503.01	465.97	437.86	415.98	398.62	384.63	373.20	363.79
28000	2511.41	1341.72	954.26	762.34	648.62	573.97	521.64	483.23	454.08	431.39	413.39	398.87	387.03	377.26
29000	2601.10	1389.64	988.34	789.57	671.78	594.47	540.27	500.48	470.29	446.80	428.15	413.12	400.85	390.73
30000	2690.80	1437.56	1022.42	816.79	694.95	614.97	558.90	517.74	486.51	462.20	442.91	427.36	414.67	404.21
31000	2780.49	1485.48	1056.50	844.02	718.11	635.47	577.53	535.00	502.73	477.61	457.68	441.61	428.49	417.68
32000	2870.18	1533.40	1090.58	871.25	741.28	655.97	596.16	552.26	518.94	493.02	472.44	455.85	442.32	431.15
33000	2959.88	1581.31	1124.66	898.47	764.44	676.47	614.79	569.51	535.16	508.42	487.20	470.10	456.14	444.63
34000	3049.57	1629.23	1158.74	925.70	787.60	696.96	633.41	586.77	551.38	523.83	501.97	484.34	469.96	458.10
35000	3139.26	1677.15	1192.83	952.92	810.77	717.46	652.04	604.03	567.59	539.24	516.73	498.59	483.78	471.57
36000	3228.95	1725.07	1226.91	980.15	833.93	737.96	670.67	621.29	583.81	554.64	531.49	512.83	497.60	485.05
37000	3318.65	1772.99	1260.99	1007.38	857.10	758.46	689.30	638.55	600.03	570.05	546.26	527.08	511.43	498.52
38000	3408.34	1820.91	1295.07	1034.60	880.26	778.96	707.93	655.80	616.24	585.46	561.02	541.32	525.25	511.99
39000	3498.03	1868.82	1329.15	1061.83	903.43	799.46	726.56	673.06	632.46	600.86	575.78	555.57	539.07	525.47
40000	3587.73	1916.74	1363.23	1089.06	926.59	819.96	745.19	690.32	648.68	616.27	590.55	569.82	552.89	538.94
41000	3677.42	1964.66	1397.31	1116.28	949.76	840.46	763.82	707.58	664.89	631.68	605.31	584.06	566.71	552.41
42000	3767.11	2012.58	1431.39	1143.51	972.92	860.95	782.45	724.84	681.11	647.08	620.08	598.31	580.54	565.89
43000	3856.81	2060.50	1465.47	1170.73	996.09	881.45	801.08	742.09	697.33	662.49	634.84	612.55	594.36	579.36
44000	3946.50	2108.42	1499.55	1197.96	1019.25	901.95	819.71	759.35	713.55	677.90	649.60	626.80	608.18	592.83
45000	4036.19	2156.34	1533.63	1225.19	1042.42	922.45	838.34	776.61	729.76	693.30	664.37	641.04	622.00	606.31
46000	4125.88	2204.25	1567.71	1252.41	1065.58	942.95	856.97	793.87	745.98	708.71	679.13	655.29	635.83	619.78
47000	4215.58	2252.17	1601.79	1279.64	1088.75	963.45	875.60	811.13	762.20	724.12	693.89	669.53	649.65	633.25
48000	4305.27	2300.09	1635.87	1306.87	1111.91	983.95	894.23	828.38	778.41	739.52	708.66	683.78	663.47	646.73
49000	4394.96	2348.01	1669.95	1334.09	1135.08	1004.45	912.86	845.64	794.63	754.93	723.42	698.02	677.29	660.20
50000	4484.66	2395.93	1704.03	1361.32	1158.24	1024.94	931.49	862.90	810.85	770.34	738.18	712.27	691.11	673.67
55000	4933.12	2635.52	1874.44	1497.45	1274.06	1127.44	1024.64	949.19	891.93	847.37	812.00	783.49	760.23	741.04
60000	5381.59	2875.11	2044.84	1633.58	1389.89	1229.93	1117.79	1035.48	973.01	924.40	885.82	854.72	829.34	808.41
65000	5830.05	3114.70	2215.24	1769.71	1505.71	1332.43	1210.94	1121.77	1054.10	1001.44	959.64	925.95	898.45	875.77
70000	6278.52	3354.30	2385.65	1905.84	1621.53	1434.92	1304.08	1208.06	1135.18	1078.47	1033.46	997.17	967.56	943.14
75000	6726.98	3593.89	2556.05	2041.97	1737.36	1537.41	1397.23	1294.35	1216.27	1155.50	1107.27	1068.40	1036.67	1010.51
80000	7175.45	3833.48	2726.45	2178.11	1853.18	1639.91	1490.38	1380.63	1297.35	1232.53	1181.09	1139.63	1105.78	1077.87
85000	7623.91	4073.07	2896.85	2314.24	1969.00	1742.40	1583.53	1466.92	1378.44	1309.57	1254.91	1210.85	1174.89	1145.24
90000	8072.38	4312.67	3067.26	2450.37	2084.83	1844.90	1676.68	1553.21	1459.52	1386.60	1328.73	1282.08	1244.00	1212.61
95000	8520.84	4552.26	3237.66	2586.50	2200.65	1947.39	1769.83	1639.50	1540.60	1463.63	1402.55	1353.30	1313.11	1279.97
100000	8969.31	4791.85	3408.06	2722.63	2316.47	2049.88	1862.98	1725.79	1621.69	1540.67	1476.36	1424.53	1382.22	1347.34

TERM	15 Years	16 Years	17 Years	18 Years	19 Years	20 Years	21 Years	22 Years	23 Years	24 Years	25 Years	30 Years	35 Years	40 Years
AMOUNT														
5	.07	.07	.07	.07	.07	.07	.07	.07	.07	.06	.06	.06	.06	.06
10	.14	.13	.13	.13	.13	.13	.13	.13	.13	.12	.12	.12	.12	.12
15	.20	.20	.20	.19	.19	.19	.19	.19	.19	.18	.18	.18	.18	.18
25	.33	.33	.32	.32	.32	.31	.31	.31	.31	.30	.30	.30	.29	.29
50	.66	.65	.64	.63	.63	.62	.61	.61	.61	.60	.60	.59	.58	.58
75	.99	.98	.96	.95	.94	.93	.92	.92	.91	.90	.90	.88	.87	.87
100	1.32	1.30	1.28	1.26	1.25	1.23	1.22	1.21	1.21	1.20	1.19	1.17	1.16	1.16
200	2.64	2.59	2.55	2.52	2.49	2.46	2.44	2.42	2.41	2.39	2.38	2.34	2.32	2.31
300	3.96	3.89	3.83	3.77	3.73	3.69	3.66	3.63	3.61	3.59	3.57	3.51	3.48	3.47
400	5.28	5.18	5.10	5.03	4.97	4.92	4.88	4.84	4.81	4.78	4.76	4.68	4.64	4.62
500	6.60	6.48	6.37	6.29	6.21	6.15	6.10	6.05	6.01	5.98	5.95	5.85	5.80	5.78
600	7.91	7.77	7.65	7.54	7.45	7.38	7.31	7.26	7.21	7.17	7.14	7.02	6.96	6.93
700	9.23	9.06	8.92	8.80	8.70	8.61	8.53	8.47	8.41	8.37	8.32	8.19	8.12	8.09
800	10.55	10.36	10.19	10.06	9.94	9.84	9.75	9.68	9.61	9.56	9.51	9.36	9.28	9.24
900	11.87	11.65	11.47	11.31	11.18	11.07	10.97	10.89	10.82	10.75	10.70	10.53	10.44	10.40
1000	13.19	12.95	12.74	12.57	12.42	12.30	12.19	12.10	12.02	11.95	11.89	11.70	11.60	11.55
2000	26.37	25.89	25.48	25.13	24.84	24.59	24.37	24.19	24.03	23.89	23.77	23.39	23.20	23.10
3000	39.55	38.83	38.21	37.69	37.25	36.88	36.55	36.28	36.04	35.84	35.66	35.08	34.79	34.65
4000	52.74	51.77	50.95	50.26	49.67	49.17	48.74	48.37	48.05	47.78	47.54	46.77	46.39	46.20
5000	65.92	64.71	63.68	62.82	62.08	61.46	60.92	60.46	60.06	59.72	59.43	58.46	57.98	57.74
6000	79.10	77.65	76.42	75.38	74.50	73.75	73.10	72.08	72.08	71.67	71.31	70.15	69.58	69.29
7000	92.29	90.59	89.16	87.94	86.91	86.04	85.29	84.64	84.09	83.61	83.20	81.84	81.17	80.84
8000	105.47	103.53	101.89	100.51	99.33	98.33	97.47	96.73	96.10	95.55	95.08	93.53	92.77	92.39
9000	118.65	116.47	114.63	113.07	111.75	110.62	109.65	108.82	108.11	107.50	106.97	105.22	104.36	103.93
10000	131.84	129.41	127.36	125.63	124.16	122.91	121.83	120.91	120.12	119.44	118.85	116.91	115.96	115.48
11000	145.02	142.35	140.10	138.20	136.58	135.20	134.02	133.00	132.13	131.38	130.74	128.60	127.55	127.03
12000	158.20	155.29	152.84	150.76	148.99	147.49	146.20	145.09	144.15	143.33	142.62	140.29	139.15	138.58
13000	171.39	168.23	165.57	163.32	161.41	159.78	158.38	157.19	156.16	155.27	154.51	151.98	150.74	150.13
14000	184.57	181.17	178.31	175.88	173.82	172.07	170.57	169.28	168.17	167.21	166.39	163.67	162.34	161.67
15000	197.75	194.11	191.04	188.45	186.24	184.36	182.75	181.37	180.18	179.16	178.28	175.36	173.93	173.22
16000	210.94	207.05	203.78	201.01	198.66	196.65	194.93	193.46	192.19	191.10	190.16	187.05	185.53	184.77
17000	224.12	219.99	216.52	213.57	211.07	208.94	207.11	205.55	204.20	203.05	202.05	198.75	197.12	196.32
18000	237.30	232.93	229.25	226.14	223.49	221.23	219.30	217.64	216.22	214.99	213.93	210.44	208.72	207.86
19000	250.49	245.87	241.99	238.70	235.90	233.52	231.48	229.73	228.23	226.93	225.82	222.13	220.31	219.41
20000	263.67	258.81	254.72	251.26	248.32	245.81	243.66	241.82	240.24	238.88	237.70	233.82	231.91	230.96
21000	276.85	271.75	267.46	263.82	260.73	258.10	255.85	253.91	252.25	250.82	249.59	245.51	243.50	242.51
22000	290.04	284.69	280.20	276.39	273.15	270.39	268.03	266.00	264.26	262.76	261.47	257.20	255.10	254.06
23000	303.22	297.64	292.93	288.95	285.57	282.68	280.21	278.09	276.27	274.71	273.36	268.89	266.69	265.60
24000	316.40	310.58	305.67	301.51	297.98	294.97	292.39	290.18	288.29	286.65	285.24	280.58	278.29	277.15
25000	329.59	323.52	318.40	314.08	310.40	307.26	304.58	302.28	300.30	298.59	297.12	292.27	289.88	288.70
26000	342.77	336.46	331.14	326.64	322.81	319.55	316.76	314.37	312.31	310.54	309.01	303.96	301.48	300.25
27000	355.95	349.40	343.87	339.20	335.23	331.84	328.94	326.46	324.32	322.48	320.89	315.65	313.08	311.79
28000	369.14	362.34	356.61	351.76	347.64	344.13	341.13	338.55	336.33	334.42	332.78	327.34	324.67	323.34
29000	382.32	375.28	369.35	364.33	360.06	356.42	353.31	350.64	348.34	346.37	344.66	339.03	336.27	334.89
30000	395.50	388.22	382.08	376.89	372.48	368.71	365.49	362.73	360.36	358.31	356.55	350.72	347.86	346.44
31000	408.69	401.16	394.82	389.45	384.89	381.00	377.67	374.82	372.37	370.26	368.43	362.41	359.46	357.98
32000	421.87	414.10	407.55	402.01	397.31	393.29	389.86	386.91	384.38	382.20	380.32	374.10	371.05	369.53
33000	435.05	427.04	420.29	414.58	409.72	405.58	402.04	399.00	396.39	394.14	392.20	385.79	382.65	381.08
34000	448.24	439.98	433.03	427.14	422.14	417.87	414.22	411.09	408.40	406.09	404.09	397.49	394.24	392.63
35000	461.42	452.92	445.76	439.70	434.55	430.16	426.41	423.18	420.41	418.03	415.97	409.18	405.84	404.18
36000	474.60	465.86	458.50	452.27	446.97	442.45	438.59	435.27	432.43	429.97	427.86	420.87	417.43	415.72
37000	487.79	478.80	471.23	464.83	459.39	454.74	450.77	447.37	444.44	441.92	439.74	432.56	429.03	427.27
38000	500.97	491.74	483.97	477.39	471.80	467.03	462.95	459.46	456.45	453.86	451.63	444.25	440.62	438.82
39000	514.15	504.68	496.71	489.95	484.22	479.32	475.14	471.55	468.46	465.80	463.51	455.94	452.22	450.37
40000	527.34	517.62	509.44	502.52	496.63	491.61	487.32	483.64	480.47	477.75	475.40	467.63	463.81	461.91
41000	540.52	530.56	522.18	515.08	509.05	503.90	499.50	495.73	492.48	489.69	487.28	479.32	475.41	473.46
42000	553.70	543.50	534.91	527.64	521.46	516.19	511.69	507.82	504.50	501.63	499.17	491.01	487.00	485.01
43000	566.89	556.44	547.65	540.21	533.88	528.48	523.87	519.91	516.51	513.58	511.05	502.70	498.60	496.56
44000	580.07	569.38	560.39	552.77	546.30	540.77	536.05	532.00	528.52	525.52	522.94	514.39	510.19	508.11
45000	593.25	582.33	573.12	565.33	558.71	553.06	548.23	544.09	540.53	537.47	534.82	526.08	521.79	519.65
46000	606.44	595.27	585.86	577.89	571.13	565.36	560.42	556.18	552.54	549.41	546.71	537.77	533.38	531.20
47000	619.62	608.21	598.59	590.46	583.54	577.65	572.60	568.27	564.56	561.35	558.59	549.46	544.98	542.75
48000	632.80	621.15	611.33	603.02	595.96	589.94	584.78	580.36	576.57	573.30	570.47	561.15	556.57	554.30
49000	645.99	634.09	624.06	615.58	608.37	602.23	596.97	592.46	588.58	585.24	582.36	572.84	568.17	565.84
50000	659.17	647.03	636.80	628.15	620.79	614.52	609.15	604.55	600.59	597.18	594.24	584.53	579.76	577.39
55000	725.09	711.73	700.48	690.96	682.87	675.97	670.06	665.00	660.65	656.90	653.67	642.99	637.74	635.13
60000	791.00	776.43	764.16	753.77	744.95	737.42	730.98	725.45	720.71	716.62	713.09	701.44	695.72	692.87
65000	856.92	841.13	827.84	816.59	807.02	798.87	791.89	785.91	780.77	776.34	772.52	759.89	753.69	750.61
70000	922.84	905.84	891.52	879.40	869.10	860.32	852.81	846.36	840.82	836.05	831.94	818.35	811.67	808.35
75000	988.75	970.54	955.20	942.22	931.18	921.77	913.72	906.82	900.88	895.77	891.36	876.80	869.64	866.09
80000	1054.67	1035.24	1018.88	1005.03	993.26	983.22	974.64	967.27	960.94	955.49	950.79	935.25	927.62	923.82
85000	1120.59	1099.94	1082.56	1067.84	1055.34	1044.67	1035.55	1027.73	1021.00	1015.21	1010.21	993.71	985.60	981.56
90000	1186.50	1164.65	1146.24	1130.66	1117.42	1106.12	1096.46	1088.18	1081.06	1074.93	1069.64	1052.16	1043.57	1039.30
95000	1252.42	1229.35	1209.92	1193.47	1179.50	1167.58	1157.38	1148.63	1141.12	1134.64	1129.06	1110.61	1101.55	1097.04
100000	1318.34	1294.05	1273.60	1256.29	1241.57	1229.03	1218.29	1209.09	1201.18	1194.36	1188.48	1169.06	1159.52	1154.78

MONTHLY PAYMENT
REQUIRED TO AMORTIZE A LOAN

TERM AMOUNT	1 Year	2 Years	3 Years	4 Years	5 Years	6 Years	7 Years	8 Years	9 Years	10 Years	11 Years	12 Years	13 Years	14 Years
5	.45	.24	.18	.14	.12	.11	.10	.09	.09	.08	.08	.08	.07	.07
10	.90	.48	.35	.28	.24	.21	.19	.18	.17	.16	.15	.15	.14	.14
15	1.35	.72	.52	.41	.35	.31	.29	.26	.25	.24	.23	.22	.21	.21
25	2.25	1.20	.86	.69	.59	.52	.47	.44	.41	.39	.38	.36	.35	.34
50	4.49	2.40	1.71	1.37	1.17	1.03	.94	.87	.82	.78	.75	.72	.70	.68
75	6.73	3.60	2.56	2.05	1.75	1.55	1.41	1.30	1.22	1.16	1.12	1.08	1.05	1.02
100	8.98	4.80	3.42	2.73	2.33	2.06	1.87	1.74	1.63	1.55	1.49	1.43	1.39	1.36
200	17.95	9.60	6.83	5.46	4.65	4.11	3.74	3.47	3.26	3.10	2.97	2.86	2.78	2.71
300	26.93	14.39	10.24	8.18	6.97	6.17	5.61	5.20	4.88	4.64	4.45	4.29	4.17	4.06
400	35.90	19.19	13.65	10.91	9.29	8.22	7.47	6.93	6.51	6.19	5.93	5.72	5.55	5.41
500	44.87	23.98	17.06	13.64	11.61	10.27	9.34	8.66	8.14	7.73	7.41	7.15	6.94	6.77
600	53.84	28.78	20.48	16.36	13.93	12.33	11.21	10.39	9.76	9.28	8.89	8.58	8.33	8.12
700	62.81	33.57	23.89	19.09	16.25	14.38	13.07	12.12	11.39	10.82	10.37	10.01	9.71	9.47
800	71.79	38.37	27.30	21.82	18.57	16.44	14.94	13.85	13.01	12.37	11.85	11.44	11.10	10.82
900	80.76	43.16	30.71	24.54	20.89	18.49	16.81	15.58	14.64	13.91	13.33	12.87	12.49	12.18
1000	89.73	47.96	34.12	27.27	23.21	20.54	18.68	17.31	16.27	15.46	14.81	14.30	13.88	13.53
2000	179.46	95.91	68.24	54.53	46.41	41.08	37.35	34.61	32.53	30.91	29.62	28.59	27.75	27.05
3000	269.19	143.87	102.36	81.80	69.62	61.62	56.02	51.91	48.79	46.36	44.43	42.88	41.62	40.57
4000	358.92	191.82	136.47	109.06	92.82	82.16	74.69	69.21	65.05	61.81	59.24	57.17	55.49	54.10
5000	448.65	239.77	170.59	136.32	116.02	102.70	93.36	86.51	81.31	77.26	74.05	71.47	69.36	67.62
6000	538.37	287.73	204.71	163.59	139.23	123.24	112.03	103.81	97.57	92.71	88.86	85.76	83.23	81.14
7000	628.10	335.68	238.82	190.85	162.43	143.78	130.70	121.11	113.83	108.17	103.67	100.05	97.10	94.66
8000	717.83	383.64	272.94	218.12	185.63	164.32	149.37	138.41	130.09	123.62	118.48	114.34	110.97	108.19
9000	807.56	431.59	307.06	245.38	208.84	184.85	168.04	155.71	146.35	139.07	133.29	128.64	124.84	121.71
10000	897.29	479.54	341.17	272.64	232.04	205.39	186.72	173.01	162.61	154.52	148.10	142.93	138.71	135.23
11000	987.02	527.50	375.29	299.91	255.24	225.93	205.39	190.31	178.87	169.97	162.91	157.22	152.58	148.75
12000	1076.74	575.45	409.41	327.17	278.45	246.47	224.06	207.61	195.13	185.42	177.72	171.51	166.45	162.28
13000	1166.47	623.41	443.53	354.43	301.65	267.01	242.73	224.91	211.39	200.88	192.53	185.81	180.32	175.80
14000	1256.20	671.36	477.64	381.70	324.85	287.55	261.40	242.21	227.65	216.33	207.34	200.10	194.19	189.32
15000	1345.93	719.31	511.76	408.96	348.06	308.09	280.07	259.51	243.91	231.78	222.15	214.39	208.06	202.84
16000	1435.66	767.27	545.88	436.23	371.26	328.63	298.74	276.81	260.17	247.23	236.96	228.68	221.93	216.37
17000	1525.39	815.22	579.99	463.49	394.46	349.17	317.41	294.11	276.44	262.68	251.77	242.98	235.80	229.89
18000	1615.11	863.17	614.11	490.75	417.67	369.70	336.08	311.41	292.70	278.13	266.58	257.27	249.67	243.41
19000	1704.84	911.13	648.23	518.02	440.87	390.24	354.75	328.71	308.96	293.58	281.39	271.56	263.54	256.93
20000	1794.57	959.08	682.34	545.28	464.07	410.78	373.43	346.01	325.22	309.04	296.20	285.85	277.41	270.46
21000	1884.30	1007.04	716.46	572.55	487.28	431.32	392.10	363.31	341.48	324.49	311.01	300.15	291.28	283.98
22000	1974.03	1054.99	750.58	599.81	510.48	451.86	410.77	380.61	357.74	339.94	325.82	314.44	305.15	297.50
23000	2063.76	1102.94	784.69	627.07	533.69	472.40	429.44	397.92	374.00	355.39	340.63	328.73	319.03	311.03
24000	2153.48	1150.90	818.81	654.34	556.89	492.94	448.11	415.22	390.26	370.84	355.44	343.02	332.90	324.55
25000	2243.21	1198.85	852.93	681.60	580.09	513.48	466.78	432.52	406.52	386.29	370.25	357.32	346.77	338.07
26000	2332.94	1246.81	887.05	708.86	603.30	534.02	485.45	449.82	422.78	401.75	385.06	371.61	360.64	351.59
27000	2422.67	1294.76	921.16	736.13	626.50	554.55	504.12	467.12	439.04	417.20	399.87	385.90	374.51	365.12
28000	2512.40	1342.71	955.28	763.39	649.70	575.09	522.79	484.42	455.30	432.65	414.68	400.19	388.38	378.64
29000	2602.13	1390.67	989.40	790.66	672.91	595.63	541.46	501.72	471.56	448.10	429.49	414.49	402.25	392.16
30000	2691.85	1438.62	1023.51	817.92	696.11	616.17	560.14	519.02	487.82	463.55	444.30	428.78	416.12	405.68
31000	2781.58	1486.57	1057.63	845.18	719.31	636.71	578.81	536.32	504.08	479.00	459.11	443.07	429.99	419.21
32000	2871.31	1534.53	1091.75	872.45	742.52	657.25	597.48	553.62	520.34	494.46	473.91	457.36	443.86	432.73
33000	2961.04	1582.48	1125.86	899.71	765.72	677.79	616.15	570.92	536.61	509.91	488.72	471.66	457.73	446.25
34000	3050.77	1630.44	1159.98	926.97	788.92	698.33	634.82	588.22	552.87	525.36	503.53	485.95	471.60	459.77
35000	3140.50	1678.39	1194.10	954.24	812.13	718.87	653.49	605.52	569.13	540.81	518.34	500.24	485.47	473.30
36000	3230.22	1726.34	1228.22	981.50	835.33	739.40	672.16	622.82	585.39	556.26	533.15	514.53	499.34	486.82
37000	3319.95	1774.30	1262.33	1008.77	858.53	759.94	690.83	640.12	601.65	571.71	547.96	528.83	513.21	500.34
38000	3409.68	1822.25	1296.45	1036.03	881.74	780.48	709.50	657.42	617.91	587.16	562.77	543.12	527.08	513.86
39000	3499.41	1870.21	1330.57	1063.29	904.94	801.02	728.18	674.72	634.17	602.62	577.58	557.41	540.95	527.39
40000	3589.14	1918.16	1364.68	1090.56	928.14	821.56	746.85	692.02	650.43	618.07	592.39	571.70	554.82	540.91
41000	3678.87	1966.11	1398.80	1117.82	951.35	842.10	765.52	709.32	666.69	633.52	607.20	586.00	568.69	554.43
42000	3768.59	2014.07	1432.92	1145.09	974.55	862.64	784.19	726.62	682.95	648.97	622.01	600.29	582.56	567.96
43000	3858.32	2062.02	1467.03	1172.35	997.76	883.18	802.86	743.92	699.21	664.42	636.82	614.58	596.43	581.48
44000	3948.05	2109.97	1501.15	1199.61	1020.96	903.72	821.53	761.22	715.47	679.87	651.63	628.87	610.30	595.00
45000	4037.78	2157.93	1535.27	1226.88	1044.16	924.25	840.20	778.52	731.73	695.33	666.44	643.17	624.18	608.52
46000	4127.51	2205.88	1569.38	1254.14	1067.37	944.79	858.87	795.83	747.99	710.78	681.25	657.46	638.05	622.05
47000	4217.24	2253.84	1603.50	1281.40	1090.57	965.33	877.54	813.13	764.25	726.23	696.06	671.75	651.92	635.57
48000	4306.96	2301.79	1637.62	1308.67	1113.77	985.87	896.21	830.43	780.51	741.68	710.87	686.04	665.79	649.09
49000	4396.69	2349.74	1671.74	1335.93	1136.98	1006.41	914.89	847.73	796.77	757.13	725.68	700.34	679.66	662.61
50000	4486.42	2397.70	1705.85	1363.20	1160.18	1026.95	933.56	865.03	813.04	772.58	740.49	714.63	693.53	676.14
55000	4935.06	2637.47	1876.44	1499.51	1276.20	1129.64	1026.91	951.53	894.34	849.84	814.54	786.09	762.88	743.75
60000	5383.70	2877.24	2047.02	1635.83	1392.21	1232.34	1120.27	1038.03	975.64	927.10	888.59	857.55	832.23	811.36
65000	5832.35	3117.01	2217.61	1772.15	1508.23	1335.03	1213.62	1124.53	1056.94	1004.36	962.63	929.01	901.58	878.98
70000	6280.99	3356.77	2388.19	1908.47	1624.25	1437.73	1306.98	1211.04	1138.25	1081.62	1036.68	1000.48	970.94	946.59
75000	6729.63	3596.54	2558.78	2044.79	1740.27	1540.42	1400.33	1297.54	1219.55	1158.87	1110.73	1071.94	1040.29	1014.20
80000	7178.27	3836.31	2729.36	2181.11	1856.28	1643.11	1493.69	1384.04	1300.85	1236.13	1184.78	1143.40	1109.64	1081.82
85000	7626.91	4076.08	2899.95	2317.43	1972.30	1745.81	1587.04	1470.54	1382.16	1313.39	1258.83	1214.86	1178.99	1149.43
90000	8075.55	4315.85	3070.53	2453.75	2088.32	1848.50	1680.40	1557.04	1463.46	1390.65	1332.88	1286.33	1248.35	1217.04
95000	8524.20	4555.62	3241.12	2590.07	2204.34	1951.20	1773.75	1643.55	1544.76	1467.90	1406.92	1357.79	1317.70	1284.65
100000	8972.84	4795.39	3411.70	2726.39	2320.35	2053.89	1867.11	1730.05	1626.07	1545.16	1480.97	1429.25	1387.05	1352.27

MONTHLY PAYMENT
REQUIRED TO AMORTIZE A LOAN

13.875%

TERM AMOUNT	15 Years	16 Years	17 Years	18 Years	19 Years	20 Years	21 Years	22 Years	23 Years	24 Years	25 Years	30 Years	35 Years	40 Years
5	.07	.07	.07	.07	.07	.07	.07	.07	.07	.07	.06	.06	.06	.06
10	.14	.13	.13	.13	.13	.13	.13	.13	.13	.13	.12	.12	.12	.12
15	.20	.20	.20	.19	.19	.19	.19	.19	.19	.19	.18	.18	.18	.18
25	.34	.33	.32	.32	.32	.31	.31	.31	.31	.31	.30	.30	.30	.30
50	.67	.65	.64	.64	.63	.62	.62	.61	.61	.61	.60	.59	.59	.59
75	1.00	.98	.96	.95	.94	.93	.92	.92	.91	.91	.90	.89	.88	.88
100	1.33	1.30	1.28	1.27	1.25	1.24	1.23	1.22	1.21	1.21	1.20	1.18	1.17	1.17
200	2.65	2.60	2.56	2.53	2.50	2.47	2.45	2.43	2.42	2.41	2.39	2.35	2.34	2.33
300	3.98	3.90	3.84	3.79	3.75	3.71	3.68	3.65	3.63	3.61	3.59	3.53	3.50	3.49
400	5.30	5.20	5.12	5.05	4.99	4.94	4.90	4.86	4.83	4.81	4.78	4.70	4.67	4.65
500	6.62	6.50	6.40	6.31	6.24	6.18	6.12	6.08	6.04	6.01	5.98	5.88	5.83	5.81
600	7.95	7.80	7.68	7.57	7.49	7.41	7.35	7.29	7.25	7.21	7.17	7.05	7.00	6.97
700	9.27	9.10	8.96	8.84	8.73	8.65	8.57	8.51	8.45	8.41	8.36	8.23	8.16	8.13
800	10.59	10.40	10.24	10.10	9.98	9.88	9.80	9.72	9.66	9.61	9.56	9.40	9.33	9.29
900	11.92	11.70	11.51	11.36	11.23	11.12	11.02	10.94	10.87	10.81	10.75	10.58	10.50	10.45
1000	13.24	13.00	12.79	12.62	12.47	12.35	12.24	12.15	12.07	12.01	11.95	11.75	11.66	11.61
2000	26.47	25.99	25.58	25.24	24.94	24.69	24.48	24.30	24.14	24.01	23.89	23.50	23.32	23.22
3000	39.71	38.98	38.37	37.85	37.41	37.04	36.72	36.44	36.21	36.01	35.83	35.25	34.97	34.83
4000	52.94	51.97	51.16	50.47	49.88	49.38	48.96	48.59	48.28	48.01	47.77	47.00	46.63	46.44
5000	66.17	64.96	63.94	63.08	62.35	61.73	61.19	60.74	60.34	60.01	59.72	58.75	58.28	58.05
6000	79.41	77.95	76.73	75.70	74.82	74.07	73.43	72.88	72.41	72.01	71.66	70.50	69.94	69.66
7000	92.64	90.95	89.52	88.31	87.29	86.42	85.67	85.03	84.48	84.01	83.60	82.25	81.60	81.27
8000	105.87	103.94	102.31	100.93	99.76	98.76	97.91	97.18	96.55	96.01	95.54	94.00	93.25	92.88
9000	119.11	116.93	115.10	113.55	112.23	111.11	110.15	109.32	108.62	108.01	107.48	105.75	104.91	104.49
10000	132.34	129.92	127.88	126.16	124.70	123.45	122.38	121.47	120.68	120.01	119.43	117.50	116.56	116.10
11000	145.57	142.91	140.67	138.78	137.17	135.79	134.62	133.62	132.75	132.01	131.37	129.25	128.22	127.70
12000	158.81	155.90	153.46	151.39	149.64	148.14	146.86	145.76	144.82	144.01	143.31	141.00	139.87	139.31
13000	172.04	168.90	166.25	164.01	162.11	160.48	159.10	157.91	156.89	156.01	155.25	152.75	151.53	150.92
14000	185.27	181.89	179.04	176.62	174.57	172.83	171.34	170.06	168.96	168.01	167.19	164.50	163.19	162.53
15000	198.51	194.88	191.82	189.24	187.04	185.17	183.57	182.20	181.02	180.01	179.14	176.25	174.84	174.14
16000	211.74	207.87	204.61	201.86	199.51	197.52	195.81	194.35	193.09	192.01	191.08	188.00	186.50	185.75
17000	224.98	220.86	217.40	214.47	211.98	209.86	208.05	206.49	205.16	204.01	203.02	199.75	198.15	197.36
18000	238.21	233.85	230.19	227.09	224.45	222.21	220.29	218.64	217.23	216.01	214.96	211.50	209.81	208.97
19000	251.44	246.85	242.98	239.70	236.92	234.55	232.52	230.79	229.30	228.01	226.90	223.25	221.46	220.58
20000	264.68	259.84	255.76	252.32	249.39	246.90	244.76	242.93	241.36	240.01	238.85	235.00	233.12	232.19
21000	277.91	272.83	268.55	264.93	261.86	259.24	257.00	255.08	253.43	252.01	250.79	246.75	244.78	243.80
22000	291.14	285.82	281.34	277.55	274.33	271.58	269.24	267.23	265.50	264.01	262.73	258.50	256.43	255.40
23000	304.38	298.81	294.13	290.16	286.80	283.93	281.48	279.37	277.57	276.01	274.67	270.25	268.09	267.01
24000	317.61	311.80	306.92	302.78	299.27	296.27	293.71	291.52	289.63	288.01	286.61	282.00	279.74	278.62
25000	330.84	324.79	319.70	315.40	311.74	308.62	305.95	303.67	301.70	300.01	298.56	293.75	291.40	290.23
26000	344.08	337.79	332.49	328.01	324.21	320.96	318.19	315.81	313.77	312.01	310.50	305.50	303.05	301.84
27000	357.31	350.78	345.28	340.63	336.68	333.31	330.43	327.96	325.84	324.01	322.44	317.25	314.71	313.45
28000	370.54	363.77	358.07	353.24	349.14	345.65	342.67	340.11	337.91	336.01	334.38	329.00	326.37	325.06
29000	383.78	376.76	370.85	365.86	361.61	358.00	354.90	352.25	349.97	348.01	346.32	340.75	338.02	336.67
30000	397.01	389.75	383.64	378.47	374.08	370.34	367.14	364.40	362.04	360.01	358.27	352.50	349.68	348.28
31000	410.24	402.74	396.43	391.09	386.55	382.69	379.38	376.54	374.11	372.01	370.21	364.25	361.33	359.89
32000	423.48	415.74	409.22	403.71	399.02	395.03	391.62	388.69	386.18	384.02	382.15	376.00	372.99	371.50
33000	436.71	428.73	422.01	416.32	411.49	407.37	403.85	400.84	398.25	396.02	394.09	387.75	384.64	383.10
34000	449.95	441.72	434.79	428.94	423.96	419.72	416.09	412.98	410.31	408.02	406.03	399.50	396.30	394.71
35000	463.18	454.71	447.58	441.55	436.43	432.06	428.33	425.13	422.38	420.02	417.98	411.25	407.96	406.32
36000	476.41	467.70	460.37	454.17	448.90	444.41	440.57	437.28	434.45	432.02	429.92	423.00	419.61	417.93
37000	489.65	480.69	473.16	466.78	461.37	456.75	452.81	449.42	446.52	444.02	441.86	434.75	431.27	429.54
38000	502.88	493.69	485.95	479.40	473.84	469.10	465.04	461.57	458.59	456.02	453.80	446.50	442.92	441.15
39000	516.11	506.68	498.73	492.01	486.31	481.44	477.28	473.72	470.65	468.02	465.74	458.25	454.58	452.76
40000	529.35	519.67	511.52	504.63	498.78	493.79	489.52	485.86	482.72	480.02	477.69	470.00	466.23	464.37
41000	542.58	532.66	524.31	517.25	511.25	506.13	501.76	498.01	494.79	492.02	489.63	481.75	477.89	475.98
42000	555.81	545.65	537.10	529.86	523.71	518.48	514.00	510.16	506.86	504.02	501.57	493.50	489.55	487.59
43000	569.05	558.64	549.89	542.48	536.18	530.82	526.23	522.30	518.92	516.02	513.51	505.25	501.20	499.20
44000	582.28	571.64	562.67	555.09	548.65	543.16	538.47	534.45	530.99	528.02	525.45	517.00	512.86	510.80
45000	595.51	584.63	575.46	567.71	561.12	555.51	550.71	546.59	543.06	540.02	537.40	528.75	524.51	522.41
46000	608.75	597.62	588.25	580.32	573.59	567.85	562.94	558.74	555.13	552.02	549.34	540.50	536.17	534.02
47000	621.98	610.61	601.04	592.94	586.06	580.20	575.18	570.89	567.20	564.02	561.28	552.25	547.82	545.63
48000	635.21	623.60	613.83	605.56	598.53	592.54	587.42	583.03	579.26	576.02	573.22	564.00	559.48	557.24
49000	648.45	636.59	626.61	618.17	611.00	604.89	599.66	595.18	591.33	588.02	585.17	575.75	571.14	568.85
50000	661.68	649.58	639.40	630.79	623.47	617.23	611.90	607.33	603.40	600.02	597.11	587.50	582.79	580.46
55000	727.85	714.54	703.34	693.86	685.82	678.95	673.09	668.06	663.74	660.02	656.82	646.25	641.07	638.50
60000	794.02	779.50	767.28	756.94	748.16	740.68	734.28	728.79	724.08	720.02	716.53	705.00	699.35	696.55
65000	860.18	844.46	831.22	820.02	810.51	802.40	795.47	789.52	784.42	780.03	776.24	763.75	757.63	754.60
70000	926.35	909.42	895.16	883.10	872.85	864.12	856.66	850.26	844.76	840.03	835.95	822.49	815.91	812.64
75000	992.52	974.37	959.10	946.18	935.20	925.84	917.85	910.99	905.10	900.03	895.66	881.24	874.19	870.69
80000	1058.69	1039.33	1023.04	1009.26	997.55	987.57	979.03	971.72	965.44	960.03	955.37	939.99	932.46	928.73
85000	1124.86	1104.29	1086.98	1072.33	1059.89	1049.29	1040.22	1032.45	1025.78	1020.03	1015.08	998.74	990.74	986.78
90000	1191.02	1169.25	1150.92	1135.41	1122.24	1111.01	1101.41	1093.18	1086.12	1080.03	1074.79	1057.49	1049.02	1044.82
95000	1257.19	1234.21	1214.86	1198.49	1184.59	1172.74	1162.60	1153.92	1146.46	1140.03	1134.50	1116.24	1107.30	1102.87
100000	1323.36	1299.16	1278.80	1261.57	1246.93	1234.46	1223.79	1214.65	1206.80	1200.04	1194.21	1174.99	1165.58	1160.91

13.900%

TERM AMOUNT	1 Year	2 Years	3 Years	4 Years	5 Years	6 Years	7 Years	8 Years	9 Years	10 Years	11 Years	12 Years	13 Years	14 Years
5	.45	.24	.18	.14	.12	.11	.10	.09	.09	.08	.08	.08	.07	.07
10	.90	.48	.35	.28	.24	.21	.19	.18	.17	.16	.15	.15	.14	.14
15	1.35	.72	.52	.41	.35	.31	.29	.26	.25	.24	.23	.22	.21	.21
25	2.25	1.20	.86	.69	.59	.52	.47	.44	.41	.39	.38	.36	.35	.34
50	4.49	2.40	1.71	1.37	1.17	1.03	.94	.87	.82	.78	.75	.72	.70	.68
75	6.74	3.60	2.56	2.05	1.75	1.55	1.41	1.30	1.23	1.16	1.12	1.08	1.05	1.02
100	8.98	4.80	3.42	2.73	2.33	2.06	1.87	1.74	1.63	1.55	1.49	1.44	1.39	1.36
200	17.95	9.60	6.83	5.46	4.65	4.12	3.74	3.47	3.26	3.10	2.97	2.87	2.78	2.71
300	26.93	14.39	10.24	8.19	6.97	6.17	5.61	5.20	4.89	4.64	4.45	4.30	4.17	4.07
400	35.90	19.19	13.66	10.92	9.29	8.23	7.48	6.93	6.52	6.19	5.94	5.73	5.56	5.42
500	44.88	23.99	17.07	13.64	11.61	10.28	9.35	8.66	8.14	7.74	7.42	7.16	6.95	6.77
600	53.85	28.78	20.48	16.37	13.93	12.34	11.22	10.39	9.77	9.28	8.90	8.59	8.34	8.13
700	62.82	33.58	23.90	19.10	16.26	14.39	13.08	12.13	11.40	10.83	10.38	10.02	9.73	9.48
800	71.80	38.38	27.31	21.83	18.58	16.45	14.95	13.86	13.03	12.38	11.87	11.45	11.11	10.84
900	80.77	43.17	30.72	24.55	20.90	18.50	16.82	15.59	14.65	13.92	13.35	12.88	12.50	12.19
1000	89.75	47.97	34.13	27.28	23.22	20.56	18.69	17.32	16.28	15.47	14.83	14.31	13.89	13.54
2000	179.49	95.94	68.26	54.56	46.44	41.11	37.37	34.63	32.56	30.94	29.66	28.62	27.78	27.08
3000	269.23	143.90	102.39	81.83	69.65	61.66	56.06	51.95	48.83	46.40	44.48	42.93	41.66	40.62
4000	358.97	191.87	136.52	109.11	92.87	82.21	74.74	69.26	65.11	61.87	59.31	57.24	55.55	54.16
5000	448.71	239.83	170.65	136.39	116.09	102.77	93.43	86.58	81.38	77.34	74.13	71.55	69.44	67.70
6000	538.45	287.80	204.78	163.66	139.30	123.32	112.11	103.89	97.66	92.80	88.96	85.85	83.32	81.24
7000	628.19	335.76	238.91	190.94	162.52	143.87	130.80	121.21	113.93	108.27	103.78	100.16	97.21	94.78
8000	717.93	383.73	273.04	218.22	185.74	164.42	149.48	138.52	130.21	123.74	118.61	114.47	111.10	108.32
9000	807.67	431.70	307.17	245.49	208.95	184.98	168.17	155.84	146.48	139.20	133.43	128.78	124.98	121.86
10000	897.41	479.66	341.30	272.77	232.17	205.53	186.85	173.15	162.76	154.67	148.26	143.09	138.87	135.40
11000	987.15	527.63	375.42	300.04	255.39	226.08	205.54	190.47	179.03	170.14	163.08	157.40	152.76	148.93
12000	1076.89	575.59	409.55	327.32	278.60	246.63	224.22	207.78	195.31	185.60	177.91	171.70	166.64	162.47
13000	1166.63	623.56	443.68	354.60	301.82	267.18	242.91	225.10	211.58	201.07	192.73	186.01	180.53	176.01
14000	1256.37	671.52	477.81	381.87	325.04	287.74	261.59	242.41	227.86	216.54	207.56	200.32	194.42	189.55
15000	1346.11	719.49	511.94	409.15	348.25	308.29	280.28	259.72	244.13	232.00	222.38	214.63	208.30	203.09
16000	1435.85	767.46	546.07	436.43	371.47	328.84	298.96	277.04	260.41	247.47	237.21	228.94	222.19	216.63
17000	1525.59	815.42	580.20	463.70	394.68	349.39	317.65	294.35	276.68	262.94	252.03	243.24	236.08	230.17
18000	1615.33	863.39	614.33	490.98	417.90	369.95	336.33	311.67	292.96	278.40	266.86	257.55	249.96	243.71
19000	1705.07	911.35	648.46	518.26	441.12	390.50	355.02	328.98	309.23	293.87	281.68	271.86	263.85	257.25
20000	1794.81	959.32	682.59	545.53	464.33	411.05	373.70	346.30	325.51	309.34	296.51	286.17	277.74	270.79
21000	1884.55	1007.28	716.72	572.81	487.55	431.60	392.39	363.61	341.78	324.80	311.33	300.48	291.62	284.33
22000	1974.29	1055.25	750.84	600.08	510.77	452.15	411.07	380.93	358.06	340.27	326.16	314.79	305.51	297.86
23000	2064.03	1103.22	784.97	627.36	533.98	472.71	429.76	398.24	374.33	355.74	340.98	329.09	319.40	311.40
24000	2153.77	1151.18	819.10	654.64	557.20	493.26	448.44	415.56	390.61	371.20	355.81	343.40	333.28	324.94
25000	2243.51	1199.15	853.23	681.91	580.42	513.81	467.13	432.87	406.89	386.67	370.63	357.71	347.17	338.48
26000	2333.25	1247.11	887.36	709.19	603.63	534.36	485.81	450.19	423.16	402.14	385.46	372.02	361.06	352.02
27000	2422.99	1295.08	921.49	736.47	626.85	554.92	504.49	467.50	439.44	417.60	400.28	386.33	374.94	365.56
28000	2512.73	1343.04	955.62	763.74	650.07	575.47	523.18	484.81	455.71	433.07	415.11	400.63	388.83	379.10
29000	2602.47	1391.01	989.75	791.02	673.28	596.02	541.86	502.13	471.99	448.54	429.93	414.94	402.71	392.64
30000	2692.21	1438.97	1023.88	818.30	696.50	616.57	560.55	519.44	488.26	464.00	444.76	429.25	416.60	406.18
31000	2781.95	1486.94	1058.01	845.57	719.71	637.12	579.23	536.76	504.54	479.47	459.58	443.56	430.49	419.72
32000	2871.69	1534.91	1092.14	872.85	742.93	657.68	597.92	554.07	520.81	494.94	474.41	457.87	444.37	433.26
33000	2961.43	1582.87	1126.26	900.12	766.15	678.23	616.60	571.39	537.09	510.40	489.23	472.18	458.26	446.79
34000	3051.17	1630.84	1160.39	927.40	789.36	698.78	635.29	588.70	553.36	525.87	504.06	486.48	472.15	460.33
35000	3140.91	1678.80	1194.52	954.68	812.58	719.33	653.97	606.02	569.64	541.34	518.88	500.79	486.03	473.87
36000	3230.65	1726.77	1228.65	981.95	835.80	739.89	672.66	623.33	585.91	556.80	533.71	515.10	499.92	487.41
37000	3320.39	1774.73	1262.78	1009.23	859.01	760.44	691.34	640.65	602.19	572.27	548.53	529.41	513.81	500.95
38000	3410.13	1822.70	1296.91	1036.51	882.23	780.99	710.03	657.96	618.46	587.73	563.36	543.72	527.69	514.49
39000	3499.87	1870.67	1331.04	1063.78	905.45	801.54	728.71	675.28	634.74	603.20	578.18	558.02	541.58	528.03
40000	3589.61	1918.63	1365.17	1091.06	928.66	822.09	747.40	692.59	651.01	618.67	593.01	572.33	555.47	541.57
41000	3679.35	1966.60	1399.30	1118.33	951.88	842.65	766.08	709.91	667.29	634.13	607.83	586.64	569.35	555.11
42000	3769.09	2014.56	1433.43	1145.61	975.10	863.20	784.77	727.22	683.56	649.60	622.66	600.95	583.24	568.65
43000	3858.83	2062.53	1467.56	1172.89	998.31	883.75	803.45	744.53	699.84	665.07	637.48	615.26	597.13	582.18
44000	3948.57	2110.49	1501.68	1200.16	1021.53	904.30	822.14	761.85	716.11	680.53	652.31	629.57	611.01	595.72
45000	4038.31	2158.46	1535.81	1227.44	1044.74	924.86	840.82	779.16	732.39	696.00	667.13	643.87	624.90	609.26
46000	4128.05	2206.43	1569.94	1254.72	1067.96	945.41	859.51	796.48	748.66	711.47	681.96	658.18	638.79	622.80
47000	4217.79	2254.39	1604.07	1281.99	1091.18	965.96	878.19	813.79	764.94	726.93	696.78	672.49	652.67	636.34
48000	4307.53	2302.36	1638.20	1309.27	1114.39	986.51	896.88	831.11	781.22	742.40	711.61	686.80	666.56	649.88
49000	4397.27	2350.32	1672.33	1336.55	1137.61	1007.06	915.56	848.42	797.49	757.87	726.43	701.11	680.45	663.42
50000	4487.01	2398.29	1706.46	1363.82	1160.83	1027.62	934.25	865.74	813.77	773.33	741.26	715.41	694.33	676.96
55000	4935.71	2638.12	1877.10	1500.20	1276.91	1130.38	1027.67	952.31	895.14	850.67	815.38	786.96	763.77	744.65
60000	5384.41	2877.94	2047.75	1636.59	1392.99	1233.14	1121.09	1038.88	976.52	928.00	889.51	858.50	833.20	812.35
65000	5833.11	3117.77	2218.40	1772.97	1509.07	1335.90	1214.52	1125.46	1057.89	1005.33	963.63	930.04	902.63	880.04
70000	6281.81	3357.60	2389.04	1909.35	1625.16	1438.66	1307.94	1212.03	1139.27	1082.67	1037.76	1001.58	972.06	947.74
75000	6730.51	3597.43	2559.69	2045.73	1741.24	1541.42	1401.37	1298.60	1220.65	1160.00	1111.88	1073.12	1041.50	1015.43
80000	7179.21	3837.26	2730.33	2182.11	1857.32	1644.18	1494.79	1385.18	1302.02	1237.33	1186.01	1144.66	1110.93	1083.13
85000	7627.91	4077.09	2900.98	2318.49	1973.40	1746.94	1588.21	1471.75	1383.40	1314.66	1260.14	1216.20	1180.36	1150.83
90000	8076.61	4316.91	3071.62	2454.88	2089.48	1849.71	1681.64	1558.32	1464.77	1392.00	1334.26	1287.74	1249.79	1218.52
95000	8525.31	4556.74	3242.27	2591.26	2205.57	1952.47	1775.06	1644.90	1546.15	1469.33	1408.39	1359.28	1319.23	1286.22
100000	8974.01	4796.57	3412.91	2727.64	2321.65	2055.23	1868.49	1731.47	1627.53	1546.66	1482.51	1430.82	1388.66	1353.91

TERM	15 Years	16 Years	17 Years	18 Years	19 Years	20 Years	21 Years	22 Years	23 Years	24 Years	25 Years	30 Years	35 Years	40 Years
AMOUNT														
5	.07	.07	.07	.07	.07	.07	.07	.07	.07	.07	.06	.06	.06	.06
10	.14	.14	.13	.13	.13	.13	.13	.13	.13	.13	.12	.12	.12	.12
15	.20	.20	.20	.19	.19	.19	.19	.19	.19	.19	.18	.18	.18	.18
25	.34	.33	.33	.32	.32	.31	.31	.31	.31	.31	.30	.30	.30	.30
50	.67	.66	.65	.64	.63	.62	.62	.61	.61	.61	.60	.59	.59	.59
75	1.00	.98	.97	.95	.94	.93	.92	.92	.91	.91	.90	.89	.88	.88
100	1.33	1.31	1.29	1.27	1.25	1.24	1.23	1.22	1.21	1.21	1.20	1.18	1.17	1.17
200	2.66	2.61	2.57	2.53	2.50	2.48	2.46	2.44	2.42	2.41	2.40	2.36	2.34	2.33
300	3.98	3.91	3.85	3.79	3.75	3.71	3.68	3.65	3.63	3.61	3.59	3.54	3.51	3.49
400	5.31	5.21	5.13	5.06	5.00	4.95	4.91	4.87	4.84	4.81	4.79	4.71	4.68	4.66
500	6.63	6.51	6.41	6.32	6.25	6.19	6.13	6.09	6.05	6.01	5.99	5.89	5.84	5.82
600	7.96	7.81	7.69	7.58	7.50	7.42	7.36	7.30	7.26	7.22	7.18	7.07	7.01	6.98
700	9.28	9.11	8.97	8.85	8.75	8.66	8.58	8.52	8.47	8.42	8.38	8.24	8.18	8.15
800	10.61	10.41	10.25	10.11	9.99	9.90	9.81	9.74	9.67	9.62	9.57	9.42	9.35	9.31
900	11.93	11.71	11.53	11.37	11.24	11.13	11.04	10.95	10.88	10.82	10.77	10.60	10.51	10.47
1000	13.26	13.01	12.81	12.64	12.49	12.37	12.26	12.17	12.09	12.02	11.97	11.77	11.68	11.63
2000	26.51	26.02	25.62	25.27	24.98	24.73	24.52	24.33	24.18	24.04	23.93	23.54	23.36	23.26
3000	39.76	39.03	38.42	37.90	37.47	37.09	36.77	36.50	36.26	36.06	35.89	35.31	35.03	34.89
4000	53.01	52.04	51.23	50.54	49.95	49.46	49.03	48.66	48.35	48.08	47.85	47.08	46.71	46.52
5000	66.26	65.05	64.03	63.17	62.44	61.82	61.29	60.83	60.44	60.10	59.81	58.85	58.38	58.15
6000	79.51	78.06	76.84	75.80	74.93	74.18	73.54	72.99	72.52	72.12	71.77	70.62	70.06	69.78
7000	92.76	91.07	89.64	88.44	87.42	86.54	85.80	85.16	84.61	84.14	83.73	82.39	81.74	81.41
8000	106.01	104.07	102.45	101.07	99.90	98.91	98.05	97.32	96.70	96.16	95.69	94.16	93.41	93.04
9000	119.26	117.08	115.25	113.70	112.39	111.27	110.31	109.49	108.78	108.18	107.66	105.93	105.09	104.67
10000	132.51	130.09	128.06	126.34	124.88	123.63	122.57	121.65	120.87	120.20	119.62	117.70	116.76	116.30
11000	145.76	143.10	140.86	138.97	137.36	135.99	134.82	133.82	132.96	132.22	131.58	129.47	128.44	127.93
12000	159.01	156.11	153.67	151.60	149.85	148.36	147.08	145.98	145.04	144.24	143.54	141.24	140.12	139.56
13000	172.26	169.12	166.47	164.24	162.34	160.72	159.34	158.15	157.13	156.26	155.50	153.01	151.79	151.19
14000	185.51	182.13	179.28	176.87	174.83	173.08	171.59	170.31	169.22	168.27	167.46	164.78	163.47	162.82
15000	198.76	195.13	192.08	189.50	187.31	185.44	183.85	182.48	181.30	180.29	179.42	176.55	175.14	174.45
16000	212.01	208.14	204.89	202.14	199.80	197.81	196.10	194.64	193.39	192.31	191.38	188.32	186.82	186.08
17000	225.26	221.15	217.69	214.77	212.29	210.17	208.36	206.81	205.48	204.33	203.34	200.09	198.50	197.71
18000	238.51	234.16	230.50	227.40	224.77	222.53	220.62	218.97	217.56	216.35	215.31	211.86	210.17	209.34
19000	251.76	247.17	243.31	240.04	237.26	234.90	232.87	231.14	229.65	228.37	227.27	223.63	221.85	220.97
20000	265.01	260.18	256.11	252.67	249.75	247.26	245.13	243.30	241.74	240.39	239.23	235.40	233.52	232.60
21000	278.26	273.19	268.92	265.30	262.24	259.62	257.39	255.47	253.82	252.41	251.19	247.17	245.20	244.23
22000	291.51	286.20	281.72	277.94	271.72	271.98	269.64	267.63	265.91	264.43	263.15	258.94	256.88	255.86
23000	304.76	299.20	294.53	290.57	287.21	284.35	281.90	279.80	278.00	276.45	275.11	270.71	268.55	267.48
24000	318.01	312.21	307.33	303.20	299.70	296.71	294.15	291.96	290.08	288.47	287.07	282.48	280.23	279.11
25000	331.26	325.22	320.14	315.84	312.18	309.07	306.41	304.13	302.17	300.49	299.03	294.25	291.90	290.74
26000	344.51	338.23	332.94	328.47	324.67	321.43	318.67	316.29	314.26	312.51	310.99	306.01	303.58	302.37
27000	357.76	351.24	345.75	341.10	337.16	333.80	330.92	328.46	326.34	324.52	322.96	317.78	315.26	314.00
28000	371.01	364.25	358.55	353.74	349.65	346.16	343.18	340.62	338.43	336.54	334.92	329.55	326.93	325.63
29000	384.26	377.26	371.36	366.37	362.13	358.52	355.44	352.79	350.52	348.56	346.88	341.32	338.61	337.26
30000	397.51	390.26	384.16	379.00	374.62	370.88	367.69	364.95	362.60	360.58	358.84	353.09	350.28	348.89
31000	410.76	403.27	396.97	391.64	387.11	383.25	379.95	377.12	374.69	372.60	370.80	364.86	361.96	360.52
32000	424.01	416.28	409.77	404.27	399.59	395.61	392.20	389.28	386.78	384.62	382.76	376.63	373.63	372.15
33000	437.26	429.29	422.58	416.90	412.08	407.97	404.46	401.45	398.86	396.64	394.72	388.40	385.31	383.78
34000	450.52	442.30	435.38	429.54	424.57	420.33	416.72	413.61	410.95	408.66	406.68	400.17	396.99	395.41
35000	463.77	455.31	448.19	442.17	437.06	432.70	428.97	425.78	423.04	420.68	418.65	411.94	408.66	407.04
36000	477.02	468.32	460.99	454.80	449.54	445.06	441.23	437.94	435.12	432.70	430.61	423.71	420.34	418.67
37000	490.27	481.33	473.80	467.44	462.03	457.42	453.48	450.11	447.21	444.72	442.57	435.48	432.01	430.30
38000	503.52	494.33	486.61	480.07	474.52	469.79	465.74	462.27	459.30	456.74	454.53	447.25	443.69	441.93
39000	516.77	507.34	499.41	492.70	487.00	482.15	478.00	474.44	471.38	468.76	466.49	459.02	455.37	453.56
40000	530.02	520.35	512.22	505.34	499.49	494.51	490.25	486.60	483.47	480.77	478.45	470.79	467.04	465.19
41000	543.27	533.36	525.02	517.97	511.98	506.87	502.51	498.77	495.56	492.79	490.41	482.56	478.72	476.82
42000	556.52	546.37	537.83	530.60	524.47	519.24	514.77	510.93	507.64	504.81	502.37	494.33	490.39	488.45
43000	569.77	559.38	550.63	543.23	536.95	531.60	527.02	523.10	519.73	516.83	514.33	506.10	502.07	500.08
44000	583.02	572.39	563.44	555.87	549.44	543.96	539.28	535.26	531.82	528.85	526.30	517.87	513.75	511.71
45000	596.27	585.39	576.24	568.50	561.93	556.32	551.53	547.43	543.90	540.87	538.26	529.64	525.42	523.33
46000	609.52	598.40	589.05	581.13	574.41	568.69	563.79	559.59	555.99	552.89	550.22	541.41	537.10	534.96
47000	622.77	611.41	601.85	593.77	586.90	581.05	576.05	571.76	568.08	564.91	562.18	553.18	548.77	546.59
48000	636.02	624.42	614.66	606.40	599.39	593.41	588.30	583.92	580.16	576.93	574.14	564.95	560.45	558.22
49000	649.27	637.43	627.46	619.03	611.88	605.77	600.56	596.09	592.25	588.95	586.10	576.72	572.13	569.85
50000	662.52	650.44	640.27	631.67	624.36	618.14	612.82	608.25	604.34	600.97	598.06	588.49	583.80	581.48
55000	728.77	715.48	704.29	694.83	686.80	679.95	674.10	669.08	664.77	661.06	657.87	647.33	642.18	639.63
60000	795.02	780.52	768.32	758.00	749.23	741.76	735.38	729.90	725.20	721.16	717.67	706.18	700.56	697.78
65000	861.27	845.57	832.35	821.17	811.67	803.58	796.66	790.73	785.64	781.26	777.48	765.03	758.94	755.93
70000	927.53	910.61	896.37	884.33	874.11	865.39	857.94	851.55	846.07	841.35	837.29	823.88	817.32	814.07
75000	993.78	975.65	960.40	947.50	936.54	927.20	919.22	912.38	906.50	901.45	897.09	882.73	875.70	872.22
80000	1060.03	1040.70	1024.43	1010.67	998.98	989.02	980.50	973.20	966.94	961.54	956.90	941.57	934.08	930.37
85000	1126.28	1105.74	1088.45	1073.83	1061.41	1050.83	1041.78	1034.03	1027.37	1021.64	1016.70	1000.42	992.46	988.52
90000	1192.53	1170.78	1152.48	1137.00	1123.85	1112.64	1103.06	1094.85	1087.80	1081.74	1076.51	1059.27	1050.84	1046.66
95000	1258.78	1235.83	1216.51	1200.16	1186.28	1174.46	1164.35	1155.68	1148.24	1141.83	1136.31	1118.12	1109.22	1104.81
100000	1325.03	1300.87	1280.53	1263.33	1248.72	1236.27	1225.63	1216.50	1208.67	1201.93	1196.12	1176.97	1167.60	1162.96

MONTHLY PAYMENT
REQUIRED TO AMORTIZE A LOAN

TERM	1 Year	2 Years	3 Years	4 Years	5 Years	6 Years	7 Years	8 Years	9 Years	10 Years	11 Years	12 Years	13 Years	14 Years
AMOUNT														
5	.45	.25	.18	.14	.12	.11	.10	.09	.09	.08	.08	.08	.07	.07
10	.90	.49	.35	.28	.24	.21	.19	.18	.17	.16	.15	.15	.14	.14
15	1.35	.73	.52	.41	.35	.31	.29	.27	.25	.24	.23	.22	.21	.21
25	2.25	1.21	.86	.69	.59	.52	.47	.44	.41	.39	.38	.36	.35	.35
50	4.49	2.41	1.71	1.37	1.17	1.04	.94	.87	.82	.78	.75	.72	.70	.69
75	6.74	3.61	2.57	2.05	1.75	1.55	1.41	1.31	1.23	1.17	1.12	1.08	1.05	1.03
100	8.98	4.81	3.42	2.74	2.33	2.07	1.88	1.74	1.64	1.56	1.49	1.44	1.40	1.37
200	17.96	9.61	6.84	5.47	4.66	4.13	3.75	3.48	3.27	3.11	2.98	2.88	2.80	2.73
300	26.94	14.41	10.26	8.20	6.99	6.19	5.63	5.22	4.91	4.66	4.47	4.32	4.19	4.09
400	35.92	19.21	15.00	10.94	9.31	8.25	7.50	6.95	6.54	6.22	5.96	5.75	5.59	5.45
500	44.90	24.01	17.09	13.67	11.64	10.31	9.38	8.69	8.17	7.77	7.45	7.19	6.98	6.81
600	53.88	28.81	20.51	16.40	13.97	12.37	11.25	10.43	9.81	9.32	8.94	8.63	8.38	8.17
700	62.86	33.61	23.93	19.13	16.29	14.43	13.12	12.17	11.44	10.87	10.43	10.06	9.77	9.53
800	71.83	38.42	27.35	21.87	18.62	16.49	15.00	13.90	13.07	12.43	11.91	11.50	11.17	10.89
900	80.81	43.22	30.76	24.60	20.95	18.55	16.87	15.64	14.71	13.98	13.40	12.94	12.56	12.25
1000	89.79	48.02	34.18	27.33	23.27	20.61	18.75	17.38	16.34	15.53	14.89	14.38	13.96	13.61
2000	179.58	96.03	68.36	54.66	46.54	41.22	37.49	34.75	32.67	31.06	29.78	28.75	27.91	27.21
3000	269.37	144.04	102.54	81.98	69.81	61.82	56.23	52.12	49.01	46.58	44.66	43.12	41.86	40.82
4000	359.15	192.06	136.72	109.31	93.08	82.43	74.97	69.49	65.34	62.11	59.55	57.49	55.81	54.42
5000	448.94	240.07	170.89	136.64	116.35	103.03	93.71	86.86	81.67	77.64	74.44	71.86	69.76	68.03
6000	538.73	288.08	205.07	163.96	139.61	123.64	112.45	104.23	98.01	93.16	89.32	86.23	83.71	81.63
7000	628.51	336.10	239.25	191.29	162.88	144.25	131.19	121.61	114.34	108.69	104.21	100.60	97.66	95.24
8000	718.30	384.11	273.43	218.62	186.15	164.85	149.93	138.98	130.67	124.22	119.10	114.98	111.61	108.84
9000	808.09	432.12	307.60	245.94	209.42	185.46	168.67	156.35	147.01	139.74	133.98	129.35	125.56	122.45
10000	897.88	480.13	341.78	273.27	232.69	206.06	187.41	173.72	163.34	155.27	148.87	143.72	139.52	136.05
11000	987.66	528.15	375.96	300.60	255.96	226.67	206.15	191.09	179.68	170.80	163.76	158.09	153.47	149.66
12000	1077.45	576.16	410.14	327.92	279.22	247.27	224.89	208.46	196.01	186.32	178.64	172.46	167.42	163.26
13000	1167.24	624.17	444.31	355.25	302.49	267.88	243.63	225.83	212.34	201.85	193.53	186.83	181.37	176.87
14000	1257.02	672.19	478.49	382.58	325.76	288.49	262.37	243.21	228.68	217.38	208.42	201.20	195.32	190.47
15000	1346.81	720.20	512.67	409.90	349.03	309.09	281.11	260.58	245.01	232.90	223.30	215.57	209.27	204.08
16000	1436.60	768.21	546.85	437.23	372.30	329.70	299.85	277.95	261.34	248.43	238.19	229.95	223.22	217.68
17000	1526.39	816.22	581.02	464.56	395.57	350.30	318.59	295.32	277.68	263.96	253.08	244.32	237.17	231.29
18000	1616.17	864.24	615.20	491.88	418.83	370.91	337.33	312.69	294.01	279.48	267.96	258.69	251.12	244.89
19000	1705.96	912.25	649.38	519.21	442.10	391.51	356.07	330.06	310.35	295.01	282.85	273.06	265.07	258.50
20000	1795.75	960.26	683.56	546.53	465.37	412.12	374.81	347.44	326.68	310.54	297.74	287.43	279.03	272.10
21000	1885.53	1008.28	717.74	573.86	488.64	432.73	393.55	364.81	343.01	326.06	312.62	301.80	292.98	285.71
22000	1975.32	1056.29	751.91	601.19	511.91	453.33	412.29	382.18	359.35	341.59	327.51	316.17	306.93	299.31
23000	2065.11	1104.30	786.09	628.51	535.17	473.94	431.03	399.55	375.68	357.12	342.40	330.54	320.88	312.92
24000	2154.90	1152.31	820.27	655.84	558.44	494.54	449.77	416.92	392.01	372.64	357.28	344.92	334.83	326.52
25000	2244.68	1200.33	854.45	683.17	581.71	515.15	468.51	434.29	408.35	388.17	372.17	359.29	348.78	340.13
26000	2334.47	1248.34	888.62	710.49	604.98	535.75	487.25	451.66	424.68	403.70	387.06	373.66	362.73	353.73
27000	2424.26	1296.35	922.80	737.82	628.25	556.36	505.99	469.04	441.01	419.22	401.94	388.03	376.68	367.34
28000	2514.04	1344.37	956.98	765.15	651.52	576.97	524.73	486.41	457.35	434.75	416.83	402.40	390.63	380.94
29000	2603.83	1392.38	991.16	792.47	674.78	597.57	543.47	503.78	473.68	450.28	431.72	416.77	404.58	394.55
30000	2693.62	1440.39	1025.33	819.80	698.05	618.18	562.21	521.15	490.02	465.80	446.60	431.14	418.54	408.15
31000	2783.41	1488.40	1059.51	847.13	721.32	638.78	580.95	538.52	506.35	481.33	461.49	445.51	432.49	421.76
32000	2873.19	1536.42	1093.69	874.45	744.59	659.39	599.69	555.89	522.68	496.86	476.38	459.89	446.44	435.36
33000	2962.98	1584.43	1127.87	901.78	767.86	679.99	618.43	573.26	539.02	512.38	491.26	474.26	460.39	448.97
34000	3052.77	1632.44	1162.04	929.11	791.13	700.60	637.17	590.64	555.35	527.91	506.15	488.63	474.34	462.57
35000	3142.55	1680.46	1196.22	956.43	814.39	721.21	655.91	608.01	571.68	543.44	521.04	503.00	488.29	476.18
36000	3232.34	1728.47	1230.40	983.76	837.66	741.81	674.65	625.38	588.02	558.96	535.92	517.37	502.24	489.78
37000	3322.13	1776.48	1264.58	1011.08	860.93	762.42	693.39	642.75	604.35	574.49	550.81	531.74	516.19	503.39
38000	3411.92	1824.49	1298.75	1038.41	884.20	783.02	712.13	660.12	620.69	590.02	565.70	546.11	530.14	516.99
39000	3501.70	1872.51	1332.93	1065.74	907.47	803.63	730.87	677.49	637.02	605.54	580.58	560.48	544.10	530.60
40000	3591.49	1920.52	1367.11	1093.06	930.74	824.23	749.61	694.87	653.35	621.07	595.47	574.86	558.05	544.20
41000	3681.28	1968.53	1401.29	1120.39	954.00	844.84	768.35	712.24	669.69	636.60	610.36	589.23	572.00	557.81
42000	3771.06	2016.55	1435.47	1147.72	977.27	865.45	787.09	729.61	686.02	652.12	625.24	603.60	585.95	571.41
43000	3860.85	2064.56	1469.64	1175.04	1000.54	886.05	805.83	746.98	702.35	667.65	640.13	617.97	599.90	585.02
44000	3950.64	2112.57	1503.82	1202.37	1023.81	906.66	824.57	764.35	718.69	683.18	655.02	632.34	613.85	598.62
45000	4040.43	2160.58	1538.00	1229.70	1047.08	927.26	843.31	781.72	735.02	698.70	669.90	646.71	627.80	612.23
46000	4130.21	2208.60	1572.18	1257.02	1070.34	947.87	862.05	799.09	751.36	714.23	684.79	661.08	641.75	625.83
47000	4220.00	2256.61	1606.35	1284.35	1093.61	968.47	880.79	816.47	767.69	729.76	699.68	675.45	655.70	639.44
48000	4309.79	2304.62	1640.53	1311.68	1116.88	989.08	899.53	833.84	784.02	745.28	714.56	689.83	669.65	653.04
49000	4399.57	2352.64	1674.71	1339.00	1140.15	1009.69	918.27	851.21	800.36	760.81	729.45	704.20	683.61	666.64
50000	4489.36	2400.65	1708.89	1366.33	1163.42	1030.29	937.01	868.58	816.69	776.34	744.34	718.57	697.56	680.25
55000	4938.30	2640.71	1879.77	1502.96	1279.76	1133.32	1030.71	955.44	898.36	853.97	818.77	790.42	767.31	748.27
60000	5387.23	2880.78	2050.66	1639.59	1396.10	1236.35	1124.41	1042.30	980.03	931.60	893.20	862.28	837.07	816.30
65000	5836.17	3120.84	2221.55	1776.23	1512.44	1339.38	1218.11	1129.15	1061.70	1009.24	967.64	934.14	906.82	884.32
70000	6285.10	3360.91	2392.44	1912.86	1628.78	1442.41	1311.81	1216.01	1143.36	1086.87	1042.07	1005.99	976.58	952.35
75000	6734.04	3600.97	2563.33	2049.49	1745.12	1545.44	1405.51	1302.87	1225.03	1164.50	1116.50	1077.85	1046.33	1020.37
80000	7182.97	3841.04	2734.22	2186.12	1861.47	1648.46	1499.21	1389.73	1306.70	1242.14	1190.94	1149.71	1116.09	1088.40
85000	7631.91	4081.10	2905.10	2322.76	1977.81	1751.49	1592.91	1476.58	1388.37	1319.77	1265.37	1221.56	1185.84	1156.42
90000	8080.85	4321.16	3075.99	2459.39	2094.15	1854.52	1686.61	1563.44	1470.04	1397.40	1339.80	1293.42	1255.60	1224.45
95000	8529.78	4561.23	3246.88	2596.02	2210.49	1957.55	1780.31	1650.30	1551.71	1475.04	1414.24	1365.28	1325.35	1292.47
100000	8978.72	4801.29	3417.77	2732.65	2326.83	2060.58	1874.01	1737.16	1633.38	1552.67	1488.67	1437.13	1395.11	1360.49

TERM	15 Years	16 Years	17 Years	18 Years	19 Years	20 Years	21 Years	22 Years	23 Years	24 Years	25 Years	30 Years	35 Years	40 Years
AMOUNT														
5	.07	.07	.07	.07	.07	.07	.07	.07	.07	.07	.07	.06	.06	.06
10	.14	.14	.13	.13	.13	.13	.13	.13	.13	.13	.13	.12	.12	.12
15	.20	.20	.20	.20	.19	.19	.19	.19	.19	.19	.19	.18	.18	.18
25	.34	.33	.33	.32	.32	.32	.31	.31	.31	.31	.31	.30	.30	.30
50	.67	.66	.65	.64	.63	.63	.62	.62	.61	.61	.61	.60	.59	.59
75	1.00	.99	.97	.96	.95	.94	.93	.92	.92	.91	.91	.89	.89	.88
100	1.34	1.31	1.29	1.28	1.26	1.25	1.24	1.23	1.22	1.21	1.21	1.19	1.18	1.18
200	2.67	2.62	2.58	2.55	2.52	2.49	2.47	2.45	2.44	2.42	2.41	2.37	2.36	2.35
300	4.00	3.93	3.87	3.82	3.77	3.74	3.70	3.68	3.65	3.63	3.62	3.56	3.53	3.52
400	5.33	5.24	5.15	5.09	5.03	4.98	4.94	4.90	4.87	4.84	4.82	4.74	4.71	4.69
500	6.66	6.54	6.44	6.36	6.28	6.22	6.17	6.12	6.09	6.05	6.02	5.93	5.88	5.86
600	8.00	7.85	7.73	7.63	7.54	7.47	7.40	7.35	7.30	7.26	7.23	7.11	7.06	7.03
700	9.33	9.16	9.02	8.90	8.80	8.71	8.64	8.57	8.52	8.47	8.43	8.30	8.23	8.20
800	10.66	10.47	10.30	10.17	10.05	9.95	9.87	9.80	9.73	9.68	9.64	9.48	9.41	9.37
900	11.99	11.77	11.59	11.44	11.31	11.20	11.10	11.02	10.95	10.89	10.84	10.67	10.59	10.55
1000	13.32	13.08	12.88	12.71	12.56	12.44	12.33	12.24	12.17	12.10	12.04	11.85	11.76	11.72
2000	26.64	26.16	25.75	25.41	25.12	24.88	24.66	24.48	24.33	24.20	24.08	23.70	23.52	23.43
3000	39.96	39.24	38.63	38.12	37.68	37.31	36.99	36.72	36.49	36.29	36.12	35.55	35.28	35.14
4000	53.27	52.31	51.50	50.82	50.24	49.75	49.32	48.96	48.65	48.39	48.16	47.40	47.03	46.85
5000	66.59	65.39	64.38	63.52	62.80	62.18	61.65	61.20	60.81	60.48	60.19	59.25	58.79	58.56
6000	79.91	78.47	77.25	76.23	75.36	74.62	73.98	73.44	72.98	72.58	72.23	71.10	70.55	70.27
7000	93.23	91.54	90.13	88.93	87.92	87.05	86.31	85.68	85.14	84.67	84.27	82.95	82.30	81.98
8000	106.54	104.62	103.00	101.64	100.48	99.49	98.64	97.92	97.30	96.77	96.31	94.79	94.06	93.70
9000	119.86	117.70	115.88	114.34	113.03	111.92	110.97	110.16	109.46	108.86	108.34	106.64	105.82	105.41
10000	133.18	130.77	128.75	127.04	125.59	124.36	123.30	122.40	121.62	120.96	120.38	118.49	117.57	117.12
11000	146.50	143.85	141.63	139.75	138.15	136.79	135.63	134.64	133.78	133.05	132.42	130.34	129.33	128.83
12000	159.81	156.93	154.50	152.45	150.71	149.23	147.96	146.88	145.95	145.15	144.46	142.19	141.09	140.54
13000	173.13	170.01	167.38	165.15	163.27	161.66	160.29	159.12	158.11	157.24	156.49	154.04	152.84	152.25
14000	186.45	183.08	180.25	177.86	175.83	174.10	172.62	171.36	170.27	169.34	168.53	165.89	164.60	163.96
15000	199.77	196.16	193.13	190.56	188.39	186.53	184.95	183.59	182.43	181.43	180.57	177.74	176.36	175.68
16000	213.08	209.24	206.00	203.27	200.95	198.97	197.28	195.83	194.59	193.53	192.61	189.58	188.11	187.39
17000	226.40	222.31	218.88	215.97	213.50	211.40	209.61	208.07	206.75	205.62	204.64	201.43	199.87	199.10
18000	239.72	235.39	231.75	220.67	226.06	223.84	221.94	220.31	218.92	217.72	216.68	213.28	211.63	210.81
19000	253.04	248.47	244.63	241.38	238.62	236.27	234.27	232.55	231.08	229.81	228.72	225.13	223.38	222.52
20000	266.35	261.54	257.50	254.08	251.18	248.71	246.60	244.79	243.24	241.91	240.76	236.98	235.14	234.23
21000	279.67	274.62	270.38	266.79	263.74	261.14	258.93	257.03	255.40	254.00	252.79	248.83	246.90	245.94
22000	292.99	287.70	283.25	279.49	276.30	273.58	271.26	269.27	267.56	266.10	264.83	260.68	258.65	257.66
23000	306.31	300.78	296.12	292.19	288.86	286.01	283.59	281.51	279.72	278.19	276.87	272.53	270.41	269.37
24000	319.62	313.85	309.00	304.90	301.42	298.45	295.92	293.75	291.89	290.29	288.91	284.37	282.17	281.08
25000	332.94	326.93	321.87	317.60	313.97	310.89	308.25	305.99	304.05	302.38	300.95	296.22	293.92	292.79
26000	346.26	340.01	334.75	330.30	326.53	323.32	320.58	318.23	316.21	314.48	312.98	308.07	305.68	304.50
27000	359.58	353.00	347.62	343.01	339.09	335.76	332.91	330.47	328.37	326.57	325.02	319.92	317.44	316.21
28000	372.89	366.16	360.50	355.71	351.65	348.19	345.24	342.71	340.53	338.67	337.06	331.77	329.19	327.92
29000	386.21	379.24	373.37	368.42	364.21	360.63	357.57	354.94	352.70	350.76	349.10	343.62	340.95	339.64
30000	399.53	392.31	386.25	381.12	376.77	373.06	369.90	367.18	364.86	362.86	361.13	355.47	352.71	351.35
31000	412.84	405.39	399.12	393.82	389.33	385.50	382.22	379.42	377.02	374.95	373.17	367.32	364.46	363.06
32000	426.16	418.47	412.00	406.53	401.89	397.93	394.55	391.66	389.18	387.05	385.21	379.16	376.22	374.77
33000	439.48	431.55	424.87	419.23	414.44	410.37	406.88	403.90	401.34	399.14	397.25	391.01	387.98	386.48
34000	452.80	444.62	437.75	431.94	427.00	422.80	419.21	416.14	413.50	411.24	409.28	402.86	399.73	398.19
35000	466.11	457.70	450.62	444.64	439.56	435.24	431.54	428.38	425.67	423.33	421.32	414.71	411.49	409.90
36000	479.43	470.78	463.50	457.34	452.12	447.67	443.87	440.62	437.83	435.43	433.36	426.56	423.25	421.62
37000	492.75	483.85	476.37	470.05	464.68	460.11	456.20	452.86	449.99	447.52	445.40	438.41	435.00	433.33
38000	506.07	496.93	489.25	482.75	477.24	472.54	468.53	465.10	462.15	459.62	457.43	450.26	446.76	445.04
39000	519.38	510.01	502.12	495.45	489.80	484.98	480.86	477.34	474.31	471.71	469.47	462.10	458.52	456.75
40000	532.70	523.08	515.00	508.16	502.36	497.41	493.19	489.58	486.47	483.81	481.51	473.95	470.27	468.46
41000	546.02	536.16	527.87	520.86	514.91	509.85	505.52	501.82	498.64	495.90	493.55	485.80	482.03	480.17
42000	559.34	549.24	540.75	533.57	527.47	522.28	517.85	514.06	510.80	508.00	505.58	497.65	493.79	491.88
43000	572.65	562.32	553.62	546.27	540.03	534.72	530.18	526.29	522.96	520.09	517.62	509.50	505.54	503.60
44000	585.97	575.39	566.49	558.97	552.59	547.15	542.51	538.53	535.12	532.19	529.66	521.35	517.30	515.31
45000	599.29	588.47	579.37	571.68	565.15	559.59	554.84	550.77	547.28	544.28	541.70	533.20	529.06	527.02
46000	612.61	601.55	592.24	584.38	577.71	572.02	567.17	563.01	559.44	556.38	553.74	545.05	540.81	538.73
47000	625.92	614.62	605.12	597.09	590.27	584.46	579.50	575.25	571.61	568.47	565.77	556.89	552.57	550.44
48000	639.24	627.70	617.99	609.79	602.83	596.89	591.83	587.49	583.77	580.57	577.81	568.74	564.33	562.15
49000	652.56	640.78	630.87	622.49	615.38	609.33	604.16	599.73	595.93	592.66	589.85	580.59	576.08	573.86
50000	665.88	653.85	643.74	635.20	627.94	621.77	616.49	611.97	608.09	604.76	601.89	592.44	587.84	585.58
55000	732.46	719.24	708.12	698.72	690.74	683.94	678.14	673.17	668.90	665.23	662.07	651.68	646.63	644.13
60000	799.05	784.62	772.49	762.23	753.53	746.12	739.79	734.36	729.71	725.71	722.26	710.93	705.41	702.69
65000	865.64	850.01	836.86	825.75	816.32	808.29	801.43	795.56	790.52	786.18	782.45	770.17	764.19	761.25
70000	932.22	915.39	901.24	889.27	879.12	870.47	863.08	856.76	851.33	846.66	842.64	829.42	822.98	819.80
75000	998.81	980.78	965.61	952.79	941.91	932.65	924.73	917.95	912.13	907.13	902.83	888.66	881.76	878.36
80000	1065.40	1046.16	1029.99	1016.31	1004.71	994.82	986.38	979.15	972.94	967.61	963.01	947.90	940.54	936.92
85000	1131.99	1111.55	1094.36	1079.83	1067.50	1057.00	1048.03	1040.35	1033.75	1028.08	1023.20	1007.15	999.33	995.47
90000	1198.57	1176.93	1158.73	1143.35	1130.29	1119.17	1109.68	1101.54	1094.56	1088.56	1083.39	1066.39	1058.11	1054.03
95000	1265.16	1242.32	1223.11	1206.87	1193.09	1181.35	1171.32	1162.74	1155.37	1149.03	1143.58	1125.63	1116.89	1112.59
100000	1331.75	1307.70	1287.48	1270.39	1255.88	1243.53	1232.97	1223.93	1216.18	1209.51	1203.77	1184.88	1175.68	1171.15

14%

MONTHLY PAYMENT
REQUIRED TO AMORTIZE A LOAN

TERM AMOUNT	1 Year	2 Years	3 Years	4 Years	5 Years	6 Years	7 Years	8 Years	9 Years	10 Years	11 Years	12 Years	13 Years	14 Years
5	.45	.25	.18	.14	.12	.11	.10	.09	.09	.08	.08	.08	.08	.07
10	.90	.49	.35	.28	.24	.21	.19	.18	.17	.16	.16	.15	.15	.14
15	1.35	.73	.52	.42	.35	.31	.29	.27	.25	.24	.23	.22	.22	.21
25	2.25	1.21	.86	.69	.59	.52	.47	.44	.41	.39	.38	.37	.36	.35
50	4.50	2.41	1.72	1.37	1.17	1.04	.94	.88	.82	.78	.75	.73	.71	.69
75	6.74	3.61	2.57	2.06	1.75	1.55	1.41	1.31	1.23	1.17	1.13	1.09	1.06	1.03
100	8.99	4.81	3.43	2.74	2.34	2.07	1.88	1.75	1.64	1.56	1.50	1.45	1.41	1.37
200	17.97	9.62	6.85	5.48	4.67	4.14	3.76	3.49	3.28	3.12	2.99	2.89	2.81	2.74
300	26.96	14.42	10.27	8.22	7.00	6.20	5.64	5.23	4.92	4.68	4.49	4.34	4.21	4.11
400	35.94	19.23	13.70	10.96	9.33	8.27	7.52	6.98	6.56	6.24	5.98	5.78	5.61	5.47
500	44.92	24.04	17.12	13.69	11.67	10.33	9.40	8.72	8.20	7.80	7.48	7.22	7.01	6.84
600	53.91	28.84	20.54	16.43	14.00	12.40	11.28	10.46	9.84	9.36	8.97	8.67	8.41	8.21
700	62.89	33.65	23.96	19.17	16.33	14.47	13.16	12.20	11.48	10.92	10.47	10.11	9.82	9.57
800	71.87	38.45	27.39	21.91	18.66	16.53	15.04	13.95	13.12	12.47	11.96	11.55	11.22	10.94
900	80.86	43.26	30.81	24.64	20.99	18.60	16.92	15.69	14.76	14.03	13.46	13.00	12.62	12.31
1000	89.84	48.07	34.23	27.38	23.33	20.66	18.80	17.43	16.40	15.59	14.95	14.44	14.02	13.68
2000	179.67	96.13	68.46	54.76	46.65	41.32	37.60	34.86	32.79	31.18	29.90	28.87	28.04	27.35
3000	269.51	144.19	102.68	82.13	69.97	61.98	56.39	52.29	49.18	46.77	44.85	43.31	42.05	41.02
4000	359.34	192.25	136.91	109.51	93.29	82.64	75.19	69.72	65.57	62.35	59.80	57.74	56.07	54.69
5000	449.18	240.31	171.14	136.89	116.61	103.30	93.98	87.15	81.97	77.94	74.75	72.18	70.08	68.36
6000	539.01	288.37	205.36	164.27	139.93	123.96	112.78	104.58	98.36	93.53	89.70	86.61	84.10	82.03
7000	628.84	336.43	239.59	191.64	163.25	144.62	131.57	122.00	114.75	109.11	104.64	101.05	98.11	95.70
8000	718.68	384.49	273.81	219.02	186.57	165.28	150.37	139.43	131.14	124.70	119.59	115.48	112.13	109.37
9000	808.51	432.55	308.04	246.39	209.89	185.94	169.16	156.86	147.54	140.29	134.54	129.92	126.15	123.04
10000	898.35	480.61	342.27	273.77	233.21	206.60	187.96	174.29	163.93	155.87	149.49	144.35	140.16	136.71
11000	988.18	528.67	376.49	301.15	256.53	227.26	206.75	191.72	180.32	171.46	164.44	158.78	154.18	150.38
12000	1078.02	576.73	410.72	328.52	279.85	247.92	225.55	209.15	196.71	187.05	179.39	173.22	168.19	164.06
13000	1167.85	624.79	444.95	355.90	303.17	268.58	244.34	226.57	213.10	202.63	194.33	187.65	182.21	177.73
14000	1257.68	672.85	479.17	383.28	326.49	289.24	263.14	244.00	229.50	218.22	209.28	202.09	196.22	191.40
15000	1347.52	720.91	513.40	410.65	349.81	309.89	281.93	261.43	245.89	233.81	224.23	216.52	210.24	205.07
16000	1437.35	768.97	547.62	438.03	373.13	330.55	300.73	278.86	262.28	249.39	239.18	230.96	224.26	218.74
17000	1527.19	817.03	581.85	465.41	396.45	351.21	319.53	296.29	278.67	264.98	254.13	245.39	238.27	232.41
18000	1617.02	865.09	616.08	492.78	419.77	371.87	338.32	313.72	295.07	280.57	269.08	259.83	252.29	246.08
19000	1706.85	913.15	650.30	520.16	443.09	392.53	357.12	331.15	311.46	296.15	284.02	274.26	266.30	259.75
20000	1796.69	961.21	684.53	547.54	466.41	413.19	375.91	348.57	327.85	311.74	298.97	288.69	280.32	273.42
21000	1886.52	1009.27	718.76	574.91	489.73	433.85	394.71	366.00	344.24	327.33	313.92	303.13	294.33	287.09
22000	1976.36	1057.33	752.98	602.29	513.05	454.51	413.50	383.43	360.64	342.92	328.87	317.56	308.35	300.76
23000	2066.19	1105.39	787.21	629.67	536.37	475.17	432.30	400.86	377.03	358.50	343.82	332.00	322.36	314.43
24000	2156.03	1153.45	821.43	657.04	559.69	495.83	451.09	418.29	393.42	374.09	358.77	346.43	336.38	328.11
25000	2245.86	1201.51	855.66	684.42	583.01	516.49	469.89	435.72	409.81	389.68	373.71	360.87	350.40	341.78
26000	2335.69	1249.57	889.89	711.80	606.33	537.15	488.68	453.14	426.20	405.26	388.66	375.30	364.41	355.45
27000	2425.53	1297.63	924.11	739.17	629.65	557.81	507.48	470.57	442.60	420.85	403.61	389.74	378.43	369.12
28000	2515.36	1345.69	958.34	766.55	652.97	578.47	526.27	488.00	458.99	436.44	418.56	404.17	392.44	382.79
29000	2605.20	1393.75	992.57	793.93	676.29	599.13	545.07	505.43	475.38	452.02	433.51	418.60	406.46	396.46
30000	2695.03	1441.81	1026.79	821.30	699.61	619.78	563.86	522.86	491.77	467.61	448.46	433.04	420.47	410.13
31000	2784.86	1489.87	1061.02	848.68	722.93	640.44	582.66	540.29	508.17	483.20	463.40	447.47	434.49	423.80
32000	2874.70	1537.93	1095.24	876.06	746.25	661.10	601.45	557.72	524.56	498.78	478.35	461.91	448.51	437.47
33000	2964.53	1585.99	1129.47	903.44	769.57	681.76	620.25	575.14	540.95	514.37	493.30	476.34	462.52	451.14
34000	3054.37	1634.05	1163.70	930.81	792.89	702.42	639.05	592.57	557.34	529.96	508.25	490.78	476.54	464.81
35000	3144.20	1682.11	1197.92	958.19	816.21	723.08	657.84	610.00	573.74	545.54	523.20	505.21	490.55	478.49
36000	3234.04	1730.17	1232.15	985.56	839.53	743.74	676.64	627.43	590.13	561.13	538.15	519.65	504.57	492.16
37000	3323.87	1778.23	1266.38	1012.94	862.85	764.40	695.43	644.86	606.52	576.72	553.10	534.08	518.58	505.83
38000	3413.70	1826.29	1300.60	1040.32	886.17	785.06	714.23	662.29	622.91	592.30	568.04	548.51	532.60	519.50
39000	3503.54	1874.35	1334.83	1067.70	909.49	805.72	733.02	679.71	639.30	607.89	582.99	562.95	546.62	533.17
40000	3593.37	1922.41	1369.05	1095.07	932.81	826.38	751.82	697.14	655.70	623.48	597.94	577.38	560.63	546.84
41000	3683.21	1970.47	1403.28	1122.45	956.13	847.04	770.61	714.57	672.09	639.06	612.89	591.82	574.65	560.51
42000	3773.04	2018.53	1437.51	1149.83	979.45	867.70	789.41	732.00	688.48	654.65	627.84	606.25	588.66	574.18
43000	3862.87	2066.59	1471.73	1177.20	1002.77	888.36	808.20	749.43	704.87	670.24	642.79	620.69	602.68	587.85
44000	3952.71	2114.65	1505.96	1204.58	1026.09	909.02	827.00	766.86	721.27	685.83	657.73	635.12	616.69	601.52
45000	4042.54	2162.71	1540.18	1231.96	1049.41	929.67	845.79	784.29	737.66	701.41	672.68	649.56	630.71	615.19
46000	4132.38	2210.77	1574.41	1259.33	1072.73	950.33	864.59	801.71	754.05	717.00	687.63	663.99	644.72	628.86
47000	4222.21	2258.83	1608.64	1286.71	1096.05	970.99	883.38	819.14	770.44	732.59	702.58	678.42	658.74	642.54
48000	4312.05	2306.89	1642.86	1314.09	1119.37	991.65	902.18	836.57	786.84	748.17	717.53	692.86	672.76	656.21
49000	4401.88	2354.95	1677.09	1341.46	1142.69	1012.31	920.97	854.00	803.23	763.76	732.48	707.29	686.77	669.88
50000	4491.71	2403.01	1711.32	1368.84	1166.01	1032.97	939.77	871.43	819.62	779.35	747.42	721.73	700.79	683.55
55000	4940.88	2643.31	1882.45	1505.72	1282.61	1136.27	1033.75	958.57	901.58	857.28	822.17	793.90	770.87	751.90
60000	5390.06	2883.61	2053.58	1642.60	1399.21	1239.56	1127.72	1045.71	983.54	935.21	896.91	866.07	840.94	820.26
65000	5839.23	3123.91	2224.71	1779.49	1515.81	1342.86	1221.70	1132.85	1065.50	1013.15	971.65	938.25	911.02	888.61
70000	6288.40	3364.21	2395.84	1916.37	1632.41	1446.16	1315.68	1220.00	1147.47	1091.08	1046.39	1010.42	981.10	956.97
75000	6737.57	3604.52	2566.97	2053.25	1749.01	1549.45	1409.65	1307.14	1229.43	1169.02	1121.13	1082.59	1051.18	1025.32
80000	7186.74	3844.82	2738.10	2190.14	1865.62	1652.75	1503.63	1394.28	1311.39	1246.95	1195.88	1154.76	1121.26	1093.67
85000	7635.91	4085.12	2909.23	2327.02	1982.22	1756.05	1597.61	1481.42	1393.35	1324.89	1270.62	1226.93	1191.33	1162.03
90000	8085.08	4325.42	3080.36	2463.90	2098.82	1859.34	1691.58	1568.57	1475.31	1402.82	1345.36	1299.11	1261.41	1230.38
95000	8534.25	4565.72	3251.50	2600.79	2215.42	1962.64	1785.56	1655.71	1557.27	1480.75	1420.10	1371.28	1331.49	1298.74
100000	8983.42	4806.02	3422.63	2737.67	2332.02	2065.94	1879.53	1742.85	1639.23	1558.69	1494.84	1443.45	1401.57	1367.09

MONTHLY PAYMENT
REQUIRED TO AMORTIZE A LOAN

14.100%

TERM	15 Years	16 Years	17 Years	18 Years	19 Years	20 Years	21 Years	22 Years	23 Years	24 Years	25 Years	30 Years	35 Years	40 Years
AMOUNT
5	.07	.07	.07	.07	.07	.07	.07	.07	.07	.07	.07	.06	.06	.06
10	.14	.14	.13	.13	.13	.13	.13	.13	.13	.13	.13	.12	.12	.12
15	.21	.20	.20	.20	.19	.19	.19	.19	.19	.19	.19	.18	.18	.18
25	.34	.33	.33	.32	.32	.32	.32	.31	.31	.31	.31	.30	.30	.30
50	.67	.66	.65	.64	.64	.63	.63	.62	.62	.61	.61	.60	.60	.59
75	1.01	.99	.98	.96	.95	.94	.94	.93	.92	.92	.91	.90	.89	.89
100	1.34	1.32	1.30	1.28	1.27	1.26	1.25	1.24	1.23	1.22	1.22	1.20	1.19	1.18
200	2.68	2.63	2.59	2.56	2.53	2.51	2.49	2.47	2.45	2.44	2.43	2.39	2.37	2.36
300	4.02	3.95	3.89	3.84	3.79	3.76	3.73	3.70	3.68	3.66	3.64	3.58	3.56	3.54
400	5.36	5.26	5.18	5.11	5.06	5.01	4.97	4.93	4.90	4.87	4.85	4.78	4.74	4.72
500	6.70	6.58	6.48	6.39	6.32	6.26	6.21	6.16	6.12	6.09	6.06	5.97	5.92	5.90
600	8.04	7.89	7.77	7.67	7.58	7.51	7.45	7.39	7.35	7.31	7.27	7.16	7.11	7.08
700	9.37	9.21	9.07	8.95	8.85	8.76	8.69	8.62	8.57	8.52	8.48	8.35	8.29	8.26
800	10.71	10.52	10.36	10.22	10.11	10.01	9.93	9.86	9.79	9.74	9.70	9.55	9.48	9.44
900	12.05	11.84	11.65	11.50	11.37	11.26	11.17	11.09	11.02	10.96	10.91	10.74	10.66	10.62
1000	13.39	13.15	12.95	12.78	12.64	12.51	12.41	12.32	12.24	12.18	12.12	11.93	11.84	11.80
2000	26.77	26.30	25.89	25.55	25.27	25.02	24.81	24.63	24.48	24.35	24.23	23.86	23.68	23.59
3000	40.16	39.44	38.84	38.33	37.90	37.53	37.21	36.95	36.72	36.52	36.35	35.79	35.52	35.38
4000	53.54	52.59	51.78	51.10	50.53	50.04	49.62	49.26	48.95	48.69	48.46	47.72	47.36	47.18
5000	66.93	65.73	64.73	63.88	63.16	62.54	62.02	61.57	61.19	60.86	60.58	59.64	59.19	58.97
6000	80.31	78.88	77.67	76.65	75.79	75.05	74.42	73.89	73.43	73.03	72.69	71.57	71.03	70.76
7000	93.70	92.02	90.62	89.43	88.42	87.56	86.83	86.20	85.66	85.20	84.80	83.50	82.87	82.56
8000	107.08	105.17	103.56	102.20	101.05	100.07	99.23	98.51	97.90	97.37	96.92	95.43	94.71	94.35
9000	120.47	118.31	116.50	114.98	113.68	112.58	111.63	110.83	110.14	109.54	109.03	107.36	106.54	106.14
10000	133.85	131.46	129.45	127.75	126.31	125.08	124.04	123.14	122.37	121.71	121.15	119.28	118.38	117.94
11000	147.24	144.61	142.39	140.53	138.94	137.59	136.44	135.46	134.61	133.89	133.26	131.21	130.22	129.73
12000	160.62	157.75	155.34	153.30	151.57	150.10	148.84	147.77	146.85	146.06	145.38	143.14	142.06	141.52
13000	174.01	170.90	168.28	166.07	164.20	162.61	161.25	160.08	159.09	158.23	157.49	155.07	153.89	153.32
14000	187.39	184.04	181.23	178.85	176.83	175.12	173.65	172.40	171.32	170.40	169.60	167.00	165.73	165.11
15000	200.78	197.19	194.17	191.62	189.46	187.62	186.05	184.71	183.56	182.57	181.72	178.92	177.57	176.90
16000	214.16	210.33	207.12	204.40	202.09	200.13	198.46	197.02	195.80	194.74	193.83	190.85	189.41	188.70
17000	227.54	223.48	220.06	217.17	214.72	212.64	210.86	209.34	208.03	206.91	205.95	202.78	201.24	200.49
18000	240.93	236.62	233.00	229.95	227.35	225.15	223.26	221.65	220.27	219.08	218.06	214.71	213.08	212.28
19000	254.31	249.77	245.95	242.72	239.98	237.66	235.67	233.97	232.51	231.25	230.17	226.64	224.92	224.08
20000	267.70	262.91	258.89	255.50	252.61	250.16	248.07	246.28	244.74	243.42	242.29	238.56	236.76	235.87
21000	281.08	276.06	271.84	268.27	265.25	262.67	260.47	258.59	256.98	255.60	254.40	250.49	248.59	247.66
22000	294.47	289.21	284.78	281.05	277.88	275.18	272.88	270.91	269.22	267.77	266.52	262.42	260.43	259.46
23000	307.85	302.35	297.73	293.82	290.51	287.69	285.28	283.22	281.45	279.94	278.63	274.35	272.27	271.25
24000	321.24	315.50	310.67	306.59	303.14	300.19	297.68	295.53	293.69	292.11	290.75	286.27	284.11	283.04
25000	334.62	328.64	323.61	319.37	315.77	312.70	310.09	307.85	305.93	304.28	302.86	298.20	295.95	294.84
26000	348.01	341.79	336.56	332.14	328.40	325.21	322.49	320.16	318.17	316.45	314.97	310.13	307.78	306.63
27000	361.39	354.93	349.50	344.92	341.03	337.72	334.89	332.48	330.40	328.62	327.09	322.06	319.62	318.42
28000	374.78	368.08	362.45	357.69	353.66	350.23	347.30	344.79	342.64	340.79	339.20	333.99	331.46	330.22
29000	388.16	381.22	375.39	370.47	366.29	362.73	359.70	357.10	354.88	352.96	351.32	345.91	343.30	342.01
30000	401.55	394.37	388.34	383.24	378.92	375.24	372.10	369.42	367.11	365.13	363.43	357.84	355.13	353.80
31000	414.93	407.51	401.28	396.02	391.55	387.75	384.51	381.73	379.35	377.30	375.54	369.77	366.97	365.60
32000	428.31	420.66	414.23	408.79	404.18	400.26	396.91	394.04	391.59	389.48	387.66	381.70	378.81	377.39
33000	441.70	433.81	427.17	421.57	416.81	412.77	409.31	406.36	403.82	401.65	399.77	393.63	390.65	389.18
34000	455.08	446.95	440.11	434.34	429.44	425.27	421.72	418.67	416.06	413.82	411.89	405.55	402.48	400.98
35000	468.47	460.10	453.06	447.11	442.07	437.78	434.12	430.99	428.30	425.99	424.00	417.48	414.32	412.77
36000	481.85	473.24	466.00	459.89	454.70	450.29	446.52	443.30	440.53	438.16	436.12	429.41	426.16	424.56
37000	495.24	486.39	478.95	472.66	467.33	462.80	458.93	455.61	452.77	450.33	448.23	441.34	438.00	436.36
38000	508.62	499.53	491.89	485.44	479.96	475.31	471.33	467.93	465.01	462.50	460.34	453.27	449.83	448.15
39000	522.01	512.68	504.84	498.21	492.59	487.81	483.73	480.24	477.25	474.67	472.46	465.19	461.67	459.94
40000	535.39	525.82	517.78	510.99	505.22	500.32	496.14	492.55	489.48	486.84	484.57	477.12	473.51	471.74
41000	548.78	538.97	530.72	523.76	517.86	512.83	508.54	504.87	501.72	499.01	496.69	489.05	485.35	483.53
42000	562.16	552.11	543.67	536.54	530.49	525.34	517.18	513.96	511.19	508.80	500.98	497.18	495.32
43000	575.55	565.26	556.61	549.31	543.12	537.84	533.35	529.49	526.19	523.36	520.92	512.91	509.02	507.12
44000	588.93	578.41	569.56	562.09	555.75	550.35	545.75	541.81	538.43	535.53	533.03	524.83	520.86	518.91
45000	602.31	591.55	582.50	574.86	568.38	562.86	558.15	554.12	550.67	547.70	545.14	536.76	532.70	530.70
46000	615.70	604.70	595.45	587.63	581.01	575.37	570.55	566.44	562.90	559.87	557.26	548.69	544.53	542.50
47000	629.08	617.84	608.39	600.41	593.64	587.88	582.96	578.75	575.14	572.04	569.37	560.62	556.37	554.29
48000	642.47	630.99	621.34	613.18	606.27	600.38	595.36	591.06	587.38	584.21	581.49	572.54	568.21	566.08
49000	655.85	644.13	634.28	625.96	618.90	612.89	607.76	603.38	599.61	596.38	593.60	584.47	580.05	577.88
50000	669.24	657.28	647.22	638.73	631.53	625.40	620.17	615.69	611.85	608.55	605.71	596.40	591.89	589.67
55000	736.16	723.01	711.95	702.61	694.68	687.94	682.17	677.26	673.04	669.41	666.29	656.04	651.07	648.64
60000	803.09	788.73	776.67	766.48	757.83	750.48	744.20	738.83	734.22	730.26	726.86	715.68	710.26	707.60
65000	870.01	854.46	841.39	830.35	820.99	813.02	806.22	800.40	795.41	791.12	787.43	775.32	769.45	766.57
70000	936.93	920.19	906.11	894.22	884.14	875.56	868.23	861.97	856.59	851.97	848.00	834.96	828.64	825.54
75000	1003.86	985.91	970.83	958.10	947.29	938.10	930.25	923.53	917.77	912.83	908.57	894.60	887.83	884.50
80000	1070.78	1051.64	1035.56	1021.97	1010.44	1000.64	992.27	985.10	978.96	973.68	969.14	954.24	947.01	943.47
85000	1137.70	1117.37	1100.28	1085.84	1073.60	1063.18	1054.28	1046.67	1040.14	1034.54	1029.71	1013.88	1006.20	1002.44
90000	1204.63	1183.10	1165.00	1149.71	1136.75	1125.72	1116.30	1108.24	1101.33	1095.39	1090.28	1073.52	1065.39	1061.40
95000	1271.55	1248.82	1229.72	1213.59	1199.90	1188.26	1178.31	1169.81	1162.51	1156.25	1150.85	1133.16	1124.58	1120.37
100000	1338.47	1314.55	1294.44	1277.46	1263.05	1250.80	1240.33	1231.38	1223.70	1217.10	1211.42	1192.80	1183.77	1179.34

MONTHLY PAYMENT
REQUIRED TO AMORTIZE A LOAN

TERM	1 Year	2 Years	3 Years	4 Years	5 Years	6 Years	7 Years	8 Years	9 Years	10 Years	11 Years	12 Years	13 Years	14 Years
AMOUNT														
5	.45	.25	.18	.14	.12	.11	.10	.09	.09	.08	.08	.08	.08	.07
10	.90	.49	.35	.28	.24	.21	.19	.18	.17	.16	.15	.15	.15	.14
15	1.35	.73	.52	.42	.35	.32	.29	.27	.25	.24	.23	.22	.22	.21
25	2.25	1.21	.86	.69	.59	.52	.48	.44	.42	.40	.38	.37	.36	.35
50	4.50	2.41	1.72	1.37	1.17	1.04	.95	.88	.83	.79	.75	.73	.71	.69
75	6.74	3.61	2.57	2.06	1.75	1.56	1.42	1.31	1.24	1.18	1.13	1.09	1.06	1.03
100	8.99	4.81	3.43	2.74	2.34	2.07	1.89	1.75	1.65	1.57	1.50	1.45	1.41	1.37
200	17.97	9.62	6.85	5.48	4.67	4.14	3.77	3.49	3.29	3.13	3.00	2.90	2.81	2.74
300	26.96	14.43	10.28	8.22	7.00	6.21	5.65	5.24	4.93	4.69	4.49	4.34	4.21	4.11
400	35.94	19.23	13.70	10.96	9.34	8.27	7.53	6.98	6.57	6.25	5.99	5.79	5.62	5.48
500	44.93	24.04	17.12	13.70	11.67	10.34	9.41	8.73	8.21	7.81	7.49	7.23	7.02	6.85
600	53.91	28.85	20.55	16.44	14.00	12.41	11.29	10.47	9.85	9.37	8.98	8.68	8.42	8.22
700	62.90	33.66	23.97	19.18	16.34	14.48	13.17	12.21	11.49	10.93	10.48	10.12	9.83	9.59
800	71.88	38.46	27.40	21.92	18.67	16.54	15.05	13.96	13.13	12.49	11.98	11.57	11.23	10.95
900	80.87	43.27	30.82	24.66	21.00	18.61	16.93	15.70	14.77	14.05	13.47	13.01	12.63	12.32
1000	89.85	48.08	34.24	27.39	23.34	20.68	18.81	17.45	16.41	15.61	14.97	14.46	14.04	13.69
2000	179.70	96.15	68.48	54.78	46.67	41.35	37.62	34.89	32.82	31.21	29.93	28.91	28.07	27.38
3000	269.54	144.22	102.72	82.17	70.00	62.02	56.43	52.33	49.23	46.81	44.90	43.36	42.10	41.07
4000	359.39	192.29	136.96	109.56	93.34	82.70	75.24	69.78	65.63	62.41	59.86	57.81	56.13	54.75
5000	449.23	240.36	171.20	136.95	116.67	103.37	94.05	87.22	82.04	78.01	74.82	72.26	70.16	68.44
6000	539.08	288.44	205.44	164.34	140.00	124.04	112.86	104.66	98.45	93.62	89.79	86.71	84.20	82.13
7000	628.93	336.51	239.67	191.73	163.34	144.71	131.67	122.10	114.85	109.22	104.75	101.16	98.23	95.82
8000	718.77	384.58	273.91	219.12	186.67	165.39	150.48	139.55	131.26	124.82	119.72	115.61	112.26	109.50
9000	808.62	432.65	308.15	246.51	210.00	186.06	169.29	156.99	147.67	140.42	134.68	130.06	126.29	123.19
10000	898.46	480.72	342.39	273.90	233.34	206.73	188.10	174.43	164.07	156.02	149.64	144.51	140.32	136.88
11000	988.31	528.80	376.63	301.29	256.67	227.41	206.91	191.87	180.48	171.63	164.61	158.96	154.36	150.57
12000	1078.16	576.87	410.87	328.68	280.00	248.08	225.71	209.32	196.89	187.23	179.57	173.41	168.39	164.25
13000	1168.00	624.94	445.10	356.06	303.34	268.75	244.52	226.76	213.30	202.83	194.53	187.86	182.42	177.94
14000	1257.85	673.01	479.34	383.45	326.67	289.42	263.33	244.20	229.70	218.43	209.50	202.31	196.45	191.63
15000	1347.69	721.08	513.58	410.84	350.00	310.10	282.14	261.65	246.11	234.03	224.46	216.76	210.48	205.32
16000	1437.54	769.16	547.82	438.23	373.33	330.77	300.95	279.09	262.52	249.64	239.43	231.21	224.51	219.00
17000	1527.39	817.23	582.06	465.62	396.67	351.44	319.76	296.53	278.92	265.24	254.39	245.66	238.55	232.69
18000	1617.23	865.30	616.30	493.01	420.00	372.11	338.57	313.97	295.33	280.84	269.35	260.11	252.58	246.38
19000	1707.08	913.37	650.53	520.40	443.33	392.79	357.38	331.42	311.74	296.44	284.32	274.56	266.61	260.07
20000	1796.92	961.44	684.77	547.79	466.67	413.46	376.19	348.86	328.14	312.04	299.28	289.01	280.64	273.75
21000	1886.77	1009.52	719.01	575.18	490.00	434.13	395.00	366.30	344.55	327.64	314.25	303.46	294.67	287.44
22000	1976.62	1057.59	753.25	602.57	513.33	454.81	413.81	383.74	360.96	343.25	329.21	317.91	308.71	301.13
23000	2066.46	1105.66	787.49	629.96	536.67	475.48	432.62	401.19	377.37	358.85	344.17	332.36	322.74	314.81
24000	2156.31	1153.73	821.73	657.35	560.00	496.15	451.42	418.63	393.77	374.45	359.14	346.81	336.77	328.50
25000	2246.15	1201.80	855.96	684.74	583.33	516.82	470.23	436.07	410.18	390.05	374.10	361.26	350.80	342.19
26000	2336.00	1249.88	890.20	712.12	606.67	537.50	489.04	453.52	426.59	405.65	389.06	375.71	364.83	355.88
27000	2425.85	1297.95	924.44	739.51	630.00	558.17	507.85	470.96	442.99	421.26	404.03	390.16	378.86	369.56
28000	2515.69	1346.02	958.68	766.90	653.33	578.84	526.66	488.40	459.40	436.86	418.99	404.61	392.90	383.25
29000	2605.54	1394.09	992.92	794.29	676.67	599.51	545.47	505.84	475.81	452.46	433.96	419.06	406.93	396.94
30000	2695.38	1442.16	1027.16	821.68	700.00	620.19	564.28	523.29	492.21	468.06	448.92	433.51	420.96	410.63
31000	2785.23	1490.24	1061.39	849.07	723.33	640.86	583.09	540.73	508.62	483.66	463.88	447.96	434.99	424.31
32000	2875.08	1538.31	1095.63	876.46	746.66	661.53	601.90	558.17	525.03	499.27	478.85	462.41	449.02	438.00
33000	2964.92	1586.38	1129.87	903.85	770.00	682.21	620.71	575.61	541.43	514.87	493.81	476.86	463.06	451.69
34000	3054.77	1634.45	1164.11	931.24	793.33	702.88	639.52	593.06	557.84	530.47	508.78	491.31	477.09	465.38
35000	3144.61	1682.52	1198.35	958.63	816.66	723.55	658.32	610.50	574.25	546.07	523.74	505.76	491.12	479.06
36000	3234.46	1730.60	1232.59	986.02	840.00	744.22	677.13	627.94	590.66	561.67	538.70	520.22	505.15	492.75
37000	3324.30	1778.67	1266.82	1013.41	863.33	764.90	695.94	645.39	607.07	577.27	553.67	534.67	519.18	506.44
38000	3414.15	1826.74	1301.06	1040.80	886.66	785.57	714.75	662.83	623.47	592.88	568.63	549.12	533.21	520.13
39000	3504.00	1874.81	1335.30	1068.18	910.00	806.24	733.56	680.27	639.88	608.48	583.59	563.57	547.25	533.81
40000	3593.84	1922.88	1369.54	1095.57	933.33	826.91	752.37	697.71	656.28	624.08	598.56	578.02	561.28	547.50
41000	3683.69	1970.96	1403.78	1122.96	956.66	847.59	771.18	715.16	672.69	639.68	613.52	592.47	575.31	561.19
42000	3773.53	2019.03	1438.02	1150.35	980.00	868.26	789.99	732.60	689.10	655.28	628.49	606.92	589.34	574.87
43000	3863.38	2067.10	1472.26	1177.74	1003.33	888.93	808.80	750.04	705.50	670.89	643.45	621.37	603.37	588.56
44000	3953.23	2115.17	1506.49	1205.13	1026.66	909.61	827.61	767.48	721.91	686.49	658.41	635.82	617.41	602.25
45000	4043.07	2163.24	1540.73	1232.52	1049.99	930.28	846.42	784.93	738.32	702.09	673.38	650.27	631.44	615.94
46000	4132.92	2211.32	1574.97	1259.91	1073.33	950.95	865.23	802.37	754.73	717.69	688.34	664.72	645.47	629.62
47000	4222.76	2259.39	1609.21	1287.30	1096.66	971.62	884.03	819.81	771.13	733.29	703.30	679.17	659.50	643.31
48000	4312.61	2307.46	1643.45	1314.69	1119.99	992.30	902.84	837.26	787.54	748.90	718.27	693.62	673.53	657.00
49000	4402.46	2355.53	1677.69	1342.08	1143.33	1012.97	921.65	854.70	803.95	764.50	733.23	708.07	687.56	670.69
50000	4492.30	2403.60	1711.92	1369.47	1166.66	1033.64	940.46	872.14	820.35	780.10	748.20	722.52	701.60	684.37
55000	4941.53	2643.96	1883.12	1506.41	1283.33	1137.01	1034.51	959.35	902.39	858.11	823.02	794.77	771.76	752.81
60000	5390.76	2884.32	2054.31	1643.36	1399.99	1240.37	1128.55	1046.57	984.42	936.12	897.83	867.02	841.91	821.25
65000	5839.99	3124.68	2225.50	1780.30	1516.66	1343.73	1222.60	1133.78	1066.46	1014.13	972.65	939.27	912.07	889.68
70000	6289.22	3365.04	2396.69	1917.25	1633.32	1447.10	1316.64	1221.00	1148.49	1092.14	1047.47	1011.52	982.23	958.12
75000	6738.45	3605.40	2567.88	2054.20	1749.99	1550.46	1410.69	1308.21	1230.53	1170.15	1122.29	1083.78	1052.39	1026.56
80000	7187.68	3845.76	2739.07	2191.14	1866.65	1653.82	1504.74	1395.42	1312.56	1248.16	1197.11	1156.03	1122.55	1094.99
85000	7636.91	4086.12	2910.27	2328.09	1983.32	1757.19	1598.78	1482.64	1394.60	1326.17	1271.93	1228.28	1192.71	1163.43
90000	8086.14	4326.48	3081.46	2465.03	2099.98	1860.55	1692.83	1569.85	1476.63	1404.18	1346.75	1300.53	1262.87	1231.87
95000	8535.37	4566.84	3252.65	2601.98	2216.65	1963.91	1786.87	1657.06	1558.67	1482.18	1421.57	1372.78	1333.03	1300.31
100000	8984.60	4807.20	3423.84	2738.93	2333.32	2067.28	1880.92	1744.28	1640.70	1560.19	1496.39	1445.03	1403.19	1368.74

TERM AMOUNT	15 Years	16 Years	17 Years	18 Years	19 Years	20 Years	21 Years	22 Years	23 Years	24 Years	25 Years	30 Years	35 Years	40 Years
5	.07	.07	.07	.07	.07	.07	.07	.07	.07	.07	.07	.06	.06	.06
10	.14	.14	.13	.13	.13	.13	.13	.13	.13	.13	.13	.12	.12	.12
15	.21	.20	.20	.20	.19	.19	.19	.19	.19	.19	.19	.18	.18	.18
25	.34	.33	.33	.32	.32	.32	.32	.31	.31	.31	.31	.30	.30	.30
50	.68	.66	.65	.64	.64	.63	.63	.62	.62	.61	.61	.60	.60	.60
75	1.01	.99	.98	.96	.95	.94	.94	.93	.92	.92	.92	.90	.89	.89
100	1.35	1.32	1.30	1.28	1.27	1.26	1.25	1.24	1.23	1.22	1.22	1.20	1.19	1.19
200	2.69	2.64	2.60	2.56	2.53	2.51	2.49	2.47	2.46	2.44	2.43	2.39	2.38	2.37
300	4.03	3.95	3.89	3.84	3.80	3.76	3.73	3.70	3.68	3.66	3.65	3.59	3.56	3.55
400	5.37	5.27	5.19	5.12	5.06	5.02	4.97	4.94	4.91	4.88	4.86	4.78	4.75	4.73
500	6.71	6.59	6.49	6.40	6.33	6.27	6.22	6.17	6.13	6.10	6.07	5.98	5.93	5.91
600	8.05	7.90	7.78	7.68	7.59	7.52	7.46	7.40	7.36	7.32	7.29	7.17	7.12	7.09
700	9.39	9.22	9.08	8.96	8.86	8.77	8.70	8.64	8.58	8.54	8.50	8.37	8.31	8.27
800	10.73	10.54	10.37	10.24	10.12	10.03	9.94	9.87	9.81	9.76	9.71	9.56	9.49	9.46
900	12.07	11.85	11.67	11.52	11.39	11.28	11.18	11.10	11.04	10.98	10.93	10.76	10.68	10.64
1000	13.41	13.17	12.97	12.80	12.65	12.53	12.43	12.34	12.26	12.19	12.14	11.95	11.86	11.82
2000	26.81	26.33	25.93	25.59	25.30	25.06	24.85	24.67	24.52	24.38	24.27	23.90	23.72	23.63
3000	40.21	39.49	38.89	38.38	37.95	37.58	37.27	37.00	36.77	36.57	36.41	35.85	35.58	35.45
4000	53.61	52.66	51.85	51.17	50.60	50.11	49.69	49.33	49.03	48.76	48.54	47.80	47.44	47.26
5000	67.01	65.82	64.81	63.97	63.25	62.64	62.11	61.67	61.28	60.95	60.67	59.74	59.29	59.07
6000	80.41	78.98	77.78	76.76	75.90	75.16	74.54	74.00	73.54	73.14	72.81	71.69	71.15	70.89
7000	93.82	92.14	90.74	89.55	88.54	87.69	86.96	86.33	85.80	85.33	84.94	83.64	83.01	82.70
8000	107.22	105.31	103.70	102.34	101.19	100.21	99.38	98.66	98.05	97.52	97.07	95.59	94.87	94.52
9000	120.62	118.47	116.66	115.14	113.84	112.74	111.80	111.00	110.31	109.71	109.21	107.53	106.73	106.33
10000	134.02	131.63	129.62	127.93	126.49	125.27	124.22	123.33	122.56	121.90	121.34	119.48	118.58	118.14
11000	147.42	144.79	142.59	140.72	139.14	137.79	136.64	135.66	134.82	134.09	133.47	131.43	130.44	129.96
12000	160.82	157.96	155.55	153.51	151.79	150.32	149.07	147.99	147.07	146.28	145.61	143.38	142.30	141.77
13000	174.22	171.12	168.51	166.30	164.43	162.84	161.49	160.33	159.33	158.47	157.74	155.33	154.16	153.58
14000	187.63	184.28	181.47	179.10	177.08	175.37	173.91	172.66	171.59	170.66	169.87	167.27	166.01	165.40
15000	201.03	197.44	194.43	191.89	189.73	187.90	186.33	184.99	183.84	182.85	182.01	179.22	177.87	177.21
16000	214.43	210.61	207.39	204.68	202.38	200.42	198.75	197.32	196.10	195.04	194.14	191.17	189.73	189.03
17000	227.83	223.77	220.36	217.47	215.03	212.95	211.17	209.65	208.35	207.23	206.27	203.12	201.59	200.84
18000	241.23	236.93	233.32	230.27	227.68	225.47	223.60	221.99	220.61	219.42	218.41	215.06	213.45	212.65
19000	254.63	250.09	246.28	243.06	240.33	238.00	236.02	234.32	232.86	231.61	230.54	227.01	225.30	224.47
20000	268.04	263.26	259.24	255.85	252.97	250.53	248.44	246.65	245.12	243.80	242.67	238.96	237.16	236.28
21000	281.44	276.42	272.20	268.64	265.62	263.05	260.86	258.98	257.38	255.99	254.81	250.91	249.02	248.09
22000	294.84	289.58	285.16	281.43	278.27	275.58	273.28	271.32	269.63	268.18	266.94	262.85	260.88	259.91
23000	308.24	302.74	298.13	294.23	290.92	288.11	285.70	283.65	281.89	280.37	279.07	274.80	272.74	271.72
24000	321.64	315.91	311.09	307.02	303.57	300.63	298.13	295.98	294.14	292.56	291.21	286.75	284.59	283.54
25000	335.04	329.07	324.05	319.81	316.22	313.16	310.55	308.31	306.40	304.75	303.34	298.70	296.45	295.35
26000	348.44	342.23	337.01	332.60	328.86	325.68	322.97	320.65	318.65	316.94	315.47	310.65	308.31	307.16
27000	361.85	355.40	349.97	345.40	341.51	338.21	335.39	332.98	330.91	329.13	327.61	322.59	320.17	318.98
28000	375.25	368.56	362.94	358.19	354.16	350.74	347.81	345.31	343.17	341.32	339.74	334.54	332.02	330.79
29000	388.65	381.72	375.90	370.98	366.81	363.26	360.23	357.64	355.42	353.51	351.87	346.49	343.88	342.60
30000	402.05	394.88	388.86	383.77	379.46	375.79	372.66	369.98	367.68	365.70	364.01	358.44	355.74	354.42
31000	415.45	408.05	401.82	396.56	392.11	388.31	385.08	382.31	379.93	377.89	376.14	370.38	367.60	366.23
32000	428.85	421.21	414.78	409.36	404.76	400.84	397.50	394.64	392.19	390.08	388.27	382.33	379.46	378.05
33000	442.25	434.37	427.74	422.15	417.40	413.37	409.92	406.97	404.44	402.27	400.41	394.28	391.31	389.86
34000	455.66	447.53	440.71	434.94	430.05	425.89	422.34	419.30	416.70	414.46	412.54	406.23	403.17	401.67
35000	469.06	460.70	453.67	447.73	442.70	438.42	434.76	431.64	428.96	426.65	424.67	418.18	415.03	413.49
36000	482.46	473.86	466.63	460.53	455.35	450.94	447.19	443.97	441.21	438.84	436.81	430.12	426.89	425.30
37000	495.86	487.02	479.59	473.32	468.00	463.47	459.61	456.30	453.47	451.03	448.94	442.07	438.74	437.11
38000	509.26	500.18	492.55	486.11	480.65	476.00	472.03	468.63	465.72	463.22	461.07	454.02	450.60	448.93
39000	522.66	513.35	505.52	498.90	493.29	488.52	484.45	480.97	477.98	475.41	473.21	465.97	462.46	460.74
40000	536.07	526.51	518.48	511.69	505.94	501.05	496.87	493.30	490.23	487.60	485.34	477.91	474.32	472.56
41000	549.47	539.67	531.44	524.49	518.59	513.57	509.30	505.63	502.49	499.79	497.47	489.86	486.18	484.37
42000	562.87	552.83	544.40	537.28	531.24	526.10	521.72	517.96	514.75	511.98	509.61	501.81	498.03	496.18
43000	576.27	566.00	557.36	550.07	543.89	538.63	534.14	530.30	527.00	524.17	521.74	513.76	509.89	508.00
44000	589.67	579.16	570.32	562.86	556.54	551.15	546.56	542.63	539.26	536.36	533.87	525.70	521.75	519.81
45000	603.07	592.32	583.29	575.66	569.19	563.68	558.98	554.96	551.51	548.55	546.01	537.65	533.61	531.63
46000	616.47	605.48	596.25	588.45	581.83	576.21	571.40	567.29	563.77	560.74	558.14	549.60	545.47	543.44
47000	629.88	618.65	609.21	601.24	594.48	588.73	583.82	579.63	576.03	572.93	570.27	561.55	557.32	555.25
48000	643.28	631.81	622.17	614.03	607.13	601.26	596.25	591.96	588.28	585.12	582.41	573.50	569.18	567.07
49000	656.68	644.97	635.13	626.83	619.78	613.78	608.67	604.29	600.54	597.31	594.54	585.44	581.04	578.88
50000	670.08	658.14	648.10	639.62	632.43	626.31	621.09	616.62	612.79	609.50	606.67	597.39	592.90	590.69
55000	737.09	723.95	712.90	703.58	695.67	688.94	683.20	678.28	674.07	670.45	667.34	657.13	652.19	649.76
60000	804.10	789.76	777.71	767.54	758.91	751.57	745.31	739.95	735.35	731.40	728.01	716.87	711.47	708.83
65000	871.10	855.57	842.52	831.50	822.15	814.20	807.41	801.61	796.63	792.35	788.67	776.61	770.76	767.90
70000	938.11	921.39	907.33	895.46	885.40	876.83	869.52	863.27	857.91	853.30	849.34	836.35	830.05	826.97
75000	1005.12	987.20	972.14	959.42	948.64	939.46	931.63	924.93	919.19	914.25	910.01	896.08	889.34	886.04
80000	1072.18	1053.01	1036.95	1023.38	1011.88	1002.09	993.74	986.59	980.46	975.20	970.67	955.82	948.63	945.11
85000	1139.13	1118.83	1101.76	1087.35	1075.12	1064.72	1055.85	1048.25	1041.74	1036.15	1031.34	1015.56	1007.92	1004.18
90000	1206.14	1184.64	1166.57	1151.31	1138.37	1127.35	1117.96	1109.92	1103.02	1097.10	1092.01	1075.30	1067.21	1063.25
95000	1273.15	1250.45	1231.38	1215.27	1201.61	1189.98	1180.06	1171.58	1164.30	1158.05	1152.67	1135.04	1126.50	1122.31
100000	1340.16	1316.27	1296.19	1279.23	1264.85	1252.61	1242.17	1233.24	1225.58	1219.00	1213.34	1194.78	1185.79	1181.38

MONTHLY PAYMENT
REQUIRED TO AMORTIZE A LOAN

TERM AMOUNT	1 Year	2 Years	3 Years	4 Years	5 Years	6 Years	7 Years	8 Years	9 Years	10 Years	11 Years	12 Years	13 Years	14 Years
5	.45	.25	.18	.14	.12	.11	.10	.09	.09	.08	.08	.08	.08	.07
10	.90	.49	.35	.28	.24	.21	.19	.18	.17	.16	.16	.15	.15	.14
15	1.35	.73	.52	.42	.36	.32	.29	.27	.25	.24	.23	.22	.22	.21
25	2.25	1.21	.86	.69	.59	.52	.48	.44	.42	.40	.38	.37	.36	.35
50	4.50	2.41	1.72	1.38	1.17	1.04	.95	.88	.83	.79	.76	.73	.71	.69
75	6.75	3.61	2.58	2.06	1.76	1.56	1.42	1.32	1.24	1.18	1.13	1.09	1.06	1.04
100	8.99	4.82	3.43	2.75	2.34	2.08	1.89	1.75	1.65	1.57	1.51	1.45	1.41	1.38
200	17.98	9.63	6.86	5.49	4.68	4.15	3.78	3.50	3.30	3.13	3.01	2.90	2.82	2.75
300	26.97	14.44	10.29	8.23	7.02	6.22	5.66	5.25	4.94	4.70	4.51	4.35	4.23	4.13
400	35.96	19.25	13.71	10.98	9.35	8.29	7.55	7.00	6.59	6.26	6.01	5.80	5.64	5.50
500	44.95	24.06	17.14	13.72	11.69	10.36	9.43	8.75	8.23	7.83	7.51	7.25	7.05	6.87
600	53.93	28.87	20.57	16.46	14.03	12.43	11.32	10.50	9.88	9.39	9.01	8.70	8.45	8.25
700	62.92	33.68	24.00	19.20	16.37	14.50	13.20	12.24	11.52	10.96	10.51	10.15	9.86	9.62
800	71.91	38.49	27.42	21.95	18.70	16.58	15.09	13.99	13.17	12.52	12.01	11.60	11.27	10.99
900	80.90	43.30	30.85	24.69	21.04	18.65	16.97	15.74	14.81	14.09	13.51	13.05	12.68	12.37
1000	89.89	48.11	34.28	27.43	23.38	20.72	18.86	17.49	16.46	15.65	15.02	14.50	14.09	13.74
2000	179.77	96.22	68.55	54.86	46.75	41.43	37.71	34.98	32.91	31.30	30.03	29.00	28.17	27.48
3000	269.65	144.33	102.83	82.29	70.12	62.14	56.56	52.46	49.36	46.95	45.04	43.50	42.25	41.22
4000	359.53	192.43	137.10	109.71	93.49	82.86	75.41	69.95	65.81	62.59	60.05	58.00	56.33	54.95
5000	449.41	240.54	171.38	137.14	116.87	103.57	94.26	87.43	82.26	78.24	75.06	72.49	70.41	68.69
6000	539.29	288.65	205.65	164.57	140.24	124.28	113.11	104.92	98.71	93.89	90.07	86.99	84.49	82.43
7000	629.17	336.76	239.93	191.99	163.61	145.00	131.96	122.40	115.16	109.53	105.08	101.49	98.57	96.16
8000	719.05	384.86	274.20	219.42	186.98	165.71	150.81	139.89	131.61	125.18	120.09	115.99	112.65	109.90
9000	808.94	432.97	308.48	246.85	210.35	186.42	169.66	157.37	148.06	140.83	135.10	130.49	126.73	123.64
10000	898.82	481.08	342.75	274.27	233.73	207.13	188.51	174.86	164.51	156.48	150.11	144.98	140.81	137.37
11000	988.70	529.19	377.03	301.70	257.10	227.85	207.36	192.35	180.97	172.12	165.12	159.48	154.89	151.11
12000	1078.58	577.29	411.30	329.13	280.47	248.56	226.21	209.83	197.42	187.77	180.13	173.98	168.97	164.85
13000	1168.46	625.40	445.58	356.55	303.84	269.27	245.06	227.32	213.87	203.42	195.14	188.48	183.05	178.59
14000	1258.34	673.51	479.85	383.98	327.21	289.99	263.91	244.80	230.32	219.06	210.15	202.97	197.13	192.32
15000	1348.22	721.62	514.13	411.41	350.59	310.70	282.77	262.29	246.77	234.71	225.16	217.47	211.21	206.06
16000	1438.11	769.72	548.40	438.84	373.96	331.41	301.62	279.77	263.22	250.36	240.17	231.97	225.29	219.80
17000	1527.99	817.83	582.68	466.26	397.33	352.13	320.47	297.26	279.67	266.01	255.18	246.47	239.37	233.53
18000	1617.87	865.94	616.95	493.69	420.70	372.84	339.32	314.74	296.12	281.65	270.19	260.97	253.45	247.27
19000	1707.75	914.05	651.23	521.12	444.07	393.55	358.17	332.23	312.57	297.30	285.20	275.46	267.53	261.01
20000	1797.63	962.15	685.50	548.54	467.45	414.26	377.02	349.72	329.02	312.95	300.21	289.96	281.61	274.74
21000	1887.51	1010.26	719.78	575.97	490.82	434.98	395.87	367.20	345.48	328.59	315.22	304.46	295.69	288.48
22000	1977.39	1058.37	754.05	603.40	514.19	455.69	414.72	384.69	361.93	344.24	330.23	318.96	309.77	302.22
23000	2067.27	1106.48	788.33	630.82	537.56	476.40	433.57	402.17	378.38	359.89	345.24	333.45	323.85	315.96
24000	2157.15	1154.58	822.60	658.25	560.93	497.12	452.42	419.66	394.83	375.54	360.25	347.95	337.93	329.69
25000	2247.04	1202.69	856.88	685.68	584.31	517.83	471.27	437.14	411.28	391.18	375.26	362.45	352.01	343.43
26000	2336.92	1250.80	891.15	713.10	607.68	538.54	490.12	454.63	427.73	406.83	390.27	376.95	366.10	357.17
27000	2426.80	1298.91	925.43	740.53	631.05	559.26	508.97	472.11	444.18	422.48	405.28	391.45	380.18	370.90
28000	2516.68	1347.01	959.70	767.96	654.42	579.97	527.82	489.60	460.63	438.12	420.29	405.94	394.26	384.64
29000	2606.56	1395.12	993.98	795.39	677.79	600.68	546.67	507.08	477.08	453.77	435.30	420.44	408.34	398.38
30000	2696.44	1443.23	1028.25	822.81	701.17	621.39	565.53	524.57	493.53	469.42	450.31	434.94	422.42	412.11
31000	2786.32	1491.34	1062.53	850.24	724.54	642.11	584.38	542.06	509.99	485.07	465.32	449.44	436.50	425.85
32000	2876.20	1539.44	1096.80	877.67	747.91	662.82	603.23	559.54	526.44	500.71	480.33	463.93	450.58	439.59
33000	2966.09	1587.55	1131.08	905.09	771.28	683.53	622.08	577.03	542.89	516.36	495.34	478.43	464.66	453.32
34000	3055.97	1635.66	1165.35	932.52	794.66	704.25	640.93	594.51	559.34	532.01	510.35	492.93	478.74	467.06
35000	3145.85	1683.76	1199.62	959.95	818.03	724.96	659.78	612.00	575.79	547.65	525.36	507.43	492.82	480.80
36000	3235.73	1731.87	1233.90	987.37	841.40	745.67	678.63	629.48	592.24	563.30	540.37	521.93	506.90	494.54
37000	3325.61	1779.98	1268.17	1014.80	864.77	766.39	697.48	646.97	608.69	578.95	555.38	536.42	520.98	508.27
38000	3415.49	1828.09	1302.45	1042.23	888.14	787.10	716.33	664.45	625.14	594.60	570.39	550.92	535.06	522.01
39000	3505.37	1876.19	1336.72	1069.65	911.52	807.81	735.18	681.94	641.59	610.24	585.40	565.42	549.14	535.75
40000	3595.25	1924.30	1371.00	1097.08	934.89	828.52	754.03	699.43	658.04	625.89	600.41	579.92	563.22	549.48
41000	3685.14	1972.41	1405.27	1124.51	958.26	849.24	772.88	716.91	674.50	641.54	615.42	594.41	577.30	563.22
42000	3775.02	2020.52	1439.55	1151.94	981.63	869.95	791.73	734.40	690.95	657.18	630.43	608.91	591.38	576.96
43000	3864.90	2068.62	1473.82	1179.36	1005.00	890.66	810.58	751.88	707.40	672.83	645.44	623.41	605.46	590.69
44000	3954.78	2116.73	1508.10	1206.79	1028.38	911.38	829.43	769.37	723.85	688.48	660.45	637.91	619.54	604.43
45000	4044.66	2164.84	1542.37	1234.22	1051.75	932.09	848.29	786.85	740.30	704.13	675.46	652.41	633.62	618.17
46000	4134.54	2212.95	1576.65	1261.64	1075.12	952.80	867.14	804.34	756.75	719.77	690.47	666.90	647.70	631.91
47000	4224.42	2261.05	1610.92	1289.07	1098.49	973.52	885.99	821.82	773.20	735.42	705.49	681.40	661.78	645.64
48000	4314.30	2309.16	1645.20	1316.50	1121.86	994.23	904.84	839.31	789.65	751.07	720.50	695.90	675.86	659.38
49000	4404.19	2357.27	1679.47	1343.92	1145.24	1014.94	923.69	856.80	806.10	766.71	735.51	710.40	689.94	673.12
50000	4494.07	2405.38	1713.75	1371.35	1168.61	1035.65	942.54	874.28	822.55	782.36	750.52	724.89	704.02	686.85
55000	4943.47	2645.91	1885.12	1508.49	1285.47	1139.22	1036.79	961.71	904.81	860.60	825.57	797.38	774.43	755.54
60000	5392.88	2886.45	2056.50	1645.62	1402.33	1242.78	1131.05	1049.14	987.06	938.83	900.62	869.87	844.83	824.22
65000	5842.29	3126.99	2227.87	1782.75	1519.19	1346.35	1225.30	1136.56	1069.32	1017.07	975.67	942.36	915.23	892.91
70000	6291.69	3367.52	2399.24	1919.89	1636.05	1449.91	1319.55	1223.99	1151.57	1095.30	1050.72	1014.85	985.63	961.59
75000	6741.10	3608.06	2570.62	2057.02	1752.91	1553.48	1413.81	1311.42	1233.83	1173.54	1125.77	1087.34	1056.03	1030.28
80000	7190.50	3848.60	2741.99	2194.16	1869.77	1657.04	1508.06	1398.85	1316.08	1251.77	1200.82	1159.83	1126.44	1098.96
85000	7639.91	4089.14	2913.37	2331.29	1986.63	1760.61	1602.31	1486.27	1398.34	1330.01	1275.87	1232.32	1196.84	1167.65
90000	8089.32	4329.67	3084.74	2468.43	2103.49	1864.17	1696.57	1573.70	1480.59	1408.25	1350.92	1304.81	1267.24	1236.33
95000	8538.72	4570.21	3256.12	2605.56	2220.35	1967.74	1790.82	1661.13	1562.85	1486.48	1425.98	1377.29	1337.64	1305.02
100000	8988.13	4810.75	3427.49	2742.70	2337.21	2071.30	1885.07	1748.56	1645.10	1564.72	1501.03	1449.78	1408.04	1373.70

TERM	15 Years	16 Years	17 Years	18 Years	19 Years	20 Years	21 Years	22 Years	23 Years	24 Years	25 Years	30 Years	35 Years	40 Years
AMOUNT														
5	.07	.07	.07	.07	.07	.07	.07	.07	.07	.07	.07	.07	.06	.06
10	.14	.14	.14	.13	.13	.13	.13	.13	.13	.13	.13	.13	.12	.12
15	.21	.20	.20	.20	.20	.19	.19	.19	.19	.19	.19	.19	.18	.18
25	.34	.34	.33	.33	.32	.32	.32	.31	.31	.31	.31	.31	.30	.30
50	.68	.67	.66	.65	.64	.63	.63	.62	.62	.62	.61	.61	.60	.60
75	1.01	1.00	.98	.97	.96	.95	.94	.93	.93	.92	.92	.91	.90	.90
100	1.35	1.33	1.31	1.29	1.28	1.26	1.25	1.24	1.24	1.23	1.22	1.21	1.20	1.19
200	2.70	2.65	2.61	2.57	2.55	2.52	2.50	2.48	2.47	2.45	2.44	2.41	2.39	2.38
300	4.04	3.97	3.91	3.86	3.82	3.78	3.75	3.72	3.70	3.68	3.66	3.61	3.58	3.57
400	5.39	5.29	5.21	5.14	5.09	5.04	5.00	4.96	4.93	4.90	4.88	4.81	4.77	4.76
500	6.73	6.61	6.51	6.43	6.36	6.30	6.24	6.20	6.16	6.13	6.10	6.01	5.96	5.94
600	8.08	7.93	7.81	7.71	7.63	7.55	7.49	7.44	7.39	7.35	7.32	7.21	7.16	7.13
700	9.42	9.25	9.11	9.00	8.90	8.81	8.74	8.68	8.62	8.58	8.54	8.41	8.35	8.32
800	10.77	10.58	10.42	10.28	10.17	10.07	9.99	9.92	9.85	9.80	9.76	9.61	9.54	9.51
900	12.11	11.90	11.72	11.57	11.44	11.33	11.23	11.15	11.09	11.03	10.98	10.81	10.73	10.69
1000	13.46	13.22	13.02	12.85	12.71	12.59	12.48	12.39	12.32	12.25	12.20	12.01	11.92	11.88
2000	26.91	26.43	26.03	25.70	25.41	25.17	24.96	24.78	24.63	24.50	24.39	24.02	23.84	23.76
3000	40.36	39.65	39.05	38.54	38.11	37.75	37.44	37.17	36.94	36.75	36.58	36.03	35.76	35.63
4000	53.81	52.86	52.06	51.39	50.81	50.33	49.91	49.56	49.25	48.99	48.77	48.03	47.68	47.51
5000	67.27	66.08	65.08	64.23	63.52	62.91	62.39	61.95	61.57	61.24	60.96	60.04	59.60	59.38
6000	80.72	79.29	78.09	77.08	76.22	75.49	74.87	74.33	73.88	73.49	73.15	72.05	71.52	71.26
7000	94.17	92.50	91.10	89.92	88.92	88.07	87.34	86.72	86.19	85.73	85.34	84.06	83.43	83.13
8000	107.62	105.72	104.12	102.77	101.62	100.65	99.82	99.11	98.50	97.98	97.53	96.06	95.35	95.01
9000	121.07	118.93	117.13	115.61	114.33	113.23	112.30	111.50	110.82	110.23	109.72	108.07	107.27	106.88
10000	134.53	132.15	130.15	128.46	127.03	125.81	124.77	123.89	123.13	122.47	121.91	120.08	119.19	118.76
11000	147.98	145.36	143.16	141.30	139.73	138.39	137.25	136.28	135.44	134.72	134.10	132.08	131.11	130.63
12000	161.43	158.57	156.17	154.15	152.43	150.97	149.73	148.66	147.75	146.97	146.30	144.09	143.03	142.51
13000	174.88	171.79	169.19	167.00	165.14	163.55	162.21	161.05	160.06	159.22	158.49	156.10	154.95	154.38
14000	188.33	185.00	182.20	179.84	177.84	176.14	174.68	173.44	172.38	171.46	170.68	168.11	166.86	166.26
15000	201.79	198.22	195.22	192.69	190.54	188.72	187.16	185.83	184.69	183.71	182.87	180.11	178.78	178.13
16000	215.24	211.43	208.23	205.53	203.24	201.30	199.64	198.22	197.00	195.96	195.06	192.12	190.70	190.01
17000	228.69	224.64	221.25	218.38	215.95	213.88	212.11	210.61	209.31	208.20	207.25	204.13	202.62	201.88
18000	242.14	237.86	234.26	231.22	228.65	226.46	224.59	222.99	221.63	220.45	219.44	216.13	214.54	213.76
19000	255.59	251.07	247.27	244.07	241.35	239.04	237.07	235.38	233.94	232.70	231.63	228.14	226.46	225.63
20000	269.05	264.29	260.29	256.91	254.05	251.62	249.54	247.77	246.25	244.94	243.82	240.15	238.38	237.51
21000	282.50	277.50	273.30	269.76	266.75	264.20	262.02	260.16	258.56	257.19	256.01	252.16	250.29	249.39
22000	295.95	290.71	286.32	282.60	279.46	276.78	274.50	272.55	270.87	269.44	268.20	264.16	262.21	261.26
23000	309.40	303.93	299.33	295.45	292.16	289.36	286.98	284.94	283.19	281.69	280.40	276.17	274.13	273.14
24000	322.85	317.14	312.34	308.29	304.86	301.94	299.45	297.32	295.50	293.93	292.59	288.18	286.05	285.01
25000	336.31	330.36	325.36	321.14	317.56	314.52	311.93	309.71	307.81	306.18	304.78	300.18	297.97	296.89
26000	349.76	343.57	338.37	333.99	330.27	327.10	324.41	322.10	320.12	318.43	316.97	312.19	309.89	308.76
27000	363.21	356.79	351.39	346.83	342.97	339.68	336.88	334.49	332.44	330.67	329.16	324.20	321.81	320.64
28000	376.66	370.00	364.40	359.68	355.67	352.27	349.36	346.88	344.75	342.92	341.35	336.21	333.72	332.51
29000	390.11	383.21	377.42	372.52	368.37	364.85	361.84	359.26	357.06	355.17	353.54	348.21	345.64	344.39
30000	403.57	396.43	390.43	385.37	381.08	377.43	374.31	371.65	369.37	367.41	365.73	360.22	357.56	356.26
31000	417.02	409.64	403.44	398.21	393.78	390.01	386.79	384.04	381.68	379.66	377.92	372.23	369.48	368.14
32000	430.47	422.86	416.46	411.06	406.48	402.59	399.27	396.43	394.00	391.91	390.11	384.24	381.40	380.01
33000	443.92	436.07	429.47	423.90	419.18	415.17	411.75	408.82	406.31	404.16	402.30	396.24	393.32	391.89
34000	457.37	449.28	442.49	436.75	431.89	427.75	424.22	421.21	418.62	416.40	414.50	408.25	405.24	403.76
35000	470.83	462.50	455.50	449.59	444.59	440.33	436.70	433.59	430.93	428.65	426.69	420.26	417.15	415.64
36000	484.28	475.71	468.51	462.44	457.29	452.91	449.18	445.98	443.25	440.90	438.88	432.26	429.07	427.51
37000	497.73	488.93	481.53	475.28	469.99	465.49	461.65	458.37	455.56	453.14	451.07	444.27	440.99	439.39
38000	511.18	502.14	494.54	488.13	482.69	478.07	474.13	470.76	467.87	465.39	463.26	456.28	452.91	451.26
39000	524.64	515.35	507.56	500.98	495.40	490.65	486.61	483.15	480.18	477.64	475.45	468.29	464.83	463.14
40000	538.09	528.57	520.57	513.82	508.10	503.23	499.08	495.54	492.49	489.88	487.64	480.29	476.75	475.01
41000	551.54	541.78	533.59	526.67	520.80	515.81	511.56	507.92	504.81	502.13	499.83	492.30	488.66	486.89
42000	564.99	555.00	546.60	539.51	533.50	528.40	524.04	520.31	517.12	514.38	512.02	504.31	500.58	498.77
43000	578.44	568.21	559.61	552.36	546.21	540.98	536.52	532.70	529.43	526.63	524.21	516.31	512.50	510.64
44000	591.90	581.42	572.63	565.20	558.91	553.56	548.99	545.09	541.74	538.87	536.40	528.32	524.42	522.52
45000	605.35	594.64	585.64	578.05	571.61	566.14	561.47	557.48	554.06	551.12	548.59	540.33	536.34	534.39
46000	618.80	607.85	598.66	590.89	584.31	578.72	573.95	569.87	566.37	563.37	560.79	552.34	548.26	546.27
47000	632.25	621.07	611.67	603.74	597.02	591.30	586.42	582.25	578.68	575.61	572.98	564.34	560.18	558.14
48000	645.70	634.28	624.68	616.58	609.72	603.88	598.90	594.64	590.99	587.86	585.17	576.35	572.09	570.02
49000	659.16	647.49	637.70	629.43	622.42	616.46	611.38	607.03	603.31	600.11	597.36	588.36	584.01	581.89
50000	672.61	660.71	650.71	642.27	635.12	629.04	623.85	619.42	615.62	612.35	609.55	600.36	595.93	593.77
55000	739.87	726.78	715.78	706.50	698.64	691.95	686.24	681.36	677.18	673.59	670.50	660.40	655.52	653.14
60000	807.13	792.85	780.85	770.73	762.15	754.85	748.62	743.30	738.74	734.82	731.46	720.44	715.12	712.52
65000	874.39	858.92	845.92	834.96	825.66	817.75	811.01	805.24	800.30	796.06	792.41	780.47	774.71	771.90
70000	941.65	924.99	911.00	899.18	889.17	880.66	873.39	867.18	861.86	857.29	853.37	840.51	834.30	831.27
75000	1008.91	991.06	976.07	963.41	952.68	943.56	935.78	929.12	923.42	918.53	914.32	900.54	893.90	890.65
80000	1076.17	1057.13	1041.14	1027.64	1016.19	1006.46	998.16	991.07	984.98	979.76	975.28	960.58	953.49	950.02
85000	1143.43	1123.20	1106.21	1091.86	1079.71	1069.37	1060.55	1053.01	1046.55	1041.00	1036.23	1020.62	1013.08	1009.40
90000	1210.69	1189.27	1171.28	1156.09	1143.22	1132.27	1122.93	1114.95	1108.11	1102.23	1097.18	1080.65	1072.67	1068.78
95000	1277.95	1255.34	1236.35	1220.32	1206.73	1195.17	1185.32	1176.89	1169.67	1163.47	1158.14	1140.69	1132.27	1128.15
100000	1345.21	1321.41	1301.42	1284.54	1270.24	1258.08	1247.70	1238.83	1231.23	1224.70	1219.09	1200.72	1191.86	1187.53

MONTHLY PAYMENT
REQUIRED TO AMORTIZE A LOAN

TERM	1 Year	2 Years	3 Years	4 Years	5 Years	6 Years	7 Years	8 Years	9 Years	10 Years	11 Years	12 Years	13 Years	14 Years
AMOUNT														
5	.45	.25	.18	.14	.12	.11	.10	.09	.09	.08	.08	.08	.08	.07
10	.90	.49	.35	.28	.24	.21	.19	.18	.17	.16	.16	.15	.15	.14
15	1.35	.73	.52	.42	.36	.32	.29	.27	.25	.24	.23	.22	.22	.21
25	2.25	1.21	.86	.69	.59	.52	.48	.44	.42	.40	.38	.37	.36	.35
50	4.50	2.41	1.72	1.38	1.17	1.04	.95	.88	.83	.79	.76	.73	.71	.69
75	6.75	3.61	2.58	2.06	1.76	1.56	1.42	1.32	1.24	1.18	1.13	1.09	1.06	1.04
100	9.00	4.82	3.43	2.75	2.34	2.08	1.89	1.76	1.65	1.57	1.51	1.46	1.42	1.38
200	17.99	9.63	6.86	5.50	4.68	4.15	3.78	3.51	3.30	3.14	3.01	2.91	2.83	2.76
300	26.98	14.44	10.29	8.24	7.02	6.23	5.67	5.26	4.95	4.71	4.52	4.36	4.24	4.14
400	35.97	19.26	13.72	10.99	9.36	8.30	7.56	7.01	6.60	6.28	6.02	5.82	5.65	5.51
500	44.96	24.07	17.15	13.73	11.70	10.37	9.44	8.76	8.25	7.84	7.53	7.27	7.06	6.89
600	53.95	28.88	20.58	16.48	14.04	12.45	11.33	10.51	9.89	9.41	9.03	8.72	8.47	8.27
700	62.94	33.70	24.01	19.22	16.38	14.52	13.22	12.26	11.54	10.98	10.53	10.18	9.88	9.64
800	71.93	38.51	27.44	21.97	18.72	16.60	15.11	14.02	13.19	12.55	12.04	11.63	11.30	11.02
900	80.92	43.32	30.87	24.71	21.06	18.67	17.00	15.77	14.84	14.11	13.54	13.08	12.71	12.40
1000	89.91	48.14	34.30	27.46	23.40	20.74	18.88	17.52	16.49	15.68	15.05	14.53	14.12	13.78
2000	179.81	96.27	68.60	54.91	46.80	41.48	37.76	35.03	32.97	31.36	30.09	29.06	28.23	27.55
3000	269.72	144.40	102.90	82.36	70.20	62.22	56.64	52.55	49.45	47.04	45.13	43.59	42.34	41.32
4000	359.62	192.53	137.20	109.81	93.60	82.96	75.52	70.06	65.93	62.71	60.17	58.12	56.46	55.09
5000	449.53	240.66	171.50	137.27	117.00	103.70	94.40	87.58	82.41	78.39	75.21	72.65	70.57	68.86
6000	539.43	288.79	205.80	164.72	140.39	124.44	113.28	105.09	98.89	94.07	90.25	87.18	84.68	82.63
7000	629.34	336.92	240.10	192.17	163.79	145.18	132.15	122.60	115.37	109.75	105.29	101.71	98.79	96.40
8000	719.24	385.05	274.40	219.62	187.19	165.92	151.03	140.12	131.85	125.42	120.33	116.24	112.91	110.17
9000	809.15	433.18	308.70	247.07	210.59	186.66	169.91	157.63	148.33	141.10	135.38	130.77	127.02	123.94
10000	899.05	481.32	343.00	274.53	233.99	207.40	188.79	175.15	164.81	156.78	150.42	145.30	141.13	137.71
11000	988.96	529.45	377.30	301.98	257.38	228.14	207.67	192.66	181.29	172.46	165.46	159.83	155.25	151.48
12000	1078.86	577.58	411.60	329.43	280.78	248.88	226.55	210.17	197.77	188.13	180.50	174.36	169.36	165.25
13000	1168.77	625.71	445.89	356.88	304.18	269.62	245.42	227.69	214.25	203.81	195.54	188.89	183.47	179.02
14000	1258.67	673.84	480.19	384.33	327.58	290.36	264.30	245.20	230.73	219.49	210.58	203.42	197.58	192.79
15000	1348.58	721.97	514.49	411.79	350.98	311.10	283.18	262.72	247.21	235.16	225.62	217.95	211.70	206.56
16000	1438.48	770.10	548.79	439.24	374.37	331.84	302.06	280.23	263.69	250.84	240.66	232.48	225.81	220.33
17000	1528.39	818.23	583.09	466.69	397.77	352.58	320.94	297.74	280.17	266.52	255.71	247.01	239.92	234.10
18000	1618.29	866.36	617.39	494.14	421.17	373.32	339.82	315.26	296.65	282.20	270.75	261.54	254.04	247.87
19000	1708.20	914.50	651.69	521.59	444.57	394.06	358.69	332.77	313.13	297.87	285.79	276.07	268.15	261.64
20000	1798.10	962.63	685.99	549.05	467.97	414.80	377.57	350.29	329.61	313.55	300.83	290.59	282.26	275.41
21000	1888.01	1010.76	720.29	576.50	491.36	435.54	396.45	367.80	346.09	329.23	315.87	305.12	296.37	289.18
22000	1977.91	1058.89	754.59	603.95	514.76	456.28	415.33	385.31	362.57	344.91	330.91	319.65	310.49	302.95
23000	2067.82	1107.02	788.89	631.40	538.16	477.02	434.21	402.83	379.05	360.58	345.95	334.18	324.60	316.72
24000	2157.72	1155.15	823.19	658.85	561.56	497.76	453.09	420.34	395.53	376.26	360.99	348.71	338.71	330.49
25000	2247.62	1203.28	857.48	686.31	584.96	518.50	471.96	437.86	412.01	391.94	376.03	363.24	352.83	344.26
26000	2337.53	1251.41	891.78	713.76	608.35	539.24	490.84	455.37	428.49	407.62	391.08	377.77	366.94	358.03
27000	2427.43	1299.54	926.08	741.21	631.75	559.98	509.72	472.89	444.98	423.29	406.12	392.30	381.05	371.80
28000	2517.34	1347.68	960.38	768.66	655.15	580.72	528.60	490.40	461.46	438.97	421.16	406.83	395.16	385.57
29000	2607.24	1395.81	994.68	796.11	678.55	601.46	547.48	507.91	477.94	454.65	436.20	421.36	409.28	399.34
30000	2697.15	1443.94	1028.98	823.57	701.95	622.20	566.36	525.43	494.42	470.32	451.24	435.89	423.39	413.11
31000	2787.05	1492.07	1063.28	851.02	725.34	642.94	585.24	542.94	510.90	486.00	466.28	450.42	437.50	426.88
32000	2876.96	1540.20	1097.58	878.47	748.74	663.68	604.11	560.46	527.38	501.68	481.32	464.95	451.61	440.65
33000	2966.86	1588.33	1131.88	905.92	772.14	684.42	622.99	577.97	543.86	517.36	496.36	479.48	465.73	454.42
34000	3056.77	1636.46	1166.18	933.37	795.54	705.16	641.87	595.48	560.34	533.03	511.41	494.01	479.84	468.19
35000	3146.67	1684.59	1200.48	960.83	818.94	725.90	660.75	613.00	576.82	548.71	526.45	508.54	493.95	481.96
36000	3236.58	1732.72	1234.78	988.28	842.34	746.64	679.63	630.51	593.30	564.39	541.49	523.07	508.07	495.73
37000	3326.48	1780.85	1269.07	1015.73	865.73	767.38	698.51	648.03	609.78	580.07	556.53	537.60	522.18	509.50
38000	3416.39	1828.99	1303.37	1043.18	889.13	788.12	717.38	665.54	626.26	595.74	571.57	552.13	536.29	523.27
39000	3506.29	1877.12	1337.67	1070.63	912.53	808.86	736.26	683.05	642.74	611.42	586.61	566.66	550.40	537.04
40000	3596.20	1925.25	1371.97	1098.09	935.93	829.60	755.14	700.57	659.22	627.10	601.65	581.18	564.52	550.81
41000	3686.10	1973.38	1406.27	1125.54	959.33	850.34	774.02	718.08	675.70	642.77	616.69	595.71	578.63	564.58
42000	3776.01	2021.51	1440.57	1152.99	982.72	871.08	792.90	735.60	692.18	658.45	631.73	610.24	592.74	578.35
43000	3865.91	2069.64	1474.87	1180.44	1006.12	891.82	811.78	753.11	708.66	674.13	646.78	624.77	606.86	592.12
44000	3955.82	2117.77	1509.17	1207.90	1029.52	912.56	830.65	770.62	725.14	689.81	661.82	639.30	620.97	605.89
45000	4045.72	2165.90	1543.47	1235.35	1052.92	933.30	849.53	788.14	741.62	705.48	676.86	653.83	635.08	619.66
46000	4135.63	2214.03	1577.77	1262.80	1076.32	954.04	868.41	805.65	758.10	721.16	691.90	668.36	649.19	633.43
47000	4225.53	2262.17	1612.07	1290.25	1099.71	974.78	887.29	823.17	774.58	736.84	706.94	682.89	663.31	647.20
48000	4315.44	2310.30	1646.37	1317.70	1123.11	995.52	906.17	840.68	791.06	752.52	721.98	697.42	677.42	660.97
49000	4405.34	2358.43	1680.66	1345.16	1146.51	1016.26	925.05	858.19	807.54	768.19	737.02	711.95	691.53	674.74
50000	4495.24	2406.56	1714.96	1372.61	1169.91	1037.00	943.92	875.71	824.02	783.87	752.06	726.48	705.65	688.51
55000	4944.77	2647.21	1886.46	1509.87	1286.90	1140.70	1038.32	963.28	906.43	862.26	827.27	799.13	776.21	757.36
60000	5394.29	2887.87	2057.96	1647.13	1403.89	1244.40	1132.71	1050.85	988.83	940.64	902.48	871.77	846.77	826.21
65000	5843.82	3128.52	2229.45	1784.39	1520.88	1348.09	1227.10	1138.42	1071.23	1019.03	977.68	944.42	917.34	895.06
70000	6293.34	3369.18	2400.95	1921.65	1637.87	1451.79	1321.49	1225.99	1153.63	1097.42	1052.89	1017.07	987.90	963.91
75000	6742.86	3609.84	2572.44	2058.91	1754.86	1555.49	1415.88	1313.56	1236.03	1175.80	1128.09	1089.72	1058.47	1032.76
80000	7192.39	3850.49	2743.94	2196.17	1871.85	1659.19	1510.28	1401.13	1318.44	1254.19	1203.30	1162.36	1129.03	1101.61
85000	7641.91	4091.15	2915.44	2333.43	1988.84	1762.89	1604.67	1488.70	1400.84	1332.58	1278.51	1235.01	1199.59	1170.46
90000	8091.44	4331.80	3086.93	2470.69	2105.83	1866.59	1699.06	1576.27	1483.24	1410.96	1353.71	1307.66	1270.16	1239.31
95000	8540.96	4572.46	3258.43	2607.95	2222.82	1970.29	1793.45	1663.84	1565.64	1489.35	1428.92	1380.31	1340.72	1308.16
100000	8990.48	4813.11	3429.92	2745.21	2339.81	2073.99	1887.84	1751.41	1648.04	1567.74	1504.12	1452.95	1411.29	1377.01

TERM	15 Years	16 Years	17 Years	18 Years	19 Years	20 Years	21 Years	22 Years	23 Years	24 Years	25 Years	30 Years	35 Years	40 Years
AMOUNT														
5	.07	.07	.07	.07	.07	.07	.07	.07	.07	.07	.07	.07	.06	.06
10	.14	.14	.14	.13	.13	.13	.13	.13	.13	.13	.13	.13	.12	.12
15	.21	.20	.20	.20	.20	.19	.19	.19	.19	.19	.19	.19	.18	.18
25	.34	.34	.33	.33	.32	.32	.32	.32	.31	.31	.31	.31	.30	.30
50	.68	.67	.66	.65	.64	.64	.63	.63	.62	.62	.62	.61	.60	.60
75	1.02	1.00	.98	.97	.96	.95	.94	.94	.93	.93	.92	.91	.90	.90
100	1.35	1.33	1.31	1.29	1.28	1.27	1.26	1.25	1.24	1.23	1.23	1.21	1.20	1.20
200	2.70	2.65	2.61	2.58	2.55	2.53	2.51	2.49	2.47	2.46	2.45	2.41	2.40	2.39
300	4.05	3.98	3.92	3.87	3.83	3.79	3.76	3.73	3.71	3.69	3.67	3.62	3.59	3.58
400	5.40	5.30	5.22	5.16	5.10	5.05	5.01	4.98	4.94	4.92	4.90	4.82	4.79	4.77
500	6.75	6.63	6.53	6.45	6.37	6.31	6.26	6.22	6.18	6.15	6.12	6.03	5.98	5.96
600	8.10	7.95	7.83	7.73	7.65	7.58	7.51	7.46	7.41	7.38	7.34	7.23	7.18	7.15
700	9.45	9.28	9.14	9.02	8.92	8.84	8.76	8.70	8.65	8.60	8.57	8.44	8.38	8.35
800	10.79	10.60	10.44	10.31	10.20	10.10	10.02	9.95	9.88	9.83	9.79	9.64	9.57	9.54
900	12.14	11.93	11.75	11.60	11.47	11.36	11.27	11.19	11.12	11.06	11.01	10.85	10.77	10.73
1000	13.49	13.25	13.05	12.89	12.74	12.62	12.52	12.43	12.35	12.29	12.23	12.05	11.96	11.92
2000	26.98	26.50	26.10	25.77	25.48	25.24	25.03	24.86	24.70	24.58	24.46	24.10	23.92	23.84
3000	40.46	39.75	39.15	38.65	38.22	37.86	37.55	37.28	37.05	36.86	36.69	36.15	35.88	35.75
4000	53.95	53.00	52.20	51.53	50.96	50.47	50.06	49.71	49.40	49.15	48.92	48.19	47.84	47.67
5000	67.43	66.25	65.25	64.41	63.70	63.09	62.57	62.13	61.75	61.43	61.15	60.24	59.80	59.59
6000	80.92	79.50	78.30	77.29	76.44	75.71	75.09	74.56	74.10	73.72	73.38	72.29	71.76	71.50
7000	94.41	92.74	91.35	90.17	89.17	88.33	87.60	86.98	86.45	86.00	85.61	84.33	83.72	83.42
8000	107.89	105.99	104.40	103.05	101.91	100.94	100.12	99.41	98.80	98.29	97.84	96.38	95.68	95.33
9000	121.38	119.24	117.45	115.93	114.65	113.56	112.63	111.84	111.15	110.57	110.07	108.43	107.64	107.25
10000	134.86	132.49	130.50	128.81	127.39	126.18	125.14	124.26	123.50	122.86	122.30	120.47	119.60	119.17
11000	148.35	145.74	143.54	141.69	140.13	138.79	137.66	136.69	135.85	135.14	134.53	132.52	131.55	131.08
12000	161.83	158.99	156.59	154.58	152.87	151.41	150.17	149.11	148.20	147.43	146.76	144.57	143.51	143.00
13000	175.32	172.23	169.64	167.46	165.60	164.03	162.69	161.54	160.55	159.71	158.99	156.61	155.47	154.92
14000	188.81	185.48	182.69	180.34	178.34	176.65	175.20	173.96	172.90	172.00	171.21	168.66	167.43	166.83
15000	202.29	198.73	195.74	193.22	191.08	189.26	187.71	186.39	185.25	184.28	183.44	180.71	179.39	178.75
16000	215.78	211.98	208.79	206.10	203.82	201.88	200.23	198.81	197.60	196.57	195.67	192.75	191.35	190.66
17000	229.26	225.23	221.84	218.98	216.56	214.50	212.74	211.24	209.95	208.85	207.90	204.80	203.31	202.58
18000	242.75	230.40	234.89	231.86	229.30	227.11	225.25	223.67	222.30	221.14	220.13	216.85	215.27	214.50
19000	256.24	251.73	247.94	244.74	242.03	239.73	237.77	236.09	234.65	233.42	232.36	228.90	227.23	226.41
20000	269.72	264.97	260.99	257.62	254.77	252.35	250.28	248.52	247.00	245.71	244.59	240.94	239.19	238.33
21000	283.21	278.22	274.04	270.50	267.51	264.97	262.80	260.94	259.35	257.99	256.82	252.99	251.14	250.25
22000	296.69	291.47	287.08	283.38	280.25	277.58	275.31	273.37	271.70	270.28	269.05	265.04	263.10	262.16
23000	310.18	304.72	300.13	296.27	292.99	290.20	287.82	285.79	284.05	282.56	281.28	277.08	275.06	274.08
24000	323.66	317.97	313.18	309.15	305.73	302.82	300.34	298.22	296.40	294.85	293.51	289.13	287.02	285.99
25000	337.15	331.22	326.23	322.03	318.46	315.43	312.85	310.64	308.75	307.13	305.74	301.18	298.98	297.91
26000	350.64	344.46	339.28	334.91	331.20	328.05	325.37	323.07	321.10	319.42	317.97	313.22	310.94	309.83
27000	364.12	357.71	352.33	347.79	343.94	340.67	337.88	335.50	333.45	331.70	330.20	325.27	322.90	321.74
28000	377.61	370.96	365.38	360.67	356.68	353.29	350.39	347.92	345.80	343.99	342.42	337.32	334.86	333.66
29000	391.09	384.21	378.43	373.55	369.42	365.90	362.91	360.35	358.15	356.27	354.65	349.36	346.82	345.58
30000	404.58	397.46	391.48	386.43	382.16	378.52	375.42	372.77	370.50	368.56	366.88	361.41	358.78	357.49
31000	418.06	410.71	404.53	399.31	394.89	391.14	387.94	385.20	382.85	380.84	379.11	373.46	370.73	369.41
32000	431.55	423.95	417.58	412.19	407.63	403.76	400.45	397.62	395.20	393.13	391.34	385.50	382.69	381.32
33000	445.04	437.20	430.62	425.07	420.37	416.37	412.96	410.05	407.55	405.41	403.57	397.55	394.65	393.24
34000	458.52	450.45	443.67	437.95	433.11	428.99	425.48	422.47	419.90	417.70	415.80	409.60	406.61	405.16
35000	472.01	463.70	456.72	450.84	445.85	441.61	437.99	434.90	432.25	429.98	428.03	421.65	418.57	417.07
36000	485.49	476.95	469.77	463.72	458.59	454.22	450.50	447.33	444.60	442.27	440.26	433.69	430.53	428.99
37000	498.98	490.20	482.82	476.60	471.32	466.84	463.02	459.75	456.95	454.55	452.49	445.74	442.49	440.91
38000	512.47	503.45	495.87	489.48	484.06	479.46	475.53	472.18	469.30	466.84	464.72	457.79	454.45	452.82
39000	525.95	516.69	508.92	502.36	496.80	492.08	488.05	484.60	481.65	479.12	476.95	469.83	466.41	464.74
40000	539.44	529.94	521.97	515.24	509.54	504.69	500.56	497.03	494.00	491.41	489.18	481.88	478.37	476.65
41000	552.92	543.19	535.02	528.12	522.28	517.31	513.07	509.45	506.35	503.69	501.41	493.93	490.33	488.57
42000	566.41	556.44	548.07	541.00	535.02	529.93	525.59	521.88	518.70	515.98	513.63	505.97	502.28	500.49
43000	579.89	569.69	561.12	553.88	547.75	542.54	538.10	534.31	531.05	528.26	525.86	518.02	514.24	512.40
44000	593.38	582.94	574.16	566.76	560.49	555.16	550.62	546.73	543.40	540.55	538.09	530.07	526.20	524.32
45000	606.87	596.18	587.21	579.64	573.23	567.78	563.13	559.16	555.75	552.83	550.32	542.11	538.16	536.24
46000	620.35	609.43	600.26	592.53	585.97	580.40	575.64	571.58	568.10	565.12	562.55	554.16	550.12	548.15
47000	633.84	622.68	613.31	605.41	598.71	593.01	588.16	584.01	580.45	577.40	574.78	566.21	562.08	560.07
48000	647.32	635.93	626.36	618.29	611.45	605.63	600.67	596.43	592.80	589.69	587.01	578.25	574.04	571.98
49000	660.81	649.18	639.41	631.17	624.18	618.25	613.19	608.86	605.15	601.97	599.24	590.30	586.00	583.90
50000	674.29	662.43	652.46	644.05	636.92	630.86	625.70	621.28	617.50	614.26	611.47	602.35	597.96	595.82
55000	741.72	728.67	717.70	708.45	700.61	693.95	688.27	683.41	679.25	675.68	672.62	662.58	657.75	655.40
60000	809.15	794.91	782.95	772.86	764.31	757.04	750.84	745.54	741.00	737.11	733.76	722.82	717.55	714.98
65000	876.58	861.15	848.20	837.26	828.00	820.12	813.41	807.67	802.75	798.53	794.91	783.05	777.34	774.56
70000	944.01	927.40	913.44	901.67	891.69	883.21	875.98	869.80	864.50	859.96	856.05	843.29	837.14	834.14
75000	1011.44	993.64	978.69	966.07	955.38	946.29	938.55	931.92	926.25	921.38	917.20	903.52	896.93	893.72
80000	1078.87	1059.88	1043.93	1030.47	1019.07	1009.38	1001.12	994.05	988.00	982.81	978.35	963.75	956.73	953.30
85000	1146.30	1126.12	1109.18	1094.88	1082.76	1072.47	1063.69	1056.18	1049.75	1044.23	1039.49	1023.99	1016.52	1012.88
90000	1213.73	1192.36	1174.42	1159.28	1146.46	1135.55	1126.25	1118.31	1111.50	1105.66	1100.64	1084.22	1076.32	1072.47
95000	1281.16	1258.61	1239.67	1223.69	1210.15	1198.64	1188.82	1180.44	1173.25	1167.09	1161.79	1144.46	1136.11	1132.05
100000	1348.58	1324.85	1304.91	1288.09	1273.84	1261.72	1251.39	1242.56	1235.00	1228.51	1222.93	1204.69	1195.91	1191.63

MONTHLY PAYMENT
REQUIRED TO AMORTIZE A LOAN

TERM	1 Year	2 Years	3 Years	4 Years	5 Years	6 Years	7 Years	8 Years	9 Years	10 Years	11 Years	12 Years	13 Years	14 Years
AMOUNT														
5	.45	.25	.18	.14	.12	.11	.10	.09	.09	.08	.08	.08	.08	.07
10	.90	.49	.35	.28	.24	.21	.19	.18	.17	.16	.16	.15	.15	.14
15	1.35	.73	.52	.42	.36	.32	.29	.27	.25	.24	.23	.22	.22	.21
25	2.25	1.21	.86	.69	.59	.52	.48	.44	.42	.40	.38	.37	.36	.35
50	4.50	2.41	1.72	1.38	1.18	1.04	.95	.88	.83	.79	.76	.73	.71	.70
75	6.75	3.62	2.58	2.07	1.76	1.56	1.42	1.32	1.24	1.18	1.14	1.10	1.07	1.04
100	9.00	4.82	3.44	2.75	2.35	2.08	1.90	1.76	1.66	1.58	1.51	1.46	1.42	1.39
200	17.99	9.64	6.87	5.50	4.69	4.16	3.79	3.51	3.31	3.15	3.02	2.92	2.83	2.77
300	26.98	14.45	10.30	8.25	7.03	6.24	5.68	5.27	4.96	4.72	4.53	4.37	4.25	4.15
400	35.98	19.27	13.73	11.00	9.37	8.31	7.57	7.02	6.61	6.29	6.03	5.83	5.66	5.53
500	44.97	24.08	17.17	13.74	11.72	10.39	9.46	8.78	8.26	7.86	7.54	7.29	7.08	6.91
600	53.96	28.90	20.60	16.49	14.06	12.47	11.35	10.53	9.91	9.43	9.05	8.74	8.49	8.29
700	62.95	33.71	24.03	19.24	16.40	14.54	13.24	12.28	11.56	11.00	10.56	10.20	9.91	9.67
800	71.95	38.53	27.46	21.99	18.74	16.62	15.13	14.04	13.21	12.57	12.06	11.65	11.32	11.05
900	80.94	43.34	30.90	24.73	21.09	18.70	17.02	15.79	14.86	14.14	13.57	13.11	12.74	12.43
1000	89.93	48.16	34.33	27.48	23.43	20.77	18.91	17.55	16.51	15.71	15.08	14.57	14.15	13.81
2000	179.86	96.31	68.65	54.96	46.85	41.54	37.82	35.09	33.02	31.42	30.15	29.13	28.30	27.61
3000	269.79	144.47	102.98	82.44	70.28	62.31	56.72	52.63	49.53	47.13	45.22	43.69	42.44	41.41
4000	359.72	192.62	137.30	109.91	93.70	83.07	75.63	70.18	66.04	62.84	60.29	58.25	56.59	55.22
5000	449.65	240.78	171.62	137.39	117.13	103.84	94.54	87.72	82.55	78.54	75.37	72.81	70.73	69.02
6000	539.58	288.93	205.95	164.87	140.55	124.61	113.44	105.26	99.06	94.25	90.44	87.37	84.88	82.82
7000	629.50	337.09	240.27	192.35	163.97	145.37	132.35	122.80	115.57	109.96	105.51	101.93	99.02	96.63
8000	719.43	385.24	274.59	219.82	187.40	166.14	151.25	140.35	132.08	125.67	120.58	116.49	113.17	110.43
9000	809.36	433.40	308.92	247.30	210.82	186.91	170.16	157.89	148.59	141.37	135.65	131.06	127.31	124.23
10000	899.29	481.55	343.24	274.78	234.25	207.67	189.07	175.43	165.10	157.08	150.73	145.62	141.46	138.04
11000	989.22	529.71	377.56	302.25	257.67	228.44	207.97	192.97	181.61	172.79	165.80	160.18	155.60	151.84
12000	1079.15	577.86	411.89	329.73	281.09	249.21	226.88	210.52	198.12	188.50	180.87	174.74	169.75	165.64
13000	1169.07	626.02	446.21	357.21	304.52	269.97	245.78	228.06	214.63	204.20	195.94	189.30	183.89	179.45
14000	1259.00	674.17	480.53	384.69	327.94	290.74	264.69	245.60	231.14	219.91	211.02	203.86	198.04	193.25
15000	1348.93	722.33	514.86	412.16	351.37	311.51	283.60	263.14	247.65	235.62	226.09	218.42	212.18	207.05
16000	1438.86	770.48	549.18	439.64	374.79	332.27	302.50	280.69	264.16	251.33	241.16	232.98	226.33	220.86
17000	1528.79	818.64	583.50	467.12	398.21	353.04	321.41	298.23	280.67	267.03	256.23	247.55	240.47	234.66
18000	1618.72	866.79	617.83	494.59	421.64	373.81	340.32	315.77	297.18	282.74	271.30	262.11	254.62	248.46
19000	1708.64	914.94	652.15	522.07	445.06	394.57	359.22	333.32	313.69	298.45	286.38	276.67	268.76	262.27
20000	1798.57	963.10	686.48	549.55	468.49	415.34	378.13	350.86	330.20	314.16	301.45	291.23	282.91	276.07
21000	1888.50	1011.25	720.80	577.03	491.91	436.11	397.03	368.40	346.71	329.86	316.52	305.79	297.06	289.87
22000	1978.43	1059.41	755.12	604.50	515.33	456.87	415.94	385.94	363.22	345.57	331.59	320.35	311.20	303.68
23000	2068.36	1107.56	789.45	631.58	538.76	477.64	434.85	403.49	379.73	361.28	346.66	334.91	325.35	317.48
24000	2158.29	1155.72	823.77	659.46	562.18	498.41	453.75	421.03	396.24	376.99	361.74	349.47	339.49	331.28
25000	2248.21	1203.87	858.09	686.94	585.61	519.17	472.66	438.57	412.75	392.69	376.81	364.04	353.64	345.08
26000	2338.14	1252.03	892.42	714.41	609.03	539.94	491.56	456.11	429.26	408.40	391.88	378.60	367.78	358.89
27000	2428.07	1300.18	926.74	741.89	632.46	560.71	510.47	473.66	445.77	424.11	406.95	393.16	381.93	372.69
28000	2518.00	1348.34	961.06	769.37	655.88	581.47	529.38	491.20	462.28	439.82	422.03	407.72	396.07	386.49
29000	2607.93	1396.49	995.39	796.84	679.30	602.24	548.28	508.74	478.79	455.52	437.10	422.28	410.22	400.30
30000	2697.86	1444.65	1029.71	824.32	702.73	623.01	567.19	526.28	495.30	471.23	452.17	436.84	424.36	414.10
31000	2787.78	1492.80	1064.03	851.80	726.15	643.77	586.09	543.83	511.81	486.94	467.24	451.40	438.51	427.90
32000	2877.71	1540.96	1098.36	879.28	749.58	664.54	605.00	561.37	528.32	502.65	482.31	465.96	452.65	441.71
33000	2967.64	1589.11	1132.68	906.75	773.00	685.31	623.91	578.91	544.83	518.35	497.39	480.53	466.80	455.51
34000	3057.57	1637.27	1167.00	934.23	796.42	706.07	642.81	596.46	561.34	534.06	512.46	495.09	480.94	469.31
35000	3147.50	1685.42	1201.33	961.71	819.85	726.84	661.72	614.00	577.85	549.77	527.53	509.65	495.09	483.12
36000	3237.43	1733.58	1235.65	989.18	843.27	747.61	680.63	631.54	594.36	565.48	542.60	524.21	509.23	496.92
37000	3327.35	1781.73	1269.98	1016.66	866.70	768.37	699.53	649.08	610.87	581.18	557.68	538.77	523.38	510.72
38000	3417.28	1829.88	1304.30	1044.14	890.12	789.14	718.44	666.63	627.38	596.89	572.75	553.33	537.52	524.53
39000	3507.21	1878.04	1338.62	1071.62	913.54	809.91	737.34	684.17	643.89	612.60	587.82	567.89	551.67	538.33
40000	3597.14	1926.19	1372.95	1099.09	936.97	830.67	756.25	701.71	660.40	628.31	602.89	582.45	565.82	552.13
41000	3687.07	1974.35	1407.27	1126.57	960.39	851.44	775.16	719.25	676.91	644.01	617.96	597.02	579.96	565.94
42000	3777.00	2022.50	1441.59	1154.05	983.82	872.21	794.06	736.80	693.42	659.72	633.04	611.58	594.11	579.74
43000	3866.92	2070.66	1475.92	1181.52	1007.24	892.97	812.97	754.34	709.93	675.43	648.11	626.14	608.25	593.54
44000	3956.85	2118.81	1510.24	1209.00	1030.66	913.74	831.87	771.88	726.44	691.14	663.18	640.70	622.40	607.35
45000	4046.78	2166.97	1544.56	1236.48	1054.09	934.51	850.78	789.42	742.95	706.84	678.25	655.26	636.54	621.15
46000	4136.71	2215.12	1578.89	1263.96	1077.51	955.27	869.69	806.97	759.46	722.55	693.32	669.82	650.69	634.95
47000	4226.64	2263.28	1613.21	1291.43	1100.94	976.04	888.59	824.51	775.97	738.26	708.40	684.38	664.83	648.75
48000	4316.57	2311.43	1647.53	1318.91	1124.36	996.81	907.50	842.05	792.48	753.97	723.47	698.94	678.98	662.56
49000	4406.49	2359.59	1681.86	1346.39	1147.78	1017.57	926.41	859.60	808.99	769.67	738.54	713.51	693.12	676.36
50000	4496.42	2407.74	1716.18	1373.87	1171.21	1038.34	945.31	877.14	825.49	785.38	753.61	728.07	707.27	690.16
55000	4946.06	2648.52	1887.80	1511.25	1288.33	1142.17	1039.84	964.85	908.04	863.92	828.97	800.87	777.99	759.18
60000	5395.71	2889.29	2059.42	1648.64	1405.45	1246.01	1134.37	1052.57	990.59	942.46	904.34	873.68	848.72	828.20
65000	5845.35	3130.06	2231.03	1786.02	1522.57	1349.84	1228.90	1140.28	1073.14	1020.99	979.70	946.49	919.45	897.21
70000	6294.99	3370.84	2402.65	1923.41	1639.69	1453.68	1323.43	1227.99	1155.69	1099.53	1055.06	1019.29	990.17	966.23
75000	6744.63	3611.61	2574.27	2060.80	1756.81	1557.51	1417.96	1315.71	1238.24	1178.07	1130.42	1092.10	1060.90	1035.24
80000	7194.27	3852.38	2745.89	2198.18	1873.93	1661.34	1512.50	1403.42	1320.79	1256.61	1205.78	1164.90	1131.63	1104.26
85000	7643.91	4093.16	2917.50	2335.57	1991.05	1765.18	1607.03	1491.13	1403.34	1335.14	1281.14	1237.71	1202.35	1173.28
90000	8093.56	4333.93	3089.12	2472.95	2108.17	1869.01	1701.56	1578.85	1485.89	1413.68	1356.50	1310.52	1273.08	1242.29
95000	8543.20	4574.70	3260.74	2610.34	2225.29	1972.84	1796.09	1666.56	1568.44	1492.22	1431.86	1383.32	1343.80	1311.31
100000	8992.84	4815.48	3432.36	2747.73	2342.41	2076.68	1890.62	1754.27	1650.98	1570.76	1507.22	1456.13	1414.53	1380.32

TERM / AMOUNT	15 Years	16 Years	17 Years	18 Years	19 Years	20 Years	21 Years	22 Years	23 Years	24 Years	25 Years	30 Years	35 Years	40 Years
5	.07	.07	.07	.07	.07	.07	.07	.07	.07	.07	.07	.07	.06	.06
10	.14	.14	.14	.13	.13	.13	.13	.13	.13	.13	.13	.13	.12	.12
15	.21	.20	.20	.20	.20	.19	.19	.19	.19	.19	.19	.19	.18	.18
25	.34	.34	.33	.33	.32	.32	.32	.32	.31	.31	.31	.31	.30	.30
50	.68	.67	.66	.65	.64	.64	.63	.63	.62	.62	.62	.61	.60	.60
75	1.02	1.00	.99	.97	.96	.95	.95	.93	.93	.93	.91	.90	.90	.90
100	1.36	1.33	1.31	1.30	1.28	1.27	1.26	1.25	1.24	1.24	1.23	1.21	1.20	1.20
200	2.71	2.66	2.62	2.59	2.56	2.54	2.52	2.50	2.48	2.47	2.46	2.42	2.40	2.40
300	4.06	3.99	3.93	3.88	3.84	3.80	3.77	3.74	3.72	3.70	3.69	3.63	3.60	3.59
400	5.41	5.32	5.24	5.17	5.11	5.07	5.03	4.99	4.96	4.93	4.91	4.84	4.80	4.79
500	6.76	6.65	6.55	6.46	6.39	6.33	6.28	6.24	6.20	6.17	6.14	6.05	6.00	5.98
600	8.12	7.97	7.86	7.75	7.67	7.60	7.54	7.48	7.44	7.40	7.37	7.26	7.20	7.18
700	9.47	9.30	9.16	9.05	8.95	8.86	8.79	8.73	8.68	8.63	8.59	8.47	8.40	8.38
800	10.82	10.63	10.47	10.34	10.22	10.13	10.05	9.98	9.92	9.86	9.82	9.67	9.60	9.57
900	12.17	11.96	11.78	11.63	11.50	11.39	11.30	11.22	11.15	11.10	11.05	10.88	10.80	10.77
1000	13.52	13.29	13.09	12.92	12.78	12.66	12.56	12.47	12.39	12.33	12.27	12.09	12.00	11.96
2000	27.04	26.57	26.17	25.84	25.55	25.31	25.11	24.93	24.78	24.65	24.54	24.18	24.00	23.92
3000	40.56	39.85	39.26	38.75	38.33	37.97	37.66	37.39	37.17	36.97	36.81	36.26	36.00	35.88
4000	54.08	53.14	52.34	51.67	51.10	50.62	50.21	49.86	49.56	49.30	49.08	48.35	48.00	47.83
5000	67.60	66.42	65.43	64.59	63.88	63.27	62.76	62.32	61.94	61.62	61.34	60.44	60.00	59.79
6000	81.12	79.70	78.51	77.50	76.65	75.93	75.31	74.78	74.33	73.94	73.61	72.52	72.00	71.75
7000	94.64	92.98	91.59	90.42	89.43	88.58	87.86	87.25	86.72	86.27	85.88	84.61	84.00	83.71
8000	108.16	106.27	104.68	103.34	102.20	101.23	100.41	99.71	99.11	98.59	98.15	96.70	96.00	95.66
9000	121.68	119.55	117.76	116.25	114.97	113.89	112.96	112.17	111.49	110.91	110.41	108.78	108.00	107.62
10000	135.20	132.83	130.85	129.17	127.75	126.54	125.51	124.63	123.88	123.24	122.68	120.87	120.00	119.58
11000	148.72	146.12	143.93	142.09	140.52	139.20	138.06	137.10	136.27	135.56	134.95	132.96	132.00	131.53
12000	162.24	159.40	157.01	155.00	153.30	151.85	150.61	149.56	148.66	147.88	147.22	145.04	144.00	143.49
13000	175.76	172.68	170.10	167.92	166.07	164.50	163.17	162.02	161.04	160.21	159.48	157.13	156.00	155.45
14000	189.28	185.96	183.18	180.83	178.85	177.16	175.72	174.49	173.43	172.53	171.75	169.22	168.00	167.41
15000	202.80	199.25	196.27	193.75	191.62	189.81	188.27	186.95	185.82	184.85	184.02	181.30	180.00	179.36
16000	216.32	212.53	209.35	206.67	204.39	202.46	200.82	199.41	198.21	197.18	196.29	193.39	192.00	191.32
17000	229.84	225.81	222.43	219.58	217.17	215.12	213.37	211.87	210.60	209.50	208.56	205.48	204.00	203.28
18000	243.36	239.10	235.52	232.50	229.94	227.77	225.92	224.34	222.98	221.82	220.82	217.56	216.00	215.24
19000	256.88	252.38	248.60	245.42	242.72	240.42	238.47	236.80	235.37	234.14	233.09	229.65	228.00	227.19
20000	270.40	265.66	261.69	258.33	255.49	253.08	251.02	249.26	247.76	246.47	245.36	241.74	240.00	239.15
21000	283.92	278.94	274.77	271.25	268.27	265.73	263.57	261.73	260.15	258.79	257.63	253.82	252.00	251.11
22000	297.44	292.23	287.85	284.17	281.04	278.39	276.12	274.19	272.53	271.11	269.89	265.91	263.99	263.06
23000	310.96	305.51	300.94	297.08	293.82	291.04	288.67	286.65	284.92	283.44	282.16	278.00	275.99	275.02
24000	324.47	318.79	314.02	310.00	306.59	303.69	301.22	299.12	297.31	295.76	294.43	290.08	287.99	286.98
25000	337.99	332.08	327.11	322.91	319.36	316.35	313.78	311.58	309.70	308.08	306.70	302.17	299.99	298.94
26000	351.51	345.36	340.19	335.83	332.14	329.00	326.33	324.04	322.08	320.41	318.96	314.26	311.99	310.89
27000	365.03	358.64	353.27	348.75	344.91	341.65	338.88	336.50	334.47	332.73	331.23	326.34	323.99	322.85
28000	378.55	371.92	366.36	361.66	357.69	354.31	351.43	348.97	346.86	345.05	343.50	338.43	335.99	334.81
29000	392.07	385.21	379.44	374.58	370.46	366.96	363.98	361.43	359.25	357.38	355.77	350.52	347.99	346.76
30000	405.59	398.49	392.53	387.50	383.24	379.62	376.53	373.89	371.64	369.70	368.04	362.60	359.99	358.72
31000	419.11	411.77	405.61	400.41	396.01	392.27	389.08	386.36	384.02	382.02	380.30	374.69	371.99	370.68
32000	432.63	425.06	418.69	413.33	408.78	404.92	401.63	398.82	396.41	394.35	392.57	386.78	383.99	382.64
33000	446.15	438.34	431.78	426.25	421.56	417.58	414.18	411.28	408.80	406.67	404.84	398.86	395.99	394.59
34000	459.67	451.62	444.86	439.16	434.33	430.23	426.73	423.74	421.19	418.99	417.11	410.95	407.99	406.55
35000	473.19	464.90	457.95	452.08	447.11	442.88	439.28	436.21	433.57	431.31	429.37	423.03	419.99	418.51
36000	486.71	478.19	471.03	464.99	459.88	455.54	451.83	448.67	445.96	443.64	441.64	435.12	431.99	430.47
37000	500.23	491.47	484.11	477.91	472.66	468.19	464.39	461.13	458.35	455.96	453.91	447.21	443.99	442.42
38000	513.75	504.75	497.20	490.83	485.43	480.84	476.94	473.60	470.74	468.28	466.18	459.29	455.99	454.38
39000	527.27	518.03	510.28	503.74	498.21	493.50	489.49	486.06	483.12	480.61	478.44	471.38	467.99	466.34
40000	540.79	531.32	523.37	516.66	510.98	506.15	502.04	498.52	495.51	492.93	490.71	483.47	479.99	478.29
41000	554.31	544.60	536.45	529.58	523.75	518.81	514.59	510.99	507.90	505.25	502.98	495.55	491.99	490.25
42000	567.83	557.88	549.54	542.49	536.53	531.46	527.14	523.45	520.29	517.58	515.25	507.64	503.99	502.21
43000	581.35	571.17	562.62	555.41	549.30	544.11	539.69	535.91	532.68	529.90	527.52	519.73	515.98	514.17
44000	594.87	584.45	575.70	568.33	562.08	556.77	552.24	548.37	545.06	542.22	539.78	531.81	527.98	526.12
45000	608.39	597.73	588.79	581.24	574.85	569.42	564.79	560.84	557.45	554.55	552.05	543.90	539.98	538.08
46000	621.91	611.01	601.87	594.16	587.63	582.07	577.34	573.30	569.84	566.87	564.32	555.99	551.98	550.04
47000	635.42	624.30	614.96	607.07	600.40	594.73	589.89	585.76	582.23	579.19	576.59	568.07	563.98	561.99
48000	648.94	637.58	628.04	619.99	613.17	607.38	602.44	598.23	594.61	591.52	588.85	580.16	575.98	573.95
49000	662.46	650.86	641.12	632.91	625.95	620.04	615.00	610.69	607.00	603.84	601.12	592.25	587.98	585.91
50000	675.98	664.15	654.21	645.82	638.72	632.69	627.55	623.15	619.39	616.16	613.39	604.33	599.98	597.87
55000	743.58	730.56	719.63	710.41	702.60	695.96	690.30	685.47	681.33	677.78	674.73	664.77	659.98	657.65
60000	811.18	796.97	785.05	774.99	766.47	759.23	753.05	747.78	743.27	739.39	736.07	725.20	719.98	717.44
65000	878.78	863.39	850.47	839.57	830.34	822.49	815.81	810.10	805.20	801.01	797.40	785.63	779.97	777.23
70000	946.38	929.80	915.89	904.15	894.21	885.76	878.56	872.41	867.14	862.62	858.74	846.06	839.97	837.01
75000	1013.97	996.22	981.31	968.73	958.08	949.03	941.32	934.73	929.08	924.24	920.08	906.50	899.97	896.80
80000	1081.57	1062.63	1046.73	1033.32	1021.95	1012.30	1004.07	997.04	991.02	985.86	981.42	966.93	959.97	956.58
85000	1149.17	1129.04	1112.15	1097.90	1085.83	1075.57	1066.82	1059.35	1052.96	1047.47	1042.76	1027.36	1019.97	1016.37
90000	1216.77	1195.46	1177.57	1162.48	1149.70	1138.84	1129.58	1121.67	1114.90	1109.09	1104.10	1087.80	1079.96	1076.16
95000	1284.36	1261.87	1242.99	1227.06	1213.57	1202.10	1192.33	1183.98	1176.84	1170.70	1165.44	1148.23	1139.96	1135.94
100000	1351.96	1328.29	1308.41	1291.64	1277.44	1265.37	1255.09	1246.30	1238.77	1232.32	1226.77	1208.66	1199.96	1195.73

MONTHLY PAYMENT
REQUIRED TO AMORTIZE A LOAN

TERM	1 Year	2 Years	3 Years	4 Years	5 Years	6 Years	7 Years	8 Years	9 Years	10 Years	11 Years	12 Years	13 Years	14 Years
AMOUNT														
5	.45	.25	.18	.14	.12	.11	.10	.09	.09	.08	.08	.08	.08	.07
10	.90	.49	.35	.28	.24	.21	.19	.18	.17	.16	.16	.15	.15	.14
15	1.35	.73	.52	.42	.36	.32	.29	.27	.25	.24	.23	.22	.22	.21
25	2.25	1.21	.86	.69	.59	.53	.48	.44	.42	.40	.38	.37	.36	.35
50	4.50	2.41	1.72	1.38	1.18	1.05	.95	.88	.83	.79	.76	.74	.71	.70
75	6.75	3.62	2.58	2.07	1.76	1.57	1.43	1.32	1.25	1.19	1.14	1.10	1.07	1.04
100	9.00	4.82	3.44	2.76	2.35	2.09	1.90	1.76	1.66	1.58	1.52	1.47	1.42	1.39
200	18.00	9.64	6.88	5.51	4.70	4.17	3.79	3.52	3.32	3.16	3.03	2.93	2.84	2.78
300	26.99	14.46	10.31	8.26	7.04	6.25	5.69	5.28	4.97	4.73	4.54	4.39	4.26	4.16
400	35.99	19.28	13.75	11.01	9.39	8.33	7.58	7.04	6.63	6.31	6.05	5.85	5.68	5.55
500	44.99	24.10	17.19	13.76	11.74	10.41	9.48	8.80	8.28	7.88	7.56	7.31	7.10	6.93
600	53.98	28.92	20.62	16.51	14.08	12.49	11.37	10.56	9.94	9.46	9.08	8.77	8.52	8.32
700	62.98	33.74	24.06	19.27	16.43	14.57	13.27	12.31	11.59	11.03	10.59	10.23	9.94	9.70
800	71.98	38.56	27.49	22.02	18.78	16.65	15.16	14.07	13.25	12.61	12.10	11.69	11.35	11.09
900	80.97	43.38	30.93	24.77	21.12	18.73	17.06	15.83	14.90	14.18	13.61	13.15	12.78	12.47
1000	89.97	48.20	34.37	27.52	23.47	20.81	18.95	17.59	16.56	15.76	15.12	14.61	14.20	13.86
2000	179.93	96.39	68.73	55.03	46.93	41.62	37.90	35.18	33.11	31.51	30.24	29.22	28.39	27.71
3000	269.90	144.58	103.09	82.55	70.39	62.43	56.85	52.76	49.67	47.26	45.36	43.83	42.59	41.56
4000	359.86	192.77	137.45	110.06	93.86	83.23	75.80	70.35	66.22	63.02	60.48	58.44	56.78	55.42
5000	449.82	240.96	171.81	137.58	117.32	104.04	94.74	87.93	82.77	78.77	75.60	73.05	70.97	69.27
6000	539.79	289.15	206.17	165.09	140.78	124.85	113.69	105.52	99.33	94.52	90.72	87.66	85.17	83.12
7000	629.75	337.34	240.53	192.61	164.25	145.65	132.64	123.10	115.88	110.28	105.84	102.27	99.36	96.98
8000	719.71	385.53	274.89	220.12	187.71	166.46	151.59	140.69	132.44	126.03	120.95	116.88	113.56	110.83
9000	809.68	433.72	309.25	247.64	211.17	187.27	170.54	158.28	148.99	141.78	136.07	131.49	127.75	124.68
10000	899.64	481.91	343.61	275.15	234.64	208.08	189.48	175.86	165.54	157.53	151.19	146.09	141.94	138.53
11000	989.61	530.10	377.97	302.67	258.10	228.88	208.43	193.45	182.10	173.29	166.31	160.70	156.14	152.39
12000	1079.57	578.29	412.33	330.18	281.56	249.69	227.38	211.03	198.65	189.04	181.43	175.31	170.33	166.24
13000	1169.53	626.48	446.69	357.70	305.03	270.50	246.33	228.62	215.21	204.79	196.55	189.92	184.53	180.09
14000	1259.50	674.67	481.05	385.21	328.49	291.30	265.27	246.20	231.76	220.55	211.67	204.53	198.72	193.95
15000	1349.46	722.86	515.41	412.73	351.95	312.11	284.22	263.79	248.31	236.30	226.79	219.14	212.91	207.80
16000	1439.42	771.05	549.77	440.24	375.41	332.92	303.17	281.37	264.87	252.05	241.90	233.75	227.11	221.65
17000	1529.39	819.24	584.13	467.76	398.88	353.73	322.12	298.96	281.42	267.80	257.02	248.36	241.30	235.51
18000	1619.35	867.43	618.49	495.27	422.34	374.53	341.07	316.55	297.98	283.56	272.14	262.97	255.50	249.36
19000	1709.31	915.62	652.85	522.79	445.80	395.34	360.01	334.13	314.53	299.31	287.26	277.57	269.69	263.21
20000	1799.28	963.81	687.21	550.30	469.27	416.15	378.96	351.72	331.08	315.06	302.38	292.18	283.88	277.06
21000	1889.24	1012.00	721.57	577.82	492.73	436.95	397.91	369.30	347.64	330.82	317.50	306.79	298.08	290.92
22000	1979.21	1060.19	755.93	605.33	516.19	457.76	416.86	386.89	364.19	346.57	332.62	321.40	312.27	304.77
23000	2069.17	1108.38	790.29	632.85	539.66	478.57	435.80	404.47	380.75	362.32	347.74	336.01	326.47	318.62
24000	2159.13	1156.57	824.65	660.36	563.12	499.37	454.75	422.06	397.30	378.07	362.85	350.62	340.66	332.48
25000	2249.10	1204.76	859.01	687.88	586.58	520.18	473.70	439.64	413.85	393.83	377.97	365.23	354.85	346.33
26000	2339.06	1252.95	893.37	715.39	610.05	540.99	492.65	457.23	430.41	409.58	393.09	379.84	369.05	360.18
27000	2429.02	1301.14	927.73	742.91	633.51	561.80	511.60	474.82	446.96	425.33	408.21	394.45	383.24	374.03
28000	2518.99	1349.33	962.09	770.42	656.97	582.60	530.54	492.40	463.52	441.09	423.33	409.05	397.44	387.89
29000	2608.95	1397.52	996.45	797.94	680.44	603.41	549.49	509.99	480.07	456.84	438.45	423.66	411.63	401.74
30000	2698.91	1445.71	1030.81	825.45	703.90	624.22	568.44	527.57	496.62	472.59	453.57	438.27	425.82	415.59
31000	2788.88	1493.90	1065.17	852.97	727.36	645.02	587.39	545.16	513.18	488.35	468.69	452.88	440.02	429.45
32000	2878.84	1542.09	1099.53	880.48	750.82	665.83	606.33	562.74	529.73	504.10	483.80	467.49	454.21	443.30
33000	2968.81	1590.28	1133.89	908.00	774.29	686.64	625.28	580.33	546.29	519.85	498.92	482.10	468.41	457.15
34000	3058.77	1638.47	1168.25	935.51	797.75	707.45	644.23	597.92	562.84	535.60	514.04	496.71	482.60	471.01
35000	3148.73	1686.66	1202.61	963.03	821.21	728.25	663.18	615.50	579.39	551.36	529.16	511.32	496.79	484.86
36000	3238.70	1734.85	1236.97	990.54	844.68	749.06	682.13	633.09	595.95	567.11	544.28	525.93	510.99	498.71
37000	3328.66	1783.04	1271.33	1018.06	868.14	769.87	701.07	650.67	612.50	582.86	559.40	540.53	525.18	512.56
38000	3418.62	1831.23	1305.69	1045.57	891.60	790.67	720.02	668.26	629.06	598.62	574.52	555.14	539.38	526.42
39000	3508.59	1879.42	1340.05	1073.09	915.07	811.48	738.97	685.84	645.61	614.37	589.63	569.75	553.57	540.27
40000	3598.55	1927.61	1374.41	1100.60	938.53	832.29	757.92	703.43	662.16	630.12	604.75	584.36	567.76	554.12
41000	3688.51	1975.80	1408.77	1128.12	961.99	853.10	776.86	721.01	678.72	645.87	619.87	598.97	581.96	567.98
42000	3778.48	2023.99	1443.13	1155.63	985.46	873.90	795.81	738.60	695.27	661.63	634.99	613.58	596.15	581.83
43000	3868.44	2072.18	1477.49	1183.15	1008.92	894.71	814.76	756.19	711.83	677.38	650.11	628.19	610.35	595.68
44000	3958.41	2120.38	1511.85	1210.66	1032.38	915.52	833.71	773.77	728.38	693.13	665.23	642.80	624.54	609.53
45000	4048.37	2168.57	1546.21	1238.18	1055.85	936.32	852.66	791.36	744.93	708.89	680.35	657.41	638.73	623.39
46000	4138.33	2216.76	1580.57	1265.69	1079.31	957.13	871.60	808.94	761.49	724.64	695.47	672.01	652.93	637.24
47000	4228.30	2264.95	1614.93	1293.21	1102.77	977.94	890.55	826.53	778.04	740.39	710.58	686.62	667.12	651.09
48000	4318.26	2313.14	1649.29	1320.72	1126.23	998.74	909.50	844.11	794.60	756.14	725.70	701.23	681.32	664.95
49000	4408.22	2361.33	1683.65	1348.24	1149.70	1019.55	928.45	861.70	811.15	771.90	740.82	715.84	695.51	678.80
50000	4498.19	2409.52	1718.01	1375.75	1173.16	1040.36	947.39	879.28	827.70	787.65	755.94	730.45	709.70	692.65
55000	4948.01	2650.47	1889.81	1513.33	1290.48	1144.39	1042.13	967.21	910.47	866.41	831.53	803.49	780.67	761.92
60000	5397.82	2891.42	2061.61	1650.90	1407.79	1248.43	1136.87	1055.14	993.24	945.18	907.13	876.54	851.64	831.18
65000	5847.64	3132.37	2233.41	1788.48	1525.11	1352.47	1231.61	1143.07	1076.01	1023.94	982.72	949.58	922.61	900.45
70000	6297.46	3373.32	2405.21	1926.05	1642.42	1456.50	1326.35	1231.00	1158.78	1102.71	1058.32	1022.63	993.58	969.71
75000	6747.28	3614.27	2577.01	2063.63	1759.74	1560.54	1421.09	1318.92	1241.55	1181.47	1133.91	1095.67	1064.55	1038.98
80000	7197.10	3855.22	2748.81	2201.20	1877.05	1664.57	1515.83	1406.85	1324.32	1260.24	1209.50	1168.72	1135.52	1108.24
85000	7646.92	4096.17	2920.61	2338.78	1994.37	1768.61	1610.57	1494.78	1407.09	1339.00	1285.10	1241.76	1206.49	1177.51
90000	8096.73	4337.13	3092.41	2476.35	2111.69	1872.64	1705.31	1582.71	1489.86	1417.77	1360.69	1314.81	1277.46	1246.77
95000	8546.55	4578.08	3264.21	2613.93	2229.00	1976.68	1800.04	1670.64	1572.63	1496.53	1436.28	1387.85	1348.43	1316.03
100000	8996.37	4819.03	3436.01	2751.50	2346.32	2080.71	1894.78	1758.56	1655.40	1575.30	1511.88	1460.89	1419.40	1385.30

TERM	15 Years	16 Years	17 Years	18 Years	19 Years	20 Years	21 Years	22 Years	23 Years	24 Years	25 Years	30 Years	35 Years	40 Years
AMOUNT														
5	.07	.07	.07	.07	.07	.07	.07	.07	.07	.07	.07	.07	.07	.07
10	.14	.14	.14	.13	.13	.13	.13	.13	.13	.13	.13	.13	.13	.13
15	.21	.21	.20	.20	.20	.20	.19	.19	.19	.19	.19	.19	.19	.19
25	.34	.34	.33	.33	.33	.32	.32	.32	.32	.31	.31	.31	.31	.31
50	.68	.67	.66	.65	.65	.64	.64	.63	.63	.62	.62	.61	.61	.61
75	1.02	1.01	.99	.98	.97	.96	.95	.94	.94	.93	.93	.92	.91	.91
100	1.36	1.34	1.32	1.30	1.29	1.28	1.27	1.26	1.25	1.24	1.24	1.22	1.21	1.21
200	2.72	2.67	2.63	2.60	2.57	2.55	2.53	2.51	2.49	2.48	2.47	2.43	2.42	2.41
300	4.08	4.01	3.95	3.90	3.85	3.82	3.79	3.76	3.74	3.72	3.70	3.65	3.62	3.61
400	5.43	5.34	5.26	5.19	5.14	5.09	5.05	5.01	4.98	4.96	4.94	4.86	4.83	4.81
500	6.79	6.67	6.57	6.49	6.42	6.36	6.31	6.26	6.23	6.20	6.17	6.08	6.04	6.01
600	8.15	8.01	7.89	7.79	7.70	7.63	7.57	7.52	7.47	7.43	7.40	7.29	7.24	7.22
700	9.50	9.34	9.20	9.08	8.98	8.90	8.83	8.77	8.72	8.67	8.63	8.51	8.45	8.42
800	10.86	10.67	10.51	10.38	10.27	10.17	10.09	10.02	9.96	9.91	9.87	9.72	9.65	9.62
900	12.22	12.01	11.83	11.68	11.55	11.44	11.35	11.27	11.20	11.15	11.10	10.94	10.86	10.82
1000	13.58	13.34	13.14	12.97	12.83	12.71	12.61	12.52	12.45	12.39	12.33	12.15	12.07	12.02
2000	27.15	26.67	26.28	25.94	25.66	25.42	25.22	25.04	24.89	24.77	24.66	24.30	24.13	24.04
3000	40.72	40.01	39.41	38.91	38.49	38.13	37.82	37.56	37.34	37.15	36.98	36.44	36.19	36.06
4000	54.29	53.34	52.55	51.88	51.32	50.84	50.43	50.08	49.78	49.53	49.31	48.59	48.25	48.08
5000	67.86	66.68	65.69	64.85	64.15	63.55	63.04	62.60	62.23	61.91	61.63	60.74	60.31	60.10
6000	81.43	80.01	78.82	77.82	76.98	76.26	75.64	75.12	74.67	74.29	73.96	72.88	72.37	72.12
7000	95.00	93.35	91.96	90.79	89.80	88.96	88.25	87.64	87.12	86.67	86.28	85.03	84.43	84.14
8000	108.57	106.68	105.10	103.76	102.63	101.67	100.86	100.16	99.56	99.05	98.61	97.17	96.49	96.15
9000	122.14	120.02	118.23	116.73	115.46	114.38	113.46	112.68	112.00	111.43	110.93	109.32	108.55	108.17
10000	135.71	133.35	131.37	129.70	128.29	127.09	126.07	125.20	124.45	123.81	123.26	121.47	120.61	120.19
11000	149.28	146.68	144.51	142.67	141.12	139.80	138.67	137.71	136.89	136.19	135.58	133.61	132.67	132.21
12000	162.85	160.02	157.64	155.64	153.95	152.51	151.28	150.23	149.34	148.57	147.91	145.76	144.73	144.23
13000	176.42	173.35	170.78	168.61	166.77	165.22	163.89	162.75	161.78	160.95	160.23	157.90	156.79	156.25
14000	189.99	186.69	183.92	181.58	179.60	177.92	176.49	175.27	174.23	173.33	172.56	170.05	168.85	168.27
15000	203.56	200.02	197.05	194.55	192.43	190.63	189.10	187.79	186.67	185.71	184.89	182.20	180.91	180.29
16000	217.13	213.36	210.19	207.52	205.26	203.34	201.71	200.31	199.11	198.09	197.21	194.34	192.97	192.30
17000	230.70	226.69	223.33	220.49	218.09	216.05	214.31	212.83	211.56	210.47	209.54	206.49	205.03	204.32
18000	244.27	240.03	236.46	233.46	230.92	228.76	226.92	225.35	224.00	222.85	221.86	218.64	217.09	216.34
19000	257.84	253.36	249.60	246.43	243.75	241.47	239.52	237.87	236.45	235.23	234.19	230.70	229.15	228.36
20000	271.41	266.69	262.74	259.40	256.57	254.17	252.13	250.39	248.89	247.61	246.51	242.93	241.21	240.38
21000	284.98	280.03	275.87	272.37	269.40	266.88	264.74	262.90	261.34	259.99	258.84	255.07	253.27	252.40
22000	298.55	293.36	289.01	285.34	282.23	279.59	277.34	275.42	273.78	272.37	271.16	267.22	265.33	264.42
23000	312.12	306.70	302.15	298.31	295.06	292.30	289.95	287.94	286.22	284.75	283.49	279.37	277.39	276.44
24000	325.69	320.03	315.28	311.28	307.89	305.01	302.56	300.46	298.67	297.13	295.81	291.51	289.45	288.45
25000	339.26	333.37	328.42	324.25	320.72	317.72	315.16	312.98	311.11	309.51	308.14	303.66	301.51	300.47
26000	352.83	346.70	341.56	337.22	333.54	330.43	327.77	325.50	323.56	321.89	320.46	315.80	313.57	312.49
27000	366.40	360.04	354.69	350.19	346.37	343.13	340.38	338.02	336.00	334.27	332.79	327.95	325.63	324.51
28000	379.97	373.37	367.83	363.16	359.20	355.84	352.98	350.54	348.45	346.65	345.12	340.10	337.69	336.53
29000	393.54	386.70	380.97	376.13	372.03	368.55	365.59	363.06	360.89	359.03	357.44	352.24	349.75	348.55
30000	407.11	400.04	394.10	389.10	384.86	381.26	378.19	375.58	373.34	371.41	369.77	364.39	361.81	360.57
31000	420.68	413.37	407.24	402.07	397.69	393.97	390.80	388.09	385.78	383.80	382.09	376.54	373.87	372.59
32000	434.25	426.71	420.37	415.04	410.52	406.68	403.41	400.61	398.22	396.18	394.42	388.68	385.94	384.60
33000	447.82	440.04	433.51	428.01	423.34	419.38	416.01	413.13	410.67	408.56	406.74	400.83	398.00	396.62
34000	461.40	453.38	446.65	440.97	436.17	432.09	428.62	425.65	423.11	420.94	419.07	412.97	410.06	408.64
35000	474.97	466.71	459.78	453.94	449.00	444.80	441.23	438.17	435.56	433.32	431.39	425.12	422.12	420.66
36000	488.54	480.05	472.92	466.91	461.83	457.51	453.83	450.69	448.00	445.70	443.72	437.27	434.18	432.68
37000	502.11	493.38	486.06	479.88	474.66	470.22	466.44	463.21	460.45	458.08	456.04	449.41	446.24	444.70
38000	515.68	506.71	499.19	492.85	487.49	482.93	479.04	475.73	472.89	470.46	468.37	461.56	458.30	456.72
39000	529.25	520.05	512.33	505.82	500.31	495.64	491.65	488.25	485.33	482.84	480.69	473.70	470.36	468.74
40000	542.82	533.38	525.47	518.79	513.14	508.34	504.26	500.77	497.78	495.22	493.02	485.85	482.42	480.75
41000	556.39	546.72	538.60	531.76	525.97	521.05	516.86	513.28	510.22	507.60	505.35	498.00	494.48	492.77
42000	569.96	560.05	551.74	544.73	538.80	533.76	529.47	525.80	522.67	519.98	517.67	510.14	506.54	504.79
43000	583.53	573.39	564.88	557.70	551.63	546.47	542.08	538.32	535.11	532.36	530.00	522.29	518.60	516.81
44000	597.10	586.72	578.01	570.67	564.46	559.18	554.68	550.84	547.56	544.74	542.32	534.44	530.66	528.83
45000	610.67	600.06	591.15	583.64	577.29	571.89	567.29	563.36	560.00	557.12	554.65	546.58	542.72	540.85
46000	624.24	613.39	604.29	596.61	590.11	584.60	579.89	575.88	572.44	569.50	566.97	558.73	554.78	552.87
47000	637.81	626.72	617.42	609.58	602.94	597.30	592.50	588.40	584.89	581.88	579.30	570.87	566.84	564.89
48000	651.38	640.06	630.56	622.55	615.77	610.01	605.11	600.92	597.33	594.26	591.62	583.02	578.90	576.90
49000	664.95	653.39	643.70	635.52	628.60	622.72	617.71	613.44	609.78	606.64	603.95	595.17	590.96	588.92
50000	678.52	666.73	656.83	648.49	641.43	635.43	630.32	625.96	622.22	619.02	616.27	607.31	603.02	600.94
55000	746.37	733.40	722.52	713.34	705.57	698.97	693.35	688.55	684.44	680.92	677.90	668.04	663.32	661.04
60000	814.22	800.07	788.20	778.19	769.71	762.51	756.38	751.15	746.67	742.82	739.53	728.77	723.62	721.13
65000	882.07	866.74	853.88	843.04	833.85	826.06	819.41	813.74	808.89	804.73	801.15	789.50	783.92	781.22
70000	949.93	933.42	919.56	907.88	898.00	889.60	882.45	876.34	871.11	866.63	862.78	850.24	844.23	841.32
75000	1017.78	1000.09	985.25	972.73	962.14	953.14	945.48	938.93	933.33	928.53	924.41	910.97	904.53	901.41
80000	1085.63	1066.76	1050.93	1037.58	1026.28	1016.68	1008.51	1001.53	995.55	990.43	986.03	971.70	964.83	961.50
85000	1153.48	1133.43	1116.61	1102.43	1090.42	1080.23	1071.54	1064.12	1057.77	1052.33	1047.66	1032.43	1025.13	1021.60
90000	1221.33	1200.11	1182.30	1167.28	1154.57	1143.77	1134.57	1126.72	1120.00	1114.23	1109.29	1093.16	1085.43	1081.69
95000	1289.18	1266.78	1247.98	1232.13	1218.71	1207.31	1197.60	1189.31	1182.22	1176.14	1170.91	1153.89	1145.74	1141.79
100000	1357.04	1333.45	1313.66	1296.98	1282.85	1270.85	1260.63	1251.91	1244.44	1238.04	1232.54	1214.62	1206.04	1201.88

MONTHLY PAYMENT
REQUIRED TO AMORTIZE A LOAN

TERM	1 Year	2 Years	3 Years	4 Years	5 Years	6 Years	7 Years	8 Years	9 Years	10 Years	11 Years	12 Years	13 Years	14 Years
AMOUNT														
5	.45	.25	.18	.14	.12	.11	.10	.09	.09	.08	.08	.08	.08	.07
10	.90	.49	.35	.28	.24	.21	.19	.18	.17	.16	.16	.15	.15	.14
15	1.35	.73	.52	.42	.36	.32	.29	.27	.25	.24	.23	.22	.22	.21
25	2.25	1.21	.86	.69	.59	.53	.48	.44	.42	.40	.38	.37	.36	.35
50	4.50	2.42	1.72	1.38	1.18	1.05	.95	.88	.83	.79	.76	.74	.72	.70
75	6.75	3.62	2.58	2.07	1.77	1.57	1.43	1.32	1.25	1.19	1.14	1.10	1.07	1.05
100	9.00	4.83	3.44	2.76	2.35	2.09	1.90	1.76	1.66	1.58	1.52	1.47	1.43	1.39
200	18.00	9.65	6.88	5.51	4.70	4.17	3.80	3.52	3.32	3.16	3.03	2.93	2.85	2.78
300	27.00	14.47	10.32	8.26	7.05	6.25	5.69	5.28	4.98	4.74	4.55	4.39	4.27	4.17
400	36.00	19.29	13.75	11.02	9.40	8.33	7.59	7.04	6.63	6.31	6.06	5.86	5.69	5.56
500	44.99	24.11	17.19	13.77	11.74	10.42	9.49	8.80	8.29	7.89	7.57	7.32	7.11	6.94
600	53.99	28.93	20.63	16.52	14.09	12.50	11.38	10.56	9.95	9.47	9.09	8.78	8.53	8.33
700	62.99	33.75	24.07	19.27	16.44	14.58	13.28	12.32	11.60	11.04	10.60	10.24	9.95	9.71
800	71.99	38.57	27.50	22.03	18.79	16.66	15.17	14.08	13.26	12.62	12.11	11.70	11.37	11.10
900	80.98	43.39	30.94	24.78	21.13	18.74	17.07	15.84	14.92	14.20	13.63	13.17	12.79	12.49
1000	89.98	48.21	34.38	27.53	23.48	20.83	18.97	17.60	16.57	15.77	15.14	14.63	14.22	13.87
2000	179.96	96.41	68.75	55.06	46.96	41.65	37.93	35.20	33.14	31.54	30.27	29.25	28.43	27.74
3000	269.93	144.61	103.12	82.59	70.43	62.47	56.89	52.80	49.71	47.31	45.41	43.88	42.64	41.61
4000	359.91	192.81	137.49	110.12	93.91	83.29	75.85	70.40	66.28	63.08	60.54	58.50	56.85	55.48
5000	449.88	241.02	171.87	137.64	117.39	104.11	94.81	88.00	82.85	78.85	75.68	73.13	71.06	69.35
6000	539.86	289.22	206.24	165.17	140.86	124.93	113.78	105.60	99.42	94.61	90.81	87.75	85.27	83.22
7000	629.83	337.42	240.61	192.70	164.34	145.75	132.74	123.20	115.99	110.38	105.94	102.38	99.48	97.09
8000	719.81	385.62	274.98	220.23	187.81	166.57	151.70	140.80	132.55	126.15	121.08	117.00	113.69	110.96
9000	809.78	433.82	309.36	247.75	211.29	187.39	170.66	158.40	149.12	141.92	136.21	131.63	127.90	124.83
10000	899.76	482.03	343.73	275.28	234.77	208.21	189.62	176.00	165.69	157.69	151.35	146.25	142.11	138.70
11000	989.73	530.23	378.10	302.81	258.24	229.03	208.58	193.60	182.26	173.45	166.48	160.88	156.32	152.57
12000	1079.71	578.43	412.47	330.34	281.72	249.85	227.55	211.20	198.83	189.22	181.62	175.50	170.53	166.44
13000	1169.69	626.63	446.84	357.86	305.19	270.67	246.51	228.80	215.40	204.99	196.75	190.13	184.74	180.31
14000	1259.66	674.83	481.22	385.39	328.67	291.49	265.47	246.40	231.97	220.76	211.88	204.75	198.95	194.18
15000	1349.64	723.04	515.59	412.92	352.15	312.31	284.43	264.00	248.54	236.53	227.02	219.38	213.16	208.05
16000	1439.61	771.24	549.96	440.45	375.62	333.13	303.39	281.60	265.10	252.29	242.15	234.00	227.37	221.92
17000	1529.59	819.44	584.33	467.97	399.10	353.95	322.35	299.20	281.67	268.06	257.29	248.63	241.58	235.79
18000	1619.56	867.64	618.71	495.50	422.58	374.77	341.32	316.80	298.24	283.83	272.42	263.25	255.79	249.66
19000	1709.54	915.84	653.08	523.03	446.05	395.60	360.28	334.40	314.81	299.60	287.56	277.88	270.00	263.53
20000	1799.51	964.05	687.45	550.56	469.53	416.42	379.24	352.00	331.38	315.37	302.69	292.50	284.21	277.40
21000	1889.49	1012.25	721.82	578.08	493.00	437.24	398.20	369.60	347.95	331.13	317.82	307.13	298.42	291.27
22000	1979.46	1060.45	756.19	605.61	516.48	458.06	417.16	387.20	364.52	346.90	332.96	321.75	312.63	305.14
23000	2069.44	1108.65	790.57	633.14	539.96	478.88	436.12	404.80	381.09	362.67	348.09	336.38	326.84	319.00
24000	2159.42	1156.85	824.94	660.67	563.43	499.70	455.09	422.40	397.65	378.44	363.23	351.00	341.05	332.87
25000	2249.39	1205.06	859.31	688.19	586.91	520.52	474.05	440.00	414.22	394.21	378.36	365.62	355.26	346.74
26000	2339.37	1253.26	893.68	715.72	610.38	541.34	493.01	457.60	430.79	409.97	393.50	380.25	369.47	360.61
27000	2429.34	1301.46	928.06	743.25	633.86	562.16	511.97	475.20	447.36	425.74	408.63	394.87	383.68	374.48
28000	2519.32	1349.66	962.43	770.78	657.34	582.98	530.93	492.80	463.93	441.51	423.76	409.50	397.89	388.35
29000	2609.29	1397.86	996.80	798.30	680.81	603.80	549.89	510.40	480.50	457.28	438.90	424.12	412.10	402.22
30000	2699.27	1446.07	1031.17	825.83	704.29	624.62	568.86	528.00	497.07	473.05	454.03	438.75	426.31	416.09
31000	2789.24	1494.27	1065.54	853.36	727.77	645.44	587.82	545.60	513.63	488.81	469.17	453.37	440.52	429.96
32000	2879.22	1542.47	1099.92	880.89	751.24	666.26	606.78	563.20	530.20	504.58	484.30	468.00	454.73	443.83
33000	2969.19	1590.67	1134.29	908.41	774.72	687.08	625.74	580.80	546.77	520.35	499.44	482.62	468.94	457.70
34000	3059.17	1638.88	1168.66	935.94	798.19	707.90	644.70	598.40	563.34	536.12	514.57	497.25	483.15	471.57
35000	3149.15	1687.08	1203.03	963.47	821.67	728.72	663.66	616.00	579.91	551.89	529.70	511.87	497.36	485.44
36000	3239.12	1735.28	1237.41	991.00	845.15	749.54	682.63	633.60	596.48	567.65	544.84	526.50	511.57	499.31
37000	3329.10	1783.48	1271.78	1018.52	868.62	770.36	701.59	651.20	613.05	583.42	559.97	541.12	525.78	513.18
38000	3419.07	1831.68	1306.15	1046.05	892.10	791.19	720.55	668.80	629.62	599.19	575.11	555.75	539.99	527.05
39000	3509.05	1879.89	1340.52	1073.58	915.57	812.01	739.51	686.40	646.18	614.96	590.24	570.37	554.20	540.92
40000	3599.02	1928.09	1374.89	1101.11	939.05	832.83	758.47	704.00	662.75	630.73	605.37	585.00	568.42	554.79
41000	3689.00	1976.29	1409.27	1128.63	962.53	853.65	777.43	721.60	679.32	646.49	620.51	599.62	582.63	568.66
42000	3778.97	2024.49	1443.64	1156.16	986.00	874.47	796.40	739.20	695.89	662.26	635.64	614.25	596.84	582.53
43000	3868.95	2072.69	1478.01	1183.69	1009.48	895.29	815.36	756.80	712.46	678.03	650.78	628.87	611.05	596.40
44000	3958.92	2120.90	1512.38	1211.22	1032.96	916.11	834.32	774.40	729.03	693.80	665.91	643.50	625.26	610.27
45000	4048.90	2169.10	1546.76	1238.74	1056.43	936.93	853.28	792.00	745.60	709.57	681.05	658.12	639.47	624.13
46000	4138.87	2217.30	1581.13	1266.27	1079.91	957.75	872.24	809.60	762.17	725.34	696.18	672.75	653.68	638.00
47000	4228.85	2265.50	1615.50	1293.80	1103.38	978.57	891.20	827.20	778.73	741.10	711.31	687.37	667.89	651.87
48000	4318.83	2313.70	1649.87	1321.33	1126.86	999.39	910.17	844.80	795.30	756.87	726.45	702.00	682.10	665.74
49000	4408.80	2361.91	1684.24	1348.86	1150.34	1020.21	929.13	862.40	811.87	772.64	741.58	716.62	696.31	679.61
50000	4498.78	2410.11	1718.62	1376.38	1173.81	1041.03	948.09	880.00	828.44	788.41	756.72	731.24	710.52	693.48
55000	4948.65	2651.12	1890.48	1514.02	1291.19	1145.13	1042.90	968.00	911.28	867.25	832.39	804.37	781.57	762.83
60000	5398.53	2892.13	2062.34	1651.66	1408.57	1249.24	1137.71	1056.00	994.13	946.09	908.06	877.49	852.62	832.18
65000	5848.41	3133.14	2234.20	1789.30	1525.95	1353.34	1232.51	1144.00	1076.97	1024.93	983.73	950.62	923.67	901.53
70000	6298.29	3374.15	2406.06	1926.93	1643.34	1457.44	1327.32	1232.00	1159.81	1103.77	1059.40	1023.74	994.72	970.87
75000	6748.16	3615.16	2577.92	2064.57	1760.72	1561.55	1422.13	1320.00	1242.66	1182.61	1135.07	1096.86	1065.77	1040.22
80000	7198.04	3856.17	2749.78	2202.21	1878.10	1665.65	1516.94	1408.00	1325.50	1261.45	1210.74	1169.99	1136.83	1109.57
85000	7647.92	4097.18	2921.64	2339.85	1995.48	1769.75	1611.75	1496.00	1408.35	1340.29	1286.42	1243.11	1207.88	1178.92
90000	8097.79	4338.19	3093.51	2477.48	2112.86	1873.85	1706.56	1584.00	1491.19	1419.13	1362.09	1316.24	1278.93	1248.26
95000	8547.67	4579.20	3265.37	2615.12	2230.24	1977.96	1801.36	1672.00	1574.03	1497.97	1437.76	1389.36	1349.98	1317.61
100000	8997.55	4820.21	3437.23	2752.76	2347.62	2082.06	1896.17	1760.00	1656.88	1576.81	1513.43	1462.48	1421.03	1386.96

TERM	15 Years	16 Years	17 Years	18 Years	19 Years	20 Years	21 Years	22 Years	23 Years	24 Years	25 Years	30 Years	35 Years	40 Years
AMOUNT														
5	.07	.07	.07	.07	.07	.07	.07	.07	.07	.07	.07	.07	.07	.07
10	.14	.14	.14	.13	.13	.13	.13	.13	.13	.13	.13	.13	.13	.13
15	.21	.21	.20	.20	.20	.20	.19	.19	.19	.19	.19	.19	.19	.19
25	.34	.34	.33	.33	.33	.32	.32	.32	.32	.31	.31	.31	.31	.31
50	.68	.67	.66	.65	.65	.64	.64	.63	.63	.62	.62	.61	.61	.61
75	1.02	1.01	.99	.98	.97	.96	.95	.95	.94	.93	.93	.92	.91	.91
100	1.36	1.34	1.32	1.30	1.29	1.28	1.27	1.26	1.25	1.24	1.24	1.22	1.21	1.21
200	2.72	2.68	2.64	2.60	2.57	2.55	2.53	2.51	2.50	2.48	2.47	2.44	2.42	2.41
300	4.08	4.01	3.95	3.90	3.86	3.82	3.79	3.77	3.74	3.72	3.71	3.65	3.63	3.62
400	5.44	5.35	5.27	5.20	5.14	5.09	5.05	5.02	4.99	4.96	4.94	4.87	4.84	4.82
500	6.80	6.68	6.58	6.50	6.43	6.37	6.32	6.27	6.24	6.20	6.18	6.09	6.05	6.02
600	8.16	8.02	7.90	7.80	7.71	7.64	7.58	7.53	7.48	7.44	7.41	7.30	7.25	7.23
700	9.52	9.35	9.21	9.10	9.00	8.91	8.84	8.78	8.73	8.68	8.65	8.52	8.46	8.43
800	10.87	10.69	10.53	10.39	10.28	10.19	10.10	10.04	9.98	9.92	9.88	9.74	9.67	9.64
900	12.23	12.02	11.84	11.69	11.57	11.46	11.37	11.29	11.22	11.16	11.12	10.95	10.88	10.84
1000	13.59	13.36	13.16	12.99	12.85	12.73	12.63	12.54	12.47	12.40	12.35	12.17	12.09	12.04
2000	27.18	26.71	26.31	25.98	25.70	25.46	25.25	25.08	24.93	24.80	24.69	24.34	24.17	24.08
3000	40.77	40.06	39.47	38.97	38.54	38.19	37.88	37.62	37.39	37.20	37.04	36.50	36.25	36.12
4000	54.35	53.41	52.62	51.95	51.39	50.91	50.50	50.16	49.86	49.60	49.38	48.67	48.33	48.16
5000	67.94	66.76	65.78	64.94	64.24	63.64	63.13	62.69	62.32	62.00	61.73	60.84	60.41	60.20
6000	81.53	80.12	78.93	77.93	77.08	76.37	75.75	75.23	74.78	74.40	74.07	73.00	72.49	72.24
7000	95.12	93.47	92.08	90.92	89.93	89.09	88.38	87.77	87.25	86.80	86.42	85.17	84.57	84.28
8000	108.70	106.82	105.24	103.90	102.78	101.82	101.00	100.31	99.71	99.20	98.76	97.33	96.65	96.32
9000	122.29	120.17	118.39	116.89	115.62	114.55	113.63	112.84	112.17	111.60	111.11	109.50	108.73	108.36
10000	135.88	133.52	131.55	129.88	128.47	127.27	126.25	125.38	124.64	124.00	123.45	121.67	120.81	120.40
11000	149.46	146.87	144.70	142.87	141.32	140.00	138.88	137.92	137.10	136.40	135.80	133.83	132.89	132.44
12000	163.05	160.23	157.85	155.85	154.16	152.73	151.50	150.46	149.56	148.80	148.14	146.00	144.97	144.48
13000	176.64	173.58	171.01	168.84	167.01	165.45	164.13	163.00	162.03	161.20	160.48	158.16	157.05	156.52
14000	190.23	186.93	184.16	181.83	179.86	178.18	176.75	175.53	174.49	173.60	172.83	170.33	169.13	168.55
15000	203.81	200.28	197.32	194.82	192.70	190.91	189.38	188.07	186.95	186.00	185.17	182.50	181.21	180.59
16000	217.40	213.63	210.47	207.80	205.55	203.63	202.00	200.61	199.42	198.40	197.52	194.66	193.29	192.63
17000	230.99	226.98	223.62	220.79	218.40	216.36	214.63	213.15	211.88	210.79	209.86	206.83	205.38	204.67
18000	244.58	240.34	236.78	233.78	231.24	229.09	227.25	225.68	224.34	223.19	222.21	218.99	217.46	216.71
19000	258.16	253.69	249.93	246.77	244.09	241.81	239.88	238.22	236.81	235.59	234.55	231.16	229.54	228.75
20000	271.75	267.04	263.09	259.75	256.94	254.54	252.50	250.76	249.27	247.99	246.90	243.33	241.62	240.79
21000	285.34	280.39	276.24	272.74	269.78	267.27	265.13	263.30	261.73	260.39	259.24	255.49	253.70	252.83
22000	298.92	293.74	289.39	285.73	282.63	279.99	277.75	275.84	274.20	272.79	271.59	267.66	265.78	264.87
23000	312.51	307.09	302.55	290.72	295.47	292.72	290.38	288.37	286.66	285.19	283.93	279.82	277.86	276.91
24000	326.10	320.45	315.70	311.70	308.32	305.45	303.00	300.91	299.12	297.59	296.28	291.99	289.94	288.95
25000	339.69	333.80	328.86	324.69	321.17	318.17	315.62	313.45	311.59	309.99	308.62	304.16	302.02	300.99
26000	353.27	347.15	342.01	337.68	334.01	330.90	328.25	325.99	324.05	322.39	320.96	316.32	314.10	313.03
27000	366.86	360.50	355.17	350.67	346.86	343.63	340.87	338.52	336.51	334.79	333.31	328.49	326.18	325.07
28000	380.45	373.85	368.32	363.65	359.71	356.35	353.50	351.06	348.98	347.19	345.65	340.65	338.26	337.10
29000	394.03	387.20	381.47	376.64	372.55	369.08	366.12	363.60	361.44	359.59	358.00	352.82	350.34	349.14
30000	407.62	400.56	394.63	389.63	385.40	381.81	378.75	376.14	373.90	371.99	370.34	364.99	362.42	361.18
31000	421.21	413.91	407.78	402.62	398.25	394.53	391.37	388.67	386.37	384.39	382.69	377.15	374.50	373.22
32000	434.80	427.26	420.94	415.60	411.09	407.26	404.00	401.21	398.83	396.79	395.03	389.32	386.58	385.26
33000	448.38	440.61	434.09	428.59	423.94	419.99	416.62	413.75	411.29	409.19	407.38	401.48	398.66	397.30
34000	461.97	453.96	447.24	441.58	436.79	432.72	429.25	426.29	423.76	421.58	419.72	413.65	410.75	409.34
35000	475.56	467.31	460.40	454.57	449.63	445.44	441.87	438.83	436.22	433.98	432.07	425.82	422.83	421.38
36000	489.15	480.67	473.55	467.55	462.48	458.17	454.50	451.36	448.68	446.38	444.41	437.98	434.91	433.42
37000	502.73	494.02	486.71	480.54	475.33	470.90	467.12	463.90	461.15	458.78	456.76	450.15	446.99	445.46
38000	516.32	507.37	499.86	493.53	488.17	483.62	479.75	476.44	473.61	471.18	469.10	462.31	459.07	457.50
39000	529.91	520.72	513.01	506.52	501.02	496.35	492.37	488.98	486.07	483.58	481.44	474.48	471.15	469.54
40000	543.49	534.07	526.17	519.50	513.87	509.08	505.00	501.51	498.53	495.98	493.79	486.65	483.23	481.58
41000	557.08	547.42	539.32	532.49	526.71	521.80	517.62	514.05	511.00	508.38	506.13	498.81	495.31	493.61
42000	570.67	560.78	552.48	545.48	539.56	534.53	530.25	526.59	523.46	520.78	518.48	510.98	507.39	505.65
43000	584.26	574.13	565.63	558.47	552.40	547.26	542.87	539.13	535.92	533.18	530.82	523.14	519.47	517.69
44000	597.84	587.48	578.78	571.45	565.25	559.98	555.50	551.67	548.39	545.58	543.17	535.31	531.55	529.73
45000	611.43	600.83	591.94	584.44	578.10	572.71	568.12	564.20	560.85	557.98	555.51	547.48	543.63	541.77
46000	625.02	614.18	605.09	597.43	590.94	585.44	580.75	576.74	573.31	570.38	567.86	559.64	555.71	553.81
47000	638.60	627.53	618.25	610.42	603.79	598.16	593.37	589.28	585.78	582.78	580.20	571.81	567.79	565.85
48000	652.19	640.89	631.40	623.40	616.64	610.89	605.99	601.82	598.24	595.18	592.55	583.97	579.87	577.89
49000	665.78	654.24	644.55	636.39	629.48	623.62	618.62	614.35	610.70	607.58	604.89	596.14	591.95	589.93
50000	679.37	667.59	657.71	649.38	642.33	636.34	631.24	626.89	623.17	619.98	617.24	608.31	604.03	601.97
55000	747.30	734.35	723.48	714.32	706.56	699.98	694.37	689.58	685.48	681.97	678.96	669.14	664.44	662.16
60000	815.24	801.11	789.25	779.25	770.80	763.61	757.49	752.27	747.80	743.97	740.68	729.97	724.84	722.36
65000	883.17	867.87	855.02	844.19	835.03	827.24	820.62	814.96	810.12	805.97	802.40	790.80	785.24	782.56
70000	951.11	934.62	920.79	909.13	899.26	890.88	883.74	877.65	872.43	867.96	864.13	851.63	845.65	842.75
75000	1019.05	1001.38	986.56	974.07	963.49	954.51	946.86	940.33	934.75	929.96	925.85	912.46	906.05	902.95
80000	1086.98	1068.14	1052.33	1039.00	1027.73	1018.15	1009.99	1003.02	997.06	991.96	987.57	973.29	966.45	963.15
85000	1154.92	1134.90	1118.10	1103.94	1091.96	1081.78	1073.11	1065.71	1059.38	1053.95	1049.30	1034.12	1026.86	1023.34
90000	1222.86	1201.66	1183.87	1168.88	1156.19	1145.41	1136.24	1128.40	1121.70	1115.95	1111.02	1094.95	1087.26	1083.54
95000	1290.79	1268.42	1249.64	1233.82	1220.42	1209.05	1199.36	1191.09	1184.01	1177.95	1172.74	1155.78	1147.66	1143.73
100000	1358.73	1335.17	1315.41	1298.75	1284.66	1272.68	1262.48	1253.78	1246.33	1239.95	1234.47	1216.61	1208.06	1203.93

MONTHLY PAYMENT
REQUIRED TO AMORTIZE A LOAN

TERM AMOUNT	1 Year	2 Years	3 Years	4 Years	5 Years	6 Years	7 Years	8 Years	9 Years	10 Years	11 Years	12 Years	13 Years	14 Years
5	.46	.25	.18	.14	.12	.11	.10	.09	.09	.08	.08	.08	.11	.07
10	.91	.49	.35	.28	.24	.21	.20	.18	.17	.16	.16	.15	.15	.14
15	1.36	.73	.52	.42	.36	.32	.29	.27	.25	.24	.23	.23	.22	.21
25	2.26	1.21	.87	.69	.59	.53	.48	.45	.42	.40	.38	.37	.36	.35
50	4.51	2.42	1.73	1.38	1.18	1.05	.96	.89	.84	.80	.76	.74	.72	.70
75	6.76	3.62	2.59	2.07	1.77	1.57	1.43	1.33	1.25	1.19	1.14	1.11	1.08	1.05
100	9.01	4.83	3.45	2.76	2.36	2.09	1.91	1.77	1.67	1.59	1.52	1.47	1.43	1.40
200	18.01	9.65	6.89	5.52	4.71	4.18	3.81	3.54	3.33	3.17	3.04	2.94	2.86	2.79
300	27.01	14.48	10.33	8.28	7.06	6.27	5.71	5.30	4.99	4.75	4.56	4.41	4.29	4.19
400	36.01	19.30	13.77	11.04	9.42	8.35	7.61	7.07	6.66	6.34	6.09	5.88	5.72	5.58
500	45.02	24.13	17.22	13.79	11.77	10.44	9.51	8.83	8.32	7.92	7.60	7.35	7.14	6.97
600	54.02	28.95	20.66	16.55	14.12	12.53	11.42	10.60	9.98	9.50	9.12	8.82	8.57	8.37
700	63.02	33.78	24.10	19.31	16.47	14.62	13.32	12.37	11.64	11.09	10.64	10.29	10.00	9.76
800	72.02	38.60	27.54	22.07	18.83	16.70	15.22	14.13	13.31	12.67	12.16	11.76	11.43	11.15
900	81.03	43.43	30.98	24.83	21.18	18.79	17.12	15.90	14.97	14.25	13.68	13.22	12.85	12.55
1000	90.03	48.25	34.43	27.58	23.53	20.88	19.02	17.66	16.63	15.83	15.20	14.69	14.28	13.94
2000	180.05	96.50	68.85	55.16	47.06	41.75	38.04	35.32	33.26	31.66	30.40	29.38	28.56	27.88
3000	270.07	144.75	103.27	82.74	70.59	62.63	57.06	52.98	49.89	47.49	45.59	44.07	42.83	41.81
4000	360.10	193.00	137.69	110.32	94.12	83.50	76.07	70.63	66.52	63.32	60.79	58.76	57.11	55.75
5000	450.12	241.25	172.11	137.89	117.65	104.38	95.09	88.29	83.14	79.15	75.99	73.45	71.38	69.69
6000	540.14	289.50	206.53	165.47	141.17	125.25	114.11	105.95	99.77	94.98	91.18	88.14	85.66	83.62
7000	630.16	337.75	240.95	193.05	164.70	146.13	133.13	123.61	116.40	110.81	106.38	102.82	99.93	97.56
8000	720.19	386.00	275.37	220.63	188.23	167.00	152.14	141.26	133.03	126.63	121.58	117.51	114.21	111.49
9000	810.21	434.25	309.79	248.21	211.76	187.87	171.16	158.92	149.65	142.46	136.77	132.20	128.48	125.43
10000	900.23	482.50	344.21	275.78	235.29	208.75	190.18	176.58	166.28	158.29	151.97	146.89	142.76	139.37
11000	990.25	530.75	378.64	303.36	258.82	229.62	209.20	194.23	182.91	174.12	167.17	161.58	157.03	153.30
12000	1080.28	579.00	413.06	330.94	282.34	250.50	228.21	211.89	199.54	189.95	182.36	176.27	171.31	167.24
13000	1170.30	627.25	447.48	358.52	305.87	271.37	247.23	229.55	216.17	205.78	197.56	190.96	185.58	181.17
14000	1260.32	675.50	481.90	386.10	329.40	292.25	266.25	247.21	232.79	221.61	212.76	205.64	199.86	195.11
15000	1350.34	723.75	516.32	413.67	352.93	313.12	285.26	264.86	249.42	237.44	227.95	220.33	214.14	209.05
16000	1440.37	772.00	550.74	441.25	376.46	334.00	304.28	282.52	266.05	253.26	243.15	235.02	228.41	222.98
17000	1530.39	820.25	585.16	468.83	399.99	354.87	323.30	300.18	282.68	269.09	258.34	249.71	242.69	236.92
18000	1620.41	868.49	619.58	496.41	423.51	375.74	342.32	317.84	299.30	284.92	273.54	264.40	256.96	250.85
19000	1710.43	916.74	654.00	523.99	447.04	396.62	361.33	335.49	315.93	300.75	288.74	279.09	271.24	264.79
20000	1800.46	964.99	688.42	551.56	470.57	417.49	380.35	353.15	332.56	316.58	303.93	293.77	285.51	278.73
21000	1890.48	1013.24	722.85	579.14	494.10	438.37	399.37	370.81	349.19	332.41	319.13	308.46	299.79	292.66
22000	1980.50	1061.49	757.27	606.72	517.63	459.24	418.39	388.46	365.81	348.24	334.33	323.15	314.06	306.60
23000	2070.52	1109.74	791.69	634.30	541.16	480.12	437.40	406.12	382.44	364.06	349.52	337.84	328.34	320.53
24000	2160.55	1157.99	826.11	661.88	564.68	500.99	456.42	423.78	399.07	379.89	364.72	352.53	342.61	334.47
25000	2250.57	1206.24	860.53	689.45	588.21	521.87	475.44	441.44	415.70	395.72	379.92	367.22	356.89	348.41
26000	2340.59	1254.49	894.95	717.03	611.74	542.74	494.45	459.09	432.33	411.55	395.11	381.91	371.16	362.34
27000	2430.61	1302.74	929.37	744.61	635.27	563.61	513.47	476.75	448.95	427.38	410.31	396.59	385.44	376.28
28000	2520.64	1350.99	963.79	772.19	658.80	584.49	532.49	494.41	465.58	443.21	425.51	411.28	399.72	390.21
29000	2610.66	1399.24	998.21	799.77	682.33	605.36	551.51	512.07	482.21	459.04	440.70	425.97	413.99	404.15
30000	2700.68	1447.49	1032.63	827.34	705.85	626.24	570.52	529.72	498.84	474.87	455.90	440.66	428.27	418.09
31000	2790.70	1495.73	1067.06	854.92	729.38	647.11	589.54	547.38	515.46	490.69	471.09	455.35	442.54	432.02
32000	2880.73	1543.99	1101.48	882.50	752.91	667.99	608.56	565.04	532.09	506.52	486.29	470.04	456.82	445.96
33000	2970.75	1592.24	1135.90	910.08	776.44	688.86	627.58	582.69	548.72	522.35	501.49	484.73	471.09	459.89
34000	3060.77	1640.49	1170.32	937.66	799.97	709.74	646.59	600.35	565.35	538.18	516.68	499.41	485.37	473.83
35000	3150.79	1688.74	1204.74	965.23	823.49	730.61	665.61	618.01	581.98	554.01	531.88	514.10	499.64	487.77
36000	3240.82	1736.98	1239.16	992.81	847.02	751.48	684.63	635.67	598.60	569.84	547.08	528.79	513.92	501.70
37000	3330.84	1785.23	1273.58	1020.39	870.55	772.36	703.65	653.32	615.23	585.67	562.27	543.48	528.19	515.64
38000	3420.86	1833.48	1308.00	1047.97	894.08	793.23	722.66	670.98	631.86	601.49	577.47	558.17	542.47	529.57
39000	3510.88	1881.73	1342.42	1075.55	917.61	814.11	741.68	688.64	648.49	617.32	592.67	572.86	556.74	543.51
40000	3600.91	1929.98	1376.84	1103.12	941.14	834.98	760.70	706.30	665.11	633.15	607.86	587.54	571.02	557.45
41000	3690.93	1978.23	1411.27	1130.70	964.66	855.86	779.71	723.95	681.74	648.98	623.06	602.23	585.30	571.38
42000	3780.95	2026.48	1445.69	1158.28	988.19	876.73	798.73	741.61	698.37	664.81	638.26	616.92	599.57	585.32
43000	3870.97	2074.73	1480.11	1185.86	1011.72	897.61	817.75	759.27	715.00	680.64	653.45	631.61	613.85	599.25
44000	3961.00	2122.98	1514.53	1213.43	1035.25	918.48	836.77	776.92	731.62	696.47	668.65	646.30	628.12	613.19
45000	4051.02	2171.23	1548.95	1241.01	1058.78	939.35	855.78	794.58	748.25	712.30	683.84	660.99	642.40	627.13
46000	4141.04	2219.48	1583.37	1268.59	1082.31	960.23	874.80	812.24	764.88	728.12	699.04	675.68	656.67	641.06
47000	4231.06	2267.73	1617.79	1296.17	1105.83	981.10	893.82	829.90	781.51	743.95	714.24	690.36	670.95	655.00
48000	4321.09	2315.98	1652.21	1323.75	1129.36	1001.98	912.84	847.55	798.14	759.78	729.43	705.05	685.22	668.93
49000	4411.11	2364.23	1686.63	1351.32	1152.89	1022.85	931.85	865.21	814.76	775.61	744.63	719.74	699.50	682.87
50000	4501.13	2412.48	1721.05	1378.90	1176.42	1043.73	950.87	882.87	831.39	791.44	759.83	734.43	713.77	696.81
55000	4951.25	2653.72	1893.16	1516.79	1294.06	1148.10	1045.96	971.15	914.53	870.58	835.81	807.87	785.15	766.49
60000	5401.36	2894.97	2065.26	1654.68	1411.70	1252.47	1141.04	1059.44	997.67	949.73	911.79	881.31	856.53	836.17
65000	5851.47	3136.22	2237.37	1792.57	1529.34	1356.84	1236.13	1147.73	1080.81	1028.87	987.77	954.76	927.90	905.85
70000	6301.58	3377.46	2409.47	1930.46	1646.98	1461.21	1331.22	1236.01	1163.95	1108.01	1063.76	1028.20	999.28	975.53
75000	6751.70	3618.71	2581.58	2068.35	1764.63	1565.59	1426.30	1324.30	1247.08	1187.16	1139.74	1101.64	1070.66	1045.21
80000	7201.81	3859.96	2753.68	2206.24	1882.27	1669.96	1521.39	1412.59	1330.22	1266.30	1215.72	1175.08	1142.04	1114.89
85000	7651.92	4101.21	2925.79	2344.13	1999.91	1774.33	1616.48	1500.87	1413.36	1345.44	1291.70	1248.53	1213.41	1184.57
90000	8102.03	4342.45	3097.89	2482.02	2117.55	1878.70	1711.56	1589.16	1496.50	1424.59	1367.68	1321.97	1284.79	1254.25
95000	8552.15	4583.70	3270.00	2619.91	2235.19	1983.08	1806.65	1677.44	1579.64	1503.73	1443.67	1395.41	1356.17	1323.93
100000	9002.26	4824.95	3442.10	2757.80	2352.83	2087.45	1901.74	1765.73	1662.78	1582.87	1519.65	1468.85	1427.54	1393.61

TERM	15 Years	16 Years	17 Years	18 Years	19 Years	20 Years	21 Years	22 Years	23 Years	24 Years	25 Years	30 Years	35 Years	40 Years
AMOUNT														
5	.07	.07	.07	.07	.07	.07	.07	.07	.07	.07	.07	.07	.07	.07
10	.14	.14	.14	.14	.13	.13	.13	.13	.13	.13	.13	.13	.13	.13
15	.21	.21	.20	.20	.20	.20	.20	.19	.19	.19	.19	.19	.19	.19
25	.35	.34	.34	.33	.33	.32	.32	.32	.32	.32	.32	.31	.31	.31
50	.69	.68	.67	.66	.65	.64	.64	.64	.63	.63	.63	.62	.61	.61
75	1.03	1.01	1.00	.98	.97	.96	.96	.95	.95	.94	.94	.92	.92	.91
100	1.37	1.35	1.33	1.31	1.30	1.28	1.27	1.27	1.26	1.25	1.25	1.23	1.22	1.22
200	2.74	2.69	2.65	2.62	2.59	2.56	2.54	2.53	2.51	2.50	2.49	2.45	2.44	2.43
300	4.10	4.03	3.97	3.92	3.88	3.84	3.81	3.79	3.77	3.75	3.73	3.68	3.65	3.64
400	5.47	5.37	5.29	5.23	5.17	5.12	5.08	5.05	5.02	5.00	4.97	4.90	4.87	4.85
500	6.83	6.72	6.62	6.53	6.46	6.40	6.35	6.31	6.27	6.24	6.22	6.13	6.09	6.07
600	8.20	8.06	7.94	7.84	7.76	7.68	7.62	7.57	7.53	7.49	7.46	7.35	7.30	7.28
700	9.56	9.40	9.26	9.15	9.05	8.96	8.89	8.83	8.78	8.74	8.70	8.58	8.52	8.49
800	10.93	10.74	10.58	10.45	10.34	10.24	10.16	10.10	10.04	9.99	9.94	9.80	9.73	9.70
900	12.29	12.08	11.91	11.76	11.63	11.52	11.43	11.36	11.29	11.23	11.18	11.03	10.95	10.91
1000	13.66	13.43	13.23	13.06	12.92	12.80	12.70	12.62	12.54	12.48	12.43	12.25	12.17	12.13
2000	27.32	26.85	26.45	26.12	25.84	25.60	25.40	25.23	25.08	24.96	24.85	24.50	24.33	24.25
3000	40.97	40.27	39.68	39.18	38.76	38.40	38.10	37.84	37.62	37.43	37.27	36.74	36.49	36.37
4000	54.63	53.69	52.90	52.24	51.68	51.20	50.80	50.46	50.16	49.91	49.69	48.99	48.65	48.49
5000	68.28	67.11	66.13	65.30	64.60	64.00	63.50	63.07	62.70	62.38	62.11	61.23	60.81	60.61
6000	81.94	80.53	79.35	78.36	77.52	76.80	76.20	75.68	75.24	74.86	74.53	73.48	72.98	72.73
7000	95.59	93.95	92.57	91.42	90.44	89.60	88.90	88.29	87.78	87.34	86.96	85.72	85.14	84.85
8000	109.25	107.37	105.80	104.47	103.36	102.40	101.60	100.91	100.32	99.81	99.38	97.97	97.30	96.98
9000	122.90	120.79	119.02	117.53	116.27	115.20	114.29	113.52	112.86	112.29	111.80	110.22	109.46	109.10
10000	136.56	134.21	132.25	130.59	129.19	128.00	126.99	126.13	125.39	124.76	124.22	122.46	121.62	121.22
11000	150.21	147.63	145.47	143.65	142.11	140.80	139.69	138.74	137.93	137.24	136.64	134.71	133.78	133.34
12000	163.87	161.05	158.70	156.71	155.03	153.60	152.39	151.36	150.47	149.71	149.06	146.95	145.95	145.46
13000	177.52	174.47	171.92	169.77	167.95	166.40	165.09	163.97	163.01	162.19	161.49	159.20	158.11	157.58
14000	191.18	187.89	185.14	182.83	180.87	179.20	177.79	176.58	175.55	174.67	173.91	171.44	170.27	169.70
15000	204.83	201.32	198.37	195.89	193.79	192.00	190.49	189.19	188.09	187.14	186.33	183.69	182.43	181.82
16000	218.49	214.74	211.59	208.94	206.71	204.80	203.19	201.81	200.63	199.62	198.75	195.93	194.59	193.95
17000	232.14	228.16	224.02	222.00	219.62	217.60	215.89	214.42	213.17	212.09	211.17	208.18	206.75	206.07
18000	245.80	241.58	238.04	235.06	232.54	230.40	228.58	227.03	225.71	224.57	223.59	220.43	218.92	218.19
19000	259.45	255.00	251.27	248.12	245.46	243.20	241.28	239.65	238.24	237.04	236.02	232.67	231.08	230.31
20000	273.11	268.42	264.49	261.18	258.38	256.00	253.98	252.26	250.78	249.52	248.44	244.92	243.24	242.43
21000	286.76	281.84	277.71	274.24	271.30	268.80	266.68	264.87	263.32	262.00	260.86	257.16	255.40	254.55
22000	300.42	295.26	290.94	287.30	284.22	281.60	279.38	277.48	275.86	274.47	273.28	269.41	267.56	266.67
23000	314.07	308.68	304.16	300.36	297.14	294.40	292.08	290.10	288.40	286.95	285.70	281.65	279.72	278.80
24000	327.73	322.10	317.39	313.41	310.06	307.20	304.78	302.71	300.94	299.42	298.12	293.90	291.89	290.92
25000	341.38	335.52	330.61	326.47	322.97	320.00	317.48	315.32	313.48	311.90	310.55	306.14	304.05	303.04
26000	355.04	348.94	343.84	339.53	335.89	332.80	330.18	327.93	326.02	324.38	322.97	318.39	316.21	315.16
27000	368.69	362.36	357.06	352.59	348.81	345.60	342.87	340.55	338.56	336.85	335.39	330.64	328.37	327.28
28000	382.35	375.78	370.28	365.65	361.73	358.40	355.57	353.16	351.09	349.33	347.81	342.88	340.53	339.40
29000	396.00	389.21	383.51	378.71	374.65	371.20	368.27	365.77	363.63	361.80	360.23	355.13	352.69	351.52
30000	409.66	402.63	396.73	391.77	387.57	384.00	380.97	378.38	376.17	374.28	372.65	367.37	364.86	363.64
31000	423.31	416.05	409.96	404.83	400.49	396.80	393.67	391.00	388.71	386.75	385.08	379.62	377.02	375.77
32000	436.97	429.47	423.18	417.88	413.41	409.60	406.37	403.61	401.25	399.23	397.50	391.86	389.18	387.89
33000	450.62	442.89	436.41	430.94	426.32	422.40	419.07	416.22	413.79	411.71	409.92	404.11	401.34	400.01
34000	464.28	456.31	449.63	444.00	439.24	435.20	431.77	428.83	426.33	424.18	422.34	416.35	413.50	412.13
35000	477.93	469.73	462.85	457.06	452.16	448.00	444.47	441.45	438.87	436.66	434.76	428.60	425.66	424.25
36000	491.59	483.15	476.08	470.12	465.08	460.80	457.16	454.06	451.41	449.13	447.18	440.85	437.83	436.37
37000	505.24	496.57	489.30	483.18	478.00	473.60	469.86	466.67	463.94	461.61	459.61	453.09	449.99	448.49
38000	518.90	509.99	502.53	496.24	490.92	486.40	482.56	479.29	476.48	474.08	472.03	465.34	462.15	460.62
39000	532.55	523.41	515.75	509.30	503.84	499.20	495.26	491.90	489.02	486.56	484.45	477.58	474.31	472.74
40000	546.21	536.83	528.97	522.35	516.76	512.00	507.96	504.51	501.56	499.04	496.87	489.83	486.47	484.86
41000	559.86	550.25	542.20	535.41	529.69	524.80	520.66	517.12	514.10	511.51	509.29	502.07	498.63	496.98
42000	573.52	563.67	555.42	548.47	542.59	537.60	533.36	529.74	526.64	523.99	521.71	514.32	510.80	509.10
43000	587.17	577.10	568.65	561.53	555.51	550.40	546.06	542.35	539.18	536.46	534.14	526.56	522.96	521.22
44000	600.83	590.52	581.87	574.59	568.43	563.20	558.76	554.96	551.72	548.94	546.56	538.81	535.12	533.34
45000	614.48	603.94	595.10	587.65	581.35	576.00	571.45	567.57	564.26	561.42	558.98	551.06	547.28	545.46
46000	628.14	617.36	608.32	600.71	594.27	588.80	584.15	580.19	576.80	573.89	571.40	563.30	559.44	557.59
47000	641.79	630.78	621.54	613.77	607.19	601.60	596.85	592.80	589.33	586.37	583.82	575.55	571.61	569.71
48000	655.45	644.20	634.77	626.82	620.11	614.40	609.55	605.41	601.87	598.84	596.24	587.79	583.77	581.83
49000	669.10	657.62	647.99	639.88	633.02	627.20	622.25	618.02	614.41	611.32	608.66	600.04	595.93	593.95
50000	682.76	671.04	661.22	652.94	645.94	640.00	634.95	630.64	626.95	623.79	621.09	612.28	608.09	606.07
55000	751.03	738.14	727.34	718.24	710.54	704.00	698.44	693.70	689.65	686.17	683.19	673.51	668.90	666.68
60000	819.31	805.25	793.46	783.53	775.13	768.00	761.94	756.76	752.34	748.55	745.30	734.74	729.71	727.28
65000	887.58	872.35	859.58	848.82	839.72	832.00	825.43	819.83	815.03	810.93	807.41	795.97	790.52	787.89
70000	955.86	939.45	925.70	914.12	904.32	896.00	888.93	882.89	877.73	873.31	869.52	857.19	851.32	848.50
75000	1024.13	1006.56	991.82	979.41	968.91	960.00	952.42	945.95	940.42	935.69	931.63	918.42	912.13	909.10
80000	1092.41	1073.66	1057.94	1044.70	1033.51	1024.00	1015.92	1009.02	1003.12	998.07	993.74	979.65	972.94	969.71
85000	1160.68	1140.76	1124.07	1110.00	1098.10	1088.00	1079.41	1072.08	1065.81	1060.45	1055.84	1040.88	1033.75	1030.32
90000	1228.96	1207.87	1190.19	1175.29	1162.69	1152.00	1142.90	1135.14	1128.51	1122.83	1117.95	1102.11	1094.56	1090.92
95000	1297.23	1274.97	1256.31	1240.59	1227.29	1216.00	1206.40	1198.21	1191.20	1185.20	1180.06	1163.33	1155.37	1151.53
100000	1365.51	1342.08	1322.43	1305.88	1291.88	1280.00	1269.89	1261.27	1253.90	1247.58	1242.17	1224.56	1216.18	1212.14

MONTHLY PAYMENT
14.600%
REQUIRED TO AMORTIZE A LOAN

TERM AMOUNT	1 Year	2 Years	3 Years	4 Years	5 Years	6 Years	7 Years	8 Years	9 Years	10 Years	11 Years	12 Years	13 Years	14 Years
5	.46	.25	.18	.14	.12	.11	.10	.09	.09	.08	.08	.08	.08	.08
10	.91	.49	.35	.28	.24	.21	.20	.18	.17	.16	.16	.15	.15	.15
15	1.36	.73	.52	.42	.36	.32	.29	.27	.26	.24	.23	.23	.22	.22
25	2.26	1.21	.87	.70	.59	.53	.48	.45	.42	.40	.39	.37	.36	.36
50	4.51	2.42	1.73	1.39	1.18	1.05	.96	.89	.84	.80	.77	.74	.72	.71
75	6.76	3.63	2.59	2.08	1.77	1.57	1.44	1.33	1.26	1.20	1.15	1.11	1.08	1.06
100	9.01	4.83	3.45	2.77	2.36	2.10	1.91	1.78	1.67	1.59	1.53	1.48	1.44	1.41
200	18.02	9.66	6.90	5.53	4.72	4.19	3.82	3.55	3.34	3.18	3.06	2.96	2.87	2.81
300	27.03	14.49	10.35	8.29	7.08	6.28	5.73	5.32	5.01	4.77	4.58	4.43	4.31	4.21
400	36.03	19.32	13.79	11.06	9.44	8.38	7.63	7.09	6.68	6.36	6.11	5.91	5.74	5.61
500	45.04	24.15	17.24	13.82	11.80	10.47	9.54	8.86	8.35	7.95	7.63	7.38	7.18	7.01
600	54.05	28.98	20.69	16.58	14.15	12.56	11.45	10.63	10.02	9.54	9.16	8.86	8.61	8.41
700	63.05	33.81	24.13	19.34	16.51	14.65	13.36	12.41	11.69	11.13	10.69	10.33	10.04	9.81
800	72.06	38.64	27.58	22.11	18.87	16.75	15.26	14.18	13.35	12.72	12.21	11.81	11.48	11.21
900	81.07	43.47	31.03	24.87	21.23	18.84	17.17	15.95	15.02	14.31	13.74	13.28	12.91	12.61
1000	90.07	48.30	34.47	27.63	23.59	20.93	19.08	17.72	16.69	15.89	15.26	14.76	14.35	14.01
2000	180.14	96.60	68.94	55.26	47.17	41.86	38.15	35.43	33.38	31.78	30.52	29.51	28.69	28.01
3000	270.21	144.90	103.41	82.89	70.75	62.79	57.22	53.15	50.07	47.67	45.78	44.26	43.03	42.01
4000	360.28	193.19	137.88	110.52	94.33	83.72	76.30	70.86	66.75	63.56	61.04	59.01	57.37	56.02
5000	450.35	241.49	172.35	138.15	117.91	104.65	95.37	88.58	83.44	79.45	76.30	73.77	71.71	70.02
6000	540.42	289.79	206.82	165.78	141.49	125.58	114.44	106.29	100.13	95.34	91.56	88.52	86.05	84.02
7000	630.49	338.08	241.29	193.40	165.07	146.50	133.52	124.01	116.81	111.23	106.82	103.27	100.39	98.02
8000	720.56	386.38	275.76	221.03	188.65	167.43	152.59	141.72	133.50	127.12	122.07	118.02	114.73	112.03
9000	810.63	434.68	310.23	248.66	212.23	188.36	171.66	159.44	150.19	143.01	137.33	132.78	129.07	126.03
10000	900.70	482.97	344.70	276.29	235.81	209.29	190.74	177.15	166.87	158.90	152.59	147.53	143.41	140.03
11000	990.77	531.27	379.17	303.92	259.39	230.22	209.81	194.87	183.56	174.79	167.85	162.28	157.75	154.03
12000	1080.84	579.57	413.64	331.55	282.97	251.15	228.88	212.58	200.25	190.68	183.11	177.03	172.09	168.04
13000	1170.91	627.86	448.11	359.17	306.55	272.07	247.95	230.30	216.93	206.57	198.37	191.78	186.43	182.04
14000	1260.98	676.16	482.58	386.80	330.13	293.00	267.03	248.01	233.62	222.46	213.63	206.54	200.77	196.04
15000	1351.05	724.46	517.05	414.43	353.71	313.93	286.10	265.73	250.31	238.35	228.89	221.29	215.11	210.04
16000	1441.12	772.75	551.52	442.06	377.29	334.86	305.17	283.44	266.99	254.24	244.14	236.04	229.46	224.05
17000	1531.19	821.05	585.99	469.69	400.87	355.79	324.25	301.15	283.68	270.13	259.40	250.79	243.80	238.05
18000	1621.26	869.35	620.46	497.32	424.45	376.72	343.32	318.87	300.37	286.01	274.66	265.55	258.14	252.05
19000	1711.33	917.64	654.93	524.94	448.03	397.64	362.39	336.58	317.05	301.90	289.92	280.30	272.48	266.06
20000	1801.40	965.94	689.40	552.57	471.61	418.57	381.47	354.30	333.74	317.79	305.18	295.05	286.82	280.06
21000	1891.47	1014.24	723.87	580.20	495.20	439.50	400.54	372.01	350.43	333.68	320.44	309.80	301.16	294.06
22000	1981.54	1062.54	758.34	607.83	518.78	460.43	419.61	389.73	367.12	349.57	335.70	324.56	315.50	308.06
23000	2071.61	1110.83	792.81	635.46	542.36	481.36	438.68	407.44	383.80	365.46	350.96	339.31	329.84	322.07
24000	2161.68	1159.13	827.28	663.09	565.94	502.29	457.76	425.16	400.49	381.35	366.21	354.06	344.18	336.07
25000	2251.75	1207.43	861.75	690.72	589.52	523.21	476.83	442.87	417.18	397.24	381.47	368.81	358.52	350.07
26000	2341.82	1255.72	896.22	718.34	613.10	544.14	495.90	460.59	433.86	413.13	396.73	383.56	372.86	364.07
27000	2431.89	1304.02	930.69	745.97	636.68	565.07	514.98	478.30	450.55	429.02	411.99	398.32	387.20	378.08
28000	2521.96	1352.32	965.16	773.60	660.26	586.00	534.05	496.02	467.24	444.91	427.25	413.07	401.54	392.08
29000	2612.03	1400.61	999.63	801.23	683.84	606.93	553.12	513.73	483.92	460.80	442.51	427.82	415.88	406.08
30000	2702.10	1448.91	1034.10	828.86	707.42	627.86	572.20	531.45	500.61	476.69	457.77	442.57	430.22	420.08
31000	2792.16	1497.21	1068.57	856.49	731.00	648.79	591.27	549.16	517.30	492.58	473.03	457.33	444.56	434.09
32000	2882.23	1545.50	1103.04	884.11	754.58	669.71	610.34	566.88	533.98	508.47	488.28	472.08	458.91	448.09
33000	2972.30	1593.80	1137.51	911.74	778.16	690.64	629.41	584.59	550.67	524.36	503.54	486.83	473.25	462.09
34000	3062.37	1642.10	1171.98	939.37	801.74	711.57	648.49	602.30	567.36	540.25	518.80	501.58	487.59	476.10
35000	3152.44	1690.39	1206.45	967.00	825.32	732.50	667.56	620.02	584.04	556.13	534.06	516.34	501.93	490.10
36000	3242.51	1738.69	1240.92	994.63	848.90	753.43	686.63	637.73	600.73	572.02	549.32	531.09	516.27	504.10
37000	3332.58	1786.99	1275.39	1022.26	872.48	774.36	705.71	655.45	617.42	587.91	564.58	545.84	530.61	518.10
38000	3422.65	1835.28	1309.86	1049.88	896.06	795.28	724.78	673.16	634.10	603.80	579.84	560.59	544.95	532.11
39000	3512.72	1883.58	1344.33	1077.51	919.64	816.21	743.85	690.88	650.79	619.69	595.10	575.34	559.29	546.11
40000	3602.79	1931.88	1378.80	1105.14	943.22	837.14	762.93	708.59	667.48	635.58	610.35	590.10	573.63	560.11
41000	3692.86	1980.17	1413.27	1132.77	966.80	858.07	782.00	726.31	684.17	651.47	625.61	604.85	587.97	574.11
42000	3782.93	2028.47	1447.74	1160.40	990.39	879.00	801.07	744.02	700.85	667.36	640.87	619.60	602.31	588.12
43000	3873.00	2076.77	1482.21	1188.03	1013.97	899.93	820.14	761.74	717.54	683.25	656.13	634.35	616.65	602.12
44000	3963.07	2125.07	1516.67	1215.65	1037.55	920.85	839.22	779.45	734.23	699.14	671.39	649.11	630.99	616.12
45000	4053.14	2173.36	1551.14	1243.28	1061.13	941.78	858.29	797.17	750.91	715.03	686.65	663.86	645.33	630.12
46000	4143.21	2221.66	1585.61	1270.91	1084.71	962.71	877.36	814.88	767.60	730.92	701.91	678.61	659.67	644.13
47000	4233.28	2269.96	1620.08	1298.54	1108.29	983.64	896.44	832.60	784.29	746.81	717.17	693.36	674.01	658.13
48000	4323.35	2318.25	1654.55	1326.17	1131.87	1004.57	915.51	850.31	800.97	762.70	732.42	708.12	688.36	672.13
49000	4413.42	2366.55	1689.02	1353.80	1155.45	1025.50	934.58	868.03	817.66	778.59	747.68	722.87	702.70	686.13
50000	4503.49	2414.85	1723.49	1381.43	1179.03	1046.42	953.66	885.74	834.35	794.48	762.94	737.62	717.04	700.14
55000	4953.84	2656.33	1895.84	1519.57	1296.93	1151.07	1049.02	974.31	917.78	873.92	839.24	811.38	788.74	770.15
60000	5404.19	2897.81	2068.19	1657.71	1414.83	1255.71	1144.39	1062.89	1001.22	953.37	915.53	885.14	860.44	840.16
65000	5854.53	3139.30	2240.54	1795.85	1532.74	1360.35	1239.75	1151.46	1084.65	1032.82	991.82	958.90	932.15	910.18
70000	6304.88	3380.78	2412.89	1933.99	1650.64	1464.99	1335.12	1240.03	1168.08	1112.26	1068.12	1032.67	1003.85	980.19
75000	6755.23	3622.27	2585.24	2072.14	1768.54	1569.63	1430.48	1328.61	1251.52	1191.71	1144.41	1106.43	1075.55	1050.20
80000	7205.58	3863.75	2757.59	2210.28	1886.44	1674.28	1525.85	1417.18	1334.95	1271.16	1220.70	1180.19	1147.26	1120.22
85000	7655.93	4105.23	2929.94	2348.42	2004.35	1778.92	1621.21	1505.75	1418.39	1350.61	1297.00	1253.95	1218.96	1190.23
90000	8106.28	4346.72	3102.28	2486.56	2122.25	1883.56	1716.58	1594.33	1501.82	1430.05	1373.29	1327.71	1290.66	1260.24
95000	8556.62	4588.20	3274.63	2624.70	2240.15	1988.20	1811.94	1682.90	1585.25	1509.50	1449.59	1401.47	1362.36	1330.26
100000	9006.97	4829.69	3446.98	2762.85	2358.05	2092.84	1907.31	1771.47	1668.69	1588.95	1525.88	1475.24	1434.07	1400.27

TERM	15 Years	16 Years	17 Years	18 Years	19 Years	20 Years	21 Years	22 Years	23 Years	24 Years	25 Years	30 Years	35 Years	40 Years
AMOUNT														
5	.07	.07	.07	.07	.07	.07	.07	.07	.07	.07	.07	.07	.07	.07
10	.14	.14	.14	.14	.13	.13	.13	.13	.13	.13	.13	.13	.13	.13
15	.21	.21	.20	.20	.20	.20	.20	.20	.19	.19	.19	.19	.19	.19
25	.35	.34	.34	.33	.33	.33	.32	.32	.32	.32	.32	.31	.31	.31
50	.69	.68	.67	.66	.65	.65	.64	.64	.64	.63	.63	.62	.62	.62
75	1.03	1.02	1.00	.99	.98	.97	.96	.96	.95	.95	.94	.93	.92	.92
100	1.38	1.35	1.33	1.32	1.30	1.29	1.28	1.27	1.27	1.26	1.25	1.24	1.23	1.23
200	2.75	2.70	2.66	2.63	2.60	2.58	2.56	2.54	2.53	2.52	2.50	2.47	2.45	2.45
300	4.12	4.05	3.99	3.94	3.90	3.87	3.84	3.81	3.79	3.77	3.75	3.70	3.68	3.67
400	5.49	5.40	5.32	5.26	5.20	5.15	5.11	5.08	5.05	5.03	5.00	4.94	4.90	4.89
500	6.87	6.75	6.65	6.57	6.50	6.44	6.39	6.35	6.31	6.28	6.25	6.17	6.13	6.11
600	8.24	8.10	7.98	7.88	7.80	7.73	7.67	7.62	7.57	7.54	7.50	7.40	7.35	7.33
700	9.61	9.45	9.31	9.20	9.10	9.02	8.95	8.89	8.84	8.79	8.75	8.63	8.58	8.55
800	10.98	10.80	10.64	10.51	10.40	10.30	10.22	10.16	10.10	10.05	10.00	9.87	9.80	9.77
900	12.36	12.15	11.97	11.82	11.70	11.59	11.50	11.42	11.36	11.30	11.25	11.10	11.02	10.99
1000	13.73	13.49	13.30	13.14	13.00	12.88	12.78	12.69	12.62	12.56	12.50	12.33	12.25	12.21
2000	27.45	26.98	26.59	25.99	25.99	25.75	25.55	25.38	25.23	25.11	25.00	24.66	24.49	24.41
3000	41.17	40.47	39.89	39.40	38.98	38.62	38.32	38.07	37.85	37.66	37.50	36.98	36.73	36.62
4000	54.90	53.96	53.18	52.53	51.97	51.50	51.10	50.76	50.46	50.21	50.00	49.31	48.98	48.82
5000	68.62	67.45	66.48	65.66	64.96	64.37	63.87	63.44	63.08	62.77	62.50	61.63	61.22	61.02
6000	82.34	80.94	79.77	78.79	77.95	77.24	76.64	76.13	75.69	75.32	75.00	73.96	73.46	73.23
7000	96.07	94.43	93.07	91.92	90.94	90.12	89.42	88.82	88.31	87.87	87.50	86.28	85.71	85.43
8000	109.79	107.92	106.36	105.05	103.93	102.99	102.19	101.51	100.92	100.42	100.00	98.61	97.95	97.63
9000	123.51	121.41	119.66	118.18	116.93	115.86	114.96	114.19	113.54	112.98	112.49	110.93	110.19	109.84
10000	137.23	134.90	132.95	131.31	129.92	128.74	127.74	126.88	126.15	125.53	124.99	123.26	122.43	122.04
11000	150.96	148.39	146.24	144.44	142.91	141.61	140.51	139.57	138.77	138.08	137.49	135.58	134.68	134.24
12000	164.68	161.88	159.54	157.57	155.90	154.48	153.28	152.26	151.38	150.63	149.99	147.91	146.92	146.45
13000	178.40	175.37	172.03	170.70	168.89	167.36	166.06	164.94	164.00	163.18	162.49	160.23	159.16	158.65
14000	192.13	188.86	186.13	183.83	181.88	180.23	178.83	177.63	176.61	175.74	174.99	172.56	171.41	170.85
15000	205.85	202.35	199.42	196.96	194.87	193.10	191.60	190.32	189.23	188.29	187.49	184.88	183.65	183.06
16000	219.57	215.84	212.72	210.09	207.86	205.98	204.37	203.01	201.84	200.84	199.99	197.21	195.89	195.26
17000	233.29	229.33	226.01	223.22	220.05	210.05	217.15	215.70	214.46	213.39	212.48	209.53	208.13	207.46
18000	247.02	242.82	239.31	236.35	233.85	231.72	229.92	228.38	227.07	225.95	224.98	221.86	220.38	219.67
19000	260.74	256.31	252.60	249.48	246.84	244.60	242.69	241.07	239.68	238.50	237.48	234.18	232.62	231.87
20000	274.46	269.80	265.90	262.61	259.83	257.47	255.47	253.76	252.30	251.05	249.98	246.51	244.86	244.07
21000	288.19	283.29	279.19	275.74	272.82	270.34	268.24	266.45	264.91	263.60	262.48	258.83	257.11	256.28
22000	301.91	296.78	292.48	288.87	285.81	283.22	281.01	279.13	277.53	276.15	274.98	271.16	269.35	268.48
23000	315.63	310.27	305.78	302.00	298.80	296.09	293.79	291.82	290.14	288.71	207.48	283.48	281.59	280.68
24000	329.36	323.76	319.07	315.13	311.79	308.96	306.56	304.51	302.76	301.26	299.98	295.81	293.83	292.89
25000	343.08	337.25	332.37	328.26	324.78	321.84	319.33	317.20	315.37	313.81	312.47	308.13	306.08	305.09
26000	356.80	350.74	345.66	341.39	337.78	334.71	332.11	329.88	327.99	326.36	324.97	320.46	318.32	317.29
27000	370.52	364.23	358.96	354.52	350.77	347.58	344.88	342.57	340.60	338.92	337.47	332.78	330.56	329.50
28000	384.25	377.72	372.25	367.65	363.76	360.46	357.65	355.26	353.22	351.47	349.97	345.11	342.81	341.70
29000	397.97	391.21	385.55	380.78	376.75	373.33	370.42	367.95	365.83	364.02	362.47	357.44	355.05	353.90
30000	411.69	404.70	398.84	393.91	389.74	386.20	383.20	380.64	378.45	376.57	374.97	369.76	367.29	366.11
31000	425.42	418.19	412.14	407.04	402.73	399.08	395.97	393.32	391.06	389.13	387.47	382.09	379.53	378.31
32000	439.14	431.68	425.43	420.17	415.72	411.95	408.74	406.01	403.68	401.68	399.97	394.41	391.78	390.52
33000	452.86	445.17	438.72	433.30	428.71	424.82	421.52	418.70	416.29	414.23	412.46	406.74	404.02	402.72
34000	466.58	458.66	452.02	446.43	441.70	437.70	434.29	431.39	428.91	426.78	424.96	419.06	416.26	414.92
35000	480.31	472.15	465.31	459.56	454.70	450.57	447.06	444.07	441.52	439.33	437.46	431.39	428.51	427.13
36000	494.03	485.64	478.61	472.69	467.69	463.44	459.84	456.76	454.13	451.89	449.96	443.71	440.75	439.33
37000	507.75	499.13	491.90	485.82	480.68	476.32	472.61	469.45	466.75	464.44	462.46	456.04	452.99	451.53
38000	521.48	512.62	505.20	498.95	493.67	489.19	485.38	482.14	479.36	476.99	474.96	468.36	465.23	463.74
39000	535.20	526.11	518.49	512.08	506.66	502.06	498.16	494.82	491.98	489.54	487.46	480.69	477.48	475.94
40000	548.92	539.60	531.79	525.21	519.65	514.94	510.93	507.51	504.59	502.10	499.96	493.01	489.72	488.14
41000	562.64	553.09	545.08	538.34	532.64	527.81	523.70	520.20	517.21	514.65	512.45	505.34	501.96	500.35
42000	576.37	566.58	558.38	551.47	545.63	540.68	536.48	532.89	529.82	527.20	524.95	517.66	514.21	512.55
43000	590.09	580.07	571.67	564.60	558.62	553.56	549.25	545.58	542.44	539.75	537.45	529.99	526.45	524.75
44000	603.81	593.56	584.96	577.73	571.62	566.43	562.02	558.26	555.05	552.30	549.95	542.31	538.69	536.96
45000	617.54	607.05	598.26	590.86	584.61	579.30	574.79	570.95	567.67	564.86	562.45	554.64	550.93	549.16
46000	631.26	620.54	611.55	603.99	597.60	592.18	587.57	583.64	580.28	577.41	574.95	566.96	563.18	561.36
47000	644.98	634.03	624.85	617.12	610.59	605.05	600.34	596.33	592.90	589.96	587.45	579.29	575.42	573.57
48000	658.71	647.52	638.14	630.25	623.58	617.92	613.11	609.01	605.51	602.51	599.95	591.61	587.66	585.77
49000	672.43	661.01	651.44	643.38	636.57	630.80	625.89	621.70	618.13	615.07	612.44	603.94	599.91	597.97
50000	686.15	674.50	664.73	656.51	649.56	643.67	638.66	634.39	630.74	627.62	624.94	616.26	612.15	610.18
55000	754.77	741.95	731.20	722.16	714.52	708.04	702.53	697.83	693.81	690.38	687.44	677.89	673.36	671.19
60000	823.38	809.40	797.68	787.81	779.47	772.40	766.39	761.27	756.89	753.14	749.93	739.52	734.58	732.21
65000	891.99	876.84	864.15	853.46	844.43	836.77	830.26	824.70	819.96	815.90	812.42	801.14	795.79	793.23
70000	960.61	944.29	930.62	919.11	909.39	901.14	894.12	888.14	883.03	878.66	874.92	862.77	857.01	854.25
75000	1029.22	1011.74	997.10	984.76	974.34	965.50	957.99	951.58	946.11	941.43	937.41	924.39	918.22	915.26
80000	1097.84	1079.19	1063.57	1050.41	1039.30	1029.87	1021.85	1015.02	1009.18	1004.19	999.91	986.02	979.44	976.28
85000	1166.45	1146.64	1130.04	1116.07	1104.25	1094.24	1085.72	1078.46	1072.26	1066.95	1062.40	1047.65	1040.65	1037.30
90000	1235.07	1214.09	1196.51	1181.72	1169.21	1158.60	1149.58	1141.90	1135.33	1129.71	1124.89	1109.27	1101.86	1098.31
95000	1303.68	1281.54	1262.99	1247.37	1234.16	1222.97	1213.45	1205.33	1198.40	1192.47	1187.39	1170.90	1163.08	1159.33
100000	1372.30	1348.99	1329.46	1313.02	1299.12	1287.34	1277.32	1268.77	1261.48	1255.23	1249.88	1232.52	1224.29	1220.35

MONTHLY PAYMENT
REQUIRED TO AMORTIZE A LOAN

TERM	1 Year	2 Years	3 Years	4 Years	5 Years	6 Years	7 Years	8 Years	9 Years	10 Years	11 Years	12 Years	13 Years	14 Years
AMOUNT														
5	.46	.25	.18	.14	.12	.11	.10	.09	.09	.08	.08	.00	.08	.08
10	.91	.49	.35	.28	.24	.21	.20	.18	.17	.16	.16	.15	.15	.15
15	1.36	.73	.52	.42	.36	.32	.29	.27	.26	.24	.23	.23	.22	.22
25	2.26	1.21	.87	.70	.59	.53	.48	.45	.42	.40	.39	.37	.36	.36
50	4.51	2.42	1.73	1.39	1.18	1.05	.96	.89	.84	.80	.77	.74	.72	.71
75	6.76	3.63	2.59	2.08	1.77	1.58	1.44	1.33	1.26	1.20	1.15	1.11	1.08	1.06
100	9.01	4.84	3.45	2.77	2.36	2.10	1.91	1.78	1.68	1.60	1.53	1.48	1.44	1.41
200	18.02	9.67	6.90	5.53	4.72	4.19	3.82	3.55	3.35	3.19	3.06	2.96	2.88	2.81
300	27.03	14.50	10.35	8.30	7.08	6.29	5.73	5.32	5.02	4.78	4.59	4.44	4.31	4.21
400	36.04	19.33	13.80	11.06	9.44	8.38	7.64	7.10	6.69	6.37	6.11	5.91	5.75	5.61
500	45.05	24.16	17.25	13.83	11.80	10.48	9.55	8.87	8.36	7.96	7.64	7.39	7.18	7.01
600	54.05	28.99	20.69	16.59	14.16	12.57	11.46	10.64	10.03	9.55	9.17	8.87	8.62	8.42
700	63.06	33.82	24.14	19.35	16.52	14.66	13.37	12.42	11.70	11.14	10.70	10.34	10.05	9.82
800	72.07	38.65	27.59	22.12	18.88	16.76	15.27	14.19	13.37	12.73	12.22	11.82	11.49	11.22
900	81.08	43.48	31.04	24.88	21.24	18.85	17.18	15.96	15.04	14.32	13.75	13.30	12.93	12.62
1000	90.09	48.31	34.49	27.65	23.60	20.95	19.09	17.73	16.71	15.91	15.28	14.77	14.36	14.02
2000	180.17	96.62	68.97	55.29	47.19	41.89	38.18	35.46	33.41	31.81	30.55	29.54	28.72	28.04
3000	270.25	144.93	103.45	82.93	70.79	62.83	57.27	53.19	50.11	47.72	45.83	44.31	43.08	42.06
4000	360.33	193.24	137.93	110.57	94.38	83.77	76.35	70.92	66.81	63.62	61.10	59.08	57.43	56.08
5000	450.41	241.55	172.41	138.21	117.97	104.71	95.44	88.65	83.51	79.53	76.38	73.85	71.79	70.10
6000	540.49	289.86	206.90	165.85	141.57	125.66	114.53	106.38	100.21	95.43	91.65	88.61	86.15	84.12
7000	630.58	338.17	241.38	193.49	165.16	146.60	133.61	124.11	116.92	111.34	106.93	103.38	100.50	98.14
8000	720.66	386.47	275.86	221.13	188.75	167.54	152.70	141.84	133.62	127.24	122.20	118.15	114.86	112.16
9000	810.74	434.78	310.34	248.77	212.35	188.48	171.79	159.57	150.32	143.15	137.47	132.92	129.22	126.18
10000	900.82	483.09	344.82	276.42	235.94	209.42	190.87	177.30	167.02	159.05	152.75	147.69	143.57	140.20
11000	990.90	531.40	379.31	304.06	259.53	230.37	209.96	195.02	183.72	174.96	168.02	162.46	157.93	154.22
12000	1080.98	579.71	413.79	331.70	283.13	251.31	229.05	212.75	200.42	190.86	183.30	177.22	172.29	168.24
13000	1171.06	628.02	448.27	359.34	306.72	272.25	248.14	230.48	217.13	206.77	198.57	191.99	186.65	182.26
14000	1261.15	676.33	482.75	386.98	330.31	293.19	267.22	248.21	233.83	222.67	213.85	206.76	201.00	196.28
15000	1351.23	724.64	517.23	414.62	353.91	314.13	286.31	265.94	250.53	238.57	229.12	221.53	215.36	210.29
16000	1441.31	772.94	551.72	442.26	377.50	335.08	305.40	283.67	267.23	254.48	244.39	236.30	229.72	224.31
17000	1531.39	821.25	586.20	469.90	401.10	356.02	324.48	301.40	283.93	270.38	259.67	251.07	244.07	238.33
18000	1621.47	869.56	620.68	497.54	424.69	376.96	343.57	319.13	300.63	286.29	274.94	265.83	258.43	252.35
19000	1711.55	917.87	655.16	525.18	448.28	397.90	362.66	336.86	317.34	302.19	290.22	280.60	272.79	266.37
20000	1801.63	966.18	689.64	552.83	471.88	418.84	381.74	354.59	334.04	318.10	305.49	295.37	287.14	280.39
21000	1891.72	1014.49	724.13	580.47	495.47	439.78	400.83	372.32	350.74	334.00	320.77	310.14	301.50	294.41
22000	1981.80	1062.80	758.61	608.11	519.06	460.73	419.92	390.04	367.44	349.91	336.04	324.91	315.86	308.43
23000	2071.88	1111.10	793.09	635.75	542.66	481.67	439.01	407.77	384.14	365.81	351.31	339.68	330.22	322.45
24000	2161.96	1159.41	827.57	663.39	566.25	502.61	458.09	425.50	400.84	381.72	366.59	354.44	344.57	336.47
25000	2252.04	1207.72	862.05	691.03	589.84	523.55	477.18	443.23	417.55	397.62	381.86	369.21	358.93	350.49
26000	2342.12	1256.03	896.54	718.67	613.44	544.49	496.27	460.96	434.25	413.53	397.14	383.98	373.29	364.51
27000	2432.20	1304.34	931.02	746.31	637.03	565.44	515.35	478.69	450.95	429.43	412.41	398.75	387.64	378.53
28000	2522.29	1352.65	965.50	773.95	660.62	586.38	534.44	496.42	467.65	445.33	427.69	413.52	402.00	392.55
29000	2612.37	1400.96	999.98	801.59	684.22	607.32	553.53	514.15	484.35	461.24	442.96	428.28	416.36	406.57
30000	2702.45	1449.27	1034.46	829.24	707.81	628.26	572.61	531.88	501.05	477.14	458.24	443.05	430.71	420.58
31000	2792.53	1497.57	1068.95	856.88	731.40	649.20	591.70	549.61	517.76	493.05	473.51	457.82	445.07	434.60
32000	2882.61	1545.88	1103.43	884.52	755.00	670.15	610.79	567.34	534.46	508.95	488.78	472.59	459.43	448.62
33000	2972.69	1594.19	1137.91	912.16	778.59	691.09	629.87	585.06	551.16	524.86	504.06	487.36	473.78	462.64
34000	3062.77	1642.50	1172.39	939.80	802.19	712.03	648.96	602.79	567.86	540.76	519.33	502.13	488.14	476.66
35000	3152.86	1690.81	1206.87	967.44	825.78	732.97	668.05	620.52	584.56	556.67	534.61	516.89	502.50	490.68
36000	3242.94	1739.12	1241.36	995.08	849.37	753.91	687.14	638.25	601.26	572.57	549.88	531.66	516.86	504.70
37000	3333.02	1787.43	1275.84	1022.72	872.97	774.86	706.22	655.98	617.97	588.48	565.16	546.43	531.21	518.72
38000	3423.10	1835.73	1310.32	1050.36	896.56	795.80	725.31	673.71	634.67	604.38	580.43	561.20	545.57	532.74
39000	3513.18	1884.04	1344.80	1078.01	920.15	816.74	744.40	691.44	651.37	620.29	595.70	575.97	559.93	546.76
40000	3603.26	1932.35	1379.28	1105.65	943.75	837.68	763.48	709.17	668.07	636.19	610.98	590.74	574.28	560.78
41000	3693.34	1980.66	1413.77	1133.29	967.34	858.62	782.57	726.90	684.77	652.09	626.25	605.50	588.64	574.80
42000	3783.43	2028.97	1448.25	1160.93	990.93	879.56	801.66	744.63	701.47	668.00	641.53	620.27	603.00	588.82
43000	3873.51	2077.28	1482.73	1188.57	1014.53	900.51	820.74	762.36	718.18	683.90	656.80	635.04	617.35	602.84
44000	3963.59	2125.59	1517.21	1216.21	1038.12	921.45	839.83	780.08	734.88	699.81	672.08	649.81	631.71	616.86
45000	4053.67	2173.90	1551.69	1243.85	1061.71	942.39	858.92	797.81	751.58	715.71	687.35	664.58	646.07	630.87
46000	4143.75	2222.20	1586.18	1271.49	1085.31	963.33	878.01	815.54	768.28	731.62	702.62	679.35	660.43	644.89
47000	4233.83	2270.51	1620.66	1299.13	1108.90	984.27	897.09	833.27	784.98	747.52	717.90	694.11	674.78	658.91
48000	4323.91	2318.82	1655.14	1326.77	1132.50	1005.22	916.18	851.00	801.68	763.43	733.17	708.88	689.14	672.93
49000	4414.00	2367.13	1689.62	1354.42	1156.09	1026.16	935.27	868.73	818.38	779.33	748.45	723.65	703.50	686.95
50000	4504.08	2415.44	1724.10	1382.06	1179.68	1047.10	954.35	886.46	835.09	795.24	763.72	738.42	717.85	700.97
55000	4954.49	2656.98	1896.51	1520.26	1297.65	1151.81	1049.79	975.10	918.59	874.76	840.09	812.26	789.64	771.07
60000	5404.89	2898.53	2068.92	1658.47	1415.62	1256.52	1145.22	1063.75	1002.10	954.28	916.47	886.10	861.42	841.16
65000	5855.30	3140.07	2241.33	1796.67	1533.59	1361.23	1240.66	1152.39	1085.61	1033.81	992.84	959.94	933.21	911.26
70000	6305.71	3381.61	2413.74	1934.88	1651.55	1465.94	1336.09	1241.04	1169.12	1113.33	1069.21	1033.78	1004.99	981.36
75000	6756.11	3623.16	2586.15	2073.08	1769.52	1570.65	1431.53	1329.69	1252.63	1192.85	1145.58	1107.63	1076.78	1051.45
80000	7206.52	3864.70	2758.56	2211.29	1887.49	1675.36	1526.96	1418.33	1336.14	1272.37	1221.95	1181.47	1148.56	1121.55
85000	7656.93	4106.24	2930.97	2349.49	2005.46	1780.07	1622.40	1506.98	1419.64	1351.90	1298.32	1255.31	1220.35	1191.65
90000	8107.34	4347.79	3103.38	2487.70	2123.42	1884.78	1717.83	1595.62	1503.15	1431.42	1374.70	1329.15	1292.13	1261.74
95000	8557.74	4589.33	3275.79	2625.90	2241.39	1989.49	1813.27	1684.27	1586.66	1510.94	1451.07	1402.99	1363.92	1331.84
100000	9008.15	4830.87	3448.20	2764.11	2359.36	2094.19	1908.70	1772.91	1670.17	1590.47	1527.44	1476.83	1435.70	1401.94

TERM AMOUNT	15 Years	16 Years	17 Years	18 Years	19 Years	20 Years	21 Years	22 Years	23 Years	24 Years	25 Years	30 Years	35 Years	40 Years
5	.07	.07	.07	.07	.07	.07	.07	.07	.07	.07	.07	.07	.07	.07
10	.14	.14	.14	.14	.14	.13	.13	.13	.13	.13	.13	.13	.13	.13
15	.21	.21	.20	.20	.20	.20	.20	.20	.19	.19	.19	.19	.19	.19
25	.35	.34	.34	.33	.33	.33	.32	.32	.32	.32	.32	.31	.31	.31
50	.69	.68	.67	.66	.66	.65	.64	.64	.64	.63	.63	.62	.62	.62
75	1.04	1.02	1.00	.99	.98	.97	.96	.96	.95	.95	.94	.93	.92	.92
100	1.38	1.36	1.34	1.32	1.31	1.29	1.28	1.28	1.27	1.26	1.26	1.24	1.23	1.23
200	2.75	2.71	2.67	2.63	2.61	2.58	2.56	2.55	2.53	2.52	2.51	2.47	2.46	2.45
300	4.13	4.06	4.00	3.95	3.91	3.87	3.84	3.82	3.80	3.78	3.76	3.71	3.68	3.67
400	5.50	5.41	5.33	5.26	5.21	5.16	5.12	5.09	5.06	5.03	5.01	4.94	4.91	4.89
500	6.87	6.76	6.66	6.58	6.51	6.45	6.40	6.36	6.32	6.29	6.26	6.18	6.14	6.12
600	8.25	8.11	7.99	7.89	7.81	7.74	7.68	7.63	7.59	7.55	7.52	7.41	7.36	7.34
700	9.62	9.46	9.32	9.21	9.11	9.03	8.96	8.90	8.85	8.80	8.77	8.65	8.59	8.56
800	11.00	10.81	10.65	10.52	10.41	10.32	10.24	10.17	10.11	10.06	10.02	9.88	9.82	9.78
900	12.37	12.16	11.99	11.84	11.71	11.61	11.52	11.44	11.38	11.32	11.27	11.12	11.04	11.01
1000	13.74	13.51	13.32	13.15	13.01	12.90	12.80	12.71	12.64	12.58	12.52	12.35	12.27	12.23
2000	27.48	27.02	26.63	26.30	26.02	25.79	25.59	25.42	25.27	25.15	25.04	24.70	24.53	24.45
3000	41.22	40.53	39.94	39.45	39.03	38.68	38.38	38.12	37.91	37.72	37.56	37.04	36.79	36.68
4000	54.96	54.03	53.25	52.60	52.04	51.57	51.17	50.83	50.54	50.29	50.08	49.39	49.06	48.90
5000	68.70	67.54	66.57	65.74	65.05	64.46	63.96	63.54	63.17	62.86	62.60	61.73	61.32	61.12
6000	82.44	81.05	79.88	78.89	78.06	77.36	76.76	76.24	75.81	75.43	75.11	74.08	73.58	73.35
7000	96.18	94.56	93.19	92.04	91.07	90.25	89.55	88.95	88.44	88.00	87.63	86.42	85.85	85.57
8000	109.92	108.06	106.50	105.19	104.08	103.14	102.34	101.66	101.07	100.58	100.15	98.77	98.11	97.80
9000	123.66	121.57	119.81	118.34	117.09	116.03	115.13	114.36	113.71	113.15	112.67	111.11	110.37	110.02
10000	137.40	135.08	133.13	131.48	130.10	128.92	127.92	127.07	126.34	125.72	125.19	123.46	122.64	122.24
11000	151.14	148.58	146.44	144.63	143.11	141.81	140.71	139.78	138.98	138.29	137.70	135.80	134.90	134.47
12000	164.88	162.09	159.75	157.78	156.12	154.71	153.51	152.48	151.61	150.86	150.22	148.15	147.16	146.69
13000	178.62	175.60	173.06	170.93	169.13	167.60	166.30	165.19	164.24	163.43	162.74	160.49	159.43	158.92
14000	192.36	189.11	186.37	184.08	182.13	180.49	179.09	177.90	176.88	176.00	175.26	172.84	171.69	171.14
15000	206.10	202.61	199.69	197.22	195.14	193.38	191.88	190.60	189.51	188.58	187.78	185.18	183.95	183.36
16000	219.84	216.12	213.00	210.37	208.15	206.27	204.67	203.31	202.14	201.15	200.29	197.53	196.22	195.59
17000	233.58	229.63	226.31	223.52	221.16	219.16	217.46	216.01	214.78	213.72	212.81	209.87	208.48	207.81
18000	247.32	243.13	239.62	236.67	234.17	232.06	230.26	228.72	227.41	226.29	225.33	222.22	220.74	220.04
19000	261.06	256.64	252.94	249.82	247.18	244.95	243.05	241.43	240.04	238.86	237.85	234.56	233.01	232.26
20000	274.80	270.15	266.25	262.96	260.19	257.84	255.84	254.13	252.68	251.43	250.37	246.91	245.27	244.48
21000	288.54	283.66	279.56	276.11	273.20	270.73	268.63	266.84	265.31	264.00	262.88	259.25	257.53	256.71
22000	302.28	297.16	292.87	289.26	286.21	283.62	281.42	279.55	277.95	276.58	275.40	271.60	269.80	268.93
23000	316.02	310.67	306.18	302.41	299.22	296.51	294.21	292.25	290.58	289.15	287.92	283.94	282.06	281.16
24000	329.76	324.18	319.50	315.56	312.23	309.41	307.01	304.96	303.21	301.72	300.44	296.29	294.32	293.38
25000	343.50	337.68	332.81	328.70	325.24	322.30	319.80	317.67	315.85	314.29	312.96	308.63	306.58	305.60
26000	357.24	351.19	346.12	341.85	338.25	335.19	332.59	330.37	328.48	326.86	325.47	320.98	318.85	317.83
27000	370.98	364.70	359.43	355.00	351.26	348.08	345.38	343.08	341.11	339.43	337.99	333.32	331.11	330.05
28000	384.72	378.21	372.74	368.15	364.26	360.97	358.17	355.79	353.75	352.00	350.51	345.67	343.37	342.28
29000	398.46	391.71	386.06	381.30	377.27	373.86	370.96	368.49	366.38	364.58	363.03	358.01	355.64	354.50
30000	412.20	405.22	399.37	394.44	390.28	386.76	383.76	381.20	379.02	377.15	375.55	370.36	367.90	366.72
31000	425.94	418.73	412.68	407.59	403.29	399.65	396.55	393.91	391.65	389.72	388.06	382.70	380.16	378.95
32000	439.68	432.23	425.99	420.74	416.30	412.54	409.34	406.61	404.28	402.29	400.58	395.05	392.43	391.17
33000	453.42	445.74	439.31	433.89	429.31	425.43	422.13	419.32	416.92	414.86	413.10	407.39	404.69	403.40
34000	467.16	459.25	452.62	447.04	442.32	438.32	434.92	432.02	429.55	427.43	425.62	419.74	416.95	415.62
35000	480.90	472.76	465.93	460.18	455.33	451.21	447.71	444.73	442.18	440.00	438.14	432.08	429.22	427.84
36000	494.64	486.26	479.24	473.33	468.34	464.11	460.51	457.44	454.82	452.58	450.66	444.43	441.48	440.07
37000	508.38	499.77	492.55	486.48	481.35	477.00	473.30	470.14	467.45	465.15	463.17	456.77	453.74	452.29
38000	522.12	513.28	505.87	499.63	494.36	489.89	486.09	482.85	480.08	477.72	475.69	469.12	466.01	464.52
39000	535.86	526.78	519.18	512.78	507.37	502.78	498.88	495.56	492.72	490.29	488.21	481.46	478.27	476.74
40000	549.60	540.29	532.49	525.92	520.38	515.67	511.67	508.26	505.35	502.86	500.73	493.81	490.53	488.96
41000	563.34	553.80	545.80	539.07	533.39	528.56	524.46	520.97	517.99	515.43	513.25	506.15	502.80	501.19
42000	577.08	567.31	559.11	552.22	546.39	541.46	537.26	533.68	530.62	528.00	525.76	518.50	515.06	513.41
43000	590.82	580.81	572.43	565.37	559.40	554.35	550.05	546.38	543.25	540.58	538.28	530.84	527.32	525.64
44000	604.56	594.32	585.74	578.52	572.41	567.24	562.84	559.09	555.89	553.15	550.80	543.19	539.59	537.86
45000	618.30	607.83	599.05	591.66	585.42	580.13	575.63	571.80	568.52	565.72	563.32	555.53	551.85	550.08
46000	632.04	621.33	612.36	604.81	598.43	593.02	588.42	584.50	581.15	578.29	575.84	567.88	564.11	562.31
47000	645.78	634.84	625.68	617.96	611.44	605.91	601.21	597.21	593.79	590.86	588.35	580.22	576.37	574.53
48000	659.52	648.35	638.99	631.11	624.45	618.81	614.01	609.91	606.42	603.43	600.87	592.57	588.64	586.76
49000	673.26	661.86	652.30	644.26	637.46	631.70	626.80	622.62	619.05	616.00	613.39	604.91	600.90	598.98
50000	687.00	675.36	665.61	657.40	650.47	644.59	639.59	635.33	631.69	628.58	625.91	617.26	613.16	611.20
55000	755.70	742.90	732.17	723.14	715.52	709.05	703.55	698.86	694.86	691.43	688.50	678.99	674.48	672.32
60000	824.40	810.43	798.73	788.88	780.56	773.51	767.51	762.39	758.03	754.29	751.09	740.71	735.80	733.44
65000	893.10	877.97	865.29	854.62	845.61	837.96	831.46	825.92	821.19	817.15	813.68	802.44	797.11	794.56
70000	961.80	945.51	931.85	920.36	910.65	902.42	895.42	889.46	884.36	880.00	876.27	864.16	858.43	855.68
75000	1030.50	1013.04	998.41	986.10	975.70	966.88	959.38	952.99	947.53	942.86	938.86	925.89	919.74	916.80
80000	1099.20	1080.58	1064.98	1051.84	1040.75	1031.34	1023.34	1016.52	1010.70	1005.72	1001.45	987.61	981.06	977.92
85000	1167.90	1148.11	1131.54	1117.58	1105.79	1095.80	1087.30	1080.05	1073.87	1068.57	1064.04	1049.34	1042.38	1039.04
90000	1236.60	1215.65	1198.10	1183.32	1170.84	1160.26	1151.26	1143.59	1137.04	1131.43	1126.63	1111.06	1103.69	1100.16
95000	1305.30	1283.18	1264.66	1249.06	1235.89	1224.71	1215.21	1207.12	1200.20	1194.29	1189.22	1172.79	1165.01	1161.28
100000	1374.00	1350.72	1331.22	1314.80	1300.93	1289.17	1279.17	1270.65	1263.37	1257.15	1251.81	1234.51	1226.32	1222.40

MONTHLY PAYMENT
REQUIRED TO AMORTIZE A LOAN

TERM	1 Year	2 Years	3 Years	4 Years	5 Years	6 Years	7 Years	8 Years	9 Years	10 Years	11 Years	12 Years	13 Years	14 Years
AMOUNT														
5	.46	.25	.18	.14	.12	.11	.10	.09	.09	.08	.08	.08	.08	.08
10	.91	.49	.35	.28	.24	.21	.20	.18	.17	.16	.16	.15	.15	.15
15	1.36	.73	.52	.42	.36	.32	.29	.27	.26	.24	.23	.23	.22	.22
25	2.26	1.21	.87	.70	.60	.53	.48	.45	.42	.40	.39	.38	.37	.36
50	4.51	2.42	1.73	1.39	1.19	1.05	.96	.89	.84	.80	.77	.75	.73	.71
75	6.76	3.63	2.59	2.08	1.78	1.58	1.44	1.34	1.26	1.20	1.15	1.12	1.09	1.06
100	9.02	4.84	3.46	2.77	2.37	2.10	1.92	1.78	1.68	1.60	1.54	1.49	1.45	1.41
200	18.03	9.67	6.91	5.54	4.73	4.20	3.83	3.56	3.35	3.20	3.07	2.97	2.89	2.82
300	27.04	14.51	10.36	8.31	7.09	6.30	5.74	5.34	5.03	4.79	4.60	4.45	4.33	4.23
400	36.05	19.34	15.81	11.08	9.46	8.40	7.66	7.11	6.70	6.39	6.13	5.93	5.77	5.63
500	45.06	24.18	17.26	13.84	11.82	10.50	9.57	8.89	8.38	7.98	7.67	7.41	7.21	7.04
600	54.08	29.01	20.72	16.61	14.18	12.59	11.48	10.67	10.05	9.58	9.20	8.89	8.65	8.45
700	63.09	33.85	24.17	19.38	16.55	14.69	13.40	12.45	11.73	11.17	10.73	10.38	10.09	9.85
800	72.10	38.68	27.62	22.15	18.91	16.79	15.31	14.22	13.40	12.77	12.26	11.86	11.53	11.26
900	81.11	43.51	31.07	24.92	21.27	18.89	17.22	16.00	15.08	14.36	13.79	13.34	12.97	12.67
1000	90.12	48.35	34.52	27.68	23.64	20.99	19.13	17.78	16.75	15.96	15.33	14.82	14.41	14.07
2000	180.24	96.69	69.04	55.36	47.27	41.97	38.26	35.55	33.50	31.91	30.65	29.64	28.82	28.14
3000	270.36	145.04	103.56	83.04	70.90	62.95	57.39	53.32	50.24	47.86	45.97	44.45	43.22	42.21
4000	360.47	193.38	138.08	110.72	94.54	83.93	76.52	71.09	66.99	63.81	61.29	59.27	57.63	56.28
5000	450.59	241.73	172.60	138.40	118.17	104.92	95.65	88.87	83.74	79.76	76.61	74.09	72.04	70.35
6000	540.71	290.07	207.12	166.08	141.80	125.90	114.78	106.64	100.48	95.71	91.93	88.90	86.44	84.42
7000	630.82	338.41	241.64	193.76	165.43	146.88	133.91	124.41	117.23	111.66	107.25	103.72	100.85	98.49
8000	720.94	386.76	276.15	221.44	189.07	167.86	153.04	142.18	133.97	127.61	122.57	118.53	115.25	112.56
9000	811.06	435.10	310.67	249.12	212.70	188.85	172.16	159.96	150.72	143.56	137.90	133.35	129.66	126.63
10000	901.17	483.45	345.19	276.79	236.33	209.83	191.29	177.73	167.47	159.51	153.22	148.17	144.07	140.70
11000	991.29	531.79	379.71	304.47	259.97	230.81	210.42	195.50	184.21	175.46	168.54	162.98	158.47	154.77
12000	1081.41	580.14	414.23	332.15	283.60	251.79	229.55	213.27	200.96	191.41	183.86	177.80	172.88	168.84
13000	1171.52	628.48	448.75	359.83	307.23	272.78	248.68	231.04	217.70	207.36	199.18	192.62	187.28	182.91
14000	1261.64	676.82	483.27	387.51	330.86	293.76	267.81	248.82	234.45	223.31	214.50	207.43	201.69	196.98
15000	1351.76	725.17	517.78	415.19	354.50	314.74	286.94	266.59	251.20	239.26	229.82	222.25	216.10	211.05
16000	1441.87	773.51	552.30	442.87	378.13	335.72	306.07	284.36	267.94	255.21	245.14	237.06	230.50	225.12
17000	1531.99	821.86	586.82	470.55	401.76	356.71	325.20	302.13	284.69	271.16	260.46	251.88	244.91	239.18
18000	1622.11	870.20	621.34	498.23	425.39	377.69	344.32	319.91	301.43	287.11	275.79	266.70	259.31	253.25
19000	1712.22	918.55	655.86	525.90	449.03	398.67	363.45	337.68	318.18	303.06	291.11	281.51	273.72	267.32
20000	1802.34	966.89	690.38	553.58	472.66	419.65	382.58	355.45	334.93	319.01	306.43	296.33	288.13	281.39
21000	1892.46	1015.23	724.90	581.26	496.29	440.64	401.71	373.22	351.67	334.96	321.75	311.15	302.53	295.46
22000	1982.57	1063.58	759.41	608.94	519.93	461.62	420.84	390.99	368.42	350.91	337.07	325.96	316.94	309.53
23000	2072.69	1111.92	793.93	636.62	543.56	482.60	439.97	408.77	385.16	366.86	352.39	340.78	331.34	323.60
24000	2162.81	1160.27	828.45	664.30	567.19	503.58	459.10	426.54	401.91	382.81	367.71	355.59	345.75	337.67
25000	2252.93	1208.61	862.97	691.98	590.82	524.57	478.23	444.31	418.66	398.76	383.03	370.41	360.16	351.74
26000	2343.04	1256.96	897.49	719.66	614.46	545.55	497.35	462.08	435.40	414.71	398.36	385.23	374.56	365.81
27000	2433.16	1305.30	932.01	747.34	638.09	566.53	516.48	479.86	452.15	430.66	413.68	400.04	388.97	379.88
28000	2523.28	1353.64	966.53	775.01	661.72	587.51	535.61	497.63	468.89	446.61	429.00	414.86	403.37	393.95
29000	2613.39	1401.99	1001.04	802.69	685.35	608.50	554.74	515.40	485.64	462.56	444.32	429.68	417.78	408.02
30000	2703.51	1450.33	1035.56	830.37	708.99	629.48	573.87	533.17	502.39	478.51	459.64	444.49	432.19	422.09
31000	2793.63	1498.68	1070.08	858.05	732.62	650.46	593.00	550.94	519.13	494.46	474.96	459.31	446.59	436.16
32000	2883.74	1547.02	1104.60	885.73	756.25	671.44	612.13	568.72	535.88	510.41	490.28	474.12	461.00	450.23
33000	2973.86	1595.36	1139.12	913.41	779.89	692.43	631.26	586.49	552.62	526.36	505.60	488.94	475.40	464.30
34000	3063.98	1643.71	1173.64	941.09	803.52	713.41	650.39	604.26	569.37	542.31	520.92	503.76	489.81	478.36
35000	3154.09	1692.05	1208.16	968.77	827.15	734.39	669.51	622.03	586.12	558.26	536.25	518.57	504.22	492.43
36000	3244.21	1740.40	1242.67	996.45	850.78	755.37	688.64	639.81	602.86	574.21	551.57	533.39	518.62	506.50
37000	3334.33	1788.74	1277.19	1024.12	874.42	776.36	707.77	657.58	619.61	590.17	566.89	548.21	533.03	520.57
38000	3424.44	1837.09	1311.71	1051.80	898.05	797.34	726.90	675.35	636.36	606.12	582.21	563.02	547.43	534.64
39000	3514.56	1885.43	1346.23	1079.48	921.68	818.32	746.03	693.12	653.10	622.07	597.53	577.84	561.84	548.71
40000	3604.68	1933.77	1380.75	1107.16	945.31	839.30	765.16	710.89	669.85	638.02	612.85	592.65	576.25	562.78
41000	3694.79	1982.12	1415.27	1134.84	968.95	860.28	784.29	728.67	686.59	653.97	628.17	607.47	590.65	576.85
42000	3784.91	2030.46	1449.79	1162.52	992.58	881.27	803.42	746.44	703.34	669.92	643.49	622.29	605.06	590.92
43000	3875.03	2078.81	1484.30	1190.20	1016.21	902.25	822.54	764.21	720.09	685.87	658.82	637.10	619.46	604.99
44000	3965.14	2127.15	1518.82	1217.88	1039.85	923.23	841.67	781.98	736.83	701.82	674.14	651.92	633.87	619.06
45000	4055.26	2175.50	1553.34	1245.56	1063.48	944.21	860.80	799.76	753.58	717.77	689.46	666.74	648.28	633.13
46000	4145.38	2223.84	1587.86	1273.24	1087.11	965.20	879.93	817.53	770.32	733.72	704.78	681.55	662.68	647.20
47000	4235.49	2272.18	1622.38	1300.91	1110.74	986.18	899.06	835.30	787.07	749.67	720.10	696.37	677.09	661.27
48000	4325.61	2320.53	1656.90	1328.59	1134.38	1007.16	918.19	853.07	803.82	765.62	735.42	711.18	691.49	675.34
49000	4415.73	2368.87	1691.42	1356.27	1158.01	1028.14	937.32	870.84	820.56	781.57	750.74	726.00	705.90	689.41
50000	4505.85	2417.22	1725.93	1383.95	1181.64	1049.13	956.45	888.62	837.31	797.52	766.06	740.82	720.31	703.47
55000	4956.43	2658.94	1898.53	1522.35	1299.81	1154.04	1052.09	977.48	921.04	877.27	842.67	814.90	792.34	773.82
60000	5407.01	2900.66	2071.12	1660.74	1417.97	1258.95	1147.73	1066.34	1004.77	957.02	919.28	888.98	864.37	844.17
65000	5857.60	3142.38	2243.71	1799.13	1536.13	1363.86	1243.38	1155.20	1088.50	1036.77	995.88	963.06	936.40	914.52
70000	6308.18	3384.10	2416.31	1937.53	1654.30	1468.78	1339.02	1244.06	1172.23	1116.52	1072.49	1037.14	1008.43	984.86
75000	6758.77	3625.82	2588.90	2075.92	1772.46	1573.69	1434.67	1332.92	1255.96	1196.28	1149.09	1111.22	1080.46	1055.21
80000	7209.35	3867.54	2761.49	2214.32	1890.62	1678.60	1530.31	1421.78	1339.69	1276.03	1225.70	1185.30	1152.49	1125.56
85000	7659.93	4109.27	2934.09	2352.71	2008.79	1783.51	1625.96	1510.64	1423.42	1355.78	1302.30	1259.39	1224.52	1195.90
90000	8110.52	4350.99	3106.68	2491.11	2126.95	1888.42	1721.60	1599.51	1507.15	1435.53	1378.91	1333.47	1296.55	1266.25
95000	8561.10	4592.71	3279.27	2629.50	2245.12	1993.34	1817.24	1688.37	1590.88	1515.28	1455.52	1407.55	1368.58	1336.60
100000	9011.69	4834.43	3451.86	2767.90	2363.28	2098.25	1912.89	1777.23	1674.61	1595.03	1532.12	1481.63	1440.61	1406.94

TERM	15 Years	16 Years	17 Years	18 Years	19 Years	20 Years	21 Years	22 Years	23 Years	24 Years	25 Years	30 Years	35 Years	40 Years
AMOUNT														
5	.07	.07	.07	.07	.07	.07	.07	.07	.07	.07	.07	.07	.07	.07
10	.14	.14	.14	.14	.14	.13	.13	.13	.13	.13	.13	.13	.13	.13
15	.21	.21	.21	.20	.20	.20	.20	.20	.20	.19	.19	.19	.19	.19
25	.35	.34	.34	.34	.33	.33	.33	.32	.32	.32	.32	.32	.31	.31
50	.69	.68	.67	.67	.66	.65	.65	.64	.64	.64	.63	.63	.62	.62
75	1.04	1.02	1.01	1.00	.98	.98	.97	.96	.96	.95	.95	.94	.93	.93
100	1.38	1.36	1.34	1.33	1.31	1.30	1.29	1.28	1.27	1.27	1.26	1.25	1.24	1.23
200	2.76	2.72	2.68	2.65	2.62	2.59	2.57	2.56	2.54	2.53	2.52	2.49	2.47	2.46
300	4.14	4.07	4.01	3.97	3.92	3.89	3.86	3.83	3.81	3.79	3.78	3.73	3.70	3.69
400	5.52	5.43	5.35	5.29	5.23	5.18	5.14	5.11	5.08	5.06	5.04	4.97	4.93	4.92
500	6.90	6.78	6.69	6.61	6.54	6.48	6.43	6.39	6.35	6.32	6.29	6.21	6.17	6.15
600	8.28	8.14	8.02	7.93	7.84	7.77	7.71	7.66	7.62	7.58	7.55	7.45	7.40	7.38
700	9.66	9.50	9.36	9.25	9.15	9.07	9.00	8.94	8.89	8.85	8.81	8.69	8.63	8.60
800	11.04	10.85	10.70	10.57	10.46	10.36	10.28	10.22	10.16	10.11	10.07	9.93	9.86	9.83
900	12.42	12.21	12.03	11.89	11.76	11.66	11.57	11.49	11.43	11.37	11.32	11.17	11.10	11.06
1000	13.80	13.56	13.37	13.21	13.07	12.95	12.85	12.77	12.70	12.63	12.58	12.41	12.33	12.29
2000	27.59	27.12	26.73	26.41	26.13	25.90	25.70	25.53	25.39	25.26	25.16	24.81	24.65	24.58
3000	41.38	40.68	40.10	39.61	39.20	38.85	38.55	38.29	38.08	37.89	37.73	37.22	36.98	36.86
4000	55.17	54.24	53.46	52.81	52.26	51.79	51.39	51.06	50.77	50.52	50.31	49.62	49.30	49.15
5000	68.96	67.80	66.83	66.01	65.32	64.74	64.24	63.82	63.46	63.15	62.88	62.03	61.63	61.43
6000	82.75	81.36	80.19	79.21	78.39	77.69	77.09	76.58	76.15	75.78	75.46	74.43	73.95	73.72
7000	96.54	94.92	93.56	92.42	91.45	90.63	89.94	89.34	88.84	88.41	88.04	86.84	86.27	86.00
8000	110.33	108.48	106.92	105.62	104.51	103.58	102.78	102.11	101.53	101.04	100.61	99.24	98.60	98.29
9000	124.12	122.04	120.29	118.82	117.58	116.53	115.63	114.87	114.22	113.66	113.19	111.65	110.92	110.58
10000	137.91	135.60	133.65	132.02	130.64	129.47	128.48	127.63	126.91	126.29	125.76	124.05	123.25	122.86
11000	151.71	149.16	147.02	145.22	143.71	142.42	141.33	140.40	139.60	138.92	138.34	136.46	135.57	135.15
12000	165.50	162.71	160.38	158.42	156.77	155.37	154.17	153.16	152.29	151.55	150.92	148.86	147.89	147.43
13000	179.29	176.27	173.75	171.63	169.83	168.31	167.02	165.92	164.98	164.18	163.49	161.27	160.22	159.72
14000	193.08	189.83	187.11	184.83	182.90	181.26	179.87	178.68	177.67	176.81	176.07	173.67	172.54	172.00
15000	206.87	203.39	200.48	198.03	195.96	194.21	192.72	191.45	190.36	189.44	188.64	186.08	184.87	184.29
16000	220.66	216.95	213.84	211.23	209.02	207.15	205.56	204.21	203.05	202.07	201.22	198.48	197.19	196.57
17000	234.45	230.51	227.21	224.45	222.09	220.10	218.41	216.97	215.75	214.70	213.80	210.89	209.51	208.86
18000	248.24	244.07	240.57	237.63	235.15	233.05	231.26	229.74	228.44	227.32	226.37	223.29	221.84	221.15
19000	262.03	257.63	253.94	250.04	248.21	245.99	244.11	242.50	241.13	239.95	238.95	235.70	234.16	233.43
20000	275.82	271.19	267.30	264.04	261.28	258.94	256.95	255.26	253.82	252.58	251.52	248.10	246.49	245.72
21000	289.62	284.75	280.67	277.24	274.34	271.89	269.80	268.02	266.51	265.21	264.10	260.51	258.81	258.00
22000	303.41	298.31	294.03	290.44	287.41	284.83	282.65	280.79	279.20	277.84	276.68	272.91	271.14	270.29
23000	317.20	311.86	307.40	303.64	300.47	297.78	295.50	293.55	291.89	290.47	289.25	285.32	283.46	282.57
24000	330.99	325.42	320.76	316.84	313.53	310.73	308.34	306.31	304.58	303.10	301.83	297.72	295.78	294.86
25000	344.78	338.98	334.13	330.05	326.60	323.67	321.19	319.08	317.27	315.73	314.40	310.13	308.11	307.14
26000	358.57	352.54	347.49	343.25	339.66	336.62	334.04	331.84	329.96	328.36	326.98	322.53	320.43	319.43
27000	372.36	366.10	360.86	356.45	352.72	349.57	346.89	344.60	342.65	340.98	339.56	334.94	332.76	331.72
28000	386.15	379.66	374.22	369.65	365.79	362.51	359.73	357.36	355.34	353.61	352.13	347.34	345.08	344.00
29000	399.94	393.22	387.59	382.85	378.85	375.46	372.58	370.13	368.03	366.24	364.71	359.75	357.40	356.29
30000	413.73	406.78	400.95	396.05	391.92	388.41	385.43	382.89	380.72	378.87	377.28	372.15	369.73	368.57
31000	427.52	420.34	414.32	409.26	404.98	401.36	398.28	395.65	393.41	391.50	389.86	384.56	382.05	380.86
32000	441.32	433.90	427.68	422.46	418.04	414.30	411.12	408.42	406.10	404.13	402.44	396.96	394.38	393.14
33000	455.11	447.46	441.05	435.66	431.11	427.25	423.97	421.18	418.80	416.76	415.01	409.37	406.70	405.43
34000	468.90	461.01	454.41	448.86	444.17	440.20	436.82	433.94	431.49	429.39	427.59	421.77	419.02	417.71
35000	482.69	474.57	467.78	462.06	457.23	453.14	449.67	446.70	444.18	442.02	440.16	434.18	431.35	430.00
36000	496.48	488.13	481.14	475.26	470.30	466.09	462.51	459.47	456.87	454.64	452.74	446.58	443.67	442.29
37000	510.27	501.69	494.51	488.47	483.36	479.04	475.36	472.23	469.56	467.27	465.32	458.99	456.00	454.57
38000	524.06	515.25	507.87	501.67	496.42	491.98	488.21	484.99	482.25	479.90	477.89	471.39	468.32	466.86
39000	537.85	528.81	521.24	514.87	509.49	504.93	501.06	497.76	494.94	492.53	490.47	483.80	480.65	479.14
40000	551.64	542.37	534.60	528.07	522.55	517.88	513.90	510.52	507.63	505.16	503.04	496.20	492.97	491.43
41000	565.43	555.93	547.97	541.27	535.62	530.82	526.75	523.28	520.32	517.79	515.62	508.61	505.29	503.71
42000	579.23	569.49	561.33	554.47	548.68	543.77	539.60	536.04	533.01	530.42	528.20	521.01	517.62	516.00
43000	593.02	583.05	574.70	567.67	561.74	556.72	552.44	548.81	545.70	543.05	540.77	533.41	529.94	528.29
44000	606.81	596.61	588.06	580.88	574.81	569.66	565.29	561.57	558.39	555.67	553.35	545.82	542.27	540.57
45000	620.60	610.16	601.43	594.08	587.87	582.61	578.14	574.33	571.08	568.30	565.92	558.22	554.59	552.86
46000	634.39	623.72	614.79	607.28	600.93	595.56	590.99	587.10	583.77	580.93	578.50	570.63	566.91	565.14
47000	648.18	637.28	628.16	620.48	614.00	608.50	603.83	599.86	596.46	593.56	591.08	583.03	579.24	577.43
48000	661.97	650.84	641.52	633.68	627.06	621.45	616.68	612.62	609.15	606.19	603.65	595.44	591.56	589.71
49000	675.76	664.40	654.89	646.88	640.13	634.40	629.53	625.38	621.84	618.82	616.23	607.84	603.89	602.00
50000	689.55	677.96	668.25	660.09	653.19	647.34	642.38	638.15	634.54	631.45	628.80	620.25	616.21	614.28
55000	758.51	745.76	735.08	726.09	718.51	712.08	706.61	701.96	697.99	694.59	691.68	682.27	677.83	675.71
60000	827.46	813.55	801.90	792.10	783.83	776.81	770.85	765.77	761.44	757.74	754.56	744.30	739.45	737.14
65000	896.42	881.35	868.73	858.11	849.14	841.55	835.09	829.59	824.89	820.88	817.44	806.32	801.07	798.57
70000	965.37	949.14	935.55	924.12	914.46	906.28	899.33	893.40	888.35	884.03	880.32	868.35	862.69	860.00
75000	1034.33	1016.94	1002.38	990.13	979.78	971.01	963.56	957.22	951.80	947.17	943.20	930.37	924.31	921.42
80000	1103.28	1084.73	1069.20	1056.14	1045.10	1035.75	1027.80	1021.03	1015.25	1010.31	1006.08	992.40	985.93	982.85
85000	1172.24	1152.53	1136.03	1122.14	1110.42	1100.48	1092.04	1084.85	1078.71	1073.46	1068.96	1054.42	1047.55	1044.28
90000	1241.19	1220.33	1202.85	1188.15	1175.74	1165.21	1156.27	1148.66	1142.16	1136.60	1131.84	1116.44	1109.18	1105.71
95000	1310.15	1288.12	1269.68	1254.16	1241.05	1229.95	1220.51	1212.47	1205.61	1199.75	1194.72	1178.47	1170.80	1167.14
100000	1379.10	1355.92	1336.50	1320.17	1306.37	1294.68	1284.75	1276.29	1269.07	1262.89	1257.60	1240.49	1232.42	1228.56

14.750%

MONTHLY PAYMENT
REQUIRED TO AMORTIZE A LOAN

TERM AMOUNT	1 Year	2 Years	3 Years	4 Years	5 Years	6 Years	7 Years	8 Years	9 Years	10 Years	11 Years	12 Years	13 Years	14 Years
5	.46	.25	.18	.14	.12	.11	.10	.09	.09	.08	.08	.08	.08	.08
10	.91	.49	.35	.28	.24	.22	.20	.18	.17	.16	.16	.15	.15	.15
15	1.36	.73	.52	.42	.36	.32	.29	.27	.26	.24	.24	.23	.22	.22
25	2.26	1.21	.87	.70	.60	.53	.48	.45	.42	.40	.39	.38	.37	.36
50	4.51	2.42	1.73	1.39	1.19	1.06	.96	.90	.84	.80	.77	.75	.73	.71
75	6.77	3.63	2.60	2.08	1.78	1.58	1.44	1.34	1.26	1.20	1.16	1.12	1.09	1.06
100	9.02	4.84	3.46	2.78	2.37	2.11	1.92	1.79	1.68	1.60	1.54	1.49	1.45	1.42
200	18.03	9.68	6.91	5.55	4.74	4.21	3.84	3.57	3.36	3.20	3.08	2.97	2.89	2.83
300	27.05	14.52	10.37	8.32	7.10	6.31	5.75	5.35	5.04	4.80	4.61	4.46	4.34	4.24
400	36.06	19.35	13.82	11.09	9.47	8.41	7.67	7.12	6.72	6.40	6.15	5.94	5.78	5.65
500	45.08	24.19	17.28	13.86	11.83	10.51	9.58	8.91	8.39	8.00	7.68	7.43	7.22	7.06
600	54.09	29.03	20.73	16.63	14.20	12.61	11.50	10.69	10.07	9.59	9.22	8.91	8.67	8.47
700	63.10	33.86	24.19	19.40	16.57	14.71	13.41	12.47	11.75	11.19	10.75	10.40	10.11	9.88
800	72.12	38.70	27.64	22.17	18.93	16.81	15.33	14.25	13.43	12.79	12.29	11.88	11.56	11.29
900	81.13	43.54	31.09	24.94	21.30	18.91	17.25	16.03	15.10	14.39	13.82	13.37	13.00	12.70
1000	90.15	48.37	34.55	27.71	23.66	21.01	19.16	17.81	16.78	15.99	15.36	14.85	14.44	14.11
2000	180.29	96.74	69.09	55.41	47.32	42.02	38.32	35.61	33.56	31.97	30.71	29.70	28.88	28.21
3000	270.43	145.11	103.63	83.12	70.98	63.03	57.48	53.41	50.33	47.95	46.06	44.55	43.32	42.31
4000	360.57	193.48	138.18	110.82	94.64	84.04	76.63	71.21	67.11	63.93	61.41	59.40	57.76	56.42
5000	450.71	241.84	172.72	138.53	118.30	105.05	95.79	89.01	83.88	79.91	76.77	74.25	72.20	70.52
6000	540.85	290.21	207.26	166.23	141.96	126.06	114.95	106.81	100.66	95.89	92.12	89.09	86.64	84.62
7000	630.99	338.58	241.81	193.93	165.62	147.07	134.10	124.61	117.43	111.87	107.47	103.94	101.08	98.72
8000	721.13	386.95	276.35	221.64	189.28	168.08	153.26	142.41	134.21	127.85	122.82	118.79	115.51	112.83
9000	811.27	435.32	310.89	249.34	212.94	189.09	172.42	160.21	150.99	143.83	138.18	133.64	129.95	126.93
10000	901.41	483.68	345.44	277.05	236.59	210.10	191.57	178.02	167.76	159.81	153.53	148.49	144.39	141.03
11000	991.55	532.05	379.98	304.75	260.25	231.11	210.73	195.82	184.54	175.79	168.88	163.34	158.83	155.14
12000	1081.69	580.42	414.52	332.46	283.91	252.12	229.89	213.62	201.31	191.77	184.23	178.18	173.27	169.24
13000	1171.83	628.79	449.06	360.16	307.57	273.13	249.04	231.42	218.09	207.75	199.59	193.03	187.71	183.34
14000	1261.97	677.16	483.61	387.86	331.23	294.14	268.20	249.22	234.86	223.74	214.94	207.88	202.15	197.44
15000	1352.11	725.52	518.15	415.57	354.89	315.15	287.36	267.02	251.64	239.72	230.29	222.73	216.59	211.55
16000	1442.25	773.89	552.69	443.27	378.55	336.16	306.51	284.82	268.42	255.70	245.64	237.58	231.02	225.65
17000	1532.39	822.26	587.24	470.98	402.21	357.17	325.67	302.62	285.19	271.68	261.00	252.43	245.46	239.75
18000	1622.53	870.63	621.78	498.68	425.87	378.18	344.83	320.42	301.97	287.66	276.35	267.27	259.90	253.86
19000	1712.67	919.00	656.32	526.38	449.52	399.19	363.98	338.22	318.74	303.64	291.70	282.12	274.34	267.96
20000	1802.81	967.36	690.87	554.09	473.18	420.19	383.14	356.03	335.52	319.62	307.05	296.97	288.78	282.06
21000	1892.95	1015.73	725.41	581.79	496.84	441.20	402.30	373.83	352.29	335.60	322.41	311.82	303.22	296.16
22000	1983.09	1064.10	759.95	609.50	520.50	462.21	421.45	391.63	369.07	351.58	337.76	326.67	317.66	310.27
23000	2073.23	1112.47	794.49	637.20	544.16	483.22	440.61	409.43	385.85	367.56	353.11	341.51	332.10	324.37
24000	2163.37	1160.84	829.04	664.91	567.82	504.23	459.77	427.23	402.62	383.54	368.46	356.36	346.53	338.47
25000	2253.51	1209.20	863.58	692.61	591.48	525.24	478.92	445.03	419.40	399.52	383.82	371.21	360.97	352.58
26000	2343.66	1257.57	898.12	720.31	615.14	546.25	498.08	462.83	436.17	415.50	399.17	386.06	375.41	366.68
27000	2433.80	1305.94	932.67	748.02	638.80	567.26	517.24	480.63	452.95	431.49	414.52	400.91	389.85	380.78
28000	2523.94	1354.31	967.21	775.72	662.45	588.27	536.39	498.43	469.72	447.47	429.87	415.76	404.29	394.88
29000	2614.08	1402.68	1001.75	803.43	686.11	609.28	555.55	516.23	486.50	463.45	445.23	430.60	418.73	408.99
30000	2704.22	1451.04	1036.30	831.13	709.77	630.29	574.71	534.04	503.28	479.43	460.58	445.45	433.17	423.09
31000	2794.36	1499.41	1070.84	858.83	733.43	651.30	593.86	551.84	520.05	495.41	475.93	460.30	447.61	437.19
32000	2884.50	1547.78	1105.38	886.54	757.09	672.31	613.02	569.64	536.83	511.39	491.28	475.15	462.04	451.30
33000	2974.64	1596.15	1139.92	914.24	780.75	693.32	632.18	587.44	553.60	527.37	506.64	490.00	476.48	465.40
34000	3064.78	1644.52	1174.47	941.95	804.41	714.33	651.33	605.24	570.38	543.35	521.99	504.85	490.92	479.50
35000	3154.92	1692.88	1209.01	969.65	828.07	735.34	670.49	623.04	587.15	559.33	537.34	519.69	505.36	493.60
36000	3245.06	1741.25	1243.55	997.36	851.73	756.35	689.65	640.84	603.93	575.31	552.69	534.54	519.80	507.71
37000	3335.20	1789.62	1278.10	1025.06	875.38	777.36	708.81	658.64	620.71	591.29	568.04	549.39	534.24	521.81
38000	3425.34	1837.99	1312.64	1052.76	899.04	798.37	727.96	676.44	637.48	607.27	583.40	564.24	548.68	535.91
39000	3515.48	1886.36	1347.18	1080.47	922.70	819.37	747.12	694.25	654.26	623.25	598.75	579.09	563.12	550.01
40000	3605.62	1934.72	1381.73	1108.17	946.36	840.38	766.28	712.05	671.03	639.23	614.10	593.94	577.55	564.12
41000	3695.76	1983.09	1416.27	1135.88	970.02	861.39	785.43	729.85	687.81	655.22	629.45	608.78	591.99	578.22
42000	3785.90	2031.46	1450.81	1163.58	993.68	882.40	804.59	747.65	704.58	671.20	644.81	623.63	606.43	592.32
43000	3876.04	2079.83	1485.36	1191.29	1017.34	903.41	823.75	765.45	721.36	687.18	660.16	638.48	620.87	606.43
44000	3966.18	2128.19	1519.90	1218.99	1041.00	924.42	842.90	783.25	738.14	703.16	675.51	653.33	635.31	620.53
45000	4056.32	2176.56	1554.44	1246.69	1064.66	945.43	862.06	801.05	754.91	719.14	690.86	668.18	649.75	634.63
46000	4146.46	2224.93	1588.98	1274.40	1088.31	966.44	881.22	818.85	771.69	735.12	706.22	683.02	664.19	648.73
47000	4236.60	2273.30	1623.53	1302.10	1111.97	987.45	900.37	836.65	788.46	751.10	721.57	697.87	678.63	662.84
48000	4326.74	2321.67	1658.07	1329.81	1135.63	1008.46	919.53	854.45	805.24	767.08	736.92	712.72	693.06	676.94
49000	4416.88	2370.03	1692.61	1357.51	1159.29	1029.47	938.69	872.26	822.01	783.06	752.27	727.57	707.50	691.04
50000	4507.02	2418.40	1727.16	1385.21	1182.95	1050.48	957.84	890.06	838.79	799.04	767.63	742.42	721.94	705.15
55000	4957.73	2660.24	1899.87	1523.74	1301.24	1155.53	1053.63	979.06	922.67	878.95	844.39	816.66	794.14	775.66
60000	5408.43	2902.08	2072.59	1662.26	1419.54	1260.57	1149.41	1068.07	1006.55	958.85	921.15	890.90	866.33	846.17
65000	5859.13	3143.92	2245.30	1800.78	1537.83	1365.62	1245.19	1157.07	1090.43	1038.75	997.91	965.14	938.52	916.69
70000	6309.83	3385.76	2418.02	1939.30	1656.13	1470.67	1340.98	1246.08	1174.30	1118.66	1074.68	1039.38	1010.72	987.20
75000	6760.53	3627.60	2590.73	2077.82	1774.42	1575.72	1436.76	1335.08	1258.18	1198.56	1151.44	1113.62	1082.91	1057.72
80000	7211.24	3869.44	2763.45	2216.34	1892.72	1680.76	1532.55	1424.09	1342.06	1278.46	1228.20	1187.87	1155.10	1128.23
85000	7661.94	4111.28	2936.16	2354.86	2011.01	1785.81	1628.33	1513.09	1425.94	1358.37	1304.96	1262.11	1227.30	1198.74
90000	8112.64	4353.12	3108.88	2493.38	2129.31	1890.86	1724.11	1602.10	1509.82	1438.27	1381.72	1336.35	1299.49	1269.26
95000	8563.34	4594.96	3281.59	2631.90	2247.60	1995.91	1819.90	1691.10	1593.70	1518.18	1458.49	1410.59	1371.68	1339.77
100000	9014.04	4836.80	3454.31	2770.42	2365.90	2100.95	1915.68	1780.11	1677.58	1598.08	1535.25	1484.83	1443.88	1410.29

TERM / AMOUNT	15 Years	16 Years	17 Years	18 Years	19 Years	20 Years	21 Years	22 Years	23 Years	24 Years	25 Years	30 Years	35 Years	40 Years
5	.07	.07	.07	.07	.07	.07	.07	.07	.07	.07	.07	.07	.07	.07
10	.14	.14	.14	.14	.14	.13	.13	.13	.13	.13	.13	.13	.13	.13
15	.21	.21	.21	.20	.20	.20	.20	.20	.20	.20	.19	.19	.19	.19
25	.35	.34	.34	.34	.33	.33	.33	.33	.32	.32	.32	.32	.31	.31
50	.70	.68	.68	.67	.66	.65	.65	.65	.64	.64	.64	.63	.62	.62
75	1.04	1.02	1.01	1.00	.99	.98	.97	.97	.96	.96	.95	.94	.93	.93
100	1.39	1.36	1.35	1.33	1.31	1.30	1.29	1.29	1.28	1.27	1.27	1.25	1.24	1.24
200	2.77	2.72	2.69	2.65	2.62	2.60	2.58	2.57	2.55	2.54	2.53	2.49	2.48	2.47
300	4.15	4.08	4.03	3.98	3.93	3.90	3.87	3.85	3.82	3.81	3.79	3.74	3.71	3.70
400	5.54	5.44	5.37	5.30	5.24	5.20	5.16	5.13	5.10	5.07	5.05	4.98	4.95	4.94
500	6.92	6.80	6.71	6.62	6.55	6.50	6.45	6.41	6.37	6.34	6.31	6.23	6.19	6.17
600	8.30	8.16	8.05	7.95	7.86	7.80	7.74	7.69	7.64	7.61	7.57	7.47	7.42	7.40
700	9.68	9.52	9.39	9.27	9.17	9.09	9.02	8.97	8.92	8.87	8.84	8.72	8.66	8.63
800	11.07	10.88	10.73	10.59	10.48	10.39	10.31	10.25	10.19	10.14	10.10	9.96	9.90	9.87
900	12.45	12.24	12.07	11.92	11.79	11.69	11.60	11.53	11.46	11.41	11.36	11.21	11.13	11.10
1000	13.83	13.60	13.41	13.24	13.10	12.99	12.89	12.81	12.73	12.67	12.62	12.45	12.37	12.33
2000	27.66	27.19	26.81	26.48	26.20	25.97	25.77	25.61	25.46	25.34	25.23	24.89	24.73	24.66
3000	41.48	40.79	40.21	39.72	39.30	38.96	38.66	38.41	38.19	38.01	37.85	37.34	37.10	36.99
4000	55.31	54.38	53.61	52.95	52.40	51.94	51.54	51.21	50.92	50.67	50.46	49.78	49.46	49.31
5000	69.13	67.97	67.01	66.19	65.50	64.92	64.43	64.01	63.65	63.34	63.08	62.23	61.83	61.64
6000	82.96	81.57	80.41	79.43	78.60	77.91	77.31	76.81	76.38	76.01	75.69	74.67	74.19	73.97
7000	96.78	95.16	93.81	92.67	91.70	90.89	90.20	89.61	89.11	88.68	88.31	87.12	86.56	86.29
8000	110.61	108.76	107.21	105.90	104.80	103.87	103.08	102.41	101.83	101.34	100.92	99.56	98.92	98.62
9000	124.43	122.35	120.61	119.14	117.90	116.86	115.97	115.21	114.56	114.01	113.54	112.01	111.29	110.95
10000	138.26	135.94	134.01	132.38	131.00	129.84	128.85	128.01	127.29	126.68	126.15	124.45	123.65	123.27
11000	152.08	149.54	147.41	145.62	144.10	142.82	141.74	140.81	140.02	139.34	138.77	136.90	136.02	135.60
12000	165.91	163.13	160.81	158.85	157.20	155.81	154.62	153.61	152.75	152.01	151.38	149.34	148.38	147.93
13000	179.73	176.72	174.21	172.09	170.30	168.79	167.51	166.41	165.48	164.68	164.00	161.79	160.75	160.25
14000	193.56	190.32	187.61	185.33	183.40	181.77	180.39	179.21	178.21	177.35	176.61	174.23	173.11	172.58
15000	207.38	203.91	201.01	198.57	196.50	194.76	193.27	192.01	190.93	190.01	189.22	186.68	185.48	184.91
16000	221.21	217.51	214.41	211.80	209.60	207.74	206.16	204.81	203.66	202.68	201.84	199.12	197.84	197.23
17000	235.03	231.10	227.81	225.04	222.70	220.73	219.04	217.61	216.39	215.35	214.45	211.57	210.21	209.56
18000	248.86	244.69	241.21	238.28	235.80	233.71	231.93	230.41	229.12	228.01	227.07	224.01	222.57	221.89
19000	262.68	258.29	254.61	251.52	248.90	246.69	244.81	243.21	241.85	240.68	239.68	236.46	234.94	234.21
20000	276.51	271.88	268.01	264.75	262.00	259.68	257.70	256.01	254.58	253.35	252.30	248.90	247.30	246.54
21000	290.33	285.47	281.41	277.99	275.10	272.66	270.58	268.81	267.31	266.02	264.91	261.34	259.66	258.87
22000	304.16	299.07	294.81	291.23	288.20	285.64	283.47	281.61	280.03	278.68	277.53	273.79	272.03	271.19
23000	317.98	312.66	308.21	304.47	301.30	298.63	296.35	294.42	292.76	291.35	290.14	286.23	284.39	283.52
24000	331.81	326.26	321.61	317.70	314.40	311.61	309.24	307.22	305.49	304.02	302.76	298.68	296.76	295.85
25000	345.63	339.85	335.01	330.94	327.50	324.59	322.12	320.02	318.22	316.69	315.37	311.12	309.12	308.17
26000	359.46	353.44	348.41	344.18	340.60	337.58	335.01	332.82	330.95	329.35	327.99	323.57	321.49	320.50
27000	373.28	367.04	361.81	357.42	353.70	350.56	347.89	345.62	343.68	342.02	340.60	336.01	333.85	332.83
28000	387.11	380.63	375.21	370.65	366.80	363.54	360.78	358.42	356.41	354.69	353.22	348.46	346.22	345.15
29000	400.93	394.23	388.61	383.89	379.90	376.53	373.66	371.22	369.13	367.35	365.83	360.90	358.58	357.48
30000	414.76	407.82	402.01	397.13	393.00	389.51	386.54	384.02	381.86	380.02	378.44	373.35	370.95	369.81
31000	428.58	421.41	415.41	410.37	406.10	402.50	399.43	396.82	394.59	392.69	391.06	385.79	383.31	382.13
32000	442.41	435.01	428.81	423.60	419.20	415.48	412.31	409.62	407.32	405.36	403.67	398.24	395.68	394.46
33000	456.23	448.60	442.21	436.84	432.30	428.46	425.20	422.42	420.05	418.02	416.29	410.68	408.04	406.79
34000	470.06	462.19	455.61	450.08	445.40	441.45	438.08	435.22	432.78	430.69	428.90	423.13	420.41	419.11
35000	483.88	475.79	469.01	463.31	458.50	454.43	450.97	448.02	445.51	443.36	441.52	435.57	432.77	431.44
36000	497.71	489.38	482.41	476.55	471.60	467.41	463.85	460.82	458.23	456.02	454.13	448.02	445.14	443.77
37000	511.53	502.98	495.81	489.79	484.70	480.40	476.74	473.62	470.96	468.69	466.75	460.46	457.50	456.09
38000	525.36	516.57	509.21	503.03	497.80	493.38	489.62	486.42	483.69	481.36	479.36	472.91	469.87	468.42
39000	539.18	530.16	522.61	516.26	510.90	506.36	502.51	499.22	496.42	494.03	491.98	485.35	482.23	480.75
40000	553.01	543.76	536.01	529.50	524.00	519.35	515.39	512.02	509.15	506.69	504.59	497.80	494.59	493.07
41000	566.83	557.35	549.41	542.74	537.10	532.33	528.28	524.82	521.88	519.36	517.21	510.24	506.96	505.40
42000	580.66	570.94	562.81	555.98	550.20	545.31	541.16	537.62	534.61	532.03	529.82	522.68	519.32	517.73
43000	594.48	584.54	576.21	569.21	563.30	558.30	554.05	550.42	547.33	544.69	542.43	535.13	531.69	530.05
44000	608.31	598.13	589.61	582.45	576.40	571.28	566.93	563.22	560.06	557.36	555.05	547.57	544.05	542.38
45000	622.13	611.73	603.01	595.69	589.50	584.26	579.81	576.03	572.79	570.03	567.66	560.02	556.42	554.71
46000	635.96	625.32	616.42	608.93	602.60	597.25	592.70	588.83	585.52	582.70	580.28	572.46	568.78	567.03
47000	649.78	638.91	629.82	622.16	615.70	610.23	605.58	601.63	598.25	595.36	592.89	584.91	581.15	579.36
48000	663.61	652.51	643.22	635.40	628.80	623.22	618.47	614.43	610.98	608.03	605.51	597.35	593.51	591.69
49000	677.43	666.10	656.62	648.64	641.90	636.20	631.35	627.23	623.71	620.70	618.12	609.80	605.88	604.01
50000	691.26	679.69	670.02	661.88	655.00	649.18	644.24	640.03	636.44	633.37	630.74	622.24	618.24	616.34
55000	760.38	747.66	737.02	728.06	720.50	714.10	708.66	704.03	700.08	696.70	693.81	684.47	680.07	677.97
60000	829.51	815.63	804.02	794.25	786.00	779.02	773.08	768.03	763.72	760.04	756.88	746.69	741.89	739.61
65000	898.63	883.60	871.02	860.44	851.50	843.94	837.51	832.03	827.36	823.37	819.96	808.91	803.71	801.24
70000	967.76	951.57	938.02	926.62	917.00	908.85	901.93	896.04	891.01	886.71	883.03	871.14	865.54	862.87
75000	1036.88	1019.54	1005.02	992.81	982.50	973.77	966.35	960.04	954.65	950.05	946.10	933.36	927.36	924.51
80000	1106.01	1087.51	1072.02	1059.00	1048.00	1038.69	1030.78	1024.04	1018.29	1013.38	1009.18	995.58	989.18	986.14
85000	1175.13	1155.48	1139.02	1125.19	1113.50	1103.61	1095.20	1088.04	1081.94	1076.72	1072.25	1057.81	1051.01	1047.77
90000	1244.26	1223.45	1206.02	1191.37	1179.00	1168.52	1159.62	1152.05	1145.58	1140.05	1135.32	1120.03	1112.83	1109.41
95000	1313.38	1291.42	1273.03	1257.56	1244.50	1233.44	1224.05	1216.05	1209.22	1203.39	1198.40	1182.26	1174.66	1171.04
100000	1382.51	1359.38	1340.03	1323.75	1310.00	1298.36	1288.47	1280.05	1272.87	1266.73	1261.47	1244.48	1236.48	1232.67

MONTHLY PAYMENT
REQUIRED TO AMORTIZE A LOAN

TERM AMOUNT	1 Year	2 Years	3 Years	4 Years	5 Years	6 Years	7 Years	8 Years	9 Years	10 Years	11 Years	12 Years	13 Years	14 Years
5	.46	.25	.18	.14	.12	.11	.10	.09	.09	.09	.08	.08	.08	.08
10	.91	.49	.35	.28	.24	.22	.20	.18	.17	.17	.16	.15	.15	.15
15	1.36	.73	.52	.42	.36	.32	.29	.27	.26	.25	.24	.23	.22	.22
25	2.26	1.21	.87	.70	.60	.53	.48	.45	.43	.41	.39	.38	.37	.36
50	4.51	2.42	1.73	1.39	1.19	1.06	.96	.90	.85	.81	.77	.75	.73	.71
75	6.77	3.63	2.60	2.08	1.78	1.58	1.44	1.34	1.27	1.21	1.16	1.12	1.09	1.07
100	9.02	4.84	3.46	2.78	2.37	2.11	1.92	1.79	1.69	1.61	1.54	1.49	1.45	1.42
200	18.04	9.68	6.92	5.55	4.74	4.21	3.84	3.57	3.37	3.21	3.08	2.98	2.90	2.83
300	27.05	14.52	10.38	8.32	7.11	6.32	5.76	5.35	5.05	4.81	4.62	4.47	4.35	4.25
400	36.07	19.36	13.83	11.10	9.48	8.42	7.68	7.14	6.73	6.41	6.16	5.96	5.79	5.66
500	45.09	24.20	17.29	13.87	11.85	10.52	9.60	8.92	8.41	8.01	7.70	7.45	7.24	7.07
600	54.10	29.04	20.75	16.64	14.22	12.63	11.52	10.70	10.09	9.61	9.24	8.93	8.69	8.49
700	63.12	33.88	24.20	19.42	16.58	14.73	13.43	12.49	11.77	11.21	10.77	10.42	10.14	9.90
800	72.14	38.72	27.66	22.19	18.95	16.83	15.35	14.27	13.45	12.81	12.31	11.91	11.58	11.31
900	81.15	43.56	31.12	24.96	21.32	18.94	17.27	16.05	15.13	14.42	13.85	13.40	13.03	12.73
1000	90.17	48.40	34.57	27.73	23.69	21.04	19.19	17.83	16.81	16.02	15.39	14.89	14.48	14.14
2000	180.33	96.79	69.14	55.46	47.38	42.08	38.37	35.66	33.62	32.03	30.77	29.77	28.95	28.28
3000	270.50	145.18	103.71	83.19	71.06	63.11	57.56	53.49	50.42	48.04	46.16	44.65	43.42	42.41
4000	360.66	193.57	138.27	110.92	94.75	84.15	76.74	71.32	67.23	64.05	61.54	59.53	57.89	56.55
5000	450.82	241.96	172.84	138.65	118.43	105.19	95.93	89.15	84.03	80.06	76.92	74.41	72.36	70.69
6000	540.99	290.36	207.41	166.38	142.12	126.22	115.11	106.98	100.84	96.07	92.31	89.29	86.83	84.82
7000	631.15	338.75	241.98	194.11	165.80	147.26	134.30	124.81	117.64	112.08	107.69	104.17	101.31	98.96
8000	721.32	387.14	276.54	221.84	189.49	168.30	153.48	142.64	134.45	128.09	123.07	119.05	115.78	113.10
9000	811.48	435.53	311.11	249.57	213.17	189.33	172.67	160.47	151.25	144.11	138.46	133.93	130.25	127.23
10000	901.64	483.92	345.68	277.30	236.86	210.37	191.85	178.30	168.06	160.12	153.84	148.81	144.72	141.37
11000	991.81	532.31	380.25	305.03	260.54	231.41	211.04	196.13	184.86	176.13	169.23	163.69	159.19	155.50
12000	1081.97	580.71	414.81	332.76	284.23	252.44	230.22	213.96	201.67	192.14	184.61	178.57	173.66	169.64
13000	1172.14	629.10	449.38	360.49	307.91	273.48	249.41	231.79	218.47	208.15	199.99	193.45	188.13	183.78
14000	1262.30	677.49	483.95	388.22	331.60	294.52	268.59	249.62	235.28	224.16	215.38	208.33	202.61	197.91
15000	1352.46	725.88	518.52	415.95	355.28	315.55	287.78	267.45	252.09	240.17	230.76	223.21	217.08	212.05
16000	1442.63	774.27	553.08	443.68	378.97	336.59	306.96	285.28	268.89	256.18	246.14	238.09	231.55	226.19
17000	1532.79	822.66	587.65	471.41	402.65	357.63	326.15	303.11	285.70	272.20	261.53	252.97	246.02	240.32
18000	1622.96	871.06	622.22	499.14	426.34	378.66	345.33	320.94	302.50	288.21	276.91	267.85	260.49	254.46
19000	1713.12	919.45	656.79	526.86	450.02	399.70	364.51	338.77	319.31	304.22	292.30	282.73	274.96	268.59
20000	1803.28	967.84	691.35	554.59	473.71	420.74	383.70	356.60	336.11	320.23	307.68	297.61	289.44	282.73
21000	1893.45	1016.23	725.92	582.32	497.39	441.77	402.88	374.43	352.92	336.24	323.06	312.49	303.91	296.87
22000	1983.61	1064.62	760.49	610.05	521.08	462.81	422.07	392.26	369.72	352.25	338.45	327.37	318.38	311.00
23000	2073.78	1113.01	795.06	637.78	544.76	483.85	441.25	410.09	386.53	368.26	353.83	342.25	332.85	325.14
24000	2163.94	1161.41	829.62	665.51	568.45	504.88	460.44	427.92	403.33	384.27	369.21	357.13	347.32	339.28
25000	2254.10	1209.80	864.19	693.24	592.13	525.92	479.62	445.75	420.14	400.29	384.60	372.01	361.79	353.41
26000	2344.27	1258.19	898.76	720.97	615.82	546.96	498.81	463.58	436.94	416.30	399.98	386.89	376.26	367.55
27000	2434.43	1306.58	933.33	748.70	639.50	567.99	517.99	481.41	453.75	432.31	415.37	401.77	390.74	381.68
28000	2524.60	1354.97	967.89	776.43	663.19	589.03	537.18	499.24	470.56	448.32	430.75	416.65	405.21	395.82
29000	2614.76	1403.36	1002.46	804.16	686.87	610.06	556.36	517.07	487.36	464.33	446.13	431.53	419.68	409.96
30000	2704.92	1451.76	1037.03	831.89	710.56	631.10	575.55	534.90	504.17	480.34	461.52	446.41	434.15	424.09
31000	2795.09	1500.15	1071.60	859.62	734.24	652.14	594.73	552.73	520.97	496.35	476.90	461.29	448.62	438.23
32000	2885.25	1548.54	1106.16	887.35	757.93	673.17	613.92	570.56	537.78	512.36	492.28	476.17	463.09	452.37
33000	2975.42	1596.93	1140.73	915.08	781.61	694.21	633.10	588.39	554.58	528.38	507.67	491.05	477.56	466.50
34000	3065.58	1645.32	1175.30	942.81	805.30	715.25	652.29	606.22	571.39	544.39	523.05	505.93	492.04	480.64
35000	3155.74	1693.71	1209.87	970.54	828.98	736.28	671.47	624.05	588.19	560.40	538.44	520.82	506.51	494.77
36000	3245.91	1742.11	1244.43	998.27	852.67	757.32	690.65	641.88	605.00	576.41	553.82	535.70	520.98	508.91
37000	3336.07	1790.50	1279.00	1026.00	876.35	778.36	709.84	659.71	621.80	592.42	569.20	550.58	535.45	523.05
38000	3426.24	1838.89	1313.57	1053.72	900.04	799.39	729.02	677.54	638.61	608.43	584.59	565.46	549.92	537.18
39000	3516.40	1887.28	1348.14	1081.45	923.72	820.43	748.21	695.37	655.41	624.44	599.97	580.34	564.39	551.32
40000	3606.56	1935.67	1382.70	1109.18	947.41	841.47	767.39	713.20	672.22	640.45	615.35	595.22	578.87	565.46
41000	3696.73	1984.06	1417.27	1136.91	971.09	862.50	786.58	731.03	689.03	656.47	630.74	610.10	593.34	579.59
42000	3786.89	2032.46	1451.84	1164.64	994.78	883.54	805.76	748.86	705.83	672.48	646.12	624.98	607.81	593.73
43000	3877.06	2080.85	1486.41	1192.37	1018.46	904.58	824.95	766.69	722.64	688.49	661.50	639.86	622.28	607.86
44000	3967.22	2129.24	1520.97	1220.10	1042.15	925.61	844.13	784.52	739.44	704.50	676.89	654.74	636.75	622.00
45000	4057.38	2177.63	1555.54	1247.83	1065.83	946.65	863.32	802.35	756.25	720.51	692.27	669.62	651.22	636.14
46000	4147.55	2226.02	1590.11	1275.56	1089.52	967.69	882.50	820.18	773.05	736.52	707.66	684.50	665.69	650.27
47000	4237.71	2274.41	1624.68	1303.29	1113.20	988.72	901.69	838.01	789.86	752.53	723.04	699.38	680.17	664.41
48000	4327.88	2322.81	1659.24	1331.02	1136.89	1009.76	920.87	855.84	806.66	768.54	738.42	714.26	694.64	678.55
49000	4418.04	2371.20	1693.81	1358.75	1160.57	1030.80	940.06	873.67	823.47	784.56	753.81	729.14	709.11	692.68
50000	4508.20	2419.59	1728.38	1386.48	1184.26	1051.83	959.24	891.50	840.27	800.57	769.19	744.02	723.58	706.82
55000	4959.02	2661.55	1901.22	1525.13	1302.68	1157.02	1055.16	980.65	924.30	880.62	846.11	818.42	795.94	777.50
60000	5409.84	2903.51	2074.05	1663.77	1421.11	1262.20	1151.09	1069.80	1008.33	960.68	923.03	892.82	868.30	848.18
65000	5860.66	3145.46	2246.89	1802.42	1539.54	1367.38	1247.01	1158.95	1092.35	1040.74	999.95	967.22	940.65	918.86
70000	6311.48	3387.42	2419.73	1941.07	1657.96	1472.56	1342.94	1248.10	1176.38	1120.79	1076.87	1041.63	1013.01	989.54
75000	6762.30	3629.38	2592.57	2079.72	1776.39	1577.75	1438.86	1337.24	1260.41	1200.85	1153.78	1116.03	1085.37	1060.23
80000	7213.12	3871.34	2765.40	2218.36	1894.81	1682.93	1534.78	1426.39	1344.44	1280.90	1230.70	1190.43	1157.73	1130.91
85000	7663.94	4113.30	2938.24	2357.01	2013.24	1788.11	1630.71	1515.54	1428.46	1360.96	1307.62	1264.83	1230.08	1201.59
90000	8114.76	4355.26	3111.08	2495.66	2131.66	1893.29	1726.63	1604.69	1512.49	1441.02	1384.54	1339.23	1302.44	1272.27
95000	8565.58	4597.21	3283.91	2634.30	2250.09	1998.48	1822.55	1693.84	1596.52	1521.07	1461.46	1413.63	1374.80	1342.95
100000	9016.40	4839.17	3456.75	2772.95	2368.51	2103.66	1918.48	1782.99	1680.54	1601.13	1538.38	1488.03	1447.16	1413.63

TERM AMOUNT	15 Years	16 Years	17 Years	18 Years	19 Years	20 Years	21 Years	22 Years	23 Years	24 Years	25 Years	30 Years	35 Years	40 Years
5	.07	.07	.07	.07	.07	.07	.07	.07	.07	.07	.07	.07	.07	.07
10	.14	.14	.14	.14	.14	.14	.13	.13	.13	.13	.13	.13	.13	.13
15	.21	.21	.21	.20	.20	.20	.20	.20	.20	.20	.19	.19	.19	.19
25	.35	.35	.34	.34	.33	.33	.33	.33	.32	.32	.32	.32	.32	.31
50	.70	.69	.68	.67	.66	.66	.65	.65	.64	.64	.64	.63	.63	.62
75	1.04	1.03	1.01	1.00	.99	.98	.97	.97	.96	.96	.95	.94	.94	.93
100	1.39	1.37	1.35	1.33	1.32	1.31	1.30	1.29	1.28	1.28	1.27	1.25	1.25	1.24
200	2.78	2.73	2.69	2.66	2.63	2.61	2.59	2.57	2.56	2.55	2.54	2.50	2.49	2.48
300	4.16	4.09	4.04	3.99	3.95	3.91	3.88	3.86	3.83	3.82	3.80	3.75	3.73	3.72
400	5.55	5.46	5.38	5.31	5.26	5.21	5.17	5.14	5.11	5.09	5.07	5.00	4.97	4.95
500	6.93	6.82	6.72	6.64	6.57	6.52	6.47	6.42	6.39	6.36	6.33	6.25	6.21	6.19
600	8.32	8.18	8.07	7.97	7.89	7.82	7.76	7.71	7.66	7.63	7.60	7.50	7.45	7.43
700	9.71	9.54	9.41	9.30	9.20	9.12	9.05	8.99	8.94	8.90	8.86	8.74	8.69	8.66
800	11.09	10.91	10.75	10.62	10.51	10.42	10.34	10.28	10.22	10.17	10.13	9.99	9.93	9.90
900	12.48	12.27	12.10	11.95	11.83	11.72	11.63	11.56	11.49	11.44	11.39	11.24	11.17	11.14
1000	13.86	13.63	13.44	13.28	13.14	13.03	12.93	12.84	12.77	12.71	12.66	12.49	12.41	12.37
2000	27.72	27.26	26.88	26.55	26.28	26.05	25.85	25.68	25.54	25.42	25.31	24.97	24.82	24.74
3000	41.58	40.89	40.31	39.82	39.41	39.07	38.77	38.52	38.30	38.12	37.96	37.46	37.22	37.11
4000	55.44	54.52	53.75	53.10	52.55	52.09	51.69	51.36	51.07	50.83	50.62	49.94	49.63	49.48
5000	69.30	68.15	67.18	66.37	65.69	65.11	64.61	64.20	63.84	63.53	63.27	62.43	62.03	61.84
6000	83.16	81.78	80.62	79.64	78.82	78.13	77.54	77.03	76.60	76.24	75.92	74.91	74.44	74.21
7000	97.02	95.40	94.05	92.92	91.96	91.15	90.46	89.87	89.37	88.94	88.58	87.40	86.84	86.58
8000	110.88	109.03	107.49	106.19	105.10	104.17	103.38	102.71	102.14	101.65	101.23	99.88	99.25	98.95
9000	124.74	122.66	120.92	119.46	118.23	117.19	116.30	115.55	114.90	114.36	113.88	112.37	111.65	111.31
10000	138.60	136.29	134.36	132.74	131.37	130.21	129.22	128.39	127.67	127.06	126.54	124.85	124.06	123.68
11000	152.46	149.92	147.80	146.01	144.50	143.23	142.15	141.22	140.44	139.77	139.19	137.34	136.46	136.05
12000	166.31	163.55	161.23	159.28	157.64	156.25	155.07	154.06	153.20	152.47	151.84	149.82	140.07	140.42
13000	180.17	177.18	174.67	172.56	170.78	169.27	167.99	166.90	165.97	165.18	164.50	162.31	161.28	160.79
14000	194.03	190.80	188.10	185.83	183.91	182.29	180.91	179.74	178.74	177.88	177.15	174.79	173.69	173.15
15000	207.89	204.43	201.54	199.10	197.05	195.31	193.83	192.58	191.50	190.59	189.80	187.27	186.09	185.52
16000	221.75	218.06	214.97	212.38	210.19	208.33	206.76	205.41	204.27	203.29	202.46	199.76	198.49	197.89
17000	235.61	231.69	228.41	225.65	223.32	221.35	219.68	218.25	217.04	216.00	215.11	212.24	210.90	210.26
18000	249.47	245.32	241.84	238.92	236.46	234.37	232.60	231.09	229.80	228.71	227.76	224.73	223.30	222.62
19000	263.33	258.95	255.28	252.20	249.60	247.39	245.52	243.93	242.57	241.41	240.42	237.21	235.71	234.99
20000	277.19	272.58	268.72	265.47	262.73	260.41	258.44	256.77	255.34	254.12	253.07	249.70	248.11	247.36
21000	291.05	286.20	282.15	278.74	275.87	273.43	271.36	269.61	268.10	266.82	265.72	262.18	260.52	259.73
22000	304.91	299.83	295.59	292.02	289.00	286.45	284.29	282.44	280.87	279.53	278.38	274.67	272.92	272.10
23000	318.77	313.46	309.02	305.29	302.14	299.47	297.21	295.28	293.64	292.23	291.03	287.15	285.33	284.46
24000	332.62	327.09	322.46	318.56	315.28	312.49	310.13	308.12	306.40	304.94	303.68	299.64	297.73	296.83
25000	346.48	340.72	335.89	331.84	328.41	325.51	323.05	320.96	319.17	317.64	316.34	312.12	310.14	309.20
26000	360.34	354.35	349.33	345.11	341.55	338.53	335.97	333.80	331.94	330.35	328.99	324.61	322.55	321.57
27000	374.20	367.97	362.76	358.38	354.69	351.55	348.90	346.63	344.70	343.06	341.64	337.09	334.95	333.93
28000	388.06	381.60	376.20	371.66	367.82	364.58	361.82	359.47	357.47	355.76	354.30	349.58	347.36	346.30
29000	401.92	395.23	389.63	384.93	380.96	377.60	374.74	372.31	370.24	368.47	366.95	362.06	359.76	358.67
30000	415.78	408.86	403.07	398.20	394.09	390.62	387.66	385.15	383.00	381.17	379.60	374.54	372.17	371.04
31000	429.64	422.49	416.51	411.48	407.23	403.64	400.58	397.99	395.77	393.88	392.26	387.03	384.57	383.41
32000	443.50	436.12	429.94	424.75	420.37	416.66	413.51	410.82	408.54	406.58	404.91	399.51	396.98	395.77
33000	457.36	449.75	443.38	438.02	433.50	429.68	426.43	423.66	421.30	419.29	417.56	412.00	409.38	408.14
34000	471.22	463.37	456.81	451.30	446.64	442.70	439.35	436.50	434.07	431.99	430.22	424.48	421.79	420.51
35000	485.07	477.00	470.25	464.57	459.78	455.72	452.27	449.34	446.84	444.70	442.87	436.97	434.19	432.88
36000	498.93	490.63	483.68	477.84	472.91	468.74	465.19	462.18	459.60	457.41	455.52	449.45	446.60	445.24
37000	512.79	504.26	497.12	491.12	486.05	481.76	478.12	475.01	472.37	470.11	468.18	461.94	459.00	457.61
38000	526.65	517.89	510.55	504.39	499.19	494.78	491.04	487.85	485.14	482.82	480.83	474.42	471.41	469.98
39000	540.51	531.52	523.99	517.66	512.32	507.80	503.96	500.69	497.90	495.52	493.48	486.91	483.82	482.35
40000	554.37	545.15	537.43	530.94	525.46	520.82	516.88	513.53	510.67	508.23	506.14	499.39	496.22	494.72
41000	568.23	558.77	550.86	544.21	538.59	533.84	529.80	526.37	523.44	520.93	518.79	511.88	508.63	507.08
42000	582.09	572.40	564.30	557.48	551.73	546.86	542.72	539.21	536.20	533.64	531.44	524.36	521.03	519.45
43000	595.95	586.03	577.73	570.76	564.87	559.88	555.65	552.04	548.97	546.34	544.10	536.85	533.44	531.82
44000	609.81	599.66	591.17	584.03	578.00	572.90	568.57	564.88	561.74	559.05	556.75	549.33	545.84	544.19
45000	623.67	613.29	604.60	597.30	591.14	585.92	581.49	577.72	574.50	571.76	569.40	561.81	558.25	556.55
46000	637.53	626.92	618.04	610.57	604.28	598.94	594.41	590.56	587.27	584.46	582.06	574.30	570.65	568.92
47000	651.38	640.55	631.47	623.85	617.41	611.96	607.33	603.40	600.04	597.17	594.71	586.78	583.06	581.29
48000	665.24	654.17	644.91	637.12	630.55	624.98	620.26	616.23	612.80	609.87	607.36	599.27	595.46	593.66
49000	679.10	667.80	658.35	650.39	643.68	638.00	633.18	629.07	625.57	622.58	620.02	611.75	607.87	606.03
50000	692.96	681.43	671.78	663.67	656.82	651.02	646.10	641.91	638.34	635.28	632.67	624.24	620.27	618.39
55000	762.26	749.57	738.96	730.03	722.50	716.12	710.71	706.10	702.17	698.81	695.94	686.66	682.30	680.23
60000	831.55	817.72	806.14	796.40	788.18	781.23	775.32	770.29	766.00	762.34	759.20	749.08	744.33	742.07
65000	900.85	885.86	873.31	862.77	853.87	846.33	839.93	834.48	829.84	825.87	822.47	811.51	806.36	803.91
70000	970.14	954.00	940.49	929.13	919.55	911.43	904.54	898.67	893.67	889.39	885.74	873.93	868.38	865.75
75000	1039.44	1022.14	1007.67	995.50	985.23	976.53	969.15	962.86	957.50	952.92	949.00	936.35	930.41	927.59
80000	1108.74	1090.29	1074.85	1061.87	1050.91	1041.63	1033.76	1027.05	1021.33	1016.45	1012.27	998.78	992.44	989.43
85000	1178.03	1158.43	1142.02	1128.23	1116.59	1106.74	1098.37	1091.24	1085.17	1079.98	1075.54	1061.20	1054.46	1051.27
90000	1247.33	1226.57	1209.20	1194.60	1182.27	1171.84	1162.98	1155.43	1149.00	1143.51	1138.80	1123.62	1116.49	1113.10
95000	1316.62	1294.71	1276.38	1260.96	1247.96	1236.94	1227.59	1219.62	1212.83	1207.03	1202.07	1186.05	1178.52	1174.94
100000	1385.92	1362.86	1343.56	1327.33	1313.64	1302.04	1292.19	1283.81	1276.67	1270.56	1265.34	1248.47	1240.54	1236.78

MONTHLY PAYMENT
REQUIRED TO AMORTIZE A LOAN

TERM AMOUNT	1 Year	2 Years	3 Years	4 Years	5 Years	6 Years	7 Years	8 Years	9 Years	10 Years	11 Years	12 Years	13 Years	14 Years
5	.46	.25	.18	.14	.12	.11	.10	.09	.09	.09	.08	.08	.08	.08
10	.91	.49	.35	.28	.24	.22	.20	.18	.17	.17	.16	.15	.15	.15
15	1.36	.73	.52	.42	.36	.32	.29	.27	.26	.25	.24	.23	.22	.22
25	2.26	1.22	.87	.70	.60	.53	.49	.45	.43	.41	.39	.38	.37	.36
50	4.51	2.43	1.74	1.39	1.19	1.06	.97	.90	.85	.81	.78	.75	.73	.71
75	6.77	3.64	2.60	2.09	1.78	1.59	1.45	1.35	1.27	1.21	1.16	1.12	1.09	1.07
100	9.02	4.85	3.47	2.78	2.38	2.11	1.93	1.79	1.69	1.61	1.55	1.50	1.46	1.42
200	18.04	9.69	6.93	5.56	4.75	4.22	3.85	3.58	3.37	3.22	3.09	2.99	2.91	2.84
300	27.06	14.53	10.39	8.34	7.12	6.33	5.77	5.37	5.06	4.82	4.63	4.48	4.36	4.26
400	36.08	19.38	13.85	11.11	9.49	8.44	7.70	7.15	6.74	6.43	6.18	5.98	5.81	5.68
500	45.10	24.22	17.31	13.89	11.87	10.54	9.62	8.94	8.43	8.03	7.72	7.47	7.27	7.10
600	54.12	29.06	20.77	16.67	14.24	12.65	11.54	10.73	10.11	9.64	9.26	8.96	8.72	8.52
700	63.14	33.90	24.23	19.44	16.61	14.76	13.46	12.52	11.80	11.24	10.81	10.45	10.17	9.94
800	72.16	38.75	27.69	22.22	18.98	16.87	15.39	14.30	13.48	12.85	12.35	11.95	11.62	11.35
900	81.18	43.59	31.15	25.00	21.36	18.97	17.31	16.09	15.17	14.46	13.89	13.44	13.07	12.77
1000	90.20	48.43	34.61	27.77	23.73	21.08	19.23	17.88	16.85	16.06	15.44	14.93	14.53	14.19
2000	180.40	96.86	69.21	55.54	47.45	42.16	38.46	35.75	33.70	32.12	30.87	29.86	29.05	28.38
3000	270.60	145.29	103.82	83.31	71.18	63.24	57.69	53.62	50.55	48.18	46.30	44.79	43.57	42.56
4000	360.80	193.71	138.42	111.07	94.90	84.31	76.91	71.50	67.40	64.23	61.73	59.72	58.09	56.75
5000	451.00	242.14	173.03	138.84	118.63	105.39	96.14	89.37	84.25	80.29	77.16	74.65	72.61	70.94
6000	541.20	290.57	207.63	166.61	142.35	126.47	115.37	107.24	101.10	96.35	92.59	89.58	87.13	85.12
7000	631.40	339.00	242.23	194.38	166.08	147.55	134.59	125.12	117.95	112.40	108.02	104.50	101.65	99.31
8000	721.60	387.42	276.84	222.14	189.80	168.62	153.82	142.99	134.80	128.46	123.45	119.43	116.17	113.50
9000	811.80	435.85	311.44	249.91	213.52	189.70	173.05	160.86	151.65	144.52	138.88	134.36	130.69	127.68
10000	902.00	484.28	346.05	277.68	237.25	210.78	192.27	178.74	168.50	160.58	154.31	149.29	145.21	141.87
11000	992.20	532.71	380.65	305.45	260.97	231.85	211.50	196.61	185.35	176.63	169.74	164.22	159.73	156.06
12000	1082.40	581.13	415.25	333.21	284.70	252.93	230.73	214.48	202.20	192.69	185.17	179.15	174.25	170.24
13000	1172.60	629.56	449.86	360.98	308.42	274.01	249.95	232.36	219.05	208.75	200.60	194.07	188.77	184.43
14000	1262.80	677.99	484.46	388.75	332.15	295.09	269.18	250.23	235.90	224.80	216.03	209.00	203.29	198.62
15000	1353.00	726.41	519.07	416.52	355.87	316.16	288.41	268.10	252.75	240.86	231.47	223.93	217.82	212.80
16000	1443.19	774.84	553.67	444.28	379.59	337.24	307.63	285.98	269.60	256.92	246.90	238.86	232.34	226.99
17000	1533.39	823.27	588.28	472.05	403.32	358.32	326.86	303.85	286.45	272.97	262.33	253.79	246.86	241.18
18000	1623.59	871.70	622.88	499.82	427.04	379.39	346.09	321.72	303.30	289.03	277.76	268.72	261.38	255.36
19000	1713.79	920.12	657.48	527.59	450.77	400.47	365.31	339.59	320.15	305.09	293.19	283.64	275.90	269.55
20000	1803.99	968.55	692.09	555.35	474.49	421.55	384.54	357.47	337.00	321.15	308.62	298.57	290.42	283.74
21000	1894.19	1016.98	726.69	583.12	498.22	442.63	403.77	375.34	353.85	337.20	324.05	313.50	304.94	297.92
22000	1984.39	1065.41	761.30	610.89	521.94	463.70	422.99	393.21	370.70	353.26	339.48	328.43	319.46	312.11
23000	2074.59	1113.83	795.90	638.66	545.67	484.78	442.22	411.09	387.55	369.32	354.91	343.36	333.98	326.29
24000	2164.79	1162.26	830.50	666.42	569.39	505.86	461.45	428.96	404.40	385.37	370.34	358.29	348.50	340.48
25000	2254.99	1210.69	865.11	694.19	593.11	526.93	480.67	446.83	421.25	401.43	385.77	373.22	363.02	354.67
26000	2345.19	1259.11	899.71	721.96	616.84	548.01	499.90	464.71	438.10	417.49	401.20	388.14	377.54	368.85
27000	2435.39	1307.54	934.32	749.73	640.56	569.09	519.13	482.58	454.95	433.54	416.63	403.07	392.06	383.04
28000	2525.59	1355.97	968.92	777.49	664.29	590.17	538.35	500.45	471.80	449.60	432.06	418.00	406.58	397.23
29000	2615.79	1404.40	1003.53	805.26	688.01	611.24	557.58	518.33	488.65	465.66	447.50	432.93	421.11	411.41
30000	2705.99	1452.82	1038.13	833.03	711.74	632.32	576.81	536.20	505.50	481.72	462.93	447.86	435.63	425.60
31000	2796.18	1501.25	1072.73	860.80	735.46	653.40	596.03	554.07	522.35	497.77	478.36	462.79	450.15	439.79
32000	2886.38	1549.68	1107.34	888.56	759.18	674.48	615.26	571.95	539.20	513.83	493.79	477.71	464.67	453.97
33000	2976.58	1598.11	1141.94	916.33	782.91	695.55	634.49	589.82	556.05	529.89	509.22	492.64	479.19	468.16
34000	3066.78	1646.53	1176.55	944.10	806.63	716.63	653.71	607.69	572.90	545.94	524.65	507.57	493.71	482.35
35000	3156.98	1694.96	1211.15	971.86	830.36	737.71	672.94	625.57	589.75	562.00	540.08	522.50	508.23	496.53
36000	3247.18	1743.39	1245.75	999.63	854.08	758.78	692.17	643.44	606.60	578.06	555.51	537.43	522.75	510.72
37000	3337.38	1791.81	1280.36	1027.40	877.81	779.86	711.39	661.31	623.45	594.12	570.94	552.36	537.27	524.91
38000	3427.58	1840.24	1314.96	1055.17	901.53	800.94	730.62	679.18	640.30	610.17	586.37	567.28	551.79	539.09
39000	3517.78	1888.67	1349.57	1082.93	925.26	822.02	749.85	697.06	657.15	626.23	601.80	582.21	566.31	553.28
40000	3607.98	1937.10	1384.17	1110.70	948.98	843.09	769.07	714.93	674.00	642.29	617.23	597.14	580.83	567.47
41000	3698.18	1985.52	1418.78	1138.47	972.70	864.17	788.30	732.80	690.85	658.34	632.66	612.07	595.35	581.65
42000	3788.38	2033.95	1453.38	1166.24	996.43	885.25	807.53	750.68	707.70	674.40	648.09	627.00	609.87	595.84
43000	3878.58	2082.38	1487.98	1194.00	1020.15	906.32	826.75	768.55	724.55	690.46	663.53	641.93	624.40	610.02
44000	3968.78	2130.81	1522.59	1221.77	1043.88	927.40	845.98	786.42	741.40	706.51	678.96	656.86	638.92	624.21
45000	4058.98	2179.23	1557.19	1249.54	1067.60	948.48	865.21	804.30	758.25	722.57	694.39	671.78	653.44	638.40
46000	4149.17	2227.66	1591.80	1277.31	1091.33	969.56	884.43	822.17	775.10	738.63	709.82	686.71	667.96	652.58
47000	4239.37	2276.09	1626.40	1305.07	1115.05	990.63	903.66	840.04	791.95	754.69	725.25	701.64	682.48	666.77
48000	4329.57	2324.51	1661.00	1332.84	1138.77	1011.71	922.89	857.92	808.80	770.74	740.68	716.57	697.00	680.96
49000	4419.77	2372.94	1695.61	1360.61	1162.50	1032.79	942.11	875.79	825.65	786.80	756.11	731.50	711.52	695.14
50000	4509.97	2421.37	1730.21	1388.38	1186.22	1053.86	961.34	893.66	842.50	802.86	771.54	746.43	726.04	709.33
55000	4960.97	2663.51	1903.23	1527.21	1304.85	1159.25	1057.47	983.03	926.75	883.14	848.69	821.07	798.64	780.26
60000	5411.97	2905.64	2076.25	1666.05	1423.47	1264.64	1153.61	1072.39	1011.00	963.43	925.85	895.71	871.25	851.20
65000	5862.96	3147.78	2249.27	1804.89	1542.09	1370.02	1249.74	1161.76	1095.25	1043.71	1003.00	970.35	943.85	922.13
70000	6313.96	3389.91	2422.30	1943.72	1660.71	1475.41	1345.87	1251.13	1179.50	1124.00	1080.15	1044.99	1016.45	993.06
75000	6764.96	3632.05	2595.32	2082.56	1779.33	1580.79	1442.01	1340.49	1263.75	1204.28	1157.31	1119.64	1089.06	1063.99
80000	7215.95	3874.19	2768.34	2221.40	1897.95	1686.18	1538.14	1429.86	1348.00	1284.57	1234.46	1194.28	1161.66	1134.93
85000	7666.95	4116.32	2941.36	2360.24	2016.58	1791.57	1634.27	1519.22	1432.25	1364.85	1311.61	1268.92	1234.27	1205.86
90000	8117.95	4358.46	3114.38	2499.07	2135.20	1896.95	1730.41	1608.59	1516.50	1445.14	1388.77	1343.56	1306.87	1276.79
95000	8568.94	4600.60	3287.40	2637.91	2253.82	2002.34	1826.54	1697.95	1600.75	1525.42	1465.92	1418.20	1379.47	1347.72
100000	9019.94	4842.73	3460.42	2776.75	2372.44	2107.72	1922.67	1787.32	1685.00	1605.71	1543.07	1492.85	1452.08	1418.66

TERM / AMOUNT	15 Years	16 Years	17 Years	18 Years	19 Years	20 Years	21 Years	22 Years	23 Years	24 Years	25 Years	30 Years	35 Years	40 Years
5	.07	.07	.07	.07	.07	.07	.07	.07	.07	.07	.07	.07	.07	.07
10	.14	.14	.14	.14	.14	.14	.13	.13	.13	.13	.13	.13	.13	.13
15	.21	.21	.21	.20	.20	.20	.20	.20	.20	.20	.20	.19	.19	.19
25	.35	.35	.34	.34	.33	.33	.33	.33	.33	.32	.32	.32	.32	.32
50	.70	.69	.68	.67	.66	.66	.65	.65	.65	.64	.64	.63	.63	.63
75	1.05	1.03	1.02	1.00	.99	.99	.98	.97	.97	.96	.96	.95	.94	.94
100	1.40	1.37	1.35	1.34	1.32	1.31	1.30	1.29	1.29	1.28	1.28	1.26	1.25	1.25
200	2.79	2.74	2.70	2.67	2.64	2.62	2.60	2.58	2.57	2.56	2.55	2.51	2.50	2.49
300	4.18	4.11	4.05	4.00	3.96	3.93	3.90	3.87	3.85	3.83	3.82	3.77	3.74	3.73
400	5.57	5.48	5.40	5.34	5.28	5.24	5.20	5.16	5.13	5.11	5.09	5.02	4.99	4.98
500	6.96	6.85	6.75	6.67	6.60	6.54	6.49	6.45	6.42	6.39	6.36	6.28	6.24	6.22
600	8.35	8.21	8.10	8.00	7.92	7.85	7.79	7.74	7.70	7.66	7.63	7.53	7.48	7.46
700	9.74	9.58	9.45	9.33	9.24	9.16	9.09	9.03	8.98	8.94	8.90	8.79	8.73	8.71
800	11.13	10.95	10.80	10.67	10.56	10.47	10.39	10.32	10.26	10.22	10.17	10.04	9.98	9.95
900	12.52	12.32	12.14	12.00	11.88	11.77	11.69	11.61	11.55	11.49	11.45	11.30	11.22	11.19
1000	13.92	13.69	13.49	13.33	13.20	13.08	12.98	12.90	12.83	12.77	12.72	12.55	12.47	12.43
2000	27.83	27.37	26.98	26.66	26.39	26.16	25.96	25.79	25.65	25.53	25.43	25.09	24.94	24.86
3000	41.74	41.05	40.47	39.99	39.58	39.23	38.94	38.69	38.48	38.29	38.14	37.64	37.40	37.29
4000	55.65	54.73	53.96	53.31	52.77	52.31	51.92	51.58	51.30	51.06	50.85	50.18	49.87	49.72
5000	69.56	68.41	67.45	66.64	65.96	65.38	64.89	64.48	64.12	63.82	63.56	62.73	62.34	62.15
6000	83.47	82.09	80.94	79.97	79.15	78.46	77.87	77.37	76.95	76.58	76.27	75.27	74.80	74.58
7000	97.38	95.77	94.42	93.29	92.34	91.53	90.85	90.27	89.77	89.35	88.98	87.82	87.27	87.01
8000	111.29	109.45	107.91	106.62	105.53	104.61	103.83	103.16	102.59	102.11	101.70	100.36	99.74	99.44
9000	125.20	123.13	121.40	119.95	118.72	117.69	116.81	116.06	115.42	114.87	114.41	112.91	112.20	111.87
10000	139.11	136.81	134.89	133.28	131.91	130.76	129.78	128.95	128.24	127.64	127.12	125.45	124.67	124.30
11000	153.02	150.49	148.38	146.60	145.10	143.84	142.76	141.85	141.07	140.40	139.83	137.99	137.14	136.73
12000	166.93	164.17	161.87	159.93	158.30	156.91	155.74	154.74	153.89	153.16	152.54	150.54	149.60	149.16
13000	180.84	177.85	175.36	173.26	171.49	169.99	168.72	167.64	166.71	165.93	165.25	163.08	162.07	161.59
14000	194.75	191.53	188.84	186.58	184.68	183.06	181.69	180.53	179.54	178.69	177.96	175.63	174.53	174.02
15000	208.66	205.21	202.33	199.91	197.87	196.14	194.67	193.42	192.36	191.45	190.68	188.17	187.00	186.45
16000	222.57	218.90	215.82	213.24	211.06	209.22	207.65	206.32	205.18	204.22	203.39	200.72	199.47	198.88
17000	236.48	232.58	229.31	226.57	224.25	222.29	220.63	219.21	218.01	216.98	216.10	213.26	211.93	211.31
18000	250.39	246.26	242.80	239.89	237.44	235.37	233.61	232.11	230.83	229.74	228.81	225.81	224.40	223.73
19000	264.30	259.94	256.29	253.22	250.63	248.44	246.59	245.00	243.66	242.51	241.52	238.35	236.87	236.16
20000	278.21	273.62	269.78	266.55	263.82	261.52	259.56	257.90	256.48	255.27	254.23	250.90	249.33	248.59
21000	292.12	287.30	283.26	279.87	277.01	274.59	272.54	270.79	269.30	268.03	266.94	263.44	261.80	261.02
22000	306.03	300.98	296.75	293.20	290.20	287.67	285.52	283.69	282.13	280.79	279.66	275.98	274.27	273.45
23000	319.94	314.66	310.24	306.53	303.40	300.74	298.49	296.58	294.95	293.56	292.37	288.53	286.73	285.88
24000	333.85	328.34	323.73	319.85	316.59	313.82	311.47	309.48	307.77	306.32	305.08	301.07	299.20	298.31
25000	347.76	342.02	337.22	333.18	329.78	324.45	324.45	322.37	320.60	319.08	317.79	313.62	311.66	310.74
26000	361.67	355.70	350.71	346.51	342.97	339.97	337.43	335.27	333.42	331.85	330.50	326.16	324.13	323.17
27000	375.58	369.38	364.19	359.84	356.16	353.05	350.41	348.16	346.25	344.61	343.21	338.71	336.60	335.60
28000	389.49	383.06	377.68	373.16	369.35	366.12	363.38	361.05	359.07	357.37	355.92	351.25	349.06	348.03
29000	403.41	396.74	391.17	386.49	382.54	379.20	376.36	373.95	371.89	370.14	368.64	363.80	361.53	360.46
30000	417.32	410.42	404.66	399.82	395.73	392.27	389.34	386.84	384.72	382.90	381.35	376.34	374.00	372.89
31000	431.23	424.11	418.15	413.14	408.92	405.35	402.32	399.74	397.54	395.66	394.06	388.89	386.46	385.32
32000	445.14	437.79	431.64	426.47	422.11	418.43	415.30	412.63	410.36	408.43	406.77	401.43	398.93	397.75
33000	459.05	451.47	445.13	439.80	435.30	431.50	428.27	425.53	423.19	421.19	419.48	413.97	411.40	410.18
34000	472.96	465.15	458.61	453.13	448.50	444.58	441.25	438.42	436.01	433.95	432.19	426.52	423.86	422.61
35000	486.87	478.83	472.10	466.45	461.69	457.65	454.23	451.32	448.83	446.72	444.90	439.06	436.33	435.04
36000	500.78	492.51	485.59	479.78	474.88	470.73	467.21	464.21	461.66	459.48	457.62	451.61	448.80	447.46
37000	514.69	506.19	499.08	493.11	488.07	483.80	480.18	477.11	474.48	472.24	470.33	464.15	461.26	459.89
38000	528.60	519.87	512.57	506.43	501.26	496.88	493.16	490.00	487.31	485.01	483.04	476.70	473.73	472.32
39000	542.51	533.55	526.06	519.76	514.45	509.95	506.14	502.90	500.13	497.77	495.75	489.24	486.19	484.75
40000	556.42	547.23	539.55	533.09	527.64	523.03	519.12	515.79	512.95	510.53	508.46	501.79	498.66	497.18
41000	570.33	560.91	553.03	546.41	540.83	536.11	532.10	528.68	525.78	523.29	521.17	514.33	511.13	509.61
42000	584.24	574.59	566.52	559.74	554.02	549.18	545.07	541.58	538.60	536.06	533.88	526.88	523.59	522.04
43000	598.15	588.27	580.01	573.07	567.21	562.26	558.05	554.47	551.42	548.82	546.60	539.42	536.06	534.47
44000	612.06	601.95	593.50	586.40	580.40	575.33	571.03	567.37	564.25	561.58	559.31	551.96	548.53	546.90
45000	625.97	615.63	606.99	599.72	593.59	588.41	584.01	580.26	577.07	574.35	572.02	564.51	560.99	559.33
46000	639.88	629.31	620.48	613.05	606.79	601.48	596.98	593.16	589.90	587.11	584.73	577.05	573.46	571.76
47000	653.79	643.00	633.97	626.38	619.98	614.56	609.96	606.05	602.72	599.87	597.44	589.60	585.93	584.19
48000	667.70	656.68	647.45	639.70	633.17	627.64	622.94	618.95	615.54	612.64	610.15	602.14	598.39	596.62
49000	681.61	670.36	660.94	653.03	646.36	640.71	635.92	631.84	628.37	625.40	622.86	614.69	610.86	609.05
50000	695.52	684.04	674.43	666.36	659.55	653.79	648.90	644.74	641.19	638.16	635.57	627.23	623.32	621.48
55000	765.07	752.44	741.87	732.99	725.50	719.16	713.79	709.21	705.31	701.98	699.13	689.95	685.66	683.62
60000	834.63	820.84	809.32	799.63	791.46	784.54	778.67	773.68	769.43	765.79	762.69	752.68	747.99	745.77
65000	904.18	889.25	876.76	866.26	857.41	849.92	843.56	838.16	833.55	829.61	826.25	815.40	810.32	807.92
70000	973.73	957.65	944.20	932.90	923.37	915.30	908.45	902.63	897.66	893.43	889.80	878.12	872.65	870.07
75000	1043.28	1026.05	1011.64	999.54	989.32	980.68	973.34	967.10	961.78	957.24	953.36	940.85	934.98	932.21
80000	1112.83	1094.46	1079.09	1066.17	1055.28	1046.06	1038.23	1031.57	1025.90	1021.06	1016.92	1003.57	997.32	994.36
85000	1182.39	1162.86	1146.53	1132.81	1121.23	1111.43	1103.12	1096.05	1090.02	1084.87	1080.47	1066.29	1059.65	1056.51
90000	1251.94	1231.26	1213.97	1199.44	1187.18	1176.81	1168.01	1160.52	1154.14	1148.69	1144.03	1129.01	1121.98	1118.65
95000	1321.49	1299.67	1281.41	1266.08	1253.14	1242.19	1232.90	1224.99	1218.26	1212.51	1207.59	1191.74	1184.31	1180.80
100000	1391.04	1368.07	1348.86	1332.71	1319.09	1307.57	1297.79	1289.47	1282.38	1276.32	1271.14	1254.46	1246.64	1242.95

MONTHLY PAYMENT
REQUIRED TO AMORTIZE A LOAN

TERM AMOUNT	1 Year	2 Years	3 Years	4 Years	5 Years	6 Years	7 Years	8 Years	9 Years	10 Years	11 Years	12 Years	13 Years	14 Years
5	.46	.25	.18	.14	.12	.11	.10	.09	.09	.09	.08	.08	.08	.08
10	.91	.49	.35	.28	.24	.22	.20	.18	.17	.17	.16	.15	.15	.15
15	1.36	.73	.52	.42	.36	.32	.29	.27	.26	.25	.24	.23	.22	.22
25	2.26	1.22	.87	.70	.60	.53	.49	.45	.43	.41	.39	.38	.37	.36
50	4.52	2.43	1.74	1.39	1.19	1.06	.97	.90	.85	.81	.78	.75	.73	.72
75	6.77	3.64	2.60	2.09	1.79	1.59	1.45	1.35	1.27	1.21	1.16	1.13	1.10	1.07
100	9.03	4.85	3.47	2.78	2.38	2.11	1.93	1.79	1.69	1.61	1.55	1.50	1.46	1.43
200	18.05	9.69	6.93	5.56	4.75	4.22	3.85	3.58	3.38	3.22	3.09	2.99	2.91	2.85
300	27.07	14.54	10.39	8.34	7.13	6.33	5.78	5.37	5.06	4.83	4.64	4.49	4.37	4.27
400	36.09	19.38	13.85	11.12	9.50	8.44	7.70	7.16	6.75	6.43	6.18	5.98	5.82	5.69
500	45.11	24.22	17.31	13.90	11.87	10.55	9.63	8.95	8.44	8.04	7.73	7.48	7.27	7.11
600	54.13	29.07	20.77	16.67	14.25	12.66	11.55	10.74	10.12	9.65	9.27	8.97	8.73	8.53
700	63.15	33.91	24.24	19.45	16.62	14.77	13.47	12.53	11.81	11.26	10.82	10.47	10.18	9.95
800	72.17	38.76	27.70	22.23	18.99	16.88	15.40	14.32	13.50	12.86	12.36	11.96	11.63	11.37
900	81.20	43.60	31.16	25.01	21.37	18.99	17.32	16.10	15.18	14.47	13.91	13.46	13.09	12.79
1000	90.22	48.44	34.62	27.79	23.74	21.10	19.25	17.89	16.87	16.08	15.45	14.95	14.54	14.21
2000	180.43	96.88	69.24	55.57	47.48	42.19	38.49	35.78	33.73	32.15	30.90	29.89	29.08	28.41
3000	270.64	145.32	103.85	83.35	71.22	63.28	57.73	53.67	50.60	48.22	46.34	44.84	43.62	42.61
4000	360.85	193.76	138.47	111.13	94.95	84.37	76.97	71.56	67.46	64.29	61.79	59.78	58.15	56.82
5000	451.06	242.20	173.09	138.91	118.69	105.46	96.21	89.44	84.33	80.37	77.24	74.73	72.69	71.02
6000	541.27	290.64	207.70	166.69	142.43	126.55	115.45	107.33	101.19	96.44	92.68	89.67	87.23	85.22
7000	631.48	339.08	242.32	194.47	166.17	147.64	134.69	125.22	118.06	112.51	108.13	104.62	101.76	99.43
8000	721.69	387.52	276.94	222.25	189.90	168.73	153.93	143.11	134.92	128.58	123.58	119.56	116.30	113.63
9000	811.91	435.96	311.55	250.03	213.64	189.82	173.17	160.99	151.79	144.66	139.02	134.51	130.84	127.83
10000	902.12	484.40	346.17	277.81	237.38	210.91	192.41	178.88	168.65	160.73	154.47	149.45	145.38	142.04
11000	992.33	532.84	380.79	305.59	261.12	232.00	211.65	196.77	185.52	176.80	169.92	164.39	159.91	156.24
12000	1082.54	581.27	415.40	333.37	284.85	253.09	230.89	214.66	202.38	192.87	185.36	179.34	174.45	170.44
13000	1172.75	629.71	450.02	361.15	308.59	274.18	250.13	232.54	219.25	208.95	200.81	194.28	188.99	184.65
14000	1262.96	678.15	484.63	388.93	332.33	295.28	269.37	250.43	236.11	225.02	216.25	209.23	203.52	198.85
15000	1353.17	726.59	519.25	416.71	356.07	316.37	288.62	268.32	252.98	241.09	231.70	224.17	218.06	213.05
16000	1443.38	775.03	553.87	444.49	379.80	337.46	307.86	286.21	269.84	257.16	247.15	239.12	232.60	227.26
17000	1533.59	823.47	588.48	472.27	403.54	358.55	327.10	304.09	286.71	273.23	262.59	254.06	247.14	241.46
18000	1623.81	871.91	623.10	500.05	427.28	379.64	346.34	321.98	303.57	289.31	278.04	269.01	261.67	255.66
19000	1714.02	920.35	657.72	527.83	451.02	400.73	365.58	339.87	320.44	305.38	293.49	283.95	276.21	269.87
20000	1804.23	968.79	692.33	555.61	474.75	421.82	384.82	357.76	337.30	321.45	308.93	298.89	290.75	284.07
21000	1894.44	1017.23	726.95	583.39	498.49	442.91	404.06	375.64	354.17	337.52	324.38	313.84	305.28	298.27
22000	1984.65	1065.67	761.57	611.17	522.23	464.00	423.30	393.53	371.03	353.60	339.83	328.78	319.82	312.48
23000	2074.86	1114.11	796.18	638.95	545.97	485.09	442.54	411.42	387.90	369.67	355.27	343.73	334.36	326.68
24000	2165.07	1162.54	830.80	666.73	569.70	506.18	461.78	429.31	404.76	385.74	370.72	358.67	348.90	340.88
25000	2255.28	1210.98	865.41	694.51	593.44	527.27	481.02	447.19	421.63	401.81	386.16	373.62	363.43	355.09
26000	2345.49	1259.42	900.03	722.29	617.18	548.36	500.26	465.08	438.49	417.89	401.61	388.56	377.97	369.29
27000	2435.71	1307.86	934.65	750.07	640.92	569.46	519.50	482.97	455.35	433.96	417.06	403.51	392.51	383.49
28000	2525.92	1356.30	969.26	777.85	664.65	590.55	538.74	500.86	472.22	450.03	432.50	418.45	407.04	397.70
29000	2616.13	1404.74	1003.88	805.63	688.39	611.64	557.99	518.74	489.08	466.10	447.95	433.39	421.58	411.90
30000	2706.34	1453.18	1038.50	833.41	712.13	632.73	577.23	536.63	505.95	482.17	463.40	448.34	436.12	426.10
31000	2796.55	1501.62	1073.11	861.19	735.87	653.82	596.47	554.52	522.81	498.25	478.84	463.28	450.66	440.31
32000	2886.76	1550.06	1107.73	888.97	759.60	674.91	615.71	572.41	539.68	514.32	494.29	478.23	465.19	454.51
33000	2976.97	1598.50	1142.35	916.75	783.34	696.00	634.95	590.30	556.54	530.39	509.74	493.17	479.73	468.71
34000	3067.18	1646.94	1176.96	944.53	807.08	717.09	654.19	608.18	573.41	546.46	525.18	508.12	494.27	482.92
35000	3157.39	1695.38	1211.58	972.31	830.82	738.18	673.43	626.07	590.27	562.54	540.63	523.06	508.80	497.12
36000	3247.61	1743.81	1246.19	1000.09	854.55	759.27	692.67	643.96	607.14	578.61	556.07	538.01	523.34	511.32
37000	3337.82	1792.25	1280.81	1027.87	878.29	780.36	711.91	661.85	624.00	594.68	571.52	552.95	537.88	525.53
38000	3428.03	1840.69	1315.43	1055.65	902.03	801.45	731.15	679.73	640.87	610.75	586.97	567.89	552.42	539.73
39000	3518.24	1889.13	1350.04	1083.43	925.77	822.54	750.39	697.62	657.73	626.83	602.41	582.84	566.95	553.93
40000	3608.45	1937.57	1384.66	1111.21	949.50	843.63	769.63	715.51	674.60	642.90	617.86	597.78	581.49	568.14
41000	3698.66	1986.01	1419.28	1138.99	973.24	864.73	788.87	733.40	691.46	658.97	633.31	612.73	596.03	582.34
42000	3788.87	2034.45	1453.89	1166.77	996.98	885.82	808.11	751.28	708.33	675.04	648.75	627.67	610.56	596.54
43000	3879.08	2082.89	1488.51	1194.55	1020.72	906.91	827.35	769.17	725.19	691.11	664.20	642.62	625.10	610.75
44000	3969.29	2131.33	1523.13	1222.33	1044.45	928.00	846.60	787.06	742.06	707.19	679.65	657.56	639.64	624.95
45000	4059.51	2179.77	1557.74	1250.11	1068.19	949.09	865.84	804.95	758.92	723.26	695.09	672.51	654.18	639.15
46000	4149.72	2228.21	1592.36	1277.89	1091.93	970.18	885.08	822.83	775.79	739.33	710.54	687.45	668.71	653.36
47000	4239.93	2276.65	1626.97	1305.67	1115.67	991.27	904.32	840.72	792.65	755.40	725.98	702.40	683.25	667.56
48000	4330.14	2325.08	1661.59	1333.45	1139.40	1012.36	923.56	858.61	809.52	771.48	741.43	717.34	697.79	681.76
49000	4420.35	2373.52	1696.21	1361.23	1163.14	1033.45	942.80	876.50	826.38	787.55	756.88	732.28	712.32	695.97
50000	4510.56	2421.96	1730.82	1389.01	1186.88	1054.54	962.04	894.38	843.25	803.62	772.32	747.23	726.86	710.17
55000	4961.62	2664.16	1903.91	1527.91	1305.57	1160.00	1058.24	983.82	927.57	883.98	849.56	821.95	799.55	781.18
60000	5412.67	2906.35	2076.99	1666.81	1424.25	1265.45	1154.45	1073.26	1011.89	964.34	926.79	896.67	872.23	852.20
65000	5863.73	3148.55	2250.07	1805.71	1542.94	1370.90	1250.65	1162.70	1096.22	1044.71	1004.02	971.40	944.92	923.22
70000	6314.78	3390.75	2423.15	1944.61	1661.63	1476.36	1346.85	1252.14	1180.54	1125.07	1081.25	1046.12	1017.60	994.23
75000	6765.84	3632.94	2596.23	2083.51	1780.32	1581.81	1443.06	1341.57	1264.87	1205.43	1158.48	1120.84	1090.29	1065.25
80000	7216.90	3875.14	2769.32	2222.41	1899.00	1687.26	1539.26	1431.01	1349.19	1285.79	1235.72	1195.56	1162.98	1136.27
85000	7667.95	4117.33	2942.40	2361.31	2017.69	1792.72	1635.46	1520.45	1433.51	1366.15	1312.95	1270.29	1235.66	1207.28
90000	8119.01	4359.53	3115.48	2500.20	2136.38	1898.17	1731.67	1609.89	1517.84	1446.51	1390.18	1345.01	1308.35	1278.30
95000	8570.06	4601.72	3288.56	2639.11	2255.06	2003.63	1827.87	1699.33	1602.16	1526.87	1467.41	1419.73	1381.03	1349.32
100000	9021.12	4843.92	3461.64	2778.01	2373.75	2109.08	1924.07	1788.76	1686.49	1607.24	1544.64	1494.45	1453.72	1420.33

MONTHLY PAYMENT
REQUIRED TO AMORTIZE A LOAN

14.900%

TERM / AMOUNT	15 Years	16 Years	17 Years	18 Years	19 Years	20 Years	21 Years	22 Years	23 Years	24 Years	25 Years	30 Years	35 Years	40 Years
5	.07	.07	.07	.07	.07	.07	.07	.07	.07	.07	.07	.07	.07	.07
10	.14	.14	.14	.14	.14	.14	.13	.13	.13	.13	.13	.13	.13	.13
15	.21	.21	.21	.21	.20	.20	.20	.20	.20	.20	.20	.19	.19	.19
25	.35	.35	.34	.34	.34	.33	.33	.33	.33	.32	.32	.32	.32	.32
50	.70	.69	.68	.67	.67	.66	.65	.65	.65	.64	.64	.63	.63	.63
75	1.05	1.03	1.02	1.01	1.00	.99	.98	.97	.97	.96	.96	.95	.94	.94
100	1.40	1.37	1.36	1.34	1.33	1.31	1.30	1.30	1.29	1.28	1.28	1.26	1.25	1.25
200	2.79	2.74	2.71	2.67	2.65	2.62	2.60	2.59	2.57	2.56	2.55	2.52	2.50	2.49
300	4.18	4.11	4.06	4.01	3.97	3.93	3.90	3.88	3.86	3.84	3.82	3.77	3.75	3.74
400	5.58	5.48	5.41	5.34	5.29	5.24	5.20	5.17	5.14	5.12	5.10	5.03	5.00	4.98
500	6.97	6.85	6.76	6.68	6.61	6.55	6.50	6.46	6.43	6.40	6.37	6.29	6.25	6.23
600	8.36	8.22	8.11	8.01	7.93	7.86	7.80	7.75	7.71	7.67	7.64	7.54	7.50	7.47
700	9.75	9.59	9.46	9.35	9.25	9.17	9.10	9.04	8.99	8.95	8.92	8.80	8.75	8.72
800	11.15	10.96	10.81	10.68	10.57	10.48	10.40	10.34	10.28	10.23	10.19	10.06	9.99	9.96
900	12.54	12.33	12.16	12.02	11.89	11.79	11.70	11.63	11.56	11.51	11.46	11.31	11.24	11.21
1000	13.93	13.70	13.51	13.35	13.21	13.10	13.00	12.92	12.85	12.79	12.74	12.57	12.49	12.45
2000	27.86	27.40	27.02	26.70	26.42	26.19	26.00	25.83	25.69	25.57	25.47	25.13	24.98	24.90
3000	41.79	41.10	40.52	40.04	39.63	39.29	38.99	38.75	38.53	38.35	38.20	37.70	37.47	37.35
4000	55.71	54.80	54.03	53.39	52.84	52.38	51.99	51.66	51.38	51.13	50.93	50.26	49.95	49.80
5000	69.64	68.50	67.54	66.73	66.05	65.48	64.99	64.57	64.22	63.92	63.66	62.83	62.44	62.25
6000	83.57	82.19	81.04	80.08	79.26	78.57	77.98	77.49	77.06	76.70	76.39	75.39	74.93	74.70
7000	97.50	95.89	94.55	93.42	92.47	91.66	90.98	90.40	89.90	89.48	89.12	87.96	87.41	87.15
8000	111.42	109.59	108.05	106.77	105.68	104.76	103.98	103.31	102.75	102.26	101.85	100.52	99.90	99.60
9000	125.35	123.29	121.56	120.11	118.89	117.85	116.97	116.23	115.59	115.05	114.58	113.09	112.39	112.05
10000	139.28	136.99	135.07	133.46	132.10	130.95	129.97	129.14	128.43	127.83	127.31	125.65	124.87	124.50
11000	153.21	150.68	148.57	146.80	145.30	144.04	142.97	142.05	141.28	140.61	140.04	138.21	137.36	136.95
12000	167.13	164.38	162.08	160.15	158.51	157.13	155.96	154.97	154.12	153.39	152.77	150.78	149.85	149.40
13000	181.06	178.08	175.59	173.49	171.72	170.23	167.00	167.00	166.96	166.18	165.50	163.34	162.33	161.85
14000	194.99	191.78	189.09	186.84	184.93	183.32	181.96	180.79	179.80	178.96	178.24	175.91	174.82	174.30
15000	208.92	205.48	202.60	200.18	198.14	196.42	194.95	193.71	192.65	191.74	190.97	188.47	187.31	186.75
16000	222.84	219.17	216.10	213.53	211.35	209.51	207.95	206.62	205.49	204.52	203.70	201.04	199.79	199.20
17000	236.77	232.87	229.61	226.87	224.56	222.60	220.95	219.53	218.33	217.31	216.43	213.60	212.28	211.65
18000	250.70	246.57	243.12	240.22	237.77	235.70	233.94	232.45	231.17	230.09	229.16	226.17	224.77	224.10
19000	264.63	260.27	256.62	253.56	248.79	248.79	246.94	245.36	244.02	242.87	241.89	238.73	237.25	236.55
20000	278.55	273.97	270.13	266.91	264.19	261.89	259.93	258.27	256.86	255.65	254.62	251.30	249.74	249.00
21000	292.48	287.66	283.64	280.25	277.40	274.98	272.93	271.19	269.70	268.43	267.35	263.86	262.23	261.45
22000	306.41	301.36	297.14	293.60	290.60	288.07	285.93	284.10	282.55	281.22	280.08	276.42	274.71	273.90
23000	320.34	315.06	310.65	306.94	303.81	301.17	298.92	297.02	295.39	294.00	292.81	288.99	287.20	286.35
24000	334.26	328.76	324.15	320.29	317.02	314.26	311.92	309.93	308.23	306.78	305.54	301.55	299.69	298.80
25000	348.19	342.46	337.66	333.63	330.23	327.36	324.92	322.84	321.07	319.56	318.27	314.12	312.17	311.25
26000	362.12	356.15	351.17	346.98	343.44	340.45	337.91	335.76	333.92	332.35	331.00	326.68	324.66	323.70
27000	376.05	369.85	364.67	360.32	356.65	353.54	350.91	348.67	346.76	345.13	343.74	339.25	337.15	336.15
28000	389.97	383.55	378.18	373.67	369.86	366.64	363.91	361.58	359.60	357.91	356.47	351.81	349.63	348.60
29000	403.90	397.25	391.68	387.01	383.07	379.73	376.90	374.50	372.44	370.69	369.20	364.38	362.12	361.05
30000	417.83	410.95	405.19	400.36	396.28	392.83	389.90	387.41	385.29	383.48	381.93	376.94	374.61	373.50
31000	431.76	424.64	418.70	413.70	409.49	405.92	400.32	400.32	398.13	396.26	394.66	389.50	387.09	385.95
32000	445.68	438.34	432.20	427.05	422.70	419.02	415.89	413.24	410.97	409.04	407.39	402.07	399.58	398.40
33000	459.61	452.04	445.71	440.39	435.90	432.11	428.89	426.15	423.82	421.82	420.12	414.63	412.07	410.85
34000	473.54	465.74	459.22	453.74	449.11	445.20	441.89	439.06	436.66	434.61	432.85	427.20	424.55	423.30
35000	487.47	479.44	472.72	467.08	462.32	458.30	454.88	451.98	449.50	447.39	445.58	439.76	437.04	435.75
36000	501.39	493.13	486.23	480.43	475.53	471.39	467.88	464.89	462.34	460.17	458.31	452.33	449.53	448.20
37000	515.32	506.83	499.73	493.77	488.74	484.49	480.87	477.80	475.19	472.95	471.04	464.89	462.01	460.65
38000	529.25	520.53	513.24	507.12	501.95	497.58	493.87	490.72	488.03	485.74	483.77	477.46	474.50	473.10
39000	543.18	534.23	526.75	520.46	515.16	510.67	506.87	503.63	500.87	498.52	496.50	490.02	486.99	485.55
40000	557.10	547.93	540.25	533.81	528.37	523.77	519.86	516.54	513.72	511.30	509.24	502.59	499.47	498.00
41000	571.03	561.62	553.76	547.15	541.58	536.86	532.86	529.46	526.56	524.08	521.97	515.15	511.96	510.45
42000	584.96	575.32	567.27	560.50	554.79	549.96	545.86	542.37	539.40	536.86	534.70	527.71	524.45	522.90
43000	598.89	589.02	580.77	573.84	568.00	563.05	558.85	555.28	552.24	549.65	547.43	540.28	536.93	535.35
44000	612.81	602.72	594.28	587.19	581.20	576.14	571.85	568.20	565.09	562.43	560.16	552.84	549.42	547.80
45000	626.74	616.42	607.78	600.53	594.41	589.24	584.85	581.11	577.93	575.21	572.89	565.41	561.91	560.25
46000	640.67	630.11	621.29	613.88	607.62	602.33	597.84	594.02	590.77	587.99	585.62	577.97	574.40	572.70
47000	654.59	643.81	634.80	627.22	620.83	615.43	610.84	606.94	603.61	600.78	598.35	590.54	586.88	585.15
48000	668.52	657.51	648.30	640.57	634.04	628.52	623.84	619.85	616.46	613.56	611.08	603.10	599.37	597.60
49000	682.45	671.21	661.81	653.91	647.25	641.61	636.83	632.77	629.30	626.34	623.81	615.67	611.86	610.05
50000	696.38	684.91	675.31	667.26	660.46	654.71	649.83	645.68	642.14	639.12	636.54	628.23	624.34	622.50
55000	766.01	753.40	742.85	733.98	726.50	720.18	714.81	710.25	706.36	703.04	700.20	691.05	686.78	684.75
60000	835.65	821.89	810.38	800.71	792.55	785.65	779.79	774.81	770.57	766.95	763.85	753.88	749.21	747.00
65000	905.29	890.38	877.91	867.43	858.60	851.12	844.78	839.38	834.78	830.86	827.50	816.70	811.64	809.25
70000	974.93	958.87	945.44	934.16	924.64	916.59	909.76	903.95	899.00	894.77	891.16	879.52	874.08	871.50
75000	1044.56	1027.36	1012.97	1000.88	990.69	982.06	974.74	968.52	963.21	958.68	954.81	942.34	936.51	933.75
80000	1114.20	1095.85	1080.50	1067.61	1056.73	1047.53	1039.72	1033.08	1027.43	1022.60	1018.47	1005.17	998.94	996.00
85000	1183.84	1164.34	1148.03	1133.34	1122.78	1113.00	1104.71	1097.65	1091.64	1086.51	1082.12	1067.99	1061.38	1058.25
90000	1253.47	1232.83	1215.56	1201.06	1188.82	1178.47	1169.69	1162.22	1155.85	1150.42	1145.77	1130.81	1123.81	1120.50
95000	1323.11	1301.32	1283.09	1267.78	1254.87	1243.94	1234.67	1226.79	1220.07	1214.33	1209.43	1193.63	1186.25	1182.75
100000	1392.75	1369.81	1350.62	1334.51	1320.91	1309.41	1299.65	1291.35	1284.28	1278.24	1273.08	1256.46	1248.68	1245.00

15.000%

MONTHLY PAYMENT
REQUIRED TO AMORTIZE A LOAN

TERM / AMOUNT	1 Year	2 Years	3 Years	4 Years	5 Years	6 Years	7 Years	8 Years	9 Years	10 Years	11 Years	12 Years	13 Years	14 Years
5	.46	.25	.18	.14	.12	.11	.10	.09	.09	.09	.08	.08	.08	.08
10	.91	.49	.35	.28	.24	.22	.20	.18	.17	.17	.16	.16	.15	.15
15	1.36	.73	.52	.42	.36	.32	.29	.27	.26	.25	.24	.23	.22	.22
25	2.26	1.22	.87	.70	.60	.53	.49	.45	.43	.41	.39	.38	.37	.36
50	4.52	2.43	1.74	1.40	1.19	1.06	.97	.90	.85	.81	.78	.76	.74	.72
75	6.77	3.64	2.60	2.09	1.79	1.59	1.45	1.35	1.27	1.22	1.17	1.13	1.10	1.08
100	9.03	4.85	3.47	2.79	2.38	2.12	1.93	1.80	1.70	1.62	1.56	1.51	1.47	1.43
200	18.06	9.70	6.94	5.57	4.76	4.23	3.86	3.59	3.39	3.23	3.11	3.01	2.93	2.86
300	27.08	14.55	10.40	8.35	7.14	6.35	5.79	5.39	5.08	4.85	4.66	4.51	4.39	4.29
400	36.11	19.40	13.87	11.14	9.52	8.46	7.72	7.18	6.77	6.46	6.21	6.01	5.85	5.71
500	45.13	24.25	17.34	13.92	11.90	10.58	9.65	8.98	8.47	8.07	7.76	7.51	7.31	7.14
600	54.16	29.10	20.80	16.70	14.28	12.69	11.58	10.77	10.16	9.69	9.31	9.01	8.77	8.57
700	63.19	33.95	24.27	19.49	16.66	14.81	13.51	12.57	11.85	11.30	10.86	10.51	10.23	9.99
800	72.21	38.79	27.74	22.27	19.04	16.92	15.44	14.36	13.54	12.91	12.41	12.01	11.69	11.42
900	81.24	43.64	31.20	25.05	21.42	19.04	17.37	16.16	15.24	14.53	13.96	13.51	13.15	12.85
1000	90.26	48.49	34.67	27.84	23.79	21.15	19.30	17.95	16.93	16.14	15.51	15.01	14.61	14.28
2000	180.52	96.98	69.34	55.67	47.58	42.30	38.60	35.90	33.85	32.27	31.02	30.02	29.21	28.55
3000	270.78	145.46	104.00	83.50	71.37	63.44	57.90	53.84	50.78	48.41	46.53	45.03	43.81	42.82
4000	361.04	193.95	138.67	111.33	95.16	84.59	71.79	71.79	67.70	64.54	62.04	60.04	58.42	57.09
5000	451.30	242.44	173.33	139.16	118.95	105.73	96.49	89.73	84.63	80.67	77.55	75.05	73.02	71.36
6000	541.55	290.92	208.00	166.99	142.74	126.88	115.79	107.68	101.55	96.81	93.06	90.06	87.62	85.63
7000	631.81	339.41	242.66	194.82	166.53	148.02	135.08	125.62	118.48	112.94	108.57	105.07	102.23	99.90
8000	722.07	387.90	277.33	222.65	190.32	169.17	154.38	143.57	135.40	129.07	124.08	120.08	116.83	114.17
9000	812.33	436.38	311.99	250.48	214.11	190.31	173.68	161.51	152.32	145.21	139.59	135.08	131.43	128.44
10000	902.59	484.87	346.66	278.31	237.90	211.46	192.97	179.46	169.25	161.34	155.10	150.09	146.03	142.71
11000	992.85	533.36	381.32	306.14	261.69	232.60	212.27	197.40	186.17	177.47	170.61	165.10	160.64	156.98
12000	1083.10	581.84	415.99	333.97	285.48	253.75	231.57	215.35	203.10	193.61	186.11	180.11	175.24	171.25
13000	1173.36	630.33	450.65	361.80	309.27	274.89	250.86	233.30	220.02	209.74	201.62	195.12	189.84	185.52
14000	1263.62	678.82	485.32	389.64	333.06	296.04	270.16	251.24	236.95	225.87	217.13	210.13	204.45	199.79
15000	1353.88	727.30	519.98	417.47	356.85	317.18	289.46	269.19	253.87	242.01	232.64	225.14	219.05	214.06
16000	1444.14	775.79	554.65	445.30	380.64	338.33	308.75	287.13	270.79	258.14	248.15	240.15	233.65	228.33
17000	1534.40	824.28	589.32	473.13	404.43	359.47	328.05	305.08	287.72	274.27	263.66	255.15	248.25	242.60
18000	1624.65	872.76	623.98	500.96	428.22	380.62	347.35	323.02	304.64	290.41	279.17	270.16	262.86	256.87
19000	1714.91	921.25	658.65	528.79	452.01	401.76	366.64	340.97	321.57	306.54	294.68	285.17	277.46	271.14
20000	1805.17	969.74	693.31	556.62	475.80	422.91	385.94	358.91	338.49	322.67	310.19	300.18	292.06	285.41
21000	1895.43	1018.22	727.98	584.45	499.59	444.05	405.24	376.86	355.42	338.81	325.70	315.19	306.67	299.68
22000	1985.69	1066.71	762.64	612.28	523.38	465.20	424.53	394.80	372.34	354.94	341.21	330.20	321.27	313.95
23000	2075.95	1115.20	797.31	640.11	547.17	486.34	443.83	412.75	389.26	371.08	356.72	345.21	335.87	328.22
24000	2166.20	1163.68	831.97	667.94	570.96	507.49	463.13	430.69	406.19	387.21	372.22	360.22	350.47	342.49
25000	2256.46	1212.17	866.64	695.77	594.75	528.63	482.42	448.64	423.11	403.34	387.73	375.22	365.08	356.76
26000	2346.72	1260.66	901.30	723.60	618.54	549.78	501.72	466.59	440.04	419.48	403.24	390.23	379.68	371.04
27000	2436.98	1309.14	935.97	751.44	642.33	570.92	521.02	484.53	456.96	435.61	418.75	405.24	394.28	385.31
28000	2527.24	1357.63	970.63	779.27	666.12	592.07	540.31	502.48	473.89	451.74	434.26	420.25	408.89	399.58
29000	2617.50	1406.12	1005.30	807.10	689.91	613.21	559.61	520.42	490.81	467.88	449.77	435.26	423.49	413.85
30000	2707.75	1454.60	1039.96	834.93	713.70	634.36	578.91	538.37	507.74	484.01	465.28	450.27	438.09	428.12
31000	2798.01	1503.09	1074.63	862.76	737.49	655.50	598.20	556.31	524.66	500.14	480.79	465.28	452.69	442.39
32000	2888.27	1551.58	1109.30	890.59	761.28	676.65	617.50	574.26	541.58	516.28	496.30	480.29	467.30	456.66
33000	2978.53	1600.06	1143.96	918.42	785.07	697.79	636.80	592.20	558.51	532.41	511.81	495.29	481.90	470.93
34000	3068.79	1648.55	1178.63	946.25	808.86	718.94	656.09	610.15	575.43	548.54	527.32	510.30	496.50	485.20
35000	3159.05	1697.04	1213.29	974.08	832.65	740.08	675.39	628.09	592.36	564.68	542.83	525.31	511.11	499.47
36000	3249.30	1745.52	1247.96	1001.91	856.44	761.23	694.69	646.04	609.28	580.81	558.33	540.32	525.71	513.74
37000	3339.56	1794.01	1282.62	1029.74	880.23	782.37	713.98	663.98	626.21	596.94	573.84	555.33	540.31	528.01
38000	3429.82	1842.50	1317.29	1057.57	904.02	803.52	733.28	681.93	643.13	613.08	589.35	570.34	554.91	542.28
39000	3520.08	1890.98	1351.95	1085.40	927.81	824.66	752.58	699.88	660.05	629.21	604.86	585.35	569.52	556.55
40000	3610.34	1939.47	1386.62	1113.23	951.60	845.81	771.88	717.82	676.98	645.34	620.37	600.36	584.12	570.82
41000	3700.60	1987.96	1421.28	1141.07	975.39	866.95	791.17	735.77	693.90	661.48	635.88	615.36	598.72	585.09
42000	3790.85	2036.44	1455.95	1168.90	999.18	888.10	810.47	753.71	710.83	677.61	651.39	630.37	613.33	599.36
43000	3881.11	2084.93	1490.61	1196.73	1022.97	909.24	829.77	771.66	727.75	693.75	666.90	645.38	627.93	613.63
44000	3971.37	2133.42	1525.28	1224.56	1046.76	930.39	849.06	789.60	744.68	709.88	682.41	660.39	642.53	627.90
45000	4061.63	2181.90	1559.94	1252.39	1070.55	951.53	868.36	807.55	761.60	726.01	697.92	675.40	657.13	642.17
46000	4151.89	2230.39	1594.61	1280.22	1094.34	972.68	887.66	825.49	778.52	742.15	713.43	690.41	671.74	656.44
47000	4242.15	2278.88	1629.28	1308.05	1118.13	993.82	906.95	843.44	795.45	758.28	728.94	705.42	686.34	670.71
48000	4332.40	2327.36	1663.94	1335.88	1141.92	1014.97	926.25	861.38	812.37	774.41	744.44	720.43	700.94	684.98
49000	4422.66	2375.85	1698.61	1363.71	1165.71	1036.11	945.55	879.33	829.30	790.55	759.95	735.43	715.55	699.25
50000	4512.92	2424.34	1733.27	1391.54	1189.50	1057.26	964.84	897.28	846.22	806.68	775.46	750.44	730.15	713.52
55000	4964.21	2666.77	1906.60	1530.70	1308.45	1162.98	1061.33	987.00	930.84	887.35	853.01	825.49	803.16	784.88
60000	5415.50	2909.20	2079.92	1669.85	1427.40	1268.71	1157.81	1076.73	1015.47	968.01	930.55	900.53	876.18	856.23
65000	5866.80	3151.64	2253.25	1809.00	1546.35	1374.43	1254.29	1166.46	1100.09	1048.68	1008.10	975.57	949.19	927.58
70000	6318.09	3394.07	2426.58	1948.16	1665.30	1480.16	1350.78	1256.18	1184.71	1129.35	1085.65	1050.62	1022.21	998.93
75000	6769.38	3636.50	2599.90	2087.31	1784.25	1585.88	1447.26	1345.91	1269.33	1210.02	1163.19	1125.66	1095.22	1070.28
80000	7220.67	3878.94	2773.23	2226.46	1903.20	1691.61	1543.75	1435.64	1353.95	1290.68	1240.74	1200.71	1168.24	1141.64
85000	7671.96	4121.37	2946.56	2365.62	2022.15	1797.33	1640.23	1525.36	1438.57	1371.35	1318.28	1275.75	1241.25	1212.99
90000	8123.25	4363.80	3119.88	2504.77	2141.10	1903.06	1736.71	1615.09	1523.20	1452.02	1395.83	1350.79	1314.26	1284.34
95000	8574.55	4606.24	3293.21	2643.93	2260.05	2008.78	1833.20	1704.82	1607.82	1532.69	1473.37	1425.84	1387.28	1355.69
100000	9025.84	4848.67	3466.54	2783.08	2379.00	2114.51	1929.68	1794.55	1692.44	1613.35	1550.92	1500.88	1460.29	1427.04

15.000%

TERM AMOUNT	15 Years	16 Years	17 Years	18 Years	19 Years	20 Years	21 Years	22 Years	23 Years	24 Years	25 Years	30 Years	35 Years	40 Years
5	.07	.07	.07	.07	.07	.07	.07	.07	.07	.07	.07	.07	.07	.07
10	.14	.14	.14	.14	.14	.14	.14	.13	.13	.13	.13	.13	.13	.13
15	.21	.21	.21	.21	.20	.20	.20	.20	.20	.20	.20	.19	.19	.19
25	.35	.35	.34	.34	.34	.33	.33	.33	.33	.33	.33	.32	.32	.32
50	.70	.69	.68	.68	.67	.66	.66	.65	.65	.65	.65	.64	.63	.63
75	1.05	1.04	1.02	1.01	1.00	.99	.99	.98	.97	.97	.97	.95	.95	.94
100	1.40	1.38	1.36	1.35	1.33	1.32	1.31	1.30	1.30	1.29	1.29	1.27	1.26	1.26
200	2.80	2.76	2.72	2.69	2.66	2.64	2.62	2.60	2.59	2.58	2.57	2.53	2.52	2.51
300	4.20	4.14	4.08	4.03	3.99	3.96	3.93	3.90	3.88	3.86	3.85	3.80	3.78	3.76
400	5.60	5.51	5.44	5.37	5.32	5.27	5.23	5.20	5.17	5.15	5.13	5.06	5.03	5.02
500	7.00	6.89	6.79	6.71	6.65	6.59	6.54	6.50	6.46	6.43	6.41	6.33	6.29	6.27
600	8.40	8.27	8.15	8.06	7.97	7.91	7.85	7.80	7.76	7.72	7.69	7.59	7.55	7.52
700	9.80	9.64	9.51	9.40	9.30	9.22	9.15	9.10	9.05	9.01	8.97	8.86	8.80	8.78
800	11.20	11.02	10.87	10.74	10.63	10.54	10.46	10.40	10.34	10.29	10.25	10.12	10.06	10.03
900	12.60	12.40	12.22	12.08	11.96	11.86	11.77	11.70	11.63	11.58	11.53	11.38	11.32	11.28
1000	14.00	13.77	13.58	13.42	13.29	13.17	13.08	12.99	12.92	12.86	12.81	12.65	12.57	12.54
2000	28.00	27.54	27.16	26.84	26.57	26.34	26.15	25.98	25.84	25.72	25.62	25.29	25.14	25.07
3000	41.99	41.31	40.74	40.26	39.85	39.51	39.22	38.97	38.76	38.58	38.43	37.94	37.71	37.60
4000	55.99	55.08	54.31	53.67	53.13	52.68	52.29	51.96	51.68	51.44	51.24	50.58	50.28	50.13
5000	69.98	68.84	67.89	67.09	66.41	65.84	65.36	64.95	64.60	64.30	64.05	63.23	62.85	62.67
6000	83.98	82.61	81.47	80.51	79.70	79.01	78.43	77.94	77.52	77.16	76.85	75.87	75.41	75.20
7000	97.98	96.38	95.04	93.92	92.98	92.18	91.50	90.93	90.44	90.02	89.66	88.52	87.98	87.73
8000	111.97	110.15	108.62	107.34	106.26	105.35	104.57	103.92	103.36	102.88	102.47	101.16	100.55	100.26
9000	125.97	123.91	122.20	120.76	119.54	118.52	117.65	116.91	116.28	115.74	115.28	113.80	113.12	112.80
10000	139.96	137.68	135.78	134.17	132.82	131.68	130.72	129.89	129.19	128.60	128.09	126.45	125.69	125.33
11000	153.96	151.45	149.35	147.59	146.11	144.85	143.79	142.88	142.11	141.46	140.90	139.09	138.25	137.86
12000	167.96	165.22	162.93	161.01	159.39	158.02	156.86	155.87	155.03	154.32	153.70	151.74	150.82	150.39
13000	181.95	178.99	176.51	174.42	172.67	171.19	169.93	168.86	167.95	167.18	166.51	164.38	163.39	162.92
14000	195.95	192.75	190.08	187.84	185.95	184.36	183.00	181.85	180.87	180.04	179.32	177.03	175.96	175.46
15000	209.94	206.52	203.66	201.26	199.23	197.52	196.07	194.84	193.79	192.89	192.13	189.67	188.53	187.99
16000	223.94	220.29	217.24	214.68	212.52	210.69	209.14	207.83	206.71	205.75	204.94	202.32	201.10	200.52
17000	237.93	234.06	230.81	228.09	225.80	223.86	222.21	220.82	219.63	218.61	217.75	214.96	213.66	213.05
18000	251.93	247.82	244.39	241.51	239.08	237.03	235.29	233.81	232.55	231.47	230.55	227.60	226.23	225.59
19000	265.93	261.59	257.97	254.93	252.36	250.20	248.36	246.80	245.47	244.33	243.36	240.25	238.80	238.12
20000	279.92	275.36	271.55	268.34	265.64	263.36	261.43	259.78	258.30	257.19	256.17	252.89	251.37	250.65
21000	293.92	289.13	285.12	281.76	278.93	276.53	274.50	272.77	271.30	270.05	268.98	265.54	263.94	263.18
22000	307.91	302.89	298.70	295.18	292.21	289.70	287.57	285.76	284.22	282.91	281.79	278.18	276.50	275.71
23000	321.91	316.66	312.28	308.59	305.49	302.87	300.64	298.75	297.14	295.77	294.60	290.83	289.07	288.25
24000	335.91	330.43	325.85	322.01	318.77	316.03	313.71	311.74	310.06	308.63	307.40	303.47	301.64	300.78
25000	349.90	344.20	339.43	335.43	332.05	329.20	326.78	324.73	322.98	321.49	320.21	316.12	314.21	313.31
26000	363.90	357.97	353.01	348.84	345.34	342.37	339.86	337.72	335.90	334.35	333.02	328.76	326.78	325.84
27000	377.89	371.73	366.58	362.26	358.62	355.54	352.93	350.71	348.82	347.21	345.83	341.40	339.34	338.38
28000	391.89	385.50	380.16	375.68	371.90	368.71	366.00	363.70	361.74	360.07	358.64	354.05	351.91	350.91
29000	405.89	399.27	393.74	389.10	385.18	381.87	379.07	376.69	374.66	372.92	371.45	366.69	364.48	363.44
30000	419.88	413.04	407.32	402.51	398.46	395.04	392.14	389.67	387.57	385.78	384.25	379.34	377.05	375.97
31000	433.88	426.80	420.89	415.93	411.75	408.21	405.21	402.66	400.49	398.64	397.06	391.98	389.62	388.50
32000	447.87	440.57	434.47	429.35	425.03	421.38	418.28	415.65	413.41	411.50	409.87	404.63	402.19	401.04
33000	461.87	454.34	448.05	442.76	438.31	434.55	431.35	428.64	426.33	424.36	422.68	417.27	414.75	413.57
34000	475.86	468.11	461.62	456.18	451.59	447.71	444.42	441.63	439.25	437.22	435.49	429.92	427.32	426.10
35000	489.86	481.87	475.20	469.60	464.87	460.88	457.50	454.62	452.17	450.08	448.30	442.56	439.89	438.63
36000	503.86	495.64	488.78	483.01	478.16	474.05	470.57	467.61	465.09	462.94	461.10	455.20	452.46	451.17
37000	517.85	509.41	502.35	496.43	491.44	487.22	483.64	480.60	478.01	475.80	473.91	467.85	465.03	463.70
38000	531.85	523.18	515.93	509.85	504.72	500.39	496.71	493.59	490.93	488.66	486.72	480.49	477.59	476.23
39000	545.84	536.95	529.51	523.26	518.00	513.55	509.78	506.58	503.85	501.52	499.53	493.14	490.16	488.76
40000	559.84	550.71	543.09	536.68	531.28	526.72	522.85	519.56	516.76	514.38	512.34	505.78	502.73	501.29
41000	573.84	564.48	556.66	550.10	544.57	539.89	535.92	532.55	529.68	527.24	525.15	518.43	515.30	513.83
42000	587.83	578.25	570.24	563.52	557.85	553.06	548.99	545.54	542.60	540.10	537.95	531.07	527.87	526.36
43000	601.83	592.02	583.82	576.93	571.13	566.22	562.07	558.53	555.52	552.95	550.76	543.72	540.43	538.89
44000	615.82	605.78	597.39	590.35	584.41	579.39	575.14	571.52	568.44	565.81	563.57	556.36	553.00	551.42
45000	629.82	619.55	610.97	603.77	597.69	592.56	588.21	584.51	581.36	578.67	576.38	569.00	565.57	563.96
46000	643.82	633.32	624.55	617.18	610.98	605.73	601.28	597.50	594.28	591.53	589.19	581.65	578.14	576.49
47000	657.81	647.09	638.12	630.60	624.26	618.90	614.35	610.49	607.20	604.39	602.00	594.29	590.71	589.02
48000	671.81	660.85	651.70	644.02	637.54	632.06	627.42	623.48	620.12	617.25	614.80	606.94	603.28	601.55
49000	685.80	674.62	665.28	657.43	650.82	645.23	640.49	636.46	633.04	630.11	627.61	619.58	615.84	614.08
50000	699.80	688.39	678.86	670.85	664.10	658.40	653.56	649.45	645.95	642.97	640.42	632.23	628.41	626.62
55000	769.78	757.23	746.74	737.93	730.51	724.24	718.92	714.40	710.55	707.27	704.46	695.45	691.25	689.28
60000	839.76	826.07	814.63	805.02	796.92	790.08	784.28	779.34	775.14	771.56	768.50	758.67	754.09	751.94
65000	909.74	894.91	882.51	872.10	863.33	855.92	849.63	844.29	839.74	835.86	832.54	821.89	816.93	814.60
70000	979.72	963.74	950.40	939.19	929.74	921.76	914.99	909.23	904.33	900.16	896.59	885.12	879.77	877.26
75000	1049.70	1032.58	1018.28	1006.27	996.15	987.60	980.34	974.18	968.93	964.45	960.63	948.34	942.61	939.92
80000	1119.67	1101.42	1086.17	1073.36	1062.56	1053.44	1045.70	1039.12	1033.52	1028.75	1024.67	1011.56	1005.46	1002.58
85000	1189.65	1170.26	1154.05	1140.44	1128.97	1119.28	1111.05	1104.07	1098.12	1093.04	1088.71	1074.78	1068.30	1065.25
90000	1259.63	1239.10	1221.94	1207.53	1195.38	1185.12	1176.41	1169.01	1162.71	1157.34	1152.75	1138.00	1131.14	1127.91
95000	1329.61	1307.94	1289.82	1274.61	1261.79	1250.96	1241.77	1233.96	1227.31	1221.64	1216.79	1201.23	1193.98	1190.57
100000	1399.59	1376.77	1357.71	1341.70	1328.20	1316.79	1307.12	1298.90	1291.90	1285.93	1280.84	1264.45	1256.82	1253.23

15%

MONTHLY PAYMENT
REQUIRED TO AMORTIZE A LOAN

TERM	1 Year	2 Years	3 Years	4 Years	5 Years	6 Years	7 Years	8 Years	9 Years	10 Years	11 Years	12 Years	13 Years	14 Years
AMOUNT														
5	.46	.25	.18	.14	.12	.11	.10	.10	.09	.09	.08	.08	.08	.08
10	.91	.49	.35	.28	.24	.22	.20	.19	.17	.17	.16	.16	.15	.15
15	1.36	.73	.53	.42	.36	.32	.30	.28	.26	.25	.24	.23	.23	.22
25	2.26	1.22	.87	.70	.60	.53	.49	.46	.43	.41	.39	.38	.37	.36
50	4.52	2.43	1.74	1.40	1.20	1.06	.97	.91	.85	.81	.78	.76	.74	.72
75	6.78	3.65	2.61	2.10	1.79	1.59	1.46	1.36	1.28	1.22	1.17	1.14	1.11	1.08
100	9.04	4.86	3.48	2.79	2.39	2.12	1.94	1.81	1.70	1.62	1.56	1.51	1.47	1.44
200	18.07	9.71	6.95	5.58	4.77	4.24	3.88	3.61	3.40	3.24	3.12	3.02	2.94	2.87
300	27.10	14.57	10.42	8.37	7.16	6.36	5.81	5.41	5.10	4.86	4.68	4.53	4.41	4.31
400	36.13	19.42	13.89	11.16	9.54	8.48	7.75	7.21	6.80	6.48	6.23	6.03	5.87	5.74
500	45.16	24.27	17.36	13.95	11.93	10.60	9.68	9.01	8.50	8.10	7.79	7.54	7.34	7.17
600	54.19	29.13	20.83	16.73	14.31	12.72	11.62	10.81	10.20	9.72	9.35	9.05	8.81	8.61
700	63.22	33.98	24.31	19.52	16.69	14.84	13.55	12.61	11.89	11.34	10.91	10.56	10.27	10.04
800	72.25	38.83	27.78	22.31	19.08	16.96	15.49	14.41	13.59	12.96	12.46	12.06	11.74	11.48
900	81.28	43.69	31.25	25.10	21.46	19.08	17.42	16.21	15.29	14.58	14.02	13.57	13.21	12.91
1000	90.31	48.54	34.72	27.89	23.85	21.20	19.36	18.01	16.99	16.20	15.58	15.08	14.67	14.34
2000	180.62	97.07	69.43	55.77	47.69	42.40	38.71	36.01	33.97	32.39	31.15	30.15	29.34	28.68
3000	270.92	145.61	104.15	83.65	71.53	63.60	58.06	54.01	50.96	48.59	46.72	45.22	44.01	43.02
4000	361.23	194.14	138.86	111.53	95.37	84.80	77.42	72.02	67.94	64.78	62.29	60.30	58.68	57.36
5000	451.53	242.68	173.58	139.41	119.22	106.00	96.77	90.02	84.92	80.98	77.87	75.37	73.35	71.69
6000	541.84	291.21	208.29	167.29	143.06	127.20	116.12	108.02	101.91	97.17	93.44	90.44	88.02	86.03
7000	632.14	339.74	243.01	195.18	166.90	148.40	135.48	126.03	118.89	113.37	109.01	105.52	102.69	100.37
8000	722.45	388.28	277.72	223.06	190.74	169.60	154.83	144.03	135.88	129.56	124.58	120.59	117.35	114.71
9000	812.75	436.81	312.43	250.94	214.59	190.80	174.18	162.03	152.86	145.76	140.15	135.66	132.02	129.04
10000	903.06	485.35	347.15	278.82	238.43	212.00	193.53	180.04	169.84	161.95	155.73	150.74	146.69	143.38
11000	993.37	533.88	381.86	306.70	262.27	233.20	212.89	198.04	186.83	178.15	171.30	165.81	161.36	157.72
12000	1083.67	582.42	416.58	334.58	286.11	254.40	232.24	216.04	203.81	194.34	186.87	180.88	176.03	172.06
13000	1173.98	630.95	451.29	362.46	309.96	275.60	251.59	234.05	220.80	210.54	202.44	195.96	190.70	186.39
14000	1264.28	679.48	486.01	390.35	333.80	296.80	270.95	252.05	237.78	226.73	218.01	211.03	205.37	200.73
15000	1354.59	728.02	520.72	418.23	357.64	318.00	290.30	270.05	254.76	242.93	233.59	226.10	220.04	215.07
16000	1444.89	776.55	555.43	446.11	381.48	339.19	309.65	288.06	271.75	259.12	249.16	241.18	234.70	229.41
17000	1535.20	825.09	590.15	473.99	405.33	360.39	329.00	306.06	288.73	275.32	264.73	256.25	249.37	243.75
18000	1625.50	873.62	624.86	501.87	429.17	381.59	348.36	324.06	305.72	291.51	280.30	271.32	264.04	258.08
19000	1715.81	922.15	659.58	529.75	453.01	402.79	367.71	342.07	322.70	307.71	295.87	286.40	278.71	272.42
20000	1806.12	970.69	694.29	557.63	476.85	423.99	387.06	360.07	339.68	323.90	311.45	301.47	293.38	286.76
21000	1896.42	1019.22	729.01	585.52	500.70	445.19	406.42	378.07	356.67	340.10	327.02	316.54	308.05	301.10
22000	1986.73	1067.76	763.72	613.40	524.54	466.39	425.77	396.08	373.65	356.29	342.59	331.62	322.72	315.43
23000	2077.03	1116.29	798.43	641.28	548.38	487.59	445.12	414.08	390.64	372.49	358.16	346.69	337.39	329.77
24000	2167.34	1164.83	833.15	669.16	572.22	508.79	464.47	432.08	407.62	388.68	373.73	361.76	352.05	344.11
25000	2257.64	1213.36	867.86	697.04	596.07	529.99	483.83	450.09	424.60	404.87	389.31	376.83	366.72	358.45
26000	2347.95	1261.89	902.58	724.92	619.91	551.19	503.18	468.09	441.59	421.07	404.88	391.91	381.39	372.78
27000	2438.25	1310.43	937.29	752.80	643.75	572.39	522.53	486.09	458.57	437.26	420.45	406.98	396.06	387.12
28000	2528.56	1358.96	972.01	780.69	667.59	593.59	541.89	504.10	475.56	453.46	436.02	422.05	410.73	401.46
29000	2618.86	1407.50	1006.72	808.57	691.44	614.79	561.24	522.10	492.54	469.65	451.59	437.13	425.40	415.80
30000	2709.17	1456.03	1041.43	836.45	715.28	635.99	580.59	540.10	509.52	485.85	467.17	452.20	440.07	430.13
31000	2799.48	1504.56	1076.15	864.33	739.12	657.19	599.94	558.11	526.51	502.04	482.74	467.27	454.74	444.47
32000	2889.78	1553.10	1110.86	892.21	762.96	678.38	619.30	576.11	543.49	518.24	498.31	482.35	469.40	458.81
33000	2980.09	1601.63	1145.58	920.09	786.81	699.58	638.65	594.11	560.48	534.43	513.88	497.42	484.07	473.15
34000	3070.39	1650.17	1180.29	947.97	810.65	720.78	658.00	612.12	577.46	550.63	529.45	512.49	498.74	487.49
35000	3160.70	1698.70	1215.01	975.86	834.49	741.98	677.36	630.12	594.44	566.82	545.03	527.57	513.41	501.82
36000	3251.00	1747.24	1249.72	1003.74	858.33	763.18	696.71	648.12	611.43	583.02	560.60	542.64	528.08	516.16
37000	3341.31	1795.77	1284.43	1031.62	882.18	784.38	716.06	666.13	628.41	599.21	576.17	557.71	542.75	530.50
38000	3431.61	1844.30	1319.15	1059.50	906.02	805.58	735.42	684.13	645.40	615.41	591.74	572.79	557.42	544.84
39000	3521.92	1892.84	1353.86	1087.38	929.86	826.78	754.77	702.13	662.38	631.60	607.31	587.86	572.09	559.17
40000	3612.23	1941.37	1388.58	1115.26	953.70	847.98	774.12	720.14	679.36	647.80	622.89	602.93	586.75	573.51
41000	3702.53	1989.91	1423.29	1143.15	977.55	869.18	793.47	738.14	696.35	663.99	638.46	618.01	601.42	587.85
42000	3792.84	2038.44	1458.01	1171.03	1001.39	890.38	812.83	756.14	713.33	680.19	654.03	633.08	616.09	602.19
43000	3883.14	2086.97	1492.72	1198.91	1025.23	911.58	832.18	774.15	730.32	696.38	669.60	648.15	630.76	616.52
44000	3973.45	2135.51	1527.44	1226.79	1049.07	932.78	851.53	792.15	747.30	712.58	685.17	663.23	645.43	630.86
45000	4063.75	2184.04	1562.15	1254.67	1072.92	953.98	870.89	810.15	764.28	728.77	700.75	678.30	660.10	645.20
46000	4154.06	2232.58	1596.86	1282.55	1096.76	975.18	890.24	828.16	781.27	744.97	716.32	693.37	674.77	659.54
47000	4244.36	2281.11	1631.58	1310.43	1120.60	996.37	909.59	846.16	798.25	761.16	731.89	708.44	689.44	673.87
48000	4334.67	2329.65	1666.29	1338.32	1144.44	1017.57	928.94	864.16	815.24	777.35	747.46	723.52	704.10	688.21
49000	4424.97	2378.18	1701.01	1366.20	1168.29	1038.77	948.30	882.17	832.22	793.55	763.03	738.59	718.77	702.55
50000	4515.28	2426.71	1735.72	1394.08	1192.13	1059.97	967.65	900.17	849.20	809.74	778.61	753.66	733.44	716.89
55000	4966.81	2669.38	1909.29	1533.49	1311.34	1165.97	1064.41	990.19	934.12	890.72	856.47	829.03	806.79	788.58
60000	5418.34	2912.06	2082.86	1672.89	1430.55	1271.97	1161.18	1080.20	1019.04	971.69	934.33	904.40	880.13	860.26
65000	5869.86	3154.73	2256.44	1812.30	1549.76	1377.96	1257.94	1170.22	1103.96	1052.67	1012.19	979.76	953.47	931.95
70000	6321.39	3397.40	2430.01	1951.71	1668.98	1483.96	1354.71	1260.24	1188.88	1133.64	1090.05	1055.13	1026.82	1003.64
75000	6772.92	3640.07	2603.58	2091.11	1788.19	1589.96	1451.47	1350.25	1273.80	1214.61	1167.91	1130.49	1100.16	1075.33
80000	7224.45	3882.74	2777.15	2230.52	1907.40	1695.95	1548.24	1440.27	1358.72	1295.59	1245.77	1205.86	1173.50	1147.02
85000	7675.97	4125.41	2950.72	2369.93	2026.61	1801.95	1645.00	1530.29	1443.64	1376.56	1323.63	1281.23	1246.85	1218.71
90000	8127.50	4368.08	3124.29	2509.34	2145.83	1907.95	1741.77	1620.30	1528.56	1457.54	1401.49	1356.59	1320.19	1290.39
95000	8579.03	4610.75	3297.87	2648.74	2265.04	2013.94	1838.53	1710.32	1613.48	1538.51	1479.35	1431.96	1393.54	1362.08
100000	9030.56	4853.42	3471.44	2788.15	2384.25	2119.94	1935.30	1800.34	1698.40	1619.48	1557.21	1507.32	1466.88	1433.77

MONTHLY PAYMENT
REQUIRED TO AMORTIZE A LOAN

TERM	15 Years	16 Years	17 Years	18 Years	19 Years	20 Years	21 Years	22 Years	23 Years	24 Years	25 Years	30 Years	35 Years	40 Years
AMOUNT														
5	.08	.07	.07	.07	.07	.07	.07	.07	.07	.07	.07	.07	.07	.07
10	.15	.14	.14	.14	.14	.14	.14	.14	.13	.13	.13	.13	.13	.13
15	.22	.21	.21	.21	.21	.20	.20	.20	.20	.20	.20	.20	.19	.19
25	.36	.35	.35	.34	.34	.34	.33	.33	.33	.33	.33	.32	.32	.32
50	.71	.70	.69	.68	.67	.67	.66	.66	.65	.65	.65	.64	.64	.64
75	1.06	1.04	1.03	1.02	1.01	1.00	.99	.98	.98	.98	.97	.96	.95	.95
100	1.41	1.39	1.37	1.35	1.34	1.33	1.32	1.31	1.30	1.30	1.29	1.28	1.27	1.27
200	2.82	2.77	2.73	2.70	2.68	2.65	2.63	2.62	2.60	2.59	2.58	2.55	2.53	2.53
300	4.22	4.16	4.10	4.05	4.01	3.98	3.95	3.92	3.90	3.89	3.87	3.82	3.80	3.79
400	5.63	5.54	5.46	5.40	5.35	5.30	5.26	5.23	5.20	5.18	5.16	5.09	5.06	5.05
500	7.04	6.92	6.83	6.75	6.68	6.63	6.58	6.54	6.50	6.47	6.45	6.37	6.33	6.31
600	8.44	8.31	8.19	8.10	8.02	7.95	7.89	7.84	7.80	7.77	7.74	7.64	7.59	7.57
700	9.85	9.69	9.56	9.45	9.35	9.27	9.21	9.15	9.10	9.06	9.03	8.91	8.86	8.84
800	11.26	11.07	10.92	10.80	10.69	10.60	10.52	10.46	10.40	10.35	10.31	10.18	10.12	10.10
900	12.66	12.46	12.29	12.15	12.02	11.92	11.84	11.76	11.70	11.65	11.60	11.46	11.39	11.36
1000	14.07	13.84	13.65	13.49	13.36	13.25	13.15	13.07	13.00	12.94	12.89	12.73	12.65	12.62
2000	28.13	27.68	27.30	26.98	26.71	26.49	26.30	26.13	26.00	25.88	25.78	25.45	25.30	25.23
3000	42.20	41.52	40.95	40.47	40.07	39.73	39.44	39.20	38.99	38.81	38.66	38.18	37.95	37.85
4000	56.26	55.35	54.60	53.96	53.42	52.97	52.59	52.26	51.99	51.75	51.55	50.90	50.60	50.46
5000	70.33	69.19	68.24	67.45	66.78	66.21	65.73	65.33	64.98	64.69	64.43	63.63	63.25	63.08
6000	84.39	83.03	81.89	80.94	80.13	79.46	78.88	78.39	77.98	77.62	77.32	76.35	75.90	75.69
7000	98.46	96.87	95.54	94.43	93.49	92.70	92.03	91.46	90.97	90.56	90.21	89.08	88.55	88.31
8000	112.52	110.70	109.19	107.92	106.84	105.94	105.17	104.52	103.97	103.50	103.09	101.80	101.20	100.92
9000	126.58	124.54	122.84	121.41	120.20	119.18	118.32	117.59	116.96	116.43	115.98	114.52	113.85	113.54
10000	140.65	138.38	136.48	134.89	133.55	132.42	131.46	130.65	129.96	129.37	128.86	127.25	126.50	126.15
11000	154.71	152.22	150.13	148.38	146.91	145.67	144.61	143.72	142.95	142.30	141.75	139.97	139.15	138.76
12000	168.78	166.05	163.78	161.87	160.26	158.91	157.76	156.78	155.95	155.24	154.64	152.70	151.80	151.38
13000	182.84	179.89	177.43	175.36	173.62	172.15	170.90	169.84	168.94	168.18	167.52	165.42	164.45	163.99
14000	196.91	193.73	191.08	188.85	186.97	185.39	184.05	182.91	181.94	181.11	180.41	178.15	177.10	176.61
15000	210.97	207.57	204.72	202.34	200.33	198.63	197.19	195.97	194.93	194.05	193.29	190.87	189.75	189.22
16000	225.04	221.40	218.37	215.83	213.68	211.87	210.34	209.04	207.93	206.99	206.18	203.60	202.40	201.84
17000	239.10	235.24	232.02	229.32	227.04	225.12	223.49	222.10	220.93	219.92	219.07	216.32	215.05	214.45
18000	253.16	249.08	245.67	242.81	240.39	238.36	236.63	235.17	233.92	232.86	231.95	229.04	227.70	227.07
19000	267.23	262.92	259.32	256.29	253.75	251.60	249.78	248.23	246.92	245.79	244.84	241.77	240.35	239.68
20000	281.29	276.75	272.96	269.78	267.10	264.84	262.92	261.30	259.91	258.73	257.72	254.49	253.00	252.30
21000	295.36	290.59	286.61	283.27	280.46	278.08	276.07	274.36	272.91	271.67	270.61	267.22	265.65	264.91
22000	309.42	304.43	300.26	296.76	293.81	291.33	289.22	287.43	285.90	284.60	283.50	279.94	278.30	277.52
23000	323.49	318.27	313.91	310.25	307.17	304.57	302.36	300.49	298.90	297.54	296.38	292.67	290.95	290.14
24000	337.55	332.10	327.56	323.74	320.52	317.81	315.51	313.56	311.89	310.48	309.27	305.39	303.59	302.75
25000	351.62	345.94	341.20	337.23	333.88	331.05	328.65	326.62	324.89	323.41	322.15	318.12	316.24	315.37
26000	365.68	359.78	354.85	350.72	347.23	344.29	341.80	339.68	337.88	336.35	335.04	330.84	328.89	327.98
27000	379.74	373.62	368.50	364.21	360.59	357.53	354.95	352.75	350.88	349.29	347.93	343.56	341.54	340.60
28000	393.81	387.45	382.15	377.69	373.94	370.78	368.09	365.81	363.87	362.22	360.81	356.29	354.19	353.21
29000	407.87	401.29	395.80	391.18	387.30	384.02	381.24	378.88	376.87	375.16	373.70	369.01	366.84	365.83
30000	421.94	415.13	409.44	404.67	400.65	397.26	394.38	391.94	389.86	388.09	386.58	381.74	379.49	378.44
31000	436.00	428.97	423.09	418.16	414.01	410.50	407.53	405.01	402.86	401.03	399.47	394.46	392.14	391.06
32000	450.07	442.80	436.74	431.65	427.36	423.74	420.68	418.07	415.86	413.97	412.36	407.19	404.79	403.67
33000	464.13	456.64	450.39	445.14	440.72	436.99	433.82	431.14	428.85	426.90	425.24	419.91	417.44	416.28
34000	478.20	470.48	464.03	458.63	454.07	450.23	446.97	444.20	441.85	439.84	438.13	432.64	430.09	428.90
35000	492.26	484.32	477.68	472.12	467.43	463.47	460.11	457.27	454.84	452.78	451.01	445.36	442.74	441.51
36000	506.32	498.15	491.33	485.61	480.78	476.71	473.26	470.33	467.84	465.71	463.90	458.08	455.39	454.13
37000	520.39	511.99	504.98	499.10	494.14	489.95	486.41	483.39	480.83	478.65	476.78	470.81	468.04	466.74
38000	534.45	525.83	518.63	512.58	507.49	503.20	499.55	496.46	493.83	491.58	489.67	483.53	480.69	479.36
39000	548.52	539.67	532.27	526.07	520.85	516.44	512.70	509.52	506.82	504.52	502.56	496.26	493.34	491.97
40000	562.58	553.50	545.92	539.56	534.20	529.68	525.84	522.59	519.82	517.46	515.44	508.98	505.99	504.59
41000	576.65	567.34	559.57	553.05	547.56	542.92	538.99	535.65	532.81	530.39	528.33	521.71	518.64	517.20
42000	590.71	581.18	573.22	566.54	560.91	556.16	552.14	548.72	545.81	543.33	541.21	534.43	531.29	529.82
43000	604.78	595.02	586.87	580.03	574.27	569.40	565.28	561.78	558.80	556.27	554.10	547.16	543.94	542.43
44000	618.84	608.85	600.51	593.52	587.62	582.65	578.43	574.85	571.80	569.20	566.99	559.88	556.59	555.04
45000	632.90	622.69	614.16	607.01	600.98	595.89	591.57	587.91	584.79	582.14	579.87	572.60	569.24	567.66
46000	646.97	636.53	627.81	620.50	614.33	609.13	604.72	600.98	597.79	595.08	592.76	585.33	581.89	580.27
47000	661.03	650.37	641.46	633.98	627.69	622.37	617.87	614.04	610.79	608.01	605.64	598.05	594.54	592.89
48000	675.10	664.20	655.11	647.47	641.04	635.61	631.01	627.11	623.78	620.95	618.53	610.78	607.18	605.50
49000	689.16	678.04	668.75	660.96	654.40	648.86	644.16	640.17	636.78	633.88	631.42	623.50	619.83	618.12
50000	703.23	691.88	682.40	674.45	667.75	662.10	657.30	653.23	649.77	646.82	644.30	636.23	632.48	630.73
55000	773.55	761.07	750.64	741.90	734.53	728.31	723.03	718.56	714.75	711.50	708.73	699.85	695.73	693.80
60000	843.87	830.25	818.88	809.34	801.30	794.52	788.76	783.88	779.72	776.18	773.16	763.47	758.98	756.88
65000	914.19	899.44	887.12	876.78	868.08	860.72	854.49	849.20	844.70	840.87	837.59	827.09	822.23	819.95
70000	984.51	968.63	955.36	944.23	934.85	926.93	920.22	914.53	909.68	905.55	902.02	890.72	885.48	883.02
75000	1054.84	1037.82	1023.60	1011.67	1001.63	993.14	985.95	979.85	974.65	970.23	966.45	954.34	948.72	946.09
80000	1125.16	1107.00	1091.84	1079.12	1068.40	1059.35	1051.68	1045.17	1039.63	1034.90	1030.88	1017.96	1011.97	1009.17
85000	1195.48	1176.19	1160.08	1146.56	1135.18	1125.56	1117.41	1110.49	1104.61	1099.59	1095.31	1081.58	1075.22	1072.24
90000	1265.80	1245.38	1228.32	1214.01	1201.95	1191.77	1183.14	1175.82	1169.58	1164.27	1159.74	1145.21	1138.47	1135.31
95000	1336.13	1314.57	1296.56	1281.45	1268.73	1257.98	1248.87	1241.14	1234.56	1228.95	1224.17	1208.83	1201.71	1198.39
100000	1406.45	1383.75	1364.80	1348.90	1335.50	1324.19	1314.60	1306.46	1299.54	1293.64	1288.60	1272.45	1264.96	1261.46

MONTHLY PAYMENT
REQUIRED TO AMORTIZE A LOAN

TERM AMOUNT	1 Year	2 Years	3 Years	4 Years	5 Years	6 Years	7 Years	8 Years	9 Years	10 Years	11 Years	12 Years	13 Years	14 Years
5	.46	.25	.18	.14	.12	.11	.10	.10	.09	.09	.08	.08	.08	.08
10	.91	.49	.35	.28	.24	.22	.20	.19	.17	.17	.16	.16	.15	.15
15	1.36	.73	.53	.42	.36	.32	.30	.28	.26	.25	.24	.23	.23	.22
25	2.26	1.22	.87	.70	.60	.54	.49	.46	.43	.41	.39	.38	.37	.36
50	4.52	2.43	1.74	1.40	1.20	1.07	.97	.91	.85	.82	.78	.76	.74	.72
75	6.78	3.65	2.61	2.10	1.79	1.60	1.46	1.36	1.28	1.22	1.17	1.14	1.11	1.08
100	9.04	4.86	3.48	2.79	2.39	2.13	1.94	1.81	1.70	1.63	1.56	1.51	1.47	1.44
200	18.07	9.71	6.95	5.58	4.78	4.25	3.88	3.61	3.40	3.25	3.12	3.02	2.94	2.88
300	27.10	14.57	10.42	8.37	7.16	6.37	5.82	5.41	5.10	4.87	4.68	4.53	4.41	4.31
400	36.13	19.42	13.90	11.16	9.55	8.49	7.75	7.21	6.80	6.49	6.24	6.04	5.88	5.75
500	45.16	24.28	17.37	13.95	11.93	10.61	9.69	9.01	8.50	8.11	7.80	7.55	7.35	7.18
600	54.20	29.13	20.84	16.74	14.32	12.73	11.63	10.82	10.20	9.73	9.36	9.06	8.82	8.62
700	63.23	33.99	24.31	19.53	16.70	14.85	13.56	12.62	11.90	11.35	10.92	10.57	10.28	10.05
800	72.26	38.84	27.79	22.32	19.09	16.98	15.50	14.42	13.60	12.97	12.48	12.08	11.75	11.49
900	81.29	43.70	31.26	25.11	21.48	19.10	17.44	16.22	15.30	14.59	14.03	13.59	13.22	12.92
1000	90.32	48.55	34.73	27.90	23.86	21.22	19.37	18.02	17.00	16.22	15.59	15.09	14.69	14.36
2000	180.64	97.10	69.46	55.79	47.72	42.43	38.74	36.04	34.00	32.43	31.18	30.18	29.38	28.71
3000	270.96	145.64	104.18	83.69	71.57	63.64	58.11	54.06	51.00	48.64	46.77	45.27	44.06	43.07
4000	361.27	194.19	138.91	111.58	95.43	84.86	77.47	72.08	68.00	64.85	62.36	60.36	58.75	57.42
5000	451.59	242.74	173.64	139.48	119.28	106.07	96.84	90.09	85.00	81.06	77.94	75.45	73.43	71.78
6000	541.91	291.28	208.36	167.37	143.14	127.28	116.21	108.11	102.00	97.27	93.53	90.54	88.12	86.13
7000	632.23	339.83	243.09	195.26	166.99	148.50	135.57	126.13	119.00	113.48	109.12	105.63	102.80	100.49
8000	722.54	388.37	277.82	223.16	190.85	169.71	154.94	144.15	136.00	129.69	124.71	120.72	117.49	114.84
9000	812.86	436.92	312.54	251.05	214.71	190.92	174.31	162.17	153.00	145.90	140.30	135.81	132.17	129.20
10000	903.18	485.47	347.27	278.95	238.56	212.13	193.67	180.18	169.99	162.11	155.88	150.90	146.86	143.55
11000	993.50	534.01	382.00	306.84	262.42	233.35	213.04	198.20	186.99	178.32	171.47	165.99	161.54	157.90
12000	1083.81	582.56	416.72	334.73	286.27	254.56	232.41	216.22	203.99	194.53	187.06	181.08	176.23	172.26
13000	1174.13	631.10	451.45	362.63	310.13	275.77	251.78	234.24	220.99	210.74	202.65	196.17	190.91	186.61
14000	1264.45	679.65	486.18	390.52	333.98	296.99	271.14	252.25	237.99	226.95	218.23	211.26	205.60	200.97
15000	1354.76	728.20	520.90	418.42	357.84	318.20	290.51	270.27	254.99	243.16	233.82	226.34	220.28	215.32
16000	1445.08	776.74	555.63	446.31	381.69	339.41	309.88	288.29	271.99	259.37	249.41	241.43	234.97	229.68
17000	1535.40	825.29	590.36	474.21	405.55	360.63	329.24	306.31	288.99	275.58	265.00	256.52	249.65	244.03
18000	1625.72	873.83	625.08	502.10	429.41	381.84	348.61	324.33	305.99	291.79	280.59	271.61	264.34	258.39
19000	1716.03	922.38	659.81	529.99	453.26	403.05	367.98	342.34	322.98	308.00	296.17	286.70	279.02	272.74
20000	1806.35	970.93	694.54	557.89	477.12	424.26	387.34	360.36	339.98	324.21	311.76	301.79	293.71	287.09
21000	1896.67	1019.47	729.26	585.78	500.97	445.48	406.71	378.38	356.98	340.42	327.35	316.88	308.39	301.45
22000	1986.99	1068.02	763.99	613.68	524.83	466.69	426.08	396.40	373.98	356.63	342.94	331.97	323.08	315.80
23000	2077.30	1116.56	798.72	641.57	548.68	487.90	445.44	414.41	390.98	372.84	358.52	347.06	337.77	330.16
24000	2167.62	1165.11	833.44	669.46	572.54	509.12	464.81	432.43	407.98	389.05	374.11	362.15	352.45	344.51
25000	2257.94	1213.66	868.17	697.36	596.39	530.33	484.18	450.45	424.98	405.26	389.70	377.24	367.14	358.87
26000	2348.25	1262.20	902.90	725.25	620.25	551.54	503.55	468.47	441.98	421.47	405.29	392.33	381.82	373.22
27000	2438.57	1310.75	937.62	753.15	644.11	572.75	522.91	486.49	458.98	437.68	420.88	407.42	396.51	387.58
28000	2528.89	1359.29	972.35	781.04	667.96	593.97	542.28	504.50	475.97	453.89	436.46	422.51	411.19	401.93
29000	2619.21	1407.84	1007.08	808.94	691.82	615.18	561.65	522.52	492.97	470.10	452.05	437.59	425.88	416.28
30000	2709.52	1456.39	1041.80	836.83	715.67	636.39	581.01	540.54	509.97	486.31	467.64	452.68	440.56	430.64
31000	2799.84	1504.93	1076.53	864.72	739.53	657.61	600.38	558.56	526.97	502.52	483.23	467.77	455.25	444.99
32000	2890.16	1553.48	1111.26	892.62	763.38	678.82	619.75	576.58	543.97	518.73	498.81	482.86	469.93	459.35
33000	2980.48	1602.02	1145.98	920.51	787.24	700.03	639.11	594.59	560.97	534.94	514.40	497.95	484.62	473.70
34000	3070.79	1650.57	1180.71	948.41	811.10	721.25	658.48	612.61	577.97	551.15	529.99	513.04	499.30	488.06
35000	3161.11	1699.12	1215.44	976.30	834.95	742.46	677.85	630.63	594.97	567.36	545.58	528.13	513.99	502.41
36000	3251.43	1747.66	1250.16	1004.19	858.81	763.67	697.22	648.65	611.97	583.57	561.17	543.22	528.67	516.77
37000	3341.75	1796.21	1284.89	1032.09	882.66	784.88	716.58	666.66	628.96	599.78	576.75	558.31	543.36	531.12
38000	3432.06	1844.76	1319.61	1059.98	906.52	806.10	735.95	684.68	645.96	615.99	592.34	573.40	558.04	545.48
39000	3522.38	1893.30	1354.34	1087.88	930.37	827.31	755.32	702.70	662.96	632.20	607.93	588.49	572.73	559.83
40000	3612.70	1941.85	1389.07	1115.77	954.23	848.52	774.68	720.72	679.96	648.41	623.52	603.58	587.41	574.18
41000	3703.01	1990.39	1423.79	1143.67	978.08	869.74	794.05	738.74	696.96	664.62	639.10	618.67	602.10	588.54
42000	3793.33	2038.94	1458.52	1171.56	1001.94	890.95	813.42	756.75	713.96	680.83	654.69	633.76	616.78	602.89
43000	3883.65	2087.49	1493.25	1199.45	1025.80	912.16	832.78	774.77	730.96	697.04	670.28	648.85	631.47	617.25
44000	3973.97	2136.03	1527.97	1227.35	1049.65	933.38	852.15	792.79	747.96	713.25	685.87	663.93	646.16	631.60
45000	4064.28	2184.58	1562.70	1255.24	1073.51	954.59	871.52	810.81	764.96	729.46	701.46	679.02	660.84	645.96
46000	4154.60	2233.12	1597.43	1283.14	1097.36	975.80	890.88	828.82	781.95	745.67	717.04	694.11	675.53	660.31
47000	4244.92	2281.67	1632.15	1311.03	1121.22	997.01	910.25	846.84	798.95	761.88	732.63	709.20	690.21	674.67
48000	4335.24	2330.22	1666.88	1338.92	1145.07	1018.23	929.62	864.86	815.95	778.09	748.22	724.29	704.90	689.02
49000	4425.55	2378.76	1701.61	1366.82	1168.93	1039.44	948.99	882.88	832.95	794.30	763.81	739.38	719.58	703.37
50000	4515.87	2427.31	1736.33	1394.71	1192.78	1060.65	968.35	900.90	849.95	810.51	779.39	754.47	734.27	717.73
55000	4967.46	2670.04	1909.97	1534.18	1312.06	1166.72	1065.19	990.98	934.94	891.56	857.33	829.92	807.69	789.50
60000	5419.04	2912.77	2083.60	1673.65	1431.34	1272.78	1162.02	1081.07	1019.94	972.61	935.27	905.36	881.12	861.27
65000	5870.63	3155.50	2257.23	1813.13	1550.62	1378.85	1258.86	1171.16	1104.93	1053.66	1013.21	980.81	954.55	933.05
70000	6322.22	3398.23	2430.87	1952.60	1669.90	1484.91	1355.69	1261.25	1189.93	1134.71	1091.15	1056.26	1027.97	1004.82
75000	6773.80	3640.96	2604.50	2092.07	1789.17	1590.98	1452.53	1351.34	1274.92	1215.76	1169.09	1131.70	1101.40	1076.59
80000	7225.39	3883.69	2778.13	2231.54	1908.45	1697.04	1549.36	1441.43	1359.92	1296.82	1247.03	1207.15	1174.82	1148.36
85000	7676.98	4126.42	2951.76	2371.01	2027.73	1803.11	1646.20	1531.52	1444.91	1377.87	1324.97	1282.60	1248.25	1220.14
90000	8128.56	4369.15	3125.40	2510.48	2147.01	1909.17	1743.03	1621.61	1529.91	1458.92	1402.91	1358.04	1321.68	1291.91
95000	8580.15	4611.88	3299.03	2649.95	2266.29	2015.24	1839.87	1711.70	1614.90	1539.97	1480.84	1433.49	1395.10	1363.68
100000	9031.74	4854.61	3472.66	2789.42	2385.56	2121.30	1936.70	1801.79	1699.89	1621.02	1558.78	1508.94	1468.53	1435.45

TERM	15 Years	16 Years	17 Years	18 Years	19 Years	20 Years	21 Years	22 Years	23 Years	24 Years	25 Years	30 Years	35 Years	40 Years
AMOUNT														
5	.08	.07	.07	.07	.07	.07	.07	.07	.07	.07	.07	.07	.07	.07
10	.15	.14	.14	.14	.14	.14	.14	.14	.14	.13	.13	.13	.13	.13
15	.22	.21	.21	.21	.21	.20	.20	.20	.20	.20	.20	.20	.20	.19
25	.36	.35	.35	.34	.34	.34	.33	.33	.33	.33	.33	.32	.32	.32
50	.71	.70	.69	.68	.67	.67	.66	.66	.66	.65	.65	.64	.64	.64
75	1.06	1.04	1.03	1.02	1.01	1.00	.99	.99	.98	.98	.97	.96	.96	.95
100	1.41	1.39	1.37	1.36	1.34	1.33	1.32	1.31	1.31	1.30	1.30	1.28	1.27	1.27
200	2.82	2.78	2.74	2.71	2.68	2.66	2.64	2.62	2.61	2.60	2.59	2.55	2.54	2.53
300	4.23	4.16	4.10	4.06	4.02	3.98	3.95	3.93	3.91	3.89	3.88	3.83	3.81	3.80
400	5.64	5.55	5.47	5.41	5.35	5.31	5.27	5.24	5.21	5.19	5.17	5.10	5.07	5.06
500	7.05	6.93	6.84	6.76	6.69	6.64	6.59	6.55	6.51	6.48	6.46	6.38	6.34	6.32
600	8.45	8.32	8.20	8.11	8.03	7.96	7.90	7.86	7.81	7.78	7.75	7.65	7.61	7.59
700	9.86	9.70	9.57	9.46	9.37	9.29	9.22	9.16	9.12	9.07	9.04	8.93	8.87	8.85
800	11.27	11.09	10.94	10.81	10.70	10.61	10.54	10.47	10.42	10.37	10.33	10.20	10.14	10.11
900	12.68	12.47	12.30	12.16	12.04	11.94	11.85	11.78	11.72	11.67	11.62	11.48	11.41	11.38
1000	14.09	13.86	13.67	13.51	13.38	13.27	13.17	13.09	13.02	12.96	12.91	12.75	12.67	12.64
2000	28.17	27.71	27.34	27.02	26.75	26.53	26.33	26.17	26.03	25.92	25.82	25.49	25.34	25.28
3000	42.25	41.57	41.00	40.53	40.12	39.79	39.50	39.26	39.05	38.87	38.72	38.24	38.01	37.91
4000	56.33	55.42	54.67	54.03	53.50	53.05	52.66	52.34	52.06	51.83	51.63	50.98	50.68	50.55
5000	70.41	69.28	68.33	67.54	66.87	66.31	65.83	65.42	65.08	64.78	64.53	63.73	63.35	63.18
6000	84.49	83.13	82.00	81.05	80.24	79.57	78.99	78.51	78.09	77.74	77.44	76.47	76.02	75.82
7000	98.58	96.99	95.66	94.55	93.62	92.83	92.16	91.59	91.11	90.69	90.34	89.22	88.69	88.45
8000	112.66	110.84	109.33	108.06	106.99	106.09	105.32	104.67	104.12	103.65	103.25	101.96	101.36	101.09
9000	126.74	124.70	123.00	121.57	120.36	119.35	118.49	117.76	117.13	116.61	116.15	114.71	114.03	113.72
10000	140.82	138.55	136.66	135.07	133.74	132.61	131.65	130.84	130.15	129.56	129.06	127.45	126.70	126.36
11000	154.90	152.41	150.33	148.58	147.11	145.87	144.82	143.92	143.16	142.52	141.96	140.19	139.37	138.99
12000	168.98	166.26	163.99	162.09	160.48	159.13	157.98	157.01	156.18	155.47	154.87	152.94	152.04	151.63
13000	183.07	180.12	177.66	175.60	173.86	172.39	171.15	170.09	169.19	168.43	167.77	165.68	164.71	164.26
14000	197.15	193.97	191.32	189.10	187.23	185.65	184.31	183.17	182.21	181.38	180.68	178.43	177.38	176.90
15000	211.23	207.83	204.99	202.61	200.60	198.91	197.48	196.26	195.22	194.34	193.59	191.17	190.05	189.53
16000	225.31	221.68	218.66	216.12	213.98	212.17	210.64	209.34	208.24	207.29	206.49	203.92	202.72	202.17
17000	239.39	235.54	232.32	229.62	227.35	225.43	223.80	222.42	221.25	220.25	219.40	216.66	215.39	214.80
18000	253.47	249.39	245.99	243.13	240.72	238.69	236.97	235.51	234.26	233.21	232.30	229.41	228.06	227.44
19000	267.56	263.25	259.65	256.64	254.10	251.95	250.13	248.59	247.28	246.16	245.21	242.15	240.73	240.07
20000	281.64	277.10	273.32	270.14	267.47	265.21	263.30	261.68	260.29	259.12	258.11	254.89	253.40	252.71
21000	295.72	290.96	286.98	283.65	280.84	278.47	276.46	274.76	273.31	272.07	271.02	267.64	266.07	265.34
22000	309.80	304.81	300.65	297.16	294.22	291.73	289.63	287.84	286.32	285.03	283.92	280.38	278.74	277.98
23000	323.88	318.67	314.32	310.66	307.59	304.99	302.79	300.93	299.34	297.98	296.83	293.13	291.41	290.61
24000	337.96	332.52	327.98	324.17	320.96	318.25	315.96	314.01	312.35	310.94	309.73	305.87	304.08	303.25
25000	352.04	346.38	341.65	337.68	334.34	331.51	329.12	327.09	325.37	323.89	322.64	318.62	316.75	315.88
26000	366.13	360.23	355.31	351.19	347.71	344.77	342.29	340.18	338.38	336.85	335.54	331.36	329.42	328.52
27000	380.21	374.09	368.98	364.69	361.08	358.03	355.26	353.26	351.39	349.81	348.45	344.11	342.09	341.15
28000	394.29	387.94	382.64	378.20	374.46	371.29	368.62	366.34	364.41	362.76	361.36	356.85	354.76	353.79
29000	408.37	401.80	396.31	391.71	387.83	384.56	381.78	379.43	377.42	375.72	374.26	369.59	367.43	366.42
30000	422.45	415.65	409.98	405.21	401.20	397.82	394.95	392.51	390.44	388.67	387.17	382.34	380.10	379.06
31000	436.53	429.51	423.64	418.72	414.58	411.08	408.11	405.59	403.45	401.63	400.07	395.08	392.77	391.69
32000	450.62	443.36	437.31	432.23	427.95	424.34	421.28	418.68	416.47	414.58	412.98	407.83	405.44	404.33
33000	464.70	457.22	450.97	445.73	441.32	437.60	434.44	431.76	429.48	427.54	425.88	420.57	418.11	416.96
34000	478.78	471.07	464.64	459.24	454.70	450.86	447.60	444.84	442.50	440.49	438.79	433.32	430.78	429.60
35000	492.86	484.93	478.30	472.75	468.07	464.12	460.77	457.93	455.51	453.45	451.69	446.06	443.45	442.23
36000	506.94	498.78	491.97	486.25	481.44	477.38	473.93	471.01	468.52	466.41	464.60	458.81	456.12	454.87
37000	521.02	512.64	505.64	499.76	494.82	490.64	487.10	484.09	481.54	479.36	477.50	471.55	468.79	467.50
38000	535.11	526.49	519.30	513.27	508.19	503.90	500.26	497.18	494.55	492.32	490.41	484.29	481.46	480.14
39000	549.19	540.35	532.97	526.78	521.56	517.16	513.43	510.26	507.57	505.27	503.31	497.04	494.13	492.77
40000	563.27	554.20	546.63	540.28	534.94	530.42	526.59	523.35	520.58	518.23	516.22	509.78	506.80	505.41
41000	577.35	568.06	560.30	553.79	548.31	543.68	539.76	536.43	533.60	531.18	529.13	522.53	519.47	518.04
42000	591.43	581.91	573.96	567.30	561.68	556.94	552.92	549.51	546.61	544.14	542.03	535.27	532.14	530.68
43000	605.51	595.77	587.63	580.80	575.06	570.20	566.09	562.60	559.63	557.10	554.94	548.02	544.81	543.31
44000	619.59	609.62	601.30	594.31	588.43	583.46	579.25	575.68	572.64	570.05	567.84	560.76	557.47	555.95
45000	633.68	623.48	614.96	607.82	601.80	596.72	592.42	588.76	585.65	583.01	580.75	573.51	570.15	568.58
46000	647.76	637.33	628.63	621.32	615.18	609.98	605.58	601.85	598.67	595.96	593.65	586.25	582.82	581.22
47000	661.84	651.19	642.29	634.83	628.55	623.24	618.75	614.93	611.68	608.92	606.56	598.99	595.49	593.86
48000	675.92	665.04	655.96	648.34	641.92	636.50	631.91	628.01	624.70	621.87	619.46	611.74	608.16	606.49
49000	690.00	678.90	669.62	661.85	655.30	649.76	645.08	641.10	637.71	634.83	632.37	624.48	620.83	619.13
50000	704.08	692.75	683.29	675.35	668.67	663.02	658.24	654.18	650.73	647.78	645.27	637.23	633.50	631.76
55000	774.49	762.03	751.62	742.89	735.53	729.32	724.06	719.60	715.80	712.56	709.80	700.95	696.85	694.94
60000	844.90	831.30	819.95	810.42	802.40	795.63	789.89	785.02	780.87	777.34	774.33	764.67	760.20	758.11
65000	915.31	900.58	888.28	877.96	869.27	861.93	855.71	850.43	845.94	842.12	838.85	828.39	823.55	821.29
70000	985.72	969.85	956.60	945.49	936.13	928.23	921.53	915.85	911.02	906.90	903.38	892.12	886.90	884.46
75000	1056.12	1039.13	1024.93	1013.03	1003.00	994.53	987.36	981.27	976.09	971.67	967.91	955.84	950.25	947.64
80000	1126.53	1108.40	1093.26	1080.56	1069.87	1060.83	1053.18	1046.69	1041.16	1036.45	1032.43	1019.56	1013.60	1010.81
85000	1196.94	1177.68	1161.59	1148.10	1136.73	1127.13	1119.00	1112.10	1106.23	1101.23	1096.96	1083.28	1076.95	1073.99
90000	1267.35	1246.95	1229.92	1215.63	1203.60	1193.44	1184.83	1177.52	1171.30	1166.01	1161.49	1147.01	1140.30	1137.16
95000	1337.76	1316.22	1298.25	1283.16	1270.47	1259.74	1250.65	1242.94	1236.38	1230.79	1226.02	1210.73	1203.65	1200.34
100000	1408.16	1385.50	1366.57	1350.70	1337.33	1326.04	1316.48	1308.36	1301.45	1295.56	1290.54	1274.45	1267.00	1263.52

MONTHLY PAYMENT
REQUIRED TO AMORTIZE A LOAN

TERM	1 Year	2 Years	3 Years	4 Years	5 Years	6 Years	7 Years	8 Years	9 Years	10 Years	11 Years	12 Years	13 Years	14 Years
AMOUNT														
5	.46	.25	.18	.14	.12	.11	.10	.10	.09	.09	.08	.08	.08	.08
10	.91	.49	.35	.28	.24	.22	.20	.19	.18	.17	.16	.16	.15	.15
15	1.36	.73	.53	.42	.36	.32	.30	.28	.26	.25	.24	.23	.23	.22
25	2.26	1.22	.87	.70	.60	.54	.49	.46	.43	.41	.40	.38	.37	.37
50	4.52	2.43	1.74	1.40	1.20	1.07	.98	.91	.86	.82	.79	.76	.74	.73
75	6.78	3.65	2.61	2.10	1.80	1.60	1.46	1.36	1.28	1.22	1.18	1.14	1.11	1.09
100	9.04	4.86	3.48	2.80	2.39	2.13	1.95	1.81	1.71	1.63	1.57	1.52	1.48	1.45
200	18.08	9.72	6.96	5.59	4.78	4.26	3.89	3.62	3.41	3.26	3.13	3.03	2.95	2.89
300	27.11	14.58	10.43	8.38	7.17	6.38	5.83	5.42	5.12	4.88	4.70	4.55	4.43	4.33
400	36.15	19.44	13.91	11.18	9.56	8.51	7.77	7.23	6.82	6.51	6.26	6.06	5.90	5.77
500	45.18	24.30	17.39	13.97	11.95	10.63	9.71	9.04	8.53	8.13	7.82	7.57	7.37	7.21
600	54.22	29.15	20.86	16.76	14.34	12.76	11.65	10.84	10.23	9.76	9.39	9.09	8.85	8.65
700	63.25	34.01	24.34	19.56	16.73	14.88	13.59	12.65	11.94	11.38	10.95	10.60	10.32	10.09
800	72.29	38.87	27.82	22.35	19.12	17.01	15.53	14.45	13.64	13.01	12.51	12.12	11.79	11.53
900	81.32	43.73	31.29	25.14	21.51	19.13	17.47	16.26	15.34	14.64	14.08	13.63	13.27	12.97
1000	90.36	48.59	34.77	27.94	23.90	21.26	19.41	18.07	17.05	16.26	15.64	15.14	14.74	14.41
2000	180.71	97.17	69.53	55.87	47.80	42.51	38.82	36.13	34.09	32.52	31.28	30.28	29.47	28.82
3000	271.06	145.75	104.30	83.80	71.69	63.77	58.23	54.19	51.14	48.77	46.91	45.42	44.21	43.22
4000	361.42	194.33	139.06	111.73	95.59	85.02	77.64	72.25	68.18	65.03	62.55	60.56	58.94	57.63
5000	451.77	242.91	173.82	139.67	119.48	106.27	97.05	90.31	85.22	81.29	78.18	75.69	73.68	72.03
6000	542.12	291.50	208.59	167.60	143.38	127.53	116.46	108.37	102.27	97.54	93.82	90.83	88.41	86.44
7000	632.47	340.08	243.35	195.53	167.27	148.78	135.87	126.43	119.31	113.80	109.45	105.97	103.15	100.84
8000	722.83	388.66	278.11	223.46	191.17	170.04	155.28	144.50	136.35	130.05	125.09	121.11	117.88	115.25
9000	813.18	437.24	312.88	251.40	215.06	191.29	174.69	162.56	153.40	146.31	140.72	136.24	132.62	129.65
10000	903.53	485.82	347.64	279.33	238.96	212.54	194.10	180.62	170.44	162.57	156.36	151.38	147.35	144.06
11000	993.88	534.40	382.40	307.26	262.85	233.80	213.51	198.68	187.49	178.82	171.99	166.52	162.09	158.46
12000	1084.24	582.99	417.17	335.19	286.75	255.05	232.91	216.74	204.53	195.08	187.63	181.66	176.82	172.87
13000	1174.59	631.57	451.93	363.12	310.64	276.30	252.32	234.80	221.57	211.34	203.26	196.80	191.56	187.27
14000	1264.94	680.15	486.69	391.06	334.54	297.56	271.73	252.86	238.62	227.59	218.90	211.93	206.29	201.68
15000	1355.30	728.73	521.46	418.99	358.43	318.81	291.14	270.92	255.66	243.85	234.53	227.07	221.03	216.08
16000	1445.65	777.31	556.22	446.92	382.33	340.07	310.55	288.99	272.70	260.10	250.17	242.21	235.76	230.49
17000	1536.00	825.89	590.98	474.85	406.22	361.32	329.96	307.05	289.75	276.36	265.80	257.35	250.50	244.89
18000	1626.35	874.48	625.75	502.79	430.12	382.57	349.37	325.11	306.79	292.62	281.44	272.48	265.23	259.30
19000	1716.71	923.06	660.51	530.72	454.01	403.83	368.78	343.17	323.84	308.87	297.07	287.62	279.97	273.70
20000	1807.06	971.64	695.27	558.65	477.91	425.08	388.19	361.23	340.88	325.13	312.71	302.76	294.70	288.11
21000	1897.41	1020.22	730.04	586.58	501.80	446.33	407.60	379.29	357.92	341.39	328.34	317.90	309.43	302.51
22000	1987.76	1068.80	764.80	614.51	525.70	467.59	427.01	397.35	374.97	357.64	343.98	333.03	324.17	316.92
23000	2078.12	1117.38	799.56	642.45	549.59	488.84	446.42	415.42	392.01	373.90	359.61	348.17	338.90	331.32
24000	2168.47	1165.97	834.33	670.38	573.49	510.10	465.82	433.48	409.05	390.15	375.25	363.31	353.64	345.73
25000	2258.82	1214.55	869.09	698.31	597.38	531.35	485.23	451.54	426.10	406.41	390.88	378.45	368.37	360.13
26000	2349.18	1263.13	903.85	726.24	621.28	552.60	504.64	469.60	443.14	422.67	406.52	393.59	383.11	374.54
27000	2439.53	1311.71	938.62	754.18	645.17	573.86	524.05	487.66	460.19	438.92	422.15	408.72	397.84	388.94
28000	2529.88	1360.29	973.38	782.11	669.07	595.11	543.46	505.72	477.23	455.18	437.79	423.86	412.58	403.35
29000	2620.23	1408.88	1008.14	810.04	692.96	616.36	562.87	523.78	494.27	471.43	453.42	439.00	427.31	417.75
30000	2710.59	1457.46	1042.91	837.97	716.86	637.62	582.28	541.84	511.32	487.69	469.06	454.14	442.05	432.16
31000	2800.94	1506.04	1077.67	865.90	740.75	658.87	601.69	559.91	528.36	503.95	484.69	469.27	456.78	446.56
32000	2891.29	1554.62	1112.43	893.84	764.65	680.13	621.10	577.97	545.40	520.20	500.33	484.41	471.52	460.97
33000	2981.64	1603.20	1147.20	921.77	788.54	701.38	640.51	596.03	562.45	536.46	515.96	499.55	486.25	475.37
34000	3072.00	1651.78	1181.96	949.70	812.44	722.63	659.92	614.09	579.49	552.72	531.60	514.69	500.99	489.78
35000	3162.35	1700.37	1216.72	977.63	836.33	743.89	679.32	632.15	596.53	568.97	547.23	529.83	515.72	504.18
36000	3252.70	1748.95	1251.49	1005.57	860.23	765.14	698.73	650.21	613.58	585.23	562.87	544.96	530.46	518.59
37000	3343.06	1797.53	1286.25	1033.50	884.12	786.39	718.14	668.27	630.62	601.48	578.50	560.10	545.19	532.99
38000	3433.41	1846.11	1321.01	1061.43	908.02	807.65	737.55	686.34	647.67	617.74	594.14	575.24	559.93	547.40
39000	3523.76	1894.69	1355.78	1089.36	931.91	828.90	756.96	704.40	664.71	634.00	609.77	590.38	574.66	561.80
40000	3614.11	1943.27	1390.54	1117.29	955.81	850.16	776.37	722.46	681.75	650.25	625.41	605.51	589.39	576.21
41000	3704.47	1991.86	1425.30	1145.23	979.70	871.41	795.78	740.52	698.80	666.51	641.04	620.65	604.13	590.61
42000	3794.82	2040.44	1460.07	1173.16	1003.60	892.66	815.19	758.58	715.84	682.77	656.68	635.79	618.86	605.02
43000	3885.17	2089.02	1494.83	1201.09	1027.49	913.92	834.60	776.64	732.88	699.02	672.31	650.93	633.60	619.42
44000	3975.52	2137.60	1529.59	1229.02	1051.39	935.17	854.01	794.70	749.93	715.28	687.95	666.06	648.33	633.83
45000	4065.88	2186.18	1564.36	1256.96	1075.28	956.42	873.42	812.76	766.97	731.53	703.58	681.20	663.07	648.23
46000	4156.23	2234.76	1599.12	1284.89	1099.18	977.68	892.83	830.83	784.02	747.79	719.22	696.34	677.80	662.64
47000	4246.58	2283.35	1633.88	1312.82	1123.07	998.93	912.23	848.89	801.06	764.05	734.85	711.48	692.54	677.04
48000	4336.94	2331.93	1668.65	1340.75	1146.97	1020.19	931.64	866.95	818.10	780.30	750.49	726.62	707.27	691.45
49000	4427.29	2380.51	1703.41	1368.68	1170.86	1041.44	951.05	885.01	835.15	796.56	766.12	741.75	722.01	705.85
50000	4517.64	2429.09	1738.17	1396.62	1194.76	1062.69	970.46	903.07	852.19	812.81	781.76	756.89	736.74	720.26
55000	4969.40	2672.00	1911.99	1536.28	1314.23	1168.96	1067.51	993.38	937.41	894.10	859.93	832.58	810.42	792.28
60000	5421.17	2914.91	2085.81	1675.94	1433.71	1275.23	1164.55	1083.68	1022.63	975.38	938.11	908.27	884.09	864.31
65000	5872.93	3157.82	2259.62	1815.60	1553.18	1381.50	1261.60	1173.99	1107.85	1056.66	1016.28	983.96	957.76	936.33
70000	6324.69	3400.73	2433.44	1955.26	1672.66	1487.77	1358.64	1264.30	1193.06	1137.94	1094.46	1059.65	1031.44	1008.36
75000	6776.46	3643.63	2607.26	2094.92	1792.13	1594.04	1455.69	1354.60	1278.28	1219.22	1172.63	1135.33	1105.11	1080.38
80000	7228.22	3886.54	2781.07	2234.58	1911.61	1700.31	1552.74	1444.91	1363.50	1300.50	1250.81	1211.02	1178.78	1152.41
85000	7679.99	4129.45	2954.89	2374.25	2031.08	1806.58	1649.78	1535.22	1448.72	1381.78	1328.98	1286.71	1252.46	1224.43
90000	8131.75	4372.36	3128.71	2513.91	2150.56	1912.85	1746.83	1625.52	1533.94	1463.06	1407.16	1362.40	1326.13	1296.46
95000	8583.51	4615.27	3302.52	2653.57	2270.03	2019.11	1843.87	1715.83	1619.16	1544.34	1485.33	1438.09	1399.81	1368.48
100000	9035.28	4858.18	3476.34	2793.23	2389.51	2125.38	1940.92	1806.14	1704.38	1625.62	1563.51	1513.78	1473.48	1440.51

TERM AMOUNT	15 Years	16 Years	17 Years	18 Years	19 Years	20 Years	21 Years	22 Years	23 Years	24 Years	25 Years	30 Years	35 Years	40 Years
5	.08	.07	.07	.07	.07	.07	.07	.07	.07	.07	.07	.07	.07	.07
10	.15	.14	.14	.14	.14	.14	.14	.14	.14	.14	.13	.13	.13	.13
15	.22	.21	.21	.21	.21	.20	.20	.20	.20	.20	.20	.20	.20	.20
25	.36	.35	.35	.34	.34	.34	.34	.33	.33	.33	.33	.33	.32	.32
50	.71	.70	.69	.68	.68	.67	.67	.66	.66	.66	.65	.65	.64	.64
75	1.06	1.05	1.03	1.02	1.01	1.00	1.00	.99	.99	.98	.98	.97	.96	.96
100	1.42	1.40	1.38	1.36	1.35	1.34	1.33	1.32	1.31	1.31	1.30	1.29	1.28	1.27
200	2.83	2.79	2.75	2.72	2.69	2.67	2.65	2.63	2.62	2.61	2.60	2.57	2.55	2.54
300	4.24	4.18	4.12	4.07	4.03	4.00	3.97	3.95	3.93	3.91	3.89	3.85	3.82	3.81
400	5.66	5.57	5.49	5.43	5.38	5.33	5.29	5.26	5.23	5.21	5.19	5.13	5.10	5.08
500	7.07	6.96	6.86	6.79	6.72	6.66	6.62	6.58	6.54	6.51	6.49	6.41	6.37	6.35
600	8.48	8.35	8.24	8.14	8.06	7.99	7.94	7.89	7.85	7.81	7.78	7.69	7.64	7.62
700	9.90	9.74	9.61	9.50	9.40	9.33	9.26	9.20	9.16	9.11	9.08	8.97	8.92	8.89
800	11.31	11.13	10.98	10.85	10.75	10.66	10.58	10.52	10.46	10.42	10.38	10.25	10.19	10.16
900	12.72	12.52	12.35	12.21	12.09	11.99	11.90	11.83	11.77	11.72	11.67	11.53	11.46	11.43
1000	14.14	13.91	13.72	13.57	13.43	13.32	13.23	13.15	13.08	13.02	12.97	12.81	12.74	12.70
2000	28.27	27.82	27.44	27.13	26.86	26.64	26.45	26.29	26.15	26.03	25.93	25.61	25.47	25.40
3000	42.40	41.73	41.16	40.69	40.29	39.95	39.67	39.43	39.22	39.05	38.90	38.42	38.20	38.10
4000	56.54	55.63	54.88	54.25	53.72	53.27	52.89	52.57	52.29	52.06	51.86	51.22	50.93	50.79
5000	70.67	69.54	68.60	67.81	67.15	66.58	66.11	65.71	65.36	65.07	64.82	64.03	63.66	63.49
6000	84.80	83.45	82.32	81.37	80.57	79.90	79.33	78.85	78.44	78.09	77.79	76.83	76.39	76.19
7000	98.94	97.36	96.04	94.93	94.00	93.22	92.55	91.99	91.51	91.10	90.75	89.64	89.12	88.88
8000	113.07	111.26	109.76	108.49	107.43	106.53	105.77	105.13	104.58	104.11	103.71	102.44	101.85	101.58
9000	127.20	125.17	123.48	122.05	120.86	119.85	118.99	118.27	117.65	117.13	116.68	115.25	114.58	114.28
10000	141.34	139.08	137.20	135.62	134.29	133.16	132.21	131.41	130.72	130.14	129.64	128.05	127.32	126.97
11000	155.47	152.99	150.91	149.18	147.71	146.48	145.44	144.55	143.79	143.15	142.61	140.85	140.05	139.67
12000	169.60	166.89	164.63	162.74	161.14	159.80	158.66	157.69	156.87	156.17	155.57	153.66	152.78	152.37
13000	183.74	180.80	178.35	176.30	174.57	173.11	171.88	170.83	169.94	169.18	168.53	166.46	165.51	165.06
14000	197.87	194.71	192.07	189.86	188.00	186.43	185.10	183.97	183.01	182.19	181.50	179.27	178.24	177.76
15000	212.00	208.62	205.79	203.42	201.43	199.74	198.32	197.11	196.08	195.21	194.46	192.07	190.97	190.46
16000	226.13	222.52	219.51	216.98	214.86	213.06	211.54	210.25	209.15	208.22	207.42	204.88	203.70	203.15
17000	240.27	236.43	233.23	230.54	228.28	226.38	224.76	223.39	222.23	221.23	220.39	217.68	216.43	215.85
18000	254.40	250.34	246.95	244.10	241.71	239.69	237.98	236.53	235.30	234.25	233.35	230.49	229.16	228.55
19000	268.53	264.25	260.67	257.67	255.14	253.01	251.20	249.67	248.37	247.26	246.31	243.29	241.90	241.25
20000	282.67	278.15	274.39	271.23	268.57	266.32	264.42	262.81	261.44	260.27	259.28	256.10	254.63	253.94
21000	296.80	292.06	288.10	284.79	282.00	279.64	277.64	275.95	274.51	273.29	272.24	268.90	267.36	266.64
22000	310.93	305.97	301.82	298.35	295.42	292.96	290.86	289.09	287.58	286.30	285.21	281.70	280.09	279.34
23000	325.07	319.87	315.54	311.91	308.85	306.27	304.09	302.23	300.66	299.31	298.17	294.51	292.82	292.03
24000	339.20	333.78	329.26	325.47	322.28	319.59	317.31	315.37	313.73	312.33	311.13	307.31	305.55	304.73
25000	353.33	347.69	342.98	339.03	335.71	332.90	330.53	328.51	326.80	325.34	324.10	320.12	318.28	317.43
26000	367.47	361.60	356.70	352.59	349.14	346.22	343.75	341.65	339.87	338.35	337.06	332.92	331.01	330.12
27000	381.60	375.50	370.42	366.15	362.56	359.53	356.97	354.79	352.94	351.37	350.02	345.73	343.74	342.82
28000	395.73	389.41	384.14	379.71	375.99	372.85	370.19	367.93	366.01	364.38	362.99	358.53	356.48	355.52
29000	409.87	403.32	397.86	393.28	389.42	386.17	383.41	381.07	379.09	377.39	375.95	371.34	369.21	368.21
30000	424.00	417.23	411.58	406.84	402.85	399.48	396.63	394.21	392.16	390.41	388.92	384.14	381.94	380.91
31000	438.13	431.13	425.29	420.40	416.28	412.80	409.85	407.35	405.23	403.42	401.88	396.95	394.67	393.61
32000	452.26	445.04	439.01	433.96	429.71	426.11	423.07	420.49	418.30	416.43	414.84	409.75	407.40	406.30
33000	466.40	458.95	452.73	447.52	443.13	439.43	436.29	433.64	431.37	429.45	427.81	422.55	420.13	419.00
34000	480.53	472.86	466.45	461.08	456.56	452.75	449.52	446.78	444.45	442.46	440.77	435.36	432.86	431.70
35000	494.66	486.76	480.17	474.64	469.99	466.06	462.74	459.92	457.52	455.48	453.73	448.16	445.59	444.39
36000	508.80	500.67	493.89	488.20	483.42	479.38	475.96	473.06	470.59	468.49	466.70	460.97	458.32	457.09
37000	522.93	514.58	507.61	501.76	496.85	492.69	489.18	486.20	483.66	481.50	479.66	473.77	471.05	469.79
38000	537.06	528.49	521.33	515.33	510.27	506.01	502.40	499.34	496.73	494.52	492.62	486.58	483.79	482.49
39000	551.20	542.39	535.05	528.89	523.70	519.33	515.62	512.48	509.80	507.53	505.59	499.38	496.52	495.18
40000	565.33	556.30	548.77	542.45	537.13	532.64	528.84	525.62	522.88	520.54	518.55	512.19	509.25	507.88
41000	579.46	570.21	562.48	556.01	550.56	545.96	542.06	538.76	535.95	533.56	531.52	524.99	521.98	520.58
42000	593.60	584.12	576.20	569.57	563.99	559.27	555.28	551.90	549.02	546.57	544.48	537.79	534.71	533.27
43000	607.73	598.02	589.92	583.13	577.41	572.59	568.50	565.04	562.09	559.58	557.44	550.60	547.44	545.97
44000	621.86	611.93	603.64	596.69	590.84	585.91	581.72	578.18	575.16	572.60	570.41	563.40	560.17	558.67
45000	635.99	625.84	617.36	610.25	604.27	599.22	594.95	591.32	588.24	585.61	583.37	576.21	572.90	571.36
46000	650.13	639.74	631.08	623.81	617.70	612.54	608.17	604.46	601.31	598.62	596.33	589.01	585.63	584.06
47000	664.26	653.65	644.80	637.37	631.13	625.85	621.39	617.60	614.38	611.64	609.30	601.82	598.37	596.76
48000	678.39	667.56	658.52	650.94	644.56	639.17	634.61	630.74	627.45	624.65	622.26	614.62	611.10	609.45
49000	692.53	681.47	672.24	664.50	657.98	652.48	647.83	643.88	640.52	637.66	635.23	627.43	623.83	622.15
50000	706.66	695.37	685.96	678.06	671.41	665.80	661.05	657.02	653.59	650.68	648.19	640.23	636.56	634.85
55000	777.33	764.91	754.55	745.86	738.55	732.38	727.15	722.72	718.95	715.74	713.01	704.25	700.21	698.33
60000	847.99	834.45	823.15	813.67	805.69	798.96	793.26	788.42	784.31	780.81	777.83	768.28	763.87	761.82
65000	918.66	903.99	891.74	881.47	872.83	865.54	859.36	854.12	849.67	845.88	842.64	832.30	827.52	825.30
70000	989.32	973.52	960.34	949.28	939.97	932.12	925.47	919.83	915.03	910.95	907.46	896.32	891.18	888.78
75000	1059.99	1043.06	1028.93	1017.08	1007.11	998.70	991.57	985.53	980.39	976.01	972.28	960.34	954.84	952.27
80000	1130.65	1112.60	1097.53	1084.89	1074.26	1065.28	1057.68	1051.23	1045.75	1041.08	1037.10	1024.37	1018.49	1015.75
85000	1201.32	1182.13	1166.12	1152.69	1141.40	1131.86	1123.78	1116.93	1111.11	1106.15	1101.92	1088.39	1082.15	1079.24
90000	1271.98	1251.67	1234.72	1220.50	1208.54	1198.44	1189.89	1182.63	1176.47	1171.21	1166.74	1152.41	1145.80	1142.72
95000	1342.65	1321.21	1303.31	1288.31	1275.68	1265.02	1255.99	1248.33	1241.82	1236.28	1231.55	1216.43	1209.46	1206.21
100000	1413.32	1390.74	1371.91	1356.11	1342.82	1331.60	1322.10	1314.04	1307.18	1301.35	1296.37	1280.46	1273.11	1269.69

TERM	1 Year	2 Years	3 Years	4 Years	5 Years	6 Years	7 Years	8 Years	9 Years	10 Years	11 Years	12 Years	13 Years	14 Years
AMOUNT														
5	.46	.25	.18	.14	.12	.11	.10	.10	.09	.09	.08	.08	.08	.08
10	.91	.49	.35	.28	.24	.22	.20	.19	.18	.17	.16	.16	.15	.15
15	1.36	.73	.53	.42	.36	.32	.30	.28	.26	.25	.24	.23	.23	.22
25	2.26	1.22	.87	.70	.60	.54	.49	.46	.43	.41	.40	.38	.37	.37
50	4.52	2.44	1.74	1.40	1.20	1.07	.98	.91	.86	.82	.79	.76	.74	.73
75	6.78	3.65	2.61	2.10	1.80	1.60	1.46	1.36	1.29	1.23	1.18	1.14	1.11	1.09
100	9.04	4.87	3.48	2.80	2.40	2.13	1.95	1.81	1.71	1.63	1.57	1.52	1.48	1.45
200	18.08	9.73	6.96	5.60	4.79	4.26	3.89	3.62	3.42	3.26	3.14	3.04	2.96	2.89
300	27.12	14.59	10.44	8.39	7.18	6.39	5.84	5.43	5.13	4.89	4.70	4.56	4.44	4.34
400	36.16	19.45	13.92	11.19	9.57	8.52	7.78	7.24	6.83	6.52	6.27	6.07	5.91	5.78
500	45.19	24.31	17.40	13.98	11.97	10.65	9.72	9.05	8.54	8.15	7.84	7.59	7.39	7.22
600	54.23	29.17	20.88	16.78	14.36	12.77	11.67	10.86	10.25	9.78	9.40	9.11	8.87	8.67
700	63.27	34.03	24.36	19.58	16.75	14.90	13.61	12.67	11.96	11.41	10.97	10.62	10.34	10.11
800	72.31	38.89	27.84	22.37	19.14	17.03	15.55	14.48	13.66	13.03	12.54	12.14	11.82	11.56
900	81.34	43.75	31.31	25.17	21.53	19.16	17.50	16.29	15.37	14.66	14.10	13.66	13.30	13.00
1000	90.38	48.61	34.79	27.96	23.93	21.29	19.44	18.10	17.08	16.29	15.67	15.18	14.77	14.44
2000	180.76	97.22	69.58	55.92	47.85	42.57	38.88	36.19	34.15	32.58	31.34	30.35	29.54	28.88
3000	271.13	145.82	104.37	83.88	71.77	63.85	58.32	54.28	51.23	48.87	47.00	45.52	44.31	43.32
4000	361.51	194.43	139.16	111.84	95.69	85.13	77.75	72.37	68.30	65.15	62.67	60.69	59.08	57.76
5000	451.89	243.03	173.94	139.79	119.61	106.41	97.19	90.46	85.37	81.44	78.34	75.86	73.84	72.20
6000	542.26	291.64	208.73	167.75	143.53	127.69	116.63	108.55	102.45	97.73	94.00	91.03	88.61	86.64
7000	632.64	340.24	243.52	195.71	167.45	148.97	136.07	126.64	119.52	114.01	109.67	106.20	103.38	101.08
8000	723.02	388.85	278.31	223.67	191.38	170.25	155.50	144.73	136.59	130.30	125.34	121.37	118.15	115.52
9000	813.39	437.45	313.10	251.62	215.30	191.53	174.94	162.82	153.67	146.59	141.00	136.54	132.92	129.95
10000	903.77	486.06	347.88	279.58	239.22	212.82	194.38	180.91	170.74	162.87	156.67	151.71	147.68	144.39
11000	994.14	534.67	382.67	307.54	263.14	234.10	213.82	199.00	187.81	179.16	172.34	166.88	162.45	158.83
12000	1084.52	583.27	417.46	335.50	287.06	255.38	233.25	217.09	204.89	195.45	188.00	182.05	177.22	173.27
13000	1174.90	631.88	452.25	363.45	310.98	276.66	252.69	235.18	221.96	211.74	203.67	197.22	191.99	187.71
14000	1265.27	680.48	487.04	391.41	334.90	297.94	272.13	253.27	239.04	228.02	219.34	212.39	206.75	202.15
15000	1355.65	729.09	521.82	419.37	358.83	319.22	291.56	271.36	256.11	244.31	235.00	227.56	221.52	216.59
16000	1446.03	777.69	556.61	447.33	382.75	340.50	311.00	289.45	273.18	260.60	250.67	242.73	236.29	231.03
17000	1536.40	826.30	591.40	475.28	406.67	361.78	330.44	307.54	290.26	276.88	266.34	257.90	251.06	245.46
18000	1626.78	874.90	626.19	503.24	430.59	383.06	349.88	325.63	307.33	293.17	282.00	273.07	265.83	259.90
19000	1717.16	923.51	660.97	531.20	454.51	404.34	369.31	343.72	324.40	309.46	297.67	288.24	280.59	274.34
20000	1807.53	972.12	695.76	559.16	478.43	425.63	388.75	361.81	341.48	325.74	313.34	303.41	295.36	288.78
21000	1897.91	1020.72	730.55	587.12	502.35	446.91	408.19	379.90	358.55	342.03	329.00	318.58	310.13	303.22
22000	1988.28	1069.33	765.34	615.07	526.27	468.19	427.63	397.99	375.62	358.32	344.67	333.75	324.90	317.66
23000	2078.66	1117.93	800.13	643.03	550.20	489.47	447.06	416.08	392.70	374.60	360.34	348.92	339.66	332.10
24000	2169.04	1166.54	834.91	670.99	574.12	510.75	466.50	434.17	409.77	390.89	376.00	364.09	354.43	346.54
25000	2259.41	1215.14	869.70	698.95	598.04	532.03	485.94	452.26	426.85	407.18	391.67	379.26	369.20	360.97
26000	2349.79	1263.75	904.49	726.90	621.96	553.31	505.37	470.35	443.92	423.47	407.34	394.43	383.97	375.41
27000	2440.17	1312.35	939.28	754.86	645.88	574.59	524.81	488.44	460.99	439.75	423.00	409.60	398.74	389.85
28000	2530.54	1360.96	974.07	782.82	669.80	595.87	544.25	506.54	478.07	456.04	438.67	424.77	413.50	404.29
29000	2620.92	1409.56	1008.85	810.78	693.72	617.15	563.69	524.63	495.14	472.33	454.34	439.94	428.27	418.73
30000	2711.29	1458.17	1043.64	838.73	717.65	638.44	583.12	542.72	512.21	488.61	470.00	455.11	443.04	433.17
31000	2801.67	1506.78	1078.43	866.69	741.57	659.72	602.56	560.81	529.29	504.90	485.67	470.28	457.81	447.61
32000	2892.05	1555.38	1113.22	894.65	765.49	681.00	622.00	578.90	546.36	521.19	501.34	485.45	472.57	462.05
33000	2982.42	1603.99	1148.01	922.61	789.41	702.28	641.44	596.99	563.43	537.47	517.00	500.62	487.34	476.48
34000	3072.80	1652.59	1182.79	950.56	813.33	723.56	660.87	615.08	580.51	553.76	532.67	515.79	502.11	490.92
35000	3163.18	1701.20	1217.58	978.52	837.25	744.84	680.31	633.17	597.58	570.05	548.34	530.96	516.88	505.36
36000	3253.55	1749.80	1252.37	1006.48	861.17	766.12	699.75	651.26	614.66	586.33	564.00	546.13	531.65	519.80
37000	3343.93	1798.41	1287.16	1034.44	885.10	787.40	719.18	669.35	631.73	602.62	579.67	561.30	546.41	534.24
38000	3434.31	1847.01	1321.94	1062.40	909.02	808.68	738.62	687.44	648.80	618.91	595.34	576.47	561.18	548.68
39000	3524.68	1895.62	1356.73	1090.35	932.94	829.96	758.06	705.53	665.88	635.20	611.00	591.64	575.95	563.12
40000	3615.06	1944.23	1391.52	1118.31	956.86	851.25	777.50	723.62	682.95	651.48	626.67	606.81	590.72	577.56
41000	3705.43	1992.83	1426.31	1146.27	980.78	872.53	796.93	741.71	700.02	667.77	642.34	621.98	605.48	591.99
42000	3795.81	2041.44	1461.10	1174.23	1004.70	893.81	816.37	759.80	717.10	684.06	658.00	637.15	620.25	606.43
43000	3886.19	2090.04	1495.88	1202.18	1028.62	915.09	835.81	777.89	734.17	700.34	673.67	652.32	635.02	620.87
44000	3976.56	2138.65	1530.67	1230.14	1052.54	936.37	855.25	795.98	751.24	716.63	689.33	667.49	649.79	635.31
45000	4066.94	2187.25	1565.46	1258.10	1076.47	957.65	874.68	814.07	768.32	732.92	705.00	682.66	664.56	649.75
46000	4157.32	2235.86	1600.25	1286.06	1100.39	978.93	894.12	832.16	785.39	749.20	720.67	697.83	679.32	664.19
47000	4247.69	2284.46	1635.04	1314.01	1124.31	1000.21	913.56	850.25	802.46	765.49	736.33	713.00	694.09	678.63
48000	4338.07	2333.07	1669.82	1341.97	1148.23	1021.49	932.99	868.34	819.54	781.78	752.00	728.17	708.86	693.07
49000	4428.44	2381.68	1704.61	1369.93	1172.15	1042.77	952.43	886.43	836.61	798.06	767.67	743.34	723.63	707.50
50000	4518.82	2430.28	1739.40	1397.89	1196.07	1064.06	971.87	904.52	853.69	814.35	783.33	758.51	738.39	721.94
55000	4970.70	2673.31	1913.34	1537.68	1315.68	1170.46	1069.06	994.98	939.05	895.79	861.67	834.36	812.23	794.14
60000	5422.58	2916.34	2087.28	1677.46	1435.29	1276.87	1166.24	1085.43	1024.42	977.22	940.00	910.21	886.07	866.33
65000	5874.47	3159.36	2261.22	1817.25	1554.89	1383.27	1263.43	1175.88	1109.79	1058.66	1018.33	986.06	959.91	938.52
70000	6326.35	3402.39	2435.16	1957.04	1674.50	1489.68	1360.61	1266.33	1195.16	1140.09	1096.67	1061.91	1033.75	1010.72
75000	6778.23	3645.42	2609.10	2096.83	1794.11	1596.08	1457.80	1356.78	1280.53	1221.53	1175.00	1137.76	1107.59	1082.91
80000	7230.11	3888.45	2783.04	2236.62	1913.71	1702.49	1554.99	1447.23	1365.89	1302.96	1253.33	1213.61	1181.43	1155.11
85000	7681.99	4131.47	2956.97	2376.40	2033.32	1808.89	1652.17	1537.69	1451.26	1384.39	1331.67	1289.46	1255.27	1227.30
90000	8133.87	4374.50	3130.91	2516.19	2152.93	1915.30	1749.36	1628.14	1536.63	1465.83	1410.00	1365.31	1329.11	1299.49
95000	8585.76	4617.53	3304.85	2655.98	2272.53	2021.70	1846.55	1718.59	1622.00	1547.26	1488.33	1441.16	1402.94	1371.69
100000	9037.64	4860.56	3478.79	2795.77	2392.14	2128.11	1943.73	1809.04	1707.37	1628.70	1566.66	1517.01	1476.78	1443.88

TERM	15 Years	16 Years	17 Years	18 Years	19 Years	20 Years	21 Years	22 Years	23 Years	24 Years	25 Years	30 Years	35 Years	40 Years
AMOUNT														
5	.08	.07	.07	.07	.07	.07	.07	.07	.07	.07	.07	.07	.07	.07
10	.15	.14	.14	.14	.14	.14	.14	.14	.14	.14	.14	.13	.13	.13
15	.22	.21	.21	.21	.21	.21	.20	.20	.20	.20	.20	.20	.20	.20
25	.36	.35	.35	.34	.34	.34	.34	.33	.33	.33	.33	.33	.32	.32
50	.71	.70	.69	.68	.68	.67	.67	.66	.66	.66	.66	.65	.64	.64
75	1.07	1.05	1.04	1.02	1.01	1.01	1.00	.99	.99	.98	.98	.97	.96	.96
100	1.42	1.40	1.38	1.36	1.35	1.34	1.33	1.32	1.32	1.31	1.31	1.29	1.28	1.28
200	2.84	2.79	2.76	2.72	2.70	2.68	2.66	2.64	2.63	2.62	2.61	2.57	2.56	2.55
300	4.26	4.19	4.13	4.08	4.04	4.01	3.98	3.96	3.94	3.92	3.91	3.86	3.84	3.83
400	5.67	5.58	5.51	5.44	5.39	5.35	5.31	5.28	5.25	5.23	5.21	5.14	5.11	5.10
500	7.09	6.98	6.88	6.80	6.74	6.68	6.63	6.59	6.56	6.53	6.51	6.43	6.39	6.37
600	8.51	8.37	8.26	8.16	8.08	8.02	7.96	7.91	7.87	7.84	7.81	7.71	7.67	7.65
700	9.92	9.76	9.63	9.52	9.43	9.35	9.29	9.23	9.18	9.14	9.11	9.00	8.95	8.92
800	11.34	11.16	11.01	10.88	10.78	10.69	10.61	10.55	10.49	10.45	10.41	10.28	10.22	10.20
900	12.76	12.55	12.38	12.24	12.12	12.02	11.94	11.87	11.80	11.75	11.71	11.57	11.50	11.47
1000	14.17	13.95	13.76	13.60	13.47	13.36	13.26	13.18	13.12	13.06	13.01	12.85	12.78	12.74
2000	28.34	27.89	27.51	27.20	26.93	26.71	26.52	26.36	26.23	26.11	26.01	25.69	25.55	25.48
3000	42.51	41.83	41.27	40.80	40.40	40.06	39.78	39.54	39.34	39.16	39.01	38.54	38.32	38.22
4000	56.67	55.77	55.02	54.39	53.86	53.42	53.04	52.72	52.45	52.21	52.02	51.38	51.09	50.96
5000	70.84	69.72	68.78	67.99	67.33	66.77	66.30	65.90	65.56	65.27	65.02	64.23	63.86	63.70
6000	85.01	83.66	82.53	81.59	80.79	80.12	79.56	79.07	78.67	78.32	78.02	77.07	76.64	76.43
7000	99.18	97.60	96.29	95.19	94.26	93.48	92.81	92.25	91.78	91.37	91.02	89.92	89.41	89.17
8000	113.34	111.54	110.04	108.78	107.72	106.83	106.07	105.43	104.89	104.42	104.03	102.76	102.18	101.91
9000	127.51	125.49	123.80	122.38	121.19	120.18	119.33	118.61	118.00	117.47	117.03	115.61	114.95	114.65
10000	141.68	139.43	137.55	135.98	134.65	133.53	132.59	131.79	131.11	130.53	130.03	128.45	127.72	127.39
11000	155.85	153.37	151.31	149.57	148.12	146.89	145.85	144.97	144.22	143.58	143.03	141.30	140.50	140.12
12000	170.01	167.31	165.06	163.17	161.58	160.24	159.11	158.14	157.33	156.63	156.04	154.14	153.27	152.86
13000	184.18	181.26	178.81	176.77	175.05	173.59	172.36	171.32	170.44	169.68	169.04	166.98	166.04	165.60
14000	198.35	195.20	192.57	190.37	188.51	186.95	185.62	184.50	183.55	182.73	182.04	179.83	178.81	178.34
15000	212.52	209.14	206.32	203.96	201.98	200.30	198.88	197.68	196.66	195.79	195.04	192.67	191.58	191.08
16000	226.68	223.08	220.08	217.56	215.44	213.65	212.14	210.86	209.77	208.84	208.05	205.52	204.35	203.81
17000	240.85	237.03	233.83	231.16	228.91	227.01	225.40	224.03	222.88	221.89	221.05	218.36	217.13	216.55
18000	255.02	250.97	247.59	244.75	242.37	240.36	238.66	237.21	235.99	234.94	234.05	231.21	229.90	229.29
19000	269.19	264.91	261.34	258.35	255.84	253.71	251.91	250.39	249.10	247.99	247.05	244.05	242.67	242.03
20000	283.35	278.85	275.10	271.95	269.30	267.06	265.17	263.57	262.21	261.05	260.06	256.90	255.44	254.77
21000	297.52	292.80	288.85	285.55	282.76	280.42	278.43	276.75	275.32	274.10	273.06	269.74	268.21	267.50
22000	311.69	306.74	302.61	299.14	296.23	293.77	291.69	289.93	288.43	287.15	286.06	282.59	280.99	280.24
23000	325.86	320.68	316.36	312.74	309.69	307.12	304.95	303.10	301.54	300.20	299.06	295.43	293.76	292.98
24000	340.02	334.62	330.11	326.34	323.16	320.48	318.21	316.28	314.65	313.25	312.07	308.28	306.53	305.72
25000	354.19	348.56	343.87	339.93	336.62	333.83	331.47	329.46	327.76	326.31	325.07	321.12	319.30	318.46
26000	368.36	362.51	357.62	353.53	350.09	347.18	344.72	342.64	340.87	339.36	338.07	333.96	332.07	331.19
27000	382.53	376.45	371.38	367.13	363.55	360.54	357.98	355.82	353.98	352.41	351.07	346.81	344.84	343.93
28000	396.69	390.39	385.13	380.73	377.02	373.89	371.24	368.99	367.09	365.46	364.08	359.65	357.62	356.67
29000	410.86	404.33	398.89	394.32	390.48	387.24	384.50	382.17	380.20	378.51	377.08	372.50	370.39	369.41
30000	425.03	418.28	412.64	407.92	403.95	400.59	397.76	395.35	393.31	391.57	390.08	385.34	383.16	382.15
31000	439.20	432.22	426.40	421.52	417.41	413.95	411.02	408.53	406.42	404.62	403.09	398.19	395.93	394.88
32000	453.36	446.16	440.15	435.11	430.88	427.30	424.27	421.71	419.53	417.67	416.09	411.03	408.70	407.62
33000	467.53	460.10	453.91	448.71	444.34	440.65	437.53	434.89	432.64	430.72	429.09	423.88	421.48	420.36
34000	481.70	474.05	467.66	462.31	457.81	454.01	450.79	448.06	445.75	443.77	442.09	436.72	434.25	433.10
35000	495.87	487.99	481.42	475.91	471.27	467.36	464.05	461.24	458.86	456.83	455.10	449.57	447.02	445.84
36000	510.03	501.93	495.17	489.50	484.74	480.71	477.31	474.42	471.97	469.88	468.10	462.41	459.79	458.57
37000	524.20	515.87	508.92	503.10	498.20	494.07	490.57	487.60	485.08	482.93	481.10	475.25	472.56	471.31
38000	538.37	529.82	522.68	516.70	511.67	507.42	503.82	500.78	498.19	495.98	494.10	488.10	485.33	484.05
39000	552.54	543.76	536.43	530.29	525.13	520.77	517.08	513.95	511.30	509.03	507.11	500.94	498.11	496.79
40000	566.70	557.70	550.19	543.89	538.59	534.12	530.34	527.13	524.41	522.09	520.11	513.79	510.88	509.53
41000	580.87	571.64	563.94	557.49	552.06	547.48	543.60	540.31	537.52	535.14	533.11	526.63	523.65	522.26
42000	595.04	585.59	577.70	571.09	565.52	560.83	556.86	553.49	550.63	548.19	546.11	539.48	536.42	535.00
43000	609.21	599.53	591.45	584.68	578.99	574.18	570.12	566.67	563.74	561.24	559.12	552.32	549.19	547.74
44000	623.37	613.47	605.21	598.28	592.45	587.54	583.38	579.85	576.85	574.29	572.12	565.17	561.97	560.48
45000	637.54	627.41	618.96	611.88	605.92	600.89	596.63	593.02	589.96	587.35	585.12	578.01	574.74	573.22
46000	651.71	641.36	632.72	625.47	619.38	614.24	609.89	606.20	603.07	600.40	598.12	590.86	587.51	585.95
47000	665.88	655.30	646.47	639.07	632.85	627.60	623.15	619.38	616.18	613.45	611.13	603.70	600.28	598.69
48000	680.04	669.24	660.22	652.67	646.31	640.95	636.41	632.56	629.29	626.50	624.13	616.55	613.05	611.43
49000	694.21	683.18	673.98	666.27	659.78	654.30	649.67	645.74	642.40	639.55	637.13	629.39	625.83	624.17
50000	708.38	697.12	687.73	679.86	673.24	667.65	662.93	658.92	655.51	652.61	650.13	642.23	638.60	636.91
55000	779.22	766.84	756.51	747.85	740.57	734.42	729.22	724.81	721.06	717.87	715.15	706.46	702.46	700.60
60000	850.05	836.55	825.28	815.84	807.89	801.18	795.51	790.70	786.61	783.13	780.16	770.68	766.32	764.29
65000	920.89	906.26	894.05	883.82	875.21	867.95	861.80	856.59	852.16	848.39	845.17	834.90	830.17	827.98
70000	991.73	975.97	962.83	951.81	942.54	934.71	928.09	922.48	917.71	913.65	910.19	899.13	894.03	891.67
75000	1062.57	1045.68	1031.60	1019.79	1009.86	1001.48	994.39	988.37	983.26	978.91	975.20	963.35	957.89	955.36
80000	1133.40	1115.40	1100.37	1087.78	1077.18	1068.24	1060.68	1054.26	1048.81	1044.17	1040.21	1027.57	1021.75	1019.05
85000	1204.24	1185.11	1169.14	1155.76	1144.51	1135.01	1126.97	1120.15	1114.36	1109.43	1105.22	1091.79	1085.61	1082.74
90000	1275.08	1254.82	1237.92	1223.75	1211.83	1201.77	1193.26	1186.04	1179.91	1174.69	1170.24	1156.02	1149.47	1146.43
95000	1345.92	1324.53	1306.69	1291.74	1279.16	1268.54	1259.55	1251.93	1245.46	1239.95	1235.25	1220.24	1213.33	1210.12
100000	1416.75	1394.24	1375.46	1359.72	1346.48	1335.30	1325.85	1317.83	1311.01	1305.21	1300.26	1284.46	1277.19	1273.81

MONTHLY PAYMENT
REQUIRED TO AMORTIZE A LOAN

TERM / AMOUNT	1 Year	2 Years	3 Years	4 Years	5 Years	6 Years	7 Years	8 Years	9 Years	10 Years	11 Years	12 Years	13 Years	14 Years
5	.46	.25	.18	.14	.12	.11	.10	.10	.09	.09	.08	.08	.08	.08
10	.91	.49	.35	.28	.24	.22	.20	.19	.18	.17	.16	.16	.15	.15
15	1.36	.73	.53	.42	.36	.32	.30	.28	.26	.25	.24	.23	.23	.22
25	2.26	1.22	.88	.70	.60	.54	.49	.46	.43	.41	.40	.39	.38	.37
50	4.52	2.44	1.75	1.40	1.20	1.07	.98	.91	.86	.82	.79	.77	.75	.73
75	6.78	3.65	2.62	2.10	1.80	1.60	1.46	1.36	1.29	1.23	1.18	1.15	1.12	1.09
100	9.04	4.87	3.49	2.80	2.40	2.14	1.95	1.82	1.72	1.64	1.57	1.53	1.49	1.45
200	18.08	9.73	6.97	5.60	4.79	4.27	3.90	3.63	3.43	3.27	3.14	3.05	2.97	2.90
300	27.12	14.59	10.45	8.40	7.19	6.40	5.84	5.44	5.14	4.90	4.71	4.57	4.45	4.35
400	36.16	19.46	13.93	11.20	9.58	8.53	7.79	7.25	6.85	6.53	6.28	6.09	5.93	5.79
500	45.20	24.32	17.41	14.00	11.98	10.66	9.74	9.06	8.56	8.16	7.85	7.61	7.41	7.24
600	54.24	29.18	20.89	16.79	14.37	12.79	11.68	10.88	10.27	9.80	9.42	9.13	8.89	8.69
700	63.28	34.05	24.37	19.59	16.77	14.92	13.63	12.69	11.98	11.43	10.99	10.65	10.37	10.14
800	72.32	38.91	27.85	22.39	19.16	17.05	15.58	14.50	13.69	13.06	12.56	12.17	11.85	11.58
900	81.36	43.77	31.34	25.19	21.56	19.18	17.52	16.31	15.40	14.69	14.13	13.69	13.33	13.03
1000	90.40	48.63	34.82	27.99	23.95	21.31	19.47	18.12	17.11	16.32	15.70	15.21	14.81	14.48
2000	180.80	97.26	69.63	55.97	47.90	42.62	38.94	36.24	34.21	32.64	31.40	30.41	29.61	28.95
3000	271.20	145.89	104.44	83.95	71.85	63.93	58.40	54.36	51.32	48.96	47.10	45.61	44.41	43.42
4000	361.60	194.52	139.25	111.94	95.80	85.24	77.87	72.48	68.42	65.28	62.80	60.81	59.21	57.90
5000	452.00	243.15	174.07	139.92	119.74	106.55	97.33	90.60	85.52	81.59	78.50	76.02	74.01	72.37
6000	542.40	291.78	208.88	167.90	143.69	127.85	116.80	108.72	102.63	97.91	94.19	91.22	88.81	86.84
7000	632.80	340.41	243.69	195.89	167.64	149.16	136.26	126.84	119.73	114.23	109.89	106.42	103.61	101.31
8000	723.20	389.04	278.50	223.87	191.59	170.47	155.73	144.96	136.83	130.55	125.59	121.62	118.41	115.79
9000	813.60	437.67	313.32	251.85	215.53	191.78	175.19	163.08	153.94	146.86	141.29	136.83	133.21	130.26
10000	904.00	486.30	348.13	279.84	239.48	213.09	194.66	181.20	171.04	163.18	156.99	152.03	148.01	144.73
11000	994.40	534.93	382.94	307.82	263.43	234.40	214.12	199.32	188.14	179.50	172.68	167.23	162.81	159.20
12000	1084.80	583.56	417.75	335.80	287.38	255.70	233.59	217.44	205.25	195.82	188.38	182.43	177.62	173.68
13000	1175.20	632.19	452.57	363.78	311.33	277.01	253.06	235.56	222.35	212.14	204.08	197.64	192.42	188.15
14000	1265.60	680.82	487.38	391.77	335.27	298.32	272.52	253.68	239.45	228.45	219.78	212.84	207.22	202.62
15000	1356.00	729.44	522.19	419.75	359.22	319.63	291.99	271.80	256.56	244.77	235.48	228.04	222.02	217.09
16000	1446.40	778.07	557.00	447.73	383.17	340.94	311.45	289.92	273.66	261.09	251.18	243.24	236.82	231.57
17000	1536.80	826.70	591.82	475.72	407.12	362.25	330.92	308.04	290.77	277.41	266.87	258.45	251.62	246.04
18000	1627.20	875.33	626.63	503.70	431.06	383.55	350.38	326.15	307.87	293.72	282.57	273.65	266.42	260.51
19000	1717.60	923.96	661.44	531.68	455.01	404.86	369.85	344.27	324.97	310.04	298.27	288.85	281.22	274.98
20000	1808.00	972.59	696.25	559.67	478.96	426.17	389.31	362.39	342.08	326.36	313.97	304.05	296.02	289.46
21000	1898.40	1021.22	731.07	587.65	502.91	447.48	408.78	380.51	359.18	342.68	329.67	319.25	310.82	303.93
22000	1988.80	1069.85	765.88	615.63	526.85	468.79	428.24	398.63	376.28	358.99	345.36	334.46	325.62	318.40
23000	2079.20	1118.48	800.69	643.62	550.80	490.10	447.71	416.75	393.39	375.31	361.06	349.66	340.42	332.87
24000	2169.60	1167.11	835.50	671.60	574.75	511.40	467.18	434.87	410.49	391.63	376.76	364.86	355.23	347.35
25000	2260.00	1215.74	870.32	699.58	598.70	532.71	486.64	452.99	427.59	407.95	392.46	380.06	370.03	361.82
26000	2350.40	1264.37	905.13	727.56	622.65	554.02	506.11	471.11	444.70	424.27	408.16	395.27	384.83	376.29
27000	2440.80	1313.00	939.94	755.55	646.59	575.33	525.57	489.23	461.80	440.58	423.86	410.47	399.63	390.76
28000	2531.20	1361.63	974.75	783.53	670.54	596.64	545.04	507.35	478.90	456.90	439.55	425.67	414.43	405.24
29000	2621.60	1410.25	1009.57	811.51	694.49	617.94	564.50	525.47	496.01	473.22	455.25	440.87	429.23	419.71
30000	2712.00	1458.88	1044.38	839.50	718.44	639.25	583.97	543.59	513.11	489.54	470.95	456.08	444.03	434.18
31000	2802.40	1507.51	1079.19	867.48	742.38	660.56	603.43	561.71	530.21	505.85	486.65	471.28	458.83	448.65
32000	2892.80	1556.14	1114.00	895.46	766.33	681.87	622.90	579.83	547.32	522.17	502.35	486.48	473.63	463.13
33000	2983.20	1604.77	1148.81	923.45	790.28	703.18	642.36	597.95	564.42	538.49	518.04	501.68	488.43	477.60
34000	3073.60	1653.40	1183.63	951.43	814.23	724.49	661.83	616.07	581.53	554.81	533.74	516.89	503.23	492.07
35000	3164.00	1702.03	1218.44	979.41	838.17	745.79	681.30	634.19	598.63	571.12	549.44	532.09	518.04	506.54
36000	3254.40	1750.66	1253.25	1007.40	862.12	767.10	700.76	652.30	615.73	587.44	565.14	547.29	532.84	521.02
37000	3344.80	1799.29	1288.06	1035.38	886.07	788.41	720.23	670.42	632.84	603.76	580.84	562.49	547.64	535.49
38000	3435.20	1847.92	1322.88	1063.36	910.02	809.72	739.69	688.54	649.94	620.08	596.54	577.70	562.44	549.96
39000	3525.60	1896.55	1357.69	1091.34	933.97	831.03	759.16	706.66	667.04	636.40	612.23	592.90	577.24	564.43
40000	3616.00	1945.18	1392.50	1119.33	957.91	852.34	778.62	724.78	684.15	652.71	627.93	608.10	592.04	578.91
41000	3706.40	1993.81	1427.31	1147.31	981.86	873.64	798.09	742.90	701.25	669.03	643.63	623.30	606.84	593.38
42000	3796.80	2042.44	1462.13	1175.29	1005.81	894.95	817.55	761.02	718.35	685.35	659.33	638.50	621.64	607.85
43000	3887.20	2091.07	1496.94	1203.28	1029.76	916.26	837.02	779.14	735.46	701.67	675.03	653.71	636.44	622.32
44000	3977.60	2139.69	1531.75	1231.26	1053.70	937.57	856.48	797.26	752.56	717.98	690.72	668.91	651.24	636.80
45000	4068.00	2188.32	1566.56	1259.24	1077.65	958.88	875.95	815.38	769.66	734.30	706.42	684.11	666.04	651.27
46000	4158.40	2236.95	1601.38	1287.23	1101.60	980.19	895.42	833.50	786.77	750.62	722.12	699.31	680.84	665.74
47000	4248.80	2285.58	1636.19	1315.21	1125.55	1001.49	914.88	851.62	803.87	766.94	737.82	714.52	695.65	680.21
48000	4339.20	2334.21	1671.00	1343.19	1149.49	1022.80	934.35	869.74	820.98	783.25	753.52	729.72	710.45	694.69
49000	4429.60	2382.84	1705.81	1371.17	1173.44	1044.11	953.81	887.86	838.08	799.57	769.22	744.92	725.25	709.16
50000	4520.00	2431.47	1740.63	1399.16	1197.39	1065.42	973.28	905.98	855.18	815.89	784.91	760.12	740.05	723.63
55000	4972.00	2674.62	1914.69	1539.07	1317.13	1171.96	1070.61	996.57	940.70	897.48	863.40	836.14	814.05	795.99
60000	5424.00	2917.76	2088.75	1678.99	1436.87	1278.50	1167.93	1087.17	1026.22	979.07	941.89	912.15	888.06	868.36
65000	5876.00	3160.91	2262.81	1818.90	1556.61	1385.04	1265.26	1177.77	1111.74	1060.66	1020.39	988.16	962.06	940.72
70000	6328.00	3404.06	2436.87	1958.82	1676.34	1491.58	1362.59	1268.37	1197.25	1142.24	1098.88	1064.17	1036.07	1013.08
75000	6780.00	3647.20	2610.94	2098.73	1796.08	1598.13	1459.91	1358.96	1282.77	1223.83	1177.37	1140.18	1110.07	1085.44
80000	7232.00	3890.35	2785.00	2238.65	1915.82	1704.67	1557.24	1449.56	1368.29	1305.42	1255.86	1216.20	1184.07	1157.81
85000	7684.00	4133.50	2959.06	2378.56	2035.56	1811.21	1654.57	1540.16	1453.81	1387.01	1334.35	1292.25	1258.08	1230.17
90000	8136.00	4376.64	3133.12	2518.48	2155.30	1917.75	1751.90	1630.75	1539.32	1468.60	1412.84	1368.22	1332.08	1302.53
95000	8588.00	4619.79	3307.18	2658.40	2275.04	2024.29	1849.22	1721.35	1624.84	1550.19	1491.33	1444.23	1406.09	1374.90
100000	9040.00	4862.94	3481.25	2798.31	2394.77	2130.83	1946.55	1811.95	1710.36	1631.78	1569.82	1520.24	1480.09	1447.26

TERM	15 Years	16 Years	17 Years	18 Years	19 Years	20 Years	21 Years	22 Years	23 Years	24 Years	25 Years	30 Years	35 Years	40 Years
AMOUNT														
5	.08	.07	.07	.07	.07	.07	.07	.07	.07	.07	.07	.07	.07	.07
10	.15	.14	.14	.14	.14	.14	.14	.14	.14	.14	.14	.13	.13	.13
15	.22	.21	.21	.21	.21	.21	.20	.20	.20	.20	.20	.20	.20	.20
25	.36	.35	.35	.35	.34	.34	.34	.34	.33	.33	.33	.33	.33	.32
50	.72	.70	.69	.69	.68	.67	.67	.67	.66	.66	.66	.65	.65	.64
75	1.07	1.05	1.04	1.03	1.02	1.01	1.00	1.00	.99	.99	.98	.97	.97	.96
100	1.43	1.40	1.38	1.37	1.36	1.34	1.33	1.33	1.32	1.31	1.31	1.29	1.29	1.28
200	2.85	2.80	2.76	2.73	2.71	2.68	2.66	2.65	2.63	2.62	2.61	2.58	2.57	2.56
300	4.27	4.20	4.14	4.09	4.06	4.02	3.99	3.97	3.95	3.93	3.92	3.87	3.85	3.84
400	5.69	5.60	5.52	5.46	5.41	5.36	5.32	5.29	5.26	5.24	5.22	5.16	5.13	5.12
500	7.11	6.99	6.90	6.82	6.76	6.70	6.65	6.61	6.58	6.55	6.53	6.45	6.41	6.39
600	8.53	8.39	8.28	8.18	8.11	8.04	7.98	7.93	7.89	7.86	7.83	7.74	7.69	7.67
700	9.95	9.79	9.66	9.55	9.46	9.38	9.31	9.26	9.21	9.17	9.13	9.02	8.97	8.95
800	11.37	11.19	11.04	10.91	10.81	10.72	10.64	10.58	10.52	10.48	10.44	10.31	10.26	10.23
900	12.79	12.58	12.42	12.27	12.16	12.06	11.97	11.90	11.84	11.79	11.74	11.60	11.54	11.51
1000	14.21	13.98	13.80	13.64	13.51	13.40	13.30	13.22	13.15	13.10	13.05	12.89	12.82	12.78
2000	28.41	27.96	27.59	27.27	27.01	26.79	26.60	26.44	26.30	26.19	26.09	25.77	25.63	25.56
3000	42.61	41.94	41.38	40.90	40.51	40.18	39.89	39.65	39.45	39.28	39.13	38.66	38.44	38.34
4000	56.81	55.91	55.17	54.54	54.01	53.57	53.19	52.87	52.60	52.37	52.17	51.54	51.26	51.12
5000	71.01	69.89	68.96	68.17	67.51	66.96	66.48	66.09	65.75	65.46	65.21	64.43	64.07	63.90
6000	85.22	83.87	82.75	81.80	81.01	80.35	79.78	79.30	78.90	78.55	78.25	77.31	76.88	76.68
7000	99.42	97.85	96.54	95.44	94.51	93.74	93.08	92.52	92.04	91.64	91.30	90.20	89.69	89.46
8000	113.62	111.82	110.33	109.07	108.02	107.13	106.37	105.73	105.19	104.73	104.34	103.08	102.51	102.24
9000	127.82	125.80	124.12	122.70	121.52	120.52	119.67	118.95	118.34	117.82	117.38	115.97	115.32	115.02
10000	142.02	139.78	137.91	136.34	135.02	133.91	132.96	132.17	131.49	130.91	130.42	128.85	128.13	127.80
11000	156.23	153.76	151.70	149.97	148.52	147.30	146.26	145.38	144.64	144.00	143.46	141.74	140.94	140.58
12000	170.43	167.73	165.49	163.60	162.02	160.69	159.56	158.60	157.79	157.09	156.50	154.62	153.76	153.36
13000	184.63	181.71	179.28	177.24	175.52	174.08	172.85	171.81	170.93	170.18	169.54	167.51	166.57	166.13
14000	198.83	195.69	193.07	190.87	189.02	187.47	186.15	185.03	184.08	183.27	182.59	180.39	179.38	178.91
15000	213.03	209.67	206.86	204.50	202.53	200.86	199.44	198.25	197.23	196.36	195.63	193.28	192.19	191.69
16000	227.24	223.64	220.65	218.14	216.03	214.25	212.74	211.46	210.38	209.46	208.67	206.16	205.01	204.47
17000	241.44	237.62	234.44	231.77	229.53	227.64	226.04	224.68	223.53	222.55	221.71	219.04	217.82	217.25
18000	255.64	251.60	248.23	245.40	243.03	241.03	239.33	237.90	236.68	235.64	234.75	231.93	230.63	230.03
19000	269.84	265.58	262.02	259.04	256.53	254.42	252.63	251.11	249.82	248.73	247.79	244.81	243.44	242.81
20000	284.04	279.55	275.81	272.67	270.03	267.81	265.92	264.33	262.97	261.82	260.84	257.70	256.26	255.59
21000	298.25	293.53	289.60	286.30	283.53	281.20	279.22	277.54	276.12	274.91	273.88	270.58	269.07	268.37
22000	312.45	307.51	303.39	299.94	297.04	294.59	292.52	290.76	289.27	288.00	286.92	283.47	281.88	281.15
23000	326.65	321.49	317.18	313.57	310.54	307.98	305.81	303.98	302.42	301.09	299.96	296.35	294.70	293.93
24000	340.85	335.46	330.97	327.20	324.04	321.37	319.11	317.19	315.57	314.18	313.00	309.24	307.51	306.71
25000	355.05	349.44	344.76	340.84	337.54	334.76	332.40	330.41	328.71	327.27	326.04	322.12	320.32	319.49
26000	369.25	363.42	358.55	354.47	351.04	348.15	345.70	343.62	341.86	340.36	339.08	335.01	333.13	332.26
27000	383.46	377.40	372.34	368.10	364.54	361.54	359.00	356.84	355.01	353.45	352.13	347.89	345.95	345.04
28000	397.66	391.37	386.13	381.74	378.04	374.93	372.29	370.06	368.16	366.54	365.17	360.78	358.76	357.82
29000	411.86	405.35	399.92	395.37	391.55	388.32	385.59	383.27	381.31	379.63	378.21	373.66	371.57	370.60
30000	426.06	419.33	413.71	409.00	405.05	401.71	398.88	396.49	394.46	392.72	391.25	386.55	384.38	383.38
31000	440.26	433.31	427.50	422.64	418.55	415.10	412.18	409.71	407.60	405.82	404.29	399.43	397.20	396.16
32000	454.47	447.28	441.29	436.27	432.05	428.49	425.48	422.92	420.75	418.91	417.33	412.31	410.01	408.94
33000	468.67	461.26	455.08	449.90	445.55	441.88	438.77	436.14	433.90	432.00	430.37	425.20	422.82	421.72
34000	482.87	475.24	468.87	463.54	459.05	455.27	452.07	449.35	447.05	445.09	443.42	438.08	435.63	434.50
35000	497.07	489.21	482.66	477.17	472.55	468.66	465.36	462.57	460.20	458.18	456.46	450.97	448.45	447.28
36000	511.27	503.19	496.45	490.80	486.06	482.05	478.66	475.79	473.35	471.27	469.50	463.85	461.26	460.06
37000	525.48	517.17	510.24	504.44	499.56	495.44	491.96	489.00	486.49	484.36	482.54	476.74	474.07	472.84
38000	539.68	531.15	524.03	518.07	513.06	508.83	505.25	502.22	499.64	497.45	495.58	489.62	486.88	485.61
39000	553.88	545.12	537.82	531.70	526.56	522.22	518.55	515.43	512.79	510.54	508.62	502.51	499.70	498.39
40000	568.00	559.10	551.61	545.34	540.06	535.61	531.84	528.65	525.94	523.63	521.67	515.39	512.51	511.17
41000	582.28	573.08	565.40	558.97	553.56	549.00	545.14	541.87	539.09	536.72	534.71	528.28	525.32	523.95
42000	596.49	587.06	579.19	572.60	567.06	562.39	558.43	555.08	552.24	549.81	547.75	541.16	538.13	536.73
43000	610.69	601.03	592.98	586.24	580.56	575.78	571.73	568.30	565.38	562.90	560.79	554.05	550.95	549.51
44000	624.89	615.01	606.77	599.87	594.07	589.17	585.03	581.51	578.53	575.99	573.83	566.93	563.76	562.29
45000	639.09	628.99	620.56	613.50	607.57	602.56	598.32	594.73	591.68	589.08	586.87	579.82	576.57	575.07
46000	653.29	642.97	634.35	627.14	621.07	615.95	611.62	607.95	604.83	602.18	599.91	592.70	589.39	587.85
47000	667.50	656.94	648.14	640.77	634.57	629.34	624.91	621.16	617.98	615.27	612.96	605.58	602.20	600.63
48000	681.70	670.92	661.93	654.40	648.07	642.73	638.21	634.38	631.13	628.36	626.00	618.47	615.01	613.41
49000	695.90	684.90	675.72	668.04	661.57	656.12	651.51	647.60	644.27	641.45	639.04	631.35	627.82	626.19
50000	710.10	698.88	689.51	681.67	675.07	669.51	664.80	660.81	657.42	654.54	652.08	644.24	640.64	638.97
55000	781.11	768.76	758.47	749.84	742.58	736.46	731.28	726.89	723.16	719.99	717.29	708.66	704.70	702.86
60000	852.12	838.65	827.42	818.00	810.09	803.41	797.76	792.97	788.91	785.44	782.50	773.09	768.76	766.76
65000	923.13	908.54	896.37	886.17	877.60	870.36	864.24	859.05	854.65	850.90	847.70	837.51	832.83	830.65
70000	994.14	978.42	965.32	954.34	945.10	937.31	930.72	925.13	920.39	916.35	912.91	901.93	896.89	894.55
75000	1065.15	1048.31	1034.27	1022.50	1012.61	1004.26	997.20	991.21	986.13	981.80	978.12	966.36	960.95	958.45
80000	1136.16	1118.20	1103.22	1090.67	1080.12	1071.21	1063.68	1057.30	1051.87	1047.26	1043.33	1030.78	1025.01	1022.34
85000	1207.17	1188.09	1172.17	1158.84	1147.62	1138.16	1130.16	1123.38	1117.61	1112.71	1108.53	1095.20	1089.08	1086.24
90000	1278.18	1257.97	1241.12	1227.00	1215.13	1205.11	1196.64	1189.46	1183.36	1178.16	1173.74	1159.63	1153.14	1150.13
95000	1349.19	1327.86	1310.07	1295.17	1282.64	1272.06	1263.12	1255.54	1249.10	1243.62	1238.95	1224.05	1217.20	1214.03
100000	1420.20	1397.75	1379.02	1363.34	1350.14	1339.01	1329.60	1321.62	1314.84	1309.07	1304.16	1288.47	1281.27	1277.93

MONTHLY PAYMENT
REQUIRED TO AMORTIZE A LOAN

TERM	1 Year	2 Years	3 Years	4 Years	5 Years	6 Years	7 Years	8 Years	9 Years	10 Years	11 Years	12 Years	13 Years	14 Years
AMOUNT														
5	.46	.25	.18	.15	.12	.11	.10	.10	.09	.09	.08	.08	.08	.08
10	.91	.49	.35	.29	.24	.22	.20	.19	.18	.17	.16	.16	.15	.15
15	1.36	.73	.53	.43	.36	.33	.30	.28	.26	.25	.24	.23	.23	.22
25	2.27	1.22	.88	.71	.60	.54	.49	.46	.43	.41	.40	.39	.38	.37
50	4.53	2.44	1.75	1.41	1.20	1.07	.98	.91	.86	.82	.79	.77	.75	.73
75	6.79	3.65	2.62	2.11	1.80	1.61	1.47	1.37	1.29	1.23	1.19	1.15	1.12	1.09
100	9.05	4.87	3.49	2.81	2.40	2.14	1.96	1.82	1.72	1.64	1.58	1.53	1.49	1.46
200	18.09	9.74	6.97	5.61	4.80	4.27	3.91	3.64	3.43	3.28	3.15	3.06	2.98	2.91
300	27.14	14.60	10.46	8.41	7.20	6.41	5.86	5.45	5.15	4.91	4.73	4.58	4.46	4.36
400	36.18	19.47	13.94	11.21	9.60	8.54	7.81	7.27	6.86	6.55	6.30	6.11	5.95	5.81
500	45.22	24.34	17.43	14.02	12.00	10.68	9.76	9.09	8.58	8.19	7.88	7.63	7.43	7.27
600	54.27	29.20	20.91	16.82	14.40	12.81	11.71	10.90	10.29	9.82	9.45	9.16	8.92	8.72
700	63.31	34.07	24.40	19.62	16.80	14.95	13.66	12.72	12.01	11.46	11.03	10.68	10.40	10.17
800	72.35	38.94	27.88	22.42	19.19	17.08	15.61	14.54	13.72	13.10	12.60	12.21	11.89	11.62
900	81.40	43.80	31.37	25.22	21.59	19.22	17.56	16.35	15.44	14.73	14.18	13.73	13.37	13.08
1000	90.44	48.67	34.85	28.03	23.99	21.35	19.51	18.17	17.15	16.37	15.75	15.26	14.86	14.53
2000	180.88	97.34	69.70	56.05	47.98	42.70	39.02	36.33	34.30	32.73	31.50	30.51	29.71	29.05
3000	271.31	146.00	104.55	84.07	71.97	64.05	58.53	54.49	51.45	49.10	47.24	45.76	44.56	43.57
4000	361.75	194.67	139.40	112.09	95.95	85.40	78.04	72.66	68.60	65.46	62.99	61.01	59.41	58.10
5000	452.18	243.33	174.25	140.11	119.94	106.75	97.54	90.82	85.75	81.82	78.73	76.26	74.26	72.62
6000	542.62	292.00	209.10	168.13	143.93	128.10	117.05	108.98	102.90	98.19	94.48	91.51	89.11	87.14
7000	633.05	340.66	243.95	196.15	167.92	149.45	136.56	127.15	120.04	114.55	110.22	106.76	103.96	101.67
8000	723.49	389.33	278.80	224.17	191.90	170.80	156.07	145.31	137.19	130.92	125.97	122.01	118.81	116.19
9000	813.92	437.99	313.65	252.20	215.89	192.15	175.57	163.47	154.34	147.28	141.72	137.26	133.66	130.71
10000	904.36	486.66	348.50	280.22	239.88	213.50	195.08	181.64	171.49	163.64	157.46	152.51	148.51	145.24
11000	994.79	535.32	383.35	308.24	263.86	234.85	214.59	199.80	188.64	180.01	173.21	167.77	163.36	159.76
12000	1085.23	583.99	418.20	336.26	287.85	256.20	234.10	217.96	205.79	196.37	188.95	183.02	178.21	174.28
13000	1175.66	632.65	453.05	364.28	311.84	277.54	253.61	236.12	222.94	212.74	204.70	198.27	193.06	188.81
14000	1266.10	681.32	487.89	392.30	335.83	298.89	273.11	254.29	240.08	229.10	220.44	213.52	207.91	203.33
15000	1356.54	729.98	522.74	420.32	359.81	320.24	292.62	272.45	257.23	245.46	236.19	228.77	222.76	217.85
16000	1446.97	778.65	557.59	448.34	383.80	341.59	312.13	290.61	274.38	261.83	251.93	244.02	237.61	232.38
17000	1537.41	827.31	592.44	476.37	407.79	362.94	331.64	308.78	291.53	278.19	267.68	259.27	252.46	246.90
18000	1627.84	875.98	627.29	504.39	431.78	384.29	351.14	326.94	308.68	294.56	283.43	274.52	267.31	261.42
19000	1718.28	924.64	662.14	532.41	455.76	405.64	370.65	345.10	325.83	310.92	299.17	289.77	282.16	275.95
20000	1808.71	973.31	696.99	560.43	479.75	426.99	390.16	363.27	342.97	327.28	314.92	305.02	297.02	290.47
21000	1899.15	1021.97	731.84	588.45	503.74	448.34	409.67	381.43	360.12	343.65	330.66	320.27	311.87	304.99
22000	1989.58	1070.64	766.69	616.47	527.72	469.69	429.18	399.59	377.27	360.01	346.41	335.53	326.72	319.52
23000	2080.02	1119.30	801.54	644.49	551.71	491.04	448.68	417.76	394.42	376.37	362.15	350.78	341.57	334.04
24000	2170.45	1167.97	836.39	672.51	575.70	512.39	468.19	435.92	411.57	392.74	377.90	366.03	356.42	348.56
25000	2260.89	1216.63	871.24	700.54	599.69	533.73	487.70	454.08	428.72	409.10	393.64	381.28	371.27	363.09
26000	2351.32	1265.30	906.09	728.56	623.67	555.08	507.21	472.24	445.87	425.47	409.39	396.53	386.12	377.61
27000	2441.76	1313.96	940.93	756.58	647.66	576.43	526.71	490.41	463.01	441.83	425.14	411.78	400.97	392.13
28000	2532.20	1362.63	975.78	784.60	671.65	597.78	546.22	508.57	480.16	458.19	440.88	427.03	415.82	406.66
29000	2622.63	1411.29	1010.63	812.62	695.63	619.13	565.73	526.73	497.31	474.56	456.63	442.28	430.67	421.18
30000	2713.07	1459.96	1045.48	840.64	719.62	640.48	585.24	544.90	514.46	490.92	472.37	457.53	445.52	435.70
31000	2803.50	1508.62	1080.33	868.66	743.61	661.83	604.75	563.06	531.61	507.29	488.12	472.78	460.37	450.23
32000	2893.94	1557.29	1115.18	896.68	767.60	683.18	624.25	581.22	548.76	523.65	503.86	488.04	475.22	464.75
33000	2984.37	1605.95	1150.03	924.70	791.58	704.53	643.76	599.39	565.91	540.01	519.61	503.29	490.07	479.27
34000	3074.81	1654.62	1184.88	952.73	815.57	725.88	663.27	617.55	583.05	556.38	535.35	518.54	504.92	493.79
35000	3165.24	1703.28	1219.73	980.75	839.56	747.23	682.78	635.71	600.20	572.74	551.10	533.79	519.77	508.32
36000	3255.68	1751.95	1254.58	1008.77	863.55	768.58	702.28	653.88	617.35	589.11	566.85	549.04	534.62	522.84
37000	3346.11	1800.61	1289.43	1036.79	887.53	789.93	721.79	672.04	634.50	605.47	582.59	564.29	549.47	537.36
38000	3436.55	1849.28	1324.28	1064.81	911.52	811.27	741.30	690.20	651.65	621.83	598.34	579.54	564.32	551.89
39000	3526.98	1897.94	1359.13	1092.83	935.51	832.62	760.81	708.36	668.80	638.20	614.08	594.79	579.18	566.41
40000	3617.42	1946.61	1393.98	1120.85	959.49	853.97	780.31	726.53	685.94	654.56	629.83	610.04	594.03	580.93
41000	3707.85	1995.27	1428.82	1148.87	983.48	875.32	799.82	744.69	703.09	670.93	645.57	625.29	608.88	595.46
42000	3798.29	2043.94	1463.67	1176.90	1007.47	896.67	819.33	762.85	720.24	687.29	661.32	640.54	623.73	609.98
43000	3888.73	2092.60	1498.52	1204.92	1031.46	918.02	838.84	781.02	737.39	703.65	677.06	655.80	638.58	624.50
44000	3979.16	2141.27	1533.37	1232.94	1055.44	939.37	858.35	799.18	754.54	720.02	692.81	671.05	653.43	639.03
45000	4069.60	2189.93	1568.22	1260.96	1079.43	960.72	877.85	817.34	771.69	736.38	708.56	686.30	668.28	653.55
46000	4160.03	2238.60	1603.07	1288.98	1103.42	982.07	897.36	835.51	788.84	752.74	724.30	701.55	683.13	668.07
47000	4250.47	2287.26	1637.92	1317.00	1127.40	1003.42	916.87	853.67	805.98	769.11	740.05	716.80	697.98	682.60
48000	4340.90	2335.93	1672.77	1345.02	1151.39	1024.77	936.38	871.83	823.13	785.47	755.79	732.05	712.83	697.12
49000	4431.34	2384.59	1707.62	1373.04	1175.38	1046.12	955.88	890.00	840.28	801.84	771.54	747.30	727.68	711.64
50000	4521.77	2433.26	1742.47	1401.07	1199.37	1067.46	975.39	908.16	857.43	818.20	787.28	762.55	742.53	726.17
55000	4973.95	2676.58	1916.71	1541.17	1319.30	1174.21	1072.93	998.97	943.17	900.02	866.01	838.81	816.78	798.78
60000	5426.13	2919.91	2090.96	1681.28	1439.24	1280.96	1170.47	1089.79	1028.91	981.84	944.74	915.06	891.04	871.40
65000	5878.30	3163.23	2265.21	1821.38	1559.17	1387.70	1268.01	1180.60	1114.66	1063.66	1023.47	991.32	965.29	944.02
70000	6330.48	3406.56	2439.45	1961.49	1679.11	1494.45	1365.55	1271.42	1200.40	1145.48	1102.20	1067.57	1039.54	1016.63
75000	6782.66	3649.88	2613.70	2101.60	1799.05	1601.19	1463.09	1362.24	1286.14	1227.30	1180.92	1143.83	1113.79	1089.25
80000	7234.83	3893.21	2787.94	2241.70	1918.98	1707.94	1560.62	1453.05	1371.88	1309.12	1259.65	1220.08	1188.05	1161.86
85000	7687.01	4136.53	2962.19	2381.81	2038.92	1814.69	1658.16	1543.87	1457.63	1390.94	1338.38	1296.34	1262.30	1234.48
90000	8139.19	4379.86	3136.44	2521.91	2158.86	1921.43	1755.70	1634.68	1543.37	1472.76	1417.11	1372.59	1336.55	1307.10
95000	8591.36	4623.18	3310.68	2662.02	2278.79	2028.18	1853.24	1725.50	1629.11	1554.58	1495.83	1448.84	1410.80	1379.71
100000	9043.54	4866.51	3484.93	2802.13	2398.73	2134.92	1950.78	1816.31	1714.85	1636.40	1574.56	1525.10	1485.06	1452.33

TERM	15 Years	16 Years	17 Years	18 Years	19 Years	20 Years	21 Years	22 Years	23 Years	24 Years	25 Years	30 Years	35 Years	40 Years
AMOUNT														
5	.08	.08	.07	.07	.07	.07	.07	.07	.07	.07	.07	.07	.07	.07
10	.15	.15	.14	.14	.14	.14	.14	.14	.14	.14	.14	.13	.13	.13
15	.22	.22	.21	.21	.21	.21	.21	.20	.20	.20	.20	.20	.20	.20
25	.36	.36	.35	.35	.34	.34	.34	.34	.34	.33	.33	.33	.33	.33
50	.72	.71	.70	.69	.68	.68	.67	.67	.67	.66	.66	.65	.65	.65
75	1.07	1.06	1.04	1.03	1.02	1.01	1.01	1.00	1.00	.99	.99	.98	.97	.97
100	1.43	1.41	1.39	1.37	1.36	1.35	1.34	1.33	1.33	1.32	1.31	1.30	1.29	1.29
200	2.86	2.81	2.77	2.74	2.72	2.69	2.68	2.66	2.65	2.63	2.62	2.59	2.58	2.57
300	4.28	4.21	4.16	4.11	4.07	4.04	4.01	3.99	3.97	3.95	3.93	3.89	3.87	3.86
400	5.71	5.62	5.54	5.48	5.43	5.38	5.35	5.31	5.29	5.26	5.24	5.18	5.15	5.14
500	7.13	7.02	6.93	6.85	6.78	6.73	6.68	6.64	6.61	6.58	6.55	6.48	6.44	6.43
600	8.56	8.42	8.31	8.22	8.14	8.07	8.02	7.97	7.93	7.89	7.86	7.77	7.73	7.71
700	9.98	9.83	9.70	9.59	9.49	9.42	9.35	9.30	9.25	9.21	9.17	9.07	9.02	8.99
800	11.41	11.23	11.08	10.96	10.85	10.76	10.69	10.62	10.57	10.52	10.48	10.36	10.30	10.28
900	12.83	12.63	12.46	12.32	12.21	12.11	12.02	11.95	11.89	11.84	11.79	11.66	11.59	11.56
1000	14.26	14.04	13.85	13.69	13.56	13.45	13.36	13.28	13.21	13.15	13.10	12.95	12.88	12.85
2000	28.51	28.07	27.69	27.38	27.12	26.90	26.71	26.55	26.42	26.30	26.20	25.89	25.75	25.69
3000	42.77	42.10	41.54	41.07	40.67	40.34	40.06	39.82	39.62	39.45	39.30	38.84	38.63	38.53
4000	57.02	56.13	55.38	54.76	54.23	53.79	53.41	53.10	52.83	52.60	52.40	51.78	51.50	51.37
5000	71.27	70.16	69.22	68.44	67.79	67.23	66.77	66.37	66.03	65.75	65.50	64.73	64.37	64.21
6000	85.53	84.19	83.07	82.13	81.34	80.68	80.12	79.64	79.24	78.90	78.60	77.67	77.25	77.05
7000	99.78	98.22	96.91	95.82	94.90	94.13	93.47	92.92	92.45	92.05	91.70	90.62	90.12	89.89
8000	114.03	112.25	110.75	109.51	108.46	107.57	106.82	106.19	105.65	105.19	104.80	103.56	103.00	102.73
9000	128.29	126.28	124.60	123.19	122.01	121.02	120.18	119.46	118.86	118.34	117.90	116.51	115.87	115.57
10000	142.54	140.31	138.44	136.88	135.57	134.46	133.53	132.74	132.06	131.49	131.00	129.45	128.74	128.41
11000	156.79	154.34	152.29	150.57	149.13	147.91	146.88	146.01	145.27	144.64	144.10	142.40	141.62	141.26
12000	171.05	168.37	166.13	164.26	162.68	161.35	160.23	159.28	158.47	157.79	157.20	155.34	154.49	154.10
13000	185.30	182.40	179.97	177.94	176.24	174.80	173.58	172.55	171.68	170.94	170.30	168.29	167.36	166.94
14000	199.56	196.43	193.82	191.63	189.79	188.25	186.94	185.83	184.89	184.09	183.40	181.23	180.24	179.78
15000	213.81	210.46	207.66	205.32	203.35	201.69	200.29	199.10	198.09	197.23	196.50	194.18	193.11	192.62
16000	228.06	224.49	221.50	219.01	216.91	215.14	213.64	212.37	211.30	210.38	209.60	207.12	205.99	205.46
17000	242.32	238.52	235.35	232.69	230.46	228.58	226.99	225.65	224.50	223.53	222.70	220.07	218.86	218.30
18000	256.57	252.55	249.19	246.38	244.02	242.03	240.35	238.92	237.71	236.68	235.80	233.01	231.73	231.14
19000	270.82	266.58	263.03	260.07	257.58	255.48	253.70	252.19	250.92	249.83	248.90	245.96	244.61	243.98
20000	285.08	280.61	276.88	273.76	271.13	268.92	267.05	265.47	264.12	262.98	262.00	258.90	257.48	256.82
21000	299.33	294.64	290.72	287.44	284.69	282.37	280.40	278.74	277.33	276.13	275.10	271.85	270.35	269.67
22000	313.58	308.67	304.57	301.13	298.25	295.81	293.76	292.01	290.53	289.27	288.20	284.79	283.23	282.51
23000	327.84	322.70	318.41	314.82	311.80	309.26	307.11	305.29	303.74	302.42	301.30	297.74	296.10	295.35
24000	342.09	336.73	332.25	328.51	325.36	322.70	320.46	318.56	316.94	315.57	314.40	310.68	308.98	308.19
25000	356.35	350.76	346.10	342.19	338.92	336.15	333.81	331.83	330.15	328.72	327.50	323.63	321.85	321.03
26000	370.60	364.79	359.94	355.88	352.47	349.60	347.16	345.10	343.36	341.87	340.60	336.57	334.72	333.87
27000	384.85	378.82	373.78	369.57	366.03	363.04	360.52	358.38	356.56	355.02	353.70	349.52	347.60	346.71
28000	399.11	392.85	387.63	383.26	379.58	376.49	373.87	371.65	369.77	368.17	366.80	362.46	360.47	359.55
29000	413.36	406.88	401.47	396.95	393.14	389.93	387.22	384.92	382.97	381.32	379.90	375.40	373.35	372.39
30000	427.61	420.91	415.31	410.63	406.70	403.38	400.57	398.20	396.18	394.46	393.00	388.35	386.22	385.23
31000	441.87	434.94	429.16	424.32	420.25	416.83	413.93	411.47	409.39	407.61	406.10	401.29	399.09	398.08
32000	456.12	448.97	443.00	438.01	433.81	430.27	427.28	424.74	422.59	420.76	419.20	414.24	411.97	410.92
33000	470.37	463.00	456.85	451.70	447.37	443.72	440.63	438.02	435.80	433.91	432.30	427.18	424.84	423.76
34000	484.63	477.03	470.69	465.38	460.92	457.16	453.98	451.29	449.00	447.06	445.40	440.13	437.71	436.60
35000	498.88	491.06	484.53	479.07	474.48	470.61	467.34	464.56	462.21	460.21	458.50	453.07	450.59	449.44
36000	513.13	505.09	498.38	492.76	488.04	484.05	480.69	477.84	475.41	473.36	471.60	466.02	463.46	462.28
37000	527.39	519.12	512.22	506.45	501.59	497.50	494.04	491.11	488.62	486.50	484.70	478.96	476.34	475.12
38000	541.64	533.15	526.06	520.13	515.15	510.95	507.39	504.38	501.83	499.65	497.80	491.91	489.21	487.96
39000	555.90	547.18	539.91	533.82	528.71	524.39	520.74	517.65	515.03	512.80	510.90	504.85	502.08	500.80
40000	570.15	561.21	553.75	547.51	542.26	537.84	534.10	530.93	528.24	525.95	524.00	517.80	514.96	513.64
41000	584.40	575.24	567.59	561.20	555.82	551.28	547.45	544.20	541.44	539.10	537.10	530.74	527.83	526.49
42000	598.66	589.27	581.44	574.88	569.37	564.73	560.80	557.47	554.65	552.25	550.20	543.69	540.70	539.33
43000	612.91	603.30	595.28	588.57	582.93	578.17	574.15	570.75	567.86	565.40	563.30	556.63	553.58	552.17
44000	627.16	617.33	609.13	602.26	596.49	591.62	587.51	584.02	581.06	578.54	576.40	569.58	566.45	565.01
45000	641.42	631.36	622.97	615.95	610.04	605.07	600.86	597.29	594.27	591.69	589.50	582.52	579.33	577.85
46000	655.67	645.39	636.81	629.63	623.60	618.51	614.21	610.57	607.47	604.84	602.60	595.47	592.20	590.69
47000	669.92	659.42	650.66	643.32	637.16	631.96	627.56	623.84	620.68	617.99	615.70	608.41	605.07	603.53
48000	684.18	673.45	664.50	657.01	650.71	645.40	640.92	637.11	633.88	631.14	628.80	621.36	617.95	616.37
49000	698.43	687.48	678.34	670.70	664.27	658.85	654.27	650.39	647.09	644.29	641.90	634.30	630.82	629.21
50000	712.69	701.51	692.19	684.38	677.83	672.30	667.62	663.66	660.30	657.44	655.00	647.25	643.70	642.05
55000	783.95	771.66	761.41	752.82	745.61	739.52	734.38	730.02	726.33	723.18	720.50	711.97	708.06	706.26
60000	855.22	841.81	830.62	821.26	813.39	806.75	801.14	796.39	792.35	788.92	786.00	776.69	772.43	770.46
65000	926.49	911.96	899.84	889.70	881.17	873.98	867.90	862.75	858.38	854.67	851.50	841.42	836.80	834.67
70000	997.76	982.11	969.06	958.14	948.95	941.21	934.67	929.12	924.41	920.41	917.00	906.14	901.17	898.87
75000	1069.03	1052.26	1038.28	1026.57	1016.74	1008.44	1001.43	995.49	990.44	986.15	982.50	970.87	965.54	963.08
80000	1140.29	1122.41	1107.50	1095.01	1084.52	1075.67	1068.19	1061.85	1056.47	1051.90	1048.00	1035.59	1029.91	1027.28
85000	1211.56	1192.56	1176.72	1163.45	1152.30	1142.90	1134.95	1128.22	1122.50	1117.64	1113.50	1100.32	1094.28	1091.49
90000	1282.83	1262.71	1245.93	1231.89	1220.08	1210.13	1201.71	1194.58	1188.53	1183.38	1179.00	1165.04	1158.65	1155.69
95000	1354.10	1332.86	1315.15	1300.33	1287.86	1277.36	1268.47	1260.95	1254.56	1249.13	1244.50	1229.76	1223.02	1219.90
100000	1425.37	1403.01	1384.37	1368.76	1355.65	1344.59	1335.24	1327.31	1320.59	1314.87	1310.00	1294.49	1287.39	1284.10

MONTHLY PAYMENT
REQUIRED TO AMORTIZE A LOAN

TERM	1 Year	2 Years	3 Years	4 Years	5 Years	6 Years	7 Years	8 Years	9 Years	10 Years	11 Years	12 Years	13 Years	14 Years
AMOUNT														
5	.48	.25	.18	.15	.13	.11	.10	.10	.09	.09	.08	.08	.08	.08
10	.91	.49	.35	.29	.25	.22	.20	.19	.18	.17	.16	.16	.15	.14
15	1.36	.74	.53	.43	.37	.33	.30	.28	.26	.25	.24	.23	.23	.22
25	2.27	1.22	.88	.71	.61	.54	.49	.46	.43	.41	.40	.39	.38	.37
50	4.53	2.44	1.75	1.41	1.21	1.07	.98	.91	.86	.82	.79	.77	.75	.73
75	6.79	3.66	2.62	2.11	1.81	1.61	1.47	1.37	1.29	1.23	1.19	1.15	1.12	1.10
100	9.05	4.87	3.49	2.81	2.41	2.14	1.96	1.82	1.72	1.64	1.58	1.53	1.49	1.46
200	18.09	9.74	6.98	5.61	4.81	4.28	3.91	3.64	3.44	3.28	3.16	3.06	2.98	2.91
300	27.14	14.61	10.46	8.42	7.21	6.41	5.86	5.46	5.15	4.92	4.73	4.59	4.47	4.37
400	36.18	19.40	13.95	11.22	9.61	8.55	7.81	7.28	6.87	6.56	6.31	6.11	5.95	5.82
500	45.23	24.34	17.44	14.02	12.01	10.69	9.77	9.09	8.59	8.19	7.89	7.64	7.44	7.28
600	54.27	29.21	20.92	16.83	14.41	12.82	11.72	10.91	10.30	9.83	9.46	9.17	8.93	8.73
700	63.32	34.08	24.41	19.63	16.81	14.96	13.67	12.73	12.02	11.47	11.04	10.69	10.41	10.18
800	72.36	38.95	27.89	22.43	19.21	17.10	15.62	14.55	13.74	13.11	12.61	12.22	11.90	11.64
900	81.41	43.81	31.38	25.24	21.61	19.23	17.57	16.36	15.45	14.75	14.19	13.75	13.39	13.09
1000	90.45	48.68	34.87	28.04	24.01	21.37	19.53	18.18	17.17	16.38	15.77	15.27	14.87	14.55
2000	180.90	97.36	69.73	56.07	48.01	42.73	39.05	36.36	34.33	32.76	31.53	30.54	29.74	29.09
3000	271.35	146.04	104.59	84.11	72.01	64.09	58.57	54.54	51.50	49.14	47.29	45.81	44.61	43.63
4000	361.79	194.71	139.45	112.14	96.01	85.46	78.09	72.72	68.66	65.52	63.05	61.07	59.47	58.17
5000	452.24	243.39	174.31	140.17	120.01	106.82	97.61	90.89	85.82	81.90	78.81	76.34	74.34	72.71
6000	542.69	292.07	209.17	168.21	144.01	128.18	117.14	109.07	102.99	98.28	94.57	91.61	89.21	87.25
7000	633.14	340.74	244.04	196.24	168.01	149.54	136.66	127.25	120.15	114.66	110.33	106.88	104.07	101.79
8000	723.58	389.42	278.90	224.28	192.01	170.91	156.18	145.43	137.31	131.04	126.10	122.14	118.94	116.33
9000	814.03	438.10	313.76	252.31	216.01	192.27	175.70	163.60	154.48	147.42	141.86	137.41	133.81	130.87
10000	904.48	486.77	348.62	280.34	240.01	213.63	195.22	181.78	171.64	163.80	157.62	152.68	148.68	145.41
11000	994.92	535.45	383.48	308.38	264.01	235.00	214.75	199.96	188.80	180.18	173.38	167.94	163.54	159.95
12000	1085.37	584.13	418.34	336.41	288.01	256.36	234.27	218.14	205.97	196.56	189.14	183.21	178.41	174.49
13000	1175.82	632.80	453.20	364.45	312.01	277.72	253.79	236.31	223.13	212.94	204.90	198.48	193.28	189.03
14000	1266.27	681.48	488.07	392.48	336.01	299.08	273.31	254.49	240.29	229.32	220.66	213.75	208.14	203.57
15000	1356.71	730.16	522.93	420.51	360.01	320.45	292.83	272.67	257.46	245.69	236.43	229.01	223.01	218.11
16000	1447.16	778.84	557.79	448.55	384.01	341.81	312.35	290.85	274.62	262.07	252.19	244.28	237.88	232.65
17000	1537.61	827.51	592.65	476.58	408.01	363.17	331.88	309.02	291.78	278.45	267.95	259.55	252.75	247.19
18000	1628.05	876.19	627.51	504.62	432.01	384.54	351.40	327.20	308.95	294.83	283.71	274.81	267.61	261.73
19000	1718.50	924.87	662.37	532.65	456.01	405.90	370.92	345.38	326.11	311.21	299.47	290.08	282.48	276.27
20000	1808.95	973.54	697.24	560.68	480.01	427.26	390.44	363.56	343.27	327.59	315.23	305.35	297.35	290.81
21000	1899.40	1022.22	732.10	588.72	504.01	448.62	409.96	381.74	360.44	343.97	330.99	320.62	312.21	305.35
22000	1989.84	1070.90	766.96	616.75	528.01	469.99	429.49	399.91	377.60	360.35	346.76	335.88	327.08	319.89
23000	2080.29	1119.57	801.82	644.79	552.01	491.35	449.01	418.09	394.77	376.73	362.52	351.15	341.95	334.43
24000	2170.74	1168.25	836.68	672.82	576.01	512.71	468.53	436.27	411.93	393.11	378.28	366.42	356.82	348.97
25000	2261.18	1216.93	871.54	700.85	600.02	534.08	488.05	454.45	429.09	409.49	394.04	381.68	371.68	363.51
26000	2351.63	1265.60	906.40	728.89	624.02	555.44	507.57	472.62	446.26	425.87	409.80	396.95	386.55	378.05
27000	2442.08	1314.28	941.27	756.92	648.02	576.80	527.10	490.80	463.42	442.25	425.56	412.22	401.42	392.59
28000	2532.53	1362.96	976.13	784.96	672.02	598.16	546.62	508.98	480.58	458.63	441.32	427.49	416.28	407.13
29000	2622.97	1411.64	1010.99	812.99	696.02	619.53	566.14	527.16	497.75	475.01	457.09	442.75	431.15	421.67
30000	2713.42	1460.31	1045.85	841.02	720.02	640.89	585.66	545.33	514.91	491.38	472.85	458.02	446.02	436.21
31000	2803.87	1508.99	1080.71	869.06	744.02	662.25	605.18	563.51	532.07	507.76	488.61	473.29	460.88	450.75
32000	2894.31	1557.67	1115.57	897.09	768.02	683.62	624.70	581.69	549.24	524.14	504.37	488.55	475.75	465.29
33000	2984.76	1606.34	1150.44	925.12	792.02	704.98	644.23	599.87	566.40	540.52	520.13	503.82	490.62	479.83
34000	3075.21	1655.02	1185.30	953.16	816.02	726.34	663.75	618.04	583.56	556.90	535.89	519.09	505.49	494.37
35000	3165.66	1703.70	1220.16	981.19	840.02	747.70	683.27	636.22	600.73	573.28	551.65	534.36	520.35	508.91
36000	3256.10	1752.37	1255.02	1009.23	864.02	769.07	702.79	654.40	617.89	589.66	567.42	549.62	535.22	523.45
37000	3346.55	1801.05	1289.88	1037.26	888.02	790.43	722.31	672.58	635.05	606.04	583.18	564.89	550.09	537.99
38000	3437.00	1849.73	1324.74	1065.29	912.02	811.79	741.84	690.75	652.22	622.42	598.94	580.16	564.95	552.53
39000	3527.44	1898.40	1359.60	1093.33	936.02	833.16	761.36	708.93	669.38	638.80	614.70	595.42	579.82	567.07
40000	3617.89	1947.08	1394.47	1121.36	960.02	854.52	780.88	727.11	686.54	655.18	630.46	610.69	594.69	581.61
41000	3708.34	1995.76	1429.33	1149.40	984.02	875.88	800.40	745.29	703.71	671.56	646.22	625.96	609.56	596.15
42000	3798.79	2044.44	1464.19	1177.43	1008.02	897.24	819.92	763.47	720.87	687.94	661.98	641.23	624.42	610.69
43000	3889.23	2093.11	1499.05	1205.46	1032.02	918.61	839.44	781.64	738.03	704.32	677.75	656.49	639.29	625.23
44000	3979.68	2141.79	1533.91	1233.50	1056.02	939.97	858.97	799.82	755.20	720.70	693.51	671.76	654.16	639.77
45000	4070.13	2190.47	1568.77	1261.53	1080.02	961.33	878.49	818.00	772.36	737.07	709.27	687.03	669.02	654.31
46000	4160.57	2239.14	1603.64	1289.57	1104.02	982.70	898.01	836.18	789.53	753.45	725.03	702.29	683.89	668.85
47000	4251.02	2287.82	1638.50	1317.60	1128.02	1004.06	917.53	854.35	806.69	769.83	740.79	717.56	698.76	683.39
48000	4341.47	2336.50	1673.36	1345.63	1152.02	1025.42	937.05	872.53	823.85	786.21	756.55	732.83	713.63	697.93
49000	4431.92	2385.17	1708.22	1373.67	1176.03	1046.78	956.58	890.71	841.02	802.59	772.31	748.10	728.49	712.47
50000	4522.36	2433.85	1743.08	1401.70	1200.03	1068.15	976.10	908.89	858.18	818.97	788.07	763.36	743.36	727.01
55000	4974.60	2677.24	1917.39	1541.87	1320.03	1174.96	1073.71	999.77	944.00	900.87	866.88	839.70	817.70	799.71
60000	5426.84	2920.62	2091.70	1682.04	1440.03	1281.78	1171.32	1090.66	1029.81	982.76	945.69	916.03	892.03	872.41
65000	5879.07	3164.00	2266.00	1822.21	1560.03	1388.59	1268.93	1181.55	1115.63	1064.66	1024.50	992.37	966.37	945.11
70000	6331.31	3407.39	2440.31	1962.38	1680.03	1495.40	1366.54	1272.44	1201.45	1146.56	1103.30	1068.71	1040.70	1017.82
75000	6783.54	3650.77	2614.62	2102.55	1800.04	1602.22	1464.14	1363.33	1287.27	1228.45	1182.11	1145.04	1115.04	1090.52
80000	7235.78	3894.16	2788.93	2242.72	1920.04	1709.03	1561.75	1454.22	1373.08	1310.35	1260.92	1221.38	1189.37	1163.22
85000	7688.01	4137.54	2963.24	2382.89	2040.04	1815.85	1659.36	1545.10	1458.90	1392.25	1339.72	1297.71	1263.71	1235.92
90000	8140.25	4380.93	3137.54	2523.06	2160.04	1922.66	1756.97	1635.99	1544.72	1474.14	1418.53	1374.05	1338.04	1308.62
95000	8592.49	4624.31	3311.85	2663.23	2280.04	2029.48	1854.58	1726.88	1630.54	1556.04	1497.34	1450.38	1412.38	1381.32
100000	9044.72	4867.70	3486.16	2803.40	2400.05	2136.29	1952.19	1817.77	1716.35	1637.94	1576.14	1526.72	1486.71	1454.02

TERM	15 Years	16 Years	17 Years	18 Years	19 Years	20 Years	21 Years	22 Years	23 Years	24 Years	25 Years	30 Years	35 Years	40 Years
AMOUNT														
5	.08	.08	.07	.07	.07	.07	.07	.07	.07	.07	.07	.07	.07	.07
10	.15	.15	.14	.14	.14	.14	.14	.14	.14	.14	.14	.13	.13	.13
15	.22	.22	.21	.21	.21	.21	.21	.20	.20	.20	.20	.20	.20	.20
25	.36	.36	.35	.35	.34	.34	.34	.34	.34	.33	.33	.33	.33	.33
50	.72	.71	.70	.69	.68	.68	.67	.67	.67	.66	.66	.65	.65	.65
75	1.08	1.06	1.04	1.03	1.02	1.01	1.01	1.00	1.00	.99	.99	.98	.97	.97
100	1.43	1.41	1.39	1.38	1.36	1.35	1.34	1.33	1.33	1.32	1.32	1.30	1.29	1.29
200	2.86	2.81	2.78	2.75	2.72	2.70	2.68	2.66	2.65	2.64	2.63	2.60	2.58	2.58
300	4.29	4.22	4.16	4.12	4.08	4.04	4.02	3.99	3.97	3.96	3.94	3.89	3.87	3.86
400	5.71	5.62	5.55	5.49	5.43	5.39	5.35	5.32	5.29	5.27	5.25	5.19	5.16	5.15
500	7.14	7.03	6.94	6.86	6.79	6.74	6.69	6.65	6.62	6.59	6.56	6.49	6.45	6.44
600	8.57	8.43	8.32	8.23	8.15	8.08	8.03	7.98	7.94	7.91	7.88	7.78	7.74	7.72
700	9.99	9.84	9.71	9.60	9.51	9.43	9.36	9.31	9.26	9.22	9.19	9.08	9.03	9.01
800	11.42	11.24	11.09	10.97	10.86	10.78	10.70	10.64	10.58	10.54	10.50	10.38	10.32	10.29
900	12.85	12.65	12.48	12.34	12.22	12.12	12.04	11.97	11.91	11.86	11.81	11.67	11.61	11.58
1000	14.28	14.05	13.87	13.71	13.58	13.47	13.38	13.30	13.23	13.17	13.12	12.97	12.90	12.87
2000	28.55	28.10	27.73	27.42	27.15	26.93	26.75	26.59	26.45	26.34	26.24	25.93	25.79	25.73
3000	42.82	42.15	41.59	41.12	40.73	40.40	40.12	39.88	39.68	39.51	39.36	38.90	38.69	38.59
4000	57.09	56.20	55.45	54.83	54.30	53.86	53.49	53.17	52.90	52.68	52.48	51.86	51.58	51.45
5000	71.36	70.24	69.31	68.53	67.88	67.33	66.86	66.47	66.13	65.84	65.60	64.83	64.48	64.31
6000	85.63	84.29	83.17	82.24	81.45	80.79	80.23	79.76	79.35	79.01	78.72	77.79	77.37	77.17
7000	99.90	98.34	97.04	95.94	95.03	94.26	93.60	93.05	92.58	92.18	91.84	90.76	90.26	90.04
8000	114.17	112.39	110.90	109.65	108.60	107.72	106.97	106.34	105.80	105.35	104.96	103.72	103.16	102.90
9000	128.44	126.43	124.76	123.36	122.18	121.18	120.34	119.63	119.03	118.52	118.08	116.69	116.05	115.76
10000	142.71	140.48	138.62	137.06	135.75	134.65	133.72	132.93	132.25	131.68	131.20	129.65	128.95	128.62
11000	156.98	154.53	152.48	150.77	149.33	148.11	147.09	146.22	145.48	144.85	144.32	142.62	141.84	141.48
12000	171.26	168.58	166.34	164.47	162.90	161.58	160.46	159.51	158.70	158.02	157.44	155.58	154.74	154.34
13000	185.53	182.62	180.20	178.18	176.48	175.04	173.83	172.80	171.93	171.19	170.56	168.55	167.63	167.21
14000	199.80	196.67	194.07	191.88	190.05	188.51	187.20	186.09	185.15	184.36	183.68	181.51	180.52	180.07
15000	214.07	210.72	207.93	205.59	203.63	201.97	200.57	199.39	198.38	197.52	196.80	194.48	193.42	192.93
16000	228.34	224.77	221.79	219.30	217.20	215.44	213.94	212.68	211.60	210.69	209.92	207.44	206.31	205.79
17000	242.61	238.81	235.65	233.00	230.78	228.90	227.31	225.97	224.83	223.86	223.04	220.41	219.21	218.65
18000	256.80	252.86	249.51	246.71	244.35	242.36	240.68	239.26	238.05	237.03	236.15	233.37	232.10	231.51
19000	271.15	266.91	263.37	260.41	257.93	255.83	254.06	252.55	251.28	250.20	249.27	246.34	244.99	244.38
20000	285.42	280.96	277.23	274.12	271.50	269.29	267.43	265.85	264.50	263.36	262.39	259.30	257.89	257.24
21000	299.69	295.00	291.10	287.82	285.08	282.76	280.80	279.14	277.73	276.53	275.51	272.27	270.78	270.10
22000	313.96	309.05	304.96	301.53	298.65	296.22	294.17	292.43	290.95	289.70	288.63	285.23	283.68	282.96
23000	328.23	323.10	318.82	315.24	312.22	309.69	307.54	305.72	304.18	302.87	301.75	298.20	296.57	295.82
24000	342.51	337.15	332.68	328.94	325.80	323.15	320.91	319.01	317.40	316.04	314.87	311.16	309.47	308.68
25000	356.78	351.19	346.54	342.65	339.37	336.61	334.28	332.31	330.63	329.20	327.99	324.13	322.36	321.54
26000	371.05	365.24	360.40	356.35	352.95	350.08	347.65	345.60	343.85	342.37	341.11	337.09	335.25	334.41
27000	385.32	379.29	374.27	370.06	366.52	363.54	361.02	358.89	357.08	355.54	354.23	350.06	348.15	347.27
28000	399.59	393.34	388.13	383.76	380.10	377.01	374.40	372.18	370.30	368.71	367.35	363.02	361.04	360.13
29000	413.86	407.38	401.99	397.47	393.67	390.47	387.77	385.48	383.53	381.88	380.47	375.99	373.94	372.99
30000	428.13	421.43	415.85	411.18	407.25	403.94	401.14	398.77	396.75	395.04	393.59	388.95	386.83	385.85
31000	442.40	435.48	429.71	424.88	420.82	417.40	414.51	412.06	409.98	408.21	406.71	401.92	399.73	398.71
32000	456.67	449.53	443.57	438.59	434.40	430.87	427.88	425.35	423.20	421.38	419.83	414.88	412.62	411.58
33000	470.94	463.58	457.43	452.29	447.97	444.33	441.25	438.64	436.43	434.55	432.95	427.85	425.51	424.44
34000	485.21	477.62	471.30	466.00	461.55	457.79	454.62	451.94	449.65	447.72	446.07	440.81	438.41	437.30
35000	499.48	491.67	485.16	479.70	475.12	471.26	467.99	465.23	462.88	460.88	459.19	453.78	451.30	450.16
36000	513.76	505.72	499.02	493.41	488.70	484.72	481.36	478.52	476.10	474.05	472.30	466.74	464.20	463.02
37000	528.03	519.77	512.88	507.12	502.27	498.19	494.74	491.81	489.33	487.22	485.42	479.71	477.09	475.88
38000	542.30	533.81	526.74	520.82	515.85	511.65	508.11	505.10	502.55	500.39	498.54	492.67	489.98	488.75
39000	556.57	547.86	540.60	534.53	529.42	525.12	521.48	518.40	515.78	513.56	511.66	505.64	502.88	501.61
40000	570.84	561.91	554.46	548.23	543.00	538.58	534.85	531.69	529.00	526.72	524.78	518.60	515.77	514.47
41000	585.11	575.96	568.33	561.94	556.57	552.05	548.22	544.98	542.23	539.89	537.90	531.57	528.67	527.33
42000	599.38	590.00	582.19	575.64	570.15	565.51	561.59	558.27	555.45	553.06	551.02	544.53	541.56	540.19
43000	613.65	604.05	596.05	589.35	583.72	578.97	574.96	571.56	568.68	566.23	564.14	557.50	554.46	553.05
44000	627.92	618.10	609.91	603.06	597.29	592.44	588.33	584.86	581.90	579.40	577.26	570.46	567.35	565.91
45000	642.19	632.15	623.77	616.76	610.87	605.90	601.70	598.15	595.13	592.56	590.38	583.42	580.24	578.78
46000	656.46	646.19	637.63	630.47	624.44	619.37	615.08	611.44	608.35	605.73	603.50	596.39	593.14	591.64
47000	670.73	660.24	651.50	644.17	638.02	632.83	628.45	624.73	621.58	618.90	616.62	609.35	606.03	604.50
48000	685.01	674.29	665.36	657.88	651.59	646.30	641.82	638.02	634.80	632.07	629.74	622.32	618.93	617.36
49000	699.28	688.34	679.22	671.58	665.17	659.76	655.19	651.32	648.03	645.24	642.86	635.28	631.82	630.22
50000	713.55	702.38	693.08	685.29	678.74	673.22	668.56	664.61	661.25	658.40	655.98	648.25	644.72	643.08
55000	784.90	772.62	762.39	753.82	746.62	740.55	735.42	731.07	727.38	724.24	721.57	713.07	709.19	707.39
60000	856.26	842.86	831.69	822.35	814.49	807.87	802.27	797.53	793.50	790.08	787.17	777.90	773.66	771.70
65000	927.61	913.10	901.00	890.88	882.36	875.19	869.13	863.99	859.63	855.92	852.77	842.72	838.13	836.01
70000	998.96	983.34	970.31	959.40	950.24	942.51	935.98	930.45	925.75	921.76	918.37	907.55	902.60	900.32
75000	1070.32	1053.57	1039.62	1027.93	1018.11	1009.83	1002.84	996.91	991.88	987.60	983.96	972.37	967.07	964.62
80000	1141.67	1123.81	1108.92	1096.46	1085.99	1077.16	1069.69	1063.37	1058.00	1053.44	1049.56	1037.20	1031.54	1028.93
85000	1213.03	1194.05	1178.23	1164.99	1153.86	1144.48	1136.55	1129.83	1124.13	1119.28	1115.16	1102.02	1096.01	1093.24
90000	1284.38	1264.05	1247.54	1233.52	1221.73	1211.80	1203.40	1196.29	1190.25	1185.12	1180.75	1166.84	1160.48	1157.55
95000	1355.74	1334.53	1316.85	1302.05	1289.61	1279.12	1270.26	1262.75	1256.38	1250.96	1246.35	1231.67	1224.95	1221.86
100000	1427.09	1404.76	1386.15	1370.57	1357.48	1346.44	1337.12	1329.21	1322.50	1316.80	1311.95	1296.49	1289.43	1286.16

MONTHLY PAYMENT
REQUIRED TO AMORTIZE A LOAN

TERM	1 Year	2 Years	3 Years	4 Years	5 Years	6 Years	7 Years	8 Years	9 Years	10 Years	11 Years	12 Years	13 Years	14 Years
AMOUNT														
5	.46	.25	.18	.15	.13	.11	.10	.10	.09	.09	.08	.08	.08	.08
10	.91	.49	.35	.29	.25	.22	.20	.19	.18	.17	.16	.16	.15	.15
15	1.36	.74	.53	.43	.37	.33	.30	.28	.26	.25	.24	.23	.23	.22
25	2.27	1.22	.88	.71	.61	.54	.49	.46	.44	.42	.40	.39	.38	.37
50	4.53	2.44	1.75	1.41	1.21	1.08	.98	.92	.87	.83	.80	.77	.75	.74
75	6.79	3.66	2.62	2.11	1.81	1.61	1.47	1.37	1.30	1.24	1.19	1.15	1.13	1.10
100	9.05	4.88	3.50	2.81	2.41	2.15	1.96	1.83	1.73	1.65	1.59	1.54	1.50	1.47
200	18.10	9.75	6.99	5.62	4.82	4.29	3.92	3.65	3.45	3.29	3.17	3.07	2.99	2.93
300	27.15	14.62	10.48	8.43	7.22	6.43	5.88	5.48	5.17	4.94	4.75	4.60	4.49	4.39
400	36.20	19.49	13.97	11.24	9.63	8.57	7.84	7.30	6.89	6.58	6.33	6.14	5.98	5.85
500	45.25	24.37	17.46	14.05	12.03	10.71	9.79	9.12	8.62	8.23	7.92	7.67	7.47	7.31
600	54.30	29.24	20.95	16.86	14.44	12.86	11.75	10.95	10.34	9.87	9.50	9.20	8.97	8.77
700	63.35	34.11	24.44	19.66	16.84	15.00	13.71	12.77	12.06	11.51	11.08	10.74	10.46	10.23
800	72.40	38.98	27.93	22.47	19.25	17.14	15.67	14.59	13.78	13.16	12.66	12.27	11.95	11.69
900	81.45	43.86	31.42	25.28	21.65	19.28	17.63	16.42	15.51	14.80	14.25	13.80	13.45	13.15
1000	90.50	48.73	34.92	28.09	24.06	21.42	19.58	18.24	17.23	16.45	15.83	15.34	14.94	14.61
2000	180.99	97.45	69.83	56.17	48.11	42.84	39.16	36.48	34.45	32.89	31.65	30.67	29.87	29.22
3000	271.49	146.18	104.74	84.26	72.16	64.26	58.74	54.71	51.68	49.33	47.48	46.00	44.81	43.83
4000	361.98	194.90	139.65	112.34	96.22	85.67	78.32	72.95	68.90	65.77	63.30	61.33	59.74	58.44
5000	452.48	243.63	174.56	140.43	120.27	107.09	97.90	91.18	86.12	82.21	79.13	76.67	74.67	73.04
6000	542.97	292.35	209.47	168.51	144.32	128.51	117.48	109.42	103.35	98.65	94.95	92.00	89.61	87.65
7000	633.47	341.08	244.38	196.60	168.38	149.93	137.05	127.66	120.57	115.09	110.78	107.33	104.54	102.26
8000	723.96	389.80	279.29	224.68	192.43	171.34	156.63	145.89	137.79	131.53	126.60	122.66	119.47	116.87
9000	814.45	438.53	314.20	252.77	216.48	192.76	176.21	164.13	155.02	147.97	142.43	137.99	134.41	131.48
10000	904.95	487.25	349.11	280.85	240.54	214.18	195.79	182.36	172.24	164.42	158.25	153.33	149.34	146.08
11000	995.44	535.97	384.02	308.94	264.59	235.60	215.37	200.60	189.46	180.86	174.08	168.66	164.27	160.69
12000	1085.94	584.70	418.93	337.02	288.64	257.01	234.95	218.84	206.69	197.30	189.90	183.99	179.21	175.30
13000	1176.43	633.42	453.84	365.11	312.70	278.43	254.52	237.07	223.91	213.74	205.73	199.32	194.14	189.91
14000	1266.93	682.15	488.75	393.19	336.75	299.85	274.10	255.31	241.13	230.18	221.55	214.65	209.07	204.52
15000	1357.42	730.87	523.67	421.28	360.80	321.27	293.68	273.54	258.36	246.62	237.38	229.99	224.01	219.12
16000	1447.92	779.60	558.58	449.36	384.86	342.68	313.26	291.78	275.58	263.06	253.20	245.32	238.94	233.73
17000	1538.41	828.32	593.49	477.45	408.91	364.10	332.84	310.02	292.80	279.50	269.03	260.65	253.87	248.34
18000	1628.90	877.05	628.40	505.53	432.96	385.52	352.42	328.25	310.03	295.94	284.85	275.98	268.81	262.95
19000	1719.40	925.77	663.31	533.62	457.02	406.94	371.99	346.49	327.25	312.39	300.68	291.31	283.74	277.56
20000	1809.89	974.50	698.22	561.70	481.07	428.35	391.57	364.72	344.48	328.83	316.50	306.65	298.67	292.16
21000	1900.39	1023.22	733.13	589.79	505.12	449.77	411.15	382.96	361.70	345.27	332.32	321.98	313.61	306.77
22000	1990.88	1071.94	768.04	617.87	529.18	471.19	430.73	401.20	378.92	361.71	348.15	337.31	328.54	321.38
23000	2081.38	1120.67	802.95	645.96	553.23	492.61	450.31	419.43	396.15	378.15	363.97	352.64	343.47	335.99
24000	2171.87	1169.39	837.86	674.04	577.28	514.02	469.89	437.67	413.37	394.59	379.80	367.97	358.41	350.59
25000	2262.37	1218.12	872.77	702.13	601.33	535.44	489.46	455.90	430.59	411.03	395.62	383.31	373.34	365.20
26000	2352.86	1266.84	907.68	730.21	625.39	556.86	509.04	474.14	447.82	427.47	411.45	398.64	388.27	379.81
27000	2443.35	1315.57	942.59	758.30	649.44	578.28	528.62	492.37	465.04	443.91	427.27	413.97	403.21	394.42
28000	2533.85	1364.29	977.50	786.38	673.49	599.69	548.20	510.61	482.26	460.35	443.10	429.30	418.14	409.03
29000	2624.34	1413.02	1012.41	814.47	697.55	621.11	567.78	528.85	499.49	476.80	458.92	444.63	433.08	423.63
30000	2714.84	1461.74	1047.33	842.55	721.60	642.53	587.36	547.08	516.71	493.24	474.75	459.97	448.01	438.24
31000	2805.33	1510.47	1082.24	870.64	745.65	663.95	606.93	565.32	533.93	509.68	490.57	475.30	462.94	452.85
32000	2895.83	1559.19	1117.15	898.72	769.71	685.36	626.51	583.55	551.16	526.12	506.40	490.63	477.88	467.46
33000	2986.32	1607.91	1152.06	926.81	793.76	706.78	646.09	601.79	568.38	542.56	522.22	505.96	492.81	482.07
34000	3076.82	1656.64	1186.97	954.89	817.81	728.20	665.67	620.03	585.60	559.00	538.05	521.29	507.74	496.67
35000	3167.31	1705.36	1221.88	982.98	841.87	749.62	685.25	638.26	602.83	575.44	553.87	536.63	522.68	511.28
36000	3257.80	1754.09	1256.79	1011.06	865.92	771.03	704.83	656.50	620.05	591.88	569.70	551.96	537.61	525.89
37000	3348.30	1802.81	1291.70	1039.14	889.97	792.45	724.40	674.73	637.28	608.32	585.52	567.29	552.54	540.50
38000	3438.79	1851.54	1326.61	1067.23	914.03	813.87	743.98	692.97	654.50	624.77	601.35	582.62	567.48	555.11
39000	3529.29	1900.26	1361.52	1095.31	938.08	835.29	763.56	711.21	671.72	641.21	617.17	597.95	582.41	569.71
40000	3619.78	1948.99	1396.43	1123.40	962.13	856.70	783.14	729.44	688.95	657.65	632.99	613.29	597.34	584.32
41000	3710.28	1997.71	1431.34	1151.48	986.19	878.12	802.72	747.68	706.17	674.09	648.82	628.62	612.28	598.93
42000	3800.77	2046.44	1466.25	1179.57	1010.24	899.54	822.30	765.91	723.39	690.53	664.64	643.95	627.21	613.54
43000	3891.26	2095.16	1501.16	1207.65	1034.29	920.96	841.87	784.15	740.62	706.97	680.47	659.28	642.14	628.14
44000	3981.76	2143.88	1536.08	1235.74	1058.35	942.37	861.45	802.39	757.84	723.41	696.29	674.61	657.08	642.75
45000	4072.25	2192.61	1570.99	1263.82	1082.40	963.79	881.03	820.62	775.06	739.85	712.12	689.95	672.01	657.36
46000	4162.75	2241.33	1605.90	1291.91	1106.45	985.21	900.61	838.86	792.29	756.29	727.94	705.28	686.94	671.97
47000	4253.24	2290.06	1640.81	1319.99	1130.51	1006.63	920.19	857.09	809.51	772.73	743.77	720.61	701.88	686.58
48000	4343.74	2338.78	1675.72	1348.08	1154.56	1028.04	939.77	875.33	826.73	789.18	759.59	735.94	716.81	701.18
49000	4434.23	2387.51	1710.63	1376.16	1178.61	1049.46	959.34	893.57	843.96	805.62	775.42	751.28	731.74	715.79
50000	4524.73	2436.23	1745.54	1404.25	1202.66	1070.88	978.92	911.80	861.18	822.06	791.24	766.61	746.68	730.40
55000	4977.20	2679.85	1920.09	1544.67	1322.93	1177.97	1076.81	1002.98	947.30	904.26	870.37	843.27	821.35	803.44
60000	5429.67	2923.48	2094.65	1685.10	1443.20	1285.05	1174.71	1094.16	1033.42	986.47	949.49	919.93	896.01	876.48
65000	5882.14	3167.10	2269.20	1825.52	1563.46	1392.14	1272.60	1185.34	1119.53	1068.67	1028.61	996.59	970.68	949.52
70000	6334.61	3410.72	2443.75	1965.95	1683.73	1499.23	1370.49	1276.52	1205.65	1150.88	1107.74	1073.25	1045.35	1022.56
75000	6787.09	3654.35	2618.31	2106.37	1803.99	1606.32	1468.38	1367.70	1291.77	1233.08	1186.86	1149.91	1120.01	1095.60
80000	7239.56	3897.97	2792.86	2246.79	1924.26	1713.40	1566.27	1458.88	1377.89	1315.29	1265.98	1226.57	1194.68	1168.64
85000	7692.03	4141.59	2967.41	2387.22	2044.53	1820.49	1664.16	1550.06	1464.00	1397.49	1345.11	1303.23	1269.35	1241.68
90000	8144.50	4385.21	3141.97	2527.64	2164.79	1927.58	1762.06	1641.24	1550.12	1479.70	1424.23	1379.89	1344.02	1314.72
95000	8596.97	4628.84	3316.52	2668.07	2285.06	2034.67	1859.95	1732.42	1636.24	1561.91	1503.36	1456.55	1418.68	1387.76
100000	9049.45	4872.46	3491.07	2808.49	2405.32	2141.75	1957.84	1823.60	1722.36	1644.11	1582.48	1533.21	1493.35	1460.79

TERM AMOUNT	15 Years	16 Years	17 Years	18 Years	19 Years	20 Years	21 Years	22 Years	23 Years	24 Years	25 Years	30 Years	35 Years	40 Years
5	.08	.08	.07	.07	.07	.07	.07	.07	.07	.07	.07	.07	.07	.07
10	.15	.15	.14	.14	.14	.14	.14	.14	.14	.14	.14	.14	.13	.13
15	.22	.22	.21	.21	.21	.21	.21	.21	.20	.20	.20	.20	.20	.20
25	.36	.36	.35	.35	.35	.34	.34	.34	.34	.34	.33	.33	.33	.33
50	.72	.71	.70	.69	.69	.68	.68	.67	.67	.67	.66	.66	.65	.65
75	1.08	1.06	1.05	1.04	1.03	1.02	1.01	1.01	1.00	1.00	.99	.98	.98	.98
100	1.44	1.42	1.40	1.38	1.37	1.36	1.35	1.34	1.34	1.33	1.32	1.31	1.30	1.30
200	2.87	2.83	2.79	2.76	2.73	2.71	2.69	2.68	2.67	2.65	2.64	2.61	2.60	2.59
300	4.31	4.24	4.18	4.14	4.10	4.07	4.04	4.02	4.00	3.98	3.96	3.92	3.90	3.89
400	5.74	5.65	5.58	5.52	5.46	5.42	5.38	5.35	5.33	5.30	5.28	5.22	5.20	5.18
500	7.17	7.06	6.97	6.89	6.83	6.77	6.73	6.69	6.66	6.63	6.60	6.53	6.49	6.48
600	8.61	8.48	8.36	8.27	8.19	8.13	8.07	8.03	7.99	7.95	7.92	7.83	7.79	7.77
700	10.04	9.89	9.76	9.65	9.56	9.48	9.42	9.36	9.32	9.28	9.24	9.14	9.09	9.07
800	11.48	11.30	11.15	11.03	10.92	10.84	10.76	10.70	10.65	10.60	10.56	10.44	10.39	10.36
900	12.91	12.71	12.54	12.41	12.29	12.19	12.11	12.04	11.98	11.93	11.88	11.75	11.68	11.65
1000	14.34	14.12	13.94	13.78	13.65	13.54	13.45	13.37	13.31	13.25	13.20	13.05	12.98	12.95
2000	28.68	28.24	27.87	27.56	27.30	27.08	26.90	26.74	26.61	26.50	26.40	26.10	25.96	25.89
3000	43.02	42.36	41.80	41.34	40.95	40.62	40.34	40.11	39.91	39.74	39.60	39.14	38.93	38.84
4000	57.36	56.48	55.74	55.12	54.60	54.16	53.79	53.48	53.21	52.99	52.79	52.19	51.91	51.78
5000	71.70	70.59	69.67	68.90	68.25	67.70	67.24	66.85	66.51	66.23	65.99	65.23	64.88	64.72
6000	86.04	84.71	83.60	82.67	81.89	81.24	80.68	80.21	79.82	79.48	79.19	78.28	77.86	77.67
7000	100.38	98.83	97.54	96.45	95.54	94.78	94.13	93.58	93.12	92.72	92.39	91.32	90.84	90.61
8000	114.72	112.95	111.47	110.23	109.19	108.32	107.58	106.95	106.42	105.97	105.58	104.37	103.81	103.56
9000	129.06	127.07	125.40	124.01	122.84	121.85	121.02	120.32	119.72	119.21	118.78	117.41	116.79	116.50
10000	143.40	141.18	139.33	137.79	136.49	135.39	134.47	133.69	133.02	132.46	131.98	130.46	129.76	129.44
11000	157.74	155.30	153.27	151.57	150.14	148.93	147.92	147.05	146.32	145.70	145.18	143.50	142.74	142.39
12000	172.08	169.42	167.20	165.34	163.78	162.47	161.36	160.42	159.63	158.95	158.37	156.55	155.72	155.33
13000	186.42	183.54	181.13	179.12	177.43	176.01	174.81	173.79	172.93	172.20	171.57	169.59	168.69	168.28
14000	200.76	197.66	195.07	192.90	191.08	189.55	188.25	187.16	186.23	185.44	184.77	182.64	181.67	181.22
15000	215.10	211.77	209.00	206.68	204.73	203.09	201.70	200.53	199.53	198.69	197.97	195.68	194.64	194.16
16000	229.44	225.89	222.93	220.46	218.38	216.63	215.15	213.89	212.83	211.93	211.16	208.73	207.62	207.11
17000	243.78	240.01	236.86	234.23	232.03	230.16	228.59	227.26	226.13	225.18	224.36	221.77	220.59	220.05
18000	258.12	254.13	250.80	248.01	245.67	243.70	242.04	240.63	239.44	238.42	237.56	234.82	233.57	233.00
19000	272.46	268.24	264.73	261.79	259.32	257.24	255.49	254.00	252.74	251.67	250.76	247.86	246.55	245.94
20000	286.80	282.36	278.66	275.57	272.97	270.78	268.93	267.37	266.04	264.91	263.95	260.91	259.52	258.88
21000	301.14	296.48	292.60	289.35	286.62	284.32	282.38	280.74	279.34	278.16	277.15	273.95	272.50	271.83
22000	315.48	310.60	306.53	303.13	300.27	297.86	295.83	294.10	292.64	291.40	290.35	287.00	285.47	284.77
23000	329.82	324.72	320.46	316.90	313.91	311.40	309.27	307.47	305.95	304.65	303.55	300.04	298.45	297.72
24000	344.16	338.83	334.40	330.68	327.56	324.94	322.72	320.84	319.25	317.89	316.74	313.09	311.43	310.66
25000	358.50	352.95	348.33	344.46	341.21	338.48	336.16	334.21	332.55	331.14	329.94	326.13	324.40	323.60
26000	372.84	367.07	362.26	358.24	354.86	352.01	349.61	347.58	345.85	344.39	343.14	339.18	337.38	336.55
27000	387.18	381.19	376.19	372.02	368.51	365.55	363.06	360.94	359.15	357.63	356.34	352.22	350.35	349.49
28000	401.52	395.31	390.13	385.79	382.16	379.09	376.50	374.31	372.45	370.88	369.53	365.27	363.33	362.44
29000	415.86	409.42	404.06	399.57	395.80	392.63	389.95	387.68	385.76	384.12	382.73	378.31	376.30	375.38
30000	430.20	423.54	417.99	413.35	409.45	406.17	403.40	401.05	399.06	397.37	395.93	391.36	389.28	388.32
31000	444.54	437.66	431.93	427.13	423.10	419.71	416.84	414.42	412.36	410.61	409.13	404.41	402.26	401.27
32000	458.88	451.78	445.86	440.91	436.75	433.25	430.29	427.78	425.66	423.86	422.32	417.45	415.23	414.21
33000	473.22	465.89	459.79	454.69	450.40	446.79	443.74	441.15	438.96	437.10	435.52	430.50	428.21	427.16
34000	487.56	480.01	473.72	468.46	464.05	460.32	457.18	454.52	452.26	450.35	448.72	443.54	441.18	440.10
35000	501.90	494.13	487.66	482.24	477.69	473.86	470.63	467.89	465.57	463.59	461.92	456.59	454.16	453.04
36000	516.24	508.25	501.59	496.02	491.34	487.40	484.07	481.26	478.87	476.84	475.11	469.63	467.14	465.99
37000	530.58	522.37	515.52	509.80	504.99	500.94	497.52	494.63	492.17	490.08	488.31	482.68	480.11	478.93
38000	544.92	536.48	529.46	523.58	518.64	514.48	510.97	507.99	505.47	503.33	501.51	495.72	493.09	491.88
39000	559.26	550.60	543.39	537.35	532.29	528.02	524.41	521.36	518.77	516.58	514.71	508.77	506.06	504.82
40000	573.60	564.72	557.32	551.13	545.94	541.56	537.86	534.73	532.08	529.82	527.90	521.81	519.04	517.76
41000	587.94	578.84	571.25	564.91	559.58	555.10	551.31	548.10	545.38	543.07	541.10	534.86	532.01	530.71
42000	602.28	592.96	585.19	578.69	573.23	568.63	564.75	561.47	558.68	556.31	554.30	547.90	544.99	543.65
43000	616.62	607.07	599.12	592.47	586.88	582.17	578.20	574.83	571.98	569.56	567.50	560.95	557.97	556.60
44000	630.96	621.19	613.05	606.25	600.53	595.71	591.65	588.20	585.28	582.80	580.69	573.99	570.94	569.54
45000	645.30	635.31	626.99	620.02	614.18	609.25	605.09	601.57	598.58	596.05	593.89	587.04	583.92	582.48
46000	659.64	649.43	640.92	633.80	627.82	622.79	618.54	614.94	611.89	609.29	607.09	600.08	596.89	595.43
47000	673.98	663.54	654.85	647.58	641.47	636.33	631.98	628.31	625.19	622.54	620.29	613.13	609.87	608.37
48000	688.32	677.66	668.79	661.36	655.12	649.87	645.43	641.67	638.49	635.78	633.48	626.17	622.85	621.32
49000	702.66	691.78	682.72	675.14	668.77	663.41	658.88	655.04	651.79	649.03	646.68	639.22	635.82	634.26
50000	717.00	705.90	696.65	688.91	682.42	676.95	672.32	668.41	665.09	662.27	659.88	652.26	648.80	647.20
55000	788.70	776.49	766.32	757.81	750.66	744.64	739.56	735.25	731.60	728.50	725.86	717.49	713.68	711.92
60000	860.40	847.08	835.98	826.70	818.90	812.33	806.79	802.09	798.11	794.73	791.85	782.72	778.56	776.64
65000	932.10	917.67	905.65	895.59	887.14	880.03	874.02	868.93	864.62	860.96	857.84	847.94	843.44	841.36
70000	1003.80	988.26	975.31	964.48	955.38	947.72	941.25	935.77	931.13	927.18	923.83	913.17	908.31	906.08
75000	1075.50	1058.85	1044.97	1033.37	1023.62	1015.42	1008.48	1002.61	997.64	993.41	989.81	978.39	973.19	970.80
80000	1147.20	1129.43	1114.64	1102.26	1091.87	1083.11	1075.71	1069.45	1064.15	1059.64	1055.80	1043.62	1038.07	1035.52
85000	1218.90	1200.02	1184.30	1171.15	1160.11	1150.80	1142.95	1136.29	1130.65	1125.86	1121.79	1108.84	1102.95	1100.24
90000	1290.60	1270.61	1253.97	1240.04	1228.35	1218.50	1210.18	1203.14	1197.16	1192.09	1187.78	1174.07	1167.83	1164.97
95000	1362.30	1341.20	1323.63	1308.93	1296.59	1286.19	1277.41	1269.98	1263.67	1258.32	1253.76	1239.30	1232.71	1229.68
100000	1434.00	1411.79	1393.30	1377.82	1364.83	1353.89	1344.64	1336.82	1330.18	1324.54	1319.75	1304.52	1297.59	1294.40

MONTHLY PAYMENT
REQUIRED TO AMORTIZE A LOAN

TERM	1 Year	2 Years	3 Years	4 Years	5 Years	6 Years	7 Years	8 Years	9 Years	10 Years	11 Years	12 Years	13 Years	14 Years
AMOUNT														
5	.46	.25	.18	.15	.13	.11	.10	.10	.09	.09	.08	.08	.08	.08
10	.91	.49	.35	.29	.25	.22	.20	.19	.18	.17	.16	.16	.15	.15
15	1.36	.74	.53	.43	.37	.33	.30	.28	.26	.25	.24	.24	.23	.23
25	2.27	1.22	.88	.71	.61	.54	.50	.46	.44	.42	.40	.39	.38	.37
50	4.53	2.44	1.75	1.41	1.21	1.08	.99	.92	.87	.83	.80	.77	.75	.74
75	6.80	3.66	2.63	2.12	1.81	1.62	1.48	1.38	1.30	1.24	1.20	1.16	1.13	1.11
100	9.06	4.88	3.50	2.82	2.42	2.15	1.97	1.83	1.73	1.66	1.59	1.54	1.50	1.47
200	18.11	9.76	7.00	5.63	4.83	4.30	3.93	3.66	3.46	3.31	3.18	3.08	3.00	2.94
300	27.17	14.64	10.49	8.45	7.24	6.45	5.90	5.49	5.19	4.96	4.77	4.62	4.50	4.41
400	36.22	19.51	13.99	11.26	9.65	8.59	7.86	7.32	6.92	6.61	6.36	6.16	6.00	5.88
500	45.28	24.39	17.48	14.07	12.06	10.74	9.82	9.15	8.65	8.26	7.95	7.70	7.50	7.34
600	54.33	29.27	20.98	16.89	14.47	12.89	11.79	10.98	10.38	9.91	9.54	9.24	9.00	8.81
700	63.38	34.15	24.48	19.70	16.88	15.04	13.75	12.81	12.10	11.56	11.13	10.78	10.50	10.28
800	72.44	39.02	27.97	22.51	19.29	17.18	15.71	14.64	13.83	13.21	12.72	12.32	12.00	11.75
900	81.49	43.90	31.47	25.33	21.70	19.33	17.68	16.47	15.56	14.86	14.30	13.86	13.50	13.21
1000	90.55	48.78	34.96	28.14	24.11	21.48	19.64	18.30	17.29	16.51	15.89	15.40	15.00	14.68
2000	181.09	97.55	69.92	56.28	48.22	42.95	39.27	36.59	34.57	33.01	31.78	30.80	30.00	29.36
3000	271.63	146.32	104.88	84.41	72.32	64.42	58.91	54.89	51.86	49.51	47.67	46.20	45.00	44.03
4000	362.17	195.09	139.84	112.55	96.43	85.89	78.54	73.18	69.14	66.02	63.56	61.59	60.00	58.71
5000	452.71	243.87	174.80	140.68	120.54	107.37	98.18	91.48	86.42	82.52	79.45	76.99	75.00	73.38
6000	543.26	292.64	209.76	168.82	144.64	128.84	117.81	109.77	103.71	99.02	95.33	92.39	90.00	88.06
7000	633.80	341.41	244.72	196.96	168.75	150.31	137.45	128.07	120.99	115.53	111.22	107.78	105.00	102.74
8000	724.34	390.18	279.68	225.09	192.85	171.78	157.08	146.36	138.27	132.03	127.11	123.18	120.00	117.41
9000	814.88	438.95	314.64	253.23	216.96	193.25	176.72	164.65	155.56	148.53	143.00	138.58	135.00	132.09
10000	905.42	487.73	349.60	281.36	241.07	214.73	196.35	182.95	172.84	165.03	158.89	153.98	150.00	146.76
11000	995.96	536.50	384.56	309.50	265.17	236.20	215.99	201.24	190.13	181.54	174.78	169.37	165.00	161.44
12000	1086.51	585.27	419.52	337.64	289.28	257.67	235.62	219.54	207.41	198.04	190.66	184.77	180.00	176.11
13000	1177.05	634.04	454.48	365.77	313.38	279.14	255.26	237.83	224.69	214.54	206.55	200.17	195.00	190.79
14000	1267.59	682.82	489.44	393.91	337.49	300.62	274.89	256.13	241.98	231.05	222.44	215.56	210.00	205.47
15000	1358.13	731.59	524.40	422.04	361.60	322.09	294.53	274.42	259.26	247.55	238.33	230.96	225.00	220.14
16000	1448.67	780.36	559.36	450.18	385.70	343.56	314.16	292.71	276.54	264.05	254.22	246.36	240.00	234.82
17000	1539.21	829.13	594.32	478.31	409.81	365.03	333.80	311.01	293.83	280.55	270.10	261.75	255.00	249.49
18000	1629.76	877.90	629.28	506.45	433.91	386.50	353.43	329.30	311.11	297.06	285.99	277.15	270.00	264.17
19000	1720.30	926.68	664.24	534.59	458.02	407.98	373.07	347.60	328.39	313.56	301.88	292.55	285.00	278.84
20000	1810.84	975.45	699.20	562.72	482.13	429.45	392.70	365.89	345.68	330.06	317.77	307.95	300.00	293.52
21000	1901.38	1024.22	734.16	590.86	506.23	450.92	412.34	384.19	362.96	346.57	333.66	323.34	315.00	308.20
22000	1991.92	1072.99	769.12	618.99	530.34	472.39	431.97	402.48	380.25	363.07	349.55	338.74	330.00	322.87
23000	2082.46	1121.77	804.08	647.13	554.44	493.87	451.61	420.77	397.53	379.57	365.43	354.14	345.00	337.55
24000	2173.01	1170.54	839.04	675.27	578.55	515.34	471.24	439.07	414.81	396.07	381.32	369.53	360.00	352.22
25000	2263.55	1219.31	874.00	703.40	602.66	536.81	490.88	457.36	432.10	412.58	397.21	384.93	375.00	366.90
26000	2354.09	1268.08	908.96	731.54	626.76	558.28	510.51	475.66	449.38	429.08	413.10	400.33	390.00	381.57
27000	2444.63	1316.85	943.92	759.67	650.87	579.75	530.15	493.95	466.66	445.58	428.99	415.73	405.00	396.25
28000	2535.17	1365.63	978.88	787.81	674.97	601.23	549.78	512.25	483.95	462.09	444.87	431.12	420.00	410.93
29000	2625.71	1414.40	1013.84	815.94	699.08	622.70	569.42	530.54	501.23	478.59	460.76	446.52	435.00	425.60
30000	2716.26	1463.17	1048.80	844.08	723.19	644.17	589.05	548.83	518.52	495.09	476.65	461.92	450.00	440.28
31000	2806.80	1511.94	1083.76	872.22	747.29	665.64	608.69	567.13	535.80	511.59	492.54	477.31	465.00	454.95
32000	2897.34	1560.72	1118.72	900.35	771.40	687.12	628.32	585.42	553.08	528.10	508.43	492.71	480.00	469.63
33000	2987.88	1609.49	1153.68	928.49	795.50	708.59	647.96	603.72	570.37	544.60	524.32	508.11	495.00	484.31
34000	3078.42	1658.26	1188.64	956.62	819.61	730.06	667.59	622.01	587.65	561.10	540.20	523.50	510.00	498.98
35000	3168.96	1707.03	1223.60	984.76	843.72	751.53	687.23	640.31	604.93	577.61	556.09	538.90	525.00	513.66
36000	3259.51	1755.80	1258.56	1012.90	867.82	773.00	706.86	658.60	622.22	594.11	571.98	554.30	540.00	528.33
37000	3350.05	1804.58	1293.52	1041.03	891.93	794.48	726.50	676.89	639.50	610.61	587.87	569.70	555.00	543.01
38000	3440.59	1853.35	1328.48	1069.17	916.03	815.95	746.13	695.19	656.78	627.11	603.76	585.09	570.00	557.68
39000	3531.13	1902.12	1363.44	1097.30	940.14	837.42	765.77	713.48	674.07	643.62	619.65	600.49	585.00	572.36
40000	3621.67	1950.89	1398.40	1125.44	964.25	858.89	785.40	731.78	691.35	660.12	635.53	615.89	600.00	587.04
41000	3712.21	1999.67	1433.36	1153.57	988.35	880.37	805.04	750.07	708.64	676.62	651.42	631.28	615.00	601.71
42000	3802.76	2048.44	1468.32	1181.71	1012.46	901.84	824.67	768.37	725.92	693.13	667.31	646.68	630.00	616.39
43000	3893.30	2097.21	1503.28	1209.85	1036.56	923.31	844.31	786.66	743.20	709.63	683.20	662.08	645.00	631.06
44000	3983.84	2145.98	1538.24	1237.98	1060.67	944.78	863.94	804.95	760.49	726.13	699.09	677.48	660.00	645.74
45000	4074.38	2194.75	1573.20	1266.12	1084.78	966.25	883.58	823.25	777.77	742.64	714.97	692.87	675.00	660.41
46000	4164.92	2243.53	1608.16	1294.25	1108.88	987.73	903.21	841.54	795.05	759.14	730.86	708.27	690.00	675.09
47000	4255.46	2292.30	1643.12	1322.39	1132.99	1009.20	922.85	859.84	812.34	775.64	746.75	723.67	705.00	689.77
48000	4346.01	2341.07	1678.08	1350.53	1157.09	1030.67	942.48	878.13	829.62	792.14	762.64	739.06	720.00	704.44
49000	4436.55	2389.84	1713.04	1378.66	1181.20	1052.14	962.12	896.43	846.90	808.65	778.53	754.46	735.00	719.12
50000	4527.09	2438.62	1748.00	1406.80	1205.31	1073.62	981.75	914.72	864.19	825.15	794.42	769.86	750.00	733.79
55000	4979.80	2682.48	1922.80	1547.48	1325.84	1180.98	1079.93	1006.19	950.61	907.66	873.86	846.84	825.00	807.17
60000	5432.51	2926.34	2097.60	1688.16	1446.37	1288.34	1178.10	1097.66	1037.03	990.18	953.30	923.83	900.00	880.55
65000	5885.21	3170.20	2272.40	1828.83	1566.90	1395.70	1276.27	1189.14	1123.44	1072.69	1032.74	1000.81	975.00	953.93
70000	6337.92	3414.06	2447.20	1969.51	1687.43	1503.06	1374.45	1280.61	1209.86	1155.21	1112.18	1077.80	1050.00	1027.31
75000	6790.63	3657.92	2622.00	2110.19	1807.96	1610.42	1472.62	1372.08	1296.28	1237.72	1191.62	1154.78	1125.00	1100.69
80000	7243.34	3901.78	2796.79	2250.87	1928.49	1717.78	1570.80	1463.55	1382.70	1320.24	1271.06	1231.77	1200.00	1174.07
85000	7696.05	4145.64	2971.59	2391.55	2049.02	1825.14	1668.97	1555.02	1469.12	1402.75	1350.50	1308.75	1275.00	1247.45
90000	8148.76	4389.50	3146.39	2532.23	2169.55	1932.50	1767.15	1646.49	1555.54	1485.27	1429.94	1385.74	1350.00	1320.82
95000	8601.46	4633.36	3321.19	2672.91	2290.08	2039.86	1865.32	1737.96	1641.95	1567.78	1509.38	1462.72	1425.00	1394.20
100000	9054.17	4877.23	3495.99	2813.59	2410.61	2147.23	1963.50	1829.44	1728.37	1650.29	1588.83	1539.71	1500.00	1467.58

TERM AMOUNT	15 Years	16 Years	17 Years	18 Years	19 Years	20 Years	21 Years	22 Years	23 Years	24 Years	25 Years	30 Years	35 Years	40 Years
5	.08	.08	.08	.07	.07	.07	.07	.07	.07	.07	.07	.07	.07	.07
10	.15	.15	.15	.14	.14	.14	.14	.14	.14	.14	.14	.14	.14	.14
15	.22	.22	.22	.21	.21	.21	.21	.21	.21	.20	.20	.20	.20	.20
25	.37	.36	.36	.35	.35	.35	.34	.34	.34	.34	.34	.33	.33	.33
50	.73	.71	.71	.70	.69	.69	.68	.68	.67	.67	.67	.66	.66	.66
75	1.09	1.07	1.06	1.04	1.03	1.03	1.02	1.01	1.01	1.00	1.00	.99	.98	.98
100	1.45	1.42	1.41	1.39	1.38	1.37	1.36	1.35	1.34	1.34	1.33	1.32	1.31	1.31
200	2.89	2.84	2.81	2.78	2.75	2.73	2.71	2.69	2.68	2.67	2.66	2.63	2.62	2.61
300	4.33	4.26	4.21	4.16	4.12	4.09	4.06	4.04	4.02	4.00	3.99	3.94	3.92	3.91
400	5.77	5.68	5.61	5.55	5.49	5.45	5.41	5.38	5.36	5.33	5.32	5.26	5.23	5.22
500	7.21	7.10	7.01	6.93	6.87	6.81	6.77	6.73	6.69	6.67	6.64	6.57	6.53	6.52
600	8.65	8.52	8.41	8.32	8.24	8.17	8.12	8.07	8.03	8.00	7.97	7.88	7.84	7.82
700	10.09	9.94	9.81	9.70	9.61	9.53	9.47	9.42	9.37	9.33	9.30	9.19	9.15	9.12
800	11.53	11.36	11.21	11.09	10.98	10.90	10.82	10.76	10.71	10.66	10.63	10.51	10.45	10.43
900	12.97	12.77	12.61	12.47	12.35	12.26	12.17	12.10	12.05	12.00	11.95	11.82	11.76	11.73
1000	14.41	14.19	14.01	13.86	13.73	13.62	13.53	13.45	13.38	13.33	13.28	13.13	13.06	13.03
2000	28.82	28.38	28.01	27.71	27.45	27.23	27.05	26.89	26.76	26.65	26.56	26.26	26.12	26.06
3000	43.23	42.57	42.02	41.56	41.17	40.85	40.57	40.34	40.14	39.97	39.83	39.38	39.18	39.08
4000	57.64	56.76	56.02	55.41	54.89	54.46	54.09	53.78	53.52	53.30	53.11	52.51	52.24	52.11
5000	72.05	70.95	70.03	69.26	68.61	68.07	67.61	67.23	66.90	66.62	66.38	65.63	65.29	65.14
6000	86.46	85.13	84.03	83.11	82.34	81.69	81.14	80.67	80.28	79.94	79.66	78.76	78.35	78.16
7000	100.87	99.32	98.04	96.96	96.06	95.30	94.66	94.11	93.66	93.27	92.93	91.88	91.41	91.19
8000	115.28	113.51	112.04	110.81	109.78	108.91	108.18	107.56	107.03	106.59	106.21	105.01	104.47	104.22
9000	129.69	127.70	126.05	124.66	123.50	122.53	121.70	121.00	120.41	119.91	119.49	118.13	117.52	117.24
10000	144.10	141.89	140.05	138.51	137.22	136.14	135.22	134.45	133.79	133.23	132.76	131.26	130.58	130.27
11000	158.50	156.08	154.05	152.36	150.95	149.75	148.74	147.89	147.17	146.56	146.04	144.39	143.64	143.30
12000	172.91	170.26	168.06	166.21	164.67	163.37	162.27	161.34	160.55	159.88	159.31	157.51	156.70	156.32
13000	187.32	184.45	182.06	180.07	178.39	176.98	175.79	174.78	173.93	173.20	172.59	170.64	169.75	169.35
14000	201.73	198.64	196.07	193.92	192.11	190.59	189.31	188.22	187.31	186.53	185.86	183.76	182.81	182.38
15000	216.14	212.83	210.07	207.77	205.83	204.21	202.83	201.67	200.68	199.85	199.14	196.89	195.87	195.40
16000	230.55	227.02	224.08	221.62	219.55	217.82	216.35	215.11	214.06	213.17	212.41	210.01	208.93	208.43
17000	244.96	241.21	238.08	235.47	233.28	231.43	229.87	228.56	227.44	226.49	225.69	223.14	221.98	221.45
18000	259.37	255.39	252.09	249.32	247.00	245.05	243.40	242.00	240.82	239.82	238.97	236.26	235.04	234.48
19000	273.78	269.58	266.09	263.17	260.72	258.66	256.92	255.45	254.20	253.14	252.24	249.39	248.10	247.51
20000	288.19	283.77	280.09	277.02	274.44	272.27	270.44	268.89	267.58	266.46	265.52	262.52	261.16	260.53
21000	302.60	297.96	294.10	290.87	288.16	285.89	283.96	282.33	280.96	279.79	278.79	275.64	274.21	273.56
22000	317.00	312.15	308.10	304.72	301.89	299.50	297.48	295.78	294.33	293.11	292.07	288.77	287.27	286.59
23000	331.41	326.34	322.11	318.57	315.61	313.11	311.00	309.22	307.71	306.44	305.34	301.89	300.33	299.61
24000	345.82	340.52	336.11	332.42	329.33	326.73	324.53	322.67	321.09	319.75	318.62	315.02	313.39	312.64
25000	360.23	354.71	350.12	346.28	343.05	340.34	338.05	336.11	334.47	333.08	331.89	328.14	326.44	325.67
26000	374.64	368.90	364.12	360.13	356.77	353.95	351.57	349.56	347.85	346.40	345.17	341.27	339.50	338.69
27000	389.05	383.09	378.13	373.98	370.50	367.57	365.09	363.00	361.23	359.72	358.45	354.39	352.56	351.72
28000	403.46	397.28	392.13	387.83	384.22	381.18	378.61	376.44	374.61	373.05	371.72	367.52	365.62	364.75
29000	417.87	411.46	406.13	401.68	397.94	394.79	392.14	389.89	387.99	386.37	385.00	380.65	378.67	377.77
30000	432.28	425.65	420.14	415.53	411.66	408.41	405.66	403.33	401.36	399.69	398.27	393.77	391.73	390.80
31000	446.69	439.84	434.14	429.38	425.38	422.02	419.18	416.78	414.74	413.02	411.55	406.90	404.79	403.82
32000	461.10	454.03	448.15	443.23	439.10	435.63	432.70	430.22	428.12	426.34	424.82	420.02	417.85	416.85
33000	475.50	468.22	462.15	457.08	452.83	449.25	446.22	443.67	441.50	439.66	438.10	433.15	430.90	429.88
34000	489.91	482.41	476.16	470.93	466.55	462.86	459.74	457.11	454.88	452.98	451.37	446.27	443.96	442.90
35000	504.32	496.59	490.16	484.78	480.27	476.47	473.27	470.55	468.26	466.31	464.65	459.40	457.02	455.93
36000	518.73	510.78	504.17	498.63	493.99	490.09	486.79	484.00	481.64	479.63	477.93	472.52	470.08	468.96
37000	533.14	524.97	518.17	512.49	507.71	503.70	500.31	497.44	495.01	492.95	491.20	485.65	483.13	481.98
38000	547.55	539.16	532.18	526.34	521.44	517.31	513.83	510.89	508.39	506.28	504.48	498.77	496.19	495.01
39000	561.96	553.35	546.18	540.19	535.16	530.93	527.35	524.33	521.77	519.60	517.75	511.90	509.25	508.04
40000	576.37	567.54	560.18	554.04	548.88	544.54	540.87	537.78	535.15	532.92	531.03	525.03	522.31	521.06
41000	590.78	581.72	574.19	567.89	562.60	558.15	554.40	551.22	548.53	546.24	544.30	538.15	535.36	534.09
42000	605.19	595.91	588.19	581.74	576.32	571.77	567.92	564.66	561.91	559.57	557.58	551.28	548.42	547.12
43000	619.60	610.10	602.20	595.59	590.05	585.38	581.44	578.11	575.29	572.89	570.85	564.40	561.48	560.14
44000	634.00	624.29	616.20	609.44	603.77	598.99	594.96	591.55	588.66	586.21	584.13	577.53	574.54	573.17
45000	648.41	638.48	630.21	623.29	617.49	612.61	608.48	605.00	602.04	599.54	597.41	590.65	587.59	586.19
46000	662.82	652.67	644.21	637.14	631.21	626.22	622.00	618.44	615.42	612.86	610.68	603.78	600.65	599.22
47000	677.23	666.85	658.22	650.99	644.93	639.83	635.53	631.89	628.80	626.18	623.96	616.90	613.71	612.25
48000	691.64	681.04	672.22	664.84	658.65	653.45	649.05	645.33	642.18	639.50	637.23	630.03	626.77	625.27
49000	706.05	695.23	686.22	678.69	672.38	667.06	662.57	658.77	655.56	652.83	650.51	643.16	639.82	638.30
50000	720.46	709.42	700.23	692.55	686.10	680.67	676.09	672.22	668.94	666.15	663.78	656.28	652.88	651.33
55000	792.50	780.36	770.25	761.80	754.71	748.74	743.70	739.44	735.83	732.76	730.16	721.91	718.17	716.46
60000	864.55	851.30	840.27	831.05	823.32	816.81	811.31	806.66	802.72	799.38	796.54	787.54	783.46	781.59
65000	936.60	922.24	910.30	900.31	891.93	884.87	878.92	873.88	869.62	865.99	862.92	853.16	848.74	846.72
70000	1008.64	993.18	980.32	969.56	960.54	952.94	946.53	941.10	936.51	932.61	929.29	918.79	914.03	911.86
75000	1080.69	1064.13	1050.34	1038.82	1029.15	1021.01	1014.14	1008.32	1003.40	999.22	995.67	984.42	979.32	976.99
80000	1152.73	1135.07	1120.36	1108.07	1097.75	1089.07	1081.74	1075.55	1070.29	1065.84	1062.05	1050.05	1044.61	1042.12
85000	1224.78	1206.01	1190.39	1177.32	1166.36	1157.14	1149.35	1142.77	1137.19	1132.45	1128.43	1115.67	1109.90	1107.25
90000	1296.82	1276.95	1260.41	1246.58	1234.97	1225.21	1216.96	1209.99	1204.08	1199.07	1194.81	1181.30	1175.18	1172.38
95000	1368.87	1347.89	1330.43	1315.83	1303.58	1293.27	1284.57	1277.21	1270.97	1265.68	1261.18	1246.93	1240.47	1237.52
100000	1440.91	1418.83	1400.45	1385.09	1372.19	1361.34	1352.18	1344.43	1337.87	1332.30	1327.56	1312.56	1305.76	1302.65

MONTHLY PAYMENT
REQUIRED TO AMORTIZE A LOAN

TERM AMOUNT	1 Year	2 Years	3 Years	4 Years	5 Years	6 Years	7 Years	8 Years	9 Years	10 Years	11 Years	12 Years	13 Years	14 Years
5	.46	.25	.18	.15	.13	.11	.10	.10	.09	.09	.08	.08	.08	.08
10	.91	.49	.35	.29	.25	.22	.20	.19	.18	.17	.16	.16	.16	.15
15	1.36	.74	.53	.43	.37	.33	.30	.28	.26	.25	.24	.24	.23	.23
25	2.27	1.22	.88	.71	.61	.54	.50	.46	.44	.42	.40	.39	.38	.37
50	4.53	2.44	1.75	1.41	1.21	1.08	.99	.92	.87	.83	.80	.78	.76	.74
75	6.80	3.66	2.63	2.12	1.81	1.62	1.48	1.38	1.30	1.24	1.20	1.16	1.13	1.11
100	9.06	4.88	3.50	2.82	2.42	2.15	1.97	1.84	1.73	1.66	1.60	1.55	1.51	1.47
200	18.12	9.76	7.00	5.63	4.83	4.30	3.93	3.67	3.46	3.31	3.19	3.09	3.01	2.94
300	27.17	14.64	10.50	8.45	7.24	6.45	5.90	5.50	5.19	4.96	4.78	4.63	4.51	4.41
400	36.23	19.52	15.99	11.24	9.65	8.60	7.86	7.33	6.92	6.61	6.37	6.17	6.01	5.88
500	45.28	24.40	17.49	14.08	12.06	10.75	9.83	9.16	8.65	8.26	7.96	7.71	7.51	7.35
600	54.34	29.28	20.99	16.89	14.48	12.90	11.79	10.99	10.38	9.92	9.55	9.25	9.01	8.82
700	63.39	34.15	24.49	19.71	16.89	15.05	13.76	12.82	12.11	11.57	11.14	10.79	10.52	10.29
800	72.45	39.03	27.98	22.52	19.30	17.19	15.72	14.65	13.84	13.22	12.73	12.34	12.02	11.76
900	81.50	43.91	31.48	25.34	21.71	19.34	17.69	16.48	15.57	14.87	14.32	13.88	13.52	13.23
1000	90.56	48.79	34.98	28.15	24.12	21.49	19.65	18.31	17.30	16.52	15.91	15.42	15.02	14.70
2000	181.11	97.57	69.95	56.30	48.24	42.98	39.30	36.62	34.60	33.04	31.81	30.83	30.04	29.39
3000	271.67	146.36	104.92	84.45	72.36	64.46	58.95	54.93	51.90	49.56	47.72	46.24	45.05	44.08
4000	362.22	195.14	139.89	112.60	96.48	85.95	78.60	73.24	69.20	66.08	63.62	61.66	60.07	58.78
5000	452.77	243.93	174.87	140.75	120.60	107.43	98.25	91.55	86.50	82.60	79.53	77.07	75.09	73.47
6000	543.33	292.71	209.84	168.90	144.72	128.92	117.90	109.86	103.80	99.12	95.43	92.48	90.10	88.16
7000	633.88	341.49	244.81	197.05	168.84	150.41	137.55	128.17	121.10	115.63	111.33	107.90	105.12	102.85
8000	724.43	390.28	279.78	225.19	192.96	171.89	157.20	146.48	138.39	132.15	127.24	123.31	120.14	117.55
9000	814.99	439.06	314.75	253.34	217.08	193.38	176.85	164.79	155.69	148.67	143.14	138.72	135.15	132.24
10000	905.54	487.85	349.73	281.49	241.20	214.86	196.50	183.09	172.99	165.19	159.05	154.14	150.17	146.93
11000	996.09	536.63	384.70	309.64	265.32	236.35	216.14	201.40	190.29	181.71	174.95	169.55	165.19	161.63
12000	1086.65	585.41	419.67	337.79	289.44	257.84	235.79	219.71	207.59	198.23	190.85	184.96	180.20	176.32
13000	1177.20	634.20	454.64	365.94	313.56	279.32	255.44	238.02	224.89	214.74	206.76	200.38	195.22	191.01
14000	1267.75	682.98	489.62	394.09	337.67	300.81	275.09	256.33	242.19	231.26	222.66	215.79	210.24	205.70
15000	1358.31	731.77	524.59	422.23	361.79	322.29	294.74	274.64	259.49	247.78	238.57	231.20	225.25	220.40
16000	1448.86	780.55	559.56	450.38	385.91	343.78	314.39	292.95	276.78	264.30	254.47	246.62	240.27	235.09
17000	1539.41	829.34	594.53	478.53	410.03	365.27	334.04	311.26	294.08	280.82	270.37	262.03	255.29	249.78
18000	1629.97	878.12	629.50	506.68	434.15	386.75	353.69	329.57	311.38	297.34	286.28	277.44	270.30	264.47
19000	1720.52	926.90	664.48	534.83	458.27	408.24	373.34	347.87	328.68	313.85	302.18	292.86	285.32	279.17
20000	1811.07	975.69	699.45	562.98	482.39	429.72	392.99	366.18	345.98	330.37	318.09	308.27	300.34	293.86
21000	1901.63	1024.47	734.42	591.13	506.51	451.21	412.64	384.49	363.28	346.89	333.99	323.68	315.35	308.55
22000	1992.18	1073.26	769.39	619.27	530.63	472.69	432.28	402.80	380.58	363.41	349.89	339.10	330.37	323.25
23000	2082.74	1122.04	804.37	647.42	554.75	494.18	451.93	421.11	397.88	379.93	365.80	354.51	345.39	337.94
24000	2173.29	1170.82	839.34	675.57	578.87	515.67	471.58	439.42	415.17	396.45	381.70	369.92	360.40	352.63
25000	2263.84	1219.61	874.31	703.72	602.99	537.15	491.23	457.73	432.47	412.96	397.61	385.34	375.42	367.32
26000	2354.40	1268.39	909.28	731.87	627.11	558.64	510.88	476.04	449.77	429.48	413.51	400.75	390.44	382.02
27000	2444.95	1317.18	944.25	760.02	651.22	580.12	530.53	494.35	467.07	446.00	429.42	416.16	405.45	396.71
28000	2535.50	1365.96	979.23	788.17	675.34	601.61	550.18	512.65	484.37	462.52	445.32	431.58	420.47	411.40
29000	2626.06	1414.74	1014.20	816.31	699.46	623.10	569.83	530.96	501.67	479.04	461.22	446.99	435.49	426.09
30000	2716.61	1463.53	1049.17	844.46	723.58	644.58	589.48	549.27	518.97	495.56	477.13	462.40	450.50	440.79
31000	2807.16	1512.31	1084.14	872.61	747.70	666.07	609.13	567.58	536.27	512.07	493.03	477.82	465.52	455.48
32000	2897.72	1561.10	1119.11	900.76	771.82	687.55	628.78	585.89	553.56	528.59	508.94	493.23	480.54	470.17
33000	2988.27	1609.88	1154.09	928.91	795.94	709.04	648.42	604.20	570.86	545.11	524.84	508.64	495.55	484.87
34000	3078.82	1658.67	1189.06	957.06	820.06	730.53	668.07	622.51	588.16	561.63	540.74	524.06	510.57	499.56
35000	3169.38	1707.45	1224.03	985.21	844.18	752.01	687.72	640.82	605.46	578.15	556.65	539.47	525.59	514.25
36000	3259.93	1756.23	1259.00	1013.35	868.30	773.50	707.37	659.13	622.76	594.67	572.55	554.88	540.60	528.94
37000	3350.48	1805.02	1293.98	1041.50	892.42	794.98	727.02	677.44	640.06	611.18	588.46	570.30	555.62	543.64
38000	3441.04	1853.80	1328.95	1069.65	916.54	816.47	746.67	695.74	657.36	627.70	604.36	585.71	570.63	558.33
39000	3531.59	1902.59	1363.92	1097.80	940.66	837.96	766.32	714.05	674.66	644.22	620.26	601.12	585.65	573.02
40000	3622.14	1951.37	1398.89	1125.95	964.78	859.44	785.97	732.36	691.95	660.74	636.17	616.54	600.67	587.72
41000	3712.70	2000.15	1433.86	1154.10	988.89	880.93	805.62	750.67	709.25	677.26	652.07	631.95	615.68	602.41
42000	3803.25	2048.94	1468.84	1182.25	1013.01	902.41	825.27	768.98	726.55	693.78	667.98	647.36	630.70	617.10
43000	3893.81	2097.72	1503.81	1210.39	1037.13	923.90	844.92	787.29	743.85	710.29	683.88	662.78	645.72	631.79
44000	3984.36	2146.51	1538.78	1238.54	1061.25	945.38	864.56	805.60	761.15	726.81	699.78	678.19	660.73	646.49
45000	4074.91	2195.29	1573.75	1266.69	1085.37	966.87	884.21	823.91	778.45	743.33	715.69	693.60	675.75	661.18
46000	4165.47	2244.07	1608.73	1294.84	1109.49	988.36	903.86	842.22	795.75	759.85	731.59	709.02	690.77	675.87
47000	4256.02	2292.86	1643.70	1322.99	1133.61	1009.84	923.51	860.52	813.04	776.37	747.50	724.43	705.78	690.56
48000	4346.57	2341.64	1678.67	1351.14	1157.73	1031.33	943.16	878.83	830.34	792.89	763.40	739.84	720.80	705.26
49000	4437.13	2390.43	1713.64	1379.29	1181.85	1052.81	962.81	897.14	847.64	809.40	779.31	755.26	735.82	719.95
50000	4527.68	2439.21	1748.61	1407.43	1205.97	1074.30	982.46	915.45	864.94	825.92	795.21	770.67	750.83	734.64
55000	4980.45	2683.13	1923.47	1548.18	1326.56	1181.73	1080.70	1007.00	951.43	908.52	874.73	847.74	825.92	808.11
60000	5433.21	2927.05	2098.34	1688.92	1447.16	1289.16	1178.95	1098.54	1037.93	991.11	954.25	924.80	901.00	881.57
65000	5885.98	3170.97	2273.20	1829.66	1567.76	1396.59	1277.20	1190.08	1124.42	1073.70	1033.77	1001.87	976.08	955.03
70000	6338.75	3414.89	2448.06	1970.41	1688.35	1504.02	1375.44	1281.63	1210.92	1156.29	1113.29	1078.94	1051.17	1028.50
75000	6791.52	3658.81	2622.92	2111.15	1808.95	1611.45	1473.69	1373.17	1297.41	1238.88	1192.81	1156.00	1126.25	1101.96
80000	7244.28	3902.73	2797.78	2251.89	1929.55	1718.88	1571.93	1464.72	1383.90	1321.47	1272.33	1233.07	1201.33	1175.43
85000	7697.05	4146.66	2972.64	2392.64	2050.14	1826.31	1670.18	1556.26	1470.40	1404.07	1351.85	1310.14	1276.41	1248.89
90000	8149.82	4390.58	3147.50	2533.38	2170.74	1933.74	1768.42	1647.81	1556.89	1486.66	1431.37	1387.20	1351.50	1322.35
95000	8602.59	4634.50	3322.36	2674.12	2291.33	2041.17	1866.67	1739.35	1643.38	1569.25	1510.89	1464.27	1426.58	1395.82
100000	9055.35	4878.42	3497.22	2814.86	2411.93	2148.60	1964.91	1830.90	1729.88	1651.84	1590.41	1541.34	1501.66	1469.28

TERM	15 Years	16 Years	17 Years	18 Years	19 Years	20 Years	21 Years	22 Years	23 Years	24 Years	25 Years	30 Years	35 Years	40 Years
AMOUNT														
5	.08	.08	.08	.07	.07	.07	.07	.07	.07	.07	.07	.07	.07	.07
10	.15	.15	.15	.14	.14	.14	.14	.14	.14	.14	.14	.14	.14	.14
15	.22	.22	.22	.21	.21	.21	.21	.21	.21	.21	.20	.20	.20	.20
25	.37	.36	.36	.35	.35	.35	.34	.34	.34	.34	.34	.33	.33	.33
50	.73	.72	.71	.70	.69	.69	.68	.68	.67	.67	.67	.66	.66	.66
75	1.09	1.07	1.06	1.05	1.04	1.03	1.02	1.01	1.01	1.01	1.00	.99	.99	.98
100	1.45	1.43	1.41	1.39	1.38	1.37	1.36	1.35	1.34	1.34	1.33	1.32	1.31	1.31
200	2.89	2.85	2.81	2.78	2.75	2.73	2.71	2.70	2.68	2.67	2.67	2.63	2.62	2.61
300	4.33	4.27	4.21	4.17	4.13	4.09	4.07	4.04	4.02	4.01	3.99	3.95	3.93	3.92
400	5.78	5.69	5.61	5.55	5.50	5.46	5.42	5.39	5.36	5.34	5.32	5.26	5.24	5.22
500	7.22	7.11	7.02	6.94	6.88	6.82	6.78	6.74	6.70	6.68	6.65	6.58	6.54	6.53
600	8.66	8.53	8.42	8.33	8.25	8.18	8.13	8.08	8.04	8.01	7.98	7.89	7.85	7.83
700	10.10	9.95	9.82	9.71	9.62	9.55	9.48	9.43	9.38	9.34	9.31	9.21	9.16	9.14
800	11.55	11.37	11.22	11.10	11.00	10.91	10.84	10.78	10.72	10.68	10.64	10.52	10.47	10.44
900	12.99	12.79	12.63	12.49	12.37	12.27	12.19	12.12	12.06	12.01	11.97	11.84	11.78	11.75
1000	14.43	14.21	14.03	13.87	13.75	13.64	13.55	13.47	13.40	13.35	13.30	13.15	13.08	13.05
2000	28.86	28.42	28.05	27.74	27.49	27.27	27.09	26.93	26.80	26.69	26.60	26.30	26.16	26.10
3000	43.28	42.62	42.07	41.61	41.23	40.90	40.63	40.39	40.20	40.03	39.89	39.44	39.24	39.15
4000	57.71	56.83	56.09	55.48	54.97	54.53	54.17	53.86	53.60	53.37	53.19	52.59	52.32	52.19
5000	72.14	71.03	70.12	69.35	68.71	68.16	67.71	67.32	66.99	66.72	66.48	65.73	65.39	65.24
6000	86.56	85.24	84.14	83.22	82.45	81.80	81.25	80.78	80.39	80.06	79.78	78.88	78.47	78.29
7000	100.99	99.45	98.16	97.09	96.19	95.43	94.79	94.25	93.79	93.40	93.07	92.02	91.55	91.33
8000	115.42	113.65	112.18	110.96	109.93	109.06	108.33	107.71	107.19	106.74	106.37	105.17	104.63	104.38
9000	129.84	127.86	126.21	124.83	123.67	122.69	121.87	121.17	120.59	120.09	119.66	118.32	117.71	117.43
10000	144.27	142.06	140.23	138.69	137.41	136.32	135.41	134.64	133.98	133.43	132.96	131.46	130.78	130.48
11000	158.70	156.27	154.25	152.56	151.15	149.96	148.95	148.10	147.38	146.77	146.25	144.61	143.86	143.52
12000	173.12	170.48	168.27	166.43	164.89	163.59	162.49	161.56	160.78	160.11	159.55	157.75	156.94	156.57
13000	187.55	184.68	182.30	180.30	178.63	177.22	176.03	175.03	174.18	173.45	172.84	170.90	170.02	169.62
14000	201.97	198.89	196.32	194.17	192.37	190.85	189.57	188.49	187.57	186.80	186.14	184.04	183.10	182.66
15000	216.40	213.09	210.34	208.04	206.11	204.48	203.11	201.95	200.97	200.14	199.43	197.19	196.17	195.71
16000	230.83	227.30	224.36	221.91	219.85	218.12	216.65	215.42	214.37	213.48	212.73	210.33	209.25	208.76
17000	245.25	241.51	238.39	235.78	233.59	231.75	230.20	228.88	227.77	226.82	226.02	223.48	222.33	221.80
18000	259.68	255.71	252.41	249.65	247.33	245.38	243.74	242.34	241.17	240.17	239.32	236.63	235.41	234.85
19000	274.11	269.92	266.43	263.52	261.07	259.01	257.28	255.81	254.56	253.51	252.61	249.77	248.49	247.90
20000	288.53	284.12	280.45	277.38	274.81	272.64	270.82	269.27	267.96	266.85	265.91	262.92	261.56	260.95
21000	302.96	298.33	294.48	291.25	288.55	286.28	284.36	282.73	281.36	280.19	279.20	276.06	274.64	273.99
22000	317.39	312.53	308.50	305.12	302.29	299.91	297.90	296.20	294.76	293.54	292.50	289.21	287.72	287.04
23000	331.81	326.74	322.52	318.99	316.03	313.54	311.44	309.66	308.16	306.88	305.79	302.35	300.80	300.09
24000	346.24	340.95	336.54	332.86	329.77	327.17	324.98	323.12	321.55	320.22	319.09	315.50	313.88	313.13
25000	360.66	355.15	350.56	346.73	343.51	340.80	338.52	336.59	334.95	333.56	332.38	328.65	326.95	326.18
26000	375.09	369.36	364.59	360.60	357.25	354.44	352.06	350.05	348.35	346.90	345.68	341.79	340.03	339.23
27000	389.52	383.56	378.61	374.47	370.99	368.07	365.60	363.51	361.75	360.25	358.97	354.94	353.11	352.28
28000	403.94	397.77	392.63	388.34	384.73	381.70	379.14	376.98	375.14	373.59	372.27	368.08	366.19	365.32
29000	418.37	411.98	406.65	402.21	398.47	395.33	392.68	390.44	388.54	386.93	385.56	381.23	379.27	378.37
30000	432.80	426.18	420.68	416.07	412.21	408.96	406.22	403.90	401.94	400.27	398.86	394.37	392.34	391.42
31000	447.22	440.39	434.70	429.94	425.95	422.60	419.76	417.37	415.34	413.62	412.15	407.52	405.42	404.46
32000	461.65	454.59	448.72	443.81	439.69	436.23	433.30	430.83	428.74	426.96	425.45	420.66	418.50	417.51
33000	476.08	468.80	462.74	457.68	453.43	449.86	446.84	444.29	442.13	440.30	438.74	433.81	431.58	430.56
34000	490.50	483.01	476.77	471.55	467.17	463.49	460.39	457.76	455.53	453.64	452.04	446.96	444.66	443.60
35000	504.93	497.21	490.79	485.42	480.92	477.12	473.93	471.22	468.93	466.99	465.33	460.10	457.73	456.65
36000	519.36	511.42	504.81	499.29	494.66	490.76	487.47	484.68	482.33	480.33	478.63	473.25	470.81	469.70
37000	533.78	525.62	518.83	513.16	508.40	504.39	501.01	498.15	495.73	493.67	491.92	486.39	483.89	482.75
38000	548.21	539.83	532.86	527.03	522.14	518.02	514.55	511.61	509.12	507.01	505.22	499.54	496.97	495.79
39000	562.63	554.03	546.88	540.90	535.88	531.65	528.09	525.07	522.52	520.35	518.51	512.68	510.05	508.84
40000	577.06	568.24	560.90	554.76	549.62	545.28	541.63	538.54	535.92	533.70	531.81	525.83	523.12	521.89
41000	591.49	582.45	574.92	568.63	563.36	558.92	555.17	552.00	549.32	547.04	545.10	538.98	536.20	534.93
42000	605.91	596.65	588.95	582.50	577.10	572.55	568.71	565.46	562.71	560.38	558.40	552.12	549.28	547.98
43000	620.34	610.86	602.97	596.37	590.84	586.18	582.25	578.93	576.11	573.72	571.69	565.27	562.36	561.03
44000	634.77	625.06	616.99	610.24	604.58	599.81	595.79	592.39	589.51	587.07	584.99	578.41	575.44	574.08
45000	649.19	639.27	631.01	624.11	618.32	613.44	609.33	605.85	602.91	600.41	598.28	591.56	588.51	587.12
46000	663.62	653.48	645.03	637.98	632.06	627.08	622.87	619.32	616.31	613.75	611.58	604.70	601.59	600.17
47000	678.05	667.68	659.06	651.85	645.80	640.71	636.41	632.78	629.70	627.09	624.87	617.85	614.67	613.22
48000	692.47	681.89	673.08	665.72	659.54	654.34	649.95	646.24	643.10	640.44	638.17	630.99	627.75	626.26
49000	706.90	696.09	687.10	679.59	673.28	667.97	663.49	659.71	656.50	653.78	651.47	644.14	640.82	639.31
50000	721.32	710.30	701.12	693.45	687.02	681.60	677.03	673.17	669.90	667.12	664.76	657.29	653.90	652.36
55000	793.46	781.33	771.24	762.80	755.72	749.76	744.74	740.49	736.89	733.83	731.24	723.01	719.29	717.59
60000	865.59	852.36	841.35	832.14	824.42	817.92	812.44	807.80	803.88	800.54	797.71	788.74	784.68	782.83
65000	937.72	923.39	911.46	901.49	893.12	886.08	880.14	875.12	870.87	867.25	864.19	854.47	850.07	848.06
70000	1009.85	994.42	981.57	970.83	961.83	954.24	947.85	942.44	937.85	933.97	930.66	920.20	915.46	913.30
75000	1081.98	1065.45	1051.68	1040.18	1030.53	1022.40	1015.55	1009.75	1004.84	1000.68	997.14	985.93	980.85	978.53
80000	1154.12	1136.48	1121.80	1109.52	1099.23	1090.56	1083.25	1077.07	1071.83	1067.39	1063.61	1051.65	1046.24	1043.77
85000	1226.25	1207.51	1191.91	1178.87	1167.93	1158.72	1150.96	1144.39	1138.82	1134.10	1130.09	1117.38	1111.63	1109.00
90000	1298.38	1278.54	1262.02	1248.21	1236.63	1226.88	1218.66	1211.70	1205.81	1200.81	1196.56	1183.11	1177.02	1174.24
95000	1370.51	1349.56	1332.13	1317.56	1305.33	1295.04	1286.36	1279.02	1272.80	1267.52	1263.04	1248.84	1242.41	1239.48
100000	1442.64	1420.59	1402.24	1386.90	1374.03	1363.20	1354.06	1346.34	1339.79	1334.24	1329.52	1314.57	1307.80	1304.71

MONTHLY PAYMENT
REQUIRED TO AMORTIZE A LOAN

TERM AMOUNT	1 Year	2 Years	3 Years	4 Years	5 Years	6 Years	7 Years	8 Years	9 Years	10 Years	11 Years	12 Years	13 Years	14 Years
5	.46	.25	.18	.15	.13	.11	.10	.10	.09	.09	.08	.08	.08	.08
10	.91	.49	.36	.29	.25	.22	.20	.19	.18	.17	.16	.16	.16	.15
15	1.36	.74	.53	.43	.37	.33	.30	.28	.27	.25	.24	.24	.23	.23
25	2.27	1.23	.88	.71	.61	.54	.50	.46	.44	.42	.40	.39	.38	.37
50	4.53	2.45	1.76	1.41	1.21	1.08	.99	.92	.87	.83	.80	.78	.76	.74
75	6.80	3.67	2.63	2.12	1.82	1.62	1.48	1.38	1.31	1.25	1.20	1.16	1.13	1.11
100	9.06	4.89	3.51	2.82	2.42	2.16	1.97	1.84	1.74	1.66	1.60	1.55	1.51	1.48
200	18.12	9.77	7.01	5.64	4.84	4.31	3.94	3.68	3.47	3.32	3.20	3.10	3.02	2.95
300	27.18	14.65	10.51	8.46	7.25	6.46	5.91	5.51	5.21	4.97	4.79	4.64	4.52	4.43
400	36.24	19.53	14.01	11.28	9.67	8.62	7.88	7.35	6.94	6.63	6.39	6.19	6.03	5.90
500	45.30	24.41	17.51	14.10	12.08	10.77	9.85	9.18	8.68	8.29	7.98	7.74	7.54	7.38
600	54.36	29.30	21.01	16.92	14.50	12.92	11.82	11.02	10.41	9.94	9.58	9.28	9.04	8.85
700	63.42	34.18	24.51	19.74	16.92	15.07	13.79	12.85	12.15	11.60	11.17	10.83	10.55	10.33
800	72.48	39.06	28.01	22.55	19.33	17.23	15.76	14.69	13.88	13.26	12.77	12.37	12.06	11.80
900	81.54	43.94	31.51	25.37	21.75	19.38	17.73	16.52	15.61	14.91	14.36	13.92	13.56	13.27
1000	90.59	48.82	35.01	28.19	24.16	21.53	19.70	18.36	17.35	16.57	15.96	15.47	15.07	14.75
2000	181.18	97.64	70.02	56.38	48.32	43.06	39.39	36.71	34.69	33.13	31.91	30.93	30.14	29.49
3000	271.77	146.46	105.03	84.57	72.48	64.59	59.08	55.06	52.04	49.70	47.86	46.39	45.20	44.24
4000	362.36	195.28	140.04	112.75	96.64	86.11	78.77	73.42	69.38	66.26	63.81	61.85	60.27	58.98
5000	452.95	244.10	175.05	140.94	120.80	107.64	98.46	91.77	86.72	82.83	79.76	77.32	75.34	73.72
6000	543.54	292.92	210.06	169.13	144.96	129.17	118.15	110.12	104.07	99.39	95.72	92.78	90.40	88.47
7000	634.13	341.74	245.07	197.31	169.12	150.69	137.85	128.47	121.41	115.96	111.67	108.24	105.47	103.21
8000	724.72	390.56	280.08	225.50	193.28	172.22	157.54	146.83	138.76	132.52	127.62	123.70	120.54	117.96
9000	815.31	439.38	315.09	253.69	217.44	193.75	177.23	165.18	156.10	149.09	143.57	139.16	135.60	132.70
10000	905.89	488.20	350.10	281.87	241.59	215.28	196.92	183.53	173.44	165.65	159.52	154.63	150.67	147.44
11000	996.48	537.02	385.11	310.06	265.75	236.80	216.61	201.89	190.79	182.22	175.47	170.09	165.74	162.19
12000	1087.07	585.84	420.11	338.25	289.91	258.33	236.30	220.24	208.13	198.78	191.43	185.55	180.80	176.93
13000	1177.66	634.66	455.12	366.43	314.07	279.86	256.00	238.59	225.48	215.35	207.38	201.01	195.87	191.67
14000	1268.25	683.48	490.13	394.62	338.23	301.38	275.69	256.94	242.82	231.91	223.33	216.48	210.94	206.42
15000	1358.84	732.30	525.14	422.81	362.39	322.91	295.38	275.30	260.16	248.48	239.28	231.94	226.00	221.16
16000	1449.43	781.12	560.15	450.99	386.55	344.44	315.07	293.65	277.51	265.04	255.23	247.40	241.07	235.91
17000	1540.02	829.94	595.16	479.18	410.71	365.96	334.76	312.00	294.85	281.61	271.19	262.86	256.14	250.65
18000	1630.61	878.76	630.17	507.37	434.87	387.49	354.45	330.36	312.20	298.17	287.14	278.32	271.20	265.39
19000	1721.20	927.58	665.18	535.56	459.02	409.02	374.15	348.71	329.54	314.74	303.09	293.79	286.27	280.14
20000	1811.78	976.40	700.19	563.74	483.18	430.55	393.84	367.06	346.88	331.30	319.04	309.25	301.34	294.88
21000	1902.37	1025.22	735.20	591.93	507.34	452.07	413.53	385.41	364.23	347.87	334.99	324.71	316.40	309.62
22000	1992.96	1074.04	770.21	620.12	531.50	473.60	433.22	403.77	381.57	364.43	350.94	340.17	331.47	324.37
23000	2083.55	1122.86	805.21	648.30	555.66	495.13	452.91	422.12	398.91	381.00	366.90	355.64	346.54	339.11
24000	2174.14	1171.68	840.22	676.49	579.82	516.65	472.60	440.47	416.26	397.56	382.85	371.10	361.60	353.86
25000	2264.73	1220.50	875.23	704.68	603.98	538.18	492.29	458.82	433.60	414.13	398.80	386.56	376.67	368.60
26000	2355.32	1269.32	910.24	732.86	628.14	559.71	511.99	477.18	450.95	430.69	414.75	402.02	391.73	383.34
27000	2445.91	1318.14	945.25	761.05	652.30	581.23	531.68	495.53	468.29	447.26	430.70	417.48	406.80	398.09
28000	2536.50	1366.96	980.26	789.24	676.46	602.76	551.37	513.88	485.63	463.82	446.65	432.95	421.87	412.83
29000	2627.08	1415.78	1015.27	817.42	700.61	624.29	571.06	532.24	502.98	480.39	462.61	448.41	436.93	427.57
30000	2717.67	1464.60	1050.28	845.61	724.77	645.82	590.75	550.59	520.32	496.95	478.56	463.87	452.00	442.32
31000	2808.26	1513.42	1085.29	873.80	748.93	667.34	610.44	568.94	537.67	513.51	494.51	479.33	467.07	457.06
32000	2898.85	1562.24	1120.30	901.98	773.09	688.87	630.14	587.29	555.01	530.08	510.46	494.79	482.13	471.81
33000	2989.44	1611.06	1155.31	930.17	797.25	710.40	649.83	605.65	572.35	546.64	526.41	510.26	497.20	486.55
34000	3080.03	1659.88	1190.31	958.36	821.41	731.92	669.52	624.00	589.70	563.21	542.37	525.72	512.27	501.29
35000	3170.62	1708.70	1225.32	986.55	845.57	753.45	689.21	642.35	607.04	579.77	558.32	541.18	527.33	516.04
36000	3261.21	1757.52	1260.33	1014.73	869.73	774.98	708.90	660.71	624.39	596.34	574.27	556.64	542.40	530.78
37000	3351.80	1806.34	1295.34	1042.92	893.89	796.50	728.59	679.06	641.73	612.90	590.22	572.11	557.47	545.52
38000	3442.39	1855.16	1330.35	1071.11	918.04	818.03	748.29	697.41	659.07	629.47	606.17	587.57	572.53	560.27
39000	3532.97	1903.98	1365.36	1099.29	942.20	839.56	767.98	715.76	676.42	646.03	622.12	603.03	587.60	575.01
40000	3623.56	1952.80	1400.37	1127.48	966.36	861.09	787.67	734.12	693.76	662.60	638.08	618.49	602.67	589.76
41000	3714.15	2001.62	1435.38	1155.67	990.52	882.61	807.36	752.47	711.11	679.16	654.03	633.95	617.73	604.50
42000	3804.74	2050.44	1470.39	1183.85	1014.68	904.14	827.05	770.82	728.45	695.73	669.98	649.42	632.80	619.24
43000	3895.33	2099.26	1505.40	1212.04	1038.84	925.67	846.74	789.17	745.79	712.29	685.93	664.88	647.87	633.99
44000	3985.92	2148.08	1540.41	1240.23	1063.00	947.19	866.43	807.53	763.14	728.86	701.88	680.34	662.93	648.73
45000	4076.51	2196.90	1575.41	1268.41	1087.16	968.72	886.13	825.88	780.48	745.42	717.84	695.80	678.00	663.47
46000	4167.10	2245.72	1610.42	1296.60	1111.32	990.25	905.82	844.23	797.82	761.99	733.79	711.27	693.07	678.22
47000	4257.69	2294.54	1645.43	1324.79	1135.48	1011.77	925.51	862.59	815.17	778.55	749.74	726.73	708.13	692.96
48000	4348.27	2343.36	1680.44	1352.97	1159.63	1033.30	945.20	880.94	832.51	795.12	765.69	742.19	723.20	707.71
49000	4438.86	2392.18	1715.45	1381.16	1183.79	1054.83	964.89	899.29	849.86	811.68	781.64	757.65	738.27	722.45
50000	4529.45	2441.00	1750.46	1409.35	1207.95	1076.36	984.58	917.64	867.20	828.25	797.59	773.11	753.33	737.19
55000	4982.40	2685.10	1925.51	1550.28	1328.75	1183.99	1083.04	1009.41	953.92	911.07	877.35	850.42	828.66	810.91
60000	5435.34	2929.20	2100.55	1691.22	1449.54	1291.63	1181.50	1101.17	1040.64	993.90	957.11	927.74	904.00	884.63
65000	5888.29	3173.30	2275.60	1832.15	1570.34	1399.26	1279.96	1192.94	1127.36	1076.72	1036.87	1005.05	979.33	958.35
70000	6341.23	3417.40	2450.64	1973.09	1691.13	1506.90	1378.42	1284.70	1214.08	1159.54	1116.63	1082.36	1054.66	1032.07
75000	6794.18	3661.50	2625.69	2114.02	1811.93	1614.53	1476.87	1376.46	1300.80	1242.37	1196.39	1159.67	1130.00	1105.79
80000	7247.12	3905.60	2800.73	2254.95	1932.72	1722.17	1575.33	1468.23	1387.52	1325.19	1276.15	1236.98	1205.33	1179.51
85000	7700.07	4149.70	2975.78	2395.89	2053.52	1829.80	1673.79	1559.99	1474.24	1408.02	1355.91	1314.29	1280.66	1253.22
90000	8153.01	4393.80	3150.82	2536.82	2174.31	1937.44	1772.25	1651.76	1560.96	1490.84	1435.67	1391.60	1355.99	1326.94
95000	8605.96	4637.89	3325.87	2677.76	2295.10	2045.07	1870.71	1743.52	1647.68	1573.66	1515.42	1468.91	1431.33	1400.66
100000	9058.90	4881.99	3500.92	2818.69	2415.90	2152.71	1969.16	1835.28	1734.40	1656.49	1595.18	1546.22	1506.66	1474.38

TERM	15 Years	16 Years	17 Years	18 Years	19 Years	20 Years	21 Years	22 Years	23 Years	24 Years	25 Years	30 Years	35 Years	40 Years
AMOUNT														
5	.08	.08	.08	.07	.07	.07	.07	.07	.07	.07	.07	.07	.07	.07
10	.15	.15	.15	.14	.14	.14	.14	.14	.14	.14	.14	.14	.14	.14
15	.22	.22	.22	.21	.21	.21	.21	.21	.21	.21	.21	.20	.20	.20
25	.37	.36	.36	.35	.35	.35	.34	.34	.34	.34	.34	.34	.33	.33
50	.73	.72	.71	.70	.69	.69	.68	.68	.68	.68	.67	.67	.66	.66
75	1.09	1.07	1.06	1.05	1.04	1.03	1.02	1.02	1.01	1.01	1.01	1.00	.99	.99
100	1.45	1.43	1.41	1.40	1.38	1.37	1.36	1.36	1.35	1.35	1.34	1.33	1.32	1.32
200	2.90	2.86	2.82	2.79	2.76	2.74	2.72	2.71	2.70	2.69	2.68	2.65	2.63	2.63
300	4.35	4.28	4.23	4.18	4.14	4.11	4.08	4.06	4.04	4.03	4.01	3.97	3.95	3.94
400	5.80	5.71	5.64	5.57	5.52	5.48	5.44	5.41	5.39	5.37	5.35	5.29	5.26	5.25
500	7.24	7.13	7.04	6.97	6.90	6.85	6.80	6.77	6.73	6.71	6.68	6.61	6.57	6.56
600	8.69	8.56	8.45	8.36	8.28	8.22	8.16	8.12	8.08	8.05	8.02	7.93	7.89	7.87
700	10.14	9.99	9.86	9.75	9.66	9.59	9.52	9.47	9.42	9.39	9.35	9.25	9.20	9.18
800	11.59	11.41	11.27	11.14	11.04	10.96	10.88	10.82	10.77	10.73	10.69	10.57	10.52	10.49
900	13.04	12.84	12.67	12.54	12.42	12.32	12.24	12.17	12.12	12.07	12.02	11.89	11.83	11.80
1000	14.48	14.26	14.08	13.93	13.80	13.69	13.60	13.53	13.46	13.41	13.36	13.21	13.14	13.11
2000	28.96	28.52	28.16	27.85	27.60	27.38	27.20	27.05	26.92	26.81	26.71	26.42	26.28	26.22
3000	43.44	42.78	42.23	41.78	41.39	41.07	40.80	40.57	40.37	40.21	40.07	39.62	39.42	39.33
4000	57.92	57.04	56.31	55.70	55.19	54.76	54.39	54.09	53.83	53.61	53.42	52.83	52.56	52.44
5000	72.40	71.30	70.39	69.62	68.98	68.44	67.99	67.61	67.28	67.01	66.77	66.03	65.70	65.55
6000	86.88	85.56	84.46	83.55	82.78	82.13	81.59	81.13	80.74	80.41	80.13	79.24	78.84	78.66
7000	101.35	99.82	98.54	97.47	96.57	95.82	95.19	94.65	94.19	93.81	93.48	92.45	91.98	91.77
8000	115.83	114.08	112.61	111.39	110.37	109.51	108.78	108.17	107.65	107.21	106.84	105.65	105.12	104.88
9000	130.31	128.33	126.69	125.32	124.17	123.20	122.38	121.69	121.11	120.61	120.19	118.86	118.26	117.99
10000	144.79	142.59	140.77	139.24	137.96	136.88	135.98	135.21	134.56	134.01	133.54	132.06	131.40	131.09
11000	159.27	156.85	154.84	153.16	151.76	150.57	149.57	148.73	148.02	147.41	146.90	145.27	144.54	144.20
12000	173.75	171.11	168.92	167.09	165.55	164.26	163.17	162.25	161.47	160.81	160.25	158.48	157.68	157.31
13000	188.22	185.37	182.99	181.01	179.35	177.95	176.77	175.77	174.93	174.21	173.60	171.68	170.82	170.42
14000	202.70	199.63	197.07	194.93	193.14	191.64	190.37	189.29	188.38	187.61	186.96	184.89	183.95	183.53
15000	217.18	213.89	211.15	208.86	206.94	205.32	203.96	202.81	201.84	201.01	200.31	198.09	197.09	196.64
16000	231.66	228.15	225.22	222.78	220.73	219.01	217.56	216.33	215.29	214.41	213.67	211.30	210.23	209.75
17000	246.14	242.40	239.30	236.71	234.53	232.70	231.16	229.85	228.75	227.81	227.02	224.51	223.37	222.86
18000	260.62	256.66	253.38	250.63	248.33	246.39	244.75	243.37	242.21	241.21	240.37	237.71	236.51	235.97
19000	275.09	270.92	267.45	264.55	262.12	260.08	258.35	256.89	255.66	254.61	253.73	250.92	249.65	249.07
20000	289.57	285.18	281.53	278.48	275.92	273.76	271.95	270.42	269.12	268.02	267.08	264.12	262.79	262.18
21000	304.05	299.44	295.60	292.40	289.71	287.45	285.55	283.94	282.57	281.42	280.43	277.33	275.93	275.29
22000	318.53	313.70	309.68	306.32	303.51	301.14	299.14	297.46	296.03	294.82	293.79	290.54	289.07	288.40
23000	333.01	327.96	323.76	320.25	317.30	314.83	312.74	310.98	309.48	308.22	307.14	303.74	302.21	301.51
24000	347.49	342.22	337.83	334.17	331.10	328.52	326.34	324.50	322.94	321.62	320.50	316.95	315.35	314.62
25000	361.96	356.47	351.91	348.09	344.89	342.20	339.94	338.02	336.39	335.02	333.85	330.15	328.49	327.73
26000	376.44	370.73	365.98	362.02	358.69	355.89	353.53	351.54	349.85	348.42	347.20	343.36	341.63	340.84
27000	390.92	384.99	380.06	375.94	372.49	369.58	367.13	365.06	363.31	361.82	360.56	356.57	354.76	353.95
28000	405.40	399.25	394.14	389.86	386.28	383.27	380.73	378.58	376.76	375.22	373.91	369.77	367.90	367.05
29000	419.88	413.51	408.21	403.79	400.08	396.96	394.32	392.10	390.22	388.62	387.26	382.98	381.04	380.16
30000	434.36	427.77	422.29	417.71	413.87	410.64	407.92	405.62	403.67	402.02	400.62	396.18	394.18	393.27
31000	448.83	442.03	436.37	431.64	427.67	424.33	421.52	419.14	417.13	415.42	413.97	409.39	407.32	406.38
32000	463.31	456.29	450.44	445.56	441.46	438.02	435.12	432.66	430.50	428.82	427.33	422.60	420.46	419.49
33000	477.79	470.55	464.52	459.48	455.26	451.71	448.71	446.18	444.04	442.22	440.68	435.80	433.60	432.60
34000	492.27	484.80	478.59	473.41	469.06	465.40	462.31	459.70	457.49	455.62	454.03	449.01	446.74	445.71
35000	506.75	499.06	492.67	487.33	482.85	479.08	475.91	473.22	470.95	469.02	467.39	462.21	459.88	458.82
36000	521.23	513.32	506.75	501.25	496.65	492.77	489.50	486.74	484.41	482.42	480.74	475.42	473.02	471.93
37000	535.71	527.58	520.82	515.18	510.44	506.46	503.10	500.26	497.86	495.82	494.09	488.62	486.16	485.03
38000	550.18	541.84	534.90	529.10	524.24	520.15	516.70	513.78	511.32	509.22	507.45	501.83	499.30	498.14
39000	564.66	556.10	548.97	543.02	538.03	533.84	530.30	527.31	524.77	522.63	520.80	515.04	512.44	511.25
40000	579.14	570.36	563.05	556.95	551.83	547.52	543.89	540.83	538.23	536.03	534.16	528.24	525.58	524.36
41000	593.62	584.62	577.13	570.87	565.62	561.21	557.49	554.35	551.68	549.43	547.51	541.45	538.71	537.47
42000	608.10	598.87	591.20	584.79	579.42	574.90	571.09	567.87	565.14	562.83	560.86	554.65	551.85	550.58
43000	622.58	613.13	605.28	598.72	593.22	588.59	584.69	581.39	578.60	576.23	574.22	567.86	564.99	563.69
44000	637.05	627.39	619.36	612.64	607.01	602.28	598.28	594.91	592.05	589.63	587.57	581.07	578.13	576.80
45000	651.53	641.65	633.43	626.56	620.81	615.96	611.88	608.43	605.51	603.03	600.92	594.27	591.27	589.91
46000	666.01	655.91	647.51	640.49	634.60	629.65	625.48	621.95	618.96	616.43	614.28	607.48	604.41	603.01
47000	680.49	670.17	661.58	654.41	648.40	643.34	639.07	635.47	632.42	629.83	627.63	620.68	617.55	616.12
48000	694.97	684.43	675.66	668.34	662.19	657.03	652.67	648.99	645.87	643.23	640.99	633.89	630.69	629.23
49000	709.45	698.69	689.74	682.26	675.99	670.72	666.27	662.51	659.33	656.63	654.34	647.10	643.83	642.34
50000	723.92	712.94	703.81	696.18	689.78	684.40	679.87	676.03	672.78	670.03	667.69	660.30	656.97	655.45
55000	796.32	784.24	774.19	765.80	758.76	752.84	747.85	743.63	740.06	737.03	734.46	726.33	722.66	721.00
60000	868.71	855.53	844.57	835.42	827.74	821.28	815.84	811.24	807.34	804.04	801.23	792.36	788.36	786.54
65000	941.10	926.83	914.95	905.04	896.72	889.72	883.82	878.84	874.62	871.04	868.00	858.39	854.06	852.08
70000	1013.49	998.12	985.34	974.65	965.70	958.16	951.81	946.44	941.90	938.04	934.77	924.42	919.75	917.63
75000	1085.88	1069.42	1055.72	1044.27	1034.67	1026.60	1019.80	1014.04	1009.17	1005.04	1001.54	990.45	985.45	983.17
80000	1158.28	1140.71	1126.10	1113.89	1103.65	1095.04	1087.78	1081.65	1076.45	1072.05	1068.31	1056.48	1051.15	1048.72
85000	1230.67	1212.00	1196.48	1183.51	1172.63	1163.48	1155.77	1149.25	1143.73	1139.05	1135.07	1122.51	1116.84	1114.26
90000	1303.06	1283.30	1266.86	1253.12	1241.61	1231.92	1223.75	1216.85	1211.01	1206.05	1201.84	1188.54	1182.54	1179.81
95000	1375.45	1354.59	1337.24	1322.74	1310.59	1300.36	1291.74	1284.45	1278.29	1273.05	1268.61	1254.57	1248.23	1245.35
100000	1447.84	1425.89	1407.62	1392.36	1379.56	1368.80	1359.73	1352.06	1345.56	1340.06	1335.38	1320.60	1313.93	1310.90

MONTHLY PAYMENT
REQUIRED TO AMORTIZE A LOAN

TERM	1 Year	2 Years	3 Years	4 Years	5 Years	6 Years	7 Years	8 Years	9 Years	10 Years	11 Years	12 Years	13 Years	14 Years
AMOUNT														
5	.46	.26	.18	.15	.13	.11	.10	.10	.09	.09	.08	.08	.08	.08
10	.91	.49	.36	.29	.25	.22	.20	.19	.18	.17	.16	.16	.16	.15
15	1.36	.74	.53	.43	.37	.33	.30	.28	.27	.25	.24	.24	.23	.23
25	2.27	1.23	.88	.71	.61	.54	.50	.46	.44	.42	.40	.39	.38	.37
50	4.54	2.45	1.76	1.42	1.21	1.08	.99	.92	.87	.83	.80	.78	.76	.74
75	6.80	3.67	2.63	2.12	1.82	1.62	1.48	1.38	1.31	1.25	1.20	1.17	1.14	1.11
100	9.07	4.89	3.51	2.83	2.42	2.16	1.98	1.84	1.74	1.66	1.60	1.55	1.51	1.48
200	18.13	9.77	7.01	5.65	4.84	4.32	3.95	3.68	3.48	3.32	3.20	3.10	3.02	2.96
300	27.19	14.66	10.52	8.47	7.26	6.47	5.92	5.52	5.22	4.98	4.80	4.65	4.53	4.44
400	36.25	19.54	14.02	11.29	9.68	8.63	7.89	7.36	6.95	6.64	6.40	6.20	6.04	5.92
500	45.31	24.43	17.52	14.11	12.10	10.78	9.86	9.20	8.69	8.30	8.00	7.75	7.55	7.39
600	54.37	29.31	21.03	16.93	14.52	12.94	11.84	11.03	10.43	9.96	9.60	9.30	9.06	8.87
700	63.43	34.20	24.53	19.75	16.93	15.09	13.81	12.87	12.17	11.62	11.19	10.85	10.57	10.35
800	72.50	39.08	28.03	22.57	19.35	17.25	15.78	14.71	13.90	13.28	12.79	12.40	12.08	11.83
900	81.56	43.96	31.54	25.40	21.77	19.40	17.75	16.55	15.64	14.94	14.39	13.95	13.59	13.31
1000	90.62	48.85	35.04	28.22	24.19	21.56	19.72	18.39	17.38	16.60	15.99	15.50	15.10	14.78
2000	181.23	97.69	70.07	56.43	48.38	43.11	39.44	36.77	34.75	33.20	31.97	30.99	30.20	29.56
3000	271.84	146.54	105.11	84.64	72.56	64.67	59.16	55.15	52.13	49.79	47.96	46.49	45.30	44.34
4000	362.46	195.38	140.14	112.85	96.75	86.22	78.88	73.53	69.50	66.39	63.94	61.98	60.40	59.12
5000	453.07	244.22	175.17	141.07	120.93	107.78	98.60	91.92	86.88	82.98	79.92	77.48	75.50	73.89
6000	543.68	293.07	210.21	169.28	145.12	129.33	118.32	110.30	104.25	99.58	95.91	92.97	90.60	88.67
7000	634.29	341.91	245.24	197.49	169.30	150.89	138.04	128.68	121.62	116.18	111.89	108.47	105.70	103.45
8000	724.91	390.75	280.27	225.70	193.49	172.44	157.76	147.06	139.00	132.77	127.87	123.96	120.80	118.23
9000	815.52	439.60	315.31	253.92	217.67	193.99	177.48	165.44	156.37	149.37	143.86	139.46	135.90	133.01
10000	906.13	488.44	350.34	282.13	241.86	215.55	197.20	183.83	173.75	165.96	159.84	154.95	151.00	147.78
11000	996.74	537.29	385.38	310.34	266.04	237.10	216.92	202.21	191.12	182.56	175.82	170.45	166.10	162.56
12000	1087.36	586.13	420.41	338.55	290.23	258.66	236.64	220.59	208.49	199.16	191.81	185.94	181.20	177.34
13000	1177.97	634.97	455.44	366.77	314.42	280.21	256.36	238.97	225.87	215.75	207.79	201.44	196.30	192.12
14000	1268.58	683.82	490.48	394.98	338.60	301.77	276.08	257.35	243.24	232.35	223.78	216.93	211.40	206.89
15000	1359.19	732.66	525.51	423.19	362.79	323.32	295.80	275.74	260.62	248.94	239.76	232.43	226.50	221.67
16000	1449.81	781.50	560.54	451.40	386.97	344.88	315.52	294.12	277.99	265.54	255.74	247.92	241.60	236.45
17000	1540.42	830.35	595.58	479.62	411.16	366.43	335.24	312.50	295.36	282.13	271.73	263.42	256.70	251.23
18000	1631.03	879.19	630.61	507.83	435.34	387.98	354.96	330.88	312.74	298.73	287.71	278.91	271.80	266.01
19000	1721.64	928.04	665.65	536.04	459.53	409.54	374.68	349.26	330.11	315.33	303.69	294.41	286.90	280.78
20000	1812.26	976.88	700.68	564.25	483.71	431.09	394.40	367.65	347.49	331.92	319.68	309.90	302.00	295.56
21000	1902.87	1025.72	735.71	592.47	507.90	452.65	414.12	386.03	364.86	348.52	335.66	325.40	317.10	310.34
22000	1993.48	1074.57	770.75	620.68	532.08	474.20	433.84	404.41	382.23	365.11	351.64	340.89	332.20	325.12
23000	2084.09	1123.41	805.78	648.89	556.27	495.76	453.56	422.79	399.61	381.71	367.63	356.39	347.30	339.89
24000	2174.71	1172.25	840.81	677.10	580.46	517.31	473.28	441.17	416.98	398.31	383.61	371.88	362.40	354.67
25000	2265.32	1221.10	875.85	705.32	604.64	538.87	493.00	459.56	434.36	414.90	399.60	387.37	377.50	369.45
26000	2355.93	1269.94	910.88	733.53	628.83	560.42	512.72	477.94	451.73	431.50	415.58	402.87	392.60	384.23
27000	2446.55	1318.79	945.92	761.74	653.01	581.97	532.44	496.32	469.10	448.09	431.56	418.36	407.70	399.01
28000	2537.16	1367.63	980.95	789.95	677.20	603.53	552.16	514.70	486.48	464.69	447.55	433.86	422.80	413.78
29000	2627.77	1416.47	1015.98	818.16	701.38	625.08	571.88	533.08	503.85	481.28	463.53	449.35	437.90	428.56
30000	2718.38	1465.32	1051.02	846.38	725.57	646.64	591.60	551.47	521.23	497.88	479.51	464.85	453.00	443.34
31000	2809.00	1514.16	1086.05	874.59	749.75	668.19	611.32	569.85	538.60	514.48	495.50	480.34	468.10	458.12
32000	2899.61	1563.00	1121.08	902.80	773.94	689.75	631.04	588.23	555.98	531.07	511.48	495.84	483.20	472.89
33000	2990.22	1611.85	1156.12	931.01	798.12	711.30	650.76	606.61	573.35	547.67	527.46	511.33	498.30	487.67
34000	3080.83	1660.69	1191.15	959.23	822.31	732.86	670.48	625.00	590.72	564.26	543.45	526.83	513.40	502.45
35000	3171.45	1709.54	1226.19	987.44	846.49	754.41	690.20	643.38	608.10	580.86	559.43	542.32	528.50	517.23
36000	3262.06	1758.38	1261.22	1015.65	870.68	775.96	709.92	661.76	625.47	597.46	575.41	557.82	543.60	532.01
37000	3352.67	1807.22	1296.25	1043.86	894.87	797.52	729.64	680.14	642.85	614.05	591.40	573.31	558.70	546.78
38000	3443.28	1856.07	1331.29	1072.08	919.05	819.07	749.36	698.52	660.22	630.65	607.38	588.81	573.80	561.56
39000	3533.90	1904.91	1366.32	1100.29	943.24	840.63	769.08	716.91	677.59	647.24	623.37	604.30	588.90	576.34
40000	3624.51	1953.75	1401.35	1128.50	967.42	862.18	788.80	735.29	694.97	663.84	639.35	619.80	604.00	591.12
41000	3715.12	2002.60	1436.39	1156.71	991.61	883.74	808.52	753.67	712.34	680.43	655.33	635.29	619.10	605.89
42000	3805.73	2051.44	1471.42	1184.93	1015.79	905.29	828.24	772.05	729.72	697.03	671.32	650.79	634.20	620.67
43000	3896.35	2100.29	1506.44	1213.14	1039.98	926.85	847.96	790.43	747.09	713.63	687.30	666.28	649.30	635.45
44000	3986.96	2149.13	1541.49	1241.35	1064.16	948.40	867.68	808.82	764.46	730.22	703.28	681.78	664.40	650.23
45000	4077.57	2197.97	1576.52	1269.56	1088.35	969.95	887.40	827.20	781.84	746.82	719.27	697.27	679.50	665.01
46000	4168.18	2246.82	1611.56	1297.78	1112.53	991.51	907.12	845.58	799.21	763.41	735.25	712.77	694.60	679.78
47000	4258.80	2295.66	1646.59	1325.99	1136.72	1013.06	926.84	863.96	816.59	780.01	751.23	728.26	709.70	694.56
48000	4349.41	2344.50	1681.62	1354.20	1160.91	1034.62	946.56	882.34	833.96	796.61	767.22	743.75	724.80	709.34
49000	4440.02	2393.35	1716.66	1382.41	1185.09	1056.17	966.28	900.73	851.33	813.20	783.20	759.25	739.90	724.12
50000	4530.63	2442.19	1751.69	1410.63	1209.28	1077.73	986.00	919.11	868.71	829.80	799.19	774.74	755.00	738.90
55000	4983.70	2686.41	1926.86	1551.69	1330.20	1185.50	1084.60	1011.02	955.58	912.78	879.10	852.22	830.50	812.78
60000	5436.76	2930.63	2102.03	1692.75	1451.13	1293.27	1183.20	1102.93	1042.45	995.76	959.02	929.69	906.00	886.67
65000	5889.82	3174.85	2277.20	1833.81	1572.06	1401.04	1281.80	1194.84	1129.32	1078.74	1038.94	1007.17	981.50	960.56
70000	6342.89	3419.07	2452.37	1974.87	1692.98	1508.82	1380.40	1286.75	1216.19	1161.71	1118.86	1084.64	1057.00	1034.45
75000	6795.95	3663.29	2627.53	2115.94	1813.91	1616.59	1479.00	1378.66	1303.06	1244.69	1198.78	1162.11	1132.50	1108.34
80000	7249.01	3907.50	2802.70	2257.00	1934.84	1724.36	1577.60	1470.57	1389.93	1327.67	1278.69	1239.59	1208.00	1182.23
85000	7702.08	4151.72	2977.87	2398.06	2055.77	1832.13	1676.20	1562.48	1476.80	1410.65	1358.61	1317.06	1283.49	1256.12
90000	8155.14	4395.94	3153.04	2539.12	2176.69	1939.90	1774.80	1654.39	1563.67	1493.63	1438.53	1394.54	1358.99	1330.01
95000	8608.20	4640.16	3328.21	2680.18	2297.62	2047.68	1873.40	1746.30	1650.54	1576.61	1518.45	1472.01	1434.49	1403.90
100000	9061.26	4884.38	3503.38	2821.25	2418.55	2155.45	1972.00	1838.21	1737.41	1659.59	1598.37	1549.48	1509.99	1477.79

TERM AMOUNT	15 Years	16 Years	17 Years	18 Years	19 Years	20 Years	21 Years	22 Years	23 Years	24 Years	25 Years	30 Years	35 Years	40 Years
5	.08	.08	.08	.07	.07	.07	.07	.07	.07	.07	.07	.07	.07	.07
10	.15	.15	.15	.14	.14	.14	.14	.14	.14	.14	.14	.14	.14	.14
15	.22	.22	.22	.21	.21	.21	.21	.21	.21	.21	.21	.20	.20	.20
25	.37	.36	.36	.35	.35	.35	.35	.34	.34	.34	.34	.34	.33	.33
50	.73	.72	.71	.70	.70	.69	.69	.68	.68	.68	.67	.67	.66	.66
75	1.09	1.08	1.06	1.05	1.04	1.03	1.03	1.02	1.02	1.01	1.01	1.00	.99	.99
100	1.46	1.43	1.42	1.40	1.39	1.38	1.37	1.36	1.35	1.35	1.34	1.33	1.32	1.32
200	2.91	2.86	2.83	2.80	2.77	2.75	2.73	2.72	2.70	2.69	2.68	2.65	2.64	2.64
300	4.36	4.29	4.24	4.19	4.15	4.12	4.10	4.07	4.05	4.04	4.02	3.98	3.96	3.95
400	5.81	5.72	5.65	5.59	5.54	5.50	5.46	5.43	5.40	5.38	5.36	5.30	5.28	5.27
500	7.26	7.15	7.06	6.98	6.92	6.87	6.82	6.78	6.75	6.72	6.70	6.63	6.60	6.58
600	8.71	8.58	8.47	8.38	8.30	8.24	8.19	8.14	8.10	8.07	8.04	7.95	7.91	7.90
700	10.16	10.01	9.88	9.78	9.69	9.61	9.55	9.50	9.45	9.41	9.38	9.28	9.23	9.21
800	11.62	11.44	11.29	11.17	11.07	10.99	10.91	10.85	10.80	10.76	10.72	10.60	10.55	10.53
900	13.07	12.87	12.71	12.57	12.45	12.36	12.28	12.21	12.15	12.10	12.06	11.93	11.87	11.84
1000	14.52	14.30	14.12	13.96	13.84	13.73	13.64	13.56	13.50	13.44	13.40	13.25	13.19	13.16
2000	29.03	28.59	28.23	27.92	27.67	27.46	27.28	27.12	26.99	26.88	26.79	26.50	26.37	26.31
3000	43.54	42.89	42.34	41.88	41.50	41.18	40.91	40.68	40.49	40.32	40.18	39.74	39.55	39.46
4000	58.06	57.18	56.45	55.04	55.34	54.91	54.55	54.24	53.98	53.76	53.58	52.99	52.73	52.61
5000	72.57	71.48	70.57	69.80	69.17	68.63	68.18	67.80	67.48	67.20	66.97	66.24	65.91	65.76
6000	87.08	85.77	84.68	83.76	83.00	82.36	81.82	81.36	80.97	80.64	80.36	79.48	79.09	78.91
7000	101.60	100.06	98.79	97.72	96.83	96.08	95.45	94.92	94.46	94.08	93.76	92.73	92.27	92.06
8000	116.11	114.36	112.90	111.68	110.67	109.81	109.09	108.47	107.96	107.52	107.15	105.97	105.45	105.21
9000	130.62	128.65	127.01	125.64	124.50	123.53	122.72	122.03	121.45	120.96	120.54	119.22	118.63	118.36
10000	145.14	142.95	141.13	139.60	138.33	137.26	136.36	135.59	134.95	134.40	133.93	132.47	131.81	131.51
11000	159.65	157.24	155.24	153.56	152.16	150.98	149.99	149.15	148.44	147.84	147.33	145.71	144.99	144.66
12000	174.16	171.53	169.35	167.52	166.00	164.71	163.63	162.71	161.93	161.28	160.72	158.96	158.17	157.81
13000	188.68	185.83	183.46	181.48	179.83	178.43	177.26	176.27	175.43	174.72	174.11	172.21	171.35	170.96
14000	203.19	200.12	197.57	195.44	193.66	192.16	190.90	189.83	188.92	188.16	187.51	185.45	184.53	184.11
15000	217.70	214.42	211.69	209.40	207.49	205.89	204.53	203.39	202.42	201.60	200.90	198.70	197.71	197.26
16000	232.21	228.71	225.80	223.36	221.33	219.61	218.17	216.94	215.91	215.03	214.29	211.94	210.89	210.41
17000	246.73	243.00	239.91	237.32	235.16	233.34	231.80	230.50	229.40	228.47	227.68	225.19	224.07	223.56
18000	261.24	257.30	254.02	251.28	248.99	247.06	245.44	244.06	242.90	241.91	241.08	238.44	237.25	236.71
19000	275.75	271.59	268.13	265.24	262.82	260.79	259.07	257.62	256.39	255.35	254.47	251.68	250.43	249.86
20000	290.27	285.89	282.25	279.20	276.66	274.51	272.71	271.18	269.89	268.79	267.86	264.93	263.61	263.01
21000	304.78	300.18	296.36	293.16	290.49	288.24	286.34	284.74	283.38	282.23	281.26	278.17	276.79	276.16
22000	319.29	314.48	310.47	307.12	304.32	301.96	299.98	298.30	296.88	295.67	294.65	291.42	289.97	289.31
23000	333.81	328.77	324.58	321.08	318.15	315.69	313.61	311.85	310.37	309.11	308.04	304.67	303.15	302.46
24000	348.32	343.06	338.69	335.04	331.99	329.41	327.25	325.41	323.86	322.55	321.43	317.91	316.33	315.61
25000	362.83	357.36	352.81	349.00	345.82	343.14	340.88	338.97	337.36	335.99	334.83	331.16	329.51	328.76
26000	377.35	371.65	366.92	362.96	359.65	356.86	354.52	352.53	350.85	349.43	348.22	344.41	342.69	341.91
27000	391.86	385.95	381.03	376.92	373.48	370.59	368.15	366.09	364.35	362.87	361.61	357.65	355.87	355.06
28000	406.37	400.24	395.14	390.88	387.32	384.31	381.79	379.65	377.84	376.31	375.01	370.90	369.05	368.21
29000	420.88	414.53	409.25	404.84	401.15	398.04	395.42	393.21	391.33	389.75	388.40	384.14	382.23	381.36
30000	435.40	428.83	423.37	418.80	414.98	411.77	409.06	406.77	404.83	403.19	401.79	397.39	395.41	394.51
31000	449.91	443.12	437.48	432.76	428.81	425.49	422.69	420.32	418.32	416.63	415.18	410.64	408.59	407.66
32000	464.42	457.42	451.59	446.72	442.65	439.22	436.33	433.88	431.82	430.06	428.58	423.88	421.77	420.81
33000	478.94	471.71	465.70	460.68	456.48	452.94	449.96	447.44	445.31	443.50	441.97	437.13	434.95	433.96
34000	493.45	486.00	479.81	474.64	470.31	466.67	463.60	461.00	458.80	456.94	455.36	450.37	448.13	447.11
35000	507.96	500.30	493.93	488.60	484.14	480.39	477.23	474.56	472.30	470.38	468.76	463.62	461.31	460.26
36000	522.48	514.59	508.04	502.56	497.98	494.12	490.87	488.12	485.79	483.82	482.15	476.87	474.49	473.41
37000	536.99	528.89	522.15	516.52	511.81	507.84	504.50	501.68	499.29	497.26	495.54	490.11	487.67	486.56
38000	551.50	543.18	536.26	530.48	525.64	521.57	518.14	515.24	512.78	510.70	508.94	503.36	500.85	499.71
39000	566.02	557.48	550.37	544.44	539.47	535.29	531.77	528.79	526.28	524.14	522.33	516.61	514.03	512.86
40000	580.53	571.77	564.49	558.40	553.31	549.02	545.41	542.35	539.77	537.58	535.72	529.85	527.21	526.01
41000	595.04	586.06	578.60	572.36	567.14	562.74	559.04	555.91	553.26	551.02	549.11	543.10	540.39	539.16
42000	609.55	600.36	592.71	586.32	580.97	576.47	572.68	569.47	566.76	564.46	562.51	556.34	553.57	552.31
43000	624.07	614.65	606.82	600.28	594.80	590.19	586.31	583.03	580.25	577.90	575.90	569.59	566.75	565.46
44000	638.58	628.95	620.93	614.24	608.64	603.92	599.95	596.59	593.75	591.34	589.29	582.84	579.93	578.61
45000	653.09	643.24	635.05	628.20	622.47	617.65	613.58	610.15	607.24	604.78	602.69	596.08	593.11	591.76
46000	667.61	657.53	649.16	642.16	636.30	631.37	627.22	623.70	620.73	618.22	616.08	609.33	606.29	604.91
47000	682.12	671.83	663.27	656.12	650.13	645.10	640.85	637.26	634.23	631.65	629.47	622.58	619.47	618.06
48000	696.63	686.12	677.38	670.08	663.97	658.82	654.49	650.82	647.72	645.09	642.86	635.82	632.65	631.21
49000	711.15	700.42	691.49	684.04	677.80	672.55	668.12	664.38	661.22	658.53	656.26	649.07	645.83	644.36
50000	725.66	714.71	705.61	698.00	691.63	686.27	681.76	677.94	674.71	671.97	669.65	662.31	659.01	657.51
55000	798.22	786.18	776.17	767.80	760.79	754.90	749.93	745.73	742.18	739.17	736.61	728.54	724.91	723.26
60000	870.79	857.65	846.73	837.60	829.96	823.53	818.11	813.53	809.65	806.37	803.58	794.78	790.81	789.01
65000	943.36	929.12	917.29	907.40	899.12	892.15	886.28	881.32	877.12	873.56	870.54	861.01	856.71	854.77
70000	1015.92	1000.59	987.85	977.20	968.28	960.78	954.46	949.11	944.59	940.76	937.51	927.24	922.61	920.52
75000	1088.49	1072.06	1058.41	1047.00	1037.44	1029.41	1022.63	1016.91	1012.06	1007.96	1004.47	993.48	988.52	986.27
80000	1161.05	1143.53	1128.97	1116.80	1106.61	1098.03	1090.81	1084.70	1079.53	1075.15	1071.44	1059.70	1054.42	1052.02
85000	1233.62	1215.00	1199.53	1186.60	1175.77	1166.66	1158.98	1152.49	1147.00	1142.35	1138.40	1125.93	1120.32	1117.77
90000	1306.18	1286.47	1270.09	1256.40	1244.93	1235.29	1227.16	1220.29	1214.47	1209.55	1205.37	1192.16	1186.22	1183.52
95000	1378.75	1357.95	1340.65	1326.20	1314.09	1303.91	1295.33	1288.08	1281.94	1276.74	1272.33	1258.39	1252.12	1249.27
100000	1451.31	1429.42	1411.21	1396.00	1383.26	1372.54	1363.51	1355.87	1349.42	1343.94	1339.29	1324.62	1318.02	1315.02

MONTHLY PAYMENT
REQUIRED TO AMORTIZE A LOAN

TERM	1 Year	2 Years	3 Years	4 Years	5 Years	6 Years	7 Years	8 Years	9 Years	10 Years	11 Years	12 Years	13 Years	14 Years
AMOUNT														
5	.46	.25	.18	.15	.13	.11	.10	.10	.09	.09	.09	.08	.08	.08
10	.91	.49	.36	.29	.25	.22	.20	.19	.18	.17	.17	.16	.16	.15
15	1.36	.74	.53	.43	.37	.33	.30	.28	.27	.25	.25	.24	.23	.23
25	2.27	1.23	.88	.71	.61	.54	.50	.47	.44	.42	.41	.39	.38	.38
50	4.54	2.45	1.76	1.42	1.22	1.08	.99	.93	.88	.84	.81	.78	.76	.75
75	6.80	3.67	2.63	2.12	1.82	1.62	1.49	1.39	1.31	1.25	1.21	1.17	1.14	1.12
100	9.07	4.89	3.51	2.83	2.43	2.16	1.98	1.85	1.75	1.67	1.61	1.56	1.52	1.49
200	18.13	9.78	7.02	5.65	4.85	4.32	3.95	3.69	3.49	3.33	3.21	3.11	3.03	2.97
300	27.20	14.67	10.52	8.48	7.27	6.48	5.93	5.53	5.23	4.99	4.81	4.66	4.54	4.45
400	36.26	19.55	14.03	11.30	9.69	8.64	7.90	7.37	6.97	6.66	6.41	6.22	6.06	5.93
500	45.32	24.44	17.53	14.12	12.11	10.80	9.88	9.21	8.71	8.32	8.01	7.77	7.57	7.41
600	54.39	29.33	21.04	16.95	14.53	12.95	11.85	11.05	10.45	9.98	9.61	9.32	9.08	8.89
700	63.45	34.21	24.55	19.77	16.95	15.11	13.83	12.89	12.19	11.64	11.22	10.87	10.60	10.37
800	72.51	39.10	28.05	22.60	19.37	17.27	15.80	14.73	13.93	13.31	12.82	12.43	12.11	11.85
900	81.58	43.99	31.56	25.42	21.80	19.43	17.78	16.58	15.67	14.97	14.42	13.98	13.62	13.34
1000	90.64	48.87	35.06	28.24	24.22	21.59	19.75	18.42	17.41	16.63	16.02	15.53	15.14	14.82
2000	181.28	97.74	70.12	56.48	48.43	43.17	39.50	36.83	34.81	33.26	32.04	31.06	30.27	29.63
3000	271.91	146.61	105.18	84.72	72.64	64.75	59.25	55.24	52.22	49.89	48.05	46.59	45.40	44.44
4000	362.55	195.48	140.24	112.96	96.85	86.33	79.00	73.65	69.62	66.51	64.07	62.11	60.54	59.25
5000	453.19	244.34	175.30	141.19	121.06	107.91	98.75	92.06	87.03	83.14	80.08	77.64	75.67	74.06
6000	543.82	293.21	210.36	169.43	145.28	129.50	118.49	110.47	104.43	99.77	96.10	93.17	90.80	88.88
7000	634.46	342.08	245.41	197.67	169.49	151.08	138.24	128.88	121.83	116.39	112.11	108.70	105.94	103.69
8000	725.09	390.95	280.47	225.91	193.70	172.66	157.99	147.30	139.24	133.02	128.13	124.22	121.07	118.50
9000	815.73	439.81	315.53	254.15	217.91	194.24	177.74	165.71	156.64	149.65	144.14	139.75	136.20	133.31
10000	906.37	488.68	350.59	282.38	242.12	215.82	197.49	184.12	174.05	166.27	160.16	155.28	151.34	148.12
11000	997.00	537.55	385.65	310.62	266.34	237.41	217.24	202.53	191.45	182.90	176.18	170.81	166.47	162.94
12000	1087.64	586.42	420.71	338.86	290.55	258.99	236.98	220.94	208.86	199.53	192.19	186.33	181.60	177.75
13000	1178.28	635.28	455.76	367.10	314.76	280.57	256.73	239.35	226.26	216.15	208.21	201.86	196.74	192.56
14000	1268.91	684.15	490.82	395.34	338.97	302.15	276.48	257.76	243.66	232.78	224.22	217.39	211.87	207.37
15000	1359.55	733.02	525.88	423.57	363.18	323.73	296.23	276.18	261.07	249.41	240.24	232.92	227.00	222.18
16000	1450.18	781.89	560.94	451.81	387.40	345.32	315.98	294.59	278.47	266.04	256.25	248.44	242.14	236.99
17000	1540.82	830.75	596.00	480.05	411.61	366.90	335.73	313.00	295.88	282.66	272.27	263.97	257.27	251.81
18000	1631.46	879.62	631.06	508.29	435.82	388.48	355.47	331.41	313.28	299.29	288.28	279.50	272.40	266.62
19000	1722.09	928.49	666.11	536.53	460.03	410.06	375.22	349.82	330.69	315.92	304.30	295.03	287.54	281.43
20000	1812.73	977.36	701.17	564.76	484.24	431.64	394.97	368.23	348.09	332.54	320.31	310.55	302.67	296.24
21000	1903.37	1026.22	736.23	593.00	508.46	453.22	414.72	386.64	365.49	349.17	336.33	326.08	317.80	311.05
22000	1994.00	1075.09	771.29	621.24	532.67	474.81	434.47	405.05	382.90	365.80	352.35	341.61	332.94	325.87
23000	2084.64	1123.96	806.35	649.48	556.88	496.39	454.22	423.47	400.30	382.42	368.36	357.14	348.07	340.68
24000	2175.27	1172.83	841.41	677.72	581.09	517.97	473.96	441.88	417.71	399.05	384.38	372.66	363.20	355.49
25000	2265.91	1221.70	876.46	705.95	605.30	539.55	493.71	460.29	435.11	415.68	400.39	388.19	378.34	370.30
26000	2356.55	1270.56	911.52	734.19	629.51	561.13	513.46	478.70	452.52	432.30	416.41	403.72	393.47	385.11
27000	2447.18	1319.43	946.58	762.43	653.73	582.72	533.21	497.11	469.92	448.93	432.42	419.25	408.60	399.93
28000	2537.82	1368.30	981.64	790.67	677.94	604.30	552.96	515.52	487.32	465.56	448.44	434.77	423.74	414.74
29000	2628.46	1417.17	1016.70	818.91	702.15	625.88	572.71	533.93	504.73	482.18	464.45	450.30	438.87	429.55
30000	2719.09	1466.03	1051.76	847.14	726.36	647.46	592.45	552.35	522.13	498.81	480.47	465.83	454.00	444.36
31000	2809.73	1514.90	1086.81	875.38	750.57	669.04	612.20	570.76	539.54	515.44	496.48	481.36	469.14	459.17
32000	2900.36	1563.77	1121.87	903.62	774.79	690.63	631.95	589.17	556.94	532.07	512.50	496.88	484.27	473.98
33000	2991.00	1612.64	1156.93	931.86	799.00	712.21	651.70	607.58	574.35	548.69	528.52	512.41	499.40	488.80
34000	3081.64	1661.50	1191.99	960.10	823.21	733.79	671.45	625.99	591.75	565.32	544.53	527.94	514.54	503.61
35000	3172.27	1710.37	1227.05	988.33	847.42	755.37	691.20	644.40	609.15	581.95	560.55	543.46	529.67	518.42
36000	3262.91	1759.24	1262.11	1016.57	871.63	776.95	710.94	662.81	626.56	598.57	576.56	558.99	544.80	533.23
37000	3353.55	1808.11	1297.16	1044.81	895.85	798.53	730.69	681.23	643.96	615.20	592.58	574.52	559.94	548.04
38000	3444.18	1856.97	1332.22	1073.05	920.06	820.12	750.44	699.64	661.37	631.83	608.59	590.05	575.07	562.86
39000	3534.82	1905.84	1367.28	1101.29	944.27	841.70	770.19	718.05	678.77	648.45	624.61	605.57	590.20	577.67
40000	3625.45	1954.71	1402.34	1129.52	968.48	863.28	789.94	736.46	696.18	665.08	640.62	621.10	605.34	592.48
41000	3716.09	2003.58	1437.40	1157.76	992.69	884.86	809.69	754.87	713.58	681.71	656.64	636.63	620.47	607.29
42000	3806.73	2052.44	1472.46	1186.00	1016.91	906.44	829.43	773.28	730.98	698.33	672.65	652.16	635.60	622.10
43000	3897.36	2101.31	1507.52	1214.24	1041.12	928.03	849.18	791.69	748.39	714.96	688.67	667.68	650.73	636.92
44000	3988.00	2150.18	1542.57	1242.48	1065.33	949.61	868.93	810.10	765.79	731.59	704.69	683.21	665.87	651.73
45000	4078.64	2199.05	1577.63	1270.71	1089.54	971.19	888.68	828.52	783.20	748.21	720.70	698.74	681.00	666.54
46000	4169.27	2247.91	1612.69	1298.95	1113.75	992.77	908.43	846.93	800.60	764.84	736.72	714.27	696.13	681.35
47000	4259.91	2296.78	1647.75	1327.19	1137.97	1014.35	928.18	865.34	818.01	781.47	752.73	729.79	711.27	696.16
48000	4350.54	2345.65	1682.81	1355.43	1162.18	1035.94	947.92	883.75	835.41	798.10	768.75	745.32	726.40	710.97
49000	4441.18	2394.52	1717.87	1383.66	1186.39	1057.52	967.67	902.16	852.81	814.72	784.76	760.85	741.53	725.79
50000	4531.82	2443.39	1752.92	1411.90	1210.60	1079.10	987.42	920.57	870.22	831.35	800.78	776.38	756.67	740.60
55000	4985.00	2687.72	1928.22	1553.09	1331.66	1187.01	1086.16	1012.63	957.24	914.48	880.86	854.01	832.33	814.66
60000	5438.18	2932.06	2103.51	1694.28	1452.72	1294.92	1184.90	1104.69	1044.26	997.62	960.93	931.65	908.00	888.72
65000	5891.36	3176.40	2278.80	1835.47	1573.78	1402.83	1283.65	1196.74	1131.28	1080.75	1041.01	1009.29	983.67	962.78
70000	6344.54	3420.74	2454.09	1976.66	1694.84	1510.74	1382.39	1288.80	1218.30	1163.89	1121.09	1086.92	1059.33	1036.84
75000	6797.72	3665.08	2629.38	2117.85	1815.90	1618.65	1481.13	1380.86	1305.32	1247.02	1201.16	1164.56	1135.00	1110.90
80000	7250.90	3909.41	2804.67	2259.04	1936.96	1726.56	1579.87	1472.91	1392.35	1330.16	1281.24	1242.20	1210.67	1184.95
85000	7704.09	4153.75	2979.97	2400.23	2058.02	1834.46	1678.61	1564.97	1479.37	1413.29	1361.32	1319.84	1286.33	1259.01
90000	8157.27	4398.09	3155.26	2541.42	2179.08	1942.37	1777.35	1657.03	1566.39	1496.42	1441.40	1397.47	1362.00	1333.07
95000	8610.45	4642.43	3330.55	2682.61	2300.14	2050.28	1876.10	1749.08	1653.41	1579.56	1521.47	1475.11	1437.66	1407.13
100000	9063.63	4886.77	3505.84	2823.80	2421.20	2158.19	1974.84	1841.14	1740.43	1662.69	1601.55	1552.75	1513.33	1481.19

TERM AMOUNT	15 Years	16 Years	17 Years	18 Years	19 Years	20 Years	21 Years	22 Years	23 Years	24 Years	25 Years	30 Years	35 Years	40 Years
5	.08	.08	.08	.07	.07	.07	.07	.07	.07	.07	.07	.07	.07	.07
10	.15	.15	.15	.14	.14	.14	.14	.14	.14	.14	.14	.14	.14	.14
15	.22	.22	.22	.21	.21	.21	.21	.21	.21	.21	.21	.20	.20	.20
25	.37	.36	.36	.35	.35	.35	.35	.34	.34	.34	.34	.34	.34	.33
50	.73	.72	.71	.70	.70	.69	.69	.68	.68	.68	.68	.67	.67	.66
75	1.10	1.08	1.07	1.05	1.05	1.04	1.03	1.02	1.02	1.02	1.01	1.00	1.00	.99
100	1.46	1.44	1.42	1.40	1.39	1.38	1.37	1.36	1.36	1.35	1.35	1.33	1.33	1.32
200	2.91	2.87	2.83	2.80	2.78	2.76	2.74	2.72	2.71	2.70	2.69	2.66	2.65	2.64
300	4.37	4.30	4.25	4.20	4.17	4.13	4.11	4.08	4.06	4.05	4.03	3.99	3.97	3.96
400	5.82	5.74	5.66	5.60	5.55	5.51	5.47	5.44	5.42	5.40	5.38	5.32	5.29	5.28
500	7.28	7.17	7.08	7.00	6.94	6.89	6.84	6.80	6.77	6.74	6.72	6.65	6.62	6.60
600	8.73	8.60	8.49	8.40	8.33	8.26	8.21	8.16	8.12	8.09	8.06	7.98	7.94	7.92
700	10.19	10.04	9.91	9.80	9.71	9.64	9.58	9.52	9.48	9.44	9.41	9.31	9.26	9.24
800	11.64	11.47	11.32	11.20	11.10	11.02	10.94	10.88	10.83	10.79	10.75	10.63	10.58	10.56
900	13.10	12.90	12.74	12.60	12.49	12.39	12.31	12.24	12.18	12.14	12.09	11.96	11.90	11.88
1000	14.55	14.33	14.15	14.00	13.87	13.77	13.68	13.60	13.54	13.48	13.44	13.29	13.23	13.20
2000	29.10	28.66	28.30	28.00	27.74	27.53	27.35	27.20	27.07	26.96	26.87	26.58	26.45	26.39
3000	43.65	42.99	42.45	41.99	41.61	41.29	41.02	40.80	40.60	40.44	40.30	39.86	39.67	39.58
4000	58.20	57.32	56.60	55.99	55.48	55.06	54.70	54.39	54.14	53.92	53.73	53.15	52.89	52.77
5000	72.74	71.65	70.74	69.99	69.35	68.82	68.37	67.99	67.67	67.40	67.17	66.44	66.11	65.96
6000	87.29	85.98	84.89	83.98	83.22	82.58	82.04	81.59	81.20	80.87	80.60	79.72	79.33	79.15
7000	101.84	100.31	99.04	97.98	97.09	96.34	95.71	95.18	94.73	94.35	94.03	93.01	92.55	92.34
8000	116.39	114.64	113.19	111.98	110.96	110.11	109.39	108.78	108.27	107.83	107.46	106.30	105.77	105.54
9000	130.94	128.97	127.34	125.97	124.83	123.87	123.06	122.38	121.80	121.31	120.89	119.58	118.99	118.73
10000	145.48	143.30	141.48	139.97	138.70	137.63	136.73	135.97	135.33	134.79	134.33	132.87	132.22	131.92
11000	160.03	157.63	155.63	153.97	152.57	151.39	150.41	149.57	148.86	148.27	147.76	146.16	145.44	145.11
12000	174.58	171.96	169.78	167.96	166.44	165.16	164.08	163.17	162.40	161.74	161.19	159.44	158.66	158.30
13000	189.13	186.29	183.93	181.96	180.31	178.92	177.75	176.76	175.93	175.22	174.62	172.73	171.88	171.49
14000	203.67	200.62	198.08	195.95	194.18	192.68	191.42	190.36	189.46	188.70	188.05	186.01	185.10	184.68
15000	218.22	214.95	212.22	209.95	208.05	206.45	205.10	203.96	202.99	202.18	201.49	199.30	198.32	197.88
16000	232.77	229.28	226.37	223.95	221.92	220.21	218.77	217.56	216.53	215.66	214.92	212.59	211.54	211.07
17000	247.32	243.61	240.52	237.94	235.79	233.97	232.44	231.15	230.06	229.13	228.35	225.87	224.76	224.26
18000	261.87	257.94	254.67	251.94	249.65	247.73	246.12	244.75	243.59	242.61	241.78	239.16	237.98	237.45
19000	276.41	272.26	268.82	265.94	263.52	261.50	259.79	258.35	257.13	256.09	255.21	252.45	251.20	250.64
20000	290.96	286.59	282.96	279.93	277.39	275.26	273.46	271.94	270.66	269.57	268.65	265.73	264.43	263.83
21000	305.51	300.92	297.11	293.93	291.26	289.02	287.13	285.54	284.19	283.05	282.08	279.02	277.65	277.02
22000	320.06	315.25	311.26	307.93	305.13	302.78	300.81	299.14	297.72	296.53	295.51	292.31	290.87	290.22
23000	334.60	329.58	325.41	321.92	319.00	316.55	314.48	312.73	311.26	310.00	308.94	305.59	304.09	303.41
24000	349.15	343.91	339.56	335.92	332.87	330.31	328.15	326.33	324.79	323.48	322.37	318.88	317.31	316.60
25000	363.70	358.24	353.70	349.92	346.74	344.07	341.83	339.93	338.32	336.96	335.81	332.17	330.53	329.79
26000	378.25	372.57	367.85	363.91	360.61	357.84	355.50	353.52	351.85	350.44	349.24	345.45	343.75	342.98
27000	392.80	386.90	382.00	377.91	374.48	371.60	369.17	367.12	365.39	363.92	362.67	358.74	356.97	356.17
28000	407.34	401.23	396.15	391.90	388.35	385.36	382.84	380.72	378.92	377.40	376.10	372.02	370.19	369.36
29000	421.89	415.56	410.30	405.90	402.22	399.12	396.52	394.31	392.45	390.87	389.53	385.31	383.41	382.56
30000	436.44	429.89	424.44	419.90	416.09	412.89	410.19	407.91	405.98	404.35	402.97	398.60	396.64	395.75
31000	450.99	444.22	438.59	433.89	429.96	426.65	423.86	421.51	419.52	417.83	416.40	411.88	409.86	408.94
32000	465.53	458.55	452.74	447.89	443.83	440.41	437.53	435.11	433.05	431.31	429.83	425.17	423.08	422.13
33000	480.08	472.88	466.89	461.89	457.70	454.17	451.21	448.70	446.58	444.79	443.26	438.46	436.30	435.32
34000	494.63	487.21	481.04	475.88	471.57	467.94	464.88	462.30	460.11	458.26	456.69	451.74	449.52	448.51
35000	509.18	501.54	495.18	489.88	485.44	481.70	478.55	475.90	473.65	471.74	470.13	465.03	462.74	461.70
36000	523.73	515.87	509.33	503.88	499.30	495.46	492.23	489.49	487.18	485.22	483.56	478.32	475.96	474.90
37000	538.27	530.19	523.48	517.87	513.17	509.23	505.90	503.09	500.71	498.70	496.99	491.60	489.18	488.09
38000	552.82	544.52	537.63	531.87	527.04	522.99	519.57	516.69	514.25	512.18	510.42	504.89	502.40	501.28
39000	567.37	558.85	551.77	545.86	540.91	536.75	533.24	530.28	527.78	525.66	523.85	518.18	515.63	514.47
40000	581.92	573.18	565.92	559.86	554.78	550.51	546.92	543.88	541.31	539.13	537.29	531.46	528.85	527.66
41000	596.46	587.51	580.07	573.86	568.65	564.28	560.59	557.48	554.84	552.61	550.72	544.75	542.07	540.85
42000	611.01	601.84	594.22	587.85	582.52	578.04	574.26	571.07	568.38	566.09	564.15	558.03	555.29	554.04
43000	625.56	616.17	608.37	601.85	596.39	591.80	587.94	584.67	581.91	579.57	577.58	571.32	568.51	567.24
44000	640.11	630.50	622.51	615.85	610.26	605.56	601.61	598.27	595.44	593.05	591.02	584.61	581.73	580.43
45000	654.66	644.83	636.66	629.84	624.13	619.33	615.28	611.86	608.97	606.52	604.45	597.89	594.95	593.62
46000	669.20	659.16	650.81	643.84	638.00	633.09	628.95	625.46	622.51	620.00	617.88	611.18	608.17	606.81
47000	683.75	673.49	664.96	657.84	651.87	646.85	642.63	639.06	636.04	633.48	631.31	624.47	621.39	620.00
48000	698.30	687.82	679.11	671.83	665.74	660.62	656.30	652.66	649.57	646.96	644.74	637.75	634.61	633.19
49000	712.85	702.15	693.25	685.83	679.61	674.38	669.97	666.25	663.10	660.44	658.18	651.04	647.84	646.38
50000	727.40	716.48	707.40	699.83	693.48	688.14	683.65	679.85	676.64	673.92	671.61	664.33	661.06	659.58
55000	800.13	788.12	778.14	769.81	762.82	756.95	752.01	747.83	744.30	741.31	738.77	730.76	727.16	725.53
60000	872.87	859.77	848.88	839.79	832.17	825.77	820.37	815.82	811.96	808.70	805.93	797.19	793.27	791.49
65000	945.61	931.42	919.62	909.77	901.52	894.58	888.74	883.80	879.63	876.09	873.09	863.62	859.37	857.45
70000	1018.35	1003.07	990.36	979.75	970.87	963.40	957.10	951.79	947.29	943.48	940.25	930.05	925.48	923.40
75000	1091.09	1074.71	1061.10	1049.74	1040.21	1032.21	1025.47	1019.77	1014.95	1010.87	1007.41	996.49	991.58	989.36
80000	1163.83	1146.36	1131.84	1119.72	1109.56	1101.02	1093.83	1087.76	1082.62	1078.26	1074.57	1062.92	1057.69	1055.32
85000	1236.57	1218.01	1202.58	1189.70	1178.91	1169.84	1162.19	1155.74	1150.28	1145.65	1141.73	1129.35	1123.79	1121.27
90000	1309.31	1289.66	1273.32	1259.68	1248.25	1238.65	1230.56	1223.72	1217.94	1213.05	1208.89	1195.78	1189.90	1187.23
95000	1382.05	1361.30	1344.06	1329.66	1317.60	1307.46	1298.92	1291.71	1285.61	1280.44	1276.05	1262.21	1256.00	1253.19
100000	1454.79	1432.95	1414.80	1399.65	1386.95	1376.28	1367.29	1359.69	1353.27	1347.83	1343.21	1328.65	1322.11	1319.15

MONTHLY PAYMENT
REQUIRED TO AMORTIZE A LOAN

TERM / AMOUNT	1 Year	2 Years	3 Years	4 Years	5 Years	6 Years	7 Years	8 Years	9 Years	10 Years	11 Years	12 Years	13 Years	14 Years
5	.46	.25	.18	.15	.13	.11	.10	.10	.09	.09	.09	.08	.08	.00
10	.91	.49	.36	.29	.25	.22	.20	.19	.18	.17	.17	.16	.16	.15
15	1.37	.74	.53	.43	.37	.33	.30	.28	.27	.26	.25	.24	.23	.23
25	2.27	1.23	.88	.71	.61	.55	.50	.47	.44	.42	.41	.39	.38	.38
50	4.54	2.45	1.76	1.42	1.22	1.09	.99	.93	.88	.84	.81	.78	.76	.75
75	6.81	3.67	2.64	2.13	1.82	1.63	1.49	1.39	1.31	1.26	1.21	1.17	1.14	1.12
100	9.07	4.90	3.51	2.83	2.43	2.17	1.98	1.85	1.75	1.67	1.61	1.56	1.52	1.49
200	18.14	9.79	7.02	5.66	4.86	4.33	3.96	3.70	3.49	3.34	3.22	3.12	3.04	2.98
300	27.21	14.68	10.53	8.49	7.28	6.49	5.94	5.54	5.24	5.01	4.82	4.68	4.56	4.46
400	36.27	19.57	14.04	11.32	9.71	8.65	7.92	7.39	6.98	6.67	6.43	6.24	6.08	5.95
500	45.34	24.46	17.55	14.14	12.13	10.82	9.90	9.23	8.73	8.34	8.04	7.79	7.60	7.44
600	54.41	29.35	21.06	16.97	14.56	12.98	11.88	11.08	10.47	10.01	9.64	9.35	9.12	8.92
700	63.48	34.24	24.57	19.80	16.98	15.14	13.86	12.92	12.22	11.68	11.25	10.91	10.63	10.41
800	72.54	39.13	28.08	22.63	19.41	17.30	15.84	14.77	13.96	13.34	12.86	12.47	12.15	11.90
900	81.61	44.02	31.59	25.45	21.83	19.47	17.82	16.61	15.71	15.01	14.46	14.02	13.67	13.38
1000	90.68	48.91	35.10	28.28	24.26	21.63	19.80	18.46	17.45	16.68	16.07	15.58	15.19	14.87
2000	181.35	97.81	70.20	56.56	48.51	43.25	39.59	36.92	34.90	33.35	32.13	31.16	30.37	29.73
3000	272.02	146.72	105.29	84.83	72.76	64.87	59.38	55.37	52.35	50.03	48.19	46.73	45.56	44.59
4000	362.69	195.62	140.39	113.11	97.01	86.50	79.17	73.83	69.80	66.70	64.26	62.31	60.74	59.46
5000	453.36	244.52	175.48	141.39	121.26	108.12	98.96	92.28	87.25	83.37	80.32	77.89	75.92	74.32
6000	544.04	293.43	210.58	169.66	145.52	129.74	118.75	110.74	104.70	100.05	96.38	93.46	91.11	89.18
7000	634.71	342.33	245.67	197.94	169.77	151.37	138.54	129.19	122.15	116.72	112.45	109.04	106.29	104.05
8000	725.38	391.23	280.77	226.22	194.02	172.99	158.33	147.65	139.60	133.39	128.51	124.62	121.47	118.91
9000	816.05	440.14	315.86	254.49	218.27	194.61	178.12	166.10	157.05	150.07	144.57	140.19	136.66	133.77
10000	906.72	489.04	350.96	282.77	242.52	216.24	197.91	184.56	174.50	166.74	160.64	155.77	151.84	148.64
11000	997.39	537.94	386.05	311.04	266.77	237.86	217.71	203.01	191.95	183.41	176.70	171.35	167.02	163.50
12000	1088.07	586.85	421.15	339.32	291.03	259.48	237.50	221.47	209.40	200.09	192.76	186.92	182.21	178.36
13000	1178.74	635.75	456.24	367.60	315.28	281.11	257.29	239.92	226.85	216.76	208.83	202.50	197.39	193.22
14000	1269.41	684.65	491.34	395.87	339.53	302.73	277.08	258.38	244.30	233.43	224.89	218.08	212.57	208.09
15000	1360.08	733.56	526.44	424.15	363.78	324.35	296.87	276.84	261.75	250.11	240.95	233.65	227.76	222.95
16000	1450.75	782.46	561.53	452.43	388.03	345.97	316.66	295.29	279.20	266.78	257.02	249.23	242.94	237.81
17000	1541.42	831.36	596.63	480.70	412.28	367.60	336.45	313.75	296.65	283.45	273.08	264.80	258.12	252.68
18000	1632.10	880.27	631.72	508.98	436.54	389.22	356.24	332.20	314.10	300.13	289.14	280.38	273.31	267.54
19000	1722.77	929.17	666.82	537.25	460.79	410.84	376.03	350.66	331.55	316.80	305.21	295.96	288.49	282.40
20000	1813.44	978.07	701.91	565.53	485.04	432.47	395.82	369.11	349.00	333.47	321.27	311.53	303.67	297.27
21000	1904.11	1026.98	737.01	593.81	509.29	454.09	415.61	387.57	366.45	350.15	337.33	327.11	318.86	312.13
22000	1994.78	1075.88	772.10	622.08	533.54	475.71	435.41	406.02	383.90	366.82	353.40	342.69	334.04	326.99
23000	2085.45	1124.78	807.20	650.36	557.79	497.34	455.20	424.48	401.35	383.50	369.46	358.26	349.22	341.85
24000	2176.13	1173.69	842.29	678.64	582.05	518.96	474.99	442.93	418.79	400.17	385.52	373.84	364.41	356.72
25000	2266.80	1222.59	877.39	706.91	606.30	540.58	494.78	461.39	436.24	416.84	401.59	389.42	379.59	371.58
26000	2357.47	1271.49	912.48	735.19	630.55	562.21	514.57	479.84	453.69	433.52	417.65	404.99	394.77	386.44
27000	2448.14	1320.40	947.58	763.47	654.80	583.83	534.36	498.30	471.14	450.19	433.71	420.57	409.96	401.31
28000	2538.81	1369.30	982.67	791.74	679.05	605.45	554.15	516.75	488.59	466.86	449.78	436.15	425.14	416.17
29000	2629.48	1418.20	1017.77	820.00	703.30	627.07	573.94	535.21	506.04	483.54	465.84	451.72	440.32	431.03
30000	2720.16	1467.11	1052.87	848.29	727.56	648.70	593.73	553.67	523.49	500.21	481.90	467.30	455.51	445.90
31000	2810.83	1516.01	1087.96	876.57	751.81	670.32	613.52	572.12	540.94	516.88	497.97	482.87	470.69	460.76
32000	2901.50	1564.91	1123.06	904.85	776.06	691.94	633.31	590.58	558.39	533.56	514.03	498.45	485.87	475.62
33000	2992.17	1613.82	1158.15	933.12	800.31	713.57	653.11	609.03	575.84	550.23	530.09	514.03	501.06	490.49
34000	3082.84	1662.72	1193.25	961.40	824.56	735.19	672.90	627.49	593.29	566.90	546.16	529.60	516.24	505.35
35000	3173.52	1711.62	1228.34	989.68	848.81	756.81	692.69	645.94	610.74	583.58	562.22	545.18	531.42	520.21
36000	3264.19	1760.53	1263.44	1017.95	873.07	778.44	712.48	664.40	628.19	600.25	578.28	560.76	546.61	535.07
37000	3354.86	1809.43	1298.53	1046.23	897.32	800.06	732.27	682.85	645.64	616.92	594.35	576.33	561.79	549.94
38000	3445.53	1858.33	1333.63	1074.50	921.57	821.68	752.06	701.31	663.09	633.60	610.41	591.91	576.97	564.80
39000	3536.20	1907.24	1368.72	1102.78	945.82	843.31	771.85	719.76	680.54	650.27	626.47	607.49	592.16	579.66
40000	3626.87	1956.14	1403.82	1131.06	970.07	864.93	791.64	738.22	697.99	666.94	642.54	623.06	607.34	594.53
41000	3717.55	2005.04	1438.91	1159.33	994.32	886.55	811.43	756.67	715.44	683.62	658.60	638.64	622.52	609.39
42000	3808.22	2053.95	1474.01	1187.61	1018.58	908.17	831.22	775.13	732.89	700.29	674.66	654.22	637.71	624.25
43000	3898.89	2102.85	1509.11	1215.89	1042.83	929.80	851.02	793.59	750.34	716.97	690.73	669.79	652.89	639.12
44000	3989.56	2151.75	1544.20	1244.16	1067.08	951.42	870.81	812.04	767.79	733.64	706.79	685.37	668.07	653.98
45000	4080.23	2200.66	1579.30	1272.44	1091.33	973.04	890.60	830.50	785.24	750.31	722.85	700.94	683.26	668.84
46000	4170.90	2249.56	1614.39	1300.71	1115.58	994.67	910.39	848.95	802.69	766.99	738.92	716.52	698.44	683.70
47000	4261.58	2298.47	1649.49	1328.99	1139.83	1016.29	930.18	867.41	820.14	783.66	754.98	732.10	713.62	698.57
48000	4352.25	2347.37	1684.58	1357.27	1164.09	1037.91	949.97	885.86	837.58	800.33	771.04	747.67	728.81	713.43
49000	4442.92	2396.27	1719.68	1385.54	1188.34	1059.54	969.76	904.32	855.03	817.01	787.11	763.25	743.99	728.29
50000	4533.59	2445.18	1754.77	1413.82	1212.59	1081.16	989.55	922.77	872.48	833.68	803.17	778.83	759.17	743.16
55000	4986.95	2689.69	1930.25	1555.20	1333.85	1189.27	1088.51	1015.05	959.73	917.05	883.49	856.71	835.09	817.47
60000	5440.31	2934.21	2105.73	1696.58	1455.11	1297.39	1187.46	1107.33	1046.98	1000.41	963.80	934.59	911.01	891.79
65000	5893.67	3178.73	2281.20	1837.96	1576.36	1405.51	1286.42	1199.60	1134.23	1083.78	1044.12	1012.47	986.92	966.10
70000	6347.03	3423.24	2456.68	1979.35	1697.62	1513.62	1385.37	1291.88	1221.48	1167.15	1124.44	1090.36	1062.84	1040.42
75000	6800.38	3667.76	2632.16	2120.73	1818.88	1621.74	1484.33	1384.16	1308.72	1250.52	1204.75	1168.24	1138.76	1114.73
80000	7253.74	3912.28	2807.63	2262.11	1940.14	1729.85	1583.24	1476.43	1395.97	1333.88	1285.07	1246.12	1214.67	1189.05
85000	7707.10	4156.79	2983.11	2403.49	2061.40	1837.97	1682.23	1568.71	1483.22	1417.25	1365.39	1324.00	1290.59	1263.36
90000	8160.46	4401.31	3158.59	2544.87	2182.66	1946.08	1781.19	1660.99	1570.47	1500.62	1445.70	1401.88	1366.51	1337.68
95000	8613.82	4645.83	3334.06	2686.25	2303.92	2054.20	1880.14	1753.26	1657.72	1583.99	1526.02	1479.77	1442.43	1411.99
100000	9067.18	4890.35	3509.54	2827.64	2425.17	2162.31	1979.10	1845.54	1744.96	1667.35	1606.34	1557.65	1518.34	1486.31

TERM AMOUNT	15 Years	16 Years	17 Years	18 Years	19 Years	20 Years	21 Years	22 Years	23 Years	24 Years	25 Years	30 Years	35 Years	40 Years
5	.08	.08	.08	.08	.07	.07	.07	.07	.07	.07	.07	.07	.07	.07
10	.15	.15	.15	.15	.14	.14	.14	.14	.14	.14	.14	.14	.14	.14
15	.22	.22	.22	.22	.21	.21	.21	.21	.21	.21	.21	.21	.20	.20
25	.37	.36	.36	.36	.35	.35	.35	.35	.34	.34	.34	.34	.34	.34
50	.73	.72	.72	.71	.70	.70	.69	.69	.68	.68	.68	.67	.67	.67
75	1.10	1.08	1.07	1.06	1.05	1.04	1.03	1.03	1.02	1.02	1.02	1.01	1.00	1.00
100	1.46	1.44	1.43	1.41	1.40	1.39	1.38	1.37	1.36	1.36	1.35	1.34	1.33	1.33
200	2.92	2.88	2.85	2.82	2.79	2.77	2.75	2.74	2.72	2.71	2.70	2.67	2.66	2.66
300	4.38	4.32	4.27	4.22	4.18	4.15	4.12	4.10	4.08	4.07	4.05	4.01	3.99	3.98
400	5.84	5.76	5.69	5.63	5.57	5.53	5.50	5.47	5.44	5.42	5.40	5.34	5.32	5.31
500	7.30	7.20	7.11	7.03	6.97	6.91	6.87	6.83	6.80	6.77	6.75	6.68	6.65	6.63
600	8.76	8.63	8.53	8.44	8.36	8.30	8.24	8.20	8.16	8.13	8.10	8.01	7.97	7.96
700	10.22	10.07	9.95	9.84	9.75	9.68	9.62	9.56	9.52	9.48	9.45	9.35	9.30	9.28
800	11.68	11.51	11.37	11.25	11.14	11.06	10.99	10.93	10.88	10.83	10.80	10.68	10.63	10.61
900	13.14	12.95	12.79	12.65	12.54	12.44	12.36	12.29	12.24	12.19	12.15	12.02	11.96	11.93
1000	14.60	14.39	14.21	14.06	13.93	13.82	13.73	13.66	13.60	13.54	13.50	13.35	13.29	13.26
2000	29.20	28.77	28.41	28.11	27.85	27.64	27.46	27.31	27.19	27.08	26.99	26.70	26.57	26.51
3000	43.80	43.15	42.61	42.16	41.78	41.46	41.19	40.97	40.78	40.61	40.48	40.05	39.85	39.76
4000	58.40	57.54	56.81	56.21	55.70	55.28	54.92	54.62	54.37	54.15	53.97	53.39	53.13	53.02
5000	73.00	71.92	71.01	70.26	69.63	69.10	68.65	68.28	67.96	67.69	67.46	66.74	66.42	66.27
6000	87.60	86.30	85.22	84.31	83.55	82.92	82.38	81.93	81.55	81.22	80.95	80.09	79.70	79.52
7000	102.20	100.68	99.42	98.36	97.48	96.74	96.11	95.58	95.14	94.76	94.44	93.43	92.98	92.78
8000	116.80	115.07	113.62	112.41	111.40	110.56	109.84	109.24	108.73	108.30	107.93	106.78	106.26	106.03
9000	131.40	129.45	127.82	126.47	125.33	124.37	123.57	122.89	122.32	121.83	121.42	120.13	119.55	119.28
10000	146.00	143.83	142.02	140.52	139.25	138.19	137.30	136.55	135.91	135.37	134.91	133.47	132.83	132.54
11000	160.60	158.21	156.23	154.57	153.18	152.01	151.03	150.20	149.50	148.91	148.40	146.82	146.11	145.79
12000	175.20	172.60	170.43	168.62	167.10	165.83	164.76	163.86	163.09	162.44	161.89	160.17	159.39	159.04
13000	189.80	186.98	184.63	182.67	181.03	179.65	178.49	177.51	176.68	175.90	175.39	173.51	172.68	172.30
14000	204.40	201.36	198.83	196.72	194.95	193.47	192.22	191.16	190.27	189.52	188.88	186.86	185.96	185.55
15000	219.00	215.74	213.03	210.77	208.88	207.29	205.95	204.82	203.86	203.05	202.37	200.21	199.24	198.80
16000	233.60	230.13	227.23	224.82	222.80	221.11	219.68	218.47	217.45	216.59	215.86	213.55	212.52	212.06
17000	248.20	244.51	241.44	238.87	236.73	234.93	233.41	232.13	231.04	230.13	229.35	226.90	225.81	225.31
18000	262.80	258.89	255.64	252.93	250.65	248.74	247.14	245.78	244.63	243.66	242.84	240.25	239.09	238.56
19000	277.40	273.27	269.84	266.98	264.58	262.56	260.87	259.44	258.22	257.20	256.33	253.59	252.37	251.82
20000	292.00	287.66	284.04	281.03	278.50	276.38	274.60	273.09	271.82	270.74	269.82	266.94	265.65	265.07
21000	306.60	302.04	298.24	295.08	292.43	290.20	288.33	286.74	285.41	284.27	283.31	280.29	278.94	278.32
22000	321.20	316.42	312.45	309.13	306.35	304.02	302.06	300.40	299.00	297.81	296.80	293.64	292.22	291.58
23000	335.80	330.80	326.65	323.18	320.28	317.84	315.79	314.05	312.59	311.35	310.29	306.98	305.50	304.83
24000	350.40	345.19	340.85	337.23	334.20	331.66	329.51	327.71	326.18	324.88	323.78	320.33	318.78	318.08
25000	365.00	359.57	355.05	351.28	348.13	345.48	343.24	341.36	339.77	338.42	337.28	333.68	332.06	331.34
26000	379.60	373.95	369.25	365.33	362.05	359.30	356.97	355.01	353.36	351.96	350.77	347.02	345.35	344.59
27000	394.20	388.33	383.46	379.39	375.98	373.11	370.70	368.67	366.95	365.49	364.26	360.37	358.63	357.84
28000	408.80	402.72	397.66	393.44	389.90	386.93	384.43	382.32	380.54	379.03	377.75	373.72	371.91	371.10
29000	423.40	417.10	411.86	407.49	403.83	400.75	398.16	395.98	394.13	392.57	391.24	387.06	385.19	384.35
30000	438.00	431.48	426.06	421.54	417.75	414.57	411.89	409.63	407.72	406.10	404.73	400.41	398.48	397.60
31000	452.60	445.86	440.26	435.59	431.68	428.39	425.62	423.29	421.31	419.64	418.22	413.76	411.76	410.86
32000	467.20	460.25	454.46	449.64	445.60	442.21	439.35	436.94	434.90	433.17	431.71	427.10	425.04	424.11
33000	481.80	474.63	468.67	463.69	459.53	456.03	453.08	450.59	448.49	446.71	445.20	440.45	438.32	437.36
34000	496.40	489.01	482.87	477.74	473.45	469.85	466.81	464.25	462.08	460.25	458.69	453.80	451.61	450.62
35000	511.00	503.39	497.07	491.79	487.38	483.67	480.54	477.90	475.67	473.78	472.18	467.14	464.89	463.87
36000	525.60	517.78	511.27	505.85	501.30	497.48	494.27	491.56	489.26	487.32	485.67	480.49	478.17	477.12
37000	540.20	532.16	525.47	519.90	515.23	511.30	508.00	505.21	502.85	500.86	499.17	493.84	491.45	490.38
38000	554.80	546.54	539.68	533.95	529.15	525.12	521.73	518.87	516.44	514.39	512.66	507.18	504.74	503.63
39000	569.40	560.92	553.88	548.00	543.08	538.94	535.46	532.52	530.03	527.93	526.15	520.53	518.02	516.88
40000	584.00	575.31	568.08	562.05	557.00	552.76	549.19	546.17	543.63	541.47	539.64	533.88	531.30	530.14
41000	598.60	589.69	582.28	576.10	570.93	566.58	562.92	559.83	557.22	555.00	553.13	547.22	544.58	543.39
42000	613.20	604.07	596.48	590.15	584.85	580.40	576.65	573.48	570.81	568.54	566.62	560.57	557.87	556.64
43000	627.80	618.45	610.69	604.20	598.78	594.22	590.38	587.14	584.40	582.08	580.11	573.92	571.15	569.90
44000	642.40	632.84	624.89	618.25	612.70	608.03	604.11	600.79	597.99	595.61	593.60	587.27	584.43	583.15
45000	657.00	647.22	639.09	632.31	626.63	621.85	617.84	614.44	611.58	609.15	607.09	600.61	597.71	596.40
46000	671.60	661.60	653.29	646.36	640.55	635.67	631.57	628.10	625.17	622.69	620.58	613.96	610.99	609.66
47000	686.20	675.98	667.49	660.41	654.48	649.49	645.29	641.75	638.76	636.22	634.07	627.31	624.28	622.91
48000	700.80	690.37	681.69	674.46	668.40	663.31	659.02	655.41	652.35	649.76	647.56	640.65	637.56	636.16
49000	715.40	704.75	695.90	688.51	682.32	677.13	672.75	669.06	665.94	663.30	661.06	654.00	650.84	649.42
50000	730.00	719.13	710.10	702.56	696.25	690.95	686.48	682.72	679.53	676.83	674.55	667.35	664.12	662.67
55000	803.00	791.04	781.11	772.82	765.87	760.04	755.13	750.99	747.48	744.52	742.00	734.08	730.54	728.94
60000	876.00	862.96	852.12	843.07	835.50	829.14	823.78	819.26	815.44	812.20	809.45	800.81	796.95	795.20
65000	949.00	934.87	923.13	913.33	905.12	898.23	892.43	887.53	883.39	879.88	876.91	867.55	863.36	861.47
70000	1022.00	1006.78	994.14	983.58	974.75	967.33	961.07	955.80	951.34	947.56	944.36	934.28	929.77	927.74
75000	1095.00	1078.69	1065.14	1053.84	1044.37	1036.42	1029.72	1024.07	1019.29	1015.25	1011.82	1001.02	996.18	994.00
80000	1168.00	1150.61	1136.15	1124.10	1114.00	1105.51	1098.37	1092.34	1087.25	1082.93	1079.27	1067.75	1062.60	1060.27
85000	1241.00	1222.52	1207.16	1194.35	1183.62	1174.61	1167.02	1160.61	1155.20	1150.61	1146.73	1134.48	1129.01	1126.54
90000	1314.00	1294.43	1278.17	1264.61	1253.25	1243.70	1235.67	1228.88	1223.15	1218.30	1214.18	1201.22	1195.42	1192.80
95000	1387.00	1366.34	1349.18	1334.86	1322.87	1312.80	1304.31	1297.16	1291.10	1285.98	1281.63	1267.95	1261.83	1259.07
100000	1460.00	1438.26	1420.19	1405.12	1392.49	1381.89	1372.96	1365.43	1359.06	1353.66	1349.09	1334.69	1328.24	1325.34

MONTHLY PAYMENT
REQUIRED TO AMORTIZE A LOAN

TERM AMOUNT	1 Year	2 Years	3 Years	4 Years	5 Years	6 Years	7 Years	8 Years	9 Years	10 Years	11 Years	12 Years	13 Years	14 Years
5	.46	.25	.18	.15	.13	.11	.10	.10	.09	.09	.09	.08	.08	.08
10	.91	.49	.36	.29	.25	.22	.20	.19	.18	.17	.17	.16	.16	.15
15	1.37	.74	.53	.43	.37	.33	.30	.28	.27	.26	.25	.24	.23	.23
25	2.27	1.23	.88	.71	.61	.55	.50	.47	.44	.42	.41	.39	.39	.38
50	4.54	2.45	1.76	1.42	1.22	1.09	1.00	.93	.88	.84	.81	.78	.77	.75
75	6.81	3.67	2.64	2.13	1.82	1.63	1.49	1.39	1.31	1.26	1.21	1.17	1.15	1.12
100	9.07	4.90	3.52	2.83	2.43	2.17	1.99	1.85	1.75	1.67	1.61	1.56	1.53	1.49
200	18.14	9.79	7.03	5.66	4.86	4.33	3.97	3.70	3.50	3.34	3.22	3.12	3.05	2.98
300	27.21	14.68	10.54	8.49	7.28	6.50	5.95	5.55	5.24	5.01	4.83	4.68	4.57	4.47
400	36.28	19.57	14.05	11.32	9.71	8.66	7.93	7.39	6.99	6.68	6.44	6.24	6.09	5.96
500	45.35	24.46	17.56	14.15	12.14	10.82	9.91	9.24	8.74	8.35	8.04	7.80	7.61	7.45
600	54.42	29.35	21.07	16.98	14.56	12.99	11.89	11.09	10.48	10.02	9.65	9.36	9.13	8.93
700	63.48	34.25	24.58	19.81	16.99	15.15	13.87	12.93	12.23	11.69	11.26	10.92	10.65	10.42
800	72.55	39.14	28.09	22.64	19.42	17.31	15.85	14.78	13.98	13.36	12.87	12.48	12.17	11.91
900	81.62	44.03	31.60	25.47	21.84	19.48	17.83	16.63	15.72	15.03	14.48	14.04	13.69	13.40
1000	90.69	48.92	35.11	28.29	24.27	21.64	19.81	18.48	17.47	16.69	16.08	15.60	15.21	14.89
2000	181.37	97.84	70.22	56.58	48.53	43.28	39.62	36.95	34.93	33.38	32.16	31.19	30.41	29.77
3000	272.06	146.75	105.33	84.87	72.80	64.92	59.42	55.42	52.40	50.07	48.24	46.78	45.61	44.65
4000	362.74	195.67	140.44	113.16	97.06	86.55	79.23	73.89	69.86	66.76	64.32	62.38	60.81	59.53
5000	453.42	244.58	175.54	141.45	121.33	108.19	99.03	92.36	87.33	83.45	80.40	77.97	76.01	74.41
6000	544.11	293.50	210.65	169.74	145.59	129.83	118.84	110.83	104.79	100.14	96.48	93.56	91.21	89.29
7000	634.79	342.41	245.76	198.03	169.86	151.46	138.64	129.30	122.26	116.83	112.56	109.15	106.41	104.17
8000	725.47	391.33	280.87	226.32	194.12	173.10	158.45	147.77	139.72	133.52	128.64	124.75	121.61	119.05
9000	816.16	440.24	315.97	254.61	218.39	194.74	178.25	166.24	157.19	150.21	144.72	140.34	136.81	133.93
10000	906.84	489.16	351.08	282.90	242.65	216.37	198.06	184.71	174.65	166.90	160.80	155.93	152.01	148.81
11000	997.52	538.07	386.19	311.19	266.92	238.01	217.86	203.18	192.12	183.58	176.88	171.53	167.21	163.69
12000	1088.21	586.99	421.30	339.47	291.18	259.65	237.67	221.65	209.58	200.27	192.96	187.12	182.41	178.57
13000	1178.89	635.90	456.40	367.76	315.45	281.28	257.47	240.12	227.05	216.96	209.04	202.71	197.61	193.45
14000	1269.57	684.82	491.51	396.05	339.71	302.92	277.28	258.59	244.51	233.65	225.11	218.30	212.81	208.33
15000	1360.26	733.74	526.62	424.34	363.98	324.56	297.08	277.06	261.98	250.34	241.19	233.90	228.01	223.21
16000	1450.94	782.65	561.73	452.63	388.24	346.19	316.89	295.53	279.44	267.03	257.27	249.49	243.21	238.09
17000	1541.63	831.57	596.84	480.92	412.51	367.83	336.69	314.00	296.90	283.72	273.35	265.08	258.41	252.97
18000	1632.31	880.48	631.94	509.21	436.77	389.47	356.50	332.47	314.37	300.41	289.43	280.68	273.61	267.85
19000	1722.99	929.40	667.05	537.50	461.04	411.10	376.30	350.94	331.83	317.10	305.51	296.27	288.81	282.73
20000	1813.68	978.31	702.16	565.79	485.30	432.74	396.11	369.41	349.30	333.79	321.59	311.86	304.01	297.61
21000	1904.36	1027.23	737.27	594.08	509.57	454.38	415.91	387.88	366.76	350.47	337.67	327.45	319.21	312.49
22000	1995.04	1076.14	772.37	622.37	533.83	476.02	435.72	406.35	384.23	367.16	353.75	343.05	334.41	327.37
23000	2085.73	1125.06	807.48	650.65	558.10	497.65	455.52	424.82	401.69	383.85	369.83	358.64	349.61	342.25
24000	2176.41	1173.97	842.59	678.94	582.36	519.29	475.33	443.29	419.16	400.54	385.91	374.23	364.81	357.13
25000	2267.09	1222.89	877.70	707.23	606.63	540.93	495.13	461.76	436.62	417.23	401.99	389.82	380.01	372.01
26000	2357.78	1271.80	912.80	735.52	630.89	562.56	514.94	480.23	454.09	433.92	418.07	405.42	395.21	386.89
27000	2448.46	1320.72	947.91	763.81	655.16	584.20	534.74	498.70	471.55	450.61	434.15	421.01	410.41	401.77
28000	2539.14	1369.63	983.02	792.10	679.42	605.84	554.55	517.17	489.02	467.30	450.22	436.60	425.61	416.65
29000	2629.83	1418.55	1018.13	820.39	703.69	627.47	574.35	535.64	506.48	483.99	466.30	452.20	440.81	431.53
30000	2720.51	1467.47	1053.24	848.68	727.95	649.11	594.16	554.11	523.95	500.68	482.38	467.79	456.01	446.41
31000	2811.19	1516.38	1088.34	876.97	752.22	670.75	613.96	572.58	541.41	517.37	498.46	483.38	471.21	461.29
32000	2901.88	1565.30	1123.45	905.26	776.48	692.38	633.77	591.05	558.88	534.05	514.54	498.97	486.41	476.17
33000	2992.56	1614.21	1158.56	933.55	800.75	714.02	653.57	609.52	576.34	550.74	530.62	514.57	501.61	491.05
34000	3083.25	1663.13	1193.67	961.83	825.01	735.66	673.38	627.99	593.80	567.43	546.70	530.16	516.81	505.93
35000	3173.93	1712.04	1228.77	990.12	849.28	757.29	693.19	646.46	611.27	584.12	562.78	545.75	532.01	520.81
36000	3264.61	1760.96	1263.88	1018.41	873.54	778.93	712.99	664.93	628.73	600.81	578.86	561.35	547.21	535.69
37000	3355.30	1809.87	1298.99	1046.70	897.81	800.57	732.80	683.40	646.20	617.50	594.94	576.94	562.41	550.57
38000	3445.98	1858.79	1334.10	1074.99	922.07	822.20	752.60	701.87	663.66	634.19	611.02	592.53	577.61	565.45
39000	3536.66	1907.70	1369.20	1103.28	946.34	843.84	772.41	720.34	681.13	650.88	627.10	608.12	592.81	580.33
40000	3627.35	1956.62	1404.31	1131.57	970.60	865.48	792.21	738.81	698.59	667.57	643.18	623.72	608.01	595.21
41000	3718.03	2005.53	1439.42	1159.86	994.87	887.11	812.02	757.28	716.06	684.26	659.25	639.31	623.21	610.09
42000	3808.71	2054.45	1474.53	1188.15	1019.13	908.75	831.82	775.75	733.52	700.94	675.33	654.90	638.41	624.97
43000	3899.40	2103.36	1509.64	1216.44	1043.40	930.39	851.63	794.22	750.99	717.63	691.41	670.49	653.61	639.85
44000	3990.08	2152.28	1544.74	1244.73	1067.66	952.03	871.43	812.69	768.45	734.32	707.49	686.09	668.81	654.73
45000	4080.76	2201.20	1579.85	1273.01	1091.93	973.66	891.24	831.16	785.92	751.01	723.57	701.68	684.01	669.61
46000	4171.45	2250.11	1614.96	1301.30	1116.19	995.30	911.04	849.63	803.38	767.70	739.65	717.27	699.21	684.49
47000	4262.13	2299.03	1650.07	1329.59	1140.46	1016.94	930.85	868.10	820.85	784.39	755.73	732.87	714.41	699.37
48000	4352.82	2347.94	1685.17	1357.88	1164.72	1038.57	950.65	886.57	838.31	801.08	771.81	748.46	729.61	714.25
49000	4443.50	2396.86	1720.28	1386.17	1188.99	1060.21	970.46	905.04	855.78	817.77	787.89	764.05	744.81	729.13
50000	4534.18	2445.77	1755.39	1414.46	1213.25	1081.85	990.26	923.51	873.24	834.46	803.97	779.64	760.01	744.01
55000	4987.60	2690.35	1930.93	1555.91	1334.58	1190.03	1089.29	1015.86	960.56	917.90	884.36	857.61	836.01	818.41
60000	5441.02	2934.93	2106.47	1697.35	1455.90	1298.21	1188.31	1108.21	1047.89	1001.35	964.76	935.57	912.01	892.81
65000	5894.44	3179.50	2282.00	1838.80	1577.23	1406.40	1287.34	1200.56	1135.21	1084.79	1045.16	1013.54	988.01	967.21
70000	6347.85	3424.08	2457.54	1980.24	1698.55	1514.58	1386.37	1292.91	1222.53	1168.24	1125.55	1091.50	1064.01	1041.61
75000	6801.27	3668.66	2633.08	2121.69	1819.88	1622.77	1485.39	1385.26	1309.86	1251.68	1205.95	1169.46	1140.01	1116.01
80000	7254.69	3913.23	2808.62	2263.13	1941.20	1730.95	1584.42	1477.61	1397.18	1335.13	1286.35	1247.43	1216.01	1190.41
85000	7708.11	4157.81	2984.16	2404.58	2062.53	1839.13	1683.44	1569.96	1484.50	1418.57	1366.74	1325.39	1292.01	1264.81
90000	8161.52	4402.39	3159.70	2546.02	2183.85	1947.32	1782.47	1662.31	1571.83	1502.02	1447.14	1403.36	1368.01	1339.21
95000	8614.94	4646.96	3335.23	2687.47	2305.18	2055.50	1881.49	1754.66	1659.15	1585.46	1527.54	1481.32	1444.01	1413.61
100000	9068.36	4891.54	3510.77	2828.91	2426.50	2163.69	1980.52	1847.01	1746.48	1668.91	1607.93	1559.28	1520.01	1488.02

TERM AMOUNT	15 Years	16 Years	17 Years	18 Years	19 Years	20 Years	21 Years	22 Years	23 Years	24 Years	25 Years	30 Years	35 Years	40 Years
5	.08	.08	.08	.08	.07	.07	.07	.07	.07	.07	.07	.07	.07	.07
10	.15	.15	.15	.15	.14	.14	.14	.14	.14	.14	.14	.14	.14	.14
15	.22	.22	.22	.22	.21	.21	.21	.21	.21	.21	.21	.21	.20	.20
25	.37	.37	.36	.36	.35	.35	.35	.35	.35	.34	.34	.34	.34	.34
50	.74	.73	.72	.71	.70	.70	.69	.69	.69	.68	.68	.67	.67	.67
75	1.10	1.09	1.07	1.06	1.05	1.04	1.04	1.03	1.03	1.02	1.02	1.01	1.00	1.00
100	1.47	1.45	1.43	1.41	1.40	1.39	1.38	1.37	1.37	1.36	1.36	1.34	1.34	1.33
200	2.93	2.89	2.85	2.82	2.79	2.77	2.75	2.74	2.73	2.72	2.71	2.68	2.67	2.66
300	4.39	4.33	4.27	4.23	4.19	4.16	4.13	4.11	4.09	4.07	4.06	4.02	4.00	3.99
400	5.85	5.77	5.69	5.63	5.58	5.54	5.50	5.47	5.45	5.43	5.41	5.35	5.33	5.31
500	7.31	7.21	7.11	7.04	6.98	6.92	6.88	6.84	6.81	6.78	6.76	6.69	6.66	6.64
600	8.78	8.65	8.54	8.45	8.37	8.31	8.25	8.21	8.17	8.14	8.11	8.03	7.99	7.97
700	10.24	10.09	9.96	9.85	9.77	9.69	9.63	9.58	9.53	9.49	9.46	9.36	9.32	9.30
800	11.70	11.53	11.38	11.26	11.16	11.08	11.00	10.94	10.89	10.85	10.81	10.70	10.65	10.62
900	13.16	12.97	12.80	12.67	12.55	12.46	12.38	12.31	12.25	12.21	12.16	12.04	11.98	11.95
1000	14.62	14.41	14.22	14.07	13.95	13.84	13.75	13.68	13.61	13.56	13.52	13.37	13.31	13.28
2000	29.24	28.81	28.44	28.14	27.89	27.68	27.50	27.35	27.22	27.12	27.03	26.74	26.61	26.55
3000	43.86	43.21	42.66	42.21	41.84	41.52	41.25	41.03	40.83	40.67	40.54	40.11	39.91	39.83
4000	58.47	57.61	56.88	56.28	55.78	55.36	55.00	54.70	54.44	54.23	54.05	53.47	53.22	53.10
5000	73.09	72.01	71.10	70.35	69.72	69.19	68.75	68.37	68.05	67.79	67.56	66.84	66.52	66.37
6000	87.71	86.41	85.32	84.42	83.67	83.03	82.50	82.05	81.66	81.34	81.07	80.21	79.82	79.65
7000	102.33	100.81	99.54	98.49	97.61	96.87	96.24	95.72	95.27	94.90	94.58	93.57	93.12	92.92
8000	116.94	115.21	113.76	112.56	111.55	110.71	109.99	109.39	108.88	108.45	108.09	106.94	106.43	106.20
9000	131.56	129.61	127.98	126.63	125.50	124.54	123.74	123.07	122.49	122.01	121.60	120.31	119.73	119.47
10000	146.18	144.01	142.20	140.70	139.44	138.38	137.49	136.74	136.10	135.57	135.11	133.67	133.03	132.74
11000	160.80	158.41	156.42	154.77	153.38	152.22	151.24	150.41	149.71	149.12	148.62	147.04	146.34	146.02
12000	175.41	172.81	170.64	168.84	167.33	166.06	164.99	164.09	163.32	162.68	162.13	160.41	159.64	159.29
13000	190.03	187.21	184.86	182.91	181.27	179.89	178.74	177.76	176.93	176.23	175.64	173.78	172.94	172.57
14000	204.65	201.61	199.08	196.98	195.21	193.73	192.48	191.43	190.54	189.79	189.15	187.14	186.24	185.84
15000	219.27	216.01	213.30	211.05	209.16	207.57	206.23	205.11	204.15	203.35	202.66	200.51	199.55	199.11
16000	233.88	230.41	227.52	225.12	223.10	221.41	219.98	218.78	217.76	216.90	216.17	213.88	212.85	212.39
17000	248.50	244.81	241.74	239.18	237.04	235.24	233.73	232.45	231.37	230.46	229.68	227.24	226.15	225.66
18000	263.12	259.21	255.96	253.25	250.99	249.08	247.48	246.13	244.98	244.01	243.19	240.61	239.46	238.94
19000	277.73	273.61	270.18	267.32	264.93	262.92	261.23	259.80	258.59	257.57	256.70	253.98	252.76	252.21
20000	292.35	288.01	284.40	281.39	278.87	276.76	274.98	273.47	272.20	271.13	270.21	267.34	266.06	265.48
21000	306.97	302.41	298.62	295.46	292.82	290.59	288.72	287.15	285.81	284.68	283.72	280.71	279.36	278.76
22000	321.59	316.81	312.84	309.53	306.76	304.43	302.47	300.82	299.42	298.24	297.23	294.08	292.67	292.03
23000	336.20	331.21	327.06	323.60	320.70	318.27	316.22	314.49	313.03	311.79	310.74	307.45	305.97	305.31
24000	350.82	345.61	341.28	337.67	334.65	332.11	329.97	328.17	326.64	325.35	324.26	320.81	319.27	318.58
25000	365.44	360.01	355.50	351.74	348.59	345.94	343.72	341.84	340.25	338.91	337.77	334.18	332.58	331.85
26000	380.06	374.41	369.72	365.81	362.53	359.78	357.47	355.51	353.86	352.46	351.28	347.55	345.88	345.13
27000	394.67	388.81	383.94	379.88	376.48	373.62	371.21	369.19	367.47	366.02	364.79	360.91	359.18	358.40
28000	409.29	403.21	398.16	393.95	390.42	387.46	384.96	382.86	381.08	379.57	378.30	374.28	372.48	371.68
29000	423.91	417.61	412.38	408.02	404.36	401.30	398.71	396.53	394.69	393.13	391.81	387.65	385.79	384.95
30000	438.53	432.01	426.60	422.09	418.31	415.13	412.46	410.21	408.30	406.69	405.32	401.01	399.09	398.22
31000	453.14	446.41	440.82	436.16	432.25	428.97	426.21	423.88	421.91	420.24	418.83	414.38	412.39	411.50
32000	467.76	460.81	455.04	450.23	446.19	442.81	439.96	437.55	435.52	433.80	432.34	427.75	425.70	424.77
33000	482.38	475.21	469.26	464.29	460.14	456.65	453.71	451.23	449.13	447.35	445.85	441.11	439.00	438.04
34000	496.99	489.61	483.48	478.36	474.08	470.48	467.45	464.90	462.74	460.91	459.36	454.48	452.30	451.32
35000	511.61	504.01	497.70	492.43	488.02	484.32	481.20	478.57	476.35	474.47	472.87	467.85	465.60	464.59
36000	526.23	518.41	511.92	506.50	501.97	498.16	494.95	492.25	489.96	488.02	486.38	481.22	478.91	477.87
37000	540.85	532.81	526.14	520.57	515.91	512.00	508.70	505.92	503.57	501.58	499.89	494.58	492.21	491.14
38000	555.46	547.21	540.36	534.64	529.85	525.83	522.45	519.59	517.18	515.13	513.40	507.95	505.51	504.41
39000	570.08	561.61	554.58	548.71	543.80	539.67	536.20	533.27	530.79	528.69	526.91	521.32	518.82	517.69
40000	584.70	576.01	568.80	562.78	557.74	553.51	549.95	546.94	544.40	542.25	540.42	534.68	532.12	530.96
41000	599.32	590.41	583.02	576.85	571.68	567.35	563.69	560.61	558.01	555.80	553.93	548.05	545.42	544.24
42000	613.93	604.81	597.24	590.92	585.63	581.18	577.44	574.29	571.62	569.36	567.44	561.42	558.72	557.51
43000	628.55	619.21	611.46	604.99	599.57	595.02	591.19	587.96	585.23	582.91	580.95	574.78	572.03	570.78
44000	643.17	633.61	625.68	619.06	613.51	608.86	604.94	601.63	598.84	596.47	594.46	588.15	585.33	584.06
45000	657.79	648.01	639.90	633.13	627.46	622.70	618.69	615.31	612.45	610.03	607.97	601.52	598.63	597.33
46000	672.40	662.41	654.12	647.20	641.40	636.53	632.44	628.98	626.06	623.58	621.48	614.89	611.94	610.61
47000	687.02	676.82	668.34	661.27	655.34	650.37	646.18	642.65	639.67	637.14	635.00	628.25	625.24	623.88
48000	701.64	691.22	682.56	675.34	669.29	664.21	659.93	656.33	653.28	650.69	648.51	641.62	638.54	637.15
49000	716.25	705.62	696.78	689.40	683.23	678.05	673.68	670.00	666.89	664.25	662.02	654.99	651.84	650.43
50000	730.87	720.02	711.00	703.47	697.17	691.88	687.43	683.67	680.50	677.81	675.53	668.35	665.15	663.70
55000	803.96	792.02	782.10	773.82	766.89	761.07	756.17	752.04	748.54	745.59	743.08	735.19	731.66	730.07
60000	877.05	864.02	853.20	844.17	836.61	830.26	824.92	820.41	816.59	813.37	810.63	802.02	798.18	796.44
65000	950.13	936.02	924.30	914.51	906.33	899.45	893.66	888.77	884.64	881.15	878.18	868.86	864.69	862.81
70000	1023.22	1008.02	995.39	984.86	976.04	968.64	962.40	957.14	952.69	948.93	945.73	935.69	931.20	929.18
75000	1096.31	1080.02	1066.49	1055.21	1045.76	1037.82	1031.14	1025.51	1020.74	1016.71	1013.29	1002.53	997.72	995.55
80000	1169.39	1152.02	1137.59	1125.56	1115.48	1107.01	1099.89	1093.87	1088.79	1084.49	1080.84	1069.36	1064.23	1061.92
85000	1242.48	1224.02	1208.69	1195.90	1185.19	1176.20	1168.63	1162.24	1156.84	1152.27	1148.39	1136.20	1130.75	1128.29
90000	1315.57	1296.02	1279.79	1266.25	1254.91	1245.39	1237.37	1230.61	1224.89	1220.05	1215.94	1203.03	1197.26	1194.66
95000	1388.65	1368.03	1350.89	1336.60	1324.63	1314.58	1306.11	1298.97	1292.94	1287.83	1283.50	1269.87	1263.77	1261.03
100000	1461.74	1440.03	1421.99	1406.94	1394.34	1383.76	1374.86	1367.34	1360.99	1355.61	1351.05	1336.70	1330.29	1327.40

MONTHLY PAYMENT
REQUIRED TO AMORTIZE A LOAN

TERM AMOUNT	1 Year	2 Years	3 Years	4 Years	5 Years	6 Years	7 Years	8 Years	9 Years	10 Years	11 Years	12 Years	13 Years	14 Years
5	.46	.25	.18	.15	.13	.11	.10	.10	.09	.09	.09	.08	.08	.08
10	.91	.49	.36	.29	.25	.22	.20	.19	.18	.17	.17	.16	.16	.15
15	1.37	.74	.53	.43	.37	.33	.30	.28	.27	.26	.25	.24	.23	.23
25	2.27	1.23	.88	.71	.61	.55	.50	.47	.44	.42	.41	.40	.39	.38
50	4.54	2.45	1.76	1.42	1.22	1.09	1.00	.93	.88	.84	.81	.79	.77	.75
75	6.81	3.68	2.64	2.13	1.83	1.63	1.49	1.39	1.32	1.26	1.22	1.18	1.15	1.13
100	9.08	4.90	3.52	2.84	2.44	2.17	1.99	1.86	1.76	1.68	1.62	1.57	1.53	1.50
200	18.15	9.80	7.04	5.67	4.87	4.34	3.98	3.71	3.51	3.36	3.23	3.14	3.06	2.99
300	27.22	14.69	10.55	8.51	7.30	6.51	5.96	5.56	5.26	5.03	4.85	4.70	4.59	4.49
400	36.30	19.59	14.07	11.34	9.73	8.68	7.95	7.42	7.02	6.71	6.46	6.27	6.11	5.98
500	45.37	24.49	17.58	14.18	12.16	10.85	9.94	9.27	8.77	8.38	8.08	7.83	7.64	7.48
600	54.44	29.38	21.10	17.01	14.60	13.02	11.92	11.12	10.52	10.06	9.69	9.40	9.17	8.97
700	63.52	34.28	24.61	19.84	17.03	15.19	13.91	12.98	12.27	11.73	11.31	10.97	10.69	10.47
800	72.59	39.18	28.13	22.68	19.46	17.36	15.89	14.83	14.03	13.41	12.92	12.53	12.22	11.96
900	81.66	44.07	31.65	25.51	21.89	19.53	17.88	16.68	15.78	15.08	14.53	14.10	13.75	13.46
1000	90.74	48.97	35.16	28.35	24.32	21.70	19.87	18.53	17.53	16.76	16.15	15.66	15.27	14.95
2000	181.47	97.93	70.32	56.69	48.64	43.39	39.73	37.06	35.06	33.51	32.29	31.32	30.54	29.90
3000	272.20	146.89	105.48	85.03	72.96	65.08	59.59	55.59	52.58	50.26	48.43	46.98	45.81	44.85
4000	362.93	195.86	140.63	113.37	97.28	86.77	79.45	74.12	70.11	67.01	64.58	62.64	61.07	59.80
5000	453.66	244.82	175.79	141.71	121.60	108.46	99.32	92.65	87.63	83.76	80.72	78.30	76.34	74.75
6000	544.39	293.78	210.95	170.05	145.91	130.16	119.18	111.18	105.16	100.51	96.86	93.95	91.61	89.70
7000	635.12	342.75	246.10	198.39	170.23	151.85	139.04	129.71	122.68	117.26	113.01	109.61	106.87	104.64
8000	725.85	391.71	281.26	226.73	194.55	173.54	158.90	148.24	140.21	134.02	129.15	125.27	122.14	119.59
9000	816.58	440.67	316.42	255.07	218.87	195.23	178.76	166.76	157.73	150.77	145.29	140.93	137.41	134.54
10000	907.31	489.64	351.58	283.41	243.19	216.92	198.63	185.29	175.26	167.52	161.44	156.59	152.68	149.49
11000	998.04	538.60	386.73	311.75	267.50	238.62	218.49	203.82	192.78	184.27	177.58	172.25	167.94	164.44
12000	1088.78	587.56	421.89	340.09	291.82	260.31	238.35	222.35	210.31	201.02	193.72	187.90	183.21	179.39
13000	1179.51	636.53	457.05	368.43	316.14	282.00	258.21	240.88	227.83	217.77	209.87	203.56	198.48	194.33
14000	1270.24	685.49	492.20	396.77	340.46	303.69	278.07	259.41	245.36	234.52	226.01	219.22	213.74	209.28
15000	1360.97	734.45	527.36	425.11	364.78	325.38	297.94	277.94	262.88	251.27	242.15	234.88	229.01	224.23
16000	1451.70	783.41	562.52	453.45	389.09	347.07	317.80	296.47	280.41	268.03	258.30	250.54	244.28	239.18
17000	1542.43	832.38	597.67	481.79	413.41	368.77	337.66	314.99	297.93	284.78	274.44	266.20	259.54	254.13
18000	1633.16	881.34	632.83	510.13	437.73	390.46	357.52	333.52	315.46	301.53	290.58	281.85	274.81	269.08
19000	1723.89	930.30	667.99	538.47	462.05	412.15	377.38	352.05	332.98	318.28	306.73	297.51	290.08	284.03
20000	1814.62	979.27	703.15	566.81	486.37	433.84	397.25	370.58	350.51	335.03	322.87	313.17	305.35	298.97
21000	1905.35	1028.23	738.30	595.15	510.68	455.53	417.11	389.11	368.04	351.78	339.01	328.83	320.61	313.92
22000	1996.08	1077.19	773.46	623.49	535.00	477.23	436.97	407.64	385.56	368.53	355.15	344.49	335.88	328.87
23000	2086.81	1126.16	808.62	651.83	559.32	498.92	456.83	426.17	403.09	385.29	371.30	360.14	351.15	343.82
24000	2177.55	1175.12	843.77	680.17	583.64	520.61	476.69	444.70	420.61	402.04	387.44	375.80	366.41	358.77
25000	2268.28	1224.08	878.93	708.51	607.96	542.30	496.56	463.22	438.14	418.79	403.58	391.46	381.68	373.72
26000	2359.01	1273.05	914.09	736.85	632.27	563.99	516.42	481.75	455.66	435.54	419.73	407.12	396.95	388.66
27000	2449.74	1322.01	949.24	765.19	656.59	585.68	536.28	500.28	473.19	452.29	435.87	422.78	412.22	403.61
28000	2540.47	1370.97	984.40	793.53	680.91	607.38	556.14	518.81	490.71	469.04	452.01	438.44	427.48	418.56
29000	2631.20	1419.94	1019.56	821.87	705.23	629.07	576.00	537.34	508.24	485.79	468.16	454.09	442.75	433.51
30000	2721.93	1468.90	1054.72	850.21	729.55	650.76	595.87	555.87	525.76	502.54	484.30	469.75	458.02	448.46
31000	2812.66	1517.86	1089.87	878.55	753.86	672.45	615.73	574.40	543.29	519.30	500.44	485.41	473.28	463.41
32000	2903.39	1566.82	1125.03	906.89	778.18	694.14	635.59	592.93	560.81	536.05	516.59	501.07	488.55	478.36
33000	2994.12	1615.79	1160.19	935.23	802.50	715.84	655.45	611.45	578.34	552.80	532.73	516.73	503.82	493.30
34000	3084.85	1664.75	1195.34	963.57	826.82	737.53	675.32	629.98	595.86	569.55	548.87	532.39	519.08	508.25
35000	3175.59	1713.71	1230.50	991.91	851.14	759.22	695.18	648.51	613.39	586.30	565.02	548.04	534.35	523.20
36000	3266.32	1762.68	1265.66	1020.26	875.46	780.91	715.04	667.04	630.91	603.05	581.16	563.70	549.62	538.15
37000	3357.05	1811.64	1300.82	1048.60	899.77	802.60	734.90	685.57	648.44	619.80	597.30	579.36	564.89	553.10
38000	3447.78	1860.60	1335.97	1076.94	924.09	824.29	754.76	704.10	665.96	636.55	613.45	595.02	580.15	568.05
39000	3538.51	1909.57	1371.13	1105.28	948.41	845.99	774.63	722.63	683.49	653.31	629.59	610.68	595.42	582.99
40000	3629.24	1958.53	1406.29	1133.62	972.73	867.68	794.49	741.16	701.02	670.06	645.73	626.34	610.69	597.94
41000	3719.97	2007.49	1441.44	1161.96	997.05	889.37	814.35	759.69	718.54	686.81	661.88	641.99	625.95	612.89
42000	3810.70	2056.46	1476.60	1190.30	1021.36	911.06	834.21	778.21	736.07	703.56	678.02	657.65	641.22	627.84
43000	3901.43	2105.42	1511.76	1218.64	1045.68	932.75	854.07	796.74	753.59	720.31	694.16	673.31	656.49	642.79
44000	3992.16	2154.38	1546.91	1246.98	1070.00	954.45	873.94	815.27	771.12	737.06	710.30	688.97	671.75	657.74
45000	4082.89	2203.35	1582.07	1275.32	1094.32	976.14	893.80	833.80	788.64	753.81	726.45	704.63	687.02	672.69
46000	4173.62	2252.31	1617.23	1303.66	1118.64	997.83	913.66	852.33	806.17	770.57	742.59	720.28	702.29	687.63
47000	4264.36	2301.27	1652.39	1332.00	1142.95	1019.52	933.52	870.86	823.69	787.32	758.73	735.94	717.56	702.58
48000	4355.09	2350.23	1687.54	1360.34	1167.27	1041.21	953.38	889.39	841.22	804.07	774.88	751.60	732.82	717.53
49000	4445.82	2399.20	1722.70	1388.68	1191.59	1062.91	973.25	907.92	858.74	820.82	791.02	767.26	748.09	732.48
50000	4536.55	2448.16	1757.86	1417.02	1215.91	1084.60	993.11	926.44	876.27	837.57	807.16	782.92	763.36	747.43
55000	4990.20	2692.98	1933.64	1558.72	1337.50	1193.06	1092.42	1019.09	963.89	921.33	887.88	861.21	839.69	822.17
60000	5443.86	2937.79	2109.43	1700.42	1459.09	1301.52	1191.73	1111.73	1051.52	1005.08	968.60	939.50	916.03	896.91
65000	5897.51	3182.61	2285.21	1842.12	1580.68	1409.97	1291.04	1204.38	1139.15	1088.84	1049.31	1017.79	992.36	971.65
70000	6351.17	3427.42	2461.00	1983.82	1702.27	1518.43	1390.35	1297.02	1226.77	1172.60	1130.03	1096.08	1068.70	1046.40
75000	6804.82	3672.24	2636.78	2125.53	1823.86	1626.89	1489.66	1389.66	1314.40	1256.35	1210.74	1174.37	1145.03	1121.14
80000	7258.47	3917.05	2812.57	2267.23	1945.45	1735.35	1588.97	1482.31	1402.03	1340.11	1291.46	1252.67	1221.37	1195.88
85000	7712.13	4161.87	2988.35	2408.93	2067.04	1843.81	1688.28	1574.95	1489.65	1423.87	1372.17	1330.96	1297.70	1270.62
90000	8165.78	4406.68	3164.14	2550.63	2188.63	1952.27	1787.59	1667.60	1577.28	1507.62	1452.89	1409.25	1374.04	1345.37
95000	8619.44	4651.50	3339.92	2692.33	2310.22	2060.73	1886.90	1760.24	1664.90	1591.38	1533.61	1487.54	1450.37	1420.11
100000	9073.09	4896.32	3515.71	2834.03	2431.81	2169.19	1986.21	1852.88	1752.53	1675.14	1614.32	1565.83	1526.71	1494.85

TERM	15 Years	16 Years	17 Years	18 Years	19 Years	20 Years	21 Years	22 Years	23 Years	24 Years	25 Years	30 Years	35 Years	40 Years
AMOUNT														
5	.08	.08	.08	.08	.08	.07	.07	.07	.07	.07	.07	.07	.07	.07
10	.15	.15	.15	.15	.15	.14	.14	.14	.14	.14	.14	.14	.14	.14
15	.23	.22	.22	.22	.22	.21	.21	.21	.21	.21	.21	.21	.21	.21
25	.37	.37	.36	.36	.36	.35	.35	.35	.35	.35	.34	.34	.34	.34
50	.74	.73	.72	.71	.71	.70	.70	.69	.69	.69	.68	.68	.67	.67
75	1.11	1.09	1.08	1.07	1.06	1.05	1.04	1.04	1.03	1.03	1.02	1.01	1.01	1.01
100	1.47	1.45	1.43	1.42	1.41	1.40	1.39	1.38	1.37	1.37	1.36	1.35	1.34	1.34
200	2.94	2.90	2.86	2.83	2.81	2.79	2.77	2.75	2.74	2.73	2.72	2.69	2.68	2.68
300	4.41	4.35	4.29	4.25	4.21	4.18	4.15	4.13	4.11	4.10	4.08	4.04	4.02	4.01
400	5.88	5.79	5.72	5.66	5.61	5.57	5.53	5.50	5.48	5.46	5.44	5.38	5.36	5.35
500	7.35	7.24	7.15	7.08	7.01	6.96	6.92	6.88	6.85	6.82	6.80	6.73	6.70	6.68
600	8.82	8.69	8.58	8.49	8.42	8.35	8.30	8.25	8.22	8.19	8.16	8.07	8.04	8.02
700	10.29	10.13	10.01	9.90	9.82	9.74	9.68	9.63	9.59	9.55	9.52	9.42	9.37	9.35
800	11.75	11.58	11.44	11.32	11.22	11.14	11.06	11.00	10.95	10.91	10.88	10.76	10.71	10.69
900	13.22	13.03	12.87	12.73	12.62	12.53	12.45	12.38	12.32	12.28	12.24	12.11	12.05	12.03
1000	14.69	14.48	14.30	14.15	14.02	13.92	13.83	13.75	13.69	13.64	13.59	13.45	13.39	13.36
2000	29.38	28.95	28.59	28.29	28.04	27.83	27.65	27.50	27.38	27.27	27.18	26.90	26.77	26.72
3000	44.07	43.42	42.88	42.43	42.06	41.74	41.48	41.25	41.07	40.91	40.77	40.35	40.16	40.07
4000	58.75	57.89	57.17	56.57	56.07	55.66	55.30	55.00	54.75	54.54	54.36	53.80	53.54	53.43
5000	73.44	72.36	71.46	70.72	70.09	69.57	69.13	68.75	68.44	68.17	67.95	67.24	66.93	66.79
6000	88.13	86.83	85.76	84.86	84.11	83.48	82.95	82.50	82.13	81.81	81.54	80.69	80.31	80.14
7000	102.81	101.30	100.05	99.00	98.13	97.39	96.78	96.25	95.81	95.44	95.13	94.14	93.70	93.50
8000	117.50	115.77	114.34	113.14	112.14	111.31	110.60	110.00	109.50	109.08	108.72	107.59	107.08	106.86
9000	132.19	130.24	128.63	127.29	126.16	125.22	124.42	123.75	123.19	122.71	122.30	121.03	120.47	120.21
10000	146.88	144.72	142.92	141.43	140.18	139.13	138.25	137.50	136.88	136.34	135.89	134.48	133.85	133.57
11000	161.56	159.19	157.22	155.57	154.20	153.04	152.07	151.25	150.56	149.98	149.48	147.93	147.24	146.93
12000	176.25	173.66	171.51	169.71	168.21	166.96	165.90	165.00	164.25	163.61	163.07	161.38	160.62	160.28
13000	190.94	188.13	185.80	183.86	182.23	180.87	179.72	178.75	177.94	177.25	176.66	174.82	174.01	173.64
14000	205.62	202.60	200.09	198.00	196.25	194.78	193.55	192.50	191.62	190.88	190.25	188.27	187.39	187.00
15000	220.31	217.07	214.38	212.14	210.27	208.69	207.37	206.25	205.31	204.51	203.84	201.72	200.78	200.35
16000	235.00	231.54	228.68	226.28	224.28	222.61	221.19	220.00	219.00	218.15	217.43	215.17	214.16	213.71
17000	249.68	246.01	242.97	240.43	238.30	236.52	235.02	233.75	232.69	231.78	231.02	228.61	227.54	227.07
18000	264.37	260.48	257.26	254.57	252.32	250.43	248.84	247.50	246.37	245.42	244.61	242.06	240.93	240.42
19000	279.06	274.96	271.55	268.71	266.34	264.34	262.67	261.25	260.06	259.05	258.19	255.51	254.31	253.78
20000	293.75	289.43	285.84	282.85	280.35	278.26	276.49	275.00	273.75	272.68	271.78	268.96	267.70	267.13
21000	308.43	303.90	300.13	297.00	294.37	292.17	290.32	288.75	287.43	286.32	285.37	282.40	281.08	280.49
22000	323.12	318.37	314.43	311.14	308.39	306.08	304.14	302.50	301.12	299.95	298.96	295.85	294.47	293.85
23000	337.81	332.84	328.72	325.28	322.41	319.99	317.96	316.25	314.81	313.58	312.55	309.30	307.85	307.20
24000	352.49	347.31	343.01	339.42	336.42	333.91	331.79	330.00	328.49	327.22	326.14	322.75	321.24	320.56
25000	367.18	361.78	357.30	353.57	350.44	347.82	345.61	343.75	342.18	340.85	339.73	336.19	334.62	333.92
26000	381.87	376.25	371.59	367.71	364.46	361.73	359.44	357.50	355.87	354.49	353.32	349.64	348.01	347.27
27000	396.55	390.72	385.89	381.85	378.48	375.64	373.26	371.25	369.56	368.12	366.91	363.09	361.39	360.63
28000	411.24	405.20	400.18	395.99	392.49	389.56	387.09	385.00	383.24	381.75	380.49	376.54	374.78	373.99
29000	425.93	419.67	414.47	410.14	406.51	403.47	400.91	398.75	396.93	395.39	394.08	389.98	388.16	387.34
30000	440.62	434.14	428.76	424.28	420.53	417.38	414.73	412.50	410.62	409.02	407.67	403.43	401.55	400.70
31000	455.30	448.61	443.05	438.42	434.55	431.29	428.56	426.25	424.30	422.66	421.26	416.88	414.93	414.06
32000	469.99	463.08	457.35	452.56	448.56	445.21	442.38	440.00	437.99	436.29	434.85	430.33	428.32	427.41
33000	484.68	477.55	471.64	466.71	462.58	459.12	456.21	453.75	451.68	449.92	448.44	443.77	441.70	440.77
34000	499.36	492.02	485.93	480.85	476.60	473.03	470.03	467.50	465.37	463.56	462.03	457.22	455.08	454.13
35000	514.05	506.49	500.22	494.99	490.62	486.94	483.86	481.25	479.05	477.19	475.62	470.67	468.47	467.48
36000	528.74	520.96	514.51	509.13	504.63	500.86	497.68	495.00	492.74	490.83	489.21	484.12	481.85	480.84
37000	543.42	535.44	528.80	523.28	518.65	514.77	511.50	508.75	506.43	504.46	502.79	497.57	495.24	494.19
38000	558.11	549.91	543.10	537.42	532.67	528.68	525.33	522.50	520.11	518.09	516.38	511.01	508.62	507.55
39000	572.80	564.38	557.39	551.56	546.69	542.59	539.15	536.25	533.80	531.73	529.97	524.46	522.01	520.91
40000	587.49	578.85	571.68	565.70	560.70	556.51	552.98	550.00	547.49	545.36	543.56	537.91	535.39	534.26
41000	602.17	593.32	585.97	579.85	574.72	570.42	566.80	563.75	561.17	559.00	557.15	551.36	548.78	547.62
42000	616.86	607.79	600.26	593.99	588.74	584.33	580.63	577.50	574.86	572.63	570.74	564.80	562.16	560.98
43000	631.55	622.26	614.56	608.13	602.76	598.25	594.45	591.25	588.55	586.26	584.33	578.25	575.55	574.33
44000	646.23	636.73	628.85	622.27	616.77	612.16	608.27	605.00	602.24	599.90	597.92	591.70	588.93	587.69
45000	660.92	651.20	643.14	636.42	630.79	626.07	622.10	618.75	615.92	613.53	611.51	605.15	602.32	601.05
46000	675.61	665.68	657.43	650.56	644.81	639.98	635.92	632.50	629.61	627.16	625.09	618.59	615.70	614.40
47000	690.29	680.15	671.72	664.70	658.83	653.90	649.75	646.25	643.30	640.80	638.68	632.04	629.09	627.76
48000	704.98	694.62	686.02	678.84	672.84	667.81	663.57	660.00	656.98	654.43	652.27	645.49	642.47	641.12
49000	719.67	709.09	700.31	692.99	686.86	681.72	677.40	673.75	670.67	668.07	665.86	658.94	655.86	654.47
50000	734.36	723.56	714.60	707.13	700.88	695.63	691.22	687.50	684.36	681.70	679.45	672.38	669.24	667.83
55000	807.79	795.92	786.06	777.84	770.97	765.20	760.34	756.25	752.79	749.87	747.39	739.62	736.16	734.61
60000	881.23	868.27	857.52	848.55	841.05	834.76	829.46	825.00	821.23	818.04	815.34	806.86	803.09	801.39
65000	954.66	940.63	928.98	919.27	911.14	904.32	898.58	893.75	889.66	886.21	883.28	874.10	870.01	868.18
70000	1028.10	1012.98	1000.44	989.98	981.23	973.88	967.71	962.50	958.10	954.38	951.23	941.33	936.93	934.96
75000	1101.53	1085.34	1071.90	1060.69	1051.31	1043.45	1036.83	1031.25	1026.53	1022.55	1019.17	1008.57	1003.86	1001.74
80000	1174.97	1157.69	1143.36	1131.40	1121.40	1113.01	1105.95	1100.00	1094.97	1090.72	1087.12	1075.81	1070.78	1068.52
85000	1248.40	1230.05	1214.82	1202.12	1191.49	1182.57	1175.07	1168.75	1163.41	1158.89	1155.06	1143.05	1137.70	1135.31
90000	1321.84	1302.40	1286.27	1272.83	1261.58	1252.14	1244.19	1237.50	1231.84	1227.06	1223.01	1210.29	1204.63	1202.09
95000	1395.27	1374.76	1357.73	1343.54	1331.66	1321.70	1313.31	1306.25	1300.28	1295.23	1290.95	1277.52	1271.55	1268.87
100000	1468.71	1447.12	1429.19	1414.25	1401.75	1391.26	1382.44	1375.00	1368.71	1363.40	1358.89	1344.76	1338.47	1335.65

16%

MONTHLY PAYMENT
REQUIRED TO AMORTIZE A LOAN

TERM	1 Year	2 Years	3 Years	4 Years	5 Years	6 Years	7 Years	8 Years	9 Years	10 Years	11 Years	12 Years	13 Years	14 Years
AMOUNT														
5	.46	.25	.18	.15	.13	.11	.10	.10	.09	.09	.09	.08	.08	.08
10	.91	.50	.36	.29	.25	.22	.20	.19	.18	.17	.17	.16	.16	.16
15	1.37	.74	.53	.43	.37	.33	.30	.28	.27	.26	.25	.24	.24	.23
25	2.27	1.23	.89	.71	.61	.55	.50	.47	.44	.43	.41	.40	.39	.38
50	4.54	2.46	1.77	1.42	1.22	1.09	1.00	.93	.88	.85	.82	.79	.77	.76
75	6.81	3.68	2.65	2.13	1.83	1.64	1.50	1.40	1.32	1.27	1.22	1.18	1.16	1.13
100	9.08	4.91	3.53	2.84	2.44	2.18	2.00	1.86	1.76	1.69	1.63	1.58	1.54	1.51
200	18.16	9.81	7.05	5.68	4.88	4.35	3.99	3.72	3.52	3.37	3.25	3.15	3.07	3.01
300	27.24	14.71	10.57	8.52	7.32	6.53	5.98	5.58	5.28	5.05	4.87	4.72	4.61	4.51
400	36.32	19.61	14.09	11.36	9.75	8.70	7.97	7.44	7.04	6.73	6.49	6.29	6.14	6.01
500	45.39	24.51	17.61	14.20	12.19	10.88	9.96	9.30	8.80	8.41	8.11	7.87	7.67	7.51
600	54.47	29.41	21.13	17.04	14.63	13.05	11.96	11.16	10.56	10.09	9.73	9.44	9.21	9.02
700	63.55	34.31	24.65	19.88	17.06	15.23	13.95	13.02	12.32	11.77	11.35	11.01	10.74	10.52
800	72.63	39.21	28.17	22.72	19.50	17.40	15.94	14.88	14.07	13.46	12.97	12.58	12.27	12.02
900	81.71	44.11	31.69	25.56	21.94	19.58	17.93	16.73	15.83	15.14	14.59	14.16	13.81	13.52
1000	90.78	49.02	35.21	28.40	24.38	21.75	19.92	18.59	17.59	16.82	16.21	15.73	15.34	15.02
2000	181.56	98.03	70.42	56.79	48.75	43.50	39.84	37.18	35.18	33.63	32.42	31.45	30.67	30.04
3000	272.34	147.04	105.62	85.18	73.12	65.25	59.76	55.77	52.76	50.45	48.63	47.18	46.01	45.06
4000	363.12	196.05	140.83	113.57	97.49	86.99	79.68	74.36	70.35	67.26	64.83	62.90	61.34	60.07
5000	453.90	245.06	176.04	141.96	121.86	108.74	99.60	92.94	87.93	84.07	81.04	78.62	76.68	75.09
6000	544.67	294.07	211.24	170.35	146.23	130.49	119.52	111.53	105.52	100.89	97.25	94.35	92.01	90.11
7000	635.45	343.08	246.45	198.75	170.60	152.23	139.44	130.12	123.11	117.70	113.46	110.07	107.34	105.12
8000	726.23	392.09	281.66	227.14	194.97	173.98	159.36	148.71	140.69	134.51	129.66	125.80	122.68	120.14
9000	817.01	441.10	316.86	255.53	219.35	195.73	179.28	167.29	158.28	151.33	145.87	141.52	138.01	135.16
10000	907.79	490.11	352.07	283.92	243.72	217.47	199.20	185.88	175.86	168.14	162.08	157.24	153.35	150.17
11000	998.57	539.12	387.28	312.31	268.09	239.22	219.11	204.47	193.45	184.96	178.28	172.97	168.68	165.19
12000	1089.34	588.14	422.48	340.70	292.46	260.97	239.03	223.06	211.04	201.77	194.49	188.69	184.01	180.21
13000	1180.12	637.15	457.69	369.09	316.83	282.72	258.95	241.64	228.62	218.58	210.70	204.41	199.35	195.23
14000	1270.90	686.16	492.89	397.49	341.20	304.46	278.87	260.23	246.21	235.40	226.91	220.14	214.68	210.24
15000	1361.68	735.17	528.10	425.88	365.57	326.21	298.79	278.82	263.79	252.21	243.11	235.86	230.02	225.26
16000	1452.46	784.18	563.31	454.27	389.94	347.96	318.71	297.41	281.38	269.02	259.32	251.59	245.35	240.28
17000	1543.23	833.19	598.51	482.66	414.32	369.70	338.63	315.99	298.97	285.84	275.53	267.31	260.68	255.29
18000	1634.01	882.20	633.72	511.05	438.69	391.45	358.55	334.58	316.55	302.65	291.73	283.03	276.02	270.31
19000	1724.79	931.21	668.93	539.44	463.06	413.20	378.47	353.17	334.14	319.47	307.94	298.76	291.35	285.33
20000	1815.57	980.22	704.13	567.84	487.43	434.94	398.39	371.76	351.72	336.28	324.15	314.48	306.69	300.34
21000	1906.35	1029.23	739.34	596.23	511.80	456.69	418.31	390.35	369.31	353.09	340.36	330.21	322.02	315.36
22000	1997.13	1078.24	774.55	624.62	536.17	478.44	438.22	408.93	386.89	369.91	356.56	345.93	337.36	330.38
23000	2087.90	1127.26	809.75	653.01	560.54	500.18	458.14	427.52	404.48	386.72	372.77	361.65	352.69	345.39
24000	2178.68	1176.27	844.96	681.40	584.91	521.93	478.06	446.11	422.07	403.53	388.98	377.38	368.02	360.41
25000	2269.46	1225.28	880.17	709.79	609.29	543.68	497.98	464.70	439.65	420.35	405.18	393.10	383.36	375.43
26000	2360.24	1274.29	915.37	738.18	633.66	565.43	517.90	483.28	457.24	437.16	421.39	408.82	398.69	390.45
27000	2451.02	1323.30	950.58	766.58	658.03	587.17	537.82	501.87	474.82	453.97	437.60	424.55	414.03	405.46
28000	2541.79	1372.31	985.78	794.97	682.40	608.92	557.74	520.46	492.41	470.79	453.81	440.27	429.36	420.48
29000	2632.57	1421.32	1020.99	823.36	706.77	630.67	577.66	539.05	510.00	487.60	470.01	456.00	444.69	435.50
30000	2723.35	1470.33	1056.20	851.75	731.14	652.41	597.58	557.63	527.58	504.42	486.22	471.72	460.03	450.51
31000	2814.13	1519.34	1091.40	880.14	755.51	674.16	617.50	576.22	545.17	521.23	502.43	487.44	475.36	465.53
32000	2904.91	1568.35	1126.61	908.53	779.88	695.91	637.41	594.81	562.75	538.04	518.64	503.17	490.70	480.55
33000	2995.69	1617.36	1161.82	936.93	804.26	717.65	657.33	613.40	580.34	554.86	534.84	518.89	506.03	495.56
34000	3086.46	1666.38	1197.02	965.32	828.63	739.40	677.25	631.98	597.93	571.67	551.05	534.62	521.36	510.58
35000	3177.24	1715.39	1232.23	993.71	853.00	761.15	697.17	650.57	615.51	588.48	567.26	550.34	536.70	525.60
36000	3268.02	1764.40	1267.44	1022.10	877.37	782.89	717.09	669.16	633.10	605.30	583.46	566.06	552.03	540.61
37000	3358.80	1813.41	1302.64	1050.49	901.74	804.64	737.01	687.75	650.68	622.11	599.67	581.79	567.37	555.63
38000	3449.58	1862.42	1337.85	1078.88	926.11	826.39	756.93	706.34	668.27	638.93	615.88	597.51	582.70	570.65
39000	3540.35	1911.43	1373.06	1107.27	950.48	848.14	776.85	724.92	685.86	655.74	632.09	613.23	598.04	585.67
40000	3631.13	1960.44	1408.26	1135.67	974.85	869.88	796.77	743.51	703.44	672.55	648.29	628.96	613.37	600.68
41000	3721.91	2009.45	1443.47	1164.06	999.23	891.63	816.69	762.10	721.03	689.37	664.50	644.68	628.70	615.70
42000	3812.69	2058.46	1478.67	1192.45	1023.60	913.38	836.61	780.69	738.61	706.18	680.71	660.41	644.04	630.72
43000	3903.47	2107.47	1513.88	1220.84	1047.97	935.12	856.52	799.27	756.20	722.99	696.91	676.13	659.37	645.73
44000	3994.25	2156.48	1549.09	1249.23	1072.34	956.87	876.44	817.86	773.78	739.81	713.12	691.85	674.71	660.75
45000	4085.03	2205.50	1584.29	1277.62	1096.71	978.62	896.36	836.45	791.37	756.62	729.33	707.58	690.04	675.77
46000	4175.80	2254.51	1619.50	1306.02	1121.08	1000.36	916.28	855.04	808.96	773.43	745.54	723.30	705.37	690.78
47000	4266.58	2303.52	1654.71	1334.41	1145.45	1022.11	936.20	873.62	826.54	790.25	761.74	739.03	720.71	705.80
48000	4357.36	2352.53	1689.91	1362.80	1169.82	1043.86	956.12	892.21	844.13	807.06	777.95	754.75	736.04	720.82
49000	4448.14	2401.54	1725.12	1391.19	1194.19	1065.60	976.04	910.80	861.71	823.88	794.16	770.47	751.38	735.83
50000	4538.91	2450.55	1760.33	1419.58	1218.57	1087.35	995.96	929.39	879.30	840.69	810.36	786.20	766.71	750.85
55000	4992.81	2695.60	1936.36	1561.54	1340.42	1196.09	1095.55	1022.33	967.23	924.76	891.40	864.82	843.38	825.94
60000	5446.70	2940.66	2112.39	1703.50	1462.28	1304.82	1195.15	1115.26	1055.16	1008.83	972.44	943.44	920.05	901.02
65000	5900.59	3185.71	2288.42	1845.45	1584.13	1413.56	1294.74	1208.20	1143.09	1092.89	1053.47	1022.05	996.72	976.11
70000	6354.48	3430.77	2464.45	1987.41	1705.99	1522.29	1394.34	1301.14	1231.02	1176.96	1134.51	1100.67	1073.39	1051.19
75000	6808.37	3675.82	2640.49	2129.37	1827.85	1631.03	1493.93	1394.08	1318.95	1261.03	1215.54	1179.29	1150.06	1126.27
80000	7262.26	3920.88	2816.52	2271.33	1949.70	1739.76	1593.53	1487.02	1406.88	1345.10	1296.58	1257.91	1226.73	1201.36
85000	7716.15	4165.93	2992.55	2413.28	2071.56	1848.49	1693.13	1579.95	1494.81	1429.17	1377.62	1336.53	1303.41	1276.44
90000	8170.04	4410.99	3168.58	2555.24	2193.42	1957.23	1792.72	1672.89	1582.74	1513.24	1458.65	1415.15	1380.08	1351.53
95000	8623.93	4656.04	3344.62	2697.20	2315.27	2065.96	1892.32	1765.83	1670.67	1597.31	1539.69	1493.77	1456.75	1426.61
100000	9077.82	4901.10	3520.65	2839.16	2437.13	2174.70	1991.91	1858.77	1758.59	1681.37	1620.72	1572.39	1533.42	1501.70

TERM	15 Years	16 Years	17 Years	18 Years	19 Years	20 Years	21 Years	22 Years	23 Years	24 Years	25 Years	30 Years	35 Years	40 Years
AMOUNT														
5	.08	.08	.08	.08	.08	.07	.07	.07	.07	.07	.07	.07	.07	.07
10	.15	.15	.15	.15	.15	.14	.14	.14	.14	.14	.14	.14	.14	.14
15	.23	.22	.22	.22	.22	.21	.21	.21	.21	.21	.21	.21	.21	.21
25	.37	.37	.36	.36	.36	.35	.35	.35	.35	.35	.35	.34	.34	.34
50	.74	.73	.72	.72	.71	.70	.70	.70	.69	.69	.69	.68	.68	.68
75	1.11	1.10	1.08	1.07	1.06	1.05	1.05	1.04	1.04	1.03	1.03	1.02	1.01	1.01
100	1.48	1.46	1.44	1.43	1.41	1.40	1.40	1.39	1.38	1.38	1.37	1.36	1.35	1.35
200	2.96	2.91	2.88	2.85	2.82	2.80	2.79	2.77	2.76	2.75	2.74	2.71	2.70	2.69
300	4.43	4.37	4.31	4.27	4.23	4.20	4.18	4.15	4.13	4.12	4.11	4.06	4.04	4.04
400	5.91	5.82	5.75	5.69	5.64	5.60	5.57	5.54	5.51	5.49	5.47	5.42	5.39	5.38
500	7.38	7.28	7.19	7.11	7.05	7.00	6.96	6.92	6.89	6.86	6.84	6.77	6.74	6.72
600	8.86	8.73	8.62	8.53	8.46	8.40	8.35	8.30	8.26	8.23	8.21	8.12	8.08	8.07
700	10.33	10.18	10.06	9.96	9.87	9.80	9.74	9.68	9.64	9.60	9.57	9.47	9.43	9.41
800	11.81	11.64	11.50	11.38	11.28	11.20	11.13	11.07	11.02	10.97	10.94	10.83	10.78	10.76
900	13.29	13.09	12.93	12.80	12.69	12.59	12.52	12.45	12.39	12.35	12.31	12.18	12.12	12.10
1000	14.76	14.55	14.37	14.22	14.10	13.99	13.91	13.83	13.77	13.72	13.67	13.53	13.47	13.44
2000	29.52	29.09	28.73	28.44	28.19	27.98	27.81	27.66	27.53	27.43	27.34	27.06	26.94	26.88
3000	44.28	43.63	43.10	42.65	42.28	41.97	41.71	41.48	41.30	41.14	41.01	40.59	40.40	40.32
4000	59.03	58.17	57.46	56.87	56.37	55.96	55.61	55.31	55.06	54.85	54.67	54.12	53.87	53.76
5000	73.79	72.72	71.83	71.08	70.46	69.94	69.51	69.14	68.83	68.56	68.34	67.65	67.34	67.20
6000	88.55	87.26	86.19	85.30	84.55	83.93	83.41	82.96	82.59	82.28	82.01	81.17	80.80	80.64
7000	103.30	101.80	100.55	99.51	98.65	97.92	97.31	96.79	96.36	95.99	95.68	94.70	94.27	94.08
8000	118.06	116.34	114.92	113.73	112.74	111.91	111.21	110.62	110.12	109.70	109.34	108.23	107.74	107.52
9000	132.82	130.88	129.28	127.95	126.83	125.89	125.11	124.44	123.88	123.41	123.01	121.76	121.20	120.96
10000	147.57	145.43	143.65	142.16	140.92	139.88	139.01	138.27	137.65	137.12	136.68	135.29	134.67	134.40
11000	162.33	159.97	158.01	156.38	155.01	153.87	152.91	152.10	151.41	150.84	150.35	148.82	148.14	147.83
12000	177.09	174.51	172.37	170.59	169.10	167.86	166.81	165.92	165.18	164.55	164.01	162.34	161.60	161.27
13000	191.84	189.05	186.74	184.81	183.20	181.84	180.71	179.75	178.94	178.26	177.68	175.87	175.07	174.71
14000	206.60	203.59	201.10	199.02	197.29	195.83	194.61	193.58	192.71	191.97	191.35	189.40	188.54	188.15
15000	221.36	218.14	215.47	213.24	211.38	209.82	208.51	207.40	206.47	205.68	205.02	202.93	202.00	201.59
16000	236.11	232.68	229.83	227.46	225.47	223.81	222.41	221.23	220.24	219.40	218.68	216.46	215.47	215.03
17000	250.87	247.22	244.19	241.67	239.56	237.79	236.31	235.06	234.00	233.11	232.35	229.99	228.94	228.47
18000	265.63	261.76	258.56	255.89	253.66	251.78	250.21	248.88	247.76	246.82	246.02	243.51	242.40	241.91
19000	280.38	276.31	272.92	270.10	267.75	265.77	264.11	262.71	261.53	260.53	259.69	257.04	255.87	255.35
20000	295.14	290.85	287.29	284.32	281.84	279.76	278.01	276.54	275.29	274.24	273.35	270.57	269.34	268.79
21000	309.90	305.39	301.65	298.53	295.93	293.75	291.91	290.36	289.06	287.95	287.02	284.10	282.80	282.23
22000	324.65	319.93	316.01	312.75	310.02	307.73	305.81	304.19	302.82	301.67	300.69	297.63	296.27	295.66
23000	339.41	334.47	330.38	326.97	324.11	321.72	319.71	318.02	316.59	315.38	314.36	311.15	309.74	309.10
24000	354.17	349.02	344.74	341.18	338.20	335.71	333.61	331.84	330.35	329.09	328.02	324.68	323.20	322.54
25000	368.92	363.56	359.11	355.40	352.30	349.70	347.51	345.67	344.12	342.80	341.69	338.21	336.67	335.98
26000	383.68	378.10	373.47	369.61	366.39	363.68	361.41	359.50	357.88	356.51	355.36	351.74	350.14	349.42
27000	398.44	392.64	387.83	383.83	380.48	377.67	375.31	373.32	371.64	370.23	369.03	365.27	363.60	362.86
28000	413.20	407.18	402.20	398.04	394.57	391.66	389.21	387.15	385.41	383.94	382.69	378.80	377.07	376.30
29000	427.95	421.73	416.56	412.26	408.66	405.65	403.11	400.98	399.17	397.65	396.36	392.32	390.54	389.74
30000	442.71	436.27	430.93	426.48	422.75	419.63	417.01	414.80	412.94	411.36	410.03	405.85	404.00	403.18
31000	457.47	450.81	445.29	440.69	436.85	433.62	430.91	428.63	426.70	425.07	423.70	419.38	417.47	416.62
32000	472.22	465.35	459.65	454.91	450.94	447.61	444.81	442.45	440.47	438.79	437.36	432.91	430.94	430.05
33000	486.98	479.89	474.02	469.12	465.03	461.60	458.71	456.28	454.23	452.50	451.03	446.44	444.40	443.49
34000	501.74	494.44	488.38	483.34	479.12	475.58	472.61	470.11	467.99	466.21	464.70	459.97	457.87	456.93
35000	516.49	508.98	502.75	497.55	493.21	489.57	486.51	483.93	481.76	479.92	478.37	473.49	471.34	470.37
36000	531.25	523.52	517.11	511.77	507.30	503.56	500.41	497.76	495.52	493.63	492.03	487.02	484.80	483.81
37000	546.01	538.06	531.47	525.98	521.40	517.55	514.31	511.59	509.29	507.34	505.70	500.55	498.27	497.25
38000	560.76	552.61	545.84	540.20	535.49	531.54	528.21	525.41	523.05	521.06	519.37	514.08	511.74	510.69
39000	575.52	567.15	560.20	554.42	549.58	545.52	542.11	539.24	536.82	534.77	533.04	527.61	525.20	524.13
40000	590.28	581.69	574.57	568.63	563.67	559.51	556.01	553.07	550.58	548.48	546.70	541.13	538.67	537.57
41000	605.03	596.23	588.93	582.85	577.76	573.50	569.91	566.89	564.35	562.19	560.37	554.66	552.14	551.01
42000	619.79	610.77	603.29	597.06	591.85	587.49	583.81	580.72	578.11	575.90	574.04	568.19	565.60	564.45
43000	634.55	625.32	617.66	611.28	605.95	601.47	597.71	594.55	591.87	589.62	587.70	581.72	579.07	577.88
44000	649.30	639.86	632.02	625.49	620.04	615.46	611.61	608.37	605.64	603.33	601.37	595.25	592.53	591.32
45000	664.06	654.40	646.39	639.71	634.13	629.45	625.51	622.20	619.40	617.04	615.04	608.78	606.00	604.76
46000	678.82	668.94	660.75	653.93	648.22	643.44	639.41	636.03	633.17	630.75	628.71	622.30	619.47	618.20
47000	693.57	683.48	675.11	668.14	662.31	657.42	653.31	649.85	646.93	644.46	642.37	635.83	632.93	631.64
48000	708.33	698.03	689.48	682.36	676.40	671.41	667.22	663.68	660.70	658.18	656.04	649.36	646.40	645.08
49000	723.09	712.57	703.84	696.57	690.50	685.40	681.12	677.51	674.46	671.89	669.71	662.89	659.87	658.52
50000	737.84	727.11	718.21	710.79	704.59	699.39	695.02	691.33	688.23	685.60	683.38	676.42	673.33	671.96
55000	811.63	799.82	790.03	781.87	775.05	769.33	764.52	760.47	757.05	754.16	751.71	744.06	740.67	739.15
60000	885.41	872.53	861.85	852.95	845.50	839.26	834.02	829.60	825.87	822.72	820.05	811.70	808.00	806.35
65000	959.20	945.24	933.67	924.02	915.96	909.20	903.52	898.73	894.69	891.28	888.39	879.34	875.33	873.54
70000	1032.98	1017.95	1005.49	995.10	986.42	979.14	973.02	967.86	963.51	959.84	956.73	946.98	942.67	940.74
75000	1106.76	1090.66	1077.31	1066.18	1056.88	1049.08	1042.52	1037.00	1032.34	1028.40	1025.06	1014.62	1010.00	1007.93
80000	1180.55	1163.37	1149.13	1137.26	1127.34	1119.02	1112.02	1106.13	1101.16	1096.96	1093.40	1082.26	1077.33	1075.13
85000	1254.33	1236.08	1220.95	1208.34	1197.79	1188.95	1181.52	1175.26	1169.98	1165.52	1161.74	1149.91	1144.66	1142.33
90000	1328.12	1308.79	1292.77	1279.42	1268.25	1258.89	1251.02	1244.40	1238.80	1234.07	1230.07	1217.55	1212.00	1209.52
95000	1401.90	1381.51	1364.59	1350.49	1338.71	1328.83	1320.52	1313.53	1307.62	1302.63	1298.41	1285.19	1279.33	1276.72
100000	1475.68	1454.22	1436.41	1421.57	1409.17	1398.77	1390.03	1382.66	1376.45	1371.19	1366.75	1352.83	1346.66	1343.91

MONTHLY PAYMENT
REQUIRED TO AMORTIZE A LOAN

TERM	1 Year	2 Years	3 Years	4 Years	5 Years	6 Years	7 Years	8 Years	9 Years	10 Years	11 Years	12 Years	13 Years	14 Years
AMOUNT														
5	.46	.25	.18	.15	.13	.11	.10	.10	.09	.09	.09	.08	.08	.08
10	.91	.50	.36	.29	.25	.22	.20	.19	.18	.17	.17	.16	.16	.16
15	1.37	.74	.53	.43	.37	.33	.30	.28	.27	.26	.25	.24	.24	.23
25	2.27	1.23	.89	.72	.61	.55	.50	.47	.45	.43	.41	.40	.39	.38
50	4.54	2.46	1.77	1.43	1.22	1.09	1.00	.94	.89	.85	.82	.79	.77	.76
75	6.81	3.68	2.65	2.14	1.83	1.64	1.50	1.40	1.33	1.27	1.22	1.19	1.16	1.13
100	9.08	4.91	3.53	2.85	2.44	2.18	2.00	1.87	1.77	1.69	1.63	1.58	1.54	1.51
200	18.16	9.81	7.05	5.69	4.88	4.36	3.99	3.73	3.53	3.37	3.25	3.15	3.08	3.01
300	27.24	14.71	10.57	8.53	7.32	6.53	5.98	5.59	5.29	5.05	4.87	4.73	4.61	4.52
400	36.32	19.61	14.09	11.37	9.76	8.71	7.98	7.45	7.05	6.74	6.49	6.30	6.15	6.02
500	45.40	24.52	17.61	14.21	12.20	10.89	9.97	9.31	8.81	8.42	8.12	7.88	7.68	7.52
600	54.48	29.42	21.14	17.05	14.64	13.06	11.96	11.17	10.57	10.10	9.74	9.45	9.22	9.03
700	63.56	34.32	24.66	19.89	17.07	15.24	13.96	13.03	12.33	11.79	11.36	11.02	10.75	10.53
800	72.64	39.22	28.18	22.73	19.51	17.41	15.95	14.89	14.09	13.47	12.98	12.60	12.29	12.03
900	81.72	44.13	31.70	25.57	21.95	19.59	17.94	16.75	15.85	15.15	14.61	14.17	13.82	13.54
1000	90.80	49.03	35.22	28.41	24.39	21.77	19.94	18.61	17.61	16.83	16.23	15.75	15.36	15.04
2000	181.59	98.05	70.44	56.81	48.77	43.53	39.87	37.21	35.21	33.66	32.45	31.49	30.71	30.07
3000	272.38	147.07	105.66	85.22	73.16	65.29	59.80	55.81	52.81	50.49	48.67	47.23	46.06	45.11
4000	363.17	196.10	140.88	113.62	97.54	87.05	79.74	74.41	70.41	67.32	64.90	62.97	61.41	60.14
5000	453.96	245.12	176.10	142.03	121.93	108.81	99.67	93.02	88.01	84.15	81.12	78.71	76.76	75.18
6000	544.75	294.14	211.32	170.43	146.31	130.57	119.60	111.62	105.61	100.98	97.34	94.45	92.11	90.21
7000	635.54	343.17	246.54	198.84	170.70	152.33	139.54	130.22	123.21	117.81	113.57	110.19	107.46	105.24
8000	726.33	392.19	281.76	227.24	195.08	174.09	159.47	148.82	140.81	134.64	129.79	125.93	122.81	120.28
9000	817.12	441.21	316.97	255.64	219.47	195.85	179.40	167.43	158.41	151.47	146.01	141.67	138.16	135.31
10000	907.91	490.23	352.19	284.05	243.85	217.61	199.34	186.03	176.02	168.30	162.24	157.41	153.51	150.35
11000	998.70	539.26	387.41	312.45	268.23	239.37	219.27	204.63	193.62	185.13	178.46	173.15	168.86	165.38
12000	1089.49	588.28	422.63	340.86	292.62	261.13	239.20	223.23	211.22	201.96	194.68	188.89	184.22	180.41
13000	1180.28	637.30	457.85	369.26	317.00	282.89	259.14	241.84	228.82	218.79	210.91	204.63	199.57	195.45
14000	1271.07	686.33	493.07	397.67	341.39	304.66	279.07	260.44	246.42	235.62	227.13	220.37	214.92	210.48
15000	1361.86	735.35	528.29	426.07	365.77	326.42	299.00	279.04	264.02	252.44	243.35	236.11	230.27	225.52
16000	1452.65	784.37	563.51	454.47	390.16	348.18	318.94	297.64	281.62	269.27	259.58	251.85	245.62	240.55
17000	1543.44	833.39	598.72	482.88	414.54	369.94	338.87	316.25	299.22	286.10	275.80	267.59	260.97	255.58
18000	1634.23	882.42	633.94	511.28	438.93	391.70	358.80	334.85	316.82	302.93	292.02	283.33	276.32	270.62
19000	1725.02	931.44	669.16	539.69	463.31	413.46	378.74	353.45	334.43	319.76	308.25	299.07	291.67	285.65
20000	1815.81	980.46	704.38	568.09	487.70	435.22	398.67	372.05	352.03	336.59	324.47	314.81	307.02	300.69
21000	1906.60	1029.49	739.60	596.50	512.08	456.98	418.60	390.65	369.63	353.42	340.69	330.55	322.37	315.72
22000	1997.39	1078.51	774.82	624.90	536.46	478.74	438.54	409.26	387.23	370.25	356.92	346.29	337.72	330.75
23000	2088.18	1127.53	810.04	653.30	560.85	500.50	458.47	427.86	404.83	387.08	373.14	362.03	353.08	345.79
24000	2178.97	1176.55	845.26	681.71	585.23	522.26	478.40	446.46	422.43	403.91	389.36	377.77	368.43	360.82
25000	2269.76	1225.58	880.47	710.11	609.62	544.02	498.34	465.06	440.03	420.74	405.59	393.51	383.78	375.86
26000	2360.55	1274.60	915.69	738.52	634.00	565.78	518.27	483.67	457.63	437.57	421.81	409.25	399.13	390.89
27000	2451.34	1323.62	950.91	766.92	658.39	587.54	538.20	502.27	475.23	454.40	438.03	424.99	414.48	405.92
28000	2542.13	1372.65	986.13	795.33	682.77	609.31	558.14	520.87	492.84	471.23	454.26	440.73	429.83	420.96
29000	2632.92	1421.67	1021.35	823.73	707.16	631.07	578.07	539.47	510.44	488.05	470.48	456.47	445.18	435.99
30000	2723.71	1470.69	1056.57	852.14	731.54	652.83	598.00	558.08	528.04	504.88	486.70	472.21	460.53	451.03
31000	2814.50	1519.71	1091.79	880.54	755.93	674.59	617.94	576.68	545.64	521.71	502.92	487.95	475.88	466.06
32000	2905.29	1568.74	1127.01	908.94	780.31	696.35	637.87	595.28	563.24	538.54	519.15	503.69	491.23	481.09
33000	2996.08	1617.76	1162.22	937.35	804.69	718.11	657.80	613.88	580.84	555.37	535.37	519.43	506.58	496.13
34000	3086.87	1666.78	1197.44	965.75	829.08	739.87	677.74	632.49	598.44	572.20	551.59	535.17	521.94	511.16
35000	3177.66	1715.81	1232.66	994.16	853.46	761.63	697.67	651.09	616.04	589.03	567.82	550.91	537.29	526.20
36000	3268.45	1764.83	1267.88	1022.56	877.85	783.39	717.60	669.69	633.64	605.86	584.04	566.65	552.64	541.23
37000	3359.24	1813.85	1303.10	1050.97	902.23	805.15	737.54	688.29	651.24	622.69	600.26	582.39	567.99	556.27
38000	3450.03	1862.87	1338.32	1079.37	926.62	826.91	757.47	706.89	668.85	639.52	616.49	598.13	583.34	571.30
39000	3540.82	1911.90	1373.54	1107.77	951.00	848.67	777.40	725.50	686.45	656.35	632.71	613.88	598.69	586.33
40000	3631.61	1960.92	1408.76	1136.18	975.39	870.43	797.34	744.10	704.05	673.18	648.93	629.62	614.04	601.37
41000	3722.40	2009.94	1443.97	1164.58	999.77	892.19	817.27	762.70	721.65	690.01	665.16	645.36	629.39	616.40
42000	3813.19	2058.97	1479.19	1192.99	1024.16	913.96	837.20	781.30	739.25	706.84	681.38	661.10	644.74	631.44
43000	3903.98	2107.99	1514.41	1221.39	1048.54	935.72	857.14	799.91	756.85	723.66	697.60	676.84	660.09	646.47
44000	3994.77	2157.01	1549.63	1249.80	1072.92	957.48	877.07	818.51	774.45	740.49	713.83	692.58	675.44	661.50
45000	4085.56	2206.03	1584.85	1278.20	1097.31	979.24	897.00	837.11	792.05	757.32	730.05	708.32	690.80	676.54
46000	4176.35	2255.06	1620.07	1306.60	1121.69	1001.00	916.94	855.71	809.65	774.15	746.27	724.06	706.15	691.57
47000	4267.14	2304.08	1655.29	1335.01	1146.08	1022.76	936.87	874.32	827.26	790.98	762.50	739.80	721.50	706.61
48000	4357.93	2353.10	1690.51	1363.41	1170.46	1044.52	956.80	892.92	844.86	807.81	778.72	755.54	736.85	721.64
49000	4448.72	2402.13	1725.73	1391.82	1194.85	1066.28	976.74	911.52	862.46	824.64	794.94	771.28	752.20	736.67
50000	4539.51	2451.15	1760.94	1420.22	1219.23	1088.04	996.67	930.12	880.06	841.47	811.17	787.02	767.55	751.71
55000	4993.46	2696.26	1937.04	1562.24	1341.15	1196.84	1096.34	1023.14	968.06	925.62	892.28	865.72	844.30	826.88
60000	5447.41	2941.38	2113.13	1704.27	1463.08	1305.65	1196.00	1116.15	1056.07	1009.76	973.40	944.42	921.06	902.05
65000	5901.36	3186.49	2289.23	1846.29	1585.00	1414.45	1295.67	1209.16	1144.07	1093.91	1054.51	1023.12	997.81	977.22
70000	6355.31	3431.61	2465.32	1988.31	1706.92	1523.26	1395.34	1302.17	1232.08	1178.06	1135.63	1101.82	1074.57	1052.39
75000	6809.26	3676.72	2641.41	2130.33	1828.84	1632.06	1495.00	1395.18	1320.09	1262.20	1216.75	1180.52	1151.32	1127.56
80000	7263.21	3921.83	2817.51	2272.35	1950.77	1740.86	1594.67	1488.19	1408.09	1346.35	1297.86	1259.23	1228.08	1202.73
85000	7717.16	4166.95	2993.60	2414.37	2072.69	1849.67	1694.34	1581.21	1496.10	1430.50	1378.98	1337.93	1304.83	1277.90
90000	8171.11	4412.06	3169.69	2556.40	2194.61	1958.47	1794.00	1674.22	1584.10	1514.64	1460.09	1416.63	1381.59	1353.07
95000	8625.06	4657.18	3345.79	2698.42	2316.53	2067.27	1893.67	1767.23	1672.11	1598.79	1541.21	1495.33	1458.34	1428.24
100000	9079.01	4902.29	3521.88	2840.44	2438.46	2176.08	1993.34	1860.24	1760.11	1682.93	1622.33	1574.03	1535.10	1503.41

TERM	15 Years	16 Years	17 Years	18 Years	19 Years	20 Years	21 Years	22 Years	23 Years	24 Years	25 Years	30 Years	35 Years	40 Years
AMOUNT														
5	.08	.08	.08	.08	.08	.08	.07	.07	.07	.07	.07	.07	.07	.07
10	.15	.15	.15	.15	.15	.15	.14	.14	.14	.14	.14	.14	.14	.14
15	.23	.22	.22	.22	.22	.22	.21	.21	.21	.21	.21	.21	.21	.21
25	.37	.37	.36	.36	.36	.36	.35	.35	.35	.35	.35	.34	.34	.34
50	.74	.73	.72	.72	.71	.71	.70	.70	.69	.69	.69	.68	.68	.68
75	1.11	1.10	1.08	1.07	1.06	1.06	1.05	1.04	1.04	1.03	1.03	1.02	1.02	1.01
100	1.48	1.46	1.44	1.43	1.42	1.41	1.40	1.39	1.38	1.38	1.37	1.36	1.35	1.35
200	2.96	2.92	2.88	2.85	2.83	2.81	2.79	2.77	2.76	2.75	2.74	2.71	2.70	2.70
300	4.44	4.37	4.32	4.28	4.24	4.21	4.18	4.16	4.14	4.12	4.11	4.07	4.05	4.04
400	5.91	5.83	5.76	5.70	5.65	5.61	5.57	5.54	5.52	5.50	5.48	5.42	5.40	5.39
500	7.39	7.28	7.20	7.12	7.06	7.01	6.96	6.93	6.90	6.87	6.85	6.78	6.75	6.73
600	8.87	8.74	8.63	8.55	8.47	8.41	8.36	8.31	8.28	8.24	8.22	8.13	8.10	8.08
700	10.35	10.20	10.07	9.97	9.88	9.81	9.75	9.70	9.65	9.62	9.59	9.49	9.45	9.43
800	11.82	11.65	11.51	11.39	11.29	11.21	11.14	11.08	11.03	10.99	10.95	10.84	10.79	10.77
900	13.30	13.11	12.95	12.82	12.70	12.61	12.53	12.47	12.41	12.36	12.32	12.20	12.14	12.12
1000	14.78	14.56	14.39	14.24	14.12	14.01	13.92	13.85	13.79	13.74	13.69	13.55	13.49	13.46
2000	29.55	29.12	28.77	28.47	28.23	28.02	27.84	27.70	27.57	27.47	27.38	27.10	26.98	26.92
3000	44.33	43.68	43.15	42.71	42.34	42.02	41.76	41.54	41.36	41.20	41.07	40.65	40.47	40.38
4000	59.10	58.24	57.53	56.94	56.45	56.03	55.68	55.39	55.14	54.93	54.75	54.20	53.95	53.84
5000	73.88	72.80	71.92	71.17	70.56	70.04	69.60	69.23	68.92	68.66	68.44	67.75	67.44	67.30
6000	88.65	87.36	86.30	85.41	84.67	84.04	83.52	83.08	82.71	82.39	82.13	81.30	80.93	80.76
7000	103.42	101.92	100.68	99.64	98.78	98.05	97.44	96.93	96.49	96.12	95.81	94.84	94.41	94.22
8000	118.20	116.48	115.06	113.88	112.89	112.06	111.36	110.77	110.28	109.86	109.50	108.39	107.90	107.68
9000	132.97	131.04	129.44	128.11	127.00	126.06	125.28	124.62	124.06	123.59	123.19	121.94	121.39	121.14
10000	147.75	145.60	143.83	142.34	141.11	140.07	139.20	138.46	137.84	137.32	136.88	135.49	134.88	134.60
11000	162.52	160.16	158.21	156.58	155.22	154.08	153.12	152.31	151.63	151.05	150.56	149.04	148.36	148.06
12000	177.30	174.72	172.59	170.81	169.33	168.08	167.04	166.15	165.41	164.78	164.25	162.59	161.85	161.52
13000	192.07	189.28	186.97	185.05	183.44	182.09	180.95	180.00	179.19	178.51	177.94	176.13	175.34	174.98
14000	206.84	203.84	201.35	199.28	197.55	196.09	194.87	193.85	192.98	192.24	191.62	189.68	188.82	188.44
15000	221.62	218.40	215.74	213.51	211.66	210.10	208.79	207.69	206.76	205.98	205.31	203.23	202.31	201.90
16000	236.39	232.96	230.12	227.75	225.77	224.11	222.71	221.54	220.55	219.71	219.00	216.78	215.80	215.36
17000	251.17	247.52	244.50	241.98	239.88	238.11	236.63	235.38	234.33	233.44	232.69	230.33	229.29	228.82
18000	265.94	262.08	258.88	256.22	252.12	250.55	249.23	248.11	247.17	246.37	243.88	242.77	242.28	
19000	280.72	276.64	273.26	270.45	268.10	266.13	264.47	263.07	261.90	260.60	257.42	256.26	255.74	
20000	295.49	291.20	287.65	284.68	282.21	280.13	278.39	276.92	275.68	274.63	273.75	270.97	269.75	269.20
21000	310.26	305.76	302.03	298.92	296.32	294.14	292.31	290.77	289.46	288.36	287.43	284.52	283.23	282.66
22000	325.04	320.32	316.41	313.15	310.43	308.15	306.23	304.61	303.25	302.10	301.12	298.07	296.72	296.12
23000	339.81	334.88	330.79	327.39	324.54	322.15	320.15	318.46	317.03	315.83	314.81	311.62	310.21	309.58
24000	354.59	349.44	345.17	341.62	338.65	336.16	334.07	332.30	330.82	329.56	328.50	325.17	323.69	323.04
25000	369.36	364.00	359.56	355.85	352.76	350.17	347.99	346.15	344.60	343.29	342.18	338.72	337.18	336.50
26000	384.14	378.56	373.94	370.09	366.87	364.17	361.90	359.99	358.38	357.02	355.87	352.26	350.67	349.96
27000	398.91	393.12	388.32	384.32	380.98	378.18	375.82	373.84	372.17	370.75	369.56	365.81	364.16	363.42
28000	413.68	407.68	402.70	398.56	395.09	392.18	389.74	387.69	385.95	384.48	383.24	379.36	377.64	376.88
29000	428.46	422.24	417.09	412.79	409.20	406.19	403.66	401.53	399.73	398.22	396.93	392.91	391.13	390.34
30000	443.23	436.80	431.47	427.02	423.31	420.20	417.58	415.38	413.52	411.95	410.62	406.46	404.62	403.80
31000	458.01	451.36	445.85	441.26	437.42	434.20	431.50	429.22	427.30	425.68	424.30	420.01	418.10	417.26
32000	472.78	465.92	460.23	455.49	451.53	448.21	445.42	443.07	441.09	439.41	437.99	433.55	431.59	430.72
33000	487.56	480.48	474.61	469.73	465.64	462.22	459.34	456.91	454.87	453.14	451.68	447.10	445.08	444.18
34000	502.33	495.04	489.00	483.96	479.75	476.22	473.26	470.76	468.65	466.87	465.37	460.65	458.57	457.64
35000	517.10	509.60	503.38	498.19	493.86	490.23	487.18	484.61	482.44	480.60	479.05	474.20	472.05	471.09
36000	531.88	524.16	517.76	512.43	507.97	504.24	501.10	498.45	496.22	494.34	492.74	487.75	485.54	484.55
37000	546.65	538.72	532.14	526.66	522.08	518.24	515.02	512.30	510.00	508.07	506.43	501.30	499.03	498.01
38000	561.43	553.28	546.52	540.90	536.19	532.25	528.93	526.14	523.79	521.80	520.11	514.84	512.51	511.47
39000	576.20	567.84	560.91	555.13	550.30	546.26	542.85	539.99	537.57	535.53	533.80	528.39	526.00	524.93
40000	590.98	582.40	575.29	569.36	564.41	560.26	556.77	553.83	551.36	549.26	547.49	541.94	539.49	538.39
41000	605.75	596.96	589.67	583.60	578.52	574.27	570.69	567.68	565.14	562.99	561.18	555.49	552.97	551.85
42000	620.52	611.52	604.05	597.83	592.63	588.27	584.61	581.53	578.92	576.72	574.86	569.04	566.46	565.31
43000	635.30	626.08	618.43	612.07	606.74	602.28	598.53	595.37	592.71	590.45	588.55	582.59	579.95	578.77
44000	650.07	640.64	632.82	626.30	620.85	616.29	612.45	609.22	606.49	604.19	602.24	596.14	593.44	592.23
45000	664.85	655.20	647.20	640.53	634.96	630.29	626.37	623.06	620.27	617.92	615.92	609.68	606.92	605.69
46000	679.62	669.76	661.58	654.77	649.07	644.30	640.29	636.91	634.06	631.65	629.61	623.23	620.41	619.15
47000	694.39	684.32	675.96	669.00	663.18	658.31	654.21	650.75	647.84	645.38	643.30	636.78	633.90	632.61
48000	709.17	698.88	690.34	683.24	677.29	672.31	668.13	664.60	661.63	659.11	656.99	650.33	647.38	646.07
49000	723.94	713.44	704.73	697.47	691.41	686.32	682.05	678.45	675.41	672.84	670.67	663.88	660.87	659.53
50000	738.72	728.00	719.11	711.70	705.52	700.33	695.97	692.29	689.19	686.57	684.36	677.43	674.36	672.99
55000	812.59	800.80	791.02	782.87	776.07	770.36	765.56	761.52	758.11	755.23	752.79	745.17	741.79	740.29
60000	886.46	873.60	862.93	854.04	846.62	840.39	835.16	830.75	827.03	823.89	821.23	812.91	809.23	807.59
65000	960.33	946.40	934.84	925.21	917.17	910.42	904.75	899.98	895.95	892.55	889.67	880.65	876.66	874.89
70000	1034.20	1019.20	1006.75	996.38	987.72	980.45	974.35	969.21	964.87	961.20	958.10	948.39	944.10	942.18
75000	1108.07	1092.00	1078.66	1067.55	1058.27	1050.49	1043.95	1038.44	1033.79	1029.86	1026.54	1016.14	1011.54	1009.48
80000	1181.95	1164.80	1150.57	1138.72	1128.82	1120.52	1113.54	1107.66	1102.71	1098.52	1094.97	1083.88	1078.97	1076.78
85000	1255.82	1237.59	1222.48	1209.89	1199.37	1190.55	1183.14	1176.89	1171.62	1167.17	1163.41	1151.62	1146.41	1144.08
90000	1329.69	1310.39	1294.39	1281.06	1269.92	1260.58	1252.73	1246.12	1240.54	1235.83	1231.84	1219.36	1213.84	1211.38
95000	1403.56	1383.19	1366.30	1352.23	1340.47	1330.62	1322.33	1315.35	1309.46	1304.49	1300.28	1287.10	1281.28	1278.68
100000	1477.43	1455.99	1438.21	1423.40	1411.03	1400.65	1391.93	1384.58	1378.38	1373.14	1368.71	1354.85	1348.71	1345.98

MONTHLY PAYMENT
REQUIRED TO AMORTIZE A LOAN

TERM	1 Year	2 Years	3 Years	4 Years	5 Years	6 Years	7 Years	8 Years	9 Years	10 Years	11 Years	12 Years	13 Years	14 Years
AMOUNT														
5	.46	.25	.18	.15	.13	.11	.10	.10	.09	.09	.09	.08	.08	.08
10	.91	.50	.36	.29	.25	.22	.20	.19	.18	.17	.17	.16	.16	.16
15	1.37	.74	.53	.43	.37	.33	.30	.28	.27	.26	.25	.24	.24	.23
25	2.28	1.23	.89	.72	.62	.55	.50	.47	.45	.43	.41	.40	.39	.38
50	4.55	2.46	1.77	1.43	1.23	1.10	1.00	.94	.89	.85	.82	.79	.78	.76
75	6.82	3.68	2.65	2.14	1.84	1.64	1.50	1.40	1.33	1.27	1.23	1.19	1.16	1.14
100	9.09	4.91	3.53	2.85	2.45	2.19	2.00	1.87	1.77	1.69	1.63	1.58	1.55	1.51
200	18.17	9.82	7.06	5.69	4.89	4.37	4.00	3.73	3.53	3.38	3.26	3.16	3.09	3.02
300	27.25	14.72	10.58	8.54	7.33	6.55	6.00	5.60	5.30	5.07	4.89	4.74	4.63	4.53
400	36.33	19.63	14.11	11.38	9.77	8.73	8.00	7.46	7.06	6.76	6.51	6.32	6.17	6.04
500	45.42	24.53	17.63	14.23	12.22	10.91	9.99	9.33	8.83	8.44	8.14	7.90	7.71	7.55
600	54.50	29.44	21.16	17.07	14.66	13.09	11.99	11.19	10.59	10.13	9.77	9.48	9.25	9.06
700	63.58	34.35	24.68	19.91	17.10	15.27	13.99	13.06	12.36	11.82	11.39	11.06	10.79	10.56
800	72.67	39.25	28.21	22.76	19.54	17.45	15.99	14.92	14.12	13.51	13.02	12.64	12.33	12.07
900	81.75	44.16	31.74	25.60	21.99	19.63	17.98	16.79	15.89	15.19	14.65	14.22	13.87	13.58
1000	90.83	49.06	35.26	28.45	24.43	21.81	19.98	18.65	17.65	16.88	16.28	15.79	15.41	15.09
2000	181.66	98.12	70.52	56.89	48.85	43.61	39.96	37.30	35.30	33.76	32.55	31.58	30.81	30.18
3000	272.48	147.18	105.77	85.33	73.28	65.41	59.93	55.94	52.94	50.63	48.82	47.37	46.21	45.26
4000	363.31	196.24	141.03	113.78	97.70	87.21	79.91	74.59	70.59	67.51	65.09	63.16	61.61	60.35
5000	454.13	245.30	176.28	142.22	122.13	109.02	99.89	93.24	88.24	84.39	81.36	78.95	77.01	75.43
6000	544.96	294.36	211.54	170.66	146.55	130.82	119.86	111.88	105.88	101.26	97.63	94.74	92.41	90.52
7000	635.78	343.42	246.80	199.10	170.98	152.62	139.84	130.53	123.53	118.14	113.90	110.53	107.81	105.60
8000	726.61	392.47	282.05	227.55	195.40	174.42	159.81	149.18	141.18	135.01	130.18	126.32	123.22	120.69
9000	817.43	441.53	317.31	255.99	219.83	196.22	179.79	167.82	158.82	151.89	146.45	142.11	138.62	135.77
10000	908.26	490.59	352.56	284.43	244.25	218.03	199.77	186.47	176.47	168.77	162.72	157.90	154.02	150.86
11000	999.09	539.65	387.82	312.88	268.67	239.83	219.74	205.12	194.12	185.64	178.99	173.69	169.42	165.95
12000	1089.91	588.71	423.08	341.32	293.10	261.63	239.72	223.76	211.76	202.52	195.26	189.48	184.82	181.03
13000	1180.74	637.77	458.33	369.76	317.52	283.43	259.69	242.41	229.41	219.40	211.53	205.27	200.22	196.12
14000	1271.56	686.83	493.59	398.20	341.95	305.23	279.67	261.06	247.06	236.27	227.80	221.06	215.62	211.20
15000	1362.39	735.89	528.84	426.65	366.37	327.04	299.65	279.70	264.70	253.15	244.07	236.85	231.02	226.29
16000	1453.21	784.94	564.10	455.09	390.80	348.84	319.62	298.35	282.35	270.02	260.35	252.64	246.43	241.37
17000	1544.04	834.00	599.35	483.53	415.22	370.64	339.60	317.00	300.00	286.90	276.62	268.43	261.83	256.46
18000	1634.86	883.06	634.61	511.98	439.65	392.44	359.58	335.64	317.64	303.78	292.89	284.22	277.23	271.54
19000	1725.69	932.12	669.87	540.42	464.07	414.24	379.55	354.29	335.29	320.65	309.16	300.01	292.63	286.63
20000	1816.52	981.18	705.12	568.86	488.49	436.05	399.53	372.94	352.94	337.53	325.43	315.80	308.03	301.72
21000	1907.34	1030.24	740.38	597.30	512.92	457.85	419.50	391.58	370.58	354.40	341.70	331.59	323.43	316.80
22000	1998.17	1079.30	775.63	625.75	537.34	479.65	439.48	410.23	388.23	371.28	357.97	347.37	338.83	331.89
23000	2088.99	1128.36	810.89	654.19	561.77	501.45	459.46	428.88	405.88	388.16	374.25	363.16	354.24	346.97
24000	2179.82	1177.41	846.15	682.63	586.19	523.26	479.43	447.52	423.52	405.03	390.52	378.95	369.64	362.06
25000	2270.64	1226.47	881.40	711.08	610.62	545.06	499.41	466.17	441.17	421.91	406.79	394.74	385.04	377.14
26000	2361.47	1275.53	916.66	739.52	635.04	566.86	519.38	484.82	458.82	438.79	423.06	410.53	400.44	392.23
27000	2452.29	1324.59	951.91	767.96	659.47	588.66	539.36	503.46	476.46	455.66	439.33	426.32	415.84	407.31
28000	2543.12	1373.65	987.17	796.40	683.89	610.46	559.34	522.11	494.11	472.54	455.60	442.11	431.24	422.40
29000	2633.95	1422.71	1022.42	824.85	708.31	632.27	579.31	540.76	511.76	489.41	471.87	457.90	446.64	437.48
30000	2724.77	1471.77	1057.68	853.29	732.74	654.07	599.29	559.40	529.40	506.29	488.14	473.69	462.04	452.57
31000	2815.60	1520.83	1092.94	881.73	757.16	675.87	619.27	578.05	547.05	523.17	504.42	489.48	477.45	467.66
32000	2906.42	1569.88	1128.19	910.18	781.59	697.67	639.24	596.70	564.70	540.04	520.69	505.27	492.85	482.74
33000	2997.25	1618.94	1163.45	938.62	806.01	719.47	659.22	615.34	582.34	556.92	536.96	521.06	508.25	497.83
34000	3088.07	1668.00	1198.70	967.06	830.44	741.28	679.19	633.99	599.99	573.79	553.23	536.85	523.65	512.91
35000	3178.90	1717.06	1233.96	995.50	854.86	763.08	699.17	652.64	617.64	590.67	569.50	552.64	539.05	528.00
36000	3269.72	1766.12	1269.22	1023.95	879.29	784.88	719.15	671.28	635.28	607.55	585.77	568.43	554.45	543.08
37000	3360.55	1815.18	1304.47	1052.39	903.71	806.68	739.12	689.93	652.93	624.42	602.04	584.22	569.85	558.17
38000	3451.38	1864.24	1339.73	1080.83	928.13	828.48	759.10	708.58	670.58	641.30	618.32	600.01	585.25	573.25
39000	3542.20	1913.30	1374.98	1109.27	952.56	850.29	779.07	727.22	688.22	658.18	634.59	615.80	600.66	588.34
40000	3633.03	1962.35	1410.24	1137.72	976.98	872.09	799.05	745.87	705.87	675.05	650.86	631.59	616.06	603.43
41000	3723.85	2011.41	1445.50	1166.16	1001.41	893.89	819.03	764.51	723.52	691.93	667.13	647.38	631.46	618.51
42000	3814.68	2060.47	1480.75	1194.60	1025.83	915.69	839.00	783.16	741.16	708.80	683.40	663.17	646.86	633.60
43000	3905.50	2109.53	1516.01	1223.05	1050.26	937.50	858.98	801.81	758.81	725.68	699.67	678.96	662.26	648.68
44000	3996.33	2158.59	1551.26	1251.49	1074.68	959.30	878.96	820.45	776.46	742.56	715.94	694.74	677.66	663.77
45000	4087.15	2207.65	1586.52	1279.93	1099.11	981.10	898.93	839.10	794.10	759.43	732.21	710.53	693.06	678.85
46000	4177.98	2256.71	1621.77	1308.37	1123.53	1002.90	918.91	857.75	811.75	776.31	748.49	726.32	708.47	693.94
47000	4268.80	2305.77	1657.03	1336.82	1147.95	1024.70	938.88	876.39	829.40	793.18	764.76	742.11	723.87	709.02
48000	4359.63	2354.82	1692.29	1365.26	1172.38	1046.51	958.86	895.04	847.04	810.06	781.03	757.90	739.27	724.11
49000	4450.46	2403.88	1727.54	1393.70	1196.80	1068.31	978.84	913.69	864.69	826.94	797.30	773.69	754.67	739.20
50000	4541.28	2452.94	1762.80	1422.15	1221.23	1090.11	998.81	932.33	882.34	843.81	813.57	789.48	770.07	754.28
55000	4995.41	2698.23	1939.08	1564.36	1343.35	1199.12	1098.69	1025.57	970.57	928.19	894.93	868.43	847.08	829.71
60000	5449.54	2943.53	2115.36	1706.57	1465.47	1308.13	1198.57	1118.80	1058.80	1012.57	976.28	947.38	924.08	905.14
65000	5903.66	3188.82	2291.64	1848.79	1587.59	1417.14	1298.45	1212.03	1147.04	1096.96	1057.64	1026.33	1001.09	980.56
70000	6357.79	3434.12	2467.91	1991.00	1709.72	1526.15	1398.33	1305.27	1235.27	1181.34	1139.00	1105.27	1078.10	1055.99
75000	6811.92	3679.41	2644.19	2133.22	1831.84	1635.16	1498.22	1398.50	1323.50	1265.72	1220.35	1184.22	1155.10	1131.42
80000	7266.05	3924.70	2820.47	2275.43	1953.96	1744.17	1598.10	1491.73	1411.74	1350.10	1301.71	1263.17	1232.11	1206.85
85000	7720.17	4170.00	2996.75	2417.64	2076.08	1853.18	1697.98	1584.96	1499.97	1434.48	1383.07	1342.12	1309.12	1282.27
90000	8174.30	4415.29	3173.03	2559.86	2198.21	1962.19	1797.86	1678.20	1588.20	1518.86	1464.42	1421.06	1386.12	1357.70
95000	8628.43	4660.58	3349.31	2702.07	2320.33	2071.20	1897.74	1771.43	1676.44	1603.24	1545.78	1500.01	1463.13	1433.13
100000	9082.56	4905.88	3525.59	2844.29	2442.45	2180.22	1997.62	1864.66	1764.67	1687.62	1627.14	1578.96	1540.14	1508.56

TERM	15 Years	16 Years	17 Years	18 Years	19 Years	20 Years	21 Years	22 Years	23 Years	24 Years	25 Years	30 Years	35 Years	40 Years
AMOUNT														
5	.08	.08	.08	.08	.08	.08	.07	.07	.07	.07	.07	.07	.07	.07
10	.15	.15	.15	.15	.15	.15	.14	.14	.14	.14	.14	.14	.14	.14
15	.23	.22	.22	.22	.22	.22	.21	.21	.21	.21	.21	.21	.21	.21
25	.38	.37	.37	.36	.36	.36	.35	.35	.35	.35	.35	.35	.34	.34
50	.75	.74	.73	.72	.71	.71	.70	.70	.70	.69	.69	.69	.68	.68
75	1.12	1.10	1.09	1.08	1.07	1.06	1.05	1.05	1.04	1.04	1.04	1.03	1.02	1.02
100	1.49	1.47	1.45	1.43	1.42	1.41	1.40	1.40	1.39	1.38	1.38	1.37	1.36	1.36
200	2.97	2.93	2.89	2.86	2.84	2.82	2.80	2.79	2.77	2.76	2.75	2.73	2.71	2.71
300	4.45	4.39	4.34	4.29	4.25	4.22	4.20	4.18	4.16	4.14	4.13	4.09	4.07	4.06
400	5.94	5.85	5.78	5.72	5.67	5.63	5.60	5.57	5.54	5.52	5.50	5.45	5.42	5.41
500	7.42	7.31	7.22	7.15	7.09	7.04	6.99	6.96	6.93	6.90	6.88	6.81	6.78	6.77
600	8.90	8.77	8.67	8.58	8.50	8.44	8.39	8.35	8.31	8.28	8.25	8.17	8.13	8.12
700	10.38	10.23	10.11	10.01	9.92	9.85	9.79	9.74	9.69	9.66	9.63	9.53	9.49	9.47
800	11.87	11.70	11.55	11.44	11.34	11.26	11.19	11.13	11.08	11.04	11.00	10.89	10.84	10.82
900	13.35	13.16	13.00	12.87	12.75	12.66	12.58	12.52	12.46	12.42	12.38	12.25	12.20	12.17
1000	14.83	14.62	14.44	14.29	14.17	14.07	13.98	13.91	13.85	13.79	13.75	13.61	13.55	13.53
2000	29.66	29.23	28.88	28.58	28.34	28.13	27.96	27.81	27.69	27.58	27.50	27.22	27.10	27.05
3000	44.49	43.84	43.31	42.87	42.50	42.19	41.93	41.71	41.53	41.37	41.24	40.83	40.65	40.57
4000	59.31	58.46	57.75	57.16	56.67	56.26	55.91	55.62	55.37	55.16	54.99	54.44	54.20	54.09
5000	74.14	73.07	72.19	71.45	70.83	70.32	69.89	69.52	69.21	68.95	68.74	68.05	67.75	67.61
6000	88.97	87.68	86.62	85.74	85.00	84.38	83.86	83.42	83.06	82.74	82.48	81.66	81.30	81.13
7000	103.79	102.30	101.06	100.03	99.17	98.44	97.84	97.33	96.90	96.53	96.23	95.27	94.84	94.66
8000	118.62	116.91	115.50	114.32	113.33	112.51	111.81	111.23	110.74	110.32	109.97	108.88	108.39	108.18
9000	133.45	131.52	129.93	128.61	127.50	126.57	125.79	125.13	124.58	124.11	123.72	122.49	121.94	121.70
10000	148.27	146.14	144.37	142.89	141.66	140.63	139.77	139.04	138.42	137.90	137.47	136.09	135.49	135.22
11000	163.10	160.75	158.80	157.18	155.83	154.70	153.74	152.94	152.27	151.69	151.21	149.70	149.04	148.74
12000	177.93	175.36	173.24	171.47	170.00	168.76	167.72	166.84	166.11	165.48	164.96	163.31	162.59	162.26
13000	192.75	189.98	187.68	185.76	184.16	182.82	181.70	180.75	179.95	179.27	178.70	176.92	176.14	175.79
14000	207.58	204.59	202.11	200.05	198.33	196.88	195.67	194.65	193.79	193.06	192.45	190.53	189.68	189.31
15000	222.41	219.20	216.55	214.34	212.49	210.95	209.65	208.55	207.63	206.85	206.20	204.14	203.23	202.83
16000	237.23	233.82	230.99	228.63	226.66	225.01	223.62	222.46	221.47	220.64	219.94	217.75	216.78	216.35
17000	252.06	248.43	245.42	242.92	240.83	239.07	237.60	236.36	235.32	234.43	233.69	231.36	230.33	229.87
18000	266.89	263.04	259.86	257.21	254.99	253.14	251.58	250.26	249.16	248.22	247.43	244.97	243.88	243.39
19000	281.71	277.66	274.29	271.50	269.16	267.20	265.55	264.17	263.00	262.01	261.18	258.58	257.43	256.92
20000	296.54	292.27	288.73	285.78	283.32	281.26	279.53	278.07	276.84	275.80	274.93	272.18	270.98	270.44
21000	311.37	306.88	303.17	300.07	297.49	295.32	293.51	291.97	290.68	289.59	288.67	285.79	284.52	283.96
22000	326.19	321.50	317.60	314.36	311.66	309.39	307.48	305.88	304.53	303.38	302.42	299.40	298.07	297.48
23000	341.02	336.11	332.04	328.65	325.82	323.45	321.46	319.78	318.37	317.17	316.16	313.01	311.62	311.00
24000	355.85	350.72	346.48	342.94	339.99	337.51	335.43	333.68	332.21	330.96	329.91	326.62	325.17	324.52
25000	370.67	365.34	360.91	357.23	354.15	351.58	349.41	347.59	346.05	344.75	343.66	340.23	338.72	338.05
26000	385.50	379.95	375.35	371.52	368.32	365.64	363.39	361.49	359.89	358.54	357.40	353.84	352.27	351.57
27000	400.33	394.56	389.78	385.81	382.49	379.70	377.36	375.39	373.74	372.33	371.15	367.45	365.82	365.09
28000	415.15	409.18	404.22	400.10	396.65	393.76	391.34	389.30	387.58	386.12	384.89	381.06	379.36	378.61
29000	429.98	423.79	418.66	414.39	410.82	407.83	405.32	403.20	401.42	399.91	398.64	394.66	392.91	392.13
30000	444.81	438.40	433.09	428.67	424.98	421.89	419.29	417.10	415.26	413.70	412.39	408.27	406.46	405.65
31000	459.63	453.02	447.53	442.96	439.15	435.95	433.27	431.01	429.10	427.49	426.13	421.88	420.01	419.18
32000	474.46	467.63	461.97	457.25	453.31	450.02	447.24	444.91	442.94	441.28	439.88	435.49	433.56	432.70
33000	489.29	482.24	476.40	471.54	467.48	464.08	461.22	458.81	456.79	455.07	453.63	449.10	447.11	446.22
34000	504.11	496.85	490.84	485.83	481.65	478.14	475.20	472.72	470.63	468.86	467.37	462.71	460.65	459.74
35000	518.94	511.47	505.28	500.12	495.81	492.20	489.17	486.62	484.47	482.65	481.12	476.32	474.20	473.26
36000	533.77	526.08	519.71	514.41	509.98	506.27	503.15	500.52	498.31	496.44	494.86	489.93	487.75	486.78
37000	548.59	540.69	534.15	528.70	524.14	520.33	517.12	514.43	512.15	510.23	508.61	503.54	501.30	500.31
38000	563.42	555.31	548.58	542.99	538.31	534.39	531.10	528.33	526.00	524.02	522.36	517.15	514.85	513.83
39000	578.25	569.92	563.02	557.28	552.48	548.46	545.08	542.23	539.84	537.81	536.10	530.75	528.40	527.35
40000	593.07	584.53	577.46	571.56	566.64	562.52	559.05	556.14	553.68	551.60	549.85	544.36	541.95	540.87
41000	607.90	599.15	591.89	585.85	580.81	576.58	573.03	570.04	567.52	565.39	563.59	557.97	555.49	554.39
42000	622.73	613.76	606.33	600.14	594.97	590.64	587.01	583.94	581.36	579.18	577.34	571.58	569.04	567.91
43000	637.55	628.37	620.77	614.43	609.14	604.71	600.98	597.85	595.20	592.97	591.09	585.19	582.59	581.44
44000	652.38	642.99	635.20	628.72	623.31	618.77	614.96	611.75	609.05	606.76	604.83	598.80	596.14	594.96
45000	667.21	657.60	649.64	643.01	637.47	632.83	628.93	625.65	622.89	620.55	618.58	612.41	609.69	608.48
46000	682.03	672.21	664.07	657.30	651.64	646.89	642.91	639.56	636.73	634.34	632.32	626.02	623.24	622.00
47000	696.86	686.83	678.51	671.59	665.80	660.96	656.89	653.46	650.57	648.13	646.07	639.63	636.79	635.52
48000	711.69	701.44	692.95	685.88	679.97	675.02	670.86	667.36	664.41	661.92	659.82	653.24	650.33	649.04
49000	726.51	716.05	707.38	700.17	694.14	689.08	684.84	681.27	678.26	675.71	673.56	666.84	663.88	662.57
50000	741.34	730.67	721.82	714.45	708.30	703.15	698.82	695.17	692.10	689.50	687.31	680.45	677.43	676.09
55000	815.47	803.73	794.00	785.90	779.13	773.46	768.70	764.69	761.31	758.45	756.04	748.50	745.17	743.70
60000	889.61	876.80	866.18	857.34	849.96	843.77	838.58	834.20	830.52	827.40	824.77	816.54	812.92	811.30
65000	963.74	949.87	938.36	928.79	920.79	914.09	908.46	903.72	899.73	896.35	893.50	884.59	880.66	878.91
70000	1037.87	1022.93	1010.55	1000.23	991.62	984.40	978.34	973.24	968.93	965.30	962.23	952.63	948.40	946.52
75000	1112.01	1096.00	1082.73	1071.68	1062.45	1054.72	1048.22	1042.75	1038.14	1034.25	1030.96	1020.68	1016.14	1014.13
80000	1186.14	1169.06	1154.91	1143.12	1133.28	1125.03	1118.10	1112.27	1107.35	1103.20	1099.69	1088.72	1083.89	1081.74
85000	1260.27	1242.13	1227.09	1214.57	1204.11	1195.34	1187.98	1181.79	1176.56	1172.15	1168.42	1156.77	1151.63	1149.35
90000	1334.41	1315.20	1299.27	1286.01	1274.94	1265.66	1257.86	1251.30	1245.77	1241.10	1237.15	1224.81	1219.37	1216.95
95000	1408.54	1388.26	1371.45	1357.46	1345.77	1335.97	1327.75	1320.82	1314.98	1310.05	1305.88	1292.86	1287.11	1284.56
100000	1482.67	1461.33	1443.63	1428.90	1416.60	1406.29	1397.63	1390.34	1384.19	1379.00	1374.61	1360.90	1354.86	1352.17

16.250%

MONTHLY PAYMENT
REQUIRED TO AMORTIZE A LOAN

TERM	1 Year	2 Years	3 Years	4 Years	5 Years	6 Years	7 Years	8 Years	9 Years	10 Years	11 Years	12 Years	13 Years	14 Years
AMOUNT														
5	.46	.25	.18	.15	.13	.11	.11	.10	.09	.09	.09	.08	.08	.08
10	.91	.50	.36	.29	.25	.22	.21	.19	.18	.17	.17	.16	.16	.16
15	1.37	.74	.53	.43	.37	.33	.31	.29	.27	.26	.25	.24	.24	.23
25	2.28	1.23	.89	.72	.62	.55	.51	.47	.45	.43	.41	.40	.39	.38
50	4.55	2.46	1.77	1.43	1.23	1.10	1.01	.94	.89	.85	.82	.80	.78	.76
75	6.82	3.69	2.65	2.14	1.84	1.64	1.51	1.41	1.33	1.27	1.23	1.19	1.16	1.14
100	9.09	4.91	3.53	2.85	2.45	2.19	2.01	1.87	1.77	1.70	1.64	1.59	1.55	1.52
200	18.17	9.82	7.06	5.70	4.90	4.37	4.01	3.74	3.54	3.39	3.27	3.17	3.09	3.03
300	27.26	14.73	10.59	8.55	7.34	6.55	6.01	5.61	5.31	5.08	4.90	4.75	4.64	4.54
400	36.34	19.64	14.12	11.39	9.79	8.74	8.01	7.48	7.08	6.77	6.53	6.33	6.18	6.05
500	45.43	24.55	17.65	14.24	12.23	10.92	10.01	9.34	8.84	8.46	8.16	7.92	7.72	7.56
600	54.51	29.45	21.17	17.09	14.68	13.10	12.01	11.21	10.61	10.15	9.79	9.50	9.27	9.08
700	63.60	34.36	24.70	19.93	17.12	15.29	14.01	13.08	12.38	11.84	11.42	11.08	10.81	10.59
800	72.68	39.27	28.23	22.78	19.57	17.47	16.01	14.95	14.15	13.53	13.05	12.66	12.35	12.10
900	81.77	44.18	31.76	25.63	22.01	19.65	18.01	16.81	15.91	15.22	14.68	14.25	13.90	13.61
1000	90.85	49.09	35.29	28.47	24.46	21.83	20.01	18.68	17.68	16.91	16.31	15.83	15.44	15.12
2000	181.70	98.17	70.57	56.94	48.91	43.66	40.01	37.36	35.36	33.82	32.61	31.65	30.87	30.24
3000	272.55	147.25	105.85	85.41	73.36	65.49	60.02	56.03	53.04	50.73	48.92	47.47	46.31	45.36
4000	363.40	196.34	141.13	113.88	97.81	87.32	80.02	74.71	70.71	67.63	65.22	63.29	61.74	60.48
5000	454.25	245.42	176.41	142.35	122.26	109.15	100.03	93.39	88.39	84.54	81.52	79.12	77.18	75.60
6000	545.10	294.50	211.69	170.82	146.71	130.98	120.03	112.06	106.07	101.45	97.83	94.94	92.61	90.72
7000	635.95	343.58	246.97	199.28	171.16	152.81	140.04	130.74	123.74	118.36	114.13	110.76	108.05	105.84
8000	726.80	392.67	282.25	227.75	195.61	174.64	160.04	149.41	141.42	135.26	130.43	126.58	123.48	120.96
9000	817.65	441.75	317.53	256.22	220.06	196.47	180.05	168.09	159.10	152.17	146.74	142.41	138.92	136.08
10000	908.50	490.83	352.81	284.69	244.52	218.30	200.05	186.77	176.78	169.08	163.04	158.23	154.35	151.20
11000	999.35	539.91	388.09	313.16	268.97	240.13	220.06	205.44	194.45	185.99	179.34	174.05	169.79	166.32
12000	1090.20	589.00	423.37	341.63	293.42	261.96	240.06	224.12	212.13	202.89	195.65	189.87	185.22	181.44
13000	1181.04	638.08	458.65	370.10	317.87	283.79	260.07	242.79	229.81	219.80	211.95	205.70	200.66	196.56
14000	1271.89	687.16	493.93	398.56	342.32	305.62	280.07	261.47	247.48	236.71	228.25	221.52	216.09	211.68
15000	1362.74	736.24	529.21	427.03	366.77	327.45	300.08	280.15	265.16	253.62	244.56	237.34	231.53	226.80
16000	1453.59	785.33	564.49	455.50	391.22	349.28	320.08	298.82	282.84	270.52	260.86	253.16	246.96	241.92
17000	1544.44	834.41	599.77	483.97	415.67	371.11	340.09	317.50	300.51	287.43	277.16	268.99	262.40	257.04
18000	1635.29	883.49	635.06	512.44	440.12	392.94	360.09	336.17	318.19	304.34	293.47	284.81	277.83	272.16
19000	1726.14	932.58	670.34	540.91	464.58	414.77	380.09	354.85	335.87	321.25	309.77	300.63	293.27	287.28
20000	1816.99	981.66	705.62	569.37	489.03	436.60	400.10	373.53	353.55	338.15	326.07	316.45	308.70	302.40
21000	1907.84	1030.74	740.90	597.84	513.48	458.43	420.10	392.20	371.22	355.06	342.38	332.28	324.14	317.52
22000	1998.69	1079.82	776.18	626.31	537.93	480.26	440.11	410.88	388.90	371.97	358.68	348.10	339.57	332.64
23000	2089.54	1128.91	811.46	654.78	562.38	502.09	460.11	429.56	406.58	388.88	374.98	363.92	355.01	347.76
24000	2180.39	1177.99	846.74	683.25	586.83	523.92	480.12	448.23	424.25	405.78	391.29	379.74	370.44	362.88
25000	2271.24	1227.07	882.02	711.72	611.28	545.75	500.12	466.91	441.93	422.69	407.59	395.57	385.88	378.00
26000	2362.08	1276.15	917.30	740.19	635.73	567.58	520.13	485.58	459.61	439.60	423.89	411.39	401.31	393.12
27000	2452.93	1325.24	952.58	768.65	660.18	589.41	540.13	504.26	477.29	456.51	440.20	427.21	416.75	408.24
28000	2543.78	1374.32	987.86	797.12	684.64	611.24	560.14	522.94	494.96	473.41	456.50	443.03	432.18	423.36
29000	2634.63	1423.40	1023.14	825.59	709.09	633.07	580.14	541.61	512.64	490.32	472.80	458.86	447.62	438.48
30000	2725.48	1472.48	1058.42	854.06	733.54	654.90	600.15	560.29	530.32	507.23	489.11	474.68	463.05	453.60
31000	2816.33	1521.57	1093.70	882.53	757.99	676.73	620.15	578.96	547.99	524.14	505.41	490.50	478.49	468.72
32000	2907.18	1570.65	1128.98	911.00	782.44	698.56	640.16	597.64	565.67	541.04	521.71	506.32	493.92	483.84
33000	2998.03	1619.73	1164.26	939.46	806.89	720.39	660.16	616.32	583.35	557.95	538.02	522.15	509.36	498.96
34000	3088.88	1668.82	1199.54	967.93	831.34	742.22	680.17	634.99	601.02	574.86	554.32	537.97	524.79	514.08
35000	3179.73	1717.90	1234.83	996.40	855.79	764.05	700.17	653.67	618.70	591.77	570.63	553.79	540.23	529.20
36000	3270.58	1766.98	1270.11	1024.87	880.24	785.87	720.17	672.34	636.38	608.67	586.93	569.61	555.66	544.32
37000	3361.43	1816.06	1305.39	1053.34	904.70	807.70	740.18	691.02	654.06	625.58	603.23	585.44	571.10	559.44
38000	3452.27	1865.15	1340.67	1081.81	929.15	829.53	760.18	709.70	671.73	642.49	619.54	601.26	586.53	574.56
39000	3543.12	1914.23	1375.95	1110.28	953.60	851.36	780.19	728.37	689.41	659.40	635.84	617.08	601.97	589.68
40000	3633.97	1963.31	1411.23	1138.74	978.05	873.19	800.19	747.05	707.09	676.30	652.14	632.90	617.40	604.80
41000	3724.82	2012.39	1446.51	1167.21	1002.50	895.02	820.20	765.72	724.76	693.21	668.45	648.73	632.84	619.92
42000	3815.67	2061.48	1481.79	1195.68	1026.95	916.85	840.20	784.40	742.44	710.12	684.75	664.55	648.27	635.04
43000	3906.52	2110.56	1517.07	1224.15	1051.40	938.68	860.21	803.08	760.12	727.02	701.05	680.37	663.71	650.16
44000	3997.37	2159.64	1552.35	1252.62	1075.85	960.51	880.21	821.75	777.80	743.93	717.36	696.19	679.14	665.28
45000	4088.22	2208.72	1587.63	1281.09	1100.30	982.34	900.22	840.43	795.47	760.84	733.66	712.01	694.58	680.40
46000	4179.07	2257.81	1622.91	1309.56	1124.76	1004.17	920.22	859.11	813.15	777.75	749.96	727.84	710.01	695.52
47000	4269.92	2306.89	1658.19	1338.02	1149.21	1026.00	940.23	877.78	830.83	794.65	766.27	743.66	725.45	710.64
48000	4360.77	2355.97	1693.47	1366.49	1173.66	1047.83	960.23	896.46	848.50	811.56	782.57	759.48	740.88	725.76
49000	4451.62	2405.05	1728.75	1394.96	1198.11	1069.66	980.24	915.13	866.18	828.47	798.87	775.30	756.32	740.88
50000	4542.47	2454.14	1764.03	1423.43	1222.56	1091.49	1000.24	933.81	883.86	845.38	815.18	791.13	771.75	756.00
55000	4996.71	2699.55	1940.44	1565.77	1344.81	1200.64	1100.26	1027.19	972.24	929.91	896.69	870.24	848.93	831.60
60000	5450.96	2944.96	2116.84	1708.11	1467.07	1309.79	1200.29	1120.57	1060.63	1014.45	978.21	949.35	926.10	907.20
65000	5905.20	3190.38	2293.24	1850.46	1589.33	1418.94	1300.31	1213.95	1149.01	1098.99	1059.73	1028.46	1003.28	982.80
70000	6359.45	3435.79	2469.65	1992.80	1711.58	1528.09	1400.34	1307.33	1237.40	1183.53	1141.25	1107.58	1080.45	1058.39
75000	6813.70	3681.20	2646.05	2135.14	1833.84	1637.23	1500.36	1400.71	1325.78	1268.06	1222.76	1186.69	1157.63	1133.99
80000	7267.94	3926.62	2822.45	2277.48	1956.09	1746.38	1600.38	1494.09	1414.17	1352.60	1304.28	1265.80	1234.80	1209.59
85000	7722.19	4172.03	2998.85	2419.83	2078.35	1855.53	1700.41	1587.47	1502.55	1437.14	1385.80	1344.91	1311.98	1285.19
90000	8176.43	4417.44	3175.26	2562.17	2200.60	1964.68	1800.43	1680.85	1590.94	1521.67	1467.31	1424.02	1389.15	1360.79
95000	8630.68	4662.86	3351.66	2704.51	2322.86	2073.83	1900.45	1774.23	1679.33	1606.21	1548.83	1503.14	1466.32	1436.39
100000	9084.93	4908.27	3528.06	2846.85	2445.11	2182.98	2000.48	1867.61	1767.71	1690.75	1630.35	1582.25	1543.50	1511.99

TERM	15 Years	16 Years	17 Years	18 Years	19 Years	20 Years	21 Years	22 Years	23 Years	24 Years	25 Years	30 Years	35 Years	40 Years
AMOUNT														
5	.08	.08	.08	.08	.08	.08	.08	.07	.07	.07	.07	.07	.07	.07
10	.15	.15	.15	.15	.15	.15	.15	.14	.14	.14	.14	.14	.14	.14
15	.23	.22	.22	.22	.22	.22	.22	.21	.21	.21	.21	.21	.21	.21
25	.38	.37	.37	.36	.36	.36	.36	.35	.35	.35	.35	.35	.34	.34
50	.75	.74	.73	.72	.72	.71	.71	.70	.70	.70	.69	.69	.68	.68
75	1.12	1.10	1.09	1.08	1.07	1.06	1.06	1.05	1.05	1.04	1.04	1.03	1.02	1.02
100	1.49	1.47	1.45	1.44	1.43	1.42	1.41	1.40	1.39	1.39	1.38	1.37	1.36	1.36
200	2.98	2.93	2.90	2.87	2.85	2.83	2.81	2.79	2.78	2.77	2.76	2.73	2.72	2.72
300	4.46	4.40	4.35	4.30	4.27	4.24	4.21	4.19	4.17	4.15	4.14	4.10	4.08	4.07
400	5.95	5.86	5.79	5.74	5.69	5.65	5.61	5.58	5.56	5.54	5.52	5.46	5.44	5.43
500	7.44	7.33	7.24	7.17	7.11	7.06	7.01	6.98	6.95	6.92	6.90	6.83	6.80	6.79
600	8.92	8.79	8.69	8.60	8.53	8.47	8.41	8.37	8.33	8.30	8.28	8.19	8.16	8.14
700	10.41	10.26	10.14	10.03	9.95	9.88	9.81	9.76	9.72	9.69	9.65	9.56	9.52	9.50
800	11.89	11.72	11.58	11.47	11.37	11.29	11.22	11.16	11.11	11.07	11.03	10.92	10.88	10.86
900	13.38	13.19	13.03	12.90	12.79	12.70	12.62	12.55	12.50	12.45	12.41	12.29	12.24	12.21
1000	14.87	14.65	14.48	14.33	14.21	14.11	14.02	13.95	13.89	13.83	13.79	13.65	13.59	13.57
2000	29.73	29.30	28.95	28.66	28.41	28.21	28.03	27.89	27.77	27.66	27.58	27.30	27.18	27.13
3000	44.59	43.95	43.42	42.98	42.61	42.31	42.05	41.83	41.65	41.49	41.36	40.95	40.77	40.69
4000	59.45	58.60	57.89	57.31	56.82	56.41	56.06	55.77	55.53	55.32	55.15	54.60	54.36	54.26
5000	74.31	73.25	72.37	71.63	71.02	70.51	70.08	69.71	69.41	69.15	68.93	68.25	67.95	67.82
6000	89.18	87.90	86.84	85.96	85.22	84.61	84.09	83.66	83.29	82.98	82.72	81.90	81.54	81.38
7000	104.04	102.55	101.31	100.28	99.43	98.71	98.10	97.60	97.17	96.81	96.50	95.55	95.13	94.95
8000	118.90	117.20	115.78	114.61	113.63	112.81	112.12	111.54	111.05	110.64	110.29	109.20	108.72	108.51
9000	133.76	131.84	130.26	128.94	127.83	126.91	126.13	125.48	124.93	124.47	124.07	122.85	122.31	122.07
10000	148.62	146.49	144.73	143.26	142.04	141.01	140.15	139.42	138.81	138.30	137.86	136.50	135.90	135.63
11000	163.48	161.14	159.20	157.59	156.24	155.11	154.16	153.36	152.69	152.12	151.64	150.15	149.49	149.20
12000	178.35	175.79	173.67	171.91	170.44	169.21	168.18	167.31	166.57	165.95	165.43	163.80	163.08	162.76
13000	193.21	190.44	188.15	186.24	184.65	183.31	182.19	181.25	180.45	179.78	179.22	177.45	176.67	176.32
14000	208.07	205.09	202.62	200.56	198.85	197.41	196.20	195.19	194.33	193.61	193.01	191.10	190.26	189.89
15000	222.93	219.74	217.09	214.89	213.05	211.51	210.22	209.13	208.21	207.44	206.79	204.75	203.85	203.45
16000	237.79	234.39	231.56	229.22	227.25	225.61	224.23	223.07	222.09	221.27	220.57	218.39	217.44	217.01
17000	252.65	249.04	246.04	243.54	241.46	239.71	238.25	237.01	235.98	235.10	234.36	232.04	231.03	230.58
18000	267.52	263.68	260.51	257.87	255.66	253.81	252.26	250.96	249.86	248.93	248.14	245.69	244.62	244.14
19000	282.38	278.33	274.98	272.19	269.86	267.91	266.28	264.90	263.74	262.76	261.93	259.34	258.21	257.70
20000	297.24	292.98	289.45	286.52	284.07	282.01	280.29	278.84	277.62	276.59	275.71	272.99	271.79	271.26
21000	312.10	307.63	303.93	300.84	298.27	296.11	294.30	292.78	291.50	290.41	289.50	286.64	285.38	284.83
22000	326.96	322.28	318.40	315.17	312.47	310.22	308.32	306.72	305.38	304.24	303.28	300.29	298.97	298.39
23000	341.82	336.93	332.87	329.50	326.68	324.32	322.33	320.66	319.26	318.07	317.07	313.94	312.56	311.95
24000	356.69	351.58	347.34	343.82	340.88	338.42	336.35	334.61	333.14	331.90	330.85	327.59	326.15	325.52
25000	371.55	366.23	361.82	358.15	355.08	352.52	350.36	348.55	347.02	345.73	344.64	341.24	339.74	339.08
26000	386.41	380.87	376.29	372.47	369.29	366.62	364.38	362.49	360.90	359.56	358.43	354.89	353.33	352.64
27000	401.27	395.52	390.76	386.80	383.49	380.72	378.43	374.43	374.78	373.39	372.21	368.54	366.92	366.21
28000	416.13	410.17	405.23	401.12	397.69	394.82	392.40	390.37	388.66	387.22	386.00	382.19	380.51	379.77
29000	430.99	424.82	419.71	415.45	411.90	408.92	406.42	404.32	402.54	401.05	399.78	395.84	394.10	393.33
30000	445.86	439.47	434.18	429.78	426.10	423.02	420.43	418.26	416.42	414.88	413.57	409.49	407.69	406.89
31000	460.72	454.12	448.65	444.10	440.30	437.12	434.45	432.20	430.30	428.70	427.35	423.13	421.28	420.46
32000	475.58	468.77	463.12	458.43	454.50	451.22	448.46	446.14	444.18	442.53	441.14	436.78	434.87	434.02
33000	490.44	483.42	477.60	472.75	468.71	465.32	462.48	460.08	458.07	456.36	454.92	450.43	448.46	447.58
34000	505.30	498.07	492.07	487.08	482.91	479.42	476.49	474.02	471.95	470.19	468.71	464.08	462.05	461.15
35000	520.16	512.71	506.54	501.40	497.11	493.52	490.50	487.97	485.83	484.02	482.49	477.73	475.64	474.71
36000	535.03	527.36	521.01	515.73	511.32	507.62	504.52	501.91	499.71	497.85	496.28	491.38	489.23	488.27
37000	549.89	542.01	535.49	530.06	525.52	521.72	518.53	515.85	513.59	511.68	510.07	505.03	502.82	501.83
38000	564.75	556.66	549.96	544.38	539.72	535.82	532.55	529.79	527.47	525.51	523.85	518.68	516.41	515.40
39000	579.61	571.31	564.43	558.71	553.93	549.92	546.56	543.73	541.35	539.34	537.64	532.33	530.00	528.96
40000	594.47	585.96	578.90	573.03	568.13	564.02	560.50	557.67	555.23	553.17	551.42	545.98	543.58	542.52
41000	609.33	600.61	593.38	587.36	582.33	578.12	574.59	571.62	569.11	566.99	565.21	559.63	557.17	556.09
42000	624.20	615.26	607.85	601.68	596.54	592.22	588.60	585.56	582.99	580.82	578.99	573.28	570.76	569.65
43000	639.06	629.91	622.32	616.01	610.74	606.32	602.62	599.50	596.87	594.65	592.78	586.93	584.35	583.21
44000	653.92	644.55	636.79	630.34	624.94	620.43	616.63	613.44	610.75	608.48	606.56	600.58	597.94	596.78
45000	668.78	659.20	651.27	644.66	639.15	634.53	630.65	627.38	624.63	622.31	620.35	614.23	611.53	610.34
46000	683.64	673.85	665.74	658.99	653.35	648.63	644.66	641.32	638.51	636.14	634.13	627.87	625.12	623.90
47000	698.50	688.50	680.21	673.31	667.55	662.73	658.68	655.27	652.39	649.97	647.92	641.52	638.71	637.46
48000	713.37	703.15	694.68	687.64	681.75	676.83	672.69	669.21	666.27	663.80	661.70	655.17	652.30	651.03
49000	728.23	717.80	709.16	701.96	695.96	690.93	686.70	683.15	680.15	677.63	675.49	668.82	665.89	664.59
50000	743.09	732.45	723.63	716.29	710.16	705.03	700.72	697.09	694.04	691.46	689.28	682.47	679.48	678.15
55000	817.40	805.69	795.99	787.92	781.18	775.53	770.79	766.80	763.44	760.60	758.20	750.72	747.43	745.97
60000	891.71	878.94	868.35	859.55	852.19	846.03	840.86	836.51	832.84	829.75	827.13	818.97	815.37	813.78
65000	966.01	952.18	940.72	931.17	923.21	916.53	910.93	906.22	902.24	898.89	896.06	887.21	883.32	881.60
70000	1040.32	1025.42	1013.08	1002.80	994.22	987.04	981.00	975.93	971.65	968.04	964.98	955.46	951.27	949.41
75000	1114.63	1098.67	1085.44	1074.43	1065.24	1057.54	1051.07	1045.64	1041.05	1037.18	1033.91	1023.71	1019.22	1017.23
80000	1188.94	1171.91	1157.80	1146.06	1136.25	1128.04	1121.15	1115.34	1110.45	1106.33	1102.84	1091.95	1087.17	1085.04
85000	1263.25	1245.16	1230.16	1217.69	1207.27	1198.54	1191.22	1185.05	1179.86	1175.47	1171.77	1160.20	1155.11	1152.86
90000	1337.56	1318.40	1302.53	1289.32	1278.29	1269.05	1261.29	1254.76	1249.26	1244.62	1240.69	1228.45	1223.06	1220.67
95000	1411.86	1391.64	1374.89	1360.95	1349.30	1339.55	1331.36	1324.47	1318.66	1313.76	1309.62	1296.69	1291.01	1288.49
100000	1486.17	1464.89	1447.25	1432.57	1420.32	1410.05	1401.43	1394.18	1388.07	1382.91	1378.55	1364.94	1358.96	1356.30

MONTHLY PAYMENT
REQUIRED TO AMORTIZE A LOAN

TERM AMOUNT	1 Year	2 Years	3 Years	4 Years	5 Years	6 Years	7 Years	8 Years	9 Years	10 Years	11 Years	12 Years	13 Years	14 Years
5	.46	.25	.18	.15	.13	.11	.11	.10	.09	.09	.09	.08	.08	.08
10	.91	.50	.36	.29	.25	.22	.21	.19	.18	.17	.17	.16	.16	.16
15	1.37	.74	.53	.43	.37	.33	.31	.29	.27	.26	.25	.24	.24	.23
25	2.28	1.23	.89	.72	.62	.55	.51	.47	.45	.43	.41	.40	.39	.38
50	4.55	2.46	1.77	1.43	1.23	1.10	1.01	.94	.89	.85	.82	.80	.78	.76
75	6.82	3.69	2.65	2.14	1.84	1.64	1.51	1.41	1.33	1.28	1.23	1.19	1.17	1.14
100	9.09	4.92	3.54	2.85	2.45	2.19	2.01	1.88	1.78	1.70	1.64	1.59	1.55	1.52
200	18.18	9.83	7.07	5.70	4.90	4.38	4.01	3.75	3.55	3.39	3.27	3.18	3.10	3.04
300	27.27	14.74	10.60	8.55	7.35	6.56	6.01	5.62	5.32	5.09	4.91	4.76	4.65	4.55
400	36.35	19.65	14.13	11.40	9.80	8.75	8.02	7.49	7.09	6.78	6.54	6.35	6.19	6.07
500	45.44	24.56	17.66	14.25	12.24	10.93	10.02	9.36	8.88	8.47	8.17	7.93	7.74	7.58
600	54.53	29.47	21.19	17.10	14.69	13.12	12.02	11.23	10.63	10.17	9.81	9.52	9.29	9.10
700	63.62	34.38	24.72	19.95	17.14	15.31	14.03	13.10	12.40	11.86	11.44	11.10	10.83	10.61
800	72.70	39.29	28.25	22.80	19.59	17.49	16.03	14.97	14.17	13.56	13.07	12.69	12.38	12.13
900	81.79	44.20	31.78	25.65	22.03	19.68	18.03	16.84	15.94	15.25	14.71	14.27	13.93	13.64
1000	90.88	49.11	35.31	28.50	24.48	21.86	20.04	18.71	17.71	16.94	16.34	15.86	15.47	15.16
2000	181.75	98.22	70.62	56.99	48.96	43.72	40.07	37.42	35.42	33.88	32.68	31.72	30.94	30.31
3000	272.62	147.32	105.92	85.49	73.44	65.58	60.10	56.12	53.13	50.82	49.01	47.57	46.41	45.47
4000	363.50	196.43	141.23	113.98	97.92	87.43	80.14	74.83	70.83	67.76	65.35	63.43	61.88	60.62
5000	454.37	245.54	176.53	142.48	122.39	109.29	100.17	93.53	88.54	84.70	81.68	79.28	77.35	75.78
6000	545.24	294.64	211.84	170.97	146.87	131.15	120.20	112.24	106.25	101.64	98.02	95.14	92.82	90.93
7000	636.12	343.75	247.14	199.46	171.35	153.01	140.24	130.94	123.96	118.58	114.35	110.99	108.29	106.08
8000	726.99	392.86	282.45	227.96	195.83	174.86	160.27	149.65	141.66	135.51	130.69	126.85	123.75	121.24
9000	817.86	441.96	317.75	256.45	220.30	196.72	180.30	168.36	159.37	152.45	147.03	142.70	139.22	136.39
10000	908.73	491.07	353.06	284.95	244.78	218.58	200.34	187.06	177.08	169.39	163.36	158.56	154.69	151.55
11000	999.61	540.18	388.36	313.44	269.26	240.44	220.37	205.77	194.79	186.33	179.70	174.41	170.16	166.70
12000	1090.48	589.28	423.67	341.93	293.74	262.29	240.40	224.47	212.49	203.27	196.03	190.27	185.63	181.86
13000	1181.35	638.39	458.97	370.43	318.22	284.15	260.44	243.18	230.20	220.21	212.37	206.12	201.10	197.01
14000	1272.23	687.50	494.28	398.92	342.69	306.01	280.47	261.88	247.91	237.15	228.70	221.98	216.57	212.16
15000	1363.10	736.60	529.58	427.42	367.17	327.87	300.50	280.59	265.62	254.09	245.04	237.84	232.03	227.32
16000	1453.97	785.71	564.89	455.91	391.65	349.72	320.54	299.29	283.32	271.02	261.37	253.69	247.50	242.47
17000	1544.84	834.82	600.20	484.41	416.13	371.58	340.57	318.00	301.03	287.96	277.71	269.55	262.97	257.63
18000	1635.72	883.92	635.50	512.90	440.60	393.44	360.60	336.71	318.74	304.90	294.05	285.40	278.44	272.78
19000	1726.59	933.03	670.81	541.39	465.08	415.29	380.64	355.41	336.45	321.84	310.38	301.26	293.91	287.94
20000	1817.46	982.14	706.11	569.89	489.56	437.15	400.67	374.12	354.15	338.78	326.72	317.11	309.38	303.09
21000	1908.34	1031.24	741.42	598.38	514.04	459.01	420.70	392.82	371.86	355.72	343.05	332.97	324.85	318.24
22000	1999.21	1080.35	776.72	626.88	538.52	480.87	440.74	411.53	389.57	372.66	359.39	348.82	340.31	333.40
23000	2090.08	1129.46	812.03	655.37	562.99	502.72	460.77	430.23	407.28	389.60	375.72	364.68	355.78	348.55
24000	2180.95	1178.56	847.33	683.86	587.47	524.58	480.80	448.94	424.98	406.53	392.06	380.53	371.25	363.71
25000	2271.83	1227.67	882.64	712.36	611.95	546.44	500.84	467.65	442.69	423.47	408.39	396.39	386.72	378.86
26000	2362.70	1276.78	917.94	740.85	636.43	568.30	520.87	486.35	460.40	440.41	424.73	412.24	402.19	394.01
27000	2453.57	1325.88	953.25	769.35	660.90	590.15	540.90	505.06	478.11	457.35	441.07	428.10	417.66	409.17
28000	2544.45	1374.99	988.55	797.84	685.38	612.01	560.94	523.76	495.81	474.29	457.40	443.95	433.13	424.32
29000	2635.32	1424.10	1023.86	826.34	709.86	633.87	580.97	542.47	513.52	491.23	473.74	459.81	448.59	439.48
30000	2726.19	1473.20	1059.16	854.83	734.34	655.73	601.00	561.17	531.23	508.17	490.07	475.67	464.06	454.63
31000	2817.06	1522.31	1094.47	883.32	758.82	677.58	621.04	579.88	548.94	525.11	506.41	491.52	479.53	469.79
32000	2907.94	1571.42	1129.78	911.82	783.29	699.44	641.07	598.58	566.64	542.04	522.74	507.38	495.00	484.94
33000	2998.81	1620.52	1165.08	940.31	807.77	721.30	661.10	617.29	584.35	558.98	539.08	523.23	510.47	500.09
34000	3089.68	1669.63	1200.39	968.81	832.25	743.15	681.14	636.00	602.06	575.92	555.41	539.09	525.94	515.25
35000	3180.56	1718.74	1235.69	997.30	856.73	765.01	701.17	654.70	619.77	592.86	571.75	554.94	541.41	530.40
36000	3271.43	1767.84	1271.00	1025.79	881.20	786.87	721.20	673.41	637.47	609.80	588.09	570.80	556.88	545.56
37000	3362.30	1816.95	1306.30	1054.29	905.68	808.73	741.24	692.11	655.18	626.74	604.42	586.65	572.34	560.71
38000	3453.17	1866.05	1341.61	1082.78	930.16	830.58	761.27	710.82	672.89	643.68	620.76	602.51	587.81	575.87
39000	3544.05	1915.16	1376.91	1111.28	954.64	852.44	781.30	729.52	690.60	660.62	637.09	618.36	603.28	591.02
40000	3634.92	1964.27	1412.22	1139.77	979.11	874.30	801.34	748.23	708.30	677.55	653.43	634.22	618.75	606.17
41000	3725.79	2013.37	1447.52	1168.27	1003.59	896.16	821.37	766.94	726.01	694.49	669.76	650.07	634.22	621.33
42000	3816.67	2062.48	1482.83	1196.76	1028.07	918.01	841.40	785.64	743.72	711.43	686.10	665.93	649.69	636.48
43000	3907.54	2111.59	1518.13	1225.25	1052.55	939.87	861.44	804.35	761.43	728.37	702.43	681.79	665.16	651.64
44000	3998.41	2160.69	1553.44	1253.75	1077.03	961.73	881.47	823.05	779.13	745.31	718.77	697.64	680.62	666.79
45000	4089.28	2209.80	1588.74	1282.24	1101.50	983.59	901.50	841.76	796.84	762.25	735.11	713.50	696.09	681.94
46000	4180.16	2258.91	1624.05	1310.74	1125.98	1005.44	921.54	860.46	814.55	779.19	751.44	729.35	711.56	697.10
47000	4271.03	2308.01	1659.36	1339.23	1150.46	1027.30	941.57	879.17	832.26	796.13	767.78	745.21	727.03	712.25
48000	4361.90	2357.12	1694.66	1367.72	1174.94	1049.16	961.60	897.87	849.96	813.06	784.11	761.06	742.50	727.41
49000	4452.78	2406.23	1729.97	1396.22	1199.41	1071.02	981.64	916.58	867.67	830.00	800.45	776.92	757.97	742.56
50000	4543.65	2455.33	1765.27	1424.71	1223.89	1092.87	1001.67	935.29	885.38	846.94	816.78	792.77	773.44	757.72
55000	4998.01	2700.87	1941.80	1567.18	1346.28	1202.16	1101.84	1028.81	973.92	931.64	898.46	872.05	850.78	833.49
60000	5452.38	2946.40	2118.32	1709.65	1468.67	1311.45	1202.00	1122.34	1062.45	1016.33	980.14	951.33	928.12	909.26
65000	5906.74	3191.93	2294.85	1852.13	1591.06	1420.73	1302.17	1215.87	1150.99	1101.02	1061.82	1030.60	1005.46	985.03
70000	6361.11	3437.47	2471.38	1994.60	1713.45	1530.02	1402.34	1309.40	1239.53	1185.72	1143.49	1109.88	1082.81	1060.80
75000	6815.47	3683.00	2647.90	2137.07	1835.84	1639.31	1502.50	1402.93	1328.07	1270.41	1225.17	1189.16	1160.15	1136.57
80000	7269.84	3928.53	2824.43	2279.54	1958.22	1748.59	1602.67	1496.45	1416.60	1355.10	1306.85	1268.43	1237.49	1212.34
85000	7724.20	4174.06	3000.96	2422.01	2080.61	1857.88	1702.84	1589.98	1505.14	1439.80	1388.53	1347.71	1314.84	1288.11
90000	8178.56	4419.60	3177.48	2564.48	2203.00	1967.17	1803.00	1683.51	1593.68	1524.49	1470.21	1426.99	1392.18	1363.88
95000	8632.93	4665.13	3354.01	2706.95	2325.39	2076.45	1903.17	1777.04	1682.22	1609.19	1551.88	1506.26	1469.52	1439.66
100000	9087.29	4910.66	3530.54	2849.42	2447.78	2185.74	2003.34	1870.57	1770.75	1693.88	1633.56	1585.54	1546.87	1515.43

TERM	15 Years	16 Years	17 Years	18 Years	19 Years	20 Years	21 Years	22 Years	23 Years	24 Years	25 Years	30 Years	35 Years	40 Years
AMOUNT														
5	.08	.08	.08	.08	.08	.08	.08	.07	.07	.07	.07	.07	.07	.07
10	.15	.15	.15	.15	.15	.15	.15	.14	.14	.14	.14	.14	.14	.14
15	.23	.23	.22	.22	.22	.22	.22	.21	.21	.21	.21	.21	.21	.21
25	.38	.37	.37	.36	.36	.36	.36	.35	.35	.35	.35	.35	.35	.35
50	.75	.74	.73	.72	.72	.71	.71	.70	.70	.70	.70	.69	.69	.69
75	1.12	1.11	1.09	1.08	1.07	1.07	1.06	1.05	1.05	1.05	1.04	1.03	1.03	1.03
100	1.49	1.47	1.46	1.44	1.43	1.42	1.41	1.40	1.40	1.39	1.39	1.37	1.37	1.37
200	2.98	2.94	2.91	2.88	2.85	2.83	2.82	2.80	2.79	2.78	2.77	2.74	2.73	2.73
300	4.47	4.41	4.36	4.31	4.28	4.25	4.22	4.20	4.18	4.17	4.15	4.11	4.09	4.09
400	5.96	5.88	5.81	5.75	5.70	5.66	5.63	5.60	5.57	5.55	5.53	5.48	5.46	5.45
500	7.45	7.35	7.26	7.19	7.13	7.07	7.03	7.00	6.96	6.94	6.92	6.85	6.82	6.81
600	8.94	8.82	8.71	8.62	8.55	8.49	8.44	8.39	8.36	8.33	8.30	8.22	8.18	8.17
700	10.43	10.28	10.16	10.06	9.97	9.90	9.84	9.79	9.75	9.71	9.68	9.59	9.55	9.53
800	11.92	11.75	11.61	11.49	11.40	11.32	11.25	11.19	11.14	11.10	11.06	10.96	10.91	10.89
900	13.41	13.22	13.06	12.93	12.82	12.73	12.65	12.59	12.53	12.49	12.45	12.33	12.27	12.25
1000	14.90	14.69	14.51	14.37	14.25	14.14	14.06	13.99	13.92	13.87	13.83	13.69	13.64	13.61
2000	29.80	29.37	29.02	28.73	28.49	28.28	28.11	27.97	27.84	27.74	27.65	27.38	27.27	27.21
3000	44.70	44.06	43.53	43.09	42.73	42.42	42.16	41.95	41.76	41.61	41.48	41.07	40.90	40.82
4000	59.59	58.74	58.04	57.45	56.97	56.56	56.21	55.93	55.68	55.48	55.30	54.76	54.53	54.42
5000	74.49	73.43	72.55	71.82	71.21	70.70	70.27	69.91	69.60	69.35	69.13	68.45	68.16	68.03
6000	89.39	88.11	87.06	86.18	85.45	84.83	84.32	83.89	83.52	83.21	82.95	82.14	81.79	81.63
7000	104.28	102.80	101.57	100.54	99.69	98.97	98.37	97.87	97.44	97.08	96.78	95.83	95.42	95.23
8000	119.18	117.48	116.07	114.90	113.93	113.11	112.42	111.85	111.36	110.95	110.60	109.52	109.05	108.84
9000	134.08	132.17	130.58	129.27	128.17	127.25	126.48	125.83	125.28	124.82	124.43	123.21	122.68	122.44
10000	148.97	146.85	145.09	143.63	142.41	141.39	140.53	139.81	139.20	138.69	138.25	136.90	136.31	136.05
11000	163.87	161.53	159.60	157.99	156.65	155.52	154.58	153.79	153.12	152.55	152.08	150.59	149.94	149.65
12000	178.77	176.22	174.11	172.35	170.89	169.66	168.63	167.77	167.04	166.42	165.90	164.28	163.57	163.26
13000	193.66	190.90	188.62	186.72	185.13	183.80	182.69	181.75	180.96	180.29	179.73	177.97	177.20	176.86
14000	208.56	205.59	203.13	201.08	199.37	197.94	196.74	195.73	194.88	194.16	193.55	191.66	190.83	190.46
15000	223.46	220.27	217.63	215.44	213.61	212.08	210.79	209.71	208.80	208.03	207.38	205.35	204.46	204.07
16000	238.35	234.96	232.14	229.80	227.85	226.21	224.84	223.69	222.72	221.89	221.20	219.04	218.09	217.67
17000	253.25	249.64	246.65	244.17	242.09	240.35	238.89	237.67	236.63	235.76	235.03	232.73	231.72	231.28
18000	268.15	264.33	261.16	258.53	256.33	254.49	252.95	251.65	250.55	249.63	248.85	246.42	245.35	244.88
19000	283.04	279.01	275.67	272.89	270.57	268.63	267.00	265.63	264.47	263.50	262.68	260.11	258.98	258.49
20000	297.94	293.69	290.18	287.25	284.81	282.77	281.05	279.61	278.39	277.37	276.50	273.80	272.61	272.09
21000	312.84	308.38	304.69	301.62	299.05	296.91	295.10	293.59	292.31	291.24	290.33	287.49	286.25	285.69
22000	327.73	323.06	319.20	315.98	313.29	311.04	309.16	307.57	306.23	305.10	304.15	301.18	299.88	299.30
23000	342.63	337.75	333.70	330.34	327.53	325.18	323.21	321.55	320.15	318.97	317.97	314.87	313.51	312.90
24000	357.53	352.43	348.21	344.70	341.77	339.32	337.26	335.53	334.07	332.84	331.80	328.56	327.14	326.51
25000	372.42	367.12	362.72	359.07	356.01	353.46	351.31	349.51	347.99	346.71	345.62	342.25	340.77	340.11
26000	387.32	381.80	377.23	373.43	370.25	367.60	365.37	363.49	361.91	360.58	359.45	355.94	354.40	353.72
27000	402.22	396.49	391.74	387.79	384.49	381.73	379.42	377.47	375.83	374.44	373.27	369.63	368.03	367.32
28000	417.11	411.17	406.25	402.15	398.73	395.87	393.47	391.45	389.75	388.31	387.10	383.32	381.66	380.92
29000	432.01	425.85	420.76	416.52	412.97	410.01	407.52	405.43	403.67	402.18	400.92	397.01	395.29	394.53
30000	446.91	440.54	435.26	430.88	427.21	424.15	421.57	419.41	417.59	416.05	414.75	410.70	408.92	408.13
31000	461.80	455.22	449.77	445.24	441.46	438.29	435.63	433.39	431.51	429.92	428.57	424.39	422.55	421.74
32000	476.70	469.91	464.28	459.60	455.70	452.42	449.68	447.37	445.43	443.78	442.40	438.08	436.18	435.34
33000	491.60	484.59	478.79	473.96	469.94	466.56	463.73	461.35	459.34	457.65	456.22	451.77	449.81	448.95
34000	506.49	499.28	493.30	488.33	484.18	480.70	477.78	475.33	473.26	471.52	470.05	465.46	463.44	462.55
35000	521.39	513.96	507.81	502.69	498.42	494.84	491.84	489.31	487.18	485.39	483.87	479.15	477.07	476.15
36000	536.29	528.65	522.32	517.05	512.66	508.98	505.89	503.29	501.10	499.26	497.70	492.84	490.70	489.76
37000	551.18	543.33	536.83	531.41	526.90	523.12	519.94	517.27	515.02	513.12	511.52	506.53	504.33	503.36
38000	566.08	558.01	551.33	545.78	541.14	537.25	533.99	531.25	528.94	526.99	525.35	520.22	517.96	516.97
39000	580.98	572.70	565.84	560.14	555.38	551.39	548.05	545.23	542.86	540.86	539.17	533.91	531.59	530.57
40000	595.87	587.38	580.35	574.50	569.62	565.53	562.10	559.21	556.78	554.73	553.00	547.59	545.22	544.18
41000	610.77	602.07	594.86	588.86	583.86	579.67	576.15	573.19	570.70	568.60	566.82	561.28	558.86	557.78
42000	625.67	616.75	609.37	603.23	598.10	593.81	590.20	587.17	584.62	582.47	580.65	574.97	572.49	571.38
43000	640.56	631.44	623.88	617.59	612.34	607.94	604.25	601.15	598.54	596.33	594.47	588.66	586.12	584.99
44000	655.46	646.12	638.39	631.95	626.58	622.08	618.31	615.13	612.46	610.20	608.30	602.35	599.75	598.59
45000	670.36	660.81	652.89	646.31	640.82	636.22	632.36	629.11	626.38	624.07	622.12	616.04	613.38	612.20
46000	685.25	675.49	667.40	660.68	655.06	650.36	646.41	643.09	640.30	637.94	635.94	629.73	627.01	625.80
47000	700.15	690.18	681.91	675.04	669.30	664.50	660.46	657.07	654.22	651.81	649.77	643.42	640.64	639.41
48000	715.05	704.86	696.42	689.40	683.54	678.63	674.52	671.05	668.14	665.67	663.59	657.11	654.27	653.01
49000	729.94	719.54	710.93	703.76	697.78	692.77	688.57	685.03	682.05	679.54	677.42	670.80	667.90	666.61
50000	744.84	734.23	725.44	718.13	712.02	706.91	702.62	699.01	695.97	693.41	691.24	684.49	681.53	680.22
55000	819.32	807.65	797.98	789.94	783.22	777.60	772.88	768.91	765.57	762.75	760.37	752.94	749.68	748.24
60000	893.81	881.07	870.52	861.75	854.42	848.29	843.14	838.82	835.17	832.09	829.49	821.39	817.83	816.26
65000	968.29	954.50	943.07	933.56	925.63	918.98	913.41	908.72	904.77	901.43	898.62	889.84	885.99	884.28
70000	1042.77	1027.92	1015.61	1005.37	996.83	989.67	983.67	978.62	974.36	970.77	967.74	958.29	954.14	952.30
75000	1117.26	1101.34	1088.15	1077.19	1068.03	1060.36	1053.93	1048.52	1043.96	1040.11	1036.86	1026.74	1022.29	1020.33
80000	1191.74	1174.76	1160.70	1149.00	1139.23	1131.05	1124.19	1118.42	1113.56	1109.45	1105.99	1095.18	1090.44	1088.35
85000	1266.22	1248.19	1233.24	1220.81	1210.43	1201.74	1194.45	1188.32	1183.15	1178.79	1175.11	1163.63	1158.60	1156.37
90000	1340.71	1321.61	1305.78	1292.62	1281.63	1272.44	1264.71	1258.22	1252.75	1248.13	1244.24	1232.08	1226.75	1224.39
95000	1415.19	1395.03	1378.33	1364.43	1352.84	1343.13	1334.98	1328.12	1322.35	1317.47	1313.36	1300.53	1294.90	1292.41
100000	1489.68	1468.45	1450.87	1436.25	1424.04	1413.82	1405.24	1398.02	1391.94	1386.82	1382.48	1368.98	1363.05	1360.43

MONTHLY PAYMENT
REQUIRED TO AMORTIZE A LOAN

TERM	1 Year	2 Years	3 Years	4 Years	5 Years	6 Years	7 Years	8 Years	9 Years	10 Years	11 Years	12 Years	13 Years	14 Years
AMOUNT														
5	.46	.25	.18	.15	.13	.11	.11	.10	.09	.09	.09	.08	.08	.08
10	.91	.50	.36	.29	.25	.22	.21	.19	.18	.17	.17	.16	.16	.16
15	1.37	.74	.54	.43	.37	.33	.31	.29	.27	.26	.25	.24	.24	.23
25	2.28	1.23	.89	.72	.62	.55	.51	.47	.45	.43	.41	.40	.39	.39
50	4.55	2.46	1.77	1.43	1.23	1.10	1.01	.94	.89	.85	.82	.80	.78	.77
75	6.82	3.69	2.66	2.14	1.84	1.65	1.51	1.41	1.34	1.28	1.23	1.20	1.17	1.15
100	9.10	4.92	3.54	2.86	2.46	2.19	2.01	1.88	1.78	1.70	1.64	1.60	1.56	1.53
200	18.19	9.83	7.07	5.71	4.91	4.38	4.02	3.75	3.56	3.40	3.28	3.19	3.11	3.05
300	27.28	14.75	10.61	8.56	7.36	6.57	6.03	5.63	5.33	5.10	4.92	4.78	4.66	4.57
400	36.37	19.66	14.14	11.42	9.81	8.76	8.04	7.50	7.11	6.80	6.56	6.37	6.21	6.09
500	45.46	24.58	17.68	14.27	12.26	10.95	10.04	9.38	8.88	8.50	8.20	7.98	7.76	7.61
600	54.55	29.49	21.21	17.12	14.72	13.14	12.05	11.25	10.66	10.20	9.84	9.55	9.32	9.13
700	63.64	34.40	24.74	19.98	17.17	15.33	14.06	13.13	12.43	11.90	11.47	11.14	10.87	10.65
800	72.73	39.32	28.28	22.83	19.62	17.52	16.07	15.00	14.21	13.59	13.11	12.73	12.42	12.17
900	81.82	44.23	31.81	25.68	22.07	19.71	18.07	16.88	15.98	15.29	14.75	14.32	13.97	13.69
1000	90.91	49.15	35.35	28.54	24.52	21.90	20.08	18.75	17.76	16.99	16.39	15.91	15.52	15.21
2000	181.82	98.29	70.69	57.07	49.04	43.80	40.16	37.50	35.51	33.98	32.77	31.81	31.04	30.42
3000	272.73	147.43	106.03	85.60	73.56	65.70	60.23	56.25	53.26	50.96	49.16	47.72	46.56	45.62
4000	363.64	196.57	141.37	114.14	98.08	87.60	80.31	75.00	71.02	67.95	65.54	63.62	62.08	60.83
5000	454.55	245.72	176.72	142.67	122.59	109.50	100.39	93.75	88.77	84.93	81.92	79.53	77.60	76.03
6000	545.46	294.86	212.06	171.20	147.11	131.40	120.46	112.50	106.52	101.92	98.31	95.43	93.12	91.24
7000	636.36	344.00	247.40	199.73	171.63	153.30	140.54	131.25	124.28	118.91	114.69	111.34	108.64	106.45
8000	727.27	393.14	282.74	228.27	196.15	175.20	160.61	150.00	142.03	135.89	131.08	127.24	124.16	121.65
9000	818.18	442.29	318.09	256.80	220.66	197.09	180.69	168.75	159.78	152.88	147.46	143.15	139.68	136.86
10000	909.09	491.43	353.43	285.33	245.18	218.99	200.77	187.50	177.54	169.86	163.84	159.05	155.20	152.06
11000	1000.00	540.57	388.77	313.86	269.70	240.89	220.84	206.25	195.29	186.85	180.23	174.96	170.72	167.27
12000	1090.91	589.71	424.11	342.40	294.22	262.79	240.92	225.00	213.04	203.83	196.61	190.86	186.24	182.47
13000	1181.81	638.86	459.46	370.93	318.74	284.69	261.00	243.75	230.80	220.82	212.99	206.77	201.75	197.68
14000	1272.72	688.00	494.80	399.46	343.25	306.59	281.07	262.50	248.55	237.81	229.38	222.67	217.27	212.89
15000	1363.63	737.14	530.14	428.00	367.77	328.49	301.15	281.25	266.30	254.79	245.76	238.58	232.79	228.09
16000	1454.54	786.28	565.48	456.53	392.29	350.39	321.22	300.00	284.06	271.78	262.15	254.48	248.31	243.30
17000	1545.45	835.43	600.83	485.06	416.81	372.29	341.30	318.75	301.81	288.76	278.53	270.39	263.83	258.50
18000	1636.36	884.57	636.17	513.59	441.32	394.18	361.38	337.50	319.56	305.75	294.91	286.29	279.35	273.71
19000	1727.26	933.71	671.51	542.13	465.84	416.08	381.45	356.25	337.32	322.73	311.30	302.20	294.87	288.92
20000	1818.17	982.85	706.85	570.66	490.36	437.98	401.53	375.00	355.07	339.72	327.68	318.10	310.39	304.12
21000	1909.08	1032.00	742.20	599.19	514.88	459.88	421.61	393.75	372.82	356.71	344.07	334.01	325.91	319.33
22000	1999.99	1081.14	777.54	627.72	539.40	481.78	441.68	412.50	390.58	373.69	360.45	349.91	341.43	334.53
23000	2090.90	1130.28	812.88	656.26	563.91	503.68	461.76	431.25	408.33	390.68	376.83	365.82	356.95	349.74
24000	2181.81	1179.42	848.22	684.79	588.43	525.58	481.83	450.00	426.08	407.66	393.22	381.72	372.47	364.94
25000	2272.72	1228.57	883.57	713.32	612.95	547.48	501.91	468.75	443.83	424.65	409.60	397.62	387.98	380.15
26000	2363.62	1277.71	918.91	741.86	637.47	569.37	521.99	487.50	461.59	441.63	425.98	413.53	403.50	395.36
27000	2454.53	1326.85	954.25	770.39	661.98	591.27	542.06	506.25	479.34	458.62	442.37	429.43	419.02	410.56
28000	2545.44	1375.99	989.59	798.92	686.50	613.17	562.14	525.00	497.09	475.61	458.75	445.34	434.54	425.77
29000	2636.35	1425.14	1024.94	827.45	711.02	635.07	582.22	543.75	514.85	492.59	475.14	461.24	450.06	440.97
30000	2727.26	1474.28	1060.28	855.99	735.54	656.97	602.29	562.50	532.60	509.58	491.52	477.15	465.58	456.18
31000	2818.17	1523.42	1095.62	884.52	760.06	678.87	622.37	581.25	550.35	526.56	507.90	493.05	481.10	471.39
32000	2909.07	1572.56	1130.96	913.05	784.57	700.77	642.44	600.00	568.11	543.55	524.29	508.96	496.62	486.59
33000	2999.98	1621.71	1166.31	941.58	809.09	722.67	662.52	618.75	585.86	560.53	540.67	524.86	512.14	501.80
34000	3090.89	1670.85	1201.65	970.12	833.61	744.57	682.60	637.50	603.61	577.52	557.05	540.77	527.66	517.00
35000	3181.80	1719.99	1236.99	998.65	858.13	766.46	702.67	656.25	621.37	594.51	573.44	556.67	543.18	532.21
36000	3272.71	1769.13	1272.33	1027.18	882.64	788.36	722.75	675.00	639.12	611.49	589.82	572.58	558.69	547.41
37000	3363.62	1818.28	1307.68	1055.72	907.16	810.26	742.83	693.75	656.87	628.48	606.21	588.48	574.21	562.62
38000	3454.52	1867.42	1343.02	1084.25	931.68	832.16	762.90	712.50	674.63	645.46	622.59	604.39	589.73	577.83
39000	3545.43	1916.56	1378.36	1112.78	956.20	854.06	782.98	731.25	692.38	662.45	638.97	620.29	605.25	593.03
40000	3636.34	1965.70	1413.70	1141.31	980.72	875.96	803.05	750.00	710.13	679.44	655.36	636.20	620.77	608.24
41000	3727.25	2014.85	1449.05	1169.85	1005.23	897.86	823.13	768.75	727.89	696.42	671.74	652.10	636.29	623.44
42000	3818.16	2063.99	1484.39	1198.38	1029.75	919.76	843.21	787.50	745.64	713.41	688.13	668.01	651.81	638.65
43000	3909.07	2113.13	1519.73	1226.91	1054.27	941.65	863.28	806.25	763.39	730.39	704.51	683.91	667.33	653.86
44000	3999.98	2162.27	1555.07	1255.44	1078.79	963.55	883.36	825.00	781.15	747.38	720.89	699.82	682.85	669.06
45000	4090.88	2211.42	1590.42	1283.98	1103.30	985.45	903.44	843.75	798.90	764.36	737.28	715.72	698.37	684.27
46000	4181.79	2260.56	1625.76	1312.51	1127.82	1007.35	923.51	862.50	816.65	781.35	753.66	731.63	713.89	699.47
47000	4272.70	2309.70	1661.10	1341.04	1152.34	1029.25	943.59	881.25	834.40	798.34	770.04	747.53	729.41	714.68
48000	4363.61	2358.84	1696.44	1369.57	1176.86	1051.15	963.66	900.00	852.16	815.32	786.43	763.44	744.92	729.88
49000	4454.52	2407.99	1731.79	1398.11	1201.38	1073.05	983.74	918.75	869.91	832.31	802.81	779.34	760.44	745.09
50000	4545.44	2457.13	1767.13	1426.64	1225.89	1094.95	1003.82	937.50	887.66	849.29	819.20	795.24	775.96	760.30
55000	4999.97	2702.84	1943.84	1569.30	1348.48	1204.44	1104.20	1031.25	976.43	934.22	901.12	874.77	853.56	836.33
60000	5454.51	2948.55	2120.55	1711.97	1471.07	1313.93	1204.58	1125.00	1065.20	1019.15	983.03	954.29	931.15	912.35
65000	5909.05	3194.27	2297.26	1854.63	1593.66	1423.43	1304.96	1218.75	1153.96	1104.08	1064.95	1033.82	1008.75	988.38
70000	6363.59	3439.98	2473.98	1997.29	1716.25	1532.92	1405.34	1312.50	1242.73	1189.01	1146.87	1113.34	1086.35	1064.41
75000	6818.14	3685.69	2650.69	2139.96	1838.84	1642.42	1505.72	1406.25	1331.49	1273.94	1228.79	1192.86	1163.94	1140.44
80000	7272.68	3931.40	2827.40	2282.62	1961.43	1751.91	1606.10	1500.00	1420.26	1358.87	1310.71	1272.39	1241.54	1216.47
85000	7727.22	4177.12	3004.10	2425.28	2084.01	1861.41	1706.49	1593.75	1509.03	1443.79	1392.63	1351.91	1319.13	1292.50
90000	8181.76	4422.83	3180.83	2567.95	2206.60	1970.90	1806.87	1687.50	1597.79	1528.72	1474.55	1431.44	1396.73	1368.53
95000	8636.30	4668.54	3357.54	2710.61	2329.19	2080.39	1907.25	1781.25	1686.56	1613.65	1556.47	1510.96	1474.33	1444.56
100000	9090.85	4914.25	3534.25	2853.28	2451.78	2189.89	2007.63	1875.00	1775.32	1698.58	1638.39	1590.48	1551.92	1520.59

TERM	15 Years	16 Years	17 Years	18 Years	19 Years	20 Years	21 Years	22 Years	23 Years	24 Years	25 Years	30 Years	35 Years	40 Years
AMOUNT														
5	.08	.08	.08	.08	.08	.08	.08	.08	.07	.07	.07	.07	.07	.07
10	.15	.15	.15	.15	.15	.15	.15	.15	.14	.14	.14	.14	.14	.14
15	.23	.23	.22	.22	.22	.22	.22	.22	.21	.21	.21	.21	.21	.21
25	.38	.37	.37	.37	.36	.36	.36	.36	.35	.35	.35	.35	.35	.35
50	.75	.74	.73	.73	.72	.71	.71	.71	.70	.70	.70	.69	.69	.69
75	1.13	1.11	1.10	1.09	1.08	1.07	1.06	1.06	1.05	1.05	1.05	1.04	1.03	1.03
100	1.50	1.48	1.46	1.45	1.43	1.42	1.42	1.41	1.40	1.40	1.39	1.38	1.37	1.37
200	2.99	2.95	2.92	2.89	2.86	2.84	2.83	2.81	2.80	2.79	2.78	2.76	2.74	2.74
300	4.49	4.43	4.37	4.33	4.29	4.26	4.24	4.22	4.20	4.18	4.17	4.13	4.11	4.10
400	5.98	5.90	5.83	5.77	5.72	5.68	5.65	5.62	5.60	5.58	5.56	5.51	5.48	5.47
500	7.48	7.37	7.29	7.21	7.15	7.10	7.06	7.02	6.99	6.97	6.95	6.88	6.85	6.84
600	8.97	8.85	8.74	8.66	8.58	8.52	8.47	8.43	8.39	8.36	8.34	8.26	8.22	8.20
700	10.47	10.32	10.20	10.10	10.01	9.94	9.88	9.83	9.79	9.75	9.72	9.63	9.59	9.57
800	11.96	11.80	11.66	11.54	11.44	11.36	11.29	11.24	11.19	11.15	11.11	11.01	10.96	10.94
900	13.46	13.27	13.11	12.98	12.87	12.78	12.70	12.64	12.58	12.54	12.50	12.38	12.33	12.30
1000	14.95	14.74	14.57	14.42	14.30	14.20	14.11	14.04	13.98	13.93	13.89	13.76	13.70	13.67
2000	29.90	29.48	29.13	28.84	28.60	28.39	28.22	28.08	27.96	27.86	27.77	27.51	27.39	27.34
3000	44.85	44.22	43.69	43.26	42.89	42.59	42.33	42.12	41.94	41.79	41.66	41.26	41.08	41.00
4000	59.80	58.96	58.26	57.68	57.19	56.78	56.44	56.16	55.92	55.71	55.54	55.01	54.77	54.67
5000	74.75	73.69	72.82	72.09	71.49	70.98	70.55	70.19	69.89	69.64	69.42	68.76	68.46	68.34
6000	89.70	88.43	87.38	86.51	85.78	85.17	84.66	84.23	83.87	83.57	83.31	82.51	82.16	82.00
7000	104.65	103.17	101.95	100.93	100.08	99.37	98.77	98.27	97.85	97.49	97.19	96.26	95.85	95.67
8000	119.60	117.91	116.51	115.35	114.37	113.56	112.88	112.31	111.83	111.42	111.08	110.01	109.54	109.34
9000	134.55	132.65	131.07	129.76	128.67	127.76	126.99	126.35	125.80	125.35	124.96	123.76	123.23	123.00
10000	149.50	147.38	145.64	144.18	142.97	141.95	141.10	140.38	139.78	139.27	138.84	137.51	136.92	136.67
11000	164.45	162.12	160.20	158.60	157.26	156.15	155.21	154.42	153.76	153.20	152.73	151.26	150.62	150.33
12000	179.40	176.86	174.76	173.02	171.56	170.34	169.32	168.46	167.74	167.13	166.61	165.01	164.31	164.00
13000	194.35	191.60	189.32	187.43	185.86	184.54	183.43	182.50	181.71	181.05	180.50	178.76	178.00	177.67
14000	209.30	206.34	203.89	201.85	200.15	198.73	197.54	196.54	195.69	194.98	194.38	192.51	191.69	191.33
15000	224.24	221.07	218.45	216.27	214.45	212.92	211.65	210.57	209.67	208.91	208.26	206.26	205.38	205.00
16000	239.19	235.81	233.01	230.69	228.74	227.12	225.76	224.61	223.65	222.83	222.15	220.01	219.08	218.67
17000	254.14	250.55	247.58	245.10	243.04	241.31	239.87	238.65	237.62	236.76	236.03	233.76	232.77	232.33
18000	269.09	265.29	262.14	259.52	257.34	255.51	253.98	252.69	251.60	250.69	249.91	247.51	246.46	246.00
19000	284.04	280.03	276.70	273.94	271.63	269.70	268.08	266.72	265.58	264.61	263.80	261.26	260.15	259.66
20000	298.99	294.76	291.27	288.36	285.93	283.90	282.19	280.76	279.56	278.54	277.68	275.01	273.84	273.33
21000	313.94	309.50	305.83	302.77	300.23	298.09	296.30	294.80	293.53	292.47	291.57	288.76	287.54	287.00
22000	328.89	324.24	320.39	317.19	314.52	312.29	310.41	308.84	307.51	306.39	305.45	302.51	301.23	300.66
23000	343.84	338.98	334.95	331.61	328.82	326.48	324.52	322.88	321.49	320.32	319.33	316.26	314.92	314.33
24000	358.79	353.72	349.52	346.03	343.11	340.68	338.63	336.91	335.47	334.25	333.22	330.01	328.61	328.00
25000	373.74	368.45	364.08	360.44	357.41	354.87	352.74	350.95	349.44	348.17	347.10	343.76	342.30	341.66
26000	388.69	383.19	378.64	374.86	371.71	369.07	366.85	364.99	363.42	362.10	360.99	357.51	356.00	355.33
27000	403.64	397.93	393.21	389.28	386.00	383.26	380.96	379.03	377.40	376.03	374.87	371.26	369.69	368.99
28000	418.59	412.67	407.77	403.70	400.30	397.46	395.07	393.07	391.38	389.95	388.75	385.02	383.38	382.66
29000	433.53	427.41	422.33	418.11	414.59	411.65	409.18	407.10	405.36	403.88	402.64	398.77	397.07	396.33
30000	448.48	442.14	436.90	432.53	428.89	425.84	423.29	421.14	419.33	417.81	416.52	412.52	410.76	409.99
31000	463.43	456.88	451.46	446.95	443.19	440.04	437.40	435.18	433.31	431.73	430.40	426.27	424.46	423.66
32000	478.38	471.62	466.02	461.37	457.48	454.23	451.51	449.22	447.29	445.66	444.29	440.02	438.15	437.33
33000	493.33	486.36	480.58	475.78	471.78	468.43	465.62	463.25	461.27	459.59	458.17	453.77	451.84	450.99
34000	508.28	501.10	495.15	490.20	486.08	482.62	479.73	477.29	475.24	473.52	472.06	467.52	465.53	464.66
35000	523.23	515.83	509.71	504.62	500.37	496.82	493.84	491.33	489.22	487.44	485.94	481.27	479.22	478.32
36000	538.18	530.57	524.27	519.04	514.67	511.01	507.95	505.37	503.20	501.37	499.82	495.02	492.91	491.99
37000	553.13	545.31	538.84	533.45	528.96	525.21	522.06	519.41	517.18	515.30	513.71	508.77	506.61	505.66
38000	568.08	560.05	553.40	547.87	543.26	539.40	536.16	533.44	531.15	529.22	527.59	522.52	520.30	519.32
39000	583.03	574.79	567.96	562.29	557.56	553.60	550.27	547.48	545.13	543.15	541.48	536.27	533.99	532.99
40000	597.98	589.52	582.53	576.71	571.85	567.79	564.38	561.52	559.11	557.08	555.36	550.02	547.68	546.66
41000	612.93	604.26	597.09	591.13	586.15	581.99	578.49	575.56	573.09	571.00	569.24	563.77	561.38	560.32
42000	627.88	619.00	611.65	605.54	600.45	596.18	592.60	589.60	587.06	584.93	583.13	577.52	575.07	573.99
43000	642.82	633.74	626.21	619.96	614.74	610.37	606.71	603.63	601.04	598.86	597.01	591.27	588.76	587.65
44000	657.77	648.48	640.78	634.38	629.04	624.57	620.82	617.67	615.02	612.78	610.90	605.02	602.45	601.32
45000	672.72	663.21	655.34	648.80	643.33	638.76	634.93	631.71	629.00	626.71	624.78	618.77	616.14	614.99
46000	687.67	677.95	669.90	663.21	657.63	652.96	649.04	645.75	642.97	640.64	638.66	632.52	629.84	628.65
47000	702.62	692.69	684.47	677.63	671.93	667.15	663.15	659.79	656.95	654.56	652.55	646.27	643.53	642.32
48000	717.57	707.43	699.03	692.05	686.22	681.35	677.26	673.82	670.93	668.49	666.43	660.02	657.22	655.99
49000	732.52	722.17	713.59	706.47	700.52	695.54	691.37	687.86	684.91	682.42	680.31	673.77	670.91	669.65
50000	747.47	736.90	728.16	720.88	714.81	709.74	705.48	701.90	698.88	696.34	694.20	687.52	684.60	683.32
55000	822.22	810.59	800.97	792.97	786.30	780.71	776.03	772.09	768.77	765.98	763.62	756.28	753.06	751.65
60000	896.96	884.28	873.79	865.06	857.78	851.68	846.57	842.28	838.66	835.61	833.04	825.03	821.52	819.98
65000	971.71	957.97	946.60	937.15	929.26	922.66	917.12	912.47	908.55	905.25	902.46	893.78	889.98	888.31
70000	1046.46	1031.66	1019.42	1009.23	1000.74	993.63	987.67	982.66	978.44	974.88	971.88	962.53	958.44	956.64
75000	1121.20	1105.35	1092.23	1081.32	1072.22	1064.60	1058.22	1052.85	1048.32	1044.51	1041.30	1031.28	1026.90	1024.97
80000	1195.95	1179.04	1165.05	1153.41	1143.70	1135.58	1128.76	1123.04	1118.21	1114.15	1110.71	1100.03	1095.36	1093.31
85000	1270.69	1252.73	1237.86	1225.50	1215.18	1206.55	1199.31	1193.22	1188.10	1183.78	1180.13	1168.79	1163.82	1161.64
90000	1345.44	1326.42	1310.68	1297.59	1286.66	1277.52	1269.86	1263.41	1257.99	1253.41	1249.55	1237.54	1232.28	1229.97
95000	1420.19	1400.11	1383.49	1369.67	1358.14	1348.50	1340.40	1333.60	1327.88	1323.05	1318.97	1306.29	1300.74	1298.30
100000	1494.93	1473.80	1456.31	1441.76	1429.63	1419.47	1410.95	1403.79	1397.76	1392.68	1388.39	1375.04	1369.20	1366.63

MONTHLY PAYMENT
REQUIRED TO AMORTIZE A LOAN

TERM AMOUNT	1 Year	2 Years	3 Years	4 Years	5 Years	6 Years	7 Years	8 Years	9 Years	10 Years	11 Years	12 Years	13 Years	14 Years
5	.46	.25	.18	.15	.13	.11	.11	.10	.09	.09	.09	.08	.08	.08
10	.91	.50	.36	.29	.25	.22	.21	.19	.18	.18	.17	.16	.16	.16
15	1.37	.74	.54	.43	.37	.33	.31	.29	.27	.26	.25	.24	.24	.23
25	2.28	1.23	.89	.72	.62	.55	.51	.47	.45	.43	.41	.40	.39	.39
50	4.55	2.46	1.77	1.43	1.23	1.10	1.01	.94	.89	.86	.82	.80	.78	.77
75	6.82	3.69	2.66	2.15	1.84	1.65	1.51	1.41	1.34	1.28	1.23	1.20	1.17	1.15
100	9.10	4.92	3.54	2.86	2.46	2.20	2.01	1.88	1.78	1.71	1.64	1.60	1.56	1.53
200	18.19	9.84	7.08	5.71	4.91	4.39	4.02	3.76	3.56	3.41	3.28	3.19	3.11	3.05
300	27.28	14.75	10.61	8.57	7.36	6.58	6.03	5.63	5.34	5.11	4.92	4.78	4.67	4.57
400	36.37	19.67	14.15	11.42	9.82	8.77	8.04	7.51	7.11	6.81	6.56	6.37	6.22	6.09
500	45.47	24.58	17.68	14.28	12.27	10.96	10.05	9.39	8.89	8.51	8.20	7.97	7.77	7.62
600	54.56	29.50	21.22	17.13	14.72	13.15	12.06	11.26	10.67	10.21	9.84	9.56	9.33	9.14
700	63.65	34.41	24.75	19.99	17.18	15.34	14.07	13.14	12.44	11.91	11.48	11.15	10.88	10.66
800	72.74	39.33	28.29	22.84	19.63	17.54	16.08	15.02	14.22	13.61	13.12	12.74	12.43	12.18
900	81.83	44.24	31.82	25.70	22.08	19.73	18.09	16.89	16.00	15.31	14.76	14.33	13.99	13.71
1000	90.93	49.16	35.36	28.55	24.54	21.92	20.10	18.77	17.77	17.01	16.40	15.93	15.54	15.23
2000	181.85	98.31	70.71	57.10	49.07	43.83	40.19	37.53	35.54	34.01	32.80	31.85	31.08	30.45
3000	272.77	147.47	106.07	85.64	73.60	65.74	60.28	56.30	53.31	51.01	49.20	47.77	46.61	45.67
4000	363.69	196.62	141.42	114.19	98.13	87.66	80.37	75.06	71.08	68.01	65.60	63.69	62.15	60.90
5000	454.61	245.78	176.78	142.73	122.66	109.57	100.46	93.83	88.85	85.01	82.00	79.61	77.69	76.12
6000	545.53	294.93	212.13	171.28	147.19	131.48	120.55	112.59	106.62	102.01	98.40	95.53	93.22	91.34
7000	636.45	344.09	247.49	199.82	171.72	153.39	140.64	131.36	124.38	119.02	114.80	111.45	108.76	106.57
8000	727.37	393.24	282.84	228.37	196.25	175.31	160.73	150.12	142.15	136.02	131.20	127.38	124.29	121.79
9000	818.29	442.40	318.20	256.92	220.78	197.22	180.82	168.89	159.92	153.02	147.60	143.30	139.83	137.01
10000	909.21	491.55	353.55	285.46	245.32	219.13	200.91	187.65	177.69	170.02	164.00	159.22	155.37	152.24
11000	1000.13	540.70	388.91	314.01	269.85	241.04	221.00	206.42	195.46	187.02	180.40	175.14	170.90	167.46
12000	1091.05	589.86	424.26	342.55	294.38	262.96	241.09	225.18	213.23	204.02	196.80	191.06	186.44	182.68
13000	1181.97	639.01	459.62	371.10	318.91	284.87	261.18	243.95	230.99	221.02	213.20	206.98	201.97	197.90
14000	1272.89	688.17	494.97	399.64	343.44	306.78	281.27	262.71	248.76	238.03	229.60	222.90	217.51	213.13
15000	1363.81	737.32	530.33	428.19	367.97	328.70	301.36	281.48	266.53	255.03	246.00	238.82	233.05	228.35
16000	1454.73	786.48	565.68	456.73	392.50	350.61	321.45	300.24	284.30	272.03	262.40	254.75	248.58	243.57
17000	1545.65	835.63	601.04	485.28	417.03	372.52	341.54	319.01	302.07	289.03	278.80	270.67	264.12	258.80
18000	1636.57	884.79	636.39	513.83	441.56	394.43	361.64	337.77	319.84	306.03	295.20	286.59	279.65	274.02
19000	1727.49	933.94	671.75	542.37	466.10	416.35	381.73	356.54	337.61	323.03	311.60	302.51	295.19	289.24
20000	1818.41	983.09	707.10	570.92	490.63	438.26	401.82	375.30	355.37	340.03	328.00	318.43	310.73	304.47
21000	1909.33	1032.25	742.46	599.46	515.16	460.17	421.91	394.06	373.14	357.04	344.40	334.35	326.26	319.69
22000	2000.25	1081.40	777.81	628.01	539.69	482.08	442.00	412.83	390.91	374.04	360.80	350.27	341.80	334.91
23000	2091.17	1130.56	813.17	656.55	564.22	504.00	462.09	431.59	408.68	391.04	377.20	366.19	357.33	350.13
24000	2182.09	1179.71	848.52	685.10	588.75	525.91	482.18	450.36	426.45	408.04	393.60	382.12	372.87	365.36
25000	2273.01	1228.87	883.88	713.64	613.28	547.82	502.27	469.12	444.22	425.04	410.00	398.04	388.41	380.58
26000	2363.93	1278.02	919.23	742.19	637.81	569.73	522.36	487.89	461.98	442.04	426.40	413.96	403.94	395.80
27000	2454.85	1327.18	954.59	770.74	662.34	591.65	542.45	506.65	479.75	459.04	442.80	429.88	419.48	411.03
28000	2545.77	1376.33	989.94	799.28	686.88	613.56	562.54	525.42	497.52	476.05	459.20	445.80	435.01	426.25
29000	2636.69	1425.48	1025.30	827.83	711.41	635.47	582.63	544.18	515.29	493.05	475.60	461.72	450.55	441.47
30000	2727.61	1474.64	1060.65	856.37	735.94	657.38	602.72	562.95	533.06	510.05	492.00	477.64	466.09	456.70
31000	2818.53	1523.79	1096.00	884.92	760.47	679.30	622.81	581.71	550.83	527.05	508.40	493.57	481.62	471.92
32000	2909.45	1572.95	1131.36	913.46	785.00	701.21	642.90	600.48	568.59	544.05	524.80	509.49	497.16	487.14
33000	3000.37	1622.10	1166.71	942.01	809.53	723.12	662.99	619.24	586.36	561.05	541.20	525.41	512.69	502.37
34000	3091.29	1671.26	1202.07	970.55	834.06	745.04	683.08	638.01	604.13	578.05	557.60	541.33	528.23	517.59
35000	3182.21	1720.41	1237.42	999.10	858.59	766.95	703.17	656.77	621.90	595.06	574.00	557.25	543.77	532.81
36000	3273.13	1769.57	1272.78	1027.65	883.12	788.86	723.27	675.54	639.67	612.06	590.40	573.17	559.30	548.03
37000	3364.05	1818.72	1308.13	1056.19	907.66	810.77	743.36	694.30	657.44	629.06	606.80	589.09	574.84	563.26
38000	3454.97	1867.87	1343.49	1084.74	932.19	832.69	763.45	713.07	675.21	646.06	623.20	605.01	590.37	578.48
39000	3545.89	1917.03	1378.84	1113.28	956.72	854.60	783.54	731.83	692.97	663.06	639.60	620.94	605.91	593.70
40000	3636.82	1966.18	1414.20	1141.83	981.25	876.51	803.63	750.59	710.74	680.06	656.00	636.86	621.45	608.93
41000	3727.74	2015.34	1449.55	1170.37	1005.78	898.42	823.72	769.36	728.51	697.06	672.40	652.78	636.98	624.15
42000	3818.66	2064.49	1484.91	1198.92	1030.31	920.34	843.81	788.12	746.28	714.07	688.80	668.70	652.52	639.37
43000	3909.58	2113.65	1520.26	1227.46	1054.84	942.25	863.90	806.89	764.05	731.07	705.20	684.62	668.05	654.60
44000	4000.50	2162.80	1555.62	1256.01	1079.37	964.16	883.99	825.65	781.82	748.07	721.60	700.54	683.59	669.82
45000	4091.42	2211.96	1590.97	1284.56	1103.90	986.07	904.08	844.42	799.58	765.07	738.00	716.46	699.13	685.04
46000	4182.34	2261.11	1626.33	1313.10	1128.44	1007.99	924.17	863.18	817.35	782.07	754.40	732.38	714.66	700.26
47000	4273.26	2310.26	1661.68	1341.65	1152.97	1029.90	944.26	881.95	835.12	799.07	770.80	748.31	730.20	715.49
48000	4364.18	2359.42	1697.04	1370.19	1177.50	1051.81	964.35	900.71	852.89	816.07	787.20	764.23	745.73	730.71
49000	4455.10	2408.57	1732.39	1398.74	1202.03	1073.73	984.44	919.48	870.66	833.08	803.60	780.15	761.27	745.93
50000	4546.02	2457.73	1767.75	1427.28	1226.56	1095.64	1004.53	938.24	888.43	850.08	820.00	796.07	776.81	761.16
55000	5000.62	2703.50	1944.52	1570.01	1349.22	1205.20	1104.99	1032.07	977.27	935.08	902.00	875.68	854.49	837.27
60000	5455.22	2949.27	2121.30	1712.74	1471.87	1314.77	1205.44	1125.89	1066.11	1020.09	984.00	955.28	932.17	913.39
65000	5909.82	3195.04	2298.07	1855.47	1594.53	1424.33	1305.89	1219.71	1154.95	1105.10	1066.00	1034.89	1009.85	989.50
70000	6364.42	3440.82	2474.84	1998.19	1717.18	1533.89	1406.34	1313.54	1243.80	1190.11	1148.00	1114.50	1087.53	1065.62
75000	6819.02	3686.59	2651.62	2140.92	1839.84	1643.46	1506.80	1407.36	1332.64	1275.11	1230.00	1194.10	1165.21	1141.73
80000	7273.63	3932.36	2828.39	2283.65	1962.49	1753.02	1607.25	1501.19	1421.48	1360.12	1312.00	1273.71	1242.89	1217.85
85000	7728.23	4178.13	3005.17	2426.38	2085.15	1862.58	1707.70	1595.01	1510.32	1445.13	1394.00	1353.31	1320.57	1293.96
90000	8182.83	4423.91	3181.94	2569.11	2207.80	1972.15	1808.16	1688.83	1599.16	1530.13	1476.00	1432.92	1398.25	1370.08
95000	8637.43	4669.68	3358.71	2711.83	2330.46	2081.71	1908.61	1782.66	1688.01	1615.14	1558.00	1512.53	1475.93	1446.19
100000	9092.03	4915.45	3535.49	2854.56	2453.12	2191.27	2009.06	1876.48	1776.85	1700.15	1640.00	1592.13	1553.61	1522.31

TERM	15 Years	16 Years	17 Years	18 Years	19 Years	20 Years	21 Years	22 Years	23 Years	24 Years	25 Years	30 Years	35 Years	40 Years
AMOUNT														
5	.08	.08	.08	.08	.08	.08	.08	.08	.07	.07	.07	.07	.07	.07
10	.15	.15	.15	.15	.15	.15	.15	.15	.14	.14	.14	.14	.14	.14
15	.23	.23	.22	.22	.22	.22	.22	.22	.21	.21	.21	.21	.21	.21
25	.38	.37	.37	.37	.36	.36	.36	.36	.35	.35	.35	.35	.35	.35
50	.75	.74	.73	.73	.72	.72	.71	.71	.70	.70	.70	.69	.69	.69
75	1.13	1.11	1.10	1.09	1.08	1.07	1.06	1.06	1.05	1.05	1.05	1.04	1.03	1.03
100	1.50	1.48	1.46	1.45	1.44	1.43	1.42	1.41	1.40	1.40	1.40	1.38	1.38	1.37
200	3.00	2.96	2.92	2.89	2.87	2.85	2.83	2.82	2.80	2.79	2.79	2.76	2.75	2.74
300	4.50	4.43	4.38	4.34	4.30	4.27	4.24	4.22	4.20	4.19	4.18	4.14	4.12	4.11
400	5.99	5.91	5.84	5.78	5.73	5.69	5.66	5.63	5.60	5.58	5.57	5.51	5.49	5.48
500	7.49	7.38	7.30	7.22	7.16	7.11	7.07	7.03	7.00	6.98	6.96	6.89	6.86	6.85
600	8.99	8.86	8.75	8.67	8.59	8.53	8.48	8.44	8.40	8.37	8.35	8.27	8.23	8.22
700	10.48	10.33	10.21	10.11	10.03	9.95	9.89	9.84	9.80	9.77	9.74	9.64	9.60	9.59
800	11.98	11.81	11.67	11.55	11.46	11.38	11.31	11.25	11.20	11.16	11.13	11.02	10.97	10.95
900	13.48	13.29	13.13	13.00	12.89	12.80	12.72	12.66	12.60	12.56	12.52	12.40	12.35	12.32
1000	14.97	14.76	14.59	14.44	14.32	14.22	14.13	14.06	14.00	13.95	13.91	13.78	13.72	13.69
2000	29.94	29.52	29.17	28.88	28.63	28.43	28.26	28.12	28.00	27.90	27.81	27.55	27.43	27.38
3000	44.91	44.27	43.75	43.31	42.95	42.65	42.39	42.18	42.00	41.84	41.72	41.32	41.14	41.07
4000	59.87	59.03	58.33	57.75	57.26	56.86	56.52	56.23	55.99	55.79	55.62	55.09	54.85	54.75
5000	74.84	73.78	72.91	72.18	71.58	71.07	70.65	70.29	69.99	69.74	69.52	68.86	68.57	68.44
6000	89.81	88.54	87.49	86.62	85.89	85.29	84.78	84.35	83.99	83.68	83.43	82.63	82.28	82.13
7000	104.77	103.30	102.07	101.06	100.21	99.50	98.90	98.40	97.98	97.63	97.33	96.40	95.99	95.81
8000	119.74	118.05	116.65	115.49	114.52	113.71	113.03	112.46	111.98	111.58	111.23	110.17	109.70	109.50
9000	134.71	132.81	131.24	129.93	128.84	127.93	127.16	126.52	125.98	125.52	125.14	123.94	123.42	123.19
10000	149.67	147.56	145.82	144.36	143.15	142.14	141.29	140.58	139.98	139.47	139.04	137.71	137.13	136.87
11000	164.64	162.32	160.40	158.80	157.47	156.35	155.42	154.63	153.97	153.41	152.94	151.48	150.84	150.56
12000	179.61	177.07	174.98	173.24	171.78	170.57	169.55	168.69	167.97	167.36	166.85	165.25	164.55	164.25
13000	194.57	191.83	189.56	187.67	186.10	184.78	183.68	182.75	181.97	181.31	180.75	179.02	178.27	177.94
14000	209.54	206.59	204.14	202.11	200.41	198.99	197.80	196.80	195.96	195.25	194.66	192.79	191.98	191.62
15000	224.51	221.34	218.72	216.54	214.73	213.21	211.93	210.86	209.96	209.20	208.56	206.56	205.69	205.31
16000	239.47	236.10	233.30	230.98	229.04	227.42	226.06	224.92	223.96	223.15	222.46	220.33	219.40	219.00
17000	254.44	250.85	247.88	245.42	243.36	241.63	240.19	238.98	237.95	237.09	236.37	234.10	233.12	232.68
18000	269.41	265.61	262.47	259.85	257.67	255.85	254.32	253.03	251.95	251.04	250.27	247.88	246.83	246.37
19000	284.37	280.37	277.05	274.29	271.99	270.06	268.45	267.09	265.95	264.99	264.17	261.65	260.54	260.06
20000	299.34	295.12	291.63	288.72	286.30	284.28	282.58	281.15	279.95	278.93	278.08	275.42	274.25	273.74
21000	314.31	309.88	306.21	303.16	300.62	298.49	296.70	295.20	293.94	292.88	291.98	289.19	287.97	287.43
22000	329.28	324.63	320.79	317.60	314.93	312.70	310.83	309.26	307.94	306.82	305.88	302.96	301.68	301.12
23000	344.24	339.39	335.37	332.03	329.25	326.92	324.96	323.32	321.94	320.77	319.79	316.73	315.39	314.80
24000	359.21	354.14	349.95	346.47	343.56	341.13	339.09	337.38	335.93	334.72	333.69	330.50	329.10	328.49
25000	374.18	368.90	364.53	360.90	357.88	355.34	353.22	351.43	349.93	348.66	347.59	344.27	342.82	342.18
26000	389.14	383.66	379.12	375.34	372.19	369.56	367.35	365.49	363.93	362.61	361.50	358.04	356.53	355.87
27000	404.11	398.41	393.70	389.78	386.51	383.77	381.48	379.55	377.92	376.56	375.40	371.81	370.24	369.55
28000	419.08	413.17	408.28	404.21	400.82	397.98	395.60	393.60	391.92	390.50	389.31	385.58	383.95	383.24
29000	434.04	427.92	422.86	418.65	415.14	412.20	409.73	407.66	405.92	404.45	403.21	399.35	397.67	396.93
30000	449.01	442.68	437.44	433.08	429.45	426.41	423.86	421.72	419.92	418.40	417.11	413.12	411.38	410.61
31000	463.98	457.44	452.02	447.52	443.76	440.62	437.99	435.78	433.91	432.34	431.02	426.89	425.09	424.30
32000	478.94	472.19	466.60	461.96	458.08	454.84	452.12	449.83	447.91	446.29	444.92	440.66	438.80	437.99
33000	493.91	486.95	481.18	476.39	472.39	469.05	466.25	463.89	461.91	460.23	458.82	454.43	452.52	451.67
34000	508.88	501.70	495.76	490.83	486.71	483.26	480.38	477.95	475.90	474.18	472.73	468.20	466.23	465.36
35000	523.84	516.46	510.35	505.26	501.02	497.48	494.50	492.00	489.90	488.13	486.63	481.98	479.94	479.05
36000	538.81	531.21	524.93	519.70	515.34	511.69	508.63	506.06	503.90	502.07	500.53	495.75	493.65	492.73
37000	553.78	545.97	539.51	534.14	529.65	525.90	522.76	520.12	517.89	516.02	514.44	509.52	507.37	506.42
38000	568.74	560.73	554.09	548.57	543.97	540.12	536.89	534.18	531.89	529.97	528.34	523.29	521.08	520.11
39000	583.71	575.48	568.67	563.01	558.28	554.33	551.02	548.23	545.89	543.91	542.24	537.06	534.79	533.80
40000	598.68	590.24	583.25	577.44	572.60	568.55	565.15	562.29	559.89	557.86	556.15	550.83	548.50	547.48
41000	613.65	604.99	597.83	591.88	586.91	582.76	579.27	576.35	573.88	571.80	570.05	564.60	562.22	561.17
42000	628.61	619.75	612.41	606.32	601.23	596.97	593.40	590.40	587.88	585.75	583.96	578.37	575.93	574.86
43000	643.58	634.51	626.99	620.75	615.54	611.19	607.53	604.46	601.88	599.70	597.86	592.14	589.64	588.54
44000	658.55	649.26	641.58	635.19	629.86	625.40	621.66	618.52	615.87	613.64	611.76	605.91	603.35	602.23
45000	673.51	664.02	656.16	649.62	644.17	639.61	635.79	632.58	629.87	627.59	625.67	619.68	617.07	615.92
46000	688.48	678.77	670.74	664.06	658.49	653.83	649.92	646.63	643.87	641.54	639.57	633.45	630.78	629.60
47000	703.45	693.53	685.32	678.49	672.80	668.04	664.05	660.69	657.86	655.48	653.47	647.22	644.49	643.29
48000	718.41	708.28	699.90	692.93	687.12	682.25	678.17	674.75	671.86	669.43	667.38	660.99	658.20	656.98
49000	733.38	723.04	714.48	707.37	701.43	696.47	692.30	688.80	685.86	683.38	681.28	674.76	671.92	670.66
50000	748.35	737.80	729.06	721.80	715.75	710.68	706.43	702.86	699.86	697.32	695.18	688.53	685.63	684.35
55000	823.18	811.58	801.97	793.98	787.32	781.75	777.07	773.15	769.84	767.05	764.70	757.39	754.19	752.79
60000	898.02	885.35	874.87	866.16	858.90	852.82	847.72	843.43	839.83	836.79	834.22	826.24	822.75	821.22
65000	972.85	959.13	947.78	938.34	930.47	923.88	918.36	913.72	909.81	906.52	903.74	895.09	891.32	889.66
70000	1047.68	1032.91	1020.69	1010.52	1002.04	994.95	989.00	984.00	979.80	976.25	973.26	963.95	959.88	958.09
75000	1122.52	1106.69	1093.59	1082.70	1073.62	1066.02	1059.64	1054.29	1049.78	1045.98	1042.77	1032.80	1028.44	1026.52
80000	1197.35	1180.47	1166.50	1154.88	1145.19	1137.09	1130.29	1124.57	1119.77	1115.71	1112.29	1101.65	1097.00	1094.96
85000	1272.19	1254.25	1239.40	1227.06	1216.77	1208.15	1200.93	1194.86	1189.75	1185.44	1181.81	1170.50	1165.57	1163.39
90000	1347.02	1328.03	1312.31	1299.24	1288.34	1279.22	1271.57	1265.15	1259.74	1255.18	1251.33	1239.36	1234.13	1231.83
95000	1421.85	1401.81	1385.21	1371.42	1359.91	1350.29	1342.22	1335.43	1329.72	1324.91	1320.84	1308.21	1302.69	1300.26
100000	1496.69	1475.59	1458.12	1443.60	1431.49	1421.36	1412.86	1405.72	1399.71	1394.64	1390.36	1377.06	1371.25	1368.70

MONTHLY PAYMENT
REQUIRED TO AMORTIZE A LOAN

TERM AMOUNT	1 Year	2 Years	3 Years	4 Years	5 Years	6 Years	7 Years	8 Years	9 Years	10 Years	11 Years	12 Years	13 Years	14 Years
5	.46	.25	.18	.15	.13	.11	.11	.10	.09	.09	.09	.08	.08	.08
10	.91	.50	.36	.29	.25	.22	.21	.19	.18	.18	.17	.16	.16	.16
15	1.37	.74	.54	.43	.37	.33	.31	.29	.27	.26	.25	.24	.24	.23
25	2.28	1.24	.89	.72	.62	.55	.51	.48	.45	.43	.42	.40	.40	.39
50	4.55	2.47	1.78	1.43	1.23	1.10	1.01	.95	.90	.86	.83	.80	.79	.77
75	6.83	3.70	2.66	2.15	1.85	1.65	1.52	1.42	1.34	1.28	1.24	1.20	1.18	1.15
100	9.10	4.93	3.55	2.86	2.46	2.20	2.02	1.89	1.79	1.71	1.65	1.60	1.57	1.53
200	18.20	9.85	7.09	5.72	4.92	4.40	4.03	3.77	3.57	3.42	3.30	3.20	3.13	3.06
300	27.30	14.77	10.63	8.58	7.38	6.60	6.05	5.65	5.35	5.12	4.94	4.80	4.69	4.59
400	36.39	19.69	14.17	11.44	9.84	8.79	8.06	7.53	7.14	6.83	6.59	6.40	6.25	6.12
500	45.49	24.61	17.71	14.30	12.30	10.99	10.08	9.42	8.92	8.54	8.24	8.00	7.81	7.65
600	54.59	29.53	21.25	17.16	14.76	13.19	12.09	11.30	10.70	10.24	9.88	9.60	9.37	9.18
700	63.68	34.45	24.79	20.02	17.21	15.38	14.11	13.18	12.49	11.95	11.53	11.20	10.93	10.71
800	72.78	39.37	28.33	22.88	19.67	17.58	16.12	15.06	14.27	13.66	13.18	12.79	12.49	12.24
900	81.88	44.29	31.87	25.74	22.13	19.78	18.14	16.95	16.05	15.36	14.82	14.39	14.05	13.77
1000	90.97	49.21	35.41	28.60	24.59	21.97	20.15	18.83	17.83	17.07	16.47	15.99	15.61	15.30
2000	181.94	98.41	70.81	57.20	49.17	43.94	40.30	37.65	35.66	34.13	32.93	31.98	31.21	30.59
3000	272.91	147.61	106.22	85.80	73.76	65.91	60.45	56.48	53.49	51.20	49.40	47.97	46.82	45.88
4000	363.88	196.81	141.62	114.39	98.34	87.88	80.60	75.30	71.32	68.26	65.86	63.95	62.42	61.17
5000	454.84	246.02	177.03	142.99	122.93	109.85	100.74	94.12	89.15	85.33	82.33	79.94	78.02	76.46
6000	545.81	295.22	212.43	171.59	147.51	131.81	120.89	112.95	106.98	102.39	98.79	95.93	93.63	91.76
7000	636.78	344.42	247.84	200.18	172.10	153.78	141.04	131.77	124.81	119.45	115.26	111.92	109.23	107.05
8000	727.75	393.62	283.24	228.78	196.68	175.75	161.19	150.60	142.64	136.52	131.72	127.90	124.83	122.34
9000	818.71	442.83	318.64	257.38	221.27	197.72	181.34	169.42	160.47	153.58	148.18	143.89	140.44	137.63
10000	909.68	492.03	354.05	285.98	245.85	219.69	201.48	188.24	178.30	170.65	164.65	159.88	156.04	152.92
11000	1000.65	541.23	389.45	314.57	270.43	241.65	221.63	207.07	196.13	187.71	181.11	175.87	171.64	168.22
12000	1091.62	590.43	424.86	343.17	295.02	263.62	241.78	225.89	213.96	204.78	197.58	191.85	187.25	183.51
13000	1182.58	639.64	460.26	371.77	319.60	285.59	261.93	244.72	231.79	221.84	214.04	207.84	202.85	198.80
14000	1273.55	688.84	495.67	400.36	344.19	307.56	282.08	263.54	249.62	238.90	230.51	223.83	218.45	214.09
15000	1364.52	738.04	531.07	428.96	368.77	329.53	302.22	282.36	267.45	255.97	246.97	239.82	234.06	229.38
16000	1455.49	787.24	566.48	457.56	393.36	351.49	322.37	301.19	285.28	273.03	263.44	255.80	249.66	244.68
17000	1546.45	836.44	601.88	486.15	417.94	373.46	342.52	320.01	303.11	290.10	279.90	271.79	265.27	259.97
18000	1637.42	885.65	637.28	514.75	442.53	395.43	362.67	338.84	320.94	307.16	296.36	287.78	280.87	275.26
19000	1728.39	934.85	672.69	543.35	467.11	417.40	382.81	357.66	338.77	324.23	312.83	303.76	296.47	290.55
20000	1819.36	984.05	708.09	571.95	491.70	439.37	402.96	376.48	356.59	341.29	329.29	319.75	312.08	305.84
21000	1910.33	1033.25	743.50	600.54	516.28	461.33	423.11	395.31	374.42	358.35	345.76	335.74	327.68	321.14
22000	2001.29	1082.46	778.90	629.14	540.86	483.30	443.26	414.13	392.25	375.42	362.22	351.73	343.28	336.43
23000	2092.26	1131.66	814.31	657.74	565.45	505.27	463.41	432.96	410.08	392.48	378.69	367.71	358.89	351.72
24000	2183.23	1180.86	849.71	686.33	590.03	527.24	483.55	451.78	427.91	409.55	395.15	383.70	374.49	367.01
25000	2274.20	1230.06	885.11	714.93	614.62	549.21	503.70	470.60	445.74	426.61	411.61	399.69	390.09	382.30
26000	2365.16	1279.27	920.52	743.53	639.20	571.17	523.85	489.43	463.57	443.67	428.08	415.68	405.70	397.60
27000	2456.13	1328.47	955.92	772.12	663.79	593.14	544.00	508.25	481.40	460.74	444.54	431.66	421.30	412.89
28000	2547.10	1377.67	991.33	800.72	688.37	615.11	564.15	527.08	499.23	477.80	461.01	447.65	436.90	428.18
29000	2638.07	1426.87	1026.73	829.32	712.96	637.08	584.29	545.90	517.06	494.87	477.47	463.64	452.51	443.47
30000	2729.03	1476.08	1062.14	857.92	737.54	659.05	604.44	564.72	534.89	511.93	493.94	479.63	468.11	458.76
31000	2820.00	1525.28	1097.54	886.51	762.13	681.01	624.59	583.55	552.72	529.00	510.40	495.61	483.72	474.06
32000	2910.97	1574.48	1132.95	915.11	786.71	702.98	644.74	602.37	570.55	546.06	526.87	511.60	499.32	489.35
33000	3001.94	1623.68	1168.35	943.71	811.29	724.95	664.89	621.20	588.38	563.12	543.33	527.59	514.92	504.64
34000	3092.90	1672.88	1203.75	972.30	835.88	746.92	685.03	640.02	606.21	580.19	559.79	543.57	530.53	519.93
35000	3183.87	1722.09	1239.16	1000.90	860.46	768.89	705.18	658.84	624.04	597.25	576.26	559.56	546.13	535.22
36000	3274.84	1771.29	1274.56	885.05	790.86	725.33	677.67	641.87	614.32	592.72	575.55	561.73	550.52	—
37000	3365.81	1820.49	1309.97	1058.09	909.63	812.82	745.48	696.49	659.70	631.38	609.19	591.54	577.34	565.81
38000	3456.78	1869.69	1345.37	1086.69	934.22	834.79	765.62	715.32	677.53	648.45	625.65	607.52	592.94	581.10
39000	3547.74	1918.90	1380.78	1115.29	958.80	856.76	785.77	734.14	695.35	665.51	642.12	623.51	608.54	596.39
40000	3638.71	1968.10	1416.18	1143.89	983.39	878.73	805.92	752.96	713.18	682.57	658.58	639.50	624.15	611.68
41000	3729.68	2017.30	1451.58	1172.48	1007.97	900.70	826.07	771.79	731.01	699.64	675.04	655.49	639.75	626.98
42000	3820.65	2066.50	1486.99	1201.08	1032.55	922.66	846.22	790.61	748.84	716.70	691.51	671.47	655.35	642.27
43000	3911.61	2115.71	1522.39	1229.68	1057.14	944.63	866.36	809.44	766.67	733.77	707.97	687.46	670.96	657.56
44000	4002.58	2164.91	1557.80	1258.27	1081.72	966.60	886.51	828.26	784.50	750.83	724.44	703.45	686.56	672.85
45000	4093.55	2214.11	1593.20	1286.87	1106.31	988.57	906.66	847.08	802.33	767.90	740.90	719.44	702.17	688.14
46000	4184.52	2263.31	1628.61	1315.47	1130.89	1010.54	926.81	865.91	820.16	784.96	757.37	735.42	717.77	703.44
47000	4275.48	2312.52	1664.01	1344.06	1155.48	1032.50	946.96	884.73	837.99	802.02	773.83	751.41	733.37	718.73
48000	4366.45	2361.72	1699.42	1372.66	1180.06	1054.47	967.10	903.56	855.82	819.09	790.30	767.40	748.98	734.02
49000	4457.42	2410.92	1734.82	1401.26	1204.65	1076.44	987.25	922.38	873.65	836.15	806.76	783.38	764.58	749.31
50000	4548.39	2460.12	1770.22	1429.86	1229.23	1098.41	1007.40	941.20	891.48	853.22	823.22	799.37	780.18	764.60
55000	5003.23	2706.13	1947.25	1572.84	1352.15	1208.25	1108.14	1035.32	980.63	938.54	905.55	879.31	858.20	841.06
60000	5458.06	2952.15	2124.27	1715.83	1475.08	1318.09	1208.88	1129.44	1069.77	1023.86	987.87	959.25	936.22	917.52
65000	5912.90	3198.16	2301.29	1858.81	1598.00	1427.93	1309.62	1223.56	1158.92	1109.18	1070.19	1039.18	1014.24	993.98
70000	6367.74	3444.17	2478.31	2001.80	1720.92	1537.77	1410.36	1317.68	1248.07	1194.50	1152.51	1119.12	1092.25	1070.44
75000	6822.58	3690.18	2655.33	2144.78	1843.84	1647.61	1511.10	1411.80	1337.22	1279.82	1234.83	1199.06	1170.27	1146.90
80000	7277.42	3936.19	2832.36	2287.77	1966.77	1757.45	1611.84	1505.92	1426.36	1365.14	1317.16	1278.99	1248.29	1223.36
85000	7732.25	4182.20	3009.38	2430.75	2089.69	1867.29	1712.58	1600.04	1515.51	1450.46	1399.48	1358.93	1326.31	1299.82
90000	8187.09	4428.22	3186.40	2573.74	2212.61	1977.13	1813.32	1694.16	1604.66	1535.79	1481.80	1438.87	1404.33	1376.28
95000	8641.93	4674.23	3363.42	2716.72	2335.53	2086.97	1914.05	1788.28	1693.81	1621.11	1564.12	1518.80	1482.34	1452.74
100000	9096.77	4920.24	3540.44	2859.71	2458.46	2196.81	2014.79	1882.40	1782.95	1706.43	1646.44	1598.74	1560.36	1529.20

TERM AMOUNT	15 Years	16 Years	17 Years	18 Years	19 Years	20 Years	21 Years	22 Years	23 Years	24 Years	25 Years	30 Years	35 Years	40 Years
5	.08	.08	.08	.08	.08	.08	.08	.08	.08	.08	.07	.07	.07	.07
10	.16	.15	.15	.15	.15	.15	.15	.15	.15	.15	.14	.14	.14	.14
15	.23	.23	.22	.22	.22	.22	.22	.22	.22	.22	.21	.21	.21	.21
25	.38	.38	.37	.37	.36	.36	.36	.36	.36	.36	.35	.35	.35	.35
50	.76	.75	.74	.73	.72	.72	.72	.71	.71	.71	.70	.70	.69	.69
75	1.13	1.12	1.10	1.09	1.08	1.08	1.07	1.07	1.06	1.06	1.05	1.04	1.04	1.04
100	1.51	1.49	1.47	1.46	1.44	1.43	1.43	1.42	1.41	1.41	1.40	1.39	1.38	1.38
200	3.01	2.97	2.94	2.91	2.88	2.86	2.85	2.83	2.82	2.81	2.80	2.78	2.76	2.76
300	4.52	4.45	4.40	4.36	4.32	4.29	4.27	4.25	4.23	4.21	4.20	4.16	4.14	4.14
400	6.02	5.94	5.87	5.81	5.76	5.72	5.69	5.66	5.63	5.61	5.60	5.55	5.52	5.51
500	7.52	7.42	7.33	7.26	7.20	7.15	7.11	7.07	7.04	7.02	7.00	6.93	6.90	6.89
600	9.03	8.90	8.80	8.71	8.64	8.58	8.53	8.49	8.45	8.42	8.39	8.32	8.28	8.27
700	10.53	10.38	10.26	10.16	10.08	10.01	9.95	9.90	9.86	9.82	9.79	9.70	9.66	9.64
800	12.03	11.87	11.73	11.61	11.52	11.44	11.37	11.31	11.26	11.22	11.19	11.09	11.04	11.02
900	13.54	13.35	13.19	13.06	12.96	12.87	12.79	12.73	12.67	12.63	12.59	12.47	12.42	12.40
1000	15.04	14.83	14.66	14.51	14.39	14.29	14.21	14.14	14.08	14.03	13.99	13.86	13.80	13.77
2000	30.08	29.66	29.31	29.02	28.78	28.58	28.41	28.27	28.15	28.05	27.97	27.71	27.59	27.54
3000	45.12	44.49	43.97	43.53	43.17	42.87	42.62	42.41	42.23	42.08	41.95	41.56	41.39	41.31
4000	60.15	59.31	58.62	58.04	57.56	57.16	56.82	56.54	56.30	56.10	55.93	55.41	55.18	55.08
5000	75.19	74.14	73.27	72.55	71.95	71.45	71.03	70.68	70.38	70.13	69.92	69.26	68.98	68.85
6000	90.23	88.97	87.93	87.06	86.34	85.74	85.23	84.81	84.45	84.15	83.90	83.11	82.77	82.62
7000	105.26	103.80	102.58	101.57	100.73	100.03	99.44	98.94	98.53	98.18	97.88	96.97	96.57	96.39
8000	120.30	118.62	117.24	116.08	115.12	114.32	113.64	113.08	112.60	112.20	111.86	110.82	110.36	110.16
9000	135.34	133.45	131.89	130.59	129.51	128.61	127.85	127.21	126.68	126.23	125.85	124.67	124.16	123.93
10000	150.38	148.28	146.54	145.10	143.90	142.90	142.05	141.35	140.75	140.25	139.83	138.52	137.95	137.70
11000	165.41	163.11	161.20	159.61	158.29	157.18	156.26	155.48	154.83	154.28	153.81	152.37	151.74	151.47
12000	180.45	177.93	175.85	174.12	172.68	171.47	170.46	169.62	168.90	168.30	167.79	166.22	165.54	165.24
13000	195.49	192.76	190.50	188.63	187.07	185.76	184.67	183.75	182.98	182.33	181.78	180.07	179.33	179.01
14000	210.52	207.59	205.16	203.14	201.46	200.05	198.87	197.88	197.05	196.35	195.76	193.93	193.13	192.78
15000	225.56	222.41	219.81	217.65	215.85	214.34	213.08	212.02	211.13	210.37	209.74	207.78	206.92	206.55
16000	240.60	237.24	234.47	232.16	230.24	228.63	227.28	226.15	225.20	224.40	223.72	221.63	220.72	220.32
17000	255.64	252.07	249.12	246.67	244.63	242.92	241.49	240.29	239.28	238.42	237.71	235.48	234.51	234.09
18000	270.67	266.90	263.77	261.18	259.02	257.21	255.69	254.42	253.35	252.45	251.69	249.33	248.31	247.86
19000	285.71	281.72	278.43	275.69	273.40	271.50	269.90	268.55	267.42	266.47	265.67	263.18	262.10	261.63
20000	300.75	296.55	293.08	290.20	287.79	285.79	284.10	282.69	281.50	280.50	279.65	277.03	275.90	275.40
21000	315.78	311.38	307.73	304.71	302.18	300.07	298.31	296.82	295.57	294.52	293.64	290.89	289.69	289.17
22000	330.82	326.21	322.39	319.22	316.57	314.36	312.51	310.96	309.65	308.55	307.62	304.74	303.48	302.94
23000	345.86	341.03	337.04	333.73	330.96	328.65	326.72	325.09	323.72	322.57	321.60	318.59	317.28	316.71
24000	360.90	355.86	351.70	348.24	345.35	342.94	340.92	339.23	337.80	336.60	335.58	332.44	331.07	330.48
25000	375.93	370.69	366.35	362.75	359.74	357.23	355.13	353.36	351.87	350.62	349.57	346.29	344.87	344.24
26000	390.97	385.51	381.00	377.25	374.13	371.52	369.33	367.49	365.95	364.65	363.55	360.14	358.66	358.01
27000	406.01	400.34	395.66	391.76	388.52	385.81	383.54	381.63	380.02	378.67	377.53	373.99	372.46	371.78
28000	421.04	415.17	410.31	406.27	402.91	400.10	397.74	395.76	394.10	392.70	391.51	387.85	386.25	385.55
29000	436.08	430.00	424.96	420.78	417.30	414.39	411.95	409.90	408.17	406.72	405.50	401.70	400.05	399.32
30000	451.12	444.82	439.62	435.29	431.69	428.68	426.15	424.03	422.25	420.74	419.48	415.55	413.84	413.09
31000	466.15	459.65	454.27	449.80	446.08	442.96	440.36	438.16	436.32	434.77	433.46	429.40	427.64	426.86
32000	481.19	474.48	468.93	464.31	460.47	457.25	454.56	452.30	450.40	448.79	447.44	443.25	441.43	440.63
33000	496.23	489.31	483.58	478.82	474.86	471.54	468.76	466.43	464.47	462.82	461.43	457.10	455.22	454.40
34000	511.27	504.13	498.23	493.33	489.25	485.83	482.97	480.57	478.55	476.84	475.41	470.96	469.02	468.17
35000	526.30	518.96	512.89	507.84	503.64	500.12	497.17	494.70	492.62	490.87	489.39	484.81	482.81	481.94
36000	541.34	533.79	527.54	522.35	518.03	514.41	511.38	508.84	506.70	504.89	503.37	498.66	496.61	495.71
37000	556.38	548.61	542.19	536.86	532.41	528.70	525.58	522.97	520.77	518.92	517.36	512.51	510.40	509.48
38000	571.41	563.44	556.85	551.37	546.80	542.99	539.79	537.10	534.84	532.94	531.34	526.36	524.20	523.25
39000	586.45	578.27	571.50	565.88	561.19	557.28	553.99	551.24	548.92	546.97	545.32	540.21	537.99	537.02
40000	601.49	593.10	586.16	580.39	575.58	571.57	568.20	565.37	562.99	560.99	559.30	554.06	551.79	550.79
41000	616.53	607.92	600.81	594.90	589.97	585.85	582.40	579.51	577.07	575.02	573.29	567.92	565.58	564.56
42000	631.56	622.75	615.46	609.41	604.36	600.14	596.61	593.64	591.14	589.04	587.27	581.77	579.38	578.33
43000	646.60	637.58	630.12	623.92	618.75	614.43	610.81	607.77	605.22	603.07	601.25	595.62	593.17	592.10
44000	661.64	652.41	644.77	638.43	633.14	628.72	625.02	621.91	619.29	617.09	615.23	609.47	606.96	605.87
45000	676.67	667.23	659.42	652.94	647.53	643.01	639.22	636.04	633.37	631.11	629.22	623.32	620.76	619.64
46000	691.71	682.06	674.08	667.45	661.92	657.30	653.43	650.18	647.44	645.14	643.20	637.17	634.55	633.41
47000	706.75	696.89	688.73	681.96	676.31	671.59	667.63	664.31	661.52	659.16	657.18	651.02	648.35	647.18
48000	721.79	711.72	703.39	696.47	690.70	685.88	681.84	678.45	675.59	673.19	671.16	664.88	662.14	660.95
49000	736.82	726.54	718.04	710.98	705.09	700.17	696.04	692.58	689.67	687.21	685.14	678.73	675.94	674.72
50000	751.86	741.37	732.69	725.49	719.48	714.46	710.25	706.71	703.74	701.24	699.13	692.58	689.73	688.48
55000	827.04	815.51	805.96	798.03	791.42	785.90	781.27	777.38	774.12	771.36	769.04	761.84	758.70	757.33
60000	902.23	889.64	879.23	870.58	863.37	857.35	852.30	848.06	844.49	841.48	838.95	831.09	827.68	826.18
65000	977.42	963.78	952.50	943.13	935.32	928.79	923.32	918.73	914.86	911.61	908.86	900.35	896.65	895.03
70000	1052.60	1037.92	1025.77	1015.68	1007.27	1000.24	994.34	989.40	985.24	981.73	978.78	969.61	965.62	963.88
75000	1127.79	1112.05	1099.04	1088.23	1079.21	1071.68	1065.37	1060.07	1055.61	1051.85	1048.69	1038.87	1034.60	1032.72
80000	1202.97	1186.19	1172.31	1160.77	1151.16	1143.13	1136.39	1130.74	1125.98	1121.98	1118.60	1108.12	1103.57	1101.57
85000	1278.16	1260.33	1245.57	1233.32	1223.11	1214.57	1207.42	1201.41	1196.36	1192.10	1188.51	1177.38	1172.54	1170.42
90000	1353.34	1334.46	1318.84	1305.87	1295.06	1286.02	1278.44	1272.08	1266.73	1262.22	1258.43	1246.64	1241.51	1239.27
95000	1428.53	1408.60	1392.11	1378.42	1367.00	1357.46	1349.46	1342.75	1337.10	1332.35	1328.34	1315.90	1310.49	1308.12
100000	1503.71	1482.73	1465.38	1450.97	1438.95	1428.91	1420.49	1413.42	1407.48	1402.47	1398.25	1385.15	1379.46	1376.96

MONTHLY PAYMENT
REQUIRED TO AMORTIZE A LOAN

TERM AMOUNT	1 Year	2 Years	3 Years	4 Years	5 Years	6 Years	7 Years	8 Years	9 Years	10 Years	11 Years	12 Years	13 Years	14 Years
5	.46	.25	.18	.15	.13	.12	.11	.10	.09	.09	.09	.09	.08	.08
10	.92	.50	.36	.29	.25	.23	.21	.19	.18	.18	.17	.17	.16	.16
15	1.37	.74	.54	.43	.37	.34	.31	.29	.27	.26	.25	.25	.24	.24
25	2.28	1.24	.89	.72	.62	.56	.51	.48	.45	.43	.42	.41	.40	.39
50	4.56	2.47	1.78	1.44	1.24	1.11	1.02	.95	.90	.86	.83	.81	.79	.77
75	6.83	3.70	2.66	2.15	1.85	1.66	1.52	1.42	1.35	1.29	1.24	1.21	1.18	1.16
100	9.11	4.93	3.55	2.87	2.47	2.21	2.03	1.89	1.79	1.72	1.66	1.61	1.57	1.54
200	18.21	9.86	7.10	5.73	4.93	4.41	4.05	3.78	3.58	3.43	3.31	3.22	3.14	3.08
300	27.31	14.78	10.64	8.60	7.40	6.61	6.07	5.67	5.37	5.14	4.96	4.82	4.71	4.61
400	36.41	19.71	14.19	11.46	9.86	8.81	8.09	7.56	7.16	6.86	6.62	6.43	6.27	6.15
500	45.51	24.63	17.73	14.33	12.32	11.02	10.11	9.45	8.95	8.57	8.27	8.03	7.84	7.69
600	54.61	29.56	21.28	17.19	14.79	13.22	12.13	11.33	10.74	10.28	9.92	9.64	9.41	9.22
700	63.72	34.48	24.82	20.06	17.25	15.42	14.15	13.22	12.53	11.99	11.58	11.24	10.97	10.76
800	72.82	39.41	28.37	22.92	19.72	17.62	16.17	15.11	14.32	13.71	13.23	12.85	12.54	12.29
900	81.92	44.33	31.91	25.79	22.18	19.83	18.19	17.00	16.11	15.42	14.88	14.45	14.11	13.83
1000	91.02	49.26	35.46	28.65	24.64	22.03	20.21	18.89	17.90	17.13	16.53	16.06	15.68	15.37
2000	182.04	98.51	70.91	57.30	49.28	44.05	40.42	37.77	35.79	34.26	33.06	32.11	31.35	30.73
3000	273.05	147.76	106.37	85.95	73.92	66.08	60.62	56.65	53.68	51.39	49.59	48.17	47.02	46.09
4000	364.07	197.01	141.82	114.60	98.56	88.10	80.83	75.54	71.57	68.51	66.12	64.22	62.69	61.45
5000	455.08	246.26	177.27	143.25	123.20	110.12	101.03	94.42	89.46	85.64	82.65	80.27	78.36	76.81
6000	546.10	295.51	212.73	171.90	147.83	132.15	121.24	113.30	107.35	102.77	99.18	96.33	94.03	92.17
7000	637.11	344.76	248.18	200.54	172.47	154.17	141.44	132.19	125.24	119.89	115.71	112.38	109.70	107.53
8000	728.13	394.01	283.64	229.19	197.11	176.19	161.65	151.07	143.13	137.02	132.24	128.43	125.37	122.89
9000	819.14	443.26	319.09	257.84	221.75	198.22	181.85	169.95	161.02	154.15	148.77	144.49	141.05	138.25
10000	910.16	492.51	354.54	286.49	246.39	220.24	202.06	188.84	178.91	171.28	165.29	160.54	156.72	153.62
11000	1001.17	541.76	390.00	315.14	271.02	242.26	222.26	207.72	196.80	188.40	181.82	176.59	172.39	168.98
12000	1092.19	591.01	425.45	343.79	295.66	264.29	242.47	226.60	214.69	205.53	198.35	192.65	188.06	184.34
13000	1183.20	640.26	460.91	372.44	320.30	286.31	262.67	245.49	232.58	222.66	214.88	208.70	203.73	199.70
14000	1274.22	689.51	496.36	401.08	344.94	308.33	282.88	264.37	250.47	239.78	231.41	224.75	219.40	215.06
15000	1365.23	738.76	531.81	429.73	369.58	330.36	303.08	283.25	268.36	256.91	247.94	240.81	235.07	230.42
16000	1456.25	788.01	567.27	458.38	394.21	352.38	323.29	302.14	286.26	274.04	264.47	256.86	250.74	245.78
17000	1547.26	837.26	602.72	487.03	418.85	374.40	343.50	321.02	304.15	291.17	281.00	272.91	266.42	261.14
18000	1638.28	886.51	638.18	515.68	443.49	396.43	363.70	339.90	322.04	308.29	297.53	288.97	282.09	276.50
19000	1729.29	935.76	673.63	544.33	468.13	418.45	383.91	358.79	339.93	325.42	314.06	305.02	297.76	291.86
20000	1820.31	985.01	709.08	572.98	492.77	440.48	404.11	377.67	357.82	342.55	330.58	321.07	313.43	307.23
21000	1911.32	1034.26	744.54	601.62	517.40	462.50	424.32	396.55	375.71	359.67	347.11	337.13	329.10	322.59
22000	2002.34	1083.51	779.99	630.27	542.04	484.52	444.52	415.44	393.60	376.80	363.64	353.18	344.77	337.95
23000	2093.35	1132.76	815.45	658.92	566.68	506.55	464.73	434.32	411.49	393.93	380.17	369.24	360.44	353.31
24000	2184.37	1182.01	850.90	687.57	591.32	528.57	484.93	453.20	429.38	411.06	396.70	385.29	376.11	368.67
25000	2275.38	1231.26	886.35	716.22	615.96	550.59	505.14	472.09	447.27	428.18	413.23	401.34	391.79	384.03
26000	2366.40	1280.51	921.81	744.87	640.59	572.62	525.34	490.97	465.16	445.31	429.76	417.40	407.46	399.39
27000	2457.41	1329.76	957.26	773.51	665.23	594.64	545.55	509.85	483.05	462.44	446.29	433.45	423.13	414.75
28000	2548.43	1379.01	992.72	802.16	689.87	616.66	565.75	528.74	500.94	479.56	462.82	449.50	438.80	430.11
29000	2639.44	1428.26	1028.17	830.81	714.51	638.69	585.96	547.62	518.83	496.69	479.34	465.56	454.47	445.47
30000	2730.46	1477.51	1063.62	859.46	739.15	660.71	606.16	566.50	536.72	513.82	495.87	481.61	470.14	460.84
31000	2821.47	1526.76	1099.08	888.11	763.78	682.73	626.37	585.39	554.61	530.95	512.40	497.66	485.81	476.20
32000	2912.49	1576.01	1134.53	916.76	788.42	704.76	646.57	604.27	572.51	548.07	528.93	513.72	501.48	491.56
33000	3003.50	1625.26	1169.99	945.41	813.06	726.78	666.78	623.15	590.40	565.20	545.46	529.77	517.16	506.92
34000	3094.52	1674.51	1205.44	974.05	837.70	748.80	686.99	642.04	608.29	582.33	561.99	545.82	532.83	522.28
35000	3185.53	1723.76	1240.89	1002.70	862.34	770.83	707.19	660.92	626.18	599.45	578.52	561.88	548.50	537.64
36000	3276.55	1773.02	1276.35	1031.35	886.97	792.85	727.40	679.80	644.07	616.58	595.05	577.93	564.17	553.00
37000	3367.56	1822.27	1311.80	1060.00	911.61	814.88	747.60	698.69	661.96	633.71	611.58	593.98	579.84	568.36
38000	3458.58	1871.52	1347.26	1088.65	936.25	836.90	767.81	717.57	679.85	650.84	628.11	610.04	595.51	583.72
39000	3549.59	1920.77	1382.71	1117.30	960.89	858.92	788.01	736.45	697.74	667.96	644.63	626.09	611.18	599.09
40000	3640.61	1970.02	1418.16	1145.95	985.53	880.95	808.22	755.34	715.63	685.09	661.16	642.14	626.85	614.45
41000	3731.62	2019.27	1453.62	1174.59	1010.16	902.97	828.42	774.22	733.52	702.22	677.69	658.20	642.52	629.81
42000	3822.64	2068.52	1489.07	1203.24	1034.80	924.99	848.63	793.10	751.41	719.34	694.22	674.25	658.20	645.17
43000	3913.65	2117.77	1524.53	1231.89	1059.44	947.02	868.83	811.99	769.30	736.47	710.75	690.31	673.87	660.53
44000	4004.67	2167.02	1559.98	1260.54	1084.08	969.04	889.04	830.87	787.19	753.60	727.28	706.36	689.54	675.89
45000	4095.68	2216.27	1595.43	1289.19	1108.72	991.06	909.24	849.75	805.08	770.73	743.81	722.41	705.21	691.25
46000	4186.70	2265.52	1630.89	1317.84	1133.35	1013.09	929.45	868.64	822.97	787.85	760.34	738.47	720.88	706.61
47000	4277.71	2314.77	1666.34	1346.49	1157.99	1035.11	949.65	887.52	840.86	804.98	776.87	754.52	736.55	721.97
48000	4368.73	2364.02	1701.80	1375.14	1182.63	1057.13	969.86	906.40	858.76	822.11	793.39	770.57	752.22	737.33
49000	4459.74	2413.27	1737.25	1403.78	1207.27	1079.16	990.06	925.29	876.65	839.23	809.92	786.63	767.89	752.70
50000	4550.76	2462.52	1772.70	1432.43	1231.91	1101.18	1010.27	944.17	894.54	856.36	826.45	802.68	783.57	768.06
55000	5005.83	2708.77	1949.97	1575.67	1355.10	1211.30	1111.30	1038.59	983.99	942.00	909.10	882.95	861.92	844.86
60000	5460.91	2955.02	2127.24	1718.92	1478.29	1321.42	1212.32	1133.00	1073.44	1027.63	991.74	963.21	940.28	921.67
65000	5915.98	3201.27	2304.51	1862.16	1601.48	1431.53	1313.35	1227.42	1162.90	1113.27	1074.39	1043.48	1018.63	998.47
70000	6371.06	3447.52	2481.78	2005.40	1724.67	1541.65	1414.38	1321.83	1252.35	1198.90	1157.03	1123.75	1096.99	1075.28
75000	6826.13	3693.78	2659.05	2148.64	1847.86	1651.77	1515.40	1416.25	1341.80	1284.54	1239.68	1204.02	1175.35	1152.08
80000	7281.21	3940.03	2836.32	2291.89	1971.05	1761.89	1616.43	1510.67	1431.26	1370.18	1322.32	1284.28	1253.70	1228.89
85000	7736.28	4186.28	3013.59	2435.13	2094.24	1872.00	1717.46	1605.08	1520.71	1455.81	1404.97	1364.55	1332.06	1305.69
90000	8191.36	4432.53	3190.86	2578.37	2217.43	1982.12	1818.48	1699.50	1610.16	1541.45	1487.61	1444.82	1410.41	1382.50
95000	8646.43	4678.78	3368.13	2721.61	2340.62	2092.24	1919.51	1793.92	1699.61	1627.08	1570.26	1525.09	1488.77	1459.30
100000	9101.51	4925.03	3545.40	2864.86	2463.81	2202.36	2020.54	1888.33	1789.07	1712.72	1652.90	1605.35	1567.13	1536.11

TERM	15 Years	16 Years	17 Years	18 Years	19 Years	20 Years	21 Years	22 Years	23 Years	24 Years	25 Years	30 Years	35 Years	40 Years
AMOUNT														
5	.08	.08	.08	.08	.08	.08	.08	.08	.08	.08	.08	.07	.07	.07
10	.16	.15	.15	.15	.15	.15	.15	.15	.15	.15	.15	.14	.14	.14
15	.23	.23	.23	.22	.22	.22	.22	.22	.22	.22	.22	.21	.21	.21
25	.38	.38	.37	.37	.37	.36	.36	.36	.36	.36	.36	.35	.35	.35
50	.76	.75	.74	.74	.73	.73	.72	.72	.72	.71	.71	.71	.70	.70
75	1.14	1.12	1.11	1.10	1.09	1.08	1.08	1.07	1.07	1.06	1.06	1.05	1.05	1.04
100	1.52	1.49	1.48	1.46	1.45	1.44	1.43	1.43	1.42	1.42	1.41	1.40	1.39	1.39
200	3.03	2.98	2.95	2.92	2.90	2.88	2.86	2.85	2.84	2.83	2.82	2.79	2.78	2.78
300	4.54	4.47	4.42	4.38	4.34	4.31	4.29	4.27	4.25	4.24	4.22	4.18	4.17	4.16
400	6.05	5.96	5.90	5.84	5.79	5.75	5.72	5.69	5.67	5.65	5.63	5.58	5.56	5.55
500	7.56	7.45	7.37	7.30	7.24	7.19	7.15	7.11	7.08	7.06	7.04	6.97	6.94	6.93
600	9.07	8.94	8.84	8.76	8.68	8.62	8.57	8.53	8.50	8.47	8.44	8.36	8.33	8.32
700	10.58	10.43	10.31	10.21	10.13	10.06	10.00	9.95	9.91	9.88	9.85	9.76	9.72	9.70
800	12.09	11.92	11.79	11.67	11.58	11.50	11.43	11.37	11.33	11.29	11.25	11.15	11.11	11.09
900	13.60	13.41	13.26	13.13	13.02	12.93	12.86	12.80	12.74	12.70	12.66	12.54	12.49	12.47
1000	15.11	14.90	14.73	14.59	14.47	14.37	14.29	14.22	14.16	14.11	14.07	13.94	13.88	13.86
2000	30.22	29.80	29.46	29.17	28.93	28.73	28.57	28.43	28.31	28.21	28.13	27.87	27.76	27.71
3000	45.33	44.70	44.18	43.76	43.40	43.10	42.85	42.64	42.46	42.31	42.19	41.80	41.63	41.56
4000	60.43	59.60	58.91	58.34	57.86	57.46	57.13	56.85	56.62	56.42	56.25	55.73	55.51	55.41
5000	75.54	74.50	73.64	72.92	72.33	71.83	71.41	71.06	70.77	70.52	70.31	69.67	69.39	69.27
6000	90.65	89.40	88.36	87.51	86.79	86.19	85.69	85.27	84.92	84.62	84.37	83.60	83.26	83.12
7000	105.76	104.30	103.09	102.09	101.25	100.56	99.97	99.48	99.07	98.73	98.43	97.53	97.14	96.97
8000	120.86	119.20	117.82	116.67	115.72	114.92	114.25	113.70	113.23	112.83	112.50	111.46	111.02	110.82
9000	135.97	134.09	132.54	131.26	130.18	129.29	128.54	127.91	127.38	126.93	126.56	125.40	124.89	124.68
10000	151.08	148.99	147.27	145.84	144.65	143.65	142.82	142.12	141.53	141.04	140.62	139.33	138.77	138.53
11000	166.19	163.89	162.00	160.42	159.11	158.02	157.10	156.33	155.68	155.14	154.68	153.26	152.65	152.38
12000	181.29	178.79	176.72	175.01	173.58	172.38	171.38	170.54	169.84	169.24	168.74	167.19	166.52	166.23
13000	196.40	193.69	191.45	189.59	188.04	186.74	185.66	184.75	183.99	183.34	182.80	181.13	180.40	180.08
14000	211.51	208.59	206.18	204.17	202.50	201.11	199.94	198.96	198.14	197.45	196.86	195.06	194.28	193.94
15000	226.62	223.49	220.90	218.76	216.97	215.47	214.22	213.17	212.29	211.55	210.93	208.99	208.15	207.79
16000	241.72	238.39	235.63	233.34	231.43	229.84	228.50	227.39	226.45	225.65	224.99	222.92	222.03	221.64
17000	256.83	253.29	250.36	247.92	245.90	244.20	242.79	241.60	240.60	239.76	239.05	236.86	235.91	235.49
18000	271.94	268.18	265.08	262.51	260.36	258.57	257.07	255.81	254.75	253.86	253.11	250.79	249.78	249.35
19000	287.05	283.08	279.81	277.09	274.82	272.93	271.35	270.02	268.90	267.96	267.17	264.72	263.66	263.20
20000	302.15	297.98	294.53	291.67	289.29	287.30	285.63	284.23	283.06	282.07	281.23	278.65	277.54	277.05
21000	317.26	312.88	309.26	306.26	303.75	301.66	299.91	298.44	297.21	296.17	295.29	292.59	291.41	290.90
22000	332.37	327.78	323.99	320.84	318.22	316.03	314.19	312.65	311.36	310.27	309.36	306.52	305.29	304.76
23000	347.48	342.68	338.71	335.42	332.68	330.39	328.47	326.07	325.51	324.38	323.42	320.45	319.17	318.61
24000	362.58	357.58	353.44	350.01	347.15	344.76	342.75	341.08	339.67	338.48	337.48	334.38	333.04	332.46
25000	377.69	372.48	368.17	364.59	361.61	359.12	357.04	355.29	353.82	352.58	351.54	348.32	346.92	346.31
26000	392.80	387.38	382.89	379.17	376.07	373.48	371.32	369.50	367.97	366.68	365.60	362.25	360.80	360.16
27000	407.91	402.27	397.62	393.76	390.54	387.85	385.60	383.71	382.12	380.79	379.66	376.18	374.67	374.02
28000	423.01	417.17	412.35	408.34	405.00	402.21	399.88	397.92	396.28	394.89	393.72	390.11	388.55	387.87
29000	438.12	432.07	427.07	422.92	419.47	416.58	414.16	412.13	410.43	408.99	407.79	404.05	402.43	401.72
30000	453.23	446.97	441.80	437.51	433.93	430.94	428.44	426.34	424.58	423.10	421.85	417.98	416.30	415.57
31000	468.34	461.87	456.53	452.09	448.39	445.31	442.72	440.56	438.73	437.20	435.91	431.91	430.18	429.43
32000	483.44	476.77	471.25	466.67	462.86	459.67	457.00	454.77	452.89	451.30	449.97	445.84	444.06	443.28
33000	498.55	491.67	485.98	481.26	477.32	474.04	471.29	468.98	467.04	465.41	464.03	459.78	457.93	457.13
34000	513.66	506.57	500.71	495.84	491.79	488.40	485.57	483.19	481.19	479.51	478.09	473.71	471.81	470.98
35000	528.77	521.47	515.43	510.42	506.25	502.77	499.85	497.40	495.34	493.61	492.15	487.64	485.69	484.83
36000	543.87	536.36	530.16	525.01	520.72	517.13	514.13	511.61	509.50	507.72	506.22	501.57	499.56	498.69
37000	558.98	551.26	544.88	539.59	535.18	531.50	528.41	525.82	523.65	521.82	520.28	515.50	513.44	512.54
38000	574.09	566.16	559.61	554.17	549.64	545.86	542.69	540.03	537.80	535.92	534.34	529.44	527.32	526.39
39000	589.20	581.06	574.34	568.76	564.11	560.22	556.97	554.25	551.95	550.02	548.40	543.37	541.19	540.24
40000	604.30	595.96	589.06	583.34	578.57	574.59	571.25	568.46	566.11	564.13	562.46	557.30	555.07	554.10
41000	619.41	610.86	603.79	597.92	593.04	588.95	585.54	582.67	580.26	578.23	576.52	571.23	568.95	567.95
42000	634.52	625.76	618.52	612.51	607.50	603.32	599.82	596.88	594.41	592.33	590.58	585.17	582.82	581.80
43000	649.63	640.66	633.24	627.09	621.96	617.68	614.10	611.09	608.56	606.44	604.65	599.10	596.70	595.65
44000	664.73	655.56	647.97	641.67	636.43	632.05	628.38	625.30	622.72	620.54	618.71	613.03	610.58	609.51
45000	679.84	670.45	662.70	656.26	650.89	646.41	642.66	639.51	636.87	634.64	632.77	626.96	624.45	623.36
46000	694.95	685.35	677.42	670.84	665.36	660.78	656.94	653.73	651.02	648.75	646.83	640.90	638.33	637.21
47000	710.06	700.25	692.15	685.42	679.82	675.14	671.22	667.94	665.17	662.85	660.89	654.83	652.21	651.06
48000	725.16	715.15	706.88	700.01	694.29	689.51	685.50	682.15	679.33	676.95	674.95	668.76	666.08	664.91
49000	740.27	730.05	721.60	714.59	708.75	703.87	699.79	696.36	693.48	691.06	689.01	682.69	679.96	678.77
50000	755.38	744.95	736.33	729.17	723.21	718.24	714.07	710.57	707.63	705.16	703.07	696.63	693.84	692.62
55000	830.91	819.44	809.96	802.09	795.53	790.06	785.47	781.63	778.39	775.67	773.38	766.29	763.22	761.88
60000	906.45	893.94	883.59	875.01	867.86	861.88	856.88	852.68	849.16	846.19	843.69	835.95	832.60	831.14
65000	981.99	968.43	957.23	947.92	940.18	933.70	928.29	923.74	919.92	916.70	914.00	905.61	901.99	900.40
70000	1057.53	1042.93	1030.86	1020.84	1012.50	1005.53	999.69	994.80	990.68	987.22	984.30	975.28	971.37	969.66
75000	1133.06	1117.42	1104.49	1093.76	1084.82	1077.35	1071.10	1065.85	1061.44	1057.74	1054.61	1044.94	1040.75	1038.93
80000	1208.60	1191.92	1178.12	1166.67	1157.14	1149.17	1142.50	1136.91	1132.21	1128.25	1124.92	1114.60	1110.13	1108.19
85000	1284.14	1266.41	1251.76	1239.59	1229.46	1221.00	1213.91	1207.97	1202.97	1198.77	1195.22	1184.26	1179.52	1177.45
90000	1359.68	1340.90	1325.39	1312.51	1301.78	1292.82	1285.32	1279.02	1273.73	1269.28	1265.53	1253.92	1248.90	1246.71
95000	1435.21	1415.40	1399.02	1385.42	1374.10	1364.64	1356.72	1350.08	1344.50	1339.80	1335.84	1323.59	1318.28	1315.97
100000	1510.75	1489.89	1472.65	1458.34	1446.42	1436.47	1428.13	1421.14	1415.26	1410.31	1406.14	1393.25	1387.67	1385.23

MONTHLY PAYMENT
REQUIRED TO AMORTIZE A LOAN

TERM	1 Year	2 Years	3 Years	4 Years	5 Years	6 Years	7 Years	8 Years	9 Years	10 Years	11 Years	12 Years	13 Years	14 Years
AMOUNT														
5	.46	.25	.18	.15	.13	.12	.11	.10	.09	.09	.09	.09	.08	.08
10	.92	.50	.36	.29	.25	.23	.21	.19	.18	.18	.17	.17	.16	.16
15	1.37	.74	.54	.43	.37	.34	.31	.29	.27	.26	.25	.25	.24	.24
25	2.28	1.24	.89	.72	.62	.56	.51	.48	.45	.43	.42	.41	.40	.39
50	4.56	2.47	1.78	1.44	1.24	1.11	1.02	.95	.90	.86	.83	.81	.79	.77
75	6.83	3.70	2.66	2.15	1.85	1.66	1.52	1.42	1.35	1.29	1.25	1.21	1.18	1.16
100	9.11	4.93	3.55	2.87	2.47	2.21	2.03	1.89	1.80	1.72	1.66	1.61	1.57	1.54
200	18.21	9.86	7.10	5.74	4.94	4.41	4.05	3.78	3.59	3.43	3.31	3.22	3.14	3.08
300	27.31	14.78	10.64	8.60	7.40	6.62	6.07	5.67	5.38	5.15	4.97	4.83	4.71	4.62
400	36.42	19.71	14.19	11.47	9.87	8.82	8.09	7.56	7.17	6.86	6.62	6.43	6.28	6.16
500	45.52	24.64	17.74	14.34	12.33	11.02	10.11	9.45	8.96	8.58	8.28	8.04	7.85	7.69
600	54.62	29.56	21.28	17.20	14.80	13.23	12.14	11.34	10.75	10.29	9.93	9.65	9.42	9.23
700	63.72	34.49	24.83	20.07	17.26	15.43	14.16	13.23	12.54	12.01	11.59	11.25	10.99	10.77
800	72.83	39.41	28.38	22.93	19.73	17.63	16.18	15.12	14.33	13.72	13.24	12.86	12.56	12.31
900	81.93	44.34	31.92	25.80	22.19	19.84	18.20	17.01	16.12	15.43	14.90	14.47	14.12	13.85
1000	91.03	49.27	35.47	28.67	24.66	22.04	20.22	18.90	17.91	17.15	16.55	16.08	15.69	15.38
2000	182.06	98.53	70.94	57.33	49.31	44.08	40.44	37.80	35.82	34.29	33.10	32.15	31.38	30.76
3000	273.09	147.79	106.40	85.99	73.96	66.12	60.66	56.70	53.72	51.43	49.64	48.22	47.07	46.14
4000	364.11	197.05	141.87	114.65	98.61	88.15	80.88	75.60	71.63	68.58	66.19	64.29	62.76	61.52
5000	455.14	246.32	177.34	143.31	123.26	110.19	101.10	94.50	89.53	85.72	82.73	80.36	78.45	76.90
6000	546.17	295.58	212.80	171.97	147.91	132.23	121.32	113.39	107.44	102.86	99.28	96.43	94.13	92.27
7000	637.19	344.84	248.27	200.63	172.56	154.27	141.54	132.29	125.35	120.01	115.82	112.50	109.82	107.65
8000	728.22	394.10	283.74	229.30	197.22	176.30	161.76	151.19	143.25	137.15	132.37	128.57	125.51	123.03
9000	819.25	443.37	319.20	257.96	221.87	198.34	181.98	170.09	161.16	154.29	148.91	144.64	141.20	138.41
10000	910.27	492.63	354.67	286.62	246.52	220.38	202.20	188.99	179.06	171.43	165.46	160.71	156.89	153.79
11000	1001.30	541.89	390.14	315.28	271.17	242.42	222.42	207.88	196.97	188.58	182.00	176.78	172.57	169.17
12000	1092.33	591.15	425.60	343.94	295.82	264.45	242.64	226.78	214.88	205.72	198.55	192.85	188.26	184.54
13000	1183.35	640.41	461.07	372.60	320.47	286.49	262.86	245.68	232.78	222.86	215.09	208.92	203.95	199.92
14000	1274.38	689.68	496.53	401.26	345.12	308.53	283.08	264.58	250.69	240.01	231.64	224.99	219.64	215.30
15000	1365.41	738.94	532.00	429.93	369.78	330.57	303.30	283.48	268.59	257.15	248.18	241.06	235.33	230.68
16000	1456.44	788.20	567.47	458.59	394.43	352.60	323.52	302.38	286.50	274.29	264.73	257.13	251.02	246.06
17000	1547.46	837.46	602.93	487.25	419.08	374.64	343.74	321.27	304.41	291.43	281.27	273.20	266.70	261.44
18000	1638.49	886.73	638.40	515.91	443.73	396.68	363.96	340.17	322.31	308.58	297.82	289.27	282.39	276.81
19000	1729.52	935.99	673.87	544.57	468.38	418.72	384.18	359.07	340.22	325.72	314.36	305.34	298.08	292.19
20000	1820.54	985.25	709.33	573.23	493.03	440.75	404.40	377.97	358.12	342.86	330.91	321.41	313.77	307.57
21000	1911.57	1034.51	744.80	601.89	517.68	462.79	424.62	396.87	376.03	360.01	347.45	337.48	329.46	322.95
22000	2002.60	1083.77	780.27	630.56	542.34	484.83	444.84	415.76	393.94	377.15	364.00	353.55	345.14	338.33
23000	2093.62	1133.04	815.73	659.22	566.99	506.87	465.06	434.66	411.84	394.29	380.54	369.62	360.83	353.71
24000	2184.65	1182.30	851.20	687.88	591.64	528.90	485.28	453.56	429.75	411.43	397.09	385.69	376.52	369.08
25000	2275.68	1231.56	886.66	716.54	616.29	550.94	505.50	472.46	447.65	428.58	413.63	401.76	392.21	384.46
26000	2366.70	1280.82	922.13	745.20	640.94	572.98	525.72	491.36	465.56	445.72	430.18	417.83	407.90	399.84
27000	2457.73	1330.09	957.60	773.86	665.59	595.01	545.94	510.25	483.47	462.86	446.72	433.90	423.59	415.22
28000	2548.76	1379.35	993.06	802.52	690.24	617.05	566.16	529.15	501.37	480.01	463.27	449.97	439.27	430.60
29000	2639.78	1428.61	1028.53	831.19	714.90	639.09	586.38	548.05	519.28	497.15	479.81	466.04	454.96	445.98
30000	2730.81	1477.87	1064.00	859.85	739.55	661.13	606.60	566.95	537.18	514.29	496.36	482.11	470.65	461.35
31000	2821.84	1527.14	1099.46	888.51	764.20	683.16	626.81	585.85	555.09	531.43	512.90	498.18	486.34	476.73
32000	2912.87	1576.40	1134.93	917.17	788.85	705.20	647.03	604.75	572.99	548.58	529.45	514.25	502.03	492.11
33000	3003.89	1625.66	1170.40	945.83	813.50	727.24	667.25	623.64	590.90	565.72	545.99	530.32	517.71	507.49
34000	3094.92	1674.92	1205.86	974.49	838.15	749.28	687.47	642.54	608.81	582.86	562.54	546.39	533.40	522.87
35000	3185.95	1724.18	1241.33	1003.15	862.80	771.31	707.69	661.44	626.71	600.01	579.08	562.46	549.09	538.25
36000	3276.97	1773.45	1276.79	1031.82	887.45	793.35	727.91	680.34	644.62	617.15	595.63	578.53	564.78	553.62
37000	3368.00	1822.71	1312.26	1060.48	912.11	815.39	748.13	699.24	662.52	634.29	612.17	594.60	580.47	569.00
38000	3459.03	1871.97	1347.73	1089.14	936.76	837.43	768.35	718.13	680.43	651.43	628.72	610.67	596.15	584.38
39000	3550.05	1921.23	1383.19	1117.80	961.41	859.46	788.57	737.03	698.34	668.58	645.26	626.74	611.84	599.76
40000	3641.08	1970.50	1418.66	1146.46	986.06	881.50	808.79	755.93	716.24	685.72	661.81	642.81	627.53	615.14
41000	3732.11	2019.76	1454.13	1175.12	1010.71	903.54	829.01	774.83	734.15	702.86	678.35	658.88	643.22	630.52
42000	3823.13	2069.02	1489.59	1203.78	1035.36	925.58	849.23	793.73	752.05	720.01	694.90	674.95	658.91	645.89
43000	3914.16	2118.28	1525.06	1232.45	1060.01	947.61	869.45	812.62	769.96	737.15	711.44	691.02	674.60	661.27
44000	4005.19	2167.54	1560.53	1261.11	1084.67	969.65	889.67	831.52	787.87	754.29	727.99	707.09	690.28	676.65
45000	4096.21	2216.81	1595.99	1289.77	1109.32	991.69	909.89	850.42	805.77	771.43	744.54	723.16	705.97	692.03
46000	4187.24	2266.07	1631.46	1318.43	1133.97	1013.73	930.11	869.32	823.68	788.58	761.08	739.23	721.66	707.41
47000	4278.27	2315.33	1666.92	1347.09	1158.62	1035.76	950.33	888.22	841.58	805.72	777.63	755.30	737.35	722.79
48000	4369.30	2364.59	1702.39	1375.75	1183.27	1057.80	970.55	907.12	859.49	822.86	794.17	771.37	753.04	738.16
49000	4460.32	2413.86	1737.86	1404.41	1207.92	1079.84	990.77	926.01	877.40	840.01	810.72	787.44	768.72	753.54
50000	4551.35	2463.12	1773.32	1433.07	1232.57	1101.88	1010.99	944.91	895.30	857.15	827.26	803.51	784.41	768.92
55000	5006.48	2709.43	1950.66	1576.38	1355.83	1212.06	1112.09	1039.40	984.83	942.86	909.99	883.86	862.85	845.81
60000	5461.62	2955.74	2127.99	1719.69	1479.09	1322.25	1213.19	1133.89	1074.36	1028.58	992.71	964.21	941.29	922.70
65000	5916.75	3202.05	2305.32	1863.00	1602.35	1432.44	1314.28	1228.38	1163.89	1114.29	1075.44	1044.56	1019.73	999.60
70000	6371.89	3448.36	2482.65	2006.30	1725.60	1542.62	1415.38	1322.87	1253.42	1200.01	1158.16	1124.91	1098.18	1076.49
75000	6827.02	3694.68	2659.98	2149.61	1848.86	1652.81	1516.48	1417.36	1342.95	1285.72	1240.89	1205.26	1176.62	1153.38
80000	7282.16	3940.99	2837.32	2292.92	1972.12	1763.00	1617.58	1511.86	1432.48	1371.43	1323.61	1285.61	1255.06	1230.27
85000	7737.29	4187.30	3014.65	2436.22	2095.37	1873.18	1718.68	1606.35	1522.01	1457.15	1406.34	1365.96	1333.50	1307.16
90000	8192.42	4433.61	3191.98	2579.53	2218.63	1983.37	1819.77	1700.84	1611.54	1542.86	1489.07	1446.31	1411.94	1384.05
95000	8647.56	4679.92	3369.31	2722.84	2341.89	2093.56	1920.87	1795.33	1701.07	1628.58	1571.79	1526.66	1490.38	1460.94
100000	9102.69	4926.23	3546.64	2866.14	2465.14	2203.75	2021.97	1889.82	1790.60	1714.29	1654.52	1607.01	1568.82	1537.84

TERM AMOUNT	15 Years	16 Years	17 Years	18 Years	19 Years	20 Years	21 Years	22 Years	23 Years	24 Years	25 Years	30 Years	35 Years	40 Years
5	.08	.08	.08	.08	.08	.08	.08	.08	.08	.08	.08	.07	.07	.07
10	.16	.15	.15	.15	.15	.15	.15	.15	.15	.15	.15	.14	.14	.14
15	.23	.23	.23	.22	.22	.22	.22	.22	.22	.22	.22	.21	.21	.21
25	.38	.38	.37	.37	.37	.36	.36	.36	.36	.36	.36	.35	.35	.35
50	.76	.75	.74	.74	.73	.72	.72	.72	.71	.71	.71	.70	.70	.70
75	1.14	1.12	1.11	1.10	1.09	1.08	1.08	1.07	1.07	1.06	1.06	1.05	1.05	1.05
100	1.52	1.50	1.48	1.47	1.45	1.44	1.44	1.43	1.42	1.42	1.42	1.40	1.39	1.39
200	3.03	2.99	2.95	2.93	2.90	2.88	2.87	2.85	2.84	2.83	2.82	2.80	2.78	2.78
300	4.54	4.48	4.43	4.39	4.35	4.32	4.30	4.27	4.26	4.24	4.23	4.19	4.17	4.17
400	6.06	5.97	5.90	5.85	5.80	5.76	5.73	5.70	5.67	5.65	5.64	5.59	5.56	5.55
500	7.57	7.46	7.38	7.31	7.25	7.20	7.16	7.12	7.09	7.07	7.05	6.98	6.95	6.94
600	9.08	8.96	8.85	8.77	8.69	8.64	8.59	8.54	8.51	8.48	8.45	8.38	8.34	8.33
700	10.59	10.45	10.33	10.23	10.14	10.07	10.02	9.97	9.93	9.89	9.86	9.77	9.73	9.72
800	12.11	11.94	11.80	11.69	11.59	11.51	11.45	11.39	11.34	11.30	11.27	11.17	11.12	11.10
900	13.62	13.43	13.28	13.15	13.04	12.95	12.88	12.81	12.76	12.72	12.68	12.56	12.51	12.49
1000	15.13	14.92	14.75	14.61	14.49	14.39	14.31	14.24	14.18	14.13	14.09	13.96	13.90	13.88
2000	30.26	29.84	29.49	29.21	28.97	28.77	28.61	28.47	28.35	28.25	28.17	27.91	27.80	27.75
3000	45.38	44.76	44.24	43.81	43.45	43.16	42.91	42.70	42.52	42.37	42.25	41.86	41.70	41.62
4000	60.51	59.67	58.98	58.41	57.94	57.54	57.21	56.93	56.69	56.50	56.33	55.82	55.59	55.50
5000	75.63	74.59	73.73	73.01	72.42	71.92	71.51	71.16	70.86	70.62	70.41	69.77	69.49	69.37
6000	90.76	89.51	88.47	87.62	86.90	86.31	85.81	85.39	85.04	84.74	84.49	83.72	83.39	83.24
7000	105.88	104.42	103.22	102.22	101.39	100.69	100.11	99.62	99.21	98.86	98.57	97.67	97.28	97.12
8000	121.01	119.34	117.96	116.82	115.87	115.07	114.41	113.85	113.38	112.99	112.65	111.63	111.18	110.99
9000	136.13	134.26	132.71	131.42	130.35	129.46	128.71	128.08	127.55	127.11	126.74	125.58	125.08	124.86
10000	151.26	149.17	147.45	146.02	144.83	143.84	143.01	142.31	141.72	141.23	140.82	139.53	138.98	138.73
11000	166.38	164.09	162.20	160.63	159.32	158.22	157.31	156.54	155.90	155.35	154.90	153.48	152.87	152.61
12000	181.51	179.01	176.94	175.23	173.80	172.61	171.61	170.77	170.07	169.48	168.98	167.44	166.77	166.48
13000	196.63	193.92	191.69	189.83	188.28	186.99	185.91	185.00	184.24	183.60	183.06	181.39	180.67	180.35
14000	211.76	208.84	206.43	204.43	202.77	201.37	200.21	199.23	198.41	197.72	197.14	195.34	194.56	194.23
15000	226.88	223.76	221.18	219.03	217.25	215.76	214.51	213.46	212.58	211.85	211.22	209.30	208.46	208.10
16000	242.01	238.67	235.92	233.63	231.73	230.14	228.81	227.69	226.76	225.97	225.30	223.25	222.36	221.97
17000	257.13	253.59	250.66	248.24	246.21	244.52	243.11	241.93	240.93	240.09	239.38	237.20	236.26	235.85
18000	272.26	268.51	265.41	262.84	260.70	250.91	257.41	256.16	255.10	254.21	253.47	251.15	250.15	249.72
19000	287.38	283.42	280.15	277.44	275.18	273.29	271.71	270.39	269.27	268.34	267.55	265.11	264.05	263.59
20000	302.51	298.34	294.90	292.04	289.66	287.68	286.01	284.62	283.44	282.46	281.63	279.06	277.95	277.46
21000	317.63	313.26	309.64	306.64	304.15	302.06	300.31	298.85	297.62	296.58	295.71	293.01	291.84	291.34
22000	332.76	328.17	324.39	321.25	318.63	316.44	314.61	313.08	311.79	310.70	309.79	306.96	305.74	305.21
23000	347.88	343.09	339.13	335.85	333.11	330.03	328.91	327.31	325.96	324.83	323.87	320.92	319.64	319.08
24000	363.01	358.01	353.00	350.45	347.59	345.21	343.21	341.54	340.13	338.95	337.95	334.87	333.54	332.96
25000	378.13	372.92	368.62	365.05	362.08	359.59	357.51	355.77	354.30	353.07	352.03	348.82	347.43	346.83
26000	393.26	387.84	383.37	379.65	376.56	373.98	371.81	370.00	368.48	367.19	366.11	362.77	361.33	360.70
27000	408.38	402.76	390.11	394.25	391.04	388.36	386.11	384.23	382.65	381.32	380.20	376.73	375.23	374.57
28000	423.51	417.68	412.86	408.86	405.53	402.74	400.42	398.46	396.82	395.44	394.28	390.68	389.12	388.45
29000	438.63	432.59	427.60	423.46	420.01	417.13	414.72	412.69	410.99	409.56	408.36	404.63	403.02	402.32
30000	453.76	447.51	442.35	438.06	434.49	431.51	429.02	426.92	425.16	423.69	422.44	418.59	416.92	416.19
31000	468.88	462.43	457.09	452.66	448.97	445.89	443.32	441.15	439.34	437.81	436.52	432.54	430.82	430.07
32000	484.01	477.34	471.83	467.26	463.46	460.28	457.62	455.30	453.51	451.93	450.60	446.49	444.71	443.94
33000	499.13	492.26	486.58	481.87	477.94	474.66	471.92	469.61	467.68	466.05	464.68	460.44	458.61	457.81
34000	514.26	507.18	501.32	496.47	492.42	489.04	486.22	483.85	481.85	480.18	478.76	474.40	472.51	471.69
35000	529.38	522.09	516.07	511.07	506.91	503.43	500.52	498.08	496.02	494.30	492.85	488.35	486.40	485.56
36000	544.51	537.01	530.81	525.67	521.39	517.81	514.82	512.31	510.20	508.42	506.93	502.30	500.30	499.43
37000	559.63	551.93	545.56	540.27	535.87	532.20	529.12	526.54	524.37	522.54	521.01	516.25	514.20	513.30
38000	574.76	566.84	560.30	554.87	550.35	546.58	543.42	540.77	538.54	536.67	535.09	530.21	528.10	527.18
39000	589.88	581.76	575.05	569.48	564.84	560.96	557.72	555.00	552.71	550.79	549.17	544.16	541.99	541.05
40000	605.01	596.68	589.79	584.08	579.32	575.35	572.02	569.23	566.88	564.91	563.25	558.11	555.89	554.92
41000	620.13	611.59	604.54	598.68	593.80	589.73	586.32	583.46	581.06	579.04	577.33	572.06	569.79	568.80
42000	635.26	626.51	619.28	613.28	608.29	604.11	600.62	597.69	595.23	593.16	591.41	586.02	583.68	582.67
43000	650.38	641.43	634.03	627.88	622.77	618.50	614.92	611.92	609.40	607.28	605.49	599.97	597.58	596.54
44000	665.51	656.34	648.77	642.49	637.25	632.88	629.22	626.15	623.57	621.40	619.58	613.92	611.48	610.42
45000	680.63	671.26	663.52	657.09	651.73	647.26	643.52	640.38	637.74	635.53	633.66	627.88	625.38	624.29
46000	695.76	686.18	678.26	671.69	666.22	661.65	657.82	654.61	651.92	649.65	647.74	641.83	639.27	638.16
47000	710.88	701.09	693.00	686.29	680.70	676.03	672.12	668.84	666.09	663.77	661.82	655.78	653.17	652.03
48000	726.01	716.01	707.75	700.89	695.18	690.41	686.42	683.07	680.26	677.89	675.90	669.73	667.07	665.91
49000	741.13	730.93	722.49	715.49	709.67	704.80	700.72	697.30	694.43	692.02	689.98	683.69	680.96	679.78
50000	756.26	745.84	737.24	730.10	724.15	719.18	715.02	711.54	708.60	706.14	704.06	697.64	694.86	693.65
55000	831.88	820.43	810.96	803.11	796.56	791.10	786.52	782.69	779.46	776.75	774.47	767.40	764.35	763.02
60000	907.51	895.01	884.69	876.11	868.98	863.02	858.03	853.84	850.32	847.37	844.87	837.17	833.83	832.38
65000	983.13	969.60	958.41	949.12	941.39	934.93	929.53	924.99	921.18	917.98	915.28	906.93	903.32	901.75
70000	1058.76	1044.18	1032.13	1022.13	1013.81	1006.85	1001.03	996.15	992.04	988.59	985.69	976.69	972.80	971.11
75000	1134.38	1118.76	1105.86	1095.14	1086.22	1078.77	1072.53	1067.30	1062.90	1059.21	1056.09	1046.46	1042.29	1040.48
80000	1210.01	1193.35	1179.58	1168.15	1158.63	1150.69	1144.03	1138.45	1133.76	1129.82	1126.50	1116.22	1111.78	1109.84
85000	1285.63	1267.93	1253.30	1241.16	1231.05	1222.60	1215.54	1209.61	1204.62	1200.43	1196.90	1185.98	1181.26	1179.21
90000	1361.26	1342.52	1327.03	1314.17	1303.46	1294.52	1287.04	1280.76	1275.48	1271.05	1267.31	1255.75	1250.75	1248.57
95000	1436.89	1417.10	1400.75	1387.18	1375.88	1366.44	1358.54	1351.91	1346.34	1341.66	1337.71	1325.51	1320.23	1317.94
100000	1512.51	1491.68	1474.47	1460.19	1448.29	1438.36	1430.04	1423.07	1417.20	1412.27	1408.12	1395.27	1389.72	1387.30

MONTHLY PAYMENT
REQUIRED TO AMORTIZE A LOAN

TERM	1 Year	2 Years	3 Years	4 Years	5 Years	6 Years	7 Years	8 Years	9 Years	10 Years	11 Years	12 Years	13 Years	14 Years
AMOUNT														
5	.46	.25	.18	.15	.13	.12	.11	.10	.09	.09	.09	.09	.08	.08
10	.92	.50	.36	.29	.25	.23	.21	.19	.18	.10	.17	.17	.16	.16
15	1.37	.74	.54	.44	.38	.34	.31	.29	.27	.26	.25	.25	.24	.24
25	2.28	1.24	.89	.72	.62	.56	.51	.48	.45	.43	.42	.41	.40	.39
50	4.56	2.47	1.78	1.44	1.24	1.11	1.02	.95	.90	.86	.83	.81	.79	.78
75	6.83	3.70	2.67	2.16	1.86	1.66	1.52	1.43	1.35	1.29	1.25	1.21	1.19	1.16
100	9.11	4.93	3.56	2.88	2.47	2.21	2.03	1.90	1.80	1.72	1.66	1.62	1.58	1.55
200	18.22	9.86	7.11	5.75	4.94	4.42	4.06	3.79	3.60	3.44	3.32	3.23	3.15	3.09
300	27.32	14.79	10.66	8.62	7.41	6.63	6.08	5.69	5.39	5.16	4.98	4.84	4.73	4.63
400	36.43	19.72	14.21	11.49	9.88	8.84	8.11	7.58	7.19	6.88	6.64	6.45	6.30	6.18
500	45.54	24.65	17.76	14.36	12.35	11.04	10.14	9.48	8.98	8.60	8.30	8.06	7.87	7.72
600	54.64	29.58	21.31	17.23	14.82	13.25	12.16	11.37	10.78	10.32	9.96	9.68	9.45	9.26
700	63.75	34.51	24.86	20.10	17.29	15.46	14.19	13.26	12.57	12.04	11.62	11.29	11.02	10.81
800	72.85	39.44	28.41	22.97	19.76	17.67	16.22	15.16	14.37	13.76	13.28	12.90	12.60	12.35
900	81.96	44.37	31.96	25.84	22.23	19.88	18.24	17.05	16.16	15.48	14.94	14.51	14.17	13.89
1000	91.07	49.30	35.51	28.71	24.70	22.08	20.27	18.95	17.96	17.20	16.60	16.12	15.74	15.44
2000	182.13	98.60	71.01	57.41	49.39	44.16	40.53	37.89	35.91	34.39	33.19	32.24	31.48	30.87
3000	273.19	147.90	106.52	86.11	74.08	66.24	60.79	56.83	53.86	51.58	49.79	48.36	47.22	46.30
4000	364.25	197.20	142.02	114.81	98.77	88.32	81.06	75.78	71.81	68.77	66.38	64.48	62.96	61.73
5000	455.32	246.50	177.52	143.51	123.46	110.40	101.32	94.72	89.76	85.96	82.97	80.60	78.70	77.16
6000	546.38	295.79	213.03	172.21	148.15	132.48	121.58	113.66	107.72	103.15	99.57	96.72	94.44	92.59
7000	637.44	345.09	248.53	200.91	172.85	154.56	141.84	132.60	125.67	120.34	116.16	112.84	110.18	108.02
8000	728.50	394.39	284.03	229.61	197.54	176.64	162.11	151.55	143.62	137.53	132.75	128.96	125.92	123.45
9000	819.57	443.69	319.54	258.31	222.23	198.72	182.37	170.49	161.57	154.72	149.35	145.08	141.66	138.88
10000	910.63	492.99	355.04	287.01	246.92	220.80	202.63	189.43	179.52	171.91	165.94	161.20	157.39	154.31
11000	1001.69	542.29	390.54	315.71	271.61	242.87	222.90	208.37	197.48	189.10	182.53	177.32	173.13	169.74
12000	1092.75	591.58	426.05	344.41	296.30	264.95	243.16	227.32	215.43	206.29	199.13	193.44	188.87	185.17
13000	1183.82	640.88	461.55	373.11	321.00	287.03	263.42	246.26	233.38	223.48	215.72	209.56	204.61	200.60
14000	1274.88	690.18	497.06	401.81	345.69	309.11	283.68	265.20	251.33	240.67	232.32	225.68	220.35	216.03
15000	1365.94	739.48	532.56	430.51	370.38	331.19	303.95	284.15	269.28	257.86	248.91	241.80	236.09	231.46
16000	1457.00	788.78	568.06	459.21	395.07	353.27	324.21	303.09	287.23	275.05	265.50	257.92	251.83	246.89
17000	1548.07	838.08	603.57	487.91	419.76	375.35	344.47	322.03	305.19	292.24	282.10	274.04	267.57	262.32
18000	1639.13	887.37	639.07	516.61	444.45	397.43	364.74	340.97	323.14	309.43	298.69	290.16	283.31	277.75
19000	1730.19	936.67	674.57	545.31	469.14	419.51	385.00	359.92	341.09	326.62	315.28	306.28	299.05	293.18
20000	1821.25	985.97	710.08	574.01	493.84	441.59	405.26	378.86	359.04	343.81	331.88	322.40	314.78	308.61
21000	1912.32	1035.27	745.58	602.71	518.53	463.67	425.52	397.80	376.99	361.00	348.47	338.52	330.52	324.04
22000	2003.38	1084.57	781.08	631.41	543.22	485.74	445.79	416.74	394.95	378.19	365.06	354.64	346.26	339.47
23000	2094.44	1133.86	816.59	660.11	567.91	507.82	466.05	435.69	412.90	395.38	381.66	370.76	362.00	354.90
24000	2185.50	1183.16	852.09	688.81	592.60	529.90	486.31	454.63	430.85	412.57	398.25	386.88	377.74	370.33
25000	2276.57	1232.46	887.60	717.51	617.29	551.98	506.58	473.57	448.80	429.76	414.85	403.00	393.48	385.76
26000	2367.63	1281.76	923.10	746.21	641.99	574.06	526.84	492.51	466.75	446.95	431.44	419.12	409.22	401.19
27000	2458.69	1331.06	958.60	774.91	666.68	596.14	547.10	511.46	484.71	464.14	448.03	435.24	424.96	416.62
28000	2549.75	1380.36	994.11	803.61	691.37	618.22	567.36	530.40	502.66	481.33	464.63	451.36	440.70	432.05
29000	2640.82	1429.65	1029.61	832.31	716.06	640.30	587.63	549.34	520.61	498.52	481.22	467.48	456.44	447.48
30000	2731.88	1478.95	1065.11	861.01	740.75	662.38	607.89	568.29	538.56	515.71	497.81	483.60	472.17	462.91
31000	2822.94	1528.25	1100.62	889.71	765.44	684.46	628.15	587.23	556.51	532.90	514.41	499.72	487.91	478.34
32000	2914.00	1577.55	1136.12	918.41	790.13	706.54	648.41	606.17	574.46	550.09	531.00	515.84	503.65	493.77
33000	3005.07	1626.85	1171.62	947.11	814.83	728.61	668.68	625.11	592.42	567.28	547.59	531.96	519.39	509.20
34000	3096.13	1676.15	1207.13	975.81	839.52	750.69	688.94	644.06	610.37	584.47	564.19	548.08	535.13	524.63
35000	3187.19	1725.44	1242.63	1004.51	864.21	772.77	709.20	663.00	628.32	601.66	580.78	564.20	550.87	540.06
36000	3278.25	1774.74	1278.13	1033.21	888.90	794.85	729.47	681.94	646.27	618.85	597.38	580.32	566.61	555.49
37000	3369.32	1824.04	1313.64	1061.91	913.59	816.93	749.73	700.88	664.22	636.04	613.97	596.44	582.35	570.92
38000	3460.38	1873.34	1349.14	1090.61	938.28	839.01	769.99	719.83	682.18	653.23	630.56	612.56	598.09	586.35
39000	3551.44	1922.64	1384.65	1119.31	962.98	861.09	790.25	738.77	700.13	670.42	647.16	628.68	613.83	601.78
40000	3642.50	1971.93	1420.15	1148.01	987.67	883.17	810.52	757.71	718.08	687.61	663.75	644.80	629.56	617.21
41000	3733.57	2021.23	1455.65	1176.71	1012.36	905.25	830.78	776.66	736.03	704.80	680.34	660.92	645.30	632.64
42000	3824.63	2070.53	1491.16	1205.41	1037.05	927.33	851.04	795.60	753.98	721.99	696.94	677.03	661.04	648.07
43000	3915.69	2119.83	1526.66	1234.11	1061.74	949.40	871.31	814.54	771.94	739.18	713.53	693.15	676.78	663.50
44000	4006.75	2169.13	1562.16	1262.81	1086.43	971.48	891.57	833.48	789.89	756.37	730.12	709.27	692.52	678.93
45000	4097.81	2218.43	1597.67	1291.51	1111.12	993.56	911.83	852.43	807.84	773.56	746.72	725.39	708.26	694.36
46000	4188.88	2267.72	1633.17	1320.21	1135.82	1015.64	932.09	871.37	825.79	790.75	763.31	741.51	724.00	709.79
47000	4279.94	2317.02	1668.67	1348.91	1160.51	1037.72	952.36	890.31	843.74	807.94	779.91	757.63	739.74	725.22
48000	4371.00	2366.32	1704.18	1377.61	1185.20	1059.80	972.62	909.25	861.69	825.13	796.50	773.75	755.48	740.65
49000	4462.06	2415.62	1739.68	1406.31	1209.89	1081.88	992.88	928.20	879.65	842.32	813.09	789.87	771.22	756.08
50000	4553.13	2464.92	1775.19	1435.01	1234.58	1103.96	1013.15	947.14	897.60	859.51	829.69	805.99	786.95	771.51
55000	5008.44	2711.41	1952.70	1578.51	1358.04	1214.35	1114.46	1041.85	987.36	945.46	912.65	886.59	865.65	848.67
60000	5463.75	2957.90	2130.22	1722.01	1481.50	1324.75	1215.77	1136.57	1077.12	1031.41	995.62	967.19	944.34	925.82
65000	5919.06	3204.39	2307.74	1865.51	1604.96	1435.14	1317.09	1231.28	1166.88	1117.36	1078.59	1047.79	1023.04	1002.97
70000	6374.38	3450.88	2485.26	2009.01	1728.41	1545.54	1418.40	1325.99	1256.64	1203.31	1161.56	1128.39	1101.73	1080.12
75000	6829.69	3697.37	2662.78	2152.51	1851.87	1655.93	1519.72	1420.71	1346.40	1289.26	1244.53	1208.99	1180.43	1157.27
80000	7285.00	3943.86	2840.29	2296.01	1975.33	1766.33	1621.03	1515.42	1436.15	1375.22	1327.50	1289.59	1259.12	1234.42
85000	7740.31	4190.36	3017.81	2439.51	2098.79	1876.73	1722.34	1610.13	1525.91	1461.17	1410.46	1370.18	1337.82	1311.57
90000	8195.63	4436.85	3195.33	2583.01	2222.24	1987.12	1823.66	1704.85	1615.67	1547.12	1493.43	1450.78	1416.51	1388.72
95000	8650.94	4683.34	3372.85	2726.51	2345.70	2097.52	1924.97	1799.56	1705.43	1633.07	1576.40	1531.38	1495.21	1465.87
100000	9106.25	4929.83	3550.37	2870.01	2469.16	2207.91	2026.29	1894.27	1795.19	1719.02	1659.37	1611.98	1573.90	1543.02

MONTHLY PAYMENT
REQUIRED TO AMORTIZE A LOAN

16.700%

TERM	15 Years	16 Years	17 Years	18 Years	19 Years	20 Years	21 Years	22 Years	23 Years	24 Years	25 Years	30 Years	35 Years	40 Years
AMOUNT														
5	.08	.08	.08	.08	.08	.08	.08	.08	.08	.08	.08	.08	.07	.07
10	.16	.15	.15	.15	.15	.15	.15	.15	.15	.15	.15	.15	.14	.14
15	.23	.23	.23	.22	.22	.22	.22	.22	.22	.22	.22	.22	.21	.21
25	.38	.38	.37	.37	.37	.37	.36	.36	.36	.36	.36	.36	.35	.35
50	.76	.75	.74	.74	.73	.73	.72	.72	.72	.71	.71	.71	.70	.70
75	1.14	1.13	1.11	1.10	1.10	1.09	1.08	1.08	1.07	1.07	1.07	1.06	1.05	1.05
100	1.52	1.50	1.48	1.47	1.46	1.45	1.44	1.43	1.43	1.42	1.42	1.41	1.40	1.40
200	3.04	3.00	2.96	2.94	2.91	2.89	2.88	2.86	2.85	2.84	2.83	2.81	2.80	2.79
300	4.56	4.50	4.44	4.40	4.37	4.34	4.31	4.29	4.27	4.26	4.25	4.21	4.19	4.19
400	6.08	5.99	5.92	5.87	5.82	5.78	5.75	5.72	5.70	5.68	5.66	5.61	5.59	5.58
500	7.59	7.49	7.40	7.33	7.27	7.23	7.18	7.15	7.12	7.10	7.08	7.01	6.98	6.97
600	9.11	8.99	8.88	8.80	8.73	8.67	8.62	8.58	8.54	8.51	8.49	8.41	8.38	8.37
700	10.63	10.48	10.36	10.27	10.18	10.11	10.06	10.01	9.97	9.93	9.90	9.81	9.78	9.76
800	12.15	11.98	11.84	11.73	11.64	11.56	11.49	11.44	11.39	11.35	11.32	11.22	11.17	11.15
900	13.67	13.48	13.32	13.20	13.09	13.00	12.93	12.86	12.81	12.77	12.73	12.62	12.57	12.55
1000	15.18	14.98	14.80	14.66	14.54	14.45	14.36	14.29	14.24	14.19	14.15	14.02	13.96	13.94
2000	30.36	29.95	29.60	29.32	29.08	28.89	28.72	28.58	28.47	28.37	28.29	28.03	27.92	27.87
3000	45.54	44.92	44.40	43.98	43.62	43.33	43.08	42.87	42.70	42.55	42.43	42.05	41.88	41.81
4000	60.72	59.89	59.20	58.63	58.16	57.77	57.44	57.16	56.93	56.73	56.57	56.06	55.84	55.74
5000	75.89	74.86	74.00	73.29	72.70	72.21	71.79	71.45	71.16	70.91	70.71	70.07	69.80	69.68
6000	91.07	89.83	88.80	87.95	87.24	86.65	86.15	85.74	85.39	85.09	84.85	84.09	83.76	83.61
7000	106.25	104.80	103.60	102.61	101.78	101.09	100.51	100.02	99.62	99.28	98.99	98.10	97.72	97.55
8000	121.43	119.77	118.40	117.26	116.32	115.53	114.87	114.31	113.85	113.46	113.13	112.11	111.67	111.48
9000	136.61	134.74	133.20	131.92	130.86	129.97	129.22	128.60	128.08	127.64	127.27	126.13	125.63	125.42
10000	151.78	149.71	148.00	146.58	145.39	144.41	143.58	142.89	142.31	141.82	141.41	140.14	139.59	139.35
11000	166.96	164.68	162.80	161.23	159.93	158.85	157.94	157.18	156.54	156.00	155.55	154.15	153.55	153.29
12000	182.14	179.65	177.60	175.89	174.47	173.29	172.30	171.47	170.77	170.18	169.69	168.17	167.51	167.22
13000	197.32	194.62	192.40	190.55	189.01	187.73	186.66	185.76	185.00	184.37	183.83	182.18	181.47	181.16
14000	212.50	209.59	207.20	205.21	203.55	202.17	201.01	200.04	199.23	198.55	197.97	196.19	195.43	195.09
15000	227.67	224.56	221.99	219.86	218.09	216.61	215.37	214.33	213.46	212.73	212.11	210.21	209.39	209.03
16000	242.85	239.53	236.79	234.52	232.63	231.05	229.73	228.62	227.69	226.91	226.25	224.22	223.34	222.96
17000	258.03	254.50	251.59	249.18	247.17	245.49	244.09	242.91	241.92	241.09	240.39	238.23	237.30	236.90
18000	273.21	269.40	266.39	263.84	261.71	259.93	258.44	257.20	256.15	255.27	254.53	252.25	251.26	250.83
19000	288.39	284.45	281.19	278.49	276.25	274.37	272.80	271.49	270.38	269.45	268.67	266.26	265.22	264.77
20000	303.56	299.42	295.99	293.15	290.78	288.81	287.16	285.70	284.61	283.64	282.81	280.27	279.18	278.70
21000	318.74	314.39	310.79	307.81	305.32	303.25	301.52	300.06	298.84	297.82	296.95	294.29	293.14	292.64
22000	333.92	329.36	325.59	322.46	319.86	317.69	315.88	314.35	313.07	312.00	311.09	308.30	307.10	306.57
23000	349.10	344.33	340.39	337.12	334.40	332.13	330.23	328.64	327.30	326.18	325.23	322.31	321.06	320.51
24000	364.28	359.30	355.19	351.78	348.94	346.57	344.59	342.93	341.54	340.36	339.38	336.33	335.01	334.44
25000	379.45	374.27	369.99	366.44	363.48	361.01	358.95	357.22	355.77	354.54	353.52	350.34	348.97	348.38
26000	394.63	389.24	384.79	381.09	378.02	375.45	373.31	371.51	370.00	368.73	367.66	364.35	362.93	362.31
27000	409.81	404.21	399.59	395.75	392.56	389.89	387.66	385.80	384.23	382.91	381.80	378.37	376.89	376.25
28000	424.99	419.18	414.39	410.41	407.10	404.33	402.02	400.08	398.46	397.09	395.94	392.38	390.85	390.18
29000	440.16	434.15	429.18	425.06	421.64	418.77	416.38	414.37	412.69	411.27	410.08	406.39	404.81	404.12
30000	455.34	449.12	443.98	439.72	436.17	433.21	430.74	428.66	426.92	425.45	424.22	420.41	418.77	418.05
31000	470.52	464.09	458.78	454.38	450.71	447.65	445.10	442.95	441.15	439.63	438.36	434.42	432.73	431.99
32000	485.70	479.06	473.58	469.04	465.25	462.09	459.45	457.24	455.38	453.81	452.50	448.43	446.68	445.92
33000	500.88	494.03	488.38	483.69	479.79	476.54	473.81	471.53	469.61	468.00	466.64	462.45	460.64	459.86
34000	516.05	509.00	503.18	498.35	494.33	490.98	488.17	485.82	483.84	482.18	480.78	476.46	474.60	473.79
35000	531.23	523.98	517.98	513.01	508.87	505.42	502.53	500.10	498.07	496.36	494.92	490.48	488.56	487.73
36000	546.41	538.95	532.78	527.67	523.41	519.86	516.88	514.39	512.30	510.54	509.06	504.49	502.52	501.66
37000	561.59	553.92	547.58	542.32	537.95	534.30	531.24	528.68	526.53	524.72	523.20	518.50	516.48	515.60
38000	576.77	568.89	562.38	556.98	552.49	548.74	545.60	542.97	540.76	538.90	537.34	532.52	530.44	529.53
39000	591.94	583.86	577.18	571.64	567.03	563.18	559.96	557.26	554.99	553.09	551.48	546.53	544.40	543.47
40000	607.12	598.83	591.98	586.29	581.56	577.62	574.31	571.55	569.22	567.27	565.62	560.54	558.35	557.40
41000	622.30	613.80	606.78	600.95	596.10	592.06	588.67	585.83	583.45	581.45	579.76	574.56	572.31	571.34
42000	637.48	628.77	621.58	615.61	610.64	606.50	603.03	600.12	597.68	595.63	593.90	588.57	586.27	585.27
43000	652.66	643.74	636.37	630.27	625.18	620.94	617.39	614.41	611.91	609.81	608.04	602.58	600.23	599.21
44000	667.83	658.71	651.17	644.92	639.72	635.38	631.75	628.70	626.14	623.99	622.18	616.60	614.19	613.14
45000	683.01	673.68	665.97	659.58	654.26	649.82	646.10	642.99	640.37	638.18	636.32	630.61	628.15	627.08
46000	698.19	688.65	680.77	674.24	668.80	664.26	660.46	657.28	654.60	652.36	650.46	644.62	642.11	641.01
47000	713.37	703.62	695.57	688.89	683.34	678.70	674.82	671.57	668.83	666.54	664.61	658.64	656.07	654.95
48000	728.55	718.59	710.37	703.55	697.88	693.14	689.18	685.85	683.07	680.72	678.75	672.65	670.02	668.88
49000	743.72	733.56	725.17	718.21	712.42	707.58	703.53	700.14	697.30	694.90	692.89	686.66	683.98	682.82
50000	758.90	748.53	739.97	732.87	726.95	722.02	717.89	714.43	711.53	709.08	707.03	700.68	697.94	696.75
55000	834.79	823.39	813.97	806.15	799.65	794.22	789.68	785.87	782.68	779.99	777.73	770.74	767.74	766.43
60000	910.68	898.24	887.96	879.44	872.34	866.42	861.47	857.32	853.83	850.90	848.43	840.81	837.53	836.10
65000	986.57	973.09	961.96	952.73	945.04	938.62	933.26	928.76	924.98	921.81	919.13	910.88	907.32	905.78
70000	1062.46	1047.95	1035.96	1026.01	1017.73	1010.83	1005.05	1000.20	996.13	992.71	989.83	980.95	977.12	975.45
75000	1138.35	1122.80	1109.95	1099.30	1090.43	1083.03	1076.84	1071.65	1067.29	1063.62	1060.54	1051.01	1046.91	1045.13
80000	1214.24	1197.65	1183.95	1172.58	1163.12	1155.23	1148.62	1143.09	1138.44	1134.53	1131.24	1121.08	1116.70	1114.80
85000	1290.13	1272.50	1257.95	1245.87	1235.82	1227.43	1220.41	1214.53	1209.59	1205.44	1201.94	1191.15	1186.50	1184.48
90000	1366.02	1347.36	1331.94	1319.16	1308.51	1299.63	1292.20	1285.97	1280.74	1276.35	1272.64	1261.21	1256.29	1254.15
95000	1441.91	1422.21	1405.94	1392.44	1381.21	1371.83	1363.99	1357.42	1351.90	1347.25	1343.35	1331.28	1326.08	1323.83
100000	1517.80	1497.06	1479.93	1465.73	1453.90	1444.04	1435.78	1428.86	1423.05	1418.16	1414.05	1401.35	1395.88	1393.50

MONTHLY PAYMENT
REQUIRED TO AMORTIZE A LOAN

TERM AMOUNT	1 Year	2 Years	3 Years	4 Years	5 Years	6 Years	7 Years	8 Years	9 Years	10 Years	11 Years	12 Years	13 Years	14 Years
5	.46	.25	.18	.15	.13	.12	.11	.10	.09	.09	.09	.09	.08	.08
10	.92	.50	.36	.29	.25	.23	.21	.19	.18	.18	.17	.17	.16	.16
15	1.37	.74	.54	.44	.38	.34	.31	.29	.27	.26	.25	.25	.24	.24
25	2.28	1.24	.89	.72	.62	.56	.51	.48	.45	.44	.42	.41	.40	.39
50	4.56	2.47	1.78	1.44	1.24	1.11	1.02	.95	.90	.87	.84	.81	.79	.78
75	6.84	3.70	2.67	2.16	1.86	1.66	1.53	1.43	1.35	1.30	1.25	1.22	1.19	1.16
100	9.11	4.94	3.56	2.88	2.48	2.22	2.03	1.90	1.80	1.73	1.67	1.62	1.58	1.55
200	18.22	9.87	7.11	5.75	4.95	4.43	4.06	3.80	3.60	3.45	3.33	3.24	3.16	3.10
300	27.33	14.80	10.66	8.62	7.42	6.64	6.09	5.70	5.40	5.17	4.99	4.85	4.74	4.64
400	36.44	19.73	14.22	11.50	9.89	8.85	8.12	7.59	7.20	6.89	6.66	6.47	6.31	6.19
500	45.55	24.67	17.77	14.37	12.36	11.06	10.15	9.49	9.00	8.62	8.32	8.08	7.89	7.74
600	54.66	29.60	21.32	17.24	14.84	13.27	12.18	11.39	10.79	10.34	9.98	9.70	9.47	9.28
700	63.77	34.53	24.87	20.11	17.31	15.48	14.21	13.29	12.59	12.06	11.64	11.31	11.05	10.83
800	72.87	39.46	28.43	22.99	19.78	17.69	16.24	15.18	14.39	13.78	13.31	12.93	12.62	12.38
900	81.98	44.40	31.98	25.86	22.25	19.90	18.27	17.08	16.19	15.50	14.97	14.54	14.20	13.92
1000	91.09	49.33	35.53	28.73	24.72	22.11	20.30	18.98	17.99	17.23	16.63	16.16	15.78	15.47
2000	182.18	98.65	71.06	57.46	49.44	44.22	40.59	37.95	35.97	34.45	33.26	32.31	31.55	30.93
3000	273.26	147.97	106.59	86.18	74.16	66.33	60.88	56.92	53.95	51.67	49.88	48.46	47.32	46.40
4000	364.35	197.29	142.12	114.91	98.88	88.43	81.17	75.89	71.94	68.89	66.51	64.62	63.10	61.86
5000	455.44	246.62	177.65	143.63	123.60	110.54	101.46	94.87	89.92	86.11	83.14	80.77	78.87	77.33
6000	546.52	295.94	213.18	172.36	148.32	132.65	121.75	113.84	107.90	103.34	99.76	96.92	94.64	92.79
7000	637.61	345.26	248.70	201.09	173.03	154.75	142.05	132.81	125.88	120.56	116.39	113.08	110.42	108.26
8000	728.69	394.58	284.23	229.81	197.75	176.86	162.34	151.78	143.87	137.78	133.01	129.23	126.19	123.72
9000	819.78	443.91	319.76	258.54	222.47	198.97	182.63	170.76	161.85	155.00	149.64	145.38	141.96	139.19
10000	910.87	493.23	355.29	287.26	247.19	221.07	202.92	189.73	179.83	172.22	166.27	161.53	157.73	154.65
11000	1001.95	542.55	390.82	315.99	271.91	243.18	223.21	208.70	197.81	189.44	182.89	177.69	173.51	170.12
12000	1093.04	591.87	426.35	344.72	296.63	265.29	243.50	227.67	215.80	206.67	199.52	193.84	189.28	185.58
13000	1184.13	641.19	461.87	373.44	321.34	287.39	263.80	246.65	233.78	223.89	216.14	209.99	205.05	201.05
14000	1275.21	690.52	497.40	402.17	346.06	309.50	284.09	265.62	251.76	241.11	232.77	226.15	220.83	216.51
15000	1366.30	739.84	532.93	430.89	370.78	331.61	304.38	284.59	269.74	258.33	249.40	242.30	236.60	231.98
16000	1457.38	789.16	568.46	459.62	395.50	353.71	324.67	303.56	287.73	275.55	266.02	258.45	252.37	247.44
17000	1548.47	838.48	603.99	488.34	420.22	375.82	344.96	322.54	305.71	292.77	282.65	274.60	268.14	262.91
18000	1639.56	887.81	639.52	517.07	444.94	397.93	365.25	341.51	323.69	310.00	299.27	290.76	283.92	278.37
19000	1730.64	937.13	675.05	545.80	469.65	420.04	385.55	360.48	341.67	327.22	315.90	306.91	299.69	293.84
20000	1821.73	986.45	710.57	574.52	494.37	442.14	405.84	379.45	359.66	344.44	332.53	323.06	315.46	309.30
21000	1912.81	1035.77	746.10	603.25	519.09	464.25	426.13	398.43	377.64	361.66	349.15	339.22	331.24	324.77
22000	2003.90	1085.09	781.63	631.97	543.81	486.36	446.42	417.40	395.62	378.88	365.78	355.37	347.01	340.23
23000	2094.99	1134.42	817.16	660.70	568.53	508.46	466.71	436.37	413.60	396.10	382.40	371.52	362.78	355.70
24000	2186.07	1183.74	852.69	689.43	593.25	530.57	487.00	455.34	431.59	413.33	399.03	387.68	378.55	371.16
25000	2277.16	1233.06	888.22	718.15	617.96	552.68	507.29	474.32	449.57	430.55	415.66	403.83	394.33	386.63
26000	2368.24	1282.38	923.74	746.88	642.68	574.78	527.59	493.29	467.55	447.77	432.28	419.98	410.10	402.09
27000	2459.33	1331.71	959.27	775.60	667.40	596.89	547.88	512.26	485.53	464.99	448.91	436.13	425.87	417.56
28000	2550.42	1381.03	994.80	804.33	692.12	619.00	568.17	531.23	503.52	482.21	465.53	452.29	441.65	433.02
29000	2641.50	1430.35	1030.33	833.06	716.84	641.10	588.46	550.21	521.50	499.43	482.16	468.44	457.42	448.48
30000	2732.59	1479.67	1065.86	861.78	741.56	663.21	608.75	569.18	539.48	516.66	498.79	484.59	473.19	463.95
31000	2823.68	1528.99	1101.39	890.51	766.27	685.32	629.04	588.15	557.46	533.88	515.41	500.75	488.97	479.41
32000	2914.76	1578.32	1136.91	919.23	790.99	707.42	649.34	607.12	575.45	551.10	532.04	516.90	504.74	494.88
33000	3005.85	1627.64	1172.44	947.96	815.71	729.53	669.63	626.10	593.43	568.32	548.66	533.05	520.51	510.34
34000	3096.93	1676.96	1207.97	976.68	840.43	751.64	689.92	645.07	611.41	585.54	565.29	549.20	536.28	525.81
35000	3188.02	1726.28	1243.50	1005.41	865.15	773.75	710.21	664.04	629.39	602.76	581.92	565.36	552.06	541.27
36000	3279.11	1775.61	1279.03	1034.14	889.87	795.85	730.50	683.01	647.38	619.99	598.54	581.51	567.83	556.74
37000	3370.19	1824.93	1314.56	1062.86	914.58	817.96	750.79	701.98	665.36	637.21	615.17	597.66	583.60	572.20
38000	3461.28	1874.25	1350.09	1091.59	939.30	840.07	771.09	720.96	683.34	654.43	631.79	613.82	599.38	587.67
39000	3552.36	1923.57	1385.61	1120.31	964.02	862.17	791.38	739.93	701.32	671.65	648.42	629.97	615.15	603.13
40000	3643.45	1972.89	1421.14	1149.04	988.74	884.28	811.67	758.90	719.31	688.87	665.05	646.12	630.92	618.60
41000	3734.54	2022.22	1456.67	1177.77	1013.46	906.39	831.96	777.87	737.29	706.09	681.67	662.28	646.69	634.06
42000	3825.62	2071.54	1492.20	1206.49	1038.18	928.49	852.25	796.85	755.27	723.32	698.30	678.43	662.47	649.53
43000	3916.71	2120.86	1527.73	1235.22	1062.89	950.60	872.54	815.82	773.25	740.54	714.92	694.58	678.24	664.99
44000	4007.80	2170.18	1563.26	1263.94	1087.61	972.71	892.83	834.79	791.24	757.76	731.55	710.73	694.01	680.46
45000	4098.88	2219.51	1598.78	1292.67	1112.33	994.81	913.13	853.76	809.22	774.98	748.18	726.89	709.79	695.92
46000	4189.97	2268.83	1634.31	1321.39	1137.05	1016.92	933.42	872.74	827.20	792.20	764.80	743.04	725.56	711.39
47000	4281.05	2318.15	1669.84	1350.12	1161.77	1039.03	953.71	891.71	845.18	809.42	781.43	759.19	741.33	726.85
48000	4372.14	2367.47	1705.37	1378.85	1186.49	1061.13	974.00	910.68	863.17	826.65	798.05	775.35	757.10	742.32
49000	4463.23	2416.79	1740.90	1407.57	1211.20	1083.24	994.29	929.65	881.15	843.87	814.68	791.50	772.88	757.78
50000	4554.31	2466.12	1776.43	1436.30	1235.92	1105.35	1014.58	948.63	899.13	861.09	831.31	807.65	788.65	773.25
55000	5009.74	2712.73	1954.07	1579.93	1359.51	1215.88	1116.04	1043.49	989.04	947.20	914.44	888.42	867.51	850.57
60000	5465.17	2959.34	2131.71	1723.56	1483.11	1326.42	1217.50	1138.35	1078.96	1033.31	997.57	969.18	946.38	927.89
65000	5920.60	3205.95	2309.35	1867.19	1606.70	1436.95	1318.96	1233.21	1168.87	1119.41	1080.70	1049.95	1025.24	1005.22
70000	6376.04	3452.56	2487.00	2010.82	1730.29	1547.49	1420.42	1328.07	1258.78	1205.52	1163.83	1130.71	1104.11	1082.54
75000	6831.47	3699.17	2664.64	2154.44	1853.88	1658.02	1521.87	1422.94	1348.69	1291.63	1246.96	1211.48	1182.97	1159.87
80000	7286.90	3945.78	2842.28	2298.07	1977.47	1768.55	1623.33	1517.80	1438.61	1377.74	1330.09	1292.24	1261.84	1237.19
85000	7742.33	4192.39	3019.92	2441.70	2101.06	1879.09	1724.79	1612.66	1528.52	1463.85	1413.22	1373.00	1340.70	1314.52
90000	8197.76	4439.01	3197.56	2585.33	2224.66	1989.62	1826.25	1707.52	1618.43	1549.96	1496.35	1453.77	1419.57	1391.84
95000	8653.19	4685.62	3375.21	2728.96	2348.25	2100.16	1927.71	1802.39	1708.35	1636.06	1579.48	1534.53	1498.43	1469.16
100000	9108.62	4932.23	3552.85	2872.59	2471.84	2210.69	2029.16	1897.25	1798.26	1722.17	1662.61	1615.30	1577.30	1546.49

TERM	15 Years	16 Years	17 Years	18 Years	19 Years	20 Years	21 Years	22 Years	23 Years	24 Years	25 Years	30 Years	35 Years	40 Years
AMOUNT														
5	.08	.08	.08	.08	.08	.08	.08	.08	.08	.08	.08	.08	.07	.07
10	.16	.16	.15	.15	.15	.15	.15	.15	.15	.15	.15	.15	.14	.14
15	.23	.23	.23	.23	.22	.22	.22	.22	.22	.22	.22	.22	.21	.21
25	.39	.38	.38	.37	.37	.37	.36	.36	.36	.36	.36	.36	.35	.35
50	.77	.76	.75	.74	.73	.73	.72	.72	.72	.72	.71	.71	.70	.70
75	1.15	1.13	1.12	1.11	1.10	1.09	1.08	1.08	1.08	1.07	1.07	1.06	1.05	1.05
100	1.53	1.51	1.49	1.47	1.46	1.45	1.44	1.44	1.43	1.43	1.42	1.41	1.40	1.40
200	3.05	3.01	2.97	2.94	2.92	2.90	2.88	2.87	2.86	2.85	2.84	2.82	2.80	2.80
300	4.57	4.51	4.46	4.41	4.38	4.35	4.32	4.30	4.29	4.27	4.26	4.22	4.20	4.20
400	6.09	6.01	5.94	5.88	5.84	5.80	5.76	5.74	5.71	5.69	5.68	5.63	5.60	5.60
500	7.61	7.51	7.42	7.35	7.29	7.24	7.20	7.17	7.14	7.12	7.09	7.03	7.00	6.99
600	9.13	9.01	8.91	8.82	8.75	8.69	8.64	8.60	8.57	8.54	8.51	8.44	8.40	8.39
700	10.65	10.51	10.39	10.29	10.21	10.14	10.08	10.03	9.99	9.96	9.93	9.84	9.80	9.79
800	12.18	12.01	11.87	11.76	11.67	11.59	11.52	11.47	11.42	11.38	11.35	11.25	11.20	11.19
900	13.70	13.51	13.36	13.23	13.12	13.04	12.96	12.90	12.85	12.80	12.77	12.65	12.60	12.58
1000	15.22	15.01	14.84	14.70	14.58	14.48	14.40	14.33	14.27	14.23	14.18	14.06	14.00	13.98
2000	30.43	30.02	29.68	29.39	29.16	28.96	28.80	28.66	28.54	28.45	28.36	28.11	28.00	27.96
3000	45.64	45.02	44.51	44.09	43.73	43.44	43.19	42.99	42.81	42.67	42.54	42.17	42.00	41.93
4000	60.86	60.03	59.35	58.78	58.31	57.92	57.59	57.31	57.08	56.89	56.72	56.22	56.00	55.91
5000	76.07	75.04	74.18	73.48	72.89	72.40	71.99	71.64	71.35	71.11	70.90	70.27	70.00	69.89
6000	91.28	90.04	89.02	88.17	87.46	86.87	86.38	85.97	85.62	85.33	85.08	84.33	84.00	83.86
7000	106.50	105.05	103.86	102.86	102.04	101.35	100.78	100.30	99.89	99.55	99.26	98.38	98.00	97.84
8000	121.71	120.06	118.69	117.56	116.62	115.83	115.17	114.62	114.16	113.77	113.44	112.44	112.00	111.82
9000	136.92	135.06	133.53	132.25	131.19	130.31	129.57	128.95	128.43	127.99	127.62	126.49	126.00	125.79
10000	152.14	150.07	148.36	146.95	145.77	144.79	143.97	143.28	142.70	142.21	141.80	140.54	140.00	139.77
11000	167.35	165.08	163.20	161.64	160.35	159.27	158.36	157.60	156.97	156.43	155.98	154.60	154.00	153.74
12000	182.56	180.08	178.03	176.34	174.92	173.74	172.76	171.93	171.24	170.66	170.16	168.65	168.00	167.72
13000	197.78	195.09	192.87	191.03	189.50	188.22	187.15	186.26	185.51	184.88	184.34	182.71	182.00	181.70
14000	212.99	210.10	207.71	205.72	204.08	202.70	201.55	200.59	199.78	199.10	198.52	196.76	196.00	195.67
15000	228.20	225.10	222.54	220.42	218.65	217.18	215.95	214.91	214.05	213.32	212.70	210.81	210.00	209.65
16000	243.42	240.11	237.38	235.11	233.23	231.66	230.34	229.24	228.32	227.54	226.88	224.87	224.00	223.63
17000	258.63	255.11	252.21	249.81	247.80	246.13	244.74	243.57	242.58	241.76	241.06	238.92	238.00	237.60
18000	273.84	270.12	267.05	264.50	262.38	260.61	259.13	257.89	256.85	255.98	255.24	252.98	252.00	251.58
19000	289.06	285.13	281.88	279.19	276.96	275.09	273.53	272.22	271.12	270.20	269.42	267.03	266.00	265.56
20000	304.27	300.13	296.72	293.89	291.53	289.57	287.93	286.55	285.39	284.42	283.60	281.08	280.00	279.53
21000	319.48	315.14	311.56	308.58	306.11	304.05	302.32	300.88	299.66	298.64	297.78	295.14	294.00	293.51
22000	334.70	330.15	326.39	323.28	320.69	318.53	316.72	315.20	313.93	312.86	311.96	309.19	308.00	307.48
23000	349.91	345.15	341.23	337.97	335.26	333.00	331.11	329.53	328.20	327.08	326.14	323.25	322.00	321.46
24000	365.12	360.16	356.06	352.67	349.84	347.48	345.51	343.86	342.47	341.31	340.32	337.30	336.00	335.44
25000	380.34	375.17	370.90	367.36	364.42	361.96	359.91	358.18	356.74	355.53	354.50	351.35	350.00	349.41
26000	395.55	390.17	385.73	382.05	378.99	376.44	374.30	372.51	371.01	369.75	368.68	365.41	364.00	363.39
27000	410.76	405.18	400.57	396.75	393.57	390.92	388.70	386.84	385.28	383.97	382.86	379.46	378.00	377.37
28000	425.97	420.19	415.41	411.44	408.15	405.39	403.09	401.17	399.55	398.19	397.04	393.52	392.00	391.34
29000	441.19	435.19	430.24	426.14	422.72	419.87	417.49	415.49	413.82	412.41	411.22	407.57	406.00	405.32
30000	456.40	450.20	445.08	440.83	437.30	434.35	431.89	429.82	428.09	426.63	425.40	421.62	420.00	419.30
31000	471.61	465.21	459.91	455.53	451.87	448.83	446.28	444.15	442.36	440.85	439.58	435.68	434.00	433.27
32000	486.83	480.21	474.75	470.22	466.45	463.31	460.68	458.47	456.63	455.07	453.76	449.73	448.00	447.25
33000	502.04	495.22	489.58	484.91	481.03	477.79	475.07	472.80	470.90	469.29	467.94	463.79	462.00	461.22
34000	517.25	510.22	504.42	499.61	495.60	492.26	489.47	487.13	485.16	483.51	482.12	477.84	476.00	475.20
35000	532.47	525.23	519.26	514.30	510.18	506.74	503.87	501.46	499.43	497.73	496.30	491.89	490.00	489.18
36000	547.68	540.24	534.09	529.00	524.76	521.22	518.26	515.78	513.70	511.96	510.48	505.95	504.00	503.15
37000	562.89	555.24	548.93	543.69	539.33	535.70	532.66	530.11	527.97	526.18	524.66	520.00	518.00	517.13
38000	578.11	570.25	563.76	558.38	553.91	550.18	547.05	544.44	542.24	540.40	538.84	534.06	532.00	531.11
39000	593.32	585.26	578.60	573.08	568.49	564.65	561.45	558.77	556.51	554.62	553.02	548.11	546.00	545.08
40000	608.53	600.26	593.44	587.77	583.06	579.13	575.85	573.09	570.78	568.84	567.20	562.16	560.00	559.06
41000	623.75	615.27	608.27	602.47	597.64	593.61	590.24	587.42	585.05	583.06	581.38	576.22	574.00	573.04
42000	638.96	630.28	623.11	617.16	612.22	608.09	604.64	601.75	599.32	597.28	595.56	590.27	588.00	587.01
43000	654.17	645.28	637.94	631.86	626.79	622.57	619.03	616.07	613.59	611.50	609.74	604.33	602.00	600.99
44000	669.39	660.29	652.78	646.55	641.37	637.05	633.43	630.40	627.86	625.72	623.92	618.38	616.00	614.96
45000	684.60	675.30	667.61	661.24	655.95	651.52	647.83	644.73	642.13	639.94	638.10	632.43	630.00	628.94
46000	699.81	690.30	682.45	675.94	670.52	666.00	662.22	659.06	656.40	654.16	652.28	646.49	644.00	642.92
47000	715.03	705.31	697.29	690.63	685.10	680.48	676.62	673.38	670.67	668.38	666.46	660.54	658.00	656.89
48000	730.24	720.32	712.12	705.33	699.67	694.96	691.01	687.71	684.94	682.61	680.64	674.59	672.00	670.87
49000	745.45	735.32	726.96	720.02	714.25	709.44	705.41	702.04	699.21	696.83	694.82	688.65	686.00	684.85
50000	760.67	750.33	741.79	734.72	728.83	723.91	719.81	716.36	713.48	711.05	709.00	702.70	699.99	698.82
55000	836.73	825.36	815.97	808.19	801.71	796.31	791.79	788.00	784.82	782.15	779.90	772.97	769.99	768.70
60000	912.80	900.39	890.15	881.66	874.59	868.70	863.77	859.64	856.17	853.26	850.80	843.24	839.99	838.59
65000	988.86	975.43	964.33	955.13	947.47	941.09	935.75	931.27	927.52	924.36	921.70	913.51	909.99	908.47
70000	1064.93	1050.46	1038.51	1028.60	1020.36	1013.48	1007.73	1002.91	998.86	995.46	992.60	983.78	979.99	978.35
75000	1141.00	1125.49	1112.69	1102.07	1093.24	1085.87	1079.71	1074.54	1070.21	1066.57	1063.50	1054.05	1049.99	1048.23
80000	1217.06	1200.52	1186.87	1175.54	1166.12	1158.26	1151.69	1146.18	1141.56	1137.67	1134.40	1124.32	1119.99	1118.11
85000	1293.13	1275.55	1261.04	1249.01	1239.00	1230.65	1223.67	1217.82	1212.90	1208.78	1205.30	1194.59	1189.99	1188.00
90000	1369.19	1350.59	1335.22	1322.48	1311.89	1303.04	1295.65	1289.45	1284.25	1279.88	1276.20	1264.86	1259.99	1257.88
95000	1445.26	1425.62	1409.40	1395.95	1384.77	1375.43	1367.63	1361.09	1355.60	1350.98	1347.10	1335.13	1329.99	1327.76
100000	1521.33	1500.65	1483.58	1469.43	1457.65	1447.82	1439.61	1432.72	1426.95	1422.09	1418.00	1405.40	1399.98	1397.64

MONTHLY PAYMENT
REQUIRED TO AMORTIZE A LOAN

TERM	1 Year	2 Years	3 Years	4 Years	5 Years	6 Years	7 Years	8 Years	9 Years	10 Years	11 Years	12 Years	13 Years	14 Years
AMOUNT														
5	.46	.25	.18	.15	.13	.12	.11	.10	.10	.09	.09	.09	.08	.08
10	.92	.50	.36	.29	.25	.23	.21	.20	.19	.18	.17	.17	.16	.16
15	1.37	.75	.54	.44	.38	.34	.31	.29	.28	.26	.25	.25	.24	.24
25	2.28	1.24	.89	.72	.62	.56	.51	.48	.46	.44	.42	.41	.40	.39
50	4.56	2.47	1.78	1.44	1.24	1.11	1.02	.96	.91	.87	.84	.81	.80	.78
75	6.84	3.71	2.67	2.16	1.86	1.67	1.53	1.43	1.36	1.30	1.25	1.22	1.19	1.17
100	9.12	4.94	3.56	2.88	2.48	2.22	2.04	1.91	1.81	1.73	1.67	1.62	1.59	1.55
200	18.23	9.87	7.12	5.76	4.95	4.43	4.07	3.81	3.61	3.46	3.34	3.24	3.17	3.10
300	27.34	14.81	10.67	8.63	7.43	6.65	6.10	5.71	5.41	5.18	5.00	4.86	4.75	4.65
400	36.45	19.74	14.23	11.51	9.90	8.86	8.13	7.61	7.21	6.91	6.67	6.48	6.33	6.20
500	45.56	24.68	17.78	14.38	12.38	11.07	10.17	9.51	9.01	8.63	8.33	8.10	7.91	7.75
600	54.67	29.61	21.34	17.26	14.85	13.29	12.20	11.41	10.81	10.36	10.00	9.72	9.49	9.30
700	63.78	34.55	24.89	20.13	17.33	15.50	14.23	13.31	12.61	12.08	11.67	11.34	11.07	10.85
800	72.89	39.48	28.45	23.01	19.80	17.71	16.26	15.21	14.42	13.81	13.33	12.95	12.65	12.40
900	82.00	44.42	32.00	25.88	22.28	19.93	18.29	17.11	16.22	15.53	15.00	14.57	14.23	13.95
1000	91.11	49.35	35.56	28.76	24.75	22.14	20.33	19.01	18.02	17.26	16.66	16.19	15.81	15.50
2000	182.22	98.70	71.11	57.51	49.50	44.27	40.65	38.01	36.03	34.51	33.32	32.38	31.62	31.00
3000	273.33	148.04	106.66	86.26	74.24	66.41	60.97	57.01	54.04	51.76	49.98	48.56	47.43	46.50
4000	364.44	197.39	142.22	115.01	98.99	88.54	81.29	76.01	72.06	69.02	66.64	64.75	63.23	62.00
5000	455.55	246.74	177.77	143.76	123.73	110.68	101.61	95.02	90.07	86.27	83.30	80.94	79.04	77.50
6000	546.66	296.08	213.32	172.52	148.48	132.81	121.93	114.02	108.08	103.52	99.96	97.12	94.85	93.00
7000	637.77	345.43	248.88	201.27	173.22	154.95	142.25	133.02	126.10	120.78	116.61	113.31	110.65	108.50
8000	728.88	394.77	284.43	230.02	197.97	177.08	162.57	152.02	144.11	138.03	133.27	129.49	126.46	124.00
9000	819.99	444.12	319.98	258.77	222.71	199.22	182.89	171.02	162.12	155.28	149.93	145.68	142.27	139.50
10000	911.10	493.47	355.54	287.52	247.46	221.35	203.21	190.03	180.14	172.54	166.59	161.87	158.07	155.00
11000	1002.21	542.81	391.09	316.27	272.20	243.49	223.53	209.03	198.15	189.79	183.25	178.05	173.88	170.50
12000	1093.32	592.16	426.64	345.03	296.95	265.62	243.85	228.03	216.16	207.04	199.91	194.24	189.69	186.00
13000	1184.43	641.51	462.20	373.78	321.69	287.76	264.17	247.03	234.18	224.30	216.56	210.42	205.49	201.50
14000	1275.54	690.85	497.75	402.53	346.44	309.89	284.49	266.04	252.19	241.55	233.22	226.61	221.30	217.00
15000	1366.65	740.20	533.30	431.28	371.18	332.03	304.81	285.04	270.20	258.80	249.88	242.80	237.11	232.50
16000	1457.76	789.54	568.86	460.03	395.93	354.16	325.13	304.04	288.22	276.06	266.54	258.98	252.91	248.00
17000	1548.87	838.89	604.41	488.78	420.67	376.29	345.45	323.04	306.23	293.31	283.20	275.17	268.72	263.50
18000	1639.98	888.24	639.96	517.54	445.42	398.43	365.77	342.04	324.24	310.56	299.86	291.36	284.53	279.00
19000	1731.09	937.58	675.52	546.29	470.16	420.56	386.09	361.05	342.26	327.82	316.52	307.54	300.34	294.50
20000	1822.20	986.93	711.07	575.04	494.91	442.70	406.41	380.05	360.27	345.07	333.17	323.73	316.14	309.99
21000	1913.31	1036.28	746.62	603.79	519.65	464.83	426.73	399.05	378.28	362.32	349.83	339.91	331.95	325.49
22000	2004.42	1085.62	782.18	632.54	544.40	486.97	447.05	418.05	396.30	379.58	366.49	356.10	347.76	340.99
23000	2095.53	1134.97	817.73	661.29	569.14	509.10	467.37	437.06	414.31	396.83	383.15	372.29	363.56	356.49
24000	2186.64	1184.31	853.28	690.05	593.89	531.24	487.69	456.06	432.32	414.08	399.81	388.47	379.37	371.99
25000	2277.75	1233.66	888.84	718.80	618.63	553.37	508.01	475.06	450.34	431.34	416.47	404.66	395.18	387.49
26000	2368.86	1283.01	924.39	747.55	643.38	575.51	528.34	494.06	468.35	448.59	433.12	420.84	410.98	402.99
27000	2459.97	1332.35	959.94	776.30	668.12	597.64	548.66	513.06	486.36	465.84	449.78	437.03	426.79	418.49
28000	2551.08	1381.70	995.50	805.05	692.87	619.78	568.98	532.07	504.37	483.10	466.44	453.22	442.60	433.99
29000	2642.19	1431.05	1031.05	833.80	717.61	641.91	589.30	551.07	522.39	500.35	483.10	469.40	458.40	449.49
30000	2733.30	1480.39	1066.60	862.56	742.36	664.05	609.62	570.07	540.40	517.60	499.76	485.59	474.21	464.99
31000	2824.41	1529.74	1102.16	891.31	767.11	686.18	629.94	589.07	558.41	534.86	516.42	501.78	490.02	480.49
32000	2915.52	1579.08	1137.71	920.06	791.85	708.31	650.26	608.07	576.43	552.11	533.07	517.96	505.82	495.99
33000	3006.63	1628.43	1173.26	948.81	816.60	730.45	670.58	627.08	594.44	569.36	549.73	534.15	521.63	511.49
34000	3097.74	1677.78	1208.82	977.56	841.34	752.58	690.90	646.08	612.45	586.62	566.39	550.33	537.44	526.99
35000	3188.85	1727.12	1244.37	1006.31	866.09	774.72	711.22	665.08	630.47	603.87	583.05	566.52	553.25	542.49
36000	3279.96	1776.47	1279.92	1035.07	890.83	796.85	731.54	684.08	648.48	621.12	599.71	582.71	569.05	557.99
37000	3371.07	1825.82	1315.48	1063.82	915.58	818.99	751.86	703.09	666.49	638.37	616.37	598.89	584.86	573.49
38000	3462.18	1875.16	1351.03	1092.57	940.32	841.12	772.18	722.09	684.51	655.63	633.03	615.08	600.67	588.99
39000	3553.29	1924.51	1386.58	1121.32	965.07	863.26	792.50	741.09	702.52	672.88	649.68	631.26	616.47	604.48
40000	3644.40	1973.85	1422.14	1150.07	989.81	885.39	812.82	760.09	720.53	690.13	666.34	647.45	632.28	619.98
41000	3735.51	2023.20	1457.69	1178.82	1014.56	907.53	833.14	779.09	738.55	707.39	683.00	663.64	648.09	635.48
42000	3826.62	2072.55	1493.24	1207.58	1039.30	929.66	853.46	798.10	756.56	724.64	699.66	679.82	663.89	650.98
43000	3917.73	2121.89	1528.80	1236.33	1064.05	951.80	873.78	817.10	774.57	741.89	716.32	696.01	679.70	666.48
44000	4008.84	2171.24	1564.35	1265.08	1088.79	973.93	894.10	836.10	792.59	759.15	732.98	712.20	695.51	681.98
45000	4099.95	2220.58	1599.90	1293.83	1113.54	996.07	914.42	855.10	810.60	776.40	749.63	728.38	711.31	697.48
46000	4191.06	2269.93	1635.46	1322.58	1138.28	1018.20	934.74	874.11	828.61	793.65	766.29	744.57	727.12	712.98
47000	4282.17	2319.28	1671.01	1351.33	1163.03	1040.34	955.06	893.11	846.63	810.91	782.95	760.75	742.93	728.48
48000	4373.28	2368.62	1706.56	1380.09	1187.77	1062.47	975.38	912.11	864.64	828.16	799.61	776.94	758.73	743.98
49000	4464.39	2417.97	1742.12	1408.84	1212.52	1084.60	995.70	931.11	882.65	845.41	816.27	793.13	774.54	759.48
50000	4555.50	2467.32	1777.67	1437.59	1237.26	1106.74	1016.02	950.11	900.67	862.67	832.93	809.31	790.35	774.98
55000	5011.05	2714.05	1955.43	1581.35	1360.99	1217.41	1117.63	1045.13	990.73	948.93	916.22	890.24	869.38	852.48
60000	5466.60	2960.78	2133.20	1725.11	1484.71	1328.09	1219.23	1140.14	1080.80	1035.20	999.51	971.17	948.42	929.97
65000	5922.15	3207.51	2310.97	1868.86	1608.44	1438.76	1320.83	1235.15	1170.86	1121.47	1082.80	1052.10	1027.45	1007.47
70000	6377.70	3454.24	2488.73	2012.62	1732.17	1549.43	1422.43	1330.16	1260.93	1207.73	1166.09	1133.03	1106.49	1084.97
75000	6833.24	3700.97	2666.50	2156.38	1855.89	1660.11	1524.03	1425.17	1351.00	1294.00	1249.39	1213.97	1185.52	1162.47
80000	7288.79	3947.70	2844.27	2300.14	1979.62	1770.78	1625.64	1520.18	1441.06	1380.26	1332.68	1294.90	1264.55	1239.96
85000	7744.34	4194.43	3022.03	2443.90	2103.34	1881.45	1727.24	1615.19	1531.13	1466.53	1415.97	1375.83	1343.59	1317.46
90000	8199.89	4441.16	3199.80	2587.66	2227.07	1992.13	1828.84	1710.20	1621.19	1552.80	1499.26	1456.76	1422.62	1394.96
95000	8655.44	4687.90	3377.57	2731.41	2350.80	2102.80	1930.44	1805.21	1711.26	1639.06	1582.56	1537.69	1501.66	1472.46
100000	9110.99	4934.63	3555.33	2875.17	2474.52	2213.47	2032.04	1900.22	1801.33	1725.33	1665.85	1618.62	1580.69	1549.95

TERM AMOUNT	15 Years	16 Years	17 Years	18 Years	19 Years	20 Years	21 Years	22 Years	23 Years	24 Years	25 Years	30 Years	35 Years	40 Years
5	.08	.08	.08	.08	.08	.08	.08	.08	.08	.08	.08	.08	.08	.08
10	.16	.16	.15	.15	.15	.15	.15	.15	.15	.15	.15	.15	.15	.15
15	.23	.23	.23	.23	.22	.22	.22	.22	.22	.22	.22	.22	.22	.22
25	.39	.38	.38	.37	.37	.37	.37	.36	.36	.36	.36	.36	.36	.36
50	.77	.76	.75	.74	.74	.73	.73	.72	.72	.72	.72	.71	.71	.71
75	1.15	1.13	1.12	1.11	1.10	1.09	1.09	1.08	1.08	1.07	1.07	1.06	1.06	1.06
100	1.53	1.51	1.49	1.48	1.47	1.46	1.45	1.44	1.44	1.43	1.43	1.41	1.41	1.41
200	3.05	3.01	2.98	2.95	2.93	2.91	2.89	2.88	2.87	2.86	2.85	2.82	2.81	2.81
300	4.58	4.52	4.47	4.42	4.39	4.36	4.34	4.31	4.30	4.28	4.27	4.23	4.22	4.21
400	6.10	6.02	5.95	5.90	5.85	5.81	5.78	5.75	5.73	5.71	5.69	5.64	5.62	5.61
500	7.63	7.53	7.44	7.37	7.31	7.26	7.22	7.19	7.16	7.14	7.11	7.05	7.03	7.01
600	9.15	9.03	8.93	8.84	8.77	8.71	8.67	8.62	8.59	8.56	8.54	8.46	8.43	8.42
700	10.68	10.53	10.42	10.32	10.23	10.17	10.11	10.06	10.02	9.99	9.96	9.87	9.83	9.82
800	12.20	12.04	11.90	11.79	11.70	11.62	11.55	11.50	11.45	11.41	11.38	11.28	11.24	11.22
900	13.73	13.54	13.39	13.26	13.16	13.07	13.00	12.93	12.88	12.84	12.80	12.69	12.64	12.62
1000	15.25	15.05	14.88	14.74	14.62	14.52	14.44	14.37	14.31	14.27	14.22	14.10	14.05	14.02
2000	30.50	30.09	29.75	29.47	29.23	29.04	28.87	28.74	28.62	28.53	28.44	28.19	28.09	28.04
3000	45.75	45.13	44.62	44.20	43.85	43.55	43.31	43.10	42.93	42.79	42.66	42.29	42.13	42.06
4000	61.00	60.17	59.49	58.93	58.46	58.07	57.74	57.47	57.24	57.05	56.88	56.38	56.17	56.08
5000	76.25	75.22	74.37	73.66	73.07	72.59	72.18	71.83	71.55	71.31	71.10	70.48	70.21	70.09
6000	91.50	90.26	89.24	88.39	87.69	87.10	86.61	86.20	85.86	85.57	85.32	84.57	84.25	84.11
7000	106.74	105.30	104.11	103.12	102.30	101.62	101.05	100.57	100.16	99.83	99.54	98.67	98.29	98.13
8000	121.99	120.34	118.98	117.85	116.92	116.13	115.48	114.93	114.47	114.09	113.76	112.76	112.33	112.15
9000	137.24	135.39	133.86	132.59	131.53	130.65	129.91	129.30	128.78	128.35	127.98	126.86	126.37	126.16
10000	152.49	150.43	148.73	147.32	146.14	145.17	144.35	143.66	143.09	142.61	142.20	140.95	140.41	140.18
11000	167.74	165.47	163.60	162.05	160.76	159.68	158.78	158.03	157.40	156.87	156.42	155.04	154.45	154.20
12000	182.99	180.51	178.47	176.78	175.37	174.20	173.22	172.40	171.71	171.13	170.64	169.14	168.50	168.22
13000	198.24	195.56	193.34	191.51	189.99	188.71	187.65	186.76	186.01	185.39	184.86	183.23	182.54	182.24
14000	213.48	210.60	208.22	206.24	204.60	203.23	202.09	201.13	200.32	199.65	199.08	197.33	196.58	196.25
15000	228.73	225.64	223.09	220.97	219.21	217.75	216.52	215.49	214.63	213.91	213.30	211.42	210.62	210.27
16000	243.98	240.68	237.96	235.70	233.83	232.26	230.95	229.86	228.94	228.17	227.52	225.52	224.66	224.29
17000	259.23	255.73	252.83	250.44	248.44	246.78	245.39	244.22	243.25	242.43	241.74	239.61	238.70	238.31
18000	274.48	270.77	267.71	265.17	263.06	261.29	259.82	258.59	257.56	256.69	255.96	253.71	252.74	252.32
19000	289.73	285.81	282.58	279.90	277.67	275.81	274.26	272.96	271.86	270.95	270.18	267.80	266.78	266.34
20000	304.98	300.85	297.45	294.63	292.28	290.33	288.69	287.32	286.17	285.21	284.40	281.89	280.82	280.36
21000	320.22	315.90	312.32	309.36	306.90	304.84	303.13	301.69	300.48	299.47	298.62	295.99	294.86	294.38
22000	335.47	330.94	327.19	324.09	321.51	319.36	317.56	316.05	314.79	313.73	312.83	310.08	308.90	308.39
23000	350.72	345.98	342.07	338.82	336.13	333.88	331.99	330.42	329.10	327.99	327.05	324.18	322.95	322.41
24000	365.97	361.02	356.94	353.55	350.74	348.39	346.43	344.79	343.41	342.25	341.27	338.27	336.99	336.43
25000	381.22	376.06	371.81	368.29	365.35	362.91	360.86	359.15	357.72	356.51	355.49	352.37	351.03	350.45
26000	396.47	391.11	386.68	383.02	379.97	377.42	375.30	373.52	372.02	370.77	369.71	366.46	365.07	364.47
27000	411.72	406.15	401.56	397.75	394.58	391.94	389.73	387.88	386.33	385.03	383.93	380.56	379.11	378.48
28000	426.96	421.19	416.43	412.48	409.19	406.46	404.17	402.25	400.64	399.29	398.15	394.65	393.15	392.50
29000	442.21	436.23	431.30	427.21	423.81	420.97	418.60	416.61	414.95	413.55	412.37	408.75	407.19	406.52
30000	457.46	451.28	446.17	441.94	438.42	435.49	433.04	430.98	429.26	427.81	426.59	422.84	421.23	420.54
31000	472.71	466.32	461.04	456.67	453.04	450.00	447.47	445.35	443.57	442.07	440.81	436.93	435.27	434.55
32000	487.96	481.36	475.92	471.40	467.65	464.52	461.90	459.71	457.87	456.33	455.03	451.03	449.31	448.57
33000	503.21	496.40	490.79	486.13	482.26	479.04	476.34	474.08	472.18	470.59	469.25	465.12	463.35	462.59
34000	518.45	511.45	505.66	500.87	496.88	493.55	490.77	488.44	486.49	484.85	483.47	479.22	477.39	476.61
35000	533.70	526.49	520.53	515.60	511.49	508.07	505.21	502.81	500.80	499.11	497.69	493.31	491.44	490.63
36000	548.95	541.53	535.41	530.33	526.11	522.58	519.64	517.18	515.11	513.37	511.91	507.41	505.48	504.64
37000	564.20	556.57	550.28	545.06	540.72	537.10	534.08	531.54	529.42	527.63	526.13	521.50	519.52	518.66
38000	579.45	571.62	565.15	559.79	555.33	551.62	548.51	545.91	543.72	541.89	540.35	535.60	533.56	532.68
39000	594.70	586.66	580.02	574.52	569.95	566.13	562.94	560.27	558.03	556.15	554.57	549.69	547.60	546.70
40000	609.95	601.70	594.89	589.25	584.56	580.65	577.38	574.64	572.34	570.41	568.79	563.78	561.64	560.71
41000	625.19	616.74	609.77	603.98	599.18	595.17	591.81	589.01	586.65	584.67	583.01	577.88	575.68	574.73
42000	640.44	631.79	624.64	618.72	613.79	609.68	606.25	603.37	600.96	598.93	597.23	591.97	589.72	588.75
43000	655.69	646.83	639.51	633.45	628.40	624.20	620.68	617.74	615.27	613.19	611.44	606.07	603.76	602.77
44000	670.94	661.87	654.38	648.18	643.02	638.71	635.12	632.10	629.57	627.45	625.66	620.16	617.80	616.78
45000	686.19	676.91	669.26	662.91	657.63	653.23	649.55	646.47	643.88	641.71	639.88	634.26	631.84	630.80
46000	701.44	691.95	684.13	677.64	672.25	667.75	664.83	660.83	658.19	655.97	654.10	648.35	645.89	644.82
47000	716.69	707.00	699.00	692.37	686.86	682.26	678.42	675.20	672.50	670.23	668.32	662.45	659.93	658.84
48000	731.93	722.04	713.87	707.10	701.47	696.78	692.85	689.57	686.81	684.49	682.54	676.54	673.97	672.86
49000	747.18	737.08	728.74	721.83	716.09	711.29	707.29	703.93	701.12	698.75	696.76	690.64	688.01	686.87
50000	762.43	752.12	743.62	736.57	730.70	725.81	721.72	718.30	715.43	713.01	710.98	704.73	702.05	700.89
55000	838.67	827.34	817.98	810.22	803.77	798.39	793.89	790.13	786.97	784.31	782.08	775.20	772.25	770.98
60000	914.92	902.55	892.34	883.88	876.84	870.97	866.07	861.96	858.51	855.61	853.18	845.67	842.46	841.07
65000	991.16	977.76	966.70	957.53	949.91	943.55	938.24	933.79	930.05	926.91	924.27	916.15	912.66	911.16
70000	1067.40	1052.97	1041.06	1031.19	1022.98	1016.13	1010.41	1005.61	1001.59	998.21	995.37	986.62	982.87	981.25
75000	1143.64	1128.18	1115.42	1104.85	1096.05	1088.71	1082.58	1077.44	1073.14	1069.51	1066.47	1057.09	1053.07	1051.33
80000	1219.89	1203.40	1189.78	1178.50	1169.12	1161.29	1154.75	1149.27	1144.68	1140.82	1137.57	1127.56	1123.28	1121.42
85000	1296.13	1278.61	1264.15	1252.16	1242.19	1233.87	1226.92	1221.10	1216.22	1212.12	1208.67	1198.04	1193.48	1191.51
90000	1372.37	1353.82	1338.51	1325.81	1315.26	1306.45	1299.10	1292.93	1287.76	1283.42	1279.76	1268.51	1263.68	1261.60
95000	1448.61	1429.03	1412.87	1399.47	1388.33	1379.04	1371.27	1364.76	1359.30	1354.72	1350.86	1338.98	1333.89	1331.69
100000	1524.86	1504.24	1487.23	1473.13	1461.40	1451.62	1443.44	1436.59	1430.85	1426.02	1421.96	1409.45	1404.09	1401.78

MONTHLY PAYMENT
REQUIRED TO AMORTIZE A LOAN

TERM AMOUNT	1 Year	2 Years	3 Years	4 Years	5 Years	6 Years	7 Years	8 Years	9 Years	10 Years	11 Years	12 Years	13 Years	14 Years
5	.46	.25	.18	.15	.13	.12	.11	.10	.10	.09	.09	.09	.08	.08
10	.92	.50	.36	.29	.25	.23	.21	.20	.19	.18	.17	.17	.16	.16
15	1.37	.75	.54	.44	.38	.34	.31	.29	.28	.26	.26	.25	.24	.24
25	2.28	1.24	.89	.72	.62	.56	.51	.48	.46	.44	.42	.41	.40	.39
50	4.56	2.47	1.78	1.44	1.24	1.11	1.02	.96	.91	.87	.84	.82	.80	.78
75	6.84	3.71	2.67	2.16	1.86	1.67	1.53	1.43	1.36	1.30	1.26	1.22	1.19	1.17
100	9.12	4.94	3.56	2.88	2.48	2.22	2.04	1.91	1.81	1.74	1.68	1.63	1.59	1.56
200	18.23	9.88	7.12	5.76	4.96	4.44	4.08	3.81	3.62	3.47	3.35	3.25	3.18	3.12
300	27.35	14.82	10.68	8.64	7.44	6.66	6.11	5.72	5.42	5.20	5.02	4.88	4.76	4.67
400	36.46	19.76	14.24	11.52	9.92	8.88	8.15	7.62	7.23	6.93	6.69	6.50	6.35	6.23
500	45.58	24.70	17.80	14.40	12.40	11.09	10.19	9.53	9.03	8.66	8.36	8.13	7.93	7.78
600	54.69	29.63	21.36	17.28	14.88	13.31	12.22	11.43	10.84	10.39	10.03	9.75	9.52	9.34
700	63.81	34.57	24.92	20.16	17.35	15.53	14.26	13.34	12.65	12.12	11.70	11.37	11.11	10.89
800	72.92	39.51	28.48	23.04	19.83	17.75	16.30	15.24	14.45	13.85	13.37	12.99	12.69	12.45
900	82.04	44.45	32.04	25.92	22.31	19.96	18.33	17.15	16.26	15.58	15.04	14.62	14.28	14.00
1000	91.15	49.39	35.60	28.80	24.79	22.18	20.37	19.05	18.06	17.31	16.71	16.24	15.86	15.56
2000	182.30	98.77	71.19	57.59	49.58	44.36	40.73	38.10	36.12	34.61	33.42	32.48	31.72	31.11
3000	273.44	148.15	106.78	86.38	74.36	66.53	61.10	57.15	54.18	51.91	50.13	48.71	47.58	46.66
4000	364.59	197.53	142.37	115.17	99.15	88.71	81.46	76.19	72.24	69.21	66.83	64.95	63.44	62.21
5000	455.73	246.92	177.96	143.96	123.93	110.89	101.82	95.24	90.30	86.51	83.54	81.18	79.29	77.76
6000	546.88	296.30	213.55	172.75	148.72	133.06	122.19	114.29	108.36	103.81	100.25	97.42	95.15	93.31
7000	638.02	345.68	249.14	201.54	173.50	155.24	142.55	133.33	126.42	121.11	116.95	113.66	111.01	108.87
8000	729.17	395.06	284.73	230.33	198.29	177.42	162.91	152.38	144.48	138.41	133.66	129.89	126.87	124.42
9000	820.31	444.45	320.32	259.12	223.07	199.59	183.28	171.43	162.54	155.71	150.37	146.13	142.73	139.97
10000	911.46	493.83	355.91	287.91	247.86	221.77	203.64	190.47	180.60	173.01	167.08	162.36	158.58	155.52
11000	1002.60	543.21	391.50	316.70	272.64	243.95	224.00	209.52	198.66	190.31	183.78	178.60	174.44	171.07
12000	1093.75	592.59	427.09	345.49	297.43	266.12	244.37	228.57	216.72	207.61	200.49	194.84	190.30	186.62
13000	1184.90	641.97	462.68	374.28	322.22	288.30	264.73	247.61	234.78	224.91	217.20	211.07	206.16	202.17
14000	1276.04	691.36	498.27	403.07	347.00	310.48	285.10	266.66	252.83	242.21	233.90	227.31	222.01	217.73
15000	1367.19	740.74	533.86	431.86	371.79	332.65	305.46	285.71	270.89	259.51	250.61	243.54	237.87	233.28
16000	1458.33	790.12	569.45	460.65	396.57	354.83	325.82	304.75	288.95	276.82	267.32	259.78	253.73	248.83
17000	1549.48	839.50	605.04	489.44	421.36	377.00	346.19	323.80	307.01	294.12	284.03	276.02	269.59	264.38
18000	1640.62	888.89	640.63	518.23	446.14	399.18	366.55	342.85	325.07	311.42	300.73	292.25	285.45	279.93
19000	1731.77	938.27	676.23	547.02	470.93	421.36	386.91	361.90	343.13	328.72	317.44	308.49	301.30	295.48
20000	1822.91	987.65	711.82	575.81	495.71	443.53	407.28	380.94	361.19	346.02	334.15	324.72	317.16	311.04
21000	1914.06	1037.03	747.41	604.60	520.50	465.71	427.64	399.99	379.25	363.32	350.85	340.96	333.02	326.59
22000	2005.20	1086.41	783.00	633.39	545.28	487.89	448.00	419.04	397.31	380.62	367.56	357.20	348.88	342.14
23000	2096.35	1135.80	818.59	662.18	570.07	510.06	468.37	438.08	415.37	397.92	384.27	373.43	364.74	357.69
24000	2187.50	1185.18	854.18	690.97	594.85	532.24	488.73	457.13	433.43	415.22	400.97	389.67	380.59	373.24
25000	2278.64	1234.56	889.77	719.77	619.64	554.42	509.10	476.18	451.49	432.52	417.68	405.90	396.45	388.79
26000	2369.79	1283.94	925.36	748.56	644.43	576.59	529.46	495.22	469.55	449.82	434.39	422.14	412.31	404.34
27000	2460.93	1333.33	960.95	777.35	669.21	598.77	549.82	514.27	487.61	467.12	451.10	438.38	428.17	419.90
28000	2552.08	1382.71	996.54	806.14	694.00	620.95	570.19	533.32	505.66	484.42	467.80	454.61	444.02	435.45
29000	2643.22	1432.09	1032.13	834.93	718.78	643.12	590.55	552.36	523.72	501.72	484.51	470.85	459.88	451.00
30000	2734.37	1481.47	1067.72	863.72	743.57	665.30	610.91	571.41	541.78	519.02	501.22	487.08	475.74	466.55
31000	2825.51	1530.85	1103.31	892.51	768.35	687.47	631.28	590.46	559.84	536.32	517.92	503.32	491.60	482.10
32000	2916.66	1580.24	1138.90	921.30	793.14	709.65	651.64	609.50	577.90	553.63	534.63	519.56	507.46	497.65
33000	3007.80	1629.62	1174.49	950.09	817.92	731.83	672.00	628.55	595.96	570.93	551.34	535.79	523.31	513.21
34000	3098.95	1679.00	1210.08	978.88	842.71	754.00	692.37	647.60	614.02	588.23	568.05	552.03	539.17	528.76
35000	3190.10	1728.38	1245.67	1007.67	867.49	776.18	712.73	666.65	632.08	605.53	584.75	568.26	555.03	544.31
36000	3281.24	1777.77	1281.26	1036.46	892.28	798.36	733.10	685.69	650.14	622.83	601.46	584.50	570.89	559.86
37000	3372.39	1827.15	1316.86	1065.25	917.07	820.53	753.46	704.74	668.20	640.13	618.17	600.74	586.75	575.41
38000	3463.53	1876.53	1352.45	1094.04	941.85	842.71	773.82	723.79	686.26	657.43	634.87	616.97	602.60	590.96
39000	3554.68	1925.91	1388.04	1122.83	966.64	864.89	794.19	742.83	704.32	674.73	651.58	633.21	618.46	606.51
40000	3645.82	1975.29	1423.63	1151.62	991.42	887.06	814.55	761.88	722.38	692.03	668.29	649.44	634.32	622.07
41000	3736.97	2024.68	1459.22	1180.41	1016.21	909.24	834.91	780.93	740.44	709.33	685.00	665.68	650.18	637.62
42000	3828.11	2074.06	1494.81	1209.20	1040.99	931.42	855.28	799.97	758.49	726.63	701.70	681.92	666.03	653.17
43000	3919.26	2123.44	1530.40	1237.99	1065.78	953.59	875.64	819.02	776.55	743.93	718.41	698.15	681.89	668.72
44000	4010.40	2172.82	1565.99	1266.78	1090.56	975.77	896.00	838.07	794.61	761.23	735.12	714.39	697.75	684.27
45000	4101.55	2222.21	1601.58	1295.57	1115.35	997.94	916.37	857.11	812.67	778.53	751.82	730.62	713.61	699.82
46000	4192.70	2271.59	1637.17	1324.36	1140.13	1020.12	936.73	876.16	830.73	795.83	768.53	746.86	729.47	715.37
47000	4283.84	2320.97	1672.76	1353.15	1164.92	1042.30	957.10	895.21	848.79	813.13	785.24	763.10	745.32	730.93
48000	4374.99	2370.35	1708.35	1381.94	1189.70	1064.47	977.46	914.25	866.85	830.44	801.94	779.33	761.18	746.48
49000	4466.13	2419.73	1743.94	1410.74	1214.49	1086.65	997.82	933.30	884.91	847.74	818.65	795.57	777.04	762.03
50000	4557.28	2469.12	1779.53	1439.53	1239.28	1108.83	1018.19	952.35	902.97	865.04	835.36	811.80	792.90	777.58
55000	5013.00	2716.03	1957.49	1583.48	1363.20	1219.71	1120.00	1047.58	993.27	951.54	918.89	892.98	872.19	855.34
60000	5468.73	2962.94	2135.44	1727.43	1487.13	1330.59	1221.82	1142.82	1083.56	1038.04	1002.43	974.16	951.48	933.10
65000	5924.46	3209.85	2313.39	1871.38	1611.06	1441.47	1323.64	1238.05	1173.86	1124.55	1085.97	1055.34	1030.76	1010.85
70000	6380.19	3456.76	2491.34	2015.33	1734.98	1552.36	1425.46	1333.29	1264.15	1211.05	1169.50	1136.52	1110.05	1088.61
75000	6835.91	3703.67	2669.30	2159.29	1858.91	1663.24	1527.28	1428.52	1354.45	1297.55	1253.04	1217.70	1189.34	1166.37
80000	7291.64	3950.58	2847.25	2303.24	1982.84	1774.12	1629.10	1523.75	1444.75	1384.06	1336.57	1298.88	1268.63	1244.13
85000	7747.37	4197.49	3025.20	2447.19	2106.77	1885.00	1730.91	1618.99	1535.04	1470.56	1420.11	1380.06	1347.92	1321.88
90000	8203.10	4444.41	3203.15	2591.14	2230.69	1995.88	1832.73	1714.22	1625.34	1557.06	1503.64	1461.24	1427.21	1399.64
95000	8658.82	4691.32	3381.11	2735.09	2354.62	2106.77	1934.55	1809.46	1715.64	1643.57	1587.18	1542.42	1506.50	1477.40
100000	9114.55	4938.23	3559.06	2879.05	2478.55	2217.65	2036.37	1904.69	1805.93	1730.07	1670.71	1623.60	1585.79	1555.16

TERM AMOUNT	15 Years	16 Years	17 Years	18 Years	19 Years	20 Years	21 Years	22 Years	23 Years	24 Years	25 Years	30 Years	35 Years	40 Years
5	.08	.08	.08	.08	.08	.08	.08	.08	.08	.08	.08	.08	.08	.08
10	.16	.16	.15	.15	.15	.15	.15	.15	.15	.15	.15	.15	.15	.15
15	.23	.23	.23	.23	.23	.22	.22	.22	.22	.22	.22	.22	.22	.22
25	.39	.38	.38	.37	.37	.37	.37	.37	.36	.36	.36	.36	.36	.36
50	.77	.76	.75	.74	.74	.73	.73	.73	.72	.72	.72	.71	.71	.71
75	1.15	1.14	1.12	1.11	1.11	1.10	1.09	1.09	1.08	1.08	1.08	1.07	1.06	1.06
100	1.54	1.51	1.50	1.48	1.47	1.46	1.45	1.45	1.44	1.44	1.43	1.42	1.42	1.41
200	3.07	3.02	2.99	2.96	2.94	2.92	2.90	2.89	2.88	2.87	2.86	2.84	2.83	2.82
300	4.60	4.53	4.48	4.44	4.41	4.38	4.35	4.33	4.32	4.30	4.29	4.25	4.24	4.23
400	6.13	6.04	5.98	5.92	5.87	5.83	5.80	5.77	5.75	5.73	5.72	5.67	5.65	5.64
500	7.66	7.55	7.47	7.40	7.34	7.29	7.25	7.22	7.19	7.16	7.14	7.08	7.06	7.04
600	9.19	9.06	8.96	8.88	8.81	8.75	8.70	8.66	8.63	8.60	8.57	8.50	8.47	8.45
700	10.72	10.57	10.45	10.36	10.27	10.21	10.15	10.10	10.06	10.03	10.00	9.91	9.88	9.86
800	12.25	12.08	11.95	11.83	11.74	11.66	11.60	11.54	11.50	11.46	11.43	11.33	11.29	11.27
900	13.78	13.59	13.44	13.31	13.21	13.12	13.05	12.99	12.94	12.89	12.86	12.74	12.70	12.68
1000	15.31	15.10	14.93	14.79	14.68	14.58	14.50	14.43	14.37	14.32	14.28	14.16	14.11	14.08
2000	30.61	30.20	29.86	29.58	29.35	29.15	28.99	28.85	28.74	28.64	28.56	28.32	28.21	28.16
3000	45.91	45.29	44.79	44.37	44.02	43.72	43.48	43.28	43.11	42.96	42.84	42.47	42.31	42.24
4000	61.21	60.39	59.71	59.15	58.69	58.30	57.97	57.70	57.47	57.28	57.12	56.63	56.42	56.32
5000	76.51	75.49	74.64	73.94	73.36	72.87	72.46	72.12	71.84	71.60	71.40	70.78	70.52	70.40
6000	91.81	90.58	89.57	88.73	88.03	87.44	86.96	86.55	86.21	85.92	85.68	84.94	84.62	84.48
7000	107.12	105.68	104.49	103.51	102.70	102.02	101.45	100.97	100.57	100.24	99.96	99.09	98.72	98.56
8000	122.42	120.78	119.42	118.30	117.37	116.59	115.94	115.40	114.94	114.56	114.24	113.25	112.83	112.64
9000	137.72	135.87	134.35	133.09	132.04	131.16	130.43	129.82	129.31	128.88	128.52	127.40	126.93	126.72
10000	153.02	150.97	149.28	147.87	146.71	145.74	144.92	144.24	143.67	143.20	142.79	141.56	141.03	140.80
11000	168.32	166.06	164.20	162.66	161.38	160.31	159.42	158.67	158.04	157.52	157.07	155.71	155.13	154.88
12000	183.62	181.16	179.13	177.45	176.05	174.88	173.91	173.09	172.41	171.83	171.35	169.87	169.24	168.96
13000	198.93	196.26	194.06	192.23	190.72	189.45	188.40	187.52	186.78	186.15	185.63	184.02	183.34	183.04
14000	214.23	211.35	208.99	207.02	205.39	204.03	202.89	201.94	201.14	200.47	199.91	198.18	197.44	197.12
15000	229.53	226.45	223.91	221.81	220.06	218.60	217.38	216.36	215.51	214.79	214.19	212.33	211.54	211.20
16000	244.83	241.55	238.84	236.59	234.73	233.17	231.87	230.79	229.88	229.11	228.47	226.49	225.65	225.28
17000	260.13	256.64	253.76	251.38	249.40	247.75	246.37	245.21	244.24	243.43	242.75	240.65	239.75	239.36
18000	275.43	271.74	268.69	266.17	264.07	262.32	260.86	259.64	258.61	257.75	257.03	254.80	253.85	253.44
19000	290.73	286.84	283.62	280.95	278.74	276.89	275.35	274.06	272.98	272.07	271.30	268.96	267.95	267.52
20000	306.04	301.93	298.55	295.74	293.41	291.47	289.84	288.48	287.34	286.39	285.58	283.11	282.06	281.60
21000	321.34	317.03	313.47	310.53	308.08	306.04	304.33	302.91	301.71	300.71	299.86	297.27	296.16	295.68
22000	336.64	332.12	328.40	325.31	322.75	320.61	318.83	317.33	316.08	315.03	314.14	311.42	310.26	309.76
23000	351.94	347.22	343.33	340.10	337.42	335.18	333.32	331.75	330.44	329.34	328.42	325.58	324.36	323.04
24000	367.24	362.32	358.25	354.89	352.09	349.76	347.81	346.18	344.81	343.66	342.70	339.73	338.47	337.92
25000	382.54	377.41	373.18	369.67	366.76	364.33	362.30	360.60	359.18	357.98	356.98	353.89	352.57	352.00
26000	397.85	392.51	388.11	384.46	381.43	378.90	376.79	375.03	373.55	372.30	371.26	368.04	366.67	366.08
27000	413.15	407.61	403.03	399.25	396.10	393.48	391.29	389.45	387.91	386.62	385.54	382.20	380.77	380.16
28000	428.45	422.70	417.96	414.03	410.77	408.05	405.78	403.87	402.28	400.94	399.81	396.35	394.88	394.24
29000	443.75	437.80	432.89	428.82	425.44	422.62	420.27	418.30	416.65	415.26	414.09	410.51	408.98	408.32
30000	459.05	452.89	447.82	443.61	440.11	437.20	434.76	432.72	431.01	429.58	428.37	424.66	423.08	422.40
31000	474.35	467.99	462.74	458.39	454.78	451.77	449.25	447.15	445.38	443.90	442.65	438.82	437.18	436.48
32000	489.66	483.09	477.67	473.18	469.45	466.34	463.74	461.57	459.75	458.22	456.93	452.98	451.29	450.56
33000	504.96	498.18	492.60	487.97	484.12	480.91	478.24	475.99	474.11	472.54	471.21	467.13	465.39	464.64
34000	520.26	513.28	507.52	502.75	498.79	495.49	492.73	490.42	488.48	486.85	485.49	481.29	479.49	478.72
35000	535.56	528.38	522.45	517.54	513.46	510.06	507.22	504.84	502.85	501.17	499.77	495.44	493.59	492.80
36000	550.86	543.47	537.38	532.33	528.13	524.63	521.71	519.27	517.21	515.49	514.05	509.60	507.70	506.88
37000	566.16	558.57	552.30	547.12	542.80	539.21	536.20	533.69	531.58	529.81	528.32	523.75	521.80	520.96
38000	581.46	573.67	567.23	561.90	557.47	553.78	550.70	548.11	545.95	544.13	542.60	537.91	535.90	535.04
39000	596.77	588.76	582.16	576.69	572.14	568.35	565.19	562.54	560.32	558.45	556.88	552.06	550.00	549.12
40000	612.07	603.86	597.09	591.48	586.81	582.93	579.68	576.96	574.68	572.77	571.16	566.22	564.11	563.20
41000	627.37	618.95	612.01	606.26	601.48	597.50	594.17	591.39	589.05	587.09	585.44	580.37	578.21	577.28
42000	642.67	634.05	626.94	621.05	616.15	612.07	608.66	605.81	603.42	601.41	599.72	594.53	592.31	591.36
43000	657.97	649.15	641.87	635.84	630.82	626.65	623.15	620.23	617.78	615.73	614.00	608.68	606.41	605.44
44000	673.27	664.24	656.79	650.62	645.49	641.22	637.65	634.66	632.15	630.05	628.28	622.84	620.52	619.52
45000	688.57	679.34	671.72	665.41	660.16	655.79	652.14	649.08	646.52	644.37	642.56	636.99	634.62	633.60
46000	703.88	694.44	686.65	680.20	674.83	670.36	666.63	663.50	660.88	658.68	656.83	651.15	648.72	647.67
47000	719.18	709.53	701.57	694.98	689.50	684.94	681.12	677.93	675.25	673.00	671.11	665.30	662.82	661.75
48000	734.48	724.63	716.50	709.77	704.17	699.51	695.61	692.35	689.62	687.32	685.39	679.46	676.93	675.83
49000	749.78	739.72	731.43	724.56	718.84	714.08	710.11	706.78	703.99	701.64	699.67	693.62	691.03	689.91
50000	765.08	754.82	746.36	739.34	733.51	728.66	724.60	721.20	718.35	715.96	713.95	707.77	705.13	703.99
55000	841.59	830.30	820.99	813.28	806.87	801.52	797.06	793.32	790.19	787.56	785.35	778.55	775.64	774.39
60000	918.10	905.78	895.63	887.21	880.22	874.39	869.52	865.44	862.02	859.15	856.74	849.32	846.16	844.79
65000	994.61	981.27	970.26	961.14	953.57	947.25	941.98	937.56	933.86	930.75	928.13	920.10	916.67	915.19
70000	1071.11	1056.75	1044.90	1035.08	1026.92	1020.12	1014.43	1009.68	1005.69	1002.34	999.53	990.88	987.18	985.59
75000	1147.62	1132.23	1119.53	1109.01	1100.27	1092.98	1086.89	1081.80	1077.53	1073.94	1070.92	1061.65	1057.69	1055.99
80000	1224.13	1207.71	1194.17	1182.95	1173.62	1165.85	1159.35	1153.92	1149.36	1145.53	1142.32	1132.43	1128.21	1126.39
85000	1300.64	1283.19	1268.80	1256.88	1246.97	1238.71	1231.81	1226.04	1221.19	1217.13	1213.71	1203.21	1198.72	1196.79
90000	1377.14	1358.67	1343.44	1330.81	1320.32	1311.58	1304.27	1298.16	1293.03	1288.73	1285.11	1273.98	1269.23	1267.19
95000	1453.65	1434.16	1418.07	1404.75	1393.67	1384.44	1376.73	1370.28	1364.86	1360.32	1356.50	1344.76	1339.74	1337.58
100000	1530.16	1509.64	1492.71	1478.68	1467.02	1457.31	1449.19	1442.40	1436.70	1431.92	1427.90	1415.54	1410.26	1407.98

MONTHLY PAYMENT
REQUIRED TO AMORTIZE A LOAN

TERM	1 Year	2 Years	3 Years	4 Years	5 Years	6 Years	7 Years	8 Years	9 Years	10 Years	11 Years	12 Years	13 Years	14 Years
AMOUNT														
5	.46	.25	.18	.15	.13	.12	.11	.10	.10	.09	.09	.09	.08	.08
10	.92	.50	.36	.29	.25	.23	.21	.20	.19	.18	.17	.17	.16	.16
15	1.37	.75	.54	.44	.38	.34	.31	.29	.28	.26	.26	.25	.24	.24
25	2.28	1.24	.90	.73	.62	.56	.51	.48	.46	.44	.42	.41	.40	.39
50	4.56	2.47	1.79	1.45	1.24	1.11	1.02	.96	.91	.87	.84	.82	.80	.78
75	6.84	3.71	2.68	2.17	1.86	1.67	1.53	1.43	1.36	1.30	1.26	1.22	1.20	1.17
100	9.12	4.94	3.57	2.89	2.48	2.22	2.04	1.91	1.81	1.74	1.68	1.63	1.59	1.56
200	18.24	9.88	7.13	5.77	4.96	4.44	4.08	3.82	3.62	3.47	3.35	3.26	3.18	3.12
300	27.35	14.82	10.69	8.65	7.44	6.66	6.12	5.72	5.43	5.20	5.02	4.88	4.77	4.68
400	36.47	19.76	14.25	11.53	9.92	8.88	8.16	7.63	7.23	6.93	6.69	6.51	6.35	6.23
500	45.58	24.70	17.81	14.41	12.40	11.10	10.19	9.54	9.04	8.66	8.37	8.13	7.94	7.79
600	54.70	29.64	21.37	17.29	14.88	13.32	12.23	11.44	10.85	10.39	10.04	9.76	9.53	9.35
700	63.82	34.58	24.93	20.17	17.36	15.54	14.27	13.35	12.66	12.13	11.71	11.38	11.12	10.90
800	72.93	39.52	28.49	23.05	19.84	17.76	16.31	15.25	14.46	13.86	13.38	13.01	12.70	12.46
900	82.05	44.46	32.05	25.93	22.32	19.98	18.35	17.16	16.27	15.59	15.06	14.63	14.29	14.02
1000	91.16	49.40	35.61	28.81	24.80	22.20	20.38	19.07	18.08	17.32	16.73	16.26	15.88	15.57
2000	182.32	98.79	71.21	57.61	49.60	44.39	40.76	38.13	36.15	34.64	33.45	32.51	31.75	31.14
3000	273.48	148.19	106.81	86.41	74.40	66.58	61.14	57.19	54.23	51.95	50.17	48.76	47.63	46.71
4000	364.63	197.58	142.42	115.22	99.20	88.77	81.52	76.25	72.30	69.27	66.90	65.02	63.50	62.28
5000	455.79	246.98	178.02	144.02	124.00	110.96	101.90	95.31	90.38	86.59	83.62	81.27	79.38	77.85
6000	546.95	296.37	213.62	172.82	148.80	133.15	122.27	114.38	108.45	103.90	100.34	97.52	95.25	93.42
7000	638.11	345.76	249.23	201.63	173.60	155.34	142.65	133.44	126.53	121.22	117.07	113.77	111.13	108.99
8000	729.26	395.16	284.83	230.43	198.40	177.53	163.03	152.50	144.60	138.54	133.79	130.03	127.00	124.56
9000	820.42	444.55	320.43	259.23	223.19	199.72	183.41	171.56	162.68	155.85	150.51	146.28	142.88	140.12
10000	911.58	493.95	356.03	288.04	247.99	221.91	203.79	190.62	180.75	173.17	167.24	162.53	158.75	155.69
11000	1002.74	543.34	391.64	316.84	272.79	244.10	224.16	209.68	198.83	190.49	183.96	178.78	174.63	171.26
12000	1093.89	592.74	427.24	345.64	297.59	266.29	244.54	228.75	216.90	207.80	200.68	195.04	190.50	186.83
13000	1185.05	642.13	462.84	374.45	322.39	288.48	264.92	247.81	234.98	225.12	217.41	211.29	206.38	202.40
14000	1276.21	691.52	498.45	403.25	347.19	310.67	285.30	266.87	253.05	242.44	234.13	227.54	222.25	217.97
15000	1367.36	740.92	534.05	432.05	371.99	332.86	305.68	285.93	271.12	259.75	250.85	243.79	238.13	233.54
16000	1458.52	790.31	569.65	460.86	396.79	355.05	326.05	304.99	289.20	277.07	267.58	260.05	254.00	249.11
17000	1549.68	839.71	605.26	489.66	421.59	377.24	346.43	324.06	307.27	294.38	284.30	276.30	269.88	264.68
18000	1640.84	889.10	640.86	518.46	446.38	399.43	366.81	343.12	325.35	311.70	301.02	292.55	285.75	280.24
19000	1731.99	938.50	676.46	547.27	471.18	421.62	387.19	362.18	343.42	329.02	317.75	308.80	301.63	295.81
20000	1823.15	987.89	712.06	576.07	495.98	443.81	407.57	381.24	361.50	346.33	334.47	325.06	317.50	311.38
21000	1914.31	1037.28	747.67	604.87	520.78	466.00	427.94	400.30	379.57	363.65	351.19	341.31	333.38	326.95
22000	2005.47	1086.68	783.27	633.68	545.58	488.19	448.32	419.36	397.65	380.97	367.92	357.56	349.25	342.52
23000	2096.62	1136.07	818.87	662.48	570.38	510.38	468.70	438.43	415.72	398.28	384.64	373.82	365.13	358.09
24000	2187.78	1185.47	854.48	691.28	595.18	532.57	489.08	457.49	433.80	415.60	401.36	390.07	381.00	373.66
25000	2278.94	1234.86	890.08	720.09	619.98	554.76	509.46	476.55	451.87	432.92	418.09	406.32	396.88	389.23
26000	2370.09	1284.25	925.68	748.89	644.77	576.95	529.83	495.61	469.95	450.23	434.81	422.57	412.75	404.80
27000	2461.25	1333.65	961.29	777.69	669.57	599.14	550.21	514.67	488.02	467.55	451.53	438.83	428.63	420.36
28000	2552.41	1383.04	996.89	806.50	694.37	621.34	570.59	533.73	506.10	484.87	468.26	455.08	444.50	435.93
29000	2643.57	1432.44	1032.49	835.30	719.17	643.53	590.97	552.80	524.17	502.18	484.98	471.33	460.38	451.50
30000	2734.72	1481.83	1068.09	864.10	743.97	665.72	611.35	571.86	542.24	519.50	501.70	487.58	476.25	467.07
31000	2825.88	1531.23	1103.70	892.91	768.77	687.91	631.72	590.92	560.32	536.81	518.43	503.84	492.13	482.64
32000	2917.04	1580.62	1139.30	921.71	793.57	710.10	652.10	609.98	578.39	554.13	535.15	520.09	508.00	498.21
33000	3008.20	1630.01	1174.90	950.51	818.37	732.29	672.48	629.04	596.47	571.45	551.87	536.34	523.88	513.78
34000	3099.35	1679.41	1210.51	979.32	843.17	754.48	692.86	648.11	614.54	588.76	568.60	552.59	539.75	529.35
35000	3190.51	1728.80	1246.11	1008.12	867.96	776.67	713.24	667.17	632.62	606.08	585.32	568.85	555.62	544.92
36000	3281.67	1778.20	1281.71	1036.92	892.76	798.86	733.61	686.23	650.69	623.40	602.04	585.10	571.50	560.48
37000	3372.83	1827.59	1317.32	1065.73	917.56	821.05	753.99	705.29	668.77	640.71	618.77	601.35	587.37	576.05
38000	3463.98	1876.99	1352.92	1094.53	942.36	843.24	774.37	724.35	686.84	658.03	635.49	617.60	603.25	591.62
39000	3555.14	1926.38	1388.52	1123.33	967.16	865.43	794.75	743.41	704.92	675.35	652.21	633.86	619.12	607.19
40000	3646.30	1975.77	1424.12	1152.14	991.96	887.62	815.13	762.48	722.99	692.66	668.94	650.11	635.00	622.76
41000	3737.45	2025.17	1459.73	1180.94	1016.76	909.81	835.51	781.54	741.07	709.98	685.66	666.36	650.87	638.33
42000	3828.61	2074.56	1495.33	1209.74	1041.56	932.00	855.88	800.60	759.14	727.30	702.38	682.62	666.75	653.90
43000	3919.77	2123.96	1530.93	1238.55	1066.36	954.19	876.26	819.66	777.21	744.61	719.11	698.87	682.62	669.47
44000	4010.93	2173.35	1566.54	1267.35	1091.15	976.38	896.64	838.72	795.29	761.93	735.83	715.12	698.50	685.04
45000	4102.08	2222.75	1602.14	1296.15	1115.95	998.57	917.02	857.78	813.36	779.25	752.55	731.37	714.37	700.60
46000	4193.24	2272.14	1637.74	1324.96	1140.75	1020.76	937.40	876.85	831.44	796.56	769.28	747.63	730.25	716.17
47000	4284.40	2321.53	1673.35	1353.76	1165.55	1042.95	957.77	895.91	849.51	813.88	786.00	763.88	746.12	731.74
48000	4375.56	2370.93	1708.95	1382.56	1190.35	1065.14	978.15	914.97	867.59	831.19	802.72	780.13	762.00	747.31
49000	4466.71	2420.32	1744.55	1411.37	1215.15	1087.33	998.53	934.03	885.66	848.51	819.45	796.38	777.87	762.88
50000	4557.87	2469.72	1780.15	1440.17	1239.95	1109.52	1018.91	953.09	903.74	865.83	836.17	812.64	793.75	778.45
55000	5013.66	2716.69	1958.17	1584.19	1363.94	1220.48	1120.80	1048.40	994.11	952.41	919.79	893.90	873.12	856.29
60000	5469.44	2963.66	2136.18	1728.20	1487.94	1331.43	1222.69	1143.71	1084.48	1038.99	1003.40	975.16	952.50	934.14
65000	5925.23	3210.63	2314.20	1872.22	1611.93	1442.38	1324.58	1239.02	1174.86	1125.57	1087.02	1056.43	1031.87	1011.98
70000	6381.02	3457.60	2492.21	2016.24	1735.92	1553.33	1426.47	1334.33	1265.23	1212.16	1170.64	1137.69	1111.24	1089.83
75000	6836.80	3704.57	2670.23	2160.25	1859.92	1664.28	1528.36	1429.64	1355.60	1298.74	1254.25	1218.95	1190.62	1167.67
80000	7292.59	3951.54	2848.24	2304.27	1983.91	1775.23	1630.25	1524.95	1445.98	1385.32	1337.87	1300.22	1269.99	1245.52
85000	7748.38	4198.51	3026.26	2448.29	2107.91	1886.19	1732.14	1620.26	1536.35	1471.90	1421.49	1381.48	1349.37	1323.36
90000	8204.16	4445.49	3204.27	2592.30	2231.90	1997.14	1834.03	1715.56	1626.72	1558.49	1505.10	1462.74	1428.74	1401.20
95000	8659.95	4692.46	3382.29	2736.32	2355.89	2108.09	1935.92	1810.87	1717.10	1645.07	1588.72	1544.00	1508.12	1479.05
100000	9115.74	4939.43	3560.30	2880.34	2479.89	2219.04	2037.81	1906.18	1807.47	1731.65	1672.34	1625.27	1587.49	1556.89

MONTHLY PAYMENT
REQUIRED TO AMORTIZE A LOAN

16.900%

TERM	15 Years	16 Years	17 Years	18 Years	19 Years	20 Years	21 Years	22 Years	23 Years	24 Years	25 Years	30 Years	35 Years	40 Years
AMOUNT														
5	.08	.08	.08	.08	.08	.08	.08	.08	.08	.08	.08	.08	.08	.08
10	.16	.16	.15	.15	.15	.15	.15	.15	.15	.15	.15	.15	.15	.15
15	.23	.23	.23	.23	.23	.22	.22	.22	.22	.22	.22	.22	.22	.22
25	.39	.38	.38	.38	.37	.37	.37	.37	.36	.36	.36	.36	.36	.36
50	.77	.76	.75	.75	.74	.73	.73	.73	.72	.72	.72	.71	.71	.71
75	1.15	1.14	1.13	1.12	1.11	1.10	1.09	1.09	1.08	1.08	1.08	1.07	1.06	1.06
100	1.54	1.52	1.50	1.49	1.47	1.46	1.46	1.45	1.44	1.44	1.43	1.42	1.42	1.42
200	3.07	3.03	2.99	2.97	2.94	2.92	2.91	2.89	2.88	2.87	2.86	2.84	2.83	2.83
300	4.60	4.54	4.49	4.45	4.41	4.38	4.36	4.34	4.32	4.31	4.29	4.26	4.24	4.24
400	6.13	6.05	5.98	5.93	5.88	5.84	5.81	5.78	5.76	5.74	5.72	5.68	5.65	5.65
500	7.66	7.56	7.48	7.41	7.35	7.30	7.26	7.23	7.20	7.17	7.15	7.09	7.07	7.06
600	9.20	9.07	8.97	8.89	8.82	8.76	8.71	8.67	8.64	8.61	8.58	8.51	8.48	8.47
700	10.73	10.59	10.47	10.37	10.29	10.22	10.16	10.12	10.08	10.04	10.01	9.93	9.89	9.88
800	12.26	12.10	11.96	11.85	11.76	11.68	11.61	11.56	11.51	11.48	11.44	11.35	11.30	11.29
900	13.79	13.61	13.46	13.33	13.23	13.14	13.06	13.00	12.95	12.91	12.87	12.76	12.72	12.70
1000	15.32	15.12	14.95	14.81	14.69	14.60	14.52	14.45	14.39	14.34	14.30	14.18	14.13	14.11
2000	30.64	30.23	29.90	29.62	29.38	29.19	29.03	28.89	28.78	28.68	28.60	28.36	28.25	28.21
3000	45.96	45.35	44.84	44.42	44.07	43.78	43.54	43.33	43.16	43.02	42.90	42.53	42.37	42.31
4000	61.28	60.46	59.79	59.23	58.76	58.37	58.05	57.78	57.55	57.36	57.20	56.71	56.50	56.41
5000	76.60	75.58	74.73	74.03	73.45	72.97	72.56	72.22	71.94	71.70	71.50	70.88	70.62	70.51
6000	91.92	90.69	89.68	88.84	88.14	87.56	87.07	86.66	86.32	86.04	85.80	85.06	84.74	84.61
7000	107.24	105.81	104.62	103.64	102.83	102.15	101.58	101.11	100.71	100.38	100.10	99.23	98.87	98.71
8000	122.56	120.92	119.57	118.45	117.52	116.74	116.09	115.55	115.10	114.72	114.39	113.41	112.99	112.81
9000	137.88	136.03	134.51	133.25	132.21	131.33	130.60	129.99	129.48	129.05	128.69	127.59	127.11	126.91
10000	153.20	151.15	149.46	148.06	146.89	145.93	145.12	144.44	143.87	143.39	142.99	141.76	141.24	141.01
11000	168.52	166.26	164.40	162.86	161.58	160.52	159.63	158.88	158.26	157.73	157.29	155.94	155.36	155.11
12000	183.84	181.38	179.35	177.67	176.27	175.11	174.14	173.32	172.64	172.07	171.59	170.11	169.48	169.21
13000	199.15	196.49	194.29	192.47	190.96	189.70	188.65	187.77	187.03	186.41	185.89	184.29	183.60	103.31
14000	214.47	211.61	209.24	207.28	205.65	204.29	203.16	202.21	201.42	200.75	200.19	198.46	197.73	197.41
15000	229.79	226.72	224.18	222.08	220.34	218.89	217.67	216.65	215.80	215.09	214.49	212.64	211.85	211.51
16000	245.11	241.83	239.13	236.89	235.03	233.48	232.18	231.10	230.19	229.43	228.78	226.81	225.97	225.61
17000	260.43	256.95	254.07	251.69	249.72	248.07	246.69	245.54	244.57	243.76	243.08	240.99	240.10	239.71
18000	275.75	272.06	269.02	266.50	264.41	262.66	261.20	259.98	258.96	258.10	257.38	255.17	254.22	253.81
19000	291.07	287.18	283.97	281.31	279.10	277.25	275.71	274.43	273.35	272.44	271.68	269.34	268.34	267.91
20000	306.39	302.29	298.91	296.11	293.78	291.85	290.23	288.87	287.73	286.78	285.98	283.52	282.47	282.01
21000	321.71	317.41	313.86	310.92	308.47	306.44	304.74	303.31	302.12	301.12	300.28	297.69	296.59	296.11
22000	337.03	332.52	328.80	325.72	323.16	321.03	319.25	317.76	316.51	315.46	314.58	311.87	310.71	310.22
23000	352.35	347.63	343.75	340.53	337.85	335.62	333.76	332.20	330.89	329.80	328.88	326.04	324.04	324.32
24000	367.67	362.75	358.69	355.33	352.54	350.21	348.27	346.64	345.28	344.14	343.17	340.22	338.96	338.42
25000	382.99	377.86	373.64	370.14	367.23	364.81	362.78	361.09	359.67	358.47	357.47	354.39	353.08	352.52
26000	398.30	392.98	388.58	384.94	381.92	379.40	377.29	375.53	374.05	372.81	371.77	368.57	367.20	366.62
27000	413.62	408.09	403.53	399.75	396.61	393.99	391.80	389.97	388.44	387.15	386.07	382.75	381.33	380.72
28000	428.94	423.21	418.47	414.55	411.30	408.58	406.31	404.42	402.83	401.49	400.37	396.92	395.45	394.82
29000	444.26	438.32	433.42	429.36	425.98	423.17	420.82	418.86	417.21	415.83	414.67	411.10	409.57	408.92
30000	459.58	453.43	448.36	444.16	440.67	437.77	435.34	433.30	431.60	430.17	428.97	425.27	423.70	423.02
31000	474.90	468.55	463.31	458.97	455.36	452.36	449.85	447.75	445.99	444.51	443.27	439.45	437.82	437.12
32000	490.22	483.66	478.25	473.77	470.05	466.95	464.36	462.19	460.37	458.85	457.56	453.62	451.94	451.22
33000	505.54	498.78	493.20	488.58	484.74	481.54	478.87	476.63	474.76	473.18	471.86	467.80	466.07	465.32
34000	520.86	513.89	508.14	503.38	499.43	496.13	493.38	491.08	489.14	487.52	486.16	481.98	480.19	479.42
35000	536.18	529.01	523.09	518.19	514.12	510.73	507.89	505.52	503.53	501.86	500.46	496.15	494.31	493.52
36000	551.50	544.12	538.04	533.00	528.81	525.32	522.40	519.96	517.92	516.20	514.76	510.33	508.43	507.62
37000	566.82	559.23	552.98	547.80	543.50	539.91	536.91	534.41	532.30	530.54	529.06	524.50	522.56	521.72
38000	582.14	574.35	567.93	562.61	558.19	554.50	551.42	548.85	546.69	544.88	543.36	538.68	536.68	535.82
39000	597.45	589.46	582.87	577.41	572.87	569.09	565.94	563.29	561.08	559.22	557.65	552.85	550.80	549.92
40000	612.77	604.58	597.82	592.22	587.56	583.69	580.45	577.74	575.46	573.56	571.95	567.03	564.93	564.02
41000	628.09	619.69	612.76	607.02	602.25	598.28	594.96	592.18	589.85	587.90	586.25	581.20	579.05	578.12
42000	643.41	634.81	627.71	621.83	616.94	612.87	609.47	606.62	604.24	602.23	600.55	595.38	593.17	592.22
43000	658.73	649.92	642.65	636.63	631.63	627.46	623.98	621.07	618.62	616.57	614.85	609.56	607.30	606.33
44000	674.05	665.03	657.60	651.44	646.32	642.05	638.49	635.51	633.01	630.91	629.15	623.73	621.42	620.43
45000	689.37	680.15	672.54	666.24	661.01	656.65	653.00	649.95	647.40	645.25	643.45	637.91	635.54	634.53
46000	704.69	695.26	687.49	681.05	675.70	671.24	667.51	664.40	661.78	659.59	657.75	652.08	649.67	648.63
47000	720.01	710.38	702.43	695.85	690.39	685.83	682.02	678.84	676.17	673.93	672.04	666.26	663.79	662.73
48000	735.33	725.49	717.38	710.66	705.07	700.42	696.53	693.28	690.56	688.27	686.34	680.43	677.91	676.83
49000	750.65	740.61	732.32	725.46	719.76	715.01	711.05	707.73	704.94	702.61	700.64	694.61	692.03	690.93
50000	765.97	755.72	747.27	740.27	734.45	729.61	725.56	722.17	719.33	716.94	714.94	708.78	706.16	705.03
55000	842.56	831.29	822.00	814.30	807.90	802.57	798.11	794.38	791.26	788.64	786.43	779.66	776.77	775.53
60000	919.16	906.86	896.72	888.32	881.34	875.53	870.67	866.60	863.19	860.33	857.93	850.54	847.39	846.03
65000	995.75	982.44	971.45	962.35	954.79	948.49	943.22	938.82	935.13	932.03	929.42	921.42	918.00	916.54
70000	1072.35	1058.01	1046.17	1036.38	1028.23	1021.45	1015.78	1011.03	1007.06	1003.72	1000.91	992.30	988.62	987.04
75000	1148.95	1133.58	1120.90	1110.40	1101.68	1094.41	1088.33	1083.25	1078.99	1075.41	1072.41	1063.17	1059.23	1057.54
80000	1225.54	1209.15	1195.63	1184.43	1175.12	1167.37	1160.89	1155.47	1150.92	1147.11	1143.90	1134.05	1129.85	1128.04
85000	1302.14	1284.72	1270.35	1258.45	1248.57	1240.33	1233.44	1227.68	1222.85	1218.80	1215.40	1204.93	1200.46	1198.54
90000	1378.74	1360.29	1345.08	1332.48	1322.01	1313.29	1306.00	1299.90	1294.79	1290.50	1286.89	1275.85	1271.08	1269.05
95000	1455.33	1435.86	1419.81	1406.51	1395.46	1386.25	1378.55	1372.12	1366.72	1362.19	1358.38	1346.69	1341.70	1339.55
100000	1531.93	1511.44	1494.53	1480.53	1468.90	1459.21	1451.11	1444.33	1438.65	1433.88	1429.88	1417.56	1412.31	1410.05

17.000%

TERM AMOUNT	1 Year	2 Years	3 Years	4 Years	5 Years	6 Years	7 Years	8 Years	9 Years	10 Years	11 Years	12 Years	13 Years	14 Years
5	.46	.25	.18	.15	.13	.12	.11	.10	.10	.09	.09	.09	.08	.08
10	.92	.50	.36	.29	.25	.23	.21	.20	.19	.18	.17	.17	.16	.16
15	1.37	.75	.54	.44	.38	.34	.31	.29	.28	.27	.26	.25	.24	.24
25	2.29	1.24	.90	.73	.63	.56	.52	.48	.46	.44	.42	.41	.40	.40
50	4.57	2.48	1.79	1.45	1.25	1.12	1.03	.96	.91	.87	.84	.82	.80	.79
75	6.85	3.71	2.68	2.17	1.87	1.67	1.54	1.44	1.37	1.31	1.26	1.23	1.20	1.18
100	9.13	4.95	3.57	2.89	2.49	2.23	2.05	1.92	1.82	1.74	1.68	1.64	1.60	1.57
200	18.25	9.89	7.14	5.78	4.98	4.45	4.09	3.83	3.63	3.48	3.36	3.27	3.19	3.13
300	27.37	14.84	10.70	8.66	7.46	6.68	6.14	5.74	5.45	5.22	5.04	4.90	4.79	4.70
400	36.49	19.78	14.27	11.55	9.95	8.90	8.18	7.65	7.26	6.96	6.72	6.53	6.38	6.26
500	45.61	24.73	17.83	14.43	12.43	11.13	10.22	9.57	9.07	8.69	8.40	8.16	7.98	7.82
600	54.73	29.67	21.40	17.32	14.92	13.35	12.27	11.48	10.89	10.43	10.08	9.80	9.57	9.39
700	63.85	34.61	24.96	20.20	17.40	15.58	14.31	13.39	12.70	12.17	11.76	11.43	11.17	10.95
800	72.97	39.56	28.53	23.09	19.89	17.80	16.35	15.30	14.51	13.91	13.44	13.06	12.76	12.52
900	82.09	44.50	32.09	25.97	22.37	20.03	18.40	17.21	16.33	15.65	15.11	14.69	14.35	14.08
1000	91.21	49.45	35.66	28.86	24.86	22.25	20.44	19.13	18.14	17.38	16.79	16.32	15.95	15.64
2000	182.41	98.89	71.31	57.72	49.71	44.50	40.88	38.25	36.28	34.76	33.58	32.64	31.89	31.28
3000	273.62	148.33	106.96	86.57	74.56	66.74	61.31	57.37	54.41	52.14	50.37	48.96	47.83	46.92
4000	364.82	197.77	142.62	115.43	99.42	88.99	81.75	76.49	72.55	69.52	67.16	65.28	63.78	62.56
5000	456.03	247.22	178.27	144.28	124.27	111.24	102.18	95.61	90.69	86.90	83.95	81.60	79.72	78.20
6000	547.23	296.66	213.92	173.14	149.12	133.48	122.62	114.73	108.82	104.28	100.73	97.92	95.66	93.84
7000	638.44	346.10	249.57	201.99	173.97	155.73	143.06	133.86	126.96	121.66	117.52	114.24	111.61	109.47
8000	729.64	395.54	285.23	230.85	198.83	177.97	163.49	152.98	145.09	139.04	134.31	130.56	127.55	125.11
9000	820.85	444.99	320.88	259.70	223.68	200.22	183.93	172.10	163.23	156.42	151.10	146.88	143.49	140.75
10000	912.05	494.43	356.53	288.56	248.53	222.47	204.36	191.22	181.37	173.80	167.89	163.20	159.43	156.39
11000	1003.26	543.87	392.19	317.41	273.38	244.71	224.80	210.34	199.50	191.18	184.68	179.52	175.38	172.03
12000	1094.46	593.31	427.84	346.27	298.24	266.96	245.23	229.46	217.64	208.56	201.46	195.84	191.32	187.67
13000	1185.67	642.75	463.49	375.12	323.09	289.20	265.67	248.58	235.78	225.94	218.25	212.15	207.26	203.30
14000	1276.87	692.20	499.14	403.98	347.94	311.45	286.11	267.71	253.91	243.32	235.04	228.47	223.21	218.94
15000	1368.08	741.64	534.80	432.83	372.79	333.70	306.54	286.83	272.05	260.70	251.83	244.79	239.15	234.58
16000	1459.28	791.08	570.45	461.69	397.65	355.94	326.98	305.95	290.18	278.08	268.62	261.11	255.09	250.22
17000	1550.49	840.52	606.10	490.54	422.50	378.19	347.41	325.07	308.32	295.46	285.41	277.43	271.04	265.86
18000	1641.69	889.97	641.75	519.40	447.35	400.44	367.85	344.19	326.46	312.84	302.19	293.75	286.98	281.50
19000	1732.90	939.41	677.41	548.25	472.20	422.68	388.29	363.31	344.59	330.22	318.98	310.07	302.92	297.13
20000	1824.10	988.85	713.06	577.11	497.06	444.93	408.72	382.43	362.73	347.60	335.77	326.39	318.86	312.77
21000	1915.30	1038.29	748.71	605.96	521.91	467.17	429.16	401.56	380.86	364.98	352.56	342.71	334.81	328.41
22000	2006.51	1087.73	784.37	634.82	546.76	489.42	449.59	420.68	399.00	382.36	369.35	359.03	350.75	344.05
23000	2097.71	1137.18	820.02	663.67	571.61	511.67	470.03	439.80	417.14	399.74	386.14	375.35	366.69	359.69
24000	2188.92	1186.62	855.67	692.53	596.47	533.91	490.46	458.92	435.27	417.12	402.92	391.67	382.64	375.33
25000	2280.12	1236.06	891.32	721.38	621.32	556.16	510.90	478.04	453.41	434.50	419.71	407.99	398.58	390.96
26000	2371.33	1285.50	926.98	750.24	646.17	578.40	531.34	497.16	471.55	451.88	436.50	424.30	414.52	406.60
27000	2462.53	1334.95	962.63	779.09	671.02	600.65	551.77	516.28	489.68	469.26	453.29	440.62	430.46	422.24
28000	2553.74	1384.39	998.28	807.95	695.88	622.90	572.21	535.41	507.82	486.64	470.08	456.94	446.41	437.88
29000	2644.94	1433.83	1033.93	836.80	720.73	645.14	592.64	554.53	525.95	504.02	486.87	473.26	462.35	453.52
30000	2736.15	1483.27	1069.59	865.66	745.58	667.39	613.08	573.65	544.09	521.40	503.65	489.58	478.29	469.16
31000	2827.35	1532.72	1105.24	894.51	770.43	689.64	633.51	592.77	562.23	538.78	520.44	505.90	494.24	484.79
32000	2918.56	1582.16	1140.89	923.37	795.29	711.88	653.95	611.89	580.36	556.16	537.23	522.22	510.18	500.43
33000	3009.76	1631.60	1176.55	952.22	820.14	734.13	674.39	631.01	598.50	573.54	554.02	538.54	526.12	516.07
34000	3100.97	1681.04	1212.20	981.08	844.99	756.37	694.82	650.13	616.64	590.92	570.81	554.86	542.07	531.71
35000	3192.17	1730.48	1247.85	1009.93	869.85	778.62	715.26	669.26	634.77	608.30	587.60	571.18	558.01	547.35
36000	3283.38	1779.93	1283.50	1038.79	894.70	800.87	735.69	688.38	652.91	625.68	604.38	587.50	573.95	562.99
37000	3374.58	1829.37	1319.16	1067.64	919.55	823.11	756.13	707.50	671.04	643.06	621.17	603.82	589.89	578.63
38000	3465.79	1878.81	1354.81	1096.50	944.40	845.36	776.57	726.62	689.18	660.44	637.96	620.14	605.84	594.26
39000	3556.99	1928.25	1390.46	1125.35	969.26	867.60	797.00	745.74	707.32	677.82	654.75	636.45	621.78	609.90
40000	3648.20	1977.70	1426.11	1154.21	994.11	889.85	817.44	764.86	725.45	695.20	671.54	652.77	637.72	625.54
41000	3739.40	2027.14	1461.77	1183.06	1018.96	912.10	837.87	783.98	743.59	712.58	688.33	669.09	653.67	641.18
42000	3830.60	2076.58	1497.42	1211.92	1043.81	934.34	858.31	803.11	761.72	729.96	705.11	685.41	669.61	656.82
43000	3921.81	2126.02	1533.07	1240.77	1068.67	956.59	878.74	822.23	779.86	747.33	721.90	701.73	685.55	672.46
44000	4013.01	2175.46	1568.73	1269.63	1093.52	978.83	899.18	841.35	798.00	764.71	738.69	718.05	701.49	688.09
45000	4104.22	2224.91	1604.38	1298.48	1118.37	1001.08	919.62	860.47	816.13	782.09	755.48	734.37	717.44	703.73
46000	4195.42	2274.35	1640.03	1327.34	1143.22	1023.33	940.05	879.59	834.27	799.47	772.27	750.69	733.38	719.37
47000	4286.63	2323.79	1675.68	1356.19	1168.08	1045.57	960.49	898.71	852.41	816.85	789.06	767.01	749.32	735.01
48000	4377.83	2373.23	1711.34	1385.05	1192.93	1067.82	980.92	917.83	870.54	834.23	805.84	783.33	765.27	750.65
49000	4469.04	2422.68	1746.99	1413.90	1217.78	1090.07	1001.36	936.96	888.68	851.61	822.63	799.65	781.21	766.29
50000	4560.24	2472.12	1782.64	1442.76	1242.63	1112.31	1021.80	956.08	906.81	868.99	839.42	815.97	797.15	781.92
55000	5016.27	2719.33	1960.91	1587.03	1366.90	1223.54	1123.97	1051.69	997.50	955.89	923.36	897.56	876.87	860.12
60000	5472.29	2966.54	2139.17	1731.31	1491.16	1334.77	1226.15	1147.29	1088.18	1042.79	1007.30	979.16	956.58	938.31
65000	5928.31	3213.75	2317.43	1875.58	1615.42	1446.00	1328.33	1242.90	1178.86	1129.69	1091.25	1060.75	1036.30	1016.50
70000	6384.34	3460.96	2495.70	2019.86	1739.69	1557.23	1430.51	1338.51	1269.54	1216.59	1175.19	1142.35	1116.01	1094.69
75000	6840.36	3708.17	2673.96	2164.13	1863.95	1668.46	1532.69	1434.11	1360.22	1303.49	1259.13	1223.95	1195.73	1172.88
80000	7296.39	3955.39	2852.22	2308.41	1988.21	1779.70	1634.87	1529.72	1450.90	1390.39	1343.07	1305.54	1275.44	1251.08
85000	7752.41	4202.60	3030.49	2452.68	2112.47	1890.93	1737.05	1625.33	1541.58	1477.29	1427.01	1387.14	1355.16	1329.27
90000	8208.43	4449.81	3208.75	2596.96	2236.74	2002.16	1839.23	1720.94	1632.26	1564.18	1510.95	1468.74	1434.87	1407.46
95000	8664.46	4697.02	3387.01	2741.23	2361.00	2113.39	1941.41	1816.54	1722.94	1651.08	1594.90	1550.33	1514.59	1485.65
100000	9120.48	4944.23	3565.28	2885.51	2485.26	2224.62	2043.59	1912.15	1813.62	1737.98	1678.84	1631.93	1594.30	1563.84

TERM	15 Years	16 Years	17 Years	18 Years	19 Years	20 Years	21 Years	22 Years	23 Years	24 Years	25 Years	30 Years	35 Years	40 Years
AMOUNT														
5	.08	.08	.08	.08	.08	.08	.08	.08	.08	.08	.08	.08	.08	.08
10	.16	.16	.16	.15	.15	.15	.15	.15	.15	.15	.15	.15	.15	.15
15	.24	.23	.23	.23	.23	.23	.22	.22	.22	.22	.22	.22	.22	.22
25	.39	.38	.38	.38	.37	.37	.37	.37	.37	.37	.36	.36	.36	.36
50	.77	.76	.76	.75	.74	.74	.73	.73	.73	.73	.72	.72	.72	.71
75	1.16	1.14	1.13	1.12	1.11	1.11	1.10	1.09	1.09	1.09	1.08	1.07	1.07	1.07
100	1.54	1.52	1.51	1.49	1.48	1.47	1.46	1.46	1.45	1.45	1.44	1.43	1.43	1.42
200	3.08	3.04	3.01	2.98	2.96	2.94	2.92	2.91	2.90	2.89	2.88	2.86	2.85	2.84
300	4.62	4.56	4.51	4.47	4.43	4.41	4.38	4.36	4.34	4.33	4.32	4.28	4.27	4.26
400	6.16	6.08	6.01	5.96	5.91	5.87	5.84	5.81	5.79	5.77	5.76	5.71	5.69	5.68
500	7.70	7.60	7.51	7.44	7.39	7.34	7.30	7.27	7.24	7.21	7.19	7.13	7.11	7.10
600	9.24	9.12	9.02	8.93	8.86	8.81	8.76	8.72	8.68	8.66	8.63	8.56	8.53	8.51
700	10.78	10.64	10.52	10.42	10.34	10.27	10.22	10.17	10.13	10.10	10.07	9.98	9.95	9.93
800	12.32	12.15	12.02	11.91	11.82	11.74	11.68	11.62	11.58	11.54	11.51	11.41	11.37	11.35
900	13.86	13.67	13.52	13.40	13.29	13.21	13.13	13.07	13.02	12.98	12.95	12.84	12.79	12.77
1000	15.40	15.19	15.02	14.88	14.77	14.67	14.59	14.53	14.47	14.42	14.38	14.26	14.21	14.19
2000	30.79	30.38	30.04	29.76	29.53	29.34	29.18	29.05	28.93	28.84	28.76	28.52	28.42	28.37
3000	46.18	45.56	45.06	44.64	44.30	44.01	43.77	43.57	43.40	43.26	43.14	42.78	42.62	42.55
4000	61.57	60.75	60.08	59.52	59.06	58.68	58.36	58.09	57.86	57.68	57.52	57.03	56.83	56.74
5000	76.96	75.94	75.10	74.40	73.83	73.35	72.94	72.61	72.33	72.09	71.89	71.29	71.03	70.92
6000	92.35	91.12	90.12	89.28	88.59	88.01	87.53	87.13	86.79	86.51	86.27	85.55	85.24	85.10
7000	107.74	106.31	105.13	104.16	103.35	102.68	102.12	101.65	101.26	100.93	100.65	99.80	99.44	99.29
8000	123.13	121.50	120.15	119.04	118.12	117.35	116.71	116.17	115.72	115.35	115.03	114.06	113.65	113.47
9000	138.52	136.68	135.17	133.92	132.88	132.02	131.30	130.69	130.19	129.76	129.41	128.32	127.85	127.65
10000	153.91	151.87	150.19	148.80	147.65	146.69	145.88	145.21	144.65	144.18	143.78	142.57	142.06	141.84
11000	169.30	167.05	165.21	163.68	162.41	161.35	160.47	159.73	159.12	158.60	158.16	156.83	156.26	156.02
12000	184.69	182.24	180.23	178.56	177.17	176.02	175.06	174.25	173.58	173.02	172.54	171.09	170.47	170.20
13000	200.08	197.43	195.24	193.44	191.94	190.69	189.65	188.77	188.04	187.43	186.92	185.34	184.67	184.39
14000	215.47	212.61	210.26	208.32	206.70	205.36	204.23	203.30	202.51	201.85	201.30	199.60	198.88	198.57
15000	230.86	227.80	225.28	223.20	221.47	220.03	218.82	217.82	216.97	216.27	215.67	213.86	213.08	212.75
16000	246.25	242.99	240.30	238.08	236.23	234.69	233.41	232.34	231.44	230.69	230.05	228.11	227.29	226.94
17000	261.64	258.17	255.32	252.96	250.99	249.36	248.00	246.86	245.90	245.10	244.43	242.37	241.49	241.12
18000	277.03	273.36	270.34	267.84	265.76	264.03	262.59	261.38	260.37	259.52	258.81	256.63	255.70	255.30
19000	292.42	288.55	285.36	282.71	280.52	278.70	277.17	275.90	274.83	273.94	273.19	270.88	269.90	269.49
20000	307.81	303.73	300.37	297.59	295.29	293.37	291.76	290.42	289.30	288.36	287.56	285.14	284.11	283.67
21000	323.20	318.92	315.39	312.47	310.05	308.03	306.35	304.94	303.76	302.77	301.94	299.40	298.32	297.85
22000	338.59	334.10	330.41	327.35	324.81	322.70	320.94	319.46	318.23	317.19	316.32	313.65	312.52	312.04
23000	353.98	349.29	345.43	342.23	339.58	337.37	335.52	333.98	332.69	331.61	330.70	327.91	326.73	326.22
24000	369.37	364.48	360.45	357.11	354.34	352.04	350.11	348.50	347.16	346.03	345.08	342.17	340.93	340.40
25000	384.76	379.66	375.47	371.99	369.11	366.71	364.70	363.02	361.62	360.44	359.45	356.42	355.14	354.59
26000	400.15	394.85	390.48	386.87	383.87	381.37	379.29	377.54	376.08	374.86	373.83	370.68	369.34	368.77
27000	415.54	410.04	405.50	401.75	398.64	396.04	393.88	392.07	390.55	389.28	388.21	384.94	383.55	382.95
28000	430.93	425.22	420.52	416.63	413.40	410.71	408.46	406.59	405.01	403.70	402.59	399.19	397.75	397.14
29000	446.32	440.41	435.54	431.51	428.16	425.38	423.05	421.11	419.48	418.11	416.97	413.45	411.96	411.32
30000	461.71	455.60	450.56	446.39	442.93	440.05	437.64	435.63	433.94	432.53	431.34	427.71	426.16	425.50
31000	477.10	470.78	465.58	461.27	457.69	454.71	452.23	450.15	448.41	446.95	445.72	441.96	440.37	439.69
32000	492.49	485.97	480.59	476.15	472.46	469.38	466.82	464.67	462.87	461.37	460.10	456.22	454.57	453.87
33000	507.88	501.15	495.61	491.03	487.22	484.05	481.40	479.19	477.34	475.78	474.48	470.48	468.78	468.05
34000	523.27	516.34	510.63	505.91	501.98	498.72	495.99	493.71	491.80	490.20	488.86	484.73	482.98	482.24
35000	538.66	531.53	525.65	520.79	516.75	513.39	510.58	508.23	506.27	504.62	503.23	498.99	497.19	496.42
36000	554.05	546.71	540.67	535.67	531.51	528.05	525.17	522.75	520.73	519.04	517.61	513.25	511.39	510.60
37000	569.44	561.90	555.69	550.55	546.28	542.72	539.75	537.27	535.20	533.45	531.99	527.50	525.60	524.78
38000	584.83	577.09	570.71	565.42	561.04	557.39	554.34	551.79	549.66	547.87	546.37	541.76	539.80	538.97
39000	600.22	592.27	585.72	580.30	575.80	572.06	568.93	566.31	564.12	562.29	560.75	556.02	554.01	553.15
40000	615.61	607.46	600.74	595.18	590.57	586.73	583.52	580.84	578.59	576.71	575.12	570.28	568.22	567.33
41000	631.00	622.64	615.76	610.06	605.33	601.39	598.11	595.36	593.05	591.12	589.50	584.53	582.42	581.52
42000	646.39	637.83	630.78	624.94	620.10	616.06	612.69	609.88	607.52	605.54	603.88	598.79	596.63	595.70
43000	661.78	653.02	645.80	639.82	634.86	630.73	627.28	624.40	621.98	619.96	618.26	613.05	610.83	609.88
44000	677.17	668.20	660.82	654.70	649.62	645.40	641.87	638.92	636.45	634.38	632.64	627.30	625.04	624.07
45000	692.56	683.39	675.83	669.58	664.39	660.07	656.46	653.44	650.91	648.79	647.01	641.56	639.24	638.25
46000	707.95	698.58	690.85	684.46	679.15	674.73	671.04	667.96	665.38	663.21	661.39	655.82	653.45	652.43
47000	723.34	713.76	705.87	699.34	693.92	689.40	685.63	682.48	679.84	677.63	675.77	670.07	667.65	666.62
48000	738.73	728.95	720.89	714.22	708.68	704.07	700.22	697.00	694.31	692.05	690.15	684.33	681.86	680.80
49000	754.12	744.14	735.91	729.10	723.45	718.74	714.81	711.52	708.77	706.46	704.53	698.59	696.06	694.98
50000	769.51	759.32	750.93	743.98	738.21	733.41	729.40	726.04	723.24	720.88	718.90	712.84	710.27	709.17
55000	846.46	835.25	826.02	818.38	812.03	806.75	802.34	798.65	795.56	792.97	790.79	784.13	781.29	780.08
60000	923.41	911.19	901.11	892.77	885.85	880.09	875.27	871.25	867.88	865.06	862.68	855.41	852.32	851.00
65000	1000.36	987.12	976.20	967.17	959.67	953.43	948.21	943.85	940.20	937.14	934.57	926.69	923.35	921.92
70000	1077.31	1063.05	1051.30	1041.57	1033.49	1026.77	1021.15	1016.46	1012.53	1009.23	1006.46	997.98	994.37	992.83
75000	1154.26	1138.98	1126.39	1115.97	1107.31	1100.11	1094.09	1089.06	1084.85	1081.32	1078.35	1069.26	1065.40	1063.75
80000	1231.21	1214.91	1201.48	1190.36	1181.13	1173.45	1167.03	1161.67	1157.17	1153.41	1150.24	1140.55	1136.43	1134.66
85000	1308.16	1290.84	1276.57	1264.76	1254.95	1246.79	1239.97	1234.27	1229.50	1225.49	1222.13	1211.83	1207.45	1205.58
90000	1385.11	1366.78	1351.66	1339.16	1328.77	1320.13	1312.91	1306.87	1301.82	1297.58	1294.02	1283.11	1278.48	1276.50
95000	1462.06	1442.71	1426.76	1413.56	1402.59	1393.47	1385.85	1379.48	1374.14	1369.67	1365.91	1354.40	1349.50	1347.41
100000	1539.01	1518.64	1501.85	1487.95	1476.41	1466.81	1458.79	1452.08	1446.47	1441.76	1437.80	1425.68	1420.53	1418.33

17%

MONTHLY PAYMENT
REQUIRED TO AMORTIZE A LOAN

TERM AMOUNT	1 Year	2 Years	3 Years	4 Years	5 Years	6 Years	7 Years	8 Years	9 Years	10 Years	11 Years	12 Years	13 Years	14 Years
5	.46	.25	.18	.15	.13	.12	.11	.10	.10	.09	.09	.09	.09	.08
10	.92	.50	.36	.29	.25	.23	.21	.20	.19	.18	.17	.17	.17	.16
15	1.37	.75	.54	.44	.38	.34	.31	.29	.28	.27	.26	.25	.25	.24
25	2.29	1.24	.90	.73	.63	.56	.52	.48	.46	.44	.43	.41	.41	.40
50	4.57	2.48	1.79	1.45	1.25	1.12	1.03	.96	.91	.88	.85	.82	.81	.79
75	6.85	3.72	2.68	2.17	1.87	1.68	1.54	1.44	1.37	1.31	1.27	1.23	1.21	1.18
100	9.13	4.95	3.58	2.90	2.50	2.24	2.05	1.92	1.82	1.75	1.69	1.64	1.61	1.58
200	18.26	9.90	7.15	5.79	4.99	4.47	4.10	3.84	3.64	3.49	3.38	3.28	3.21	3.15
300	27.38	14.85	10.72	8.68	7.48	6.70	6.15	5.76	5.46	5.24	5.06	4.92	4.81	4.72
400	36.51	19.80	14.29	11.57	9.97	8.93	8.20	7.68	7.28	6.98	6.75	6.56	6.41	6.29
500	45.63	24.75	17.86	14.46	12.46	11.16	10.25	9.60	9.10	8.73	8.43	8.20	8.01	7.86
600	54.76	29.70	21.43	17.35	14.95	13.39	12.30	11.51	10.92	10.47	10.12	9.84	9.61	9.43
700	63.88	34.65	25.00	20.24	17.44	15.62	14.35	13.43	12.74	12.22	11.80	11.48	11.21	11.00
800	73.01	39.60	28.57	23.13	19.93	17.85	16.40	15.35	14.56	13.96	13.49	13.11	12.81	12.57
900	82.13	44.55	32.14	26.02	22.42	20.08	18.45	17.27	16.38	15.70	15.17	14.75	14.42	14.14
1000	91.26	49.50	35.71	28.91	24.91	22.31	20.50	19.19	18.20	17.45	16.86	16.39	16.02	15.71
2000	182.51	98.99	71.41	57.82	49.82	44.61	40.99	38.37	36.40	34.89	33.71	32.78	32.03	31.42
3000	273.76	148.48	107.11	86.73	74.72	66.91	61.49	57.55	54.60	52.33	50.57	49.16	48.04	47.13
4000	365.01	197.97	142.82	115.63	99.63	89.21	81.98	76.73	72.80	69.78	67.42	65.55	64.05	62.84
5000	456.27	247.46	178.52	144.54	124.54	111.51	102.47	95.91	90.99	87.22	84.27	81.93	80.06	78.55
6000	547.52	296.95	214.22	173.45	149.44	133.82	122.97	115.09	109.19	104.66	101.13	98.32	96.07	94.25
7000	638.77	346.44	249.92	202.35	174.35	156.12	143.46	134.27	127.39	122.11	117.98	114.71	112.08	109.96
8000	730.02	395.93	285.63	231.26	199.26	178.42	163.95	153.45	145.59	139.55	134.83	131.09	128.09	125.67
9000	821.27	445.42	321.33	260.17	224.16	200.72	184.45	172.64	163.79	156.99	151.69	147.48	144.11	141.38
10000	912.53	494.91	357.03	289.07	249.07	223.02	204.94	191.82	181.98	174.44	168.54	163.86	160.12	157.09
11000	1003.78	544.40	392.73	317.98	273.98	245.33	225.44	211.00	200.18	191.88	185.39	180.25	176.13	172.79
12000	1095.03	593.89	428.44	346.89	298.88	267.63	245.93	230.18	218.38	209.32	202.25	196.64	192.14	188.50
13000	1186.28	643.38	464.14	375.79	323.79	289.93	266.42	249.36	236.58	226.77	219.10	213.02	208.15	204.21
14000	1277.54	692.87	499.84	404.70	348.69	312.23	286.92	268.54	254.77	244.21	235.95	229.41	224.16	219.92
15000	1368.79	742.36	535.54	433.61	373.60	334.53	307.41	287.72	272.97	261.65	252.81	245.79	240.17	235.63
16000	1460.04	791.85	571.25	462.51	398.51	356.84	327.90	306.90	291.17	279.10	269.66	262.18	256.18	251.33
17000	1551.29	841.34	606.95	491.42	423.41	379.14	348.40	326.09	309.37	296.54	286.51	278.57	272.19	267.04
18000	1642.54	890.83	642.65	520.33	448.32	401.44	368.89	345.27	327.57	313.98	303.37	294.95	288.21	282.75
19000	1733.80	940.32	678.35	549.23	473.23	423.74	389.38	364.45	345.76	331.43	320.22	311.34	304.22	298.46
20000	1825.05	989.81	714.06	578.14	498.13	446.04	409.88	383.63	363.96	348.87	337.07	327.72	320.23	314.17
21000	1916.30	1039.30	749.76	607.05	523.04	468.35	430.37	402.81	382.16	366.31	353.93	344.11	336.24	329.87
22000	2007.55	1088.79	785.46	635.95	547.95	490.65	450.87	421.99	400.36	383.76	370.78	360.50	352.25	345.58
23000	2098.81	1138.28	821.16	664.86	572.85	512.95	471.36	441.17	418.55	401.20	387.63	376.88	368.26	361.29
24000	2190.06	1187.77	856.87	693.77	597.76	535.25	491.85	460.35	436.75	418.64	404.49	393.27	384.27	377.00
25000	2281.31	1237.26	892.57	722.68	622.66	557.55	512.35	479.54	454.95	436.08	421.34	409.65	400.28	392.71
26000	2372.56	1286.75	928.27	751.58	647.57	579.86	532.84	498.72	473.15	453.53	438.19	426.04	416.30	408.41
27000	2463.81	1336.24	963.97	780.49	672.48	602.16	553.33	517.90	491.35	470.97	455.05	442.43	432.31	424.12
28000	2555.07	1385.73	999.68	809.40	697.38	624.46	573.83	537.08	509.54	488.41	471.90	458.81	448.32	439.83
29000	2646.32	1435.22	1035.38	838.30	722.29	646.76	594.32	556.26	527.74	505.86	488.75	475.20	464.33	455.54
30000	2737.57	1484.71	1071.08	867.21	747.20	669.06	614.81	575.44	545.94	523.30	505.61	491.58	480.34	471.25
31000	2828.82	1534.21	1106.78	896.12	772.10	691.37	635.31	594.62	564.14	540.74	522.46	507.97	496.35	486.95
32000	2920.08	1583.70	1142.49	925.02	797.01	713.67	655.80	613.80	582.34	558.19	539.31	524.36	512.36	502.66
33000	3011.33	1633.19	1178.19	953.93	821.92	735.97	676.30	632.99	600.53	575.63	556.17	540.74	528.37	518.37
34000	3102.58	1682.68	1213.89	982.84	846.82	758.27	696.79	652.17	618.73	593.07	573.02	557.13	544.38	534.08
35000	3193.83	1732.17	1249.59	1011.74	871.73	780.57	717.28	671.35	636.93	610.52	589.88	573.51	560.40	549.79
36000	3285.08	1781.66	1285.30	1040.65	896.63	802.88	737.78	690.53	655.13	627.96	606.73	589.90	576.41	565.49
37000	3376.34	1831.15	1321.00	1069.56	921.54	825.18	758.27	709.71	673.32	645.40	623.58	606.28	592.42	581.20
38000	3467.59	1880.64	1356.70	1098.46	946.45	847.48	778.76	728.89	691.52	662.85	640.44	622.67	608.43	596.91
39000	3558.84	1930.13	1392.40	1127.37	971.35	869.78	799.26	748.07	709.72	680.29	657.29	639.06	624.44	612.62
40000	3650.09	1979.62	1428.11	1156.28	996.26	892.08	819.75	767.25	727.92	697.73	674.14	655.44	640.45	628.33
41000	3741.35	2029.11	1463.81	1185.18	1021.17	914.39	840.24	786.44	746.12	715.18	691.00	671.83	656.46	644.03
42000	3832.60	2078.60	1499.51	1214.09	1046.07	936.69	860.74	805.62	764.31	732.62	707.85	688.21	672.47	659.74
43000	3923.85	2128.09	1535.21	1243.00	1070.98	958.99	881.23	824.80	782.51	750.06	724.70	704.60	688.49	675.45
44000	4015.10	2177.58	1570.92	1271.90	1095.89	981.29	901.73	843.98	800.71	767.51	741.56	720.99	704.50	691.16
45000	4106.35	2227.07	1606.62	1300.81	1120.79	1003.59	922.22	863.16	818.91	784.95	758.41	737.37	720.51	706.87
46000	4197.61	2276.55	1642.32	1329.72	1145.70	1025.90	942.71	882.34	837.10	802.39	775.26	753.76	736.52	722.57
47000	4288.86	2326.05	1678.02	1358.62	1170.60	1048.20	963.21	901.52	855.30	819.83	792.12	770.14	752.53	738.28
48000	4380.11	2375.54	1713.73	1387.53	1195.51	1070.50	983.70	920.70	873.50	837.28	808.97	786.53	768.54	753.99
49000	4471.36	2425.03	1749.43	1416.44	1220.42	1092.80	1004.19	939.88	891.70	854.72	825.82	802.92	784.55	769.70
50000	4562.62	2474.52	1785.13	1445.35	1245.32	1115.10	1024.69	959.07	909.90	872.16	842.68	819.30	800.56	785.41
55000	5018.88	2721.97	1963.64	1589.88	1369.86	1226.61	1127.16	1054.97	1000.89	959.38	926.94	901.23	880.62	863.95
60000	5475.14	2969.42	2142.16	1734.41	1494.39	1338.12	1229.62	1150.88	1091.87	1046.60	1011.21	983.16	960.67	942.49
65000	5931.40	3216.88	2320.67	1878.95	1618.92	1449.63	1332.09	1246.78	1182.86	1133.81	1095.48	1065.09	1040.73	1021.03
70000	6387.66	3464.33	2499.18	2023.48	1743.45	1561.14	1434.56	1342.69	1273.85	1221.03	1179.75	1147.02	1120.79	1099.57
75000	6843.92	3711.78	2677.69	2168.02	1867.98	1672.65	1537.03	1438.60	1364.84	1308.24	1264.01	1228.95	1200.84	1178.11
80000	7300.18	3959.23	2856.21	2312.55	1992.52	1784.16	1639.50	1534.50	1455.83	1395.46	1348.28	1310.88	1280.90	1256.65
85000	7756.44	4206.68	3034.72	2457.08	2117.05	1895.67	1741.96	1630.41	1546.82	1482.68	1432.55	1392.81	1360.95	1335.19
90000	8212.70	4454.13	3213.23	2601.62	2241.58	2007.18	1844.43	1726.32	1637.81	1569.89	1516.81	1474.74	1441.01	1413.73
95000	8668.97	4701.59	3391.74	2746.15	2366.11	2118.69	1946.90	1822.22	1728.80	1657.11	1601.08	1556.67	1521.07	1492.27
100000	9125.23	4949.04	3570.26	2890.69	2490.64	2230.20	2049.37	1918.13	1819.79	1744.32	1685.35	1638.60	1601.12	1570.81

TERM AMOUNT	15 Years	16 Years	17 Years	18 Years	19 Years	20 Years	21 Years	22 Years	23 Years	24 Years	25 Years	30 Years	35 Years	40 Years
5	.08	.08	.08	.08	.08	.08	.08	.08	.08	.08	.08	.08	.08	.08
10	.16	.16	.16	.15	.15	.15	.15	.15	.15	.15	.15	.15	.15	.15
15	.24	.23	.23	.23	.23	.23	.22	.22	.22	.22	.22	.22	.22	.22
25	.39	.39	.38	.38	.38	.37	.37	.37	.37	.37	.37	.36	.36	.36
50	.78	.77	.76	.75	.75	.74	.74	.73	.73	.73	.73	.72	.72	.72
75	1.16	1.15	1.14	1.13	1.12	1.11	1.10	1.10	1.10	1.09	1.09	1.08	1.08	1.07
100	1.55	1.53	1.51	1.50	1.49	1.48	1.47	1.46	1.46	1.45	1.45	1.44	1.43	1.43
200	3.10	3.06	3.02	3.00	2.97	2.95	2.94	2.92	2.91	2.90	2.90	2.87	2.86	2.86
300	4.64	4.58	4.53	4.49	4.46	4.43	4.40	4.38	4.37	4.35	4.34	4.31	4.29	4.28
400	6.19	6.11	6.04	5.99	5.94	5.90	5.87	5.84	5.82	5.80	5.79	5.74	5.72	5.71
500	7.74	7.63	7.55	7.48	7.42	7.38	7.34	7.30	7.28	7.25	7.23	7.17	7.15	7.14
600	9.28	9.16	9.06	8.98	8.91	8.85	8.80	8.76	8.73	8.70	8.68	8.61	8.58	8.56
700	10.83	10.69	10.57	10.47	10.39	10.33	10.27	10.22	10.18	10.15	10.13	10.04	10.01	9.99
800	12.37	12.21	12.08	11.97	11.88	11.80	11.74	11.68	11.64	11.60	11.57	11.48	11.44	11.42
900	13.92	13.74	13.59	13.46	13.36	13.27	13.20	13.14	13.09	13.05	13.02	12.91	12.86	12.84
1000	15.47	15.26	15.10	14.96	14.84	14.75	14.67	14.60	14.55	14.50	14.46	14.34	14.29	14.27
2000	30.93	30.52	30.19	29.91	29.68	29.49	29.33	29.20	29.09	29.00	28.92	28.68	28.58	28.54
3000	46.39	45.78	45.28	44.87	44.52	44.24	44.00	43.80	43.63	43.49	43.38	43.02	42.87	42.80
4000	61.85	61.04	60.37	59.82	59.36	58.98	58.66	58.40	58.18	57.99	57.83	57.36	57.16	57.07
5000	77.31	76.30	75.46	74.77	74.20	73.73	73.33	73.00	72.72	72.49	72.29	71.69	71.44	71.34
6000	92.77	91.56	90.56	89.73	89.04	88.47	87.99	87.60	87.26	86.98	86.75	86.03	85.73	85.60
7000	108.23	106.81	105.65	104.68	103.88	103.21	102.66	102.19	101.80	101.48	101.21	100.37	100.02	99.87
8000	123.69	122.07	120.74	119.64	118.72	117.96	117.32	116.79	116.35	115.98	115.66	114.71	114.31	114.13
9000	139.15	137.33	135.83	134.59	133.56	132.70	131.99	131.39	130.89	130.47	130.12	129.05	128.59	128.40
10000	154.61	152.59	150.92	149.54	148.40	147.45	146.65	145.99	145.43	144.97	144.58	143.38	142.88	142.67
11000	170.08	167.85	166.01	164.50	163.24	162.19	161.32	160.59	159.98	159.46	159.04	157.72	157.17	156.93
12000	185.54	183.11	181.11	179.45	178.08	176.93	175.98	175.19	174.52	173.96	173.49	172.06	171.46	171.20
13000	201.00	198.37	196.20	194.40	192.92	191.68	190.65	189.78	189.06	188.46	187.95	186.40	185.74	185.46
14000	216.46	213.62	211.29	209.36	207.76	206.42	205.31	204.38	203.60	202.95	202.41	200.74	200.03	199.73
15000	231.92	228.88	226.38	224.31	222.59	221.17	219.98	218.98	218.15	217.45	216.86	215.07	214.32	214.00
16000	247.38	244.14	241.47	239.27	237.43	235.91	234.64	233.58	232.69	231.95	231.32	229.41	228.61	228.26
17000	262.84	259.40	256.56	254.22	252.27	250.65	249.30	248.18	247.23	246.44	245.78	243.75	242.89	242.53
18000	278.30	274.66	271.66	269.17	267.11	265.40	263.97	262.78	261.78	260.94	260.24	258.09	257.18	256.79
19000	293.76	289.92	286.75	284.13	281.95	280.14	278.63	277.37	276.32	275.44	274.69	272.43	271.47	271.06
20000	309.22	305.17	301.84	299.08	296.79	294.89	293.30	291.97	290.86	289.93	289.15	286.76	285.76	285.33
21000	324.69	320.43	316.93	314.03	311.63	309.63	307.96	306.57	305.40	304.43	303.61	301.10	300.04	299.59
22000	340.15	335.69	332.02	328.99	326.47	324.38	322.63	321.17	319.95	318.92	318.07	315.44	314.33	313.86
23000	355.61	350.95	347.11	343.94	341.31	339.12	337.29	335.77	334.49	333.42	332.52	329.78	328.62	328.12
24000	371.07	366.21	362.21	358.90	356.15	353.86	351.96	350.37	349.03	347.92	346.98	344.12	342.91	342.39
25000	386.53	381.47	377.30	373.85	370.99	368.61	366.62	364.96	363.58	362.41	361.44	358.45	357.19	356.66
26000	401.99	396.73	392.39	388.80	385.83	383.35	381.29	379.56	378.12	376.91	375.89	372.79	371.48	370.92
27000	417.45	411.98	407.48	403.76	400.67	398.10	395.95	394.16	392.66	391.41	390.35	387.13	385.77	385.19
28000	432.91	427.24	422.57	418.71	415.51	412.84	410.62	408.76	407.20	405.90	404.81	401.47	400.06	399.45
29000	448.37	442.50	437.66	433.66	430.35	427.58	425.28	423.36	421.75	420.40	419.27	415.81	414.34	413.72
30000	463.83	457.76	452.76	448.62	445.18	442.33	439.95	437.96	436.29	434.89	433.72	430.14	428.63	427.99
31000	479.30	473.02	467.85	463.57	460.02	457.07	454.61	452.55	450.83	449.39	448.18	444.48	442.92	442.25
32000	494.76	488.28	482.94	478.53	474.86	471.82	469.28	467.15	465.38	463.89	462.64	458.82	457.21	456.52
33000	510.22	503.53	498.03	493.48	489.70	486.56	483.94	481.75	479.92	478.38	477.10	473.16	471.49	470.78
34000	525.68	518.79	513.12	508.43	504.54	501.30	498.60	496.35	494.46	492.88	491.55	487.50	485.78	485.05
35000	541.14	534.05	528.21	523.39	519.38	516.05	513.27	510.95	509.00	507.38	506.01	501.83	500.07	499.32
36000	556.60	549.31	543.31	538.34	534.22	530.79	527.93	525.55	523.55	521.87	520.47	516.17	514.36	513.58
37000	572.06	564.57	558.40	553.29	549.06	545.54	542.60	540.14	538.09	536.37	534.92	530.51	528.64	527.85
38000	587.52	579.83	573.49	568.25	563.90	560.28	557.26	554.74	552.63	550.87	549.38	544.85	542.93	542.11
39000	602.98	595.09	588.58	583.20	578.74	575.02	571.93	569.34	567.18	565.36	563.84	559.19	557.22	556.38
40000	618.44	610.34	603.67	598.16	593.58	589.77	586.59	583.94	581.72	579.86	578.30	573.52	571.51	570.65
41000	633.90	625.60	618.76	613.11	608.42	604.51	601.26	598.54	596.26	594.36	592.75	587.86	585.79	584.91
42000	649.37	640.86	633.86	628.06	623.26	619.26	615.92	613.14	610.80	608.85	607.21	602.20	600.08	599.18
43000	664.83	656.12	648.95	643.02	638.10	634.00	630.59	627.73	625.35	623.35	621.67	616.54	614.37	613.44
44000	680.29	671.38	664.04	657.97	652.94	648.75	645.25	642.33	639.89	637.84	636.13	630.88	628.66	627.71
45000	695.75	686.64	679.13	672.92	667.77	663.49	659.92	656.93	654.43	652.34	650.58	645.21	642.94	641.98
46000	711.21	701.90	694.22	687.88	682.61	678.23	674.58	671.53	668.98	666.84	665.04	659.55	657.23	656.24
47000	726.67	717.15	709.31	702.83	697.45	692.98	689.25	686.13	683.52	681.33	679.50	673.89	671.52	670.51
48000	742.13	732.41	724.41	717.79	712.29	707.72	703.91	700.73	698.06	695.83	693.96	688.23	685.81	684.77
49000	757.59	747.67	739.50	732.74	727.13	722.47	718.58	715.32	712.60	710.32	708.41	702.57	700.09	699.04
50000	773.05	762.93	754.59	747.69	741.97	737.21	733.24	729.92	727.15	724.82	722.87	716.90	714.38	713.31
55000	850.36	839.22	830.05	822.46	816.17	810.93	806.56	802.91	799.86	797.30	795.16	788.59	785.82	784.64
60000	927.66	915.51	905.51	897.23	890.36	884.65	879.89	875.91	872.58	869.78	867.44	860.28	857.26	855.97
65000	1004.97	991.81	980.97	972.00	964.56	958.37	953.21	948.90	945.29	942.27	939.73	931.97	928.69	927.30
70000	1082.27	1068.10	1056.42	1046.77	1038.76	1032.09	1026.53	1021.89	1018.00	1014.75	1012.02	1003.66	1000.13	998.63
75000	1159.58	1144.39	1131.88	1121.54	1112.95	1105.81	1099.86	1094.88	1090.72	1087.23	1084.30	1075.35	1071.57	1069.96
80000	1236.88	1220.68	1207.34	1196.31	1187.15	1179.53	1173.18	1167.87	1163.43	1159.71	1156.59	1147.04	1143.01	1141.29
85000	1314.19	1296.98	1282.80	1271.07	1261.35	1253.25	1246.50	1240.87	1236.15	1232.19	1228.87	1218.73	1214.44	1212.62
90000	1391.49	1373.27	1358.26	1345.84	1335.54	1326.97	1319.83	1313.86	1308.86	1304.67	1301.16	1290.42	1285.88	1283.95
95000	1468.80	1449.56	1433.72	1420.61	1409.74	1400.69	1393.15	1386.85	1381.57	1377.16	1373.45	1362.11	1357.32	1355.28
100000	1546.10	1525.85	1509.17	1495.38	1483.94	1474.41	1466.47	1459.84	1454.29	1449.64	1445.73	1433.80	1428.76	1426.61

MONTHLY PAYMENT
REQUIRED TO AMORTIZE A LOAN

TERM	1 Year	2 Years	3 Years	4 Years	5 Years	6 Years	7 Years	8 Years	9 Years	10 Years	11 Years	12 Years	13 Years	14 Years
AMOUNT														
5	.46	.25	.18	.15	.13	.12	.11	.10	.10	.09	.09	.09	.09	.08
10	.92	.50	.36	.29	.25	.23	.21	.20	.19	.18	.17	.17	.17	.16
15	1.37	.75	.54	.44	.38	.34	.31	.29	.28	.27	.26	.25	.25	.24
25	2.29	1.24	.90	.73	.63	.56	.52	.48	.46	.44	.43	.42	.41	.40
50	4.57	2.48	1.79	1.45	1.25	1.12	1.03	.96	.92	.88	.85	.83	.81	.79
75	6.85	3.72	2.68	2.17	1.87	1.68	1.54	1.44	1.37	1.31	1.27	1.24	1.21	1.18
100	9.13	4.96	3.58	2.90	2.50	2.24	2.06	1.92	1.83	1.75	1.69	1.65	1.61	1.58
200	18.26	9.91	7.15	5.79	4.99	4.47	4.11	3.84	3.65	3.50	3.38	3.29	3.21	3.15
300	27.38	14.86	10.72	8.68	7.48	6.70	6.16	5.76	5.47	5.24	5.07	4.93	4.81	4.72
400	36.51	19.81	14.29	11.57	9.97	8.93	8.21	7.68	7.29	6.99	6.75	6.57	6.42	6.30
500	45.64	24.76	17.86	14.46	12.46	11.16	10.26	9.60	9.11	8.73	8.44	8.21	8.02	7.87
600	54.76	29.71	21.43	17.36	14.96	13.39	12.31	11.52	10.93	10.48	10.13	9.85	9.62	9.44
700	63.89	34.66	25.01	20.25	17.45	15.63	14.36	13.44	12.75	12.23	11.81	11.49	11.22	11.01
800	73.02	39.61	28.58	23.14	19.94	17.86	16.41	15.36	14.58	13.97	13.50	13.13	12.83	12.59
900	82.14	44.56	32.15	26.03	22.43	20.09	18.46	17.28	16.40	15.72	15.19	14.77	14.43	14.16
1000	91.27	49.51	35.72	28.92	24.92	22.32	20.51	19.20	18.22	17.46	16.87	16.41	16.03	15.73
2000	182.53	99.01	71.43	57.84	49.84	44.64	41.02	38.40	36.43	34.92	33.74	32.81	32.06	31.46
3000	273.80	148.51	107.15	86.76	74.76	66.95	61.53	57.59	54.64	52.38	50.61	49.21	48.09	47.18
4000	365.06	198.01	142.86	115.68	99.68	89.27	82.04	76.79	72.86	69.84	67.48	65.62	64.12	62.91
5000	456.33	247.52	178.58	144.60	124.60	111.58	102.55	95.99	91.07	87.30	84.35	82.02	80.15	78.63
6000	547.59	297.02	214.29	173.52	149.52	133.90	123.05	115.18	109.28	104.76	101.22	98.42	96.17	94.36
7000	638.85	346.52	250.01	202.44	174.44	156.22	143.56	134.38	127.50	122.22	118.09	114.82	112.20	110.08
8000	730.12	396.02	285.72	231.36	199.36	178.53	164.07	153.57	145.71	139.68	134.96	131.23	128.23	125.81
9000	821.38	445.53	321.44	260.28	224.28	200.85	184.58	172.77	163.92	157.14	151.83	147.63	144.26	141.53
10000	912.65	495.03	357.15	289.20	249.20	223.16	205.09	191.97	182.14	174.60	168.70	164.03	160.29	157.26
11000	1003.91	544.53	392.87	318.12	274.12	245.48	225.59	211.16	200.35	192.05	185.57	180.43	176.32	172.98
12000	1095.17	594.03	428.58	347.04	299.04	267.80	246.10	230.36	218.56	209.51	202.44	196.84	192.34	188.71
13000	1186.44	643.54	464.30	375.96	323.96	290.11	266.61	249.56	236.78	226.97	219.31	213.24	208.37	204.44
14000	1277.70	693.04	500.01	404.88	348.88	312.43	287.12	268.75	254.99	244.43	236.18	229.64	224.40	220.16
15000	1368.97	742.54	535.73	433.80	373.80	334.74	307.63	287.95	273.20	261.89	253.05	246.04	240.43	235.89
16000	1460.23	792.04	571.44	462.72	398.72	357.06	328.13	307.14	291.42	279.35	269.92	262.45	256.46	251.61
17000	1551.49	841.54	607.16	491.64	423.64	379.38	348.64	326.34	309.63	296.81	286.79	278.85	272.49	267.34
18000	1642.76	891.05	642.87	520.56	448.56	401.69	369.15	345.54	327.84	314.27	303.66	295.25	288.51	283.06
19000	1734.02	940.55	678.59	549.48	473.48	424.01	389.66	364.73	346.06	331.73	320.53	311.66	304.54	298.79
20000	1825.29	990.05	714.30	578.40	498.40	446.32	410.17	383.93	364.27	349.19	337.40	328.06	320.57	314.51
21000	1916.55	1039.56	750.02	607.32	523.32	468.64	430.68	403.12	382.48	366.65	354.27	344.46	336.60	330.24
22000	2007.81	1089.06	785.73	636.24	548.24	490.96	451.18	422.32	400.70	384.10	371.14	360.86	352.63	345.96
23000	2099.08	1138.56	821.45	665.16	573.16	513.27	471.69	441.52	418.91	401.56	388.01	377.27	368.65	361.69
24000	2190.34	1188.06	857.16	694.08	598.08	535.59	492.20	460.71	437.12	419.02	404.88	393.67	384.68	377.42
25000	2281.61	1237.56	892.88	723.00	623.00	557.90	512.71	479.91	455.34	436.48	421.75	410.07	400.71	393.14
26000	2372.87	1287.07	928.59	751.92	647.92	580.22	533.22	499.11	473.55	453.94	438.62	426.47	416.74	408.87
27000	2464.14	1336.57	964.31	780.84	672.84	602.54	553.72	518.30	491.76	471.40	455.49	442.88	432.77	424.59
28000	2555.40	1386.07	1000.02	809.76	697.76	624.85	574.23	537.50	509.98	488.86	472.36	459.28	448.80	440.32
29000	2646.66	1435.57	1035.74	838.68	722.68	647.17	594.74	556.69	528.19	506.32	489.23	475.68	464.82	456.04
30000	2737.93	1485.08	1071.45	867.60	747.60	669.48	615.25	575.89	546.40	523.78	506.10	492.08	480.85	471.77
31000	2829.19	1534.58	1107.17	896.52	772.52	691.80	635.76	595.09	564.62	541.24	522.97	508.49	496.88	487.49
32000	2920.46	1584.08	1142.88	925.44	797.44	714.12	656.26	614.28	582.83	558.69	539.84	524.89	512.91	503.22
33000	3011.72	1633.58	1178.60	954.36	822.36	736.43	676.77	633.48	601.04	576.15	556.71	541.29	528.94	518.94
34000	3102.98	1683.08	1214.31	983.28	847.28	758.75	697.28	652.68	619.26	593.61	573.58	557.69	544.97	534.67
35000	3194.25	1732.59	1250.03	1012.20	872.20	781.06	717.79	671.87	637.47	611.07	590.45	574.10	560.99	550.39
36000	3285.51	1782.09	1285.74	1041.12	897.12	803.38	738.30	691.07	655.68	628.53	607.32	590.50	577.02	566.12
37000	3376.78	1831.59	1321.46	1070.04	922.04	825.69	758.81	710.26	673.90	645.99	624.18	606.90	593.05	581.85
38000	3468.04	1881.09	1357.17	1098.96	946.96	848.01	779.31	729.46	692.11	663.45	641.05	623.31	609.08	597.57
39000	3559.30	1930.60	1392.89	1127.88	971.88	870.33	799.82	748.66	710.32	680.91	657.92	639.71	625.11	613.30
40000	3650.57	1980.10	1428.60	1156.80	996.80	892.64	820.33	767.85	728.53	698.37	674.79	656.11	641.13	629.02
41000	3741.83	2029.60	1464.32	1185.71	1021.72	914.96	840.84	787.05	746.75	715.83	691.66	672.51	657.16	644.75
42000	3833.10	2079.10	1500.03	1214.63	1046.64	937.27	861.35	806.24	764.96	733.29	708.53	688.92	673.19	660.47
43000	3924.36	2128.61	1535.75	1243.55	1071.56	959.59	881.85	825.44	783.17	750.74	725.40	705.32	689.22	676.20
44000	4015.62	2178.11	1571.46	1272.47	1096.48	981.91	902.36	844.64	801.39	768.20	742.27	721.72	705.25	691.92
45000	4106.89	2227.61	1607.18	1301.39	1121.40	1004.22	922.87	863.83	819.60	785.66	759.14	738.12	721.28	707.65
46000	4198.15	2277.11	1642.89	1330.31	1146.32	1026.54	943.38	883.03	837.81	803.12	776.01	754.53	737.30	723.37
47000	4289.42	2326.62	1678.61	1359.23	1171.24	1048.85	963.89	902.23	856.03	820.58	792.88	770.93	753.33	739.10
48000	4380.68	2376.12	1714.32	1388.15	1196.16	1071.17	984.39	921.42	874.24	838.04	809.75	787.33	769.36	754.83
49000	4471.95	2425.62	1750.04	1417.07	1221.08	1093.49	1004.90	940.62	892.45	855.50	826.62	803.73	785.39	770.55
50000	4563.21	2475.12	1785.75	1445.99	1246.00	1115.80	1025.41	959.81	910.67	872.96	843.49	820.14	801.42	786.28
55000	5019.53	2722.63	1964.33	1590.59	1370.60	1227.38	1127.95	1055.79	1001.73	960.25	927.84	902.15	881.56	864.90
60000	5475.85	2970.15	2142.90	1735.19	1495.20	1338.96	1230.49	1151.78	1092.80	1047.55	1012.19	984.16	961.70	943.53
65000	5932.17	3217.66	2321.48	1879.79	1619.79	1450.54	1333.03	1247.76	1183.87	1134.84	1096.54	1066.18	1041.84	1022.16
70000	6388.49	3465.17	2500.05	2024.39	1744.39	1562.12	1435.57	1343.74	1274.93	1222.14	1180.89	1148.19	1121.98	1100.78
75000	6844.81	3712.68	2678.63	2168.99	1868.99	1673.70	1538.11	1439.72	1366.00	1309.43	1265.23	1230.20	1202.12	1179.41
80000	7301.13	3960.19	2857.20	2313.59	1993.59	1785.28	1640.65	1535.70	1457.06	1396.73	1349.58	1312.22	1282.26	1258.04
85000	7757.45	4207.70	3035.78	2458.18	2118.19	1896.86	1743.19	1631.68	1548.13	1484.02	1433.93	1394.23	1362.41	1336.67
90000	8213.77	4455.22	3214.35	2602.78	2242.79	2008.44	1845.73	1727.66	1639.20	1571.32	1518.28	1476.24	1442.55	1415.29
95000	8670.09	4702.73	3392.93	2747.38	2367.39	2120.02	1948.28	1823.64	1730.26	1658.62	1602.63	1558.26	1522.69	1493.92
100000	9126.41	4950.24	3571.50	2891.98	2491.99	2231.60	2050.82	1919.62	1821.33	1745.91	1686.98	1640.27	1602.83	1572.55

TERM	15 Years	16 Years	17 Years	18 Years	19 Years	20 Years	21 Years	22 Years	23 Years	24 Years	25 Years	30 Years	35 Years	40 Years
AMOUNT														
5	.08	.08	.08	.08	.08	.08	.08	.08	.08	.08	.08	.08	.08	.08
10	.16	.16	.16	.15	.15	.15	.15	.15	.15	.15	.15	.15	.15	.15
15	.24	.23	.23	.23	.23	.23	.23	.22	.22	.22	.22	.22	.22	.22
25	.39	.39	.38	.38	.38	.37	.37	.37	.37	.37	.37	.36	.36	.36
50	.78	.77	.76	.75	.75	.74	.74	.74	.73	.73	.73	.72	.72	.72
75	1.17	1.15	1.14	1.13	1.12	1.11	1.11	1.10	1.10	1.09	1.09	1.08	1.08	1.08
100	1.55	1.53	1.52	1.50	1.49	1.48	1.47	1.47	1.46	1.46	1.45	1.44	1.44	1.43
200	3.10	3.06	3.03	3.00	2.98	2.96	2.94	2.93	2.92	2.91	2.90	2.88	2.87	2.86
300	4.65	4.59	4.54	4.50	4.46	4.43	4.41	4.39	4.37	4.36	4.35	4.31	4.30	4.29
400	6.20	6.12	6.05	5.99	5.95	5.91	5.88	5.85	5.83	5.81	5.80	5.75	5.73	5.72
500	7.74	7.64	7.56	7.49	7.43	7.39	7.35	7.31	7.29	7.26	7.24	7.18	7.16	7.15
600	9.29	9.17	9.07	8.99	8.92	8.86	8.82	8.78	8.74	8.71	8.69	8.62	8.59	8.58
700	10.84	10.70	10.58	10.49	10.41	10.34	10.28	10.24	10.20	10.17	10.14	10.06	10.02	10.01
800	12.39	12.23	12.09	11.98	11.89	11.82	11.75	11.70	11.65	11.62	11.59	11.49	11.45	11.43
900	13.94	13.75	13.60	13.48	13.38	13.29	13.22	13.16	13.11	13.07	13.03	12.93	12.88	12.86
1000	15.48	15.28	15.12	14.98	14.86	14.77	14.69	14.62	14.57	14.52	14.48	14.36	14.31	14.29
2000	30.96	30.56	30.23	29.95	29.72	29.53	29.37	29.24	29.13	29.04	28.96	28.72	28.62	28.58
3000	46.44	45.83	45.34	44.92	44.58	44.29	44.06	43.86	43.69	43.55	43.44	43.08	42.93	42.87
4000	61.92	61.11	60.45	59.89	59.44	59.06	58.74	58.48	58.25	58.07	57.91	57.44	57.24	57.15
5000	77.40	76.39	75.56	74.87	74.30	73.82	73.42	73.09	72.82	72.59	72.39	71.80	71.55	71.44
6000	92.88	91.66	90.67	89.84	89.15	88.58	88.11	87.71	87.38	87.10	86.87	86.15	85.85	85.73
7000	108.36	106.94	105.78	104.81	104.01	103.35	102.79	102.33	101.94	101.62	101.34	100.51	100.16	100.01
8000	123.83	122.22	120.89	119.78	118.87	118.11	117.48	116.95	116.50	116.13	115.82	114.87	114.47	114.30
9000	139.31	137.49	136.00	134.76	133.73	132.87	132.16	131.56	131.07	130.65	130.30	129.23	128.78	128.59
10000	154.79	152.77	151.11	149.73	148.59	147.64	146.84	146.18	145.63	145.17	144.78	143.59	143.09	142.87
11000	170.27	168.05	166.22	164.70	163.44	162.40	161.53	160.80	160.19	159.68	159.25	157.95	157.39	157.16
12000	185.75	183.32	181.33	179.67	178.30	177.16	176.21	175.42	174.75	174.20	173.73	172.30	171.70	171.45
13000	201.23	198.60	196.44	194.65	193.16	191.93	190.90	190.04	189.32	188.71	188.21	186.66	186.01	185.73
14000	216.71	213.00	211.55	209.62	208.02	206.69	205.58	204.65	203.88	203.23	202.68	201.02	200.32	200.02
15000	232.19	229.15	226.66	224.59	222.88	221.45	220.26	219.27	218.44	217.75	217.16	215.38	214.63	214.31
16000	247.66	244.43	241.77	239.56	237.74	236.22	234.95	233.89	233.00	232.26	231.64	229.74	228.93	228.59
17000	263.14	259.71	256.88	254.53	252.59	250.98	249.63	248.51	247.57	246.78	246.12	244.10	243.24	242.88
18000	278.62	274.98	271.99	269.51	267.45	265.74	264.32	263.12	262.13	261.29	260.59	258.45	257.55	257.17
19000	294.10	290.26	287.10	284.48	282.31	280.50	279.00	277.74	276.69	275.81	275.07	272.81	271.86	271.45
20000	309.58	305.54	302.21	299.45	297.17	295.27	293.68	292.36	291.25	290.33	289.55	287.17	286.17	285.74
21000	325.06	320.81	317.32	314.42	312.03	310.03	308.37	306.98	305.82	304.84	304.02	301.53	300.47	300.03
22000	340.54	336.09	332.43	329.40	326.88	324.79	323.05	321.60	320.38	319.36	318.50	315.89	314.78	314.31
23000	356.02	351.37	347.54	344.37	341.74	339.56	337.74	336.21	334.94	333.87	332.98	330.25	329.09	328.60
24000	371.49	366.64	362.65	359.34	356.60	354.32	352.42	350.83	349.50	348.39	347.46	344.60	343.40	342.89
25000	386.97	381.92	377.76	374.31	371.46	369.08	367.10	365.45	364.07	362.91	361.93	358.96	357.71	357.17
26000	402.45	397.19	392.87	389.29	386.32	383.85	381.79	380.07	378.63	377.42	376.41	373.32	372.01	371.46
27000	417.93	412.47	407.98	404.26	401.17	398.61	396.47	394.68	393.19	391.94	390.89	387.68	386.32	385.75
28000	433.41	427.75	423.09	419.23	416.03	413.37	411.16	409.30	407.75	406.45	405.36	402.04	400.63	400.03
29000	448.89	443.02	438.20	434.20	430.89	428.14	425.84	423.92	422.31	420.97	419.84	416.39	414.94	414.32
30000	464.37	458.30	453.31	449.18	445.75	442.90	440.52	438.54	436.88	435.49	434.32	430.75	429.25	428.61
31000	479.85	473.58	468.42	464.15	460.61	457.66	455.21	453.16	451.44	450.00	448.80	445.11	443.56	442.89
32000	495.32	488.85	483.53	479.12	475.47	472.43	469.89	467.77	466.00	464.52	463.27	459.47	457.86	457.18
33000	510.80	504.13	498.64	494.09	490.32	487.19	484.57	482.39	480.56	479.03	477.75	473.83	472.17	471.47
34000	526.28	519.41	513.75	509.06	505.18	501.95	499.26	497.01	495.13	493.55	492.23	488.19	486.48	485.75
35000	541.76	534.68	528.86	524.04	520.04	516.71	513.94	511.63	509.69	508.07	506.70	502.54	500.79	500.04
36000	557.24	549.96	543.97	539.01	534.90	531.48	528.63	526.24	524.25	522.58	521.18	516.90	515.10	514.33
37000	572.72	565.24	559.08	553.98	549.76	546.24	543.31	540.86	538.81	537.10	535.66	531.26	529.40	528.61
38000	588.20	580.51	574.19	568.95	564.61	561.00	557.99	555.48	553.38	551.61	550.14	545.62	543.71	542.90
39000	603.68	595.79	589.30	583.93	579.47	575.77	572.68	570.10	567.94	566.13	564.61	559.98	558.02	557.19
40000	619.15	611.07	604.41	598.90	594.33	590.53	587.36	584.72	582.50	580.65	579.09	574.34	572.33	571.47
41000	634.63	626.34	619.52	613.87	609.19	605.29	602.05	599.33	597.06	595.16	593.57	588.69	586.64	585.76
42000	650.11	641.62	634.63	628.84	624.05	620.06	616.73	613.95	611.63	609.68	608.04	603.05	600.94	600.05
43000	665.59	656.90	649.74	643.82	638.91	634.82	631.41	628.57	626.19	624.19	622.52	617.41	615.25	614.33
44000	681.07	672.17	664.85	658.79	653.76	649.58	646.10	643.19	640.75	638.71	637.00	631.77	629.56	628.62
45000	696.55	687.45	679.96	673.76	668.62	664.35	660.78	657.80	655.31	653.23	651.48	646.13	643.87	642.91
46000	712.03	702.73	695.07	688.73	683.48	679.11	675.47	672.42	669.88	667.74	665.95	660.49	658.18	657.19
47000	727.50	718.00	710.18	703.71	698.34	693.87	690.15	687.04	684.44	682.26	680.43	674.84	672.48	671.48
48000	742.98	733.28	725.29	718.68	713.20	708.64	704.83	701.66	699.00	696.77	694.91	689.20	686.79	685.77
49000	758.46	748.56	740.40	733.65	728.05	723.40	719.52	716.28	713.56	711.29	709.38	703.56	701.10	700.05
50000	773.94	763.83	755.51	748.62	742.91	738.16	734.20	730.89	728.13	725.81	723.86	717.92	715.41	714.34
55000	851.33	840.21	831.06	823.48	817.20	811.98	807.62	803.98	800.94	798.39	796.25	789.71	786.95	785.77
60000	928.73	916.60	906.61	898.35	891.49	885.79	881.04	877.07	873.75	870.97	868.63	861.50	858.49	857.21
65000	1006.12	992.98	982.16	973.21	965.78	959.61	954.46	950.16	946.56	943.55	941.02	933.29	930.03	928.64
70000	1083.52	1069.36	1057.71	1048.07	1040.08	1033.42	1027.88	1023.25	1019.37	1016.13	1013.40	1005.08	1001.57	1000.08
75000	1160.91	1145.75	1133.26	1122.93	1114.37	1107.24	1101.30	1096.34	1092.19	1088.71	1085.79	1076.88	1073.11	1071.51
80000	1238.30	1222.13	1208.81	1197.79	1188.66	1181.06	1174.72	1169.43	1165.00	1161.29	1158.18	1148.67	1144.65	1142.94
85000	1315.70	1298.51	1284.36	1272.66	1262.95	1254.87	1248.14	1242.51	1237.81	1233.87	1230.56	1220.46	1216.19	1214.38
90000	1393.09	1374.89	1359.91	1347.52	1337.24	1328.69	1321.56	1315.60	1310.62	1306.45	1302.95	1292.05	1287.73	1285.81
95000	1470.48	1451.28	1435.46	1422.38	1411.53	1402.50	1394.98	1388.69	1383.43	1379.03	1375.33	1364.04	1359.27	1357.24
100000	1547.88	1527.66	1511.01	1497.24	1485.82	1476.32	1468.40	1461.78	1456.25	1451.61	1447.72	1435.83	1430.81	1428.68

TERM	1 Year	2 Years	3 Years	4 Years	5 Years	6 Years	7 Years	8 Years	9 Years	10 Years	11 Years	12 Years	13 Years	14 Years
AMOUNT														
5	.46	.26	.18	.15	.13	.12	.11	.10	.10	.09	.09	.09	.09	.08
10	.92	.50	.36	.29	.25	.23	.21	.20	.19	.18	.17	.17	.17	.16
15	1.37	.75	.54	.44	.38	.34	.31	.29	.28	.27	.26	.25	.25	.24
25	2.29	1.24	.90	.73	.63	.56	.52	.49	.46	.44	.43	.42	.41	.40
50	4.57	2.48	1.79	1.45	1.25	1.12	1.03	.97	.92	.88	.85	.83	.81	.79
75	6.85	3.72	2.69	2.18	1.88	1.68	1.55	1.45	1.37	1.32	1.27	1.24	1.21	1.19
100	9.13	4.96	3.58	2.90	2.50	2.24	2.06	1.93	1.83	1.76	1.70	1.65	1.61	1.58
200	18.26	9.91	7.16	5.80	5.00	4.48	4.12	3.85	3.66	3.51	3.39	3.30	3.22	3.16
300	27.39	14.87	10.73	8.69	7.49	6.71	6.17	5.78	5.48	5.26	5.08	4.94	4.83	4.74
400	36.52	19.82	14.31	11.59	9.99	8.95	8.23	7.70	7.31	7.01	6.77	6.59	6.44	6.32
500	45.65	24.77	17.88	14.48	12.49	11.18	10.28	9.63	9.13	8.76	8.46	8.23	8.04	7.89
600	54.78	29.73	21.46	17.38	14.98	13.42	12.34	11.55	10.96	10.51	10.16	9.88	9.65	9.47
700	63.91	34.68	25.03	20.28	17.48	15.66	14.39	13.47	12.79	12.26	11.85	11.52	11.26	11.05
800	73.04	39.64	28.61	23.17	19.97	17.89	16.45	15.40	14.61	14.01	13.54	13.17	12.87	12.63
900	82.17	44.59	32.18	26.07	22.47	20.13	18.50	17.32	16.44	15.76	15.23	14.81	14.48	14.20
1000	91.30	49.54	35.76	28.96	24.97	22.36	20.56	19.25	18.26	17.51	16.92	16.46	16.08	15.78
2000	182.60	99.08	71.51	57.92	49.93	44.72	41.11	38.49	36.52	35.02	33.84	32.91	32.16	31.56
3000	273.90	148.62	107.26	86.88	74.89	67.08	61.66	57.73	54.78	52.53	50.76	49.36	48.24	47.34
4000	365.20	198.16	143.01	115.84	99.85	89.44	82.21	76.97	73.04	70.03	67.68	65.82	64.32	63.12
5000	456.50	247.70	178.77	144.80	124.81	111.79	102.76	96.21	91.30	87.54	84.60	82.27	80.40	78.89
6000	547.80	297.24	214.52	173.76	149.77	134.15	123.31	115.45	109.56	105.05	101.52	98.72	96.48	94.67
7000	639.10	346.77	250.27	202.72	174.73	156.51	143.87	134.69	127.82	122.55	118.44	115.17	112.56	110.45
8000	730.40	396.31	286.02	231.67	199.69	178.87	164.42	153.93	146.08	140.06	135.35	131.63	128.64	126.23
9000	821.70	445.85	321.78	260.63	224.65	201.23	184.97	173.17	164.34	157.57	152.27	148.08	144.72	142.00
10000	913.00	495.39	357.53	289.59	249.61	223.58	205.52	192.42	182.60	175.07	169.19	164.53	160.80	157.78
11000	1004.30	544.93	393.28	318.55	274.57	245.94	226.07	211.66	200.86	192.58	186.11	180.99	176.88	173.56
12000	1095.60	594.47	429.03	347.51	299.53	268.30	246.62	230.90	219.12	210.09	203.03	197.44	192.96	189.34
13000	1186.90	644.00	464.79	376.47	324.49	290.66	267.18	250.14	237.38	227.59	219.95	213.89	209.04	205.12
14000	1278.20	693.54	500.54	405.43	349.45	313.02	287.73	269.38	255.64	245.10	236.87	230.34	225.12	220.89
15000	1369.50	743.08	536.29	434.38	374.41	335.37	308.28	288.62	273.90	262.61	253.78	246.80	241.20	236.67
16000	1460.80	792.62	572.04	463.34	399.37	357.73	328.83	307.86	292.16	280.11	270.70	263.25	257.28	252.45
17000	1552.10	842.16	607.79	492.30	424.33	380.09	349.38	327.10	310.42	297.62	287.62	279.70	273.36	268.23
18000	1643.40	891.70	643.55	521.26	449.29	402.45	369.93	346.34	328.68	315.13	304.54	296.15	289.44	284.00
19000	1734.70	941.23	679.30	550.22	474.25	424.80	390.48	365.59	346.94	332.63	321.46	312.61	305.52	299.78
20000	1826.00	990.77	715.05	579.18	499.21	447.16	411.04	384.83	365.20	350.14	338.38	329.06	321.59	315.56
21000	1917.30	1040.31	750.80	608.14	524.17	469.52	431.59	404.07	383.46	367.65	355.30	345.51	337.67	331.34
22000	2008.60	1089.85	786.56	637.09	549.13	491.88	452.14	423.31	401.72	385.15	372.22	361.97	353.75	347.12
23000	2099.90	1139.39	822.31	666.05	574.09	514.24	472.69	442.55	419.97	402.66	389.13	378.42	369.83	362.89
24000	2191.20	1188.93	858.06	695.01	599.05	536.59	493.24	461.79	438.23	420.17	406.05	394.87	385.91	378.67
25000	2282.50	1238.47	893.81	723.97	624.01	558.95	513.79	481.03	456.49	437.67	422.97	411.32	401.99	394.45
26000	2373.80	1288.00	929.57	752.93	648.97	581.31	534.35	500.27	474.75	455.18	439.89	427.78	418.07	410.23
27000	2465.10	1337.54	965.32	781.89	673.93	603.67	554.90	519.51	493.01	472.69	456.81	444.23	434.15	426.00
28000	2556.40	1387.08	1001.07	810.85	698.89	626.03	575.45	538.76	511.27	490.19	473.73	460.68	450.23	441.78
29000	2647.70	1436.62	1036.82	839.80	723.85	648.38	596.00	558.00	529.53	507.70	490.65	477.14	466.31	457.56
30000	2739.00	1486.16	1072.58	868.76	748.81	670.74	616.55	577.24	547.79	525.21	507.56	493.59	482.39	473.34
31000	2830.30	1535.70	1108.33	897.72	773.77	693.10	637.10	596.48	566.05	542.71	524.48	510.04	498.47	489.11
32000	2921.60	1585.23	1144.08	926.68	798.73	715.46	657.65	615.72	584.31	560.22	541.40	526.49	514.55	504.89
33000	3012.89	1634.77	1179.83	955.64	823.69	737.81	678.21	634.96	602.57	577.73	558.32	542.95	530.63	520.67
34000	3104.19	1684.31	1215.58	984.60	848.65	760.17	698.76	654.20	620.83	595.23	575.24	559.40	546.71	536.45
35000	3195.49	1733.85	1251.34	1013.56	873.61	782.53	719.31	673.44	639.09	612.74	592.16	575.85	562.79	552.23
36000	3286.79	1783.39	1287.09	1042.52	898.57	804.89	739.86	692.68	657.35	630.25	609.08	592.30	578.87	568.00
37000	3378.09	1832.93	1322.84	1071.47	923.53	827.25	760.41	711.93	675.61	647.75	626.00	608.76	594.95	583.78
38000	3469.39	1882.46	1358.59	1100.43	948.49	849.60	780.96	731.17	693.87	665.26	642.91	625.21	611.03	599.56
39000	3560.69	1932.00	1394.35	1129.39	973.45	871.96	801.52	750.41	712.13	682.77	659.83	641.66	627.11	615.34
40000	3651.99	1981.54	1430.10	1158.35	998.41	894.32	822.07	769.65	730.39	700.27	676.75	658.12	643.18	631.11
41000	3743.29	2031.08	1465.85	1187.31	1023.37	916.68	842.62	788.89	748.65	717.78	693.67	674.57	659.26	646.89
42000	3834.59	2080.62	1501.60	1216.27	1048.34	939.04	863.17	808.13	766.91	735.29	710.59	691.02	675.34	662.67
43000	3925.89	2130.16	1537.36	1245.23	1073.30	961.39	883.72	827.37	785.17	752.79	727.51	707.47	691.42	678.45
44000	4017.19	2179.70	1573.11	1274.18	1098.26	983.75	904.27	846.61	803.43	770.30	744.43	723.93	707.50	694.23
45000	4108.49	2229.23	1608.86	1303.14	1123.22	1006.11	924.82	865.85	821.68	787.81	761.34	740.38	723.58	710.00
46000	4199.79	2278.77	1644.61	1332.10	1148.18	1028.47	945.38	885.09	839.94	805.31	778.26	756.83	739.66	725.78
47000	4291.09	2328.31	1680.37	1361.06	1173.14	1050.83	965.93	904.34	858.20	822.82	795.18	773.28	755.74	741.56
48000	4382.39	2377.85	1716.12	1390.02	1198.10	1073.18	986.48	923.58	876.46	840.33	812.10	789.74	771.82	757.34
49000	4473.69	2427.39	1751.87	1418.98	1223.06	1095.54	1007.03	942.82	894.72	857.83	829.02	806.19	787.90	773.11
50000	4564.99	2476.93	1787.62	1447.94	1248.02	1117.90	1027.58	962.06	912.98	875.34	845.94	822.64	803.98	788.89
55000	5021.49	2724.62	1966.38	1592.73	1372.82	1229.69	1130.34	1058.26	1004.28	962.87	930.53	904.91	884.38	867.78
60000	5477.99	2972.31	2145.15	1737.52	1497.62	1341.48	1233.10	1154.47	1095.58	1050.41	1015.12	987.17	964.77	946.67
65000	5934.49	3220.00	2323.91	1882.32	1622.42	1453.27	1335.86	1250.68	1186.88	1137.94	1099.72	1069.43	1045.17	1025.56
70000	6390.98	3467.69	2502.67	2027.11	1747.22	1565.06	1438.61	1346.88	1278.17	1225.47	1184.31	1151.70	1125.57	1104.45
75000	6847.48	3715.39	2681.43	2171.90	1872.02	1676.85	1541.37	1443.09	1369.47	1313.01	1268.90	1233.96	1205.97	1183.34
80000	7303.98	3963.08	2860.19	2316.69	1996.82	1788.64	1644.13	1539.29	1460.77	1400.54	1353.50	1316.23	1286.36	1262.22
85000	7760.48	4210.77	3038.95	2461.49	2121.63	1900.42	1746.89	1635.50	1552.07	1488.07	1438.09	1398.49	1366.76	1341.11
90000	8216.98	4458.46	3217.72	2606.28	2246.43	2012.21	1849.64	1731.70	1643.37	1575.61	1522.68	1480.75	1447.16	1420.00
95000	8673.48	4706.15	3396.48	2751.07	2371.23	2124.00	1952.40	1827.91	1734.66	1663.14	1607.28	1563.02	1527.56	1498.89
100000	9129.97	4953.85	3575.24	2895.87	2496.03	2235.79	2055.16	1924.11	1825.96	1750.68	1691.87	1645.28	1607.95	1577.78

TERM	15 Years	16 Years	17 Years	18 Years	19 Years	20 Years	21 Years	22 Years	23 Years	24 Years	25 Years	30 Years	35 Years	40 Years
AMOUNT														
5	.08	.08	.08	.08	.08	.08	.08	.08	.08	.08	.08	.08	.08	.08
10	.16	.16	.16	.16	.15	.15	.15	.15	.15	.15	.15	.15	.15	.15
15	.24	.23	.23	.23	.23	.23	.23	.23	.22	.22	.22	.22	.22	.22
25	.39	.39	.38	.38	.38	.38	.37	.37	.37	.37	.37	.37	.36	.36
50	.78	.77	.76	.76	.75	.75	.74	.74	.74	.73	.73	.73	.72	.72
75	1.17	1.15	1.14	1.13	1.12	1.12	1.11	1.11	1.10	1.10	1.10	1.09	1.08	1.08
100	1.56	1.54	1.52	1.51	1.50	1.49	1.48	1.47	1.47	1.46	1.46	1.45	1.44	1.44
200	3.11	3.07	3.04	3.01	2.99	2.97	2.95	2.94	2.93	2.92	2.91	2.89	2.88	2.87
300	4.66	4.60	4.55	4.51	4.48	4.45	4.43	4.41	4.39	4.38	4.37	4.33	4.32	4.31
400	6.22	6.14	6.07	6.02	5.97	5.93	5.90	5.88	5.85	5.84	5.82	5.77	5.75	5.74
500	7.77	7.67	7.59	7.52	7.46	7.42	7.38	7.34	7.32	7.29	7.27	7.21	7.19	7.18
600	9.32	9.20	9.10	9.02	8.95	8.90	8.85	8.81	8.78	8.75	8.73	8.66	8.63	8.61
700	10.88	10.74	10.62	10.52	10.45	10.38	10.32	10.28	10.24	10.21	10.18	10.10	10.06	10.05
800	12.43	12.27	12.14	12.03	11.94	11.86	11.80	11.75	11.70	11.67	11.63	11.54	11.50	11.48
900	13.98	13.80	13.65	13.53	13.43	13.34	13.27	13.21	13.16	13.12	13.09	12.98	12.94	12.92
1000	15.54	15.34	15.17	15.03	14.92	14.83	14.75	14.68	14.63	14.58	14.54	14.42	14.37	14.35
2000	31.07	30.67	30.34	30.06	29.83	29.65	29.49	29.36	29.25	29.16	29.08	28.84	28.74	28.70
3000	46.60	46.00	45.50	45.09	44.75	44.47	44.23	44.03	43.87	43.73	43.62	43.26	43.11	43.05
4000	62.13	61.33	60.67	60.12	59.66	59.29	58.97	58.71	58.49	58.31	58.15	57.68	57.48	57.40
5000	77.67	76.66	75.83	75.15	74.58	74.11	73.71	73.39	73.11	72.88	72.69	72.10	71.85	71.75
6000	93.20	91.99	91.00	90.17	89.49	88.93	88.45	88.06	87.73	87.46	87.23	86.52	86.22	86.10
7000	108.73	107.32	106.16	105.20	104.41	103.75	103.20	102.74	102.35	102.03	101.76	100.94	100.59	100.45
8000	124.26	122.65	121.33	120.23	119.32	118.57	117.94	117.41	116.97	116.61	116.30	115.36	114.96	114.80
9000	139.79	137.98	136.49	135.26	134.24	133.39	132.68	132.09	131.60	131.18	130.84	129.78	129.33	129.14
10000	155.33	153.31	151.66	150.29	149.15	148.21	147.42	146.77	146.22	145.76	145.37	144.20	143.70	143.49
11000	170.86	168.64	166.82	165.31	164.07	163.03	162.16	161.44	160.84	160.33	159.91	158.62	158.07	157.84
12000	186.39	183.97	181.99	180.34	178.98	177.85	176.90	176.12	175.46	174.91	174.45	173.04	172.44	172.19
13000	201.92	199.30	197.15	195.37	193.90	192.67	191.65	190.79	190.08	189.48	188.98	187.45	186.81	186.54
14000	217.45	214.64	212.32	210.40	208.81	207.49	206.39	205.47	204.70	204.06	203.52	201.87	201.18	200.89
15000	232.99	229.97	227.48	225.43	223.72	222.31	221.13	220.15	219.32	218.63	218.06	216.29	215.55	215.24
16000	248.52	245.30	242.65	240.46	238.64	237.13	235.87	234.82	233.94	233.21	232.59	230.71	229.92	229.59
17000	264.05	260.63	257.81	255.48	253.55	251.95	250.61	249.50	248.56	247.78	247.13	245.13	244.29	243.94
18000	279.58	275.96	272.98	270.51	268.47	266.77	265.35	264.17	263.19	262.36	261.67	259.55	258.66	258.28
19000	295.11	291.29	288.14	285.54	283.38	281.59	280.10	278.85	277.81	276.93	276.20	273.97	273.03	272.63
20000	310.65	306.62	303.31	300.57	298.30	296.41	294.84	293.53	292.43	291.51	290.74	288.39	287.40	286.98
21000	326.18	321.95	318.47	315.60	313.21	311.23	309.58	308.20	307.05	306.08	305.28	302.81	301.77	301.33
22000	341.71	337.28	333.64	330.62	328.13	326.05	324.32	322.88	321.67	320.66	319.81	317.23	316.14	315.68
23000	357.24	352.61	348.80	345.65	343.04	340.07	339.06	337.55	336.29	335.23	334.35	331.65	330.51	330.03
24000	372.77	367.94	363.97	360.68	357.96	355.69	353.80	352.23	350.91	349.81	348.89	346.07	344.88	344.38
25000	388.31	383.27	379.13	375.71	372.87	370.51	368.55	366.91	365.53	364.38	363.42	360.49	359.25	358.73
26000	403.84	398.60	394.30	390.74	387.79	385.33	383.29	381.58	380.15	378.96	377.96	374.90	373.62	373.07
27000	419.37	413.93	409.46	405.77	402.70	400.15	398.03	396.26	394.78	393.54	392.50	389.32	387.99	387.42
28000	434.90	429.27	424.63	420.79	417.62	414.97	412.77	410.93	409.40	408.11	407.03	403.74	402.36	401.77
29000	450.43	444.60	439.79	435.82	432.53	429.79	427.51	425.61	424.02	422.69	421.57	418.16	416.73	416.12
30000	465.97	459.93	454.96	450.85	447.44	444.61	442.25	440.29	438.64	437.26	436.11	432.58	431.10	430.47
31000	481.50	475.26	470.12	465.88	462.36	459.43	457.00	454.96	453.26	451.84	450.64	447.00	445.47	444.82
32000	497.03	490.59	485.29	480.91	477.27	474.25	471.74	469.64	467.88	466.41	465.18	461.42	459.84	459.17
33000	512.56	505.92	500.45	495.93	492.19	489.07	486.48	484.31	482.50	480.99	479.72	475.84	474.21	473.52
34000	528.09	521.25	515.62	510.96	507.10	503.89	501.22	498.99	497.12	495.56	494.25	490.26	488.58	487.87
35000	543.63	536.58	530.78	525.99	522.02	518.72	515.96	513.67	511.75	510.14	508.79	504.68	502.95	502.21
36000	559.16	551.91	545.95	541.02	536.93	533.54	530.70	528.34	526.37	524.71	523.33	519.10	517.32	516.56
37000	574.69	567.24	561.11	556.05	551.85	548.36	545.45	543.02	540.99	539.29	537.86	533.52	531.69	530.91
38000	590.22	582.57	576.28	571.07	566.76	563.18	560.19	557.69	555.61	553.86	552.40	547.94	546.06	545.26
39000	605.75	597.90	591.44	586.10	581.68	578.00	574.93	572.37	570.23	568.44	566.94	562.35	560.43	559.61
40000	621.29	613.23	606.61	601.13	596.59	592.82	589.67	587.05	584.85	583.01	581.47	576.77	574.80	573.96
41000	636.82	628.57	621.77	616.16	611.51	607.64	604.41	601.72	599.47	597.59	596.01	591.19	589.17	588.31
42000	652.35	643.90	636.94	631.19	626.42	622.46	619.15	616.40	614.09	612.16	610.55	605.61	603.54	602.66
43000	667.88	659.23	652.10	646.22	641.34	637.28	633.90	631.07	628.71	626.74	625.08	620.03	617.91	617.00
44000	683.41	674.56	667.27	661.24	656.25	652.10	648.64	645.75	643.34	641.31	639.62	634.45	632.27	631.35
45000	698.95	689.89	682.43	676.27	671.16	666.92	663.38	660.43	657.96	655.89	654.16	648.87	646.64	645.70
46000	714.48	705.22	697.60	691.30	686.08	681.74	678.12	675.10	672.58	670.46	668.69	663.29	661.01	660.05
47000	730.01	720.55	712.76	706.33	700.99	696.56	692.86	689.78	687.20	685.04	683.23	677.71	675.38	674.40
48000	745.54	735.88	727.93	721.36	715.91	711.38	707.60	704.45	701.82	699.61	697.77	692.13	689.75	688.75
49000	761.07	751.21	743.09	736.38	730.82	726.20	722.35	719.13	716.44	714.19	712.30	706.55	704.12	703.10
50000	776.61	766.54	758.26	751.41	745.74	741.02	737.09	733.81	731.06	728.76	726.84	720.97	718.49	717.45
55000	854.27	843.20	834.08	826.55	820.31	815.12	810.80	807.19	804.17	801.64	799.52	793.06	790.34	789.19
60000	931.93	919.85	909.91	901.69	894.88	889.22	884.50	880.57	877.27	874.52	872.21	865.16	862.19	860.93
65000	1009.59	996.50	985.73	976.84	969.46	963.32	958.21	953.95	950.38	947.39	944.89	937.25	934.04	932.68
70000	1087.25	1073.16	1061.56	1051.98	1044.03	1037.43	1031.92	1027.33	1023.49	1020.27	1017.57	1009.35	1005.89	1004.42
75000	1164.91	1149.81	1137.38	1127.12	1118.60	1111.53	1105.63	1100.71	1096.59	1093.14	1090.26	1081.45	1077.74	1076.17
80000	1242.57	1226.46	1213.21	1202.26	1193.18	1185.63	1179.34	1174.09	1169.70	1166.02	1162.94	1153.54	1149.59	1147.91
85000	1320.23	1303.12	1289.04	1277.40	1267.75	1259.73	1253.05	1247.47	1242.80	1238.90	1235.62	1225.64	1221.44	1219.66
90000	1397.89	1379.77	1364.86	1352.54	1342.32	1333.83	1326.75	1320.85	1315.91	1311.77	1308.31	1297.73	1293.28	1291.40
95000	1475.55	1456.42	1440.69	1427.68	1416.90	1407.93	1400.46	1394.23	1389.01	1384.65	1380.99	1369.83	1365.13	1363.14
100000	1553.21	1533.08	1516.51	1502.82	1491.47	1482.03	1474.17	1467.61	1462.12	1457.52	1453.67	1441.93	1436.98	1434.89

MONTHLY PAYMENT
REQUIRED TO AMORTIZE A LOAN

TERM	1 Year	2 Years	3 Years	4 Years	5 Years	6 Years	7 Years	8 Years	9 Years	10 Years	11 Years	12 Years	13 Years	14 Years
AMOUNT														
5	.46	.25	.18	.15	.13	.12	.11	.10	.10	.09	.09	.09	.09	.08
10	.92	.50	.36	.29	.25	.23	.21	.20	.19	.18	.17	.17	.17	.16
15	1.37	.75	.54	.44	.38	.34	.31	.29	.28	.27	.26	.25	.25	.24
25	2.29	1.24	.90	.73	.63	.56	.52	.49	.46	.44	.43	.42	.41	.40
50	4.57	2.48	1.79	1.45	1.25	1.12	1.03	.97	.92	.88	.85	.83	.81	.80
75	6.85	3.72	2.69	2.18	1.88	1.68	1.55	1.45	1.38	1.32	1.28	1.24	1.21	1.19
100	9.14	4.96	3.58	2.90	2.50	2.24	2.06	1.93	1.83	1.76	1.70	1.65	1.62	1.59
200	18.27	9.92	7.16	5.80	5.00	4.48	4.12	3.86	3.66	3.51	3.40	3.30	3.23	3.17
300	27.40	14.87	10.74	8.70	7.50	6.72	6.18	5.79	5.49	5.27	5.09	4.95	4.84	4.75
400	36.53	19.83	14.32	11.60	10.00	8.96	8.24	7.71	7.32	7.02	6.79	6.60	6.45	6.33
500	45.67	24.79	17.89	14.50	12.50	11.20	10.30	9.64	9.15	8.77	8.48	8.25	8.06	7.91
600	54.80	29.74	21.47	17.40	15.00	13.44	12.35	11.57	10.98	10.53	10.18	9.90	9.67	9.49
700	63.93	34.70	25.05	20.29	17.50	15.68	14.41	13.49	12.81	12.28	11.87	11.55	11.28	11.07
800	73.06	39.65	28.63	23.19	19.99	17.91	16.47	15.42	14.64	14.04	13.57	13.19	12.90	12.66
900	82.20	44.61	32.20	26.09	22.49	20.15	18.53	17.35	16.47	15.79	15.26	14.84	14.51	14.24
1000	91.33	49.57	35.78	28.99	24.99	22.39	20.59	19.28	18.30	17.54	16.96	16.49	16.12	15.82
2000	182.65	99.13	71.56	57.97	49.98	44.78	41.17	38.55	36.59	35.08	33.91	32.98	32.23	31.63
3000	273.98	148.69	107.34	86.96	74.97	67.16	61.75	57.82	54.88	52.62	50.86	49.46	48.35	47.44
4000	365.30	198.25	143.11	115.94	99.95	89.55	82.33	77.09	73.17	70.16	67.81	65.95	64.46	63.26
5000	456.62	247.82	178.89	144.93	124.94	111.93	102.91	96.36	91.46	87.70	84.76	82.44	80.57	79.07
6000	547.95	297.38	214.67	173.91	149.93	134.32	123.49	115.63	109.75	105.24	101.71	98.92	96.69	94.88
7000	639.27	346.94	250.45	202.90	174.92	156.71	144.07	134.90	128.04	122.77	118.66	115.41	112.80	110.69
8000	730.59	396.50	286.22	231.88	199.90	179.09	164.65	154.17	146.33	140.31	135.62	131.89	128.91	126.51
9000	821.92	446.07	322.00	260.87	224.89	201.48	185.23	173.44	164.62	157.85	152.57	148.38	145.03	142.32
10000	913.24	495.63	357.78	289.85	249.88	223.86	205.81	192.72	182.91	175.39	169.52	164.87	161.14	158.13
11000	1004.56	545.19	393.56	318.84	274.86	246.25	226.39	211.99	201.20	192.93	186.47	181.35	177.26	173.94
12000	1095.89	594.75	429.33	347.82	299.85	268.64	246.97	231.26	219.49	210.47	203.42	197.84	193.37	189.76
13000	1187.21	644.32	465.11	376.80	324.84	291.02	267.55	250.53	237.78	228.01	220.37	214.33	209.48	205.57
14000	1278.53	693.88	500.89	405.79	349.83	313.41	288.13	269.80	256.07	245.54	237.32	230.81	225.60	221.38
15000	1369.86	743.44	536.66	434.77	374.81	335.79	308.71	289.07	274.36	263.08	254.27	247.30	241.71	237.19
16000	1461.18	793.00	572.44	463.76	399.80	358.18	329.29	308.34	292.65	280.62	271.23	263.78	257.82	253.01
17000	1552.50	842.57	608.22	492.74	424.79	380.56	349.87	327.61	310.94	298.16	288.18	280.27	273.94	268.82
18000	1643.83	892.13	644.00	521.73	449.77	402.95	370.45	346.88	329.23	315.70	305.13	296.76	290.05	284.63
19000	1735.15	941.69	679.77	550.71	474.76	425.34	391.04	366.15	347.52	333.24	322.08	313.24	306.17	300.45
20000	1826.47	991.25	715.55	579.70	499.75	447.72	411.62	385.43	365.81	350.78	339.03	329.73	322.28	316.26
21000	1917.80	1040.82	751.33	608.68	524.74	470.11	432.20	404.70	384.10	368.31	355.98	346.22	338.39	332.07
22000	2009.12	1090.38	787.11	637.67	549.72	492.49	452.78	423.97	402.40	385.85	372.93	362.70	354.51	347.88
23000	2100.44	1139.94	822.88	666.65	574.71	514.88	473.36	443.24	420.69	403.39	389.88	379.19	370.62	363.70
24000	2191.77	1189.50	858.66	695.63	599.70	537.27	493.94	462.51	438.98	420.93	406.84	395.67	386.73	379.51
25000	2283.09	1239.07	894.44	724.62	624.68	559.65	514.52	481.78	457.27	438.47	423.79	412.16	402.85	395.32
26000	2374.41	1288.63	930.21	753.60	649.67	582.04	535.10	501.05	475.56	456.01	440.74	428.65	418.96	411.13
27000	2465.74	1338.19	965.99	782.59	674.66	604.42	555.68	520.32	493.85	473.54	457.69	445.13	435.07	426.95
28000	2557.06	1387.75	1001.77	811.57	699.65	626.81	576.26	539.59	512.14	491.08	474.64	461.62	451.19	442.76
29000	2648.38	1437.32	1037.55	840.56	724.63	649.19	596.84	558.87	530.43	508.62	491.59	478.11	467.30	458.57
30000	2739.71	1486.88	1073.32	869.54	749.62	671.58	617.42	578.14	548.72	526.16	508.54	494.59	483.42	474.38
31000	2831.03	1536.44	1109.10	898.53	774.61	693.97	638.00	597.41	567.01	543.70	525.50	511.08	499.53	490.20
32000	2922.35	1586.00	1144.88	927.51	799.60	716.35	658.58	616.68	585.30	561.24	542.45	527.56	515.64	506.01
33000	3013.68	1635.57	1180.66	956.50	824.58	738.74	679.16	635.95	603.60	578.78	559.40	544.05	531.76	521.82
34000	3105.00	1685.13	1216.43	985.48	849.57	761.12	699.74	655.22	621.88	596.31	576.35	560.54	547.87	537.63
35000	3196.33	1734.69	1252.21	1014.46	874.56	783.51	720.32	674.49	640.17	613.85	593.30	577.02	563.98	553.45
36000	3287.65	1784.25	1287.99	1043.45	899.54	805.90	740.90	693.76	658.46	631.39	610.25	593.51	580.10	569.26
37000	3378.97	1833.82	1323.76	1072.43	924.53	828.28	761.49	713.03	676.75	648.93	627.20	609.99	596.21	585.07
38000	3470.30	1883.38	1359.54	1101.42	949.52	850.67	782.07	732.30	695.04	666.47	644.15	626.48	612.33	600.89
39000	3561.62	1932.94	1395.32	1130.40	974.51	873.05	802.65	751.58	713.33	684.01	661.11	642.97	628.44	616.70
40000	3652.94	1982.50	1431.10	1159.39	999.49	895.44	823.23	770.85	731.62	701.55	678.06	659.45	644.55	632.51
41000	3744.27	2032.07	1466.87	1188.37	1024.48	917.83	843.81	790.12	749.91	719.08	695.01	675.94	660.67	648.32
42000	3835.59	2081.63	1502.65	1217.36	1049.47	940.21	864.39	809.39	768.20	736.62	711.96	692.43	676.78	664.14
43000	3926.91	2131.19	1538.43	1246.34	1074.45	962.60	884.97	828.66	786.49	754.16	728.91	708.91	692.89	679.95
44000	4018.24	2180.75	1574.21	1275.33	1099.44	984.98	905.55	847.93	804.79	771.70	745.86	725.40	709.01	695.76
45000	4109.56	2230.32	1609.98	1304.31	1124.43	1007.37	926.13	867.20	823.08	789.24	762.81	741.88	725.12	711.57
46000	4200.88	2279.88	1645.76	1333.29	1149.42	1029.75	946.71	886.47	841.37	806.78	779.76	758.37	741.23	727.39
47000	4292.21	2329.44	1681.54	1362.28	1174.40	1052.14	967.29	905.74	859.66	824.31	796.72	774.86	757.35	743.20
48000	4383.53	2379.00	1717.31	1391.26	1199.39	1074.53	987.87	925.02	877.95	841.85	813.67	791.34	773.46	759.01
49000	4474.85	2428.57	1753.09	1420.25	1224.38	1096.91	1008.45	944.29	896.24	859.39	830.62	807.83	789.58	774.82
50000	4566.18	2478.13	1788.87	1449.23	1249.36	1119.30	1029.03	963.56	914.53	876.93	847.57	824.32	805.69	790.64
55000	5022.79	2725.94	1967.76	1594.16	1374.30	1231.23	1131.93	1059.91	1005.98	964.62	932.33	906.75	886.26	869.70
60000	5479.41	2973.75	2146.64	1739.08	1499.24	1343.16	1234.84	1156.27	1097.43	1052.32	1017.08	989.18	966.83	948.76
65000	5936.03	3221.57	2325.53	1884.00	1624.17	1455.09	1337.74	1252.62	1188.88	1140.01	1101.84	1071.61	1047.40	1027.83
70000	6392.65	3469.38	2504.41	2028.92	1749.11	1567.02	1440.64	1348.98	1280.34	1227.70	1186.60	1154.04	1127.96	1106.89
75000	6849.26	3717.19	2683.30	2173.85	1874.04	1678.94	1543.55	1445.33	1371.79	1315.39	1271.35	1236.47	1208.53	1185.95
80000	7305.88	3965.00	2862.19	2318.77	1998.98	1790.87	1646.45	1541.69	1463.24	1403.09	1356.11	1318.90	1289.10	1265.02
85000	7762.50	4212.82	3041.07	2463.69	2123.92	1902.80	1749.35	1638.04	1554.69	1490.78	1440.87	1401.33	1369.67	1344.08
90000	8219.11	4460.63	3219.96	2608.61	2248.85	2014.73	1852.25	1734.40	1646.15	1578.47	1525.62	1483.76	1450.24	1423.14
95000	8675.73	4708.44	3398.85	2753.54	2373.79	2126.66	1955.16	1830.75	1737.60	1666.16	1610.38	1566.20	1530.81	1502.21
100000	9132.35	4956.25	3577.73	2898.46	2498.72	2238.59	2058.06	1927.11	1829.05	1753.86	1695.13	1648.63	1611.37	1581.27

TERM	15 Years	16 Years	17 Years	18 Years	19 Years	20 Years	21 Years	22 Years	23 Years	24 Years	25 Years	30 Years	35 Years	40 Years
AMOUNT														
5	.08	.08	.08	.08	.08	.08	.08	.08	.08	.08	.08	.08	.08	.08
10	.16	.16	.16	.16	.15	.15	.15	.15	.15	.15	.15	.15	.15	.15
15	.24	.24	.23	.23	.23	.23	.23	.23	.22	.22	.22	.22	.22	.22
25	.39	.39	.39	.38	.38	.38	.37	.37	.37	.37	.37	.37	.37	.36
50	.78	.77	.77	.76	.75	.75	.74	.74	.74	.74	.73	.73	.73	.72
75	1.17	1.16	1.15	1.13	1.13	1.12	1.11	1.11	1.10	1.10	1.10	1.09	1.09	1.08
100	1.56	1.54	1.53	1.51	1.50	1.49	1.48	1.48	1.47	1.47	1.46	1.45	1.45	1.44
200	3.12	3.08	3.05	3.02	3.00	2.98	2.96	2.95	2.94	2.93	2.92	2.90	2.89	2.88
300	4.68	4.62	4.57	4.52	4.49	4.46	4.44	4.42	4.40	4.39	4.38	4.34	4.33	4.32
400	6.23	6.15	6.09	6.03	5.99	5.95	5.92	5.89	5.87	5.85	5.84	5.79	5.77	5.76
500	7.79	7.69	7.61	7.54	7.48	7.43	7.40	7.36	7.34	7.31	7.29	7.23	7.21	7.20
600	9.35	9.23	9.13	9.04	8.98	8.92	8.87	8.83	8.80	8.77	8.75	8.68	8.65	8.64
700	10.90	10.76	10.65	10.55	10.47	10.41	10.35	10.31	10.27	10.24	10.21	10.13	10.09	10.08
800	12.46	12.30	12.17	12.06	11.97	11.89	11.83	11.78	11.73	11.70	11.67	11.57	11.53	11.52
900	14.02	13.84	13.69	13.56	13.46	13.38	13.31	13.25	13.20	13.16	13.12	13.02	12.97	12.96
1000	15.57	15.37	15.21	15.07	14.96	14.86	14.79	14.72	14.67	14.62	14.58	14.46	14.42	14.40
2000	31.14	30.74	30.41	30.14	29.91	29.72	29.57	29.43	29.33	29.23	29.16	28.92	28.83	28.79
3000	46.71	46.11	45.61	45.20	44.86	44.58	44.35	44.15	43.99	43.85	43.73	43.38	43.24	43.18
4000	62.28	61.47	60.81	60.27	59.81	59.44	59.13	58.86	58.65	58.46	58.31	57.84	57.65	57.57
5000	77.84	76.84	76.01	75.33	74.77	74.30	73.91	73.58	73.31	73.08	72.89	72.30	72.06	71.96
6000	93.41	92.21	91.22	90.40	89.72	89.16	88.69	88.29	87.97	87.69	87.46	86.76	86.47	86.35
7000	108.98	107.57	106.42	105.46	104.67	104.01	103.47	103.01	102.63	102.31	102.04	101.22	100.88	100.74
8000	124.55	122.94	121.62	120.53	119.62	118.87	118.25	117.72	117.29	116.92	116.62	115.68	115.29	115.13
9000	140.11	138.31	136.82	135.59	134.58	133.73	133.03	132.44	131.95	131.54	131.19	130.14	129.70	129.52
10000	155.68	153.67	152.02	150.66	149.53	148.59	147.81	147.15	146.61	146.15	145.77	144.60	144.11	143.91
11000	171.25	169.04	167.22	165.72	164.48	163.45	162.59	161.87	161.27	160.77	160.35	159.06	158.53	158.30
12000	186.82	184.41	182.43	180.79	179.43	178.31	177.37	176.58	175.93	175.38	174.92	173.52	172.94	172.69
13000	202.38	199.77	197.63	195.86	194.39	193.16	192.15	191.30	190.59	190.00	189.50	187.98	187.35	187.08
14000	217.95	215.14	212.83	210.92	209.34	208.02	206.93	206.01	205.25	204.61	204.07	202.44	201.76	201.47
15000	233.52	230.51	228.03	225.99	224.29	222.88	221.71	220.73	219.91	219.23	218.65	216.90	216.17	215.86
16000	249.09	245.88	243.23	241.05	239.24	237.74	236.49	235.44	234.57	233.84	233.23	231.36	230.58	230.25
17000	264.65	261.24	258.44	256.12	254.20	252.60	251.27	250.16	249.23	248.45	247.80	245.82	244.99	244.64
18000	280.22	276.61	273.64	271.18	269.15	267.46	266.05	264.87	263.89	263.07	262.38	260.28	259.40	259.03
19000	295.79	291.98	288.84	286.25	284.10	282.31	280.83	279.59	278.55	277.68	276.96	274.74	273.81	273.42
20000	311.36	307.34	304.04	301.31	299.05	297.17	295.61	294.30	293.21	292.30	291.53	289.20	288.22	287.81
21000	326.92	322.71	319.24	316.38	314.00	312.03	310.39	309.02	307.87	306.91	306.11	303.66	302.63	302.20
22000	342.49	338.08	334.44	331.44	328.96	326.89	325.17	323.73	322.53	321.53	320.69	318.12	317.05	316.59
23000	358.06	353.44	349.65	346.51	343.91	341.75	339.95	338.45	337.19	336.14	335.26	332.58	331.46	330.98
24000	373.63	368.81	364.85	361.57	358.86	356.61	354.73	353.16	351.85	350.76	349.84	347.04	345.87	345.37
25000	389.19	384.18	380.05	376.64	373.81	371.47	369.51	367.88	366.51	365.37	364.42	361.50	360.28	359.76
26000	404.76	399.54	395.25	391.71	388.77	386.32	384.29	382.59	381.17	379.99	378.99	375.96	374.69	374.15
27000	420.33	414.91	410.45	406.77	403.72	401.18	399.07	397.31	395.83	394.60	393.57	390.42	389.10	388.54
28000	435.90	430.28	425.66	421.84	418.67	416.04	413.85	412.02	410.49	409.22	408.14	404.88	403.51	402.93
29000	451.46	445.65	440.86	436.90	433.62	430.90	428.63	426.74	425.15	423.83	422.72	419.34	417.92	417.32
30000	467.03	461.01	456.06	451.97	448.58	445.76	443.41	441.45	439.81	438.45	437.30	433.80	432.33	431.71
31000	482.60	476.38	471.26	467.03	463.53	460.62	458.19	456.17	454.48	453.06	451.87	448.26	446.74	446.10
32000	498.17	491.75	486.46	482.10	478.48	475.47	472.97	470.88	469.14	467.67	466.45	462.72	461.15	460.49
33000	513.73	507.11	501.66	497.16	493.43	490.33	487.75	485.60	483.80	482.29	481.03	477.18	475.57	474.88
34000	529.30	522.48	516.87	512.23	508.39	505.19	502.53	500.31	498.46	496.90	495.60	491.64	489.98	489.27
35000	544.87	537.85	532.07	527.29	523.34	520.05	517.31	515.03	513.12	511.52	510.18	506.10	504.39	503.66
36000	560.44	553.21	547.27	542.36	538.29	534.91	532.09	529.74	527.78	526.13	524.76	520.56	518.80	518.05
37000	576.01	568.58	562.47	557.42	553.24	549.77	546.87	544.46	542.44	540.75	539.33	535.02	533.21	532.44
38000	591.57	583.95	577.67	572.49	568.19	564.62	561.65	559.17	557.10	555.36	553.91	549.48	547.62	546.83
39000	607.14	599.31	592.87	587.56	583.15	579.48	576.43	573.89	571.76	569.98	568.49	563.94	562.03	561.22
40000	622.71	614.68	608.08	602.62	598.10	594.34	591.21	588.60	586.42	584.59	583.06	578.40	576.44	575.61
41000	638.28	630.05	623.28	617.69	613.05	609.20	605.99	603.32	601.08	599.21	597.64	592.86	590.85	590.00
42000	653.84	645.41	638.48	632.75	628.00	624.06	620.77	618.03	615.74	613.82	612.21	607.32	605.26	604.39
43000	669.41	660.78	653.68	647.82	642.96	638.92	635.55	632.75	630.40	628.44	626.79	621.78	619.67	618.78
44000	684.98	676.15	668.88	662.88	657.91	653.78	650.33	647.46	645.06	643.05	641.37	636.24	634.09	633.18
45000	700.55	691.52	684.09	677.95	672.86	668.63	665.11	662.18	659.72	657.67	655.94	650.70	648.50	647.57
46000	716.11	706.88	699.29	693.01	687.81	683.49	679.89	676.89	674.38	672.28	670.52	665.16	662.91	661.96
47000	731.68	722.25	714.49	708.08	702.77	698.35	694.67	691.61	689.04	686.89	685.10	679.62	677.32	676.35
48000	747.25	737.62	729.69	723.14	717.72	713.21	709.45	706.32	703.70	701.51	699.67	694.08	691.73	690.74
49000	762.82	752.98	744.89	738.21	732.67	728.07	724.23	721.03	718.36	716.12	714.25	708.54	706.14	705.13
50000	778.38	768.35	760.09	753.27	747.62	742.93	739.01	735.75	733.02	730.74	728.83	723.00	720.55	719.52
55000	856.22	845.18	836.10	828.60	822.38	817.22	812.91	809.32	806.32	803.81	801.71	795.30	792.61	791.47
60000	934.06	922.02	912.11	903.93	897.15	891.51	886.82	882.90	879.62	876.89	874.59	867.60	864.66	863.42
65000	1011.90	998.85	988.12	979.26	971.91	965.80	960.72	956.47	952.93	949.96	947.47	939.90	936.71	935.37
70000	1089.73	1075.69	1064.13	1054.58	1046.67	1040.09	1034.62	1030.05	1026.23	1023.03	1020.35	1012.20	1008.77	1007.32
75000	1167.57	1152.52	1140.14	1129.91	1121.43	1114.39	1108.52	1103.62	1099.53	1096.11	1093.24	1084.49	1080.82	1079.27
80000	1245.41	1229.36	1216.15	1205.24	1196.19	1188.68	1182.42	1177.20	1172.83	1169.18	1166.12	1156.79	1152.88	1151.22
85000	1323.25	1306.19	1292.16	1280.56	1270.96	1262.97	1256.32	1250.77	1246.13	1242.26	1239.00	1229.09	1224.93	1223.17
90000	1401.09	1383.03	1368.17	1355.89	1345.72	1337.26	1330.22	1324.35	1319.43	1315.33	1311.88	1301.39	1296.99	1295.13
95000	1478.92	1459.86	1444.17	1431.22	1420.48	1411.55	1404.12	1397.92	1392.74	1388.40	1384.76	1373.69	1369.04	1367.08
100000	1556.76	1536.69	1520.18	1506.54	1495.24	1485.85	1478.02	1471.49	1466.04	1461.47	1457.65	1445.99	1441.10	1439.03

MONTHLY PAYMENT
REQUIRED TO AMORTIZE A LOAN

TERM AMOUNT	1 Year	2 Years	3 Years	4 Years	5 Years	6 Years	7 Years	8 Years	9 Years	10 Years	11 Years	12 Years	13 Years	14 Years
5	.46	.25	.18	.15	.13	.12	.11	.10	.10	.09	.09	.09	.09	.08
10	.92	.50	.36	.30	.26	.23	.21	.20	.19	.18	.17	.17	.17	.16
15	1.38	.75	.54	.44	.38	.34	.31	.29	.28	.27	.26	.25	.25	.24
25	2.29	1.24	.90	.73	.63	.57	.52	.49	.46	.44	.43	.42	.41	.40
50	4.57	2.48	1.80	1.46	1.26	1.13	1.04	.97	.92	.88	.85	.83	.81	.80
75	6.86	3.72	2.69	2.18	1.88	1.69	1.55	1.45	1.38	1.32	1.28	1.24	1.22	1.19
100	9.14	4.96	3.59	2.91	2.51	2.25	2.07	1.94	1.84	1.76	1.70	1.66	1.62	1.59
200	18.27	9.92	7.17	5.81	5.01	4.49	4.13	3.87	3.67	3.52	3.40	3.31	3.23	3.17
300	27.41	14.88	10.75	8.71	7.51	6.73	6.19	5.80	5.50	5.28	5.10	4.96	4.85	4.76
400	36.54	19.84	14.33	11.61	10.01	8.97	8.25	7.73	7.33	7.03	6.80	6.61	6.46	6.34
500	45.68	24.80	17.91	14.51	12.51	11.21	10.31	9.66	9.17	8.79	8.50	8.26	8.08	7.93
600	54.81	29.76	21.49	17.41	15.01	13.45	12.37	11.59	11.00	10.55	10.20	9.92	9.69	9.51
700	63.95	34.72	25.07	20.31	17.51	15.69	14.43	13.52	12.83	12.30	11.89	11.57	11.31	11.10
800	73.08	39.67	28.65	23.21	20.02	17.94	16.49	15.45	14.66	14.06	13.59	13.22	12.92	12.68
900	82.22	44.63	32.23	26.11	22.52	20.18	18.55	17.38	16.49	15.82	15.29	14.87	14.54	14.27
1000	91.35	49.59	35.81	29.02	25.02	22.42	20.61	19.31	18.33	17.58	16.99	16.52	16.15	15.85
2000	182.70	99.18	71.61	58.03	50.03	44.83	41.22	38.61	36.65	35.15	33.97	33.04	32.30	31.70
3000	274.05	148.76	107.41	87.04	75.05	67.25	61.83	57.91	54.97	52.72	50.96	49.56	48.45	47.55
4000	365.39	198.35	143.21	116.05	100.06	89.66	82.44	77.21	73.29	70.29	67.94	66.08	64.60	63.40
5000	456.74	247.94	179.02	145.06	125.08	112.07	103.05	96.51	91.61	87.86	84.92	82.60	80.74	79.24
6000	548.09	297.52	214.82	174.07	150.09	134.49	123.66	115.81	109.93	105.43	101.91	99.12	96.89	95.09
7000	639.44	347.11	250.62	203.08	175.10	156.90	144.27	135.11	128.25	123.00	118.89	115.64	113.04	110.94
8000	730.78	396.70	286.42	232.09	200.12	179.32	164.88	154.41	146.58	140.57	135.88	132.16	129.19	126.79
9000	822.13	446.28	322.22	261.10	225.13	201.73	185.49	173.71	164.90	158.14	152.86	148.68	145.34	142.63
10000	913.48	495.87	358.03	290.11	250.15	224.14	206.10	193.02	183.22	175.71	169.84	165.20	161.48	158.48
11000	1004.82	545.46	393.83	319.12	275.16	246.56	226.71	212.32	201.54	193.28	186.83	181.72	177.63	174.33
12000	1096.17	595.04	429.63	348.13	300.18	268.97	247.32	231.62	219.86	210.85	203.81	198.24	193.78	190.18
13000	1187.52	644.63	465.43	377.14	325.19	291.39	267.93	250.92	238.18	228.42	220.80	214.76	209.93	206.02
14000	1278.87	694.22	501.24	406.15	350.20	313.80	288.54	270.22	256.50	245.99	237.78	231.28	226.08	221.87
15000	1370.21	743.80	537.04	435.16	375.22	336.21	309.15	289.52	274.83	263.56	254.76	247.80	242.22	237.72
16000	1461.56	793.39	572.84	464.17	400.23	358.63	329.76	308.82	293.15	281.13	271.75	264.32	258.37	253.57
17000	1552.91	842.98	608.64	493.18	425.25	381.04	350.37	328.12	311.47	298.70	288.73	280.84	274.52	269.41
18000	1644.25	892.56	644.44	522.19	450.26	403.45	370.98	347.42	329.79	316.27	305.72	297.36	290.67	285.26
19000	1735.60	942.15	680.25	551.20	475.27	425.87	391.59	366.72	348.11	333.84	322.70	313.88	306.82	301.11
20000	1826.95	991.74	716.05	580.21	500.29	448.28	412.20	386.03	366.43	351.41	339.68	330.40	322.96	316.96
21000	1918.30	1041.32	751.85	609.23	525.30	470.70	432.81	405.33	384.75	368.98	356.67	346.92	339.11	332.80
22000	2009.64	1090.91	787.65	638.24	550.32	493.11	453.42	424.63	403.08	386.55	373.65	363.44	355.26	348.65
23000	2100.99	1140.50	823.46	667.25	575.33	515.52	474.02	443.93	421.40	404.12	390.64	379.96	371.41	364.50
24000	2192.34	1190.08	859.26	696.26	600.35	537.94	494.63	463.23	439.72	421.69	407.62	396.48	387.56	380.35
25000	2283.68	1239.67	895.06	725.27	625.36	560.35	515.24	482.53	458.04	439.26	424.60	413.00	403.70	396.19
26000	2375.03	1289.25	930.86	754.28	650.37	582.77	535.85	501.83	476.36	456.83	441.59	429.52	419.85	412.04
27000	2466.38	1338.84	966.66	783.29	675.39	605.18	556.46	521.13	494.68	474.40	458.57	446.04	436.00	427.89
28000	2557.73	1388.43	1002.47	812.30	700.40	627.59	577.07	540.43	513.00	491.97	475.56	462.56	452.15	443.74
29000	2649.07	1438.01	1038.27	841.31	725.42	650.01	597.68	559.74	531.33	509.54	492.54	479.08	468.29	459.58
30000	2740.42	1487.60	1074.07	870.32	750.43	672.42	618.29	579.04	549.65	527.11	509.52	495.60	484.44	475.43
31000	2831.77	1537.19	1109.87	899.33	775.44	694.83	638.90	598.34	567.97	544.69	526.51	512.12	500.59	491.28
32000	2923.11	1586.77	1145.68	928.34	800.46	717.25	659.51	617.64	586.29	562.26	543.49	528.64	516.74	507.13
33000	3014.46	1636.36	1181.48	957.35	825.47	739.66	680.12	636.94	604.61	579.83	560.48	545.15	532.89	522.97
34000	3105.81	1685.95	1217.28	986.36	850.49	762.08	700.73	656.24	622.93	597.40	577.46	561.67	549.03	538.82
35000	3197.16	1735.53	1253.08	1015.37	875.50	784.49	721.34	675.54	641.25	614.97	594.44	578.19	565.18	554.67
36000	3288.50	1785.12	1288.88	1044.38	900.52	806.90	741.95	694.84	659.57	632.54	611.43	594.71	581.33	570.52
37000	3379.85	1834.71	1324.69	1073.39	925.53	829.32	762.56	714.14	677.90	650.11	628.41	611.23	597.48	586.37
38000	3471.20	1884.29	1360.49	1102.40	950.54	851.73	783.17	733.44	696.22	667.68	645.40	627.75	613.63	602.21
39000	3562.55	1933.88	1396.29	1131.41	975.56	874.15	803.78	752.75	714.54	685.25	662.38	644.27	629.77	618.06
40000	3653.89	1983.47	1432.09	1160.42	1000.57	896.56	824.39	772.05	732.86	702.82	679.36	660.79	645.92	633.91
41000	3745.24	2033.05	1467.90	1189.43	1025.59	918.97	845.00	791.35	751.18	720.39	696.35	677.31	662.07	649.76
42000	3836.59	2082.64	1503.70	1218.45	1050.60	941.39	865.61	810.65	769.50	737.96	713.33	693.83	678.22	665.60
43000	3927.93	2132.23	1539.50	1247.46	1075.61	963.80	886.22	829.95	787.82	755.53	730.32	710.35	694.37	681.45
44000	4019.28	2181.81	1575.30	1276.47	1100.63	986.21	906.83	849.25	806.15	773.10	747.30	726.87	710.51	697.30
45000	4110.63	2231.40	1611.10	1305.48	1125.64	1008.63	927.43	868.55	824.47	790.67	764.28	743.39	726.66	713.15
46000	4201.98	2280.99	1646.91	1334.49	1150.66	1031.04	948.04	887.85	842.79	808.24	781.27	759.91	742.81	728.99
47000	4293.32	2330.57	1682.71	1363.50	1175.67	1053.46	968.65	907.15	861.11	825.81	798.25	776.43	758.96	744.84
48000	4384.67	2380.16	1718.51	1392.51	1200.69	1075.87	989.26	926.45	879.43	843.38	815.24	792.95	775.11	760.69
49000	4476.02	2429.75	1754.31	1421.52	1225.70	1098.28	1009.87	945.76	897.75	860.95	832.22	809.47	791.25	776.54
50000	4567.36	2479.33	1790.12	1450.53	1250.71	1120.70	1030.48	965.06	916.07	878.52	849.20	825.99	807.40	792.38
55000	5024.10	2727.26	1969.13	1595.58	1375.78	1232.77	1133.53	1061.56	1007.68	966.37	934.12	908.59	888.14	871.62
60000	5480.84	2975.20	2148.14	1740.63	1500.86	1344.84	1236.58	1158.07	1099.29	1054.22	1019.04	991.19	968.88	950.86
65000	5937.57	3223.13	2327.15	1885.69	1625.93	1456.91	1339.63	1254.57	1190.90	1142.08	1103.96	1073.78	1049.62	1030.10
70000	6394.31	3471.06	2506.16	2030.74	1751.00	1568.98	1442.67	1351.08	1282.50	1229.93	1188.88	1156.38	1130.36	1109.34
75000	6851.04	3719.00	2685.17	2175.79	1876.07	1681.04	1545.72	1447.58	1374.11	1317.78	1273.80	1238.98	1211.10	1188.57
80000	7307.78	3966.93	2864.18	2320.84	2001.14	1793.11	1648.77	1544.09	1465.72	1405.63	1358.72	1321.58	1291.84	1267.81
85000	7764.52	4214.86	3043.19	2465.90	2126.21	1905.18	1751.82	1640.59	1557.32	1493.48	1443.64	1404.18	1372.58	1347.05
90000	8221.25	4462.79	3222.20	2610.95	2251.28	2017.25	1854.86	1737.10	1648.93	1581.33	1528.56	1486.78	1453.32	1426.29
95000	8677.99	4710.73	3401.22	2756.00	2376.35	2129.32	1957.91	1833.60	1740.54	1669.19	1613.48	1569.38	1534.06	1505.52
100000	9134.72	4958.66	3580.23	2901.05	2501.42	2241.39	2060.96	1930.11	1832.14	1757.04	1698.40	1651.97	1614.80	1584.76

MONTHLY PAYMENT
REQUIRED TO AMORTIZE A LOAN

17.300%

TERM	15 Years	16 Years	17 Years	18 Years	19 Years	20 Years	21 Years	22 Years	23 Years	24 Years	25 Years	30 Years	35 Years	40 Years
AMOUNT														
5	.08	.08	.08	.08	.08	.08	.08	.08	.08	.08	.08	.08	.08	.08
10	.16	.16	.16	.16	.15	.15	.15	.15	.15	.15	.15	.15	.15	.15
15	.24	.24	.23	.23	.23	.23	.23	.23	.23	.22	.22	.22	.22	.22
25	.40	.39	.39	.38	.38	.38	.38	.37	.37	.37	.37	.37	.37	.37
50	.79	.78	.77	.76	.75	.75	.75	.74	.74	.74	.74	.73	.73	.73
75	1.18	1.16	1.15	1.14	1.13	1.12	1.12	1.11	1.11	1.10	1.10	1.09	1.09	1.09
100	1.57	1.55	1.53	1.52	1.50	1.49	1.49	1.48	1.47	1.47	1.47	1.46	1.45	1.45
200	3.13	3.09	3.05	3.03	3.00	2.98	2.97	2.96	2.94	2.94	2.93	2.91	2.90	2.89
300	4.69	4.63	4.58	4.54	4.50	4.47	4.45	4.43	4.41	4.40	4.39	4.36	4.34	4.33
400	6.25	6.17	6.10	6.05	6.00	5.96	5.93	5.91	5.88	5.87	5.85	5.81	5.79	5.78
500	7.81	7.71	7.62	7.56	7.50	7.45	7.41	7.38	7.35	7.33	7.31	7.26	7.23	7.22
600	9.37	9.25	9.15	9.07	9.00	8.94	8.90	8.86	8.82	8.80	8.77	8.71	8.68	8.66
700	10.93	10.79	10.67	10.58	10.50	10.43	10.38	10.33	10.29	10.26	10.24	10.16	10.12	10.11
800	12.49	12.33	12.20	12.09	12.00	11.92	11.86	11.81	11.76	11.73	11.70	11.61	11.57	11.55
900	14.05	13.87	13.72	13.60	13.50	13.41	13.34	13.28	13.23	13.19	13.16	13.06	13.01	12.99
1000	15.61	15.41	15.24	15.11	15.00	14.90	14.82	14.76	14.70	14.66	14.62	14.51	14.46	14.44
2000	31.21	30.81	30.48	30.21	29.99	29.80	29.64	29.51	29.40	29.31	29.24	29.01	28.91	28.87
3000	46.81	46.21	45.72	45.31	44.98	44.69	44.46	44.27	44.10	43.97	43.85	43.51	43.36	43.30
4000	62.42	61.62	60.96	60.42	59.97	59.59	59.28	59.02	58.80	58.62	58.47	58.01	57.81	57.73
5000	78.02	77.02	76.20	75.52	74.96	74.49	74.10	73.77	73.50	73.28	73.09	72.51	72.27	72.16
6000	93.62	92.42	91.44	90.62	89.95	89.38	88.92	88.53	88.20	87.93	87.70	87.01	86.72	86.59
7000	109.23	107.83	106.67	105.72	104.94	104.28	103.74	103.28	102.90	102.58	102.32	101.51	101.17	101.03
8000	124.83	123.23	121.91	120.83	119.93	119.18	118.55	118.04	117.60	117.24	116.93	116.01	115.62	115.46
9000	140.43	138.63	137.15	135.93	134.92	134.07	133.37	132.79	132.30	131.89	131.55	130.51	130.07	129.89
10000	156.04	154.04	152.39	151.03	149.91	148.97	148.19	147.54	147.00	146.55	146.17	145.01	144.53	144.32
11000	171.64	169.44	167.63	166.13	164.90	163.87	163.01	162.30	161.70	161.20	160.78	159.51	158.98	158.75
12000	187.24	184.84	182.87	181.24	179.89	178.76	177.83	177.05	176.40	175.85	175.40	174.01	173.43	173.18
13000	202.85	200.25	198.11	196.34	194.88	193.66	192.65	191.80	191.10	190.51	190.02	188.51	187.88	187.62
14000	218.45	215.65	213.34	211.44	209.87	208.56	207.47	206.56	205.80	205.16	204.63	203.01	202.33	202.05
15000	234.05	231.05	228.58	226.54	224.86	223.45	222.29	221.31	220.50	219.82	219.25	217.51	216.79	216.48
16000	249.66	246.45	243.82	241.65	239.85	238.35	237.10	236.07	235.20	234.47	233.86	232.01	231.24	230.91
17000	265.26	261.86	259.06	256.75	254.84	253.25	251.92	250.82	249.90	249.13	248.48	246.51	245.69	245.34
18000	280.06	277.26	274.30	271.05	269.83	268.14	266.74	265.57	264.60	263.78	263.10	261.01	260.14	259.77
19000	296.47	292.66	289.54	286.96	284.82	283.04	281.56	280.33	279.30	278.43	277.71	275.51	274.59	274.21
20000	312.07	308.07	304.78	302.06	299.81	297.94	296.30	295.08	294.00	293.09	292.33	290.02	289.05	288.64
21000	327.67	323.47	320.01	317.16	314.80	312.83	311.20	309.83	308.70	307.74	306.94	304.52	303.50	303.07
22000	343.27	338.87	335.25	332.26	329.79	327.73	326.02	324.59	323.39	322.40	321.56	319.02	317.95	317.50
23000	358.88	354.28	350.49	347.37	344.78	342.63	340.84	339.34	338.09	337.05	336.18	333.52	332.40	331.93
24000	374.48	369.68	365.73	362.47	359.77	357.52	355.65	354.10	352.79	351.70	350.79	348.02	346.85	346.36
25000	390.08	385.08	380.97	377.57	374.76	372.42	370.47	368.85	367.49	366.36	365.41	362.52	361.31	360.80
26000	405.69	400.49	396.21	392.67	389.75	387.32	385.29	383.60	382.19	381.01	380.03	377.02	375.76	375.23
27000	421.29	415.89	411.45	407.78	404.74	402.21	400.11	398.36	396.89	395.67	394.64	391.52	390.21	389.66
28000	436.89	431.29	426.68	422.88	419.73	417.11	414.93	413.11	411.59	410.32	409.26	406.02	404.66	404.09
29000	452.50	446.69	441.92	437.98	434.72	432.01	429.75	427.86	426.29	424.98	423.87	420.52	419.12	418.52
30000	468.10	462.10	457.16	453.08	449.71	446.90	444.57	442.62	440.99	439.63	438.49	435.02	433.57	432.95
31000	483.70	477.50	472.40	468.19	464.70	461.80	459.39	457.37	455.69	454.28	453.11	449.52	448.02	447.39
32000	499.31	492.90	487.64	483.29	479.69	476.70	474.20	472.13	470.39	468.94	467.72	464.02	462.47	461.82
33000	514.91	508.31	502.88	498.39	494.68	491.59	489.02	486.88	485.09	483.59	482.34	478.52	476.92	476.25
34000	530.51	523.71	518.12	513.50	509.67	506.49	503.84	501.63	499.79	498.25	496.95	493.02	491.38	490.68
35000	546.12	539.11	533.35	528.60	524.66	521.39	518.66	516.39	514.49	512.90	511.57	507.52	505.83	505.11
36000	561.72	554.52	548.59	543.70	539.65	536.28	533.48	531.14	529.19	527.55	526.19	522.02	520.28	519.54
37000	577.32	569.92	563.83	558.80	554.64	551.18	548.30	545.89	543.89	542.21	540.80	536.52	534.73	533.98
38000	592.93	585.32	579.07	573.91	569.63	566.07	563.12	560.65	558.59	556.86	555.42	551.02	549.18	548.41
39000	608.53	600.73	594.31	589.01	584.62	580.97	577.94	575.40	573.29	571.52	570.04	565.53	563.64	562.84
40000	624.13	616.13	609.55	604.11	599.61	595.87	592.75	590.16	587.99	586.17	584.65	580.03	578.09	577.27
41000	639.73	631.53	624.78	619.21	614.60	610.76	607.57	604.91	602.69	600.83	599.27	594.53	592.54	591.70
42000	655.34	646.93	640.02	634.32	629.59	625.66	622.39	619.66	617.39	615.48	613.88	609.03	606.99	606.13
43000	670.94	662.34	655.26	649.42	644.58	640.56	637.21	634.42	632.08	630.13	628.50	623.53	621.44	620.57
44000	686.54	677.74	670.50	664.52	659.57	655.45	652.03	649.17	646.78	644.79	643.12	638.03	635.90	635.00
45000	702.15	693.14	685.74	679.62	674.56	670.35	666.85	663.93	661.48	659.44	657.73	652.53	650.35	649.43
46000	717.75	708.55	700.98	694.73	689.55	685.25	681.67	678.68	676.18	674.10	672.35	667.03	664.80	663.86
47000	733.35	723.95	716.22	709.83	704.54	700.14	696.48	693.43	690.88	688.75	686.96	681.53	679.25	678.29
48000	748.96	739.35	731.45	724.93	719.53	715.04	711.30	708.19	705.58	703.40	701.58	696.03	693.70	692.72
49000	764.56	754.76	746.69	740.04	734.52	729.94	726.12	722.94	720.28	718.06	716.20	710.53	708.16	707.16
50000	780.16	770.16	761.93	755.14	749.51	744.83	740.94	737.69	734.98	732.71	730.81	725.03	722.61	721.59
55000	858.18	847.17	838.12	830.65	824.46	819.32	815.03	811.46	808.48	805.98	803.89	797.53	794.87	793.75
60000	936.19	924.19	914.32	906.16	899.41	893.80	889.13	885.23	881.98	879.25	876.97	870.04	867.13	865.90
65000	1014.21	1001.21	990.51	981.68	974.36	968.28	963.22	959.00	955.47	952.53	950.06	942.54	939.39	938.06
70000	1092.23	1078.22	1066.70	1057.19	1049.31	1042.77	1037.32	1032.77	1028.97	1025.80	1023.14	1015.04	1011.65	1010.22
75000	1170.24	1155.24	1142.90	1132.70	1124.26	1117.25	1111.41	1106.54	1102.47	1099.07	1096.22	1087.54	1083.91	1082.38
80000	1248.26	1232.25	1219.09	1208.22	1199.21	1191.73	1185.50	1180.31	1175.97	1172.34	1169.30	1160.05	1156.17	1154.54
85000	1326.28	1309.27	1295.28	1283.73	1274.16	1266.21	1259.60	1254.08	1249.47	1245.61	1242.38	1232.55	1228.43	1226.69
90000	1404.29	1386.28	1371.47	1359.24	1349.11	1340.70	1333.69	1327.85	1322.96	1318.88	1315.46	1305.05	1300.69	1298.85
95000	1482.31	1463.30	1447.67	1434.76	1424.06	1415.18	1407.78	1401.61	1396.46	1392.15	1388.54	1377.55	1372.95	1371.01
100000	1560.32	1540.31	1523.86	1510.27	1499.01	1489.66	1481.88	1475.38	1469.96	1465.42	1461.62	1450.06	1445.21	1443.17

MONTHLY PAYMENT
REQUIRED TO AMORTIZE A LOAN

TERM	1 Year	2 Years	3 Years	4 Years	5 Years	6 Years	7 Years	8 Years	9 Years	10 Years	11 Years	12 Years	13 Years	14 Years
AMOUNT														
5	.46	.25	.18	.15	.13	.12	.11	.10	.10	.09	.09	.09	.09	.08
10	.92	.50	.36	.30	.26	.23	.21	.20	.19	.18	.18	.17	.17	.16
15	1.38	.75	.54	.44	.38	.34	.31	.30	.28	.27	.26	.25	.25	.24
25	2.29	1.25	.90	.73	.63	.57	.52	.49	.46	.45	.43	.42	.41	.40
50	4.57	2.49	1.80	1.46	1.26	1.13	1.04	.97	.92	.89	.86	.83	.81	.80
75	6.86	3.73	2.69	2.18	1.88	1.69	1.55	1.46	1.38	1.33	1.28	1.25	1.22	1.20
100	9.14	4.97	3.59	2.91	2.51	2.25	2.07	1.94	1.84	1.77	1.71	1.66	1.62	1.60
200	18.28	9.93	7.17	5.81	5.02	4.50	4.14	3.87	3.68	3.53	3.41	3.32	3.24	3.19
300	27.42	14.89	10.76	8.72	7.52	6.74	6.20	5.81	5.52	5.29	5.11	4.98	4.86	4.78
400	36.56	19.85	14.34	11.62	10.03	8.99	8.27	7.74	7.35	7.05	6.82	6.63	6.48	6.37
500	45.70	24.82	17.92	14.53	12.53	11.23	10.33	9.68	9.19	8.81	8.52	8.29	8.10	7.96
600	54.83	29.78	21.51	17.43	15.04	13.48	12.40	11.61	11.03	10.58	10.22	9.95	9.72	9.55
700	63.97	34.74	25.09	20.34	17.54	15.72	14.46	13.55	12.86	12.34	11.93	11.60	11.34	11.14
800	73.11	39.70	28.68	23.24	20.05	17.97	16.53	15.48	14.70	14.10	13.63	13.26	12.96	12.73
900	82.25	44.67	32.26	26.15	22.55	20.22	18.59	17.42	16.54	15.86	15.33	14.92	14.58	14.32
1000	91.39	49.63	35.84	29.05	25.06	22.46	20.66	19.35	18.37	17.62	17.04	16.57	16.20	15.91
2000	182.77	99.25	71.68	58.10	50.11	44.92	41.31	38.70	36.74	35.24	34.07	33.14	32.40	31.81
3000	274.15	148.87	107.52	87.15	75.17	67.37	61.96	58.04	55.11	52.86	51.10	49.71	48.60	47.71
4000	365.54	198.50	143.36	116.20	100.22	89.83	82.62	77.39	73.48	70.48	68.14	66.28	64.80	63.61
5000	456.92	248.12	179.20	145.25	125.28	112.28	103.27	96.74	91.84	88.10	85.17	82.85	81.00	79.51
6000	548.30	297.74	215.04	174.30	150.33	134.74	123.92	116.08	110.21	105.71	102.20	99.42	97.20	95.41
7000	639.68	347.36	250.88	203.35	175.39	157.20	144.58	135.43	128.58	123.33	119.24	115.99	113.40	111.31
8000	731.07	396.99	286.72	232.40	200.44	179.65	165.23	154.77	146.95	140.95	136.27	132.56	129.60	127.21
9000	822.45	446.61	322.56	261.45	225.50	202.11	185.88	174.12	165.32	158.57	153.30	149.13	145.80	143.11
10000	913.83	496.23	358.40	290.50	250.55	224.56	206.54	193.47	183.68	176.19	170.34	165.70	162.00	159.01
11000	1005.22	545.85	394.24	319.55	275.61	247.02	227.19	212.81	202.05	193.80	187.37	182.27	178.20	174.91
12000	1096.60	595.48	430.08	348.60	300.66	269.48	247.84	232.16	220.42	211.42	204.40	198.84	194.40	190.81
13000	1187.98	645.10	465.92	377.65	325.72	291.93	268.50	251.50	238.79	229.04	221.43	215.41	210.60	206.71
14000	1279.36	694.72	501.76	406.70	350.77	314.39	289.15	270.85	257.15	246.66	238.47	231.98	226.80	222.61
15000	1370.75	744.34	537.60	435.75	375.82	336.84	309.80	290.20	275.52	264.28	255.50	248.55	242.99	238.51
16000	1462.13	793.97	573.44	464.80	400.88	359.30	330.45	309.54	293.89	281.89	272.53	265.12	259.19	254.41
17000	1553.51	843.59	609.28	493.85	425.93	381.76	351.11	328.89	312.26	299.51	289.57	281.69	275.39	270.31
18000	1644.90	893.21	645.12	522.89	450.99	404.21	371.76	348.23	330.63	317.13	306.60	298.26	291.59	286.21
19000	1736.28	942.84	680.96	551.94	476.04	426.67	392.41	367.58	348.99	334.75	323.63	314.83	307.79	302.11
20000	1827.66	992.46	716.80	580.99	501.10	449.12	413.07	386.93	367.36	352.37	340.67	331.40	323.99	318.01
21000	1919.04	1042.08	752.64	610.04	526.15	471.58	433.72	406.27	385.73	369.99	357.70	347.97	340.19	333.91
22000	2010.43	1091.70	788.48	639.09	551.21	494.03	454.37	425.62	404.10	387.60	374.73	364.54	356.39	349.81
23000	2101.81	1141.33	824.32	668.14	576.26	516.49	475.03	444.96	422.46	405.22	391.76	381.11	372.59	365.71
24000	2193.19	1190.95	860.16	697.19	601.32	538.95	495.68	464.31	440.83	422.84	408.80	397.68	388.79	381.61
25000	2284.58	1240.57	896.00	726.24	626.37	561.40	516.33	483.66	459.20	440.46	425.83	414.25	404.99	397.51
26000	2375.96	1290.19	931.84	755.29	651.43	583.86	536.99	503.00	477.57	458.08	442.86	430.82	421.19	413.41
27000	2467.34	1339.82	967.68	784.34	676.48	606.31	557.64	522.35	495.94	475.69	459.90	447.39	437.39	429.31
28000	2558.72	1389.44	1003.51	813.39	701.54	628.77	578.29	541.69	514.30	493.31	476.93	463.96	453.59	445.21
29000	2650.11	1439.06	1039.35	842.44	726.59	651.23	598.94	561.04	532.67	510.93	493.96	480.53	469.79	461.11
30000	2741.49	1488.68	1075.19	871.49	751.64	673.68	619.60	580.39	551.04	528.55	511.00	497.10	485.98	477.01
31000	2832.87	1538.31	1111.03	900.54	776.70	696.14	640.25	599.73	569.41	546.17	528.03	513.67	502.18	492.91
32000	2924.25	1587.93	1146.87	929.59	801.75	718.59	660.90	619.08	587.78	563.78	545.06	530.24	518.38	508.81
33000	3015.64	1637.55	1182.71	958.64	826.81	741.05	681.56	638.42	606.14	581.40	562.10	546.81	534.58	524.71
34000	3107.02	1687.17	1218.55	987.69	851.86	763.51	702.21	657.77	624.51	599.02	579.13	563.38	550.78	540.61
35000	3198.40	1736.80	1254.39	1016.73	876.92	785.96	722.86	677.12	642.88	616.64	596.16	579.95	566.98	556.51
36000	3289.79	1786.42	1290.23	1045.78	901.97	808.42	743.52	696.46	661.25	634.26	613.19	596.52	583.18	572.41
37000	3381.17	1836.04	1326.07	1074.83	927.03	830.87	764.17	715.81	679.61	651.88	630.23	613.09	599.38	588.31
38000	3472.55	1885.67	1361.91	1103.88	952.08	853.33	784.82	735.16	697.98	669.49	647.26	629.66	615.58	604.21
39000	3563.93	1935.29	1397.75	1132.93	977.14	875.78	805.48	754.50	716.35	687.11	664.29	646.23	631.78	620.11
40000	3655.32	1984.91	1433.59	1161.98	1002.19	898.24	826.13	773.85	734.72	704.73	681.33	662.80	647.98	636.01
41000	3746.70	2034.53	1469.43	1191.03	1027.25	920.70	846.78	793.19	753.09	722.35	698.36	679.37	664.18	651.91
42000	3838.08	2084.16	1505.27	1220.08	1052.30	943.15	867.44	812.54	771.45	739.97	715.39	695.94	680.38	667.81
43000	3929.47	2133.78	1541.11	1249.13	1077.36	965.61	888.09	831.89	789.82	757.58	732.43	712.51	696.58	683.71
44000	4020.85	2183.40	1576.95	1278.18	1102.41	988.06	908.74	851.23	808.19	775.20	749.46	729.08	712.78	699.61
45000	4112.23	2233.02	1612.79	1307.23	1127.46	1010.52	929.39	870.58	826.56	792.82	766.49	745.65	728.97	715.51
46000	4203.61	2282.65	1648.63	1336.28	1152.52	1032.98	950.05	889.92	844.92	810.44	783.52	762.22	745.17	731.41
47000	4295.00	2332.27	1684.47	1365.33	1177.57	1055.43	970.70	909.27	863.29	828.06	800.56	778.79	761.37	747.31
48000	4386.38	2381.89	1720.31	1394.38	1202.63	1077.89	991.35	928.62	881.66	845.67	817.59	795.36	777.57	763.21
49000	4477.76	2431.51	1756.15	1423.43	1227.68	1100.34	1012.01	947.96	900.03	863.29	834.62	811.93	793.77	779.11
50000	4569.15	2481.14	1791.99	1452.48	1252.74	1122.80	1032.66	967.31	918.40	880.91	851.66	828.50	809.97	795.01
55000	5026.06	2729.25	1971.19	1597.72	1378.01	1235.08	1135.93	1064.04	1010.24	969.00	936.82	911.35	890.97	874.51
60000	5482.97	2977.36	2150.38	1742.97	1503.28	1347.36	1239.19	1160.77	1102.07	1057.09	1021.99	994.20	971.96	954.01
65000	5939.89	3225.48	2329.58	1888.22	1628.56	1459.64	1342.46	1257.50	1193.91	1145.18	1107.15	1077.05	1052.96	1033.51
70000	6396.80	3473.59	2508.78	2033.46	1753.83	1571.92	1445.72	1354.23	1285.75	1233.27	1192.32	1159.90	1133.96	1113.01
75000	6853.72	3721.70	2687.98	2178.71	1879.10	1684.20	1548.99	1450.96	1377.59	1321.36	1277.48	1242.75	1214.95	1192.51
80000	7310.63	3969.82	2867.18	2323.96	2004.38	1796.48	1652.25	1547.69	1469.43	1409.45	1362.65	1325.60	1295.95	1272.01
85000	7767.54	4217.93	3046.37	2469.21	2129.65	1908.76	1755.52	1644.42	1561.27	1497.54	1447.81	1408.45	1376.95	1351.51
90000	8224.46	4466.04	3225.57	2614.45	2254.92	2021.04	1858.78	1741.15	1653.11	1585.63	1532.98	1491.30	1457.94	1431.01
95000	8681.37	4714.16	3404.77	2759.70	2380.20	2133.32	1962.05	1837.88	1744.95	1673.73	1618.14	1574.15	1538.94	1510.51
100000	9138.29	4962.27	3583.97	2904.95	2505.47	2245.59	2065.32	1934.61	1836.79	1761.82	1703.31	1657.00	1619.94	1590.01

MONTHLY PAYMENT
REQUIRED TO AMORTIZE A LOAN

17.375%

TERM AMOUNT	15 Years	16 Years	17 Years	18 Years	19 Years	20 Years	21 Years	22 Years	23 Years	24 Years	25 Years	30 Years	35 Years	40 Years
5	.08	.08	.08	.08	.08	.08	.08	.08	.08	.08	.08	.08	.08	.08
10	.16	.16	.16	.16	.16	.15	.15	.15	.15	.15	.15	.15	.15	.15
15	.24	.24	.23	.23	.23	.23	.23	.23	.23	.23	.23	.22	.22	.22
25	.40	.39	.39	.38	.38	.38	.38	.38	.37	.37	.37	.37	.37	.37
50	.79	.78	.77	.76	.76	.75	.75	.75	.74	.74	.74	.73	.73	.73
75	1.18	1.16	1.15	1.14	1.13	1.13	1.12	1.12	1.11	1.11	1.11	1.10	1.09	1.09
100	1.57	1.55	1.53	1.52	1.51	1.50	1.49	1.49	1.48	1.48	1.47	1.46	1.46	1.45
200	3.14	3.10	3.06	3.04	3.01	3.00	2.98	2.97	2.96	2.95	2.94	2.92	2.91	2.90
300	4.70	4.64	4.59	4.55	4.52	4.49	4.47	4.45	4.43	4.42	4.41	4.37	4.36	4.35
400	6.27	6.19	6.12	6.07	6.02	5.99	5.96	5.93	5.91	5.89	5.88	5.83	5.81	5.80
500	7.83	7.73	7.65	7.58	7.53	7.48	7.44	7.41	7.38	7.36	7.34	7.29	7.26	7.25
600	9.40	9.28	9.18	9.10	9.03	8.98	8.93	8.89	8.86	8.83	8.81	8.74	8.71	8.70
700	10.96	10.83	10.71	10.62	10.54	10.47	10.42	10.37	10.34	10.30	10.28	10.20	10.16	10.15
800	12.53	12.37	12.24	12.13	12.04	11.97	11.91	11.85	11.81	11.78	11.75	11.65	11.62	11.60
900	14.10	13.92	13.77	13.65	13.55	13.46	13.39	13.34	13.29	13.25	13.21	13.11	13.07	13.05
1000	15.66	15.46	15.30	15.16	15.05	14.96	14.88	14.82	14.76	14.72	14.68	14.57	14.52	14.50
2000	31.32	30.92	30.59	30.32	30.10	29.91	29.76	29.63	29.52	29.43	29.36	29.13	29.03	28.99
3000	46.97	46.38	45.89	45.48	45.15	44.87	44.63	44.44	44.28	44.15	44.03	43.69	43.55	43.49
4000	62.63	61.83	61.18	60.64	60.19	59.82	59.51	59.25	59.04	58.86	58.71	58.25	58.06	57.98
5000	78.29	77.29	76.47	75.80	75.24	74.77	74.39	74.07	73.80	73.57	73.38	72.81	72.57	72.47
6000	93.94	92.75	91.77	90.96	90.29	89.73	89.26	88.88	88.56	88.29	88.06	87.37	87.09	86.97
7000	109.60	108.21	107.06	106.12	105.33	104.68	104.14	103.69	103.31	103.00	102.74	101.94	101.60	101.46
8000	125.26	123.66	122.35	121.27	120.38	119.64	119.02	118.50	118.07	117.71	117.41	116.50	116.12	115.96
9000	140.91	139.12	137.65	136.43	135.43	134.59	133.89	133.31	132.83	132.43	132.09	131.06	130.63	130.45
10000	156.57	154.58	152.94	151.59	150.47	149.54	148.77	148.13	147.59	147.14	146.76	145.62	145.14	144.94
11000	172.23	170.04	168.24	166.75	165.52	164.50	163.65	162.94	162.35	161.85	161.44	160.18	159.66	159.44
12000	187.88	185.49	183.53	181.91	180.57	179.45	178.52	177.75	177.11	176.57	176.11	174.74	174.17	173.93
13000	203.54	200.95	198.82	197.07	195.61	194.41	193.40	192.56	191.86	191.28	190.79	189.30	188.68	188.43
14000	219.20	216.41	214.12	212.23	210.66	209.36	208.28	207.38	206.62	205.99	205.47	203.87	203.20	202.92
15000	234.85	231.87	229.41	227.38	225.71	224.31	223.15	222.19	221.38	220.71	220.14	218.43	217.71	217.41
16000	250.51	247.32	244.70	242.54	240.75	239.27	238.03	237.00	236.14	235.42	234.82	232.99	232.23	231.91
17000	266.17	262.78	260.00	257.70	255.80	254.22	252.91	251.81	250.90	250.13	249.49	247.55	246.74	246.40
18000	281.82	278.24	275.29	272.86	270.85	269.17	267.78	266.62	265.66	264.85	264.17	262.11	261.25	260.89
19000	297.48	293.70	290.59	288.02	285.89	284.13	282.66	281.44	280.41	279.56	278.85	276.67	275.77	275.39
20000	313.14	309.15	305.88	303.18	300.94	299.08	297.54	296.25	295.17	294.27	293.52	291.24	290.28	289.88
21000	328.79	324.61	321.17	318.34	315.99	314.04	312.41	311.06	309.93	308.99	308.20	305.80	304.80	304.37
22000	344.45	340.07	336.47	333.49	331.03	328.99	327.29	325.87	324.69	323.70	322.87	320.36	319.31	318.87
23000	360.11	355.53	351.76	348.65	346.08	343.94	342.17	340.68	339.45	338.41	337.55	334.92	333.82	333.36
24000	375.76	370.98	367.05	363.81	361.13	358.90	357.04	355.50	354.21	353.13	352.22	349.48	348.34	347.86
25000	391.42	386.44	382.35	378.97	376.17	373.85	371.92	370.31	368.96	367.84	366.90	364.04	362.85	362.35
26000	407.08	401.90	397.64	394.13	391.22	388.81	386.80	385.12	383.72	382.55	381.58	378.60	377.36	376.84
27000	422.73	417.36	412.94	409.29	406.27	403.76	401.67	399.93	398.48	397.27	396.25	393.17	391.88	391.34
28000	438.39	432.81	428.23	424.45	421.31	418.71	416.55	414.75	413.24	411.98	410.93	407.73	406.39	405.83
29000	454.05	448.27	443.52	439.60	436.36	433.67	431.43	429.56	428.00	426.69	425.60	422.29	420.91	420.32
30000	469.70	463.73	458.82	454.76	451.41	448.62	446.30	444.37	442.76	441.41	440.28	436.85	435.42	434.82
31000	485.36	479.19	474.11	469.92	466.45	463.57	461.18	459.18	457.51	456.12	454.95	451.41	449.93	449.31
32000	501.02	494.64	489.40	485.08	481.50	478.53	476.06	473.99	472.27	470.83	469.63	465.97	464.45	463.81
33000	516.67	510.10	504.70	500.24	496.55	493.48	490.93	488.81	487.03	485.55	484.31	480.54	478.96	478.30
34000	532.33	525.56	519.99	515.40	511.59	508.44	505.81	503.62	501.79	500.26	498.98	495.10	493.47	492.79
35000	547.99	541.02	535.28	530.56	526.64	523.39	520.69	518.43	516.55	514.97	513.66	509.66	507.99	507.29
36000	563.64	556.47	550.58	545.71	541.69	538.34	535.56	533.24	531.31	529.69	528.33	524.22	522.50	521.78
37000	579.30	571.93	565.87	560.87	556.73	553.30	550.44	548.05	546.07	544.40	543.01	538.78	537.02	536.27
38000	594.96	587.39	581.17	576.03	571.78	568.25	565.31	562.87	560.82	559.12	557.69	553.34	551.53	550.77
39000	610.61	602.84	596.46	591.19	586.83	583.21	580.19	577.68	575.58	573.83	572.36	567.90	566.04	565.26
40000	626.27	618.30	611.75	606.35	601.87	598.16	595.07	592.49	590.34	588.54	587.04	582.47	580.56	579.76
41000	641.93	633.76	627.05	621.51	616.92	613.11	609.94	607.30	605.10	603.26	601.71	597.03	595.07	594.25
42000	657.58	649.22	642.34	636.67	631.97	628.07	624.82	622.12	619.86	617.97	616.39	611.59	609.59	608.74
43000	673.24	664.67	657.63	651.82	647.01	643.02	639.70	636.93	634.62	632.68	631.06	626.15	624.10	623.24
44000	688.90	680.13	672.93	666.98	662.06	657.97	654.57	651.74	649.37	647.40	645.74	640.71	638.61	637.73
45000	704.55	695.59	688.22	682.14	677.11	672.93	669.45	666.55	664.13	662.11	660.42	655.27	653.13	652.22
46000	720.21	711.05	703.52	697.30	692.15	687.88	684.33	681.36	678.89	676.82	675.09	669.83	667.64	666.72
47000	735.86	726.50	718.81	712.46	707.20	702.84	699.20	696.18	693.65	691.54	689.77	684.40	682.15	681.21
48000	751.52	741.96	734.10	727.62	722.25	717.79	714.08	710.99	708.41	706.25	704.44	698.96	696.67	695.71
49000	767.18	757.42	749.40	742.78	737.29	732.74	728.96	725.80	723.17	720.96	719.12	713.52	711.18	710.20
50000	782.83	772.88	764.69	757.93	752.34	747.70	743.83	740.61	737.92	735.68	733.80	728.08	725.70	724.69
55000	861.12	850.16	841.16	833.73	827.57	822.47	818.22	814.67	811.72	809.24	807.17	800.89	798.26	797.16
60000	939.40	927.45	917.63	909.52	902.81	897.24	892.60	888.73	885.51	882.81	880.55	873.70	870.83	869.63
65000	1017.68	1004.74	994.10	985.31	978.04	972.01	966.98	962.80	959.30	956.38	953.93	946.50	943.40	942.10
70000	1095.97	1082.03	1070.56	1061.11	1053.28	1046.77	1041.37	1036.86	1033.09	1029.94	1027.31	1019.31	1015.97	1014.57
75000	1174.25	1159.31	1147.03	1136.90	1128.51	1121.54	1115.75	1110.92	1106.88	1103.51	1100.69	1092.12	1088.54	1087.04
80000	1252.53	1236.60	1223.50	1212.69	1203.74	1196.31	1190.13	1184.98	1180.68	1177.08	1174.07	1164.93	1161.11	1159.51
85000	1330.82	1313.89	1299.97	1288.49	1278.98	1271.08	1264.51	1259.04	1254.47	1250.65	1247.45	1237.73	1233.68	1231.98
90000	1409.10	1391.17	1376.44	1364.28	1354.21	1345.85	1338.90	1333.10	1328.26	1324.21	1320.83	1310.54	1306.25	1304.44
95000	1487.38	1468.46	1452.91	1440.07	1429.44	1420.62	1413.28	1407.16	1402.05	1397.78	1394.21	1383.35	1378.82	1376.91
100000	1565.66	1545.75	1529.38	1515.86	1504.68	1495.39	1487.66	1481.22	1475.84	1471.35	1467.59	1456.16	1451.39	1449.38

MONTHLY PAYMENT
REQUIRED TO AMORTIZE A LOAN

TERM	1 Year	2 Years	3 Years	4 Years	5 Years	6 Years	7 Years	8 Years	9 Years	10 Years	11 Years	12 Years	13 Years	14 Years
AMOUNT														
5	.46	.25	.18	.15	.13	.12	.11	.10	.10	.09	.09	.09	.09	.08
10	.92	.50	.36	.30	.26	.23	.21	.20	.19	.18	.18	.17	.17	.16
15	1.38	.75	.54	.44	.38	.34	.32	.30	.28	.27	.26	.25	.25	.24
25	2.29	1.25	.90	.73	.63	.57	.52	.49	.46	.45	.43	.42	.41	.40
50	4.57	2.49	1.80	1.46	1.26	1.13	1.04	.97	.92	.89	.86	.83	.82	.80
75	6.86	3.73	2.69	2.18	1.89	1.69	1.56	1.46	1.38	1.33	1.28	1.25	1.22	1.20
100	9.14	4.97	3.59	2.91	2.51	2.25	2.07	1.94	1.84	1.77	1.71	1.66	1.63	1.60
200	18.28	9.93	7.18	5.82	5.02	4.50	4.14	3.88	3.68	3.53	3.41	3.32	3.25	3.19
300	27.42	14.90	10.76	8.72	7.53	6.75	6.21	5.81	5.52	5.30	5.12	4.98	4.87	4.78
400	36.56	19.86	14.35	11.63	10.03	8.99	8.27	7.75	7.36	7.06	6.82	6.64	6.49	6.37
500	45.70	24.82	17.93	14.54	12.54	11.24	10.34	9.69	9.20	8.82	8.53	8.30	8.11	7.96
600	54.84	29.79	21.52	17.44	15.05	13.49	12.41	11.62	11.03	10.59	10.23	9.96	9.73	9.56
700	63.98	34.75	25.10	20.35	17.55	15.73	14.47	13.56	12.87	12.35	11.94	11.62	11.36	11.15
800	73.12	39.71	28.69	23.25	20.06	17.98	16.54	15.49	14.71	14.11	13.64	13.27	12.98	12.74
900	82.26	44.68	32.27	26.16	22.57	20.23	18.61	17.43	16.55	15.88	15.35	14.93	14.60	14.33
1000	91.40	49.64	35.86	29.07	25.07	22.47	20.67	19.37	18.39	17.64	17.05	16.59	16.22	15.92
2000	182.79	99.27	71.71	58.13	50.14	44.94	41.34	38.73	36.77	35.27	34.10	33.18	32.44	31.84
3000	274.19	148.91	107.56	87.19	75.21	67.41	62.01	58.09	55.15	52.91	51.15	49.77	48.65	47.76
4000	365.58	198.54	143.41	116.25	100.28	89.88	82.68	77.45	73.54	70.54	68.20	66.35	64.87	63.68
5000	456.98	248.18	179.27	145.32	125.35	112.35	103.34	96.81	91.92	88.18	85.25	82.94	81.09	79.59
6000	548.37	297.81	215.12	174.38	150.41	134.82	124.01	116.17	110.30	105.81	102.30	99.53	97.30	95.51
7000	639.77	347.45	250.97	203.44	175.48	157.29	144.68	135.53	128.69	123.44	119.35	116.11	113.52	111.43
8000	731.16	397.08	286.82	232.50	200.55	179.76	165.35	154.89	147.07	141.08	136.40	132.70	129.74	127.35
9000	822.56	446.72	322.67	261.57	225.62	202.23	186.01	174.25	165.45	158.71	153.45	149.29	145.95	143.26
10000	913.95	496.35	358.53	290.63	250.69	224.70	206.68	193.62	183.84	176.35	170.50	165.87	162.17	159.18
11000	1005.35	545.99	394.38	319.69	275.75	247.17	227.35	212.98	202.22	193.98	187.55	182.46	178.39	175.10
12000	1096.74	595.62	430.23	348.75	300.82	269.64	248.02	232.34	220.60	211.61	204.60	199.05	194.60	191.02
13000	1188.14	645.26	466.08	377.82	325.89	292.11	268.68	251.70	238.99	229.25	221.65	215.63	210.82	206.93
14000	1279.53	694.89	501.93	406.88	350.96	314.58	289.35	271.06	257.37	246.88	238.70	232.22	227.04	222.85
15000	1370.93	744.53	537.79	435.94	376.03	337.05	310.02	290.42	275.75	264.52	255.75	248.81	243.25	238.77
16000	1462.32	794.16	573.64	465.00	401.10	359.52	330.69	309.78	294.14	282.15	272.80	265.39	259.47	254.69
17000	1553.71	843.79	609.49	494.07	426.16	381.99	351.35	329.14	312.52	299.78	289.84	281.98	275.68	270.60
18000	1645.11	893.43	645.34	523.13	451.23	404.46	372.02	348.50	330.90	317.42	306.89	298.57	291.90	286.52
19000	1736.50	943.06	681.20	552.19	476.30	426.93	392.69	367.87	349.29	335.05	323.94	315.15	308.12	302.44
20000	1827.90	992.70	717.05	581.25	501.37	449.40	413.36	387.23	367.67	352.69	340.99	331.74	324.33	318.36
21000	1919.29	1042.33	752.90	610.32	526.44	471.87	434.03	406.59	386.05	370.32	358.04	348.33	340.55	334.27
22000	2010.69	1091.97	788.75	639.38	551.50	494.34	454.69	425.95	404.44	387.95	375.09	364.91	356.77	350.19
23000	2102.08	1141.60	824.60	668.44	576.57	516.81	475.36	445.31	422.82	405.59	392.14	381.50	372.98	366.11
24000	2193.48	1191.24	860.46	697.50	601.64	539.28	496.03	464.67	441.20	423.22	409.19	398.09	389.20	382.03
25000	2284.87	1240.87	896.31	726.57	626.71	561.75	516.70	484.03	459.59	440.86	426.24	414.67	405.42	397.94
26000	2376.27	1290.51	932.16	755.63	651.78	584.22	537.36	503.39	477.97	458.49	443.29	431.26	421.63	413.86
27000	2467.66	1340.14	968.01	784.69	676.85	606.69	558.03	522.75	496.35	476.12	460.34	447.85	437.85	429.78
28000	2559.06	1389.78	1003.86	813.75	701.91	629.16	578.70	542.12	514.74	493.76	477.39	464.44	454.07	445.70
29000	2650.45	1439.41	1039.72	842.81	726.98	651.63	599.37	561.48	533.12	511.39	494.44	481.02	470.28	461.61
30000	2741.85	1489.05	1075.57	871.88	752.05	674.10	620.03	580.84	551.50	529.03	511.49	497.61	486.50	477.53
31000	2833.24	1538.68	1111.42	900.94	777.12	696.57	640.70	600.20	569.89	546.66	528.54	514.19	502.72	493.45
32000	2924.64	1588.31	1147.27	930.00	802.19	719.04	661.37	619.56	588.27	564.29	545.59	530.78	518.93	509.37
33000	3016.03	1637.95	1183.12	959.06	827.25	741.51	682.04	638.92	606.65	581.93	562.64	547.37	535.15	525.28
34000	3107.42	1687.58	1218.98	988.13	852.32	763.98	702.70	658.28	625.04	599.56	579.68	563.95	551.36	541.20
35000	3198.82	1737.22	1254.83	1017.19	877.39	786.45	723.37	677.64	643.42	617.20	596.73	580.54	567.58	557.12
36000	3290.21	1786.85	1290.68	1046.25	902.46	808.92	744.04	697.00	661.80	634.83	613.78	597.13	583.80	573.04
37000	3381.61	1836.49	1326.53	1075.31	927.53	831.39	764.71	716.36	680.19	652.46	630.83	613.71	600.01	588.95
38000	3473.00	1886.12	1362.39	1104.38	952.60	853.86	785.37	735.73	698.57	670.10	647.88	630.30	616.23	604.87
39000	3564.40	1935.76	1398.24	1133.44	977.66	876.33	806.04	755.09	716.95	687.73	664.93	646.89	632.45	620.79
40000	3655.79	1985.39	1434.09	1162.50	1002.73	898.80	826.71	774.45	735.34	705.37	681.98	663.47	648.66	636.71
41000	3747.19	2035.03	1469.94	1191.56	1027.80	921.27	847.38	793.81	753.72	723.00	699.03	680.06	664.88	652.62
42000	3838.58	2084.66	1505.79	1220.63	1052.87	943.74	868.05	813.17	772.10	740.64	716.08	696.65	681.10	668.54
43000	3929.98	2134.30	1541.65	1249.69	1077.94	966.21	888.71	832.53	790.49	758.27	733.13	713.23	697.31	684.46
44000	4021.37	2183.93	1577.50	1278.75	1103.00	988.68	909.38	851.89	808.87	775.90	750.18	729.82	713.53	700.38
45000	4112.77	2233.57	1613.35	1307.81	1128.07	1011.15	930.05	871.25	827.25	793.54	767.23	746.41	729.75	716.29
46000	4204.16	2283.20	1649.20	1336.88	1153.14	1033.62	950.72	890.61	845.64	811.17	784.28	762.99	745.96	732.21
47000	4295.56	2332.83	1685.05	1365.94	1178.21	1056.09	971.38	909.98	864.02	828.81	801.33	779.58	762.18	748.13
48000	4386.95	2382.47	1720.91	1395.00	1203.28	1078.56	992.05	929.34	882.40	846.44	818.38	796.17	778.40	764.05
49000	4478.34	2432.10	1756.76	1424.06	1228.34	1101.03	1012.72	948.70	900.79	864.07	835.43	812.75	794.61	779.96
50000	4569.74	2481.74	1792.61	1453.13	1253.41	1123.50	1033.39	968.06	919.17	881.71	852.48	829.34	810.83	795.88
55000	5026.71	2729.91	1971.87	1598.44	1378.75	1235.85	1136.72	1064.86	1011.09	969.88	937.72	912.27	891.91	875.47
60000	5483.69	2978.09	2151.13	1743.75	1504.09	1348.20	1240.06	1161.67	1103.00	1058.05	1022.97	995.21	972.99	955.06
65000	5940.66	3226.26	2330.39	1889.06	1629.44	1460.55	1343.40	1258.48	1194.92	1146.22	1108.22	1078.14	1054.08	1034.64
70000	6397.63	3474.43	2509.65	2034.37	1754.78	1572.90	1446.74	1355.28	1286.84	1234.39	1193.46	1161.08	1135.16	1114.23
75000	6854.61	3722.61	2688.91	2179.69	1880.12	1685.25	1550.08	1452.09	1378.75	1322.56	1278.71	1244.01	1216.24	1193.82
80000	7311.58	3970.78	2868.17	2325.00	2005.46	1797.60	1653.42	1548.89	1470.67	1410.73	1363.96	1326.94	1297.32	1273.41
85000	7768.55	4218.95	3047.44	2470.31	2130.80	1909.95	1756.75	1645.70	1562.59	1498.90	1449.20	1409.88	1378.41	1352.99
90000	8225.53	4467.13	3226.70	2615.62	2256.14	2022.30	1860.09	1742.50	1654.50	1587.07	1534.45	1492.81	1459.49	1432.58
95000	8682.50	4715.30	3405.96	2760.93	2381.48	2134.65	1963.43	1839.31	1746.42	1675.24	1619.70	1575.74	1540.57	1512.17
100000	9139.47	4963.47	3585.22	2906.25	2506.82	2247.00	2066.77	1936.11	1838.34	1763.41	1704.95	1658.68	1621.65	1591.76

MONTHLY PAYMENT
REQUIRED TO AMORTIZE A LOAN

17.400%

TERM	15 Years	16 Years	17 Years	18 Years	19 Years	20 Years	21 Years	22 Years	23 Years	24 Years	25 Years	30 Years	35 Years	40 Years
AMOUNT														
5	.08	.08	.08	.08	.08	.08	.08	.08	.08	.08	.08	.08	.08	.08
10	.16	.16	.16	.16	.16	.15	.15	.15	.15	.15	.15	.15	.15	.15
15	.24	.24	.23	.23	.23	.23	.23	.23	.23	.23	.23	.22	.22	.22
25	.40	.39	.39	.38	.38	.38	.38	.38	.37	.37	.37	.37	.37	.37
50	.79	.78	.77	.76	.76	.75	.75	.75	.74	.74	.74	.73	.73	.73
75	1.18	1.17	1.15	1.14	1.13	1.13	1.12	1.12	1.11	1.11	1.11	1.10	1.10	1.09
100	1.57	1.55	1.54	1.52	1.51	1.50	1.49	1.49	1.48	1.48	1.47	1.46	1.46	1.46
200	3.14	3.10	3.07	3.04	3.02	3.00	2.98	2.97	2.96	2.95	2.94	2.92	2.91	2.91
300	4.71	4.65	4.60	4.56	4.52	4.50	4.47	4.45	4.44	4.42	4.41	4.38	4.37	4.36
400	6.27	6.20	6.13	6.08	6.03	5.99	5.96	5.94	5.92	5.90	5.88	5.84	5.82	5.81
500	7.84	7.74	7.66	7.59	7.54	7.49	7.45	7.42	7.39	7.37	7.35	7.30	7.27	7.26
600	9.41	9.29	9.19	9.11	9.04	8.99	8.94	8.90	8.87	8.84	8.82	8.75	8.73	8.71
700	10.98	10.84	10.72	10.63	10.55	10.49	10.43	10.39	10.35	10.32	10.29	10.21	10.18	10.17
800	12.54	12.39	12.25	12.15	12.06	11.98	11.92	11.87	11.83	11.79	11.76	11.67	11.63	11.62
900	14.11	13.93	13.79	13.66	13.56	13.48	13.41	13.35	13.31	13.26	13.23	13.13	13.09	13.07
1000	15.68	15.48	15.32	15.18	15.07	14.98	14.90	14.84	14.78	14.74	14.70	14.59	14.54	14.52
2000	31.35	30.96	30.63	30.36	30.14	29.95	29.80	29.67	29.56	29.47	29.40	29.17	29.07	29.03
3000	47.03	46.43	45.94	45.54	45.20	44.92	44.69	44.50	44.34	44.20	44.09	43.75	43.61	43.55
4000	62.70	61.91	61.25	60.71	60.27	59.90	59.59	59.33	59.12	58.94	58.79	58.33	58.14	58.06
5000	78.38	77.38	76.57	75.89	75.33	74.87	74.48	74.16	73.90	73.67	73.48	72.91	72.68	72.58
6000	94.05	92.86	91.88	91.07	90.40	89.84	89.38	88.99	88.67	88.40	88.18	87.50	87.21	87.09
7000	109.73	108.33	107.19	106.25	105.46	104.82	104.28	103.83	103.45	103.14	102.87	102.08	101.75	101.61
8000	125.40	123.81	122.50	121.42	120.53	119.79	119.17	118.66	118.23	117.87	117.57	116.66	116.28	116.12
9000	141.07	139.29	137.81	136.60	135.60	134.76	134.07	133.49	133.01	132.60	132.27	131.24	130.81	130.64
10000	156.75	154.76	153.13	151.78	150.66	149.73	148.96	148.32	147.79	147.34	146.96	145.82	145.35	145.15
11000	172.42	170.24	168.44	166.95	165.73	164.71	163.86	163.15	162.56	162.07	161.66	160.41	159.88	159.66
12000	188.10	185.71	183.75	182.13	180.79	179.68	178.76	177.98	177.34	176.80	176.35	174.99	174.42	174.18
13000	203.77	201.19	199.06	197.31	195.86	194.65	193.65	192.82	192.12	191.54	191.05	189.57	188.95	188.69
14000	219.45	216.66	214.37	212.49	210.92	209.63	208.55	207.65	206.90	206.27	205.74	204.15	203.49	203.21
15000	235.12	232.14	229.69	227.66	225.99	224.60	223.44	222.48	221.68	221.00	220.44	218.73	218.02	217.72
16000	250.80	247.61	245.00	242.84	241.05	239.57	238.34	237.31	236.45	235.74	235.14	233.31	232.56	232.24
17000	266.47	263.09	260.31	258.02	256.12	254.55	253.23	252.14	251.23	250.47	249.83	247.90	247.09	246.75
18000	282.14	278.57	275.62	273.20	271.19	269.52	268.13	266.97	266.01	265.20	264.53	262.48	261.62	261.27
19000	297.82	294.04	290.94	288.37	286.25	284.49	283.03	281.81	280.79	279.94	279.22	277.06	276.16	275.78
20000	313.49	309.52	306.25	303.55	301.32	299.46	297.92	296.64	295.57	294.67	293.92	291.64	290.69	290.29
21000	329.17	324.99	321.56	318.73	316.38	314.44	312.82	311.47	310.34	309.40	308.61	306.22	305.23	304.81
22000	344.84	340.47	336.87	333.90	331.45	329.41	327.71	326.30	325.12	324.14	323.31	320.81	319.76	319.32
23000	360.52	355.94	352.18	349.08	346.51	344.38	342.61	341.13	339.90	338.87	338.01	335.39	334.30	333.84
24000	376.19	371.42	367.50	364.26	361.58	359.36	357.51	355.96	354.68	353.60	352.70	349.97	348.83	348.35
25000	391.87	386.89	382.81	379.44	376.65	374.33	372.40	370.80	369.46	368.33	367.40	364.55	363.36	362.87
26000	407.54	402.37	398.12	394.61	391.71	389.30	387.30	385.63	384.23	383.07	382.09	379.13	377.90	377.38
27000	423.21	417.85	413.43	409.79	406.78	404.27	402.19	400.46	399.01	397.80	396.79	393.72	392.43	391.90
28000	438.89	433.32	428.74	424.97	421.84	419.25	417.09	415.29	413.79	412.53	411.48	408.30	406.97	406.41
29000	454.56	448.80	444.06	440.15	436.91	434.22	431.99	430.12	428.57	427.27	426.18	422.88	421.50	420.92
30000	470.24	464.27	459.37	455.32	451.97	449.19	446.88	444.95	443.35	442.00	440.88	437.46	436.04	435.44
31000	485.91	479.75	474.68	470.50	467.04	464.17	461.78	459.79	458.12	456.73	455.57	452.04	450.57	449.95
32000	501.59	495.22	489.99	485.68	482.10	479.14	476.67	474.62	472.90	471.47	470.27	466.62	465.11	464.47
33000	517.26	510.70	505.30	500.85	497.17	494.11	491.57	489.45	487.68	486.20	484.96	481.21	479.64	478.98
34000	532.94	526.17	520.62	516.03	512.24	509.09	506.46	504.28	502.46	500.93	499.66	495.79	494.17	493.50
35000	548.61	541.65	535.93	531.21	527.30	524.06	521.36	519.11	517.24	515.67	514.35	510.37	508.71	508.01
36000	564.28	557.13	551.24	546.39	542.37	539.03	536.26	533.94	532.01	530.40	529.05	524.95	523.24	522.53
37000	579.96	572.60	566.55	561.56	557.43	554.00	551.15	548.78	546.79	545.13	543.75	539.53	537.78	537.04
38000	595.63	588.08	581.87	576.74	572.50	568.98	566.05	563.61	561.57	559.87	558.44	554.12	552.31	551.56
39000	611.31	603.55	597.18	591.92	587.56	583.95	580.94	578.44	576.35	574.60	573.14	568.70	566.85	566.07
40000	626.98	619.03	612.49	607.10	602.63	598.92	595.84	593.27	591.13	589.33	587.83	583.28	581.38	580.58
41000	642.66	634.50	627.80	622.27	617.70	613.90	610.74	608.10	605.90	604.07	602.53	597.86	595.92	595.10
42000	658.33	649.98	643.11	637.45	632.76	628.87	625.63	622.93	620.68	618.80	617.22	612.44	610.45	609.61
43000	674.00	665.45	658.43	652.63	647.83	643.84	640.53	637.76	635.46	633.53	631.92	627.03	624.98	624.13
44000	689.68	680.93	673.74	667.80	662.89	658.81	655.42	652.60	650.24	648.27	646.62	641.61	639.52	638.64
45000	705.35	696.41	689.05	682.98	677.96	673.79	670.32	667.43	665.02	663.00	661.31	656.19	654.05	653.16
46000	721.03	711.88	704.36	698.16	693.02	688.76	685.21	682.26	679.79	677.73	676.01	670.77	668.59	667.67
47000	736.70	727.36	719.67	713.34	708.09	703.73	700.11	697.09	694.57	692.46	690.70	685.35	683.12	682.19
48000	752.38	742.83	734.99	728.51	723.15	718.71	715.01	711.92	709.35	707.20	705.40	699.93	697.66	696.70
49000	768.05	758.31	750.30	743.69	738.22	733.68	729.90	726.75	724.13	721.93	720.09	714.52	712.19	711.21
50000	783.73	773.78	765.61	758.87	753.29	748.65	744.80	741.59	738.91	736.66	734.79	729.10	726.72	725.73
55000	862.10	851.16	842.17	834.75	828.61	823.52	819.28	815.74	812.80	810.33	808.27	802.01	799.40	798.30
60000	940.47	928.54	918.73	910.64	903.94	898.38	893.76	889.90	886.69	884.00	881.75	874.92	872.07	870.87
65000	1018.84	1005.92	995.29	986.53	979.27	973.25	968.24	964.06	960.58	957.66	955.23	947.83	944.74	943.45
70000	1097.21	1083.29	1071.85	1062.41	1054.60	1048.11	1042.72	1038.22	1034.47	1031.33	1028.70	1020.74	1017.41	1016.02
75000	1175.59	1160.67	1148.41	1138.30	1129.93	1122.98	1117.20	1112.38	1108.36	1104.99	1102.18	1093.64	1090.08	1088.59
80000	1253.96	1238.05	1224.97	1214.19	1205.25	1197.84	1191.67	1186.54	1182.25	1178.66	1175.66	1166.55	1162.76	1161.16
85000	1332.33	1315.43	1301.53	1290.07	1280.58	1272.71	1266.15	1260.69	1256.14	1252.33	1249.14	1239.46	1235.43	1233.74
90000	1410.70	1392.81	1378.10	1365.96	1355.91	1347.57	1340.63	1334.85	1330.03	1325.99	1322.62	1312.37	1308.10	1306.31
95000	1489.07	1470.18	1454.66	1441.84	1431.24	1422.44	1415.11	1409.01	1403.92	1399.66	1396.10	1385.28	1380.77	1378.88
100000	1567.45	1547.56	1531.22	1517.73	1506.57	1497.30	1489.59	1483.17	1477.81	1473.32	1469.57	1458.19	1453.44	1451.45

MONTHLY PAYMENT
REQUIRED TO AMORTIZE A LOAN

TERM AMOUNT	1 Year	2 Years	3 Years	4 Years	5 Years	6 Years	7 Years	8 Years	9 Years	10 Years	11 Years	12 Years	13 Years	14 Years
5	.46	.25	.18	.15	.13	.12	.11	.10	.10	.09	.09	.09	.09	.08
10	.92	.50	.36	.30	.26	.23	.21	.20	.19	.18	.18	.17	.17	.16
15	1.38	.75	.54	.44	.38	.34	.32	.30	.28	.27	.26	.25	.25	.24
25	2.29	1.25	.90	.73	.63	.57	.52	.49	.47	.45	.43	.42	.41	.40
50	4.58	2.49	1.80	1.46	1.26	1.13	1.04	.98	.93	.89	.86	.84	.82	.80
75	6.86	3.73	2.70	2.19	1.89	1.69	1.56	1.46	1.39	1.33	1.29	1.25	1.23	1.20
100	9.15	4.97	3.60	2.92	2.52	2.26	2.08	1.95	1.85	1.77	1.72	1.67	1.63	1.60
200	18.29	9.94	7.19	5.83	5.03	4.51	4.15	3.89	3.69	3.54	3.43	3.34	3.26	3.20
300	27.44	14.91	10.78	8.74	7.54	6.76	6.22	5.83	5.54	5.31	5.14	5.00	4.89	4.80
400	36.58	19.88	14.37	11.65	10.05	9.02	8.30	7.77	7.38	7.08	6.85	6.67	6.52	6.40
500	45.73	24.85	17.96	14.56	12.57	11.27	10.37	9.72	9.23	8.85	8.56	8.33	8.15	8.00
600	54.87	29.81	21.55	17.47	15.08	13.52	12.44	11.66	11.07	10.62	10.27	10.00	9.78	9.60
700	64.01	34.78	25.14	20.39	17.59	15.77	14.51	13.60	12.92	12.39	11.99	11.66	11.40	11.20
800	73.16	39.75	28.73	23.30	20.10	18.03	16.59	15.54	14.76	14.16	13.70	13.33	13.03	12.80
900	82.30	44.72	32.32	26.21	22.61	20.28	18.66	17.48	16.61	15.93	15.41	14.99	14.66	14.39
1000	91.45	49.69	35.91	29.12	25.13	22.53	20.73	19.43	18.45	17.70	17.12	16.66	16.29	15.99
2000	182.89	99.37	71.81	58.23	50.25	45.06	41.46	38.85	36.90	35.40	34.23	33.31	32.58	31.98
3000	274.33	149.05	107.71	87.35	75.37	67.58	62.18	58.27	55.34	53.10	51.35	49.97	48.86	47.97
4000	365.77	198.74	143.61	116.46	100.49	90.11	82.91	77.69	73.79	70.80	68.46	66.62	65.15	63.96
5000	457.22	248.42	179.52	145.58	125.62	112.64	103.63	97.11	92.23	88.49	85.58	83.27	81.43	79.94
6000	548.66	298.10	215.42	174.69	150.74	135.16	124.36	116.53	110.68	106.19	102.69	99.93	97.72	95.93
7000	640.10	347.78	251.32	203.81	175.86	157.69	145.09	135.95	129.12	123.89	119.81	116.58	114.00	111.92
8000	731.54	397.47	287.22	232.92	200.98	180.21	165.81	155.37	147.57	141.59	136.92	133.24	130.29	127.91
9000	822.98	447.15	323.12	262.03	226.10	202.74	186.54	174.80	166.01	159.29	154.04	149.89	146.57	143.89
10000	914.43	496.83	359.03	291.15	251.23	225.27	207.26	194.22	184.46	176.98	171.15	166.54	162.86	159.88
11000	1005.87	546.52	394.93	320.26	276.35	247.79	227.99	213.64	202.90	194.68	188.27	183.20	179.14	175.87
12000	1097.31	596.20	430.83	349.38	301.47	270.32	248.71	233.06	221.35	212.38	205.38	199.85	195.43	191.86
13000	1188.75	645.88	466.73	378.49	326.59	292.84	269.44	252.48	239.79	230.08	222.50	216.51	211.71	207.84
14000	1280.20	695.56	502.63	407.61	351.72	315.37	290.17	271.90	258.24	247.78	239.61	233.16	228.00	223.83
15000	1371.64	745.25	538.54	436.72	376.84	337.90	310.89	291.32	276.69	265.47	256.73	249.81	244.28	239.82
16000	1463.08	794.93	574.44	465.83	401.96	360.42	331.62	310.74	295.13	283.17	273.84	266.47	260.57	255.81
17000	1554.52	844.61	610.34	494.95	427.08	382.95	352.34	330.17	313.58	300.87	290.96	283.12	276.85	271.79
18000	1645.96	894.30	646.24	524.06	452.20	405.47	373.07	349.59	332.02	318.57	308.07	299.77	293.14	287.78
19000	1737.41	943.98	682.14	553.18	477.33	428.00	393.80	369.01	350.47	336.26	325.19	316.43	309.42	303.77
20000	1828.85	993.66	718.05	582.29	502.45	450.52	414.52	388.43	368.91	353.96	342.30	333.08	325.71	319.76
21000	1920.29	1043.34	753.95	611.41	527.57	473.05	435.25	407.85	387.36	371.66	359.42	349.74	341.99	335.74
22000	2011.73	1093.03	789.85	640.52	552.69	495.58	455.97	427.27	405.80	389.36	376.53	366.39	358.28	351.73
23000	2103.18	1142.71	825.75	669.64	577.82	518.10	476.70	446.69	424.25	407.06	393.65	383.04	374.56	367.72
24000	2194.62	1192.39	861.65	698.75	602.94	540.63	497.42	466.11	442.69	424.75	410.76	399.70	390.85	383.71
25000	2286.06	1242.08	897.56	727.86	628.06	563.16	518.15	485.54	461.14	442.45	427.88	416.35	407.13	399.69
26000	2377.50	1291.76	933.46	756.98	653.18	585.68	538.88	504.96	479.58	460.15	444.99	433.01	423.42	415.68
27000	2468.94	1341.44	969.36	786.09	678.30	608.21	559.60	524.38	498.03	477.85	462.11	449.66	439.70	431.67
28000	2560.39	1391.12	1005.26	815.21	703.43	630.73	580.33	543.80	516.47	495.55	479.22	466.31	455.99	447.66
29000	2651.83	1440.81	1041.16	844.32	728.55	653.26	601.05	563.22	534.92	513.24	496.34	482.97	472.27	463.65
30000	2743.27	1490.49	1077.07	873.44	753.67	675.79	621.78	582.64	553.37	530.94	513.45	499.62	488.56	479.63
31000	2834.71	1540.17	1112.97	902.55	778.79	698.31	642.50	602.06	571.81	548.64	530.57	516.27	504.84	495.62
32000	2926.16	1589.86	1148.87	931.66	803.92	720.84	663.23	621.48	590.26	566.34	547.68	532.93	521.13	511.61
33000	3017.60	1639.54	1184.77	960.78	829.04	743.36	683.96	640.90	608.70	584.03	564.80	549.58	537.41	527.60
34000	3109.04	1689.22	1220.68	989.89	854.16	765.89	704.68	660.33	627.15	601.73	581.91	566.24	553.70	543.58
35000	3200.48	1738.90	1256.58	1019.01	879.28	788.42	725.41	679.75	645.59	619.43	599.03	582.89	569.98	559.57
36000	3291.92	1788.59	1292.48	1048.12	904.40	810.94	746.13	699.17	664.04	637.13	616.14	599.54	586.27	575.56
37000	3383.37	1838.27	1328.38	1077.24	929.53	833.47	766.86	718.59	682.48	654.83	633.26	616.20	602.55	591.55
38000	3474.81	1887.95	1364.28	1106.35	954.65	855.99	787.59	738.01	700.93	672.52	650.37	632.85	618.84	607.53
39000	3566.25	1937.64	1400.19	1135.47	979.77	878.52	808.31	757.43	719.37	690.22	667.49	649.51	635.12	623.52
40000	3657.69	1987.32	1436.09	1164.58	1004.89	901.05	829.04	776.85	737.82	707.92	684.60	666.16	651.41	639.51
41000	3749.14	2037.00	1471.99	1193.69	1030.02	923.57	849.76	796.27	756.26	725.62	701.72	682.81	667.70	655.50
42000	3840.58	2086.68	1507.89	1222.81	1055.14	946.10	870.49	815.70	774.71	743.32	718.83	699.47	683.98	671.48
43000	3932.02	2136.37	1543.79	1251.92	1080.26	968.62	891.21	835.12	793.15	761.01	735.95	716.12	700.27	687.47
44000	4023.46	2186.05	1579.70	1281.04	1105.38	991.15	911.94	854.54	811.60	778.71	753.06	732.78	716.55	703.46
45000	4114.90	2235.73	1615.60	1310.15	1130.50	1013.68	932.67	873.96	830.05	796.41	770.18	749.43	732.84	719.45
46000	4206.35	2285.42	1651.50	1339.27	1155.63	1036.20	953.39	893.38	848.49	814.11	787.29	766.08	749.12	735.43
47000	4297.79	2335.10	1687.40	1368.38	1180.75	1058.73	974.12	912.80	866.94	831.81	804.41	782.74	765.41	751.42
48000	4389.23	2384.78	1723.30	1397.49	1205.87	1081.26	994.84	932.22	885.38	849.50	821.52	799.39	781.69	767.41
49000	4480.67	2434.46	1759.21	1426.61	1230.99	1103.78	1015.57	951.64	903.83	867.20	838.64	816.04	797.98	783.40
50000	4572.12	2484.15	1795.11	1455.72	1256.12	1126.31	1036.29	971.07	922.27	884.90	855.75	832.70	814.26	799.38
55000	5029.33	2732.56	1974.62	1601.30	1381.73	1238.94	1139.92	1068.17	1014.50	973.39	941.33	915.97	895.69	879.32
60000	5486.54	2980.98	2154.13	1746.87	1507.34	1351.57	1243.55	1165.28	1106.73	1061.88	1026.90	999.24	977.11	959.26
65000	5943.75	3229.39	2333.64	1892.44	1632.95	1464.20	1347.18	1262.38	1198.95	1150.37	1112.48	1082.51	1058.54	1039.20
70000	6400.96	3477.80	2513.15	2038.01	1758.56	1576.83	1450.81	1359.49	1291.18	1238.86	1198.05	1165.78	1139.96	1119.14
75000	6858.17	3726.22	2692.66	2183.58	1884.17	1689.46	1554.44	1456.60	1383.41	1327.35	1283.63	1249.05	1221.39	1199.07
80000	7315.38	3974.63	2872.17	2329.15	2009.78	1802.09	1658.07	1553.70	1475.63	1415.84	1369.20	1332.31	1302.81	1279.01
85000	7772.59	4223.05	3051.68	2474.73	2135.39	1914.72	1761.70	1650.81	1567.86	1504.32	1454.77	1415.58	1384.24	1358.95
90000	8229.80	4471.46	3231.19	2620.30	2261.00	2027.35	1865.33	1747.91	1660.09	1592.81	1540.35	1498.85	1465.67	1438.89
95000	8687.01	4719.88	3410.70	2765.87	2386.62	2139.98	1968.96	1845.02	1752.31	1681.30	1625.92	1582.12	1547.09	1518.83
100000	9144.23	4968.29	3590.21	2911.44	2512.23	2252.61	2072.58	1942.13	1844.54	1769.79	1711.50	1665.39	1628.52	1598.76

TERM AMOUNT	15 Years	16 Years	17 Years	18 Years	19 Years	20 Years	21 Years	22 Years	23 Years	24 Years	25 Years	30 Years	35 Years	40 Years
5	.08	.08	.08	.08	.08	.08	.08	.08	.08	.08	.08	.08	.08	.08
10	.16	.16	.16	.16	.16	.16	.15	.15	.15	.15	.15	.15	.15	.15
15	.24	.24	.24	.23	.23	.23	.23	.23	.23	.23	.23	.22	.22	.22
25	.40	.39	.39	.39	.38	.38	.38	.38	.38	.38	.37	.37	.37	.37
50	.79	.78	.77	.77	.76	.76	.75	.75	.75	.75	.74	.74	.74	.73
75	1.19	1.17	1.16	1.15	1.14	1.13	1.13	1.12	1.12	1.12	1.11	1.10	1.10	1.10
100	1.58	1.56	1.54	1.53	1.52	1.51	1.50	1.50	1.49	1.49	1.48	1.47	1.47	1.46
200	3.15	3.11	3.08	3.06	3.03	3.01	3.00	2.99	2.98	2.97	2.96	2.94	2.93	2.92
300	4.73	4.67	4.62	4.58	4.55	4.52	4.50	4.48	4.46	4.45	4.44	4.40	4.39	4.38
400	6.30	6.22	6.16	6.11	6.06	6.02	5.99	5.97	5.95	5.93	5.92	5.87	5.85	5.84
500	7.88	7.78	7.70	7.63	7.58	7.53	7.49	7.46	7.43	7.41	7.39	7.34	7.31	7.30
600	9.45	9.33	9.24	9.16	9.09	9.03	8.99	8.95	8.92	8.89	8.87	8.80	8.78	8.76
700	11.03	10.89	10.78	10.68	10.60	10.54	10.49	10.44	10.40	10.37	10.35	10.27	10.24	10.22
800	12.60	12.44	12.31	12.21	12.12	12.04	11.98	11.93	11.89	11.85	11.83	11.74	11.70	11.68
900	14.18	14.00	13.85	13.73	13.63	13.55	13.48	13.42	13.38	13.34	13.30	13.20	13.16	13.14
1000	15.75	15.55	15.39	15.26	15.15	15.05	14.98	14.91	14.86	14.82	14.78	14.67	14.62	14.60
2000	31.50	31.10	30.78	30.51	30.29	30.10	29.95	29.82	29.72	29.63	29.56	29.33	29.24	29.20
3000	47.24	46.65	46.16	45.76	45.43	45.15	44.92	44.73	44.57	44.44	44.33	43.99	43.86	43.80
4000	62.99	62.20	61.55	61.01	60.57	60.20	59.90	59.64	59.43	59.25	59.11	58.66	58.47	58.39
5000	78.73	77.75	76.93	76.26	75.71	75.25	74.87	74.55	74.29	74.07	73.88	73.32	73.09	72.99
6000	94.48	93.29	92.32	91.52	90.85	90.30	89.84	89.46	89.14	88.88	88.66	87.98	87.71	87.59
7000	110.23	108.84	107.71	106.77	105.99	105.35	104.82	104.37	104.00	103.69	103.43	102.65	102.32	102.19
8000	125.97	124.39	123.09	122.02	121.13	120.40	119.79	119.28	118.86	118.50	118.21	117.31	116.94	116.78
9000	141.72	139.94	138.48	137.27	136.28	135.45	134.76	134.19	133.71	133.32	132.98	131.97	131.56	131.38
10000	157.46	155.49	153.86	152.52	151.42	150.50	149.74	149.10	148.57	148.13	147.76	146.64	146.17	145.98
11000	173.21	171.03	169.25	167.78	166.56	165.55	164.71	164.01	163.43	162.94	162.53	161.30	160.79	160.58
12000	188.95	186.58	184.63	183.03	181.70	180.60	179.68	178.92	178.28	177.75	177.31	175.96	175.41	175.17
13000	204.70	202.13	200.02	198.28	196.84	195.65	194.66	193.83	193.14	192.56	192.08	190.63	190.02	189.77
14000	220.45	217.68	215.41	213.53	211.98	210.70	209.63	208.74	208.00	207.38	206.86	205.29	204.64	204.37
15000	236.19	233.23	230.79	228.78	227.12	225.75	224.60	223.65	222.85	222.19	221.63	219.95	219.26	218.97
16000	251.94	248.78	246.18	244.04	242.26	240.80	239.57	238.56	237.71	237.00	236.41	234.62	233.87	233.56
17000	267.68	264.32	261.56	259.29	257.41	255.85	254.55	253.47	252.57	251.81	251.19	249.28	248.49	248.16
18000	283.43	279.87	276.95	274.54	272.55	270.89	269.52	268.38	267.42	266.63	265.96	263.94	263.11	262.76
19000	299.17	295.42	292.34	289.79	287.69	285.94	284.49	283.29	282.28	281.44	280.74	278.61	277.72	277.35
20000	314.92	310.97	307.72	305.04	302.83	300.99	299.47	298.20	297.14	296.25	295.51	293.27	292.34	291.95
21000	330.67	326.52	323.11	320.30	317.97	316.04	314.44	313.11	311.99	311.06	310.29	307.93	306.96	306.55
22000	346.41	342.06	338.49	335.55	333.11	331.09	329.41	328.02	326.85	325.88	325.06	322.60	321.57	321.15
23000	362.16	357.61	353.88	350.80	348.25	346.14	344.39	342.92	341.71	340.69	339.84	337.26	336.19	335.74
24000	377.90	373.16	369.26	366.05	363.39	361.19	359.36	357.83	356.56	355.50	354.61	351.92	350.81	350.34
25000	393.65	388.71	384.65	381.30	378.54	376.24	374.33	372.74	371.42	370.31	369.39	366.59	365.42	364.94
26000	409.40	404.26	400.04	396.56	393.68	391.29	389.31	387.65	386.28	385.12	384.16	381.25	380.04	379.54
27000	425.14	419.80	415.42	411.81	408.82	406.34	404.28	402.56	401.13	399.94	398.94	395.91	394.66	394.13
28000	440.89	435.35	430.81	427.06	423.96	421.39	419.25	417.47	415.99	414.75	413.71	410.58	409.27	408.73
29000	456.63	450.90	446.19	442.31	439.10	436.44	434.22	432.38	430.84	429.56	428.49	425.24	423.89	423.33
30000	472.38	466.45	461.58	457.56	454.24	451.49	449.20	447.29	445.70	444.37	443.26	439.90	438.51	437.93
31000	488.12	482.00	476.96	472.82	469.38	466.54	464.17	462.20	460.56	459.19	458.04	454.57	453.12	452.52
32000	503.87	497.55	492.35	488.07	484.52	481.59	479.14	477.11	475.41	474.00	472.81	469.23	467.74	467.12
33000	519.62	513.09	507.74	503.32	499.67	496.64	494.12	492.02	490.27	488.81	487.59	483.89	482.36	481.72
34000	535.36	528.64	523.12	518.57	514.81	511.69	509.09	506.93	505.13	503.62	502.37	498.56	496.97	496.31
35000	551.11	544.19	538.51	533.82	529.95	526.73	524.06	521.84	519.98	518.44	517.14	513.22	511.59	510.91
36000	566.85	559.74	553.89	549.08	545.09	541.78	539.04	536.75	534.84	533.25	531.92	527.88	526.21	525.51
37000	582.60	575.29	569.28	564.33	560.23	556.83	554.01	551.66	549.70	548.06	546.69	542.55	540.82	540.11
38000	598.34	590.83	584.67	579.58	575.37	571.88	568.98	566.57	564.55	562.87	561.47	557.21	555.44	554.70
39000	614.09	606.38	600.05	594.83	590.51	586.93	583.96	581.48	579.41	577.68	576.24	571.87	570.06	569.30
40000	629.84	621.93	615.44	610.08	605.65	601.98	598.93	596.39	594.27	592.50	591.02	586.54	584.68	583.90
41000	645.58	637.48	630.82	625.33	620.80	617.03	613.90	611.30	609.12	607.31	605.79	601.20	599.29	598.50
42000	661.33	653.03	646.21	640.59	635.94	632.08	628.88	626.21	623.98	622.12	620.57	615.86	613.91	613.09
43000	677.07	668.57	661.59	655.84	651.08	647.13	643.85	641.12	638.84	636.93	635.34	630.52	628.53	627.69
44000	692.82	684.12	676.98	671.09	666.22	662.18	658.82	656.03	653.69	651.75	650.12	645.19	643.14	642.29
45000	708.57	699.67	692.37	686.34	681.36	677.23	673.79	670.93	668.55	666.56	664.89	659.85	657.76	656.89
46000	724.31	715.22	707.75	701.59	696.50	692.28	688.77	685.84	683.41	681.37	679.67	674.51	672.38	671.48
47000	740.06	730.77	723.14	716.85	711.64	707.33	703.74	700.75	698.26	696.18	694.44	689.18	686.99	686.08
48000	755.80	746.32	738.52	732.10	726.78	722.38	718.71	715.66	713.12	711.00	709.22	703.84	701.61	700.68
49000	771.55	761.86	753.91	747.35	741.93	737.43	733.69	730.57	727.98	725.81	723.99	718.50	716.23	715.27
50000	787.29	777.41	769.29	762.60	757.07	752.48	748.66	745.48	742.83	740.62	738.77	733.17	730.84	729.87
55000	866.02	855.15	846.22	838.86	832.77	827.72	823.53	820.03	817.12	814.68	812.65	806.48	803.93	802.86
60000	944.75	932.89	923.15	915.12	908.48	902.97	898.39	894.58	891.40	888.74	886.52	879.80	877.01	875.85
65000	1023.48	1010.63	1000.08	991.38	984.19	978.22	973.26	969.13	965.68	962.80	960.40	953.12	950.09	948.83
70000	1102.21	1088.37	1077.01	1067.64	1059.89	1053.46	1048.12	1043.67	1039.96	1036.87	1034.28	1026.43	1023.18	1021.82
75000	1180.94	1166.11	1153.94	1143.90	1135.60	1128.71	1122.99	1118.22	1114.25	1110.93	1108.15	1099.75	1096.26	1094.81
80000	1259.67	1243.86	1230.87	1220.16	1211.30	1203.96	1197.85	1192.77	1188.53	1184.99	1182.03	1173.07	1169.35	1167.79
85000	1338.40	1321.60	1307.80	1296.42	1287.01	1279.21	1272.72	1267.32	1262.81	1259.05	1255.91	1246.38	1242.43	1240.78
90000	1417.13	1399.34	1384.73	1372.68	1362.72	1354.45	1347.58	1341.86	1337.09	1333.11	1329.78	1319.70	1315.51	1313.77
95000	1495.85	1477.08	1461.66	1448.94	1438.42	1429.70	1422.45	1416.41	1411.38	1407.17	1403.66	1393.01	1388.60	1386.75
100000	1574.58	1554.82	1538.58	1525.20	1514.13	1504.95	1497.32	1490.96	1485.66	1481.23	1477.53	1466.33	1461.68	1459.74

MONTHLY PAYMENT
REQUIRED TO AMORTIZE A LOAN

TERM	1 Year	2 Years	3 Years	4 Years	5 Years	6 Years	7 Years	8 Years	9 Years	10 Years	11 Years	12 Years	13 Years	14 Years
AMOUNT
5	.46	.25	.18	.15	.13	.12	.11	.10	.10	.09	.09	.09	.09	.09
10	.92	.50	.36	.30	.26	.23	.21	.20	.19	.18	.10	.17	.17	.17
15	1.38	.75	.54	.44	.38	.34	.32	.30	.28	.27	.26	.26	.25	.25
25	2.29	1.25	.90	.73	.63	.57	.52	.49	.47	.45	.43	.42	.41	.41
50	4.58	2.49	1.80	1.46	1.26	1.13	1.04	.98	.93	.89	.86	.84	.82	.81
75	6.87	3.73	2.70	2.19	1.89	1.70	1.56	1.47	1.39	1.34	1.29	1.26	1.23	1.21
100	9.15	4.98	3.60	2.92	2.52	2.26	2.08	1.95	1.86	1.78	1.72	1.68	1.64	1.61
200	18.30	9.95	7.20	5.84	5.04	4.52	4.16	3.90	3.71	3.56	3.44	3.35	3.28	3.22
300	27.45	14.92	10.79	8.75	7.56	6.78	6.24	5.85	5.56	5.33	5.16	5.02	4.91	4.82
400	36.60	19.90	14.39	11.67	10.08	9.04	8.32	7.80	7.41	7.11	6.88	6.69	6.55	6.43
500	45.75	24.87	17.98	14.59	12.59	11.30	10.40	9.75	9.26	8.89	8.60	8.37	8.18	8.03
600	54.90	29.84	21.58	17.50	15.11	13.55	12.48	11.69	11.11	10.66	10.31	10.04	9.82	9.64
700	64.05	34.82	25.17	20.42	17.63	15.81	14.55	13.64	12.96	12.44	12.03	11.71	11.45	11.25
800	73.20	39.79	28.77	23.34	20.15	18.07	16.63	15.59	14.81	14.21	13.75	13.38	13.09	12.85
900	82.35	44.76	32.36	26.25	22.66	20.33	18.71	17.54	16.66	15.99	15.47	15.05	14.72	14.46
1000	91.49	49.74	35.96	29.17	25.18	22.59	20.79	19.49	18.51	17.77	17.19	16.73	16.36	16.06
2000	182.98	99.47	71.91	58.34	50.36	45.17	41.57	38.97	37.02	35.53	34.37	33.45	32.71	32.12
3000	274.47	149.20	107.86	87.50	75.53	67.75	62.36	58.45	55.53	53.29	51.55	50.17	49.07	48.18
4000	365.96	198.93	143.81	116.67	100.71	90.33	83.14	77.93	74.03	71.05	68.73	66.89	65.42	64.24
5000	457.45	248.66	179.77	145.84	125.89	112.92	103.93	97.41	92.54	88.81	85.91	83.61	81.77	80.29
6000	548.94	298.39	215.72	175.00	151.06	135.50	124.71	116.89	111.05	106.58	103.09	100.33	98.13	96.35
7000	640.43	348.12	251.67	204.17	176.24	158.08	145.49	136.38	129.56	124.34	120.27	117.05	114.48	112.41
8000	731.92	397.85	287.62	233.34	201.42	180.66	166.28	155.86	148.06	142.10	137.45	133.77	130.84	128.47
9000	823.41	447.58	323.57	262.50	226.59	203.25	187.06	175.34	166.57	159.86	154.63	150.50	147.19	144.52
10000	914.90	497.32	359.53	291.67	251.77	225.83	207.85	194.82	185.08	177.62	171.81	167.22	163.54	160.58
11000	1006.39	547.05	395.48	320.84	276.94	248.41	228.63	214.30	203.59	195.38	188.99	183.94	179.90	176.64
12000	1097.88	596.78	431.43	350.00	302.12	270.99	249.41	233.78	222.09	213.15	206.17	200.66	196.25	192.70
13000	1189.37	646.51	467.38	379.17	327.30	293.57	270.20	253.26	240.60	230.91	223.35	217.38	212.61	208.76
14000	1280.86	696.24	503.33	408.33	352.47	316.16	290.98	272.75	259.11	248.67	240.53	234.10	228.96	224.81
15000	1372.35	745.97	539.29	437.50	377.65	338.74	311.77	292.23	277.62	266.43	257.71	250.82	245.31	240.87
16000	1463.84	795.70	575.24	466.67	402.83	361.32	332.55	311.71	296.12	284.19	274.89	267.54	261.67	256.93
17000	1555.33	845.43	611.19	495.83	428.00	383.90	353.33	331.19	314.63	301.96	292.07	284.26	278.02	272.99
18000	1646.82	895.16	647.14	525.00	453.18	406.49	374.12	350.67	333.14	319.72	309.26	300.99	294.37	289.04
19000	1738.31	944.89	683.09	554.17	478.36	429.07	394.90	370.15	351.65	337.48	326.44	317.71	310.73	305.10
20000	1829.80	994.63	719.05	583.33	503.53	451.65	415.69	389.63	370.15	355.24	343.62	334.43	327.08	321.16
21000	1921.29	1044.36	755.00	612.50	528.71	474.23	436.47	409.12	388.66	373.00	360.80	351.15	343.44	337.22
22000	2012.78	1094.09	790.95	641.67	553.88	496.81	457.25	428.60	407.17	390.76	377.98	367.87	359.79	353.28
23000	2104.27	1143.82	826.90	670.83	579.06	519.40	478.04	448.08	425.68	408.53	395.16	384.59	376.14	369.33
24000	2195.76	1193.55	862.85	700.00	604.24	541.98	498.82	467.56	444.18	426.29	412.34	401.31	392.50	385.39
25000	2287.25	1243.28	898.81	729.16	629.41	564.56	519.61	487.04	462.69	444.05	429.52	418.03	408.85	401.45
26000	2378.74	1293.01	934.76	758.33	654.59	587.14	540.39	506.52	481.20	461.81	446.70	434.75	425.21	417.51
27000	2470.23	1342.74	970.71	787.50	679.77	609.73	561.17	526.00	499.71	479.57	463.88	451.48	441.56	433.56
28000	2561.72	1392.47	1006.66	816.66	704.94	632.31	581.96	545.49	518.21	497.34	481.06	468.20	457.91	449.62
29000	2653.21	1442.21	1042.61	845.83	730.12	654.89	602.74	564.97	536.72	515.10	498.24	484.92	474.27	465.68
30000	2744.70	1491.94	1078.57	875.00	755.29	677.47	623.53	584.45	555.23	532.86	515.42	501.64	490.62	481.74
31000	2836.19	1541.67	1114.52	904.16	780.47	700.05	644.31	603.93	573.74	550.62	532.60	518.36	506.98	497.80
32000	2927.68	1591.40	1150.47	933.33	805.65	722.64	665.09	623.41	592.24	568.38	549.78	535.08	523.33	513.85
33000	3019.17	1641.13	1186.42	962.50	830.82	745.22	685.88	642.89	610.75	586.14	566.96	551.80	539.68	529.91
34000	3110.66	1690.86	1222.37	991.66	856.00	767.80	706.66	662.37	629.26	603.91	584.14	568.52	556.04	545.97
35000	3202.15	1740.59	1258.33	1020.83	881.18	790.38	727.45	681.86	647.77	621.67	601.33	585.24	572.39	562.03
36000	3293.64	1790.32	1294.28	1050.00	906.35	812.97	748.23	701.34	666.27	639.43	618.51	601.97	588.74	578.08
37000	3385.13	1840.05	1330.23	1079.16	931.53	835.55	769.01	720.82	684.78	657.19	635.69	618.69	605.10	594.14
38000	3476.61	1889.78	1366.18	1108.33	956.71	858.13	789.80	740.30	703.29	674.95	652.87	635.41	621.45	610.20
39000	3568.10	1939.52	1402.14	1137.49	981.88	880.71	810.58	759.78	721.80	692.72	670.05	652.13	637.81	626.26
40000	3659.59	1989.25	1438.09	1166.66	1007.06	903.29	831.37	779.26	740.30	710.48	687.23	668.85	654.16	642.32
41000	3751.08	2038.98	1474.04	1195.83	1032.23	925.88	852.15	798.74	758.81	728.24	704.41	685.57	670.51	658.37
42000	3842.57	2088.71	1509.99	1224.99	1057.41	948.46	872.93	818.23	777.32	746.00	721.59	702.29	686.87	674.43
43000	3934.06	2138.44	1545.94	1254.16	1082.59	971.04	893.72	837.71	795.83	763.76	738.77	719.01	703.22	690.49
44000	4025.55	2188.17	1581.90	1283.33	1107.76	993.62	914.50	857.19	814.33	781.52	755.95	735.73	719.58	706.55
45000	4117.04	2237.90	1617.85	1312.49	1132.94	1016.21	935.29	876.67	832.84	799.29	773.13	752.46	735.93	722.60
46000	4208.53	2287.63	1653.80	1341.66	1158.12	1038.79	956.07	896.15	851.35	817.05	790.31	769.18	752.28	738.66
47000	4300.02	2337.36	1689.75	1370.83	1183.29	1061.37	976.85	915.63	869.86	834.81	807.49	785.90	768.64	754.72
48000	4391.51	2387.10	1725.70	1399.99	1208.47	1083.95	997.64	935.11	888.36	852.57	824.67	802.62	784.99	770.78
49000	4483.00	2436.83	1761.66	1429.16	1233.65	1106.54	1018.42	954.60	906.87	870.33	841.85	819.34	801.35	786.84
50000	4574.49	2486.56	1797.61	1458.32	1258.82	1129.12	1039.21	974.08	925.38	888.10	859.03	836.06	817.70	802.89
55000	5031.94	2735.21	1977.37	1604.16	1384.70	1242.03	1143.13	1071.48	1017.91	976.90	944.94	919.67	899.47	883.18
60000	5489.39	2983.87	2157.13	1749.99	1510.58	1354.94	1247.05	1168.89	1110.45	1065.71	1030.84	1003.27	981.24	963.47
65000	5946.84	3232.52	2336.89	1895.82	1636.47	1467.85	1350.97	1266.30	1202.99	1154.52	1116.74	1086.88	1063.01	1043.76
70000	6404.29	3481.18	2516.65	2041.65	1762.35	1580.76	1454.89	1363.71	1295.53	1243.33	1202.65	1170.48	1144.78	1124.05
75000	6861.74	3729.83	2696.41	2187.48	1888.23	1693.67	1558.81	1461.11	1388.06	1332.14	1288.55	1254.09	1226.55	1204.34
80000	7319.18	3978.49	2876.17	2333.32	2014.11	1806.58	1662.73	1558.52	1480.60	1420.95	1374.45	1337.69	1308.32	1284.63
85000	7776.63	4227.14	3055.93	2479.15	2139.99	1919.50	1766.65	1655.93	1573.14	1509.76	1460.35	1421.30	1390.09	1364.91
90000	8234.08	4475.80	3235.69	2624.98	2265.87	2032.41	1870.57	1753.33	1665.68	1598.57	1546.26	1504.91	1471.85	1445.20
95000	8691.53	4724.45	3415.45	2770.81	2391.76	2145.32	1974.49	1850.74	1758.21	1687.38	1632.16	1588.51	1553.62	1525.49
100000	9148.98	4973.11	3595.21	2916.64	2517.64	2258.23	2078.41	1948.15	1850.75	1776.19	1718.06	1672.12	1635.39	1605.78

TERM	15 Years	16 Years	17 Years	18 Years	19 Years	20 Years	21 Years	22 Years	23 Years	24 Years	25 Years	30 Years	35 Years	40 Years
AMOUNT														
5	.08	.08	.08	.08	.08	.08	.08	.08	.08	.08	.08	.08	.08	.08
10	.16	.16	.16	.16	.16	.16	.16	.15	.15	.15	.15	.15	.15	.15
15	.24	.24	.24	.23	.23	.23	.23	.23	.23	.23	.23	.23	.23	.23
25	.40	.40	.39	.39	.39	.38	.38	.38	.38	.38	.38	.37	.37	.37
50	.80	.79	.78	.77	.77	.76	.76	.75	.75	.75	.75	.74	.74	.74
75	1.19	1.18	1.16	1.15	1.15	1.14	1.13	1.13	1.13	1.12	1.12	1.11	1.11	1.11
100	1.59	1.57	1.55	1.54	1.53	1.52	1.51	1.50	1.50	1.49	1.49	1.48	1.47	1.47
200	3.17	3.13	3.10	3.07	3.05	3.03	3.02	3.00	2.99	2.98	2.98	2.95	2.94	2.94
300	4.75	4.69	4.64	4.60	4.57	4.54	4.52	4.50	4.49	4.47	4.46	4.43	4.41	4.41
400	6.33	6.25	6.19	6.14	6.09	6.06	6.03	6.00	5.98	5.96	5.95	5.90	5.88	5.88
500	7.91	7.82	7.73	7.67	7.61	7.57	7.53	7.50	7.47	7.45	7.43	7.38	7.35	7.35
600	9.50	9.38	9.28	9.20	9.14	9.08	9.04	9.00	8.97	8.94	8.92	8.85	8.82	8.81
700	11.08	10.94	10.83	10.73	10.66	10.59	10.54	10.50	10.46	10.43	10.40	10.33	10.29	10.28
800	12.66	12.50	12.37	12.27	12.18	12.11	12.05	12.00	11.95	11.92	11.89	11.80	11.76	11.75
900	14.24	14.06	13.92	13.80	13.70	13.62	13.55	13.49	13.45	13.41	13.37	13.28	13.23	13.22
1000	15.82	15.63	15.46	15.33	15.22	15.13	15.06	14.99	14.94	14.90	14.86	14.75	14.70	14.69
2000	31.64	31.25	30.92	30.66	30.44	30.26	30.11	29.98	29.88	29.79	29.71	29.49	29.40	29.37
3000	47.46	46.87	46.38	45.99	45.66	45.38	45.16	44.97	44.81	44.68	44.57	44.24	44.10	44.05
4000	63.27	62.49	61.84	61.31	60.87	60.51	60.21	59.96	59.75	59.57	59.42	58.98	58.80	58.73
5000	79.09	78.11	77.30	76.64	76.09	75.63	75.26	74.94	74.68	74.46	74.28	73.73	73.50	73.41
6000	94.91	93.73	92.76	91.97	91.31	90.76	90.31	89.93	89.62	89.35	89.13	88.47	88.20	88.09
7000	110.73	109.35	108.22	107.29	106.52	105.89	105.36	104.92	104.55	104.25	103.99	103.22	102.90	102.77
8000	126.54	124.97	123.68	122.62	121.74	121.01	120.41	119.91	119.49	119.14	118.84	117.96	117.60	117.45
9000	142.36	140.59	139.14	137.95	136.96	136.14	135.46	134.89	134.42	134.03	133.70	132.71	132.30	132.13
10000	158.18	156.21	154.60	153.27	152.17	151.26	150.51	149.88	149.36	148.92	148.55	147.45	147.00	146.81
11000	173.99	171.83	170.06	168.60	167.39	166.39	165.56	164.87	164.29	163.81	163.41	162.20	161.70	161.49
12000	189.81	187.45	185.52	183.93	182.61	181.52	180.61	179.86	179.23	178.70	178.26	176.94	176.39	176.17
13000	205.63	203.08	200.98	199.25	197.83	196.64	195.66	194.04	194.16	193.59	193.12	191.69	191.09	190.85
14000	221.45	218.70	216.44	214.58	213.04	211.77	210.71	209.83	209.10	208.49	207.97	206.43	205.79	205.53
15000	237.26	234.32	231.90	229.91	228.26	226.89	225.76	224.82	224.03	223.38	222.83	221.18	220.49	220.21
16000	253.08	249.94	247.36	245.23	243.48	242.02	240.81	239.81	238.97	238.27	237.68	235.92	235.19	234.89
17000	268.90	265.56	262.82	260.56	258.69	257.15	255.86	254.79	253.90	253.16	252.54	250.66	249.89	249.57
18000	284.72	281.18	278.28	275.89	273.91	272.27	270.91	269.78	268.84	268.05	267.39	265.41	264.59	264.25
19000	300.53	296.80	293.74	291.21	289.13	287.40	285.96	284.77	283.77	282.94	282.25	280.15	279.29	278.93
20000	316.35	312.42	309.20	306.54	304.34	302.52	301.01	299.76	298.71	297.83	297.10	294.90	293.99	293.61
21000	332.17	328.04	324.66	321.87	319.56	317.65	316.06	314.74	313.64	312.73	311.96	309.64	308.69	308.29
22000	347.98	343.66	340.12	337.19	334.78	332.78	331.11	329.73	328.58	327.62	326.81	324.39	323.39	322.97
23000	363.80	359.28	355.58	352.52	350.00	347.90	346.16	344.72	343.51	342.51	341.67	339.13	338.09	337.65
24000	379.62	374.90	371.03	367.85	365.21	363.03	361.22	359.71	358.45	357.40	356.52	353.88	352.78	352.33
25000	395.44	390.53	386.49	383.17	380.43	378.15	376.27	374.69	373.38	372.29	371.38	368.62	367.48	367.01
26000	411.25	406.15	401.95	398.50	395.65	393.28	391.32	389.68	388.32	387.18	386.23	383.37	382.18	381.69
27000	427.07	421.77	417.41	413.83	410.86	408.41	406.37	404.67	403.25	402.07	401.09	398.11	396.88	396.37
28000	442.89	437.39	432.87	429.15	426.08	423.53	421.42	419.66	418.19	416.97	415.94	412.86	411.58	411.05
29000	458.71	453.01	448.33	444.48	441.30	438.66	436.47	434.64	433.13	431.86	430.80	427.60	426.28	425.73
30000	474.52	468.63	463.79	459.81	456.51	453.78	451.52	449.63	448.06	446.75	445.65	442.35	440.98	440.41
31000	490.34	484.25	479.25	475.13	471.73	468.91	466.57	464.62	463.00	461.64	460.51	457.09	455.68	455.09
32000	506.16	499.87	494.71	490.46	486.95	484.04	481.62	479.61	477.93	476.53	475.36	471.84	470.38	469.77
33000	521.97	515.49	510.17	505.79	502.16	499.16	496.67	494.59	492.87	491.42	490.22	486.58	485.08	484.45
34000	537.79	531.11	525.63	521.11	517.38	514.29	511.72	509.58	507.80	506.31	505.07	501.32	499.78	499.13
35000	553.61	546.73	541.09	536.44	532.60	529.41	526.77	524.57	522.74	521.21	519.93	516.07	514.47	513.81
36000	569.43	562.35	556.55	551.77	547.82	544.54	541.82	539.56	537.67	536.10	534.78	530.81	529.17	528.49
37000	585.24	577.97	572.01	567.09	563.03	559.67	556.87	554.54	552.61	550.99	549.64	545.56	543.87	543.17
38000	601.06	593.60	587.47	582.42	578.25	574.79	571.92	569.53	567.54	565.88	564.49	560.30	558.57	557.85
39000	616.88	609.22	602.93	597.75	593.47	589.92	586.97	584.52	582.48	580.77	579.35	575.05	573.27	572.53
40000	632.70	624.84	618.39	613.07	608.68	605.04	602.02	599.51	597.41	595.66	594.20	589.79	587.97	587.21
41000	648.51	640.46	633.85	628.40	623.90	620.17	617.07	614.49	612.35	610.56	609.06	604.54	602.67	601.89
42000	664.33	656.08	649.31	643.73	639.12	635.30	632.12	629.48	627.28	625.45	623.91	619.28	617.37	616.57
43000	680.15	671.70	664.77	659.06	654.33	650.42	647.17	644.47	642.22	640.34	638.77	634.03	632.07	631.25
44000	695.96	687.32	680.23	674.38	669.55	665.55	662.22	659.46	657.15	655.23	653.62	648.77	646.77	645.93
45000	711.78	702.94	695.69	689.71	684.77	680.67	677.27	674.45	672.09	670.12	668.48	663.52	661.47	660.61
46000	727.60	718.56	711.15	705.04	699.99	695.80	692.32	689.43	687.02	685.01	683.33	678.26	676.17	675.29
47000	743.42	734.18	726.61	720.36	715.20	710.93	707.37	704.42	701.96	699.90	698.19	693.01	690.86	689.97
48000	759.23	749.80	742.06	735.69	730.42	726.05	722.43	719.41	716.89	714.80	713.04	707.75	705.56	704.65
49000	775.05	765.42	757.52	751.02	745.64	741.18	737.48	734.40	731.83	729.69	727.90	722.49	720.26	719.33
50000	790.87	781.05	772.98	766.34	760.85	756.30	752.53	749.38	746.76	744.58	742.75	737.24	734.96	734.02
55000	869.95	859.15	850.28	842.98	836.94	831.93	827.78	824.32	821.44	819.04	817.03	810.96	808.46	807.42
60000	949.04	937.25	927.58	919.61	913.02	907.56	903.03	899.26	896.12	893.49	891.30	884.69	881.95	880.82
65000	1028.13	1015.36	1004.88	996.24	989.11	983.19	978.28	974.20	970.79	967.95	965.58	958.41	955.45	954.22
70000	1107.21	1093.46	1082.18	1072.88	1065.19	1058.82	1053.53	1049.13	1045.47	1042.41	1039.85	1032.13	1028.94	1027.62
75000	1186.30	1171.57	1159.47	1149.51	1141.28	1134.45	1128.79	1124.07	1120.14	1116.87	1114.13	1105.86	1102.44	1101.02
80000	1265.39	1249.67	1236.77	1226.14	1217.36	1210.08	1204.04	1199.01	1194.82	1191.32	1188.40	1179.58	1175.94	1174.42
85000	1344.47	1327.77	1314.07	1302.78	1293.45	1285.71	1279.29	1273.95	1269.49	1265.78	1262.68	1253.30	1249.43	1247.82
90000	1423.56	1405.88	1391.37	1379.41	1369.53	1361.34	1354.54	1348.89	1344.17	1340.24	1336.95	1327.03	1322.93	1321.22
95000	1502.64	1483.98	1468.67	1456.05	1445.62	1436.97	1429.80	1423.82	1418.85	1414.69	1411.23	1400.75	1396.42	1394.62
100000	1581.73	1562.09	1545.96	1532.68	1521.70	1512.60	1505.05	1498.76	1493.52	1489.15	1485.50	1474.47	1469.92	1468.03

MONTHLY PAYMENT
REQUIRED TO AMORTIZE A LOAN

TERM AMOUNT	1 Year	2 Years	3 Years	4 Years	5 Years	6 Years	7 Years	8 Years	9 Years	10 Years	11 Years	12 Years	13 Years	14 Years
5	.46	.25	.18	.15	.13	.12	.11	.10	.10	.09	.09	.09	.09	.09
10	.92	.50	.36	.30	.26	.23	.21	.20	.19	.18	.18	.17	.17	.17
15	1.38	.75	.54	.44	.38	.34	.32	.30	.28	.27	.26	.26	.25	.25
25	2.29	1.25	.90	.73	.63	.57	.52	.49	.47	.45	.43	.42	.41	.41
50	4.58	2.49	1.80	1.46	1.26	1.13	1.04	.98	.93	.89	.86	.84	.82	.81
75	6.87	3.74	2.70	2.19	1.89	1.70	1.56	1.47	1.39	1.34	1.29	1.26	1.23	1.21
100	9.16	4.98	3.60	2.92	2.52	2.26	2.08	1.95	1.86	1.78	1.72	1.68	1.64	1.61
200	18.31	9.95	7.20	5.84	5.04	4.52	4.16	3.90	3.71	3.56	3.44	3.35	3.28	3.22
300	27.46	14.93	10.79	8.76	7.56	6.78	6.24	5.85	5.56	5.34	5.16	5.03	4.92	4.83
400	36.61	19.90	14.39	11.68	10.08	9.04	8.32	7.80	7.41	7.12	6.88	6.70	6.55	6.44
500	45.76	24.88	17.99	14.59	12.60	11.30	10.40	9.75	9.27	8.89	8.60	8.37	8.19	8.04
600	54.91	29.85	21.58	17.51	15.12	13.56	12.48	11.70	11.12	10.67	10.32	10.05	9.83	9.65
700	64.06	34.83	25.18	20.43	17.64	15.82	14.56	13.65	12.97	12.45	12.04	11.72	11.46	11.26
800	73.21	39.80	28.78	23.35	20.16	18.08	16.64	15.60	14.82	14.23	13.76	13.40	13.10	12.87
900	82.36	44.77	32.37	26.27	22.68	20.34	18.72	17.55	16.68	16.01	15.48	15.07	14.74	14.47
1000	91.51	49.75	35.97	29.18	25.19	22.60	20.80	19.50	18.53	17.78	17.20	16.74	16.38	16.08
2000	183.01	99.49	71.93	58.36	50.38	45.20	41.60	39.00	37.05	35.56	34.40	33.48	32.75	32.16
3000	274.51	149.23	107.90	87.54	75.57	67.79	62.40	58.49	55.57	53.34	51.60	50.22	49.12	48.23
4000	366.01	198.98	143.86	116.72	100.76	90.39	83.20	77.99	74.10	71.12	68.79	66.96	65.49	64.31
5000	457.51	248.72	179.83	145.90	125.95	112.99	104.00	97.49	92.62	88.89	85.99	83.69	81.86	80.38
6000	549.01	298.46	215.79	175.08	151.14	135.58	124.80	116.98	111.14	106.67	103.19	100.43	98.23	96.46
7000	640.52	348.21	251.76	204.26	176.33	158.18	145.60	136.48	129.67	124.45	120.38	117.17	114.60	112.53
8000	732.02	397.95	287.72	233.44	201.52	180.78	166.39	155.98	148.19	142.23	137.58	133.91	130.97	128.61
9000	823.52	447.69	323.69	262.62	226.71	203.37	187.19	175.47	166.71	160.01	154.78	150.65	147.34	144.68
10000	915.02	497.44	359.65	291.80	251.90	225.97	207.99	194.97	185.23	177.78	171.98	167.38	163.72	160.76
11000	1006.52	547.18	395.62	320.98	277.09	248.56	228.79	214.47	203.76	195.56	189.17	184.12	180.09	176.83
12000	1098.02	596.92	431.58	350.16	302.28	271.16	249.59	233.96	222.28	213.34	206.37	200.86	196.46	192.91
13000	1189.53	646.67	467.54	379.34	327.47	293.76	270.39	253.46	240.80	231.12	223.57	217.60	212.83	208.98
14000	1281.03	696.41	503.51	408.52	352.66	316.35	291.19	272.96	259.33	248.89	240.76	234.34	229.20	225.06
15000	1372.53	746.15	539.47	437.70	377.85	338.95	311.98	292.45	277.85	266.67	257.96	251.07	245.57	241.13
16000	1464.03	795.89	575.44	466.88	403.04	361.55	332.78	311.95	296.37	284.45	275.16	267.81	261.94	257.21
17000	1555.53	845.64	611.40	496.05	428.23	384.14	353.58	331.45	314.90	302.23	292.35	284.55	278.31	273.29
18000	1647.03	895.38	647.37	525.23	453.42	406.74	374.38	350.94	333.42	320.01	309.55	301.29	294.68	289.36
19000	1738.54	945.12	683.33	554.41	478.61	429.33	395.18	370.44	351.94	337.78	326.75	318.03	311.06	305.44
20000	1830.04	994.87	719.30	583.59	503.80	451.93	415.98	389.94	370.46	355.56	343.95	334.76	327.43	321.51
21000	1921.54	1044.61	755.26	612.77	528.99	474.53	436.78	409.43	388.99	373.34	361.14	351.50	343.80	337.59
22000	2013.04	1094.35	791.23	641.95	554.18	497.12	457.57	428.93	407.51	391.12	378.34	368.24	360.17	353.66
23000	2104.54	1144.10	827.19	671.13	579.37	519.72	478.37	448.42	426.03	408.89	395.54	384.98	376.54	369.74
24000	2196.04	1193.84	863.15	700.31	604.56	542.32	499.17	467.92	444.56	426.67	412.73	401.72	392.91	385.81
25000	2287.55	1243.58	899.12	729.49	629.75	564.91	519.97	487.42	463.08	444.45	429.93	418.45	409.28	401.89
26000	2379.05	1293.33	935.08	758.67	654.94	587.51	540.77	506.91	481.60	462.23	447.13	435.19	425.65	417.96
27000	2470.55	1343.07	971.05	787.85	680.13	610.11	561.57	526.41	500.13	480.01	464.32	451.93	442.02	434.04
28000	2562.05	1392.81	1007.01	817.03	705.32	632.70	582.37	545.91	518.65	497.78	481.52	468.67	458.40	450.11
29000	2653.55	1442.55	1042.98	846.21	730.51	655.30	603.16	565.40	537.17	515.56	498.72	485.41	474.77	466.19
30000	2745.05	1492.30	1078.94	875.39	755.70	677.89	623.96	584.90	555.69	533.34	515.92	502.14	491.14	482.26
31000	2836.56	1542.04	1114.91	904.57	780.89	700.49	644.76	604.40	574.22	551.12	533.11	518.88	507.51	498.34
32000	2928.06	1591.78	1150.87	933.75	806.08	723.09	665.56	623.89	592.74	568.89	550.31	535.62	523.88	514.42
33000	3019.56	1641.53	1186.84	962.93	831.27	745.68	686.36	643.39	611.26	586.67	567.51	552.36	540.25	530.49
34000	3111.06	1691.27	1222.80	992.10	856.46	768.28	707.16	662.89	629.79	604.45	584.70	569.10	556.62	546.57
35000	3202.56	1741.01	1258.76	1021.28	881.65	790.88	727.96	682.38	648.31	622.23	601.90	585.83	572.99	562.64
36000	3294.06	1790.76	1294.73	1050.46	906.84	813.47	748.76	701.88	666.83	640.01	619.10	602.57	589.36	578.72
37000	3385.56	1840.50	1330.69	1079.64	932.03	836.07	769.55	721.38	685.36	657.78	636.29	619.31	605.74	594.79
38000	3477.07	1890.24	1366.66	1108.82	957.22	858.66	790.35	740.87	703.88	675.56	653.49	636.05	622.11	610.87
39000	3568.57	1939.99	1402.62	1138.00	982.41	881.26	811.15	760.37	722.40	693.34	670.69	652.79	638.48	626.94
40000	3660.07	1989.73	1438.59	1167.18	1007.60	903.86	831.95	779.87	740.92	711.12	687.89	669.52	654.85	643.02
41000	3751.57	2039.47	1474.55	1196.36	1032.79	926.45	852.75	799.36	759.45	728.89	705.08	686.26	671.22	659.09
42000	3843.07	2089.22	1510.52	1225.54	1057.98	949.05	873.55	818.86	777.97	746.67	722.28	703.00	687.59	675.17
43000	3934.57	2138.96	1546.48	1254.72	1083.17	971.65	894.35	838.35	796.49	764.45	739.48	719.74	703.96	691.24
44000	4026.08	2188.70	1582.45	1283.90	1108.36	994.24	915.14	857.85	815.02	782.23	756.67	736.47	720.33	707.32
45000	4117.58	2238.44	1618.41	1313.08	1133.55	1016.84	935.94	877.35	833.54	800.01	773.87	753.21	736.70	723.39
46000	4209.08	2288.19	1654.37	1342.26	1158.74	1039.44	956.74	896.84	852.06	817.78	791.07	769.95	753.08	739.47
47000	4300.58	2337.93	1690.34	1371.44	1183.93	1062.03	977.54	916.34	870.59	835.56	808.26	786.69	769.45	755.54
48000	4392.08	2387.67	1726.30	1400.62	1209.12	1084.63	998.34	935.84	889.11	853.34	825.46	803.43	785.82	771.62
49000	4483.58	2437.42	1762.27	1429.80	1234.31	1107.22	1019.14	955.33	907.63	871.12	842.66	820.16	802.19	787.70
50000	4575.09	2487.16	1798.23	1458.98	1259.50	1129.82	1039.94	974.83	926.15	888.90	859.86	836.90	818.56	803.77
55000	5032.59	2735.88	1978.06	1604.87	1385.45	1242.80	1143.93	1072.31	1018.77	977.78	945.84	920.59	900.42	884.15
60000	5490.10	2984.59	2157.88	1750.77	1511.40	1355.78	1247.92	1169.80	1111.38	1066.67	1031.83	1004.28	982.27	964.52
65000	5947.61	3233.31	2337.70	1896.67	1637.35	1468.77	1351.91	1267.28	1204.00	1155.56	1117.81	1087.97	1064.13	1044.90
70000	6405.12	3482.02	2517.52	2042.56	1763.30	1581.75	1455.91	1364.76	1296.61	1244.45	1203.80	1171.66	1145.98	1125.28
75000	6862.63	3730.74	2697.35	2188.46	1889.25	1694.73	1559.90	1462.24	1389.23	1333.34	1289.78	1255.35	1227.84	1205.65
80000	7320.13	3979.45	2877.17	2334.36	2015.19	1807.71	1663.89	1559.73	1481.84	1422.23	1375.77	1339.04	1309.69	1286.03
85000	7777.64	4228.17	3056.99	2480.25	2141.14	1920.69	1767.89	1657.21	1574.46	1511.12	1461.75	1422.73	1391.55	1366.41
90000	8235.15	4476.88	3236.82	2626.15	2267.09	2033.67	1871.88	1754.69	1667.07	1600.01	1547.74	1506.42	1473.40	1446.78
95000	8692.66	4725.60	3416.64	2772.05	2393.04	2146.65	1975.87	1852.17	1759.69	1688.90	1633.72	1590.11	1555.26	1527.16
100000	9150.17	4974.31	3596.46	2917.95	2518.99	2259.64	2079.87	1949.66	1852.30	1777.79	1719.71	1673.80	1637.11	1607.54

MONTHLY PAYMENT
REQUIRED TO AMORTIZE A LOAN

17.625%

TERM AMOUNT	15 Years	16 Years	17 Years	18 Years	19 Years	20 Years	21 Years	22 Years	23 Years	24 Years	25 Years	30 Years	35 Years	40 Years
5	.08	.08	.08	.08	.08	.08	.08	.08	.08	.08	.08	.08	.08	.08
10	.16	.16	.16	.16	.16	.16	.16	.16	.15	.15	.15	.15	.15	.15
15	.24	.24	.24	.24	.23	.23	.23	.23	.23	.23	.23	.23	.23	.23
25	.40	.40	.39	.39	.39	.38	.38	.38	.38	.38	.38	.37	.37	.37
50	.80	.79	.78	.77	.77	.76	.76	.76	.75	.75	.75	.74	.74	.74
75	1.19	1.18	1.17	1.16	1.15	1.14	1.14	1.13	1.13	1.12	1.12	1.11	1.11	1.11
100	1.59	1.57	1.55	1.54	1.53	1.52	1.51	1.51	1.50	1.50	1.49	1.48	1.48	1.48
200	3.17	3.13	3.10	3.07	3.05	3.03	3.02	3.01	3.00	2.99	2.98	2.96	2.95	2.95
300	4.76	4.70	4.65	4.61	4.58	4.55	4.53	4.51	4.49	4.48	4.47	4.43	4.42	4.42
400	6.34	6.26	6.20	6.14	6.10	6.06	6.03	6.01	5.99	5.97	5.95	5.91	5.89	5.89
500	7.92	7.82	7.74	7.68	7.62	7.58	7.54	7.51	7.48	7.46	7.44	7.39	7.36	7.36
600	9.51	9.39	9.29	9.21	9.15	9.09	9.05	9.01	8.98	8.95	8.93	8.86	8.84	8.83
700	11.09	10.95	10.84	10.75	10.67	10.61	10.55	10.51	10.47	10.44	10.42	10.34	10.31	10.30
800	12.67	12.52	12.39	12.28	12.19	12.12	12.06	12.01	11.97	11.93	11.90	11.82	11.78	11.77
900	14.26	14.08	13.94	13.82	13.72	13.64	13.57	13.51	13.46	13.43	13.39	13.29	13.25	13.24
1000	15.84	15.64	15.48	15.35	15.24	15.15	15.07	15.01	14.96	14.92	14.88	14.77	14.72	14.71
2000	31.68	31.28	30.96	30.70	30.48	30.30	30.14	30.02	29.91	29.83	29.75	29.54	29.44	29.41
3000	47.51	46.92	46.44	46.04	45.71	45.44	45.21	45.03	44.87	44.74	44.63	44.30	44.16	44.11
4000	63.35	62.56	61.92	61.39	60.95	60.59	60.28	60.03	59.82	59.65	59.50	59.07	58.88	58.81
5000	79.18	78.20	77.40	76.73	76.18	75.73	75.35	75.04	74.78	74.56	74.38	73.83	73.60	73.51
6000	95.02	93.84	92.87	92.08	91.42	90.88	90.42	90.05	89.73	89.47	89.25	88.60	88.32	88.21
7000	110.85	109.48	108.35	107.42	106.66	106.02	105.49	105.05	104.69	104.38	104.13	103.36	103.04	102.91
8000	126.69	125.12	123.83	122.77	121.89	121.17	120.56	120.06	119.64	119.30	119.00	118.13	117.76	117.61
9000	142.52	140.76	139.31	138.11	137.13	136.31	135.63	135.07	134.60	134.21	133.88	132.89	132.48	132.31
10000	158.36	156.39	154.79	153.46	152.36	151.46	150.70	150.08	149.55	149.12	148.75	147.66	147.20	147.01
11000	174.19	172.03	170.26	168.81	167.60	166.60	165.77	165.08	164.51	164.03	163.63	162.42	161.92	161.72
12000	190.03	187.67	185.74	184.15	182.84	181.75	180.84	180.09	179.46	178.94	178.50	177.19	176.64	176.42
13000	205.86	203.31	201.22	199.50	198.07	196.89	195.91	195.10	194.42	193.85	193.38	191.95	191.36	191.12
14000	221.70	218.95	216.70	214.84	213.31	212.04	210.98	210.10	209.37	208.76	208.25	206.72	206.08	205.82
15000	237.53	234.59	232.18	230.19	228.54	227.18	226.05	225.11	224.33	223.67	223.13	221.48	220.80	220.52
16000	253.37	250.23	247.65	245.53	243.78	242.33	241.12	240.12	239.28	238.59	238.00	236.25	235.52	235.22
17000	269.20	265.87	263.13	260.88	259.02	257.47	256.19	255.13	254.24	253.50	252.88	251.01	250.24	249.92
18000	285.04	281.51	278.61	276.22	272.25	272.62	271.26	270.13	269.19	268.41	267.75	265.78	264.96	264.62
19000	300.87	297.15	294.09	291.57	289.49	287.76	286.33	285.14	284.15	283.32	282.63	280.54	279.68	279.32
20000	316.71	312.78	309.57	306.91	304.72	302.91	301.40	300.15	299.10	298.23	297.50	295.31	294.40	294.02
21000	332.54	328.42	325.04	322.26	319.96	318.05	316.47	315.15	314.06	313.14	312.38	310.07	309.12	308.72
22000	348.38	344.06	340.52	337.61	335.19	333.20	331.54	330.16	329.01	328.05	327.25	324.84	323.84	323.43
23000	364.21	359.70	356.00	352.95	350.43	348.34	346.61	345.17	343.97	342.96	342.13	339.60	338.56	338.13
24000	380.05	375.34	371.48	368.30	365.67	363.49	361.68	360.17	358.92	357.88	357.00	354.37	353.28	352.03
25000	395.88	390.98	386.96	383.64	380.90	378.63	376.75	375.18	373.88	372.79	371.88	369.13	368.00	367.53
26000	411.72	406.62	402.43	398.99	396.14	393.78	391.82	390.19	388.83	387.70	386.75	383.90	382.72	382.23
27000	427.55	422.26	417.91	414.33	411.37	408.92	406.89	405.20	403.79	402.61	401.63	398.66	397.44	396.93
28000	443.39	437.90	433.39	429.68	426.61	424.07	421.96	420.20	418.74	417.52	416.50	413.43	412.16	411.63
29000	459.22	453.54	448.87	445.02	441.85	439.21	437.03	435.21	433.70	432.43	431.38	428.19	426.88	426.33
30000	475.06	469.17	464.35	460.37	457.08	454.36	452.10	450.22	448.65	447.34	446.25	442.96	441.60	441.03
31000	490.89	484.81	479.82	475.71	472.32	469.50	467.17	465.22	463.61	462.25	461.13	457.72	456.32	455.73
32000	506.73	500.45	495.30	491.06	487.55	484.65	482.24	480.23	478.56	477.17	476.00	472.49	471.04	470.43
33000	522.56	516.09	510.78	506.41	502.79	499.79	497.31	495.24	493.51	492.08	490.88	487.25	485.76	485.14
34000	538.40	531.73	526.26	521.75	518.03	514.94	512.38	510.25	508.47	506.99	505.75	502.02	500.48	499.84
35000	554.23	547.37	541.74	537.10	533.26	530.08	527.45	525.25	523.42	521.90	520.63	516.78	515.20	514.54
36000	570.07	563.01	557.21	552.44	548.50	545.23	542.52	540.26	538.38	536.81	535.50	531.55	529.92	529.24
37000	585.91	578.65	572.69	567.79	563.73	560.37	557.59	555.27	553.33	551.72	550.38	546.31	544.64	543.94
38000	601.74	594.29	588.17	583.13	578.97	575.52	572.66	570.27	568.29	566.63	565.25	561.08	559.35	558.64
39000	617.58	609.93	603.65	598.48	594.21	590.67	587.73	585.28	583.24	581.54	580.13	575.84	574.07	573.34
40000	633.41	625.56	619.13	613.82	609.44	605.81	602.80	600.29	598.20	596.46	595.00	590.61	588.79	588.04
41000	649.25	641.20	634.60	629.17	624.68	620.96	617.87	615.29	613.15	611.37	609.88	605.37	603.51	602.74
42000	665.08	656.84	650.08	644.51	639.91	636.10	632.94	630.30	628.11	626.28	624.75	620.14	618.23	617.44
43000	680.92	672.48	665.56	659.86	655.15	651.25	648.00	645.31	643.06	641.19	639.63	634.90	632.95	632.14
44000	696.75	688.12	681.04	675.21	669.38	666.39	663.07	660.32	658.02	656.10	654.50	649.67	647.67	646.85
45000	712.59	703.76	696.52	690.55	685.62	681.54	678.14	675.32	672.97	671.01	669.38	664.43	662.39	661.55
46000	728.42	719.40	711.99	705.90	700.86	696.68	693.21	690.33	687.93	685.92	684.25	679.20	677.11	676.25
47000	744.26	735.04	727.47	721.24	716.09	711.83	708.28	705.34	702.88	700.83	699.13	693.96	691.83	690.95
48000	760.09	750.68	742.95	736.59	731.33	726.97	723.35	720.34	717.84	715.75	714.00	708.73	706.55	705.65
49000	775.93	766.32	758.43	751.93	746.56	742.12	738.42	735.35	732.79	730.66	728.87	723.49	721.27	720.35
50000	791.76	781.95	773.91	767.28	761.80	757.26	753.49	750.36	747.75	745.57	743.75	738.26	735.99	735.05
55000	870.94	860.15	851.30	844.01	837.98	832.99	828.84	825.39	822.52	820.13	818.12	812.08	809.59	808.56
60000	950.11	938.34	928.69	920.73	914.16	908.71	904.19	900.43	897.30	894.68	892.50	885.91	883.19	882.06
65000	1029.29	1016.54	1006.08	997.46	990.34	984.44	979.54	975.46	972.07	969.24	966.87	959.73	956.79	955.56
70000	1108.46	1094.73	1083.47	1074.19	1066.52	1060.16	1054.89	1050.50	1046.84	1043.79	1041.25	1033.56	1030.39	1029.07
75000	1187.64	1172.93	1160.86	1150.91	1142.70	1135.89	1130.24	1125.54	1121.62	1118.35	1115.62	1107.38	1103.99	1102.57
80000	1266.82	1251.12	1238.25	1227.64	1218.88	1211.62	1205.59	1200.57	1196.39	1192.91	1190.00	1181.21	1177.58	1176.08
85000	1345.99	1329.32	1315.64	1304.37	1295.06	1287.34	1280.94	1275.61	1271.17	1267.46	1264.37	1255.03	1251.18	1249.58
90000	1425.17	1407.51	1393.03	1381.10	1371.24	1363.07	1356.28	1350.64	1345.94	1342.02	1338.75	1328.86	1324.78	1323.09
95000	1504.34	1485.71	1470.42	1457.82	1447.42	1438.79	1431.63	1425.68	1420.71	1416.58	1413.12	1402.69	1398.38	1396.59
100000	1583.52	1563.90	1547.81	1534.55	1523.60	1514.52	1506.98	1500.71	1495.49	1491.13	1487.49	1476.51	1471.98	1470.10

17.700%

MONTHLY PAYMENT
REQUIRED TO AMORTIZE A LOAN

TERM AMOUNT	1 Year	2 Years	3 Years	4 Years	5 Years	6 Years	7 Years	8 Years	9 Years	10 Years	11 Years	12 Years	13 Years	14 Years
5	.46	.25	.19	.15	.13	.12	.11	.10	.10	.09	.09	.09	.09	.09
10	.92	.50	.37	.30	.26	.23	.21	.20	.19	.18	.18	.17	.17	.17
15	1.38	.75	.55	.44	.38	.34	.32	.30	.28	.27	.26	.26	.25	.25
25	2.29	1.25	.91	.74	.64	.57	.53	.49	.47	.45	.44	.42	.42	.41
50	4.58	2.49	1.81	1.47	1.27	1.14	1.05	.98	.93	.90	.87	.84	.83	.81
75	6.87	3.74	2.71	2.20	1.90	1.70	1.57	1.47	1.40	1.34	1.30	1.26	1.24	1.21
100	9.16	4.98	3.61	2.93	2.53	2.27	2.09	1.96	1.86	1.79	1.73	1.68	1.65	1.62
200	18.31	9.96	7.21	5.85	5.05	4.53	4.17	3.91	3.72	3.57	3.45	3.36	3.29	3.23
300	27.47	14.94	10.81	8.77	7.57	6.80	6.26	5.87	5.58	5.35	5.18	5.04	4.93	4.84
400	36.62	19.92	14.41	11.69	10.10	9.06	8.34	7.82	7.43	7.14	6.90	6.72	6.57	6.46
500	45.77	24.89	18.01	14.61	12.62	11.32	10.43	9.78	9.29	8.92	8.63	8.40	8.22	8.07
600	54.93	29.87	21.61	17.54	15.14	13.59	12.51	11.73	11.15	10.70	10.35	10.08	9.86	9.68
700	64.08	34.85	25.21	20.46	17.67	15.85	14.59	13.68	13.00	12.48	12.08	11.76	11.50	11.29
800	73.23	39.83	28.81	23.38	20.19	18.12	16.68	15.64	14.86	14.27	13.80	13.44	13.14	12.91
900	82.39	44.81	32.41	26.30	22.71	20.38	18.76	17.59	16.72	16.05	15.53	15.11	14.79	14.52
1000	91.54	49.78	36.01	29.22	25.24	22.64	20.85	19.55	18.57	17.83	17.25	16.79	16.43	16.13
2000	183.08	99.56	72.01	58.44	50.47	45.28	41.69	39.09	37.14	35.66	34.50	33.58	32.85	32.26
3000	274.62	149.34	108.01	87.66	75.70	67.92	62.53	58.63	55.71	53.48	51.74	50.37	49.27	48.39
4000	366.15	199.12	144.01	116.88	100.93	90.56	83.37	78.17	74.28	71.31	68.99	67.16	65.70	64.52
5000	457.69	248.90	180.02	146.10	126.16	113.20	104.22	97.71	92.85	89.13	86.24	83.95	82.12	80.65
6000	549.23	298.68	216.02	175.32	151.39	135.84	125.06	117.26	111.42	106.96	103.48	100.74	98.54	96.77
7000	640.77	348.46	252.02	204.53	176.62	158.47	145.90	136.80	129.99	124.79	120.73	117.52	114.96	112.90
8000	732.30	398.24	288.02	233.75	201.85	181.11	166.74	156.34	148.56	142.61	137.98	134.31	131.39	129.03
9000	823.84	448.02	324.02	262.97	227.08	203.75	187.59	175.88	167.13	160.44	155.22	151.10	147.81	145.16
10000	915.38	497.80	360.03	292.19	252.31	226.39	208.43	195.42	185.70	178.26	172.47	167.89	164.23	161.29
11000	1006.92	547.58	396.03	321.41	277.54	249.03	229.27	214.96	204.27	196.09	189.71	184.68	180.66	177.41
12000	1098.45	597.36	432.03	350.63	302.77	271.67	250.11	234.51	222.84	213.91	206.96	201.47	197.08	193.54
13000	1189.99	647.14	468.03	379.85	328.00	294.31	270.96	254.05	241.41	231.74	224.21	218.26	213.50	209.67
14000	1281.53	696.91	504.03	409.06	353.23	316.94	291.80	273.59	259.98	249.57	241.45	235.04	229.92	225.80
15000	1373.07	746.69	540.04	438.28	378.46	339.58	312.64	293.13	278.55	267.39	258.70	251.83	246.35	241.93
16000	1464.60	796.47	576.04	467.50	403.69	362.22	333.48	312.67	297.12	285.22	275.95	268.62	262.77	258.05
17000	1556.14	846.25	612.04	496.72	428.92	384.86	354.33	332.21	315.69	303.04	293.19	285.41	279.19	274.18
18000	1647.68	896.03	648.04	525.94	454.15	407.50	375.17	351.76	334.26	320.87	310.44	302.20	295.61	290.31
19000	1739.21	945.81	684.04	555.16	479.38	430.14	396.01	371.30	352.83	338.70	327.69	318.99	312.04	306.44
20000	1830.75	995.59	720.05	584.37	504.62	452.78	416.85	390.84	371.40	356.52	344.93	335.77	328.46	322.57
21000	1922.29	1045.37	756.05	613.59	529.85	475.41	437.69	410.38	389.97	374.35	362.18	352.56	344.88	338.69
22000	2013.83	1095.15	792.05	642.81	555.08	498.05	458.54	429.92	408.54	392.17	379.42	369.35	361.31	354.82
23000	2105.36	1144.93	828.05	672.03	580.31	520.69	479.38	449.47	427.11	410.00	396.67	386.14	377.73	370.95
24000	2196.90	1194.71	864.05	701.25	605.54	543.33	500.22	469.01	445.68	427.82	413.92	402.93	394.15	387.08
25000	2288.44	1244.49	900.06	730.47	630.77	565.97	521.06	488.55	464.25	445.65	431.16	419.72	410.57	403.21
26000	2379.97	1294.27	936.06	759.69	656.00	588.61	541.91	508.09	482.82	463.48	448.41	436.51	427.00	419.33
27000	2471.51	1344.05	972.06	788.90	681.23	611.25	562.75	527.63	501.39	481.30	465.66	453.29	443.42	435.46
28000	2563.05	1393.82	1008.06	818.12	706.46	633.88	583.59	547.17	519.96	499.13	482.90	470.08	459.84	451.59
29000	2654.59	1443.60	1044.07	847.34	731.69	656.52	604.43	566.72	538.53	516.95	500.15	486.87	476.26	467.72
30000	2746.12	1493.38	1080.07	876.56	756.92	679.16	625.28	586.26	557.10	534.78	517.39	503.66	492.69	483.85
31000	2837.66	1543.16	1116.07	905.78	782.15	701.80	646.12	605.80	575.66	552.61	534.64	520.45	509.11	499.97
32000	2929.20	1592.94	1152.07	935.00	807.38	724.44	666.96	625.34	594.23	570.43	551.89	537.24	525.53	516.10
33000	3020.74	1642.72	1188.07	964.21	832.61	747.08	687.80	644.88	612.80	588.26	569.13	554.02	541.96	532.23
34000	3112.27	1692.50	1224.08	993.43	857.84	769.71	708.65	664.42	631.37	606.08	586.38	570.81	558.38	548.36
35000	3203.81	1742.28	1260.08	1022.65	883.07	792.35	729.49	683.97	649.94	623.91	603.63	587.60	574.80	564.49
36000	3295.35	1792.06	1296.08	1051.87	908.30	814.99	750.33	703.51	668.51	641.73	620.87	604.39	591.22	580.61
37000	3386.88	1841.84	1332.08	1081.09	933.53	837.63	771.17	723.05	687.08	659.56	638.12	621.18	607.65	596.74
38000	3478.42	1891.62	1368.08	1110.31	958.76	860.27	792.01	742.59	705.65	677.39	655.37	637.97	624.07	612.87
39000	3569.96	1941.40	1404.09	1139.53	983.99	882.91	812.86	762.13	724.22	695.21	672.61	654.76	640.49	629.00
40000	3661.50	1991.18	1440.09	1168.74	1009.23	905.55	833.70	781.67	742.79	713.04	689.86	671.54	656.92	645.13
41000	3753.03	2040.96	1476.09	1197.96	1034.46	928.18	854.54	801.22	761.36	730.86	707.10	688.33	673.34	661.25
42000	3844.57	2090.73	1512.09	1227.18	1059.69	950.82	875.38	820.76	779.93	748.69	724.35	705.12	689.76	677.38
43000	3936.11	2140.51	1548.09	1256.40	1084.92	973.46	896.23	840.30	798.50	766.52	741.60	721.91	706.18	693.51
44000	4027.65	2190.29	1584.10	1285.62	1110.15	996.10	917.07	859.84	817.07	784.34	758.84	738.70	722.61	709.64
45000	4119.18	2240.07	1620.10	1314.84	1135.38	1018.74	937.91	879.38	835.64	802.17	776.09	755.49	739.03	725.77
46000	4210.72	2289.85	1656.10	1344.05	1160.61	1041.38	958.75	898.93	854.21	819.99	793.34	772.28	755.45	741.89
47000	4302.26	2339.63	1692.10	1373.27	1185.84	1064.02	979.60	918.47	872.78	837.82	810.58	789.06	771.87	758.02
48000	4393.79	2389.41	1728.10	1402.49	1211.07	1086.65	1000.44	938.01	891.35	855.64	827.83	805.85	788.30	774.15
49000	4485.33	2439.19	1764.11	1431.71	1236.30	1109.29	1021.28	957.55	909.92	873.47	845.07	822.64	804.72	790.28
50000	4576.87	2488.97	1800.11	1460.93	1261.53	1131.93	1042.12	977.09	928.49	891.30	862.32	839.43	821.14	806.41
55000	5034.56	2737.86	1980.12	1607.02	1387.68	1245.12	1146.34	1074.80	1021.34	980.43	948.55	923.37	903.26	887.05
60000	5492.24	2986.76	2160.13	1753.11	1513.84	1358.32	1250.55	1172.51	1114.19	1069.55	1034.78	1007.31	985.37	967.69
65000	5949.93	3235.66	2340.14	1899.21	1639.99	1471.51	1354.76	1270.22	1207.03	1158.68	1121.02	1091.26	1067.48	1048.33
70000	6407.61	3484.55	2520.15	2045.30	1766.14	1584.70	1458.97	1367.93	1299.88	1247.81	1207.25	1175.20	1149.60	1128.97
75000	6865.30	3733.45	2700.16	2191.39	1892.29	1697.89	1563.18	1465.64	1392.73	1336.94	1293.48	1259.14	1231.71	1209.61
80000	7322.99	3982.35	2880.17	2337.48	2018.45	1811.09	1667.39	1563.34	1485.58	1426.07	1379.71	1343.08	1313.83	1290.25
85000	7780.67	4231.24	3060.18	2483.57	2144.60	1924.28	1771.61	1661.05	1578.43	1515.20	1465.94	1427.03	1395.94	1370.89
90000	8238.36	4480.14	3240.19	2629.67	2270.75	2037.47	1875.82	1758.76	1671.28	1604.33	1552.17	1510.97	1478.05	1451.53
95000	8696.05	4729.04	3420.20	2775.76	2396.90	2150.66	1980.03	1856.47	1764.12	1693.46	1638.41	1594.91	1560.17	1532.17
100000	9153.73	4977.93	3600.21	2921.85	2523.06	2263.86	2084.24	1954.18	1856.97	1782.59	1724.64	1678.85	1642.28	1612.81

TERM	15 Years	16 Years	17 Years	18 Years	19 Years	20 Years	21 Years	22 Years	23 Years	24 Years	25 Years	30 Years	35 Years	40 Years
AMOUNT														
5	.08	.08	.08	.08	.08	.08	.08	.08	.08	.08	.08	.08	.08	.08
10	.16	.16	.16	.16	.16	.16	.16	.16	.16	.15	.15	.15	.15	.15
15	.24	.24	.24	.24	.23	.23	.23	.23	.23	.23	.23	.23	.23	.23
25	.40	.40	.39	.39	.39	.39	.38	.38	.38	.38	.38	.38	.37	.37
50	.80	.79	.78	.78	.77	.77	.76	.76	.76	.75	.75	.75	.74	.74
75	1.20	1.18	1.17	1.16	1.15	1.15	1.14	1.13	1.13	1.13	1.13	1.12	1.11	1.11
100	1.59	1.57	1.56	1.55	1.53	1.53	1.52	1.51	1.51	1.50	1.50	1.49	1.48	1.48
200	3.18	3.14	3.11	3.09	3.06	3.05	3.03	3.02	3.01	3.00	2.99	2.97	2.96	2.96
300	4.77	4.71	4.67	4.63	4.59	4.57	4.54	4.52	4.51	4.50	4.49	4.45	4.44	4.43
400	6.36	6.28	6.22	6.17	6.12	6.09	6.06	6.03	6.01	5.99	5.98	5.94	5.92	5.91
500	7.95	7.85	7.77	7.71	7.65	7.61	7.57	7.54	7.51	7.49	7.47	7.42	7.40	7.39
600	9.54	9.42	9.33	9.25	9.18	9.13	9.08	9.04	9.01	8.99	8.97	8.90	8.87	8.86
700	11.13	10.99	10.88	10.79	10.71	10.65	10.59	10.55	10.51	10.48	10.46	10.38	10.35	10.34
800	12.72	12.56	12.43	12.33	12.24	12.17	12.11	12.06	12.02	11.98	11.95	11.87	11.83	11.82
900	14.30	14.13	13.99	13.87	13.77	13.69	13.62	13.56	13.52	13.48	13.45	13.35	13.31	13.29
1000	15.89	15.70	15.54	15.41	15.30	15.21	15.13	15.07	15.02	14.98	14.94	14.83	14.79	14.77
2000	31.78	31.39	31.07	30.81	30.59	30.41	30.26	30.14	30.03	29.95	29.87	29.66	29.57	29.53
3000	47.67	47.09	46.61	46.21	45.88	45.61	45.39	45.20	45.05	44.92	44.81	44.48	44.35	44.29
4000	63.56	62.78	62.14	61.61	61.18	60.82	60.52	60.27	60.06	59.89	59.74	59.31	59.13	59.06
5000	79.45	78.47	77.67	77.01	76.47	76.02	75.64	75.33	75.07	74.86	74.68	74.14	73.91	73.82
6000	95.34	94.17	93.21	92.41	91.76	91.22	90.77	90.40	90.09	89.83	89.61	88.96	88.69	88.58
7000	111.23	109.86	108.74	107.82	107.05	106.42	105.90	105.46	105.10	104.80	104.55	103.79	103.48	103.35
8000	127.12	125.55	124.27	123.22	122.35	121.63	121.03	120.53	120.12	119.77	119.48	118.61	118.26	118.11
9000	143.00	141.25	139.81	138.62	137.64	136.83	136.16	135.60	135.13	134.74	134.42	133.44	133.04	132.87
10000	158.89	156.94	155.34	154.02	152.93	152.03	151.28	150.66	150.14	149.71	149.35	148.27	147.82	147.64
11000	174.78	172.63	170.87	169.42	168.23	167.23	166.41	165.73	165.16	164.68	164.29	163.09	162.60	162.40
12000	190.67	188.33	186.41	184.82	183.52	182.44	181.54	180.79	180.17	179.65	179.22	177.92	177.38	177.16
13000	206.56	204.02	201.94	200.23	198.81	197.64	196.67	195.86	195.19	194.62	194.16	192.75	192.17	191.93
14000	222.45	219.72	217.47	215.63	214.10	212.84	211.79	210.92	210.20	209.60	209.09	207.57	206.95	206.69
15000	238.34	235.41	233.01	231.03	229.40	228.04	226.92	225.99	225.21	224.57	224.03	222.40	221.73	221.45
16000	254.23	251.10	248.54	246.43	244.69	243.25	241.06	240.23	239.54	238.96	237.22	236.51	236.21
17000	270.12	266.80	264.07	261.83	259.98	258.45	257.18	256.12	255.24	254.51	253.89	252.05	251.29	250.98
18000	286.00	282.49	279.61	277.23	275.27	273.65	272.31	271.19	270.25	269.48	268.83	266.88	266.07	265.74
19000	301.89	298.18	295.14	292.64	290.57	288.85	287.43	286.25	285.27	284.45	283.76	281.70	280.85	280.50
20000	317.78	313.88	310.67	308.04	305.86	304.06	302.56	301.32	300.28	299.42	298.70	296.53	295.64	295.27
21000	333.67	329.57	326.21	323.44	321.15	319.26	317.69	316.38	315.30	314.39	313.63	311.35	310.42	310.03
22000	349.56	345.26	341.74	338.84	336.45	334.46	332.82	331.45	330.31	329.36	328.57	326.18	325.20	324.79
23000	365.45	360.96	357.27	354.24	351.74	349.67	347.95	346.51	345.32	344.33	343.50	341.01	339.98	339.56
24000	381.34	376.65	372.81	369.64	367.03	364.87	363.07	361.58	360.34	359.30	358.44	355.83	354.76	354.32
25000	397.23	392.34	388.34	385.05	382.32	380.07	378.20	376.65	375.35	374.27	373.37	370.66	369.54	369.08
26000	413.11	408.04	403.88	400.45	397.62	395.27	393.33	391.71	390.37	389.24	388.31	385.49	384.33	383.85
27000	429.00	423.73	419.41	415.85	412.91	410.48	408.46	406.78	405.38	404.21	403.24	400.31	399.11	398.61
28000	444.89	439.43	434.94	431.25	428.20	425.68	423.58	421.84	420.39	419.19	418.18	415.14	413.89	413.37
29000	460.78	455.12	450.48	446.65	443.50	440.88	438.71	436.91	435.41	434.16	433.11	429.96	428.67	428.13
30000	476.67	470.81	466.01	462.05	458.79	456.08	453.84	451.97	450.42	449.13	448.05	444.79	443.45	442.90
31000	492.56	486.51	481.54	477.46	474.08	471.29	468.97	467.04	465.44	464.10	462.98	459.62	458.23	457.66
32000	508.45	502.20	497.08	492.86	489.37	486.49	484.10	482.11	480.45	479.07	477.92	474.44	473.01	472.42
33000	524.34	517.89	512.61	508.26	504.67	501.69	499.22	497.17	495.46	494.04	492.85	489.27	487.80	487.19
34000	540.23	533.59	528.14	523.66	519.96	516.89	514.35	512.24	510.48	509.01	507.78	504.09	502.58	501.95
35000	556.11	549.28	543.68	539.06	535.25	532.10	529.48	527.30	525.49	523.98	522.72	518.92	517.36	516.71
36000	572.00	564.97	559.21	554.46	550.54	547.30	544.61	542.37	540.50	538.95	537.65	533.75	532.14	531.48
37000	587.89	580.67	574.74	569.87	565.84	562.50	559.73	557.43	555.52	553.92	552.59	548.57	546.92	546.24
38000	603.78	596.36	590.28	585.27	581.13	577.70	574.86	572.50	570.53	568.89	567.52	563.40	561.70	561.00
39000	619.67	612.05	605.81	600.67	596.42	592.91	589.99	587.57	585.55	583.86	582.46	578.23	576.49	575.77
40000	635.56	627.75	621.34	616.07	611.72	608.11	605.12	602.63	600.56	598.83	597.39	593.05	591.27	590.53
41000	651.45	643.44	636.88	631.47	627.01	623.31	620.25	617.70	615.57	613.80	612.33	607.88	606.05	605.29
42000	667.34	659.14	652.41	646.87	642.30	638.52	635.37	632.76	630.59	628.78	627.26	622.70	620.83	620.05
43000	683.22	674.83	667.94	662.28	657.59	653.72	650.50	647.83	645.60	643.75	642.20	637.53	635.61	634.82
44000	699.11	690.52	683.48	677.68	672.89	668.92	665.63	662.89	660.62	658.72	657.13	652.36	650.39	649.58
45000	715.00	706.22	699.01	693.08	688.18	684.12	680.76	677.96	675.63	673.69	672.07	667.18	665.17	664.34
46000	730.89	721.91	714.54	708.48	703.47	699.33	695.89	693.02	690.64	688.66	687.00	682.01	679.96	679.11
47000	746.78	737.60	730.08	723.88	718.77	714.53	711.01	708.09	705.66	703.63	701.94	696.83	694.74	693.87
48000	762.67	753.30	745.61	739.28	734.06	729.73	726.14	723.16	720.67	718.60	716.87	711.66	709.52	708.63
49000	778.56	768.99	761.14	754.69	749.35	744.93	741.27	738.22	735.68	733.57	731.81	726.49	724.30	723.40
50000	794.45	784.68	776.68	770.09	764.64	760.14	756.40	753.29	750.70	748.54	746.74	741.31	739.08	738.16
55000	873.89	863.15	854.35	847.10	841.11	836.15	832.04	828.62	825.77	823.39	821.41	815.44	812.99	811.97
60000	953.34	941.62	932.01	924.10	917.57	912.16	907.67	903.94	900.84	898.25	896.09	889.58	886.90	885.79
65000	1032.78	1020.09	1009.68	1001.11	994.04	988.18	983.31	979.27	975.91	973.10	970.76	963.71	960.81	959.61
70000	1112.22	1098.56	1087.35	1078.12	1070.50	1064.19	1058.95	1054.60	1050.98	1047.96	1045.43	1037.84	1034.71	1033.42
75000	1191.67	1177.02	1165.01	1155.13	1146.96	1140.20	1134.59	1129.93	1126.05	1122.81	1120.11	1111.97	1108.62	1107.24
80000	1271.11	1255.49	1242.68	1232.14	1223.43	1216.22	1210.23	1205.26	1201.11	1197.66	1194.78	1186.10	1182.53	1181.05
85000	1350.56	1333.96	1320.35	1309.14	1299.89	1292.23	1285.87	1280.58	1276.18	1272.52	1269.45	1260.23	1256.44	1254.87
90000	1430.00	1412.43	1398.02	1386.15	1376.35	1368.24	1361.51	1355.91	1351.25	1347.37	1344.13	1334.36	1330.34	1328.68
95000	1509.44	1490.90	1475.68	1463.16	1452.82	1444.25	1437.15	1431.24	1426.32	1422.22	1418.80	1408.49	1404.25	1402.50
100000	1588.89	1569.36	1553.35	1540.17	1529.28	1520.27	1512.79	1506.57	1501.39	1497.08	1493.48	1482.62	1478.16	1476.31

MONTHLY PAYMENT
REQUIRED TO AMORTIZE A LOAN

TERM	1 Year	2 Years	3 Years	4 Years	5 Years	6 Years	7 Years	8 Years	9 Years	10 Years	11 Years	12 Years	13 Years	14 Years
AMOUNT														
5	.46	.25	.19	.15	.13	.12	.11	.10	.10	.09	.09	.09	.09	.09
10	.92	.50	.37	.30	.26	.23	.21	.20	.19	.18	.18	.17	.17	.17
15	1.38	.75	.55	.44	.38	.35	.32	.30	.28	.27	.26	.26	.25	.25
25	2.29	1.25	.91	.74	.64	.57	.53	.49	.47	.45	.44	.43	.42	.41
50	4.58	2.50	1.81	1.47	1.27	1.14	1.05	.98	.94	.90	.87	.85	.83	.81
75	6.87	3.74	2.71	2.20	1.90	1.71	1.57	1.47	1.40	1.34	1.30	1.27	1.24	1.22
100	9.16	4.99	3.61	2.93	2.53	2.27	2.09	1.96	1.87	1.79	1.73	1.69	1.65	1.62
200	18.32	9.97	7.21	5.85	5.06	4.54	4.18	3.92	3.73	3.58	3.46	3.37	3.30	3.24
300	27.47	14.95	10.81	8.78	7.58	6.81	6.27	5.88	5.59	5.36	5.19	5.05	4.94	4.85
400	36.63	19.93	14.42	11.70	10.11	9.07	8.35	7.83	7.45	7.15	6.92	6.73	6.59	6.47
500	45.79	24.91	18.02	14.63	12.63	11.34	10.44	9.79	9.31	8.93	8.64	8.42	8.23	8.09
600	54.94	29.89	21.62	17.55	15.16	13.61	12.53	11.75	11.17	10.72	10.37	10.10	9.88	9.70
700	64.10	34.87	25.22	20.48	17.69	15.87	14.62	13.71	13.03	12.51	12.10	11.78	11.53	11.32
800	73.25	39.85	28.83	23.40	20.21	18.14	16.70	15.66	14.89	14.29	13.83	13.46	13.17	12.94
900	82.41	44.83	32.43	26.33	22.74	20.41	18.79	17.62	16.75	16.08	15.56	15.14	14.82	14.55
1000	91.57	49.81	36.03	29.25	25.26	22.67	20.88	19.58	18.61	17.86	17.28	16.83	16.46	16.17
2000	183.13	99.61	72.06	58.49	50.52	45.34	41.75	39.15	37.21	35.72	34.56	33.65	32.92	32.33
3000	274.69	149.42	108.09	87.74	75.78	68.01	62.62	58.72	55.81	53.58	51.84	50.47	49.38	48.49
4000	366.25	199.22	144.11	116.98	101.04	90.67	83.49	78.29	74.41	71.44	69.12	67.29	65.83	64.66
5000	457.81	249.02	180.14	146.23	126.29	113.34	104.36	97.86	93.01	89.29	86.40	84.12	82.29	80.82
6000	549.37	298.83	216.17	175.47	151.55	136.01	125.23	117.44	111.61	107.15	103.68	100.94	98.75	96.98
7000	640.93	348.63	252.19	204.72	176.81	158.67	146.11	137.01	130.21	125.01	120.96	117.76	115.21	113.15
8000	732.49	398.43	288.22	233.96	202.07	181.34	166.98	156.58	148.81	142.87	138.24	134.58	131.66	129.31
9000	824.05	448.24	324.25	263.21	227.32	204.01	187.85	176.15	167.41	160.73	155.52	151.40	148.12	145.47
10000	915.62	498.04	360.28	292.45	252.58	226.67	208.72	195.72	186.01	178.58	172.80	168.23	164.58	161.64
11000	1007.18	547.84	396.30	321.69	277.84	249.34	229.59	215.30	204.61	196.44	190.08	185.05	181.03	177.80
12000	1098.74	597.65	432.33	350.94	303.10	272.01	250.46	234.87	223.21	214.30	207.36	201.87	197.49	193.96
13000	1190.30	647.45	468.36	380.18	328.35	294.67	271.34	254.44	241.82	232.16	224.64	218.69	213.95	210.13
14000	1281.86	697.25	504.38	409.43	353.61	317.34	292.21	274.01	260.42	250.02	241.91	235.52	230.41	226.29
15000	1373.42	747.06	540.41	438.67	378.87	340.01	313.08	293.58	279.02	267.87	259.19	252.34	246.86	242.45
16000	1464.98	796.86	576.44	467.92	404.13	362.67	333.95	313.16	297.62	285.73	276.47	269.16	263.32	258.62
17000	1556.54	846.66	612.47	497.16	429.38	385.34	354.82	332.73	316.22	303.59	293.75	285.98	279.78	274.78
18000	1648.10	896.47	648.49	526.41	454.64	408.01	375.69	352.30	334.82	321.45	311.03	302.80	296.24	290.94
19000	1739.67	946.27	684.52	555.65	479.90	430.67	396.56	371.87	353.42	339.30	328.31	319.63	312.69	307.11
20000	1831.23	996.07	720.55	584.90	505.16	453.34	417.44	391.44	372.02	357.16	345.59	336.45	329.15	323.27
21000	1922.79	1045.88	756.57	614.14	530.42	476.01	438.31	411.02	390.62	375.02	362.87	353.27	345.61	339.43
22000	2014.35	1095.68	792.60	643.38	555.67	498.67	459.18	430.59	409.22	392.88	380.15	370.09	362.06	355.60
23000	2105.91	1145.48	828.63	672.63	580.93	521.34	480.05	450.16	427.82	410.74	397.43	386.92	378.52	371.76
24000	2197.47	1195.29	864.66	701.87	606.19	544.01	500.92	469.73	446.42	428.59	414.71	403.74	394.98	387.92
25000	2289.03	1245.09	900.68	731.12	631.45	566.67	521.79	489.30	465.03	446.45	431.99	420.56	411.44	404.09
26000	2380.59	1294.89	936.71	760.36	656.70	589.34	542.67	508.88	483.63	464.31	449.27	437.38	427.89	420.25
27000	2472.15	1344.70	972.74	789.61	681.96	612.01	563.54	528.45	502.23	482.17	466.54	454.20	444.35	436.41
28000	2563.71	1394.50	1008.76	818.85	707.22	634.67	584.41	548.02	520.83	500.03	483.82	471.03	460.81	452.57
29000	2655.28	1444.30	1044.79	848.10	732.48	657.34	605.28	567.59	539.43	517.88	501.10	487.85	477.26	468.74
30000	2746.84	1494.11	1080.82	877.34	757.73	680.01	626.15	587.16	558.03	535.74	518.38	504.67	493.72	484.90
31000	2838.40	1543.91	1116.85	906.59	782.99	702.67	647.02	606.73	576.63	553.60	535.66	521.49	510.18	501.06
32000	2929.96	1593.71	1152.87	935.83	808.25	725.34	667.89	626.31	595.23	571.46	552.94	538.32	526.64	517.23
33000	3021.52	1643.52	1188.90	965.07	833.51	748.01	688.77	645.88	613.83	589.32	570.22	555.14	543.09	533.39
34000	3113.08	1693.32	1224.93	994.32	858.76	770.67	709.64	665.45	632.43	607.17	587.50	571.96	559.55	549.55
35000	3204.64	1743.12	1260.95	1023.56	884.02	793.34	730.51	685.02	651.03	625.03	604.78	588.78	576.01	565.72
36000	3296.20	1792.93	1296.98	1052.81	909.28	816.01	751.38	704.59	669.63	642.89	622.06	605.60	592.47	581.88
37000	3387.76	1842.73	1333.01	1082.05	934.54	838.67	772.25	724.17	688.24	660.75	639.34	622.43	608.92	598.04
38000	3479.33	1892.53	1369.04	1111.30	959.79	861.34	793.12	743.74	706.84	678.60	656.62	639.25	625.38	614.21
39000	3570.89	1942.34	1405.06	1140.54	985.05	884.01	814.00	763.31	725.44	696.46	673.90	656.07	641.84	630.37
40000	3662.45	1992.14	1441.09	1169.79	1010.31	906.67	834.87	782.88	744.04	714.32	691.17	672.89	658.29	646.53
41000	3754.01	2041.94	1477.12	1199.03	1035.57	929.34	855.74	802.45	762.64	732.18	708.45	689.72	674.75	662.70
42000	3845.57	2091.75	1513.14	1228.28	1060.83	952.01	876.61	822.03	781.24	750.04	725.73	706.54	691.21	678.86
43000	3937.13	2141.55	1549.17	1257.52	1086.08	974.67	897.48	841.60	799.84	767.89	743.01	723.36	707.67	695.02
44000	4028.69	2191.35	1585.20	1286.76	1111.34	997.34	918.35	861.17	818.44	785.75	760.29	740.18	724.12	711.19
45000	4120.25	2241.16	1621.22	1316.01	1136.60	1020.01	939.23	880.74	837.04	803.61	777.57	757.00	740.58	727.35
46000	4211.81	2290.96	1657.25	1345.25	1161.86	1042.67	960.10	900.31	855.64	821.47	794.85	773.83	757.04	743.51
47000	4303.37	2340.76	1693.28	1374.50	1187.11	1065.34	980.97	919.89	874.24	839.33	812.13	790.65	773.49	759.68
48000	4394.94	2390.57	1729.31	1403.74	1212.37	1088.01	1001.84	939.46	892.84	857.18	829.41	807.47	789.95	775.84
49000	4486.50	2440.37	1765.33	1432.99	1237.63	1110.67	1022.71	959.03	911.44	875.04	846.69	824.29	806.41	792.00
50000	4578.06	2490.17	1801.36	1462.23	1262.89	1133.34	1043.58	978.60	930.05	892.90	863.97	841.12	822.87	808.17
55000	5035.86	2739.19	1981.50	1608.45	1389.17	1246.67	1147.94	1076.46	1023.05	982.19	950.36	925.23	905.15	888.98
60000	5493.67	2988.21	2161.63	1754.68	1515.46	1360.01	1252.30	1174.32	1116.05	1071.48	1036.76	1009.34	987.44	969.80
65000	5951.47	3237.23	2341.77	1900.90	1641.75	1473.34	1356.66	1272.18	1209.06	1160.77	1123.16	1093.45	1069.73	1050.61
70000	6409.28	3486.24	2521.90	2047.12	1768.04	1586.67	1461.01	1370.04	1302.06	1250.06	1209.55	1177.56	1152.01	1131.43
75000	6867.08	3735.26	2702.04	2193.34	1894.33	1700.01	1565.37	1467.90	1395.07	1339.35	1295.95	1261.67	1234.30	1212.25
80000	7324.89	3984.28	2882.17	2339.57	2020.61	1813.34	1669.73	1565.76	1488.07	1428.64	1382.34	1345.78	1316.58	1293.06
85000	7782.69	4233.29	3062.31	2485.79	2146.90	1926.67	1774.09	1663.62	1581.07	1517.93	1468.74	1429.89	1398.87	1373.88
90000	8240.50	4482.31	3242.44	2632.01	2273.19	2040.01	1878.44	1761.48	1674.08	1607.21	1555.14	1514.00	1481.16	1454.69
95000	8698.31	4731.33	3422.58	2778.23	2399.48	2153.34	1982.80	1859.34	1767.08	1696.50	1641.53	1598.11	1563.44	1535.51
100000	9156.11	4980.34	3602.72	2924.46	2525.77	2266.67	2087.16	1957.20	1860.09	1785.79	1727.93	1682.23	1645.73	1616.33

TERM	15 Years	16 Years	17 Years	18 Years	19 Years	20 Years	21 Years	22 Years	23 Years	24 Years	25 Years	30 Years	35 Years	40 Years
AMOUNT														
5	.08	.08	.08	.08	.08	.08	.08	.08	.08	.08	.08	.08	.08	.08
10	.16	.16	.16	.16	.16	.16	.16	.16	.16	.16	.15	.15	.15	.15
15	.24	.24	.24	.24	.23	.23	.23	.23	.23	.23	.23	.23	.23	.23
25	.40	.40	.39	.39	.39	.39	.38	.38	.38	.38	.38	.38	.38	.38
50	.80	.79	.78	.78	.77	.77	.76	.76	.76	.76	.75	.75	.75	.75
75	1.20	1.18	1.17	1.16	1.15	1.15	1.14	1.14	1.13	1.13	1.13	1.12	1.12	1.12
100	1.60	1.58	1.56	1.55	1.54	1.53	1.52	1.52	1.51	1.51	1.50	1.49	1.49	1.49
200	3.19	3.15	3.12	3.09	3.07	3.05	3.04	3.03	3.02	3.01	3.00	2.98	2.97	2.97
300	4.78	4.72	4.68	4.64	4.60	4.58	4.55	4.54	4.52	4.51	4.50	4.47	4.45	4.45
400	6.37	6.30	6.23	6.18	6.14	6.10	6.07	6.05	6.03	6.01	5.99	5.95	5.93	5.93
500	7.97	7.87	7.79	7.72	7.67	7.63	7.59	7.56	7.53	7.51	7.49	7.44	7.42	7.41
600	9.56	9.44	9.35	9.27	9.20	9.15	9.10	9.07	9.04	9.01	8.99	8.93	8.90	8.89
700	11.15	11.02	10.90	10.81	10.74	10.67	10.62	10.58	10.54	10.51	10.49	10.41	10.38	10.37
800	12.74	12.59	12.46	12.36	12.27	12.20	12.14	12.09	12.05	12.01	11.98	11.90	11.86	11.85
900	14.34	14.16	14.02	13.90	13.80	13.72	13.65	13.60	13.55	13.51	13.48	13.39	13.35	13.33
1000	15.93	15.74	15.58	15.44	15.34	15.25	15.17	15.11	15.06	15.02	14.98	14.87	14.83	14.81
2000	31.85	31.47	31.15	30.88	30.67	30.49	30.34	30.21	30.11	30.03	29.95	29.74	29.65	29.61
3000	47.78	47.20	46.72	46.32	46.00	45.73	45.50	45.32	45.16	45.04	44.93	44.61	44.47	44.42
4000	63.70	62.93	62.29	61.76	61.33	60.97	60.67	60.42	60.22	60.05	59.90	59.47	59.29	59.22
5000	79.63	78.66	77.86	77.20	76.66	76.21	75.84	75.53	75.27	75.06	74.88	74.34	74.12	74.03
6000	95.55	94.39	93.43	92.64	91.99	91.45	91.00	90.63	90.32	90.07	89.85	89.21	88.94	88.83
7000	111.48	110.12	109.00	108.08	107.32	106.69	106.17	105.74	105.38	105.08	104.83	104.07	103.76	103.64
8000	127.40	125.85	124.57	123.52	122.65	121.93	121.34	120.84	120.43	120.09	119.80	118.94	118.59	118.44
9000	143.33	141.58	140.14	138.96	137.98	137.17	136.50	135.95	135.48	135.10	134.78	133.81	133.41	133.25
10000	159.25	157.31	155.71	154.40	153.31	152.41	151.67	151.05	150.54	150.11	149.75	148.67	148.23	148.05
11000	175.18	173.04	171.28	169.84	168.64	167.66	166.84	166.16	165.59	165.12	164.73	163.54	163.06	162.85
12000	191.10	188.77	186.85	185.27	183.97	182.90	182.00	181.26	180.64	180.13	179.70	178.41	177.88	177.66
13000	207.03	204.50	202.42	200.71	199.30	198.14	197.17	196.37	195.70	195.14	194.67	193.27	192.70	192.46
14000	222.95	220.23	217.99	216.15	214.64	213.38	212.34	211.47	210.75	210.15	209.65	208.14	207.52	207.27
15000	238.87	235.96	233.56	231.59	229.97	228.62	227.50	226.58	225.80	225.16	224.62	223.01	222.35	222.07
16000	254.80	251.69	249.13	247.03	245.30	243.86	242.67	241.68	240.86	240.17	239.60	237.88	237.17	236.88
17000	270.72	267.42	264.70	262.47	260.63	259.10	257.84	256.79	255.91	255.18	254.57	252.74	251.99	251.68
18000	286.65	283.15	280.27	277.91	275.96	274.34	273.00	271.89	270.96	270.19	269.55	267.61	266.81	266.49
19000	302.57	298.88	295.84	293.35	291.29	289.58	288.17	286.99	286.02	285.20	284.52	282.48	281.64	281.29
20000	318.50	314.61	311.41	308.79	306.62	304.82	303.34	302.10	301.07	300.21	299.50	297.34	296.46	296.10
21000	334.42	330.34	326.98	324.23	321.95	320.07	318.50	317.20	316.12	315.22	314.47	312.21	311.28	310.90
22000	350.35	346.07	342.55	339.67	337.28	335.31	333.67	332.31	331.18	330.23	329.45	327.08	326.11	325.70
23000	366.27	361.80	358.13	355.10	352.61	350.55	340.04	347.41	346.23	345.24	344.42	341.94	340.93	340.51
24000	382.20	377.53	373.70	370.54	367.94	365.79	364.00	362.52	361.28	360.25	359.40	356.81	355.75	355.31
25000	398.12	393.26	389.27	385.98	383.27	381.03	379.17	377.62	376.34	375.26	374.37	371.68	370.57	370.12
26000	414.05	408.99	404.84	401.42	398.60	396.27	394.34	392.73	391.39	390.27	389.34	386.54	385.40	384.92
27000	429.97	424.72	420.41	416.86	413.93	411.51	409.50	407.83	406.44	405.28	404.32	401.41	400.22	399.73
28000	445.90	440.45	435.98	432.30	429.27	426.75	424.67	422.94	421.50	420.30	419.29	416.28	415.04	414.53
29000	461.82	456.18	451.55	447.74	444.60	441.99	439.84	438.04	436.55	435.31	434.27	431.15	429.86	429.34
30000	477.74	471.91	467.12	463.18	459.93	457.23	455.00	453.15	451.60	450.32	449.24	446.01	444.69	444.14
31000	493.67	487.64	482.69	478.62	475.26	472.48	470.17	468.25	466.66	465.33	464.22	460.88	459.51	458.95
32000	509.59	503.37	498.26	494.06	490.59	487.72	485.33	483.36	481.71	480.34	479.19	475.75	474.33	473.75
33000	525.52	519.10	513.83	509.50	505.92	502.96	500.50	498.46	496.76	495.35	494.17	490.61	489.16	488.55
34000	541.44	534.83	529.40	524.94	521.25	518.20	515.67	513.57	511.82	510.36	509.14	505.48	503.98	503.36
35000	557.37	550.56	544.97	540.37	536.58	533.44	530.83	528.67	526.87	525.37	524.12	520.35	518.80	518.16
36000	573.29	566.29	560.54	555.81	551.91	548.68	546.00	543.77	541.92	540.38	539.09	535.21	533.62	532.97
37000	589.22	582.02	576.11	571.25	567.24	563.92	561.17	558.88	556.98	555.39	554.07	550.08	548.45	547.77
38000	605.14	597.75	591.68	586.69	582.57	579.16	576.33	573.98	572.03	570.40	569.04	564.95	563.27	562.58
39000	621.07	613.48	607.25	602.13	597.90	594.40	591.50	589.09	587.08	585.41	584.01	579.81	578.09	577.38
40000	636.99	629.21	622.82	617.57	613.23	609.64	606.67	604.19	602.13	600.42	598.99	594.68	592.92	592.19
41000	652.92	644.94	638.39	633.01	628.56	624.89	621.83	619.30	617.19	615.43	613.96	609.55	607.74	606.99
42000	668.84	660.67	653.96	648.45	643.90	640.13	637.00	634.40	632.24	630.44	628.94	624.42	622.56	621.80
43000	684.77	676.40	669.53	663.89	659.23	655.37	652.17	649.51	647.29	645.45	643.91	639.28	637.38	636.60
44000	700.69	692.13	685.10	679.33	674.56	670.61	667.33	664.61	662.35	660.46	658.89	654.15	652.21	651.40
45000	716.61	707.86	700.68	694.77	689.89	685.85	682.50	679.72	677.40	675.47	673.86	669.02	667.03	666.21
46000	732.54	723.59	716.25	710.20	705.22	701.09	697.67	694.82	692.45	690.48	688.84	683.88	681.85	681.01
47000	748.46	739.32	731.82	725.64	720.55	716.33	712.83	709.93	707.51	705.49	703.81	698.75	696.67	695.82
48000	764.39	755.05	747.39	741.08	735.88	731.57	728.00	725.03	722.56	720.50	718.79	713.62	711.50	710.62
49000	780.31	770.78	762.96	756.52	751.21	746.81	743.17	740.14	737.61	735.51	733.76	728.48	726.32	725.43
50000	796.24	786.51	778.53	771.96	766.54	762.05	758.33	755.24	752.67	750.52	748.73	743.35	741.14	740.23
55000	875.86	865.16	856.38	849.16	843.19	838.26	834.17	830.76	827.93	825.58	823.61	817.69	815.26	814.25
60000	955.48	943.81	934.23	926.35	919.85	914.46	910.00	906.29	903.20	900.63	898.48	892.02	889.37	888.28
65000	1035.11	1022.46	1012.08	1003.55	996.50	990.67	985.83	981.81	978.47	975.68	973.35	966.35	963.48	962.30
70000	1114.73	1101.11	1089.94	1080.74	1073.16	1066.87	1061.66	1057.34	1053.73	1050.73	1048.23	1040.69	1037.60	1036.32
75000	1194.36	1179.76	1167.79	1157.94	1149.81	1143.08	1137.50	1132.86	1129.00	1125.78	1123.10	1115.02	1111.71	1110.35
80000	1273.98	1258.41	1245.64	1235.14	1226.46	1219.28	1213.33	1208.38	1204.26	1200.83	1197.97	1189.36	1185.83	1184.37
85000	1353.60	1337.06	1323.49	1312.33	1303.12	1295.49	1289.16	1283.91	1279.53	1275.89	1272.85	1263.69	1259.94	1258.39
90000	1433.23	1415.71	1401.35	1389.53	1379.77	1371.69	1365.00	1359.43	1354.80	1350.94	1347.72	1338.03	1334.05	1332.41
95000	1512.85	1494.36	1479.20	1466.72	1456.42	1447.90	1440.83	1434.95	1430.06	1425.99	1422.59	1412.36	1408.17	1406.44
100000	1592.47	1573.01	1557.05	1543.92	1533.08	1524.10	1516.66	1510.48	1505.33	1501.04	1497.46	1486.70	1482.28	1480.46

MONTHLY PAYMENT
REQUIRED TO AMORTIZE A LOAN

TERM AMOUNT	1 Year	2 Years	3 Years	4 Years	5 Years	6 Years	7 Years	8 Years	9 Years	10 Years	11 Years	12 Years	13 Years	14 Years
5	.46	.25	.19	.15	.13	.12	.11	.10	.10	.09	.09	.09	.09	.09
10	.92	.50	.37	.30	.26	.23	.21	.20	.19	.18	.18	.17	.17	.17
15	1.38	.75	.55	.44	.38	.35	.32	.30	.28	.27	.26	.26	.25	.25
25	2.29	1.25	.91	.74	.64	.57	.53	.50	.47	.45	.44	.43	.42	.41
50	4.58	2.50	1.81	1.47	1.27	1.14	1.05	.99	.94	.90	.87	.85	.83	.81
75	6.87	3.74	2.71	2.20	1.90	1.71	1.57	1.48	1.40	1.35	1.30	1.27	1.24	1.22
100	9.16	4.99	3.61	2.93	2.53	2.27	2.10	1.97	1.87	1.79	1.74	1.69	1.65	1.62
200	18.32	9.97	7.22	5.86	5.06	4.54	4.19	3.93	3.73	3.58	3.47	3.38	3.30	3.24
300	27.48	14.95	10.82	8.79	7.59	6.81	6.28	5.89	5.59	5.37	5.20	5.06	4.95	4.86
400	36.64	19.94	14.43	11.71	10.12	9.08	8.37	7.85	7.46	7.16	6.93	6.75	6.60	6.48
500	45.80	24.92	18.03	14.64	12.65	11.35	10.46	9.81	9.32	8.95	8.66	8.43	8.25	8.10
600	54.96	29.90	21.64	17.57	15.18	13.62	12.55	11.77	11.18	10.74	10.39	10.12	9.90	9.72
700	64.11	34.88	25.24	20.49	17.70	15.89	14.64	13.73	13.05	12.53	12.12	11.80	11.55	11.34
800	73.27	39.87	28.85	23.42	20.23	18.16	16.73	15.69	14.91	14.32	13.85	13.49	13.20	12.96
900	82.43	44.85	32.45	26.35	22.76	20.43	18.82	17.65	16.77	16.11	15.59	15.18	14.85	14.58
1000	91.59	49.83	36.06	29.28	25.29	22.70	20.91	19.61	18.64	17.89	17.32	16.86	16.50	16.20
2000	183.17	99.66	72.11	58.55	50.57	45.39	41.81	39.21	37.27	35.78	34.63	33.72	32.99	32.40
3000	274.76	149.49	108.16	87.82	75.86	68.09	62.71	58.81	55.90	53.67	51.94	50.57	49.48	48.60
4000	366.34	199.32	144.21	117.09	101.14	90.78	83.61	78.41	74.53	71.56	69.25	67.43	65.97	64.80
5000	457.93	249.14	180.27	146.36	126.43	113.48	104.51	98.02	93.16	89.45	86.57	84.28	82.46	81.00
6000	549.51	298.97	216.32	175.63	151.71	136.17	125.41	117.62	111.80	107.34	103.88	101.14	98.96	97.20
7000	641.10	348.80	252.37	204.90	177.00	158.87	146.31	137.22	130.43	125.23	121.19	118.00	115.45	113.39
8000	732.68	398.63	288.42	234.17	202.28	181.56	167.21	156.82	149.06	143.12	138.50	134.85	131.94	129.59
9000	824.27	448.45	324.47	263.44	227.57	204.26	188.11	176.42	167.69	161.01	155.81	151.71	148.43	145.79
10000	915.85	498.28	360.53	292.71	252.85	226.95	209.01	196.03	186.32	178.90	173.13	168.56	164.92	161.99
11000	1007.44	548.11	396.58	321.98	278.14	249.65	229.91	215.63	204.96	196.79	190.44	185.42	181.41	178.19
12000	1099.02	597.94	432.63	351.25	303.42	272.34	250.81	235.23	223.59	214.68	207.75	202.28	197.91	194.39
13000	1190.61	647.76	468.68	380.52	328.71	295.04	271.72	254.83	242.22	232.57	225.06	219.13	214.40	210.58
14000	1282.19	697.59	504.74	409.79	353.99	317.73	292.62	274.44	260.85	250.46	242.38	235.99	230.89	226.78
15000	1373.78	747.42	540.79	439.06	379.28	340.43	313.52	294.04	279.48	268.35	259.69	252.84	247.38	242.98
16000	1465.36	797.25	576.84	468.33	404.56	363.12	334.42	313.64	298.12	286.24	277.00	269.70	263.87	259.18
17000	1556.95	847.07	612.89	497.61	429.85	385.82	355.32	333.24	316.75	304.13	294.31	286.56	280.36	275.38
18000	1648.53	896.90	648.94	526.88	455.13	408.51	376.22	352.84	335.38	322.02	311.62	303.41	296.86	291.58
19000	1740.12	946.73	685.00	556.15	480.42	431.21	397.12	372.45	354.01	339.91	328.94	320.27	313.35	307.77
20000	1831.70	996.56	721.05	585.42	505.70	453.90	418.02	392.05	372.64	357.80	346.25	337.12	329.84	323.97
21000	1923.29	1046.38	757.10	614.69	530.98	476.60	438.92	411.65	391.28	375.69	363.56	353.98	346.33	340.17
22000	2014.87	1096.21	793.15	643.96	556.27	499.29	459.82	431.25	409.91	393.58	380.87	370.84	362.82	356.37
23000	2106.46	1146.04	829.20	673.23	581.55	521.99	480.72	450.85	428.54	411.47	398.18	387.69	379.31	372.57
24000	2198.04	1195.87	865.26	702.50	606.84	544.68	501.62	470.46	447.17	429.36	415.50	404.55	395.81	388.77
25000	2289.63	1245.69	901.31	731.77	632.12	567.38	522.52	490.06	465.80	447.25	432.81	421.40	412.30	404.97
26000	2381.21	1295.52	937.36	761.04	657.41	590.07	543.43	509.66	484.44	465.14	450.12	438.26	428.79	421.16
27000	2472.80	1345.35	973.41	790.31	682.69	612.77	564.33	529.26	503.07	483.03	467.43	455.12	445.28	437.36
28000	2564.38	1395.18	1009.47	819.58	707.98	635.46	585.23	548.87	521.70	500.92	484.75	471.97	461.77	453.56
29000	2655.97	1445.00	1045.52	848.85	733.26	658.16	606.13	568.47	540.33	518.81	502.06	488.83	478.27	469.76
30000	2747.55	1494.83	1081.57	878.12	758.55	680.85	627.03	588.07	558.96	536.70	519.37	505.68	494.76	485.96
31000	2839.13	1544.66	1117.62	907.39	783.83	703.55	647.93	607.67	577.60	554.59	536.68	522.54	511.25	502.16
32000	2930.72	1594.49	1153.67	936.66	809.12	726.24	668.83	627.27	596.23	572.48	553.99	539.40	527.74	518.35
33000	3022.30	1644.31	1189.73	965.93	834.40	748.94	689.73	646.88	614.86	590.37	571.31	556.25	544.23	534.55
34000	3113.89	1694.14	1225.78	995.21	859.69	771.63	710.63	666.48	633.49	608.26	588.62	573.11	560.72	550.75
35000	3205.47	1743.97	1261.83	1024.48	884.97	794.33	731.53	686.08	652.12	626.15	605.93	589.96	577.22	566.95
36000	3297.06	1793.80	1297.88	1053.75	910.26	817.02	752.43	705.68	670.76	644.04	623.24	606.82	593.71	583.15
37000	3388.64	1843.62	1333.93	1083.02	935.54	839.72	773.33	725.28	689.39	661.93	640.56	623.68	610.20	599.35
38000	3480.23	1893.45	1369.99	1112.29	960.83	862.41	794.23	744.89	708.02	679.82	657.87	640.53	626.69	615.54
39000	3571.81	1943.28	1406.04	1141.56	986.11	885.11	815.14	764.49	726.65	697.71	675.18	657.39	643.18	631.74
40000	3663.40	1993.11	1442.09	1170.83	1011.40	907.80	836.04	784.09	745.28	715.60	692.49	674.24	659.67	647.94
41000	3754.98	2042.93	1478.14	1200.10	1036.68	930.49	856.94	803.69	763.92	733.49	709.80	691.10	676.17	664.14
42000	3846.57	2092.76	1514.20	1229.37	1061.96	953.19	877.84	823.30	782.55	751.38	727.12	707.95	692.66	680.34
43000	3938.15	2142.59	1550.25	1258.64	1087.25	975.88	898.74	842.90	801.18	769.27	744.43	724.81	709.15	696.54
44000	4029.74	2192.42	1586.30	1287.91	1112.53	998.58	919.64	862.50	819.81	787.16	761.74	741.67	725.64	712.74
45000	4121.32	2242.24	1622.35	1317.18	1137.82	1021.27	940.54	882.10	838.44	805.05	779.05	758.52	742.13	728.93
46000	4212.91	2292.07	1658.40	1346.45	1163.10	1043.97	961.44	901.70	857.08	822.94	796.36	775.38	758.62	745.13
47000	4304.49	2341.90	1694.46	1375.72	1188.39	1066.66	982.34	921.31	875.71	840.83	813.68	792.23	775.12	761.33
48000	4396.08	2391.73	1730.51	1404.99	1213.67	1089.36	1003.24	940.91	894.34	858.72	830.99	809.09	791.61	777.53
49000	4487.66	2441.55	1766.56	1434.26	1238.96	1112.05	1024.14	960.51	912.97	876.61	848.30	825.95	808.10	793.73
50000	4579.25	2491.38	1802.61	1463.53	1264.24	1134.75	1045.04	980.11	931.60	894.50	865.61	842.80	824.59	809.93
55000	5037.17	2740.52	1982.87	1609.89	1390.67	1248.22	1149.55	1078.12	1024.76	983.95	952.17	927.08	907.05	890.92
60000	5495.10	2989.66	2163.13	1756.24	1517.09	1361.70	1254.05	1176.13	1117.92	1073.40	1038.74	1011.36	989.51	971.91
65000	5953.02	3238.79	2343.39	1902.59	1643.51	1475.17	1358.56	1274.14	1211.08	1162.85	1125.30	1095.64	1071.97	1052.90
70000	6410.94	3487.93	2523.66	2048.95	1769.94	1588.65	1463.06	1372.16	1304.24	1252.30	1211.86	1179.92	1154.43	1133.89
75000	6868.87	3737.07	2703.92	2195.30	1896.36	1702.12	1567.56	1470.17	1397.40	1341.75	1298.42	1264.20	1236.89	1214.89
80000	7326.79	3986.21	2884.18	2341.65	2022.79	1815.59	1672.07	1568.18	1490.56	1431.20	1384.98	1348.48	1319.34	1295.88
85000	7784.72	4235.34	3064.44	2488.01	2149.21	1929.07	1776.57	1666.19	1583.72	1520.65	1471.54	1432.76	1401.80	1376.87
90000	8242.64	4484.48	3244.70	2634.36	2275.63	2042.54	1881.07	1764.20	1676.88	1610.10	1558.10	1517.04	1484.26	1457.86
95000	8700.56	4733.62	3424.96	2780.71	2402.06	2156.02	1985.58	1862.21	1770.04	1699.55	1644.66	1601.32	1566.72	1538.85
100000	9158.49	4982.76	3605.22	2927.06	2528.48	2269.49	2090.08	1960.22	1863.20	1789.00	1731.22	1685.60	1649.18	1619.85

TERM	15 Years	16 Years	17 Years	18 Years	19 Years	20 Years	21 Years	22 Years	23 Years	24 Years	25 Years	30 Years	35 Years	40 Years
AMOUNT														
5	.08	.08	.08	.08	.08	.08	.08	.08	.08	.08	.08	.08	.08	.08
10	.16	.16	.16	.16	.16	.16	.16	.16	.16	.16	.16	.15	.15	.15
15	.24	.24	.24	.24	.24	.23	.23	.23	.23	.23	.23	.23	.23	.23
25	.40	.40	.40	.39	.39	.39	.39	.38	.38	.38	.38	.38	.38	.38
50	.80	.79	.79	.78	.77	.77	.77	.76	.76	.76	.76	.75	.75	.75
75	1.20	1.19	1.18	1.17	1.16	1.15	1.15	1.14	1.14	1.13	1.13	1.12	1.12	1.12
100	1.60	1.58	1.57	1.55	1.54	1.53	1.53	1.52	1.51	1.51	1.51	1.50	1.49	1.49
200	3.20	3.16	3.13	3.10	3.08	3.06	3.05	3.03	3.02	3.02	3.01	2.99	2.98	2.97
300	4.79	4.73	4.69	4.65	4.62	4.59	4.57	4.55	4.53	4.52	4.51	4.48	4.46	4.46
400	6.39	6.31	6.25	6.20	6.15	6.12	6.09	6.06	6.04	6.03	6.01	5.97	5.95	5.94
500	7.99	7.89	7.81	7.74	7.69	7.64	7.61	7.58	7.55	7.53	7.51	7.46	7.44	7.43
600	9.58	9.46	9.37	9.29	9.23	9.17	9.13	9.09	9.06	9.04	9.01	8.95	8.92	8.91
700	11.18	11.04	10.93	10.84	10.76	10.70	10.65	10.61	10.57	10.54	10.52	10.44	10.41	10.40
800	12.77	12.62	12.49	12.39	12.30	12.23	12.17	12.12	12.08	12.05	12.02	11.93	11.90	11.88
900	14.37	14.19	14.05	13.93	13.84	13.76	13.69	13.63	13.59	13.55	13.52	13.42	13.38	13.37
1000	15.97	15.77	15.61	15.48	15.37	15.28	15.21	15.15	15.10	15.06	15.02	14.91	14.87	14.85
2000	31.93	31.54	31.22	30.96	30.74	30.56	30.42	30.29	30.19	30.11	30.03	29.82	29.73	29.70
3000	47.89	47.30	46.83	46.43	46.11	45.84	45.62	45.44	45.28	45.16	45.05	44.73	44.60	44.54
4000	63.85	63.07	62.43	61.91	61.48	61.12	60.83	60.58	60.38	60.21	60.06	59.64	59.46	59.39
5000	79.81	78.84	78.04	77.39	76.85	76.40	76.03	75.72	75.47	75.26	75.08	74.54	74.32	74.23
6000	95.77	94.60	93.65	92.86	92.22	91.68	91.24	90.87	90.56	90.31	90.09	89.45	89.19	89.08
7000	111.73	110.37	109.26	108.34	107.59	106.96	106.44	106.01	105.65	105.36	105.11	104.36	104.05	103.93
8000	127.69	126.14	124.86	123.82	122.95	122.24	121.65	121.16	120.75	120.41	120.12	119.27	118.92	118.77
9000	143.65	141.90	140.47	139.29	138.32	137.52	136.85	136.30	135.84	135.46	135.14	134.17	133.78	133.62
10000	159.61	157.67	156.08	154.77	153.69	152.80	152.06	151.44	150.93	150.51	150.15	149.08	148.64	148.46
11000	175.57	173.44	171.69	170.25	169.06	168.08	167.26	166.59	166.02	165.56	165.16	163.99	163.51	163.31
12000	191.53	189.20	187.29	185.72	184.43	183.36	182.47	181.73	181.12	180.61	180.10	178.90	178.37	178.16
13000	207.49	204.97	202.90	201.20	199.80	198.64	197.67	196.87	196.21	195.66	195.19	193.80	193.24	193.00
14000	223.45	220.74	218.51	216.68	215.17	213.92	212.88	212.02	211.30	210.71	210.21	208.71	208.10	207.85
15000	239.41	236.50	234.12	232.15	230.54	229.20	228.08	227.16	226.39	225.76	225.22	223.62	222.96	222.69
16000	255.37	252.27	249.72	247.63	245.90	244.47	243.29	242.31	241.49	240.81	240.24	238.53	237.83	237.54
17000	271.33	268.04	265.33	263.11	261.27	259.75	258.50	257.45	256.58	255.86	255.25	253.44	252.69	252.39
18000	287.29	283.80	280.94	278.58	276.64	275.03	273.70	272.59	271.67	270.91	270.27	268.34	267.56	267.23
19000	303.25	299.57	296.55	294.06	292.01	290.31	288.91	287.74	286.77	285.96	285.28	283.25	282.42	282.08
20000	319.22	315.33	312.15	309.54	307.38	305.59	304.11	302.88	301.86	301.01	300.30	298.16	297.28	296.92
21000	335.18	331.10	327.76	325.01	322.75	320.87	319.32	318.02	316.95	316.06	315.31	313.07	312.15	311.77
22000	351.14	346.87	343.37	340.49	338.12	336.15	334.52	333.17	332.04	331.11	330.32	327.97	327.01	326.62
23000	367.10	362.63	358.97	355.97	353.48	351.43	349.73	348.31	347.14	346.16	345.34	342.88	341.88	341.46
24000	383.06	378.40	374.58	371.44	368.85	366.71	364.93	363.46	362.23	361.21	360.35	357.79	356.74	356.31
25000	399.02	394.17	390.19	386.92	384.22	381.99	380.14	378.60	377.32	376.26	375.37	372.70	371.60	371.15
26000	414.98	409.93	405.80	402.40	399.59	397.27	395.34	393.74	392.41	391.31	390.38	387.60	386.47	386.00
27000	430.94	425.70	421.41	417.87	414.96	412.55	410.55	408.89	407.51	406.36	405.40	402.51	401.33	400.85
28000	446.90	441.47	437.01	433.35	430.33	427.83	425.75	424.03	422.60	421.41	420.41	417.42	416.20	415.69
29000	462.86	457.23	452.62	448.83	445.70	443.11	440.96	439.18	437.69	436.46	435.43	432.33	431.06	430.54
30000	478.82	473.00	468.23	464.30	461.07	458.39	456.16	454.32	452.78	451.51	450.44	447.24	445.92	445.38
31000	494.78	488.77	483.84	479.78	476.43	473.67	471.37	469.46	467.88	466.56	465.45	462.14	460.79	460.23
32000	510.74	504.53	499.44	495.26	491.80	488.94	486.58	484.61	482.97	481.61	480.47	477.05	475.65	475.08
33000	526.70	520.30	515.05	510.73	507.17	504.22	501.78	499.75	498.06	496.66	495.48	491.96	490.52	489.92
34000	542.66	536.07	530.66	526.21	522.54	519.50	516.99	514.89	513.15	511.71	510.50	506.87	505.38	504.77
35000	558.62	551.83	546.27	541.69	537.91	534.78	532.19	530.04	528.25	526.76	525.51	521.77	520.24	519.61
36000	574.58	567.60	561.87	557.16	553.28	550.06	547.40	545.18	543.34	541.81	540.53	536.68	535.11	534.46
37000	590.54	583.36	577.48	572.64	568.65	565.34	562.60	560.33	558.43	556.86	555.54	551.59	549.97	549.31
38000	606.50	599.13	593.09	588.12	584.02	580.62	577.81	575.47	573.53	571.91	570.56	566.50	564.84	564.15
39000	622.47	614.90	608.70	603.59	599.38	595.90	593.01	590.61	588.62	586.96	585.57	581.40	579.70	579.00
40000	638.43	630.66	624.30	619.07	614.75	611.18	608.22	605.76	603.71	602.01	600.59	596.31	594.56	593.84
41000	654.39	646.43	639.91	634.55	630.12	626.46	623.42	620.90	618.80	617.06	615.60	611.22	609.43	608.69
42000	670.35	662.20	655.52	650.02	645.49	641.74	638.63	636.04	633.90	632.11	630.61	626.13	624.29	623.54
43000	686.31	677.96	671.13	665.50	660.86	657.02	653.83	651.19	648.99	647.16	645.63	641.04	639.16	638.38
44000	702.27	693.73	686.73	680.98	676.23	672.30	669.04	666.33	664.08	662.21	660.64	655.95	654.02	653.23
45000	718.23	709.50	702.34	696.45	691.60	687.58	684.24	681.48	679.17	677.26	675.66	670.85	668.88	668.07
46000	734.19	725.26	717.95	711.93	706.96	702.86	699.45	696.62	694.27	692.31	690.67	685.76	683.75	682.92
47000	750.15	741.03	733.56	727.41	722.33	718.14	714.65	711.76	709.36	707.36	705.69	700.67	698.61	697.77
48000	766.11	756.80	749.16	742.88	737.70	733.41	729.86	726.91	724.45	722.41	720.70	715.57	713.48	712.61
49000	782.07	772.56	764.77	758.36	753.07	748.69	745.07	742.05	739.54	737.46	735.72	730.48	728.34	727.46
50000	798.03	788.33	780.38	773.84	768.44	763.97	760.27	757.20	754.64	752.51	750.73	745.39	743.20	742.30
55000	877.83	867.16	858.41	851.22	845.28	840.37	836.30	832.91	830.10	827.76	825.80	819.93	817.52	816.53
60000	957.64	945.99	936.45	928.60	922.13	916.77	912.32	908.63	905.56	903.01	900.88	894.47	891.84	890.76
65000	1037.44	1024.83	1014.49	1005.99	998.97	993.16	988.35	984.35	981.03	978.26	975.95	969.00	966.16	964.99
70000	1117.24	1103.66	1092.53	1083.37	1075.81	1069.56	1064.38	1060.07	1056.49	1053.51	1051.02	1043.54	1040.48	1039.22
75000	1197.04	1182.49	1170.56	1160.75	1152.66	1145.96	1140.40	1135.79	1131.95	1128.76	1126.09	1118.08	1114.80	1113.45
80000	1276.85	1261.32	1248.60	1238.14	1229.50	1222.35	1216.43	1211.51	1207.42	1204.01	1201.17	1192.62	1189.12	1187.68
85000	1356.65	1340.16	1326.64	1315.52	1306.34	1298.75	1292.46	1287.23	1282.88	1279.26	1276.24	1267.16	1263.44	1261.91
90000	1436.45	1418.99	1404.68	1392.90	1383.19	1375.15	1368.48	1362.95	1358.34	1354.51	1351.31	1341.70	1337.76	1336.14
95000	1516.25	1497.82	1482.71	1470.29	1460.03	1451.55	1444.51	1438.67	1433.81	1429.76	1426.38	1416.24	1412.08	1410.37
100000	1596.06	1576.65	1560.75	1547.67	1536.87	1527.94	1520.54	1514.39	1509.27	1505.01	1501.46	1490.77	1486.40	1484.60

MONTHLY PAYMENT
REQUIRED TO AMORTIZE A LOAN

TERM	1 Year	2 Years	3 Years	4 Years	5 Years	6 Years	7 Years	8 Years	9 Years	10 Years	11 Years	12 Years	13 Years	14 Years
AMOUNT														
5	.46	.25	.19	.15	.13	.12	.11	.10	.10	.09	.09	.09	.09	.09
10	.92	.50	.37	.30	.26	.23	.21	.20	.19	.18	.18	.17	.17	.17
15	1.38	.75	.55	.44	.38	.35	.32	.30	.29	.27	.27	.26	.25	.25
25	2.30	1.25	.91	.74	.64	.57	.53	.50	.47	.45	.44	.43	.42	.41
50	4.59	2.50	1.81	1.47	1.27	1.14	1.05	.99	.94	.90	.87	.85	.83	.82
75	6.88	3.74	2.71	2.20	1.90	1.71	1.58	1.48	1.41	1.35	1.31	1.27	1.25	1.22
100	9.17	4.99	3.61	2.94	2.54	2.28	2.10	1.97	1.87	1.80	1.74	1.70	1.66	1.63
200	18.33	9.98	7.22	5.87	5.07	4.55	4.19	3.93	3.74	3.59	3.48	3.39	3.31	3.26
300	27.49	14.96	10.83	8.80	7.60	6.83	6.29	5.90	5.61	5.39	5.21	5.08	4.97	4.88
400	36.65	19.95	14.44	11.73	10.14	9.10	8.38	7.86	7.48	7.18	6.95	6.77	6.62	6.51
500	45.82	24.94	18.05	14.66	12.67	11.37	10.48	9.83	9.34	8.97	8.69	8.46	8.28	8.13
600	54.98	29.92	21.66	17.59	15.20	13.65	12.57	11.79	11.21	10.77	10.42	10.15	9.93	9.76
700	64.14	34.91	25.27	20.52	17.73	15.92	14.67	13.76	13.08	12.56	12.16	11.84	11.59	11.38
800	73.30	39.90	28.88	23.45	20.27	18.19	16.76	15.72	14.95	14.36	13.89	13.53	13.24	13.01
900	82.46	44.88	32.49	26.38	22.80	20.47	18.86	17.69	16.82	16.15	15.63	15.22	14.89	14.63
1000	91.63	49.87	36.09	29.31	25.33	22.74	20.95	19.65	18.68	17.94	17.37	16.91	16.55	16.26
2000	183.25	99.73	72.18	58.62	50.66	45.48	41.89	39.30	37.36	35.88	34.73	33.82	33.09	32.51
3000	274.87	149.60	108.27	87.93	75.98	68.22	62.84	58.95	56.04	53.82	52.09	50.72	49.64	48.76
4000	366.49	199.46	144.36	117.24	101.31	90.95	83.78	78.60	74.72	71.76	69.45	67.63	66.18	65.01
5000	458.11	249.32	180.45	146.55	126.63	113.69	104.73	98.24	93.40	89.70	86.81	84.54	82.72	81.26
6000	549.73	299.19	216.54	175.86	151.96	136.43	125.67	117.89	112.08	107.63	104.17	101.44	99.27	97.51
7000	641.35	349.05	252.63	205.17	177.28	159.17	146.62	137.54	130.76	125.57	121.54	118.35	115.81	113.76
8000	732.97	398.91	288.72	234.48	202.61	181.90	167.56	157.19	149.44	143.51	138.90	135.26	132.35	130.02
9000	824.59	448.78	324.81	263.79	227.93	204.64	188.51	176.83	168.11	161.45	156.26	152.16	148.90	146.27
10000	916.21	498.64	360.90	293.10	253.26	227.38	209.45	196.48	186.79	179.39	173.62	169.07	165.44	162.52
11000	1007.83	548.51	396.99	322.41	278.59	250.11	230.40	216.13	205.47	197.32	190.98	185.98	181.98	178.77
12000	1099.45	598.37	433.08	351.72	303.91	272.85	251.34	235.78	224.15	215.26	208.34	202.88	198.53	195.02
13000	1191.07	648.23	469.17	381.03	329.24	295.59	272.29	255.42	242.83	233.20	225.71	219.79	215.07	211.27
14000	1282.69	698.10	505.26	410.34	354.56	318.33	293.23	275.07	261.51	251.14	243.07	236.70	231.61	227.52
15000	1374.31	747.96	541.35	439.65	379.89	341.06	314.17	294.72	280.19	269.08	260.43	253.60	248.16	243.77
16000	1465.93	797.82	577.44	468.96	405.21	363.80	335.12	314.37	298.87	287.01	277.79	270.51	264.70	260.03
17000	1557.55	847.69	613.53	498.27	430.54	386.54	356.06	334.01	317.54	304.95	295.15	287.42	281.25	276.28
18000	1649.17	897.55	649.62	527.58	455.86	409.27	377.01	353.66	336.22	322.89	312.51	304.32	297.79	292.53
19000	1740.79	947.42	685.71	556.89	481.19	432.01	397.95	373.31	354.90	340.83	329.88	321.23	314.33	308.78
20000	1832.42	997.28	721.80	586.20	506.51	454.75	418.90	392.96	373.58	358.77	347.24	338.14	330.88	325.03
21000	1924.04	1047.14	757.89	615.51	531.84	477.49	439.84	412.60	392.26	376.71	364.60	355.04	347.42	341.28
22000	2015.66	1097.01	793.98	644.82	557.17	500.22	460.79	432.25	410.94	394.64	381.96	371.95	363.96	357.53
23000	2107.28	1146.87	830.07	674.13	582.49	522.96	481.73	451.90	429.62	412.58	399.32	388.86	380.51	373.78
24000	2198.90	1196.73	866.16	703.44	607.82	545.70	502.68	471.55	448.30	430.52	416.68	405.76	397.05	390.04
25000	2290.52	1246.60	902.25	732.75	633.14	568.43	523.62	491.19	466.97	448.46	434.05	422.67	413.59	406.29
26000	2382.14	1296.46	938.34	762.06	658.47	591.17	544.57	510.84	485.65	466.40	451.41	439.58	430.14	422.54
27000	2473.76	1346.33	974.43	791.37	683.79	613.91	565.51	530.49	504.33	484.33	468.77	456.48	446.68	438.79
28000	2565.38	1396.19	1010.52	820.68	709.12	636.65	586.46	550.14	523.01	502.27	486.13	473.39	463.22	455.04
29000	2657.00	1446.05	1046.61	849.99	734.44	659.38	607.40	569.78	541.69	520.21	503.49	490.30	479.77	471.29
30000	2748.62	1495.92	1082.70	879.30	759.77	682.12	628.34	589.43	560.37	538.15	520.85	507.20	496.31	487.54
31000	2840.24	1545.78	1118.79	908.61	785.09	704.86	649.29	609.08	579.05	556.09	538.22	524.11	512.85	503.79
32000	2931.86	1595.64	1154.88	937.92	810.42	727.59	670.23	628.73	597.73	574.02	555.58	541.02	529.40	520.05
33000	3023.48	1645.51	1190.97	967.23	835.75	750.33	691.18	648.37	616.40	591.96	572.94	557.92	545.94	536.30
34000	3115.10	1695.37	1227.06	996.54	861.07	773.07	712.12	668.02	635.08	609.90	590.30	574.83	562.49	552.55
35000	3206.72	1745.24	1263.15	1025.85	886.40	795.81	733.07	687.67	653.76	627.84	607.66	591.74	579.03	568.80
36000	3298.34	1795.10	1299.23	1055.16	911.72	818.54	754.01	707.32	672.44	645.78	625.02	608.64	595.57	585.05
37000	3389.96	1844.96	1335.32	1084.46	937.05	841.28	774.96	726.96	691.12	663.72	642.39	625.55	612.12	601.30
38000	3481.58	1894.83	1371.41	1113.77	962.37	864.02	795.90	746.61	709.80	681.65	659.75	642.46	628.66	617.55
39000	3573.21	1944.69	1407.50	1143.08	987.70	886.76	816.85	766.26	728.48	699.59	677.11	659.36	645.20	633.80
40000	3664.83	1994.55	1443.59	1172.39	1013.02	909.49	837.79	785.91	747.16	717.53	694.47	676.27	661.75	650.06
41000	3756.45	2044.42	1479.68	1201.70	1038.35	932.23	858.74	805.55	765.83	735.47	711.83	693.18	678.29	666.31
42000	3848.07	2094.28	1515.77	1231.01	1063.68	954.97	879.68	825.20	784.51	753.41	729.19	710.08	694.83	682.56
43000	3939.69	2144.15	1551.86	1260.32	1089.00	977.70	900.62	844.85	803.19	771.34	746.55	726.99	711.38	698.81
44000	4031.31	2194.01	1587.95	1289.63	1114.33	1000.44	921.57	864.50	821.87	789.28	763.92	743.90	727.92	715.06
45000	4122.93	2243.87	1624.04	1318.94	1139.65	1023.18	942.51	884.14	840.55	807.22	781.28	760.80	744.46	731.31
46000	4214.55	2293.74	1660.13	1348.25	1164.98	1045.92	963.46	903.79	859.23	825.16	798.64	777.71	761.01	747.56
47000	4306.17	2343.60	1696.22	1377.56	1190.30	1068.65	984.40	923.44	877.91	843.10	816.00	794.62	777.55	763.81
48000	4397.79	2393.46	1732.31	1406.87	1215.63	1091.39	1005.35	943.09	896.59	861.03	833.36	811.52	794.09	780.07
49000	4489.41	2443.33	1768.40	1436.18	1240.95	1114.13	1026.29	962.73	915.26	878.97	850.72	828.43	810.64	796.32
50000	4581.03	2493.19	1804.49	1465.49	1266.28	1136.86	1047.24	982.38	933.94	896.91	868.09	845.34	827.18	812.57
55000	5039.13	2742.51	1984.94	1612.04	1392.91	1250.55	1151.96	1080.62	1027.34	986.60	954.89	929.87	909.90	893.83
60000	5497.24	2991.83	2165.39	1758.59	1519.53	1364.24	1256.68	1178.86	1120.73	1076.29	1041.70	1014.40	992.62	975.08
65000	5955.34	3241.15	2345.84	1905.14	1646.16	1477.92	1361.41	1277.09	1214.13	1165.98	1128.51	1098.94	1075.33	1056.34
70000	6413.44	3490.47	2526.29	2051.69	1772.79	1591.61	1466.13	1375.33	1307.52	1255.67	1215.32	1183.47	1158.05	1137.59
75000	6871.54	3739.78	2706.73	2198.23	1899.42	1705.29	1570.85	1473.57	1400.91	1345.36	1302.13	1268.00	1240.77	1218.85
80000	7329.65	3989.10	2887.18	2344.78	2026.04	1818.98	1675.58	1571.81	1494.31	1435.05	1388.94	1352.53	1323.49	1300.11
85000	7787.75	4238.42	3067.63	2491.33	2152.67	1932.67	1780.30	1670.04	1587.70	1524.75	1475.74	1437.07	1406.21	1381.36
90000	8245.85	4487.74	3248.08	2637.88	2279.30	2046.35	1885.02	1768.28	1681.09	1614.44	1562.55	1521.60	1488.92	1462.62
95000	8703.95	4737.06	3428.53	2784.43	2405.93	2160.04	1989.75	1866.52	1774.49	1704.13	1649.36	1606.13	1571.64	1543.88
100000	9162.06	4986.38	3608.98	2930.98	2532.55	2273.72	2094.47	1964.76	1867.88	1793.82	1736.17	1690.67	1654.36	1625.13

TERM	15 Years	16 Years	17 Years	18 Years	19 Years	20 Years	21 Years	22 Years	23 Years	24 Years	25 Years	30 Years	35 Years	40 Years
AMOUNT														
5	.09	.08	.08	.08	.08	.08	.08	.08	.08	.08	.08	.08	.08	.08
10	.17	.16	.16	.16	.16	.16	.16	.16	.16	.16	.16	.15	.15	.15
15	.25	.24	.24	.24	.24	.24	.23	.23	.23	.23	.23	.23	.23	.23
25	.41	.40	.40	.39	.39	.39	.39	.39	.38	.38	.38	.38	.38	.38
50	.81	.80	.79	.78	.78	.77	.77	.77	.76	.76	.76	.75	.75	.75
75	1.21	1.19	1.18	1.17	1.16	1.16	1.15	1.15	1.14	1.14	1.14	1.13	1.12	1.12
100	1.61	1.59	1.57	1.56	1.55	1.54	1.53	1.53	1.52	1.52	1.51	1.50	1.50	1.50
200	3.21	3.17	3.14	3.11	3.09	3.07	3.06	3.05	3.04	3.03	3.02	3.00	2.99	2.99
300	4.81	4.75	4.70	4.66	4.63	4.61	4.58	4.57	4.55	4.54	4.53	4.50	4.48	4.48
400	6.41	6.33	6.27	6.22	6.18	6.14	6.11	6.09	6.07	6.05	6.03	5.99	5.98	5.97
500	8.01	7.92	7.84	7.77	7.72	7.67	7.64	7.61	7.58	7.56	7.54	7.49	7.47	7.46
600	9.61	9.50	9.40	9.32	9.26	9.21	9.16	9.13	9.10	9.07	9.05	8.99	8.96	8.95
700	11.22	11.08	10.97	10.88	10.80	10.74	10.69	10.65	10.61	10.58	10.56	10.48	10.45	10.44
800	12.82	12.66	12.54	12.43	12.35	12.27	12.22	12.17	12.13	12.09	12.06	11.98	11.95	11.93
900	14.42	14.24	14.10	13.98	13.89	13.81	13.74	13.69	13.64	13.60	13.57	13.48	13.44	13.42
1000	16.02	15.83	15.67	15.54	15.43	15.34	15.27	15.21	15.16	15.11	15.08	14.97	14.93	14.91
2000	32.03	31.65	31.33	31.07	30.86	30.68	30.53	30.41	30.31	30.22	30.15	29.94	29.86	29.82
3000	48.05	47.47	46.99	46.60	46.28	46.02	45.80	45.61	45.46	45.33	45.23	44.91	44.78	44.73
4000	64.06	63.29	62.66	62.14	61.71	61.35	61.06	60.81	60.61	60.44	60.30	59.88	59.71	59.64
5000	80.08	79.11	78.32	77.67	77.13	76.69	76.32	76.02	75.76	75.55	75.38	74.85	74.63	74.55
6000	96.09	94.93	93.98	93.20	92.56	92.03	91.59	91.22	90.92	90.66	90.45	89.82	89.56	89.45
7000	112.11	110.75	109.65	108.74	107.98	107.36	106.85	106.42	106.07	105.77	105.53	104.79	104.49	104.36
8000	128.12	126.57	125.31	124.27	123.41	122.70	122.11	121.62	121.22	120.88	120.60	119.76	119.41	119.27
9000	144.13	142.40	140.97	139.80	138.84	138.04	137.38	136.83	136.37	135.99	135.67	134.72	134.34	134.18
10000	160.15	158.22	156.64	155.33	154.26	153.37	152.64	152.03	151.52	151.10	150.75	149.69	149.26	149.09
11000	176.16	174.04	172.30	170.87	169.69	168.71	167.90	167.23	166.67	166.21	165.82	164.66	164.19	163.99
12000	192.18	189.86	187.96	186.40	185.11	184.05	183.17	182.43	181.83	181.32	180.90	179.63	179.11	178.90
13000	208.19	205.68	203.62	201.93	200.54	199.39	198.43	197.64	196.98	196.43	195.97	194.60	194.04	193.81
14000	224.21	221.50	219.29	217.47	215.96	214.72	213.69	212.84	212.13	211.54	211.05	209.57	208.97	208.72
15000	240.22	237.32	234.95	233.00	231.39	230.06	228.96	228.04	227.28	226.65	226.12	224.54	223.89	223.63
16000	256.23	253.14	250.61	248.53	246.82	245.40	244.22	243.24	242.43	241.76	241.20	239.51	238.82	238.54
17000	272.25	268.97	266.28	264.07	262.24	260.73	259.48	258.45	257.59	256.87	256.27	254.48	253.74	253.44
18000	288.26	284.79	281.94	279.60	277.67	276.07	274.75	273.65	272.74	271.98	271.34	269.44	268.67	268.35
19000	304.28	300.61	297.60	295.13	293.09	291.41	290.01	288.85	287.89	287.09	286.42	284.41	283.60	283.26
20000	320.29	316.43	313.27	310.66	308.52	306.74	305.27	304.05	303.04	302.20	301.49	299.38	298.52	298.17
21000	336.31	332.25	328.93	326.20	323.94	322.08	320.54	319.26	318.19	317.31	316.57	314.35	313.45	313.08
22000	352.32	348.07	344.59	341.73	339.37	337.42	335.80	334.46	333.34	332.42	331.64	329.32	328.37	327.98
23000	368.34	363.89	360.25	357.26	354.80	352.76	351.07	349.66	348.50	347.52	346.72	344.29	343.30	342.89
24000	384.35	379.71	375.92	372.80	370.22	368.09	366.33	364.86	363.65	362.63	361.79	359.26	358.22	357.80
25000	400.36	395.54	391.58	388.33	385.65	383.43	381.59	380.07	378.80	377.74	376.86	374.23	373.15	372.71
26000	416.38	411.36	407.24	403.86	401.07	398.77	396.86	395.27	393.95	392.85	391.94	389.20	388.08	387.62
27000	432.39	427.18	422.91	419.39	416.50	414.10	412.12	410.47	409.10	407.96	407.01	404.16	403.00	402.53
28000	448.41	443.00	438.57	434.93	431.92	429.44	427.38	425.67	424.25	423.07	422.09	419.13	417.93	417.43
29000	464.42	458.82	454.23	450.46	447.35	444.78	442.65	440.88	439.41	438.18	437.16	434.10	432.85	432.34
30000	480.44	474.64	469.90	465.99	462.78	460.11	457.91	456.08	454.56	453.29	452.24	449.07	447.78	447.25
31000	496.45	490.46	485.56	481.53	478.20	475.45	473.17	471.28	469.71	468.40	467.31	464.04	462.71	462.16
32000	512.46	506.28	501.22	497.06	493.63	490.79	488.44	486.48	484.86	483.51	482.39	479.01	477.63	477.07
33000	528.48	522.10	516.88	512.59	509.05	506.13	503.70	501.69	500.01	498.62	497.46	493.98	492.56	491.97
34000	544.49	537.93	532.55	528.13	524.48	521.46	518.96	516.89	515.17	513.73	512.53	508.95	507.48	506.88
35000	560.51	553.75	548.21	543.66	539.90	536.80	534.23	532.09	530.32	528.84	527.61	523.91	522.41	521.79
36000	576.52	569.57	563.87	559.19	555.33	552.14	549.49	547.29	545.47	543.95	542.68	538.88	537.33	536.70
37000	592.54	585.39	579.54	574.72	570.76	567.47	564.75	562.50	560.62	559.06	557.76	553.85	552.26	551.61
38000	608.55	601.21	595.20	590.26	586.18	582.81	580.02	577.70	575.77	574.17	572.83	568.82	567.19	566.52
39000	624.56	617.03	610.86	605.79	601.61	598.15	595.28	592.90	590.92	589.28	587.91	583.79	582.11	581.42
40000	640.58	632.85	626.53	621.32	617.03	613.48	610.54	608.10	606.08	604.39	602.98	598.76	597.04	596.33
41000	656.59	648.67	642.19	636.86	632.46	628.82	625.81	623.31	621.23	619.50	618.06	613.73	611.96	611.24
42000	672.61	664.50	657.85	652.39	647.88	644.16	641.07	638.51	636.38	634.61	633.13	628.70	626.89	626.15
43000	688.62	680.32	673.51	667.92	663.31	659.50	656.34	653.71	651.53	649.72	648.20	643.67	641.82	641.06
44000	704.64	696.14	689.18	683.45	678.73	674.83	671.60	668.91	666.68	664.83	663.28	658.63	656.74	655.96
45000	720.65	711.96	704.84	698.99	694.16	690.17	686.86	684.12	681.83	679.94	678.35	673.60	671.67	670.87
46000	736.67	727.78	720.50	714.52	709.59	705.51	702.13	699.32	696.99	695.04	693.43	688.57	686.59	685.78
47000	752.68	743.60	736.17	730.05	725.01	720.84	717.39	714.52	712.14	710.15	708.50	703.54	701.52	700.69
48000	768.69	759.42	751.83	745.59	740.44	736.18	732.65	729.72	727.29	725.26	723.58	718.51	716.44	715.60
49000	784.71	775.24	767.49	761.12	755.86	751.52	747.92	744.93	742.44	740.37	738.65	733.48	731.37	730.51
50000	800.72	791.07	783.16	776.65	771.29	766.85	763.18	760.13	757.59	755.48	753.72	748.45	746.30	745.41
55000	880.79	870.17	861.47	854.32	848.42	843.54	839.50	836.14	833.35	831.03	829.10	823.29	820.93	819.95
60000	960.87	949.28	939.79	931.98	925.55	920.22	915.81	912.15	909.11	906.58	904.47	898.14	895.55	894.50
65000	1040.94	1028.38	1018.10	1009.65	1002.67	996.91	992.13	988.17	984.87	982.13	979.84	972.98	970.18	969.04
70000	1121.01	1107.49	1096.42	1087.31	1079.80	1073.59	1068.45	1064.18	1060.63	1057.67	1055.21	1047.82	1044.81	1043.58
75000	1201.08	1186.60	1174.73	1164.98	1156.93	1150.28	1144.77	1140.19	1136.39	1133.22	1130.59	1122.67	1119.44	1118.12
80000	1281.15	1265.70	1253.05	1242.64	1234.06	1226.96	1221.08	1216.20	1212.15	1208.77	1205.96	1197.51	1194.07	1192.66
85000	1361.23	1344.81	1331.36	1320.31	1311.19	1303.65	1297.40	1292.22	1287.91	1284.32	1281.33	1272.36	1268.70	1267.20
90000	1441.30	1423.91	1409.68	1397.97	1388.32	1380.33	1373.72	1368.23	1363.66	1359.87	1356.70	1347.20	1343.33	1341.74
95000	1521.37	1503.02	1487.99	1475.63	1465.44	1457.02	1450.04	1444.24	1439.42	1435.41	1432.07	1422.05	1417.96	1416.28
100000	1601.44	1582.13	1566.31	1553.30	1542.57	1533.70	1526.35	1520.25	1515.18	1510.96	1507.44	1496.89	1492.59	1490.82

17.900%

TERM	1 Year	2 Years	3 Years	4 Years	5 Years	6 Years	7 Years	8 Years	9 Years	10 Years	11 Years	12 Years	13 Years	14 Years
AMOUNT														
5	.46	.25	.19	.15	.13	.12	.11	.10	.10	.09	.09	.09	.09	.09
10	.92	.50	.37	.30	.26	.23	.21	.20	.19	.18	.18	.17	.17	.17
15	1.38	.75	.55	.44	.39	.35	.32	.30	.29	.27	.27	.26	.25	.25
25	2.30	1.25	.91	.74	.64	.57	.53	.50	.47	.45	.44	.43	.42	.41
50	4.59	2.50	1.81	1.47	1.27	1.14	1.05	.99	.94	.90	.87	.85	.83	.82
75	6.88	3.75	2.71	2.20	1.91	1.71	1.58	1.48	1.41	1.35	1.31	1.27	1.25	1.23
100	9.17	4.99	3.62	2.94	2.54	2.28	2.10	1.97	1.87	1.80	1.74	1.70	1.66	1.63
200	18.33	9.98	7.23	5.87	5.07	4.56	4.20	3.94	3.74	3.60	3.48	3.39	3.32	3.26
300	27.49	14.97	10.84	8.80	7.61	6.83	6.29	5.90	5.61	5.39	5.22	5.08	4.97	4.89
400	36.66	19.96	14.45	11.73	10.14	9.11	8.39	7.87	7.48	7.19	6.96	6.77	6.63	6.51
500	45.82	24.94	18.06	14.67	12.67	11.38	10.48	9.84	9.35	8.98	8.69	8.47	8.29	8.14
600	54.98	29.93	21.67	17.60	15.21	13.66	12.58	11.80	11.22	10.78	10.43	10.16	9.94	9.77
700	64.15	34.92	25.28	20.53	17.74	15.93	14.68	13.77	13.09	12.57	12.17	11.85	11.60	11.39
800	73.31	39.91	28.89	23.46	20.28	18.21	16.77	15.74	14.96	14.37	13.91	13.54	13.25	13.02
900	82.47	44.89	32.50	26.40	22.81	20.48	18.87	17.70	16.83	16.16	15.65	15.24	14.91	14.65
1000	91.64	49.88	36.11	29.33	25.34	22.76	20.96	19.67	18.70	17.96	17.38	16.93	16.57	16.27
2000	183.27	99.76	72.21	58.65	50.68	45.51	41.92	39.33	37.39	35.91	34.76	33.85	33.13	32.54
3000	274.90	149.63	108.31	87.97	76.02	68.26	62.88	58.99	56.09	53.87	52.14	50.78	49.69	48.81
4000	366.53	199.51	144.41	117.30	101.36	91.01	83.84	78.66	74.78	71.82	69.52	67.70	66.25	65.08
5000	458.17	249.38	180.52	146.62	126.70	113.76	104.80	98.32	93.48	89.78	86.90	84.62	82.81	81.35
6000	549.80	299.26	216.62	175.94	152.04	136.51	125.76	117.98	112.17	107.73	104.27	101.55	99.37	97.62
7000	641.43	349.14	252.72	205.26	177.38	159.26	146.72	137.64	130.87	125.68	121.65	118.47	115.93	113.89
8000	733.06	399.01	288.82	234.59	202.72	182.02	167.68	157.31	149.56	143.64	139.03	135.39	132.49	130.16
9000	824.70	448.89	324.93	263.91	228.06	204.77	188.64	176.97	168.25	161.59	156.41	152.32	149.05	146.43
10000	916.33	498.76	361.03	293.23	253.40	227.52	209.60	196.63	186.95	179.55	173.79	169.24	165.61	162.69
11000	1007.96	548.64	397.13	322.56	278.73	250.27	230.56	216.29	205.64	197.50	191.16	186.16	182.17	178.96
12000	1099.59	598.51	433.23	351.88	304.07	273.02	251.52	235.96	224.34	215.46	208.54	203.09	198.73	195.23
13000	1191.23	648.39	469.33	381.20	329.41	295.77	272.48	255.62	243.03	233.41	225.92	220.01	215.30	211.50
14000	1282.86	698.27	505.44	410.52	354.75	318.52	293.43	275.28	261.73	251.36	243.30	236.93	231.86	227.77
15000	1374.49	748.14	541.54	439.85	380.09	341.27	314.39	294.94	280.42	269.32	260.68	253.86	248.42	244.04
16000	1466.12	798.02	577.64	469.17	405.43	364.03	335.35	314.61	299.12	287.27	278.05	270.78	264.98	260.31
17000	1557.76	847.89	613.74	498.49	430.77	386.78	356.31	334.27	317.81	305.23	295.43	287.70	281.54	276.58
18000	1649.39	897.77	649.85	527.81	456.11	409.53	377.27	353.93	336.50	323.18	312.81	304.63	298.10	292.85
19000	1741.02	947.65	685.95	557.14	481.45	432.28	398.23	373.60	355.20	341.13	330.19	321.55	314.66	309.11
20000	1832.65	997.52	722.05	586.46	506.79	455.03	419.19	393.26	373.89	359.09	347.57	338.48	331.22	325.38
21000	1924.29	1047.40	758.15	615.78	532.13	477.78	440.15	412.92	392.59	377.04	364.95	355.40	347.78	341.65
22000	2015.92	1097.27	794.25	645.11	557.46	500.53	461.11	432.58	411.28	395.00	382.32	372.32	364.34	357.92
23000	2107.55	1147.15	830.36	674.43	582.80	523.28	482.07	452.25	429.98	412.95	399.70	389.25	380.90	374.19
24000	2199.18	1197.02	866.46	703.75	608.14	546.04	503.03	471.91	448.67	430.91	417.08	406.17	397.46	390.46
25000	2290.82	1246.90	902.56	733.07	633.48	568.79	523.99	491.57	467.36	448.86	434.46	423.09	414.03	406.73
26000	2382.45	1296.78	938.66	762.40	658.82	591.54	544.95	511.23	486.06	466.81	451.84	440.02	430.59	423.00
27000	2474.08	1346.65	974.77	791.72	684.16	614.29	565.91	530.90	504.75	484.77	469.21	456.94	447.15	439.27
28000	2565.71	1396.53	1010.87	821.04	709.50	637.04	586.86	550.56	523.45	502.72	486.59	473.86	463.71	455.53
29000	2657.34	1446.40	1046.97	850.37	734.84	659.79	607.82	570.22	542.14	520.68	503.97	490.79	480.27	471.80
30000	2748.98	1496.28	1083.07	879.69	760.18	682.54	628.78	589.88	560.84	538.63	521.35	507.71	496.83	488.07
31000	2840.61	1546.15	1119.17	909.01	785.52	705.30	649.74	609.55	579.53	556.58	538.73	524.63	513.39	504.34
32000	2932.24	1596.03	1155.28	938.33	810.85	728.05	670.70	629.21	598.23	574.54	556.10	541.56	529.95	520.61
33000	3023.87	1645.91	1191.38	967.66	836.19	750.80	691.66	648.87	616.92	592.49	573.48	558.48	546.51	536.88
34000	3115.51	1695.78	1227.48	996.98	861.53	773.55	712.62	668.53	635.61	610.45	590.86	575.40	563.07	553.15
35000	3207.14	1745.66	1263.58	1026.30	886.87	796.30	733.58	688.20	654.31	628.40	608.24	592.33	579.63	569.42
36000	3298.77	1795.53	1299.69	1055.62	912.21	819.05	754.54	707.86	673.00	646.36	625.62	609.25	596.19	585.69
37000	3390.40	1845.41	1335.79	1084.95	937.55	841.80	775.50	727.52	691.70	664.31	643.00	626.18	612.76	601.95
38000	3482.04	1895.29	1371.89	1114.27	962.89	864.55	796.46	747.19	710.39	682.26	660.37	643.10	629.32	618.22
39000	3573.67	1945.16	1407.99	1143.59	988.23	887.31	817.42	766.85	729.09	700.22	677.75	660.02	645.88	634.49
40000	3665.30	1995.04	1444.10	1172.92	1013.57	910.06	838.38	786.51	747.78	718.17	695.13	676.95	662.44	650.76
41000	3756.93	2044.91	1480.20	1202.24	1038.91	932.81	859.33	806.17	766.47	736.13	712.51	693.87	679.00	667.03
42000	3848.57	2094.79	1516.30	1231.56	1064.25	955.56	880.29	825.84	785.17	754.08	729.89	710.79	695.56	683.30
43000	3940.20	2144.66	1552.40	1260.88	1089.58	978.31	901.25	845.50	803.86	772.04	747.26	727.72	712.12	699.57
44000	4031.83	2194.54	1588.50	1290.21	1114.92	1001.06	922.21	865.16	822.56	789.99	764.64	744.64	728.68	715.84
45000	4123.46	2244.42	1624.61	1319.53	1140.26	1023.81	943.17	884.82	841.25	807.94	782.02	761.56	745.24	732.11
46000	4215.10	2294.29	1660.71	1348.85	1165.60	1046.56	964.13	904.49	859.95	825.90	799.40	778.49	761.80	748.37
47000	4306.73	2344.17	1696.81	1378.18	1190.94	1069.32	985.09	924.15	878.64	843.85	816.78	795.41	778.36	764.64
48000	4398.36	2394.04	1732.91	1407.50	1216.28	1092.07	1006.05	943.81	897.34	861.81	834.15	812.33	794.92	780.91
49000	4489.99	2443.92	1769.02	1436.82	1241.62	1114.82	1027.01	963.47	916.03	879.76	851.53	829.26	811.49	797.18
50000	4581.63	2493.79	1805.12	1466.14	1266.96	1137.57	1047.97	983.14	934.72	897.71	868.91	846.18	828.05	813.45
55000	5039.79	2743.17	1985.63	1612.76	1393.65	1251.33	1152.76	1081.45	1028.20	987.49	955.80	930.80	910.85	894.79
60000	5497.95	2992.55	2166.14	1759.37	1520.35	1365.08	1257.56	1179.76	1121.67	1077.26	1042.69	1015.42	993.65	976.14
65000	5956.11	3241.93	2346.65	1905.99	1647.04	1478.84	1362.36	1278.08	1215.14	1167.03	1129.58	1100.03	1076.46	1057.48
70000	6414.27	3491.31	2527.16	2052.60	1773.74	1592.60	1467.15	1376.39	1308.61	1256.80	1216.47	1184.65	1159.26	1138.83
75000	6872.44	3740.69	2707.67	2199.21	1900.43	1706.35	1571.95	1474.70	1402.08	1346.57	1303.36	1269.27	1242.07	1220.17
80000	7330.60	3990.07	2888.19	2345.83	2027.13	1820.11	1676.75	1573.02	1495.56	1436.34	1390.25	1353.89	1324.87	1301.52
85000	7788.76	4239.45	3068.70	2492.44	2153.83	1933.87	1781.54	1671.33	1589.03	1526.11	1477.15	1438.50	1407.67	1382.86
90000	8246.92	4488.83	3249.21	2639.05	2280.52	2047.62	1886.34	1769.64	1682.50	1615.88	1564.04	1523.12	1490.48	1464.21
95000	8705.08	4738.21	3429.72	2785.67	2407.22	2161.38	1991.14	1867.96	1775.97	1705.65	1650.93	1607.74	1573.28	1545.55
100000	9163.25	4987.58	3610.23	2932.28	2533.91	2275.13	2095.93	1966.27	1869.44	1795.42	1737.82	1692.36	1656.09	1626.90

TERM AMOUNT	15 Years	16 Years	17 Years	18 Years	19 Years	20 Years	21 Years	22 Years	23 Years	24 Years	25 Years	30 Years	35 Years	40 Years
5	.09	.08	.08	.08	.08	.08	.08	.08	.08	.08	.08	.08	.08	.08
10	.17	.16	.16	.16	.16	.16	.16	.16	.16	.16	.16	.15	.15	.15
15	.25	.24	.24	.24	.24	.24	.23	.23	.23	.23	.23	.23	.23	.23
25	.41	.40	.40	.39	.39	.39	.39	.39	.38	.38	.38	.38	.38	.38
50	.81	.80	.79	.78	.78	.78	.77	.77	.76	.76	.76	.75	.75	.75
75	1.21	1.19	1.18	1.17	1.16	1.16	1.15	1.15	1.14	1.14	1.14	1.13	1.13	1.12
100	1.61	1.59	1.57	1.56	1.55	1.54	1.53	1.53	1.52	1.52	1.51	1.50	1.50	1.50
200	3.21	3.17	3.14	3.12	3.09	3.08	3.06	3.05	3.04	3.03	3.02	3.00	2.99	2.99
300	4.81	4.76	4.71	4.67	4.64	4.61	4.59	4.57	4.56	4.54	4.53	4.50	4.49	4.48
400	6.42	6.34	6.28	6.23	6.18	6.15	6.12	6.09	6.07	6.06	6.04	6.00	5.98	5.98
500	8.02	7.92	7.85	7.78	7.73	7.68	7.65	7.62	7.59	7.57	7.55	7.50	7.48	7.47
600	9.62	9.51	9.41	9.34	9.27	9.22	9.17	9.14	9.11	9.08	9.06	9.00	8.97	8.96
700	11.23	11.09	10.98	10.89	10.82	10.75	10.70	10.66	10.63	10.60	10.57	10.50	10.47	10.46
800	12.83	12.68	12.55	12.45	12.36	12.29	12.23	12.18	12.14	12.11	12.08	12.00	11.96	11.95
900	14.43	14.26	14.12	14.00	13.91	13.83	13.76	13.70	13.66	13.62	13.59	13.50	13.46	13.44
1000	16.04	15.84	15.69	15.56	15.45	15.36	15.29	15.23	15.18	15.13	15.10	14.99	14.95	14.93
2000	32.07	31.68	31.37	31.11	30.89	30.72	30.57	30.45	30.35	30.26	30.19	29.98	29.90	29.86
3000	48.10	47.52	47.05	46.66	46.34	46.07	45.85	45.67	45.52	45.39	45.29	44.97	44.84	44.79
4000	64.13	63.36	62.73	62.21	61.78	61.43	61.14	60.89	60.69	60.52	60.38	59.96	59.79	59.72
5000	80.17	79.20	78.41	77.76	77.23	76.79	76.42	76.12	75.86	75.65	75.48	74.95	74.74	74.65
6000	96.20	95.04	94.09	93.32	92.67	92.14	91.70	91.34	91.03	90.78	90.57	89.94	89.68	89.58
7000	112.23	110.88	109.78	108.87	108.12	107.50	106.99	106.56	106.21	105.91	105.67	104.93	104.63	104.51
8000	128.26	126.72	125.46	124.42	123.56	122.85	122.27	121.78	121.38	121.04	120.76	119.92	119.58	119.44
9000	144.30	142.56	141.14	139.97	139.01	138.21	137.55	137.00	136.55	136.17	135.85	134.91	134.52	134.37
10000	160.33	158.40	156.82	155.52	154.45	153.57	152.83	152.23	151.72	151.30	150.95	149.90	149.47	149.29
11000	176.36	174.24	172.50	171.07	169.90	168.92	168.12	167.45	166.89	166.43	166.04	164.89	164.42	164.22
12000	192.39	190.08	188.18	186.63	185.34	184.28	183.40	182.67	182.06	181.56	181.14	179.88	179.36	179.15
13000	208.43	205.92	203.87	202.18	200.79	199.64	198.68	197.89	197.23	196.69	196.23	194.87	194.31	194.08
14000	224.46	221.76	219.55	217.73	216.23	214.99	213.97	213.11	212.41	211.82	211.33	209.85	209.26	209.01
15000	240.49	237.60	235.23	233.28	231.68	230.35	229.25	228.34	227.58	226.95	226.42	224.84	224.20	223.94
16000	256.52	253.44	250.91	248.83	247.12	245.70	244.53	243.56	242.75	242.08	241.51	239.83	239.15	238.87
17000	272.55	269.28	266.59	264.38	262.56	261.06	259.81	258.78	257.92	257.21	256.61	254.82	254.09	253.80
18000	288.59	285.12	282.27	279.94	278.01	276.42	275.10	274.00	273.09	272.33	271.70	269.81	269.04	268.73
19000	304.62	300.95	297.95	295.49	293.45	291.77	290.38	289.22	288.26	287.46	286.80	284.80	283.99	283.65
20000	320.65	316.79	313.64	311.04	308.90	307.13	305.66	304.45	303.43	302.59	301.89	299.79	298.93	298.58
21000	336.68	332.63	329.32	326.59	324.34	322.49	320.95	319.67	318.61	317.72	316.99	314.78	313.88	313.51
22000	352.72	348.47	345.00	342.14	339.79	337.84	336.23	334.89	333.78	332.85	332.00	329.77	328.83	328.44
23000	368.75	364.31	360.68	357.69	355.23	353.20	351.51	350.11	348.95	347.90	347.18	344.76	343.77	343.37
24000	384.78	380.15	376.36	373.25	370.68	368.55	366.79	365.33	364.12	363.11	362.27	359.75	358.72	358.30
25000	400.81	395.99	392.04	388.80	386.12	383.91	382.08	380.56	379.29	378.24	377.36	374.74	373.67	373.23
26000	416.85	411.83	407.73	404.35	401.57	399.27	397.36	395.78	394.46	393.37	392.46	389.73	388.61	388.16
27000	432.88	427.67	423.41	419.90	417.01	414.62	412.64	411.00	409.64	408.50	407.55	404.71	403.56	403.09
28000	448.91	443.51	439.09	435.45	432.46	429.98	427.93	426.22	424.81	423.63	422.65	419.70	418.51	418.01
29000	464.94	459.35	454.77	451.01	447.90	445.33	443.21	441.44	439.98	438.76	437.74	434.69	433.45	432.94
30000	480.97	475.19	470.45	466.56	463.35	460.69	458.49	456.67	455.15	453.89	452.84	449.68	448.40	447.87
31000	497.01	491.03	486.13	482.11	478.79	476.05	473.77	471.89	470.32	469.02	467.93	464.67	463.34	462.80
32000	513.04	506.87	501.81	497.66	494.24	491.40	489.06	487.11	485.49	484.15	483.02	479.66	478.29	477.73
33000	529.07	522.71	517.50	513.21	509.68	506.76	504.34	502.33	500.66	499.28	498.12	494.65	493.24	492.66
34000	545.10	538.55	533.18	528.76	525.12	522.12	519.62	517.55	515.84	514.41	513.21	509.64	508.18	507.59
35000	561.14	554.39	548.86	544.32	540.57	537.47	534.91	532.78	531.01	529.53	528.31	524.63	523.13	522.52
36000	577.17	570.23	564.54	559.87	556.01	552.83	550.19	548.00	546.18	544.66	543.40	539.62	538.08	537.45
37000	593.20	586.07	580.22	575.42	571.46	568.18	565.47	563.22	561.35	559.79	558.50	554.61	553.02	552.37
38000	609.23	601.90	595.90	590.97	586.90	583.54	580.75	578.44	576.52	574.92	573.59	569.60	567.97	567.30
39000	625.27	617.74	611.59	606.52	602.35	598.90	596.04	593.67	591.69	590.05	588.69	584.59	582.92	582.23
40000	641.30	633.50	627.27	622.07	617.79	614.25	611.32	608.89	606.86	605.18	603.78	599.58	597.86	597.16
41000	657.33	649.42	642.95	637.63	633.24	629.61	626.60	624.11	622.04	620.31	618.87	614.56	612.81	612.09
42000	673.36	665.26	658.63	653.18	648.68	644.97	641.89	639.33	637.21	635.44	633.97	629.55	627.76	627.02
43000	689.39	681.10	674.31	668.73	664.13	660.32	657.17	654.55	652.38	650.57	649.06	644.54	642.70	641.95
44000	705.43	696.94	689.99	684.28	679.57	675.68	672.45	669.78	667.55	665.70	664.16	659.53	657.65	656.88
45000	721.46	712.78	705.67	699.83	695.02	691.03	687.74	685.00	682.72	680.83	679.25	674.52	672.59	671.81
46000	737.49	728.62	721.36	715.38	710.46	706.39	703.02	700.22	697.89	695.96	694.35	689.51	687.54	686.73
47000	753.52	744.46	737.04	730.94	725.91	721.75	718.30	715.44	713.07	711.09	709.44	704.50	702.49	701.66
48000	769.56	760.30	752.72	746.49	741.35	737.10	733.58	730.66	728.24	726.22	724.53	719.49	717.43	716.59
49000	785.59	776.14	768.40	762.04	756.79	752.46	748.87	745.89	743.41	741.35	739.63	734.48	732.38	731.52
50000	801.62	791.98	784.08	777.59	772.24	767.81	764.15	761.11	758.58	756.48	754.72	749.47	747.33	746.45
55000	881.78	871.18	862.49	855.35	849.46	844.60	840.56	837.22	834.44	832.12	830.20	824.41	822.06	821.09
60000	961.94	950.37	940.90	933.11	926.69	921.38	916.98	913.33	910.29	907.77	905.67	899.36	896.79	895.74
65000	1042.11	1029.57	1019.31	1010.87	1003.91	998.16	993.39	989.44	986.15	983.42	981.14	974.31	971.52	970.38
70000	1122.27	1108.77	1097.71	1088.63	1081.13	1074.94	1069.81	1065.55	1062.01	1059.06	1056.61	1049.25	1046.26	1045.03
75000	1202.43	1187.96	1176.12	1166.39	1158.36	1151.72	1146.22	1141.66	1137.87	1134.71	1132.08	1124.20	1120.99	1119.67
80000	1282.59	1267.16	1254.53	1244.14	1235.58	1228.50	1222.64	1217.77	1213.72	1210.36	1207.55	1199.15	1195.72	1194.32
85000	1362.75	1346.36	1332.94	1321.90	1312.80	1305.28	1299.05	1293.88	1289.58	1286.01	1283.03	1274.09	1270.45	1268.96
90000	1442.91	1425.56	1411.34	1399.66	1390.03	1382.06	1375.47	1369.99	1365.44	1361.65	1358.50	1349.04	1345.18	1343.61
95000	1523.07	1504.75	1489.75	1477.42	1467.25	1458.84	1451.88	1446.10	1441.30	1437.30	1433.97	1423.98	1419.92	1418.25
100000	1603.24	1583.95	1568.16	1555.18	1544.47	1535.63	1528.29	1522.21	1517.15	1512.95	1509.44	1498.93	1494.65	1492.89

TERM AMOUNT	1 Year	2 Years	3 Years	4 Years	5 Years	6 Years	7 Years	8 Years	9 Years	10 Years	11 Years	12 Years	13 Years	14 Years
5	.46	.25	.19	.15	.13	.12	.11	.10	.10	.10	.09	.09	.09	.09
10	.92	.50	.37	.30	.26	.23	.22	.20	.19	.19	.18	.17	.17	.17
15	1.38	.75	.55	.45	.39	.35	.32	.30	.29	.28	.27	.26	.25	.25
25	2.30	1.25	.91	.74	.64	.58	.53	.50	.47	.46	.44	.43	.42	.41
50	4.59	2.50	1.81	1.47	1.27	1.15	1.06	.99	.94	.91	.88	.85	.84	.82
75	6.88	3.75	2.72	2.21	1.91	1.72	1.58	1.48	1.41	1.36	1.31	1.28	1.25	1.23
100	9.17	5.00	3.62	2.94	2.54	2.29	2.11	1.98	1.88	1.81	1.75	1.70	1.67	1.64
200	18.34	9.99	7.24	5.88	5.08	4.57	4.21	3.95	3.76	3.61	3.49	3.40	3.33	3.27
300	27.51	14.98	10.85	8.82	7.62	6.85	6.31	5.92	5.63	5.41	5.24	5.10	4.99	4.91
400	36.68	19.97	14.47	11.76	10.16	9.13	8.41	7.89	7.51	7.21	6.98	6.80	6.66	6.54
500	45.84	24.97	18.08	14.69	12.70	11.41	10.51	9.87	9.38	9.01	8.73	8.50	8.32	8.17
600	55.01	29.96	21.70	17.63	15.24	13.69	12.62	11.84	11.26	10.82	10.47	10.20	9.98	9.81
700	64.18	34.95	25.31	20.57	17.78	15.97	14.72	13.81	13.13	12.62	12.22	11.90	11.65	11.44
800	73.35	39.94	28.93	23.51	20.32	18.25	16.82	15.78	15.01	14.42	13.96	13.60	13.31	13.08
900	82.52	44.94	32.54	26.44	22.86	20.53	18.92	17.76	16.89	16.22	15.70	15.30	14.97	14.71
1000	91.68	49.93	36.16	29.38	25.40	22.81	21.02	19.73	18.76	18.02	17.45	17.00	16.64	16.34
2000	183.36	99.85	72.31	58.75	50.79	45.62	42.04	39.45	37.52	36.04	34.89	33.99	33.27	32.68
3000	275.04	149.78	108.46	88.13	76.19	68.43	63.06	59.17	56.28	54.06	52.34	50.98	49.90	49.02
4000	366.72	199.70	144.61	117.50	101.58	91.24	84.08	78.90	75.03	72.08	69.78	67.97	66.53	65.36
5000	458.40	249.63	180.77	146.88	126.97	114.04	105.09	98.62	93.79	90.10	87.23	84.96	83.16	81.70
6000	550.08	299.55	216.92	176.26	152.37	136.85	126.11	118.34	112.55	108.12	104.67	101.95	99.79	98.04
7000	641.76	349.47	253.07	205.63	177.76	159.66	147.13	138.07	131.30	126.13	122.11	118.94	116.42	114.38
8000	733.44	399.40	289.22	235.01	203.15	182.47	168.15	157.79	150.06	144.15	139.56	135.93	133.05	130.72
9000	825.12	449.32	325.38	264.38	228.55	205.28	189.17	177.51	168.82	162.17	157.00	152.93	149.68	147.06
10000	916.80	499.25	361.53	293.75	253.94	228.08	210.18	197.24	187.57	180.19	174.45	169.92	166.31	163.40
11000	1008.48	549.17	397.68	323.13	279.33	250.89	231.20	216.96	206.33	198.21	191.89	186.91	182.94	179.74
12000	1100.16	599.09	433.83	352.50	304.73	273.70	252.22	236.68	225.09	216.23	209.34	203.90	199.57	196.08
13000	1191.84	649.02	469.99	381.88	330.12	296.51	273.24	256.41	243.84	234.25	226.78	220.89	216.20	212.42
14000	1283.52	698.94	506.14	411.25	355.51	319.31	294.25	276.13	262.60	252.26	244.22	237.88	232.83	228.76
15000	1375.20	748.87	542.29	440.63	380.91	342.12	315.27	295.85	281.36	270.28	261.67	254.87	249.46	245.10
16000	1466.88	798.79	578.44	470.00	406.30	364.93	336.29	315.58	300.12	288.30	279.11	271.86	266.09	261.44
17000	1558.56	848.71	614.60	499.38	431.69	387.74	357.31	335.30	318.87	306.32	296.56	288.86	282.72	277.78
18000	1650.48	898.64	650.75	528.75	457.09	410.55	378.33	355.02	337.63	324.34	314.00	305.85	299.35	294.12
19000	1741.92	948.56	686.90	558.13	482.48	433.35	399.34	374.75	356.39	342.36	331.44	322.84	315.98	310.46
20000	1833.60	998.49	723.05	587.50	507.87	456.16	420.36	394.47	375.14	360.38	348.89	339.83	332.61	326.80
21000	1925.28	1048.41	759.21	616.88	533.27	478.97	441.38	414.19	393.90	378.39	366.33	356.82	349.24	343.13
22000	2016.96	1098.34	795.36	646.25	558.66	501.78	462.40	433.92	412.66	396.41	383.78	373.81	365.87	359.47
23000	2108.64	1148.26	831.51	675.63	584.05	524.58	483.42	453.64	431.41	414.43	401.22	390.80	382.50	375.81
24000	2200.32	1198.18	867.66	705.00	609.45	547.39	504.43	473.36	450.17	432.45	418.67	407.79	399.13	392.15
25000	2292.00	1248.11	903.81	734.38	634.84	570.20	525.45	493.09	468.93	450.47	436.11	424.78	415.76	408.49
26000	2383.68	1298.03	939.97	763.75	660.23	593.01	546.47	512.81	487.68	468.49	453.55	441.78	432.39	424.83
27000	2475.36	1347.96	976.12	793.13	685.63	615.82	567.49	532.53	506.44	486.51	471.00	458.77	449.02	441.17
28000	2567.04	1397.88	1012.27	822.50	711.02	638.62	588.50	552.25	525.20	504.52	488.44	475.76	465.65	457.51
29000	2658.72	1447.80	1048.42	851.88	736.41	661.43	609.52	571.98	543.95	522.54	505.89	492.75	482.28	473.85
30000	2750.40	1497.73	1084.58	881.25	761.81	684.24	630.54	591.70	562.71	540.56	523.33	509.74	498.91	490.19
31000	2842.08	1547.65	1120.73	910.63	787.20	707.05	651.56	611.42	581.47	558.58	540.77	526.73	515.54	506.53
32000	2933.76	1597.58	1156.88	940.00	812.59	729.85	672.58	631.15	600.23	576.60	558.22	543.72	532.17	522.87
33000	3025.44	1647.50	1193.03	969.38	837.99	752.66	693.59	650.87	618.98	594.62	575.66	560.71	548.80	539.21
34000	3117.12	1697.42	1229.19	998.75	863.38	775.47	714.61	670.59	637.74	612.63	593.11	577.71	565.43	555.55
35000	3208.80	1747.35	1265.34	1028.13	888.77	798.28	735.63	690.32	656.50	630.65	610.55	594.70	582.06	571.89
36000	3300.48	1797.27	1301.49	1057.51	914.17	821.09	756.65	710.04	675.25	648.67	628.00	611.69	598.69	588.23
37000	3392.16	1847.20	1337.64	1086.88	939.56	843.89	777.67	729.76	694.01	666.69	645.44	628.68	615.32	604.57
38000	3483.84	1897.12	1373.80	1116.26	964.96	866.70	798.68	749.49	712.77	684.71	662.88	645.67	631.95	620.91
39000	3575.52	1947.05	1409.95	1145.63	990.35	889.51	819.70	769.21	731.52	702.73	680.33	662.66	648.58	637.25
40000	3667.20	1996.97	1446.10	1175.01	1015.74	912.32	840.72	788.93	750.28	720.75	697.77	679.65	665.21	653.59
41000	3758.88	2046.89	1482.25	1204.38	1041.14	935.12	861.74	808.66	769.04	738.76	715.22	696.64	681.84	669.92
42000	3850.56	2096.82	1518.41	1233.76	1066.53	957.93	882.75	828.38	787.79	756.78	732.66	713.64	698.47	686.26
43000	3942.24	2146.74	1554.56	1263.13	1091.92	980.74	903.77	848.10	806.55	774.80	750.10	730.63	715.10	702.60
44000	4033.92	2196.67	1590.71	1292.51	1117.32	1003.55	924.79	867.83	825.31	792.82	767.55	747.62	731.73	718.94
45000	4125.60	2246.59	1626.86	1321.88	1142.71	1026.36	945.81	887.55	844.06	810.84	784.99	764.61	748.36	735.28
46000	4217.28	2296.51	1663.02	1351.26	1168.10	1049.16	966.83	907.27	862.82	828.86	802.44	781.60	764.99	751.62
47000	4308.96	2346.44	1699.17	1380.63	1193.50	1071.97	987.84	927.00	881.58	846.88	819.88	798.59	781.62	767.96
48000	4400.64	2396.36	1735.32	1410.01	1218.89	1094.78	1008.86	946.72	900.34	864.89	837.33	815.58	798.25	784.30
49000	4492.32	2446.29	1771.47	1439.38	1244.28	1117.59	1029.88	966.44	919.09	882.91	854.77	832.57	814.88	800.64
50000	4584.00	2496.21	1807.62	1468.76	1269.68	1140.39	1050.90	986.17	937.85	900.93	872.21	849.56	831.51	816.98
55000	5042.40	2745.83	1988.39	1615.63	1396.64	1254.43	1155.99	1084.78	1031.63	991.02	959.43	934.52	914.66	898.68
60000	5500.80	2995.45	2169.15	1762.51	1523.61	1368.47	1261.08	1183.40	1125.42	1081.12	1046.66	1019.48	997.81	980.38
65000	5959.20	3245.07	2349.91	1909.38	1650.58	1482.51	1366.16	1282.01	1219.20	1171.21	1133.88	1104.43	1080.96	1062.07
70000	6417.60	3494.69	2530.67	2056.25	1777.54	1596.55	1471.25	1380.63	1312.99	1261.30	1221.10	1189.39	1164.11	1143.77
75000	6876.00	3744.31	2711.43	2203.13	1904.51	1710.59	1576.34	1479.25	1406.77	1351.39	1308.32	1274.34	1247.26	1225.47
80000	7334.40	3993.93	2892.20	2350.00	2031.48	1824.63	1681.43	1577.86	1500.56	1441.49	1395.54	1359.30	1330.41	1307.17
85000	7792.80	4243.55	3072.96	2496.88	2158.45	1938.67	1786.52	1676.48	1594.34	1531.58	1482.76	1444.26	1413.56	1388.86
90000	8251.20	4493.17	3253.72	2643.75	2285.41	2052.71	1891.61	1775.09	1688.12	1621.67	1569.98	1529.21	1496.71	1470.56
95000	8709.60	4742.79	3434.48	2790.63	2412.38	2166.75	1996.70	1873.71	1781.91	1711.76	1657.20	1614.17	1579.86	1552.26
100000	9168.00	4992.42	3615.24	2937.50	2539.35	2280.78	2101.79	1972.33	1875.69	1801.86	1744.42	1699.12	1663.01	1633.96

TERM	15 Years	16 Years	17 Years	18 Years	19 Years	20 Years	21 Years	22 Years	23 Years	24 Years	25 Years	30 Years	35 Years	40 Years
AMOUNT														
5	.09	.08	.08	.08	.08	.08	.08	.08	.08	.08	.08	.08	.08	.08
10	.17	.16	.16	.16	.16	.16	.16	.16	.16	.16	.16	.16	.16	.16
15	.25	.24	.24	.24	.24	.24	.24	.23	.23	.23	.23	.23	.23	.23
25	.41	.40	.40	.40	.39	.39	.39	.39	.39	.39	.38	.38	.38	.38
50	.81	.80	.79	.79	.78	.78	.77	.77	.77	.77	.76	.76	.76	.76
75	1.21	1.20	1.19	1.18	1.17	1.16	1.16	1.15	1.15	1.15	1.14	1.14	1.13	1.13
100	1.62	1.60	1.58	1.57	1.56	1.55	1.54	1.54	1.53	1.53	1.53	1.52	1.51	1.51
200	3.23	3.19	3.16	3.13	3.11	3.09	3.08	3.07	3.06	3.05	3.04	3.02	3.01	3.01
300	4.84	4.78	4.73	4.69	4.66	4.63	4.61	4.60	4.58	4.57	4.56	4.53	4.51	4.51
400	6.45	6.37	6.31	6.26	6.21	6.18	6.15	6.13	6.11	6.09	6.07	6.03	6.02	6.01
500	8.06	7.96	7.88	7.82	7.77	7.72	7.69	7.66	7.63	7.61	7.59	7.54	7.52	7.51
600	9.67	9.55	9.46	9.38	9.32	9.26	9.22	9.19	9.16	9.13	9.11	9.05	9.02	9.01
700	11.28	11.14	11.03	10.94	10.87	10.81	10.76	10.72	10.68	10.65	10.63	10.55	10.53	10.51
800	12.89	12.74	12.61	12.51	12.42	12.35	12.29	12.25	12.21	12.17	12.14	12.06	12.03	12.01
900	14.50	14.33	14.19	14.07	13.97	13.89	13.83	13.78	13.73	13.69	13.66	13.57	13.53	13.52
1000	16.11	15.92	15.76	15.63	15.53	15.44	15.37	15.31	15.26	15.21	15.18	15.08	15.03	15.02
2000	32.21	31.83	31.52	31.26	31.05	30.87	30.73	30.61	30.51	30.42	30.35	30.15	30.06	30.03
3000	48.32	47.74	47.27	46.89	46.57	46.30	46.09	45.91	45.76	45.63	45.53	45.22	45.09	45.04
4000	64.42	63.66	63.03	62.51	62.09	61.74	61.45	61.21	61.01	60.84	60.70	60.29	60.12	60.05
5000	80.53	79.57	78.78	78.14	77.61	77.17	76.81	76.51	76.26	76.05	75.88	75.36	75.15	75.06
6000	96.63	95.48	94.54	93.77	93.13	92.60	92.17	91.81	91.51	91.26	91.05	90.43	90.18	90.08
7000	112.73	111.39	110.30	109.39	108.65	108.04	107.53	107.11	106.76	106.47	106.23	105.50	105.21	105.09
8000	128.84	127.31	126.05	125.02	124.17	123.47	122.89	122.41	122.01	121.68	121.40	120.57	120.24	120.10
9000	144.94	143.22	141.81	140.65	139.69	138.90	138.25	137.71	137.26	136.89	136.57	135.64	135.27	135.11
10000	161.05	159.13	157.56	156.27	155.21	154.34	153.61	153.01	152.51	152.09	151.75	150.71	150.29	150.12
11000	177.15	175.04	173.32	171.90	170.73	169.77	168.97	168.31	167.76	167.30	166.92	165.78	165.32	165.14
12000	193.26	190.96	189.07	187.53	186.25	185.20	184.33	183.61	183.01	182.51	182.10	180.86	180.35	180.15
13000	209.36	206.87	204.83	203.15	201.78	200.64	199.69	198.91	198.26	197.72	197.27	195.93	195.38	195.16
14000	225.46	222.78	220.59	218.78	217.30	216.07	215.05	214.21	213.51	212.93	212.45	211.00	210.41	210.17
15000	241.57	238.69	236.34	234.41	232.82	231.50	230.41	229.51	228.76	228.14	227.62	226.07	225.44	225.18
16000	257.67	254.61	252.10	250.04	248.34	246.93	245.77	244.81	244.01	243.35	242.79	241.14	240.47	240.19
17000	273.78	270.52	267.85	265.66	263.86	262.37	261.13	260.11	259.26	258.56	257.97	256.21	255.50	255.21
18000	289.88	286.43	283.61	281.29	279.38	277.80	276.49	275.41	274.51	273.76	273.14	271.28	270.53	270.22
19000	305.99	302.34	299.36	296.92	294.90	293.23	291.86	290.71	289.76	288.97	288.32	286.35	285.55	285.23
20000	322.09	318.26	315.12	312.54	310.42	308.67	307.22	306.01	305.01	304.18	303.49	301.42	300.58	300.24
21000	338.19	334.17	330.88	328.17	325.94	324.10	322.58	321.31	320.26	319.39	318.67	316.49	315.61	315.25
22000	354.30	350.08	346.63	343.80	341.46	339.53	337.94	336.61	335.51	334.60	333.84	331.56	330.64	330.27
23000	370.40	365.99	362.39	359.42	356.98	354.97	353.30	351.91	350.76	349.81	349.01	346.63	345.67	345.28
24000	386.51	381.91	378.14	375.05	372.50	370.40	368.66	367.21	366.01	365.02	364.19	361.71	360.70	360.29
25000	402.61	397.82	393.90	390.68	388.02	385.83	384.02	382.51	381.27	380.23	379.36	376.78	375.73	375.30
26000	418.71	413.73	409.65	406.30	403.55	401.27	399.38	397.81	396.52	395.44	394.54	391.85	390.76	390.31
27000	434.82	429.64	425.41	421.93	419.07	416.70	414.74	413.12	411.77	410.64	409.71	406.92	405.79	405.32
28000	450.92	445.56	441.17	437.56	434.59	432.13	430.10	428.42	427.02	425.85	424.89	421.99	420.81	420.34
29000	467.03	461.47	456.92	453.19	450.11	447.57	445.46	443.72	442.27	441.06	440.06	437.06	435.84	435.35
30000	483.13	477.38	472.68	468.81	465.63	463.00	460.82	459.02	457.52	456.27	455.23	452.13	450.87	450.36
31000	499.24	493.29	488.43	484.44	481.15	478.43	476.18	474.32	472.77	471.48	470.41	467.20	465.90	465.37
32000	515.34	509.21	504.19	500.07	496.67	493.86	491.54	489.62	488.02	486.69	485.58	482.27	480.93	480.38
33000	531.44	525.12	519.94	515.69	512.19	509.30	506.90	504.92	503.27	501.90	500.76	497.34	495.96	495.40
34000	547.55	541.03	535.70	531.32	527.71	524.73	522.26	520.22	518.52	517.11	515.93	512.41	510.99	510.41
35000	563.65	556.94	551.46	546.95	543.23	540.16	537.62	535.52	533.77	532.32	531.11	527.48	526.02	525.42
36000	579.76	572.86	567.21	562.57	558.75	555.60	552.98	550.82	549.02	547.52	546.28	542.56	541.05	540.43
37000	595.86	588.77	582.97	578.20	574.27	571.03	568.35	566.12	564.27	562.73	561.45	557.63	556.08	555.44
38000	611.96	604.68	598.72	593.83	589.79	586.46	583.71	581.42	579.52	577.94	576.63	572.70	571.10	570.45
39000	628.07	620.59	614.48	609.45	605.32	601.90	599.07	596.72	594.77	593.15	591.80	587.77	586.13	585.47
40000	644.17	636.51	630.23	625.08	620.84	617.33	614.43	612.02	610.02	608.36	606.98	602.84	601.16	600.48
41000	660.28	652.42	645.99	640.71	636.36	632.76	629.79	627.32	625.27	623.57	622.15	617.91	616.19	615.49
42000	676.38	668.33	661.75	656.34	651.88	648.20	645.15	642.62	640.52	638.78	637.33	632.98	631.22	630.50
43000	692.49	684.24	677.50	671.96	667.40	663.63	660.51	657.92	655.77	653.99	652.50	648.05	646.25	645.51
44000	708.59	700.16	693.26	687.59	682.92	679.06	675.87	673.22	671.02	669.20	667.67	663.12	661.28	660.53
45000	724.69	716.07	709.01	703.22	698.44	694.50	691.23	688.52	686.27	684.40	682.85	678.19	676.31	675.54
46000	740.80	731.98	724.77	718.84	713.96	709.93	706.59	703.82	701.52	699.61	698.02	693.26	691.34	690.55
47000	756.90	747.90	740.52	734.47	729.48	725.36	721.95	719.12	716.77	714.82	713.20	708.34	706.36	705.56
48000	773.01	763.81	756.28	750.10	745.00	740.79	737.31	734.42	732.02	730.03	728.37	723.41	721.39	720.57
49000	789.11	779.72	772.04	765.72	760.52	756.23	752.67	749.72	747.28	745.24	743.55	738.48	736.42	735.58
50000	805.22	795.63	787.79	781.35	776.04	771.66	768.03	765.02	762.53	760.45	758.72	753.55	751.45	750.60
55000	885.74	875.20	866.57	859.49	853.65	848.83	844.84	841.53	838.78	836.49	834.59	828.90	826.60	825.66
60000	966.26	954.76	945.35	937.62	931.25	925.99	921.64	918.03	915.03	912.54	910.46	904.26	901.74	900.71
65000	1046.78	1034.32	1024.13	1015.75	1008.86	1003.16	998.44	994.53	991.28	988.58	986.33	979.61	976.88	975.77
70000	1127.30	1113.88	1102.91	1093.89	1086.46	1080.32	1075.24	1071.03	1067.53	1064.63	1062.21	1054.96	1052.03	1050.83
75000	1207.82	1193.45	1181.68	1172.02	1164.06	1157.49	1152.05	1147.53	1143.79	1140.67	1138.08	1130.32	1127.17	1125.89
80000	1288.34	1273.01	1260.46	1250.16	1241.67	1234.65	1228.85	1224.04	1220.04	1216.71	1213.95	1205.67	1202.32	1200.95
85000	1368.86	1352.57	1339.24	1328.29	1319.27	1311.82	1305.65	1300.54	1296.29	1292.76	1289.82	1281.03	1277.46	1276.01
90000	1449.38	1432.14	1418.02	1406.43	1396.88	1388.99	1382.45	1377.04	1372.54	1368.80	1365.69	1356.38	1352.61	1351.07
95000	1529.91	1511.70	1496.80	1484.56	1474.48	1466.15	1459.26	1453.54	1448.79	1444.85	1441.56	1431.74	1427.75	1426.13
100000	1610.43	1591.26	1575.58	1562.70	1552.08	1543.32	1536.06	1530.04	1525.05	1520.89	1517.43	1507.09	1502.90	1501.19

18%

MONTHLY PAYMENT
REQUIRED TO AMORTIZE A LOAN

TERM	1 Year	2 Years	3 Years	4 Years	5 Years	6 Years	7 Years	8 Years	9 Years	10 Years	11 Years	12 Years	13 Years	14 Years
AMOUNT														
5	.46	.25	.19	.15	.13	.12	.11	.10	.10	.10	.09	.09	.09	.09
10	.92	.50	.37	.30	.26	.23	.22	.20	.19	.19	.18	.18	.17	.17
15	1.38	.75	.55	.45	.39	.35	.32	.30	.29	.28	.27	.26	.26	.25
25	2.30	1.25	.91	.74	.64	.58	.53	.50	.48	.46	.44	.43	.42	.42
50	4.59	2.50	1.82	1.48	1.28	1.15	1.06	.99	.95	.91	.88	.86	.84	.83
75	6.88	3.75	2.72	2.21	1.91	1.72	1.59	1.49	1.42	1.36	1.32	1.28	1.26	1.24
100	9.18	5.00	3.63	2.95	2.55	2.29	2.11	1.98	1.89	1.81	1.76	1.71	1.67	1.65
200	18.35	10.00	7.25	5.89	5.09	4.58	4.22	3.96	3.77	3.62	3.51	3.42	3.34	3.29
300	27.52	15.00	10.87	8.83	7.64	6.86	6.33	5.94	5.65	5.43	5.26	5.12	5.01	4.93
400	36.70	19.99	14.49	11.78	10.18	9.15	8.44	7.92	7.53	7.24	7.01	6.83	6.68	6.57
500	45.87	24.99	18.11	14.72	12.73	11.44	10.56	9.90	9.41	9.05	8.76	8.53	8.35	8.21
600	55.04	29.99	21.73	17.66	15.27	13.72	12.65	11.88	11.30	10.85	10.51	10.24	10.02	9.85
700	64.21	34.99	25.35	20.60	17.82	16.01	14.76	13.85	13.18	12.66	12.26	11.95	11.69	11.49
800	73.39	39.98	28.97	23.55	20.36	18.30	16.87	15.83	15.06	14.47	14.01	13.65	13.36	13.13
900	82.56	44.98	32.59	26.49	22.91	20.58	18.97	17.81	16.94	16.28	15.76	15.36	15.03	14.77
1000	91.73	49.98	36.21	29.43	25.45	22.87	21.08	19.79	18.82	18.09	17.52	17.06	16.70	16.42
2000	183.46	99.95	72.41	58.86	50.90	45.73	42.16	39.57	37.64	36.17	35.03	34.12	33.40	32.83
3000	275.19	149.92	108.61	88.29	76.35	68.60	63.23	59.36	56.46	54.25	52.54	51.18	50.10	49.24
4000	366.92	199.89	144.82	117.71	101.80	91.46	84.31	79.14	75.28	72.34	70.05	68.24	66.80	65.65
5000	458.64	249.87	181.02	147.14	127.24	114.33	105.39	98.92	94.10	90.42	87.56	85.30	83.50	82.06
6000	550.37	299.84	217.22	176.57	152.69	137.19	126.46	118.71	112.92	108.50	105.07	102.36	100.20	98.47
7000	642.10	349.81	253.42	206.00	178.14	160.06	147.54	138.49	131.74	126.59	122.58	119.42	116.90	114.88
8000	733.83	399.78	289.63	235.42	203.59	182.92	168.62	158.28	150.56	144.67	140.09	136.48	133.60	131.29
9000	825.55	449.76	325.83	264.85	229.04	205.78	189.69	178.06	169.38	162.75	157.60	153.54	150.30	147.70
10000	917.28	499.73	362.03	294.28	254.48	228.65	210.77	197.84	188.20	180.83	175.11	170.59	167.00	164.11
11000	1009.01	549.70	398.23	323.71	279.93	251.51	231.85	217.63	207.02	198.92	192.62	187.65	183.70	180.52
12000	1100.74	599.67	434.44	353.13	305.38	274.38	252.92	237.41	225.84	217.00	210.13	204.71	200.40	196.93
13000	1192.46	649.65	470.64	382.56	330.83	297.24	274.00	257.20	244.66	235.08	227.64	221.77	217.10	213.34
14000	1284.19	699.62	506.84	411.99	356.28	320.11	295.08	276.98	263.48	253.17	245.15	238.83	233.80	229.75
15000	1375.92	749.59	543.04	441.41	381.72	342.97	316.15	296.76	282.30	271.25	262.66	255.89	250.49	246.16
16000	1467.65	799.56	579.25	470.84	407.17	365.83	337.23	316.55	301.12	289.33	280.17	272.95	267.19	262.57
17000	1559.37	849.54	615.45	500.27	432.62	388.70	358.31	336.33	319.94	307.42	297.68	290.01	283.89	278.98
18000	1651.10	899.51	651.65	529.70	458.07	411.56	379.38	356.11	338.76	325.50	315.19	307.07	300.59	295.39
19000	1742.83	949.48	687.85	559.12	483.51	434.43	400.46	375.90	357.58	343.58	332.70	324.13	317.29	311.80
20000	1834.56	999.45	724.06	588.55	508.96	457.29	421.53	395.68	376.39	361.66	350.21	341.18	333.99	328.21
21000	1926.28	1049.43	760.26	617.98	534.41	480.16	442.61	415.47	395.21	379.75	367.72	358.24	350.69	344.62
22000	2018.01	1099.40	796.46	647.41	559.86	503.02	463.69	435.25	414.03	397.83	385.23	375.30	367.39	361.03
23000	2109.74	1149.37	832.66	676.83	585.31	525.89	484.76	455.03	432.85	415.91	402.74	392.36	384.09	377.44
24000	2201.47	1199.34	868.87	706.26	610.75	548.75	505.84	474.82	451.67	434.00	420.25	409.42	400.79	393.85
25000	2293.19	1249.32	905.07	735.69	636.20	571.61	526.92	494.60	470.49	452.08	437.76	426.48	417.49	410.26
26000	2384.92	1299.29	941.27	765.11	661.65	594.48	547.99	514.39	489.31	470.16	455.27	443.54	434.19	426.67
27000	2476.65	1349.26	977.47	794.54	687.10	617.34	569.07	534.17	508.13	488.24	472.78	460.60	450.89	443.08
28000	2568.38	1399.23	1013.68	823.97	712.55	640.21	590.15	553.95	526.95	506.33	490.29	477.66	467.59	459.49
29000	2660.11	1449.21	1049.88	853.40	737.99	663.07	611.22	573.74	545.77	524.41	507.80	494.72	484.28	475.90
30000	2751.83	1499.18	1086.08	882.82	763.44	685.94	632.30	593.52	564.59	542.49	525.32	511.77	500.98	492.31
31000	2843.56	1549.15	1122.29	912.25	788.89	708.80	653.38	613.31	583.41	560.58	542.83	528.83	517.68	508.72
32000	2935.29	1599.12	1158.49	941.68	814.34	731.66	674.45	633.09	602.23	578.66	560.34	545.89	534.38	525.13
33000	3027.02	1649.10	1194.69	971.11	839.78	754.53	695.53	652.87	621.05	596.74	577.85	562.95	551.08	541.54
34000	3118.74	1699.07	1230.89	1000.53	865.23	777.39	716.61	672.66	639.87	614.83	595.36	580.01	567.78	557.95
35000	3210.47	1749.04	1267.10	1029.96	890.68	800.26	737.68	692.44	658.69	632.91	612.87	597.07	584.48	574.36
36000	3302.20	1799.01	1303.30	1059.39	916.13	823.12	758.76	712.22	677.51	650.99	630.38	614.13	601.18	590.77
37000	3393.93	1848.99	1339.50	1088.81	941.58	845.99	779.84	732.01	696.33	669.07	647.89	631.19	617.88	607.18
38000	3485.65	1898.96	1375.70	1118.24	967.02	868.85	800.91	751.79	715.15	687.16	665.40	648.25	634.58	623.59
39000	3577.38	1948.93	1411.91	1147.67	992.47	891.71	821.99	771.58	733.96	705.24	682.91	665.31	651.28	640.00
40000	3669.11	1998.90	1448.11	1177.10	1017.92	914.58	843.06	791.36	752.78	723.32	700.42	682.36	667.98	656.41
41000	3760.84	2048.87	1484.31	1206.52	1043.37	937.44	864.14	811.14	771.60	741.41	717.93	699.42	684.68	672.82
42000	3852.56	2098.85	1520.51	1235.95	1068.82	960.31	885.22	830.93	790.42	759.49	735.44	716.48	701.38	689.23
43000	3944.29	2148.82	1556.72	1265.38	1094.26	983.17	906.29	850.71	809.24	777.57	752.95	733.54	718.08	705.64
44000	4036.02	2198.79	1592.92	1294.81	1119.71	1006.04	927.37	870.50	828.06	795.65	770.46	750.60	734.77	722.05
45000	4127.75	2248.76	1629.12	1324.23	1145.16	1028.90	948.45	890.28	846.88	813.74	787.97	767.66	751.47	738.46
46000	4219.47	2298.74	1665.32	1353.66	1170.61	1051.77	969.52	910.06	865.70	831.82	805.48	784.72	768.17	754.87
47000	4311.20	2348.71	1701.53	1383.09	1196.05	1074.63	990.60	929.85	884.52	849.90	822.99	801.78	784.87	771.28
48000	4402.93	2398.68	1737.73	1412.51	1221.50	1097.49	1011.68	949.63	903.34	867.99	840.50	818.84	801.57	787.69
49000	4494.66	2448.65	1773.93	1441.94	1246.95	1120.36	1032.75	969.42	922.16	886.07	858.01	835.89	818.27	804.11
50000	4586.38	2498.63	1810.13	1471.37	1272.40	1143.22	1053.83	989.20	940.98	904.15	875.52	852.95	834.97	820.52
55000	5045.02	2748.49	1991.15	1618.51	1399.64	1257.54	1159.21	1088.12	1035.08	994.57	963.07	938.25	918.47	902.57
60000	5503.66	2998.35	2172.16	1765.64	1526.88	1371.87	1264.59	1187.04	1129.17	1084.98	1050.63	1023.54	1001.96	984.62
65000	5962.30	3248.21	2353.17	1912.78	1654.12	1486.19	1369.98	1285.96	1223.27	1175.40	1138.18	1108.84	1085.46	1066.67
70000	6420.94	3498.08	2534.19	2059.91	1781.36	1600.51	1475.36	1384.88	1317.37	1265.81	1225.73	1194.13	1168.96	1148.72
75000	6879.57	3747.94	2715.20	2207.05	1908.59	1714.83	1580.74	1483.80	1411.47	1356.23	1313.28	1279.43	1252.45	1230.77
80000	7338.21	3997.80	2896.21	2354.19	2035.83	1829.15	1686.12	1582.72	1505.56	1446.64	1400.83	1364.72	1335.95	1312.82
85000	7796.85	4247.66	3077.22	2501.32	2163.07	1943.48	1791.51	1681.64	1599.66	1537.06	1488.38	1450.02	1419.45	1394.87
90000	8255.49	4497.52	3258.24	2648.46	2290.31	2057.80	1896.89	1780.55	1693.76	1627.47	1575.94	1535.31	1502.94	1476.92
95000	8714.13	4747.39	3439.25	2795.60	2417.55	2172.12	2002.27	1879.47	1787.86	1717.89	1663.49	1620.61	1586.44	1558.97
100000	9172.76	4997.25	3620.26	2942.73	2544.79	2286.44	2107.65	1978.39	1881.95	1808.30	1751.04	1705.90	1669.94	1641.03

TERM	15 Years	16 Years	17 Years	18 Years	19 Years	20 Years	21 Years	22 Years	23 Years	24 Years	25 Years	30 Years	35 Years	40 Years
AMOUNT														
5	.09	.08	.08	.08	.08	.08	.08	.08	.08	.08	.08	.08	.08	.08
10	.17	.16	.16	.16	.16	.16	.16	.16	.16	.16	.16	.16	.16	.16
15	.25	.24	.24	.24	.24	.24	.24	.24	.23	.23	.23	.23	.23	.23
25	.41	.40	.40	.40	.39	.39	.39	.39	.39	.39	.39	.38	.38	.38
50	.81	.80	.80	.79	.78	.78	.78	.77	.77	.77	.77	.76	.76	.76
75	1.22	1.20	1.19	1.18	1.17	1.17	1.16	1.16	1.15	1.15	1.15	1.14	1.14	1.14
100	1.62	1.60	1.58	1.58	1.56	1.56	1.55	1.54	1.54	1.53	1.53	1.52	1.52	1.51
200	3.24	3.20	3.17	3.15	3.12	3.11	3.09	3.08	3.07	3.06	3.06	3.04	3.03	3.02
300	4.86	4.80	4.75	4.72	4.68	4.66	4.64	4.62	4.60	4.59	4.58	4.55	4.54	4.53
400	6.48	6.40	6.34	6.29	6.24	6.21	6.18	6.16	6.14	6.12	6.11	6.07	6.05	6.04
500	8.09	8.00	7.92	7.86	7.80	7.76	7.72	7.69	7.67	7.65	7.63	7.58	7.56	7.55
600	9.71	9.60	9.50	9.43	9.36	9.31	9.27	9.23	9.20	9.18	9.16	9.10	9.07	9.06
700	11.33	11.20	11.09	11.00	10.92	10.86	10.81	10.77	10.74	10.71	10.68	10.61	10.58	10.57
800	12.95	12.79	12.67	12.57	12.48	12.41	12.36	12.31	12.27	12.24	12.21	12.13	12.09	12.08
900	14.56	14.39	14.25	14.14	14.04	13.96	13.90	13.85	13.80	13.76	13.73	13.64	13.61	13.59
1000	16.18	15.99	15.84	15.71	15.60	15.52	15.44	15.38	15.33	15.29	15.26	15.16	15.12	15.10
2000	32.36	31.98	31.67	31.41	31.20	31.03	30.88	30.76	30.66	30.58	30.51	30.31	30.23	30.19
3000	48.53	47.96	47.50	47.11	46.80	46.54	46.32	46.14	45.99	45.87	45.77	45.46	45.34	45.29
4000	64.71	63.95	63.33	62.81	62.39	62.05	61.76	61.52	61.32	61.16	61.02	60.61	60.45	60.38
5000	80.89	79.93	79.16	78.52	77.99	77.56	77.20	76.90	76.65	76.45	76.28	75.77	75.56	75.48
6000	97.06	95.92	94.99	94.22	93.59	93.07	92.63	92.28	91.98	91.74	91.53	90.92	90.67	90.57
7000	113.24	111.91	110.82	109.92	109.18	108.58	108.07	107.66	107.31	107.03	106.79	106.07	105.78	105.67
8000	129.41	127.89	126.65	125.62	124.78	124.09	123.51	123.04	122.64	122.31	122.04	121.22	120.90	120.76
9000	145.59	143.88	142.48	141.32	140.38	139.60	138.95	138.41	137.97	137.60	137.29	136.38	136.01	135.86
10000	161.77	159.86	158.31	157.03	155.97	155.11	154.39	153.79	153.30	152.89	152.55	151.53	151.12	150.95
11000	177.94	175.85	174.14	172.73	171.57	170.62	169.83	169.17	168.63	168.18	167.80	166.68	166.23	166.05
12000	194.12	191.83	189.97	188.43	187.17	186.13	185.26	184.55	183.96	183.47	183.06	181.83	181.34	181.14
13000	210.30	207.82	205.80	204.13	202.77	201.64	200.70	199.93	199.29	198.75	198.31	196.99	196.45	196.24
14000	226.47	223.81	221.63	219.84	218.36	217.15	216.14	215.31	214.62	214.04	213.57	212.14	211.56	211.33
15000	242.65	239.79	237.46	235.54	233.96	232.66	231.58	230.69	229.95	229.33	228.82	227.29	226.68	226.43
16000	258.82	255.78	253.29	251.24	249.56	248.17	247.02	246.07	245.28	244.62	244.07	242.44	241.79	241.52
17000	275.00	271.76	269.12	266.94	265.15	263.68	262.46	261.44	260.60	259.91	259.33	257.60	256.90	256.62
18000	291.18	287.75	284.95	282.64	280.75	279.19	277.89	276.82	275.93	275.20	274.58	272.75	272.01	271.71
19000	307.35	303.73	300.78	298.35	296.35	294.70	293.33	292.20	291.26	290.48	289.84	287.90	287.12	286.81
20000	323.53	319.72	316.61	314.05	311.94	310.21	308.77	307.58	306.59	305.77	305.09	303.05	302.23	301.90
21000	339.71	335.71	332.44	329.75	327.54	325.72	324.21	322.96	321.92	321.06	320.35	318.21	317.34	317.00
22000	355.88	351.69	348.27	345.45	343.14	341.23	339.65	338.34	337.25	336.35	335.60	333.36	332.46	332.09
23000	372.06	367.68	364.10	361.16	358.74	356.74	355.09	353.72	352.58	351.64	350.85	348.51	347.57	347.18
24000	388.23	383.66	379.93	376.06	374.33	372.25	370.52	369.10	367.91	366.93	366.11	363.66	362.68	362.28
25000	404.41	399.65	395.76	392.56	389.93	387.76	385.96	384.47	383.24	382.21	381.36	378.82	377.79	377.37
26000	420.59	415.63	411.59	408.26	405.53	403.27	401.40	399.85	398.57	397.50	396.62	393.97	392.90	392.47
27000	436.76	431.62	427.42	423.96	421.12	418.78	416.84	415.23	413.90	412.79	411.87	409.12	408.01	407.56
28000	452.94	447.61	443.25	439.67	436.72	434.29	432.28	430.61	429.23	428.08	427.13	424.27	423.12	422.66
29000	469.12	463.59	459.08	455.37	452.32	449.80	447.72	445.99	444.56	443.37	442.38	439.43	438.24	437.75
30000	485.29	479.58	474.91	471.07	467.91	465.31	463.15	461.37	459.89	458.66	457.63	454.58	453.35	452.85
31000	501.47	495.56	490.74	486.77	483.51	480.82	478.59	476.75	475.22	473.95	472.89	469.73	468.46	467.94
32000	517.64	511.55	506.57	502.48	499.11	496.33	494.03	492.13	490.55	489.23	488.14	484.88	483.57	483.04
33000	533.82	527.53	522.40	518.18	514.70	511.84	509.47	507.50	505.88	504.52	503.40	500.04	498.68	498.13
34000	550.00	543.52	538.23	533.88	530.30	527.35	524.91	522.88	521.20	519.81	518.65	515.19	513.79	513.23
35000	566.17	559.51	554.06	549.58	545.90	542.86	540.35	538.26	536.53	535.10	533.91	530.34	528.90	528.32
36000	582.35	575.49	569.89	565.28	561.50	558.37	555.78	553.64	551.86	550.39	549.16	545.49	544.02	543.42
37000	598.52	591.48	585.72	580.99	577.09	573.88	571.22	569.02	567.19	565.68	564.41	560.65	559.13	558.51
38000	614.70	607.46	601.55	596.69	592.69	589.39	586.66	584.40	582.52	580.96	579.67	575.80	574.24	573.61
39000	630.88	623.45	617.38	612.39	608.29	604.90	602.10	599.78	597.85	596.25	594.92	590.95	589.35	588.70
40000	647.05	639.44	633.21	628.09	623.88	620.41	617.54	615.16	613.18	611.54	610.18	606.10	604.46	603.80
41000	663.23	655.42	649.04	643.80	639.48	635.92	632.97	630.53	628.51	626.83	625.43	621.26	619.57	618.89
42000	679.41	671.41	664.87	659.50	655.08	651.43	648.41	645.91	643.84	642.12	640.69	636.41	634.68	633.99
43000	695.58	687.39	680.70	675.20	670.67	666.94	663.85	661.29	659.17	657.41	655.94	651.56	649.80	649.08
44000	711.76	703.38	696.53	690.90	686.27	682.45	679.29	676.67	674.50	672.69	671.19	666.71	664.91	664.17
45000	727.93	719.36	712.36	706.60	701.87	697.96	694.73	692.05	689.83	687.98	686.45	681.87	680.02	679.27
46000	744.11	735.35	728.19	722.31	717.47	713.47	710.17	707.43	705.16	703.27	701.70	697.02	695.13	694.36
47000	760.29	751.34	744.02	738.01	733.06	728.98	725.60	722.81	720.49	718.56	716.96	712.17	710.24	709.46
48000	776.46	767.32	759.85	753.71	748.66	744.49	741.04	738.19	735.82	733.85	732.21	727.32	725.35	724.55
49000	792.64	783.31	775.68	769.41	764.26	760.00	756.48	753.57	751.15	749.14	747.47	742.48	740.46	739.65
50000	808.82	799.29	791.51	785.11	779.85	775.51	771.92	768.94	766.48	764.42	762.72	757.63	755.58	754.74
55000	889.70	879.22	870.66	863.63	857.84	853.06	849.11	845.84	843.12	840.87	838.99	833.39	831.13	830.22
60000	970.58	959.15	949.81	942.14	935.82	930.61	926.30	922.73	919.77	917.31	915.26	909.15	906.69	905.69
65000	1051.46	1039.08	1028.96	1020.65	1013.81	1008.16	1003.49	999.63	996.42	993.75	991.53	984.92	982.25	981.16
70000	1132.34	1119.01	1108.11	1099.16	1091.79	1085.71	1080.69	1076.52	1073.06	1070.19	1067.81	1060.68	1057.80	1056.64
75000	1213.22	1198.94	1187.26	1177.67	1169.78	1163.26	1157.88	1153.41	1149.71	1146.63	1144.08	1136.44	1133.36	1132.11
80000	1294.10	1278.87	1266.41	1256.18	1247.76	1240.81	1235.07	1230.31	1226.36	1223.08	1220.35	1212.20	1208.92	1207.59
85000	1374.98	1358.79	1345.56	1334.69	1325.75	1318.36	1312.26	1307.20	1303.00	1299.52	1296.62	1287.97	1284.48	1283.06
90000	1455.86	1438.72	1424.71	1413.20	1403.73	1395.92	1389.45	1384.09	1379.65	1375.96	1372.89	1363.73	1360.03	1358.53
95000	1536.75	1518.65	1503.86	1491.71	1481.72	1473.47	1466.64	1460.99	1456.30	1452.40	1449.16	1439.49	1435.59	1434.01
100000	1617.63	1598.58	1583.01	1570.22	1559.70	1551.02	1543.83	1537.88	1532.95	1528.84	1525.43	1515.25	1511.15	1509.48

MONTHLY PAYMENT
REQUIRED TO AMORTIZE A LOAN

TERM AMOUNT	1 Year	2 Years	3 Years	4 Years	5 Years	6 Years	7 Years	8 Years	9 Years	10 Years	11 Years	12 Years	13 Years	14 Years
5	.46	.25	.19	.15	.13	.12	.11	.10	.10	.10	.09	.09	.09	.09
10	.92	.50	.37	.30	.26	.23	.22	.20	.19	.19	.18	.18	.17	.17
15	1.38	.75	.55	.45	.39	.35	.32	.30	.29	.28	.27	.26	.26	.25
25	2.30	1.25	.91	.74	.64	.58	.53	.50	.48	.46	.44	.43	.42	.42
50	4.59	2.50	1.82	1.48	1.28	1.15	1.06	.99	.95	.91	.88	.86	.84	.83
75	6.89	3.75	2.72	2.21	1.91	1.72	1.59	1.49	1.42	1.36	1.32	1.29	1.26	1.24
100	9.18	5.00	3.63	2.95	2.55	2.29	2.11	1.98	1.89	1.81	1.76	1.71	1.68	1.65
200	18.35	10.00	7.25	5.89	5.10	4.58	4.22	3.96	3.77	3.62	3.51	3.42	3.35	3.29
300	27.53	15.00	10.87	8.84	7.64	6.87	6.33	5.94	5.66	5.43	5.26	5.13	5.02	4.93
400	36.70	20.00	14.49	11.78	10.19	9.16	8.44	7.92	7.54	7.24	7.02	6.84	6.69	6.58
500	45.87	25.00	18.11	14.73	12.74	11.44	10.55	9.90	9.42	9.05	8.77	8.54	8.36	8.22
600	55.05	30.00	21.73	17.67	15.28	13.73	12.66	11.88	11.31	10.86	10.52	10.25	10.03	9.86
700	64.22	34.99	25.36	20.61	17.83	16.02	14.77	13.86	13.19	12.67	12.27	11.96	11.71	11.50
800	73.40	39.99	28.98	23.56	20.37	18.31	16.88	15.84	15.07	14.48	14.03	13.67	13.38	13.15
900	82.57	44.99	32.60	26.50	22.92	20.60	18.99	17.82	16.96	16.29	15.78	15.37	15.05	14.79
1000	91.74	49.99	36.22	29.45	25.47	22.88	21.10	19.80	18.84	18.10	17.53	17.08	16.72	16.43
2000	183.48	99.97	72.44	58.89	50.93	45.76	42.19	39.60	37.68	36.20	35.06	34.16	33.44	32.86
3000	275.22	149.96	108.65	88.33	76.39	68.64	63.28	59.40	56.51	54.30	52.59	51.23	50.15	49.29
4000	366.96	199.94	144.87	117.77	101.85	91.52	84.37	79.20	75.35	72.40	70.11	68.31	66.87	65.72
5000	458.70	249.93	181.08	147.21	127.31	114.40	105.46	99.00	94.18	90.50	87.64	85.38	83.59	82.14
6000	550.44	299.91	217.30	176.65	152.77	137.28	126.55	118.80	113.02	108.60	105.17	102.46	100.30	98.57
7000	642.18	349.90	253.51	206.09	178.24	160.15	147.64	138.60	131.85	126.70	122.69	119.54	117.02	115.00
8000	733.92	399.88	289.73	235.53	203.70	183.03	168.73	158.40	150.69	144.80	140.22	136.61	133.74	131.43
9000	825.66	449.87	325.94	264.97	229.16	205.91	189.83	178.20	169.52	162.90	157.75	153.69	150.45	147.86
10000	917.40	499.85	362.16	294.41	254.62	228.79	210.92	198.00	188.36	181.00	175.27	170.76	167.17	164.28
11000	1009.14	549.83	398.37	323.85	280.08	251.67	232.01	217.79	207.19	199.09	192.80	187.84	183.89	180.71
12000	1100.88	599.82	434.59	353.29	305.54	274.55	253.10	237.59	226.03	217.19	210.33	204.92	200.60	197.14
13000	1192.62	649.80	470.80	382.73	331.00	297.43	274.19	257.39	244.86	235.29	227.85	221.99	217.32	213.57
14000	1284.36	699.79	507.02	412.17	356.47	320.30	295.28	277.19	263.70	253.39	245.38	239.07	234.04	230.00
15000	1376.10	749.77	543.23	441.61	381.93	343.18	316.37	296.99	282.53	271.49	262.91	256.14	250.75	246.42
16000	1467.84	799.76	579.45	471.05	407.39	366.06	337.46	316.79	301.37	289.59	280.44	273.22	267.47	262.85
17000	1559.58	849.74	615.66	500.49	432.85	388.94	358.55	336.59	320.20	307.69	297.96	290.30	284.19	279.28
18000	1651.32	899.73	651.88	529.93	458.31	411.82	379.65	356.39	339.04	325.79	315.49	307.37	300.90	295.71
19000	1743.06	949.71	688.09	559.37	483.77	434.70	400.74	376.19	357.87	343.89	333.02	324.45	317.62	312.14
20000	1834.79	999.70	724.31	588.81	509.23	457.58	421.83	395.99	376.71	361.99	350.54	341.52	334.34	328.56
21000	1926.53	1049.68	760.52	618.25	534.70	480.45	442.92	415.79	395.54	380.09	368.07	358.60	351.05	344.99
22000	2018.27	1099.66	796.74	647.69	560.16	503.33	464.01	435.58	414.38	398.18	385.60	375.68	367.77	361.42
23000	2110.01	1149.65	832.95	677.13	585.62	526.21	485.10	455.38	433.21	416.28	403.12	392.75	384.49	377.85
24000	2201.75	1199.63	869.17	706.57	611.08	549.09	506.19	475.18	452.05	434.38	420.65	409.83	401.20	394.27
25000	2293.49	1249.62	905.38	736.01	636.54	571.97	527.28	494.98	470.88	452.48	438.18	426.90	417.92	410.70
26000	2385.23	1299.60	941.60	765.45	662.00	594.85	548.38	514.78	489.72	470.58	455.70	443.98	434.64	427.13
27000	2476.97	1349.59	977.81	794.89	687.46	617.72	569.47	534.58	508.55	488.68	473.23	461.06	451.35	443.56
28000	2568.71	1399.57	1014.03	824.34	712.93	640.60	590.56	554.38	527.39	506.78	490.76	478.13	468.07	459.99
29000	2660.45	1449.56	1050.24	853.78	738.39	663.48	611.65	574.18	546.22	524.88	508.28	495.21	484.79	476.41
30000	2752.19	1499.54	1086.46	883.22	763.85	686.36	632.74	593.98	565.06	542.98	525.81	512.28	501.50	492.84
31000	2843.93	1549.53	1122.67	912.66	789.31	709.24	653.83	613.78	583.89	561.08	543.34	529.36	518.22	509.27
32000	2935.67	1599.51	1158.89	942.10	814.77	732.12	674.92	633.58	602.73	579.18	560.87	546.44	534.94	525.70
33000	3027.41	1649.49	1195.10	971.54	840.23	755.00	696.01	653.37	621.56	597.27	578.39	563.51	551.65	542.13
34000	3119.15	1699.48	1231.32	1000.98	865.70	777.87	717.10	673.17	640.40	615.37	595.92	580.59	568.37	558.55
35000	3210.89	1749.46	1267.53	1030.42	891.16	800.75	738.20	692.97	659.24	633.47	613.45	597.66	585.09	574.98
36000	3302.63	1799.45	1303.75	1059.86	916.62	823.63	759.29	712.77	678.07	651.57	630.97	614.74	601.80	591.41
37000	3394.37	1849.43	1339.96	1089.30	942.08	846.51	780.38	732.57	696.91	669.67	648.50	631.81	618.52	607.84
38000	3486.11	1899.42	1376.18	1118.74	967.54	869.39	801.47	752.37	715.74	687.77	666.03	648.89	635.24	624.27
39000	3577.85	1949.40	1412.40	1148.18	993.00	892.27	822.56	772.17	734.58	705.87	683.55	665.97	651.95	640.69
40000	3669.58	1999.39	1448.61	1177.62	1018.46	915.15	843.65	791.97	753.41	723.97	701.08	683.04	668.67	657.12
41000	3761.32	2049.37	1484.83	1207.06	1043.93	938.02	864.74	811.77	772.25	742.07	718.61	700.12	685.39	673.55
42000	3853.06	2099.35	1521.04	1236.50	1069.39	960.90	885.83	831.57	791.08	760.17	736.13	717.19	702.10	689.98
43000	3944.80	2149.34	1557.26	1265.94	1094.85	983.78	906.93	851.36	809.92	778.27	753.66	734.27	718.82	706.40
44000	4036.54	2199.32	1593.47	1295.38	1120.31	1006.66	928.02	871.16	828.75	796.36	771.19	751.35	735.54	722.83
45000	4128.28	2249.31	1629.69	1324.82	1145.77	1029.54	949.11	890.96	847.59	814.46	788.72	768.42	752.25	739.26
46000	4220.02	2299.29	1665.90	1354.26	1171.23	1052.42	970.20	910.76	866.42	832.56	806.24	785.50	768.97	755.69
47000	4311.76	2349.28	1702.12	1383.70	1196.69	1075.30	991.29	930.56	885.26	850.66	823.77	802.57	785.69	772.12
48000	4403.50	2399.26	1738.33	1413.14	1222.16	1098.17	1012.38	950.36	904.09	868.76	841.30	819.65	802.40	788.54
49000	4495.24	2449.25	1774.55	1442.58	1247.62	1121.05	1033.47	970.16	922.93	886.86	858.82	836.73	819.12	804.97
50000	4586.98	2499.23	1810.76	1472.02	1273.08	1143.93	1054.56	989.96	941.76	904.96	876.35	853.80	835.84	821.40
55000	5045.68	2749.15	1991.84	1619.22	1400.39	1258.32	1160.02	1088.95	1035.94	995.45	963.98	939.18	919.42	903.54
60000	5504.37	2999.08	2172.91	1766.43	1527.69	1372.72	1265.48	1187.95	1130.11	1085.95	1051.62	1024.56	1003.00	985.68
65000	5963.07	3249.00	2353.99	1913.63	1655.00	1487.11	1370.93	1286.94	1224.29	1176.44	1139.25	1109.94	1086.59	1067.82
70000	6421.77	3498.92	2535.06	2060.83	1782.31	1601.50	1476.39	1385.94	1318.47	1266.94	1226.89	1195.32	1170.17	1149.96
75000	6880.47	3748.84	2716.14	2208.03	1909.62	1715.89	1581.84	1484.93	1412.64	1357.44	1314.52	1280.70	1253.75	1232.10
80000	7339.16	3998.77	2897.22	2355.23	2036.92	1830.29	1687.30	1583.93	1506.82	1447.93	1402.16	1366.08	1337.34	1314.24
85000	7797.86	4248.69	3078.29	2502.44	2164.23	1944.68	1792.75	1682.93	1600.99	1538.43	1489.79	1451.46	1420.92	1396.38
90000	8256.56	4498.61	3259.37	2649.64	2291.54	2059.07	1898.21	1781.92	1695.17	1628.92	1577.43	1536.84	1504.50	1478.52
95000	8715.26	4748.53	3440.44	2796.84	2418.85	2173.46	2003.67	1880.92	1789.34	1719.42	1665.06	1622.22	1588.09	1560.66
100000	9173.95	4998.46	3621.52	2944.04	2546.15	2287.86	2109.12	1979.91	1883.52	1809.91	1752.69	1707.60	1671.67	1642.79

TERM AMOUNT	15 Years	16 Years	17 Years	18 Years	19 Years	20 Years	21 Years	22 Years	23 Years	24 Years	25 Years	30 Years	35 Years	40 Years
5	.09	.09	.08	.08	.08	.08	.08	.08	.08	.08	.08	.08	.08	.08
10	.17	.17	.16	.16	.16	.16	.16	.16	.16	.16	.16	.16	.16	.16
15	.25	.25	.24	.24	.24	.24	.24	.24	.24	.23	.23	.23	.23	.23
25	.41	.41	.40	.40	.40	.39	.39	.39	.39	.39	.39	.38	.38	.38
50	.81	.81	.80	.79	.79	.78	.78	.77	.77	.77	.77	.76	.76	.76
75	1.22	1.21	1.19	1.18	1.18	1.17	1.16	1.16	1.16	1.15	1.15	1.14	1.14	1.14
100	1.62	1.61	1.59	1.58	1.57	1.55	1.55	1.54	1.54	1.54	1.53	1.52	1.52	1.52
200	3.24	3.21	3.17	3.15	3.13	3.11	3.10	3.08	3.07	3.07	3.06	3.04	3.03	3.03
300	4.86	4.81	4.76	4.72	4.69	4.66	4.64	4.62	4.61	4.60	4.59	4.56	4.54	4.54
400	6.48	6.41	6.34	6.29	6.25	6.22	6.19	6.16	6.14	6.13	6.11	6.07	6.06	6.05
500	8.10	8.01	7.93	7.87	7.81	7.77	7.73	7.70	7.68	7.66	7.64	7.59	7.57	7.56
600	9.72	9.61	9.51	9.44	9.37	9.32	9.28	9.24	9.21	9.19	9.17	9.11	9.08	9.07
700	11.34	11.21	11.10	11.01	10.94	10.88	10.83	10.78	10.75	10.72	10.70	10.63	10.60	10.59
800	12.96	12.81	12.68	12.58	12.50	12.43	12.37	12.32	12.28	12.25	12.22	12.14	12.11	12.10
900	14.58	14.41	14.27	14.15	14.06	13.98	13.92	13.86	13.82	13.78	13.75	13.66	13.62	13.61
1000	16.20	16.01	15.85	15.73	15.62	15.53	15.46	15.40	15.35	15.31	15.28	15.18	15.14	15.12
2000	32.39	32.01	31.70	31.45	31.24	31.06	30.92	30.80	30.70	30.62	30.55	30.35	30.27	30.24
3000	48.59	48.02	47.55	47.17	46.85	46.59	46.38	46.20	46.05	45.93	45.83	45.52	45.40	45.35
4000	64.78	64.02	63.40	62.89	62.47	62.12	61.84	61.60	61.40	61.24	61.10	60.70	60.53	60.47
5000	80.98	80.03	79.25	78.61	78.09	77.65	77.29	77.00	76.75	76.55	76.38	75.87	75.67	75.58
6000	97.17	96.03	95.10	94.33	93.70	93.18	92.75	92.40	92.10	91.85	91.65	91.04	90.80	90.70
7000	113.36	112.03	110.95	110.05	109.32	108.71	108.21	107.79	107.45	107.16	106.93	106.22	105.93	105.81
8000	129.56	128.04	126.79	125.77	124.93	124.24	123.67	123.19	122.80	122.47	122.20	121.39	121.06	120.93
9000	145.75	144.04	142.64	141.49	140.55	139.77	139.12	138.59	138.15	137.78	137.47	136.56	136.19	136.04
10000	161.95	160.05	158.49	157.22	156.17	155.30	154.58	153.99	153.50	153.09	152.75	151.73	151.33	151.16
11000	178.14	176.05	174.34	172.94	171.78	170.83	170.04	169.39	168.85	168.40	168.02	166.91	166.46	166.28
12000	194.34	192.05	190.19	188.66	187.40	186.36	185.50	184.79	184.19	183.70	183.30	182.08	181.59	181.39
13000	210.53	208.06	206.04	204.38	203.01	201.89	200.96	200.18	199.54	199.01	198.57	197.25	196.72	196.51
14000	226.72	224.06	221.89	220.10	218.63	217.42	216.41	215.58	214.89	214.32	213.85	212.43	211.85	211.62
15000	242.92	240.07	237.73	235.82	234.25	232.95	231.87	230.98	230.24	229.63	229.12	227.60	226.99	226.74
16000	259.11	256.07	253.58	251.54	249.86	248.48	247.33	246.38	245.59	244.94	244.39	242.77	242.12	241.85
17000	275.31	272.07	269.43	267.26	265.48	264.00	262.79	261.78	260.94	260.25	259.67	257.94	257.25	256.97
18000	291.50	288.08	285.28	282.98	281.09	279.53	278.24	277.18	276.29	275.55	274.94	273.12	272.38	272.08
19000	307.70	304.08	301.13	298.70	296.71	295.06	293.70	292.57	291.64	290.86	290.22	288.29	287.51	287.20
20000	323.89	320.09	316.98	314.43	312.33	310.59	309.16	307.97	306.99	306.17	305.49	303.46	302.65	302.31
21000	340.08	336.09	332.83	330.15	327.94	326.12	324.62	323.37	322.34	321.48	320.77	318.64	317.78	317.43
22000	356.28	352.09	348.67	345.87	343.56	341.65	340.08	338.77	337.69	336.79	336.04	333.81	332.91	332.55
23000	372.47	368.10	364.52	361.59	359.17	357.18	355.53	354.17	353.04	352.10	351.31	348.98	348.04	347.66
24000	388.67	384.10	380.37	377.31	374.79	372.71	370.99	369.57	368.38	367.40	366.59	364.15	363.17	362.78
25000	404.86	400.11	396.22	393.03	390.41	388.24	386.45	384.96	383.73	382.71	381.86	379.33	378.31	377.89
26000	421.05	416.11	412.07	408.75	406.02	403.77	401.91	400.36	399.08	398.02	397.14	394.50	393.44	393.01
27000	437.25	432.11	427.92	424.47	421.64	419.30	417.36	415.76	414.43	413.33	412.41	409.67	408.57	408.12
28000	453.44	448.12	443.77	440.19	437.25	434.83	432.82	431.16	429.78	428.64	427.69	424.85	423.70	423.24
29000	469.64	464.12	459.61	455.91	452.87	450.36	448.28	446.56	445.13	443.95	442.96	440.02	438.83	438.35
30000	485.83	480.13	475.46	471.64	468.49	465.89	463.74	461.96	460.48	459.25	458.23	455.19	453.97	453.47
31000	502.03	496.13	491.31	487.36	484.10	481.42	479.19	477.36	475.83	474.56	473.51	470.37	469.10	468.59
32000	518.22	512.14	507.16	503.08	499.72	496.95	494.65	492.75	491.18	489.87	488.78	485.54	484.23	483.70
33000	534.41	528.14	523.01	518.80	515.33	512.47	510.11	508.15	506.53	505.18	504.06	500.71	499.36	498.82
34000	550.61	544.14	538.86	534.52	530.95	528.00	525.57	523.55	521.88	520.49	519.33	515.88	514.49	513.93
35000	566.80	560.15	554.71	550.24	546.57	543.53	541.03	538.95	537.23	535.79	534.61	531.06	529.63	529.05
36000	583.00	576.15	570.55	565.96	562.18	559.06	556.48	554.35	552.57	551.10	549.88	546.23	544.76	544.16
37000	599.19	592.16	586.40	581.68	577.80	574.59	571.94	569.75	567.92	566.41	565.15	561.40	559.89	559.28
38000	615.39	608.16	602.25	597.40	593.41	590.12	587.40	585.14	583.27	581.72	580.43	576.58	575.02	574.39
39000	631.58	624.16	618.10	613.13	609.03	605.65	602.86	600.54	598.62	597.03	595.70	591.75	590.16	589.51
40000	647.77	640.17	633.95	628.85	624.65	621.18	618.31	615.94	613.97	612.34	610.98	606.92	605.29	604.62
41000	663.97	656.17	649.80	644.57	640.26	636.71	633.77	631.34	629.32	627.64	626.25	622.09	620.42	619.74
42000	680.16	672.18	665.65	660.29	655.88	652.24	649.23	646.74	644.67	642.95	641.53	637.27	635.55	634.86
43000	696.36	688.18	681.49	676.01	671.49	667.77	664.77	662.14	660.02	658.26	656.80	652.44	650.68	649.97
44000	712.55	704.18	697.34	691.73	687.11	683.30	680.15	677.53	675.37	673.57	672.07	667.61	665.82	665.09
45000	728.75	720.19	713.19	707.45	702.72	698.83	695.60	692.93	690.72	688.88	687.35	682.79	680.95	680.20
46000	744.94	736.19	729.04	723.17	718.34	714.36	711.06	708.33	706.07	704.19	702.62	697.96	696.08	695.32
47000	761.13	752.20	744.89	738.89	733.96	729.89	726.52	723.73	721.42	719.49	717.90	713.13	711.21	710.43
48000	777.33	768.20	760.74	754.61	749.57	745.42	741.98	739.13	736.76	734.80	733.17	728.30	726.34	725.55
49000	793.52	784.20	776.59	770.34	765.19	760.94	757.43	754.53	752.11	750.11	748.45	743.48	741.48	740.66
50000	809.72	800.21	792.44	786.06	780.81	776.47	772.89	769.92	767.46	765.42	763.72	758.65	756.61	755.78
55000	890.69	880.23	871.68	864.66	858.89	854.12	850.18	846.92	844.21	841.96	840.09	834.52	832.27	831.36
60000	971.66	960.25	950.92	943.27	936.97	931.77	927.47	923.91	920.95	918.50	916.46	910.38	907.93	906.93
65000	1052.63	1040.27	1030.16	1021.87	1015.05	1009.41	1004.76	1000.90	997.70	995.04	992.83	986.24	983.59	982.51
70000	1133.60	1120.29	1109.41	1100.48	1093.13	1087.06	1082.05	1077.89	1074.45	1071.58	1069.21	1062.11	1059.25	1058.09
75000	1214.57	1200.31	1188.65	1179.08	1171.21	1164.71	1159.34	1154.88	1151.19	1148.13	1145.58	1137.97	1134.91	1133.67
80000	1295.54	1280.33	1267.89	1257.69	1249.29	1242.36	1236.62	1231.88	1227.94	1224.67	1221.95	1213.84	1210.57	1209.24
85000	1376.51	1360.35	1347.14	1336.29	1327.37	1320.00	1313.91	1308.87	1304.68	1301.21	1298.32	1289.70	1286.23	1284.82
90000	1457.49	1440.37	1426.38	1414.90	1405.45	1397.65	1391.20	1385.86	1381.43	1377.75	1374.69	1365.57	1361.89	1360.40
95000	1538.46	1520.39	1505.62	1493.50	1483.53	1475.30	1468.49	1462.85	1458.18	1454.29	1451.06	1441.43	1437.55	1435.98
100000	1619.43	1600.41	1584.87	1572.11	1561.61	1552.94	1545.78	1539.84	1534.92	1530.83	1527.43	1517.30	1513.21	1511.55

18.200%

TERM AMOUNT	1 Year	2 Years	3 Years	4 Years	5 Years	6 Years	7 Years	8 Years	9 Years	10 Years	11 Years	12 Years	13 Years	14 Years
5	.46	.26	.19	.15	.13	.12	.11	.10	.10	.10	.09	.09	.09	.09
10	.92	.51	.37	.30	.26	.23	.22	.20	.19	.19	.18	.18	.17	.17
15	1.38	.76	.55	.45	.39	.35	.32	.30	.29	.28	.27	.26	.26	.25
25	2.30	1.26	.91	.74	.64	.58	.53	.50	.48	.46	.44	.43	.42	.42
50	4.59	2.51	1.82	1.48	1.28	1.15	1.06	1.00	.95	.91	.88	.86	.84	.83
75	6.89	3.76	2.72	2.22	1.92	1.72	1.59	1.49	1.42	1.37	1.32	1.29	1.26	1.24
100	9.18	5.01	3.63	2.95	2.56	2.30	2.12	1.99	1.89	1.82	1.76	1.72	1.68	1.65
200	18.36	10.01	7.26	5.90	5.11	4.59	4.23	3.97	3.78	3.63	3.52	3.43	3.36	3.30
300	27.54	15.01	10.88	8.85	7.66	6.88	6.35	5.96	5.67	5.45	5.28	5.14	5.04	4.95
400	36.72	20.01	14.51	11.80	10.21	9.17	8.46	7.94	7.56	7.26	7.04	6.86	6.71	6.60
500	45.89	25.02	18.13	14.74	12.76	11.47	10.57	9.93	9.45	9.08	8.79	8.57	8.39	8.25
600	55.07	30.02	21.76	17.69	15.31	13.76	12.69	11.91	11.33	10.89	10.55	10.28	10.07	9.89
700	64.25	35.02	25.38	20.64	17.86	16.05	14.80	13.90	13.22	12.71	12.31	11.99	11.74	11.54
800	73.43	40.02	29.01	23.59	20.41	18.34	16.91	15.88	15.11	14.52	14.07	13.71	13.42	13.19
900	82.60	45.02	32.63	26.54	22.96	20.63	19.03	17.87	17.00	16.34	15.82	15.42	15.10	14.84
1000	91.78	50.03	36.26	29.48	25.51	22.93	21.14	19.85	18.89	18.15	17.58	17.13	16.77	16.49
2000	183.56	100.05	72.51	58.96	51.01	45.85	42.28	39.69	37.77	36.30	35.16	34.26	33.54	32.97
3000	275.33	150.07	108.76	88.44	76.51	68.77	63.41	59.54	56.65	54.45	52.73	51.39	50.31	49.45
4000	367.11	200.09	145.02	117.92	102.01	91.69	84.55	79.38	75.53	72.59	70.31	68.51	67.08	65.93
5000	458.88	250.11	181.27	147.40	127.52	114.61	105.68	99.23	94.42	90.74	87.89	85.64	83.85	82.41
6000	550.66	300.13	217.52	176.88	153.02	137.53	126.82	119.07	113.30	108.89	105.46	102.77	100.62	98.89
7000	642.43	350.15	253.77	206.36	178.52	160.45	147.95	138.92	132.18	127.04	123.04	119.89	117.39	115.37
8000	734.21	400.17	290.03	235.84	204.02	183.37	169.09	158.76	151.06	145.18	140.62	137.02	134.15	131.85
9000	825.98	450.19	326.28	265.32	229.53	206.29	190.22	178.61	169.94	163.33	158.19	154.15	150.92	148.33
10000	917.76	500.21	362.53	294.80	255.03	229.21	211.36	198.45	188.83	181.48	175.77	171.27	167.69	164.82
11000	1009.53	550.23	398.79	324.28	280.53	252.14	232.49	218.30	207.71	199.63	193.35	188.40	184.46	181.30
12000	1101.31	600.25	435.04	353.76	306.03	275.06	253.63	238.14	226.59	217.77	210.92	205.53	201.23	197.78
13000	1193.08	650.28	471.29	383.24	331.54	297.98	274.76	257.99	245.47	235.92	228.50	222.65	218.00	214.26
14000	1284.86	700.30	507.54	412.72	357.04	320.90	295.90	277.83	264.36	254.07	246.08	239.78	234.77	230.74
15000	1376.63	750.32	543.80	442.20	382.54	343.82	317.03	297.67	283.24	272.22	263.65	256.91	251.54	247.22
16000	1468.41	800.34	580.05	471.68	408.04	366.74	338.17	317.52	302.12	290.36	281.23	274.03	268.30	263.70
17000	1560.18	850.36	616.30	501.16	433.54	389.66	359.30	337.36	321.00	308.51	298.81	291.16	285.07	280.18
18000	1651.96	900.38	652.56	530.64	459.05	412.58	380.44	357.21	339.88	326.66	316.38	308.29	301.84	296.66
19000	1743.73	950.40	688.81	560.12	484.55	435.50	401.57	377.05	358.77	344.81	333.96	325.42	318.61	313.14
20000	1835.51	1000.42	725.06	589.60	510.05	458.42	422.71	396.90	377.65	362.95	351.54	342.54	335.38	329.63
21000	1927.28	1050.44	761.31	619.08	535.55	481.35	443.84	416.74	396.53	381.10	369.11	359.67	352.15	346.11
22000	2019.06	1100.46	797.57	648.56	561.06	504.27	464.98	436.59	415.41	399.25	386.69	376.80	368.92	362.59
23000	2110.83	1150.48	833.82	678.04	586.56	527.19	486.12	456.43	434.30	417.40	404.27	393.92	385.69	379.07
24000	2202.61	1200.50	870.07	707.52	612.06	550.11	507.25	476.28	453.18	435.54	421.84	411.05	402.45	395.55
25000	2294.39	1250.52	906.33	737.00	637.56	573.03	528.39	496.12	472.06	453.69	439.42	428.18	419.22	412.03
26000	2386.16	1300.55	942.58	766.47	663.07	595.95	549.52	515.97	490.94	471.84	457.00	445.30	435.99	428.51
27000	2477.94	1350.57	978.83	795.95	688.57	618.87	570.66	535.81	509.82	489.99	474.57	462.43	452.76	444.99
28000	2569.71	1400.59	1015.08	825.43	714.07	641.79	591.79	555.65	528.71	508.13	492.15	479.56	469.53	461.47
29000	2661.49	1450.61	1051.34	854.91	739.57	664.71	612.93	575.50	547.59	526.28	509.73	496.68	486.30	477.95
30000	2753.26	1500.63	1087.59	884.39	765.08	687.63	634.06	595.34	566.47	544.43	527.30	513.81	503.07	494.44
31000	2845.04	1550.65	1123.84	913.87	790.58	710.56	655.20	615.19	585.35	562.58	544.88	530.94	519.83	510.92
32000	2936.81	1600.67	1160.09	943.35	816.08	733.48	676.33	635.03	604.23	580.72	562.46	548.06	536.60	527.40
33000	3028.59	1650.69	1196.35	972.83	841.58	756.40	697.47	654.88	623.12	598.87	580.03	565.19	553.37	543.88
34000	3120.36	1700.71	1232.60	1002.31	867.08	779.32	718.60	674.72	642.00	617.02	597.61	582.32	570.14	560.36
35000	3212.14	1750.73	1268.85	1031.79	892.59	802.24	739.74	694.57	660.88	635.17	615.19	599.45	586.91	576.84
36000	3303.91	1800.75	1305.11	1061.27	918.09	825.16	760.87	714.41	679.76	653.31	632.76	616.57	603.68	593.32
37000	3395.69	1850.77	1341.36	1090.75	943.59	848.08	782.01	734.26	698.65	671.46	650.34	633.70	620.45	609.80
38000	3487.46	1900.80	1377.61	1120.23	969.09	871.00	803.14	754.10	717.53	689.61	667.92	650.83	637.22	626.28
39000	3579.24	1950.82	1413.86	1149.71	994.60	893.92	824.28	773.95	736.41	707.76	685.49	667.95	653.98	642.76
40000	3671.01	2000.84	1450.12	1179.19	1020.10	916.84	845.41	793.79	755.29	725.90	703.07	685.08	670.75	659.25
41000	3762.79	2050.86	1486.37	1208.67	1045.60	939.77	866.55	813.64	774.17	744.05	720.65	702.21	687.52	675.73
42000	3854.56	2100.88	1522.62	1238.15	1071.10	962.69	887.68	833.48	793.06	762.20	738.22	719.33	704.29	692.21
43000	3946.34	2150.90	1558.88	1267.63	1096.61	985.61	908.82	853.32	811.94	780.35	755.80	736.46	721.06	708.69
44000	4038.11	2200.92	1595.13	1297.11	1122.11	1008.53	929.95	873.17	830.82	798.49	773.38	753.59	737.83	725.17
45000	4129.89	2250.94	1631.38	1326.59	1147.61	1031.45	951.09	893.01	849.70	816.64	790.95	770.71	754.60	741.65
46000	4221.66	2300.96	1667.63	1356.07	1173.11	1054.37	972.23	912.86	868.59	834.79	808.53	787.84	771.37	758.13
47000	4313.44	2350.98	1703.89	1385.55	1198.62	1077.29	993.36	932.70	887.47	852.94	826.11	804.97	788.13	774.61
48000	4405.21	2401.00	1740.14	1415.03	1224.12	1100.21	1014.50	952.55	906.35	871.08	843.68	822.09	804.90	791.09
49000	4496.99	2451.02	1776.39	1444.51	1249.62	1123.13	1035.63	972.39	925.23	889.23	861.26	839.22	821.67	807.57
50000	4588.77	2501.04	1812.65	1473.99	1275.12	1146.05	1056.77	992.24	944.11	907.38	878.83	856.35	838.44	824.06
55000	5047.64	2751.15	1993.91	1621.38	1402.63	1260.66	1162.44	1091.46	1038.52	998.12	966.72	941.98	922.28	906.46
60000	5506.52	3001.25	2175.17	1768.78	1530.15	1375.26	1268.12	1190.68	1132.94	1088.85	1054.60	1027.62	1006.13	988.87
65000	5965.39	3251.36	2356.44	1916.18	1657.66	1489.87	1373.79	1289.91	1227.35	1179.59	1142.48	1113.25	1089.97	1071.27
70000	6424.27	3501.46	2537.70	2063.58	1785.17	1604.47	1479.47	1389.13	1321.76	1270.33	1230.37	1198.89	1173.81	1153.68
75000	6883.15	3751.56	2718.97	2210.98	1912.68	1719.08	1585.15	1488.35	1416.17	1361.07	1318.25	1284.52	1257.66	1236.08
80000	7342.02	4001.67	2900.23	2358.37	2040.19	1833.68	1690.82	1587.58	1510.58	1451.80	1406.13	1370.15	1341.50	1318.49
85000	7800.90	4251.77	3081.49	2505.77	2167.70	1948.29	1796.50	1686.80	1604.99	1542.54	1494.02	1455.79	1425.35	1400.89
90000	8259.77	4501.88	3262.76	2653.17	2295.22	2062.89	1902.18	1786.02	1699.40	1633.28	1581.90	1541.42	1509.19	1483.30
95000	8718.65	4751.98	3444.02	2800.57	2422.73	2177.50	2007.85	1885.25	1793.81	1724.02	1669.78	1627.06	1593.03	1565.70
100000	9177.53	5002.08	3625.29	2947.97	2550.24	2292.10	2113.53	1984.47	1888.22	1814.75	1757.66	1712.69	1676.88	1648.11

TERM	15 Years	16 Years	17 Years	18 Years	19 Years	20 Years	21 Years	22 Years	23 Years	24 Years	25 Years	30 Years	35 Years	40 Years
AMOUNT														
5	.09	.09	.08	.08	.08	.08	.08	.08	.08	.08	.08	.08	.08	.08
10	.17	.17	.16	.16	.16	.16	.16	.16	.16	.16	.16	.16	.16	.16
15	.25	.25	.24	.24	.24	.24	.24	.24	.24	.24	.24	.23	.23	.23
25	.41	.41	.40	.40	.40	.39	.39	.39	.39	.39	.39	.39	.38	.38
50	.82	.81	.80	.79	.79	.78	.78	.78	.78	.77	.77	.77	.76	.76
75	1.22	1.21	1.20	1.19	1.18	1.17	1.17	1.16	1.16	1.16	1.16	1.15	1.14	1.14
100	1.63	1.61	1.60	1.58	1.57	1.56	1.56	1.55	1.55	1.54	1.54	1.53	1.52	1.52
200	3.25	3.22	3.19	3.16	3.14	3.12	3.11	3.10	3.09	3.08	3.07	3.05	3.04	3.04
300	4.88	4.82	4.78	4.74	4.71	4.68	4.66	4.64	4.63	4.62	4.61	4.58	4.56	4.56
400	6.50	6.43	6.37	6.32	6.27.	6.24	6.21	6.19	6.17	6.15	6.14	6.10	6.08	6.08
500	8.13	8.03	7.96	7.89	7.84	7.80	7.76	7.73	7.71	7.69	7.67	7.62	7.60	7.59
600	9.75	9.64	9.55	9.47	9.41	9.36	9.31	9.28	9.25	9.23	9.21	9.15	9.12	9.11
700	11.38	11.25	11.14	11.05	10.98	10.92	10.87	10.83	10.79	10.76	10.74	10.67	10.64	10.63
800	13.00	12.85	12.73	12.63	12.54	12.47	12.42	12.37	12.33	12.30	12.27	12.19	12.16	12.15
900	14.63	14.46	14.32	14.20	14.11	14.03	13.97	13.92	13.87	13.84	13.81	13.72	13.68	13.66
1000	16.25	16.06	15.91	15.78	15.68	15.59	15.52	15.46	15.41	15.37	15.34	15.24	15.20	15.18
2000	32.50	32.12	31.81	31.56	31.35	31.18	31.04	30.92	30.82	30.74	30.67	30.47	30.39	30.36
3000	48.75	48.18	47.72	47.34	47.02	46.77	46.55	46.38	46.23	46.11	46.01	45.71	45.59	45.54
4000	65.00	64.24	63.62	63.12	62.70	62.35	62.07	61.83	61.64	61.48	61.34	60.94	60.78	60.72
5000	81.25	80.30	79.53	78.89	78.37	77.94	77.59	77.29	77.05	76.84	76.68	76.18	75.97	75.89
6000	97.49	96.36	95.43	94.67	94.04	93.53	93.10	92.75	92.46	92.21	92.01	91.41	91.17	91.07
7000	113.74	112.42	111.34	110.45	109.72	109.12	108.62	108.21	107.86	107.58	107.35	106.64	106.36	106.25
8000	129.99	128.48	127.24	126.23	125.39	124.70	124.13	123.66	123.27	122.95	122.68	121.88	121.56	121.43
9000	146.24	144.54	143.14	142.00	141.06	140.29	139.65	139.12	138.68	138.32	138.01	137.11	136.75	136.60
10000	162.49	160.60	159.05	157.78	156.74	155.88	155.17	154.58	154.09	153.68	153.35	152.35	151.94	151.78
11000	178.74	176.65	174.95	173.56	172.41	171.46	170.68	170.03	169.50	169.05	168.68	167.58	167.14	166.96
12000	194.98	192.71	190.86	189.34	188.08	187.05	186.20	185.49	184.91	184.42	184.02	182.82	182.33	182.14
13000	211.23	208.77	206.76	205.11	203.76	202.64	201.71	200.95	200.32	199.79	199.35	198.05	197.53	197.32
14000	227.48	224.83	222.67	220.89	219.43	218.23	217.23	216.41	215.72	215.16	214.69	213.28	212.72	212.49
15000	243.73	240.89	238.57	236.67	235.10	233.81	232.75	231.86	231.13	230.52	230.02	228.52	227.91	227.67
16000	259.98	256.95	254.48	252.45	250.78	249.40	248.26	247.32	246.54	245.89	245.35	243.75	243.11	242.85
17000	276.23	273.01	270.38	268.22	266.45	264.99	263.78	262.78	261.95	261.26	260.69	258.99	258.30	258.03
18000	292.47	289.07	286.28	284.00	282.12	280.57	279.29	278.24	277.36	276.63	276.02	274.22	273.50	273.20
19000	308.72	305.13	302.19	299.78	297.80	296.16	294.81	293.69	292.77	292.00	291.36	289.45	288.69	288.38
20000	324.97	321.19	318.09	315.56	313.47	311.75	310.33	309.15	308.17	307.36	306.69	304.69	303.88	303.56
21000	341.22	337.24	334.00	331.33	329.14	327.34	325.84	324.61	323.58	322.73	322.03	319.92	319.08	318.74
22000	357.47	353.30	349.90	347.11	344.82	342.92	341.36	340.06	338.99	338.10	337.36	335.16	334.27	333.91
23000	373.72	369.36	365.81	362.89	360.49	358.51	356.88	355.52	354.40	353.47	352.69	350.39	349.47	349.09
24000	389.96	385.42	381.71	378.67	376.16	374.10	372.39	370.98	369.81	368.84	368.03	365.63	364.66	364.27
25000	406.21	401.40	397.61	394.44	391.84	389.69	387.91	386.44	385.22	384.20	383.36	380.86	379.85	379.45
26000	422.46	417.54	413.52	410.22	407.51	405.27	403.42	401.89	400.63	399.57	398.70	396.09	395.05	394.63
27000	438.71	433.60	429.42	426.00	423.18	420.86	418.94	417.35	416.03	414.94	414.03	411.33	410.24	409.80
28000	454.96	449.66	445.33	441.78	438.86	436.45	434.46	432.81	431.44	430.31	429.37	426.56	425.44	424.98
29000	471.21	465.72	461.23	457.55	454.53	452.03	449.97	448.27	446.85	445.68	444.70	441.80	440.63	440.16
30000	487.45	481.78	477.14	473.33	470.20	467.62	465.49	463.72	462.26	461.04	460.04	457.03	455.82	455.34
31000	503.70	497.84	493.04	489.11	485.88	483.21	481.00	479.18	477.67	476.41	475.37	472.26	471.02	470.51
32000	519.95	513.89	508.95	504.89	501.55	498.80	496.52	494.64	493.08	491.78	490.70	487.50	486.21	485.69
33000	536.20	529.95	524.85	520.66	517.22	514.38	512.04	510.09	508.48	507.15	506.04	502.73	501.41	500.87
34000	552.45	546.01	540.75	536.44	532.90	529.97	527.55	525.55	523.89	522.52	521.37	517.97	516.60	516.05
35000	568.70	562.07	556.66	552.22	548.57	545.56	543.07	541.01	539.30	537.88	536.71	533.20	531.79	531.23
36000	584.94	578.13	572.56	568.00	564.24	561.14	558.58	556.47	554.71	553.25	552.04	548.44	546.99	546.40
37000	601.19	594.19	588.47	583.78	579.91	576.73	574.10	571.92	570.12	568.62	567.38	563.67	562.18	561.58
38000	617.44	610.25	604.37	599.55	595.59	592.32	589.62	587.38	585.53	583.99	582.71	578.90	577.38	576.76
39000	633.69	626.31	620.28	615.33	611.26	607.91	605.13	602.84	600.94	599.36	598.04	594.14	592.57	591.94
40000	649.94	642.37	636.18	631.11	626.93	623.49	620.65	618.30	616.34	614.72	613.38	609.37	607.76	607.11
41000	666.19	658.43	652.09	646.89	642.61	639.08	636.17	633.75	631.75	630.09	628.71	624.61	622.96	622.29
42000	682.43	674.48	667.99	662.66	658.28	654.67	651.68	649.21	647.16	645.46	644.05	639.84	638.15	637.47
43000	698.68	690.54	683.89	678.44	673.95	670.25	667.20	664.67	662.57	660.83	659.38	655.07	653.35	652.65
44000	714.93	706.60	699.80	694.22	689.63	685.84	682.71	680.12	677.98	676.20	674.72	670.31	668.54	667.82
45000	731.18	722.66	715.70	710.00	705.30	701.43	698.23	695.58	693.39	691.56	690.05	685.54	683.73	683.00
46000	747.43	738.72	731.61	725.77	720.97	717.02	713.75	711.04	708.79	706.93	705.38	700.78	698.93	698.18
47000	763.68	754.78	747.51	741.55	736.65	732.60	729.26	726.50	724.20	722.30	720.72	716.01	714.12	713.36
48000	779.92	770.84	763.42	757.33	752.32	748.19	744.78	741.95	739.61	737.67	736.05	731.25	729.31	728.54
49000	796.17	786.90	779.32	773.11	767.99	763.78	760.29	757.41	755.02	753.04	751.39	746.48	744.51	743.71
50000	812.42	802.96	795.22	788.88	783.67	779.37	775.81	772.87	770.43	768.40	766.72	761.71	759.70	758.89
55000	893.66	883.25	874.75	867.77	862.03	857.30	853.39	850.15	847.47	845.24	843.39	837.88	835.67	834.78
60000	974.90	963.55	954.27	946.66	940.40	935.24	930.97	927.44	924.51	922.08	920.07	914.06	911.64	910.67
65000	1056.15	1043.84	1033.79	1025.55	1018.77	1013.17	1008.55	1004.73	1001.56	998.92	996.74	990.23	987.61	986.56
70000	1137.39	1124.14	1113.31	1104.43	1097.13	1091.11	1086.13	1082.01	1078.60	1075.76	1073.41	1066.40	1063.58	1062.45
75000	1218.63	1204.43	1192.83	1183.32	1175.50	1169.05	1163.71	1159.30	1155.64	1152.60	1150.08	1142.57	1139.55	1138.33
80000	1299.87	1284.73	1272.36	1262.21	1253.86	1246.98	1241.29	1236.59	1232.68	1229.44	1226.75	1218.74	1215.52	1214.22
85000	1381.11	1365.02	1351.88	1341.10	1332.23	1324.92	1318.87	1313.87	1309.72	1306.28	1303.42	1294.91	1291.49	1290.11
90000	1462.35	1445.32	1431.40	1419.99	1410.60	1402.85	1396.45	1391.16	1386.77	1383.12	1380.10	1371.08	1367.46	1366.00
95000	1543.59	1525.61	1510.92	1498.87	1488.96	1480.79	1474.04	1468.44	1463.81	1459.96	1456.77	1447.25	1443.43	1441.89
100000	1624.84	1605.91	1590.44	1577.76	1567.33	1558.73	1551.62	1545.73	1540.85	1536.80	1533.44	1523.42	1519.40	1517.78

MONTHLY PAYMENT
REQUIRED TO AMORTIZE A LOAN

TERM / AMOUNT	1 Year	2 Years	3 Years	4 Years	5 Years	6 Years	7 Years	8 Years	9 Years	10 Years	11 Years	12 Years	13 Years	14 Years
5	.46	.26	.19	.15	.13	.12	.11	.10	.10	.10	.09	.09	.09	.09
10	.92	.51	.37	.30	.26	.23	.22	.20	.19	.19	.18	.18	.17	.17
15	1.38	.76	.55	.45	.39	.35	.32	.30	.29	.28	.27	.26	.26	.25
25	2.30	1.26	.91	.74	.64	.58	.53	.50	.48	.46	.45	.43	.43	.42
50	4.59	2.51	1.82	1.48	1.28	1.15	1.06	1.00	.95	.91	.89	.86	.85	.83
75	6.89	3.76	2.73	2.22	1.92	1.73	1.59	1.50	1.42	1.37	1.33	1.29	1.27	1.24
100	9.18	5.01	3.63	2.96	2.56	2.30	2.12	1.99	1.90	1.82	1.77	1.72	1.69	1.66
200	18.36	10.01	7.26	5.91	5.11	4.59	4.24	3.98	3.79	3.64	3.53	3.44	3.37	3.31
300	27.54	15.02	10.89	8.86	7.66	6.89	6.35	5.97	5.68	5.46	5.29	5.15	5.05	4.96
400	36.72	20.02	14.52	11.81	10.22	9.18	8.47	7.96	7.57	7.28	7.05	6.87	6.73	6.61
500	45.90	25.03	18.14	14.76	12.77	11.48	10.59	9.94	9.46	9.09	8.81	8.59	8.41	8.26
600	55.08	30.03	21.77	17.71	15.32	13.77	12.70	11.93	11.35	10.91	10.57	10.30	10.09	9.91
700	64.26	35.04	25.40	20.66	17.88	16.07	14.82	13.92	13.24	12.73	12.33	12.02	11.77	11.57
800	73.44	40.04	29.03	23.61	20.43	18.36	16.94	15.91	15.14	14.55	14.09	13.73	13.45	13.22
900	82.62	45.05	32.66	26.56	22.98	20.66	19.05	17.89	17.03	16.37	15.85	15.45	15.13	14.87
1000	91.80	50.05	36.28	29.51	25.53	22.95	21.17	19.88	18.92	18.18	17.61	17.17	16.81	16.52
2000	183.60	100.09	72.56	59.02	51.06	45.90	42.33	39.76	37.83	36.36	35.22	34.33	33.61	33.04
3000	275.40	150.14	108.84	88.52	76.59	68.85	63.50	59.63	56.75	54.54	52.83	51.49	50.42	49.55
4000	367.20	200.18	145.12	118.03	102.12	91.80	84.66	79.51	75.66	72.72	70.44	68.65	67.22	66.07
5000	459.00	250.23	181.39	147.53	127.65	114.75	105.83	99.38	94.57	90.90	88.05	85.81	84.02	82.59
6000	550.80	300.27	217.67	177.04	153.18	137.70	126.99	119.26	113.49	109.08	105.66	102.97	100.83	99.10
7000	642.60	350.32	253.95	206.55	178.71	160.65	148.16	139.13	132.40	127.26	123.27	120.13	117.63	115.62
8000	734.40	400.36	290.23	236.05	204.24	183.60	169.32	159.01	151.31	145.44	140.88	137.29	134.43	132.14
9000	826.20	450.41	326.51	265.56	229.77	206.55	190.49	178.88	170.23	163.62	158.49	154.45	151.24	148.65
10000	918.00	500.45	362.78	295.06	255.30	229.50	211.65	198.76	189.14	181.80	176.10	171.61	168.04	165.17
11000	1009.79	550.50	399.06	324.57	280.83	252.45	232.82	218.63	208.05	199.98	193.71	188.77	184.84	181.69
12000	1101.59	600.54	435.34	354.07	306.36	275.40	253.98	238.51	226.97	218.16	211.32	205.94	201.65	198.20
13000	1193.39	650.59	471.62	383.58	331.89	298.35	275.15	258.38	245.88	236.34	228.93	223.10	218.45	214.72
14000	1285.19	700.63	507.90	413.09	357.42	321.30	296.31	278.26	264.79	254.52	246.54	240.26	235.25	231.24
15000	1376.99	750.68	544.17	442.59	382.95	344.25	317.47	298.13	283.71	272.70	264.15	257.42	252.06	247.75
16000	1468.79	800.72	580.45	472.10	408.46	367.19	338.64	318.01	302.62	290.88	281.76	274.58	268.86	264.27
17000	1560.59	850.77	616.73	501.60	434.01	390.14	359.80	337.88	321.54	309.06	299.37	291.74	285.66	280.78
18000	1652.39	900.81	653.01	531.11	459.54	413.09	380.97	357.76	340.45	327.24	316.98	308.90	302.47	297.30
19000	1744.19	950.86	689.29	560.62	485.07	436.04	402.13	377.63	359.36	345.42	334.59	326.06	319.27	313.82
20000	1835.99	1000.90	725.56	590.12	510.60	458.99	423.30	397.51	378.28	363.60	352.20	343.22	336.07	330.33
21000	1927.78	1050.95	761.84	619.63	536.13	481.94	444.46	417.38	397.19	381.78	369.81	360.38	352.88	346.85
22000	2019.58	1100.99	798.12	649.13	561.66	504.89	465.63	437.26	416.10	399.96	387.42	377.54	369.68	363.37
23000	2111.38	1151.04	834.40	678.64	587.19	527.84	486.79	457.13	435.02	418.14	405.03	394.70	386.48	379.88
24000	2203.18	1201.08	870.68	708.14	612.72	550.79	507.96	477.01	453.93	436.32	422.64	411.87	403.29	396.40
25000	2294.98	1251.13	906.95	737.65	638.25	573.74	529.12	496.88	472.84	454.50	440.25	429.03	420.09	412.92
26000	2386.78	1301.17	943.23	767.16	663.78	596.69	550.29	516.76	491.76	472.68	457.86	446.19	436.89	429.43
27000	2478.58	1351.22	979.51	796.66	689.30	619.64	571.45	536.63	510.67	490.86	475.47	463.35	453.70	445.95
28000	2570.38	1401.26	1015.79	826.17	714.83	642.59	592.61	556.51	529.58	509.04	493.08	480.51	470.50	462.47
29000	2662.18	1451.31	1052.07	855.67	740.36	665.54	613.78	576.38	548.50	527.22	510.69	497.67	487.30	478.98
30000	2753.98	1501.35	1088.34	885.18	765.89	688.49	634.94	596.26	567.41	545.40	528.30	514.83	504.11	495.50
31000	2845.77	1551.40	1124.62	914.68	791.42	711.43	656.11	616.13	586.33	563.58	545.91	531.99	520.91	512.02
32000	2937.57	1601.44	1160.90	944.19	816.95	734.38	677.27	636.01	605.24	581.76	563.52	549.15	537.72	528.53
33000	3029.37	1651.49	1197.18	973.70	842.48	757.33	698.44	655.88	624.15	599.94	581.13	566.31	554.52	545.05
34000	3121.17	1701.53	1233.45	1003.20	868.01	780.28	719.60	675.76	643.07	618.12	598.74	583.47	571.32	561.56
35000	3212.97	1751.58	1269.73	1032.71	893.54	803.23	740.77	695.63	661.98	636.30	616.35	600.63	588.13	578.08
36000	3304.77	1801.62	1306.01	1062.21	919.07	826.18	761.93	715.51	680.89	654.48	633.96	617.80	604.93	594.60
37000	3396.57	1851.67	1342.29	1091.72	944.60	849.13	783.10	735.38	699.81	672.66	651.57	634.96	621.73	611.11
38000	3488.37	1901.71	1378.57	1121.23	970.13	872.08	804.26	755.26	718.72	690.84	669.18	652.12	638.54	627.63
39000	3580.17	1951.76	1414.84	1150.73	995.66	895.03	825.43	775.13	737.63	709.02	686.79	669.28	655.34	644.15
40000	3671.97	2001.80	1451.12	1180.24	1021.19	917.98	846.59	795.01	756.55	727.20	704.40	686.44	672.14	660.66
41000	3763.76	2051.85	1487.40	1209.74	1046.72	940.93	867.75	814.88	775.46	745.38	722.01	703.60	688.95	677.18
42000	3855.56	2101.89	1523.68	1239.25	1072.25	963.88	888.92	834.76	794.37	763.56	739.62	720.76	705.75	693.70
43000	3947.36	2151.94	1559.96	1268.75	1097.78	986.83	910.08	854.63	813.29	781.74	757.22	737.92	722.55	710.21
44000	4039.16	2201.98	1596.23	1298.26	1123.31	1009.78	931.25	874.51	832.20	799.92	774.83	755.08	739.36	726.73
45000	4130.96	2252.03	1632.51	1327.77	1148.84	1032.73	952.41	894.38	851.12	818.10	792.44	772.24	756.16	743.25
46000	4222.76	2302.07	1668.79	1357.27	1174.37	1055.67	973.58	914.26	870.03	836.27	810.05	789.40	772.96	759.76
47000	4314.56	2352.12	1705.07	1386.78	1199.90	1078.62	994.74	934.13	888.94	854.45	827.66	806.56	789.77	776.28
48000	4406.36	2402.16	1741.35	1416.28	1225.43	1101.57	1015.91	954.01	907.86	872.63	845.27	823.73	806.57	792.79
49000	4498.16	2452.21	1777.62	1445.79	1250.96	1124.52	1037.07	973.88	926.77	890.81	862.88	840.89	823.37	809.31
50000	4589.96	2502.25	1813.90	1475.29	1276.49	1147.47	1058.24	993.76	945.68	908.99	880.49	858.05	840.18	825.83
55000	5048.95	2752.48	1995.29	1622.82	1404.13	1262.22	1164.06	1093.13	1040.25	999.89	968.54	943.85	924.19	908.41
60000	5507.95	3002.70	2176.68	1770.35	1531.78	1376.97	1269.88	1192.51	1134.82	1090.79	1056.59	1029.66	1008.21	990.99
65000	5966.94	3252.93	2358.07	1917.88	1659.43	1491.71	1375.71	1291.88	1229.39	1181.69	1144.64	1115.46	1092.23	1073.57
70000	6425.94	3503.15	2539.46	2065.41	1787.08	1606.46	1481.53	1391.26	1323.95	1272.59	1232.69	1201.26	1176.25	1156.16
75000	6884.93	3753.38	2720.85	2212.94	1914.73	1721.21	1587.35	1490.63	1418.52	1363.49	1320.74	1287.07	1260.26	1238.74
80000	7343.93	4003.60	2902.24	2360.47	2042.37	1835.95	1693.18	1590.01	1513.09	1454.39	1408.79	1372.87	1344.28	1321.32
85000	7802.92	4253.83	3083.63	2508.00	2170.02	1950.70	1799.00	1689.38	1607.66	1545.29	1496.84	1458.68	1428.30	1403.90
90000	8261.92	4504.05	3265.02	2655.53	2297.67	2065.45	1904.82	1788.76	1702.23	1636.19	1584.88	1544.48	1512.32	1486.49
95000	8720.91	4754.28	3446.41	2803.06	2425.32	2180.19	2010.64	1888.13	1796.79	1727.08	1672.93	1630.29	1596.33	1569.07
100000	9179.91	5004.50	3627.80	2950.58	2552.97	2294.94	2116.47	1987.51	1891.36	1817.98	1760.98	1716.09	1680.35	1651.65

MONTHLY PAYMENT
REQUIRED TO AMORTIZE A LOAN

18.250%

TERM	15 Years	16 Years	17 Years	18 Years	19 Years	20 Years	21 Years	22 Years	23 Years	24 Years	25 Years	30 Years	35 Years	40 Years
AMOUNT														
5	.09	.09	.08	.08	.08	.08	.08	.08	.08	.08	.08	.08	.08	.08
10	.17	.17	.16	.16	.16	.16	.16	.16	.16	.16	.16	.16	.16	.16
15	.25	.25	.24	.24	.24	.24	.24	.24	.24	.24	.24	.23	.23	.23
25	.41	.41	.40	.40	.40	.40	.39	.39	.39	.39	.39	.39	.39	.39
50	.82	.81	.80	.80	.79	.79	.78	.78	.78	.78	.77	.77	.77	.77
75	1.23	1.21	1.20	1.19	1.18	1.18	1.17	1.17	1.16	1.16	1.16	1.15	1.15	1.15
100	1.63	1.61	1.60	1.59	1.58	1.57	1.56	1.55	1.55	1.55	1.54	1.53	1.53	1.53
200	3.26	3.22	3.19	3.17	3.15	3.13	3.12	3.10	3.09	3.09	3.08	3.06	3.05	3.05
300	4.89	4.83	4.79	4.75	4.72	4.69	4.67	4.65	4.64	4.63	4.62	4.59	4.58	4.57
400	6.52	6.44	6.38	6.33	6.29	6.26	6.23	6.20	6.18	6.17	6.15	6.12	6.10	6.09
500	8.15	8.05	7.98	7.91	7.86	7.82	7.78	7.75	7.73	7.71	7.69	7.64	7.62	7.61
600	9.78	9.66	9.57	9.49	9.43	9.38	9.34	9.30	9.27	9.25	9.23	9.17	9.15	9.14
700	11.40	11.27	11.16	11.08	11.00	10.94	10.89	10.85	10.82	10.79	10.77	10.70	10.67	10.66
800	13.03	12.88	12.76	12.66	12.57	12.51	12.45	12.40	12.36	12.33	12.30	12.23	12.19	12.18
900	14.66	14.49	14.35	14.24	14.15	14.07	14.00	13.95	13.91	13.87	13.84	13.75	13.72	13.70
1000	16.29	16.10	15.95	15.82	15.72	15.63	15.56	15.50	15.45	15.41	15.38	15.28	15.24	15.22
2000	32.57	32.20	31.89	31.64	31.43	31.26	31.12	31.00	30.90	30.82	30.75	30.56	30.48	30.44
3000	48.86	48.29	47.83	47.45	47.14	46.88	46.67	46.49	46.35	46.23	46.13	45.83	45.71	45.66
4000	65.14	64.39	63.77	63.27	62.85	62.51	62.23	61.99	61.80	61.64	61.50	61.11	60.95	60.88
5000	81.43	80.48	79.71	79.08	78.56	78.13	77.78	77.49	77.25	77.04	76.88	76.38	76.18	76.10
6000	97.71	96.58	95.65	94.90	94.27	93.76	93.34	92.98	92.69	92.45	92.25	91.66	91.42	91.32
7000	114.00	112.68	111.60	110.71	109.98	109.39	108.89	108.48	108.14	107.06	107.69	106.93	106.65	106.54
8000	130.28	128.77	127.54	126.53	125.70	125.01	124.45	123.98	123.59	123.27	123.00	122.21	121.89	121.76
9000	146.56	144.87	143.48	142.34	141.41	140.64	140.00	139.47	139.04	138.68	138.37	137.48	137.12	136.98
10000	162.85	160.96	159.42	158.16	157.12	156.26	155.56	154.97	154.49	154.08	153.75	152.76	152.36	152.20
11000	179.13	177.06	175.36	173.97	172.83	171.89	171.11	170.47	169.93	169.49	169.12	168.03	167.59	167.42
12000	195.42	193.15	191.30	189.79	188.54	187.51	186.67	185.96	185.38	184.90	184.50	183.31	182.83	182.64
13000	211.70	209.25	207.25	205.60	204.25	203.14	202.22	201.46	200.83	200.31	199.87	198.58	198.06	197.85
14000	227.99	225.35	223.19	221.42	219.96	218.77	217.78	216.96	216.28	215.71	215.25	213.86	213.30	213.07
15000	244.27	241.44	239.13	237.23	235.68	234.39	233.33	232.45	231.73	231.12	230.62	229.13	228.53	228.29
16000	260.56	257.54	255.07	253.05	251.39	250.02	248.89	247.95	247.17	246.53	246.00	244.41	243.77	243.51
17000	276.84	273.63	271.01	268.86	267.10	265.64	264.44	263.45	262.62	261.94	261.37	259.68	259.00	258.73
18000	293.12	289.73	286.95	284.68	282.81	281.27	280.00	278.94	278.07	277.35	276.74	274.96	274.24	273.95
19000	309.41	305.82	302.90	300.50	298.52	296.89	295.55	294.44	293.52	292.75	292.12	290.23	289.47	289.17
20000	325.69	321.92	318.84	316.31	314.23	312.52	311.11	309.94	308.97	308.16	307.49	305.51	304.71	304.39
21000	341.98	338.02	334.78	332.13	329.94	328.15	326.66	325.43	324.41	323.57	322.87	320.78	319.94	319.61
22000	358.26	354.11	350.72	347.94	345.66	343.77	342.22	340.93	339.86	338.98	338.24	336.06	335.18	334.83
23000	374.55	370.21	366.66	363.76	361.37	359.40	357.77	356.42	355.31	354.38	353.62	351.33	350.42	350.05
24000	390.83	386.30	382.60	379.57	377.08	375.02	373.33	371.92	370.76	369.79	368.99	366.61	365.65	365.27
25000	407.12	402.40	398.55	395.39	392.79	390.65	388.88	387.42	386.21	385.20	384.36	381.88	380.89	380.48
26000	423.40	418.49	414.49	411.20	408.50	406.28	404.44	402.91	401.65	400.61	399.74	397.16	396.12	395.70
27000	439.68	434.59	430.43	427.02	424.21	421.90	419.99	418.41	417.10	416.02	415.11	412.43	411.36	410.92
28000	455.97	450.69	446.37	442.83	439.92	437.53	435.55	433.91	432.55	431.42	430.49	427.71	426.59	426.14
29000	472.25	466.78	462.31	458.65	455.64	453.15	451.10	449.40	448.00	446.83	445.86	442.98	441.83	441.36
30000	488.54	482.88	478.25	474.46	471.35	468.78	466.66	464.90	463.45	462.24	461.24	458.26	457.06	456.58
31000	504.82	498.97	494.20	490.28	487.06	484.40	482.21	480.40	478.89	477.65	476.61	473.53	472.30	471.80
32000	521.11	515.07	510.14	506.09	502.77	500.03	497.77	495.89	494.34	493.05	491.99	488.81	487.53	487.02
33000	537.39	531.16	526.08	521.91	518.48	515.66	513.32	511.39	509.79	508.46	507.36	504.08	502.77	502.24
34000	553.67	547.26	542.02	537.72	534.19	531.28	528.88	526.89	525.24	523.87	522.73	519.36	518.00	517.46
35000	569.96	563.36	557.96	553.54	549.90	546.91	544.43	542.38	540.69	539.28	538.11	534.63	533.24	532.68
36000	586.24	579.45	573.90	569.36	565.62	562.53	559.99	557.88	556.13	554.69	553.48	549.91	548.47	547.90
37000	602.53	595.55	589.85	585.17	581.33	578.16	575.54	573.38	571.58	570.09	568.86	565.18	563.71	563.12
38000	618.81	611.64	605.79	600.99	597.04	593.78	591.10	588.87	587.03	585.50	584.23	580.46	578.94	578.33
39000	635.10	627.74	621.73	616.80	612.75	609.41	606.65	604.37	602.48	600.91	599.61	595.73	594.18	593.55
40000	651.38	643.83	637.67	632.62	628.46	625.04	622.21	619.87	617.93	616.32	614.98	611.01	609.41	608.77
41000	667.67	659.93	653.61	648.43	644.17	640.66	637.76	635.36	633.37	631.72	630.35	626.28	624.65	623.99
42000	683.95	676.03	669.55	664.25	659.88	656.29	653.32	650.86	648.82	647.13	645.73	641.56	639.88	639.21
43000	700.23	692.12	685.49	680.06	675.60	671.91	668.87	666.36	664.27	662.54	661.10	656.83	655.12	654.43
44000	716.52	708.22	701.44	695.88	691.31	687.54	684.43	681.85	679.72	677.95	676.48	672.11	670.36	669.65
45000	732.80	724.31	717.38	711.69	707.02	703.17	699.98	697.35	695.17	693.36	691.85	687.38	685.59	684.87
46000	749.09	740.41	733.32	727.51	722.73	718.79	715.54	712.84	710.61	708.76	707.23	702.66	700.83	700.09
47000	765.37	756.50	749.26	743.32	738.44	734.42	731.09	728.34	726.06	724.17	722.60	717.93	716.06	715.31
48000	781.66	772.60	765.20	759.14	754.15	750.04	746.65	743.84	741.51	739.58	737.98	733.21	731.30	730.53
49000	797.94	788.70	781.14	774.95	769.86	765.67	762.20	759.33	756.96	754.99	753.35	748.48	746.53	745.75
50000	814.23	804.79	797.09	790.77	785.58	781.29	777.76	774.83	772.41	770.39	768.72	763.76	761.77	760.96
55000	895.65	885.27	876.79	869.85	864.13	859.42	855.53	852.31	849.65	847.43	845.60	840.13	837.94	837.06
60000	977.07	965.75	956.50	948.92	942.69	937.55	933.31	929.80	926.89	924.47	922.47	916.51	914.12	913.16
65000	1058.49	1046.23	1036.21	1028.00	1021.25	1015.68	1011.08	1007.28	1004.13	1001.51	999.34	992.88	990.29	989.25
70000	1139.91	1126.71	1115.92	1107.08	1099.80	1093.81	1088.86	1084.76	1081.37	1078.55	1076.21	1069.26	1066.47	1065.35
75000	1221.34	1207.18	1195.63	1186.15	1178.36	1171.94	1166.63	1162.24	1158.61	1155.59	1153.08	1145.63	1142.65	1141.44
80000	1302.76	1287.66	1275.34	1265.23	1256.92	1250.07	1244.41	1239.73	1235.85	1232.63	1229.96	1222.01	1218.82	1217.54
85000	1384.18	1368.14	1355.04	1344.30	1335.48	1328.20	1322.18	1317.21	1313.09	1309.67	1306.83	1298.38	1295.00	1293.64
90000	1465.60	1448.62	1434.75	1423.38	1414.03	1406.33	1399.96	1394.69	1390.33	1386.71	1383.70	1374.76	1371.18	1369.73
95000	1547.02	1529.10	1514.46	1502.46	1492.59	1484.45	1477.73	1472.17	1467.57	1463.75	1460.57	1451.13	1447.35	1445.83
100000	1628.45	1609.58	1594.17	1581.53	1571.15	1562.58	1555.51	1549.66	1544.81	1540.78	1537.44	1527.51	1523.53	1521.92

427

MONTHLY PAYMENT
REQUIRED TO AMORTIZE A LOAN

TERM	1 Year	2 Years	3 Years	4 Years	5 Years	6 Years	7 Years	8 Years	9 Years	10 Years	11 Years	12 Years	13 Years	14 Years
AMOUNT														
5	.46	.26	.19	.15	.13	.12	.11	.10	.10	.10	.09	.09	.09	.09
10	.92	.51	.37	.30	.26	.23	.22	.20	.19	.19	.18	.18	.17	.17
15	1.38	.76	.55	.45	.39	.35	.32	.30	.29	.28	.27	.26	.26	.25
25	2.30	1.26	.91	.74	.64	.58	.53	.50	.48	.46	.45	.43	.43	.42
50	4.60	2.51	1.82	1.48	1.28	1.15	1.06	1.00	.95	.92	.89	.86	.85	.83
75	6.89	3.76	2.73	2.22	1.92	1.73	1.59	1.50	1.43	1.37	1.33	1.29	1.27	1.25
100	9.19	5.01	3.64	2.96	2.56	2.30	2.12	2.00	1.90	1.83	1.77	1.72	1.69	1.66
200	18.37	10.02	7.27	5.91	5.12	4.60	4.24	3.99	3.79	3.65	3.53	3.44	3.37	3.32
300	27.55	15.03	10.90	8.86	7.67	6.90	6.36	5.98	5.69	5.47	5.30	5.16	5.06	4.97
400	36.73	20.03	14.53	11.82	10.23	9.20	8.48	7.97	7.58	7.29	7.06	6.88	6.74	6.63
500	45.92	25.04	18.16	14.77	12.78	11.49	10.60	9.96	9.48	9.11	8.82	8.60	8.42	8.28
600	55.10	30.05	21.79	17.72	15.34	13.79	12.72	11.95	11.37	10.93	10.59	10.32	10.11	9.94
700	64.28	35.05	25.42	20.68	17.89	16.09	14.84	13.94	13.27	12.75	12.36	12.04	11.79	11.59
800	73.46	40.06	29.05	23.63	20.45	18.39	16.96	15.93	15.16	14.57	14.12	13.76	13.48	13.25
900	82.65	45.07	32.68	26.58	23.01	20.68	19.08	17.92	17.06	16.40	15.88	15.48	15.16	14.90
1000	91.83	50.07	36.31	29.54	25.56	22.98	21.20	19.91	18.95	18.22	17.65	17.20	16.84	16.56
2000	183.65	100.14	72.61	59.07	51.12	45.96	42.39	39.82	37.89	36.43	35.29	34.39	33.68	33.11
3000	275.47	150.21	108.91	88.60	76.68	68.94	63.59	59.72	56.84	54.64	52.93	51.59	50.52	49.66
4000	367.30	200.28	145.22	118.13	102.23	91.92	84.78	79.63	75.78	72.85	70.58	68.78	67.36	66.21
5000	459.12	250.35	181.52	147.66	127.79	114.89	105.98	99.53	94.73	91.07	88.22	85.98	84.20	82.76
6000	550.94	300.42	217.82	177.20	153.35	137.87	127.17	119.44	113.67	109.28	105.86	103.17	101.03	99.32
7000	642.76	350.49	254.13	206.73	178.90	160.85	148.36	139.34	132.62	127.49	123.51	120.37	117.87	115.87
8000	734.59	400.56	290.43	236.26	204.46	183.83	169.56	159.25	151.56	145.70	141.15	137.56	134.71	132.42
9000	826.41	450.63	326.73	265.79	230.02	206.80	190.75	179.15	170.51	163.91	158.79	154.76	151.55	148.97
10000	918.23	500.70	363.04	295.32	255.57	229.78	211.95	199.06	189.45	182.13	176.43	171.95	168.39	165.52
11000	1010.06	550.77	399.34	324.86	281.13	252.76	233.14	218.97	208.40	200.34	194.08	189.15	185.23	182.08
12000	1101.88	600.84	435.64	354.39	306.69	275.74	254.33	238.87	227.34	218.55	211.72	206.34	202.06	198.63
13000	1193.70	650.90	471.94	383.92	332.24	298.72	275.53	258.78	246.29	236.76	229.36	223.54	218.90	215.18
14000	1285.52	700.97	508.25	413.45	357.80	321.69	296.72	278.68	265.23	254.97	247.01	240.73	235.74	231.73
15000	1377.35	751.04	544.55	442.98	383.36	344.67	317.92	298.59	284.18	273.19	264.65	257.93	252.58	248.28
16000	1469.17	801.11	580.85	472.52	408.92	367.65	339.11	318.49	303.12	291.40	282.29	275.12	269.42	264.84
17000	1560.99	851.18	617.16	502.05	434.47	390.63	360.30	338.40	322.07	309.61	299.94	292.32	286.25	281.39
18000	1652.82	901.25	653.46	531.58	460.03	413.60	381.50	358.30	341.01	327.82	317.58	309.51	303.09	297.94
19000	1744.64	951.32	689.76	561.11	485.59	436.58	402.69	378.21	359.96	346.03	335.22	326.71	319.93	314.49
20000	1836.46	1001.39	726.07	590.64	511.14	459.56	423.89	398.11	378.90	364.25	352.86	343.90	336.77	331.04
21000	1928.28	1051.46	762.37	620.18	536.70	482.54	445.08	418.02	397.85	382.46	370.51	361.10	353.61	347.60
22000	2020.11	1101.53	798.67	649.71	562.26	505.51	466.27	437.93	416.79	400.67	388.15	378.29	370.45	364.15
23000	2111.93	1151.60	834.98	679.24	587.81	528.49	487.47	457.83	435.74	418.88	405.79	395.49	387.28	380.70
24000	2203.75	1201.67	871.28	708.77	613.37	551.47	508.66	477.74	454.68	437.10	423.44	412.68	404.12	397.25
25000	2295.58	1251.73	907.58	738.30	638.93	574.45	529.86	497.64	473.63	455.31	441.08	429.88	420.96	413.80
26000	2387.40	1301.80	943.88	767.84	664.48	597.43	551.05	517.55	492.57	473.52	458.72	447.07	437.80	430.35
27000	2479.22	1351.87	980.19	797.37	690.04	620.40	572.24	537.45	511.52	491.73	476.36	464.27	454.64	446.91
28000	2571.04	1401.94	1016.49	826.90	715.60	643.38	593.44	557.36	530.46	509.94	494.01	481.46	471.47	463.46
29000	2662.87	1452.01	1052.79	856.43	741.16	666.36	614.63	577.26	549.41	528.16	511.65	498.66	488.31	480.01
30000	2754.69	1502.08	1089.10	885.96	766.71	689.34	635.83	597.17	568.35	546.37	529.29	515.85	505.15	496.56
31000	2846.51	1552.15	1125.40	915.50	792.27	712.31	657.02	617.08	587.30	564.58	546.94	533.05	521.99	513.11
32000	2938.34	1602.22	1161.70	945.03	817.83	735.29	678.21	636.98	606.24	582.79	564.58	550.24	538.83	529.67
33000	3030.16	1652.29	1198.01	974.56	843.38	758.27	699.41	656.89	625.19	601.00	582.22	567.44	555.67	546.22
34000	3121.98	1702.36	1234.31	1004.09	868.94	781.25	720.60	676.79	644.13	619.22	599.87	584.63	572.50	562.77
35000	3213.80	1752.43	1270.61	1033.62	894.50	804.22	741.80	696.70	663.08	637.43	617.51	601.82	589.34	579.32
36000	3305.63	1802.50	1306.92	1063.16	920.05	827.20	762.99	716.60	682.02	655.64	635.15	619.02	606.18	595.87
37000	3397.45	1852.56	1343.22	1092.69	945.61	850.18	784.18	736.51	700.97	673.85	652.79	636.21	623.02	612.43
38000	3489.27	1902.63	1379.52	1122.22	971.17	873.16	805.38	756.41	719.91	692.06	670.44	653.41	639.86	628.98
39000	3581.10	1952.70	1415.82	1151.75	996.72	896.14	826.57	776.32	738.86	710.28	688.08	670.60	656.70	645.53
40000	3672.92	2002.77	1452.13	1181.28	1022.28	919.11	847.77	796.22	757.80	728.49	705.72	687.80	673.53	662.08
41000	3764.74	2052.84	1488.43	1210.82	1047.84	942.09	868.96	816.13	776.75	746.70	723.37	704.99	690.37	678.63
42000	3856.56	2102.91	1524.73	1240.35	1073.40	965.07	890.15	836.04	795.69	764.91	741.01	722.19	707.21	695.19
43000	3948.39	2152.98	1561.04	1269.88	1098.95	988.05	911.35	855.94	814.64	783.13	758.65	739.38	724.05	711.74
44000	4040.21	2203.05	1597.34	1299.41	1124.51	1011.02	932.54	875.85	833.58	801.34	776.30	756.58	740.89	728.29
45000	4132.03	2253.12	1633.64	1328.94	1150.07	1034.00	953.74	895.75	852.53	819.55	793.94	773.77	757.72	744.84
46000	4223.86	2303.19	1669.95	1358.48	1175.62	1056.98	974.93	915.66	871.47	837.76	811.58	790.97	774.56	761.39
47000	4315.68	2353.26	1706.25	1388.01	1201.18	1079.96	996.13	935.56	890.42	855.97	829.22	808.16	791.40	777.95
48000	4407.50	2403.33	1742.55	1417.54	1226.74	1102.94	1017.32	955.47	909.36	874.19	846.87	825.36	808.24	794.50
49000	4499.32	2453.39	1778.86	1447.07	1252.29	1125.91	1038.51	975.37	928.31	892.40	864.51	842.55	825.08	811.05
50000	4591.15	2503.46	1815.16	1476.60	1277.85	1148.89	1059.71	995.28	947.25	910.61	882.15	859.75	841.92	827.60
55000	5050.26	2753.81	1996.67	1624.26	1405.64	1263.78	1165.68	1094.81	1041.98	1001.67	970.37	945.72	926.11	910.36
60000	5509.37	3004.16	2178.19	1771.92	1533.42	1378.67	1271.65	1194.33	1136.70	1092.73	1058.58	1031.70	1010.30	993.12
65000	5968.49	3254.50	2359.70	1919.58	1661.20	1493.56	1377.62	1293.86	1231.43	1183.79	1146.80	1117.67	1094.49	1075.88
70000	6427.60	3504.85	2541.22	2067.24	1788.99	1608.44	1483.59	1393.39	1326.15	1274.85	1235.01	1203.64	1178.68	1158.64
75000	6886.72	3755.19	2722.74	2214.90	1916.77	1723.33	1589.56	1492.92	1420.88	1365.91	1323.23	1289.62	1262.87	1241.40
80000	7345.83	4005.54	2904.25	2362.56	2044.56	1838.22	1695.53	1592.44	1515.60	1456.97	1411.44	1375.59	1347.06	1324.16
85000	7804.95	4255.88	3085.77	2510.22	2172.34	1953.11	1801.50	1691.97	1610.33	1548.03	1499.66	1461.57	1431.25	1406.92
90000	8264.06	4506.23	3267.28	2657.88	2300.13	2068.00	1907.47	1791.50	1705.05	1639.09	1587.87	1547.54	1515.44	1489.68
95000	8723.17	4756.58	3448.80	2805.54	2427.91	2182.89	2013.44	1891.03	1799.78	1730.15	1676.09	1633.52	1599.64	1572.44
100000	9182.29	5006.92	3630.31	2953.20	2555.70	2297.78	2119.41	1990.55	1894.50	1821.22	1764.30	1719.49	1683.83	1655.20

TERM	15 Years	16 Years	17 Years	18 Years	19 Years	20 Years	21 Years	22 Years	23 Years	24 Years	25 Years	30 Years	35 Years	40 Years
AMOUNT														
5	.09	.09	.08	.08	.08	.08	.08	.08	.08	.08	.08	.08	.08	.08
10	.17	.17	.16	.16	.16	.16	.16	.16	.16	.16	.16	.16	.16	.16
15	.25	.25	.24	.24	.24	.24	.24	.24	.24	.24	.24	.23	.23	.23
25	.41	.41	.40	.40	.40	.40	.39	.39	.39	.39	.39	.39	.39	.39
50	.82	.81	.80	.80	.79	.79	.78	.78	.78	.78	.78	.77	.77	.77
75	1.23	1.21	1.20	1.19	1.19	1.18	1.17	1.17	1.17	1.16	1.16	1.15	1.15	1.15
100	1.64	1.62	1.60	1.59	1.58	1.57	1.56	1.56	1.55	1.55	1.55	1.54	1.53	1.53
200	3.27	3.23	3.20	3.18	3.15	3.14	3.12	3.11	3.10	3.09	3.09	3.07	3.06	3.06
300	4.90	4.84	4.80	4.76	4.73	4.70	4.68	4.67	4.65	4.64	4.63	4.60	4.59	4.58
400	6.53	6.46	6.40	6.35	6.30	6.27	6.24	6.22	6.20	6.18	6.17	6.13	6.12	6.11
500	8.17	8.07	7.99	7.93	7.88	7.84	7.80	7.77	7.75	7.73	7.71	7.66	7.64	7.64
600	9.80	9.68	9.59	9.52	9.45	9.40	9.36	9.33	9.30	9.27	9.25	9.19	9.17	9.16
700	11.43	11.30	11.19	11.10	11.03	10.97	10.92	10.88	10.85	10.82	10.80	10.73	10.70	10.69
800	13.06	12.91	12.79	12.69	12.60	12.54	12.48	12.43	12.40	12.36	12.34	12.26	12.23	12.21
900	14.69	14.52	14.39	14.27	14.18	14.10	14.04	13.99	13.94	13.91	13.88	13.79	13.75	13.74
1000	16.33	16.14	15.98	15.86	15.75	15.67	15.60	15.54	15.49	15.45	15.42	15.32	15.28	15.27
2000	32.65	32.27	31.96	31.71	31.50	31.33	31.19	31.08	30.98	30.90	30.83	30.64	30.56	30.53
3000	48.97	48.40	47.94	47.56	47.25	47.00	46.79	46.61	46.47	46.35	46.25	45.95	45.83	45.79
4000	65.29	64.53	63.92	63.42	63.00	62.66	62.38	62.15	61.96	61.80	61.66	61.27	61.11	61.05
5000	81.61	80.67	79.90	79.27	78.75	78.33	77.98	77.68	77.44	77.24	77.08	76.58	76.39	76.31
6000	97.93	96.80	95.88	95.12	94.50	93.99	93.57	93.22	92.93	92.69	92.49	91.90	91.66	91.57
7000	114.25	112.93	111.86	110.98	110.25	109.66	109.16	108.76	108.42	108.14	107.91	107.22	106.94	106.83
8000	130.57	129.06	127.84	126.83	126.00	125.32	124.76	124.29	123.91	123.59	123.32	122.53	122.22	122.09
9000	146.89	145.20	143.81	142.68	141.75	140.98	140.35	139.83	139.39	139.03	138.74	137.85	137.49	137.35
10000	163.21	161.33	159.79	158.54	157.50	156.65	155.95	155.36	154.88	154.48	154.15	153.16	152.77	152.61
11000	179.53	177.46	175.77	174.39	173.25	172.31	171.54	170.90	170.37	169.93	169.56	168.48	168.05	167.87
12000	195.85	193.59	191.75	190.24	189.00	187.98	187.13	186.43	185.86	185.38	184.98	183.80	183.32	183.13
13000	212.17	209.73	207.73	206.09	204.75	203.64	202.73	201.97	201.34	200.82	200.39	199.11	198.60	198.39
14000	228.49	225.86	223.71	221.95	220.50	219.31	218.32	217.51	216.83	216.27	215.81	214.43	213.88	213.65
15000	244.81	241.99	239.69	237.80	236.25	234.97	233.92	233.04	232.32	231.72	231.22	229.74	229.15	228.92
16000	261.13	258.12	255.67	253.65	252.00	250.64	249.51	248.58	247.81	247.17	246.64	245.06	244.43	244.18
17000	277.45	274.26	271.65	269.51	267.75	266.30	265.10	264.11	263.29	262.61	262.05	260.38	259.71	259.44
18000	293.77	290.39	287.62	285.36	283.50	281.96	280.70	279.65	278.78	278.06	277.47	275.69	274.98	274.70
19000	310.09	306.52	303.60	301.21	299.25	297.63	296.29	295.19	294.27	293.51	292.88	291.01	290.26	289.96
20000	326.42	322.65	319.58	317.07	315.00	313.29	311.89	310.72	309.76	308.96	308.29	306.32	305.54	305.22
21000	342.74	338.79	335.56	332.92	330.75	328.96	327.48	326.26	325.24	324.41	323.71	321.64	320.81	320.48
22000	359.06	354.92	351.54	348.77	346.50	344.62	343.07	341.79	340.73	339.85	339.12	336.95	336.09	335.74
23000	375.38	371.05	367.52	364.62	362.25	360.29	358.67	357.33	356.22	355.30	354.54	352.27	351.36	351.00
24000	391.70	387.18	383.50	380.48	378.00	375.95	374.26	372.86	371.71	370.75	369.95	367.59	366.64	366.26
25000	408.02	403.32	399.48	396.33	393.75	391.61	389.86	388.40	387.19	386.20	385.37	382.90	381.92	381.52
26000	424.34	419.45	415.46	412.18	409.49	407.28	405.45	403.94	402.68	401.64	400.78	398.22	397.19	396.78
27000	440.66	435.58	431.43	428.04	425.24	422.94	421.04	419.47	418.17	417.09	416.20	413.53	412.47	412.04
28000	456.98	451.71	447.41	443.89	440.99	438.61	436.64	435.01	433.66	432.54	431.61	428.85	427.75	427.30
29000	473.30	467.85	463.39	459.74	456.74	454.27	452.23	450.54	449.15	447.99	447.02	444.17	443.02	442.56
30000	489.62	483.98	479.37	475.60	472.49	469.94	467.83	466.08	464.63	463.43	462.44	459.48	458.30	457.83
31000	505.94	500.11	495.35	491.45	488.24	485.60	483.42	481.61	480.12	478.88	477.85	474.80	473.58	473.09
32000	522.26	516.24	511.33	507.30	503.99	501.27	499.01	497.15	495.61	494.33	493.27	490.11	488.85	488.35
33000	538.58	532.38	527.31	523.16	519.74	516.93	514.61	512.69	511.10	509.78	508.68	505.43	504.13	503.61
34000	554.90	548.51	543.29	539.01	535.49	532.59	530.20	528.22	526.58	525.22	524.10	520.75	519.41	518.87
35000	571.22	564.64	559.27	554.86	551.24	548.26	545.80	543.76	542.07	540.67	539.51	536.06	534.68	534.13
36000	587.54	580.77	575.24	570.71	566.99	563.92	561.39	559.29	557.56	556.12	554.93	551.38	549.96	549.39
37000	603.86	596.91	591.22	586.57	582.74	579.59	576.98	574.83	573.05	571.57	570.34	566.69	565.24	564.65
38000	620.18	613.04	607.20	602.42	598.49	595.25	592.58	590.37	588.53	587.01	585.75	582.01	580.51	579.91
39000	636.51	629.17	623.18	618.27	614.24	610.92	608.17	605.90	604.02	602.46	601.17	597.32	595.79	595.17
40000	652.83	645.30	639.16	634.13	629.99	626.58	623.77	621.44	619.51	617.91	616.58	612.64	611.07	610.43
41000	669.15	661.43	655.14	649.98	645.74	642.24	639.36	636.97	635.00	633.36	632.00	627.96	626.34	625.69
42000	685.47	677.57	671.12	665.83	661.49	657.91	654.95	652.51	650.48	648.81	647.41	643.27	641.62	640.95
43000	701.79	693.70	687.10	681.69	677.24	673.57	670.55	668.04	665.97	664.25	662.83	658.59	656.89	656.21
44000	718.11	709.83	703.08	697.54	692.99	689.24	686.14	683.58	681.46	679.70	678.24	673.90	672.17	671.47
45000	734.43	725.96	719.05	713.39	708.74	704.90	701.74	699.12	696.95	695.15	693.66	689.22	687.45	686.74
46000	750.75	742.10	735.03	729.24	724.49	720.57	717.33	714.65	712.43	710.60	709.07	704.54	702.72	702.00
47000	767.07	758.23	751.01	745.10	740.24	736.23	732.92	730.19	727.92	726.04	724.48	719.85	718.00	717.26
48000	783.39	774.36	766.99	760.95	755.99	751.90	748.52	745.72	743.41	741.49	739.90	735.17	733.28	732.52
49000	799.71	790.49	782.97	776.80	771.74	767.56	764.11	761.26	758.90	756.94	755.31	750.48	748.55	747.78
50000	816.03	806.63	798.95	792.66	787.49	783.22	779.71	776.79	774.38	772.39	770.73	765.80	763.83	763.04
55000	897.63	887.29	878.84	871.92	866.23	861.55	857.68	854.47	851.82	849.62	847.80	842.38	840.21	839.34
60000	979.24	967.95	958.74	951.19	944.98	939.87	935.65	932.15	929.26	926.86	924.87	918.96	916.60	915.65
65000	1060.84	1048.61	1038.63	1030.45	1023.73	1018.19	1013.62	1009.83	1006.70	1004.10	1001.94	995.54	992.98	991.95
70000	1142.44	1129.28	1118.53	1109.72	1102.48	1096.51	1091.59	1087.51	1084.14	1081.34	1079.02	1072.12	1069.36	1068.25
75000	1224.04	1209.94	1198.42	1188.98	1181.23	1174.83	1169.56	1165.19	1161.57	1158.58	1156.09	1148.70	1145.74	1144.56
80000	1305.65	1290.60	1278.32	1268.25	1259.97	1253.16	1247.53	1242.87	1239.01	1235.81	1233.16	1225.28	1222.13	1220.86
85000	1387.25	1371.26	1358.21	1347.51	1338.72	1331.48	1325.50	1320.55	1316.45	1313.05	1310.23	1301.86	1298.51	1297.16
90000	1468.85	1451.92	1438.10	1426.78	1417.47	1409.80	1403.47	1398.23	1393.89	1390.29	1387.31	1378.44	1374.89	1373.47
95000	1550.45	1532.59	1518.00	1506.04	1496.22	1488.12	1481.44	1475.91	1471.33	1467.53	1464.38	1455.02	1451.27	1449.77
100000	1632.06	1613.25	1597.89	1585.31	1574.97	1566.44	1559.41	1553.59	1548.76	1544.77	1541.45	1531.59	1527.66	1526.07

MONTHLY PAYMENT
REQUIRED TO AMORTIZE A LOAN

TERM AMOUNT	1 Year	2 Years	3 Years	4 Years	5 Years	6 Years	7 Years	8 Years	9 Years	10 Years	11 Years	12 Years	13 Years	14 Years
5	.46	.26	.19	.15	.13	.12	.11	.10	.10	.10	.09	.09	.09	.09
10	.92	.51	.37	.30	.26	.24	.22	.20	.19	.19	.18	.18	.17	.17
15	1.38	.76	.55	.45	.39	.35	.32	.30	.29	.28	.27	.26	.26	.25
25	2.30	1.26	.91	.74	.64	.58	.54	.50	.48	.46	.45	.44	.43	.42
50	4.60	2.51	1.82	1.48	1.28	1.16	1.07	1.00	.95	.92	.89	.87	.85	.84
75	6.89	3.76	2.73	2.22	1.92	1.73	1.60	1.50	1.43	1.37	1.33	1.30	1.27	1.25
100	9.19	5.02	3.64	2.96	2.56	2.31	2.13	2.00	1.90	1.83	1.77	1.73	1.69	1.67
200	18.38	10.03	7.27	5.92	5.12	4.61	4.25	4.00	3.80	3.66	3.54	3.45	3.38	3.33
300	27.56	15.04	10.91	8.88	7.68	6.91	6.38	5.99	5.70	5.48	5.31	5.18	5.07	4.99
400	36.75	20.05	14.54	11.83	10.24	9.21	8.50	7.99	7.60	7.31	7.08	6.90	6.76	6.65
500	45.93	25.06	18.18	14.79	12.80	11.52	10.62	9.98	9.50	9.14	8.85	8.63	8.45	8.31
600	55.12	30.07	21.81	17.75	15.36	13.82	12.75	11.98	11.40	10.96	10.62	10.35	10.14	9.97
700	64.31	35.08	25.44	20.70	17.92	16.12	14.87	13.97	13.30	12.79	12.39	12.08	11.83	11.63
800	73.49	40.09	29.08	23.66	20.48	18.42	17.00	15.97	15.20	14.61	14.16	13.80	13.52	13.29
900	82.68	45.10	32.71	26.62	23.04	20.72	19.12	17.96	17.10	16.44	15.93	15.53	15.21	14.95
1000	91.86	50.11	36.35	29.58	25.60	23.03	21.24	19.96	19.00	18.27	17.70	17.25	16.90	16.61
2000	183.72	100.22	72.69	59.15	51.20	46.05	42.48	39.91	37.99	36.53	35.39	34.50	33.79	33.22
3000	275.58	150.32	109.03	88.72	76.80	69.07	63.72	59.86	56.98	54.79	53.08	51.74	50.68	49.82
4000	367.44	200.43	145.37	118.29	102.40	92.09	84.96	79.81	75.97	73.05	70.78	68.99	67.57	66.43
5000	459.30	250.53	181.71	147.86	127.99	115.11	106.20	99.76	94.97	91.31	88.47	86.23	84.46	83.03
6000	551.16	300.64	218.05	177.43	153.59	138.13	127.43	119.71	113.96	109.57	106.16	103.48	101.35	99.64
7000	643.01	350.74	254.39	207.00	179.19	161.15	148.67	139.66	132.95	127.83	123.85	120.73	118.24	116.24
8000	734.87	400.85	290.73	236.58	204.79	184.17	169.91	159.61	151.94	146.09	141.55	137.97	135.13	132.85
9000	826.73	450.95	327.07	266.15	230.39	207.19	191.15	179.57	170.93	164.35	159.24	155.22	152.02	149.45
10000	918.59	501.06	363.41	295.72	255.98	230.21	212.39	199.52	189.93	182.61	176.93	172.46	168.91	166.06
11000	1010.45	551.17	399.75	325.29	281.58	253.23	233.63	219.47	208.92	200.87	194.63	189.71	185.80	182.66
12000	1102.30	601.27	436.09	354.86	307.18	276.25	254.86	239.42	227.91	219.13	212.32	206.96	202.69	199.27
13000	1194.17	651.38	472.44	384.43	332.78	299.27	276.10	259.37	246.90	237.39	230.01	224.20	219.58	215.87
14000	1286.02	701.48	508.78	414.00	358.38	322.29	297.34	279.32	265.89	255.65	247.70	241.45	236.47	232.48
15000	1377.88	751.59	545.12	443.57	383.97	345.31	318.58	299.27	284.89	273.91	265.40	258.69	253.36	249.08
16000	1469.74	801.69	581.46	473.15	409.57	368.33	339.82	319.22	303.88	292.18	283.09	275.94	270.25	265.69
17000	1561.60	851.80	617.80	502.72	435.17	391.35	361.05	339.18	322.87	310.44	300.78	293.19	287.14	282.29
18000	1653.46	901.90	654.14	532.29	460.77	414.37	382.29	359.13	341.86	328.70	318.48	310.43	304.03	298.90
19000	1745.32	952.01	690.48	561.86	486.36	437.39	403.53	379.08	360.86	346.96	336.17	327.68	320.92	315.50
20000	1837.18	1002.11	726.82	591.43	511.96	460.41	424.77	399.03	379.85	365.22	353.86	344.92	337.81	332.11
21000	1929.03	1052.22	763.16	621.00	537.56	483.43	446.01	418.98	398.84	383.48	371.55	362.17	354.70	348.71
22000	2020.89	1102.33	799.50	650.57	563.16	506.45	467.25	438.93	417.83	401.74	389.25	379.42	371.59	365.32
23000	2112.75	1152.43	835.84	680.15	588.76	529.47	488.48	458.88	436.82	420.00	406.94	396.66	388.48	381.92
24000	2204.61	1202.54	872.18	709.72	614.35	552.49	509.72	478.83	455.82	438.26	424.63	413.91	405.37	398.53
25000	2296.47	1252.64	908.52	739.29	639.95	575.51	530.96	498.78	474.81	456.52	442.33	431.15	422.27	415.13
26000	2388.33	1302.75	944.87	768.86	665.55	598.53	552.20	518.74	493.80	474.78	460.02	448.40	439.16	431.74
27000	2480.19	1352.85	981.21	798.43	691.15	621.55	573.44	538.69	512.79	493.04	477.71	465.64	456.05	448.34
28000	2572.04	1402.96	1017.55	828.00	716.75	644.57	594.67	558.64	531.78	511.30	495.40	482.89	472.94	464.95
29000	2663.90	1453.06	1053.89	857.57	742.34	667.59	615.91	578.59	550.78	529.56	513.10	500.14	489.83	481.55
30000	2755.76	1503.17	1090.23	887.14	767.94	690.61	637.15	598.54	569.77	547.82	530.79	517.38	506.72	498.16
31000	2847.62	1553.27	1126.57	916.72	793.54	713.63	658.39	618.49	588.76	566.08	548.48	534.63	523.61	514.77
32000	2939.48	1603.38	1162.91	946.29	819.14	736.65	679.63	638.44	607.75	584.35	566.17	551.87	540.50	531.37
33000	3031.34	1653.49	1199.25	975.86	844.73	759.67	700.87	658.39	626.74	602.61	583.87	569.12	557.39	547.98
34000	3123.20	1703.59	1235.59	1005.43	870.33	782.69	722.10	678.35	645.74	620.87	601.56	586.37	574.28	564.58
35000	3215.05	1753.70	1271.93	1035.00	895.93	805.72	743.34	698.30	664.73	639.13	619.25	603.61	591.17	581.19
36000	3306.91	1803.80	1308.27	1064.57	921.53	828.74	764.58	718.25	683.72	657.39	636.95	620.86	608.06	597.79
37000	3398.77	1853.91	1344.61	1094.14	947.13	851.76	785.82	738.20	702.71	675.65	654.64	638.10	624.95	614.40
38000	3490.63	1904.01	1380.96	1123.72	972.72	874.78	807.06	758.15	721.71	693.91	672.33	655.35	641.84	631.00
39000	3582.49	1954.12	1417.30	1153.29	998.32	897.80	828.30	778.10	740.70	712.17	690.02	672.60	658.73	647.61
40000	3674.35	2004.22	1453.64	1182.86	1023.92	920.82	849.53	798.05	759.69	730.43	707.72	689.84	675.62	664.21
41000	3766.21	2054.33	1489.98	1212.43	1049.52	943.84	870.77	818.00	778.68	748.69	725.41	707.09	692.51	680.82
42000	3858.06	2104.44	1526.32	1242.00	1075.12	966.86	892.01	837.95	797.67	766.95	743.10	724.33	709.40	697.42
43000	3949.92	2154.54	1562.66	1271.57	1100.71	989.88	913.25	857.91	816.67	785.21	760.80	741.58	726.29	714.03
44000	4041.78	2204.65	1599.00	1301.14	1126.31	1012.90	934.49	877.86	835.66	803.47	778.49	758.83	743.18	730.63
45000	4133.64	2254.75	1635.34	1330.71	1151.91	1035.92	955.72	897.81	854.65	821.73	796.18	776.07	760.07	747.24
46000	4225.50	2304.86	1671.68	1360.29	1177.51	1058.94	976.96	917.76	873.64	839.99	813.87	793.32	776.96	763.84
47000	4317.36	2354.96	1708.02	1389.86	1203.10	1081.96	998.20	937.71	892.63	858.26	831.57	810.56	793.85	780.45
48000	4409.22	2405.07	1744.36	1419.43	1228.70	1104.98	1019.44	957.66	911.63	876.52	849.26	827.81	810.74	797.05
49000	4501.07	2455.17	1780.70	1449.00	1254.30	1128.00	1040.68	977.61	930.62	894.78	866.95	845.05	827.64	813.66
50000	4592.93	2505.28	1817.04	1478.57	1279.90	1151.02	1061.92	997.56	949.61	913.04	884.65	862.30	844.53	830.26
55000	5052.23	2755.81	1998.75	1626.43	1407.89	1266.12	1168.11	1097.32	1044.57	1004.34	973.11	948.53	928.98	913.29
60000	5511.52	3006.33	2180.45	1774.28	1535.88	1381.22	1274.30	1197.08	1139.53	1095.64	1061.57	1034.76	1013.43	996.32
65000	5970.81	3256.86	2362.16	1922.14	1663.87	1496.33	1380.49	1296.83	1234.49	1186.95	1150.04	1120.99	1097.88	1079.34
70000	6430.10	3507.39	2543.86	2070.00	1791.86	1611.43	1486.68	1396.59	1329.45	1278.25	1238.50	1207.22	1182.33	1162.37
75000	6889.40	3757.92	2725.56	2217.85	1919.85	1726.53	1592.87	1496.34	1424.41	1369.55	1326.97	1293.45	1266.79	1245.39
80000	7348.69	4008.44	2907.27	2365.71	2047.83	1841.63	1699.06	1596.10	1519.37	1460.86	1415.43	1379.68	1351.24	1328.42
85000	7807.98	4258.97	3088.97	2513.57	2175.82	1956.73	1805.25	1695.86	1614.33	1552.16	1503.89	1465.91	1435.69	1411.44
90000	8267.28	4509.50	3270.68	2661.42	2303.81	2071.83	1911.44	1795.61	1709.30	1643.46	1592.36	1552.14	1520.14	1494.47
95000	8726.57	4760.03	3452.38	2809.28	2431.80	2186.93	2017.63	1895.37	1804.26	1734.77	1680.82	1638.37	1604.59	1577.50
100000	9185.86	5010.55	3634.08	2957.14	2559.79	2302.03	2123.83	1995.12	1899.22	1826.07	1769.29	1724.60	1689.05	1660.52

TERM	15 Years	16 Years	17 Years	18 Years	19 Years	20 Years	21 Years	22 Years	23 Years	24 Years	25 Years	30 Years	35 Years	40 Years
AMOUNT														
5	.09	.09	.09	.08	.08	.08	.08	.08	.08	.08	.08	.08	.08	.08
10	.17	.17	.17	.16	.16	.16	.16	.16	.16	.16	.16	.16	.16	.16
15	.25	.25	.25	.24	.24	.24	.24	.24	.24	.24	.24	.24	.24	.23
25	.41	.41	.41	.40	.40	.40	.40	.39	.39	.39	.39	.39	.39	.39
50	.82	.81	.81	.80	.80	.79	.79	.78	.78	.78	.78	.77	.77	.77
75	1.23	1.22	1.21	1.20	1.19	1.18	1.18	1.17	1.17	1.17	1.17	1.16	1.16	1.15
100	1.64	1.62	1.61	1.60	1.59	1.58	1.57	1.56	1.56	1.56	1.55	1.54	1.54	1.54
200	3.28	3.24	3.21	3.19	3.17	3.15	3.14	3.12	3.11	3.11	3.10	3.08	3.07	3.07
300	4.92	4.86	4.82	4.78	4.75	4.72	4.70	4.68	4.67	4.66	4.65	4.62	4.61	4.60
400	6.55	6.48	6.42	6.37	6.33	6.29	6.27	6.24	6.22	6.21	6.19	6.16	6.14	6.13
500	8.19	8.10	8.02	7.96	7.91	7.87	7.83	7.80	7.78	7.76	7.74	7.69	7.67	7.67
600	9.83	9.72	9.63	9.55	9.49	9.44	9.40	9.36	9.33	9.31	9.29	9.23	9.21	9.20
700	11.47	11.34	11.23	11.14	11.07	11.01	10.96	10.92	10.89	10.86	10.84	10.77	10.74	10.73
800	13.10	12.96	12.83	12.73	12.65	12.58	12.53	12.48	12.44	12.41	12.38	12.31	12.28	12.26
900	14.74	14.57	14.44	14.32	14.23	14.16	14.09	14.04	14.00	13.96	13.93	13.84	13.81	13.80
1000	16.38	16.19	16.04	15.91	15.81	15.73	15.66	15.60	15.55	15.51	15.48	15.38	15.34	15.33
2000	32.75	32.38	32.07	31.82	31.62	31.45	31.31	31.19	31.10	31.02	30.95	30.76	30.68	30.65
3000	49.13	48.57	48.11	47.73	47.43	47.17	46.96	46.79	46.65	46.53	46.43	46.14	46.02	45.97
4000	65.50	64.76	64.14	63.64	63.23	62.89	62.61	62.38	62.19	62.03	61.90	61.51	61.36	61.30
5000	81.88	80.94	80.18	79.55	79.04	78.62	78.27	77.98	77.74	77.54	77.38	76.89	76.70	76.62
6000	98.25	97.13	96.21	95.46	94.85	94.34	93.92	93.57	93.29	93.05	92.85	92.27	92.04	91.94
7000	114.63	113.32	112.25	111.37	110.65	110.06	109.57	109.17	108.83	108.56	108.33	107.65	107.37	107.27
8000	131.00	129.51	128.28	127.28	126.46	125.78	125.22	124.76	124.38	124.06	123.80	123.02	122.71	122.59
9000	147.38	145.69	144.32	143.19	142.27	141.51	140.88	140.36	139.93	139.57	139.28	138.40	138.05	137.91
10000	163.75	161.88	160.35	159.10	158.07	157.23	156.53	155.95	155.47	155.08	154.75	153.78	153.39	153.23
11000	180.13	178.07	176.39	175.01	173.88	172.95	172.18	171.55	171.02	170.59	170.23	169.15	168.73	168.56
12000	196.50	194.26	192.42	190.92	189.69	188.67	187.83	187.14	186.57	186.09	185.70	184.53	184.07	183.88
13000	212.88	210.44	208.46	206.83	205.50	204.40	203.49	202.74	202.12	201.60	201.17	199.91	199.40	199.20
14000	229.25	226.63	224.49	222.74	221.30	220.12	219.14	218.33	217.66	217.11	216.65	215.29	214.74	214.53
15000	245.63	242.82	240.53	238.65	237.11	235.84	234.79	233.93	233.21	232.62	232.12	230.66	230.08	229.85
16000	262.00	259.01	256.56	254.56	252.92	251.56	250.44	249.52	248.76	248.12	247.60	246.04	245.42	245.17
17000	278.38	275.19	272.60	270.47	268.72	267.28	266.10	265.12	264.30	263.63	263.07	261.42	260.76	260.49
18000	294.75	291.38	288.63	286.38	284.53	283.01	281.75	280.71	279.85	279.14	278.55	276.79	276.10	275.82
19000	311.13	307.57	304.67	302.29	300.34	298.73	297.40	296.31	295.40	294.65	294.02	292.17	291.44	291.14
20000	327.50	323.76	320.70	318.20	316.14	314.45	313.05	311.90	310.94	310.15	309.50	307.55	306.77	306.46
21000	343.87	339.94	336.74	334.11	331.95	330.17	328.71	327.49	326.49	325.66	324.97	322.93	322.11	321.79
22000	360.25	356.13	352.77	350.02	347.76	345.90	344.36	343.09	342.04	341.17	340.45	338.30	337.45	337.11
23000	376.62	372.32	368.81	365.93	363.56	361.62	360.01	358.68	357.59	356.68	355.92	353.68	352.79	352.43
24000	393.00	388.51	384.84	381.84	379.37	377.34	375.66	374.28	373.13	372.18	371.39	369.06	368.13	367.75
25000	409.37	404.69	400.88	397.75	395.18	393.06	391.32	389.87	388.68	387.69	386.87	384.44	383.47	383.08
26000	425.75	420.88	416.91	413.66	410.99	408.79	406.97	405.47	404.23	403.20	402.34	399.81	398.80	398.40
27000	442.12	437.07	432.94	429.57	426.79	424.51	422.62	421.06	419.77	418.70	417.82	415.19	414.14	413.72
28000	458.50	453.26	448.98	445.48	442.60	440.23	438.27	436.66	435.32	434.21	433.29	430.57	429.48	429.05
29000	474.87	469.44	465.01	461.39	458.41	455.95	453.93	452.25	450.87	449.72	448.77	445.94	444.82	444.37
30000	491.25	485.63	481.05	477.30	474.21	471.67	469.58	467.85	466.41	465.23	464.24	461.32	460.16	459.69
31000	507.62	501.82	497.08	493.21	490.02	487.40	485.23	483.44	481.96	480.73	479.72	476.70	475.50	475.02
32000	524.00	518.01	513.12	509.12	505.83	503.12	500.88	499.04	497.51	496.24	495.19	492.08	490.83	490.34
33000	540.37	534.19	529.15	525.03	521.63	518.84	516.54	514.63	513.06	511.75	510.67	507.45	506.17	505.66
34000	556.75	550.38	545.19	540.93	537.44	534.56	532.19	530.23	528.60	527.26	526.14	522.83	521.51	520.98
35000	573.12	566.57	561.22	556.84	553.25	550.29	547.84	545.82	544.15	542.76	541.61	538.21	536.85	536.31
36000	589.50	582.76	577.26	572.75	569.05	566.01	563.49	561.42	559.70	558.27	557.09	553.58	552.19	551.63
37000	605.87	598.94	593.29	588.66	584.86	581.73	579.15	577.01	575.24	573.78	572.56	568.96	567.53	566.95
38000	622.25	615.13	609.33	604.57	600.67	597.45	594.80	592.61	590.79	589.29	588.04	584.34	582.87	582.28
39000	638.62	631.32	625.36	620.48	616.48	613.18	610.45	608.20	606.34	604.79	603.51	599.72	598.20	597.60
40000	654.99	647.51	641.40	636.39	632.28	628.90	626.10	623.80	621.88	620.30	618.99	615.09	613.54	612.92
41000	671.37	663.69	657.43	652.30	648.09	644.62	641.76	639.39	637.43	635.81	634.46	630.47	628.88	628.24
42000	687.74	679.88	673.47	668.21	663.90	660.34	657.41	654.98	652.98	651.32	649.94	645.85	644.22	643.57
43000	704.12	696.07	689.50	684.12	679.70	676.06	673.06	670.58	668.53	666.82	665.41	661.23	659.56	658.89
44000	720.49	712.26	705.54	700.03	695.51	691.79	688.71	686.17	684.07	682.33	680.89	676.60	674.90	674.21
45000	736.87	728.44	721.57	715.94	711.32	707.51	704.37	701.77	699.62	697.84	696.36	691.98	690.23	689.54
46000	753.24	744.63	737.61	731.85	727.12	723.23	720.02	717.36	715.17	713.35	711.84	707.36	705.57	704.86
47000	769.62	760.82	753.64	747.76	742.93	738.95	735.67	732.96	730.71	728.85	727.31	722.73	720.91	720.18
48000	785.99	777.01	769.68	763.67	758.74	754.68	751.32	748.55	746.26	744.36	742.78	738.11	736.25	735.50
49000	802.37	793.19	785.71	779.58	774.54	770.40	766.98	764.15	761.81	759.87	758.26	753.49	751.59	750.83
50000	818.74	809.38	801.75	795.49	790.35	786.12	782.63	779.74	777.35	775.38	773.73	768.87	766.93	766.15
55000	900.62	890.32	881.92	875.04	869.39	864.73	860.89	857.72	855.09	852.91	851.11	845.75	843.62	842.77
60000	982.49	971.26	962.09	954.59	948.42	943.34	939.15	935.69	932.82	930.45	928.48	922.64	920.31	919.38
65000	1064.36	1052.20	1042.27	1034.14	1027.46	1021.96	1017.42	1013.66	1010.56	1007.99	1005.85	999.52	997.00	995.99
70000	1146.24	1133.13	1122.44	1113.68	1106.49	1100.57	1095.68	1091.64	1088.29	1085.52	1083.22	1076.41	1073.70	1072.61
75000	1228.11	1214.07	1202.62	1193.23	1185.53	1179.18	1173.94	1169.61	1166.03	1163.06	1160.60	1153.30	1150.39	1149.22
80000	1309.98	1295.01	1282.79	1272.78	1264.56	1257.79	1252.20	1247.59	1243.76	1240.60	1237.97	1230.18	1227.08	1225.84
85000	1391.86	1375.95	1362.96	1352.33	1343.59	1336.40	1330.47	1325.56	1321.50	1318.13	1315.34	1307.07	1303.77	1302.45
90000	1473.73	1456.88	1443.14	1431.88	1422.63	1415.01	1408.73	1403.53	1399.23	1395.67	1392.72	1383.95	1380.46	1379.07
95000	1555.61	1537.82	1523.31	1511.43	1501.66	1493.62	1486.99	1481.51	1476.97	1473.21	1470.09	1460.84	1457.16	1455.68
100000	1637.48	1618.76	1603.49	1590.98	1580.70	1572.24	1565.25	1559.48	1554.70	1550.75	1547.46	1537.73	1533.85	1532.30

MONTHLY PAYMENT
REQUIRED TO AMORTIZE A LOAN

TERM	1 Year	2 Years	3 Years	4 Years	5 Years	6 Years	7 Years	8 Years	9 Years	10 Years	11 Years	12 Years	13 Years	14 Years
AMOUNT														
5	.46	.26	.19	.15	.13	.12	.11	.10	.10	.10	.09	.09	.09	.09
10	.92	.51	.37	.30	.26	.24	.22	.20	.20	.19	.18	.18	.17	.17
15	1.38	.76	.55	.45	.39	.35	.32	.30	.29	.28	.27	.26	.26	.25
25	2.30	1.26	.91	.74	.65	.58	.54	.50	.48	.46	.45	.44	.43	.42
50	4.60	2.51	1.82	1.48	1.29	1.16	1.07	1.00	.96	.92	.89	.87	.85	.84
75	6.90	3.76	2.73	2.22	1.93	1.73	1.60	1.50	1.43	1.38	1.33	1.30	1.27	1.25
100	9.19	5.02	3.64	2.96	2.57	2.31	2.13	2.00	1.91	1.83	1.78	1.73	1.70	1.67
200	18.38	10.03	7.28	5.92	5.13	4.61	4.26	4.00	3.81	3.66	3.55	3.46	3.39	3.33
300	27.57	15.04	10.91	8.88	7.69	6.92	6.38	5.99	5.71	5.49	5.32	5.18	5.08	4.99
400	36.75	20.05	14.55	11.84	10.25	9.22	8.51	7.99	7.61	7.32	7.09	6.91	6.77	6.65
500	45.94	25.06	18.18	14.80	12.81	11.52	10.63	9.99	9.51	9.14	8.86	8.64	8.46	8.32
600	55.13	30.08	21.82	17.76	15.37	13.83	12.76	11.98	11.41	10.97	10.63	10.36	10.15	9.98
700	64.31	35.09	25.45	20.71	17.93	16.13	14.88	13.98	13.31	12.80	12.40	12.09	11.84	11.64
800	73.50	40.10	29.09	23.67	20.49	18.43	17.01	15.98	15.21	14.63	14.17	13.82	13.53	13.30
900	82.69	45.11	32.72	26.63	23.06	20.74	19.13	17.97	17.11	16.45	15.94	15.54	15.22	14.97
1000	91.88	50.12	36.36	29.59	25.62	23.04	21.26	19.97	19.01	18.28	17.71	17.27	16.91	16.63
2000	183.75	100.24	72.71	59.17	51.23	46.07	42.51	39.94	38.02	36.56	35.42	34.53	33.82	33.25
3000	275.62	150.36	109.07	88.76	76.84	69.11	63.76	59.90	57.03	54.84	53.13	51.79	50.73	49.87
4000	367.49	200.48	145.42	118.34	102.45	92.14	85.02	79.87	76.04	73.11	70.84	69.06	67.64	66.50
5000	459.36	250.59	181.77	147.93	128.06	115.18	106.27	99.84	95.04	91.39	88.55	86.32	84.54	83.12
6000	551.23	300.71	218.13	177.51	153.67	138.21	127.52	119.80	114.05	109.67	106.26	103.58	101.45	99.74
7000	643.10	350.83	254.48	207.10	179.29	161.25	148.78	139.77	133.06	127.94	123.97	120.85	118.36	116.37
8000	734.97	400.95	290.83	236.68	204.90	184.28	170.03	159.74	152.07	146.22	141.68	138.11	135.27	132.99
9000	826.84	451.06	327.19	266.26	230.51	207.32	191.28	179.70	171.08	164.50	159.39	155.37	152.18	149.61
10000	918.71	501.18	363.54	295.85	256.12	230.35	212.53	199.67	190.08	182.77	177.10	172.63	169.08	166.23
11000	1010.58	551.30	399.89	325.43	281.73	253.38	233.79	219.64	209.09	201.05	194.81	189.90	185.99	182.86
12000	1102.45	601.42	436.25	355.02	307.34	276.42	255.04	239.60	228.10	219.33	212.52	207.16	202.90	199.48
13000	1194.32	651.53	472.60	384.60	332.95	299.45	276.29	259.57	247.11	237.60	230.23	224.42	219.81	216.10
14000	1286.19	701.65	508.95	414.19	358.57	322.49	297.55	279.53	266.11	255.88	247.94	241.69	236.71	232.73
15000	1378.06	751.77	545.31	443.77	384.18	345.52	318.80	299.50	285.12	274.16	265.65	258.95	253.62	249.35
16000	1469.93	801.89	581.66	473.36	409.79	368.56	340.05	319.47	304.13	292.43	283.36	276.21	270.53	265.97
17000	1561.80	852.00	618.01	502.94	435.40	391.59	361.30	339.43	323.14	310.71	301.07	293.48	287.44	282.59
18000	1653.67	902.12	654.37	532.52	461.01	414.63	382.56	359.40	342.15	328.99	318.77	310.74	304.35	299.22
19000	1745.54	952.24	690.72	562.11	486.62	437.66	403.81	379.37	361.15	347.26	336.48	328.00	321.25	315.84
20000	1837.41	1002.36	727.07	591.69	512.24	460.69	425.06	399.33	380.16	365.54	354.19	345.26	338.16	332.46
21000	1929.28	1052.47	763.43	621.28	537.85	483.73	446.32	419.30	399.17	383.82	371.90	362.53	355.07	349.09
22000	2021.16	1102.59	799.78	650.86	563.46	506.76	467.57	439.27	418.18	402.10	389.61	379.79	371.98	365.71
23000	2113.03	1152.71	836.13	680.45	589.07	529.80	488.82	459.23	437.19	420.37	407.32	397.05	388.88	382.33
24000	2204.90	1202.83	872.49	710.03	614.68	552.83	510.08	479.20	456.19	438.65	425.03	414.32	405.79	398.96
25000	2296.77	1252.94	908.84	739.62	640.29	575.87	531.33	499.17	475.20	456.93	442.74	431.58	422.70	415.58
26000	2388.64	1303.06	945.19	769.20	665.90	598.90	552.58	519.13	494.21	475.20	460.45	448.84	439.61	432.20
27000	2480.51	1353.18	981.55	798.78	691.52	621.94	573.83	539.10	513.22	493.48	478.16	466.10	456.52	448.82
28000	2572.38	1403.30	1017.90	828.37	717.13	644.97	595.09	559.06	532.22	511.76	495.87	483.37	473.42	465.45
29000	2664.25	1453.42	1054.25	857.95	742.74	668.01	616.34	579.03	551.23	530.03	513.58	500.63	490.33	482.07
30000	2756.12	1503.53	1090.61	887.54	768.35	691.04	637.59	599.00	570.24	548.31	531.29	517.89	507.24	498.69
31000	2847.99	1553.65	1126.96	917.12	793.96	714.07	658.85	618.96	589.25	566.59	549.00	535.16	524.15	515.32
32000	2939.86	1603.77	1163.31	946.71	819.57	737.11	680.10	638.93	608.26	584.86	566.71	552.42	541.06	531.94
33000	3031.73	1653.89	1199.67	976.29	845.19	760.14	701.35	658.90	627.26	603.14	584.42	569.68	557.96	548.56
34000	3123.60	1704.00	1236.02	1005.88	870.80	783.18	722.60	678.86	646.27	621.42	602.13	586.95	574.87	565.18
35000	3215.47	1754.12	1272.37	1035.46	896.41	806.21	743.86	698.83	665.28	639.69	619.83	604.21	591.78	581.81
36000	3307.34	1804.24	1308.73	1065.04	922.02	829.25	765.11	718.80	684.29	657.97	637.54	621.47	608.69	598.43
37000	3399.21	1854.36	1345.08	1094.63	947.63	852.28	786.36	738.76	703.30	676.25	655.25	638.73	625.59	615.05
38000	3491.08	1904.47	1381.43	1124.21	973.24	875.32	807.62	758.73	722.30	694.52	672.96	656.00	642.50	631.68
39000	3582.95	1954.59	1417.79	1153.80	998.85	898.35	828.87	778.70	741.31	712.80	690.67	673.26	659.41	648.30
40000	3674.82	2004.71	1454.14	1183.38	1024.47	921.38	850.12	798.66	760.32	731.08	708.38	690.52	676.32	664.92
41000	3766.69	2054.83	1490.49	1212.97	1050.08	944.42	871.38	818.63	779.33	749.36	726.09	707.79	693.23	681.55
42000	3858.56	2104.94	1526.85	1242.55	1075.69	967.45	892.63	838.59	798.33	767.63	743.80	725.05	710.13	698.17
43000	3950.44	2155.06	1563.20	1272.14	1101.30	990.49	913.88	858.56	817.34	785.91	761.51	742.31	727.04	714.79
44000	4042.31	2205.18	1599.55	1301.72	1126.91	1013.52	935.13	878.53	836.35	804.19	779.22	759.57	743.95	731.41
45000	4134.18	2255.30	1635.91	1331.30	1152.52	1036.56	956.39	898.49	855.36	822.46	796.93	776.84	760.86	748.04
46000	4226.05	2305.41	1672.26	1360.89	1178.14	1059.59	977.64	918.46	874.37	840.74	814.64	794.10	777.76	764.66
47000	4317.92	2355.53	1708.61	1390.47	1203.75	1082.63	998.89	938.43	893.37	859.02	832.35	811.36	794.67	781.28
48000	4409.79	2405.65	1744.97	1420.06	1229.36	1105.66	1020.15	958.39	912.38	877.29	850.06	828.63	811.58	797.91
49000	4501.66	2455.77	1781.32	1449.64	1254.97	1128.70	1041.40	978.36	931.39	895.57	867.77	845.89	828.49	814.53
50000	4593.53	2505.88	1817.67	1479.23	1280.58	1151.73	1062.65	998.33	950.40	913.85	885.48	863.15	845.40	831.15
55000	5052.88	2756.47	1999.44	1627.15	1408.64	1266.90	1168.92	1098.16	1045.44	1005.23	974.02	949.47	929.94	914.27
60000	5512.23	3007.06	2181.21	1775.07	1536.70	1382.07	1275.18	1197.99	1140.48	1096.61	1062.57	1035.78	1014.47	997.38
65000	5971.59	3257.65	2362.97	1922.99	1664.75	1497.25	1381.45	1297.82	1235.51	1188.00	1151.12	1122.10	1099.01	1080.50
70000	6430.94	3508.24	2544.74	2070.92	1792.81	1612.42	1487.71	1397.65	1330.55	1279.38	1239.66	1208.41	1183.55	1163.61
75000	6890.29	3758.82	2726.51	2218.84	1920.87	1727.59	1593.98	1497.49	1425.59	1370.77	1328.21	1294.73	1268.09	1246.73
80000	7349.64	4009.41	2908.27	2366.76	2048.93	1842.76	1700.24	1597.32	1520.63	1462.15	1416.76	1381.04	1352.63	1329.84
85000	7808.99	4260.00	3090.04	2514.68	2176.98	1957.94	1806.51	1697.15	1615.67	1553.54	1505.31	1467.36	1437.17	1412.95
90000	8268.35	4510.59	3271.81	2662.60	2305.04	2073.11	1912.77	1796.98	1710.71	1644.92	1593.85	1553.67	1521.71	1496.07
95000	8727.70	4761.18	3453.58	2810.53	2433.10	2188.28	2019.03	1896.81	1805.75	1736.30	1682.40	1639.98	1606.25	1579.18
100000	9187.05	5011.76	3635.34	2958.45	2561.16	2303.45	2125.30	1996.65	1900.79	1827.69	1770.95	1726.30	1690.79	1662.30

MONTHLY PAYMENT
REQUIRED TO AMORTIZE A LOAN

18.400%

TERM	15 Years	16 Years	17 Years	18 Years	19 Years	20 Years	21 Years	22 Years	23 Years	24 Years	25 Years	30 Years	35 Years	40 Years
AMOUNT														
5	.09	.09	.09	.08	.08	.08	.08	.08	.08	.08	.08	.08	.08	.08
10	.17	.17	.17	.16	.16	.16	.16	.16	.16	.16	.16	.16	.16	.16
15	.25	.25	.25	.24	.24	.24	.24	.24	.24	.24	.24	.24	.24	.24
25	.41	.41	.41	.40	.40	.40	.40	.40	.39	.39	.39	.39	.39	.39
50	.82	.82	.81	.80	.80	.79	.79	.79	.78	.78	.78	.77	.77	.77
75	1.23	1.22	1.21	1.20	1.19	1.19	1.18	1.18	1.17	1.17	1.17	1.16	1.16	1.16
100	1.64	1.63	1.61	1.60	1.59	1.58	1.57	1.57	1.56	1.56	1.55	1.54	1.54	1.54
200	3.28	3.25	3.22	3.19	3.17	3.15	3.14	3.13	3.12	3.11	3.10	3.08	3.08	3.07
300	4.92	4.87	4.82	4.78	4.75	4.73	4.71	4.69	4.68	4.66	4.65	4.62	4.61	4.61
400	6.56	6.49	6.43	6.38	6.34	6.30	6.27	6.25	6.23	6.22	6.20	6.16	6.15	6.14
500	8.20	8.11	8.03	7.97	7.92	7.88	7.84	7.81	7.79	7.77	7.75	7.70	7.68	7.68
600	9.84	9.73	9.64	9.56	9.50	9.45	9.41	9.37	9.35	9.32	9.30	9.24	9.22	9.21
700	11.48	11.35	11.24	11.16	11.08	11.02	10.98	10.94	10.90	10.87	10.85	10.78	10.76	10.75
800	13.12	12.97	12.85	12.75	12.67	12.60	12.54	12.50	12.46	12.43	12.40	12.32	12.29	12.28
900	14.76	14.59	14.45	14.34	14.25	14.17	14.11	14.06	14.02	13.98	13.95	13.86	13.83	13.81
1000	16.40	16.21	16.06	15.93	15.83	15.75	15.68	15.62	15.57	15.53	15.50	15.40	15.36	15.35
2000	32.79	32.42	32.11	31.86	31.66	31.49	31.35	31.23	31.14	31.06	30.99	30.80	30.72	30.69
3000	49.18	48.62	48.17	47.79	47.48	47.23	47.02	46.85	46.71	46.59	46.49	46.20	46.08	46.04
4000	65.58	64.83	64.22	63.72	63.31	62.97	62.69	62.46	62.27	62.11	61.98	61.60	61.44	61.38
5000	81.97	81.03	80.27	79.65	79.14	78.71	78.36	78.08	77.84	77.64	77.48	76.99	76.80	76.72
6000	98.36	97.24	96.33	95.58	94.96	94.45	94.04	93.69	93.41	93.17	92.97	92.39	92.16	92.07
7000	114.75	113.45	112.38	111.51	110.79	110.20	109.71	109.31	108.97	108.70	108.47	107.79	107.52	107.41
8000	131.15	129.65	128.43	127.43	126.61	125.94	125.38	124.92	124.54	124.22	123.96	123.19	122.88	122.75
9000	147.54	145.86	144.49	143.36	142.44	141.68	141.05	140.53	140.11	139.75	139.46	138.58	138.24	138.10
10000	163.93	162.06	160.54	159.29	158.27	157.42	156.72	156.15	155.67	155.28	154.95	153.98	153.60	153.44
11000	180.33	178.27	176.59	175.22	174.09	173.16	172.40	171.76	171.24	170.81	170.45	169.38	168.95	168.79
12000	196.72	194.48	192.65	191.15	189.92	188.90	188.07	187.38	186.81	186.33	185.94	184.78	184.31	184.13
13000	213.11	210.68	208.70	207.08	205.74	204.65	203.74	202.99	202.37	201.86	201.44	200.17	199.67	199.47
14000	229.50	226.89	224.75	223.01	221.57	220.39	219.41	218.61	217.94	217.39	216.93	215.57	215.03	214.82
15000	245.90	243.09	240.81	238.93	237.40	236.13	235.08	234.22	233.51	232.92	232.42	230.97	230.39	230.16
16000	262.29	259.30	256.86	254.86	253.22	251.87	250.76	249.84	249.07	248.44	247.92	246.37	245.75	245.50
17000	278.68	275.51	272.91	270.79	269.05	267.61	266.43	265.45	264.64	263.97	263.41	261.77	261.11	260.85
18000	295.08	291.71	288.97	286.72	284.87	283.35	282.10	281.06	280.21	279.50	278.91	277.16	276.47	276.19
19000	311.47	307.92	305.02	302.65	300.70	299.10	297.77	296.68	295.77	295.02	294.40	292.56	291.83	291.53
20000	327.86	324.12	321.07	318.58	316.53	314.84	313.44	312.29	311.34	310.55	309.90	307.96	307.19	306.88
21000	344.25	340.33	337.13	334.51	332.35	330.58	329.12	327.91	326.91	326.08	325.39	323.36	322.55	322.22
22000	360.65	356.54	353.18	350.43	348.18	346.32	344.79	343.52	342.47	341.61	340.89	338.75	337.90	337.57
23000	377.04	372.74	369.23	366.36	364.00	362.06	360.46	359.14	358.04	357.13	356.38	354.15	353.26	352.91
24000	393.43	388.95	385.29	382.29	379.03	377.80	376.13	374.75	373.61	372.66	371.88	369.55	368.62	368.25
25000	409.83	405.15	401.34	398.22	395.66	393.55	391.80	390.37	389.17	388.19	387.37	384.95	383.98	383.60
26000	426.22	421.36	417.39	414.15	411.48	409.29	407.48	405.98	404.74	403.72	402.87	400.34	399.34	398.94
27000	442.61	437.57	433.45	430.08	427.31	425.03	423.15	421.59	420.31	419.24	418.36	415.74	414.70	414.28
28000	459.00	453.77	449.50	446.01	443.13	440.77	438.82	437.21	435.88	434.77	433.85	431.14	430.06	429.63
29000	475.40	469.98	465.56	461.93	458.96	456.51	454.49	452.82	451.44	450.30	449.35	446.54	445.42	444.97
30000	491.79	486.18	481.61	477.86	474.79	472.25	470.16	468.44	467.01	465.83	464.84	461.93	460.78	460.31
31000	508.18	502.39	497.66	493.79	490.61	488.00	485.84	484.05	482.58	481.35	480.34	477.33	476.14	475.66
32000	524.58	518.59	513.72	509.72	506.44	503.74	501.51	499.67	498.14	496.88	495.83	492.73	491.50	491.00
33000	540.97	534.80	529.77	525.65	522.26	519.48	517.18	515.28	513.71	512.41	511.33	508.13	506.85	506.35
34000	557.36	551.01	545.82	541.58	538.09	535.22	532.85	530.90	529.28	527.93	526.82	523.53	522.21	521.69
35000	573.75	567.21	561.88	557.51	553.92	550.96	548.52	546.51	544.84	543.46	542.32	538.92	537.57	537.03
36000	590.15	583.42	577.93	573.43	569.74	566.70	564.20	562.12	560.41	558.99	557.81	554.32	552.93	552.38
37000	606.54	599.62	593.98	589.36	585.57	582.45	579.87	577.74	575.98	574.52	573.31	569.72	568.29	567.72
38000	622.93	615.83	610.04	605.29	601.40	598.19	595.54	593.35	591.54	590.04	588.80	585.12	583.65	583.06
39000	639.33	632.04	626.09	621.22	617.22	613.93	611.21	608.97	607.11	605.57	604.30	600.51	599.01	598.41
40000	655.72	648.24	642.14	637.15	633.05	629.67	626.88	624.58	622.68	621.10	619.79	615.91	614.37	613.75
41000	672.11	664.45	658.20	653.08	648.87	645.41	642.56	640.20	638.24	636.63	635.28	631.31	629.73	629.09
42000	688.50	680.65	674.25	669.01	664.70	661.15	658.23	655.81	653.81	652.15	650.78	646.71	645.09	644.44
43000	704.90	696.86	690.30	684.93	680.53	676.90	673.90	671.43	669.38	667.68	666.27	662.10	660.45	659.78
44000	721.29	713.07	706.36	700.86	696.35	692.64	689.57	687.04	684.94	683.21	681.77	677.50	675.80	675.13
45000	737.68	729.27	722.41	716.79	712.18	708.38	705.24	702.65	700.51	698.74	697.26	692.90	691.16	690.47
46000	754.07	745.48	738.46	732.72	728.00	724.12	720.92	718.27	716.08	714.26	712.76	708.30	706.52	705.81
47000	770.47	761.68	754.52	748.65	743.83	739.86	736.59	733.88	731.64	729.79	728.25	723.69	721.88	721.16
48000	786.86	777.89	770.57	764.58	759.66	755.60	752.26	749.50	747.21	745.32	743.75	739.09	737.24	736.50
49000	803.25	794.10	786.62	780.51	775.48	771.34	767.93	765.11	762.78	760.84	759.24	754.49	752.60	751.84
50000	819.65	810.30	802.68	796.43	791.31	787.09	783.60	780.73	778.34	776.37	774.74	769.89	767.96	767.19
55000	901.61	891.33	882.94	876.08	870.44	865.79	861.96	858.80	856.18	854.01	852.21	846.88	844.75	843.91
60000	983.57	972.36	963.21	955.72	949.57	944.50	940.32	936.87	934.01	931.65	929.68	923.86	921.55	920.62
65000	1065.54	1053.39	1043.48	1035.36	1028.70	1023.21	1018.68	1014.94	1011.85	1009.28	1007.16	1000.85	998.35	997.34
70000	1147.50	1134.42	1123.75	1115.01	1107.83	1101.92	1097.04	1093.01	1089.68	1086.92	1084.63	1077.84	1075.14	1074.06
75000	1229.47	1215.45	1204.01	1194.65	1186.96	1180.63	1175.40	1171.09	1167.51	1164.56	1162.10	1154.83	1151.94	1150.78
80000	1311.43	1296.48	1284.28	1274.29	1266.09	1259.34	1253.76	1249.16	1245.35	1242.19	1239.57	1231.82	1228.73	1227.50
85000	1393.40	1377.51	1364.55	1353.94	1345.22	1338.05	1332.12	1327.23	1323.18	1319.83	1317.05	1308.81	1305.53	1304.22
90000	1475.36	1458.54	1444.82	1433.58	1424.35	1416.75	1410.48	1405.30	1401.02	1397.47	1394.52	1385.79	1382.32	1380.93
95000	1557.32	1539.57	1525.08	1513.22	1503.48	1495.46	1488.84	1483.38	1478.85	1475.10	1471.99	1462.78	1459.12	1457.65
100000	1639.29	1620.60	1605.35	1592.86	1582.61	1574.17	1567.20	1561.45	1556.68	1552.74	1549.47	1539.77	1535.91	1534.37

18.500%

TERM	1 Year	2 Years	3 Years	4 Years	5 Years	6 Years	7 Years	8 Years	9 Years	10 Years	11 Years	12 Years	13 Years	14 Years
AMOUNT														
5	.46	.26	.19	.15	.13	.12	.11	.11	.10	.10	.09	.09	.09	.09
10	.92	.51	.37	.30	.26	.24	.22	.21	.20	.19	.18	.18	.17	.17
15	1.38	.76	.55	.45	.39	.35	.32	.31	.29	.28	.27	.26	.26	.26
25	2.30	1.26	.92	.75	.65	.58	.54	.51	.48	.46	.45	.44	.43	.42
50	4.60	2.51	1.83	1.49	1.29	1.16	1.07	1.01	.96	.92	.89	.87	.85	.84
75	6.90	3.77	2.74	2.23	1.93	1.74	1.60	1.51	1.44	1.38	1.34	1.30	1.28	1.26
100	9.20	5.02	3.65	2.97	2.57	2.31	2.14	2.01	1.91	1.84	1.78	1.74	1.70	1.67
200	18.39	10.04	7.29	5.93	5.14	4.62	4.27	4.01	3.82	3.67	3.56	3.47	3.40	3.34
300	27.58	15.05	10.93	8.90	7.70	6.93	6.40	6.01	5.73	5.51	5.34	5.20	5.10	5.01
400	36.77	20.07	14.57	11.86	10.27	9.24	8.53	8.02	7.63	7.34	7.12	6.94	6.80	6.68
500	45.96	25.09	18.21	14.82	12.84	11.55	10.66	10.02	9.54	9.18	8.89	8.67	8.49	8.35
600	55.16	30.10	21.85	17.79	15.40	13.86	12.79	12.02	11.45	11.01	10.67	10.40	10.19	10.02
700	64.35	35.12	25.49	20.75	17.97	16.17	14.92	14.02	13.35	12.84	12.45	12.14	11.89	11.69
800	73.54	40.14	29.13	23.71	20.54	18.48	17.05	16.03	15.26	14.68	14.23	13.87	13.59	13.36
900	82.73	45.15	32.77	26.68	23.10	20.79	19.19	18.03	17.17	16.51	16.00	15.60	15.28	15.03
1000	91.92	50.17	36.41	29.64	25.67	23.10	21.32	20.03	19.08	18.35	17.78	17.34	16.98	16.70
2000	183.84	100.34	72.81	59.28	51.34	46.19	42.63	40.06	38.15	36.69	35.56	34.67	33.96	33.39
3000	275.76	150.50	109.22	88.92	77.00	69.28	63.94	60.09	57.22	55.03	53.33	52.00	50.94	50.09
4000	367.68	200.67	145.62	118.55	102.67	92.37	85.25	80.11	76.29	73.37	71.11	69.33	67.92	66.78
5000	459.60	250.84	182.02	148.19	128.34	115.46	106.56	100.14	95.36	91.71	88.88	86.66	84.89	83.48
6000	551.51	301.00	218.43	177.83	154.00	138.55	127.88	120.17	114.43	110.05	106.66	103.99	101.87	100.17
7000	643.43	351.17	254.83	207.46	179.67	161.64	149.19	140.20	133.50	128.40	124.44	121.32	118.85	116.86
8000	735.35	401.33	291.23	237.10	205.33	184.74	170.50	160.22	152.57	146.74	142.21	138.65	135.83	133.56
9000	827.27	451.50	327.64	266.74	231.00	207.83	191.81	180.25	171.64	165.08	159.99	155.99	152.80	150.25
10000	919.19	501.67	364.04	296.37	256.67	230.92	213.12	200.28	190.71	183.42	177.76	173.32	169.78	166.95
11000	1011.10	551.83	400.45	326.01	282.33	254.01	234.44	220.31	209.78	201.76	195.54	190.65	186.76	183.64
12000	1103.02	602.00	436.85	355.65	308.00	277.10	255.75	240.33	228.85	220.10	213.32	207.98	203.74	200.33
13000	1194.94	652.16	473.25	385.28	333.67	300.19	277.06	260.36	247.93	238.45	231.09	225.31	220.71	217.03
14000	1286.86	702.33	509.66	414.92	359.33	323.28	298.37	280.39	267.00	256.79	248.87	242.64	237.69	233.72
15000	1378.78	752.50	546.06	444.56	385.00	346.38	319.68	300.42	286.07	275.13	266.64	259.97	254.67	250.42
16000	1470.69	802.66	582.46	474.20	410.66	369.47	341.00	320.44	305.14	293.47	284.42	277.30	271.65	267.11
17000	1562.61	852.83	618.87	503.83	436.33	392.56	362.31	340.47	324.21	311.81	302.20	294.63	288.62	283.80
18000	1654.53	902.99	655.27	533.47	462.00	415.65	383.62	360.50	343.28	330.15	319.97	311.97	305.60	300.50
19000	1746.45	953.16	691.68	563.11	487.66	438.74	404.93	380.53	362.35	348.50	337.75	329.30	322.58	317.19
20000	1838.37	1003.33	728.08	592.74	513.33	461.83	426.24	400.55	381.42	366.84	355.52	346.63	339.56	333.89
21000	1930.29	1053.49	764.48	622.38	539.00	484.92	447.56	420.58	400.49	385.18	373.30	363.96	356.53	350.58
22000	2022.20	1103.66	800.89	652.02	564.66	508.01	468.87	440.61	419.56	403.52	391.08	381.29	373.51	367.27
23000	2114.12	1153.82	837.29	681.65	590.33	531.11	490.18	460.64	438.63	421.86	408.85	398.62	390.49	383.97
24000	2206.04	1203.99	873.69	711.29	615.99	554.20	511.49	480.66	457.70	440.20	426.63	415.95	407.47	400.66
25000	2297.96	1254.16	910.10	740.93	641.66	577.29	532.80	500.69	476.78	458.55	444.40	433.28	424.44	417.36
26000	2389.88	1304.32	946.50	770.56	667.33	600.38	554.11	520.72	495.85	476.89	462.18	450.61	441.42	434.05
27000	2481.79	1354.49	982.91	800.20	692.99	623.47	575.43	540.75	514.92	495.23	479.96	467.95	458.40	450.74
28000	2573.71	1404.65	1019.31	829.84	718.66	646.56	596.74	560.77	533.99	513.57	497.73	485.28	475.38	467.44
29000	2665.63	1454.82	1055.71	859.48	744.33	669.65	618.05	580.80	553.06	531.91	515.51	502.61	492.35	484.13
30000	2757.55	1504.99	1092.12	889.11	769.99	692.75	639.36	600.83	572.13	550.25	533.28	519.94	509.33	500.83
31000	2849.47	1555.15	1128.52	918.75	795.66	715.84	660.67	620.86	591.20	568.60	551.06	537.27	526.31	517.52
32000	2941.38	1605.32	1164.92	948.39	821.32	738.93	681.99	640.88	610.27	586.94	568.84	554.60	543.29	534.21
33000	3033.30	1655.48	1201.33	978.02	846.99	762.02	703.30	660.91	629.34	605.28	586.61	571.93	560.26	550.91
34000	3125.22	1705.65	1237.73	1007.66	872.66	785.11	724.61	680.94	648.41	623.62	604.39	589.26	577.24	567.60
35000	3217.14	1755.82	1274.14	1037.30	898.32	808.20	745.92	700.97	667.48	641.96	622.16	606.59	594.22	584.30
36000	3309.06	1805.98	1310.54	1066.93	923.99	831.29	767.23	720.99	686.55	660.30	639.94	623.93	611.20	600.99
37000	3400.98	1856.15	1346.94	1096.57	949.65	854.39	788.55	741.02	705.63	678.65	657.72	641.26	628.17	617.68
38000	3492.89	1906.31	1383.35	1126.21	975.32	877.48	809.86	761.05	724.70	696.99	675.49	658.59	645.15	634.38
39000	3584.81	1956.48	1419.75	1155.84	1000.99	900.57	831.17	781.08	743.77	715.33	693.27	675.92	662.13	651.07
40000	3676.73	2006.65	1456.15	1185.48	1026.65	923.66	852.48	801.10	762.84	733.67	711.04	693.25	679.11	667.77
41000	3768.65	2056.81	1492.56	1215.12	1052.32	946.75	873.79	821.13	781.91	752.01	728.82	710.58	696.08	684.46
42000	3860.57	2106.98	1528.96	1244.76	1077.99	969.84	895.11	841.16	800.98	770.35	746.60	727.91	713.06	701.16
43000	3952.48	2157.14	1565.36	1274.39	1103.65	992.93	916.42	861.18	820.05	788.70	764.37	745.24	730.04	717.85
44000	4044.40	2207.31	1601.77	1304.03	1129.32	1016.02	937.73	881.21	839.12	807.04	782.15	762.58	747.02	734.54
45000	4136.32	2257.48	1638.17	1333.67	1154.98	1039.12	959.04	901.24	858.19	825.38	799.92	779.91	763.99	751.24
46000	4228.24	2307.64	1674.58	1363.30	1180.65	1062.21	980.35	921.27	877.26	843.72	817.70	797.24	780.97	767.93
47000	4320.16	2357.81	1710.98	1392.94	1206.32	1085.30	1001.67	941.29	896.33	862.06	835.48	814.57	797.95	784.63
48000	4412.07	2407.97	1747.38	1422.58	1231.98	1108.39	1022.98	961.32	915.40	880.40	853.25	831.90	814.93	801.32
49000	4503.99	2458.14	1783.79	1452.21	1257.65	1131.48	1044.29	981.35	934.47	898.75	871.03	849.23	831.90	818.01
50000	4595.91	2508.31	1820.19	1481.85	1283.32	1154.57	1065.60	1001.38	953.55	917.09	888.80	866.56	848.88	834.71
55000	5055.50	2759.14	2002.21	1630.04	1411.65	1270.03	1172.16	1101.51	1048.90	1008.80	977.68	953.22	933.77	918.18
60000	5515.09	3009.97	2184.23	1778.22	1539.98	1385.49	1278.72	1201.65	1144.25	1100.50	1066.56	1039.87	1018.66	1001.65
65000	5974.68	3260.80	2366.25	1926.40	1668.31	1500.94	1385.28	1301.79	1239.61	1192.21	1155.44	1126.53	1103.54	1085.12
70000	6434.27	3511.63	2548.27	2074.59	1796.64	1616.40	1491.84	1401.93	1334.96	1283.92	1244.32	1213.18	1188.43	1168.59
75000	6893.86	3762.46	2730.28	2222.77	1924.97	1731.86	1598.40	1502.06	1430.32	1375.63	1333.20	1299.84	1273.32	1252.06
80000	7353.45	4013.29	2912.30	2370.96	2053.30	1847.31	1704.96	1602.20	1525.67	1467.34	1422.08	1386.50	1358.21	1335.53
85000	7813.05	4264.12	3094.32	2519.14	2181.63	1962.77	1811.52	1702.34	1621.02	1559.05	1510.96	1473.15	1443.10	1419.00
90000	8272.64	4514.95	3276.34	2667.33	2309.96	2078.23	1918.08	1802.47	1716.38	1650.75	1599.84	1559.81	1527.98	1502.47
95000	8732.23	4765.78	3458.36	2815.51	2438.29	2193.68	2024.64	1902.61	1811.73	1742.46	1688.72	1646.46	1612.87	1585.94
100000	9191.82	5016.61	3640.38	2963.70	2566.63	2309.14	2131.20	2002.75	1907.09	1834.17	1777.60	1733.12	1697.76	1669.41

TERM	15 Years	16 Years	17 Years	18 Years	19 Years	20 Years	21 Years	22 Years	23 Years	24 Years	25 Years	30 Years	35 Years	40 Years
AMOUNT														
5	.09	.09	.09	.09	.08	.08	.08	.08	.08	.08	.08	.08	.08	.08
10	.17	.17	.17	.17	.16	.16	.16	.16	.16	.16	.16	.16	.16	.16
15	.25	.25	.25	.25	.24	.24	.24	.24	.24	.24	.24	.24	.24	.24
25	.42	.41	.41	.41	.40	.40	.40	.40	.40	.40	.39	.39	.39	.39
50	.83	.82	.81	.81	.80	.80	.79	.79	.79	.79	.78	.78	.78	.78
75	1.24	1.23	1.21	1.21	1.20	1.19	1.19	1.18	1.18	1.18	1.17	1.17	1.16	1.16
100	1.65	1.63	1.62	1.61	1.60	1.59	1.58	1.57	1.57	1.57	1.56	1.55	1.55	1.55
200	3.30	3.26	3.23	3.21	3.19	3.17	3.16	3.14	3.13	3.13	3.12	3.10	3.09	3.09
300	4.94	4.89	4.84	4.81	4.78	4.75	4.73	4.71	4.70	4.69	4.68	4.65	4.64	4.63
400	6.59	6.52	6.46	6.41	6.37	6.33	6.31	6.28	6.26	6.25	6.23	6.20	6.18	6.18
500	8.24	8.14	8.07	8.01	7.96	7.91	7.88	7.85	7.83	7.81	7.79	7.74	7.73	7.72
600	9.88	9.77	9.68	9.61	9.55	9.50	9.46	9.42	9.39	9.37	9.35	9.29	9.27	9.26
700	11.53	11.40	11.29	11.21	11.14	11.08	11.03	10.99	10.96	10.93	10.91	10.84	10.81	10.80
800	13.18	13.03	12.91	12.81	12.73	12.66	12.61	12.56	12.52	12.49	12.46	12.39	12.36	12.35
900	14.82	14.66	14.52	14.41	14.32	14.24	14.18	14.13	14.09	14.05	14.02	13.94	13.90	13.89
1000	16.47	16.28	16.13	16.01	15.91	15.82	15.76	15.70	15.65	15.61	15.58	15.48	15.45	15.43
2000	32.94	32.56	32.26	32.01	31.81	31.64	31.51	31.39	31.30	31.22	31.15	30.96	30.89	30.86
3000	49.40	48.84	48.39	48.02	47.71	47.46	47.26	47.08	46.94	46.83	46.73	46.44	46.33	46.28
4000	65.87	65.12	64.52	64.02	63.62	63.28	63.01	62.78	62.59	62.43	62.30	61.92	61.77	61.71
5000	82.33	81.40	80.65	80.03	79.52	79.10	78.76	78.47	78.24	78.04	77.88	77.40	77.21	77.14
6000	98.80	97.68	96.77	96.03	95.42	94.92	94.51	94.16	93.88	93.65	93.45	92.88	92.66	92.56
7000	115.26	113.96	112.90	112.03	111.32	110.74	110.26	109.86	109.53	109.25	109.03	108.36	108.10	107.99
8000	131.73	130.24	129.03	128.04	127.23	126.56	126.01	125.55	125.17	124.86	124.60	123.84	123.54	123.42
9000	148.19	146.52	145.16	144.04	143.13	142.38	141.76	141.24	140.82	140.47	140.18	139.32	138.98	138.84
10000	164.66	162.80	161.29	160.05	159.03	158.19	157.51	156.94	156.47	156.08	155.75	154.80	154.42	154.27
11000	181.12	179.08	177.41	176.05	174.93	174.01	173.26	172.63	172.11	171.68	171.33	170.28	169.86	169.70
12000	197.59	195.36	193.54	192.06	190.84	189.83	189.01	188.32	187.76	187.29	186.90	185.76	185.31	185.12
13000	214.05	211.64	209.67	208.06	206.74	205.65	204.76	204.02	203.40	202.90	202.48	201.24	200.75	200.55
14000	230.52	227.92	225.80	224.06	222.64	221.47	220.51	219.71	219.05	218.50	218.05	216.72	216.19	215.98
15000	246.98	244.20	241.93	240.07	238.54	237.29	236.26	235.40	234.70	234.11	233.63	232.20	231.63	231.40
16000	263.45	260.48	258.05	256.07	254.45	253.11	252.01	251.09	250.34	249.72	249.20	247.68	247.07	246.83
17000	279.91	276.76	274.18	272.08	270.35	268.93	267.76	266.79	265.99	265.33	264.78	263.16	262.51	262.26
18000	296.38	293.04	290.31	288.08	286.25	284.75	283.51	282.48	281.63	280.93	280.35	278.64	277.96	277.68
19000	312.84	309.32	306.44	304.09	302.15	300.57	299.26	298.17	297.28	296.54	295.93	294.11	293.40	293.11
20000	329.31	325.60	322.57	320.09	318.06	316.38	315.01	313.87	312.93	312.15	311.50	309.59	308.84	308.54
21000	345.77	341.87	338.70	336.09	333.96	332.20	330.76	329.56	328.57	327.75	327.08	325.07	324.28	323.96
22000	362.24	358.15	354.82	352.10	349.86	348.02	346.51	345.25	344.22	343.36	342.65	340.55	339.72	339.39
23000	378.71	374.43	370.95	368.10	365.76	363.84	362.26	360.95	359.86	358.97	358.23	356.03	355.16	354.82
24000	395.17	390.71	387.08	384.11	381.67	379.66	378.01	376.64	375.51	374.58	373.80	371.51	370.61	370.24
25000	411.64	406.99	403.21	400.11	397.57	395.48	393.76	392.33	391.16	390.18	389.38	386.99	386.05	385.67
26000	428.10	423.27	419.34	416.12	413.47	411.30	409.51	408.03	406.80	405.79	404.95	402.47	401.49	401.10
27000	444.57	439.55	435.46	432.12	429.38	427.12	425.26	423.72	422.45	421.40	420.53	417.95	416.93	416.52
28000	461.03	455.83	451.59	448.12	445.28	442.94	441.01	439.41	438.09	437.00	436.10	433.43	432.37	431.95
29000	477.50	472.11	467.72	464.13	461.18	458.76	456.76	455.11	453.74	452.61	451.68	448.91	447.81	447.38
30000	493.96	488.39	483.85	480.13	477.08	474.57	472.51	470.80	469.39	468.22	467.25	464.39	463.26	462.80
31000	510.43	504.67	499.98	496.14	492.99	490.39	488.26	486.49	485.03	483.83	482.83	479.87	478.70	478.23
32000	526.89	520.95	516.10	512.14	508.89	506.21	504.01	502.18	500.68	499.43	498.40	495.35	494.14	493.66
33000	543.36	537.23	532.23	528.15	524.79	522.03	519.76	517.88	516.32	515.04	513.97	510.83	509.58	509.08
34000	559.82	553.51	548.36	544.15	540.69	537.85	535.51	533.57	531.97	530.65	529.55	526.31	525.02	524.51
35000	576.29	569.79	564.49	560.15	556.60	553.67	551.26	549.26	547.62	546.25	545.12	541.79	540.46	539.94
36000	592.75	586.07	580.62	576.16	572.50	569.49	567.01	564.96	563.26	561.86	560.70	557.27	555.91	555.36
37000	609.22	602.35	596.75	592.16	588.40	585.31	582.76	580.65	578.91	577.47	576.27	572.74	571.35	570.79
38000	625.68	618.63	612.87	608.17	604.30	601.13	598.51	596.34	594.56	593.08	591.85	588.22	586.79	586.22
39000	642.15	634.91	629.00	624.17	620.21	616.94	614.26	612.04	610.20	608.68	607.42	603.70	602.23	601.64
40000	658.61	651.19	645.13	640.17	636.11	632.76	630.01	627.73	625.85	624.29	623.00	619.18	617.67	617.07
41000	675.08	667.47	661.26	656.18	652.01	648.58	645.76	643.42	641.49	639.90	638.57	634.66	633.11	632.50
42000	691.54	683.74	677.39	672.18	667.91	664.40	661.51	659.12	657.14	655.50	654.15	650.14	648.56	647.92
43000	708.01	700.02	693.51	688.19	683.82	680.22	677.26	674.81	672.79	671.11	669.72	665.62	664.00	663.35
44000	724.48	716.30	709.64	704.19	699.72	696.04	693.01	690.50	688.43	686.72	685.30	681.10	679.44	678.78
45000	740.94	732.58	725.77	720.20	715.62	711.86	708.76	706.20	704.08	702.32	700.87	696.58	694.88	694.20
46000	757.41	748.86	741.90	736.20	731.52	727.68	724.51	721.89	719.72	717.93	716.45	712.06	710.32	709.63
47000	773.87	765.14	758.03	752.20	747.43	743.50	740.26	737.58	735.37	733.54	732.02	727.54	725.76	725.06
48000	790.34	781.42	774.15	768.21	763.33	759.32	756.01	753.27	751.02	749.15	747.60	743.02	741.21	740.48
49000	806.80	797.70	790.28	784.21	779.23	775.13	771.76	768.97	766.66	764.75	763.17	758.50	756.65	755.91
50000	823.27	813.98	806.41	800.22	795.13	790.95	787.51	784.66	782.31	780.36	778.75	773.98	772.09	771.34
55000	905.59	895.38	887.05	880.24	874.65	870.05	866.26	863.13	860.54	858.40	856.62	851.37	849.30	848.47
60000	987.92	976.78	967.69	960.26	954.16	949.14	945.01	941.59	938.77	936.43	934.50	928.77	926.51	925.60
65000	1070.25	1058.17	1048.33	1040.28	1033.67	1028.24	1023.76	1020.06	1017.00	1014.47	1012.37	1006.17	1003.71	1002.74
70000	1152.57	1139.57	1128.97	1120.30	1113.19	1107.33	1102.51	1098.52	1095.23	1092.50	1090.24	1083.57	1080.92	1079.87
75000	1234.90	1220.97	1209.61	1200.32	1192.70	1186.43	1181.26	1176.99	1173.46	1170.54	1168.12	1160.96	1158.13	1157.00
80000	1317.22	1302.37	1290.26	1280.35	1272.21	1265.52	1260.01	1255.45	1251.69	1248.57	1245.99	1238.36	1235.34	1234.14
85000	1399.55	1383.76	1370.90	1360.37	1351.73	1344.62	1338.76	1333.92	1329.92	1326.61	1323.87	1315.76	1312.55	1311.27
90000	1481.88	1465.16	1451.54	1440.39	1431.24	1423.71	1417.51	1412.39	1408.15	1404.65	1401.74	1393.16	1389.76	1388.40
95000	1564.20	1546.56	1532.18	1520.41	1510.75	1502.81	1496.26	1490.85	1486.38	1482.68	1479.61	1470.55	1466.96	1465.54
100000	1646.53	1627.96	1612.82	1600.43	1590.26	1581.90	1575.01	1569.32	1564.61	1560.72	1557.49	1547.95	1544.17	1542.67

MONTHLY PAYMENT
REQUIRED TO AMORTIZE A LOAN

TERM AMOUNT	1 Year	2 Years	3 Years	4 Years	5 Years	6 Years	7 Years	8 Years	9 Years	10 Years	11 Years	12 Years	13 Years	14 Years
5	.46	.26	.19	.15	.13	.12	.11	.11	.10	.10	.09	.09	.09	.09
10	.92	.51	.37	.30	.26	.24	.22	.21	.20	.19	.18	.18	.18	.17
15	1.38	.76	.55	.45	.39	.35	.33	.31	.29	.28	.27	.27	.26	.26
25	2.30	1.26	.92	.75	.65	.58	.54	.51	.48	.47	.45	.44	.43	.42
50	4.60	2.52	1.83	1.49	1.29	1.16	1.07	1.01	.96	.93	.90	.87	.86	.84
75	6.90	3.77	2.74	2.23	1.93	1.74	1.61	1.51	1.44	1.39	1.34	1.31	1.28	1.26
100	9.20	5.03	3.65	2.97	2.58	2.32	2.14	2.01	1.92	1.85	1.79	1.74	1.71	1.68
200	18.40	10.05	7.30	5.94	5.15	4.63	4.28	4.02	3.83	3.69	3.57	3.48	3.41	3.36
300	27.59	15.07	10.94	8.91	7.72	6.95	6.42	6.03	5.75	5.53	5.36	5.22	5.12	5.03
400	36.79	20.09	14.59	11.88	10.29	9.26	8.55	8.04	7.66	7.37	7.14	6.96	6.82	6.71
500	45.99	25.11	18.23	14.85	12.87	11.58	10.69	10.05	9.57	9.21	8.93	8.70	8.53	8.39
600	55.18	30.13	21.88	17.82	15.44	13.89	12.83	12.06	11.49	11.05	10.71	10.44	10.23	10.06
700	64.38	35.16	25.52	20.79	18.01	16.21	14.96	14.07	13.40	12.89	12.49	12.18	11.94	11.74
800	73.58	40.18	29.17	23.76	20.58	18.52	17.10	16.08	15.31	14.73	14.28	13.92	13.64	13.42
900	82.77	45.20	32.81	26.73	23.15	20.84	19.24	18.08	17.23	16.57	16.06	15.66	15.35	15.09
1000	91.97	50.22	36.46	29.69	25.73	23.15	21.38	20.09	19.14	18.41	17.85	17.40	17.05	16.77
2000	183.94	100.43	72.91	59.38	51.45	46.30	42.75	40.18	38.27	36.82	35.69	34.80	34.10	33.54
3000	275.90	150.65	109.37	89.07	77.17	69.45	64.12	60.27	57.41	55.22	53.53	52.20	51.15	50.30
4000	367.87	200.86	145.82	118.76	102.89	92.60	85.49	80.36	76.54	73.63	71.38	69.60	68.19	67.07
5000	459.83	251.08	182.28	148.45	128.61	115.75	106.86	100.45	95.67	92.04	89.22	87.00	85.24	83.83
6000	551.80	301.29	218.73	178.14	154.33	138.89	128.23	120.54	114.81	110.44	107.06	104.40	102.29	100.60
7000	643.77	351.51	255.18	207.83	180.05	162.04	149.60	140.62	133.94	128.85	124.90	121.80	119.34	117.36
8000	735.73	401.72	291.64	237.52	205.77	185.19	170.97	160.71	153.08	147.26	142.75	139.20	136.38	134.13
9000	827.70	451.94	328.09	267.21	231.49	208.34	192.34	180.80	172.21	165.66	160.59	156.60	153.43	150.89
10000	919.66	502.15	364.55	296.90	257.21	231.49	213.71	200.89	191.34	184.07	178.43	174.00	170.48	167.66
11000	1011.63	552.36	401.00	326.59	282.94	254.64	235.09	220.98	210.48	202.48	196.27	191.40	187.53	184.42
12000	1103.59	602.58	437.45	356.28	308.66	277.78	256.46	241.07	229.61	220.88	214.12	208.80	204.57	201.19
13000	1195.56	652.79	473.91	385.97	334.38	300.93	277.83	261.16	248.75	239.29	231.96	226.20	221.62	217.95
14000	1287.53	703.01	510.36	415.66	360.10	324.08	299.20	281.24	267.88	257.70	249.80	243.60	238.67	234.72
15000	1379.49	753.22	546.82	445.35	385.82	347.23	320.57	301.33	287.01	276.10	267.64	261.00	255.72	251.48
16000	1471.46	803.44	583.27	475.04	411.54	370.38	341.94	321.42	306.15	294.51	285.49	278.40	272.76	268.25
17000	1563.42	853.65	619.72	504.73	437.26	393.53	363.31	341.51	325.28	312.92	303.33	295.80	289.81	285.01
18000	1655.39	903.87	656.18	534.42	462.98	416.67	384.68	361.60	344.41	331.32	321.17	313.19	306.86	301.78
19000	1747.35	954.08	692.63	564.10	488.70	439.82	406.05	381.69	363.55	349.73	339.02	330.59	323.90	318.55
20000	1839.32	1004.29	729.09	593.79	514.42	462.97	427.42	401.78	382.68	368.14	356.86	347.99	340.95	335.31
21000	1931.29	1054.51	765.54	623.48	540.15	486.12	448.80	421.86	401.82	386.54	374.70	365.39	358.00	352.08
22000	2023.25	1104.72	802.00	653.17	565.87	509.27	470.17	441.95	420.95	404.95	392.54	382.79	375.05	368.84
23000	2115.22	1154.94	838.45	682.86	591.59	532.42	491.54	462.04	440.08	423.36	410.39	400.19	392.09	385.61
24000	2207.18	1205.15	874.90	712.55	617.31	555.56	512.91	482.13	459.22	441.76	428.23	417.59	409.14	402.37
25000	2299.15	1255.37	911.36	742.24	643.03	578.71	534.28	502.22	478.35	460.17	446.07	434.99	426.19	419.14
26000	2391.12	1305.58	947.81	771.93	668.75	601.86	555.65	522.31	497.49	478.58	463.91	452.39	443.24	435.90
27000	2483.08	1355.80	984.27	801.62	694.47	625.01	577.02	542.40	516.62	496.98	481.76	469.79	460.28	452.67
28000	2575.05	1406.01	1020.72	831.31	720.19	648.16	598.39	562.48	535.75	515.39	499.60	487.19	477.33	469.43
29000	2667.01	1456.23	1057.17	861.00	745.91	671.31	619.76	582.57	554.89	533.80	517.44	504.59	494.38	486.20
30000	2758.98	1506.44	1093.63	890.69	771.63	694.45	641.13	602.66	574.02	552.20	535.28	521.99	511.43	502.96
31000	2850.94	1556.65	1130.08	920.38	797.35	717.60	662.51	622.75	593.16	570.61	553.13	539.39	528.47	519.73
32000	2942.91	1606.87	1166.54	950.07	823.08	740.75	683.88	642.84	612.29	589.02	570.97	556.79	545.52	536.49
33000	3034.88	1657.08	1202.99	979.76	848.80	763.90	705.25	662.93	631.42	607.42	588.81	574.19	562.57	553.26
34000	3126.84	1707.30	1239.44	1009.45	874.52	787.05	726.62	683.02	650.56	625.83	606.66	591.59	579.61	570.02
35000	3218.81	1757.51	1275.90	1039.14	900.24	810.19	747.99	703.10	669.69	644.24	624.50	608.99	596.66	586.79
36000	3310.77	1807.73	1312.35	1068.83	925.96	833.34	769.36	723.19	688.82	662.64	642.34	626.38	613.71	603.55
37000	3402.74	1857.94	1348.81	1098.51	951.68	856.49	790.73	743.28	707.96	681.05	660.18	643.78	630.76	620.32
38000	3494.70	1908.16	1385.26	1128.20	977.40	879.64	812.10	763.37	727.09	699.45	678.03	661.18	647.80	637.09
39000	3586.67	1958.37	1421.71	1157.89	1003.12	902.79	833.47	783.46	746.23	717.86	695.87	678.58	664.85	653.85
40000	3678.64	2008.58	1458.17	1187.58	1028.84	925.94	854.84	803.55	765.36	736.27	713.71	695.98	681.90	670.62
41000	3770.60	2058.80	1494.62	1217.27	1054.56	949.08	876.22	823.64	784.49	754.67	731.55	713.38	698.95	687.38
42000	3862.57	2109.01	1531.08	1246.96	1080.29	972.23	897.59	843.72	803.63	773.08	749.40	730.78	715.99	704.15
43000	3954.53	2159.23	1567.53	1276.65	1106.01	995.38	918.96	863.81	822.76	791.49	767.24	748.18	733.04	720.91
44000	4046.50	2209.44	1603.99	1306.34	1131.73	1018.53	940.33	883.90	841.90	809.89	785.08	765.58	750.09	737.68
45000	4138.47	2259.66	1640.44	1336.03	1157.45	1041.68	961.70	903.99	861.03	828.30	802.92	782.98	767.14	754.44
46000	4230.43	2309.87	1676.89	1365.72	1183.17	1064.83	983.07	924.08	880.16	846.71	820.77	800.38	784.18	771.21
47000	4322.40	2360.09	1713.35	1395.41	1208.89	1087.97	1004.44	944.17	899.30	865.11	838.61	817.78	801.23	787.97
48000	4414.36	2410.30	1749.80	1425.10	1234.61	1111.12	1025.81	964.26	918.43	883.52	856.45	835.18	818.28	804.74
49000	4506.33	2460.52	1786.26	1454.79	1260.33	1134.27	1047.18	984.34	937.57	901.93	874.30	852.58	835.33	821.50
50000	4598.29	2510.73	1822.71	1484.48	1286.05	1157.42	1068.55	1004.43	956.70	920.33	892.14	869.98	852.37	838.27
55000	5058.12	2761.80	2004.98	1632.92	1414.66	1273.16	1175.41	1104.88	1052.37	1012.37	981.35	956.97	937.61	922.09
60000	5517.95	3012.87	2187.25	1781.37	1543.26	1388.90	1282.26	1205.32	1148.04	1104.40	1070.56	1043.97	1022.85	1005.92
65000	5977.78	3263.95	2369.52	1929.82	1671.87	1504.64	1389.12	1305.76	1243.71	1196.43	1159.78	1130.97	1108.08	1089.75
70000	6437.61	3515.02	2551.79	2078.27	1800.47	1620.38	1495.97	1406.20	1339.38	1288.47	1248.99	1217.97	1193.32	1173.57
75000	6897.44	3766.09	2734.06	2226.71	1929.08	1736.13	1602.83	1506.65	1435.05	1380.50	1338.20	1304.96	1278.56	1257.40
80000	7357.27	4017.16	2916.33	2375.16	2057.68	1851.87	1709.68	1607.09	1530.72	1472.53	1427.42	1391.96	1363.79	1341.23
85000	7817.10	4268.24	3098.60	2523.61	2186.29	1967.61	1816.54	1707.53	1626.39	1564.56	1516.63	1478.96	1449.03	1425.05
90000	8276.93	4519.31	3280.87	2672.06	2314.89	2083.35	1923.39	1807.97	1722.05	1656.60	1605.84	1565.95	1534.27	1508.88
95000	8736.75	4770.38	3463.14	2820.50	2443.50	2199.09	2030.25	1908.42	1817.72	1748.63	1695.06	1652.95	1619.50	1592.71
100000	9196.58	5021.45	3645.41	2968.95	2572.10	2314.83	2137.10	2008.86	1913.39	1840.66	1784.27	1739.95	1704.74	1676.53

TERM AMOUNT	15 Years	16 Years	17 Years	18 Years	19 Years	20 Years	21 Years	22 Years	23 Years	24 Years	25 Years	30 Years	35 Years	40 Years
5	.09	.09	.09	.09	.08	.08	.08	.08	.08	.08	.08	.08	.08	.08
10	.17	.17	.17	.17	.16	.16	.16	.16	.16	.16	.16	.16	.16	.16
15	.25	.25	.25	.25	.24	.24	.24	.24	.24	.24	.24	.24	.24	.24
25	.42	.41	.41	.41	.40	.40	.40	.40	.40	.40	.40	.39	.39	.39
50	.83	.82	.82	.81	.80	.80	.80	.79	.79	.79	.79	.78	.78	.78
75	1.25	1.23	1.22	1.21	1.20	1.20	1.19	1.19	1.18	1.18	1.18	1.17	1.17	1.17
100	1.66	1.64	1.63	1.61	1.60	1.59	1.59	1.58	1.58	1.57	1.57	1.56	1.56	1.56
200	3.31	3.28	3.25	3.22	3.20	3.18	3.17	3.16	3.15	3.14	3.14	3.12	3.11	3.11
300	4.97	4.91	4.87	4.83	4.80	4.77	4.75	4.74	4.72	4.71	4.70	4.67	4.66	4.66
400	6.62	6.55	6.49	6.44	6.40	6.36	6.34	6.31	6.30	6.28	6.27	6.23	6.21	6.21
500	8.27	8.18	8.11	8.04	7.99	7.95	7.92	7.89	7.87	7.85	7.83	7.79	7.77	7.76
600	9.93	9.82	9.73	9.65	9.59	9.54	9.50	9.47	9.44	9.42	9.40	9.34	9.32	9.31
700	11.58	11.45	11.35	11.26	11.19	11.13	11.08	11.05	11.01	10.99	10.96	10.90	10.87	10.86
800	13.24	13.09	12.97	12.87	12.79	12.72	12.67	12.62	12.59	12.55	12.53	12.45	12.42	12.41
900	14.89	14.72	14.59	14.48	14.39	14.31	14.25	14.20	14.16	14.12	14.09	14.01	13.98	13.96
1000	16.54	16.36	16.21	16.08	15.98	15.90	15.83	15.78	15.73	15.69	15.66	15.57	15.53	15.51
2000	33.08	32.71	32.41	32.16	31.96	31.80	31.66	31.55	31.46	31.38	31.32	31.13	31.05	31.02
3000	49.62	49.06	48.61	48.24	47.94	47.69	47.49	47.32	47.18	47.07	46.97	46.69	46.58	46.53
4000	66.16	65.42	64.82	64.32	63.92	63.59	63.32	63.09	62.91	62.75	62.63	62.25	62.10	62.04
5000	82.69	81.77	81.02	80.40	79.90	79.49	79.15	78.86	78.63	78.44	78.28	77.81	77.63	77.55
6000	99.23	98.12	97.22	96.48	95.88	95.38	94.97	94.64	94.36	94.13	93.94	93.37	93.15	93.06
7000	115.77	114.48	113.43	112.56	111.86	111.28	110.80	110.41	110.08	109.81	109.59	108.93	108.68	108.57
8000	132.31	130.83	129.63	128.64	127.84	127.18	126.63	126.18	125.81	125.50	125.25	124.50	124.20	124.08
9000	148.84	147.18	145.83	144.72	143.82	143.07	142.46	141.95	141.53	141.19	140.90	140.06	139.72	139.59
10000	165.38	163.54	162.03	160.80	159.80	158.97	158.29	157.72	157.26	156.87	156.56	155.62	155.25	155.10
11000	181.92	179.89	178.24	176.88	175.78	174.87	174.11	173.50	172.98	172.56	172.21	171.18	170.77	170.61
12000	198.46	196.24	194.44	192.96	191.76	190.76	189.94	189.27	188.71	188.25	187.87	186.74	186.30	186.12
13000	215.00	212.60	210.64	209.04	207.73	206.66	205.77	205.04	204.44	203.94	203.52	202.30	201.82	201.63
14000	231.53	228.95	226.85	225.12	223.71	222.55	221.60	220.81	220.16	219.62	219.18	217.86	217.35	217.14
15000	248.07	245.30	243.05	241.20	239.69	238.45	237.43	236.58	235.89	235.31	234.83	233.42	232.87	232.65
16000	264.61	261.66	259.25	257.28	255.67	254.35	253.26	252.36	251.61	251.00	250.49	248.99	248.39	248.16
17000	281.15	278.01	275.45	273.36	271.65	270.24	269.08	268.13	267.34	266.68	266.14	264.55	263.92	263.67
18000	297.68	294.36	291.66	289.44	287.63	286.14	284.91	283.90	283.06	282.37	281.80	280.11	279.44	279.18
19000	314.22	310.72	307.86	305.52	303.61	302.04	300.74	299.67	298.79	298.06	297.45	295.67	294.97	294.69
20000	330.76	327.07	324.06	321.60	319.59	317.93	316.57	315.44	314.51	313.74	313.11	311.23	310.49	310.20
21000	347.30	343.42	340.27	337.68	335.57	333.83	332.40	331.21	330.24	329.43	328.76	326.79	326.02	325.71
22000	363.84	359.78	356.47	353.76	351.55	349.73	348.22	346.99	345.96	345.12	344.42	342.35	341.54	341.22
23000	380.37	376.13	372.67	369.84	367.53	365.62	364.05	362.76	361.69	360.80	360.07	357.91	357.06	356.73
24000	396.91	392.48	388.87	385.92	383.51	381.52	379.88	378.53	377.41	376.49	375.73	373.48	372.59	372.24
25000	413.45	408.84	405.08	402.00	399.49	397.41	395.71	394.30	393.14	392.18	391.38	389.04	388.11	387.75
26000	429.99	425.19	421.28	418.08	415.46	413.31	411.54	410.07	408.87	407.87	407.04	404.60	403.64	403.26
27000	446.52	441.54	437.48	434.16	431.44	429.21	427.37	425.85	424.59	423.55	422.69	420.16	419.16	418.77
28000	463.06	457.89	453.69	450.24	447.42	445.10	443.19	441.62	440.32	439.24	438.35	435.72	434.69	434.28
29000	479.60	474.25	469.89	466.32	463.40	461.00	459.02	457.39	456.04	454.93	454.00	451.28	450.21	449.78
30000	496.14	490.60	486.09	482.40	479.38	476.90	474.85	473.16	471.77	470.61	469.66	466.84	465.73	465.29
31000	512.67	506.95	502.29	498.48	495.36	492.79	490.68	488.93	487.49	486.30	485.31	482.40	481.26	480.80
32000	529.21	523.31	518.50	514.56	511.34	508.69	506.51	504.71	503.22	501.99	500.97	497.97	496.78	496.31
33000	545.75	539.66	534.70	530.64	527.32	524.59	522.33	520.48	518.94	517.67	516.62	513.53	512.31	511.82
34000	562.29	556.01	550.90	546.72	543.30	540.48	538.16	536.25	534.67	533.36	532.28	529.09	527.83	527.33
35000	578.83	572.37	567.11	562.80	559.28	556.38	553.99	552.02	550.39	549.05	547.93	544.65	543.36	542.84
36000	595.36	588.72	583.31	578.88	575.26	572.27	569.82	567.79	566.12	564.74	563.59	560.21	558.88	558.35
37000	611.90	605.07	599.51	594.96	591.24	588.17	585.65	583.56	581.84	580.42	579.24	575.77	574.40	573.86
38000	628.44	621.43	615.71	611.04	607.22	604.07	601.48	599.34	597.57	596.11	594.90	591.33	589.93	589.37
39000	644.98	637.78	631.92	627.12	623.19	619.96	617.30	615.11	613.30	611.80	610.55	606.89	605.45	604.88
40000	661.51	654.13	648.12	643.20	639.17	635.86	633.13	630.88	629.02	627.48	626.21	622.46	620.98	620.39
41000	678.05	670.49	664.32	659.28	655.15	651.76	648.96	646.65	644.75	643.17	641.87	638.02	636.50	635.90
42000	694.59	686.84	680.53	675.36	671.13	667.65	664.79	662.42	660.47	658.86	657.52	653.58	652.03	651.41
43000	711.13	703.19	696.73	691.44	687.11	683.55	680.62	678.20	676.20	674.54	673.18	669.14	667.55	666.92
44000	727.67	719.55	712.93	707.52	703.09	699.45	696.44	693.97	691.92	690.23	688.83	684.70	683.07	682.43
45000	744.20	735.90	729.14	723.60	719.07	715.34	712.27	709.74	707.65	705.92	704.49	700.26	698.60	697.94
46000	760.74	752.25	745.34	739.68	735.05	731.24	728.10	725.51	723.37	721.60	720.14	715.82	714.12	713.45
47000	777.28	768.61	761.54	755.76	751.03	747.14	743.93	741.28	739.10	737.29	735.80	731.38	729.65	728.96
48000	793.82	784.96	777.74	771.84	767.01	763.03	759.76	757.06	754.82	752.98	751.45	746.95	745.17	744.47
49000	810.35	801.31	793.95	787.92	782.99	778.93	775.58	772.83	770.55	768.67	767.11	762.51	760.70	759.98
50000	826.89	817.67	810.15	804.00	798.97	794.82	791.41	788.60	786.27	784.35	782.76	778.07	776.22	775.49
55000	909.58	899.43	891.16	884.40	878.86	874.31	870.55	867.46	864.90	862.79	861.04	855.88	853.84	853.04
60000	992.27	981.20	972.18	964.80	958.76	953.79	949.69	946.32	943.53	941.22	939.31	933.68	931.46	930.58
65000	1074.96	1062.96	1053.19	1045.20	1038.65	1033.27	1028.84	1025.18	1022.16	1019.66	1017.59	1011.49	1009.08	1008.13
70000	1157.65	1144.73	1134.21	1125.60	1118.55	1112.75	1107.98	1104.04	1100.78	1098.09	1095.86	1089.29	1086.71	1085.68
75000	1240.34	1226.50	1215.22	1206.00	1198.45	1192.23	1187.12	1182.90	1179.41	1176.53	1174.14	1167.10	1164.33	1163.23
80000	1323.02	1308.26	1296.24	1286.40	1278.34	1271.72	1266.26	1261.76	1258.04	1254.96	1252.41	1244.91	1241.95	1240.78
85000	1405.71	1390.03	1377.25	1366.80	1358.24	1351.20	1345.40	1340.62	1336.66	1333.40	1330.69	1322.71	1319.57	1318.32
90000	1488.40	1471.79	1458.27	1447.20	1438.13	1430.68	1424.54	1419.47	1415.29	1411.83	1408.97	1400.52	1397.19	1395.87
95000	1571.09	1553.56	1539.28	1527.60	1518.03	1510.16	1503.68	1498.33	1493.92	1490.27	1487.24	1478.33	1474.81	1473.42
100000	1653.78	1635.33	1620.29	1608.00	1597.93	1589.64	1582.82	1577.19	1572.54	1568.70	1565.52	1556.13	1552.43	1550.97

MONTHLY PAYMENT
REQUIRED TO AMORTIZE A LOAN

TERM AMOUNT	1 Year	2 Years	3 Years	4 Years	5 Years	6 Years	7 Years	8 Years	9 Years	10 Years	11 Years	12 Years	13 Years	14 Years
5	.46	.26	.19	.15	.13	.12	.11	.11	.10	.10	.09	.09	.09	.09
10	.92	.51	.37	.30	.26	.24	.22	.21	.20	.19	.18	.18	.18	.17
15	1.38	.76	.55	.45	.39	.35	.33	.31	.29	.28	.27	.27	.26	.26
25	2.30	1.26	.92	.75	.65	.58	.54	.51	.48	.47	.45	.44	.43	.42
50	4.60	2.52	1.83	1.49	1.29	1.16	1.07	1.01	.96	.93	.90	.88	.86	.84
75	6.90	3.77	2.74	2.23	1.94	1.74	1.61	1.51	1.44	1.39	1.34	1.31	1.28	1.26
100	9.20	5.03	3.65	2.98	2.58	2.32	2.14	2.02	1.92	1.85	1.79	1.75	1.71	1.68
200	18.40	10.05	7.30	5.95	5.15	4.64	4.28	4.03	3.83	3.69	3.58	3.49	3.42	3.36
300	27.60	15.07	10.95	8.92	7.73	6.95	6.42	6.04	5.75	5.53	5.36	5.23	5.12	5.04
400	36.80	20.10	14.59	11.89	10.30	9.27	8.56	8.05	7.66	7.37	7.15	6.97	6.83	6.72
500	45.99	25.12	18.24	14.86	12.87	11.59	10.70	10.06	9.58	9.22	8.93	8.71	8.54	8.40
600	55.19	30.14	21.89	17.83	15.45	13.90	12.84	12.07	11.49	11.06	10.72	10.45	10.24	10.07
700	64.39	35.16	25.53	20.80	18.02	16.22	14.98	14.08	13.41	12.90	12.51	12.20	11.95	11.75
800	73.59	40.19	29.18	23.77	20.59	18.54	17.11	16.09	15.32	14.74	14.29	13.94	13.66	13.43
900	82.78	45.21	32.83	26.74	23.17	20.85	19.25	18.10	17.24	16.59	16.08	15.68	15.36	15.11
1000	91.98	50.23	36.47	29.71	25.74	23.17	21.39	20.11	19.15	18.43	17.86	17.42	17.07	16.79
2000	183.96	100.46	72.94	59.41	51.47	46.33	42.78	40.21	38.30	36.85	35.72	34.84	34.13	33.57
3000	275.94	150.68	109.41	89.11	77.21	69.49	64.16	60.32	57.45	55.27	53.58	52.25	51.20	50.35
4000	367.92	200.91	145.87	118.82	102.94	92.66	85.55	80.42	76.60	73.70	71.44	69.67	68.26	67.14
5000	459.89	251.14	182.34	148.52	128.68	115.82	106.93	100.52	95.75	92.12	89.30	87.09	85.33	83.92
6000	551.87	301.36	218.81	178.22	154.41	138.98	128.32	120.63	114.90	110.54	107.16	104.50	102.39	100.70
7000	643.85	351.59	255.27	207.92	180.15	162.14	149.71	140.73	134.05	128.96	125.02	121.92	119.46	117.49
8000	735.83	401.82	291.74	237.63	205.88	185.31	171.09	160.84	153.20	147.39	142.88	139.34	136.52	134.27
9000	827.80	452.04	328.21	267.33	231.62	208.47	192.48	180.94	172.35	165.81	160.74	156.75	153.59	151.05
10000	919.78	502.27	364.67	297.03	257.35	231.63	213.86	201.04	191.50	184.23	178.60	174.17	170.65	167.84
11000	1011.76	552.50	401.14	326.73	283.09	254.79	235.25	221.15	210.65	202.66	196.46	191.59	187.72	184.62
12000	1103.74	602.72	437.61	356.44	308.82	277.96	256.63	241.25	229.80	221.08	214.32	209.00	204.78	201.40
13000	1195.72	652.95	474.07	386.14	334.56	301.12	278.02	261.35	248.95	239.50	232.18	226.42	221.85	218.19
14000	1287.69	703.18	510.54	415.84	360.29	324.28	299.41	281.46	268.10	257.92	250.04	243.84	238.91	234.97
15000	1379.67	753.40	547.01	445.54	386.02	347.44	320.79	301.56	287.25	276.35	267.90	261.25	255.98	251.75
16000	1471.65	803.63	583.47	475.25	411.76	370.61	342.18	321.67	306.40	294.77	285.75	278.67	273.04	268.53
17000	1563.63	853.86	619.94	504.95	437.49	393.77	363.56	341.77	325.55	313.19	303.61	296.09	290.11	285.32
18000	1655.60	904.08	656.41	534.65	463.23	416.93	384.95	361.87	344.70	331.62	321.47	313.50	307.17	302.10
19000	1747.58	954.31	692.87	564.35	488.96	440.09	406.33	381.98	363.85	350.04	339.33	330.92	324.24	318.88
20000	1839.56	1004.54	729.34	594.06	514.70	463.26	427.72	402.08	383.00	368.46	357.19	348.34	341.30	335.67
21000	1931.54	1054.76	765.81	623.76	540.43	486.42	449.11	422.19	402.15	386.88	375.05	365.75	358.37	352.45
22000	2023.51	1104.99	802.27	653.46	566.17	509.58	470.49	442.29	421.30	405.31	392.91	383.17	375.43	369.23
23000	2115.49	1155.22	838.74	683.16	591.90	532.74	491.88	462.39	440.45	423.73	410.77	400.59	392.50	386.02
24000	2207.47	1205.44	875.21	712.87	617.64	555.91	513.26	482.50	459.60	442.15	428.63	418.00	406.56	402.80
25000	2299.45	1255.67	911.67	742.57	643.37	579.07	534.65	502.60	478.75	460.58	446.49	435.42	426.63	419.58
26000	2391.43	1305.90	948.14	772.27	669.11	602.23	556.03	522.70	497.90	479.00	464.35	452.83	443.69	436.37
27000	2483.40	1356.12	984.61	801.98	694.84	625.39	577.42	542.81	517.05	497.42	482.21	470.25	460.76	453.15
28000	2575.38	1406.35	1021.07	831.68	720.58	648.56	598.81	562.91	536.20	515.84	500.07	487.67	477.82	469.93
29000	2667.36	1456.58	1057.54	861.38	746.31	671.72	620.19	583.02	555.35	534.27	517.93	505.09	494.88	486.71
30000	2759.34	1506.80	1094.01	891.08	772.04	694.88	641.58	603.12	574.49	552.69	535.79	522.50	511.95	503.50
31000	2851.31	1557.03	1130.47	920.79	797.78	718.04	662.96	623.22	593.64	571.11	553.64	539.92	529.01	520.28
32000	2943.29	1607.26	1166.94	950.49	823.51	741.21	684.35	643.33	612.79	589.54	571.50	557.33	546.08	537.06
33000	3035.27	1657.48	1203.41	980.19	849.25	764.37	705.73	663.43	631.94	607.96	589.36	574.75	563.14	553.85
34000	3127.25	1707.71	1239.87	1009.89	874.98	787.53	727.12	683.54	651.09	626.38	607.22	592.17	580.21	570.63
35000	3219.22	1757.94	1276.34	1039.60	900.72	810.69	748.51	703.64	670.24	644.80	625.08	609.58	597.27	587.41
36000	3311.20	1808.16	1312.81	1069.30	926.45	833.86	769.89	723.74	689.39	663.23	642.94	627.00	614.34	604.20
37000	3403.18	1858.39	1349.27	1099.00	952.19	857.02	791.28	743.85	708.54	681.65	660.80	644.42	631.40	620.98
38000	3495.16	1908.62	1385.74	1128.70	977.92	880.18	812.66	763.95	727.69	700.07	678.66	661.83	648.47	637.76
39000	3587.14	1958.84	1422.21	1158.41	1003.66	903.34	834.05	784.05	746.84	718.50	696.52	679.25	665.53	654.55
40000	3679.11	2009.07	1458.67	1188.11	1029.39	926.51	855.44	804.16	765.99	736.92	714.38	696.67	682.60	671.33
41000	3771.09	2059.30	1495.14	1217.81	1055.13	949.67	876.82	824.26	785.14	755.34	732.24	714.08	699.66	688.11
42000	3863.07	2109.52	1531.61	1247.51	1080.86	972.83	898.21	844.37	804.29	773.76	750.10	731.50	716.73	704.89
43000	3955.05	2159.75	1568.07	1277.22	1106.59	995.99	919.59	864.47	823.44	792.19	767.96	748.92	733.79	721.68
44000	4047.02	2209.98	1604.54	1306.92	1132.33	1019.16	940.98	884.57	842.59	810.61	785.82	766.33	750.86	738.46
45000	4139.00	2260.20	1641.01	1336.62	1158.06	1042.32	962.36	904.68	861.74	829.03	803.68	783.75	767.92	755.24
46000	4230.98	2310.43	1677.47	1366.32	1183.80	1065.48	983.75	924.78	880.89	847.45	821.53	801.17	784.99	772.03
47000	4322.96	2360.66	1713.94	1396.03	1209.53	1088.64	1005.14	944.89	900.04	865.88	839.39	818.58	802.05	788.81
48000	4414.93	2410.88	1750.41	1425.73	1235.27	1111.81	1026.52	964.99	919.19	884.30	857.25	836.00	819.12	805.59
49000	4506.91	2461.11	1786.87	1455.43	1261.00	1134.97	1047.91	985.09	938.34	902.72	875.11	853.42	836.18	822.38
50000	4598.89	2511.34	1823.34	1485.13	1286.74	1158.13	1069.29	1005.20	957.49	921.15	892.97	870.83	853.25	839.16
55000	5058.78	2762.47	2005.67	1633.65	1415.41	1273.94	1176.22	1105.72	1053.24	1013.26	982.27	957.91	938.57	923.07
60000	5518.67	3013.60	2188.01	1782.16	1544.08	1389.76	1283.15	1206.24	1148.98	1105.37	1071.57	1045.00	1023.89	1006.99
65000	5978.56	3264.73	2370.34	1930.67	1672.76	1505.57	1390.08	1306.75	1244.73	1197.49	1160.86	1132.08	1109.22	1090.91
70000	6438.44	3515.87	2552.67	2079.19	1801.43	1621.38	1497.01	1407.27	1340.48	1289.60	1250.16	1219.16	1194.54	1174.82
75000	6898.33	3767.00	2735.01	2227.70	1930.10	1737.19	1603.94	1507.79	1436.23	1381.72	1339.46	1306.24	1279.87	1258.74
80000	7358.22	4018.13	2917.34	2376.21	2058.78	1853.01	1710.87	1608.31	1531.98	1473.83	1428.75	1393.33	1365.19	1342.65
85000	7818.11	4269.27	3099.67	2524.73	2187.45	1968.82	1817.79	1708.83	1627.73	1565.94	1518.05	1480.41	1450.51	1426.57
90000	8278.00	4520.40	3282.01	2673.24	2316.12	2084.63	1924.72	1809.35	1723.47	1658.06	1607.35	1567.49	1535.84	1510.48
95000	8737.89	4771.53	3464.34	2821.75	2444.80	2200.45	2031.65	1909.87	1819.22	1750.17	1696.64	1654.58	1621.16	1594.40
100000	9197.78	5022.67	3646.67	2970.26	2573.47	2316.26	2138.58	2010.39	1914.97	1842.29	1785.94	1741.66	1706.49	1678.31

TERM	15 Years	16 Years	17 Years	18 Years	19 Years	20 Years	21 Years	22 Years	23 Years	24 Years	25 Years	30 Years	35 Years	40 Years
AMOUNT														
5	.09	.09	.09	.09	.08	.08	.08	.08	.08	.08	.08	.08	.08	.08
10	.17	.17	.17	.17	.16	.16	.16	.16	.16	.16	.16	.16	.16	.16
15	.25	.25	.25	.25	.24	.24	.24	.24	.24	.24	.24	.24	.24	.24
25	.42	.41	.41	.41	.40	.40	.40	.40	.40	.40	.40	.39	.39	.39
50	.83	.82	.82	.81	.80	.80	.80	.79	.79	.79	.79	.78	.78	.78
75	1.25	1.23	1.22	1.21	1.20	1.20	1.19	1.19	1.19	1.18	1.18	1.17	1.17	1.17
100	1.66	1.64	1.63	1.61	1.60	1.60	1.59	1.58	1.58	1.58	1.57	1.56	1.56	1.56
200	3.32	3.28	3.25	3.22	3.20	3.19	3.17	3.16	3.15	3.15	3.14	3.12	3.11	3.11
300	4.97	4.92	4.87	4.83	4.80	4.78	4.76	4.74	4.73	4.72	4.71	4.68	4.67	4.66
400	6.63	6.55	6.49	6.44	6.40	6.37	6.34	6.32	6.30	6.29	6.28	6.24	6.22	6.22
500	8.28	8.19	8.12	8.05	8.00	7.96	7.93	7.90	7.88	7.86	7.84	7.80	7.78	7.77
600	9.94	9.83	9.74	9.66	9.60	9.55	9.51	9.48	9.45	9.43	9.41	9.35	9.33	9.32
700	11.59	11.47	11.36	11.27	11.20	11.15	11.10	11.06	11.03	11.00	10.98	10.91	10.89	10.88
800	13.25	13.10	12.98	12.88	12.80	12.74	12.68	12.64	12.60	12.57	12.55	12.47	12.44	12.43
900	14.91	14.74	14.60	14.49	14.40	14.33	14.27	14.22	14.18	14.14	14.11	14.03	14.00	13.98
1000	16.56	16.38	16.23	16.10	16.00	15.92	15.85	15.80	15.75	15.71	15.68	15.59	15.55	15.54
2000	33.12	32.75	32.45	32.20	32.00	31.84	31.70	31.59	31.50	31.42	31.36	31.17	31.09	31.07
3000	49.67	49.12	48.67	48.30	48.00	47.75	47.55	47.38	47.24	47.13	47.03	46.75	46.64	46.60
4000	66.23	65.49	64.89	64.40	64.00	63.67	63.40	63.17	62.99	62.83	62.71	62.33	62.18	62.13
5000	82.78	81.86	81.11	80.50	80.00	79.58	79.24	78.96	78.73	78.54	78.38	77.91	77.73	77.66
6000	99.34	98.23	97.33	96.60	96.00	95.50	95.09	94.75	94.48	94.25	94.06	93.50	93.27	93.19
7000	115.90	114.61	113.56	112.70	111.99	111.42	110.94	110.55	110.22	109.95	109.73	109.08	108.82	108.72
8000	132.45	130.98	129.78	128.80	127.99	127.33	126.79	126.34	125.97	125.66	125.41	124.66	124.36	124.25
9000	149.01	147.35	146.00	144.90	143.99	143.25	142.63	142.13	141.71	141.37	141.08	140.24	139.91	139.78
10000	165.56	163.72	162.22	160.99	159.99	159.16	158.48	157.92	157.46	157.07	156.76	155.82	155.45	155.31
11000	182.12	180.09	178.44	177.09	175.99	175.08	174.33	173.71	173.20	172.78	172.43	171.40	171.00	170.84
12000	198.68	196.46	194.66	193.19	191.99	190.99	190.18	189.50	188.95	188.49	188.11	186.99	186.54	186.37
13000	215.23	212.84	210.89	209.29	207.98	206.91	206.03	205.30	204.69	204.19	203.78	202.57	202.09	201.90
14000	231.79	229.21	227.11	225.39	223.98	222.83	221.87	221.09	220.44	219.90	219.46	218.15	217.63	217.43
15000	248.34	245.58	243.33	241.49	239.98	238.74	237.72	236.88	236.18	235.61	235.13	233.73	233.18	232.96
16000	264.90	261.95	259.55	257.59	255.98	254.66	253.57	252.67	251.93	251.32	250.81	249.31	248.72	248.49
17000	281.46	278.32	275.77	273.69	271.98	270.57	269.42	268.46	267.67	267.02	266.48	264.89	264.27	264.02
18000	298.01	294.69	291.99	289.79	287.98	286.49	285.26	284.25	283.42	282.73	282.16	280.48	279.81	279.55
19000	314.57	311.07	308.22	305.88	303.97	302.40	301.11	300.05	299.16	298.44	297.83	296.06	295.36	295.08
20000	331.12	327.44	324.44	321.98	319.97	318.32	316.96	315.84	314.91	314.14	313.51	311.64	310.90	310.61
21000	347.68	343.81	340.66	338.08	335.97	334.24	332.81	331.63	330.65	329.85	329.18	327.22	326.45	326.14
22000	364.23	360.18	356.88	354.18	351.97	350.15	348.65	347.42	346.40	345.56	344.86	342.80	341.99	341.67
23000	380.79	376.55	373.10	370.28	367.97	366.07	364.50	363.21	362.15	361.26	360.53	358.38	357.54	357.20
24000	397.35	392.92	389.32	386.30	383.97	381.98	380.35	379.00	377.89	376.97	376.21	373.97	373.08	372.73
25000	413.90	409.30	405.54	402.48	399.96	397.90	396.20	394.79	393.64	392.68	391.89	389.55	388.63	388.26
26000	430.46	425.67	421.77	418.58	415.96	413.81	412.05	410.59	409.38	408.38	407.56	405.13	404.17	403.80
27000	447.01	442.04	437.99	434.68	431.96	429.73	427.89	426.38	425.13	424.09	423.24	420.71	419.72	419.33
28000	463.57	458.41	454.21	450.78	447.96	445.65	443.74	442.17	440.87	439.80	438.91	436.29	435.26	434.86
29000	480.13	474.78	470.43	466.87	463.96	461.56	459.59	457.96	456.62	455.51	454.59	451.88	450.81	450.39
30000	496.68	491.15	486.65	482.97	479.96	477.48	475.44	473.75	472.36	471.21	470.26	467.46	466.35	465.92
31000	513.24	507.53	502.87	499.07	495.95	493.39	491.28	489.54	488.11	486.92	485.94	483.04	481.90	481.45
32000	529.79	523.90	519.10	515.17	511.95	509.31	507.13	505.34	503.85	502.63	501.61	498.62	497.44	496.98
33000	546.35	540.27	535.32	531.27	527.95	525.22	522.98	521.13	519.60	518.33	517.29	514.20	512.99	512.51
34000	562.91	556.64	551.54	547.37	543.95	541.14	538.83	536.92	535.34	534.04	532.96	529.78	528.53	528.04
35000	579.46	573.01	567.76	563.47	559.95	557.06	554.67	552.71	551.09	549.75	548.64	545.37	544.08	543.57
36000	596.02	589.38	583.98	579.57	575.95	572.97	570.52	568.50	566.83	565.45	564.31	560.95	559.62	559.10
37000	612.57	605.76	600.20	595.67	591.95	588.89	586.37	584.29	582.58	581.16	579.99	576.53	575.17	574.63
38000	629.13	622.13	616.43	611.76	607.94	604.80	602.22	600.09	598.32	596.87	595.66	592.11	590.71	590.16
39000	645.68	638.50	632.65	627.86	623.94	620.72	618.07	615.88	614.07	612.57	611.34	607.69	606.26	605.69
40000	662.24	654.87	648.87	643.96	639.94	636.64	633.91	631.67	629.81	628.28	627.01	623.27	621.80	621.22
41000	678.80	671.24	665.09	660.06	655.94	652.55	649.76	647.46	645.56	643.99	642.69	638.86	637.35	636.75
42000	695.35	687.61	681.31	676.16	671.94	668.47	665.61	663.25	661.30	659.70	658.36	654.44	652.89	652.28
43000	711.91	703.99	697.53	692.26	687.94	684.38	681.46	679.04	677.05	675.40	674.04	670.02	668.44	667.81
44000	728.46	720.36	713.76	708.36	703.93	700.30	697.30	694.83	692.80	691.11	689.71	685.60	683.98	683.34
45000	745.02	736.73	729.98	724.46	719.93	716.21	713.15	710.63	708.54	706.82	705.39	701.18	699.53	698.87
46000	761.58	753.10	746.20	740.56	735.93	732.13	729.00	726.42	724.29	722.52	721.06	716.76	715.07	714.40
47000	778.13	769.47	762.42	756.66	751.93	748.05	744.85	742.21	740.03	738.23	736.74	732.35	730.62	729.93
48000	794.69	785.84	778.64	772.75	767.93	763.96	760.69	758.00	755.78	753.94	752.41	747.93	746.16	745.46
49000	811.24	802.22	794.86	788.85	783.93	779.88	776.54	773.79	771.52	769.64	768.09	763.51	761.71	760.99
50000	827.80	818.59	811.08	804.95	799.92	795.79	792.39	789.58	787.27	785.35	783.77	779.09	777.25	776.52
55000	910.58	900.45	892.19	885.45	879.92	875.37	871.63	868.54	865.99	863.89	862.14	857.00	854.98	854.18
60000	993.36	982.30	973.30	965.94	959.91	954.95	950.87	947.50	944.72	942.42	940.52	934.91	932.70	931.83
65000	1076.14	1064.16	1054.41	1046.44	1039.90	1034.53	1030.11	1026.46	1023.45	1020.95	1018.89	1012.82	1010.43	1009.48
70000	1158.92	1146.02	1135.52	1126.93	1119.89	1114.11	1109.35	1105.42	1102.17	1099.49	1097.27	1090.73	1088.15	1087.13
75000	1241.70	1227.88	1216.62	1207.43	1199.88	1193.69	1188.58	1184.37	1180.90	1178.02	1175.65	1168.64	1165.88	1164.78
80000	1324.48	1309.74	1297.73	1287.92	1279.88	1273.27	1267.82	1263.33	1259.62	1256.56	1254.02	1246.54	1243.60	1242.44
85000	1407.26	1391.60	1378.84	1368.41	1359.87	1352.84	1347.06	1342.29	1338.35	1335.09	1332.40	1324.45	1321.33	1320.09
90000	1490.03	1473.45	1459.95	1448.91	1439.86	1432.42	1426.30	1421.25	1417.08	1413.63	1410.77	1402.36	1399.05	1397.74
95000	1572.81	1555.31	1541.06	1529.40	1519.85	1512.00	1505.54	1500.21	1495.80	1492.16	1489.15	1480.27	1476.78	1475.39
100000	1655.59	1637.17	1622.16	1609.90	1599.84	1591.58	1584.78	1579.16	1574.53	1570.70	1567.53	1558.18	1554.50	1553.04

MONTHLY PAYMENT
REQUIRED TO AMORTIZE A LOAN

TERM AMOUNT	1 Year	2 Years	3 Years	4 Years	5 Years	6 Years	7 Years	8 Years	9 Years	10 Years	11 Years	12 Years	13 Years	14 Years
5	.47	.26	.19	.15	.13	.12	.11	.11	.10	.10	.09	.09	.09	.09
10	.93	.51	.37	.30	.26	.24	.22	.21	.20	.19	.18	.18	.18	.17
15	1.39	.76	.55	.45	.39	.35	.33	.31	.29	.28	.27	.27	.26	.26
25	2.31	1.26	.92	.75	.65	.59	.54	.51	.48	.47	.45	.44	.43	.43
50	4.61	2.52	1.83	1.49	1.29	1.17	1.08	1.01	.96	.93	.90	.88	.86	.85
75	6.91	3.77	2.74	2.24	1.94	1.75	1.61	1.52	1.44	1.39	1.35	1.32	1.29	1.27
100	9.21	5.03	3.66	2.98	2.58	2.33	2.15	2.02	1.92	1.85	1.80	1.75	1.72	1.69
200	18.41	10.06	7.31	5.95	5.16	4.65	4.29	4.03	3.84	3.70	3.59	3.50	3.43	3.37
300	27.61	15.08	10.96	8.93	7.74	6.97	6.43	6.05	5.76	5.55	5.38	5.25	5.14	5.06
400	36.81	20.11	14.61	11.90	10.32	9.29	8.58	8.06	7.68	7.39	7.17	6.99	6.85	6.74
500	46.01	25.14	18.26	14.88	12.89	11.61	10.72	10.08	9.60	9.24	8.96	8.74	8.56	8.42
600	55.21	30.16	21.91	17.85	15.47	13.93	12.86	12.09	11.52	11.09	10.75	10.49	10.28	10.11
700	64.41	35.19	25.56	20.82	18.05	16.25	15.01	14.11	13.44	12.94	12.54	12.23	11.99	11.79
800	73.62	40.22	29.21	23.80	20.63	18.57	17.15	16.12	15.36	14.78	14.33	13.98	13.70	13.47
900	82.82	45.24	32.86	26.77	23.20	20.89	19.29	18.14	17.28	16.63	16.12	15.73	15.41	15.16
1000	92.02	50.27	36.51	29.75	25.78	23.21	21.44	20.15	19.20	18.48	17.91	17.47	17.12	16.84
2000	184.03	100.53	73.01	59.49	51.56	46.42	42.87	40.30	38.40	36.95	35.82	34.94	34.24	33.68
3000	276.05	150.79	109.52	89.23	77.33	69.62	64.30	60.45	57.60	55.42	53.73	52.41	51.36	50.51
4000	368.06	201.06	146.02	118.97	103.11	92.83	85.73	80.60	76.79	73.89	71.64	69.88	68.47	67.35
5000	460.07	251.32	182.53	148.72	128.88	116.03	107.16	100.75	95.99	92.36	89.55	87.34	85.59	84.19
6000	552.09	301.58	219.03	178.46	154.66	139.24	128.59	120.90	115.19	110.83	107.46	104.81	102.71	101.02
7000	644.10	351.85	255.54	208.20	180.44	162.44	150.02	141.05	134.38	129.31	125.37	122.28	119.83	117.86
8000	736.11	402.11	292.04	237.94	206.21	185.65	171.45	161.20	153.58	147.78	143.28	139.75	136.94	134.70
9000	828.13	452.37	328.55	267.68	231.99	208.85	192.88	181.35	172.78	166.25	161.19	157.22	154.06	151.53
10000	920.14	502.63	365.05	297.43	257.76	232.06	214.31	201.50	191.98	184.72	179.10	174.68	171.18	168.37
11000	1012.15	552.90	401.55	327.17	283.54	255.26	235.74	221.65	211.17	203.19	197.01	192.15	188.29	185.21
12000	1104.17	603.16	438.06	356.91	309.31	278.47	257.17	241.80	230.37	221.66	214.92	209.62	205.41	202.04
13000	1196.18	653.42	474.56	386.65	335.09	301.67	278.60	261.95	249.57	240.14	232.83	227.09	222.53	218.88
14000	1288.19	703.69	511.07	416.39	360.87	324.88	300.03	282.10	268.76	258.61	250.74	244.55	239.65	235.72
15000	1380.21	753.95	547.57	446.14	386.64	348.08	321.46	302.25	287.96	277.08	268.65	262.02	256.76	252.55
16000	1472.22	804.21	584.08	475.88	412.42	371.29	342.89	322.40	307.16	295.55	286.56	279.49	273.88	269.39
17000	1564.23	854.48	620.58	505.62	438.19	394.49	364.32	342.55	326.35	314.02	304.47	296.96	291.00	286.23
18000	1656.25	904.74	657.09	535.36	463.97	417.70	385.75	362.70	345.55	332.49	322.37	314.43	308.12	303.06
19000	1748.26	955.00	693.59	565.10	489.74	440.91	407.18	382.85	364.75	350.97	340.28	331.89	325.23	319.90
20000	1840.27	1005.26	730.10	594.85	515.52	464.11	428.61	403.00	383.95	369.44	358.19	349.36	342.35	336.74
21000	1932.29	1055.53	766.60	624.59	541.30	487.32	450.04	423.15	403.14	387.91	376.10	366.83	359.47	353.57
22000	2024.30	1105.79	803.10	654.33	567.07	510.52	471.47	443.30	422.34	406.38	394.01	384.30	376.58	370.41
23000	2116.31	1156.05	839.61	684.07	592.85	533.73	492.90	463.45	441.54	424.85	411.92	401.77	393.70	387.25
24000	2208.33	1206.32	876.11	713.81	618.62	556.93	514.33	483.60	460.73	443.32	429.83	419.23	410.82	404.08
25000	2300.34	1256.58	912.62	743.56	644.40	580.14	535.76	503.75	479.93	461.79	447.74	436.70	427.94	420.92
26000	2392.36	1306.84	949.12	773.30	670.17	603.34	557.19	523.90	499.13	480.27	465.65	454.17	445.05	437.76
27000	2484.37	1357.11	985.63	803.04	695.95	626.55	578.62	544.05	518.33	498.74	483.56	471.64	462.17	454.59
28000	2576.38	1407.37	1022.13	832.78	721.73	649.75	600.05	564.20	537.52	517.21	501.47	489.10	479.29	471.43
29000	2668.40	1457.63	1058.64	862.52	747.50	672.96	621.48	584.35	556.72	535.68	519.38	506.57	496.41	488.27
30000	2760.41	1507.89	1095.14	892.27	773.28	696.16	642.91	604.50	575.92	554.15	537.29	524.04	513.52	505.10
31000	2852.42	1558.16	1131.65	922.01	799.05	719.37	664.34	624.65	595.11	572.62	555.20	541.51	530.64	521.94
32000	2944.44	1608.42	1168.15	951.75	824.83	742.57	685.77	644.80	614.31	591.10	573.11	558.98	547.76	538.78
33000	3036.45	1658.68	1204.65	981.49	850.61	765.78	707.20	664.95	633.51	609.57	591.02	576.44	564.87	555.61
34000	3128.46	1708.95	1241.16	1011.23	876.38	788.98	728.63	685.10	652.70	628.04	608.93	593.91	581.99	572.45
35000	3220.48	1759.21	1277.66	1040.98	902.16	812.19	750.06	705.25	671.90	646.51	626.83	611.38	599.11	589.29
36000	3312.49	1809.47	1314.17	1070.72	927.93	835.40	771.49	725.40	691.10	664.98	644.74	628.85	616.23	606.12
37000	3404.50	1859.74	1350.67	1100.46	953.71	858.60	792.92	745.55	710.30	683.45	662.65	646.32	633.34	622.96
38000	3496.52	1910.00	1387.18	1130.20	979.48	881.81	814.35	765.70	729.49	701.93	680.56	663.78	650.46	639.80
39000	3588.53	1960.26	1423.68	1159.94	1005.26	905.01	835.78	785.85	748.69	720.40	698.47	681.25	667.58	656.63
40000	3680.54	2010.52	1460.19	1189.69	1031.04	928.22	857.21	805.99	767.89	738.87	716.38	698.72	684.70	673.47
41000	3772.56	2060.79	1496.69	1219.43	1056.81	951.42	878.64	826.14	787.08	757.34	734.29	716.19	701.81	690.31
42000	3864.57	2111.05	1533.19	1249.17	1082.59	974.63	900.07	846.29	806.28	775.81	752.20	733.65	718.93	707.14
43000	3956.58	2161.31	1569.70	1278.91	1108.36	997.83	921.50	866.44	825.48	794.28	770.11	751.12	736.05	723.98
44000	4048.60	2211.58	1606.20	1308.65	1134.14	1021.04	942.93	886.59	844.67	812.76	788.02	768.59	753.16	740.81
45000	4140.61	2261.84	1642.71	1338.40	1159.91	1044.24	964.36	906.74	863.87	831.23	805.93	786.06	770.28	757.65
46000	4232.62	2312.10	1679.21	1368.14	1185.69	1067.45	985.79	926.89	883.07	849.70	823.84	803.53	787.40	774.49
47000	4324.64	2362.37	1715.72	1397.88	1211.47	1090.65	1007.22	947.04	902.27	868.17	841.75	820.99	804.52	791.32
48000	4416.65	2412.63	1752.22	1427.62	1237.24	1113.86	1028.65	967.19	921.46	886.64	859.66	838.46	821.63	808.16
49000	4508.66	2462.89	1788.73	1457.37	1263.02	1137.06	1050.08	987.34	940.66	905.11	877.57	855.93	838.75	825.00
50000	4600.68	2513.15	1825.23	1487.11	1288.79	1160.27	1071.51	1007.49	959.86	923.58	895.48	873.40	855.87	841.83
55000	5060.75	2764.47	2007.75	1635.82	1417.67	1276.30	1178.66	1108.24	1055.84	1015.94	985.02	960.74	941.45	926.02
60000	5520.81	3015.78	2190.28	1784.53	1546.55	1392.32	1285.81	1208.99	1151.83	1108.30	1074.57	1048.08	1027.04	1010.20
65000	5980.88	3267.10	2372.80	1933.24	1675.43	1508.35	1392.96	1309.74	1247.81	1200.66	1164.12	1135.41	1112.63	1094.38
70000	6440.95	3518.41	2555.32	2081.95	1804.31	1624.38	1500.11	1410.49	1343.80	1293.02	1253.66	1222.75	1198.21	1178.57
75000	6901.01	3769.73	2737.84	2230.66	1933.19	1740.40	1607.26	1511.24	1439.78	1385.37	1343.21	1310.09	1283.80	1262.75
80000	7361.08	4021.04	2920.37	2379.37	2062.07	1856.43	1714.41	1611.98	1535.77	1477.73	1432.76	1397.43	1369.39	1346.93
85000	7821.15	4272.36	3102.89	2528.08	2190.94	1972.45	1821.57	1712.73	1631.75	1570.09	1522.31	1484.77	1454.97	1431.11
90000	8281.22	4523.67	3285.41	2676.79	2319.82	2088.48	1928.72	1813.48	1727.74	1662.45	1611.85	1572.11	1540.56	1515.30
95000	8741.28	4774.99	3467.93	2825.50	2448.70	2204.51	2035.87	1914.23	1823.72	1754.81	1701.40	1659.45	1626.15	1599.48
100000	9201.35	5026.30	3650.46	2974.21	2577.58	2320.53	2143.02	2014.98	1919.71	1847.16	1790.95	1746.79	1711.73	1683.66

TERM	15 Years	16 Years	17 Years	18 Years	19 Years	20 Years	21 Years	22 Years	23 Years	24 Years	25 Years	30 Years	35 Years	40 Years
AMOUNT														
5	.09	.09	.09	.09	.09	.08	.08	.08	.08	.08	.08	.08	.08	.08
10	.17	.17	.17	.17	.17	.16	.16	.16	.16	.16	.16	.16	.16	.16
15	.25	.25	.25	.25	.25	.24	.24	.24	.24	.24	.24	.24	.24	.24
25	.42	.42	.41	.41	.41	.40	.40	.40	.40	.40	.40	.40	.40	.39
50	.84	.83	.82	.81	.81	.80	.80	.80	.80	.79	.79	.79	.79	.78
75	1.25	1.24	1.23	1.22	1.21	1.20	1.20	1.19	1.19	1.19	1.19	1.18	1.18	1.17
100	1.67	1.65	1.63	1.62	1.61	1.60	1.60	1.59	1.59	1.58	1.58	1.57	1.57	1.56
200	3.33	3.29	3.26	3.24	3.22	3.20	3.19	3.18	3.17	3.16	3.15	3.13	3.13	3.12
300	4.99	4.93	4.89	4.85	4.82	4.80	4.78	4.76	4.75	4.74	4.73	4.70	4.69	4.68
400	6.65	6.58	6.52	6.47	6.43	6.39	6.37	6.35	6.33	6.31	6.30	6.26	6.25	6.24
500	8.31	8.22	8.14	8.08	8.03	7.99	7.96	7.93	7.91	7.89	7.87	7.83	7.81	7.80
600	9.97	9.86	9.77	9.70	9.64	9.59	9.55	9.52	9.49	9.47	9.45	9.39	9.37	9.36
700	11.63	11.50	11.40	11.31	11.24	11.19	11.14	11.10	11.07	11.04	11.02	10.96	10.93	10.92
800	13.29	13.15	13.03	12.93	12.85	12.78	12.73	12.69	12.65	12.62	12.59	12.52	12.49	12.48
900	14.95	14.79	14.65	14.55	14.46	14.38	14.32	14.27	14.23	14.20	14.17	14.08	14.05	14.04
1000	16.62	16.43	16.28	16.16	16.06	15.98	15.91	15.86	15.81	15.77	15.74	15.65	15.61	15.60
2000	33.23	32.86	32.56	32.32	32.12	31.95	31.82	31.71	31.61	31.54	31.48	31.29	31.22	31.19
3000	49.84	49.29	48.84	48.47	48.17	47.93	47.72	47.56	47.42	47.31	47.21	46.93	46.83	46.78
4000	66.45	65.71	65.12	64.63	64.23	63.90	63.63	63.41	63.22	63.07	62.95	62.58	62.43	62.38
5000	83.06	82.14	81.39	80.78	80.28	79.87	79.54	79.26	79.03	78.84	78.68	78.22	78.04	77.97
6000	99.67	98.57	97.67	96.94	96.34	95.85	95.44	95.11	94.83	94.61	94.42	93.86	93.65	93.56
7000	116.28	114.99	113.95	113.10	112.40	111.82	111.35	110.96	110.64	110.37	110.15	109.51	109.25	109.15
8000	132.89	131.42	130.23	129.25	128.45	127.80	127.26	126.81	126.44	126.14	125.89	125.15	124.86	124.75
9000	149.50	147.85	146.50	145.41	144.51	143.77	143.16	142.66	142.25	141.91	141.62	140.79	140.47	140.34
10000	166.11	164.27	162.78	161.56	160.56	159.74	159.07	158.51	158.05	157.67	157.36	156.44	156.07	155.93
11000	182.72	180.70	179.06	177.72	176.62	175.72	174.98	174.36	173.86	173.44	173.10	172.08	171.68	171.52
12000	199.33	197.13	195.34	193.87	192.68	191.69	190.88	190.21	189.66	189.21	188.83	187.72	187.29	187.12
13000	215.94	213.56	211.62	210.03	208.73	207.67	206.79	206.06	205.47	204.97	204.57	203.37	202.90	202.71
14000	232.55	229.98	227.89	226.19	224.79	223.64	222.69	221.92	221.27	220.74	220.30	219.01	218.50	218.30
15000	249.16	246.41	244.17	242.34	240.84	239.61	238.60	237.77	237.08	236.51	236.04	234.65	234.11	233.89
16000	265.77	262.84	260.45	258.50	256.90	255.59	254.51	253.62	252.88	252.27	251.77	250.30	249.72	249.49
17000	282.38	279.26	276.73	274.65	272.96	271.56	270.41	269.47	268.69	268.04	267.51	265.94	265.32	265.08
18000	298.99	295.69	293.00	290.81	289.01	287.53	286.32	285.32	284.49	283.81	283.24	281.58	280.93	280.67
19000	315.60	312.12	309.28	306.97	305.07	303.51	302.23	301.17	300.30	299.58	298.98	297.22	296.54	296.27
20000	332.21	328.54	325.56	323.12	321.12	319.48	318.13	317.02	316.10	315.34	314.71	312.87	312.14	311.86
21000	348.82	344.97	341.84	339.28	337.18	335.46	334.04	332.87	331.91	331.11	330.45	328.51	327.75	327.45
22000	365.43	361.40	358.12	355.43	353.24	351.43	349.95	348.72	347.71	346.88	346.19	344.15	343.36	343.04
23000	382.04	377.83	374.39	371.59	369.29	367.40	365.85	364.57	363.52	362.64	361.92	359.80	358.96	358.64
24000	398.65	394.25	390.67	387.74	385.35	383.38	381.76	380.42	379.32	378.41	377.66	375.44	374.57	374.23
25000	415.26	410.68	406.95	403.90	401.40	399.35	397.66	396.27	395.12	394.18	393.39	391.08	390.18	389.82
26000	431.87	427.11	423.23	420.06	417.46	415.33	413.57	412.12	410.93	409.94	409.13	406.73	405.79	405.41
27000	448.48	443.53	439.50	436.21	433.51	431.30	429.48	427.97	426.73	425.71	424.86	422.37	421.39	421.01
28000	465.09	459.96	455.78	452.37	449.57	447.27	445.38	443.83	442.54	441.48	440.60	438.01	437.00	436.60
29000	481.71	476.39	472.06	468.52	465.63	463.25	461.29	459.68	458.34	457.24	456.33	453.66	452.61	452.19
30000	498.32	492.81	488.34	484.68	481.68	479.22	477.20	475.53	474.15	473.01	472.07	469.30	468.21	467.78
31000	514.93	509.24	504.62	500.84	497.74	495.20	493.10	491.38	489.95	488.78	487.80	484.94	483.82	483.38
32000	531.54	525.67	520.89	516.99	513.79	511.17	509.01	507.23	505.76	504.54	503.54	500.59	499.43	498.97
33000	548.15	542.10	537.17	533.15	529.85	527.14	524.92	523.08	521.56	520.31	519.28	516.23	515.03	514.56
34000	564.76	558.52	553.45	549.30	545.91	543.12	540.82	538.93	537.37	536.08	535.01	531.87	530.64	530.16
35000	581.37	574.95	569.73	565.46	561.96	559.09	556.73	554.78	553.17	551.84	550.75	547.51	546.25	545.75
36000	597.98	591.38	586.00	581.61	578.02	575.06	572.63	570.63	568.98	567.61	566.48	563.16	561.85	561.34
37000	614.59	607.80	602.28	597.77	594.07	591.04	588.54	586.48	584.78	583.38	582.22	578.80	577.46	576.93
38000	631.20	624.23	618.56	613.93	610.13	607.01	604.45	602.33	600.59	599.15	597.95	594.44	593.07	592.53
39000	647.81	640.66	634.84	630.08	626.19	622.99	620.35	618.18	616.39	614.91	613.69	610.09	608.68	600.12
40000	664.42	657.08	651.11	646.24	642.24	638.96	636.26	634.03	632.20	630.68	629.42	625.73	624.28	623.71
41000	681.03	673.51	667.39	662.39	658.30	654.93	652.17	649.88	648.00	646.45	645.16	641.37	639.89	639.30
42000	697.64	689.94	683.67	678.55	674.35	670.91	668.07	665.74	663.81	662.21	660.89	657.02	655.50	654.90
43000	714.25	706.37	699.95	694.71	690.41	686.88	683.98	681.59	679.61	677.98	676.63	672.66	671.10	670.49
44000	730.86	722.79	716.23	710.86	706.47	702.86	699.89	697.44	695.42	693.75	692.37	688.30	686.71	686.08
45000	747.47	739.22	732.50	727.02	722.52	718.83	715.79	713.29	711.22	709.51	708.10	703.95	702.32	701.67
46000	764.08	755.65	748.78	743.17	738.58	734.80	731.70	729.14	727.03	725.28	723.84	719.59	717.92	717.27
47000	780.69	772.07	765.06	759.33	754.63	750.78	747.60	744.99	742.83	741.05	739.57	735.23	733.53	732.86
48000	797.30	788.50	781.34	775.48	770.69	766.75	763.51	760.84	758.64	756.81	755.31	750.88	749.14	748.45
49000	813.91	804.93	797.61	791.64	786.75	782.73	779.42	776.69	774.44	772.58	771.04	766.52	764.74	764.05
50000	830.52	821.35	813.89	807.80	802.80	798.70	795.32	792.54	790.24	788.35	786.78	782.16	780.35	779.64
55000	913.57	903.49	895.28	888.58	883.08	878.57	874.86	871.79	869.27	867.18	865.46	860.38	858.39	857.60
60000	996.63	985.62	976.67	969.35	963.36	958.44	954.39	951.05	948.29	946.02	944.13	938.59	936.42	935.56
65000	1079.68	1067.76	1058.06	1050.13	1043.64	1038.31	1033.92	1030.30	1027.32	1024.85	1022.81	1016.81	1014.46	1013.53
70000	1162.73	1149.89	1139.45	1130.91	1123.92	1118.18	1113.45	1109.56	1106.34	1103.68	1101.49	1095.02	1092.49	1091.49
75000	1245.78	1232.03	1220.84	1211.69	1204.20	1198.05	1192.98	1188.81	1185.36	1182.52	1180.16	1173.24	1170.52	1169.45
80000	1328.83	1314.16	1302.22	1292.47	1284.48	1277.92	1272.51	1268.06	1264.39	1261.35	1258.84	1251.46	1248.56	1247.42
85000	1411.88	1396.30	1383.61	1373.25	1364.76	1357.78	1352.05	1347.32	1343.41	1340.19	1337.52	1329.67	1326.59	1325.38
90000	1494.94	1478.43	1465.00	1454.03	1445.04	1437.65	1431.58	1426.57	1422.44	1419.02	1416.20	1407.89	1404.63	1403.34
95000	1577.99	1560.57	1546.39	1534.81	1525.32	1517.52	1511.11	1505.82	1501.46	1497.86	1494.87	1486.10	1482.66	1481.31
100000	1661.04	1642.70	1627.78	1615.59	1605.60	1597.39	1590.64	1585.08	1580.48	1576.69	1573.55	1564.32	1560.70	1559.27

MONTHLY PAYMENT
REQUIRED TO AMORTIZE A LOAN

TERM AMOUNT	1 Year	2 Years	3 Years	4 Years	5 Years	6 Years	7 Years	8 Years	9 Years	10 Years	11 Years	12 Years	13 Years	14 Years
5	.47	.26	.19	.15	.13	.12	.11	.11	.10	.10	.09	.09	.09	.09
10	.93	.51	.37	.30	.26	.24	.22	.21	.20	.19	.18	.18	.18	.17
15	1.39	.76	.55	.45	.39	.35	.33	.31	.29	.28	.27	.27	.26	.26
25	2.31	1.26	.92	.75	.65	.59	.54	.51	.49	.47	.45	.44	.43	.43
50	4.61	2.52	1.83	1.49	1.30	1.17	1.08	1.01	.97	.93	.90	.88	.86	.85
75	6.91	3.78	2.74	2.24	1.94	1.75	1.61	1.52	1.45	1.39	1.35	1.32	1.29	1.27
100	9.21	5.03	3.66	2.98	2.59	2.33	2.15	2.02	1.93	1.86	1.80	1.76	1.72	1.69
200	18.41	10.06	7.31	5.96	5.17	4.65	4.30	4.04	3.85	3.71	3.59	3.51	3.44	3.38
300	27.62	15.09	10.96	8.94	7.75	6.98	6.44	6.06	5.77	5.56	5.39	5.26	5.15	5.07
400	36.82	20.12	14.62	11.91	10.33	9.30	8.59	8.08	7.70	7.41	7.18	7.01	6.87	6.75
500	46.02	25.15	18.27	14.89	12.91	11.62	10.73	10.10	9.62	9.26	8.98	8.76	8.58	8.44
600	55.23	30.18	21.92	17.87	15.49	13.95	12.88	12.11	11.54	11.11	10.77	10.51	10.30	10.13
700	64.43	35.21	25.58	20.84	18.07	16.27	15.03	14.13	13.47	12.96	12.56	12.26	12.01	11.82
800	73.63	40.23	29.23	23.82	20.65	18.59	17.17	16.15	15.39	14.81	14.36	14.01	13.73	13.50
900	82.84	45.26	32.88	26.80	23.23	20.92	19.32	18.17	17.31	16.66	16.15	15.76	15.44	15.19
1000	92.04	50.29	36.53	29.77	25.81	23.24	21.46	20.19	19.23	18.51	17.95	17.51	17.16	16.88
2000	184.08	100.58	73.06	59.54	51.61	46.47	42.92	40.37	38.46	37.01	35.89	35.01	34.31	33.75
3000	276.12	150.87	109.59	89.31	77.41	69.71	64.38	60.55	57.69	55.52	53.83	52.51	51.46	50.62
4000	368.15	201.15	146.12	119.08	103.22	92.94	85.84	80.73	76.92	74.02	71.78	70.01	68.61	67.49
5000	460.19	251.44	182.65	148.85	129.02	116.17	107.30	100.91	96.15	92.53	89.72	87.52	85.77	84.37
6000	552.23	301.73	219.18	178.62	154.82	139.41	128.76	121.09	115.38	111.03	107.66	105.02	102.92	101.24
7000	644.27	352.02	255.71	208.38	180.63	162.64	150.22	141.27	134.61	129.53	125.60	122.52	120.07	118.11
8000	736.30	402.30	292.24	238.15	206.43	185.88	171.68	161.45	153.83	148.04	143.55	140.02	137.22	134.98
9000	828.34	452.59	328.77	267.92	232.23	209.11	193.14	181.63	173.06	166.54	161.49	157.52	154.38	151.86
10000	920.38	502.88	365.30	297.69	258.04	232.34	214.60	201.81	192.29	185.05	179.43	175.03	171.53	168.73
11000	1012.42	553.16	401.83	327.46	283.84	255.58	236.06	221.99	211.52	203.55	197.38	192.53	188.68	185.60
12000	1104.45	603.45	438.36	357.23	309.64	278.81	257.52	242.17	230.75	222.05	215.32	210.03	205.83	202.47
13000	1196.49	653.74	474.89	386.99	335.45	302.04	278.98	262.35	249.98	240.56	233.26	227.53	222.98	219.34
14000	1288.53	704.03	511.42	416.76	361.25	325.28	300.44	282.53	269.21	259.06	251.20	245.03	240.14	236.22
15000	1380.56	754.31	547.95	446.53	387.05	348.51	321.90	302.71	288.43	277.57	269.15	262.54	257.29	253.09
16000	1472.60	804.60	584.48	476.30	412.86	371.75	343.36	322.89	307.66	296.07	287.09	280.04	274.44	269.96
17000	1564.64	854.89	621.01	506.07	438.66	394.98	364.82	343.07	326.89	314.58	305.03	297.54	291.59	286.83
18000	1656.68	905.18	657.54	535.84	464.46	418.21	386.28	363.25	346.12	333.08	322.98	315.04	308.75	303.71
19000	1748.71	955.46	694.07	565.60	490.27	441.45	407.74	383.43	365.35	351.58	340.92	332.54	325.90	320.58
20000	1840.75	1005.75	730.60	595.37	516.07	464.68	429.20	403.61	384.58	370.09	358.86	350.05	343.05	337.45
21000	1932.79	1056.04	767.13	625.14	541.87	487.92	450.66	423.79	403.81	388.59	376.80	367.55	360.20	354.32
22000	2024.83	1106.32	803.66	654.91	567.68	511.15	472.12	443.97	423.04	407.10	394.75	385.05	377.35	371.20
23000	2116.86	1156.61	840.19	684.68	593.48	534.38	493.58	464.15	442.26	425.60	412.69	402.55	394.51	388.07
24000	2208.90	1206.90	876.72	714.45	619.28	557.62	515.04	484.33	461.49	444.10	430.63	420.05	411.66	404.94
25000	2300.94	1257.19	913.25	744.21	645.08	580.85	536.50	504.51	480.72	462.61	448.58	437.56	428.81	421.81
26000	2392.97	1307.47	949.78	773.98	670.89	604.08	557.96	524.69	499.95	481.11	466.52	455.06	445.96	438.68
27000	2485.01	1357.76	986.31	803.75	696.69	627.32	579.42	544.88	519.18	499.62	484.46	472.56	463.12	455.56
28000	2577.05	1408.05	1022.84	833.52	722.49	650.55	600.88	565.06	538.41	518.12	502.40	490.06	480.27	472.43
29000	2669.09	1458.33	1059.37	863.29	748.30	673.79	622.34	585.24	557.64	536.63	520.35	507.57	497.42	489.30
30000	2761.12	1508.62	1095.90	893.06	774.10	697.02	643.80	605.42	576.86	555.13	538.29	525.07	514.57	506.17
31000	2853.16	1558.91	1132.43	922.82	799.90	720.25	665.26	625.60	596.09	573.63	556.23	542.57	531.73	523.05
32000	2945.20	1609.20	1168.96	952.59	825.71	743.49	686.72	645.78	615.32	592.14	574.18	560.07	548.88	539.92
33000	3037.24	1659.48	1205.49	982.36	851.51	766.72	708.18	665.96	634.55	610.64	592.12	577.57	566.03	556.79
34000	3129.27	1709.77	1242.02	1012.13	877.31	789.95	729.64	686.14	653.78	629.15	610.06	595.08	583.18	573.66
35000	3221.31	1760.06	1278.55	1041.90	903.12	813.19	751.10	706.32	673.01	647.65	628.00	612.58	600.33	590.53
36000	3313.35	1810.35	1315.08	1071.67	928.92	836.42	772.55	726.50	692.24	666.15	645.95	630.08	617.49	607.41
37000	3405.39	1860.63	1351.61	1101.43	954.72	859.66	794.01	746.68	711.47	684.66	663.89	647.58	634.64	624.28
38000	3497.42	1910.92	1388.14	1131.20	980.53	882.89	815.47	766.86	730.69	703.16	681.83	665.08	651.79	641.15
39000	3589.46	1961.21	1424.67	1160.97	1006.33	906.12	836.93	787.04	749.92	721.67	699.78	682.59	668.94	658.02
40000	3681.50	2011.49	1461.19	1190.74	1032.13	929.36	858.39	807.22	769.15	740.17	717.72	700.09	686.10	674.90
41000	3773.53	2061.78	1497.72	1220.51	1057.94	952.59	879.85	827.40	788.38	758.67	735.66	717.59	703.25	691.77
42000	3865.57	2112.07	1534.25	1250.28	1083.74	975.83	901.31	847.58	807.61	777.18	753.60	735.09	720.40	708.64
43000	3957.61	2162.36	1570.78	1280.04	1109.54	999.06	922.77	867.76	826.84	795.68	771.55	752.59	737.55	725.51
44000	4049.65	2212.64	1607.31	1309.81	1135.35	1022.29	944.23	887.94	846.07	814.19	789.49	770.10	754.70	742.39
45000	4141.68	2262.93	1643.84	1339.58	1161.15	1045.53	965.69	908.12	865.29	832.69	807.43	787.60	771.86	759.26
46000	4233.72	2313.22	1680.37	1369.35	1186.95	1068.76	987.15	928.30	884.52	851.20	825.38	805.10	789.01	776.13
47000	4325.76	2363.51	1716.90	1399.12	1212.75	1091.99	1008.61	948.48	903.75	869.70	843.32	822.60	806.16	793.00
48000	4417.80	2413.79	1753.43	1428.89	1238.56	1115.23	1030.07	968.66	922.98	888.20	861.26	840.10	823.31	809.87
49000	4509.83	2464.08	1789.96	1458.65	1264.36	1138.46	1051.53	988.84	942.21	906.71	879.20	857.61	840.47	826.75
50000	4601.87	2514.37	1826.49	1488.42	1290.16	1161.70	1072.99	1009.02	961.44	925.21	897.15	875.11	857.62	843.62
55000	5062.06	2765.80	2009.14	1637.26	1419.18	1277.86	1180.29	1109.93	1057.58	1017.73	986.86	962.62	943.38	927.98
60000	5522.24	3017.24	2191.79	1786.11	1548.20	1394.03	1287.59	1210.83	1153.72	1110.25	1076.58	1050.13	1029.14	1012.34
65000	5982.43	3268.68	2374.44	1934.95	1677.21	1510.20	1394.89	1311.73	1249.87	1202.77	1166.29	1137.64	1114.90	1096.70
70000	6442.62	3520.11	2557.09	2083.79	1806.23	1626.37	1502.19	1412.63	1346.01	1295.29	1256.00	1225.15	1200.66	1181.06
75000	6902.80	3771.55	2739.74	2232.63	1935.24	1742.54	1609.48	1513.53	1442.15	1387.82	1345.72	1312.66	1286.42	1265.43
80000	7362.99	4022.98	2922.38	2381.47	2064.26	1858.71	1716.78	1614.44	1538.30	1480.34	1435.43	1400.17	1372.19	1349.79
85000	7823.18	4274.42	3105.03	2530.32	2193.28	1974.88	1824.08	1715.34	1634.44	1572.86	1525.15	1487.68	1457.95	1434.15
90000	8283.36	4525.86	3287.68	2679.16	2322.29	2091.05	1931.38	1816.24	1730.58	1665.38	1614.86	1575.19	1543.71	1518.51
95000	8743.55	4777.29	3470.33	2828.00	2451.31	2207.22	2038.68	1917.14	1826.73	1757.90	1704.58	1662.70	1629.47	1602.87
100000	9203.74	5028.73	3652.98	2976.84	2580.32	2323.39	2145.98	2018.04	1922.87	1850.42	1794.29	1750.21	1715.23	1687.23

MONTHLY PAYMENT
REQUIRED TO AMORTIZE A LOAN

18.750%

TERM AMOUNT	15 Years	16 Years	17 Years	18 Years	19 Years	20 Years	21 Years	22 Years	23 Years	24 Years	25 Years	30 Years	35 Years	40 Years
5	.09	.09	.09	.09	.09	.09	.08	.08	.08	.08	.08	.08	.08	.08
10	.17	.17	.17	.17	.17	.17	.16	.16	.16	.16	.16	.16	.16	.16
15	.25	.25	.25	.25	.25	.25	.24	.24	.24	.24	.24	.24	.24	.24
25	.42	.42	.41	.41	.41	.41	.40	.40	.40	.40	.40	.40	.40	.40
50	.84	.83	.82	.81	.81	.81	.80	.80	.80	.80	.79	.79	.79	.79
75	1.25	1.24	1.23	1.22	1.21	1.21	1.20	1.20	1.19	1.19	1.19	1.18	1.18	1.18
100	1.67	1.65	1.64	1.62	1.61	1.61	1.60	1.59	1.59	1.59	1.58	1.57	1.57	1.57
200	3.33	3.30	3.27	3.24	3.22	3.21	3.21	3.18	3.17	3.17	3.16	3.14	3.13	3.13
300	5.00	4.94	4.90	4.86	4.83	4.81	4.79	4.77	4.76	4.75	4.74	4.71	4.70	4.70
400	6.66	6.59	6.53	6.48	6.44	6.41	6.38	6.36	6.34	6.33	6.32	6.28	6.26	6.26
500	8.33	8.24	8.16	8.10	8.05	8.01	7.98	7.95	7.93	7.91	7.89	7.85	7.83	7.82
600	9.99	9.88	9.79	9.72	9.66	9.61	9.57	9.54	9.51	9.49	9.47	9.42	9.39	9.39
700	11.66	11.53	11.43	11.34	11.27	11.21	11.17	11.13	11.10	11.07	11.05	10.98	10.96	10.95
800	13.32	13.18	13.06	12.96	12.88	12.82	12.76	12.72	12.68	12.65	12.63	12.55	12.52	12.51
900	14.99	14.82	14.69	14.58	14.49	14.42	14.36	14.31	14.27	14.23	14.20	14.12	14.09	14.08
1000	16.65	16.47	16.32	16.20	16.10	16.02	15.95	15.90	15.85	15.81	15.78	15.69	15.65	15.64
2000	33.30	32.93	32.64	32.39	32.19	32.03	31.90	31.79	31.69	31.62	31.56	31.37	31.30	31.27
3000	49.95	49.40	48.95	48.59	48.29	48.04	47.84	47.68	47.54	47.43	47.33	47.06	46.95	46.91
4000	66.59	65.86	65.27	64.78	64.38	64.06	63.79	63.57	63.38	63.23	63.11	62.74	62.60	62.54
5000	83.24	82.32	81.58	80.97	80.48	80.07	79.73	79.46	79.23	79.04	78.88	78.43	78.25	78.18
6000	99.89	98.79	97.90	97.17	96.57	96.08	95.68	95.35	95.07	94.85	94.66	94.11	93.89	93.81
7000	116.53	115.25	114.21	113.36	112.67	112.09	111.62	111.24	110.92	110.65	110.43	109.79	109.54	109.44
8000	133.18	131.72	130.53	129.56	128.76	128.11	127.57	127.13	126.76	126.46	126.21	125.48	125.19	125.08
9000	149.83	148.18	146.84	145.75	144.85	144.12	143.51	143.02	142.61	142.27	141.99	141.16	140.84	140.71
10000	166.47	164.64	163.16	161.94	160.95	160.13	159.46	158.91	158.45	158.07	157.76	156.85	156.49	156.35
11000	183.12	181.11	179.47	178.14	177.04	176.14	175.41	174.80	174.29	173.88	173.54	172.53	172.14	171.98
12000	199.77	197.57	195.79	194.33	193.14	192.16	191.35	190.69	190.14	189.69	189.31	188.21	187.78	187.61
13000	216.41	214.04	212.10	210.52	209.23	208.17	207.30	206.58	206.98	205.49	205.09	203.90	203.43	203.25
14000	233.06	230.50	228.42	226.72	225.33	224.18	223.24	222.47	221.83	221.30	220.86	219.58	219.08	218.88
15000	249.71	246.96	244.73	242.91	241.42	240.19	239.19	238.36	237.67	237.11	236.64	235.27	234.73	234.52
16000	266.35	263.43	261.05	259.11	257.51	256.21	255.13	254.25	253.52	252.91	252.42	250.95	250.38	250.15
17000	283.00	279.89	277.36	275.30	273.61	272.22	271.08	270.14	269.36	268.72	268.19	266.63	266.03	265.79
18000	299.65	296.36	293.68	291.49	289.70	288.23	287.02	286.03	285.21	284.53	283.97	282.32	281.67	281.42
19000	316.29	312.82	309.99	307.69	305.80	304.25	302.97	301.92	301.05	300.33	299.74	298.00	297.32	297.05
20000	332.94	329.28	326.31	323.88	321.89	320.26	318.91	317.81	316.90	316.14	315.52	313.69	312.97	312.69
21000	349.59	345.75	342.62	340.07	337.99	336.27	334.86	333.70	332.74	331.95	331.29	329.37	328.62	328.32
22000	366.23	362.21	358.94	356.27	354.08	352.28	350.81	349.59	348.58	347.75	347.07	345.05	344.27	343.96
23000	382.88	378.68	375.25	372.46	370.17	368.30	366.75	365.48	364.43	363.56	362.84	360.74	359.91	359.59
24000	399.53	395.14	391.57	388.66	386.27	384.31	382.70	381.37	380.27	379.37	378.62	376.42	375.56	375.22
25000	416.17	411.60	407.89	404.85	402.36	400.32	398.64	397.26	396.12	395.18	394.40	392.11	391.21	390.86
26000	432.82	428.07	424.20	421.04	418.46	416.33	414.59	413.15	411.96	410.98	410.17	407.79	406.86	406.49
27000	449.47	444.53	440.52	437.24	434.55	432.35	430.53	429.04	427.81	426.79	425.95	423.48	422.51	422.13
28000	466.11	460.99	456.83	453.43	450.65	448.36	446.48	444.93	443.65	442.60	441.72	439.16	438.16	437.76
29000	482.76	477.46	473.15	469.62	466.74	464.37	462.42	460.82	459.50	458.40	457.50	454.84	453.80	453.40
30000	499.41	493.92	489.46	485.82	482.83	480.38	478.37	476.71	475.34	474.21	473.27	470.53	469.45	469.03
31000	516.05	510.39	505.78	502.01	498.93	496.40	494.32	492.60	491.18	490.02	489.05	486.21	485.10	484.66
32000	532.70	526.85	522.09	518.21	515.02	512.41	510.26	508.49	507.03	505.82	504.83	501.90	500.75	500.30
33000	549.35	543.31	538.41	534.40	531.12	528.42	526.21	524.38	522.87	521.63	520.60	517.58	516.40	515.93
34000	565.99	559.78	554.72	550.59	547.21	544.44	542.15	540.27	538.72	537.44	536.38	533.26	532.05	531.57
35000	582.64	576.24	571.04	566.79	563.31	560.45	558.10	556.16	554.56	553.24	552.15	548.95	547.69	547.20
36000	599.29	592.71	587.35	582.98	579.40	576.46	574.04	572.05	570.41	569.05	567.93	564.63	563.34	562.83
37000	615.93	609.17	603.67	599.17	595.49	592.47	589.99	587.94	586.25	584.86	583.70	580.32	578.99	578.47
38000	632.58	625.63	619.98	615.37	611.59	608.49	605.93	603.83	602.10	600.66	599.48	596.00	594.64	594.10
39000	649.23	642.10	636.30	631.56	627.68	624.50	621.88	619.72	617.94	616.47	615.26	611.68	610.29	609.74
40000	665.87	658.56	652.61	647.76	643.78	640.51	637.82	635.61	633.79	632.28	631.03	627.37	625.94	625.37
41000	682.52	675.03	668.93	663.95	659.87	656.52	653.77	651.50	649.63	648.08	646.81	643.05	641.58	641.01
42000	699.17	691.49	685.24	680.14	675.97	672.54	669.72	667.39	665.47	663.89	662.58	658.74	657.23	656.64
43000	715.81	707.95	701.56	696.34	692.06	688.55	685.66	683.28	681.32	679.70	678.36	674.42	672.88	672.27
44000	732.46	724.42	717.87	712.53	708.15	704.56	701.61	699.17	697.16	695.50	694.13	690.10	688.53	687.91
45000	749.11	740.88	734.19	728.72	724.25	720.57	717.55	715.06	713.01	711.31	709.91	705.79	704.18	703.54
46000	765.75	757.35	750.50	744.92	740.34	736.59	733.50	730.95	728.85	727.12	725.68	721.47	719.82	719.18
47000	782.40	773.81	766.82	761.11	756.44	752.60	749.44	746.84	744.70	742.93	741.46	737.16	735.47	734.81
48000	799.05	790.27	783.14	777.31	772.53	768.61	765.39	762.73	760.54	758.73	757.24	752.84	751.12	750.44
49000	815.69	806.74	799.45	793.50	788.63	784.63	781.33	778.62	776.39	774.54	773.01	768.52	766.77	766.08
50000	832.34	823.20	815.77	809.69	804.72	800.64	797.28	794.51	792.23	790.35	788.79	784.21	782.42	781.71
55000	915.57	905.52	897.34	890.66	885.19	880.70	877.01	873.96	871.45	869.38	867.67	862.63	860.66	859.88
60000	998.81	987.84	978.92	971.63	965.66	960.76	956.73	953.41	950.68	948.43	946.54	941.05	938.90	938.05
65000	1082.04	1070.16	1060.49	1052.60	1046.14	1040.83	1036.46	1032.87	1029.90	1027.45	1025.42	1019.47	1017.14	1016.23
70000	1165.27	1152.48	1142.07	1133.57	1126.61	1120.89	1116.19	1112.32	1109.12	1106.48	1104.30	1097.89	1095.38	1094.40
75000	1248.51	1234.80	1223.65	1214.54	1207.08	1200.95	1195.92	1191.77	1188.34	1185.52	1183.18	1176.31	1173.62	1172.57
80000	1331.74	1317.12	1305.22	1295.51	1287.55	1281.02	1275.64	1271.22	1267.57	1264.55	1262.06	1254.73	1251.87	1250.74
85000	1414.97	1399.44	1386.80	1376.48	1368.02	1361.08	1355.37	1350.67	1346.79	1343.58	1340.94	1333.15	1330.11	1328.91
90000	1498.21	1481.76	1468.37	1457.44	1448.49	1441.14	1435.10	1430.12	1426.01	1422.62	1419.81	1411.57	1408.35	1407.08
95000	1581.44	1564.08	1549.95	1538.41	1528.96	1521.21	1514.83	1509.57	1505.23	1501.65	1498.69	1489.99	1486.59	1485.25
100000	1664.67	1646.40	1631.53	1619.38	1609.44	1601.27	1594.55	1589.02	1584.46	1580.69	1577.57	1568.41	1564.83	1563.42

443

MONTHLY PAYMENT
REQUIRED TO AMORTIZE A LOAN

TERM	1 Year	2 Years	3 Years	4 Years	5 Years	6 Years	7 Years	8 Years	9 Years	10 Years	11 Years	12 Years	13 Years	14 Years
AMOUNT														
5	.47	.26	.19	.15	.13	.12	.11	.11	.10	.10	.09	.09	.09	.09
10	.93	.51	.37	.30	.26	.24	.22	.21	.20	.19	.18	.18	.18	.17
15	1.39	.76	.55	.45	.39	.35	.33	.31	.29	.28	.27	.27	.26	.26
25	2.31	1.26	.92	.75	.65	.59	.54	.51	.49	.47	.45	.44	.43	.43
50	4.61	2.52	1.83	1.49	1.30	1.17	1.08	1.02	.97	.93	.90	.88	.86	.85
75	6.91	3.78	2.75	2.24	1.94	1.75	1.62	1.52	1.45	1.40	1.35	1.32	1.29	1.27
100	9.21	5.04	3.66	2.98	2.59	2.33	2.15	2.03	1.93	1.86	1.80	1.76	1.72	1.70
200	18.42	10.07	7.32	5.96	5.17	4.66	4.30	4.05	3.86	3.71	3.60	3.51	3.44	3.39
300	27.62	15.10	10.97	8.94	7.75	6.98	6.45	6.07	5.78	5.57	5.40	5.27	5.16	5.08
400	36.83	20.13	14.63	11.92	10.34	9.31	8.60	8.09	7.71	7.42	7.20	7.02	6.88	6.77
500	46.04	25.16	18.28	14.90	12.92	11.64	10.75	10.11	9.64	9.27	8.99	8.77	8.60	8.46
600	55.24	30.19	21.94	17.88	15.50	13.96	12.90	12.13	11.56	11.13	10.79	10.53	10.32	10.15
700	64.45	35.22	25.59	20.86	18.09	16.29	15.05	14.15	13.49	12.98	12.59	12.28	12.04	11.84
800	73.65	40.25	29.25	23.84	20.67	18.61	17.20	16.17	15.41	14.83	14.39	14.03	13.75	13.53
900	82.86	45.29	32.90	26.82	23.25	20.94	19.35	18.19	17.34	16.69	16.18	15.79	15.47	15.22
1000	92.07	50.32	36.56	29.80	25.84	23.27	21.49	20.22	19.27	18.54	17.98	17.54	17.19	16.91
2000	184.13	100.63	73.11	59.59	51.67	46.53	42.98	40.43	38.53	37.08	35.96	35.08	34.38	33.82
3000	276.19	150.94	109.67	89.39	77.50	69.79	64.47	60.64	57.79	55.62	53.93	52.61	51.57	50.73
4000	368.25	201.25	146.22	119.18	103.33	93.05	85.96	80.85	77.05	74.15	71.91	70.15	68.75	67.64
5000	460.31	251.56	182.78	148.98	129.16	116.32	107.45	101.06	96.31	92.69	89.89	87.69	85.94	84.55
6000	552.37	301.87	219.33	178.77	154.99	139.58	128.94	121.27	115.57	111.23	107.86	105.22	103.13	101.45
7000	644.43	352.19	255.89	208.57	180.82	162.84	150.43	141.48	134.83	129.76	125.84	122.76	120.32	118.36
8000	736.49	402.50	292.44	238.36	206.65	186.10	171.92	161.69	154.09	148.30	143.82	140.30	137.50	135.27
9000	828.56	452.81	329.00	268.16	232.48	209.37	193.41	181.90	173.35	166.84	161.79	157.83	154.69	152.18
10000	920.62	503.12	365.55	297.95	258.31	232.63	214.90	202.12	192.61	185.37	179.77	175.37	171.88	169.09
11000	1012.68	553.43	402.11	327.75	284.14	255.89	236.39	222.33	211.87	203.91	197.74	192.90	189.07	185.99
12000	1104.74	603.74	438.66	357.54	309.97	279.15	257.88	242.54	231.13	222.45	215.72	210.44	206.25	202.90
13000	1196.80	654.05	475.22	387.34	335.80	302.42	279.37	262.75	250.39	240.98	233.70	227.98	223.44	219.81
14000	1288.86	704.37	511.77	417.13	361.63	325.68	300.86	282.96	269.65	259.52	251.67	245.51	240.63	236.72
15000	1380.92	754.68	548.33	446.93	387.46	348.94	322.35	303.17	288.91	278.06	269.65	263.05	257.81	253.63
16000	1472.98	804.99	584.88	476.72	413.30	372.20	343.83	323.38	308.17	296.59	287.63	280.59	275.00	270.53
17000	1565.04	855.30	621.44	506.51	439.13	395.47	365.32	343.59	327.43	315.13	305.60	298.12	292.19	287.44
18000	1657.11	905.61	657.99	536.31	464.96	418.73	386.81	363.80	346.69	333.67	323.58	315.66	309.38	304.35
19000	1749.17	955.92	694.55	566.10	490.79	441.99	408.30	384.01	365.95	352.20	341.55	333.20	326.56	321.26
20000	1841.23	1006.24	731.10	595.90	516.62	465.25	429.79	404.23	385.21	370.74	359.53	350.73	343.75	338.17
21000	1933.29	1056.55	767.66	625.69	542.45	488.51	451.28	424.44	404.47	389.28	377.51	368.27	360.94	355.07
22000	2025.35	1106.86	804.21	655.49	568.28	511.78	472.77	444.65	423.73	407.81	395.48	385.80	378.13	371.98
23000	2117.41	1157.17	840.77	685.28	594.11	535.04	494.26	464.86	442.99	426.35	413.46	403.34	395.31	388.89
24000	2209.47	1207.48	877.32	715.08	619.94	558.30	515.75	485.07	462.25	444.89	431.44	420.88	412.50	405.80
25000	2301.53	1257.79	913.88	744.87	645.77	581.56	537.24	505.28	481.51	463.42	449.41	438.41	429.69	422.71
26000	2393.60	1308.10	950.43	774.67	671.60	604.83	558.73	525.49	500.77	481.96	467.39	455.95	446.87	439.61
27000	2485.66	1358.42	986.99	804.46	697.43	628.09	580.22	545.70	520.03	500.50	485.36	473.49	464.06	456.52
28000	2577.72	1408.73	1023.54	834.26	723.26	651.35	601.71	565.91	539.29	519.03	503.34	491.02	481.25	473.43
29000	2669.78	1459.04	1060.10	864.05	749.09	674.61	623.20	586.12	558.55	537.57	521.32	508.56	498.44	490.34
30000	2761.84	1509.35	1096.65	893.85	774.92	697.88	644.69	606.34	577.81	556.11	539.29	526.10	515.62	507.25
31000	2853.90	1559.66	1133.21	923.64	800.75	721.14	666.17	626.55	597.07	574.64	557.27	543.63	532.81	524.15
32000	2945.96	1609.97	1169.76	953.43	826.59	744.40	687.66	646.76	616.33	593.18	575.25	561.17	550.00	541.06
33000	3038.02	1660.28	1206.32	983.23	852.42	767.66	709.15	666.97	635.59	611.72	593.22	578.70	567.19	557.97
34000	3130.08	1710.60	1242.87	1013.02	878.25	790.93	730.64	687.18	654.86	630.25	611.20	596.24	584.37	574.88
35000	3222.15	1760.91	1279.43	1042.82	904.08	814.19	752.13	707.39	674.12	648.79	629.18	613.78	601.56	591.79
36000	3314.21	1811.22	1315.98	1072.61	929.91	837.45	773.62	727.60	693.38	667.33	647.15	631.31	618.75	608.69
37000	3406.27	1861.53	1352.54	1102.41	955.74	860.71	795.11	747.81	712.64	685.86	665.13	648.85	635.93	625.60
38000	3498.33	1911.84	1389.09	1132.20	981.57	883.97	816.60	768.02	731.90	704.40	683.10	666.39	653.12	642.51
39000	3590.39	1962.15	1425.65	1162.00	1007.40	907.24	838.09	788.24	751.16	722.94	701.08	683.92	670.31	659.42
40000	3682.45	2012.47	1462.20	1191.79	1033.23	930.50	859.58	808.45	770.42	741.47	719.06	701.46	687.50	676.33
41000	3774.51	2062.78	1498.76	1221.59	1059.06	953.76	881.07	828.66	789.68	760.01	737.03	719.00	704.68	693.23
42000	3866.57	2113.09	1535.31	1251.38	1084.89	977.02	902.56	848.87	808.94	778.55	755.01	736.53	721.87	710.14
43000	3958.63	2163.40	1571.87	1281.18	1110.72	1000.29	924.05	869.08	828.20	797.08	772.99	754.07	739.06	727.05
44000	4050.70	2213.71	1608.42	1310.97	1136.55	1023.55	945.54	889.29	847.46	815.62	790.96	771.60	756.25	743.96
45000	4142.76	2264.02	1644.98	1340.77	1162.38	1046.81	967.03	909.50	866.72	834.16	808.94	789.14	773.43	760.87
46000	4234.82	2314.33	1681.53	1370.56	1188.21	1070.07	988.51	929.71	885.98	852.69	826.91	806.68	790.62	777.77
47000	4326.88	2364.65	1718.09	1400.36	1214.04	1093.34	1010.00	949.92	905.24	871.23	844.89	824.21	807.81	794.68
48000	4418.94	2414.96	1754.64	1430.15	1239.88	1116.60	1031.49	970.13	924.50	889.77	862.87	841.75	824.99	811.59
49000	4511.00	2465.27	1791.20	1459.94	1265.71	1139.86	1052.98	990.35	943.76	908.30	880.84	859.29	842.18	828.50
50000	4603.06	2515.58	1827.75	1489.74	1291.54	1163.12	1074.47	1010.56	963.02	926.84	898.82	876.82	859.37	845.41
55000	5063.37	2767.14	2010.53	1638.71	1420.69	1279.43	1181.92	1111.61	1059.32	1019.52	988.70	964.50	945.31	929.95
60000	5523.67	3018.70	2193.30	1787.69	1549.84	1395.75	1289.37	1212.67	1155.62	1112.21	1078.58	1052.19	1031.24	1014.49
65000	5983.98	3270.25	2376.08	1936.66	1679.00	1512.06	1396.81	1313.72	1251.92	1204.89	1168.46	1139.87	1117.18	1099.03
70000	6444.29	3521.81	2558.85	2085.63	1808.15	1628.37	1504.26	1414.78	1348.23	1297.57	1258.35	1227.55	1203.11	1183.57
75000	6904.59	3773.37	2741.63	2234.61	1937.30	1744.68	1611.71	1515.83	1444.53	1390.26	1348.23	1315.23	1289.04	1268.11
80000	7364.90	4024.93	2924.40	2383.58	2066.46	1860.99	1719.15	1616.89	1540.83	1482.94	1438.11	1402.91	1374.99	1352.65
85000	7825.20	4276.48	3107.18	2532.55	2195.61	1977.31	1826.60	1717.94	1637.13	1575.63	1527.99	1490.59	1460.92	1437.19
90000	8285.51	4528.04	3289.95	2681.53	2324.76	2093.62	1934.05	1819.00	1733.43	1668.31	1617.87	1578.28	1546.86	1521.73
95000	8745.82	4779.60	3472.73	2830.50	2453.91	2209.93	2041.49	1920.05	1829.73	1760.99	1707.75	1665.96	1632.80	1606.27
100000	9206.12	5031.16	3655.50	2979.47	2583.07	2326.24	2148.94	2021.11	1926.03	1853.68	1797.63	1753.64	1718.73	1690.81

TERM	15 Years	16 Years	17 Years	18 Years	19 Years	20 Years	21 Years	22 Years	23 Years	24 Years	25 Years	30 Years	35 Years	40 Years
AMOUNT														
5	.09	.09	.09	.09	.09	.09	.08	.08	.08	.08	.08	.08	.08	.08
10	.17	.17	.17	.17	.17	.17	.16	.16	.16	.16	.16	.16	.16	.16
15	.26	.25	.25	.25	.25	.25	.24	.24	.24	.24	.24	.24	.24	.24
25	.42	.42	.41	.41	.41	.41	.40	.40	.40	.40	.40	.40	.40	.40
50	.84	.83	.82	.82	.81	.81	.80	.80	.80	.80	.80	.79	.79	.79
75	1.26	1.24	1.23	1.22	1.21	1.21	1.20	1.20	1.20	1.19	1.19	1.18	1.18	1.18
100	1.67	1.66	1.64	1.63	1.62	1.61	1.60	1.60	1.59	1.59	1.59	1.58	1.57	1.57
200	3.34	3.31	3.28	3.25	3.23	3.22	3.20	3.19	3.18	3.17	3.17	3.15	3.14	3.14
300	5.01	4.96	4.91	4.87	4.84	4.82	4.80	4.78	4.77	4.76	4.75	4.72	4.71	4.71
400	6.68	6.61	6.55	6.50	6.46	6.43	6.40	6.38	6.36	6.34	6.33	6.30	6.28	6.28
500	8.35	8.26	8.18	8.12	8.07	8.03	8.00	7.97	7.95	7.93	7.91	7.87	7.85	7.84
600	10.01	9.91	9.82	9.74	9.68	9.64	9.60	9.56	9.54	9.51	9.49	9.44	9.42	9.41
700	11.68	11.56	11.45	11.37	11.30	11.24	11.19	11.16	11.12	11.10	11.08	11.01	10.99	10.98
800	13.35	13.21	13.09	12.99	12.91	12.85	12.79	12.75	12.71	12.68	12.66	12.59	12.56	12.55
900	15.02	14.86	14.72	14.61	14.52	14.45	14.39	14.34	14.30	14.27	14.24	14.16	14.13	14.11
1000	16.69	16.51	16.36	16.24	16.14	16.06	15.99	15.93	15.89	15.85	15.82	15.73	15.69	15.68
2000	33.37	33.01	32.71	32.47	32.27	32.11	31.97	31.86	31.77	31.70	31.64	31.46	31.38	31.36
3000	50.05	49.51	49.06	48.70	48.40	48.16	47.96	47.79	47.66	47.55	47.45	47.18	47.07	47.03
4000	66.74	66.01	65.42	64.93	64.54	64.21	63.94	63.72	63.54	63.39	63.27	62.91	62.76	62.71
5000	83.42	82.51	81.77	81.16	80.67	80.26	79.93	79.65	79.43	79.24	79.08	78.63	78.45	78.38
6000	100.10	99.01	98.12	97.40	96.80	96.31	95.91	95.58	95.31	95.09	94.90	94.36	94.14	94.06
7000	116.79	115.51	114.47	113.63	112.93	112.37	111.90	111.51	111.19	110.93	110.72	110.08	109.83	109.73
8000	133.47	132.01	130.83	129.86	129.07	128.42	127.88	127.44	127.08	126.78	126.53	125.81	125.52	125.41
9000	150.15	148.51	147.18	146.09	145.20	144.47	143.87	143.37	142.96	142.63	142.35	141.53	141.21	141.09
10000	166.84	165.01	163.53	162.32	161.33	160.52	159.85	159.30	158.85	158.47	158.16	157.26	156.90	156.76
11000	183.52	181.51	179.88	178.55	177.46	176.57	175.84	175.23	174.73	174.32	173.98	172.98	172.59	172.44
12000	200.20	198.02	196.24	194.79	193.60	192.62	191.82	191.16	190.62	190.17	189.80	188.71	188.28	188.11
13000	216.88	214.52	212.59	211.02	209.73	208.67	207.81	207.09	206.50	206.01	205.61	204.43	203.97	203.79
14000	233.57	231.02	228.94	227.25	225.86	224.73	223.02	223.02	222.38	221.86	221.43	220.16	219.66	219.46
15000	250.25	247.52	245.30	243.48	242.00	240.78	239.77	238.95	238.27	237.71	237.24	235.88	235.35	235.14
16000	266.93	264.02	261.65	259.71	258.13	256.83	255.76	254.88	254.15	253.55	253.06	251.61	251.04	250.82
17000	283.62	280.52	278.00	275.94	274.26	272.88	271.74	270.81	270.04	269.40	268.87	267.33	266.73	266.49
18000	300.30	297.02	294.35	292.18	290.39	288.93	287.73	286.74	285.92	285.25	284.69	283.06	282.42	282.17
19000	316.98	313.52	310.71	308.41	306.53	304.98	303.71	302.67	301.81	301.09	300.51	298.78	298.11	297.84
20000	333.67	330.02	327.06	324.64	322.66	321.03	319.70	318.60	317.69	316.94	316.32	314.51	313.80	313.52
21000	350.35	346.52	343.41	340.87	338.79	337.09	335.68	334.53	333.57	332.79	332.14	330.23	329.49	329.19
22000	367.03	363.02	359.76	357.10	354.92	353.14	351.67	350.46	349.46	348.63	347.95	345.96	345.18	344.87
23000	383.72	379.53	376.12	373.34	371.06	369.19	367.65	366.39	365.34	364.48	363.77	361.68	360.87	360.55
24000	400.40	396.03	392.47	389.57	387.19	385.24	383.64	382.32	381.23	380.33	379.59	377.41	376.55	376.22
25000	417.08	412.53	408.82	405.80	403.32	401.29	399.62	398.25	397.11	396.18	395.40	393.13	392.24	391.90
26000	433.76	429.03	425.18	422.03	419.46	417.34	415.61	414.18	413.00	412.02	411.22	408.86	407.93	407.57
27000	450.45	445.53	441.53	438.26	435.59	433.39	431.59	430.10	428.88	427.87	427.03	424.58	423.62	423.25
28000	467.13	462.03	457.88	454.49	451.72	449.45	447.58	446.03	444.76	443.72	442.85	440.31	439.31	438.92
29000	483.81	478.53	474.23	470.73	467.85	465.50	463.56	461.96	460.65	459.56	458.66	456.03	455.00	454.60
30000	500.50	495.03	490.59	486.96	483.99	481.55	479.54	477.89	476.53	475.41	474.48	471.76	470.69	470.28
31000	517.18	511.53	506.94	503.19	500.12	497.60	495.53	493.82	492.42	491.26	490.30	487.48	486.38	485.95
32000	533.86	528.03	523.29	519.42	516.25	513.65	511.51	509.75	508.30	507.10	506.11	503.21	502.07	501.63
33000	550.55	544.53	539.64	535.65	532.38	529.70	527.50	525.68	524.19	522.95	521.93	518.93	517.76	517.30
34000	567.23	561.03	556.00	551.88	548.52	545.75	543.48	541.61	540.07	538.80	537.74	534.66	533.45	532.98
35000	583.91	577.54	572.35	568.12	564.65	561.81	559.47	557.54	555.95	554.64	553.56	550.38	549.14	548.65
36000	600.59	594.04	588.70	584.35	580.78	577.86	575.45	573.47	571.84	570.49	569.38	566.11	564.83	564.33
37000	617.28	610.54	605.05	600.58	596.92	593.91	591.44	589.40	587.72	586.34	585.19	581.83	580.52	580.00
38000	633.96	627.04	621.41	616.81	613.05	609.96	607.42	605.33	603.61	602.18	601.01	597.56	596.21	595.68
39000	650.64	643.54	637.76	633.04	629.18	626.01	623.41	621.26	619.49	618.03	616.82	613.28	611.90	611.36
40000	667.33	660.04	654.11	649.27	645.31	642.06	639.39	637.19	635.38	633.88	632.64	629.01	627.59	627.03
41000	684.01	676.54	670.47	665.51	661.45	658.11	655.38	653.12	651.26	649.72	648.46	644.73	643.28	642.71
42000	700.69	693.04	686.82	681.74	677.58	674.17	671.36	669.05	667.14	665.57	664.27	660.46	658.97	658.38
43000	717.38	709.54	703.17	697.97	693.71	690.22	687.34	684.98	683.03	681.42	680.09	676.18	674.66	674.06
44000	734.06	726.04	719.52	714.20	709.84	706.27	703.33	700.91	698.91	697.26	695.90	691.91	690.35	689.73
45000	750.74	742.54	735.88	730.43	725.98	722.32	719.31	716.84	714.80	713.11	711.72	707.63	706.04	705.41
46000	767.43	759.05	752.23	746.67	742.11	738.37	735.30	732.77	730.68	728.96	727.53	723.36	721.73	721.09
47000	784.11	775.55	768.58	762.90	758.24	754.42	751.28	748.70	746.56	744.80	743.35	739.08	737.42	736.76
48000	800.79	792.05	784.93	779.13	774.38	770.48	767.27	764.63	762.45	760.65	759.17	754.81	753.10	752.44
49000	817.47	808.55	801.29	795.36	790.51	786.53	783.25	780.56	778.33	776.50	774.98	770.53	768.79	768.11
50000	834.16	825.05	817.64	811.59	806.64	802.58	799.24	796.49	794.22	792.35	790.80	786.26	784.48	783.79
55000	917.57	907.55	899.40	892.75	887.30	882.84	879.16	876.13	873.64	871.58	869.88	864.88	862.93	862.17
60000	1000.99	990.06	981.17	973.91	967.97	963.09	959.08	955.78	953.06	950.81	948.96	943.51	941.38	940.55
65000	1084.40	1072.56	1062.93	1055.07	1048.63	1043.35	1039.01	1035.43	1032.48	1030.05	1028.04	1022.13	1019.83	1018.92
70000	1167.82	1155.07	1144.69	1136.23	1129.30	1123.61	1118.93	1115.08	1111.90	1109.28	1107.11	1100.76	1098.28	1097.30
75000	1251.23	1237.57	1226.46	1217.39	1209.96	1203.86	1198.85	1194.73	1191.32	1188.52	1186.19	1179.38	1176.72	1175.68
80000	1334.65	1320.08	1308.22	1298.54	1290.62	1284.12	1278.78	1274.38	1270.75	1267.75	1265.27	1258.01	1255.17	1254.06
85000	1418.06	1402.58	1389.98	1379.70	1371.29	1364.38	1358.70	1354.02	1350.17	1346.98	1344.35	1336.63	1333.62	1332.44
90000	1501.48	1485.08	1471.75	1460.86	1451.95	1444.64	1438.62	1433.67	1429.59	1426.22	1423.43	1415.26	1412.07	1410.82
95000	1584.90	1567.59	1553.51	1542.02	1532.61	1524.89	1518.55	1513.32	1509.01	1505.45	1502.51	1493.88	1490.52	1489.19
100000	1668.31	1650.09	1635.27	1623.18	1613.28	1605.15	1598.47	1592.97	1588.43	1584.69	1581.59	1572.51	1568.96	1567.57

MONTHLY PAYMENT
REQUIRED TO AMORTIZE A LOAN

TERM	1 Year	2 Years	3 Years	4 Years	5 Years	6 Years	7 Years	8 Years	9 Years	10 Years	11 Years	12 Years	13 Years	14 Years
AMOUNT														
5	.47	.26	.19	.15	.13	.12	.11	.11	.10	.10	.10	.09	.09	.09
10	.93	.51	.37	.30	.26	.24	.22	.21	.20	.19	.19	.18	.18	.17
15	1.39	.76	.55	.45	.39	.35	.33	.31	.29	.28	.28	.27	.26	.26
25	2.31	1.26	.92	.75	.65	.59	.54	.51	.49	.47	.46	.44	.44	.43
50	4.61	2.52	1.83	1.50	1.30	1.17	1.08	1.02	.97	.93	.91	.88	.87	.85
75	6.91	3.78	2.75	2.24	1.95	1.75	1.62	1.52	1.45	1.40	1.36	1.32	1.30	1.28
100	9.21	5.04	3.66	2.99	2.59	2.34	2.16	2.03	1.94	1.86	1.81	1.76	1.73	1.70
200	18.42	10.07	7.32	5.97	5.18	4.67	4.31	4.06	3.87	3.72	3.61	3.52	3.45	3.40
300	27.63	15.11	10.98	8.96	7.77	7.00	6.47	6.08	5.80	5.58	5.41	5.28	5.18	5.09
400	36.84	20.14	14.64	11.94	10.36	9.33	8.62	8.11	7.73	7.44	7.22	7.04	6.90	6.79
500	46.05	25.18	18.30	14.92	12.94	11.66	10.77	10.13	9.66	9.30	9.02	8.80	8.62	8.49
600	55.26	30.21	21.96	17.91	15.53	13.99	12.93	12.16	11.59	11.16	10.82	10.56	10.35	10.18
700	64.47	35.25	25.62	20.89	18.12	16.32	15.08	14.18	13.52	13.01	12.62	12.32	12.07	11.88
800	73.68	40.28	29.28	23.87	20.70	18.65	17.23	16.21	15.45	14.87	14.43	14.08	13.80	13.57
900	82.89	45.32	32.94	26.86	23.29	20.98	19.39	18.24	17.38	16.73	16.23	15.83	15.52	15.27
1000	92.10	50.35	36.60	29.84	25.88	23.31	21.54	20.26	19.31	18.59	18.03	17.59	17.24	16.97
2000	184.20	100.70	73.19	59.67	51.75	46.62	43.07	40.52	38.62	37.18	36.06	35.18	34.48	33.93
3000	276.30	151.05	109.78	89.51	77.62	69.92	64.61	60.78	57.93	55.76	54.08	52.77	51.72	50.89
4000	368.39	201.40	146.38	119.34	103.49	93.23	86.14	81.03	77.24	74.35	72.11	70.36	68.96	67.85
5000	460.49	251.74	182.97	149.18	129.36	116.53	107.67	101.29	96.54	92.93	90.14	87.94	86.20	84.81
6000	552.59	302.09	219.56	179.01	155.24	139.84	129.21	121.55	115.85	111.52	108.16	105.53	103.44	101.77
7000	644.68	352.44	256.15	208.84	181.11	163.14	150.74	141.80	135.16	130.10	126.19	123.12	120.68	118.74
8000	736.78	402.79	292.75	238.68	206.98	186.45	172.28	162.06	154.47	148.69	144.22	140.71	137.92	135.70
9000	828.88	453.14	329.34	268.51	232.85	209.75	193.81	182.32	173.78	167.28	162.24	158.30	155.15	152.66
10000	920.97	503.48	365.93	298.35	258.72	233.06	215.34	202.58	193.08	185.86	180.27	175.88	172.40	169.62
11000	1013.07	553.83	402.53	328.18	284.60	256.36	236.88	222.83	212.39	204.45	198.30	193.47	189.64	186.58
12000	1105.17	604.18	439.12	358.02	310.47	279.67	258.41	243.09	231.70	223.03	216.32	211.06	206.88	203.54
13000	1197.27	654.53	475.71	387.85	336.34	302.97	279.94	263.35	251.01	241.62	234.35	228.65	224.12	220.51
14000	1289.36	704.88	512.30	417.68	362.21	326.28	301.48	283.60	270.31	260.20	252.38	246.23	241.36	237.47
15000	1381.46	755.22	548.90	447.52	388.08	349.58	323.01	303.86	289.62	278.79	270.40	263.82	258.60	254.43
16000	1473.56	805.57	585.49	477.35	413.95	372.89	344.55	324.12	308.93	297.37	288.43	281.41	275.84	271.39
17000	1565.65	855.92	622.08	507.19	439.83	396.19	366.08	344.37	328.24	315.96	306.46	299.00	293.08	288.35
18000	1657.75	906.27	658.68	537.02	465.70	419.50	387.61	364.63	347.55	334.55	324.48	316.59	310.32	305.31
19000	1749.85	956.62	695.27	566.85	491.57	442.80	409.15	384.89	366.85	353.13	342.51	334.17	327.56	322.28
20000	1841.94	1006.96	731.86	596.69	517.44	466.11	430.68	405.15	386.16	371.72	360.54	351.76	344.80	339.24
21000	1934.04	1057.31	768.45	626.52	543.31	489.41	452.21	425.40	405.47	390.30	378.56	369.35	362.04	356.20
22000	2026.14	1107.66	805.05	656.36	569.19	512.72	473.75	445.66	424.78	408.89	396.59	386.94	379.28	373.16
23000	2118.23	1158.01	841.64	686.19	595.06	536.02	495.28	465.92	444.08	427.47	414.61	404.52	396.52	390.12
24000	2210.33	1208.35	878.23	716.03	620.93	559.33	516.82	486.17	463.39	446.06	432.64	422.11	413.76	407.08
25000	2302.43	1258.70	914.83	745.86	646.80	582.64	538.35	506.43	482.70	464.65	450.67	439.70	431.00	424.05
26000	2394.53	1309.05	951.42	775.69	672.67	605.94	559.88	526.69	502.01	483.23	468.69	457.29	448.24	441.01
27000	2486.62	1359.40	988.01	805.53	698.54	629.25	581.42	546.95	521.32	501.82	486.72	474.88	465.48	457.97
28000	2578.72	1409.75	1024.60	835.36	724.42	652.55	602.95	567.20	540.62	520.40	504.75	492.46	482.72	474.93
29000	2670.82	1460.09	1061.20	865.20	750.29	675.86	624.49	587.46	559.93	538.99	522.77	510.05	499.96	491.89
30000	2762.91	1510.44	1097.79	895.03	776.16	699.16	646.02	607.72	579.24	557.57	540.80	527.64	517.20	508.85
31000	2855.01	1560.79	1134.38	924.87	802.03	722.47	667.55	627.97	598.55	576.16	558.83	545.23	534.44	525.82
32000	2947.11	1611.14	1170.98	954.70	827.90	745.77	689.09	648.23	617.85	594.74	576.85	562.81	551.68	542.78
33000	3039.20	1661.49	1207.57	984.53	853.78	769.08	710.62	668.49	637.16	613.33	594.88	580.40	568.92	559.74
34000	3131.30	1711.83	1244.16	1014.37	879.65	792.38	732.15	688.74	656.47	631.92	612.91	597.99	586.16	576.70
35000	3223.40	1762.18	1280.75	1044.20	905.52	815.69	753.69	709.00	675.78	650.50	630.93	615.58	603.40	593.66
36000	3315.49	1812.53	1317.35	1074.04	931.39	838.99	775.22	729.26	695.09	669.09	648.96	633.17	620.64	610.62
37000	3407.59	1862.88	1353.94	1103.87	957.26	862.30	796.76	749.52	714.39	687.67	666.99	650.75	637.88	627.59
38000	3499.69	1913.23	1390.53	1133.70	983.13	885.60	818.29	769.77	733.70	706.26	685.01	668.34	655.12	644.55
39000	3591.79	1963.57	1427.13	1163.54	1009.01	908.91	839.82	790.03	753.01	724.84	703.04	685.93	672.36	661.51
40000	3683.88	2013.92	1463.72	1193.37	1034.88	932.21	861.36	810.29	772.32	743.43	721.07	703.52	689.60	678.47
41000	3775.98	2064.27	1500.31	1223.21	1060.75	955.52	882.89	830.54	791.62	762.02	739.09	721.10	706.84	695.43
42000	3868.08	2114.62	1536.90	1253.04	1086.62	978.82	904.42	850.80	810.93	780.60	757.12	738.69	724.07	712.39
43000	3960.17	2164.97	1573.50	1282.88	1112.49	1002.13	925.96	871.06	830.24	799.19	775.14	756.28	741.32	729.36
44000	4052.27	2215.31	1610.09	1312.71	1138.37	1025.43	947.49	891.32	849.55	817.77	793.17	773.87	758.56	746.32
45000	4144.37	2265.66	1646.68	1342.54	1164.24	1048.74	969.03	911.57	868.86	836.36	811.20	791.46	775.80	763.28
46000	4236.46	2316.01	1683.28	1372.38	1190.11	1072.04	990.56	931.83	888.16	854.94	829.22	809.04	793.04	780.24
47000	4328.56	2366.36	1719.87	1402.21	1215.98	1095.35	1012.09	952.09	907.47	873.53	847.25	826.63	810.28	797.20
48000	4420.66	2416.70	1756.46	1432.05	1241.85	1118.66	1033.63	972.34	926.78	892.11	865.28	844.22	827.52	814.16
49000	4512.75	2467.05	1793.05	1461.88	1267.72	1141.96	1055.16	992.60	946.09	910.70	883.30	861.81	844.76	831.13
50000	4604.85	2517.40	1829.65	1491.71	1293.60	1165.27	1076.70	1012.86	965.39	929.29	901.33	879.39	862.00	848.09
55000	5065.34	2769.14	2012.61	1640.89	1422.96	1281.79	1184.36	1114.14	1061.93	1022.21	991.46	967.33	948.20	932.90
60000	5525.82	3020.88	2195.58	1790.06	1552.31	1398.32	1292.03	1215.43	1158.47	1115.14	1081.60	1055.27	1034.40	1017.70
65000	5986.31	3272.62	2378.54	1939.23	1681.67	1514.84	1399.70	1316.71	1255.01	1208.07	1171.73	1143.21	1120.60	1102.51
70000	6446.79	3524.36	2561.50	2088.40	1811.03	1631.37	1507.37	1418.00	1351.55	1301.00	1261.86	1231.15	1206.80	1187.32
75000	6907.27	3776.10	2744.47	2237.57	1940.39	1747.90	1615.04	1519.28	1448.09	1393.93	1351.99	1319.09	1292.99	1272.13
80000	7367.76	4027.84	2927.43	2386.74	2069.75	1864.42	1722.71	1620.57	1544.63	1486.85	1442.13	1407.03	1379.19	1356.94
85000	7828.24	4279.58	3110.40	2535.91	2199.11	1980.95	1830.38	1721.85	1641.17	1579.78	1532.26	1494.97	1465.39	1441.74
90000	8288.73	4531.32	3293.36	2685.08	2328.47	2097.47	1938.05	1823.14	1737.71	1672.71	1622.39	1582.91	1551.59	1526.55
95000	8749.21	4783.06	3476.33	2834.25	2457.83	2214.00	2045.72	1924.43	1834.25	1765.64	1712.52	1670.84	1637.79	1611.36
100000	9209.70	5034.80	3659.29	2983.42	2587.19	2330.53	2153.39	2025.71	1930.78	1858.57	1802.66	1758.78	1723.99	1696.17

MONTHLY PAYMENT
REQUIRED TO AMORTIZE A LOAN

18.875%

TERM AMOUNT	15 Years	16 Years	17 Years	18 Years	19 Years	20 Years	21 Years	22 Years	23 Years	24 Years	25 Years	30 Years	35 Years	40 Years
5	.09	.09	.09	.09	.09	.09	.09	.08	.08	.08	.08	.08	.08	.08
10	.17	.17	.17	.17	.17	.17	.17	.16	.16	.16	.16	.16	.16	.16
15	.26	.25	.25	.25	.25	.25	.25	.24	.24	.24	.24	.24	.24	.24
25	.42	.42	.42	.41	.41	.41	.41	.40	.40	.40	.40	.40	.40	.40
50	.84	.83	.83	.82	.81	.81	.81	.80	.80	.80	.80	.79	.79	.79
75	1.26	1.25	1.24	1.23	1.22	1.21	1.21	1.20	1.20	1.20	1.20	1.19	1.19	1.19
100	1.68	1.66	1.65	1.63	1.62	1.62	1.61	1.60	1.60	1.60	1.59	1.58	1.58	1.58
200	3.35	3.32	3.29	3.26	3.24	3.23	3.21	3.20	3.19	3.19	3.18	3.16	3.16	3.15
300	5.03	4.97	4.93	4.89	4.86	4.84	4.82	4.80	4.79	4.78	4.77	4.74	4.73	4.73
400	6.70	6.63	6.57	6.52	6.48	6.45	6.42	6.40	6.38	6.37	6.36	6.32	6.31	6.30
500	8.37	8.28	8.21	8.15	8.10	8.06	8.03	8.00	7.98	7.96	7.94	7.90	7.88	7.87
600	10.05	9.94	9.85	9.78	9.72	9.67	9.63	9.60	9.57	9.55	9.53	9.48	9.46	9.45
700	11.72	11.59	11.49	11.41	11.34	11.28	11.24	11.20	11.17	11.14	11.12	11.06	11.03	11.02
800	13.40	13.25	13.13	13.04	12.96	12.89	12.84	12.80	12.76	12.73	12.71	12.63	12.61	12.60
900	15.07	14.91	14.77	14.66	14.58	14.50	14.44	14.39	14.35	14.32	14.29	14.21	14.18	14.17
1000	16.74	16.56	16.41	16.29	16.20	16.11	16.05	15.99	15.95	15.91	15.88	15.79	15.76	15.74
2000	33.48	33.12	32.82	32.58	32.39	32.22	32.09	31.98	31.89	31.82	31.76	31.58	31.51	31.48
3000	50.22	49.67	49.23	48.87	48.58	48.33	48.14	47.97	47.84	47.73	47.63	47.36	47.26	47.22
4000	66.96	66.23	65.64	65.16	64.77	64.44	64.18	63.96	63.78	63.63	63.51	63.15	63.01	62.96
5000	83.69	82.79	82.05	81.45	80.96	80.55	80.22	79.95	79.72	79.54	79.39	78.94	78.76	78.69
6000	100.43	99.34	98.46	97.74	97.15	96.66	96.27	95.94	95.67	95.45	95.26	94.72	94.51	94.43
7000	117.17	115.90	114.87	114.03	113.34	112.77	112.32	111.93	111.61	111.35	111.14	110.51	110.27	110.17
8000	133.91	132.46	131.28	130.31	129.53	128.88	128.35	127.92	127.56	127.26	127.01	126.30	126.02	125.91
9000	150.64	149.01	147.69	146.60	145.72	144.99	144.40	143.90	143.50	143.17	142.89	142.08	141.77	141.65
10000	167.38	165.57	164.09	162.89	161.91	161.10	160.44	159.89	159.44	159.07	158.77	157.87	157.52	157.38
11000	184.12	182.12	180.50	179.18	178.10	177.21	176.48	175.88	175.39	174.98	174.64	173.66	173.27	173.12
12000	200.86	198.68	196.91	195.47	194.29	193.32	192.53	191.87	191.33	190.89	190.52	189.44	189.02	188.86
13000	217.59	215.24	213.32	211.76	210.48	209.43	208.57	207.86	207.28	206.79	206.40	205.23	204.78	204.60
14000	234.33	231.79	229.73	228.05	226.67	225.54	224.61	223.85	223.22	222.70	222.27	221.02	220.53	220.34
15000	251.07	248.35	246.14	244.34	242.86	241.65	240.66	239.84	239.16	238.61	238.15	236.80	236.28	236.07
16000	267.81	264.91	262.55	260.62	259.05	257.76	256.70	255.83	255.11	254.51	254.02	252.59	252.03	251.81
17000	284.55	281.46	278.96	276.91	275.24	273.87	272.74	271.82	271.05	270.42	269.90	268.38	267.78	267.55
18000	301.28	298.02	295.37	293.20	291.43	289.90	288.79	287.80	287.00	286.33	285.78	284.16	283.53	283.29
19000	318.02	314.58	311.78	309.49	307.62	306.09	304.83	303.79	302.94	302.23	301.65	299.95	299.29	299.03
20000	334.76	331.13	328.18	325.78	323.81	322.20	320.87	319.78	318.88	318.14	317.53	315.73	315.04	314.76
21000	351.50	347.69	344.59	342.07	340.00	338.31	336.92	335.77	334.83	334.05	333.40	331.52	330.79	330.50
22000	368.23	364.24	361.00	358.36	356.19	354.42	352.96	351.76	350.77	349.95	349.28	347.31	346.54	346.24
23000	384.97	380.80	377.41	374.65	372.38	370.53	369.00	367.75	366.71	365.86	365.16	363.09	362.29	361.98
24000	401.71	397.36	393.82	390.93	388.57	386.64	385.05	383.74	382.66	381.77	381.03	378.88	378.04	377.72
25000	418.45	413.91	410.23	407.22	404.76	402.75	401.09	399.73	398.60	397.68	396.91	394.67	393.79	393.45
26000	435.18	430.47	426.64	423.51	420.95	418.86	417.13	415.72	414.54	413.58	412.79	410.45	409.55	409.19
27000	451.92	447.03	443.05	439.80	437.14	434.97	433.18	431.70	430.49	429.49	428.66	426.24	425.30	424.93
28000	468.66	463.58	459.46	456.09	453.34	451.08	449.22	447.69	446.43	445.40	444.54	442.03	441.05	440.67
29000	485.40	480.14	475.87	472.38	469.53	467.19	465.26	463.68	462.38	461.30	460.41	457.81	456.80	456.41
30000	502.13	496.70	492.27	488.67	485.72	483.30	481.31	479.67	478.32	477.21	476.29	473.60	472.55	472.14
31000	518.87	513.25	508.68	504.96	501.91	499.41	497.35	495.66	494.27	493.12	492.17	489.39	488.30	487.88
32000	535.61	529.81	525.09	521.24	518.10	515.52	513.39	511.65	510.21	509.02	508.04	505.17	504.06	503.62
33000	552.35	546.36	541.50	537.53	534.29	531.62	529.44	527.64	526.15	524.93	523.92	520.96	519.81	519.36
34000	569.09	562.92	557.91	553.82	550.48	547.73	545.48	543.63	542.10	540.84	539.80	536.75	535.56	535.10
35000	585.82	579.48	574.32	570.11	566.67	563.84	561.52	559.61	558.04	556.74	555.67	552.53	551.31	550.83
36000	602.56	596.03	590.73	586.40	582.86	579.95	577.57	575.60	573.99	572.65	571.55	568.32	567.06	566.57
37000	619.30	612.59	607.14	602.69	599.05	596.06	593.61	591.59	589.93	588.56	587.42	584.10	582.81	582.31
38000	636.04	629.15	623.55	618.98	615.24	612.17	609.65	607.58	605.87	604.46	603.30	599.89	598.57	598.05
39000	652.77	645.70	639.95	635.27	631.43	628.28	625.70	623.57	621.82	620.37	619.18	615.68	614.32	613.78
40000	669.51	662.26	656.36	651.55	647.62	644.39	641.74	639.56	637.76	636.28	635.05	631.46	630.07	629.52
41000	686.25	678.82	672.77	667.84	663.81	660.50	657.78	655.55	653.70	652.18	650.93	647.25	645.82	645.26
42000	702.99	695.37	689.18	684.13	680.00	676.61	673.83	671.54	669.65	668.09	666.80	663.04	661.57	661.00
43000	719.72	711.93	705.59	700.40	696.19	692.72	689.87	687.53	685.59	684.00	682.68	678.82	677.32	676.74
44000	736.46	728.48	722.00	716.71	712.38	708.83	705.91	703.51	701.54	699.90	698.56	694.61	693.07	692.47
45000	753.20	745.04	738.41	733.00	728.57	724.94	721.96	719.50	717.48	715.81	714.43	710.40	708.83	708.21
46000	769.94	761.60	754.82	749.29	744.76	741.05	738.00	735.49	733.42	731.72	730.31	726.18	724.58	723.95
47000	786.67	778.15	771.23	765.58	760.95	757.16	754.05	751.48	749.37	747.62	746.19	741.97	740.33	739.69
48000	803.41	794.71	787.64	781.86	777.14	773.27	770.09	767.47	765.31	763.53	762.06	757.76	756.08	755.43
49000	820.15	811.27	804.04	798.15	793.33	789.38	786.13	783.46	781.26	779.44	777.94	773.54	771.83	771.16
50000	836.89	827.82	820.45	814.44	809.52	805.49	802.18	799.45	797.20	795.35	793.81	789.33	787.58	786.90
55000	920.58	910.60	902.50	895.89	890.48	886.04	882.39	879.39	876.92	874.88	873.20	868.26	866.34	865.59
60000	1004.26	993.39	984.54	977.33	971.43	966.59	962.61	959.34	956.64	954.41	952.58	947.19	945.10	944.28
65000	1087.95	1076.17	1066.59	1058.77	1052.38	1047.14	1042.83	1039.28	1036.36	1033.95	1031.96	1026.13	1023.86	1022.97
70000	1171.64	1158.95	1148.63	1140.22	1133.33	1127.68	1123.04	1119.22	1116.08	1113.48	1111.34	1105.06	1102.62	1101.66
75000	1255.33	1241.73	1230.68	1221.66	1214.28	1208.23	1203.26	1199.17	1195.80	1193.02	1190.72	1183.99	1181.37	1180.35
80000	1339.02	1324.51	1312.72	1303.10	1295.23	1288.78	1283.48	1279.11	1275.52	1272.55	1270.10	1262.92	1260.13	1259.04
85000	1422.71	1407.30	1394.77	1384.55	1376.19	1369.33	1363.69	1359.06	1355.24	1352.08	1349.48	1341.86	1338.89	1337.73
90000	1506.39	1490.08	1476.81	1465.99	1457.14	1449.88	1443.91	1439.00	1434.96	1431.62	1428.86	1420.79	1417.65	1416.42
95000	1590.08	1572.86	1558.86	1547.44	1538.09	1530.43	1524.13	1518.95	1514.67	1511.15	1508.24	1499.72	1496.41	1495.11
100000	1673.77	1655.64	1640.90	1628.88	1619.04	1610.97	1604.35	1598.89	1594.39	1590.69	1587.62	1578.65	1575.16	1573.80

18.900%

TERM AMOUNT	1 Year	2 Years	3 Years	4 Years	5 Years	6 Years	7 Years	8 Years	9 Years	10 Years	11 Years	12 Years	13 Years	14 Years
5	.47	.26	.19	.15	.13	.12	.11	.11	.10	.10	.10	.09	.09	.09
10	.93	.51	.37	.30	.26	.24	.22	.21	.20	.19	.19	.18	.18	.17
15	1.39	.76	.55	.45	.39	.35	.33	.31	.29	.28	.28	.27	.26	.26
25	2.31	1.26	.92	.75	.65	.59	.54	.51	.49	.47	.46	.45	.44	.43
50	4.61	2.52	1.84	1.50	1.30	1.17	1.08	1.02	.97	.94	.91	.89	.87	.85
75	6.91	3.78	2.75	2.24	1.95	1.75	1.62	1.53	1.45	1.40	1.36	1.33	1.30	1.28
100	9.22	5.04	3.67	2.99	2.59	2.34	2.16	2.03	1.94	1.87	1.81	1.77	1.73	1.70
200	18.43	10.08	7.33	5.97	5.18	4.67	4.31	4.06	3.87	3.73	3.61	3.53	3.46	3.40
300	27.64	15.11	10.99	8.96	7.77	7.00	6.47	6.09	5.80	5.59	5.42	5.29	5.18	5.10
400	36.85	20.15	14.65	11.94	10.36	9.33	8.62	8.11	7.73	7.45	7.22	7.05	6.91	6.80
500	46.06	25.19	18.31	14.93	12.95	11.66	10.78	10.14	9.67	9.31	9.03	8.81	8.63	8.49
600	55.27	30.22	21.97	17.91	15.54	14.00	12.93	12.17	11.60	11.17	10.83	10.57	10.36	10.19
700	64.48	35.26	25.63	20.90	18.12	16.33	15.09	14.20	13.53	13.03	12.64	12.33	12.09	11.89
800	73.69	40.29	29.29	23.88	20.71	18.66	17.24	16.22	15.46	14.89	14.44	14.09	13.81	13.59
900	82.90	45.33	32.95	26.87	23.30	20.99	19.40	18.25	17.40	16.75	16.24	15.85	15.54	15.29
1000	92.11	50.37	36.61	29.85	25.89	23.32	21.55	20.28	19.33	18.61	18.05	17.61	17.26	16.98
2000	184.22	100.73	73.22	59.70	51.78	46.64	43.10	40.55	38.65	37.21	36.09	35.21	34.52	33.96
3000	276.33	151.09	109.82	89.55	77.66	69.96	64.65	60.82	57.98	55.81	54.13	52.82	51.78	50.94
4000	368.44	201.45	146.43	119.39	103.55	93.28	86.20	81.09	77.30	74.41	72.18	70.42	69.03	67.92
5000	460.55	251.81	183.03	149.24	129.43	116.60	107.75	101.37	96.62	93.01	90.22	88.03	86.29	84.90
6000	552.66	302.17	219.64	179.09	155.32	139.92	129.30	121.64	115.95	111.62	108.26	105.63	103.55	101.88
7000	644.77	352.53	256.24	208.94	181.20	163.24	150.85	141.91	135.27	130.22	126.31	123.24	120.81	118.86
8000	736.88	402.89	292.85	238.78	207.09	186.56	172.39	162.18	154.59	148.82	144.35	140.84	138.06	135.84
9000	828.98	453.25	329.45	268.63	232.98	209.88	193.94	182.46	173.92	167.42	162.39	158.45	155.32	152.82
10000	921.09	503.61	366.06	298.48	258.86	233.20	215.49	202.73	193.24	186.02	180.44	176.05	172.58	169.80
11000	1013.20	553.97	402.67	328.33	284.75	256.52	237.04	223.00	212.57	204.63	198.48	193.66	189.84	186.78
12000	1105.31	604.33	439.27	358.17	310.63	279.84	258.59	243.27	231.89	223.23	216.52	211.26	207.09	203.76
13000	1197.42	654.69	475.88	388.02	336.52	303.16	280.14	263.55	251.21	241.83	234.57	228.87	224.35	220.74
14000	1289.53	705.05	512.48	417.87	362.40	326.48	301.69	283.82	270.54	260.43	252.61	246.47	241.61	237.72
15000	1381.64	755.41	549.09	447.72	388.29	349.80	323.23	304.09	289.86	279.03	270.65	264.08	258.87	254.70
16000	1473.75	805.77	585.69	477.56	414.17	373.12	344.78	324.36	309.18	297.64	288.70	281.68	276.12	271.68
17000	1565.86	856.13	622.30	507.41	440.06	396.44	366.33	344.64	328.51	316.24	306.74	299.29	293.38	288.66
18000	1657.96	906.49	658.90	537.26	465.95	419.76	387.88	364.91	347.83	334.84	324.78	316.89	310.64	305.64
19000	1750.07	956.85	695.51	567.11	491.83	443.08	409.43	385.18	367.15	353.44	342.83	334.50	327.90	322.62
20000	1842.18	1007.21	732.11	596.95	517.72	466.40	430.98	405.45	386.48	372.04	360.87	352.10	345.15	339.60
21000	1934.29	1057.57	768.72	626.80	543.60	489.71	452.53	425.73	405.80	390.65	378.91	369.71	362.41	356.58
22000	2026.40	1107.93	805.33	656.65	569.49	513.03	474.08	446.00	425.13	409.25	396.96	387.31	379.67	373.55
23000	2118.51	1158.29	841.93	680.49	595.37	536.35	495.62	466.27	444.45	427.85	415.00	404.92	396.93	390.53
24000	2210.62	1208.65	878.54	716.34	621.26	559.67	517.17	486.54	463.77	446.45	433.04	422.52	414.18	407.51
25000	2302.73	1259.01	915.14	746.19	647.14	582.99	538.72	506.82	483.10	465.05	451.09	440.13	431.44	424.49
26000	2394.84	1309.37	951.75	776.04	673.03	606.31	560.27	527.09	502.42	483.66	469.13	457.73	448.70	441.47
27000	2486.94	1359.73	988.35	805.88	698.92	629.63	581.82	547.36	521.74	502.26	487.17	475.34	465.95	458.45
28000	2579.05	1410.09	1024.96	835.73	724.80	652.95	603.37	567.63	541.07	520.86	505.22	492.94	483.21	475.43
29000	2671.16	1460.45	1061.56	865.58	750.69	676.27	624.92	587.90	560.39	539.46	523.26	510.55	500.47	492.41
30000	2763.27	1510.81	1098.17	895.43	776.57	699.59	646.46	608.18	579.71	558.06	541.30	528.15	517.73	509.39
31000	2855.38	1561.17	1134.77	925.27	802.46	722.91	668.01	628.45	599.04	576.66	559.35	545.76	534.98	526.37
32000	2947.49	1611.53	1171.38	955.12	828.34	746.23	689.56	648.72	618.36	595.27	577.39	563.36	552.24	543.35
33000	3039.60	1661.89	1207.99	984.97	854.23	769.55	711.11	668.99	637.69	613.87	595.43	580.97	569.50	560.33
34000	3131.71	1712.25	1244.59	1014.82	880.11	792.87	732.66	689.27	657.01	632.47	613.48	598.57	586.76	577.31
35000	3223.82	1762.61	1281.20	1044.66	906.00	816.19	754.21	709.54	676.33	651.07	631.52	616.18	604.01	594.29
36000	3315.92	1812.97	1317.80	1074.51	931.89	839.51	775.76	729.81	695.66	669.67	649.56	633.78	621.27	611.27
37000	3408.03	1863.33	1354.41	1104.36	957.77	862.83	797.30	750.08	714.98	688.28	667.61	651.39	638.53	628.25
38000	3500.14	1913.69	1391.01	1134.21	983.66	886.15	818.85	770.36	734.30	706.88	685.65	668.99	655.79	645.23
39000	3592.25	1964.05	1427.62	1164.05	1009.54	909.47	840.40	790.63	753.63	725.48	703.69	686.60	673.04	662.21
40000	3684.36	2014.41	1464.22	1193.90	1035.43	932.79	861.95	810.90	772.95	744.08	721.74	704.20	690.30	679.19
41000	3776.47	2064.77	1500.83	1223.75	1061.31	956.10	883.50	831.17	792.27	762.68	739.78	721.81	707.56	696.17
42000	3868.58	2115.13	1537.44	1253.59	1087.20	979.42	905.05	851.45	811.60	781.29	757.82	739.41	724.82	713.15
43000	3960.69	2165.49	1574.04	1283.44	1113.08	1002.74	926.60	871.72	830.92	799.89	775.87	757.02	742.07	730.12
44000	4052.79	2215.85	1610.65	1313.29	1138.97	1026.06	948.15	891.99	850.25	818.49	793.91	774.62	759.33	747.10
45000	4144.90	2266.21	1647.25	1343.14	1164.86	1049.38	969.69	912.26	869.57	837.09	811.95	792.23	776.59	764.08
46000	4237.01	2316.57	1683.86	1372.98	1190.74	1072.70	991.24	932.54	888.89	855.69	829.99	809.83	793.85	781.06
47000	4329.12	2366.93	1720.46	1402.83	1216.63	1096.02	1012.79	952.81	908.22	874.30	848.04	827.44	811.10	798.04
48000	4421.23	2417.29	1757.07	1432.68	1242.51	1119.34	1034.34	973.08	927.54	892.90	866.08	845.04	828.36	815.02
49000	4513.34	2467.65	1793.67	1462.53	1268.40	1142.66	1055.89	993.35	946.86	911.50	884.12	862.65	845.62	832.00
50000	4605.45	2518.01	1830.28	1492.37	1294.28	1165.98	1077.44	1013.63	966.19	930.10	902.17	880.25	862.88	848.98
55000	5065.99	2769.81	2013.31	1641.61	1423.71	1282.58	1185.18	1114.99	1062.81	1023.11	992.38	968.28	949.16	933.88
60000	5526.54	3021.61	2196.33	1790.85	1553.14	1399.18	1292.92	1216.35	1159.42	1116.12	1082.60	1056.30	1035.45	1018.78
65000	5987.08	3273.41	2379.36	1940.08	1682.57	1515.77	1400.67	1317.71	1256.04	1209.13	1172.82	1144.33	1121.74	1103.67
70000	6447.63	3525.21	2562.39	2089.32	1811.99	1632.37	1508.41	1419.07	1352.66	1302.14	1263.03	1232.35	1208.02	1188.57
75000	6908.17	3777.01	2745.42	2238.56	1941.42	1748.97	1616.15	1520.44	1449.28	1395.15	1353.25	1320.38	1294.31	1273.47
80000	7368.71	4028.81	2928.44	2387.80	2070.85	1865.57	1723.90	1621.80	1545.90	1488.16	1443.47	1408.40	1380.60	1358.37
85000	7829.26	4280.61	3111.47	2537.03	2200.28	1982.16	1831.64	1723.16	1642.51	1581.17	1533.68	1496.43	1466.88	1443.26
90000	8289.80	4532.41	3294.50	2686.27	2329.71	2098.76	1939.38	1824.52	1739.13	1674.18	1623.90	1584.45	1553.17	1528.16
95000	8750.35	4784.21	3477.53	2835.51	2459.13	2215.36	2047.13	1925.88	1835.75	1767.19	1714.11	1672.47	1639.46	1613.06
100000	9210.89	5036.01	3660.55	2984.74	2588.56	2331.96	2154.87	2027.25	1932.37	1860.20	1804.33	1760.50	1725.75	1697.96

TERM	15 Years	16 Years	17 Years	18 Years	19 Years	20 Years	21 Years	22 Years	23 Years	24 Years	25 Years	30 Years	35 Years	40 Years
AMOUNT														
5	.09	.09	.09	.09	.09	.09	.09	.09	.08	.08	.08	.08	.08	.08
10	.17	.17	.17	.17	.17	.17	.17	.17	.16	.16	.16	.16	.16	.16
15	.26	.25	.25	.25	.25	.25	.25	.25	.24	.24	.24	.24	.24	.24
25	.42	.42	.42	.41	.41	.41	.41	.41	.40	.40	.40	.40	.40	.40
50	.84	.83	.83	.82	.82	.81	.81	.81	.80	.80	.80	.80	.79	.79
75	1.26	1.25	1.24	1.23	1.22	1.21	1.21	1.21	1.20	1.20	1.20	1.19	1.19	1.19
100	1.68	1.66	1.65	1.64	1.63	1.62	1.61	1.61	1.60	1.60	1.59	1.59	1.58	1.58
200	3.36	3.32	3.29	3.27	3.25	3.23	3.22	3.21	3.20	3.19	3.18	3.17	3.16	3.16
300	5.03	4.98	4.93	4.90	4.87	4.84	4.82	4.81	4.79	4.78	4.77	4.75	4.74	4.73
400	6.71	6.63	6.58	6.53	6.49	6.46	6.43	6.41	6.39	6.38	6.36	6.33	6.31	6.31
500	8.38	8.29	8.22	8.16	8.11	8.07	8.04	8.01	7.99	7.97	7.95	7.91	7.89	7.88
600	10.06	9.95	9.86	9.79	9.73	9.68	9.64	9.61	9.58	9.56	9.54	9.49	9.47	9.46
700	11.73	11.61	11.50	11.42	11.35	11.30	11.25	11.21	11.18	11.15	11.13	11.07	11.05	11.04
800	13.41	13.26	13.15	13.05	12.97	12.91	12.86	12.81	12.78	12.75	12.72	12.65	12.62	12.61
900	15.09	14.92	14.79	14.68	14.59	14.52	14.46	14.41	14.37	14.34	14.31	14.23	14.20	14.19
1000	16.76	16.58	16.43	16.31	16.21	16.13	16.07	16.01	15.97	15.93	15.90	15.81	15.78	15.76
2000	33.52	33.15	32.86	32.62	32.42	32.26	32.13	32.02	31.93	31.86	31.80	31.62	31.55	31.52
3000	50.27	49.73	49.29	48.93	48.63	48.39	48.19	48.03	47.90	47.79	47.69	47.43	47.32	47.28
4000	67.03	66.30	65.72	65.24	64.84	64.52	64.26	64.04	63.86	63.71	63.59	63.23	63.09	63.04
5000	83.78	82.88	82.14	81.54	81.05	80.65	80.32	80.05	79.82	79.64	79.49	79.04	78.87	78.80
6000	100.54	99.45	98.57	97.85	97.26	96.78	96.38	96.06	95.79	95.57	95.38	94.85	94.64	94.56
7000	117.30	116.03	115.00	114.16	113.47	112.91	112.45	112.07	111.75	111.49	111.28	110.65	110.41	110.32
8000	134.05	132.60	131.43	130.47	129.68	129.04	128.51	128.07	127.72	127.42	127.18	126.46	126.18	126.07
9000	150.81	149.18	147.85	146.77	145.89	145.17	144.57	144.08	143.68	143.35	143.07	142.27	141.96	141.83
10000	167.56	165.75	164.28	163.08	162.10	161.30	160.64	160.09	159.64	159.27	158.97	158.07	157.73	157.59
11000	184.32	182.33	180.71	179.39	178.31	177.43	176.70	176.10	175.61	175.20	174.86	173.88	173.50	173.35
12000	201.08	198.90	197.14	195.70	194.52	193.55	192.76	192.11	191.57	191.13	190.76	189.69	189.27	189.11
13000	217.83	215.48	213.57	212.01	210.73	209.68	208.82	208.12	207.53	207.05	206.66	205.50	205.04	204.87
14000	234.59	232.05	229.99	228.31	226.94	225.81	224.89	224.13	223.50	222.98	222.55	221.30	220.82	220.63
15000	251.34	248.63	246.42	244.62	243.15	241.94	240.95	240.13	239.46	238.91	238.45	237.11	236.59	236.39
16000	268.10	265.20	262.85	260.93	259.36	258.07	257.01	256.14	255.43	254.83	254.35	252.92	252.36	252.14
17000	284.85	281.78	279.28	277.24	275.57	274.20	273.08	272.15	271.39	270.76	270.24	268.72	268.13	267.90
18000	301.61	298.35	295.70	293.54	291.78	290.33	289.14	288.16	287.35	286.69	286.14	284.53	283.91	283.66
19000	318.37	314.93	312.13	309.85	307.99	306.46	305.20	304.17	303.32	302.61	302.03	300.34	299.68	299.42
20000	335.12	331.50	328.56	326.16	324.20	322.59	321.27	320.18	319.28	318.54	317.93	316.14	315.45	315.18
21000	351.88	348.08	344.99	342.47	340.41	338.72	337.33	336.19	335.24	334.47	333.83	331.95	331.22	330.94
22000	368.63	364.65	361.42	358.78	356.62	354.85	353.39	352.19	351.21	350.39	349.72	347.76	346.99	346.70
23000	385.39	381.23	377.84	375.08	372.83	370.97	369.45	368.20	367.17	366.32	365.62	363.57	362.77	362.46
24000	402.15	397.80	394.27	391.39	389.04	387.10	385.52	384.21	383.14	382.25	381.52	379.37	378.54	378.21
25000	418.90	414.38	410.70	407.70	405.24	403.23	401.58	400.22	399.10	398.18	397.41	395.18	394.31	393.97
26000	435.66	430.95	427.13	424.01	421.45	419.36	417.64	416.23	415.06	414.10	413.31	410.99	410.08	409.73
27000	452.41	447.53	443.55	440.31	437.66	435.49	433.71	432.24	431.03	430.03	429.21	426.79	425.86	425.49
28000	469.17	464.10	459.98	456.62	453.87	451.62	449.77	448.25	446.99	445.96	445.10	442.60	441.63	441.25
29000	485.92	480.68	476.41	472.93	470.08	467.75	465.83	464.25	462.95	461.88	461.00	458.41	457.40	457.01
30000	502.68	497.25	492.84	489.24	486.29	483.88	481.90	480.26	478.92	477.81	476.89	474.21	473.17	472.77
31000	519.44	513.83	509.27	505.55	502.50	500.01	497.96	496.27	494.88	493.74	492.79	490.02	488.94	488.52
32000	536.19	530.40	525.69	521.85	518.71	516.14	514.02	512.28	510.85	509.66	508.69	505.83	504.72	504.28
33000	552.95	546.98	542.12	538.16	534.92	532.27	530.08	528.29	526.81	525.59	524.58	521.63	520.49	520.04
34000	569.70	563.55	558.55	554.47	551.13	548.39	546.15	544.30	542.77	541.52	540.48	537.44	536.26	535.80
35000	586.46	580.12	574.98	570.78	567.34	564.52	562.21	560.31	558.74	557.44	556.38	553.25	552.03	551.56
36000	603.22	596.70	591.40	587.08	583.55	580.65	578.27	576.31	574.70	573.37	572.27	569.06	567.81	567.32
37000	619.97	613.27	607.83	603.39	599.76	596.78	594.34	592.32	590.66	589.30	588.17	584.86	583.58	583.08
38000	636.73	629.85	624.26	619.70	615.97	612.91	610.40	608.33	606.63	605.22	604.06	600.67	599.35	598.84
39000	653.48	646.42	640.69	636.01	632.18	629.04	626.46	624.34	622.59	621.15	619.96	616.48	615.12	614.59
40000	670.24	663.00	657.11	652.31	648.39	645.17	642.53	640.35	638.56	637.08	635.86	632.28	630.90	630.35
41000	687.00	679.57	673.54	668.62	664.60	661.30	658.59	656.36	654.52	653.00	651.75	648.09	646.67	646.11
42000	703.75	696.15	689.97	684.93	680.81	677.43	674.65	672.37	670.48	668.93	667.65	663.90	662.44	661.87
43000	720.51	712.72	706.40	701.24	697.02	693.56	690.71	688.37	686.45	684.86	683.55	679.70	678.21	677.63
44000	737.26	729.30	722.83	717.55	713.23	709.69	706.78	704.38	702.41	700.78	699.44	695.51	693.98	693.39
45000	754.02	745.87	739.25	733.85	729.44	725.82	722.84	720.39	718.38	716.71	715.34	711.32	709.76	709.15
46000	770.77	762.45	755.68	750.16	745.65	741.94	738.90	736.40	734.34	732.64	731.23	727.13	725.53	724.91
47000	787.53	779.02	772.11	766.47	761.86	758.07	754.97	752.41	750.30	748.57	747.13	742.93	741.30	740.66
48000	804.29	795.60	788.54	782.78	778.07	774.20	771.03	768.42	766.27	764.49	763.03	758.74	757.07	756.42
49000	821.04	812.17	804.96	799.08	794.28	790.33	787.09	784.43	782.23	780.42	778.92	774.55	772.85	772.18
50000	837.80	828.75	821.39	815.39	810.48	806.46	803.16	800.44	798.19	796.35	794.82	790.35	788.62	787.94
55000	921.58	911.62	903.53	896.93	891.53	887.11	883.47	880.48	878.01	875.98	874.30	869.39	867.48	866.73
60000	1005.36	994.50	985.67	978.47	972.58	967.75	963.79	960.52	957.83	955.61	953.78	948.42	946.34	945.53
65000	1089.14	1077.37	1067.81	1060.01	1053.63	1048.40	1044.10	1040.56	1037.65	1035.25	1033.26	1027.46	1025.20	1024.32
70000	1172.92	1160.24	1149.95	1141.55	1134.68	1129.04	1124.42	1120.61	1117.47	1114.88	1112.75	1106.49	1104.06	1103.11
75000	1256.69	1243.12	1232.09	1223.09	1215.72	1209.69	1204.73	1200.65	1197.29	1194.52	1192.23	1185.53	1182.92	1181.91
80000	1340.47	1325.99	1314.22	1304.62	1296.77	1290.33	1285.05	1280.69	1277.11	1274.15	1271.71	1264.56	1261.79	1260.70
85000	1424.25	1408.87	1396.36	1386.16	1377.82	1370.98	1365.36	1360.74	1356.93	1353.78	1351.19	1343.60	1340.65	1339.50
90000	1508.03	1491.74	1478.50	1467.70	1458.87	1451.63	1445.68	1440.78	1436.75	1433.42	1430.67	1422.63	1419.51	1418.29
95000	1591.81	1574.62	1560.64	1549.24	1539.92	1532.27	1525.99	1520.82	1516.56	1513.05	1510.15	1501.67	1498.37	1497.08
100000	1675.59	1657.49	1642.78	1630.78	1620.96	1612.92	1606.31	1600.87	1596.38	1592.69	1589.64	1580.70	1577.23	1575.88

MONTHLY PAYMENT
REQUIRED TO AMORTIZE A LOAN

TERM	1 Year	2 Years	3 Years	4 Years	5 Years	6 Years	7 Years	8 Years	9 Years	10 Years	11 Years	12 Years	13 Years	14 Years
AMOUNT														
5	.47	.26	.19	.15	.13	.12	.11	.11	.10	.10	.10	.09	.09	.09
10	.93	.51	.37	.30	.26	.24	.22	.21	.20	.19	.19	.18	.18	.18
15	1.39	.76	.55	.45	.39	.36	.33	.31	.30	.29	.28	.27	.26	.26
25	2.31	1.27	.92	.75	.65	.59	.55	.51	.49	.47	.46	.45	.44	.43
50	4.61	2.53	1.84	1.50	1.30	1.17	1.09	1.02	.97	.94	.91	.89	.87	.86
75	6.92	3.79	2.75	2.25	1.95	1.76	1.63	1.53	1.46	1.41	1.36	1.33	1.30	1.28
100	9.22	5.05	3.67	3.00	2.60	2.34	2.17	2.04	1.94	1.87	1.82	1.77	1.74	1.71
200	18.44	10.09	7.34	5.99	5.19	4.68	4.33	4.07	3.88	3.74	3.63	3.54	3.47	3.42
300	27.65	15.13	11.00	8.98	7.79	7.02	6.49	6.11	5.82	5.61	5.44	5.31	5.20	5.12
400	36.87	20.17	14.67	11.97	10.39	9.36	8.65	8.14	7.76	7.47	7.25	7.07	6.94	6.83
500	46.08	25.21	18.33	14.96	11.69	10.81	10.17	9.70	9.34	9.06	8.84	8.67	8.53	
600	55.30	30.25	22.00	17.95	15.57	14.03	12.97	12.21	11.64	11.21	10.87	10.61	10.40	10.24
700	64.51	35.29	25.66	20.94	18.16	16.37	15.13	14.24	13.58	13.07	12.68	12.38	12.13	11.94
800	73.73	40.33	29.33	23.93	20.76	18.71	17.29	16.27	15.51	14.94	14.49	14.14	13.87	13.65
900	82.95	45.37	33.00	26.92	23.35	21.04	19.45	18.31	17.45	16.81	16.30	15.91	15.60	15.35
1000	92.16	50.41	36.66	29.91	25.95	23.38	21.61	20.34	19.39	18.67	18.12	17.68	17.33	17.06
2000	184.32	100.82	73.32	59.81	51.89	46.76	43.22	40.67	38.78	37.34	36.23	35.35	34.66	34.11
3000	276.47	151.23	109.97	89.71	77.83	70.14	64.83	61.01	58.17	56.01	54.34	53.03	51.99	51.16
4000	368.63	201.64	146.63	119.61	103.77	93.51	86.44	81.34	77.55	74.67	72.45	70.70	69.32	68.21
5000	460.79	252.05	183.29	149.51	129.71	116.89	108.05	101.67	96.94	93.34	90.56	88.37	86.64	85.26
6000	552.94	302.46	219.94	175.41	155.65	140.27	129.65	122.01	116.33	112.01	108.67	106.05	103.97	102.31
7000	645.10	352.87	256.60	209.31	181.59	163.64	151.26	142.34	135.71	130.68	126.78	123.72	121.30	119.36
8000	737.26	403.27	293.25	239.21	207.53	187.02	172.87	162.68	155.10	149.34	144.89	141.39	138.63	136.41
9000	829.41	453.68	329.91	269.11	233.47	210.40	194.48	183.01	174.49	168.01	163.00	159.07	155.95	153.47
10000	921.57	504.09	366.57	299.01	259.41	233.77	216.09	203.34	193.88	186.68	181.11	176.74	173.28	170.52
11000	1013.73	554.50	403.22	328.91	285.35	257.15	237.69	223.68	213.26	205.34	199.22	194.42	190.61	187.57
12000	1105.88	604.91	439.88	358.81	311.29	280.53	259.30	244.01	232.65	224.01	217.33	212.09	207.94	204.62
13000	1198.04	655.32	476.53	388.71	337.23	303.90	280.91	264.35	252.04	242.68	235.44	229.76	225.26	221.67
14000	1290.20	705.73	513.19	418.61	363.17	327.28	302.52	284.68	271.42	261.35	253.55	247.44	242.59	238.72
15000	1382.35	756.13	549.85	448.51	389.11	350.66	324.13	305.01	290.81	280.01	271.66	265.11	259.92	255.77
16000	1474.51	806.54	586.50	478.41	415.05	374.03	345.73	325.35	310.20	298.68	289.77	282.78	277.25	272.82
17000	1566.67	856.95	623.16	508.31	440.99	397.41	367.34	345.68	329.59	317.35	307.88	300.46	294.57	289.87
18000	1658.82	907.36	659.81	538.21	466.93	420.79	388.95	366.01	348.97	336.02	325.99	318.13	311.90	306.93
19000	1750.98	957.77	696.47	568.11	492.88	444.16	410.56	386.35	368.36	354.68	344.10	335.80	329.23	323.98
20000	1843.14	1008.18	733.13	598.01	518.82	467.54	432.17	406.68	387.75	373.35	362.21	353.48	346.56	341.03
21000	1935.29	1058.59	769.78	627.91	544.76	490.92	453.77	427.02	407.13	392.02	380.32	371.15	363.89	358.08
22000	2027.45	1108.99	806.44	657.81	570.70	514.29	475.38	447.35	426.52	410.68	398.43	388.83	381.21	375.13
23000	2119.61	1159.40	843.09	687.71	596.64	537.67	496.99	467.68	445.91	429.35	416.54	406.50	398.54	392.18
24000	2211.76	1209.81	879.75	717.61	622.58	561.05	518.60	488.02	465.29	448.02	434.65	424.17	415.87	409.23
25000	2303.92	1260.22	916.41	747.51	648.52	584.42	540.21	508.35	484.68	466.69	452.76	441.85	433.20	426.28
26000	2396.08	1310.63	953.06	777.41	674.46	607.80	561.81	528.69	504.07	485.35	470.87	459.52	450.52	443.33
27000	2488.23	1361.04	989.72	807.31	700.40	631.18	583.42	549.02	523.46	504.02	488.98	477.19	467.85	460.39
28000	2580.39	1411.45	1026.37	837.21	726.34	654.55	605.03	569.35	542.84	522.69	507.09	494.87	485.18	477.44
29000	2672.55	1461.85	1063.03	867.11	752.28	677.93	626.64	589.69	562.23	541.35	525.20	512.54	502.51	494.49
30000	2764.70	1512.26	1099.69	897.01	778.22	701.31	648.25	610.02	581.62	560.02	543.31	530.21	519.83	511.54
31000	2856.86	1562.67	1136.34	926.91	804.16	724.68	669.85	630.35	601.00	578.69	561.43	547.89	537.16	528.59
32000	2949.02	1613.08	1173.00	956.81	830.10	748.06	691.46	650.69	620.39	597.36	579.54	565.56	554.49	545.64
33000	3041.17	1663.49	1209.65	986.71	856.04	771.44	713.07	671.02	639.78	616.02	597.65	583.24	571.82	562.69
34000	3133.33	1713.90	1246.31	1016.61	881.98	794.81	734.68	691.36	659.17	634.69	615.76	600.91	589.14	579.74
35000	3225.49	1764.31	1282.97	1046.51	907.92	818.19	756.29	711.69	678.55	653.36	633.87	618.58	606.47	596.80
36000	3317.64	1814.72	1319.62	1076.41	933.86	841.57	777.89	732.02	697.94	672.03	651.98	636.26	623.80	613.85
37000	3409.80	1865.12	1356.28	1106.31	959.81	864.94	799.50	752.36	717.33	690.69	670.09	653.93	641.13	630.90
38000	3501.96	1915.53	1392.93	1136.21	985.75	888.32	821.11	772.69	736.71	709.36	688.20	671.60	658.45	647.95
39000	3594.11	1965.94	1429.59	1166.11	1011.69	911.70	842.72	793.03	756.10	728.03	706.31	689.28	675.78	665.00
40000	3686.27	2016.35	1466.25	1196.01	1037.63	935.07	864.33	813.36	775.49	746.69	724.42	706.95	693.11	682.05
41000	3778.42	2066.76	1502.90	1225.91	1063.57	958.45	885.93	833.69	794.88	765.36	742.53	724.62	710.44	699.10
42000	3870.58	2117.17	1539.56	1255.81	1089.51	981.83	907.54	854.03	814.26	784.03	760.64	742.30	727.77	716.15
43000	3962.74	2167.58	1576.21	1285.71	1115.45	1005.20	929.15	874.36	833.65	802.70	778.75	759.97	745.09	733.20
44000	4054.89	2217.98	1612.87	1315.61	1141.39	1028.58	950.76	894.70	853.04	821.36	796.86	777.65	762.42	750.26
45000	4147.05	2268.39	1649.53	1345.51	1167.33	1051.96	972.37	915.03	872.42	840.03	814.97	795.32	779.75	767.31
46000	4239.21	2318.80	1686.18	1375.41	1193.27	1075.33	993.97	935.36	891.81	858.70	833.08	812.99	797.08	784.36
47000	4331.36	2369.21	1722.84	1405.31	1219.21	1098.71	1015.58	955.70	911.20	877.37	851.19	830.67	814.40	801.41
48000	4423.52	2419.62	1759.49	1435.21	1245.15	1122.09	1037.19	976.03	930.58	896.03	869.30	848.34	831.73	818.46
49000	4515.68	2470.03	1796.15	1465.11	1271.09	1145.46	1058.80	996.36	949.97	914.70	887.41	866.01	849.06	835.51
50000	4607.83	2520.44	1832.81	1495.01	1297.03	1168.84	1080.41	1016.70	969.36	933.37	905.52	883.69	866.39	852.56
55000	5068.62	2772.48	2016.09	1644.51	1426.74	1285.72	1188.45	1118.37	1066.29	1026.70	996.07	972.06	953.02	937.82
60000	5529.40	3024.52	2199.37	1794.01	1556.44	1402.61	1296.49	1220.04	1163.23	1120.04	1086.62	1060.42	1039.66	1023.07
65000	5990.18	3276.57	2382.65	1943.51	1686.14	1519.49	1404.53	1321.71	1260.17	1213.38	1177.18	1148.79	1126.30	1108.33
70000	6450.97	3528.61	2565.93	2093.01	1815.84	1636.38	1512.57	1423.38	1357.10	1306.71	1267.73	1237.16	1212.94	1193.59
75000	6911.75	3780.65	2749.21	2242.51	1945.55	1753.26	1620.61	1525.04	1454.04	1400.05	1358.28	1325.53	1299.58	1278.84
80000	7372.53	4032.69	2932.49	2392.01	2075.25	1870.14	1728.65	1626.71	1550.97	1493.38	1448.83	1413.90	1386.22	1364.10
85000	7833.31	4284.74	3115.77	2541.52	2204.95	1987.03	1836.69	1728.38	1647.91	1586.72	1539.38	1502.27	1472.85	1449.35
90000	8294.10	4536.78	3299.05	2691.02	2334.65	2103.91	1944.73	1830.05	1744.84	1680.06	1629.93	1590.63	1559.49	1534.61
95000	8754.88	4788.82	3482.33	2840.52	2464.36	2220.79	2052.77	1931.72	1841.78	1773.39	1720.49	1679.00	1646.13	1619.86
100000	9215.66	5040.87	3665.61	2990.02	2594.06	2337.68	2160.81	2033.39	1938.71	1866.73	1811.04	1767.37	1732.77	1705.12

TERM	15 Years	16 Years	17 Years	18 Years	19 Years	20 Years	21 Years	22 Years	23 Years	24 Years	25 Years	30 Years	35 Years	40 Years
AMOUNT														
5	.09	.09	.09	.09	.09	.09	.09	.09	.09	.09	.08	.08	.08	.08
10	.17	.17	.17	.17	.17	.17	.17	.17	.17	.17	.16	.16	.16	.16
15	.26	.25	.25	.25	.25	.25	.25	.25	.25	.25	.24	.24	.24	.24
25	.43	.42	.42	.41	.41	.41	.41	.41	.41	.41	.40	.40	.40	.40
50	.85	.84	.83	.82	.82	.82	.81	.81	.81	.81	.80	.80	.80	.80
75	1.27	1.25	1.24	1.23	1.23	1.22	1.22	1.21	1.21	1.21	1.20	1.20	1.19	1.19
100	1.69	1.67	1.66	1.64	1.63	1.63	1.62	1.61	1.61	1.61	1.60	1.59	1.59	1.59
200	3.37	3.33	3.31	3.28	3.26	3.25	3.23	3.22	3.21	3.21	3.20	3.18	3.18	3.17
300	5.05	5.00	4.96	4.92	4.89	4.87	4.85	4.83	4.82	4.81	4.80	4.77	4.76	4.76
400	6.74	6.66	6.61	6.56	6.52	6.49	6.46	6.44	6.42	6.41	6.40	6.36	6.35	6.34
500	8.42	8.33	8.26	8.20	8.15	8.11	8.08	8.05	8.03	8.01	7.99	7.95	7.93	7.93
600	10.10	9.99	9.91	9.84	9.78	9.73	9.69	9.66	9.63	9.61	9.59	9.54	9.52	9.51
700	11.79	11.66	11.56	11.47	11.41	11.35	11.30	11.27	11.24	11.21	11.19	11.13	11.10	11.09
800	13.47	13.32	13.21	13.11	13.03	12.97	12.92	12.88	12.84	12.81	12.79	12.72	12.69	12.68
900	15.15	14.99	14.86	14.75	14.66	14.59	14.53	14.48	14.44	14.41	14.38	14.31	14.27	14.26
1000	16.83	16.65	16.51	16.39	16.29	16.21	16.15	16.09	16.05	16.01	15.98	15.89	15.86	15.85
2000	33.66	33.30	33.01	32.77	32.58	32.42	32.29	32.18	32.09	32.02	31.96	31.78	31.71	31.69
3000	50.49	49.95	49.51	49.16	48.86	48.63	48.43	48.27	48.14	48.03	47.94	47.67	47.57	47.53
4000	67.32	66.60	66.02	65.54	65.15	64.83	64.57	64.36	64.18	64.03	63.91	63.56	63.42	63.37
5000	84.15	83.25	82.52	81.92	81.44	81.04	80.71	80.44	80.22	80.04	79.89	79.45	79.28	79.21
6000	100.98	99.90	99.02	98.31	97.72	97.25	96.85	96.53	96.27	96.05	95.87	95.34	95.13	95.06
7000	117.81	116.55	115.53	114.69	114.01	113.45	112.99	112.62	112.31	112.05	111.84	111.23	110.99	110.90
8000	134.64	133.20	132.03	131.08	130.30	129.66	129.14	128.71	128.35	128.06	127.82	127.12	126.84	126.74
9000	151.46	149.85	148.53	147.46	146.58	145.87	145.28	144.79	144.40	144.07	143.80	143.01	142.70	142.58
10000	168.29	166.49	165.03	163.84	162.87	162.07	161.42	160.88	160.44	160.07	159.77	158.89	158.55	158.42
11000	185.12	183.14	181.54	180.23	179.16	178.28	177.56	176.97	176.48	176.08	175.75	174.78	174.41	174.26
12000	201.95	199.79	198.04	196.61	195.44	194.49	193.70	193.06	192.53	192.09	191.73	190.67	190.26	190.11
13000	218.78	216.44	214.54	212.99	211.73	210.69	209.84	209.14	208.57	208.09	207.70	206.56	206.12	205.95
14000	235.61	233.09	231.05	229.38	228.02	226.90	225.98	225.23	224.61	224.10	223.68	222.45	221.97	221.79
15000	252.44	249.74	247.55	245.76	244.30	243.11	242.13	241.32	240.66	240.11	239.66	238.34	237.83	237.63
16000	269.27	266.39	264.05	262.15	260.59	259.31	258.27	257.41	256.70	256.12	255.63	254.23	253.68	253.47
17000	286.09	283.04	280.55	278.53	276.88	275.52	274.41	273.49	272.74	272.12	271.61	270.12	269.54	269.31
18000	302.92	299.69	297.06	294.91	293.16	291.73	290.55	289.58	288.79	288.13	287.59	286.01	285.39	285.16
19000	319.75	316.33	313.56	311.30	309.45	307.94	306.69	305.67	304.83	304.14	303.56	301.89	301.25	301.00
20000	336.58	332.98	330.06	327.68	325.74	324.14	322.83	321.76	320.87	320.14	319.54	317.78	317.10	316.84
21000	353.41	349.63	346.57	344.07	342.02	340.35	338.97	337.85	336.92	336.15	335.52	333.67	332.96	332.68
22000	370.24	366.28	363.07	360.45	358.31	356.56	355.12	353.93	352.96	352.16	351.49	349.56	348.81	348.52
23000	387.07	382.93	379.57	376.83	374.60	372.76	371.26	370.02	369.00	368.16	367.47	365.45	364.67	364.37
24000	403.90	399.58	396.07	393.22	390.88	388.97	387.40	386.11	385.05	384.17	383.45	381.34	380.52	380.21
25000	420.72	416.23	412.58	409.60	407.17	405.18	403.54	402.20	401.09	400.18	399.43	397.23	396.38	396.05
26000	437.55	432.88	429.08	425.98	423.46	421.38	419.68	418.28	417.13	416.18	415.40	413.12	412.23	411.89
27000	454.38	449.53	445.58	442.37	439.74	437.59	435.82	434.37	433.18	432.19	431.38	429.01	428.09	427.73
28000	471.21	466.17	462.09	458.75	456.03	453.80	451.96	450.46	449.22	448.20	447.36	444.89	443.94	443.57
29000	488.04	482.82	478.59	475.14	472.32	470.00	468.11	466.55	465.26	464.20	463.33	460.78	459.80	459.42
30000	504.87	499.47	495.09	491.52	488.60	486.21	484.25	482.63	481.31	480.21	479.31	476.67	475.65	475.26
31000	521.70	516.12	511.59	507.90	504.89	502.42	500.39	498.72	497.35	496.22	495.29	492.56	491.51	491.10
32000	538.53	532.77	528.10	524.29	521.17	518.62	516.53	514.81	513.39	512.23	511.26	508.45	507.36	506.94
33000	555.35	549.42	544.60	540.67	537.46	534.83	532.67	530.90	529.44	528.23	527.24	524.34	523.22	522.78
34000	572.18	566.07	561.10	557.06	553.75	551.04	548.81	546.98	545.48	544.24	543.22	540.23	539.07	538.62
35000	589.01	582.72	577.61	573.44	570.03	567.24	564.95	563.07	561.52	560.25	559.19	556.12	554.93	554.47
36000	605.84	599.37	594.11	589.82	586.32	583.45	581.10	579.16	577.57	576.25	575.17	572.01	570.78	570.31
37000	622.67	616.02	610.61	606.21	602.61	599.66	597.24	595.25	593.61	592.26	591.15	587.90	586.64	586.15
38000	639.50	632.66	627.11	622.59	618.89	615.87	613.38	611.34	609.65	608.27	607.12	603.78	602.49	601.99
39000	656.33	649.31	643.62	638.97	635.18	632.07	629.52	627.42	625.70	624.27	623.10	619.67	618.35	617.83
40000	673.16	665.96	660.12	655.36	651.47	648.28	645.66	643.51	641.74	640.28	639.08	635.56	634.20	633.67
41000	689.98	682.61	676.62	671.74	667.75	664.49	661.80	659.60	657.78	656.29	655.05	651.45	650.06	649.52
42000	706.81	699.26	693.13	688.13	684.04	680.69	677.94	675.69	673.83	672.29	671.03	667.34	665.91	665.36
43000	723.64	715.91	709.63	704.51	700.33	696.90	694.09	691.77	689.87	688.30	687.01	683.23	681.77	681.20
44000	740.47	732.56	726.13	720.89	716.61	713.11	710.23	707.86	705.91	704.31	702.98	699.12	697.62	697.04
45000	757.30	749.21	742.63	737.28	732.90	729.31	726.37	723.95	721.96	720.31	718.96	715.01	713.48	712.88
46000	774.13	765.86	759.14	753.66	749.19	745.52	742.51	740.04	738.00	736.32	734.94	730.90	729.33	728.73
47000	790.96	782.50	775.64	770.05	765.47	761.73	758.65	756.12	754.04	752.33	750.91	746.78	745.19	744.57
48000	807.79	799.15	792.14	786.43	781.76	777.93	774.79	772.21	770.09	768.34	766.89	762.67	761.04	760.41
49000	824.61	815.80	808.65	802.81	798.05	794.14	790.93	788.30	786.13	784.34	782.87	778.56	776.90	776.25
50000	841.44	832.45	825.15	819.20	814.33	810.35	807.08	804.39	802.17	800.35	798.85	794.45	792.75	792.09
55000	925.59	915.70	907.66	901.12	895.77	891.38	887.78	884.83	882.39	880.38	878.73	873.90	872.03	871.30
60000	1009.73	998.94	990.18	983.04	977.20	972.42	968.49	965.26	962.61	960.42	958.61	953.34	951.30	950.51
65000	1093.87	1082.19	1072.69	1064.95	1058.63	1053.45	1049.20	1045.70	1042.82	1040.45	1038.50	1032.79	1030.58	1029.72
70000	1178.02	1165.43	1155.21	1146.87	1140.06	1134.48	1129.90	1126.14	1123.04	1120.49	1118.38	1112.23	1109.85	1108.93
75000	1262.16	1248.67	1237.72	1228.79	1221.50	1215.52	1210.61	1206.58	1203.26	1200.52	1198.27	1191.67	1189.13	1188.14
80000	1346.31	1331.92	1320.24	1310.71	1302.93	1296.55	1291.32	1287.02	1283.47	1280.56	1278.15	1271.12	1268.40	1267.34
85000	1430.45	1415.16	1402.75	1392.63	1384.36	1377.59	1372.03	1367.45	1363.69	1360.59	1358.03	1350.56	1347.68	1346.55
90000	1514.59	1498.41	1485.26	1474.55	1465.79	1458.62	1452.73	1447.89	1443.91	1440.63	1437.92	1430.01	1426.95	1425.76
95000	1598.74	1581.65	1567.78	1556.47	1547.23	1539.66	1533.44	1528.33	1524.13	1520.66	1517.80	1509.45	1506.23	1504.97
100000	1682.88	1664.90	1650.29	1638.39	1628.66	1620.69	1614.15	1608.77	1604.34	1600.69	1597.69	1588.90	1585.50	1584.18

19%

451

MONTHLY PAYMENT
REQUIRED TO AMORTIZE A LOAN

TERM	1 Year	2 Years	3 Years	4 Years	5 Years	6 Years	7 Years	8 Years	9 Years	10 Years	11 Years	12 Years	13 Years	14 Years
AMOUNT														
5	.47	.26	.19	.15	.13	.12	.11	.11	.10	.10	.10	.09	.09	.09
10	.93	.51	.37	.30	.26	.24	.22	.21	.20	.19	.19	.18	.18	.18
15	1.39	.76	.56	.45	.39	.36	.33	.31	.30	.29	.28	.27	.27	.26
25	2.31	1.27	.92	.75	.65	.59	.55	.51	.49	.47	.46	.45	.44	.43
50	4.62	2.53	1.84	1.50	1.30	1.18	1.09	1.02	.98	.94	.91	.89	.87	.86
75	6.92	3.79	2.76	2.25	1.95	1.76	1.63	1.53	1.46	1.41	1.37	1.34	1.31	1.29
100	9.23	5.05	3.68	3.00	2.60	2.35	2.17	2.04	1.95	1.88	1.82	1.78	1.74	1.72
200	18.45	10.10	7.35	6.00	5.20	4.69	4.34	4.08	3.90	3.75	3.64	3.55	3.48	3.43
300	27.67	15.14	11.02	8.99	7.80	7.04	6.51	6.12	5.84	5.62	5.46	5.33	5.22	5.14
400	36.89	20.19	14.69	11.99	10.40	9.38	8.67	8.16	7.79	7.50	7.28	7.10	6.96	6.85
500	46.11	25.23	18.36	14.98	13.00	11.72	10.84	10.20	9.73	9.37	9.09	8.88	8.70	8.57
600	55.33	30.28	22.03	17.98	15.60	14.07	13.01	12.24	11.68	11.24	10.91	10.65	10.44	10.28
700	64.55	35.33	25.70	20.97	18.20	16.41	15.17	14.28	13.62	13.12	12.73	12.42	12.18	11.99
800	73.77	40.37	29.37	23.97	20.80	18.75	17.34	16.32	15.57	14.99	14.55	14.20	13.92	13.70
900	82.99	45.42	33.04	26.96	23.40	21.10	19.51	18.36	17.51	16.86	16.36	15.97	15.66	15.42
1000	92.21	50.46	36.71	29.96	26.00	23.44	21.67	20.40	19.46	18.74	18.18	17.75	17.40	17.13
2000	184.41	100.92	73.42	59.91	52.00	46.87	43.34	40.80	38.91	37.47	36.36	35.49	34.80	34.25
3000	276.62	151.38	110.12	89.86	77.99	70.31	65.01	61.19	58.36	56.20	54.54	53.23	52.20	51.37
4000	368.82	201.83	146.83	119.82	103.99	93.74	86.67	81.59	77.81	74.94	72.71	70.97	69.60	68.50
5000	461.03	252.29	183.54	149.77	129.98	117.18	108.34	101.98	97.26	93.67	90.89	88.72	86.99	85.62
6000	553.23	302.75	220.24	179.72	155.98	140.61	130.01	122.38	116.71	112.40	109.07	106.46	104.39	102.74
7000	645.44	353.21	256.95	209.68	181.97	164.04	151.68	142.77	136.16	131.13	127.25	124.20	121.79	119.87
8000	737.64	403.66	293.66	239.63	207.97	187.48	173.34	163.17	155.61	149.87	145.42	141.94	139.19	136.99
9000	829.84	454.12	330.36	269.58	233.97	210.91	195.01	183.56	175.06	168.60	163.60	159.69	156.59	154.11
10000	922.05	504.58	367.07	299.53	259.96	234.35	216.68	203.96	194.51	187.33	181.78	177.43	173.98	171.23
11000	1014.25	555.03	403.78	329.49	285.96	257.78	238.35	224.35	213.96	206.06	199.96	195.17	191.38	188.36
12000	1106.46	605.49	440.48	359.44	311.95	281.21	260.01	244.75	233.41	224.80	218.13	212.91	208.78	205.48
13000	1198.66	655.95	477.19	389.39	337.95	304.65	281.68	265.15	252.86	243.53	236.31	230.66	226.18	222.60
14000	1290.87	706.41	513.90	419.35	363.94	328.08	303.35	285.54	272.31	262.26	254.49	248.40	243.58	239.73
15000	1383.07	756.86	550.60	449.30	389.94	351.52	325.02	305.94	291.76	280.99	272.67	266.14	260.97	256.85
16000	1475.27	807.32	587.31	479.25	415.93	374.95	346.68	326.33	311.21	299.73	290.84	283.88	278.37	273.97
17000	1567.48	857.78	624.02	509.20	441.93	398.38	368.35	346.73	330.67	318.46	309.02	301.63	295.77	291.09
18000	1659.68	908.23	660.72	539.16	467.93	421.82	390.02	367.12	350.12	337.19	327.20	319.37	313.17	308.22
19000	1751.89	958.69	697.43	569.11	493.92	445.25	411.69	387.52	369.57	355.93	345.38	337.11	330.57	325.34
20000	1844.09	1009.15	734.14	599.06	519.92	468.69	433.35	407.91	389.02	374.66	363.55	354.85	347.96	342.46
21000	1936.30	1059.61	770.84	629.02	545.91	492.12	455.02	428.31	408.47	393.39	381.73	372.60	365.36	359.59
22000	2028.50	1110.06	807.55	658.97	571.91	515.55	476.69	448.70	427.92	412.12	399.91	390.34	382.76	376.71
23000	2120.70	1160.52	844.26	688.92	597.90	538.99	498.36	469.10	447.37	430.86	418.09	408.08	400.16	393.83
24000	2212.91	1210.98	880.96	718.87	623.90	562.42	520.02	489.49	466.82	449.59	436.26	425.82	417.56	410.95
25000	2305.11	1261.44	917.67	748.83	649.90	585.86	541.69	509.89	486.27	468.32	454.44	443.57	434.95	428.08
26000	2397.32	1311.89	954.38	778.78	675.89	609.29	563.36	530.29	505.72	487.05	472.62	461.31	452.35	445.20
27000	2489.52	1362.35	991.08	808.73	701.89	632.72	585.03	550.68	525.17	505.79	490.80	479.05	469.75	462.32
28000	2581.73	1412.81	1027.79	838.69	727.88	656.16	606.69	571.08	544.62	524.52	508.97	496.79	487.15	479.45
29000	2673.93	1463.26	1064.50	868.64	753.88	679.59	628.36	591.47	564.07	543.25	527.15	514.54	504.55	496.57
30000	2766.13	1513.72	1101.20	898.59	779.87	703.03	650.03	611.87	583.52	561.98	545.33	532.28	521.94	513.69
31000	2858.34	1564.18	1137.91	928.55	805.87	726.46	671.70	632.26	602.97	580.72	563.51	550.02	539.34	530.81
32000	2950.54	1614.64	1174.62	958.50	831.86	749.89	693.36	652.66	622.42	599.45	581.68	567.76	556.74	547.94
33000	3042.75	1665.09	1211.32	988.45	857.86	773.33	715.03	673.05	641.88	618.18	599.86	585.51	574.14	565.06
34000	3134.95	1715.55	1248.03	1018.40	883.86	796.76	736.70	693.45	661.33	636.91	618.04	603.25	591.54	582.18
35000	3227.16	1766.01	1284.74	1048.36	909.85	820.20	758.37	713.84	680.78	655.65	636.22	620.99	608.93	599.31
36000	3319.36	1816.46	1321.44	1078.31	935.85	843.63	780.03	734.24	700.23	674.38	654.39	638.73	626.33	616.43
37000	3411.56	1866.92	1358.15	1108.26	961.84	867.06	801.70	754.64	719.68	693.11	672.57	656.48	643.73	633.55
38000	3503.77	1917.38	1394.86	1138.22	987.84	890.50	823.37	775.03	739.13	711.85	690.75	674.22	661.13	650.67
39000	3595.97	1967.84	1431.56	1168.17	1013.83	913.93	845.04	795.43	758.58	730.58	708.93	691.96	678.52	667.80
40000	3688.18	2018.29	1468.27	1198.12	1039.83	937.37	866.70	815.82	778.03	749.31	727.10	709.70	695.92	684.92
41000	3780.38	2068.75	1504.98	1228.07	1065.82	960.80	888.37	836.22	797.48	768.04	745.28	727.45	713.32	702.04
42000	3872.59	2119.21	1541.68	1258.03	1091.82	984.23	910.04	856.61	816.93	786.78	763.46	745.19	730.72	719.17
43000	3964.79	2169.67	1578.39	1287.98	1117.82	1007.67	931.71	877.01	836.38	805.51	781.64	762.93	748.12	736.29
44000	4056.99	2220.12	1615.10	1317.93	1143.81	1031.10	953.37	897.40	855.83	824.24	799.81	780.67	765.51	753.41
45000	4149.20	2270.58	1651.80	1347.89	1169.81	1054.54	975.04	917.80	875.28	842.97	817.99	798.42	782.91	770.53
46000	4241.40	2321.04	1688.51	1377.84	1195.80	1077.97	996.71	938.19	894.73	861.71	836.17	816.16	800.31	787.66
47000	4333.61	2371.49	1725.22	1407.79	1221.80	1101.40	1018.38	958.59	914.18	880.44	854.35	833.90	817.71	804.78
48000	4425.81	2421.95	1761.92	1437.74	1247.79	1124.84	1040.04	978.98	933.63	899.17	872.52	851.64	835.11	821.90
49000	4518.02	2472.41	1798.63	1467.70	1273.79	1148.27	1061.71	999.38	953.09	917.90	890.70	869.39	852.50	839.03
50000	4610.22	2522.87	1835.34	1497.65	1299.79	1171.71	1083.38	1019.78	972.54	936.64	908.88	887.13	869.90	856.15
55000	5071.24	2775.15	2018.87	1647.42	1429.76	1288.88	1191.72	1121.75	1069.79	1030.30	999.77	975.84	956.89	941.76
60000	5532.26	3027.44	2202.40	1797.18	1559.74	1406.05	1300.05	1223.73	1167.04	1123.96	1090.65	1064.55	1043.88	1027.38
65000	5993.29	3279.72	2385.93	1946.94	1689.72	1523.22	1408.39	1325.71	1264.29	1217.63	1181.54	1153.26	1130.87	1112.99
70000	6454.31	3532.01	2569.47	2096.71	1819.70	1640.39	1516.73	1427.68	1361.55	1311.29	1272.43	1241.98	1217.86	1198.61
75000	6915.33	3784.30	2753.00	2246.47	1949.68	1757.56	1625.07	1529.66	1458.80	1404.95	1363.32	1330.69	1304.85	1284.22
80000	7376.35	4036.58	2936.53	2396.24	2079.65	1874.73	1733.40	1631.64	1556.05	1498.62	1454.20	1419.40	1391.84	1369.83
85000	7837.37	4288.87	3120.07	2546.00	2209.63	1991.90	1841.74	1733.61	1653.31	1592.28	1545.09	1508.11	1478.83	1455.45
90000	8298.39	4541.15	3303.60	2695.77	2339.61	2109.07	1950.08	1835.59	1750.56	1685.94	1635.98	1596.83	1565.82	1541.06
95000	8759.41	4793.44	3487.13	2845.53	2469.59	2226.24	2058.42	1937.57	1847.81	1779.61	1726.87	1685.54	1652.81	1626.68
100000	9220.44	5045.73	3670.66	2995.30	2599.57	2343.41	2166.75	2039.55	1945.07	1873.27	1817.75	1774.25	1739.80	1712.29

TERM	15 Years	16 Years	17 Years	18 Years	19 Years	20 Years	21 Years	22 Years	23 Years	24 Years	25 Years	30 Years	35 Years	40 Years
AMOUNT														
5	.09	.09	.09	.09	.09	.09	.09	.09	.09	.09	.09	.08	.08	.08
10	.17	.17	.17	.17	.17	.17	.17	.17	.17	.17	.17	.16	.16	.16
15	.26	.26	.25	.25	.25	.25	.25	.25	.25	.25	.25	.24	.24	.24
25	.43	.42	.42	.42	.41	.41	.41	.41	.41	.41	.41	.40	.40	.40
50	.85	.84	.83	.83	.82	.82	.82	.81	.81	.81	.81	.80	.80	.80
75	1.27	1.26	1.25	1.24	1.23	1.23	1.22	1.22	1.21	1.21	1.21	1.20	1.20	1.20
100	1.70	1.68	1.66	1.65	1.64	1.63	1.63	1.62	1.62	1.61	1.61	1.60	1.60	1.60
200	3.39	3.35	3.32	3.30	3.28	3.26	3.25	3.24	3.23	3.22	3.22	3.20	3.19	3.19
300	5.08	5.02	4.98	4.94	4.91	4.89	4.87	4.86	4.84	4.83	4.82	4.80	4.79	4.78
400	6.77	6.69	6.64	6.59	6.55	6.52	6.49	6.47	6.45	6.44	6.43	6.39	6.38	6.37
500	8.46	8.37	8.29	8.24	8.19	8.15	8.11	8.09	8.07	8.05	8.03	7.99	7.97	7.97
600	10.15	10.04	9.95	9.88	9.82	9.78	9.74	9.71	9.68	9.66	9.64	9.59	9.57	9.56
700	11.84	11.71	11.61	11.53	11.46	11.40	11.36	11.32	11.29	11.27	11.25	11.18	11.16	11.15
800	13.53	13.38	13.27	13.17	13.10	13.03	12.98	12.94	12.90	12.87	12.85	12.78	12.76	12.74
900	15.22	15.06	14.93	14.82	14.73	14.66	14.60	14.56	14.52	14.48	14.46	14.38	14.35	14.34
1000	16.91	16.73	16.58	16.47	16.37	16.29	16.22	16.17	16.13	16.09	16.06	15.98	15.94	15.93
2000	33.81	33.45	33.16	32.93	32.73	32.57	32.44	32.34	32.25	32.18	32.12	31.95	31.88	31.85
3000	50.71	50.17	49.74	49.39	49.10	48.86	48.66	48.51	48.37	48.27	48.18	47.92	47.82	47.78
4000	67.61	66.90	66.32	65.85	65.46	65.14	64.88	64.67	64.50	64.35	64.23	63.89	63.76	63.70
5000	84.51	83.62	82.90	82.31	81.82	81.43	81.10	80.84	80.62	80.44	80.29	79.86	79.69	79.63
6000	101.42	100.34	99.47	98.77	98.19	97.71	97.32	97.01	96.74	96.53	96.35	95.83	95.63	95.55
7000	118.32	117.07	116.05	115.23	114.55	114.00	113.54	113.17	112.87	112.61	112.41	111.80	111.57	111.48
8000	135.22	133.79	132.63	131.69	130.91	130.28	129.76	129.34	128.99	128.70	128.46	127.77	127.51	127.40
9000	152.12	150.51	149.21	148.15	147.28	146.57	145.98	145.51	145.11	144.79	144.52	143.74	143.44	143.33
10000	169.02	167.24	165.79	164.61	163.64	162.85	162.20	161.67	161.24	160.88	160.58	159.71	159.38	159.25
11000	185.92	183.96	182.36	181.07	180.00	179.14	178.42	177.84	177.36	176.96	176.64	175.69	175.32	175.18
12000	202.83	200.68	198.94	197.53	196.37	195.42	194.64	194.01	193.48	193.05	192.69	191.66	191.26	191.10
13000	219.73	217.41	215.52	213.99	212.73	211.71	210.86	210.17	209.60	209.14	208.75	207.63	207.19	207.03
14000	236.63	234.13	232.10	230.45	229.10	227.99	227.08	226.34	225.73	225.22	224.81	223.60	223.13	222.95
15000	253.53	250.85	248.68	246.91	245.46	244.27	243.30	242.51	241.85	241.31	240.87	239.57	239.07	238.88
16000	270.43	267.57	265.25	263.37	261.82	260.56	259.52	258.67	257.97	257.40	256.92	255.54	255.01	254.80
17000	287.33	284.30	281.83	279.83	278.19	276.84	275.74	274.84	274.10	273.48	272.98	271.51	270.95	270.73
18000	304.24	301.02	298.41	296.29	294.55	293.13	291.96	291.01	290.22	289.57	289.04	287.48	286.88	286.65
19000	321.14	317.74	314.99	312.75	310.91	309.41	308.18	307.17	306.34	305.66	305.09	303.45	302.82	302.58
20000	338.04	334.47	331.57	329.21	327.28	325.70	324.40	323.34	322.47	321.75	321.15	319.42	318.76	318.50
21000	354.94	351.19	348.15	345.67	343.64	341.98	340.62	339.51	338.59	337.83	337.21	335.39	334.70	334.43
22000	371.84	367.91	364.72	362.13	360.00	358.27	356.84	355.67	354.71	353.92	353.27	351.37	350.63	350.35
23000	388.75	384.64	381.30	378.59	376.37	374.55	373.06	371.84	370.83	370.01	369.32	367.34	366.57	366.28
24000	405.65	401.36	397.88	395.05	392.73	390.84	309.28	388.01	386.96	386.09	385.38	383.31	382.51	382.20
25000	422.55	418.08	414.46	411.51	409.09	407.12	405.50	404.17	403.08	402.18	401.44	399.28	398.45	398.12
26000	439.45	434.81	431.04	427.97	425.46	423.41	421.72	420.34	419.20	418.27	417.50	415.25	414.38	414.05
27000	456.35	451.53	447.61	444.43	441.82	439.69	437.94	436.51	435.33	434.35	433.55	431.22	430.32	429.97
28000	473.25	468.25	464.19	460.89	458.19	455.98	454.16	452.67	451.45	450.44	449.61	447.19	446.26	445.90
29000	490.16	484.97	480.77	477.35	474.55	472.26	470.38	468.84	467.57	466.53	465.67	463.16	462.20	461.82
30000	507.06	501.70	497.35	493.81	490.91	488.54	486.60	485.01	483.70	482.62	481.73	479.13	478.13	477.75
31000	523.96	518.42	513.93	510.27	507.28	504.83	502.82	501.17	499.82	498.70	497.78	495.10	494.07	493.67
32000	540.86	535.14	530.50	526.73	523.64	521.11	519.04	517.34	515.94	514.79	513.84	511.07	510.01	509.60
33000	557.76	551.87	547.08	543.19	540.00	537.40	535.26	533.51	532.06	530.88	529.90	527.05	525.95	525.52
34000	574.66	568.59	563.66	559.65	556.37	553.68	551.48	549.67	548.19	546.96	545.95	543.02	541.89	541.45
35000	591.57	585.31	580.24	576.11	572.73	569.97	567.70	565.84	564.31	563.05	562.01	558.99	557.82	557.37
36000	608.47	602.04	596.82	592.57	589.09	586.25	583.92	582.01	580.43	579.14	578.07	574.96	573.76	573.30
37000	625.37	618.76	613.39	609.03	605.46	602.54	600.14	598.17	596.56	595.22	594.13	590.93	589.70	589.22
38000	642.27	635.48	629.97	625.49	621.82	618.82	616.36	614.34	612.68	611.31	610.18	606.90	605.64	605.15
39000	659.17	652.21	646.55	641.95	638.19	635.11	632.58	630.51	628.80	627.40	626.24	622.87	621.57	621.07
40000	676.08	668.93	663.13	658.41	654.55	651.39	648.80	646.68	644.93	643.49	642.30	638.84	637.51	637.00
41000	692.98	685.65	679.71	674.87	670.91	667.68	665.02	662.84	661.05	659.57	658.36	654.81	653.45	652.92
42000	709.88	702.37	696.29	691.33	687.28	683.96	681.24	679.01	677.17	675.66	674.41	670.78	669.39	668.85
43000	726.78	719.10	712.86	707.79	703.64	700.25	697.46	695.18	693.29	691.75	690.47	686.75	685.32	684.77
44000	743.68	735.82	729.44	724.25	720.00	716.53	713.68	711.34	709.42	707.83	706.53	702.73	701.26	700.70
45000	760.58	752.54	746.02	740.71	736.37	732.81	729.90	727.51	725.54	723.92	722.59	718.70	717.20	716.62
46000	777.49	769.27	762.60	757.17	752.73	749.10	746.12	743.68	741.66	740.01	738.64	734.67	733.14	732.55
47000	794.39	785.99	779.18	773.63	769.09	765.38	762.34	759.84	757.79	756.09	754.70	750.64	749.07	748.47
48000	811.29	802.71	795.75	790.09	785.46	781.67	778.56	776.01	773.91	772.18	770.76	766.61	765.01	764.40
49000	828.19	819.44	812.33	806.55	801.82	797.95	794.78	792.18	790.03	788.27	786.82	782.58	780.95	780.32
50000	845.09	836.16	828.91	823.01	818.18	814.24	811.00	808.34	806.16	804.36	802.87	798.55	796.89	796.24
55000	929.60	919.78	911.80	905.31	900.00	895.66	892.10	889.18	886.77	884.79	883.16	878.41	876.58	875.87
60000	1014.11	1003.39	994.69	987.61	981.82	977.08	973.20	970.01	967.39	965.23	963.45	958.26	956.26	955.49
65000	1098.62	1087.01	1077.58	1069.91	1063.64	1058.51	1054.30	1050.84	1048.00	1045.66	1043.73	1038.11	1035.95	1035.12
70000	1183.13	1170.62	1160.47	1152.21	1145.46	1139.93	1135.40	1131.68	1128.62	1126.10	1124.02	1117.97	1115.64	1114.74
75000	1267.64	1254.24	1243.36	1234.51	1227.27	1221.35	1216.50	1212.51	1209.23	1206.53	1204.31	1197.82	1195.33	1194.36
80000	1352.15	1337.85	1326.25	1316.81	1309.09	1302.78	1297.60	1293.35	1289.85	1286.97	1284.59	1277.68	1275.02	1273.99
85000	1436.65	1421.47	1409.14	1399.11	1390.91	1384.20	1378.70	1374.18	1370.46	1367.40	1364.88	1357.53	1354.71	1353.61
90000	1521.16	1505.08	1492.03	1481.41	1472.73	1465.62	1459.80	1455.01	1451.08	1447.84	1445.17	1437.39	1434.39	1433.24
95000	1605.67	1588.70	1574.92	1563.71	1554.55	1547.05	1540.90	1535.85	1531.69	1528.27	1525.45	1517.24	1514.08	1512.86
100000	1690.18	1672.31	1657.81	1646.01	1636.36	1628.47	1622.00	1616.68	1612.31	1608.71	1605.74	1597.10	1593.77	1592.48

MONTHLY PAYMENT
REQUIRED TO AMORTIZE A LOAN

TERM AMOUNT	1 Year	2 Years	3 Years	4 Years	5 Years	6 Years	7 Years	8 Years	9 Years	10 Years	11 Years	12 Years	13 Years	14 Years
5	.47	.26	.19	.15	.14	.12	.11	.11	.10	.10	.10	.09	.09	.09
10	.93	.51	.37	.30	.27	.24	.22	.21	.20	.19	.19	.18	.18	.18
15	1.39	.76	.56	.45	.40	.36	.33	.31	.30	.29	.28	.27	.27	.26
25	2.31	1.27	.92	.75	.66	.59	.55	.52	.49	.47	.46	.45	.44	.43
50	4.62	2.53	1.84	1.50	1.31	1.18	1.09	1.03	.98	.94	.91	.89	.88	.86
75	6.92	3.79	2.76	2.25	1.96	1.76	1.63	1.54	1.46	1.41	1.37	1.34	1.31	1.29
100	9.23	5.05	3.68	3.00	2.61	2.35	2.17	2.05	1.95	1.88	1.82	1.78	1.75	1.72
200	18.45	10.10	7.35	6.00	5.21	4.69	4.34	4.09	3.90	3.75	3.64	3.56	3.49	3.43
300	27.67	15.15	11.02	8.99	7.81	7.04	6.51	6.13	5.84	5.63	5.46	5.33	5.23	5.15
400	36.89	20.19	14.69	11.99	10.41	9.38	8.68	8.17	7.79	7.50	7.28	7.11	6.97	6.86
500	46.11	25.24	18.36	14.99	13.01	11.73	10.85	10.21	9.74	9.38	9.10	8.88	8.71	8.58
600	55.33	30.29	22.04	17.98	15.61	14.07	13.01	12.25	11.68	11.25	10.92	10.66	10.45	10.29
700	64.56	35.33	25.71	20.98	18.21	16.42	15.18	14.29	13.63	13.13	12.74	12.44	12.20	12.00
800	73.78	40.38	29.38	23.98	20.81	18.76	17.35	16.33	15.58	15.00	14.56	14.21	13.94	13.72
900	83.00	45.43	33.05	26.97	23.41	21.11	19.52	18.37	17.52	16.88	16.38	15.99	15.68	15.43
1000	92.22	50.47	36.72	29.97	26.01	23.45	21.69	20.42	19.47	18.75	18.20	17.76	17.42	17.15
2000	184.44	100.94	73.44	59.94	52.02	46.90	43.37	40.83	38.94	37.50	36.39	35.52	34.84	34.29
3000	276.65	151.41	110.16	89.90	78.03	70.35	65.05	61.24	58.40	56.25	54.59	53.28	52.25	51.43
4000	368.87	201.88	146.88	119.87	104.04	93.80	86.73	81.65	77.87	75.00	72.78	71.04	69.67	68.57
5000	461.09	252.35	183.60	149.84	130.05	117.25	108.42	102.06	97.34	93.75	90.98	88.80	87.08	85.71
6000	553.30	302.82	220.32	179.80	156.06	140.70	130.10	122.47	116.80	112.50	109.17	106.56	104.50	102.85
7000	645.52	353.29	257.04	209.77	182.07	164.14	151.78	142.88	136.27	131.25	127.37	124.32	121.91	119.99
8000	737.73	403.76	293.76	239.73	208.08	187.59	173.46	163.29	155.74	150.00	145.56	142.08	139.33	137.13
9000	829.95	454.23	330.48	269.70	234.09	211.04	195.15	183.70	175.20	168.75	163.75	159.84	156.74	154.27
10000	922.17	504.70	367.20	299.67	260.10	234.49	216.83	204.11	194.67	187.50	181.95	177.60	174.16	171.41
11000	1014.38	555.17	403.92	329.63	286.11	257.94	238.51	224.52	214.14	206.24	200.14	195.36	191.58	188.55
12000	1106.60	605.64	440.64	359.60	312.12	281.39	260.19	244.93	233.60	224.99	218.34	213.12	208.99	205.69
13000	1198.82	656.11	477.36	389.56	338.13	304.83	281.88	265.35	253.07	243.74	236.53	230.88	226.41	222.84
14000	1291.03	706.58	514.07	419.53	364.14	328.28	303.56	285.76	272.54	262.49	254.73	248.64	243.82	239.98
15000	1383.25	757.05	550.79	449.50	390.15	351.73	325.24	306.17	292.00	281.24	272.92	266.40	261.24	257.12
16000	1475.46	807.51	587.51	479.46	416.16	375.18	346.92	326.58	311.47	299.99	291.11	284.16	278.65	274.26
17000	1567.68	857.98	624.23	509.43	442.16	398.63	368.61	346.99	330.94	318.74	309.31	301.92	296.07	291.40
18000	1659.90	908.45	660.95	539.40	468.17	422.08	390.29	367.40	350.40	337.49	327.50	319.68	313.48	308.54
19000	1752.11	958.92	697.67	569.36	494.18	445.52	411.97	387.81	369.87	356.24	345.70	337.44	330.90	325.68
20000	1844.33	1009.39	734.39	599.33	520.19	468.97	433.65	408.22	389.34	374.99	363.89	355.20	348.32	342.82
21000	1936.55	1059.86	771.11	629.29	546.20	492.42	455.33	428.63	408.80	393.73	382.09	372.96	365.73	359.96
22000	2028.76	1110.33	807.83	659.26	572.21	515.87	477.02	449.04	428.27	412.48	400.28	390.72	383.15	377.10
23000	2120.98	1160.80	844.55	669.23	598.22	539.32	498.70	469.45	447.73	431.23	418.47	408.48	400.56	394.24
24000	2213.19	1211.27	881.27	719.19	624.23	562.77	520.38	489.86	467.20	449.98	436.67	426.24	417.98	411.38
25000	2305.41	1261.74	917.99	749.16	650.24	586.21	542.06	510.28	486.67	468.73	454.86	444.00	435.39	428.53
26000	2397.63	1312.21	954.71	779.12	676.25	609.66	563.75	530.69	506.13	487.48	473.06	461.76	452.81	445.67
27000	2489.84	1362.68	991.42	809.09	702.26	633.11	585.43	551.10	525.60	506.23	491.25	479.52	470.22	462.81
28000	2582.06	1413.15	1028.14	839.06	728.27	656.56	607.11	571.51	545.07	524.98	509.45	497.28	487.64	479.95
29000	2674.28	1463.62	1064.86	869.02	754.28	680.01	628.79	591.92	564.53	543.73	527.64	515.04	505.06	497.09
30000	2766.49	1514.09	1101.58	898.99	780.29	703.46	650.48	612.33	584.00	562.48	545.83	532.79	522.47	514.23
31000	2858.71	1564.56	1138.30	928.95	806.30	726.90	672.16	632.74	603.47	581.22	564.03	550.55	539.89	531.37
32000	2950.92	1615.02	1175.02	958.92	832.31	750.35	693.84	653.15	622.93	599.97	582.22	568.31	557.30	548.51
33000	3043.14	1665.49	1211.74	988.89	858.31	773.80	715.52	673.56	642.40	618.72	600.42	586.07	574.72	565.65
34000	3135.36	1715.96	1248.46	1018.85	884.32	797.25	737.21	693.97	661.87	637.47	618.61	603.83	592.13	582.79
35000	3227.57	1766.43	1285.18	1048.82	910.33	820.70	758.89	714.38	681.33	656.22	636.81	621.59	609.55	599.93
36000	3319.79	1816.90	1321.90	1078.79	936.34	844.15	780.57	734.79	700.80	674.97	655.00	639.35	626.96	617.07
37000	3412.01	1867.37	1358.62	1108.75	962.35	867.59	802.25	755.21	720.27	693.72	673.19	657.11	644.38	634.21
38000	3504.22	1917.84	1395.34	1138.72	988.36	891.04	823.93	775.62	739.73	712.47	691.39	674.87	661.80	651.36
39000	3596.44	1968.31	1432.06	1168.68	1014.37	914.49	845.62	796.03	759.20	731.22	709.58	692.63	679.21	668.50
40000	3688.65	2018.78	1468.78	1198.65	1040.38	937.94	867.30	816.44	778.67	749.97	727.78	710.39	696.63	685.64
41000	3780.87	2069.25	1505.49	1228.62	1066.39	961.39	888.98	836.85	798.13	768.71	745.97	728.15	714.04	702.78
42000	3873.09	2119.72	1542.21	1258.58	1092.40	984.84	910.66	857.26	817.60	787.46	764.17	745.91	731.46	719.92
43000	3965.30	2170.19	1578.93	1288.55	1118.41	1008.28	932.35	877.67	837.06	806.21	782.36	763.67	748.87	737.06
44000	4057.52	2220.66	1615.65	1318.51	1144.42	1031.73	954.03	898.08	856.53	824.96	800.55	781.43	766.29	754.20
45000	4149.74	2271.13	1652.37	1348.48	1170.43	1055.18	975.71	918.49	876.00	843.71	818.75	799.19	783.70	771.34
46000	4241.95	2321.60	1689.09	1378.45	1196.44	1078.63	997.39	938.90	895.46	862.46	836.94	816.95	801.12	788.48
47000	4334.17	2372.07	1725.81	1408.41	1222.45	1102.08	1019.08	959.31	914.93	881.21	855.14	834.71	818.54	805.62
48000	4426.38	2422.53	1762.53	1438.38	1248.46	1125.53	1040.76	979.72	934.40	899.96	873.33	852.47	835.95	822.76
49000	4518.60	2473.00	1799.25	1468.34	1274.46	1148.97	1062.44	1000.13	953.86	918.71	891.53	870.23	853.37	839.90
50000	4610.82	2523.47	1835.97	1498.31	1300.47	1172.42	1084.12	1020.55	973.33	937.46	909.72	887.99	870.78	857.05
55000	5071.90	2775.82	2019.56	1648.14	1430.52	1289.66	1192.53	1122.60	1070.66	1031.20	1000.69	976.79	957.86	942.75
60000	5532.98	3028.17	2203.16	1797.97	1560.57	1406.91	1300.95	1224.65	1168.00	1124.95	1091.66	1065.59	1044.94	1028.45
65000	5994.06	3280.51	2386.76	1947.80	1690.61	1524.15	1409.36	1326.71	1265.33	1218.69	1182.63	1154.38	1132.02	1114.16
70000	6455.14	3532.86	2570.35	2097.63	1820.66	1641.39	1517.77	1428.76	1362.66	1312.44	1273.61	1243.18	1219.10	1199.86
75000	6916.22	3785.21	2753.95	2247.46	1950.71	1758.63	1626.18	1530.82	1459.99	1406.18	1364.58	1331.98	1306.17	1285.57
80000	7377.30	4037.55	2937.55	2397.29	2080.76	1875.87	1734.59	1632.87	1557.33	1499.93	1455.55	1420.78	1393.25	1371.27
85000	7838.39	4289.90	3121.14	2547.13	2210.80	1993.11	1843.01	1734.92	1654.66	1593.67	1546.52	1509.58	1480.33	1456.97
90000	8299.47	4542.25	3304.74	2696.96	2340.85	2110.36	1951.42	1836.98	1751.99	1687.42	1637.49	1598.38	1567.40	1542.68
95000	8760.55	4794.60	3488.33	2846.79	2470.90	2227.60	2059.83	1939.03	1849.32	1781.16	1728.46	1687.17	1654.48	1628.38
100000	9221.63	5046.94	3671.93	2996.62	2600.94	2344.84	2168.24	2041.09	1946.66	1874.91	1819.43	1775.97	1741.56	1714.09

TERM	15 Years	16 Years	17 Years	18 Years	19 Years	20 Years	21 Years	22 Years	23 Years	24 Years	25 Years	30 Years	35 Years	40 Years
AMOUNT														
5	.09	.09	.09	.09	.09	.09	.09	.09	.09	.09	.09	.08	.08	.08
10	.17	.17	.17	.17	.17	.17	.17	.17	.17	.17	.17	.16	.16	.16
15	.26	.26	.25	.25	.25	.25	.25	.25	.25	.25	.25	.24	.24	.24
25	.43	.42	.42	.42	.41	.41	.41	.41	.41	.41	.41	.40	.40	.40
50	.85	.84	.83	.83	.82	.82	.82	.81	.81	.81	.81	.80	.80	.80
75	1.27	1.26	1.25	1.24	1.23	1.23	1.22	1.22	1.22	1.21	1.21	1.20	1.20	1.20
100	1.70	1.68	1.66	1.65	1.64	1.64	1.63	1.62	1.62	1.62	1.61	1.60	1.60	1.60
200	3.39	3.35	3.32	3.30	3.28	3.27	3.25	3.24	3.23	3.23	3.22	3.20	3.20	3.19
300	5.08	5.03	4.98	4.95	4.92	4.90	4.88	4.86	4.85	4.84	4.83	4.80	4.79	4.79
400	6.77	6.70	6.64	6.60	6.56	6.53	6.50	6.48	6.46	6.45	6.44	6.40	6.39	6.38
500	8.47	8.38	8.30	8.24	8.20	8.16	8.12	8.10	8.08	8.06	8.04	8.00	7.98	7.98
600	10.16	10.05	9.96	9.89	9.83	9.79	9.75	9.72	9.69	9.67	9.65	9.60	9.58	9.57
700	11.85	11.72	11.62	11.54	11.47	11.42	11.37	11.34	11.31	11.28	11.26	11.20	11.18	11.17
800	13.54	13.40	13.28	13.19	13.11	13.05	13.00	12.95	12.92	12.89	12.87	12.80	12.77	12.76
900	15.23	15.07	14.94	14.84	14.75	14.68	14.62	14.57	14.53	14.50	14.47	14.40	14.37	14.36
1000	16.93	16.75	16.60	16.48	16.39	16.31	16.24	16.19	16.15	16.11	16.08	16.00	15.96	15.95
2000	33.85	33.49	33.20	32.96	32.77	32.61	32.48	32.38	32.29	32.22	32.16	31.99	31.92	31.90
3000	50.77	50.23	49.80	49.44	49.15	48.92	48.72	48.56	48.43	48.33	48.24	47.98	47.88	47.84
4000	67.69	66.97	66.39	65.92	65.54	65.22	64.96	64.75	64.58	64.43	64.31	63.97	63.84	63.79
5000	84.61	83.71	82.99	82.40	81.92	81.53	81.20	80.94	80.72	80.54	80.39	79.96	79.80	79.73
6000	101.53	100.45	99.59	98.88	98.30	97.83	97.44	97.12	96.86	96.65	96.47	95.95	95.76	95.68
7000	118.45	117.20	116.18	115.36	114.69	114.13	113.68	113.31	113.01	112.75	112.55	111.94	111.71	111.62
8000	135.37	133.94	132.78	131.84	131.07	130.44	129.92	129.50	129.15	128.86	128.62	127.94	127.67	127.57
9000	152.29	150.68	149.38	148.32	147.45	146.74	146.16	145.68	145.29	144.97	144.70	143.93	143.63	143.52
10000	169.21	167.42	165.97	164.80	163.83	163.05	162.40	161.87	161.43	161.08	160.78	159.92	159.59	159.46
11000	186.13	184.16	182.57	181.27	180.22	179.35	178.64	178.06	177.58	177.18	176.86	175.91	175.55	175.41
12000	203.05	200.90	199.17	197.75	196.60	195.65	194.88	194.24	193.72	193.29	192.93	191.90	191.51	191.35
13000	219.97	217.65	215.76	214.23	212.98	211.96	211.12	210.43	209.86	209.40	209.01	207.89	207.46	207.30
14000	236.89	234.39	232.36	230.71	229.37	228.26	227.36	226.62	226.01	225.50	225.09	223.88	223.42	223.24
15000	253.81	251.13	248.96	247.19	245.75	244.57	243.60	242.80	242.15	241.61	241.17	239.88	239.38	239.19
16000	270.73	267.87	265.56	263.67	262.13	260.87	259.84	258.99	258.29	257.72	257.24	255.87	255.34	255.13
17000	287.65	284.61	282.15	280.15	278.51	277.18	276.08	275.18	274.44	273.83	273.32	271.86	271.30	271.08
18000	304.57	301.35	298.75	296.63	294.90	293.48	292.32	291.36	290.58	289.93	289.40	287.85	287.26	287.03
19000	321.49	318.10	315.35	313.11	311.28	309.78	308.56	307.55	306.72	306.04	305.48	303.84	303.21	302.97
20000	338.41	334.84	331.94	329.59	327.66	326.09	324.80	323.74	322.86	322.15	321.55	319.83	319.17	318.92
21000	355.33	351.58	348.54	346.07	344.05	342.39	341.04	339.92	339.01	338.25	337.63	335.82	335.13	334.86
22000	372.25	368.32	365.14	362.54	360.43	358.70	357.28	356.11	355.15	354.36	353.71	351.82	351.09	350.81
23000	389.17	385.06	381.73	379.02	376.81	375.00	373.51	372.30	371.29	370.47	369.79	367.81	367.05	366.75
24000	406.09	401.80	398.33	395.50	393.19	391.30	389.75	388.48	387.44	386.57	385.86	383.80	383.01	382.70
25000	423.01	418.55	414.93	411.98	409.58	407.61	405.99	404.67	403.58	402.68	401.94	399.79	398.96	398.64
26000	439.93	435.29	431.52	428.46	425.96	423.91	422.23	420.86	419.72	418.79	418.02	415.78	414.92	414.59
27000	456.85	452.03	448.12	444.94	442.34	440.22	438.47	437.04	435.86	434.90	434.10	431.77	430.88	430.54
28000	473.77	468.77	464.72	461.42	458.73	456.52	454.71	453.23	452.01	451.00	450.17	447.76	446.84	446.48
29000	490.69	485.51	481.32	477.90	475.11	472.82	470.95	469.41	468.15	467.11	466.25	463.76	462.80	462.43
30000	507.61	502.25	497.91	494.38	491.49	489.13	487.19	485.60	484.29	483.22	482.33	479.75	478.76	478.37
31000	524.53	519.00	514.51	510.86	507.87	505.43	503.43	501.79	500.44	499.32	498.41	495.74	494.71	494.32
32000	541.45	535.74	531.11	527.34	524.26	521.74	519.67	517.97	516.58	515.43	514.48	511.73	510.67	510.26
33000	558.37	552.48	547.70	543.81	540.64	538.04	535.91	534.16	532.72	531.54	530.56	527.72	526.63	526.21
34000	575.29	569.22	564.30	560.29	557.02	554.35	552.15	550.35	548.87	547.65	546.64	543.71	542.59	542.15
35000	592.21	585.96	580.90	576.77	573.41	570.65	568.39	566.53	565.01	563.75	562.72	559.70	558.55	558.10
36000	609.13	602.70	597.49	593.25	589.79	586.95	584.63	582.72	581.15	579.86	578.79	575.70	574.51	574.05
37000	626.05	619.45	614.09	609.73	606.17	603.26	600.87	598.91	597.29	595.97	594.87	591.69	590.46	589.99
38000	642.97	636.19	630.69	626.21	622.55	619.56	617.11	615.09	613.44	612.07	610.95	607.68	606.42	605.94
39000	659.89	652.93	647.28	642.69	638.94	635.87	633.35	631.28	629.58	628.18	627.03	623.67	622.38	621.88
40000	676.81	669.67	663.88	659.17	655.32	652.17	649.59	647.47	645.72	644.29	643.10	639.66	638.34	637.83
41000	693.73	686.41	680.48	675.65	671.70	668.47	665.83	663.65	661.87	660.39	659.18	655.65	654.30	653.77
42000	710.65	703.15	697.08	692.13	688.09	684.78	682.07	679.84	678.01	676.50	675.26	671.64	670.26	669.72
43000	727.57	719.90	713.67	708.61	704.47	701.08	698.31	696.03	694.15	692.61	691.34	687.64	686.21	685.66
44000	744.49	736.64	730.27	725.08	720.65	717.39	714.55	712.21	710.29	708.72	707.41	703.63	702.17	701.61
45000	761.41	753.38	746.87	741.56	737.23	733.69	730.79	728.40	726.44	724.82	723.49	719.62	718.13	717.56
46000	778.33	770.12	763.46	756.04	753.62	749.99	747.02	744.59	742.58	740.93	739.57	735.61	734.09	733.50
47000	795.25	786.86	780.06	774.52	770.00	766.30	763.26	760.77	758.72	757.04	755.65	751.60	750.05	749.45
48000	812.17	803.60	796.66	791.00	786.38	782.60	779.50	776.96	774.87	773.14	771.72	767.59	766.01	765.39
49000	829.09	820.35	813.25	807.48	802.77	798.91	795.74	793.15	791.01	789.25	787.80	783.58	781.96	781.34
50000	846.01	837.09	829.85	823.96	819.15	815.21	811.98	809.33	807.15	805.36	803.88	799.58	797.92	797.28
55000	930.61	920.80	912.84	906.35	901.06	896.73	893.18	890.26	887.87	885.89	884.27	879.53	877.71	877.01
60000	1015.21	1004.50	995.82	988.75	982.98	978.25	974.38	971.20	968.58	966.43	964.65	959.49	957.51	956.74
65000	1099.81	1088.21	1078.80	1071.15	1064.89	1059.77	1055.58	1052.13	1049.30	1046.96	1045.04	1039.44	1037.30	1036.47
70000	1184.41	1171.92	1161.79	1153.54	1146.81	1141.29	1136.77	1133.06	1130.01	1127.50	1125.43	1119.40	1117.09	1116.19
75000	1269.01	1255.63	1244.77	1235.94	1228.72	1222.81	1217.97	1214.00	1210.73	1208.03	1205.82	1199.36	1196.88	1195.92
80000	1353.61	1339.34	1327.76	1318.33	1310.63	1304.33	1299.17	1294.93	1291.44	1288.57	1286.20	1279.32	1276.67	1275.65
85000	1438.21	1423.05	1410.74	1400.73	1392.55	1385.86	1380.37	1375.86	1372.16	1369.11	1366.59	1359.28	1356.46	1355.38
90000	1522.81	1506.75	1493.73	1483.12	1474.46	1467.38	1461.57	1456.79	1452.87	1449.64	1446.98	1439.23	1436.26	1435.11
95000	1607.41	1590.46	1576.71	1565.52	1556.38	1548.90	1542.76	1537.73	1533.58	1530.18	1527.37	1519.19	1516.05	1514.83
100000	1692.01	1674.17	1659.70	1647.91	1638.29	1630.42	1623.96	1618.66	1614.30	1610.71	1607.75	1599.15	1595.84	1594.56

MONTHLY PAYMENT
REQUIRED TO AMORTIZE A LOAN

TERM AMOUNT	1 Year	2 Years	3 Years	4 Years	5 Years	6 Years	7 Years	8 Years	9 Years	10 Years	11 Years	12 Years	13 Years	14 Years
5	.47	.26	.19	.16	.14	.12	.11	.11	.10	.10	.10	.09	.09	.09
10	.93	.51	.37	.31	.27	.24	.22	.21	.20	.19	.19	.18	.18	.18
15	1.39	.76	.56	.46	.40	.36	.33	.31	.30	.29	.28	.27	.27	.26
25	2.31	1.27	.92	.76	.66	.59	.55	.52	.49	.47	.46	.45	.44	.43
50	4.62	2.53	1.84	1.51	1.31	1.18	1.09	1.03	.98	.94	.92	.90	.88	.86
75	6.92	3.79	2.76	2.26	1.96	1.77	1.63	1.54	1.47	1.41	1.37	1.34	1.32	1.29
100	9.23	5.06	3.68	3.01	2.61	2.35	2.18	2.05	1.96	1.88	1.83	1.79	1.75	1.72
200	18.46	10.11	7.36	6.01	5.22	4.70	4.35	4.10	3.91	3.76	3.65	3.57	3.50	3.44
300	27.68	15.16	11.03	9.01	7.82	7.05	6.52	6.14	5.86	5.64	5.48	5.35	5.25	5.16
400	36.91	20.21	14.71	12.01	10.43	9.40	8.70	8.19	7.81	7.52	7.30	7.13	6.99	6.88
500	46.13	25.26	18.38	15.01	13.03	11.75	10.87	10.23	9.76	9.40	9.13	8.91	8.74	8.60
600	55.36	30.31	22.06	18.01	15.64	14.10	13.04	12.28	11.71	11.28	10.95	10.69	10.49	10.32
700	64.58	35.36	25.74	21.01	18.24	16.45	15.21	14.32	13.66	13.16	12.78	12.47	12.23	12.04
800	73.81	40.41	29.41	24.01	20.85	18.80	17.39	16.37	15.62	15.04	14.60	14.25	13.98	13.76
900	83.03	45.46	33.09	27.01	23.45	21.15	19.56	18.42	17.57	16.92	16.43	16.04	15.73	15.48
1000	92.26	50.51	36.76	30.01	26.06	23.50	21.73	20.46	19.52	18.80	18.25	17.82	17.47	17.20
2000	184.51	101.02	73.52	60.02	52.11	46.99	43.46	40.92	39.03	37.60	36.49	35.63	34.94	34.39
3000	276.76	151.52	110.28	90.02	78.16	70.48	65.19	61.38	58.55	56.40	54.74	53.44	52.41	51.59
4000	369.01	202.03	147.03	120.03	104.21	93.97	86.91	81.83	78.06	75.20	72.98	71.25	69.88	68.78
5000	461.27	252.53	183.79	150.03	130.26	117.46	108.64	102.29	97.58	94.00	91.23	89.06	87.35	85.98
6000	553.52	303.04	220.55	180.04	156.31	140.95	130.37	122.75	117.09	112.79	109.47	106.87	104.82	103.17
7000	645.77	353.55	257.31	210.05	182.36	164.44	152.09	143.20	136.60	131.59	127.72	124.68	122.28	120.37
8000	738.02	404.05	294.06	240.05	208.41	187.94	173.82	163.66	156.12	150.39	145.96	142.50	139.75	137.56
9000	830.27	454.56	330.82	270.06	234.46	211.43	195.55	184.12	175.63	169.19	164.21	160.31	157.22	154.76
10000	922.53	505.06	367.58	300.06	260.51	234.92	217.28	204.58	195.15	187.99	182.45	178.12	174.69	171.95
11000	1014.78	555.57	404.33	330.07	286.56	258.41	239.00	225.03	214.66	206.78	200.70	195.93	192.16	189.15
12000	1107.03	606.08	441.09	360.08	312.61	281.90	260.73	245.49	234.18	225.58	218.94	213.74	209.63	206.34
13000	1199.28	656.58	477.85	390.08	338.66	305.39	282.46	265.95	253.69	244.38	237.19	231.55	227.09	223.54
14000	1291.53	707.09	514.61	420.09	364.72	328.88	304.18	286.40	273.20	263.18	255.43	249.36	244.56	240.73
15000	1383.79	757.59	551.36	450.09	390.77	352.38	325.91	306.86	292.72	281.98	273.68	267.18	262.03	257.93
16000	1476.04	808.10	588.12	480.10	416.82	375.87	347.64	327.32	312.23	300.78	291.92	284.99	279.50	275.12
17000	1568.29	858.60	624.88	510.11	442.87	399.36	369.36	347.77	331.75	319.57	310.17	302.80	296.97	292.31
18000	1660.54	909.11	661.63	540.11	468.92	422.85	391.09	368.23	351.26	338.37	328.41	320.61	314.44	309.51
19000	1752.79	959.62	698.39	570.11	494.97	446.34	412.82	388.69	370.78	357.17	346.66	338.42	331.90	326.70
20000	1845.05	1010.12	735.15	600.12	521.02	469.83	434.55	409.15	390.29	375.97	364.90	356.23	349.37	343.90
21000	1937.30	1060.63	771.91	630.13	547.07	493.32	456.27	429.60	409.80	394.77	383.14	374.04	366.84	361.09
22000	2029.55	1111.13	808.66	660.13	573.12	516.82	478.00	450.06	429.32	413.56	401.39	391.85	384.31	378.29
23000	2121.80	1161.64	845.42	690.14	599.17	540.31	499.73	470.52	448.83	432.36	419.63	409.67	401.78	395.48
24000	2214.05	1212.15	882.18	720.14	625.22	563.80	521.45	490.97	468.35	451.16	437.88	427.48	419.25	412.68
25000	2306.31	1262.65	918.94	750.15	651.27	587.29	543.18	511.43	487.86	469.96	456.12	445.29	436.71	429.87
26000	2398.56	1313.16	955.69	780.15	677.32	610.78	564.91	531.89	507.38	488.76	474.37	463.10	454.18	447.07
27000	2490.81	1363.66	992.45	810.16	703.37	634.27	586.63	552.35	526.89	507.55	492.61	480.91	471.65	464.26
28000	2583.06	1414.17	1029.21	840.17	729.43	657.76	608.36	572.80	546.40	526.35	510.86	498.72	489.12	481.46
29000	2675.31	1464.67	1065.96	870.17	755.48	681.25	630.09	593.26	565.92	545.15	529.10	516.53	506.59	498.65
30000	2767.57	1515.18	1102.72	900.18	781.53	704.75	651.82	613.72	585.43	563.95	547.35	534.35	524.06	515.85
31000	2859.82	1565.69	1139.48	930.18	807.58	728.24	673.54	634.17	604.95	582.75	565.59	552.16	541.52	533.04
32000	2952.07	1616.19	1176.24	960.19	833.63	751.73	695.27	654.63	624.46	601.55	583.84	569.97	558.99	550.23
33000	3044.32	1666.70	1212.99	990.20	859.68	775.22	717.00	675.09	643.97	620.34	602.08	587.78	576.46	567.43
34000	3136.57	1717.20	1249.75	1020.20	885.73	798.71	738.72	695.54	663.49	639.14	620.33	605.59	593.93	584.62
35000	3228.83	1767.71	1286.51	1050.21	911.78	822.20	760.45	716.00	683.00	657.94	638.57	623.40	611.40	601.82
36000	3321.08	1818.22	1323.26	1080.21	937.83	845.69	782.18	736.46	702.52	676.74	656.82	641.21	628.87	619.01
37000	3413.33	1868.72	1360.02	1110.22	963.88	869.19	803.90	756.92	722.03	695.54	675.06	659.03	646.33	636.21
38000	3505.58	1919.23	1396.78	1140.22	989.93	892.68	825.63	777.37	741.55	714.33	693.31	676.84	663.80	653.40
39000	3597.84	1969.73	1433.54	1170.23	1015.98	916.17	847.36	797.83	761.06	733.13	711.55	694.65	681.27	670.60
40000	3690.09	2020.24	1470.29	1200.24	1042.03	939.66	869.09	818.29	780.57	751.93	729.80	712.46	698.74	687.79
41000	3782.34	2070.74	1507.05	1230.24	1068.08	963.15	890.81	838.74	800.09	770.73	748.04	730.27	716.21	704.99
42000	3874.59	2121.25	1543.81	1260.25	1094.14	986.64	912.54	859.20	819.60	789.53	766.28	748.08	733.68	722.18
43000	3966.84	2171.76	1580.57	1290.25	1120.19	1010.13	934.27	879.66	839.12	808.33	784.53	765.89	751.14	739.38
44000	4059.10	2222.26	1617.32	1320.26	1146.24	1033.63	955.99	900.11	858.63	827.12	802.77	783.70	768.61	756.57
45000	4151.35	2272.77	1654.08	1350.26	1172.29	1057.12	977.72	920.57	878.15	845.92	821.02	801.52	786.08	773.77
46000	4243.60	2323.27	1690.84	1380.27	1198.34	1080.61	999.45	941.03	897.66	864.72	839.26	819.33	803.55	790.96
47000	4335.85	2373.78	1727.59	1410.28	1224.39	1104.10	1021.17	961.49	917.17	883.52	857.51	837.14	821.02	808.15
48000	4428.10	2424.29	1764.35	1440.28	1250.44	1127.59	1042.90	981.94	936.69	902.32	875.75	854.95	838.49	825.35
49000	4520.36	2474.79	1801.11	1470.29	1276.49	1151.08	1064.63	1002.40	956.20	921.11	894.00	872.76	855.95	842.54
50000	4612.61	2525.30	1837.87	1500.29	1302.54	1174.57	1086.36	1022.86	975.72	939.91	912.24	890.57	873.42	859.74
55000	5073.87	2777.83	2021.65	1650.32	1432.79	1292.03	1194.99	1125.14	1073.29	1033.90	1003.47	979.63	960.77	945.71
60000	5535.13	3030.36	2205.44	1800.35	1563.05	1409.49	1303.63	1227.43	1170.86	1127.89	1094.69	1068.69	1048.11	1031.69
65000	5996.39	3282.88	2389.22	1950.38	1693.30	1526.94	1412.26	1329.71	1268.43	1221.88	1185.91	1157.74	1135.45	1117.66
70000	6457.65	3535.41	2573.01	2100.41	1823.56	1644.40	1520.90	1432.00	1366.00	1315.88	1277.14	1246.80	1222.79	1203.63
75000	6918.91	3787.94	2756.80	2250.44	1953.81	1761.86	1629.53	1534.28	1463.57	1409.87	1368.36	1335.86	1310.13	1289.61
80000	7380.17	4040.47	2940.58	2400.47	2084.06	1879.31	1738.17	1636.57	1561.14	1503.86	1459.59	1424.91	1397.47	1375.58
85000	7841.43	4293.00	3124.37	2550.49	2214.32	1996.77	1846.80	1738.85	1658.72	1597.85	1550.81	1513.97	1484.82	1461.55
90000	8302.69	4545.53	3308.15	2700.52	2344.57	2114.23	1955.44	1841.14	1756.29	1691.84	1642.03	1603.03	1572.16	1547.53
95000	8763.95	4798.06	3491.94	2850.55	2474.82	2231.69	2064.07	1943.42	1853.86	1785.83	1733.26	1692.08	1659.50	1633.50
100000	9225.21	5050.59	3675.73	3000.58	2605.08	2349.14	2172.71	2045.71	1951.43	1879.82	1824.48	1781.14	1746.84	1719.47

TERM	15 Years	16 Years	17 Years	18 Years	19 Years	20 Years	21 Years	22 Years	23 Years	24 Years	25 Years	30 Years	35 Years	40 Years
AMOUNT														
5	.09	.09	.09	.09	.09	.09	.09	.09	.09	.09	.09	.09	.09	.09
10	.17	.17	.17	.17	.17	.17	.17	.17	.17	.17	.17	.17	.17	.17
15	.26	.26	.25	.25	.25	.25	.25	.25	.25	.25	.25	.25	.25	.25
25	.43	.42	.42	.42	.42	.41	.41	.41	.41	.41	.41	.41	.41	.41
50	.85	.84	.84	.83	.83	.82	.82	.82	.82	.81	.81	.81	.81	.81
75	1.28	1.26	1.25	1.25	1.24	1.23	1.23	1.22	1.22	1.22	1.22	1.21	1.21	1.21
100	1.70	1.68	1.67	1.66	1.65	1.64	1.63	1.63	1.63	1.62	1.62	1.61	1.61	1.61
200	3.40	3.36	3.34	3.31	3.29	3.28	3.26	3.25	3.25	3.24	3.23	3.22	3.21	3.21
300	5.10	5.04	5.00	4.97	4.94	4.91	4.89	4.88	4.87	4.86	4.85	4.82	4.81	4.81
400	6.79	6.72	6.67	6.62	6.58	6.55	6.52	6.50	6.49	6.47	6.46	6.43	6.41	6.41
500	8.49	8.40	8.33	8.27	8.23	8.19	8.15	8.13	8.11	8.09	8.07	8.03	8.02	8.01
600	10.19	10.08	10.00	9.93	9.87	9.82	9.78	9.75	9.73	9.71	9.69	9.64	9.62	9.61
700	11.89	11.76	11.66	11.58	11.51	11.46	11.41	11.38	11.35	11.32	11.30	11.24	11.22	11.21
800	13.58	13.44	13.33	13.23	13.16	13.10	13.04	13.00	12.97	12.94	12.92	12.85	12.82	12.81
900	15.28	15.12	14.99	14.89	14.80	14.73	14.67	14.63	14.59	14.56	14.53	14.45	14.42	14.41
1000	16.98	16.80	16.66	16.54	16.45	16.37	16.30	16.25	16.21	16.17	16.14	16.06	16.03	16.01
2000	33.95	33.60	33.31	33.08	32.89	32.73	32.60	32.50	32.41	32.34	32.28	32.11	32.05	32.02
3000	50.93	50.40	49.97	49.61	49.33	49.09	48.90	48.74	48.61	48.51	48.42	48.16	48.07	48.03
4000	67.90	67.19	66.62	66.15	65.77	65.46	65.20	64.99	64.82	64.67	64.56	64.22	64.09	64.04
5000	84.88	83.99	83.27	82.69	82.21	81.82	81.50	81.23	81.02	80.84	80.69	80.27	80.11	80.04
6000	101.85	100.79	99.93	99.22	98.65	98.18	97.80	97.48	97.22	97.01	96.83	96.32	96.13	96.05
7000	118.83	117.59	116.58	115.76	115.09	114.54	114.09	113.73	113.42	113.18	112.97	112.38	112.15	112.06
8000	135.80	134.38	133.23	132.30	131.53	130.91	130.39	129.97	129.63	129.34	129.11	128.43	128.17	128.07
9000	152.78	151.18	149.89	148.83	147.97	147.27	146.69	146.22	145.83	145.51	145.25	144.48	144.19	144.08
10000	169.75	167.98	166.54	165.37	164.41	163.63	162.99	162.46	162.03	161.68	161.38	160.53	160.21	160.08
11000	186.73	184.78	183.19	181.90	180.85	179.99	179.29	178.71	178.24	177.84	177.52	176.59	176.23	176.09
12000	203.70	201.57	199.85	198.44	197.29	196.36	195.59	194.96	194.44	194.01	193.66	192.64	192.25	192.10
13000	220.68	218.37	216.50	214.98	213.73	212.72	211.89	211.20	210.64	210.18	209.80	208.69	208.27	208.11
14000	237.65	235.17	233.15	231.51	230.17	229.00	228.18	227.45	226.84	226.35	225.94	224.75	224.29	224.12
15000	254.63	251.97	249.81	248.05	246.62	245.44	244.48	243.69	243.05	242.51	242.07	240.80	240.31	240.12
16000	271.60	268.76	266.46	264.59	263.06	261.81	260.78	259.94	259.25	258.68	258.21	256.85	256.33	256.13
17000	288.58	285.56	283.11	281.12	279.50	278.17	277.08	276.19	275.45	274.85	274.35	272.91	272.35	272.14
18000	305.55	302.36	299.77	297.66	295.94	294.53	293.38	292.43	291.65	291.01	290.49	288.96	288.37	288.15
19000	322.53	319.15	316.42	314.19	312.38	310.89	309.68	308.68	307.86	307.18	306.63	305.01	304.39	304.15
20000	339.50	335.95	333.07	330.73	328.82	327.26	325.97	324.92	324.06	323.35	322.76	321.06	320.41	320.16
21000	356.48	352.75	349.73	347.27	345.26	343.62	342.27	341.17	340.26	339.52	338.90	337.12	336.43	336.17
22000	373.45	369.55	366.38	363.80	361.70	359.98	358.57	357.42	356.47	355.68	355.04	353.17	352.45	352.18
23000	390.43	386.34	383.03	380.34	378.14	376.34	374.87	373.66	372.67	371.85	371.18	369.22	368.47	368.19
24000	407.40	403.14	399.69	396.88	394.58	392.71	391.17	389.91	388.87	388.02	387.32	385.28	384.49	384.19
25000	424.38	419.94	416.34	413.41	411.02	409.07	407.47	406.15	405.07	404.19	403.45	401.33	400.51	400.20
26000	441.35	436.74	432.99	429.95	427.46	425.43	423.77	422.40	421.28	420.35	419.59	417.38	416.54	416.21
27000	458.33	453.53	449.65	446.48	443.90	441.79	440.06	438.65	437.48	436.52	435.73	433.43	432.56	432.22
28000	475.30	470.33	466.30	463.02	460.34	458.16	456.36	454.89	453.68	452.69	451.87	449.49	448.58	448.23
29000	492.28	487.13	482.95	479.56	476.79	474.52	472.66	471.14	469.88	468.85	468.01	465.54	464.60	464.23
30000	509.25	503.93	499.61	496.09	493.23	490.88	488.96	487.38	486.09	485.02	484.14	481.59	480.62	480.24
31000	526.23	520.72	516.26	512.63	509.67	507.24	505.26	503.63	502.29	501.19	500.28	497.65	496.64	496.25
32000	543.20	537.52	532.91	529.17	526.11	523.61	521.56	519.87	518.49	517.36	516.42	513.70	512.66	512.26
33000	560.18	554.32	549.57	545.70	542.55	539.97	537.86	536.12	534.70	533.52	532.56	529.75	528.68	528.26
34000	577.15	571.11	566.22	562.24	558.99	556.33	554.15	552.37	550.90	549.69	548.70	545.81	544.70	544.27
35000	594.12	587.91	582.87	578.78	575.43	572.69	570.45	568.61	567.10	565.86	564.83	561.86	560.72	560.28
36000	611.10	604.71	599.53	595.31	591.87	589.06	586.75	584.86	583.30	582.02	580.97	577.91	576.74	576.29
37000	628.07	621.51	616.18	611.85	608.31	605.42	603.05	601.10	599.51	598.19	597.11	593.96	592.76	592.30
38000	645.05	638.30	632.83	628.38	624.75	621.78	619.35	617.35	615.71	614.36	613.25	610.02	608.78	608.30
39000	662.02	655.10	649.49	644.92	641.19	638.14	635.65	633.60	631.91	630.53	629.39	626.07	624.80	624.31
40000	679.00	671.90	666.14	661.46	657.63	654.51	651.94	649.84	648.11	646.69	645.52	642.12	640.82	640.32
41000	695.97	688.70	682.79	677.99	674.07	670.87	668.24	666.09	664.32	662.86	661.66	658.18	656.84	656.33
42000	712.95	705.49	699.45	694.53	690.51	687.23	684.54	682.33	680.52	679.03	677.80	674.23	672.86	672.34
43000	729.92	722.29	716.10	711.07	706.96	703.59	700.84	698.58	696.72	695.19	693.94	690.28	688.88	688.34
44000	746.90	739.09	732.76	727.60	723.40	719.96	717.14	714.83	712.93	711.36	710.08	706.33	704.90	704.35
45000	763.87	755.89	749.41	744.14	739.84	736.32	733.44	731.07	729.13	727.53	726.21	722.39	720.92	720.36
46000	780.85	772.68	766.06	760.67	756.28	752.68	749.74	747.32	745.33	743.70	742.35	738.44	736.94	736.37
47000	797.82	789.48	782.72	777.21	772.72	769.04	766.03	763.56	761.53	759.86	758.49	754.49	752.96	752.37
48000	814.80	806.28	799.37	793.75	789.16	785.41	782.33	779.81	777.74	776.03	774.63	770.55	768.98	768.38
49000	831.77	823.08	816.02	810.28	805.60	801.77	798.63	796.06	793.94	792.20	790.76	786.60	785.00	784.39
50000	848.75	839.87	832.68	826.82	822.04	818.13	814.93	812.30	810.14	808.37	806.90	802.65	801.02	800.40
55000	933.62	923.86	915.94	909.50	904.24	899.94	896.42	893.53	891.16	889.20	887.59	882.92	881.13	880.44
60000	1018.50	1007.85	999.21	992.18	986.45	981.76	977.91	974.76	972.17	970.04	968.28	963.18	961.23	960.48
65000	1103.37	1091.83	1082.48	1074.86	1068.65	1063.57	1059.41	1055.99	1053.18	1050.87	1048.97	1043.45	1041.33	1040.52
70000	1188.24	1175.82	1165.74	1157.55	1150.85	1145.38	1140.90	1137.22	1134.20	1131.71	1129.66	1123.71	1121.43	1120.56
75000	1273.12	1259.81	1249.01	1240.23	1233.06	1227.20	1222.39	1218.45	1215.21	1212.55	1210.35	1203.98	1201.53	1200.59
80000	1357.99	1343.79	1332.28	1322.91	1315.26	1309.01	1303.88	1299.68	1296.22	1293.38	1291.04	1284.24	1281.64	1280.63
85000	1442.87	1427.78	1415.55	1405.59	1397.47	1390.82	1385.38	1380.91	1377.24	1374.22	1371.73	1364.51	1361.74	1360.67
90000	1527.74	1511.77	1498.81	1488.27	1479.67	1472.63	1466.87	1462.14	1458.25	1455.05	1452.42	1444.77	1441.84	1440.71
95000	1612.62	1595.75	1582.08	1570.95	1561.87	1554.45	1548.36	1543.37	1539.26	1535.89	1533.11	1525.03	1521.94	1520.75
100000	1697.49	1679.74	1665.35	1653.63	1644.08	1636.26	1629.85	1624.60	1620.28	1616.73	1613.80	1605.30	1602.04	1600.79

MONTHLY PAYMENT
REQUIRED TO AMORTIZE A LOAN

TERM AMOUNT	1 Year	2 Years	3 Years	4 Years	5 Years	6 Years	7 Years	8 Years	9 Years	10 Years	11 Years	12 Years	13 Years	14 Years
5	.47	.26	.19	.16	.14	.12	.11	.11	.10	.10	.10	.09	.09	.09
10	.93	.51	.37	.31	.27	.24	.22	.21	.20	.19	.19	.18	.18	.18
15	1.39	.76	.56	.46	.40	.36	.33	.31	.30	.29	.28	.27	.27	.26
25	2.31	1.27	.92	.76	.66	.59	.55	.52	.49	.48	.46	.45	.44	.44
50	4.62	2.53	1.84	1.51	1.31	1.18	1.09	1.03	.98	.95	.92	.90	.88	.87
75	6.93	3.79	2.76	2.26	1.96	1.77	1.64	1.54	1.47	1.42	1.38	1.34	1.32	1.30
100	9.23	5.06	3.68	3.01	2.61	2.36	2.18	2.05	1.96	1.89	1.83	1.79	1.76	1.73
200	18.46	10.11	7.36	6.01	5.22	4.71	4.36	4.10	3.91	3.77	3.66	3.57	3.51	3.45
300	27.69	15.16	11.04	9.01	7.83	7.06	6.53	6.15	5.87	5.65	5.49	5.36	5.26	5.17
400	36.92	20.22	14.72	12.02	10.44	9.41	8.71	8.20	7.82	7.54	7.32	7.14	7.01	6.90
500	46.14	25.27	18.40	15.02	13.04	11.77	10.88	10.25	9.78	9.42	9.14	8.93	8.76	8.62
600	55.37	30.32	22.07	18.02	15.65	14.12	13.06	12.30	11.73	11.30	10.97	10.71	10.51	10.34
700	64.60	35.38	25.75	21.03	18.26	16.47	15.23	14.35	13.69	13.19	12.80	12.50	12.26	12.07
800	73.83	40.43	29.43	24.03	20.87	18.82	17.41	16.40	15.64	15.07	14.63	14.28	14.01	13.79
900	83.05	45.48	33.11	27.03	23.48	21.17	19.59	18.44	17.60	16.95	16.46	16.07	15.76	15.51
1000	92.28	50.54	36.79	30.04	26.08	23.53	21.76	20.49	19.55	18.84	18.28	17.85	17.51	17.24
2000	184.56	101.07	73.57	60.07	52.16	47.05	43.52	40.98	39.10	37.67	36.56	35.70	35.01	34.47
3000	276.83	151.60	110.35	90.10	78.24	70.57	65.28	61.47	58.64	56.50	54.84	53.54	52.52	51.70
4000	369.11	202.13	147.14	120.13	104.32	94.09	87.03	81.96	78.19	75.33	73.12	71.39	70.02	68.93
5000	461.38	252.66	183.92	150.17	130.40	117.61	108.79	102.44	97.74	94.16	91.40	89.23	87.52	86.16
6000	553.66	303.19	220.70	180.20	156.47	141.13	130.55	122.93	117.28	112.99	109.68	107.08	105.03	103.39
7000	645.94	353.72	257.48	210.23	182.55	164.65	152.30	143.42	136.83	131.82	127.95	124.93	122.53	120.62
8000	738.21	404.25	294.27	240.26	208.63	188.17	174.06	163.91	156.37	150.65	146.23	142.77	140.03	137.85
9000	830.49	454.78	331.05	270.29	234.71	211.69	195.82	184.40	175.92	169.48	164.51	160.62	157.54	155.08
10000	922.76	505.31	367.83	300.33	260.79	235.21	217.57	204.88	195.47	188.31	182.79	178.46	175.04	172.31
11000	1015.04	555.84	404.61	330.36	286.87	258.73	239.33	225.37	215.01	207.15	201.07	196.31	192.54	189.54
12000	1107.32	606.37	441.40	360.39	312.94	282.25	261.09	245.86	234.56	225.98	219.35	214.16	210.05	206.77
13000	1199.59	656.90	478.18	390.42	339.02	305.77	282.84	266.35	254.10	244.81	237.62	232.00	227.55	224.00
14000	1291.87	707.43	514.96	420.46	365.10	329.29	304.60	286.84	273.65	263.64	255.90	249.85	245.06	241.23
15000	1384.14	757.96	551.74	450.49	391.18	352.81	326.36	307.32	293.20	282.47	274.18	267.69	262.56	258.46
16000	1476.42	808.49	588.53	480.52	417.26	376.33	348.11	327.81	312.74	301.30	292.46	285.54	280.06	275.69
17000	1568.70	859.02	625.31	510.55	443.34	399.85	369.87	348.30	332.29	320.13	310.74	303.38	297.57	292.93
18000	1660.97	909.55	662.09	540.58	469.41	423.37	391.63	368.79	351.83	338.96	329.02	321.23	315.07	310.16
19000	1753.25	960.08	698.87	570.62	495.49	446.89	413.38	389.27	371.38	357.79	347.29	339.08	332.57	327.39
20000	1845.52	1010.61	735.66	600.65	521.57	470.41	435.14	409.76	390.93	376.62	365.57	356.92	350.08	344.62
21000	1937.80	1061.14	772.44	630.68	547.65	493.93	456.90	430.25	410.47	395.45	383.85	374.77	367.58	361.85
22000	2030.08	1111.67	809.22	660.71	573.73	517.45	478.66	450.74	430.02	414.29	402.13	392.61	385.08	379.08
23000	2122.35	1162.20	846.00	690.75	599.81	540.97	500.41	471.23	449.56	433.12	420.41	410.46	402.59	396.31
24000	2214.63	1212.73	882.79	720.78	625.88	564.49	522.17	491.71	469.11	451.95	438.69	428.31	420.09	413.54
25000	2306.90	1263.26	919.57	750.81	651.96	588.01	543.93	512.20	488.66	470.78	456.97	446.15	437.60	430.77
26000	2399.18	1313.79	956.35	780.84	678.04	611.53	565.68	532.69	508.20	489.61	475.24	464.00	455.10	448.00
27000	2491.46	1364.32	993.13	810.87	704.12	635.05	587.44	553.18	527.75	508.44	493.52	481.84	472.60	465.23
28000	2583.73	1414.85	1029.92	840.91	730.20	658.57	609.20	573.67	547.30	527.27	511.80	499.69	490.11	482.46
29000	2676.01	1465.38	1066.70	870.94	756.28	682.09	630.95	594.15	566.84	546.10	530.08	517.53	507.61	499.69
30000	2768.28	1515.91	1103.48	900.97	782.35	705.61	652.71	614.64	586.39	564.93	548.36	535.38	525.11	516.92
31000	2860.56	1566.44	1140.26	931.00	808.43	729.13	674.47	635.13	605.93	583.76	566.64	553.23	542.62	534.15
32000	2952.83	1616.97	1177.05	961.04	834.51	752.65	696.22	655.62	625.48	602.59	584.91	571.07	560.12	551.38
33000	3045.11	1667.50	1213.83	991.07	860.59	776.17	717.98	676.11	645.03	621.43	603.19	588.92	577.62	568.62
34000	3137.39	1718.03	1250.61	1021.10	886.67	799.69	739.74	696.59	664.57	640.26	621.47	606.76	595.13	585.85
35000	3229.66	1768.56	1287.39	1051.13	912.75	823.21	761.49	717.08	684.12	659.09	639.75	624.61	612.63	603.08
36000	3321.94	1819.09	1324.18	1081.16	938.82	846.73	783.25	737.57	703.66	677.92	658.03	642.46	630.13	620.31
37000	3414.21	1869.62	1360.96	1111.20	964.90	870.25	805.01	758.06	723.21	696.75	676.31	660.30	647.64	637.54
38000	3506.49	1920.15	1397.74	1141.23	990.98	893.77	826.76	778.54	742.76	715.58	694.58	678.15	665.14	654.77
39000	3598.77	1970.68	1434.52	1171.26	1017.06	917.29	848.52	799.03	762.30	734.41	712.86	695.99	682.65	672.00
40000	3691.04	2021.21	1471.31	1201.29	1043.14	940.81	870.28	819.52	781.85	753.24	731.14	713.84	700.15	689.23
41000	3783.32	2071.74	1508.09	1231.33	1069.22	964.33	892.03	840.01	801.39	772.07	749.42	731.68	717.65	706.46
42000	3875.59	2122.27	1544.87	1261.36	1095.29	987.85	913.79	860.50	820.94	790.90	767.70	749.53	735.16	723.69
43000	3967.87	2172.80	1581.65	1291.39	1121.37	1011.37	935.55	880.98	840.49	809.74	785.98	767.38	752.66	740.92
44000	4060.15	2223.33	1618.44	1321.42	1147.45	1034.89	957.31	901.47	860.03	828.57	804.26	785.22	770.16	758.15
45000	4152.42	2273.86	1655.22	1351.45	1173.53	1058.41	979.06	921.96	879.58	847.40	822.53	803.07	787.67	775.38
46000	4244.70	2324.39	1692.00	1381.49	1199.61	1081.93	1000.82	942.45	899.12	866.23	840.81	820.91	805.17	792.61
47000	4336.97	2374.92	1728.78	1411.52	1225.69	1105.45	1022.58	962.94	918.67	885.06	859.09	838.76	822.67	809.84
48000	4429.25	2425.45	1765.57	1441.55	1251.76	1128.97	1044.33	983.42	938.22	903.89	877.37	856.61	840.18	827.07
49000	4521.53	2475.98	1802.35	1471.58	1277.84	1152.49	1066.09	1003.91	957.76	922.72	895.65	874.45	857.68	844.31
50000	4613.80	2526.51	1839.13	1501.62	1303.92	1176.01	1087.85	1024.40	977.31	941.55	913.93	892.30	875.19	861.54
55000	5075.18	2779.16	2023.04	1651.78	1434.31	1293.61	1196.63	1126.84	1075.04	1035.71	1005.32	981.53	962.70	947.69
60000	5536.56	3031.81	2206.96	1801.94	1564.70	1411.21	1305.41	1229.28	1172.77	1129.86	1096.71	1070.76	1050.22	1033.84
65000	5997.94	3284.47	2390.87	1952.10	1695.09	1528.81	1414.20	1331.72	1270.50	1224.02	1188.10	1159.98	1137.74	1120.00
70000	6459.32	3537.12	2574.78	2102.26	1825.49	1646.41	1522.98	1434.16	1368.23	1318.17	1279.49	1249.21	1225.26	1206.15
75000	6920.70	3789.77	2758.70	2252.42	1955.88	1764.01	1631.77	1536.60	1465.96	1412.32	1370.89	1338.44	1312.78	1292.30
80000	7382.08	4042.42	2942.61	2402.58	2086.27	1881.61	1740.55	1639.04	1563.69	1506.48	1462.28	1427.67	1400.29	1378.45
85000	7843.46	4295.07	3126.52	2552.74	2216.66	1999.21	1849.33	1741.48	1661.42	1600.63	1553.67	1516.90	1487.81	1464.61
90000	8304.84	4547.72	3310.43	2702.90	2347.05	2116.81	1958.12	1843.92	1759.15	1694.79	1645.06	1606.13	1575.33	1550.76
95000	8766.22	4800.37	3494.35	2853.06	2477.44	2234.41	2066.90	1946.35	1856.88	1788.94	1736.46	1695.36	1662.85	1636.91
100000	9227.60	5053.02	3678.26	3003.23	2607.84	2352.01	2175.69	2048.79	1954.61	1883.10	1827.85	1784.59	1750.37	1723.07

TERM	15 Years	16 Years	17 Years	18 Years	19 Years	20 Years	21 Years	22 Years	23 Years	24 Years	25 Years	30 Years	35 Years	40 Years
AMOUNT														
5	.09	.09	.09	.09	.09	.09	.09	.09	.09	.09	.09	.09	.09	.09
10	.18	.17	.17	.17	.17	.17	.17	.17	.17	.17	.17	.17	.17	.17
15	.26	.26	.26	.25	.25	.25	.25	.25	.25	.25	.25	.25	.25	.25
25	.43	.43	.42	.42	.42	.42	.41	.41	.41	.41	.41	.41	.41	.41
50	.86	.85	.84	.83	.83	.83	.82	.82	.82	.82	.81	.81	.81	.81
75	1.28	1.27	1.26	1.25	1.24	1.24	1.23	1.23	1.22	1.22	1.22	1.21	1.21	1.21
100	1.71	1.69	1.67	1.66	1.65	1.65	1.64	1.63	1.63	1.63	1.62	1.61	1.61	1.61
200	3.41	3.37	3.34	3.32	3.30	3.29	3.27	3.26	3.25	3.25	3.24	3.22	3.22	3.21
300	5.11	5.06	5.01	4.98	4.95	4.93	4.91	4.89	4.88	4.87	4.86	4.83	4.82	4.82
400	6.81	6.74	6.68	6.63	6.60	6.57	6.54	6.52	6.50	6.49	6.48	6.44	6.43	6.42
500	8.51	8.42	8.35	8.29	8.24	8.21	8.17	8.15	8.13	8.11	8.09	8.05	8.04	8.03
600	10.21	10.11	10.02	9.95	9.89	9.85	9.81	9.78	9.75	9.73	9.71	9.66	9.64	9.63
700	11.91	11.79	11.69	11.61	11.54	11.49	11.44	11.40	11.37	11.35	11.33	11.27	11.25	11.24
800	13.61	13.47	13.36	13.26	13.19	13.13	13.08	13.03	13.00	12.97	12.95	12.88	12.85	12.84
900	15.32	15.16	15.03	14.92	14.84	14.77	14.71	14.66	14.62	14.59	14.57	14.49	14.46	14.45
1000	17.02	16.84	16.70	16.58	16.48	16.41	16.34	16.29	16.25	16.21	16.18	16.10	16.07	16.05
2000	34.03	33.67	33.39	33.15	32.96	32.81	32.68	32.58	32.49	32.42	32.36	32.19	32.13	32.10
3000	51.04	50.51	50.08	49.73	49.44	49.21	49.02	48.86	48.73	48.63	48.54	48.29	48.19	48.15
4000	68.05	67.34	66.77	66.30	65.92	65.61	65.36	65.15	64.98	64.83	64.72	64.38	64.25	64.20
5000	85.06	84.18	83.46	82.88	82.40	82.01	81.69	81.43	81.22	81.04	80.90	80.47	80.31	80.25
6000	102.07	101.01	100.15	99.45	98.88	98.41	98.03	97.72	97.46	97.25	97.07	96.57	96.38	96.30
7000	119.09	117.85	116.84	116.03	115.36	114.82	114.37	114.00	113.70	113.46	113.25	112.66	112.44	112.35
8000	136.10	134.68	133.53	132.60	131.84	131.22	130.71	130.29	129.95	129.66	129.43	128.76	128.50	128.40
9000	153.11	151.52	150.22	149.18	148.32	147.62	147.05	146.57	146.19	145.87	145.61	144.85	144.56	144.45
10000	170.12	168.35	166.92	165.75	164.80	164.02	163.38	162.86	162.43	162.08	161.79	160.94	160.62	160.50
11000	187.13	185.18	183.61	182.32	181.28	180.42	179.72	179.15	178.67	178.29	177.97	177.04	176.68	176.55
12000	204.14	202.02	200.30	198.90	197.76	196.82	196.06	195.43	194.92	194.49	194.14	193.13	192.75	192.60
13000	221.15	218.85	216.99	215.47	214.24	213.22	212.40	211.72	211.16	210.70	210.32	209.23	208.81	208.65
14000	238.17	235.69	233.68	232.05	230.72	229.63	228.73	228.00	227.40	226.91	226.50	225.32	224.87	224.70
15000	255.18	252.52	250.37	248.62	247.19	246.03	245.07	244.29	243.64	243.11	242.68	241.41	240.93	240.75
16000	272.19	269.36	267.06	265.20	263.67	262.43	261.41	260.57	259.89	259.32	258.86	257.51	256.99	256.80
17000	289.20	286.19	283.75	281.77	280.15	278.83	277.75	276.86	276.13	275.53	275.04	273.60	273.05	272.84
18000	306.21	303.03	300.44	298.35	296.63	295.23	294.09	293.14	292.37	291.74	291.21	289.70	289.12	288.89
19000	323.22	319.86	317.14	314.92	313.11	311.63	310.42	309.43	308.61	307.94	307.39	305.79	305.18	304.94
20000	340.23	336.70	333.83	331.49	329.59	328.04	326.76	325.72	324.86	324.15	323.57	321.88	321.24	320.99
21000	357.25	353.53	350.52	348.07	346.07	344.44	343.10	342.00	341.10	340.36	339.75	337.98	337.30	337.04
22000	374.26	370.36	367.21	364.64	362.55	360.84	359.44	358.29	357.34	356.57	355.93	354.07	353.36	353.09
23000	391.27	387.20	383.90	381.22	379.03	377.24	375.77	374.57	373.59	372.77	372.11	370.17	369.43	369.14
24000	408.28	404.03	400.59	397.79	395.51	393.64	392.11	390.86	389.83	388.98	388.28	386.26	385.49	385.19
25000	425.29	420.87	417.28	414.37	411.99	410.04	408.45	407.14	406.07	405.19	404.46	402.35	401.55	401.24
26000	442.30	437.70	433.97	430.94	428.47	426.44	424.79	423.43	422.31	421.40	420.64	418.45	417.61	417.29
27000	459.31	454.54	450.66	447.52	444.95	442.85	441.13	439.71	438.56	437.60	436.82	434.54	433.67	433.34
28000	476.33	471.37	467.36	464.09	461.43	459.25	457.46	456.00	454.80	453.81	453.00	450.64	449.73	449.39
29000	493.34	488.21	484.05	480.66	477.90	475.65	473.80	472.29	471.04	470.02	469.17	466.73	465.80	465.44
30000	510.35	505.04	500.74	497.24	494.38	492.05	490.14	488.57	487.28	486.22	485.35	482.82	481.86	481.49
31000	527.36	521.87	517.43	513.81	510.86	508.45	506.48	504.86	503.53	502.43	501.53	498.92	497.92	497.54
32000	544.37	538.71	534.12	530.39	527.34	524.85	522.81	521.14	519.77	518.64	517.71	515.01	513.98	513.59
33000	561.38	555.54	550.81	546.96	543.82	541.26	539.15	537.43	536.01	534.85	533.89	531.11	530.04	529.63
34000	578.39	572.38	567.50	563.54	560.30	557.66	555.49	553.71	552.25	551.05	550.07	547.20	546.10	545.68
35000	595.41	589.21	584.19	580.11	576.78	574.06	571.83	570.00	568.50	567.26	566.24	563.29	562.17	561.73
36000	612.42	606.05	600.88	596.69	593.26	590.46	588.17	586.28	584.74	583.47	582.42	579.39	578.23	577.78
37000	629.43	622.88	617.58	613.26	609.74	606.86	604.50	602.57	600.98	599.68	598.60	595.48	594.29	593.83
38000	646.44	639.72	634.27	629.83	626.22	623.26	620.84	618.86	617.22	615.88	614.78	611.58	610.35	609.88
39000	663.45	656.55	650.96	646.41	642.70	639.66	637.18	635.14	633.47	632.09	630.96	627.67	626.41	625.93
40000	680.46	673.39	667.65	662.98	659.18	656.07	653.52	651.43	649.71	648.30	647.14	643.76	642.48	641.98
41000	697.47	690.22	684.34	679.56	675.66	672.47	669.85	667.71	665.95	664.51	663.31	659.86	658.54	658.03
42000	714.49	707.05	701.03	696.13	692.14	688.87	686.19	684.00	682.19	680.71	679.49	675.95	674.60	674.08
43000	731.50	723.89	717.72	712.71	708.62	705.27	702.53	700.28	698.44	696.92	695.67	692.05	690.66	690.13
44000	748.51	740.72	734.41	729.28	725.09	721.67	718.87	716.57	714.68	713.13	711.85	708.14	706.72	706.18
45000	765.52	757.56	751.10	745.86	741.57	738.07	735.21	732.85	730.92	729.33	728.03	724.23	722.78	722.23
46000	782.53	774.39	767.80	762.43	758.05	754.47	751.54	749.14	747.17	745.54	744.21	740.33	738.85	738.28
47000	799.54	791.23	784.49	779.00	774.53	770.88	767.88	765.43	763.41	761.75	760.38	756.42	754.91	754.33
48000	816.55	808.06	801.18	795.58	791.01	787.28	784.22	781.71	779.65	777.96	776.56	772.52	770.97	770.38
49000	833.57	824.90	817.87	812.15	807.49	803.68	800.56	798.00	795.89	794.16	792.74	788.61	787.03	786.43
50000	850.58	841.73	834.56	828.73	823.97	820.08	816.90	814.28	812.14	810.37	808.92	804.70	803.09	802.47
55000	935.63	925.90	918.02	911.60	906.37	902.09	898.58	895.71	893.35	891.41	889.81	885.17	883.40	882.72
60000	1020.69	1010.08	1001.47	994.47	988.76	984.10	980.27	977.14	974.56	972.44	970.70	965.64	963.71	962.97
65000	1105.75	1094.25	1084.93	1077.34	1071.16	1066.10	1061.96	1058.57	1055.77	1053.48	1051.59	1046.11	1044.02	1043.22
70000	1190.81	1178.42	1168.38	1160.22	1153.56	1148.11	1143.65	1139.99	1136.99	1134.52	1132.48	1126.58	1124.33	1123.46
75000	1275.86	1262.59	1251.84	1243.09	1235.95	1230.12	1225.34	1221.42	1218.20	1215.55	1213.38	1207.05	1204.64	1203.71
80000	1360.92	1346.77	1335.29	1325.96	1318.35	1312.13	1307.03	1302.85	1299.41	1296.59	1294.27	1287.52	1284.95	1283.96
85000	1445.98	1430.94	1418.75	1408.83	1400.75	1394.13	1388.72	1384.28	1380.63	1377.63	1375.16	1367.99	1365.25	1364.20
90000	1531.03	1515.11	1502.20	1491.71	1483.14	1476.14	1470.41	1465.70	1461.84	1458.66	1456.05	1448.46	1445.56	1444.45
95000	1616.09	1599.28	1585.66	1574.58	1565.54	1558.15	1552.10	1547.13	1543.05	1539.70	1536.94	1528.93	1525.87	1524.70
100000	1701.15	1683.46	1669.12	1657.45	1647.94	1640.16	1633.79	1628.56	1624.27	1620.74	1617.83	1609.40	1606.18	1604.94

MONTHLY PAYMENT
REQUIRED TO AMORTIZE A LOAN

TERM	1 Year	2 Years	3 Years	4 Years	5 Years	6 Years	7 Years	8 Years	9 Years	10 Years	11 Years	12 Years	13 Years	14 Years
AMOUNT														
5	.47	.26	.19	.16	.14	.12	.11	.11	.10	.10	.10	.09	.09	.09
10	.93	.51	.37	.31	.27	.24	.22	.21	.20	.19	.19	.18	.18	.18
15	1.39	.76	.56	.46	.40	.36	.33	.31	.30	.29	.28	.27	.27	.26
25	2.31	1.27	.93	.76	.66	.59	.55	.52	.49	.48	.46	.45	.44	.44
50	4.62	2.53	1.85	1.51	1.31	1.18	1.09	1.03	.98	.95	.92	.90	.88	.87
75	6.93	3.80	2.77	2.26	1.96	1.77	1.64	1.54	1.47	1.42	1.38	1.35	1.32	1.30
100	9.23	5.06	3.69	3.01	2.62	2.36	2.18	2.06	1.96	1.89	1.84	1.79	1.76	1.73
200	18.46	10.12	7.37	6.02	5.23	4.71	4.36	4.11	3.92	3.78	3.67	3.58	3.51	3.46
300	27.69	15.17	11.05	9.02	7.84	7.07	6.54	6.16	5.88	5.66	5.50	5.37	5.27	5.18
400	36.92	20.23	14.73	12.03	10.45	9.42	8.72	8.21	7.84	7.55	7.33	7.16	7.02	6.91
500	46.15	25.28	18.41	15.03	13.06	11.78	10.90	10.26	9.79	9.44	9.18	8.95	8.77	8.64
600	55.38	30.34	22.09	18.04	15.67	14.13	13.08	12.32	11.75	11.32	10.99	10.73	10.53	10.36
700	64.61	35.39	25.77	21.05	18.28	16.49	15.26	14.37	13.71	13.21	12.82	12.52	12.28	12.09
800	73.84	40.45	29.45	24.05	20.89	18.84	17.43	16.42	15.67	15.10	14.65	14.31	14.04	13.82
900	83.07	45.50	33.13	27.06	23.50	21.20	19.61	18.47	17.63	16.98	16.49	16.10	15.79	15.54
1000	92.30	50.56	36.81	30.06	26.11	23.55	21.79	20.52	19.58	18.87	18.32	17.89	17.54	17.27
2000	184.60	101.11	73.62	60.12	52.22	47.10	43.58	41.04	39.16	37.73	36.63	35.77	35.08	34.54
3000	276.90	151.67	110.43	90.18	78.32	70.65	65.36	61.56	58.74	56.60	54.94	53.65	52.62	51.80
4000	369.20	202.22	147.24	120.24	104.43	94.20	87.15	82.08	78.32	75.46	73.25	71.53	70.16	69.07
5000	461.50	252.78	184.04	150.30	130.53	117.75	108.94	102.60	97.89	94.32	91.57	89.41	87.70	86.34
6000	553.80	303.33	220.85	180.36	156.64	141.30	130.72	123.12	117.47	113.19	109.88	107.29	105.24	103.60
7000	646.10	353.89	257.66	210.42	182.75	164.85	152.51	143.64	137.05	132.05	128.19	125.17	122.78	120.87
8000	738.40	404.44	294.47	240.47	208.85	188.40	174.30	164.16	156.63	150.91	146.50	143.05	140.32	138.14
9000	830.70	455.00	331.28	270.53	234.96	211.94	196.08	184.67	176.21	169.78	164.81	160.93	157.85	155.40
10000	923.00	505.55	368.08	300.59	261.06	235.49	217.87	205.19	195.78	188.64	183.13	178.81	175.39	172.67
11000	1015.30	556.10	404.89	330.65	287.17	259.04	239.66	225.71	215.36	207.51	201.44	196.69	192.93	189.94
12000	1107.60	606.66	441.70	360.71	313.28	282.59	261.44	246.23	234.94	226.37	219.75	214.57	210.47	207.20
13000	1199.90	657.21	478.51	390.77	339.38	306.14	283.23	266.75	254.52	245.23	238.06	232.45	228.01	224.47
14000	1292.20	707.77	515.32	420.83	365.49	329.69	305.02	287.27	274.10	264.10	256.37	250.33	245.55	241.74
15000	1384.50	758.32	552.12	450.88	391.59	353.24	326.80	307.79	293.67	282.96	274.69	268.21	263.09	259.00
16000	1476.80	808.88	588.93	480.94	417.70	376.79	348.59	328.31	313.25	301.82	293.00	286.09	280.63	276.27
17000	1569.10	859.43	625.74	511.00	443.81	400.33	370.38	348.82	332.83	320.69	311.31	303.97	298.17	293.54
18000	1661.40	909.99	662.55	541.06	469.91	423.88	392.16	369.34	352.41	339.55	329.62	321.85	315.70	310.80
19000	1753.70	960.54	699.35	571.12	496.02	447.43	413.95	389.86	371.99	358.42	347.94	339.73	333.24	328.07
20000	1846.00	1011.09	736.16	601.18	522.12	470.98	435.74	410.38	391.56	377.28	366.25	357.61	350.78	345.34
21000	1938.30	1061.65	772.97	631.24	548.23	494.53	457.52	430.90	411.14	396.14	384.56	375.49	368.32	362.60
22000	2030.60	1112.20	809.78	661.30	574.33	518.08	479.31	451.42	430.72	415.01	402.87	393.37	385.86	379.87
23000	2122.90	1162.76	846.59	691.35	600.44	541.63	501.10	471.94	450.30	433.87	421.18	411.25	403.40	397.14
24000	2215.20	1213.31	883.39	721.41	626.55	565.18	522.88	492.46	469.88	452.73	439.50	429.13	420.94	414.40
25000	2307.50	1263.87	920.20	751.47	652.65	588.73	544.67	512.97	489.45	471.60	457.81	447.01	438.48	431.67
26000	2399.80	1314.42	957.01	781.53	678.76	612.27	566.46	533.49	509.03	490.46	476.12	464.89	456.02	448.94
27000	2492.10	1364.98	993.82	811.59	704.86	635.82	588.24	554.01	528.61	509.33	494.43	482.77	473.55	466.20
28000	2584.40	1415.53	1030.63	841.65	730.97	659.37	610.03	574.53	548.19	528.19	512.74	500.65	491.09	483.47
29000	2676.70	1466.09	1067.43	871.71	757.08	682.92	631.82	595.05	567.77	547.05	531.06	518.54	508.63	500.74
30000	2769.00	1516.64	1104.24	901.76	783.18	706.47	653.60	615.57	587.34	565.92	549.37	536.42	526.17	518.00
31000	2861.30	1567.19	1141.05	931.82	809.29	730.02	675.39	636.09	606.92	584.78	567.68	554.30	543.71	535.27
32000	2953.60	1617.75	1177.86	961.88	835.39	753.57	697.18	656.61	626.50	603.64	585.99	572.18	561.25	552.54
33000	3045.90	1668.30	1214.66	991.94	861.50	777.12	718.96	677.12	646.08	622.51	604.30	590.06	578.79	569.80
34000	3138.20	1718.86	1251.47	1022.00	887.61	800.66	740.75	697.64	665.66	641.37	622.62	607.94	596.33	587.07
35000	3230.50	1769.41	1288.28	1052.06	913.71	824.21	762.54	718.16	685.23	660.24	640.93	625.82	613.87	604.34
36000	3322.80	1819.97	1325.09	1082.12	939.82	847.76	784.32	738.68	704.81	679.10	659.24	643.70	631.40	621.60
37000	3415.10	1870.52	1361.90	1112.18	965.92	871.31	806.11	759.20	724.39	697.96	677.55	661.58	648.94	638.87
38000	3507.40	1921.08	1398.70	1142.23	992.03	894.86	827.90	779.72	743.97	716.83	695.87	679.46	666.48	656.14
39000	3599.70	1971.63	1435.51	1172.29	1018.14	918.41	849.68	800.24	763.55	735.69	714.18	697.34	684.02	673.40
40000	3692.00	2022.18	1472.32	1202.35	1044.24	941.96	871.47	820.76	783.12	754.55	732.49	715.22	701.56	690.67
41000	3784.30	2072.74	1509.13	1232.41	1070.35	965.51	893.26	841.27	802.70	773.42	750.80	733.10	719.10	707.94
42000	3876.60	2123.29	1545.94	1262.47	1096.45	989.05	915.04	861.79	822.28	792.28	769.11	750.98	736.64	725.20
43000	3968.90	2173.85	1582.74	1292.53	1122.56	1012.60	936.83	882.31	841.86	811.15	787.43	768.86	754.18	742.47
44000	4061.20	2224.40	1619.55	1322.59	1148.66	1036.15	958.62	902.83	861.43	830.01	805.74	786.74	771.72	759.74
45000	4153.50	2274.96	1656.36	1352.64	1174.77	1059.70	980.40	923.35	881.01	848.87	824.05	804.62	789.25	777.00
46000	4245.80	2325.51	1693.17	1382.70	1200.88	1083.25	1002.19	943.87	900.59	867.74	842.36	822.50	806.79	794.27
47000	4338.10	2376.07	1729.98	1412.76	1226.98	1106.80	1023.98	964.39	920.17	886.60	860.67	840.38	824.33	811.53
48000	4430.40	2426.62	1766.78	1442.82	1253.09	1130.35	1045.76	984.91	939.75	905.46	878.99	858.26	841.87	828.80
49000	4522.70	2477.18	1803.59	1472.88	1279.19	1153.90	1067.55	1005.42	959.32	924.33	897.30	876.14	859.41	846.07
50000	4615.00	2527.73	1840.40	1502.94	1305.30	1177.45	1089.34	1025.94	978.90	943.19	915.61	894.02	876.95	863.33
55000	5076.49	2780.50	2024.44	1653.23	1435.83	1295.19	1198.27	1128.54	1076.79	1037.51	1007.17	983.42	964.64	949.67
60000	5537.99	3033.27	2208.48	1803.52	1566.36	1412.93	1307.20	1231.13	1174.68	1131.83	1098.73	1072.83	1052.34	1036.00
65000	5999.49	3286.05	2392.52	1953.82	1696.89	1530.68	1416.14	1333.72	1272.57	1226.15	1190.29	1162.23	1140.03	1122.33
70000	6460.99	3538.82	2576.56	2104.11	1827.42	1648.42	1525.07	1436.32	1370.46	1320.47	1281.85	1251.63	1227.73	1208.67
75000	6922.49	3791.59	2760.60	2254.40	1957.95	1766.17	1634.00	1538.91	1468.35	1414.79	1373.41	1341.03	1315.42	1295.00
80000	7383.99	4044.36	2944.64	2404.70	2088.48	1883.91	1742.94	1641.51	1566.24	1509.10	1464.97	1430.43	1403.12	1381.33
85000	7845.49	4297.14	3128.67	2554.99	2219.01	2001.65	1851.87	1744.10	1664.13	1603.42	1556.53	1519.84	1490.81	1467.67
90000	8306.99	4549.91	3312.71	2705.28	2349.54	2119.40	1960.80	1846.69	1762.02	1697.74	1648.10	1609.24	1578.50	1554.00
95000	8768.49	4802.68	3496.75	2855.58	2480.07	2237.14	2069.74	1949.29	1859.91	1792.06	1739.66	1698.64	1666.20	1640.33
100000	9229.99	5055.45	3680.79	3005.87	2610.60	2354.89	2178.67	2051.88	1957.80	1886.38	1831.22	1788.04	1753.89	1726.66

TERM	15 Years	16 Years	17 Years	18 Years	19 Years	20 Years	21 Years	22 Years	23 Years	24 Years	25 Years	30 Years	35 Years	40 Years
AMOUNT														
5	.09	.09	.09	.09	.09	.09	.09	.09	.09	.09	.09	.09	.09	.09
10	.18	.17	.17	.17	.17	.17	.17	.17	.17	.17	.17	.17	.17	.17
15	.26	.26	.26	.25	.25	.25	.25	.25	.25	.25	.25	.25	.25	.25
25	.43	.43	.42	.42	.42	.42	.41	.41	.41	.41	.41	.41	.41	.41
50	.86	.85	.84	.84	.83	.83	.82	.82	.82	.82	.82	.82	.81	.81
75	1.28	1.27	1.26	1.25	1.24	1.24	1.23	1.23	1.23	1.22	1.22	1.22	1.21	1.21
100	1.71	1.69	1.68	1.67	1.66	1.65	1.64	1.64	1.63	1.63	1.63	1.62	1.62	1.61
200	3.41	3.38	3.35	3.33	3.31	3.29	3.28	3.27	3.26	3.25	3.25	3.23	3.23	3.22
300	5.12	5.07	5.02	4.99	4.96	4.94	4.92	4.90	4.89	4.88	4.87	4.85	4.84	4.83
400	6.82	6.75	6.70	6.65	6.61	6.58	6.56	6.54	6.52	6.50	6.49	6.46	6.45	6.44
500	8.53	8.44	8.37	8.31	8.26	8.23	8.19	8.17	8.15	8.13	8.11	8.07	8.06	8.05
600	10.23	10.13	10.04	9.97	9.92	9.87	9.83	9.80	9.77	9.75	9.74	9.69	9.67	9.66
700	11.94	11.82	11.72	11.63	11.57	11.51	11.47	11.43	11.40	11.38	11.36	11.30	11.28	11.27
800	13.64	13.50	13.39	13.30	13.22	13.16	13.11	13.07	13.03	13.00	12.98	12.91	12.89	12.88
900	15.35	15.19	15.06	14.96	14.87	14.80	14.74	14.70	14.66	14.63	14.60	14.53	14.50	14.49
1000	17.05	16.88	16.73	16.62	16.52	16.45	16.38	16.33	16.29	16.25	16.22	16.14	16.11	16.10
2000	34.10	33.75	33.46	33.23	33.04	32.89	32.76	32.66	32.57	32.50	32.44	32.28	32.21	32.19
3000	51.15	50.62	50.19	49.84	49.56	49.33	49.14	48.98	48.85	48.75	48.66	48.41	48.31	48.28
4000	68.20	67.49	66.92	66.46	66.08	65.77	65.51	65.31	65.14	64.99	64.88	64.55	64.42	64.37
5000	85.25	84.36	83.65	83.07	82.59	82.21	81.89	81.63	81.42	81.24	81.10	80.68	80.52	80.46
6000	102.29	101.24	100.38	99.68	99.11	98.65	98.27	97.96	97.70	97.49	97.32	96.82	96.62	96.55
7000	119.34	118.11	117.11	116.29	115.63	115.09	114.64	114.28	113.98	113.74	113.54	112.95	112.73	112.64
8000	136.39	134.98	133.84	132.91	132.15	131.53	131.02	130.61	130.27	129.98	129.75	129.09	128.83	128.73
9000	153.44	151.85	150.56	149.52	148.67	147.97	147.40	146.93	146.55	146.23	145.97	145.22	144.93	144.82
10000	170.49	168.72	167.29	166.13	165.18	164.41	163.78	163.26	162.83	162.48	162.19	161.36	161.04	160.91
11000	187.53	185.59	184.02	182.74	181.70	180.85	180.15	179.58	179.11	178.73	178.41	177.49	177.14	177.01
12000	204.58	202.47	200.75	199.36	198.22	197.29	196.53	195.90	195.40	194.97	194.63	193.63	193.24	193.10
13000	221.63	219.34	217.48	215.97	214.74	213.73	212.91	212.23	211.68	211.22	210.85	209.76	209.35	209.19
14000	238.68	236.21	234.21	232.58	231.26	230.17	229.28	228.56	227.96	227.47	227.07	225.90	225.45	225.28
15000	255.73	253.08	250.94	249.19	247.77	246.61	245.66	244.88	244.24	243.72	243.28	242.03	241.55	241.37
16000	272.77	269.95	267.67	265.81	264.29	263.05	262.04	261.21	260.53	259.96	259.50	258.17	257.66	257.46
17000	289.82	286.82	284.39	282.42	280.81	279.49	278.42	277.53	276.81	276.21	275.72	274.30	273.76	273.55
18000	306.87	303.70	301.12	299.03	297.33	295.93	294.79	293.86	293.09	292.46	291.94	290.44	289.86	289.64
19000	323.92	320.57	317.85	315.65	313.85	312.37	311.17	310.18	309.37	308.71	308.16	306.57	305.96	305.73
20000	340.97	337.44	334.58	332.26	330.36	328.82	327.55	326.51	325.66	324.95	324.38	322.71	322.07	321.82
21000	358.01	354.31	351.31	348.87	346.88	345.26	343.92	342.83	341.94	341.20	340.60	338.84	338.17	337.91
22000	375.06	371.18	368.04	365.48	363.40	361.70	360.30	359.16	358.22	357.45	356.81	354.98	354.27	354.01
23000	392.11	388.05	384.77	382.10	379.92	378.14	376.68	375.48	374.50	373.70	373.03	371.11	370.38	370.10
24000	409.16	404.93	401.50	398.71	396.43	394.58	393.06	391.81	390.79	389.94	389.25	387.25	386.48	386.19
25000	426.21	421.80	418.23	415.32	412.95	411.02	409.43	408.13	407.07	406.19	405.47	403.38	402.58	402.28
26000	443.25	438.67	434.95	431.93	429.47	427.46	425.81	424.46	423.35	422.44	421.69	419.52	418.69	418.37
27000	460.30	455.54	451.68	448.55	445.99	443.90	442.19	440.78	439.63	438.69	437.91	435.65	434.79	434.46
28000	477.35	472.41	468.41	465.16	462.51	460.34	458.56	457.11	455.92	454.93	454.13	451.79	450.89	450.55
29000	494.40	489.28	485.14	481.77	479.02	476.78	474.94	473.43	472.20	471.18	470.34	467.92	467.00	466.64
30000	511.45	506.16	501.87	498.38	495.54	493.22	491.32	489.76	488.48	487.43	486.56	484.06	483.10	482.73
31000	528.49	523.03	518.60	515.00	512.06	509.66	507.70	506.09	504.76	503.68	502.78	500.19	499.20	498.82
32000	545.54	539.90	535.33	531.61	528.58	526.10	524.07	522.41	521.05	519.92	519.00	516.33	515.31	514.91
33000	562.59	556.77	552.06	548.22	545.10	542.54	540.45	538.74	537.33	536.17	535.22	532.46	531.41	531.01
34000	579.64	573.64	568.78	564.83	561.61	558.98	556.83	555.06	553.61	552.42	551.44	548.60	547.51	547.10
35000	596.69	590.51	585.51	581.45	578.13	575.42	573.20	571.39	569.89	568.67	567.66	564.73	563.61	563.19
36000	613.73	607.39	602.24	598.06	594.65	591.86	589.58	587.71	586.18	584.91	583.87	580.87	579.72	579.28
37000	630.78	624.26	618.97	614.67	611.17	608.30	605.96	604.04	602.46	601.16	600.09	597.00	595.82	595.37
38000	647.83	641.13	635.70	631.29	627.69	624.74	622.34	620.36	618.74	617.41	616.31	613.14	611.92	611.46
39000	664.88	658.00	652.43	647.90	644.20	641.18	638.71	636.69	635.02	633.66	632.53	629.27	628.03	627.55
40000	681.93	674.87	669.16	664.51	660.72	657.63	655.09	653.01	651.31	649.90	648.75	645.41	644.13	643.64
41000	698.97	691.74	685.89	681.12	677.24	674.07	671.47	669.34	667.59	666.15	664.97	661.54	660.23	659.73
42000	716.02	708.62	702.62	697.74	693.76	690.51	687.84	685.66	683.87	682.40	681.19	677.68	676.34	675.82
43000	733.07	725.49	719.34	714.35	710.28	706.95	704.22	700.15	700.15	698.65	697.41	693.81	692.44	691.91
44000	750.12	742.36	736.07	730.96	726.79	723.39	720.60	718.31	716.44	714.89	713.62	709.95	708.54	708.01
45000	767.17	759.23	752.80	747.57	743.31	739.83	736.98	734.64	732.72	731.14	729.84	726.08	724.65	724.10
46000	784.21	776.10	769.53	764.19	759.83	756.27	753.35	750.96	749.00	747.39	746.06	742.22	740.75	740.19
47000	801.26	792.97	786.26	780.80	776.35	772.71	769.73	767.29	765.28	763.63	762.28	758.35	756.85	756.28
48000	818.31	809.85	802.99	797.41	792.86	789.15	786.11	783.61	781.57	779.88	778.50	774.49	772.96	772.37
49000	835.36	826.72	819.72	814.02	809.38	805.59	802.48	799.94	797.85	796.13	794.72	790.62	789.06	788.46
50000	852.41	843.59	836.45	830.64	825.90	822.03	818.86	816.26	814.13	812.38	810.94	806.76	805.16	804.55
55000	937.65	927.95	920.09	913.70	908.49	904.23	900.75	897.89	895.54	893.61	892.03	887.43	885.68	885.01
60000	1022.89	1012.31	1003.73	996.76	991.08	986.44	982.63	979.51	976.96	974.85	973.12	968.11	966.19	965.46
65000	1108.13	1096.67	1087.38	1079.83	1073.67	1068.64	1064.52	1061.14	1058.37	1056.09	1054.21	1048.78	1046.71	1045.92
70000	1193.37	1181.02	1171.02	1162.89	1156.26	1150.84	1146.40	1142.77	1139.78	1137.33	1135.31	1129.46	1127.22	1126.37
75000	1278.61	1265.38	1254.67	1245.95	1238.85	1233.04	1228.29	1224.39	1221.19	1218.56	1216.40	1210.13	1207.74	1206.82
80000	1363.85	1349.74	1338.31	1329.02	1321.44	1315.25	1310.18	1306.02	1302.61	1299.80	1297.49	1290.81	1288.26	1287.28
85000	1449.09	1434.10	1421.95	1412.08	1404.03	1397.45	1392.06	1387.64	1384.02	1381.04	1378.59	1371.48	1368.77	1367.73
90000	1534.33	1518.46	1505.60	1495.14	1486.62	1479.65	1473.95	1469.27	1465.43	1462.28	1459.68	1452.16	1449.29	1448.19
95000	1619.57	1602.82	1589.24	1578.21	1569.21	1561.85	1555.83	1550.90	1546.84	1543.51	1540.77	1532.83	1529.80	1528.64
100000	1704.81	1687.17	1672.89	1661.27	1651.80	1644.06	1637.72	1632.52	1628.26	1624.75	1621.87	1613.51	1610.32	1609.10

MONTHLY PAYMENT
REQUIRED TO AMORTIZE A LOAN

TERM	1 Year	2 Years	3 Years	4 Years	5 Years	6 Years	7 Years	8 Years	9 Years	10 Years	11 Years	12 Years	13 Years	14 Years
AMOUNT														
5	.47	.26	.19	.16	.14	.12	.11	.11	.10	.10	.10	.09	.09	.09
10	.93	.51	.37	.31	.27	.24	.22	.21	.20	.19	.19	.18	.18	.18
15	1.39	.76	.56	.46	.40	.36	.33	.31	.30	.29	.28	.27	.27	.26
25	2.31	1.27	.93	.76	.66	.59	.55	.52	.50	.48	.46	.45	.44	.44
50	4.62	2.53	1.85	1.51	1.31	1.18	1.10	1.03	.99	.95	.92	.90	.88	.87
75	6.93	3.80	2.77	2.26	1.97	1.77	1.64	1.55	1.48	1.42	1.38	1.35	1.32	1.30
100	9.24	5.06	3.69	3.01	2.62	2.36	2.19	2.06	1.97	1.90	1.84	1.80	1.76	1.74
200	18.47	10.12	7.37	6.02	5.23	4.72	4.37	4.12	3.93	3.79	3.68	3.59	3.52	3.47
300	27.71	15.18	11.06	9.03	7.85	7.08	6.55	6.17	5.89	5.68	5.51	5.38	5.28	5.20
400	36.94	20.24	14.74	12.04	10.46	9.44	8.74	8.23	7.86	7.57	7.35	7.18	7.04	6.93
500	46.17	25.30	18.43	15.05	13.08	11.80	10.92	10.29	9.82	9.46	9.19	8.97	8.80	8.67
600	55.41	30.36	22.11	18.06	15.69	14.16	13.10	12.34	11.78	11.35	11.02	10.76	10.56	10.40
700	64.64	35.42	25.80	21.07	18.31	16.52	15.29	14.40	13.74	13.24	12.86	12.56	12.32	12.13
800	73.87	40.48	29.48	24.08	20.92	18.88	17.47	16.46	15.71	15.14	14.70	14.35	14.08	13.86
900	83.11	45.54	33.17	27.09	23.54	21.24	19.65	18.51	17.67	17.03	16.53	16.14	15.84	15.59
1000	92.34	50.60	36.85	30.10	26.15	23.60	21.84	20.57	19.63	18.92	18.37	17.94	17.60	17.33
2000	184.68	101.19	73.70	60.20	52.30	47.19	43.67	41.14	39.26	37.83	36.73	35.87	35.19	34.65
3000	277.01	151.78	110.54	90.30	78.45	70.78	65.50	61.70	58.88	56.74	55.09	53.80	52.78	51.97
4000	369.35	202.37	147.39	120.40	104.59	94.37	87.33	82.27	78.51	75.66	73.46	71.73	70.37	69.29
5000	461.68	252.96	184.23	150.50	130.74	117.96	109.16	102.83	98.13	94.57	91.82	89.67	87.96	86.61
6000	554.02	303.55	221.08	180.60	156.89	141.56	130.99	123.40	117.76	113.48	110.18	107.60	105.56	103.93
7000	646.35	354.14	257.93	210.69	183.04	165.15	152.82	143.96	137.39	132.40	128.54	125.53	123.15	121.25
8000	738.69	404.73	294.77	240.79	209.18	188.74	174.66	164.53	157.01	151.31	146.91	143.46	140.74	138.57
9000	831.03	455.32	331.62	270.89	235.33	212.33	196.49	185.09	176.64	170.22	165.27	161.39	158.33	155.89
10000	923.36	505.91	368.46	300.99	261.48	235.92	218.32	205.66	196.26	189.14	183.63	179.33	175.92	173.21
11000	1015.70	556.51	405.31	331.09	287.63	259.52	240.15	226.22	215.89	208.05	201.99	197.26	193.52	190.53
12000	1108.03	607.10	442.16	361.19	313.77	283.11	261.98	246.79	235.51	226.96	220.36	215.19	211.11	207.85
13000	1200.37	657.69	479.00	391.28	339.92	306.70	283.81	267.35	255.14	245.87	238.72	233.12	228.70	225.17
14000	1292.70	708.28	515.85	421.38	366.07	330.29	305.64	287.92	274.77	264.79	257.08	251.06	246.29	242.49
15000	1385.04	758.87	552.69	451.48	392.21	353.88	327.48	308.48	294.39	283.70	275.45	268.99	263.88	259.81
16000	1477.38	809.46	589.54	481.58	418.36	377.48	349.31	329.05	314.02	302.61	293.81	286.92	281.47	277.13
17000	1569.71	860.05	626.39	511.68	444.51	401.07	371.14	349.61	333.64	321.53	312.17	304.85	299.07	294.46
18000	1662.05	910.64	663.23	541.78	470.66	424.66	392.97	370.18	353.27	340.44	330.53	322.78	316.66	311.78
19000	1754.38	961.23	700.08	571.87	496.80	448.25	414.80	390.74	372.90	359.35	348.90	340.72	334.25	329.10
20000	1846.72	1011.82	736.92	601.97	522.95	471.84	436.63	411.31	392.52	378.27	367.26	358.65	351.84	346.42
21000	1939.05	1062.42	773.77	632.07	549.10	495.44	458.46	431.87	412.15	397.18	385.62	376.58	369.43	363.74
22000	2031.39	1113.01	810.61	662.17	575.25	519.03	480.30	452.44	431.77	416.09	403.98	394.51	387.03	381.06
23000	2123.72	1163.60	847.46	692.27	601.39	542.62	502.13	473.00	451.40	435.00	422.35	412.44	404.62	398.38
24000	2216.06	1214.19	884.31	722.37	627.54	566.21	523.96	493.57	471.02	453.92	440.71	430.38	422.21	415.70
25000	2308.40	1264.78	921.15	752.46	653.69	589.80	545.79	514.13	490.65	472.83	459.07	448.31	439.80	433.02
26000	2400.73	1315.37	958.00	782.56	679.84	613.40	567.62	534.70	510.28	491.74	477.44	466.24	457.39	450.34
27000	2493.07	1365.96	994.84	812.66	705.98	636.99	589.45	555.26	529.90	510.66	495.80	484.17	474.98	467.66
28000	2585.40	1416.55	1031.69	842.76	732.13	660.58	611.28	575.83	549.53	529.57	514.16	502.11	492.58	484.98
29000	2677.74	1467.14	1068.54	872.86	758.28	684.17	633.12	596.39	569.15	548.48	532.52	520.04	510.17	502.30
30000	2770.07	1517.74	1105.38	902.96	784.42	707.76	654.95	616.96	588.78	567.40	550.89	537.97	527.76	519.62
31000	2862.41	1568.33	1142.23	933.05	810.57	731.35	676.78	637.52	608.40	586.31	569.25	555.90	545.35	536.94
32000	2954.75	1618.92	1179.07	963.15	836.72	754.95	698.61	658.09	628.03	605.22	587.61	573.83	562.94	554.26
33000	3047.08	1669.51	1215.92	993.25	862.87	778.54	720.44	678.65	647.66	624.13	605.97	591.77	580.54	571.58
34000	3139.42	1720.10	1252.77	1023.35	889.01	802.13	742.27	699.22	667.28	643.05	624.34	609.70	598.13	588.91
35000	3231.75	1770.69	1289.61	1053.45	915.16	825.72	764.10	719.78	686.91	661.96	642.70	627.63	615.72	606.23
36000	3324.09	1821.28	1326.46	1083.55	941.31	849.31	785.94	740.35	706.53	680.87	661.06	645.56	633.31	623.55
37000	3416.42	1871.87	1363.30	1113.64	967.46	872.91	807.77	760.91	726.16	699.79	679.42	663.50	650.90	640.87
38000	3508.76	1922.46	1400.15	1143.74	993.60	896.50	829.60	781.48	745.79	718.70	697.79	681.43	668.49	658.19
39000	3601.10	1973.05	1436.99	1173.84	1019.75	920.09	851.43	802.04	765.41	737.61	716.15	699.36	686.09	675.51
40000	3693.43	2023.65	1473.84	1203.94	1045.90	943.68	873.26	822.61	785.04	756.53	734.51	717.29	703.68	692.83
41000	3785.77	2074.24	1510.69	1234.04	1072.05	967.27	895.09	843.17	804.66	775.44	752.88	735.22	721.27	710.15
42000	3878.10	2124.83	1547.53	1264.14	1098.19	990.87	916.92	863.74	824.29	794.35	771.24	753.16	738.86	727.47
43000	3970.44	2175.42	1584.38	1294.23	1124.34	1014.46	938.76	884.30	843.91	813.26	789.60	771.09	756.45	744.79
44000	4062.77	2226.01	1621.22	1324.33	1150.49	1038.05	960.59	904.87	863.54	832.18	807.96	789.02	774.05	762.11
45000	4155.11	2276.60	1658.07	1354.43	1176.63	1061.64	982.42	925.43	883.17	851.09	826.33	806.95	791.64	779.43
46000	4247.44	2327.19	1694.92	1384.53	1202.78	1085.23	1004.25	946.00	902.79	870.00	844.69	824.88	809.23	796.75
47000	4339.78	2377.78	1731.76	1414.63	1228.93	1108.83	1026.08	966.57	922.42	888.92	863.05	842.82	826.82	814.07
48000	4432.12	2428.37	1768.61	1444.73	1255.08	1132.42	1047.91	987.13	942.04	907.83	881.41	860.75	844.41	831.39
49000	4524.45	2478.96	1805.45	1474.82	1281.22	1156.01	1069.74	1007.70	961.67	926.74	899.78	878.68	862.00	848.71
50000	4616.79	2529.55	1842.30	1504.92	1307.37	1179.60	1091.58	1028.26	981.29	945.66	918.14	896.61	879.60	866.03
55000	5078.47	2782.51	2026.53	1655.41	1438.11	1297.56	1200.73	1131.09	1079.42	1040.22	1009.95	986.27	967.56	952.64
60000	5540.14	3035.46	2210.76	1805.91	1568.84	1415.52	1309.89	1233.91	1177.55	1134.79	1101.77	1075.94	1055.52	1039.24
65000	6001.82	3288.42	2394.99	1956.40	1699.58	1533.48	1419.05	1336.74	1275.68	1229.35	1193.58	1165.60	1143.47	1125.84
70000	6463.50	3541.37	2579.22	2106.89	1830.32	1651.44	1528.20	1439.56	1373.81	1323.92	1285.39	1255.26	1231.43	1212.45
75000	6925.18	3794.33	2763.45	2257.38	1961.05	1769.40	1637.36	1542.39	1471.94	1418.48	1377.21	1344.92	1319.39	1299.05
80000	7386.86	4047.28	2947.68	2407.87	2091.79	1887.36	1746.52	1645.21	1570.07	1513.05	1469.02	1434.58	1407.35	1385.65
85000	7848.53	4300.24	3131.91	2558.37	2222.53	2005.32	1855.67	1748.04	1668.20	1607.61	1560.83	1524.24	1495.31	1472.26
90000	8310.21	4553.19	3316.14	2708.86	2353.26	2123.28	1964.83	1850.86	1766.33	1702.18	1652.65	1613.90	1583.27	1558.86
95000	8771.89	4806.15	3500.37	2859.35	2484.00	2241.24	2073.99	1953.69	1864.46	1796.74	1744.46	1703.56	1671.23	1645.46
100000	9233.57	5059.10	3684.59	3009.84	2614.74	2359.20	2183.15	2056.52	1962.58	1891.31	1836.27	1793.22	1759.19	1732.06

TERM	15 Years	16 Years	17 Years	18 Years	19 Years	20 Years	21 Years	22 Years	23 Years	24 Years	25 Years	30 Years	35 Years	40 Years
AMOUNT														
5	.09	.09	.09	.09	.09	.09	.09	.09	.09	.09	.09	.09	.09	.09
10	.18	.17	.17	.17	.17	.17	.17	.17	.17	.17	.17	.17	.17	.17
15	.26	.26	.26	.26	.25	.25	.25	.25	.25	.25	.25	.25	.25	.25
25	.43	.43	.42	.42	.42	.42	.42	.41	.41	.41	.41	.41	.41	.41
50	.86	.85	.84	.84	.83	.83	.83	.82	.82	.82	.82	.81	.81	.81
75	1.29	1.27	1.26	1.26	1.25	1.24	1.24	1.23	1.23	1.23	1.23	1.22	1.22	1.22
100	1.72	1.70	1.68	1.67	1.66	1.65	1.65	1.64	1.64	1.64	1.63	1.62	1.62	1.62
200	3.43	3.39	3.36	3.34	3.32	3.30	3.29	3.27	3.28	3.27	3.26	3.24	3.24	3.24
300	5.14	5.08	5.04	5.01	4.98	4.95	4.94	4.92	4.91	4.90	4.89	4.86	4.85	4.85
400	6.85	6.78	6.72	6.67	6.64	6.60	6.58	6.56	6.54	6.53	6.52	6.48	6.47	6.47
500	8.56	8.47	8.40	8.34	8.29	8.25	8.22	8.20	8.18	8.16	8.14	8.10	8.09	8.08
600	10.27	10.16	10.08	10.01	9.95	9.90	9.87	9.84	9.81	9.79	9.77	9.72	9.70	9.70
700	11.98	11.85	11.75	11.67	11.61	11.55	11.51	11.47	11.44	11.42	11.40	11.34	11.32	11.31
800	13.69	13.55	13.43	13.34	13.27	13.20	13.15	13.11	13.08	13.05	13.03	12.96	12.94	12.93
900	15.40	15.24	15.11	15.01	14.92	14.85	14.80	14.75	14.71	14.68	14.66	14.58	14.55	14.54
1000	17.11	16.93	16.79	16.67	16.58	16.50	16.44	16.39	16.35	16.31	16.28	16.20	16.17	16.16
2000	34.21	33.86	33.58	33.34	33.16	33.00	32.88	32.77	32.69	32.62	32.56	32.40	32.34	32.31
3000	51.31	50.79	50.36	50.01	49.73	49.50	49.31	49.16	49.03	48.93	48.84	48.59	48.50	48.46
4000	68.42	67.72	67.15	66.68	66.31	66.00	65.75	65.54	65.37	65.24	65.12	64.79	64.67	64.62
5000	85.52	84.64	83.93	83.35	82.88	82.50	82.19	81.93	81.72	81.54	81.40	80.99	80.83	80.77
6000	102.62	101.57	100.72	100.02	99.46	99.00	98.62	98.31	98.06	97.85	97.68	97.18	97.00	96.92
7000	119.73	118.50	117.50	116.69	116.04	115.50	115.06	114.70	114.40	114.16	113.96	113.38	113.16	113.08
8000	136.83	135.43	134.29	133.36	132.61	132.00	131.49	131.08	130.74	130.47	130.24	129.58	129.33	129.23
9000	153.93	152.35	151.07	150.03	149.19	148.50	147.93	147.47	147.09	146.77	146.52	145.77	145.49	145.38
10000	171.03	169.28	167.86	166.70	165.76	165.00	164.37	163.85	163.43	163.08	162.80	161.97	161.66	161.54
11000	188.14	186.21	184.64	183.37	182.34	181.49	180.80	180.24	179.77	179.39	179.08	178.17	177.82	177.69
12000	205.24	203.14	201.43	200.04	198.92	197.99	197.24	196.62	196.11	195.70	195.35	194.36	193.99	193.84
13000	222.34	220.06	218.22	216.71	215.49	214.49	213.68	213.01	212.46	212.00	211.63	210.56	210.15	210.00
14000	239.45	236.99	235.00	233.38	232.07	230.99	230.11	229.39	228.80	228.31	227.91	226.76	226.32	226.15
15000	256.55	253.92	251.79	250.05	248.64	247.49	246.55	245.77	245.14	244.62	244.19	242.95	242.48	242.30
16000	273.65	270.85	268.57	266.72	265.22	263.99	262.98	262.16	261.48	260.93	260.47	259.15	258.65	258.46
17000	290.76	287.77	285.36	283.39	281.79	280.49	279.42	278.54	277.83	277.24	276.75	275.35	274.81	274.61
18000	307.86	304.70	302.14	300.06	298.37	296.99	295.86	294.93	294.17	293.54	293.03	291.54	290.98	290.76
19000	324.96	321.63	318.93	316.73	314.95	313.49	312.29	311.31	310.51	309.85	309.31	307.74	307.14	306.92
20000	342.06	338.56	335.71	333.40	331.52	329.99	328.73	327.70	326.85	326.16	325.59	323.94	323.31	323.07
21000	359.17	355.48	352.50	350.07	348.10	346.48	345.16	344.08	343.19	342.47	341.87	340.13	339.47	339.22
22000	376.27	372.41	369.28	366.74	364.67	362.98	361.60	360.47	359.54	358.77	358.15	356.33	355.64	355.38
23000	393.37	389.34	386.07	383.41	381.25	379.48	378.04	376.85	375.88	375.08	374.42	372.53	371.80	371.53
24000	410.48	406.27	402.86	400.08	397.83	395.98	394.47	393.24	392.22	391.39	390.70	388.72	387.97	387.68
25000	427.58	423.19	419.64	416.75	414.40	412.48	410.91	409.62	408.56	407.70	406.98	404.92	404.13	403.84
26000	444.68	440.12	436.43	433.42	430.98	428.98	427.35	426.01	424.91	424.00	423.26	421.12	420.30	419.99
27000	461.79	457.05	453.21	450.09	447.55	445.48	443.78	442.39	441.25	440.31	439.54	437.31	436.47	436.14
28000	478.89	473.98	470.00	466.76	464.13	461.98	460.22	458.77	457.59	456.62	455.82	453.51	452.63	452.30
29000	495.99	490.90	486.78	483.43	480.71	478.48	476.65	475.16	473.93	472.93	472.10	469.71	468.80	468.45
30000	513.09	507.83	503.57	500.10	497.28	494.98	493.09	491.54	490.28	489.23	488.38	485.90	484.96	484.60
31000	530.20	524.76	520.35	516.77	513.86	511.47	509.53	507.93	506.62	505.54	504.66	502.10	501.13	500.76
32000	547.30	541.69	537.14	533.44	530.43	527.97	525.96	524.31	522.96	521.85	520.94	518.29	517.29	516.91
33000	564.40	558.61	553.92	550.11	547.01	544.47	542.40	540.70	539.30	538.16	537.22	534.49	533.46	533.06
34000	581.51	575.54	570.71	566.78	563.58	560.97	558.83	557.08	555.65	554.47	553.50	550.69	549.62	549.22
35000	598.61	592.47	587.49	583.45	580.16	577.47	575.27	573.47	571.99	570.77	569.77	566.88	565.79	565.37
36000	615.71	609.40	604.28	600.12	596.74	593.97	591.71	589.85	588.33	587.08	586.05	583.08	581.95	581.52
37000	632.82	626.32	621.07	616.79	613.31	610.47	608.14	606.24	604.67	603.39	602.33	599.28	598.12	597.67
38000	649.92	643.25	637.85	633.46	629.89	626.97	624.58	622.62	621.02	619.70	618.61	615.47	614.28	613.83
39000	667.02	660.18	654.64	650.13	646.46	643.47	641.02	639.01	637.36	636.00	634.89	631.67	630.45	629.98
40000	684.12	677.11	671.42	666.80	663.04	659.97	657.45	655.39	653.70	652.31	651.17	647.87	646.61	646.13
41000	701.23	694.03	688.21	683.47	679.62	676.46	673.89	671.78	670.04	668.62	667.45	664.06	662.78	662.29
42000	718.33	710.96	704.99	700.14	696.19	692.96	690.32	688.16	686.38	684.93	683.73	680.26	678.94	678.44
43000	735.43	727.89	721.78	716.81	712.77	709.46	706.76	704.54	702.73	701.23	700.01	696.46	695.11	694.59
44000	752.54	744.82	738.56	733.48	729.34	725.96	723.20	720.93	719.07	717.54	716.29	712.65	711.27	710.75
45000	769.64	761.74	755.35	750.15	745.92	742.46	739.63	737.31	735.41	733.85	732.57	728.85	727.44	726.90
46000	786.74	778.67	772.13	766.82	762.49	758.96	756.07	753.70	751.75	750.16	748.84	745.05	743.60	743.05
47000	803.85	795.60	788.92	783.49	779.07	775.46	772.50	770.08	768.10	766.47	765.12	761.24	759.77	759.21
48000	820.95	812.53	805.71	800.16	795.65	791.96	788.94	786.47	784.44	782.77	781.40	777.44	775.93	775.36
49000	838.05	829.45	822.49	816.83	812.22	808.46	805.38	802.85	800.78	799.08	797.68	793.64	792.10	791.51
50000	855.15	846.38	839.28	833.50	828.80	824.96	821.81	819.24	817.12	815.39	813.96	809.83	808.26	807.67
55000	940.67	931.02	923.20	916.85	911.68	907.45	903.99	901.16	898.84	896.93	895.36	890.82	889.09	888.43
60000	1026.18	1015.66	1007.13	1000.20	994.56	989.95	986.17	983.08	980.55	978.46	976.75	971.80	969.92	969.20
65000	1111.70	1100.29	1091.06	1083.55	1077.44	1072.44	1068.36	1065.01	1062.26	1060.00	1058.15	1052.78	1050.74	1049.97
70000	1197.21	1184.93	1174.98	1166.90	1160.32	1154.94	1150.54	1146.93	1143.97	1141.54	1139.54	1133.76	1131.57	1130.73
75000	1282.73	1269.57	1258.91	1250.25	1243.19	1237.43	1232.72	1228.85	1225.68	1223.08	1220.94	1214.75	1212.40	1211.50
80000	1368.24	1354.21	1342.84	1333.60	1326.07	1319.93	1314.90	1310.78	1307.39	1304.62	1302.34	1295.73	1293.22	1292.26
85000	1453.76	1438.84	1426.77	1416.95	1408.95	1402.42	1397.08	1392.70	1389.11	1386.16	1383.73	1376.71	1374.05	1373.03
90000	1539.27	1523.48	1510.69	1500.30	1491.83	1484.92	1479.26	1474.62	1470.82	1467.69	1465.13	1457.70	1454.87	1453.80
95000	1624.79	1608.12	1594.62	1583.65	1574.71	1567.41	1561.44	1556.55	1552.53	1549.23	1546.52	1538.68	1535.70	1534.56
100000	1710.30	1692.76	1678.55	1667.00	1657.59	1649.91	1643.62	1638.47	1634.24	1630.77	1627.92	1619.66	1616.52	1615.33

TERM	1 Year	2 Years	3 Years	4 Years	5 Years	6 Years	7 Years	8 Years	9 Years	10 Years	11 Years	12 Years	13 Years	14 Years
AMOUNT														
5	.47	.26	.19	.16	.14	.12	.11	.11	.10	.10	.10	.09	.09	.09
10	.93	.51	.37	.31	.27	.24	.22	.21	.20	.19	.19	.18	.18	.18
15	1.39	.76	.56	.46	.40	.36	.33	.31	.30	.29	.28	.27	.27	.27
25	2.31	1.27	.93	.76	.66	.60	.55	.52	.50	.48	.46	.45	.45	.44
50	4.62	2.54	1.85	1.51	1.31	1.19	1.10	1.03	.99	.95	.92	.90	.89	.87
75	6.93	3.80	2.77	2.26	1.97	1.78	1.64	1.55	1.48	1.42	1.38	1.35	1.33	1.31
100	9.24	5.07	3.69	3.02	2.62	2.37	2.19	2.06	1.97	1.90	1.84	1.80	1.77	1.74
200	18.47	10.13	7.38	6.03	5.24	4.73	4.37	4.12	3.93	3.79	3.68	3.59	3.53	3.47
300	27.71	15.19	11.06	9.04	7.85	7.09	6.56	6.18	5.90	5.68	5.52	5.39	5.29	5.21
400	36.94	20.25	14.75	12.05	10.47	9.45	8.74	8.24	7.86	7.58	7.36	7.18	7.05	6.94
500	46.18	25.31	18.43	15.06	13.09	11.81	10.93	10.30	9.83	9.47	9.19	8.98	8.81	8.67
600	55.41	30.37	22.12	18.07	15.70	14.17	13.11	12.35	11.79	11.36	11.03	10.77	10.57	10.41
700	64.65	35.43	25.81	21.08	18.32	16.53	15.30	14.41	13.75	13.26	12.87	12.57	12.33	12.14
800	73.88	40.49	29.49	24.09	20.93	18.89	17.48	16.47	15.72	15.15	14.71	14.36	14.09	13.88
900	83.12	45.55	33.18	27.11	23.55	21.25	19.67	18.53	17.68	17.04	16.55	16.16	15.85	15.61
1000	92.35	50.61	36.86	30.12	26.17	23.61	21.85	20.59	19.65	18.93	18.38	17.95	17.61	17.34
2000	184.70	101.21	73.72	60.23	52.33	47.22	43.70	41.17	39.29	37.86	36.76	35.90	35.22	34.68
3000	277.05	151.81	110.58	90.34	78.49	70.82	65.54	61.75	58.93	56.79	55.14	53.85	52.83	52.02
4000	369.40	202.42	147.44	120.45	104.65	94.43	87.39	82.33	78.57	75.72	73.52	71.80	70.44	69.36
5000	461.74	253.02	184.30	150.56	130.81	118.04	109.24	102.91	98.21	94.65	91.90	89.75	88.05	86.70
6000	554.09	303.62	221.16	180.67	156.97	141.64	131.08	123.49	117.86	113.58	110.28	107.70	105.66	104.04
7000	646.44	354.23	258.02	210.79	183.13	165.25	152.93	144.07	137.50	132.51	128.66	125.65	123.27	121.38
8000	738.79	404.83	294.87	240.90	209.29	188.86	174.78	164.65	157.14	151.44	147.04	143.60	140.88	138.71
9000	831.13	455.43	331.73	271.01	235.46	212.46	196.62	185.23	176.78	170.37	165.42	161.55	158.49	156.05
10000	923.48	506.04	368.59	301.12	261.62	236.07	218.47	205.81	196.42	189.30	183.80	179.50	176.10	173.39
11000	1015.83	556.64	405.45	331.23	287.78	259.67	240.31	226.39	216.06	208.23	202.18	197.45	193.71	190.73
12000	1108.18	607.24	442.31	361.34	313.94	283.28	262.16	246.97	235.71	227.16	220.56	215.40	211.32	208.07
13000	1200.52	657.85	479.17	391.46	340.10	306.89	284.01	267.55	255.35	246.09	238.94	233.35	228.93	225.41
14000	1292.87	708.45	516.03	421.57	366.26	330.49	305.85	288.13	274.99	265.02	257.32	251.30	246.54	242.75
15000	1385.22	759.05	552.88	451.68	392.42	354.10	327.70	308.71	294.63	283.95	275.70	269.25	264.15	260.08
16000	1477.57	809.66	589.74	481.79	418.58	377.71	349.55	329.29	314.27	302.88	294.08	287.20	281.76	277.42
17000	1569.91	860.26	626.60	511.90	444.74	401.31	371.39	349.87	333.91	321.81	312.46	305.15	299.37	294.76
18000	1662.26	910.86	663.46	542.01	470.91	424.92	393.24	370.46	353.56	340.73	330.84	323.10	316.98	312.10
19000	1754.61	961.47	700.32	572.13	497.07	448.52	415.09	391.04	373.20	359.66	349.22	341.04	334.59	329.44
20000	1846.96	1012.07	737.18	602.24	523.23	472.13	436.93	411.62	392.84	378.59	367.60	358.99	352.19	346.78
21000	1939.30	1062.67	774.04	632.35	549.39	495.74	458.78	432.20	412.48	397.52	385.98	376.94	369.80	364.12
22000	2031.65	1113.27	810.89	662.46	575.55	519.34	480.62	452.78	432.12	416.45	404.36	394.89	387.41	381.45
23000	2124.00	1163.88	847.75	692.57	601.71	542.95	502.47	473.36	451.77	435.38	422.74	412.84	405.02	398.79
24000	2216.35	1214.48	884.61	722.68	627.87	566.56	524.32	493.94	471.41	454.31	441.11	430.79	422.63	416.13
25000	2308.69	1265.08	921.47	752.80	654.03	590.16	546.16	514.52	491.05	473.24	459.49	448.74	440.24	433.47
26000	2401.04	1315.69	958.33	782.91	680.19	613.77	568.01	535.10	510.69	492.17	477.87	466.69	457.85	450.81
27000	2493.39	1366.29	995.19	813.02	706.36	637.38	589.86	555.68	530.33	511.10	496.25	484.64	475.46	468.15
28000	2585.74	1416.89	1032.05	843.13	732.52	660.98	611.70	576.26	549.97	530.03	514.63	502.59	493.07	485.49
29000	2678.09	1467.50	1068.90	873.24	758.68	684.59	633.55	596.84	569.62	548.96	533.01	520.54	510.68	502.82
30000	2770.43	1518.10	1105.76	903.35	784.84	708.19	655.40	617.42	589.26	567.89	551.39	538.49	528.29	520.16
31000	2862.78	1568.70	1142.62	933.46	811.00	731.80	677.24	638.00	608.90	586.82	569.77	556.44	545.90	537.50
32000	2955.13	1619.31	1179.48	963.58	837.16	755.41	699.09	658.58	628.54	605.75	588.15	574.39	563.51	554.84
33000	3047.48	1669.91	1216.34	993.69	863.32	779.01	720.93	679.16	648.18	624.68	606.53	592.34	581.12	572.18
34000	3139.82	1720.51	1253.20	1023.80	889.48	802.62	742.78	699.74	667.82	643.61	624.91	610.29	598.73	589.52
35000	3232.17	1771.12	1290.06	1053.91	915.64	826.23	764.63	720.32	687.47	662.54	643.29	628.24	616.34	606.86
36000	3324.52	1821.72	1326.91	1084.02	941.81	849.83	786.47	740.91	707.11	681.46	661.67	646.19	633.95	624.19
37000	3416.87	1872.32	1363.77	1114.13	967.97	873.44	808.32	761.49	726.75	700.39	680.05	664.13	651.56	641.53
38000	3509.21	1922.93	1400.63	1144.25	994.13	897.04	830.17	782.07	746.39	719.32	698.43	682.08	669.17	658.87
39000	3601.56	1973.53	1437.49	1174.36	1020.29	920.65	852.01	802.65	766.03	738.25	716.81	700.03	686.78	676.21
40000	3693.91	2024.13	1474.35	1204.47	1046.45	944.26	873.86	823.23	785.68	757.18	735.19	717.98	704.38	693.55
41000	3786.26	2074.74	1511.21	1234.58	1072.61	967.86	895.70	843.81	805.32	776.11	753.57	735.93	721.99	710.89
42000	3878.60	2125.34	1548.07	1264.69	1098.77	991.47	917.55	864.39	824.96	795.04	771.95	753.88	739.60	728.23
43000	3970.95	2175.94	1584.92	1294.80	1124.93	1015.08	939.40	884.97	844.60	813.97	790.33	771.83	757.21	745.56
44000	4063.30	2226.54	1621.78	1324.92	1151.10	1038.68	961.24	905.55	864.24	832.90	808.71	789.78	774.82	762.90
45000	4155.65	2277.15	1658.64	1355.03	1177.26	1062.29	983.09	926.13	883.88	851.83	827.09	807.73	792.43	780.24
46000	4247.99	2327.75	1695.50	1385.14	1203.42	1085.90	1004.94	946.71	903.53	870.76	845.47	825.68	810.04	797.58
47000	4340.34	2378.35	1732.36	1415.25	1229.58	1109.50	1026.78	967.29	923.17	889.69	863.84	843.63	827.65	814.92
48000	4432.69	2428.96	1769.22	1445.36	1255.74	1133.11	1048.63	987.87	942.81	908.62	882.22	861.58	845.26	832.26
49000	4525.04	2479.56	1806.08	1475.47	1281.90	1156.71	1070.48	1008.45	962.45	927.55	900.60	879.53	862.87	849.60
50000	4617.38	2530.16	1842.93	1505.59	1308.06	1180.32	1092.32	1029.03	982.09	946.48	918.98	897.48	880.48	866.94
55000	5079.12	2783.18	2027.23	1656.14	1438.87	1298.35	1201.55	1131.94	1080.30	1041.12	1010.88	987.22	968.53	953.63
60000	5540.86	3036.20	2211.52	1806.70	1569.67	1416.38	1310.79	1234.84	1178.51	1135.77	1102.78	1076.97	1056.57	1040.32
65000	6002.60	3289.21	2395.81	1957.26	1700.48	1534.42	1420.02	1337.74	1276.72	1230.42	1194.68	1166.72	1144.62	1127.01
70000	6464.34	3542.23	2580.11	2107.82	1831.29	1652.45	1529.25	1440.64	1374.93	1325.07	1286.58	1256.47	1232.67	1213.71
75000	6926.07	3795.24	2764.40	2258.38	1962.09	1770.48	1638.48	1543.55	1473.14	1419.71	1378.47	1346.21	1320.72	1300.40
80000	7387.81	4048.26	2948.69	2408.93	2092.90	1888.51	1747.71	1646.45	1571.35	1514.36	1470.37	1435.96	1408.76	1387.09
85000	7849.55	4301.27	3132.98	2559.49	2223.70	2006.54	1856.94	1749.35	1669.55	1609.01	1562.27	1525.71	1496.81	1473.79
90000	8311.29	4554.29	3317.28	2710.05	2354.51	2124.57	1966.18	1852.26	1767.76	1703.65	1654.17	1615.46	1584.86	1560.48
95000	8773.03	4807.31	3501.57	2860.61	2485.31	2242.60	2075.41	1955.16	1865.97	1798.30	1746.06	1705.20	1672.91	1647.17
100000	9234.76	5060.32	3685.86	3011.17	2616.12	2360.64	2184.64	2058.06	1964.18	1892.95	1837.96	1794.95	1760.95	1733.87

TERM	15 Years	16 Years	17 Years	18 Years	19 Years	20 Years	21 Years	22 Years	23 Years	24 Years	25 Years	30 Years	35 Years	40 Years
AMOUNT														
5	.09	.09	.09	.09	.09	.09	.09	.09	.09	.09	.09	.09	.09	.09
10	.18	.17	.17	.17	.17	.17	.17	.17	.17	.17	.17	.17	.17	.17
15	.26	.26	.26	.26	.25	.25	.25	.25	.25	.25	.25	.25	.25	.25
25	.43	.43	.43	.42	.42	.42	.42	.42	.41	.41	.41	.41	.41	.41
50	.86	.85	.85	.84	.83	.83	.83	.83	.82	.82	.82	.82	.81	.81
75	1.29	1.28	1.27	1.26	1.25	1.24	1.24	1.24	1.23	1.23	1.23	1.22	1.22	1.22
100	1.72	1.70	1.69	1.67	1.66	1.66	1.65	1.65	1.64	1.64	1.64	1.63	1.62	1.62
200	3.43	3.39	3.37	3.34	3.32	3.31	3.30	3.29	3.28	3.27	3.26	3.25	3.24	3.24
300	5.14	5.09	5.05	5.01	4.98	4.96	4.94	4.93	4.91	4.90	4.89	4.87	4.86	4.86
400	6.85	6.78	6.73	6.68	6.64	6.61	6.59	6.57	6.55	6.54	6.52	6.49	6.48	6.47
500	8.57	8.48	8.41	8.35	8.30	8.26	8.23	8.21	8.19	8.17	8.15	8.11	8.10	8.09
600	10.28	10.17	10.09	10.02	9.96	9.92	9.88	9.85	9.82	9.80	9.78	9.74	9.72	9.71
700	11.99	11.87	11.77	11.69	11.62	11.57	11.52	11.49	11.46	11.43	11.41	11.36	11.34	11.33
800	13.70	13.56	13.45	13.36	13.28	13.22	13.17	13.13	13.09	13.07	13.04	12.98	12.95	12.94
900	15.41	15.26	15.13	15.03	14.94	14.87	14.82	14.77	14.73	14.70	14.67	14.60	14.57	14.56
1000	17.13	16.95	16.81	16.69	16.60	16.52	16.46	16.41	16.37	16.33	16.30	16.22	16.19	16.18
2000	34.25	33.90	33.61	33.38	33.20	33.04	32.92	32.81	32.73	32.66	32.60	32.44	32.38	32.35
3000	51.37	50.84	50.42	50.07	49.79	49.56	49.37	49.22	49.09	48.99	48.90	48.66	48.56	48.53
4000	68.49	67.79	67.22	66.76	66.39	66.08	65.83	65.62	65.45	65.32	65.20	64.87	64.75	64.70
5000	85.61	84.74	84.03	83.45	82.98	82.60	82.28	82.03	81.82	81.64	81.50	81.09	80.93	80.88
6000	102.73	101.68	100.83	100.14	99.58	99.12	98.74	98.43	98.18	97.97	97.80	97.31	97.12	97.05
7000	119.85	118.63	117.64	116.83	116.17	115.63	115.20	114.84	114.54	114.30	114.10	113.52	113.31	113.22
8000	136.98	135.57	134.44	133.52	132.77	132.15	131.65	131.24	130.90	130.63	130.40	129.74	129.49	129.40
9000	154.10	152.52	151.24	150.21	149.36	148.67	148.11	147.65	147.27	146.95	146.70	145.96	145.68	145.57
10000	171.22	169.47	168.05	166.90	165.96	165.19	164.56	164.05	163.63	163.28	163.00	162.18	161.86	161.75
11000	188.34	186.41	184.85	183.58	182.55	181.71	181.02	180.45	179.99	179.61	179.30	178.39	178.05	177.92
12000	205.46	203.36	201.66	200.27	199.15	198.23	197.48	196.86	196.35	195.94	195.60	194.61	194.24	194.09
13000	222.58	220.30	218.46	216.96	215.74	214.75	213.93	213.26	212.72	212.27	211.90	210.83	210.43	210.27
14000	239.70	237.25	235.27	233.65	232.34	231.26	230.39	229.67	229.08	228.59	228.20	227.04	226.61	226.44
15000	256.82	254.20	252.07	250.34	248.93	247.78	246.84	246.07	245.44	244.92	244.49	243.26	242.79	242.62
16000	273.95	271.14	268.87	267.03	265.53	264.30	263.30	262.48	261.80	261.25	260.79	259.48	258.98	258.79
17000	291.07	288.09	285.68	283.72	282.12	280.82	279.75	278.88	278.16	277.58	277.09	275.70	275.17	274.96
18000	308.19	305.04	302.48	300.41	298.72	297.34	296.21	295.29	294.53	293.90	293.39	291.91	291.35	291.14
19000	325.31	321.98	319.29	317.10	315.31	313.86	312.67	311.69	310.89	310.23	309.69	308.13	307.54	307.31
20000	342.43	338.93	336.09	333.79	331.91	330.38	329.12	328.09	327.25	326.56	325.99	324.35	323.72	323.49
21000	359.55	355.87	352.90	350.48	348.50	346.89	345.58	344.50	343.61	342.89	342.29	340.56	339.91	339.66
22000	376.67	372.82	369.70	367.16	365.10	363.41	362.03	360.90	359.98	359.22	358.59	356.78	356.09	355.83
23000	393.80	389.77	386.50	383.85	381.69	379.93	378.49	377.31	376.34	375.54	374.89	373.00	372.28	372.01
24000	410.92	406.71	403.31	400.54	398.29	396.45	394.95	393.71	392.70	391.87	391.19	389.22	388.47	388.18
25000	428.04	423.66	420.11	417.23	414.88	412.97	411.40	410.12	409.06	408.20	407.49	405.43	404.65	404.36
26000	445.16	440.60	436.92	433.92	431.48	429.49	427.86	426.52	425.43	424.53	423.79	421.65	420.84	420.53
27000	462.28	457.55	453.72	450.61	448.08	446.01	444.31	442.93	441.79	440.85	440.09	437.87	437.02	436.70
28000	479.40	474.50	470.53	467.30	464.67	462.52	460.77	459.33	458.15	457.18	456.39	454.08	453.21	452.88
29000	496.52	491.44	487.33	483.99	481.27	479.04	477.22	475.73	474.51	473.51	472.68	470.30	469.40	469.05
30000	513.64	508.39	504.13	500.68	497.86	495.56	493.68	492.14	490.88	489.84	488.98	486.52	485.58	485.23
31000	530.77	525.34	520.94	517.37	514.46	512.08	510.14	508.54	507.24	506.16	505.28	502.73	501.77	501.40
32000	547.89	542.28	537.74	534.06	531.05	528.60	526.59	524.95	523.60	522.49	521.58	518.95	517.95	517.57
33000	565.01	559.23	554.55	550.74	547.65	545.12	543.05	541.35	539.96	538.82	537.88	535.17	534.14	533.75
34000	582.13	576.17	571.35	567.43	564.24	561.64	559.50	557.76	556.32	555.15	554.18	551.39	550.33	549.92
35000	599.25	593.12	588.16	584.12	580.84	578.15	575.96	574.16	572.69	571.48	570.48	567.60	566.51	566.10
36000	616.37	610.07	604.96	600.81	597.43	594.67	592.42	590.57	589.05	587.80	586.78	583.82	582.70	582.27
37000	633.49	627.01	621.76	617.50	614.03	611.19	608.87	606.97	605.41	604.13	603.08	600.04	598.88	598.44
38000	650.62	643.96	638.57	634.19	630.62	627.71	625.33	623.37	621.77	620.46	619.38	616.25	615.07	614.62
39000	667.74	660.90	655.37	650.88	647.22	644.23	641.78	639.78	638.14	636.79	635.68	632.47	631.25	630.79
40000	684.86	677.85	672.18	667.57	663.81	660.75	658.24	656.18	654.50	653.11	651.98	648.69	647.44	646.97
41000	701.98	694.80	688.98	684.26	680.41	677.27	674.69	672.59	670.86	669.44	668.28	664.91	663.63	663.14
42000	719.10	711.74	705.79	700.95	697.00	693.78	691.15	688.99	687.22	685.77	684.58	681.12	679.81	679.31
43000	736.22	728.69	722.59	717.63	713.60	710.30	707.61	705.40	703.59	702.10	700.88	697.34	696.00	695.49
44000	753.34	745.64	739.39	734.32	730.19	726.82	724.06	721.80	719.95	718.43	717.17	713.56	712.18	711.66
45000	770.46	762.58	756.20	751.01	746.79	743.34	740.52	738.21	736.31	734.75	733.47	729.77	728.37	727.84
46000	787.59	779.53	773.00	767.70	763.38	759.86	756.97	754.61	752.67	751.08	749.77	745.99	744.56	744.01
47000	804.71	796.47	789.81	784.39	779.98	776.38	773.43	771.02	769.03	767.41	766.07	762.21	760.74	760.18
48000	821.83	813.42	806.61	801.08	796.57	792.89	789.89	787.42	785.40	783.74	782.37	778.43	776.93	776.36
49000	838.95	830.37	823.42	817.77	813.17	809.41	806.34	803.82	801.76	800.06	798.67	794.64	793.11	792.53
50000	856.07	847.31	840.22	834.46	829.76	825.93	822.80	820.23	818.12	816.39	814.97	810.86	809.30	808.71
55000	941.68	932.04	924.24	917.90	912.74	908.52	905.08	902.25	899.93	898.03	896.47	891.94	890.23	889.58
60000	1027.28	1016.77	1008.26	1001.35	995.72	991.12	987.36	984.27	981.75	979.67	977.96	973.03	971.16	970.45
65000	1112.89	1101.50	1092.28	1084.79	1078.69	1073.71	1069.63	1066.30	1063.56	1061.31	1059.46	1054.12	1052.09	1051.32
70000	1198.50	1186.23	1176.31	1168.24	1161.67	1156.30	1151.91	1148.32	1145.37	1142.95	1140.96	1135.20	1133.02	1132.19
75000	1284.10	1270.97	1260.33	1251.69	1244.64	1238.90	1234.19	1230.34	1227.18	1224.59	1222.45	1216.29	1213.95	1213.06
80000	1369.71	1355.70	1344.35	1335.13	1327.62	1321.49	1316.47	1312.36	1308.99	1306.22	1303.95	1297.37	1294.88	1293.93
85000	1455.32	1440.43	1428.37	1418.58	1410.60	1404.08	1398.75	1394.38	1390.80	1387.86	1385.45	1378.46	1375.81	1374.80
90000	1540.92	1525.16	1512.39	1502.02	1493.57	1486.67	1481.03	1476.41	1472.62	1469.50	1466.94	1459.54	1456.74	1455.67
95000	1626.53	1609.89	1596.41	1585.47	1576.55	1569.27	1563.31	1558.43	1554.43	1551.14	1548.44	1540.63	1537.66	1536.54
100000	1712.14	1694.62	1680.44	1668.91	1659.52	1651.86	1645.59	1640.45	1636.24	1632.78	1629.94	1621.71	1618.59	1617.41

19.500%

TERM	1 Year	2 Years	3 Years	4 Years	5 Years	6 Years	7 Years	8 Years	9 Years	10 Years	11 Years	12 Years	13 Years	14 Years
AMOUNT														
5	.47	.26	.19	.16	.14	.12	.11	.11	.10	.10	.10	.10	.09	.09
10	.93	.51	.37	.31	.27	.24	.22	.21	.20	.19	.19	.19	.18	.18
15	1.39	.76	.56	.46	.40	.36	.33	.31	.30	.29	.28	.28	.27	.27
25	2.31	1.27	.93	.76	.66	.60	.55	.52	.50	.48	.47	.46	.45	.44
50	4.62	2.54	1.85	1.51	1.32	1.19	1.10	1.04	.99	.95	.93	.91	.89	.88
75	6.93	3.80	2.77	2.27	1.97	1.78	1.65	1.55	1.48	1.43	1.39	1.36	1.33	1.31
100	9.24	5.07	3.70	3.02	2.63	2.37	2.20	2.07	1.98	1.90	1.85	1.81	1.77	1.75
200	18.48	10.14	7.39	6.04	5.25	4.74	4.39	4.13	3.95	3.80	3.69	3.61	3.54	3.49
300	27.72	15.20	11.08	9.05	7.87	7.10	6.58	6.20	5.92	5.70	5.54	5.41	5.31	5.23
400	36.96	20.27	14.77	12.07	10.49	9.47	8.77	8.26	7.89	7.60	7.38	7.21	7.08	6.97
500	46.20	25.33	18.46	15.09	13.11	11.84	10.96	10.33	9.86	9.50	9.23	9.01	8.85	8.71
600	55.44	30.40	22.15	18.10	15.73	14.20	13.15	12.39	11.83	11.40	11.07	10.82	10.61	10.45
700	64.68	35.46	25.84	21.12	18.36	16.57	15.34	14.45	13.80	13.30	12.92	12.62	12.38	12.19
800	73.92	40.53	29.53	24.14	20.98	18.94	17.53	16.52	15.77	15.20	14.76	14.42	14.15	13.93
900	83.16	45.59	33.22	27.15	23.60	21.30	19.72	18.58	17.74	17.10	16.61	16.22	15.92	15.67
1000	92.40	50.66	36.91	30.17	26.22	23.67	21.91	20.65	19.71	19.00	18.45	18.02	17.69	17.42
2000	184.80	101.31	73.82	60.33	52.44	47.33	43.82	41.29	39.42	38.00	36.90	36.04	35.37	34.83
3000	277.19	151.96	110.73	90.50	78.65	71.00	65.72	61.93	59.12	56.99	55.35	54.06	53.05	52.24
4000	369.59	202.61	147.64	120.66	104.87	94.66	87.63	82.57	78.83	75.99	73.79	72.08	70.73	69.65
5000	461.98	253.26	184.55	150.83	131.09	118.32	109.54	103.22	98.53	94.98	92.24	90.10	88.41	87.06
6000	554.38	303.92	221.46	180.99	157.30	141.99	131.44	123.86	118.24	113.98	110.69	108.12	106.09	104.47
7000	646.77	354.57	258.37	211.16	183.52	165.65	153.35	144.50	137.94	132.97	129.13	126.14	123.77	121.88
8000	739.17	405.22	295.28	241.32	209.74	189.32	175.25	165.14	157.65	151.97	147.58	144.15	141.45	139.29
9000	831.56	455.87	332.19	271.49	235.95	212.98	197.16	185.79	177.36	170.96	166.03	162.17	159.13	156.70
10000	923.96	506.52	369.10	301.65	262.17	236.64	219.07	206.43	197.06	189.96	184.48	180.19	176.81	174.11
11000	1016.35	557.18	406.01	331.82	288.39	260.31	240.97	227.07	216.77	208.95	202.92	198.21	194.49	191.52
12000	1108.75	607.83	442.92	361.98	314.60	283.97	262.88	247.71	236.47	227.95	221.37	216.23	212.17	208.93
13000	1201.14	658.48	479.83	392.14	340.82	307.64	284.78	268.36	256.18	246.94	239.82	234.25	229.85	226.34
14000	1293.94	709.13	516.74	422.31	367.04	331.30	306.69	289.00	275.88	265.94	258.26	252.27	247.53	243.75
15000	1385.94	759.78	553.64	452.47	393.25	354.96	328.60	309.64	295.59	284.93	276.71	270.28	265.21	261.17
16000	1478.33	810.44	590.55	482.64	419.47	378.63	350.50	330.28	315.30	303.93	295.16	288.30	282.89	278.58
17000	1570.73	861.09	627.46	512.80	445.68	402.29	372.41	350.93	335.00	322.92	313.61	306.32	300.57	295.99
18000	1663.12	911.74	664.37	542.97	471.90	425.95	394.32	371.57	354.71	341.92	332.05	324.34	318.25	313.40
19000	1755.52	962.39	701.28	573.13	498.12	449.62	416.22	392.21	374.41	360.91	350.50	342.36	335.93	330.81
20000	1847.91	1013.04	738.19	603.30	524.33	473.28	438.13	412.85	394.12	379.91	368.95	360.38	353.61	348.22
21000	1940.31	1063.69	775.10	633.46	550.55	496.95	460.03	433.50	413.82	398.90	387.39	378.40	371.29	365.63
22000	2032.70	1114.35	812.01	663.63	576.77	520.61	481.94	454.14	433.53	417.90	405.84	396.42	388.97	383.04
23000	2125.10	1165.00	848.92	693.79	602.98	544.27	503.85	474.78	453.24	436.90	424.29	414.43	406.65	400.45
24000	2217.49	1215.65	885.83	723.96	629.20	567.94	525.75	495.42	472.94	455.89	442.74	432.45	424.33	417.86
25000	2309.89	1266.30	922.74	754.12	655.42	591.60	547.66	516.07	492.65	474.89	461.18	450.47	442.01	435.27
26000	2402.28	1316.95	959.65	784.28	681.63	615.27	569.56	536.71	512.35	493.88	479.63	468.49	459.69	452.68
27000	2494.68	1367.61	996.56	814.45	707.85	638.93	591.47	557.35	532.06	512.88	498.08	486.51	477.37	470.09
28000	2587.08	1418.26	1033.47	844.61	734.07	662.59	613.38	577.99	551.76	531.87	516.52	504.53	495.05	487.50
29000	2679.47	1468.91	1070.38	874.78	760.28	686.26	635.28	598.64	571.47	550.87	534.97	522.55	512.73	504.92
30000	2771.87	1519.56	1107.28	904.94	786.50	709.92	657.19	619.28	591.17	569.86	553.42	540.56	530.41	522.33
31000	2864.26	1570.21	1144.19	935.11	812.71	733.59	679.09	639.92	610.88	588.86	571.87	558.58	548.09	539.74
32000	2956.66	1620.87	1181.10	965.27	838.93	757.25	701.00	660.56	630.59	607.85	590.31	576.60	565.77	557.15
33000	3049.05	1671.52	1218.01	995.44	865.15	780.91	722.91	681.21	650.29	626.85	608.76	594.62	583.45	574.56
34000	3141.45	1722.17	1254.92	1025.60	891.36	804.58	744.81	701.85	670.00	645.84	627.21	612.64	601.13	591.97
35000	3233.84	1772.82	1291.83	1055.77	917.58	828.24	766.72	722.49	689.70	664.84	645.65	630.66	618.81	609.38
36000	3326.24	1823.47	1328.74	1085.93	943.80	851.90	788.63	743.13	709.41	683.83	664.10	648.68	636.49	626.79
37000	3418.63	1874.12	1365.65	1116.10	970.01	875.57	810.53	763.78	729.11	702.83	682.55	666.70	654.17	644.20
38000	3511.03	1924.78	1402.56	1146.26	996.23	899.23	832.44	784.42	748.82	721.82	701.00	684.71	671.85	661.61
39000	3603.42	1975.43	1439.47	1176.42	1022.45	922.90	854.34	805.06	768.53	740.82	719.44	702.73	689.53	679.02
40000	3695.82	2026.08	1476.38	1206.59	1048.66	946.56	876.25	825.70	788.23	759.81	737.89	720.75	707.21	696.43
41000	3788.22	2076.73	1513.29	1236.75	1074.88	970.22	898.16	846.35	807.94	778.81	756.34	738.77	724.89	713.84
42000	3880.61	2127.38	1550.20	1266.92	1101.10	993.89	920.06	866.99	827.64	797.80	774.78	756.79	742.57	731.25
43000	3973.01	2178.04	1587.11	1297.08	1127.31	1017.55	941.97	887.63	847.35	816.80	793.23	774.81	760.25	748.67
44000	4065.40	2228.69	1624.01	1327.25	1153.53	1041.22	963.87	908.27	867.05	835.79	811.68	792.83	777.93	766.08
45000	4157.80	2279.34	1660.92	1357.41	1179.75	1064.88	985.78	928.92	886.76	854.79	830.13	810.84	795.61	783.49
46000	4250.19	2329.99	1697.83	1387.58	1205.96	1088.54	1007.69	949.56	906.47	873.79	848.57	828.86	813.29	800.90
47000	4342.59	2380.64	1734.74	1417.74	1232.18	1112.21	1029.59	970.20	926.17	892.78	867.02	846.88	830.97	818.31
48000	4434.98	2431.30	1771.65	1447.91	1258.39	1135.87	1051.50	990.84	945.88	911.78	885.47	864.90	848.65	835.72
49000	4527.38	2481.95	1808.56	1478.07	1284.61	1159.54	1073.40	1011.49	965.58	930.77	903.91	882.92	866.34	853.13
50000	4619.77	2532.60	1845.47	1508.24	1310.83	1183.20	1095.31	1032.13	985.29	949.77	922.36	900.94	884.02	870.54
55000	5081.75	2785.86	2030.02	1659.06	1441.91	1301.52	1204.84	1135.34	1083.82	1044.74	1014.60	991.03	972.42	957.59
60000	5543.73	3039.12	2214.56	1809.88	1572.99	1419.84	1314.37	1238.55	1182.34	1139.72	1106.83	1081.12	1060.82	1044.65
65000	6005.70	3292.38	2399.11	1960.70	1704.07	1538.16	1423.90	1341.76	1280.87	1234.69	1199.07	1171.22	1149.22	1131.70
70000	6467.68	3545.64	2583.66	2111.53	1835.16	1656.48	1533.43	1444.98	1379.40	1329.67	1291.30	1261.31	1237.62	1218.75
75000	6929.66	3798.90	2768.20	2262.35	1966.24	1774.80	1642.96	1548.19	1477.93	1424.65	1383.54	1351.40	1326.02	1305.81
80000	7391.63	4052.16	2952.75	2413.17	2097.32	1893.12	1752.49	1651.40	1576.46	1519.62	1475.78	1441.50	1414.42	1392.86
85000	7853.61	4305.41	3137.30	2564.00	2228.40	2011.44	1862.03	1754.61	1674.99	1614.60	1568.01	1531.59	1502.82	1479.92
90000	8315.59	4558.67	3321.84	2714.82	2359.49	2129.75	1971.56	1857.83	1773.51	1709.57	1660.25	1621.68	1591.22	1566.97
95000	8777.57	4811.93	3506.39	2865.64	2490.57	2248.07	2081.09	1961.04	1872.04	1804.55	1752.48	1711.78	1679.63	1654.02
100000	9239.54	5065.19	3690.94	3016.47	2621.65	2366.39	2190.62	2064.25	1970.57	1899.53	1844.72	1801.87	1768.03	1741.08

TERM	15 Years	16 Years	17 Years	18 Years	19 Years	20 Years	21 Years	22 Years	23 Years	24 Years	25 Years	30 Years	35 Years	40 Years
AMOUNT														
5	.09	.09	.09	.09	.09	.09	.09	.09	.09	.09	.09	.09	.09	.09
10	.18	.18	.17	.17	.17	.17	.17	.17	.17	.17	.17	.17	.17	.17
15	.26	.26	.26	.26	.26	.25	.25	.25	.25	.25	.25	.25	.25	.25
25	.43	.43	.43	.42	.42	.42	.42	.42	.42	.42	.41	.41	.41	.41
50	.86	.86	.85	.84	.84	.83	.83	.83	.83	.83	.82	.82	.82	.82
75	1.29	1.28	1.27	1.26	1.26	1.25	1.25	1.24	1.24	1.24	1.23	1.23	1.23	1.22
100	1.72	1.71	1.69	1.68	1.67	1.66	1.66	1.65	1.65	1.65	1.64	1.63	1.63	1.63
200	3.44	3.41	3.38	3.36	3.34	3.32	3.31	3.30	3.29	3.29	3.28	3.26	3.26	3.26
300	5.16	5.11	5.07	5.03	5.01	4.98	4.97	4.95	4.94	4.93	4.92	4.89	4.89	4.88
400	6.88	6.81	6.76	6.71	6.67	6.64	6.62	6.60	6.58	6.57	6.56	6.52	6.51	6.51
500	8.60	8.52	8.44	8.39	8.34	8.30	8.27	8.25	8.23	8.21	8.20	8.15	8.14	8.13
600	10.32	10.22	10.13	10.06	10.01	9.96	9.93	9.90	9.87	9.85	9.83	9.78	9.77	9.76
700	12.04	11.92	11.82	11.74	11.68	11.62	11.58	11.54	11.51	11.49	11.47	11.41	11.39	11.38
800	13.76	13.62	13.51	13.42	13.34	13.28	13.23	13.19	13.16	13.13	13.11	13.04	13.02	13.01
900	15.48	15.32	15.20	15.09	15.01	14.94	14.89	14.84	14.80	14.77	14.75	14.67	14.65	14.64
1000	17.20	17.03	16.88	16.77	16.68	16.60	16.54	16.49	16.45	16.41	16.39	16.30	16.27	16.26
2000	34.39	34.05	33.76	33.54	33.35	33.20	33.07	32.97	32.89	32.82	32.77	32.60	32.54	32.52
3000	51.59	51.07	50.64	50.30	50.02	49.79	49.61	49.46	49.33	49.23	49.15	48.90	48.81	48.78
4000	68.78	68.09	67.52	67.07	66.70	66.39	66.14	65.94	65.77	65.64	65.53	65.20	65.08	65.03
5000	85.98	85.11	84.40	83.83	83.37	82.99	82.68	82.42	82.22	82.05	81.91	81.50	81.35	81.29
6000	103.17	102.13	101.28	100.60	100.04	99.58	99.21	98.91	98.66	98.45	98.29	97.80	97.62	97.55
7000	120.37	119.15	118.16	117.36	116.71	116.18	115.75	115.39	115.10	114.86	114.67	114.10	113.89	113.80
8000	137.56	136.17	135.04	134.13	133.39	132.78	132.28	131.88	131.54	131.27	131.05	130.40	130.15	130.06
9000	154.76	153.19	151.92	150.90	150.06	149.37	148.82	148.36	147.99	147.68	147.43	146.70	146.42	146.32
10000	171.95	170.21	168.80	167.66	166.73	165.97	165.35	164.84	164.43	164.09	163.81	163.00	162.69	162.58
11000	189.15	187.23	185.68	184.43	183.40	182.57	181.89	181.33	180.87	180.49	180.19	179.30	178.96	178.83
12000	206.34	204.25	202.56	201.19	200.08	199.16	198.42	197.81	197.31	196.90	196.57	195.60	195.23	195.09
13000	223.54	221.27	219.44	217.96	216.75	215.76	214.95	214.29	213.75	213.31	212.95	211.89	211.50	211.35
14000	240.73	238.29	236.32	234.72	233.42	232.36	231.49	230.78	230.20	229.72	229.33	228.19	227.77	227.60
15000	257.93	255.32	253.20	251.49	250.09	248.95	248.02	247.26	246.64	246.13	245.71	244.49	244.04	243.86
16000	275.12	272.34	270.08	268.25	266.77	265.55	264.56	263.75	263.08	262.53	262.09	260.79	260.30	260.12
17000	292.31	289.36	286.96	285.02	283.44	282.15	281.09	280.23	279.52	278.94	278.47	277.09	276.57	276.38
18000	309.51	306.38	303.84	301.79	300.11	298.74	297.63	296.71	295.97	295.35	294.85	293.39	292.84	292.63
19000	326.70	323.40	320.72	318.55	316.78	315.34	314.16	313.20	312.41	311.76	311.23	309.69	309.11	308.89
20000	343.90	340.42	337.60	335.32	333.46	331.94	330.70	329.68	328.85	328.17	327.61	325.99	325.38	325.15
21000	361.09	357.44	354.48	352.08	350.13	348.53	347.23	346.17	345.29	344.57	343.99	342.29	341.65	341.40
22000	378.29	374.46	371.36	368.85	366.80	365.13	363.77	362.65	361.73	360.98	360.37	358.59	357.92	357.66
23000	395.48	391.48	388.24	385.61	383.47	381.73	380.30	379.13	378.18	377.39	376.75	374.89	374.18	373.92
24000	412.68	408.50	405.12	402.38	400.15	398.32	396.84	395.62	394.62	393.80	393.13	391.19	390.45	390.18
25000	429.87	425.52	422.00	419.14	416.82	414.92	413.37	412.10	411.06	410.21	409.51	407.49	406.72	406.43
26000	447.07	442.54	438.88	435.91	433.49	431.52	429.90	428.58	427.50	426.62	425.89	423.78	422.99	422.69
27000	464.26	459.56	455.76	452.68	450.16	448.11	446.44	445.07	443.95	443.02	442.27	440.08	439.26	438.95
28000	481.46	476.58	472.64	469.44	466.84	464.71	462.97	461.55	460.39	459.43	458.65	456.38	455.53	455.20
29000	498.65	493.60	489.52	486.21	483.51	481.31	479.51	478.04	476.83	475.84	475.03	472.68	471.80	471.46
30000	515.85	510.63	506.40	502.97	500.18	497.90	496.04	494.52	493.27	492.25	491.41	488.98	488.07	487.72
31000	533.04	527.65	523.28	519.74	516.85	514.50	512.58	511.00	509.71	508.66	507.79	505.28	504.33	503.97
32000	550.24	544.67	540.16	536.50	533.53	531.10	529.11	527.49	526.16	525.06	524.17	521.58	520.60	520.23
33000	567.43	561.69	557.04	553.27	550.20	547.69	545.65	543.97	542.60	541.47	540.55	537.88	536.87	536.49
34000	584.62	578.71	573.92	570.03	566.87	564.29	562.18	560.46	559.04	557.88	556.93	554.18	553.14	552.75
35000	601.82	595.73	590.80	586.80	583.54	580.89	578.72	576.94	575.48	574.29	573.31	570.48	569.41	569.00
36000	619.01	612.75	607.68	603.57	600.22	597.48	595.25	593.42	591.93	590.70	589.69	586.78	585.68	585.26
37000	636.21	629.77	624.56	620.33	616.89	614.08	611.79	609.91	608.37	607.10	606.07	603.08	601.95	601.52
38000	653.40	646.79	641.44	637.10	633.56	630.68	628.32	626.39	624.81	623.51	622.45	619.37	618.21	617.77
39000	670.60	663.81	658.32	653.86	650.23	647.27	644.85	642.87	641.25	639.92	638.83	635.67	634.48	634.03
40000	687.79	680.83	675.20	670.63	666.91	663.87	661.39	659.36	657.69	656.33	655.21	651.97	650.75	650.29
41000	704.99	697.85	692.08	687.39	683.58	680.47	677.92	675.84	674.14	672.74	671.59	668.27	667.02	666.55
42000	722.18	714.87	708.96	704.16	700.25	697.06	694.46	692.33	690.58	689.14	687.97	684.57	683.29	682.80
43000	739.38	731.89	725.84	720.93	716.92	713.66	710.99	708.81	707.02	705.55	704.35	700.87	699.56	699.06
44000	756.57	748.91	742.72	737.69	733.60	730.26	727.53	725.29	723.46	721.96	720.73	717.17	715.83	715.32
45000	773.77	765.94	759.60	754.46	750.27	746.85	744.06	741.78	739.91	738.37	737.11	733.47	732.10	731.57
46000	790.96	782.96	776.48	771.22	766.94	763.45	760.60	758.26	756.35	754.78	753.49	749.77	748.36	747.83
47000	808.16	799.98	793.36	787.99	783.61	780.05	777.13	774.75	772.79	771.19	769.87	766.07	764.63	764.09
48000	825.35	817.00	810.24	804.75	800.29	796.64	793.67	791.23	789.23	787.59	786.25	782.37	780.90	780.35
49000	842.55	834.02	827.12	821.52	816.96	813.24	810.20	807.71	805.67	804.00	802.63	798.67	797.17	796.60
50000	859.74	851.04	844.00	838.28	833.63	829.84	826.74	824.20	822.12	820.41	819.01	814.97	813.44	812.86
55000	945.71	936.14	928.40	922.11	917.00	912.82	909.41	906.62	904.33	902.45	900.91	896.46	894.78	894.15
60000	1031.69	1021.25	1012.80	1005.94	1000.36	995.80	992.08	989.04	986.54	984.49	982.81	977.96	976.13	975.43
65000	1117.66	1106.35	1097.20	1089.77	1083.72	1078.79	1074.75	1071.45	1068.75	1066.53	1064.71	1059.45	1057.47	1056.72
70000	1203.63	1191.45	1181.60	1173.60	1167.08	1161.77	1157.43	1153.87	1150.96	1148.57	1146.61	1140.95	1138.81	1138.00
75000	1289.61	1276.56	1266.00	1257.42	1250.45	1244.75	1240.10	1236.29	1233.17	1230.61	1228.51	1222.45	1220.16	1219.29
80000	1375.58	1361.66	1350.40	1341.25	1333.81	1327.74	1322.77	1318.71	1315.38	1312.65	1310.41	1303.94	1301.50	1300.57
85000	1461.55	1446.76	1434.79	1425.08	1417.17	1410.72	1405.45	1401.13	1397.59	1394.69	1392.31	1385.44	1382.84	1381.86
90000	1547.53	1531.87	1519.19	1508.91	1500.53	1493.70	1488.12	1483.55	1479.81	1476.73	1474.21	1466.93	1464.19	1463.14
95000	1633.50	1616.97	1603.59	1592.74	1583.90	1576.69	1570.79	1565.97	1562.02	1558.77	1556.11	1548.43	1545.53	1544.43
100000	1719.48	1702.07	1687.99	1676.56	1667.26	1659.67	1653.47	1648.39	1644.23	1640.81	1638.01	1629.93	1626.87	1625.71

TERM AMOUNT	1 Year	2 Years	3 Years	4 Years	5 Years	6 Years	7 Years	8 Years	9 Years	10 Years	11 Years	12 Years	13 Years	14 Years
5	.47	.26	.19	.16	.14	.12	.11	.11	.10	.10	.10	.10	.09	.09
10	.93	.51	.37	.31	.27	.24	.22	.21	.20	.20	.19	.19	.18	.18
15	1.39	.77	.56	.46	.40	.36	.33	.32	.30	.29	.28	.28	.27	.27
25	2.32	1.27	.93	.76	.66	.60	.55	.52	.50	.48	.47	.46	.45	.44
50	4.63	2.54	1.85	1.52	1.32	1.19	1.10	1.04	.99	.96	.93	.91	.89	.88
75	6.94	3.81	2.78	2.27	1.98	1.78	1.65	1.56	1.49	1.43	1.39	1.36	1.34	1.32
100	9.25	5.08	3.70	3.03	2.63	2.38	2.20	2.08	1.98	1.91	1.86	1.81	1.78	1.75
200	18.49	10.15	7.40	6.05	5.26	4.75	4.40	4.15	3.96	3.82	3.71	3.62	3.56	3.50
300	27.74	15.22	11.09	9.07	7.89	7.12	6.59	6.22	5.94	5.72	5.56	5.43	5.33	5.25
400	36.98	20.29	14.79	12.09	10.51	9.49	8.79	8.29	7.91	7.63	7.41	7.24	7.11	7.00
500	46.23	25.36	18.49	15.11	13.14	11.87	10.99	10.36	9.89	9.54	9.26	9.05	8.88	8.75
600	55.47	30.43	22.18	18.14	15.77	14.24	13.18	12.43	11.87	11.44	11.11	10.86	10.66	10.49
700	64.72	35.50	25.88	21.16	18.40	16.61	15.38	14.50	13.84	13.35	12.97	12.67	12.43	12.24
800	73.96	40.57	29.57	24.18	21.02	18.98	17.58	16.57	15.82	15.25	14.82	14.48	14.21	13.99
900	83.20	45.64	33.27	27.20	23.65	21.35	19.77	18.64	17.80	17.16	16.67	16.28	15.98	15.74
1000	92.45	50.71	36.97	30.22	26.28	23.73	21.97	20.71	19.77	19.07	18.52	18.09	17.76	17.49
2000	184.89	101.41	73.93	60.44	52.55	47.45	43.94	41.41	39.54	38.13	37.03	36.18	35.51	34.97
3000	277.33	152.11	110.89	90.66	78.82	71.17	65.90	62.12	59.31	57.19	55.55	54.27	53.26	52.45
4000	369.78	202.81	147.85	120.88	105.09	94.89	87.87	82.82	79.08	76.25	74.06	72.36	71.01	69.94
5000	462.22	253.51	184.81	151.09	131.36	118.61	109.83	103.53	98.85	95.31	92.58	90.44	88.76	87.42
6000	554.66	304.21	221.77	181.31	157.64	142.33	131.80	124.23	118.62	114.37	111.09	108.53	106.51	104.90
7000	647.11	354.91	258.73	211.53	183.91	166.06	153.77	144.94	138.39	133.43	129.61	126.62	124.26	122.39
8000	739.55	405.61	295.69	241.75	210.18	189.78	175.73	165.64	158.16	152.49	148.12	144.71	142.01	139.87
9000	831.99	456.31	332.65	271.96	236.45	213.50	197.70	186.34	177.93	171.55	166.64	162.80	159.76	157.35
10000	924.44	507.01	369.61	302.18	262.72	237.22	219.66	207.05	197.70	190.62	185.15	180.88	177.52	174.83
11000	1016.88	557.71	406.57	332.40	288.99	260.94	241.63	227.75	217.47	209.68	203.67	198.97	195.27	192.32
12000	1109.32	608.41	443.53	362.62	315.27	284.66	263.60	248.46	237.24	228.74	222.18	217.06	213.02	209.80
13000	1201.77	659.11	480.49	392.83	341.54	308.38	285.56	269.16	257.01	247.80	240.70	235.15	230.77	227.28
14000	1294.21	709.81	517.45	423.05	367.81	332.11	307.53	289.87	276.78	266.86	259.21	253.24	248.52	244.77
15000	1386.65	760.51	554.41	453.27	394.08	355.83	329.49	310.57	296.55	285.92	277.73	271.32	266.27	262.25
16000	1479.10	811.21	591.37	483.49	420.35	379.55	351.46	331.28	316.32	304.98	296.24	289.41	284.02	279.73
17000	1571.54	861.92	628.33	513.71	446.63	403.27	373.43	351.98	336.09	324.04	314.76	307.50	301.77	297.21
18000	1663.98	912.62	665.29	543.92	472.90	426.99	395.39	372.68	355.86	343.10	333.27	325.59	319.52	314.70
19000	1756.43	963.32	702.25	574.14	499.17	450.71	417.36	393.39	375.63	362.17	351.79	343.68	337.27	332.18
20000	1848.87	1014.02	739.21	604.36	525.44	474.44	439.32	414.09	395.40	381.23	370.30	361.76	355.03	349.66
21000	1941.31	1064.72	776.17	634.58	551.71	498.16	461.29	434.80	415.17	400.29	388.82	379.85	372.78	367.15
22000	2033.75	1115.42	813.13	664.79	577.98	521.88	483.26	455.50	434.94	419.35	407.33	397.94	390.53	384.63
23000	2126.20	1166.12	850.09	695.01	604.26	545.60	505.22	476.21	454.71	438.41	425.84	416.03	408.28	402.11
24000	2218.64	1216.82	887.05	725.23	630.53	569.32	527.19	496.91	474.48	457.47	444.36	434.12	426.03	419.59
25000	2311.08	1267.52	924.01	755.45	656.80	593.04	549.15	517.62	494.25	476.53	462.87	452.20	443.78	437.08
26000	2403.53	1318.22	960.97	785.66	683.07	616.76	571.12	538.32	514.02	495.59	481.39	470.29	461.53	454.56
27000	2495.97	1368.92	997.93	815.88	709.34	640.49	593.09	559.02	533.79	514.65	499.90	488.38	479.28	472.04
28000	2588.41	1419.62	1034.89	846.10	735.62	664.21	615.05	579.73	553.56	533.72	518.42	506.47	497.03	489.53
29000	2680.86	1470.32	1071.85	876.32	761.89	687.93	637.02	600.43	573.32	552.78	536.93	524.56	514.78	507.01
30000	2773.30	1521.02	1108.81	906.53	788.16	711.65	658.98	621.14	593.09	571.84	555.45	542.64	532.54	524.49
31000	2865.74	1571.72	1145.77	936.75	814.43	735.37	680.95	641.84	612.86	590.90	573.96	560.73	550.29	541.98
32000	2958.19	1622.42	1182.73	966.97	840.70	759.09	702.92	662.55	632.63	609.96	592.48	578.82	568.04	559.46
33000	3050.63	1673.13	1219.69	997.19	866.97	782.82	724.88	683.25	652.40	629.02	610.99	596.91	585.79	576.94
34000	3143.07	1723.83	1256.65	1027.41	893.25	806.54	746.85	703.96	672.17	648.08	629.51	615.00	603.54	594.42
35000	3235.52	1774.53	1293.61	1057.62	919.52	830.26	768.81	724.66	691.94	667.14	648.02	633.08	621.29	611.91
36000	3327.96	1825.23	1330.57	1087.84	945.79	853.98	790.78	745.36	711.71	686.20	666.54	651.17	639.04	629.39
37000	3420.40	1875.93	1367.53	1118.06	972.06	877.70	812.75	766.07	731.48	705.27	685.05	669.26	656.79	646.87
38000	3512.85	1926.63	1404.49	1148.28	998.33	901.42	834.71	786.77	751.25	724.33	703.57	687.35	674.54	664.36
39000	3605.29	1977.33	1441.45	1178.49	1024.61	925.14	856.68	807.48	771.02	743.39	722.08	705.43	692.29	681.84
40000	3697.73	2028.03	1478.41	1208.71	1050.88	948.87	878.64	828.18	790.79	762.45	740.60	723.52	710.05	699.32
41000	3790.18	2078.73	1515.37	1238.93	1077.15	972.59	900.61	848.89	810.56	781.51	759.11	741.61	727.80	716.80
42000	3882.62	2129.43	1552.33	1269.15	1103.42	996.31	922.58	869.59	830.33	800.57	777.63	759.70	745.55	734.29
43000	3975.06	2180.13	1589.29	1299.36	1129.69	1020.03	944.54	890.30	850.10	819.63	796.14	777.79	763.30	751.77
44000	4067.50	2230.83	1626.25	1329.58	1155.96	1043.75	966.51	911.00	869.87	838.69	814.66	795.87	781.05	769.25
45000	4159.95	2281.53	1663.21	1359.80	1182.24	1067.47	988.47	931.70	889.64	857.75	833.17	813.96	798.80	786.74
46000	4252.39	2332.23	1700.17	1390.02	1208.51	1091.20	1010.44	952.41	909.41	876.82	851.68	832.05	816.55	804.22
47000	4344.83	2382.93	1737.13	1420.23	1234.78	1114.92	1032.41	973.11	929.18	895.88	870.20	850.14	834.30	821.70
48000	4437.28	2433.63	1774.09	1450.45	1261.05	1138.64	1054.37	993.82	948.95	914.94	888.71	868.23	852.05	839.18
49000	4529.72	2484.33	1811.05	1480.67	1287.32	1162.36	1076.34	1014.52	968.72	934.00	907.23	886.31	869.81	856.67
50000	4622.16	2535.04	1848.01	1510.89	1313.60	1186.08	1098.30	1035.23	988.49	953.06	925.74	904.40	887.56	874.15
55000	5084.38	2788.54	2032.81	1661.98	1444.95	1304.69	1208.13	1138.75	1087.34	1048.37	1018.32	994.84	976.31	961.56
60000	5546.60	3042.04	2217.61	1813.06	1576.31	1423.30	1317.96	1242.27	1186.18	1143.67	1110.89	1085.28	1065.07	1048.98
65000	6008.81	3295.54	2402.44	1964.15	1707.67	1541.90	1427.79	1345.79	1285.03	1238.98	1203.47	1175.72	1153.82	1136.39
70000	6471.03	3549.05	2587.21	2115.24	1839.03	1660.51	1537.62	1449.32	1383.88	1334.28	1296.04	1266.16	1242.58	1223.81
75000	6933.24	3802.55	2772.01	2266.33	1970.39	1779.12	1647.45	1552.84	1482.73	1429.59	1388.61	1356.60	1331.33	1311.22
80000	7395.46	4056.05	2956.81	2417.42	2101.75	1897.73	1757.28	1656.36	1581.58	1524.89	1481.19	1447.04	1420.09	1398.64
85000	7857.67	4309.56	3141.61	2568.51	2233.11	2016.34	1867.11	1759.88	1680.42	1620.20	1573.76	1537.48	1508.84	1486.05
90000	8319.89	4563.06	3326.41	2719.59	2364.47	2134.94	1976.94	1863.40	1779.27	1715.50	1666.34	1627.92	1597.60	1573.47
95000	8782.11	4816.56	3511.22	2870.68	2495.83	2253.55	2086.77	1966.93	1878.12	1810.81	1758.91	1718.36	1686.35	1660.88
100000	9244.32	5070.07	3696.01	3021.77	2627.19	2372.16	2196.60	2070.45	1976.97	1906.12	1851.48	1808.80	1775.11	1748.30

TERM	15 Years	16 Years	17 Years	18 Years	19 Years	20 Years	21 Years	22 Years	23 Years	24 Years	25 Years	30 Years	35 Years	40 Years
AMOUNT														
5	.09	.09	.09	.09	.09	.09	.09	.09	.09	.09	.09	.09	.09	.09
10	.18	.18	.17	.17	.17	.17	.17	.17	.17	.17	.17	.17	.17	.17
15	.26	.26	.26	.26	.26	.26	.25	.25	.25	.25	.25	.25	.25	.25
25	.44	.43	.43	.43	.42	.42	.42	.42	.42	.42	.42	.41	.41	.41
50	.87	.86	.85	.85	.84	.84	.84	.83	.83	.83	.83	.82	.82	.82
75	1.30	1.29	1.28	1.27	1.26	1.26	1.25	1.25	1.24	1.24	1.24	1.23	1.23	1.23
100	1.73	1.71	1.70	1.69	1.68	1.67	1.67	1.66	1.66	1.65	1.65	1.64	1.64	1.64
200	3.46	3.42	3.40	3.37	3.35	3.34	3.33	3.32	3.31	3.30	3.30	3.28	3.28	3.27
300	5.19	5.13	5.09	5.06	5.03	5.01	4.99	4.97	4.96	4.95	4.94	4.92	4.91	4.91
400	6.91	6.84	6.79	6.74	6.70	6.67	6.65	6.63	6.61	6.60	6.59	6.56	6.55	6.54
500	8.64	8.55	8.48	8.43	8.38	8.34	8.31	8.29	8.27	8.25	8.24	8.20	8.18	8.18
600	10.37	10.26	10.18	10.11	10.05	10.01	9.97	9.54	9.92	9.90	9.88	9.83	9.82	9.81
700	12.09	11.97	11.87	11.79	11.73	11.68	11.63	11.60	11.57	11.55	11.53	11.47	11.45	11.44
800	13.82	13.68	13.57	13.48	13.40	13.34	13.30	13.26	13.22	13.20	13.17	13.11	13.09	13.08
900	15.55	15.39	15.26	15.16	15.08	15.01	14.96	14.91	14.87	14.84	14.82	14.75	14.72	14.71
1000	17.27	17.10	16.96	16.85	16.75	16.68	16.62	16.57	16.53	16.49	16.47	16.39	16.36	16.35
2000	34.54	34.20	33.92	33.69	33.50	33.35	33.23	33.13	33.05	32.98	32.93	32.77	32.71	32.69
3000	51.81	51.29	50.87	50.53	50.25	50.03	49.85	49.69	49.57	49.47	49.39	49.15	49.06	49.03
4000	69.08	68.39	67.83	67.37	67.00	66.70	66.46	66.26	66.09	65.96	65.85	65.53	65.41	65.37
5000	86.35	85.48	84.78	84.22	83.75	83.38	83.07	82.82	82.62	82.45	82.31	81.91	81.76	81.71
6000	103.61	102.58	101.74	101.06	100.50	100.05	99.69	99.38	99.14	98.94	98.77	98.29	98.11	98.05
7000	120.88	119.67	118.69	117.90	117.25	116.73	116.30	115.95	115.66	115.42	115.23	114.67	114.47	114.39
8000	138.15	136.77	135.65	134.74	134.00	133.40	132.91	132.51	132.18	131.91	131.69	131.06	130.82	130.73
9000	155.42	153.86	152.60	151.58	150.75	150.08	149.53	149.07	148.70	148.40	148.15	147.44	147.17	147.07
10000	172.69	170.96	169.56	168.43	167.50	166.75	166.14	165.64	165.23	164.89	164.61	163.82	163.52	163.41
11000	189.95	188.05	186.52	185.27	184.25	183.43	182.75	182.20	181.75	181.38	181.07	180.20	179.87	179.75
12000	207.22	205.15	203.47	202.11	201.00	200.10	199.37	198.76	198.27	197.87	197.54	196.58	196.22	196.09
13000	224.49	222.24	220.43	218.95	217.75	216.78	215.98	215.33	214.79	214.36	214.00	212.96	212.57	212.43
14000	241.76	239.34	237.38	235.80	234.50	233.45	232.59	231.89	231.32	230.84	230.46	229.34	228.93	228.77
15000	259.03	256.43	254.34	252.64	251.25	250.13	249.21	248.45	247.84	247.33	246.92	245.73	245.28	245.11
16000	276.30	273.53	271.29	269.48	268.00	266.80	265.82	265.02	264.36	263.82	263.38	262.11	261.63	261.45
17000	293.56	290.62	288.25	286.32	284.75	283.48	282.43	281.58	280.88	280.31	279.84	270.49	277.90	277.79
18000	310.83	307.72	305.20	303.16	301.50	300.15	299.05	298.14	297.40	296.80	296.30	294.87	294.33	294.13
19000	328.10	324.82	322.16	320.01	318.25	316.83	315.66	314.71	313.93	313.29	312.76	311.25	310.68	310.47
20000	345.37	341.91	339.12	336.85	335.00	333.50	332.27	331.27	330.45	329.77	329.22	327.63	327.03	326.81
21000	362.64	359.01	356.07	353.69	351.75	350.18	348.89	347.83	346.97	346.26	345.68	344.01	343.39	343.15
22000	379.90	376.10	373.03	370.53	368.50	366.85	365.50	364.40	363.49	362.75	362.14	360.39	359.74	359.49
23000	397.17	393.20	389.98	387.30	385.25	383.53	382.11	380.96	380.01	379.24	378.60	376.78	376.09	375.83
24000	414.44	410.29	406.94	404.22	402.00	400.20	398.73	397.52	396.54	395.73	395.07	393.16	392.44	392.17
25000	431.71	427.39	423.89	421.06	418.75	416.88	415.34	414.09	413.06	412.22	411.53	409.54	408.79	408.51
26000	448.98	444.48	440.85	437.90	435.50	433.55	431.95	430.65	429.58	428.71	427.99	425.92	425.14	424.85
27000	466.25	461.58	457.80	454.74	452.25	450.23	448.57	447.21	446.10	445.19	444.45	442.30	441.49	441.19
28000	483.51	478.67	474.76	471.59	469.00	466.90	465.18	463.78	462.63	461.68	460.91	458.68	457.85	457.53
29000	500.78	495.77	491.72	488.43	485.75	483.57	481.80	480.34	479.15	478.17	477.37	475.06	474.20	473.87
30000	518.05	512.86	508.67	505.27	502.50	500.25	498.41	496.90	495.67	494.66	493.83	491.45	490.55	490.21
31000	535.32	529.96	525.63	522.11	519.25	516.92	515.02	513.47	512.19	511.15	510.29	507.83	506.90	506.55
32000	552.59	547.05	542.58	538.95	536.00	533.60	531.64	530.03	528.71	527.64	526.75	524.21	523.25	522.89
33000	569.85	564.15	559.54	555.80	552.75	550.27	548.25	546.59	545.24	544.13	543.21	540.59	539.60	539.23
34000	587.12	581.24	576.49	572.64	569.50	566.95	564.86	563.16	561.76	560.61	559.67	556.97	555.95	555.57
35000	604.39	598.34	593.45	589.48	586.25	583.62	581.48	579.72	578.28	577.10	576.14	573.35	572.31	571.91
36000	621.66	615.44	610.40	606.32	603.00	600.30	598.09	596.28	594.80	593.59	592.60	589.73	588.66	588.25
37000	638.93	632.53	627.36	623.17	619.75	616.97	614.70	612.85	611.33	610.08	609.06	606.11	605.01	604.59
38000	656.20	649.63	644.32	640.01	636.50	633.65	631.32	629.41	627.85	626.57	625.52	622.50	621.36	620.93
39000	673.46	666.72	661.27	656.85	653.25	650.32	647.93	645.97	644.37	643.06	641.98	638.88	637.71	637.27
40000	690.73	683.82	678.23	673.69	670.00	667.00	664.54	662.54	660.89	659.54	658.44	655.26	654.06	653.61
41000	708.00	700.91	695.18	690.53	686.75	683.67	681.16	679.10	677.41	676.03	674.90	671.64	670.41	669.95
42000	725.27	718.01	712.14	707.38	703.50	700.35	697.77	695.66	693.94	692.52	691.36	688.02	686.77	686.29
43000	742.54	735.10	729.09	724.22	720.25	717.02	714.38	712.23	710.46	709.01	707.82	704.40	703.12	702.63
44000	759.80	752.20	746.05	741.06	737.00	733.70	731.00	728.79	726.98	725.50	724.28	720.78	719.47	718.97
45000	777.07	769.29	763.00	757.90	753.75	750.37	747.61	745.35	743.50	741.99	740.74	737.17	735.82	735.31
46000	794.34	786.39	779.96	774.75	770.50	767.05	764.22	761.92	760.02	758.48	757.20	753.55	752.17	751.65
47000	811.61	803.48	796.92	791.59	787.25	783.72	780.84	778.48	776.55	774.96	773.67	769.93	768.52	767.99
48000	828.88	820.58	813.87	808.43	804.00	800.40	797.45	795.04	793.07	791.45	790.13	786.31	784.88	784.33
49000	846.15	837.67	830.83	825.27	820.75	817.07	814.06	811.60	809.59	807.94	806.59	802.69	801.23	800.67
50000	863.41	854.77	847.78	842.11	837.50	833.75	830.68	828.17	826.11	824.43	823.05	819.07	817.58	817.01
55000	949.75	940.25	932.56	926.32	921.25	917.12	913.74	910.98	908.72	906.87	905.35	900.98	899.34	898.72
60000	1036.10	1025.72	1017.34	1010.54	1005.00	1000.49	996.81	993.80	991.34	989.31	987.66	982.89	981.09	980.42
65000	1122.44	1111.20	1102.11	1094.75	1088.75	1083.87	1079.88	1076.62	1073.95	1071.76	1069.96	1064.79	1062.85	1062.12
70000	1208.78	1196.68	1186.89	1178.96	1172.50	1167.24	1162.95	1159.43	1156.56	1154.20	1152.27	1146.70	1144.61	1143.82
75000	1295.12	1282.15	1271.67	1263.17	1256.25	1250.62	1246.01	1242.25	1239.17	1236.64	1234.57	1228.61	1226.36	1225.52
80000	1381.46	1367.63	1356.45	1347.38	1340.00	1333.99	1329.08	1325.07	1321.78	1319.08	1316.87	1310.51	1308.12	1307.22
85000	1467.80	1453.10	1441.23	1431.59	1423.75	1417.37	1412.15	1407.88	1404.39	1401.53	1399.18	1392.42	1389.88	1388.92
90000	1554.14	1538.58	1526.00	1515.80	1507.50	1500.74	1495.22	1490.70	1487.00	1483.97	1481.48	1474.33	1471.64	1470.62
95000	1640.48	1624.06	1610.78	1600.01	1591.25	1584.11	1578.28	1573.52	1569.61	1566.41	1563.79	1556.23	1553.39	1552.32
100000	1726.82	1709.53	1695.56	1684.22	1675.00	1667.49	1661.35	1656.33	1652.22	1648.85	1646.09	1638.14	1635.15	1634.02

19.625%

MONTHLY PAYMENT
REQUIRED TO AMORTIZE A LOAN

TERM	1 Year	2 Years	3 Years	4 Years	5 Years	6 Years	7 Years	8 Years	9 Years	10 Years	11 Years	12 Years	13 Years	14 Years
AMOUNT														
5	.47	.26	.19	.16	.14	.12	.11	.11	.10	.10	.10	.10	.09	.09
10	.93	.51	.37	.31	.27	.24	.22	.21	.20	.20	.19	.19	.18	.18
15	1.39	.77	.56	.46	.40	.36	.33	.32	.30	.29	.28	.28	.27	.27
25	2.32	1.27	.93	.76	.66	.60	.55	.52	.50	.48	.47	.46	.45	.44
50	4.63	2.54	1.85	1.52	1.32	1.19	1.10	1.04	.99	.96	.93	.91	.89	.88
75	6.94	3.81	2.78	2.27	1.98	1.79	1.65	1.56	1.49	1.44	1.39	1.36	1.34	1.32
100	9.25	5.08	3.70	3.03	2.63	2.38	2.20	2.08	1.98	1.91	1.86	1.82	1.78	1.76
200	18.50	10.15	7.40	6.05	5.26	4.75	4.40	4.15	3.96	3.82	3.71	3.63	3.56	3.51
300	27.74	15.22	11.10	9.07	7.89	7.13	6.60	6.22	5.94	5.73	5.56	5.44	5.34	5.26
400	36.99	20.29	14.79	12.10	10.52	9.50	8.80	8.29	7.92	7.64	7.42	7.25	7.11	7.01
500	46.23	25.36	18.49	15.12	13.15	11.87	11.00	10.36	9.90	9.54	9.27	9.06	8.89	8.76
600	55.48	30.43	22.19	18.14	15.78	14.25	13.19	12.44	11.88	11.45	11.12	10.87	10.67	10.51
700	64.72	35.50	25.89	21.17	18.40	16.62	15.39	14.51	13.85	13.36	12.98	12.68	12.44	12.26
800	73.97	40.58	29.58	24.19	21.03	18.99	17.59	16.58	15.83	15.27	14.83	14.49	14.22	14.01
900	83.21	45.65	33.28	27.21	23.66	21.37	19.79	18.65	17.81	17.17	16.68	16.30	16.00	15.76
1000	92.46	50.72	36.98	30.24	26.29	23.74	21.99	20.72	19.79	19.08	18.54	18.11	17.77	17.51
2000	184.92	101.43	73.95	60.47	52.58	47.48	43.97	41.44	39.58	38.16	37.07	36.22	35.54	35.01
3000	277.37	152.14	110.92	90.70	78.86	71.21	65.95	62.16	59.36	57.24	55.60	54.32	53.31	52.51
4000	369.83	202.86	147.90	120.93	105.15	94.95	87.93	82.88	79.15	76.32	74.13	72.43	71.08	70.01
5000	462.28	253.57	184.87	151.16	131.43	118.68	109.91	103.60	98.93	95.39	92.66	90.53	88.85	87.51
6000	554.74	304.28	221.84	181.39	157.72	142.42	131.89	124.32	118.72	114.47	111.20	108.64	106.62	105.01
7000	647.19	354.99	258.81	211.62	184.00	166.16	153.87	145.04	138.50	133.55	129.73	126.74	124.39	122.51
8000	739.65	405.71	295.79	241.85	210.29	189.89	175.85	165.76	158.29	152.63	148.26	146.85	142.15	140.01
9000	832.10	456.42	332.76	272.08	236.58	213.63	197.83	186.48	178.08	171.70	166.79	162.95	159.92	157.51
10000	924.56	507.13	369.73	302.31	262.86	237.36	219.81	207.20	197.86	190.78	185.32	181.06	177.69	175.01
11000	1017.01	557.85	406.71	332.55	289.15	261.10	241.80	227.92	217.65	209.86	203.85	199.16	195.46	192.52
12000	1109.47	608.56	443.68	362.78	315.43	284.84	263.78	248.64	237.43	228.94	222.39	217.27	213.23	210.02
13000	1201.92	659.27	480.65	393.01	341.72	308.57	285.76	269.36	257.22	248.01	240.92	235.37	231.00	227.52
14000	1294.38	709.98	517.62	423.24	368.00	332.31	307.74	290.08	277.00	267.09	259.45	253.48	248.77	245.02
15000	1386.83	760.70	554.60	453.47	394.29	356.04	329.72	310.80	296.79	286.17	277.98	271.58	266.54	262.52
16000	1479.29	811.41	591.57	483.70	420.58	379.78	351.70	331.52	316.58	305.25	296.51	289.69	284.30	280.02
17000	1571.74	862.12	628.54	513.93	446.86	403.52	373.68	352.24	336.36	324.32	315.04	307.79	302.07	297.52
18000	1664.20	912.84	665.52	544.16	473.15	427.25	395.66	372.96	356.15	343.40	333.58	325.90	319.84	315.02
19000	1756.65	963.55	702.49	574.39	499.43	450.99	417.64	393.68	375.93	362.48	352.11	344.01	337.61	332.52
20000	1849.11	1014.26	739.46	604.62	525.72	474.72	439.62	414.40	395.72	381.56	370.64	362.11	355.38	350.02
21000	1941.56	1064.97	776.43	634.85	552.00	498.46	461.61	435.12	415.50	400.63	389.17	380.22	373.15	367.53
22000	2034.02	1115.69	813.41	665.09	578.29	522.20	483.59	455.84	435.29	419.71	407.70	398.32	390.92	385.03
23000	2126.47	1166.40	850.38	695.32	604.58	545.93	505.57	476.56	455.08	438.79	426.23	416.43	408.69	402.53
24000	2218.93	1217.11	887.35	725.55	630.86	569.67	527.55	497.28	474.86	457.87	444.77	434.53	426.45	420.03
25000	2311.38	1267.82	924.32	755.78	657.15	593.40	549.53	518.00	494.65	476.94	463.30	452.64	444.22	437.53
26000	2403.84	1318.54	961.30	786.01	683.43	617.14	571.51	538.72	514.43	496.02	481.83	470.74	461.99	455.03
27000	2496.29	1369.25	998.27	816.24	709.72	640.88	593.49	559.44	534.22	515.10	500.36	488.85	479.76	472.53
28000	2588.75	1419.96	1035.24	846.47	736.00	664.61	615.47	580.16	554.00	534.18	518.89	506.95	497.53	490.03
29000	2681.20	1470.68	1072.22	876.70	762.29	688.35	637.45	600.88	573.79	553.26	537.42	525.06	515.30	507.53
30000	2773.66	1521.39	1109.19	906.93	788.57	712.08	659.43	621.60	593.57	572.33	555.96	543.16	533.07	525.03
31000	2866.11	1572.10	1146.16	937.16	814.86	735.82	681.41	642.32	613.36	591.41	574.49	561.27	550.84	542.54
32000	2958.57	1622.81	1183.13	967.39	841.15	759.56	703.40	663.04	633.15	610.49	593.02	579.37	568.60	560.04
33000	3051.02	1673.53	1220.11	997.63	867.43	783.29	725.38	683.76	652.93	629.57	611.55	597.48	586.37	577.54
34000	3143.48	1724.24	1257.08	1027.86	893.72	807.03	747.36	704.48	672.72	648.64	630.08	615.58	604.14	595.04
35000	3235.93	1774.95	1294.05	1058.09	920.00	830.76	769.34	725.20	692.50	667.72	648.61	633.69	621.91	612.54
36000	3328.39	1825.67	1331.03	1088.32	946.29	854.50	791.32	745.92	712.29	686.80	667.15	651.80	639.68	630.04
37000	3420.84	1876.38	1368.00	1118.55	972.57	878.24	813.30	766.64	732.07	705.88	685.68	669.90	657.45	647.54
38000	3513.30	1927.09	1404.97	1148.78	998.86	901.97	835.28	787.36	751.86	724.95	704.21	688.01	675.22	665.04
39000	3605.75	1977.80	1441.94	1179.01	1025.15	925.71	857.26	808.08	771.65	744.03	722.74	706.11	692.99	682.54
40000	3698.21	2028.52	1478.92	1209.24	1051.43	949.44	879.24	828.80	791.43	763.11	741.27	724.22	710.75	700.04
41000	3790.67	2079.23	1515.89	1239.47	1077.72	973.18	901.22	849.52	811.22	782.19	759.80	742.32	728.52	717.54
42000	3883.12	2129.94	1552.86	1269.70	1104.00	996.92	923.21	870.24	831.00	801.26	778.34	760.43	746.29	735.05
43000	3975.58	2180.66	1589.83	1299.93	1130.29	1020.65	945.19	890.96	850.79	820.34	796.87	778.53	764.06	752.55
44000	4068.03	2231.37	1626.81	1330.17	1156.57	1044.39	967.17	911.68	870.57	839.42	815.40	796.64	781.83	770.05
45000	4160.49	2282.08	1663.78	1360.40	1182.86	1068.12	989.15	932.40	890.36	858.50	833.93	814.74	799.60	787.55
46000	4252.94	2332.79	1700.75	1390.63	1209.15	1091.86	1011.13	953.12	910.15	877.57	852.46	832.85	817.37	805.05
47000	4345.40	2383.51	1737.73	1420.86	1235.43	1115.59	1033.11	973.84	929.93	896.65	871.00	850.95	835.14	822.55
48000	4437.85	2434.22	1774.70	1451.09	1261.72	1139.33	1055.09	994.56	949.72	915.73	889.53	869.06	852.90	840.05
49000	4530.31	2484.93	1811.67	1481.32	1288.00	1163.07	1077.07	1015.28	969.50	934.81	908.06	887.16	870.67	857.55
50000	4622.76	2535.64	1848.64	1511.55	1314.29	1186.80	1099.05	1036.00	989.29	953.88	926.59	905.27	888.44	875.05
55000	5085.04	2789.21	2033.51	1662.71	1445.72	1305.48	1208.96	1139.60	1088.22	1049.27	1019.25	995.80	977.29	962.56
60000	5547.31	3042.77	2218.37	1813.86	1577.14	1424.16	1318.86	1243.20	1187.14	1144.66	1111.91	1086.32	1066.13	1050.06
65000	6009.59	3296.34	2403.24	1965.02	1708.57	1542.84	1428.77	1346.80	1286.07	1240.05	1204.57	1176.85	1154.97	1137.57
70000	6471.86	3549.90	2588.10	2116.17	1840.00	1661.52	1538.67	1450.40	1385.00	1335.44	1297.22	1267.37	1243.82	1225.07
75000	6934.14	3803.46	2772.96	2267.32	1971.43	1780.20	1648.58	1554.00	1483.93	1430.82	1389.88	1357.90	1332.66	1312.58
80000	7396.42	4057.03	2957.83	2418.48	2102.86	1898.88	1758.48	1657.60	1582.86	1526.21	1482.54	1448.43	1421.50	1400.08
85000	7858.69	4310.59	3142.69	2569.63	2234.29	2017.56	1868.39	1761.20	1681.79	1621.60	1575.20	1538.95	1510.35	1487.59
90000	8320.97	4564.16	3327.56	2720.79	2365.71	2136.24	1978.29	1864.80	1780.71	1716.99	1667.86	1629.48	1599.19	1575.09
95000	8783.24	4817.72	3512.42	2871.94	2497.14	2254.92	2088.20	1968.40	1879.64	1812.38	1760.52	1720.01	1688.04	1662.60
100000	9245.52	5071.28	3697.28	3023.10	2628.57	2373.60	2198.10	2072.00	1978.57	1907.76	1853.18	1810.53	1776.88	1750.10

TERM	15 Years	16 Years	17 Years	18 Years	19 Years	20 Years	21 Years	22 Years	23 Years	24 Years	25 Years	30 Years	35 Years	40 Years
AMOUNT														
5	.09	.09	.09	.09	.09	.09	.09	.09	.09	.09	.09	.09	.09	.09
10	.18	.18	.17	.17	.17	.17	.17	.17	.17	.17	.17	.17	.17	.17
15	.26	.26	.26	.26	.26	.26	.25	.25	.25	.25	.25	.25	.25	.25
25	.44	.43	.43	.43	.42	.42	.42	.42	.42	.42	.42	.42	.41	.41
50	.87	.86	.85	.85	.84	.84	.84	.83	.83	.83	.83	.83	.82	.82
75	1.30	1.29	1.28	1.27	1.26	1.26	1.25	1.25	1.25	1.24	1.24	1.24	1.23	1.23
100	1.73	1.72	1.70	1.69	1.68	1.67	1.67	1.66	1.66	1.66	1.65	1.65	1.64	1.64
200	3.46	3.43	3.40	3.38	3.36	3.34	3.33	3.32	3.31	3.31	3.30	3.29	3.28	3.28
300	5.19	5.14	5.10	5.06	5.04	5.01	4.99	4.98	4.97	4.96	4.95	4.93	4.92	4.91
400	6.92	6.85	6.79	6.75	6.71	6.68	6.66	6.64	6.62	6.61	6.60	6.57	6.55	6.55
500	8.65	8.56	8.49	8.44	8.39	8.35	8.32	8.30	8.28	8.26	8.25	8.21	8.19	8.19
600	10.38	10.27	10.19	10.12	10.07	10.02	9.98	9.95	9.93	9.91	9.89	9.85	9.83	9.82
700	12.11	11.98	11.89	11.81	11.74	11.69	11.65	11.61	11.58	11.56	11.54	11.49	11.47	11.46
800	13.83	13.70	13.58	13.49	13.42	13.36	13.31	13.27	13.24	13.21	13.19	13.13	13.10	13.09
900	15.56	15.41	15.28	15.18	15.10	15.03	14.97	14.93	14.89	14.86	14.84	14.77	14.74	14.73
1000	17.29	17.12	16.98	16.87	16.77	16.70	16.64	16.59	16.55	16.51	16.49	16.41	16.38	16.37
2000	34.58	34.23	33.95	33.73	33.54	33.39	33.27	33.17	33.09	33.02	32.97	32.81	32.75	32.73
3000	51.86	51.35	50.93	50.59	50.31	50.09	49.90	49.75	49.63	49.53	49.45	49.21	49.12	49.09
4000	69.15	68.46	67.90	67.45	67.08	66.78	66.54	66.34	66.17	66.04	65.93	65.61	65.49	65.45
5000	86.44	85.57	84.88	84.31	83.85	83.48	83.17	82.92	82.72	82.55	82.41	82.01	81.87	81.81
6000	103.72	102.69	101.85	101.17	100.62	100.17	99.80	99.50	99.26	99.06	98.89	98.42	98.24	98.17
7000	121.01	119.80	118.83	118.03	117.39	116.87	116.44	116.09	115.80	115.57	115.37	114.82	114.61	114.53
8000	138.30	136.92	135.80	134.90	134.16	133.56	133.07	132.67	132.34	132.07	131.85	131.22	130.98	130.89
9000	155.58	154.03	152.78	151.76	150.93	150.25	149.70	149.25	148.88	148.58	148.33	147.62	147.35	147.25
10000	172.87	171.14	169.75	168.62	167.70	166.95	166.34	165.84	165.43	165.09	164.82	164.02	163.73	163.61
11000	190.16	188.26	186.72	185.48	184.47	183.64	182.97	182.42	181.97	181.60	181.30	180.43	180.10	179.98
12000	207.44	205.37	203.70	202.34	201.24	200.34	199.60	199.00	198.51	198.11	197.78	196.83	196.47	196.34
13000	224.73	222.49	220.67	219.20	218.01	217.03	216.24	215.59	215.05	214.62	214.26	213.23	212.84	212.70
14000	242.02	239.60	237.65	236.06	234.78	233.73	232.87	232.17	231.60	231.13	230.74	229.63	229.22	229.06
15000	259.30	256.71	254.62	252.93	251.55	250.42	249.50	248.75	248.14	247.63	247.22	246.03	245.59	245.42
16000	276.59	273.83	271.60	269.79	268.31	267.12	266.14	265.34	264.68	264.14	263.70	262.44	261.96	261.78
17000	293.88	290.94	288.57	286.65	285.08	283.81	282.77	281.92	281.22	280.65	280.18	278.84	278.33	278.14
18000	311.16	308.06	305.55	303.51	301.85	300.50	299.40	298.50	297.76	297.16	296.66	295.24	294.70	294.50
19000	328.45	325.17	322.52	320.37	318.62	317.20	316.04	315.08	314.31	313.67	313.15	311.64	311.08	310.86
20000	345.74	342.28	339.49	337.23	335.39	333.89	332.67	331.67	330.85	330.18	329.63	328.04	327.45	327.22
21000	363.02	359.40	356.47	354.09	352.16	350.59	349.30	348.25	347.39	346.69	346.11	344.44	343.82	343.59
22000	380.31	376.51	373.44	370.95	368.93	367.28	365.93	364.83	363.93	363.19	362.59	360.85	360.19	359.95
23000	397.60	393.63	390.42	387.82	385.70	383.98	382.57	381.42	380.47	379.70	379.07	377.25	376.56	376.31
24000	414.88	410.74	407.39	404.68	402.47	400.67	399.20	398.00	397.02	396.21	395.55	393.65	392.94	392.67
25000	432.17	427.85	424.37	421.54	419.24	417.36	415.83	414.58	413.56	412.72	412.03	410.05	409.31	409.03
26000	449.46	444.97	441.34	438.40	436.01	434.06	432.47	431.17	430.10	429.23	428.51	426.45	425.68	425.39
27000	466.74	462.08	458.32	455.26	452.78	450.75	449.10	447.75	446.64	445.74	444.99	442.86	442.05	441.75
28000	484.03	479.20	475.29	472.12	469.55	467.45	465.73	464.33	463.19	462.25	461.47	459.26	458.43	458.11
29000	501.32	496.31	492.26	488.98	486.32	484.14	482.37	480.92	479.73	478.75	477.96	475.66	474.80	474.47
30000	518.60	513.42	509.24	505.85	503.09	500.84	499.00	497.50	496.27	495.26	494.44	492.06	491.17	490.83
31000	535.89	530.54	526.21	522.71	519.85	517.53	515.63	514.08	512.81	511.77	510.92	508.46	507.54	507.19
32000	553.17	547.65	543.19	539.57	536.62	534.23	532.27	530.67	529.35	528.28	527.40	524.87	523.91	523.56
33000	570.46	564.77	560.16	556.43	553.39	550.92	548.90	547.25	545.90	544.79	543.88	541.27	540.29	539.92
34000	587.75	581.88	577.14	573.29	570.16	567.61	565.53	563.83	562.44	561.30	560.36	557.67	556.66	556.28
35000	605.03	598.99	594.11	590.15	586.93	584.31	582.17	580.41	578.98	577.81	576.84	574.07	573.03	572.64
36000	622.32	616.11	611.09	607.01	603.70	601.00	598.80	597.00	595.52	594.31	593.32	590.47	589.40	589.00
37000	639.61	633.22	628.06	623.87	620.47	617.70	615.43	613.58	612.07	610.82	609.80	606.87	605.78	605.36
38000	656.89	650.34	645.03	640.74	637.24	634.39	632.07	630.16	628.61	627.33	626.29	623.28	622.15	621.72
39000	674.18	667.45	662.01	657.60	654.01	651.09	648.70	646.75	645.15	643.84	642.77	639.68	638.52	638.00
40000	691.47	684.56	678.98	674.46	670.78	667.78	665.33	663.33	661.69	660.35	659.25	656.08	654.89	654.44
41000	708.75	701.68	695.96	691.32	687.55	684.47	681.97	679.91	678.23	676.86	675.73	672.48	671.26	670.80
42000	726.04	718.79	712.93	708.18	704.32	701.17	698.60	696.50	694.78	693.37	692.21	688.88	687.64	687.17
43000	743.33	735.91	729.91	725.04	721.09	717.86	715.23	713.08	711.32	709.87	708.69	705.29	704.01	703.53
44000	760.61	753.02	746.88	741.90	737.86	734.56	731.86	729.66	727.86	726.38	725.17	721.69	720.38	719.89
45000	777.90	770.13	763.86	758.77	754.63	751.25	748.50	746.25	744.40	742.89	741.65	738.09	736.75	736.25
46000	795.19	787.25	780.83	775.63	771.40	767.95	765.13	762.83	760.94	759.40	758.13	754.49	753.12	752.61
47000	812.47	804.36	797.80	792.49	788.16	784.64	781.76	779.41	777.49	775.91	774.62	770.89	769.50	768.97
48000	829.76	821.48	814.78	809.35	804.93	801.34	798.40	796.00	794.03	792.42	791.10	787.30	785.87	785.33
49000	847.05	838.59	831.75	826.21	821.70	818.03	815.03	812.58	810.57	808.93	807.58	803.70	802.24	801.69
50000	864.33	855.70	848.73	843.07	838.47	834.72	831.66	829.16	827.11	825.43	824.06	820.10	818.61	818.05
55000	950.77	941.27	933.60	927.38	922.32	918.20	914.83	912.08	909.82	907.98	906.46	902.11	900.47	899.86
60000	1037.20	1026.84	1018.47	1011.69	1006.17	1001.67	998.00	994.99	992.53	990.52	988.87	984.12	982.33	981.66
65000	1123.63	1112.41	1103.35	1095.99	1090.01	1085.14	1081.16	1077.91	1075.25	1073.06	1071.27	1066.13	1064.20	1063.47
70000	1210.06	1197.98	1188.22	1180.30	1173.86	1168.61	1164.33	1160.82	1157.96	1155.61	1153.68	1148.14	1146.06	1145.27
75000	1296.50	1283.55	1273.09	1264.61	1257.71	1252.08	1247.49	1243.74	1240.67	1238.15	1236.09	1230.15	1227.92	1227.08
80000	1382.93	1369.12	1357.96	1348.91	1341.55	1335.56	1330.66	1326.66	1323.38	1320.69	1318.49	1312.16	1309.78	1308.88
85000	1469.36	1454.69	1442.83	1433.22	1425.40	1419.03	1413.82	1409.57	1406.09	1403.24	1400.90	1394.17	1391.64	1390.69
90000	1555.79	1540.26	1527.71	1517.53	1509.25	1502.50	1496.99	1492.49	1488.80	1485.78	1483.30	1476.17	1473.50	1472.49
95000	1642.23	1625.83	1612.58	1601.83	1593.09	1585.97	1580.16	1575.40	1571.51	1568.32	1565.71	1558.18	1555.36	1554.30
100000	1728.66	1711.40	1697.45	1686.14	1676.94	1669.44	1663.32	1658.32	1654.22	1650.86	1648.11	1640.19	1637.22	1636.10

MONTHLY PAYMENT
REQUIRED TO AMORTIZE A LOAN

19.700%

TERM AMOUNT	1 Year	2 Years	3 Years	4 Years	5 Years	6 Years	7 Years	8 Years	9 Years	10 Years	11 Years	12 Years	13 Years	14 Years
5	.47	.26	.19	.16	.14	.12	.12	.11	.10	.10	.10	.10	.09	.09
10	.93	.51	.38	.31	.27	.24	.23	.21	.20	.20	.19	.19	.18	.18
15	1.39	.77	.56	.46	.40	.36	.34	.32	.30	.29	.28	.28	.27	.27
25	2.32	1.27	.93	.76	.66	.60	.56	.52	.50	.48	.47	.46	.45	.44
50	4.63	2.54	1.86	1.52	1.32	1.19	1.11	1.04	1.00	.96	.93	.91	.90	.88
75	6.94	3.81	2.78	2.28	1.98	1.79	1.66	1.56	1.49	1.44	1.40	1.37	1.34	1.32
100	9.25	5.08	3.71	3.03	2.64	2.38	2.21	2.08	1.99	1.92	1.86	1.82	1.79	1.76
200	18.50	10.15	7.41	6.06	5.27	4.76	4.41	4.16	3.97	3.83	3.72	3.64	3.57	3.52
300	27.75	15.23	11.11	9.09	7.90	7.14	6.61	6.23	5.96	5.74	5.58	5.45	5.35	5.27
400	37.00	20.30	14.81	12.11	10.54	9.52	8.82	8.31	7.94	7.66	7.44	7.27	7.13	7.03
500	46.25	25.38	18.51	15.14	13.17	11.89	11.02	10.39	9.92	9.57	9.30	9.08	8.92	8.78
600	55.50	30.45	22.21	18.17	15.80	14.27	13.22	12.46	11.91	11.48	11.15	10.90	10.70	10.54
700	64.75	35.53	25.91	21.19	18.43	16.65	15.42	14.54	13.89	13.39	13.01	12.72	12.48	12.29
800	74.00	40.60	29.61	24.22	21.07	19.03	17.63	16.62	15.87	15.31	14.87	14.53	14.26	14.05
900	83.25	45.68	33.31	27.25	23.70	21.41	19.83	18.69	17.86	17.22	16.73	16.35	16.04	15.80
1000	92.50	50.75	37.02	30.28	26.33	23.78	22.03	20.77	19.84	19.13	18.59	18.16	17.83	17.56
2000	184.99	101.50	74.03	60.55	52.66	47.56	44.06	41.54	39.67	38.26	37.17	36.32	35.65	35.12
3000	277.48	152.25	111.04	90.82	78.99	71.34	66.08	62.30	59.51	57.39	55.75	54.48	53.47	52.67
4000	369.97	203.00	148.05	121.09	105.31	95.12	88.11	83.07	79.34	76.51	74.34	72.63	71.29	70.23
5000	462.46	253.75	185.06	151.36	131.64	118.90	110.13	103.84	99.17	95.64	92.92	90.79	89.11	87.78
6000	554.95	304.50	222.07	181.63	157.97	142.68	132.16	124.60	119.01	114.77	111.50	108.95	106.94	105.34
7000	647.44	355.25	259.08	211.90	184.30	166.46	154.19	145.37	138.84	133.89	130.08	127.11	124.76	122.89
8000	739.93	406.00	296.09	242.17	210.62	190.24	176.21	166.14	158.67	153.02	148.67	145.26	142.58	140.45
9000	832.42	456.75	333.10	272.44	236.95	214.02	198.24	186.90	178.51	172.15	167.25	163.42	160.40	158.00
10000	924.91	507.50	370.11	302.71	263.28	237.80	220.26	207.67	198.34	191.28	185.83	181.58	178.22	175.56
11000	1017.41	558.25	407.12	332.98	289.60	261.58	242.29	228.44	218.18	210.40	204.41	199.74	196.05	193.11
12000	1109.90	609.00	444.14	363.25	315.93	285.36	264.32	249.20	238.01	229.53	223.00	217.89	213.87	210.67
13000	1202.39	659.75	481.15	393.52	342.26	309.14	286.34	269.97	257.84	248.66	241.58	236.05	231.69	228.22
14000	1294.88	710.50	518.16	423.80	368.59	332.91	308.37	290.74	277.68	267.78	260.16	254.21	249.51	245.78
15000	1387.37	761.25	555.17	454.07	394.91	356.69	330.39	311.50	297.51	286.91	278.74	272.37	267.33	263.33
16000	1479.86	811.99	592.18	484.34	421.24	380.47	352.42	332.27	317.34	306.04	297.33	290.52	285.16	280.89
17000	1572.35	862.74	629.19	514.61	447.57	404.25	374.45	353.04	337.18	325.17	315.91	308.68	302.98	298.44
18000	1664.84	913.49	666.20	544.88	473.90	428.03	396.47	373.80	357.01	344.29	334.49	326.84	320.80	316.00
19000	1757.33	964.24	703.21	575.15	500.22	451.81	418.50	394.57	376.85	363.42	353.07	344.99	338.62	333.55
20000	1849.82	1014.99	740.22	605.42	526.55	475.59	440.52	415.34	396.68	382.55	371.66	363.15	356.44	351.11
21000	1942.32	1065.74	777.23	635.69	552.88	499.37	462.55	436.10	416.51	401.67	390.24	381.31	374.27	368.66
22000	2034.81	1116.49	814.24	665.96	579.20	523.15	484.58	456.87	436.35	420.80	408.82	399.47	392.09	386.22
23000	2127.30	1167.24	851.26	696.23	605.53	546.93	506.60	477.63	456.18	439.93	427.40	417.62	409.91	403.77
24000	2219.79	1217.99	888.27	726.50	631.86	570.71	528.63	498.40	476.01	459.05	445.99	435.78	427.73	421.33
25000	2312.28	1268.74	925.28	756.77	658.19	594.49	550.65	519.17	495.85	478.18	464.57	453.94	445.55	438.89
26000	2404.77	1319.49	962.29	787.04	684.51	618.27	572.68	539.93	515.68	497.31	483.15	472.10	463.38	456.44
27000	2497.26	1370.24	999.30	817.32	710.84	642.04	594.70	560.70	535.52	516.44	501.73	490.25	481.20	474.00
28000	2589.75	1420.99	1036.31	847.59	737.17	665.82	616.73	581.47	555.35	535.56	520.32	508.41	499.02	491.55
29000	2682.24	1471.74	1073.32	877.86	763.49	689.60	638.76	602.23	575.18	554.69	538.90	526.57	516.84	509.11
30000	2774.73	1522.49	1110.33	908.13	789.82	713.38	660.78	623.00	595.02	573.82	557.48	544.73	534.66	526.66
31000	2867.23	1573.24	1147.34	938.40	816.15	737.16	682.81	643.77	614.85	592.94	576.06	562.88	552.48	544.22
32000	2959.72	1623.98	1184.35	968.67	842.48	760.94	704.83	664.53	634.68	612.07	594.65	581.04	570.31	561.77
33000	3052.21	1674.73	1221.36	998.94	868.80	784.72	726.86	685.30	654.52	631.20	613.23	599.20	588.13	579.33
34000	3144.70	1725.48	1258.38	1029.21	895.13	808.50	748.89	706.07	674.35	650.33	631.81	617.35	605.95	596.88
35000	3237.19	1776.23	1295.39	1059.48	921.46	832.28	770.91	726.83	694.19	669.45	650.39	635.51	623.77	614.44
36000	3329.68	1826.98	1332.40	1089.75	947.79	856.06	792.94	747.60	714.02	688.58	668.98	653.67	641.59	631.99
37000	3422.17	1877.73	1369.41	1120.02	974.11	879.84	814.96	768.37	733.85	707.71	687.56	671.83	659.42	649.55
38000	3514.66	1928.48	1406.42	1150.29	1000.44	903.62	836.99	789.13	753.69	726.83	706.14	689.98	677.24	667.10
39000	3607.15	1979.23	1443.43	1180.56	1026.77	927.40	859.02	809.90	773.52	745.96	724.72	708.14	695.06	684.66
40000	3699.64	2029.98	1480.44	1210.84	1053.09	951.17	881.04	830.67	793.35	765.09	743.31	726.30	712.88	702.21
41000	3792.14	2080.73	1517.45	1241.11	1079.42	974.95	903.07	851.43	813.19	784.22	761.89	744.46	730.70	719.77
42000	3884.63	2131.48	1554.46	1271.38	1105.75	998.73	925.09	872.20	833.02	803.34	780.47	762.61	748.53	737.32
43000	3977.12	2182.23	1591.47	1301.65	1132.08	1022.51	947.12	892.96	852.86	822.47	799.05	780.77	766.35	754.88
44000	4069.61	2232.98	1628.48	1331.92	1158.40	1046.29	969.15	913.73	872.69	841.60	817.64	798.93	784.17	772.43
45000	4162.10	2283.73	1665.50	1362.19	1184.73	1070.07	991.17	934.50	892.52	860.72	836.22	817.09	801.99	789.99
46000	4254.59	2334.48	1702.51	1392.46	1211.06	1093.85	1013.20	955.26	912.36	879.85	854.80	835.24	819.81	807.54
47000	4347.08	2385.23	1739.52	1422.73	1237.39	1117.63	1035.22	976.03	932.19	898.98	873.38	853.40	837.64	825.10
48000	4439.57	2435.97	1776.53	1453.00	1263.71	1141.41	1057.25	996.80	952.02	918.10	891.97	871.56	855.46	842.65
49000	4532.06	2486.72	1813.54	1483.27	1290.04	1165.19	1079.27	1017.56	971.86	937.23	910.55	889.71	873.28	860.21
50000	4624.55	2537.47	1850.55	1513.54	1316.37	1188.97	1101.30	1038.33	991.69	956.36	929.13	907.87	891.10	877.77
55000	5087.01	2791.22	2035.60	1664.90	1448.00	1307.86	1211.43	1142.16	1090.86	1051.99	1022.04	998.66	980.21	965.54
60000	5549.46	3044.97	2220.66	1816.25	1579.64	1426.76	1321.56	1246.00	1190.03	1147.63	1114.96	1089.45	1069.32	1053.32
65000	6011.92	3298.71	2405.71	1967.60	1711.28	1545.66	1431.69	1349.83	1289.20	1243.27	1207.87	1180.23	1158.43	1141.09
70000	6474.37	3552.46	2590.77	2118.96	1842.91	1664.55	1541.82	1453.66	1388.37	1338.90	1300.78	1271.02	1247.54	1228.87
75000	6936.83	3806.21	2775.82	2270.31	1974.55	1783.45	1651.95	1557.49	1487.53	1434.54	1393.69	1361.81	1336.65	1316.65
80000	7399.28	4059.95	2960.88	2421.67	2106.18	1902.34	1762.08	1661.33	1586.70	1530.17	1486.61	1452.59	1425.76	1404.42
85000	7861.74	4313.70	3145.93	2573.02	2237.82	2021.24	1872.21	1765.16	1685.87	1625.81	1579.52	1543.38	1514.87	1492.20
90000	8324.19	4567.45	3330.99	2724.37	2369.46	2140.14	1982.34	1868.99	1785.04	1721.44	1672.43	1634.17	1603.98	1579.97
95000	8786.65	4821.19	3516.04	2875.73	2501.09	2259.03	2092.47	1972.82	1884.21	1817.08	1765.34	1724.95	1693.09	1667.75
100000	9249.10	5074.94	3701.10	3027.08	2632.73	2377.93	2202.60	2076.66	1983.38	1912.71	1858.26	1815.74	1782.20	1755.53

TERM	15 Years	16 Years	17 Years	18 Years	19 Years	20 Years	21 Years	22 Years	23 Years	24 Years	25 Years	30 Years	35 Years	40 Years
AMOUNT														
5	.09	.09	.09	.09	.09	.09	.09	.09	.09	.09	.09	.09	.09	.09
10	.18	.18	.18	.17	.17	.17	.17	.17	.17	.17	.17	.17	.17	.17
15	.27	.26	.26	.26	.26	.26	.26	.25	.25	.25	.25	.25	.25	.25
25	.44	.43	.43	.43	.43	.42	.42	.42	.42	.42	.42	.42	.42	.42
50	.87	.86	.86	.85	.85	.84	.84	.84	.84	.83	.83	.83	.83	.83
75	1.31	1.29	1.28	1.27	1.27	1.26	1.26	1.25	1.25	1.25	1.25	1.24	1.24	1.24
100	1.74	1.72	1.71	1.70	1.69	1.68	1.67	1.67	1.67	1.66	1.66	1.65	1.65	1.65
200	3.47	3.44	3.41	3.39	3.37	3.36	3.34	3.33	3.33	3.32	3.31	3.30	3.29	3.29
300	5.21	5.16	5.11	5.08	5.05	5.03	5.01	5.00	4.99	4.98	4.97	4.94	4.94	4.93
400	6.94	6.87	6.82	6.77	6.74	6.71	6.68	6.66	6.65	6.63	6.62	6.59	6.58	6.57
500	8.68	8.59	8.52	8.46	8.42	8.38	8.35	8.33	8.31	8.29	8.28	8.24	8.22	8.22
600	10.41	10.31	10.22	10.16	10.10	10.06	10.02	9.99	9.97	9.95	9.93	9.88	9.87	9.86
700	12.14	12.02	11.93	11.85	11.78	11.73	11.69	11.65	11.63	11.60	11.58	11.53	11.51	11.50
800	13.88	13.74	13.63	13.54	13.47	13.41	13.36	13.32	13.29	13.26	13.24	13.18	13.15	13.14
900	15.61	15.46	15.33	15.23	15.15	15.08	15.03	14.98	14.95	14.92	14.89	14.82	14.80	14.79
1000	17.35	17.18	17.04	16.92	16.83	16.76	16.70	16.65	16.61	16.57	16.55	16.47	16.44	16.43
2000	34.69	34.35	34.07	33.84	33.66	33.51	33.39	33.29	33.21	33.14	33.09	32.93	32.87	32.85
3000	52.03	51.52	51.10	50.76	50.49	50.26	50.08	49.93	49.81	49.71	49.63	49.40	49.31	49.27
4000	69.37	68.69	68.13	67.68	67.31	67.02	66.77	66.58	66.41	66.28	66.17	65.86	65.74	65.70
5000	86.71	85.86	85.16	84.60	84.14	83.77	83.47	83.22	83.02	82.85	82.71	82.32	82.18	82.12
6000	104.06	103.03	102.19	101.52	100.97	100.52	100.16	99.86	99.62	99.42	99.26	98.79	98.61	98.54
7000	121.40	120.20	119.22	118.44	117.80	117.28	116.85	116.50	116.22	115.99	115.80	115.25	115.04	114.97
8000	138.74	137.37	136.26	135.36	134.62	134.03	133.54	133.15	132.82	132.56	132.34	131.71	131.48	131.39
9000	156.08	154.54	153.29	152.27	151.45	150.78	150.24	149.79	149.42	149.13	148.88	148.18	147.91	147.81
10000	173.42	171.71	170.32	169.19	168.28	167.54	166.93	166.43	166.03	166.69	165.42	164.64	164.35	164.24
11000	190.76	188.88	187.35	186.11	185.11	184.29	183.62	183.08	182.63	182.26	181.96	181.10	180.78	180.66
12000	208.11	206.05	204.38	203.03	201.93	201.04	200.31	199.72	199.23	198.83	198.51	197.57	197.22	197.08
13000	225.45	223.22	221.41	219.95	218.76	217.79	217.01	216.36	215.83	215.40	215.05	214.03	213.65	213.51
14000	242.79	240.39	238.44	236.87	235.59	234.55	233.70	233.00	232.44	231.97	231.59	230.49	230.08	229.93
15000	260.13	257.56	255.47	253.79	252.42	251.30	250.39	249.65	249.04	248.54	248.13	246.96	246.52	246.35
16000	277.47	274.73	272.51	270.71	269.24	268.05	267.08	266.29	265.64	265.11	264.67	263.42	262.95	262.78
17000	294.81	291.90	289.54	287.63	286.07	284.81	283.78	282.93	282.24	281.68	281.21	279.88	279.39	279.20
18000	312.16	309.07	306.57	304.54	302.90	301.56	300.47	299.57	298.84	298.25	297.76	296.35	295.82	295.62
19000	329.50	326.24	323.60	321.46	319.73	318.31	317.16	316.22	315.45	314.82	314.30	312.81	312.26	312.05
20000	346.84	343.41	340.63	338.38	336.55	335.07	333.85	332.86	332.05	331.38	330.84	329.28	328.69	328.47
21000	364.18	360.58	357.66	355.30	353.38	351.82	350.54	349.50	348.65	347.95	347.38	345.74	345.12	344.89
22000	381.52	377.75	374.69	372.22	370.21	368.57	367.24	366.15	365.25	364.52	363.92	362.20	361.56	361.32
23000	398.86	394.92	391.72	389.14	387.04	385.33	383.93	382.79	381.85	381.09	380.46	378.67	377.99	377.74
24000	416.21	412.09	408.76	406.06	403.86	402.08	400.62	399.43	398.46	397.66	397.01	395.13	394.43	394.16
25000	433.55	429.26	425.79	422.98	420.69	418.83	417.31	416.07	415.06	414.23	413.55	411.59	410.86	410.59
26000	450.89	446.43	442.82	439.90	437.52	435.58	434.01	432.72	431.66	430.80	430.09	428.06	427.30	427.01
27000	468.23	463.60	459.85	456.81	454.35	452.34	450.70	449.36	448.26	447.37	446.63	444.52	443.73	443.43
28000	485.57	480.77	476.88	473.73	471.17	469.09	467.39	466.00	464.87	463.94	463.17	460.98	460.16	459.86
29000	502.92	497.94	493.91	490.65	488.00	485.84	484.08	482.64	481.47	480.50	479.71	477.45	476.60	476.28
30000	520.26	515.11	510.94	507.57	504.83	502.60	500.78	499.29	498.07	497.07	496.26	493.91	493.03	492.70
31000	537.60	532.28	527.97	524.49	521.66	519.35	517.47	515.93	514.67	513.64	512.80	510.37	509.47	509.13
32000	554.94	549.45	545.01	541.41	538.48	536.10	534.16	532.57	531.27	530.21	529.34	526.84	525.90	525.55
33000	572.28	566.62	562.04	558.33	555.31	552.86	550.85	549.22	547.88	546.78	545.88	543.30	542.34	541.97
34000	589.62	583.79	579.07	575.25	572.14	569.61	567.55	565.86	564.48	563.35	562.42	559.76	558.77	558.40
35000	606.97	600.96	596.10	592.16	588.97	586.36	584.24	582.50	581.08	579.92	578.96	576.23	575.20	574.82
36000	624.31	618.13	613.13	609.08	605.79	603.12	600.93	599.14	597.68	596.49	595.51	592.69	591.64	591.24
37000	641.65	635.30	630.16	626.00	622.62	619.87	617.62	615.79	614.29	613.06	612.05	609.16	608.07	607.67
38000	658.99	652.47	647.19	642.92	639.45	636.62	634.31	632.43	630.89	629.62	628.59	625.62	624.51	624.09
39000	676.33	669.64	664.23	659.84	656.28	653.37	651.01	649.07	647.49	646.19	645.13	642.08	640.94	640.51
40000	693.67	686.81	681.26	676.76	673.10	670.13	667.70	665.72	664.09	662.76	661.67	658.55	657.38	656.94
41000	711.02	703.98	698.29	693.68	689.93	686.88	684.39	682.36	680.69	679.33	678.21	675.01	673.81	673.36
42000	728.36	721.15	715.32	710.60	706.76	703.63	701.08	699.00	697.30	695.90	694.76	691.47	690.24	689.78
43000	745.70	738.32	732.35	727.52	723.59	720.39	717.78	715.64	713.90	712.47	711.30	707.94	706.68	706.21
44000	763.04	755.49	749.38	744.43	740.41	737.14	734.47	732.29	730.50	729.04	727.84	724.40	723.11	722.63
45000	780.38	772.66	766.41	761.35	757.24	753.89	751.16	748.93	747.10	745.61	744.38	740.86	739.55	739.05
46000	797.72	789.83	783.44	778.27	774.07	770.65	767.85	765.57	763.70	762.18	760.92	757.33	755.98	755.48
47000	815.07	807.00	800.48	795.19	790.90	787.40	784.55	782.21	780.31	778.75	777.47	773.79	772.42	771.90
48000	832.41	824.17	817.51	812.11	807.72	804.15	801.24	798.86	796.91	795.31	794.01	790.25	788.85	788.32
49000	849.75	841.34	834.54	829.03	824.55	820.91	817.93	815.50	813.51	811.88	810.55	806.72	805.28	804.75
50000	867.09	858.51	851.57	845.95	841.38	837.66	834.62	832.14	830.11	828.45	827.09	823.18	821.72	821.17
55000	953.80	944.36	936.73	930.54	925.52	921.42	918.08	915.36	913.12	911.30	909.80	905.50	903.89	903.29
60000	1040.51	1030.21	1021.88	1015.14	1009.65	1005.19	1001.55	998.57	996.14	994.14	992.51	987.82	986.06	985.40
65000	1127.22	1116.06	1107.04	1099.73	1093.79	1088.95	1085.01	1081.78	1079.15	1076.99	1075.22	1070.13	1068.23	1067.52
70000	1213.93	1201.91	1192.19	1184.32	1177.93	1172.72	1168.47	1165.00	1162.16	1159.83	1157.92	1152.45	1150.40	1149.64
75000	1300.63	1287.76	1277.35	1268.92	1262.07	1256.49	1251.93	1248.21	1245.17	1242.68	1240.63	1234.77	1232.58	1231.75
80000	1387.34	1373.61	1362.51	1353.51	1346.20	1340.25	1335.39	1331.43	1328.18	1325.52	1323.34	1317.09	1314.75	1313.87
85000	1474.05	1459.46	1447.66	1438.11	1430.34	1424.02	1418.86	1414.64	1411.19	1408.36	1406.05	1399.40	1396.92	1395.98
90000	1560.76	1545.31	1532.82	1522.70	1514.48	1507.78	1502.32	1497.85	1494.20	1491.21	1488.76	1481.72	1479.09	1478.10
95000	1647.47	1631.16	1617.98	1607.30	1598.62	1591.55	1585.78	1581.07	1577.21	1574.05	1571.47	1564.04	1561.26	1560.22
100000	1734.18	1717.01	1703.13	1691.89	1682.75	1675.31	1669.24	1664.28	1660.22	1656.90	1654.18	1646.36	1643.43	1642.33

TERM	1 Year	2 Years	3 Years	4 Years	5 Years	6 Years	7 Years	8 Years	9 Years	10 Years	11 Years	12 Years	13 Years	14 Years
AMOUNT														
5	.47	.26	.19	.16	.14	.12	.12	.11	.10	.10	.10	.10	.09	.09
10	.93	.51	.38	.31	.27	.24	.23	.21	.20	.20	.19	.19	.18	.18
15	1.39	.77	.56	.46	.40	.36	.34	.32	.30	.29	.28	.28	.27	.27
25	2.32	1.27	.93	.76	.66	.60	.56	.52	.50	.48	.47	.46	.45	.44
50	4.63	2.54	1.86	1.52	1.32	1.20	1.11	1.04	1.00	.96	.94	.91	.90	.88
75	6.94	3.81	2.78	2.28	1.98	1.79	1.66	1.56	1.49	1.44	1.40	1.37	1.34	1.32
100	9.26	5.08	3.71	3.03	2.64	2.39	2.21	2.08	1.99	1.92	1.87	1.82	1.79	1.76
200	18.51	10.16	7.41	6.06	5.28	4.77	4.42	4.16	3.98	3.84	3.73	3.64	3.58	3.52
300	27.76	15.24	11.12	9.09	7.91	7.15	6.62	6.24	5.96	5.75	5.59	5.46	5.36	5.28
400	37.01	20.31	14.82	12.12	10.55	9.53	8.83	8.31	7.95	7.67	7.45	7.28	7.15	7.04
500	46.26	25.39	18.52	15.15	13.18	11.91	11.03	10.40	9.94	9.59	9.31	9.10	8.93	8.80
600	55.51	30.47	22.23	18.18	15.82	14.29	13.24	12.48	11.92	11.50	11.17	10.92	10.72	10.56
700	64.77	35.55	25.93	21.21	18.45	16.67	15.44	14.56	13.91	13.42	13.04	12.74	12.51	12.32
800	74.02	40.62	29.63	24.24	21.09	19.05	17.65	16.64	15.90	15.33	14.90	14.56	14.29	14.08
900	83.27	45.70	33.34	27.27	23.72	21.43	19.86	18.72	17.88	17.25	16.76	16.38	16.08	15.84
1000	92.52	50.78	37.04	30.30	26.36	23.81	22.06	20.80	19.87	19.17	18.62	18.20	17.86	17.60
2000	185.03	101.55	74.08	60.60	52.71	47.62	44.12	41.60	39.74	38.33	37.24	36.39	35.72	35.19
3000	277.55	152.33	111.11	90.90	79.07	71.43	66.17	62.40	59.60	57.49	55.85	54.58	53.58	52.78
4000	370.06	203.10	148.15	121.19	105.42	95.24	88.23	83.20	79.47	76.65	74.47	72.77	71.43	70.37
5000	462.58	253.87	185.19	151.49	131.78	119.05	110.28	103.99	99.33	95.81	93.09	90.97	89.29	87.96
6000	555.09	304.65	222.22	181.79	158.13	142.85	132.34	124.79	119.20	114.97	111.70	109.16	107.15	105.55
7000	647.61	355.42	259.26	212.09	184.49	166.66	154.40	145.59	139.07	134.13	130.32	127.35	125.01	123.14
8000	740.12	406.20	296.30	242.38	210.84	190.47	176.45	166.39	158.93	153.29	148.94	145.54	142.86	140.74
9000	832.64	456.97	333.33	272.68	237.20	214.28	198.51	187.18	178.80	172.45	167.55	163.73	160.72	158.33
10000	925.15	507.74	370.37	302.98	263.55	238.09	220.56	207.98	198.66	191.61	186.17	181.93	178.58	175.92
11000	1017.67	558.52	407.40	333.28	289.91	261.89	242.62	228.78	218.53	210.77	204.79	200.12	196.44	193.51
12000	1110.18	609.29	444.44	363.57	316.26	285.70	264.68	249.58	238.39	229.93	223.40	218.31	214.29	211.10
13000	1202.70	660.06	481.48	393.87	342.62	309.51	286.73	270.37	258.26	249.09	242.02	236.50	232.15	228.69
14000	1295.21	710.84	518.51	424.17	368.97	333.32	308.79	291.17	278.13	268.25	260.64	254.69	250.01	246.28
15000	1387.73	761.61	555.55	454.46	395.33	357.13	330.84	311.97	297.99	287.41	279.25	272.89	267.87	263.88
16000	1480.24	812.39	592.59	484.76	421.68	380.94	352.90	332.77	317.86	306.57	297.87	291.08	285.72	281.47
17000	1572.76	863.16	629.62	515.06	448.04	404.74	374.96	353.56	337.72	325.73	316.48	309.27	303.58	299.06
18000	1665.27	913.93	666.66	545.36	474.39	428.55	397.01	374.36	357.59	344.89	335.10	327.46	321.44	316.65
19000	1757.79	964.71	703.70	575.65	500.75	452.36	419.07	395.16	377.46	364.05	353.72	345.65	339.30	334.24
20000	1850.30	1015.48	740.73	605.95	527.10	476.17	441.12	415.96	397.32	383.21	372.33	363.85	357.15	351.83
21000	1942.82	1066.25	777.77	636.25	553.46	499.98	463.18	436.75	417.19	402.37	390.95	382.04	375.01	369.42
22000	2035.33	1117.03	814.80	666.55	579.81	523.78	485.24	457.55	437.05	421.53	409.57	400.23	392.87	387.02
23000	2127.85	1167.80	851.84	696.84	606.17	547.59	507.29	478.35	456.92	440.69	428.18	418.42	410.73	404.61
24000	2220.36	1218.58	888.88	727.14	632.52	571.40	529.35	499.15	476.78	459.85	446.80	436.61	428.58	422.20
25000	2312.88	1269.35	925.91	757.44	658.88	595.21	551.40	519.94	496.65	479.01	465.42	454.81	446.44	439.79
26000	2405.39	1320.12	962.95	787.74	685.23	619.02	573.46	540.74	516.52	498.17	484.03	473.00	464.30	457.38
27000	2497.91	1370.90	999.99	818.03	711.59	642.82	595.51	561.54	536.38	517.33	502.65	491.19	482.16	474.97
28000	2590.42	1421.67	1037.02	848.33	737.94	666.63	617.57	582.34	556.25	536.49	521.27	509.38	500.01	492.56
29000	2682.94	1472.44	1074.06	878.63	764.30	690.44	639.63	603.13	576.11	555.65	539.88	527.57	517.87	510.16
30000	2775.45	1523.22	1111.09	908.92	790.65	714.25	661.68	623.93	595.98	574.81	558.50	545.77	535.73	527.75
31000	2867.97	1573.99	1148.13	939.22	817.01	738.06	683.74	644.73	615.84	593.97	577.11	563.96	553.58	545.34
32000	2960.48	1624.77	1185.17	969.52	843.36	761.87	705.79	665.53	635.71	613.13	595.73	582.15	571.44	562.93
33000	3053.00	1675.54	1222.20	999.82	869.72	785.67	727.85	686.32	655.58	632.29	614.35	600.34	589.30	580.52
34000	3145.51	1726.31	1259.24	1030.11	896.07	809.48	749.91	707.12	675.44	651.45	632.96	618.54	607.16	598.11
35000	3238.03	1777.09	1296.28	1060.41	922.43	833.29	771.96	727.92	695.31	670.61	651.58	636.73	625.01	615.70
36000	3330.54	1827.86	1333.31	1090.71	948.78	857.10	794.02	748.72	715.17	689.77	670.20	654.92	642.87	633.29
37000	3423.06	1878.63	1370.35	1121.01	975.14	880.91	816.07	769.51	735.04	708.93	688.81	673.11	660.73	650.89
38000	3515.57	1929.41	1407.39	1151.30	1001.49	904.71	838.13	790.31	754.91	728.09	707.43	691.30	678.59	668.48
39000	3608.09	1980.18	1444.42	1181.60	1027.85	928.52	860.19	811.11	774.77	747.25	726.05	709.50	696.44	686.07
40000	3700.60	2030.96	1481.46	1211.90	1054.20	952.33	882.24	831.91	794.64	766.41	744.66	727.69	714.30	703.66
41000	3793.12	2081.73	1518.49	1242.20	1080.56	976.14	904.30	852.71	814.50	785.57	763.28	745.88	732.16	721.25
42000	3885.63	2132.50	1555.53	1272.49	1106.91	999.95	926.35	873.50	834.37	804.73	781.90	764.07	750.02	738.84
43000	3978.15	2183.28	1592.57	1302.79	1133.27	1023.75	948.41	894.30	854.23	823.89	800.51	782.26	767.87	756.43
44000	4070.66	2234.05	1629.60	1333.09	1159.62	1047.56	970.47	915.10	874.10	843.05	819.13	800.46	785.73	774.03
45000	4163.18	2284.82	1666.64	1363.38	1185.98	1071.37	992.52	935.90	893.97	862.21	837.74	818.65	803.59	791.62
46000	4255.69	2335.60	1703.68	1393.68	1212.33	1095.18	1014.58	956.69	913.83	881.37	856.36	836.84	821.45	809.21
47000	4348.21	2386.37	1740.71	1423.98	1238.69	1118.99	1036.63	977.49	933.70	900.53	874.98	855.03	839.30	826.80
48000	4440.72	2437.15	1777.75	1454.28	1265.04	1142.80	1058.69	998.29	953.56	919.69	893.59	873.22	857.16	844.39
49000	4533.24	2487.92	1814.78	1484.57	1291.40	1166.60	1080.74	1019.09	973.43	938.85	912.21	891.42	875.02	861.98
50000	4625.75	2538.69	1851.82	1514.87	1317.75	1190.41	1102.80	1039.88	993.29	958.01	930.83	909.61	892.88	879.57
55000	5088.32	2792.56	2037.00	1666.36	1449.53	1309.45	1213.08	1143.87	1092.62	1053.81	1023.91	1000.57	982.16	967.53
60000	5550.90	3046.43	2222.18	1817.84	1581.30	1428.49	1323.36	1247.86	1191.95	1149.61	1116.99	1091.53	1071.45	1055.49
65000	6013.47	3300.30	2407.37	1969.33	1713.08	1547.53	1433.64	1351.85	1291.28	1245.41	1210.07	1182.49	1160.74	1143.45
70000	6476.05	3554.17	2592.55	2120.82	1844.85	1666.57	1543.92	1455.83	1390.61	1341.21	1303.16	1273.45	1250.02	1231.40
75000	6938.62	3808.04	2777.73	2272.30	1976.63	1785.62	1654.20	1559.82	1489.94	1437.01	1396.24	1364.41	1339.31	1319.36
80000	7401.20	4061.91	2962.91	2423.79	2108.40	1904.66	1764.48	1663.81	1589.27	1532.81	1489.32	1455.37	1428.60	1407.32
85000	7863.77	4315.77	3148.09	2575.28	2240.18	2023.70	1874.76	1767.80	1688.60	1628.61	1582.40	1546.33	1517.89	1495.27
90000	8326.35	4569.64	3333.27	2726.76	2371.95	2142.74	1985.04	1871.79	1787.93	1724.41	1675.48	1637.29	1607.17	1583.23
95000	8788.92	4823.51	3518.46	2878.25	2503.73	2261.78	2095.32	1975.77	1887.26	1820.21	1768.57	1728.25	1696.46	1671.19
100000	9251.50	5077.38	3703.64	3029.74	2635.50	2380.82	2205.60	2079.76	1986.58	1916.02	1861.65	1819.21	1785.75	1759.14

TERM	15 Years	16 Years	17 Years	18 Years	19 Years	20 Years	21 Years	22 Years	23 Years	24 Years	25 Years	30 Years	35 Years	40 Years
AMOUNT														
5	.09	.09	.09	.09	.09	.09	.09	.09	.09	.09	.09	.09	.09	.09
10	.18	.18	.18	.17	.17	.17	.17	.17	.17	.17	.17	.17	.17	.17
15	.27	.26	.26	.26	.26	.26	.26	.26	.25	.25	.25	.25	.25	.25
25	.44	.44	.43	.43	.43	.42	.42	.42	.42	.42	.42	.42	.42	.42
50	.87	.87	.86	.85	.85	.84	.84	.84	.84	.84	.83	.83	.83	.83
75	1.31	1.30	1.29	1.28	1.27	1.26	1.26	1.26	1.25	1.25	1.25	1.24	1.24	1.24
100	1.74	1.73	1.71	1.70	1.69	1.68	1.68	1.67	1.67	1.67	1.66	1.66	1.65	1.65
200	3.48	3.45	3.42	3.40	3.38	3.36	3.35	3.34	3.33	3.33	3.32	3.31	3.30	3.30
300	5.22	5.17	5.13	5.09	5.06	5.04	5.02	5.01	5.00	4.99	4.98	4.96	4.95	4.94
400	6.96	6.89	6.83	6.79	6.75	6.72	6.70	6.68	6.66	6.65	6.64	6.61	6.60	6.59
500	8.69	8.61	8.54	8.48	8.44	8.40	8.37	8.35	8.33	8.31	8.30	8.26	8.24	8.24
600	10.43	10.33	10.25	10.18	10.12	10.08	10.04	10.01	9.99	9.97	9.95	9.91	9.89	9.88
700	12.17	12.05	11.95	11.88	11.81	11.76	11.72	11.68	11.65	11.63	11.61	11.56	11.54	11.53
800	13.91	13.77	13.66	13.57	13.50	13.44	13.39	13.35	13.32	13.29	13.27	13.21	13.19	13.18
900	15.65	15.49	15.37	15.27	15.18	15.12	15.06	15.02	14.98	14.95	14.93	14.86	14.83	14.82
1000	17.38	17.21	17.07	16.96	16.87	16.80	16.74	16.69	16.65	16.61	16.59	16.51	16.48	16.47
2000	34.76	34.42	34.14	33.92	33.74	33.59	33.47	33.37	33.29	33.22	33.17	33.01	32.96	32.93
3000	52.14	51.63	51.21	50.88	50.60	50.38	50.20	50.05	49.93	49.83	49.75	49.52	49.43	49.40
4000	69.52	68.83	68.28	67.83	67.47	67.17	66.93	66.74	66.57	66.44	66.33	66.02	65.91	65.86
5000	86.90	86.04	85.35	84.79	84.34	83.97	83.66	83.42	83.22	83.05	82.92	82.53	82.38	82.33
6000	104.28	103.25	102.42	101.75	101.20	100.76	100.40	100.10	99.86	99.66	99.50	99.03	98.86	98.79
7000	121.65	120.46	119.49	118.71	118.07	117.55	117.13	116.78	116.50	116.27	116.08	115.54	115.33	115.26
8000	139.03	137.66	136.56	135.66	134.94	134.34	133.86	133.47	133.14	132.88	132.66	132.04	131.81	131.72
9000	156.41	154.87	153.63	152.62	151.80	151.14	150.59	150.15	149.78	149.49	149.24	148.55	148.29	148.19
10000	173.79	172.08	170.70	169.58	168.67	167.93	167.32	166.83	166.43	166.10	165.83	165.05	164.76	164.65
11000	191.17	189.29	187.77	186.53	185.53	184.72	184.06	183.51	183.07	182.71	182.41	181.56	181.24	181.12
12000	208.55	206.49	204.84	203.49	202.40	201.51	200.79	200.20	199.71	199.32	198.99	198.06	197.71	197.58
13000	225.93	223.70	221.90	220.45	219.27	218.30	217.52	216.88	216.35	215.92	215.57	214.56	214.19	214.05
14000	243.30	240.91	238.97	237.41	236.13	235.10	234.25	233.56	233.00	232.53	232.16	231.07	230.68	230.51
15000	260.68	258.12	256.04	254.36	253.00	251.89	250.98	250.24	249.64	249.14	248.74	247.57	247.14	246.98
16000	278.06	275.32	273.11	271.32	269.87	268.68	267.71	266.93	266.28	265.75	265.32	264.08	263.62	263.44
17000	295.44	292.53	290.18	288.28	286.73	285.47	284.45	283.61	282.92	282.36	281.90	280.58	280.09	279.91
18000	312.82	309.74	307.25	305.24	303.60	302.27	301.18	300.29	299.56	298.97	298.48	297.09	296.57	296.37
19000	330.20	326.95	324.32	322.19	320.46	319.06	317.91	316.97	316.21	315.50	315.07	313.59	313.04	312.84
20000	347.58	344.15	341.39	339.15	337.33	335.85	334.64	333.66	332.85	332.19	331.65	330.10	329.52	329.30
21000	364.95	361.36	358.46	356.11	354.20	352.64	351.37	350.34	349.49	348.80	348.23	346.60	345.99	345.77
22000	382.33	378.57	375.53	373.06	371.06	369.43	368.11	367.02	366.13	365.41	364.81	363.11	362.47	362.23
23000	399.71	395.78	392.60	390.02	387.93	386.23	384.84	383.70	382.78	382.02	381.39	379.61	378.95	378.70
24000	417.09	412.98	409.67	406.98	404.80	403.02	401.57	400.39	399.42	398.63	397.98	396.12	395.42	395.16
25000	434.47	430.19	426.73	423.94	421.66	419.81	418.30	417.07	416.06	415.23	414.56	412.62	411.90	411.63
26000	451.85	447.40	443.80	440.89	438.53	436.60	435.03	433.75	432.70	431.84	431.14	429.12	428.37	428.09
27000	469.23	464.60	460.87	457.85	455.39	453.40	451.76	450.43	449.34	448.45	447.72	445.63	444.85	444.56
28000	486.60	481.81	477.94	474.81	472.26	470.19	468.50	467.12	465.99	465.06	464.31	462.13	461.32	461.02
29000	503.98	499.02	495.01	491.76	489.13	486.98	485.23	483.80	482.63	481.67	480.89	478.64	477.80	477.49
30000	521.36	516.23	512.08	508.72	505.99	503.77	501.96	500.48	499.27	498.28	497.47	495.14	494.28	493.95
31000	538.74	533.43	529.15	525.68	522.86	520.56	518.69	517.16	515.91	514.89	514.05	511.65	510.75	510.42
32000	556.12	550.64	546.22	542.64	539.73	537.36	535.42	533.85	532.56	531.50	530.63	528.15	527.23	526.88
33000	573.50	567.85	563.29	559.59	556.59	554.15	552.16	550.53	549.20	548.11	547.22	544.66	543.70	543.34
34000	590.88	585.06	580.36	576.55	573.46	570.94	568.89	567.21	565.84	564.72	563.80	561.16	560.18	559.81
35000	608.25	602.26	597.43	593.51	590.32	587.73	585.62	583.89	582.48	581.33	580.38	577.67	576.65	576.27
36000	625.63	619.47	614.50	610.47	607.19	604.53	602.35	600.58	599.12	597.94	596.96	594.18	593.13	592.74
37000	643.01	636.68	631.56	627.42	624.06	621.32	619.08	617.26	615.77	614.54	613.54	610.68	609.61	609.20
38000	660.39	653.89	648.63	644.38	640.92	638.11	635.81	633.94	632.41	631.15	630.13	627.18	626.08	625.67
39000	677.77	671.09	665.70	661.34	657.79	654.90	652.55	650.62	649.05	647.76	646.71	643.68	642.56	642.13
40000	695.15	688.30	682.77	678.29	674.66	671.69	669.28	667.31	665.69	664.37	663.29	660.19	659.03	658.60
41000	712.53	705.51	699.84	695.25	691.52	688.49	686.01	683.99	682.33	680.98	679.87	676.69	675.51	675.06
42000	729.90	722.72	716.91	712.21	708.39	705.28	702.74	700.67	698.98	697.59	696.46	693.20	691.98	691.53
43000	747.28	739.92	733.98	729.17	725.25	722.07	719.47	717.35	715.62	714.20	713.04	709.70	708.46	707.99
44000	764.66	757.13	751.05	746.12	742.12	738.86	736.21	734.04	732.26	730.81	729.62	726.21	724.93	724.46
45000	782.04	774.34	768.12	763.08	758.99	755.66	752.94	750.72	748.90	747.42	746.20	742.71	741.41	740.92
46000	799.42	791.55	785.19	780.04	775.85	772.45	769.67	767.40	765.55	764.03	762.78	759.22	757.89	757.39
47000	816.80	808.75	802.26	796.99	792.72	789.24	786.40	784.08	782.19	780.64	779.37	775.72	774.36	773.85
48000	834.18	825.96	819.33	813.95	809.59	806.03	803.13	800.77	798.83	797.25	795.95	792.23	790.84	790.32
49000	851.55	843.17	836.40	830.91	826.45	822.82	819.87	817.45	815.47	813.86	812.53	808.73	807.31	806.78
50000	868.93	860.37	853.46	847.87	843.32	839.62	836.60	834.13	832.11	830.46	829.11	825.24	823.79	823.25
55000	955.83	946.41	938.81	932.65	927.65	923.58	920.26	917.54	915.33	913.51	912.02	907.76	906.17	905.57
60000	1042.72	1032.45	1024.16	1017.44	1011.98	1007.54	1003.92	1000.96	998.54	996.56	994.93	990.28	988.55	987.90
65000	1129.61	1118.49	1109.50	1102.22	1096.31	1091.50	1087.57	1084.37	1081.75	1079.60	1077.84	1072.80	1070.92	1070.22
70000	1216.50	1204.52	1194.85	1187.01	1180.64	1175.46	1171.23	1167.78	1164.96	1162.65	1160.76	1155.33	1153.30	1152.54
75000	1303.40	1290.56	1280.19	1271.80	1264.98	1259.42	1254.89	1251.19	1248.17	1245.69	1243.67	1237.85	1235.68	1234.87
80000	1390.29	1376.60	1365.54	1356.58	1349.31	1343.38	1338.55	1334.61	1331.38	1328.74	1326.58	1320.37	1318.06	1317.19
85000	1477.18	1462.63	1450.89	1441.37	1433.64	1427.34	1422.21	1418.02	1414.59	1411.79	1409.49	1402.90	1400.44	1399.52
90000	1564.07	1548.67	1536.23	1526.16	1517.97	1511.31	1505.87	1501.43	1497.80	1494.83	1492.40	1485.42	1482.82	1481.84
95000	1650.97	1634.71	1621.58	1610.94	1602.30	1595.27	1589.53	1584.84	1581.01	1577.88	1575.31	1567.94	1565.19	1564.17
100000	1737.86	1720.74	1706.92	1695.73	1686.63	1679.23	1673.19	1668.26	1664.22	1660.92	1658.22	1650.47	1647.57	1646.49

MONTHLY PAYMENT
REQUIRED TO AMORTIZE A LOAN

TERM	1 Year	2 Years	3 Years	4 Years	5 Years	6 Years	7 Years	8 Years	9 Years	10 Years	11 Years	12 Years	13 Years	14 Years
AMOUNT														
5	.47	.26	.19	.16	.14	.12	.12	.11	.10	.10	.10	.10	.09	.09
10	.93	.51	.38	.31	.27	.24	.23	.21	.20	.20	.19	.19	.18	.10
15	1.39	.77	.56	.46	.40	.36	.34	.32	.30	.29	.28	.28	.27	.27
25	2.32	1.27	.93	.76	.66	.60	.56	.53	.50	.48	.47	.46	.45	.45
50	4.63	2.54	1.86	1.52	1.32	1.20	1.11	1.05	1.00	.96	.94	.92	.90	.89
75	6.95	3.81	2.78	2.28	1.98	1.79	1.66	1.57	1.50	1.44	1.40	1.37	1.35	1.33
100	9.26	5.08	3.71	3.04	2.64	2.39	2.21	2.09	1.99	1.92	1.87	1.83	1.79	1.77
200	18.51	10.16	7.42	6.07	5.28	4.77	4.42	4.17	3.98	3.84	3.74	3.65	3.58	3.53
300	27.77	15.24	11.12	9.10	7.92	7.16	6.63	6.25	5.97	5.76	5.60	5.47	5.37	5.29
400	37.02	20.32	14.83	10.13	10.56	9.54	8.84	8.34	7.96	7.68	7.47	7.30	7.16	7.06
500	46.27	25.40	18.54	15.17	13.20	11.92	11.05	10.42	9.95	9.60	9.33	9.12	8.95	8.82
600	55.53	30.48	22.24	18.20	15.83	14.31	13.26	12.50	11.94	11.52	11.20	10.94	10.74	10.58
700	64.78	35.56	25.95	21.23	18.47	16.69	15.47	14.59	13.93	13.44	13.06	12.76	12.53	12.34
800	74.04	40.64	29.65	24.26	21.11	19.07	17.67	16.67	15.92	15.36	14.93	14.59	14.32	14.11
900	83.29	45.72	33.36	27.30	23.75	21.46	19.88	18.75	17.91	17.28	16.79	16.41	16.11	15.87
1000	92.54	50.80	37.07	30.33	26.39	23.84	22.09	20.83	19.90	19.20	18.66	18.23	17.90	17.63
2000	185.08	101.60	74.13	60.65	52.77	47.68	44.18	41.66	39.80	38.39	37.31	36.46	35.79	35.26
3000	277.62	152.40	111.19	90.98	79.15	71.52	66.26	62.49	59.70	57.58	55.96	54.69	53.68	52.89
4000	370.16	203.20	148.25	121.30	105.54	95.35	88.35	83.32	79.60	76.78	74.61	72.91	71.58	70.52
5000	462.70	254.00	185.31	151.62	131.92	119.19	110.43	104.15	99.49	95.97	93.26	91.14	89.47	88.14
6000	555.24	304.79	222.38	181.95	158.30	143.03	132.52	124.98	119.39	115.16	111.91	109.37	107.36	105.77
7000	647.78	355.59	259.44	212.27	184.68	166.86	154.61	145.81	139.29	134.36	130.56	127.59	125.26	123.40
8000	740.32	406.39	296.50	242.60	211.07	190.70	176.69	166.63	159.19	153.55	149.21	145.82	143.15	141.03
9000	832.85	457.19	333.56	272.92	237.45	214.54	198.78	187.46	179.09	172.74	167.86	164.05	161.04	158.65
10000	925.39	507.99	370.62	303.24	263.83	238.38	220.86	208.29	198.98	191.94	186.51	182.27	178.93	176.28
11000	1017.93	558.78	407.68	333.57	290.21	262.21	242.95	229.12	218.88	211.13	205.16	200.50	196.83	193.91
12000	1110.47	609.58	444.75	363.89	316.60	286.05	265.04	249.95	238.78	230.32	223.81	218.73	214.72	211.54
13000	1203.01	660.38	481.81	394.22	342.98	309.89	287.12	270.78	258.68	249.52	242.46	236.95	232.61	229.16
14000	1295.55	711.18	518.87	424.54	369.36	333.72	309.21	291.61	278.58	268.71	261.11	255.18	250.51	246.79
15000	1388.09	761.98	555.93	454.86	395.75	357.56	331.29	312.43	298.47	287.90	279.76	273.41	268.40	264.42
16000	1480.63	812.78	592.99	485.19	422.13	381.40	353.38	333.26	318.37	307.10	298.41	291.63	286.29	282.05
17000	1573.16	863.57	630.05	515.51	448.51	405.23	375.47	354.09	338.27	326.29	317.06	309.86	304.18	299.67
18000	1665.70	914.37	667.12	545.84	474.89	429.07	397.55	374.92	358.17	345.48	335.71	328.09	322.08	317.30
19000	1758.24	965.17	704.18	576.16	501.28	452.91	419.64	395.75	378.06	364.67	354.36	346.31	339.97	334.93
20000	1850.78	1015.97	741.24	606.48	527.66	476.75	441.72	416.58	397.96	383.87	373.01	364.54	357.86	352.56
21000	1943.32	1066.77	778.30	636.81	554.04	500.58	463.81	437.41	417.86	403.06	391.66	382.77	375.76	370.18
22000	2035.86	1117.56	815.36	667.13	580.42	524.42	485.90	458.24	437.76	422.25	410.31	401.00	393.65	387.81
23000	2128.40	1168.36	852.43	697.45	606.81	548.26	507.98	479.06	457.66	441.45	428.96	419.22	411.54	405.44
24000	2220.94	1219.16	889.49	727.78	633.19	572.09	530.07	499.89	477.55	460.64	447.61	437.45	429.44	423.07
25000	2313.48	1269.96	926.55	758.10	659.57	595.93	552.15	520.72	497.45	479.83	466.26	455.68	447.33	440.69
26000	2406.01	1320.76	963.61	788.43	685.96	619.77	574.24	541.55	517.35	499.03	484.91	473.90	465.22	458.32
27000	2498.55	1371.56	1000.67	818.75	712.34	643.60	596.33	562.38	537.25	518.22	503.56	492.13	483.11	475.95
28000	2591.09	1422.35	1037.73	849.07	738.72	667.44	618.41	583.21	557.15	537.41	522.22	510.36	501.01	493.58
29000	2683.63	1473.15	1074.80	879.40	765.10	691.28	640.50	604.04	577.04	556.61	540.87	528.58	518.90	511.21
30000	2776.17	1523.95	1111.86	909.72	791.49	715.12	662.58	624.86	596.94	575.80	559.52	546.81	536.79	528.83
31000	2868.71	1574.75	1148.92	940.05	817.87	738.95	684.67	645.69	616.84	594.99	578.17	565.04	554.69	546.46
32000	2961.25	1625.55	1185.98	970.37	844.25	762.79	706.75	666.52	636.74	614.19	596.82	583.26	572.58	564.09
33000	3053.79	1676.34	1223.04	1000.69	870.63	786.63	728.84	687.35	656.64	633.38	615.47	601.49	590.47	581.72
34000	3146.32	1727.14	1260.10	1031.02	897.02	810.46	750.93	708.18	676.53	652.57	634.12	619.72	608.36	599.34
35000	3238.86	1777.94	1297.17	1061.34	923.40	834.30	773.01	729.01	696.43	671.77	652.77	637.94	626.26	616.97
36000	3331.40	1828.74	1334.23	1091.67	949.78	858.14	795.10	749.84	716.33	690.96	671.42	656.17	644.15	634.60
37000	3423.94	1879.54	1371.29	1121.99	976.17	881.98	817.18	770.66	736.23	710.15	690.07	674.40	662.04	652.23
38000	3516.48	1930.33	1408.35	1152.31	1002.55	905.81	839.27	791.49	756.12	729.34	708.72	692.62	679.94	669.85
39000	3609.02	1981.13	1445.41	1182.64	1028.93	929.65	861.36	812.32	776.02	748.54	727.37	710.85	697.83	687.48
40000	3701.56	2031.93	1482.48	1212.96	1055.31	953.49	883.44	833.15	795.92	767.73	746.02	729.08	715.72	705.11
41000	3794.10	2082.73	1519.54	1243.29	1081.70	977.32	905.53	853.98	815.82	786.92	764.67	747.30	733.62	722.74
42000	3886.64	2133.53	1556.60	1273.61	1108.08	1001.16	927.61	874.81	835.72	806.12	783.32	765.53	751.51	740.36
43000	3979.17	2184.33	1593.66	1303.93	1134.46	1025.00	949.70	895.64	855.61	825.31	801.97	783.76	769.40	757.99
44000	4071.71	2235.12	1630.72	1334.26	1160.84	1048.83	971.79	916.47	875.51	844.50	820.62	801.99	787.29	775.62
45000	4164.25	2285.92	1667.78	1364.58	1187.23	1072.67	993.87	937.29	895.41	863.70	839.27	820.21	805.19	793.25
46000	4256.79	2336.72	1704.85	1394.90	1213.61	1096.51	1015.96	958.12	915.31	882.89	857.92	838.44	823.08	810.87
47000	4349.33	2387.52	1741.91	1425.23	1239.99	1120.35	1038.04	978.95	935.21	902.08	876.57	856.67	840.97	828.50
48000	4441.87	2438.32	1778.97	1455.55	1266.38	1144.18	1060.13	999.78	955.10	921.28	895.22	874.89	858.87	846.13
49000	4534.41	2489.11	1816.03	1485.88	1292.76	1168.02	1082.22	1020.61	975.00	940.47	913.87	893.12	876.76	863.76
50000	4626.95	2539.91	1853.09	1516.20	1319.14	1191.86	1104.30	1041.44	994.90	959.66	932.52	911.35	894.65	881.38
55000	5089.64	2793.90	2038.40	1667.82	1451.05	1311.04	1214.73	1145.58	1094.39	1055.63	1025.78	1002.48	984.12	969.52
60000	5552.33	3047.89	2223.71	1819.44	1582.97	1430.23	1325.16	1249.72	1193.88	1151.59	1119.03	1093.61	1073.58	1057.66
65000	6015.03	3301.88	2409.02	1971.06	1714.88	1549.41	1435.59	1353.87	1293.37	1247.56	1212.28	1184.75	1163.05	1145.80
70000	6477.72	3555.88	2594.33	2122.68	1846.80	1668.60	1546.02	1458.01	1392.86	1343.53	1305.53	1275.88	1252.51	1233.94
75000	6940.42	3809.87	2779.64	2274.30	1978.71	1787.78	1656.45	1562.15	1492.35	1439.49	1398.78	1367.02	1341.97	1322.07
80000	7403.11	4063.86	2964.95	2425.92	2110.62	1906.97	1766.88	1666.30	1591.84	1535.46	1492.03	1458.15	1431.44	1410.21
85000	7865.80	4317.85	3150.25	2577.54	2242.54	2026.15	1877.31	1770.44	1691.33	1631.43	1585.29	1549.28	1520.90	1498.35
90000	8328.50	4571.84	3335.56	2729.16	2374.45	2145.34	1987.74	1874.58	1790.82	1727.39	1678.54	1640.42	1610.37	1586.49
95000	8791.19	4825.83	3520.87	2880.78	2506.36	2264.52	2098.17	1978.73	1890.30	1823.35	1771.79	1731.55	1699.83	1674.63
100000	9253.89	5079.82	3706.18	3032.40	2638.28	2383.71	2208.60	2082.87	1989.79	1919.32	1865.04	1822.69	1789.30	1762.76

TERM	15 Years	16 Years	17 Years	18 Years	19 Years	20 Years	21 Years	22 Years	23 Years	24 Years	25 Years	30 Years	35 Years	40 Years
AMOUNT														
5	.09	.09	.09	.09	.09	.09	.09	.09	.09	.09	.09	.09	.09	.09
10	.18	.18	.18	.17	.17	.17	.17	.17	.17	.17	.17	.17	.17	.17
15	.27	.26	.26	.26	.26	.26	.26	.26	.26	.25	.25	.25	.25	.25
25	.44	.44	.43	.43	.43	.43	.42	.42	.42	.42	.42	.42	.42	.42
50	.88	.87	.86	.85	.85	.85	.84	.84	.84	.84	.84	.84	.83	.83
75	1.31	1.30	1.29	1.28	1.27	1.27	1.26	1.26	1.26	1.25	1.25	1.25	1.24	1.24
100	1.75	1.73	1.72	1.70	1.70	1.69	1.68	1.68	1.67	1.67	1.67	1.66	1.66	1.66
200	3.49	3.45	3.43	3.40	3.39	3.37	3.36	3.35	3.34	3.33	3.33	3.31	3.31	3.31
300	5.23	5.18	5.14	5.10	5.08	5.05	5.04	5.02	5.01	5.00	4.99	4.97	4.96	4.96
400	6.97	6.90	6.85	6.80	6.77	6.74	6.71	6.69	6.68	6.66	6.65	6.62	6.61	6.61
500	8.71	8.63	8.56	8.50	8.46	8.42	8.39	8.37	8.35	8.33	8.32	8.28	8.26	8.26
600	10.45	10.35	10.27	10.20	10.15	10.10	10.07	10.04	10.01	9.99	9.98	9.93	9.92	9.91
700	12.20	12.08	11.98	11.90	11.84	11.79	11.74	11.71	11.68	11.66	11.64	11.59	11.57	11.56
800	13.94	13.80	13.69	13.60	13.53	13.47	13.42	13.38	13.35	13.32	13.30	13.24	13.22	13.21
900	15.68	15.53	15.40	15.30	15.22	15.15	15.10	15.06	15.02	14.99	14.97	14.90	14.87	14.86
1000	17.42	17.25	17.11	17.00	16.91	16.84	16.78	16.73	16.69	16.65	16.63	16.55	16.52	16.51
2000	34.84	34.49	34.22	34.00	33.82	33.67	33.55	33.45	33.37	33.30	33.25	33.10	33.04	33.02
3000	52.25	51.74	51.33	50.99	50.72	50.50	50.32	50.17	50.05	49.95	49.87	49.64	49.56	49.52
4000	69.67	68.98	68.43	67.99	67.63	67.33	67.09	66.89	66.73	66.60	66.50	66.19	66.07	66.03
5000	87.08	86.23	85.54	84.98	84.53	84.16	83.86	83.62	83.42	83.25	83.12	82.73	82.59	82.54
6000	104.50	103.47	102.65	101.98	101.44	100.99	100.63	100.34	100.10	99.90	99.74	99.28	99.11	99.04
7000	121.91	120.72	119.75	118.97	118.34	117.82	117.40	117.06	116.78	116.55	116.36	115.82	115.62	115.55
8000	139.33	137.96	136.86	135.97	135.25	134.66	134.18	133.78	133.46	133.20	132.99	132.37	132.14	132.06
9000	156.74	155.21	153.97	152.97	152.15	151.49	150.95	150.51	150.15	149.85	149.61	148.92	148.66	148.56
10000	174.16	172.45	171.08	169.96	169.06	168.32	167.72	167.23	166.83	166.50	166.23	165.46	165.18	165.07
11000	191.57	189.70	188.18	186.96	185.96	185.15	184.49	183.95	183.51	183.15	182.85	182.01	181.69	181.58
12000	208.99	206.94	205.29	203.95	202.87	201.98	201.26	200.67	200.19	199.80	199.48	198.55	198.21	198.08
13000	226.41	224.19	222.40	220.95	219.77	218.81	218.03	217.39	216.87	216.45	216.10	215.10	214.73	214.59
14000	243.82	241.43	239.50	237.94	236.68	235.64	234.80	234.12	233.56	233.10	232.72	231.64	231.24	231.09
15000	261.24	258.68	256.61	254.94	253.58	252.48	251.58	250.84	250.24	249.75	249.34	248.19	247.76	247.60
16000	278.65	275.92	273.72	271.93	270.49	269.31	268.35	267.56	266.92	266.40	265.97	264.74	264.28	264.11
17000	296.07	293.17	290.83	288.93	287.39	286.14	285.12	284.28	283.60	283.05	282.59	281.28	280.80	280.61
18000	313.48	310.41	307.93	305.93	304.30	302.97	301.89	301.01	300.29	299.69	299.21	297.83	297.31	297.12
19000	330.90	327.66	325.04	322.92	321.20	319.80	318.66	317.73	316.97	316.34	315.83	314.37	313.83	313.63
20000	348.31	344.90	342.15	339.92	338.11	336.63	335.43	334.45	333.65	332.99	332.46	330.92	330.35	330.13
21000	365.73	362.15	359.25	356.91	355.01	353.46	352.20	351.17	350.33	349.64	349.08	347.46	346.86	346.64
22000	383.14	379.39	376.36	373.91	371.92	370.30	368.97	367.90	367.01	366.29	365.70	364.01	363.38	363.15
23000	400.56	396.64	393.47	390.90	388.82	387.13	385.75	384.62	383.70	382.94	382.32	380.56	379.90	379.65
24000	417.97	413.88	410.58	407.90	405.73	403.96	402.52	401.34	400.38	399.59	398.95	397.10	396.42	396.16
25000	435.39	431.13	427.68	424.90	422.63	420.79	419.29	418.06	417.06	416.24	415.57	413.65	412.93	412.66
26000	452.81	448.37	444.79	441.89	439.54	437.62	436.06	434.78	433.74	432.89	432.19	430.19	429.45	429.17
27000	470.22	465.61	461.90	458.89	456.44	454.45	452.83	451.51	450.43	449.54	448.82	446.74	445.97	445.68
28000	487.64	482.86	479.00	475.88	473.35	471.28	469.60	468.23	467.11	466.19	465.44	463.28	462.48	462.18
29000	505.05	500.10	496.11	492.88	490.25	488.12	486.37	484.95	483.79	482.84	482.06	479.83	479.00	478.69
30000	522.47	517.35	513.22	509.87	507.16	504.95	503.15	501.67	500.47	499.49	498.68	496.38	495.52	495.20
31000	539.88	534.59	530.33	526.87	524.06	521.78	519.92	518.40	517.15	516.14	515.31	512.92	512.03	511.70
32000	557.30	551.84	547.43	543.86	540.97	538.61	536.69	535.12	533.84	532.79	531.93	529.47	528.55	528.21
33000	574.71	569.08	564.54	560.86	557.87	555.44	553.46	551.84	550.52	549.44	548.55	546.01	545.07	544.72
34000	592.13	586.33	581.65	577.86	574.78	572.27	570.23	568.56	567.20	566.09	565.17	562.56	561.59	561.22
35000	609.54	603.57	598.75	594.85	591.68	589.10	587.00	585.29	583.88	582.74	581.80	579.10	578.10	577.73
36000	626.96	620.82	615.86	611.85	608.59	605.94	603.77	602.01	600.57	599.38	598.42	595.65	594.62	594.24
37000	644.37	638.06	632.97	628.84	625.49	622.77	620.54	618.73	617.25	616.03	615.04	612.20	611.14	610.74
38000	661.79	655.31	650.08	645.84	642.40	639.60	637.32	635.45	633.93	632.68	631.66	628.74	627.65	627.25
39000	679.21	672.55	667.18	662.83	659.30	656.43	654.09	652.17	650.61	649.33	648.29	645.29	644.17	643.75
40000	696.62	689.80	684.29	679.83	676.21	673.26	670.86	668.90	667.29	665.98	664.91	661.83	660.69	660.26
41000	714.04	707.04	701.40	696.83	693.11	690.09	687.63	685.62	683.98	682.63	681.53	678.38	677.21	676.77
42000	731.45	724.29	718.50	713.82	710.02	706.92	704.40	702.34	700.66	699.28	698.15	694.92	693.72	693.27
43000	748.87	741.53	735.61	730.82	726.92	723.76	721.17	719.06	717.34	715.93	714.78	711.47	710.24	709.78
44000	766.28	758.78	752.72	747.81	743.83	740.59	737.94	735.79	734.02	732.58	731.40	728.02	726.76	726.29
45000	783.70	776.02	769.83	764.81	760.73	757.42	754.72	752.51	750.71	749.23	748.02	744.56	743.27	742.79
46000	801.11	793.27	786.93	781.80	777.64	774.25	771.49	769.23	767.39	765.88	764.64	761.11	759.79	759.30
47000	818.53	810.51	804.04	798.80	794.54	791.08	788.26	785.95	784.07	782.53	781.27	777.65	776.31	775.81
48000	835.94	827.76	821.15	815.79	811.45	807.91	805.03	802.68	800.75	799.18	797.89	794.20	792.83	792.31
49000	853.36	845.00	838.25	832.79	828.35	824.74	821.80	819.40	817.43	815.83	814.51	810.74	809.34	808.82
50000	870.77	862.25	855.36	849.79	845.26	841.57	838.57	836.12	834.12	832.48	831.13	827.29	825.86	825.32
55000	957.85	948.47	940.90	934.76	929.78	925.73	922.43	919.73	917.53	915.72	914.25	910.02	908.45	907.86
60000	1044.93	1034.69	1026.43	1019.74	1014.31	1009.89	1006.29	1003.34	1000.94	998.97	997.36	992.75	991.03	990.39
65000	1132.01	1120.92	1111.97	1104.72	1098.83	1094.05	1090.14	1086.95	1084.35	1082.22	1080.47	1075.48	1073.62	1072.92
70000	1219.08	1207.14	1197.50	1189.70	1183.36	1178.20	1174.00	1170.57	1167.76	1165.47	1163.59	1158.20	1156.20	1155.45
75000	1306.16	1293.37	1283.04	1274.68	1267.89	1262.36	1257.86	1254.18	1251.17	1248.71	1246.70	1240.93	1238.79	1237.98
80000	1393.24	1379.59	1368.57	1359.65	1352.41	1346.52	1341.71	1337.79	1334.58	1331.96	1329.81	1323.66	1321.37	1320.52
85000	1480.31	1465.81	1454.11	1444.63	1436.94	1430.67	1425.57	1421.40	1417.99	1415.21	1412.93	1406.39	1403.96	1403.05
90000	1567.39	1552.04	1539.65	1529.61	1521.46	1514.83	1509.43	1505.01	1501.41	1498.45	1496.04	1489.12	1486.54	1485.58
95000	1654.47	1638.26	1625.18	1614.59	1605.99	1598.99	1593.28	1588.62	1584.82	1581.70	1579.15	1571.85	1569.13	1568.11
100000	1741.54	1724.49	1710.72	1699.57	1690.51	1683.14	1677.14	1672.24	1668.23	1664.95	1662.26	1654.58	1651.71	1650.64

MONTHLY PAYMENT
REQUIRED TO AMORTIZE A LOAN

TERM AMOUNT	1 Year	2 Years	3 Years	4 Years	5 Years	6 Years	7 Years	8 Years	9 Years	10 Years	11 Years	12 Years	13 Years	14 Years
5	.47	.26	.19	.16	.14	.12	.12	.11	.10	.10	.10	.10	.09	.09
10	.93	.51	.38	.31	.27	.24	.23	.21	.20	.20	.19	.19	.18	.18
15	1.39	.77	.56	.46	.40	.36	.34	.32	.30	.29	.29	.28	.27	.27
25	2.32	1.28	.93	.76	.67	.60	.56	.53	.50	.49	.47	.46	.45	.45
50	4.63	2.55	1.86	1.52	1.33	1.20	1.11	1.05	1.00	.97	.94	.92	.90	.89
75	6.95	3.82	2.79	2.28	1.99	1.80	1.66	1.57	1.50	1.45	1.41	1.38	1.35	1.33
100	9.26	5.09	3.71	3.04	2.65	2.39	2.22	2.09	2.00	1.93	1.88	1.83	1.80	1.77
200	18.52	10.17	7.42	6.08	5.29	4.78	4.43	4.18	3.99	3.85	3.75	3.66	3.59	3.54
300	27.78	15.26	11.13	9.11	7.93	7.17	6.64	6.27	5.99	5.78	5.62	5.49	5.39	5.31
400	37.03	20.34	14.84	12.15	10.57	9.56	8.86	8.36	7.98	7.70	7.49	7.32	7.18	7.08
500	46.29	25.42	18.55	15.19	13.22	11.95	11.07	10.44	9.98	9.63	9.36	9.14	8.98	8.85
600	55.55	30.51	22.26	18.22	15.86	14.33	13.28	12.53	11.97	11.55	11.23	10.97	10.77	10.61
700	64.81	35.59	25.97	21.26	18.50	16.72	15.50	14.62	13.97	13.47	13.10	12.80	12.57	12.38
800	74.06	40.67	29.68	24.30	21.14	19.11	17.71	16.71	15.96	15.40	14.97	14.63	14.36	14.15
900	83.32	45.76	33.39	27.33	23.79	21.50	19.92	18.79	17.96	17.32	16.84	16.46	16.16	15.92
1000	92.58	50.84	37.10	30.37	26.43	23.89	22.14	20.88	19.95	19.25	18.71	18.28	17.95	17.69
2000	185.15	101.67	74.20	60.73	52.85	47.77	44.27	41.76	39.90	38.49	37.41	36.56	35.90	35.37
3000	277.73	152.51	111.30	91.10	79.28	71.65	66.40	62.63	59.84	57.73	56.11	54.84	53.84	53.05
4000	370.30	203.34	148.40	121.46	105.70	95.53	88.53	83.51	79.79	76.98	74.81	73.12	71.79	70.73
5000	462.88	254.18	185.50	151.82	132.13	119.41	110.66	104.38	99.74	96.22	93.51	91.40	89.74	88.41
6000	555.45	305.01	222.60	182.19	158.55	143.29	132.79	125.26	119.68	115.46	112.21	109.68	107.69	106.10
7000	648.03	355.85	259.70	212.55	184.98	167.17	154.92	146.13	139.63	134.70	130.91	127.96	125.63	123.78
8000	740.60	406.68	296.80	242.92	211.40	191.05	177.05	167.01	159.57	153.95	149.62	146.24	143.57	141.46
9000	833.18	457.52	333.90	273.28	237.82	214.93	199.18	187.88	179.52	173.19	168.32	164.52	161.52	159.14
10000	925.75	508.35	371.00	303.64	264.25	238.81	221.31	208.76	199.47	192.43	187.02	182.80	179.47	176.82
11000	1018.33	559.19	408.10	334.01	290.67	262.69	243.45	229.63	219.41	211.68	205.72	201.07	197.41	194.51
12000	1110.90	610.02	445.20	364.37	317.10	286.57	265.58	250.51	239.36	230.92	224.42	219.35	215.36	212.19
13000	1203.48	660.86	482.30	394.73	343.52	310.45	287.71	271.38	259.30	250.16	243.12	237.63	233.31	229.87
14000	1296.05	711.69	519.40	425.10	369.95	334.33	309.84	292.26	279.25	269.40	261.82	255.91	251.25	247.55
15000	1388.63	762.53	556.50	455.46	396.37	358.21	331.97	313.13	299.20	288.65	280.52	274.19	269.20	265.23
16000	1481.20	813.36	593.60	485.83	422.80	382.09	354.10	334.01	319.14	307.89	299.23	292.47	287.14	282.92
17000	1573.77	864.20	630.70	516.19	449.22	405.97	376.23	354.89	339.09	327.13	317.93	310.75	305.09	300.60
18000	1666.35	915.03	667.80	546.55	475.64	429.85	398.36	375.76	359.03	346.37	336.63	329.03	323.04	318.28
19000	1758.92	965.87	704.90	576.92	502.07	453.73	420.49	396.64	378.98	365.62	355.33	347.31	340.98	335.96
20000	1851.50	1016.70	742.00	607.28	528.49	477.61	442.62	417.51	398.93	384.86	374.03	365.59	358.93	353.64
21000	1944.07	1067.53	779.10	637.64	554.92	501.49	464.76	438.39	418.87	404.10	392.73	383.86	376.88	371.33
22000	2036.65	1118.37	816.20	668.01	581.34	525.37	486.89	459.26	438.82	423.35	411.43	402.14	394.82	389.01
23000	2129.22	1169.20	853.30	698.37	607.77	549.25	509.02	480.14	458.76	442.59	430.14	420.42	412.77	406.69
24000	2221.80	1220.04	890.40	728.74	634.19	573.14	531.15	501.01	478.71	461.83	448.84	438.70	430.71	424.37
25000	2314.37	1270.87	927.50	759.10	660.61	597.02	553.28	521.89	498.66	481.07	467.54	456.98	448.66	442.05
26000	2406.95	1321.71	964.60	789.46	687.04	620.90	575.41	542.76	518.60	500.32	486.24	475.26	466.61	459.74
27000	2499.52	1372.54	1001.70	819.83	713.46	644.78	597.54	563.64	538.55	519.56	504.94	493.54	484.55	477.42
28000	2592.10	1423.38	1038.80	850.19	739.89	668.66	619.67	584.51	558.50	538.80	523.64	511.82	502.50	495.10
29000	2684.67	1474.21	1075.90	880.56	766.31	692.54	641.80	605.39	578.44	558.05	542.34	530.10	520.45	512.78
30000	2777.25	1525.05	1113.00	910.92	792.74	716.42	663.93	626.26	598.39	577.29	561.04	548.38	538.39	530.46
31000	2869.82	1575.88	1150.10	941.28	819.16	740.30	686.07	647.14	618.33	596.53	579.75	566.65	556.34	548.15
32000	2962.40	1626.72	1187.20	971.65	845.59	764.18	708.20	668.02	638.28	615.77	598.45	584.93	574.28	565.83
33000	3054.97	1677.55	1224.30	1002.01	872.01	788.06	730.33	688.89	658.23	635.02	617.15	603.21	592.23	583.51
34000	3147.54	1728.39	1261.40	1032.37	898.43	811.94	752.46	709.77	678.17	654.26	635.85	621.49	610.18	601.19
35000	3240.12	1779.22	1298.50	1062.74	924.86	835.82	774.59	730.64	698.12	673.50	654.55	639.77	628.12	618.87
36000	3332.69	1830.06	1335.60	1093.10	951.28	859.70	796.72	751.52	718.06	692.74	673.25	658.05	646.07	636.56
37000	3425.27	1880.89	1372.70	1123.47	977.71	883.58	818.85	772.39	738.01	711.99	691.95	676.33	664.02	654.24
38000	3517.84	1931.73	1409.80	1153.83	1004.13	907.46	840.98	793.27	757.96	731.23	710.65	694.61	681.96	671.92
39000	3610.42	1982.56	1446.90	1184.19	1030.56	931.34	863.11	814.14	777.90	750.47	729.36	712.89	699.91	689.60
40000	3702.99	2033.40	1484.00	1214.56	1056.98	955.22	885.24	835.02	797.85	769.72	748.06	731.17	717.85	707.28
41000	3795.57	2084.23	1521.10	1244.92	1083.40	979.10	907.38	855.89	817.79	788.96	766.76	749.44	735.80	724.96
42000	3888.14	2135.06	1558.20	1275.28	1109.83	1002.98	929.51	876.77	837.74	808.20	785.46	767.72	753.75	742.65
43000	3980.72	2185.90	1595.30	1305.65	1136.25	1026.86	951.64	897.64	857.69	827.44	804.16	786.00	771.69	760.33
44000	4073.29	2236.73	1632.40	1336.01	1162.68	1050.74	973.77	918.52	877.63	846.69	822.86	804.28	789.64	778.01
45000	4165.87	2287.57	1669.50	1366.38	1189.10	1074.62	995.90	939.39	897.58	865.93	841.56	822.56	807.59	795.69
46000	4258.44	2338.40	1706.60	1396.74	1215.53	1098.50	1018.03	960.27	917.52	885.17	860.27	840.84	825.53	813.37
47000	4351.02	2389.24	1743.70	1427.10	1241.95	1122.38	1040.16	981.14	937.47	904.41	878.97	859.12	843.48	831.06
48000	4443.59	2440.07	1780.80	1457.47	1268.38	1146.27	1062.29	1002.02	957.42	923.66	897.67	877.40	861.42	848.74
49000	4536.16	2490.91	1817.90	1487.83	1294.80	1170.15	1084.42	1022.90	977.36	942.90	916.37	895.68	879.37	866.42
50000	4628.74	2541.74	1855.00	1518.20	1321.22	1194.03	1106.55	1043.77	997.31	962.14	935.07	913.96	897.32	884.10
55000	5091.61	2795.92	2040.50	1670.01	1453.35	1313.43	1217.21	1148.15	1097.04	1058.36	1028.58	1005.35	987.05	972.51
60000	5554.49	3050.09	2226.00	1821.83	1585.47	1432.83	1327.86	1252.52	1196.77	1154.57	1122.08	1096.75	1076.78	1060.92
65000	6017.36	3304.26	2411.50	1973.65	1717.59	1552.23	1438.52	1356.90	1296.50	1250.78	1215.59	1188.14	1166.51	1149.33
70000	6480.23	3558.44	2597.00	2125.47	1849.71	1671.63	1549.17	1461.28	1396.23	1347.00	1309.10	1279.54	1256.24	1237.74
75000	6943.11	3812.61	2782.50	2277.29	1981.83	1791.04	1659.83	1565.65	1495.96	1443.21	1402.60	1370.93	1345.97	1326.15
80000	7405.98	4066.79	2968.00	2429.11	2113.96	1910.44	1770.48	1670.03	1595.69	1539.43	1496.11	1462.33	1435.70	1414.56
85000	7868.85	4320.96	3153.50	2580.93	2246.08	2029.84	1881.14	1774.41	1695.42	1635.64	1589.62	1553.72	1525.44	1502.97
90000	8331.73	4575.13	3339.00	2732.75	2378.20	2149.24	1991.79	1878.78	1795.15	1731.85	1683.12	1645.12	1615.17	1591.38
95000	8794.60	4829.31	3524.50	2884.57	2510.32	2268.65	2102.45	1983.16	1894.88	1828.07	1776.63	1736.51	1704.90	1679.79
100000	9257.47	5083.48	3710.00	3036.39	2642.44	2388.05	2213.10	2087.54	1994.61	1924.28	1870.14	1827.91	1794.63	1768.20

MONTHLY PAYMENT
REQUIRED TO AMORTIZE A LOAN

TERM AMOUNT	15 Years	16 Years	17 Years	18 Years	19 Years	20 Years	21 Years	22 Years	23 Years	24 Years	25 Years	30 Years	35 Years	40 Years
5	.09	.09	.09	.09	.09	.09	.09	.09	.09	.09	.09	.09	.09	.09
10	.18	.18	.18	.18	.17	.17	.17	.17	.17	.17	.17	.17	.17	.17
15	.27	.26	.26	.26	.26	.26	.26	.26	.26	.26	.26	.25	.25	.25
25	.44	.44	.43	.43	.43	.43	.43	.42	.42	.42	.42	.42	.42	.42
50	.88	.87	.86	.86	.85	.85	.85	.84	.84	.84	.84	.84	.83	.83
75	1.32	1.30	1.29	1.28	1.28	1.27	1.27	1.26	1.26	1.26	1.26	1.25	1.25	1.25
100	1.75	1.74	1.72	1.71	1.70	1.69	1.69	1.68	1.68	1.68	1.67	1.67	1.66	1.66
200	3.50	3.47	3.44	3.42	3.40	3.38	3.37	3.36	3.35	3.34	3.33	3.33	3.32	3.32
300	5.25	5.20	5.15	5.12	5.09	5.07	5.05	5.04	5.03	5.02	5.01	4.99	4.98	4.98
400	6.99	6.93	6.87	6.83	6.79	6.76	6.74	6.72	6.70	6.69	6.68	6.65	6.64	6.63
500	8.74	8.66	8.59	8.53	8.49	8.45	8.42	8.40	8.38	8.36	8.35	8.31	8.29	8.29
600	10.49	10.39	10.30	10.24	10.18	10.14	10.10	10.07	10.05	10.03	10.01	9.97	9.95	9.95
700	12.23	12.12	12.02	11.94	11.88	11.83	11.79	11.75	11.72	11.70	11.68	11.63	11.61	11.60
800	13.98	13.85	13.74	13.65	13.58	13.52	13.47	13.43	13.40	13.37	13.35	13.29	13.27	13.26
900	15.73	15.58	15.45	15.35	15.27	15.21	15.15	15.11	15.07	15.04	15.02	14.95	14.93	14.92
1000	17.48	17.31	17.17	17.06	16.97	16.90	16.84	16.79	16.75	16.71	16.69	16.61	16.58	16.57
2000	34.95	34.61	34.33	34.11	33.93	33.79	33.67	33.57	33.49	33.42	33.37	33.22	33.16	33.14
3000	52.42	51.91	51.50	51.16	50.89	50.68	50.50	50.35	50.23	50.13	50.05	49.83	49.74	49.71
4000	69.89	69.21	68.66	68.22	67.86	67.57	67.33	67.13	66.97	66.84	66.74	66.43	66.32	66.28
5000	87.36	86.51	85.83	85.27	84.82	84.46	84.16	83.92	83.72	83.55	83.42	83.04	82.90	82.85
6000	104.83	103.81	102.99	102.32	101.78	101.35	100.99	100.70	100.46	100.26	100.10	99.65	99.48	99.42
7000	122.30	121.11	120.15	119.38	118.75	118.24	117.82	117.48	117.20	116.97	116.79	116.26	116.06	115.99
8000	139.77	138.41	137.32	136.43	135.71	135.13	134.65	134.26	133.94	133.68	133.47	132.86	132.64	132.55
9000	157.24	155.71	154.48	153.48	152.67	152.02	151.48	151.04	150.69	150.39	150.15	149.47	149.22	149.12
10000	174.71	173.01	171.65	170.54	169.64	168.91	168.31	167.83	167.43	167.10	166.84	166.08	165.80	165.69
11000	192.18	190.32	188.81	187.59	186.60	185.80	185.14	184.61	184.17	183.81	183.52	182.69	182.38	182.26
12000	209.65	207.62	205.97	204.64	203.56	202.69	201.97	201.39	200.91	200.52	200.20	199.29	198.96	198.83
13000	227.12	224.92	223.14	221.70	220.53	219.58	218.80	218.17	217.66	217.23	216.89	215.90	215.53	215.40
14000	244.59	242.22	240.30	238.75	237.49	236.47	235.63	234.95	234.40	233.94	233.57	232.51	232.11	231.97
15000	262.07	259.52	257.47	255.80	254.45	253.36	252.46	251.74	251.14	250.65	250.25	249.12	248.69	248.54
16000	279.54	276.82	274.63	272.86	271.42	270.25	269.29	268.52	267.88	267.36	266.94	265.72	265.27	265.10
17000	297.01	294.12	291.79	289.91	288.38	287.14	286.13	285.30	284.62	284.07	283.62	282.33	281.85	281.67
18000	314.48	311.42	308.96	306.96	305.34	304.03	302.96	302.08	301.37	300.78	300.30	298.94	298.43	298.24
19000	331.95	328.72	326.12	324.02	322.31	320.92	319.79	318.86	318.11	317.49	316.99	315.55	315.01	314.81
20000	349.42	346.02	343.29	341.07	339.27	337.81	336.62	335.65	334.85	334.20	333.67	332.15	331.59	331.38
21000	366.89	363.33	360.45	358.12	356.23	354.70	353.45	352.43	351.59	350.91	350.35	348.76	348.17	347.95
22000	384.36	380.63	377.61	375.18	373.20	371.59	370.28	369.21	368.34	367.62	367.04	365.37	364.75	364.52
23000	401.83	397.93	394.78	392.23	390.16	388.48	387.11	385.99	385.08	384.33	383.72	381.97	381.33	381.09
24000	419.30	415.23	411.94	409.28	407.12	405.37	403.94	402.77	401.82	401.04	400.40	398.58	397.91	397.65
25000	436.77	432.53	429.11	426.34	424.09	422.26	420.77	419.56	418.56	417.75	417.09	415.19	414.49	414.22
26000	454.24	449.83	446.27	443.39	441.05	439.15	437.60	436.34	435.30	434.46	433.77	431.80	431.06	430.79
27000	471.71	467.13	463.43	460.44	458.01	456.04	454.43	453.12	452.05	451.17	450.45	448.40	447.64	447.36
28000	489.18	484.43	480.60	477.50	474.98	472.93	471.26	469.90	468.79	467.88	467.14	465.01	464.22	463.93
29000	506.65	501.73	497.76	494.55	491.94	489.82	488.09	486.68	485.53	484.59	483.82	481.62	480.80	480.50
30000	524.13	519.03	514.93	511.60	508.90	506.71	504.92	503.47	502.27	501.30	500.50	498.23	497.38	497.07
31000	541.60	536.33	532.09	528.66	525.87	523.60	521.75	520.25	519.02	518.01	517.19	514.83	513.96	513.64
32000	559.07	553.64	549.25	545.71	542.83	540.49	538.58	537.03	535.76	534.72	533.87	531.44	530.54	530.20
33000	576.54	570.94	566.42	562.76	559.79	557.38	555.42	553.81	552.50	551.43	550.55	548.05	547.12	546.77
34000	594.01	588.24	583.58	579.81	576.76	574.27	572.25	570.59	569.24	568.14	567.24	564.66	563.70	563.34
35000	611.48	605.54	600.75	596.87	593.72	591.16	589.08	587.38	585.99	584.85	583.92	581.26	580.28	579.91
36000	628.95	622.84	617.91	613.92	610.68	608.05	605.91	604.16	602.73	601.56	600.60	597.87	596.86	596.48
37000	646.42	640.14	635.07	630.97	627.65	624.94	622.74	620.94	619.47	618.27	617.29	614.48	613.44	613.05
38000	663.89	657.44	652.24	648.03	644.61	641.83	639.57	637.72	636.21	634.98	633.97	631.09	630.02	629.62
39000	681.36	674.74	669.40	665.08	661.57	658.72	656.40	654.50	652.95	651.69	650.65	647.69	646.59	646.19
40000	698.83	692.04	686.57	682.13	678.54	675.61	673.23	671.29	669.70	668.40	667.34	664.30	663.17	662.75
41000	716.30	709.34	703.73	699.19	695.50	692.50	690.06	688.07	686.44	685.11	684.02	680.91	679.75	679.32
42000	733.77	726.65	720.89	716.24	712.46	709.39	706.89	704.85	703.18	701.82	700.70	697.51	696.33	695.89
43000	751.24	743.95	738.06	733.29	729.43	726.28	723.72	721.63	719.92	718.53	717.39	714.12	712.91	712.46
44000	768.72	761.25	755.22	750.35	746.39	743.17	740.55	738.41	736.67	735.24	734.07	730.73	729.49	729.03
45000	786.19	778.55	772.39	767.40	763.35	760.06	757.38	755.20	753.41	751.95	750.75	747.34	746.07	745.60
46000	803.66	795.85	789.55	784.45	780.32	776.95	774.21	771.98	770.15	768.66	767.44	763.94	762.65	762.17
47000	821.13	813.15	806.71	801.51	797.28	793.84	791.04	788.76	786.89	785.37	784.12	780.55	779.23	778.74
48000	838.60	830.45	823.88	818.56	814.24	810.73	807.87	805.54	803.64	802.08	800.80	797.16	795.81	795.30
49000	856.07	847.75	841.04	835.61	831.21	827.62	824.70	822.32	820.38	818.79	817.49	813.77	812.39	811.87
50000	873.54	865.05	858.21	852.67	848.17	844.51	841.54	839.11	837.12	835.50	834.17	830.37	828.97	828.44
55000	960.89	951.56	944.03	937.93	932.99	928.97	925.69	923.02	920.83	919.05	917.59	913.41	911.86	911.29
60000	1048.25	1038.06	1029.85	1023.20	1017.80	1013.42	1009.84	1006.93	1004.54	1002.60	1001.00	996.45	994.76	994.13
65000	1135.60	1124.57	1115.67	1108.47	1102.62	1097.87	1093.99	1090.84	1088.26	1086.15	1084.42	1079.48	1077.65	1076.97
70000	1222.95	1211.07	1201.49	1193.73	1187.44	1182.32	1178.15	1174.75	1171.97	1169.69	1167.84	1162.52	1160.55	1159.82
75000	1310.31	1297.58	1287.31	1279.00	1272.25	1266.77	1262.30	1258.66	1255.68	1253.24	1251.25	1245.56	1243.45	1242.66
80000	1397.66	1384.08	1373.13	1364.26	1357.07	1351.22	1346.45	1342.57	1339.39	1336.79	1334.67	1328.60	1326.34	1325.50
85000	1485.01	1470.59	1458.95	1449.53	1441.89	1435.67	1430.61	1426.48	1423.10	1420.34	1418.09	1411.63	1409.24	1408.35
90000	1572.37	1557.09	1544.77	1534.80	1526.70	1520.12	1514.76	1510.39	1506.81	1503.89	1501.50	1494.67	1492.13	1491.19
95000	1659.72	1643.60	1630.59	1620.06	1611.52	1604.57	1598.91	1594.30	1590.52	1587.44	1584.92	1577.71	1575.03	1574.03
100000	1747.07	1730.10	1716.41	1705.33	1696.34	1689.02	1683.07	1678.21	1674.24	1670.99	1668.33	1660.74	1657.93	1656.88

MONTHLY PAYMENT
REQUIRED TO AMORTIZE A LOAN

TERM AMOUNT	1 Year	2 Years	3 Years	4 Years	5 Years	6 Years	7 Years	8 Years	9 Years	10 Years	11 Years	12 Years	13 Years	14 Years
5	.47	.26	.19	.16	.14	.12	.12	.11	.10	.10	.10	.10	.09	.09
10	.93	.51	.38	.31	.27	.24	.23	.21	.20	.20	.19	.19	.18	.18
15	1.39	.77	.56	.46	.40	.36	.34	.32	.30	.29	.29	.28	.27	.27
25	2.32	1.28	.93	.76	.67	.60	.56	.53	.50	.49	.47	.46	.45	.45
50	4.63	2.55	1.86	1.52	1.33	1.20	1.11	1.05	1.00	.97	.94	.92	.90	.89
75	6.95	3.82	2.79	2.28	1.99	1.80	1.67	1.57	1.50	1.45	1.41	1.38	1.35	1.33
100	9.26	5.09	3.72	3.04	2.65	2.39	2.22	2.09	2.00	1.93	1.88	1.83	1.80	1.78
200	18.52	10.17	7.43	6.08	5.29	4.78	4.43	4.18	4.00	3.86	3.75	3.66	3.60	3.55
300	27.78	15.26	11.14	9.12	7.94	7.17	6.65	6.27	5.99	5.78	5.62	5.49	5.39	5.32
400	37.04	20.34	14.85	12.16	10.58	9.56	8.86	8.36	7.99	7.71	7.49	7.32	7.19	7.09
500	46.30	25.43	18.56	15.19	13.22	11.95	11.08	10.45	9.99	9.63	9.36	9.15	8.99	8.86
600	55.56	30.51	22.27	18.23	15.87	14.34	13.29	12.54	11.98	11.56	11.24	10.98	10.78	10.63
700	64.82	35.60	25.98	21.27	18.51	16.73	15.51	14.63	13.98	13.49	13.11	12.81	12.58	12.40
800	74.07	40.68	29.70	24.31	21.16	19.12	17.72	16.72	15.97	15.41	14.98	14.64	14.38	14.17
900	83.33	45.77	33.41	27.34	23.80	21.51	19.94	18.81	17.97	17.34	16.85	16.47	16.17	15.94
1000	92.59	50.85	37.12	30.38	26.44	23.90	22.15	20.90	19.97	19.26	18.72	18.30	17.97	17.71
2000	185.18	101.70	74.23	60.76	52.88	47.79	44.30	41.79	39.93	38.52	37.44	36.60	35.93	35.41
3000	277.76	152.55	111.34	91.14	79.32	71.69	66.44	62.68	59.89	57.78	56.16	54.89	53.90	53.11
4000	370.35	203.39	148.46	121.51	105.76	95.58	88.59	83.57	79.85	77.04	74.88	73.19	71.86	70.81
5000	462.94	254.24	185.57	151.89	132.20	119.48	110.74	104.46	99.82	96.30	93.60	91.49	89.83	88.51
6000	555.52	305.09	222.68	182.27	158.63	143.37	132.88	125.35	119.78	115.56	112.31	109.78	107.79	106.21
7000	648.11	355.93	259.79	212.64	185.07	167.27	155.03	146.24	139.74	134.82	131.03	128.08	125.75	123.91
8000	740.70	406.78	296.91	243.02	211.51	191.16	177.17	167.13	159.70	154.08	149.75	146.38	143.72	141.61
9000	833.28	457.63	334.02	273.40	237.95	215.06	199.32	188.02	179.66	173.34	168.47	164.67	161.68	159.31
10000	925.87	508.47	371.13	303.78	264.39	238.95	221.47	208.91	199.63	192.60	187.19	182.97	179.65	177.01
11000	1018.46	559.32	408.24	334.15	290.83	262.85	243.61	229.80	219.59	211.86	205.91	201.27	197.61	194.71
12000	1111.04	610.17	445.36	364.53	317.26	286.74	265.76	250.70	239.55	231.12	224.62	219.56	215.57	212.41
13000	1203.63	661.02	482.47	394.91	343.70	310.64	287.90	271.59	259.51	250.38	243.34	237.86	233.54	230.11
14000	1296.22	711.86	519.58	425.28	370.14	334.53	310.05	292.48	279.48	269.64	262.06	256.15	251.50	247.81
15000	1388.80	762.71	556.69	455.66	396.58	358.43	332.20	313.37	299.44	288.89	280.78	274.45	269.47	265.51
16000	1481.39	813.56	593.81	486.04	423.02	382.32	354.34	334.26	319.40	308.15	299.50	292.75	287.43	283.21
17000	1573.98	864.40	630.92	516.42	449.46	406.22	376.49	355.15	339.36	327.41	318.22	311.04	305.39	300.91
18000	1666.56	915.25	668.03	546.79	475.89	430.11	398.63	376.04	359.32	346.67	336.93	329.34	323.36	318.61
19000	1759.15	966.10	705.15	577.17	502.33	454.01	420.78	396.93	379.29	365.93	355.65	347.64	341.32	336.31
20000	1851.74	1016.94	742.26	607.55	528.77	477.90	442.93	417.82	399.25	385.19	374.37	365.93	359.29	354.01
21000	1944.32	1067.79	779.37	637.92	555.21	501.80	465.07	438.71	419.21	404.45	393.09	384.23	377.25	371.71
22000	2036.91	1118.64	816.48	668.30	581.65	525.69	487.22	459.60	439.17	423.71	411.81	402.53	395.21	389.41
23000	2129.50	1169.49	853.60	698.68	608.09	549.59	509.36	480.50	459.13	442.97	430.53	420.82	413.18	407.11
24000	2222.08	1220.33	890.71	729.06	634.52	573.48	531.51	501.39	479.10	462.23	449.24	439.12	431.14	424.81
25000	2314.67	1271.18	927.82	759.43	660.96	597.38	553.66	522.28	499.06	481.49	467.96	457.42	449.11	442.51
26000	2407.26	1322.03	964.93	789.81	687.40	621.27	575.80	543.17	519.02	500.75	486.68	475.71	467.07	460.21
27000	2499.84	1372.87	1002.05	820.19	713.84	645.17	597.95	564.06	538.98	520.01	505.40	494.01	485.03	477.91
28000	2592.43	1423.72	1039.16	850.56	740.28	669.06	620.09	584.95	558.95	539.27	524.12	512.30	503.00	495.61
29000	2685.02	1474.57	1076.27	880.94	766.71	692.96	642.24	605.84	578.91	558.53	542.84	530.60	520.96	513.31
30000	2777.60	1525.41	1113.38	911.32	793.15	716.85	664.39	626.73	598.87	577.78	561.55	548.90	538.93	531.01
31000	2870.19	1576.26	1150.50	941.70	819.59	740.75	686.53	647.62	618.83	597.04	580.27	567.19	556.89	548.71
32000	2962.78	1627.11	1187.61	972.07	846.03	764.64	708.68	668.51	638.79	616.30	598.99	585.49	574.85	566.41
33000	3055.36	1677.95	1224.72	1002.45	872.47	788.54	730.82	689.40	658.76	635.56	617.71	603.79	592.82	584.11
34000	3147.95	1728.80	1261.84	1032.83	898.91	812.43	752.97	710.29	678.72	654.82	636.43	622.08	610.78	601.81
35000	3240.54	1779.65	1298.95	1063.20	925.34	836.33	775.12	731.19	698.68	674.08	655.15	640.38	628.75	619.51
36000	3333.12	1830.50	1336.06	1093.58	951.78	860.22	797.26	752.08	718.64	693.34	673.86	658.68	646.71	637.21
37000	3425.71	1881.34	1373.17	1123.96	978.22	884.12	819.41	772.97	738.60	712.60	692.58	676.97	664.67	654.91
38000	3518.30	1932.19	1410.29	1154.34	1004.66	908.01	841.55	793.86	758.57	731.86	711.30	695.27	682.64	672.61
39000	3610.88	1983.04	1447.40	1184.71	1031.10	931.91	863.70	814.75	778.53	751.12	730.02	713.56	700.60	690.31
40000	3703.47	2033.88	1484.51	1215.09	1057.54	955.80	885.85	835.64	798.49	770.38	748.74	731.86	718.57	708.01
41000	3796.06	2084.73	1521.62	1245.47	1083.97	979.70	907.99	856.53	818.45	789.64	767.46	750.16	736.53	725.71
42000	3888.64	2135.58	1558.74	1275.84	1110.41	1003.59	930.14	877.42	838.42	808.90	786.17	768.45	754.49	743.41
43000	3981.23	2186.42	1595.85	1306.22	1136.85	1027.49	952.28	898.31	858.38	828.16	804.89	786.75	772.46	761.11
44000	4073.82	2237.27	1632.96	1336.60	1163.29	1051.38	974.43	919.20	878.34	847.41	823.61	805.05	790.42	778.81
45000	4166.40	2288.12	1670.07	1366.97	1189.73	1075.28	996.58	940.09	898.30	866.67	842.33	823.34	808.39	796.51
46000	4258.99	2338.97	1707.19	1397.35	1216.17	1099.17	1018.72	960.99	918.26	885.93	861.05	841.64	826.35	814.21
47000	4351.58	2389.81	1744.30	1427.73	1242.60	1123.07	1040.87	981.88	938.23	905.19	879.77	859.94	844.31	831.91
48000	4444.16	2440.66	1781.41	1458.11	1269.04	1146.96	1063.01	1002.77	958.19	924.45	898.48	878.23	862.28	849.61
49000	4536.75	2491.51	1818.52	1488.48	1295.48	1170.85	1085.16	1023.66	978.15	943.71	917.20	896.53	880.24	867.31
50000	4629.34	2542.35	1855.64	1518.86	1321.92	1194.75	1107.31	1044.55	998.11	962.97	935.92	914.83	898.21	885.01
55000	5092.27	2796.59	2041.20	1670.75	1454.11	1314.22	1218.04	1149.00	1097.92	1059.27	1029.51	1006.31	988.03	973.51
60000	5555.20	3050.82	2226.76	1822.63	1586.30	1433.70	1328.77	1253.46	1197.73	1155.56	1123.10	1097.79	1077.85	1062.01
65000	6018.14	3305.06	2412.33	1974.52	1718.49	1553.17	1439.50	1357.91	1297.54	1251.86	1216.69	1189.27	1167.67	1150.51
70000	6481.07	3559.29	2597.89	2126.40	1850.68	1672.65	1550.23	1462.37	1397.36	1348.16	1310.29	1280.75	1257.49	1239.01
75000	6944.00	3813.53	2783.45	2278.29	1982.88	1792.12	1660.96	1566.82	1497.17	1444.45	1403.88	1372.24	1347.31	1327.51
80000	7406.94	4067.76	2969.02	2430.17	2115.07	1911.60	1771.69	1671.28	1596.98	1540.75	1497.47	1463.72	1437.13	1416.01
85000	7869.87	4322.00	3154.58	2582.06	2247.26	2031.07	1882.42	1775.73	1696.79	1637.05	1591.06	1555.20	1526.95	1504.51
90000	8332.80	4576.23	3340.14	2733.94	2379.45	2150.55	1993.15	1880.18	1796.60	1733.34	1684.65	1646.68	1616.77	1593.01
95000	8795.74	4830.47	3525.71	2885.83	2511.64	2270.02	2103.88	1984.64	1896.41	1829.64	1778.24	1738.16	1706.59	1681.51
100000	9258.67	5084.70	3711.27	3037.72	2643.83	2389.49	2214.61	2089.09	1996.22	1925.94	1871.84	1829.65	1796.41	1770.01

TERM AMOUNT	15 Years	16 Years	17 Years	18 Years	19 Years	20 Years	21 Years	22 Years	23 Years	24 Years	25 Years	30 Years	35 Years	40 Years
5	.09	.09	.09	.09	.09	.09	.09	.09	.09	.09	.09	.09	.09	.09
10	.18	.18	.18	.18	.17	.17	.17	.17	.17	.17	.17	.17	.17	.17
15	.27	.26	.26	.26	.26	.26	.26	.26	.26	.26	.26	.25	.25	.25
25	.44	.44	.43	.43	.43	.43	.43	.43	.42	.42	.42	.42	.42	.42
50	.88	.87	.86	.86	.85	.85	.85	.85	.84	.84	.84	.84	.83	.83
75	1.32	1.30	1.29	1.29	1.28	1.27	1.27	1.27	1.26	1.26	1.26	1.25	1.25	1.25
100	1.75	1.74	1.72	1.71	1.70	1.70	1.69	1.69	1.68	1.68	1.68	1.67	1.66	1.66
200	3.50	3.47	3.44	3.42	3.40	3.39	3.38	3.37	3.36	3.35	3.35	3.33	3.32	3.32
300	5.25	5.20	5.16	5.13	5.10	5.08	5.06	5.05	5.03	5.02	5.02	4.99	4.98	4.98
400	7.00	6.93	6.88	6.83	6.80	6.77	6.75	6.73	6.71	6.70	6.69	6.66	6.64	6.64
500	8.75	8.66	8.60	8.54	8.50	8.46	8.43	8.41	8.39	8.37	8.36	8.32	8.30	8.30
600	10.50	10.40	10.31	10.25	10.19	10.15	10.12	10.09	10.06	10.04	10.03	9.98	9.96	9.96
700	12.25	12.13	12.03	11.96	11.89	11.84	11.80	11.77	11.74	11.72	11.70	11.64	11.62	11.62
800	14.00	13.86	13.75	13.66	13.59	13.53	13.49	13.45	13.41	13.39	13.37	13.31	13.28	13.28
900	15.75	15.59	15.47	15.37	15.29	15.22	15.17	15.13	15.09	15.06	15.04	14.97	14.94	14.94
1000	17.49	17.32	17.19	17.08	16.99	16.91	16.86	16.81	16.77	16.73	16.71	16.63	16.60	16.59
2000	34.98	34.64	34.37	34.15	33.97	33.82	33.71	33.61	33.53	33.46	33.41	33.26	33.20	33.18
3000	52.47	51.96	51.55	51.22	50.95	50.73	50.56	50.41	50.29	50.19	50.12	49.89	49.80	49.77
4000	69.96	69.28	68.74	68.29	67.94	67.64	67.41	67.21	67.05	66.92	66.82	66.52	66.40	66.36
5000	87.45	86.60	85.92	85.37	84.92	84.55	84.26	84.01	83.82	83.65	83.52	83.14	83.00	82.95
6000	104.94	103.92	103.10	102.44	101.90	101.46	101.11	100.82	100.58	100.38	100.23	99.77	99.60	99.54
7000	122.43	121.24	120.29	119.51	118.88	118.37	117.96	117.62	117.34	117.11	116.93	116.40	116.20	116.13
8000	139.92	138.56	137.47	136.58	135.87	135.28	134.81	134.42	134.10	133.84	133.63	133.03	132.80	132.72
9000	157.41	155.88	154.65	153.66	152.85	152.19	151.66	151.22	150.87	150.57	150.34	149.66	149.40	149.31
10000	174.90	173.20	171.84	170.73	169.83	169.10	168.51	168.03	167.63	167.30	167.04	166.28	166.00	165.90
11000	192.39	190.52	189.02	187.80	186.82	186.01	185.36	184.83	184.39	184.03	183.74	182.91	182.60	182.49
12000	209.87	207.84	206.20	204.87	203.80	202.92	202.21	201.63	201.15	200.76	200.45	199.54	199.20	199.08
13000	227.36	225.16	223.38	221.95	220.78	219.83	219.06	218.43	217.92	217.49	217.15	216.17	215.80	215.67
14000	244.85	242.48	240.57	239.02	237.76	236.74	235.91	235.23	234.68	234.22	233.85	232.80	232.40	232.26
15000	262.34	259.80	257.75	256.09	254.75	253.65	252.76	252.03	251.44	250.95	250.56	249.42	249.00	248.85
16000	279.83	277.12	274.93	273.16	271.73	270.56	269.61	268.84	268.20	267.68	267.26	266.05	265.60	265.44
17000	297.32	294.44	292.12	290.24	288.71	287.47	286.46	285.64	284.96	284.41	283.97	282.68	282.20	282.03
18000	314.81	311.76	309.30	307.31	305.69	304.38	303.31	302.44	301.73	301.14	300.67	299.31	298.80	298.62
19000	332.30	329.08	326.48	324.38	322.68	321.29	320.16	319.24	318.49	317.87	317.37	315.94	315.40	315.21
20000	349.79	346.40	343.67	341.45	339.66	338.20	337.01	336.04	335.25	334.60	334.08	332.56	332.00	331.80
21000	367.28	363.72	360.85	358.53	356.64	355.11	353.86	352.85	352.01	351.33	350.78	349.19	348.60	348.38
22000	384.77	381.04	378.03	375.60	373.63	372.02	370.71	369.65	368.78	368.06	367.48	365.82	365.20	364.97
23000	402.25	398.36	395.21	392.67	390.61	388.93	387.56	386.45	385.54	384.79	384.19	382.45	381.80	381.56
24000	419.74	415.68	412.40	409.74	407.59	405.84	404.41	403.25	402.30	401.52	400.89	399.08	398.40	398.15
25000	437.23	433.00	429.58	426.82	424.57	422.75	421.26	420.05	419.06	418.25	417.59	415.70	415.00	414.74
26000	454.72	450.32	446.76	443.89	441.56	439.66	438.11	436.85	435.83	434.98	434.30	432.33	431.60	431.33
27000	472.21	467.64	463.95	460.96	458.54	456.57	454.97	453.66	452.59	451.71	451.00	448.96	448.20	447.92
28000	489.70	484.96	481.13	478.03	475.52	473.48	471.82	470.46	469.35	468.44	467.70	465.59	464.80	464.51
29000	507.19	502.28	498.31	495.11	492.50	490.39	488.67	487.26	486.11	485.17	484.41	482.22	481.40	481.10
30000	524.68	519.60	515.50	512.18	509.49	507.30	505.52	504.06	502.88	501.90	501.11	498.84	498.00	497.69
31000	542.17	536.92	532.68	529.25	526.47	524.21	522.37	520.86	519.64	518.63	517.81	515.47	514.60	514.28
32000	559.66	554.24	549.86	546.32	543.45	541.12	539.22	537.67	536.40	535.36	534.52	532.10	531.20	530.87
33000	577.15	571.55	567.04	563.40	560.44	558.03	556.07	554.47	553.16	552.09	551.22	548.73	547.80	547.46
34000	594.64	588.87	584.23	580.47	577.42	574.94	572.92	571.27	569.92	568.82	567.93	565.35	564.40	564.05
35000	612.12	606.19	601.41	597.54	594.40	591.85	589.77	588.07	586.69	585.55	584.63	581.98	581.00	580.64
36000	629.61	623.51	618.59	614.61	611.38	608.76	606.62	604.87	603.45	602.28	601.33	598.61	597.60	597.23
37000	647.10	640.83	635.78	631.69	628.37	625.67	623.47	621.68	620.21	619.01	618.04	615.24	614.20	613.82
38000	664.59	658.15	652.96	648.76	645.35	642.58	640.32	638.48	636.97	635.74	634.74	631.87	630.80	630.41
39000	682.00	675.47	670.14	665.83	662.33	659.49	657.17	655.28	653.74	652.47	651.44	648.49	647.40	647.00
40000	699.57	692.79	687.33	682.90	679.31	676.40	674.02	672.08	670.50	669.20	668.15	665.12	664.00	663.59
41000	717.06	710.11	704.51	699.98	696.30	693.31	690.87	688.88	687.26	685.93	684.85	681.75	680.60	680.18
42000	734.55	727.43	721.69	717.05	713.28	710.22	707.72	705.69	704.02	702.66	701.55	698.38	697.20	696.76
43000	752.04	744.75	738.88	734.12	730.26	727.13	724.57	722.49	720.79	719.39	718.26	715.01	713.80	713.35
44000	769.53	762.07	756.06	751.19	747.25	744.04	741.42	739.29	737.55	736.12	734.96	731.63	730.40	729.94
45000	787.02	779.39	773.24	768.27	764.23	760.95	758.27	756.09	754.31	752.85	751.66	748.26	747.00	746.53
46000	804.50	796.71	790.42	785.34	781.21	777.86	775.12	772.89	771.07	769.58	768.37	764.89	763.60	763.12
47000	821.99	814.03	807.61	802.41	798.19	794.76	791.97	789.69	787.84	786.31	785.07	781.52	780.20	779.71
48000	839.48	831.35	824.79	819.48	815.18	811.67	808.82	806.50	804.60	803.04	801.77	798.15	796.80	796.30
49000	856.97	848.67	841.97	836.55	832.16	828.58	825.67	823.30	821.36	819.77	818.48	814.77	813.40	812.89
50000	874.46	865.99	859.16	853.63	849.14	845.49	842.52	840.10	838.12	836.50	835.18	831.40	830.00	829.48
55000	961.91	952.59	945.07	938.99	934.06	930.04	926.78	924.11	921.93	920.15	918.70	914.54	913.00	912.43
60000	1049.35	1039.19	1030.99	1024.35	1018.97	1014.59	1011.03	1008.12	1005.75	1003.80	1002.22	997.68	996.00	995.38
65000	1136.80	1125.78	1116.90	1109.71	1103.88	1099.14	1095.28	1092.13	1089.56	1087.45	1085.73	1080.82	1079.00	1078.32
70000	1224.24	1212.38	1202.82	1195.08	1188.80	1183.69	1179.53	1176.14	1173.37	1171.10	1169.25	1163.96	1162.00	1161.27
75000	1311.69	1298.98	1288.73	1280.44	1273.71	1268.24	1263.78	1260.15	1257.18	1254.75	1252.77	1247.10	1245.00	1244.22
80000	1399.14	1385.58	1374.65	1365.80	1358.62	1352.79	1348.03	1344.16	1340.99	1338.40	1336.29	1330.24	1328.00	1327.17
85000	1486.58	1472.18	1460.56	1451.16	1443.54	1437.34	1432.29	1428.17	1424.80	1422.05	1419.81	1413.38	1411.00	1410.11
90000	1574.03	1558.78	1546.48	1536.53	1528.45	1521.89	1516.54	1512.18	1508.62	1505.70	1503.32	1496.52	1494.00	1493.06
95000	1661.47	1645.38	1632.39	1621.89	1613.36	1606.43	1600.79	1596.19	1592.43	1589.35	1586.84	1579.66	1577.00	1576.01
100000	1748.92	1731.97	1718.31	1707.25	1698.28	1690.98	1685.04	1680.20	1676.24	1673.00	1670.36	1662.80	1660.00	1658.96

MONTHLY PAYMENT
REQUIRED TO AMORTIZE A LOAN

TERM	1 Year	2 Years	3 Years	4 Years	5 Years	6 Years	7 Years	8 Years	9 Years	10 Years	11 Years	12 Years	13 Years	14 Years
AMOUNT														
5	.47	.26	.19	.16	.14	.12	.12	.11	.11	.10	.10	.10	.10	.09
10	.93	.51	.38	.31	.27	.24	.23	.21	.21	.20	.19	.19	.19	.18
15	1.39	.77	.56	.46	.40	.36	.34	.32	.31	.29	.29	.28	.28	.27
25	2.32	1.28	.93	.77	.67	.60	.56	.53	.51	.49	.47	.46	.46	.45
50	4.64	2.55	1.86	1.53	1.33	1.20	1.12	1.05	1.01	.97	.94	.92	.91	.89
75	6.95	3.82	2.79	2.29	1.99	1.80	1.67	1.58	1.51	1.45	1.41	1.38	1.36	1.34
100	9.27	5.09	3.72	3.05	2.65	2.40	2.23	2.10	2.01	1.94	1.88	1.84	1.81	1.78
200	18.53	10.18	7.44	6.09	5.30	4.80	4.45	4.20	4.01	3.87	3.76	3.68	3.61	3.56
300	27.80	15.27	11.15	9.13	7.95	7.19	6.67	6.29	6.01	5.80	5.64	5.51	5.42	5.34
400	37.06	20.36	14.87	12.18	10.60	9.59	8.89	8.39	8.02	7.74	7.52	7.35	7.22	7.11
500	46.32	25.45	18.59	15.22	13.25	11.98	11.11	10.48	10.02	9.67	9.40	9.19	9.02	8.89
600	55.59	30.54	22.30	18.26	15.90	14.38	13.33	12.58	12.02	11.60	11.28	11.02	10.83	10.67
700	64.85	35.63	26.02	21.31	18.55	16.77	15.55	14.67	14.02	13.53	13.16	12.86	12.63	12.45
800	74.11	40.72	29.74	24.35	21.20	19.17	17.77	16.77	16.03	15.47	15.03	14.70	14.43	14.22
900	83.38	45.81	33.45	27.39	23.85	21.56	19.99	18.86	18.03	17.40	16.91	16.53	16.24	16.00
1000	92.64	50.90	37.17	30.44	26.50	23.96	22.21	20.96	20.03	19.33	18.79	18.37	18.04	17.78
2000	185.27	101.80	74.33	60.87	52.99	47.91	44.42	41.91	40.06	38.66	37.58	36.74	36.08	35.55
3000	277.91	152.69	111.50	91.30	79.49	71.86	66.62	62.86	60.08	57.98	56.36	55.10	54.11	53.32
4000	370.54	203.59	148.66	121.73	105.98	95.82	88.83	83.82	80.11	77.31	75.15	73.47	72.15	71.10
5000	463.18	254.48	185.82	152.16	132.47	119.77	111.04	104.77	100.14	96.63	93.94	91.84	90.18	88.87
6000	555.81	305.38	222.99	182.59	158.97	143.72	133.24	125.72	120.16	115.96	112.72	110.20	108.22	106.64
7000	648.45	356.28	260.15	213.02	185.46	167.67	155.45	146.68	140.19	135.28	131.51	128.57	126.25	124.41
8000	741.08	407.17	297.31	243.45	211.96	191.63	177.65	167.63	160.22	154.61	150.30	146.93	144.29	142.19
9000	833.72	458.07	334.48	273.88	238.45	215.58	199.86	188.58	180.24	173.94	169.08	165.30	162.32	159.96
10000	926.35	508.96	371.64	304.31	264.94	239.53	222.07	209.54	200.27	193.26	187.87	183.67	180.36	177.73
11000	1018.98	559.86	408.80	334.74	291.44	263.49	244.27	230.49	220.30	212.59	206.65	202.03	198.39	195.50
12000	1111.62	610.75	445.97	365.17	317.93	287.44	266.48	251.44	240.32	231.91	225.44	220.40	216.43	213.28
13000	1204.25	661.65	483.13	395.60	344.43	311.39	288.69	272.40	260.35	251.24	244.23	238.76	234.46	231.05
14000	1296.89	712.55	520.30	426.03	370.92	335.34	310.89	293.35	280.38	270.56	263.01	257.13	252.50	248.82
15000	1389.52	763.44	557.46	456.46	397.41	359.30	333.10	314.30	300.40	289.89	281.80	275.50	270.53	266.59
16000	1482.16	814.34	594.62	486.89	423.91	383.25	355.30	335.26	320.43	309.21	300.59	293.86	288.57	284.37
17000	1574.79	865.23	631.79	517.32	450.40	407.20	377.51	356.21	340.46	328.54	319.37	312.23	306.60	302.14
18000	1667.43	916.13	668.95	547.75	476.89	431.16	399.72	377.16	360.48	347.87	338.16	330.59	324.64	319.91
19000	1760.06	967.03	706.11	578.18	503.39	455.11	421.92	398.12	380.51	367.19	356.95	348.96	342.67	337.69
20000	1852.70	1017.92	743.28	608.61	529.88	479.06	444.13	419.07	400.54	386.52	375.73	367.33	360.71	355.46
21000	1945.33	1068.82	780.44	639.04	556.38	503.01	466.34	440.02	420.56	405.84	394.52	385.69	378.74	373.23
22000	2037.96	1119.71	817.60	669.47	582.87	526.97	488.54	460.98	440.59	425.17	413.30	404.06	396.78	391.00
23000	2130.60	1170.61	854.77	699.90	609.36	550.92	510.75	481.93	460.61	444.49	432.09	422.42	414.82	408.78
24000	2223.23	1221.50	891.93	730.33	635.86	574.87	532.95	502.88	480.64	463.82	450.88	440.79	432.85	426.55
25000	2315.87	1272.40	929.09	760.76	662.35	598.83	555.16	523.84	500.67	483.14	469.66	459.16	450.89	444.32
26000	2408.50	1323.30	966.26	791.19	688.85	622.78	577.37	544.79	520.69	502.47	488.45	477.52	468.92	462.09
27000	2501.14	1374.19	1003.42	821.62	715.34	646.73	599.57	565.74	540.72	521.80	507.24	495.89	486.96	479.87
28000	2593.77	1425.09	1040.59	852.06	741.83	670.68	621.78	586.69	560.75	541.12	526.02	514.26	504.99	497.64
29000	2686.41	1475.98	1077.75	882.49	768.33	694.64	643.98	607.65	580.77	560.45	544.81	532.62	523.03	515.41
30000	2779.04	1526.88	1114.91	912.92	794.82	718.59	666.19	628.60	600.80	579.77	563.60	550.99	541.06	533.18
31000	2871.67	1577.77	1152.08	943.35	821.32	742.54	688.40	649.55	620.83	599.10	582.38	569.35	559.10	550.96
32000	2964.31	1628.67	1189.24	973.78	847.81	766.50	710.60	670.51	640.85	618.42	601.17	587.72	577.13	568.73
33000	3056.94	1679.57	1226.40	1004.21	874.30	790.45	732.81	691.46	660.88	637.75	619.95	606.09	595.17	586.50
34000	3149.58	1730.46	1263.57	1034.64	900.80	814.40	755.02	712.41	680.91	657.07	638.74	624.45	613.20	604.28
35000	3242.21	1781.36	1300.73	1065.07	927.29	838.35	777.22	733.37	700.93	676.40	657.53	642.82	631.24	622.05
36000	3334.85	1832.25	1337.89	1095.50	953.78	862.31	799.43	754.32	720.96	695.73	676.31	661.18	649.27	639.82
37000	3427.48	1883.15	1375.06	1125.93	980.28	886.26	821.63	775.27	740.99	715.05	695.10	679.55	667.31	657.59
38000	3520.12	1934.05	1412.22	1156.36	1006.77	910.21	843.84	796.23	761.01	734.38	713.89	697.92	685.34	675.37
39000	3612.75	1984.94	1449.38	1186.79	1033.27	934.17	866.05	817.18	781.04	753.70	732.67	716.28	703.38	693.14
40000	3705.39	2035.84	1486.55	1217.22	1059.76	958.12	888.25	838.13	801.07	773.03	751.46	734.65	721.41	710.91
41000	3798.02	2086.73	1523.71	1247.65	1086.25	982.07	910.46	859.09	821.09	792.35	770.24	753.01	739.45	728.68
42000	3890.65	2137.63	1560.88	1278.08	1112.75	1006.02	932.67	880.04	841.12	811.68	789.03	771.38	757.48	746.46
43000	3983.29	2188.52	1598.04	1308.51	1139.24	1029.98	954.87	900.99	861.14	831.00	807.82	789.75	775.52	764.23
44000	4075.92	2239.42	1635.20	1338.94	1165.74	1053.93	977.08	921.95	881.17	850.33	826.60	808.11	793.55	782.00
45000	4168.56	2290.32	1672.37	1369.37	1192.23	1077.88	999.28	942.90	901.20	869.66	845.39	826.48	811.59	799.77
46000	4261.19	2341.21	1709.53	1399.80	1218.72	1101.84	1021.49	963.85	921.22	888.98	864.18	844.84	829.62	817.55
47000	4353.83	2392.11	1746.69	1430.23	1245.22	1125.79	1043.70	984.81	941.25	908.31	882.96	863.21	847.66	835.32
48000	4446.46	2443.00	1783.86	1460.66	1271.71	1149.74	1065.90	1005.76	961.28	927.63	901.75	881.58	865.70	853.09
49000	4539.10	2493.90	1821.02	1491.09	1298.21	1173.69	1088.11	1026.71	981.30	946.96	920.54	899.94	883.73	870.87
50000	4631.73	2544.80	1858.18	1521.52	1324.70	1197.65	1110.32	1047.67	1001.33	966.28	939.32	918.31	901.77	888.64
55000	5094.90	2799.27	2044.00	1673.67	1457.17	1317.41	1221.35	1152.43	1101.46	1062.91	1033.25	1010.14	991.94	977.50
60000	5558.08	3053.75	2229.82	1825.83	1589.64	1437.17	1332.38	1257.20	1201.60	1159.54	1127.19	1101.97	1082.12	1066.36
65000	6021.25	3308.23	2415.64	1977.98	1722.11	1556.94	1443.41	1361.96	1301.73	1256.17	1221.12	1193.80	1172.29	1155.23
70000	6484.42	3562.71	2601.46	2130.13	1854.58	1676.70	1554.44	1466.73	1401.86	1352.79	1315.05	1285.63	1262.47	1244.09
75000	6947.59	3817.19	2787.27	2282.28	1987.05	1796.47	1665.47	1571.50	1501.99	1449.42	1408.98	1377.46	1352.65	1332.95
80000	7410.77	4071.67	2973.09	2434.43	2119.52	1916.23	1776.50	1676.26	1602.13	1546.05	1502.91	1469.29	1442.82	1421.82
85000	7873.94	4326.15	3158.91	2586.59	2251.99	2036.00	1887.53	1781.03	1702.26	1642.68	1596.84	1561.12	1533.00	1510.68
90000	8337.11	4580.63	3344.73	2738.74	2384.45	2155.76	1998.56	1885.79	1802.39	1739.31	1690.78	1652.95	1623.18	1599.54
95000	8800.28	4835.11	3530.55	2890.89	2516.92	2275.52	2109.59	1990.56	1902.52	1835.93	1784.71	1744.78	1713.35	1688.41
100000	9263.46	5089.59	3716.36	3043.04	2649.39	2395.29	2220.62	2095.33	2002.66	1932.56	1878.64	1836.61	1803.53	1777.27

TERM	15 Years	16 Years	17 Years	18 Years	19 Years	20 Years	21 Years	22 Years	23 Years	24 Years	25 Years	30 Years	35 Years	40 Years
AMOUNT														
5	.09	.09	.09	.09	.09	.09	.09	.09	.09	.09	.09	.09	.09	.09
10	.18	.18	.18	.18	.18	.17	.17	.17	.17	.17	.17	.17	.17	.17
15	.27	.27	.26	.26	.26	.26	.26	.26	.26	.26	.26	.26	.26	.26
25	.44	.44	.44	.43	.43	.43	.43	.43	.43	.43	.42	.42	.42	.42
50	.88	.87	.87	.86	.86	.85	.85	.85	.85	.85	.84	.84	.84	.84
75	1.32	1.31	1.30	1.29	1.28	1.28	1.27	1.27	1.27	1.27	1.26	1.26	1.26	1.26
100	1.76	1.74	1.73	1.72	1.71	1.70	1.70	1.69	1.69	1.69	1.68	1.68	1.67	1.67
200	3.52	3.48	3.46	3.43	3.42	3.40	3.39	3.38	3.37	3.37	3.36	3.35	3.34	3.34
300	5.27	5.22	5.18	5.15	5.12	5.10	5.08	5.07	5.06	5.05	5.04	5.02	5.01	5.01
400	7.03	6.96	6.91	6.86	6.83	6.80	6.78	6.76	6.74	6.73	6.72	6.69	6.68	6.67
500	8.79	8.70	8.63	8.58	8.54	8.50	8.47	8.45	8.43	8.41	8.40	8.36	8.35	8.34
600	10.54	10.44	10.36	10.29	10.24	10.20	10.16	10.13	10.11	10.09	10.08	10.03	10.01	10.01
700	12.30	12.18	12.09	12.01	11.95	11.90	11.86	11.82	11.79	11.77	11.75	11.70	11.68	11.68
800	14.06	13.92	13.81	13.72	13.65	13.60	13.55	13.51	13.48	13.45	13.43	13.37	13.35	13.34
900	15.81	15.66	15.54	15.44	15.36	15.29	15.24	15.20	15.16	15.13	15.11	15.04	15.02	15.01
1000	17.57	17.40	17.26	17.15	17.07	16.99	16.93	16.89	16.85	16.82	16.79	16.72	16.69	16.68
2000	35.13	34.79	34.52	34.30	34.13	33.98	33.86	33.77	33.69	33.63	33.57	33.43	33.37	33.35
3000	52.69	52.19	51.78	51.45	51.19	50.97	50.79	50.65	50.53	50.44	50.36	50.14	50.05	50.02
4000	70.26	69.58	69.04	68.60	68.25	67.96	67.72	67.53	67.38	67.25	67.14	66.85	66.74	66.70
5000	87.82	86.98	86.30	85.75	85.31	84.95	84.65	84.41	84.22	84.06	83.93	83.56	83.42	83.37
6000	105.38	104.37	103.56	102.90	102.37	101.93	101.58	101.29	101.06	100.87	100.71	100.27	100.10	100.04
7000	122.95	121.77	120.82	120.05	119.43	118.92	118.51	118.18	117.90	117.68	117.50	116.98	116.78	116.71
8000	140.51	139.16	138.08	137.20	136.49	135.91	135.44	135.06	134.75	134.49	134.28	133.69	133.47	133.39
9000	158.07	156.56	155.34	154.35	153.55	152.90	152.37	151.94	151.59	151.30	151.07	150.40	150.15	150.06
10000	175.63	173.95	172.60	171.50	170.61	169.89	169.30	168.82	168.43	168.11	167.85	167.11	166.83	166.73
11000	193.20	191.35	189.85	188.65	187.67	186.88	186.23	185.70	185.27	184.92	184.63	183.82	183.52	183.40
12000	210.76	208.74	207.11	205.80	204.73	203.86	203.16	202.58	202.12	201.73	201.42	200.53	200.20	200.08
13000	228.32	226.14	224.37	222.95	221.79	220.85	220.09	219.47	218.96	218.54	218.20	217.24	216.88	216.75
14000	245.89	243.53	241.63	240.10	238.85	237.84	237.02	236.35	235.80	235.35	234.99	233.95	233.56	233.42
15000	263.45	260.92	258.89	257.25	255.91	254.83	253.95	253.23	252.64	252.16	251.77	250.66	250.25	250.09
16000	281.01	278.32	276.15	274.39	272.97	271.82	270.88	270.11	269.49	268.97	268.56	267.37	266.93	266.77
17000	298.58	295.71	293.41	291.54	290.03	288.81	287.81	286.99	286.33	285.79	285.34	284.08	283.61	283.44
18000	316.14	313.11	310.67	308.69	307.09	305.79	304.74	303.87	303.17	302.60	302.13	300.79	300.30	300.11
19000	333.70	330.50	327.93	325.84	324.15	322.78	321.67	320.76	320.01	319.41	318.91	317.50	316.98	316.79
20000	351.26	347.90	345.19	342.99	341.21	339.77	338.59	337.64	336.86	336.22	335.70	334.21	333.66	333.46
21000	368.83	365.29	362.44	360.14	358.27	356.76	355.52	354.52	353.70	353.03	352.48	350.92	350.34	350.13
22000	386.39	382.69	379.70	377.29	375.34	373.75	372.45	371.40	370.54	369.84	369.26	367.63	367.03	366.80
23000	403.95	400.08	396.96	394.44	392.40	390.73	389.38	388.28	387.38	386.65	386.05	384.34	383.71	383.48
24000	421.52	417.48	414.22	411.59	409.46	407.72	406.31	405.16	404.23	403.46	402.83	401.05	400.39	400.15
25000	439.08	434.87	431.48	428.74	426.52	424.71	423.24	422.04	421.07	420.27	419.62	417.76	417.07	416.82
26000	456.64	452.27	448.74	445.89	443.58	441.70	440.17	438.93	437.91	437.08	436.40	434.47	433.76	433.49
27000	474.21	469.66	466.00	463.04	460.64	458.69	457.10	455.81	454.75	453.89	453.19	451.18	450.44	450.17
28000	491.77	487.06	483.26	480.19	477.70	475.68	474.03	472.69	471.60	470.70	469.97	467.89	467.12	466.84
29000	509.33	504.45	500.52	497.34	494.76	492.66	490.96	489.57	488.44	487.51	486.76	484.60	483.81	483.51
30000	526.89	521.84	517.78	514.49	511.82	509.65	507.89	506.45	505.28	504.32	503.54	501.31	500.49	500.18
31000	544.46	539.24	535.03	531.64	528.88	526.64	524.82	523.33	522.12	521.13	520.33	518.02	517.17	516.86
32000	562.02	556.63	552.29	548.78	545.94	543.63	541.75	540.22	538.97	537.94	537.11	534.73	533.85	533.53
33000	579.58	574.03	569.55	565.93	563.00	560.62	558.68	557.10	555.81	554.75	553.89	551.44	550.54	550.20
34000	597.15	591.42	586.81	583.08	580.06	577.61	575.61	573.98	572.65	571.57	570.68	568.15	567.22	566.87
35000	614.71	608.82	604.07	600.23	597.12	594.59	592.54	590.86	589.49	588.38	587.46	584.86	583.90	583.55
36000	632.27	626.21	621.33	617.38	614.18	611.58	609.47	607.74	606.34	605.19	604.25	601.57	600.59	600.22
37000	649.83	643.61	638.59	634.53	631.24	628.57	626.40	624.62	623.18	622.00	621.03	618.28	617.27	616.89
38000	667.40	661.00	655.85	651.68	648.30	645.56	643.33	641.51	640.02	638.81	637.82	634.99	633.95	633.57
39000	684.96	678.40	673.11	668.83	665.36	662.55	660.25	658.39	656.86	655.62	654.60	651.70	650.63	650.24
40000	702.52	695.79	690.37	685.90	682.42	679.53	677.18	675.27	673.71	672.43	671.39	668.41	667.32	666.91
41000	720.09	713.19	707.63	703.13	699.48	696.52	694.11	692.15	690.55	689.24	688.17	685.12	684.00	683.58
42000	737.65	730.58	724.88	720.28	716.54	713.51	711.04	709.03	707.39	706.05	704.95	701.83	700.68	700.26
43000	755.21	747.98	742.14	737.43	733.60	730.50	727.97	725.91	724.23	722.86	721.74	718.54	717.36	716.93
44000	772.78	765.37	759.40	754.58	750.67	747.49	744.90	742.79	741.08	739.52	738.52	735.25	734.05	733.60
45000	790.34	782.76	776.66	771.73	767.73	764.48	761.83	759.68	757.92	756.48	755.31	751.96	750.73	750.27
46000	807.90	800.16	793.92	788.88	784.79	781.46	778.76	776.56	774.76	773.29	772.09	768.67	767.41	766.95
47000	825.46	817.55	811.18	806.03	801.85	798.45	795.69	793.44	791.60	790.10	788.88	785.38	784.10	783.62
48000	843.03	834.95	828.44	823.17	818.91	815.44	812.62	810.32	808.45	806.91	805.66	802.09	800.78	800.29
49000	860.59	852.34	845.70	840.32	835.97	832.43	829.55	827.20	825.29	823.72	822.45	818.80	817.46	816.96
50000	878.15	869.74	862.96	857.47	853.03	849.42	846.48	844.08	842.13	840.53	839.23	835.51	834.14	833.64
55000	965.97	956.71	949.25	943.22	938.33	934.36	931.13	928.49	926.34	924.59	923.15	919.07	917.56	917.00
60000	1053.78	1043.68	1035.55	1028.97	1023.63	1019.30	1015.77	1012.90	1010.56	1008.64	1007.08	1002.62	1000.97	1000.36
65000	1141.60	1130.66	1121.84	1114.71	1108.94	1104.24	1100.42	1097.31	1094.77	1092.69	1091.00	1086.17	1084.39	1083.73
70000	1229.41	1217.63	1208.14	1200.46	1194.24	1189.18	1185.07	1181.72	1178.98	1176.75	1174.92	1169.72	1167.80	1167.09
75000	1317.23	1304.60	1294.43	1286.21	1279.54	1274.12	1269.72	1266.12	1263.19	1260.80	1258.84	1253.27	1251.21	1250.45
80000	1405.04	1391.58	1380.73	1371.95	1364.84	1359.06	1354.36	1350.53	1347.41	1344.85	1342.77	1336.82	1334.63	1333.82
85000	1492.86	1478.55	1467.02	1457.70	1450.14	1444.01	1439.01	1434.94	1431.62	1428.91	1426.69	1420.37	1418.04	1417.18
90000	1580.67	1565.52	1553.32	1543.45	1535.45	1528.95	1523.66	1519.35	1515.83	1512.96	1510.61	1503.92	1501.46	1500.54
95000	1668.49	1652.50	1639.61	1629.19	1620.75	1613.89	1608.31	1603.76	1600.04	1597.01	1594.53	1587.47	1584.87	1583.91
100000	1756.30	1739.47	1725.91	1714.94	1706.05	1698.83	1692.95	1688.16	1684.26	1681.06	1678.46	1671.02	1668.28	1667.27

20%

MONTHLY PAYMENT
REQUIRED TO AMORTIZE A LOAN

TERM	1 Year	2 Years	3 Years	4 Years	5 Years	6 Years	7 Years	8 Years	9 Years	10 Years	11 Years	12 Years	13 Years	14 Years
AMOUNT														
5	.47	.26	.19	.16	.14	.13	.12	.11	.11	.10	.10	.10	.10	.09
10	.93	.51	.38	.31	.27	.25	.23	.22	.21	.20	.19	.19	.19	.18
15	1.40	.77	.56	.46	.40	.37	.34	.32	.31	.30	.29	.28	.28	.27
25	2.32	1.28	.94	.77	.67	.61	.56	.53	.51	.49	.48	.47	.46	.45
50	4.64	2.55	1.87	1.53	1.33	1.21	1.12	1.06	1.01	.97	.95	.93	.91	.90
75	6.96	3.83	2.80	2.29	2.00	1.81	1.67	1.58	1.51	1.46	1.42	1.39	1.36	1.34
100	9.27	5.10	3.73	3.05	2.66	2.41	2.23	2.11	2.01	1.94	1.89	1.85	1.82	1.79
200	18.54	10.19	7.45	6.10	5.31	4.81	4.46	4.21	4.02	3.88	3.78	3.69	3.63	3.57
300	27.81	15.29	11.17	9.15	7.97	7.21	6.68	6.31	6.03	5.82	5.66	5.54	5.44	5.36
400	37.08	20.38	14.89	12.20	10.62	9.61	8.91	8.41	8.04	7.76	7.55	7.38	7.25	7.14
500	46.35	25.48	18.61	15.25	13.28	12.01	11.14	10.51	10.05	9.70	9.43	9.22	9.06	8.93
600	55.61	30.57	22.33	18.30	15.93	14.41	13.36	12.61	12.06	11.64	11.32	11.07	10.87	10.71
700	64.88	35.67	26.06	21.34	18.59	16.81	15.59	14.72	14.07	13.58	13.20	12.91	12.68	12.50
800	74.15	40.76	29.78	24.39	21.24	19.21	17.82	16.82	16.08	15.52	15.09	14.75	14.49	14.28
900	83.42	45.86	33.50	27.44	23.90	21.61	20.04	18.92	18.09	17.46	16.97	16.60	16.30	16.07
1000	92.69	50.95	37.22	30.49	26.55	24.02	22.27	21.02	20.10	19.40	18.86	18.44	18.11	17.85
2000	185.37	101.89	74.43	60.97	53.10	48.03	44.54	42.04	40.19	38.79	37.71	36.88	36.22	35.70
3000	278.05	152.84	111.65	91.46	79.65	72.04	66.80	63.05	60.28	58.18	56.57	55.31	54.32	53.54
4000	370.73	203.78	148.86	121.94	106.20	96.05	89.07	84.07	80.37	77.57	75.42	73.75	72.43	71.39
5000	463.42	254.73	186.08	152.42	132.75	120.06	111.34	105.08	100.46	96.96	94.28	92.18	90.54	89.23
6000	556.10	305.67	223.29	182.91	159.30	144.07	133.60	126.10	120.55	116.36	113.13	110.62	108.64	107.08
7000	648.78	356.62	260.51	213.39	185.85	168.08	155.87	147.11	140.64	135.75	131.99	129.06	126.75	124.92
8000	741.46	407.56	297.72	243.87	212.40	192.09	178.14	168.13	160.73	155.14	150.84	147.49	144.86	142.77
9000	834.15	458.51	334.94	274.36	238.95	216.10	200.40	189.15	180.82	174.53	169.70	165.93	162.96	160.61
10000	926.83	509.45	372.15	304.84	265.50	240.11	222.67	210.16	200.91	193.92	188.55	184.36	181.07	178.46
11000	1019.51	560.40	409.37	335.33	292.05	264.12	244.94	231.18	221.01	213.32	207.40	202.80	199.18	196.30
12000	1112.19	611.34	446.58	365.81	318.60	288.13	267.20	252.19	241.10	232.71	226.26	221.24	217.28	214.15
13000	1204.88	662.29	483.79	396.29	345.15	312.15	289.47	273.21	261.19	252.10	245.11	239.67	235.39	231.99
14000	1297.56	713.23	521.01	426.78	371.70	336.16	311.74	294.22	281.28	271.49	263.97	258.11	253.50	249.84
15000	1390.24	764.18	558.22	457.26	398.25	360.17	334.00	315.24	301.37	290.88	282.82	276.54	271.60	267.68
16000	1482.92	815.12	595.44	487.74	424.80	384.18	356.27	336.25	321.46	310.28	301.68	294.98	289.71	285.53
17000	1575.61	866.06	632.65	518.23	451.35	408.19	378.53	357.27	341.55	329.67	320.53	313.41	307.82	303.38
18000	1668.29	917.01	669.87	548.71	477.90	432.20	400.80	378.29	361.64	349.06	339.39	331.85	325.92	321.22
19000	1760.97	967.95	707.08	579.19	504.45	456.21	423.07	399.30	381.73	368.45	358.24	350.29	344.03	339.07
20000	1853.65	1018.90	744.30	609.68	531.00	480.22	445.33	420.32	401.82	387.84	377.09	368.72	362.14	356.91
21000	1946.33	1069.84	781.51	640.16	557.55	504.23	467.60	441.33	421.91	407.24	395.95	387.16	380.24	374.76
22000	2039.02	1120.79	818.73	670.65	584.10	528.24	489.87	462.35	442.01	426.63	414.80	405.59	398.35	392.60
23000	2131.70	1171.73	855.94	701.13	610.64	552.25	512.13	483.36	462.10	446.02	433.66	424.03	416.45	410.45
24000	2224.38	1222.68	893.15	731.61	637.19	576.26	534.40	504.38	482.19	465.41	452.51	442.47	434.56	428.29
25000	2317.06	1273.62	930.37	762.10	663.74	600.28	556.67	525.40	502.28	484.80	471.37	460.90	452.67	446.14
26000	2409.75	1324.57	967.58	792.58	690.29	624.29	578.93	546.41	522.37	504.19	490.22	479.34	470.77	463.98
27000	2502.43	1375.51	1004.80	823.06	716.84	648.30	601.20	567.43	542.46	523.59	509.08	497.77	488.88	481.83
28000	2595.11	1426.46	1042.01	853.55	743.39	672.31	623.47	588.44	562.55	542.98	527.93	516.21	506.99	499.67
29000	2687.79	1477.40	1079.23	884.03	769.94	696.32	645.73	609.46	582.64	562.37	546.78	534.64	525.09	517.52
30000	2780.48	1528.35	1116.44	914.52	796.49	720.33	668.00	630.47	602.73	581.76	565.64	553.08	543.20	535.36
31000	2873.16	1579.29	1153.66	945.00	823.04	744.34	690.26	651.49	622.82	601.15	584.49	571.52	561.31	553.21
32000	2965.84	1630.23	1190.87	975.48	849.59	768.35	712.53	672.50	642.92	620.55	603.35	589.95	579.41	571.06
33000	3058.52	1681.18	1228.09	1005.97	876.14	792.36	734.80	693.52	663.01	639.94	622.20	608.39	597.52	588.90
34000	3151.21	1732.12	1265.30	1036.45	902.69	816.37	757.06	714.54	683.10	659.33	641.06	626.82	615.63	606.75
35000	3243.89	1783.07	1302.51	1066.93	929.24	840.38	779.33	735.55	703.19	678.72	659.91	645.26	633.73	624.59
36000	3336.57	1834.01	1339.73	1097.42	955.79	864.39	801.60	756.57	723.28	698.11	678.77	663.70	651.84	642.44
37000	3429.25	1884.96	1376.94	1127.90	982.34	888.41	823.86	777.58	743.37	717.51	697.62	682.13	669.95	660.28
38000	3521.94	1935.90	1414.16	1158.38	1008.89	912.42	846.13	798.60	763.46	736.90	716.47	700.57	688.05	678.13
39000	3614.62	1986.85	1451.37	1188.87	1035.44	936.43	868.40	819.61	783.55	756.29	735.33	719.00	706.16	695.97
40000	3707.30	2037.79	1488.59	1219.35	1061.99	960.44	890.66	840.63	803.64	775.68	754.18	737.44	724.27	713.82
41000	3799.98	2088.74	1525.80	1249.84	1088.54	984.45	912.93	861.64	823.73	795.07	773.04	755.88	742.37	731.66
42000	3892.66	2139.68	1563.02	1280.32	1115.09	1008.46	935.20	882.66	843.82	814.47	791.89	774.31	760.48	749.51
43000	3985.35	2190.63	1600.23	1310.80	1141.64	1032.47	957.46	903.68	863.92	833.86	810.75	792.75	778.58	767.35
44000	4078.03	2241.57	1637.45	1341.29	1168.19	1056.48	979.73	924.69	884.01	853.25	829.60	811.18	796.69	785.20
45000	4170.71	2292.52	1674.66	1371.77	1194.74	1080.49	1002.00	945.71	904.10	872.64	848.46	829.62	814.80	803.04
46000	4263.39	2343.46	1711.87	1402.25	1221.28	1104.50	1024.26	966.72	924.19	892.03	867.31	848.05	832.90	820.89
47000	4356.08	2394.40	1749.09	1432.74	1247.83	1128.51	1046.53	987.74	944.28	911.43	886.17	866.49	851.01	838.74
48000	4448.76	2445.35	1786.30	1463.22	1274.38	1152.52	1068.79	1008.75	964.37	930.82	905.02	884.93	869.12	856.58
49000	4541.44	2496.29	1823.52	1493.70	1300.93	1176.54	1091.06	1029.77	984.46	950.21	923.87	903.36	887.22	874.43
50000	4634.12	2547.24	1860.73	1524.19	1327.48	1200.55	1113.33	1050.79	1004.55	969.60	942.73	921.80	905.33	892.27
55000	5097.54	2801.96	2046.81	1676.61	1460.23	1320.60	1224.66	1155.86	1105.01	1066.56	1037.00	1013.98	995.86	981.50
60000	5560.95	3056.69	2232.88	1829.03	1592.98	1440.65	1335.99	1260.94	1205.46	1163.52	1131.27	1106.16	1086.40	1070.72
65000	6024.36	3311.41	2418.95	1981.44	1725.73	1560.71	1447.32	1366.02	1305.92	1260.48	1225.55	1198.34	1176.93	1159.95
70000	6487.77	3566.13	2605.02	2133.86	1858.47	1680.76	1558.66	1471.10	1406.37	1357.44	1319.82	1290.52	1267.46	1249.18
75000	6951.18	3820.86	2791.10	2286.28	1991.22	1800.82	1669.99	1576.18	1506.83	1454.40	1414.09	1382.69	1357.99	1338.40
80000	7414.59	4075.58	2977.17	2438.70	2123.97	1920.87	1781.32	1681.25	1607.28	1551.36	1508.36	1474.87	1448.53	1427.63
85000	7878.01	4330.30	3163.24	2591.12	2256.72	2040.93	1892.65	1786.33	1707.73	1648.32	1602.63	1567.05	1539.06	1516.86
90000	8341.42	4585.03	3349.32	2743.54	2389.47	2160.98	2003.99	1891.41	1808.19	1745.28	1696.91	1659.23	1629.59	1606.08
95000	8804.83	4839.75	3535.39	2895.95	2522.21	2281.03	2115.32	1996.49	1908.64	1842.24	1791.18	1751.41	1720.12	1695.31
100000	9268.24	5094.47	3721.46	3048.37	2654.96	2401.09	2226.65	2101.57	2009.10	1939.20	1885.45	1843.59	1810.66	1784.54

MONTHLY PAYMENT
REQUIRED TO AMORTIZE A LOAN

20.100%

TERM	15 Years	16 Years	17 Years	18 Years	19 Years	20 Years	21 Years	22 Years	23 Years	24 Years	25 Years	30 Years	35 Years	40 Years
AMOUNT														
5	.09	.09	.09	.09	.09	.09	.09	.09	.09	.09	.09	.09	.09	.09
10	.18	.18	.18	.18	.18	.18	.18	.17	.17	.17	.17	.17	.17	.17
15	.27	.27	.27	.26	.26	.26	.26	.26	.26	.26	.26	.26	.26	.26
25	.45	.44	.44	.44	.43	.43	.43	.43	.43	.43	.43	.42	.42	.42
50	.89	.88	.87	.87	.86	.86	.86	.85	.85	.85	.85	.84	.84	.84
75	1.33	1.32	1.31	1.30	1.29	1.29	1.28	1.28	1.27	1.27	1.27	1.26	1.26	1.26
100	1.77	1.75	1.74	1.73	1.72	1.71	1.71	1.70	1.70	1.69	1.69	1.68	1.68	1.68
200	3.53	3.50	3.47	3.45	3.43	3.42	3.41	3.40	3.39	3.38	3.38	3.36	3.36	3.36
300	5.30	5.25	5.21	5.17	5.15	5.13	5.11	5.09	5.08	5.07	5.06	5.04	5.03	5.03
400	7.06	6.99	6.94	6.90	6.86	6.83	6.81	6.79	6.77	6.76	6.75	6.72	6.71	6.71
500	8.82	8.74	8.67	8.62	8.57	8.54	8.51	8.49	8.47	8.45	8.44	8.40	8.39	8.38
600	10.59	10.49	10.41	10.34	10.29	10.25	10.21	10.18	10.16	10.14	10.12	10.08	10.06	10.06
700	12.35	12.23	12.14	12.06	12.00	11.95	11.91	11.88	11.85	11.83	11.81	11.76	11.74	11.73
800	14.11	13.98	13.87	13.79	13.72	13.66	13.61	13.57	13.54	13.52	13.50	13.44	13.42	13.41
900	15.88	15.73	15.61	15.51	15.43	15.37	15.31	15.27	15.24	15.21	15.18	15.12	15.09	15.09
1000	17.64	17.47	17.34	17.23	17.14	17.07	17.01	16.97	16.93	16.90	16.87	16.80	16.77	16.76
2000	35.28	34.94	34.68	34.46	34.28	34.14	34.02	33.93	33.85	33.79	33.74	33.59	33.54	33.52
3000	52.92	52.41	52.01	51.68	51.42	51.21	51.03	50.89	50.77	50.68	50.60	50.38	50.30	50.27
4000	70.55	69.88	69.35	68.91	68.56	68.27	68.04	67.85	67.70	67.57	67.47	67.17	67.07	67.03
5000	88.19	87.35	86.68	86.14	85.70	85.34	85.05	84.81	84.62	84.46	84.33	83.97	83.83	83.78
6000	105.83	104.82	104.02	103.36	102.83	102.41	102.06	101.77	101.54	101.35	101.20	100.76	100.60	100.54
7000	123.46	122.29	121.35	120.59	119.97	119.47	119.07	118.73	118.46	118.24	118.06	117.55	117.36	117.30
8000	141.10	139.76	138.69	137.82	137.11	136.54	136.07	135.70	135.39	135.13	134.93	134.34	134.13	134.05
9000	158.74	157.23	156.02	155.04	154.25	153.61	153.08	152.66	152.31	152.03	151.79	151.14	150.90	150.81
10000	176.37	174.70	173.36	172.27	171.39	170.67	170.09	169.62	169.23	168.92	168.66	167.93	167.66	167.56
11000	194.01	192.17	190.69	189.49	188.53	187.74	187.10	186.58	186.15	185.81	185.53	184.72	184.43	184.32
12000	211.65	209.64	208.03	206.72	205.66	204.81	204.11	203.54	203.08	202.70	202.39	201.51	201.19	201.07
13000	229.28	227.11	225.36	223.95	222.80	221.87	221.12	220.50	220.00	219.59	219.26	218.31	217.96	217.83
14000	246.92	244.58	242.70	241.17	239.94	238.94	238.13	237.46	236.92	236.48	236.12	235.10	234.72	234.59
15000	264.56	262.05	260.03	258.40	257.08	256.01	255.13	254.42	253.85	253.37	252.99	251.89	251.49	251.34
16000	282.20	279.52	277.37	275.63	274.22	273.07	272.14	271.39	270.77	270.26	269.85	268.68	268.26	268.10
17000	299.83	296.99	294.70	292.85	291.36	290.14	289.15	288.35	287.69	287.16	286.72	285.48	285.02	284.85
18000	317.47	314.46	312.04	310.08	308.49	307.21	306.16	305.31	304.61	304.05	303.58	302.27	301.79	301.61
19000	335.11	331.93	329.37	327.31	325.63	324.27	323.17	322.27	321.54	320.94	320.45	319.06	318.55	318.36
20000	352.74	349.40	346.71	344.53	342.77	341.34	340.18	339.23	338.46	337.83	337.32	335.85	335.32	335.12
21000	370.38	366.87	364.04	361.76	359.91	358.41	357.19	356.19	355.38	354.72	354.18	352.65	352.08	351.88
22000	388.02	384.34	381.38	378.98	377.05	375.47	374.20	373.15	372.30	371.61	371.05	369.44	368.85	368.63
23000	405.65	401.81	398.71	396.21	394.19	392.54	391.20	390.12	389.23	388.50	387.91	386.23	385.61	385.39
24000	423.29	419.28	416.05	413.44	411.32	409.61	408.21	407.08	406.15	405.39	404.78	403.02	402.38	402.14
25000	440.93	436.75	433.38	430.66	428.46	426.67	425.22	424.04	423.07	422.29	421.64	419.82	419.15	418.90
26000	458.56	454.22	450.72	447.89	445.60	443.74	442.23	441.00	440.00	439.18	438.51	436.61	435.91	435.66
27000	476.20	471.69	468.05	465.12	462.74	460.81	459.24	457.96	456.92	456.07	455.37	453.40	452.68	452.41
28000	493.84	489.16	485.39	482.34	479.88	477.87	476.25	474.92	473.84	472.96	472.24	470.19	469.44	469.17
29000	511.47	506.63	502.72	499.57	497.01	494.94	493.26	491.88	490.76	489.85	489.11	486.99	486.21	485.92
30000	529.11	524.10	520.06	516.80	514.15	512.01	510.26	508.84	507.69	506.74	505.97	503.78	502.97	502.68
31000	546.75	541.57	537.39	534.02	531.29	529.07	527.27	525.81	524.61	523.63	522.84	520.57	519.74	519.43
32000	564.39	559.04	554.73	551.25	548.43	546.14	544.28	542.77	541.53	540.52	539.70	537.36	536.51	536.19
33000	582.02	576.51	572.06	568.47	565.57	563.21	561.29	559.73	558.45	557.42	556.57	554.16	553.27	552.95
34000	599.66	593.98	589.40	585.70	582.71	580.28	578.30	576.69	575.38	574.31	573.43	570.95	570.04	569.70
35000	617.30	611.45	606.73	602.93	599.84	597.34	595.31	593.65	592.30	591.20	590.30	587.74	586.80	586.46
36000	634.93	628.91	624.07	620.15	616.98	614.41	612.32	610.61	609.22	608.09	607.16	604.53	603.57	603.21
37000	652.57	646.38	641.40	637.38	634.12	631.48	629.32	627.57	626.15	624.98	624.03	621.33	620.33	619.97
38000	670.21	663.85	658.74	654.61	651.26	648.54	646.33	644.53	643.07	641.87	640.90	638.12	637.10	636.72
39000	687.84	681.32	676.07	671.83	668.40	665.61	663.34	661.50	659.99	658.76	657.76	654.91	653.87	653.48
40000	705.48	698.79	693.41	689.06	685.54	682.68	680.35	678.46	676.91	675.65	674.63	671.70	670.63	670.24
41000	723.12	716.26	710.74	706.29	702.67	699.74	697.36	695.42	693.84	692.55	691.49	688.50	687.40	686.99
42000	740.75	733.73	728.08	723.51	719.81	716.81	714.37	712.38	710.76	709.44	708.36	705.29	704.16	703.75
43000	758.39	751.20	745.41	740.74	736.95	733.88	731.38	729.34	727.68	726.33	725.22	722.08	720.93	720.50
44000	776.03	768.67	762.75	757.96	754.09	750.94	748.39	746.30	744.60	743.22	742.09	738.87	737.69	737.26
45000	793.67	786.14	780.08	775.19	771.23	768.01	765.39	763.26	761.53	760.11	758.95	755.67	754.46	754.01
46000	811.30	803.61	797.42	792.42	788.37	785.08	782.40	780.23	778.45	777.00	775.82	772.46	771.22	770.77
47000	828.94	821.08	814.75	809.64	805.50	802.14	799.41	797.19	795.37	793.89	792.69	789.25	787.99	787.53
48000	846.58	838.55	832.09	826.87	822.64	819.21	816.42	814.15	812.30	810.78	809.55	806.04	804.76	804.28
49000	864.21	856.02	849.43	844.10	839.78	836.28	833.43	831.11	829.22	827.68	826.42	822.84	821.52	821.04
50000	881.85	873.49	866.76	861.32	856.92	853.34	850.44	848.07	846.14	844.57	843.28	839.63	838.29	837.79
55000	970.03	960.84	953.44	947.45	942.61	938.68	935.48	932.88	930.75	929.02	927.61	923.59	922.12	921.57
60000	1058.22	1048.19	1040.11	1033.59	1028.30	1024.01	1020.52	1017.68	1015.37	1013.48	1011.94	1007.55	1005.94	1005.35
65000	1146.40	1135.54	1126.79	1119.72	1113.99	1109.35	1105.57	1102.49	1099.98	1097.94	1096.27	1091.52	1089.77	1089.13
70000	1234.59	1222.89	1213.46	1205.85	1199.68	1194.68	1190.61	1187.30	1184.60	1182.39	1180.59	1175.48	1173.60	1172.91
75000	1322.77	1310.23	1300.14	1291.98	1285.38	1280.01	1275.65	1272.10	1269.21	1266.85	1264.92	1259.44	1257.43	1256.69
80000	1410.96	1397.58	1386.81	1378.11	1371.07	1365.35	1360.70	1356.91	1353.82	1351.30	1349.25	1343.40	1341.26	1340.47
85000	1499.14	1484.93	1473.49	1464.25	1456.76	1450.68	1445.74	1441.72	1438.44	1435.76	1433.58	1427.36	1425.09	1424.25
90000	1587.33	1572.28	1560.16	1550.38	1542.45	1536.01	1530.78	1526.52	1523.05	1520.22	1517.90	1511.33	1508.91	1508.02
95000	1675.51	1659.63	1646.84	1636.51	1628.14	1621.35	1615.83	1611.33	1607.66	1604.67	1602.23	1595.29	1592.74	1591.80
100000	1763.69	1746.98	1733.52	1722.64	1713.83	1706.68	1700.87	1696.14	1692.28	1689.13	1686.56	1679.25	1676.57	1675.58

MONTHLY PAYMENT
REQUIRED TO AMORTIZE A LOAN

TERM / AMOUNT	1 Year	2 Years	3 Years	4 Years	5 Years	6 Years	7 Years	8 Years	9 Years	10 Years	11 Years	12 Years	13 Years	14 Years
5	.47	.26	.19	.16	.14	.13	.12	.11	.11	.10	.10	.10	.10	.09
10	.93	.51	.38	.31	.27	.25	.23	.22	.21	.20	.19	.19	.19	.18
15	1.40	.77	.56	.46	.40	.37	.34	.32	.31	.30	.29	.28	.28	.27
25	2.32	1.28	.94	.77	.67	.61	.56	.53	.51	.49	.48	.47	.46	.45
50	4.64	2.55	1.87	1.53	1.33	1.21	1.12	1.06	1.01	.98	.95	.93	.91	.90
75	6.96	3.83	2.80	2.29	2.00	1.81	1.68	1.58	1.51	1.46	1.42	1.39	1.36	1.34
100	9.27	5.10	3.73	3.05	2.66	2.41	2.23	2.11	2.02	1.95	1.89	1.85	1.82	1.79
200	18.54	10.20	7.45	6.10	5.32	4.81	4.46	4.21	4.03	3.89	3.78	3.70	3.63	3.58
300	27.81	15.29	11.17	9.15	7.97	7.21	6.69	6.31	6.04	5.83	5.67	5.54	5.44	5.36
400	37.08	20.39	14.90	12.20	10.63	9.62	8.92	8.42	8.05	7.77	7.55	7.39	7.25	7.15
500	46.35	25.48	18.62	15.25	13.29	12.02	11.15	10.52	10.08	9.71	9.44	9.23	9.07	8.94
600	55.62	30.58	22.34	18.30	15.94	14.42	13.37	12.62	12.07	11.65	11.33	11.08	10.88	10.72
700	64.89	35.67	26.06	21.35	18.60	16.82	15.60	14.73	14.08	13.59	13.22	12.92	12.69	12.51
800	74.16	40.77	29.79	24.40	21.26	19.23	17.83	16.83	16.09	15.53	15.10	14.77	14.50	14.30
900	83.43	45.87	33.51	27.45	23.91	21.63	20.06	18.93	18.10	17.47	16.99	16.61	16.32	16.08
1000	92.70	50.96	37.23	30.50	26.57	24.03	22.29	21.04	20.11	19.41	18.88	18.46	18.13	17.87
2000	185.39	101.92	74.46	61.00	53.13	48.06	44.57	42.07	40.22	38.82	37.75	36.91	36.25	35.73
3000	278.09	152.88	111.69	91.50	79.70	72.08	66.85	63.10	60.33	58.23	56.62	55.36	54.38	53.60
4000	370.78	203.83	148.91	121.99	106.26	96.11	89.13	84.13	80.43	77.64	75.49	73.82	72.50	71.46
5000	463.48	254.79	186.14	152.49	132.82	120.13	111.41	105.16	100.54	97.05	94.36	92.27	90.63	89.32
6000	556.17	305.75	223.37	182.99	159.39	144.16	133.69	126.19	120.65	116.46	113.23	110.72	108.75	107.19
7000	648.87	356.70	260.60	213.48	185.95	168.18	155.98	147.22	140.75	135.86	132.11	129.18	126.88	125.05
8000	741.56	407.66	297.82	243.98	212.51	192.21	178.26	168.25	160.86	155.27	150.98	147.63	145.00	142.91
9000	834.25	458.62	335.05	274.48	239.08	216.23	200.54	189.29	180.97	174.68	169.85	166.08	163.12	160.78
10000	926.95	509.57	372.28	304.98	265.64	240.26	222.82	210.32	201.08	194.09	188.72	184.54	181.25	178.64
11000	1019.64	560.53	409.51	335.47	292.20	264.28	245.10	231.35	221.18	213.50	207.59	202.99	199.37	196.50
12000	1112.34	611.49	446.73	365.97	318.77	288.31	267.38	252.38	241.29	232.91	226.46	221.44	217.50	214.37
13000	1205.03	662.44	483.96	396.47	345.33	312.33	289.66	273.41	261.40	252.32	245.33	239.90	235.62	232.23
14000	1297.73	713.40	521.19	426.96	371.89	336.36	311.95	294.44	281.50	271.72	264.21	258.35	253.75	250.09
15000	1390.42	764.36	558.41	457.46	398.46	360.39	334.23	315.47	301.61	291.13	283.08	276.80	271.87	267.96
16000	1483.11	815.32	595.64	487.96	425.02	384.41	356.51	336.50	321.72	310.54	301.95	295.26	289.99	285.82
17000	1575.81	866.27	632.87	518.45	451.58	408.44	378.79	357.54	341.83	329.95	320.82	313.71	308.12	303.68
18000	1668.50	917.23	670.10	548.95	478.15	432.46	401.07	378.57	361.93	349.36	339.69	332.16	326.24	321.55
19000	1761.20	968.19	707.32	579.45	504.71	456.49	423.35	399.60	382.04	368.77	358.56	350.62	344.37	339.41
20000	1853.89	1019.14	744.55	609.95	531.27	480.51	445.64	420.63	402.15	388.18	377.44	369.07	362.49	357.28
21000	1946.59	1070.10	781.78	640.44	557.84	504.54	467.92	441.66	422.25	407.58	396.31	387.52	380.62	375.14
22000	2039.28	1121.06	819.01	670.94	584.40	528.56	490.20	462.69	442.36	426.99	415.18	405.98	398.74	393.00
23000	2131.97	1172.01	856.23	701.44	610.97	552.59	512.48	483.72	462.47	446.40	434.05	424.43	416.86	410.87
24000	2224.67	1222.97	893.46	731.93	637.53	576.61	534.76	504.75	482.57	465.81	452.92	442.88	434.99	428.73
25000	2317.36	1273.93	930.69	762.43	664.09	600.64	557.04	525.79	502.68	485.22	471.79	461.34	453.11	446.59
26000	2410.06	1324.88	967.91	792.93	690.66	624.66	579.32	546.82	522.79	504.63	490.66	479.79	471.24	464.46
27000	2502.75	1375.84	1005.14	823.42	717.22	648.69	601.61	567.85	542.90	524.03	509.54	498.24	489.36	482.32
28000	2595.45	1426.80	1042.37	853.92	743.78	672.71	623.89	588.88	563.00	543.44	528.41	516.70	507.49	500.18
29000	2688.14	1477.75	1079.60	884.42	770.35	696.74	646.17	609.91	583.11	562.85	547.28	535.15	525.61	518.05
30000	2780.84	1528.71	1116.82	914.92	796.91	720.77	668.45	630.94	603.22	582.26	566.15	553.60	543.74	535.91
31000	2873.53	1579.67	1154.05	945.41	823.47	744.79	690.73	651.97	623.32	601.67	585.02	572.06	561.86	553.77
32000	2966.22	1630.63	1191.28	975.91	850.04	768.82	713.01	673.00	643.43	621.08	603.89	590.51	579.98	571.64
33000	3058.92	1681.58	1228.51	1006.41	876.60	792.84	735.30	694.04	663.54	640.49	622.76	608.96	598.11	589.50
34000	3151.61	1732.54	1265.73	1036.90	903.16	816.87	757.58	715.07	683.65	659.89	641.64	627.42	616.23	607.36
35000	3244.31	1783.50	1302.96	1067.40	929.73	840.89	779.86	736.10	703.75	679.30	660.51	645.87	634.36	625.23
36000	3337.00	1834.45	1340.19	1097.90	956.29	864.92	802.14	757.13	723.86	698.71	679.38	664.32	652.48	643.09
37000	3429.70	1865.41	1377.42	1128.39	982.85	888.94	824.42	778.16	743.97	718.12	698.25	682.78	670.61	660.95
38000	3522.39	1936.37	1414.64	1158.89	1009.42	912.97	846.70	799.19	764.07	737.53	717.12	701.23	688.73	678.82
39000	3615.08	1987.32	1451.87	1189.39	1035.98	936.99	868.98	820.22	784.18	756.94	735.99	719.68	706.85	696.68
40000	3707.78	2038.28	1489.10	1219.89	1062.54	961.02	691.27	841.25	804.29	776.35	754.87	738.14	724.98	714.55
41000	3800.47	2089.24	1526.32	1250.38	1089.11	985.04	913.55	862.28	824.39	795.75	773.74	756.59	743.10	732.41
42000	3893.17	2140.19	1563.55	1280.88	1115.67	1009.07	935.83	883.32	844.50	815.16	792.61	775.04	761.23	750.27
43000	3985.86	2191.15	1600.78	1311.38	1142.23	1033.09	958.11	904.35	864.61	834.57	811.48	793.50	779.35	768.14
44000	4078.56	2242.11	1638.01	1341.87	1168.80	1057.12	980.39	925.38	884.72	853.98	830.35	811.95	797.48	786.00
45000	4171.25	2293.06	1675.23	1372.37	1195.36	1081.15	1002.67	946.41	904.82	873.39	849.22	830.40	815.60	803.86
46000	4263.94	2344.02	1712.46	1402.87	1221.93	1105.17	1024.96	967.44	924.93	892.80	868.09	848.86	833.72	821.73
47000	4356.64	2394.98	1749.69	1433.36	1248.49	1129.20	1047.24	988.47	945.04	912.21	886.97	867.31	851.85	839.59
48000	4449.33	2445.94	1786.92	1463.86	1275.05	1153.22	1069.52	1009.50	965.14	931.61	905.84	885.76	869.97	857.45
49000	4542.03	2496.89	1824.14	1494.36	1301.62	1177.25	1091.80	1030.53	985.25	951.02	924.71	904.22	888.10	875.32
50000	4634.72	2547.85	1861.37	1524.86	1328.18	1201.27	1114.08	1051.57	1005.36	970.43	943.58	922.67	906.22	893.18
55000	5098.19	2802.63	2047.51	1677.34	1461.00	1321.40	1225.49	1156.72	1105.89	1067.47	1037.94	1014.94	996.84	982.50
60000	5561.67	3057.42	2233.64	1829.83	1593.81	1441.53	1336.90	1261.88	1206.43	1164.52	1132.30	1107.20	1087.47	1071.82
65000	6025.14	3312.20	2419.78	1982.31	1726.63	1561.65	1448.30	1367.03	1306.96	1261.56	1226.65	1199.47	1178.09	1161.13
70000	6488.61	3566.99	2605.92	2134.80	1859.45	1681.78	1559.71	1472.19	1407.50	1358.60	1321.01	1291.74	1268.71	1250.45
75000	6952.08	3821.77	2792.05	2287.28	1992.27	1801.91	1671.12	1577.35	1508.03	1455.64	1415.37	1384.00	1359.33	1339.77
80000	7415.55	4076.56	2978.19	2439.77	2125.09	1922.03	1782.53	1682.50	1608.57	1552.69	1509.73	1476.27	1449.95	1429.09
85000	7879.02	4331.34	3164.33	2592.25	2257.90	2042.16	1893.93	1787.66	1709.11	1649.73	1604.08	1568.54	1540.57	1518.40
90000	8342.50	4586.12	3350.46	2744.74	2390.72	2162.29	2005.34	1892.81	1809.64	1746.77	1698.44	1660.80	1631.20	1607.72
95000	8805.97	4840.91	3536.60	2897.22	2523.54	2282.41	2116.75	1997.97	1910.18	1843.81	1792.80	1753.07	1721.82	1697.04
100000	9269.44	5095.69	3722.74	3049.71	2656.35	2402.54	2228.16	2103.13	2010.71	1940.86	1887.16	1845.34	1812.44	1786.36

TERM	15 Years	16 Years	17 Years	18 Years	19 Years	20 Years	21 Years	22 Years	23 Years	24 Years	25 Years	30 Years	35 Years	40 Years
AMOUNT														
5	.09	.09	.09	.09	.09	.09	.09	.09	.09	.09	.09	.09	.09	.09
10	.18	.18	.18	.18	.18	.18	.18	.17	.17	.17	.17	.17	.17	.17
15	.27	.27	.27	.26	.26	.26	.26	.26	.26	.26	.26	.26	.26	.26
25	.45	.44	.44	.44	.43	.43	.43	.43	.43	.43	.43	.43	.42	.42
50	.89	.88	.87	.87	.86	.86	.86	.85	.85	.85	.85	.85	.84	.84
75	1.33	1.32	1.31	1.30	1.29	1.29	1.28	1.28	1.28	1.27	1.27	1.27	1.26	1.26
100	1.77	1.75	1.74	1.73	1.72	1.71	1.71	1.70	1.70	1.70	1.69	1.69	1.68	1.68
200	3.54	3.50	3.48	3.45	3.44	3.42	3.41	3.40	3.39	3.39	3.38	3.37	3.36	3.36
300	5.30	5.25	5.21	5.18	5.15	5.13	5.11	5.10	5.09	5.08	5.07	5.05	5.04	5.04
400	7.07	7.00	6.95	6.90	6.87	6.84	6.82	6.80	6.78	6.77	6.76	6.73	6.72	6.72
500	8.83	8.75	8.68	8.63	8.58	8.55	8.52	8.50	8.48	8.46	8.45	8.41	8.40	8.39
600	10.60	10.50	10.42	10.35	10.30	10.26	10.22	10.19	10.17	10.15	10.14	10.09	10.08	10.07
700	12.36	12.25	12.15	12.08	12.02	11.97	11.92	11.89	11.86	11.84	11.83	11.77	11.76	11.75
800	14.13	14.00	13.89	13.80	13.73	13.67	13.63	13.59	13.56	13.53	13.51	13.46	13.43	13.43
900	15.89	15.74	15.62	15.53	15.45	15.38	15.33	15.29	15.25	15.23	15.20	15.14	15.11	15.10
1000	17.66	17.49	17.36	17.25	17.16	17.09	17.03	16.99	16.95	16.92	16.89	16.82	16.79	16.78
2000	35.32	34.98	34.71	34.50	34.32	34.18	34.06	33.97	33.89	33.83	33.78	33.63	33.58	33.56
3000	52.97	52.47	52.07	51.74	51.48	51.26	51.09	50.95	50.83	50.74	50.66	50.44	50.36	50.33
4000	70.63	69.96	69.42	68.99	68.64	68.35	68.12	67.93	67.78	67.65	67.55	67.26	67.15	67.11
5000	88.28	87.45	86.78	86.23	85.79	85.44	85.15	84.91	84.72	84.56	84.43	84.07	83.94	83.89
6000	105.94	104.94	104.13	103.48	102.95	102.52	102.18	101.89	101.66	101.47	101.32	100.88	100.72	100.66
7000	123.59	122.42	121.48	120.72	120.11	119.61	119.20	118.87	118.60	118.38	118.21	117.70	117.51	117.44
8000	141.25	139.91	138.84	137.97	137.27	136.70	136.23	135.85	135.55	135.30	135.09	134.51	134.30	134.22
9000	158.90	157.40	156.19	155.22	154.42	153.78	153.26	152.84	152.49	152.21	151.98	151.32	151.08	150.99
10000	176.56	174.89	173.55	172.46	171.58	170.87	170.29	169.82	169.43	169.12	168.86	168.14	167.87	167.77
11000	194.21	192.38	190.90	189.71	188.74	187.96	187.32	186.80	186.38	186.03	185.75	184.95	184.66	184.55
12000	211.87	209.87	208.25	206.95	205.90	205.04	204.35	203.78	203.32	202.94	202.63	201.76	201.44	201.32
13000	229.52	227.36	225.61	224.20	223.06	222.13	221.37	220.76	220.26	219.85	219.52	218.57	218.23	218.10
14000	247.18	244.84	242.96	241.44	240.21	239.21	238.40	237.74	237.20	236.76	236.41	235.39	235.01	234.88
15000	264.84	262.33	260.32	258.69	257.37	256.30	255.43	254.72	254.15	253.68	253.29	252.20	251.80	251.65
16000	282.49	279.82	277.67	275.93	274.53	273.39	272.46	271.70	271.09	270.59	270.18	269.01	268.59	268.43
17000	300.15	297.31	295.03	293.18	291.69	290.47	289.49	288.69	288.03	287.50	287.06	285.83	285.37	285.21
18000	317.80	314.80	312.38	310.43	308.84	307.56	306.52	305.67	304.98	304.41	303.95	302.64	302.16	301.98
19000	335.46	332.29	329.73	327.67	326.00	324.65	323.55	322.65	321.92	321.32	320.84	319.45	318.95	318.76
20000	353.11	349.77	347.09	344.92	343.16	341.73	340.57	339.63	338.86	338.23	337.72	336.27	335.73	335.54
21000	370.77	367.26	364.44	362.16	360.32	358.82	357.60	356.61	355.80	355.14	354.61	353.08	352.52	352.31
22000	388.42	384.75	381.80	379.41	377.48	375.91	374.63	373.59	372.75	372.06	371.49	369.89	369.31	369.09
23000	406.08	402.24	399.15	396.65	394.63	392.99	391.66	390.57	389.69	388.97	388.38	386.70	386.09	385.87
24000	423.73	419.73	416.50	413.90	411.79	410.08	408.69	407.55	406.63	405.88	405.26	403.52	402.00	402.64
25000	441.39	437.22	433.86	431.15	428.95	427.17	425.72	424.54	423.57	422.79	422.15	420.33	419.66	419.42
26000	459.04	454.71	451.21	448.39	446.11	444.25	442.74	441.52	440.52	439.70	439.04	437.14	436.45	436.20
27000	476.70	472.19	468.57	465.64	463.26	461.34	459.77	458.50	457.46	456.61	455.92	453.96	453.24	452.97
28000	494.36	489.68	485.92	482.88	480.42	478.42	476.80	475.48	474.40	473.52	472.81	470.77	470.02	469.75
29000	512.01	507.17	503.27	500.13	497.58	495.51	493.83	492.46	491.35	490.44	489.69	487.58	486.81	486.53
30000	529.67	524.66	520.63	517.37	514.74	512.60	510.86	509.44	508.29	507.35	506.58	504.40	503.60	503.30
31000	547.32	542.15	537.98	534.62	531.89	529.68	527.89	526.42	525.23	524.26	523.47	521.21	520.38	520.08
32000	564.98	559.64	555.34	551.86	549.05	546.77	544.92	543.40	542.17	541.17	540.35	538.02	537.17	536.85
33000	582.63	577.13	572.69	569.11	566.21	563.86	561.94	560.39	559.12	558.08	557.24	554.84	553.96	553.63
34000	600.29	594.61	590.05	586.36	583.37	580.94	578.97	577.37	576.06	574.99	574.12	571.65	570.74	570.41
35000	617.94	612.10	607.40	603.60	600.53	598.03	596.00	594.35	593.00	591.90	591.01	588.46	587.53	587.18
36000	635.60	629.59	624.75	620.85	617.68	615.12	613.03	611.33	609.95	608.82	607.89	605.27	604.31	603.96
37000	653.25	647.08	642.11	638.09	634.84	632.20	630.06	628.31	626.89	625.73	624.78	622.09	621.10	620.74
38000	670.91	664.57	659.46	655.34	652.00	649.29	647.09	645.29	643.83	642.64	641.67	638.90	637.89	637.51
39000	688.56	682.06	676.82	672.58	669.16	666.38	664.11	662.27	660.77	659.55	658.55	655.71	654.67	654.29
40000	706.22	699.54	694.17	689.83	686.31	683.46	681.14	679.25	677.72	676.46	675.44	672.53	671.46	671.07
41000	723.88	717.03	711.52	707.08	703.47	700.55	698.17	696.24	694.66	693.37	692.32	689.34	688.25	687.84
42000	741.53	734.52	728.88	724.32	720.63	717.63	715.20	713.22	711.60	710.28	709.21	706.15	705.03	704.62
43000	759.19	752.01	746.23	741.57	737.79	734.72	732.23	730.20	728.54	727.20	726.09	722.97	721.82	721.40
44000	776.84	769.50	763.59	758.81	754.95	751.81	749.26	747.18	745.49	744.11	742.98	739.78	738.61	738.17
45000	794.50	786.99	780.94	776.06	772.10	768.89	766.28	764.16	762.43	761.02	759.87	756.59	755.39	754.95
46000	812.15	804.48	798.30	793.30	789.26	785.98	783.31	781.14	779.37	777.93	776.75	773.40	772.18	771.73
47000	829.81	821.97	815.65	810.55	806.42	803.07	800.34	798.12	796.32	794.84	793.64	790.22	788.96	788.50
48000	847.46	839.45	833.00	827.79	823.58	820.15	817.37	815.10	813.26	811.75	810.52	807.03	805.75	805.28
49000	865.12	856.94	850.36	845.04	840.73	837.24	834.40	832.09	830.20	828.66	827.41	823.84	822.54	822.06
50000	882.77	874.43	867.71	862.29	857.89	854.33	851.43	849.07	847.14	845.58	844.30	840.66	839.32	838.83
55000	971.05	961.87	954.48	948.51	943.68	939.76	936.57	933.97	931.86	930.13	928.72	924.72	923.26	922.72
60000	1059.33	1049.31	1041.25	1034.74	1029.47	1025.19	1021.71	1018.88	1016.57	1014.69	1013.15	1008.79	1007.19	1006.60
65000	1147.61	1136.76	1128.02	1120.97	1115.26	1110.62	1106.85	1103.79	1101.29	1099.25	1097.58	1092.85	1091.12	1090.48
70000	1235.88	1224.20	1214.79	1207.20	1201.05	1196.05	1192.00	1188.69	1186.00	1183.80	1182.01	1176.92	1175.05	1174.36
75000	1324.16	1311.64	1301.57	1293.43	1286.83	1281.49	1277.14	1273.60	1270.71	1268.36	1266.44	1260.98	1258.98	1258.25
80000	1412.44	1399.08	1388.34	1379.65	1372.62	1366.92	1362.28	1358.50	1355.43	1352.92	1350.87	1345.05	1342.91	1342.13
85000	1500.71	1486.53	1475.11	1465.88	1458.41	1452.35	1447.42	1443.41	1440.14	1437.48	1435.30	1429.11	1426.85	1426.01
90000	1588.99	1573.97	1561.88	1552.11	1544.20	1537.78	1532.56	1528.32	1524.86	1522.03	1519.73	1513.18	1510.78	1509.90
95000	1677.27	1661.41	1648.65	1638.34	1629.99	1623.21	1617.71	1613.22	1609.57	1606.59	1604.16	1597.24	1594.71	1593.78
100000	1765.54	1748.85	1735.42	1724.57	1715.78	1708.65	1702.85	1698.13	1694.28	1691.15	1688.59	1681.31	1678.64	1677.66

MONTHLY PAYMENT
REQUIRED TO AMORTIZE A LOAN

TERM	1 Year	2 Years	3 Years	4 Years	5 Years	6 Years	7 Years	8 Years	9 Years	10 Years	11 Years	12 Years	13 Years	14 Years
AMOUNT														
5	.47	.26	.19	.16	.14	.13	.12	.11	.11	.10	.10	.10	.10	.09
10	.93	.51	.38	.31	.27	.25	.23	.22	.21	.20	.19	.19	.19	.18
15	1.40	.77	.56	.46	.40	.37	.34	.32	.31	.30	.29	.28	.28	.27
25	2.32	1.28	.94	.77	.67	.61	.56	.53	.51	.49	.48	.47	.46	.45
50	4.64	2.55	1.87	1.53	1.34	1.21	1.12	1.06	1.01	.98	.95	.93	.91	.90
75	6.96	3.83	2.80	2.30	2.00	1.81	1.68	1.59	1.52	1.46	1.42	1.39	1.37	1.35
100	9.28	5.10	3.73	3.06	2.67	2.41	2.24	2.11	2.02	1.95	1.90	1.86	1.82	1.80
200	18.55	10.20	7.46	6.11	5.33	4.82	4.47	4.22	4.04	3.90	3.79	3.71	3.64	3.59
300	27.82	15.30	11.18	9.17	7.99	7.23	6.70	6.33	6.05	5.84	5.68	5.56	5.46	5.38
400	37.10	20.40	14.91	12.22	10.65	9.63	8.94	8.44	8.07	7.79	7.57	7.41	7.28	7.17
500	46.37	25.50	18.64	15.27	13.31	12.04	11.17	10.54	10.08	9.73	9.47	9.24	9.09	8.96
600	55.64	30.60	22.36	18.33	15.97	14.45	13.40	12.65	12.10	11.68	11.36	11.11	10.91	10.76
700	64.92	35.70	26.09	21.38	18.63	16.85	15.63	14.76	14.11	13.63	13.25	12.96	12.73	12.55
800	74.19	40.80	29.82	24.43	21.29	19.26	17.87	16.87	16.13	15.57	15.14	14.81	14.55	14.34
900	83.46	45.90	33.54	27.49	23.95	21.67	20.10	18.98	18.14	17.52	17.04	16.66	16.37	16.13
1000	92.74	51.00	37.27	30.54	26.61	24.07	22.33	21.08	20.16	19.46	18.93	18.51	18.18	17.92
2000	185.47	101.99	74.54	61.08	53.22	48.14	44.66	42.16	40.32	38.92	37.85	37.02	36.36	35.84
3000	278.20	152.99	111.80	91.62	79.82	72.21	66.99	63.24	60.47	58.38	56.77	55.52	54.54	53.76
4000	370.93	203.98	149.07	122.15	106.43	96.28	89.31	84.32	80.63	77.84	75.70	74.03	72.72	71.68
5000	463.66	254.97	186.33	152.69	133.03	120.35	111.64	105.40	100.78	97.30	94.62	92.53	90.89	89.60
6000	556.39	305.97	223.60	183.23	159.64	144.42	133.97	126.47	120.94	116.76	113.54	111.04	109.07	107.51
7000	649.12	356.96	260.86	213.76	186.24	168.49	156.29	147.55	141.09	136.21	132.46	129.55	127.25	125.43
8000	741.85	407.95	298.13	244.30	212.85	192.56	178.62	168.63	161.25	155.67	151.39	148.05	145.43	143.35
9000	834.58	458.95	335.40	274.84	239.45	216.63	200.95	189.71	181.40	175.13	170.31	166.56	163.61	161.27
10000	927.31	509.94	372.66	305.38	266.06	240.69	223.27	210.79	201.56	194.59	189.23	185.06	181.78	179.19
11000	1020.04	560.93	409.93	335.91	292.66	264.76	245.60	231.86	221.72	214.05	208.15	203.57	199.96	197.10
12000	1112.77	611.93	447.19	366.45	319.27	288.83	267.93	252.94	241.87	233.51	227.08	222.07	218.14	215.02
13000	1205.50	662.92	484.46	396.99	345.87	312.90	290.25	274.02	262.03	252.96	246.00	240.58	236.32	232.94
14000	1298.23	713.91	521.72	427.52	372.48	336.97	312.58	295.10	282.18	272.42	264.92	259.09	254.50	250.86
15000	1390.96	764.91	558.99	458.06	399.08	361.04	334.91	316.18	302.34	291.88	283.85	277.59	272.67	268.78
16000	1483.69	815.90	596.25	488.60	425.69	385.11	357.23	337.25	322.49	311.34	302.77	296.10	290.85	286.69
17000	1576.42	866.90	633.52	519.13	452.29	409.18	379.56	358.33	342.65	330.80	321.69	314.60	309.03	304.61
18000	1669.15	917.89	670.79	549.67	478.90	433.25	401.89	379.41	362.80	350.26	340.61	333.11	327.21	322.53
19000	1761.88	968.88	708.05	580.21	505.51	457.31	424.21	400.49	382.96	369.71	359.54	351.61	345.38	340.45
20000	1854.61	1019.88	745.32	610.75	532.11	481.38	446.54	421.57	403.11	389.17	378.46	370.12	363.56	358.37
21000	1947.34	1070.87	782.58	641.28	558.72	505.45	468.87	442.64	423.27	408.63	397.38	388.63	381.74	376.28
22000	2040.07	1121.86	819.85	671.82	585.32	529.52	491.19	463.72	443.43	428.09	416.30	407.13	399.92	394.20
23000	2132.80	1172.86	857.11	702.36	611.93	553.59	513.52	484.80	463.58	447.55	435.23	425.64	418.10	412.12
24000	2225.53	1223.85	894.38	732.89	638.53	577.66	535.85	505.88	483.74	467.01	454.15	444.14	436.27	430.04
25000	2318.26	1274.84	931.64	763.43	665.14	601.73	558.17	526.96	503.89	486.46	473.07	462.65	454.45	447.96
26000	2410.99	1325.84	968.91	793.97	691.74	625.80	580.50	548.04	524.05	505.92	491.99	481.15	472.63	465.88
27000	2503.72	1376.83	1006.18	824.50	718.35	649.87	602.83	569.11	544.20	525.38	510.92	499.66	490.81	483.79
28000	2596.45	1427.82	1043.44	855.04	744.95	673.93	625.15	590.19	564.36	544.84	529.84	518.17	508.99	501.71
29000	2689.18	1478.82	1080.71	885.58	771.56	698.00	647.48	611.27	584.51	564.30	548.76	536.67	527.16	519.63
30000	2781.91	1529.81	1117.97	916.12	798.16	722.07	669.81	632.35	604.67	583.76	567.69	555.18	545.34	537.55
31000	2874.64	1580.81	1155.24	946.65	824.77	746.14	692.14	653.43	624.82	603.21	586.61	573.68	563.52	555.47
32000	2967.37	1631.80	1192.50	977.19	851.37	770.21	714.46	674.50	644.98	622.67	605.53	592.19	581.70	573.38
33000	3060.10	1682.79	1229.77	1007.73	877.98	794.28	736.79	695.58	665.14	642.13	624.45	610.69	599.88	591.30
34000	3152.83	1733.79	1267.03	1038.26	904.58	818.35	759.12	716.66	685.29	661.59	643.38	629.20	618.05	609.22
35000	3245.56	1784.78	1304.30	1068.80	931.19	842.42	781.44	737.74	705.45	681.05	662.30	647.71	636.23	627.14
36000	3338.29	1835.77	1341.57	1099.34	957.80	866.49	803.77	758.82	725.60	700.51	681.22	666.21	654.41	645.06
37000	3431.02	1886.77	1378.83	1129.87	984.40	890.55	826.10	779.89	745.76	719.96	700.14	684.72	672.59	662.97
38000	3523.75	1937.76	1416.10	1160.41	1011.01	914.62	848.42	800.97	765.91	739.42	719.07	703.22	690.76	680.89
39000	3616.48	1988.75	1453.36	1190.95	1037.61	938.69	870.75	822.05	786.07	758.88	737.99	721.73	708.94	698.81
40000	3709.22	2039.75	1490.63	1221.49	1064.22	962.76	893.08	843.13	806.22	778.34	756.91	740.23	727.12	716.73
41000	3801.95	2090.74	1527.89	1252.02	1090.82	986.83	915.40	864.21	826.38	797.80	775.84	758.74	745.30	734.65
42000	3894.68	2141.73	1565.16	1282.56	1117.43	1010.90	937.73	885.28	846.53	817.26	794.76	777.25	763.48	752.56
43000	3987.41	2192.73	1602.42	1313.10	1144.03	1034.97	960.06	906.36	866.69	836.71	813.68	795.75	781.65	770.48
44000	4080.14	2243.72	1639.69	1343.63	1170.64	1059.04	982.38	927.44	886.85	856.17	832.60	814.26	799.83	788.40
45000	4172.87	2294.72	1676.96	1374.17	1197.24	1083.11	1004.71	948.52	907.00	875.63	851.53	832.76	818.01	806.32
46000	4265.60	2345.71	1714.22	1404.71	1223.85	1107.17	1027.04	969.60	927.16	895.09	870.45	851.27	836.19	824.24
47000	4358.33	2396.70	1751.49	1435.25	1250.45	1131.24	1049.36	990.68	947.31	914.55	889.37	869.77	854.37	842.15
48000	4451.06	2447.70	1788.75	1465.78	1277.06	1155.31	1071.69	1011.75	967.47	934.01	908.29	888.28	872.54	860.07
49000	4543.79	2498.69	1826.02	1496.32	1303.66	1179.38	1094.02	1032.83	987.62	953.46	927.22	906.79	890.72	877.99
50000	4636.52	2549.68	1863.28	1526.86	1330.27	1203.45	1116.34	1053.91	1007.78	972.92	946.14	925.29	908.90	895.91
55000	5100.17	2804.65	2049.61	1679.54	1463.30	1323.79	1227.98	1159.30	1108.56	1070.21	1040.75	1017.82	999.79	985.50
60000	5563.82	3059.62	2235.94	1832.23	1596.32	1444.14	1339.61	1264.69	1209.33	1167.51	1135.37	1110.35	1090.68	1075.09
65000	6027.47	3314.59	2422.27	1984.91	1729.35	1564.48	1451.25	1370.08	1310.11	1264.80	1229.98	1202.88	1181.57	1164.68
70000	6491.12	3569.55	2608.59	2137.60	1862.38	1684.83	1562.88	1475.47	1410.89	1362.09	1324.59	1295.41	1272.46	1254.27
75000	6954.77	3824.52	2794.92	2290.28	1995.40	1805.17	1674.51	1580.86	1511.67	1459.38	1419.21	1387.93	1363.35	1343.86
80000	7418.43	4079.49	2981.25	2442.97	2128.43	1925.52	1786.15	1686.25	1612.44	1556.67	1513.82	1480.46	1454.24	1433.45
85000	7882.08	4334.46	3167.58	2595.65	2261.45	2045.86	1897.78	1791.64	1713.22	1653.97	1608.43	1572.99	1545.13	1523.04
90000	8345.73	4589.43	3353.91	2748.34	2394.48	2166.21	2009.42	1897.03	1814.00	1751.26	1703.05	1665.52	1636.02	1612.63
95000	8809.38	4844.39	3540.23	2901.02	2527.51	2286.55	2121.05	2002.42	1914.77	1848.55	1797.66	1758.05	1726.90	1702.22
100000	9273.03	5099.36	3726.56	3053.71	2660.53	2406.89	2232.68	2107.81	2015.55	1945.84	1892.27	1850.58	1817.79	1791.81

MONTHLY PAYMENT
REQUIRED TO AMORTIZE A LOAN

20.200%

TERM	15 Years	16 Years	17 Years	18 Years	19 Years	20 Years	21 Years	22 Years	23 Years	24 Years	25 Years	30 Years	35 Years	40 Years
AMOUNT														
5	.09	.09	.09	.09	.09	.09	.09	.09	.09	.09	.09	.09	.09	.09
10	.18	.18	.18	.18	.18	.18	.18	.18	.18	.17	.17	.17	.17	.17
15	.27	.27	.27	.26	.26	.26	.26	.26	.26	.26	.26	.26	.26	.26
25	.45	.44	.44	.44	.44	.43	.43	.43	.43	.43	.43	.43	.43	.43
50	.89	.88	.88	.87	.87	.86	.86	.86	.86	.85	.85	.85	.85	.85
75	1.33	1.32	1.31	1.30	1.30	1.29	1.29	1.28	1.28	1.28	1.28	1.27	1.27	1.27
100	1.78	1.76	1.75	1.74	1.73	1.72	1.71	1.71	1.71	1.70	1.70	1.69	1.69	1.69
200	3.55	3.51	3.49	3.47	3.45	3.43	3.42	3.41	3.41	3.40	3.39	3.38	3.37	3.37
300	5.32	5.27	5.23	5.20	5.17	5.15	5.13	5.12	5.11	5.10	5.09	5.07	5.06	5.06
400	7.09	7.02	6.97	6.93	6.89	6.86	6.84	6.82	6.81	6.79	6.78	6.75	6.74	6.74
500	8.86	8.78	8.71	8.66	8.61	8.58	8.55	8.53	8.51	8.49	8.48	8.44	8.43	8.42
600	10.63	10.53	10.45	10.39	10.33	10.29	10.26	10.23	10.21	10.19	10.17	10.13	10.11	10.11
700	12.40	12.29	12.19	12.12	12.06	12.01	11.97	11.93	11.91	11.89	11.87	11.82	11.80	11.79
800	14.17	14.04	13.93	13.85	13.78	13.72	13.68	13.64	13.61	13.58	13.56	13.50	13.48	13.48
900	15.94	15.80	15.68	15.58	15.50	15.44	15.38	15.34	15.31	15.28	15.26	15.19	15.17	15.16
1000	17.72	17.55	17.42	17.31	17.22	17.15	17.09	17.05	17.01	16.98	16.95	16.88	16.85	16.84
2000	35.43	35.09	34.83	34.61	34.44	34.30	34.18	34.09	34.01	33.95	33.90	33.75	33.70	33.68
3000	53.14	52.64	52.24	51.92	51.65	51.44	51.27	51.13	51.01	50.92	50.84	50.63	50.55	50.52
4000	70.85	70.18	69.65	69.22	68.87	68.59	68.36	68.17	68.02	67.89	67.79	67.50	67.40	67.36
5000	88.56	87.73	87.06	86.52	86.09	85.73	85.44	85.21	85.02	84.86	84.74	84.38	84.25	84.20
6000	106.27	105.27	104.47	103.83	103.30	102.88	102.53	102.25	102.02	101.84	101.68	101.25	101.10	101.04
7000	123.98	122.82	121.88	121.13	120.52	120.02	119.62	119.29	119.03	118.81	118.63	118.13	117.94	117.88
8000	141.69	140.36	139.30	138.43	137.73	137.17	136.71	136.33	136.03	135.78	135.58	135.00	134.79	134.72
9000	159.40	157.91	156.71	155.74	154.95	154.31	153.80	153.37	153.03	152.75	152.52	151.88	151.64	151.56
10000	177.11	175.45	174.12	173.04	172.17	171.46	170.88	170.42	170.03	169.72	169.47	168.75	168.49	168.39
11000	194.82	193.00	191.53	190.34	189.38	188.60	187.97	187.46	187.04	186.70	186.42	185.63	185.34	185.23
12000	212.54	210.54	208.94	207.65	206.60	205.75	205.06	204.50	204.04	203.67	203.36	202.50	202.19	202.07
13000	230.25	228.09	226.35	224.95	223.81	222.89	222.15	221.54	221.04	220.64	220.31	219.38	219.04	218.91
14000	247.96	245.63	243.76	242.25	241.03	240.04	239.24	238.58	238.05	237.61	237.26	236.25	235.88	235.75
15000	265.67	263.18	261.17	259.56	258.25	257.19	256.32	255.62	255.05	254.58	254.20	253.13	252.73	252.59
16000	283.38	280.72	278.59	276.86	275.46	274.33	273.41	272.66	272.05	271.56	271.15	270.00	269.58	269.43
17000	301.09	298.27	296.00	294.16	292.68	291.48	290.50	289.70	289.06	288.53	288.10	286.88	286.43	286.27
18000	318.80	315.81	313.41	311.47	309.90	308.62	307.59	306.74	306.06	305.50	305.04	303.75	303.28	303.11
19000	336.51	333.36	330.82	328.77	327.11	325.77	324.67	323.79	323.06	322.47	321.99	320.63	320.13	319.94
20000	354.22	350.90	348.23	346.07	344.33	342.91	341.76	340.83	340.06	339.44	338.94	337.50	336.98	336.78
21000	371.93	368.45	365.64	363.38	361.54	360.06	358.85	357.87	357.07	356.42	355.88	354.38	353.82	353.62
22000	389.64	385.99	383.05	380.68	378.76	377.20	375.94	374.91	374.07	373.39	372.83	371.25	370.67	370.46
23000	407.36	403.54	400.46	397.98	395.98	394.35	393.03	391.95	391.07	390.36	389.78	388.12	387.52	387.30
24000	425.07	421.08	417.88	415.29	413.19	411.49	410.11	408.99	408.08	407.33	406.72	405.00	404.37	404.14
25000	442.78	438.63	435.29	432.59	430.41	428.64	427.20	426.03	425.08	424.30	423.67	421.87	421.22	420.98
26000	460.49	456.17	452.70	449.89	447.62	445.78	444.29	443.07	442.08	441.28	440.62	438.75	438.07	437.82
27000	478.20	473.72	470.11	467.20	464.84	462.93	461.38	460.11	459.09	458.25	457.56	455.62	454.92	454.66
28000	495.91	491.26	487.52	484.50	482.06	480.08	478.47	477.16	476.09	475.22	474.51	472.50	471.76	471.49
29000	513.62	508.81	504.93	501.80	499.27	497.22	495.55	494.20	493.09	492.19	491.46	489.37	488.61	488.33
30000	531.33	526.35	522.34	519.11	516.49	514.37	512.64	511.24	510.09	509.16	508.40	506.25	505.46	505.17
31000	549.04	543.90	539.75	536.41	533.71	531.51	529.73	528.28	527.10	526.14	525.35	523.12	522.31	522.01
32000	566.75	561.44	557.17	553.71	550.92	548.66	546.82	545.32	544.10	543.11	542.30	540.00	539.16	538.85
33000	584.46	578.99	574.58	571.02	568.14	565.80	563.90	562.36	561.10	560.08	559.24	556.87	556.01	555.69
34000	602.18	596.53	591.99	588.32	585.35	582.95	580.99	579.40	578.11	577.05	576.19	573.75	572.85	572.53
35000	619.89	614.08	609.40	605.62	602.57	600.09	598.08	596.44	595.11	594.02	593.14	590.62	589.70	589.37
36000	637.60	631.62	626.81	622.93	619.79	617.24	615.17	613.48	612.11	610.99	610.08	607.50	606.55	606.21
37000	655.31	649.16	644.22	640.23	637.00	634.38	632.26	630.53	629.12	627.97	627.03	624.37	623.40	623.04
38000	673.02	666.71	661.63	657.54	654.22	651.53	649.34	647.57	646.12	644.94	643.98	641.25	640.25	639.88
39000	690.73	684.25	679.04	674.84	671.43	668.67	666.43	664.61	663.12	661.91	660.92	658.12	657.10	656.72
40000	708.44	701.80	696.46	692.14	688.65	685.82	683.52	681.65	680.12	678.88	677.87	675.00	673.95	673.56
41000	726.15	719.34	713.87	709.45	705.87	702.97	700.61	698.69	697.13	695.85	694.82	691.87	690.79	690.40
42000	743.86	736.89	731.28	726.75	723.08	720.11	717.70	715.73	714.13	712.83	711.76	708.75	707.64	707.24
43000	761.57	754.43	748.69	744.05	740.30	737.26	734.78	732.77	731.13	729.80	728.71	725.62	724.49	724.08
44000	779.28	771.98	766.10	761.36	757.52	754.40	751.87	749.81	748.14	746.77	745.66	742.49	741.34	740.92
45000	797.00	789.52	783.51	778.66	774.73	771.55	768.96	766.85	765.14	763.74	762.60	759.37	758.19	757.76
46000	814.71	807.07	800.92	795.96	791.95	788.69	786.05	783.90	782.14	780.71	779.55	776.24	775.04	774.59
47000	832.42	824.61	818.33	813.27	809.16	805.84	803.13	800.94	799.15	797.69	796.50	793.12	791.89	791.43
48000	850.13	842.16	835.75	830.57	826.38	822.98	820.22	817.98	816.15	814.66	813.44	809.99	808.73	808.27
49000	867.84	859.70	853.16	847.87	843.60	840.13	837.31	835.02	833.15	831.63	830.39	826.87	825.58	825.11
50000	885.55	877.25	870.57	865.18	860.81	857.27	854.40	852.06	850.15	848.60	847.34	843.74	842.43	841.95
55000	974.10	964.97	957.62	951.69	946.89	943.00	939.84	937.27	935.17	933.46	932.07	928.12	926.67	926.15
60000	1062.66	1052.70	1044.68	1038.21	1032.97	1028.73	1025.28	1022.47	1020.18	1018.32	1016.80	1012.49	1010.92	1010.34
65000	1151.21	1140.42	1131.74	1124.73	1119.05	1114.45	1110.72	1107.68	1105.20	1103.18	1101.53	1096.86	1095.16	1094.53
70000	1239.77	1228.15	1218.79	1211.24	1205.14	1200.18	1196.16	1192.88	1190.21	1188.04	1186.27	1181.24	1179.40	1178.73
75000	1328.32	1315.87	1305.85	1297.76	1291.22	1285.91	1281.60	1278.09	1275.23	1272.90	1271.00	1265.61	1263.64	1262.92
80000	1416.88	1403.60	1392.91	1384.28	1377.30	1371.63	1367.03	1363.29	1360.24	1357.76	1355.73	1349.99	1347.89	1347.12
85000	1505.43	1491.32	1479.96	1470.80	1463.38	1457.36	1452.47	1448.50	1445.26	1442.62	1440.47	1434.36	1432.13	1431.31
90000	1593.99	1579.04	1567.02	1557.31	1549.46	1543.09	1537.91	1533.70	1530.27	1527.48	1525.20	1518.73	1516.37	1515.51
95000	1682.54	1666.77	1654.08	1643.83	1635.54	1628.81	1623.35	1618.91	1615.29	1612.34	1609.93	1603.11	1600.62	1599.70
100000	1771.10	1754.49	1741.13	1730.35	1721.62	1714.54	1708.79	1704.11	1700.30	1697.20	1694.67	1687.48	1684.86	1683.90

MONTHLY PAYMENT
REQUIRED TO AMORTIZE A LOAN

TERM AMOUNT	1 Year	2 Years	3 Years	4 Years	5 Years	6 Years	7 Years	8 Years	9 Years	10 Years	11 Years	12 Years	13 Years	14 Years
5	.47	.26	.19	.16	.14	.13	.12	.11	.11	.10	.10	.10	.10	.09
10	.93	.52	.38	.31	.27	.25	.23	.22	.21	.20	.19	.19	.19	.18
15	1.40	.77	.56	.46	.40	.37	.34	.32	.31	.30	.29	.28	.28	.27
25	2.32	1.28	.94	.77	.67	.61	.56	.53	.51	.49	.48	.47	.46	.45
50	4.64	2.56	1.87	1.53	1.34	1.21	1.12	1.06	1.01	.98	.95	.93	.92	.90
75	6.96	3.83	2.80	2.30	2.00	1.81	1.68	1.59	1.52	1.47	1.43	1.40	1.37	1.35
100	9.28	5.11	3.73	3.06	2.67	2.41	2.24	2.12	2.02	1.95	1.90	1.86	1.83	1.80
200	18.56	10.21	7.46	6.12	5.33	4.82	4.48	4.23	4.04	3.90	3.80	3.71	3.65	3.60
300	27.83	15.31	11.19	9.17	7.99	7.23	6.71	6.34	6.06	5.85	5.69	5.57	5.47	5.39
400	37.11	20.41	14.92	12.23	10.66	9.64	8.95	8.45	8.08	7.80	7.59	7.42	7.29	7.19
500	46.38	25.51	18.65	15.29	13.32	12.05	11.18	10.56	10.10	9.75	9.48	9.28	9.11	8.98
600	55.66	30.62	22.38	18.34	15.98	14.46	13.42	12.67	12.12	11.70	11.38	11.13	10.93	10.78
700	64.93	35.72	26.11	21.40	18.65	16.87	15.65	14.78	14.14	13.65	13.27	12.98	12.75	12.57
800	74.21	40.82	29.84	24.46	21.31	19.28	17.89	16.89	16.16	15.60	15.17	14.84	14.58	14.37
900	83.48	45.92	33.57	27.51	23.97	21.69	20.13	19.00	18.17	17.55	17.07	16.69	16.40	16.16
1000	92.76	51.02	37.30	30.57	26.64	24.10	22.36	21.11	20.19	19.50	18.96	18.55	18.22	17.96
2000	185.51	102.04	74.59	61.13	53.27	48.20	44.72	42.22	40.38	38.99	37.92	37.09	36.43	35.91
3000	278.27	153.06	111.88	91.70	79.90	72.30	67.08	63.33	60.57	58.48	56.88	55.63	54.65	53.87
4000	371.02	204.08	149.17	122.26	106.54	96.40	89.43	84.44	80.76	77.97	75.83	74.17	72.86	71.82
5000	463.78	255.10	186.46	152.82	133.17	120.49	111.79	105.55	100.94	97.46	94.79	92.71	91.07	89.78
6000	556.53	306.11	223.75	183.39	159.80	144.59	134.15	126.66	121.13	116.95	113.75	111.25	109.29	107.73
7000	649.28	357.13	261.04	213.95	186.44	168.69	156.50	147.77	141.32	136.45	132.70	129.79	127.50	125.69
8000	742.04	408.15	298.33	244.51	213.07	192.79	178.86	168.88	161.51	155.94	151.66	148.33	145.71	143.64
9000	834.79	459.17	335.62	275.08	239.70	216.89	201.22	189.99	181.69	175.43	170.62	166.87	163.93	161.60
10000	927.55	510.19	372.92	305.64	266.34	240.98	223.57	211.10	201.88	194.92	189.57	185.41	182.14	179.55
11000	1020.30	561.20	410.21	336.21	292.97	265.08	245.93	232.21	222.07	214.41	208.53	203.95	200.35	197.50
12000	1113.06	612.22	447.50	366.77	319.60	289.18	268.29	253.32	242.26	233.90	227.49	222.49	218.57	215.46
13000	1205.81	663.24	484.79	397.33	346.24	313.28	290.65	274.43	262.45	253.40	246.44	241.03	236.78	233.41
14000	1298.56	714.26	522.08	427.90	372.87	337.38	313.00	295.54	282.63	272.89	265.40	259.57	255.00	251.37
15000	1391.32	765.28	559.37	458.46	399.50	361.47	335.36	316.65	302.82	292.38	284.36	278.12	273.21	269.32
16000	1484.07	816.29	596.66	489.02	426.14	385.57	357.72	337.75	323.01	311.87	303.31	296.66	291.42	287.28
17000	1576.83	867.31	633.95	519.59	452.77	409.67	380.07	358.86	343.20	331.36	322.27	315.20	309.64	305.23
18000	1669.58	918.33	671.24	550.15	479.40	433.77	402.43	379.97	363.38	350.85	341.23	333.74	327.85	323.19
19000	1762.33	969.35	708.54	580.72	506.04	457.87	424.79	401.08	383.57	370.35	360.18	352.28	346.06	341.14
20000	1855.09	1020.37	745.83	611.28	532.67	481.96	447.14	422.19	403.76	389.84	379.14	370.82	364.28	359.09
21000	1947.84	1071.38	783.12	641.84	559.30	506.06	469.50	443.30	423.95	409.33	398.10	389.36	382.49	377.05
22000	2040.60	1122.40	820.41	672.41	585.93	530.16	491.86	464.41	444.14	428.82	417.06	407.90	400.70	395.00
23000	2133.35	1173.42	857.70	702.97	612.57	554.26	514.22	485.52	464.32	448.31	436.01	426.44	418.92	412.96
24000	2226.11	1224.44	894.99	733.53	639.20	578.36	536.57	506.63	484.51	467.80	454.97	444.98	437.13	430.91
25000	2318.86	1275.46	932.28	764.10	665.83	602.45	558.93	527.74	504.70	487.30	473.93	463.52	455.35	448.87
26000	2411.61	1326.47	969.57	794.66	692.47	626.55	581.29	548.85	524.89	506.79	492.88	482.06	473.56	466.82
27000	2504.37	1377.49	1006.86	825.23	719.10	650.65	603.64	569.96	545.07	526.28	511.84	500.60	491.77	484.78
28000	2597.12	1428.51	1044.16	855.79	745.73	674.75	626.00	591.07	565.26	545.77	530.80	519.15	509.99	502.73
29000	2689.88	1479.53	1081.45	886.35	772.37	698.85	648.36	612.18	585.45	565.26	549.75	537.69	528.20	520.69
30000	2782.63	1530.55	1118.74	916.92	799.00	722.94	670.71	633.29	605.64	584.75	568.71	556.23	546.41	538.64
31000	2875.39	1581.56	1156.03	947.48	825.63	747.04	693.07	654.40	625.83	604.24	587.67	574.77	564.63	556.59
32000	2968.14	1632.58	1193.32	978.04	852.27	771.14	715.43	675.50	646.01	623.74	606.62	593.31	582.84	574.55
33000	3060.89	1683.60	1230.61	1008.61	878.90	795.24	737.79	696.61	666.20	643.23	625.58	611.85	601.05	592.50
34000	3153.65	1734.62	1267.90	1039.17	905.53	819.34	760.14	717.72	686.39	662.72	644.54	630.39	619.27	610.46
35000	3246.40	1785.64	1305.19	1069.74	932.17	843.43	782.50	738.83	706.58	682.21	663.49	648.93	637.48	628.41
36000	3339.16	1836.65	1342.48	1100.30	958.80	867.53	804.86	759.94	726.76	701.70	682.45	667.47	655.70	646.37
37000	3431.91	1887.67	1379.78	1130.86	985.43	891.63	827.21	781.05	746.95	721.19	701.41	686.01	673.91	664.32
38000	3524.66	1938.69	1417.07	1161.43	1012.07	915.73	849.57	802.16	767.14	740.69	720.36	704.55	692.12	682.28
39000	3617.42	1989.71	1454.36	1191.99	1038.70	939.83	871.93	823.27	787.33	760.18	739.32	723.09	710.34	700.23
40000	3710.17	2040.73	1491.65	1222.55	1065.33	963.92	894.28	844.38	807.52	779.67	758.28	741.63	728.55	718.18
41000	3802.93	2091.74	1528.94	1253.12	1091.97	988.02	916.64	865.49	827.70	799.16	777.24	760.17	746.76	736.14
42000	3895.68	2142.76	1566.23	1283.68	1118.60	1012.12	939.00	886.60	847.89	818.65	796.19	778.71	764.98	754.09
43000	3988.44	2193.78	1603.52	1314.24	1145.23	1036.22	961.35	907.71	868.08	838.14	815.15	797.25	783.19	772.05
44000	4081.19	2244.80	1640.81	1344.81	1171.86	1060.32	983.71	928.82	888.27	857.64	834.11	815.80	801.40	790.00
45000	4173.94	2295.82	1678.10	1375.37	1198.50	1084.41	1006.07	949.93	908.45	877.13	853.06	834.34	819.62	807.96
46000	4266.70	2346.83	1715.40	1405.94	1225.13	1108.51	1028.43	971.04	928.64	896.62	872.02	852.88	837.83	825.91
47000	4359.45	2397.85	1752.69	1436.50	1251.76	1132.61	1050.78	992.15	948.83	916.11	890.98	871.42	856.04	843.87
48000	4452.21	2448.87	1789.98	1467.06	1278.40	1156.71	1073.14	1013.25	969.02	935.60	909.93	889.96	874.26	861.82
49000	4544.96	2499.89	1827.27	1497.63	1305.03	1180.81	1095.50	1034.36	989.21	955.09	928.89	908.50	892.47	879.78
50000	4637.71	2550.91	1864.56	1528.19	1331.66	1204.90	1117.85	1055.47	1009.39	974.59	947.85	927.04	910.69	897.73
55000	5101.49	2806.00	2051.01	1681.01	1464.83	1325.39	1229.64	1161.02	1110.33	1072.04	1042.63	1019.74	1001.75	987.50
60000	5565.26	3061.09	2237.47	1833.83	1598.00	1445.88	1341.42	1266.57	1211.27	1169.50	1137.42	1112.45	1092.82	1077.27
65000	6029.03	3316.18	2423.93	1986.65	1731.16	1566.37	1453.21	1372.11	1312.21	1266.96	1232.20	1205.15	1183.89	1167.05
70000	6492.80	3571.27	2610.38	2139.47	1864.33	1686.86	1564.99	1477.66	1413.15	1364.42	1326.98	1297.85	1274.96	1256.82
75000	6956.57	3826.36	2796.84	2292.28	1997.49	1807.35	1676.78	1583.21	1514.09	1461.88	1421.77	1390.56	1366.03	1346.59
80000	7420.34	4081.45	2983.29	2445.10	2130.66	1927.84	1788.56	1688.75	1615.03	1559.33	1516.55	1483.26	1457.09	1436.36
85000	7884.11	4336.54	3169.75	2597.92	2263.83	2048.33	1900.35	1794.30	1715.97	1656.79	1611.34	1575.96	1548.16	1526.14
90000	8347.88	4591.63	3356.20	2750.74	2396.99	2168.82	2012.13	1899.85	1816.90	1754.25	1706.12	1668.67	1639.23	1615.91
95000	8811.65	4846.72	3542.66	2903.56	2530.16	2289.31	2123.92	2005.39	1917.84	1851.71	1800.90	1761.37	1730.30	1705.68
100000	9275.43	5101.81	3729.11	3056.38	2663.32	2409.80	2235.70	2110.94	2018.78	1949.17	1895.69	1854.07	1821.37	1795.45

MONTHLY PAYMENT
REQUIRED TO AMORTIZE A LOAN

20.250%

TERM AMOUNT	15 Years	16 Years	17 Years	18 Years	19 Years	20 Years	21 Years	22 Years	23 Years	24 Years	25 Years	30 Years	35 Years	40 Years
5	.09	.09	.09	.09	.09	.09	.09	.09	.09	.09	.09	.09	.09	.09
10	.18	.18	.18	.18	.18	.18	.18	.18	.18	.18	.17	.17	.17	.17
15	.27	.27	.27	.27	.26	.26	.26	.26	.26	.26	.26	.26	.26	.26
25	.45	.44	.44	.44	.44	.43	.43	.43	.43	.43	.43	.43	.43	.43
50	.89	.88	.88	.87	.87	.86	.86	.86	.86	.86	.85	.85	.85	.85
75	1.34	1.32	1.31	1.31	1.30	1.29	1.29	1.29	1.28	1.28	1.28	1.27	1.27	1.27
100	1.78	1.76	1.75	1.74	1.73	1.72	1.72	1.71	1.71	1.71	1.70	1.70	1.69	1.69
200	3.55	3.52	3.49	3.47	3.46	3.44	3.43	3.42	3.41	3.41	3.40	3.39	3.38	3.38
300	5.33	5.28	5.24	5.21	5.18	5.16	5.14	5.13	5.12	5.11	5.10	5.08	5.07	5.07
400	7.10	7.04	6.98	6.94	6.91	6.88	6.86	6.84	6.82	6.81	6.80	6.77	6.76	6.76
500	8.88	8.80	8.73	8.68	8.63	8.60	8.57	8.53	8.53	8.51	8.50	8.46	8.45	8.45
600	10.65	10.55	10.47	10.41	10.36	10.32	10.28	10.25	10.23	10.21	10.20	10.15	10.14	10.13
700	12.43	12.31	12.22	12.14	12.08	12.03	11.99	11.96	11.94	11.91	11.90	11.85	11.83	11.82
800	14.20	14.07	13.96	13.88	13.81	13.75	13.71	13.67	13.64	13.61	13.59	13.54	13.52	13.51
900	15.98	15.83	15.71	15.61	15.53	15.47	15.42	15.38	15.34	15.32	15.29	15.23	15.21	15.20
1000	17.75	17.59	17.45	17.35	17.26	17.19	17.13	17.09	17.05	17.02	16.99	16.92	16.89	16.89
2000	35.50	35.17	34.90	34.69	34.52	34.37	34.26	34.17	34.09	34.03	33.98	33.84	33.78	33.77
3000	53.25	52.75	52.35	52.03	51.77	51.56	51.39	51.25	51.13	51.04	50.97	50.75	50.67	50.65
4000	71.00	70.33	69.80	69.37	69.03	68.74	68.52	68.33	68.18	68.05	67.95	67.67	67.56	67.53
5000	88.74	87.92	87.25	86.71	86.28	85.93	85.64	85.41	85.22	85.07	84.94	84.58	84.45	84.41
6000	106.49	105.50	104.70	104.06	103.54	103.11	102.77	102.49	102.26	102.08	101.93	101.50	101.34	101.29
7000	124.24	123.08	122.15	121.40	120.79	120.30	119.90	119.57	119.31	119.09	118.92	118.42	118.23	118.17
8000	141.99	140.66	139.60	138.74	138.05	137.48	137.03	136.65	136.35	136.10	135.90	135.33	135.12	135.05
9000	159.74	158.25	157.05	156.08	155.30	154.67	154.15	153.73	153.39	153.12	152.89	152.25	152.01	151.93
10000	177.48	175.83	174.50	173.42	172.56	171.85	171.28	170.82	170.44	170.13	169.88	169.16	168.90	168.81
11000	195.23	193.41	191.95	190.77	189.81	189.04	188.41	187.90	187.48	187.14	186.86	186.08	185.79	185.69
12000	212.98	210.99	209.40	208.11	207.07	206.22	205.54	204.98	204.52	204.15	203.85	203.00	202.68	202.57
13000	230.73	228.58	226.85	225.45	224.32	223.41	222.66	222.06	221.57	221.17	220.84	219.91	219.57	219.45
14000	248.48	246.16	244.30	242.79	241.58	240.59	239.79	239.14	238.61	238.18	237.83	236.83	236.46	236.33
15000	266.22	263.74	261.75	260.13	258.83	257.78	256.92	256.22	255.65	255.19	254.81	253.74	253.35	253.21
16000	283.97	281.32	279.20	277.48	276.09	274.96	274.05	273.30	272.70	272.20	271.80	270.66	270.24	270.09
17000	301.72	298.91	296.64	294.82	293.34	292.14	291.17	290.38	289.74	289.21	288.79	287.58	287.13	286.97
18000	319.47	316.49	314.09	312.16	310.60	309.33	308.30	307.46	306.78	306.23	305.77	304.49	304.02	303.85
19000	337.22	334.07	331.54	329.50	327.85	326.51	325.43	324.54	323.82	323.24	322.76	321.41	320.91	320.73
20000	354.96	351.65	348.99	346.84	345.11	343.70	342.56	341.63	340.87	340.25	339.75	338.32	337.80	337.61
21000	372.71	369.24	366.44	364.19	362.36	360.88	359.68	358.71	357.91	357.26	356.74	355.24	354.69	354.50
22000	390.46	386.82	383.89	381.53	379.62	378.07	376.81	375.79	374.95	374.28	373.72	372.16	371.58	371.38
23000	408.21	404.40	401.34	398.87	396.87	395.25	393.94	392.87	392.00	391.29	390.71	389.07	388.47	388.26
24000	425.96	421.98	418.79	416.21	414.13	412.44	411.07	409.95	409.04	408.30	407.70	405.99	405.36	405.14
25000	443.70	439.57	436.24	433.55	431.38	429.62	428.19	427.03	426.08	425.31	424.60	422.90	422.25	422.02
26000	461.45	457.15	453.69	450.90	448.64	446.81	445.32	444.11	443.13	442.33	441.67	439.82	439.14	438.90
27000	479.20	474.73	471.14	468.24	465.89	463.99	462.45	461.19	460.17	459.34	458.66	456.73	456.03	455.78
28000	496.95	492.31	488.59	485.58	483.15	481.18	479.58	478.27	477.21	476.35	475.65	473.65	472.92	472.66
29000	514.70	509.90	506.04	502.92	500.40	498.36	496.70	495.35	494.26	493.36	492.63	490.57	489.81	489.54
30000	532.44	527.48	523.49	520.26	517.66	515.55	513.83	512.44	511.30	510.37	509.62	507.48	506.70	506.42
31000	550.19	545.06	540.94	537.61	534.91	532.73	530.96	529.52	528.34	527.39	526.61	524.40	523.59	523.30
32000	567.94	562.64	558.38	554.95	552.17	549.92	548.09	546.60	545.39	544.40	543.59	541.31	540.48	540.18
33000	585.69	580.23	575.83	572.29	569.42	567.10	565.21	563.68	562.43	561.41	560.58	558.23	557.37	557.06
34000	603.44	597.81	593.28	589.63	586.68	584.28	582.34	580.76	579.47	578.42	577.57	575.15	574.26	573.94
35000	621.18	615.39	610.73	606.97	603.93	601.47	599.47	597.84	596.52	595.44	594.56	592.06	591.15	590.82
36000	638.93	632.97	628.18	624.32	621.19	618.65	616.60	614.92	613.56	612.45	611.54	608.98	608.04	607.70
37000	656.68	650.56	645.63	641.66	638.44	635.84	633.72	632.00	630.60	629.46	628.53	625.89	624.93	624.58
38000	674.43	668.14	663.08	659.00	655.70	653.02	650.85	649.08	647.64	646.47	645.52	642.81	641.82	641.46
39000	692.17	685.72	680.53	676.34	672.95	670.21	667.98	666.16	664.69	663.49	662.50	659.73	658.71	658.34
40000	709.92	703.30	697.98	693.68	690.21	687.39	685.11	683.25	681.73	680.50	679.49	676.64	675.60	675.22
41000	727.67	720.89	715.43	711.03	707.46	704.58	702.23	700.33	698.77	697.51	696.48	693.56	692.49	692.10
42000	745.42	738.47	732.88	728.37	724.72	721.76	719.36	717.41	715.82	714.52	713.47	710.47	709.38	708.99
43000	763.17	756.05	750.33	745.71	741.97	738.95	736.49	734.49	732.86	731.53	730.45	727.39	726.27	725.87
44000	780.91	773.63	767.78	763.05	759.23	756.13	753.62	751.57	749.90	748.55	747.44	744.31	743.16	742.75
45000	798.66	791.22	785.23	780.39	776.49	773.32	770.74	768.65	766.95	765.56	764.43	761.22	760.05	759.63
46000	816.41	808.80	802.68	797.74	793.74	790.50	787.87	785.73	783.99	782.57	781.41	778.14	776.94	776.51
47000	834.16	826.38	820.13	815.08	811.00	807.69	805.00	802.81	801.03	799.58	798.40	795.05	793.83	793.39
48000	851.91	843.96	837.58	832.42	828.25	824.87	822.13	819.89	818.08	816.60	815.39	811.97	810.72	810.27
49000	869.65	861.55	855.02	849.76	845.51	842.05	839.25	836.97	835.12	833.61	832.38	828.89	827.61	827.15
50000	887.40	879.13	872.47	867.10	862.76	859.24	856.38	854.06	852.16	850.62	849.36	845.80	844.50	844.03
55000	976.14	967.04	959.72	953.81	949.04	945.16	942.02	939.46	937.38	935.68	934.30	930.38	928.95	928.43
60000	1064.88	1054.95	1046.97	1040.52	1035.31	1031.09	1027.66	1024.87	1022.59	1020.74	1019.23	1014.96	1013.40	1012.83
65000	1153.62	1142.87	1134.21	1127.23	1121.59	1117.01	1113.29	1110.27	1107.81	1105.81	1104.17	1099.54	1097.85	1097.24
70000	1242.36	1230.78	1221.46	1213.94	1207.86	1202.93	1198.93	1195.68	1193.03	1190.87	1189.11	1184.12	1182.30	1181.64
75000	1331.10	1318.69	1308.71	1300.65	1294.14	1288.86	1284.57	1281.08	1278.24	1275.93	1274.04	1268.70	1266.75	1266.04
80000	1419.84	1406.60	1395.96	1387.36	1380.41	1374.78	1370.21	1366.49	1363.46	1360.99	1358.98	1353.28	1351.20	1350.44
85000	1508.58	1494.51	1483.20	1474.07	1466.69	1460.70	1455.84	1451.89	1448.67	1446.05	1443.91	1437.86	1435.65	1434.85
90000	1597.32	1582.43	1570.45	1560.78	1546.97	1546.63	1541.48	1537.30	1533.89	1531.11	1528.85	1522.44	1520.10	1519.25
95000	1686.06	1670.34	1657.70	1647.49	1639.24	1632.55	1627.12	1622.70	1619.10	1616.17	1613.79	1607.02	1604.55	1603.65
100000	1774.80	1758.25	1744.94	1734.20	1725.52	1718.47	1712.76	1708.11	1704.32	1701.24	1698.72	1691.60	1689.00	1688.05

MONTHLY PAYMENT
REQUIRED TO AMORTIZE A LOAN

TERM AMOUNT	1 Year	2 Years	3 Years	4 Years	5 Years	6 Years	7 Years	8 Years	9 Years	10 Years	11 Years	12 Years	13 Years	14 Years
5	.47	.26	.19	.16	.14	.13	.12	.11	.11	.10	.10	.10	.10	.09
10	.93	.52	.38	.31	.27	.25	.23	.22	.21	.20	.19	.19	.19	.18
15	1.40	.77	.56	.46	.40	.37	.34	.32	.31	.30	.29	.28	.28	.27
25	2.32	1.28	.94	.77	.67	.61	.56	.53	.51	.49	.48	.47	.46	.45
50	4.64	2.56	1.87	1.53	1.34	1.21	1.12	1.06	1.02	.98	.95	.93	.92	.90
75	6.96	3.83	2.80	2.30	2.00	1.81	1.68	1.59	1.52	1.47	1.43	1.40	1.37	1.35
100	9.28	5.11	3.74	3.06	2.67	2.42	2.24	2.12	2.03	1.96	1.90	1.86	1.83	1.80
200	18.56	10.21	7.47	6.12	5.34	4.83	4.48	4.23	4.05	3.91	3.80	3.72	3.65	3.60
300	27.84	15.32	11.20	9.18	8.00	7.24	6.72	6.35	6.07	5.86	5.70	5.58	5.48	5.40
400	37.12	20.42	14.93	12.24	10.67	9.66	8.96	8.46	8.09	7.81	7.60	7.44	7.30	7.20
500	46.39	25.53	18.66	15.30	13.34	12.07	11.20	10.58	10.12	9.77	9.50	9.29	9.13	9.00
600	55.67	30.63	22.39	18.36	16.00	14.48	13.44	12.69	12.14	11.72	11.40	11.15	10.95	10.80
700	64.95	35.73	26.13	21.42	18.67	16.89	15.68	14.80	14.16	13.67	13.30	13.01	12.78	12.60
800	74.23	40.84	29.86	24.48	21.33	19.31	17.91	16.92	16.18	15.62	15.20	14.87	14.60	14.40
900	83.51	45.94	33.59	27.54	24.00	21.72	20.15	19.03	18.20	17.58	17.10	16.72	16.43	16.20
1000	92.78	51.05	37.32	30.60	26.67	24.13	22.39	21.15	20.23	19.53	19.00	18.58	18.25	18.00
2000	185.56	102.09	74.64	61.19	53.33	48.26	44.78	42.29	40.45	39.05	37.99	37.16	36.50	35.99
3000	278.34	153.13	111.95	91.78	79.99	72.39	67.17	63.43	60.67	58.58	56.98	55.73	54.75	53.98
4000	371.12	204.17	149.27	122.37	106.65	96.51	89.55	84.57	80.89	78.10	75.97	74.31	73.00	71.97
5000	463.90	255.22	186.59	152.96	133.31	120.64	111.94	105.71	101.11	97.63	94.96	92.88	91.25	89.96
6000	556.67	306.26	223.90	183.55	159.97	144.77	134.33	126.85	121.33	117.15	113.95	111.46	109.50	107.95
7000	649.45	357.30	261.22	214.14	186.63	168.89	156.72	147.99	141.55	136.68	132.94	130.03	127.75	125.94
8000	742.23	408.34	298.54	244.73	213.29	193.02	179.10	169.13	161.77	156.20	151.93	148.61	146.00	143.93
9000	835.01	459.39	335.85	275.32	239.95	217.15	201.49	190.27	181.99	175.73	170.92	167.19	164.25	161.92
10000	927.79	510.43	373.17	305.91	266.62	241.28	223.88	211.41	202.21	195.25	189.92	185.76	182.50	179.91
11000	1020.56	561.47	410.49	336.50	293.28	265.40	246.26	232.55	222.43	214.78	208.91	204.34	200.75	197.91
12000	1113.34	612.51	447.80	367.09	319.94	289.53	268.65	253.69	242.65	234.30	227.90	222.91	219.00	215.90
13000	1206.12	663.56	485.12	397.68	346.60	313.66	291.04	274.83	262.87	253.83	246.89	241.49	237.25	233.89
14000	1298.90	714.60	522.44	428.27	373.26	337.78	313.43	295.97	283.09	273.35	265.88	260.06	255.50	251.88
15000	1391.68	765.64	559.75	458.86	399.92	361.91	335.81	317.11	303.31	292.88	284.87	278.64	273.75	269.87
16000	1484.46	816.68	597.07	489.45	426.58	386.04	358.20	338.26	323.53	312.40	303.86	297.22	291.99	287.86
17000	1577.23	867.73	634.39	520.04	453.24	410.16	380.59	359.40	343.75	331.93	322.85	315.79	310.24	305.85
18000	1670.01	918.77	671.70	550.63	479.90	434.29	402.97	380.54	363.97	351.45	341.84	334.37	328.49	323.84
19000	1762.79	969.81	709.02	581.22	506.57	458.42	425.36	401.68	384.19	370.98	360.83	352.94	346.74	341.83
20000	1855.57	1020.85	746.34	611.81	533.23	482.55	447.75	422.82	404.41	390.50	379.83	371.52	364.99	359.82
21000	1948.35	1071.90	783.65	642.40	559.89	506.67	470.14	443.96	424.63	410.03	398.82	390.09	383.24	377.81
22000	2041.12	1122.94	820.97	672.99	586.55	530.80	492.52	465.10	444.85	429.55	417.81	408.67	401.49	395.81
23000	2133.90	1173.98	858.29	703.58	613.21	554.93	514.91	486.24	465.07	449.08	436.80	427.25	419.74	413.80
24000	2226.68	1225.02	895.60	734.18	639.87	579.05	537.30	507.38	485.29	468.60	455.79	445.82	437.99	431.79
25000	2319.46	1276.07	932.92	764.77	666.53	603.18	559.68	528.52	505.51	488.13	474.78	464.40	456.24	449.78
26000	2412.24	1327.11	970.24	795.36	693.19	627.31	582.07	549.66	525.73	507.65	493.77	482.97	474.49	467.77
27000	2505.01	1378.15	1007.55	825.95	719.85	651.44	604.46	570.80	545.95	527.18	512.76	501.55	492.74	485.76
28000	2597.79	1429.19	1044.87	856.54	746.52	675.56	626.85	591.94	566.17	546.70	531.75	520.12	510.99	503.75
29000	2690.57	1480.24	1082.19	887.13	773.18	699.69	649.23	613.08	586.39	566.23	550.74	538.70	529.24	521.74
30000	2783.35	1531.28	1119.50	917.72	799.84	723.82	671.62	634.22	606.61	585.75	569.74	557.28	547.49	539.73
31000	2876.13	1582.32	1156.82	948.31	826.50	747.94	694.01	655.37	626.83	605.28	588.73	575.85	565.74	557.72
32000	2968.91	1633.36	1194.14	978.90	853.16	772.07	716.40	676.51	647.05	624.80	607.72	594.43	583.98	575.71
33000	3061.68	1684.41	1231.45	1009.49	879.82	796.20	738.78	697.65	667.27	644.33	626.71	613.00	602.23	593.71
34000	3154.46	1735.45	1268.77	1040.08	906.48	820.32	761.17	718.79	687.49	663.85	645.70	631.58	620.48	611.70
35000	3247.24	1786.49	1306.09	1070.67	933.14	844.45	783.56	739.93	707.71	683.38	664.69	650.15	638.73	629.69
36000	3340.02	1837.53	1343.40	1101.26	959.80	868.58	805.94	761.07	727.93	702.90	683.68	668.73	656.98	647.68
37000	3432.80	1888.58	1380.72	1131.85	986.47	892.71	828.33	782.21	748.15	722.43	702.67	687.31	675.23	665.67
38000	3525.57	1939.62	1418.04	1162.44	1013.13	916.83	850.72	803.35	768.37	741.95	721.66	705.88	693.48	683.66
39000	3618.35	1990.66	1455.35	1193.03	1039.79	940.96	873.11	824.49	788.59	761.48	740.65	724.46	711.73	701.65
40000	3711.13	2041.70	1492.67	1223.62	1066.45	965.09	895.49	845.63	808.81	781.00	759.65	743.03	729.98	719.64
41000	3803.91	2092.75	1529.99	1254.21	1093.11	989.21	917.88	866.77	829.03	800.53	778.64	761.61	748.23	737.63
42000	3896.69	2143.79	1567.30	1284.80	1119.77	1013.34	940.27	887.91	849.25	820.05	797.63	780.18	766.48	755.62
43000	3989.47	2194.83	1604.62	1315.39	1146.43	1037.47	962.65	909.05	869.47	839.58	816.62	798.76	784.73	773.62
44000	4082.24	2245.87	1641.94	1345.98	1173.09	1061.59	985.04	930.19	889.69	859.10	835.61	817.34	802.98	791.61
45000	4175.02	2296.92	1679.25	1376.57	1199.75	1085.72	1007.43	951.33	909.91	878.63	854.60	835.91	821.23	809.60
46000	4267.80	2347.96	1716.57	1407.16	1226.41	1109.85	1029.82	972.48	930.13	898.15	873.59	854.49	839.48	827.59
47000	4360.58	2399.00	1753.89	1437.76	1253.08	1133.98	1052.20	993.62	950.35	917.67	892.58	873.06	857.72	845.58
48000	4453.36	2450.04	1791.20	1468.35	1279.74	1158.10	1074.59	1014.76	970.57	937.20	911.57	891.64	875.97	863.57
49000	4546.13	2501.09	1828.52	1498.94	1306.40	1182.23	1096.98	1035.90	990.79	956.72	930.56	910.21	894.22	881.56
50000	4638.91	2552.13	1865.84	1529.53	1333.06	1206.36	1119.36	1057.04	1011.01	976.25	949.56	928.79	912.47	899.55
55000	5102.80	2807.34	2052.42	1682.48	1466.36	1326.99	1231.30	1162.74	1112.11	1073.87	1044.51	1021.67	1003.72	989.51
60000	5566.69	3062.55	2239.00	1835.43	1599.67	1447.63	1343.24	1268.44	1213.21	1171.50	1139.47	1114.55	1094.97	1079.46
65000	6030.58	3317.77	2425.59	1988.38	1732.98	1568.26	1455.17	1374.15	1314.31	1269.12	1234.42	1207.42	1186.21	1169.42
70000	6494.48	3572.98	2612.17	2141.34	1866.28	1688.90	1567.11	1479.85	1415.41	1366.75	1329.38	1300.30	1277.46	1259.37
75000	6958.37	3828.19	2798.75	2294.29	1999.59	1809.53	1679.04	1585.55	1516.51	1464.37	1424.33	1393.18	1368.71	1349.33
80000	7422.26	4083.40	2985.33	2447.24	2132.89	1930.17	1790.98	1691.26	1617.61	1562.00	1519.29	1486.06	1459.95	1439.28
85000	7886.15	4338.62	3171.92	2600.19	2266.20	2050.80	1902.92	1796.96	1718.71	1659.62	1614.24	1578.94	1551.20	1529.23
90000	8350.04	4593.83	3358.50	2753.14	2399.50	2171.44	2014.85	1902.66	1819.81	1757.25	1709.20	1671.82	1642.45	1619.19
95000	8813.93	4849.04	3545.08	2906.10	2532.81	2292.07	2126.79	2008.37	1920.91	1854.87	1804.15	1764.70	1733.69	1709.14
100000	9277.82	5104.25	3731.67	3059.05	2666.11	2412.71	2238.72	2114.07	2022.01	1952.49	1899.11	1857.57	1824.94	1799.10

TERM	15 Years	16 Years	17 Years	18 Years	19 Years	20 Years	21 Years	22 Years	23 Years	24 Years	25 Years	30 Years	35 Years	40 Years
AMOUNT														
5	.09	.09	.09	.09	.09	.09	.09	.09	.09	.09	.09	.09	.09	.09
10	.18	.18	.18	.18	.18	.18	.18	.18	.18	.18	.18	.17	.17	.17
15	.27	.27	.27	.27	.26	.26	.26	.26	.26	.26	.26	.26	.26	.26
25	.45	.45	.44	.44	.44	.44	.43	.43	.43	.43	.43	.43	.43	.43
50	.89	.89	.88	.87	.87	.87	.86	.86	.86	.86	.86	.85	.85	.85
75	1.34	1.33	1.32	1.31	1.30	1.30	1.29	1.29	1.29	1.28	1.28	1.28	1.27	1.27
100	1.78	1.77	1.75	1.74	1.73	1.73	1.72	1.72	1.71	1.71	1.71	1.70	1.70	1.70
200	3.56	3.53	3.50	3.48	3.46	3.45	3.44	3.43	3.42	3.42	3.41	3.40	3.39	3.39
300	5.34	5.29	5.25	5.22	5.19	5.17	5.16	5.14	5.13	5.12	5.11	5.09	5.08	5.08
400	7.12	7.05	7.00	6.96	6.92	6.89	6.87	6.85	6.84	6.83	6.82	6.79	6.78	6.77
500	8.90	8.82	8.75	8.70	8.65	8.62	8.59	8.57	8.55	8.53	8.52	8.48	8.47	8.47
600	10.68	10.58	10.50	10.43	10.38	10.34	10.31	10.28	10.25	10.24	10.22	10.18	10.16	10.16
700	12.45	12.34	12.25	12.17	12.11	12.06	12.02	11.99	11.96	11.94	11.92	11.87	11.86	11.85
800	14.23	14.10	14.00	13.91	13.84	13.78	13.74	13.70	13.67	13.65	13.63	13.57	13.55	13.54
900	16.01	15.86	15.74	15.65	15.57	15.51	15.46	15.41	15.38	15.35	15.33	15.27	15.24	15.23
1000	17.79	17.63	17.49	17.39	17.30	17.23	17.17	17.13	17.09	17.06	17.03	16.96	16.94	16.93
2000	35.58	35.25	34.98	34.77	34.59	34.45	34.34	34.25	34.17	34.11	34.06	33.92	33.87	33.85
3000	53.36	52.87	52.47	52.15	51.89	51.68	51.51	51.37	51.25	51.16	51.09	50.88	50.80	50.77
4000	71.15	70.49	69.96	69.53	69.18	68.90	68.67	68.49	68.34	68.22	68.12	67.83	67.73	67.69
5000	88.93	88.11	87.44	86.91	86.48	86.13	85.84	85.61	85.42	85.27	85.14	84.79	84.66	84.62
6000	106.72	105.73	104.93	104.29	103.77	103.35	103.01	102.73	102.50	102.32	102.17	101.75	101.59	101.54
7000	124.50	123.35	122.42	121.67	121.06	120.57	120.18	119.85	119.59	119.37	119.20	118.70	118.52	118.46
8000	142.29	140.97	139.91	139.05	138.36	137.80	137.34	136.97	136.67	136.43	136.23	135.66	135.46	135.38
9000	160.07	158.59	157.39	156.43	155.65	155.02	154.51	154.09	153.75	153.48	153.25	152.62	152.39	152.30
10000	177.86	176.21	174.88	173.81	172.95	172.25	171.68	171.21	170.84	170.53	170.28	169.58	169.32	169.23
11000	195.64	193.83	192.37	191.19	190.24	189.47	188.84	188.34	187.92	187.58	187.31	186.53	186.25	186.15
12000	213.43	211.45	209.86	208.57	207.53	206.69	206.01	205.46	205.00	204.64	204.34	203.49	203.18	203.07
13000	231.21	229.07	227.34	225.95	224.83	223.92	223.18	222.58	222.09	221.69	221.37	220.45	220.11	219.99
14000	249.00	246.69	244.83	243.33	242.12	241.14	240.35	239.70	239.17	238.74	238.39	237.40	237.04	236.91
15000	266.78	264.31	262.32	260.71	259.42	258.37	257.51	256.82	256.25	255.80	255.42	254.36	253.98	253.84
16000	284.57	281.93	279.81	278.09	276.71	275.59	274.68	273.94	273.34	272.85	272.45	271.32	270.91	270.76
17000	302.35	299.55	297.29	295.47	294.00	292.81	291.85	291.06	290.42	289.90	289.48	288.28	287.84	287.68
18000	320.14	317.17	314.78	312.86	311.30	310.04	309.01	308.18	307.50	306.95	306.50	305.23	304.77	304.60
19000	337.92	334.79	332.27	330.24	328.59	327.26	326.18	325.30	324.59	324.01	323.53	322.19	321.70	321.52
20000	355.71	352.41	349.76	347.62	345.89	344.49	343.35	342.42	341.67	341.06	340.56	339.15	338.63	338.45
21000	373.49	370.03	367.24	365.00	363.18	361.71	360.52	359.54	358.75	358.11	357.59	356.10	355.56	355.37
22000	391.28	387.65	384.73	382.38	380.48	378.93	377.68	376.67	375.84	375.16	374.61	373.06	372.50	372.29
23000	409.06	405.27	402.22	399.76	397.77	396.16	394.85	393.79	392.92	392.22	391.64	390.02	389.43	389.21
24000	426.85	422.89	419.71	417.14	415.06	413.38	412.02	410.91	410.00	409.27	408.67	406.98	406.36	406.13
25000	444.63	440.51	437.19	434.52	432.36	430.61	429.18	428.03	427.09	426.32	425.70	423.93	423.29	423.06
26000	462.42	458.13	454.68	451.90	449.65	447.83	446.35	445.15	444.17	443.37	442.73	440.89	440.22	439.98
27000	480.20	475.75	472.17	469.28	466.95	465.05	463.52	462.27	461.25	460.43	459.75	457.85	457.15	456.90
28000	497.99	493.37	489.66	486.66	484.24	482.28	480.69	479.39	478.34	477.48	476.78	474.80	474.08	473.82
29000	515.77	510.99	507.14	504.04	501.53	499.50	497.85	496.51	495.42	494.53	493.81	491.76	491.02	490.74
30000	533.56	528.61	524.63	521.42	518.83	516.73	515.02	513.63	512.50	511.59	510.84	508.72	507.95	507.67
31000	551.34	546.23	542.12	538.80	536.12	533.95	532.19	530.75	529.59	528.64	527.86	525.67	524.88	524.59
32000	569.13	563.85	559.61	556.18	553.42	551.17	549.35	547.87	546.67	545.69	544.89	542.63	541.81	541.51
33000	586.91	581.47	577.09	573.56	570.71	568.40	566.52	565.00	563.75	562.74	561.92	559.59	558.74	558.43
34000	604.70	599.09	594.58	590.94	588.00	585.62	583.69	582.12	580.84	579.80	578.95	576.55	575.67	575.35
35000	622.48	616.71	612.07	608.32	605.30	602.85	600.86	599.24	597.92	596.85	595.98	593.50	592.60	592.28
36000	640.27	634.33	629.56	625.71	622.59	620.07	618.02	616.36	615.00	613.90	613.00	610.46	609.54	609.20
37000	658.05	651.95	647.04	643.09	639.89	637.29	635.19	633.48	632.09	630.95	630.03	627.42	626.47	626.12
38000	675.84	669.57	664.53	660.47	657.18	654.52	652.36	650.60	649.17	648.01	647.06	644.37	643.40	643.04
39000	693.62	687.19	682.02	677.85	674.47	671.74	669.52	667.72	666.25	665.06	664.09	661.33	660.33	659.97
40000	711.41	704.81	699.51	695.23	691.77	688.97	686.69	684.84	683.34	682.11	681.11	678.29	677.26	676.89
41000	729.19	722.43	716.99	712.61	709.06	706.19	703.86	701.96	700.42	699.17	698.14	695.25	694.19	693.81
42000	746.98	740.05	734.48	729.99	726.36	723.41	721.03	719.08	717.50	716.22	715.17	712.20	711.12	710.73
43000	764.76	757.67	751.97	747.37	743.65	740.64	738.19	736.20	734.59	733.27	732.20	729.16	728.06	727.65
44000	782.55	775.29	769.46	764.75	760.95	757.86	755.36	753.33	751.67	750.32	749.22	746.12	744.99	744.58
45000	800.33	792.91	786.94	782.13	778.24	775.09	772.53	770.45	768.75	767.38	766.25	763.07	761.92	761.50
46000	818.12	810.53	804.43	799.51	795.53	792.31	789.69	787.57	785.84	784.43	783.28	780.03	778.85	778.42
47000	835.90	828.15	821.92	816.89	812.83	809.53	806.86	804.69	802.92	801.48	800.31	796.99	795.78	795.34
48000	853.69	845.77	839.41	834.27	830.12	826.76	824.03	821.81	820.00	818.53	817.34	813.95	812.71	812.26
49000	871.47	863.39	856.89	851.65	847.42	843.98	841.20	838.93	837.09	835.59	834.36	830.90	829.64	829.19
50000	889.26	881.01	874.38	869.03	864.71	861.21	858.36	856.05	854.17	852.64	851.39	847.86	846.58	846.11
55000	978.18	969.11	961.82	955.94	951.18	947.33	944.20	941.66	939.59	937.90	936.53	932.64	931.23	930.72
60000	1067.11	1057.21	1049.26	1042.84	1037.65	1033.45	1030.03	1027.26	1025.00	1023.17	1021.67	1017.43	1015.89	1015.33
65000	1156.03	1145.31	1136.69	1129.74	1124.12	1119.57	1115.87	1112.87	1110.42	1108.43	1106.81	1102.22	1100.55	1099.94
70000	1244.96	1233.41	1224.13	1216.64	1210.59	1205.69	1201.71	1198.47	1195.84	1193.69	1191.95	1187.00	1185.20	1184.55
75000	1333.88	1321.51	1311.57	1303.55	1297.06	1291.81	1287.54	1284.07	1281.25	1278.96	1277.08	1271.79	1269.86	1269.16
80000	1422.81	1409.61	1399.01	1390.45	1383.53	1377.93	1373.38	1369.68	1366.67	1364.22	1362.22	1356.57	1354.52	1353.77
85000	1511.73	1497.71	1486.44	1477.35	1470.00	1464.05	1459.21	1455.28	1452.09	1449.48	1447.36	1441.36	1439.18	1438.38
90000	1600.66	1585.81	1573.88	1564.26	1556.47	1550.17	1545.05	1540.89	1537.50	1534.75	1532.50	1526.14	1523.83	1522.99
95000	1689.58	1673.91	1661.32	1651.16	1642.94	1636.29	1630.88	1626.49	1622.92	1620.01	1617.64	1610.93	1608.49	1607.60
100000	1778.51	1762.01	1748.76	1738.06	1729.41	1722.41	1716.72	1712.10	1708.34	1705.27	1702.78	1695.71	1693.15	1692.21

MONTHLY PAYMENT
REQUIRED TO AMORTIZE A LOAN

TERM	1 Year	2 Years	3 Years	4 Years	5 Years	6 Years	7 Years	8 Years	9 Years	10 Years	11 Years	12 Years	13 Years	14 Years
AMOUNT														
5	.47	.26	.19	.16	.14	.13	.12	.11	.11	.10	.10	.10	.10	.10
10	.93	.52	.38	.31	.27	.25	.23	.22	.21	.20	.20	.19	.19	.19
15	1.40	.77	.57	.46	.41	.37	.34	.32	.31	.30	.29	.28	.28	.28
25	2.33	1.28	.94	.77	.67	.61	.57	.53	.51	.49	.48	.47	.46	.46
50	4.65	2.56	1.87	1.54	1.34	1.21	1.13	1.06	1.02	.98	.96	.94	.92	.91
75	6.97	3.84	2.81	2.30	2.01	1.82	1.69	1.59	1.53	1.47	1.43	1.40	1.38	1.36
100	9.29	5.11	3.74	3.07	2.68	2.42	2.25	2.12	2.03	1.96	1.91	1.87	1.84	1.81
200	18.57	10.22	7.48	6.13	5.35	4.84	4.49	4.24	4.06	3.92	3.81	3.73	3.67	3.61
300	27.85	15.33	11.21	9.19	8.02	7.26	6.73	6.36	6.09	5.88	5.72	5.59	5.50	5.42
400	37.13	20.44	14.95	12.26	10.69	9.67	8.98	8.48	8.11	7.83	7.62	7.46	7.33	7.22
500	46.41	25.54	18.68	15.32	13.36	12.09	11.22	10.60	10.14	9.79	9.53	9.32	9.16	9.03
600	55.69	30.65	22.42	18.38	16.03	14.51	13.46	12.72	12.17	11.75	11.43	11.18	10.99	10.83
700	64.97	35.76	26.15	21.45	18.70	16.92	15.71	14.84	14.19	13.71	13.33	13.04	12.82	12.64
800	74.26	40.87	29.89	24.51	21.37	19.34	17.95	16.96	16.22	15.66	15.24	14.91	14.65	14.44
900	83.54	45.98	33.62	27.57	24.04	21.76	20.19	19.07	18.25	17.62	17.14	16.77	16.48	16.25
1000	92.82	51.08	37.36	30.64	26.71	24.18	22.44	21.19	20.27	19.58	19.05	18.63	18.31	18.05
2000	185.63	102.16	74.71	61.27	53.41	48.35	44.87	42.38	40.54	39.15	38.09	37.26	36.61	36.10
3000	278.45	153.24	112.07	91.90	80.11	72.52	67.30	63.57	60.81	58.73	57.13	55.89	54.91	54.14
4000	371.26	204.32	149.42	122.53	106.82	96.69	89.74	84.76	81.08	78.30	76.17	74.52	73.22	72.19
5000	464.08	255.40	186.78	153.16	133.52	120.86	112.17	105.94	101.35	97.88	95.22	93.15	91.52	90.23
6000	556.89	306.48	224.13	183.79	160.22	145.03	134.60	127.13	121.62	117.45	114.26	111.77	109.82	108.28
7000	649.70	357.56	261.49	214.42	186.93	169.20	157.03	148.32	141.89	137.03	133.30	130.40	128.13	126.32
8000	742.52	408.64	298.84	245.05	213.63	193.37	179.47	169.51	162.15	156.60	152.34	149.03	146.43	144.37
9000	835.33	459.72	336.20	275.68	240.33	217.54	201.90	190.69	182.42	176.18	171.39	167.66	164.73	162.42
10000	928.15	510.80	373.55	306.31	267.03	241.71	224.33	211.88	202.69	195.75	190.43	186.29	183.04	180.46
11000	1020.96	561.88	410.91	336.94	293.74	265.88	246.76	233.07	222.96	215.33	209.47	204.92	201.34	198.51
12000	1113.77	612.96	448.26	367.57	320.44	290.05	269.20	254.26	243.23	234.90	228.51	223.54	219.64	216.55
13000	1206.59	664.03	485.62	398.20	347.14	314.22	291.63	275.44	263.50	254.48	247.55	242.17	237.94	234.60
14000	1299.40	715.11	522.97	428.83	373.85	338.39	314.06	296.63	283.77	274.05	266.60	260.80	256.25	252.64
15000	1392.22	766.19	560.33	459.46	400.55	362.57	336.49	317.82	304.03	293.63	285.64	279.43	274.55	270.69
16000	1485.03	817.27	597.68	490.09	427.25	386.74	358.93	339.01	324.30	313.20	304.68	298.06	292.85	288.74
17000	1577.84	868.35	635.04	520.72	453.96	410.91	381.36	360.20	344.57	332.78	323.72	316.68	311.16	306.78
18000	1670.66	919.43	672.39	551.35	480.66	435.08	403.79	381.38	364.84	352.35	342.77	335.31	329.46	324.83
19000	1763.47	970.51	709.75	581.98	507.36	459.25	426.22	402.57	385.11	371.93	361.81	353.94	347.76	342.87
20000	1856.29	1021.59	747.10	612.62	534.06	483.42	448.66	423.76	405.38	391.50	380.85	372.57	366.07	360.92
21000	1949.10	1072.67	784.46	643.25	560.77	507.59	471.09	444.95	425.65	411.08	399.89	391.20	384.37	378.96
22000	2041.91	1123.75	821.81	673.88	587.47	531.76	493.52	466.13	445.91	430.65	418.94	409.83	402.67	397.01
23000	2134.73	1174.83	859.17	704.51	614.17	555.93	515.95	487.32	466.18	450.23	437.98	428.45	420.97	415.05
24000	2227.54	1225.91	896.52	735.14	640.88	580.10	538.39	508.51	486.45	469.80	457.02	447.08	439.28	433.10
25000	2320.36	1276.98	933.88	765.77	667.58	604.27	560.82	529.70	506.72	489.38	476.06	465.71	457.58	451.15
26000	2413.17	1328.06	971.23	796.40	694.28	628.44	583.25	550.88	526.99	508.95	495.10	484.34	475.88	469.19
27000	2505.99	1379.14	1008.59	827.03	720.99	652.61	605.68	572.07	547.26	528.53	514.15	502.97	494.19	487.24
28000	2598.80	1430.22	1045.94	857.66	747.69	676.78	628.12	593.26	567.53	548.10	533.19	521.60	512.49	505.28
29000	2691.61	1481.30	1083.30	888.29	774.39	700.96	650.55	614.45	587.79	567.68	552.23	540.22	530.79	523.33
30000	2784.43	1532.38	1120.65	918.92	801.09	725.13	672.98	635.63	608.06	587.25	571.27	558.85	549.10	541.37
31000	2877.24	1583.46	1158.01	949.55	827.80	749.30	695.41	656.82	628.33	606.83	590.32	577.48	567.40	559.42
32000	2970.06	1634.54	1195.36	980.18	854.50	773.47	717.85	678.01	648.60	626.40	609.36	596.11	585.70	577.47
33000	3062.87	1685.62	1232.72	1010.81	881.20	797.64	740.28	699.20	668.87	645.98	628.40	614.74	604.00	595.51
34000	3155.68	1736.70	1270.07	1041.44	907.91	821.81	762.71	720.39	689.14	665.55	647.44	633.36	622.31	613.56
35000	3248.50	1787.78	1307.43	1072.07	934.61	845.98	785.14	741.57	709.41	685.12	666.49	651.99	640.61	631.60
36000	3341.31	1838.86	1344.78	1102.70	961.31	870.15	807.58	762.76	729.67	704.70	685.53	670.62	658.91	649.65
37000	3434.13	1889.93	1382.14	1133.33	988.01	894.32	830.01	783.95	749.94	724.27	704.57	689.25	677.22	667.69
38000	3526.94	1941.01	1419.49	1163.96	1014.72	918.49	852.44	805.14	770.21	743.85	723.61	707.88	695.52	685.74
39000	3619.76	1992.09	1456.85	1194.60	1041.42	942.66	874.87	826.32	790.48	763.42	742.65	726.51	713.82	703.78
40000	3712.57	2043.17	1494.20	1225.23	1068.12	966.83	897.31	847.51	810.75	783.00	761.70	745.13	732.13	721.83
41000	3805.38	2094.25	1531.56	1255.86	1094.83	991.00	919.74	868.70	831.02	802.57	780.74	763.76	750.43	739.88
42000	3898.20	2145.33	1568.91	1286.49	1121.53	1015.17	942.17	889.89	851.29	822.15	799.78	782.39	768.73	757.92
43000	3991.01	2196.41	1606.27	1317.12	1148.23	1039.34	964.60	911.07	871.56	841.72	818.82	801.02	787.04	775.97
44000	4083.82	2247.49	1643.62	1347.75	1174.94	1063.52	987.04	932.26	891.82	861.30	837.87	819.65	805.34	794.01
45000	4176.64	2298.57	1680.98	1378.38	1201.64	1087.69	1009.47	953.45	912.09	880.87	856.91	838.28	823.64	812.06
46000	4269.45	2349.65	1718.33	1409.01	1228.34	1111.86	1031.90	974.64	932.36	900.45	875.95	856.90	841.94	830.10
47000	4362.27	2400.73	1755.69	1439.64	1255.04	1136.03	1054.33	995.82	952.63	920.02	894.99	875.53	860.25	848.15
48000	4455.08	2451.81	1793.04	1470.27	1281.75	1160.20	1076.77	1017.01	972.90	939.60	914.04	894.16	878.55	866.20
49000	4547.89	2502.89	1830.40	1500.90	1308.45	1184.37	1099.20	1038.20	993.17	959.17	933.08	912.79	896.85	884.24
50000	4640.71	2553.96	1867.75	1531.53	1335.15	1208.54	1121.63	1059.39	1013.44	978.75	952.12	931.42	915.16	902.29
55000	5104.78	2809.36	2054.53	1684.68	1468.67	1329.39	1233.80	1165.33	1114.78	1076.62	1047.33	1024.56	1006.67	992.51
60000	5568.85	3064.76	2241.30	1837.84	1602.18	1450.25	1345.96	1271.26	1216.12	1174.50	1142.54	1117.70	1098.19	1082.74
65000	6032.92	3320.15	2428.08	1990.99	1735.70	1571.10	1458.12	1377.20	1317.46	1272.37	1237.75	1210.84	1189.70	1172.97
70000	6496.99	3575.55	2614.85	2144.14	1869.21	1691.95	1570.28	1483.14	1418.81	1370.24	1332.97	1303.98	1281.22	1263.20
75000	6961.06	3830.94	2801.62	2297.29	2002.73	1812.81	1682.45	1589.08	1520.15	1468.12	1428.18	1397.12	1372.73	1353.43
80000	7425.13	4086.34	2988.40	2450.44	2136.24	1933.66	1794.61	1695.02	1621.49	1565.99	1523.39	1490.26	1464.25	1443.66
85000	7889.20	4341.74	3175.17	2603.60	2269.76	2054.51	1906.77	1800.96	1722.84	1663.87	1618.60	1583.40	1555.76	1533.88
90000	8353.27	4597.13	3361.95	2756.75	2403.27	2175.37	2018.93	1906.89	1824.18	1761.74	1713.81	1676.55	1647.28	1624.11
95000	8817.34	4852.53	3548.72	2909.90	2536.79	2296.22	2131.10	2012.83	1925.52	1859.62	1809.02	1769.69	1738.79	1714.34
100000	9281.41	5107.92	3735.50	3063.06	2670.30	2417.07	2243.26	2118.77	2026.87	1957.49	1904.24	1862.83	1830.31	1804.57

MONTHLY PAYMENT
REQUIRED TO AMORTIZE A LOAN

20.375%

TERM	15 Years	16 Years	17 Years	18 Years	19 Years	20 Years	21 Years	22 Years	23 Years	24 Years	25 Years	30 Years	35 Years	40 Years
AMOUNT														
5	.09	.09	.09	.09	.09	.09	.09	.09	.09	.09	.09	.09	.09	.09
10	.18	.18	.18	.18	.18	.18	.18	.18	.18	.18	.18	.18	.17	.17
15	.27	.27	.27	.27	.27	.26	.26	.26	.26	.26	.26	.26	.26	.26
25	.45	.45	.44	.44	.44	.44	.44	.43	.43	.43	.43	.43	.43	.43
50	.90	.89	.88	.88	.87	.87	.87	.86	.86	.86	.86	.86	.85	.85
75	1.34	1.33	1.32	1.31	1.31	1.30	1.30	1.29	1.29	1.29	1.29	1.28	1.28	1.28
100	1.79	1.77	1.76	1.75	1.74	1.73	1.73	1.72	1.72	1.72	1.71	1.71	1.70	1.70
200	3.57	3.54	3.51	3.49	3.48	3.46	3.45	3.44	3.43	3.43	3.42	3.41	3.40	3.40
300	5.36	5.31	5.27	5.24	5.21	5.19	5.17	5.16	5.15	5.14	5.13	5.11	5.10	5.10
400	7.14	7.08	7.02	6.98	6.95	6.92	6.90	6.88	6.86	6.85	6.84	6.81	6.80	6.80
500	8.93	8.84	8.78	8.72	8.68	8.65	8.62	8.60	8.58	8.56	8.55	8.51	8.50	8.50
600	10.71	10.61	10.53	10.47	10.42	10.37	10.34	10.31	10.29	10.27	10.26	10.22	10.20	10.20
700	12.49	12.38	12.29	12.21	12.15	12.10	12.06	12.03	12.01	11.98	11.97	11.92	11.90	11.89
800	14.28	14.15	14.04	13.96	13.89	13.83	13.79	13.75	13.72	13.70	13.68	13.62	13.60	13.59
900	16.06	15.91	15.80	15.70	15.62	15.56	15.51	15.47	15.43	15.41	15.38	15.32	15.30	15.29
1000	17.85	17.68	17.55	17.44	17.36	17.29	17.23	17.19	17.15	17.12	17.09	17.02	17.00	16.99
2000	35.69	35.36	35.09	34.88	34.71	34.57	34.46	34.37	34.29	34.23	34.18	34.04	33.99	33.97
3000	53.53	53.03	52.64	52.32	52.06	51.85	51.68	51.55	51.44	51.34	51.27	51.06	50.99	50.96
4000	71.37	70.71	70.18	69.76	69.42	69.14	68.91	68.73	68.58	68.46	68.36	68.08	67.98	67.94
5000	89.21	88.39	87.73	87.20	86.77	86.42	86.14	85.91	85.72	85.57	85.45	85.10	84.97	84.93
6000	107.05	106.06	105.27	104.64	104.12	103.70	103.36	103.09	102.87	102.68	102.54	102.12	101.97	101.91
7000	124.89	123.74	122.82	122.07	121.47	120.99	120.59	120.27	120.01	119.80	119.63	119.14	118.96	118.90
8000	142.73	141.42	140.36	139.51	138.83	138.27	137.82	137.45	137.15	136.91	136.71	136.16	135.95	135.88
9000	160.57	159.09	157.91	156.95	156.18	155.55	155.04	154.63	154.30	154.02	153.80	153.17	152.95	152.86
10000	178.41	176.77	175.45	174.39	173.53	172.84	172.27	171.81	171.44	171.14	170.89	170.19	169.94	169.85
11000	196.25	194.45	193.00	191.83	190.88	190.12	189.50	188.99	188.58	188.25	187.98	187.21	186.93	186.83
12000	214.09	212.12	210.54	209.27	208.24	207.40	206.72	206.18	205.73	205.36	205.07	204.23	203.93	203.82
13000	231.93	229.80	228.09	226.71	225.59	224.68	223.95	223.36	222.87	222.48	222.16	221.25	220.92	220.80
14000	249.77	247.48	245.63	244.14	242.94	241.97	241.18	240.54	240.02	239.59	239.25	238.27	237.92	237.79
15000	267.61	265.15	263.18	261.58	260.29	259.25	258.40	257.72	257.16	256.70	256.33	255.29	254.91	254.77
16000	285.46	282.83	280.72	279.02	277.65	276.53	275.63	274.90	274.30	273.82	273.42	272.31	271.90	271.76
17000	303.30	300.51	298.27	296.46	295.00	293.82	292.86	292.08	291.45	290.93	290.51	289.33	288.90	288.74
18000	321.14	318.18	315.81	313.90	312.35	311.10	310.08	309.26	308.59	308.04	307.60	306.34	305.89	305.72
19000	338.98	335.86	333.36	331.34	329.70	328.38	327.31	326.44	325.73	325.16	324.69	323.36	322.88	322.71
20000	356.82	353.54	350.90	348.77	347.06	345.67	344.54	343.62	342.88	342.27	341.78	340.38	339.88	339.69
21000	374.66	371.21	368.44	366.21	364.41	362.95	361.76	360.80	360.02	359.38	358.87	357.40	356.87	356.68
22000	392.50	388.89	385.99	383.65	381.76	380.23	378.99	377.98	377.16	376.50	375.95	374.42	373.86	373.66
23000	410.34	406.57	403.53	401.09	399.11	397.52	396.22	395.16	394.31	393.61	393.04	391.44	390.86	390.65
24000	428.18	424.24	421.08	418.53	416.47	414.80	413.44	412.35	411.45	410.72	410.13	408.46	407.85	407.63
25000	446.02	441.92	438.62	435.97	433.82	432.08	430.67	429.53	428.59	427.84	427.22	425.48	424.84	424.62
26000	463.86	459.60	456.17	453.41	451.17	449.36	447.90	446.71	445.74	444.95	444.31	442.50	441.84	441.60
27000	481.70	477.27	473.71	470.04	468.53	466.65	465.12	463.89	462.88	462.06	461.40	459.51	458.83	458.58
28000	499.54	494.95	491.26	488.28	485.88	483.93	481.07	480.03	479.18	478.49	476.53	475.83	475.57	475.57
29000	517.38	512.63	508.80	505.72	503.23	501.21	499.58	498.25	497.17	496.29	495.57	493.55	492.82	492.55
30000	535.22	530.30	526.35	523.16	520.58	518.50	516.80	515.43	514.31	513.40	512.66	510.57	509.81	509.54
31000	553.06	547.98	543.89	540.60	537.94	535.78	534.03	532.61	531.46	530.52	529.75	527.59	526.81	526.52
32000	570.91	565.66	561.44	558.04	555.29	553.06	551.26	549.79	548.60	547.63	546.84	544.61	543.80	543.51
33000	588.75	583.33	578.98	575.47	572.64	570.35	568.48	566.97	565.74	564.74	563.93	561.63	560.79	560.49
34000	606.59	601.01	596.53	592.91	589.99	587.63	585.71	584.15	582.89	581.86	581.02	578.65	577.79	577.48
35000	624.43	618.68	614.07	610.35	607.35	604.91	602.94	601.33	600.03	598.97	598.11	595.66	594.78	594.46
36000	642.27	636.36	631.62	627.79	624.70	622.20	620.16	618.52	617.17	616.08	615.19	612.68	611.77	611.44
37000	660.11	654.04	649.16	645.23	642.05	639.48	637.39	635.70	634.32	633.20	632.28	629.70	628.77	628.43
38000	677.95	671.71	666.71	662.67	659.40	656.76	654.62	652.88	651.46	650.31	649.37	646.72	645.76	645.41
39000	695.79	689.39	684.25	680.11	676.76	674.04	671.84	670.06	668.61	667.42	666.46	663.74	662.76	662.40
40000	713.63	707.07	701.79	697.54	694.11	691.33	689.07	687.24	685.75	684.54	683.55	680.76	679.75	679.38
41000	731.47	724.74	719.34	714.98	711.46	708.61	706.30	704.42	702.89	701.65	700.64	697.78	696.74	696.37
42000	749.31	742.42	736.88	732.42	728.81	725.89	723.52	721.60	720.04	718.76	717.73	714.80	713.74	713.35
43000	767.15	760.10	754.43	749.86	746.17	743.18	740.75	738.78	737.18	735.88	734.81	731.82	730.73	730.33
44000	784.99	777.77	771.97	767.30	763.52	760.46	757.98	755.96	754.32	752.99	751.90	748.83	747.72	747.32
45000	802.83	795.45	789.52	784.74	780.87	777.74	775.20	773.14	771.47	770.10	768.99	765.85	764.72	764.30
46000	820.67	813.13	807.06	802.17	798.22	795.03	792.43	790.32	788.61	787.22	786.08	782.87	781.71	781.29
47000	838.51	830.80	824.61	819.61	815.58	812.31	809.66	807.50	805.75	804.33	803.17	799.89	798.70	798.27
48000	856.36	848.48	842.15	837.05	832.93	829.59	826.88	824.69	822.90	821.44	820.26	816.91	815.70	815.26
49000	874.20	866.16	859.70	854.49	850.28	846.88	844.11	841.87	840.04	838.56	837.35	833.93	832.69	832.24
50000	892.04	883.83	877.24	871.93	867.64	864.16	861.34	859.05	857.18	855.67	854.43	850.95	849.68	849.23
55000	981.24	972.22	964.97	959.12	954.40	950.57	947.47	944.95	942.90	941.24	939.88	936.04	934.65	934.15
60000	1070.44	1060.60	1052.69	1046.31	1041.16	1036.99	1033.60	1030.86	1028.62	1026.80	1025.32	1021.14	1019.62	1019.07
65000	1159.65	1148.98	1140.41	1133.51	1127.92	1123.40	1119.74	1116.76	1114.34	1112.37	1110.76	1106.23	1104.59	1103.99
70000	1248.85	1237.36	1228.14	1220.70	1214.69	1209.82	1205.87	1202.66	1200.06	1197.93	1196.21	1191.32	1189.56	1188.91
75000	1338.05	1325.75	1315.86	1307.89	1301.45	1296.23	1292.00	1288.57	1285.77	1283.50	1281.65	1276.42	1274.52	1273.84
80000	1427.26	1414.13	1403.58	1395.08	1388.21	1382.65	1378.14	1374.47	1371.49	1369.07	1367.09	1361.51	1359.49	1358.76
85000	1516.46	1502.51	1491.31	1482.28	1474.98	1469.07	1464.27	1460.38	1457.21	1454.63	1452.53	1446.61	1444.46	1443.68
90000	1605.66	1590.90	1579.03	1569.48	1561.74	1555.48	1550.40	1546.28	1542.93	1540.20	1537.98	1531.70	1529.43	1528.60
95000	1694.87	1679.28	1666.76	1656.66	1648.50	1641.90	1636.54	1632.19	1628.65	1625.77	1623.42	1616.80	1614.40	1613.52
100000	1784.07	1767.66	1754.48	1743.85	1735.27	1728.31	1722.67	1718.09	1714.36	1711.33	1708.86	1701.89	1699.36	1698.45

MONTHLY PAYMENT
REQUIRED TO AMORTIZE A LOAN

TERM	1 Year	2 Years	3 Years	4 Years	5 Years	6 Years	7 Years	8 Years	9 Years	10 Years	11 Years	12 Years	13 Years	14 Years
AMOUNT														
5	.47	.26	.19	.16	.14	.13	.12	.11	.11	.10	.10	.10	.10	.10
10	.93	.52	.38	.31	.27	.25	.23	.22	.21	.20	.20	.19	.19	.19
15	1.40	.77	.57	.46	.41	.37	.34	.32	.31	.30	.29	.28	.28	.28
25	2.33	1.28	.94	.77	.67	.61	.57	.54	.51	.49	.48	.47	.46	.46
50	4.65	2.56	1.87	1.54	1.34	1.21	1.13	1.07	1.02	.98	.96	.94	.92	.91
75	6.97	3.84	2.81	2.30	2.01	1.82	1.69	1.60	1.53	1.47	1.43	1.40	1.38	1.36
100	9.29	5.11	3.74	3.07	2.68	2.42	2.25	2.13	2.03	1.96	1.91	1.87	1.84	1.81
200	18.57	10.22	7.48	6.13	5.35	4.84	4.49	4.25	4.06	3.92	3.82	3.73	3.67	3.62
300	27.85	15.33	11.22	9.20	8.02	7.26	6.74	6.37	6.09	5.88	5.72	5.60	5.50	5.42
400	37.14	20.44	14.95	12.26	10.69	9.68	8.98	8.49	8.12	7.84	7.63	7.46	7.33	7.23
500	46.42	25.55	18.69	15.33	13.36	12.10	11.23	10.61	10.15	9.80	9.53	9.33	9.17	9.04
600	55.70	30.66	22.43	18.39	16.04	14.52	13.47	12.73	12.18	11.76	11.44	11.19	11.00	10.84
700	64.98	35.77	26.16	21.46	18.71	16.93	15.72	14.85	14.20	13.72	13.35	13.06	12.83	12.65
800	74.27	40.88	29.90	24.52	21.38	19.35	17.96	16.97	16.23	15.68	15.25	14.92	14.66	14.46
900	83.55	45.99	33.64	27.58	24.05	21.77	20.21	19.09	18.26	17.64	17.16	16.79	16.49	16.26
1000	92.83	51.10	37.37	30.65	26.72	24.19	22.45	21.21	20.29	19.60	19.06	18.65	18.33	18.07
2000	185.66	102.19	74.74	61.29	53.44	48.38	44.90	42.41	40.57	39.19	38.12	37.30	36.65	36.13
3000	278.48	153.28	112.11	91.94	80.16	72.56	67.35	63.61	60.86	58.78	57.18	55.94	54.97	54.20
4000	371.31	204.37	149.48	122.58	106.87	96.75	89.80	84.82	81.14	78.37	76.24	74.59	73.29	72.26
5000	464.14	255.46	186.84	153.22	133.59	120.93	112.24	106.02	101.43	97.96	95.30	93.23	91.61	90.32
6000	556.96	306.55	224.21	183.87	160.31	145.12	134.69	127.22	121.71	117.55	114.36	111.88	109.93	108.39
7000	649.79	357.64	261.58	214.51	187.02	169.30	157.14	148.43	142.00	137.15	133.42	130.53	128.25	126.45
8000	742.61	408.74	298.95	245.16	213.74	193.49	179.59	169.63	162.28	156.74	152.48	149.17	146.57	144.52
9000	835.44	459.83	336.31	275.80	240.46	217.67	202.03	190.83	182.57	176.33	171.54	167.82	164.89	162.58
10000	928.27	510.92	373.68	306.44	267.17	241.86	224.48	212.04	202.85	195.92	190.60	186.46	183.21	180.64
11000	1021.09	562.01	411.05	337.09	293.89	266.04	246.93	233.24	223.14	215.51	209.66	205.11	201.54	198.71
12000	1113.92	613.10	448.42	367.73	320.61	290.23	269.38	254.44	243.42	235.10	228.72	223.75	219.86	216.77
13000	1206.74	664.19	485.79	398.38	347.33	314.41	291.82	275.65	263.71	254.69	247.78	242.40	238.18	234.84
14000	1299.57	715.28	523.15	429.02	374.04	338.60	314.27	296.85	283.99	274.29	266.84	261.05	256.50	252.90
15000	1392.40	766.38	560.52	459.66	400.76	362.78	336.72	318.05	304.28	293.88	285.90	279.69	274.82	270.96
16000	1485.22	817.47	597.89	490.31	427.48	386.97	359.17	339.26	324.56	313.47	304.96	298.34	293.14	289.03
17000	1578.05	868.56	635.26	520.95	454.19	411.15	381.62	360.46	344.85	333.06	324.02	316.98	311.46	307.09
18000	1670.87	919.65	672.62	551.59	480.91	435.34	404.06	381.66	365.13	352.65	343.07	335.63	329.78	325.15
19000	1763.70	970.74	709.99	582.24	507.63	459.52	426.51	402.87	385.42	372.24	362.13	354.27	348.10	343.22
20000	1856.53	1021.83	747.36	612.88	534.34	483.71	448.96	424.07	405.70	391.84	381.19	372.92	366.42	361.28
21000	1949.35	1072.92	784.73	643.53	561.06	507.90	471.41	445.27	425.99	411.43	400.25	391.57	384.74	379.35
22000	2042.18	1124.02	822.09	674.17	587.78	532.08	493.85	466.48	446.27	431.02	419.31	410.21	403.07	397.41
23000	2135.00	1175.11	859.46	704.81	614.49	556.27	516.30	487.68	466.56	450.61	438.37	428.86	421.39	415.47
24000	2227.83	1226.20	896.83	735.46	641.21	580.45	538.75	508.88	486.84	470.20	457.43	447.50	439.71	433.54
25000	2320.66	1277.29	934.20	766.10	667.93	604.64	561.20	530.09	507.12	489.79	476.49	466.15	458.03	451.60
26000	2413.48	1328.38	971.57	796.75	694.65	628.82	583.64	551.29	527.41	509.38	495.55	484.79	476.35	469.67
27000	2506.31	1379.47	1008.93	827.39	721.36	653.01	606.09	572.49	547.69	528.98	514.61	503.44	494.67	487.73
28000	2599.13	1430.56	1046.30	858.03	748.08	677.19	628.54	593.70	567.98	548.57	533.67	522.09	512.99	505.79
29000	2691.96	1481.66	1083.67	888.68	774.80	701.38	650.99	614.90	588.26	568.16	552.73	540.73	531.31	523.86
30000	2784.79	1532.75	1121.04	919.32	801.51	725.56	673.44	636.10	608.55	587.75	571.79	559.38	549.63	541.92
31000	2877.61	1583.84	1158.40	949.97	828.23	749.75	695.88	657.31	628.83	607.34	590.85	578.02	567.95	559.99
32000	2970.44	1634.93	1195.77	980.61	854.95	773.93	718.33	678.51	649.12	626.93	609.91	596.67	586.27	578.05
33000	3063.26	1686.02	1233.14	1011.25	881.66	798.12	740.78	699.71	669.40	646.52	628.97	615.31	604.60	596.11
34000	3156.09	1737.11	1270.51	1041.90	908.38	822.30	763.23	720.92	689.69	666.12	648.03	633.96	622.92	614.18
35000	3248.92	1788.20	1307.87	1072.54	935.10	846.49	785.67	742.12	709.97	685.71	667.08	652.61	641.24	632.24
36000	3341.74	1839.30	1345.24	1103.18	961.81	870.67	808.12	763.32	730.26	705.30	686.14	671.25	659.56	650.30
37000	3434.57	1890.39	1382.61	1133.83	988.53	894.86	830.57	784.53	750.54	724.89	705.20	689.90	677.88	668.37
38000	3527.40	1941.48	1419.98	1164.47	1015.25	919.04	853.02	805.73	770.83	744.48	724.26	708.54	696.20	686.43
39000	3620.22	1992.57	1457.35	1195.12	1041.97	943.23	875.46	826.93	791.11	764.07	743.32	727.19	714.52	704.50
40000	3713.05	2043.66	1494.71	1225.76	1068.68	967.42	897.91	848.14	811.40	783.67	762.38	745.83	732.84	722.56
41000	3805.87	2094.75	1532.08	1256.40	1095.40	991.60	920.36	869.34	831.68	803.26	781.44	764.48	751.16	740.62
42000	3898.70	2145.84	1569.45	1287.05	1122.12	1015.79	942.81	890.54	851.97	822.85	800.50	783.13	769.48	758.69
43000	3991.53	2196.94	1606.82	1317.69	1148.83	1039.97	965.26	911.75	872.25	842.44	819.56	801.77	787.80	776.75
44000	4084.35	2248.03	1644.18	1348.34	1175.55	1064.16	987.70	932.95	892.54	862.03	838.62	820.42	806.13	794.82
45000	4177.18	2299.12	1681.55	1378.98	1202.27	1088.34	1010.15	954.15	912.82	881.62	857.68	839.06	824.45	812.88
46000	4270.00	2350.21	1718.92	1409.62	1228.98	1112.53	1032.60	975.36	933.11	901.21	876.74	857.71	842.77	830.94
47000	4362.83	2401.30	1756.29	1440.27	1255.70	1136.71	1055.05	996.56	953.39	920.81	895.80	876.36	861.09	849.01
48000	4455.66	2452.39	1793.66	1470.91	1282.42	1160.90	1077.49	1017.76	973.67	940.40	914.86	895.00	879.41	867.07
49000	4548.48	2503.48	1831.02	1501.56	1309.14	1185.08	1099.94	1038.97	993.96	959.99	933.92	913.65	897.73	885.13
50000	4641.31	2554.58	1868.39	1532.20	1335.85	1209.27	1122.39	1060.17	1014.24	979.58	952.98	932.29	916.05	903.20
55000	5105.44	2810.03	2055.23	1685.42	1469.44	1330.19	1234.63	1166.19	1115.67	1077.54	1048.27	1025.52	1007.66	993.52
60000	5569.57	3065.49	2242.07	1838.64	1603.02	1451.12	1346.87	1272.20	1217.09	1175.50	1143.57	1118.75	1099.26	1083.84
65000	6033.70	3320.95	2428.91	1991.86	1736.61	1572.05	1459.10	1378.22	1318.52	1273.45	1238.87	1211.98	1190.87	1174.16
70000	6497.83	3576.40	2615.74	2145.08	1870.19	1692.97	1571.34	1484.24	1419.94	1371.41	1334.16	1305.21	1282.47	1264.48
75000	6961.96	3831.86	2802.58	2298.30	2003.78	1813.90	1683.58	1590.25	1521.36	1469.37	1429.46	1398.44	1374.07	1354.80
80000	7426.09	4087.32	2989.42	2451.52	2137.36	1934.83	1795.82	1696.27	1622.79	1567.33	1524.76	1491.66	1465.68	1445.12
85000	7890.22	4342.78	3176.26	2604.74	2270.94	2055.75	1908.06	1802.29	1724.21	1665.28	1620.06	1584.89	1557.28	1535.43
90000	8354.35	4598.23	3363.10	2757.95	2404.53	2176.68	2020.30	1908.30	1825.64	1763.24	1715.35	1678.12	1648.89	1625.75
95000	8818.48	4853.69	3549.94	2911.17	2538.11	2297.60	2132.53	2014.32	1927.06	1861.20	1810.65	1771.35	1740.49	1716.07
100000	9282.61	5109.15	3736.78	3064.39	2671.70	2418.53	2244.77	2120.34	2028.48	1959.16	1905.95	1864.58	1832.10	1806.39

TERM	15 Years	16 Years	17 Years	18 Years	19 Years	20 Years	21 Years	22 Years	23 Years	24 Years	25 Years	30 Years	35 Years	40 Years
AMOUNT														
5	.09	.09	.09	.09	.09	.09	.09	.09	.09	.09	.09	.09	.09	.09
10	.18	.18	.18	.18	.18	.18	.18	.18	.18	.18	.18	.18	.18	.18
15	.27	.27	.27	.27	.27	.26	.26	.26	.26	.26	.26	.26	.26	.26
25	.45	.45	.44	.44	.44	.44	.44	.44	.43	.43	.43	.43	.43	.43
50	.90	.89	.88	.88	.87	.87	.87	.87	.86	.86	.86	.86	.86	.86
75	1.34	1.33	1.32	1.31	1.31	1.30	1.30	1.30	1.29	1.29	1.29	1.28	1.28	1.28
100	1.79	1.77	1.76	1.75	1.74	1.74	1.73	1.72	1.72	1.72	1.72	1.71	1.71	1.71
200	3.58	3.54	3.52	3.50	3.48	3.47	3.45	3.45	3.44	3.43	3.43	3.41	3.41	3.41
300	5.36	5.31	5.27	5.24	5.22	5.20	5.18	5.17	5.15	5.15	5.14	5.12	5.11	5.11
400	7.15	7.08	7.03	6.99	6.95	6.93	6.90	6.89	6.87	6.86	6.85	6.82	6.81	6.81
500	8.93	8.85	8.79	8.73	8.69	8.66	8.63	8.61	8.59	8.57	8.56	8.52	8.51	8.51
600	10.72	10.62	10.54	10.48	10.43	10.39	10.35	10.33	10.30	10.29	10.27	10.23	10.21	10.21
700	12.51	12.39	12.30	12.23	12.17	12.12	12.08	12.05	12.02	12.00	11.98	11.93	11.92	11.91
800	14.29	14.16	14.06	13.97	13.90	13.85	13.80	13.77	13.74	13.71	13.69	13.64	13.62	13.61
900	16.08	15.93	15.81	15.72	15.64	15.58	15.53	15.49	15.45	15.43	15.40	15.34	15.32	15.31
1000	17.86	17.70	17.57	17.46	17.38	17.31	17.25	17.21	17.17	17.14	17.11	17.04	17.02	17.01
2000	35.72	35.40	35.13	34.92	34.75	34.61	34.50	34.41	34.33	34.27	34.22	34.08	34.03	34.02
3000	53.58	53.09	52.70	52.38	52.12	51.91	51.74	51.61	51.50	51.41	51.33	51.12	51.05	51.02
4000	71.44	70.79	70.26	69.84	69.49	69.22	68.99	68.81	68.66	68.54	68.44	68.16	68.06	68.03
5000	89.30	88.48	87.82	87.29	86.87	86.52	86.24	86.01	85.82	85.67	85.55	85.20	85.08	85.03
6000	107.16	106.18	105.39	104.75	104.24	103.82	103.48	103.21	102.99	102.81	102.66	102.24	102.09	102.04
7000	125.02	123.87	122.95	122.21	121.61	121.12	120.73	120.41	120.15	119.94	119.77	119.28	119.11	119.04
8000	142.88	141.57	140.52	139.67	138.98	138.43	137.98	137.61	137.31	137.07	136.88	136.32	136.12	136.05
9000	160.74	159.26	158.08	157.13	156.35	155.73	155.22	154.81	154.48	154.21	153.98	153.36	153.13	153.05
10000	178.60	176.96	175.64	174.58	173.73	173.03	172.47	172.01	171.64	171.34	171.09	170.40	170.15	170.06
11000	196.46	194.65	193.21	192.04	191.10	190.34	189.72	189.21	188.81	188.47	188.20	187.44	187.16	187.06
12000	214.32	212.35	210.77	209.50	208.47	207.64	206.96	206.41	205.97	205.61	205.31	204.48	204.18	204.07
13000	232.17	230.05	228.33	226.96	225.84	224.94	224.21	223.62	223.13	222.74	222.42	221.52	221.19	221.07
14000	250.03	247.74	245.90	244.41	243.21	242.24	241.46	240.82	240.30	239.87	239.53	238.56	238.21	238.08
15000	267.89	265.44	263.46	261.87	260.59	259.55	258.70	258.02	257.46	257.01	256.64	255.60	255.22	255.08
16000	285.75	283.13	281.03	279.33	277.96	276.85	275.95	275.22	274.62	274.14	273.75	272.64	272.23	272.09
17000	303.61	300.83	298.59	296.79	295.33	294.15	293.20	292.42	291.79	291.27	290.86	289.68	289.25	289.09
18000	321.47	318.52	316.15	314.25	312.70	311.45	310.44	309.62	308.95	308.41	307.96	306.71	306.26	306.10
19000	339.33	336.22	333.72	331.70	330.08	328.76	327.69	326.82	326.12	325.54	325.07	323.75	323.28	323.10
20000	357.19	353.91	351.28	349.16	347.45	346.06	344.94	344.02	343.28	342.67	342.18	340.79	340.29	340.11
21000	375.05	371.61	368.85	366.62	364.82	363.36	362.18	361.22	360.44	359.81	359.29	357.83	357.31	357.11
22000	392.91	389.30	386.41	384.08	382.19	380.67	379.43	378.42	377.61	376.94	376.40	374.87	374.32	374.12
23000	410.77	407.00	403.97	401.53	399.56	397.97	396.67	395.62	394.77	394.08	393.51	391.91	391.33	391.12
24000	428.63	424.69	421.54	418.99	416.94	415.27	413.92	412.82	411.93	411.21	410.62	408.95	408.35	408.13
25000	446.48	442.39	439.10	436.45	434.31	432.57	431.17	430.03	429.10	428.34	427.73	425.99	425.36	425.14
26000	464.34	460.09	456.66	453.91	451.68	449.88	448.41	447.23	446.26	445.48	444.84	443.03	442.38	442.14
27000	482.20	477.78	474.23	471.37	469.05	467.18	465.66	464.43	463.42	462.61	461.94	460.07	459.39	459.15
28000	500.06	495.48	491.79	488.82	486.42	484.48	482.91	481.63	480.59	479.74	479.05	477.11	476.41	476.15
29000	517.92	513.17	509.36	506.28	503.80	501.78	500.15	498.83	497.75	496.88	496.16	494.15	493.42	493.16
30000	535.78	530.87	526.92	523.74	521.17	519.09	517.40	516.03	514.92	514.01	513.27	511.19	510.43	510.16
31000	553.64	548.56	544.48	541.20	538.54	536.39	534.65	533.23	532.08	531.14	530.38	528.23	527.45	527.17
32000	571.50	566.26	562.05	558.65	555.91	553.69	551.89	550.43	549.24	548.28	547.49	545.27	544.46	544.17
33000	589.36	583.95	579.61	576.11	573.28	571.00	569.14	567.63	566.41	565.41	564.60	562.31	561.48	561.18
34000	607.22	601.65	597.18	593.57	590.66	588.30	586.39	584.83	583.57	582.54	581.71	579.35	578.49	578.18
35000	625.08	619.34	614.74	611.03	608.03	605.60	603.63	602.03	600.73	599.68	598.82	596.39	595.51	595.19
36000	642.94	637.04	632.30	628.49	625.40	622.90	620.88	619.23	617.90	616.81	615.92	613.42	612.52	612.19
37000	660.80	654.73	649.87	645.94	642.77	640.21	638.13	636.44	635.06	633.94	633.03	630.46	629.53	629.20
38000	678.65	672.43	667.43	663.40	660.15	657.51	655.37	653.64	652.23	651.08	650.14	647.50	646.55	646.20
39000	696.51	690.13	684.99	680.86	677.52	674.81	672.62	670.84	669.39	668.21	667.25	664.54	663.56	663.21
40000	714.37	707.82	702.56	698.32	694.89	692.12	689.87	688.04	686.55	685.34	684.36	681.58	680.58	680.21
41000	732.23	725.52	720.12	715.77	712.26	709.42	707.11	705.24	703.72	702.48	701.47	698.62	697.59	697.22
42000	750.09	743.21	737.69	733.23	729.63	726.72	724.36	722.44	720.88	719.61	718.58	715.66	714.61	714.22
43000	767.95	760.91	755.25	750.69	747.01	744.02	741.60	739.64	738.04	736.74	735.69	732.70	731.62	731.23
44000	785.81	778.60	772.81	768.15	764.38	761.33	758.85	756.84	755.21	753.88	752.80	749.74	748.64	748.23
45000	803.67	796.30	790.38	785.61	781.75	778.63	776.10	774.04	772.37	771.01	769.90	766.78	765.65	765.24
46000	821.53	813.99	807.94	803.06	799.12	795.93	793.34	791.24	789.53	788.15	787.01	783.82	782.66	782.24
47000	839.39	831.69	825.50	820.52	816.49	813.23	810.59	808.44	806.70	805.28	804.12	800.86	799.68	799.25
48000	857.25	849.38	843.07	837.98	833.87	830.54	827.84	825.64	823.86	822.41	821.23	817.90	816.69	816.25
49000	875.11	867.08	860.63	855.44	851.24	847.84	845.08	842.85	841.03	839.55	838.34	834.94	833.71	833.26
50000	892.96	884.78	878.20	872.89	868.61	865.14	862.33	860.05	858.19	856.68	855.45	851.98	850.72	850.27
55000	982.26	973.25	966.02	960.18	955.47	951.66	948.56	946.05	944.01	942.35	940.99	937.17	935.79	935.29
60000	1071.56	1061.73	1053.83	1047.47	1042.33	1038.17	1034.80	1032.05	1029.83	1028.01	1026.54	1022.37	1020.86	1020.32
65000	1160.85	1150.21	1141.65	1134.76	1129.19	1124.69	1121.03	1118.06	1115.65	1113.68	1112.08	1107.57	1105.94	1105.34
70000	1250.15	1238.68	1229.47	1222.05	1216.05	1211.20	1207.26	1204.06	1201.46	1199.35	1197.63	1192.77	1191.01	1190.37
75000	1339.44	1327.16	1317.29	1309.34	1302.91	1297.71	1293.49	1290.07	1287.28	1285.02	1283.17	1277.96	1276.08	1275.40
80000	1428.74	1415.64	1405.11	1396.63	1389.77	1384.23	1379.73	1376.07	1373.10	1370.68	1368.72	1363.16	1361.15	1360.42
85000	1518.04	1504.11	1492.93	1483.92	1476.63	1470.74	1465.96	1462.08	1458.92	1456.35	1454.26	1448.36	1446.23	1445.45
90000	1607.33	1592.59	1580.75	1571.21	1563.50	1557.25	1552.19	1548.08	1544.74	1542.02	1539.80	1533.55	1531.29	1530.47
95000	1696.63	1681.07	1668.57	1658.49	1650.36	1643.77	1638.42	1634.08	1630.56	1627.69	1625.35	1618.75	1616.37	1615.50
100000	1785.92	1769.55	1756.39	1745.78	1737.22	1730.28	1724.66	1720.09	1716.37	1713.35	1710.89	1703.95	1701.44	1700.53

MONTHLY PAYMENT
REQUIRED TO AMORTIZE A LOAN

TERM AMOUNT	1 Year	2 Years	3 Years	4 Years	5 Years	6 Years	7 Years	8 Years	9 Years	10 Years	11 Years	12 Years	13 Years	14 Years
5	.47	.26	.19	.16	.14	.13	.12	.11	.11	.10	.10	.10	.10	.10
10	.93	.52	.38	.31	.27	.25	.23	.22	.21	.20	.20	.19	.19	.19
15	1.40	.77	.57	.47	.41	.37	.34	.32	.31	.30	.29	.29	.28	.28
25	2.33	1.28	.94	.77	.67	.61	.57	.54	.51	.50	.48	.47	.46	.46
50	4.65	2.56	1.88	1.54	1.34	1.22	1.13	1.07	1.02	.99	.96	.94	.92	.91
75	6.97	3.84	2.81	2.31	2.01	1.82	1.69	1.60	1.53	1.48	1.44	1.41	1.38	1.37
100	9.29	5.12	3.75	3.07	2.68	2.43	2.26	2.13	2.04	1.97	1.92	1.88	1.84	1.82
200	18.58	10.23	7.49	6.14	5.36	4.85	4.51	4.26	4.07	3.94	3.83	3.75	3.68	3.63
300	27.87	15.35	11.23	9.21	8.04	7.28	6.76	6.38	6.11	5.90	5.74	5.62	5.52	5.45
400	37.15	20.46	14.97	12.28	10.71	9.70	9.01	8.51	8.14	7.87	7.66	7.49	7.36	7.26
500	46.44	25.58	18.71	15.35	13.39	12.13	11.26	10.64	10.18	9.83	9.57	9.36	9.20	9.07
600	55.73	30.69	22.46	18.42	16.07	14.55	13.51	12.76	12.21	11.80	11.48	11.23	11.04	10.89
700	65.02	35.80	26.20	21.49	18.75	16.98	15.76	14.89	14.25	13.77	13.39	13.11	12.88	12.70
800	74.30	40.92	29.94	24.56	21.42	19.40	18.01	17.02	16.28	15.73	15.31	14.98	14.72	14.51
900	83.59	46.03	33.68	27.63	24.10	21.82	20.26	19.14	18.32	17.70	17.22	16.85	16.56	16.33
1000	92.88	51.15	37.42	30.70	26.78	24.25	22.51	21.27	20.35	19.66	19.13	18.72	18.40	18.14
2000	185.75	102.29	74.84	61.40	53.55	48.49	45.02	42.54	40.70	39.32	38.26	37.44	36.79	36.28
3000	278.63	153.43	112.26	92.10	80.32	72.74	67.53	63.80	61.05	58.98	57.39	56.15	55.18	54.42
4000	371.50	204.57	149.68	122.79	107.10	96.98	90.04	85.07	81.40	78.64	76.52	74.87	73.58	72.55
5000	464.37	255.71	187.10	153.49	133.87	121.22	112.55	106.34	101.75	98.30	95.64	93.58	91.97	90.69
6000	557.25	306.85	224.52	184.19	160.64	145.47	135.05	127.60	122.10	117.95	114.77	112.30	110.36	108.83
7000	650.12	357.99	261.94	214.89	187.42	169.71	157.56	148.87	142.45	137.61	133.90	131.02	128.75	126.96
8000	743.00	409.13	299.36	245.58	214.19	193.95	180.07	170.13	162.80	157.27	153.03	149.73	147.15	145.10
9000	835.87	460.27	336.77	276.28	240.96	218.20	202.58	191.40	183.15	176.93	172.16	168.45	165.54	163.24
10000	928.74	511.41	374.19	306.98	267.73	242.44	225.09	212.67	203.50	196.59	191.28	187.16	183.93	181.37
11000	1021.62	562.55	411.61	337.68	294.51	266.68	247.60	233.93	223.85	216.25	210.41	205.88	202.32	199.51
12000	1114.49	613.69	449.03	368.37	321.28	290.93	270.10	255.20	244.20	235.90	229.54	224.60	220.72	217.65
13000	1207.37	664.83	486.45	399.07	348.05	315.17	292.61	276.46	264.55	255.56	248.67	243.31	239.11	235.78
14000	1300.24	715.97	523.87	429.77	374.83	339.41	315.12	297.73	284.90	275.22	267.80	262.03	257.50	253.92
15000	1393.11	767.11	561.29	460.47	401.60	363.66	337.63	319.00	305.25	294.88	286.92	280.74	275.89	272.06
16000	1485.99	818.25	598.71	491.16	428.37	387.90	360.14	340.26	325.60	314.54	306.05	299.46	294.29	290.20
17000	1578.86	869.39	636.13	521.86	455.14	412.15	382.65	361.53	345.95	334.19	325.18	318.18	312.68	308.33
18000	1671.74	920.53	673.54	552.56	481.92	436.39	405.15	382.79	366.30	353.85	344.31	336.89	331.07	326.47
19000	1764.61	971.67	710.96	583.26	508.69	460.63	427.66	404.06	386.65	373.51	363.44	355.61	349.46	344.61
20000	1857.48	1022.81	748.38	613.95	535.46	484.88	450.17	425.33	407.00	393.17	382.56	374.32	367.86	362.74
21000	1950.36	1073.95	785.80	644.65	562.24	509.12	472.68	446.59	427.35	412.83	401.69	393.04	386.25	380.88
22000	2043.23	1125.09	823.22	675.35	589.01	533.36	495.19	467.86	447.70	432.49	420.82	411.75	404.64	399.02
23000	2136.11	1176.23	860.64	706.05	615.78	557.61	517.69	489.12	468.05	452.14	439.95	430.47	423.03	417.15
24000	2228.98	1227.37	898.06	736.74	642.55	581.85	540.20	510.39	488.40	471.80	459.07	449.19	441.43	435.29
25000	2321.85	1278.51	935.48	767.44	669.33	606.09	562.71	531.66	508.74	491.46	478.20	467.90	459.82	453.43
26000	2414.73	1329.66	972.89	798.14	696.10	630.34	585.22	552.92	529.09	511.12	497.33	486.62	478.21	471.56
27000	2507.60	1380.80	1010.31	828.83	722.87	654.58	607.73	574.19	549.44	530.78	516.46	505.33	496.60	489.70
28000	2600.48	1431.94	1047.73	859.53	749.65	678.82	630.24	595.45	569.79	550.44	535.59	524.05	515.00	507.84
29000	2693.35	1483.08	1085.15	890.23	776.42	703.07	652.74	616.72	590.14	570.09	554.71	542.77	533.39	525.98
30000	2786.22	1534.22	1122.57	920.93	803.19	727.31	675.25	637.99	610.49	589.75	573.84	561.48	551.78	544.11
31000	2879.10	1585.36	1159.99	951.62	829.96	751.55	697.76	659.25	630.84	609.41	592.97	580.20	570.18	562.25
32000	2971.97	1636.50	1197.41	982.32	856.74	775.80	720.27	680.52	651.19	629.07	612.10	598.91	588.57	580.39
33000	3064.85	1687.64	1234.83	1013.02	883.51	800.04	742.78	701.78	671.54	648.73	631.23	617.63	606.96	598.52
34000	3157.72	1738.78	1272.25	1043.72	910.28	824.29	765.29	723.05	691.89	668.38	650.35	636.35	625.35	616.66
35000	3250.59	1789.92	1309.66	1074.41	937.06	848.53	787.79	744.32	712.24	688.04	669.48	655.06	643.75	634.80
36000	3343.47	1841.06	1347.08	1105.11	963.83	872.77	810.30	765.58	732.59	707.70	688.61	673.78	662.14	652.93
37000	3436.34	1892.20	1384.50	1135.81	990.60	897.02	832.81	786.85	752.94	727.36	707.74	692.49	680.53	671.07
38000	3529.22	1943.34	1421.92	1166.51	1017.37	921.26	855.32	808.12	773.29	747.02	726.87	711.21	698.92	689.21
39000	3622.09	1994.48	1459.34	1197.20	1044.15	945.50	877.83	829.38	793.64	766.68	745.99	729.92	717.32	707.34
40000	3714.96	2045.62	1496.76	1227.90	1070.92	969.75	900.33	850.65	813.99	786.33	765.12	748.64	735.71	725.48
41000	3807.84	2096.76	1534.18	1258.60	1097.69	993.99	922.84	871.91	834.34	805.99	784.25	767.36	754.10	743.62
42000	3900.71	2147.90	1571.60	1289.30	1124.47	1018.23	945.35	893.18	854.69	825.65	803.38	786.07	772.49	761.76
43000	3993.59	2199.04	1609.02	1319.99	1151.24	1042.48	967.86	914.45	875.04	845.31	822.51	804.79	790.89	779.89
44000	4086.46	2250.18	1646.43	1350.69	1178.01	1066.72	990.37	935.71	895.39	864.97	841.63	823.50	809.28	798.03
45000	4179.33	2301.32	1683.85	1381.39	1204.78	1090.96	1012.88	956.98	915.74	884.63	860.76	842.22	827.67	816.17
46000	4272.21	2352.46	1721.27	1412.09	1231.56	1115.21	1035.38	978.24	936.09	904.28	879.89	860.94	846.06	834.30
47000	4365.08	2403.60	1758.69	1442.78	1258.33	1139.45	1057.89	999.51	956.44	923.94	899.02	879.65	864.46	852.44
48000	4457.96	2454.74	1796.11	1473.48	1285.10	1163.69	1080.40	1020.78	976.79	943.60	918.14	898.37	882.85	870.58
49000	4550.83	2505.88	1833.53	1504.18	1311.88	1187.94	1102.91	1042.04	997.13	963.26	937.27	917.08	901.24	888.71
50000	4643.70	2557.02	1870.95	1534.87	1338.65	1212.18	1125.42	1063.31	1017.48	982.92	956.40	935.80	919.63	906.85
55000	5108.07	2812.73	2058.04	1688.36	1472.51	1333.40	1237.96	1169.64	1119.23	1081.21	1052.04	1029.38	1011.60	997.53
60000	5572.44	3068.43	2245.14	1841.85	1606.38	1454.62	1350.50	1275.97	1220.98	1179.50	1147.68	1122.96	1103.56	1088.22
65000	6036.81	3324.13	2432.23	1995.34	1740.24	1575.83	1463.04	1382.30	1322.73	1277.79	1243.32	1216.54	1195.52	1178.90
70000	6501.18	3579.83	2619.32	2148.82	1874.11	1697.05	1575.58	1488.63	1424.48	1376.08	1338.96	1310.12	1287.49	1269.59
75000	6965.55	3835.53	2806.42	2302.31	2007.97	1818.27	1688.12	1594.96	1526.22	1474.37	1434.60	1403.70	1379.45	1360.27
80000	7429.92	4091.24	2993.51	2455.80	2141.83	1939.49	1800.66	1701.29	1627.97	1572.66	1530.24	1497.28	1471.41	1450.96
85000	7894.29	4346.94	3180.61	2609.28	2275.70	2060.71	1913.21	1807.62	1729.72	1670.95	1625.88	1590.86	1563.37	1541.64
90000	8358.66	4602.64	3367.70	2762.77	2409.56	2181.92	2025.75	1913.95	1831.46	1769.25	1721.52	1684.44	1655.34	1632.33
95000	8823.03	4858.34	3554.79	2916.26	2543.43	2303.14	2138.29	2020.28	1933.22	1867.54	1817.16	1778.01	1747.30	1723.01
100000	9287.40	5114.04	3741.89	3069.74	2677.29	2424.36	2250.83	2126.61	2034.96	1965.83	1912.80	1871.59	1839.26	1813.70

TERM	15 Years	16 Years	17 Years	18 Years	19 Years	20 Years	21 Years	22 Years	23 Years	24 Years	25 Years	30 Years	35 Years	40 Years
AMOUNT														
5	.09	.09	.09	.09	.09	.09	.09	.09	.09	.09	.09	.09	.09	.09
10	.18	.18	.18	.18	.18	.18	.18	.16	.18	.18	.18	.18	.18	.18
15	.27	.27	.27	.27	.27	.27	.26	.26	.26	.26	.26	.26	.26	.26
25	.45	.45	.45	.44	.44	.44	.44	.44	.44	.44	.44	.43	.43	.43
50	.90	.89	.89	.88	.88	.87	.87	.87	.87	.87	.86	.86	.86	.86
75	1.35	1.34	1.33	1.32	1.31	1.31	1.30	1.30	1.30	1.30	1.29	1.29	1.29	1.29
100	1.80	1.78	1.77	1.76	1.75	1.74	1.74	1.73	1.73	1.73	1.72	1.72	1.71	1.71
200	3.59	3.56	3.53	3.51	3.50	3.48	3.47	3.47	3.45	3.45	3.44	3.43	3.42	3.42
300	5.39	5.34	5.30	5.27	5.24	5.22	5.20	5.19	5.18	5.17	5.16	5.14	5.13	5.13
400	7.18	7.11	7.06	7.02	6.99	6.96	6.94	6.92	6.90	6.89	6.88	6.85	6.84	6.84
500	8.97	8.89	8.83	8.77	8.73	8.70	8.67	8.65	8.63	8.61	8.60	8.57	8.55	8.55
600	10.77	10.67	10.59	10.53	10.48	10.43	10.40	10.37	10.35	10.33	10.32	10.28	10.26	10.26
700	12.56	12.44	12.35	12.28	12.22	12.17	12.13	12.10	12.08	12.06	12.04	11.99	11.97	11.97
800	14.35	14.22	14.12	14.03	13.97	13.91	13.87	13.83	13.80	13.78	13.76	13.70	13.68	13.68
900	16.15	16.00	15.88	15.79	15.71	15.65	15.60	15.56	15.52	15.50	15.48	15.41	15.39	15.38
1000	17.94	17.78	17.65	17.54	17.46	17.39	17.33	17.29	17.25	17.22	17.20	17.13	17.10	17.09
2000	35.87	35.55	35.29	35.08	34.91	34.77	34.66	34.57	34.49	34.43	34.39	34.25	34.20	34.18
3000	53.81	53.32	52.93	52.61	52.36	52.15	51.98	51.85	51.74	51.65	51.58	51.37	51.30	51.27
4000	71.74	71.09	70.57	70.15	69.81	69.53	69.31	69.13	68.98	68.86	68.77	68.49	68.39	68.36
5000	89.67	88.86	88.21	87.68	87.26	86.91	86.63	86.41	86.23	86.08	85.96	85.61	85.49	85.45
6000	107.61	106.63	105.85	105.22	104.71	104.29	103.96	103.69	103.47	103.29	103.15	102.74	102.59	102.54
7000	125.54	124.40	123.49	122.75	122.16	121.68	121.29	120.97	120.71	120.71	120.34	119.86	119.69	119.62
8000	143.47	142.17	141.13	140.29	139.61	139.06	138.61	138.25	137.96	137.72	137.53	136.98	136.78	136.71
9000	161.41	159.94	158.77	157.82	157.06	156.44	155.94	155.53	155.20	154.93	154.72	154.10	153.88	153.80
10000	179.34	177.71	176.41	175.36	174.51	173.82	173.26	172.81	172.45	172.15	171.91	171.22	170.98	170.89
11000	197.27	195.48	194.05	192.89	191.96	191.20	190.59	190.09	189.69	189.36	189.10	188.34	188.07	187.98
12000	215.21	213.25	211.69	210.43	209.41	208.58	207.92	207.37	206.93	206.58	206.29	205.47	205.17	205.07
13000	233.14	231.03	229.33	227.96	226.86	225.97	225.24	224.66	224.18	223.79	223.48	222.59	222.27	222.15
14000	251.07	248.80	246.97	245.50	244.31	243.35	242.57	241.94	241.42	241.01	240.67	239.71	239.37	239.24
15000	269.01	266.57	264.61	263.03	261.76	260.73	259.89	259.22	258.67	258.22	257.86	256.83	256.46	256.33
16000	286.94	284.34	282.25	280.57	279.21	278.11	277.22	276.50	275.91	275.43	275.05	273.95	273.56	273.42
17000	304.87	302.11	299.89	298.10	296.66	295.49	294.55	293.78	293.15	292.65	292.24	291.08	290.66	290.51
18000	322.81	319.88	317.53	315.64	314.11	312.07	311.87	311.06	310.40	309.86	309.43	308.20	307.76	307.60
19000	340.74	337.65	335.17	333.17	331.56	330.25	329.20	328.34	327.64	327.08	326.62	325.32	324.85	324.68
20000	358.67	355.42	352.81	350.71	349.01	347.64	346.52	345.62	344.89	344.29	343.81	342.44	341.95	341.77
21000	376.61	373.19	370.45	368.24	366.46	365.02	363.85	362.90	362.13	361.51	361.00	359.56	359.05	358.86
22000	394.54	390.96	388.09	385.78	383.91	382.40	381.18	380.18	379.38	378.72	378.19	376.68	376.14	375.95
23000	412.47	408.73	405.73	403.31	401.36	399.70	398.50	397.46	396.62	395.93	395.38	393.81	393.24	393.04
24000	430.41	426.50	423.37	420.85	418.81	417.16	415.83	414.74	413.86	413.15	412.57	410.93	410.34	410.13
25000	448.34	444.28	441.01	438.38	436.26	434.54	433.15	432.02	431.11	430.36	429.76	428.05	427.44	427.21
26000	466.28	462.05	458.65	455.92	453.71	451.93	450.48	449.31	448.35	447.58	446.95	445.17	444.53	444.30
27000	484.21	479.82	476.29	473.45	471.16	469.31	467.80	466.59	465.60	464.79	464.14	462.29	461.63	461.39
28000	502.14	497.59	493.93	490.99	488.61	486.69	485.13	483.87	482.84	482.01	481.33	479.42	478.73	478.48
29000	520.08	515.36	511.57	508.52	506.06	504.07	502.46	501.15	500.08	499.22	498.52	496.54	495.82	495.57
30000	538.01	533.13	529.21	526.06	523.51	521.45	519.78	518.43	517.33	516.43	515.71	513.66	512.92	512.66
31000	555.94	550.90	546.85	543.59	540.96	538.83	537.11	535.71	534.57	533.65	532.90	530.78	530.02	529.74
32000	573.88	568.67	564.49	561.13	558.41	556.21	554.43	552.99	551.82	550.86	550.09	547.90	547.12	546.83
33000	591.81	586.44	582.13	578.66	575.86	573.60	571.76	570.27	569.06	568.08	567.28	565.02	564.21	563.92
34000	609.74	604.21	599.77	596.20	593.31	590.98	589.09	587.55	586.30	585.29	584.47	582.15	581.31	581.01
35000	627.68	621.98	617.41	613.73	610.76	608.36	606.41	604.83	603.55	602.51	601.66	599.27	598.41	598.10
36000	645.61	639.75	635.05	631.27	628.21	625.74	623.74	622.11	620.79	619.72	618.85	616.39	615.51	615.19
37000	663.54	657.52	652.69	648.80	645.66	643.12	641.06	639.39	638.04	636.93	636.04	633.51	632.60	632.27
38000	681.48	675.30	670.33	666.34	663.11	660.50	658.39	656.67	655.28	654.15	653.23	650.63	649.70	649.36
39000	699.41	693.07	687.97	683.87	680.56	677.89	675.72	673.96	672.53	671.36	670.42	667.76	666.80	666.45
40000	717.34	710.84	705.61	701.41	698.01	695.27	693.04	691.24	689.77	688.58	687.61	684.88	683.89	683.54
41000	735.28	728.61	723.25	718.94	715.46	712.65	710.37	708.52	707.01	705.79	704.80	702.00	700.99	700.63
42000	753.21	746.38	740.89	736.48	732.91	730.03	727.69	725.80	724.26	723.01	721.99	719.12	718.09	717.72
43000	771.14	764.15	758.53	754.01	750.36	747.41	745.02	743.08	741.50	740.22	739.18	736.24	735.19	734.80
44000	789.08	781.92	776.17	771.55	767.81	764.79	762.35	760.36	758.75	757.43	756.37	753.36	752.28	751.89
45000	807.01	799.69	793.82	789.08	785.26	782.17	779.67	777.64	775.99	774.65	773.56	770.49	769.38	768.98
46000	824.94	817.46	811.46	806.62	802.71	799.56	797.00	794.92	793.23	791.86	790.75	787.61	786.48	786.07
47000	842.88	835.23	829.10	824.15	820.16	816.94	814.32	812.20	810.48	809.08	807.94	804.73	803.58	803.16
48000	860.81	853.00	846.74	841.69	837.61	834.32	831.65	829.48	827.72	826.29	825.13	821.85	820.67	820.25
49000	878.74	870.77	864.38	859.22	855.06	851.70	848.97	846.76	844.97	843.51	842.32	838.97	837.77	837.33
50000	896.68	888.55	882.02	876.76	872.52	869.08	866.30	864.04	862.21	860.72	859.51	856.10	854.87	854.42
55000	986.35	977.40	970.22	964.43	959.77	955.99	952.93	950.45	948.43	946.79	945.46	941.70	940.35	939.86
60000	1076.01	1066.25	1058.42	1052.11	1047.02	1042.90	1039.56	1036.85	1034.65	1032.86	1031.41	1027.31	1025.84	1025.31
65000	1165.68	1155.11	1146.62	1139.79	1134.27	1129.81	1126.19	1123.26	1120.87	1118.94	1117.36	1112.92	1111.33	1110.75
70000	1255.35	1243.96	1234.82	1227.46	1221.52	1216.71	1212.82	1209.66	1207.09	1205.01	1203.31	1198.53	1196.81	1196.19
75000	1345.02	1332.82	1323.02	1315.14	1308.77	1303.62	1299.45	1296.06	1293.31	1291.08	1289.26	1284.14	1282.30	1281.63
80000	1434.68	1421.67	1411.22	1402.81	1396.02	1390.53	1386.08	1382.47	1379.53	1377.15	1375.21	1369.75	1367.78	1367.07
85000	1524.35	1510.52	1499.42	1490.49	1483.27	1477.44	1472.71	1468.87	1465.75	1463.22	1461.16	1455.36	1453.27	1452.52
90000	1614.02	1599.38	1587.63	1578.16	1570.52	1564.34	1559.34	1555.27	1551.98	1549.29	1547.11	1540.97	1538.76	1537.96
95000	1703.68	1688.23	1675.83	1665.84	1657.77	1651.25	1645.97	1641.68	1638.20	1635.36	1633.06	1626.58	1624.24	1623.40
100000	1793.35	1777.09	1764.03	1753.51	1745.03	1738.16	1732.60	1728.08	1724.42	1721.44	1719.01	1712.19	1709.73	1708.84

MONTHLY PAYMENT
REQUIRED TO AMORTIZE A LOAN

TERM	1 Year	2 Years	3 Years	4 Years	5 Years	6 Years	7 Years	8 Years	9 Years	10 Years	11 Years	12 Years	13 Years	14 Years
AMOUNT														
5	.47	.26	.19	.16	.14	.13	.12	.11	.11	.10	.10	.10	.10	.10
10	.93	.52	.38	.31	.27	.25	.23	.22	.21	.20	.20	.19	.19	.19
15	1.40	.77	.57	.47	.41	.37	.34	.32	.31	.30	.29	.29	.28	.28
25	2.33	1.28	.94	.77	.68	.61	.57	.54	.52	.50	.48	.47	.47	.46
50	4.65	2.56	1.88	1.54	1.35	1.22	1.13	1.07	1.03	.99	.96	.94	.93	.92
75	6.97	3.84	2.82	2.31	2.02	1.83	1.70	1.60	1.54	1.48	1.44	1.41	1.39	1.37
100	9.30	5.12	3.75	3.08	2.69	2.44	2.26	2.14	2.05	1.98	1.92	1.88	1.85	1.83
200	18.59	10.24	7.50	6.16	5.37	4.87	4.52	4.27	4.09	3.95	3.84	3.76	3.70	3.65
300	27.88	15.36	11.25	9.23	8.05	7.30	6.78	6.40	6.13	5.92	5.76	5.64	5.54	5.47
400	37.17	20.48	14.99	12.31	10.74	9.73	9.03	8.54	8.17	7.90	7.68	7.52	7.39	7.29
500	46.47	25.60	18.74	15.38	13.42	12.16	11.29	10.67	10.21	9.87	9.60	9.40	9.24	9.11
600	55.76	30.72	22.49	18.46	16.10	14.59	13.55	12.80	12.25	11.84	11.52	11.28	11.08	10.93
700	65.05	35.84	26.23	21.53	18.79	17.02	15.80	14.94	14.30	13.81	13.44	13.16	12.93	12.75
800	74.34	40.96	29.98	24.61	21.47	19.45	18.06	17.07	16.34	15.79	15.36	15.03	14.78	14.57
900	83.63	46.08	33.73	27.68	24.15	21.88	20.32	19.20	18.38	17.76	17.28	16.91	16.62	16.39
1000	92.93	51.19	37.48	30.76	26.83	24.31	22.57	21.33	20.42	19.73	19.20	18.79	18.47	18.22
2000	185.85	102.38	74.95	61.51	53.66	48.61	45.14	42.66	40.83	39.46	38.40	37.58	36.93	36.43
3000	278.77	153.57	112.42	92.26	80.49	72.91	67.71	63.99	61.25	59.18	57.59	56.36	55.40	54.64
4000	371.69	204.76	149.89	123.01	107.32	97.21	90.28	85.32	81.66	78.91	76.79	75.15	73.86	72.85
5000	464.61	255.95	187.36	153.76	134.15	121.51	112.85	106.65	102.08	98.63	95.99	93.94	92.33	91.06
6000	557.54	307.14	224.83	184.51	160.98	145.82	135.42	127.98	122.49	118.36	115.18	112.72	110.79	109.27
7000	650.46	358.33	262.30	215.26	187.81	170.12	157.99	149.31	142.91	138.08	134.38	131.51	129.26	127.48
8000	743.38	409.52	299.77	246.01	214.64	194.42	180.56	170.64	163.32	157.81	153.58	150.29	147.72	145.69
9000	836.30	460.71	337.24	276.76	241.46	218.72	203.12	191.96	183.74	177.53	172.77	169.08	166.18	163.90
10000	929.22	511.90	374.71	307.51	268.29	243.02	225.69	213.29	204.15	197.26	191.97	187.87	184.65	182.11
11000	1022.15	563.09	412.18	338.27	295.12	267.33	248.26	234.62	224.56	216.98	211.17	206.65	203.11	200.32
12000	1115.07	614.28	449.65	369.02	321.95	291.63	270.83	255.95	244.98	236.71	230.36	225.44	221.58	218.53
13000	1207.99	665.47	487.12	399.77	348.78	315.93	293.40	277.28	265.39	256.43	249.56	244.22	240.04	236.74
14000	1300.91	716.66	524.59	430.52	375.61	340.23	315.97	298.61	285.81	276.16	268.76	263.01	258.51	254.95
15000	1393.83	767.85	562.06	461.27	402.44	364.53	338.54	319.94	306.22	295.88	287.95	281.80	276.97	273.16
16000	1486.76	819.04	599.53	492.02	429.27	388.84	361.11	341.27	326.64	315.61	307.15	300.58	295.43	291.37
17000	1579.68	870.22	637.00	522.77	456.10	413.14	383.68	362.60	347.05	335.33	326.35	319.37	313.90	309.58
18000	1672.60	921.41	674.47	553.52	482.92	437.44	406.24	383.92	367.47	355.06	345.54	338.16	332.36	327.79
19000	1765.52	972.60	711.94	584.27	509.75	461.74	428.81	405.25	387.88	374.78	364.74	356.94	350.83	346.00
20000	1858.44	1023.79	749.41	615.02	536.58	486.04	451.38	426.58	408.29	394.51	383.94	375.73	369.29	364.21
21000	1951.37	1074.98	786.88	645.78	563.41	510.34	473.95	447.91	428.71	414.23	403.13	394.51	387.76	382.42
22000	2044.29	1126.17	824.35	676.53	590.24	534.65	496.52	469.24	449.12	433.96	422.33	413.30	406.22	400.63
23000	2137.21	1177.36	861.82	707.28	617.07	558.95	519.09	490.57	469.54	453.68	441.52	432.09	424.68	418.84
24000	2230.13	1228.55	899.29	738.03	643.90	583.25	541.66	511.90	489.95	473.41	460.72	450.87	443.15	437.05
25000	2323.05	1279.74	936.76	768.78	670.73	607.55	564.23	533.23	510.37	493.13	479.92	469.66	461.61	455.26
26000	2415.97	1330.93	974.23	799.53	697.55	631.85	586.80	554.56	530.78	512.86	499.11	488.44	480.08	473.47
27000	2508.90	1382.12	1011.70	830.28	724.38	656.16	609.36	575.88	551.20	532.58	518.31	507.23	498.54	491.68
28000	2601.82	1433.31	1049.17	861.03	751.21	680.46	631.93	597.21	571.61	552.31	537.51	526.02	517.01	509.89
29000	2694.74	1484.50	1086.64	891.78	778.04	704.76	654.50	618.54	592.02	572.03	556.70	544.80	535.47	528.10
30000	2787.66	1535.69	1124.11	922.53	804.87	729.06	677.07	639.87	612.44	591.76	575.90	563.59	553.93	546.31
31000	2880.58	1586.88	1161.58	953.28	831.70	753.36	699.64	661.20	632.85	611.48	595.10	582.38	572.40	564.52
32000	2973.50	1638.07	1199.05	984.04	858.53	777.67	722.21	682.53	653.27	631.21	614.29	601.16	590.86	582.73
33000	3066.43	1689.25	1236.52	1014.79	885.36	801.97	744.78	703.86	673.68	650.93	633.49	619.95	609.33	600.94
34000	3159.35	1740.44	1273.99	1045.54	912.19	826.27	767.35	725.19	694.10	670.66	652.69	638.73	627.79	619.15
35000	3252.27	1791.63	1311.46	1076.29	939.01	850.57	789.92	746.52	714.51	690.38	671.88	657.52	646.26	637.36
36000	3345.19	1842.82	1348.93	1107.04	965.84	874.87	812.48	767.84	734.93	710.11	691.08	676.31	664.72	655.57
37000	3438.12	1894.01	1386.40	1137.79	992.67	899.17	835.05	789.17	755.34	729.83	710.28	695.09	683.19	673.78
38000	3531.04	1945.20	1423.87	1168.54	1019.50	923.48	857.62	810.50	775.75	749.56	729.47	713.88	701.65	691.99
39000	3623.96	1996.39	1461.34	1199.29	1046.33	947.78	880.19	831.83	796.17	769.28	748.67	732.66	720.11	710.20
40000	3716.88	2047.58	1498.81	1230.04	1073.16	972.08	902.76	853.16	816.58	789.01	767.87	751.45	738.58	728.41
41000	3809.80	2098.77	1536.28	1260.79	1099.99	996.38	925.33	874.49	837.00	808.73	787.06	770.24	757.04	746.62
42000	3902.73	2149.96	1573.75	1291.55	1126.82	1020.68	947.90	895.82	857.41	828.46	806.26	789.02	775.51	764.83
43000	3995.65	2201.15	1611.22	1322.30	1153.65	1044.99	970.47	917.15	877.83	848.18	825.45	807.81	793.97	783.04
44000	4088.57	2252.34	1648.69	1353.05	1180.47	1069.29	993.04	938.48	898.24	867.91	844.65	826.59	812.44	801.25
45000	4181.49	2303.53	1686.16	1383.80	1207.30	1093.59	1015.60	959.80	918.66	887.63	863.85	845.38	830.90	819.46
46000	4274.41	2354.72	1723.63	1414.55	1234.13	1117.89	1038.17	981.13	939.07	907.36	883.04	864.17	849.36	837.67
47000	4367.33	2405.91	1761.10	1445.30	1260.96	1142.19	1060.74	1002.46	959.48	927.08	902.24	882.95	867.83	855.88
48000	4460.26	2457.10	1798.57	1476.05	1287.79	1166.50	1083.31	1023.79	979.90	946.81	921.44	901.74	886.29	874.09
49000	4553.18	2508.29	1836.04	1506.80	1314.62	1190.80	1105.88	1045.12	1000.31	966.53	940.63	920.53	904.76	892.30
50000	4646.10	2559.47	1873.51	1537.55	1341.45	1215.10	1128.45	1066.45	1020.73	986.26	959.83	939.31	923.22	910.51
55000	5110.71	2815.42	2060.86	1691.31	1475.59	1336.61	1241.29	1173.09	1122.80	1084.88	1055.81	1033.24	1015.54	1001.56
60000	5575.32	3071.37	2248.21	1845.06	1609.74	1458.12	1354.14	1279.74	1224.87	1183.51	1151.80	1127.17	1107.87	1092.61
65000	6039.93	3327.32	2435.56	1998.82	1743.88	1579.63	1466.98	1386.38	1326.95	1282.13	1247.78	1221.10	1200.19	1183.66
70000	6504.54	3583.26	2622.91	2152.57	1878.02	1701.14	1579.83	1493.03	1429.02	1380.76	1343.76	1315.03	1292.51	1274.71
75000	6969.15	3839.21	2810.26	2306.33	2012.17	1822.65	1692.67	1599.67	1531.09	1479.38	1439.74	1408.97	1384.83	1365.76
80000	7433.76	4095.16	2997.61	2460.08	2146.31	1944.16	1805.52	1706.32	1633.16	1578.01	1535.73	1502.90	1477.15	1456.81
85000	7898.37	4351.10	3184.96	2613.84	2280.46	2065.67	1918.36	1812.96	1735.23	1676.63	1631.71	1596.83	1569.47	1547.86
90000	8362.98	4607.05	3372.31	2767.59	2414.60	2187.17	2031.20	1919.60	1837.31	1775.26	1727.69	1690.76	1661.79	1638.91
95000	8827.59	4863.00	3559.66	2921.35	2548.74	2308.68	2144.05	2026.25	1939.38	1873.88	1823.67	1784.69	1754.12	1729.96
100000	9292.20	5118.94	3747.01	3075.10	2682.89	2430.19	2256.89	2132.89	2041.45	1972.51	1919.66	1878.62	1846.44	1821.01

TERM	15 Years	16 Years	17 Years	18 Years	19 Years	20 Years	21 Years	22 Years	23 Years	24 Years	25 Years	30 Years	35 Years	40 Years
AMOUNT														
5	.10	.09	.09	.09	.09	.09	.09	.09	.09	.09	.09	.09	.09	.09
10	.19	.18	.18	.18	.18	.18	.18	.18	.18	.18	.18	.18	.18	.18
15	.28	.27	.27	.27	.27	.27	.27	.27	.26	.26	.26	.26	.26	.26
25	.46	.45	.45	.45	.44	.44	.44	.44	.44	.44	.44	.44	.43	.43
50	.91	.90	.89	.89	.88	.88	.88	.87	.87	.87	.87	.87	.86	.86
75	1.36	1.34	1.33	1.33	1.32	1.31	1.31	1.31	1.30	1.30	1.30	1.30	1.29	1.29
100	1.81	1.79	1.78	1.77	1.76	1.75	1.75	1.74	1.74	1.73	1.73	1.73	1.72	1.72
200	3.61	3.57	3.55	3.53	3.51	3.50	3.49	3.48	3.47	3.46	3.46	3.45	3.44	3.44
300	5.41	5.36	5.32	5.29	5.26	5.24	5.23	5.21	5.20	5.19	5.19	5.17	5.16	5.16
400	7.21	7.14	7.09	7.05	7.02	6.99	6.97	6.95	6.93	6.92	6.91	6.89	6.88	6.87
500	9.01	8.93	8.86	8.81	8.77	8.74	8.71	8.69	8.67	8.65	8.64	8.61	8.60	8.59
600	10.81	10.71	10.64	10.57	10.52	10.48	10.45	10.42	10.40	10.38	10.37	10.33	10.31	10.31
700	12.61	12.50	12.41	12.33	12.27	12.23	12.19	12.16	12.13	12.11	12.09	12.05	12.03	12.03
800	14.41	14.28	14.18	14.09	14.03	13.97	13.93	13.89	13.86	13.84	13.82	13.77	13.75	13.74
900	16.21	16.07	15.95	15.86	15.78	15.72	15.67	15.63	15.60	15.57	15.55	15.49	15.47	15.46
1000	18.01	17.85	17.72	17.62	17.53	17.47	17.41	17.37	17.33	17.30	17.28	17.21	17.19	17.18
2000	36.02	35.70	35.44	35.23	35.06	34.93	34.82	34.73	34.65	34.60	34.55	34.41	34.37	34.35
3000	54.03	53.54	53.16	52.84	52.59	52.39	52.22	52.09	51.98	51.89	51.82	51.62	51.55	51.52
4000	72.04	71.39	70.87	70.45	70.12	69.85	69.63	69.45	69.30	69.19	69.09	68.82	68.73	68.69
5000	90.04	89.24	88.59	88.07	87.65	87.31	87.03	86.81	86.63	86.48	86.36	86.03	85.91	85.86
6000	108.05	107.08	106.31	105.68	105.18	104.77	104.44	104.17	103.95	103.78	103.63	103.23	103.09	103.03
7000	126.06	124.93	124.02	123.29	122.70	122.23	121.84	121.53	121.28	121.07	120.90	120.43	120.27	120.21
8000	144.07	142.78	141.74	140.90	140.23	139.69	139.25	138.89	138.60	138.37	138.18	137.64	137.45	137.38
9000	162.08	160.62	159.46	158.52	157.76	157.15	156.65	156.25	155.93	155.66	155.45	154.84	154.63	154.55
10000	180.08	178.47	177.17	176.13	175.29	174.61	174.06	173.61	173.25	172.96	172.72	172.05	171.81	171.72
11000	198.09	196.31	194.89	193.74	192.82	192.07	191.46	190.97	190.58	190.25	189.99	189.25	188.99	188.89
12000	216.10	214.16	212.61	211.35	210.35	209.53	208.87	208.33	207.90	207.55	207.26	206.46	206.17	206.06
13000	234.11	232.01	230.32	228.97	227.87	226.99	226.27	225.70	225.22	224.84	224.53	223.66	223.35	223.23
14000	252.11	249.85	248.04	246.58	245.40	244.45	243.68	243.06	242.55	242.14	241.80	240.86	240.53	240.41
15000	270.12	267.70	265.76	264.19	262.93	261.91	261.09	260.42	259.87	259.43	259.07	258.07	257.71	257.58
16000	288.13	285.55	283.47	281.80	280.46	279.37	278.49	277.78	277.20	276.73	276.35	275.27	274.89	274.75
17000	306.14	303.39	301.19	299.42	297.99	296.83	295.90	295.14	294.52	294.02	293.62	292.48	292.07	291.92
18000	324.15	321.24	318.91	317.03	315.52	314.29	313.30	312.50	311.85	311.32	310.89	309.68	309.25	309.09
19000	342.15	339.00	336.62	334.64	333.04	331.75	330.71	329.86	329.17	328.61	328.16	326.88	326.43	326.26
20000	360.16	356.93	354.34	352.25	350.57	349.21	348.11	347.22	346.50	345.91	345.43	344.09	343.61	343.44
21000	378.17	374.78	372.06	369.87	368.10	366.67	365.52	364.58	363.82	363.20	362.70	361.29	360.79	360.61
22000	396.18	392.62	389.77	387.48	385.63	384.13	382.92	381.94	381.15	380.50	379.97	378.50	377.97	377.78
23000	414.19	410.47	407.49	405.09	403.16	401.59	400.33	399.30	398.47	397.79	397.25	395.70	395.15	394.95
24000	432.19	428.32	425.21	422.70	420.69	419.05	417.73	416.66	415.80	415.09	414.52	412.91	412.33	412.12
25000	450.20	446.16	442.92	440.32	438.21	436.51	435.14	434.02	433.12	432.38	431.79	430.11	429.51	429.29
26000	468.21	464.01	460.64	457.93	455.74	453.98	452.54	451.39	450.44	449.68	449.06	447.31	446.69	446.46
27000	486.22	481.85	478.36	475.54	473.27	471.44	469.95	468.75	467.77	466.98	466.33	464.52	463.87	463.64
28000	504.22	499.70	496.07	493.15	490.80	488.90	487.36	486.11	485.09	484.27	483.60	481.72	481.05	480.81
29000	522.23	517.55	513.79	510.77	508.33	506.36	504.76	503.47	502.42	501.57	500.87	498.93	498.23	497.98
30000	540.24	535.39	531.51	528.38	525.86	523.82	522.17	520.83	519.74	518.86	518.14	516.13	515.41	515.15
31000	558.25	553.24	549.22	545.99	543.38	541.28	539.57	538.19	537.07	536.16	535.42	533.34	532.59	532.32
32000	576.26	571.09	566.94	563.60	560.91	558.74	556.98	555.55	554.39	553.45	552.69	550.54	549.77	549.49
33000	594.26	588.93	584.66	581.22	578.44	576.20	574.38	572.91	571.72	570.75	569.96	567.74	566.95	566.67
34000	612.27	606.78	602.37	598.83	595.97	593.66	591.79	590.27	589.04	588.04	587.23	584.95	584.13	583.84
35000	630.28	624.62	620.09	616.44	613.50	611.12	609.19	607.63	606.37	605.34	604.50	602.15	601.31	601.01
36000	648.29	642.47	637.81	634.05	631.03	628.58	626.60	624.99	623.69	622.63	621.77	619.36	618.49	618.18
37000	666.29	660.32	655.52	651.67	648.55	646.04	644.00	642.35	641.01	639.93	639.04	636.56	635.67	635.35
38000	684.30	678.16	673.24	669.28	666.08	663.50	661.41	659.71	658.34	657.22	656.31	653.76	652.85	652.52
39000	702.31	696.01	690.96	686.89	683.61	680.96	678.81	677.08	675.66	674.52	673.59	670.97	670.03	669.69
40000	720.32	713.86	708.67	704.50	701.14	698.42	696.22	694.44	692.99	691.81	690.86	688.17	687.21	686.87
41000	738.33	731.70	726.39	722.12	718.67	715.88	713.63	711.80	710.31	709.11	708.13	705.38	704.39	704.04
42000	756.33	749.55	744.11	739.73	736.20	733.34	731.03	729.16	727.64	726.40	725.40	722.58	721.57	721.21
43000	774.34	767.39	761.82	757.34	753.73	750.80	748.44	746.52	744.96	743.70	742.67	739.79	738.75	738.38
44000	792.35	785.24	779.54	774.95	771.25	768.26	765.84	763.88	762.29	760.99	759.94	756.99	755.93	755.55
45000	810.36	803.09	797.26	792.57	788.78	785.72	783.25	781.24	779.61	778.29	777.21	774.19	773.11	772.72
46000	828.37	820.93	814.97	810.18	806.31	803.18	800.65	798.60	796.94	795.58	794.49	791.40	790.29	789.90
47000	846.37	838.78	832.69	827.79	823.84	820.64	818.06	815.96	814.26	812.88	811.76	808.60	807.47	807.07
48000	864.38	856.63	850.41	845.40	841.37	838.10	835.46	833.32	831.59	830.17	829.03	825.81	824.65	824.24
49000	882.39	874.47	868.12	863.01	858.89	855.56	852.87	850.68	848.91	847.47	846.30	843.01	841.83	841.41
50000	900.40	892.32	885.84	880.63	876.42	873.02	870.27	868.04	866.23	864.76	863.57	860.22	859.01	858.58
55000	990.44	981.55	974.42	968.69	964.06	960.33	957.30	954.85	952.86	951.24	949.93	946.24	944.91	944.44
60000	1080.47	1070.78	1063.01	1056.75	1051.71	1047.63	1044.33	1041.65	1039.48	1037.72	1036.28	1032.26	1030.82	1030.30
65000	1170.51	1160.01	1151.59	1144.81	1139.35	1134.93	1131.35	1128.46	1126.10	1124.19	1122.64	1118.28	1116.72	1116.15
70000	1260.55	1249.24	1240.17	1232.88	1226.99	1222.23	1218.38	1215.26	1212.73	1210.67	1209.00	1204.30	1202.62	1202.01
75000	1350.59	1338.48	1328.76	1320.94	1314.63	1309.53	1305.41	1302.06	1299.35	1297.14	1295.35	1290.32	1288.52	1287.87
80000	1440.63	1427.71	1417.34	1409.00	1402.27	1396.84	1392.44	1388.87	1385.97	1383.62	1381.71	1376.34	1374.42	1373.73
85000	1530.67	1516.94	1505.92	1497.06	1489.92	1484.14	1479.46	1475.67	1472.59	1470.10	1468.07	1462.36	1460.32	1459.58
90000	1620.71	1606.17	1594.51	1585.13	1577.56	1571.44	1566.49	1562.48	1559.22	1556.57	1554.42	1548.38	1546.22	1545.44
95000	1710.75	1695.40	1683.09	1673.19	1665.20	1658.74	1653.52	1649.28	1645.84	1643.05	1640.78	1634.40	1632.12	1631.30
100000	1800.79	1784.63	1771.68	1761.25	1752.84	1746.04	1740.54	1736.08	1732.46	1729.52	1727.14	1720.43	1718.02	1717.16

20.625%

TERM	1 Year	2 Years	3 Years	4 Years	5 Years	6 Years	7 Years	8 Years	9 Years	10 Years	11 Years	12 Years	13 Years	14 Years
AMOUNT														
5	.47	.26	.19	.16	.14	.13	.12	.11	.11	.10	.10	.10	.10	.10
10	.93	.52	.38	.31	.27	.25	.23	.22	.21	.20	.20	.19	.19	.19
15	1.40	.77	.57	.47	.41	.37	.34	.33	.31	.30	.29	.29	.28	.28
25	2.33	1.29	.94	.77	.68	.61	.57	.54	.52	.50	.49	.48	.47	.46
50	4.65	2.57	1.88	1.54	1.35	1.22	1.13	1.07	1.03	.99	.97	.95	.93	.92
75	6.98	3.85	2.82	2.31	2.02	1.83	1.70	1.61	1.54	1.49	1.45	1.42	1.39	1.37
100	9.30	5.13	3.75	3.08	2.69	2.44	2.26	2.14	2.05	1.98	1.93	1.89	1.85	1.83
200	18.59	10.25	7.50	6.16	5.37	4.87	4.52	4.27	4.09	3.95	3.85	3.77	3.70	3.65
300	27.89	15.37	11.25	9.23	8.06	7.30	6.78	6.41	6.13	5.93	5.77	5.65	5.55	5.47
400	37.18	20.49	15.00	12.31	10.74	9.73	9.04	8.54	8.18	7.90	7.69	7.53	7.40	7.30
500	46.47	25.61	18.75	15.39	13.43	12.16	11.30	10.68	10.22	9.88	9.61	9.41	9.25	9.12
600	55.77	30.73	22.49	18.46	16.11	14.59	13.56	12.81	12.26	11.85	11.53	11.29	11.09	10.94
700	65.06	35.85	26.24	21.54	18.79	17.03	15.81	14.95	14.31	13.82	13.45	13.17	12.94	12.76
800	74.35	40.97	29.99	24.62	21.48	19.46	18.07	17.08	16.35	15.80	15.38	15.05	14.79	14.59
900	83.65	46.09	33.74	27.69	24.16	21.89	20.33	19.22	18.39	17.77	17.30	16.93	16.64	16.41
1000	92.94	51.21	37.49	30.77	26.85	24.32	22.59	21.35	20.44	19.75	19.22	18.81	18.49	18.23
2000	185.87	102.41	74.97	61.53	53.69	48.64	45.17	42.69	40.87	39.49	38.43	37.61	36.97	36.46
3000	278.81	153.61	112.45	92.30	80.53	72.95	67.76	64.04	61.30	59.23	57.65	56.42	55.45	54.69
4000	371.74	204.81	149.94	123.06	107.38	97.27	90.34	85.38	81.73	78.97	76.86	75.22	73.93	72.92
5000	464.67	256.01	187.42	153.83	134.22	121.59	112.93	106.73	102.16	98.71	96.07	94.02	92.42	91.15
6000	557.61	307.21	224.90	184.59	161.06	145.90	135.51	128.07	122.59	118.46	115.29	112.83	110.90	109.37
7000	650.54	358.42	262.38	215.36	187.90	170.22	158.09	149.42	143.02	138.20	134.50	131.63	129.38	127.60
8000	743.48	409.62	299.87	246.12	214.75	194.54	180.68	170.76	163.45	157.94	153.71	150.43	147.86	145.83
9000	836.41	460.82	337.35	276.88	241.59	218.85	203.26	192.11	183.88	177.68	172.93	169.24	166.35	164.06
10000	929.34	512.02	374.83	307.65	268.43	243.17	225.85	213.45	204.31	197.42	192.14	188.04	184.83	182.29
11000	1022.28	563.22	412.32	338.41	295.28	267.49	248.43	234.80	224.74	217.16	211.36	206.85	203.31	200.52
12000	1115.21	614.42	449.80	369.18	322.12	291.80	271.01	256.14	245.17	236.91	230.57	225.65	221.79	218.74
13000	1208.15	665.63	487.28	399.94	348.96	316.12	293.60	277.48	265.60	256.65	249.78	244.45	240.27	236.97
14000	1301.08	716.83	524.76	430.71	375.80	340.44	316.18	298.83	286.03	276.39	269.00	263.26	258.76	255.20
15000	1394.01	768.03	562.25	461.47	402.65	364.75	338.77	320.17	306.47	296.13	288.21	282.06	277.24	273.43
16000	1486.95	819.23	599.73	492.23	429.49	389.07	361.35	341.52	326.90	315.87	307.42	300.86	295.72	291.66
17000	1579.88	870.43	637.21	523.00	456.33	413.39	383.93	362.86	347.33	335.61	326.64	319.67	314.20	309.89
18000	1672.82	921.63	674.70	553.76	483.18	437.70	406.52	384.21	367.76	355.36	345.85	338.47	332.69	328.11
19000	1765.75	972.84	712.18	584.53	510.02	462.02	429.10	405.55	388.19	375.10	365.06	357.28	351.17	346.34
20000	1858.68	1024.04	749.66	615.29	536.86	486.33	451.69	426.90	408.62	394.84	384.28	376.08	369.65	364.57
21000	1951.62	1075.24	787.14	646.06	563.70	510.65	474.27	448.24	429.05	414.58	403.49	394.88	388.13	382.80
22000	2044.55	1126.44	824.63	676.82	590.55	534.97	496.85	469.59	449.48	434.32	422.71	413.69	406.62	401.03
23000	2137.48	1177.64	862.11	707.59	617.39	559.28	519.44	490.93	469.91	454.07	441.92	432.49	425.10	419.26
24000	2230.42	1228.84	899.59	738.35	644.23	583.60	542.02	512.28	490.34	473.81	461.13	451.29	443.58	437.48
25000	2323.35	1280.05	937.08	769.11	671.08	607.92	564.61	533.62	510.77	493.55	480.35	470.10	462.06	455.71
26000	2416.29	1331.25	974.56	799.88	697.92	632.23	587.19	554.96	531.20	513.29	499.56	488.90	480.54	473.94
27000	2509.22	1382.45	1012.04	830.64	724.76	656.55	609.77	576.31	551.63	533.03	518.77	507.71	499.03	492.17
28000	2602.15	1433.65	1049.52	861.41	751.60	680.87	632.36	597.65	572.06	552.77	537.99	526.51	517.51	510.40
29000	2695.09	1484.85	1087.01	892.17	778.45	705.18	654.94	619.00	592.50	572.52	557.20	545.31	535.99	528.63
30000	2788.02	1536.05	1124.49	922.94	805.29	729.50	677.53	640.34	612.93	592.26	576.42	564.12	554.47	546.85
31000	2880.96	1587.26	1161.97	953.70	832.13	753.82	700.11	661.69	633.36	612.00	595.63	582.92	572.96	565.08
32000	2973.89	1638.46	1199.45	984.46	858.98	778.13	722.69	683.03	653.79	631.74	614.84	601.72	591.44	583.31
33000	3066.82	1689.66	1236.94	1015.23	885.82	802.45	745.28	704.38	674.22	651.48	634.06	620.53	609.92	601.54
34000	3159.76	1740.86	1274.42	1045.99	912.66	826.77	767.86	725.72	694.65	671.22	653.27	639.33	628.40	619.77
35000	3252.69	1792.06	1311.90	1076.76	939.50	851.08	790.45	747.07	715.08	690.97	672.48	658.13	646.88	638.00
36000	3345.63	1843.26	1349.39	1107.52	966.35	875.40	813.03	768.41	735.51	710.71	691.70	676.94	665.37	656.22
37000	3438.56	1894.47	1386.87	1138.29	993.19	899.71	835.62	789.76	755.94	730.45	710.91	695.74	683.85	674.45
38000	3531.49	1945.67	1424.35	1169.05	1020.03	924.03	858.20	811.10	776.37	750.19	730.12	714.55	702.33	692.68
39000	3624.43	1996.87	1461.83	1199.81	1046.88	948.35	880.78	832.44	796.80	769.93	749.34	733.35	720.81	710.91
40000	3717.36	2048.07	1499.32	1230.58	1073.72	972.66	903.37	853.79	817.23	789.68	768.55	752.15	739.30	729.14
41000	3810.29	2099.27	1536.80	1261.34	1100.56	996.98	925.95	875.13	837.66	809.42	787.77	770.96	757.78	747.37
42000	3903.23	2150.47	1574.28	1292.11	1127.40	1021.30	948.54	896.48	858.09	829.16	806.98	789.76	776.26	765.59
43000	3996.16	2201.68	1611.77	1322.87	1154.25	1045.61	971.12	917.82	878.53	848.90	826.19	808.56	794.74	783.82
44000	4089.10	2252.88	1649.25	1353.64	1181.09	1069.93	993.70	939.17	898.96	868.64	845.41	827.37	813.23	802.05
45000	4182.03	2304.08	1686.73	1384.40	1207.93	1094.25	1016.29	960.51	919.39	888.38	864.62	846.17	831.71	820.28
46000	4274.96	2355.28	1724.21	1415.17	1234.78	1118.56	1038.87	981.86	939.82	908.13	883.83	864.98	850.19	838.51
47000	4367.90	2406.48	1761.70	1445.93	1261.62	1142.88	1061.46	1003.20	960.25	927.87	903.05	883.78	868.67	856.74
48000	4460.83	2457.68	1799.18	1476.69	1288.46	1167.20	1084.04	1024.55	980.68	947.61	922.26	902.58	887.15	874.96
49000	4553.77	2508.89	1836.66	1507.46	1315.30	1191.51	1106.62	1045.89	1001.11	967.35	941.47	921.39	905.64	893.19
50000	4646.70	2560.09	1874.15	1538.22	1342.15	1215.83	1129.21	1067.24	1021.54	987.09	960.69	940.19	924.12	911.42
55000	5111.37	2816.10	2061.56	1692.04	1476.36	1337.41	1242.13	1173.96	1123.69	1085.80	1056.76	1034.21	1016.53	1002.56
60000	5576.04	3072.10	2248.97	1845.87	1610.58	1458.99	1355.05	1280.68	1225.85	1184.51	1152.83	1128.23	1108.94	1093.70
65000	6040.71	3328.11	2436.39	1999.69	1744.79	1580.58	1467.97	1387.40	1328.00	1283.22	1248.89	1222.25	1201.35	1184.85
70000	6505.38	3584.12	2623.80	2153.51	1879.00	1702.16	1580.89	1494.13	1430.15	1381.93	1344.96	1316.26	1293.76	1275.99
75000	6970.05	3840.13	2811.22	2307.33	2013.22	1823.74	1693.81	1600.85	1532.31	1480.64	1441.03	1410.28	1386.18	1367.13
80000	7434.72	4096.14	2998.63	2461.15	2147.43	1945.32	1806.73	1707.57	1634.46	1579.35	1537.10	1504.30	1478.59	1458.27
85000	7899.39	4352.14	3186.04	2614.97	2281.65	2066.91	1919.65	1814.30	1736.61	1678.05	1633.17	1598.32	1571.00	1549.41
90000	8364.06	4608.15	3373.46	2768.80	2415.86	2188.49	2032.57	1921.02	1838.77	1776.76	1729.24	1692.34	1663.41	1640.55
95000	8828.73	4864.16	3560.87	2922.62	2550.07	2310.07	2145.49	2027.74	1940.92	1875.47	1825.30	1786.36	1755.82	1731.70
100000	9293.39	5120.17	3748.29	3076.44	2684.29	2431.65	2258.41	2134.47	2043.07	1974.18	1921.37	1880.38	1848.23	1822.84

TERM	15 Years	16 Years	17 Years	18 Years	19 Years	20 Years	21 Years	22 Years	23 Years	24 Years	25 Years	30 Years	35 Years	40 Years
AMOUNT														
5	.10	.09	.09	.09	.09	.09	.09	.09	.09	.09	.09	.09	.09	.09
10	.19	.18	.18	.18	.18	.18	.18	.18	.18	.18	.18	.18	.18	.18
15	.28	.27	.27	.27	.27	.27	.27	.27	.27	.26	.26	.26	.26	.26
25	.46	.45	.45	.45	.44	.44	.44	.44	.44	.44	.44	.44	.44	.43
50	.91	.90	.89	.89	.88	.88	.88	.87	.87	.87	.87	.87	.87	.86
75	1.36	1.34	1.34	1.33	1.32	1.32	1.31	1.31	1.31	1.30	1.30	1.30	1.30	1.29
100	1.81	1.79	1.78	1.77	1.76	1.75	1.75	1.74	1.74	1.74	1.73	1.73	1.73	1.72
200	3.61	3.58	3.55	3.53	3.51	3.50	3.49	3.48	3.47	3.47	3.46	3.45	3.45	3.44
300	5.41	5.36	5.33	5.29	5.27	5.25	5.23	5.22	5.21	5.20	5.19	5.17	5.17	5.16
400	7.22	7.15	7.10	7.06	7.02	7.00	6.98	6.96	6.94	6.93	6.92	6.89	6.89	6.88
500	9.02	8.94	8.87	8.82	8.78	8.75	8.72	8.70	8.68	8.66	8.65	8.62	8.61	8.60
600	10.82	10.72	10.65	10.58	10.53	10.49	10.46	10.43	10.41	10.39	10.38	10.34	10.33	10.32
700	12.62	12.51	12.42	12.35	12.29	12.24	12.20	12.17	12.15	12.13	12.11	12.06	12.05	12.04
800	14.43	14.30	14.19	14.11	14.04	13.99	13.95	13.91	13.88	13.86	13.84	13.78	13.77	13.76
900	16.23	16.08	15.97	15.87	15.80	15.74	15.69	15.65	15.62	15.59	15.57	15.51	15.49	15.48
1000	18.03	17.87	17.74	17.64	17.55	17.49	17.43	17.39	17.35	17.32	17.30	17.23	17.21	17.20
2000	36.06	35.74	35.48	35.27	35.10	34.97	34.86	34.77	34.69	34.64	34.59	34.45	34.41	34.39
3000	54.08	53.60	53.21	52.90	52.65	52.45	52.28	52.15	52.04	51.95	51.88	51.68	51.61	51.58
4000	72.11	71.47	70.95	70.53	70.20	69.93	69.71	69.53	69.38	69.27	69.17	68.90	68.81	68.77
5000	90.14	89.33	88.68	88.16	87.74	87.41	87.13	86.91	86.73	86.58	86.46	86.13	86.01	85.97
6000	108.16	107.20	106.42	105.80	105.29	104.89	104.56	104.29	104.07	103.90	103.75	103.35	103.21	103.16
7000	126.19	125.06	124.16	123.43	122.84	122.37	121.98	121.67	121.42	121.21	121.05	120.58	120.41	120.35
8000	144.22	142.93	141.89	141.06	140.39	139.85	139.41	139.05	138.76	138.53	138.34	137.80	137.61	137.54
9000	162.24	160.79	159.63	158.69	157.94	157.33	156.83	156.43	156.11	155.84	155.63	155.03	154.81	154.74
10000	180.27	178.66	177.36	176.32	175.48	174.81	174.26	173.81	173.45	173.16	172.92	172.25	172.01	171.93
11000	198.30	196.52	195.10	193.95	193.03	192.29	191.68	191.19	190.80	190.47	190.21	189.48	189.21	189.12
12000	216.32	214.39	212.84	211.59	210.58	209.77	209.11	208.57	208.14	207.79	207.50	206.70	206.42	206.31
13000	234.35	232.25	230.57	229.22	228.13	227.25	226.53	225.96	225.49	225.11	224.80	223.93	223.62	223.51
14000	252.38	250.12	248.31	246.85	245.68	244.73	243.96	243.34	242.83	242.42	242.09	241.15	240.82	240.70
15000	270.40	267.98	266.04	264.48	263.22	262.21	261.38	260.72	260.18	259.74	259.38	258.38	258.02	257.89
16000	288.43	285.85	283.78	282.11	280.77	279.69	278.81	278.10	277.52	277.05	276.67	275.60	275.22	275.08
17000	306.45	303.71	301.51	299.75	298.32	297.17	296.23	295.48	294.87	294.37	293.96	292.83	292.42	292.27
18000	324.48	321.58	319.25	317.38	315.87	314.65	313.66	312.86	312.21	311.68	311.25	310.05	309.62	309.47
19000	342.51	339.44	336.99	335.01	333.42	332.13	331.08	330.24	329.55	329.00	328.55	327.28	326.82	326.66
20000	360.53	357.31	354.72	352.64	350.96	349.61	348.51	347.62	346.90	346.31	345.84	344.50	344.02	343.85
21000	378.56	375.17	372.46	370.27	368.51	367.09	365.94	365.00	364.24	363.63	363.13	361.73	361.22	361.04
22000	396.59	393.04	390.19	387.90	386.06	384.57	383.36	382.38	381.59	380.94	380.42	378.95	378.42	378.24
23000	414.61	410.90	407.93	405.54	403.61	402.05	400.79	399.76	398.93	398.26	397.71	396.18	395.63	395.43
24000	432.64	428.77	425.67	423.17	421.15	419.53	418.21	417.14	416.28	415.58	415.00	413.40	412.83	412.62
25000	450.67	446.63	443.40	440.80	438.70	437.01	435.64	434.52	433.62	432.89	432.30	430.63	430.03	429.81
26000	468.69	464.50	461.14	458.43	456.25	454.49	453.06	451.91	450.97	450.21	449.59	447.85	447.23	447.01
27000	486.72	482.36	478.87	476.06	473.80	471.97	470.49	469.29	468.31	467.52	466.88	465.07	464.43	464.20
28000	504.75	500.23	496.61	493.70	491.35	489.45	487.91	486.67	485.66	484.84	484.17	482.30	481.63	481.39
29000	522.77	518.09	514.34	511.33	508.89	506.93	505.34	504.05	503.00	502.15	501.46	499.52	498.83	498.58
30000	540.80	535.96	532.08	528.96	526.44	524.41	522.76	521.43	520.35	519.47	518.75	516.75	516.03	515.77
31000	558.82	553.82	549.82	546.59	543.99	541.89	540.19	538.81	537.69	536.78	536.05	533.97	533.23	532.97
32000	576.85	571.69	567.55	564.22	561.54	559.37	557.61	556.19	555.04	554.10	553.34	551.20	550.43	550.16
33000	594.88	589.56	585.29	581.85	579.09	576.85	575.04	573.57	572.38	571.41	570.63	568.42	567.63	567.35
34000	612.90	607.42	603.02	599.49	596.63	594.33	592.46	590.95	589.73	588.73	587.92	585.65	584.84	584.54
35000	630.93	625.29	620.76	617.12	614.18	611.81	609.89	608.33	607.07	606.04	605.21	602.87	602.04	601.74
36000	648.96	643.15	638.50	634.75	631.73	629.29	627.31	625.71	624.41	623.36	622.50	620.10	619.24	618.93
37000	666.98	661.02	656.23	652.38	649.28	646.77	644.74	643.09	641.76	640.68	639.79	637.32	636.44	636.12
38000	685.01	678.88	673.97	670.01	666.83	664.25	662.16	660.47	659.10	657.99	657.09	654.55	653.64	653.31
39000	703.04	696.75	691.70	687.65	684.37	681.73	679.59	677.86	676.45	675.31	674.38	671.77	670.84	670.51
40000	721.06	714.61	709.44	705.28	701.92	699.21	697.02	695.24	693.79	692.62	691.67	689.00	688.04	687.70
41000	739.09	732.48	727.17	722.91	719.47	716.69	714.44	712.62	711.14	709.94	708.96	706.22	705.24	704.89
42000	757.12	750.34	744.91	740.54	737.02	734.17	731.87	730.00	728.48	727.25	726.25	723.45	722.44	722.08
43000	775.14	768.21	762.65	758.17	754.57	751.65	749.29	747.38	745.83	744.57	743.54	740.67	739.64	739.27
44000	793.17	786.07	780.38	775.80	772.11	769.13	766.72	764.76	763.17	761.88	760.84	757.90	756.84	756.47
45000	811.19	803.94	798.12	793.44	789.66	786.61	784.14	782.14	780.52	779.20	778.13	775.12	774.05	773.66
46000	829.22	821.80	815.85	811.07	807.21	804.09	801.57	799.52	797.86	796.51	795.42	792.35	791.25	790.85
47000	847.25	839.67	833.59	828.70	824.76	821.57	818.99	816.90	815.21	813.83	812.71	809.57	808.45	808.04
48000	865.27	857.53	851.33	846.33	842.30	839.05	836.42	834.28	832.55	831.15	830.00	826.80	825.65	825.24
49000	883.30	875.40	869.06	863.96	859.85	856.53	853.84	851.66	849.90	848.46	847.29	844.02	842.85	842.43
50000	901.33	893.26	886.80	881.60	877.40	874.01	871.27	869.04	867.24	865.78	864.59	861.25	860.05	859.62
55000	991.46	982.59	975.48	969.75	965.14	961.41	958.39	955.95	953.96	952.35	951.04	947.37	946.05	945.58
60000	1081.59	1071.91	1064.16	1057.91	1052.88	1048.81	1045.52	1042.85	1040.69	1038.93	1037.50	1033.49	1032.06	1031.54
65000	1171.72	1161.24	1152.83	1146.07	1140.62	1136.21	1132.65	1129.76	1127.41	1125.51	1123.96	1119.62	1118.06	1117.51
70000	1261.86	1250.57	1241.51	1234.23	1228.36	1223.61	1219.77	1216.66	1214.13	1212.08	1210.42	1205.74	1204.07	1203.47
75000	1351.99	1339.89	1330.19	1322.39	1316.10	1311.01	1306.90	1303.56	1300.86	1298.66	1296.88	1291.87	1290.07	1289.43
80000	1442.12	1429.22	1418.87	1410.55	1403.84	1398.41	1394.03	1390.47	1387.58	1385.24	1383.33	1377.99	1376.08	1375.39
85000	1532.25	1518.54	1507.55	1498.71	1491.58	1485.82	1481.15	1477.37	1474.31	1471.82	1469.79	1464.11	1462.08	1461.35
90000	1622.38	1607.87	1596.23	1586.87	1579.32	1573.22	1568.28	1564.28	1561.03	1558.39	1556.25	1550.24	1548.09	1547.31
95000	1712.52	1697.20	1684.91	1675.03	1667.06	1660.62	1655.40	1651.18	1647.75	1644.97	1642.71	1636.36	1634.09	1633.28
100000	1802.65	1786.52	1773.59	1763.19	1754.80	1748.02	1742.53	1738.08	1734.48	1731.55	1729.17	1722.49	1720.10	1719.24

MONTHLY PAYMENT
REQUIRED TO AMORTIZE A LOAN

TERM	1 Year	2 Years	3 Years	4 Years	5 Years	6 Years	7 Years	8 Years	9 Years	10 Years	11 Years	12 Years	13 Years	14 Years
AMOUNT														
5	.47	.26	.19	.16	.14	.13	.12	.11	.11	.10	.10	.10	.10	.10
10	.93	.52	.38	.31	.27	.25	.23	.22	.21	.20	.20	.19	.19	.19
15	1.40	.77	.57	.47	.41	.37	.34	.33	.31	.30	.29	.29	.28	.28
25	2.33	1.29	.94	.78	.68	.61	.57	.54	.52	.50	.49	.48	.47	.46
50	4.65	2.57	1.88	1.55	1.35	1.22	1.14	1.07	1.03	.99	.97	.95	.93	.92
75	6.98	3.85	2.82	2.32	2.02	1.83	1.70	1.61	1.54	1.49	1.45	1.42	1.40	1.38
100	9.30	5.13	3.76	3.09	2.69	2.44	2.27	2.14	2.05	1.98	1.93	1.89	1.86	1.83
200	18.60	10.25	7.51	6.17	5.38	4.88	4.53	4.28	4.10	3.96	3.86	3.78	3.71	3.66
300	27.90	15.38	11.26	9.25	8.07	7.31	6.79	6.42	6.15	5.94	5.78	5.66	5.57	5.49
400	37.19	20.50	15.01	12.33	10.76	9.75	9.06	8.56	8.20	7.92	7.71	7.55	7.42	7.32
500	46.49	25.62	18.77	15.41	13.45	12.19	11.32	10.70	10.24	9.90	9.64	9.43	9.27	9.15
600	55.79	30.75	22.52	18.49	16.14	14.62	13.58	12.84	12.29	11.88	11.56	11.32	11.13	10.97
700	65.08	35.87	26.27	21.57	18.82	17.06	15.85	14.98	14.34	13.86	13.49	13.20	12.98	12.80
800	74.38	41.00	30.02	24.65	21.51	19.49	18.11	17.12	16.39	15.84	15.42	15.09	14.83	14.63
900	83.68	46.12	33.77	27.73	24.20	21.93	20.37	19.26	18.44	17.82	17.34	16.98	16.69	16.46
1000	92.97	51.24	37.53	30.81	26.89	24.37	22.63	21.40	20.48	19.80	19.27	18.86	18.54	18.29
2000	185.94	102.48	75.05	61.61	53.77	48.73	45.26	42.79	40.96	39.59	38.54	37.72	37.08	36.57
3000	278.91	153.72	112.57	92.42	80.66	73.09	67.89	64.18	61.44	59.38	57.80	56.57	55.61	54.85
4000	371.88	204.96	150.09	123.22	107.54	97.45	90.52	85.57	81.92	79.17	77.07	75.43	74.15	73.14
5000	464.85	256.20	187.61	154.03	134.43	121.81	113.15	106.96	102.40	98.96	96.33	94.29	92.69	91.42
6000	557.82	307.44	225.13	184.83	161.31	146.17	135.78	128.36	122.88	118.76	115.60	113.14	111.22	109.70
7000	650.79	358.67	262.65	215.64	188.20	170.53	158.41	149.75	143.36	138.55	134.86	132.00	129.76	127.99
8000	743.76	409.91	300.17	246.44	215.08	194.89	181.04	171.14	163.84	158.34	154.13	150.86	148.29	146.27
9000	836.73	461.15	337.70	277.25	241.97	219.25	203.67	192.53	184.32	178.13	173.39	169.71	166.83	164.55
10000	929.70	512.39	375.22	308.05	268.85	243.61	226.30	213.92	204.80	197.92	192.66	188.57	185.37	182.84
11000	1022.67	563.63	412.74	338.86	295.74	267.97	248.93	235.31	225.28	217.72	211.92	207.43	203.90	201.12
12000	1115.64	614.87	450.26	369.66	322.62	292.33	271.56	256.71	245.76	237.51	231.19	226.28	222.44	219.40
13000	1208.61	666.10	487.78	400.46	349.51	316.69	294.19	278.10	266.24	257.30	250.45	245.14	240.97	237.69
14000	1301.58	717.34	525.30	431.27	376.39	341.05	316.82	299.49	286.72	277.09	269.72	264.00	259.51	255.97
15000	1394.55	768.58	562.82	462.07	403.28	365.41	339.45	320.88	307.20	296.88	288.98	282.85	278.05	274.25
16000	1487.52	819.82	600.34	492.88	430.16	389.77	362.08	342.27	327.68	316.68	308.25	301.71	296.58	292.54
17000	1580.49	871.06	637.87	523.68	457.05	414.13	384.71	363.67	348.16	336.47	327.51	320.56	315.12	310.82
18000	1673.46	922.30	675.39	554.49	483.93	438.49	407.34	385.06	368.63	356.26	346.78	339.42	333.66	329.10
19000	1766.43	973.53	712.91	585.29	510.82	462.85	429.97	406.45	389.11	376.05	366.04	358.28	352.19	347.39
20000	1859.40	1024.77	750.43	616.10	537.70	487.21	452.60	427.84	409.59	395.84	385.31	377.13	370.73	365.67
21000	1952.37	1076.01	787.95	646.90	564.59	511.57	475.23	449.23	430.07	415.64	404.57	395.99	389.26	383.95
22000	2045.34	1127.25	825.47	677.71	591.47	535.93	497.86	470.62	450.55	435.43	423.84	414.85	407.80	402.24
23000	2138.31	1178.49	862.99	708.51	618.36	560.29	520.49	492.02	471.03	455.22	443.10	433.70	426.34	420.52
24000	2231.28	1229.73	900.51	739.31	645.24	584.65	543.12	513.41	491.51	475.01	462.37	452.56	444.87	438.80
25000	2324.25	1280.97	938.04	770.12	672.13	609.01	565.75	534.80	511.99	494.80	481.63	471.42	463.41	457.09
26000	2417.22	1332.20	975.56	800.92	699.01	633.37	588.37	556.19	532.47	514.60	500.90	490.27	481.95	475.37
27000	2510.19	1383.44	1013.08	831.73	725.90	657.73	611.00	577.58	552.95	534.39	520.17	509.13	500.48	493.65
28000	2603.16	1434.68	1050.60	862.53	752.78	682.09	633.63	598.98	573.43	554.18	539.43	527.99	519.02	511.94
29000	2696.13	1485.92	1088.12	893.34	779.67	706.45	656.26	620.37	593.91	573.97	558.70	546.84	537.55	530.22
30000	2789.10	1537.16	1125.64	924.14	806.55	730.81	678.89	641.76	614.39	593.76	577.96	565.70	556.09	548.50
31000	2882.07	1588.40	1163.16	954.95	833.44	755.17	701.52	663.15	634.87	613.55	597.23	584.56	574.63	566.79
32000	2975.04	1639.63	1200.68	985.75	860.32	779.53	724.15	684.54	655.35	633.35	616.49	603.41	593.16	585.07
33000	3068.01	1690.87	1238.21	1016.56	887.21	803.90	746.78	705.93	675.83	653.14	635.76	622.27	611.70	603.35
34000	3160.98	1742.11	1275.73	1047.36	914.09	828.26	769.41	727.33	696.31	672.93	655.02	641.12	630.23	621.64
35000	3253.95	1793.35	1313.25	1078.16	940.98	852.62	792.04	748.72	716.79	692.72	674.29	659.98	648.77	639.92
36000	3346.92	1844.59	1350.77	1108.97	967.86	876.98	814.67	770.11	737.26	712.51	693.55	678.84	667.31	658.20
37000	3439.89	1895.83	1388.29	1139.77	994.75	901.34	837.30	791.50	757.74	732.31	712.82	697.69	685.84	676.48
38000	3532.86	1947.06	1425.81	1170.58	1021.63	925.70	859.93	812.89	778.22	752.10	732.08	716.55	704.38	694.77
39000	3625.83	1998.30	1463.33	1201.38	1048.52	950.06	882.56	834.28	798.70	771.89	751.35	735.41	722.92	713.05
40000	3718.80	2049.54	1500.85	1232.19	1075.40	974.42	905.19	855.68	819.18	791.68	770.61	754.26	741.45	731.33
41000	3811.77	2100.78	1538.37	1262.99	1102.28	998.78	927.82	877.07	839.66	811.47	789.88	773.12	759.99	749.62
42000	3904.74	2152.02	1575.90	1293.80	1129.17	1023.14	950.45	898.46	860.14	831.27	809.14	791.98	778.52	767.90
43000	3997.71	2203.26	1613.42	1324.60	1156.05	1047.50	973.08	919.85	880.62	851.06	828.41	810.83	797.06	786.18
44000	4090.68	2254.50	1650.94	1355.41	1182.94	1071.86	995.71	941.24	901.10	870.85	847.67	829.69	815.60	804.47
45000	4183.65	2305.73	1688.46	1386.21	1209.82	1096.22	1018.34	962.64	921.58	890.64	866.94	848.55	834.13	822.75
46000	4276.62	2356.97	1725.98	1417.01	1236.71	1120.58	1040.97	984.03	942.06	910.43	886.20	867.40	852.67	841.03
47000	4369.59	2408.21	1763.50	1447.82	1263.59	1144.94	1063.60	1005.42	962.54	930.23	905.47	886.26	871.21	859.32
48000	4462.56	2459.45	1801.02	1478.62	1290.48	1169.30	1086.23	1026.81	983.02	950.02	924.73	905.12	889.74	877.60
49000	4555.53	2510.69	1838.54	1509.43	1317.36	1193.66	1108.86	1048.20	1003.50	969.81	944.00	923.97	908.28	895.88
50000	4648.50	2561.93	1876.07	1540.23	1344.25	1218.02	1131.49	1069.59	1023.98	989.60	963.26	942.83	926.81	914.17
55000	5113.35	2818.12	2063.67	1694.26	1478.67	1339.82	1244.63	1176.55	1126.37	1088.56	1059.59	1037.11	1019.49	1005.58
60000	5578.20	3074.31	2251.28	1848.28	1613.10	1461.62	1357.78	1283.51	1228.77	1187.52	1155.92	1131.39	1112.18	1097.00
65000	6043.05	3330.50	2438.88	2002.30	1747.52	1583.43	1470.93	1390.47	1331.17	1286.48	1252.24	1225.68	1204.86	1188.42
70000	6507.89	3586.69	2626.49	2156.32	1881.95	1705.23	1584.08	1497.43	1433.57	1385.44	1348.57	1319.96	1297.54	1279.83
75000	6972.74	3842.89	2814.10	2310.35	2016.37	1827.03	1697.23	1604.39	1535.96	1484.40	1444.89	1414.24	1390.22	1371.25
80000	7437.59	4099.08	3001.70	2464.37	2150.80	1948.83	1810.37	1711.35	1638.36	1583.36	1541.22	1508.52	1482.90	1462.66
85000	7902.44	4355.27	3189.31	2618.39	2285.22	2070.63	1923.52	1818.31	1740.76	1682.32	1637.55	1602.80	1575.58	1554.08
90000	8367.29	4611.46	3376.91	2772.42	2419.64	2192.43	2036.67	1925.27	1843.15	1781.28	1733.87	1697.09	1668.26	1645.50
95000	8832.14	4867.65	3564.52	2926.44	2554.07	2314.23	2149.82	2032.23	1945.55	1880.24	1830.20	1791.37	1760.94	1736.91
100000	9296.99	5123.85	3752.13	3080.46	2688.49	2436.04	2262.97	2139.18	2047.95	1979.20	1926.52	1885.65	1853.62	1828.33

TERM AMOUNT	15 Years	16 Years	17 Years	18 Years	19 Years	20 Years	21 Years	22 Years	23 Years	24 Years	25 Years	30 Years	35 Years	40 Years
5	.10	.09	.09	.09	.09	.09	.09	.09	.09	.09	.09	.09	.09	.09
10	.19	.18	.18	.18	.18	.18	.18	.18	.18	.18	.18	.18	.18	.18
15	.28	.27	.27	.27	.27	.27	.27	.27	.27	.27	.27	.26	.26	.26
25	.46	.45	.45	.45	.45	.44	.44	.44	.44	.44	.44	.44	.44	.44
50	.91	.90	.89	.89	.89	.88	.88	.88	.88	.87	.87	.87	.87	.87
75	1.36	1.35	1.34	1.33	1.33	1.32	1.32	1.31	1.31	1.31	1.31	1.30	1.30	1.30
100	1.81	1.80	1.78	1.77	1.77	1.76	1.75	1.75	1.75	1.74	1.74	1.73	1.73	1.73
200	3.62	3.59	3.56	3.54	3.53	3.51	3.50	3.49	3.49	3.48	3.48	3.46	3.46	3.46
300	5.43	5.38	5.34	5.31	5.29	5.27	5.25	5.24	5.23	5.22	5.21	5.19	5.18	5.18
400	7.24	7.17	7.12	7.08	7.05	7.02	7.00	6.98	6.97	6.96	6.95	6.92	6.91	6.91
500	9.05	8.97	8.90	8.85	8.81	8.77	8.75	8.73	8.71	8.69	8.68	8.65	8.64	8.63
600	10.85	10.76	10.68	10.62	10.57	10.53	10.50	10.47	10.45	10.43	10.42	10.38	10.36	10.36
700	12.66	12.55	12.46	12.39	12.33	12.28	12.24	12.21	12.19	12.17	12.15	12.11	12.09	12.08
800	14.47	14.34	14.24	14.16	14.09	14.04	13.99	13.96	13.93	13.91	13.89	13.83	13.82	13.81
900	16.28	16.13	16.02	15.93	15.85	15.79	15.74	15.70	15.67	15.64	15.62	15.56	15.54	15.53
1000	18.09	17.93	17.80	17.69	17.61	17.54	17.49	17.45	17.41	17.38	17.36	17.29	17.27	17.26
2000	36.17	35.85	35.59	35.38	35.22	35.08	34.97	34.89	34.82	34.76	34.71	34.58	34.53	34.51
3000	54.25	53.77	53.38	53.07	52.82	52.62	52.46	52.33	52.22	52.13	52.06	51.86	51.79	51.77
4000	72.33	71.69	71.18	70.76	70.43	70.16	69.94	69.77	69.63	69.51	69.42	69.15	69.06	69.02
5000	90.42	89.61	88.97	88.45	88.04	87.70	87.43	87.21	87.03	86.89	86.77	86.44	86.32	86.28
6000	108.50	107.54	106.76	106.14	105.64	105.24	104.91	104.65	104.44	104.26	104.12	103.72	103.58	103.53
7000	126.58	125.46	124.56	123.83	123.25	122.78	122.40	122.09	121.84	121.64	121.47	121.01	120.85	120.79
8000	144.66	143.38	142.35	141.52	140.86	140.32	139.88	139.53	139.25	139.01	138.83	138.30	138.11	138.04
9000	162.75	161.30	160.14	159.21	158.46	157.86	157.37	156.97	156.65	156.39	156.18	155.58	155.37	155.30
10000	180.83	179.22	177.94	176.90	176.07	175.40	174.85	174.41	174.06	173.77	173.53	172.87	172.64	172.55
11000	198.91	197.15	195.73	194.59	193.68	192.94	192.34	191.85	191.46	191.14	190.88	190.16	189.90	189.81
12000	216.99	215.07	213.52	212.28	211.28	210.48	209.82	209.30	208.87	208.52	208.24	207.44	207.16	207.06
13000	235.07	232.99	231.32	229.97	228.89	228.02	227.31	226.74	226.27	225.89	225.59	224.73	224.43	224.32
14000	253.16	250.91	249.11	247.66	246.50	245.56	244.79	244.18	243.68	243.27	242.94	242.02	241.69	241.57
15000	271.24	268.83	266.90	265.35	264.10	263.09	262.28	261.62	261.08	260.65	260.29	259.30	258.95	258.83
16000	289.32	286.75	284.70	283.04	281.71	280.63	279.76	279.06	278.49	278.02	277.65	276.59	276.21	276.08
17000	307.40	304.68	302.49	300.73	299.32	298.17	297.25	296.50	295.89	295.40	295.00	293.88	293.48	293.33
18000	325.49	322.60	320.28	318.42	316.92	315.71	314.73	313.94	313.30	312.78	312.35	311.16	310.74	310.59
19000	343.57	340.52	338.08	336.11	334.53	333.25	332.22	331.38	330.70	330.15	329.70	328.45	328.00	327.84
20000	361.65	358.44	355.87	353.80	352.14	350.79	349.70	348.82	348.11	347.53	347.06	345.74	345.27	345.10
21000	379.73	376.36	373.66	371.49	369.74	368.33	367.19	366.26	365.51	364.90	364.41	363.02	362.53	362.35
22000	397.82	394.29	391.46	389.18	387.35	385.87	384.67	383.70	382.92	382.28	381.76	380.31	379.79	379.61
23000	415.90	412.21	409.25	406.87	404.96	403.41	402.16	401.14	400.32	399.66	399.11	397.60	397.06	396.86
24000	433.98	430.13	427.04	424.56	422.56	420.95	419.64	418.59	417.73	417.03	416.47	414.88	414.32	414.12
25000	452.06	448.05	444.84	442.25	440.17	438.49	437.13	436.03	435.13	434.41	433.82	432.17	431.58	431.37
26000	470.14	465.97	462.63	459.94	457.78	456.03	454.61	453.47	452.54	451.78	451.17	449.46	448.85	448.63
27000	488.23	483.89	480.42	477.63	475.38	473.57	472.10	470.91	469.94	469.16	468.52	466.74	466.11	465.88
28000	506.31	501.82	498.22	495.32	492.99	491.11	489.58	488.35	487.35	486.54	485.88	484.03	483.37	483.14
29000	524.39	519.74	516.01	513.01	510.60	508.65	507.07	505.79	504.75	503.91	503.23	501.32	500.64	500.39
30000	542.47	537.66	533.80	530.70	528.20	526.18	524.55	523.23	522.16	521.29	520.58	518.60	517.90	517.65
31000	560.56	555.58	551.60	548.39	545.81	543.72	542.04	540.67	539.56	538.66	537.93	535.89	535.16	534.90
32000	578.64	573.50	569.39	566.08	563.42	561.26	559.52	558.11	556.97	556.04	555.29	553.18	552.42	552.16
33000	596.72	591.43	587.18	583.77	581.02	578.80	577.01	575.55	574.37	573.42	572.64	570.46	569.69	569.41
34000	614.80	609.35	604.98	601.46	598.63	596.34	594.49	592.99	591.78	590.79	589.99	587.75	586.95	586.66
35000	632.88	627.27	622.77	619.15	616.24	613.88	611.98	610.43	609.18	608.17	607.35	605.04	604.21	603.92
36000	650.97	645.19	640.56	636.84	633.84	631.42	629.46	627.88	626.59	625.55	624.70	622.32	621.48	621.17
37000	669.05	663.11	658.36	654.53	651.45	648.96	646.95	645.32	643.99	642.92	642.05	639.61	638.74	638.43
38000	687.13	681.03	676.15	672.22	669.06	666.50	664.43	662.76	661.40	660.30	659.40	656.90	656.00	655.68
39000	705.21	698.96	693.94	689.91	686.66	684.04	681.92	680.20	678.80	677.67	676.76	674.18	673.27	672.94
40000	723.30	716.88	711.74	707.60	704.27	701.58	699.40	697.64	696.21	695.05	694.11	691.47	690.53	690.19
41000	741.38	734.80	729.53	725.29	721.87	719.12	716.89	715.08	713.61	712.43	711.46	708.76	707.79	707.45
42000	759.46	752.72	747.32	742.98	739.48	736.66	734.37	732.52	731.02	729.80	728.81	726.04	725.06	724.70
43000	777.54	770.64	765.12	760.67	757.09	754.20	751.86	749.96	748.42	747.18	746.17	743.33	742.32	741.96
44000	795.63	788.57	782.91	778.36	774.69	771.73	769.34	767.40	765.83	764.55	763.52	760.62	759.58	759.21
45000	813.71	806.49	800.70	796.05	792.30	789.27	786.83	784.84	783.23	781.93	780.87	777.90	776.84	776.47
46000	831.79	824.41	818.49	813.74	809.91	806.81	804.31	802.28	800.64	799.31	798.22	795.19	794.11	793.72
47000	849.87	842.33	836.29	831.43	827.51	824.35	821.80	819.72	818.05	816.68	815.58	812.48	811.37	810.98
48000	867.95	860.25	854.08	849.12	845.12	841.89	839.28	837.17	835.45	834.06	832.93	829.76	828.63	828.23
49000	886.04	878.18	871.87	866.81	862.73	859.43	856.77	854.61	852.86	851.43	850.28	847.05	845.90	845.49
50000	904.12	896.10	889.67	884.50	880.33	876.97	874.25	872.05	870.26	868.81	867.63	864.34	863.16	862.74
55000	994.53	985.71	978.63	972.95	968.37	964.67	961.67	959.25	957.29	955.69	954.40	950.77	949.48	949.01
60000	1084.94	1075.32	1067.60	1061.40	1056.40	1052.36	1049.10	1046.46	1044.31	1042.57	1041.16	1037.20	1035.79	1035.29
65000	1175.35	1164.92	1156.57	1149.85	1144.43	1140.06	1136.52	1133.66	1131.34	1129.45	1127.92	1123.64	1122.11	1121.56
70000	1265.76	1254.53	1245.53	1238.30	1232.47	1227.76	1223.95	1220.86	1218.36	1216.33	1214.69	1210.07	1208.42	1207.83
75000	1356.18	1344.14	1334.50	1326.75	1320.50	1315.45	1311.37	1308.07	1305.39	1303.21	1301.45	1296.50	1294.74	1294.11
80000	1446.59	1433.75	1423.47	1415.20	1408.53	1403.15	1398.80	1395.27	1392.41	1390.09	1388.21	1382.93	1381.05	1380.38
85000	1537.00	1523.36	1512.43	1503.65	1496.56	1490.85	1486.22	1482.48	1479.44	1476.98	1474.97	1469.37	1467.37	1466.65
90000	1627.41	1612.97	1601.40	1592.09	1584.60	1578.54	1573.65	1569.68	1566.46	1563.86	1561.74	1555.80	1553.68	1552.93
95000	1717.82	1702.58	1690.36	1680.54	1672.63	1666.24	1661.07	1656.88	1653.49	1650.74	1648.50	1642.23	1640.00	1639.20
100000	1808.23	1792.19	1779.33	1768.99	1760.66	1753.94	1748.50	1744.09	1740.52	1737.62	1735.26	1728.67	1726.32	1725.47

TERM AMOUNT	1 Year	2 Years	3 Years	4 Years	5 Years	6 Years	7 Years	8 Years	9 Years	10 Years	11 Years	12 Years	13 Years	14 Years
5	.47	.26	.19	.16	.14	.13	.12	.11	.11	.10	.10	.10	.10	.10
10	.93	.52	.38	.31	.27	.25	.23	.22	.21	.20	.20	.19	.19	.19
15	1.40	.77	.57	.47	.41	.37	.34	.33	.31	.30	.29	.29	.28	.28
25	2.33	1.29	.94	.78	.68	.61	.57	.54	.52	.50	.49	.48	.47	.46
50	4.65	2.57	1.88	1.55	1.35	1.22	1.14	1.08	1.03	1.00	.97	.95	.93	.92
75	6.98	3.85	2.82	2.32	2.02	1.83	1.70	1.61	1.54	1.49	1.45	1.42	1.40	1.38
100	9.30	5.13	3.76	3.09	2.70	2.44	2.27	2.15	2.06	1.99	1.93	1.89	1.86	1.84
200	18.60	10.26	7.51	6.17	5.39	4.88	4.54	4.29	4.11	3.97	3.86	3.78	3.72	3.67
300	27.90	15.38	11.27	9.25	8.08	7.32	6.80	6.43	6.16	5.95	5.79	5.67	5.58	5.50
400	37.20	20.51	15.02	12.34	10.77	9.76	9.07	8.57	8.21	7.94	7.72	7.56	7.43	7.33
500	46.50	25.64	18.78	15.42	13.46	12.20	11.33	10.72	10.26	9.92	9.65	9.45	9.29	9.16
600	55.80	30.76	22.53	18.50	16.15	14.64	13.60	12.86	12.31	11.90	11.58	11.34	11.15	11.00
700	65.10	35.89	26.29	21.59	18.84	17.08	15.87	15.00	14.36	13.88	13.51	13.23	13.01	12.83
800	74.40	41.02	30.04	24.67	21.54	19.52	18.13	17.14	16.41	15.87	15.44	15.12	14.86	14.66
900	83.70	46.14	33.80	27.75	24.23	21.96	20.40	19.29	18.47	17.85	17.37	17.01	16.72	16.49
1000	93.00	51.27	37.55	30.84	26.92	24.39	22.66	21.43	20.52	19.83	19.30	18.90	18.58	18.32
2000	185.99	102.53	75.10	61.67	53.83	48.78	45.32	42.85	41.03	39.66	38.60	37.79	37.15	36.64
3000	278.99	153.79	112.65	92.50	80.74	73.17	67.98	64.27	61.54	59.48	57.90	56.68	55.72	54.96
4000	371.98	205.06	150.19	123.33	107.66	97.56	90.64	85.70	82.05	79.31	77.20	75.57	74.29	73.28
5000	464.97	256.32	187.74	154.16	134.57	121.95	113.30	107.12	102.56	99.13	96.50	94.46	92.87	91.60
6000	557.97	307.58	225.29	184.99	161.48	146.34	135.96	128.54	123.08	118.96	115.80	113.36	111.44	109.92
7000	650.96	358.85	262.83	215.82	188.40	170.73	158.62	149.97	143.59	138.78	135.10	132.25	130.01	128.24
8000	743.96	410.11	300.38	246.66	215.31	195.12	181.28	171.39	164.10	158.61	154.40	151.14	148.58	146.56
9000	836.95	461.37	337.93	277.49	242.22	219.51	203.94	192.81	184.61	178.43	173.70	170.03	167.15	164.88
10000	929.94	512.63	375.47	308.32	269.13	243.90	226.60	214.24	205.12	198.26	193.00	188.92	185.73	183.20
11000	1022.94	563.90	413.02	339.15	296.05	268.29	249.26	235.66	225.64	218.08	212.30	207.81	204.30	201.52
12000	1115.93	615.16	450.57	369.98	322.96	292.68	271.92	257.08	246.15	237.91	231.60	226.71	222.87	219.84
13000	1208.92	666.42	488.11	400.81	349.87	317.07	294.58	278.51	266.66	257.74	250.90	245.60	241.44	238.16
14000	1301.92	717.69	525.66	431.64	376.79	341.46	317.24	299.93	287.17	277.56	270.20	264.49	260.01	256.48
15000	1394.91	768.95	563.21	462.48	403.70	365.85	339.90	321.35	307.68	297.39	289.50	283.38	278.59	274.80
16000	1487.91	820.21	600.75	493.31	430.61	390.24	362.56	342.78	328.20	317.21	308.80	302.27	297.16	293.12
17000	1580.90	871.47	638.30	524.14	457.52	414.63	385.22	364.20	348.71	337.04	328.10	321.16	315.73	311.44
18000	1673.89	922.74	675.85	554.97	484.44	439.02	407.88	385.62	369.22	356.86	347.40	340.06	334.30	329.76
19000	1766.89	974.00	713.39	585.80	511.35	463.41	430.54	407.05	389.73	376.69	366.70	358.95	352.88	348.08
20000	1859.88	1025.26	750.94	616.63	538.26	487.80	453.20	428.47	410.24	396.51	386.00	377.84	371.45	366.40
21000	1952.88	1076.53	788.49	647.46	565.18	512.19	475.86	449.89	430.76	416.34	405.30	396.73	390.02	384.72
22000	2045.87	1127.79	826.04	678.30	592.09	536.58	498.52	471.32	451.27	436.16	424.60	415.62	408.59	403.04
23000	2138.86	1179.05	863.58	709.13	619.00	560.96	521.18	492.74	471.78	455.99	443.90	434.51	427.16	421.36
24000	2231.86	1230.32	901.13	739.96	645.92	585.35	543.84	514.16	492.29	475.82	463.19	453.41	445.74	439.68
25000	2324.85	1281.58	938.68	770.79	672.83	609.74	566.50	535.59	512.80	495.64	482.49	472.30	464.31	458.00
26000	2417.84	1332.84	976.22	801.62	699.74	634.13	589.16	557.01	533.32	515.47	501.79	491.19	482.88	476.32
27000	2510.84	1384.10	1013.77	832.45	726.65	658.52	611.82	578.43	553.83	535.29	521.09	510.08	501.45	494.64
28000	2603.83	1435.37	1051.32	863.28	753.57	682.91	634.48	599.86	574.34	555.12	540.39	528.97	520.02	512.96
29000	2696.83	1486.63	1088.86	894.12	780.48	707.30	657.14	621.28	594.85	574.94	559.69	547.86	538.60	531.28
30000	2789.82	1537.89	1126.41	924.95	807.39	731.69	679.80	642.70	615.36	594.77	578.99	566.76	557.17	549.60
31000	2882.81	1589.16	1163.96	955.78	834.31	756.08	702.46	664.13	635.88	614.59	598.29	585.65	575.74	567.92
32000	2975.81	1640.42	1201.50	986.61	861.22	780.47	725.12	685.55	656.39	634.42	617.59	604.54	594.31	586.24
33000	3068.80	1691.68	1239.05	1017.44	888.13	804.86	747.78	706.97	676.90	654.24	636.89	623.43	612.89	604.56
34000	3161.80	1742.94	1276.60	1048.27	915.04	829.25	770.44	728.40	697.41	674.07	656.19	642.32	631.46	622.88
35000	3254.79	1794.21	1314.14	1079.10	941.96	853.64	793.10	749.82	717.92	693.89	675.49	661.21	650.03	641.20
36000	3347.78	1845.47	1351.69	1109.93	968.87	878.03	815.76	771.24	738.44	713.72	694.79	680.11	668.60	659.52
37000	3440.78	1896.73	1389.24	1140.77	995.78	902.42	838.42	792.67	758.95	733.55	714.09	699.00	687.17	677.84
38000	3533.77	1948.00	1426.78	1171.60	1022.70	926.81	861.08	814.09	779.46	753.37	733.39	717.89	705.75	696.16
39000	3626.76	1999.26	1464.33	1202.43	1049.61	951.20	883.74	835.51	799.97	773.20	752.69	736.78	724.32	714.48
40000	3719.76	2050.52	1501.88	1233.26	1076.52	975.59	906.40	856.94	820.48	793.02	771.99	755.67	742.89	732.80
41000	3812.75	2101.79	1539.43	1264.09	1103.43	999.98	929.06	878.36	841.00	812.85	791.29	774.56	761.46	751.12
42000	3905.75	2153.05	1576.97	1294.92	1130.35	1024.37	951.72	899.78	861.51	832.67	810.59	793.46	780.03	769.44
43000	3998.74	2204.31	1614.52	1325.75	1157.26	1048.76	974.38	921.21	882.02	852.50	829.89	812.35	798.61	787.76
44000	4091.73	2255.57	1652.07	1356.59	1184.17	1073.15	997.04	942.63	902.53	872.32	849.19	831.24	817.18	806.08
45000	4184.73	2306.84	1689.61	1387.42	1211.09	1097.53	1019.70	964.05	923.04	892.15	868.49	850.13	835.75	824.40
46000	4277.72	2358.10	1727.16	1418.25	1238.00	1121.92	1042.36	985.48	943.55	911.97	887.79	869.02	854.32	842.72
47000	4370.72	2409.36	1764.71	1449.08	1264.91	1146.31	1065.02	1006.90	964.07	931.80	907.08	887.91	872.89	861.04
48000	4463.71	2460.63	1802.25	1479.91	1291.83	1170.70	1087.68	1028.32	984.58	951.63	926.38	906.81	891.47	879.36
49000	4556.70	2511.89	1839.80	1510.74	1318.74	1195.09	1110.34	1049.75	1005.09	971.45	945.68	925.70	910.04	897.68
50000	4649.70	2563.15	1877.35	1541.57	1345.65	1219.48	1133.01	1071.17	1025.60	991.28	964.98	944.59	928.61	916.00
55000	5114.67	2819.47	2065.08	1695.73	1480.22	1341.43	1246.30	1178.29	1128.16	1090.40	1061.48	1039.05	1021.47	1007.60
60000	5579.63	3075.78	2252.81	1849.89	1614.78	1463.38	1359.60	1285.40	1230.72	1189.53	1157.98	1133.51	1114.33	1099.20
65000	6044.60	3332.10	2440.55	2004.05	1749.34	1585.33	1472.90	1392.52	1333.28	1288.66	1254.48	1227.96	1207.19	1190.80
70000	6509.57	3588.41	2628.28	2158.20	1883.91	1707.27	1586.20	1499.63	1435.84	1387.78	1350.98	1322.42	1300.05	1282.40
75000	6974.54	3844.73	2816.02	2312.36	2018.47	1829.22	1699.50	1606.75	1538.40	1486.91	1447.47	1416.88	1392.91	1374.00
80000	7439.51	4101.04	3003.75	2466.52	2153.04	1951.17	1812.80	1713.87	1640.96	1586.04	1543.97	1511.34	1485.78	1465.59
85000	7904.48	4357.35	3191.49	2620.67	2287.60	2073.12	1926.10	1820.98	1743.52	1685.17	1640.47	1605.80	1578.64	1557.19
90000	8369.45	4613.67	3379.22	2774.83	2422.17	2195.06	2039.40	1928.10	1846.08	1784.29	1736.97	1700.26	1671.50	1648.79
95000	8834.42	4869.98	3566.95	2928.99	2556.73	2317.01	2152.70	2035.22	1948.64	1883.42	1833.46	1794.71	1764.36	1740.39
100000	9299.39	5126.30	3754.69	3083.14	2691.30	2438.96	2266.00	2142.33	2051.20	1982.55	1929.96	1889.17	1857.22	1831.99

MONTHLY PAYMENT
REQUIRED TO AMORTIZE A LOAN

20.750%

TERM AMOUNT	15 Years	16 Years	17 Years	18 Years	19 Years	20 Years	21 Years	22 Years	23 Years	24 Years	25 Years	30 Years	35 Years	40 Years
5	.10	.09	.09	.09	.09	.09	.09	.09	.09	.09	.09	.09	.09	.09
10	.19	.18	.18	.18	.18	.18	.18	.18	.18	.18	.18	.18	.18	.18
15	.28	.27	.27	.27	.27	.27	.27	.27	.27	.27	.27	.26	.26	.26
25	.46	.45	.45	.45	.45	.44	.44	.44	.44	.44	.44	.44	.44	.44
50	.91	.90	.90	.89	.88	.88	.88	.88	.88	.88	.87	.87	.87	.87
75	1.36	1.35	1.34	1.33	1.33	1.32	1.32	1.32	1.31	1.31	1.31	1.30	1.30	1.30
100	1.82	1.80	1.79	1.78	1.77	1.76	1.76	1.75	1.75	1.75	1.74	1.74	1.74	1.73
200	3.63	3.60	3.57	3.55	3.53	3.52	3.51	3.50	3.49	3.49	3.48	3.47	3.47	3.46
300	5.44	5.39	5.35	5.32	5.30	5.28	5.26	5.25	5.24	5.23	5.22	5.20	5.20	5.19
400	7.25	7.19	7.14	7.10	7.06	7.04	7.01	7.00	6.98	6.97	6.96	6.94	6.93	6.92
500	9.06	8.98	8.92	8.87	8.83	8.79	8.77	8.75	8.73	8.71	8.70	8.67	8.66	8.65
600	10.88	10.78	10.70	10.64	10.59	10.55	10.52	10.49	10.47	10.45	10.44	10.40	10.39	10.38
700	12.69	12.58	12.49	12.42	12.36	12.31	12.27	12.24	12.22	12.20	12.18	12.13	12.12	12.11
800	14.50	14.37	14.27	14.19	14.12	14.07	14.02	13.99	13.96	13.94	13.92	13.87	13.85	13.84
900	16.31	16.17	16.05	15.96	15.89	15.83	15.78	15.74	15.71	15.68	15.66	15.60	15.58	15.57
1000	18.12	17.96	17.84	17.73	17.65	17.58	17.53	17.49	17.45	17.42	17.40	17.33	17.31	17.30
2000	36.24	35.92	35.67	35.46	35.30	35.16	35.05	34.97	34.90	34.84	34.79	34.66	34.61	34.60
3000	54.36	53.88	53.50	53.19	52.94	52.74	52.58	52.45	52.34	52.25	52.18	51.99	51.92	51.89
4000	72.48	71.84	71.33	70.92	70.59	70.32	70.10	69.93	69.79	69.67	69.58	69.32	69.22	69.19
5000	90.60	89.80	89.16	88.65	88.23	87.90	87.63	87.41	87.23	87.09	86.97	86.64	86.53	86.49
6000	108.72	107.76	106.99	106.38	105.88	105.48	105.15	104.89	104.68	104.50	104.36	103.97	103.83	103.78
7000	126.84	125.72	124.83	124.11	123.53	123.06	122.68	122.37	122.12	121.92	121.76	121.30	121.14	121.08
8000	144.96	143.68	142.66	141.83	141.17	140.64	140.20	139.85	139.57	139.34	139.15	138.63	138.44	138.38
9000	163.08	161.64	160.49	159.56	158.82	158.21	157.73	157.33	157.01	156.75	156.54	155.96	155.75	155.67
10000	181.20	179.60	178.32	177.29	176.46	175.79	175.25	174.81	174.46	174.17	173.94	173.28	173.05	172.97
11000	199.32	197.56	196.15	195.02	194.11	193.37	192.78	192.29	191.90	191.59	191.33	190.61	190.36	190.26
12000	217.44	215.52	213.98	212.75	211.75	210.95	210.30	209.78	209.35	209.00	208.72	207.94	207.66	207.56
13000	235.56	233.48	231.82	230.48	229.40	228.53	227.83	227.26	226.80	226.42	226.12	225.27	224.96	224.86
14000	253.68	251.44	249.65	248.21	247.05	246.11	245.35	244.74	244.24	243.84	243.51	242.59	242.27	242.15
15000	271.80	269.40	267.48	265.93	264.69	263.69	262.88	262.22	261.69	261.25	260.90	259.92	259.57	259.45
16000	289.92	287.36	285.31	283.66	282.34	281.27	280.40	279.70	279.13	278.67	278.30	277.25	276.88	276.75
17000	308.04	305.32	303.14	301.39	299.98	298.84	297.92	297.18	296.58	296.09	295.69	294.58	294.18	294.04
18000	326.16	323.28	320.97	319.12	317.63	316.42	315.45	314.66	314.02	313.50	313.08	311.91	311.49	311.34
19000	344.28	341.24	338.80	336.85	335.27	334.00	332.97	332.14	331.47	330.92	330.48	329.23	328.79	328.63
20000	362.40	359.20	356.64	354.58	352.92	351.58	350.50	349.62	348.91	348.34	347.87	346.56	346.10	345.93
21000	380.52	377.16	374.47	372.31	370.57	369.16	368.02	367.10	366.36	365.75	365.26	363.89	363.40	363.23
22000	398.63	395.12	392.30	390.03	388.21	386.74	385.55	384.58	383.80	383.17	382.66	381.22	380.71	380.52
23000	416.75	413.08	410.13	407.76	405.86	404.32	403.07	402.07	401.25	400.59	400.05	398.55	398.01	397.82
24000	434.87	431.04	427.96	425.49	423.50	421.90	420.60	419.55	418.69	418.00	417.44	415.87	415.31	415.12
25000	452.99	449.00	445.79	443.22	441.15	439.47	438.12	437.03	436.14	435.42	434.84	433.20	432.62	432.41
26000	471.11	466.96	463.63	460.95	458.79	457.05	455.65	454.51	453.59	452.84	452.23	450.53	449.92	449.71
27000	489.23	484.92	481.46	478.68	476.44	474.63	473.17	471.99	471.03	470.25	469.62	467.86	467.23	467.00
28000	507.35	502.88	499.29	496.41	494.09	492.21	490.70	489.47	488.48	487.67	487.02	485.18	484.53	484.30
29000	525.47	520.83	517.12	514.14	511.73	509.79	508.22	506.95	505.92	505.09	504.41	502.51	501.84	501.60
30000	543.59	538.79	534.95	531.86	529.38	527.37	525.75	524.43	523.37	522.50	521.80	519.84	519.14	518.89
31000	561.71	556.75	552.78	549.59	547.02	544.95	543.27	541.91	540.81	539.92	539.20	537.17	536.45	536.19
32000	579.83	574.71	570.62	567.32	564.67	562.53	560.79	559.39	558.26	557.34	556.59	554.50	553.75	553.49
33000	597.95	592.67	588.45	585.05	582.31	580.11	578.32	576.87	575.70	574.75	573.98	571.82	571.06	570.78
34000	616.07	610.63	606.28	602.78	599.96	597.68	595.84	594.35	593.15	592.17	591.37	589.15	588.36	588.08
35000	634.19	628.59	624.11	620.51	617.61	615.26	613.37	611.84	610.59	609.59	608.77	606.48	605.67	605.37
36000	652.31	646.55	641.94	638.24	635.25	632.84	630.89	629.32	628.04	627.00	626.16	623.81	622.97	622.67
37000	670.43	664.51	659.77	655.96	652.90	650.42	648.42	646.80	645.48	644.42	643.55	641.14	640.27	639.97
38000	688.55	682.47	677.60	673.69	670.54	668.00	665.94	664.28	662.93	661.84	660.95	658.46	657.58	657.26
39000	706.67	700.43	695.44	691.42	688.19	685.58	683.47	681.76	680.38	679.25	678.34	675.79	674.88	674.56
40000	724.79	718.39	713.27	709.15	705.83	703.16	700.99	699.24	697.82	696.67	695.73	693.12	692.19	691.86
41000	742.91	736.35	731.10	726.88	723.48	720.74	718.52	716.72	715.27	714.09	713.13	710.45	709.49	709.15
42000	761.03	754.31	748.93	744.61	741.13	738.31	736.04	734.20	732.71	731.50	730.52	727.77	726.80	726.45
43000	779.14	772.27	766.76	762.34	758.77	755.89	753.57	751.68	750.16	748.92	747.91	745.10	744.10	743.75
44000	797.26	790.23	784.59	780.06	776.42	773.47	771.09	769.16	767.60	766.34	765.31	762.43	761.41	761.04
45000	815.38	808.19	802.43	797.79	794.06	791.05	788.62	786.64	785.05	783.75	782.70	779.76	778.71	778.34
46000	833.50	826.15	820.26	815.52	811.71	808.63	806.14	804.13	802.49	801.17	800.09	797.09	796.02	795.63
47000	851.62	844.11	838.09	833.25	829.35	826.21	823.67	821.61	819.94	818.58	817.49	814.41	813.32	812.93
48000	869.74	862.07	855.92	850.98	847.00	843.79	841.19	839.09	837.38	836.00	834.88	831.74	830.62	830.23
49000	887.86	880.03	873.75	868.71	864.65	861.37	858.71	856.57	854.83	853.42	852.27	849.07	847.93	847.52
50000	905.98	897.99	891.58	886.44	882.29	878.94	876.24	874.05	872.27	870.83	869.67	866.40	865.23	864.82
55000	996.58	987.79	980.74	975.08	970.52	966.84	963.86	961.45	959.50	957.92	956.63	953.04	951.76	951.30
60000	1087.18	1077.58	1069.90	1063.72	1058.75	1054.73	1051.44	1048.86	1046.73	1045.00	1043.60	1039.68	1038.28	1037.78
65000	1177.77	1167.38	1159.06	1152.37	1146.98	1142.63	1139.11	1136.26	1133.96	1132.08	1130.56	1126.31	1124.80	1124.26
70000	1268.37	1257.18	1248.21	1241.01	1235.21	1230.52	1226.73	1223.67	1221.18	1219.17	1217.53	1212.95	1211.33	1210.74
75000	1358.97	1346.98	1337.37	1329.65	1323.43	1318.41	1314.34	1311.07	1308.41	1306.25	1304.50	1299.59	1297.85	1297.23
80000	1449.57	1436.78	1426.53	1418.30	1411.66	1406.31	1401.98	1398.48	1395.64	1393.33	1391.46	1386.23	1384.37	1383.71
85000	1540.17	1526.58	1515.69	1506.94	1499.89	1494.20	1489.60	1485.88	1482.86	1480.42	1478.43	1472.87	1470.89	1470.19
90000	1630.76	1616.37	1604.85	1595.58	1588.12	1582.10	1577.23	1573.28	1570.09	1567.50	1565.40	1559.51	1557.42	1556.67
95000	1721.36	1706.17	1694.00	1684.23	1676.35	1669.99	1664.85	1660.69	1657.32	1654.58	1652.36	1646.15	1643.94	1643.15
100000	1811.96	1795.97	1783.16	1772.87	1764.58	1757.88	1752.47	1748.09	1744.54	1741.66	1739.33	1732.79	1730.46	1729.63

20.800%

TERM AMOUNT	1 Year	2 Years	3 Years	4 Years	5 Years	6 Years	7 Years	8 Years	9 Years	10 Years	11 Years	12 Years	13 Years	14 Years
5	.47	.26	.19	.16	.14	.13	.12	.11	.11	.10	.10	.10	.10	.10
10	.94	.52	.38	.31	.27	.25	.23	.22	.21	.20	.20	.19	.19	.19
15	1.40	.77	.57	.47	.41	.37	.35	.33	.31	.30	.30	.29	.28	.28
25	2.33	1.29	.94	.78	.68	.62	.57	.54	.52	.50	.49	.48	.47	.46
50	4.66	2.57	1.88	1.55	1.35	1.23	1.14	1.08	1.03	1.00	.97	.95	.94	.92
75	6.98	3.85	2.82	2.32	2.03	1.84	1.71	1.61	1.55	1.49	1.46	1.42	1.40	1.38
100	9.31	5.13	3.76	3.09	2.70	2.45	2.27	2.15	2.06	1.99	1.94	1.90	1.87	1.84
200	18.61	10.26	7.52	6.18	5.39	4.89	4.54	4.30	4.11	3.98	3.87	3.79	3.73	3.68
300	27.91	15.39	11.28	9.26	8.09	7.33	6.81	6.44	6.17	5.96	5.81	5.68	5.59	5.51
400	37.21	20.52	15.03	12.35	10.78	9.77	9.08	8.59	8.22	7.95	7.74	7.58	7.45	7.35
500	46.51	25.65	18.79	15.43	13.48	12.21	11.35	10.73	10.28	9.93	9.67	9.47	9.31	9.18
600	55.82	30.78	22.55	18.52	16.17	14.66	13.62	12.88	12.33	11.92	11.61	11.36	11.17	11.02
700	65.12	35.91	26.31	21.61	18.86	17.10	15.89	15.02	14.39	13.91	13.54	13.25	13.03	12.85
800	74.42	41.03	30.06	24.69	21.56	19.54	18.16	17.17	16.44	15.89	15.47	15.15	14.89	14.69
900	83.72	46.16	33.82	27.78	24.25	21.98	20.43	19.31	18.50	17.88	17.41	17.04	16.75	16.53
1000	93.02	51.29	37.58	30.86	26.95	24.42	22.70	21.46	20.55	19.86	19.34	18.93	18.61	18.36
2000	186.04	102.58	75.15	61.72	53.89	48.84	45.39	42.91	41.09	39.72	38.67	37.86	37.22	36.72
3000	279.06	153.87	112.72	92.58	80.83	73.26	68.08	64.37	61.64	59.58	58.01	56.79	55.83	55.07
4000	372.08	205.15	150.29	123.44	107.77	97.68	90.77	85.82	82.18	79.44	77.34	75.71	74.44	73.43
5000	465.09	256.44	187.87	154.30	134.71	122.10	113.46	107.28	102.73	99.30	96.67	94.64	93.05	91.79
6000	558.11	307.73	225.44	185.15	161.65	146.52	136.15	128.73	123.27	119.16	116.01	113.57	111.65	110.14
7000	651.13	359.02	263.01	216.01	188.59	170.94	158.84	150.19	143.82	139.02	135.34	132.49	130.26	128.50
8000	744.15	410.30	300.58	246.87	215.53	195.36	181.53	171.64	164.36	158.88	154.68	151.42	148.87	146.86
9000	837.17	461.59	338.16	277.73	242.47	219.77	204.22	193.10	184.91	178.74	174.01	170.35	167.48	165.21
10000	930.18	512.88	375.73	308.59	269.41	244.19	226.91	214.55	205.45	198.59	193.34	189.27	186.09	183.57
11000	1023.20	564.17	413.30	339.45	296.36	268.61	249.60	236.01	225.99	218.45	212.68	208.20	204.69	201.93
12000	1116.22	615.45	450.87	370.30	323.30	293.03	272.29	257.46	246.54	238.31	232.01	227.13	223.30	220.28
13000	1209.24	666.74	488.45	401.16	350.24	317.45	294.98	278.92	267.08	258.17	251.35	246.05	241.91	238.64
14000	1302.25	718.03	526.02	432.02	377.18	341.87	317.67	300.37	287.63	278.03	270.68	264.98	260.52	257.00
15000	1395.27	769.32	563.59	462.88	404.12	366.29	340.36	321.83	308.17	297.89	290.01	283.91	279.13	275.35
16000	1488.29	820.60	601.16	493.74	431.06	390.71	363.05	343.28	328.72	317.75	309.35	302.84	297.73	293.71
17000	1581.31	871.89	638.74	524.59	458.00	415.12	385.74	364.74	349.26	337.61	328.68	321.76	316.34	312.07
18000	1674.33	923.18	676.31	555.45	484.94	439.54	408.43	386.19	369.81	357.47	348.02	340.69	334.95	330.42
19000	1767.34	974.47	713.88	586.31	511.88	463.96	431.12	407.65	390.35	377.32	367.35	359.62	353.56	348.78
20000	1860.36	1025.75	751.45	617.17	538.82	488.38	453.81	429.10	410.89	397.18	386.68	378.54	372.17	367.14
21000	1953.38	1077.04	789.03	648.03	565.77	512.80	476.50	450.56	431.44	417.04	406.02	397.47	390.78	385.49
22000	2046.40	1128.33	826.60	678.89	592.71	537.22	499.19	472.01	451.98	436.90	425.35	416.40	409.38	403.85
23000	2139.41	1179.62	864.17	709.74	619.65	561.64	521.88	493.46	472.53	456.76	444.69	435.32	427.99	422.21
24000	2232.43	1230.90	901.74	740.60	646.59	586.06	544.57	514.92	493.07	476.62	464.02	454.25	446.60	440.56
25000	2325.45	1282.19	939.32	771.46	673.53	610.48	567.27	536.37	513.62	496.48	483.35	473.18	465.21	458.92
26000	2418.47	1333.48	976.89	802.32	700.47	634.89	589.96	557.83	534.16	516.34	502.69	492.10	483.82	477.27
27000	2511.49	1384.77	1014.46	833.18	727.41	659.31	612.65	579.28	554.71	536.20	522.02	511.03	502.42	495.63
28000	2604.50	1436.05	1052.03	864.04	754.35	683.73	635.34	600.74	575.25	556.05	541.36	529.96	521.03	513.99
29000	2697.52	1487.34	1089.61	894.89	781.29	708.15	658.03	622.19	595.80	575.91	560.69	548.88	539.64	532.34
30000	2790.54	1538.63	1127.18	925.75	808.23	732.57	680.72	643.65	616.34	595.77	580.02	567.81	558.25	550.70
31000	2883.56	1589.92	1164.75	956.61	835.18	756.99	703.41	665.10	636.88	615.63	599.36	586.74	576.86	569.06
32000	2976.58	1641.20	1202.32	987.47	862.12	781.41	726.10	686.56	657.43	635.49	618.69	605.67	595.46	587.41
33000	3069.59	1692.49	1239.90	1018.33	889.06	805.83	748.79	708.01	677.97	655.35	638.03	624.59	614.07	605.77
34000	3162.61	1743.78	1277.47	1049.18	916.00	830.24	771.48	729.47	698.52	675.21	657.36	643.52	632.68	624.13
35000	3255.63	1795.07	1315.04	1080.04	942.94	854.66	794.17	750.92	719.06	695.07	676.69	662.45	651.29	642.48
36000	3348.65	1846.35	1352.61	1110.90	969.88	879.08	816.86	772.38	739.61	714.93	696.03	681.37	669.90	660.84
37000	3441.66	1897.64	1390.19	1141.76	996.82	903.50	839.55	793.83	760.15	734.79	715.36	700.30	688.50	679.20
38000	3534.68	1948.93	1427.76	1172.62	1023.76	927.92	862.24	815.29	780.70	754.64	734.70	719.23	707.11	697.55
39000	3627.70	2000.22	1465.33	1203.48	1050.70	952.34	884.93	836.74	801.24	774.50	754.03	738.15	725.72	715.91
40000	3720.72	2051.50	1502.90	1234.33	1077.64	976.76	907.62	858.20	821.78	794.36	773.36	757.08	744.33	734.27
41000	3813.74	2102.79	1540.48	1265.19	1104.59	1001.18	930.31	879.65	842.33	814.22	792.70	776.01	762.94	752.62
42000	3906.75	2154.08	1578.05	1296.05	1131.53	1025.59	953.00	901.11	862.87	834.08	812.03	794.93	781.55	770.98
43000	3999.77	2205.37	1615.62	1326.91	1158.47	1050.01	975.69	922.56	883.42	853.94	831.37	813.86	800.15	789.34
44000	4092.79	2256.65	1653.19	1357.77	1185.41	1074.43	998.38	944.02	903.96	873.80	850.70	832.79	818.76	807.69
45000	4185.81	2307.94	1690.77	1388.63	1212.35	1098.85	1021.07	965.47	924.51	893.66	870.03	851.72	837.37	826.05
46000	4278.82	2359.23	1728.34	1419.48	1239.29	1123.27	1043.76	986.92	945.05	913.52	889.37	870.64	855.98	844.41
47000	4371.84	2410.52	1765.91	1450.34	1266.23	1147.69	1066.45	1008.38	965.60	933.37	908.70	889.57	874.59	862.76
48000	4464.86	2461.80	1803.48	1481.20	1293.17	1172.11	1089.14	1029.83	986.14	953.23	928.04	908.50	893.19	881.12
49000	4557.88	2513.09	1841.06	1512.06	1320.11	1196.53	1111.83	1051.29	1006.69	973.09	947.37	927.42	911.80	899.48
50000	4650.90	2564.38	1878.63	1542.92	1347.05	1220.95	1134.53	1072.74	1027.23	992.95	966.70	946.35	930.41	917.83
55000	5115.98	2820.82	2066.49	1697.21	1481.76	1343.04	1247.98	1180.02	1129.95	1092.25	1063.37	1040.98	1023.45	1009.61
60000	5581.07	3077.25	2254.35	1851.50	1616.46	1465.13	1361.43	1287.29	1232.67	1191.54	1160.04	1135.62	1116.49	1101.40
65000	6046.16	3333.69	2442.21	2005.79	1751.17	1587.23	1474.88	1394.57	1335.40	1290.84	1256.71	1230.25	1209.53	1193.18
70000	6511.25	3590.13	2630.08	2160.08	1885.87	1709.32	1588.33	1501.84	1438.12	1390.13	1353.38	1324.89	1302.57	1284.96
75000	6976.34	3846.57	2817.94	2314.37	2020.58	1831.42	1701.79	1609.11	1540.84	1489.42	1450.05	1419.52	1395.61	1376.75
80000	7441.43	4103.00	3005.80	2468.66	2155.28	1953.51	1815.24	1716.39	1643.56	1588.72	1546.72	1514.16	1488.65	1468.53
85000	7906.52	4359.44	3193.66	2622.95	2289.99	2075.60	1928.69	1823.66	1746.29	1688.01	1643.39	1608.79	1581.69	1560.31
90000	8371.61	4615.88	3381.53	2777.25	2424.69	2197.70	2042.14	1930.94	1849.01	1787.31	1740.06	1703.43	1674.73	1652.09
95000	8836.70	4872.31	3569.39	2931.54	2559.40	2319.79	2155.59	2038.21	1951.73	1886.60	1836.73	1798.06	1767.77	1743.88
100000	9301.79	5128.75	3757.25	3085.83	2694.10	2441.89	2269.05	2145.48	2054.45	1985.90	1933.40	1892.69	1860.82	1835.66

MONTHLY PAYMENT
REQUIRED TO AMORTIZE A LOAN

20.800%

TERM AMOUNT	15 Years	16 Years	17 Years	18 Years	19 Years	20 Years	21 Years	22 Years	23 Years	24 Years	25 Years	30 Years	35 Years	40 Years
5	.10	.09	.09	.09	.09	.09	.09	.09	.09	.09	.09	.09	.09	.09
10	.19	.18	.18	.18	.18	.18	.18	.18	.18	.18	.18	.18	.18	.18
15	.28	.27	.27	.27	.27	.27	.27	.27	.27	.27	.27	.27	.27	.27
25	.46	.45	.45	.45	.45	.45	.44	.44	.44	.44	.44	.44	.44	.44
50	.91	.90	.90	.89	.89	.89	.88	.88	.88	.88	.88	.87	.87	.87
75	1.37	1.35	1.35	1.34	1.33	1.33	1.32	1.32	1.32	1.31	1.31	1.31	1.31	1.31
100	1.82	1.80	1.79	1.78	1.77	1.77	1.76	1.76	1.75	1.75	1.75	1.74	1.74	1.74
200	3.64	3.60	3.58	3.56	3.54	3.53	3.52	3.51	3.50	3.50	3.49	3.48	3.47	3.47
300	5.45	5.40	5.37	5.34	5.31	5.29	5.27	5.26	5.25	5.24	5.24	5.22	5.21	5.21
400	7.27	7.20	7.15	7.11	7.08	7.05	7.03	7.01	7.00	6.99	6.98	6.95	6.94	6.94
500	9.08	9.00	8.94	8.89	8.85	8.81	8.79	8.77	8.75	8.73	8.72	8.69	8.68	8.67
600	10.90	10.80	10.73	10.67	10.62	10.58	10.54	10.52	10.50	10.48	10.47	10.43	10.41	10.41
700	12.71	12.60	12.51	12.44	12.38	12.34	12.30	12.27	12.24	12.22	12.21	12.16	12.15	12.14
800	14.53	14.40	14.30	14.22	14.15	14.10	14.06	14.02	13.99	13.97	13.95	13.90	13.88	13.88
900	16.35	16.20	16.09	16.00	15.92	15.86	15.81	15.77	15.74	15.72	15.70	15.64	15.62	15.61
1000	18.16	18.00	17.87	17.77	17.69	17.62	17.57	17.53	17.49	17.46	17.44	17.37	17.35	17.34
2000	36.32	36.00	35.74	35.54	35.37	35.24	35.13	35.05	34.98	34.92	34.87	34.74	34.70	34.68
3000	54.48	54.00	53.61	53.31	53.06	52.86	52.70	52.57	52.46	52.38	52.31	52.11	52.04	52.02
4000	72.63	71.99	71.48	71.07	70.74	70.48	70.26	70.09	69.95	69.83	69.74	69.48	69.39	69.36
5000	90.79	89.99	89.35	88.84	88.43	88.10	87.83	87.61	87.43	87.29	87.17	86.85	86.74	86.69
6000	108.95	107.99	107.22	106.61	106.11	105.71	105.39	105.13	104.92	104.75	104.61	104.22	104.08	104.03
7000	127.10	125.99	125.09	124.38	123.80	123.33	122.96	122.65	122.40	122.20	122.04	121.59	121.43	121.37
8000	145.26	143.98	142.96	142.14	141.48	140.95	140.52	140.17	139.89	139.66	139.48	138.96	138.77	138.71
9000	163.42	161.98	160.83	159.91	159.17	158.57	158.09	157.69	157.38	157.12	156.91	156.33	156.12	156.05
10000	181.57	179.98	178.70	177.68	176.85	176.19	175.65	175.21	174.86	174.58	174.34	173.70	173.47	173.38
11000	199.73	197.98	196.57	195.45	194.54	193.81	193.21	192.74	192.35	192.03	191.78	191.06	190.81	190.72
12000	217.89	215.97	214.44	213.21	212.22	211.42	210.78	210.26	209.83	209.49	209.21	208.43	208.16	208.06
13000	236.04	233.97	232.31	230.98	229.91	229.04	228.34	227.78	227.32	226.95	226.65	225.80	225.50	225.40
14000	254.20	251.97	250.18	248.75	247.59	246.66	245.91	245.30	244.80	244.40	244.08	243.17	242.85	242.74
15000	272.36	269.97	268.05	266.52	265.28	264.28	263.47	262.82	262.29	261.86	261.51	260.54	260.20	260.07
16000	290.51	287.96	285.92	284.28	282.96	281.90	281.04	280.34	279.78	279.32	278.95	277.91	277.54	277.41
17000	308.67	305.96	303.79	302.05	300.65	299.52	298.60	297.86	297.26	296.78	296.38	295.28	294.89	294.75
18000	326.83	323.96	321.66	319.82	318.33	317.13	316.17	315.38	314.75	314.23	313.82	312.65	312.23	312.09
19000	344.98	341.96	339.53	337.59	336.02	334.75	333.73	332.90	332.23	331.69	331.25	330.02	329.58	329.42
20000	363.14	359.95	357.40	355.35	353.70	352.37	351.29	350.42	349.72	349.15	348.68	347.39	346.93	346.76
21000	381.30	377.95	375.27	373.12	371.39	369.99	368.86	367.94	367.20	366.60	366.12	364.76	364.27	364.10
22000	399.45	395.95	393.14	390.89	389.07	387.61	386.42	385.47	384.69	384.06	383.55	382.12	381.62	381.44
23000	417.61	413.95	411.01	408.66	406.76	405.23	403.99	402.99	402.18	401.52	400.98	399.49	398.96	398.78
24000	435.77	431.94	428.88	426.42	424.44	422.84	421.55	420.51	419.66	418.98	418.42	416.86	416.31	416.11
25000	453.93	449.94	446.75	444.19	442.13	440.46	439.12	438.03	437.15	436.43	435.85	434.23	433.66	433.45
26000	472.08	467.94	464.62	461.96	459.81	458.08	456.68	455.55	454.63	453.89	453.29	451.60	451.00	450.79
27000	490.24	485.94	482.49	479.72	477.50	475.70	474.25	473.07	472.12	471.35	470.72	468.97	468.35	468.13
28000	508.40	503.93	500.36	497.49	495.18	493.32	491.81	490.59	489.60	488.80	488.15	486.34	485.69	485.47
29000	526.55	521.93	518.23	515.26	512.87	510.94	509.37	508.11	507.09	506.26	505.59	503.71	503.04	502.80
30000	544.71	539.93	536.10	533.03	530.55	528.55	526.94	525.63	524.58	523.72	523.02	521.08	520.39	520.14
31000	562.87	557.93	553.97	550.79	548.24	546.17	544.50	543.15	542.06	541.17	540.46	538.45	537.73	537.48
32000	581.02	575.92	571.84	568.56	565.92	563.79	562.07	560.68	559.55	558.63	557.89	555.81	555.08	554.82
33000	599.18	593.92	589.71	586.33	583.61	581.41	579.63	578.20	577.03	576.09	575.32	573.18	572.42	572.15
34000	617.34	611.92	607.58	604.10	601.29	599.03	597.20	595.72	594.52	593.55	592.76	590.55	589.77	589.49
35000	635.49	629.92	625.45	621.86	618.98	616.65	614.76	613.24	612.00	611.00	610.19	607.92	607.12	606.83
36000	653.65	647.91	643.32	639.63	636.66	634.26	632.33	630.76	629.49	628.46	627.63	625.29	624.46	624.17
37000	671.81	665.91	661.19	657.40	654.35	651.88	649.89	648.28	646.98	645.92	645.06	642.66	641.81	641.51
38000	689.96	683.91	679.06	675.17	672.03	669.50	667.46	665.80	664.46	663.37	662.49	660.03	659.16	658.84
39000	708.12	701.91	696.93	692.93	689.72	687.12	685.02	683.32	681.95	680.83	679.93	677.40	676.50	676.18
40000	726.28	719.90	714.80	710.70	707.40	704.74	702.58	700.84	699.43	698.29	697.36	694.77	693.85	693.52
41000	744.43	737.90	732.67	728.47	725.08	722.35	720.15	718.36	716.92	715.75	714.79	712.14	711.19	710.86
42000	762.59	755.90	750.54	746.24	742.77	739.97	737.71	735.88	734.40	733.20	732.23	729.51	728.54	728.20
43000	780.75	773.90	768.41	764.00	760.45	757.59	755.28	753.41	751.89	750.66	749.66	746.87	745.89	745.53
44000	798.90	791.89	786.28	781.77	778.14	775.21	772.84	770.93	769.37	768.12	767.10	764.24	763.23	762.87
45000	817.06	809.89	804.15	799.54	795.82	792.83	790.41	788.45	786.86	785.57	784.53	781.61	780.58	780.21
46000	835.22	827.89	822.02	817.31	813.51	810.45	807.97	805.97	804.35	803.03	801.96	798.98	797.92	797.55
47000	853.37	845.89	839.89	835.07	831.19	828.06	825.54	823.49	821.83	820.49	819.40	816.35	815.27	814.88
48000	871.53	863.88	857.76	852.84	848.88	845.68	843.10	841.01	839.32	837.95	836.83	833.72	832.62	832.22
49000	889.69	881.88	875.63	870.61	866.56	863.30	860.66	858.53	856.80	855.40	854.27	851.09	849.96	849.56
50000	907.85	899.88	893.50	888.38	884.25	880.92	878.23	876.05	874.29	872.86	871.70	868.46	867.31	866.90
55000	998.63	989.87	982.85	977.21	972.67	969.01	966.05	963.66	961.72	960.14	958.87	955.30	954.04	953.59
60000	1089.41	1079.85	1072.20	1066.05	1061.10	1057.10	1053.87	1051.26	1049.15	1047.43	1046.04	1042.15	1040.77	1040.28
65000	1180.20	1169.84	1161.55	1154.89	1149.52	1145.19	1141.70	1138.87	1136.57	1134.72	1133.21	1128.99	1127.50	1126.97
70000	1270.98	1259.83	1250.90	1243.72	1237.95	1233.29	1229.52	1226.47	1224.00	1222.00	1220.38	1215.84	1214.23	1213.66
75000	1361.77	1349.82	1340.25	1332.56	1326.37	1321.38	1317.34	1314.08	1311.43	1309.29	1307.55	1302.68	1300.96	1300.35
80000	1452.55	1439.80	1429.60	1421.40	1414.79	1409.47	1405.16	1401.68	1398.86	1396.57	1394.72	1389.53	1387.69	1387.03
85000	1543.33	1529.79	1518.95	1510.23	1503.22	1497.56	1492.99	1489.29	1486.29	1483.86	1481.89	1476.38	1474.42	1473.72
90000	1634.12	1619.78	1608.29	1599.07	1591.64	1585.65	1580.81	1576.89	1573.72	1571.14	1569.06	1563.22	1561.15	1560.41
95000	1724.90	1709.77	1697.64	1687.91	1680.07	1673.74	1668.63	1664.49	1661.14	1658.43	1656.22	1650.07	1647.88	1647.10
100000	1815.69	1799.75	1786.99	1776.75	1768.49	1761.83	1756.45	1752.10	1748.57	1745.71	1743.39	1736.91	1734.61	1733.79

MONTHLY PAYMENT
REQUIRED TO AMORTIZE A LOAN

TERM AMOUNT	1 Year	2 Years	3 Years	4 Years	5 Years	6 Years	7 Years	8 Years	9 Years	10 Years	11 Years	12 Years	13 Years	14 Years
5	.47	.26	.19	.16	.14	.13	.12	.11	.11	.10	.10	.10	.10	.10
10	.94	.52	.38	.31	.27	.25	.23	.22	.21	.20	.20	.19	.19	.19
15	1.40	.77	.57	.47	.41	.37	.35	.33	.31	.30	.30	.29	.28	.28
25	2.33	1.29	.95	.78	.68	.62	.57	.54	.52	.50	.49	.48	.47	.47
50	4.66	2.57	1.89	1.55	1.35	1.23	1.14	1.08	1.03	1.00	.97	.95	.94	.93
75	6.98	3.85	2.83	2.32	2.03	1.84	1.71	1.62	1.55	1.50	1.46	1.43	1.40	1.39
100	9.31	5.14	3.77	3.09	2.70	2.45	2.28	2.16	2.06	2.00	1.94	1.90	1.87	1.85
200	18.62	10.27	7.53	6.18	5.40	4.90	4.55	4.31	4.12	3.99	3.88	3.80	3.74	3.69
300	27.92	15.40	11.29	9.27	8.10	7.34	6.83	6.46	6.18	5.98	5.82	5.70	5.60	5.53
400	37.23	20.53	15.05	12.36	10.80	9.79	9.10	8.61	8.24	7.97	7.76	7.60	7.47	7.37
500	46.53	25.67	18.81	15.45	13.50	12.24	11.37	10.76	10.30	9.96	9.70	9.49	9.34	9.21
600	55.84	30.80	22.57	18.54	16.19	14.68	13.65	12.91	12.36	11.95	11.64	11.39	11.20	11.05
700	65.14	35.93	26.33	21.63	18.89	17.13	15.92	15.06	14.42	13.94	13.57	13.29	13.07	12.89
800	74.45	41.06	30.09	24.72	21.59	19.58	18.19	17.21	16.48	15.93	15.51	15.19	14.93	14.73
900	83.75	46.20	33.85	27.81	24.29	22.02	20.47	19.36	18.54	17.92	17.45	17.09	16.80	16.58
1000	93.06	51.33	37.62	30.90	26.99	24.47	22.74	21.51	20.60	19.91	19.39	18.98	18.67	18.42
2000	186.11	102.65	75.23	61.80	53.97	48.93	45.48	43.01	41.19	39.82	38.78	37.96	37.33	36.83
3000	279.17	153.98	112.84	92.70	80.95	73.39	68.21	64.51	61.79	59.73	58.16	56.94	55.99	55.24
4000	372.22	205.30	150.45	123.60	107.94	97.86	90.95	86.01	82.38	79.64	77.55	75.92	74.65	73.65
5000	465.27	256.63	188.06	154.50	134.92	122.32	113.69	107.52	102.97	99.55	96.93	94.90	93.32	92.06
6000	558.33	307.95	225.67	185.40	161.90	146.78	136.42	129.02	123.57	119.46	116.32	113.88	111.98	110.47
7000	651.38	359.27	263.28	216.29	188.89	171.24	159.16	150.52	144.16	139.37	135.70	132.86	130.64	128.89
8000	744.44	410.60	300.89	247.19	215.87	195.71	181.89	172.02	164.75	159.28	155.09	151.84	149.30	147.30
9000	837.49	461.92	338.50	278.09	242.85	220.17	204.63	193.52	185.35	179.19	174.48	170.82	167.96	165.71
10000	930.54	513.25	376.11	308.99	269.84	244.63	227.37	215.03	205.94	199.10	193.86	189.80	186.63	184.12
11000	1023.60	564.57	413.73	339.89	296.82	269.09	250.10	236.53	226.53	219.01	213.25	208.78	205.29	202.53
12000	1116.65	615.90	451.34	370.79	323.80	293.56	272.84	258.03	247.13	238.92	232.63	227.76	223.95	220.94
13000	1209.70	667.22	488.95	401.69	350.79	318.02	295.57	279.53	267.72	258.82	252.02	246.74	242.61	239.36
14000	1302.76	718.54	526.56	432.58	377.77	342.48	318.31	301.03	288.31	278.73	271.40	265.72	261.27	257.77
15000	1395.81	769.87	564.17	463.48	404.75	366.95	341.05	322.54	308.91	298.64	290.79	284.70	279.94	276.18
16000	1488.87	821.19	601.78	494.38	431.73	391.41	363.78	344.04	329.50	318.55	310.17	303.68	298.60	294.59
17000	1581.92	872.52	639.39	525.28	458.72	415.87	386.52	365.54	350.09	338.46	329.56	322.66	317.26	313.00
18000	1674.97	923.84	677.00	556.18	485.70	440.33	409.25	387.04	370.69	358.37	348.95	341.64	335.92	331.41
19000	1768.03	975.17	714.61	587.08	512.68	464.80	431.99	408.54	391.28	378.28	368.33	360.62	354.59	349.82
20000	1861.08	1026.49	752.22	617.98	539.67	489.26	454.73	430.05	411.87	398.19	387.72	379.60	373.25	368.24
21000	1954.13	1077.81	789.83	648.87	566.65	513.72	477.46	451.55	432.47	418.10	407.10	398.58	391.91	386.65
22000	2047.19	1129.14	827.45	679.77	593.63	538.18	500.20	473.05	453.06	438.01	426.49	417.56	410.57	405.06
23000	2140.24	1180.46	865.06	710.67	620.62	562.65	522.93	494.55	473.65	457.92	445.87	436.54	429.23	423.47
24000	2233.30	1231.79	902.67	741.57	647.60	587.11	545.67	516.05	494.25	477.83	465.26	455.52	447.90	441.88
25000	2326.35	1283.11	940.28	772.47	674.58	611.57	568.41	537.56	514.84	497.74	484.64	474.50	466.56	460.29
26000	2419.40	1334.44	977.89	803.37	701.57	636.04	591.14	559.06	535.43	517.64	504.03	493.48	485.22	478.71
27000	2512.46	1385.76	1015.50	834.26	728.55	660.50	613.88	580.56	556.03	537.55	523.42	512.46	503.88	497.12
28000	2605.51	1437.08	1053.11	865.16	755.53	684.96	636.61	602.06	576.62	557.46	542.80	531.44	522.54	515.53
29000	2698.56	1488.41	1090.72	896.06	782.51	709.42	659.35	623.57	597.21	577.37	562.19	550.42	541.21	533.94
30000	2791.62	1539.73	1128.33	926.96	809.50	733.89	682.09	645.07	617.81	597.28	581.57	569.40	559.87	552.35
31000	2884.67	1591.06	1165.94	957.86	836.48	758.35	704.82	666.57	638.40	617.19	600.96	588.38	578.53	570.76
32000	2977.73	1642.38	1203.55	988.76	863.46	782.81	727.56	688.07	658.99	637.10	620.34	607.36	597.19	589.18
33000	3070.78	1693.71	1241.17	1019.66	890.45	807.27	750.29	709.57	679.59	657.01	639.73	626.34	615.85	607.59
34000	3163.83	1745.03	1278.78	1050.55	917.43	831.74	773.03	731.08	700.18	676.92	659.12	645.32	634.52	626.00
35000	3256.89	1796.35	1316.39	1081.45	944.41	856.20	795.77	752.58	720.77	696.83	678.50	664.30	653.18	644.41
36000	3349.94	1847.68	1354.00	1112.35	971.40	880.66	818.50	774.08	741.37	716.74	697.89	683.28	671.84	662.82
37000	3443.00	1899.00	1391.61	1143.25	998.38	905.13	841.24	795.58	761.96	736.65	717.27	702.26	690.50	681.23
38000	3536.05	1950.33	1429.22	1174.15	1025.36	929.59	863.97	817.08	782.55	756.56	736.66	721.24	709.17	699.64
39000	3629.10	2001.65	1466.83	1205.05	1052.35	954.05	886.71	838.59	803.15	776.46	756.04	740.22	727.83	718.06
40000	3722.16	2052.98	1504.44	1235.95	1079.33	978.51	909.45	860.09	823.74	796.37	775.43	759.20	746.49	736.47
41000	3815.21	2104.30	1542.05	1266.84	1106.31	1002.98	932.18	881.59	844.33	816.28	794.82	778.18	765.15	754.88
42000	3908.26	2155.62	1579.66	1297.74	1133.29	1027.44	954.92	903.09	864.93	836.19	814.20	797.16	783.81	773.29
43000	4001.32	2206.95	1617.27	1328.64	1160.28	1051.90	977.66	924.59	885.52	856.10	833.59	816.14	802.48	791.70
44000	4094.37	2258.27	1654.89	1359.54	1187.26	1076.36	1000.39	946.10	906.11	876.01	852.97	835.11	821.14	810.11
45000	4187.43	2309.60	1692.50	1390.44	1214.24	1100.83	1023.13	967.60	926.71	895.92	872.36	854.09	839.80	828.53
46000	4280.48	2360.92	1730.11	1421.34	1241.23	1125.29	1045.86	989.10	947.30	915.83	891.74	873.07	858.46	846.94
47000	4373.53	2412.25	1767.72	1452.23	1268.21	1149.75	1068.60	1010.60	967.89	935.74	911.13	892.05	877.12	865.35
48000	4466.59	2463.57	1805.33	1483.13	1295.19	1174.22	1091.34	1032.10	988.49	955.65	930.51	911.03	895.79	883.76
49000	4559.64	2514.89	1842.94	1514.03	1322.18	1198.68	1114.07	1053.61	1009.08	975.56	949.90	930.01	914.45	902.17
50000	4652.69	2566.22	1880.55	1544.93	1349.16	1223.14	1136.81	1075.11	1029.67	995.47	969.29	948.99	933.11	920.58
55000	5117.96	2822.84	2068.61	1699.42	1484.08	1345.45	1250.49	1182.62	1132.64	1095.01	1066.21	1043.89	1026.42	1012.64
60000	5583.23	3079.46	2256.66	1853.92	1618.99	1467.77	1364.17	1290.13	1235.61	1194.56	1163.14	1138.79	1119.73	1104.70
65000	6048.50	3336.08	2444.71	2008.41	1753.91	1590.08	1477.85	1397.64	1338.57	1294.10	1260.07	1233.69	1213.04	1196.76
70000	6513.77	3592.70	2632.77	2162.90	1888.82	1712.40	1591.53	1505.15	1441.54	1393.65	1357.00	1328.59	1306.35	1288.81
75000	6979.04	3849.33	2820.82	2317.39	2023.74	1834.71	1705.21	1612.66	1544.51	1493.20	1453.93	1423.49	1399.66	1380.87
80000	7444.31	4105.95	3008.88	2471.89	2158.65	1957.02	1818.89	1720.17	1647.47	1592.74	1550.85	1518.39	1492.97	1472.93
85000	7909.58	4362.57	3196.93	2626.38	2293.57	2079.34	1932.57	1827.68	1750.44	1692.29	1647.78	1613.29	1586.28	1564.99
90000	8374.85	4619.19	3384.99	2780.87	2428.48	2201.65	2046.25	1935.19	1853.41	1791.84	1744.71	1708.18	1679.59	1657.05
95000	8840.12	4875.81	3573.04	2935.36	2563.40	2323.96	2159.93	2042.70	1956.37	1891.38	1841.64	1803.08	1772.91	1749.10
100000	9305.38	5132.43	3761.10	3089.86	2698.31	2446.28	2273.61	2150.21	2059.34	1990.93	1938.57	1897.98	1866.22	1841.16

TERM	15 Years	16 Years	17 Years	18 Years	19 Years	20 Years	21 Years	22 Years	23 Years	24 Years	25 Years	30 Years	35 Years	40 Years
AMOUNT														
5	.10	.10	.09	.09	.09	.09	.09	.09	.09	.09	.09	.09	.09	.09
10	.19	.19	.18	.18	.18	.18	.18	.18	.18	.18	.18	.18	.18	.18
15	.28	.28	.27	.27	.27	.27	.27	.27	.27	.27	.27	.27	.27	.27
25	.46	.46	.45	.45	.45	.45	.45	.44	.44	.44	.44	.44	.44	.44
50	.92	.91	.90	.90	.89	.89	.89	.88	.88	.88	.88	.88	.88	.88
75	1.37	1.36	1.35	1.34	1.34	1.33	1.33	1.32	1.32	1.32	1.32	1.31	1.31	1.31
100	1.83	1.81	1.80	1.79	1.78	1.77	1.77	1.76	1.76	1.76	1.75	1.75	1.75	1.75
200	3.65	3.62	3.59	3.57	3.55	3.54	3.53	3.52	3.51	3.51	3.50	3.49	3.49	3.49
300	5.47	5.42	5.38	5.35	5.33	5.31	5.29	5.28	5.27	5.26	5.25	5.23	5.23	5.23
400	7.29	7.23	7.18	7.14	7.10	7.08	7.05	7.04	7.02	7.01	7.00	6.98	6.97	6.97
500	9.11	9.03	8.97	8.92	8.88	8.84	8.82	8.80	8.78	8.76	8.75	8.72	8.71	8.71
600	10.93	10.84	10.76	10.70	10.65	10.61	10.58	10.55	10.53	10.52	10.50	10.46	10.45	10.45
700	12.75	12.64	12.55	12.48	12.43	12.38	12.34	12.31	12.29	12.27	12.25	12.21	12.19	12.19
800	14.58	14.45	14.35	14.27	14.20	14.15	14.10	14.07	14.04	14.02	14.00	13.95	13.93	13.93
900	16.40	16.25	16.14	16.05	15.97	15.91	15.87	15.83	15.80	15.77	15.75	15.69	15.67	15.67
1000	18.22	18.06	17.93	17.83	17.75	17.68	17.63	17.59	17.55	17.52	17.50	17.44	17.41	17.41
2000	36.43	36.11	35.86	35.66	35.49	35.36	35.25	35.17	35.10	35.04	34.99	34.87	34.82	34.81
3000	54.64	54.17	53.79	53.48	53.24	53.04	52.88	52.75	52.64	52.56	52.49	52.30	52.23	52.21
4000	72.86	72.22	71.71	71.31	70.98	70.72	70.50	70.33	70.19	70.08	69.98	69.73	69.64	69.61
5000	91.07	90.28	89.64	89.13	88.72	88.39	88.13	87.91	87.74	87.59	87.48	87.16	87.05	87.01
6000	109.28	108.33	107.57	106.96	106.47	106.07	105.75	105.49	105.28	105.11	104.97	104.59	104.45	104.41
7000	127.49	126.38	125.50	124.78	124.21	123.75	123.37	123.07	122.83	122.63	122.47	122.02	121.86	121.81
8000	145.71	144.44	143.42	142.61	141.95	141.43	141.00	140.65	140.37	140.15	139.96	139.45	139.27	139.21
9000	163.92	162.49	161.35	160.44	159.70	159.10	158.62	158.23	157.92	157.67	157.46	156.88	156.68	156.61
10000	182.13	180.55	179.28	178.26	177.44	176.78	176.25	175.82	175.47	175.18	174.95	174.31	174.09	174.01
11000	200.35	198.60	197.21	196.09	195.19	194.46	193.87	193.40	193.01	192.70	192.45	191.74	191.50	191.41
12000	218.56	216.66	215.13	213.91	212.93	212.14	211.50	210.98	210.56	210.22	209.94	209.18	208.90	208.81
13000	236.77	234.71	233.06	231.74	230.67	229.81	229.12	228.56	228.10	227.74	227.44	226.61	226.31	226.21
14000	254.98	252.76	250.99	249.56	248.42	247.49	246.74	246.14	245.65	245.25	244.93	244.04	243.72	243.61
15000	273.20	270.82	268.92	267.39	266.16	265.17	264.37	263.72	263.20	262.77	262.43	261.47	261.13	261.01
16000	291.41	288.87	286.84	285.21	283.90	282.85	281.99	281.30	280.74	280.29	279.92	278.90	278.54	278.41
17000	309.62	306.93	304.77	303.04	301.65	300.52	299.62	298.88	298.29	297.81	297.42	296.33	295.95	295.81
18000	327.83	324.98	322.70	320.87	319.39	318.20	317.24	316.46	315.84	315.33	314.91	313.76	313.35	313.21
19000	346.05	343.04	340.63	338.69	337.13	335.88	334.86	334.05	333.38	332.84	332.41	331.19	330.76	330.61
20000	364.26	361.09	358.55	356.52	354.88	353.56	352.49	351.63	350.93	350.36	349.90	348.62	348.17	348.01
21000	382.47	379.14	376.48	374.34	372.62	371.23	370.11	369.21	368.47	367.88	367.40	366.05	365.58	365.41
22000	400.69	397.20	394.41	392.17	390.36	388.91	387.74	386.79	386.02	385.40	384.89	383.48	382.99	382.81
23000	418.90	415.25	412.34	409.99	408.11	406.59	405.36	404.37	403.57	402.92	402.39	400.92	400.40	400.21
24000	437.11	433.31	430.26	427.82	425.85	424.27	422.99	421.95	421.11	420.43	419.88	418.35	417.00	417.61
25000	455.32	451.36	448.19	445.64	443.60	441.94	440.61	439.53	438.66	437.95	437.38	435.78	435.21	435.01
26000	473.54	469.42	466.12	463.47	461.34	459.62	458.23	457.11	456.20	455.47	454.87	453.21	452.62	452.41
27000	491.75	487.47	484.05	481.30	479.08	477.30	475.86	474.69	473.75	472.99	472.37	470.64	470.03	469.81
28000	509.96	505.52	501.97	499.12	496.83	494.98	493.48	492.27	491.30	490.50	489.86	488.07	487.44	487.21
29000	528.18	523.58	519.90	516.95	514.57	512.65	511.11	509.86	508.84	508.02	507.36	505.50	504.85	504.61
30000	546.39	541.63	537.83	534.77	532.31	530.33	528.73	527.44	526.39	525.54	524.85	522.93	522.25	522.01
31000	564.60	559.69	555.75	552.60	550.06	548.01	546.36	545.02	543.94	543.06	542.35	540.36	539.66	539.41
32000	582.81	577.74	573.68	570.42	567.80	565.69	563.98	562.60	561.48	560.58	559.84	557.79	557.07	556.81
33000	601.03	595.80	591.61	588.25	585.54	583.36	581.60	580.18	579.03	578.09	577.34	575.22	574.48	574.21
34000	619.24	613.85	609.54	606.07	603.29	601.04	599.23	597.76	596.57	595.61	594.83	592.66	591.89	591.61
35000	637.45	631.90	627.46	623.90	621.03	618.72	616.85	615.34	614.12	613.13	612.33	610.09	609.29	609.01
36000	655.66	649.96	645.39	641.73	638.78	636.40	634.48	632.92	631.67	630.65	629.82	627.52	626.70	626.41
37000	673.88	668.01	663.32	659.55	656.52	654.07	652.10	650.50	649.21	648.16	647.32	644.95	644.11	643.81
38000	692.09	686.07	681.25	677.38	674.26	671.75	669.72	668.09	666.76	665.68	664.81	662.38	661.52	661.21
39000	710.30	704.12	699.17	695.20	692.01	689.43	687.35	685.67	684.30	683.20	682.31	679.81	678.93	678.61
40000	728.52	722.18	717.10	713.03	709.75	707.11	704.97	703.25	701.85	700.72	699.80	697.24	696.34	696.02
41000	746.73	740.23	735.03	730.85	727.49	724.79	722.60	720.83	719.40	718.24	717.30	714.67	713.74	713.42
42000	764.94	758.28	752.96	748.68	745.24	742.46	740.22	738.41	736.94	735.75	734.79	732.10	731.15	730.82
43000	783.15	776.34	770.88	766.50	762.98	760.14	757.85	755.99	754.49	753.27	752.29	749.53	748.56	748.22
44000	801.37	794.39	788.81	784.33	780.72	777.82	775.47	773.57	772.03	770.79	769.78	766.96	765.97	765.62
45000	819.58	812.45	806.74	802.16	798.47	795.50	793.09	791.15	789.58	788.31	787.28	784.40	783.38	783.02
46000	837.79	830.50	824.67	819.98	816.21	813.17	810.72	808.73	807.13	805.83	804.77	801.83	800.79	800.42
47000	856.00	848.56	842.59	837.81	833.96	830.85	828.34	826.31	824.67	823.34	822.27	819.26	818.19	817.82
48000	874.22	866.61	860.52	855.63	851.70	848.53	845.97	843.90	842.22	840.86	839.76	836.69	835.60	835.22
49000	892.43	884.66	878.45	873.46	869.44	866.21	863.59	861.48	859.77	858.38	857.26	854.12	853.01	852.62
50000	910.64	902.72	896.38	891.28	887.19	883.88	881.22	879.06	877.31	875.90	874.75	871.55	870.42	870.02
55000	1001.71	992.99	986.01	980.41	975.90	972.27	969.34	966.96	965.04	963.49	962.22	958.70	957.46	957.02
60000	1092.77	1083.26	1075.65	1069.54	1064.62	1060.66	1057.46	1054.87	1052.77	1051.08	1049.70	1045.86	1044.50	1044.02
65000	1183.83	1173.53	1165.29	1158.67	1153.34	1149.05	1145.58	1142.77	1140.50	1138.66	1137.17	1133.01	1131.54	1131.02
70000	1274.90	1263.80	1254.92	1247.80	1242.06	1237.43	1233.70	1230.68	1228.23	1226.25	1224.65	1220.17	1218.58	1218.02
75000	1365.96	1354.07	1344.56	1336.92	1330.78	1325.82	1321.82	1318.58	1315.96	1313.84	1312.12	1307.32	1305.63	1305.02
80000	1457.03	1444.35	1434.20	1426.05	1419.50	1414.21	1409.94	1406.49	1403.70	1401.43	1399.60	1394.48	1392.67	1392.03
85000	1548.09	1534.62	1523.83	1515.18	1508.21	1502.60	1498.06	1494.39	1491.43	1489.02	1487.07	1481.63	1479.71	1479.03
90000	1639.15	1624.89	1613.47	1604.31	1596.93	1590.99	1586.18	1582.30	1579.16	1576.61	1574.55	1568.79	1566.75	1566.03
95000	1730.22	1715.16	1703.11	1693.44	1685.65	1679.37	1674.30	1670.21	1666.89	1664.20	1662.02	1655.94	1653.79	1653.03
100000	1821.28	1805.43	1792.75	1782.56	1774.37	1767.76	1762.43	1758.11	1754.62	1751.79	1749.49	1743.10	1740.83	1740.03

20.900%

MONTHLY PAYMENT
REQUIRED TO AMORTIZE A LOAN

TERM	1 Year	2 Years	3 Years	4 Years	5 Years	6 Years	7 Years	8 Years	9 Years	10 Years	11 Years	12 Years	13 Years	14 Years
AMOUNT														
5	.47	.26	.19	.16	.14	.13	.12	.11	.11	.10	.10	.10	.10	.10
10	.94	.52	.38	.31	.27	.25	.23	.22	.21	.20	.20	.19	.19	.19
15	1.40	.78	.57	.47	.41	.37	.35	.33	.31	.30	.30	.29	.29	.28
25	2.33	1.29	.95	.78	.68	.62	.57	.54	.52	.50	.49	.48	.47	.47
50	4.66	2.57	1.89	1.55	1.35	1.23	1.14	1.08	1.04	1.00	.98	.95	.94	.93
75	6.98	3.86	2.83	2.32	2.03	1.84	1.71	1.62	1.55	1.50	1.46	1.43	1.41	1.39
100	9.31	5.14	3.77	3.10	2.70	2.45	2.28	2.16	2.07	2.00	1.95	1.90	1.87	1.85
200	18.62	10.27	7.53	6.19	5.40	4.90	4.56	4.31	4.13	3.99	3.89	3.80	3.74	3.69
300	27.92	15.41	11.29	9.28	8.10	7.35	6.83	6.46	6.19	5.98	5.83	5.70	5.61	5.53
400	37.23	20.54	15.05	12.37	10.80	9.80	9.11	8.61	8.25	7.98	7.77	7.60	7.48	7.38
500	46.54	25.67	18.82	15.46	13.50	12.24	11.38	10.76	10.31	9.97	9.71	9.50	9.35	9.22
600	55.84	30.81	22.58	18.55	16.20	14.69	13.66	12.92	12.37	11.96	11.65	11.40	11.21	11.06
700	65.15	35.94	26.34	21.64	18.90	17.14	15.93	15.07	14.43	13.95	13.59	13.30	13.08	12.91
800	74.46	41.07	30.10	24.73	21.60	19.59	18.21	17.22	16.49	15.95	15.53	15.20	14.95	14.75
900	83.76	46.21	33.87	27.83	24.30	22.03	20.48	19.37	18.55	17.94	17.47	17.10	16.82	16.59
1000	93.07	51.34	37.63	30.92	27.00	24.48	22.76	21.52	20.61	19.93	19.41	19.00	18.69	18.43
2000	186.14	102.68	75.25	61.83	54.00	48.96	45.51	43.04	41.22	39.86	38.81	38.00	37.37	36.86
3000	279.20	154.01	112.88	92.74	81.00	73.44	68.26	64.56	61.83	59.78	58.21	57.00	56.05	55.29
4000	372.27	205.35	150.50	123.65	107.99	97.91	91.01	86.08	82.44	79.71	77.62	75.99	74.73	73.72
5000	465.33	256.69	188.12	154.56	134.99	122.39	113.76	107.59	103.05	99.64	97.02	94.99	93.41	92.15
6000	558.40	308.02	225.75	185.48	161.99	146.87	136.51	129.11	123.66	119.56	116.42	113.99	112.09	110.58
7000	651.47	359.36	263.37	216.39	188.98	171.35	159.26	150.63	144.27	139.49	135.82	132.99	130.77	129.01
8000	744.53	410.70	300.99	247.30	215.98	195.82	182.02	172.15	164.88	159.41	155.23	151.98	149.45	147.44
9000	837.60	462.03	338.62	278.21	242.98	220.30	204.77	193.67	185.49	179.34	174.63	170.98	168.13	165.87
10000	930.66	513.37	376.24	309.12	269.98	244.78	227.52	215.18	206.10	199.27	194.03	189.98	186.81	184.30
11000	1023.73	564.71	413.87	340.04	296.97	269.26	250.27	236.70	226.71	219.19	213.44	208.98	205.49	202.73
12000	1116.79	616.04	451.49	370.95	323.97	293.73	273.02	258.22	247.32	239.12	232.84	227.97	224.17	221.16
13000	1209.86	667.38	489.11	401.86	350.97	318.21	295.77	279.74	267.93	259.04	252.24	246.97	242.85	239.59
14000	1302.93	718.72	526.74	432.77	377.96	342.69	318.52	301.25	288.54	278.97	271.64	265.97	261.53	258.02
15000	1395.99	770.05	564.36	463.68	404.96	367.17	341.27	322.77	309.15	298.90	291.05	284.97	280.21	276.45
16000	1489.06	821.39	601.98	494.60	431.96	391.64	364.03	344.29	329.76	318.82	310.45	303.96	298.89	294.88
17000	1582.12	872.73	639.61	525.51	458.96	416.12	386.78	365.81	350.37	338.75	329.85	322.96	317.57	313.31
18000	1675.19	924.06	677.23	556.42	485.95	440.60	409.53	387.33	370.98	358.67	349.26	341.96	336.25	331.74
19000	1768.25	975.40	714.86	587.33	512.95	465.07	432.28	408.84	391.59	378.60	368.66	360.96	354.93	350.17
20000	1861.32	1026.74	752.48	618.24	539.95	489.55	455.03	430.36	412.20	398.53	388.06	379.95	373.61	368.60
21000	1954.39	1078.07	790.10	649.16	566.94	514.03	477.78	451.88	432.81	418.45	407.46	398.95	392.29	387.03
22000	2047.45	1129.41	827.73	680.07	593.94	538.51	500.53	473.40	453.42	438.38	426.87	417.95	410.97	405.46
23000	2140.52	1180.75	865.35	710.98	620.94	562.98	523.28	494.92	474.03	458.30	446.27	436.95	429.65	423.89
24000	2233.58	1232.08	902.97	741.89	647.94	587.46	546.04	516.43	494.64	478.23	465.67	455.94	448.33	442.32
25000	2326.65	1283.42	940.60	772.80	674.93	611.94	568.79	537.95	515.25	498.16	485.08	474.94	467.01	460.75
26000	2419.72	1334.76	978.22	803.72	701.93	636.42	591.54	559.47	535.86	518.08	504.48	493.94	485.69	479.18
27000	2512.78	1386.09	1015.85	834.63	728.93	660.89	614.29	580.99	556.47	538.01	523.88	512.93	504.37	497.61
28000	2605.85	1437.43	1053.47	865.54	755.92	685.37	637.04	602.50	577.07	557.93	543.28	531.93	523.05	516.04
29000	2698.91	1488.76	1091.09	896.45	782.92	709.85	659.79	624.02	597.68	577.86	562.69	550.93	541.73	534.47
30000	2791.98	1540.10	1128.72	927.36	809.92	734.33	682.54	645.54	618.29	597.79	582.09	569.93	560.41	552.90
31000	2885.04	1591.44	1166.34	958.27	836.92	758.80	705.29	667.06	638.90	617.71	601.49	588.92	579.09	571.33
32000	2978.11	1642.77	1203.96	989.19	863.91	783.28	728.05	688.58	659.51	637.64	620.90	607.92	597.77	589.76
33000	3071.18	1694.11	1241.59	1020.10	890.91	807.76	750.80	710.09	680.12	657.56	640.30	626.92	616.45	608.19
34000	3164.24	1745.45	1279.21	1051.01	917.91	832.24	773.55	731.61	700.73	677.49	659.70	645.92	635.13	626.62
35000	3257.31	1796.78	1316.84	1081.92	944.90	856.71	796.30	753.13	721.34	697.42	679.10	664.91	653.81	645.05
36000	3350.37	1848.12	1354.46	1112.83	971.90	881.19	819.05	774.65	741.95	717.34	698.51	683.91	672.49	663.48
37000	3443.44	1899.46	1392.08	1143.75	998.90	905.67	841.80	796.17	762.56	737.27	717.91	702.91	691.17	681.91
38000	3536.50	1950.79	1429.71	1174.66	1025.90	930.14	864.55	817.68	783.17	757.19	737.31	721.91	709.85	700.34
39000	3629.57	2002.13	1467.33	1205.57	1052.89	954.62	887.30	839.20	803.78	777.12	756.72	740.90	728.53	718.77
40000	3722.64	2053.47	1504.95	1236.48	1079.89	979.10	910.06	860.72	824.39	797.05	776.12	759.90	747.21	737.20
41000	3815.70	2104.80	1542.58	1267.39	1106.89	1003.58	932.81	882.24	845.00	816.97	795.52	778.90	765.89	755.63
42000	3908.77	2156.14	1580.20	1298.31	1133.88	1028.05	955.56	903.75	865.61	836.90	814.92	797.90	784.57	774.06
43000	4001.83	2207.48	1617.83	1329.22	1160.88	1052.53	978.31	925.27	886.22	856.82	834.33	816.89	803.25	792.49
44000	4094.90	2258.81	1655.45	1360.13	1187.88	1077.01	1001.06	946.79	906.83	876.75	853.73	835.89	821.93	810.92
45000	4187.97	2310.15	1693.07	1391.04	1214.88	1101.49	1023.81	968.31	927.44	896.68	873.13	854.89	840.61	829.35
46000	4281.03	2361.49	1730.70	1421.95	1241.87	1125.96	1046.56	989.83	948.05	916.60	892.54	873.89	859.29	847.78
47000	4374.10	2412.82	1768.32	1452.87	1268.87	1150.44	1069.31	1011.34	968.66	936.53	911.94	892.88	877.97	866.21
48000	4467.16	2464.16	1805.94	1483.78	1295.87	1174.92	1092.07	1032.86	989.27	956.45	931.34	911.88	896.65	884.64
49000	4560.23	2515.50	1843.57	1514.69	1322.86	1199.40	1114.82	1054.38	1009.88	976.38	950.74	930.88	915.33	903.07
50000	4653.29	2566.83	1881.19	1545.60	1349.86	1223.87	1137.57	1075.90	1030.49	996.31	970.15	949.88	934.01	921.50
55000	5118.62	2823.52	2069.31	1700.16	1484.85	1346.26	1251.33	1183.49	1133.54	1095.94	1067.16	1044.86	1027.41	1013.65
60000	5583.95	3080.20	2257.43	1854.72	1619.83	1468.65	1365.08	1291.08	1236.58	1195.58	1164.18	1139.85	1120.81	1105.80
65000	6049.28	3336.88	2445.55	2009.28	1754.82	1591.03	1478.84	1398.67	1339.63	1295.20	1261.19	1234.84	1214.21	1197.95
70000	6514.61	3593.56	2633.67	2163.84	1889.80	1713.42	1592.59	1506.25	1442.68	1394.83	1358.20	1329.82	1307.61	1290.10
75000	6979.94	3850.25	2821.79	2318.40	2024.79	1835.81	1706.35	1613.84	1545.73	1494.46	1455.22	1424.81	1401.01	1382.25
80000	7445.27	4106.93	3009.90	2472.96	2159.78	1958.19	1820.11	1721.43	1648.78	1594.09	1552.23	1519.80	1494.41	1474.40
85000	7910.60	4363.61	3198.02	2627.52	2294.76	2080.58	1933.86	1829.02	1751.82	1693.72	1649.25	1614.78	1587.82	1566.55
90000	8375.93	4620.29	3386.14	2782.08	2429.75	2202.97	2047.62	1936.61	1854.87	1793.35	1746.26	1709.77	1681.22	1658.70
95000	8841.26	4876.98	3574.26	2936.64	2564.73	2325.35	2161.38	2044.20	1957.92	1892.98	1843.27	1804.76	1774.62	1750.85
100000	9306.58	5133.66	3762.38	3091.20	2699.72	2447.74	2275.13	2151.79	2060.97	1992.61	1940.29	1899.75	1868.02	1843.00

512

TERM	15 Years	16 Years	17 Years	18 Years	19 Years	20 Years	21 Years	22 Years	23 Years	24 Years	25 Years	30 Years	35 Years	40 Years
AMOUNT
5	.10	.10	.09	.09	.09	.09	.09	.09	.09	.09	.09	.09	.09	.09
10	.19	.19	.18	.18	.18	.18	.18	.18	.18	.18	.18	.18	.18	.18
15	.28	.28	.27	.27	.27	.27	.27	.27	.27	.27	.27	.27	.27	.27
25	.46	.46	.45	.45	.45	.45	.45	.45	.44	.44	.44	.44	.44	.44
50	.92	.91	.90	.90	.89	.89	.89	.89	.88	.88	.88	.88	.88	.88
75	1.37	1.36	1.35	1.34	1.34	1.33	1.33	1.33	1.32	1.32	1.32	1.31	1.31	1.31
100	1.83	1.81	1.80	1.79	1.78	1.77	1.77	1.77	1.76	1.76	1.76	1.75	1.75	1.75
200	3.65	3.62	3.59	3.57	3.56	3.54	3.54	3.53	3.52	3.51	3.51	3.50	3.49	3.49
300	5.47	5.43	5.39	5.36	5.33	5.31	5.30	5.29	5.27	5.27	5.26	5.24	5.23	5.23
400	7.30	7.23	7.18	7.14	7.11	7.08	7.06	7.05	7.03	7.02	7.01	6.99	6.98	6.97
500	9.12	9.04	8.98	8.93	8.89	8.85	8.83	8.81	8.79	8.77	8.76	8.73	8.72	8.72
600	10.94	10.85	10.77	10.71	10.66	10.62	10.59	10.57	10.54	10.53	10.51	10.48	10.46	10.46
700	12.77	12.66	12.57	12.50	12.44	12.39	12.36	12.33	12.30	12.28	12.27	12.22	12.21	12.20
800	14.59	14.46	14.36	14.28	14.22	14.16	14.12	14.09	14.06	14.04	14.02	13.97	13.95	13.94
900	16.41	16.27	16.16	16.07	15.99	15.93	15.88	15.85	15.81	15.79	15.77	15.71	15.69	15.68
1000	18.24	18.08	17.95	17.85	17.77	17.70	17.65	17.61	17.57	17.54	17.52	17.46	17.43	17.43
2000	36.47	36.15	35.90	35.69	35.53	35.40	35.29	35.21	35.14	35.08	35.04	34.91	34.86	34.85
3000	54.70	54.22	53.84	53.54	53.29	53.10	52.94	52.81	52.70	52.62	52.55	52.36	52.29	52.27
4000	72.93	72.30	71.79	71.38	71.06	70.79	70.58	70.41	70.27	70.16	70.07	69.81	69.72	69.69
5000	91.16	90.37	89.74	89.23	88.82	88.49	88.23	88.01	87.84	87.70	87.58	87.26	87.15	87.11
6000	109.39	108.44	107.68	107.07	106.58	106.19	105.87	105.61	105.40	105.23	105.10	104.71	104.58	104.53
7000	127.62	126.52	125.63	124.92	124.35	123.89	123.51	123.21	122.97	122.77	122.61	122.17	122.01	121.95
8000	145.86	144.59	143.58	142.76	142.11	141.58	141.16	140.81	140.54	140.31	140.13	139.62	139.44	139.37
9000	164.09	162.66	161.52	160.61	159.87	159.28	158.80	158.41	158.10	157.85	157.64	157.07	156.87	156.79
10000	182.32	180.74	179.47	178.45	177.64	176.98	176.45	176.02	175.67	175.39	175.16	174.52	174.30	174.22
11000	200.55	198.81	197.42	196.30	195.40	194.68	194.09	193.62	193.23	192.92	192.67	191.97	191.72	191.64
12000	218.78	216.88	215.36	214.14	213.16	212.37	211.73	211.22	210.80	210.46	210.19	209.42	209.15	209.06
13000	237.01	234.96	233.31	231.99	230.93	230.07	229.38	228.82	228.37	228.00	227.70	226.87	226.58	226.48
14000	255.24	253.03	251.26	249.83	248.69	247.77	247.02	246.42	245.93	245.54	245.22	244.33	244.01	243.90
15000	273.48	271.10	269.20	267.68	266.45	265.46	264.67	264.02	263.50	263.08	262.73	261.78	261.44	261.32
16000	291.71	289.18	287.15	285.52	284.22	283.16	282.31	281.62	281.07	280.61	280.25	279.23	278.87	278.74
17000	309.94	307.25	305.10	303.37	301.98	300.86	299.96	299.22	298.63	298.15	297.76	296.68	296.30	296.16
18000	328.17	325.32	323.04	321.21	319.74	318.56	317.60	316.82	316.20	315.69	315.28	314.13	313.73	313.58
19000	346.40	343.40	340.99	339.06	337.51	336.25	335.24	334.43	333.76	333.23	332.79	331.58	331.16	331.00
20000	364.63	361.47	358.94	356.90	355.27	353.95	352.89	352.03	351.33	350.77	350.31	349.04	348.59	348.43
21000	382.86	379.54	376.88	374.75	373.03	371.65	370.53	369.63	368.90	368.30	367.83	366.49	366.01	365.85
22000	401.10	397.62	394.83	392.59	390.80	389.35	388.18	387.23	386.46	385.84	385.34	383.94	383.44	383.27
23000	419.33	415.69	412.78	410.44	408.56	407.04	405.82	404.83	404.03	403.38	402.86	401.39	400.87	400.69
24000	437.56	433.76	430.72	428.28	426.32	424.74	423.46	422.43	421.60	420.92	420.37	418.84	418.30	418.11
25000	455.79	451.83	448.67	446.13	444.09	442.44	441.11	440.03	439.16	438.46	437.89	436.29	435.73	435.53
26000	474.02	469.91	466.62	463.97	461.85	460.14	458.75	457.63	456.73	456.00	455.40	453.74	453.16	452.95
27000	492.25	487.98	484.56	481.82	479.61	477.83	476.40	475.23	474.29	473.53	472.92	471.20	470.59	470.37
28000	510.48	506.05	502.51	499.66	497.38	495.53	494.04	492.84	491.86	491.07	490.43	488.65	488.02	487.79
29000	528.72	524.13	520.46	517.51	515.14	513.23	511.68	510.44	509.43	508.61	507.95	506.10	505.45	505.22
30000	546.95	542.20	538.40	535.35	532.90	530.92	529.33	528.04	526.99	526.15	525.46	523.55	522.88	522.64
31000	565.18	560.27	556.35	553.20	550.67	548.62	546.97	545.64	544.56	543.69	542.98	541.00	540.30	540.06
32000	583.41	578.35	574.30	571.04	568.43	566.32	564.62	563.24	562.13	561.22	560.49	558.45	557.73	557.48
33000	601.64	596.42	592.24	588.89	586.19	584.02	582.26	580.84	579.69	578.76	578.01	575.91	575.16	574.90
34000	619.87	614.49	610.19	606.73	603.95	601.71	599.91	598.44	597.26	596.30	595.52	593.36	592.59	592.32
35000	638.10	632.57	628.14	624.58	621.72	619.41	617.55	616.04	614.83	613.84	613.04	610.81	610.02	609.74
36000	656.34	650.64	646.08	642.42	639.48	637.11	635.19	633.64	632.39	631.38	630.55	628.26	627.45	627.16
37000	674.57	668.71	664.03	660.27	657.24	654.81	652.84	651.25	649.96	648.91	648.07	645.71	644.88	644.58
38000	692.80	686.79	681.98	678.11	675.01	672.50	670.48	668.85	667.52	666.45	665.58	663.16	662.31	662.00
39000	711.03	704.86	699.92	695.96	692.77	690.20	688.13	686.45	685.09	683.99	683.10	680.61	679.74	679.43
40000	729.26	722.93	717.87	713.80	710.53	707.90	705.77	704.05	702.66	701.53	700.61	698.07	697.17	696.85
41000	747.49	741.01	735.82	731.65	728.30	725.60	723.41	721.65	720.22	719.07	718.13	715.52	714.59	714.27
42000	765.72	759.08	753.76	749.49	746.06	743.29	741.06	739.25	737.79	736.60	735.65	732.97	732.02	731.69
43000	783.96	777.15	771.71	767.34	763.82	760.99	758.70	756.85	755.36	754.14	753.16	750.42	749.45	749.11
44000	802.19	795.23	789.66	785.18	781.59	778.69	776.35	774.45	772.92	771.68	770.68	767.87	766.88	766.53
45000	820.42	813.30	807.60	803.03	799.35	796.38	793.99	792.05	790.49	789.22	788.19	785.32	784.31	783.95
46000	838.65	831.37	825.55	820.87	817.11	814.08	811.63	809.66	808.05	806.76	805.71	802.77	801.74	801.37
47000	856.88	849.45	843.49	838.72	834.88	831.78	829.28	827.26	825.62	824.30	823.22	820.23	819.17	818.79
48000	875.11	867.52	861.44	856.56	852.64	849.48	846.92	844.86	843.19	841.83	840.74	837.68	836.60	836.22
49000	893.34	885.59	879.39	874.41	870.40	867.17	864.57	862.46	860.75	859.37	858.25	855.13	854.03	853.64
50000	911.58	903.66	897.33	892.25	888.17	884.87	882.21	880.06	878.32	876.91	875.77	872.58	871.46	871.06
55000	1002.73	994.03	987.07	981.48	976.98	973.36	970.43	968.07	966.15	964.60	963.34	959.84	958.60	958.16
60000	1093.89	1084.40	1076.80	1070.70	1065.80	1061.84	1058.65	1056.07	1053.98	1052.29	1050.92	1047.10	1045.75	1045.27
65000	1185.05	1174.76	1166.53	1159.93	1154.62	1150.33	1146.87	1144.08	1141.81	1139.98	1138.50	1134.35	1132.89	1132.37
70000	1276.20	1265.13	1256.27	1249.15	1243.43	1238.82	1235.09	1232.08	1229.65	1227.67	1226.07	1221.61	1220.04	1219.48
75000	1367.36	1355.49	1346.00	1338.38	1332.25	1327.30	1323.31	1320.09	1317.48	1315.36	1313.65	1308.87	1307.18	1306.58
80000	1458.52	1445.86	1435.73	1427.60	1421.06	1415.79	1411.53	1408.09	1405.31	1403.05	1401.22	1396.13	1394.33	1393.69
85000	1549.68	1536.23	1525.47	1516.83	1509.88	1504.28	1499.76	1496.10	1493.14	1490.74	1488.80	1483.38	1481.47	1480.79
90000	1640.83	1626.59	1615.20	1606.05	1598.70	1592.76	1587.99	1584.10	1580.97	1578.43	1576.38	1570.64	1568.62	1567.90
95000	1731.99	1716.96	1704.93	1695.28	1687.51	1681.25	1676.20	1672.11	1668.80	1666.12	1663.95	1657.90	1655.76	1655.00
100000	1823.15	1807.32	1794.66	1784.50	1776.33	1769.74	1764.42	1760.12	1756.63	1753.81	1751.53	1745.16	1742.91	1742.11

MONTHLY PAYMENT
REQUIRED TO AMORTIZE A LOAN

TERM	1 Year	2 Years	3 Years	4 Years	5 Years	6 Years	7 Years	8 Years	9 Years	10 Years	11 Years	12 Years	13 Years	14 Years
AMOUNT
5	.47	.26	.19	.16	.14	.13	.12	.11	.11	.10	.10	.10	.10	.10
10	.94	.52	.38	.31	.28	.25	.23	.22	.21	.20	.20	.20	.19	.19
15	1.40	.78	.57	.47	.41	.37	.35	.33	.32	.30	.30	.29	.29	.28
25	2.33	1.29	.95	.78	.68	.62	.58	.54	.52	.50	.49	.48	.47	.47
50	4.66	2.57	1.89	1.55	1.36	1.23	1.15	1.08	1.04	1.00	.98	.96	.94	.93
75	6.99	3.86	2.83	2.33	2.03	1.85	1.72	1.62	1.56	1.50	1.47	1.44	1.41	1.39
100	9.32	5.14	3.77	3.10	2.71	2.46	2.29	2.16	2.07	2.00	1.95	1.91	1.88	1.86
200	18.63	10.28	7.54	6.20	5.42	4.91	4.57	4.32	4.14	4.00	3.90	3.82	3.76	3.71
300	27.94	15.42	11.31	9.29	8.12	7.37	6.85	6.48	6.21	6.00	5.85	5.73	5.63	5.56
400	37.25	20.56	15.08	12.39	10.83	9.82	9.13	8.64	8.27	8.00	7.79	7.63	7.51	7.41
500	46.56	25.70	18.84	15.49	13.53	12.27	11.41	10.80	10.34	10.00	9.74	9.54	9.38	9.26
600	55.87	30.84	22.61	18.58	16.24	14.73	13.69	12.95	12.41	12.00	11.69	11.45	11.26	11.11
700	65.18	35.97	26.38	21.68	18.94	17.18	15.97	15.11	14.48	14.00	13.64	13.35	13.13	12.96
800	74.50	41.11	30.15	24.78	21.65	19.63	18.25	17.27	16.54	16.00	15.58	15.26	15.01	14.81
900	83.81	46.25	33.91	27.87	24.35	22.09	20.54	19.43	18.61	18.00	17.53	17.17	16.88	16.66
1000	93.12	51.39	37.68	30.97	27.06	24.54	22.82	21.59	20.68	20.00	19.48	19.07	18.76	18.51
2000	186.23	102.78	75.36	61.94	54.11	49.08	45.63	43.17	41.35	39.99	38.95	38.14	37.51	37.01
3000	279.35	154.16	113.03	92.90	81.17	73.61	68.44	64.75	62.03	59.98	58.42	57.21	56.26	55.52
4000	372.46	205.55	150.71	123.87	108.22	98.15	91.25	86.33	82.70	79.98	77.89	76.28	75.01	74.02
5000	465.57	256.93	188.38	154.83	135.27	122.68	114.07	107.91	103.38	99.97	97.36	95.35	93.77	92.52
6000	558.69	308.32	226.06	185.80	162.33	147.22	136.88	129.49	124.05	119.96	116.84	114.41	112.52	111.03
7000	651.80	359.70	263.73	216.76	189.38	171.76	159.69	151.07	144.73	139.96	136.31	133.48	131.27	129.53
8000	744.92	411.09	301.41	247.73	216.43	196.29	182.50	172.65	165.40	159.95	155.78	152.55	150.02	148.03
9000	838.03	462.48	339.08	278.70	243.49	220.83	205.32	194.23	186.08	179.94	175.25	171.62	168.78	166.54
10000	931.14	513.86	376.76	309.66	270.54	245.36	228.13	215.82	206.75	199.94	194.72	190.69	187.53	185.04
11000	1024.26	565.25	414.43	340.63	297.59	269.90	250.94	237.40	227.43	219.93	214.19	209.75	206.28	203.54
12000	1117.37	616.63	452.11	371.59	324.65	294.44	273.75	258.98	248.10	239.92	233.67	228.82	225.03	222.05
13000	1210.48	668.02	489.78	402.56	351.70	318.97	296.56	280.56	268.78	259.92	253.14	247.89	243.78	240.55
14000	1303.60	719.40	527.46	433.52	378.75	343.51	319.38	302.14	289.45	279.91	272.61	266.96	262.54	259.05
15000	1396.71	770.79	565.13	464.49	405.81	368.04	342.19	323.72	310.13	299.90	292.08	286.03	281.29	277.56
16000	1489.83	822.18	602.81	495.46	432.86	392.58	365.00	345.30	330.80	319.90	311.55	305.09	300.04	296.06
17000	1582.94	873.56	640.48	526.42	459.91	417.12	387.81	366.88	351.48	339.89	331.03	324.16	318.79	314.56
18000	1676.05	924.95	678.16	557.39	486.97	441.65	410.63	388.46	372.15	359.88	350.50	343.23	337.55	333.07
19000	1769.17	976.33	715.83	588.35	514.02	466.19	433.44	410.04	392.83	379.88	369.97	362.30	356.30	351.57
20000	1862.28	1027.72	753.51	619.32	541.07	490.72	456.25	431.63	413.50	399.87	389.44	381.37	375.05	370.07
21000	1955.39	1079.10	791.18	650.28	568.13	515.26	479.06	453.21	434.18	419.86	408.91	400.43	393.80	388.58
22000	2048.51	1130.49	828.86	681.25	595.18	539.80	501.87	474.79	454.85	439.85	428.38	419.50	412.55	407.08
23000	2141.62	1181.88	866.53	712.22	622.23	564.33	524.69	496.37	475.53	459.85	447.86	438.57	431.31	425.58
24000	2234.74	1233.26	904.21	743.18	649.29	588.87	547.50	517.95	496.20	479.84	467.33	457.64	450.06	444.09
25000	2327.85	1284.65	941.88	774.15	676.34	613.40	570.31	539.53	516.88	499.83	486.80	476.71	468.81	462.59
26000	2420.96	1336.03	979.56	805.11	703.39	637.94	593.12	561.11	537.55	519.83	506.27	495.77	487.56	481.09
27000	2514.08	1387.42	1017.23	836.08	730.45	662.48	615.94	582.69	558.23	539.82	525.74	514.84	506.32	499.60
28000	2607.19	1438.80	1054.91	867.04	757.50	687.01	638.75	604.27	578.90	559.81	545.22	533.91	525.07	518.10
29000	2700.30	1490.19	1092.58	898.01	784.55	711.55	661.56	625.85	599.58	579.81	564.69	552.98	543.82	536.60
30000	2793.42	1541.57	1130.26	928.98	811.61	736.08	684.37	647.44	620.25	599.80	584.16	572.05	562.57	555.11
31000	2886.53	1592.96	1167.93	959.94	838.66	760.62	707.18	669.02	640.93	619.79	603.63	591.11	581.32	573.61
32000	2979.65	1644.35	1205.61	990.91	865.71	785.16	730.00	690.60	661.60	639.79	623.10	610.18	600.08	592.11
33000	3072.76	1695.73	1243.28	1021.87	892.77	809.69	752.81	712.18	682.28	659.78	642.57	629.25	618.83	610.62
34000	3165.87	1747.12	1280.96	1052.84	919.82	834.23	775.62	733.76	702.95	679.77	662.05	648.32	637.58	629.12
35000	3258.99	1798.50	1318.63	1083.80	946.87	858.76	798.43	755.34	723.63	699.77	681.52	667.39	656.33	647.62
36000	3352.10	1849.89	1356.31	1114.77	973.93	883.30	821.25	776.92	744.30	719.76	700.99	686.45	675.09	666.13
37000	3445.21	1901.28	1393.98	1145.74	1000.98	907.84	844.06	798.50	764.98	739.75	720.46	705.52	693.84	684.63
38000	3538.33	1952.66	1431.66	1176.70	1028.03	932.37	866.87	820.08	785.65	759.75	739.93	724.59	712.59	703.13
39000	3631.44	2004.05	1469.33	1207.67	1055.09	956.91	889.68	841.66	806.32	779.74	759.41	743.66	731.34	721.64
40000	3724.56	2055.43	1507.01	1238.63	1082.14	981.44	912.49	863.25	827.00	799.73	778.88	762.73	750.09	740.14
41000	3817.67	2106.82	1544.68	1269.60	1109.19	1005.98	935.31	884.83	847.67	819.72	798.35	781.79	768.85	758.64
42000	3910.78	2158.20	1582.36	1300.56	1136.25	1030.52	958.12	906.41	868.35	839.72	817.82	800.86	787.60	777.15
43000	4003.90	2209.59	1620.03	1331.53	1163.30	1055.05	980.93	927.99	889.02	859.71	837.29	819.93	806.35	795.65
44000	4097.01	2260.97	1657.71	1362.50	1190.35	1079.59	1003.74	949.57	909.70	879.70	856.76	839.00	825.10	814.15
45000	4190.12	2312.36	1695.38	1393.46	1217.41	1104.12	1026.56	971.15	930.37	899.70	876.24	858.07	843.86	832.66
46000	4283.24	2363.74	1733.06	1424.43	1244.46	1128.66	1049.37	992.73	951.05	919.69	895.71	877.13	862.61	851.16
47000	4376.35	2415.13	1770.73	1455.39	1271.51	1153.20	1072.18	1014.31	971.72	939.69	915.18	896.20	881.36	869.66
48000	4469.47	2466.52	1808.41	1486.36	1298.57	1177.73	1094.99	1035.89	992.40	959.68	934.65	915.27	900.11	888.17
49000	4562.58	2517.90	1846.08	1517.32	1325.62	1202.27	1117.80	1057.47	1013.07	979.67	954.12	934.34	918.86	906.67
50000	4655.69	2569.29	1883.76	1548.29	1352.67	1226.80	1140.62	1079.06	1033.75	999.66	973.60	953.41	937.62	925.17
55000	5121.26	2826.22	2072.13	1703.12	1487.94	1349.48	1254.68	1186.96	1137.12	1099.63	1070.95	1048.75	1031.38	1017.69
60000	5586.83	3083.14	2260.51	1857.95	1623.21	1472.16	1368.74	1294.87	1240.50	1199.60	1168.31	1144.09	1125.14	1110.21
65000	6052.40	3340.07	2448.88	2012.78	1758.47	1594.84	1482.80	1402.77	1343.87	1299.56	1265.67	1239.43	1218.90	1202.73
70000	6517.97	3597.00	2637.26	2167.60	1893.74	1717.52	1596.86	1510.68	1447.25	1399.53	1363.03	1334.77	1312.66	1295.24
75000	6983.54	3853.93	2825.64	2322.43	2029.01	1840.20	1710.92	1618.58	1550.62	1499.49	1460.39	1430.11	1406.42	1387.76
80000	7449.11	4110.86	3014.01	2477.26	2164.27	1962.88	1824.98	1726.49	1653.99	1599.46	1557.75	1525.45	1500.18	1480.28
85000	7914.68	4367.79	3202.39	2632.09	2299.54	2085.56	1939.04	1834.39	1757.37	1699.42	1655.11	1620.79	1593.94	1572.79
90000	8380.25	4624.71	3390.76	2786.92	2434.81	2208.24	2053.11	1942.30	1860.74	1799.39	1752.47	1716.13	1687.71	1665.31
95000	8845.81	4881.64	3579.14	2941.75	2570.07	2330.92	2167.17	2050.20	1964.12	1899.36	1849.83	1811.47	1781.47	1757.83
100000	9311.38	5138.57	3767.51	3096.57	2705.34	2453.60	2281.23	2158.11	2067.49	1999.32	1947.19	1906.81	1875.23	1850.34

MONTHLY PAYMENT
REQUIRED TO AMORTIZE A LOAN

21.000%

TERM	15 Years	16 Years	17 Years	18 Years	19 Years	20 Years	21 Years	22 Years	23 Years	24 Years	25 Years	30 Years	35 Years	40 Years
AMOUNT														
5	.10	.10	.10	.09	.09	.09	.09	.09	.09	.09	.09	.09	.09	.09
10	.19	.19	.19	.18	.18	.18	.18	.18	.18	.18	.18	.18	.18	.18
15	.28	.28	.28	.27	.27	.27	.27	.27	.27	.27	.27	.27	.27	.27
25	.46	.46	.46	.45	.45	.45	.45	.45	.45	.45	.44	.44	.44	.44
50	.92	.91	.91	.90	.90	.89	.89	.89	.89	.89	.88	.88	.88	.88
75	1.38	1.37	1.36	1.35	1.34	1.34	1.33	1.33	1.33	1.33	1.32	1.32	1.32	1.32
100	1.84	1.82	1.81	1.80	1.79	1.78	1.78	1.77	1.77	1.77	1.76	1.76	1.76	1.76
200	3.67	3.63	3.61	3.59	3.57	3.56	3.55	3.54	3.53	3.53	3.52	3.51	3.51	3.51
300	5.50	5.45	5.41	5.38	5.36	5.34	5.32	5.31	5.30	5.29	5.28	5.27	5.26	5.26
400	7.33	7.26	7.21	7.17	7.14	7.12	7.09	7.08	7.06	7.05	7.04	7.02	7.01	7.01
500	9.16	9.08	9.02	8.97	8.93	8.89	8.87	8.85	8.83	8.81	8.80	8.77	8.76	8.76
600	10.99	10.89	10.82	10.76	10.71	10.67	10.64	10.61	10.59	10.58	10.56	10.53	10.51	10.51
700	12.82	12.71	12.62	12.55	12.49	12.45	12.41	12.38	12.36	12.34	12.32	12.28	12.26	12.26
800	14.65	14.52	14.42	14.34	14.28	14.23	14.18	14.15	14.12	14.10	14.08	14.03	14.01	14.01
900	16.48	16.34	16.23	16.14	16.06	16.00	15.96	15.92	15.89	15.86	15.84	15.79	15.77	15.76
1000	18.31	18.15	18.03	17.93	17.85	17.78	17.73	17.69	17.65	17.62	17.60	17.54	17.52	17.51
2000	36.62	36.30	36.05	35.85	35.69	35.56	35.45	35.37	35.30	35.24	35.20	35.07	35.03	35.01
3000	54.92	54.45	54.08	53.77	53.53	53.33	53.18	53.05	52.95	52.86	52.79	52.61	52.54	52.52
4000	73.23	72.60	72.10	71.70	71.37	71.11	70.90	70.73	70.59	70.48	70.39	70.14	70.05	70.02
5000	91.54	90.75	90.12	89.62	89.21	88.89	88.62	88.41	88.24	88.10	87.99	87.68	87.56	87.53
6000	109.84	108.90	108.15	107.54	107.05	106.66	106.35	106.09	105.89	105.72	105.58	105.21	105.08	105.03
7000	128.15	127.05	126.17	125.46	124.90	124.44	124.07	123.77	123.53	123.34	123.18	122.74	122.59	122.53
8000	146.45	145.20	144.19	143.39	142.74	142.22	141.80	141.46	141.18	140.96	140.78	140.28	140.10	140.04
9000	164.76	163.35	162.22	161.31	160.58	159.99	159.52	159.14	158.83	158.58	158.37	157.81	157.61	157.54
10000	183.07	181.50	180.24	179.23	178.42	177.77	177.24	176.82	176.47	176.20	175.97	175.35	175.12	175.05
11000	201.37	199.64	198.26	197.15	196.26	195.55	194.97	194.50	194.12	193.82	193.57	192.88	192.64	192.55
12000	219.68	217.79	216.29	215.08	214.10	213.32	212.69	212.18	211.77	211.43	211.16	210.41	210.15	210.06
13000	237.98	235.94	234.31	233.00	231.95	231.10	230.41	229.86	229.42	229.05	228.76	227.95	227.66	227.56
14000	256.29	254.09	252.33	250.92	249.79	248.88	248.14	247.54	247.06	246.67	246.36	245.40	245.17	245.06
15000	274.60	272.24	270.36	268.84	267.63	266.65	265.86	265.22	264.71	264.29	263.95	263.02	262.68	262.57
16000	292.90	290.39	288.38	286.77	285.47	284.43	283.59	282.91	282.36	281.91	281.55	280.55	280.20	280.07
17000	311.21	308.54	306.40	304.69	303.31	302.20	301.31	300.59	300.00	299.53	299.15	298.08	297.71	297.58
18000	329.52	326.69	324.43	322.61	321.15	319.98	319.03	318.27	317.65	317.15	316.74	315.62	315.22	315.08
19000	347.82	344.84	342.45	340.54	339.00	337.76	336.76	335.95	335.30	334.77	334.34	333.15	332.73	332.59
20000	366.13	362.98	360.47	358.46	356.84	355.53	354.48	353.63	352.94	352.39	351.94	350.69	350.24	350.09
21000	384.43	381.13	378.50	376.38	374.68	373.31	372.21	371.31	370.59	370.01	369.53	368.22	367.76	367.59
22000	402.74	399.28	396.52	394.30	392.52	391.09	389.93	388.99	388.24	387.63	387.13	385.75	385.27	385.10
23000	421.05	417.43	414.54	412.23	410.36	408.86	407.65	406.68	405.88	405.25	404.73	403.29	402.78	402.60
24000	439.35	435.58	432.57	430.15	428.20	426.64	425.38	424.36	423.53	422.86	422.32	420.82	420.29	420.11
25000	457.66	453.73	450.59	448.07	446.05	444.42	443.10	442.04	441.18	440.48	439.92	438.36	437.80	437.61
26000	475.96	471.88	468.61	465.99	463.89	462.19	460.82	459.72	458.83	458.10	457.52	455.89	455.32	455.12
27000	494.27	490.03	486.64	483.92	481.73	479.97	478.55	477.40	476.47	475.72	475.11	473.42	472.83	472.62
28000	512.58	508.18	504.66	501.84	499.57	497.75	496.27	495.08	494.12	493.34	492.71	490.96	490.34	490.12
29000	530.88	526.33	522.68	519.76	517.41	515.52	514.00	512.76	511.77	510.96	510.31	508.49	507.85	507.63
30000	549.19	544.47	540.71	537.68	535.25	533.30	531.72	530.44	529.41	528.58	527.90	526.03	525.36	525.13
31000	567.49	562.62	558.73	555.61	553.10	551.07	549.44	548.13	547.06	546.20	545.50	543.56	542.88	542.64
32000	585.80	580.77	576.75	573.53	570.94	568.85	567.17	565.81	564.71	563.82	563.10	561.09	560.39	560.14
33000	604.11	598.92	594.78	591.45	588.78	586.63	584.89	583.49	582.35	581.44	580.69	578.63	577.90	577.64
34000	622.41	617.07	612.80	609.37	606.62	604.40	602.61	601.17	600.00	599.06	598.29	596.16	595.41	595.15
35000	640.72	635.22	630.82	627.30	624.46	622.18	620.34	618.85	617.65	616.68	615.89	613.70	612.92	612.65
36000	659.03	653.37	648.85	645.22	642.30	639.96	638.06	636.53	635.30	634.29	633.48	631.23	630.44	630.16
37000	677.33	671.52	666.87	663.14	660.15	657.73	655.79	654.21	652.94	651.91	651.08	648.76	647.95	647.66
38000	695.64	689.67	684.89	681.07	677.99	675.51	673.51	671.89	670.59	669.53	668.68	666.30	665.46	665.17
39000	713.94	707.82	702.92	698.99	695.83	693.29	691.23	689.58	688.24	687.15	686.27	683.83	682.97	682.67
40000	732.25	725.96	720.94	716.91	713.67	711.06	708.96	707.26	705.88	704.77	703.87	701.37	700.48	700.17
41000	750.56	744.11	738.96	734.83	731.51	728.84	726.68	724.94	723.53	722.39	721.47	718.90	718.00	717.68
42000	768.86	762.26	756.99	752.76	749.35	746.62	744.41	742.62	741.18	740.01	739.06	736.43	735.51	735.18
43000	787.17	780.41	775.01	770.68	767.20	764.39	762.13	760.30	758.82	757.63	756.66	753.97	753.02	752.69
44000	805.47	798.56	793.03	788.60	785.04	782.17	779.85	777.98	776.47	775.25	774.26	771.50	770.53	770.19
45000	823.78	816.71	811.06	806.52	802.88	799.94	797.58	795.66	794.12	792.87	791.85	789.04	788.04	787.70
46000	842.09	834.86	829.08	824.45	820.72	817.72	815.30	813.35	811.76	810.49	809.45	806.57	805.56	805.20
47000	860.39	853.01	847.10	842.37	838.56	835.50	833.02	831.03	829.41	828.10	827.05	824.10	823.07	822.70
48000	878.70	871.16	865.13	860.29	856.40	853.27	850.75	848.71	847.06	845.72	844.64	841.64	840.58	840.21
49000	897.01	889.31	883.15	878.21	874.25	871.05	868.47	866.39	864.71	863.34	862.24	859.17	858.09	857.71
50000	915.31	907.45	901.17	896.14	892.09	888.83	886.20	884.07	882.35	880.96	879.84	876.71	875.60	875.22
55000	1006.84	998.20	991.29	985.75	981.30	977.71	974.81	972.48	970.59	969.06	967.82	964.38	963.16	962.74
60000	1098.37	1088.95	1081.41	1075.36	1070.50	1066.59	1063.43	1060.88	1058.82	1057.15	1055.80	1052.05	1050.72	1050.26
65000	1189.90	1179.69	1171.52	1164.98	1159.71	1155.47	1152.05	1149.29	1147.06	1145.25	1143.79	1139.72	1138.28	1137.78
70000	1281.43	1270.44	1261.64	1254.59	1248.92	1244.36	1240.67	1237.70	1235.29	1233.35	1231.77	1227.39	1225.84	1225.30
75000	1372.96	1361.18	1351.76	1344.20	1338.13	1333.24	1329.29	1326.10	1323.53	1321.44	1319.75	1315.06	1313.40	1312.82
80000	1464.49	1451.93	1441.88	1433.82	1427.34	1422.12	1417.91	1414.51	1411.76	1409.54	1407.74	1402.73	1400.96	1400.34
85000	1556.03	1542.67	1531.99	1523.43	1516.55	1511.00	1506.53	1502.92	1500.00	1497.63	1495.72	1490.40	1488.52	1487.86
90000	1647.56	1633.42	1622.11	1613.04	1605.75	1599.88	1595.15	1591.32	1588.23	1585.73	1583.70	1578.07	1576.08	1575.39
95000	1739.09	1724.16	1712.23	1702.66	1694.96	1688.77	1683.77	1679.73	1676.47	1673.82	1671.68	1665.74	1663.64	1662.91
100000	1830.62	1814.91	1802.34	1792.27	1784.17	1777.65	1772.39	1768.14	1764.70	1761.92	1759.67	1753.41	1751.20	1750.43

21%

515

MONTHLY PAYMENT
REQUIRED TO AMORTIZE A LOAN

TERM AMOUNT	1 Year	2 Years	3 Years	4 Years	5 Years	6 Years	7 Years	8 Years	9 Years	10 Years	11 Years	12 Years	13 Years	14 Years
5	.47	.26	.19	.16	.14	.13	.12	.11	.11	.11	.10	.10	.10	.10
10	.94	.52	.38	.32	.28	.25	.23	.22	.21	.21	.20	.20	.19	.19
15	1.40	.78	.57	.47	.41	.37	.35	.33	.32	.31	.30	.29	.29	.28
25	2.33	1.29	.95	.78	.68	.62	.58	.55	.52	.51	.49	.48	.48	.47
50	4.66	2.58	1.89	1.56	1.36	1.23	1.15	1.09	1.04	1.01	.98	.96	.95	.93
75	6.99	3.86	2.83	2.33	2.04	1.85	1.72	1.63	1.56	1.51	1.47	1.44	1.42	1.40
100	9.32	5.15	3.78	3.11	2.72	2.46	2.29	2.17	2.08	2.01	1.96	1.92	1.89	1.86
200	18.64	10.29	7.55	6.21	5.43	4.92	4.58	4.33	4.15	4.02	3.91	3.83	3.77	3.72
300	27.95	15.44	11.32	9.31	8.14	7.38	6.87	6.50	6.23	6.02	5.87	5.75	5.65	5.58
400	37.27	20.58	15.10	12.41	10.85	9.84	9.15	8.66	8.30	8.03	7.82	7.66	7.53	7.44
500	46.59	25.72	18.87	15.51	13.56	12.30	11.44	10.83	10.38	10.04	9.78	9.57	9.42	9.29
600	55.90	30.87	22.64	18.62	16.27	14.76	13.73	12.99	12.45	12.04	11.73	11.49	11.30	11.15
700	65.22	36.01	26.41	21.72	18.98	17.22	16.02	15.16	14.52	14.05	13.68	13.40	13.18	13.01
800	74.53	41.15	30.19	24.82	21.69	19.68	18.30	17.32	16.60	16.05	15.64	15.32	15.06	14.87
900	83.85	46.30	33.96	27.92	24.40	22.14	20.59	19.48	18.67	18.06	17.59	17.23	16.95	16.72
1000	93.17	51.44	37.73	31.02	27.11	24.60	22.88	21.65	20.75	20.07	19.55	19.14	18.83	18.58
2000	186.33	102.87	75.46	62.04	54.22	49.19	45.75	43.29	41.49	40.13	39.09	38.28	37.65	37.16
3000	279.49	154.31	113.18	93.06	81.33	73.79	68.62	64.94	62.23	60.19	58.63	57.42	56.48	55.74
4000	372.65	205.74	150.91	124.08	108.44	98.38	91.50	86.58	82.97	80.25	78.17	76.56	75.30	74.31
5000	465.81	257.18	188.64	155.10	135.55	122.98	114.37	108.23	103.71	100.31	97.71	95.70	94.13	92.89
6000	558.98	308.61	226.36	186.12	162.66	147.57	137.24	129.87	124.45	120.37	117.25	114.84	112.95	111.47
7000	652.14	360.05	264.09	217.14	189.77	172.17	160.12	151.51	145.19	140.43	136.79	133.98	131.78	130.04
8000	745.30	411.48	301.82	248.16	216.88	196.76	182.99	173.16	165.93	160.49	156.33	153.11	150.60	148.62
9000	838.46	462.92	339.54	279.18	243.99	221.36	205.86	194.80	186.67	180.55	175.87	172.25	169.42	167.20
10000	931.62	514.35	377.27	310.20	271.10	245.95	228.74	216.45	207.41	200.61	195.41	191.39	188.25	185.77
11000	1024.78	565.79	415.00	341.22	298.21	270.55	251.61	238.09	228.15	220.67	214.95	210.53	207.07	204.35
12000	1117.95	617.22	452.72	372.24	325.32	295.14	274.48	259.74	248.89	240.73	234.50	229.67	225.90	222.93
13000	1211.11	668.66	490.45	403.26	352.43	319.74	297.36	281.38	269.63	260.79	254.04	248.81	244.72	241.51
14000	1304.27	720.09	528.18	434.28	379.54	344.33	320.23	303.02	290.37	280.85	273.58	267.95	263.55	260.08
15000	1397.43	771.53	565.90	465.30	406.65	368.93	343.10	324.67	311.11	300.91	293.12	287.09	282.37	278.66
16000	1490.59	822.96	603.63	496.32	433.76	393.52	365.98	346.31	331.85	320.97	312.66	306.22	301.20	297.24
17000	1583.76	874.40	641.35	527.34	460.87	418.11	388.85	367.96	352.59	341.03	332.20	325.36	320.02	315.81
18000	1676.92	925.83	679.08	558.36	487.98	442.71	411.72	389.60	373.33	361.09	351.74	344.50	338.84	334.39
19000	1770.08	977.27	716.81	589.38	515.09	467.30	434.60	411.25	394.07	381.15	371.28	363.64	357.67	352.97
20000	1863.24	1028.70	754.53	620.40	542.20	491.90	457.47	432.89	414.81	401.21	390.82	382.78	376.49	371.54
21000	1956.40	1080.14	792.26	651.41	569.31	516.49	480.34	454.53	435.55	421.27	410.36	401.92	395.32	390.12
22000	2049.56	1131.57	829.99	682.43	596.42	541.09	503.22	476.18	456.29	441.33	429.90	421.06	414.14	408.70
23000	2142.73	1183.01	867.71	713.45	623.53	565.68	526.09	497.82	477.03	461.39	449.44	440.20	432.97	427.27
24000	2235.89	1234.44	905.44	744.47	650.64	590.28	548.96	519.47	497.77	481.46	468.99	459.33	451.79	445.85
25000	2329.05	1285.87	943.17	775.49	677.75	614.87	571.84	541.11	518.51	501.52	488.53	478.47	470.62	464.43
26000	2422.21	1337.31	980.89	806.51	704.86	639.47	594.71	562.76	539.25	521.58	508.07	497.61	489.44	483.01
27000	2515.37	1388.74	1018.62	837.53	731.97	664.06	617.58	584.40	559.99	541.64	527.61	516.75	508.26	501.58
28000	2608.53	1440.18	1056.35	868.55	759.07	688.66	640.46	606.04	580.73	561.70	547.15	535.89	527.09	520.16
29000	2701.70	1491.61	1094.07	899.57	786.18	713.25	663.33	627.69	601.47	581.76	566.69	555.03	545.91	538.74
30000	2794.86	1543.05	1131.80	930.59	813.29	737.85	686.20	649.33	622.21	601.82	586.23	574.17	564.74	557.31
31000	2888.02	1594.48	1169.52	961.61	840.40	762.44	709.08	670.98	642.95	621.88	605.77	593.30	583.56	575.89
32000	2981.18	1645.92	1207.25	992.63	867.51	787.04	731.95	692.62	663.69	641.94	625.31	612.44	602.39	594.47
33000	3074.34	1697.35	1244.98	1023.65	894.62	811.63	754.82	714.27	684.43	662.00	644.85	631.58	621.21	613.04
34000	3167.51	1748.79	1282.70	1054.67	921.73	836.22	777.70	735.91	705.17	682.06	664.39	650.72	640.04	631.62
35000	3260.67	1800.22	1320.43	1085.69	948.84	860.82	800.57	757.55	725.91	702.12	683.93	669.86	658.86	650.20
36000	3353.83	1851.66	1358.16	1116.71	975.95	885.41	823.44	779.20	746.65	722.18	703.48	689.00	677.68	668.78
37000	3446.99	1903.09	1395.88	1147.73	1003.06	910.01	846.32	800.84	767.39	742.24	723.02	708.14	696.51	687.35
38000	3540.15	1954.53	1433.61	1178.75	1030.17	934.60	869.19	822.49	788.13	762.30	742.56	727.28	715.33	705.93
39000	3633.31	2005.96	1471.34	1209.77	1057.28	959.20	892.06	844.13	808.87	782.36	762.10	746.41	734.16	724.51
40000	3726.48	2057.40	1509.06	1240.79	1084.39	983.79	914.94	865.77	829.61	802.42	781.64	765.55	752.98	743.08
41000	3819.64	2108.83	1546.79	1271.80	1111.50	1008.39	937.81	887.42	850.35	822.48	801.18	784.69	771.81	761.66
42000	3912.80	2160.27	1584.52	1302.82	1138.61	1032.98	960.68	909.06	871.09	842.54	820.72	803.83	790.63	780.24
43000	4005.96	2211.70	1622.24	1333.84	1165.72	1057.58	983.55	930.71	891.83	862.60	840.26	822.97	809.46	798.81
44000	4099.12	2263.14	1659.97	1364.86	1192.83	1082.17	1006.43	952.35	912.57	882.66	859.80	842.11	828.28	817.39
45000	4192.28	2314.57	1697.69	1395.88	1219.94	1106.77	1029.30	974.00	933.31	902.72	879.34	861.25	847.10	835.97
46000	4285.45	2366.00	1735.42	1426.90	1247.05	1131.36	1052.17	995.64	954.05	922.78	898.88	880.39	865.93	854.54
47000	4378.61	2417.44	1773.15	1457.92	1274.16	1155.96	1075.05	1017.28	974.79	942.84	918.42	899.52	884.75	873.12
48000	4471.77	2468.87	1810.87	1488.94	1301.27	1180.55	1097.92	1038.93	995.53	962.91	937.97	918.66	903.58	891.70
49000	4564.93	2520.31	1848.60	1519.96	1328.38	1205.15	1120.79	1060.57	1016.27	982.97	957.51	937.80	922.40	910.28
50000	4658.09	2571.74	1886.33	1550.98	1355.49	1229.74	1143.67	1082.22	1037.01	1003.03	977.05	956.94	941.23	928.85
55000	5123.90	2828.92	2074.96	1706.08	1491.04	1352.71	1258.03	1190.44	1140.72	1103.33	1074.75	1052.63	1035.35	1021.74
60000	5589.71	3086.09	2263.59	1861.18	1626.58	1475.69	1372.40	1298.66	1244.42	1203.63	1172.46	1148.33	1129.47	1114.62
65000	6055.52	3343.27	2452.22	2016.27	1762.13	1598.66	1486.77	1406.88	1348.12	1303.93	1270.16	1244.02	1223.59	1207.51
70000	6521.33	3600.44	2640.86	2171.37	1897.68	1721.63	1601.13	1515.10	1451.82	1404.23	1367.86	1339.72	1317.71	1300.39
75000	6987.14	3857.61	2829.49	2326.47	2033.23	1844.61	1715.50	1623.32	1555.52	1504.54	1465.57	1435.41	1411.84	1393.28
80000	7452.95	4114.79	3018.12	2481.57	2168.78	1967.58	1829.87	1731.54	1659.22	1604.84	1563.27	1531.10	1505.96	1486.16
85000	7918.76	4371.96	3206.75	2636.66	2304.32	2090.55	1944.23	1839.77	1762.92	1705.14	1660.98	1626.80	1600.08	1579.05
90000	8384.57	4629.14	3395.38	2791.76	2439.87	2213.53	2058.60	1947.99	1866.62	1805.44	1758.68	1722.49	1694.20	1671.93
95000	8850.37	4886.31	3584.02	2946.86	2575.42	2336.50	2172.96	2056.21	1970.32	1905.75	1856.39	1818.18	1788.33	1764.81
100000	9316.18	5143.48	3772.65	3101.96	2710.97	2459.47	2287.33	2164.43	2074.02	2006.05	1954.09	1913.88	1882.45	1857.70

TERM	15 Years	16 Years	17 Years	18 Years	19 Years	20 Years	21 Years	22 Years	23 Years	24 Years	25 Years	30 Years	35 Years	40 Years
AMOUNT														
5	.10	.10	.10	.10	.09	.09	.09	.09	.09	.09	.09	.09	.09	.09
10	.19	.19	.19	.19	.18	.18	.18	.18	.18	.18	.18	.18	.18	.18
15	.28	.28	.28	.28	.27	.27	.27	.27	.27	.27	.27	.27	.27	.27
25	.46	.46	.46	.46	.45	.45	.45	.45	.45	.45	.45	.45	.44	.44
50	.92	.92	.92	.91	.90	.90	.90	.89	.89	.89	.89	.89	.88	.88
75	1.38	1.37	1.36	1.36	1.35	1.34	1.34	1.34	1.33	1.33	1.33	1.33	1.32	1.32
100	1.84	1.83	1.82	1.81	1.80	1.79	1.79	1.78	1.78	1.78	1.77	1.77	1.76	1.76
200	3.68	3.65	3.63	3.61	3.59	3.58	3.57	3.56	3.55	3.55	3.54	3.53	3.52	3.52
300	5.52	5.47	5.44	5.41	5.38	5.36	5.35	5.33	5.32	5.32	5.31	5.29	5.28	5.28
400	7.36	7.29	7.25	7.21	7.17	7.15	7.13	7.11	7.10	7.09	7.08	7.05	7.04	7.04
500	9.20	9.12	9.06	9.01	8.97	8.93	8.91	8.89	8.87	8.86	8.84	8.81	8.80	8.80
600	11.03	10.94	10.87	10.81	10.76	10.72	10.69	10.66	10.64	10.63	10.61	10.57	10.56	10.56
700	12.87	12.76	12.68	12.61	12.55	12.50	12.47	12.44	12.41	12.40	12.38	12.34	12.32	12.32
800	14.71	14.58	14.49	14.41	14.34	14.29	14.25	14.21	14.19	14.17	14.15	14.10	14.08	14.07
900	16.55	16.41	16.30	16.21	16.13	16.08	16.03	15.99	15.96	15.94	15.92	15.86	15.84	15.83
1000	18.39	18.23	18.11	18.01	17.93	17.86	17.81	17.77	17.73	17.71	17.68	17.62	17.60	17.59
2000	36.77	36.45	36.21	36.01	35.85	35.72	35.61	35.53	35.46	35.41	35.36	35.24	35.19	35.18
3000	55.15	54.68	54.31	54.01	53.77	53.57	53.42	53.29	53.19	53.11	53.04	52.85	52.79	52.77
4000	73.53	72.90	72.41	72.01	71.69	71.43	71.22	71.05	70.92	70.81	70.72	70.47	70.38	70.35
5000	91.91	91.13	90.51	90.01	89.61	89.28	89.02	88.81	88.64	88.51	88.40	88.09	87.98	87.94
6000	110.29	109.35	108.61	108.01	107.53	107.14	106.83	106.57	106.37	106.21	106.07	105.70	105.57	105.53
7000	128.67	127.58	126.71	126.01	125.45	124.99	124.63	124.34	124.10	123.91	123.75	123.32	123.17	123.12
8000	147.05	145.80	144.81	144.01	143.37	142.85	142.43	142.10	141.83	141.61	141.43	140.94	140.76	140.70
9000	165.43	164.03	162.91	162.01	161.29	160.71	160.24	159.86	159.55	159.31	159.11	158.55	158.36	158.29
10000	183.81	182.25	181.01	180.01	179.21	178.56	178.04	177.62	177.28	177.01	176.79	176.17	175.95	175.88
11000	202.19	200.48	199.11	198.01	197.13	196.42	195.84	195.38	195.01	194.71	194.46	193.79	193.55	193.47
12000	220.58	218.70	217.21	216.01	215.05	214.27	213.65	213.14	212.74	212.41	212.14	211.40	211.14	211.05
13000	238.96	236.93	235.31	234.01	232.97	232.13	231.45	230.91	230.46	230.11	229.82	229.02	228.74	228.64
14000	257.34	255.15	253.41	252.01	250.89	249.98	249.25	248.67	248.19	247.81	247.50	246.64	246.33	246.23
15000	275.72	273.38	271.51	270.01	268.81	267.84	267.06	266.43	265.92	265.51	265.18	264.25	263.93	263.82
16000	294.10	291.60	289.61	288.01	286.73	285.69	284.86	284.19	283.65	283.21	282.85	281.87	281.52	281.40
17000	312.48	309.83	307.71	306.01	304.65	303.55	302.67	301.95	301.38	300.91	300.53	299.49	299.12	298.99
18000	330.86	328.05	325.81	324.01	322.57	321.41	320.47	319.71	319.10	318.61	318.21	317.10	316.71	316.58
19000	349.24	346.28	343.91	342.01	340.49	339.26	338.27	337.47	336.83	336.31	335.89	334.72	334.31	334.17
20000	367.62	364.50	362.01	360.01	358.41	357.12	356.08	355.24	354.56	354.01	353.57	352.34	351.90	351.75
21000	386.00	382.73	380.11	378.01	376.33	374.97	373.88	373.00	372.29	371.71	371.24	369.95	369.50	369.34
22000	404.38	400.95	398.21	396.01	394.25	392.83	391.68	390.76	390.01	389.41	388.92	387.57	387.09	386.93
23000	422.77	419.18	416.31	414.01	412.17	410.68	409.49	408.52	407.74	407.11	406.60	405.18	404.69	404.52
24000	441.15	437.40	434.41	432.01	430.09	428.54	427.29	426.28	425.47	424.81	424.28	422.80	422.28	422.10
25000	459.53	455.63	452.51	450.01	448.01	446.39	445.09	444.04	443.20	442.51	441.96	440.42	439.88	439.69
26000	477.91	473.85	470.61	468.01	465.93	464.25	462.90	461.81	460.92	460.21	459.63	458.03	457.47	457.28
27000	496.29	492.08	488.71	486.01	483.85	482.11	480.70	479.57	478.65	477.91	477.31	475.65	475.07	474.87
28000	514.67	510.30	506.81	504.02	501.77	499.96	498.50	497.33	496.38	495.61	494.99	493.27	492.66	492.45
29000	533.05	528.53	524.91	522.02	519.69	517.82	516.31	515.09	514.11	513.31	512.67	510.88	510.26	510.04
30000	551.43	546.75	543.01	540.02	537.61	535.67	534.11	532.85	531.83	531.01	530.35	528.50	527.85	527.63
31000	569.81	564.98	561.11	558.02	555.53	553.53	551.92	550.61	549.56	548.71	548.02	546.12	545.45	545.22
32000	588.19	583.20	579.21	576.02	573.45	571.38	569.72	568.38	567.29	566.41	565.70	563.73	563.04	562.80
33000	606.57	601.43	597.31	594.02	591.37	589.24	587.52	586.14	585.02	584.11	583.38	581.35	580.64	580.39
34000	624.96	619.65	615.41	612.02	609.29	607.10	605.33	603.90	602.75	601.81	601.06	598.97	598.23	597.98
35000	643.34	637.88	633.51	630.02	627.21	624.95	623.13	621.66	620.47	619.51	618.74	616.58	615.83	615.56
36000	661.72	656.10	651.61	648.02	645.13	642.81	640.93	639.42	638.20	637.21	636.41	634.20	633.42	633.15
37000	680.10	674.33	669.71	666.02	663.05	660.66	658.74	657.18	655.93	654.91	654.09	651.82	651.02	650.74
38000	698.48	692.55	687.81	684.02	680.97	678.52	676.54	674.94	673.66	672.61	671.77	669.43	668.61	668.33
39000	716.86	710.78	705.91	702.02	698.89	696.37	694.34	692.71	691.38	690.31	689.45	687.05	686.21	685.91
40000	735.24	729.00	724.01	720.02	716.81	714.23	712.15	710.47	709.11	708.01	707.13	704.67	703.80	703.50
41000	753.62	747.23	742.11	738.02	734.73	732.08	729.95	728.23	726.84	725.71	724.81	722.28	721.40	721.09
42000	772.00	765.45	760.21	756.02	752.65	749.94	747.75	745.99	744.57	743.41	742.48	739.90	738.99	738.68
43000	790.38	783.67	778.32	774.02	770.57	767.80	765.56	763.75	762.29	761.12	760.16	757.51	756.59	756.26
44000	808.76	801.90	796.42	792.02	788.49	785.65	783.36	781.51	780.02	778.82	777.84	775.13	774.18	773.85
45000	827.15	820.12	814.52	810.02	806.41	803.51	801.17	799.28	797.75	796.52	795.52	792.75	791.78	791.44
46000	845.53	838.35	832.62	828.02	824.33	821.36	818.97	817.04	815.48	814.22	813.20	810.36	809.37	809.03
47000	863.91	856.57	850.72	846.02	842.25	839.22	836.77	834.80	833.20	831.92	830.87	827.98	826.97	826.61
48000	882.29	874.80	868.82	664.02	860.17	857.07	854.58	852.56	850.93	849.62	848.55	845.60	844.56	844.20
49000	900.67	893.02	886.92	882.02	878.09	874.93	872.38	870.32	868.66	867.32	866.23	863.21	862.16	861.79
50000	919.05	911.25	905.02	900.02	896.01	892.78	890.18	888.08	886.39	885.02	883.91	880.83	879.75	879.38
55000	1010.95	1002.37	995.52	990.02	985.61	982.06	979.20	976.89	975.03	973.52	972.30	968.91	967.73	967.31
60000	1102.86	1093.50	1086.02	1080.03	1075.21	1071.34	1068.22	1065.70	1063.66	1062.02	1060.69	1057.00	1055.70	1055.25
65000	1194.76	1184.62	1176.52	1170.03	1164.81	1160.62	1157.24	1154.51	1152.30	1150.52	1149.08	1145.08	1143.68	1143.19
70000	1286.67	1275.75	1267.02	1260.03	1254.42	1249.90	1246.25	1243.32	1240.94	1239.02	1237.47	1233.16	1231.65	1231.12
75000	1378.57	1366.87	1357.52	1350.03	1344.02	1339.17	1335.27	1332.12	1329.58	1327.52	1325.86	1321.24	1319.63	1319.06
80000	1470.48	1458.00	1448.02	1440.03	1433.62	1428.45	1424.29	1420.93	1418.22	1416.02	1414.25	1409.33	1407.60	1407.00
85000	1562.38	1549.12	1538.52	1530.04	1523.22	1517.73	1513.31	1509.74	1506.86	1504.53	1502.64	1497.41	1495.58	1494.94
90000	1654.29	1640.24	1629.03	1620.04	1612.82	1607.01	1602.33	1598.55	1595.49	1593.03	1591.03	1585.49	1583.55	1582.87
95000	1746.19	1731.37	1719.53	1710.04	1702.42	1696.29	1691.34	1687.35	1684.13	1681.53	1679.42	1673.57	1671.53	1670.81
100000	1838.10	1822.49	1810.03	1800.04	1792.02	1785.56	1780.36	1776.16	1772.77	1770.03	1767.81	1761.66	1759.50	1758.75

MONTHLY PAYMENT
REQUIRED TO AMORTIZE A LOAN

TERM AMOUNT	1 Year	2 Years	3 Years	4 Years	5 Years	6 Years	7 Years	8 Years	9 Years	10 Years	11 Years	12 Years	13 Years	14 Years
5	.47	.26	.19	.16	.14	.13	.12	.11	.11	.11	.10	.10	.10	.10
10	.94	.52	.38	.32	.28	.25	.23	.22	.21	.21	.20	.20	.19	.19
15	1.40	.78	.57	.47	.41	.37	.35	.33	.32	.31	.30	.29	.29	.28
25	2.33	1.29	.95	.78	.68	.62	.58	.55	.52	.51	.49	.48	.48	.47
50	4.66	2.58	1.89	1.56	1.36	1.24	1.15	1.09	1.04	1.01	.98	.96	.95	.93
75	6.99	3.86	2.84	2.33	2.04	1.85	1.72	1.63	1.56	1.51	1.47	1.44	1.42	1.40
100	9.32	5.15	3.78	3.11	2.72	2.47	2.29	2.17	2.08	2.01	1.96	1.92	1.89	1.86
200	18.64	10.29	7.55	6.21	5.43	4.93	4.58	4.34	4.16	4.02	3.92	3.84	3.77	3.72
300	27.96	15.44	11.33	9.31	8.14	7.39	6.87	6.50	6.23	6.03	5.87	5.75	5.66	5.58
400	37.27	20.58	15.10	12.42	10.85	9.85	9.16	8.67	8.31	8.04	7.83	7.67	7.54	7.44
500	46.59	25.73	18.87	15.52	13.57	12.31	11.45	10.84	10.38	10.04	9.78	9.58	9.43	9.30
600	55.91	30.87	22.65	18.62	16.28	14.77	13.74	13.00	12.46	12.05	11.74	11.50	11.31	11.16
700	65.23	36.02	26.42	21.73	18.99	17.23	16.03	15.17	14.53	14.06	13.70	13.41	13.19	13.02
800	74.54	41.16	30.20	24.83	21.70	19.69	18.32	17.33	16.61	16.07	15.65	15.33	15.08	14.88
900	83.86	46.31	33.97	27.93	24.42	22.15	20.60	19.50	18.69	18.07	17.61	17.25	16.96	16.74
1000	93.18	51.45	37.74	31.04	27.13	24.61	22.89	21.67	20.76	20.08	19.56	19.16	18.85	18.60
2000	186.35	102.90	75.48	62.07	54.25	49.22	45.78	43.33	41.52	40.16	39.12	38.32	37.69	37.20
3000	279.53	154.35	113.22	93.10	81.38	73.83	68.67	64.99	62.27	60.24	58.68	57.47	56.53	55.79
4000	372.70	205.79	150.96	124.14	108.50	98.44	91.56	86.65	83.03	80.31	78.24	76.63	75.37	74.39
5000	465.87	257.24	188.70	155.17	135.62	123.05	114.45	108.31	103.79	100.39	97.80	95.79	94.22	92.98
6000	559.05	308.69	226.44	186.20	162.75	147.66	137.34	129.97	124.54	120.47	117.35	114.94	113.06	111.58
7000	652.22	360.13	264.18	217.24	189.87	172.27	160.22	151.63	145.30	140.55	136.91	134.10	131.90	130.17
8000	745.40	411.58	301.92	248.27	216.99	196.88	183.11	173.29	166.06	160.62	156.47	153.26	150.74	148.77
9000	838.57	463.03	339.66	279.30	244.12	221.49	206.00	194.95	186.81	180.70	176.03	172.41	169.59	167.36
10000	931.74	514.48	377.40	310.33	271.24	246.10	228.89	216.61	207.57	200.78	195.59	191.57	188.43	185.96
11000	1024.92	565.92	415.14	341.37	298.37	270.71	251.78	238.27	228.33	220.85	215.14	210.73	207.27	204.55
12000	1118.09	617.37	452.88	372.40	325.49	295.32	274.67	259.93	249.08	240.93	234.70	229.88	226.11	223.15
13000	1211.26	668.82	490.62	403.43	352.61	319.93	297.56	281.59	269.84	261.01	254.26	249.04	244.96	241.74
14000	1304.44	720.26	528.35	434.47	379.74	344.54	320.44	303.25	290.60	281.09	273.82	268.19	263.80	260.34
15000	1397.61	771.71	566.09	465.50	406.86	369.15	343.33	324.91	311.35	301.16	293.38	287.35	282.64	278.94
16000	1490.79	823.16	603.83	496.53	433.98	393.76	366.22	346.57	332.11	321.24	312.94	306.51	301.48	297.53
17000	1583.96	874.61	641.57	527.57	461.11	418.36	389.11	368.23	352.87	341.32	332.49	325.66	320.33	316.13
18000	1677.13	926.05	679.31	558.60	488.23	442.97	412.00	389.89	373.62	361.40	352.05	344.82	339.17	334.72
19000	1770.31	977.50	717.05	589.63	515.36	467.58	434.89	411.55	394.38	381.47	371.61	363.98	358.01	353.32
20000	1863.48	1028.95	754.79	620.66	542.48	492.19	457.78	433.21	415.14	401.55	391.17	383.13	376.85	371.91
21000	1956.65	1080.39	792.53	651.70	569.60	516.80	480.66	454.87	435.89	421.63	410.73	402.29	395.70	390.51
22000	2049.83	1131.84	830.27	682.73	596.73	541.41	503.55	476.53	456.65	441.70	430.28	421.45	414.54	409.10
23000	2143.00	1183.29	868.01	713.76	623.85	566.02	526.44	498.19	477.41	461.78	449.84	440.60	433.38	427.70
24000	2236.18	1234.73	905.75	744.80	650.97	590.63	549.33	519.85	498.16	481.86	469.40	459.76	452.22	446.29
25000	2329.35	1286.18	943.49	775.83	678.10	615.24	572.22	541.51	518.92	501.94	488.96	478.91	471.07	464.89
26000	2422.52	1337.63	981.23	806.86	705.22	639.85	595.11	563.17	539.67	522.01	508.52	498.07	489.91	483.48
27000	2515.70	1389.08	1018.97	837.90	732.35	664.46	618.00	584.83	560.43	542.09	528.07	517.23	508.75	502.08
28000	2608.87	1440.52	1056.70	868.93	759.47	689.07	640.88	606.49	581.19	562.17	547.63	536.38	527.59	520.67
29000	2702.04	1491.97	1094.44	899.96	786.59	713.68	663.77	628.15	601.94	582.25	567.19	555.54	546.44	539.27
30000	2795.22	1543.42	1132.18	930.99	813.72	738.29	686.66	649.81	622.70	602.32	586.75	574.70	565.28	557.87
31000	2888.39	1594.86	1169.92	962.03	840.84	762.90	709.55	671.47	643.46	622.40	606.31	593.85	584.12	576.46
32000	2981.57	1646.31	1207.66	993.06	867.96	787.51	732.44	693.13	664.21	642.48	625.87	613.01	602.96	595.06
33000	3074.74	1697.76	1245.40	1024.09	895.09	812.11	755.33	714.79	684.97	662.55	645.42	632.17	621.81	613.65
34000	3167.91	1749.21	1283.14	1055.13	922.21	836.72	778.21	736.45	705.73	682.63	664.98	651.32	640.65	632.25
35000	3261.09	1800.65	1320.88	1086.16	949.34	861.33	801.10	758.11	726.48	702.71	684.54	670.48	659.49	650.84
36000	3354.26	1852.10	1358.62	1117.19	976.46	885.94	823.99	779.77	747.24	722.79	704.10	689.64	678.33	669.44
37000	3447.43	1903.55	1396.36	1148.22	1003.58	910.55	846.88	801.43	768.00	742.86	723.66	708.79	697.18	688.03
38000	3540.61	1954.99	1434.10	1179.26	1030.71	935.16	869.77	823.09	788.75	762.94	743.21	727.95	716.02	706.63
39000	3633.78	2006.44	1471.84	1210.29	1057.83	959.77	892.66	844.75	809.51	783.02	762.77	747.10	734.86	725.22
40000	3726.96	2057.89	1509.58	1241.32	1084.95	984.38	915.55	866.41	830.27	803.10	782.33	766.26	753.70	743.82
41000	3820.13	2109.33	1547.32	1272.36	1112.08	1008.99	938.43	888.07	851.02	823.17	801.89	785.42	772.55	762.41
42000	3913.30	2160.78	1585.05	1303.39	1139.20	1033.60	961.32	909.73	871.78	843.25	821.45	804.57	791.39	781.01
43000	4006.48	2212.23	1622.79	1334.42	1166.33	1058.21	984.21	931.39	892.54	863.33	841.00	823.73	810.23	799.60
44000	4099.65	2263.68	1660.53	1365.46	1193.45	1082.82	1007.10	953.05	913.29	883.40	860.56	842.89	829.07	818.20
45000	4192.82	2315.12	1698.27	1396.49	1220.57	1107.43	1029.99	974.71	934.05	903.48	880.12	862.04	847.92	836.80
46000	4286.00	2366.57	1736.01	1427.52	1247.70	1132.04	1052.88	996.37	954.81	923.56	899.68	881.20	866.76	855.39
47000	4379.17	2418.02	1773.75	1458.55	1274.82	1156.65	1075.77	1018.03	975.56	943.64	919.24	900.36	885.60	873.99
48000	4472.35	2469.46	1811.49	1489.59	1301.94	1181.26	1098.65	1039.69	996.32	963.71	938.80	919.51	904.44	892.58
49000	4565.52	2520.91	1849.23	1520.62	1329.07	1205.86	1121.54	1061.35	1017.07	983.79	958.35	938.67	923.29	911.18
50000	4658.69	2572.36	1886.97	1551.65	1356.19	1230.47	1144.43	1083.01	1037.83	1003.87	977.91	957.82	942.13	929.77
55000	5124.56	2829.59	2075.67	1706.82	1491.81	1353.52	1258.87	1191.31	1141.61	1104.25	1075.70	1053.61	1036.34	1022.75
60000	5590.43	3086.83	2264.36	1861.98	1627.43	1476.57	1373.32	1299.61	1245.40	1204.64	1173.49	1149.39	1130.55	1115.73
65000	6056.30	3344.06	2453.06	2017.15	1763.05	1599.62	1487.76	1407.91	1349.18	1305.03	1271.28	1245.17	1224.77	1208.70
70000	6522.17	3601.30	2641.75	2172.31	1898.67	1722.66	1602.20	1516.21	1452.96	1405.41	1369.07	1340.95	1318.98	1301.68
75000	6988.04	3858.54	2830.45	2327.48	2034.26	1845.71	1716.64	1624.51	1556.74	1505.80	1466.86	1436.73	1413.19	1394.66
80000	7453.91	4115.77	3019.15	2482.64	2169.90	1968.76	1831.09	1732.81	1660.53	1606.19	1564.66	1532.52	1507.40	1487.63
85000	7919.78	4373.01	3207.84	2637.81	2305.52	2091.80	1945.53	1841.11	1764.31	1706.57	1662.45	1628.30	1601.62	1580.61
90000	8385.65	4630.24	3396.54	2792.97	2441.14	2214.85	2059.97	1949.41	1868.09	1806.96	1760.24	1724.08	1695.83	1673.59
95000	8851.51	4887.48	3585.24	2948.14	2576.76	2337.90	2174.41	2057.71	1971.88	1907.34	1858.03	1819.86	1790.04	1766.56
100000	9317.38	5144.71	3773.93	3103.30	2712.38	2460.94	2288.86	2166.01	2075.66	2007.73	1955.82	1915.64	1884.25	1859.54

TERM	15 Years	16 Years	17 Years	18 Years	19 Years	20 Years	21 Years	22 Years	23 Years	24 Years	25 Years	30 Years	35 Years	40 Years
AMOUNT														
5	.10	.10	.10	.10	.09	.09	.09	.09	.09	.09	.09	.09	.09	.09
10	.19	.19	.19	.19	.18	.18	.18	.18	.18	.18	.18	.18	.18	.18
15	.28	.28	.28	.28	.27	.27	.27	.27	.27	.27	.27	.27	.27	.27
25	.46	.46	.46	.46	.45	.45	.45	.45	.45	.45	.45	.45	.45	.45
50	.92	.92	.91	.91	.90	.90	.90	.89	.89	.89	.89	.89	.89	.89
75	1.38	1.37	1.36	1.36	1.35	1.35	1.34	1.34	1.34	1.33	1.33	1.33	1.33	1.33
100	1.84	1.83	1.82	1.81	1.80	1.79	1.79	1.78	1.78	1.78	1.77	1.77	1.77	1.77
200	3.68	3.65	3.63	3.61	3.59	3.58	3.57	3.56	3.55	3.55	3.54	3.53	3.53	3.53
300	5.52	5.48	5.44	5.41	5.39	5.37	5.35	5.34	5.33	5.32	5.31	5.30	5.29	5.29
400	7.36	7.30	7.25	7.21	7.18	7.16	7.13	7.12	7.10	7.09	7.08	7.06	7.05	7.05
500	9.20	9.13	9.06	9.01	8.97	8.94	8.92	8.90	8.88	8.87	8.85	8.82	8.81	8.81
600	11.04	10.95	10.88	10.82	10.77	10.73	10.70	10.67	10.65	10.64	10.62	10.59	10.57	10.57
700	12.88	12.78	12.69	12.62	12.56	12.52	12.48	12.45	12.43	12.41	12.39	12.35	12.34	12.33
800	14.72	14.60	14.50	14.42	14.36	14.31	14.26	14.23	14.20	14.18	14.16	14.11	14.10	14.09
900	16.56	16.42	16.31	16.22	16.15	16.09	16.05	16.01	15.98	15.95	15.93	15.88	15.86	15.85
1000	18.40	18.25	18.12	18.02	17.94	17.88	17.83	17.79	17.75	17.73	17.70	17.64	17.62	17.61
2000	36.80	36.49	36.24	36.04	35.88	35.76	35.65	35.57	35.50	35.45	35.40	35.28	35.24	35.22
3000	55.20	54.74	54.36	54.06	53.82	53.63	53.48	53.35	53.25	53.17	53.10	52.92	52.85	52.83
4000	73.60	72.98	72.48	72.08	71.76	71.51	71.30	71.13	71.00	70.89	70.80	70.55	70.47	70.44
5000	92.00	91.22	90.60	90.10	89.70	89.38	89.12	88.91	88.74	88.61	88.50	88.19	88.08	88.05
6000	110.40	109.47	108.72	108.12	107.64	107.26	106.95	106.69	106.49	106.33	106.20	105.83	105.70	105.65
7000	128.80	127.71	126.84	126.14	125.58	125.13	124.77	124.48	124.24	124.05	123.89	123.46	123.32	123.26
8000	147.20	145.96	144.96	144.16	143.52	143.01	142.59	142.26	141.99	141.77	141.59	141.10	140.93	140.87
9000	165.60	164.20	163.08	162.18	161.46	160.88	160.42	160.04	159.74	159.49	159.29	158.74	158.55	158.48
10000	184.00	182.44	181.20	180.20	179.40	178.76	178.24	177.82	177.48	177.21	176.99	176.38	176.16	176.09
11000	202.40	200.69	199.32	198.22	197.34	196.63	196.06	195.60	195.23	194.93	194.69	194.01	193.78	193.70
12000	220.80	218.93	217.44	216.24	215.28	214.51	213.89	213.38	212.98	212.65	212.39	211.65	211.39	211.30
13000	239.20	237.18	235.56	234.26	233.22	232.39	231.71	231.17	230.73	230.37	230.08	229.29	229.01	228.91
14000	257.60	255.42	253.68	252.20	251.16	250.26	249.53	248.95	248.47	248.09	247.78	246.92	246.63	246.52
15000	276.00	273.66	271.80	270.30	269.10	268.14	267.36	266.73	266.22	265.81	265.48	264.56	264.24	264.13
16000	294.40	291.91	289.92	288.32	287.04	286.01	285.18	284.51	283.97	283.53	283.18	282.20	281.86	281.74
17000	312.80	310.15	308.04	306.34	304.98	303.89	303.00	302.29	301.72	301.25	300.88	299.84	299.47	299.34
18000	331.20	328.39	326.16	324.36	322.92	321.76	320.83	320.07	319.47	318.97	318.58	317.47	317.09	316.95
19000	349.60	346.64	344.27	342.38	340.86	339.64	338.65	337.86	337.21	336.69	336.27	335.11	334.70	334.56
20000	368.00	364.88	362.39	360.40	358.80	357.51	356.48	355.64	354.96	354.42	353.97	352.75	352.32	352.17
21000	386.40	383.13	380.51	378.42	376.74	375.39	374.30	373.42	372.71	372.14	371.67	370.38	369.94	369.78
22000	404.80	401.37	398.63	396.44	394.68	393.26	392.12	391.20	390.46	389.86	389.37	388.02	387.55	387.39
23000	423.20	419.61	416.75	414.46	412.62	411.14	409.95	408.98	408.21	407.58	407.07	405.66	405.17	404.99
24000	441.60	437.86	434.87	432.48	430.56	429.01	427.77	426.76	425.95	425.30	424.77	423.30	422.78	422.60
25000	460.00	456.10	452.99	450.50	448.50	446.89	445.59	444.55	443.70	443.02	442.47	440.93	440.40	440.21
26000	478.39	474.35	471.11	468.52	466.44	464.77	463.42	462.33	461.45	460.74	460.16	458.57	458.01	457.82
27000	496.79	492.59	489.23	486.54	484.38	482.64	481.24	480.11	479.20	478.46	477.86	476.21	475.63	475.43
28000	515.19	510.83	507.35	504.56	502.32	500.52	499.06	497.89	496.94	496.18	495.56	493.84	493.25	493.04
29000	533.59	529.08	525.47	522.58	520.26	518.39	516.89	515.67	514.69	513.90	513.26	511.48	510.86	510.64
30000	551.99	547.32	543.59	540.60	538.20	536.27	534.71	533.45	532.44	531.62	530.96	529.12	528.48	528.25
31000	570.39	565.56	561.71	558.62	556.14	554.14	552.53	551.24	550.19	549.34	548.66	546.76	546.09	545.86
32000	588.79	583.81	579.83	576.64	574.08	572.02	570.36	569.02	567.94	567.06	566.35	564.39	563.71	563.47
33000	607.19	602.05	597.95	594.66	592.02	589.89	588.18	586.80	585.68	584.78	584.05	582.03	581.32	581.08
34000	625.59	620.30	616.07	612.68	609.96	607.77	606.00	604.58	603.43	602.50	601.75	599.67	598.94	598.68
35000	643.99	638.54	634.19	630.70	627.90	625.64	623.83	622.36	621.18	620.22	619.45	617.30	616.56	616.29
36000	662.39	656.78	652.31	648.72	645.84	643.52	641.65	640.14	638.93	637.94	637.15	634.94	634.17	633.90
37000	680.79	675.03	670.43	666.74	663.78	661.39	659.47	657.93	656.68	655.66	654.85	652.58	651.79	651.51
38000	699.19	693.27	688.54	684.76	681.72	679.27	677.30	675.71	674.42	673.38	672.54	670.22	669.40	669.12
39000	717.59	711.52	706.66	702.78	699.66	697.15	695.12	693.49	692.17	691.11	690.24	687.85	687.02	686.73
40000	735.99	729.76	724.78	720.80	717.60	715.02	712.95	711.27	709.92	708.83	707.94	705.49	704.63	704.33
41000	754.39	748.00	742.90	738.82	735.54	732.90	730.77	729.05	727.67	726.55	725.64	723.13	722.25	721.94
42000	772.79	766.25	761.02	756.84	753.48	750.77	748.59	746.83	745.41	744.27	743.34	740.76	739.87	739.55
43000	791.19	784.49	779.14	774.86	771.42	768.65	766.42	764.62	763.16	761.99	761.04	758.40	757.48	757.16
44000	809.59	802.73	797.26	792.88	789.36	786.52	784.24	782.40	780.91	779.71	778.74	776.04	775.10	774.77
45000	827.99	820.98	815.38	810.90	807.29	804.40	802.06	800.18	798.66	797.43	796.43	793.68	792.71	792.37
46000	846.39	839.22	833.50	828.92	825.23	822.27	819.89	817.96	816.41	815.15	814.13	811.31	810.33	809.98
47000	864.79	857.47	851.62	846.94	843.17	840.15	837.71	835.74	834.15	832.87	831.83	828.95	827.94	827.59
48000	883.19	875.71	869.74	864.96	861.11	858.02	855.53	853.52	851.90	850.59	849.53	846.59	845.56	845.20
49000	901.59	893.95	887.86	882.98	879.05	875.90	873.36	871.31	869.65	868.31	867.23	864.22	863.18	862.81
50000	919.99	912.20	905.98	901.00	896.99	893.77	891.18	889.09	887.40	886.03	884.93	881.86	880.79	880.42
55000	1011.98	1003.42	996.58	991.09	986.69	983.15	980.30	978.00	976.14	974.63	973.42	970.05	968.87	968.46
60000	1103.98	1094.64	1087.17	1081.19	1076.39	1072.53	1069.42	1066.90	1064.88	1063.24	1061.91	1058.23	1056.95	1056.50
65000	1195.98	1185.86	1177.77	1171.29	1166.09	1161.91	1158.53	1155.81	1153.61	1151.84	1150.40	1146.42	1145.03	1144.54
70000	1287.98	1277.08	1268.37	1261.39	1255.79	1251.28	1247.65	1244.72	1242.35	1240.44	1238.89	1234.60	1233.11	1232.58
75000	1379.98	1368.29	1358.96	1351.49	1345.49	1340.66	1336.77	1333.63	1331.09	1329.04	1327.39	1322.79	1321.18	1320.62
80000	1471.97	1459.51	1449.56	1441.59	1435.19	1430.04	1425.89	1422.54	1419.83	1417.65	1415.88	1410.98	1409.26	1408.66
85000	1563.97	1550.73	1540.16	1531.69	1524.89	1519.41	1515.00	1511.44	1508.57	1506.25	1504.37	1499.16	1497.34	1496.70
90000	1655.97	1641.95	1630.76	1621.79	1614.58	1608.79	1604.12	1600.35	1597.31	1594.85	1592.86	1587.35	1585.42	1584.74
95000	1747.97	1733.17	1721.35	1711.89	1704.28	1698.17	1693.24	1689.26	1686.05	1683.45	1681.35	1675.53	1673.50	1672.79
100000	1839.97	1824.39	1811.95	1801.99	1793.98	1787.54	1782.36	1778.17	1774.79	1772.06	1769.85	1763.72	1761.58	1760.83

MONTHLY PAYMENT
REQUIRED TO AMORTIZE A LOAN

TERM AMOUNT	1 Year	2 Years	3 Years	4 Years	5 Years	6 Years	7 Years	8 Years	9 Years	10 Years	11 Years	12 Years	13 Years	14 Years
5	.47	.26	.19	.16	.14	.13	.12	.11	.11	.11	.10	.10	.10	.10
10	.94	.52	.38	.32	.28	.25	.23	.22	.21	.21	.20	.20	.19	.19
15	1.40	.78	.57	.47	.41	.37	.35	.33	.32	.31	.30	.29	.29	.28
25	2.34	1.29	.95	.78	.68	.62	.58	.55	.53	.51	.50	.49	.48	.47
50	4.67	2.58	1.89	1.56	1.36	1.24	1.15	1.09	1.05	1.01	.99	.97	.95	.94
75	7.00	3.87	2.84	2.34	2.04	1.85	1.73	1.63	1.57	1.51	1.48	1.45	1.42	1.40
100	9.33	5.15	3.78	3.11	2.72	2.47	2.30	2.18	2.09	2.02	1.97	1.93	1.89	1.87
200	18.65	10.30	7.56	6.22	5.44	4.94	4.59	4.35	4.17	4.03	3.93	3.85	3.78	3.74
300	27.97	15.45	11.34	9.33	8.15	7.40	6.89	6.52	6.25	6.04	5.89	5.77	5.67	5.60
400	37.29	20.60	15.12	12.43	10.87	9.87	9.18	8.69	8.33	8.06	7.85	7.69	7.56	7.47
500	46.61	25.75	18.89	15.54	13.59	12.33	11.47	10.86	10.41	10.07	9.81	9.61	9.45	9.33
600	55.93	30.90	22.67	18.65	16.30	14.80	13.77	13.03	12.49	12.08	11.77	11.53	11.34	11.20
700	65.25	36.04	26.45	21.76	19.02	17.26	16.06	15.20	14.57	14.09	13.73	13.45	13.23	13.06
800	74.57	41.19	30.23	24.86	21.74	19.73	18.35	17.37	16.65	16.11	15.69	15.37	15.12	14.93
900	83.89	46.34	34.01	27.97	24.45	22.19	20.65	19.54	18.73	18.12	17.65	17.29	17.01	16.79
1000	93.21	51.49	37.78	31.08	27.17	24.66	22.94	21.71	20.81	20.13	19.61	19.21	18.90	18.66
2000	186.42	102.97	75.56	62.15	54.34	49.31	45.87	43.42	41.62	40.26	39.22	38.42	37.80	37.31
3000	279.63	154.46	113.34	93.23	81.50	73.97	68.81	65.13	62.42	60.39	58.83	57.63	56.70	55.96
4000	372.84	205.94	151.12	124.30	108.67	98.62	91.74	86.84	83.23	80.52	78.44	76.84	75.59	74.61
5000	466.05	257.42	188.89	155.37	135.83	123.27	114.68	108.54	104.03	100.64	98.05	96.05	94.49	93.26
6000	559.26	308.91	226.67	186.45	163.00	147.93	137.61	130.25	124.84	120.77	117.66	115.26	113.39	111.91
7000	652.47	360.39	264.45	217.52	190.17	172.58	160.55	151.96	145.64	140.90	137.27	134.47	132.28	130.56
8000	745.68	411.88	302.23	248.59	217.33	197.23	183.48	173.67	166.45	161.03	156.88	153.68	151.18	149.21
9000	838.89	463.36	340.01	279.67	244.50	221.89	206.41	195.37	187.26	181.15	176.49	172.89	170.08	167.86
10000	932.10	514.84	377.78	310.74	271.66	246.54	229.35	217.08	208.06	201.28	196.10	192.10	188.97	186.51
11000	1025.31	566.33	415.56	341.81	298.83	271.19	252.28	238.79	228.87	221.41	215.71	211.31	207.87	205.16
12000	1118.52	617.81	453.34	372.89	326.00	295.85	275.22	260.50	249.67	241.54	235.32	230.52	226.77	223.81
13000	1211.73	669.30	491.12	403.96	353.16	320.50	298.15	282.20	270.48	261.67	254.93	249.73	245.66	242.46
14000	1304.94	720.78	528.89	435.03	380.33	345.15	321.09	303.91	291.28	281.79	274.54	268.94	264.56	261.11
15000	1398.15	772.26	566.67	466.11	407.49	369.81	344.02	325.62	312.09	301.92	294.15	288.15	283.46	279.76
16000	1491.36	823.75	604.45	497.18	434.66	394.46	366.95	347.33	332.89	322.05	313.76	307.36	302.35	298.41
17000	1584.57	875.23	642.23	528.25	461.83	419.11	389.89	369.03	353.70	342.18	333.37	326.57	321.25	317.06
18000	1677.78	926.72	680.01	559.33	488.99	443.77	412.82	390.74	374.51	362.30	352.98	345.78	340.15	335.72
19000	1770.99	978.20	717.78	590.40	516.16	468.42	435.76	412.45	395.31	382.43	372.59	364.99	359.04	354.37
20000	1864.20	1029.68	755.56	621.47	543.32	493.07	458.69	434.16	416.12	402.56	392.20	384.19	377.94	373.02
21000	1957.41	1081.17	793.34	652.55	570.49	517.73	481.63	455.86	436.92	422.69	411.81	403.40	396.84	391.67
22000	2050.62	1132.65	831.12	683.62	597.66	542.38	504.56	477.57	457.73	442.82	431.42	422.61	415.73	410.32
23000	2143.83	1184.14	868.90	714.69	624.82	567.03	527.50	499.28	478.53	462.94	451.03	441.82	434.63	428.97
24000	2237.04	1235.62	906.67	745.77	651.99	591.69	550.43	520.99	499.34	483.07	470.64	461.03	453.53	447.62
25000	2330.25	1287.10	944.45	776.84	679.15	616.34	573.36	542.69	520.14	503.20	490.25	480.24	472.42	466.27
26000	2423.46	1338.59	982.23	807.91	706.32	641.00	596.30	564.40	540.95	523.33	509.86	499.45	491.32	484.92
27000	2516.67	1390.07	1020.01	838.99	733.49	665.65	619.23	586.11	561.76	543.45	529.47	518.66	510.22	503.57
28000	2609.88	1441.56	1057.78	870.06	760.65	690.30	642.17	607.82	582.56	563.58	549.08	537.87	529.11	522.22
29000	2703.09	1493.04	1095.56	901.13	787.82	714.96	665.10	629.52	603.37	583.71	568.69	557.08	548.01	540.87
30000	2796.30	1544.52	1133.34	932.21	814.98	739.61	688.04	651.23	624.17	603.84	588.30	576.29	566.91	559.52
31000	2889.51	1596.01	1171.12	963.28	842.15	764.26	710.97	672.94	644.98	623.97	607.91	595.50	585.80	578.17
32000	2982.72	1647.49	1208.90	994.35	869.32	788.92	733.90	694.65	665.78	644.09	627.52	614.71	604.70	596.82
33000	3075.93	1698.98	1246.67	1025.43	896.48	813.57	756.84	716.35	686.59	664.22	647.13	633.92	623.60	615.47
34000	3169.14	1750.46	1284.45	1056.50	923.65	838.22	779.77	738.06	707.40	684.35	666.74	653.13	642.49	634.12
35000	3262.35	1801.94	1322.23	1087.57	950.81	862.88	802.71	759.77	728.20	704.48	686.35	672.34	661.39	652.78
36000	3355.56	1853.43	1360.01	1118.65	977.98	887.53	825.64	781.48	749.01	724.60	705.96	691.55	680.29	671.43
37000	3448.77	1904.91	1397.78	1149.72	1005.15	912.18	848.58	803.19	769.81	744.73	725.57	710.76	699.18	690.08
38000	3541.98	1956.39	1435.56	1180.79	1032.31	936.84	871.51	824.89	790.62	764.86	745.18	729.97	718.08	708.73
39000	3635.19	2007.88	1473.34	1211.87	1059.48	961.49	894.45	846.60	811.42	784.99	764.79	749.18	736.98	727.38
40000	3728.40	2059.36	1511.12	1242.94	1086.64	986.14	917.38	868.31	832.23	805.12	784.40	768.38	755.87	746.03
41000	3821.61	2110.85	1548.90	1274.01	1113.81	1010.80	940.31	890.02	853.03	825.24	804.01	787.59	774.77	764.68
42000	3914.82	2162.33	1586.67	1305.09	1140.98	1035.45	963.25	911.72	873.84	845.37	823.62	806.80	793.67	783.33
43000	4008.03	2213.81	1624.45	1336.16	1168.14	1060.10	986.18	933.43	894.65	865.50	843.23	826.01	812.56	801.98
44000	4101.24	2265.30	1662.23	1367.23	1195.31	1084.76	1009.12	955.14	915.45	885.63	862.84	845.22	831.46	820.63
45000	4194.45	2316.78	1700.01	1398.31	1222.47	1109.41	1032.05	976.85	936.26	905.75	882.45	864.43	850.36	839.28
46000	4287.66	2368.27	1737.79	1429.38	1249.64	1134.06	1054.99	998.55	957.06	925.88	902.06	883.64	869.25	857.93
47000	4380.87	2419.75	1775.56	1460.45	1276.81	1158.72	1077.92	1020.26	977.87	946.01	921.67	902.85	888.15	876.58
48000	4474.07	2471.23	1813.34	1491.53	1303.97	1183.37	1100.85	1041.97	998.67	966.14	941.28	922.06	907.05	895.23
49000	4567.28	2522.72	1851.12	1522.60	1331.14	1208.03	1123.79	1063.68	1019.48	986.27	960.89	941.27	925.94	913.88
50000	4660.49	2574.20	1888.90	1553.67	1358.30	1232.68	1146.72	1085.38	1040.28	1006.39	980.50	960.48	944.84	932.53
55000	5126.54	2831.62	2077.79	1709.04	1494.13	1355.95	1261.39	1193.92	1144.31	1107.03	1078.55	1056.53	1039.32	1025.79
60000	5592.59	3089.04	2266.68	1864.41	1629.96	1479.21	1376.07	1302.46	1248.34	1207.67	1176.60	1152.57	1133.81	1119.04
65000	6058.64	3346.46	2455.56	2019.77	1765.79	1602.48	1490.74	1411.00	1352.37	1308.31	1274.65	1248.62	1228.29	1212.29
70000	6524.69	3603.88	2644.45	2175.14	1901.62	1725.75	1605.41	1519.53	1456.40	1408.95	1372.70	1344.67	1322.77	1305.55
75000	6990.74	3861.30	2833.34	2330.51	2037.45	1849.02	1720.08	1628.07	1560.42	1509.59	1470.75	1440.72	1417.26	1398.80
80000	7456.79	4118.72	3022.23	2485.87	2173.28	1972.28	1834.75	1736.61	1664.45	1610.23	1568.80	1536.76	1511.74	1492.05
85000	7922.84	4376.14	3211.12	2641.24	2309.11	2095.55	1949.43	1845.15	1768.48	1710.87	1666.85	1632.81	1606.23	1585.30
90000	8388.89	4633.56	3400.01	2796.61	2444.94	2218.82	2064.10	1953.69	1872.51	1811.50	1764.90	1728.86	1700.71	1678.56
95000	8854.94	4890.98	3588.90	2951.98	2580.77	2342.08	2178.77	2062.22	1976.54	1912.14	1862.95	1824.91	1795.19	1771.81
100000	9320.98	5148.40	3777.79	3107.34	2716.60	2465.35	2293.44	2170.76	2080.56	2012.78	1961.00	1920.95	1889.68	1865.06

TERM	15 Years	16 Years	17 Years	18 Years	19 Years	20 Years	21 Years	22 Years	23 Years	24 Years	25 Years	30 Years	35 Years	40 Years
AMOUNT														
5	.10	.10	.10	.10	.09	.09	.09	.09	.09	.09	.09	.09	.09	.09
10	.19	.19	.19	.19	.18	.18	.18	.18	.18	.18	.18	.18	.18	.18
15	.28	.28	.28	.28	.27	.27	.27	.27	.27	.27	.27	.27	.27	.27
25	.47	.46	.46	.46	.45	.45	.45	.45	.45	.45	.45	.45	.45	.45
50	.93	.92	.91	.91	.90	.90	.90	.90	.90	.89	.89	.89	.89	.89
75	1.39	1.38	1.37	1.36	1.35	1.35	1.35	1.34	1.34	1.34	1.34	1.33	1.33	1.33
100	1.85	1.84	1.82	1.81	1.80	1.80	1.79	1.79	1.79	1.78	1.78	1.77	1.77	1.77
200	3.70	3.67	3.64	3.62	3.60	3.59	3.58	3.57	3.57	3.56	3.56	3.54	3.54	3.54
300	5.54	5.50	5.46	5.43	5.40	5.39	5.37	5.36	5.35	5.34	5.33	5.31	5.31	5.31
400	7.39	7.33	7.28	7.24	7.20	7.18	7.16	7.14	7.13	7.12	7.11	7.08	7.08	7.07
500	9.23	9.16	9.09	9.04	9.00	8.97	8.95	8.93	8.91	8.90	8.88	8.85	8.84	8.84
600	11.08	10.99	10.91	10.85	10.80	10.77	10.74	10.71	10.69	10.67	10.66	10.62	10.61	10.61
700	12.92	12.82	12.73	12.66	12.60	12.56	12.52	12.49	12.47	12.45	12.44	12.39	12.38	12.37
800	14.77	14.65	14.55	14.47	14.40	14.35	14.31	14.28	14.25	14.23	14.21	14.16	14.15	14.14
900	16.62	16.48	16.36	16.28	16.20	16.15	16.10	16.06	16.03	16.01	15.99	15.93	15.92	15.91
1000	18.46	18.31	18.18	18.08	18.00	17.94	17.89	17.85	17.81	17.79	17.76	17.70	17.68	17.68
2000	36.92	36.61	36.36	36.16	36.00	35.87	35.77	35.69	35.62	35.57	35.52	35.40	35.36	35.35
3000	55.37	54.91	54.54	54.24	54.00	53.81	53.66	53.53	53.43	53.35	53.28	53.10	53.04	53.02
4000	73.83	73.21	72.71	72.32	72.00	71.74	71.54	71.37	71.24	71.13	71.04	70.80	70.72	70.69
5000	92.28	91.51	90.89	90.40	90.00	89.68	89.42	89.21	89.05	88.91	88.80	88.50	88.39	88.36
6000	110.74	109.81	109.07	108.47	108.00	107.61	107.31	107.06	106.86	106.69	106.56	106.20	106.07	106.03
7000	129.20	128.11	127.25	126.55	126.00	125.55	125.19	124.90	124.66	124.47	124.32	123.90	123.75	123.70
8000	147.65	146.41	145.42	144.63	143.99	143.48	143.07	142.74	142.47	142.26	142.08	141.60	141.43	141.37
9000	166.11	164.71	163.60	162.71	161.99	161.42	160.96	160.58	160.28	160.04	159.84	159.30	159.11	159.04
10000	184.56	183.01	181.78	180.79	179.99	179.35	178.84	178.42	178.09	177.82	177.60	177.00	176.78	176.71
11000	203.02	201.31	199.95	198.86	197.99	197.29	196.72	196.27	195.90	195.60	195.36	194.69	194.46	194.38
12000	221.47	219.62	218.13	216.94	215.99	215.22	214.61	214.11	213.71	213.38	213.12	212.39	212.14	212.05
13000	239.93	237.92	236.31	235.02	233.99	233.16	232.49	231.95	231.51	231.16	230.88	230.09	229.82	229.72
14000	258.39	256.22	254.49	253.10	251.99	251.09	250.37	249.79	249.32	248.94	248.64	247.79	247.50	247.39
15000	276.84	274.52	272.66	271.18	269.99	269.03	268.26	267.63	267.13	266.73	266.40	265.49	265.17	265.06
16000	295.30	292.82	290.84	289.26	287.98	286.96	286.14	285.48	284.94	284.51	284.16	283.19	282.85	282.73
17000	313.75	311.12	309.02	307.33	305.98	304.90	304.02	303.32	302.75	302.29	301.92	300.89	300.53	300.41
18000	332.21	329.42	327.19	325.41	323.98	322.83	321.91	321.16	320.56	320.07	319.68	318.59	318.21	318.08
19000	350.66	347.72	345.37	343.49	341.98	340.77	339.79	339.00	338.36	337.85	337.44	336.29	335.89	335.75
20000	369.12	366.02	363.55	361.57	359.98	358.70	357.67	356.84	356.17	355.63	355.20	353.99	353.56	353.42
21000	387.58	384.32	381.73	379.65	377.98	376.64	375.56	374.68	373.98	373.41	372.95	371.68	371.24	371.09
22000	406.03	402.62	399.90	397.72	395.98	394.57	393.44	392.53	391.79	391.20	390.71	389.38	388.92	388.76
23000	424.49	420.92	418.08	415.80	413.97	412.51	411.32	410.37	409.60	408.98	408.47	407.08	406.60	406.43
24000	442.94	439.23	436.26	433.88	431.97	430.44	429.21	428.21	427.41	426.76	426.23	424.78	424.28	424.10
25000	461.40	457.53	454.43	451.96	449.97	448.38	447.09	446.05	445.22	444.54	443.99	442.48	441.95	441.77
26000	479.85	475.83	472.61	470.04	467.97	466.31	464.97	463.89	463.02	462.32	461.75	460.18	459.63	459.44
27000	498.31	494.13	490.79	488.12	485.97	484.24	482.86	481.74	480.83	480.10	479.51	477.88	477.31	477.11
28000	516.77	512.43	508.97	506.19	503.97	502.18	500.74	499.58	498.64	497.88	497.27	495.58	494.99	494.78
29000	535.22	530.73	527.14	524.27	521.97	520.11	518.62	517.42	516.45	515.66	515.03	513.28	512.67	512.45
30000	553.68	549.03	545.32	542.35	539.97	538.05	536.51	535.26	534.26	533.45	532.79	530.98	530.34	530.12
31000	572.13	567.33	563.50	560.43	557.96	555.98	554.39	553.10	552.07	551.23	550.55	548.67	548.02	547.79
32000	590.59	585.63	581.67	578.51	575.96	573.92	572.27	570.95	569.87	569.01	568.31	566.37	565.70	565.46
33000	609.05	603.93	599.85	596.58	593.96	591.85	590.16	588.79	587.68	586.79	586.07	584.07	583.38	583.14
34000	627.50	622.23	618.03	614.66	611.96	609.79	608.04	606.63	605.49	604.57	603.83	601.77	601.06	600.81
35000	645.96	640.53	636.21	632.74	629.96	627.72	625.92	624.47	623.30	622.35	621.59	619.47	618.73	618.48
36000	664.41	658.84	654.38	650.82	647.96	645.66	643.81	642.31	641.11	640.13	639.35	637.17	636.41	636.15
37000	682.87	677.14	672.56	668.90	665.96	663.59	661.69	660.15	658.92	657.92	657.11	654.87	654.09	653.82
38000	701.32	695.44	690.74	686.97	683.96	681.53	679.57	678.00	676.72	675.70	674.87	672.57	671.77	671.49
39000	719.78	713.74	708.91	705.05	701.95	699.46	697.46	695.84	694.53	693.48	692.63	690.27	689.45	689.16
40000	738.24	732.04	727.09	723.13	719.95	717.40	715.34	713.68	712.34	711.26	710.39	707.97	707.12	706.83
41000	756.69	750.34	745.27	741.21	737.95	735.33	733.22	731.52	730.15	729.04	728.15	725.66	724.80	724.50
42000	775.15	768.64	763.45	759.29	755.95	753.27	751.11	749.36	747.96	746.82	745.90	743.36	742.48	742.17
43000	793.60	786.94	781.62	777.37	773.95	771.20	768.99	767.21	765.77	764.60	763.66	761.06	760.16	759.84
44000	812.06	805.24	799.80	795.44	791.95	789.14	786.87	785.05	783.57	782.39	781.42	778.76	777.84	777.51
45000	830.51	823.54	817.98	813.52	809.95	807.07	804.75	802.89	801.38	800.17	799.18	796.46	795.51	795.18
46000	848.97	841.84	836.15	831.60	827.94	825.01	822.64	820.73	819.19	817.95	816.94	814.16	813.19	812.85
47000	867.43	860.14	854.33	849.68	845.94	842.94	840.52	838.57	837.00	835.73	834.70	831.86	830.87	830.52
48000	885.88	878.45	872.51	867.76	863.94	860.88	858.41	856.42	854.81	853.51	852.46	849.56	848.55	848.19
49000	904.34	896.75	890.69	885.83	881.94	878.81	876.29	874.26	872.62	871.29	870.22	867.26	866.23	865.87
50000	922.79	915.05	908.86	903.91	899.94	896.75	894.17	892.10	890.43	889.07	887.98	884.96	883.90	883.54
55000	1015.07	1006.55	999.75	994.30	989.93	986.42	983.59	981.31	979.47	977.98	976.78	973.45	972.29	971.89
60000	1107.35	1098.06	1090.63	1084.69	1079.93	1076.09	1073.01	1070.52	1068.51	1066.89	1065.58	1061.95	1060.68	1060.24
65000	1199.63	1189.56	1181.52	1175.08	1169.92	1165.77	1162.42	1159.73	1157.55	1155.79	1154.37	1150.44	1149.07	1148.60
70000	1291.91	1281.06	1272.41	1265.48	1259.91	1255.44	1251.84	1248.94	1246.59	1244.70	1243.17	1238.94	1237.46	1236.95
75000	1384.19	1372.57	1363.29	1355.87	1349.91	1345.12	1341.26	1338.15	1335.64	1333.61	1331.97	1327.43	1325.85	1325.30
80000	1476.47	1464.07	1454.18	1446.26	1439.90	1434.79	1430.67	1427.36	1424.68	1422.51	1420.77	1415.93	1414.24	1413.65
85000	1568.75	1555.57	1545.06	1536.65	1529.89	1524.46	1520.09	1516.57	1513.72	1511.42	1509.56	1504.42	1502.63	1502.01
90000	1661.02	1647.08	1635.95	1627.04	1619.89	1614.14	1609.51	1605.77	1602.76	1600.33	1598.36	1592.92	1591.02	1590.36
95000	1753.30	1738.58	1726.84	1717.43	1709.88	1703.81	1698.92	1694.98	1691.80	1689.23	1687.16	1681.41	1679.41	1678.71
100000	1845.58	1830.09	1817.72	1807.82	1799.87	1793.49	1788.34	1784.19	1780.85	1778.14	1775.96	1769.91	1767.80	1767.07

MONTHLY PAYMENT
REQUIRED TO AMORTIZE A LOAN

TERM	1 Year	2 Years	3 Years	4 Years	5 Years	6 Years	7 Years	8 Years	9 Years	10 Years	11 Years	12 Years	13 Years	14 Years
AMOUNT														
5	.47	.26	.19	.16	.14	.13	.12	.11	.11	.11	.10	.10	.10	.10
10	.94	.52	.38	.32	.28	.25	.23	.22	.21	.21	.20	.20	.19	.19
15	1.40	.78	.57	.47	.41	.38	.35	.33	.32	.31	.30	.29	.29	.29
25	2.34	1.29	.95	.78	.68	.62	.58	.55	.53	.51	.50	.49	.48	.47
50	4.67	2.58	1.90	1.56	1.36	1.24	1.15	1.09	1.05	1.01	.99	.97	.95	.94
75	7.00	3.87	2.84	2.34	2.04	1.86	1.73	1.64	1.57	1.52	1.48	1.45	1.42	1.41
100	9.33	5.16	3.79	3.12	2.72	2.47	2.30	2.18	2.09	2.02	1.97	1.93	1.90	1.87
200	18.65	10.31	7.57	6.23	5.44	4.94	4.60	4.35	4.17	4.04	3.93	3.85	3.79	3.74
300	27.98	15.46	11.35	9.34	8.16	7.41	6.89	6.53	6.26	6.05	5.90	5.78	5.68	5.61
400	37.30	20.61	15.13	12.45	10.88	9.88	9.19	8.70	8.34	8.07	7.86	7.70	7.58	7.48
500	46.62	25.76	18.91	15.56	13.60	12.35	11.49	10.87	10.42	10.09	9.83	9.63	9.47	9.35
600	55.95	30.91	22.69	18.67	16.32	14.81	13.78	13.05	12.51	12.10	11.79	11.55	11.36	11.22
700	65.27	36.06	26.47	21.78	19.04	17.28	16.08	15.22	14.59	14.12	13.76	13.48	13.26	13.09
800	74.59	41.21	30.25	24.89	21.76	19.75	18.38	17.40	16.68	16.13	15.72	15.40	15.15	14.95
900	83.92	46.36	34.03	28.00	24.48	22.22	20.67	19.57	18.76	18.15	17.69	17.33	17.04	16.82
1000	93.24	51.51	37.81	31.11	27.20	24.69	22.97	21.74	20.84	20.17	19.65	19.25	18.94	18.69
2000	186.47	103.02	75.61	62.21	54.39	49.37	45.93	43.48	41.68	40.33	39.29	38.49	37.87	37.38
3000	279.71	154.53	113.42	93.31	81.59	74.05	68.90	65.22	62.52	60.49	58.94	57.74	56.80	56.07
4000	372.94	206.04	151.22	124.41	108.78	98.74	91.86	86.96	83.36	80.65	78.58	76.98	75.74	74.75
5000	466.17	257.55	189.02	155.51	135.98	123.42	114.83	108.70	104.20	100.81	98.23	96.23	94.67	93.44
6000	559.41	309.06	226.83	186.61	163.17	148.10	137.79	130.44	125.03	120.97	117.87	115.47	113.60	112.13
7000	652.64	360.56	264.63	217.71	190.36	172.79	160.76	152.18	145.87	141.14	137.52	134.72	132.54	130.82
8000	745.88	412.07	302.43	248.81	217.56	197.47	183.72	173.92	166.71	161.30	157.16	153.96	151.47	149.50
9000	839.11	463.58	340.24	279.91	244.75	222.15	206.69	195.66	187.55	181.46	176.81	173.21	170.40	168.19
10000	932.34	515.09	378.04	311.01	271.95	246.83	229.65	217.40	208.39	201.62	196.45	192.45	189.33	186.88
11000	1025.58	566.60	415.84	342.11	299.14	271.52	252.62	239.14	229.23	221.78	216.10	211.70	208.27	205.57
12000	1118.81	618.11	453.65	373.21	326.34	296.20	275.58	260.88	250.06	241.94	235.74	230.94	227.20	224.25
13000	1212.04	669.62	491.45	404.31	353.53	320.88	298.55	282.62	270.90	262.10	255.38	250.19	246.13	242.94
14000	1305.28	721.12	529.25	435.41	380.72	345.57	321.51	304.35	291.74	282.27	275.03	269.43	265.07	261.63
15000	1398.51	772.63	567.06	466.51	407.92	370.25	344.48	326.09	312.58	302.43	294.67	288.68	284.00	280.32
16000	1491.75	824.14	604.86	497.61	435.11	394.93	367.44	347.83	333.42	322.59	314.32	307.92	302.93	299.00
17000	1584.98	875.65	642.67	528.71	462.31	419.61	390.41	369.57	354.26	342.75	333.96	327.17	321.86	317.69
18000	1678.21	927.16	680.47	559.81	489.50	444.30	413.37	391.31	375.09	362.91	353.61	346.41	340.80	336.38
19000	1771.45	978.67	718.27	590.91	516.69	468.98	436.34	413.05	395.93	383.07	373.25	365.66	359.73	355.07
20000	1864.68	1030.18	756.08	622.01	543.89	493.66	459.30	434.79	416.77	403.23	392.90	384.90	378.66	373.75
21000	1957.91	1081.68	793.88	653.11	571.08	518.35	482.27	456.53	437.61	423.40	412.54	404.15	397.60	392.44
22000	2051.15	1133.19	831.68	684.21	598.28	543.03	505.23	478.27	458.45	443.56	432.19	423.39	416.53	411.13
23000	2144.38	1184.70	869.49	715.31	625.47	567.71	528.20	500.01	479.29	463.72	451.83	442.64	435.46	429.82
24000	2237.62	1236.21	907.29	746.41	652.67	592.39	551.16	521.75	500.13	483.88	471.48	461.88	454.39	448.50
25000	2330.85	1287.72	945.09	777.51	679.86	617.08	574.13	543.49	520.96	504.04	491.12	481.13	473.33	467.19
26000	2424.08	1339.23	982.90	808.61	707.05	641.76	597.09	565.23	541.80	524.20	510.76	500.37	492.26	485.88
27000	2517.32	1390.74	1020.70	839.71	734.25	666.44	620.06	586.97	562.64	544.36	530.41	519.62	511.19	504.57
28000	2610.55	1442.24	1058.50	870.81	761.44	691.13	643.02	608.70	583.48	564.53	550.05	538.86	530.13	523.25
29000	2703.79	1493.75	1096.31	901.91	788.64	715.81	665.99	630.44	604.32	584.69	569.70	558.11	549.06	541.94
30000	2797.02	1545.26	1134.11	933.01	815.83	740.49	688.95	652.18	625.15	604.85	589.34	577.35	567.99	560.63
31000	2890.25	1596.77	1171.92	964.11	843.02	765.17	711.92	673.92	645.99	625.01	608.99	596.60	586.92	579.32
32000	2983.49	1648.28	1209.72	995.22	870.22	789.86	734.88	695.66	666.83	645.17	628.63	615.84	605.86	598.00
33000	3076.72	1699.79	1247.52	1026.32	897.41	814.54	757.85	717.40	687.67	665.33	648.28	635.09	624.79	616.69
34000	3169.95	1751.30	1285.33	1057.42	924.61	839.22	780.81	739.14	708.51	685.50	667.92	654.33	643.72	635.38
35000	3263.19	1802.80	1323.13	1088.52	951.80	863.91	803.78	760.88	729.35	705.66	687.57	673.58	662.66	654.07
36000	3356.42	1854.31	1360.93	1119.62	979.00	888.59	826.74	782.62	750.18	725.82	707.21	692.82	681.59	672.75
37000	3449.66	1905.82	1398.74	1150.72	1006.19	913.27	849.71	804.36	771.02	745.98	726.85	712.07	700.52	691.44
38000	3542.89	1957.33	1436.54	1181.82	1033.38	937.95	872.67	826.10	791.86	766.14	746.50	731.31	719.45	710.13
39000	3636.12	2008.84	1474.34	1212.92	1060.58	962.64	895.64	847.84	812.70	786.30	766.14	750.56	738.39	728.82
40000	3729.36	2060.35	1512.15	1244.02	1087.77	987.32	918.60	869.58	833.54	806.46	785.79	769.80	757.32	747.50
41000	3822.59	2111.85	1549.95	1275.12	1114.97	1012.00	941.57	891.31	854.38	826.63	805.43	789.05	776.25	766.19
42000	3915.82	2163.36	1587.75	1306.22	1142.16	1036.69	964.53	913.05	875.21	846.79	825.08	808.29	795.19	784.88
43000	4009.06	2214.87	1625.56	1337.32	1169.35	1061.37	987.50	934.79	896.05	866.95	844.72	827.54	814.12	803.56
44000	4102.29	2266.38	1663.36	1368.42	1196.55	1086.05	1010.46	956.53	916.89	887.11	864.37	846.78	833.05	822.25
45000	4195.53	2317.89	1701.16	1399.52	1223.74	1110.73	1033.43	978.27	937.73	907.27	884.01	866.03	851.98	840.94
46000	4288.76	2369.40	1738.97	1430.62	1250.94	1135.42	1056.39	1000.01	958.57	927.43	903.66	885.27	870.92	859.63
47000	4381.99	2420.91	1776.77	1461.72	1278.13	1160.10	1079.36	1021.75	979.41	947.59	923.30	904.52	889.85	878.31
48000	4475.23	2472.41	1814.58	1492.82	1305.33	1184.78	1102.32	1043.49	1000.24	967.76	942.95	923.76	908.78	897.00
49000	4568.46	2523.92	1852.38	1523.92	1332.52	1209.47	1125.29	1065.23	1021.08	987.92	962.59	943.01	927.72	915.69
50000	4661.69	2575.43	1890.18	1555.02	1359.71	1234.15	1148.25	1086.97	1041.92	1008.08	982.23	962.25	946.65	934.38
55000	5127.86	2832.97	2079.20	1710.52	1495.68	1357.56	1263.08	1195.66	1146.11	1108.89	1080.46	1058.48	1041.31	1027.81
60000	5594.03	3090.52	2268.22	1866.02	1631.66	1480.98	1377.90	1304.36	1250.30	1209.69	1178.68	1154.70	1135.98	1121.25
65000	6060.20	3348.06	2457.24	2021.53	1767.63	1604.39	1492.73	1413.06	1354.50	1310.50	1276.90	1250.92	1230.64	1214.69
70000	6526.37	3605.60	2646.25	2177.03	1903.60	1727.81	1607.55	1521.75	1458.69	1411.31	1375.13	1347.15	1325.31	1308.13
75000	6992.54	3863.14	2835.27	2332.53	2039.57	1851.22	1722.38	1630.45	1562.88	1512.12	1473.35	1443.37	1419.97	1401.56
80000	7458.71	4120.69	3024.29	2488.03	2175.54	1974.64	1837.20	1739.15	1667.07	1612.92	1571.57	1539.60	1514.64	1495.00
85000	7924.88	4378.23	3213.31	2643.53	2311.51	2098.05	1952.03	1847.84	1771.26	1713.73	1669.80	1635.82	1609.30	1588.44
90000	8391.05	4635.77	3402.32	2799.03	2447.48	2221.46	2066.85	1956.54	1875.45	1814.54	1768.02	1732.05	1703.96	1681.87
95000	8857.22	4893.32	3591.34	2954.54	2583.45	2344.88	2181.67	2065.23	1979.65	1915.35	1866.24	1828.27	1798.63	1775.31
100000	9323.39	5150.86	3780.36	3110.04	2719.42	2468.29	2296.50	2173.93	2083.84	2016.15	1964.46	1924.50	1893.29	1868.75

TERM	15 Years	16 Years	17 Years	18 Years	19 Years	20 Years	21 Years	22 Years	23 Years	24 Years	25 Years	30 Years	35 Years	40 Years
AMOUNT														
5	.10	.10	.10	.10	.10	.09	.09	.09	.09	.09	.09	.09	.09	.09
10	.19	.19	.19	.19	.19	.18	.18	.18	.18	.18	.18	.18	.18	.18
15	.28	.28	.28	.28	.28	.27	.27	.27	.27	.27	.27	.27	.27	.27
25	.47	.46	.46	.46	.46	.45	.45	.45	.45	.45	.45	.45	.45	.45
50	.93	.92	.92	.91	.91	.90	.90	.90	.90	.90	.90	.89	.89	.89
75	1.39	1.38	1.37	1.36	1.36	1.35	1.35	1.35	1.34	1.34	1.34	1.34	1.33	1.33
100	1.85	1.84	1.83	1.82	1.81	1.80	1.80	1.79	1.79	1.79	1.79	1.78	1.78	1.78
200	3.70	3.67	3.65	3.63	3.61	3.60	3.59	3.58	3.57	3.57	3.57	3.55	3.55	3.55
300	5.55	5.51	5.47	5.44	5.42	5.40	5.38	5.37	5.36	5.35	5.35	5.33	5.32	5.32
400	7.40	7.34	7.29	7.25	7.22	7.19	7.17	7.16	7.14	7.13	7.13	7.10	7.09	7.09
500	9.25	9.17	9.11	9.06	9.02	8.99	8.97	8.95	8.93	8.92	8.91	8.88	8.86	8.86
600	11.10	11.01	10.93	10.88	10.83	10.79	10.76	10.73	10.71	10.70	10.69	10.65	10.64	10.63
700	12.95	12.84	12.76	12.69	12.63	12.59	12.55	12.52	12.50	12.48	12.47	12.42	12.41	12.40
800	14.80	14.68	14.58	14.50	14.44	14.38	14.34	14.31	14.28	14.26	14.25	14.20	14.18	14.17
900	16.65	16.51	16.40	16.31	16.24	16.18	16.14	16.10	16.07	16.04	16.03	15.97	15.95	15.95
1000	18.50	18.34	18.22	18.12	18.04	17.98	17.93	17.89	17.85	17.83	17.81	17.75	17.72	17.72
2000	36.99	36.68	36.44	36.24	36.08	35.95	35.85	35.77	35.70	35.65	35.61	35.49	35.44	35.43
3000	55.48	55.02	54.65	54.36	54.12	53.93	53.77	53.65	53.55	53.47	53.41	53.23	53.16	53.14
4000	73.98	73.36	72.87	72.47	72.16	71.90	71.70	71.53	71.40	71.29	71.21	70.97	70.88	70.85
5000	92.47	91.70	91.08	90.59	90.19	89.88	89.62	89.42	89.25	89.11	89.01	88.71	88.60	88.57
6000	110.96	110.04	109.30	108.71	108.23	107.85	107.54	107.30	107.10	106.94	106.81	106.45	106.32	106.28
7000	129.46	128.38	127.51	126.82	126.27	125.83	125.47	125.18	124.95	124.76	124.61	124.19	124.04	123.99
8000	147.95	146.72	145.73	144.94	144.31	143.80	143.39	143.06	142.80	142.58	142.41	141.93	141.76	141.70
9000	166.44	165.05	163.95	163.06	162.35	161.77	161.31	160.94	160.64	160.40	160.21	159.67	159.48	159.41
10000	184.94	183.39	182.16	181.18	180.38	179.75	179.24	178.83	178.49	178.22	178.01	177.41	177.20	177.13
11000	203.43	201.73	200.38	199.29	198.42	197.72	197.16	196.71	196.34	196.05	195.81	195.15	194.92	194.84
12000	221.92	220.07	218.59	217.41	216.46	215.70	215.08	214.59	214.19	213.87	213.61	212.89	212.64	212.55
13000	240.42	238.41	236.81	235.53	234.50	233.67	233.01	232.47	232.04	231.69	231.41	230.63	230.36	230.26
14000	258.91	256.75	255.02	253.64	252.54	251.65	250.93	250.35	249.89	249.51	249.21	248.37	248.08	247.98
15000	277.40	275.09	273.24	271.76	270.57	269.62	268.85	268.24	267.74	267.33	267.01	266.11	265.80	265.69
16000	295.90	293.43	291.46	289.88	288.61	287.60	286.78	286.12	285.59	285.16	284.81	283.85	283.52	283.40
17000	314.39	311.77	309.67	308.00	306.65	305.57	304.70	304.00	303.43	302.98	302.61	301.59	301.24	301.11
18000	332.88	330.10	327.89	326.11	324.69	323.54	322.62	321.88	321.28	320.80	320.41	319.33	318.96	318.82
19000	351.38	348.44	346.10	344.23	342.73	341.52	340.55	339.76	339.13	338.62	338.21	337.07	336.67	336.54
20000	369.87	366.78	364.32	362.35	360.76	359.49	358.47	357.65	356.98	356.44	356.01	354.81	354.39	354.25
21000	388.36	385.12	382.53	380.46	378.80	377.47	376.39	375.53	374.83	374.27	373.81	372.55	372.11	371.96
22000	406.86	403.46	400.75	398.58	396.84	395.44	394.32	393.41	392.68	392.09	391.61	390.29	389.83	389.67
23000	425.35	421.80	418.97	416.70	414.88	413.42	412.24	411.29	410.53	409.91	409.41	408.03	407.55	407.39
24000	443.84	440.14	437.18	434.81	432.92	431.39	430.16	429.17	428.38	427.73	427.21	425.77	425.27	425.10
25000	462.34	458.48	455.40	452.93	450.95	449.37	448.09	447.06	446.22	445.55	445.01	443.51	442.99	442.81
26000	480.83	476.81	473.61	471.05	468.99	467.34	466.01	464.94	464.07	463.38	462.81	461.25	460.71	460.52
27000	499.32	495.15	491.83	489.17	487.03	485.31	483.93	482.82	481.92	481.20	480.61	478.99	478.43	478.23
28000	517.82	513.49	510.04	507.28	505.07	503.29	501.86	500.70	499.77	499.02	498.41	496.73	496.15	495.95
29000	536.31	531.83	528.26	525.40	523.11	521.26	519.78	518.58	517.62	516.84	516.21	514.47	513.87	513.66
30000	554.80	550.17	546.47	543.52	541.14	539.24	537.70	536.47	535.47	534.66	534.01	532.21	531.59	531.37
31000	573.30	568.51	564.69	561.63	559.18	557.21	555.63	554.35	553.32	552.49	551.81	549.95	549.31	549.08
32000	591.79	586.85	582.91	579.75	577.22	575.19	573.55	572.23	571.17	570.31	569.61	567.69	567.03	566.80
33000	610.28	605.19	601.12	597.07	595.26	593.16	591.47	590.11	589.02	588.13	587.41	585.43	584.75	584.51
34000	628.77	623.53	619.34	615.99	613.30	611.14	609.40	607.99	606.86	605.95	605.21	603.17	602.47	602.22
35000	647.27	641.86	637.55	634.10	631.33	629.11	627.32	625.88	624.71	623.77	623.01	620.92	620.19	619.93
36000	665.76	660.20	655.77	652.22	649.37	647.08	645.24	643.76	642.56	641.60	640.81	638.66	637.91	637.64
37000	684.25	678.54	673.98	670.34	667.41	665.06	663.17	661.64	660.41	659.42	658.61	656.40	655.63	655.36
38000	702.75	696.88	692.20	688.45	685.45	683.03	681.09	679.52	678.26	677.24	676.41	674.14	673.34	673.07
39000	721.24	715.22	710.42	706.57	703.49	701.01	699.01	697.41	696.11	695.06	694.22	691.88	691.06	690.78
40000	739.73	733.56	728.63	724.69	721.52	718.98	716.94	715.29	713.96	712.88	712.02	709.62	708.78	708.49
41000	758.23	751.90	746.85	742.81	739.56	736.96	734.86	733.17	731.81	730.70	729.82	727.36	726.50	726.21
42000	776.72	770.24	765.06	760.92	757.60	754.93	752.78	751.05	749.65	748.53	747.62	745.10	744.22	743.92
43000	795.21	788.58	783.28	779.04	775.64	772.91	770.71	768.93	767.50	766.35	765.42	762.84	761.94	761.63
44000	813.71	806.91	801.49	797.16	793.68	790.88	788.63	786.82	785.35	784.17	783.22	780.58	779.66	779.34
45000	832.20	825.25	819.71	815.27	811.71	808.85	806.55	804.70	803.20	801.99	801.02	798.32	797.38	797.05
46000	850.69	843.59	837.93	833.39	829.75	826.83	824.48	822.58	821.05	819.81	818.82	816.06	815.10	814.77
47000	869.19	861.93	856.14	851.51	847.79	844.80	842.40	840.46	838.90	837.64	836.62	833.80	832.82	832.48
48000	887.68	880.27	874.36	869.62	865.83	862.78	860.32	858.34	856.75	855.46	854.42	851.54	850.54	850.19
49000	906.17	898.61	892.57	887.74	883.87	880.75	878.25	876.23	874.60	873.28	872.22	869.28	868.26	867.90
50000	924.67	916.95	910.79	905.86	901.90	898.73	896.17	894.11	892.44	891.10	890.02	887.02	885.98	885.62
55000	1017.13	1008.64	1001.87	996.44	992.09	988.60	985.79	983.52	981.69	980.21	979.02	975.72	974.58	974.18
60000	1109.60	1100.34	1092.94	1087.03	1082.28	1078.47	1075.40	1072.93	1070.93	1069.32	1068.02	1064.42	1063.17	1062.74
65000	1202.07	1192.03	1184.02	1177.61	1172.47	1168.34	1165.02	1162.34	1160.18	1158.43	1157.02	1153.12	1151.77	1151.30
70000	1294.53	1283.72	1275.10	1268.20	1262.66	1258.22	1254.63	1251.75	1249.42	1247.54	1246.02	1241.83	1240.37	1239.86
75000	1387.00	1375.42	1366.18	1358.79	1352.85	1348.09	1344.25	1341.16	1338.66	1336.65	1335.02	1330.53	1328.97	1328.42
80000	1479.46	1467.11	1457.26	1449.37	1443.04	1437.96	1433.87	1430.57	1427.91	1425.76	1424.03	1419.23	1417.56	1416.98
85000	1571.93	1558.81	1548.34	1539.96	1533.23	1527.83	1523.48	1519.98	1517.15	1514.87	1513.03	1507.93	1506.16	1505.54
90000	1664.40	1650.50	1639.41	1630.54	1623.42	1617.70	1613.10	1609.39	1606.40	1603.98	1602.03	1596.63	1594.76	1594.10
95000	1756.86	1742.20	1730.49	1721.13	1713.61	1707.58	1702.72	1698.80	1695.64	1693.09	1691.03	1685.33	1683.35	1682.67
100000	1849.33	1833.89	1821.57	1811.71	1803.80	1797.45	1792.33	1788.21	1784.88	1782.20	1780.03	1774.03	1771.95	1771.23

21.300%

TERM	1 Year	2 Years	3 Years	4 Years	5 Years	6 Years	7 Years	8 Years	9 Years	10 Years	11 Years	12 Years	13 Years	14 Years
AMOUNT														
5	.47	.26	.19	.16	.14	.13	.12	.11	.11	.11	.10	.10	.10	.10
10	.94	.52	.38	.32	.28	.25	.23	.22	.21	.21	.20	.20	.19	.19
15	1.40	.78	.57	.47	.41	.38	.35	.33	.32	.31	.30	.29	.29	.29
25	2.34	1.29	.95	.78	.69	.62	.58	.55	.53	.51	.50	.49	.48	.47
50	4.67	2.58	1.90	1.56	1.37	1.24	1.15	1.09	1.05	1.01	.99	.97	.95	.94
75	7.00	3.87	2.84	2.34	2.05	1.86	1.73	1.64	1.57	1.52	1.48	1.45	1.43	1.41
100	9.33	5.16	3.79	3.12	2.73	2.48	2.30	2.18	2.09	2.02	1.97	1.93	1.90	1.88
200	18.66	10.31	7.57	6.23	4.95	4.60	4.36	4.18	4.04	3.94	3.86	3.80	3.75
300	27.98	15.46	11.35	9.34	8.17	7.42	6.90	6.54	6.27	6.06	5.91	5.79	5.70	5.62
400	37.31	20.62	15.14	12.46	10.89	9.89	9.20	8.71	8.35	8.08	7.88	7.72	7.59	7.49
500	46.63	25.77	18.92	15.57	13.62	12.36	11.50	10.89	10.44	10.10	9.84	9.65	9.49	9.37
600	55.96	30.92	22.70	18.68	16.34	14.83	13.80	13.07	12.53	12.12	11.81	11.57	11.39	11.24
700	65.29	36.08	26.49	21.79	19.06	17.30	16.10	15.24	14.61	14.14	13.78	13.50	13.28	13.11
800	74.61	41.23	30.27	24.91	21.78	19.77	18.40	17.42	16.70	16.16	15.75	15.43	15.18	14.98
900	83.94	46.38	34.05	28.02	24.51	22.25	20.70	19.60	18.79	18.18	17.72	17.36	17.08	16.86
1000	93.26	51.54	37.83	31.13	27.23	24.72	23.00	21.78	20.88	20.20	19.68	19.29	18.97	18.73
2000	186.52	103.07	75.66	62.26	54.45	49.43	46.00	43.55	41.75	40.40	39.36	38.57	37.94	37.45
3000	279.78	154.60	113.49	93.39	81.67	74.14	68.99	65.32	62.62	60.59	59.04	57.85	56.91	56.18
4000	373.04	206.14	151.32	124.51	108.89	98.85	91.99	87.09	83.49	80.79	78.72	77.13	75.88	74.90
5000	466.29	257.67	189.15	155.64	136.12	123.57	114.98	108.86	104.36	100.98	98.40	96.41	94.85	93.63
6000	559.55	309.20	226.98	186.77	163.34	148.28	137.98	130.63	125.23	121.18	118.08	115.69	113.82	112.35
7000	652.81	360.74	264.81	217.90	190.56	172.99	160.97	152.40	146.10	141.37	137.76	134.97	132.79	131.08
8000	746.07	412.27	302.64	249.02	217.78	197.70	183.97	174.17	166.97	161.57	157.44	154.25	151.76	149.80
9000	839.33	463.80	340.47	280.15	245.01	222.42	206.96	195.94	187.84	181.76	177.12	173.53	170.73	168.52
10000	932.58	515.34	378.30	311.28	272.23	247.13	229.96	217.71	208.72	201.96	196.80	192.81	189.70	187.25
11000	1025.84	566.87	416.13	342.41	299.45	271.84	252.96	239.49	229.59	222.15	216.48	212.09	208.66	205.97
12000	1119.10	618.40	453.96	373.53	326.67	296.55	275.95	261.26	250.46	242.35	236.16	231.37	227.63	224.70
13000	1212.36	669.94	491.79	404.66	353.90	321.27	298.95	283.03	271.33	262.54	255.83	250.65	246.60	243.42
14000	1305.61	721.47	529.61	435.79	381.12	345.98	321.94	304.80	292.20	282.74	275.51	269.93	265.57	262.15
15000	1398.87	773.00	567.44	466.91	408.34	370.69	344.94	326.57	313.07	302.93	295.19	289.21	284.54	280.87
16000	1492.13	824.53	605.27	498.04	435.56	395.40	367.93	348.34	333.94	323.13	314.87	308.49	303.51	299.59
17000	1585.39	876.07	643.10	529.17	462.79	420.11	390.93	370.11	354.81	343.32	334.55	327.77	322.48	318.32
18000	1678.65	927.60	680.93	560.30	490.01	444.83	413.92	391.88	375.68	363.52	354.23	347.05	341.45	337.04
19000	1771.90	979.13	718.76	591.42	517.23	469.54	436.92	413.65	396.56	383.71	373.91	366.22	360.42	355.77
20000	1865.16	1030.67	756.59	622.55	544.45	494.25	459.92	435.42	417.43	403.91	393.59	385.61	379.39	374.49
21000	1958.42	1082.20	794.42	653.68	571.68	518.96	482.91	457.20	438.30	424.10	413.27	404.89	398.36	393.22
22000	2051.68	1133.73	832.25	684.81	598.90	543.68	505.91	478.97	459.17	444.30	432.95	424.17	417.32	411.94
23000	2144.93	1185.27	870.08	715.93	626.12	568.39	528.90	500.74	480.04	464.49	452.63	443.45	436.29	430.66
24000	2238.19	1236.80	907.91	747.06	653.34	593.10	551.90	522.51	500.91	484.69	472.31	462.73	455.26	449.39
25000	2331.45	1288.33	945.74	778.19	680.56	617.81	574.89	544.28	521.78	500.89	491.99	482.01	474.23	468.11
26000	2424.71	1339.87	983.57	809.31	707.79	642.53	597.89	566.05	542.65	525.08	511.66	501.29	493.20	486.84
27000	2517.97	1391.40	1021.40	840.44	735.01	667.24	620.88	587.82	563.52	545.28	531.34	520.57	512.17	505.56
28000	2611.22	1442.93	1059.22	871.57	762.23	691.95	643.88	609.59	584.40	565.47	551.02	539.86	531.14	524.29
29000	2704.48	1494.47	1097.05	902.70	789.45	716.66	666.88	631.36	605.27	585.67	570.70	559.14	550.11	543.01
30000	2797.74	1546.00	1134.88	933.82	816.68	741.37	689.87	653.13	626.14	605.86	590.38	578.42	569.08	561.73
31000	2891.00	1597.53	1172.71	964.95	843.90	766.09	712.87	674.91	647.01	626.06	610.06	597.70	588.05	580.46
32000	2984.26	1649.06	1210.54	996.08	871.12	790.80	735.86	696.68	667.88	646.25	629.74	616.98	607.02	599.18
33000	3077.51	1700.60	1248.37	1027.21	898.34	815.51	758.86	718.45	688.75	666.45	649.42	636.26	625.98	617.91
34000	3170.77	1752.13	1286.20	1058.33	925.57	840.22	781.85	740.22	709.62	686.64	669.10	655.54	644.95	636.63
35000	3264.03	1803.66	1324.03	1089.46	952.79	864.94	804.85	761.99	730.49	706.84	688.78	674.82	663.92	655.36
36000	3357.29	1855.20	1361.86	1120.59	980.01	889.65	827.84	783.76	751.36	727.03	708.46	694.10	682.89	674.08
37000	3450.54	1906.73	1399.69	1151.71	1007.23	914.36	850.84	805.53	772.23	747.23	728.14	713.38	701.86	692.80
38000	3543.80	1958.26	1437.52	1182.84	1034.46	939.07	873.84	827.30	793.11	767.42	747.82	732.66	720.83	711.53
39000	3637.06	2009.80	1475.35	1213.97	1061.68	963.79	896.83	849.07	813.98	787.62	767.49	751.94	739.80	730.25
40000	3730.32	2061.33	1513.18	1245.10	1088.90	988.50	919.83	870.84	834.85	807.81	787.17	771.22	758.77	748.98
41000	3823.58	2112.86	1551.01	1276.22	1116.12	1013.21	942.82	892.61	855.72	828.01	806.85	790.50	777.74	767.70
42000	3916.83	2164.40	1588.83	1307.35	1143.35	1037.92	965.82	914.39	876.59	848.20	826.53	809.78	796.71	786.43
43000	4010.09	2215.93	1626.66	1338.48	1170.57	1062.63	988.81	936.16	897.46	868.40	846.21	829.06	815.68	805.15
44000	4103.35	2267.46	1664.49	1369.61	1197.79	1087.35	1011.81	957.93	918.33	888.59	865.89	848.34	834.64	823.87
45000	4196.61	2319.00	1702.32	1400.73	1225.01	1112.06	1034.80	979.70	939.20	908.79	885.57	867.62	853.61	842.60
46000	4289.86	2370.53	1740.15	1431.86	1252.24	1136.77	1057.80	1001.47	960.07	928.98	905.25	886.90	872.58	861.32
47000	4383.12	2422.06	1777.98	1462.99	1279.46	1161.48	1080.80	1023.24	980.95	949.18	924.93	906.18	891.55	880.05
48000	4476.38	2473.59	1815.81	1494.11	1306.68	1186.20	1103.79	1045.01	1001.82	969.37	944.61	925.46	910.52	898.77
49000	4569.64	2525.13	1853.64	1525.24	1333.90	1210.91	1126.79	1066.78	1022.69	989.57	964.29	944.74	929.49	917.50
50000	4662.90	2576.66	1891.47	1556.37	1361.12	1235.62	1149.78	1088.55	1043.56	1009.77	983.97	964.02	948.46	936.22
55000	5129.18	2834.33	2080.62	1712.01	1497.24	1359.18	1264.76	1197.41	1147.91	1110.74	1082.36	1060.43	1043.30	1029.84
60000	5595.47	3091.99	2269.76	1867.64	1633.35	1482.74	1379.74	1306.26	1252.27	1211.72	1180.76	1156.83	1138.15	1123.46
65000	6061.76	3349.66	2458.91	2023.28	1769.46	1606.31	1494.72	1415.12	1356.63	1312.69	1279.15	1253.23	1233.00	1217.09
70000	6528.05	3607.32	2648.05	2178.91	1905.57	1729.87	1609.69	1523.97	1460.98	1413.67	1377.55	1349.63	1327.84	1310.71
75000	6994.34	3864.99	2837.20	2334.55	2041.68	1853.43	1724.67	1632.83	1565.34	1514.65	1475.95	1446.03	1422.69	1404.33
80000	7460.63	4122.65	3026.35	2490.19	2177.80	1976.99	1839.65	1741.68	1669.69	1615.62	1574.34	1542.43	1517.53	1497.95
85000	7926.92	4380.32	3215.49	2645.82	2313.91	2100.55	1954.63	1850.54	1774.05	1716.60	1672.74	1638.84	1612.38	1591.57
90000	8393.21	4637.99	3404.64	2801.46	2450.02	2224.11	2069.60	1959.39	1878.40	1817.57	1771.13	1735.24	1707.22	1685.19
95000	8859.50	4895.65	3593.79	2957.10	2586.13	2347.67	2184.58	2068.25	1982.76	1918.55	1869.53	1831.64	1802.07	1778.81
100000	9325.79	5153.32	3782.93	3112.73	2722.24	2471.24	2299.56	2177.10	2087.11	2019.53	1967.93	1928.04	1896.91	1872.44

TERM	15 Years	16 Years	17 Years	18 Years	19 Years	20 Years	21 Years	22 Years	23 Years	24 Years	25 Years	30 Years	35 Years	40 Years
AMOUNT														
5	.10	.10	.10	.10	.10	.10	.09	.09	.09	.09	.09	.09	.09	.09
10	.19	.19	.19	.19	.19	.19	.18	.18	.18	.18	.18	.18	.18	.18
15	.28	.28	.28	.28	.28	.28	.27	.27	.27	.27	.27	.27	.27	.27
25	.47	.46	.46	.46	.46	.46	.45	.45	.45	.45	.45	.45	.45	.45
50	.93	.92	.92	.91	.91	.91	.90	.90	.90	.90	.90	.89	.89	.89
75	1.39	1.38	1.37	1.37	1.36	1.36	1.35	1.35	1.35	1.34	1.34	1.34	1.34	1.34
100	1.86	1.84	1.83	1.82	1.81	1.81	1.80	1.80	1.79	1.79	1.79	1.78	1.78	1.78
200	3.71	3.68	3.66	3.64	3.62	3.61	3.60	3.59	3.58	3.58	3.57	3.56	3.56	3.56
300	5.56	5.52	5.48	5.45	5.43	5.41	5.39	5.38	5.37	5.36	5.36	5.34	5.33	5.33
400	7.42	7.36	7.31	7.27	7.24	7.21	7.19	7.17	7.16	7.15	7.14	7.12	7.11	7.11
500	9.27	9.19	9.13	9.08	9.04	9.01	8.99	8.97	8.95	8.94	8.93	8.90	8.89	8.88
600	11.12	11.03	10.96	10.90	10.85	10.81	10.78	10.76	10.74	10.72	10.71	10.67	10.66	10.66
700	12.98	12.87	12.78	12.71	12.66	12.61	12.58	12.55	12.53	12.51	12.49	12.45	12.44	12.43
800	14.83	14.71	14.61	14.53	14.47	14.42	14.38	14.34	14.32	14.30	14.28	14.23	14.21	14.21
900	16.68	16.54	16.43	16.35	16.27	16.22	16.17	16.14	16.11	16.08	16.06	16.01	15.99	15.98
1000	18.54	18.38	18.26	18.16	18.08	18.02	17.97	17.93	17.89	17.87	17.85	17.79	17.77	17.76
2000	37.07	36.76	36.51	36.32	36.16	36.03	35.93	35.85	35.78	35.73	35.69	35.57	35.53	35.51
3000	55.60	55.14	54.77	54.47	54.24	54.05	53.89	53.77	53.67	53.59	53.53	53.35	53.29	53.27
4000	74.13	73.51	73.02	72.63	72.31	72.06	71.86	71.69	71.56	71.46	71.37	71.13	71.05	71.02
5000	92.66	91.89	91.28	90.79	90.39	90.08	89.82	89.62	89.45	89.32	89.21	88.91	88.81	88.77
6000	111.19	110.27	109.53	108.94	108.47	108.09	107.78	107.54	107.34	107.18	107.05	106.69	106.57	106.53
7000	129.72	128.64	127.78	127.10	126.55	126.10	125.75	125.46	125.23	125.04	124.89	124.48	124.33	124.28
8000	148.25	147.02	146.04	145.25	144.62	144.12	143.71	143.38	143.12	142.91	142.73	142.26	142.09	142.04
9000	166.78	165.40	164.29	163.41	162.70	162.13	161.67	161.31	161.01	160.77	160.57	160.04	159.85	159.79
10000	185.31	183.77	182.55	181.57	180.78	180.15	179.64	179.23	178.90	178.63	178.42	177.82	177.61	177.54
11000	203.84	202.15	200.80	199.72	198.86	198.16	197.60	197.15	196.79	196.49	196.26	195.60	195.38	195.30
12000	222.37	220.53	219.06	217.88	216.93	216.17	215.56	215.07	214.68	214.36	214.10	213.38	213.14	213.05
13000	240.90	238.90	237.31	236.03	235.01	234.19	233.53	232.99	232.56	232.22	231.94	231.17	230.90	230.80
14000	259.44	257.20	255.56	254.19	253.09	252.20	251.49	250.92	250.45	250.08	249.78	248.95	248.66	248.56
15000	277.97	275.66	273.82	272.35	271.16	270.22	269.45	268.84	268.34	267.94	267.62	266.73	266.42	266.31
16000	296.50	294.03	292.07	290.50	289.24	288.23	287.42	286.76	286.23	285.81	285.46	284.51	284.18	284.07
17000	315.03	312.41	310.33	308.66	307.32	306.24	305.38	304.68	304.12	303.67	303.30	302.29	301.94	301.82
18000	333.56	330.79	328.58	326.81	325.40	324.26	323.34	322.61	322.01	321.53	321.14	320.07	319.70	319.57
19000	352.09	349.17	346.83	344.97	343.47	342.27	341.31	340.53	339.90	339.39	338.98	337.85	337.46	337.33
20000	370.62	367.54	365.09	363.13	361.55	360.29	359.27	358.45	357.79	357.26	356.83	355.64	355.22	355.08
21000	389.15	385.92	383.34	381.28	379.63	378.30	377.23	376.37	375.68	375.12	374.67	373.42	372.99	372.84
22000	407.68	404.30	401.60	399.44	397.71	396.31	395.20	394.29	393.57	392.98	392.51	391.20	390.75	390.59
23000	426.21	422.67	419.85	417.59	415.78	414.33	413.16	412.22	411.46	410.84	410.35	408.98	408.51	408.34
24000	444.74	441.05	438.11	435.75	433.86	432.34	431.12	430.14	429.35	428.71	428.19	426.76	426.27	426.10
25000	463.27	459.43	456.36	453.91	451.94	450.36	449.09	448.06	447.24	446.57	446.03	444.54	444.03	443.85
26000	481.80	477.80	474.61	472.06	470.02	468.37	467.05	465.98	465.12	464.43	463.87	462.33	461.79	461.60
27000	500.33	496.18	492.87	490.22	488.09	486.39	485.01	483.91	483.01	482.29	481.71	480.11	479.55	479.36
28000	518.87	514.56	511.12	508.37	506.17	504.40	502.98	501.83	500.90	500.16	499.55	497.89	497.31	497.11
29000	537.40	532.93	529.38	526.53	524.25	522.41	520.94	519.75	518.79	518.02	517.39	515.67	515.07	514.87
30000	555.93	551.31	547.63	544.69	542.32	540.43	538.90	537.67	536.68	535.88	535.24	533.45	532.83	532.62
31000	574.46	569.69	565.88	562.84	560.40	558.44	556.86	555.59	554.57	553.74	553.08	551.23	550.60	550.37
32000	592.99	588.06	584.14	581.00	578.48	576.46	574.83	573.52	572.46	571.61	570.92	569.01	568.36	568.13
33000	611.52	606.44	602.39	599.15	596.56	594.47	592.79	591.44	590.35	589.47	588.76	586.80	586.12	585.88
34000	630.05	624.82	620.65	617.31	614.63	612.48	610.75	609.36	608.24	607.33	606.60	604.58	603.88	603.63
35000	648.58	643.20	638.90	635.47	632.71	630.50	628.72	627.28	626.13	625.19	624.44	622.36	621.64	621.39
36000	667.11	661.57	657.16	653.62	650.79	648.51	646.68	645.21	644.02	643.06	642.28	640.14	639.40	639.14
37000	685.64	679.95	675.41	671.78	668.87	666.53	664.64	663.13	661.91	660.92	660.12	657.92	657.16	656.90
38000	704.17	698.33	693.66	689.93	686.94	684.54	682.61	681.05	679.79	678.78	677.96	675.70	674.92	674.65
39000	722.70	716.70	711.92	708.09	705.02	702.55	700.57	698.97	697.68	696.64	695.80	693.49	692.68	692.40
40000	741.23	735.08	730.17	726.25	723.10	720.57	718.53	716.89	715.57	714.51	713.65	711.27	710.44	710.16
41000	759.76	753.46	748.43	744.40	741.17	738.58	736.50	734.82	733.46	732.37	731.49	729.05	728.20	727.91
42000	778.30	771.83	766.68	762.56	759.25	756.60	754.46	752.74	751.35	750.23	749.33	746.83	745.97	745.67
43000	796.83	790.21	784.93	780.71	777.33	774.61	772.42	770.66	769.24	768.09	767.17	764.61	763.73	763.42
44000	815.36	808.59	803.19	798.87	795.41	792.62	790.39	788.58	787.13	785.96	785.01	782.39	781.49	781.17
45000	833.89	826.96	821.44	817.03	813.48	810.64	808.35	806.51	805.02	803.82	802.85	800.18	799.25	798.93
46000	852.42	845.34	839.70	835.18	831.56	828.65	826.31	824.43	822.91	821.68	820.69	817.96	817.01	816.68
47000	870.95	863.72	857.95	853.34	849.64	846.67	844.28	842.35	840.80	839.54	838.53	835.74	834.77	834.43
48000	889.48	882.09	876.21	871.49	867.72	864.68	862.24	860.27	858.69	857.41	856.37	853.52	852.53	852.19
49000	908.01	900.47	894.46	889.65	885.79	882.70	880.20	878.19	876.58	875.27	874.21	871.30	870.29	869.94
50000	926.54	918.85	912.71	907.81	903.87	900.71	898.17	896.12	894.47	893.13	892.06	889.08	888.05	887.70
55000	1019.19	1010.73	1003.98	998.59	994.26	990.78	987.98	985.73	983.91	982.44	981.26	977.99	976.86	976.46
60000	1111.85	1102.62	1095.26	1089.37	1084.64	1080.85	1077.80	1075.34	1073.36	1071.76	1070.47	1066.90	1065.66	1065.23
65000	1204.50	1194.50	1186.53	1180.15	1175.03	1170.92	1167.61	1164.95	1162.80	1161.07	1159.67	1155.81	1154.47	1154.00
70000	1297.16	1286.39	1277.80	1270.93	1265.42	1260.99	1257.43	1254.56	1252.25	1250.38	1248.88	1244.71	1243.27	1242.77
75000	1389.81	1378.27	1369.07	1361.71	1355.80	1351.06	1347.25	1344.17	1341.70	1339.70	1338.08	1333.62	1332.08	1331.54
80000	1482.46	1470.15	1460.34	1452.49	1446.19	1441.13	1437.06	1433.78	1431.14	1429.01	1427.29	1422.53	1420.88	1420.31
85000	1575.12	1562.04	1551.61	1543.27	1536.58	1531.20	1526.88	1523.40	1520.59	1518.32	1516.49	1511.44	1509.69	1509.08
90000	1667.77	1653.92	1642.88	1634.05	1626.96	1621.27	1616.69	1613.01	1610.03	1607.63	1605.70	1600.35	1598.49	1597.85
95000	1760.42	1745.81	1734.15	1724.83	1717.35	1711.34	1706.51	1702.62	1699.48	1696.95	1694.90	1689.25	1687.30	1686.62
100000	1853.08	1837.69	1825.42	1815.61	1807.74	1801.41	1796.33	1792.23	1788.93	1786.26	1784.11	1778.16	1776.10	1775.39

MONTHLY PAYMENT
REQUIRED TO AMORTIZE A LOAN

TERM	1 Year	2 Years	3 Years	4 Years	5 Years	6 Years	7 Years	8 Years	9 Years	10 Years	11 Years	12 Years	13 Years	14 Years
AMOUNT														
5	.47	.26	.19	.16	.14	.13	.12	.11	.11	.11	.10	.10	.10	.10
10	.94	.52	.38	.32	.28	.25	.24	.22	.21	.21	.20	.20	.20	.19
15	1.40	.78	.57	.47	.41	.38	.35	.33	.32	.31	.30	.30	.29	.29
25	2.34	1.29	.95	.78	.69	.62	.58	.55	.53	.51	.50	.49	.48	.47
50	4.67	2.58	1.90	1.56	1.37	1.24	1.16	1.10	1.05	1.02	.99	.97	.96	.94
75	7.00	3.87	2.85	2.34	2.05	1.86	1.73	1.64	1.57	1.52	1.48	1.46	1.43	1.41
100	9.33	5.16	3.79	3.12	2.73	2.48	2.31	2.19	2.10	2.03	1.98	1.94	1.91	1.88
200	18.66	10.32	7.58	6.24	5.46	4.96	4.61	4.37	4.19	4.05	3.95	3.87	3.81	3.76
300	27.99	15.48	11.37	9.36	8.18	7.43	6.92	6.55	6.28	6.08	5.92	5.81	5.71	5.64
400	37.32	20.63	15.15	12.47	10.91	9.91	9.22	8.73	8.37	8.10	7.90	7.74	7.61	7.52
500	46.65	25.79	18.94	15.59	13.64	12.38	11.53	10.91	10.47	10.13	9.87	9.67	9.52	9.39
600	55.98	30.95	22.73	18.71	16.36	14.86	13.83	13.10	12.56	12.15	11.84	11.61	11.42	11.27
700	65.31	36.10	26.51	21.82	19.09	17.33	16.13	15.28	14.65	14.18	13.82	13.54	13.32	13.15
800	74.64	41.26	30.30	24.94	21.82	19.81	18.44	17.46	16.74	16.20	15.79	15.47	15.22	15.03
900	83.97	46.42	34.09	28.06	24.54	22.29	20.74	19.64	18.83	18.23	17.76	17.41	17.13	16.91
1000	93.30	51.58	37.87	31.17	27.27	24.76	23.05	21.82	20.93	20.25	19.74	19.34	19.03	18.78
2000	186.59	103.15	75.74	62.34	54.53	49.52	46.09	43.64	41.85	40.50	39.47	38.67	38.05	37.56
3000	279.89	154.72	113.61	93.51	81.80	74.27	69.13	65.46	62.77	60.74	59.20	58.01	57.08	56.34
4000	373.18	206.29	151.48	124.68	109.06	99.03	92.17	87.28	83.69	80.99	78.93	77.34	76.10	75.12
5000	466.47	257.86	189.34	155.84	136.33	123.79	115.21	109.10	104.61	101.23	98.66	96.67	95.12	93.90
6000	559.77	309.43	227.21	187.01	163.59	148.54	138.25	130.92	125.53	121.48	118.39	116.01	114.15	112.68
7000	653.06	361.00	265.08	218.18	190.86	173.30	161.30	152.74	146.45	141.73	138.12	135.34	133.17	131.46
8000	746.36	412.57	302.95	249.35	218.12	198.06	184.34	174.55	167.37	161.97	157.85	154.67	152.19	150.24
9000	839.65	464.14	340.82	280.51	245.39	222.81	207.38	196.37	188.29	182.22	177.59	174.01	171.22	169.02
10000	932.94	515.71	378.68	311.68	272.65	247.57	230.42	218.19	209.21	202.46	197.32	193.34	190.24	187.80
11000	1026.24	567.28	416.55	342.85	299.92	272.33	253.46	240.01	230.13	222.71	217.05	212.67	209.26	206.58
12000	1119.53	618.85	454.42	374.02	327.18	297.08	276.50	261.83	251.05	242.96	236.78	232.01	228.29	225.36
13000	1212.83	670.42	492.29	405.19	354.45	321.84	299.54	283.65	271.97	263.20	256.51	251.34	247.31	244.14
14000	1306.12	721.99	530.16	436.35	381.71	346.60	322.59	305.47	292.89	283.45	276.24	270.68	266.33	262.92
15000	1399.41	773.56	568.02	467.52	408.98	371.35	345.63	327.28	313.81	303.69	295.97	290.01	285.36	281.70
16000	1492.71	825.13	605.89	498.69	436.24	396.11	368.67	349.10	334.73	323.94	315.70	309.34	304.38	300.48
17000	1586.00	876.70	643.76	529.86	463.51	420.87	391.71	370.92	355.65	344.18	335.44	328.68	323.40	319.26
18000	1679.29	928.27	681.63	561.02	490.77	445.62	414.75	392.74	376.57	364.43	355.17	348.01	342.43	338.04
19000	1772.59	979.84	719.49	592.19	518.03	470.38	437.79	414.56	397.49	384.68	374.90	367.34	361.45	356.82
20000	1865.88	1031.41	757.36	623.36	545.30	495.13	460.83	436.38	418.41	404.92	394.63	386.68	380.47	375.60
21000	1959.18	1082.98	795.23	654.53	572.56	519.89	483.88	458.20	439.33	425.17	414.36	406.01	399.50	394.38
22000	2052.47	1134.55	833.10	685.70	599.83	544.65	506.92	480.01	460.25	445.41	434.09	425.34	418.52	413.16
23000	2145.76	1186.12	870.97	716.86	627.09	569.40	529.96	501.83	481.17	465.66	453.82	444.68	437.54	431.94
24000	2239.06	1237.69	908.83	746.03	654.36	594.16	553.00	523.65	502.09	485.91	473.55	464.01	456.57	450.72
25000	2332.35	1289.26	946.70	779.20	681.62	618.92	576.04	545.47	523.01	506.15	493.28	483.34	475.59	469.50
26000	2425.64	1340.83	984.57	810.37	708.89	643.67	599.08	567.29	543.93	526.40	513.02	502.68	494.61	488.28
27000	2518.94	1392.40	1022.44	841.53	736.15	668.43	622.12	589.11	564.85	546.64	532.75	522.01	513.64	507.06
28000	2612.23	1443.97	1060.31	872.70	763.42	693.19	645.17	610.93	585.77	566.89	552.48	541.35	532.66	525.84
29000	2705.53	1495.54	1098.17	903.87	790.68	717.94	668.21	632.74	606.69	587.13	572.21	560.68	551.68	544.62
30000	2798.82	1547.11	1136.04	935.04	817.95	742.70	691.25	654.56	627.61	607.38	591.94	580.01	570.71	563.39
31000	2892.11	1598.68	1173.91	966.21	845.21	767.46	714.29	676.38	648.53	627.63	611.67	599.35	589.73	582.17
32000	2985.41	1650.25	1211.78	997.37	872.48	792.21	737.33	698.20	669.45	647.87	631.40	618.68	608.75	600.95
33000	3078.70	1701.82	1249.65	1028.54	899.74	816.97	760.37	720.02	690.37	668.12	651.13	638.01	627.78	619.73
34000	3172.00	1753.39	1287.51	1059.71	927.01	841.73	783.42	741.84	711.29	688.36	670.87	657.35	646.80	638.51
35000	3265.29	1804.96	1325.38	1090.88	954.27	866.48	806.46	763.66	732.21	708.61	690.60	676.68	665.82	657.29
36000	3358.58	1856.53	1363.25	1122.04	981.54	891.24	829.50	785.47	753.13	728.86	710.33	696.01	684.85	676.07
37000	3451.88	1908.10	1401.12	1153.21	1008.80	915.99	852.54	807.29	774.05	749.10	730.06	715.35	703.87	694.85
38000	3545.17	1959.67	1438.98	1184.38	1036.06	940.75	875.58	829.11	794.97	769.35	749.79	734.68	722.89	713.63
39000	3638.46	2011.24	1476.85	1215.55	1063.33	965.51	898.62	850.93	815.89	789.59	769.52	754.01	741.92	732.41
40000	3731.76	2062.81	1514.72	1246.72	1090.59	990.26	921.66	872.75	836.82	809.84	789.25	773.35	760.94	751.19
41000	3825.05	2114.38	1552.59	1277.88	1117.86	1015.02	944.71	894.57	857.74	830.08	808.98	792.68	779.97	769.97
42000	3918.35	2165.95	1590.46	1309.05	1145.12	1039.78	967.75	916.39	878.66	850.33	828.72	812.02	798.99	788.75
43000	4011.64	2217.52	1628.32	1340.22	1172.39	1064.53	990.79	938.20	899.58	870.58	848.45	831.35	818.01	807.53
44000	4104.93	2269.09	1666.19	1371.39	1199.65	1089.29	1013.83	960.02	920.50	890.82	868.18	850.68	837.04	826.31
45000	4198.23	2320.66	1704.06	1402.55	1226.92	1114.05	1036.87	981.84	941.42	911.07	887.91	870.02	856.06	845.09
46000	4291.52	2372.23	1741.93	1433.72	1254.18	1138.80	1059.91	1003.66	962.34	931.31	907.64	889.35	875.08	863.87
47000	4384.82	2423.80	1779.80	1464.89	1281.45	1163.56	1082.95	1025.48	983.26	951.56	927.37	908.68	894.11	882.65
48000	4478.11	2475.37	1817.66	1496.06	1308.71	1188.32	1106.00	1047.30	1004.18	971.81	947.10	928.02	913.13	901.43
49000	4571.40	2526.94	1855.53	1527.22	1335.98	1213.07	1129.04	1069.12	1025.10	992.05	966.83	947.35	932.15	920.21
50000	4664.70	2578.51	1893.40	1558.39	1363.24	1237.83	1152.08	1090.93	1046.02	1012.30	986.56	966.68	951.18	938.99
55000	5131.17	2836.36	2082.74	1714.23	1499.57	1361.61	1267.29	1200.03	1150.62	1113.53	1085.22	1063.35	1046.29	1032.89
60000	5597.64	3094.21	2272.08	1870.07	1635.89	1485.39	1382.49	1309.12	1255.22	1214.76	1183.88	1160.02	1141.41	1126.78
65000	6064.10	3352.06	2461.42	2025.91	1772.21	1609.18	1497.70	1418.21	1359.82	1315.98	1282.53	1256.69	1236.53	1220.68
70000	6530.57	3609.91	2650.76	2181.75	1908.54	1732.96	1612.91	1527.31	1464.42	1417.21	1381.19	1353.36	1331.64	1314.58
75000	6997.04	3867.76	2840.10	2337.59	2044.86	1856.74	1728.12	1636.40	1569.02	1518.44	1479.84	1450.02	1426.76	1408.48
80000	7463.51	4125.61	3029.44	2493.42	2181.18	1980.52	1843.32	1745.49	1673.63	1619.67	1578.50	1546.69	1521.88	1502.38
85000	7929.98	4383.46	3218.77	2649.26	2317.51	2104.30	1958.53	1854.58	1778.23	1720.90	1677.16	1643.36	1617.00	1596.28
90000	8396.45	4641.31	3408.11	2805.10	2453.83	2228.09	2073.74	1963.68	1882.83	1822.13	1775.81	1740.03	1712.11	1690.17
95000	8862.92	4899.16	3597.45	2960.94	2590.15	2351.87	2188.95	2072.77	1987.43	1923.36	1874.47	1836.70	1807.23	1784.07
100000	9329.39	5157.01	3786.79	3116.78	2726.48	2475.65	2304.15	2181.86	2092.03	2024.59	1973.12	1933.36	1902.35	1877.97

TERM	15 Years	16 Years	17 Years	18 Years	19 Years	20 Years	21 Years	22 Years	23 Years	24 Years	25 Years	30 Years	35 Years	40 Years
AMOUNT														
5	.10	.10	.10	.10	.10	.10	.10	.09	.09	.09	.09	.09	.09	.09
10	.19	.19	.19	.19	.19	.19	.19	.18	.18	.18	.18	.18	.18	.18
15	.28	.28	.28	.28	.28	.28	.28	.27	.27	.27	.27	.27	.27	.27
25	.47	.47	.46	.46	.46	.46	.46	.45	.45	.45	.45	.45	.45	.45
50	.93	.93	.92	.92	.91	.91	.91	.90	.90	.90	.90	.90	.90	.90
75	1.40	1.39	1.38	1.37	1.37	1.36	1.36	1.35	1.35	1.35	1.35	1.34	1.34	1.34
100	1.86	1.85	1.84	1.83	1.82	1.81	1.81	1.80	1.80	1.80	1.80	1.79	1.79	1.79
200	3.72	3.69	3.67	3.65	3.63	3.62	3.61	3.60	3.59	3.59	3.59	3.57	3.57	3.57
300	5.58	5.54	5.50	5.47	5.45	5.43	5.41	5.40	5.39	5.38	5.38	5.36	5.35	5.35
400	7.44	7.38	7.33	7.29	7.26	7.23	7.21	7.20	7.18	7.17	7.17	7.14	7.13	7.13
500	9.30	9.22	9.16	9.11	9.07	9.04	9.02	9.00	8.98	8.97	8.96	8.93	8.92	8.91
600	11.16	11.07	10.99	10.93	10.89	10.85	10.82	10.79	10.77	10.76	10.75	10.71	10.70	10.69
700	13.02	12.91	12.82	12.76	12.70	12.66	12.62	12.59	12.57	12.55	12.54	12.50	12.48	12.48
800	14.87	14.75	14.65	14.58	14.51	14.46	14.42	14.39	14.36	14.34	14.33	14.28	14.26	14.26
900	16.73	16.60	16.49	16.40	16.33	16.27	16.23	16.19	16.16	16.14	16.12	16.06	16.05	16.04
1000	18.59	18.44	18.32	18.22	18.14	18.08	18.03	17.99	17.95	17.93	17.91	17.85	17.83	17.82
2000	37.18	36.87	36.63	36.43	36.28	36.15	36.05	35.97	35.90	35.85	35.81	35.69	35.65	35.64
3000	55.77	55.31	54.94	54.65	54.41	54.23	54.07	53.95	53.85	53.78	53.71	53.54	53.47	53.45
4000	74.35	73.74	73.25	72.86	72.55	72.30	72.10	71.94	71.80	71.70	71.61	71.38	71.30	71.27
5000	92.94	92.17	91.56	91.08	90.69	90.37	90.12	89.92	89.75	89.62	89.52	89.22	89.12	89.09
6000	111.53	110.61	109.88	109.29	108.82	108.45	108.14	107.90	107.70	107.55	107.42	107.07	106.94	106.90
7000	130.11	129.04	128.19	127.51	126.96	126.52	126.17	125.88	125.65	125.47	125.32	124.91	124.77	124.72
8000	148.70	147.48	146.50	145.72	145.10	144.59	144.19	143.87	143.60	143.39	143.22	142.75	142.59	142.53
9000	167.29	165.91	164.81	163.94	163.23	162.67	162.21	161.85	161.55	161.32	161.12	160.60	160.41	160.35
10000	185.87	184.34	183.12	182.15	181.37	180.74	180.24	179.83	179.50	179.24	179.03	178.44	178.24	178.17
11000	204.46	202.78	201.44	200.36	199.50	198.81	198.26	197.81	197.45	197.16	196.93	196.28	196.06	195.98
12000	223.05	221.21	219.75	218.58	217.64	216.89	216.28	215.80	215.40	215.09	214.83	214.13	213.88	213.80
13000	241.64	239.65	238.06	236.79	235.78	234.96	234.31	233.78	233.35	233.01	232.73	231.97	231.71	231.62
14000	260.22	258.08	256.37	255.01	253.91	253.04	252.33	251.76	251.30	250.93	250.64	249.81	249.53	249.43
15000	278.81	276.51	274.68	273.22	272.05	271.11	270.35	269.74	269.25	268.86	268.54	267.66	267.35	267.25
16000	297.40	294.95	293.00	291.44	290.19	289.18	288.38	287.73	287.20	286.78	286.44	285.50	285.18	285.06
17000	315.98	313.38	311.31	309.65	308.32	307.26	306.40	305.71	305.15	304.70	304.34	303.34	303.00	302.88
18000	334.57	331.82	329.62	327.87	326.46	325.33	324.42	323.69	323.10	322.63	322.24	321.19	320.82	320.70
19000	353.16	350.25	347.93	346.08	344.59	343.40	342.44	341.67	341.05	340.55	340.15	339.03	338.65	338.51
20000	371.74	368.68	366.24	364.29	362.73	361.48	360.47	359.66	359.00	358.47	358.05	356.87	356.47	356.33
21000	390.33	387.12	384.56	382.51	380.87	379.55	378.49	377.64	376.95	376.40	375.95	374.72	374.29	374.15
22000	408.92	405.55	402.87	400.72	399.00	397.62	396.51	395.62	394.90	394.32	393.85	392.56	392.12	391.96
23000	427.51	423.99	421.18	418.94	417.14	415.70	414.54	413.60	412.85	412.24	411.75	410.41	409.94	409.78
24000	446.09	442.42	439.49	437.15	435.28	433.77	432.56	431.59	430.80	430.17	429.66	428.25	427.76	427.59
25000	464.68	460.85	457.80	455.37	453.41	451.84	450.58	449.57	448.75	448.09	447.56	446.09	445.59	445.41
26000	483.27	479.29	476.12	473.58	471.55	469.92	468.61	467.55	466.70	466.01	465.46	463.94	463.41	463.23
27000	501.85	497.72	494.43	491.80	489.69	487.99	486.63	485.53	484.65	483.94	483.36	481.78	481.23	481.04
28000	520.44	516.16	512.74	510.01	507.82	506.07	504.65	503.52	502.60	501.86	501.27	499.62	499.06	498.86
29000	539.03	534.59	531.05	528.22	525.96	524.14	522.68	521.50	520.55	519.78	519.17	517.47	516.88	516.68
30000	557.61	553.02	549.36	546.44	544.09	542.21	540.70	539.48	538.50	537.71	537.07	535.31	534.70	534.49
31000	576.20	571.46	567.68	564.65	562.23	560.29	558.72	557.46	556.45	555.63	554.97	553.15	552.53	552.31
32000	594.79	589.89	585.99	582.87	580.37	578.36	576.75	575.45	574.40	573.56	572.87	571.00	570.35	570.12
33000	613.38	608.33	604.30	601.08	598.50	596.43	594.77	593.43	592.35	591.48	590.78	588.84	588.17	587.94
34000	631.96	626.76	622.61	619.30	616.64	614.51	612.79	611.41	610.30	609.40	608.68	606.68	605.99	605.76
35000	650.55	645.19	640.92	637.51	634.78	632.58	630.82	629.39	628.25	627.33	626.58	624.53	623.82	623.57
36000	669.14	663.63	659.24	655.73	652.91	650.65	648.84	647.38	646.20	645.25	644.48	642.37	641.64	641.39
37000	687.72	682.06	677.55	673.94	671.05	668.73	666.86	665.36	664.15	663.17	662.38	660.21	659.46	659.21
38000	706.31	700.50	695.86	692.15	689.18	686.80	684.88	683.34	682.10	681.10	680.29	678.06	677.29	677.02
39000	724.90	718.93	714.17	710.37	707.32	704.87	702.91	701.32	700.05	699.02	698.19	695.90	695.11	694.84
40000	743.48	737.36	732.48	728.58	725.46	722.95	720.93	719.31	718.00	716.94	716.09	713.74	712.93	712.65
41000	762.07	755.80	750.80	746.80	743.59	741.02	738.95	737.29	735.95	734.87	733.99	731.59	730.76	730.47
42000	780.66	774.23	769.11	765.01	761.73	759.10	756.98	755.27	753.90	752.79	751.90	749.43	748.58	748.29
43000	799.24	792.66	787.42	783.23	779.87	777.17	775.00	773.25	771.85	770.71	769.80	767.27	766.40	766.10
44000	817.83	811.10	805.73	801.44	798.00	795.24	793.02	791.24	789.80	788.64	787.70	785.12	784.23	783.92
45000	836.42	829.53	824.04	819.66	816.14	813.32	811.05	809.22	807.75	806.56	805.60	802.96	802.05	801.73
46000	855.01	847.97	842.36	837.87	834.28	831.39	829.07	827.20	825.70	824.48	823.50	820.81	819.87	819.55
47000	873.59	866.40	860.67	856.08	852.41	849.46	847.09	845.18	843.65	842.41	841.41	838.65	837.70	837.37
48000	892.18	884.83	878.98	874.30	870.55	867.54	865.12	863.17	861.60	860.33	859.31	856.49	855.52	855.18
49000	910.77	903.27	897.29	892.51	888.68	885.61	883.14	881.15	879.55	878.25	877.21	874.34	873.34	873.00
50000	929.35	921.70	915.60	910.73	906.82	903.68	901.16	899.13	897.50	896.18	895.11	892.18	891.17	890.82
55000	1022.29	1013.87	1007.16	1001.80	997.50	994.05	991.28	989.04	987.25	985.79	984.62	981.40	980.28	979.90
60000	1115.22	1106.04	1098.72	1092.87	1088.18	1084.42	1081.39	1078.96	1076.99	1075.41	1074.13	1070.61	1069.40	1068.98
65000	1208.16	1198.21	1190.28	1183.94	1178.87	1174.79	1171.51	1168.87	1166.74	1165.03	1163.65	1159.83	1158.51	1158.06
70000	1301.09	1290.38	1281.84	1275.02	1269.55	1265.16	1261.63	1258.78	1256.49	1254.65	1253.16	1249.05	1247.63	1247.14
75000	1394.03	1382.55	1373.40	1366.09	1360.23	1355.52	1351.74	1348.70	1346.24	1344.26	1342.67	1338.27	1336.75	1336.22
80000	1486.96	1474.72	1464.96	1457.16	1450.91	1445.89	1441.86	1438.61	1435.99	1433.88	1432.18	1427.48	1425.86	1425.30
85000	1579.90	1566.89	1556.52	1548.23	1541.59	1536.26	1531.97	1528.52	1525.74	1523.50	1521.69	1516.70	1514.98	1514.38
90000	1672.83	1659.06	1648.08	1639.31	1632.27	1626.63	1622.09	1618.43	1615.49	1613.11	1611.20	1605.92	1604.10	1603.46
95000	1765.77	1751.23	1739.64	1730.38	1722.95	1717.00	1712.20	1708.35	1705.24	1702.73	1700.71	1695.14	1693.21	1692.55
100000	1858.70	1843.40	1831.20	1821.45	1813.64	1807.36	1802.32	1798.26	1794.99	1792.35	1790.22	1784.35	1782.33	1781.63

21.400%

TERM AMOUNT	1 Year	2 Years	3 Years	4 Years	5 Years	6 Years	7 Years	8 Years	9 Years	10 Years	11 Years	12 Years	13 Years	14 Years
5	.47	.26	.19	.16	.14	.13	.12	.11	.11	.11	.10	.10	.10	.10
10	.94	.52	.38	.32	.28	.25	.24	.22	.21	.21	.20	.20	.20	.19
15	1.40	.78	.57	.47	.41	.38	.35	.33	.32	.31	.30	.30	.29	.29
25	2.34	1.29	.95	.78	.69	.62	.58	.55	.53	.51	.50	.49	.48	.47
50	4.67	2.58	1.90	1.56	1.37	1.24	1.16	1.10	1.05	1.02	.99	.97	.96	.94
75	7.00	3.87	2.85	2.34	2.05	1.86	1.73	1.64	1.58	1.52	1.49	1.46	1.43	1.41
100	9.34	5.16	3.79	3.12	2.73	2.48	2.31	2.19	2.10	2.03	1.98	1.94	1.91	1.88
200	18.67	10.32	7.58	6.24	5.46	4.96	4.62	4.37	4.19	4.06	3.95	3.88	3.81	3.76
300	28.00	15.48	11.37	9.36	8.19	7.44	6.92	6.56	6.29	6.08	5.93	5.81	5.72	5.64
400	37.33	20.64	15.16	12.48	10.92	9.91	9.23	8.74	8.38	8.11	7.90	7.75	7.62	7.52
500	46.66	25.80	18.95	15.60	13.64	12.39	11.53	10.92	10.47	10.14	9.88	9.68	9.53	9.40
600	55.99	30.95	22.73	18.71	16.37	14.87	13.84	13.11	12.57	12.16	11.85	11.62	11.43	11.28
700	65.32	36.11	26.52	21.83	19.10	17.34	16.14	15.29	14.66	14.19	13.83	13.55	13.33	13.16
800	74.65	41.27	30.31	24.95	21.83	19.82	18.45	17.47	16.75	16.22	15.80	15.49	15.24	15.04
900	83.98	46.43	34.10	28.07	24.56	22.30	20.76	19.66	18.85	18.24	17.78	17.42	17.14	16.92
1000	93.31	51.59	37.89	31.19	27.28	24.78	23.06	21.84	20.94	20.27	19.75	19.36	19.05	18.80
2000	186.62	103.17	75.77	62.37	54.56	49.55	46.12	43.67	41.88	40.53	39.50	38.71	38.09	37.60
3000	279.92	154.75	113.65	93.55	81.84	74.32	69.18	65.51	62.81	60.79	59.25	58.06	57.13	56.40
4000	373.23	206.33	151.53	124.73	109.12	99.09	92.23	87.34	83.75	81.06	79.00	77.41	76.17	75.20
5000	466.53	257.92	189.41	155.91	136.40	123.86	115.29	109.18	104.69	101.32	98.75	96.76	95.21	94.00
6000	559.84	309.50	227.29	187.09	163.68	148.63	138.35	131.01	125.62	121.58	118.50	116.11	114.25	112.79
7000	653.15	361.08	265.17	218.27	190.96	173.40	161.40	152.85	146.56	141.84	138.24	135.46	133.30	131.59
8000	746.45	412.66	303.05	249.45	218.24	198.17	184.46	174.68	167.50	162.11	157.99	154.82	152.34	150.39
9000	839.76	464.25	340.93	280.64	245.51	222.95	207.52	196.52	188.43	182.37	177.74	174.17	171.38	169.19
10000	933.06	515.83	378.81	311.82	272.79	247.72	230.57	218.35	209.37	202.63	197.49	193.52	190.42	187.99
11000	1026.37	567.41	416.69	343.00	300.07	272.49	253.63	240.18	230.31	222.89	217.24	212.87	209.46	206.78
12000	1119.68	618.99	454.57	374.18	327.35	297.26	276.69	262.02	251.24	243.16	236.99	232.22	228.50	225.58
13000	1212.98	670.58	492.45	405.36	354.63	322.03	299.74	283.85	272.18	263.42	256.74	251.57	247.55	244.38
14000	1306.29	722.16	530.34	436.54	381.91	346.80	322.80	305.69	293.12	283.68	276.48	270.92	266.59	263.18
15000	1399.59	773.74	568.22	467.72	409.19	371.57	345.86	327.52	314.05	303.95	296.23	290.27	285.63	281.98
16000	1492.90	825.32	606.10	498.90	436.47	396.34	368.91	349.36	334.99	324.21	315.98	309.63	304.67	300.78
17000	1586.20	876.90	643.98	530.09	463.75	421.12	391.97	371.19	355.93	344.47	335.73	328.98	323.71	319.57
18000	1679.51	928.49	681.86	561.27	491.02	445.89	415.03	393.03	376.86	364.73	355.48	348.33	342.75	338.37
19000	1772.82	980.07	719.74	592.45	518.30	470.66	438.08	414.86	397.80	385.00	375.23	367.68	361.79	357.17
20000	1866.12	1031.65	757.62	623.64	545.58	495.43	461.14	436.69	418.74	405.26	394.98	387.03	380.84	375.97
21000	1959.43	1083.23	795.50	654.81	572.86	520.20	484.20	458.53	439.67	425.52	414.72	406.38	399.88	394.77
22000	2052.73	1134.82	833.38	685.99	600.14	544.97	507.25	480.36	460.61	445.78	434.47	425.73	418.92	413.56
23000	2146.04	1186.40	871.26	717.17	627.42	569.74	530.31	502.20	481.55	466.05	454.22	445.09	437.96	432.36
24000	2239.35	1237.98	909.14	748.35	654.70	594.51	553.37	524.03	502.48	486.31	473.97	464.44	457.00	451.16
25000	2332.65	1289.56	947.02	779.54	681.98	619.29	576.42	545.87	523.42	506.57	493.72	483.79	476.04	469.96
26000	2425.96	1341.15	984.90	810.72	709.26	644.06	599.48	567.70	544.36	526.84	513.47	503.14	495.09	488.76
27000	2519.26	1392.73	1022.79	841.90	736.53	668.83	622.54	589.54	565.29	547.10	533.22	522.49	514.13	507.55
28000	2612.57	1444.31	1060.67	873.08	763.81	693.60	645.60	611.37	586.23	567.36	552.96	541.84	533.17	526.35
29000	2705.87	1495.89	1098.55	904.26	791.09	718.37	668.65	633.20	607.17	587.62	572.71	561.19	552.21	545.15
30000	2799.18	1547.48	1136.43	935.44	818.37	743.14	691.71	655.04	628.10	607.89	592.46	580.54	571.25	563.95
31000	2892.49	1599.06	1174.31	966.62	845.65	767.91	714.77	676.87	649.04	628.15	612.21	599.90	590.29	582.75
32000	2985.79	1650.64	1212.19	997.80	872.93	792.68	737.82	698.71	669.98	648.41	631.96	619.25	609.33	601.55
33000	3079.10	1702.22	1250.07	1028.99	900.21	817.46	760.88	720.54	690.91	668.67	651.71	638.60	628.38	620.34
34000	3172.40	1753.80	1287.95	1060.17	927.49	842.23	783.94	742.38	711.85	688.94	671.46	657.95	647.42	639.14
35000	3265.71	1805.39	1325.83	1091.35	954.76	867.00	806.99	764.21	732.79	709.20	691.20	677.30	666.46	657.94
36000	3359.02	1856.97	1363.71	1122.53	982.04	891.77	830.05	786.05	753.72	729.46	710.95	696.65	685.50	676.74
37000	3452.32	1908.55	1401.59	1153.71	1009.32	916.54	853.11	807.88	774.66	749.73	730.70	716.00	704.54	695.54
38000	3545.63	1960.13	1439.47	1184.90	1036.60	941.31	876.16	829.71	795.60	769.99	750.45	735.36	723.58	714.33
39000	3638.93	2011.72	1477.35	1216.07	1063.88	966.08	899.22	851.55	816.53	790.25	770.20	754.71	742.63	733.13
40000	3732.24	2063.30	1515.24	1247.25	1091.16	990.85	922.28	873.38	837.47	810.51	789.95	774.06	761.67	751.93
41000	3825.55	2114.88	1553.12	1278.44	1118.44	1015.63	945.33	895.22	858.41	830.78	809.69	793.41	780.71	770.73
42000	3918.85	2166.46	1591.00	1309.62	1145.72	1040.40	968.39	917.05	879.34	851.04	829.44	812.76	799.75	789.53
43000	4012.16	2218.05	1628.88	1340.80	1173.00	1065.17	991.45	938.89	900.28	871.30	849.19	832.11	818.79	808.32
44000	4105.46	2269.63	1666.76	1371.98	1200.27	1089.94	1014.50	960.72	921.22	891.56	868.94	851.46	837.83	827.12
45000	4198.77	2321.21	1704.64	1403.16	1227.55	1114.71	1037.56	982.56	942.15	911.83	888.69	870.81	856.87	845.92
46000	4292.07	2372.79	1742.52	1434.34	1254.83	1139.48	1060.62	1004.39	963.09	932.09	908.44	890.17	875.92	864.72
47000	4385.38	2424.37	1780.40	1465.52	1282.11	1164.25	1083.67	1026.22	984.03	952.35	928.19	909.52	894.96	883.52
48000	4478.69	2475.96	1818.28	1496.70	1309.39	1189.02	1106.73	1048.06	1004.96	972.62	947.93	928.87	914.00	902.32
49000	4571.99	2527.54	1856.16	1527.89	1336.67	1213.79	1129.79	1069.89	1025.90	992.88	967.68	948.22	933.04	921.11
50000	4665.30	2579.12	1894.04	1559.07	1363.95	1238.57	1152.85	1091.73	1046.84	1013.14	987.43	967.57	952.08	939.91
55000	5131.83	2837.03	2083.45	1714.97	1500.34	1362.42	1268.13	1200.90	1151.52	1114.45	1086.17	1064.33	1047.29	1033.90
60000	5598.36	3094.95	2272.85	1870.88	1636.74	1486.28	1383.41	1310.07	1256.20	1215.77	1184.92	1161.08	1142.50	1127.89
65000	6064.89	3352.86	2462.25	2026.79	1773.13	1610.13	1498.70	1419.24	1360.89	1317.08	1283.66	1257.84	1237.71	1221.88
70000	6531.41	3610.77	2651.66	2182.69	1909.52	1733.99	1613.98	1528.42	1465.57	1418.40	1382.40	1354.60	1332.91	1315.87
75000	6997.94	3868.68	2841.06	2338.60	2045.92	1857.85	1729.26	1637.59	1570.25	1519.71	1481.15	1451.35	1428.12	1409.86
80000	7464.47	4126.59	3030.47	2494.50	2182.31	1981.70	1844.55	1746.76	1674.94	1621.02	1579.89	1548.11	1523.33	1503.86
85000	7931.00	4384.50	3219.87	2650.41	2318.71	2105.56	1959.83	1855.93	1779.62	1722.34	1678.63	1644.87	1618.54	1597.85
90000	8397.53	4642.42	3409.27	2806.32	2455.10	2075.12	1965.11	1883.10	1884.30	1823.65	1777.37	1741.62	1713.74	1691.84
95000	8864.06	4900.33	3598.68	2962.22	2591.50	2353.27	2190.40	2074.28	1988.99	1924.96	1876.12	1838.38	1808.95	1785.83
100000	9330.59	5158.24	3788.08	3118.13	2727.89	2477.13	2305.68	2183.45	2093.67	2026.28	1974.86	1935.14	1904.16	1879.82

TERM	15 Years	16 Years	17 Years	18 Years	19 Years	20 Years	21 Years	22 Years	23 Years	24 Years	25 Years	30 Years	35 Years	40 Years
AMOUNT														
5	.10	.10	.10	.10	.10	.10	.10	.10	.09	.09	.09	.09	.09	.09
10	.19	.19	.19	.19	.19	.19	.19	.19	.18	.18	.18	.18	.18	.18
15	.28	.28	.28	.28	.28	.28	.28	.28	.27	.27	.27	.27	.27	.27
25	.47	.47	.46	.46	.46	.46	.46	.46	.45	.45	.45	.45	.45	.45
50	.94	.93	.92	.92	.91	.91	.91	.91	.90	.90	.90	.90	.90	.90
75	1.40	1.39	1.38	1.37	1.37	1.36	1.36	1.36	1.35	1.35	1.35	1.34	1.34	1.34
100	1.87	1.85	1.84	1.83	1.82	1.81	1.81	1.81	1.80	1.80	1.80	1.79	1.79	1.79
200	3.73	3.70	3.67	3.65	3.64	3.62	3.61	3.61	3.60	3.59	3.59	3.58	3.57	3.57
300	5.59	5.54	5.50	5.48	5.45	5.43	5.42	5.41	5.40	5.39	5.38	5.36	5.36	5.36
400	7.45	7.39	7.34	7.30	7.27	7.24	7.22	7.21	7.19	7.18	7.17	7.15	7.14	7.14
500	9.31	9.23	9.17	9.12	9.08	9.05	9.03	9.01	8.99	8.98	8.97	8.94	8.93	8.92
600	11.17	11.08	11.00	10.95	10.90	10.86	10.83	10.81	10.79	10.77	10.76	10.72	10.71	10.71
700	13.03	12.92	12.84	12.77	12.71	12.67	12.64	12.61	12.58	12.57	12.55	12.51	12.50	12.49
800	14.89	14.77	14.67	14.59	14.53	14.48	14.44	14.41	14.38	14.36	14.34	14.30	14.28	14.27
900	16.75	16.61	16.50	16.42	16.35	16.29	16.24	16.21	16.18	16.15	16.14	16.08	16.06	16.06
1000	18.61	18.46	18.34	18.24	18.16	18.10	18.05	18.01	17.98	17.95	17.93	17.87	17.85	17.84
2000	37.22	36.91	36.67	36.47	36.32	36.19	36.09	36.01	35.95	35.89	35.85	35.73	35.69	35.68
3000	55.82	55.36	55.00	54.71	54.47	54.29	54.13	54.01	53.92	53.84	53.77	53.60	53.54	53.52
4000	74.43	73.82	73.33	72.94	72.63	72.38	72.18	72.02	71.89	71.78	71.70	71.46	71.38	71.35
5000	93.03	92.27	91.66	91.17	90.78	90.47	90.22	90.02	89.86	89.72	89.62	89.33	89.22	89.19
6000	111.64	110.72	109.99	109.41	108.94	108.57	108.26	108.02	107.83	107.67	107.54	107.19	107.07	107.03
7000	130.25	129.18	128.32	127.64	127.10	126.66	126.31	126.02	125.80	125.61	125.46	125.05	124.91	124.86
8000	148.85	147.63	146.65	145.88	145.25	144.75	144.35	144.03	143.77	143.55	143.39	142.92	142.76	142.70
9000	167.46	166.08	164.99	164.11	163.41	162.85	162.39	162.03	161.74	161.50	161.31	160.78	160.60	160.54
10000	186.06	184.53	183.32	182.34	181.56	180.94	180.44	180.03	179.71	179.44	179.23	178.65	178.44	178.38
11000	204.67	202.99	201.65	200.58	199.72	199.03	198.48	198.03	197.68	197.39	197.15	196.51	196.29	196.21
12000	223.27	221.44	219.98	218.81	217.88	217.13	216.52	216.04	215.65	215.33	215.08	214.37	214.13	214.05
13000	241.88	239.89	238.31	237.05	236.03	235.22	234.57	234.04	233.62	233.27	233.00	232.24	231.98	231.89
14000	260.49	258.35	256.64	255.28	254.19	253.31	252.61	252.04	251.59	251.22	250.92	250.10	249.82	249.72
15000	279.09	276.80	274.97	273.51	272.34	271.41	270.65	270.04	269.56	269.16	268.84	267.97	267.66	267.56
16000	297.70	295.25	293.30	291.75	290.50	289.50	288.70	288.05	287.53	287.10	286.77	285.83	285.51	285.40
17000	316.30	313.71	311.64	309.98	308.66	307.59	306.74	306.05	305.50	305.05	304.69	303.70	303.35	303.23
18000	334.91	332.16	329.97	328.22	326.81	325.69	324.78	324.05	323.47	322.99	322.61	321.56	321.20	321.07
19000	353.51	350.61	348.30	346.45	344.97	343.78	342.82	342.06	341.44	340.94	340.53	339.42	339.04	338.91
20000	372.12	369.06	366.63	364.68	363.12	361.87	360.87	360.06	359.41	358.88	358.46	357.29	356.88	356.75
21000	390.73	387.52	384.96	382.92	381.28	379.97	378.91	378.06	377.38	376.82	376.38	375.15	374.73	374.58
22000	409.33	405.97	403.29	401.15	399.44	398.06	396.96	396.06	395.35	394.77	394.30	393.02	392.57	392.42
23000	427.94	424.42	421.62	419.39	417.59	416.15	415.00	414.07	413.32	412.71	412.22	410.88	410.42	410.26
24000	446.54	442.88	439.95	437.62	435.75	434.25	433.04	432.07	431.29	430.65	430.15	428.74	428.26	428.09
25000	465.15	461.33	458.29	455.85	453.90	452.34	451.08	450.07	449.26	448.60	448.07	446.61	446.10	445.93
26000	483.75	479.78	476.62	474.09	472.06	470.43	469.13	468.07	467.23	466.54	465.99	464.47	463.95	463.77
27000	502.36	498.24	494.95	492.32	490.22	488.53	487.17	486.08	485.20	484.49	483.91	482.34	481.79	481.60
28000	520.97	516.69	513.28	510.56	508.37	506.62	505.21	504.08	503.17	502.43	501.84	500.20	499.64	499.44
29000	539.57	535.14	531.61	528.79	526.53	524.71	523.26	522.08	521.14	520.37	519.76	518.06	517.48	517.28
30000	558.18	553.59	549.94	547.02	544.68	542.81	541.30	540.08	539.11	538.32	537.68	535.93	535.32	535.12
31000	576.78	572.05	568.27	565.26	562.84	560.90	559.34	558.09	557.08	556.26	555.60	553.78	553.17	552.95
32000	595.39	590.50	586.60	583.49	581.00	578.99	577.39	576.09	575.05	574.20	573.53	571.66	571.01	570.79
33000	613.99	608.95	604.94	601.73	599.15	597.09	595.43	594.09	593.02	592.15	591.45	589.52	588.86	588.63
34000	632.60	627.41	623.27	619.96	617.31	615.18	613.47	612.10	610.99	610.09	609.37	607.39	606.70	606.46
35000	651.21	645.86	641.60	638.19	635.46	633.27	631.51	630.10	628.96	628.04	627.29	625.25	624.54	624.30
36000	669.81	664.31	659.93	656.43	653.62	651.37	649.56	648.10	646.93	645.98	645.22	643.11	642.39	642.14
37000	688.42	682.77	678.26	674.66	671.78	669.46	667.60	666.10	664.90	663.92	663.14	660.98	660.23	659.97
38000	707.02	701.22	696.59	692.89	689.93	687.56	685.64	684.11	682.87	681.87	681.06	678.84	678.08	677.81
39000	725.63	719.67	714.92	711.13	708.09	705.65	703.69	702.11	700.84	699.81	698.98	696.71	695.92	695.65
40000	744.23	738.12	733.25	729.36	726.24	723.74	721.73	720.11	718.81	717.75	716.91	714.57	713.76	713.49
41000	762.84	756.58	751.59	747.60	744.40	741.84	739.77	738.11	736.78	735.70	734.83	732.43	731.61	731.32
42000	781.45	775.03	769.92	765.83	762.56	759.93	757.82	756.12	754.75	753.64	752.75	750.30	749.45	749.16
43000	800.05	793.48	788.25	784.06	780.71	778.02	775.86	774.12	772.72	771.59	770.67	768.16	767.30	767.00
44000	818.66	811.94	806.58	802.30	798.87	796.12	793.90	792.12	790.69	789.53	788.60	786.03	785.14	784.83
45000	837.26	830.39	824.91	820.53	817.02	814.21	811.95	810.12	808.66	807.47	806.52	803.89	802.98	802.67
46000	855.87	848.84	843.24	838.77	835.18	832.30	829.99	828.13	826.63	825.42	824.44	821.75	820.83	820.51
47000	874.47	867.30	861.57	857.00	853.34	850.40	848.03	846.13	844.60	843.36	842.36	839.62	838.67	838.34
48000	893.08	885.75	879.90	875.23	871.49	868.49	866.08	864.13	862.57	861.30	860.29	857.48	856.52	856.18
49000	911.69	904.20	898.24	893.47	889.65	886.58	884.12	882.13	880.54	879.25	878.21	875.35	874.36	874.02
50000	930.29	922.65	916.57	911.70	907.80	904.68	902.16	900.14	898.51	897.19	896.13	893.21	892.20	891.86
55000	1023.32	1014.92	1008.22	1002.87	998.58	995.14	992.38	990.15	988.36	986.91	985.74	982.53	981.42	981.04
60000	1116.35	1107.18	1099.88	1094.04	1089.36	1085.61	1082.59	1080.16	1078.21	1076.63	1075.36	1071.85	1070.64	1070.23
65000	1209.38	1199.45	1191.54	1185.21	1180.14	1176.08	1172.81	1170.18	1168.06	1166.35	1164.97	1161.17	1159.86	1159.41
70000	1302.41	1291.71	1283.19	1276.38	1270.92	1266.54	1263.02	1260.19	1257.91	1256.07	1254.58	1250.49	1249.08	1248.60
75000	1395.44	1383.98	1374.85	1367.55	1361.70	1357.01	1353.24	1350.20	1347.76	1345.79	1344.20	1339.81	1338.30	1337.78
80000	1488.46	1476.24	1466.50	1458.72	1452.48	1447.48	1443.46	1440.22	1437.61	1435.50	1433.81	1429.13	1427.52	1426.97
85000	1581.49	1568.51	1558.16	1549.89	1543.26	1537.95	1533.67	1530.23	1527.46	1525.22	1523.42	1518.46	1516.74	1516.15
90000	1674.52	1660.77	1649.82	1641.06	1634.04	1628.41	1623.89	1620.24	1617.31	1614.94	1613.03	1607.78	1605.96	1605.34
95000	1767.55	1753.04	1741.47	1732.23	1724.82	1718.88	1714.10	1710.26	1707.16	1704.66	1702.65	1697.10	1695.18	1694.52
100000	1860.58	1845.30	1833.13	1823.40	1815.60	1809.35	1804.32	1800.27	1797.01	1794.38	1792.26	1786.42	1784.40	1783.71

21.500%

TERM	1 Year	2 Years	3 Years	4 Years	5 Years	6 Years	7 Years	8 Years	9 Years	10 Years	11 Years	12 Years	13 Years	14 Years
AMOUNT														
5	.47	.26	.19	.16	.14	.13	.12	.11	.11	.11	.10	.10	.10	.10
10	.94	.52	.38	.32	.28	.25	.24	.22	.22	.21	.20	.20	.20	.19
15	1.41	.78	.57	.47	.42	.38	.35	.33	.32	.31	.30	.30	.29	.29
25	2.34	1.30	.95	.79	.69	.63	.58	.55	.53	.51	.50	.49	.48	.48
50	4.67	2.59	1.90	1.57	1.37	1.25	1.16	1.10	1.06	1.02	1.00	.98	.96	.95
75	7.01	3.88	2.85	2.35	2.06	1.87	1.74	1.65	1.58	1.53	1.49	1.46	1.44	1.42
100	9.34	5.17	3.80	3.13	2.74	2.49	2.32	2.19	2.11	2.04	1.99	1.95	1.92	1.89
200	18.68	10.33	7.59	6.25	5.47	4.97	4.63	4.38	4.21	4.07	3.97	3.89	3.83	3.78
300	28.01	15.49	11.38	9.38	8.21	7.45	6.94	6.57	6.31	6.10	5.95	5.83	5.74	5.67
400	37.35	20.66	15.18	12.50	10.94	9.94	9.25	8.76	8.41	8.14	7.93	7.77	7.65	7.55
500	46.68	25.82	18.97	15.62	13.67	12.42	11.56	10.95	10.51	10.17	9.91	9.72	9.56	9.44
600	56.02	30.98	22.76	18.75	16.41	14.90	13.88	13.14	12.61	12.20	11.90	11.66	11.47	11.33
700	65.35	36.15	26.56	21.87	19.14	17.39	16.19	15.33	14.71	14.24	13.88	13.60	13.38	13.22
800	74.69	41.31	30.35	24.99	21.87	19.87	18.50	17.52	16.81	16.27	15.86	15.54	15.30	15.10
900	84.02	46.47	34.14	28.12	24.61	22.35	20.81	19.71	18.91	18.30	17.84	17.49	17.21	16.99
1000	93.36	51.64	37.94	31.24	27.34	24.84	23.12	21.90	21.01	20.34	19.82	19.43	19.12	18.88
2000	186.71	103.27	75.87	62.48	54.68	49.67	46.24	43.80	42.01	40.67	39.64	38.85	38.23	37.75
3000	280.07	154.90	113.80	93.71	82.01	74.50	69.36	65.70	63.01	61.00	59.46	58.27	57.35	56.62
4000	373.42	206.53	151.73	124.95	109.35	99.33	92.48	87.60	84.01	81.33	79.28	77.69	76.46	75.49
5000	466.77	258.16	189.67	156.18	136.68	124.16	115.60	109.50	105.02	101.66	99.09	97.12	95.58	94.37
6000	560.13	309.79	227.60	187.42	164.02	148.99	136.71	131.39	126.02	121.99	118.91	116.54	114.69	113.24
7000	653.48	361.43	265.53	218.65	191.35	173.82	161.83	153.29	147.02	142.32	138.73	135.96	133.80	132.11
8000	746.84	413.06	303.46	249.89	218.69	198.65	184.95	175.19	168.02	162.65	158.55	155.38	152.92	150.98
9000	840.19	464.69	341.40	281.12	246.02	223.48	208.07	197.09	189.03	182.98	178.37	174.81	172.03	169.85
10000	933.54	516.32	379.33	312.36	273.36	248.31	231.19	218.99	210.03	203.31	198.18	194.23	191.15	188.73
11000	1026.90	567.95	417.26	343.59	300.69	273.14	254.30	240.88	231.03	223.64	218.00	213.65	210.26	207.60
12000	1120.25	619.58	455.19	374.83	328.03	297.97	277.42	262.78	252.03	243.97	237.82	233.07	229.37	226.47
13000	1213.61	671.22	493.12	406.06	355.36	322.80	300.54	284.68	273.04	264.30	257.64	252.50	248.49	245.34
14000	1306.96	722.85	531.06	437.30	382.70	347.63	323.66	306.58	294.04	284.63	277.46	271.92	267.60	264.21
15000	1400.31	774.48	568.99	468.53	410.04	372.46	346.78	328.48	315.04	304.96	297.27	291.34	286.72	283.09
16000	1493.67	826.11	606.92	499.77	437.37	397.29	369.90	350.37	336.04	325.29	317.09	310.76	305.83	301.96
17000	1587.02	877.74	644.85	531.00	464.71	422.12	393.01	372.27	357.04	345.62	336.91	330.19	324.94	320.83
18000	1680.38	929.37	682.79	562.24	492.04	446.95	416.13	394.17	378.05	365.95	356.73	349.61	344.06	339.70
19000	1773.73	981.00	720.72	593.47	519.38	471.78	439.25	416.07	399.05	386.28	376.55	369.03	363.17	358.57
20000	1867.08	1032.64	758.65	624.71	546.71	496.61	462.37	437.97	420.05	406.61	396.36	388.45	382.29	377.45
21000	1960.44	1084.27	796.58	655.95	574.05	521.44	485.49	459.86	441.05	426.94	416.18	407.87	401.40	396.32
22000	2053.79	1135.90	834.52	687.18	601.38	546.27	508.60	481.76	462.06	447.27	436.00	427.30	420.51	415.19
23000	2147.14	1187.53	872.45	718.42	628.72	571.10	531.72	503.66	483.06	467.60	455.82	446.72	439.63	434.06
24000	2240.50	1239.16	910.38	749.65	656.05	595.93	554.84	525.56	504.06	487.93	475.64	466.14	458.74	452.93
25000	2333.85	1290.79	948.31	780.89	683.39	620.76	577.96	547.46	525.06	508.26	495.45	485.56	477.86	471.81
26000	2427.21	1342.43	986.24	812.12	710.72	645.59	601.08	569.35	546.07	528.59	515.27	504.99	496.97	490.68
27000	2520.56	1394.06	1024.18	843.36	738.06	670.42	624.19	591.25	567.07	548.92	535.09	524.41	516.09	509.55
28000	2613.91	1445.69	1062.11	874.59	765.40	695.25	647.31	613.15	588.07	569.25	554.91	543.83	535.20	528.42
29000	2707.27	1497.32	1100.04	905.83	792.73	720.08	670.43	635.05	609.07	589.58	574.73	563.25	554.31	547.29
30000	2800.62	1548.95	1137.97	937.06	820.07	744.91	693.55	656.95	630.07	609.92	594.54	582.68	573.43	566.17
31000	2893.98	1600.58	1175.91	968.30	847.40	769.74	716.67	678.84	651.08	630.25	614.36	602.10	592.54	585.04
32000	2987.33	1652.22	1213.84	999.53	874.74	794.57	739.79	700.74	672.08	650.58	634.18	621.52	611.66	603.91
33000	3080.68	1703.85	1251.77	1030.77	902.07	819.40	762.90	722.64	693.08	670.91	654.00	640.94	630.77	622.78
34000	3174.04	1755.48	1289.70	1062.00	929.41	844.23	786.02	744.54	714.08	691.24	673.81	660.37	649.88	641.65
35000	3267.39	1807.11	1327.63	1093.24	956.74	869.06	809.14	766.44	735.09	711.57	693.63	679.79	669.00	660.53
36000	3360.75	1858.74	1365.57	1124.47	984.08	893.89	832.26	788.33	756.09	731.90	713.45	699.21	688.11	679.40
37000	3454.10	1910.37	1403.50	1155.71	1011.41	918.72	855.38	810.23	777.09	752.23	733.27	718.63	707.23	698.27
38000	3547.45	1962.00	1441.43	1186.94	1038.75	943.55	878.49	832.13	798.09	772.56	753.09	738.06	726.34	717.14
39000	3640.81	2013.64	1479.36	1218.18	1066.08	968.38	901.61	854.03	819.10	792.89	772.90	757.48	745.45	736.01
40000	3734.16	2065.27	1517.30	1249.42	1093.42	993.21	924.73	875.93	840.10	813.22	792.72	776.90	764.57	754.89
41000	3827.52	2116.90	1555.23	1280.65	1120.76	1018.04	947.85	897.82	861.10	833.55	812.54	796.32	783.68	773.76
42000	3920.87	2168.53	1593.16	1311.89	1148.09	1042.87	970.97	919.72	882.10	853.88	832.36	815.74	802.80	792.63
43000	4014.22	2220.16	1631.09	1343.12	1175.43	1067.70	994.08	941.62	903.10	874.21	852.18	835.17	821.91	811.50
44000	4107.58	2271.79	1669.03	1374.36	1202.76	1092.53	1017.20	963.52	924.11	894.54	871.99	854.59	841.02	830.37
45000	4200.93	2323.43	1706.96	1405.59	1230.10	1117.36	1040.32	985.42	945.11	914.87	891.81	874.01	860.14	849.25
46000	4294.28	2375.06	1744.89	1436.83	1257.43	1142.19	1063.44	1007.31	966.11	935.20	911.63	893.43	879.25	868.12
47000	4387.64	2426.69	1782.82	1468.06	1284.77	1167.02	1086.56	1029.21	987.11	955.53	931.45	912.86	898.37	886.99
48000	4480.99	2478.32	1820.75	1499.30	1312.10	1191.85	1109.68	1051.11	1008.12	975.86	951.27	932.28	917.48	905.86
49000	4574.35	2529.95	1858.69	1530.53	1339.44	1216.68	1132.79	1073.01	1029.12	996.19	971.08	951.70	936.60	924.73
50000	4667.70	2581.58	1896.62	1561.77	1366.77	1241.51	1155.91	1094.91	1050.12	1016.52	990.90	971.12	955.71	943.61
55000	5134.47	2839.74	2086.28	1717.94	1503.45	1365.67	1271.50	1204.40	1155.13	1118.17	1089.99	1068.24	1051.28	1037.97
60000	5601.24	3097.90	2275.94	1874.12	1640.13	1489.82	1387.09	1313.89	1260.14	1219.83	1189.08	1165.35	1146.85	1132.33
65000	6068.01	3356.06	2465.60	2030.30	1776.80	1613.97	1502.68	1423.38	1365.16	1321.48	1288.17	1262.46	1242.42	1226.69
70000	6534.78	3614.22	2655.26	2186.47	1913.48	1738.12	1618.27	1532.87	1470.17	1423.13	1387.26	1359.57	1337.99	1321.05
75000	7001.55	3872.37	2844.93	2342.65	2050.16	1862.27	1733.87	1642.36	1575.18	1524.78	1486.35	1456.68	1433.56	1415.41
80000	7468.32	4130.53	3034.59	2498.83	2186.84	1986.42	1849.46	1751.85	1680.19	1626.43	1585.44	1553.80	1529.13	1509.77
85000	7935.09	4388.69	3224.25	2655.00	2323.51	2110.57	1965.05	1861.34	1785.20	1728.08	1684.53	1650.91	1624.70	1604.13
90000	8401.86	4646.85	3413.91	2811.08	2460.19	2234.72	2080.64	1970.83	1890.21	1829.74	1783.62	1748.02	1720.27	1698.49
95000	8868.63	4905.00	3603.57	2967.35	2596.87	2358.87	2196.23	2080.32	1995.23	1931.39	1882.71	1845.13	1815.84	1792.85
100000	9335.40	5163.16	3793.23	3123.53	2733.54	2483.02	2311.82	2189.81	2100.24	2033.04	1981.80	1942.24	1911.41	1887.21

TERM AMOUNT	15 Years	16 Years	17 Years	18 Years	19 Years	20 Years	21 Years	22 Years	23 Years	24 Years	25 Years	30 Years	35 Years	40 Years
5	.10	.10	.10	.10	.10	.10	.10	.10	.10	.10	.10	.09	.09	.09
10	.19	.19	.19	.19	.19	.19	.19	.19	.19	.19	.19	.18	.18	.18
15	.29	.28	.28	.28	.28	.28	.28	.28	.28	.28	.28	.27	.27	.27
25	.47	.47	.47	.46	.46	.46	.46	.46	.46	.46	.46	.45	.45	.45
50	.94	.93	.93	.92	.92	.91	.91	.91	.91	.91	.91	.90	.90	.90
75	1.41	1.39	1.39	1.38	1.37	1.37	1.36	1.36	1.36	1.36	1.36	1.35	1.35	1.35
100	1.87	1.86	1.85	1.84	1.83	1.82	1.82	1.81	1.81	1.81	1.81	1.80	1.80	1.80
200	3.74	3.71	3.69	3.67	3.65	3.64	3.63	3.62	3.62	3.61	3.61	3.59	3.59	3.59
300	5.61	5.56	5.53	5.50	5.48	5.46	5.44	5.43	5.42	5.41	5.41	5.39	5.38	5.38
400	7.48	7.42	7.37	7.33	7.30	7.27	7.25	7.24	7.23	7.21	7.21	7.18	7.18	7.17
500	9.35	9.27	9.21	9.16	9.12	9.09	9.07	9.05	9.03	9.02	9.01	8.98	8.97	8.97
600	11.21	11.12	11.05	10.99	10.95	10.91	10.88	10.85	10.84	10.82	10.81	10.77	10.76	10.76
700	13.08	12.98	12.89	12.82	12.77	12.73	12.69	12.66	12.64	12.62	12.61	12.57	12.55	12.55
800	14.95	14.83	14.73	14.65	14.59	14.54	14.50	14.47	14.45	14.42	14.41	14.36	14.35	14.34
900	16.82	16.68	16.57	16.49	16.42	16.36	16.32	16.28	16.25	16.23	16.21	16.16	16.14	16.13
1000	18.69	18.53	18.41	18.32	18.24	18.18	18.13	18.09	18.06	18.03	18.01	17.95	17.93	17.93
2000	37.37	37.06	36.82	36.63	36.47	36.35	36.25	36.17	36.11	36.05	36.01	35.90	35.86	35.85
3000	56.05	55.59	55.23	54.94	54.71	54.52	54.37	54.25	54.16	54.08	54.02	53.85	53.79	53.77
4000	74.73	74.12	73.64	73.25	72.94	72.70	72.50	72.34	72.21	72.10	72.02	71.79	71.71	71.69
5000	93.41	92.65	92.05	91.56	91.18	90.87	90.62	90.42	90.26	90.13	90.03	89.74	89.64	89.61
6000	112.09	111.18	110.46	109.88	109.41	109.04	108.74	108.50	108.31	108.15	108.03	107.69	107.57	107.53
7000	130.77	129.71	128.86	128.19	127.65	127.21	126.87	126.59	126.36	126.18	126.03	125.63	125.49	125.45
8000	149.45	148.24	147.27	146.50	145.88	145.39	144.99	144.67	144.41	144.20	144.04	143.58	143.42	143.37
9000	168.13	166.77	165.68	164.81	164.12	163.56	163.11	162.75	162.46	162.23	162.04	161.53	161.35	161.29
10000	186.81	185.30	184.09	183.12	182.35	181.73	181.24	180.84	180.51	180.25	180.05	179.47	179.28	179.21
11000	205.49	203.83	202.50	201.44	200.59	199.91	199.36	198.92	198.57	198.28	198.05	197.42	197.20	197.13
12000	224.18	222.36	220.91	219.75	218.82	218.08	217.48	217.00	216.62	216.30	216.05	215.37	215.13	215.05
13000	242.86	240.88	239.31	238.06	237.06	236.25	235.61	235.09	234.67	234.33	234.06	233.31	233.06	232.97
14000	261.54	259.41	257.72	256.37	255.29	254.42	253.73	253.17	252.72	252.35	252.06	251.26	250.98	250.89
15000	280.22	277.94	276.13	274.68	273.53	272.60	271.85	271.25	270.77	270.38	270.07	269.21	268.91	268.81
16000	298.90	296.47	294.54	293.00	291.76	290.77	289.97	289.33	288.82	288.40	288.07	287.15	286.84	286.73
17000	317.58	315.00	312.95	311.31	310.00	308.94	308.10	307.42	306.87	306.43	306.07	305.10	304.76	304.65
18000	336.26	333.53	331.36	329.62	328.23	327.12	326.22	325.50	324.92	324.45	324.08	323.05	322.69	322.57
19000	354.94	352.06	349.76	347.93	346.46	345.29	344.34	343.58	342.97	342.48	342.08	340.99	340.62	340.49
20000	373.62	370.59	368.17	366.24	364.70	363.46	362.47	361.67	361.02	360.50	360.09	358.94	358.55	358.41
21000	392.30	389.12	386.58	384.56	382.93	381.63	380.59	379.75	379.07	378.53	378.09	376.89	376.47	376.33
22000	410.98	407.65	404.99	402.87	401.17	399.81	398.71	397.83	397.13	396.55	396.10	394.83	394.40	394.25
23000	429.66	426.18	423.40	421.18	419.40	417.98	416.84	415.92	415.18	414.58	414.10	412.78	412.33	412.17
24000	448.35	444.71	441.81	439.49	437.64	436.15	434.96	434.00	433.23	432.60	432.10	430.73	430.25	430.09
25000	467.03	463.23	460.21	457.80	455.87	454.33	453.08	452.08	451.28	450.63	450.11	448.67	448.18	448.01
26000	485.71	481.76	478.62	476.12	474.11	472.50	471.21	470.17	469.33	468.65	468.11	466.62	466.11	465.93
27000	504.39	500.29	497.03	494.43	492.34	490.67	489.33	488.25	487.38	486.68	486.12	484.57	484.03	483.85
28000	523.07	518.82	515.44	512.74	510.58	508.84	507.45	506.33	505.43	504.70	504.12	502.51	501.96	501.77
29000	541.75	537.35	533.85	531.05	528.81	527.02	525.57	524.41	523.48	522.73	522.12	520.46	519.89	519.69
30000	560.43	555.88	552.26	549.36	547.05	545.19	543.70	542.50	541.53	540.75	540.13	538.41	537.82	537.61
31000	579.11	574.41	570.67	567.68	565.28	563.36	561.82	560.58	559.58	558.78	558.13	556.35	555.74	555.53
32000	597.79	592.94	589.07	585.99	583.52	581.54	579.94	578.66	577.63	576.80	576.14	574.30	573.67	573.45
33000	616.47	611.47	607.48	604.30	601.75	599.71	598.07	596.75	595.69	594.83	594.14	592.25	591.60	591.37
34000	635.15	630.00	625.89	622.61	619.99	617.88	616.19	614.83	613.74	612.85	612.14	610.19	609.52	609.29
35000	653.83	648.53	644.30	640.92	638.22	636.05	634.31	632.91	631.79	630.88	630.15	628.14	627.45	627.21
36000	672.52	667.06	662.71	659.23	656.46	654.23	652.44	651.00	649.84	648.90	648.15	646.09	645.38	645.13
37000	691.20	685.58	681.12	677.55	674.69	672.40	670.56	669.08	667.89	666.93	666.16	664.03	663.30	663.05
38000	709.88	704.11	699.52	695.86	692.92	690.57	688.68	687.16	685.94	684.95	684.16	681.98	681.23	680.97
39000	728.56	722.64	717.93	714.17	711.16	708.74	706.81	705.25	703.99	702.98	702.17	699.93	699.16	698.89
40000	747.24	741.17	736.34	732.48	729.39	726.92	724.93	723.33	722.04	721.00	720.17	717.87	717.09	716.81
41000	765.92	759.70	754.75	750.79	747.63	745.09	743.05	741.41	740.09	739.03	738.17	735.82	735.01	734.73
42000	784.60	778.23	773.16	769.11	765.86	763.26	761.17	759.50	758.14	757.05	756.18	753.77	752.94	752.65
43000	803.28	796.76	791.57	787.42	784.10	781.44	779.30	777.58	776.19	775.08	774.18	771.71	770.87	770.57
44000	821.96	815.29	809.97	805.73	802.33	799.61	797.42	795.66	794.25	793.10	792.19	789.66	788.79	788.49
45000	840.64	833.82	828.38	824.04	820.57	817.78	815.54	813.74	812.30	811.13	810.19	807.61	806.72	806.42
46000	859.32	852.35	846.79	842.35	838.80	835.95	833.67	831.83	830.35	829.15	828.19	825.55	824.65	824.34
47000	878.00	870.88	865.20	860.67	857.04	854.13	851.79	849.91	848.40	847.18	846.20	843.50	842.57	842.26
48000	896.69	889.41	883.61	878.98	875.27	872.30	869.91	867.99	866.45	865.20	864.20	861.45	860.50	860.18
49000	915.37	907.93	902.02	897.29	893.51	890.47	888.04	886.08	884.50	883.23	882.21	879.39	878.43	878.10
50000	934.05	926.46	920.42	915.60	911.74	908.65	906.16	904.16	902.55	901.25	900.21	897.34	896.36	896.02
55000	1027.45	1019.11	1012.47	1007.16	1002.92	999.51	996.77	994.58	992.81	991.38	990.23	987.07	985.99	985.62
60000	1120.86	1111.76	1104.51	1098.72	1094.09	1090.37	1087.39	1084.99	1083.06	1081.50	1080.25	1076.81	1075.63	1075.22
65000	1214.26	1204.40	1196.55	1190.28	1185.26	1181.24	1178.01	1175.41	1173.31	1171.63	1170.27	1166.54	1165.26	1164.82
70000	1307.66	1297.05	1288.59	1281.84	1276.44	1272.10	1268.62	1265.82	1263.57	1261.75	1260.29	1256.27	1254.90	1254.42
75000	1401.07	1389.69	1380.63	1373.40	1367.61	1362.97	1359.24	1356.24	1353.82	1351.88	1350.31	1346.01	1344.53	1344.02
80000	1494.47	1482.34	1472.68	1464.96	1458.78	1453.83	1449.85	1446.65	1444.08	1442.00	1440.33	1435.74	1434.17	1433.62
85000	1587.88	1574.98	1564.72	1556.52	1549.96	1544.69	1540.47	1537.07	1534.33	1532.13	1530.35	1525.47	1523.80	1523.22
90000	1681.28	1667.63	1656.76	1648.08	1641.13	1635.56	1631.08	1627.48	1624.59	1622.25	1620.37	1615.21	1613.44	1612.83
95000	1774.69	1760.28	1748.80	1739.64	1732.30	1726.42	1721.70	1717.90	1714.84	1712.38	1710.40	1704.94	1703.07	1702.43
100000	1868.09	1852.92	1840.84	1831.20	1823.48	1817.29	1812.31	1808.32	1805.10	1802.50	1800.42	1794.67	1792.71	1792.03

21.600%

TERM AMOUNT	1 Year	2 Years	3 Years	4 Years	5 Years	6 Years	7 Years	8 Years	9 Years	10 Years	11 Years	12 Years	13 Years	14 Years
5	.47	.26	.19	.16	.14	.13	.12	.11	.11	.11	.10	.10	.10	.10
10	.94	.52	.38	.32	.28	.25	.24	.22	.22	.21	.20	.20	.20	.19
15	1.41	.78	.57	.47	.42	.38	.35	.33	.32	.31	.30	.30	.29	.29
25	2.34	1.30	.95	.79	.69	.63	.58	.55	.53	.51	.50	.49	.48	.48
50	4.68	2.59	1.90	1.57	1.37	1.25	1.16	1.10	1.06	1.02	1.00	.98	.96	.95
75	7.01	3.88	2.85	2.35	2.06	1.87	1.74	1.65	1.59	1.53	1.50	1.47	1.44	1.43
100	9.35	5.17	3.80	3.13	2.74	2.49	2.32	2.20	2.11	2.04	1.99	1.95	1.92	1.90
200	18.69	10.34	7.60	6.26	5.48	4.98	4.64	4.40	4.22	4.08	3.98	3.90	3.84	3.79
300	28.03	15.51	11.40	9.39	8.22	7.47	6.96	6.59	6.33	6.12	5.97	5.85	5.76	5.69
400	37.37	20.68	15.20	12.52	10.96	9.96	9.28	8.79	8.43	8.16	7.96	7.80	7.68	7.58
500	46.71	25.85	19.00	15.65	13.70	12.45	11.59	10.99	10.54	10.20	9.95	9.75	9.60	9.48
600	56.05	31.01	22.80	18.78	16.44	14.94	13.91	13.18	12.65	12.24	11.94	11.70	11.52	11.37
700	65.39	36.18	26.59	21.91	19.18	17.43	16.23	15.38	14.75	14.28	13.93	13.65	13.44	13.27
800	74.73	41.35	30.39	25.04	21.92	19.92	18.55	17.57	16.86	16.32	15.91	15.60	15.35	15.16
900	84.07	46.52	34.19	28.17	24.66	22.41	20.87	19.77	18.97	18.36	17.90	17.55	17.27	17.06
1000	93.41	51.69	37.99	31.29	27.40	24.89	23.18	21.97	21.07	20.40	19.89	19.50	19.19	18.95
2000	186.81	103.37	75.97	62.58	54.79	49.78	46.36	43.93	42.14	40.80	39.78	38.99	38.38	37.90
3000	280.21	155.05	113.96	93.87	82.18	74.67	69.54	65.89	63.21	61.20	59.67	58.49	57.57	56.84
4000	373.61	206.73	151.94	125.16	109.57	99.56	92.72	87.85	84.28	81.60	79.55	77.98	76.75	75.79
5000	467.01	258.41	189.92	156.45	136.96	124.45	115.90	109.81	105.35	102.00	99.44	97.47	95.94	94.73
6000	560.42	310.09	227.91	187.74	164.36	149.34	139.08	131.78	126.41	122.39	119.33	116.97	115.13	113.68
7000	653.82	361.77	265.89	219.03	191.75	174.23	162.26	153.74	147.48	142.79	139.22	136.46	134.31	132.63
8000	747.22	413.45	303.88	250.32	219.14	199.12	185.44	175.70	168.55	163.19	159.10	155.95	153.50	151.57
9000	840.62	465.13	341.86	281.61	246.53	224.01	208.62	197.66	189.62	183.59	178.99	175.45	172.69	170.52
10000	934.02	516.81	379.84	312.90	273.92	248.90	231.80	219.62	210.69	203.99	198.88	194.94	191.87	189.46
11000	1027.43	568.49	417.83	344.19	301.32	273.79	254.98	241.58	231.75	224.38	218.77	214.43	211.06	208.41
12000	1120.83	620.18	455.81	375.48	328.71	298.68	278.16	263.55	252.82	244.78	238.65	233.93	230.25	227.36
13000	1214.23	671.86	493.79	406.77	356.10	323.57	301.34	285.51	273.89	265.18	258.54	253.42	249.43	246.30
14000	1307.63	723.54	531.78	438.06	383.49	348.45	324.52	307.47	294.96	285.58	278.43	272.91	268.62	265.25
15000	1401.03	775.22	569.76	469.34	410.88	373.34	347.70	329.43	316.03	305.98	298.32	292.41	287.81	284.19
16000	1494.44	826.90	607.75	500.63	438.28	398.23	370.88	351.39	337.09	326.37	318.20	311.90	306.99	303.14
17000	1587.84	878.58	645.73	531.92	465.67	423.12	394.06	373.35	358.16	346.77	338.09	331.39	326.18	322.09
18000	1681.24	930.26	683.71	563.21	493.06	448.01	417.24	395.32	379.23	367.17	357.98	350.89	345.37	341.03
19000	1774.64	981.94	721.70	594.50	520.45	472.90	440.42	417.28	400.30	387.57	377.87	370.38	364.55	359.98
20000	1868.04	1033.62	759.68	625.79	547.84	497.79	463.60	439.24	421.37	407.97	397.75	389.88	383.74	378.92
21000	1961.45	1085.30	797.67	657.08	575.24	522.68	486.78	461.20	442.43	428.36	417.64	409.37	402.93	397.87
22000	2054.85	1136.98	835.65	688.37	602.63	547.57	509.95	483.16	463.50	448.76	437.53	428.86	422.11	416.82
23000	2148.25	1188.66	873.63	719.66	630.02	572.46	533.13	505.12	484.57	469.16	457.42	448.36	441.30	435.76
24000	2241.65	1240.35	911.62	750.95	657.41	597.35	556.31	527.09	505.64	489.56	477.30	467.85	460.49	454.71
25000	2335.05	1292.03	949.60	782.24	684.80	622.24	579.49	549.05	526.71	509.96	497.19	487.34	479.67	473.65
26000	2428.46	1343.71	987.58	813.53	712.20	647.13	602.67	571.01	547.77	530.35	517.08	506.84	498.86	492.60
27000	2521.86	1395.39	1025.57	844.82	739.59	672.01	625.85	592.97	568.84	550.75	536.97	526.33	518.05	511.55
28000	2615.26	1447.07	1063.55	876.11	766.98	696.90	649.03	614.93	589.91	571.15	556.85	545.82	537.23	530.49
29000	2708.66	1498.75	1101.54	907.40	794.37	721.79	672.21	636.89	610.98	591.55	576.74	565.32	556.42	549.44
30000	2802.06	1550.43	1139.52	938.68	821.76	746.68	695.39	658.86	632.05	611.95	596.63	584.81	575.61	568.38
31000	2895.47	1602.11	1177.50	969.97	849.16	771.57	718.57	680.82	653.12	632.34	616.52	604.30	594.79	587.33
32000	2988.87	1653.79	1215.49	1001.26	876.55	796.46	741.75	702.78	674.18	652.74	636.40	623.80	613.98	606.28
33000	3082.27	1705.47	1253.47	1032.55	903.94	821.35	764.93	724.74	695.25	673.14	656.29	643.29	633.17	625.22
34000	3175.67	1757.15	1291.46	1063.84	931.33	846.24	788.11	746.70	716.32	693.54	676.18	662.78	652.35	644.17
35000	3269.07	1808.83	1329.44	1095.13	958.72	871.13	811.29	768.66	737.39	713.94	696.07	682.28	671.54	663.11
36000	3362.48	1860.52	1367.42	1126.42	986.12	896.02	834.47	790.63	758.46	734.33	715.95	701.77	690.73	682.06
37000	3455.88	1912.20	1405.41	1157.71	1013.51	920.91	857.65	812.59	779.52	754.73	735.84	721.27	709.91	701.01
38000	3549.28	1963.88	1443.39	1189.00	1040.90	945.80	880.83	834.55	800.59	775.13	755.73	740.76	729.10	719.95
39000	3642.68	2015.56	1481.37	1220.29	1068.29	970.69	904.01	856.51	821.66	795.53	775.61	760.25	748.29	738.90
40000	3736.08	2067.24	1519.36	1251.58	1095.68	995.57	927.19	878.47	842.73	815.93	795.50	779.75	767.47	757.84
41000	3829.49	2118.92	1557.34	1282.87	1123.08	1020.46	950.37	900.43	863.80	836.32	815.39	799.24	786.66	776.79
42000	3922.89	2170.60	1595.33	1314.16	1150.47	1045.35	973.55	922.40	884.86	856.72	835.28	818.73	805.85	795.74
43000	4016.29	2222.28	1633.31	1345.45	1177.86	1070.24	996.73	944.36	905.93	877.12	855.16	838.23	825.03	814.68
44000	4109.69	2273.96	1671.29	1376.74	1205.25	1095.13	1019.90	966.32	927.00	897.52	875.05	857.72	844.22	833.63
45000	4203.09	2325.64	1709.28	1408.02	1232.64	1120.02	1043.08	988.28	948.07	917.92	894.94	877.21	863.41	852.57
46000	4296.50	2377.32	1747.26	1439.31	1260.04	1144.91	1066.26	1010.24	969.14	938.31	914.83	896.71	882.59	871.52
47000	4389.90	2429.00	1785.25	1470.60	1287.43	1169.80	1089.44	1032.20	990.20	958.71	934.71	916.20	901.78	890.47
48000	4483.30	2480.69	1823.23	1501.89	1314.82	1194.69	1112.62	1054.17	1011.27	979.11	954.60	935.69	920.97	909.41
49000	4576.70	2532.37	1861.21	1533.18	1342.21	1219.58	1135.80	1076.13	1032.34	999.51	974.49	955.19	940.15	928.36
50000	4670.10	2584.05	1899.20	1564.47	1369.60	1244.47	1158.98	1098.09	1053.41	1019.91	994.38	974.68	959.34	947.30
55000	5137.11	2842.45	2089.12	1720.92	1506.56	1368.91	1274.88	1207.90	1158.75	1121.90	1093.81	1072.15	1055.27	1042.04
60000	5604.12	3100.86	2279.03	1877.36	1643.52	1493.36	1390.78	1317.71	1264.09	1223.89	1193.25	1169.62	1151.21	1136.77
65000	6071.13	3359.26	2468.95	2033.81	1780.48	1617.81	1506.66	1427.51	1369.43	1325.88	1292.69	1267.08	1247.14	1231.49
70000	6538.16	3617.66	2658.87	2190.26	1917.44	1742.25	1622.57	1537.32	1474.77	1427.87	1392.13	1364.55	1343.08	1326.22
75000	7005.15	3876.07	2848.79	2346.70	2054.40	1866.70	1738.47	1647.13	1580.11	1529.86	1491.56	1462.02	1439.01	1420.95
80000	7472.16	4134.47	3038.71	2503.15	2191.36	1991.14	1854.37	1756.94	1685.45	1631.85	1591.00	1559.49	1534.94	1515.68
85000	7939.17	4392.88	3228.63	2659.60	2328.32	2115.59	1970.27	1866.75	1790.79	1733.84	1690.44	1656.95	1630.88	1610.41
90000	8406.18	4651.28	3418.55	2816.04	2465.28	2240.04	2086.16	1976.56	1896.13	1835.83	1789.87	1754.42	1726.81	1705.14
95000	8873.19	4909.68	3608.47	2972.49	2602.24	2364.48	2202.06	2086.36	2001.47	1937.82	1889.31	1851.89	1822.74	1799.87
100000	9340.20	5168.09	3798.39	3128.94	2739.20	2488.93	2317.96	2196.17	2106.81	2039.81	1988.75	1949.36	1918.68	1894.60

TERM	15 Years	16 Years	17 Years	18 Years	19 Years	20 Years	21 Years	22 Years	23 Years	24 Years	25 Years	30 Years	35 Years	40 Years
AMOUNT														
5	.10	.10	.10	.10	.10	.10	.10	.10	.10	.10	.10	.10	.10	.10
10	.19	.19	.19	.19	.19	.19	.19	.19	.19	.19	.19	.19	.19	.19
15	.29	.28	.28	.28	.28	.28	.28	.28	.28	.28	.28	.28	.28	.28
25	.47	.47	.47	.46	.46	.46	.46	.46	.46	.46	.46	.46	.46	.46
50	.94	.94	.93	.92	.92	.92	.92	.91	.91	.91	.91	.91	.91	.91
75	1.41	1.40	1.39	1.38	1.38	1.37	1.37	1.37	1.36	1.36	1.36	1.36	1.36	1.36
100	1.88	1.87	1.85	1.84	1.84	1.83	1.83	1.82	1.82	1.82	1.81	1.81	1.81	1.81
200	3.76	3.73	3.70	3.68	3.67	3.66	3.65	3.64	3.63	3.63	3.62	3.61	3.61	3.61
300	5.63	5.59	5.55	5.52	5.50	5.48	5.47	5.45	5.44	5.44	5.43	5.41	5.41	5.41
400	7.51	7.45	7.40	7.36	7.33	7.31	7.29	7.27	7.26	7.25	7.24	7.22	7.21	7.21
500	9.38	9.31	9.25	9.20	9.16	9.13	9.11	9.09	9.07	9.06	9.05	9.02	9.01	9.01
600	11.26	11.17	11.10	11.04	10.99	10.96	10.93	10.90	10.88	10.87	10.86	10.82	10.81	10.81
700	13.13	13.03	12.94	12.88	12.82	12.78	12.75	12.72	12.70	12.68	12.66	12.63	12.61	12.61
800	15.01	14.89	14.79	14.72	14.66	14.61	14.57	14.54	14.51	14.49	14.47	14.43	14.41	14.41
900	16.89	16.75	16.64	16.56	16.49	16.43	16.39	16.35	16.32	16.30	16.28	16.23	16.21	16.21
1000	18.76	18.61	18.49	18.39	18.32	18.26	18.21	18.17	18.14	18.11	18.09	18.03	18.02	18.01
2000	37.52	37.22	36.98	36.78	36.63	36.51	36.41	36.33	36.27	36.22	36.18	36.06	36.03	36.01
3000	56.27	55.82	55.46	55.17	54.95	54.76	54.61	54.50	54.40	54.32	54.26	54.09	54.04	54.02
4000	75.03	74.43	73.95	73.56	73.26	73.01	72.82	72.66	72.53	72.43	72.35	72.12	72.05	72.02
5000	93.79	93.03	92.43	91.95	91.57	91.27	91.02	90.82	90.66	90.54	90.43	90.15	90.06	90.02
6000	112.54	111.64	110.92	110.34	109.89	109.52	109.22	108.99	108.80	108.64	108.52	108.18	108.07	108.03
7000	131.30	130.24	129.40	128.73	128.20	127.77	127.43	127.15	126.93	126.75	126.60	126.21	126.08	126.03
8000	150.05	148.85	147.89	147.12	146.51	146.02	145.63	145.31	145.06	144.86	144.69	144.24	144.09	144.03
9000	168.81	167.45	166.38	165.51	164.83	164.28	163.83	163.48	163.19	162.96	162.78	162.27	162.10	162.04
10000	187.57	186.06	184.86	183.90	183.14	182.53	182.04	181.64	181.32	181.07	180.86	180.30	180.11	180.04
11000	206.32	204.66	203.35	202.29	201.45	200.78	200.24	199.80	199.46	199.17	198.95	198.33	198.12	198.04
12000	225.08	223.27	221.83	220.68	219.77	219.03	218.44	217.97	217.59	217.28	217.03	216.36	216.13	216.05
13000	243.83	241.88	240.32	239.07	238.08	237.28	236.65	236.13	235.72	235.39	235.12	234.39	234.14	234.05
14000	262.59	260.48	258.80	257.46	256.39	255.54	254.85	254.30	253.85	253.49	253.20	252.42	252.15	252.05
15000	281.35	279.09	277.29	275.85	274.71	273.79	273.05	272.46	271.98	271.60	271.29	270.44	270.16	270.06
16000	300.10	297.69	295.77	294.24	293.02	292.04	291.25	290.62	290.11	289.71	289.38	288.47	288.17	288.06
17000	318.86	316.30	314.26	312.63	311.34	310.29	309.46	308.79	308.25	307.81	307.46	306.50	306.18	306.06
18000	337.61	334.90	332.75	331.02	329.65	328.55	327.66	326.95	326.38	325.92	325.55	324.53	324.19	324.07
19000	356.37	353.51	351.23	349.41	347.96	346.80	345.86	345.11	344.51	344.02	343.63	342.56	342.20	342.07
20000	375.13	372.11	369.72	367.80	366.28	365.05	364.07	363.28	362.64	362.13	361.72	360.59	360.21	360.07
21000	393.88	390.72	388.20	386.19	384.59	383.30	382.27	381.44	380.77	380.24	379.80	378.62	378.22	378.08
22000	412.64	409.32	406.69	404.58	402.90	401.55	400.47	399.60	398.91	398.34	397.89	396.65	396.23	396.08
23000	431.39	427.93	425.17	422.97	421.22	419.81	418.68	417.77	417.04	416.45	415.98	414.68	414.24	414.08
24000	450.15	446.54	443.66	441.36	439.53	438.06	436.88	435.93	435.17	434.56	434.06	432.71	432.25	432.09
25000	468.91	465.14	462.15	459.75	457.84	456.31	455.08	454.10	453.30	452.66	452.15	450.74	450.26	450.09
26000	487.66	483.75	480.63	478.14	476.16	474.56	473.29	472.26	471.43	470.77	470.23	468.77	468.27	468.09
27000	506.42	502.35	499.12	496.53	494.47	492.82	491.49	490.42	489.56	488.87	488.32	486.80	486.28	486.10
28000	525.17	520.96	517.60	514.92	512.78	511.07	509.69	508.59	507.70	506.98	506.40	504.83	504.29	504.10
29000	543.93	539.56	536.09	533.31	531.10	529.32	527.89	526.75	525.83	525.09	524.49	522.85	522.30	522.10
30000	562.69	558.17	554.57	551.70	549.41	547.57	546.10	544.91	543.96	543.19	542.58	540.88	540.31	540.11
31000	581.44	576.77	573.06	570.09	567.72	565.83	564.30	563.08	562.09	561.30	560.66	558.91	558.32	558.11
32000	600.20	595.38	591.54	588.48	586.04	584.08	582.50	581.24	580.22	579.41	578.75	576.94	576.33	576.12
33000	618.95	613.98	610.03	606.87	604.35	602.33	600.71	599.40	598.36	597.51	596.83	594.97	594.34	594.12
34000	637.71	632.59	628.52	625.26	622.67	620.58	618.91	617.57	616.49	615.62	614.92	613.00	612.35	612.12
35000	656.47	651.20	647.00	643.65	640.98	638.83	637.11	635.73	634.62	633.72	633.00	631.03	630.36	630.13
36000	675.22	669.80	665.49	662.04	659.29	657.09	655.32	653.89	652.75	651.83	651.09	649.06	648.37	648.13
37000	693.98	688.41	683.97	680.43	677.61	675.34	673.52	672.06	670.88	669.94	669.18	667.09	666.38	666.13
38000	712.73	707.01	702.46	698.82	695.92	693.59	691.72	690.22	689.02	688.04	687.26	685.12	684.39	684.14
39000	731.49	725.62	720.94	717.21	714.23	711.84	709.93	708.39	707.15	706.15	705.35	703.15	702.40	702.14
40000	750.25	744.22	739.43	735.60	732.55	730.10	728.13	726.55	725.28	724.26	723.43	721.18	720.41	720.14
41000	769.00	762.83	757.91	753.99	750.86	748.35	746.33	744.71	743.41	742.36	741.52	739.21	738.42	738.15
42000	787.76	781.43	776.40	772.38	769.17	766.60	764.54	762.88	761.54	760.47	759.60	757.24	756.43	756.15
43000	806.51	800.04	794.89	790.77	787.49	784.85	782.74	781.04	779.67	778.58	777.69	775.26	774.44	774.15
44000	825.27	818.64	813.37	809.16	805.80	803.10	800.94	799.20	797.81	796.68	795.78	793.29	792.45	792.16
45000	844.03	837.25	831.86	827.55	824.11	821.36	819.14	817.37	815.94	814.79	813.86	811.32	810.46	810.16
46000	862.78	855.85	850.34	845.94	842.43	839.61	837.35	835.53	834.07	832.89	831.95	829.35	828.47	828.16
47000	881.54	874.46	868.83	864.33	860.74	857.86	855.55	853.69	852.20	851.00	850.03	847.38	846.48	846.17
48000	900.29	893.07	887.31	882.72	879.05	876.11	873.75	871.86	870.33	869.11	868.12	865.41	864.49	864.17
49000	919.05	911.67	905.80	901.11	897.37	894.37	891.96	890.02	888.47	887.21	886.20	883.44	882.50	882.17
50000	937.81	930.28	924.29	919.50	915.68	912.62	910.16	908.19	906.60	905.32	904.29	901.47	900.51	900.18
55000	1031.59	1023.30	1016.71	1011.45	1007.25	1003.88	1001.18	999.00	997.26	995.85	994.72	991.62	990.56	990.19
60000	1125.37	1116.33	1109.14	1103.40	1098.82	1095.14	1092.19	1089.82	1087.92	1086.38	1085.15	1081.76	1080.61	1080.21
65000	1219.15	1209.36	1201.57	1195.35	1190.38	1186.40	1183.21	1180.64	1178.57	1176.91	1175.58	1171.91	1170.66	1170.23
70000	1312.93	1302.39	1294.00	1287.30	1281.95	1277.66	1274.22	1271.46	1269.23	1267.44	1266.00	1262.06	1260.71	1260.25
75000	1406.71	1395.41	1386.43	1379.25	1373.52	1368.92	1365.24	1362.28	1359.89	1357.98	1356.43	1352.20	1350.76	1350.26
80000	1500.49	1488.44	1478.85	1471.20	1465.09	1460.19	1456.25	1453.09	1450.55	1448.51	1446.86	1442.35	1440.81	1440.28
85000	1594.27	1581.47	1571.28	1563.15	1556.66	1551.45	1547.27	1543.91	1541.21	1539.04	1537.29	1532.50	1530.86	1530.30
90000	1688.05	1674.49	1663.71	1655.10	1648.22	1642.71	1638.28	1634.73	1631.87	1629.57	1627.72	1622.64	1620.91	1620.31
95000	1781.83	1767.52	1756.14	1747.05	1739.79	1733.97	1729.30	1725.55	1722.53	1720.10	1718.15	1712.79	1710.96	1710.33
100000	1875.61	1860.55	1848.57	1839.00	1831.36	1825.23	1820.31	1816.37	1813.19	1810.63	1808.58	1802.93	1801.01	1800.35

MONTHLY PAYMENT
REQUIRED TO AMORTIZE A LOAN

TERM AMOUNT	1 Year	2 Years	3 Years	4 Years	5 Years	6 Years	7 Years	8 Years	9 Years	10 Years	11 Years	12 Years	13 Years	14 Years
5	.47	.26	.19	.16	.14	.13	.12	.11	.11	.11	.10	.10	.10	.10
10	.94	.52	.38	.32	.28	.25	.24	.22	.22	.21	.20	.20	.20	.19
15	1.41	.78	.57	.47	.42	.38	.35	.33	.32	.31	.30	.30	.29	.29
25	2.34	1.30	.95	.79	.69	.63	.58	.55	.53	.52	.50	.49	.49	.48
50	4.68	2.59	1.90	1.57	1.38	1.25	1.16	1.10	1.06	1.03	1.00	.98	.97	.95
75	7.01	3.88	2.85	2.35	2.06	1.87	1.74	1.65	1.59	1.54	1.50	1.47	1.45	1.43
100	9.35	5.17	3.80	3.14	2.75	2.50	2.32	2.20	2.11	2.05	2.00	1.96	1.93	1.90
200	18.69	10.34	7.60	6.27	5.49	4.99	4.64	4.40	4.22	4.09	3.99	3.91	3.85	3.80
300	28.03	15.51	11.40	9.40	8.23	7.48	6.96	6.60	6.33	6.13	5.98	5.86	5.77	5.69
400	31.37	20.68	15.20	12.53	10.97	9.97	9.28	8.80	8.44	8.17	7.97	7.81	7.69	7.59
500	46.71	25.85	19.00	15.66	13.71	12.46	11.60	10.99	10.55	10.21	9.96	9.76	9.61	9.49
600	56.05	31.02	22.80	18.79	16.45	14.95	13.92	13.19	12.66	12.25	11.95	11.71	11.53	11.38
700	65.39	36.19	26.60	21.92	19.19	17.44	16.24	15.39	14.76	14.30	13.94	13.66	13.45	13.28
800	74.74	41.36	30.40	25.05	21.93	19.93	18.56	17.59	16.87	16.34	15.93	15.61	15.37	15.18
900	84.08	46.53	34.20	28.18	24.67	22.42	20.88	19.78	18.98	18.38	17.92	17.57	17.29	17.07
1000	93.42	51.70	38.00	31.31	27.41	24.91	23.20	21.98	21.09	20.42	19.91	19.52	19.21	18.97
2000	186.83	103.39	76.00	62.61	54.82	49.81	46.39	43.96	42.17	40.83	39.81	39.03	38.41	37.93
3000	280.25	155.08	114.00	93.91	82.22	74.72	69.59	65.94	63.26	61.25	59.72	58.54	57.62	56.90
4000	373.66	206.78	151.99	125.22	109.63	99.62	92.78	87.92	84.34	81.66	79.62	78.05	76.82	75.86
5000	467.07	258.47	189.99	156.52	137.04	124.53	115.98	109.89	105.43	102.08	99.53	97.56	96.03	94.83
6000	560.49	310.16	227.99	187.82	164.44	149.43	139.17	131.87	126.51	122.49	119.43	117.07	115.23	113.79
7000	653.90	361.86	265.98	219.12	191.85	174.33	162.37	153.85	147.60	142.91	139.34	136.58	134.44	132.76
8000	747.32	413.55	303.98	250.43	219.25	199.24	185.56	175.83	168.68	163.32	159.24	156.10	153.64	151.72
9000	840.73	465.24	341.98	281.73	246.66	224.14	208.76	197.80	189.77	183.74	179.15	175.61	172.85	170.69
10000	934.14	516.94	379.97	313.03	274.07	249.05	231.95	219.78	210.85	204.15	199.05	195.12	192.05	189.65
11000	1027.56	568.63	417.97	344.34	301.47	273.95	255.15	241.76	231.93	224.57	218.96	214.63	211.26	208.61
12000	1120.97	620.32	455.97	375.64	328.88	298.85	278.34	263.74	253.02	244.98	238.86	234.14	230.46	227.58
13000	1214.39	672.02	493.96	406.94	356.28	323.76	301.54	285.71	274.10	265.40	258.77	253.65	249.67	246.54
14000	1307.80	723.71	531.96	438.24	383.69	348.66	324.73	307.69	295.19	285.81	278.67	273.16	268.87	265.51
15000	1401.21	775.40	569.96	469.55	411.10	373.57	347.93	329.67	316.27	306.23	298.58	292.67	288.08	284.47
16000	1494.63	827.10	607.95	500.85	438.50	398.47	371.12	351.65	337.36	326.64	318.48	312.19	307.28	303.44
17000	1588.04	878.79	645.95	532.15	465.91	423.37	394.32	373.62	358.44	347.06	338.39	331.70	326.49	322.40
18000	1681.46	930.48	683.95	563.46	493.32	448.28	417.51	395.60	379.53	367.47	358.29	351.21	345.69	341.37
19000	1774.87	982.17	721.94	594.76	520.72	473.18	440.71	417.58	400.61	387.89	378.20	370.72	364.90	360.33
20000	1868.28	1033.87	759.94	626.06	548.13	498.09	463.90	439.56	421.70	408.30	398.10	390.23	384.10	379.30
21000	1961.70	1085.56	797.94	657.36	575.53	522.99	487.10	461.53	442.78	428.72	418.01	409.74	403.31	398.26
22000	2055.11	1137.25	835.93	688.67	602.94	547.89	510.29	483.51	463.86	449.13	437.91	429.25	422.51	417.22
23000	2148.53	1188.95	873.93	719.97	630.35	572.80	533.49	505.49	484.95	469.55	457.82	448.77	441.72	436.19
24000	2241.94	1240.64	911.93	751.27	657.75	597.70	556.68	527.47	506.03	489.96	477.72	468.28	460.92	455.15
25000	2335.35	1292.33	949.92	782.58	685.16	622.61	579.88	549.44	527.12	510.38	497.63	487.79	480.13	474.12
26000	2428.77	1344.03	987.92	813.88	712.56	647.51	603.07	571.42	548.20	530.79	517.53	507.30	499.33	493.08
27000	2522.18	1395.72	1025.92	845.18	739.97	672.41	626.27	593.40	569.29	551.21	537.44	526.81	518.54	512.05
28000	2615.60	1447.41	1063.91	876.48	767.38	697.32	649.46	615.38	590.37	571.62	557.34	546.32	537.74	531.01
29000	2709.01	1499.11	1101.91	907.79	794.78	722.22	672.66	637.36	611.46	592.04	577.24	565.83	556.95	549.98
30000	2802.42	1550.80	1139.91	939.09	822.19	747.13	695.85	659.33	632.54	612.45	597.15	585.34	576.15	568.94
31000	2895.84	1602.49	1177.90	970.39	849.59	772.03	719.05	681.31	653.62	632.87	617.05	604.86	595.36	587.90
32000	2989.25	1654.19	1215.90	1001.70	877.00	796.93	742.24	703.29	674.71	653.28	636.96	624.37	614.56	606.87
33000	3082.67	1705.88	1253.90	1033.00	904.41	821.84	765.44	725.27	695.79	673.70	656.86	643.88	633.77	625.83
34000	3176.08	1757.57	1291.89	1064.30	931.81	846.74	788.63	747.24	716.88	694.11	676.77	663.39	652.97	644.80
35000	3269.49	1809.27	1329.89	1095.60	959.22	871.65	811.83	769.22	737.96	714.53	696.67	682.90	672.18	663.76
36000	3362.91	1860.96	1367.89	1126.91	986.63	896.55	835.02	791.20	759.05	734.94	716.58	702.41	691.38	682.73
37000	3456.32	1912.65	1405.88	1158.21	1014.03	921.45	858.22	813.18	780.13	755.36	736.48	721.92	710.59	701.69
38000	3549.74	1964.34	1443.88	1189.51	1041.44	946.36	881.41	835.15	801.22	775.77	756.39	741.43	729.79	720.66
39000	3643.15	2016.04	1481.88	1220.82	1068.84	971.26	904.61	857.13	822.30	796.19	776.29	760.95	749.00	739.62
40000	3736.56	2067.73	1519.87	1252.12	1096.25	996.17	927.80	879.11	843.39	816.60	796.20	780.46	768.20	758.59
41000	3829.98	2119.42	1557.87	1283.42	1123.66	1021.07	951.00	901.09	864.47	837.02	816.10	799.97	787.41	777.55
42000	3923.39	2171.12	1595.87	1314.72	1151.06	1045.97	974.19	923.06	885.55	857.43	836.01	819.48	806.61	796.51
43000	4016.81	2222.81	1633.86	1346.03	1178.47	1070.88	997.39	945.04	906.64	877.85	855.91	838.99	825.82	815.48
44000	4110.22	2274.50	1671.86	1377.33	1205.87	1095.78	1020.58	967.02	927.72	898.26	875.82	858.50	845.02	834.44
45000	4203.63	2326.20	1709.86	1408.63	1233.28	1120.69	1043.78	989.00	948.81	918.68	895.72	878.01	864.22	853.41
46000	4297.05	2377.89	1747.85	1439.94	1260.69	1145.59	1066.97	1010.97	969.89	939.09	915.63	897.53	883.43	872.37
47000	4390.46	2429.58	1785.85	1471.24	1288.09	1170.49	1090.17	1032.95	990.98	959.51	935.53	917.04	902.63	891.34
48000	4483.88	2481.28	1823.85	1502.54	1315.50	1195.40	1113.36	1054.93	1012.06	979.92	955.44	936.55	921.84	910.30
49000	4577.29	2532.97	1861.84	1533.84	1342.91	1220.30	1136.56	1076.91	1033.15	1000.34	975.34	956.06	941.04	929.27
50000	4670.70	2584.66	1899.84	1565.15	1370.31	1245.21	1159.75	1098.88	1054.23	1020.75	995.25	975.57	960.25	948.23
55000	5137.77	2843.13	2089.83	1721.66	1507.34	1369.73	1275.73	1208.77	1159.65	1122.83	1094.77	1073.13	1056.27	1043.05
60000	5604.84	3101.59	2279.81	1878.18	1644.37	1494.25	1391.70	1318.66	1265.08	1224.90	1194.29	1170.68	1152.30	1137.88
65000	6071.91	3360.06	2469.79	2034.69	1781.40	1618.77	1507.67	1428.55	1370.50	1326.98	1293.82	1268.24	1248.32	1232.70
70000	6538.98	3618.53	2659.78	2191.20	1918.43	1743.29	1623.65	1538.44	1475.92	1429.05	1393.34	1365.80	1344.35	1327.52
75000	7006.05	3876.99	2849.76	2347.72	2055.46	1867.81	1739.62	1648.32	1581.34	1531.13	1492.87	1463.35	1440.37	1422.34
80000	7473.12	4135.46	3039.74	2504.23	2192.49	1992.33	1855.60	1758.21	1686.77	1633.20	1592.39	1560.91	1536.40	1517.17
85000	7940.19	4393.92	3229.73	2660.75	2329.53	2116.85	1971.57	1868.10	1792.19	1735.28	1691.91	1658.47	1632.42	1611.99
90000	8407.27	4652.39	3419.71	2817.26	2466.56	2241.37	2087.55	1977.99	1897.61	1837.35	1791.44	1756.02	1728.45	1706.81
95000	8874.34	4910.85	3609.69	2973.78	2603.59	2365.89	2203.52	2087.88	2003.03	1939.43	1890.96	1853.58	1824.47	1801.63
100000	9341.41	5169.32	3799.68	3130.29	2740.62	2490.41	2319.50	2197.76	2108.46	2041.50	1990.49	1951.14	1920.49	1896.46

TERM / AMOUNT	15 Years	16 Years	17 Years	18 Years	19 Years	20 Years	21 Years	22 Years	23 Years	24 Years	25 Years	30 Years	35 Years	40 Years
5	.10	.10	.10	.10	.10	.10	.10	.10	.10	.10	.10	.10	.10	.10
10	.19	.19	.19	.19	.19	.19	.19	.19	.19	.19	.19	.19	.19	.19
15	.29	.28	.28	.28	.28	.28	.28	.28	.28	.28	.28	.28	.28	.28
25	.47	.47	.47	.47	.46	.46	.46	.46	.46	.46	.46	.46	.46	.46
50	.94	.94	.93	.93	.92	.92	.92	.91	.91	.91	.91	.91	.91	.91
75	1.41	1.40	1.39	1.39	1.38	1.38	1.37	1.37	1.37	1.36	1.36	1.36	1.36	1.36
100	1.88	1.87	1.86	1.85	1.84	1.83	1.83	1.82	1.82	1.82	1.82	1.81	1.81	1.81
200	3.76	3.73	3.71	3.69	3.67	3.66	3.65	3.64	3.64	3.63	3.63	3.61	3.61	3.61
300	5.64	5.59	5.56	5.53	5.50	5.49	5.47	5.46	5.45	5.44	5.44	5.42	5.41	5.41
400	7.51	7.45	7.41	7.37	7.34	7.31	7.29	7.28	7.27	7.26	7.25	7.22	7.22	7.21
500	9.39	9.32	9.26	9.21	9.17	9.14	9.12	9.10	9.08	9.07	9.06	9.03	9.02	9.02
600	11.27	11.18	11.11	11.05	11.00	10.97	10.94	10.92	10.90	10.88	10.87	10.83	10.82	10.82
700	13.15	13.04	12.96	12.89	12.84	12.80	12.76	12.73	12.71	12.69	12.68	12.64	12.63	12.62
800	15.02	14.90	14.81	14.73	14.67	14.62	14.58	14.55	14.53	14.51	14.49	14.44	14.43	14.42
900	16.90	16.77	16.66	16.57	16.50	16.45	16.41	16.37	16.34	16.32	16.30	16.25	16.23	16.23
1000	18.78	18.63	18.51	18.41	18.34	18.28	18.23	18.19	18.16	18.13	18.11	18.05	18.04	18.03
2000	37.55	37.25	37.01	36.82	36.67	36.55	36.45	36.37	36.31	36.26	36.22	36.10	36.07	36.05
3000	56.33	55.88	55.52	55.23	55.00	54.82	54.67	54.56	54.46	54.38	54.32	54.15	54.10	54.08
4000	75.10	74.50	74.02	73.64	73.34	73.09	72.90	72.74	72.61	72.51	72.43	72.20	72.13	72.10
5000	93.88	93.13	92.53	92.05	91.67	91.37	91.12	90.92	90.77	90.64	90.54	90.25	90.16	90.13
6000	112.65	111.75	111.03	110.46	110.00	109.64	109.34	109.11	108.92	108.76	108.64	108.30	108.19	108.15
7000	131.43	130.38	129.54	128.87	128.34	127.91	127.57	127.29	127.07	126.89	126.75	126.35	126.22	126.17
8000	150.20	149.00	148.04	147.28	146.67	146.18	145.79	145.47	145.22	145.02	144.85	144.40	144.25	144.20
9000	168.98	167.63	166.55	165.69	165.00	164.45	164.01	163.66	163.37	163.14	162.96	162.45	162.28	162.22
10000	187.75	186.25	185.05	184.10	183.34	182.73	182.24	181.84	181.53	181.27	181.07	180.50	180.31	180.25
11000	206.53	204.87	203.56	202.51	201.67	201.00	200.46	200.03	199.68	199.40	199.17	198.55	198.34	198.27
12000	225.30	223.50	222.06	220.92	220.00	219.27	218.68	218.21	217.83	217.52	217.28	216.60	216.37	216.30
13000	244.08	242.12	240.57	239.33	238.34	237.54	236.91	236.39	235.98	235.65	235.38	234.65	234.41	234.32
14000	262.85	260.75	259.07	257.74	256.67	255.81	255.13	254.58	254.13	253.78	253.49	252.70	252.44	252.34
15000	281.63	279.37	277.58	276.15	275.00	274.09	273.35	272.76	272.29	271.90	271.60	270.75	270.47	270.37
16000	300.40	298.00	296.08	294.56	293.34	292.36	291.57	290.94	290.44	290.03	289.70	288.80	288.50	288.39
17000	319.18	316.62	314.59	312.97	311.67	310.63	309.80	309.13	308.59	308.16	307.81	306.85	306.53	306.42
18000	337.95	335.25	333.09	331.38	330.00	328.90	328.02	327.31	326.74	326.28	325.91	324.90	324.56	324.44
19000	356.73	353.87	351.60	349.79	348.34	347.18	346.24	345.50	344.89	344.41	344.02	342.95	342.59	342.47
20000	375.50	372.50	370.10	368.20	366.67	365.45	364.47	363.68	363.05	362.54	362.13	361.00	360.62	360.49
21000	394.28	391.12	388.61	386.60	385.00	383.72	382.69	381.86	381.20	380.66	380.23	379.05	378.65	378.51
22000	413.05	409.74	407.11	405.01	403.34	401.99	400.91	400.05	399.35	398.79	398.34	397.10	396.68	396.54
23000	431.83	428.37	425.62	423.42	421.67	420.26	419.14	418.23	417.50	416.92	416.45	415.15	414.71	414.56
24000	450.60	446.99	444.12	441.83	440.00	438.54	437.36	436.41	435.65	435.04	434.55	433.20	432.74	432.59
25000	469.38	465.62	462.63	460.24	458.34	456.81	455.58	454.60	453.81	453.17	452.66	451.25	450.77	450.61
26000	488.15	484.24	481.13	478.65	476.67	475.08	473.81	472.78	471.96	471.30	470.76	469.30	468.81	468.64
27000	506.93	502.87	499.64	497.06	495.00	493.35	492.03	490.97	490.11	489.42	488.87	487.35	486.84	486.66
28000	525.70	521.49	518.14	515.47	513.34	511.62	510.25	509.15	508.26	507.55	506.98	505.40	504.87	504.68
29000	544.48	540.12	536.65	533.88	531.67	529.90	528.48	527.33	526.42	525.68	525.08	523.45	522.90	522.71
30000	563.25	558.74	555.15	552.29	550.00	548.17	546.70	545.52	544.57	543.80	543.19	541.50	540.93	540.73
31000	582.03	577.36	573.66	570.70	568.34	566.44	564.92	563.70	562.72	561.93	561.29	559.55	558.96	558.76
32000	600.80	595.99	592.16	589.11	586.67	584.71	583.14	581.88	580.87	580.06	579.40	577.60	576.99	576.78
33000	619.57	614.61	610.67	607.52	605.00	602.99	601.37	600.07	599.02	598.18	597.51	595.65	595.02	594.81
34000	638.35	633.24	629.17	625.93	623.34	621.26	619.59	618.25	617.18	616.31	615.61	613.70	613.05	612.83
35000	657.12	651.86	647.68	644.34	641.67	639.53	637.81	636.44	635.33	634.44	633.72	631.75	631.08	630.85
36000	675.90	670.49	666.18	662.75	660.00	657.80	656.04	654.62	653.48	652.56	651.82	649.80	649.11	648.88
37000	694.67	689.11	684.69	681.16	678.33	676.07	674.26	672.80	671.63	670.69	669.93	667.85	667.14	666.90
38000	713.45	707.74	703.19	699.57	696.67	694.35	692.48	690.99	689.78	688.82	688.04	685.90	685.18	684.93
39000	732.22	726.36	721.70	717.98	715.00	712.62	710.71	709.17	707.94	706.94	706.14	703.95	703.21	702.95
40000	751.00	744.99	740.20	736.39	733.33	730.89	728.93	727.35	726.09	725.07	724.25	722.00	721.24	720.97
41000	769.77	763.61	758.71	754.80	751.67	749.16	747.15	745.54	744.24	743.20	742.36	740.05	739.27	739.00
42000	788.55	782.23	777.21	773.20	770.00	767.43	765.38	763.72	762.39	761.32	760.46	758.10	757.30	757.02
43000	807.32	800.86	795.72	791.61	788.33	785.71	783.60	781.91	780.54	779.45	778.57	776.15	775.33	775.05
44000	826.10	819.48	814.22	810.02	806.67	803.98	801.82	800.09	798.70	797.58	796.67	794.20	793.36	793.07
45000	844.87	838.11	832.73	828.43	825.00	822.25	820.04	818.27	816.85	815.70	814.78	812.25	811.39	811.10
46000	863.65	856.73	851.23	846.84	843.33	840.52	838.27	836.46	835.00	833.83	832.89	830.30	829.42	829.12
47000	882.42	875.36	869.74	865.25	861.67	858.80	856.49	854.64	853.15	851.96	850.99	848.35	847.45	847.14
48000	901.20	893.98	888.24	883.66	880.00	877.07	874.71	872.82	871.30	870.08	869.10	866.40	865.48	865.17
49000	919.97	912.61	906.75	902.07	898.33	895.34	892.94	891.01	889.46	888.21	887.20	884.45	883.51	883.19
50000	938.75	931.23	925.25	920.48	916.67	913.61	911.16	909.19	907.61	906.34	905.31	902.50	901.54	901.22
55000	1032.62	1024.35	1017.78	1012.53	1008.33	1004.97	1002.28	1000.11	998.37	996.97	995.84	992.75	991.70	991.34
60000	1126.50	1117.48	1110.30	1104.58	1100.00	1096.33	1093.39	1091.03	1089.13	1087.60	1086.37	1083.00	1081.85	1081.46
65000	1220.37	1210.60	1202.83	1196.62	1191.67	1187.69	1184.51	1181.95	1179.89	1178.23	1176.90	1173.25	1172.01	1171.58
70000	1314.24	1303.72	1295.35	1288.67	1283.33	1279.05	1275.62	1272.87	1270.65	1268.87	1267.43	1263.50	1262.16	1261.70
75000	1408.12	1396.84	1387.87	1380.72	1375.00	1370.41	1366.74	1363.79	1361.41	1359.50	1357.96	1353.75	1352.31	1351.82
80000	1501.99	1489.97	1480.40	1472.77	1466.66	1461.78	1457.85	1454.70	1452.17	1450.13	1448.49	1444.00	1442.47	1441.94
85000	1595.87	1583.09	1572.92	1564.81	1558.33	1553.14	1548.97	1545.62	1542.93	1540.77	1539.02	1534.25	1532.62	1532.07
90000	1689.74	1676.21	1665.45	1656.86	1650.00	1644.50	1640.08	1636.54	1633.69	1631.40	1629.55	1624.50	1622.78	1622.19
95000	1783.62	1769.33	1757.97	1748.91	1741.66	1735.86	1731.20	1727.46	1724.45	1722.03	1720.09	1714.75	1712.93	1712.31
100000	1877.49	1862.46	1850.50	1840.96	1833.33	1827.22	1822.32	1818.38	1815.21	1812.67	1810.62	1805.00	1803.08	1802.43

21.700%

TERM	1 Year	2 Years	3 Years	4 Years	5 Years	6 Years	7 Years	8 Years	9 Years	10 Years	11 Years	12 Years	13 Years	14 Years
AMOUNT														
5	.47	.26	.20	.16	.14	.13	.12	.12	.11	.11	.10	.10	.10	.10
10	.94	.52	.39	.32	.28	.25	.24	.23	.22	.21	.20	.20	.20	.20
15	1.41	.78	.58	.48	.42	.38	.35	.34	.32	.31	.30	.30	.29	.29
25	2.34	1.30	.96	.79	.69	.63	.59	.56	.53	.52	.50	.49	.49	.48
50	4.68	2.59	1.91	1.57	1.38	1.25	1.17	1.11	1.06	1.03	1.00	.98	.97	.96
75	7.01	3.88	2.86	2.36	2.06	1.88	1.75	1.66	1.59	1.54	1.50	1.47	1.45	1.43
100	9.35	5.18	3.81	3.14	2.75	2.50	2.33	2.21	2.12	2.05	2.00	1.96	1.93	1.91
200	18.70	10.35	7.61	6.27	5.49	4.99	4.65	4.41	4.23	4.10	4.00	3.92	3.86	3.81
300	28.04	15.52	11.42	9.41	8.24	7.49	6.98	6.61	6.35	6.14	5.99	5.87	5.78	5.71
400	37.39	20.70	15.22	12.54	10.98	9.98	9.30	8.82	8.46	8.19	7.99	7.83	7.71	7.61
500	46.73	25.87	19.02	15.68	13.73	12.48	11.63	11.02	10.57	10.24	9.98	9.79	9.63	9.52
600	56.08	31.04	22.83	18.81	16.47	14.97	13.95	13.22	12.69	12.28	11.98	11.74	11.56	11.42
700	65.42	36.22	26.63	21.95	19.22	17.47	16.27	15.42	14.80	14.33	13.97	13.70	13.49	13.32
800	74.77	41.39	30.43	25.08	21.96	19.96	18.60	17.63	16.91	16.38	15.97	15.66	15.41	15.22
900	84.11	46.56	34.24	28.21	24.71	22.46	20.92	19.83	19.03	18.42	17.97	17.61	17.34	17.12
1000	93.46	51.74	38.04	31.35	27.45	24.95	23.25	22.03	21.14	20.47	19.96	19.57	19.26	19.03
2000	186.91	103.47	76.08	62.69	54.90	49.90	46.49	44.06	42.27	40.94	39.92	39.13	38.52	38.05
3000	280.36	155.20	114.11	94.04	82.35	74.85	69.73	66.08	63.41	61.40	59.88	58.70	57.78	57.07
4000	373.81	206.93	152.15	125.38	109.80	99.80	92.97	88.11	84.54	81.87	79.83	78.26	77.04	76.09
5000	467.26	258.66	190.18	156.72	137.25	124.75	116.21	110.13	105.67	102.33	99.79	97.83	96.30	95.11
6000	560.71	310.39	228.22	188.07	164.70	149.70	139.45	132.16	126.81	122.80	119.75	117.39	115.56	114.13
7000	654.16	362.12	266.25	219.41	192.15	174.64	162.69	154.18	147.94	143.27	139.70	136.96	134.82	133.15
8000	747.61	413.85	304.29	250.75	219.59	199.59	185.93	176.21	169.08	163.73	159.66	156.52	154.08	152.17
9000	841.06	465.58	342.32	282.10	247.04	224.54	209.17	198.23	190.21	184.20	179.62	176.09	173.34	171.19
10000	934.51	517.31	380.36	313.44	274.49	249.49	232.42	220.26	211.34	204.66	199.58	195.65	192.60	190.21
11000	1027.96	569.04	418.39	344.78	301.94	274.44	255.66	242.28	232.48	225.13	219.53	215.22	211.86	209.23
12000	1121.41	620.77	456.43	376.13	329.39	299.39	278.90	264.31	253.61	245.59	239.49	234.78	231.12	228.25
13000	1214.86	672.50	494.47	407.47	356.84	324.33	302.14	286.34	274.75	266.06	259.45	254.35	250.38	247.27
14000	1308.31	724.23	532.50	438.81	384.29	349.28	325.38	308.36	295.88	286.53	279.40	273.91	269.64	266.29
15000	1401.76	775.96	570.54	470.16	411.73	374.23	348.62	330.39	317.01	306.99	299.36	293.48	288.90	285.31
16000	1495.21	827.69	608.57	501.50	439.18	399.18	371.86	352.41	338.15	327.46	319.32	313.04	308.16	304.33
17000	1588.66	879.42	646.61	532.84	466.63	424.13	395.10	374.44	359.28	347.92	339.27	332.61	327.42	323.35
18000	1682.11	931.15	684.64	564.19	494.08	449.08	418.34	396.46	380.42	368.39	359.23	352.17	346.67	342.37
19000	1775.56	982.88	722.68	595.53	521.53	474.02	441.58	418.49	401.55	388.86	379.19	371.74	365.93	361.39
20000	1869.01	1034.61	760.71	626.87	548.98	498.97	464.83	440.51	422.68	409.32	399.15	391.30	385.19	380.41
21000	1962.46	1086.34	798.75	658.22	576.43	523.92	488.07	462.54	443.82	429.79	419.10	410.86	404.45	399.43
22000	2055.91	1138.07	836.78	689.56	603.87	548.87	511.31	484.56	464.95	450.25	439.06	430.43	423.71	418.45
23000	2149.36	1189.80	874.82	720.90	631.32	573.82	534.55	506.59	486.08	470.72	459.02	449.99	442.97	437.47
24000	2242.81	1241.53	912.86	752.25	658.77	598.77	557.79	528.61	507.22	491.18	478.97	469.56	462.23	456.49
25000	2336.26	1293.26	950.89	783.59	686.22	623.71	581.03	550.64	528.35	511.65	498.93	489.12	481.49	475.51
26000	2429.71	1344.99	988.93	814.93	713.67	648.66	604.27	572.67	549.49	532.12	518.89	508.69	500.75	494.53
27000	2523.16	1396.72	1026.96	846.28	741.12	673.61	627.51	594.69	570.62	552.58	538.84	528.25	520.01	513.55
28000	2616.61	1448.45	1065.00	877.62	768.57	698.56	650.75	616.72	591.75	573.05	558.80	547.82	539.27	532.57
29000	2710.06	1500.18	1103.03	908.96	796.01	723.51	673.99	638.74	612.89	593.51	578.76	567.38	558.53	551.59
30000	2803.51	1551.91	1141.07	940.31	823.46	748.46	697.24	660.77	634.02	613.98	598.72	586.95	577.79	570.61
31000	2896.96	1603.64	1179.10	971.65	850.91	773.40	720.48	682.79	655.16	634.45	618.67	606.51	597.05	589.63
32000	2990.41	1655.37	1217.14	1002.99	878.36	798.35	743.72	704.82	676.29	654.91	638.63	626.08	616.31	608.65
33000	3083.86	1707.10	1255.17	1034.34	905.81	823.30	766.96	726.84	697.42	675.38	658.59	645.64	635.57	627.67
34000	3177.31	1758.83	1293.21	1065.68	933.26	848.25	790.20	748.87	718.56	695.84	678.54	665.21	654.83	646.69
35000	3270.76	1810.56	1331.25	1097.03	960.71	873.20	813.44	770.89	739.69	716.31	698.50	684.77	674.09	665.71
36000	3364.21	1862.29	1369.28	1128.37	988.16	898.15	836.68	792.92	760.83	736.77	718.46	704.34	693.34	684.73
37000	3457.66	1914.02	1407.32	1159.71	1015.60	923.09	859.92	814.94	781.96	757.24	738.41	723.90	712.60	703.75
38000	3551.11	1965.75	1445.35	1191.06	1043.05	948.04	883.16	836.97	803.09	777.71	758.37	743.47	731.86	722.77
39000	3644.56	2017.48	1483.39	1222.40	1070.50	972.99	906.41	859.00	824.23	798.17	778.33	763.03	751.12	741.79
40000	3738.01	2069.21	1521.42	1253.74	1097.95	997.94	929.65	881.02	845.36	818.64	798.29	782.59	770.38	760.81
41000	3831.46	2120.94	1559.46	1285.09	1125.40	1022.89	952.89	903.05	866.49	839.10	818.24	802.16	789.64	779.83
42000	3924.91	2172.67	1597.49	1316.43	1152.85	1047.84	976.13	925.07	887.63	859.57	838.20	821.72	808.90	798.85
43000	4018.36	2224.40	1635.53	1347.77	1180.30	1072.78	999.37	947.10	908.76	880.04	858.16	841.29	828.16	817.87
44000	4111.81	2276.13	1673.56	1379.12	1207.74	1097.73	1022.61	969.12	929.90	900.50	878.11	860.85	847.42	836.89
45000	4205.26	2327.86	1711.60	1410.46	1235.19	1122.68	1045.85	991.15	951.03	920.97	898.07	880.42	866.68	855.91
46000	4298.71	2379.59	1749.63	1441.80	1262.64	1147.63	1069.09	1013.17	972.16	941.43	918.03	899.98	885.94	874.93
47000	4392.16	2431.32	1787.67	1473.15	1290.09	1172.58	1092.33	1035.20	993.30	961.90	937.98	919.55	905.20	893.95
48000	4485.61	2483.05	1825.71	1504.49	1317.54	1197.53	1115.57	1057.22	1014.43	982.36	957.94	939.11	924.46	912.97
49000	4579.06	2534.78	1863.74	1535.83	1344.99	1222.47	1138.82	1079.25	1035.57	1002.83	977.90	958.68	943.72	931.99
50000	4672.51	2586.51	1901.78	1567.18	1372.44	1247.42	1162.06	1101.28	1056.70	1023.30	997.86	978.24	962.98	951.01
55000	5139.76	2845.16	2091.95	1723.89	1509.68	1372.17	1278.26	1211.40	1162.37	1125.62	1097.64	1076.07	1059.27	1046.11
60000	5607.01	3103.81	2282.13	1880.61	1646.92	1496.91	1394.47	1321.53	1268.04	1227.95	1197.43	1173.89	1155.57	1141.21
65000	6074.26	3362.46	2472.31	2037.33	1784.16	1621.65	1510.67	1431.66	1373.71	1330.28	1297.21	1271.71	1251.87	1236.31
70000	6541.51	3621.11	2662.49	2194.05	1921.41	1746.39	1626.88	1541.78	1479.38	1432.61	1397.00	1369.54	1348.17	1331.41
75000	7008.76	3879.76	2852.66	2350.76	2058.65	1871.13	1743.08	1651.91	1585.05	1534.94	1496.78	1467.36	1444.46	1426.51
80000	7476.01	4138.42	3042.84	2507.48	2195.89	1995.87	1859.29	1762.04	1690.72	1637.27	1596.57	1565.18	1540.76	1521.61
85000	7943.26	4397.07	3233.02	2664.20	2333.14	2120.62	1975.49	1872.16	1796.39	1739.60	1696.35	1663.01	1637.06	1616.71
90000	8410.51	4655.72	3423.19	2820.91	2470.38	2245.36	2091.70	1982.29	1902.06	1841.93	1796.14	1760.83	1733.35	1711.81
95000	8877.76	4914.37	3613.37	2977.63	2607.62	2370.10	2207.90	2092.42	2007.73	1944.26	1895.92	1858.66	1829.65	1806.91
100000	9345.01	5173.02	3803.55	3134.35	2744.87	2494.84	2324.11	2202.55	2113.39	2046.59	1995.71	1956.48	1925.95	1902.01

TERM	15 Years	16 Years	17 Years	18 Years	19 Years	20 Years	21 Years	22 Years	23 Years	24 Years	25 Years	30 Years	35 Years	40 Years
AMOUNT														
5	.10	.10	.10	.10	.10	.10	.10	.10	.10	.10	.10	.10	.10	.10
10	.19	.19	.19	.19	.19	.19	.19	.19	.19	.19	.19	.19	.19	.19
15	.29	.29	.28	.28	.28	.28	.28	.28	.28	.28	.28	.28	.28	.28
25	.48	.47	.47	.47	.46	.46	.46	.46	.46	.46	.46	.46	.46	.46
50	.95	.94	.93	.93	.92	.92	.92	.92	.92	.91	.91	.91	.91	.91
75	1.42	1.41	1.40	1.39	1.38	1.38	1.38	1.37	1.37	1.37	1.37	1.36	1.36	1.36
100	1.89	1.87	1.86	1.85	1.84	1.84	1.83	1.83	1.83	1.82	1.82	1.82	1.81	1.81
200	3.77	3.74	3.72	3.70	3.68	3.67	3.66	3.65	3.65	3.64	3.64	3.63	3.62	3.62
300	5.65	5.61	5.57	5.55	5.52	5.50	5.49	5.48	5.47	5.46	5.46	5.44	5.43	5.43
400	7.54	7.48	7.43	7.39	7.36	7.34	7.32	7.30	7.29	7.28	7.27	7.25	7.24	7.24
500	9.42	9.35	9.29	9.24	9.20	9.17	9.15	9.13	9.11	9.10	9.09	9.06	9.05	9.05
600	11.30	11.21	11.14	11.09	11.04	11.00	10.97	10.95	10.93	10.92	10.91	10.87	10.86	10.86
700	13.19	13.08	13.00	12.93	12.88	12.84	12.80	12.78	12.75	12.74	12.72	12.68	12.67	12.67
800	15.07	14.95	14.86	14.78	14.72	14.67	14.63	14.60	14.58	14.56	14.54	14.49	14.48	14.47
900	16.95	16.82	16.71	16.63	16.56	16.50	16.46	16.42	16.40	16.37	16.36	16.31	16.29	16.28
1000	18.84	18.69	18.57	18.47	18.40	18.34	18.29	18.25	18.22	18.19	18.17	18.12	18.10	18.09
2000	37.67	37.37	37.13	36.94	36.79	36.67	36.57	36.49	36.43	36.38	36.34	36.23	36.19	36.18
3000	56.50	56.05	55.69	55.41	55.18	55.00	54.85	54.74	54.64	54.57	54.51	54.34	54.28	54.26
4000	75.33	74.73	74.26	73.88	73.57	73.33	73.14	72.98	72.86	72.76	72.67	72.45	72.38	72.35
5000	94.16	93.41	92.82	92.35	91.97	91.66	91.42	91.23	91.07	90.94	90.84	90.56	90.47	90.44
6000	112.99	112.10	111.38	110.81	110.36	110.00	109.70	109.47	109.28	109.13	109.01	108.68	108.56	108.52
7000	131.82	130.78	129.95	129.28	128.75	128.33	127.99	127.71	127.49	127.32	127.18	126.79	126.66	126.61
8000	150.66	149.46	148.51	147.75	147.14	146.66	146.27	145.96	145.71	145.51	145.34	144.90	144.75	144.70
9000	169.49	168.14	167.07	166.22	165.54	164.99	164.55	164.20	163.92	163.69	163.51	163.01	162.84	162.78
10000	188.32	186.82	185.63	184.69	183.93	183.32	182.84	182.45	182.13	181.88	181.68	181.12	180.94	180.87
11000	207.15	205.50	204.20	203.15	202.32	201.65	201.12	200.69	200.35	200.07	199.85	199.24	199.03	198.96
12000	225.98	224.19	222.76	221.62	220.71	219.99	219.40	218.93	218.56	218.26	218.01	217.35	217.12	217.04
13000	244.81	242.87	241.32	240.09	239.11	238.32	237.69	237.18	236.77	236.44	236.18	235.46	235.21	235.13
14000	263.64	261.55	259.89	258.56	257.50	256.65	255.97	255.42	254.98	254.63	254.35	253.57	253.31	253.22
15000	282.47	280.23	278.45	277.03	275.89	274.98	274.25	273.67	273.20	272.82	272.52	271.68	271.40	271.30
16000	301.31	298.91	297.01	295.49	294.28	293.31	292.54	291.91	291.41	291.01	290.68	289.80	289.49	289.39
17000	320.14	317.60	315.57	313.96	312.68	311.64	310.82	310.16	309.62	309.19	308.85	307.91	307.59	307.48
18000	338.97	336.28	334.14	332.43	331.07	329.98	329.10	328.40	327.84	327.38	327.02	326.02	325.68	325.56
19000	357.00	354.96	352.70	350.90	349.46	348.31	347.39	346.64	346.05	345.57	345.18	344.13	343.77	343.65
20000	376.63	373.64	371.26	369.37	367.85	366.64	365.67	364.89	364.26	363.76	363.35	362.24	361.87	361.74
21000	395.46	392.32	389.83	387.84	386.25	384.97	383.95	383.13	382.47	381.94	381.52	380.36	379.96	379.82
22000	414.29	411.00	408.39	406.30	404.64	403.30	402.23	401.38	400.69	400.13	399.69	398.47	398.05	397.91
23000	433.12	429.69	426.95	424.77	423.03	421.64	420.52	419.62	418.90	418.32	417.85	416.58	416.15	416.00
24000	451.96	448.37	445.51	443.24	441.42	439.97	438.80	437.86	437.11	436.51	436.02	434.69	434.24	434.08
25000	470.79	467.05	464.08	461.71	459.81	458.30	457.08	456.11	455.33	454.70	454.19	452.80	452.33	452.17
26000	489.62	485.73	482.64	480.18	478.21	476.63	475.37	474.35	473.54	472.88	472.36	470.91	470.42	470.26
27000	508.45	504.41	501.20	498.64	496.60	494.96	493.65	492.60	491.75	491.07	490.52	489.03	488.52	488.34
28000	527.28	523.09	519.77	517.11	514.99	513.29	511.93	510.84	509.96	509.26	508.69	507.14	506.61	506.43
29000	546.11	541.78	538.33	535.58	533.38	531.63	530.22	529.09	528.18	527.45	526.86	525.25	524.70	524.52
30000	564.94	560.46	556.89	554.05	551.78	549.96	548.50	547.33	546.39	545.63	545.03	543.36	542.80	542.60
31000	583.78	579.14	575.45	572.52	570.17	568.29	566.78	565.57	564.60	563.82	563.19	561.47	560.89	560.69
32000	602.61	597.82	594.02	590.98	588.56	586.62	585.07	583.82	582.81	582.01	581.36	579.59	578.98	578.78
33000	621.44	616.50	612.58	609.45	606.95	604.95	603.35	602.06	601.03	600.20	599.53	597.70	597.08	596.86
34000	640.27	635.19	631.14	627.92	625.35	623.28	621.63	620.31	619.24	618.38	617.69	615.81	615.17	614.95
35000	659.10	653.87	649.71	646.39	643.74	641.62	639.92	638.55	637.45	636.57	635.86	633.92	633.26	633.04
36000	677.93	672.55	668.27	664.86	662.13	659.95	658.20	656.79	655.67	654.76	654.03	652.03	651.36	651.12
37000	696.76	691.23	686.83	683.33	680.52	678.28	676.48	675.04	673.88	672.95	672.20	670.15	669.45	669.21
38000	715.59	709.91	705.40	701.79	698.92	696.61	694.77	693.28	692.09	691.13	690.36	688.26	687.54	687.30
39000	734.43	728.59	723.96	720.26	717.31	714.94	713.05	711.53	710.30	709.32	708.53	706.37	705.63	705.38
40000	753.26	747.28	742.52	738.73	735.70	733.28	731.33	729.77	728.52	727.51	726.70	724.48	723.73	723.47
41000	772.09	765.96	761.08	757.20	754.09	751.61	749.61	748.02	746.73	745.70	744.87	742.59	741.82	741.56
42000	790.92	784.64	779.65	775.67	772.49	769.94	767.90	766.26	764.94	763.88	763.03	760.71	759.91	759.64
43000	809.75	803.32	798.21	794.13	790.88	788.27	786.18	784.50	783.16	782.07	781.20	778.82	778.01	777.73
44000	828.58	822.00	816.77	812.60	809.27	806.60	804.46	802.75	801.37	800.26	799.37	796.93	796.10	795.82
45000	847.41	840.68	835.34	831.07	827.66	824.93	822.75	820.99	819.58	818.45	817.54	815.04	814.19	813.90
46000	866.24	859.37	853.90	849.54	846.05	843.27	841.03	839.24	837.79	836.63	835.70	833.15	832.29	831.99
47000	885.08	878.05	872.46	868.01	864.45	861.60	859.31	857.48	856.01	854.82	853.87	851.26	850.38	850.08
48000	903.91	896.73	891.02	886.47	882.84	879.93	877.60	875.72	874.22	873.01	872.04	869.38	868.47	868.16
49000	922.74	915.41	909.59	904.94	901.23	898.26	895.88	893.97	892.43	891.20	890.20	887.49	886.57	886.25
50000	941.57	934.09	928.15	923.41	919.62	916.59	914.16	912.21	910.65	909.39	908.37	905.60	904.66	904.34
55000	1035.73	1027.50	1020.96	1015.75	1011.59	1008.25	1005.58	1003.43	1001.71	1000.32	999.21	996.16	995.12	994.77
60000	1129.88	1120.91	1113.78	1108.09	1103.55	1099.91	1096.99	1094.65	1092.77	1091.26	1090.05	1086.72	1085.59	1085.20
65000	1224.04	1214.32	1206.59	1200.43	1195.51	1191.57	1188.41	1185.87	1183.84	1182.20	1180.88	1177.28	1176.05	1175.64
70000	1318.20	1307.73	1299.41	1292.77	1287.47	1283.23	1279.83	1277.10	1274.90	1273.14	1271.72	1267.84	1266.52	1266.07
75000	1412.35	1401.14	1392.22	1385.11	1379.43	1374.89	1371.24	1368.32	1365.97	1364.08	1362.56	1358.40	1356.99	1356.50
80000	1506.51	1494.55	1485.04	1477.45	1471.40	1466.55	1462.66	1459.54	1457.03	1455.01	1453.39	1448.96	1447.45	1446.94
85000	1600.67	1587.96	1577.85	1569.80	1563.36	1558.21	1554.07	1550.76	1548.09	1545.95	1544.23	1539.52	1537.92	1537.37
90000	1694.82	1681.36	1670.67	1662.14	1655.32	1649.86	1645.49	1641.98	1639.16	1636.89	1635.07	1630.08	1628.38	1627.80
95000	1788.98	1774.77	1763.49	1754.48	1747.28	1741.52	1736.91	1733.20	1730.22	1727.83	1725.90	1720.64	1718.85	1718.24
100000	1883.13	1868.18	1856.29	1846.82	1839.24	1833.18	1828.32	1824.42	1821.29	1818.77	1816.74	1811.20	1809.31	1808.67

MONTHLY PAYMENT
REQUIRED TO AMORTIZE A LOAN

TERM	1 Year	2 Years	3 Years	4 Years	5 Years	6 Years	7 Years	8 Years	9 Years	10 Years	11 Years	12 Years	13 Years	14 Years
AMOUNT														
5	.47	.26	.20	.16	.14	.13	.12	.12	.11	.11	.10	.10	.10	.10
10	.94	.52	.39	.32	.28	.25	.24	.23	.22	.21	.20	.20	.20	.20
15	1.41	.78	.58	.48	.42	.38	.35	.34	.32	.31	.30	.30	.29	.29
25	2.34	1.30	.96	.79	.69	.63	.59	.56	.53	.52	.50	.50	.49	.48
50	4.68	2.59	1.91	1.57	1.38	1.25	1.17	1.11	1.06	1.03	1.00	.99	.97	.96
75	7.02	3.89	2.86	2.36	2.07	1.88	1.75	1.66	1.59	1.54	1.50	1.48	1.45	1.43
100	9.35	5.18	3.81	3.14	2.75	2.50	2.33	2.21	2.12	2.05	2.00	1.97	1.93	1.91
200	18.70	10.36	7.62	6.28	5.50	5.00	4.66	4.42	4.24	4.10	4.00	3.93	3.86	3.82
300	28.05	15.53	11.42	9.42	8.25	7.50	6.99	6.62	6.36	6.15	6.00	5.89	5.79	5.72
400	37.39	20.71	15.23	12.55	11.00	10.00	9.31	8.83	8.47	8.20	8.00	7.85	7.72	7.63
500	46.74	25.88	19.04	15.69	13.74	12.49	11.64	11.03	10.59	10.25	10.00	9.81	9.65	9.53
600	56.09	31.06	22.84	18.83	16.49	14.99	13.97	13.24	12.71	12.30	12.00	11.77	11.58	11.44
700	65.44	36.23	26.65	21.96	19.24	17.49	16.30	15.45	14.82	14.35	14.00	13.73	13.51	13.34
800	74.78	41.41	30.45	25.10	21.99	19.99	18.62	17.65	16.94	16.40	16.00	15.69	15.44	15.25
900	84.13	46.58	34.26	28.24	24.73	22.49	20.95	19.86	19.06	18.45	18.00	17.65	17.37	17.16
1000	93.48	51.76	38.07	31.38	27.48	24.98	23.28	22.06	21.17	20.50	20.00	19.61	19.30	19.06
2000	186.95	103.51	76.13	62.75	54.96	49.96	46.55	44.12	42.34	41.00	39.99	39.21	38.60	38.12
3000	280.43	155.27	114.19	94.12	82.44	74.94	69.82	66.18	63.51	61.50	59.98	58.81	57.89	57.18
4000	373.90	207.02	152.25	125.49	109.91	99.92	93.09	88.23	84.67	82.00	79.97	78.41	77.19	76.23
5000	467.38	258.78	190.31	156.86	137.39	124.89	116.36	110.29	105.84	102.50	99.96	98.01	96.48	95.29
6000	560.85	310.53	228.37	188.23	164.87	149.87	139.64	132.35	127.01	123.00	119.96	117.61	115.78	114.35
7000	654.32	362.29	266.43	219.60	192.34	174.85	162.91	154.41	148.17	143.50	139.95	137.21	135.08	133.40
8000	747.80	414.04	304.49	250.97	219.82	199.83	186.18	176.46	169.34	164.00	159.94	156.81	154.37	152.46
9000	841.27	465.80	342.56	282.34	247.30	224.81	209.45	198.52	190.51	184.50	179.93	176.41	173.67	171.52
10000	934.75	517.55	380.62	313.71	274.77	249.78	232.72	220.58	211.67	205.00	199.92	196.01	192.96	190.58
11000	1028.22	569.31	418.68	345.08	302.25	274.76	255.99	242.64	232.84	225.50	219.92	215.61	212.26	209.63
12000	1121.69	621.06	456.74	376.45	329.73	299.74	279.27	264.69	254.01	246.00	239.91	235.21	231.55	228.69
13000	1215.17	672.82	494.80	407.82	357.21	324.72	302.54	286.75	275.17	266.50	259.90	254.81	250.85	247.75
14000	1308.64	724.57	532.86	439.19	384.68	349.70	325.81	308.81	296.34	287.00	279.89	274.41	270.15	266.80
15000	1402.12	776.33	570.92	470.56	412.16	374.67	349.08	330.86	317.51	307.50	299.88	294.01	289.44	285.86
16000	1495.59	828.08	608.98	501.93	439.64	399.65	372.35	352.92	338.67	328.00	319.88	313.61	308.74	304.92
17000	1589.06	879.84	647.05	533.30	467.11	424.63	395.63	374.98	359.84	348.50	339.87	333.21	328.03	323.98
18000	1682.54	931.59	685.11	564.67	494.59	449.61	418.90	397.04	381.01	369.00	359.86	352.81	347.33	343.03
19000	1776.01	983.35	723.17	596.04	522.07	474.59	442.17	419.09	402.18	389.50	379.85	372.41	366.63	362.09
20000	1869.49	1035.10	761.23	627.42	549.54	499.56	465.44	441.15	423.34	410.00	399.84	392.01	385.92	381.15
21000	1962.96	1086.86	799.29	658.79	577.02	524.54	488.71	463.21	444.51	430.50	419.83	411.61	405.22	400.20
22000	2056.44	1138.61	837.35	690.16	604.50	549.52	511.98	485.27	465.68	451.00	439.83	431.21	424.51	419.26
23000	2149.91	1190.36	875.41	721.53	631.98	574.50	535.26	507.32	486.84	471.50	459.82	450.81	443.81	438.32
24000	2243.38	1242.12	913.49	752.90	659.45	599.48	558.53	529.38	508.01	492.00	479.81	470.41	463.10	457.38
25000	2336.86	1293.87	951.54	784.27	686.93	624.45	581.80	551.44	529.18	512.50	499.80	490.01	482.40	476.43
26000	2430.33	1345.63	989.60	815.64	714.41	649.43	605.07	573.49	550.34	533.00	519.79	509.62	501.70	495.49
27000	2523.81	1397.38	1027.66	847.01	741.88	674.41	628.34	595.55	571.51	553.50	539.78	529.22	520.99	514.55
28000	2617.28	1449.14	1065.72	878.38	769.36	699.39	651.62	617.61	592.68	574.00	559.78	548.82	540.29	533.60
29000	2710.75	1500.89	1103.78	909.75	796.84	724.37	674.89	639.67	613.84	594.50	579.77	568.42	559.58	552.66
30000	2804.23	1552.65	1141.84	941.12	824.31	749.34	698.16	661.72	635.01	615.00	599.76	588.02	578.88	571.72
31000	2897.70	1604.40	1179.90	972.49	851.79	774.32	721.43	683.78	656.18	635.50	619.75	607.62	598.18	590.78
32000	2991.18	1656.16	1217.96	1003.86	879.27	799.30	744.70	705.84	677.34	656.00	639.74	627.22	617.47	609.83
33000	3084.65	1707.91	1256.03	1035.23	906.74	824.28	767.97	727.90	698.51	676.50	659.74	646.82	636.77	628.89
34000	3178.12	1759.67	1294.09	1066.60	934.22	849.26	791.25	749.95	719.68	697.00	679.73	666.42	656.06	647.95
35000	3271.60	1811.42	1332.15	1097.97	961.70	874.23	814.52	772.01	740.84	717.50	699.72	686.02	675.36	667.00
36000	3365.07	1863.18	1370.21	1129.34	989.18	899.21	837.79	794.07	762.01	738.00	719.71	705.62	694.65	686.06
37000	3458.55	1914.93	1408.27	1160.71	1016.65	924.19	861.06	816.13	783.18	758.50	739.70	725.22	713.95	705.12
38000	3552.02	1966.69	1446.33	1192.08	1044.13	949.17	884.33	838.18	804.35	779.00	759.69	744.82	733.25	724.18
39000	3645.50	2018.44	1484.39	1223.45	1071.61	974.14	907.61	860.24	825.51	799.49	779.69	764.42	752.54	743.23
40000	3738.97	2070.20	1522.45	1254.83	1099.08	999.12	930.88	882.30	846.68	819.99	799.68	784.02	771.84	762.29
41000	3832.44	2121.95	1560.52	1286.20	1126.56	1024.10	954.15	904.35	867.85	840.49	819.67	803.62	791.13	781.35
42000	3925.92	2173.71	1598.58	1317.57	1154.04	1049.08	977.42	926.41	889.01	860.99	839.66	823.22	810.43	800.40
43000	4019.39	2225.46	1636.64	1348.94	1181.51	1074.06	1000.69	948.47	910.18	881.49	859.65	842.82	829.73	819.46
44000	4112.87	2277.22	1674.70	1380.31	1208.99	1099.03	1023.96	970.53	931.35	901.99	879.65	862.42	849.02	838.52
45000	4206.34	2328.97	1712.76	1411.68	1236.47	1124.01	1047.24	992.58	952.51	922.49	899.64	882.02	868.32	857.58
46000	4299.81	2380.72	1750.82	1443.05	1263.95	1148.99	1070.51	1014.64	973.68	942.99	919.63	901.62	887.61	876.63
47000	4393.29	2432.48	1788.88	1474.42	1291.42	1173.97	1093.78	1036.70	994.85	963.49	939.62	921.22	906.91	895.69
48000	4486.76	2484.23	1826.94	1505.79	1318.90	1198.95	1117.05	1058.76	1016.01	983.99	959.61	940.82	926.20	914.75
49000	4580.24	2535.99	1865.01	1537.16	1346.38	1223.92	1140.32	1080.81	1037.18	1004.49	979.61	960.42	945.50	933.80
50000	4673.71	2587.74	1903.07	1568.53	1373.85	1248.90	1163.60	1102.87	1058.35	1024.99	999.60	980.02	964.80	952.86
55000	5141.08	2846.52	2093.37	1725.38	1511.24	1373.79	1279.95	1213.16	1164.18	1127.49	1099.56	1078.03	1061.28	1048.15
60000	5608.45	3105.29	2283.68	1882.24	1648.62	1498.68	1396.31	1323.44	1270.02	1229.99	1199.52	1176.03	1157.75	1143.43
65000	6075.82	3364.07	2473.99	2039.09	1786.01	1623.57	1512.67	1433.73	1375.85	1332.49	1299.47	1274.03	1254.23	1238.72
70000	6543.19	3622.84	2664.29	2195.94	1923.39	1748.46	1629.03	1544.02	1481.68	1434.99	1399.43	1372.03	1350.71	1334.00
75000	7010.56	3881.61	2854.60	2352.79	2060.78	1873.35	1745.39	1654.30	1587.52	1537.49	1499.39	1470.03	1447.19	1429.29
80000	7477.93	4140.39	3044.90	2509.65	2198.16	1998.24	1861.75	1764.59	1693.35	1639.98	1599.35	1568.04	1543.67	1524.57
85000	7945.30	4399.16	3235.21	2666.50	2335.55	2123.13	1978.11	1874.88	1799.19	1742.48	1699.31	1666.04	1640.15	1619.86
90000	8412.67	4657.94	3425.52	2823.35	2472.93	2248.02	2094.47	1985.16	1905.02	1844.98	1799.27	1764.04	1736.63	1715.15
95000	8880.05	4916.71	3615.82	2980.20	2610.32	2372.91	2210.83	2095.45	2010.86	1947.48	1899.23	1862.04	1833.11	1810.43
100000	9347.42	5175.48	3806.13	3137.06	2747.70	2497.80	2327.19	2205.73	2116.69	2049.98	1999.19	1960.04	1929.59	1905.72

MONTHLY PAYMENT
REQUIRED TO AMORTIZE A LOAN

21.750%

TERM	15 Years	16 Years	17 Years	18 Years	19 Years	20 Years	21 Years	22 Years	23 Years	24 Years	25 Years	30 Years	35 Years	40 Years
AMOUNT														
5	.10	.10	.10	.10	.10	.10	.10	.10	.10	.10	.10	.10	.10	.10
10	.19	.19	.19	.19	.19	.19	.19	.19	.19	.19	.19	.19	.19	.19
15	.29	.29	.28	.28	.28	.28	.28	.28	.28	.28	.28	.28	.28	.28
25	.48	.47	.47	.47	.47	.46	.46	.46	.46	.46	.46	.46	.46	.46
50	.95	.94	.94	.93	.93	.92	.92	.92	.92	.92	.92	.91	.91	.91
75	1.42	1.41	1.40	1.39	1.39	1.38	1.38	1.38	1.37	1.37	1.37	1.37	1.37	1.36
100	1.89	1.88	1.87	1.86	1.85	1.84	1.84	1.83	1.83	1.83	1.83	1.82	1.82	1.82
200	3.78	3.75	3.73	3.71	3.69	3.68	3.67	3.66	3.66	3.65	3.65	3.64	3.63	3.63
300	5.67	5.62	5.59	5.56	5.53	5.52	5.50	5.49	5.48	5.47	5.47	5.45	5.45	5.44
400	7.55	7.49	7.45	7.41	7.38	7.35	7.33	7.32	7.31	7.30	7.29	7.27	7.26	7.26
500	9.44	9.36	9.31	9.26	9.22	9.19	9.17	9.15	9.13	9.12	9.11	9.08	9.07	9.07
600	11.33	11.24	11.17	11.11	11.06	11.03	11.00	10.98	10.96	10.94	10.93	10.90	10.89	10.88
700	13.21	13.11	13.03	12.96	12.91	12.87	12.83	12.80	12.78	12.76	12.75	12.71	12.70	12.69
800	15.10	14.98	14.89	14.81	14.75	14.70	14.66	14.63	14.61	14.59	14.57	14.53	14.51	14.51
900	16.99	16.85	16.75	16.66	16.59	16.54	16.50	16.46	16.43	16.41	16.39	16.34	16.33	16.32
1000	18.87	18.72	18.61	18.51	18.44	18.38	18.33	18.29	18.26	18.23	18.21	18.16	18.14	18.13
2000	37.74	37.44	37.21	37.02	36.87	36.75	36.65	36.57	36.51	36.46	36.42	36.31	36.27	36.26
3000	56.61	56.16	55.81	55.53	55.30	55.12	54.97	54.86	54.76	54.69	54.63	54.46	54.41	54.39
4000	75.48	74.88	74.41	74.03	73.73	73.49	73.30	73.14	73.02	72.92	72.84	72.62	72.54	72.52
5000	94.35	93.60	93.01	92.54	92.16	91.86	91.62	91.43	91.27	91.15	91.05	90.77	90.68	90.65
6000	113.22	112.32	111.61	111.05	110.60	110.23	109.94	109.71	109.52	109.37	109.25	108.92	108.81	108.77
7000	132.09	131.04	130.22	129.56	129.03	128.61	128.27	128.00	127.78	127.60	127.46	127.08	126.95	126.90
8000	150.96	149.76	148.82	148.06	147.46	146.98	146.59	146.28	146.03	145.83	145.67	145.23	145.08	145.03
9000	169.83	168.48	167.42	166.57	165.89	165.35	164.91	164.56	164.28	164.06	163.88	163.38	163.22	163.16
10000	188.69	187.20	186.02	185.08	184.32	183.72	183.24	182.85	182.54	182.29	182.09	181.54	181.35	181.29
11000	207.56	205.92	204.62	203.58	202.76	202.09	201.56	201.13	200.79	200.52	200.29	199.69	199.49	199.42
12000	226.43	224.64	223.22	222.09	221.19	220.46	219.88	219.42	219.04	218.74	218.50	217.84	217.62	217.54
13000	245.30	243.36	241.83	240.60	239.62	238.83	238.21	237.70	237.30	236.97	236.71	236.00	235.75	235.67
14000	264.17	262.08	260.43	259.11	258.05	257.21	256.53	255.99	255.55	255.20	254.92	254.15	253.89	253.80
15000	283.04	280.80	279.03	277.61	276.48	275.58	274.85	274.27	273.80	273.43	273.13	272.30	272.02	271.93
16000	301.91	299.52	297.63	296.12	294.91	293.95	293.18	292.56	292.06	291.66	291.34	290.46	290.16	290.06
17000	320.78	318.24	316.23	314.63	313.35	312.32	311.50	310.84	310.31	309.89	309.54	308.61	308.29	308.19
18000	339.65	336.96	334.83	333.13	331.78	330.69	329.82	329.12	328.56	328.11	327.75	326.76	326.43	326.31
19000	358.52	355.68	353.43	351.64	350.21	349.06	348.15	347.41	346.82	346.34	345.96	344.92	344.56	344.44
20000	377.38	374.40	372.04	370.15	368.64	367.44	366.47	365.69	365.07	364.57	364.17	363.07	362.70	362.57
21000	396.25	393.12	390.64	388.66	387.07	385.81	384.79	383.98	383.32	382.80	382.38	381.22	380.83	380.70
22000	415.12	411.84	409.24	407.16	405.51	404.18	403.12	402.26	401.58	401.03	400.58	399.38	398.97	398.83
23000	433.99	430.56	427.84	425.67	423.94	422.55	421.44	420.55	419.83	419.26	418.79	417.53	417.10	416.96
24000	452.86	449.28	446.44	444.18	442.37	440.92	439.76	438.83	438.08	437.48	437.00	435.68	435.24	435.08
25000	471.73	468.00	465.04	462.69	460.80	459.29	458.09	457.12	456.34	455.71	455.21	453.84	453.37	453.21
26000	490.60	486.72	483.65	481.19	479.23	477.66	476.41	475.40	474.59	473.94	473.42	471.99	471.50	471.34
27000	509.47	505.44	502.25	499.70	497.66	496.04	494.73	493.68	492.84	492.17	491.63	490.14	489.64	489.47
28000	528.34	524.16	520.85	518.21	516.10	514.41	513.05	511.97	511.10	510.40	509.83	508.30	507.77	507.60
29000	547.20	542.88	539.45	536.71	534.53	532.78	531.38	530.25	529.35	528.63	528.04	526.45	525.91	525.72
30000	566.07	561.60	558.05	555.22	552.96	551.15	549.70	548.54	547.60	546.85	546.25	544.60	544.04	543.85
31000	584.94	580.32	576.65	573.73	571.39	569.52	568.02	566.82	565.86	565.08	564.46	562.75	562.18	561.98
32000	603.81	599.04	595.26	592.24	589.82	587.89	586.35	585.11	584.11	583.31	582.67	580.91	580.31	580.11
33000	622.68	617.76	613.86	610.74	608.26	606.27	604.67	603.39	602.36	601.54	600.87	599.06	598.45	598.24
34000	641.55	636.48	632.46	629.25	626.69	624.64	622.99	621.68	620.62	619.77	619.08	617.21	616.58	616.37
35000	660.42	655.20	651.06	647.76	645.12	643.01	641.32	639.96	638.87	637.99	637.29	635.37	634.72	634.49
36000	679.29	673.92	669.66	666.26	663.55	661.38	659.64	658.24	657.12	656.22	655.50	653.52	652.85	652.62
37000	698.16	692.64	688.26	684.77	681.98	679.75	677.96	676.53	675.38	674.45	673.71	671.67	670.99	670.75
38000	717.03	711.36	706.86	703.28	700.42	698.12	696.29	694.81	693.63	692.68	691.92	689.83	689.12	688.88
39000	735.89	730.08	725.47	721.79	718.85	716.49	714.61	713.10	711.88	710.91	710.12	707.98	707.25	707.01
40000	754.76	748.80	744.07	740.29	737.28	734.87	732.93	731.38	730.14	729.14	728.33	726.13	725.39	725.14
41000	773.63	767.52	762.67	758.80	755.71	753.24	751.26	749.67	748.39	747.36	746.54	744.29	743.52	743.26
42000	792.50	786.24	781.27	777.31	774.14	771.61	769.58	767.95	766.64	765.59	764.75	762.44	761.66	761.39
43000	811.37	804.96	799.87	795.82	792.57	789.98	787.90	786.24	784.90	783.82	782.96	780.59	779.79	779.52
44000	830.24	823.68	818.47	814.32	811.01	808.35	806.23	804.52	803.15	802.05	801.16	798.75	797.93	797.65
45000	849.11	842.40	837.08	832.83	829.44	826.72	824.55	822.80	821.40	820.28	819.37	816.90	816.06	815.78
46000	867.98	861.12	855.68	851.34	847.87	845.10	842.87	841.09	839.66	838.51	837.58	835.05	834.20	833.91
47000	886.85	879.84	874.28	869.84	866.30	863.47	861.20	859.37	857.91	856.73	855.79	853.21	852.33	852.03
48000	905.72	898.56	892.88	888.35	884.73	881.84	879.52	877.66	876.16	874.96	874.00	871.36	870.47	870.16
49000	924.58	917.28	911.48	906.86	903.17	900.21	897.84	895.94	894.42	893.19	892.21	889.51	888.60	888.29
50000	943.45	936.00	930.08	925.37	921.60	918.58	916.17	914.23	912.67	911.42	910.41	907.67	906.73	906.42
55000	1037.80	1029.60	1023.09	1017.90	1013.76	1010.44	1007.78	1005.65	1003.94	1002.56	1001.45	998.43	997.41	997.06
60000	1132.14	1123.20	1116.10	1110.44	1105.92	1102.30	1099.40	1097.07	1095.20	1093.70	1092.49	1089.20	1088.08	1087.70
65000	1226.49	1216.80	1209.11	1202.97	1198.07	1194.15	1191.01	1188.49	1186.47	1184.84	1183.54	1179.96	1178.75	1178.34
70000	1320.83	1310.40	1302.11	1295.51	1290.23	1286.01	1282.63	1279.92	1277.74	1275.98	1274.58	1270.73	1269.43	1268.98
75000	1415.18	1404.00	1395.12	1388.05	1382.39	1377.87	1374.25	1371.34	1369.00	1367.13	1365.62	1361.50	1360.10	1359.62
80000	1509.52	1497.60	1488.13	1480.58	1474.55	1469.73	1465.86	1462.76	1460.27	1458.27	1456.66	1452.26	1450.77	1450.27
85000	1603.87	1591.20	1581.14	1573.12	1566.71	1561.59	1557.48	1554.18	1551.54	1549.41	1547.70	1543.03	1541.45	1540.91
90000	1698.21	1684.80	1674.15	1665.65	1658.87	1653.44	1649.09	1645.60	1642.80	1640.55	1638.74	1633.79	1632.12	1631.55
95000	1792.56	1778.40	1767.15	1758.19	1751.03	1745.30	1740.71	1737.03	1734.07	1731.69	1729.78	1724.56	1722.79	1722.19
100000	1886.90	1872.00	1860.16	1850.73	1843.19	1837.16	1832.33	1828.45	1825.34	1822.83	1820.82	1815.33	1813.46	1812.83

MONTHLY PAYMENT
REQUIRED TO AMORTIZE A LOAN

TERM AMOUNT	1 Year	2 Years	3 Years	4 Years	5 Years	6 Years	7 Years	8 Years	9 Years	10 Years	11 Years	12 Years	13 Years	14 Years
5	.47	.26	.20	.16	.14	.13	.12	.12	.11	.11	.11	.10	.10	.10
10	.94	.52	.39	.32	.28	.26	.24	.23	.22	.21	.21	.20	.20	.20
15	1.41	.78	.58	.48	.42	.38	.35	.34	.32	.31	.31	.30	.29	.29
25	2.34	1.30	.96	.79	.69	.63	.59	.56	.53	.52	.51	.50	.49	.48
50	4.68	2.59	1.91	1.57	1.38	1.26	1.17	1.11	1.06	1.03	1.01	.99	.97	.96
75	7.02	3.89	2.86	2.36	2.07	1.88	1.75	1.66	1.59	1.55	1.51	1.48	1.45	1.44
100	9.35	5.18	3.81	3.14	2.76	2.51	2.34	2.21	2.12	2.06	2.01	1.97	1.94	1.91
200	18.70	10.36	7.62	6.28	5.51	5.01	4.67	4.42	4.24	4.11	4.01	3.93	3.87	3.82
300	28.05	15.54	11.43	9.42	8.26	7.51	7.00	6.63	6.36	6.17	6.01	5.90	5.80	5.73
400	37.40	20.72	15.24	12.56	11.01	10.01	9.33	8.84	8.48	8.22	8.02	7.86	7.74	7.64
500	46.75	25.89	19.05	15.70	13.76	12.51	11.66	11.05	10.60	10.27	10.02	9.82	9.67	9.55
600	56.10	31.07	22.86	18.84	16.51	15.01	13.99	13.26	12.72	12.33	12.02	11.79	11.60	11.46
700	65.45	36.25	26.67	21.98	19.26	17.51	16.32	15.47	14.84	14.38	14.02	13.75	13.54	13.37
800	74.80	41.43	30.47	25.12	22.01	20.01	18.65	17.68	16.96	16.43	16.03	15.71	15.47	15.28
900	84.15	46.61	34.28	28.26	24.76	22.51	20.98	19.89	19.08	18.49	18.03	17.68	17.40	17.19
1000	93.50	51.78	38.09	31.40	27.51	25.01	23.31	22.09	21.20	20.54	20.03	19.64	19.34	19.10
2000	187.00	103.56	76.18	62.80	55.02	50.02	46.61	44.18	42.40	41.07	40.06	39.28	38.67	38.19
3000	280.50	155.34	114.27	94.20	82.52	75.03	69.91	66.27	63.60	61.61	60.09	58.91	58.00	57.29
4000	374.00	207.12	152.35	125.60	110.03	100.04	93.22	88.36	84.80	82.14	80.11	78.55	77.33	76.38
5000	467.50	258.90	190.44	156.99	137.53	125.04	116.52	110.45	106.00	102.67	100.14	98.19	96.67	95.48
6000	560.99	310.68	228.53	188.39	165.04	150.05	139.82	132.54	127.20	123.21	120.17	117.82	116.00	114.57
7000	654.49	362.46	266.61	219.79	192.54	175.06	163.12	154.63	148.40	143.74	140.19	137.46	135.33	133.66
8000	747.99	414.24	304.70	251.19	220.05	200.07	186.43	176.72	169.60	164.27	160.22	157.09	154.66	152.76
9000	841.49	466.02	342.79	282.58	247.55	225.07	209.73	198.81	190.80	184.81	180.25	176.73	174.00	171.85
10000	934.99	517.80	380.88	313.98	275.06	250.08	233.03	220.90	212.00	205.34	200.27	196.37	193.33	190.95
11000	1028.48	569.58	418.96	345.38	302.56	275.09	256.33	242.99	233.20	225.88	220.30	216.00	212.66	210.04
12000	1121.98	621.36	457.05	376.78	330.07	300.10	279.64	265.08	254.40	246.41	240.33	235.64	231.99	229.14
13000	1215.48	673.14	495.14	408.17	357.57	325.10	302.94	287.16	275.60	266.94	260.35	255.27	251.32	248.23
14000	1308.98	724.92	533.22	439.57	385.08	350.11	326.24	309.25	296.80	287.48	280.38	274.91	270.66	267.32
15000	1402.48	776.70	571.31	470.97	412.58	375.12	349.54	331.34	318.00	308.01	300.41	294.55	289.99	286.42
16000	1495.98	828.48	609.40	502.37	440.09	400.13	372.85	353.43	339.20	328.54	320.43	314.18	309.32	305.51
17000	1589.47	880.26	647.49	533.76	467.60	425.13	396.15	375.52	360.40	349.08	340.46	333.82	328.65	324.61
18000	1682.97	932.03	685.57	565.16	495.10	450.14	419.45	397.61	381.60	369.61	360.49	353.45	347.99	343.70
19000	1776.47	983.81	723.66	596.56	522.61	475.15	442.75	419.70	402.80	390.15	380.51	373.09	367.32	362.79
20000	1869.97	1035.59	761.75	627.96	550.11	500.16	466.06	441.79	424.00	410.68	400.54	392.73	386.65	381.89
21000	1963.47	1087.37	799.83	659.35	577.62	525.16	489.36	463.88	445.20	431.21	420.57	412.36	405.98	400.98
22000	2056.96	1139.15	837.92	690.75	605.12	550.17	512.66	485.97	466.40	451.75	440.59	432.00	425.31	420.08
23000	2150.46	1190.93	876.01	722.15	632.63	575.18	535.96	508.06	487.60	472.28	460.62	451.63	444.65	439.17
24000	2243.96	1242.71	914.09	753.55	660.13	600.19	559.27	530.15	508.80	492.81	480.65	471.27	463.98	458.27
25000	2337.46	1294.49	952.18	784.94	687.64	625.19	582.57	552.24	530.00	513.35	500.67	490.91	483.31	477.36
26000	2430.96	1346.27	990.27	816.34	715.14	650.20	605.87	574.32	551.20	533.88	520.70	510.54	502.64	496.45
27000	2524.46	1398.05	1028.36	847.74	742.65	675.21	629.18	596.41	572.40	554.41	540.73	530.18	521.98	515.55
28000	2617.95	1449.83	1066.44	879.14	770.15	700.22	652.48	618.50	593.60	574.95	560.75	549.81	541.31	534.64
29000	2711.45	1501.61	1104.53	910.54	797.66	725.22	675.78	640.59	614.80	595.48	580.78	569.45	560.64	553.74
30000	2804.95	1553.39	1142.62	941.93	825.16	750.23	699.08	662.68	636.00	616.02	600.81	589.09	579.97	572.83
31000	2898.45	1605.17	1180.70	973.33	852.67	775.24	722.39	684.77	657.20	636.55	620.83	608.72	599.30	591.93
32000	2991.95	1656.95	1218.79	1004.73	880.18	800.25	745.69	706.86	678.40	657.08	640.86	628.36	618.64	611.02
33000	3085.44	1708.73	1256.88	1036.13	907.68	825.25	768.99	728.95	699.60	677.62	660.89	647.99	637.97	630.11
34000	3178.94	1760.51	1294.97	1067.52	935.19	850.26	792.29	751.04	720.80	698.15	680.91	667.63	657.30	649.21
35000	3272.44	1812.29	1333.05	1098.92	962.69	875.27	815.60	773.13	742.00	718.68	700.94	687.27	676.63	668.30
36000	3365.94	1864.06	1371.14	1130.32	990.20	900.28	838.90	795.22	763.20	739.22	720.97	706.90	695.97	687.40
37000	3459.44	1915.84	1409.23	1161.72	1017.70	925.28	862.20	817.31	784.40	759.75	740.99	726.54	715.30	706.49
38000	3552.93	1967.62	1447.31	1193.11	1045.21	950.29	885.50	839.40	805.60	780.29	761.02	746.18	734.63	725.58
39000	3646.43	2019.40	1485.40	1224.51	1072.71	975.30	908.81	861.48	826.80	800.82	781.05	765.81	753.96	744.68
40000	3739.93	2071.18	1523.49	1255.91	1100.22	1000.31	932.11	883.57	848.00	821.35	801.07	785.45	773.29	763.77
41000	3833.43	2122.96	1561.57	1287.31	1127.72	1025.31	955.41	905.66	869.20	841.89	821.10	805.08	792.63	782.87
42000	3926.93	2174.74	1599.66	1318.70	1155.23	1050.32	978.71	927.75	890.40	862.42	841.13	824.72	811.96	801.96
43000	4020.43	2226.52	1637.75	1350.10	1182.73	1075.33	1002.02	949.84	911.60	882.95	861.15	844.36	831.29	821.06
44000	4113.92	2278.30	1675.84	1381.50	1210.24	1100.34	1025.32	971.93	932.80	903.49	881.18	863.99	850.62	840.15
45000	4207.42	2330.08	1713.92	1412.90	1237.74	1125.34	1048.62	994.02	954.00	924.02	901.21	883.63	869.96	859.24
46000	4300.92	2381.86	1752.01	1444.29	1265.25	1150.35	1071.92	1016.11	975.20	944.55	921.23	903.26	889.29	878.34
47000	4394.42	2433.64	1790.10	1475.69	1292.76	1175.36	1095.23	1038.20	996.40	965.09	941.26	922.90	908.62	897.43
48000	4487.92	2485.41	1828.18	1507.09	1320.26	1200.37	1118.53	1060.29	1017.60	985.62	961.29	942.54	927.95	916.53
49000	4581.41	2537.20	1866.27	1538.49	1347.77	1225.37	1141.83	1082.38	1038.80	1006.16	981.31	962.17	947.28	935.62
50000	4674.91	2588.98	1904.36	1569.88	1375.27	1250.38	1165.13	1104.47	1060.00	1026.69	1001.34	981.81	966.62	954.72
55000	5142.40	2847.87	2094.79	1726.87	1512.80	1375.42	1281.65	1214.91	1165.99	1129.36	1101.47	1079.99	1063.28	1050.19
60000	5609.89	3106.77	2285.23	1883.86	1650.32	1500.46	1398.16	1325.36	1271.99	1232.03	1201.61	1178.17	1159.94	1145.66
65000	6077.38	3365.67	2475.66	2040.85	1787.85	1625.50	1514.67	1435.80	1377.99	1334.69	1301.74	1276.35	1256.60	1241.13
70000	6544.88	3624.57	2666.10	2197.84	1925.38	1750.53	1631.19	1546.25	1483.99	1437.36	1401.87	1374.53	1353.26	1336.60
75000	7012.37	3883.46	2856.53	2354.82	2062.90	1875.57	1747.70	1656.70	1589.99	1540.03	1502.01	1472.71	1449.92	1432.07
80000	7479.86	4142.36	3046.97	2511.81	2200.43	2000.61	1864.21	1767.14	1695.99	1642.70	1602.14	1570.89	1546.58	1527.54
85000	7947.35	4401.26	3237.41	2668.80	2337.96	2125.65	1980.73	1877.59	1801.99	1745.37	1702.27	1669.07	1643.24	1623.01
90000	8414.84	4660.15	3427.84	2825.79	2475.48	2250.68	2097.24	1988.03	1907.99	1848.04	1802.41	1767.25	1739.91	1718.48
95000	8882.33	4919.05	3618.28	2982.78	2613.01	2375.72	2213.75	2098.48	2013.99	1950.71	1902.54	1865.43	1836.57	1813.95
100000	9349.82	5177.95	3808.71	3139.76	2750.54	2500.76	2330.26	2208.93	2119.99	2053.37	2002.67	1963.61	1933.23	1909.43

TERM	15 Years	16 Years	17 Years	18 Years	19 Years	20 Years	21 Years	22 Years	23 Years	24 Years	25 Years	30 Years	35 Years	40 Years
AMOUNT														
5	.10	.10	.10	.10	.10	.10	.10	.10	.10	.10	.10	.10	.10	.10
10	.19	.19	.19	.19	.19	.19	.19	.19	.19	.19	.19	.19	.19	.19
15	.29	.29	.28	.28	.28	.28	.28	.28	.28	.28	.28	.28	.28	.28
25	.48	.47	.47	.47	.47	.47	.46	.46	.46	.46	.46	.46	.46	.46
50	.95	.94	.94	.93	.93	.93	.92	.92	.92	.92	.92	.91	.91	.91
75	1.42	1.41	1.40	1.40	1.39	1.39	1.38	1.38	1.38	1.38	1.37	1.37	1.37	1.37
100	1.90	1.88	1.87	1.86	1.85	1.85	1.84	1.84	1.83	1.83	1.83	1.82	1.82	1.82
200	3.79	3.76	3.73	3.71	3.70	3.69	3.68	3.67	3.66	3.66	3.65	3.64	3.64	3.64
300	5.68	5.63	5.60	5.57	5.55	5.53	5.51	5.50	5.49	5.49	5.48	5.46	5.46	5.46
400	7.57	7.51	7.46	7.42	7.39	7.37	7.35	7.33	7.32	7.31	7.30	7.28	7.28	7.27
500	9.46	9.38	9.33	9.28	9.24	9.21	9.19	9.17	9.15	9.14	9.13	9.10	9.09	9.09
600	11.35	11.26	11.19	11.13	11.09	11.05	11.02	11.00	10.98	10.97	10.95	10.92	10.91	10.91
700	13.24	13.14	13.05	12.99	12.93	12.89	12.86	12.83	12.81	12.79	12.78	12.74	12.73	12.72
800	15.13	15.01	14.92	14.84	14.78	14.73	14.70	14.66	14.64	14.62	14.60	14.56	14.55	14.54
900	17.02	16.89	16.78	16.70	16.63	16.58	16.53	16.50	16.47	16.45	16.43	16.38	16.36	16.36
1000	18.91	18.76	18.65	18.55	18.48	18.42	18.37	18.33	18.30	18.27	18.25	18.20	18.18	18.17
2000	37.82	37.52	37.29	37.10	36.95	36.83	36.73	36.65	36.59	36.54	36.50	36.39	36.36	36.34
3000	56.72	56.28	55.93	55.64	55.42	55.24	55.09	54.98	54.89	54.81	54.75	54.59	54.53	54.51
4000	75.63	75.04	74.57	74.19	73.89	73.65	73.46	73.30	73.18	73.08	73.00	72.78	72.71	72.68
5000	94.54	93.80	93.21	92.74	92.36	92.06	91.82	91.63	91.47	91.35	91.25	90.98	90.89	90.85
6000	113.44	112.55	111.85	111.28	110.83	110.47	110.18	109.95	109.77	109.62	109.50	109.17	109.06	109.02
7000	132.35	131.31	130.49	129.83	129.30	128.88	128.55	128.28	128.06	127.89	127.75	127.37	127.24	127.19
8000	151.26	150.07	149.13	148.38	147.78	147.30	146.91	146.60	146.36	146.16	146.00	145.56	145.41	145.36
9000	170.16	168.83	167.77	166.92	166.25	165.71	165.27	164.93	164.65	164.43	164.25	163.76	163.59	163.53
10000	189.07	187.59	186.41	185.47	184.72	184.12	183.64	183.25	182.94	182.69	182.50	181.95	181.77	181.70
11000	207.98	206.35	205.05	204.01	203.19	202.53	202.00	201.58	201.24	200.96	200.74	200.14	199.94	199.87
12000	226.88	225.10	223.69	222.56	221.66	220.94	220.36	219.90	219.53	219.23	218.99	218.34	218.12	218.04
13000	245.79	243.86	242.33	241.11	240.13	239.35	238.73	238.23	237.82	237.50	237.24	236.53	236.29	236.21
14000	264.70	262.62	260.97	259.65	258.60	257.76	257.09	256.55	256.12	255.77	255.49	254.73	254.47	254.38
15000	283.60	281.38	279.61	278.20	277.07	276.17	275.45	274.88	274.41	274.04	273.74	272.92	272.65	272.55
16000	302.51	300.14	298.25	296.75	295.55	294.59	293.82	293.20	292.71	292.31	291.99	291.12	290.82	290.72
17000	321.42	318.89	316.89	315.29	314.02	313.00	312.18	311.53	311.00	310.58	310.24	309.31	309.00	308.89
18000	340.32	337.65	335.53	333.84	332.49	331.41	330.54	329.85	329.29	328.85	328.49	327.51	327.18	327.06
19000	359.23	356.41	354.17	352.38	350.96	349.82	348.91	348.18	347.59	347.12	346.74	345.70	345.35	345.23
20000	378.14	375.17	372.81	370.93	369.43	368.23	367.27	366.50	365.88	365.38	364.99	363.90	363.53	363.40
21000	397.04	393.93	391.45	389.48	387.90	386.64	385.63	384.82	384.18	383.65	383.23	382.09	381.70	381.57
22000	415.95	412.69	410.09	408.02	406.37	405.05	404.00	403.15	402.47	401.92	401.48	400.28	399.88	399.74
23000	434.86	431.44	428.73	426.57	424.85	423.47	422.36	421.47	420.76	420.19	419.73	418.48	418.06	417.91
24000	453.76	450.20	447.37	445.12	443.32	441.88	440.72	439.80	439.06	438.46	437.98	436.67	436.23	436.08
25000	472.67	468.96	466.01	463.66	461.79	460.29	459.09	458.12	457.35	456.73	456.23	454.87	454.41	454.25
26000	491.58	487.72	484.65	482.21	480.26	478.70	477.45	476.45	475.64	475.00	474.48	473.06	472.58	472.42
27000	510.48	506.48	503.29	500.76	498.73	497.11	495.81	494.77	493.94	493.27	492.73	491.26	490.76	490.59
28000	529.39	525.23	521.93	519.30	517.20	515.52	514.18	513.10	512.23	511.54	510.98	509.45	508.94	508.76
29000	548.30	543.99	540.57	537.85	535.67	533.93	532.54	531.42	530.53	529.81	529.23	527.65	527.11	526.93
30000	567.20	562.75	559.21	556.39	554.14	552.34	550.90	549.75	548.82	548.07	547.48	545.84	545.29	545.10
31000	586.11	581.51	577.85	574.94	572.62	570.76	569.27	568.07	567.11	566.34	565.72	564.04	563.46	563.27
32000	605.02	600.27	596.49	593.49	591.09	589.17	587.63	586.40	585.41	584.61	583.97	582.23	581.64	581.44
33000	623.92	619.03	615.13	612.03	609.56	607.58	605.99	604.72	603.70	602.88	602.22	600.42	599.82	599.61
34000	642.83	637.78	633.77	630.58	628.03	625.99	624.36	623.05	621.99	621.15	620.47	618.62	617.99	617.78
35000	661.74	656.54	652.41	649.13	646.50	644.40	642.72	641.37	640.29	639.42	638.72	636.81	636.17	635.95
36000	680.64	675.30	671.05	667.67	664.97	662.81	661.08	659.70	658.58	657.69	656.97	655.01	654.35	654.12
37000	699.55	694.06	689.69	686.22	683.44	681.22	679.45	678.02	676.88	675.96	675.22	673.20	672.52	672.29
38000	718.46	712.82	708.33	704.76	701.91	699.64	697.81	696.35	695.17	694.23	693.47	691.40	690.70	690.46
39000	737.36	731.57	726.97	723.31	720.39	718.05	716.17	714.67	713.46	712.49	711.72	709.59	708.87	708.63
40000	756.27	750.33	745.62	741.86	738.86	736.46	734.54	732.99	731.76	730.76	729.97	727.79	727.05	726.80
41000	775.18	769.09	764.26	760.40	757.33	754.87	752.90	751.32	750.05	749.03	748.21	745.98	745.23	744.97
42000	794.08	787.85	782.90	778.95	775.80	773.28	771.26	769.64	768.35	767.30	766.46	764.18	763.40	763.14
43000	812.99	806.61	801.54	797.50	794.27	791.69	789.63	787.97	786.64	785.57	784.71	782.37	781.58	781.31
44000	831.90	825.37	820.18	816.04	812.74	810.10	807.99	806.29	804.93	803.84	802.96	800.56	799.75	799.48
45000	850.80	844.12	838.82	834.59	831.21	828.51	826.35	824.62	823.23	822.11	821.21	818.76	817.93	817.65
46000	869.71	862.88	857.46	853.14	849.69	846.93	844.72	842.94	841.52	840.38	839.46	836.95	836.11	835.82
47000	888.62	881.64	876.10	871.68	868.16	865.34	863.08	861.27	859.81	858.65	857.71	855.15	854.28	853.99
48000	907.52	900.40	894.74	890.23	886.63	883.75	881.44	879.59	878.11	876.92	875.96	873.34	872.46	872.16
49000	926.43	919.16	913.38	908.77	905.10	902.16	899.81	897.92	896.40	895.18	894.21	891.54	890.63	890.33
50000	945.34	937.91	932.02	927.32	923.57	920.57	918.17	916.24	914.70	913.45	912.46	909.73	908.81	908.50
55000	1039.87	1031.71	1025.22	1020.05	1015.93	1012.63	1009.98	1007.87	1006.16	1004.80	1003.70	1000.70	999.69	999.35
60000	1134.40	1125.50	1118.42	1112.78	1108.28	1104.68	1101.80	1099.49	1097.63	1096.14	1094.95	1091.68	1090.57	1090.20
65000	1228.94	1219.29	1211.62	1205.52	1200.64	1196.74	1193.62	1191.11	1189.10	1187.49	1186.19	1182.65	1181.45	1181.05
70000	1323.47	1313.08	1304.82	1298.25	1293.00	1288.80	1285.43	1282.74	1280.57	1278.83	1277.44	1273.62	1272.33	1271.90
75000	1418.00	1406.87	1398.02	1390.98	1385.35	1380.85	1377.25	1374.36	1372.04	1370.18	1368.68	1364.60	1363.21	1362.75
80000	1512.54	1500.66	1491.23	1483.71	1477.71	1472.91	1469.07	1465.98	1463.51	1461.52	1459.93	1455.57	1454.09	1453.60
85000	1607.07	1594.45	1584.43	1576.44	1570.07	1564.97	1560.88	1557.61	1554.98	1552.87	1551.17	1546.54	1544.98	1544.46
90000	1701.60	1688.24	1677.63	1669.17	1662.42	1657.02	1652.70	1649.23	1646.45	1644.21	1642.42	1637.51	1635.86	1635.29
95000	1796.14	1782.03	1770.83	1761.90	1754.78	1749.08	1744.52	1740.86	1737.92	1735.56	1733.66	1728.49	1726.74	1726.14
100000	1890.67	1875.82	1864.03	1854.64	1847.14	1841.14	1836.33	1832.48	1829.39	1826.90	1824.91	1819.46	1817.62	1816.99

MONTHLY PAYMENT
REQUIRED TO AMORTIZE A LOAN

TERM / AMOUNT	1 Year	2 Years	3 Years	4 Years	5 Years	6 Years	7 Years	8 Years	9 Years	10 Years	11 Years	12 Years	13 Years	14 Years
5	.47	.26	.20	.16	.14	.13	.12	.12	.11	.11	.11	.10	.10	.10
10	.94	.52	.39	.32	.28	.26	.24	.23	.22	.21	.21	.20	.20	.20
15	1.41	.78	.58	.48	.42	.38	.36	.34	.32	.31	.31	.30	.30	.29
25	2.34	1.30	.96	.79	.69	.63	.59	.56	.54	.52	.51	.50	.49	.48
50	4.68	2.60	1.91	1.58	1.38	1.26	1.17	1.11	1.07	1.03	1.01	.99	.97	.96
75	7.02	3.89	2.86	2.36	2.07	1.88	1.76	1.67	1.60	1.55	1.51	1.48	1.46	1.44
100	9.36	5.19	3.82	3.15	2.76	2.51	2.34	2.22	2.13	2.06	2.01	1.97	1.94	1.92
200	18.71	10.37	7.63	6.29	5.51	5.02	4.67	4.43	4.25	4.12	4.02	3.94	3.88	3.83
300	28.07	15.55	11.44	9.44	8.27	7.52	7.01	6.65	6.38	6.18	6.03	5.91	5.82	5.75
400	37.42	20.73	15.26	12.58	11.02	10.03	9.34	8.86	8.50	8.24	8.04	7.88	7.76	7.66
500	46.77	25.91	19.07	15.72	13.78	12.53	11.68	11.07	10.63	10.30	10.04	9.85	9.70	9.58
600	56.13	31.09	22.88	18.87	16.53	15.04	14.01	13.29	12.75	12.36	12.05	11.82	11.64	11.49
700	65.48	36.28	26.69	22.01	19.29	17.54	16.35	15.50	14.88	14.41	14.06	13.79	13.58	13.41
800	74.83	41.46	30.51	25.16	22.04	20.05	18.68	17.71	17.00	16.47	16.07	15.76	15.51	15.32
900	84.19	46.64	34.32	28.30	24.80	22.55	21.02	19.93	19.13	18.53	18.08	17.73	17.45	17.24
1000	93.54	51.82	38.13	31.44	27.55	25.06	23.35	22.14	21.25	20.59	20.08	19.69	19.39	19.15
2000	187.07	103.64	76.26	62.88	55.10	50.11	46.70	44.28	42.50	41.17	40.16	39.38	38.78	38.30
3000	280.61	155.45	114.38	94.32	82.65	75.16	70.05	66.42	63.75	61.76	60.24	59.07	58.17	57.45
4000	374.14	207.27	152.51	125.76	110.20	100.21	93.40	88.55	85.00	82.34	80.32	78.76	77.55	76.60
5000	467.68	259.09	190.63	157.20	137.74	125.26	116.75	110.69	106.25	102.93	100.40	98.45	96.94	95.75
6000	561.21	310.90	228.76	188.63	165.29	150.32	140.10	132.83	127.50	123.51	120.48	118.14	116.33	114.90
7000	654.74	362.72	266.89	220.07	192.84	175.37	163.45	154.96	148.75	144.10	140.56	137.83	135.71	134.05
8000	748.28	414.54	305.01	251.51	220.39	200.42	186.80	177.10	170.00	164.68	160.64	157.52	155.10	153.20
9000	841.81	466.35	343.14	282.95	247.94	225.47	210.14	199.24	191.25	185.27	180.72	177.21	174.49	172.35
10000	935.35	518.17	381.26	314.39	275.48	250.52	233.49	221.38	212.50	205.85	200.79	196.90	193.87	191.50
11000	1028.88	569.99	419.39	345.83	303.03	275.58	256.84	243.51	233.75	226.44	220.87	216.59	213.26	210.65
12000	1122.42	621.80	457.51	377.26	330.58	300.63	280.19	265.65	255.00	247.02	240.95	236.28	232.65	229.80
13000	1215.95	673.62	495.64	408.70	358.13	325.68	303.54	287.79	276.25	267.61	261.03	255.97	252.03	248.95
14000	1309.48	725.44	533.77	440.14	385.68	350.73	326.89	309.92	297.50	288.19	281.11	275.66	271.42	268.10
15000	1403.02	777.25	571.89	471.58	413.22	375.78	350.24	332.06	318.74	308.77	301.19	295.35	290.81	287.25
16000	1496.55	829.07	610.02	503.02	440.77	400.84	373.59	354.20	339.99	329.36	321.27	315.04	310.20	306.40
17000	1590.09	880.88	648.14	534.46	468.32	425.89	396.93	376.34	361.24	349.94	341.35	334.73	329.58	325.55
18000	1683.62	932.70	686.27	565.89	495.87	450.94	420.28	398.47	382.49	370.53	361.43	354.42	348.97	344.70
19000	1777.16	984.52	724.40	597.33	523.41	475.99	443.63	420.61	403.74	391.11	381.51	374.11	368.36	363.85
20000	1870.69	1036.33	762.52	628.77	550.96	501.04	466.98	442.75	424.99	411.70	401.58	393.80	387.74	383.00
21000	1964.22	1088.15	800.65	660.21	578.51	526.10	490.33	464.88	446.24	432.28	421.66	413.49	407.13	402.15
22000	2057.76	1139.97	838.77	691.65	606.06	551.15	513.68	487.02	467.49	452.87	441.74	433.18	426.52	421.30
23000	2151.29	1191.78	876.90	723.08	633.61	576.20	537.03	509.16	488.74	473.45	461.82	452.87	445.90	440.45
24000	2244.83	1243.60	915.02	754.52	661.15	601.25	560.38	531.30	509.99	494.04	481.90	472.56	465.29	459.60
25000	2338.36	1295.42	953.15	785.96	688.70	626.30	583.73	553.43	531.24	514.62	501.98	492.24	484.68	478.75
26000	2431.90	1347.23	991.28	817.40	716.25	651.36	607.07	575.57	552.49	535.21	522.06	511.93	504.06	497.90
27000	2525.43	1399.05	1029.40	848.84	743.80	676.41	630.42	597.71	573.74	555.79	542.14	531.62	523.45	517.05
28000	2618.96	1450.87	1067.53	880.28	771.35	701.46	653.77	619.84	594.99	576.38	562.22	551.31	542.84	536.20
29000	2712.50	1502.68	1105.65	911.71	798.89	726.51	677.12	641.98	616.23	596.96	582.30	571.00	562.22	555.35
30000	2806.03	1554.50	1143.78	943.15	826.44	751.56	700.47	664.12	637.48	617.54	602.37	590.69	581.61	574.50
31000	2899.57	1606.31	1181.91	974.59	853.99	776.62	723.82	686.26	658.73	638.13	622.45	610.38	601.00	593.65
32000	2993.10	1658.13	1220.03	1006.03	881.54	801.67	747.17	708.39	679.98	658.71	642.53	630.07	620.39	612.80
33000	3086.63	1709.95	1258.16	1037.47	909.09	826.72	770.52	730.53	701.23	679.30	662.61	649.76	639.77	631.95
34000	3180.17	1761.76	1296.28	1068.91	936.63	851.77	793.86	752.67	722.48	699.88	682.69	669.45	659.16	651.10
35000	3273.70	1813.58	1334.41	1100.34	964.18	876.82	817.21	774.80	743.73	720.47	702.77	689.14	678.55	670.25
36000	3367.24	1865.40	1372.53	1131.78	991.73	901.88	840.56	796.94	764.98	741.05	722.85	708.83	697.93	689.40
37000	3460.77	1917.21	1410.66	1163.22	1019.28	926.93	863.91	819.08	786.23	761.64	742.93	728.52	717.32	708.55
38000	3554.31	1969.03	1448.79	1194.66	1046.82	951.98	887.26	841.22	807.48	782.22	763.01	748.21	736.71	727.70
39000	3647.84	2020.85	1486.91	1226.10	1074.37	977.03	910.61	863.35	828.73	802.81	783.09	767.90	756.09	746.85
40000	3741.37	2072.66	1525.04	1257.54	1101.92	1002.08	933.96	885.49	849.98	823.39	803.16	787.59	775.48	766.00
41000	3834.91	2124.48	1563.16	1288.97	1129.47	1027.14	957.31	907.63	871.23	843.98	823.24	807.28	794.87	785.15
42000	3928.44	2176.30	1601.29	1320.41	1157.02	1052.19	980.66	929.76	892.48	864.56	843.32	826.97	814.25	804.30
43000	4021.98	2228.11	1639.42	1351.85	1184.56	1077.24	1004.00	951.90	913.73	885.14	863.40	846.66	833.64	823.45
44000	4115.51	2279.93	1677.54	1383.29	1212.11	1102.29	1027.35	974.04	934.97	905.73	883.48	866.35	853.03	842.60
45000	4209.05	2331.75	1715.67	1414.73	1239.66	1127.34	1050.70	996.18	956.22	926.31	903.56	886.04	872.42	861.75
46000	4302.58	2383.56	1753.79	1446.16	1267.21	1152.40	1074.05	1018.31	977.47	946.90	923.64	905.73	891.80	880.90
47000	4396.11	2435.38	1791.92	1477.60	1294.76	1177.45	1097.40	1040.45	998.72	967.48	943.72	925.42	911.19	900.05
48000	4489.65	2487.19	1830.04	1509.04	1322.30	1202.50	1120.75	1062.59	1019.97	988.07	963.80	945.11	930.58	919.20
49000	4583.18	2539.01	1868.17	1540.48	1349.85	1227.55	1144.10	1084.72	1041.22	1008.65	983.88	964.80	949.96	938.35
50000	4676.72	2590.83	1906.30	1571.92	1377.40	1252.60	1167.45	1106.86	1062.47	1029.24	1003.95	984.48	969.35	957.50
55000	5144.39	2849.91	2096.92	1729.11	1515.14	1377.86	1284.19	1217.55	1168.72	1132.16	1104.35	1082.93	1066.28	1053.25
60000	5612.06	3108.99	2287.55	1886.30	1652.88	1503.12	1400.93	1328.23	1274.96	1235.08	1204.74	1181.38	1163.22	1149.00
65000	6079.73	3368.07	2478.18	2043.49	1790.62	1628.38	1517.68	1438.92	1381.21	1338.01	1305.14	1279.83	1260.15	1244.75
70000	6547.40	3627.16	2668.81	2200.68	1928.36	1753.64	1634.42	1549.60	1487.46	1440.93	1405.53	1378.28	1357.09	1340.50
75000	7015.07	3886.24	2859.44	2357.87	2066.10	1878.90	1751.17	1660.29	1593.70	1543.85	1505.93	1476.72	1454.02	1436.24
80000	7482.74	4145.32	3050.07	2515.07	2203.84	2004.16	1867.91	1770.98	1699.95	1646.78	1606.32	1575.17	1550.96	1531.99
85000	7950.41	4404.40	3240.70	2672.26	2341.58	2129.42	1984.65	1881.66	1806.20	1749.70	1706.72	1673.62	1647.89	1627.74
90000	8418.09	4663.49	3431.33	2829.45	2479.31	2254.68	2101.40	1992.35	1912.44	1852.62	1807.11	1772.07	1744.83	1723.49
95000	8885.76	4922.57	3621.96	2986.64	2617.05	2379.94	2218.14	2103.03	2018.69	1955.55	1907.51	1870.52	1841.76	1819.24
100000	9353.43	5181.65	3812.59	3143.83	2754.79	2505.20	2334.89	2213.72	2124.94	2058.47	2007.90	1968.96	1938.69	1914.99

TERM	15 Years	16 Years	17 Years	18 Years	19 Years	20 Years	21 Years	22 Years	23 Years	24 Years	25 Years	30 Years	35 Years	40 Years
AMOUNT														
5	.10	.10	.10	.10	.10	.10	.10	.10	.10	.10	.10	.10	.10	.10
10	.19	.19	.19	.19	.19	.19	.19	.19	.19	.19	.19	.19	.19	.19
15	.29	.29	.29	.28	.28	.28	.28	.28	.28	.28	.28	.28	.28	.28
25	.48	.48	.47	.47	.47	.47	.47	.46	.46	.46	.46	.46	.46	.46
50	.95	.95	.94	.94	.94	.93	.93	.92	.92	.92	.92	.92	.92	.92
75	1.43	1.42	1.41	1.40	1.39	1.39	1.39	1.38	1.38	1.38	1.38	1.37	1.37	1.37
100	1.90	1.89	1.87	1.87	1.86	1.85	1.85	1.84	1.84	1.84	1.84	1.83	1.83	1.83
200	3.80	3.77	3.74	3.73	3.71	3.70	3.69	3.68	3.68	3.67	3.67	3.66	3.65	3.65
300	5.69	5.65	5.61	5.59	5.56	5.55	5.53	5.52	5.51	5.50	5.50	5.48	5.48	5.47
400	7.59	7.53	7.48	7.45	7.42	7.39	7.37	7.36	7.35	7.34	7.33	7.31	7.30	7.30
500	9.49	9.41	9.35	9.31	9.27	9.24	9.22	9.20	9.18	9.17	9.16	9.13	9.12	9.12
600	11.38	11.29	11.22	11.17	11.12	11.09	11.06	11.04	11.02	11.00	10.99	10.96	10.95	10.94
700	13.28	13.18	13.09	13.03	12.98	12.93	12.90	12.87	12.85	12.84	12.82	12.78	12.77	12.77
800	15.18	15.06	14.96	14.89	14.83	14.78	14.74	14.71	14.69	14.67	14.65	14.61	14.60	14.59
900	17.07	16.94	16.83	16.75	16.68	16.63	16.59	16.55	16.52	16.50	16.48	16.44	16.42	16.41
1000	18.97	18.82	18.70	18.61	18.54	18.48	18.43	18.39	18.36	18.34	18.32	18.26	18.24	18.24
2000	37.93	37.64	37.40	37.21	37.07	36.95	36.85	36.78	36.71	36.67	36.63	36.52	36.48	36.47
3000	56.89	56.45	56.10	55.82	55.60	55.42	55.28	55.16	55.07	55.00	54.94	54.77	54.72	54.70
4000	75.86	75.27	74.80	74.42	74.13	73.89	73.70	73.55	73.42	73.33	73.25	73.03	72.96	72.93
5000	94.82	94.08	93.50	93.03	92.66	92.36	92.12	91.93	91.78	91.66	91.56	91.29	91.20	91.17
6000	113.78	112.90	112.19	111.63	111.19	110.83	110.55	110.32	110.13	109.99	109.87	109.54	109.44	109.40
7000	132.75	131.71	130.89	130.24	129.72	129.30	128.97	128.70	128.49	128.32	128.18	127.80	127.67	127.63
8000	151.71	150.53	149.59	148.84	148.25	147.77	147.39	147.09	146.84	146.65	146.49	146.06	145.91	145.86
9000	170.67	169.34	168.29	167.45	166.78	166.24	165.82	165.47	165.20	164.98	164.80	164.31	164.15	164.10
10000	189.64	188.16	186.99	186.05	185.31	184.72	184.24	183.86	183.55	183.31	183.11	182.57	182.39	182.33
11000	208.60	206.98	205.69	204.66	203.84	203.19	202.66	202.24	201.91	201.64	201.42	200.83	200.63	200.56
12000	227.56	225.79	224.38	223.26	222.37	221.66	221.09	220.63	220.26	219.97	219.73	219.08	218.87	218.79
13000	246.53	244.61	243.08	241.87	240.90	240.13	239.51	239.01	238.61	238.30	238.04	237.34	237.10	237.02
14000	265.49	263.42	261.78	260.47	259.43	258.60	257.93	257.40	256.97	256.63	256.35	255.60	255.34	255.26
15000	284.45	282.24	280.48	279.08	277.96	277.07	276.36	275.78	275.32	274.96	274.66	273.85	273.58	273.49
16000	303.42	301.05	299.18	297.68	296.49	295.54	294.78	294.17	293.68	293.29	292.97	292.11	291.82	291.72
17000	322.38	319.87	317.88	316.29	315.02	314.01	313.20	312.55	312.03	311.62	311.28	310.37	310.06	309.95
18000	341.34	338.68	336.57	334.89	333.55	332.48	331.63	330.94	330.39	329.95	329.59	328.62	328.30	328.19
19000	360.31	357.50	355.27	353.50	352.09	350.95	350.05	349.32	348.74	348.28	347.90	346.88	346.53	346.42
20000	379.27	376.32	373.97	372.11	370.62	369.43	368.47	367.71	367.10	366.61	366.21	365.14	364.77	364.65
21000	398.23	395.13	392.67	390.71	389.15	387.90	386.90	386.09	385.45	384.94	384.52	383.39	383.01	382.88
22000	417.20	413.95	411.37	409.31	407.68	406.37	405.32	404.48	403.81	403.27	402.83	401.65	401.25	401.12
23000	436.16	432.76	430.07	427.92	426.21	424.84	423.74	422.86	422.16	421.60	421.14	419.90	419.49	419.35
24000	455.12	451.58	448.76	446.52	444.74	443.31	442.17	441.25	440.52	439.93	439.45	438.16	437.73	437.58
25000	474.09	470.39	467.46	465.13	463.27	461.78	460.59	459.64	458.87	458.26	457.76	456.42	455.97	455.81
26000	493.05	489.21	486.16	483.73	481.80	480.25	479.01	478.02	477.22	476.59	476.07	474.67	474.20	474.04
27000	512.01	508.02	504.86	502.34	500.33	498.72	497.44	496.41	495.58	494.92	494.38	492.93	492.44	492.28
28000	530.97	526.84	523.56	520.94	518.86	517.19	515.86	514.79	513.93	513.25	512.69	511.19	510.68	510.51
29000	549.94	545.66	542.26	539.55	537.39	535.66	534.28	533.18	532.29	531.58	531.00	529.44	528.92	528.74
30000	568.90	564.47	560.95	558.15	555.92	554.14	552.71	551.56	550.64	549.91	549.31	547.70	547.16	546.97
31000	587.86	583.29	579.65	576.76	574.45	572.61	571.13	569.95	569.00	568.24	567.62	565.96	565.40	565.21
32000	606.83	602.10	598.35	595.36	592.98	591.08	589.55	588.33	587.35	586.57	585.93	584.21	583.63	583.44
33000	625.79	620.92	617.05	613.97	611.51	609.55	607.98	606.72	605.71	604.90	604.24	602.47	601.87	601.67
34000	644.75	639.73	635.75	632.57	630.04	628.02	626.40	625.10	624.06	623.23	622.55	620.73	620.11	619.90
35000	663.72	658.55	654.45	651.18	648.57	646.49	644.82	643.49	642.42	641.56	640.86	638.98	638.35	638.14
36000	682.68	677.36	673.14	669.78	667.10	664.96	663.25	661.87	660.77	659.89	659.17	657.24	656.59	656.37
37000	701.64	696.18	691.84	688.39	685.64	683.43	681.67	680.26	679.12	678.22	677.48	675.50	674.83	674.60
38000	720.61	715.00	710.54	706.99	704.17	701.90	700.09	698.64	697.48	696.55	695.80	693.75	693.06	692.83
39000	739.57	733.81	729.24	725.60	722.70	720.38	718.52	717.03	715.83	714.88	714.11	712.01	711.30	711.06
40000	758.53	752.63	747.94	744.20	741.23	738.85	736.94	735.41	734.19	733.21	732.42	730.27	729.54	729.30
41000	777.50	771.44	766.64	762.81	759.76	757.32	755.36	753.80	752.54	751.54	750.73	748.52	747.78	747.53
42000	796.46	790.26	785.33	781.41	778.29	775.79	773.79	772.18	770.90	769.87	769.04	766.78	766.02	765.76
43000	815.42	809.07	804.03	800.02	796.82	794.26	792.21	790.57	789.25	788.20	787.35	785.04	784.26	783.99
44000	834.39	827.89	822.73	818.62	815.35	812.73	810.63	808.95	807.61	806.53	805.66	803.29	802.50	802.23
45000	853.35	846.70	841.43	837.23	833.88	831.20	829.06	827.34	825.96	824.86	823.97	821.55	820.73	820.46
46000	872.31	865.52	860.13	855.83	852.41	849.67	847.48	845.72	844.32	843.19	842.28	839.80	838.97	838.69
47000	891.28	884.34	878.83	874.44	870.94	868.14	865.90	864.11	862.67	861.52	860.59	858.06	857.21	856.92
48000	910.24	903.15	897.52	893.04	889.47	886.61	884.33	882.50	881.03	879.85	878.90	876.32	875.45	875.16
49000	929.20	921.97	916.22	911.65	908.00	905.09	902.75	900.88	899.38	898.18	897.21	894.57	893.69	893.39
50000	948.16	940.78	934.92	930.25	926.53	923.56	921.17	919.27	917.73	916.51	915.52	912.83	911.93	911.62
55000	1042.98	1034.86	1028.41	1023.28	1019.18	1015.91	1013.29	1011.19	1009.51	1008.16	1007.07	1004.11	1003.12	1002.78
60000	1137.80	1128.94	1121.90	1116.30	1111.84	1108.27	1105.41	1103.12	1101.28	1099.81	1098.62	1095.40	1094.31	1093.94
65000	1232.61	1223.02	1215.40	1209.33	1204.49	1200.62	1197.53	1195.04	1193.05	1191.46	1190.17	1186.68	1185.50	1185.10
70000	1327.43	1317.09	1308.89	1302.35	1297.14	1292.98	1289.64	1286.97	1284.83	1283.11	1281.72	1277.96	1276.69	1276.27
75000	1422.25	1411.17	1402.38	1395.38	1389.80	1385.33	1381.76	1378.90	1376.60	1374.76	1373.28	1369.24	1367.89	1367.43
80000	1517.06	1505.25	1495.87	1488.40	1482.45	1477.69	1473.88	1470.82	1468.37	1466.41	1464.83	1460.53	1459.08	1458.59
85000	1611.88	1599.33	1589.36	1581.43	1575.10	1570.04	1565.99	1562.75	1560.15	1558.06	1556.38	1551.81	1550.27	1549.75
90000	1706.69	1693.40	1682.85	1674.45	1667.75	1662.40	1658.11	1654.67	1651.92	1649.71	1647.93	1643.09	1641.46	1640.91
95000	1801.51	1787.48	1776.35	1767.48	1760.41	1754.75	1750.23	1746.60	1743.69	1741.36	1739.48	1734.37	1732.65	1732.07
100000	1896.33	1881.56	1869.84	1860.50	1853.06	1847.11	1842.34	1838.53	1835.46	1833.01	1831.03	1825.66	1823.85	1823.23

MONTHLY PAYMENT
REQUIRED TO AMORTIZE A LOAN

TERM AMOUNT	1 Year	2 Years	3 Years	4 Years	5 Years	6 Years	7 Years	8 Years	9 Years	10 Years	11 Years	12 Years	13 Years	14 Years
5	.47	.26	.20	.16	.14	.13	.12	.12	.11	.11	.11	.10	.10	.10
10	.94	.52	.39	.32	.28	.26	.24	.23	.22	.21	.21	.20	.20	.20
15	1.41	.78	.58	.48	.42	.38	.36	.34	.32	.31	.31	.30	.30	.29
25	2.34	1.30	.96	.79	.69	.63	.59	.56	.54	.52	.51	.50	.49	.48
50	4.68	2.60	1.91	1.58	1.38	1.26	1.17	1.11	1.07	1.04	1.01	.99	.98	.96
75	7.02	3.89	2.87	2.36	2.07	1.89	1.76	1.67	1.60	1.55	1.51	1.48	1.46	1.44
100	9.36	5.19	3.82	3.15	2.76	2.51	2.34	2.22	2.13	2.07	2.01	1.98	1.95	1.92
200	18.71	10.37	7.63	6.30	5.52	5.02	4.68	4.44	4.26	4.13	4.02	3.95	3.89	3.84
300	28.07	15.55	11.45	9.44	8.27	7.53	7.01	6.65	6.38	6.19	6.03	5.92	5.83	5.76
400	37.42	20.74	15.26	12.59	11.03	10.03	9.35	8.87	8.51	8.25	8.04	7.89	7.77	7.67
500	46.78	25.92	19.07	15.73	13.79	12.54	11.69	11.08	10.64	10.31	10.05	9.86	9.71	9.59
600	56.13	31.10	22.89	18.88	16.54	15.05	14.02	13.30	12.76	12.37	12.06	11.83	11.65	11.51
700	65.49	36.29	26.70	22.02	19.30	17.55	16.36	15.51	14.89	14.43	14.07	13.80	13.59	13.42
800	74.84	41.47	30.52	25.17	22.05	20.06	18.70	17.73	17.02	16.49	16.08	15.77	15.53	15.34
900	84.20	46.65	34.33	28.31	24.81	22.57	21.03	19.94	19.14	18.55	18.09	17.74	17.47	17.26
1000	93.55	51.83	38.14	31.46	27.57	25.07	23.37	22.16	21.27	20.61	20.10	19.71	19.41	19.17
2000	187.10	103.66	76.28	62.91	55.13	50.14	46.73	44.31	42.54	41.21	40.20	39.42	38.82	38.34
3000	280.64	155.49	114.42	94.36	82.69	75.21	70.10	66.46	63.80	61.81	60.29	59.13	58.22	57.51
4000	374.19	207.32	152.56	125.81	110.25	100.27	93.46	88.62	85.07	82.41	80.39	78.83	77.63	76.68
5000	467.74	259.15	190.70	157.26	137.82	125.34	116.83	110.77	106.33	103.01	100.49	98.54	97.03	95.85
6000	561.28	310.98	228.84	188.72	165.38	150.41	140.19	132.92	127.60	123.61	120.58	118.25	116.44	115.02
7000	654.83	362.81	266.98	220.17	192.94	175.47	163.55	155.08	148.87	144.22	140.68	137.96	135.84	134.18
8000	748.38	414.64	305.11	251.62	220.50	200.54	186.92	177.23	170.13	164.82	160.78	157.66	155.25	153.35
9000	841.92	466.46	343.25	283.07	248.06	225.61	210.28	199.38	191.40	185.42	180.87	177.37	174.65	172.52
10000	935.47	518.29	381.39	314.52	275.63	250.67	233.65	221.54	212.66	206.02	200.97	197.08	194.06	191.69
11000	1029.01	570.12	419.53	345.97	303.19	275.74	257.01	243.69	233.93	226.62	221.07	216.79	213.46	210.86
12000	1122.56	621.95	457.67	377.43	330.75	300.81	280.38	265.84	255.19	247.22	241.16	236.49	232.87	230.03
13000	1216.11	673.78	495.81	408.88	358.31	325.87	303.74	288.00	276.46	267.83	261.26	256.20	252.27	249.19
14000	1309.65	725.61	533.95	440.33	385.87	350.94	327.10	310.15	297.73	288.43	281.36	275.91	271.68	268.36
15000	1403.20	777.44	572.09	471.78	413.44	376.01	350.47	332.30	318.99	309.03	301.45	295.62	291.08	287.53
16000	1496.75	829.27	610.22	503.23	441.00	401.07	373.83	354.45	340.26	329.63	321.55	315.32	310.49	306.70
17000	1590.29	881.09	648.36	534.69	468.56	426.14	397.20	376.61	361.52	350.23	341.64	335.03	329.89	325.87
18000	1683.84	932.92	686.50	566.14	496.12	451.21	420.56	398.76	382.79	370.83	361.74	354.74	349.30	345.04
19000	1777.38	984.75	724.64	597.59	523.68	476.27	443.93	420.91	404.06	391.44	381.84	374.45	368.70	364.21
20000	1870.93	1036.58	762.78	629.04	551.25	501.34	467.29	443.07	425.32	412.04	401.93	394.15	388.11	383.37
21000	1964.48	1088.41	800.92	660.49	578.81	526.41	490.65	465.22	446.59	432.64	422.03	413.86	407.51	402.54
22000	2058.02	1140.24	839.06	691.94	606.37	551.47	514.02	487.37	467.85	453.24	442.13	433.57	426.92	421.71
23000	2151.57	1192.07	877.20	723.40	633.93	576.54	537.38	509.53	489.12	473.84	462.22	453.28	446.32	440.88
24000	2245.12	1243.90	915.33	754.85	661.50	601.61	560.75	531.68	510.38	494.44	482.32	472.98	465.73	460.05
25000	2338.66	1295.72	953.47	786.30	689.06	626.68	584.11	553.83	531.65	515.05	502.42	492.69	485.13	479.22
26000	2432.21	1347.55	991.61	817.75	716.62	651.74	607.47	575.99	552.92	535.65	522.51	512.40	504.54	498.38
27000	2525.75	1399.38	1029.75	849.20	744.18	676.81	630.84	598.14	574.18	556.25	542.61	532.11	523.94	517.55
28000	2619.30	1451.21	1067.89	880.66	771.74	701.88	654.20	620.29	595.45	576.85	562.71	551.81	543.35	536.72
29000	2712.85	1503.04	1106.03	912.11	799.31	726.94	677.57	642.45	616.71	597.45	582.80	571.52	562.75	555.89
30000	2806.39	1554.87	1144.17	943.56	826.87	752.01	700.93	664.60	637.98	618.05	602.90	591.23	582.16	575.06
31000	2899.94	1606.70	1182.31	975.01	854.43	777.08	724.30	686.75	659.25	638.66	622.99	610.94	601.56	594.23
32000	2993.49	1658.53	1220.44	1006.46	881.99	802.14	747.66	708.90	680.51	659.26	643.09	630.64	620.97	613.39
33000	3087.03	1710.35	1258.58	1037.91	909.55	827.21	771.02	731.06	701.78	679.86	663.19	650.35	640.37	632.56
34000	3180.58	1762.18	1296.72	1069.37	937.12	852.28	794.39	753.21	723.04	700.46	683.28	670.06	659.78	651.73
35000	3274.12	1814.01	1334.86	1100.82	964.68	877.34	817.75	775.36	744.31	721.06	703.38	689.77	679.18	670.90
36000	3367.67	1865.84	1373.00	1132.27	992.24	902.41	841.12	797.52	765.57	741.66	723.48	709.47	698.59	690.07
37000	3461.22	1917.67	1411.14	1163.72	1019.80	927.48	864.48	819.67	786.84	762.27	743.57	729.18	717.99	709.24
38000	3554.76	1969.50	1449.28	1195.17	1047.36	952.54	887.85	841.82	808.11	782.87	763.67	748.89	737.40	728.41
39000	3648.31	2021.33	1487.42	1226.63	1074.93	977.61	911.21	863.98	829.37	803.47	783.77	768.60	756.80	747.57
40000	3741.86	2073.16	1525.55	1258.08	1102.49	1002.68	934.57	886.13	850.64	824.07	803.86	788.30	776.21	766.74
41000	3835.40	2124.99	1563.69	1289.53	1130.05	1027.74	957.94	908.28	871.90	844.67	823.96	808.01	795.61	785.91
42000	3928.95	2176.81	1601.83	1320.98	1157.61	1052.81	981.30	930.44	893.17	865.27	844.06	827.72	815.02	805.08
43000	4022.49	2228.64	1639.97	1352.43	1185.17	1077.88	1004.67	952.59	914.44	885.88	864.15	847.43	834.43	824.25
44000	4116.04	2280.47	1678.11	1383.88	1212.74	1102.94	1028.03	974.74	935.70	906.48	884.25	867.13	853.83	843.42
45000	4209.59	2332.30	1716.25	1415.34	1240.30	1128.01	1051.40	996.89	956.97	927.08	904.34	886.84	873.24	862.58
46000	4303.13	2384.13	1754.39	1446.79	1267.86	1153.08	1074.76	1019.05	978.23	947.68	924.44	906.55	892.64	881.75
47000	4396.68	2435.96	1792.53	1478.24	1295.42	1178.14	1098.12	1041.20	999.50	968.28	944.54	926.26	912.05	900.92
48000	4490.23	2487.79	1830.66	1509.69	1322.99	1203.21	1121.49	1063.35	1020.76	988.88	964.63	945.96	931.45	920.09
49000	4583.77	2539.62	1868.80	1541.14	1350.55	1228.28	1144.85	1085.51	1042.03	1009.49	984.73	965.67	950.86	939.26
50000	4677.32	2591.44	1906.94	1572.60	1378.11	1253.35	1168.22	1107.66	1063.30	1030.09	1004.83	985.38	970.26	958.43
55000	5145.05	2850.59	2097.64	1729.85	1515.92	1378.68	1285.04	1218.43	1169.62	1133.10	1105.31	1083.91	1067.29	1054.27
60000	5612.78	3109.73	2288.33	1887.11	1653.73	1504.01	1401.86	1329.19	1275.95	1236.10	1205.79	1182.45	1164.31	1150.11
65000	6080.51	3368.88	2479.02	2044.37	1791.54	1629.35	1518.68	1439.96	1382.28	1339.11	1306.27	1280.99	1261.34	1245.95
70000	6548.24	3628.02	2669.72	2201.63	1929.35	1754.68	1635.50	1550.72	1488.61	1442.12	1406.76	1379.53	1358.36	1341.79
75000	7015.97	3887.16	2860.41	2358.89	2067.16	1880.02	1752.32	1661.49	1594.94	1545.13	1507.24	1478.06	1455.39	1437.64
80000	7483.71	4146.31	3051.10	2516.15	2204.97	2005.35	1869.14	1772.25	1701.27	1648.14	1607.72	1576.60	1552.41	1533.48
85000	7951.44	4405.45	3241.80	2673.41	2342.78	2130.68	1985.96	1883.02	1807.60	1751.14	1708.20	1675.14	1649.44	1629.32
90000	8419.17	4664.60	3432.49	2830.67	2480.59	2256.02	2102.79	1993.78	1913.93	1854.15	1808.68	1773.68	1746.47	1725.16
95000	8886.90	4923.74	3623.19	2987.93	2618.40	2381.35	2219.61	2104.55	2020.26	1957.16	1909.17	1872.21	1843.49	1821.01
100000	9354.63	5182.88	3813.88	3145.19	2756.21	2506.69	2336.43	2215.32	2126.59	2060.17	2009.65	1970.75	1940.52	1916.85

TERM	15 Years	16 Years	17 Years	18 Years	19 Years	20 Years	21 Years	22 Years	23 Years	24 Years	25 Years	30 Years	35 Years	40 Years
AMOUNT														
5	.10	.10	.10	.10	.10	.10	.10	.10	.10	.10	.10	.10	.10	.10
10	.19	.19	.19	.19	.19	.19	.19	.19	.19	.19	.19	.19	.19	.19
15	.29	.29	.29	.28	.28	.28	.28	.28	.28	.28	.28	.28	.28	.28
25	.48	.48	.47	.47	.47	.47	.47	.47	.46	.46	.46	.46	.46	.46
50	.95	.95	.94	.94	.93	.93	.93	.93	.92	.92	.92	.92	.92	.92
75	1.43	1.42	1.41	1.40	1.40	1.39	1.39	1.39	1.38	1.38	1.38	1.38	1.37	1.37
100	1.90	1.89	1.88	1.87	1.86	1.85	1.85	1.65	1.84	1.84	1.84	1.83	1.83	1.83
200	3.80	3.77	3.75	3.73	3.72	3.70	3.69	3.69	3.68	3.68	3.67	3.66	3.66	3.66
300	5.70	5.66	5.62	5.59	5.57	5.55	5.54	5.53	5.52	5.51	5.50	5.49	5.48	5.48
400	7.60	7.54	7.49	7.45	7.43	7.40	7.38	7.37	7.35	7.35	7.34	7.32	7.31	7.31
500	9.50	9.42	9.36	9.32	9.28	9.25	9.23	9.21	9.19	9.18	9.17	9.14	9.13	9.13
600	11.39	11.31	11.24	11.18	11.14	11.10	11.07	11.05	11.03	11.02	11.00	10.97	10.96	10.96
700	13.29	13.19	13.11	13.04	12.99	12.95	12.92	12.89	12.87	12.85	12.84	12.80	12.79	12.78
800	15.19	15.07	14.98	14.90	14.85	14.80	14.76	14.73	14.70	14.69	14.67	14.63	14.61	14.61
900	17.09	16.96	16.85	16.77	16.70	16.65	16.60	16.57	16.54	16.52	16.50	16.45	16.44	16.43
1000	18.99	18.84	18.72	18.63	18.56	18.50	18.45	18.41	18.38	18.36	18.34	18.28	18.26	18.26
2000	37.97	37.67	37.44	37.25	37.11	36.99	36.89	36.82	36.75	36.71	36.67	36.56	36.52	36.51
3000	56.95	56.51	56.16	55.88	55.66	55.48	55.34	55.22	55.13	55.06	55.00	54.84	54.78	54.76
4000	75.93	75.34	74.88	74.50	74.21	73.97	73.78	73.63	73.50	73.41	73.33	73.11	73.04	73.02
5000	94.92	94.18	93.59	93.13	92.76	92.46	92.22	92.03	91.88	91.76	91.66	91.39	91.30	91.27
6000	113.90	113.01	112.31	111.75	111.31	110.95	110.67	110.44	110.25	110.11	109.99	109.67	109.56	109.52
7000	132.88	131.85	131.03	130.38	129.86	129.44	129.11	128.84	128.63	128.46	128.32	127.95	127.82	127.78
8000	151.86	150.68	149.75	149.00	148.41	147.93	147.55	147.25	147.00	146.81	146.65	146.22	146.08	146.03
9000	170.84	169.52	168.46	167.63	166.96	166.42	166.00	165.65	165.38	165.16	164.98	164.50	164.34	164.28
10000	189.83	188.35	187.18	186.25	185.51	184.91	184.44	184.06	183.75	183.51	183.31	182.78	182.60	182.54
11000	208.81	207.19	205.90	204.88	204.06	203.41	202.88	202.46	202.13	201.86	201.64	201.05	200.86	200.79
12000	227.79	226.02	224.62	223.50	222.61	221.90	221.33	220.87	220.50	220.21	219.97	219.33	219.12	219.04
13000	246.77	244.86	243.33	242.12	241.16	240.39	239.77	239.27	238.88	238.56	238.30	237.61	237.37	237.30
14000	265.75	263.69	262.05	260.75	259.71	258.88	258.21	257.68	257.25	256.91	256.63	255.89	255.63	255.55
15000	284.74	282.53	280.77	279.37	278.26	277.37	276.66	276.09	275.63	275.26	274.97	274.16	273.89	273.80
16000	303.72	301.36	299.49	298.00	296.81	295.86	295.10	294.49	294.00	293.61	293.30	292.44	292.15	292.05
17000	322.70	320.19	318.21	316.62	315.36	314.35	313.54	312.90	312.38	311.96	311.63	310.72	310.41	310.31
18000	341.68	339.03	336.92	335.25	333.91	332.84	331.99	331.30	330.75	330.31	329.96	328.99	328.67	328.56
19000	360.66	357.86	355.64	353.87	352.46	351.33	350.43	349.71	349.13	348.66	348.29	347.27	346.93	346.81
20000	379.65	376.70	374.36	372.50	371.01	369.82	368.87	368.11	367.50	367.01	366.62	365.55	365.19	365.07
21000	398.63	395.53	393.08	391.12	389.56	388.31	387.32	386.52	385.88	385.36	384.95	383.83	383.45	383.32
22000	417.61	414.37	411.79	409.75	408.11	406.80	405.76	404.92	404.25	403.71	403.28	402.10	401.71	401.57
23000	436.59	433.20	430.51	428.37	426.66	425.30	424.20	423.33	422.63	422.06	421.61	420.38	419.97	419.83
24000	455.57	452.04	449.23	446.99	445.21	443.79	442.65	441.73	441.00	440.41	439.94	438.66	438.23	438.08
25000	474.55	470.87	467.95	465.62	463.76	462.28	461.09	460.14	459.38	458.76	458.27	456.93	456.48	456.33
26000	493.54	489.71	486.66	484.24	482.31	480.77	479.53	478.54	477.75	477.11	476.60	475.21	474.74	474.59
27000	512.52	508.54	505.38	502.87	500.86	499.26	497.98	496.95	496.13	495.46	494.93	493.49	493.00	492.84
28000	531.50	527.38	524.10	521.49	519.41	517.75	516.42	515.36	514.50	513.82	513.26	511.77	511.26	511.09
29000	550.48	546.21	542.82	540.12	537.96	536.24	534.86	533.76	532.88	532.17	531.60	530.04	529.52	529.34
30000	569.47	565.05	561.54	558.74	556.51	554.73	553.31	552.17	551.25	550.52	549.93	548.32	547.78	547.60
31000	588.45	583.88	580.25	577.37	575.06	573.22	571.75	570.57	569.63	568.87	568.26	566.60	566.04	565.85
32000	607.43	602.71	598.97	595.99	593.61	591.71	590.19	588.98	588.00	587.22	586.59	584.87	584.30	584.10
33000	626.41	621.55	617.69	614.62	612.16	610.21	608.64	607.38	606.38	605.57	604.92	603.15	602.56	602.36
34000	645.40	640.38	636.41	633.24	630.71	628.70	627.08	625.79	624.75	623.92	623.25	621.43	620.82	620.61
35000	664.38	659.22	655.12	651.86	649.27	647.19	645.53	644.19	643.12	642.27	641.58	639.71	639.08	638.86
36000	683.36	678.05	673.84	670.49	667.82	665.68	663.97	662.60	661.50	660.62	659.91	657.98	657.34	657.12
37000	702.34	696.89	692.56	689.11	686.37	684.17	682.41	681.00	679.87	678.97	678.24	676.26	675.59	675.37
38000	721.32	715.72	711.28	707.74	704.92	702.66	700.86	699.41	698.25	697.32	696.57	694.54	693.85	693.62
39000	740.31	734.56	729.99	726.36	723.47	721.15	719.30	717.81	716.62	715.67	714.90	712.82	712.11	711.88
40000	759.29	753.39	748.71	744.99	742.02	739.64	737.74	736.22	735.00	734.02	733.23	731.09	730.37	730.13
41000	778.27	772.23	767.43	763.61	760.57	758.13	756.19	754.63	753.37	752.37	751.56	749.37	748.63	748.38
42000	797.25	791.06	786.15	782.24	779.12	776.62	774.63	773.03	771.75	770.72	769.89	767.65	766.89	766.64
43000	816.23	809.90	804.87	800.86	797.67	795.12	793.07	791.44	790.12	789.07	788.22	785.92	785.15	784.89
44000	835.22	828.73	823.58	819.49	816.22	813.61	811.52	809.84	808.50	807.42	806.56	804.20	803.41	803.14
45000	854.20	847.57	842.30	838.11	834.77	832.10	829.96	828.25	826.87	825.77	824.89	822.48	821.67	821.39
46000	873.18	866.40	861.02	856.74	853.32	850.59	848.40	846.65	845.25	844.12	843.22	840.76	839.93	839.65
47000	892.16	885.23	879.74	875.36	871.87	869.08	866.85	865.06	863.62	862.47	861.55	859.03	858.19	857.90
48000	911.14	904.07	898.45	893.98	890.42	887.57	885.29	883.46	882.00	880.82	879.88	877.31	876.45	876.15
49000	930.13	922.90	917.17	912.61	908.97	906.06	903.73	901.87	900.37	899.17	898.21	895.59	894.70	894.41
50000	949.11	941.74	935.89	931.23	927.52	924.55	922.18	920.27	918.75	917.52	916.54	913.86	912.96	912.66
55000	1044.02	1035.91	1029.48	1024.36	1020.27	1017.01	1014.39	1012.30	1010.62	1009.27	1008.19	1005.25	1004.26	1003.93
60000	1138.93	1130.09	1123.07	1117.48	1113.02	1109.46	1106.61	1104.33	1102.50	1101.03	1099.85	1096.64	1095.56	1095.19
65000	1233.84	1224.26	1216.65	1210.60	1205.77	1201.92	1198.83	1196.35	1194.37	1192.78	1191.50	1188.02	1186.85	1186.46
70000	1328.75	1318.43	1310.24	1303.72	1298.53	1294.37	1291.05	1288.38	1286.24	1284.53	1283.15	1279.41	1278.15	1277.72
75000	1423.66	1412.61	1403.83	1396.85	1391.28	1386.83	1383.26	1380.41	1378.12	1376.28	1374.81	1370.79	1369.44	1368.99
80000	1518.57	1506.78	1497.42	1489.97	1484.03	1479.28	1475.48	1472.43	1469.99	1468.03	1466.46	1462.18	1460.74	1460.25
85000	1613.48	1600.95	1591.01	1583.09	1576.78	1571.73	1567.70	1564.46	1561.87	1559.79	1558.11	1553.57	1552.03	1551.52
90000	1708.39	1695.13	1684.60	1676.22	1669.53	1664.19	1659.91	1656.49	1653.74	1651.54	1649.77	1644.95	1643.33	1642.78
95000	1803.30	1789.30	1778.18	1769.34	1762.28	1756.64	1752.13	1748.52	1745.62	1743.29	1741.42	1736.34	1734.63	1734.05
100000	1898.21	1883.47	1871.77	1862.46	1855.03	1849.10	1844.35	1840.54	1837.49	1835.04	1833.07	1827.72	1825.92	1825.31

MONTHLY PAYMENT
REQUIRED TO AMORTIZE A LOAN

TERM AMOUNT	1 Year	2 Years	3 Years	4 Years	5 Years	6 Years	7 Years	8 Years	9 Years	10 Years	11 Years	12 Years	13 Years	14 Years
5	.47	.26	.20	.16	.14	.13	.12	.12	.11	.11	.11	.10	.10	.10
10	.94	.52	.39	.32	.28	.26	.24	.23	.22	.21	.21	.20	.20	.20
15	1.41	.78	.58	.48	.42	.38	.36	.34	.32	.32	.31	.30	.30	.29
25	2.34	1.30	.96	.79	.70	.63	.59	.56	.54	.52	.51	.50	.49	.49
50	4.68	2.60	1.91	1.58	1.39	1.26	1.18	1.12	1.07	1.04	1.01	.99	.98	.97
75	7.02	3.90	2.87	2.37	2.08	1.89	1.76	1.67	1.60	1.56	1.52	1.49	1.47	1.45
100	9.36	5.19	3.82	3.16	2.77	2.52	2.35	2.23	2.14	2.07	2.02	1.98	1.95	1.93
200	18.72	10.38	7.64	6.31	5.53	5.03	4.69	4.45	4.27	4.14	4.04	3.96	3.90	3.85
300	28.08	15.57	11.46	9.46	8.29	7.54	7.03	6.67	6.40	6.21	6.05	5.94	5.85	5.78
400	37.44	20.76	15.28	12.61	11.05	10.06	9.38	8.89	8.54	8.27	8.07	7.92	7.80	7.70
500	46.80	25.94	19.10	15.76	13.81	12.57	11.72	11.11	10.67	10.34	10.09	9.89	9.74	9.63
600	56.16	31.13	22.92	18.91	16.58	15.08	14.06	13.34	12.80	12.41	12.10	11.87	11.69	11.55
700	65.52	36.32	26.74	22.06	19.34	17.59	16.40	15.56	14.94	14.47	14.12	13.85	13.64	13.47
800	74.88	41.51	30.56	25.21	22.10	20.11	18.75	17.78	17.07	16.54	16.14	15.83	15.59	15.40
900	84.24	46.70	34.38	28.36	24.86	22.62	21.09	20.00	19.20	18.61	18.15	17.81	17.54	17.32
1000	93.60	51.88	38.20	31.51	27.62	25.13	23.43	22.22	21.34	20.67	20.17	19.78	19.48	19.25
2000	187.19	103.76	76.39	63.02	55.24	50.26	46.86	44.44	42.67	41.34	40.34	39.56	38.96	38.49
3000	280.79	155.64	114.58	94.52	82.86	75.38	70.28	66.66	64.00	62.01	60.50	59.34	58.44	57.73
4000	374.38	207.52	152.77	126.03	110.48	100.51	93.71	88.87	85.33	82.68	80.67	79.12	77.92	76.98
5000	467.98	259.40	190.96	157.54	138.10	125.64	117.13	111.09	106.66	103.35	100.84	98.90	97.40	96.22
6000	561.57	311.27	229.15	189.04	165.72	150.76	140.56	133.31	128.00	124.02	121.00	118.68	116.87	115.46
7000	655.17	363.15	267.34	220.55	193.34	175.89	163.99	155.52	149.33	144.69	141.17	138.46	136.35	134.70
8000	748.76	415.03	305.53	252.05	220.96	201.01	187.41	177.74	170.66	165.36	161.34	158.24	155.83	153.95
9000	842.35	466.91	343.72	283.56	248.58	226.14	210.84	199.96	191.99	186.03	181.50	178.02	175.31	173.19
10000	935.95	518.79	381.91	315.07	276.19	251.27	234.26	222.18	213.32	206.70	201.67	197.79	194.79	192.43
11000	1029.54	570.66	420.10	346.57	303.81	276.39	257.69	244.39	234.66	227.37	221.83	217.57	214.26	211.68
12000	1123.14	622.54	458.29	378.08	331.43	301.52	281.12	266.61	255.99	248.04	242.00	237.35	233.74	230.92
13000	1216.73	674.42	496.48	409.58	359.05	326.64	304.54	288.83	277.32	268.71	262.17	257.13	253.22	250.16
14000	1310.33	726.30	534.67	441.09	386.67	351.77	327.97	311.04	298.65	289.38	282.33	276.91	272.70	269.40
15000	1403.92	778.18	572.86	472.60	414.29	376.90	351.39	333.26	319.98	310.05	302.50	296.69	292.18	288.65
16000	1497.52	830.06	611.05	504.10	441.91	402.02	374.82	355.48	341.32	330.72	322.67	316.47	311.65	307.89
17000	1591.11	881.93	649.24	535.61	469.53	427.15	398.25	377.70	362.65	351.39	342.83	336.25	331.13	327.13
18000	1684.70	933.81	687.43	567.11	497.15	452.28	421.67	399.91	383.98	372.06	363.00	356.03	350.61	346.37
19000	1778.30	985.69	725.62	598.62	524.76	477.40	445.10	422.13	405.31	392.73	383.16	375.80	370.09	365.62
20000	1871.89	1037.57	763.81	630.13	552.38	502.53	468.52	444.35	426.64	413.40	403.33	395.58	389.57	384.86
21000	1965.49	1089.45	802.00	661.63	580.00	527.65	491.95	466.56	447.97	434.07	423.50	415.36	409.04	404.10
22000	2059.08	1141.32	840.19	693.14	607.62	552.78	515.38	488.78	469.31	454.74	443.66	435.14	428.52	423.35
23000	2152.68	1193.20	878.39	724.64	635.24	577.91	538.80	511.00	490.64	475.41	463.83	454.92	448.00	442.59
24000	2246.27	1245.08	916.58	756.15	662.86	603.03	562.23	533.21	511.97	496.08	484.00	474.70	467.48	461.83
25000	2339.86	1296.96	954.77	787.66	690.48	628.16	585.65	555.43	533.30	516.75	504.16	494.48	486.96	481.07
26000	2433.46	1348.84	992.96	819.16	718.10	653.28	609.08	577.65	554.63	537.42	524.33	514.26	506.44	500.32
27000	2527.05	1400.72	1031.15	850.67	745.72	678.41	632.51	599.87	575.97	558.09	544.49	534.04	525.91	519.56
28000	2620.65	1452.59	1069.34	882.18	773.33	703.54	655.93	622.08	597.30	578.76	564.66	553.82	545.39	538.80
29000	2714.24	1504.47	1107.53	913.68	800.95	728.66	679.36	644.30	618.63	599.43	584.83	573.59	564.87	558.04
30000	2807.84	1556.35	1145.72	945.19	828.57	753.79	702.78	666.52	639.96	620.10	604.99	593.37	584.35	577.29
31000	2901.43	1608.23	1183.91	976.69	856.19	778.91	726.21	688.73	661.29	640.77	625.16	613.15	603.83	596.53
32000	2995.03	1660.11	1222.10	1008.20	883.81	804.04	749.64	710.95	682.63	661.44	645.33	632.93	623.30	615.77
33000	3088.62	1711.98	1260.29	1039.71	911.43	829.17	773.06	733.17	703.96	682.10	665.49	652.71	642.78	635.02
34000	3182.21	1763.86	1298.48	1071.21	939.05	854.29	796.49	755.39	725.29	702.77	685.66	672.49	662.26	654.26
35000	3275.81	1815.74	1336.67	1102.72	966.67	879.42	819.91	777.60	746.62	723.44	705.83	692.27	681.74	673.50
36000	3369.40	1867.62	1374.86	1134.22	994.29	904.55	843.34	799.82	767.95	744.11	725.99	712.05	701.22	692.74
37000	3463.00	1919.50	1413.05	1165.73	1021.90	929.67	866.76	822.04	789.29	764.78	746.16	731.83	720.69	711.99
38000	3556.59	1971.37	1451.24	1197.24	1049.52	954.80	890.19	844.25	810.62	785.45	766.32	751.60	740.17	731.23
39000	3650.19	2023.25	1489.43	1228.74	1077.14	979.92	913.62	866.47	831.95	806.12	786.49	771.38	759.65	750.47
40000	3743.78	2075.13	1527.62	1260.25	1104.76	1005.05	937.04	888.69	853.28	826.79	806.66	791.16	779.13	769.71
41000	3837.37	2127.01	1565.81	1291.75	1132.38	1030.18	960.47	910.91	874.61	847.46	826.82	810.94	798.61	788.96
42000	3930.97	2178.89	1604.00	1323.26	1160.00	1055.30	983.89	933.12	895.94	868.13	846.99	830.72	818.08	808.20
43000	4024.56	2230.77	1642.19	1354.77	1187.62	1080.43	1007.32	955.34	917.28	888.80	867.16	850.50	837.56	827.44
44000	4118.16	2282.64	1680.38	1386.27	1215.24	1105.55	1030.75	977.56	938.61	909.47	887.32	870.28	857.04	846.69
45000	4211.75	2334.52	1718.58	1417.78	1242.86	1130.68	1054.17	999.77	959.94	930.14	907.49	890.06	876.52	865.93
46000	4305.35	2386.40	1756.77	1449.28	1270.47	1155.81	1077.60	1021.99	981.27	950.81	927.65	909.84	896.00	885.17
47000	4398.94	2438.28	1794.96	1480.79	1298.09	1180.93	1101.02	1044.21	1002.60	971.48	947.82	929.61	915.48	904.41
48000	4492.54	2490.16	1833.15	1512.30	1325.71	1206.06	1124.45	1066.42	1023.94	992.15	967.99	949.39	934.95	923.66
49000	4586.13	2542.03	1871.34	1543.80	1353.33	1231.19	1147.88	1088.64	1045.27	1012.82	988.15	969.17	954.43	942.90
50000	4679.72	2593.91	1909.53	1575.31	1380.95	1256.31	1171.30	1110.86	1066.60	1033.49	1008.32	988.95	973.91	962.14
55000	5147.70	2853.30	2100.48	1732.84	1519.05	1381.94	1288.43	1221.94	1173.26	1136.84	1109.15	1087.85	1071.30	1058.36
60000	5615.67	3112.69	2291.43	1890.37	1657.14	1507.57	1405.56	1333.03	1279.92	1240.19	1209.98	1186.74	1168.69	1154.57
65000	6083.64	3372.09	2482.38	2047.90	1795.23	1633.20	1522.69	1444.12	1386.58	1343.53	1310.81	1285.64	1266.08	1250.78
70000	6551.61	3631.48	2673.34	2205.43	1933.33	1758.83	1639.82	1555.20	1493.24	1446.88	1411.65	1384.53	1363.47	1347.00
75000	7019.58	3890.87	2864.29	2362.96	2071.42	1884.46	1756.95	1666.29	1599.90	1550.23	1512.48	1483.43	1460.86	1443.21
80000	7487.56	4150.26	3055.24	2520.49	2209.52	2010.10	1874.08	1777.37	1706.56	1653.58	1613.31	1582.32	1558.25	1539.42
85000	7955.53	4409.65	3246.19	2678.02	2347.61	2135.73	1991.21	1888.46	1813.22	1756.93	1714.14	1681.21	1655.64	1635.64
90000	8423.50	4669.04	3437.15	2835.55	2485.71	2261.36	2108.34	1999.54	1919.88	1860.28	1814.97	1780.11	1753.03	1731.85
95000	8891.47	4928.43	3628.10	2993.08	2623.80	2386.99	2225.47	2110.63	2026.54	1963.63	1915.80	1879.00	1850.42	1828.06
100000	9359.44	5187.82	3819.05	3150.61	2761.90	2512.62	2342.60	2221.71	2133.20	2066.97	2016.63	1977.90	1947.81	1924.28

TERM AMOUNT	15 Years	16 Years	17 Years	18 Years	19 Years	20 Years	21 Years	22 Years	23 Years	24 Years	25 Years	30 Years	35 Years	40 Years
5	.10	.10	.10	.10	.10	.10	.10	.10	.10	.10	.10	.10	.10	.10
10	.20	.19	.19	.19	.19	.19	.19	.19	.19	.19	.19	.19	.19	.19
15	.29	.29	.29	.29	.28	.28	.28	.28	.28	.28	.28	.28	.28	.28
25	.48	.48	.47	.47	.47	.47	.47	.47	.47	.47	.47	.46	.46	.46
50	.96	.95	.94	.94	.94	.93	.93	.93	.93	.93	.93	.92	.92	.92
75	1.43	1.42	1.41	1.41	1.40	1.40	1.39	1.39	1.39	1.39	1.39	1.38	1.38	1.38
100	1.91	1.90	1.88	1.88	1.87	1.86	1.86	1.85	1.85	1.85	1.85	1.84	1.84	1.84
200	3.82	3.79	3.76	3.75	3.73	3.72	3.71	3.70	3.70	3.69	3.69	3.68	3.67	3.67
300	5.72	5.68	5.64	5.62	5.59	5.58	5.56	5.55	5.54	5.53	5.53	5.51	5.51	5.51
400	7.63	7.57	7.52	7.49	7.46	7.43	7.41	7.40	7.39	7.38	7.37	7.35	7.34	7.34
500	9.53	9.46	9.40	9.36	9.32	9.29	9.27	9.25	9.23	9.22	9.21	9.18	9.18	9.17
600	11.44	11.35	11.28	11.23	11.18	11.15	11.12	11.10	11.08	11.06	11.05	11.02	11.01	11.01
700	13.35	13.24	13.16	13.10	13.05	13.00	12.97	12.95	12.92	12.91	12.89	12.86	12.84	12.84
800	15.25	15.13	15.04	14.97	14.91	14.86	14.82	14.79	14.77	14.75	14.73	14.69	14.68	14.67
900	17.16	17.03	16.92	16.84	16.77	16.72	16.68	16.64	16.62	16.59	16.58	16.53	16.51	16.51
1000	19.06	18.92	18.80	18.71	18.63	18.58	18.53	18.49	18.46	18.44	18.42	18.36	18.35	18.34
2000	38.12	37.83	37.60	37.41	37.26	37.15	37.05	36.98	36.92	36.87	36.83	36.72	36.69	36.68
3000	57.18	56.74	56.39	56.11	55.89	55.72	55.58	55.46	55.37	55.30	55.24	55.08	55.03	55.01
4000	76.24	75.65	75.19	74.82	74.52	74.29	74.10	73.95	73.83	73.73	73.65	73.44	73.37	73.35
5000	95.29	94.56	93.98	93.52	93.15	92.86	92.62	92.44	92.28	92.16	92.07	91.80	91.72	91.69
6000	114.35	113.47	112.78	112.22	111.78	111.43	111.15	110.92	110.74	110.60	110.48	110.16	110.06	110.02
7000	133.41	132.38	131.57	130.93	130.41	130.00	129.67	129.41	129.20	129.03	128.89	128.52	128.40	128.36
8000	152.47	151.29	150.37	149.63	149.04	148.57	148.19	147.89	147.65	147.46	147.30	146.88	146.74	146.70
9000	171.52	170.21	169.16	168.33	167.67	167.14	166.72	166.38	166.11	165.89	165.72	165.24	165.09	165.03
10000	190.58	189.12	187.96	187.03	186.30	185.71	185.24	184.87	184.56	184.32	184.13	183.60	183.43	183.37
11000	209.64	208.03	206.75	205.74	204.93	204.28	203.77	203.35	203.02	202.75	202.54	201.96	201.77	201.70
12000	228.70	226.94	225.55	224.44	223.56	222.85	222.29	221.84	221.48	221.19	220.95	220.32	220.11	220.04
13000	247.75	245.85	244.34	243.14	242.19	241.42	240.81	240.32	239.93	239.62	239.37	238.68	238.45	238.38
14000	266.81	264.76	263.14	261.85	260.82	259.99	259.34	258.81	258.39	258.05	257.78	257.04	256.80	256.71
15000	285.87	283.67	281.93	280.55	279.44	278.56	277.86	277.30	276.84	276.48	276.19	275.40	275.14	275.05
16000	304.93	302.58	300.73	299.25	298.07	297.13	296.38	295.78	295.30	294.91	294.60	293.76	293.48	293.39
17000	323.98	321.50	319.52	317.95	316.70	315.71	314.91	314.27	313.76	313.35	313.02	312.12	311.82	311.72
18000	343.04	340.41	338.32	336.66	335.33	334.28	333.43	332.75	332.21	331.78	331.43	330.48	330.17	330.06
19000	362.10	359.32	357.11	355.36	353.96	352.85	351.95	351.24	350.67	350.21	349.84	348.84	348.51	348.40
20000	381.16	378.23	375.91	374.06	372.59	371.42	370.48	369.73	369.12	368.64	368.25	367.20	366.85	366.73
21000	400.21	397.14	394.70	392.77	391.22	389.99	389.00	388.21	387.58	387.07	386.67	385.56	385.19	385.07
22000	419.27	416.05	413.50	411.47	409.85	408.56	407.53	406.70	406.04	405.50	405.08	403.92	403.53	403.40
23000	438.33	434.96	432.29	430.17	428.48	427.13	426.05	425.18	424.49	423.94	423.49	422.28	421.88	421.74
24000	457.39	453.87	451.09	448.87	447.11	445.70	444.57	443.67	442.95	442.37	441.90	440.64	440.22	440.08
25000	476.44	472.79	469.88	467.58	465.74	464.27	463.10	462.16	461.40	460.80	460.32	459.00	458.56	458.41
26000	495.50	491.70	488.68	486.28	484.37	482.84	481.62	480.64	479.86	479.23	478.73	477.36	476.90	476.75
27000	514.56	510.61	507.47	504.98	503.00	501.41	500.14	499.13	498.32	497.66	497.14	495.72	495.25	495.09
28000	533.62	529.52	526.27	523.69	521.63	519.98	518.67	517.61	516.77	516.10	515.55	514.08	513.59	513.42
29000	552.67	548.43	545.07	542.39	540.26	538.55	537.19	536.10	535.23	534.53	533.97	532.44	531.93	531.76
30000	571.73	567.34	563.86	561.09	558.88	557.12	555.71	554.59	553.68	552.96	552.38	550.80	550.27	550.09
31000	590.79	586.25	582.66	579.79	577.51	575.69	574.24	573.07	572.14	571.39	570.79	569.16	568.61	568.43
32000	609.85	605.16	601.45	598.50	596.14	594.26	592.76	591.56	590.60	589.82	589.20	587.52	586.96	586.77
33000	628.90	624.08	620.25	617.20	614.77	612.83	611.29	610.04	609.05	608.25	607.61	605.88	605.30	605.10
34000	647.96	642.99	639.04	635.90	633.40	631.41	629.81	628.53	627.51	626.69	626.03	624.24	623.64	623.44
35000	667.02	661.90	657.84	654.61	652.03	649.98	648.33	647.02	645.96	645.12	644.44	642.60	641.98	641.78
36000	686.08	680.81	676.63	673.31	670.66	668.55	666.86	665.50	664.42	663.55	662.85	660.96	660.33	660.11
37000	705.13	699.72	695.43	692.01	689.29	687.12	685.38	683.99	682.87	681.98	681.26	679.32	678.67	678.45
38000	724.19	718.63	714.22	710.71	707.92	705.69	703.90	702.48	701.33	700.41	699.68	697.68	697.01	696.79
39000	743.25	737.54	733.02	729.42	726.55	724.26	722.43	720.96	719.79	718.84	718.09	716.04	715.35	715.12
40000	762.31	756.45	751.81	748.12	745.18	742.83	740.95	739.45	738.24	737.28	736.50	734.40	733.69	733.46
41000	781.36	775.37	770.61	766.82	763.81	761.40	759.47	757.93	756.70	755.71	754.91	752.76	752.04	751.79
42000	800.42	794.28	789.40	785.53	782.44	779.97	778.00	776.42	775.15	774.14	773.33	771.12	770.38	770.13
43000	819.48	813.19	808.20	804.23	801.07	798.54	796.52	794.91	793.61	792.57	791.74	789.48	788.72	788.47
44000	838.54	832.10	826.99	822.93	819.70	817.11	815.05	813.39	812.07	811.00	810.15	807.84	807.06	806.80
45000	857.60	851.01	845.79	841.63	838.32	835.68	833.57	831.88	830.52	829.44	828.56	826.20	825.41	825.14
46000	876.65	869.92	864.58	860.34	856.95	854.25	852.09	850.36	848.98	847.87	846.98	844.56	843.75	843.48
47000	895.71	888.83	883.38	879.04	875.58	872.82	870.62	868.85	867.43	866.30	865.39	862.92	862.09	861.81
48000	914.77	907.74	902.17	897.74	894.21	891.39	889.14	887.34	885.89	884.73	883.80	881.28	880.43	880.15
49000	933.83	926.66	920.97	916.45	912.84	909.96	907.66	905.82	904.35	903.16	902.21	899.64	898.77	898.48
50000	952.88	945.57	939.76	935.15	931.47	928.53	926.19	924.31	922.80	921.59	920.63	918.00	917.12	916.82
55000	1048.17	1040.12	1033.74	1028.66	1024.62	1021.39	1018.81	1016.74	1015.08	1013.75	1012.69	1009.80	1008.83	1008.50
60000	1143.46	1134.68	1127.72	1122.18	1117.76	1114.24	1111.42	1109.17	1107.36	1105.91	1104.75	1101.60	1100.54	1100.18
65000	1238.75	1229.23	1221.69	1215.69	1210.91	1207.09	1204.04	1201.60	1199.64	1198.07	1196.81	1193.40	1192.25	1191.87
70000	1334.03	1323.79	1315.67	1309.21	1304.06	1299.95	1296.66	1294.03	1291.92	1290.23	1288.87	1285.19	1283.96	1283.55
75000	1429.32	1418.35	1409.64	1402.72	1397.20	1392.80	1389.28	1386.46	1384.20	1382.39	1380.94	1376.99	1375.67	1375.23
80000	1524.61	1512.90	1503.62	1496.24	1490.35	1485.65	1481.90	1478.89	1476.48	1474.55	1473.00	1468.79	1467.38	1466.91
85000	1619.90	1607.46	1597.60	1589.75	1583.50	1578.51	1574.51	1571.32	1568.76	1566.71	1565.06	1560.59	1559.10	1558.59
90000	1715.19	1702.02	1691.57	1683.26	1676.64	1671.36	1667.13	1663.75	1661.04	1658.87	1657.12	1652.39	1650.81	1650.27
95000	1810.49	1796.57	1785.55	1776.78	1769.79	1764.21	1759.75	1756.18	1753.32	1751.03	1749.19	1744.19	1742.52	1741.96
100000	1905.76	1891.13	1879.52	1870.29	1862.94	1857.06	1852.37	1848.61	1845.60	1843.18	1841.25	1835.99	1834.23	1833.64

22%

MONTHLY PAYMENT
REQUIRED TO AMORTIZE A LOAN

TERM	1 Year	2 Years	3 Years	4 Years	5 Years	6 Years	7 Years	8 Years	9 Years	10 Years	11 Years	12 Years	13 Years	14 Years
AMOUNT														
5	.47	.26	.20	.16	.14	.13	.12	.12	.11	.11	.11	.10	.10	.10
10	.94	.52	.39	.32	.28	.26	.24	.23	.22	.21	.21	.20	.20	.20
15	1.41	.78	.58	.48	.42	.38	.36	.34	.33	.32	.31	.30	.30	.29
25	2.35	1.30	.96	.79	.70	.63	.59	.56	.54	.52	.51	.50	.49	.49
50	4.69	2.60	1.92	1.58	1.39	1.26	1.18	1.12	1.07	1.04	1.02	1.00	.98	.97
75	7.03	3.90	2.87	2.37	2.08	1.89	1.77	1.68	1.61	1.56	1.52	1.49	1.47	1.45
100	9.37	5.20	3.83	3.16	2.77	2.52	2.35	2.23	2.14	2.08	2.03	1.99	1.96	1.94
200	18.73	10.39	7.65	6.32	5.54	5.04	4.70	4.46	4.28	4.15	4.05	3.98	3.92	3.87
300	28.10	15.58	11.48	9.47	8.31	7.56	7.05	6.69	6.42	6.23	6.08	5.96	5.87	5.80
400	37.46	20.78	15.30	12.63	11.08	10.08	9.40	8.92	8.56	8.30	8.10	7.95	7.83	7.73
500	46.83	25.97	19.13	15.79	13.84	12.60	11.75	11.15	10.70	10.37	10.12	9.93	9.78	9.66
600	56.19	31.16	22.95	18.94	16.61	15.12	14.10	13.37	12.84	12.45	12.15	11.92	11.74	11.60
700	65.55	36.35	26.77	22.10	19.38	17.63	16.45	15.60	14.98	14.52	14.17	13.90	13.69	13.53
800	74.92	41.55	30.60	25.25	22.15	20.15	18.80	17.83	17.12	16.60	16.19	15.89	15.65	15.46
900	84.28	46.74	34.42	28.41	24.91	22.67	21.14	20.06	19.26	18.67	18.22	17.87	17.60	17.39
1000	93.65	51.93	38.25	31.57	27.68	25.19	23.49	22.29	21.40	20.74	20.24	19.86	19.56	19.32
2000	187.29	103.86	76.49	63.13	55.36	50.38	46.98	44.57	42.80	41.48	40.48	39.71	39.11	38.64
3000	280.93	155.79	114.73	94.69	83.03	75.56	70.47	66.85	64.20	62.22	60.71	59.56	58.66	57.96
4000	374.58	207.72	152.97	126.25	110.71	100.75	93.96	89.13	85.60	82.96	80.95	79.41	78.21	77.27
5000	468.22	259.64	191.22	157.81	138.38	125.93	117.44	111.41	107.00	103.69	101.19	99.26	97.76	96.59
6000	561.86	311.57	229.46	189.37	166.06	151.12	140.93	133.69	128.39	124.43	121.42	119.11	117.31	115.91
7000	655.50	363.50	267.70	220.93	193.74	176.30	164.42	155.97	149.79	145.17	141.66	138.96	136.86	135.22
8000	749.15	415.43	305.94	252.49	221.41	201.49	187.91	178.25	171.19	165.91	161.89	158.81	156.41	154.54
9000	842.79	467.35	344.18	284.05	249.09	226.67	211.39	200.54	192.59	186.65	182.13	178.66	175.97	173.86
10000	936.43	519.28	382.43	315.61	276.76	251.86	234.88	222.82	213.99	207.38	202.37	198.51	195.52	193.18
11000	1030.07	571.21	420.67	347.17	304.44	277.05	258.37	245.10	235.38	228.12	222.60	218.36	215.07	212.49
12000	1123.72	623.14	458.91	378.73	332.11	302.23	281.86	267.38	256.78	248.86	242.84	238.21	234.62	231.81
13000	1217.36	675.06	497.15	410.29	359.79	327.42	305.35	289.66	278.18	269.60	263.08	258.06	254.17	251.13
14000	1311.00	726.99	535.40	441.85	387.47	352.60	328.83	311.94	299.58	290.33	283.31	277.91	273.72	270.44
15000	1404.64	778.92	573.64	473.41	415.14	377.79	352.32	334.22	320.98	311.07	303.55	297.76	293.27	289.76
16000	1498.29	830.85	611.88	504.97	442.82	402.97	375.81	356.50	342.37	331.81	323.78	317.61	312.82	309.08
17000	1591.93	882.77	650.12	536.53	470.49	428.16	399.30	378.78	363.77	352.55	344.02	337.46	332.37	328.40
18000	1685.57	934.70	688.36	568.09	498.17	453.34	422.78	401.07	385.17	373.29	364.26	357.31	351.93	347.71
19000	1779.21	986.63	726.61	599.65	525.85	478.53	446.27	423.35	406.57	394.02	384.49	377.16	371.48	367.03
20000	1872.86	1038.56	764.85	631.21	553.52	503.72	469.76	445.63	427.97	414.76	404.73	397.02	391.03	386.35
21000	1966.50	1090.48	803.09	662.77	581.20	528.90	493.25	467.91	449.36	435.50	424.97	416.87	410.58	405.66
22000	2060.14	1142.41	841.33	694.33	608.87	554.09	516.74	490.19	470.76	456.24	445.20	436.72	430.13	424.98
23000	2153.78	1194.34	879.58	725.89	636.55	579.27	540.22	512.47	492.16	476.97	465.44	456.57	449.68	444.30
24000	2247.43	1246.27	917.82	757.45	664.22	604.46	563.71	534.75	513.56	497.71	485.67	476.42	469.23	463.62
25000	2341.07	1298.19	956.06	789.01	691.90	629.64	587.20	557.03	534.96	518.45	505.91	496.27	488.78	482.93
26000	2434.71	1350.12	994.30	820.58	719.58	654.83	610.69	579.31	556.35	539.19	526.15	516.12	508.33	502.25
27000	2528.35	1402.05	1032.54	852.14	747.25	680.01	634.17	601.60	577.75	559.93	546.38	535.97	527.89	521.57
28000	2622.00	1453.98	1070.79	883.70	774.93	705.20	657.66	623.88	599.15	580.66	566.62	555.82	547.44	540.88
29000	2715.64	1505.90	1109.03	915.26	802.60	730.39	681.15	646.16	620.55	601.40	586.86	575.67	566.99	560.20
30000	2809.28	1557.83	1147.27	946.82	830.28	755.57	704.64	668.44	641.95	622.14	607.09	595.52	586.54	579.52
31000	2902.92	1609.76	1185.51	978.38	857.95	780.76	728.12	690.72	663.35	642.88	627.33	615.37	606.09	598.84
32000	2996.57	1661.69	1223.76	1009.94	885.63	805.94	751.61	713.00	684.74	663.62	647.56	635.22	625.64	618.15
33000	3090.21	1713.61	1262.00	1041.50	913.31	831.13	775.10	735.28	706.14	684.35	667.80	655.07	645.19	637.47
34000	3183.85	1765.54	1300.24	1073.06	940.98	856.31	798.59	757.56	727.54	705.09	688.04	674.92	664.74	656.79
35000	3277.49	1817.47	1338.48	1104.62	968.66	881.50	822.08	779.84	748.94	725.83	708.27	694.77	684.29	676.10
36000	3371.14	1869.40	1376.72	1136.18	996.33	906.68	845.56	802.13	770.34	746.57	728.51	714.62	703.85	695.42
37000	3464.78	1921.32	1414.97	1167.74	1024.01	931.87	869.05	824.41	791.73	767.30	748.74	734.47	723.40	714.74
38000	3558.42	1973.25	1453.21	1199.30	1051.69	957.05	892.54	846.69	813.13	788.04	768.98	754.32	742.95	734.06
39000	3652.06	2025.18	1491.45	1230.86	1079.36	982.24	916.03	868.97	834.53	808.78	789.22	774.17	762.50	753.37
40000	3745.71	2077.11	1529.69	1262.42	1107.04	1007.43	939.51	891.25	855.93	829.52	809.45	794.03	782.05	772.69
41000	3839.35	2129.03	1567.94	1293.98	1134.71	1032.61	963.00	913.53	877.33	850.26	829.69	813.88	801.60	792.01
42000	3932.99	2180.96	1606.18	1325.54	1162.39	1057.80	986.49	935.81	898.72	870.99	849.93	833.73	821.15	811.32
43000	4026.63	2232.89	1644.42	1357.10	1190.06	1082.98	1009.98	958.09	920.12	891.73	870.16	853.58	840.70	830.64
44000	4120.28	2284.82	1682.66	1388.66	1217.74	1108.17	1033.47	980.37	941.52	912.47	890.40	873.43	860.26	849.96
45000	4213.92	2336.74	1720.90	1420.22	1245.42	1133.35	1056.95	1002.66	962.92	933.21	910.63	893.28	879.81	869.28
46000	4307.56	2388.67	1759.15	1451.78	1273.09	1158.54	1080.44	1024.94	984.32	953.94	930.87	913.13	899.36	888.59
47000	4401.20	2440.60	1797.39	1483.34	1300.77	1183.72	1103.93	1047.22	1005.71	974.68	951.11	932.98	918.91	907.91
48000	4494.85	2492.53	1835.63	1514.90	1328.44	1208.91	1127.42	1069.50	1027.11	995.42	971.34	952.83	938.46	927.23
49000	4588.49	2544.46	1873.87	1546.46	1356.12	1234.10	1150.90	1091.78	1048.51	1016.16	991.58	972.68	958.01	946.54
50000	4682.13	2596.38	1912.12	1578.02	1383.79	1259.28	1174.39	1114.06	1069.91	1036.90	1011.82	992.53	977.56	965.86
55000	5150.34	2856.02	2103.33	1735.83	1522.17	1385.21	1291.83	1225.47	1176.90	1140.58	1113.00	1091.78	1075.32	1062.45
60000	5618.56	3115.66	2294.54	1893.63	1660.55	1511.14	1409.27	1336.87	1283.89	1244.27	1214.18	1191.04	1173.07	1159.03
65000	6086.77	3375.30	2485.75	2051.43	1798.93	1637.06	1526.71	1448.28	1390.88	1347.96	1315.36	1290.29	1270.83	1255.62
70000	6554.98	3634.93	2676.96	2209.23	1937.31	1762.99	1644.15	1559.68	1497.87	1451.65	1416.54	1389.54	1368.58	1352.20
75000	7023.19	3894.57	2868.17	2367.03	2075.69	1888.92	1761.58	1671.09	1604.86	1555.34	1517.72	1488.79	1466.34	1448.79
80000	7491.41	4154.21	3059.38	2524.84	2214.07	2014.85	1879.02	1782.50	1711.85	1659.03	1618.90	1588.05	1564.10	1545.37
85000	7959.62	4413.85	3250.59	2682.64	2352.45	2140.77	1996.46	1893.90	1818.84	1762.72	1720.08	1687.30	1661.85	1641.96
90000	8427.83	4673.48	3441.80	2840.44	2490.83	2266.70	2113.90	2005.31	1925.83	1866.41	1821.26	1786.55	1759.61	1738.55
95000	8896.04	4933.12	3633.01	2998.24	2629.21	2392.63	2231.34	2116.71	2032.82	1970.10	1922.45	1885.80	1857.36	1835.13
100000	9364.26	5192.76	3824.23	3156.04	2767.58	2518.56	2348.78	2228.12	2139.81	2073.79	2023.63	1985.06	1955.12	1931.72

TERM	15 Years	16 Years	17 Years	18 Years	19 Years	20 Years	21 Years	22 Years	23 Years	24 Years	25 Years	30 Years	35 Years	40 Years
AMOUNT														
5	.10	.10	.10	.10	.10	.10	.10	.10	.10	.10	.10	.10	.10	.10
10	.20	.19	.19	.19	.19	.19	.19	.19	.19	.19	.19	.19	.19	.19
15	.29	.29	.29	.29	.29	.28	.28	.28	.28	.28	.28	.28	.28	.28
25	.48	.48	.48	.47	.47	.47	.47	.47	.47	.47	.47	.47	.47	.47
50	.96	.95	.95	.94	.94	.94	.94	.93	.93	.93	.93	.93	.93	.93
75	1.44	1.43	1.42	1.41	1.41	1.40	1.40	1.40	1.40	1.39	1.39	1.39	1.39	1.39
100	1.92	1.90	1.89	1.88	1.88	1.87	1.87	1.86	1.86	1.86	1.85	1.85	1.85	1.85
200	3.83	3.80	3.78	3.76	3.75	3.74	3.73	3.72	3.71	3.71	3.70	3.69	3.69	3.69
300	5.74	5.70	5.67	5.64	5.62	5.60	5.59	5.58	5.57	5.56	5.55	5.54	5.53	5.53
400	7.66	7.60	7.55	7.52	7.49	7.47	7.45	7.43	7.42	7.41	7.40	7.38	7.38	7.37
500	9.57	9.50	9.44	9.40	9.36	9.33	9.31	9.29	9.27	9.26	9.25	9.23	9.22	9.21
600	11.48	11.40	11.33	11.27	11.23	11.20	11.17	11.15	11.13	11.11	11.10	11.07	11.06	11.06
700	13.40	13.30	13.22	13.15	13.10	13.06	13.03	13.00	12.98	12.96	12.95	12.91	12.90	12.90
800	15.31	15.20	15.10	15.03	14.97	14.93	14.89	14.86	14.83	14.82	14.80	14.76	14.75	14.74
900	17.22	17.09	16.99	16.91	16.84	16.79	16.75	16.72	16.69	16.67	16.65	16.60	16.59	16.58
1000	19.14	18.99	18.88	18.79	18.71	18.66	18.61	18.57	18.54	18.52	18.50	18.45	18.43	18.42
2000	38.27	37.98	37.75	37.57	37.42	37.31	37.21	37.14	37.08	37.03	36.99	36.89	36.86	36.84
3000	57.40	56.97	56.62	56.35	56.13	55.96	55.82	55.71	55.62	55.55	55.49	55.33	55.28	55.26
4000	76.54	75.96	75.50	75.13	74.84	74.61	74.42	74.27	74.15	74.06	73.98	73.78	73.71	73.68
5000	95.67	94.94	94.37	93.91	93.55	93.26	93.02	92.84	92.69	92.57	92.48	92.22	92.13	92.10
6000	114.80	113.93	113.24	112.69	112.26	111.91	111.63	111.41	111.23	111.08	110.97	110.66	110.56	110.52
7000	133.94	132.92	132.11	131.47	130.96	130.56	130.23	129.97	129.76	129.60	129.46	129.10	128.98	128.94
8000	153.07	151.91	150.99	150.26	149.67	149.21	148.84	148.54	148.30	148.11	147.96	147.55	147.41	147.36
9000	172.20	170.90	169.86	169.04	168.38	167.86	167.44	167.11	166.84	166.62	166.45	165.99	165.83	165.78
10000	191.34	189.88	188.73	187.82	187.09	186.51	186.04	185.67	185.38	185.14	184.95	184.43	184.26	184.20
11000	210.47	208.87	207.61	206.60	205.80	205.16	204.65	204.24	203.91	203.65	203.44	202.87	202.68	202.62
12000	229.60	227.86	226.48	225.38	224.51	223.81	223.25	222.81	222.45	222.16	221.94	221.32	221.11	221.04
13000	248.74	246.85	245.35	244.16	243.21	242.46	241.86	241.37	240.99	240.68	240.43	239.76	239.53	239.46
14000	267.87	265.83	264.22	262.94	261.92	261.11	260.46	259.94	259.52	259.19	258.92	258.20	257.96	257.88
15000	287.00	284.82	283.10	281.72	280.63	279.76	279.06	278.51	278.06	277.70	277.42	276.64	276.38	276.30
16000	306.14	303.81	301.97	300.51	299.34	298.41	297.67	297.07	296.60	296.22	295.91	295.09	294.81	294.72
17000	325.27	322.80	320.84	319.29	318.05	317.06	316.27	315.64	315.14	314.73	314.41	313.53	313.24	313.14
18000	344.40	341.79	339.71	338.07	336.76	335.71	334.88	334.21	333.67	333.24	332.90	331.97	331.66	331.56
19000	363.53	360.77	358.59	356.05	355.47	354.36	353.48	352.77	352.21	351.76	351.39	350.41	350.09	349.98
20000	382.67	379.76	377.46	375.63	374.17	373.01	372.08	371.34	370.75	370.27	369.89	368.86	368.51	368.40
21000	401.80	398.75	396.33	394.41	392.88	391.66	390.69	389.91	389.28	388.78	388.38	387.30	386.94	386.82
22000	420.93	417.74	415.21	413.19	411.59	410.31	409.29	408.47	407.82	407.30	406.88	405.74	405.36	405.24
23000	440.07	436.73	434.08	431.97	430.30	428.96	427.89	427.04	426.36	425.81	425.37	424.18	423.79	423.65
24000	459.20	455.71	452.95	450.76	449.01	447.61	446.50	445.61	444.89	444.32	443.87	442.63	442.21	442.07
25000	478.33	474.70	471.82	469.54	467.72	466.26	465.10	464.17	463.43	462.84	462.36	461.07	460.64	460.49
26000	497.47	493.69	490.70	488.32	486.42	484.91	483.71	482.74	481.97	481.35	480.85	479.51	479.06	478.91
27000	516.60	512.68	509.57	507.10	505.13	503.56	502.31	501.31	500.51	499.86	499.35	497.95	497.49	497.33
28000	535.73	531.66	528.44	525.88	523.84	522.21	520.91	519.87	519.04	518.38	517.84	516.40	515.91	515.75
29000	554.87	550.65	547.31	544.66	542.55	540.86	539.52	538.44	537.58	536.89	536.34	534.84	534.34	534.17
30000	574.00	569.64	566.19	563.44	561.26	559.51	558.12	557.01	556.12	555.40	554.83	553.28	552.76	552.59
31000	593.13	588.63	585.06	582.22	579.97	578.16	576.73	575.58	574.65	573.92	573.32	571.72	571.19	571.01
32000	612.27	607.62	603.93	601.01	598.67	596.82	595.33	594.14	593.19	592.43	591.82	590.17	589.61	589.43
33000	631.40	626.60	622.81	619.79	617.38	615.47	613.93	612.71	611.73	610.94	610.31	608.61	608.04	607.85
34000	650.53	645.59	641.68	638.57	636.09	634.12	632.54	631.28	630.27	629.46	628.81	627.05	626.47	626.27
35000	669.66	664.58	660.55	657.35	654.80	652.77	651.14	649.84	648.80	647.97	647.30	645.49	644.89	644.69
36000	688.80	683.57	679.42	676.13	673.51	671.42	669.75	668.41	667.34	666.48	665.80	663.94	663.32	663.11
37000	707.93	702.56	698.30	694.91	692.22	690.07	688.35	686.98	685.88	685.00	684.29	682.38	681.74	681.53
38000	727.06	721.54	717.17	713.69	710.93	708.72	706.95	705.54	704.41	703.51	702.78	700.82	700.17	699.95
39000	746.20	740.53	736.04	732.47	729.63	727.37	725.56	724.11	722.95	722.02	721.28	719.26	718.59	718.37
40000	765.33	759.52	754.91	751.26	748.34	746.02	744.16	742.68	741.49	740.54	739.77	737.71	737.02	736.79
41000	784.46	778.51	773.79	770.04	767.05	764.67	762.76	761.24	760.02	759.05	758.27	756.15	755.44	755.21
42000	803.60	797.49	792.66	788.82	785.76	783.32	781.37	779.81	778.56	777.56	776.76	774.59	773.87	773.63
43000	822.73	816.48	811.53	807.60	804.47	801.97	799.97	798.38	797.10	796.08	795.25	793.03	792.29	792.05
44000	841.86	835.47	830.41	826.38	823.18	820.62	818.58	816.94	815.64	814.59	813.75	811.48	810.72	810.47
45000	861.00	854.46	849.28	845.16	841.88	839.27	837.18	835.51	834.17	833.10	832.24	829.92	829.14	828.89
46000	880.13	873.45	868.15	863.94	860.59	857.92	855.78	854.08	852.71	851.61	850.74	848.36	847.57	847.30
47000	899.26	892.43	887.02	882.72	879.30	876.57	874.39	872.64	871.25	870.13	869.23	866.80	865.99	865.72
48000	918.40	911.42	905.90	901.50	898.01	895.22	892.99	891.21	889.78	888.64	887.73	885.25	884.42	884.14
49000	937.53	930.41	924.77	920.29	916.72	913.87	911.60	909.78	908.32	907.15	906.22	903.69	902.85	902.56
50000	956.66	949.40	943.64	939.07	935.43	932.52	930.20	928.34	926.86	925.67	924.71	922.13	921.27	920.98
55000	1052.33	1044.34	1038.01	1032.97	1028.97	1025.77	1023.22	1021.18	1019.54	1018.23	1017.18	1014.34	1013.40	1013.08
60000	1147.99	1139.28	1132.37	1126.88	1122.51	1119.02	1116.24	1114.01	1112.23	1110.80	1109.66	1106.56	1105.52	1105.18
65000	1243.66	1234.22	1226.73	1220.79	1216.05	1212.28	1209.26	1206.85	1204.91	1203.37	1202.13	1198.77	1197.65	1197.28
70000	1339.32	1329.15	1321.10	1314.69	1309.59	1305.53	1302.28	1299.68	1297.60	1295.93	1294.60	1290.98	1289.78	1289.37
75000	1434.99	1424.09	1415.46	1408.60	1403.14	1398.78	1395.30	1392.51	1390.28	1388.50	1387.07	1383.19	1381.90	1381.47
80000	1530.66	1519.03	1509.82	1502.51	1496.68	1492.03	1488.32	1485.35	1482.97	1481.07	1479.54	1475.41	1474.03	1473.57
85000	1626.32	1613.97	1604.19	1596.41	1590.22	1585.28	1581.34	1578.18	1575.66	1573.63	1572.01	1567.62	1566.16	1565.67
90000	1721.99	1708.91	1698.55	1690.32	1683.76	1678.54	1674.36	1671.01	1668.34	1666.20	1664.48	1659.83	1658.28	1657.77
95000	1817.65	1803.85	1792.92	1784.23	1777.31	1771.79	1767.38	1763.85	1761.03	1758.76	1756.95	1752.05	1750.41	1749.86
100000	1913.32	1898.79	1887.28	1878.13	1870.85	1865.04	1860.39	1856.68	1853.71	1851.33	1849.42	1844.26	1842.54	1841.96

MONTHLY PAYMENT
REQUIRED TO AMORTIZE A LOAN

TERM	1 Year	2 Years	3 Years	4 Years	5 Years	6 Years	7 Years	8 Years	9 Years	10 Years	11 Years	12 Years	13 Years	14 Years
AMOUNT														
5	.47	.26	.20	.16	.14	.13	.12	.12	.11	.11	.11	.10	.10	.10
10	.94	.52	.39	.32	.28	.26	.24	.23	.22	.21	.21	.20	.20	.20
15	1.41	.78	.58	.48	.42	.38	.36	.34	.33	.32	.31	.30	.30	.30
25	2.35	1.30	.96	.79	.70	.64	.59	.56	.54	.52	.51	.50	.49	.49
50	4.69	2.60	1.92	1.58	1.39	1.27	1.18	1.12	1.08	1.04	1.02	1.00	.98	.97
75	7.03	3.90	2.87	2.37	2.08	1.90	1.77	1.68	1.61	1.56	1.52	1.50	1.47	1.46
100	9.37	5.20	3.83	3.16	2.77	2.53	2.36	2.23	2.15	2.08	2.03	1.99	1.96	1.94
200	18.74	10.39	7.66	6.32	5.54	5.05	4.71	4.46	4.29	4.16	4.06	3.98	3.92	3.87
300	28.10	15.59	11.48	9.48	8.31	7.57	7.06	6.69	6.43	6.23	6.08	5.97	5.88	5.81
400	37.47	20.78	15.31	12.63	11.08	10.09	9.41	8.92	8.57	8.31	8.11	7.95	7.83	7.74
500	46.83	25.97	19.13	15.79	13.85	12.61	11.76	11.15	10.71	10.38	10.13	9.94	9.79	9.67
600	56.20	31.17	22.96	18.95	16.62	15.13	14.11	13.38	12.85	12.46	12.16	11.93	11.75	11.61
700	65.56	36.36	26.78	22.11	19.39	17.65	16.46	15.61	15.00	14.53	14.18	13.91	13.70	13.54
800	74.93	41.56	30.61	25.26	22.16	20.17	18.81	17.84	17.14	16.61	16.21	15.90	15.66	15.47
900	84.29	46.75	34.43	28.42	24.93	22.69	21.16	20.07	19.28	18.68	18.23	17.89	17.62	17.41
1000	93.66	51.94	38.26	31.58	27.70	25.21	23.51	22.30	21.42	20.76	20.26	19.87	19.57	19.34
2000	187.31	103.88	76.52	63.15	55.39	50.41	47.01	44.60	42.83	41.51	40.51	39.74	39.14	38.68
3000	280.97	155.82	114.77	94.73	83.08	75.61	70.51	66.90	64.25	62.27	60.77	59.61	58.71	58.01
4000	374.62	207.76	153.03	126.30	110.77	100.81	94.02	89.19	85.66	83.02	81.02	79.48	78.28	77.35
5000	468.28	259.70	191.28	157.87	138.46	126.01	117.52	111.49	107.08	103.78	101.27	99.35	97.85	96.68
6000	561.93	311.64	229.54	189.45	166.15	151.21	141.02	133.79	128.49	124.53	121.53	119.22	117.42	116.02
7000	655.59	363.58	267.79	221.02	193.84	176.41	164.53	156.09	149.91	145.29	141.78	139.08	136.99	135.36
8000	749.24	415.52	306.05	252.60	221.53	201.61	188.03	178.38	171.32	166.04	162.03	158.95	156.56	154.69
9000	842.90	467.46	344.30	284.17	249.22	226.81	211.53	200.68	192.74	186.80	182.29	178.82	176.13	174.03
10000	936.55	519.40	382.56	315.74	276.91	252.01	235.04	222.98	214.15	207.55	202.54	198.69	195.70	193.36
11000	1030.21	571.34	420.81	347.32	304.60	277.21	258.54	245.27	235.57	228.31	222.80	218.56	215.27	212.70
12000	1123.86	623.28	459.07	378.89	332.29	302.41	282.04	267.57	256.98	249.06	243.05	238.43	234.84	232.03
13000	1217.51	675.22	497.32	410.47	359.98	327.61	305.55	289.87	278.40	269.82	263.30	258.29	254.41	251.37
14000	1311.17	727.16	535.58	442.04	387.67	352.81	329.05	312.17	299.81	290.57	283.56	278.16	273.98	270.71
15000	1404.82	779.10	573.83	473.61	415.36	378.01	352.55	334.46	321.22	311.33	303.81	298.03	293.55	290.04
16000	1498.48	831.04	612.09	505.19	443.05	403.21	376.06	356.76	342.64	332.08	324.06	317.90	313.12	309.38
17000	1592.13	882.98	650.34	536.76	470.74	428.41	399.56	379.06	364.05	352.84	344.32	337.77	332.69	328.71
18000	1685.79	934.92	688.60	568.34	498.43	453.61	423.06	401.35	385.47	373.59	364.57	357.64	352.25	348.05
19000	1779.44	986.86	726.85	599.91	526.12	478.81	446.57	423.65	406.88	394.35	384.83	377.50	371.82	367.38
20000	1873.10	1038.80	765.11	631.48	553.81	504.01	470.07	445.95	428.30	415.10	405.08	397.37	391.39	386.72
21000	1966.75	1090.74	803.36	663.06	581.50	529.21	493.57	468.25	449.71	435.86	425.33	417.24	410.96	406.06
22000	2060.41	1142.68	841.62	694.63	609.19	554.41	517.08	490.54	471.13	456.61	445.59	437.11	430.53	425.39
23000	2154.06	1194.62	879.87	726.21	636.88	579.61	540.58	512.84	492.54	477.37	465.84	456.98	450.10	444.73
24000	2247.71	1246.56	918.13	757.78	664.57	604.81	564.08	535.14	513.96	498.12	486.09	476.85	469.67	464.06
25000	2341.37	1298.50	956.38	789.35	692.26	630.01	587.58	557.43	535.37	518.88	506.35	496.72	489.24	483.40
26000	2435.02	1350.44	994.64	820.93	719.95	655.21	611.09	579.73	556.79	539.63	526.60	516.58	508.81	502.73
27000	2528.68	1402.38	1032.89	852.50	747.64	680.42	634.59	602.03	578.20	560.39	546.86	536.45	528.38	522.07
28000	2622.33	1454.32	1071.15	884.08	775.33	705.62	658.09	624.33	599.61	581.14	567.11	556.32	547.95	541.41
29000	2715.99	1506.26	1109.40	915.65	803.02	730.82	681.60	646.62	621.03	601.90	587.36	576.19	567.52	560.74
30000	2809.64	1558.20	1147.66	947.22	830.71	756.02	705.10	668.92	642.44	622.65	607.62	596.06	587.09	580.08
31000	2903.30	1610.14	1185.91	978.80	858.40	781.22	728.60	691.22	663.86	643.41	627.87	615.93	606.66	599.41
32000	2996.95	1662.08	1224.17	1010.37	886.09	806.42	752.11	713.51	685.27	664.16	648.12	635.79	626.23	618.75
33000	3090.61	1714.02	1262.42	1041.95	913.78	831.62	775.61	735.81	706.69	684.92	668.38	655.66	645.80	638.08
34000	3184.26	1765.96	1300.68	1073.52	941.47	856.82	799.11	758.11	728.10	705.67	688.63	675.53	665.37	657.42
35000	3277.91	1817.90	1338.94	1105.09	969.16	882.02	822.62	780.41	749.52	726.43	708.88	695.40	684.93	676.76
36000	3371.57	1869.84	1377.19	1136.67	996.85	907.22	846.12	802.70	770.93	747.18	729.14	715.27	704.50	696.09
37000	3465.22	1921.78	1415.45	1168.24	1024.54	932.42	869.62	825.00	792.35	767.93	749.39	735.14	724.07	715.43
38000	3558.88	1973.72	1453.70	1199.82	1052.23	957.62	893.13	847.30	813.76	788.69	769.65	755.00	743.64	734.76
39000	3652.53	2025.66	1491.96	1231.39	1079.92	982.82	916.63	869.59	835.18	809.44	789.90	774.87	763.21	754.10
40000	3746.19	2077.60	1530.21	1262.96	1107.61	1008.02	940.13	891.89	856.59	830.20	810.15	794.74	782.78	773.43
41000	3839.84	2129.54	1568.47	1294.54	1135.30	1033.22	963.64	914.19	878.00	850.95	830.41	814.61	802.35	792.77
42000	3933.50	2181.48	1606.72	1326.11	1162.99	1058.42	987.14	936.49	899.42	871.71	850.66	834.48	821.92	812.11
43000	4027.15	2233.42	1644.98	1357.69	1190.68	1083.62	1010.64	958.78	920.83	892.46	870.91	854.35	841.49	831.44
44000	4120.81	2285.36	1683.23	1389.26	1218.37	1108.82	1034.15	981.08	942.25	913.22	891.17	874.22	861.06	850.78
45000	4214.46	2337.30	1721.49	1420.83	1246.06	1134.02	1057.65	1003.38	963.66	933.97	911.42	894.08	880.63	870.11
46000	4308.11	2389.24	1759.74	1452.41	1273.75	1159.22	1081.15	1025.67	985.08	954.73	931.68	913.95	900.20	889.45
47000	4401.77	2441.18	1798.00	1483.98	1301.44	1184.42	1104.66	1047.97	1006.49	975.48	951.93	933.82	919.77	908.78
48000	4495.42	2493.12	1836.25	1515.56	1329.13	1209.62	1128.16	1070.27	1027.91	996.24	972.18	953.69	939.34	928.12
49000	4589.08	2545.06	1874.51	1547.13	1356.82	1234.82	1151.66	1092.57	1049.32	1016.99	992.44	973.56	958.91	947.46
50000	4682.73	2597.00	1912.76	1578.70	1384.51	1260.02	1175.16	1114.86	1070.74	1037.75	1012.69	993.43	978.48	966.79
55000	5151.01	2856.70	2104.04	1736.57	1522.96	1386.03	1292.68	1226.35	1177.81	1141.52	1113.96	1092.77	1076.32	1063.47
60000	5619.28	3116.40	2295.31	1894.44	1661.41	1512.03	1410.20	1337.83	1284.88	1245.30	1215.23	1192.11	1174.17	1160.15
65000	6087.55	3376.10	2486.59	2052.31	1799.86	1638.03	1527.71	1449.32	1391.96	1349.07	1316.50	1291.45	1272.02	1256.83
70000	6555.82	3635.80	2677.87	2210.18	1938.31	1764.03	1645.23	1560.81	1499.03	1452.85	1417.76	1390.79	1369.86	1353.51
75000	7024.10	3895.50	2869.14	2368.05	2076.76	1890.03	1762.74	1672.29	1606.10	1556.62	1519.03	1490.14	1467.71	1450.18
80000	7492.37	4155.20	3060.42	2525.92	2215.21	2016.04	1880.26	1783.78	1713.18	1660.39	1620.30	1589.48	1565.56	1546.86
85000	7960.64	4414.90	3251.69	2683.79	2353.66	2142.04	1997.78	1895.26	1820.25	1764.17	1721.57	1688.82	1663.41	1643.54
90000	8428.91	4674.60	3442.97	2841.66	2492.11	2268.04	2115.29	2006.75	1927.32	1867.94	1822.84	1788.16	1761.25	1740.22
95000	8897.19	4934.30	3634.24	2999.53	2630.56	2394.04	2232.81	2118.24	2034.39	1971.72	1924.11	1887.50	1859.10	1836.90
100000	9365.46	5194.00	3825.52	3157.40	2769.01	2520.04	2350.32	2229.72	2141.47	2075.49	2025.38	1986.85	1956.95	1933.58

TERM	15 Years	16 Years	17 Years	18 Years	19 Years	20 Years	21 Years	22 Years	23 Years	24 Years	25 Years	30 Years	35 Years	40 Years
AMOUNT														
5	.10	.10	.10	.10	.10	.10	.10	.10	.10	.10	.10	.10	.10	.10
10	.20	.20	.19	.19	.19	.19	.19	.19	.19	.19	.19	.19	.19	.19
15	.29	.29	.29	.29	.29	.29	.28	.28	.28	.28	.28	.28	.28	.28
25	.48	.48	.48	.48	.47	.47	.47	.47	.47	.47	.47	.47	.47	.47
50	.96	.96	.95	.95	.94	.94	.94	.93	.93	.93	.93	.93	.93	.93
75	1.44	1.43	1.42	1.42	1.41	1.41	1.40	1.40	1.40	1.40	1.39	1.39	1.39	1.39
100	1.92	1.91	1.89	1.89	1.88	1.87	1.87	1.86	1.86	1.86	1.86	1.85	1.85	1.85
200	3.84	3.81	3.78	3.77	3.75	3.74	3.73	3.72	3.72	3.71	3.71	3.70	3.69	3.69
300	5.75	5.71	5.67	5.65	5.62	5.61	5.59	5.58	5.57	5.57	5.56	5.54	5.54	5.54
400	7.67	7.61	7.56	7.53	7.50	7.47	7.45	7.44	7.43	7.42	7.41	7.39	7.38	7.38
500	9.58	9.51	9.45	9.41	9.37	9.34	9.32	9.30	9.28	9.27	9.26	9.24	9.23	9.23
600	11.50	11.41	11.34	11.29	11.24	11.21	11.18	11.16	11.14	11.13	11.11	11.08	11.07	11.07
700	13.41	13.31	13.23	13.17	13.11	13.07	13.04	13.02	13.00	12.98	12.97	12.93	12.92	12.91
800	15.33	15.21	15.12	15.05	14.99	14.94	14.90	14.87	14.85	14.83	14.82	14.78	14.76	14.76
900	17.24	17.11	17.01	16.93	16.86	16.81	16.77	16.73	16.71	16.69	16.67	16.62	16.61	16.60
1000	19.16	19.01	18.90	18.81	18.73	18.68	18.63	18.59	18.56	18.54	18.52	18.47	18.45	18.45
2000	38.31	38.02	37.79	37.61	37.46	37.35	37.25	37.18	37.12	37.07	37.03	36.93	36.90	36.89
3000	57.46	57.03	56.68	56.41	56.19	56.02	55.88	55.77	55.68	55.61	55.55	55.39	55.34	55.33
4000	76.61	76.03	75.57	75.21	74.92	74.69	74.50	74.35	74.23	74.14	74.06	73.86	73.79	73.77
5000	95.77	95.04	94.47	94.01	93.65	93.36	93.12	92.94	92.79	92.67	92.58	92.32	92.24	92.21
6000	114.92	114.05	113.36	112.81	112.37	112.03	111.75	111.53	111.35	111.21	111.09	110.78	110.68	110.65
7000	134.07	133.05	132.25	131.61	131.10	130.70	130.37	130.11	129.91	129.74	129.61	129.25	129.13	129.09
8000	153.22	152.06	151.14	150.41	149.83	149.37	149.00	148.70	148.46	148.27	148.12	147.71	147.57	147.53
9000	172.37	171.07	170.03	169.21	168.56	168.04	167.62	167.29	167.02	166.81	166.64	166.17	166.02	165.97
10000	191.53	190.08	188.93	188.01	187.29	186.71	186.24	185.87	185.58	185.34	185.15	184.64	184.47	184.41
11000	210.68	209.08	207.82	206.81	206.02	205.38	204.87	204.46	204.14	203.87	203.67	203.10	202.91	202.85
12000	229.83	228.09	226.71	225.62	224.74	224.05	223.49	223.05	222.69	222.41	222.18	221.56	221.36	221.29
13000	248.98	247.10	245.60	244.42	243.47	242.72	242.12	241.64	241.25	240.94	240.70	240.03	239.80	239.73
14000	268.13	266.10	264.49	263.22	262.20	261.39	260.74	260.22	259.81	259.48	259.21	258.49	258.25	258.17
15000	287.29	285.11	283.39	282.02	280.93	280.06	279.36	278.81	278.37	278.01	277.72	276.95	276.70	276.61
16000	306.44	304.12	302.28	300.82	299.66	298.73	297.99	297.40	296.92	296.54	296.24	295.42	295.14	295.05
17000	325.59	323.12	321.17	319.62	318.38	317.40	316.61	315.98	315.48	315.08	314.75	313.88	313.59	313.49
18000	344.74	342.13	340.06	338.42	337.11	336.07	335.24	334.57	334.04	333.61	333.27	332.34	332.03	331.93
19000	363.89	361.14	358.96	357.22	355.84	354.74	353.86	353.16	352.59	352.14	351.78	350.81	350.48	350.37
20000	383.05	380.15	377.85	376.02	374.57	373.41	372.48	371.74	371.15	370.68	370.30	369.27	368.93	368.81
21000	402.20	399.15	396.74	394.82	393.30	392.08	391.11	390.33	389.71	389.21	388.81	387.73	387.37	387.25
22000	421.35	418.16	415.63	413.62	412.03	410.75	409.73	408.92	408.27	407.74	407.33	406.20	405.82	405.69
23000	440.50	437.17	434.52	432.43	430.75	429.42	428.36	427.51	426.82	426.28	425.84	424.66	424.26	424.13
24000	459.65	456.17	453.42	451.23	449.48	448.09	446.98	446.09	445.38	444.81	444.36	443.12	442.71	442.57
25000	478.81	475.18	472.31	470.03	468.21	466.76	465.60	464.68	463.94	463.35	462.87	461.58	461.16	461.01
26000	497.96	494.19	491.20	488.83	486.94	485.43	484.23	483.27	482.50	481.88	481.39	480.05	479.60	479.45
27000	517.11	513.19	510.09	507.63	505.67	504.10	502.85	501.85	501.05	500.41	499.90	498.51	498.05	497.89
28000	536.26	532.20	528.98	526.43	524.39	522.77	521.48	520.44	519.61	518.95	518.41	516.97	516.50	516.34
29000	555.41	551.21	547.88	545.23	543.12	541.44	540.10	539.03	538.17	537.48	536.93	535.44	534.94	534.78
30000	574.57	570.22	566.77	564.03	561.85	560.11	558.72	557.61	556.73	556.01	555.44	553.90	553.39	553.22
31000	593.72	589.22	585.66	582.83	580.58	578.78	577.35	576.20	575.28	574.55	573.96	572.36	571.83	571.66
32000	612.87	608.23	604.55	601.63	599.31	597.45	595.97	594.79	593.84	593.08	592.47	590.83	590.28	590.10
33000	632.02	627.24	623.45	620.43	618.04	616.12	614.60	613.37	612.40	611.61	610.99	609.29	608.73	608.54
34000	651.17	646.24	642.34	639.23	636.76	634.79	633.22	631.96	630.95	630.15	629.50	627.75	627.17	626.98
35000	670.33	665.25	661.23	658.04	655.49	653.46	651.84	650.55	649.51	648.68	648.02	646.22	645.62	645.42
36000	689.48	684.26	680.12	676.84	674.22	672.13	670.47	669.14	668.07	667.22	666.53	664.68	664.06	663.86
37000	708.63	703.26	699.01	695.64	692.95	690.80	689.09	687.72	686.63	685.75	685.05	683.14	682.51	682.30
38000	727.78	722.27	717.91	714.44	711.68	709.47	707.72	706.31	705.18	704.28	703.56	701.61	700.96	700.74
39000	746.93	741.28	736.80	733.24	730.41	728.14	726.34	724.90	723.74	722.82	722.08	720.07	719.40	719.18
40000	766.09	760.29	755.69	752.04	749.13	746.82	744.96	743.48	742.30	741.35	740.59	738.53	737.85	737.62
41000	785.24	779.29	774.58	770.84	767.86	765.49	763.59	762.07	760.86	759.88	759.10	757.00	756.29	756.06
42000	804.39	798.30	793.47	789.64	786.59	784.16	782.21	780.66	779.41	778.42	777.62	775.46	774.74	774.50
43000	823.54	817.31	812.37	808.44	805.32	802.83	800.84	799.24	797.97	796.95	796.13	793.92	793.19	792.94
44000	842.69	836.31	831.26	827.24	824.05	821.50	819.46	817.83	816.53	815.48	814.65	812.39	811.63	811.38
45000	861.85	855.32	850.15	846.04	842.77	840.17	838.08	836.42	835.09	834.02	833.16	830.85	830.08	829.82
46000	881.00	874.33	869.04	864.85	861.50	858.84	856.71	855.01	853.64	852.55	851.68	849.31	848.52	848.26
47000	900.15	893.34	887.94	883.65	880.23	877.51	875.33	873.59	872.20	871.09	870.19	867.78	866.97	866.70
48000	919.30	912.34	906.83	902.45	898.96	896.18	893.96	892.18	890.76	889.62	888.71	886.24	885.42	885.14
49000	938.45	931.35	925.72	921.25	917.69	914.85	912.58	910.77	909.31	908.15	907.22	904.70	903.86	903.58
50000	957.61	950.36	944.61	940.05	936.42	933.52	931.20	929.35	927.87	926.69	925.74	923.16	922.31	922.02
55000	1053.37	1045.39	1039.07	1034.05	1030.06	1026.87	1024.32	1022.29	1020.66	1019.35	1018.31	1015.48	1014.54	1014.23
60000	1149.13	1140.43	1133.53	1128.06	1123.70	1120.22	1117.44	1115.22	1113.45	1112.02	1110.88	1107.80	1106.77	1106.43
65000	1244.89	1235.46	1227.99	1222.06	1217.34	1213.57	1210.56	1208.16	1206.23	1204.69	1203.46	1200.11	1199.00	1198.63
70000	1340.65	1330.50	1322.45	1316.07	1310.98	1306.92	1303.68	1301.09	1299.02	1297.36	1296.03	1292.43	1291.23	1290.83
75000	1436.41	1425.53	1416.92	1410.07	1404.62	1400.27	1396.80	1394.03	1391.81	1390.03	1388.60	1384.75	1383.46	1383.03
80000	1532.17	1520.57	1511.38	1504.07	1498.26	1493.63	1489.92	1486.96	1484.59	1482.70	1481.18	1477.06	1475.69	1475.23
85000	1627.93	1615.60	1605.84	1598.08	1591.90	1586.98	1583.04	1579.90	1577.38	1575.36	1573.75	1569.38	1567.92	1567.44
90000	1723.69	1710.64	1700.30	1692.08	1685.54	1680.33	1676.16	1672.83	1670.17	1668.03	1666.32	1661.69	1660.15	1659.64
95000	1819.45	1805.67	1794.76	1786.09	1779.18	1773.68	1769.28	1765.77	1762.95	1760.70	1758.89	1754.01	1752.38	1751.84
100000	1915.21	1900.71	1889.22	1880.09	1872.83	1867.03	1862.40	1858.70	1855.74	1853.37	1851.47	1846.33	1844.61	1844.04

22.200%

TERM / AMOUNT	1 Year	2 Years	3 Years	4 Years	5 Years	6 Years	7 Years	8 Years	9 Years	10 Years	11 Years	12 Years	13 Years	14 Years
5	.47	.26	.20	.16	.14	.13	.12	.12	.11	.11	.11	.10	.10	.10
10	.94	.52	.39	.32	.28	.26	.24	.23	.22	.21	.21	.20	.20	.20
15	1.41	.78	.58	.48	.42	.38	.36	.34	.33	.32	.31	.30	.30	.30
25	2.35	1.30	.96	.80	.70	.64	.59	.56	.54	.53	.51	.50	.50	.49
50	4.69	2.60	1.92	1.59	1.39	1.27	1.18	1.12	1.08	1.05	1.02	1.00	.99	.97
75	7.03	3.90	2.88	2.38	2.08	1.90	1.77	1.68	1.61	1.57	1.53	1.50	1.48	1.46
100	9.37	5.20	3.83	3.17	2.78	2.53	2.36	2.24	2.15	2.09	2.04	2.00	1.97	1.94
200	18.74	10.40	7.66	6.33	5.55	5.05	4.71	4.47	4.30	4.17	4.07	3.99	3.93	3.88
300	28.11	15.60	11.49	9.49	8.32	7.58	7.07	6.71	6.44	6.25	6.10	5.98	5.89	5.82
400	37.48	20.80	15.32	12.65	11.10	10.10	9.42	8.94	8.59	8.33	8.13	7.97	7.85	7.76
500	46.85	25.99	19.15	15.81	13.87	12.63	11.78	11.18	10.74	10.41	10.16	9.97	9.82	9.70
600	56.22	31.19	22.98	18.97	16.64	15.15	14.13	13.41	12.88	12.49	12.19	11.96	11.78	11.64
700	65.59	36.39	26.81	22.14	19.42	17.68	16.49	15.65	15.03	14.57	14.22	13.95	13.74	13.58
800	74.96	41.59	30.64	25.30	22.19	20.20	18.84	17.88	17.18	16.65	16.25	15.94	15.70	15.52
900	84.33	46.78	34.47	28.46	24.96	22.73	21.20	20.12	19.32	18.73	18.28	17.93	17.67	17.46
1000	93.70	51.98	38.30	31.62	27.74	25.25	23.55	22.35	21.47	20.81	20.31	19.93	19.63	19.40
2000	187.39	103.96	76.59	63.23	55.47	50.49	47.10	44.70	42.93	41.62	40.62	39.85	39.25	38.79
3000	281.08	155.94	114.89	94.85	83.20	75.74	70.65	67.04	64.40	62.42	60.92	59.77	58.88	58.18
4000	374.77	207.91	153.18	126.46	110.94	100.98	94.20	89.39	85.86	83.23	81.23	79.69	78.50	77.57
5000	468.46	259.89	191.47	158.08	138.67	126.23	117.75	111.73	107.33	104.04	101.54	99.62	98.13	96.96
6000	562.15	311.87	229.77	189.69	166.40	151.47	141.30	134.08	128.79	124.84	121.84	119.54	117.75	116.35
7000	655.84	363.84	268.06	221.31	194.13	176.72	164.85	156.42	150.26	145.65	142.15	139.46	137.37	135.75
8000	749.53	415.82	306.36	252.92	221.87	201.96	188.40	178.77	171.72	166.46	162.45	159.38	157.00	155.14
9000	843.22	467.80	344.65	284.54	249.60	227.21	211.95	201.11	193.18	187.26	182.76	179.30	176.62	174.53
10000	936.91	519.77	382.94	316.15	277.33	252.45	235.50	223.46	214.65	208.07	203.07	199.23	196.25	193.92
11000	1030.60	571.75	421.24	347.77	305.07	277.70	259.05	245.80	236.11	228.87	223.37	219.15	215.87	213.31
12000	1124.29	623.73	459.53	379.38	332.80	302.94	282.60	268.15	257.58	249.68	243.68	239.07	235.50	232.70
13000	1217.98	675.71	497.83	411.00	360.53	328.19	306.15	290.49	279.04	270.48	263.99	258.99	255.12	252.10
14000	1311.67	727.68	536.12	442.61	388.26	353.43	329.70	312.84	300.51	291.29	284.29	278.92	274.74	271.49
15000	1405.36	779.66	574.41	474.23	416.00	378.68	353.25	335.18	321.97	312.10	304.60	298.84	294.37	290.88
16000	1499.06	831.64	612.71	505.84	443.73	403.92	376.80	357.53	343.43	332.90	324.90	318.76	313.99	310.27
17000	1592.75	883.61	651.00	537.46	471.46	429.17	400.35	379.87	364.90	353.71	345.21	338.68	333.62	329.66
18000	1686.44	935.59	689.30	569.07	499.19	454.41	423.90	402.22	386.36	374.51	365.52	358.60	353.24	349.05
19000	1780.13	987.57	727.59	600.69	526.93	479.66	447.45	424.57	407.83	395.32	385.82	378.53	372.87	368.44
20000	1873.82	1039.54	765.88	632.30	554.66	504.90	471.00	446.91	429.29	416.13	406.13	398.45	392.49	387.84
21000	1967.51	1091.52	804.18	663.91	582.39	530.15	494.55	469.26	450.76	436.93	426.44	418.37	412.11	407.23
22000	2061.20	1143.50	842.47	695.53	610.13	555.39	518.10	491.60	472.22	457.74	446.74	438.29	431.74	426.62
23000	2154.89	1195.48	880.77	727.14	637.86	580.64	541.65	513.95	493.68	478.54	467.05	458.21	451.36	446.01
24000	2248.58	1247.45	919.06	758.76	665.59	605.88	565.20	536.29	515.15	499.35	487.35	478.14	470.99	465.40
25000	2342.27	1299.43	957.35	790.37	693.32	631.13	588.74	558.64	536.61	520.16	507.66	498.06	490.61	484.79
26000	2435.96	1351.41	995.65	821.99	721.06	656.37	612.29	580.98	558.08	540.96	527.97	517.98	510.24	504.19
27000	2529.65	1403.38	1033.94	853.60	748.79	681.62	635.84	603.33	579.54	561.77	548.27	537.90	529.86	523.58
28000	2623.34	1455.36	1072.24	885.22	776.52	706.86	659.39	625.67	601.01	582.57	568.58	557.83	549.48	542.97
29000	2717.03	1507.34	1110.53	916.83	804.25	732.11	682.94	648.02	622.47	603.38	588.89	577.75	569.11	562.36
30000	2810.72	1559.31	1148.82	948.45	831.99	757.35	706.49	670.36	643.93	624.19	609.19	597.67	588.73	581.75
31000	2904.42	1611.29	1187.12	980.06	859.72	782.60	730.04	692.71	665.40	644.99	629.50	617.59	608.36	601.14
32000	2998.11	1663.27	1225.41	1011.68	887.45	807.84	753.59	715.05	686.86	665.80	649.80	637.51	627.98	620.54
33000	3091.80	1715.25	1263.71	1043.29	915.19	833.09	777.14	737.40	708.33	686.60	670.11	657.44	647.61	639.93
34000	3185.49	1767.22	1302.00	1074.91	942.92	858.33	800.69	759.74	729.79	707.41	690.42	677.36	667.23	659.32
35000	3279.18	1819.20	1340.29	1106.52	970.65	883.58	824.24	782.09	751.26	728.22	710.72	697.28	686.85	678.71
36000	3372.87	1871.18	1378.59	1138.14	998.38	908.82	847.79	804.43	772.72	749.02	731.03	717.20	706.48	698.10
37000	3466.56	1923.15	1416.88	1169.75	1026.12	934.07	871.34	826.78	794.18	769.83	751.34	737.12	726.10	717.49
38000	3560.25	1975.13	1455.18	1201.37	1053.85	959.31	894.89	849.13	815.65	790.63	771.64	757.05	745.73	736.88
39000	3653.94	2027.11	1493.47	1232.98	1081.58	984.56	918.44	871.47	837.11	811.44	791.95	776.97	765.35	756.28
40000	3747.63	2079.08	1531.76	1264.60	1109.31	1009.80	941.99	893.82	858.58	832.25	812.25	796.89	784.98	775.67
41000	3841.32	2131.06	1570.06	1296.21	1137.05	1035.05	965.54	916.16	880.04	853.05	832.56	816.81	804.60	795.06
42000	3935.01	2183.04	1608.35	1327.82	1164.78	1060.29	989.09	938.51	901.51	873.86	852.87	836.74	824.22	814.45
43000	4028.70	2235.01	1646.65	1359.44	1192.51	1085.54	1012.64	960.85	922.97	894.66	873.17	856.66	843.85	833.84
44000	4122.39	2286.99	1684.94	1391.05	1220.25	1110.78	1036.19	983.20	944.44	915.47	893.48	876.58	863.47	853.23
45000	4216.08	2338.97	1723.23	1422.67	1247.98	1136.03	1059.74	1005.54	965.90	936.28	913.79	896.50	883.10	872.63
46000	4309.78	2390.95	1761.53	1454.28	1275.71	1161.27	1083.29	1027.89	987.36	957.08	934.09	916.42	902.72	892.02
47000	4403.47	2442.92	1799.82	1485.90	1303.44	1186.52	1106.84	1050.23	1008.83	977.89	954.40	936.35	922.35	911.41
48000	4497.16	2494.90	1838.12	1517.51	1331.18	1211.76	1130.39	1072.58	1030.29	998.69	974.70	956.27	941.97	930.80
49000	4590.85	2546.88	1876.41	1549.13	1358.91	1237.01	1153.94	1094.92	1051.76	1019.50	995.01	976.19	961.59	950.19
50000	4684.54	2598.85	1914.70	1580.74	1386.64	1262.25	1177.48	1117.27	1073.22	1040.31	1015.32	996.11	981.22	969.58
55000	5152.99	2858.74	2106.17	1738.82	1525.31	1388.48	1295.23	1228.99	1180.54	1144.34	1116.85	1095.72	1079.34	1066.54
60000	5621.44	3118.62	2297.64	1896.89	1663.97	1514.70	1412.98	1340.72	1287.86	1248.37	1218.38	1195.33	1177.46	1163.50
65000	6089.90	3378.51	2489.11	2054.96	1802.63	1640.93	1530.73	1452.45	1395.19	1352.40	1319.91	1294.95	1275.58	1260.46
70000	6558.35	3638.39	2680.58	2213.04	1941.30	1767.15	1648.48	1564.17	1502.51	1456.43	1421.44	1394.56	1373.70	1357.42
75000	7026.80	3898.28	2872.05	2371.11	2079.96	1893.38	1766.22	1675.90	1609.83	1560.46	1522.97	1494.17	1471.83	1454.37
80000	7495.26	4158.16	3063.52	2529.19	2218.62	2019.60	1883.97	1787.63	1717.15	1664.49	1624.50	1593.78	1569.95	1551.33
85000	7963.71	4418.05	3254.99	2687.26	2357.29	2145.83	2001.72	1899.35	1824.47	1768.52	1726.03	1693.39	1668.07	1648.29
90000	8432.16	4677.93	3446.46	2845.33	2495.95	2272.05	2119.47	2011.08	1931.79	1872.55	1827.57	1793.00	1766.19	1745.25
95000	8900.62	4937.82	3637.93	3003.41	2634.62	2398.28	2237.22	2122.81	2039.12	1976.58	1929.10	1892.61	1864.31	1842.20
100000	9369.07	5197.70	3829.40	3161.48	2773.28	2524.50	2354.96	2234.53	2146.44	2080.61	2030.63	1992.22	1962.43	1939.16

TERM AMOUNT	15 Years	16 Years	17 Years	18 Years	19 Years	20 Years	21 Years	22 Years	23 Years	24 Years	25 Years	30 Years	35 Years	40 Years
5	.10	.10	.10	.10	.10	.10	.10	.10	.10	.10	.10	.10	.10	.10
10	.20	.20	.19	.19	.19	.19	.19	.19	.19	.19	.19	.19	.19	.19
15	.29	.29	.29	.29	.29	.29	.29	.28	.28	.28	.28	.28	.28	.28
25	.49	.48	.48	.48	.47	.47	.47	.47	.47	.47	.47	.47	.47	.47
50	.97	.96	.95	.95	.94	.94	.94	.94	.94	.93	.93	.93	.93	.93
75	1.45	1.43	1.43	1.42	1.41	1.41	1.41	1.40	1.40	1.40	1.40	1.39	1.39	1.39
100	1.93	1.91	1.90	1.89	1.88	1.88	1.87	1.87	1.87	1.86	1.86	1.86	1.86	1.86
200	3.85	3.82	3.80	3.78	3.76	3.75	3.74	3.73	3.73	3.72	3.72	3.71	3.71	3.71
300	5.77	5.72	5.69	5.66	5.64	5.62	5.61	5.60	5.59	5.58	5.58	5.56	5.56	5.56
400	7.69	7.63	7.59	7.55	7.52	7.50	7.48	7.46	7.46	7.44	7.44	7.42	7.41	7.41
500	9.61	9.54	9.48	9.43	9.40	9.37	9.35	9.33	9.31	9.30	9.29	9.27	9.26	9.26
600	11.53	11.44	11.38	11.32	11.28	11.24	11.22	11.19	11.18	11.16	11.15	11.12	11.11	11.11
700	13.45	13.35	13.27	13.21	13.16	13.12	13.08	13.06	13.04	13.02	13.01	12.97	12.96	12.96
800	15.37	15.26	15.17	15.09	15.04	14.99	14.95	14.92	14.90	14.88	14.87	14.83	14.81	14.81
900	17.29	17.16	17.06	16.98	16.91	16.86	16.82	16.79	16.76	16.74	16.72	16.68	16.66	16.66
1000	19.21	19.07	18.96	18.86	18.79	18.74	18.69	18.65	18.62	18.60	18.58	18.53	18.51	18.51
2000	38.42	38.13	37.91	37.72	37.58	37.47	37.37	37.30	37.24	37.19	37.16	37.06	37.02	37.01
3000	57.63	57.20	56.86	56.58	56.37	56.20	56.06	55.95	55.86	55.79	55.73	55.58	55.53	55.51
4000	76.84	76.26	75.81	75.44	75.16	74.93	74.74	74.60	74.48	74.38	74.31	74.11	74.04	74.02
5000	96.05	95.33	94.76	94.30	93.94	93.66	93.43	93.24	93.10	92.98	92.88	92.63	92.55	92.52
6000	115.26	114.39	113.71	113.16	112.73	112.39	112.11	111.89	111.71	111.57	111.46	111.16	111.06	111.02
7000	134.47	133.46	132.66	132.02	131.52	131.12	130.79	130.54	130.33	130.17	130.04	129.68	129.56	129.52
8000	153.68	152.52	151.61	150.88	150.31	149.85	149.48	149.19	148.95	148.76	148.61	148.21	148.07	148.03
9000	172.88	171.59	170.56	169.74	169.09	168.58	168.16	167.83	167.57	167.36	167.19	166.73	166.58	166.53
10000	192.09	190.65	189.51	188.60	187.88	187.31	186.85	186.48	186.19	185.95	185.76	185.26	185.09	185.03
11000	211.30	209.72	208.46	207.46	206.67	206.04	205.53	205.13	204.81	204.55	204.34	203.78	203.60	203.54
12000	230.51	228.78	227.41	226.32	225.46	224.77	224.22	223.78	223.42	223.14	222.92	222.31	222.11	222.04
13000	249.72	247.04	246.36	245.18	244.24	243.50	242.90	242.42	242.04	241.74	241.49	240.83	240.61	240.54
14000	268.93	266.91	265.31	264.04	263.03	262.23	261.58	261.07	260.66	260.33	260.07	259.36	259.12	259.04
15000	288.14	285.97	284.26	282.90	281.82	280.96	280.27	279.72	279.28	278.93	278.64	277.88	277.63	277.55
16000	307.35	305.04	303.21	301.76	300.61	299.69	298.95	298.37	297.90	297.52	297.22	296.41	296.14	296.05
17000	326.55	324.10	322.16	320.62	319.39	318.42	317.64	317.01	316.51	316.12	315.80	314.93	314.65	314.55
18000	345.76	343.17	341.11	339.48	338.18	337.15	336.32	335.66	335.13	334.71	334.37	333.46	333.16	333.06
19000	364.97	362.23	360.06	358.34	356.97	355.88	355.00	354.31	353.75	353.31	352.95	351.98	351.66	351.56
20000	384.18	381.30	379.01	377.20	375.76	374.61	373.69	372.96	372.37	371.90	371.52	370.51	370.17	370.06
21000	403.39	400.36	397.96	396.06	394.54	393.34	392.37	391.60	390.99	390.49	390.10	389.03	388.68	388.56
22000	422.60	419.43	416.91	414.92	413.33	412.07	411.06	410.25	409.61	409.09	408.68	407.56	407.19	407.07
23000	441.81	438.49	435.86	433.78	432.12	430.80	429.74	428.90	428.22	427.68	427.25	426.09	425.70	425.57
24000	461.02	457.55	454.81	452.64	450.91	449.53	448.43	447.55	446.84	446.28	445.83	444.61	444.21	444.07
25000	480.22	476.62	473.76	471.50	469.69	468.26	467.11	466.19	465.46	464.87	464.40	463.14	462.71	462.57
26000	499.43	495.68	492.71	490.36	488.48	486.99	485.79	484.84	484.08	483.47	482.98	481.66	481.22	481.08
27000	518.64	514.75	511.66	509.22	507.27	505.72	504.48	503.49	502.70	502.06	501.56	500.19	499.73	499.58
28000	537.85	533.81	530.62	528.08	526.06	524.45	523.16	522.14	521.32	520.66	520.13	518.71	518.24	518.08
29000	557.06	552.88	549.57	546.94	544.84	543.18	541.85	540.78	539.93	539.25	538.71	537.24	536.75	536.59
30000	576.27	571.94	568.52	565.80	563.63	561.91	560.53	559.43	558.55	557.85	557.28	555.76	555.26	555.09
31000	595.48	591.01	587.47	584.66	582.42	580.64	579.22	578.08	577.17	576.44	575.86	574.29	573.77	573.59
32000	614.69	610.07	606.42	603.52	601.21	599.37	597.90	596.73	595.79	595.04	594.44	592.81	592.27	592.09
33000	633.89	629.14	625.37	622.38	620.00	618.10	616.58	615.37	614.41	613.63	613.01	611.34	610.78	610.60
34000	653.10	648.20	644.32	641.24	638.78	636.83	635.27	634.02	633.02	632.23	631.59	629.86	629.29	629.10
35000	672.31	667.26	663.27	660.09	657.57	655.56	653.95	652.67	651.64	650.82	650.16	648.39	647.80	647.60
36000	691.52	686.33	682.22	678.95	676.36	674.29	672.64	671.32	670.26	669.42	668.74	666.91	666.31	666.11
37000	710.73	705.39	701.17	697.81	695.15	693.02	691.32	689.96	688.88	688.01	687.32	685.44	684.82	684.61
38000	729.94	724.46	720.12	716.67	713.93	711.75	710.00	708.61	707.50	706.61	705.89	703.96	703.32	703.11
39000	749.15	743.52	739.07	735.53	732.72	730.40	728.69	727.26	726.12	725.20	724.47	722.49	721.83	721.61
40000	768.36	762.59	758.02	754.39	751.51	749.21	747.37	745.91	744.73	743.80	743.04	741.01	740.34	740.12
41000	787.57	781.65	776.97	773.25	770.30	767.94	766.06	764.55	763.35	762.39	761.62	759.54	758.85	758.62
42000	806.77	800.72	795.92	792.11	789.08	786.67	784.74	783.20	781.97	780.98	780.20	778.06	777.36	777.12
43000	825.98	819.78	814.87	810.97	807.87	805.40	803.43	801.85	800.59	799.58	798.77	796.59	795.87	795.63
44000	845.19	838.85	833.82	829.83	826.66	824.13	822.11	820.50	819.21	818.17	817.35	815.11	814.37	814.13
45000	864.40	857.91	852.77	848.69	845.45	842.86	840.79	839.14	837.82	836.77	835.92	833.64	832.88	832.63
46000	883.61	876.97	871.72	867.55	864.23	861.59	859.48	857.79	856.44	855.36	854.50	852.17	851.39	851.13
47000	902.82	896.04	890.67	886.41	883.02	880.32	878.16	876.44	875.06	873.96	873.08	870.69	869.90	869.64
48000	922.03	915.10	909.62	905.27	901.81	899.05	896.85	895.09	893.68	892.55	891.65	889.22	888.41	888.14
49000	941.24	934.17	928.57	924.13	920.60	917.78	915.53	913.73	912.30	911.15	910.23	907.74	906.92	906.64
50000	960.44	953.23	947.52	942.99	939.38	936.51	934.22	932.38	930.92	929.74	928.80	926.27	925.42	925.14
55000	1056.49	1048.56	1042.28	1037.29	1033.32	1030.16	1027.64	1025.62	1024.01	1022.72	1021.68	1018.89	1017.97	1017.66
60000	1152.53	1143.88	1137.03	1131.59	1127.26	1123.81	1121.06	1118.86	1117.10	1115.69	1114.56	1111.52	1110.51	1110.17
65000	1248.58	1239.20	1231.78	1225.89	1221.20	1217.46	1214.48	1212.10	1210.19	1208.66	1207.44	1204.14	1203.05	1202.69
70000	1344.62	1334.52	1326.53	1320.18	1315.14	1311.11	1307.90	1305.33	1303.28	1301.64	1300.32	1296.77	1295.59	1295.20
75000	1440.66	1429.85	1421.28	1414.48	1409.07	1404.76	1401.32	1398.57	1396.37	1394.61	1393.20	1389.40	1388.13	1387.71
80000	1536.71	1525.17	1516.03	1508.78	1503.01	1498.41	1494.74	1491.81	1489.46	1487.59	1486.08	1482.02	1480.68	1480.23
85000	1632.75	1620.49	1610.79	1603.08	1596.95	1592.06	1588.16	1585.05	1582.55	1580.56	1578.96	1574.65	1573.22	1572.74
90000	1728.80	1715.82	1705.54	1697.38	1690.89	1685.71	1681.58	1678.28	1675.64	1673.53	1671.84	1667.28	1665.76	1665.25
95000	1824.84	1811.14	1800.29	1791.68	1784.82	1779.36	1775.00	1771.52	1768.74	1766.51	1764.72	1759.90	1758.30	1757.77
100000	1920.88	1906.46	1895.04	1885.98	1878.76	1873.01	1868.43	1864.76	1861.83	1859.48	1857.60	1852.53	1850.84	1850.28

MONTHLY PAYMENT
REQUIRED TO AMORTIZE A LOAN

TERM	1 Year	2 Years	3 Years	4 Years	5 Years	6 Years	7 Years	8 Years	9 Years	10 Years	11 Years	12 Years	13 Years	14 Years
AMOUNT														
5	.47	.27	.20	.16	.14	.13	.12	.12	.11	.11	.11	.10	.10	.10
10	.94	.53	.39	.32	.28	.26	.24	.23	.22	.21	.21	.20	.20	.20
15	1.41	.79	.58	.48	.42	.38	.36	.34	.33	.32	.31	.30	.30	.30
25	2.35	1.31	.96	.80	.70	.64	.59	.56	.54	.53	.51	.50	.50	.49
50	4.69	2.61	1.92	1.59	1.39	1.27	1.18	1.12	1.08	1.05	1.02	1.00	.99	.98
75	7.03	3.91	2.88	2.38	2.09	1.90	1.77	1.68	1.62	1.57	1.53	1.50	1.48	1.46
100	9.38	5.21	3.84	3.17	2.78	2.53	2.36	2.24	2.15	2.09	2.04	2.00	1.97	1.95
200	18.75	10.41	7.67	6.33	5.56	5.06	4.72	4.48	4.30	4.17	4.07	4.00	3.94	3.89
300	28.12	15.61	11.50	9.50	8.33	7.59	7.08	6.72	6.45	6.26	6.11	5.99	5.90	5.83
400	37.49	20.81	15.33	12.66	11.11	10.11	9.44	8.96	8.60	8.34	8.14	7.99	7.87	7.70
500	46.86	26.01	19.16	15.83	13.89	12.64	11.80	11.19	10.75	10.43	10.18	9.98	9.84	9.72
600	56.23	31.21	23.00	18.99	16.66	15.17	14.15	13.43	12.90	12.51	12.21	11.98	11.80	11.66
700	65.61	36.41	26.83	22.15	19.44	17.70	16.51	15.67	15.05	14.59	14.24	13.98	13.77	13.61
800	74.98	41.61	30.66	25.32	22.21	20.22	18.87	17.91	17.20	16.68	16.28	15.97	15.73	15.55
900	84.35	46.81	34.49	28.48	24.99	22.75	21.23	20.14	19.35	18.76	18.31	17.97	17.70	17.49
1000	93.72	52.01	38.32	31.65	27.77	25.28	23.59	22.38	21.50	20.85	20.35	19.96	19.67	19.43
2000	187.43	104.01	76.64	63.29	55.53	50.55	47.17	44.76	43.00	41.69	40.69	39.92	39.33	38.86
3000	281.15	156.01	114.96	94.93	83.29	75.83	70.75	67.14	64.50	62.53	61.03	59.88	58.99	58.29
4000	374.86	208.01	153.28	126.57	111.05	101.10	94.33	89.51	85.99	83.37	81.37	79.84	78.65	77.72
5000	468.58	260.01	191.60	158.21	138.81	126.38	117.91	111.89	107.49	104.21	101.71	99.80	98.31	97.15
6000	562.29	312.02	229.92	189.86	166.57	151.65	141.49	134.27	128.99	125.05	122.05	119.75	117.97	116.58
7000	656.01	364.02	268.24	221.50	194.33	176.93	165.07	156.65	150.49	145.89	142.39	139.71	137.63	136.01
8000	749.72	416.02	306.56	253.14	222.09	202.20	188.65	179.02	171.98	166.73	162.74	159.67	157.29	155.44
9000	843.44	468.02	344.88	284.78	249.86	227.48	212.23	201.40	193.48	187.57	183.08	179.63	176.95	174.86
10000	937.15	520.02	383.20	316.42	277.62	252.75	235.81	223.78	214.98	208.41	203.42	199.59	196.61	194.29
11000	1030.87	572.02	421.52	348.07	305.38	278.03	259.39	246.16	236.48	229.25	223.76	219.54	216.27	213.72
12000	1124.58	624.03	459.84	379.71	333.14	303.30	282.97	268.53	257.97	250.09	244.10	239.50	235.94	233.15
13000	1218.30	676.03	498.16	411.35	360.90	328.58	306.55	290.91	279.47	270.93	264.44	259.46	255.60	252.58
14000	1312.01	728.03	536.48	442.99	388.66	353.85	330.13	313.29	300.97	291.77	284.78	279.42	275.26	272.01
15000	1405.73	780.03	574.80	474.63	416.42	379.13	353.71	335.67	322.47	312.61	305.12	299.38	294.92	291.44
16000	1499.44	832.03	613.12	506.28	444.18	404.40	377.29	358.04	343.96	333.45	325.47	319.33	314.58	310.87
17000	1593.16	884.03	651.44	537.92	471.95	429.68	400.87	380.42	365.46	354.29	345.81	339.29	334.24	330.30
18000	1686.87	936.04	689.76	569.56	499.71	454.95	424.46	402.80	386.96	375.13	366.15	359.25	353.90	349.72
19000	1780.59	988.04	728.08	601.20	527.47	480.22	448.04	425.17	408.46	395.97	386.49	379.21	373.56	369.15
20000	1874.30	1040.04	766.40	632.84	555.23	505.50	471.62	447.55	429.95	416.81	406.83	399.17	393.22	388.58
21000	1968.01	1092.04	804.72	664.49	582.99	530.77	495.20	469.93	451.45	437.65	427.17	419.12	412.88	408.01
22000	2061.73	1144.04	843.04	696.13	610.75	556.05	518.78	492.31	472.95	458.49	447.51	439.08	432.54	427.44
23000	2155.44	1196.05	881.36	727.77	638.51	581.32	542.36	514.68	494.45	479.33	467.85	459.04	452.21	446.87
24000	2249.16	1248.05	919.68	759.41	666.27	606.60	565.94	537.06	515.94	500.17	488.20	479.00	471.87	466.30
25000	2342.87	1300.05	958.00	791.05	694.04	631.87	589.52	559.44	537.44	521.01	508.54	498.96	491.53	485.73
26000	2436.59	1352.05	996.32	822.70	721.80	657.15	613.10	581.82	558.94	541.85	528.88	518.91	511.19	505.15
27000	2530.30	1404.05	1034.64	854.34	749.56	682.42	636.68	604.19	580.44	562.69	549.22	538.87	530.85	524.58
28000	2624.02	1456.05	1072.96	885.98	777.32	707.70	660.26	626.57	601.93	583.53	569.56	558.83	550.51	544.01
29000	2717.73	1508.05	1111.28	917.62	805.08	732.97	683.84	648.95	623.43	604.37	589.90	578.79	570.17	563.44
30000	2811.45	1560.06	1149.60	949.26	832.84	758.25	707.42	671.33	644.93	625.21	610.24	598.75	589.83	582.87
31000	2905.16	1612.06	1187.92	980.91	860.60	783.52	731.00	693.70	666.43	646.05	630.58	618.70	609.49	602.30
32000	2998.88	1664.06	1226.24	1012.55	888.36	808.80	754.58	716.08	687.92	666.89	650.93	638.66	629.15	621.73
33000	3092.59	1716.06	1264.56	1044.19	916.13	834.07	778.16	738.46	709.42	687.73	671.27	658.62	648.81	641.16
34000	3186.31	1768.06	1302.88	1075.83	943.89	859.35	801.74	760.84	730.92	708.57	691.61	678.58	668.47	660.59
35000	3280.02	1820.06	1341.20	1107.47	971.65	884.62	825.32	783.21	752.42	729.41	711.95	698.54	688.14	680.01
36000	3373.74	1872.07	1379.52	1139.12	999.41	909.90	848.91	805.59	773.91	750.25	732.29	718.49	707.80	699.44
37000	3467.45	1924.07	1417.84	1170.76	1027.17	935.17	872.49	827.97	795.41	771.09	752.63	738.45	727.46	718.87
38000	3561.17	1976.07	1456.16	1202.40	1054.93	960.44	896.07	850.34	816.91	791.93	772.97	758.41	747.12	738.30
39000	3654.88	2028.07	1494.48	1234.04	1082.69	985.72	919.65	872.72	838.41	812.77	793.31	778.37	766.78	757.73
40000	3748.59	2080.07	1532.80	1265.68	1110.45	1010.99	943.23	895.10	859.90	833.61	813.66	798.33	786.44	777.16
41000	3842.31	2132.07	1571.12	1297.33	1138.22	1036.27	966.81	917.48	881.40	854.45	834.00	818.28	806.10	796.59
42000	3936.02	2184.08	1609.44	1328.97	1165.98	1061.54	990.39	939.85	902.90	875.29	854.34	838.24	825.76	816.02
43000	4029.74	2236.08	1647.76	1360.61	1193.74	1086.82	1013.97	962.23	924.40	896.13	874.68	858.20	845.42	835.45
44000	4123.45	2288.08	1686.08	1392.25	1221.50	1112.09	1037.55	984.61	945.89	916.97	895.02	878.16	865.08	854.87
45000	4217.17	2340.08	1724.40	1423.89	1249.26	1137.37	1061.13	1006.99	967.39	937.81	915.36	898.12	884.74	874.30
46000	4310.88	2392.08	1762.72	1455.54	1277.02	1162.64	1084.71	1029.36	988.89	958.65	935.70	918.07	904.41	893.73
47000	4404.60	2444.08	1801.04	1487.18	1304.78	1187.92	1108.29	1051.74	1010.39	979.49	956.04	938.03	924.07	913.16
48000	4498.31	2496.09	1839.36	1518.82	1332.54	1213.19	1131.87	1074.12	1031.88	1000.33	976.39	957.99	943.73	932.59
49000	4592.03	2548.09	1877.68	1550.46	1360.31	1238.47	1155.45	1096.50	1053.38	1021.17	996.73	977.95	963.39	952.02
50000	4685.74	2600.09	1916.00	1582.10	1388.07	1263.74	1179.03	1118.87	1074.88	1042.01	1017.07	997.91	983.05	971.45
55000	5154.32	2860.10	2107.60	1740.31	1526.87	1390.12	1296.94	1230.76	1182.37	1146.21	1118.77	1097.70	1081.35	1068.59
60000	5622.89	3120.11	2299.20	1898.52	1665.68	1516.49	1414.84	1342.65	1289.85	1250.42	1220.48	1197.49	1179.66	1165.74
65000	6091.46	3380.12	2490.80	2056.73	1804.49	1642.86	1532.74	1454.53	1397.34	1354.62	1322.19	1297.28	1277.96	1262.88
70000	6560.04	3640.12	2682.40	2214.94	1943.29	1769.24	1650.64	1566.42	1504.83	1458.82	1423.89	1397.07	1376.27	1360.02
75000	7028.61	3900.13	2874.00	2373.15	2082.10	1895.61	1768.55	1678.31	1612.32	1563.02	1525.60	1496.86	1474.57	1457.17
80000	7497.18	4160.14	3065.60	2531.36	2220.90	2021.98	1886.45	1790.19	1719.80	1667.22	1627.31	1596.65	1572.87	1554.31
85000	7965.76	4420.15	3257.20	2689.57	2359.71	2148.36	2004.35	1902.08	1827.29	1771.42	1729.01	1696.44	1671.18	1651.46
90000	8434.33	4680.16	3448.80	2847.78	2498.52	2274.73	2122.26	2013.97	1934.78	1875.62	1830.72	1796.23	1769.48	1748.60
95000	8902.91	4940.17	3640.40	3005.99	2637.32	2401.10	2240.16	2125.85	2042.27	1979.82	1932.43	1896.02	1867.79	1845.74
100000	9371.48	5200.17	3832.00	3164.20	2776.13	2527.48	2358.06	2237.74	2149.75	2084.02	2034.13	1995.81	1966.09	1942.89

TERM	15 Years	16 Years	17 Years	18 Years	19 Years	20 Years	21 Years	22 Years	23 Years	24 Years	25 Years	30 Years	35 Years	40 Years
AMOUNT														
5	.10	.10	.10	.10	.10	.10	.10	.10	.10	.10	.10	.10	.10	.10
10	.20	.20	.19	.19	.19	.19	.19	.19	.19	.19	.19	.19	.19	.19
15	.29	.29	.29	.29	.29	.29	.29	.29	.28	.28	.28	.28	.28	.28
25	.49	.48	.48	.48	.48	.47	.47	.47	.47	.47	.47	.47	.47	.47
50	.97	.96	.95	.95	.95	.94	.94	.94	.94	.94	.94	.93	.93	.93
75	1.45	1.44	1.43	1.42	1.42	1.41	1.41	1.41	1.40	1.40	1.40	1.40	1.40	1.40
100	1.93	1.92	1.90	1.89	1.89	1.88	1.88	1.87	1.87	1.87	1.87	1.86	1.86	1.86
200	3.85	3.83	3.80	3.78	3.77	3.76	3.75	3.74	3.74	3.73	3.73	3.72	3.71	3.71
300	5.78	5.74	5.70	5.67	5.65	5.64	5.62	5.61	5.60	5.60	5.59	5.57	5.57	5.57
400	7.70	7.65	7.60	7.56	7.54	7.51	7.49	7.48	7.47	7.46	7.45	7.43	7.42	7.42
500	9.63	9.56	9.50	9.45	9.42	9.39	9.37	9.35	9.33	9.32	9.31	9.29	9.28	9.28
600	11.55	11.47	11.40	11.34	11.30	11.27	11.24	11.22	11.20	11.19	11.18	11.14	11.13	11.13
700	13.48	13.38	13.30	13.23	13.18	13.14	13.11	13.09	13.07	13.05	13.04	13.00	12.99	12.99
800	15.40	15.29	15.20	15.12	15.07	15.02	14.98	14.96	14.93	14.91	14.90	14.86	14.84	14.84
900	17.33	17.20	17.10	17.01	16.95	16.90	16.86	16.82	16.80	16.78	16.76	16.71	16.70	16.69
1000	19.25	19.11	18.99	18.90	18.83	18.77	18.73	18.69	18.66	18.64	18.62	18.57	18.55	18.55
2000	38.50	38.21	37.98	37.80	37.66	37.54	37.45	37.38	37.32	37.28	37.24	37.14	37.10	37.09
3000	57.74	57.31	56.97	56.70	56.49	56.31	56.18	56.07	55.98	55.91	55.86	55.70	55.65	55.64
4000	76.99	76.42	75.96	75.60	75.31	75.08	74.90	74.76	74.64	74.55	74.47	74.27	74.20	74.18
5000	96.24	95.52	94.95	94.50	94.14	93.85	93.63	93.45	93.30	93.18	93.09	92.84	92.75	92.73
6000	115.48	114.62	113.94	113.40	112.97	112.62	112.35	112.13	111.96	111.82	111.71	111.40	111.30	111.27
7000	134.73	133.73	132.93	132.30	131.80	131.39	131.08	130.82	130.62	130.45	130.32	129.97	129.85	129.82
8000	153.98	152.83	151.92	151.20	150.62	150.16	149.80	149.51	149.28	149.09	148.94	148.54	148.40	148.36
9000	173.22	171.93	170.91	170.10	169.45	168.93	168.52	168.20	167.93	167.72	167.56	167.10	166.95	166.90
10000	192.47	191.03	189.90	188.99	188.28	187.70	187.25	186.88	186.59	186.36	186.17	185.67	185.50	185.45
11000	211.72	210.14	208.89	207.89	207.10	206.47	205.97	205.57	205.25	205.00	204.79	204.24	204.05	203.99
12000	230.96	229.24	227.88	226.79	225.93	225.24	224.70	224.26	223.91	223.63	223.41	222.80	222.60	222.54
13000	250.21	248.34	246.86	245.69	244.76	244.01	243.42	242.95	242.57	242.27	242.02	241.37	241.15	241.08
14000	269.46	267.45	265.85	264.59	263.59	262.78	262.15	261.64	261.23	260.90	260.64	259.94	259.70	259.63
15000	288.70	286.55	284.84	283.49	282.41	281.55	280.87	280.32	279.89	279.54	279.26	278.50	278.25	278.17
16000	307.95	305.65	303.83	302.39	301.24	300.32	299.59	299.01	298.55	298.17	297.88	297.07	296.80	296.72
17000	327.20	324.75	322.82	321.29	320.07	319.09	318.32	317.70	317.20	316.81	316.49	315.64	315.35	315.26
18000	346.44	343.86	341.81	340.19	338.89	337.86	337.04	336.39	335.86	335.44	335.11	334.20	333.90	333.80
19000	365.69	362.96	360.80	359.09	357.72	356.63	355.77	355.08	354.52	354.08	353.73	352.77	352.45	352.35
20000	384.94	382.06	379.79	377.98	376.55	375.40	374.49	373.76	373.18	372.72	372.34	371.34	371.00	370.89
21000	404.18	401.17	398.78	396.88	395.38	394.17	393.22	392.45	391.84	391.35	390.96	389.90	389.55	389.44
22000	423.43	420.27	417.77	415.78	414.20	412.94	411.94	411.14	410.50	409.99	409.58	408.47	408.10	407.98
23000	442.68	439.37	436.76	434.68	433.03	431.71	430.67	429.83	429.16	428.62	428.19	427.04	426.65	426.53
24000	461.92	458.48	455.75	453.58	451.86	450.48	449.39	448.52	447.82	447.26	446.81	445.60	445.20	445.07
25000	481.17	477.58	474.74	472.48	470.68	469.25	468.11	467.20	466.48	465.89	465.43	464.17	463.75	463.62
26000	500.42	496.68	493.72	491.38	489.51	488.02	486.84	485.89	485.13	484.53	484.04	482.74	482.30	482.16
27000	519.66	515.78	512.71	510.28	508.34	506.79	505.56	504.58	503.79	503.16	502.66	501.30	500.85	500.70
28000	538.91	534.89	531.70	529.18	527.17	525.56	524.29	523.27	522.45	521.80	521.28	519.87	519.40	519.25
29000	558.16	553.99	550.69	548.07	545.99	544.33	543.01	541.96	541.11	540.44	539.89	538.44	537.95	537.79
30000	577.40	573.09	569.68	566.97	564.82	563.10	561.74	560.64	559.77	559.07	558.51	557.00	556.50	556.34
31000	596.65	592.20	588.67	585.87	583.65	581.87	580.46	579.33	578.43	577.71	577.13	575.57	575.05	574.88
32000	615.90	611.30	607.66	604.77	602.47	600.64	599.18	598.02	597.09	596.34	595.75	594.14	593.60	593.43
33000	635.14	630.40	626.65	623.67	621.30	619.41	617.91	616.71	615.75	614.98	614.36	612.70	612.15	611.97
34000	654.39	649.50	645.64	642.57	640.13	638.18	636.63	635.39	634.40	633.61	632.98	631.27	630.70	630.51
35000	673.64	668.61	664.63	661.47	658.96	656.95	655.36	654.08	653.06	652.25	651.60	649.84	649.25	649.06
36000	692.88	687.71	683.62	680.37	677.78	675.72	674.08	672.77	671.72	670.88	670.21	668.40	667.80	667.60
37000	712.13	706.81	702.61	699.27	696.61	694.49	692.81	691.46	690.38	689.52	688.83	686.97	686.35	686.15
38000	731.38	725.92	721.59	718.17	715.44	713.26	711.53	710.15	709.04	708.15	707.45	705.53	704.90	704.69
39000	750.62	745.02	740.58	737.06	734.26	732.03	730.26	728.83	727.70	726.79	726.06	724.10	723.45	723.24
40000	769.87	764.12	759.57	755.96	753.09	750.80	748.98	747.52	746.36	745.43	744.68	742.67	742.00	741.78
41000	789.12	783.23	778.56	774.86	771.92	769.57	767.70	766.21	765.02	764.06	763.30	761.23	760.55	760.33
42000	808.36	802.33	797.55	793.76	790.75	788.34	786.43	784.90	783.68	782.70	781.91	779.80	779.10	778.87
43000	827.61	821.43	816.54	812.66	809.57	807.11	805.15	803.59	802.33	801.33	800.53	798.37	797.65	797.41
44000	846.86	840.53	835.53	831.56	828.40	825.88	823.88	822.27	820.99	819.97	819.15	816.93	816.20	815.96
45000	866.10	859.64	854.52	850.46	847.23	844.65	842.60	840.96	839.65	838.60	837.76	835.50	834.75	834.50
46000	885.35	878.74	873.51	869.36	866.06	863.42	861.33	859.65	858.31	857.24	856.38	854.07	853.30	853.05
47000	904.60	897.84	892.50	888.26	884.88	882.19	880.05	878.34	876.97	875.87	875.00	872.63	871.85	871.59
48000	923.84	916.95	911.49	907.15	903.71	900.96	898.77	897.03	895.63	894.51	893.62	891.20	890.40	890.14
49000	943.09	936.05	930.48	926.05	922.54	919.73	917.50	915.71	914.29	913.15	912.23	909.77	908.95	908.68
50000	962.34	955.15	949.47	944.95	941.36	938.50	936.22	934.40	932.95	931.78	930.85	928.33	927.50	927.23
55000	1058.57	1050.67	1044.41	1039.45	1035.50	1032.35	1029.85	1027.84	1026.24	1024.96	1023.93	1021.17	1020.25	1019.95
60000	1154.80	1146.18	1139.36	1133.94	1129.64	1126.20	1123.47	1121.28	1119.53	1118.14	1117.02	1114.00	1113.00	1112.67
65000	1251.04	1241.70	1234.30	1228.44	1223.77	1220.05	1217.09	1214.72	1212.83	1211.31	1210.10	1206.83	1205.75	1205.39
70000	1347.27	1337.21	1329.25	1322.93	1317.91	1313.90	1310.71	1308.16	1306.12	1304.49	1303.19	1299.67	1298.50	1298.11
75000	1443.50	1432.73	1424.20	1417.43	1412.04	1407.75	1404.33	1401.60	1399.42	1397.67	1396.27	1392.50	1391.25	1390.84
80000	1539.74	1528.24	1519.14	1511.92	1506.18	1501.60	1497.95	1495.04	1492.71	1490.85	1489.36	1485.33	1484.00	1483.56
85000	1635.97	1623.75	1614.09	1606.42	1600.31	1595.45	1591.58	1588.48	1586.00	1584.02	1582.44	1578.16	1576.75	1576.28
90000	1732.20	1719.27	1709.03	1700.91	1694.45	1689.30	1685.20	1681.92	1679.30	1677.20	1675.52	1671.00	1669.50	1669.00
95000	1828.44	1814.78	1803.98	1795.41	1788.59	1783.15	1778.82	1775.36	1772.59	1770.38	1768.61	1763.83	1762.25	1761.72
100000	1924.67	1910.30	1898.93	1889.90	1882.72	1877.00	1872.44	1868.80	1865.89	1863.56	1861.69	1856.66	1855.00	1854.45

MONTHLY PAYMENT
REQUIRED TO AMORTIZE A LOAN

TERM	1 Year	2 Years	3 Years	4 Years	5 Years	6 Years	7 Years	8 Years	9 Years	10 Years	11 Years	12 Years	13 Years	14 Years
AMOUNT														
5	.47	.27	.20	.16	.14	.13	.12	.12	.11	.11	.11	.10	.10	.10
10	.94	.53	.39	.32	.28	.26	.24	.23	.22	.21	.21	.20	.20	.20
15	1.41	.79	.58	.48	.42	.38	.36	.34	.33	.32	.31	.30	.30	.30
25	2.35	1.31	.96	.80	.70	.64	.60	.57	.54	.53	.51	.50	.50	.49
50	4.69	2.61	1.92	1.59	1.39	1.27	1.19	1.13	1.08	1.05	1.02	1.00	.99	.98
75	7.04	3.91	2.88	2.38	2.09	1.90	1.78	1.69	1.62	1.57	1.53	1.50	1.48	1.46
100	9.38	5.21	3.84	3.17	2.78	2.54	2.37	2.25	2.16	2.09	2.04	2.00	1.97	1.95
200	18.75	10.41	7.67	6.34	5.56	5.07	4.73	4.49	4.31	4.18	4.08	4.00	3.94	3.90
300	28.13	15.61	11.51	9.51	8.34	7.60	7.09	6.73	6.46	6.27	6.12	6.00	5.91	5.84
400	37.50	20.82	15.34	12.67	11.12	10.13	9.45	8.97	8.62	8.35	8.16	8.00	7.88	7.79
500	46.87	26.02	19.18	15.84	13.90	12.66	11.81	11.21	10.77	10.44	10.19	10.00	9.85	9.74
600	56.25	31.22	23.01	19.01	16.68	15.19	14.17	13.45	12.92	12.53	12.23	12.00	11.82	11.68
700	65.62	36.42	26.85	22.17	19.46	17.72	16.53	15.69	15.08	14.62	14.27	14.00	13.79	13.63
800	75.00	41.63	30.68	25.34	22.24	20.25	16.89	17.93	17.23	16.70	16.31	16.00	15.76	15.58
900	84.37	46.83	34.52	28.51	25.02	22.78	21.26	20.17	19.38	18.79	18.34	18.00	17.73	17.52
1000	93.74	52.03	38.35	31.67	27.79	25.31	23.62	22.41	21.54	20.88	20.38	20.00	19.70	19.47
2000	187.48	104.06	76.70	63.34	55.58	50.61	47.23	44.82	43.07	41.75	40.76	39.99	39.40	38.94
3000	281.22	156.08	115.04	95.01	83.37	75.92	70.84	67.23	64.60	62.63	61.13	59.99	59.10	58.40
4000	374.96	208.11	153.39	126.68	111.16	101.22	94.45	89.64	86.13	83.50	81.51	79.98	78.79	77.87
5000	468.70	260.14	191.73	158.35	138.95	126.53	118.06	112.05	107.66	104.38	101.89	99.97	98.49	97.34
6000	562.44	312.16	230.08	190.02	166.74	151.83	141.67	134.46	129.19	125.25	122.26	119.97	118.19	116.80
7000	656.18	364.19	268.43	221.69	194.53	177.14	165.29	156.87	150.72	146.13	142.64	139.96	137.89	136.27
8000	749.92	416.22	306.77	253.36	222.32	202.44	188.90	179.28	172.25	167.00	163.02	159.96	157.58	155.73
9000	843.65	468.24	345.12	285.03	250.11	227.75	212.51	201.69	193.78	187.87	183.39	179.95	177.28	175.20
10000	937.39	520.27	383.46	316.70	277.90	253.05	236.12	224.10	215.31	208.75	203.77	199.94	196.98	194.67
11000	1031.13	572.30	421.81	348.37	305.69	278.35	259.73	246.51	236.84	229.62	224.14	219.94	216.68	214.13
12000	1124.87	624.32	460.15	380.04	333.48	303.66	283.34	268.92	258.37	250.50	244.52	239.93	236.37	233.60
13000	1218.61	676.35	498.50	411.70	361.27	328.96	306.95	291.33	279.90	271.37	264.90	259.93	256.07	253.06
14000	1312.35	728.37	536.85	443.37	389.06	354.27	330.57	313.74	301.43	292.25	285.27	279.92	275.77	272.53
15000	1406.09	780.40	575.19	475.04	416.85	379.57	354.18	336.15	322.96	313.12	305.65	299.91	295.47	292.00
16000	1499.83	832.43	613.54	506.71	444.64	404.88	377.79	358.56	344.50	333.99	326.03	319.91	315.16	311.46
17000	1593.57	884.45	651.88	538.38	472.43	430.18	401.40	380.97	366.03	354.87	346.40	339.90	334.86	330.93
18000	1687.30	936.48	690.23	570.05	500.22	455.49	425.01	403.38	387.56	375.74	366.78	359.90	354.56	350.40
19000	1781.04	988.51	728.58	601.72	528.01	480.79	448.62	425.79	409.09	396.62	387.16	379.89	374.26	369.86
20000	1874.78	1040.53	766.92	633.39	555.80	506.10	472.24	448.19	430.62	417.49	407.53	399.88	393.95	389.33
21000	1968.52	1092.56	805.27	665.06	583.59	531.40	495.85	470.60	452.15	438.37	427.91	419.88	413.65	408.79
22000	2062.26	1144.59	843.61	696.73	611.38	556.70	519.46	493.01	473.68	459.24	448.28	439.87	433.35	428.26
23000	2156.00	1196.61	881.96	728.40	639.17	582.01	543.07	515.42	495.21	480.11	468.66	459.86	453.05	447.73
24000	2249.74	1248.64	920.30	760.07	666.96	607.31	566.68	537.83	516.74	500.99	489.04	479.86	472.74	467.19
25000	2343.48	1300.67	958.65	791.73	694.75	632.62	590.29	560.24	538.27	521.86	509.41	499.85	492.44	486.66
26000	2437.21	1352.69	997.00	823.40	722.54	657.92	613.90	582.65	559.80	542.74	529.79	519.85	512.14	506.12
27000	2530.95	1404.72	1035.34	855.07	750.33	683.23	637.52	605.06	581.33	563.61	550.17	539.84	531.84	525.59
28000	2624.69	1456.74	1073.69	886.74	778.12	708.53	661.13	627.47	602.86	584.49	570.54	559.83	551.53	545.06
29000	2718.43	1508.77	1112.03	918.41	805.91	733.84	684.74	649.88	624.39	605.36	590.92	579.83	571.23	564.52
30000	2812.17	1560.80	1150.38	950.08	833.70	759.14	708.35	672.29	645.92	626.23	611.29	599.82	590.93	583.99
31000	2905.91	1612.82	1188.73	981.75	861.49	784.44	731.96	694.70	667.46	647.11	631.67	619.82	610.63	603.45
32000	2999.65	1664.85	1227.07	1013.42	889.28	809.75	755.57	717.11	688.99	667.98	652.05	639.81	630.32	622.92
33000	3093.39	1716.88	1265.42	1045.09	917.07	835.05	779.19	739.52	710.52	688.86	672.42	659.80	650.02	642.39
34000	3187.12	1768.90	1303.76	1076.76	944.86	860.36	802.80	761.93	732.05	709.73	692.80	679.80	669.72	661.85
35000	3280.86	1820.93	1342.11	1108.43	972.65	885.66	826.41	784.34	753.58	730.61	713.18	699.79	689.42	681.32
36000	3374.60	1872.96	1380.45	1140.10	1000.44	910.97	850.02	806.75	775.11	751.48	733.55	719.79	709.11	700.79
37000	3468.34	1924.98	1418.80	1171.76	1028.23	936.27	873.63	829.16	796.64	772.36	753.93	739.78	728.81	720.25
38000	3562.08	1977.01	1457.15	1203.43	1056.02	961.58	897.24	851.57	818.17	793.23	774.31	759.77	748.51	739.72
39000	3655.82	2029.04	1495.49	1235.10	1083.81	986.88	920.85	873.97	839.70	814.10	794.68	779.77	768.21	759.18
40000	3749.56	2081.06	1533.84	1266.77	1111.60	1012.19	944.47	896.38	861.23	834.98	815.06	799.76	787.90	778.65
41000	3843.30	2133.09	1572.18	1298.44	1139.38	1037.49	968.08	918.79	882.76	855.85	835.43	819.75	807.60	798.12
42000	3937.04	2185.11	1610.53	1330.11	1167.17	1062.79	991.69	941.20	904.29	876.73	855.81	839.75	827.30	817.58
43000	4030.77	2237.14	1648.88	1361.78	1194.96	1088.10	1015.30	963.61	925.82	897.60	876.19	859.74	847.00	837.05
44000	4124.51	2289.17	1687.22	1393.45	1222.75	1113.40	1038.91	986.02	947.35	918.48	896.56	879.74	866.69	856.51
45000	4218.25	2341.19	1725.57	1425.12	1250.54	1138.71	1062.52	1008.43	968.88	939.35	916.94	899.73	886.39	875.98
46000	4311.99	2393.22	1763.91	1456.79	1278.33	1164.01	1086.14	1030.84	990.42	960.22	937.32	919.72	906.09	895.45
47000	4405.73	2445.25	1802.26	1488.46	1306.12	1189.32	1109.75	1053.25	1011.95	981.10	957.69	939.72	925.79	914.91
48000	4499.47	2497.27	1840.60	1520.13	1333.91	1214.62	1133.36	1075.66	1033.48	1001.97	978.07	959.71	945.48	934.38
49000	4593.21	2549.30	1878.95	1551.79	1361.70	1239.93	1156.97	1098.07	1055.01	1022.85	998.45	979.71	965.18	953.84
50000	4686.95	2601.33	1917.30	1583.46	1389.49	1265.23	1180.58	1120.48	1076.54	1043.72	1018.82	999.70	984.88	973.31
55000	5155.64	2861.46	2109.03	1741.81	1528.44	1391.75	1298.64	1232.53	1184.19	1148.09	1120.70	1099.67	1083.37	1070.64
60000	5624.33	3121.59	2300.75	1900.16	1667.39	1518.28	1416.70	1344.57	1291.84	1252.46	1222.58	1199.64	1181.85	1167.97
65000	6093.03	3381.72	2492.48	2058.50	1806.34	1644.80	1534.75	1456.62	1399.50	1356.84	1324.47	1299.61	1280.34	1265.30
70000	6561.72	3641.85	2684.21	2216.85	1945.29	1771.32	1652.81	1568.67	1507.15	1461.21	1426.35	1399.58	1378.83	1362.63
75000	7030.42	3901.99	2875.94	2375.19	2084.24	1897.84	1770.87	1680.72	1614.80	1565.58	1528.23	1499.55	1477.32	1459.96
80000	7499.11	4162.12	3067.67	2533.54	2223.19	2024.37	1888.93	1792.76	1722.46	1669.95	1630.11	1599.52	1575.80	1557.29
85000	7967.80	4422.25	3259.40	2691.88	2362.13	2150.89	2006.99	1904.81	1830.11	1774.32	1731.99	1699.49	1674.29	1654.63
90000	8436.50	4682.38	3451.13	2850.23	2501.08	2277.41	2125.04	2016.86	1937.76	1878.69	1833.87	1799.46	1772.78	1751.96
95000	8905.19	4942.52	3642.86	3008.58	2640.03	2403.93	2243.10	2128.91	2045.42	1983.07	1935.76	1899.43	1871.27	1849.29
100000	9373.89	5202.65	3834.59	3166.92	2778.98	2530.46	2361.16	2240.95	2153.07	2087.44	2037.64	1999.39	1969.75	1946.62

TERM	15 Years	16 Years	17 Years	18 Years	19 Years	20 Years	21 Years	22 Years	23 Years	24 Years	25 Years	30 Years	35 Years	40 Years
AMOUNT														
5	.10	.10	.10	.10	.10	.10	.10	.10	.10	.10	.10	.10	.10	.10
10	.20	.20	.20	.19	.19	.19	.19	.19	.19	.19	.19	.19	.19	.19
15	.29	.29	.29	.29	.29	.29	.29	.29	.29	.29	.28	.28	.28	.28
25	.49	.48	.48	.48	.48	.48	.47	.47	.47	.47	.47	.47	.47	.47
50	.97	.96	.96	.95	.95	.95	.94	.94	.94	.94	.94	.94	.93	.93
75	1.45	1.44	1.43	1.43	1.42	1.42	1.41	1.41	1.41	1.41	1.40	1.40	1.40	1.40
100	1.93	1.92	1.91	1.90	1.89	1.89	1.88	1.88	1.87	1.87	1.87	1.87	1.86	1.86
200	3.86	3.83	3.81	3.79	3.78	3.77	3.76	3.75	3.74	3.74	3.74	3.73	3.72	3.72
300	5.79	5.75	5.71	5.69	5.67	5.65	5.63	5.62	5.61	5.61	5.60	5.59	5.58	5.58
400	7.72	7.66	7.62	7.58	7.55	7.53	7.51	7.50	7.48	7.48	7.47	7.45	7.44	7.44
500	9.65	9.58	9.52	9.47	9.44	9.41	9.39	9.37	9.35	9.34	9.33	9.31	9.30	9.30
600	11.58	11.49	11.42	11.37	11.33	11.29	11.26	11.24	11.22	11.21	11.20	11.17	11.16	11.16
700	13.50	13.40	13.32	13.26	13.21	13.17	13.14	13.11	13.09	13.08	13.07	13.03	13.02	13.02
800	15.43	15.32	15.23	15.16	15.10	15.05	15.02	14.99	14.96	14.95	14.93	14.89	14.88	14.87
900	17.36	17.23	17.13	17.05	16.99	16.93	16.89	16.86	16.83	16.81	16.80	16.75	16.74	16.73
1000	19.29	19.15	19.03	18.94	18.87	18.81	18.77	18.73	18.70	18.68	18.66	18.61	18.60	18.59
2000	38.57	38.29	38.06	37.88	37.74	37.62	37.53	37.46	37.40	37.36	37.32	37.22	37.19	37.18
3000	57.86	57.43	57.09	56.82	56.61	56.43	56.30	56.19	56.10	56.03	55.98	55.83	55.78	55.76
4000	77.14	76.57	76.12	75.76	75.47	75.24	75.06	74.92	74.80	74.71	74.64	74.44	74.37	74.35
5000	96.43	95.71	95.15	94.70	94.34	94.05	93.83	93.65	93.50	93.39	93.29	93.04	92.96	92.94
6000	115.71	114.85	114.17	113.63	113.21	112.86	112.59	112.38	112.20	112.06	111.95	111.65	111.55	111.52
7000	135.00	133.99	133.20	132.57	132.07	131.67	131.36	131.10	130.90	130.74	130.61	130.26	130.15	130.11
8000	154.28	153.14	152.23	151.51	150.94	150.48	150.12	149.83	149.60	149.42	149.27	148.87	148.74	148.69
9000	173.57	172.28	171.26	170.45	169.81	169.29	168.89	168.56	168.30	168.09	167.93	167.48	167.33	167.28
10000	192.85	191.42	190.29	189.39	188.67	188.10	187.65	187.29	187.00	186.77	186.58	186.08	185.92	185.87
11000	212.13	210.56	209.31	208.33	207.54	206.91	206.42	206.02	205.70	205.44	205.24	204.69	204.51	204.45
12000	231.42	229.70	228.34	227.26	226.41	225.72	225.18	224.75	224.40	224.12	223.90	223.30	223.10	223.04
13000	250.70	248.84	247.37	246.20	245.27	244.53	243.94	243.47	243.10	242.80	242.56	241.91	241.69	241.62
14000	269.99	267.98	266.40	265.14	264.14	263.34	262.71	262.20	261.80	261.47	261.21	260.52	260.29	260.21
15000	289.27	287.12	285.43	284.08	283.01	282.15	281.47	280.93	280.50	280.15	279.87	279.12	278.88	278.80
16000	308.56	306.27	304.45	303.02	301.87	300.96	300.24	299.66	299.20	298.83	298.53	297.73	297.47	297.38
17000	327.84	325.41	323.48	321.95	320.74	319.77	319.00	318.39	317.90	317.50	317.19	316.34	316.06	315.97
18000	347.13	344.55	342.51	340.89	339.61	338.58	337.77	337.12	336.59	336.18	335.85	334.95	334.65	334.55
19000	366.41	363.69	361.54	359.83	358.47	357.39	356.53	355.84	355.29	354.85	354.50	353.56	353.24	353.14
20000	385.70	382.83	380.57	378.77	377.34	376.20	375.30	374.57	373.99	373.53	373.16	372.16	371.83	371.73
21000	404.98	401.97	399.59	397.71	396.21	395.01	394.06	393.30	392.69	392.21	391.82	390.77	390.43	390.31
22000	424.26	421.11	418.62	416.65	415.07	413.82	412.83	412.03	411.39	410.88	410.48	409.38	409.02	408.90
23000	443.55	440.26	437.65	435.58	433.94	432.63	431.59	430.76	430.09	429.56	429.13	427.99	427.61	427.48
24000	462.83	459.40	456.68	454.52	452.81	451.44	450.35	449.49	448.79	448.24	447.79	446.60	446.20	446.07
25000	482.12	478.54	475.71	473.46	471.67	470.25	469.12	468.21	467.49	466.91	466.45	465.20	464.79	464.66
26000	501.40	497.68	494.73	492.40	490.54	489.06	487.88	486.94	486.19	485.59	485.11	483.81	483.38	483.24
27000	520.69	516.82	513.76	511.34	509.41	507.87	506.65	505.67	504.89	504.26	503.77	502.42	501.97	501.83
28000	539.97	535.96	532.79	530.27	528.28	526.68	525.41	524.40	523.59	522.94	522.42	521.03	520.57	520.41
29000	559.26	555.10	551.82	549.21	547.14	545.49	544.18	543.13	542.29	541.62	541.08	539.64	539.16	539.00
30000	578.54	574.24	570.85	568.15	566.01	564.30	562.94	561.86	560.99	560.29	559.74	558.24	557.75	557.59
31000	597.82	593.39	589.87	587.09	584.88	583.11	581.71	580.58	579.69	578.97	578.40	576.85	576.34	576.17
32000	617.11	612.53	608.90	606.03	603.74	601.92	600.47	599.31	598.39	597.65	597.05	595.46	594.93	594.76
33000	636.39	631.67	627.93	624.97	622.61	620.73	619.24	618.04	617.09	616.32	615.71	614.07	613.52	613.34
34000	655.68	650.81	646.96	643.90	641.48	639.54	638.00	636.77	635.79	635.00	634.37	632.67	632.12	631.93
35000	674.96	669.95	665.99	662.84	660.34	658.35	656.76	655.50	654.48	653.68	653.03	651.28	650.71	650.52
36000	694.25	689.09	685.02	681.78	679.21	677.16	675.53	674.23	673.18	672.35	671.69	669.89	669.30	669.10
37000	713.53	708.23	704.04	700.72	698.08	695.97	694.29	692.95	691.88	691.03	690.34	688.50	687.89	687.69
38000	732.82	727.38	723.07	719.66	716.94	714.78	713.06	711.68	710.58	709.70	709.00	707.11	706.48	706.27
39000	752.10	746.52	742.10	738.60	735.81	733.59	731.82	730.41	729.28	728.38	727.66	725.71	725.07	724.86
40000	771.39	765.66	761.13	757.53	754.68	752.40	750.59	749.14	747.98	747.06	746.32	744.32	743.66	743.45
41000	790.67	784.80	780.16	776.47	773.54	771.21	769.35	767.87	766.68	765.73	764.97	762.93	762.26	762.03
42000	809.95	803.94	799.19	795.41	792.41	790.02	788.12	786.60	785.38	784.41	783.63	781.54	780.85	780.62
43000	829.24	823.08	818.21	814.35	811.28	808.83	806.88	805.32	804.08	803.09	802.29	800.15	799.44	799.20
44000	848.52	842.22	837.24	833.29	830.14	827.64	825.65	824.05	822.78	821.76	820.95	818.75	818.03	817.79
45000	867.81	861.36	856.27	852.22	849.01	846.45	844.41	842.78	841.48	840.44	839.61	837.36	836.62	836.38
46000	887.09	880.51	875.30	871.16	867.88	865.26	863.17	861.51	860.18	859.11	858.26	855.97	855.21	854.96
47000	906.38	899.65	894.32	890.10	886.74	884.07	881.94	880.24	878.88	877.79	876.92	874.58	873.80	873.55
48000	925.66	918.79	913.35	909.04	905.61	902.88	900.70	898.97	897.58	896.47	895.58	893.19	892.40	892.13
49000	944.95	937.93	932.38	927.98	924.48	921.69	919.47	917.69	916.28	915.14	914.24	911.79	910.99	910.72
50000	964.23	957.07	951.41	946.92	943.34	940.50	938.23	936.42	934.98	933.82	932.89	930.40	929.58	929.31
55000	1060.65	1052.78	1046.55	1041.61	1037.68	1034.55	1032.06	1030.06	1028.47	1027.20	1026.18	1023.44	1022.54	1022.24
60000	1157.08	1148.48	1141.69	1136.30	1132.01	1128.60	1125.88	1123.71	1121.97	1120.58	1119.47	1116.48	1115.48	1115.17
65000	1253.50	1244.19	1236.83	1230.99	1226.35	1222.65	1219.70	1217.35	1215.47	1213.96	1212.76	1209.52	1208.45	1208.10
70000	1349.92	1339.90	1331.97	1325.68	1320.68	1316.70	1313.52	1310.99	1308.96	1307.35	1306.05	1302.56	1301.41	1301.03
75000	1446.34	1435.60	1427.11	1420.37	1415.01	1410.75	1407.35	1404.63	1402.46	1400.73	1399.34	1395.60	1394.37	1393.96
80000	1542.77	1531.31	1522.25	1515.06	1509.35	1504.80	1501.17	1498.27	1495.96	1494.11	1492.63	1488.64	1487.32	1486.89
85000	1639.19	1627.02	1617.39	1609.75	1603.68	1598.85	1594.99	1591.91	1589.46	1587.49	1585.92	1581.68	1580.28	1579.82
90000	1735.61	1722.72	1712.53	1704.44	1698.02	1692.90	1688.81	1685.56	1682.95	1680.87	1679.21	1674.72	1673.24	1672.75
95000	1832.03	1818.43	1807.67	1799.14	1792.35	1786.95	1782.64	1779.20	1776.45	1774.25	1772.49	1767.76	1766.20	1765.68
100000	1928.46	1914.14	1902.81	1893.83	1886.68	1881.00	1876.46	1872.84	1869.95	1867.63	1865.78	1860.80	1859.15	1858.61

MONTHLY PAYMENT
REQUIRED TO AMORTIZE A LOAN

TERM	1 Year	2 Years	3 Years	4 Years	5 Years	6 Years	7 Years	8 Years	9 Years	10 Years	11 Years	12 Years	13 Years	14 Years
AMOUNT														
5	.47	.27	.20	.16	.14	.13	.12	.12	.11	.11	.11	.11	.10	.10
10	.94	.53	.39	.32	.28	.26	.24	.23	.22	.21	.21	.21	.20	.20
15	1.41	.79	.58	.48	.42	.39	.36	.34	.33	.32	.31	.31	.30	.30
25	2.35	1.31	.96	.80	.70	.64	.60	.57	.54	.53	.52	.51	.50	.49
50	4.69	2.61	1.92	1.59	1.40	1.27	1.19	1.13	1.08	1.05	1.03	1.01	.99	.98
75	7.04	3.91	2.88	2.38	2.09	1.91	1.78	1.69	1.62	1.57	1.54	1.51	1.49	1.47
100	9.38	5.21	3.84	3.18	2.79	2.54	2.37	2.25	2.16	2.10	2.05	2.01	1.98	1.96
200	18.76	10.42	7.68	6.35	5.57	5.07	4.74	4.50	4.32	4.19	4.09	4.01	3.96	3.91
300	28.14	15.62	11.52	9.52	8.35	7.61	7.10	6.74	6.48	6.28	6.13	6.02	5.93	5.86
400	37.51	20.83	15.36	12.69	11.14	10.14	9.47	8.99	8.64	8.38	8.18	8.02	7.91	7.81
500	46.89	26.04	19.20	15.86	13.92	12.68	11.83	11.23	10.80	10.47	10.22	10.02	9.88	9.77
600	56.27	31.24	23.04	19.03	16.70	15.21	14.20	13.48	12.95	12.56	12.26	12.03	11.86	11.72
700	65.65	36.45	26.87	22.20	19.49	17.75	16.57	15.73	15.11	14.65	14.31	14.04	13.83	13.67
800	75.02	41.66	30.71	25.37	22.27	20.28	18.93	17.97	17.27	16.75	16.35	16.04	15.81	15.62
900	84.40	46.86	34.55	28.54	25.05	22.82	21.30	20.22	19.43	18.84	18.39	18.05	17.78	17.57
1000	93.78	52.07	38.39	31.72	27.84	25.35	23.66	22.46	21.59	20.93	20.43	20.05	19.76	19.53
2000	187.55	104.13	76.77	63.43	55.67	50.70	47.32	44.92	43.17	41.86	40.86	40.10	39.51	39.05
3000	281.33	156.20	115.16	95.14	83.50	76.05	70.98	67.38	64.75	62.78	61.29	60.15	59.26	58.57
4000	375.10	208.26	153.54	126.85	111.34	101.40	94.64	89.84	86.33	83.71	81.72	80.20	79.01	78.09
5000	468.88	260.32	191.93	158.56	139.17	126.75	118.30	112.29	107.91	104.63	102.15	100.24	98.77	97.62
6000	562.65	312.39	230.31	190.27	167.00	152.10	141.95	134.75	129.49	125.56	122.58	120.29	118.52	117.14
7000	656.43	364.45	268.70	221.98	194.83	177.45	165.61	157.21	151.07	146.48	143.01	140.34	138.27	136.66
8000	750.20	416.51	307.08	253.69	222.67	202.80	189.27	179.67	172.65	167.41	163.44	160.39	158.02	156.18
9000	843.98	468.58	345.47	285.40	250.50	228.15	212.93	202.12	194.23	188.34	183.87	180.43	177.78	175.70
10000	937.75	520.64	383.85	317.11	278.33	253.50	236.59	224.58	215.81	209.26	204.29	200.48	197.53	195.23
11000	1031.53	572.70	422.24	348.82	306.16	278.85	260.24	247.04	237.39	230.19	224.72	220.53	217.28	214.75
12000	1125.30	624.77	460.62	380.53	334.00	304.20	283.90	269.50	258.97	251.11	245.15	240.58	237.03	234.27
13000	1219.08	676.83	499.01	412.24	361.83	329.54	307.56	291.95	280.55	272.04	265.58	260.63	256.79	253.79
14000	1312.85	728.89	537.39	443.95	389.66	354.89	331.22	314.41	302.13	292.96	286.01	280.67	276.54	273.31
15000	1406.63	780.96	575.78	475.66	417.49	380.24	354.88	336.87	323.71	313.89	306.44	300.72	296.29	292.84
16000	1500.40	833.02	614.16	507.37	445.33	405.59	378.53	359.33	345.29	334.81	326.87	320.77	316.04	312.36
17000	1594.18	885.08	652.55	539.08	473.16	430.94	402.19	381.79	366.87	355.74	347.30	340.82	335.80	331.88
18000	1687.95	937.15	690.93	570.79	500.99	456.29	425.85	404.24	388.45	376.67	367.73	360.86	355.55	351.40
19000	1781.73	989.21	729.31	602.50	528.82	481.64	449.51	426.70	410.03	397.59	388.16	380.91	375.30	370.92
20000	1875.50	1041.28	767.70	634.21	556.66	506.99	473.17	449.16	431.61	418.52	408.58	400.96	395.05	390.45
21000	1969.28	1093.34	806.08	665.92	584.49	532.34	496.82	471.62	453.19	439.44	429.01	421.01	414.81	409.97
22000	2063.05	1145.40	844.47	697.63	612.32	557.69	520.48	494.07	474.78	460.37	449.44	441.06	434.56	429.49
23000	2156.83	1197.47	882.85	729.34	640.15	583.04	544.14	516.53	496.36	481.29	469.87	461.10	454.31	449.01
24000	2250.60	1249.53	921.24	761.05	667.99	608.39	567.80	538.99	517.94	502.22	490.30	481.15	474.06	468.53
25000	2344.38	1301.59	959.62	792.76	695.82	633.73	591.46	561.45	539.52	523.15	510.73	501.20	493.82	488.06
26000	2438.15	1353.66	998.01	824.47	723.65	659.08	615.11	583.90	561.10	544.07	531.16	521.25	513.57	507.58
27000	2531.93	1405.72	1036.39	856.18	751.48	684.43	638.77	606.36	582.68	565.00	551.59	541.29	533.32	527.10
28000	2625.70	1457.78	1074.78	887.89	779.32	709.78	662.43	628.82	604.26	585.92	572.02	561.34	553.07	546.62
29000	2719.48	1509.85	1113.16	919.60	807.15	735.13	686.09	651.28	625.84	606.85	592.44	581.39	572.83	566.15
30000	2813.25	1561.91	1151.55	951.31	834.98	760.48	709.75	673.74	647.42	627.77	612.87	601.44	592.58	585.67
31000	2907.03	1613.97	1189.93	983.02	862.81	785.83	733.40	696.19	669.00	648.70	633.30	621.49	612.33	605.19
32000	3000.80	1666.04	1228.32	1014.73	890.65	811.18	757.06	718.65	690.58	669.62	653.73	641.53	632.08	624.71
33000	3094.58	1718.10	1266.70	1046.44	918.48	836.53	780.72	741.11	712.16	690.55	674.16	661.58	651.84	644.23
34000	3188.35	1770.16	1305.09	1078.15	946.31	861.88	804.38	763.57	733.74	711.48	694.59	681.63	671.59	663.76
35000	3282.13	1822.23	1343.47	1109.86	974.14	887.23	828.04	786.02	755.32	732.40	715.02	701.68	691.34	683.28
36000	3375.90	1874.29	1381.86	1141.57	1001.98	912.58	851.69	808.48	776.90	753.33	735.45	721.72	711.09	702.80
37000	3469.68	1926.36	1420.24	1173.28	1029.81	937.93	875.35	830.94	798.48	774.25	755.88	741.77	730.85	722.32
38000	3563.45	1978.42	1458.62	1204.99	1057.64	963.27	899.01	853.40	820.06	795.18	776.31	761.82	750.60	741.84
39000	3657.23	2030.48	1497.01	1236.70	1085.47	988.62	922.67	875.85	841.64	816.10	796.73	781.87	770.35	761.37
40000	3751.00	2082.55	1535.39	1268.41	1113.31	1013.97	946.33	898.31	863.22	837.03	817.16	801.92	790.10	780.89
41000	3844.78	2134.61	1573.78	1300.12	1141.14	1039.32	969.98	920.77	884.80	857.96	837.59	821.96	809.86	800.41
42000	3938.55	2186.67	1612.16	1331.83	1168.97	1064.67	993.64	943.23	906.38	878.88	858.02	842.01	829.61	819.93
43000	4032.33	2238.74	1650.55	1363.54	1196.80	1090.02	1017.30	965.69	927.97	899.81	878.45	862.06	849.36	839.45
44000	4126.10	2290.80	1688.93	1395.25	1224.64	1115.37	1040.96	988.14	949.55	920.73	898.88	882.11	869.11	858.98
45000	4219.88	2342.86	1727.32	1426.96	1252.47	1140.72	1064.62	1010.60	971.13	941.66	919.31	902.15	888.87	878.50
46000	4313.65	2394.93	1765.70	1458.67	1280.30	1166.07	1088.27	1033.06	992.71	962.58	939.74	922.20	908.62	898.02
47000	4407.43	2446.99	1804.09	1490.38	1308.13	1191.42	1111.93	1055.52	1014.29	983.51	960.17	942.25	928.37	917.54
48000	4501.20	2499.05	1842.47	1522.09	1335.97	1216.77	1135.59	1077.97	1035.87	1004.43	980.60	962.30	948.12	937.06
49000	4594.98	2551.12	1880.86	1553.80	1363.80	1242.12	1159.25	1100.43	1057.45	1025.36	1001.02	982.34	967.88	956.59
50000	4688.75	2603.18	1919.24	1585.51	1391.63	1267.46	1182.91	1122.89	1079.03	1046.29	1021.45	1002.39	987.63	976.11
55000	5157.63	2863.50	2111.16	1744.06	1530.80	1394.21	1301.20	1235.18	1186.93	1150.91	1123.60	1102.63	1086.39	1073.72
60000	5626.50	3123.82	2303.09	1902.61	1669.96	1520.96	1419.49	1347.47	1294.83	1255.54	1225.74	1202.87	1185.15	1171.33
65000	6095.38	3384.13	2495.01	2061.16	1809.12	1647.70	1537.78	1459.75	1402.74	1360.17	1327.89	1303.11	1283.91	1268.94
70000	6564.25	3644.45	2686.94	2219.71	1948.28	1774.45	1656.07	1572.04	1510.64	1464.80	1430.03	1403.35	1382.68	1366.55
75000	7033.13	3904.77	2878.86	2378.26	2087.45	1901.19	1774.36	1684.33	1618.54	1569.43	1532.18	1503.59	1481.44	1464.16
80000	7502.00	4165.09	3070.78	2536.81	2226.61	2027.94	1892.65	1796.62	1726.44	1674.05	1634.32	1603.83	1580.20	1561.77
85000	7970.88	4425.40	3262.71	2695.36	2365.77	2154.69	2010.94	1908.91	1834.34	1778.68	1736.47	1704.06	1678.96	1659.38
90000	8439.75	4685.72	3454.63	2853.91	2504.93	2281.43	2129.23	2021.20	1942.25	1883.31	1838.61	1804.30	1777.73	1756.99
95000	8908.63	4946.04	3646.55	3012.46	2644.10	2408.18	2247.52	2133.49	2050.15	1987.94	1940.76	1904.54	1876.49	1854.60
100000	9377.50	5206.36	3838.48	3171.01	2783.26	2534.92	2365.81	2245.77	2158.05	2092.57	2042.90	2004.78	1975.25	1952.21

TERM	15 Years	16 Years	17 Years	18 Years	19 Years	20 Years	21 Years	22 Years	23 Years	24 Years	25 Years	30 Years	35 Years	40 Years
AMOUNT														
5	.10	.10	.10	.10	.10	.10	.10	.10	.10	.10	.10	.10	.10	.10
10	.20	.20	.20	.19	.19	.19	.19	.19	.19	.19	.19	.19	.19	.19
15	.30	.29	.29	.29	.29	.29	.29	.29	.29	.29	.29	.29	.28	.28
25	.49	.48	.48	.48	.48	.48	.48	.47	.47	.47	.47	.47	.47	.47
50	.97	.96	.96	.95	.95	.95	.95	.94	.94	.94	.94	.94	.94	.94
75	1.46	1.44	1.44	1.43	1.42	1.42	1.42	1.41	1.41	1.41	1.41	1.41	1.40	1.40
100	1.94	1.92	1.91	1.90	1.90	1.89	1.89	1.88	1.88	1.88	1.88	1.87	1.87	1.87
200	3.87	3.84	3.82	3.80	3.79	3.78	3.77	3.76	3.76	3.75	3.75	3.74	3.74	3.73
300	5.81	5.76	5.73	5.70	5.68	5.67	5.65	5.64	5.63	5.63	5.62	5.61	5.60	5.60
400	7.74	7.68	7.64	7.60	7.58	7.55	7.53	7.52	7.51	7.50	7.49	7.47	7.47	7.46
500	9.68	9.60	9.55	9.50	9.47	9.44	9.42	9.40	9.39	9.37	9.36	9.34	9.33	9.33
600	11.61	11.52	11.46	11.40	11.36	11.33	11.30	11.28	11.26	11.25	11.24	11.21	11.20	11.19
700	13.54	13.44	13.37	13.30	13.25	13.21	13.18	13.16	13.14	13.12	13.11	13.07	13.06	13.06
800	15.48	15.36	15.27	15.20	15.15	15.10	15.06	15.04	15.01	14.99	14.98	14.94	14.93	14.92
900	17.41	17.28	17.18	17.10	17.04	16.99	16.95	16.92	16.89	16.87	16.85	16.81	16.79	16.79
1000	19.35	19.20	19.09	19.00	18.93	18.87	18.83	18.79	18.77	18.74	18.72	18.67	18.66	18.65
2000	38.69	38.40	38.18	38.00	37.86	37.74	37.65	37.58	37.53	37.48	37.44	37.34	37.31	37.30
3000	58.03	57.60	57.26	57.00	56.78	56.61	56.48	56.37	56.29	56.22	56.16	56.01	55.97	55.95
4000	77.37	76.80	76.35	75.99	75.71	75.48	75.30	75.16	75.05	74.95	74.88	74.68	74.62	74.60
5000	96.71	96.00	95.44	94.99	94.64	94.35	94.13	93.95	93.81	93.69	93.60	93.35	93.27	93.25
6000	116.05	115.20	114.52	113.99	113.56	113.22	112.95	112.74	112.57	112.43	112.32	112.02	111.93	111.90
7000	135.39	134.40	133.61	132.98	132.49	132.09	131.78	131.53	131.33	131.17	131.04	130.69	130.58	130.54
8000	154.74	153.60	152.70	151.98	151.41	150.96	150.60	150.32	150.09	149.90	149.76	149.36	149.24	149.19
9000	174.08	172.80	171.78	170.98	170.34	169.83	169.43	169.11	168.85	168.64	168.48	168.03	167.89	167.84
10000	193.42	191.99	190.87	189.98	189.27	188.70	188.25	187.89	187.61	187.38	187.20	186.70	186.54	186.49
11000	212.76	211.19	209.96	208.97	208.19	207.57	207.08	206.68	206.37	206.12	205.92	205.37	205.20	205.14
12000	232.10	230.39	229.04	227.97	227.12	226.44	225.90	225.47	225.13	224.85	224.64	224.04	223.85	223.79
13000	251.44	249.59	248.13	246.97	246.05	245.31	244.73	244.26	243.89	243.59	243.35	242.71	242.50	242.43
14000	270.78	268.79	267.21	265.96	264.97	264.18	263.55	263.05	262.65	262.33	262.07	261.38	261.16	261.08
15000	290.13	287.99	286.30	284.96	283.90	283.05	282.38	281.84	281.41	281.07	280.79	280.05	279.81	279.73
16000	309.47	307.19	305.39	303.96	302.82	301.92	301.20	300.63	300.17	299.80	299.51	298.72	298.47	298.38
17000	328.81	326.39	324.47	322.96	321.75	320.79	320.03	319.42	318.93	318.54	318.23	317.39	317.12	317.03
18000	348.15	345.59	343.56	341.95	340.68	339.66	338.85	338.21	337.69	337.28	336.95	336.06	335.77	335.68
19000	367.49	364.79	362.65	360.95	359.60	358.53	357.68	357.00	356.45	356.02	355.67	354.73	354.43	354.33
20000	386.83	383.98	381.73	379.95	378.53	377.40	376.50	375.78	375.21	374.75	374.39	373.40	373.08	372.97
21000	406.17	403.18	400.82	398.94	397.46	396.27	395.33	394.57	393.97	393.49	393.11	392.07	391.73	391.62
22000	425.51	422.38	419.91	417.94	416.38	415.14	414.15	413.36	412.73	412.23	411.83	410.74	410.39	410.27
23000	444.86	441.58	438.99	436.94	435.31	434.01	432.98	432.15	431.49	430.97	430.55	429.41	429.04	428.92
24000	464.20	460.78	458.08	455.94	454.23	452.88	451.80	450.94	450.25	449.70	449.27	448.08	447.70	447.57
25000	483.54	479.98	477.16	474.93	473.16	471.75	470.63	469.73	469.01	468.44	467.98	466.75	466.35	466.22
26000	502.88	499.18	496.25	493.93	492.09	490.62	489.45	488.52	487.77	487.18	486.70	485.42	485.00	484.86
27000	522.22	518.38	515.34	512.93	511.01	509.49	508.28	507.31	506.53	505.92	505.42	504.09	503.66	503.51
28000	541.56	537.58	534.42	531.92	529.94	528.36	527.10	526.10	525.29	524.65	524.14	522.76	522.31	522.16
29000	560.90	556.77	553.51	550.92	548.87	547.23	545.93	544.89	544.05	543.39	542.86	541.43	540.97	540.81
30000	580.25	575.97	572.60	569.92	567.79	566.10	564.75	563.67	562.82	562.13	561.58	560.10	559.62	559.46
31000	599.59	595.17	591.68	588.92	586.72	584.97	583.58	582.46	581.58	580.87	580.30	578.77	578.27	578.11
32000	618.93	614.37	610.77	607.91	605.64	603.84	602.40	601.25	600.34	599.60	599.02	597.44	596.93	596.76
33000	638.27	633.57	629.86	626.91	624.57	622.71	621.22	620.04	619.10	618.34	617.74	616.11	615.58	615.40
34000	657.61	652.77	648.94	645.91	643.50	641.58	640.05	638.83	637.86	637.08	636.46	634.78	634.23	634.05
35000	676.95	671.97	668.03	664.90	662.42	660.45	658.87	657.62	656.62	655.82	655.18	653.45	652.89	652.70
36000	696.29	691.17	687.11	683.90	681.35	679.32	677.70	676.41	675.38	674.55	673.90	672.12	671.54	671.35
37000	715.64	710.37	706.20	702.90	700.28	698.19	696.52	695.20	694.14	693.29	692.61	690.79	690.20	690.00
38000	734.98	729.57	725.29	721.90	719.20	717.06	715.35	713.99	712.90	712.03	711.33	709.46	708.85	708.65
39000	754.32	748.76	744.37	740.89	738.13	735.93	734.17	732.78	731.66	730.77	730.05	728.13	727.50	727.29
40000	773.66	767.96	763.46	759.89	757.05	754.80	753.00	751.56	750.42	749.50	748.77	746.80	746.16	745.94
41000	793.00	787.16	782.55	778.89	775.98	773.67	771.82	770.35	769.18	768.24	767.49	765.47	764.81	764.59
42000	812.34	806.36	801.63	797.88	794.91	792.54	790.65	789.14	787.94	786.98	786.21	784.14	783.46	783.24
43000	831.68	825.56	820.72	816.88	813.83	811.41	809.47	807.93	806.70	805.72	804.93	802.81	802.12	801.89
44000	851.02	844.76	839.81	835.88	832.76	830.28	828.30	826.72	825.46	824.45	823.65	821.48	820.77	820.54
45000	870.37	863.96	858.89	854.88	851.69	849.15	847.12	845.51	844.22	843.19	842.37	840.15	839.43	839.19
46000	889.71	883.16	877.98	873.87	870.61	868.02	865.95	864.30	862.98	861.93	861.09	858.82	858.08	857.83
47000	909.05	902.36	897.06	892.87	889.54	886.89	884.77	883.09	881.74	880.67	879.81	877.49	876.73	876.48
48000	928.39	921.55	916.15	911.87	908.46	905.76	903.60	901.88	900.50	899.40	898.53	896.16	895.39	895.13
49000	947.73	940.75	935.24	930.86	927.39	924.63	922.42	920.66	919.26	918.14	917.24	914.83	914.04	913.78
50000	967.07	959.95	954.32	949.86	946.32	943.50	941.25	939.45	938.02	936.88	935.96	933.50	932.69	932.43
55000	1063.78	1055.95	1049.76	1044.85	1040.95	1037.84	1035.37	1033.40	1031.82	1030.57	1029.56	1026.85	1025.96	1025.67
60000	1160.49	1151.94	1145.19	1139.83	1135.58	1132.19	1129.50	1127.34	1125.63	1124.25	1123.16	1120.20	1119.23	1118.91
65000	1257.19	1247.94	1240.62	1234.82	1230.21	1226.54	1223.62	1221.29	1219.43	1217.94	1216.75	1213.55	1212.50	1212.15
70000	1353.90	1343.93	1336.05	1329.80	1324.84	1320.89	1317.74	1315.23	1313.23	1311.63	1310.35	1306.90	1305.77	1305.40
75000	1450.61	1439.93	1431.48	1424.79	1419.47	1415.24	1411.87	1409.18	1407.03	1405.31	1403.94	1400.25	1399.04	1398.64
80000	1547.31	1535.92	1526.92	1519.78	1514.10	1509.59	1505.99	1503.12	1500.83	1499.00	1497.54	1493.60	1492.31	1491.88
85000	1644.02	1631.92	1622.35	1614.76	1608.73	1603.94	1600.12	1597.07	1594.63	1592.69	1591.13	1586.95	1585.58	1585.12
90000	1740.73	1727.91	1717.78	1709.75	1703.37	1698.29	1694.24	1691.01	1688.44	1686.38	1684.73	1680.30	1678.85	1678.37
95000	1837.43	1823.91	1813.21	1804.73	1798.00	1792.64	1788.37	1784.96	1782.24	1780.06	1778.33	1773.65	1772.12	1771.61
100000	1934.14	1919.90	1908.64	1899.72	1892.63	1886.99	1882.49	1878.90	1876.04	1873.75	1871.92	1867.00	1865.38	1864.85

MONTHLY PAYMENT
REQUIRED TO AMORTIZE A LOAN

TERM	1 Year	2 Years	3 Years	4 Years	5 Years	6 Years	7 Years	8 Years	9 Years	10 Years	11 Years	12 Years	13 Years	14 Years
AMOUNT														
5	.47	.27	.20	.16	.14	.13	.12	.12	.11	.11	.11	.11	.10	.10
10	.94	.53	.39	.32	.28	.26	.24	.23	.22	.21	.21	.21	.20	.20
15	1.41	.79	.58	.48	.42	.39	.36	.34	.33	.32	.31	.31	.30	.30
25	2.35	1.31	.96	.80	.70	.64	.60	.57	.54	.53	.52	.51	.50	.49
50	4.69	2.61	1.92	1.59	1.40	1.27	1.19	1.13	1.08	1.05	1.03	1.01	.99	.98
75	7.04	3.91	2.88	2.38	2.09	1.91	1.78	1.69	1.62	1.58	1.54	1.51	1.49	1.47
100	9.38	5.21	3.84	3.18	2.79	2.54	2.37	2.25	2.16	2.10	2.05	2.01	1.98	1.96
200	18.76	10.42	7.68	6.35	5.57	5.08	4.74	4.50	4.32	4.19	4.09	4.02	3.96	3.91
300	28.14	15.63	11.52	9.52	8.36	7.61	7.11	6.75	6.48	6.29	6.14	6.02	5.94	5.87
400	37.52	20.84	15.36	12.69	11.14	10.15	9.47	8.99	8.64	8.38	8.18	8.03	7.91	7.82
500	46.90	26.04	19.20	15.87	13.93	12.69	11.84	11.24	10.80	10.48	10.23	10.04	9.89	9.78
600	56.28	31.25	23.04	19.04	16.71	15.22	14.21	13.49	12.96	12.57	12.27	12.04	11.87	11.73
700	65.66	36.46	26.88	22.21	19.50	17.76	16.58	15.74	15.12	14.66	14.32	14.05	13.84	13.68
800	75.03	41.67	30.72	25.38	22.28	20.30	18.94	17.98	17.28	16.76	16.36	16.06	15.82	15.64
900	84.41	46.87	34.56	28.56	25.07	22.83	21.31	20.23	19.44	18.85	18.41	18.06	17.80	17.59
1000	93.79	52.08	38.40	31.73	27.85	25.37	23.68	22.48	21.60	20.95	20.45	20.07	19.78	19.55
2000	187.58	104.16	76.80	63.45	55.70	50.73	47.35	44.95	43.20	41.89	40.90	40.14	39.55	39.09
3000	281.37	156.23	115.20	95.18	83.55	76.10	71.03	67.43	64.80	62.83	61.34	60.20	59.32	58.63
4000	375.15	208.31	153.60	126.90	111.39	101.46	94.70	89.90	86.39	83.78	81.79	80.27	79.09	78.17
5000	468.94	260.38	191.99	158.62	139.24	126.83	118.37	112.37	107.99	104.72	102.24	100.33	98.86	97.71
6000	562.73	312.46	230.39	190.35	167.09	152.19	142.05	134.85	129.59	125.66	122.68	120.40	118.63	117.25
7000	656.51	364.54	268.79	222.07	194.93	177.55	165.72	157.32	151.18	146.60	143.13	140.47	138.40	136.79
8000	750.30	416.61	307.19	253.79	222.78	202.92	189.39	179.80	172.78	167.55	163.58	160.53	158.17	156.33
9000	844.09	468.69	345.58	285.52	250.63	228.28	213.07	202.27	194.38	188.49	184.02	180.60	177.94	175.87
10000	937.87	520.76	383.98	317.24	278.47	253.65	236.74	224.74	215.98	209.43	204.47	200.66	197.71	195.41
11000	1031.66	572.84	422.38	348.97	306.32	279.01	260.41	247.22	237.57	230.37	224.92	220.73	217.48	214.95
12000	1125.45	624.92	460.78	380.69	334.17	304.37	284.09	269.69	259.17	251.32	245.36	240.79	237.25	234.49
13000	1219.24	676.99	499.18	412.41	362.01	329.74	307.76	292.16	280.77	272.26	265.81	260.86	257.03	254.03
14000	1313.02	729.07	537.57	444.14	389.86	355.10	331.43	314.64	302.36	293.20	286.26	280.93	276.80	273.58
15000	1406.81	781.14	575.97	475.86	417.71	380.47	355.11	337.11	323.96	314.15	306.70	300.99	296.57	293.12
16000	1500.60	833.22	614.37	507.58	445.55	405.83	378.78	359.59	345.56	335.09	327.15	321.06	316.34	312.66
17000	1594.38	885.30	652.77	539.31	473.40	431.19	402.46	382.06	367.16	356.03	347.60	341.12	336.11	332.20
18000	1688.17	937.37	691.16	571.03	501.25	456.56	426.13	404.53	388.75	376.97	368.04	361.19	355.88	351.74
19000	1781.96	989.45	729.56	602.75	529.09	481.92	449.80	427.01	410.35	397.92	388.49	381.25	375.65	371.28
20000	1875.74	1041.52	767.96	634.48	556.94	507.29	473.48	449.48	431.95	418.86	408.94	401.32	395.42	390.82
21000	1969.53	1093.60	806.36	666.20	584.79	532.65	497.15	471.95	453.54	439.80	429.38	421.39	415.19	410.36
22000	2063.32	1145.67	844.75	697.93	612.64	558.02	520.82	494.43	475.14	460.74	449.83	441.45	434.96	429.90
23000	2157.11	1197.75	883.15	729.65	640.48	583.38	544.50	516.90	496.74	481.69	470.27	461.52	454.73	449.44
24000	2250.89	1249.83	921.55	761.37	668.33	608.74	568.17	539.38	518.33	502.63	490.72	481.58	474.50	468.98
25000	2344.68	1301.90	959.95	793.10	696.18	634.11	591.84	561.85	539.93	523.57	511.17	501.65	494.27	488.52
26000	2438.47	1353.98	998.35	824.82	724.02	659.47	615.52	584.32	561.53	544.52	531.61	521.71	514.05	508.06
27000	2532.25	1406.05	1036.74	856.54	751.87	684.84	639.19	606.80	583.13	565.46	552.06	541.78	533.82	527.61
28000	2626.04	1458.13	1075.14	888.27	779.72	710.20	662.86	629.27	604.72	586.40	572.51	561.85	553.59	547.15
29000	2719.83	1510.21	1113.54	919.99	807.56	735.56	686.54	651.74	626.32	607.34	592.95	581.91	573.36	566.69
30000	2813.61	1562.28	1151.94	951.71	835.41	760.93	710.21	674.22	647.92	628.29	613.40	601.98	593.13	586.23
31000	2907.40	1614.36	1190.33	983.44	863.26	786.29	733.89	696.69	669.51	649.23	633.85	622.04	612.90	605.77
32000	3001.19	1666.43	1228.73	1015.16	891.10	811.66	757.56	719.17	691.11	670.17	654.29	642.11	632.67	625.31
33000	3094.98	1718.51	1267.13	1046.89	918.95	837.02	781.23	741.64	712.71	691.11	674.74	662.17	652.44	644.85
34000	3188.76	1770.59	1305.53	1078.61	946.80	862.38	804.91	764.11	734.31	712.06	695.19	682.24	672.21	664.39
35000	3282.55	1822.66	1343.92	1110.33	974.64	887.75	828.58	786.59	755.90	733.00	715.63	702.31	691.98	683.93
36000	3376.34	1874.74	1382.32	1142.06	1002.49	913.11	852.25	809.06	777.50	753.94	736.08	722.37	711.75	703.47
37000	3470.12	1926.81	1420.72	1173.78	1030.34	938.48	875.93	831.53	799.10	774.89	756.53	742.44	731.52	723.01
38000	3563.91	1978.89	1459.12	1205.50	1058.18	963.84	899.60	854.01	820.69	795.83	776.97	762.50	751.29	742.55
39000	3657.70	2030.97	1497.52	1237.23	1086.03	989.21	923.27	876.48	842.29	816.77	797.42	782.57	771.07	762.09
40000	3751.48	2083.04	1535.91	1268.95	1113.88	1014.57	946.95	898.96	863.89	837.71	817.87	802.63	790.84	781.63
41000	3845.27	2135.12	1574.31	1300.67	1141.72	1039.93	970.62	921.43	885.49	858.66	838.31	822.70	810.61	801.18
42000	3939.06	2187.19	1612.71	1332.40	1169.57	1065.30	994.29	943.90	907.08	879.60	858.76	842.77	830.38	820.72
43000	4032.85	2239.27	1651.11	1364.12	1197.42	1090.66	1017.97	966.38	928.68	900.54	879.21	862.83	850.15	840.26
44000	4126.63	2291.34	1689.50	1395.85	1225.27	1116.03	1041.64	988.85	950.28	921.48	899.65	882.90	869.92	859.80
45000	4220.42	2343.42	1727.90	1427.57	1253.11	1141.39	1065.31	1011.32	971.87	942.43	920.10	902.96	889.69	879.34
46000	4314.21	2395.50	1766.30	1459.29	1280.96	1166.75	1088.99	1033.80	993.47	963.37	940.54	923.03	909.46	898.88
47000	4407.99	2447.57	1804.70	1491.02	1308.81	1192.12	1112.66	1056.27	1015.07	984.31	960.99	943.09	929.23	918.42
48000	4501.78	2499.65	1843.09	1522.74	1336.65	1217.48	1136.34	1078.75	1036.66	1005.26	981.44	963.16	949.00	937.96
49000	4595.57	2551.72	1881.49	1554.46	1364.50	1242.85	1160.01	1101.22	1058.26	1026.20	1001.88	983.23	968.77	957.50
50000	4689.35	2603.80	1919.89	1586.19	1392.35	1268.21	1183.68	1123.69	1079.86	1047.14	1022.33	1003.29	988.54	977.04
55000	5158.29	2864.18	2111.88	1744.81	1531.58	1395.03	1302.05	1236.06	1187.84	1151.85	1124.56	1103.62	1087.40	1074.75
60000	5627.22	3124.56	2303.87	1903.42	1670.81	1521.85	1420.42	1348.43	1295.83	1256.57	1226.80	1203.95	1186.25	1172.45
65000	6096.16	3384.94	2495.86	2062.04	1810.05	1648.67	1538.79	1460.80	1403.82	1361.28	1329.03	1304.28	1285.11	1270.15
70000	6565.09	3645.32	2687.84	2220.66	1949.28	1775.49	1657.15	1573.17	1511.80	1466.00	1431.26	1404.61	1383.96	1367.86
75000	7034.03	3905.70	2879.83	2379.28	2088.52	1902.31	1775.52	1685.54	1619.79	1570.71	1533.49	1504.93	1482.81	1465.56
80000	7502.96	4166.08	3071.82	2537.90	2227.75	2029.13	1893.89	1797.91	1727.77	1675.42	1635.73	1605.26	1581.67	1563.26
85000	7971.90	4426.46	3263.80	2696.51	2366.98	2155.95	2012.26	1910.28	1835.76	1780.14	1737.96	1705.59	1680.52	1660.97
90000	8440.84	4686.84	3455.80	2855.13	2506.22	2282.77	2130.62	2022.64	1943.74	1884.85	1840.19	1805.92	1779.38	1758.67
95000	8909.77	4947.22	3647.79	3013.75	2645.45	2409.59	2248.99	2135.01	2051.73	1989.56	1942.42	1906.25	1878.23	1856.38
100000	9378.71	5207.59	3839.77	3172.37	2784.69	2536.42	2367.36	2247.38	2159.71	2094.28	2044.66	2006.58	1977.08	1954.08

TERM AMOUNT	15 Years	16 Years	17 Years	18 Years	19 Years	20 Years	21 Years	22 Years	23 Years	24 Years	25 Years	30 Years	35 Years	40 Years
5	.10	.10	.10	.10	.10	.10	.10	.10	.10	.10	.10	.10	.10	.10
10	.20	.20	.20	.20	.19	.19	.19	.19	.19	.19	.19	.19	.19	.19
15	.30	.29	.29	.29	.29	.29	.29	.29	.29	.29	.29	.29	.29	.29
25	.49	.49	.48	.48	.48	.48	.48	.48	.47	.47	.47	.47	.47	.47
50	.97	.97	.96	.96	.95	.95	.95	.95	.94	.94	.94	.94	.94	.94
75	1.46	1.45	1.44	1.43	1.43	1.42	1.42	1.42	1.41	1.41	1.41	1.41	1.41	1.41
100	1.94	1.93	1.92	1.91	1.90	1.89	1.89	1.89	1.88	1.88	1.88	1.87	1.87	1.87
200	3.88	3.85	3.83	3.81	3.79	3.78	3.77	3.77	3.76	3.76	3.75	3.74	3.74	3.74
300	5.81	5.77	5.74	5.71	5.69	5.67	5.66	5.65	5.64	5.63	5.63	5.61	5.61	5.61
400	7.75	7.69	7.65	7.61	7.58	7.56	7.54	7.53	7.52	7.51	7.50	7.48	7.47	7.47
500	9.69	9.61	9.56	9.51	9.48	9.45	9.43	9.41	9.40	9.38	9.37	9.35	9.34	9.34
600	11.62	11.54	11.47	11.42	11.37	11.34	11.31	11.29	11.27	11.26	11.25	11.22	11.21	11.21
700	13.56	13.46	13.38	13.32	13.27	13.23	13.20	13.17	13.15	13.14	13.12	13.09	13.08	13.07
800	15.49	15.38	15.29	15.22	15.16	15.12	15.08	15.05	15.03	15.01	15.00	14.96	14.94	14.94
900	17.43	17.30	17.20	17.12	17.06	17.01	16.97	16.93	16.91	16.89	16.87	16.83	16.81	16.81
1000	19.37	19.22	19.11	19.02	18.95	18.89	18.85	18.81	18.79	18.76	18.74	18.70	18.68	18.67
2000	38.73	38.44	38.22	38.04	37.90	37.78	37.69	37.62	37.57	37.52	37.48	37.39	37.35	37.34
3000	58.09	57.66	57.32	57.06	56.84	56.67	56.54	56.43	56.35	56.28	56.22	56.08	56.03	56.01
4000	77.45	76.88	76.43	76.07	75.79	75.56	75.38	75.24	75.13	75.04	74.96	74.77	74.70	74.68
5000	96.81	96.10	95.53	95.09	94.74	94.45	94.23	94.05	93.91	93.79	93.70	93.46	93.38	93.35
6000	116.17	115.31	114.64	114.11	113.68	113.34	113.07	112.86	112.69	112.55	112.44	112.15	112.05	112.02
7000	135.53	134.53	133.75	133.12	132.63	132.23	131.92	131.67	131.47	131.31	131.18	130.84	130.73	130.69
8000	154.89	153.75	152.85	152.14	151.57	151.12	150.76	150.48	150.25	150.07	149.92	149.53	149.40	149.36
9000	174.25	172.97	171.96	171.16	170.52	170.01	169.61	169.29	169.03	168.83	168.66	168.22	168.08	168.03
10000	193.61	192.19	191.06	190.17	189.47	188.90	188.45	188.10	187.81	187.58	187.40	186.91	186.75	186.70
11000	212.97	211.40	210.17	209.19	208.41	207.79	207.30	206.91	206.59	206.34	206.14	205.60	205.43	205.37
12000	232.33	230.62	229.27	228.21	227.36	226.68	226.14	225.72	225.37	225.10	224.88	224.29	224.10	224.04
13000	251.69	249.84	248.38	247.22	246.30	245.57	244.99	244.52	244.15	243.86	243.62	242.98	242.77	242.71
14000	271.05	269.06	267.49	266.24	265.25	264.46	263.83	263.33	262.93	262.61	262.36	261.67	261.45	261.37
15000	290.41	288.28	286.59	285.26	284.20	283.35	282.68	282.14	281.71	281.37	281.10	280.36	280.12	280.04
16000	309.77	307.50	305.70	304.27	303.14	302.24	301.52	300.95	300.50	300.13	299.84	299.06	298.80	298.71
17000	329.13	326.71	324.80	323.29	322.09	321.13	320.37	319.76	319.28	318.89	318.58	317.75	317.47	317.38
18000	348.49	345.93	343.91	342.31	341.03	340.02	339.21	338.57	338.06	337.65	337.32	336.44	336.15	336.05
19000	367.85	365.15	363.02	361.32	359.98	358.91	358.06	357.38	356.84	356.40	356.06	355.13	354.82	354.72
20000	387.21	384.37	382.12	380.34	378.93	377.80	376.90	376.19	375.62	375.16	374.80	373.82	373.50	373.39
21000	406.57	403.59	401.23	399.36	397.87	396.69	395.75	395.00	394.40	393.92	393.54	392.51	392.17	392.06
22000	425.93	422.80	420.33	418.37	416.82	415.58	414.59	413.81	413.18	412.68	412.28	411.20	410.85	410.73
23000	445.29	442.02	439.44	437.39	435.76	434.47	433.44	432.62	431.96	431.44	431.02	429.89	429.52	429.40
24000	464.65	461.24	458.54	456.41	454.71	453.36	452.28	451.43	450.74	450.19	449.76	448.58	448.19	448.07
25000	484.01	480.46	477.65	475.42	473.66	472.25	471.13	470.23	469.52	468.95	468.50	467.27	466.87	466.74
26000	503.37	499.68	496.76	494.44	492.60	491.14	489.97	489.04	488.30	487.71	487.24	485.96	485.54	485.41
27000	522.73	518.90	515.86	513.46	511.55	510.03	508.82	507.85	507.08	506.47	505.98	504.65	504.22	504.08
28000	542.09	538.11	534.97	532.47	530.49	528.92	527.66	526.66	525.86	525.22	524.71	523.34	522.89	522.74
29000	561.45	557.33	554.07	551.49	549.44	547.81	546.51	545.47	544.64	543.98	543.45	542.03	541.57	541.41
30000	580.81	576.55	573.18	570.51	568.39	566.70	565.35	564.28	563.42	562.74	562.19	560.72	560.24	560.08
31000	600.17	595.77	592.29	589.53	587.33	585.59	584.20	583.09	582.21	581.50	580.93	579.42	578.92	578.75
32000	619.53	614.99	611.39	608.54	606.28	604.48	603.04	601.90	600.99	600.26	599.67	598.11	597.59	597.42
33000	638.90	634.20	630.50	627.56	625.22	623.37	621.89	620.71	619.77	619.01	618.41	616.80	616.27	616.09
34000	658.26	653.42	649.60	646.58	644.17	642.26	640.73	639.52	638.55	637.77	637.15	635.49	634.94	634.76
35000	677.62	672.64	668.71	665.59	663.12	661.15	659.58	658.33	657.33	656.53	655.89	654.18	653.61	653.43
36000	696.98	691.86	687.81	684.61	682.06	680.04	678.42	677.14	676.11	675.29	674.63	672.87	672.29	672.10
37000	716.34	711.08	706.92	703.63	701.01	698.93	697.27	695.95	694.89	694.05	693.37	691.56	690.96	690.77
38000	735.70	730.30	726.03	722.64	719.95	717.82	716.11	714.75	713.67	712.80	712.11	710.25	709.64	709.44
39000	755.06	749.51	745.13	741.66	738.90	736.71	734.96	733.56	732.45	731.56	730.85	728.94	728.31	728.11
40000	774.42	768.73	764.24	760.68	757.85	755.60	753.80	752.37	751.23	750.32	749.59	747.63	746.99	746.78
41000	793.78	787.95	783.34	779.69	776.79	774.49	772.65	771.17	770.01	769.08	768.33	766.32	765.66	765.45
42000	813.14	807.17	802.45	798.71	795.74	793.38	791.49	789.99	788.79	787.83	787.07	785.01	784.34	784.11
43000	832.50	826.39	821.56	817.73	814.69	812.27	810.34	808.80	807.57	806.59	805.81	803.70	803.01	802.78
44000	851.86	845.60	840.66	836.74	833.63	831.16	829.18	827.61	826.35	825.35	824.55	822.39	821.69	821.45
45000	871.22	864.82	859.77	855.76	852.58	850.05	848.03	846.42	845.13	844.11	843.29	841.08	840.36	840.12
46000	890.58	884.04	878.87	874.78	871.52	868.93	866.87	865.23	863.92	862.87	862.03	859.78	859.04	858.79
47000	909.94	903.26	897.98	893.79	890.47	887.82	885.72	884.04	882.70	881.62	880.77	878.47	877.71	877.46
48000	929.30	922.48	917.08	912.81	909.42	906.71	904.56	902.85	901.48	900.38	899.51	897.16	896.38	896.13
49000	948.66	941.70	936.19	931.83	928.36	925.60	923.41	921.66	920.26	919.14	918.25	915.85	915.06	914.80
50000	968.02	960.91	955.30	950.84	947.31	944.49	942.25	940.46	939.04	937.90	936.99	934.54	933.73	933.47
55000	1064.82	1057.00	1050.83	1045.93	1042.04	1038.94	1036.48	1034.51	1032.94	1031.69	1030.68	1027.99	1027.11	1026.81
60000	1161.62	1153.10	1146.35	1141.01	1136.77	1133.39	1130.70	1128.56	1126.84	1125.48	1124.38	1121.44	1120.48	1120.16
65000	1258.43	1249.19	1241.88	1236.10	1231.50	1227.84	1224.93	1222.60	1220.75	1219.27	1218.08	1214.90	1213.85	1213.51
70000	1355.23	1345.28	1337.41	1331.18	1326.23	1322.29	1319.15	1316.65	1314.65	1313.05	1311.78	1308.35	1307.22	1306.85
75000	1452.03	1441.37	1432.94	1426.26	1420.96	1416.74	1413.38	1410.69	1408.55	1406.84	1405.48	1401.80	1400.60	1400.20
80000	1548.83	1537.46	1528.47	1521.35	1515.69	1511.19	1507.60	1504.74	1502.46	1500.63	1499.18	1495.26	1493.97	1493.55
85000	1645.63	1633.55	1624.00	1616.43	1610.42	1605.64	1601.83	1598.79	1596.36	1594.42	1592.87	1588.71	1587.34	1586.89
90000	1742.43	1729.64	1719.53	1711.51	1705.15	1700.09	1696.05	1692.83	1690.26	1688.21	1686.57	1682.16	1680.72	1680.24
95000	1839.23	1825.73	1815.06	1806.60	1799.88	1794.53	1790.28	1786.88	1784.17	1782.00	1780.27	1775.62	1774.09	1773.59
100000	1936.04	1921.82	1910.59	1901.68	1894.61	1888.98	1884.50	1880.92	1878.07	1875.79	1873.97	1869.07	1867.46	1866.93

MONTHLY PAYMENT
REQUIRED TO AMORTIZE A LOAN

TERM / AMOUNT	1 Year	2 Years	3 Years	4 Years	5 Years	6 Years	7 Years	8 Years	9 Years	10 Years	11 Years	12 Years	13 Years	14 Years
5	.47	.27	.20	.16	.14	.13	.12	.12	.11	.11	.11	.11	.10	.10
10	.94	.53	.39	.32	.28	.26	.24	.23	.22	.22	.21	.21	.20	.20
15	1.41	.79	.58	.48	.42	.39	.36	.34	.33	.32	.31	.31	.30	.30
25	2.35	1.31	.97	.80	.70	.64	.60	.57	.55	.53	.52	.51	.50	.50
50	4.70	2.61	1.93	1.59	1.40	1.28	1.19	1.13	1.09	1.06	1.03	1.01	1.00	.99
75	7.04	3.91	2.89	2.39	2.10	1.91	1.79	1.70	1.63	1.58	1.54	1.52	1.49	1.48
100	9.39	5.22	3.85	3.18	2.80	2.55	2.38	2.26	2.17	2.11	2.06	2.02	1.99	1.97
200	18.77	10.43	7.69	6.36	5.59	5.09	4.75	4.51	4.34	4.21	4.11	4.03	3.97	3.93
300	28.16	15.64	11.54	9.54	8.38	7.63	7.13	6.77	6.50	6.31	6.16	6.05	5.96	5.89
400	37.54	20.86	15.38	12.72	11.17	10.17	9.50	9.02	8.67	8.41	8.21	8.06	7.94	7.85
500	46.92	26.07	19.23	15.89	13.96	12.72	11.87	11.27	10.84	10.51	10.26	10.07	9.93	9.81
600	56.31	31.28	23.07	19.07	16.75	15.26	14.25	13.53	13.00	12.61	12.32	12.09	11.91	11.77
700	65.69	36.49	26.92	22.25	19.54	17.80	16.62	15.78	15.17	14.71	14.37	14.10	13.90	13.74
800	75.07	41.71	30.76	25.43	22.33	20.34	18.99	18.04	17.34	16.81	16.42	16.12	15.88	15.70
900	84.46	46.92	34.61	28.61	25.12	22.89	21.37	20.29	19.50	18.92	18.47	18.13	17.86	17.66
1000	93.84	52.13	38.45	31.78	27.91	25.43	23.74	22.54	21.67	21.02	20.52	20.14	19.85	19.62
2000	187.68	104.26	76.90	63.56	55.81	50.85	47.48	45.08	43.33	42.03	41.04	40.28	39.69	39.24
3000	281.51	156.38	115.35	95.34	83.72	76.28	71.21	67.62	65.00	63.04	61.56	60.42	59.54	58.85
4000	375.35	208.51	153.80	127.12	111.62	101.70	94.95	90.16	86.66	84.05	82.07	80.56	79.38	78.47
5000	469.18	260.63	192.25	158.90	139.52	127.12	118.68	112.70	108.32	105.06	102.59	100.69	99.23	98.08
6000	563.02	312.76	230.70	190.67	167.43	152.55	142.42	135.23	129.99	126.07	123.11	120.83	119.07	117.70
7000	656.85	364.88	269.15	222.45	195.33	177.97	166.15	157.77	151.65	147.08	143.62	140.97	138.91	137.31
8000	750.69	417.01	307.60	254.23	223.24	203.40	189.89	180.31	173.31	168.09	164.14	161.11	158.76	156.93
9000	844.52	469.13	346.05	286.01	251.14	228.82	213.63	202.85	194.98	189.11	184.66	181.24	178.60	176.54
10000	938.36	521.26	384.50	317.79	279.04	254.24	237.36	225.39	216.64	210.12	205.17	201.38	198.45	196.16
11000	1032.19	573.38	422.95	349.56	306.95	279.67	261.10	247.92	238.30	231.13	225.69	221.52	218.29	215.77
12000	1126.03	625.51	461.40	381.34	334.85	305.09	284.83	270.46	259.97	252.14	246.21	241.66	238.14	235.39
13000	1219.86	677.64	499.85	413.12	362.76	330.51	308.57	293.00	281.63	273.15	266.72	261.79	257.98	255.01
14000	1313.70	729.76	538.30	444.90	390.66	355.94	332.30	315.54	303.30	294.16	287.24	281.93	277.82	274.62
15000	1407.53	781.89	576.75	476.68	418.56	381.36	356.04	338.08	324.96	315.17	307.76	302.07	297.67	294.24
16000	1501.37	834.01	615.20	508.46	446.47	406.79	379.78	360.62	346.62	336.18	328.27	322.21	317.51	313.85
17000	1595.20	886.14	653.65	540.23	474.37	432.21	403.51	383.15	368.29	357.20	348.79	342.34	337.36	333.47
18000	1689.04	938.26	692.10	572.01	502.28	457.63	427.25	405.69	389.95	378.21	369.31	362.48	357.20	353.08
19000	1782.87	990.39	730.55	603.79	530.18	483.06	450.98	428.23	411.61	399.22	389.82	382.62	377.04	372.70
20000	1876.71	1042.51	769.00	635.57	558.08	508.48	474.72	450.77	433.28	420.23	410.34	402.76	396.89	392.31
21000	1970.54	1094.64	807.45	667.35	585.99	533.90	498.45	473.31	454.94	441.24	430.86	422.90	416.73	411.93
22000	2064.38	1146.76	845.90	699.12	613.89	559.33	522.19	495.84	476.60	462.25	451.37	443.03	436.58	431.54
23000	2158.21	1198.89	884.35	730.90	641.80	584.75	545.92	518.38	498.27	483.26	471.89	463.17	456.42	451.16
24000	2252.05	1251.01	922.80	762.68	669.70	610.18	569.66	540.92	519.93	504.27	492.41	483.31	476.27	470.78
25000	2345.88	1303.14	961.25	794.46	697.60	635.60	593.40	563.46	541.59	525.28	512.92	503.45	496.11	490.39
26000	2439.72	1355.27	999.69	826.24	725.51	661.02	617.13	586.00	563.26	546.30	533.44	523.58	515.95	510.01
27000	2533.55	1407.39	1038.14	858.02	753.41	686.45	640.87	608.53	584.92	567.31	553.96	543.72	535.80	529.62
28000	2627.39	1459.52	1076.59	889.79	781.32	711.87	664.60	631.07	606.59	588.32	574.47	563.86	555.64	549.24
29000	2721.23	1511.64	1115.04	921.57	809.22	737.29	688.34	653.61	628.25	609.33	594.99	584.00	575.49	568.85
30000	2815.06	1563.77	1153.49	953.35	837.12	762.72	712.07	676.15	649.91	630.34	615.51	604.13	595.33	588.47
31000	2908.90	1615.89	1191.94	985.13	865.03	788.14	735.81	698.69	671.58	651.35	636.03	624.27	615.17	608.08
32000	3002.73	1668.02	1230.39	1016.91	892.93	813.57	759.55	721.23	693.24	672.36	656.54	644.41	635.02	627.70
33000	3096.57	1720.14	1268.84	1048.68	920.84	838.99	783.28	743.76	714.90	693.37	677.06	664.55	654.86	647.31
34000	3190.40	1772.27	1307.29	1080.46	948.74	864.41	807.02	766.30	736.57	714.39	697.58	684.68	674.71	666.93
35000	3284.24	1824.39	1345.74	1112.24	976.64	889.84	830.75	788.84	758.23	735.40	718.09	704.82	694.55	686.55
36000	3378.07	1876.52	1384.19	1144.02	1004.55	915.26	854.49	811.38	779.89	756.41	738.61	724.96	714.40	706.16
37000	3471.91	1928.64	1422.64	1175.80	1032.45	940.68	878.22	833.92	801.56	777.42	759.13	745.10	734.24	725.78
38000	3565.74	1980.77	1461.09	1207.57	1060.35	966.11	901.96	856.45	823.22	798.43	779.64	765.23	754.08	745.39
39000	3659.58	2032.90	1499.54	1239.35	1088.26	991.53	925.69	878.99	844.88	819.44	800.16	785.37	773.93	765.01
40000	3753.41	2085.02	1537.99	1271.13	1116.16	1016.96	949.43	901.53	866.55	840.45	820.68	805.51	793.77	784.62
41000	3847.25	2137.15	1576.44	1302.91	1144.07	1042.38	973.17	924.07	888.21	861.46	841.19	825.65	813.62	804.24
42000	3941.08	2189.27	1614.89	1334.69	1171.97	1067.80	996.90	946.61	909.88	882.47	861.71	845.79	833.46	823.85
43000	4034.92	2241.40	1653.34	1366.47	1199.87	1093.23	1020.64	969.15	931.54	903.49	882.23	865.92	853.30	843.47
44000	4128.75	2293.52	1691.79	1398.24	1227.78	1118.65	1044.37	991.68	953.20	924.50	902.74	886.06	873.15	863.08
45000	4222.59	2345.65	1730.24	1430.02	1255.68	1144.07	1068.11	1014.22	974.87	945.51	923.26	906.20	892.99	882.70
46000	4316.42	2397.77	1768.69	1461.80	1283.59	1169.50	1091.84	1036.76	996.53	966.52	943.78	926.34	912.84	902.32
47000	4410.26	2449.90	1807.14	1493.58	1311.49	1194.92	1115.58	1059.30	1018.19	987.53	964.29	946.47	932.68	921.93
48000	4504.09	2502.02	1845.59	1525.36	1339.39	1220.35	1139.32	1081.84	1039.86	1008.54	984.81	966.61	952.53	941.55
49000	4597.93	2554.15	1884.04	1557.13	1367.30	1245.77	1163.05	1104.37	1061.52	1029.55	1005.33	986.75	972.37	961.16
50000	4691.76	2606.28	1922.49	1588.91	1395.20	1271.19	1186.79	1126.91	1083.18	1050.56	1025.84	1006.89	992.21	980.78
55000	5160.94	2866.90	2114.73	1747.80	1534.72	1398.31	1305.47	1239.60	1191.50	1155.62	1128.43	1107.57	1091.43	1078.85
60000	5630.12	3127.53	2306.98	1906.69	1674.24	1525.43	1424.14	1352.29	1299.82	1260.68	1231.01	1208.26	1190.66	1176.93
65000	6099.29	3388.16	2499.23	2065.58	1813.76	1652.55	1542.82	1464.98	1408.14	1365.73	1333.60	1308.95	1289.88	1275.01
70000	6568.47	3648.78	2691.48	2224.48	1953.28	1779.67	1661.50	1577.68	1516.46	1470.79	1436.18	1409.64	1389.10	1373.09
75000	7037.64	3909.41	2883.73	2383.37	2092.80	1906.79	1780.18	1690.37	1624.77	1575.84	1538.76	1510.33	1488.32	1471.16
80000	7506.82	4170.04	3075.97	2542.26	2232.32	2033.91	1898.86	1803.06	1733.09	1680.90	1641.35	1611.01	1587.54	1569.24
85000	7976.00	4430.66	3268.22	2701.15	2371.84	2161.03	2017.53	1915.75	1841.41	1785.96	1743.93	1711.70	1686.76	1667.32
90000	8445.17	4691.29	3460.47	2860.04	2511.36	2288.14	2136.21	2028.44	1949.73	1891.01	1846.52	1812.39	1785.98	1765.39
95000	8914.35	4951.92	3652.72	3018.93	2650.88	2415.26	2254.89	2141.13	2058.05	1996.07	1949.10	1913.08	1885.20	1863.47
100000	9383.52	5212.55	3844.97	3177.82	2790.40	2542.38	2373.57	2253.82	2166.36	2101.12	2051.68	2013.77	1984.42	1961.55

TERM AMOUNT	15 Years	16 Years	17 Years	18 Years	19 Years	20 Years	21 Years	22 Years	23 Years	24 Years	25 Years	30 Years	35 Years	40 Years
5	.10	.10	.10	.10	.10	.10	.10	.10	.10	.10	.10	.10	.10	.10
10	.20	.20	.20	.20	.20	.19	.19	.19	.19	.19	.19	.19	.19	.19
15	.30	.29	.29	.29	.29	.29	.29	.29	.29	.29	.29	.29	.29	.29
25	.49	.49	.48	.48	.48	.48	.48	.48	.48	.48	.48	.47	.47	.47
50	.98	.97	.96	.96	.96	.95	.95	.95	.95	.95	.95	.94	.94	.94
75	1.46	1.45	1.44	1.44	1.43	1.43	1.42	1.42	1.42	1.42	1.42	1.41	1.41	1.41
100	1.95	1.93	1.92	1.91	1.91	1.90	1.90	1.89	1.89	1.89	1.89	1.88	1.88	1.88
200	3.89	3.86	3.83	3.82	3.81	3.80	3.79	3.78	3.78	3.77	3.77	3.76	3.76	3.76
300	5.84	5.79	5.76	5.73	5.71	5.70	5.68	5.67	5.66	5.66	5.65	5.64	5.63	5.63
400	7.78	7.72	7.68	7.64	7.62	7.59	7.58	7.56	7.55	7.54	7.53	7.51	7.51	7.51
500	9.72	9.65	9.60	9.55	9.52	9.49	9.47	9.45	9.44	9.42	9.42	9.39	9.38	9.38
600	11.67	11.58	11.52	11.46	11.42	11.39	11.36	11.34	11.32	11.31	11.30	11.27	11.26	11.26
700	13.61	13.51	13.43	13.37	13.32	13.28	13.25	13.23	13.21	13.19	13.18	13.15	13.14	13.13
800	15.55	15.44	15.35	15.28	15.23	15.18	15.15	15.12	15.09	15.08	15.06	15.02	15.01	15.01
900	17.50	17.37	17.27	17.19	17.13	17.08	17.04	17.01	16.98	16.96	16.94	16.90	16.89	16.88
1000	19.44	19.30	19.19	19.10	19.03	18.97	18.93	18.90	18.87	18.84	18.83	18.78	18.76	18.76
2000	38.88	38.60	38.37	38.20	38.06	37.94	37.86	37.79	37.73	37.68	37.65	37.55	37.52	37.51
3000	58.31	57.89	57.56	57.29	57.08	56.91	56.78	56.68	56.59	56.52	56.47	56.33	56.28	56.26
4000	77.75	77.19	76.74	76.39	76.11	75.88	75.71	75.57	75.45	75.36	75.29	75.10	75.04	75.02
5000	97.19	96.48	95.92	95.48	95.13	94.85	94.63	94.46	94.31	94.20	94.11	93.87	93.79	93.77
6000	116.62	115.78	115.11	114.58	114.16	113.82	113.56	113.35	113.18	113.04	112.93	112.65	112.55	112.52
7000	136.06	135.07	134.29	133.67	133.18	132.79	132.48	132.24	132.04	131.88	131.76	131.42	131.31	131.27
8000	155.49	154.37	153.47	152.77	152.21	151.76	151.41	151.13	150.90	150.72	150.58	150.19	150.07	150.03
9000	174.93	173.66	172.66	171.86	171.23	170.73	170.33	170.02	169.76	169.56	169.40	168.97	168.82	168.78
10000	194.37	192.96	191.84	190.96	190.26	189.70	189.26	188.91	188.62	188.40	188.22	187.74	187.58	187.53
11000	213.80	212.25	211.03	210.05	209.28	208.67	208.18	207.80	207.49	207.24	207.04	206.51	206.34	206.28
12000	233.24	231.55	230.21	229.15	228.31	227.64	227.11	226.69	226.35	226.08	225.86	225.29	225.10	225.04
13000	252.68	250.84	249.39	248.25	247.33	246.61	246.04	245.58	245.21	244.92	244.68	244.06	243.85	243.79
14000	272.11	270.14	268.58	267.34	266.36	265.58	264.96	264.47	264.07	263.76	263.51	262.83	262.61	262.54
15000	291.55	289.43	287.76	286.44	285.39	284.55	283.89	283.36	282.93	282.60	282.33	281.61	281.37	281.29
16000	310.98	308.73	306.94	305.53	304.41	303.52	302.81	302.25	301.80	301.44	301.15	300.38	300.13	300.05
17000	330.42	328.02	326.13	324.63	323.44	322.49	321.74	321.14	320.66	320.28	319.97	319.15	318.89	318.80
18000	349.86	347.32	345.31	343.72	342.46	341.46	340.66	340.03	339.52	339.12	338.79	337.93	337.64	337.55
19000	369.29	366.61	364.49	362.82	361.49	360.43	359.59	358.92	358.38	357.95	357.61	356.70	356.40	356.30
20000	388.73	385.91	383.68	381.91	380.51	379.40	378.51	377.81	377.24	376.79	376.44	375.47	375.16	375.06
21000	408.16	405.20	402.86	401.01	399.54	398.37	397.44	396.70	396.11	395.63	395.26	394.25	393.92	393.81
22000	427.60	424.50	422.05	420.10	418.56	417.34	416.36	415.59	414.97	414.47	414.08	413.02	412.67	412.56
23000	447.04	443.79	441.23	439.20	437.59	436.31	435.29	434.48	433.83	433.31	432.90	431.79	431.43	431.31
24000	466.47	463.09	460.41	458.29	456.61	455.28	454.21	453.37	452.69	452.15	451.72	450.57	450.19	450.07
25000	485.91	482.38	479.60	477.39	475.64	474.25	473.14	472.26	471.55	470.99	470.54	469.34	468.95	468.82
26000	505.35	501.68	498.78	496.49	494.66	493.22	492.07	491.15	490.42	489.83	489.36	488.11	487.70	487.57
27000	524.78	520.97	517.96	515.58	513.69	512.19	510.99	510.04	509.28	508.67	508.19	506.89	506.46	506.32
28000	544.22	540.27	537.15	534.68	532.72	531.16	529.92	528.93	528.14	527.51	527.01	525.66	525.22	525.08
29000	563.65	559.56	556.33	553.77	551.74	550.13	548.84	547.82	547.00	546.35	545.83	544.43	543.98	543.83
30000	583.09	578.86	575.51	572.87	570.77	569.10	567.77	566.71	565.86	565.19	564.65	563.21	562.74	562.58
31000	602.53	598.15	594.70	591.96	589.79	588.07	586.69	585.60	584.72	584.03	583.47	581.98	581.49	581.33
32000	621.96	617.45	613.88	611.06	608.82	607.04	605.62	604.49	603.59	602.87	602.29	600.75	600.25	600.09
33000	641.40	636.74	633.07	630.15	627.84	626.01	624.54	623.38	622.45	621.71	621.11	619.53	619.01	618.84
34000	660.84	656.04	652.25	649.25	646.87	644.97	643.47	642.27	641.31	640.55	639.94	638.30	637.77	637.59
35000	680.27	675.33	671.43	668.34	665.89	663.94	662.39	661.16	660.17	659.39	658.76	657.07	656.52	656.34
36000	699.71	694.63	690.62	687.44	684.92	682.91	681.32	680.05	679.03	678.23	677.58	675.85	675.28	675.10
37000	719.14	713.92	709.80	706.53	703.94	701.88	700.24	698.94	697.90	697.06	696.40	694.62	694.04	693.85
38000	738.58	733.22	728.98	725.63	722.97	720.85	719.17	717.83	716.76	715.90	715.22	713.39	712.80	712.60
39000	758.02	752.51	748.17	744.73	741.99	739.82	738.10	736.72	735.62	734.74	734.04	732.17	731.55	731.35
40000	777.45	771.81	767.35	763.82	761.02	758.79	757.02	755.61	754.48	753.58	752.87	750.94	750.31	750.11
41000	796.89	791.10	786.54	782.92	780.05	777.76	775.95	774.50	773.34	772.42	771.69	769.71	769.07	768.86
42000	816.32	810.40	805.72	802.01	799.07	796.73	794.87	793.39	792.21	791.26	790.51	788.49	787.83	787.61
43000	835.76	829.69	824.90	821.11	818.10	815.70	813.80	812.28	811.07	810.10	809.33	807.26	806.58	806.36
44000	855.20	848.99	844.09	840.20	837.12	834.67	832.72	831.17	829.93	828.94	828.15	826.03	825.34	825.12
45000	874.63	868.28	863.27	859.30	856.15	853.64	851.65	850.06	848.79	847.78	846.97	844.81	844.10	843.87
46000	894.07	887.58	882.45	878.39	875.17	872.61	870.57	868.95	867.65	866.62	865.79	863.58	862.86	862.62
47000	913.51	906.87	901.64	897.49	894.20	891.58	889.50	887.84	886.52	885.46	884.62	882.35	881.62	881.37
48000	932.94	926.17	920.82	916.58	913.22	910.55	908.42	906.73	905.38	904.30	903.44	901.13	900.37	900.13
49000	952.38	945.46	940.00	935.68	932.25	929.52	927.35	925.62	924.24	923.14	922.26	919.90	919.13	918.88
50000	971.81	964.76	959.19	954.78	951.27	948.49	946.27	944.51	943.10	941.98	941.08	938.67	937.89	937.63
55000	1069.00	1061.23	1055.11	1050.25	1046.40	1043.34	1040.90	1038.96	1037.41	1036.17	1035.19	1032.54	1031.68	1031.39
60000	1166.18	1157.71	1151.02	1145.73	1141.53	1138.19	1135.53	1133.41	1131.72	1130.37	1129.30	1126.41	1125.47	1125.16
65000	1263.36	1254.19	1246.94	1241.21	1236.65	1233.04	1230.16	1227.86	1226.03	1224.57	1223.40	1220.28	1219.25	1218.92
70000	1360.54	1350.66	1342.86	1336.68	1331.78	1327.88	1324.78	1322.31	1320.34	1318.77	1317.51	1314.14	1313.04	1312.68
75000	1457.72	1447.14	1438.78	1432.16	1426.91	1422.73	1419.41	1416.76	1414.65	1412.96	1411.62	1408.01	1406.83	1406.44
80000	1554.90	1543.61	1534.70	1527.64	1522.03	1517.58	1514.04	1511.21	1508.96	1507.16	1505.73	1501.88	1500.62	1500.21
85000	1652.08	1640.09	1630.62	1623.11	1617.16	1612.43	1608.66	1605.66	1603.27	1601.36	1599.83	1595.74	1594.41	1593.97
90000	1749.26	1736.56	1726.53	1718.59	1712.29	1707.28	1703.29	1700.11	1697.58	1695.56	1693.94	1689.61	1688.20	1687.73
95000	1846.44	1833.04	1822.45	1814.07	1807.42	1802.13	1797.92	1794.56	1791.89	1789.75	1788.05	1783.48	1781.98	1781.49
100000	1943.62	1929.51	1918.37	1909.55	1902.54	1896.98	1892.54	1889.01	1886.20	1883.95	1882.16	1877.34	1875.77	1875.26

MONTHLY PAYMENT
REQUIRED TO AMORTIZE A LOAN

TERM	1 Year	2 Years	3 Years	4 Years	5 Years	6 Years	7 Years	8 Years	9 Years	10 Years	11 Years	12 Years	13 Years	14 Years
AMOUNT														
5	.47	.27	.20	.16	.14	.13	.12	.12	.11	.11	.11	.11	.10	.10
10	.94	.53	.39	.32	.28	.26	.24	.23	.22	.22	.21	.21	.20	.20
15	1.41	.79	.58	.48	.42	.39	.36	.34	.33	.32	.31	.31	.30	.30
25	2.35	1.31	.97	.80	.70	.64	.60	.57	.55	.53	.52	.51	.50	.50
50	4.70	2.61	1.93	1.60	1.40	1.28	1.19	1.14	1.09	1.06	1.03	1.02	1.00	.99
75	7.05	3.92	2.89	2.39	2.10	1.92	1.79	1.70	1.63	1.59	1.55	1.52	1.50	1.48
100	9.39	5.22	3.86	3.19	2.80	2.55	2.38	2.27	2.18	2.11	2.06	2.03	2.00	1.97
200	18.78	10.44	7.71	6.37	5.60	5.10	4.76	4.53	4.35	4.22	4.12	4.05	3.99	3.94
300	28.17	15.66	11.56	9.55	8.39	7.65	7.14	6.79	6.52	6.33	6.18	6.07	5.98	5.91
400	37.56	20.87	15.41	12.74	11.19	10.20	9.52	9.05	8.70	8.44	8.24	8.09	7.97	7.88
500	46.95	26.09	19.26	15.92	13.99	12.75	11.90	11.31	10.87	10.54	10.30	10.11	9.96	9.85
600	56.34	31.31	23.11	19.10	16.78	15.30	14.28	13.57	13.04	12.65	12.36	12.13	11.96	11.82
700	65.72	36.53	26.96	22.29	19.58	17.84	16.66	15.83	15.22	14.76	14.42	14.15	13.95	13.79
800	75.11	41.74	30.81	25.47	22.37	20.39	19.04	18.09	17.39	16.87	16.47	16.17	15.94	15.76
900	84.50	46.96	34.66	28.65	25.17	22.94	21.42	20.35	19.56	18.98	18.53	18.19	17.93	17.73
1000	93.89	52.18	38.51	31.84	27.97	25.49	23.80	22.61	21.74	21.08	20.59	20.21	19.92	19.70
2000	187.77	104.35	77.01	63.67	55.93	50.97	47.60	45.21	43.47	42.16	41.18	40.42	39.84	39.39
3000	281.66	156.53	115.51	95.50	83.89	76.46	71.40	67.81	65.20	63.24	61.77	60.63	59.76	59.08
4000	375.54	208.70	154.01	127.34	111.85	101.94	95.20	90.42	86.93	84.32	82.35	80.84	79.68	78.77
5000	469.42	260.88	192.51	159.17	139.81	127.42	118.99	113.02	108.66	105.40	102.94	101.05	99.59	98.46
6000	563.31	313.05	231.01	191.00	167.77	152.91	142.79	135.62	130.39	126.48	123.53	121.26	119.51	118.15
7000	657.19	365.23	269.52	222.83	195.73	178.39	166.59	158.22	152.12	147.56	144.11	141.47	139.43	137.84
8000	751.07	417.40	308.02	254.67	223.69	203.87	190.39	180.83	173.85	168.64	164.70	161.68	159.35	157.53
9000	844.96	469.58	346.52	286.50	251.66	229.36	214.19	203.43	195.58	189.72	185.29	181.89	179.26	177.22
10000	938.84	521.75	385.02	318.33	279.62	254.84	237.98	226.03	217.31	210.80	205.88	202.10	199.18	196.91
11000	1032.72	573.93	423.52	350.16	307.58	280.32	261.78	248.63	239.04	231.88	226.46	222.31	219.10	216.60
12000	1126.61	626.10	462.02	382.00	335.54	305.81	285.58	271.24	260.77	252.96	247.05	242.52	239.02	236.29
13000	1220.49	678.28	500.53	413.83	363.50	331.29	309.38	293.84	282.50	274.04	267.64	262.73	258.93	255.98
14000	1314.37	730.45	539.03	445.66	391.46	356.77	333.17	316.44	304.23	295.12	288.22	282.94	278.85	255.67
15000	1408.26	782.63	577.53	477.50	419.42	382.26	356.97	339.04	325.96	316.20	308.81	303.15	298.77	295.36
16000	1502.14	834.80	616.03	509.33	447.38	407.74	380.77	361.65	347.69	337.28	329.40	323.36	318.69	315.05
17000	1596.02	886.98	654.53	541.16	475.34	433.22	404.57	384.25	369.42	358.36	349.99	343.57	338.60	334.74
18000	1689.91	939.15	693.03	572.99	503.31	458.71	428.37	406.85	391.15	379.44	370.57	363.78	358.52	354.43
19000	1783.79	991.33	731.53	604.83	531.27	484.19	452.16	429.45	412.88	400.52	391.16	383.99	378.44	374.12
20000	1877.67	1043.50	770.04	636.66	559.23	509.68	475.96	452.06	434.61	421.60	411.75	404.20	398.36	393.81
21000	1971.56	1095.68	808.54	668.49	587.19	535.16	499.76	474.66	456.34	442.68	432.33	424.41	418.28	413.50
22000	2065.44	1147.85	847.04	700.32	615.15	560.64	523.56	497.26	478.07	463.76	452.92	444.62	438.19	433.19
23000	2159.32	1200.03	885.54	732.16	643.11	586.13	547.35	519.86	499.80	484.84	473.51	464.83	458.11	452.88
24000	2253.21	1252.20	924.04	763.99	671.07	611.61	571.15	542.47	521.53	505.92	494.10	485.04	478.03	472.57
25000	2347.09	1304.38	962.54	795.82	699.03	637.09	594.95	565.07	543.26	527.00	514.68	505.25	497.95	492.26
26000	2440.97	1356.55	1001.05	827.66	726.99	662.58	618.75	587.67	564.99	548.08	535.27	525.45	517.86	511.95
27000	2534.86	1408.73	1039.55	859.49	754.96	688.06	642.55	610.28	586.72	569.16	555.86	545.66	537.78	531.64
28000	2628.74	1460.90	1078.05	891.32	782.92	713.54	666.34	632.88	608.45	590.24	576.44	565.87	557.70	551.33
29000	2722.62	1513.08	1116.55	923.15	810.88	739.03	690.14	655.48	630.18	611.32	597.03	586.08	577.62	571.02
30000	2816.51	1565.25	1155.05	954.99	838.84	764.51	713.94	678.08	651.91	632.40	617.62	606.29	597.53	590.71
31000	2910.39	1617.43	1193.55	986.82	866.80	789.99	737.74	700.69	673.64	653.48	638.21	626.50	617.45	610.40
32000	3004.27	1669.60	1232.05	1018.65	894.76	815.48	761.53	723.29	695.37	674.56	658.79	646.71	637.37	630.09
33000	3098.16	1721.78	1270.56	1050.48	922.72	840.96	785.33	745.89	717.10	695.64	679.38	666.92	657.29	649.78
34000	3192.04	1773.95	1309.06	1082.32	950.68	866.44	809.13	768.49	738.83	716.72	699.97	687.13	677.20	669.47
35000	3285.92	1826.13	1347.56	1114.15	978.64	891.93	832.93	791.10	760.56	737.80	720.55	707.34	697.12	689.16
36000	3379.81	1878.30	1386.06	1145.98	1006.61	917.41	856.73	813.70	782.29	758.88	741.14	727.55	717.04	708.85
37000	3473.69	1930.48	1424.56	1177.82	1034.57	942.89	880.52	836.30	804.02	779.96	761.73	747.76	736.96	728.54
38000	3567.57	1982.65	1463.06	1209.65	1062.53	968.38	904.32	858.90	825.75	801.03	782.32	767.97	756.87	748.23
39000	3661.46	2034.83	1501.57	1241.48	1090.49	993.86	928.12	881.51	847.48	822.11	802.90	788.18	776.79	767.92
40000	3755.34	2087.00	1540.07	1273.31	1118.45	1019.35	951.92	904.11	869.21	843.19	823.49	808.39	796.71	787.61
41000	3849.22	2139.18	1578.57	1305.15	1146.41	1044.83	975.71	926.71	890.94	864.27	844.08	828.60	816.63	807.30
42000	3943.11	2191.35	1617.07	1336.98	1174.37	1070.31	999.51	949.31	912.67	885.35	864.66	848.81	836.55	826.99
43000	4036.99	2243.53	1655.57	1368.81	1202.33	1095.80	1023.31	971.92	934.40	906.43	885.25	869.02	856.46	846.68
44000	4130.87	2295.70	1694.07	1400.64	1230.29	1121.28	1047.11	994.52	956.13	927.51	905.84	889.23	876.38	866.37
45000	4224.76	2347.88	1732.57	1432.48	1258.26	1146.76	1070.91	1017.12	977.86	948.59	926.43	909.44	896.30	886.06
46000	4318.64	2400.05	1771.08	1464.31	1286.22	1172.25	1094.70	1039.72	999.59	969.67	947.01	929.65	916.22	905.76
47000	4412.52	2452.23	1809.58	1496.14	1314.18	1197.73	1118.50	1062.33	1021.32	990.75	967.60	949.86	936.13	925.45
48000	4506.41	2504.40	1848.08	1527.98	1342.14	1223.21	1142.30	1084.93	1043.05	1011.83	988.19	970.07	956.05	945.14
49000	4600.29	2556.58	1886.58	1559.81	1370.10	1248.70	1166.10	1107.53	1064.78	1032.91	1008.77	990.28	975.97	964.83
50000	4694.17	2608.75	1925.08	1591.64	1398.06	1274.18	1189.90	1130.13	1086.51	1053.99	1029.36	1010.49	995.89	984.52
55000	5163.59	2869.63	2117.59	1750.80	1537.87	1401.60	1308.88	1243.15	1195.16	1159.39	1132.30	1111.53	1095.47	1082.97
60000	5633.01	3130.50	2310.10	1909.97	1677.67	1529.02	1427.87	1356.16	1303.81	1264.79	1235.23	1212.58	1195.06	1181.42
65000	6102.43	3391.38	2502.61	2069.13	1817.48	1656.43	1546.86	1469.17	1412.47	1370.19	1338.17	1313.63	1294.65	1279.87
70000	6571.84	3652.25	2695.11	2228.30	1957.28	1783.85	1665.85	1582.19	1521.12	1475.59	1441.10	1414.68	1394.24	1378.32
75000	7041.26	3913.12	2887.62	2387.46	2097.09	1911.27	1784.84	1695.20	1629.77	1580.99	1544.04	1515.73	1493.83	1476.77
80000	7510.68	4174.00	3080.13	2546.62	2236.90	2038.69	1903.83	1808.21	1738.42	1686.38	1646.98	1616.77	1593.42	1575.22
85000	7980.09	4434.87	3272.64	2705.79	2376.70	2166.10	2022.82	1921.23	1847.07	1791.78	1749.91	1717.82	1693.00	1673.67
90000	8449.51	4695.75	3465.14	2864.95	2516.51	2293.52	2141.81	2034.24	1955.72	1897.18	1852.85	1818.87	1792.59	1772.12
95000	8918.93	4956.62	3657.65	3024.11	2656.31	2420.94	2260.80	2147.25	2064.37	2002.58	1955.78	1919.92	1892.18	1870.58
100000	9388.34	5217.50	3850.16	3183.28	2796.12	2548.36	2379.79	2260.26	2173.02	2107.98	2058.72	2020.97	1991.77	1969.03

TERM	15 Years	16 Years	17 Years	18 Years	19 Years	20 Years	21 Years	22 Years	23 Years	24 Years	25 Years	30 Years	35 Years	40 Years
AMOUNT														
5	.10	.10	.10	.10	.10	.10	.10	.10	.10	.10	.10	.10	.10	.10
10	.20	.20	.20	.20	.20	.20	.20	.19	.19	.19	.19	.19	.19	.19
15	.30	.30	.29	.29	.29	.29	.29	.29	.29	.29	.29	.29	.29	.29
25	.49	.49	.49	.48	.48	.48	.48	.48	.48	.48	.48	.48	.48	.48
50	.98	.97	.97	.96	.96	.96	.96	.95	.95	.95	.95	.95	.95	.95
75	1.47	1.46	1.45	1.44	1.44	1.43	1.43	1.43	1.43	1.42	1.42	1.42	1.42	1.42
100	1.96	1.94	1.93	1.92	1.92	1.91	1.91	1.90	1.90	1.90	1.90	1.89	1.89	1.89
200	3.91	3.88	3.86	3.84	3.83	3.81	3.81	3.80	3.79	3.79	3.79	3.78	3.77	3.77
300	5.86	5.82	5.78	5.76	5.74	5.72	5.71	5.70	5.69	5.68	5.68	5.66	5.66	5.66
400	7.81	7.75	7.71	7.67	7.65	7.62	7.61	7.59	7.58	7.57	7.57	7.55	7.54	7.54
500	9.76	9.69	9.64	9.59	9.56	9.53	9.51	9.49	9.48	9.47	9.46	9.43	9.43	9.42
600	11.71	11.63	11.56	11.51	11.47	11.43	11.41	11.39	11.37	11.36	11.35	11.32	11.31	11.31
700	13.66	13.57	13.49	13.43	13.38	13.34	13.31	13.28	13.27	13.25	13.24	13.20	13.19	13.19
800	15.61	15.50	15.41	15.34	15.29	15.24	15.21	15.18	15.16	15.14	15.13	15.09	15.08	15.07
900	17.57	17.44	17.34	17.26	17.20	17.15	17.11	17.08	17.05	17.03	17.02	16.98	16.96	16.96
1000	19.52	19.38	19.27	19.18	19.11	19.05	19.01	18.98	18.95	18.93	18.91	18.86	18.85	18.84
2000	39.03	38.75	38.53	38.35	38.21	38.10	38.02	37.95	37.89	37.85	37.81	37.72	37.69	37.68
3000	58.54	58.12	57.79	57.53	57.32	57.15	57.02	56.92	56.83	56.77	56.72	56.57	56.53	56.51
4000	78.05	77.49	77.05	76.70	76.42	76.20	76.03	75.89	75.78	75.69	75.62	75.43	75.37	75.35
5000	97.57	96.87	96.31	95.88	95.53	95.25	95.03	94.86	94.72	94.61	94.52	94.29	94.21	94.18
6000	117.08	116.24	115.57	115.05	114.63	114.30	114.04	113.83	113.66	113.53	113.43	113.14	113.05	113.02
7000	136.59	135.61	134.84	134.22	133.74	133.35	133.05	132.80	132.61	132.45	132.33	132.00	131.89	131.86
8000	156.10	154.98	154.10	153.40	152.84	152.40	152.05	151.77	151.55	151.37	151.23	150.85	150.73	150.69
9000	175.61	174.35	173.36	172.57	171.95	171.45	171.06	170.74	170.49	170.29	170.14	169.71	169.57	169.53
10000	195.13	193.73	192.62	191.75	191.05	190.50	190.06	189.72	189.44	189.22	189.04	188.57	188.41	188.36
11000	214.64	213.10	211.88	210.92	210.16	209.55	209.07	208.69	208.38	208.14	207.94	207.42	207.25	207.20
12000	234.15	232.47	231.14	230.09	229.26	228.60	228.08	227.66	227.32	227.06	226.85	226.28	226.09	226.03
13000	253.66	251.04	250.40	249.27	248.37	247.65	247.08	246.63	246.27	245.98	245.75	245.14	244.94	244.87
14000	273.17	271.21	269.67	268.44	267.47	266.70	266.09	265.60	265.21	264.90	264.65	263.99	263.78	263.71
15000	292.69	290.59	288.93	287.62	286.58	285.75	285.09	284.57	284.15	283.82	283.56	282.85	282.62	282.54
16000	312.20	309.96	308.19	306.79	305.68	304.80	304.10	303.54	303.10	302.74	302.46	301.70	301.46	301.38
17000	331.71	329.33	327.45	325.96	324.79	323.85	323.10	322.51	322.04	321.66	321.36	320.56	320.30	320.21
18000	351.22	348.70	346.71	345.14	343.89	342.90	342.11	341.48	340.98	340.58	340.27	339.42	339.14	339.05
19000	370.74	368.07	365.97	364.31	363.00	361.95	361.12	360.45	359.93	359.51	359.17	358.27	357.98	357.88
20000	390.25	387.45	385.24	383.49	382.10	381.00	380.12	379.43	378.87	378.43	378.07	377.13	376.82	376.72
21000	409.76	406.82	404.50	402.66	401.20	400.05	399.13	398.40	397.81	397.35	396.98	395.98	395.66	395.56
22000	429.27	426.19	423.76	421.83	420.31	419.10	418.13	417.37	416.76	416.27	415.88	414.84	414.50	414.39
23000	448.78	445.56	443.02	441.01	439.41	438.15	437.14	436.34	435.70	435.19	434.78	433.70	433.34	433.23
24000	468.30	464.93	462.28	460.18	458.52	457.20	456.15	455.31	454.64	454.11	453.69	452.55	452.18	452.06
25000	487.81	484.31	481.54	479.36	477.62	476.25	475.15	474.28	473.59	473.03	472.59	471.41	471.02	470.90
26000	507.32	503.68	500.80	498.53	496.73	495.30	494.16	493.25	492.53	491.95	491.49	490.26	489.87	489.73
27000	526.83	523.05	520.07	517.71	515.83	514.35	513.16	512.22	511.47	510.87	510.40	509.12	508.71	508.57
28000	546.34	542.42	539.33	536.88	534.94	533.40	532.17	531.19	530.42	529.80	529.30	527.98	527.55	527.41
29000	565.86	561.79	558.59	556.05	554.04	552.45	551.18	550.16	549.36	548.72	548.20	546.83	546.39	546.24
30000	585.37	581.17	577.85	575.23	573.15	571.50	570.18	569.14	568.30	567.64	567.11	565.69	565.23	565.08
31000	604.88	600.54	597.11	594.40	592.25	590.54	589.19	588.11	587.25	586.56	586.01	584.55	584.07	583.91
32000	624.39	619.91	616.37	613.58	611.36	609.59	608.19	607.08	606.19	605.48	604.91	603.40	602.91	602.75
33000	643.91	639.28	635.64	632.75	630.46	628.64	627.20	626.05	625.13	624.40	623.82	622.26	621.75	621.59
34000	663.42	658.66	654.90	651.92	649.57	647.69	646.20	645.02	644.07	643.32	642.72	641.11	640.59	640.42
35000	682.93	678.03	674.16	671.10	668.67	666.74	665.21	663.99	663.02	662.24	661.62	659.97	659.43	659.26
36000	702.44	697.40	693.42	690.27	687.78	685.79	684.22	682.96	681.96	681.16	680.53	678.83	678.27	678.09
37000	721.95	716.77	712.68	709.45	706.88	704.84	703.22	701.93	700.90	700.09	699.43	697.68	697.11	696.93
38000	741.47	736.14	731.94	728.62	725.99	723.89	722.23	720.90	719.85	719.01	718.33	716.54	715.95	715.76
39000	760.98	755.52	751.20	747.79	745.09	742.94	741.23	739.87	738.79	737.93	737.24	735.39	734.80	734.60
40000	780.49	774.89	770.47	766.97	764.19	761.99	760.24	758.85	757.73	756.85	756.14	754.25	753.64	753.44
41000	800.00	794.26	789.73	786.14	783.30	781.04	779.25	777.82	776.68	775.77	775.04	773.11	772.48	772.27
42000	819.51	813.63	808.99	805.32	802.40	800.09	798.25	796.79	795.62	794.69	793.95	791.96	791.32	791.11
43000	839.03	833.00	828.25	824.49	821.51	819.14	817.26	815.76	814.56	813.61	812.85	810.82	810.16	809.94
44000	858.54	852.38	847.51	843.66	840.61	838.19	836.26	834.73	833.51	832.53	831.76	829.68	829.00	828.78
45000	878.05	871.75	866.77	862.84	859.72	857.24	855.27	853.70	852.45	851.45	850.66	848.53	847.84	847.61
46000	897.56	891.12	886.04	882.01	878.82	876.29	874.28	872.67	871.39	870.37	869.56	867.39	866.68	866.45
47000	917.08	910.49	905.30	901.19	897.93	895.34	893.28	891.64	890.34	889.30	888.47	886.24	885.52	885.29
48000	936.59	929.86	924.56	920.36	917.03	914.39	912.29	910.61	909.28	908.22	907.37	905.10	904.36	904.12
49000	956.10	949.24	943.82	939.54	936.14	933.44	931.29	929.58	928.22	927.14	926.27	923.96	923.20	922.96
50000	975.61	968.61	963.08	958.71	955.24	952.49	950.30	948.56	947.17	946.06	945.18	942.81	942.04	941.79
55000	1073.17	1065.47	1059.39	1054.58	1050.77	1047.74	1045.33	1043.41	1041.88	1040.66	1039.69	1037.09	1036.25	1035.97
60000	1170.73	1162.33	1155.70	1150.45	1146.29	1142.99	1140.36	1138.27	1136.60	1135.27	1134.21	1131.37	1130.45	1130.15
65000	1268.29	1259.19	1252.00	1246.32	1241.81	1238.23	1235.39	1233.12	1231.32	1229.88	1228.73	1225.66	1224.66	1224.33
70000	1365.85	1356.05	1348.31	1342.19	1337.34	1333.48	1330.42	1327.98	1326.03	1324.48	1323.24	1319.94	1318.86	1318.51
75000	1463.41	1452.91	1444.62	1438.06	1432.86	1428.73	1425.45	1422.83	1420.75	1419.09	1417.76	1414.22	1413.06	1412.69
80000	1560.98	1549.77	1540.93	1533.93	1528.38	1523.98	1520.48	1517.69	1515.46	1513.69	1512.28	1508.50	1507.27	1506.87
85000	1658.54	1646.63	1637.24	1629.80	1623.91	1619.23	1615.50	1612.54	1610.18	1608.30	1606.80	1602.78	1601.47	1601.04
90000	1756.10	1743.49	1733.54	1725.67	1719.43	1714.48	1710.53	1707.40	1704.90	1702.90	1701.31	1697.06	1695.67	1695.22
95000	1853.66	1840.35	1829.85	1821.54	1814.96	1809.72	1805.56	1802.25	1799.61	1797.51	1795.83	1791.34	1789.88	1789.40
100000	1951.22	1937.21	1926.16	1917.41	1910.48	1904.97	1900.59	1897.11	1894.33	1892.11	1890.35	1885.62	1884.08	1883.58

MONTHLY PAYMENT
REQUIRED TO AMORTIZE A LOAN

TERM	1 Year	2 Years	3 Years	4 Years	5 Years	6 Years	7 Years	8 Years	9 Years	10 Years	11 Years	12 Years	13 Years	14 Years
AMOUNT														
5	.47	.27	.20	.16	.14	.13	.12	.12	.11	.11	.11	.11	.10	.10
10	.94	.53	.39	.32	.28	.26	.24	.23	.22	.22	.21	.21	.20	.20
15	1.41	.79	.58	.48	.42	.39	.36	.34	.33	.32	.31	.31	.30	.30
25	2.35	1.31	.97	.80	.70	.64	.60	.57	.55	.53	.52	.51	.50	.50
50	4.70	2.61	1.93	1.60	1.40	1.28	1.20	1.14	1.09	1.06	1.04	1.02	1.00	.99
75	7.05	3.92	2.89	2.39	2.10	1.92	1.79	1.70	1.64	1.59	1.55	1.52	1.50	1.48
100	9.39	5.22	3.86	3.19	2.80	2.55	2.39	2.27	2.18	2.11	2.07	2.03	2.00	1.98
200	18.78	10.44	7.71	6.37	5.60	5.10	4.77	4.53	4.35	4.22	4.13	4.05	3.99	3.95
300	28.17	15.66	11.56	9.56	8.40	7.65	7.15	6.79	6.53	6.33	6.19	6.07	5.99	5.92
400	37.56	20.88	15.41	12.74	11.20	10.20	9.53	9.05	8.70	8.44	8.25	8.10	7.98	7.89
500	46.95	26.10	19.26	15.93	13.99	12.75	11.91	11.31	10.88	10.55	10.31	10.12	9.97	9.86
600	56.34	31.32	23.11	19.11	16.79	15.30	14.29	13.58	13.05	12.66	12.37	12.14	11.97	11.83
700	65.73	36.54	26.97	22.30	19.59	17.85	16.67	15.84	15.23	14.77	14.43	14.16	13.96	13.80
800	75.12	41.75	30.82	25.48	22.39	20.40	19.06	18.10	17.40	16.88	16.49	16.19	15.95	15.77
900	84.51	46.97	34.67	28.67	25.18	22.95	21.44	20.36	19.58	18.99	18.55	18.21	17.95	17.74
1000	93.90	52.19	38.52	31.85	27.98	25.50	23.82	22.62	21.75	21.10	20.61	20.23	19.94	19.71
2000	187.80	104.38	77.03	63.70	55.96	51.00	47.63	45.24	43.50	42.20	41.21	40.46	39.88	39.42
3000	281.69	156.57	115.55	95.54	83.93	76.50	71.45	67.86	65.25	63.30	61.82	60.69	59.81	59.13
4000	375.59	208.75	154.06	127.39	111.91	102.00	95.26	90.48	86.99	84.39	82.42	80.92	79.75	78.84
5000	469.48	260.94	192.58	159.24	139.88	127.50	119.07	113.10	108.74	105.49	103.03	101.14	99.69	98.55
6000	563.38	313.13	231.09	191.08	167.86	153.00	142.89	135.72	130.49	126.59	123.63	121.37	119.62	118.26
7000	657.27	365.32	269.61	222.93	195.83	178.49	166.70	158.34	152.23	147.68	144.24	141.60	139.56	137.97
8000	751.17	417.50	308.12	254.78	223.81	203.99	190.51	180.95	173.98	168.78	164.84	161.83	159.49	157.68
9000	845.06	469.69	346.64	286.62	251.78	229.49	214.33	203.57	195.73	189.88	185.45	182.05	179.43	177.39
10000	938.96	521.88	385.15	318.47	279.76	254.99	238.14	226.19	217.47	210.97	206.05	202.28	199.37	197.09
11000	1032.85	574.07	423.66	350.32	307.73	280.49	261.95	248.81	239.22	232.07	226.66	222.51	219.30	216.80
12000	1126.75	626.25	462.18	382.16	335.71	305.99	285.77	271.43	260.97	253.17	247.26	242.74	239.24	236.51
13000	1220.65	678.44	500.69	414.01	363.69	331.48	309.58	294.05	282.71	274.26	267.87	262.96	259.17	256.22
14000	1314.54	730.63	539.21	445.85	391.66	356.98	333.39	316.67	304.46	295.36	288.47	283.19	279.11	275.93
15000	1408.44	782.81	577.72	477.70	419.64	382.48	357.21	339.29	326.21	316.46	309.08	303.42	299.05	295.64
16000	1502.33	835.00	616.24	509.55	447.61	407.98	381.02	361.90	347.95	337.56	329.68	323.65	318.98	315.35
17000	1596.23	887.19	654.75	541.39	475.59	433.48	404.83	384.52	369.70	358.65	350.29	343.87	338.92	335.06
18000	1690.12	939.38	693.27	573.24	503.56	458.98	428.65	407.14	391.45	379.75	370.89	364.10	358.85	354.77
19000	1784.02	991.56	731.78	605.09	531.54	484.48	452.46	429.76	413.19	400.85	391.50	384.33	378.79	374.47
20000	1877.91	1043.75	770.30	636.93	559.51	509.97	476.27	452.38	434.94	421.94	412.10	404.56	398.73	394.18
21000	1971.81	1095.94	808.81	668.78	587.49	535.47	500.09	475.00	456.69	443.04	432.70	424.78	418.66	413.89
22000	2065.70	1148.13	847.32	700.63	615.46	560.97	523.90	497.62	478.44	464.14	453.31	445.01	438.60	433.60
23000	2159.60	1200.31	885.84	732.47	643.44	586.47	547.71	520.24	500.18	485.23	473.91	465.24	458.53	453.31
24000	2253.50	1252.50	924.35	764.32	671.42	611.97	571.53	542.85	521.93	506.33	494.52	485.47	478.47	473.02
25000	2347.39	1304.69	962.87	796.16	699.39	637.47	595.34	565.47	543.68	527.43	515.12	505.70	498.41	492.73
26000	2441.29	1356.88	1001.38	828.01	727.37	662.96	619.15	588.09	565.42	548.52	535.73	525.92	518.34	512.44
27000	2535.18	1409.06	1039.90	859.86	755.34	688.46	642.97	610.71	587.17	569.62	556.33	546.15	538.28	532.15
28000	2629.08	1461.25	1078.41	891.70	783.32	713.96	666.78	633.33	608.92	590.72	576.94	566.38	558.21	551.85
29000	2722.97	1513.44	1116.93	923.55	811.29	739.46	690.59	655.95	630.66	611.81	597.54	586.61	578.15	571.56
30000	2816.87	1565.62	1155.44	955.40	839.27	764.96	714.41	678.57	652.41	632.91	618.15	606.83	598.09	591.27
31000	2910.76	1617.81	1193.96	987.24	867.24	790.46	738.22	701.19	674.16	654.01	638.75	627.06	618.02	610.98
32000	3004.66	1670.00	1232.47	1019.09	895.22	815.96	762.03	723.80	695.90	675.11	659.36	647.29	637.96	630.69
33000	3098.55	1722.19	1270.98	1050.94	923.19	841.45	785.85	746.42	717.65	696.20	679.96	667.52	657.89	650.40
34000	3192.45	1774.37	1309.50	1082.78	951.17	866.95	809.66	769.04	739.40	717.30	700.57	687.74	677.83	670.11
35000	3286.35	1826.56	1348.01	1114.63	979.15	892.45	833.47	791.66	761.14	738.40	721.17	707.97	697.77	689.82
36000	3380.24	1878.75	1386.53	1146.47	1007.12	917.95	857.29	814.28	782.89	759.49	741.78	728.20	717.70	709.53
37000	3474.14	1930.94	1425.04	1178.32	1035.10	943.45	881.10	836.90	804.64	780.59	762.38	748.43	737.64	729.24
38000	3568.03	1983.12	1463.56	1210.17	1063.07	968.95	904.91	859.52	826.38	801.69	782.99	768.65	757.57	748.94
39000	3661.93	2035.31	1502.07	1242.01	1091.05	994.44	928.73	882.14	848.13	822.78	803.59	788.88	777.51	768.65
40000	3755.82	2087.50	1540.59	1273.86	1119.02	1019.94	952.54	904.75	869.88	843.88	824.19	809.11	797.45	788.36
41000	3849.72	2139.68	1579.10	1305.71	1147.00	1045.44	976.35	927.37	891.62	864.98	844.80	829.34	817.38	808.07
42000	3943.61	2191.87	1617.62	1337.55	1174.97	1070.94	1000.17	949.99	913.37	886.07	865.40	849.56	837.32	827.78
43000	4037.51	2244.06	1656.13	1369.40	1202.95	1096.44	1023.98	972.61	935.12	907.17	886.01	869.79	857.25	847.49
44000	4131.40	2296.25	1694.64	1401.25	1230.92	1121.94	1047.79	995.23	956.87	928.27	906.61	890.02	877.19	867.20
45000	4225.30	2348.43	1733.16	1433.09	1258.90	1147.44	1071.61	1017.85	978.61	949.36	927.22	910.25	897.13	886.91
46000	4319.20	2400.62	1771.67	1464.94	1286.88	1172.93	1095.42	1040.47	1000.36	970.46	947.82	930.48	917.06	906.62
47000	4413.09	2452.81	1810.19	1496.78	1314.85	1198.43	1119.23	1063.08	1022.11	991.56	968.43	950.70	937.00	926.32
48000	4506.99	2505.00	1848.70	1528.63	1342.83	1223.93	1143.05	1085.70	1043.85	1012.66	989.03	970.93	956.93	946.03
49000	4600.88	2557.18	1887.22	1560.48	1370.80	1249.43	1166.86	1108.32	1065.60	1033.75	1009.64	991.16	976.87	965.74
50000	4694.78	2609.37	1925.73	1592.32	1398.78	1274.93	1190.67	1130.94	1087.35	1054.85	1030.24	1011.39	996.81	985.45
55000	5164.25	2870.31	2118.30	1751.56	1538.65	1402.42	1309.74	1244.03	1196.08	1160.33	1133.27	1112.52	1096.49	1084.00
60000	5633.73	3131.24	2310.88	1910.79	1678.53	1529.91	1428.81	1357.13	1304.81	1265.82	1236.29	1213.66	1196.17	1182.54
65000	6103.21	3392.18	2503.45	2070.02	1818.41	1657.40	1547.87	1470.22	1413.55	1371.30	1339.31	1314.80	1295.85	1281.09
70000	6572.69	3653.12	2696.02	2229.25	1958.29	1784.90	1666.94	1583.32	1522.28	1476.79	1442.34	1415.94	1395.53	1379.63
75000	7042.16	3914.05	2888.60	2388.48	2098.16	1912.39	1786.01	1696.41	1631.02	1582.27	1545.36	1517.08	1495.21	1478.17
80000	7511.64	4174.99	3081.17	2547.71	2238.04	2039.88	1905.07	1809.50	1739.75	1687.76	1648.38	1618.21	1594.89	1576.72
85000	7981.12	4435.93	3273.74	2706.95	2377.92	2167.37	2024.14	1922.60	1848.49	1793.24	1751.41	1719.35	1694.57	1675.26
90000	8450.59	4696.86	3466.31	2866.18	2517.79	2294.87	2143.21	2035.69	1957.22	1898.72	1854.43	1820.49	1794.25	1773.81
95000	8920.07	4957.80	3658.89	3025.41	2657.67	2422.36	2262.27	2148.78	2065.95	2004.21	1957.46	1921.63	1893.93	1872.35
100000	9389.55	5218.74	3851.46	3184.64	2797.55	2549.85	2381.34	2261.88	2174.69	2109.69	2060.48	2022.77	1993.61	1970.90

MONTHLY PAYMENT
REQUIRED TO AMORTIZE A LOAN

22.625%

TERM AMOUNT	15 Years	16 Years	17 Years	18 Years	19 Years	20 Years	21 Years	22 Years	23 Years	24 Years	25 Years	30 Years	35 Years	40 Years
5	.10	.10	.10	.10	.10	.10	.10	.10	.10	.10	.10	.10	.10	.10
10	.20	.20	.20	.20	.20	.20	.20	.19	.19	.19	.19	.19	.19	.19
15	.30	.30	.29	.29	.29	.29	.29	.29	.29	.29	.29	.29	.29	.29
25	.49	.49	.49	.48	.48	.48	.48	.48	.48	.48	.48	.48	.48	.48
50	.98	.97	.97	.96	.96	.96	.95	.95	.95	.95	.95	.95	.95	.95
75	1.47	1.46	1.45	1.44	1.44	1.44	1.43	1.43	1.43	1.43	1.42	1.42	1.42	1.42
100	1.96	1.94	1.93	1.92	1.92	1.91	1.91	1.90	1.90	1.90	1.90	1.89	1.89	1.89
200	3.91	3.88	3.86	3.84	3.83	3.82	3.81	3.80	3.80	3.79	3.79	3.78	3.78	3.78
300	5.86	5.82	5.79	5.76	5.74	5.73	5.71	5.70	5.69	5.69	5.68	5.67	5.66	5.66
400	7.82	7.76	7.72	7.68	7.65	7.63	7.62	7.60	7.59	7.58	7.57	7.56	7.55	7.55
500	9.77	9.70	9.65	9.60	9.57	9.54	9.52	9.50	9.49	9.48	9.47	9.44	9.44	9.43
600	11.72	11.64	11.57	11.52	11.48	11.45	11.42	11.40	11.38	11.37	11.36	11.33	11.32	11.32
700	13.68	13.58	13.50	13.44	13.39	13.35	13.32	13.30	13.28	13.26	13.25	13.22	13.21	13.20
800	15.63	15.52	15.43	15.36	15.30	15.26	15.23	15.20	15.18	15.16	15.14	15.11	15.09	15.09
900	17.58	17.46	17.36	17.28	17.22	17.17	17.13	17.10	17.07	17.05	17.04	16.99	16.98	16.98
1000	19.54	19.40	19.29	19.20	19.13	19.07	19.03	19.00	18.97	18.95	18.93	18.88	18.87	18.86
2000	39.07	38.79	38.57	38.39	38.25	38.14	38.06	37.99	37.93	37.89	37.85	37.76	37.73	37.72
3000	58.60	58.18	57.85	57.59	57.38	57.21	57.08	56.98	56.90	56.83	56.78	56.64	56.59	56.57
4000	78.13	77.57	77.13	76.78	76.50	76.28	76.11	75.97	75.86	75.77	75.70	75.51	75.45	75.43
5000	97.66	96.96	96.41	95.97	95.63	95.35	95.14	94.96	94.82	94.71	94.62	94.39	94.31	94.29
6000	117.19	116.35	115.69	115.17	114.75	114.42	114.16	113.95	113.79	113.65	113.55	113.27	113.17	113.14
7000	136.72	135.74	134.97	134.36	133.88	133.49	133.19	132.94	132.75	132.60	132.47	132.14	132.04	132.00
8000	156.25	155.14	154.25	153.56	153.00	152.56	152.21	151.93	151.71	151.54	151.40	151.02	150.90	150.86
9000	175.79	174.53	173.53	172.75	172.13	171.63	171.24	170.93	170.68	170.48	170.32	169.90	169.76	169.71
10000	195.32	193.92	192.82	191.94	191.25	190.70	190.27	189.92	189.64	189.42	189.24	188.77	188.62	188.57
11000	214.85	213.31	212.10	211.14	210.38	209.77	209.29	208.91	208.60	208.36	208.17	207.65	207.48	207.43
12000	234.38	232.70	231.38	230.33	229.50	228.84	228.32	227.90	227.57	227.30	227.09	226.53	226.34	226.28
13000	253.91	252.09	250.66	249.52	248.62	247.91	247.34	246.89	246.53	246.24	246.02	245.40	245.21	245.14
14000	273.44	271.48	269.94	268.72	267.75	266.98	266.37	265.88	265.49	265.19	264.94	264.28	264.07	264.00
15000	292.97	290.87	289.22	287.91	286.87	286.05	285.40	284.87	284.46	284.13	283.86	283.16	282.93	282.85
16000	312.50	310.27	308.50	307.11	306.00	305.12	304.42	303.86	303.42	303.07	302.79	302.03	301.79	301.71
17000	332.03	329.66	327.78	326.30	325.12	324.19	323.45	322.86	322.39	322.01	321.71	320.91	320.65	320.57
18000	351.57	349.05	347.06	345.49	344.25	343.26	342.47	341.85	341.35	340.95	340.64	339.79	339.51	339.42
19000	371.10	368.44	366.34	364.69	363.37	362.33	361.50	360.84	360.31	359.89	359.56	358.67	358.37	358.28
20000	390.63	387.83	385.63	383.88	382.50	381.40	380.53	379.83	379.28	378.83	378.48	377.54	377.24	377.14
21000	410.16	407.22	404.91	403.07	401.62	400.47	399.55	398.82	398.24	397.78	397.41	396.42	396.10	395.99
22000	429.69	426.61	424.19	422.27	420.75	419.54	418.58	417.81	417.20	416.72	416.33	415.30	414.96	414.85
23000	449.22	446.01	443.47	441.46	439.87	438.61	437.60	436.80	436.15	435.66	435.25	434.17	433.82	433.71
24000	468.75	465.40	462.75	460.66	459.00	457.68	456.63	455.79	455.13	454.60	454.18	453.05	452.68	452.56
25000	488.28	484.79	482.03	479.85	478.12	476.75	475.66	474.79	474.09	473.54	473.10	471.93	471.54	471.42
26000	507.81	504.18	501.31	499.04	497.24	495.82	494.68	493.78	493.06	492.48	492.03	490.80	490.41	490.28
27000	527.35	523.57	520.59	518.24	516.37	514.89	513.71	512.77	512.02	511.43	510.95	509.68	509.27	509.13
28000	546.88	542.96	539.87	537.43	535.49	533.96	532.73	531.76	530.98	530.37	529.87	528.56	528.13	527.99
29000	566.41	562.35	559.15	556.62	554.62	553.03	551.76	550.75	549.95	549.31	548.80	547.43	546.99	546.85
30000	585.94	581.74	578.44	575.82	573.74	572.10	570.79	569.74	568.91	568.25	567.72	566.31	565.85	565.70
31000	605.47	601.14	597.72	595.01	592.87	591.16	589.81	588.73	587.88	587.19	586.65	585.19	584.71	584.56
32000	625.00	620.53	617.00	614.21	611.99	610.23	608.84	607.72	606.84	606.13	605.57	604.06	603.57	603.42
33000	644.53	639.92	636.28	633.40	631.12	629.30	627.86	626.72	625.80	625.07	624.49	622.94	622.44	622.27
34000	664.06	659.31	655.56	652.59	650.24	648.37	646.89	645.71	644.77	644.02	643.42	641.82	641.30	641.13
35000	683.59	678.70	674.84	671.79	669.37	667.44	665.92	664.70	663.73	662.96	662.34	660.69	660.16	659.99
36000	703.13	698.09	694.12	690.98	688.49	686.51	684.94	683.69	682.69	681.90	681.27	679.57	679.02	678.84
37000	722.66	717.48	713.40	710.17	707.61	705.58	703.97	702.68	701.66	700.84	700.19	698.45	697.88	697.70
38000	742.19	736.88	732.68	729.37	726.74	724.65	722.99	721.67	720.62	719.78	719.11	717.33	716.74	716.55
39000	761.72	756.27	751.96	748.56	745.86	743.72	742.02	740.66	739.58	738.72	738.04	736.20	735.61	735.41
40000	781.25	775.66	771.25	767.76	764.99	762.79	761.05	759.65	758.55	757.66	756.96	755.08	754.47	754.27
41000	800.78	795.05	790.53	786.95	784.11	781.86	780.07	778.65	777.51	776.61	775.88	773.96	773.33	773.12
42000	820.31	814.44	809.81	806.14	803.24	800.93	799.10	797.64	796.47	795.55	794.81	792.83	792.19	791.98
43000	839.84	833.83	829.09	825.34	822.36	820.00	818.12	816.63	815.44	814.49	813.73	811.71	811.05	810.84
44000	859.37	853.22	848.37	844.53	841.49	839.07	837.15	835.62	834.40	833.43	832.66	830.59	829.91	829.69
45000	878.91	872.61	867.65	863.72	860.61	858.14	856.18	854.61	853.37	852.37	851.58	849.46	848.77	848.55
46000	898.44	892.01	886.93	882.92	879.74	877.21	875.20	873.60	872.33	871.31	870.50	868.34	867.64	867.41
47000	917.97	911.40	906.21	902.11	898.86	896.28	894.23	892.59	891.29	890.26	889.43	887.22	886.50	886.26
48000	937.50	930.79	925.49	921.31	917.99	915.35	913.25	911.58	910.26	909.20	908.35	906.09	905.36	905.12
49000	957.03	950.18	944.77	940.50	937.11	934.42	932.28	930.58	929.22	928.14	927.28	924.97	924.22	923.98
50000	976.56	969.57	964.05	959.69	956.23	953.49	951.31	949.57	948.18	947.08	946.20	943.85	943.08	942.83
55000	1074.22	1066.53	1060.46	1055.66	1051.86	1048.84	1046.44	1044.52	1043.00	1041.79	1040.82	1038.23	1037.39	1037.12
60000	1171.87	1163.48	1156.87	1151.63	1147.48	1144.19	1141.57	1139.48	1137.82	1136.49	1135.44	1132.62	1131.70	1131.40
65000	1269.53	1260.44	1253.27	1247.60	1243.10	1239.53	1236.70	1234.44	1232.64	1231.20	1230.06	1227.00	1226.01	1225.68
70000	1367.18	1357.40	1349.68	1343.57	1338.73	1334.88	1331.83	1329.39	1327.45	1325.91	1324.68	1321.38	1320.31	1319.97
75000	1464.84	1454.35	1446.08	1439.54	1434.35	1430.23	1426.96	1424.35	1422.27	1420.62	1419.30	1415.77	1414.62	1414.25
80000	1562.50	1551.31	1542.49	1535.51	1529.97	1525.58	1522.09	1519.30	1517.09	1515.32	1513.92	1510.15	1508.93	1508.53
85000	1660.15	1648.27	1638.89	1631.47	1625.60	1620.93	1617.22	1614.26	1611.91	1610.03	1608.54	1604.54	1603.24	1602.81
90000	1757.81	1745.22	1735.30	1727.44	1721.22	1716.28	1712.35	1709.22	1706.73	1704.74	1703.16	1698.92	1697.54	1697.10
95000	1855.46	1842.18	1831.70	1823.41	1816.84	1811.62	1807.48	1804.17	1801.54	1799.45	1797.78	1793.31	1791.85	1791.38
100000	1953.12	1939.14	1928.11	1919.38	1912.46	1906.97	1902.61	1899.13	1896.36	1894.15	1892.39	1887.69	1886.16	1885.66

MONTHLY PAYMENT
REQUIRED TO AMORTIZE A LOAN

TERM AMOUNT	1 Year	2 Years	3 Years	4 Years	5 Years	6 Years	7 Years	8 Years	9 Years	10 Years	11 Years	12 Years	13 Years	14 Years
5	.47	.27	.20	.16	.15	.13	.12	.12	.11	.11	.11	.11	.10	.10
10	.94	.53	.39	.32	.29	.26	.24	.23	.22	.22	.21	.21	.20	.20
15	1.41	.79	.58	.48	.43	.39	.36	.35	.32	.32	.31	.31	.30	.30
25	2.35	1.31	.97	.80	.71	.64	.60	.57	.55	.53	.52	.51	.50	.50
50	4.70	2.62	1.93	1.60	1.41	1.28	1.20	1.14	1.09	1.06	1.04	1.02	1.00	.99
75	7.05	3.92	2.90	2.40	2.11	1.92	1.79	1.71	1.64	1.59	1.55	1.53	1.50	1.49
100	9.40	5.23	3.86	3.19	2.81	2.56	2.39	2.27	2.18	2.12	2.07	2.03	2.00	1.98
200	18.79	10.45	7.72	6.38	5.61	5.11	4.78	4.54	4.36	4.23	4.14	4.06	4.00	3.96
300	28.18	15.67	11.57	9.57	8.41	7.67	7.16	6.81	6.54	6.35	6.20	6.09	6.00	5.93
400	37.58	20.89	15.43	12.76	11.21	10.22	9.55	9.07	8.72	8.46	8.27	8.12	8.00	7.91
500	46.97	26.12	19.28	15.95	14.01	12.79	11.94	11.34	10.90	10.58	10.33	10.15	10.00	9.89
600	56.36	31.34	23.14	19.14	16.82	15.33	14.32	13.61	13.08	12.69	12.40	12.17	12.00	11.86
700	65.76	36.56	26.99	22.33	19.62	17.89	16.71	15.87	15.26	14.81	14.47	14.20	14.00	13.84
800	75.15	41.78	30.85	25.51	22.42	20.44	19.09	18.14	17.44	16.92	16.53	16.23	16.00	15.82
900	84.54	47.01	34.70	28.70	25.22	22.99	21.48	20.41	19.62	19.04	18.60	18.26	18.00	17.79
1000	93.94	52.23	38.56	31.89	28.02	25.55	23.87	22.67	21.80	21.15	20.66	20.29	20.00	19.77
2000	187.87	104.45	77.11	63.78	56.04	51.09	47.73	45.34	43.60	42.30	41.32	40.57	39.99	39.54
3000	281.80	156.68	115.67	95.67	84.06	76.63	71.59	68.01	65.40	63.45	61.98	60.85	59.98	59.30
4000	375.73	208.90	154.22	127.55	112.08	102.18	95.45	90.67	87.19	84.60	82.64	81.13	79.97	79.07
5000	469.66	261.13	192.77	159.44	140.10	127.72	119.31	113.34	108.99	105.75	103.29	101.41	99.96	98.83
6000	563.59	313.35	231.33	191.33	168.12	153.26	143.17	136.01	130.79	126.90	123.95	121.70	119.95	118.60
7000	657.53	365.58	269.88	223.22	196.13	178.81	167.03	158.67	152.58	148.04	144.61	141.98	139.94	138.36
8000	751.46	417.80	308.43	255.10	224.15	204.35	190.89	181.34	174.38	169.19	165.27	162.26	159.93	158.13
9000	845.39	470.03	346.99	286.99	252.17	229.89	214.75	204.01	196.18	190.34	185.92	182.54	179.93	177.89
10000	939.32	522.25	385.54	318.88	280.19	255.44	238.61	226.68	217.97	211.49	206.58	202.82	199.92	197.66
11000	1033.25	574.47	424.09	350.77	308.21	280.98	262.47	249.34	239.77	232.64	227.24	223.10	219.91	217.42
12000	1127.18	626.70	462.65	382.65	336.23	306.52	286.33	272.01	261.57	253.79	247.90	243.39	239.90	237.19
13000	1221.12	678.92	501.20	414.54	364.24	332.07	310.19	294.68	283.36	274.93	268.55	263.67	259.89	256.95
14000	1315.05	731.15	539.75	446.43	392.26	357.61	334.05	317.34	305.16	296.08	289.21	283.95	279.88	276.72
15000	1408.98	783.37	578.31	478.31	420.28	383.15	357.91	340.01	326.96	317.23	309.87	304.23	299.87	296.48
16000	1502.91	835.60	616.86	510.20	448.30	408.70	381.77	362.68	348.75	338.38	330.53	324.51	319.86	316.25
17000	1596.84	887.82	655.42	542.09	476.32	434.24	405.63	385.35	370.55	359.53	351.18	344.79	339.85	336.01
18000	1690.77	940.05	693.97	573.98	504.34	459.78	429.49	408.01	392.35	380.68	371.84	365.08	359.85	355.78
19000	1784.71	992.27	732.52	605.86	532.35	485.33	453.35	430.68	414.14	401.82	392.50	385.36	379.84	375.54
20000	1878.64	1044.49	771.08	637.75	560.37	510.87	477.21	453.35	435.94	422.97	413.16	405.64	399.83	395.31
21000	1972.57	1096.72	809.63	669.64	588.39	536.41	501.07	476.01	457.74	444.12	433.81	425.92	419.82	415.07
22000	2066.50	1148.94	848.18	701.53	616.41	561.96	524.93	498.68	479.54	465.27	454.47	446.20	439.81	434.84
23000	2160.43	1201.17	886.74	733.41	644.43	587.50	548.79	521.35	501.33	486.42	475.13	466.48	459.80	454.60
24000	2254.36	1253.39	925.29	765.30	672.45	613.04	572.65	544.02	523.13	507.57	495.79	486.77	479.79	474.37
25000	2348.30	1305.62	963.84	797.19	700.46	638.59	596.51	566.68	544.93	528.71	516.44	507.05	499.78	494.13
26000	2442.23	1357.84	1002.40	829.08	728.48	664.13	620.37	589.35	566.72	549.86	537.10	527.33	519.78	513.90
27000	2536.16	1410.07	1040.95	860.96	756.50	689.67	644.23	612.02	588.52	571.01	557.76	547.61	539.77	533.66
28000	2630.09	1462.29	1079.50	892.85	784.52	715.22	668.09	634.68	610.32	592.16	578.42	567.89	559.76	553.43
29000	2724.02	1514.52	1118.06	924.74	812.54	740.76	691.95	657.35	632.11	613.31	599.07	588.17	579.75	573.19
30000	2817.95	1566.74	1156.61	956.62	840.56	766.30	715.81	680.02	653.91	634.46	619.73	608.46	599.74	592.96
31000	2911.88	1618.96	1195.16	988.51	868.57	791.85	739.67	702.69	675.71	655.60	640.39	628.74	619.73	612.72
32000	3005.82	1671.19	1233.72	1020.40	896.59	817.39	763.53	725.35	697.50	676.75	661.05	649.02	639.72	632.49
33000	3099.75	1723.41	1272.27	1052.29	924.61	842.93	787.39	748.02	719.30	697.90	681.70	669.30	659.71	652.25
34000	3193.68	1775.64	1310.83	1084.17	952.63	868.48	811.25	770.69	741.10	719.05	702.36	689.58	679.70	672.02
35000	3287.61	1827.86	1349.38	1116.06	980.65	894.02	835.11	793.35	762.89	740.20	723.02	709.86	699.70	691.78
36000	3381.54	1880.09	1387.93	1147.95	1008.67	919.56	858.97	816.02	784.69	761.35	743.68	730.15	719.69	711.55
37000	3475.47	1932.31	1426.49	1179.84	1036.68	945.11	882.83	838.69	806.49	782.49	764.34	750.43	739.68	731.31
38000	3569.41	1984.54	1465.04	1211.72	1064.70	970.65	906.69	861.36	828.28	803.64	784.99	770.71	759.67	751.08
39000	3663.34	2036.76	1503.59	1243.61	1092.72	996.19	930.55	884.02	850.08	824.79	805.65	790.99	779.66	770.84
40000	3757.27	2088.98	1542.15	1275.50	1120.74	1021.74	954.41	906.69	871.88	845.94	826.31	811.27	799.65	790.61
41000	3851.20	2141.21	1580.70	1307.39	1148.76	1047.28	978.27	929.36	893.68	867.09	846.97	831.55	819.64	810.37
42000	3945.13	2193.43	1619.25	1339.27	1176.78	1072.82	1002.13	952.02	915.47	888.24	867.62	851.84	839.63	830.14
43000	4039.06	2245.66	1657.81	1371.16	1204.80	1098.37	1025.99	974.69	937.27	909.39	888.28	872.12	859.63	849.90
44000	4133.00	2297.88	1696.36	1403.05	1232.81	1123.91	1049.85	997.36	959.07	930.53	908.94	892.40	879.62	869.67
45000	4226.93	2350.11	1734.91	1434.93	1260.83	1149.45	1073.71	1020.03	980.86	951.68	929.60	912.68	899.61	889.43
46000	4320.86	2402.33	1773.47	1466.82	1288.85	1175.00	1097.57	1042.69	1002.66	972.83	950.25	932.96	919.60	909.20
47000	4414.79	2454.56	1812.02	1498.71	1316.87	1200.54	1121.43	1065.36	1024.46	993.98	970.91	953.24	939.59	928.96
48000	4508.72	2506.78	1850.57	1530.60	1344.89	1226.08	1145.29	1088.03	1046.25	1015.13	991.57	973.53	959.58	948.73
49000	4602.65	2559.00	1889.13	1562.48	1372.91	1251.63	1169.15	1110.69	1068.05	1036.28	1012.23	993.81	979.57	968.49
50000	4696.58	2611.23	1927.68	1594.37	1400.92	1277.17	1193.01	1133.36	1089.85	1057.42	1032.88	1014.09	999.56	988.26
55000	5166.24	2872.35	2120.45	1753.81	1541.02	1404.89	1312.31	1246.70	1198.83	1163.17	1136.17	1115.50	1099.52	1087.08
60000	5635.90	3133.47	2313.22	1913.24	1681.11	1532.60	1431.61	1360.03	1307.81	1268.91	1239.46	1216.91	1199.48	1185.91
65000	6105.56	3394.60	2505.98	2072.68	1821.20	1660.32	1550.91	1473.37	1416.80	1374.65	1342.75	1318.31	1299.43	1284.73
70000	6575.22	3655.72	2698.75	2232.12	1961.29	1788.04	1670.21	1586.70	1525.78	1480.39	1446.04	1419.72	1399.39	1383.56
75000	7044.87	3916.84	2891.52	2391.55	2101.38	1915.75	1789.51	1700.04	1634.77	1586.13	1549.32	1521.13	1499.34	1482.39
80000	7514.53	4177.96	3084.29	2550.99	2241.48	2043.47	1908.91	1813.38	1743.75	1691.87	1652.61	1622.54	1599.30	1581.21
85000	7984.19	4439.09	3277.06	2710.43	2381.57	2171.19	2028.11	1926.71	1852.74	1797.62	1755.90	1723.95	1699.25	1680.04
90000	8453.85	4700.21	3469.82	2869.86	2521.66	2298.90	2147.41	2040.05	1961.72	1903.36	1859.19	1825.36	1799.21	1778.86
95000	8923.51	4961.33	3662.59	3029.30	2661.75	2426.62	2266.71	2153.38	2070.70	2009.10	1962.47	1926.76	1899.17	1877.69
100000	9393.17	5222.45	3855.36	3188.74	2801.84	2554.34	2386.01	2266.72	2179.69	2114.84	2065.76	2028.17	1999.12	1976.51

MONTHLY PAYMENT
REQUIRED TO AMORTIZE A LOAN

22.700%

TERM AMOUNT	15 Years	16 Years	17 Years	18 Years	19 Years	20 Years	21 Years	22 Years	23 Years	24 Years	25 Years	30 Years	35 Years	40 Years
5	.10	.10	.10	.10	.10	.10	.10	.10	.10	.10	.10	.10	.10	.10
10	.20	.20	.20	.20	.20	.20	.20	.20	.20	.20	.19	.19	.19	.19
15	.30	.30	.30	.29	.29	.29	.29	.29	.29	.29	.29	.29	.29	.29
25	.49	.49	.49	.49	.48	.48	.48	.48	.48	.48	.48	.48	.48	.48
50	.98	.98	.97	.97	.96	.96	.96	.96	.96	.96	.95	.95	.95	.95
75	1.47	1.46	1.46	1.45	1.44	1.44	1.44	1.43	1.43	1.43	1.43	1.43	1.42	1.42
100	1.96	1.95	1.94	1.93	1.92	1.92	1.91	1.91	1.91	1.91	1.90	1.90	1.90	1.90
200	3.92	3.89	3.87	3.86	3.84	3.83	3.82	3.82	3.81	3.81	3.80	3.79	3.79	3.79
300	5.88	5.84	5.81	5.78	5.76	5.74	5.73	5.72	5.71	5.71	5.70	5.69	5.68	5.68
400	7.84	7.78	7.74	7.71	7.68	7.66	7.64	7.63	7.61	7.61	7.60	7.58	7.57	7.57
500	9.80	9.73	9.67	9.63	9.60	9.57	9.55	9.53	9.52	9.51	9.50	9.47	9.47	9.46
600	11.76	11.67	11.61	11.56	11.52	11.48	11.46	11.44	11.42	11.41	11.40	11.37	11.36	11.36
700	13.72	13.62	13.54	13.48	13.43	13.40	13.37	13.34	13.32	13.31	13.29	13.26	13.25	13.25
800	15.68	15.56	15.48	15.41	15.35	15.31	15.27	15.25	15.22	15.21	15.19	15.16	15.14	15.14
900	17.63	17.51	17.41	17.33	17.27	17.22	17.18	17.15	17.13	17.11	17.09	17.05	17.04	17.03
1000	19.59	19.45	19.34	19.26	19.19	19.13	19.09	19.06	19.03	19.01	18.99	18.94	18.93	18.92
2000	39.18	38.90	38.68	38.51	38.37	38.26	38.18	38.11	38.05	38.01	37.98	37.88	37.85	37.84
3000	58.77	58.35	58.02	57.76	57.56	57.39	57.26	57.16	57.08	57.01	56.96	56.82	56.78	56.76
4000	78.36	77.80	77.36	77.02	76.74	76.52	76.35	76.21	76.10	76.02	75.95	75.76	75.70	75.68
5000	97.95	97.25	96.70	96.27	95.93	95.65	95.44	95.26	95.13	95.02	94.93	94.70	94.62	94.60
6000	117.53	116.70	116.04	115.52	115.11	114.78	114.52	114.32	114.15	114.02	113.92	113.64	113.55	113.52
7000	137.12	136.15	135.38	134.77	134.29	133.91	133.61	133.37	133.18	133.02	132.90	132.58	132.47	132.44
8000	156.71	155.60	154.72	154.03	153.48	153.04	152.70	152.42	152.20	152.03	151.89	151.52	151.40	151.36
9000	176.30	175.05	174.06	173.28	172.66	172.17	171.78	171.47	171.23	171.03	170.87	170.46	170.32	170.28
10000	195.89	194.50	193.40	192.53	191.85	191.30	190.87	190.52	190.25	190.03	189.86	189.39	189.24	189.20
11000	215.47	213.95	212.74	211.79	211.03	210.43	209.96	209.58	209.28	209.04	208.84	208.33	208.17	208.11
12000	235.06	233.39	232.08	231.04	230.22	229.56	229.04	228.63	228.30	228.04	227.83	227.27	227.09	227.03
13000	254.65	252.84	251.42	250.29	249.40	248.69	248.13	247.68	247.32	247.04	246.81	246.21	246.02	245.95
14000	274.24	272.29	270.76	269.54	268.58	267.82	267.21	266.73	266.35	266.04	265.80	265.15	264.94	264.87
15000	293.83	291.74	290.10	288.80	287.77	286.95	286.30	285.78	285.37	285.05	284.79	284.09	283.86	283.79
16000	313.42	311.19	309.44	308.05	306.95	306.08	305.39	304.84	304.40	304.05	303.77	303.03	302.79	302.71
17000	333.00	330.64	328.78	327.30	326.14	325.21	324.47	323.89	323.42	323.05	322.76	321.97	321.71	321.63
18000	352.59	350.09	348.12	346.56	345.32	344.34	343.56	342.94	342.45	342.05	341.74	340.91	340.64	340.55
19000	372.18	369.54	367.46	365.81	364.50	363.47	362.65	361.99	361.47	361.06	360.73	359.84	359.56	359.47
20000	391.77	388.99	386.79	385.06	383.69	382.60	381.73	381.04	380.50	380.06	379.71	378.78	378.48	378.39
21000	411.36	408.44	406.13	404.31	402.87	401.73	400.82	400.10	399.52	399.06	398.70	397.72	397.41	397.30
22000	430.94	427.89	425.47	423.57	422.06	420.86	419.91	419.15	418.55	418.07	417.68	416.66	416.33	416.22
23000	450.53	447.33	444.81	442.82	441.24	439.99	438.99	438.20	437.57	437.07	436.67	435.60	435.25	435.14
24000	470.12	466.78	464.15	462.07	460.43	459.12	458.08	457.25	456.59	456.07	455.65	454.54	454.18	454.06
25000	489.71	486.23	483.49	481.33	479.61	478.25	477.17	476.30	475.62	475.07	474.64	473.48	473.10	472.98
26000	509.30	505.68	502.83	500.58	498.79	497.38	496.25	495.36	494.64	494.08	493.62	492.42	492.03	491.90
27000	528.88	525.13	522.17	519.83	517.98	516.51	515.34	514.41	513.67	513.08	512.61	511.36	510.95	510.82
28000	548.47	544.58	541.51	539.08	537.16	535.64	534.42	533.46	532.69	532.08	531.59	530.29	529.87	529.74
29000	568.06	564.03	560.85	558.34	556.35	554.77	553.51	552.51	551.72	551.08	550.58	549.23	548.80	548.66
30000	587.65	583.48	580.19	577.59	575.53	573.90	572.60	571.56	570.74	570.09	569.57	568.17	567.72	567.58
31000	607.24	602.93	599.53	596.84	594.71	593.03	591.68	590.62	589.77	589.09	588.55	587.11	586.65	586.49
32000	626.83	622.38	618.87	616.10	613.90	612.16	610.77	609.67	608.79	608.09	607.54	606.05	605.57	605.41
33000	646.41	641.83	638.21	635.35	633.08	631.28	629.86	628.72	627.82	627.10	626.52	624.99	624.49	624.33
34000	666.00	661.27	657.55	654.60	652.27	650.41	648.94	647.77	646.84	646.10	645.51	643.93	643.42	643.25
35000	685.59	680.72	676.89	673.85	671.45	669.54	668.03	666.82	665.87	665.10	664.49	662.87	662.34	662.17
36000	705.18	700.17	696.23	693.11	690.64	688.67	687.12	685.88	684.89	684.10	683.48	681.81	681.27	681.09
37000	724.77	719.62	715.57	712.36	709.82	707.80	706.20	704.93	703.91	703.11	702.46	700.75	700.19	700.01
38000	744.35	739.07	734.91	731.61	729.00	726.93	725.29	723.98	722.94	722.11	721.45	719.68	719.11	718.93
39000	763.94	758.52	754.25	750.87	748.19	746.06	744.37	743.03	741.96	741.11	740.43	738.62	738.04	737.85
40000	783.53	777.97	773.58	770.12	767.37	765.19	763.46	762.08	760.99	760.11	759.42	757.56	756.96	756.77
41000	803.12	797.42	792.92	789.37	786.56	784.32	782.55	781.14	780.01	779.12	778.40	776.50	775.88	775.68
42000	822.71	816.87	812.26	808.62	805.74	803.45	801.63	800.19	799.04	798.12	797.39	795.44	794.81	794.60
43000	842.30	836.32	831.60	827.88	824.92	822.58	820.72	819.24	818.06	817.12	816.37	814.38	813.73	813.52
44000	861.88	855.77	850.94	847.13	844.11	841.71	839.81	838.29	837.09	836.13	835.36	833.32	832.66	832.44
45000	881.47	875.22	870.28	866.38	863.29	860.84	858.89	857.34	856.11	855.13	854.35	852.26	851.58	851.36
46000	901.06	894.66	889.62	885.63	882.48	879.97	877.98	876.40	875.14	874.13	873.33	871.20	870.50	870.28
47000	920.65	914.11	908.96	904.89	901.66	899.10	897.07	895.45	894.16	893.13	892.32	890.13	889.43	889.20
48000	940.24	933.56	928.30	924.14	920.85	918.23	916.15	914.50	913.18	912.14	911.30	909.07	908.35	908.12
49000	959.82	953.01	947.64	943.39	940.03	937.36	935.24	933.55	932.21	931.14	930.29	928.01	927.28	927.04
50000	979.41	972.46	966.98	962.65	959.21	956.49	954.33	952.60	951.23	950.14	949.27	946.95	946.20	945.96
55000	1077.35	1069.71	1063.68	1058.91	1055.13	1052.14	1049.76	1047.86	1046.36	1045.16	1044.20	1041.65	1040.82	1040.55
60000	1175.29	1166.95	1160.37	1155.17	1151.06	1147.79	1145.19	1143.12	1141.48	1140.17	1139.13	1136.34	1135.44	1135.15
65000	1273.23	1264.20	1257.07	1251.44	1246.98	1243.43	1240.62	1238.38	1236.60	1235.18	1234.05	1231.03	1230.06	1229.74
70000	1371.18	1361.44	1353.77	1347.70	1342.90	1339.08	1336.05	1333.64	1331.73	1330.20	1328.98	1325.73	1324.68	1324.34
75000	1469.12	1458.69	1450.47	1443.97	1438.82	1434.73	1431.49	1428.90	1426.85	1425.21	1423.91	1420.42	1419.30	1418.93
80000	1567.06	1555.93	1547.16	1540.23	1534.74	1530.38	1526.92	1524.16	1521.97	1520.22	1518.83	1515.12	1513.92	1513.53
85000	1665.00	1653.18	1643.86	1636.50	1630.66	1626.03	1622.35	1619.42	1617.09	1615.23	1613.76	1609.81	1608.54	1608.12
90000	1762.94	1750.43	1740.56	1732.76	1726.58	1721.68	1717.78	1714.68	1712.22	1710.25	1708.69	1704.51	1703.16	1702.72
95000	1860.88	1847.67	1837.26	1829.02	1822.50	1817.33	1813.21	1809.94	1807.34	1805.27	1803.61	1799.20	1797.77	1797.31
100000	1958.82	1944.92	1933.95	1925.29	1918.42	1912.97	1908.65	1905.20	1902.46	1900.28	1898.54	1893.90	1892.39	1891.91

MONTHLY PAYMENT
REQUIRED TO AMORTIZE A LOAN

TERM	1 Year	2 Years	3 Years	4 Years	5 Years	6 Years	7 Years	8 Years	9 Years	10 Years	11 Years	12 Years	13 Years	14 Years
AMOUNT														
5	.47	.27	.20	.16	.15	.13	.12	.12	.11	.11	.11	.11	.11	.10
10	.94	.53	.39	.32	.29	.26	.24	.23	.22	.22	.21	.21	.21	.20
15	1.41	.79	.58	.48	.45	.39	.36	.35	.33	.32	.31	.31	.31	.30
25	2.35	1.31	.97	.80	.71	.64	.60	.57	.55	.53	.52	.51	.51	.50
50	4.70	2.62	1.93	1.60	1.41	1.28	1.20	1.14	1.10	1.06	1.04	1.02	1.01	1.00
75	7.05	3.92	2.90	2.40	2.11	1.92	1.80	1.71	1.64	1.59	1.56	1.53	1.51	1.49
100	9.40	5.23	3.86	3.20	2.81	2.56	2.39	2.27	2.19	2.12	2.07	2.04	2.01	1.99
200	18.80	10.45	7.72	6.39	5.61	5.12	4.78	4.54	4.37	4.24	4.14	4.07	4.01	3.97
300	28.19	15.68	11.58	9.58	8.42	7.68	7.17	6.81	6.55	6.36	6.21	6.10	6.01	5.95
400	37.59	20.90	15.44	12.77	11.22	10.23	9.56	9.08	8.74	8.48	8.28	8.13	8.02	7.93
500	46.98	26.13	19.29	15.96	14.03	12.79	11.95	11.35	10.92	10.60	10.35	10.16	10.02	9.91
600	56.38	31.35	23.15	19.15	16.83	15.35	14.34	13.62	13.10	12.71	12.42	12.20	12.02	11.89
700	65.77	36.58	27.01	22.35	19.64	17.91	16.73	15.89	15.29	14.83	14.49	14.23	14.02	13.87
800	75.17	41.80	30.87	25.54	22.44	20.46	19.12	18.16	17.47	16.95	16.56	16.26	16.03	15.85
900	84.57	47.03	34.73	28.73	25.25	23.02	21.51	20.43	19.65	19.07	18.63	18.29	18.03	17.83
1000	93.96	52.25	38.58	31.92	28.05	25.58	23.90	22.70	21.84	21.19	20.70	20.32	20.03	19.81
2000	187.92	104.50	77.16	63.83	56.10	51.15	47.79	45.40	43.67	42.37	41.39	40.64	40.06	39.61
3000	281.87	156.75	115.74	95.75	84.15	76.72	71.68	68.10	65.50	63.55	62.08	60.96	60.09	59.41
4000	375.83	209.00	154.32	127.66	112.19	102.30	95.57	90.80	87.33	84.74	82.78	81.28	80.12	79.22
5000	469.78	261.25	192.90	159.58	140.24	127.87	119.46	113.50	109.16	105.92	103.47	101.59	100.14	99.02
6000	563.74	313.50	231.48	191.49	168.29	153.44	143.35	136.20	130.99	127.10	124.16	121.91	120.17	118.82
7000	657.69	365.75	270.06	223.41	196.33	179.02	167.24	158.90	152.82	148.28	144.85	142.23	140.20	138.62
8000	751.65	418.00	308.64	255.32	224.38	204.59	191.13	181.60	174.65	169.47	165.55	162.55	160.23	158.43
9000	845.61	470.25	347.22	287.24	252.43	230.16	215.03	204.30	196.48	190.65	186.24	182.86	180.26	178.23
10000	939.56	522.50	385.80	319.15	280.48	255.74	238.92	227.00	218.31	211.83	206.93	203.18	200.28	198.03
11000	1033.52	574.75	424.38	351.07	308.52	281.31	262.81	249.70	240.14	233.01	227.63	223.50	220.31	217.83
12000	1127.47	627.00	462.96	382.98	336.57	306.88	286.70	272.40	261.97	254.20	248.32	243.82	240.34	237.64
13000	1221.43	679.25	501.54	414.90	364.62	332.46	310.59	295.10	283.80	275.38	269.01	264.14	260.37	257.44
14000	1315.38	731.49	540.12	446.81	392.66	358.03	334.48	317.80	305.63	296.56	289.70	284.45	280.40	277.24
15000	1409.34	783.74	578.70	478.72	420.71	383.60	358.37	340.50	327.46	317.75	310.40	304.77	300.42	297.04
16000	1503.30	835.99	617.28	510.64	448.76	409.18	382.26	363.20	349.29	338.93	331.09	325.09	320.45	316.85
17000	1597.25	888.24	655.86	542.55	476.80	434.75	406.16	385.90	371.12	360.11	351.78	345.41	340.48	336.65
18000	1691.21	940.49	694.44	574.47	504.85	460.32	430.05	408.59	392.95	381.29	372.48	365.72	360.51	356.45
19000	1785.16	992.74	733.02	606.38	532.90	485.90	453.94	431.29	414.78	402.48	393.17	386.04	380.54	376.25
20000	1879.12	1044.99	771.60	638.30	560.95	511.47	477.83	453.99	436.61	423.66	413.86	406.36	400.56	396.06
21000	1973.07	1097.24	810.18	670.21	588.99	537.04	501.72	476.69	458.44	444.84	434.55	426.68	420.59	415.86
22000	2067.03	1149.49	848.75	702.13	617.04	562.62	525.61	499.39	480.27	466.02	455.25	447.00	440.62	435.66
23000	2160.99	1201.74	887.33	734.04	645.09	588.19	549.50	522.09	502.10	487.21	475.94	467.31	460.65	455.46
24000	2254.94	1253.99	925.91	765.96	673.13	613.76	573.39	544.79	523.93	508.39	496.63	487.63	480.68	475.27
25000	2348.90	1306.24	964.49	797.87	701.18	639.34	597.28	567.49	545.76	529.57	517.33	507.95	500.70	495.07
26000	2442.85	1358.49	1003.07	829.79	729.23	664.91	621.18	590.19	567.59	550.76	538.02	528.27	520.73	514.87
27000	2536.81	1410.74	1041.65	861.70	757.27	690.48	645.07	612.89	589.42	571.94	558.71	548.58	540.76	534.67
28000	2630.76	1462.98	1080.23	893.62	785.32	716.06	668.96	635.59	611.25	593.12	579.40	568.90	560.79	554.48
29000	2724.72	1515.23	1118.81	925.53	813.37	741.63	692.85	658.29	633.08	614.30	600.10	589.22	580.82	574.28
30000	2818.68	1567.48	1157.39	957.44	841.42	767.20	716.74	680.99	654.91	635.49	620.79	609.54	600.84	594.08
31000	2912.63	1619.73	1195.97	989.36	869.46	792.78	740.63	703.69	676.74	656.67	641.48	629.86	620.87	613.88
32000	3006.59	1671.98	1234.55	1021.27	897.51	818.35	764.52	726.39	698.57	677.85	662.18	650.17	640.90	633.69
33000	3100.54	1724.23	1273.13	1053.19	925.56	843.92	788.41	749.09	720.40	699.03	682.87	670.49	660.93	653.49
34000	3194.50	1776.48	1311.71	1085.10	953.60	869.49	812.31	771.79	742.23	720.22	703.56	690.81	680.96	673.29
35000	3288.45	1828.73	1350.29	1117.02	981.65	895.07	836.20	794.48	764.06	741.40	724.25	711.13	700.98	693.09
36000	3382.41	1880.98	1388.87	1148.93	1009.70	920.64	860.09	817.18	785.89	762.58	744.95	731.44	721.01	712.90
37000	3476.37	1933.23	1427.45	1180.85	1037.74	946.21	883.98	839.88	807.72	783.77	765.64	751.76	741.04	732.70
38000	3570.32	1985.48	1466.03	1212.76	1065.79	971.79	907.87	862.58	829.55	804.95	786.33	772.08	761.07	752.50
39000	3664.28	2037.73	1504.61	1244.68	1093.84	997.36	931.76	885.28	851.38	826.13	807.03	792.40	781.10	772.30
40000	3758.23	2089.98	1543.19	1276.59	1121.89	1022.93	955.65	907.98	873.21	847.31	827.72	812.71	801.12	792.11
41000	3852.19	2142.23	1581.77	1308.51	1149.93	1048.51	979.54	930.68	895.04	868.50	848.41	833.03	821.15	811.91
42000	3946.14	2194.47	1620.35	1340.42	1177.98	1074.08	1003.43	953.38	916.87	889.68	869.10	853.35	841.18	831.71
43000	4040.10	2246.72	1658.93	1372.34	1206.03	1099.65	1027.33	976.08	938.70	910.86	889.80	873.67	861.21	851.51
44000	4134.06	2298.97	1697.50	1404.25	1234.07	1125.23	1051.22	998.78	960.53	932.04	910.49	893.99	881.24	871.32
45000	4228.01	2351.22	1736.08	1436.16	1262.12	1150.80	1075.11	1021.48	982.36	953.23	931.18	914.30	901.26	891.12
46000	4321.97	2403.47	1774.66	1468.08	1290.17	1176.37	1099.00	1044.18	1004.19	974.41	951.87	934.62	921.29	910.92
47000	4415.92	2455.72	1813.24	1499.99	1318.22	1201.95	1122.89	1066.88	1026.02	995.59	972.57	954.94	941.32	930.72
48000	4509.88	2507.97	1851.82	1531.91	1346.26	1227.52	1146.78	1089.58	1047.85	1016.78	993.26	975.26	961.35	950.53
49000	4603.83	2560.22	1890.40	1563.82	1374.31	1253.09	1170.67	1112.28	1069.68	1037.96	1013.95	995.57	981.38	970.33
50000	4697.79	2612.47	1928.98	1595.74	1402.36	1278.67	1194.56	1134.98	1091.51	1059.14	1034.65	1015.89	1001.40	990.13
55000	5167.57	2873.71	2121.88	1755.31	1542.59	1406.53	1314.02	1248.47	1200.67	1165.05	1138.11	1117.48	1101.54	1089.14
60000	5637.35	3134.96	2314.78	1914.88	1682.83	1534.40	1433.48	1361.97	1309.82	1270.97	1241.57	1219.07	1201.68	1188.16
65000	6107.13	3396.21	2507.68	2074.46	1823.06	1662.26	1552.93	1475.47	1418.97	1376.88	1345.04	1320.66	1301.82	1287.17
70000	6576.90	3657.45	2700.57	2234.03	1963.30	1790.13	1672.39	1588.96	1528.12	1482.80	1448.50	1422.25	1401.96	1386.18
75000	7046.68	3918.70	2893.47	2393.60	2103.53	1918.00	1791.84	1702.46	1637.27	1588.71	1551.97	1523.84	1502.10	1485.19
80000	7516.46	4179.95	3086.37	2553.18	2243.77	2045.86	1911.30	1815.96	1746.42	1694.62	1655.43	1625.42	1602.24	1584.21
85000	7986.24	4441.19	3279.27	2712.75	2384.00	2173.73	2030.76	1929.46	1855.57	1800.54	1758.89	1727.01	1702.38	1683.22
90000	8456.02	4702.44	3472.16	2872.32	2524.24	2301.60	2150.21	2042.95	1964.72	1906.45	1862.36	1828.60	1802.52	1782.23
95000	8925.80	4963.69	3665.06	3031.90	2664.47	2429.46	2269.67	2156.45	2073.87	2012.36	1965.82	1930.19	1902.66	1881.24
100000	9395.58	5224.93	3857.96	3191.47	2804.71	2557.33	2389.12	2269.95	2183.02	2118.28	2069.29	2031.78	2002.80	1980.26

TERM	15 Years	16 Years	17 Years	18 Years	19 Years	20 Years	21 Years	22 Years	23 Years	24 Years	25 Years	30 Years	35 Years	40 Years
AMOUNT														
5	.10	.10	.10	.10	.10	.10	.10	.10	.10	.10	.10	.10	.10	.10
10	.20	.20	.20	.20	.20	.20	.20	.20	.20	.20	.20	.19	.19	.19
15	.30	.30	.30	.29	.29	.29	.29	.29	.29	.29	.29	.29	.29	.29
25	.50	.49	.49	.49	.49	.48	.48	.48	.48	.48	.48	.48	.48	.48
50	.99	.98	.97	.97	.97	.96	.96	.96	.96	.96	.96	.95	.95	.95
75	1.48	1.47	1.46	1.45	1.45	1.44	1.44	1.44	1.43	1.43	1.43	1.43	1.43	1.43
100	1.97	1.95	1.94	1.93	1.93	1.92	1.92	1.91	1.91	1.91	1.91	1.90	1.90	1.90
200	3.93	3.90	3.88	3.86	3.85	3.84	3.83	3.82	3.82	3.81	3.81	3.80	3.80	3.80
300	5.89	5.85	5.82	5.79	5.77	5.76	5.74	5.73	5.72	5.72	5.71	5.70	5.69	5.69
400	7.86	7.80	7.76	7.72	7.69	7.67	7.66	7.64	7.63	7.62	7.62	7.60	7.59	7.59
500	9.82	9.75	9.69	9.65	9.62	9.59	9.57	9.55	9.54	9.53	9.52	9.50	9.49	9.49
600	11.78	11.70	11.63	11.58	11.54	11.51	11.48	11.46	11.44	11.43	11.42	11.39	11.38	11.38
700	13.74	13.65	13.57	13.51	13.46	13.42	13.39	13.37	13.35	13.34	13.32	13.29	13.28	13.28
800	15.71	15.60	15.51	15.44	15.38	15.34	15.31	15.28	15.26	15.24	15.23	15.19	15.18	15.17
900	17.67	17.54	17.45	17.37	17.31	17.26	17.22	17.19	17.16	17.14	17.13	17.09	17.07	17.07
1000	19.63	19.49	19.38	19.30	19.23	19.17	19.13	19.10	19.07	19.05	19.03	18.99	18.97	18.97
2000	39.26	38.98	38.76	38.59	38.45	38.34	38.26	38.19	38.14	38.09	38.06	37.97	37.94	37.93
3000	58.88	58.47	58.14	57.88	57.68	57.51	57.39	57.28	57.20	57.14	57.08	56.95	56.90	56.89
4000	78.51	77.96	77.52	77.17	76.90	76.68	76.51	76.37	76.27	76.18	76.11	75.93	75.87	75.85
5000	98.14	97.45	96.90	96.47	96.12	95.85	95.64	95.47	95.33	95.22	95.14	94.91	94.83	94.81
6000	117.76	116.93	116.28	115.76	115.35	115.02	114.77	114.56	114.40	114.27	114.16	113.89	113.80	113.77
7000	137.39	136.42	135.65	135.05	134.57	134.19	133.89	133.65	133.46	133.31	133.19	132.87	132.76	132.73
8000	157.01	155.91	155.03	154.34	153.80	153.36	153.02	152.74	152.53	152.36	152.22	151.85	151.73	151.69
9000	176.64	175.39	174.41	173.63	173.02	172.53	172.15	171.84	171.59	171.40	171.24	170.83	170.69	170.65
10000	196.27	194.88	193.79	192.93	192.24	191.70	191.27	190.93	190.66	190.44	190.27	189.81	189.66	189.61
11000	215.89	214.37	213.17	212.22	211.47	210.87	210.40	210.02	209.72	209.48	209.29	208.79	208.62	208.57
12000	235.52	233.86	232.55	231.51	230.69	230.04	229.53	229.11	228.79	228.53	228.32	227.77	227.59	227.53
13000	255.15	253.34	251.93	250.80	249.92	249.21	248.65	248.21	247.85	247.57	247.35	246.75	246.56	246.49
14000	274.77	272.83	271.30	270.10	269.14	268.38	267.78	267.30	266.92	266.62	266.37	265.73	265.52	265.45
15000	294.40	292.32	290.68	289.39	288.36	287.55	286.91	286.39	285.98	285.66	285.40	284.71	284.49	284.41
16000	314.02	311.81	310.06	308.68	307.59	306.72	306.03	305.48	305.05	304.70	304.43	303.69	303.45	303.38
17000	333.65	331.30	329.44	327.97	326.81	325.89	325.16	324.58	324.11	323.75	323.45	322.67	322.42	322.34
18000	353.28	350.78	348.82	347.26	346.04	345.06	344.29	343.67	343.18	342.79	342.48	341.65	341.38	341.30
19000	372.90	370.27	368.20	366.56	365.26	364.23	363.41	362.76	362.24	361.83	361.51	360.63	360.35	360.26
20000	392.53	389.76	387.57	385.85	384.48	383.40	382.54	381.85	381.31	380.88	380.53	379.61	379.31	379.22
21000	412.15	409.25	406.95	405.14	403.71	402.57	401.67	400.95	400.38	399.92	399.56	398.59	398.28	398.18
22000	431.78	428.73	426.33	424.43	422.93	421.74	420.79	420.04	419.44	418.96	418.58	417.57	417.24	417.14
23000	451.41	448.22	445.71	443.73	442.15	440.91	439.92	439.13	438.51	438.01	437.61	436.55	436.21	436.10
24000	471.03	467.71	465.09	463.02	461.38	460.08	459.05	458.22	457.57	457.05	456.64	455.53	455.18	455.06
25000	490.66	487.20	484.47	482.31	480.60	479.25	478.17	477.32	476.64	476.09	475.66	474.51	474.14	474.02
26000	510.29	506.68	503.85	501.60	499.83	498.42	497.30	496.41	495.70	495.14	494.69	493.49	493.11	492.98
27000	529.91	526.17	523.22	520.89	519.05	517.59	516.43	515.50	514.77	514.18	513.72	512.47	512.07	511.94
28000	549.54	545.66	542.60	540.19	538.27	536.76	535.55	534.59	533.83	533.23	532.74	531.45	531.04	530.90
29000	569.16	565.15	561.98	559.48	557.50	555.93	554.68	553.69	552.90	552.27	551.77	550.43	550.00	549.86
30000	588.79	584.63	581.36	578.77	576.72	575.10	573.81	572.78	571.96	571.31	570.79	569.41	568.97	568.82
31000	608.42	604.12	600.74	598.06	595.95	594.27	592.93	591.87	591.03	590.36	589.82	588.39	587.93	587.78
32000	628.04	623.61	620.12	617.36	615.17	613.44	612.06	610.96	610.09	609.40	608.85	607.37	606.90	606.75
33000	647.67	643.10	639.50	636.65	634.39	632.61	631.19	630.06	629.16	628.44	627.87	626.36	625.86	625.71
34000	667.30	662.59	658.87	655.94	653.62	651.78	650.31	649.15	648.22	647.49	646.90	645.34	644.83	644.67
35000	686.92	682.07	678.25	675.23	672.84	670.95	669.44	668.24	667.29	666.53	665.93	664.32	663.80	663.63
36000	706.55	701.56	697.63	694.52	692.07	690.11	688.57	687.33	686.35	685.57	684.95	683.30	682.76	682.59
37000	726.17	721.05	717.01	713.82	711.29	709.28	707.69	706.43	705.42	704.62	703.98	702.28	701.73	701.55
38000	745.80	740.54	736.39	733.11	730.51	728.45	726.82	725.52	724.48	723.66	723.01	721.26	720.69	720.51
39000	765.43	760.02	755.77	752.40	749.74	747.62	745.95	744.61	743.55	742.70	742.03	740.24	739.66	739.47
40000	785.05	779.51	775.14	771.69	768.96	766.79	765.07	763.70	762.62	761.75	761.06	759.22	758.62	758.43
41000	804.68	799.00	794.52	790.99	788.18	785.96	784.20	782.80	781.68	780.79	780.08	778.20	777.59	777.39
42000	824.30	818.49	813.90	810.28	807.41	805.13	803.33	801.89	800.75	799.84	799.11	797.18	796.55	796.35
43000	843.93	837.97	833.28	829.57	826.63	824.30	822.45	820.98	819.81	818.88	818.14	816.16	815.52	815.31
44000	863.56	857.46	852.66	848.86	845.86	843.47	841.58	840.07	838.88	837.92	837.16	835.14	834.48	834.27
45000	883.18	876.95	872.04	868.15	865.08	862.64	860.71	859.17	857.94	856.97	856.19	854.12	853.45	853.23
46000	902.81	896.44	891.42	887.45	884.30	881.80	879.83	878.26	877.01	876.01	875.22	873.10	872.42	872.19
47000	922.44	915.93	910.79	906.74	903.53	900.98	898.96	897.35	896.07	895.05	894.24	892.08	891.38	891.16
48000	942.06	935.41	930.17	926.03	922.75	920.15	918.09	916.44	915.14	914.10	913.27	911.06	910.35	910.12
49000	961.69	954.90	949.55	945.32	941.98	939.32	937.21	935.54	934.20	933.14	932.29	930.04	929.31	929.08
50000	981.31	974.39	968.93	964.62	961.20	958.49	956.34	954.63	953.27	952.18	951.32	949.02	948.28	948.04
55000	1079.45	1071.83	1065.82	1061.08	1057.32	1054.34	1051.97	1050.09	1048.59	1047.40	1046.45	1043.92	1043.10	1042.84
60000	1177.58	1169.26	1162.71	1157.54	1153.44	1150.19	1147.61	1145.55	1143.92	1142.62	1141.58	1138.82	1137.93	1137.64
65000	1275.71	1266.70	1259.61	1254.00	1249.56	1246.04	1243.24	1241.02	1239.25	1237.84	1236.72	1233.73	1232.76	1232.45
70000	1373.84	1364.14	1356.50	1350.46	1345.68	1341.89	1338.87	1336.48	1334.57	1333.06	1331.85	1328.63	1327.59	1327.25
75000	1471.97	1461.58	1453.39	1446.92	1441.80	1437.73	1434.51	1431.94	1429.90	1428.27	1426.98	1423.53	1422.41	1422.05
80000	1570.10	1559.02	1550.28	1543.38	1537.92	1533.58	1530.14	1527.40	1525.23	1523.49	1522.11	1518.43	1517.24	1516.86
85000	1668.23	1656.46	1647.18	1639.84	1634.04	1629.43	1625.77	1622.87	1620.55	1618.71	1617.24	1613.33	1612.07	1611.66
90000	1766.36	1753.89	1744.07	1736.30	1730.16	1725.28	1721.41	1718.33	1715.88	1713.93	1712.37	1708.23	1706.90	1706.46
95000	1864.49	1851.33	1840.96	1832.77	1826.28	1821.13	1817.04	1813.79	1811.20	1809.15	1807.51	1803.13	1801.72	1801.27
100000	1962.62	1948.77	1937.85	1929.23	1922.40	1916.98	1912.67	1909.25	1906.53	1904.36	1902.64	1898.04	1896.55	1896.07

MONTHLY PAYMENT
REQUIRED TO AMORTIZE A LOAN

TERM AMOUNT	1 Year	2 Years	3 Years	4 Years	5 Years	6 Years	7 Years	8 Years	9 Years	10 Years	11 Years	12 Years	13 Years	14 Years
5	.47	.27	.20	.16	.15	.13	.12	.12	.11	.11	.11	.11	.11	.10
10	.94	.53	.39	.32	.29	.26	.24	.23	.22	.22	.21	.21	.21	.20
15	1.41	.79	.58	.48	.43	.39	.36	.35	.33	.32	.32	.31	.31	.30
25	2.35	1.31	.97	.80	.71	.65	.60	.57	.55	.54	.52	.51	.51	.50
50	4.70	2.62	1.94	1.60	1.41	1.29	1.20	1.14	1.10	1.07	1.04	1.02	1.01	1.00
75	7.05	3.93	2.90	2.40	2.11	1.93	1.80	1.71	1.64	1.60	1.56	1.53	1.51	1.49
100	9.40	5.23	3.87	3.20	2.81	2.57	2.40	2.28	2.19	2.13	2.08	2.04	2.01	1.99
200	18.80	10.46	7.73	6.39	5.62	5.13	4.79	4.55	4.38	4.25	4.15	4.08	4.02	3.97
300	28.20	15.69	11.59	9.59	8.43	7.69	7.18	6.82	6.56	6.37	6.22	6.11	6.02	5.96
400	37.60	20.91	15.45	12.78	11.24	10.25	9.57	9.10	8.75	8.49	8.30	8.15	8.03	7.94
500	46.99	26.14	19.31	15.98	14.04	12.81	11.97	11.37	10.94	10.61	10.37	10.18	10.04	9.92
600	56.39	31.37	23.17	19.17	16.85	15.37	14.36	13.64	13.12	12.74	12.44	12.22	12.04	11.91
700	65.79	36.60	27.03	22.36	19.66	17.93	16.75	15.92	15.31	14.86	14.51	14.25	14.05	13.89
800	75.19	41.82	30.89	25.56	22.47	20.49	19.14	18.19	17.50	16.98	16.59	16.29	16.06	15.88
900	84.59	47.05	34.75	28.75	25.27	23.05	21.54	20.46	19.68	19.10	18.66	18.32	18.06	17.86
1000	93.98	52.28	38.61	31.95	28.08	25.61	23.93	22.74	21.87	21.22	20.73	20.36	20.07	19.84
2000	187.96	104.55	77.22	63.89	56.16	51.21	47.85	45.47	43.73	42.44	41.46	40.71	40.13	39.68
3000	281.94	156.83	115.82	95.83	84.23	76.81	71.77	68.20	65.60	63.66	62.19	61.07	60.20	59.52
4000	375.92	209.10	154.43	127.77	112.31	102.42	95.69	90.93	87.46	84.87	82.92	81.42	80.26	79.36
5000	469.90	261.38	193.03	159.71	140.38	128.02	119.62	113.66	109.32	106.09	103.65	101.77	100.33	99.20
6000	563.88	313.65	231.64	191.66	168.46	153.62	143.54	136.40	131.19	127.31	124.37	122.13	120.39	119.04
7000	657.86	365.92	270.24	223.60	196.53	179.23	167.46	159.13	153.05	148.52	145.10	142.48	140.46	138.88
8000	751.84	418.20	308.85	255.54	224.61	204.83	191.38	181.86	174.91	169.74	165.83	162.84	160.52	158.72
9000	845.82	470.47	347.46	287.48	252.69	230.43	215.31	204.59	196.78	190.96	186.56	183.19	180.59	178.56
10000	939.80	522.75	386.06	319.42	280.76	256.04	239.23	227.32	218.64	212.18	207.29	203.54	200.65	198.40
11000	1033.78	575.02	424.67	351.37	308.84	281.64	263.15	250.05	240.50	233.39	228.01	223.90	220.72	218.24
12000	1127.76	627.29	463.27	383.31	336.91	307.24	287.07	272.79	262.37	254.61	248.74	244.25	240.78	238.08
13000	1221.74	679.57	501.88	415.25	364.99	332.85	311.00	295.52	284.23	275.83	269.47	264.60	260.85	257.92
14000	1315.72	731.84	540.48	447.19	393.06	358.45	334.92	318.25	306.10	297.04	290.20	284.96	280.91	277.76
15000	1409.70	784.12	579.09	479.13	421.14	384.05	358.84	340.98	327.96	318.26	310.93	305.31	300.98	297.60
16000	1503.68	836.39	617.69	511.08	449.22	409.66	382.76	363.71	349.82	339.48	331.65	325.67	321.04	317.44
17000	1597.66	888.66	656.30	543.02	477.29	435.26	406.68	386.44	371.69	360.70	352.38	346.02	341.11	337.28
18000	1691.64	940.94	694.91	574.96	505.37	460.86	430.61	409.18	393.55	381.91	373.11	366.37	361.17	357.12
19000	1785.62	993.21	733.51	606.90	533.44	486.47	454.53	431.91	415.41	403.13	393.84	386.73	381.24	376.96
20000	1879.60	1045.49	772.12	638.84	561.52	512.07	478.45	454.64	437.28	424.35	414.57	407.08	401.30	396.80
21000	1973.58	1097.76	810.72	670.79	589.59	537.67	502.37	477.37	459.14	445.56	435.29	427.44	421.37	416.64
22000	2067.56	1150.03	849.33	702.73	617.67	563.27	526.30	500.10	481.00	466.78	456.02	447.79	441.43	436.48
23000	2161.54	1202.31	887.93	734.67	645.75	588.88	550.22	522.83	502.87	488.00	476.75	468.14	461.50	456.32
24000	2255.52	1254.58	926.54	766.61	673.82	614.48	574.14	545.57	524.73	509.22	497.48	488.50	481.56	476.16
25000	2349.50	1306.86	965.14	798.55	701.90	640.08	598.06	568.30	546.59	530.43	518.21	508.85	501.62	496.00
26000	2443.48	1359.13	1003.75	830.50	729.97	665.69	621.99	591.03	568.46	551.65	538.94	529.20	521.69	515.84
27000	2537.46	1411.40	1042.36	862.44	758.05	691.29	645.91	613.76	590.32	572.87	559.66	549.56	541.75	535.68
28000	2631.44	1463.68	1080.96	894.38	786.12	716.89	669.83	636.49	612.19	594.08	580.39	569.91	561.82	555.52
29000	2725.42	1515.95	1119.57	926.32	814.20	742.50	693.75	659.23	634.05	615.30	601.12	590.27	581.88	575.36
30000	2819.40	1568.23	1158.17	958.26	842.28	768.10	717.68	681.96	655.91	636.52	621.85	610.62	601.95	595.20
31000	2913.38	1620.50	1196.78	990.21	870.35	793.70	741.60	704.69	677.78	657.73	642.58	630.97	622.01	615.04
32000	3007.36	1672.78	1235.38	1022.15	898.43	819.31	765.52	727.42	699.64	678.95	663.30	651.33	642.08	634.88
33000	3101.34	1725.05	1273.99	1054.09	926.50	844.91	789.44	750.15	721.50	700.17	684.03	671.68	662.14	654.72
34000	3195.32	1777.32	1312.59	1086.03	954.58	870.51	813.36	772.88	743.37	721.39	704.76	692.04	682.21	674.56
35000	3289.30	1829.60	1351.20	1117.97	982.65	896.12	837.29	795.62	765.23	742.60	725.49	712.39	702.27	694.40
36000	3383.28	1881.87	1389.81	1149.92	1010.73	921.72	861.21	818.35	787.09	763.82	746.22	732.74	722.34	714.24
37000	3477.26	1934.15	1428.41	1181.86	1038.81	947.32	885.13	841.08	808.96	785.04	766.94	753.10	742.40	734.08
38000	3571.24	1986.42	1467.02	1213.80	1066.88	972.93	909.05	863.81	830.82	806.25	787.67	773.45	762.47	753.92
39000	3665.22	2038.69	1505.62	1245.74	1094.96	998.53	932.98	886.54	852.68	827.47	808.40	793.80	782.53	773.76
40000	3759.20	2090.97	1544.23	1277.68	1123.03	1024.13	956.90	909.27	874.55	848.69	829.13	814.16	802.60	793.60
41000	3853.18	2143.24	1582.83	1309.63	1151.11	1049.74	980.82	932.01	896.41	869.91	849.86	834.51	822.66	813.44
42000	3947.16	2195.52	1621.44	1341.57	1179.18	1075.34	1004.74	954.74	918.28	891.12	870.58	854.87	842.73	833.28
43000	4041.14	2247.79	1660.04	1373.51	1207.26	1100.94	1028.67	977.47	940.14	912.34	891.31	875.22	862.79	853.12
44000	4135.12	2300.06	1698.65	1405.45	1235.34	1126.54	1052.59	1000.20	962.00	933.56	912.04	895.57	882.86	872.96
45000	4229.10	2352.34	1737.26	1437.39	1263.41	1152.15	1076.51	1022.93	983.87	954.77	932.77	915.93	902.92	892.80
46000	4323.08	2404.61	1775.86	1469.34	1291.49	1177.75	1100.43	1045.66	1005.73	975.99	953.50	936.28	922.99	912.64
47000	4417.06	2456.89	1814.47	1501.28	1319.56	1203.35	1124.36	1068.40	1027.59	997.21	974.23	956.63	943.05	932.48
48000	4511.04	2509.16	1853.07	1533.22	1347.64	1228.96	1148.28	1091.13	1049.46	1018.43	994.95	976.99	963.11	952.32
49000	4605.02	2561.43	1891.68	1565.16	1375.71	1254.56	1172.20	1113.86	1071.32	1039.64	1015.68	997.34	983.18	972.16
50000	4699.00	2613.71	1930.28	1597.10	1403.79	1280.16	1196.12	1136.59	1093.18	1060.86	1036.41	1017.70	1003.24	992.00
55000	5168.90	2875.08	2123.31	1756.81	1544.17	1408.18	1315.73	1250.25	1202.50	1166.95	1140.05	1119.47	1103.57	1091.20
60000	5638.79	3136.45	2316.34	1916.52	1684.55	1536.20	1435.35	1363.91	1311.82	1273.03	1243.69	1221.23	1203.89	1190.40
65000	6108.69	3397.82	2509.37	2076.23	1824.92	1664.21	1554.96	1477.57	1421.14	1379.12	1347.33	1323.00	1304.22	1289.60
70000	6578.59	3659.19	2702.39	2235.94	1965.30	1792.23	1674.57	1591.23	1530.46	1485.20	1450.97	1424.77	1404.54	1388.80
75000	7048.49	3920.56	2895.42	2395.65	2105.68	1920.24	1794.18	1704.89	1639.77	1591.29	1554.61	1526.54	1504.86	1488.00
80000	7518.39	4181.93	3088.45	2555.36	2246.06	2048.26	1913.79	1818.54	1749.09	1697.37	1658.25	1628.31	1605.19	1587.20
85000	7988.29	4443.30	3281.48	2715.07	2386.44	2176.27	2033.40	1932.20	1858.41	1803.46	1761.89	1730.08	1705.51	1686.40
90000	8458.19	4704.67	3474.51	2874.78	2526.82	2304.29	2153.02	2045.86	1967.73	1909.54	1865.53	1831.85	1805.84	1785.60
95000	8928.09	4966.04	3667.53	3034.49	2667.19	2432.31	2272.63	2159.52	2077.05	2015.63	1969.17	1933.62	1906.16	1884.80
100000	9397.99	5227.41	3860.56	3194.20	2807.57	2560.32	2392.24	2273.18	2186.36	2121.71	2072.81	2035.39	2006.48	1984.00

TERM	15 Years	16 Years	17 Years	18 Years	19 Years	20 Years	21 Years	22 Years	23 Years	24 Years	25 Years	30 Years	35 Years	40 Years
AMOUNT														
5	.10	.10	.10	.10	.10	.10	.10	.10	.10	.10	.10	.10	.10	.10
10	.20	.20	.20	.20	.20	.20	.20	.20	.20	.20	.20	.20	.20	.20
15	.30	.30	.30	.29	.29	.29	.29	.29	.29	.29	.29	.29	.29	.29
25	.50	.49	.49	.49	.49	.49	.48	.48	.48	.48	.48	.48	.48	.48
50	.99	.98	.98	.97	.97	.97	.96	.96	.96	.96	.96	.96	.96	.96
75	1.48	1.47	1.46	1.45	1.45	1.45	1.44	1.44	1.44	1.44	1.44	1.43	1.43	1.43
100	1.97	1.96	1.95	1.94	1.93	1.93	1.92	1.92	1.92	1.91	1.91	1.91	1.91	1.91
200	3.94	3.91	3.89	3.87	3.86	3.85	3.84	3.83	3.83	3.82	3.82	3.81	3.81	3.81
300	5.90	5.86	5.83	5.80	5.78	5.77	5.76	5.74	5.74	5.73	5.73	5.71	5.71	5.71
400	7.87	7.82	7.77	7.74	7.71	7.69	7.67	7.66	7.65	7.64	7.63	7.61	7.61	7.61
500	9.84	9.77	9.71	9.67	9.64	9.61	9.59	9.57	9.56	9.55	9.54	9.52	9.51	9.51
600	11.80	11.72	11.66	11.60	11.56	11.53	11.51	11.48	11.47	11.46	11.45	11.42	11.41	11.41
700	13.77	13.67	13.60	13.54	13.49	13.45	13.42	13.40	13.38	13.36	13.35	13.32	13.31	13.31
800	15.74	15.63	15.54	15.47	15.42	15.37	15.34	15.31	15.29	15.27	15.26	15.22	15.21	15.21
900	17.70	17.58	17.48	17.40	17.34	17.29	17.26	17.22	17.20	17.18	17.17	17.12	17.11	17.11
1000	19.67	19.53	19.42	19.34	19.27	19.21	19.17	19.14	19.11	19.09	19.07	19.03	19.01	19.01
2000	39.33	39.06	38.84	38.67	38.53	38.42	38.34	38.27	38.22	38.17	38.14	38.05	38.02	38.01
3000	59.00	58.58	58.26	58.00	57.80	57.63	57.50	57.40	57.32	57.26	57.21	57.07	57.03	57.01
4000	78.66	78.11	77.68	77.33	77.06	76.84	76.67	76.54	76.43	76.34	76.27	76.09	76.03	76.01
5000	98.33	97.64	97.09	96.66	96.32	96.05	95.84	95.67	95.53	95.43	95.34	95.11	95.04	95.02
6000	117.99	117.16	116.51	115.99	115.59	115.26	115.01	114.80	114.64	114.51	114.41	114.14	114.05	114.02
7000	137.65	136.69	135.93	135.33	134.85	134.47	134.17	133.94	133.75	133.60	133.48	133.16	133.05	133.02
8000	157.32	156.21	155.35	154.66	154.11	153.68	153.34	153.07	152.85	152.68	152.54	152.18	152.06	152.02
9000	176.98	175.74	174.76	173.99	173.38	172.89	172.51	172.20	171.96	171.76	171.61	171.20	171.07	171.03
10000	196.65	195.27	194.18	193.32	192.64	192.10	191.67	191.33	191.06	190.85	190.68	190.22	190.08	190.03
11000	216.31	214.79	213.60	212.65	211.91	211.31	210.84	210.47	210.17	209.93	209.75	209.24	209.08	209.03
12000	235.98	234.32	233.02	231.96	231.17	230.52	230.01	229.60	229.28	229.02	228.81	228.27	228.09	228.03
13000	255.64	253.85	252.43	251.32	250.43	249.73	249.18	248.73	248.38	248.10	247.88	247.29	247.10	247.03
14000	275.30	273.37	271.85	270.65	269.70	268.94	268.34	267.87	267.49	267.19	266.95	266.31	266.10	266.04
15000	294.97	292.90	291.27	289.98	288.96	288.15	287.51	287.00	286.59	286.27	286.01	285.33	285.11	285.04
16000	314.63	312.42	310.69	309.31	308.22	307.36	306.68	306.13	305.70	305.36	305.08	304.35	304.12	304.04
17000	334.30	331.95	330.10	328.64	327.49	326.57	325.84	325.27	324.81	324.44	324.15	323.37	323.12	323.04
18000	353.96	351.48	349.52	347.97	346.75	345.78	345.01	344.40	343.91	343.52	343.22	342.40	342.13	342.05
19000	373.63	371.00	368.94	367.31	366.01	364.99	364.18	363.53	363.02	362.61	362.28	361.42	361.14	361.05
20000	393.29	390.53	388.36	386.64	385.28	384.20	383.34	382.66	382.12	381.69	381.35	380.44	380.15	380.05
21000	412.95	410.06	407.77	405.97	404.54	403.41	402.51	401.80	401.23	400.78	400.42	399.46	399.15	399.05
22000	432.62	429.58	427.19	425.30	423.81	422.62	421.68	420.93	420.34	419.86	419.49	418.48	418.16	418.05
23000	452.28	449.11	446.61	444.63	443.07	441.83	440.85	440.06	439.44	438.95	438.55	437.50	437.17	437.06
24000	471.95	468.63	466.03	463.96	462.33	461.04	460.01	459.20	458.54	458.03	457.62	456.53	456.17	456.06
25000	491.61	488.16	485.44	483.30	481.60	480.25	479.18	478.33	477.65	477.12	476.69	475.55	475.18	475.06
26000	511.28	507.69	504.86	502.63	500.86	499.46	498.35	497.46	496.76	496.20	495.75	494.57	494.19	494.06
27000	530.94	527.21	524.28	521.96	520.12	518.67	517.51	516.60	515.87	515.28	514.82	513.59	513.19	513.07
28000	550.60	546.74	543.70	541.29	539.39	537.88	536.68	535.73	534.97	534.37	533.89	532.61	532.20	532.07
29000	570.27	566.27	563.11	560.62	558.65	557.09	555.85	554.86	554.08	553.45	552.96	551.63	551.21	551.07
30000	589.93	585.79	582.53	579.95	577.91	576.30	575.01	573.99	573.18	572.54	572.02	570.66	570.22	570.07
31000	609.60	605.32	601.95	599.29	597.18	595.51	594.18	593.13	592.29	591.62	591.09	589.68	589.22	589.08
32000	629.26	624.84	621.37	618.62	616.44	614.72	613.35	612.26	611.40	610.71	610.16	608.70	608.23	608.08
33000	648.92	644.37	640.78	637.95	635.71	633.93	632.52	631.39	630.50	629.79	629.23	627.72	627.24	627.08
34000	668.59	663.90	660.20	657.28	654.97	653.14	651.68	650.53	649.61	648.88	648.29	646.74	646.24	646.08
35000	688.25	683.42	679.62	676.61	674.23	672.35	670.85	669.66	668.71	667.96	667.36	665.76	665.25	665.08
36000	707.92	702.95	699.04	695.94	693.50	691.56	690.02	688.79	687.82	687.04	686.43	684.79	684.26	684.09
37000	727.58	722.48	718.45	715.28	712.76	710.77	709.18	707.93	706.93	706.13	705.50	703.81	703.26	703.09
38000	747.25	742.00	737.87	734.61	732.02	729.98	728.35	727.06	726.03	725.21	724.56	722.83	722.27	722.09
39000	766.91	761.53	757.29	753.94	751.29	749.19	747.52	746.19	745.14	744.30	743.63	741.85	741.28	741.09
40000	786.57	781.05	776.71	773.27	770.55	768.40	766.68	765.32	764.24	763.38	762.70	760.87	760.29	760.10
41000	806.24	800.58	796.12	792.60	789.81	787.61	785.85	784.46	783.35	782.47	781.76	779.89	779.29	779.10
42000	825.90	820.11	815.54	811.93	809.08	806.81	805.02	803.59	802.45	801.55	800.83	798.92	798.30	798.10
43000	845.57	839.63	834.96	831.26	828.34	826.02	824.19	822.72	821.56	820.64	819.90	817.94	817.31	817.10
44000	865.23	859.16	854.38	850.60	847.61	845.23	843.35	841.86	840.67	839.72	838.97	836.96	836.31	836.10
45000	884.90	878.69	873.79	869.93	866.87	864.44	862.52	860.99	859.77	858.80	858.03	855.98	855.32	855.11
46000	904.56	898.21	893.21	889.26	886.13	883.65	881.69	880.12	878.88	877.89	877.10	875.00	874.33	874.11
47000	924.22	917.74	912.63	908.59	905.40	902.86	900.85	899.26	897.98	896.97	896.17	894.03	893.33	893.11
48000	943.89	937.26	932.05	927.92	924.66	922.07	920.02	918.39	917.09	916.06	915.24	913.05	912.34	912.11
49000	963.55	956.79	951.46	947.25	943.92	941.28	939.19	937.52	936.20	935.14	934.30	932.07	931.35	931.12
50000	983.22	976.32	970.88	966.59	963.19	960.49	958.35	956.65	955.30	954.23	953.37	951.09	950.36	950.12
55000	1081.54	1073.95	1067.97	1063.24	1059.51	1056.54	1054.19	1052.32	1050.83	1049.65	1048.71	1046.20	1045.39	1045.13
60000	1179.86	1171.58	1165.06	1159.90	1155.82	1152.59	1150.02	1147.98	1146.36	1145.07	1144.04	1141.31	1140.43	1140.14
65000	1278.18	1269.21	1262.14	1256.56	1252.14	1248.64	1245.86	1243.65	1241.89	1240.49	1239.38	1236.42	1235.46	1235.15
70000	1376.50	1366.84	1359.23	1353.22	1348.46	1344.69	1341.69	1339.31	1337.42	1335.92	1334.72	1331.53	1330.50	1330.16
75000	1474.82	1464.47	1456.32	1449.88	1444.78	1440.74	1437.53	1434.98	1432.95	1431.34	1430.05	1426.63	1425.53	1425.17
80000	1573.14	1562.10	1553.41	1546.53	1541.10	1536.79	1533.36	1530.64	1528.48	1526.76	1525.39	1521.74	1520.57	1520.19
85000	1671.47	1659.73	1650.49	1643.19	1637.42	1632.83	1629.20	1626.31	1624.01	1622.18	1620.73	1616.85	1615.60	1615.20
90000	1769.79	1757.37	1747.58	1739.85	1733.73	1728.88	1725.03	1721.97	1719.54	1717.60	1716.06	1711.96	1710.64	1710.21
95000	1868.11	1855.00	1844.67	1836.51	1830.05	1824.93	1820.87	1817.64	1815.07	1813.03	1811.40	1807.07	1805.67	1805.22
100000	1966.43	1952.63	1941.76	1933.17	1926.37	1920.98	1916.70	1913.30	1910.60	1908.45	1906.74	1902.18	1900.71	1900.23

MONTHLY PAYMENT
REQUIRED TO AMORTIZE A LOAN

TERM	1 Year	2 Years	3 Years	4 Years	5 Years	6 Years	7 Years	8 Years	9 Years	10 Years	11 Years	12 Years	13 Years	14 Years
AMOUNT														
5	.40	.27	.20	.16	.15	.13	.12	.12	.11	.11	.11	.11	.11	.10
10	.95	.53	.39	.32	.29	.26	.24	.23	.22	.22	.21	.21	.21	.20
15	1.42	.79	.58	.48	.43	.39	.36	.35	.33	.32	.32	.31	.31	.30
25	2.36	1.31	.97	.80	.71	.65	.60	.57	.55	.54	.52	.52	.51	.50
50	4.71	2.62	1.94	1.60	1.41	1.29	1.20	1.14	1.10	1.07	1.04	1.03	1.01	1.00
75	7.06	3.93	2.90	2.40	2.11	1.93	1.80	1.71	1.65	1.60	1.56	1.54	1.51	1.50
100	9.41	5.24	3.87	3.20	2.82	2.57	2.40	2.28	2.20	2.13	2.08	2.05	2.02	1.99
200	18.81	10.47	7.73	6.40	5.63	5.13	4.80	4.56	4.39	4.26	4.16	4.09	4.03	3.98
300	28.21	15.70	11.60	9.60	8.44	7.70	7.20	6.84	6.58	6.39	6.24	6.13	6.04	5.97
400	37.61	20.93	15.46	12.80	11.25	10.26	9.59	9.12	8.77	8.51	8.32	8.17	8.05	7.96
500	47.01	26.16	19.33	16.00	14.06	12.83	11.99	11.40	10.96	10.64	10.40	10.21	10.07	9.95
600	56.41	31.39	23.19	19.19	16.88	15.39	14.35	13.67	13.15	12.77	12.47	12.25	12.08	11.94
700	65.82	36.62	27.06	22.39	19.69	17.96	16.78	15.95	15.34	14.89	14.55	14.29	14.09	13.93
800	75.22	41.85	30.92	25.59	22.50	20.52	19.18	18.23	17.54	17.02	16.63	16.33	16.10	15.92
900	84.62	47.09	34.79	28.79	25.31	23.09	21.58	20.51	19.73	19.15	18.71	18.37	18.11	17.91
1000	94.02	52.32	38.65	31.99	28.12	25.65	23.97	22.79	21.92	21.27	20.79	20.41	20.13	19.90
2000	188.04	104.63	77.29	63.97	56.24	51.30	47.94	45.57	43.83	42.54	41.57	40.82	40.25	39.80
3000	282.05	156.94	115.94	95.95	84.36	76.95	71.91	68.35	65.75	63.81	62.35	61.23	60.37	59.69
4000	376.07	209.25	154.58	127.94	112.48	102.60	95.88	91.13	87.66	85.08	83.13	81.64	80.49	79.59
5000	470.09	261.56	193.23	159.92	140.60	128.25	119.85	113.91	109.57	106.35	103.91	102.04	100.61	99.49
6000	564.10	313.87	231.87	191.90	168.72	153.89	143.82	136.69	131.49	127.62	124.69	122.45	120.73	119.38
7000	658.12	366.18	270.52	223.89	196.84	179.54	167.79	159.47	153.40	148.89	145.47	142.86	140.85	139.28
8000	752.13	418.50	309.16	255.87	224.95	205.19	191.76	182.25	175.31	170.15	166.25	163.27	160.97	159.17
9000	846.15	470.81	347.81	287.85	253.07	230.84	215.73	205.03	197.23	191.42	187.03	183.68	181.09	179.07
10000	940.17	523.12	386.45	319.84	281.19	256.49	239.70	227.81	219.14	212.69	207.82	204.08	201.21	198.97
11000	1034.18	575.43	425.10	351.82	309.31	282.13	263.67	250.59	241.06	233.96	228.60	224.49	221.33	218.86
12000	1128.20	627.74	463.74	383.80	337.43	307.78	287.63	273.37	262.97	255.23	249.38	244.90	241.45	238.76
13000	1222.21	680.05	502.38	415.78	365.55	333.43	311.60	296.15	284.88	276.50	270.16	265.31	261.57	258.66
14000	1316.23	732.36	541.03	447.77	393.67	359.08	335.57	318.93	306.80	297.77	290.94	285.72	281.69	278.55
15000	1410.25	784.67	579.67	479.75	421.79	384.73	359.54	341.71	328.71	319.04	311.72	306.12	301.81	298.45
16000	1504.26	836.99	618.32	511.73	449.90	410.37	383.51	364.49	350.62	340.30	332.50	326.53	321.93	318.34
17000	1598.28	889.30	656.96	543.72	478.02	436.02	407.48	387.27	372.54	361.57	353.28	346.94	342.05	338.24
18000	1692.29	941.61	695.61	575.70	506.14	461.67	431.45	410.05	394.45	382.84	374.06	367.35	362.17	358.14
19000	1786.31	993.92	734.25	607.68	534.26	487.32	455.42	432.83	416.37	404.11	394.84	387.76	382.29	378.03
20000	1880.33	1046.23	772.90	639.67	562.38	512.97	479.39	455.61	438.28	425.38	415.63	408.16	402.41	397.93
21000	1974.34	1098.54	811.54	671.65	590.50	538.62	503.36	478.39	460.19	446.65	436.41	428.57	422.53	417.83
22000	2068.36	1150.85	850.19	703.63	618.62	564.26	527.33	501.17	482.11	467.92	457.19	448.98	442.65	437.72
23000	2162.37	1203.16	888.83	735.61	646.74	589.91	551.30	523.95	504.02	489.18	477.97	469.39	462.77	457.62
24000	2256.39	1255.48	927.48	767.60	674.85	615.56	575.26	546.73	525.93	510.45	498.75	489.80	482.89	477.51
25000	2350.41	1307.79	966.12	799.58	702.97	641.21	599.23	569.51	547.85	531.72	519.53	510.20	503.01	497.41
26000	2444.42	1360.10	1004.76	831.56	731.09	666.86	623.20	592.29	569.76	552.99	540.31	530.61	523.13	517.31
27000	2538.44	1412.41	1043.41	863.55	759.21	692.50	647.17	615.07	591.67	574.26	561.09	551.02	543.25	537.20
28000	2632.45	1464.72	1082.05	895.53	787.33	718.15	671.14	637.85	613.59	595.53	581.87	571.43	563.37	557.10
29000	2726.47	1517.03	1120.70	927.51	815.45	743.80	695.11	660.63	635.50	616.80	602.66	591.84	583.49	577.00
30000	2820.49	1569.34	1159.34	959.50	843.57	769.45	719.08	683.41	657.42	638.07	623.44	612.24	603.61	596.89
31000	2914.50	1621.65	1197.99	991.48	871.68	795.10	743.05	706.19	679.33	659.33	644.22	632.65	623.73	616.79
32000	3008.52	1673.97	1236.63	1023.46	899.80	820.74	767.02	728.97	701.24	680.60	665.00	653.06	643.85	636.68
33000	3102.53	1726.28	1275.28	1055.44	927.92	846.39	790.99	751.75	723.16	701.87	685.78	673.47	663.97	656.58
34000	3196.55	1778.59	1313.92	1087.43	956.04	872.04	814.96	774.53	745.07	723.14	706.56	693.88	684.09	676.48
35000	3290.57	1830.90	1352.57	1119.41	984.16	897.69	838.92	797.31	766.98	744.41	727.34	714.28	704.21	696.37
36000	3384.58	1883.21	1391.21	1151.39	1012.28	923.34	862.89	820.09	788.90	765.68	748.12	734.69	724.33	716.27
37000	3478.60	1935.52	1429.86	1183.38	1040.40	948.99	886.86	842.87	810.81	786.95	768.90	755.10	744.45	736.17
38000	3572.61	1987.83	1468.50	1215.36	1068.52	974.63	910.83	865.65	832.73	808.22	789.68	775.51	764.57	756.06
39000	3666.63	2040.14	1507.14	1247.34	1096.63	1000.28	934.80	888.43	854.64	829.48	810.47	795.92	784.69	775.96
40000	3760.65	2092.46	1545.79	1279.33	1124.75	1025.93	958.77	911.21	876.55	850.75	831.25	816.32	804.81	795.85
41000	3854.66	2144.77	1584.43	1311.31	1152.87	1051.58	982.74	934.00	898.47	872.02	852.03	836.73	824.93	815.75
42000	3948.68	2197.08	1623.08	1343.29	1180.99	1077.23	1006.71	956.78	920.38	893.29	872.81	857.14	845.05	835.65
43000	4042.69	2249.39	1661.72	1375.28	1209.11	1102.87	1030.68	979.56	942.29	914.56	893.59	877.55	865.17	855.54
44000	4136.71	2301.70	1700.37	1407.26	1237.23	1128.52	1054.65	1002.34	964.21	935.83	914.37	897.96	885.29	875.44
45000	4230.73	2354.01	1739.01	1439.24	1265.35	1154.17	1078.62	1025.12	986.12	957.10	935.15	918.36	905.41	895.34
46000	4324.74	2406.32	1777.66	1471.22	1293.47	1179.82	1102.59	1047.90	1008.04	978.36	955.93	938.77	925.53	915.23
47000	4418.76	2458.63	1816.30	1503.21	1321.58	1205.47	1126.55	1070.68	1029.95	999.63	976.71	959.18	945.65	935.13
48000	4512.77	2510.95	1854.95	1535.19	1349.70	1231.11	1150.52	1093.46	1051.86	1020.90	997.49	979.59	965.77	955.02
49000	4606.79	2563.26	1893.59	1567.17	1377.82	1256.76	1174.49	1116.24	1073.78	1042.17	1018.28	1000.00	985.89	974.92
50000	4700.81	2615.57	1932.24	1599.16	1405.94	1282.41	1198.46	1139.02	1095.69	1063.44	1039.06	1020.40	1006.01	994.82
55000	5170.89	2877.12	2125.46	1759.07	1546.53	1410.65	1318.31	1252.92	1205.26	1169.79	1142.96	1122.44	1106.61	1094.30
60000	5640.97	3138.68	2318.68	1918.99	1687.13	1538.89	1438.15	1366.82	1314.83	1276.13	1246.87	1224.48	1207.21	1193.78
65000	6111.05	3400.24	2511.90	2078.90	1827.72	1667.13	1558.00	1480.72	1424.40	1382.47	1350.77	1326.52	1307.81	1293.26
70000	6581.13	3661.79	2705.13	2238.82	1968.31	1795.37	1677.84	1594.62	1533.96	1488.81	1454.68	1428.56	1408.41	1392.74
75000	7051.21	3923.35	2898.35	2398.73	2108.91	1923.61	1797.69	1708.52	1643.53	1595.16	1558.58	1530.60	1509.01	1492.22
80000	7521.29	4184.91	3091.57	2558.65	2249.50	2051.85	1917.54	1822.42	1753.10	1701.50	1662.49	1632.64	1609.61	1591.70
85000	7991.37	4446.46	3284.80	2718.56	2390.09	2180.09	2037.38	1936.33	1862.67	1807.84	1766.39	1734.68	1710.21	1691.19
90000	8461.45	4708.02	3478.02	2878.48	2530.69	2308.34	2157.23	2050.23	1972.24	1914.19	1870.30	1836.72	1810.81	1790.67
95000	8931.53	4969.58	3671.24	3038.39	2671.28	2436.58	2277.07	2164.13	2081.81	2020.53	1974.20	1938.76	1911.41	1890.15
100000	9401.61	5231.13	3864.47	3198.31	2811.88	2564.82	2396.92	2278.03	2191.37	2126.87	2078.11	2040.80	2012.01	1989.63

TERM AMOUNT	15 Years	16 Years	17 Years	18 Years	19 Years	20 Years	21 Years	22 Years	23 Years	24 Years	25 Years	30 Years	35 Years	40 Years
5	.10	.10	.10	.10	.10	.10	.10	.10	.10	.10	.10	.10	.10	.10
10	.20	.20	.20	.20	.20	.20	.20	.20	.20	.20	.20	.20	.20	.20
15	.30	.30	.30	.30	.29	.29	.29	.29	.29	.29	.29	.29	.29	.29
25	.50	.49	.49	.49	.49	.49	.49	.48	.48	.48	.48	.48	.48	.48
50	.99	.98	.98	.97	.97	.97	.97	.96	.96	.96	.96	.96	.96	.96
75	1.48	1.47	1.47	1.46	1.45	1.45	1.45	1.44	1.44	1.44	1.44	1.44	1.44	1.43
100	1.98	1.96	1.95	1.94	1.94	1.93	1.93	1.92	1.92	1.92	1.92	1.91	1.91	1.91
200	3.95	3.92	3.90	3.88	3.87	3.86	3.85	3.84	3.84	3.83	3.83	3.82	3.82	3.82
300	5.92	5.88	5.85	5.82	5.80	5.79	5.77	5.76	5.76	5.75	5.74	5.73	5.73	5.72
400	7.89	7.84	7.80	7.76	7.73	7.71	7.70	7.68	7.67	7.66	7.66	7.64	7.63	7.63
500	9.87	9.80	9.74	9.70	9.67	9.64	9.62	9.60	9.59	9.58	9.57	9.55	9.54	9.54
600	11.84	11.76	11.69	11.64	11.60	11.57	11.54	11.52	11.51	11.49	11.48	11.46	11.45	11.44
700	13.81	13.71	13.64	13.58	13.53	13.49	13.46	13.44	13.42	13.41	13.40	13.36	13.35	13.35
800	15.78	15.67	15.59	15.52	15.46	15.42	15.39	15.36	15.34	15.32	15.31	15.27	15.26	15.26
900	17.75	17.63	17.53	17.46	17.40	17.35	17.31	17.28	17.26	17.24	17.22	17.18	17.17	17.16
1000	19.73	19.59	19.48	19.40	19.33	19.27	19.23	19.20	19.17	19.15	19.13	19.09	19.07	19.07
2000	39.45	39.17	38.96	38.79	38.65	38.54	38.46	38.39	38.34	38.30	38.26	38.17	38.14	38.13
3000	59.17	58.76	58.43	58.18	57.97	57.81	57.69	57.59	57.51	57.44	57.39	57.26	57.21	57.20
4000	78.89	78.34	77.91	77.57	77.30	77.08	76.91	76.78	76.67	76.59	76.52	76.34	76.28	76.26
5000	98.61	97.93	97.39	96.96	96.62	96.35	96.14	95.97	95.84	95.73	95.65	95.42	95.35	95.33
6000	118.33	117.51	116.86	116.35	115.94	115.62	115.37	115.17	115.01	114.88	114.78	114.51	114.42	114.39
7000	138.05	137.09	136.34	135.74	135.27	134.89	134.60	134.36	134.17	134.03	133.91	133.59	133.49	133.46
8000	157.78	156.68	155.81	155.13	154.59	154.16	153.82	153.56	153.34	153.17	153.04	152.68	152.56	152.52
9000	177.50	176.26	175.29	174.52	173.91	173.43	173.05	172.75	172.51	172.32	172.16	171.76	171.63	171.59
10000	197.22	195.85	194.77	193.91	193.24	192.70	192.28	191.94	191.68	191.46	191.29	190.84	190.70	190.65
11000	216.94	215.43	214.24	213.30	212.56	211.97	211.51	211.14	210.84	210.61	210.42	209.93	209.77	209.72
12000	236.66	235.01	233.72	232.69	231.88	231.24	230.73	230.33	230.01	229.75	229.55	229.01	228.84	228.78
13000	256.38	254.60	253.19	252.08	251.21	250.51	249.96	249.52	249.18	248.90	248.68	248.09	247.91	247.85
14000	276.10	274.18	272.67	271.48	270.53	269.78	269.19	268.72	268.34	268.05	267.81	267.18	266.98	266.91
15000	295.83	293.77	292.15	290.87	289.85	289.05	288.42	287.91	287.51	287.19	286.94	286.26	286.05	285.98
16000	315.55	313.35	311.62	310.26	309.18	308.32	307.64	307.11	306.68	306.34	306.07	305.35	305.11	305.04
17000	335.27	332.93	331.10	329.65	328.50	327.59	326.87	326.30	325.84	325.48	325.19	324.43	324.18	324.11
18000	354.99	352.52	350.57	349.04	347.82	346.86	346.10	345.49	345.01	344.63	344.32	343.51	343.25	343.17
19000	374.71	372.10	370.05	368.43	367.15	366.13	365.33	364.69	364.18	363.77	363.45	362.60	362.32	362.23
20000	394.43	391.69	389.53	387.82	386.47	385.40	384.55	383.88	383.35	382.92	382.58	381.68	381.39	381.30
21000	414.15	411.27	409.00	407.21	405.79	404.67	403.78	403.07	402.51	402.07	401.71	400.76	400.46	400.36
22000	433.87	430.86	428.48	426.60	425.12	423.94	423.01	422.27	421.68	421.21	420.84	419.85	419.53	419.43
23000	453.60	450.44	447.95	445.99	444.44	443.21	442.24	441.46	440.85	440.36	439.97	438.93	438.60	438.49
24000	473.32	470.02	467.43	465.38	463.76	462.48	461.46	460.66	460.01	459.50	459.10	458.02	457.67	457.56
25000	493.04	489.61	486.91	484.77	483.09	481.75	480.69	479.85	479.18	478.65	478.22	477.10	476.74	476.62
26000	512.76	509.19	506.38	504.16	502.41	501.02	499.92	499.04	498.35	497.79	497.35	496.18	495.81	495.69
27000	532.48	528.78	525.86	523.56	521.73	520.29	519.15	518.24	517.51	516.94	516.48	515.27	514.88	514.75
28000	552.20	548.36	545.33	542.95	541.06	539.56	538.37	537.43	536.68	536.09	535.61	534.35	533.95	533.82
29000	571.92	567.94	564.81	562.34	560.38	558.83	557.60	556.62	555.85	555.23	554.74	553.44	553.02	552.88
30000	591.65	587.53	584.29	581.73	579.70	578.10	576.83	575.82	575.02	574.38	573.87	572.52	572.09	571.95
31000	611.37	607.11	603.76	601.12	599.03	597.37	596.06	595.01	594.18	593.52	593.00	591.60	591.15	591.01
32000	631.09	626.70	623.24	620.51	618.35	616.64	615.28	614.21	613.35	612.67	612.13	610.69	610.22	610.08
33000	650.81	646.28	642.71	639.90	637.67	635.91	634.51	633.40	632.52	631.81	631.26	629.77	629.29	629.14
34000	670.53	665.86	662.19	659.29	657.00	655.18	653.74	652.59	651.68	650.96	650.38	648.85	648.36	648.21
35000	690.25	685.45	681.67	678.68	676.32	674.45	672.97	671.79	670.85	670.11	669.51	667.94	667.43	667.27
36000	709.97	705.03	701.14	698.07	695.64	693.72	692.19	690.98	690.02	689.25	688.64	687.02	686.50	686.33
37000	729.70	724.62	720.62	717.46	714.97	712.99	711.42	710.17	709.18	708.40	707.77	706.11	705.57	705.40
38000	749.42	744.20	740.10	736.85	734.29	732.26	730.65	729.37	728.35	727.54	726.90	725.19	724.64	724.46
39000	769.14	763.79	759.57	756.24	753.61	751.53	749.87	748.56	747.52	746.69	746.03	744.27	743.71	743.53
40000	788.86	783.37	779.05	775.64	772.94	770.80	769.10	767.76	766.69	765.83	765.16	763.36	762.78	762.59
41000	808.58	802.95	798.52	795.03	792.26	790.07	788.33	786.95	785.85	784.98	784.29	782.44	781.85	781.66
42000	828.30	822.54	818.00	814.42	811.58	809.34	807.56	806.14	805.02	804.13	803.41	801.52	800.92	800.72
43000	848.02	842.12	837.48	833.81	830.91	828.61	826.78	825.34	824.19	823.27	822.54	820.61	819.99	819.79
44000	867.74	861.71	856.95	853.20	850.23	847.88	846.01	844.53	843.35	842.42	841.67	839.69	839.06	838.85
45000	887.47	881.29	876.43	872.59	869.55	867.15	865.24	863.72	862.52	861.56	860.80	858.78	858.13	857.92
46000	907.19	900.87	895.90	891.98	888.88	886.42	884.47	882.92	881.68	880.71	879.93	877.86	877.20	876.98
47000	926.91	920.46	915.38	911.37	908.20	905.69	903.69	902.11	900.85	899.85	899.06	896.94	896.26	896.05
48000	946.63	940.04	934.86	930.76	927.52	924.96	922.92	921.31	920.02	919.00	918.19	916.03	915.33	915.11
49000	966.35	959.63	954.33	950.15	946.85	944.23	942.15	940.50	939.19	938.15	937.32	935.11	934.40	934.18
50000	986.07	979.21	973.81	969.54	966.17	963.50	961.38	959.69	958.36	957.29	956.44	954.19	953.47	953.24
55000	1084.68	1077.13	1071.19	1066.50	1062.79	1059.85	1057.51	1055.66	1054.19	1053.02	1052.09	1049.61	1048.82	1048.56
60000	1183.29	1175.05	1168.57	1163.45	1159.40	1156.20	1153.65	1151.63	1150.03	1148.75	1147.73	1145.03	1144.17	1143.89
65000	1281.89	1272.97	1265.95	1260.40	1256.02	1252.54	1249.79	1247.60	1245.86	1244.48	1243.38	1240.45	1239.51	1239.21
70000	1380.50	1370.89	1363.33	1357.36	1352.64	1348.89	1345.93	1343.57	1341.70	1340.21	1339.02	1335.87	1334.86	1334.53
75000	1479.11	1468.81	1460.71	1454.31	1449.25	1445.24	1442.06	1439.54	1437.53	1435.93	1434.66	1431.29	1430.21	1429.86
80000	1577.71	1566.73	1558.09	1551.27	1545.87	1541.59	1538.20	1535.51	1533.37	1531.66	1530.31	1526.71	1525.55	1525.18
85000	1676.32	1664.65	1655.47	1648.22	1642.48	1637.94	1634.34	1631.47	1629.20	1627.39	1625.95	1622.13	1620.90	1620.51
90000	1774.93	1762.57	1752.85	1745.17	1739.10	1734.29	1730.47	1727.44	1725.04	1723.12	1721.60	1717.55	1716.25	1715.83
95000	1873.53	1860.50	1850.23	1842.13	1835.72	1830.64	1826.61	1823.41	1820.87	1818.85	1817.24	1812.97	1811.59	1811.15
100000	1972.14	1958.42	1947.61	1939.08	1932.33	1926.99	1922.75	1919.38	1916.71	1914.58	1912.88	1908.38	1906.94	1906.48

MONTHLY PAYMENT
REQUIRED TO AMORTIZE A LOAN

TERM AMOUNT	1 Year	2 Years	3 Years	4 Years	5 Years	6 Years	7 Years	8 Years	9 Years	10 Years	11 Years	12 Years	13 Years	14 Years
5	.48	.27	.20	.16	.15	.13	.12	.12	.11	.11	.11	.11	.11	.10
10	.95	.53	.39	.32	.29	.26	.24	.23	.22	.22	.21	.21	.21	.20
15	1.42	.79	.58	.48	.43	.39	.36	.35	.33	.32	.32	.31	.31	.30
25	2.36	1.31	.97	.80	.71	.65	.60	.57	.55	.54	.52	.52	.51	.50
50	4.71	2.62	1.94	1.60	1.41	1.29	1.20	1.14	1.10	1.07	1.04	1.03	1.01	1.00
75	7.06	3.93	2.90	2.40	2.11	1.93	1.80	1.71	1.65	1.60	1.56	1.54	1.52	1.50
100	9.41	5.24	3.87	3.20	2.82	2.57	2.40	2.28	2.20	2.13	2.08	2.05	2.02	2.00
200	18.81	10.47	7.74	6.40	5.63	5.14	4.80	4.56	4.39	4.26	4.16	4.09	4.03	3.99
300	28.21	15.70	11.60	9.60	8.44	7.70	7.20	6.84	6.58	6.39	6.24	6.13	6.05	5.98
400	37.62	20.93	15.47	12.80	11.26	10.27	9.60	9.12	8.78	8.52	8.32	8.18	8.06	7.97
500	47.02	26.17	19.33	16.00	14.07	12.84	12.00	11.40	10.97	10.65	10.40	10.22	10.07	9.96
600	56.82	31.40	23.20	19.20	16.88	15.40	14.40	13.68	13.16	12.78	12.48	12.26	12.09	11.95
700	65.82	36.63	27.07	22.40	19.70	17.97	16.79	15.96	15.36	14.91	14.56	14.30	14.10	13.95
800	75.23	41.86	30.93	25.60	22.51	20.54	19.19	18.24	17.55	17.03	16.64	16.35	16.12	15.94
900	84.63	47.10	34.80	28.80	25.32	23.10	21.59	20.52	19.74	19.16	18.72	18.39	18.13	17.93
1000	94.03	52.33	38.66	32.00	28.14	25.67	23.99	22.80	21.94	21.29	20.80	20.43	20.14	19.92
2000	188.06	104.65	77.32	64.00	56.27	51.33	47.97	45.60	43.87	42.58	41.60	40.86	40.28	39.84
3000	282.09	156.98	115.98	96.00	84.40	76.99	71.96	68.39	65.80	63.86	62.40	61.28	60.42	59.75
4000	376.12	209.30	154.64	127.99	112.54	102.66	95.94	91.19	87.73	85.15	83.20	81.71	80.56	79.67
5000	470.15	261.62	193.29	159.99	140.67	128.32	119.93	113.99	109.66	106.43	104.00	102.14	100.70	99.58
6000	564.17	313.95	231.95	191.99	168.80	153.98	143.91	136.78	131.59	127.72	124.80	122.56	120.84	119.50
7000	658.20	366.27	270.61	223.98	196.94	179.65	167.90	159.58	153.52	149.01	145.60	142.99	140.97	139.41
8000	752.23	418.59	309.27	255.98	225.07	205.31	191.88	182.38	175.45	170.29	166.39	163.41	161.11	159.33
9000	846.26	470.92	347.92	287.98	253.20	230.97	215.87	205.17	197.38	191.58	187.19	183.84	181.25	179.24
10000	940.29	523.24	386.58	319.97	281.34	256.64	239.85	227.97	219.31	212.86	207.99	204.27	201.39	199.16
11000	1034.31	575.57	425.24	351.97	309.47	282.30	263.84	250.77	241.24	234.15	228.79	224.69	221.53	219.07
12000	1128.34	627.89	463.90	383.97	337.60	307.96	287.82	273.56	263.17	255.44	249.59	245.12	241.67	238.99
13000	1222.37	680.21	502.55	415.96	365.73	333.63	311.81	296.36	285.10	276.72	270.39	265.54	261.81	258.90
14000	1316.40	732.54	541.21	447.96	393.87	359.29	335.79	319.15	307.03	298.01	291.19	285.97	281.94	278.82
15000	1410.43	784.86	579.87	479.96	422.00	384.95	359.78	341.95	328.96	319.29	311.99	306.40	302.08	298.73
16000	1504.45	837.18	618.53	511.95	450.13	410.61	383.76	364.75	350.89	340.58	332.78	326.82	322.22	318.65
17000	1598.48	889.51	657.18	543.95	478.27	436.28	407.75	387.54	372.82	361.87	353.58	347.25	342.36	338.56
18000	1692.51	941.83	695.84	575.95	506.40	461.94	431.73	410.34	394.75	383.15	374.38	367.67	362.50	358.48
19000	1786.54	994.15	734.50	607.94	534.53	487.60	455.71	433.14	416.68	404.44	395.18	388.10	382.64	378.39
20000	1880.57	1046.48	773.16	639.94	562.67	513.27	479.70	455.93	438.61	425.72	415.98	408.53	402.77	398.31
21000	1974.59	1098.80	811.82	671.94	590.80	538.93	503.68	478.73	460.54	447.01	436.78	428.95	422.91	418.22
22000	2068.62	1151.13	850.47	703.93	618.93	564.59	527.67	501.53	482.47	468.29	457.58	449.38	443.05	438.14
23000	2162.65	1203.45	889.13	735.93	647.07	590.26	551.65	524.32	504.40	489.58	478.38	469.80	463.19	458.05
24000	2256.68	1255.77	927.79	767.93	675.20	615.92	575.64	547.12	526.33	510.87	499.17	490.23	483.33	477.97
25000	2350.71	1308.10	966.45	799.92	703.33	641.58	599.62	569.92	548.27	532.15	519.97	510.66	503.47	497.88
26000	2444.73	1360.42	1005.10	831.92	731.46	667.25	623.61	592.71	570.20	553.44	540.77	531.08	523.61	517.80
27000	2538.76	1412.74	1043.76	863.92	759.60	692.91	647.59	615.51	592.13	574.72	561.57	551.51	543.74	537.71
28000	2632.79	1465.07	1082.42	895.91	787.73	718.57	671.58	638.30	614.06	596.01	582.37	571.93	563.88	557.63
29000	2726.82	1517.39	1121.08	927.91	815.86	744.24	695.56	661.10	635.99	617.30	603.17	592.36	584.02	577.54
30000	2820.85	1569.72	1159.73	959.91	844.00	769.90	719.55	683.90	657.92	638.58	623.97	612.79	604.16	597.46
31000	2914.88	1622.04	1198.39	991.90	872.13	795.56	743.53	706.69	679.85	659.87	644.76	633.21	624.30	617.37
32000	3008.90	1674.36	1237.05	1023.90	900.26	821.22	767.52	729.49	701.78	681.15	665.56	653.64	644.44	637.29
33000	3102.93	1726.69	1275.71	1055.90	928.40	846.89	791.50	752.29	723.71	702.44	686.36	674.07	664.57	657.20
34000	3196.96	1779.01	1314.36	1087.89	956.53	872.55	815.49	775.08	745.64	723.73	707.16	694.49	684.71	677.12
35000	3290.99	1831.33	1353.02	1119.89	984.66	898.21	839.47	797.88	767.57	745.01	727.96	714.92	704.85	697.03
36000	3385.02	1883.66	1391.68	1151.89	1012.79	923.88	863.46	820.68	789.50	766.30	748.76	735.34	724.99	716.95
37000	3479.04	1935.98	1430.34	1183.88	1040.93	949.54	887.44	843.47	811.43	787.58	769.56	755.77	745.13	736.86
38000	3573.07	1988.30	1468.99	1215.88	1069.06	975.20	911.42	866.27	833.36	808.87	790.36	776.20	765.27	756.78
39000	3667.10	2040.63	1507.65	1247.88	1097.19	1000.87	935.41	889.07	855.29	830.15	811.15	796.62	785.41	776.69
40000	3761.13	2092.95	1546.31	1279.87	1125.33	1026.53	959.39	911.86	877.22	851.44	831.95	817.05	805.54	796.61
41000	3855.16	2145.28	1584.97	1311.87	1153.46	1052.19	983.38	934.66	899.15	872.73	852.75	837.48	825.68	816.52
42000	3949.18	2197.60	1623.63	1343.87	1181.59	1077.86	1007.36	957.45	921.08	894.01	873.55	857.90	845.82	836.44
43000	4043.21	2249.92	1662.28	1375.86	1209.73	1103.52	1031.35	980.25	943.01	915.30	894.35	878.33	865.96	856.35
44000	4137.24	2302.25	1700.94	1407.86	1237.86	1129.18	1055.33	1003.05	964.94	936.58	915.15	898.75	886.10	876.27
45000	4231.27	2354.57	1739.60	1439.86	1265.99	1154.84	1079.32	1025.84	986.87	957.87	935.95	919.18	906.24	896.18
46000	4325.30	2406.89	1778.26	1471.85	1294.13	1180.51	1103.30	1048.64	1008.80	979.16	956.74	939.60	926.38	916.10
47000	4419.32	2459.22	1816.91	1503.85	1322.26	1206.17	1127.29	1071.44	1030.73	1000.44	977.54	960.03	946.51	936.01
48000	4513.35	2511.54	1855.57	1535.85	1350.39	1231.83	1151.27	1094.23	1052.66	1021.73	998.34	980.46	966.65	955.93
49000	4607.38	2563.86	1894.23	1567.84	1378.52	1257.50	1175.26	1117.03	1074.60	1043.01	1019.14	1000.88	986.79	975.84
50000	4701.41	2616.19	1932.89	1599.84	1406.66	1283.16	1199.24	1139.83	1096.53	1064.30	1039.94	1021.31	1006.93	995.76
55000	5171.55	2877.81	2126.17	1759.82	1547.32	1411.48	1319.17	1253.81	1206.18	1170.73	1143.93	1123.44	1107.62	1095.33
60000	5641.69	3139.43	2319.46	1919.81	1687.99	1539.79	1439.09	1367.79	1315.83	1277.16	1247.93	1225.57	1208.31	1194.91
65000	6111.83	3401.04	2512.75	2079.79	1828.65	1668.11	1559.01	1481.77	1425.48	1383.59	1351.92	1327.70	1309.01	1294.48
70000	6581.97	3662.66	2706.04	2239.77	1969.32	1796.42	1678.94	1595.75	1535.13	1490.02	1455.91	1429.83	1409.70	1394.06
75000	7052.11	3924.28	2899.33	2399.76	2109.98	1924.74	1798.86	1709.74	1644.79	1596.45	1559.91	1531.96	1510.39	1493.63
80000	7522.25	4185.90	3092.61	2559.74	2250.65	2053.05	1918.78	1823.72	1754.44	1702.88	1663.90	1634.09	1611.08	1593.21
85000	7992.39	4447.52	3285.90	2719.73	2391.31	2181.37	2038.71	1937.70	1864.09	1809.31	1767.89	1736.22	1711.78	1692.78
90000	8462.53	4709.14	3479.19	2879.71	2531.98	2309.68	2158.63	2051.68	1973.74	1915.74	1871.89	1838.35	1812.47	1792.36
95000	8932.67	4970.75	3672.48	3039.69	2672.64	2438.00	2278.55	2165.67	2083.39	2022.17	1975.88	1940.48	1913.16	1891.93
100000	9402.81	5232.37	3865.77	3199.68	2813.31	2566.32	2398.48	2279.65	2193.05	2128.59	2079.87	2042.61	2013.85	1991.51

TERM	15 Years	16 Years	17 Years	18 Years	19 Years	20 Years	21 Years	22 Years	23 Years	24 Years	25 Years	30 Years	35 Years	40 Years
AMOUNT														
5	.10	.10	.10	.10	.10	.10	.10	.10	.10	.10	.10	.10	.10	.10
10	.20	.20	.20	.20	.20	.20	.20	.20	.20	.20	.20	.20	.20	.20
15	.30	.30	.30	.30	.30	.29	.29	.29	.29	.29	.29	.29	.29	.29
25	.50	.50	.49	.49	.49	.49	.49	.49	.48	.48	.48	.48	.48	.48
50	.99	.99	.98	.98	.97	.97	.97	.97	.96	.96	.96	.96	.96	.96
75	1.49	1.48	1.47	1.46	1.46	1.45	1.45	1.45	1.44	1.44	1.44	1.44	1.44	1.44
100	1.98	1.97	1.95	1.95	1.94	1.93	1.93	1.93	1.92	1.92	1.92	1.92	1.91	1.91
200	3.95	3.93	3.90	3.89	3.87	3.86	3.85	3.85	3.84	3.84	3.83	3.83	3.82	3.82
300	5.93	5.89	5.85	5.83	5.81	5.79	5.78	5.77	5.76	5.75	5.75	5.74	5.73	5.73
400	7.90	7.85	7.80	7.77	7.74	7.72	7.70	7.69	7.68	7.67	7.66	7.65	7.64	7.64
500	9.88	9.81	9.75	9.71	9.68	9.65	9.63	9.61	9.60	9.59	9.58	9.56	9.55	9.55
600	11.85	11.77	11.70	11.65	11.61	11.58	11.55	11.53	11.52	11.50	11.49	11.47	11.46	11.46
700	13.82	13.73	13.65	13.59	13.55	13.51	13.48	13.45	13.44	13.42	13.41	13.38	13.37	13.36
800	15.80	15.69	15.60	15.53	15.48	15.44	15.40	15.38	15.35	15.34	15.32	15.29	15.28	15.27
900	17.77	17.65	17.55	17.47	17.41	17.37	17.33	17.30	17.27	17.25	17.24	17.20	17.19	17.18
1000	19.75	19.61	19.50	19.42	19.35	19.29	19.25	19.22	19.19	19.17	19.15	19.11	19.10	19.09
2000	39.49	39.21	39.00	38.83	38.69	38.58	38.50	38.43	38.38	38.34	38.30	38.21	38.19	38.18
3000	59.23	58.82	58.49	58.24	58.03	57.87	57.75	57.65	57.57	57.50	57.45	57.32	57.28	57.26
4000	78.97	78.42	77.99	77.65	77.38	77.16	77.00	76.86	76.75	76.67	76.60	76.42	76.37	76.35
5000	98.71	98.02	97.48	97.06	96.72	96.45	96.24	96.08	95.94	95.84	95.75	95.53	95.46	95.43
6000	118.45	117.63	116.98	116.47	116.06	115.74	115.49	115.29	115.13	115.00	114.90	114.63	114.55	114.52
7000	138.19	137.23	136.47	135.88	135.41	135.03	134.74	134.50	134.32	134.17	134.05	133.74	133.64	133.60
8000	157.93	156.83	155.97	155.29	154.75	154.32	153.99	153.72	153.50	153.33	153.20	152.84	152.73	152.69
9000	177.67	176.44	175.47	174.70	174.09	173.61	173.23	172.93	172.69	172.50	172.35	171.95	171.82	171.77
10000	197.41	196.04	194.96	194.11	193.44	192.90	192.48	192.15	191.88	191.67	191.50	191.05	190.91	190.86
11000	217.15	215.64	214.46	213.52	212.78	212.19	211.73	211.36	211.07	210.83	210.65	210.15	210.00	209.95
12000	236.89	235.25	233.95	232.93	232.12	231.48	230.98	230.57	230.25	230.00	229.80	229.26	229.09	229.03
13000	256.63	254.85	253.45	252.34	251.47	250.77	250.22	249.79	249.44	249.17	248.95	248.36	248.18	248.12
14000	276.37	274.45	272.94	271.75	270.81	270.06	269.47	269.00	268.63	268.33	268.10	267.47	267.27	267.20
15000	296.10	294.06	292.44	291.16	290.15	289.35	288.72	288.22	287.82	287.50	287.24	286.57	286.36	286.29
16000	315.85	313.66	311.93	310.57	309.50	308.64	307.97	307.43	307.00	306.66	306.39	305.68	305.45	305.37
17000	335.59	333.26	331.43	329.98	328.84	327.93	327.21	326.64	326.19	325.83	325.54	324.78	324.54	324.46
18000	355.33	352.87	350.93	349.39	348.18	347.22	346.46	345.85	345.38	345.00	344.69	343.89	343.63	343.54
19000	375.07	372.47	370.42	368.80	367.53	366.51	365.71	365.07	364.56	364.16	363.84	362.99	362.72	362.63
20000	394.81	392.07	389.92	388.21	386.87	385.80	384.96	384.29	383.75	383.33	382.99	382.09	381.81	381.72
21000	414.55	411.68	409.41	407.63	406.21	405.09	404.20	403.50	402.94	402.49	402.14	401.20	400.90	400.80
22000	434.29	431.28	428.91	427.04	425.55	424.38	423.45	422.71	422.13	421.66	421.29	420.30	419.99	419.89
23000	454.03	450.88	448.40	446.45	444.90	443.67	442.70	441.93	441.31	440.83	440.44	439.41	439.08	438.97
24000	473.77	470.49	467.90	465.86	464.24	462.96	461.95	461.14	460.50	459.99	459.59	458.51	458.17	458.06
25000	493.52	490.09	487.39	485.27	483.58	482.25	481.19	480.36	479.69	479.16	478.74	477.62	477.26	477.14
26000	513.26	509.69	506.89	504.68	502.93	501.54	500.44	499.57	498.88	498.33	497.89	496.72	496.35	496.23
27000	533.00	529.30	526.39	524.09	522.27	520.83	519.69	518.78	518.06	517.49	517.04	515.83	515.44	515.31
28000	552.74	548.90	545.88	543.50	541.61	540.12	538.94	538.00	537.25	536.66	536.19	534.93	534.53	534.40
29000	572.48	568.50	565.38	562.91	560.96	559.41	558.19	557.21	556.44	555.82	555.33	554.04	553.62	553.49
30000	592.22	588.11	584.87	582.32	580.30	578.70	577.43	576.43	575.63	574.99	574.48	573.14	572.71	572.57
31000	611.96	607.71	604.37	601.73	599.64	597.99	596.68	595.64	594.81	594.16	593.63	592.24	591.80	591.66
32000	631.70	627.31	623.86	621.14	618.99	617.28	615.93	614.85	614.00	613.32	612.78	611.35	610.89	610.74
33000	651.44	646.92	643.36	640.55	638.33	636.57	635.18	634.07	633.19	632.49	631.93	630.45	629.98	629.83
34000	671.18	666.52	662.85	659.96	657.67	655.86	654.42	653.28	652.38	651.65	651.08	649.56	649.07	648.91
35000	690.92	686.12	682.35	679.37	677.02	675.15	673.67	672.50	671.56	670.82	670.23	668.66	668.16	668.00
36000	710.66	705.73	701.85	698.78	696.36	694.44	692.92	691.71	690.75	689.99	689.38	687.77	687.25	687.08
37000	730.40	725.33	721.34	718.19	715.70	713.73	712.17	710.92	709.94	709.15	708.53	706.87	706.34	706.17
38000	750.14	744.93	740.84	737.60	735.05	733.02	731.41	730.14	729.12	728.32	727.68	725.98	725.43	725.25
39000	769.88	764.54	760.33	757.01	754.39	752.31	750.66	749.35	748.31	747.49	746.83	745.08	744.52	744.34
40000	789.62	784.14	779.83	776.42	773.73	771.60	769.91	768.57	767.50	766.65	765.98	764.18	763.61	763.43
41000	809.36	803.74	799.32	795.83	793.08	790.89	789.16	787.78	786.69	785.82	785.13	783.29	782.70	782.51
42000	829.10	823.35	818.82	815.25	812.42	810.18	808.40	806.99	805.87	804.98	804.28	802.39	801.79	801.60
43000	848.84	842.95	838.31	834.66	831.76	829.47	827.65	826.21	825.06	824.15	823.42	821.50	820.88	820.68
44000	868.58	862.56	857.81	854.07	851.10	848.76	846.90	845.42	844.25	843.32	842.57	840.60	839.97	839.77
45000	888.32	882.16	877.31	873.48	870.45	868.05	666.15	864.64	863.44	862.48	861.72	859.71	859.06	858.85
46000	908.06	901.76	896.80	892.89	889.79	887.34	885.39	883.85	882.62	881.65	880.87	878.81	878.15	877.94
47000	927.80	921.37	916.30	912.30	909.13	906.63	904.64	903.06	901.81	900.81	900.02	897.92	897.24	897.02
48000	947.54	940.97	935.79	931.71	928.48	925.92	923.89	922.28	921.00	919.98	919.17	917.02	916.33	916.11
49000	967.28	960.57	955.29	951.12	947.82	945.21	943.14	941.49	940.19	939.15	938.32	936.13	935.42	935.20
50000	987.03	980.18	974.78	970.53	967.16	964.50	962.38	960.71	959.37	958.31	957.47	955.23	954.51	954.28
55000	1085.73	1078.19	1072.26	1067.58	1063.88	1060.95	1058.62	1056.78	1055.31	1054.14	1053.22	1050.75	1049.96	1049.71
60000	1184.43	1176.21	1169.74	1164.63	1160.60	1157.40	1154.86	1152.85	1151.25	1149.97	1148.96	1146.28	1145.41	1145.14
65000	1283.13	1274.23	1267.22	1261.69	1257.31	1253.85	1251.10	1248.92	1247.18	1245.81	1244.71	1241.80	1240.86	1240.56
70000	1381.83	1372.24	1364.70	1358.74	1354.03	1350.30	1347.34	1344.99	1343.12	1341.64	1340.46	1337.32	1336.31	1335.99
75000	1480.54	1470.26	1462.17	1455.79	1450.74	1446.75	1443.57	1441.06	1439.06	1437.47	1436.20	1432.84	1431.77	1431.42
80000	1579.24	1568.28	1559.65	1552.84	1547.46	1543.19	1539.81	1537.13	1534.99	1533.30	1531.95	1528.37	1527.22	1526.85
85000	1677.94	1666.30	1657.13	1649.90	1644.18	1639.64	1636.05	1633.20	1630.93	1629.13	1627.69	1623.89	1622.67	1622.27
90000	1776.64	1764.31	1754.61	1746.95	1740.89	1736.09	1732.29	1729.27	1726.87	1724.96	1723.44	1719.41	1718.12	1717.70
95000	1875.34	1862.33	1852.09	1844.00	1837.61	1832.54	1828.53	1825.34	1822.80	1820.79	1819.19	1814.93	1813.57	1813.13
100000	1974.05	1960.35	1949.56	1941.05	1934.32	1928.99	1924.76	1921.41	1918.74	1916.62	1914.93	1910.46	1909.02	1908.56

MONTHLY PAYMENT
REQUIRED TO AMORTIZE A LOAN

TERM AMOUNT	1 Year	2 Years	3 Years	4 Years	5 Years	6 Years	7 Years	8 Years	9 Years	10 Years	11 Years	12 Years	13 Years	14 Years
5	.48	.27	.20	.17	.15	.13	.13	.12	.11	.11	.11	.11	.11	.10
10	.95	.53	.39	.33	.29	.26	.25	.23	.22	.22	.21	.21	.21	.20
15	1.42	.79	.59	.49	.43	.39	.37	.35	.33	.33	.32	.31	.31	.30
25	2.36	1.31	.97	.81	.71	.65	.61	.58	.55	.54	.53	.52	.51	.50
50	4.71	2.62	1.94	1.61	1.41	1.29	1.21	1.15	1.10	1.07	1.05	1.03	1.02	1.00
75	7.06	3.93	2.91	2.41	2.12	1.93	1.81	1.72	1.65	1.61	1.57	1.54	1.52	1.50
100	9.41	5.24	3.88	3.21	2.82	2.58	2.41	2.29	2.20	2.14	2.09	2.05	2.03	2.00
200	18.82	10.48	7.75	6.42	5.64	5.15	4.81	4.58	4.40	4.28	4.18	4.10	4.05	4.00
300	28.23	15.72	11.62	9.62	8.46	7.72	7.22	6.86	6.60	6.41	6.27	6.15	6.07	6.00
400	37.64	20.95	15.49	12.83	11.28	10.29	9.62	9.15	8.80	8.55	8.35	8.20	8.09	8.00
500	47.04	26.19	19.36	16.03	14.10	12.87	12.03	11.44	11.00	10.68	10.44	10.25	10.11	10.00
600	56.45	31.43	23.23	19.24	16.92	15.44	14.43	13.72	13.20	12.82	12.53	12.30	12.13	12.00
700	65.86	36.67	27.10	22.44	19.74	18.01	16.84	16.01	15.40	14.95	14.61	14.35	14.15	14.00
800	75.27	41.90	30.97	25.65	22.56	20.58	19.24	18.29	17.60	17.09	16.70	16.40	16.17	16.00
900	84.67	47.14	34.84	28.85	25.38	23.16	21.65	20.58	19.80	19.22	18.79	18.45	18.20	18.00
1000	94.08	52.38	38.71	32.06	28.20	25.73	24.05	22.87	22.00	21.36	20.87	20.50	20.22	20.00
2000	188.16	104.75	77.42	64.11	56.39	51.45	48.10	45.73	44.00	42.71	41.74	41.00	40.43	39.99
3000	282.23	157.12	116.13	96.16	84.58	77.17	72.15	68.59	66.00	64.07	62.61	61.50	60.64	59.98
4000	376.31	209.50	154.84	128.21	112.77	102.90	96.19	91.45	87.99	85.42	83.48	82.00	80.85	79.97
5000	470.39	261.87	193.55	160.26	140.96	128.62	120.24	114.31	109.99	106.78	104.35	102.50	101.07	99.96
6000	564.46	314.24	232.26	192.31	169.15	154.34	144.29	137.17	131.99	128.13	125.22	123.00	121.28	119.95
7000	658.54	366.62	270.97	224.37	197.34	180.07	168.34	160.03	153.99	149.49	146.09	143.49	141.49	139.94
8000	752.62	418.99	309.68	256.42	225.53	205.79	192.38	182.89	175.98	170.84	166.96	163.99	161.70	159.93
9000	846.69	471.36	348.39	288.47	253.72	231.51	216.43	205.76	197.98	192.20	187.83	184.49	181.92	179.92
10000	940.77	523.74	387.10	320.52	281.91	257.24	240.48	228.62	219.98	213.55	208.70	204.99	202.13	199.91
11000	1034.84	576.11	425.81	352.57	310.10	282.96	264.52	251.48	241.98	234.91	229.57	225.49	222.34	219.90
12000	1128.92	628.48	464.52	384.62	338.29	308.68	288.57	274.34	263.97	256.26	250.44	245.99	242.55	239.89
13000	1223.00	680.86	503.23	416.67	366.48	334.41	312.62	297.20	285.97	277.62	271.31	266.48	262.76	259.88
14000	1317.07	733.23	541.94	448.73	394.67	360.13	336.67	320.06	307.97	298.97	292.18	286.98	282.98	279.87
15000	1411.15	785.60	580.65	480.78	422.86	385.85	360.71	342.92	329.96	320.33	313.05	307.48	303.19	299.86
16000	1505.23	837.98	619.36	512.83	451.05	411.57	384.76	365.78	351.96	341.68	333.92	327.98	323.40	319.85
17000	1599.30	890.35	658.07	544.88	479.24	437.30	408.81	388.65	373.96	363.04	354.78	348.48	343.61	339.84
18000	1693.38	942.72	696.78	576.93	507.43	463.02	432.85	411.51	395.96	384.39	375.65	368.98	363.83	359.83
19000	1787.46	995.10	735.49	608.98	535.62	488.74	456.90	434.37	417.95	405.75	396.52	389.47	384.04	379.82
20000	1881.53	1047.47	774.20	641.03	563.81	514.47	480.95	457.23	439.95	427.10	417.39	409.97	404.25	399.81
21000	1975.61	1099.84	812.91	673.09	592.00	540.19	505.00	480.09	461.95	448.46	438.26	430.47	424.46	419.80
22000	2069.68	1152.22	851.62	705.14	620.20	565.91	529.04	502.95	483.95	469.81	459.13	450.97	444.67	439.79
23000	2163.76	1204.59	890.33	737.19	648.39	591.64	553.09	525.81	505.94	491.16	480.00	471.47	464.89	459.78
24000	2257.84	1256.96	929.04	769.24	676.58	617.36	577.14	548.67	527.94	512.52	500.87	491.97	485.10	479.77
25000	2351.91	1309.34	967.75	801.29	704.77	643.08	601.18	571.53	549.94	533.87	521.74	512.46	505.31	499.76
26000	2445.99	1361.71	1006.46	833.34	732.96	668.81	625.23	594.40	571.94	555.23	542.61	532.96	525.52	519.75
27000	2540.07	1414.08	1045.17	865.39	761.15	694.53	649.28	617.26	593.93	576.58	563.48	553.46	545.74	539.74
28000	2634.14	1466.46	1083.88	897.45	789.34	720.25	673.33	640.12	615.93	597.94	584.35	573.96	565.95	559.73
29000	2728.22	1518.83	1122.59	929.50	817.53	745.98	697.37	662.98	637.93	619.29	605.22	594.46	586.16	579.72
30000	2822.29	1571.20	1161.30	961.55	845.72	771.70	721.42	685.84	659.92	640.65	626.09	614.96	606.37	599.71
31000	2916.37	1623.58	1200.01	993.60	873.91	797.42	745.47	708.70	681.92	662.00	646.96	635.45	626.58	619.70
32000	3010.45	1675.95	1238.72	1025.65	902.10	823.14	769.52	731.56	703.92	683.36	667.83	655.95	646.80	639.69
33000	3104.52	1728.32	1277.43	1057.70	930.29	848.87	793.56	754.42	725.92	704.71	688.69	676.45	667.01	659.68
34000	3198.60	1780.70	1316.14	1089.76	958.48	874.59	817.61	777.29	747.91	726.07	709.56	696.95	687.22	679.67
35000	3292.68	1833.07	1354.85	1121.81	986.67	900.31	841.66	800.15	769.91	747.42	730.43	717.45	707.43	699.66
36000	3386.75	1885.44	1393.56	1153.86	1014.86	926.04	865.70	823.01	791.91	768.78	751.30	737.95	727.65	719.65
37000	3480.83	1937.82	1432.26	1185.91	1043.05	951.76	889.75	845.87	813.91	790.13	772.17	758.44	747.86	739.64
38000	3574.91	1990.19	1470.97	1217.96	1071.24	977.48	913.80	868.73	835.90	811.49	793.04	778.94	768.07	759.63
39000	3668.98	2042.56	1509.68	1250.01	1099.43	1003.21	937.85	891.59	857.90	832.84	813.91	799.44	788.28	779.62
40000	3763.06	2094.94	1548.39	1282.06	1127.62	1028.93	961.89	914.45	879.90	854.20	834.78	819.94	808.50	799.61
41000	3857.13	2147.31	1587.10	1314.12	1155.81	1054.65	985.94	937.31	901.90	875.55	855.65	840.44	828.71	819.60
42000	3951.21	2199.68	1625.81	1346.17	1184.00	1080.38	1009.99	960.18	923.89	896.91	876.52	860.94	848.92	839.59
43000	4045.29	2252.06	1664.52	1378.22	1212.20	1106.10	1034.03	983.04	945.89	918.26	897.39	881.44	869.13	859.58
44000	4139.36	2304.43	1703.23	1410.27	1240.39	1131.82	1058.08	1005.90	967.89	939.62	918.26	901.93	889.34	879.57
45000	4233.44	2356.80	1741.94	1442.32	1268.58	1157.54	1082.13	1028.76	989.88	960.97	939.13	922.43	909.56	899.56
46000	4327.52	2409.18	1780.65	1474.37	1296.77	1183.27	1106.18	1051.62	1011.88	982.32	960.00	942.93	929.77	919.55
47000	4421.59	2461.55	1819.36	1506.42	1324.96	1208.99	1130.22	1074.48	1033.88	1003.68	980.87	963.43	949.98	939.54
48000	4515.67	2513.92	1858.07	1538.48	1353.15	1234.71	1154.27	1097.34	1055.88	1025.03	1001.74	983.93	970.19	959.53
49000	4609.74	2566.30	1896.78	1570.53	1381.34	1260.44	1178.32	1120.20	1077.87	1046.39	1022.60	1004.43	990.41	979.52
50000	4703.82	2618.67	1935.49	1602.58	1409.53	1286.16	1202.36	1143.06	1099.87	1067.74	1043.47	1024.92	1010.62	999.51
55000	5174.20	2880.54	2129.04	1762.84	1550.48	1414.78	1322.60	1257.37	1209.86	1174.52	1147.82	1127.42	1111.68	1099.46
60000	5644.58	3142.40	2322.59	1923.09	1691.43	1543.39	1442.84	1371.68	1319.84	1281.29	1252.17	1229.91	1212.74	1199.41
65000	6114.97	3404.27	2516.14	2083.35	1832.39	1672.01	1563.07	1485.98	1429.83	1388.07	1356.51	1332.40	1313.80	1299.36
70000	6585.35	3666.14	2709.69	2243.61	1973.34	1800.62	1683.31	1600.29	1539.82	1494.84	1460.86	1434.89	1414.86	1399.31
75000	7055.73	3928.00	2903.24	2403.87	2114.29	1929.24	1803.54	1714.59	1649.80	1601.61	1565.21	1537.38	1515.92	1499.26
80000	7526.11	4189.87	3096.78	2564.12	2255.24	2057.85	1923.78	1828.90	1759.79	1708.39	1669.56	1639.88	1616.99	1599.21
85000	7996.49	4451.74	3290.33	2724.38	2396.20	2186.47	2044.02	1943.21	1869.78	1815.16	1773.90	1742.37	1718.05	1699.16
90000	8466.87	4713.60	3483.88	2884.64	2537.15	2315.08	2164.25	2057.51	1979.76	1921.94	1878.25	1844.86	1819.11	1799.11
95000	8937.26	4975.47	3677.43	3044.89	2678.10	2443.70	2284.49	2171.82	2089.75	2028.71	1982.60	1947.35	1920.17	1899.06
100000	9407.64	5237.34	3870.98	3205.15	2819.05	2572.32	2404.72	2286.12	2199.74	2135.48	2086.94	2049.84	2021.23	1999.01

TERM	15 Years	16 Years	17 Years	18 Years	19 Years	20 Years	21 Years	22 Years	23 Years	24 Years	25 Years	30 Years	35 Years	40 Years
AMOUNT														
5	.10	.10	.10	.10	.10	.10	.10	.10	.10	.10	.10	.10	.10	.10
10	.20	.20	.20	.20	.20	.20	.20	.20	.20	.20	.20	.20	.20	.20
15	.30	.30	.30	.30	.30	.30	.29	.29	.29	.29	.29	.29	.29	.29
25	.50	.50	.49	.49	.49	.49	.49	.49	.49	.49	.49	.49	.48	.48
50	1.00	.99	.98	.98	.98	.97	.97	.97	.97	.97	.97	.96	.96	.96
75	1.49	1.48	1.47	1.47	1.46	1.46	1.45	1.45	1.45	1.45	1.45	1.44	1.44	1.44
100	1.99	1.97	1.96	1.95	1.95	1.94	1.94	1.93	1.93	1.93	1.93	1.92	1.92	1.92
200	3.97	3.94	3.92	3.90	3.89	3.82	3.87	3.86	3.86	3.85	3.85	3.84	3.84	3.84
300	5.95	5.91	5.88	5.85	5.83	5.82	5.80	5.79	5.79	5.78	5.77	5.76	5.76	5.76
400	7.93	7.88	7.83	7.80	7.77	7.75	7.74	7.72	7.71	7.70	7.70	7.68	7.67	7.67
500	9.91	9.85	9.79	9.75	9.72	9.69	9.67	9.65	9.64	9.63	9.62	9.60	9.59	9.59
600	11.89	11.81	11.75	11.70	11.66	11.63	11.60	11.58	11.57	11.55	11.54	11.52	11.51	11.51
700	13.88	13.78	13.71	13.65	13.60	13.56	13.53	13.51	13.49	13.48	13.47	13.44	13.43	13.42
800	15.86	15.75	15.66	15.60	15.54	15.50	15.47	15.44	15.42	15.40	15.39	15.35	15.34	15.34
900	17.84	17.72	17.62	17.55	17.49	17.44	17.40	17.37	17.35	17.33	17.31	17.27	17.26	17.26
1000	19.82	19.69	19.58	19.49	19.43	19.38	19.33	19.30	19.27	19.25	19.24	19.19	19.18	19.17
2000	39.64	39.37	39.15	38.98	38.85	38.75	38.66	38.60	38.54	38.50	38.47	38.38	38.35	38.34
3000	59.45	59.05	58.73	58.47	58.27	58.12	57.99	57.89	57.81	57.75	57.70	57.57	57.52	57.51
4000	79.27	78.73	78.30	77.96	77.70	77.49	77.32	77.19	77.08	77.00	76.93	76.75	76.70	76.68
5000	99.09	98.41	97.87	97.45	97.12	96.86	96.65	96.48	96.35	96.24	96.16	95.94	95.87	95.85
6000	118.90	118.09	117.45	116.94	116.54	116.23	115.97	115.78	115.62	115.49	115.39	115.13	115.04	115.02
7000	138.72	137.77	137.02	136.43	135.96	135.60	135.30	135.07	134.89	134.74	134.62	134.32	134.22	134.19
8000	158.54	157.45	156.59	155.92	155.39	154.97	154.63	154.37	154.16	153.99	153.86	153.50	153.39	153.36
9000	178.35	177.13	176.17	175.41	174.81	174.34	173.96	173.66	173.42	173.24	173.09	172.69	172.56	172.52
10000	198.17	196.81	195.74	194.90	194.23	193.71	193.29	192.96	192.69	192.48	192.32	191.88	191.74	191.69
11000	217.99	216.49	215.32	214.39	213.66	213.08	212.62	212.25	211.96	211.73	211.55	211.07	210.91	210.86
12000	237.80	236.17	234.89	233.88	233.08	232.45	231.94	231.55	231.23	230.98	230.78	230.25	230.08	230.03
13000	257.62	255.85	254.46	253.37	252.50	251.82	251.27	250.84	250.50	250.23	250.01	249.44	249.26	249.20
14000	277.44	275.53	274.04	272.86	271.92	271.19	270.60	270.14	269.77	269.48	269.24	268.63	268.43	268.37
15000	297.25	295.21	293.61	292.35	291.35	290.56	289.93	289.43	289.04	288.72	288.47	287.81	287.60	287.54
16000	317.07	314.90	313.18	311.84	310.77	309.93	309.26	308.73	308.31	307.97	307.71	307.00	306.78	306.71
17000	336.89	334.58	332.76	331.32	330.19	329.30	328.59	328.02	327.57	327.22	326.94	326.19	325.95	325.87
18000	356.70	354.26	352.33	350.81	349.61	348.67	347.91	347.32	346.04	346.04	346.17	345.38	345.12	345.04
19000	376.52	373.94	371.91	370.30	369.04	368.04	367.24	366.61	366.11	365.72	365.40	364.56	364.30	364.21
20000	396.34	393.62	391.48	389.79	388.46	387.41	386.57	385.91	385.38	384.96	384.63	383.75	383.47	383.38
21000	416.15	413.30	411.05	409.28	407.88	406.78	405.90	405.20	404.65	404.21	403.86	402.94	402.64	402.55
22000	435.97	432.98	430.63	428.77	427.31	426.15	425.23	424.50	423.92	423.46	423.09	422.13	421.82	421.72
23000	455.79	452.66	450.20	448.26	446.73	445.52	444.55	443.79	443.19	442.71	442.32	441.31	440.99	440.89
24000	475.60	472.34	469.77	467.75	466.15	464.89	463.88	463.09	462.46	461.95	461.56	460.50	460.16	460.06
25000	495.42	492.02	489.35	487.24	485.57	484.26	483.21	482.38	481.73	481.20	480.79	479.69	479.34	479.22
26000	515.24	511.70	508.92	506.73	505.00	503.63	502.54	501.68	500.99	500.45	500.02	498.88	498.51	498.39
27000	535.05	531.38	528.50	526.22	524.42	523.00	521.87	520.97	520.26	519.70	519.25	518.06	517.68	517.56
28000	554.87	551.06	548.07	545.71	543.84	542.37	541.20	540.27	539.53	538.95	538.48	537.25	536.86	536.73
29000	574.69	570.74	567.64	565.20	563.27	561.74	560.52	559.56	558.80	558.19	557.71	556.44	556.03	555.90
30000	594.50	590.42	587.22	584.69	582.69	581.11	579.85	578.86	578.07	577.44	576.94	575.62	575.20	575.07
31000	614.32	610.11	606.79	604.18	602.11	600.48	599.18	598.15	597.34	596.69	596.18	594.81	594.38	594.24
32000	634.14	629.79	626.36	623.67	621.53	619.85	618.51	617.45	616.61	615.94	615.41	614.00	613.55	613.41
33000	653.95	649.47	645.94	643.15	640.96	639.22	637.84	636.74	635.88	635.19	634.64	633.19	632.72	632.57
34000	673.77	669.15	665.51	662.64	660.38	658.59	657.17	656.04	655.14	654.43	653.87	652.37	651.90	651.74
35000	693.59	688.83	685.09	682.13	679.80	677.96	676.49	675.33	674.41	673.68	673.10	671.56	671.07	670.91
36000	713.40	708.51	704.66	701.62	699.22	697.33	695.82	694.63	693.68	692.93	692.33	690.75	690.24	690.08
37000	733.22	728.19	724.23	721.11	718.65	716.70	715.15	713.92	712.95	712.18	711.56	709.94	709.42	709.25
38000	753.04	747.87	743.81	740.60	738.07	736.07	734.48	733.22	732.22	731.43	730.79	729.12	728.59	728.42
39000	772.85	767.55	763.38	760.09	757.49	755.44	753.81	752.51	751.49	750.67	750.03	748.31	747.76	747.59
40000	792.67	787.23	782.95	779.58	776.92	774.81	773.14	771.81	770.76	769.92	769.26	767.50	766.94	766.76
41000	812.49	806.91	802.53	799.07	796.34	794.18	792.46	791.10	790.03	789.17	788.49	786.68	786.11	785.92
42000	832.30	826.59	822.10	818.56	815.76	813.55	811.79	810.40	809.29	808.42	807.72	805.87	805.28	805.09
43000	852.12	846.27	841.67	838.05	835.18	832.92	831.12	829.69	828.56	827.66	826.95	825.06	824.46	824.26
44000	871.94	865.95	861.25	857.54	854.61	852.29	850.45	848.99	847.83	846.91	846.18	844.25	843.63	843.43
45000	891.75	885.63	880.82	877.03	874.03	871.66	869.78	868.28	867.10	866.16	865.41	863.43	862.80	862.60
46000	911.57	905.32	900.40	896.52	893.45	891.03	889.10	887.58	886.37	885.41	884.64	882.62	881.98	881.77
47000	931.39	925.00	919.97	916.01	912.87	910.40	908.43	906.88	905.64	904.66	903.88	901.81	901.15	900.94
48000	951.20	944.68	939.54	935.50	932.30	929.77	927.76	926.17	924.91	923.90	923.11	921.00	920.32	920.11
49000	971.02	964.36	959.12	954.99	951.72	949.14	947.09	945.47	944.18	943.15	942.34	940.18	939.50	939.28
50000	990.84	984.04	978.69	974.47	971.14	968.51	966.42	964.76	963.45	962.40	961.57	959.37	958.67	958.44
55000	1089.92	1082.44	1076.56	1071.92	1068.26	1065.36	1063.06	1061.24	1059.79	1058.64	1057.73	1055.31	1054.53	1054.29
60000	1189.00	1180.84	1174.43	1169.37	1165.37	1162.21	1159.70	1157.71	1156.13	1154.88	1153.88	1151.24	1150.40	1150.13
65000	1288.09	1279.25	1272.30	1266.82	1262.48	1259.06	1256.34	1254.19	1252.48	1251.12	1250.04	1247.18	1246.27	1245.98
70000	1387.17	1377.65	1370.17	1364.26	1359.60	1355.91	1352.98	1350.66	1348.82	1347.36	1346.20	1343.12	1342.13	1341.82
75000	1486.25	1476.05	1468.03	1461.71	1456.71	1452.76	1449.62	1447.14	1445.17	1443.60	1442.35	1439.05	1438.00	1437.66
80000	1585.34	1574.46	1565.90	1559.16	1553.83	1549.61	1546.27	1543.61	1541.51	1539.84	1538.51	1534.99	1533.87	1533.51
85000	1684.42	1672.86	1663.77	1656.60	1650.94	1646.46	1642.91	1640.09	1637.85	1636.08	1634.67	1630.93	1629.73	1629.35
90000	1783.50	1771.26	1761.64	1754.05	1748.05	1743.31	1739.55	1736.56	1734.20	1732.32	1730.82	1726.86	1725.60	1725.20
95000	1882.59	1869.67	1859.51	1851.50	1845.17	1840.16	1836.19	1833.04	1830.54	1828.56	1826.98	1822.80	1821.47	1821.04
100000	1981.67	1968.07	1957.38	1948.94	1942.28	1937.01	1932.83	1929.52	1926.89	1924.80	1923.13	1918.74	1917.33	1916.88

23%

MONTHLY PAYMENT
REQUIRED TO AMORTIZE A LOAN

TERM AMOUNT	1 Year	2 Years	3 Years	4 Years	5 Years	6 Years	7 Years	8 Years	9 Years	10 Years	11 Years	12 Years	13 Years	14 Years
5	.48	.27	.20	.17	.15	.13	.13	.12	.12	.11	.11	.11	.11	.11
10	.95	.53	.39	.33	.29	.26	.25	.23	.23	.22	.21	.21	.21	.21
15	1.42	.79	.59	.49	.43	.39	.37	.35	.34	.33	.32	.31	.31	.31
25	2.36	1.32	.97	.81	.71	.65	.61	.58	.56	.54	.53	.52	.51	.51
50	4.71	2.63	1.94	1.61	1.42	1.29	1.21	1.15	1.11	1.08	1.05	1.03	1.02	1.01
75	7.06	3.94	2.91	2.41	2.12	1.94	1.81	1.72	1.66	1.61	1.58	1.55	1.53	1.51
100	9.42	5.25	3.88	3.22	2.83	2.58	2.42	2.30	2.21	2.15	2.10	2.06	2.03	2.01
200	18.83	10.49	7.76	6.43	5.65	5.16	4.83	4.59	4.42	4.29	4.19	4.12	4.06	4.02
300	28.24	15.73	11.63	9.64	8.48	7.74	7.24	6.88	6.62	6.43	6.29	6.18	6.09	6.02
400	37.65	20.97	15.51	12.85	11.30	10.32	9.65	9.18	8.83	8.57	8.38	8.23	8.12	8.03
500	47.07	26.22	19.39	16.06	14.13	12.90	12.06	11.47	11.04	10.72	10.48	10.29	10.15	10.04
600	56.48	31.46	23.26	19.27	16.95	15.47	14.47	13.76	13.24	12.86	12.57	12.35	12.18	12.04
700	65.89	36.70	27.14	22.48	19.78	18.05	16.88	16.05	15.45	15.00	14.66	14.40	14.21	14.05
800	75.30	41.94	31.01	25.69	22.60	20.63	19.29	18.35	17.66	17.14	16.76	16.46	16.23	16.06
900	84.72	47.19	34.89	28.90	25.43	23.21	21.70	20.64	19.86	19.29	18.85	18.52	18.26	18.06
1000	94.13	52.43	38.77	32.11	28.25	25.79	24.11	22.93	22.07	21.43	20.95	20.58	20.29	20.07
2000	188.25	104.85	77.53	64.22	56.50	51.57	48.22	45.86	44.13	42.85	41.89	41.15	40.58	40.14
3000	282.38	157.27	116.29	96.32	84.75	77.35	72.33	68.78	66.20	64.28	62.83	61.72	60.86	60.20
4000	376.50	209.70	155.05	128.43	113.00	103.14	96.44	91.71	88.26	85.70	83.77	82.29	81.15	80.27
5000	470.63	262.12	193.81	160.54	141.24	128.92	120.55	114.64	110.33	107.12	104.71	102.86	101.44	100.33
6000	564.75	314.54	232.58	192.64	169.49	154.70	144.66	137.56	132.39	128.55	125.65	123.43	121.72	120.40
7000	658.88	366.97	271.34	224.75	197.74	180.49	168.77	160.49	154.46	149.97	146.59	144.00	142.01	140.46
8000	753.00	419.39	310.10	256.86	225.99	206.27	192.88	183.41	176.52	171.39	167.53	164.57	162.29	160.53
9000	847.13	471.81	348.86	288.96	254.24	232.05	216.99	206.34	198.58	192.82	188.47	185.14	182.58	180.59
10000	941.25	524.23	387.62	321.07	282.48	257.84	241.10	229.27	220.65	214.24	209.41	205.71	202.87	200.66
11000	1035.38	576.66	426.39	353.17	310.73	283.62	265.21	252.19	242.71	235.67	230.35	226.28	223.15	220.72
12000	1129.50	629.08	465.15	385.28	338.98	309.40	289.32	275.12	264.78	257.09	251.29	246.85	243.44	240.79
13000	1223.62	681.50	503.91	417.39	367.23	335.19	313.43	298.04	286.84	278.51	272.23	267.42	263.72	260.85
14000	1317.75	733.93	542.67	449.49	395.48	360.97	337.54	320.97	308.91	299.94	293.17	288.00	283.72	280.92
15000	1411.87	786.35	581.43	481.60	423.72	386.75	361.65	343.90	330.97	321.36	314.11	308.57	304.30	300.98
16000	1506.00	838.77	620.19	513.71	451.97	412.54	385.76	366.82	353.03	342.78	335.05	329.14	324.58	321.05
17000	1600.12	891.20	658.96	545.81	480.22	438.32	409.87	389.75	375.10	364.21	355.99	349.71	344.87	341.11
18000	1694.25	943.62	697.72	577.92	508.47	464.10	433.98	412.67	397.16	385.63	376.93	370.28	365.16	361.18
19000	1788.37	996.04	736.48	610.02	536.72	489.89	458.09	435.60	419.23	407.06	397.87	390.85	385.44	381.24
20000	1882.50	1048.46	775.24	642.13	564.96	515.67	482.20	458.53	441.29	428.48	418.81	411.42	405.73	401.31
21000	1976.62	1100.89	814.00	674.24	593.21	541.45	506.31	481.45	463.36	449.90	439.75	431.99	426.01	421.37
22000	2070.75	1153.31	852.77	706.34	621.46	567.23	530.42	504.38	485.42	471.33	460.69	452.56	446.30	441.44
23000	2164.87	1205.73	891.53	738.45	649.71	593.02	554.53	527.30	507.49	492.75	481.63	473.13	466.59	461.51
24000	2259.00	1258.16	930.29	770.56	677.96	618.80	578.64	550.23	529.55	514.17	502.57	493.70	486.87	481.57
25000	2353.12	1310.58	969.05	802.66	706.20	644.58	602.75	573.16	551.61	535.60	523.51	514.27	507.16	501.64
26000	2447.24	1363.00	1007.81	834.77	734.45	670.37	626.86	596.08	573.68	557.02	544.45	534.84	527.44	521.70
27000	2541.37	1415.43	1046.58	866.87	762.70	696.15	650.97	619.01	595.74	578.45	565.39	555.42	547.73	541.77
28000	2635.49	1467.85	1085.34	898.98	790.95	721.93	675.08	641.93	617.81	599.87	586.33	575.99	568.02	561.83
29000	2729.62	1520.27	1124.10	931.09	819.20	747.72	699.19	664.86	639.87	621.29	607.27	596.56	588.30	581.90
30000	2823.74	1572.69	1162.86	963.19	847.44	773.50	723.30	687.79	661.93	642.72	628.21	617.13	608.59	601.96
31000	2917.87	1625.12	1201.62	995.30	875.69	799.28	747.41	710.71	684.00	664.14	649.15	637.70	628.87	622.03
32000	3011.99	1677.54	1240.38	1027.41	903.94	825.07	771.52	733.64	706.06	685.56	670.09	658.27	649.16	642.09
33000	3106.12	1729.96	1279.15	1059.51	932.19	850.85	795.63	756.56	728.13	706.99	691.03	678.84	669.45	662.16
34000	3200.24	1782.39	1317.91	1091.62	960.44	876.63	819.74	779.49	750.19	728.41	711.97	699.41	689.73	682.22
35000	3294.37	1834.81	1356.67	1123.73	988.68	902.42	843.85	802.42	772.26	749.84	732.91	719.98	710.02	702.29
36000	3388.49	1887.23	1395.43	1155.83	1016.93	928.20	867.96	825.34	794.32	771.26	753.85	740.55	730.31	722.35
37000	3482.61	1939.65	1434.19	1187.94	1045.18	953.98	892.06	848.27	816.38	792.68	774.79	761.12	750.59	742.42
38000	3576.74	1992.08	1472.96	1220.04	1073.43	979.77	916.17	871.19	838.45	814.11	795.73	781.69	770.88	762.48
39000	3670.86	2044.50	1511.72	1252.15	1101.68	1005.55	940.28	894.12	860.51	835.53	816.67	802.26	791.16	782.55
40000	3764.99	2096.92	1550.48	1284.26	1129.92	1031.33	964.39	917.05	882.58	856.95	837.61	822.84	811.45	802.61
41000	3859.11	2149.35	1589.24	1316.36	1158.17	1057.12	988.50	939.97	904.64	878.38	858.55	843.41	831.74	822.68
42000	3953.24	2201.77	1628.00	1348.47	1186.42	1082.90	1012.61	962.90	926.71	899.80	879.49	863.98	852.02	842.74
43000	4047.36	2254.19	1666.77	1380.58	1214.67	1108.68	1036.72	985.82	948.77	921.23	900.43	884.55	872.31	862.81
44000	4141.49	2306.62	1705.53	1412.68	1242.92	1134.46	1060.83	1008.75	970.83	942.65	921.37	905.12	892.59	882.88
45000	4235.61	2359.04	1744.29	1444.79	1271.16	1160.25	1084.94	1031.68	992.90	964.07	942.31	925.69	912.88	902.94
46000	4329.74	2411.46	1783.05	1476.89	1299.41	1186.03	1109.05	1054.60	1014.96	985.50	963.25	946.26	933.17	923.01
47000	4423.86	2463.88	1821.81	1509.00	1327.66	1211.81	1133.16	1077.53	1037.03	1006.92	984.19	966.83	953.45	943.07
48000	4517.99	2516.31	1860.57	1541.11	1355.91	1237.60	1157.27	1100.45	1059.09	1028.34	1005.13	987.40	973.74	963.14
49000	4612.11	2568.73	1899.34	1573.21	1384.15	1263.38	1181.38	1123.38	1081.16	1049.77	1026.07	1007.97	994.02	983.20
50000	4706.23	2621.15	1938.10	1605.32	1412.40	1289.16	1205.49	1146.31	1103.22	1071.19	1047.01	1028.54	1014.31	1003.27
55000	5176.86	2883.27	2131.91	1765.85	1553.64	1418.08	1326.04	1260.94	1213.54	1178.31	1151.71	1131.40	1115.74	1103.59
60000	5647.48	3145.38	2325.72	1926.38	1694.88	1547.00	1446.59	1375.57	1323.86	1285.43	1256.41	1234.25	1217.17	1203.92
65000	6118.10	3407.50	2519.53	2086.91	1836.12	1675.91	1567.14	1490.20	1434.19	1392.55	1361.11	1337.11	1318.60	1304.25
70000	6588.73	3669.61	2713.34	2247.44	1977.36	1804.83	1687.69	1604.83	1544.51	1499.67	1465.82	1439.96	1420.03	1404.57
75000	7059.35	3931.73	2907.14	2407.98	2118.60	1933.74	1808.23	1719.46	1654.83	1606.79	1570.52	1542.81	1521.46	1504.90
80000	7529.97	4193.84	3100.95	2568.51	2259.84	2062.66	1928.78	1834.09	1765.15	1713.90	1675.22	1645.67	1622.89	1605.22
85000	8000.60	4455.96	3294.76	2729.04	2401.08	2191.58	2049.33	1948.72	1875.47	1821.02	1779.92	1748.52	1724.32	1705.55
90000	8471.22	4718.07	3488.57	2889.57	2542.32	2320.49	2169.88	2063.35	1985.79	1928.14	1884.62	1851.37	1825.76	1805.88
95000	8941.84	4980.19	3682.38	3050.10	2683.56	2449.41	2290.43	2177.98	2096.11	2035.26	1989.32	1954.23	1927.19	1906.20
100000	9412.46	5242.30	3876.19	3210.63	2824.80	2578.32	2410.98	2292.61	2206.44	2142.38	2094.02	2057.08	2028.62	2006.53

TERM	15 Years	16 Years	17 Years	18 Years	19 Years	20 Years	21 Years	22 Years	23 Years	24 Years	25 Years	30 Years	35 Years	40 Years
AMOUNT														
5	.10	.10	.10	.10	.10	.10	.10	.10	.10	.10	.10	.10	.10	.10
10	.20	.20	.20	.20	.20	.20	.20	.20	.20	.20	.20	.20	.20	.20
15	.30	.30	.30	.30	.30	.30	.30	.30	.30	.29	.29	.29	.29	.29
25	.50	.50	.50	.49	.49	.49	.49	.49	.49	.49	.49	.49	.49	.49
50	1.00	.99	.99	.98	.98	.98	.98	.97	.97	.97	.97	.97	.97	.97
75	1.50	1.49	1.48	1.47	1.47	1.46	1.46	1.46	1.46	1.45	1.45	1.45	1.45	1.45
100	1.99	1.98	1.97	1.96	1.96	1.95	1.95	1.94	1.94	1.94	1.94	1.93	1.93	1.93
200	3.98	3.96	3.94	3.92	3.91	3.90	3.89	3.88	3.88	3.87	3.87	3.86	3.86	3.86
300	5.97	5.93	5.90	5.88	5.86	5.84	5.83	5.82	5.81	5.80	5.80	5.79	5.78	5.78
400	7.96	7.91	7.87	7.83	7.81	7.79	7.77	7.76	7.75	7.74	7.73	7.71	7.71	7.71
500	9.95	9.88	9.83	9.79	9.76	9.73	9.71	9.69	9.68	9.67	9.66	9.64	9.63	9.63
600	11.94	11.86	11.80	11.75	11.71	11.68	11.65	11.63	11.62	11.60	11.59	11.57	11.56	11.56
700	13.93	13.84	13.76	13.70	13.66	13.62	13.59	13.57	13.55	13.54	13.52	13.49	13.48	13.48
800	15.92	15.81	15.73	15.66	15.61	15.57	15.53	15.51	15.49	15.47	15.46	15.42	15.41	15.41
900	17.91	17.79	17.69	17.62	17.56	17.51	17.47	17.44	17.42	17.40	17.39	17.35	17.34	17.33
1000	19.90	19.76	19.66	19.57	19.51	19.46	19.41	19.38	19.36	19.33	19.32	19.28	19.26	19.26
2000	39.79	39.52	39.31	39.14	39.01	38.91	38.82	38.76	38.71	38.66	38.63	38.55	38.52	38.51
3000	59.68	59.28	58.96	58.71	58.51	58.36	58.23	58.13	58.06	57.99	57.95	57.82	57.77	57.76
4000	79.58	79.04	78.61	78.28	78.01	77.81	77.64	77.51	77.41	77.32	77.26	77.09	77.03	77.01
5000	99.47	98.79	98.26	97.85	97.52	97.26	97.05	96.89	96.76	96.65	96.57	96.36	96.29	96.27
6000	119.36	118.55	117.92	117.42	117.02	116.71	116.46	116.26	116.11	115.98	115.89	115.63	115.54	115.52
7000	139.26	138.31	137.57	136.98	136.52	136.16	135.87	135.64	135.46	135.31	135.20	134.90	134.80	134.77
8000	159.15	158.07	157.22	156.55	156.02	155.61	155.28	155.01	154.81	154.64	154.51	154.17	154.06	154.02
9000	179.04	177.83	176.87	176.12	175.53	175.06	174.69	174.39	174.16	173.97	173.83	173.44	173.31	173.27
10000	198.93	197.58	196.52	195.69	195.03	194.51	194.09	193.77	193.51	193.30	193.14	192.71	192.57	192.53
11000	218.83	217.34	216.18	215.26	214.53	213.96	213.50	213.14	212.86	212.63	212.45	211.98	211.83	211.78
12000	238.72	237.10	235.83	234.83	234.03	233.41	232.91	232.52	232.21	231.96	231.77	231.25	231.08	231.03
13000	258.61	256.86	255.48	254.39	253.54	252.86	252.32	251.90	251.56	251.29	251.08	250.52	250.34	250.28
14000	278.51	276.62	275.13	273.96	273.04	272.31	271.73	271.27	270.91	270.62	270.39	269.79	269.59	269.53
15000	298.40	296.37	294.78	293.53	292.54	291.76	291.14	290.65	290.26	289.95	289.71	289.06	288.85	288.79
16000	318.29	316.13	314.44	313.10	312.04	311.21	310.55	310.02	309.61	309.28	309.02	308.33	308.11	308.04
17000	338.18	335.89	334.09	332.67	331.55	330.66	329.96	329.40	328.96	328.61	328.33	327.60	327.36	327.29
18000	358.08	355.65	353.74	352.24	351.05	350.11	349.37	348.78	348.31	347.94	347.65	346.87	346.62	346.54
19000	377.97	375.41	373.39	371.80	370.55	369.56	368.78	368.15	367.66	367.27	366.96	366.14	365.88	365.79
20000	397.86	395.16	393.04	391.37	390.05	389.01	388.18	387.53	387.01	386.60	386.27	385.41	385.13	385.05
21000	417.76	414.92	412.70	410.94	409.56	408.46	407.59	406.91	406.36	405.93	405.59	404.68	404.39	404.30
22000	437.65	434.68	432.35	430.51	429.06	427.91	427.00	426.28	425.71	425.26	424.90	423.95	423.65	423.55
23000	457.54	454.44	452.00	450.08	448.56	447.36	446.41	445.66	445.06	444.59	444.21	443.22	442.90	442.80
24000	477.44	474.20	471.65	469.65	468.06	466.81	465.82	465.03	464.41	463.92	463.53	462.49	462.16	462.05
25000	497.33	493.95	491.30	489.21	487.56	486.26	485.23	484.41	483.76	483.25	482.84	481.76	481.42	481.31
26000	517.22	513.71	510.95	508.78	507.07	505.71	504.64	503.79	503.11	502.58	502.15	501.03	500.67	500.56
27000	537.11	533.47	530.61	528.35	526.57	525.16	524.05	523.16	522.46	521.91	521.47	520.30	519.93	519.81
28000	557.01	553.23	550.26	547.92	546.07	544.61	543.46	542.54	541.81	541.24	540.78	539.57	539.18	539.06
29000	576.90	572.99	569.91	567.49	565.57	564.06	562.86	561.92	561.16	560.57	560.09	558.84	558.44	558.31
30000	596.79	592.74	589.56	587.06	585.08	583.51	582.27	581.29	580.51	579.90	579.41	578.11	577.70	577.57
31000	616.69	612.50	609.21	606.62	604.58	602.96	601.68	600.67	599.86	599.23	598.72	597.38	596.95	596.82
32000	636.58	632.26	628.87	626.19	624.08	622.41	621.09	620.04	619.21	618.55	618.03	616.65	616.21	616.07
33000	656.47	652.02	648.52	645.76	643.58	641.86	640.50	639.42	638.56	637.88	637.35	635.92	635.47	635.32
34000	676.36	671.78	668.17	665.33	663.09	661.31	659.91	658.80	657.91	657.21	656.66	655.19	654.72	654.57
35000	696.26	691.53	687.82	684.90	682.59	680.76	679.32	678.17	677.26	676.54	675.97	674.46	673.98	673.83
36000	716.15	711.29	707.47	704.47	702.09	700.21	698.73	697.55	696.62	695.87	695.29	693.73	693.24	693.08
37000	736.04	731.05	727.13	724.03	721.59	719.66	718.14	716.93	715.97	715.20	714.60	713.00	712.49	712.33
38000	755.94	750.81	746.78	743.60	741.10	739.11	737.55	736.30	735.32	734.53	733.91	732.27	731.75	731.58
39000	775.83	770.57	766.43	763.17	760.60	758.56	756.95	755.68	754.67	753.86	753.23	751.54	751.00	750.83
40000	795.72	790.32	786.08	782.74	780.10	778.01	776.36	775.05	774.02	773.19	772.54	770.81	770.26	770.09
41000	815.62	810.08	805.73	802.31	799.60	797.46	795.77	794.43	793.37	792.52	791.85	790.08	789.52	789.34
42000	835.51	829.84	825.39	821.88	819.11	816.92	815.18	813.81	812.72	811.85	811.17	809.35	808.77	808.59
43000	855.40	849.60	845.04	841.44	838.61	836.37	834.59	833.18	832.07	831.18	830.48	828.62	828.03	827.84
44000	875.29	869.36	864.69	861.01	858.11	855.82	854.00	852.56	851.42	850.51	849.79	847.89	847.29	847.09
45000	895.19	889.11	884.34	880.58	877.61	875.27	873.41	871.94	870.77	869.84	869.11	867.16	866.54	866.35
46000	915.08	908.87	903.99	900.15	897.12	894.72	892.82	891.31	890.12	889.17	888.42	886.43	885.80	885.60
47000	934.97	928.63	923.65	919.72	916.62	914.17	912.23	910.69	909.47	908.50	907.73	905.70	905.06	904.85
48000	954.87	948.39	943.30	939.29	936.12	933.62	931.63	930.06	928.82	927.83	927.05	924.97	924.31	924.10
49000	974.76	968.15	962.95	958.85	955.62	953.07	951.04	949.44	948.17	947.16	946.36	944.24	943.57	943.35
50000	994.65	987.90	982.60	978.42	975.12	972.52	970.45	968.82	967.52	966.49	965.67	963.51	962.83	962.61
55000	1094.12	1086.69	1080.86	1076.26	1072.64	1069.77	1067.50	1065.70	1064.27	1063.14	1062.24	1059.86	1059.11	1058.87
60000	1193.58	1185.48	1179.12	1174.11	1170.15	1167.02	1164.54	1162.58	1161.02	1159.79	1158.81	1156.21	1155.39	1155.13
65000	1293.05	1284.27	1277.38	1271.95	1267.66	1264.27	1261.59	1259.46	1257.77	1256.43	1255.37	1252.56	1251.67	1251.39
70000	1392.51	1383.06	1375.64	1369.79	1365.17	1361.52	1358.63	1356.34	1354.52	1353.08	1351.94	1348.91	1347.95	1347.65
75000	1491.98	1481.85	1473.90	1467.63	1462.68	1458.77	1455.68	1453.22	1451.28	1449.73	1448.51	1445.26	1444.24	1443.91
80000	1591.44	1580.64	1572.16	1565.47	1560.20	1556.02	1552.72	1550.10	1548.03	1546.38	1545.07	1541.62	1540.52	1540.17
85000	1690.90	1679.43	1670.42	1663.32	1657.71	1653.28	1649.77	1646.98	1644.78	1643.03	1641.64	1637.97	1636.80	1636.43
90000	1790.37	1778.22	1768.68	1761.16	1755.22	1750.53	1746.81	1743.87	1741.53	1739.68	1738.21	1734.32	1733.08	1732.69
95000	1889.83	1877.01	1866.94	1859.00	1852.73	1847.78	1843.86	1840.75	1838.28	1836.33	1834.77	1830.67	1829.36	1828.95
100000	1989.30	1975.80	1965.20	1956.84	1950.24	1945.03	1940.90	1937.63	1935.03	1932.97	1931.34	1927.02	1925.65	1925.21

MONTHLY PAYMENT
REQUIRED TO AMORTIZE A LOAN

TERM AMOUNT	1 Year	2 Years	3 Years	4 Years	5 Years	6 Years	7 Years	8 Years	9 Years	10 Years	11 Years	12 Years	13 Years	14 Years
5	.48	.27	.20	.17	.15	.13	.13	.12	.12	.11	.11	.11	.11	.11
10	.95	.53	.39	.33	.29	.26	.25	.23	.23	.22	.21	.21	.21	.21
15	1.42	.79	.58	.49	.43	.39	.37	.35	.34	.33	.32	.31	.31	.31
25	2.36	1.32	.97	.81	.71	.65	.61	.58	.56	.54	.53	.52	.51	.51
50	4.71	2.63	1.94	1.61	1.42	1.29	1.21	1.15	1.11	1.08	1.05	1.03	1.02	1.01
75	7.07	3.94	2.91	2.41	2.12	1.94	1.81	1.73	1.66	1.61	1.58	1.55	1.53	1.51
100	9.42	5.25	3.88	3.22	2.83	2.58	2.42	2.30	2.21	2.15	2.10	2.06	2.04	2.01
200	18.83	10.49	7.76	6.43	5.66	5.16	4.83	4.59	4.42	4.29	4.20	4.12	4.07	4.02
300	28.25	15.74	11.64	9.64	8.48	7.74	7.24	6.89	6.63	6.44	6.29	6.18	6.10	6.03
400	37.66	20.98	15.51	12.85	11.31	10.32	9.66	9.18	8.84	8.58	8.39	8.24	8.13	8.04
500	47.07	26.22	19.39	16.06	14.14	12.90	12.07	11.48	11.05	10.73	10.48	10.30	10.16	10.05
600	56.49	31.47	23.27	19.28	16.96	15.48	14.48	13.77	13.25	12.87	12.50	12.36	12.19	12.06
700	65.90	36.71	27.15	22.49	19.79	18.06	16.89	16.06	15.46	15.01	14.68	14.42	14.22	14.06
800	75.31	41.95	31.02	25.70	22.61	20.64	19.31	18.36	17.67	17.16	16.77	16.48	16.25	16.07
900	84.73	47.20	34.90	28.91	25.44	23.22	21.72	20.65	19.88	19.30	18.87	18.53	18.28	18.08
1000	94.14	52.44	38.78	32.12	28.27	25.80	24.13	22.95	22.09	21.45	20.96	20.59	20.31	20.09
2000	188.28	104.88	77.55	64.24	56.53	51.60	48.26	45.89	44.17	42.89	41.92	41.18	40.61	40.17
3000	282.41	157.31	116.33	96.36	84.79	77.40	72.38	68.83	66.25	64.33	62.88	61.77	60.92	60.26
4000	376.55	209.75	155.10	128.48	113.05	103.20	96.51	91.77	88.33	85.77	83.84	82.36	81.22	80.34
5000	470.69	262.18	193.88	160.60	141.32	129.00	120.63	114.72	110.41	107.21	104.79	102.95	101.53	100.43
6000	564.82	314.62	232.65	192.72	169.58	154.79	144.76	137.66	132.49	128.65	125.75	123.54	121.83	120.51
7000	658.96	367.05	271.43	224.84	197.84	180.59	168.88	160.60	154.57	150.09	146.71	144.13	142.14	140.59
8000	753.10	419.49	310.20	256.96	226.10	206.39	193.01	183.54	176.65	171.53	167.67	164.72	162.44	160.68
9000	847.23	471.92	348.98	289.08	254.37	232.19	217.13	206.49	198.73	192.97	188.63	185.30	182.75	180.76
10000	941.37	524.36	387.75	321.20	282.63	257.99	241.26	229.43	220.82	214.42	209.58	205.89	203.05	200.85
11000	1035.51	576.79	426.53	353.32	310.89	283.79	265.38	252.37	242.90	235.86	230.54	226.48	223.36	220.93
12000	1129.64	629.23	465.30	385.44	339.15	309.58	289.51	275.31	264.98	257.30	251.50	247.07	243.66	241.01
13000	1223.78	681.67	504.08	417.56	367.42	335.38	313.63	298.25	287.06	278.74	272.46	267.66	263.96	261.10
14000	1317.92	734.10	542.85	449.68	395.68	361.18	337.76	321.20	309.14	300.18	293.41	288.25	284.27	281.18
15000	1412.05	786.54	581.63	481.80	423.94	386.98	361.89	344.14	331.22	321.62	314.37	308.84	304.57	301.27
16000	1506.19	838.97	620.40	513.92	452.20	412.78	386.01	367.08	353.30	343.06	335.33	329.43	324.88	321.35
17000	1600.33	891.41	659.18	546.04	480.46	438.57	410.14	390.02	375.38	364.50	356.29	350.02	345.18	341.43
18000	1694.46	943.84	697.95	578.16	508.73	464.37	434.26	412.97	397.46	385.94	377.25	370.60	365.49	361.52
19000	1788.60	996.28	736.73	610.28	536.99	490.17	458.39	435.91	419.55	407.38	398.20	391.19	385.79	381.60
20000	1882.74	1048.71	775.50	642.40	565.25	515.97	482.51	458.85	441.63	428.83	419.16	411.78	406.10	401.69
21000	1976.87	1101.15	814.28	674.52	593.51	541.77	506.64	481.79	463.71	450.27	440.12	432.37	426.40	421.77
22000	2071.01	1153.58	853.05	706.64	621.78	567.57	530.76	504.73	485.79	471.71	461.08	452.96	446.71	441.85
23000	2165.15	1206.02	891.83	738.76	650.04	593.36	554.89	527.68	507.87	493.15	482.04	473.55	467.01	461.94
24000	2259.28	1258.45	930.60	770.88	678.30	619.16	579.01	550.62	529.95	514.59	502.99	494.14	487.32	482.02
25000	2353.42	1310.89	969.38	803.00	706.56	644.96	603.14	573.56	552.03	536.03	523.95	514.73	507.62	502.11
26000	2447.56	1363.33	1008.15	835.12	734.83	670.76	627.26	596.50	574.11	557.47	544.91	535.32	527.92	522.19
27000	2541.69	1415.76	1046.93	867.24	763.09	696.56	651.39	619.45	596.19	578.91	565.87	555.90	548.23	542.27
28000	2635.83	1468.20	1085.70	899.36	791.35	722.35	675.52	642.39	618.28	600.35	586.82	576.49	568.53	562.36
29000	2729.97	1520.63	1124.48	931.48	819.61	748.15	699.64	665.33	640.36	621.79	607.78	597.08	588.84	582.44
30000	2824.10	1573.07	1163.25	963.60	847.88	773.95	723.77	688.27	662.44	643.24	628.74	617.67	609.14	602.53
31000	2918.24	1625.50	1202.03	995.72	876.14	799.75	747.89	711.22	684.52	664.68	649.70	638.26	629.45	622.61
32000	3012.38	1677.94	1240.80	1027.84	904.40	825.55	772.02	734.16	706.60	686.12	670.66	658.85	649.75	642.69
33000	3106.51	1730.37	1279.58	1059.96	932.66	851.35	796.14	757.10	728.68	707.56	691.61	679.44	670.06	662.78
34000	3200.65	1782.81	1318.35	1092.08	960.92	877.14	820.27	780.04	750.76	729.00	712.57	700.03	690.36	682.86
35000	3294.79	1835.24	1357.13	1124.20	989.19	902.94	844.39	802.98	772.84	750.44	733.53	720.62	710.67	702.95
36000	3388.92	1887.68	1395.90	1156.32	1017.45	928.74	868.52	825.93	794.92	771.88	754.49	741.20	730.97	723.03
37000	3483.06	1940.11	1434.68	1188.44	1045.71	954.54	892.64	848.87	817.00	793.32	775.45	761.79	751.27	743.11
38000	3577.20	1992.55	1473.45	1220.56	1073.97	980.34	916.77	871.81	839.09	814.76	796.40	782.38	771.58	763.20
39000	3671.33	2044.99	1512.23	1252.68	1102.24	1006.14	940.89	894.75	861.17	836.20	817.36	802.97	791.88	783.28
40000	3765.47	2097.42	1551.00	1284.80	1130.50	1031.93	965.02	917.70	883.25	857.65	838.32	823.56	812.19	803.37
41000	3859.61	2149.86	1589.78	1316.92	1158.76	1057.73	989.15	940.64	905.33	879.09	859.28	844.15	832.49	823.45
42000	3953.74	2202.29	1628.55	1349.04	1187.02	1083.53	1013.27	963.58	927.41	900.53	880.23	864.74	852.80	843.53
43000	4047.88	2254.73	1667.33	1381.16	1215.29	1109.33	1037.40	986.52	949.49	921.97	901.19	885.33	873.10	863.62
44000	4142.02	2307.16	1706.10	1413.28	1243.55	1135.13	1061.52	1009.46	971.57	943.41	922.15	905.92	893.41	883.70
45000	4236.15	2359.60	1744.88	1445.40	1271.81	1160.92	1085.65	1032.41	993.65	964.85	943.11	926.50	913.71	903.79
46000	4330.29	2412.03	1783.65	1477.52	1300.07	1186.72	1109.77	1055.35	1015.73	986.29	964.07	947.09	934.02	923.87
47000	4424.43	2464.47	1822.43	1509.64	1328.33	1212.52	1133.90	1078.29	1037.82	1007.73	985.02	967.68	954.32	943.95
48000	4518.56	2516.90	1861.20	1541.76	1356.60	1238.32	1158.02	1101.23	1059.90	1029.17	1005.98	988.27	974.63	964.04
49000	4612.70	2569.34	1899.98	1573.88	1384.86	1264.12	1182.15	1124.18	1081.98	1050.61	1026.94	1008.86	994.93	984.12
50000	4706.84	2621.77	1938.75	1606.00	1413.12	1289.92	1206.27	1147.12	1104.06	1072.06	1047.90	1029.45	1015.23	1004.21
55000	5177.52	2883.95	2132.62	1766.60	1554.43	1418.91	1326.90	1261.83	1214.46	1179.26	1152.69	1132.39	1116.76	1104.63
60000	5648.20	3146.13	2326.50	1927.20	1695.75	1547.90	1447.53	1376.54	1324.87	1286.47	1257.48	1235.34	1218.28	1205.05
65000	6118.89	3408.31	2520.37	2087.80	1837.06	1676.89	1568.15	1491.25	1435.27	1393.67	1362.27	1338.28	1319.80	1305.47
70000	6589.57	3670.48	2714.25	2248.40	1978.37	1805.88	1688.78	1605.96	1545.68	1500.88	1467.05	1441.23	1421.33	1405.89
75000	7060.25	3932.66	2908.12	2409.00	2119.68	1934.87	1809.41	1720.67	1656.09	1608.08	1571.84	1544.17	1522.85	1506.31
80000	7530.94	4194.84	3102.00	2569.60	2260.99	2063.86	1930.03	1835.39	1766.49	1715.29	1676.63	1647.12	1624.37	1606.73
85000	8001.62	4457.01	3295.87	2730.20	2402.30	2192.85	2050.66	1950.10	1876.90	1822.49	1781.42	1750.06	1725.89	1707.15
90000	8472.30	4719.19	3489.75	2890.80	2543.62	2321.84	2171.29	2064.81	1987.30	1929.70	1886.21	1853.00	1827.42	1807.57
95000	8942.99	4981.37	3683.62	3051.40	2684.93	2450.83	2291.92	2179.52	2097.71	2036.90	1991.00	1955.95	1928.94	1907.99
100000	9413.67	5243.54	3877.50	3212.00	2826.24	2579.83	2412.54	2294.23	2208.11	2144.11	2095.79	2058.89	2030.46	2008.41

TERM	15 Years	16 Years	17 Years	18 Years	19 Years	20 Years	21 Years	22 Years	23 Years	24 Years	25 Years	30 Years	35 Years	40 Years
AMOUNT														
5	.10	.10	.10	.10	.10	.10	.10	.10	.10	.10	.10	.10	.10	.10
10	.20	.20	.20	.20	.20	.20	.20	.20	.20	.20	.20	.20	.20	.20
15	.30	.30	.30	.30	.30	.30	.30	.30	.30	.30	.30	.29	.29	.29
25	.50	.50	.50	.49	.49	.49	.49	.49	.49	.49	.49	.49	.49	.49
50	1.00	.99	.99	.98	.98	.98	.98	.97	.97	.97	.97	.97	.97	.97
75	1.50	1.49	1.48	1.47	1.47	1.47	1.46	1.46	1.46	1.46	1.46	1.45	1.45	1.45
100	2.00	1.98	1.97	1.96	1.96	1.95	1.95	1.94	1.94	1.94	1.94	1.93	1.93	1.93
200	3.99	3.96	3.94	3.92	3.91	3.90	3.89	3.88	3.88	3.88	3.87	3.86	3.86	3.86
300	5.98	5.94	5.91	5.88	5.86	5.85	5.83	5.82	5.82	5.81	5.81	5.79	5.79	5.79
400	7.97	7.92	7.87	7.84	7.81	7.79	7.78	7.76	7.75	7.75	7.74	7.72	7.72	7.71
500	9.96	9.89	9.84	9.80	9.77	9.74	9.72	9.70	9.69	9.68	9.67	9.65	9.64	9.64
600	11.95	11.87	11.81	11.76	11.72	11.69	11.66	11.64	11.63	11.62	11.61	11.58	11.57	11.57
700	13.94	13.85	13.78	13.72	13.67	13.63	13.61	13.58	13.56	13.55	13.54	13.51	13.50	13.50
800	15.93	15.83	15.74	15.68	15.62	15.58	15.55	15.52	15.50	15.49	15.47	15.44	15.43	15.42
900	17.93	17.80	17.71	17.63	17.58	17.53	17.49	17.46	17.44	17.42	17.41	17.37	17.35	17.35
1000	19.92	19.78	19.68	19.59	19.53	19.48	19.43	19.40	19.38	19.36	19.34	19.30	19.28	19.28
2000	39.83	39.56	39.35	39.18	39.05	38.95	38.86	38.80	38.75	38.71	38.67	38.59	38.56	38.55
3000	59.74	59.34	59.02	58.77	58.57	58.42	58.29	58.19	58.12	58.06	58.01	57.88	57.84	57.82
4000	79.65	79.11	78.69	78.36	78.09	77.89	77.72	77.59	77.49	77.41	77.34	77.17	77.11	77.10
5000	99.57	98.89	98.36	97.95	97.62	97.36	97.15	96.99	96.86	96.76	96.67	96.46	96.39	96.37
6000	119.48	118.67	118.03	117.53	117.14	116.83	116.58	116.38	116.23	116.11	116.01	115.75	115.67	115.64
7000	139.39	138.45	137.71	137.12	136.66	136.30	136.01	135.78	135.60	135.46	135.34	135.04	134.95	134.91
8000	159.30	158.22	157.38	156.71	156.18	155.77	155.44	155.18	154.97	154.81	154.68	154.33	154.22	154.19
9000	179.21	178.00	177.05	176.30	175.71	175.24	174.87	174.57	174.34	174.16	174.01	173.62	173.50	173.46
10000	199.13	197.78	196.72	195.89	195.23	194.71	194.30	193.97	193.71	193.51	193.34	192.91	192.78	192.73
11000	219.04	217.56	216.39	215.47	214.75	214.18	213.73	213.37	213.08	212.86	212.68	212.20	212.05	212.01
12000	238.95	237.33	236.06	235.06	234.27	233.65	233.15	232.76	232.45	232.21	232.01	231.50	231.33	231.28
13000	258.86	257.11	255.73	254.65	253.80	253.12	252.58	252.16	251.82	251.56	251.35	250.79	250.61	250.55
14000	278.77	276.89	275.41	274.24	273.32	272.59	272.01	271.56	271.19	270.91	270.68	270.08	269.89	269.82
15000	298.69	296.66	295.08	293.83	292.84	292.06	291.44	290.95	290.56	290.26	290.01	289.37	289.16	289.10
16000	318.60	316.44	314.75	313.41	312.36	311.53	310.87	310.35	309.94	309.61	309.35	308.66	308.44	308.37
17000	338.51	336.22	334.42	333.00	331.88	331.00	330.30	329.75	329.31	328.96	328.68	327.95	327.72	327.64
18000	358.42	356.00	354.09	352.59	351.41	350.47	349.73	349.14	348.68	348.31	348.01	347.24	346.99	346.92
19000	378.33	375.77	373.76	372.18	370.93	369.94	369.16	368.54	368.05	367.66	367.35	366.53	366.27	366.19
20000	398.25	395.55	393.43	391.77	390.45	389.41	388.59	387.94	387.42	387.01	386.68	385.82	385.55	385.46
21000	418.16	415.33	413.11	411.36	409.97	408.88	408.02	407.33	406.79	406.36	406.02	405.11	404.83	404.73
22000	438.07	435.11	432.78	430.94	429.50	428.35	427.45	426.73	426.16	425.71	425.35	424.40	424.10	424.01
23000	457.98	454.88	452.45	450.53	449.02	447.82	446.88	446.12	445.53	445.06	444.68	443.69	443.38	443.28
24000	477.89	474.66	472.12	470.12	468.54	467.29	466.30	465.52	464.90	464.41	464.02	462.99	462.66	462.55
25000	497.81	494.44	491.79	489.71	488.06	486.76	485.73	484.92	484.27	483.76	483.35	482.28	481.93	481.83
26000	517.72	514.22	511.46	509.30	507.59	506.23	505.16	504.31	503.64	503.11	502.69	501.57	501.21	501.10
27000	537.63	533.99	531.13	528.88	527.11	525.70	524.59	523.71	523.01	522.46	522.02	520.86	520.49	520.37
28000	557.54	553.77	550.81	548.47	546.63	545.17	544.02	543.11	542.38	541.81	541.35	540.15	539.77	539.64
29000	577.45	573.55	570.48	568.06	566.15	564.64	563.45	562.50	561.75	561.16	560.69	559.44	559.04	558.92
30000	597.37	593.32	590.15	587.65	585.67	584.11	582.88	581.90	581.12	580.51	580.02	578.73	578.32	578.19
31000	617.28	613.10	609.82	607.24	605.20	603.58	602.31	601.30	600.50	599.86	599.35	598.02	597.60	597.46
32000	637.19	632.88	629.49	626.82	624.72	623.05	621.74	620.69	619.87	619.21	618.69	617.31	616.88	616.74
33000	657.10	652.66	649.16	646.41	644.24	642.52	641.17	640.09	639.24	638.56	638.02	636.60	636.15	636.01
34000	677.01	672.43	668.84	666.00	663.76	662.00	660.60	659.49	658.61	657.91	657.36	655.89	655.43	655.28
35000	696.93	692.21	688.51	685.59	683.29	681.47	680.02	678.88	677.98	677.26	676.69	675.18	674.71	674.55
36000	716.84	711.99	708.18	705.18	702.81	700.94	699.45	698.28	697.35	696.61	696.02	694.48	693.98	693.83
37000	736.75	731.77	727.85	724.77	722.33	720.41	718.88	717.68	716.72	715.96	715.36	713.77	713.26	713.10
38000	756.66	751.54	747.52	744.35	741.85	739.88	738.31	737.07	736.09	735.31	734.69	733.06	732.54	732.37
39000	776.57	771.32	767.19	763.94	761.38	759.35	757.74	756.47	755.46	754.66	754.03	752.35	751.82	751.65
40000	796.49	791.10	786.86	783.53	780.90	778.82	777.17	775.87	774.83	774.01	773.36	771.64	771.09	770.92
41000	816.40	810.87	806.54	803.12	800.42	798.29	796.60	795.26	794.20	793.36	792.69	790.93	790.37	790.19
42000	836.31	830.65	826.21	822.71	819.94	817.76	816.03	814.66	813.57	812.71	812.03	810.22	809.65	809.46
43000	856.22	850.43	845.88	842.29	839.46	837.23	835.46	834.06	832.94	832.06	831.36	829.51	828.92	828.74
44000	876.13	870.21	865.55	861.88	858.99	856.70	854.89	853.45	852.31	851.41	850.69	848.80	848.20	848.01
45000	896.05	889.98	885.22	881.47	878.51	876.17	874.32	872.85	871.68	870.76	870.03	868.09	867.48	867.28
46000	915.96	909.76	904.89	901.06	898.03	895.64	893.75	892.24	891.06	890.11	889.36	887.38	886.76	886.56
47000	935.87	929.54	924.56	920.65	917.55	915.11	913.17	911.64	910.43	909.46	908.70	906.67	906.03	905.83
48000	955.78	949.32	944.24	940.23	937.08	934.58	932.60	931.04	929.80	928.81	928.03	925.97	925.31	925.10
49000	975.69	969.09	963.91	959.82	956.60	954.05	952.03	950.43	949.17	948.16	947.36	945.26	944.59	944.37
50000	995.61	988.87	983.58	979.41	976.12	973.52	971.46	969.83	968.54	967.51	966.70	964.55	963.86	963.65
55000	1095.17	1087.76	1081.94	1077.35	1073.73	1070.87	1068.61	1066.81	1065.39	1064.26	1063.37	1061.00	1060.25	1060.01
60000	1194.73	1186.64	1180.29	1175.29	1171.34	1168.22	1165.75	1163.80	1162.24	1161.01	1160.04	1157.46	1156.64	1156.38
65000	1294.29	1285.53	1278.65	1273.23	1268.96	1265.57	1262.90	1260.78	1259.10	1257.76	1256.71	1253.91	1253.02	1252.74
70000	1393.85	1384.42	1377.01	1371.17	1366.57	1362.93	1360.04	1357.76	1355.95	1354.51	1353.39	1350.36	1349.41	1349.10
75000	1493.41	1483.30	1475.37	1469.11	1464.19	1460.28	1457.19	1454.74	1452.80	1451.27	1450.04	1446.82	1445.79	1445.47
80000	1592.97	1582.19	1573.72	1567.05	1561.79	1557.63	1554.34	1551.73	1549.66	1548.02	1546.71	1543.27	1542.18	1541.83
85000	1692.53	1681.08	1672.08	1664.99	1659.40	1654.98	1651.48	1648.71	1646.51	1644.77	1643.38	1639.73	1638.57	1638.20
90000	1792.09	1779.96	1770.44	1762.94	1757.01	1752.33	1748.63	1745.69	1743.36	1741.52	1740.05	1736.18	1734.95	1734.56
95000	1891.65	1878.85	1868.80	1860.88	1854.62	1849.68	1845.77	1842.67	1840.22	1838.27	1836.72	1832.63	1831.34	1830.93
100000	1991.21	1977.74	1967.15	1958.82	1952.24	1947.03	1942.92	1939.66	1937.07	1935.02	1933.39	1929.09	1927.72	1927.29

MONTHLY PAYMENT
REQUIRED TO AMORTIZE A LOAN

TERM AMOUNT	1 Year	2 Years	3 Years	4 Years	5 Years	6 Years	7 Years	8 Years	9 Years	10 Years	11 Years	12 Years	13 Years	14 Years
5	.48	.27	.20	.17	.15	.13	.13	.12	.12	.11	.11	.11	.11	.11
10	.95	.53	.39	.33	.29	.26	.25	.23	.23	.22	.22	.21	.21	.21
15	1.42	.79	.59	.49	.43	.39	.37	.35	.34	.33	.32	.31	.31	.31
25	2.36	1.32	.98	.81	.71	.65	.61	.58	.56	.54	.53	.52	.51	.51
50	4.71	2.63	1.95	1.61	1.42	1.30	1.21	1.15	1.11	1.08	1.06	1.04	1.02	1.01
75	7.07	3.94	2.92	2.42	2.13	1.94	1.82	1.73	1.66	1.62	1.58	1.55	1.53	1.52
100	9.42	5.25	3.89	3.22	2.84	2.59	2.42	2.30	2.22	2.15	2.11	2.07	2.04	2.02
200	18.84	10.50	7.77	6.44	5.67	5.17	4.84	4.60	4.43	4.30	4.21	4.13	4.08	4.03
300	28.26	15.75	11.65	9.65	8.50	7.76	7.26	6.90	6.64	6.45	6.31	6.20	6.11	6.05
400	37.67	20.99	15.53	12.87	11.33	10.34	9.67	9.20	8.86	8.60	8.41	8.26	8.15	8.06
500	47.09	26.24	19.41	16.09	14.16	12.93	12.09	11.50	11.07	10.75	10.51	10.33	10.19	10.08
600	56.51	31.49	23.29	19.30	16.99	15.51	14.51	13.80	13.28	12.90	12.61	12.39	12.22	12.09
700	65.93	36.74	27.17	22.52	19.82	18.10	16.93	16.10	15.50	15.05	14.71	14.46	14.26	14.10
800	75.34	41.98	31.06	25.73	22.65	20.68	19.34	18.40	17.71	17.20	16.81	16.52	16.29	16.12
900	84.76	47.23	34.94	28.95	25.48	23.26	21.76	20.70	19.92	19.35	18.91	18.58	18.33	18.13
1000	94.18	52.48	38.82	32.17	28.31	25.85	24.18	23.00	22.14	21.50	21.02	20.65	20.37	20.15
2000	188.35	104.95	77.63	64.33	56.62	51.69	48.35	45.99	44.27	42.99	42.03	41.29	40.73	40.29
3000	282.52	157.42	116.45	96.49	84.92	77.53	72.52	68.98	66.40	64.48	63.04	61.93	61.09	60.43
4000	376.70	209.90	155.26	128.65	113.23	103.38	96.69	91.97	88.53	85.98	84.05	82.58	81.45	80.57
5000	470.87	262.37	194.08	160.81	141.53	129.22	120.87	114.96	110.66	107.47	105.06	103.22	101.81	100.71
6000	565.04	314.84	232.89	192.97	169.84	155.06	145.04	137.95	132.79	128.96	126.07	123.86	122.17	120.85
7000	659.22	367.31	271.70	225.13	198.14	180.91	169.21	160.94	154.92	150.45	147.08	144.51	142.53	140.99
8000	753.39	419.79	310.52	257.29	226.45	206.75	193.38	183.93	177.06	171.95	168.09	165.15	162.89	161.13
9000	847.56	472.26	349.33	289.46	254.75	232.59	217.56	206.92	199.19	193.44	189.10	185.79	183.25	181.27
10000	941.73	524.73	388.15	321.62	283.06	258.44	241.73	229.91	221.32	214.93	210.11	206.44	203.61	201.41
11000	1035.91	577.20	426.96	353.78	311.37	284.28	265.90	252.91	243.45	236.43	231.13	227.08	223.97	221.55
12000	1130.08	629.68	465.77	385.94	339.67	310.12	290.07	275.90	265.58	257.92	252.14	247.72	244.33	241.69
13000	1224.25	682.15	504.59	418.10	367.98	335.97	314.25	298.89	287.71	279.41	273.15	268.37	264.69	261.83
14000	1318.43	734.62	543.40	450.26	396.28	361.81	338.42	321.88	309.84	300.90	294.16	289.01	285.05	281.97
15000	1412.60	787.09	582.22	482.42	424.59	387.65	362.59	344.87	331.98	322.40	315.17	309.65	305.41	302.11
16000	1506.77	839.57	621.03	514.58	452.89	413.50	386.77	367.86	354.11	343.89	336.18	330.30	325.77	322.25
17000	1600.94	892.04	659.84	546.74	481.20	439.34	410.93	390.85	376.24	365.38	357.19	350.94	346.13	342.39
18000	1695.12	944.51	698.66	578.91	509.50	465.18	435.11	413.84	398.37	386.88	378.20	371.58	366.49	362.53
19000	1789.29	996.99	737.47	611.07	537.81	491.03	459.28	436.83	420.50	408.37	399.21	392.23	386.85	382.67
20000	1883.46	1049.46	776.29	643.23	566.11	516.87	483.45	459.82	442.63	429.86	420.22	412.87	407.21	402.81
21000	1977.64	1101.93	815.10	675.39	594.42	542.71	507.62	482.82	464.76	451.35	441.24	433.51	427.57	422.95
22000	2071.81	1154.40	853.91	707.55	622.73	568.56	531.80	505.81	486.90	472.85	462.25	454.16	447.93	443.10
23000	2165.98	1206.88	892.73	739.71	651.03	594.40	555.97	528.80	509.03	494.34	483.26	474.80	468.29	463.24
24000	2260.15	1259.35	931.54	771.87	679.34	620.24	580.14	551.79	531.16	515.83	504.27	495.44	488.65	483.38
25000	2354.33	1311.82	970.36	804.03	707.64	646.09	604.31	574.78	553.29	537.32	525.28	516.09	509.01	503.52
26000	2448.50	1364.29	1009.17	836.19	735.95	671.93	628.49	597.77	575.42	558.82	546.29	536.73	529.37	523.66
27000	2542.67	1416.77	1047.98	868.36	764.25	697.77	652.66	620.76	597.55	580.31	567.30	557.37	549.73	543.80
28000	2636.85	1469.24	1086.80	900.52	792.56	723.62	676.83	643.75	619.68	601.80	588.31	578.02	570.09	563.94
29000	2731.02	1521.71	1125.61	932.68	820.86	749.46	701.00	666.74	641.82	623.30	609.32	598.66	590.45	584.08
30000	2825.19	1574.18	1164.43	964.84	849.17	775.30	725.17	689.73	663.95	644.79	630.33	619.30	610.81	604.22
31000	2919.36	1626.66	1203.24	997.00	877.48	801.15	749.35	712.72	686.08	666.28	651.35	639.95	631.17	624.36
32000	3013.54	1679.13	1242.05	1029.16	905.78	826.99	773.52	735.72	708.21	687.77	672.36	660.59	651.53	644.50
33000	3107.71	1731.60	1280.87	1061.32	934.09	852.83	797.69	758.71	730.34	709.27	693.37	681.23	671.89	664.64
34000	3201.88	1784.08	1319.68	1093.48	962.39	878.68	821.86	781.70	752.47	730.76	714.38	701.88	692.25	684.78
35000	3296.06	1836.55	1358.50	1125.65	990.70	904.52	846.04	804.69	774.60	752.25	735.39	722.52	712.61	704.92
36000	3390.23	1889.02	1397.31	1157.81	1019.00	930.36	870.21	827.68	796.73	773.75	756.40	743.16	732.97	725.06
37000	3484.40	1941.49	1436.12	1189.97	1047.31	956.21	894.38	850.67	818.87	795.24	777.41	763.80	753.33	745.20
38000	3578.57	1993.97	1474.94	1222.13	1075.61	982.05	918.55	873.66	841.00	816.73	798.42	784.45	773.69	765.34
39000	3672.75	2046.44	1513.75	1254.29	1103.92	1007.89	942.73	896.65	863.13	838.22	819.43	805.09	794.05	785.48
40000	3766.92	2098.91	1552.57	1286.45	1132.22	1033.74	966.90	919.64	885.26	859.72	840.44	825.73	814.41	805.62
41000	3861.09	2151.38	1591.38	1318.61	1160.53	1059.58	991.07	942.63	907.39	881.21	861.46	846.38	834.77	825.76
42000	3955.27	2203.86	1630.19	1350.77	1188.84	1085.42	1015.24	965.63	929.52	902.70	882.47	867.02	855.13	845.90
43000	4049.44	2256.33	1669.01	1382.93	1217.14	1111.27	1039.42	988.62	951.65	924.20	903.48	887.66	875.49	866.04
44000	4143.61	2308.80	1707.82	1415.10	1245.45	1137.11	1063.59	1011.61	973.79	945.69	924.49	908.31	895.85	886.19
45000	4237.78	2361.27	1746.64	1447.26	1273.75	1162.95	1087.76	1034.60	995.92	967.18	945.50	928.95	916.21	906.33
46000	4331.96	2413.75	1785.45	1479.42	1302.06	1188.80	1111.93	1057.59	1018.05	988.67	966.51	949.59	936.57	926.47
47000	4426.13	2466.22	1824.26	1511.58	1330.36	1214.64	1136.10	1060.58	1040.18	1010.17	987.52	970.24	956.93	946.61
48000	4520.30	2518.69	1863.08	1543.74	1358.67	1240.48	1160.28	1103.57	1062.31	1031.66	1008.53	990.88	977.29	966.75
49000	4614.48	2571.17	1901.89	1575.90	1386.97	1266.33	1184.45	1126.56	1084.44	1053.15	1029.54	1011.52	997.65	986.89
50000	4708.65	2623.64	1940.71	1608.06	1415.28	1292.17	1208.62	1149.55	1106.57	1074.64	1050.55	1032.17	1018.01	1007.03
55000	5179.51	2886.00	2134.78	1768.87	1556.81	1421.39	1329.48	1264.51	1217.23	1182.11	1155.61	1135.38	1119.81	1107.73
60000	5650.38	3148.36	2328.85	1929.67	1698.33	1550.60	1450.34	1379.46	1327.89	1289.57	1260.66	1238.60	1221.61	1208.43
65000	6121.24	3410.73	2522.92	2090.48	1839.86	1679.82	1571.21	1494.42	1438.55	1397.04	1365.72	1341.82	1323.41	1309.14
70000	6592.11	3673.09	2716.99	2251.29	1981.39	1809.04	1692.07	1609.37	1549.20	1504.50	1470.77	1445.03	1425.21	1409.84
75000	7062.97	3935.45	2911.06	2412.09	2122.92	1938.25	1812.93	1724.33	1659.86	1611.96	1575.83	1548.25	1527.01	1510.54
80000	7533.83	4197.82	3105.13	2572.90	2264.44	2067.47	1933.79	1839.28	1770.52	1719.43	1680.88	1651.46	1628.81	1611.24
85000	8004.70	4460.18	3299.20	2733.70	2405.97	2196.69	2054.65	1954.24	1881.17	1826.89	1785.94	1754.68	1730.61	1711.94
90000	8475.56	4722.54	3493.27	2894.51	2547.50	2325.90	2175.51	2069.19	1991.83	1934.36	1890.99	1857.90	1832.41	1812.65
95000	8946.43	4984.91	3687.34	3055.31	2689.03	2455.12	2296.38	2184.15	2102.49	2041.82	1996.05	1961.11	1934.21	1913.35
100000	9417.29	5247.27	3881.41	3216.12	2830.55	2584.34	2417.24	2299.10	2213.14	2149.28	2101.10	2064.33	2036.01	2014.05

TERM	15 Years	16 Years	17 Years	18 Years	19 Years	20 Years	21 Years	22 Years	23 Years	24 Years	25 Years	30 Years	35 Years	40 Years
AMOUNT														
5	.10	.10	.10	.10	.10	.10	.10	.10	.10	.10	.10	.10	.10	.10
10	.20	.20	.20	.20	.20	.20	.20	.20	.20	.20	.20	.20	.20	.20
15	.30	.30	.30	.30	.30	.30	.30	.30	.30	.30	.30	.30	.30	.30
25	.50	.50	.50	.50	.49	.49	.49	.49	.49	.49	.49	.49	.49	.49
50	1.00	1.00	.99	.99	.98	.98	.98	.98	.98	.98	.97	.97	.97	.97
75	1.50	1.49	1.48	1.48	1.47	1.47	1.47	1.46	1.46	1.46	1.46	1.46	1.46	1.46
100	2.00	1.99	1.98	1.97	1.96	1.96	1.95	1.95	1.95	1.95	1.94	1.94	1.94	1.94
200	4.00	3.97	3.95	3.93	3.92	3.91	3.90	3.90	3.89	3.89	3.88	3.88	3.87	3.87
300	6.00	5.96	5.92	5.90	5.88	5.86	5.85	5.84	5.83	5.83	5.82	5.81	5.81	5.81
400	7.99	7.94	7.90	7.86	7.84	7.82	7.80	7.79	7.78	7.77	7.77	7.75	7.74	7.74
500	9.99	9.92	9.87	9.83	9.80	9.77	9.75	9.73	9.72	9.71	9.70	9.68	9.67	9.67
600	11.99	11.91	11.84	11.79	11.75	11.72	11.70	11.68	11.66	11.65	11.64	11.62	11.61	11.61
700	13.98	13.89	13.82	13.76	13.71	13.68	13.65	13.63	13.61	13.59	13.58	13.55	13.54	13.54
800	15.98	15.87	15.79	15.72	15.67	15.63	15.60	15.57	15.55	15.53	15.52	15.49	15.48	15.47
900	17.98	17.86	17.76	17.69	17.63	17.58	17.55	17.52	17.49	17.48	17.46	17.42	17.41	17.41
1000	19.97	19.84	19.74	19.65	19.59	19.54	19.49	19.46	19.44	19.42	19.40	19.36	19.34	19.34
2000	39.94	39.68	39.47	39.30	39.17	39.07	38.98	38.92	38.87	38.83	38.80	38.71	38.68	38.68
3000	59.91	59.51	59.20	58.95	58.75	58.60	58.47	58.38	58.30	58.24	58.19	58.06	58.02	58.01
4000	79.88	79.35	78.93	78.59	78.33	78.13	77.96	77.83	77.73	77.65	77.59	77.42	77.36	77.35
5000	99.85	99.18	98.66	98.24	97.92	97.66	97.45	97.29	97.16	97.06	96.98	96.77	96.70	96.68
6000	119.82	119.02	118.39	117.89	117.50	117.19	116.94	116.75	116.60	116.47	116.38	116.12	116.04	116.02
7000	139.79	138.85	138.12	137.54	137.08	136.72	136.43	136.21	136.03	135.88	135.77	135.48	135.38	135.35
8000	159.76	158.69	157.85	157.18	156.66	156.25	155.92	155.66	155.46	155.30	155.17	154.83	154.72	154.69
9000	179.73	178.52	177.58	176.83	176.24	175.78	175.41	175.12	174.89	174.71	174.56	174.18	174.06	174.02
10000	199.70	198.36	197.31	196.48	195.83	195.31	194.90	194.58	194.32	194.12	193.96	193.53	193.40	193.36
11000	219.67	218.19	217.04	216.13	215.41	214.84	214.39	214.04	213.75	213.53	213.35	212.89	212.74	212.69
12000	239.64	238.03	236.77	235.77	234.99	234.37	233.88	233.49	233.19	232.94	232.75	232.24	232.08	232.03
13000	259.61	257.86	256.50	255.42	254.57	253.90	253.37	252.95	252.62	252.35	252.15	251.59	251.42	251.36
14000	279.58	277.70	276.23	275.07	274.15	273.43	272.86	272.41	272.05	271.77	271.54	270.95	270.76	270.70
15000	299.54	297.54	295.96	294.72	293.74	292.96	292.35	291.87	291.48	291.18	290.94	290.30	290.10	290.03
16000	319.51	317.37	315.69	314.36	313.32	312.49	311.84	311.32	310.91	310.59	310.33	309.65	309.44	309.37
17000	339.48	337.21	335.42	334.01	332.90	332.02	331.33	330.78	330.35	330.00	329.73	329.01	328.78	328.71
18000	359.45	357.04	355.15	353.66	352.48	351.55	350.82	350.24	349.78	349.41	349.12	348.36	348.12	348.04
19000	379.42	376.88	374.88	373.31	372.06	371.08	370.31	369.70	369.21	368.82	368.52	367.71	367.46	367.38
20000	399.39	396.71	394.61	392.95	391.65	390.61	389.80	389.15	388.64	388.23	387.91	387.06	386.80	386.71
21000	419.36	416.55	414.34	412.60	411.23	410.15	409.29	408.61	408.07	407.65	407.31	406.42	406.14	406.05
22000	439.33	436.38	434.07	432.25	430.81	429.68	428.78	428.07	427.50	427.06	426.70	425.77	425.48	425.38
23000	459.30	456.22	453.80	451.89	450.39	449.21	448.27	447.52	446.94	446.47	446.10	445.12	444.81	444.72
24000	479.27	476.05	473.53	471.54	469.97	468.74	467.76	466.98	466.37	465.88	465.49	464.48	464.15	464.05
25000	499.24	495.89	493.26	491.19	489.56	488.27	487.25	486.44	485.80	485.29	484.89	483.83	483.49	483.39
26000	519.21	515.72	512.99	510.84	509.14	507.80	506.74	505.90	505.23	504.70	504.29	503.18	502.83	502.72
27000	539.18	535.56	532.72	530.48	528.72	527.33	526.23	525.35	524.66	524.12	523.68	522.53	522.17	522.06
28000	559.15	555.40	552.45	550.13	548.30	546.86	545.72	544.81	544.10	543.53	543.08	541.89	541.51	541.39
29000	579.12	575.23	572.18	569.78	567.89	566.39	565.21	564.27	563.53	562.94	562.47	561.24	560.85	560.73
30000	599.08	595.07	591.91	589.43	587.47	585.92	584.70	583.73	582.96	582.35	581.87	580.59	580.19	580.06
31000	619.05	614.90	611.64	609.07	607.05	605.45	604.19	603.18	602.39	601.76	601.26	599.95	599.53	599.40
32000	639.02	634.74	631.37	628.72	626.63	624.98	623.68	622.64	621.82	621.17	620.66	619.30	618.87	618.73
33000	658.99	654.57	651.10	648.37	646.21	644.51	643.16	642.10	641.25	640.58	640.05	638.65	638.21	638.07
34000	678.96	674.41	670.83	668.02	665.80	664.04	662.65	661.56	660.69	660.00	659.45	658.01	657.55	657.41
35000	698.93	694.24	690.56	687.66	685.38	683.57	682.14	681.01	680.12	679.41	678.84	677.36	676.89	676.74
36000	718.90	714.08	710.29	707.31	704.96	703.10	701.63	700.47	699.55	698.82	698.24	696.71	696.23	696.08
37000	738.87	733.91	730.02	726.96	724.54	722.63	721.12	719.93	718.98	718.23	717.63	716.06	715.57	715.41
38000	758.84	753.75	749.75	746.61	744.12	742.16	740.61	739.39	738.41	737.64	737.03	735.42	734.91	734.75
39000	778.81	773.58	769.48	766.25	763.71	761.69	760.10	758.84	757.85	757.05	756.43	754.77	754.25	754.08
40000	798.78	793.42	789.21	785.90	783.29	781.22	779.59	778.30	777.28	776.46	775.82	774.12	773.59	773.42
41000	818.75	813.25	808.94	805.55	802.87	800.76	799.08	797.76	796.71	795.88	795.22	793.48	792.93	792.75
42000	838.72	833.09	828.67	825.20	822.45	820.29	818.57	817.22	816.14	815.29	814.61	812.83	812.27	812.09
43000	858.69	852.93	848.40	844.84	842.03	839.82	838.06	836.67	835.57	834.70	834.01	832.18	831.61	831.42
44000	878.65	872.76	868.13	864.49	861.62	859.35	857.55	856.13	855.00	854.11	853.40	851.54	850.95	850.76
45000	898.62	892.60	887.86	884.14	881.20	878.88	877.04	875.59	874.44	873.52	872.80	870.89	870.28	870.09
46000	918.59	912.43	907.59	903.78	900.78	898.41	896.53	895.04	893.87	892.93	892.19	890.24	889.62	889.43
47000	938.56	932.27	927.32	923.43	920.36	917.94	916.02	914.50	913.30	912.35	911.59	909.59	908.96	908.76
48000	958.53	952.10	947.05	943.08	939.94	937.47	935.51	933.96	932.73	931.76	930.98	928.95	928.30	928.10
49000	978.50	971.94	966.78	962.73	959.53	957.00	955.00	953.42	952.16	951.17	950.38	948.30	947.64	947.43
50000	998.47	991.77	986.51	982.37	979.11	976.53	974.49	972.87	971.59	970.58	969.77	967.65	966.98	966.77
55000	1098.32	1090.95	1085.16	1080.61	1077.02	1074.18	1071.94	1070.16	1068.75	1067.64	1066.75	1064.42	1063.68	1063.45
60000	1198.16	1190.13	1183.82	1178.85	1174.93	1171.83	1169.39	1167.45	1165.91	1164.69	1163.73	1161.18	1160.38	1160.12
65000	1298.01	1289.30	1282.47	1277.09	1272.84	1269.49	1266.83	1264.74	1263.07	1261.75	1260.71	1257.95	1257.08	1256.80
70000	1397.86	1388.48	1381.12	1375.32	1370.75	1367.14	1364.28	1362.02	1360.23	1358.81	1357.68	1354.71	1353.77	1353.48
75000	1497.70	1487.66	1479.77	1473.56	1468.65	1464.79	1461.73	1459.31	1457.39	1455.87	1454.66	1451.48	1450.47	1450.15
80000	1597.55	1586.83	1578.42	1571.80	1566.57	1562.44	1559.18	1556.60	1554.55	1552.92	1551.64	1548.24	1547.17	1546.83
85000	1697.40	1686.01	1677.07	1670.03	1664.48	1660.10	1656.63	1653.88	1651.71	1649.98	1648.61	1645.01	1643.87	1643.51
90000	1797.24	1785.19	1775.72	1768.27	1762.39	1757.75	1754.08	1751.17	1748.87	1747.04	1745.59	1741.77	1740.56	1740.18
95000	1897.09	1884.36	1874.37	1866.51	1860.30	1855.40	1851.53	1848.46	1846.02	1844.10	1842.57	1838.54	1837.26	1836.86
100000	1996.94	1983.54	1973.02	1964.74	1958.21	1953.05	1948.97	1945.74	1943.18	1941.15	1939.54	1935.30	1933.96	1933.54

MONTHLY PAYMENT
REQUIRED TO AMORTIZE A LOAN

TERM	1 Year	2 Years	3 Years	4 Years	5 Years	6 Years	7 Years	8 Years	9 Years	10 Years	11 Years	12 Years	13 Years	14 Years
AMOUNT														
5	.48	.27	.20	.17	.15	.13	.13	.12	.12	.11	.11	.11	.11	.11
10	.95	.53	.39	.33	.29	.26	.25	.24	.23	.22	.22	.21	.21	.21
15	1.42	.79	.59	.49	.43	.39	.37	.35	.34	.33	.32	.32	.31	.31
25	2.36	1.32	.98	.81	.71	.65	.61	.58	.56	.54	.53	.52	.51	.51
50	4.71	2.63	1.95	1.61	1.42	1.30	1.22	1.16	1.11	1.08	1.06	1.04	1.02	1.01
75	7.07	3.94	2.92	2.42	2.13	1.95	1.82	1.73	1.67	1.62	1.58	1.56	1.53	1.52
100	9.42	5.25	3.89	3.22	2.84	2.59	2.43	2.31	2.22	2.16	2.11	2.07	2.04	2.02
200	18.84	10.50	7.77	6.44	5.67	5.18	4.85	4.61	4.44	4.31	4.21	4.14	4.08	4.04
300	28.26	15.75	11.66	9.66	8.51	7.77	7.27	6.91	6.65	6.46	6.32	6.21	6.12	6.06
400	37.68	21.00	15.54	12.88	11.34	10.35	9.69	9.21	8.87	8.62	8.42	8.28	8.16	8.08
500	47.10	26.25	19.43	16.10	14.17	12.94	12.11	11.52	11.09	10.77	10.53	10.34	10.20	10.07
600	56.52	31.50	23.31	19.32	17.01	15.53	14.53	13.82	13.30	12.92	12.63	12.41	12.24	12.11
700	65.94	36.75	27.19	22.54	19.84	18.12	16.95	16.12	15.52	15.07	14.74	14.48	14.28	14.13
800	75.36	42.00	31.08	25.76	22.67	20.70	19.37	18.42	17.74	17.23	16.84	16.55	16.32	16.15
900	84.78	47.25	34.96	28.97	25.51	23.29	21.79	20.73	19.95	19.38	18.95	18.62	18.36	18.17
1000	94.20	52.50	38.85	32.19	28.34	25.88	24.21	23.03	22.17	21.53	21.05	20.68	20.40	20.18
2000	188.40	105.00	77.69	64.38	56.67	51.75	48.41	46.05	44.33	43.06	42.10	41.36	40.80	40.36
3000	282.60	157.50	116.53	96.57	85.01	77.63	72.62	69.08	66.50	64.59	63.14	62.04	61.20	60.54
4000	376.79	210.00	155.37	128.76	113.34	103.50	96.82	92.10	88.66	86.11	84.19	82.72	81.59	80.72
5000	470.99	262.49	194.21	160.95	141.68	129.37	121.02	115.12	110.83	107.64	105.24	103.40	101.99	100.90
6000	565.19	314.99	233.05	193.14	170.01	155.25	145.23	138.15	132.99	129.17	126.28	124.08	122.39	121.07
7000	659.38	367.49	271.89	225.33	198.35	181.12	169.43	161.17	155.16	150.70	147.33	144.76	142.78	141.25
8000	753.58	419.99	310.73	257.51	226.68	206.99	193.63	184.19	177.32	172.22	168.38	165.44	163.18	161.43
9000	847.78	472.48	349.57	289.70	255.01	232.87	217.84	207.22	199.49	193.75	189.42	186.12	183.58	181.61
10000	941.98	524.98	388.41	321.89	283.35	258.74	242.04	230.24	221.65	215.28	210.47	206.80	203.98	201.79
11000	1036.17	577.48	427.25	354.08	311.68	284.61	266.25	253.26	243.82	236.81	231.52	227.48	224.37	221.96
12000	1130.37	629.98	466.09	386.27	340.02	310.49	290.45	276.29	265.98	258.33	252.56	248.16	244.77	242.14
13000	1224.57	682.47	504.93	418.46	368.35	336.36	314.65	299.31	288.15	279.86	273.61	268.84	265.17	262.32
14000	1318.76	734.97	543.77	450.65	396.69	362.23	338.86	322.33	310.31	301.39	294.66	289.52	285.56	282.50
15000	1412.96	787.47	582.61	482.83	425.02	388.11	363.06	345.36	332.48	322.92	315.70	310.20	305.96	302.68
16000	1507.16	839.97	621.45	515.02	453.35	413.98	387.26	368.38	354.64	344.44	336.75	330.88	326.36	322.85
17000	1601.35	892.46	660.29	547.21	481.69	439.85	411.47	391.40	376.81	365.97	357.79	351.56	346.75	343.03
18000	1695.55	944.96	699.13	579.40	510.02	465.73	435.67	414.43	398.97	387.50	378.84	372.24	367.15	363.21
19000	1789.75	997.46	737.97	611.59	538.36	491.60	459.87	437.45	421.14	409.02	399.89	392.92	387.55	383.39
20000	1883.95	1049.96	776.81	643.78	566.69	517.47	484.08	460.47	443.30	430.55	420.93	413.60	407.95	403.57
21000	1978.14	1102.45	815.65	675.97	595.03	543.35	508.28	483.50	465.47	452.08	441.98	434.27	428.34	423.75
22000	2072.34	1154.95	854.49	708.15	623.36	569.22	532.49	506.52	487.63	473.61	463.03	454.95	448.74	443.92
23000	2166.54	1207.45	893.33	740.34	651.69	595.09	556.69	529.54	509.80	495.13	484.07	475.63	469.14	464.10
24000	2260.73	1259.95	932.17	772.53	680.03	620.97	580.89	552.57	531.96	516.66	505.12	496.31	489.53	484.28
25000	2354.93	1312.44	971.01	804.72	708.36	646.84	605.10	575.59	554.13	538.19	526.17	516.99	509.93	504.46
26000	2449.13	1364.94	1009.85	836.91	736.70	672.71	629.30	598.61	576.29	559.72	547.21	537.67	530.33	524.64
27000	2543.32	1417.44	1048.69	869.10	765.03	698.59	653.50	621.64	598.46	581.24	568.26	558.35	550.72	544.81
28000	2637.52	1469.94	1087.52	901.29	793.37	724.46	677.71	644.66	620.62	602.77	589.31	579.03	571.12	564.99
29000	2731.72	1522.43	1126.37	933.47	821.70	750.33	701.91	667.69	642.79	624.30	610.35	599.71	591.52	585.17
30000	2825.92	1574.93	1165.21	965.66	850.03	776.21	726.11	690.71	664.95	645.83	631.40	620.39	611.92	605.35
31000	2920.11	1627.43	1204.05	997.85	878.37	802.08	750.32	713.73	687.12	667.35	652.44	641.07	632.31	625.53
32000	3014.31	1679.93	1242.89	1030.04	906.70	827.95	774.52	736.76	709.28	688.88	673.49	661.75	652.71	645.70
33000	3108.51	1732.42	1281.73	1062.23	935.04	853.83	798.73	759.78	731.45	710.41	694.54	682.43	673.11	665.88
34000	3202.70	1784.92	1320.57	1094.42	963.37	879.70	822.93	782.80	753.61	731.93	715.58	703.11	693.50	686.06
35000	3296.90	1837.42	1359.41	1126.61	991.71	905.57	847.13	805.83	775.78	753.46	736.63	723.79	713.90	706.24
36000	3391.10	1889.92	1398.25	1158.79	1020.04	931.45	871.34	828.85	797.94	774.99	757.68	744.47	734.30	726.42
37000	3485.29	1942.41	1437.09	1190.98	1048.37	957.32	895.54	851.87	820.11	796.52	778.72	765.15	754.70	746.59
38000	3579.49	1994.91	1475.93	1223.17	1076.71	983.19	919.74	874.90	842.27	818.04	799.77	785.83	775.09	766.77
39000	3673.69	2047.41	1514.77	1255.36	1105.04	1009.07	943.95	897.92	864.44	839.57	820.82	806.51	795.49	786.95
40000	3767.89	2099.91	1553.61	1287.55	1133.38	1034.94	968.15	920.94	886.60	861.10	841.86	827.19	815.89	807.13
41000	3862.08	2152.40	1592.45	1319.74	1161.71	1060.81	992.36	943.97	908.77	882.63	862.91	847.86	836.28	827.31
42000	3956.28	2204.90	1631.29	1351.93	1190.05	1086.69	1016.56	966.99	930.93	904.15	883.96	868.54	856.68	847.49
43000	4050.48	2257.40	1670.13	1384.11	1218.38	1112.56	1040.76	990.01	953.10	925.68	905.00	889.22	877.08	867.66
44000	4144.67	2309.90	1708.97	1416.30	1246.71	1138.44	1064.97	1013.04	975.26	947.21	926.05	909.90	897.47	887.84
45000	4238.87	2362.39	1747.81	1448.49	1275.05	1164.31	1089.17	1036.06	997.43	968.74	947.10	930.58	917.87	908.02
46000	4333.07	2414.89	1786.65	1480.68	1303.38	1190.18	1113.37	1059.08	1019.59	990.26	968.14	951.26	938.27	928.20
47000	4427.26	2467.39	1825.49	1512.87	1331.72	1216.06	1137.58	1082.11	1041.76	1011.79	989.19	971.94	958.67	948.38
48000	4521.46	2519.89	1864.33	1545.06	1360.05	1241.93	1161.78	1105.13	1063.92	1033.32	1010.23	992.62	979.06	968.55
49000	4615.66	2572.38	1903.17	1577.25	1388.39	1267.80	1185.98	1128.15	1086.09	1054.85	1031.28	1013.30	999.46	988.73
50000	4709.86	2624.88	1942.01	1609.43	1416.72	1293.68	1210.19	1151.18	1108.25	1076.37	1052.33	1033.98	1019.86	1008.91
55000	5180.84	2887.37	2136.21	1770.38	1558.39	1423.04	1331.21	1266.29	1219.08	1184.01	1157.56	1137.38	1121.84	1109.80
60000	5651.83	3149.86	2330.41	1931.32	1700.06	1552.41	1452.22	1381.41	1329.90	1291.65	1262.79	1240.78	1223.83	1210.69
65000	6122.81	3412.34	2524.61	2092.26	1841.73	1681.78	1573.24	1496.53	1440.73	1399.28	1368.02	1344.17	1325.81	1311.58
70000	6593.80	3674.83	2718.82	2253.21	1983.41	1811.14	1694.26	1611.65	1551.55	1506.92	1473.26	1447.57	1427.80	1412.47
75000	7064.78	3937.32	2913.02	2414.15	2125.08	1940.51	1815.28	1726.76	1662.38	1614.56	1578.49	1550.97	1529.78	1513.36
80000	7535.77	4199.81	3107.22	2575.09	2266.75	2069.88	1936.30	1841.88	1773.20	1722.19	1683.72	1654.37	1631.77	1614.25
85000	8006.75	4462.29	3301.42	2736.04	2408.42	2199.25	2057.32	1957.00	1884.03	1829.83	1788.95	1757.76	1733.75	1715.14
90000	8477.74	4724.78	3495.62	2896.98	2550.09	2328.61	2178.33	2072.12	1994.85	1937.47	1894.19	1861.16	1835.74	1816.03
95000	8948.72	4987.27	3689.82	3057.92	2691.76	2457.98	2299.35	2187.23	2105.68	2045.10	1999.42	1964.56	1937.72	1916.92
100000	9419.71	5249.76	3884.02	3218.86	2833.43	2587.35	2420.37	2302.35	2216.50	2152.74	2104.65	2067.96	2039.71	2017.82

TERM AMOUNT	15 Years	16 Years	17 Years	18 Years	19 Years	20 Years	21 Years	22 Years	23 Years	24 Years	25 Years	30 Years	35 Years	40 Years
5	.11	.10	.10	.10	.10	.10	.10	.10	.10	.10	.10	.10	.10	.10
10	.21	.20	.20	.20	.20	.20	.20	.20	.20	.20	.20	.20	.20	.20
15	.31	.30	.30	.30	.30	.30	.30	.30	.30	.30	.30	.30	.30	.30
25	.51	.50	.50	.50	.50	.49	.49	.49	.49	.49	.49	.49	.49	.49
50	1.01	1.00	.99	.99	.99	.98	.98	.98	.98	.98	.98	.97	.97	.97
75	1.51	1.50	1.49	1.48	1.48	1.47	1.47	1.47	1.47	1.46	1.46	1.46	1.46	1.46
100	2.01	1.99	1.98	1.97	1.97	1.96	1.96	1.95	1.95	1.95	1.95	1.94	1.94	1.94
200	4.01	3.98	3.96	3.94	3.93	3.92	3.91	3.90	3.90	3.90	3.89	3.88	3.88	3.88
300	6.01	5.97	5.94	5.91	5.89	5.88	5.86	5.85	5.85	5.84	5.84	5.82	5.82	5.82
400	8.01	7.95	7.91	7.88	7.85	7.83	7.82	7.80	7.79	7.79	7.78	7.76	7.76	7.76
500	10.01	9.94	9.89	9.85	9.82	9.79	9.77	9.75	9.74	9.73	9.72	9.70	9.70	9.69
600	12.01	11.93	11.87	11.82	11.78	11.75	11.72	11.70	11.69	11.68	11.67	11.64	11.63	11.63
700	14.01	13.92	13.84	13.79	13.74	13.70	13.68	13.65	13.64	13.62	13.61	13.58	13.57	13.57
800	16.01	15.90	15.82	15.75	15.70	15.66	15.63	15.60	15.58	15.57	15.55	15.52	15.51	15.51
900	18.01	17.89	17.80	17.72	17.66	17.62	17.58	17.55	17.53	17.51	17.50	17.46	17.45	17.44
1000	20.01	19.88	19.77	19.69	19.63	19.58	19.54	19.50	19.48	19.46	19.44	19.40	19.39	19.38
2000	40.02	39.75	39.54	39.38	39.25	39.15	39.07	39.00	38.95	38.91	38.88	38.79	38.77	38.76
3000	60.03	59.63	59.31	59.07	58.87	58.72	58.60	58.50	58.42	58.36	58.31	58.19	58.15	58.14
4000	80.04	79.50	79.08	78.75	78.49	78.29	78.13	78.00	77.90	77.81	77.75	77.58	77.53	77.51
5000	100.04	99.38	98.85	98.44	98.11	97.86	97.66	97.49	97.37	97.27	97.19	96.98	96.91	96.89
6000	120.05	119.25	118.62	118.13	117.74	117.43	117.19	116.99	116.84	116.72	116.62	116.37	116.29	116.27
7000	140.06	139.12	138.39	137.81	137.36	137.00	136.72	136.49	136.31	136.17	136.06	135.77	135.67	135.64
8000	160.07	159.00	158.16	157.50	156.98	156.57	156.25	155.99	155.79	155.62	155.50	155.16	155.05	155.02
9000	180.07	178.87	177.93	177.19	176.60	176.14	175.78	175.49	175.26	175.08	174.93	174.55	174.44	174.40
10000	200.08	198.75	197.70	196.87	196.22	195.71	195.31	194.98	194.73	194.53	194.37	193.95	193.82	193.77
11000	220.09	218.62	217.47	216.56	215.85	215.28	214.84	214.48	214.20	213.98	213.81	213.34	213.20	213.15
12000	240.10	238.49	237.24	236.25	235.47	234.85	234.37	233.98	233.68	233.43	233.24	232.74	232.58	232.53
13000	260.10	258.37	257.01	255.93	255.09	254.42	253.90	253.48	253.15	252.89	252.68	252.13	251.96	251.91
14000	280.11	278.24	276.78	275.62	274.71	273.99	273.43	272.98	272.62	272.34	272.12	271.53	271.34	271.28
15000	300.12	298.12	296.54	295.31	294.33	293.56	292.96	292.47	292.09	291.79	291.55	290.92	290.72	290.66
16000	320.13	317.99	316.31	315.00	313.96	313.14	312.49	311.97	311.57	311.24	310.99	310.32	310.10	310.04
17000	340.13	337.86	336.08	334.68	333.58	332.71	332.02	331.47	331.04	330.70	330.42	329.71	329.48	329.41
18000	360.14	357.74	355.85	354.37	353.20	352.28	351.55	350.97	350.51	350.15	349.86	349.10	348.87	348.79
19000	300.15	377.61	375.62	374.06	372.82	371.85	371.00	370.47	369.98	369.60	369.30	368.50	368.25	368.17
20000	400.16	397.49	395.39	393.74	392.44	391.42	390.61	389.96	389.46	389.05	388.73	387.89	387.63	387.54
21000	420.16	417.36	415.16	413.43	412.07	410.99	410.14	409.46	408.93	408.51	408.17	407.29	407.01	406.92
22000	440.17	437.23	434.93	433.12	431.69	430.56	429.67	428.96	428.40	427.96	427.61	426.68	426.39	426.30
23000	460.18	457.11	454.70	452.80	451.31	450.13	449.20	448.46	447.87	447.41	447.04	446.08	445.77	445.67
24000	480.19	476.98	474.47	472.49	470.93	469.70	468.73	467.96	467.35	466.86	466.48	465.47	465.15	465.05
25000	500.19	496.86	494.24	492.18	490.55	489.27	488.26	487.45	486.82	486.32	485.92	484.86	484.53	484.43
26000	520.20	516.73	514.01	511.86	510.18	508.84	507.79	506.95	506.29	505.77	505.35	504.26	503.91	503.81
27000	540.21	536.60	533.78	531.55	529.80	528.41	527.32	526.45	525.76	525.22	524.79	523.65	523.30	523.18
28000	560.22	556.48	553.55	551.24	549.42	547.98	546.85	545.95	545.24	544.67	544.23	543.05	542.68	542.56
29000	580.22	576.35	573.32	570.93	569.04	567.55	566.38	565.45	564.71	564.12	563.66	562.44	562.06	561.94
30000	600.23	596.23	593.08	590.61	588.66	587.12	585.91	584.94	584.18	583.58	583.10	581.84	581.44	581.31
31000	620.24	616.10	612.85	610.30	608.29	606.69	605.44	604.44	603.65	603.03	602.53	601.23	600.82	600.69
32000	640.25	635.98	632.62	629.99	627.91	626.27	624.97	623.94	623.13	622.48	621.97	620.63	620.20	620.07
33000	660.25	655.85	652.39	649.67	647.53	645.84	644.50	643.44	642.60	641.93	641.41	640.02	639.58	639.44
34000	680.26	675.72	672.16	669.36	667.15	665.41	664.03	662.94	662.07	661.39	660.84	659.41	658.96	658.82
35000	700.27	695.60	691.93	689.05	686.77	684.98	683.56	682.43	681.54	680.84	680.28	678.81	678.34	678.20
36000	720.28	715.47	711.70	708.73	706.39	704.55	703.09	701.93	701.02	700.29	699.72	698.20	697.73	697.57
37000	740.28	735.35	731.47	728.42	726.02	724.12	722.62	721.43	720.49	719.74	719.15	717.60	717.11	716.95
38000	760.29	755.22	751.24	748.11	745.64	743.69	742.15	740.93	739.96	739.20	738.59	736.99	736.49	736.33
39000	780.30	775.09	771.01	767.79	765.26	763.26	761.68	760.43	759.43	758.65	758.03	756.39	755.87	755.71
40000	800.31	794.97	790.78	787.48	784.88	782.83	781.21	779.92	778.91	778.10	777.46	775.78	775.25	775.08
41000	820.31	814.84	810.55	807.17	804.50	802.40	800.74	799.42	798.38	797.55	796.90	795.17	794.63	794.46
42000	840.32	834.72	830.32	826.86	824.13	821.97	820.27	818.92	817.85	817.01	816.34	814.57	814.01	813.84
43000	860.33	854.59	850.09	846.54	843.75	841.54	839.80	838.42	837.32	836.46	835.77	833.96	833.39	833.21
44000	880.34	874.46	869.86	866.23	863.37	861.11	859.33	857.92	856.80	855.91	855.21	853.36	852.77	852.59
45000	900.34	894.34	889.62	885.92	882.99	880.68	878.86	877.41	876.27	875.36	874.64	872.75	872.16	871.97
46000	920.35	914.21	909.39	905.60	902.61	900.25	898.39	896.91	895.74	894.82	894.08	892.15	891.54	891.34
47000	940.36	934.09	929.16	925.29	922.24	919.82	917.92	916.41	915.22	914.27	913.52	911.54	910.92	910.72
48000	960.37	953.96	948.93	944.98	941.86	939.40	937.45	935.91	934.69	933.72	932.95	930.94	930.30	930.10
49000	980.37	973.83	968.70	964.66	961.48	958.97	956.98	955.41	954.16	953.17	952.39	950.33	949.68	949.47
50000	1000.38	993.71	988.47	984.35	981.10	978.54	976.51	974.90	973.63	972.63	971.83	969.72	969.06	968.85
55000	1100.42	1093.08	1087.32	1082.79	1079.21	1076.39	1074.16	1072.39	1071.00	1069.89	1069.01	1066.70	1065.97	1065.74
60000	1200.46	1192.45	1186.16	1181.22	1177.32	1174.24	1171.81	1169.88	1168.36	1167.15	1166.19	1163.67	1162.87	1162.62
65000	1300.49	1291.82	1285.01	1279.65	1275.43	1272.10	1269.46	1267.37	1265.72	1264.41	1263.37	1260.64	1259.78	1259.51
70000	1400.53	1391.19	1383.86	1378.09	1373.54	1369.95	1367.11	1364.86	1363.08	1361.67	1360.56	1357.61	1356.68	1356.39
75000	1500.57	1490.56	1482.70	1476.52	1471.65	1467.80	1464.76	1462.35	1460.45	1458.94	1457.74	1454.58	1453.59	1453.28
80000	1600.61	1589.93	1581.55	1574.96	1569.76	1565.66	1562.41	1559.84	1557.81	1556.20	1554.92	1551.56	1550.50	1550.16
85000	1700.64	1689.30	1680.40	1673.39	1667.87	1663.51	1660.06	1657.33	1655.17	1653.46	1652.10	1648.53	1647.40	1647.04
90000	1800.68	1788.67	1779.24	1771.83	1765.98	1761.36	1757.71	1754.82	1752.53	1750.72	1749.28	1745.50	1744.31	1743.93
95000	1900.72	1888.04	1878.09	1870.26	1864.09	1859.22	1855.36	1852.31	1849.90	1847.98	1846.47	1842.47	1841.21	1840.81
100000	2000.76	1987.41	1976.94	1968.70	1962.20	1957.07	1953.01	1949.80	1947.26	1945.25	1943.65	1939.44	1938.12	1937.70

MONTHLY PAYMENT
REQUIRED TO AMORTIZE A LOAN

TERM AMOUNT	1 Year	2 Years	3 Years	4 Years	5 Years	6 Years	7 Years	8 Years	9 Years	10 Years	11 Years	12 Years	13 Years	14 Years
5	.48	.27	.20	.17	.15	.13	.13	.12	.12	.11	.11	.11	.11	.11
10	.95	.53	.39	.33	.29	.26	.25	.24	.23	.22	.22	.21	.21	.21
15	1.42	.79	.59	.49	.43	.39	.37	.35	.34	.33	.32	.32	.31	.31
25	2.36	1.32	.98	.81	.71	.65	.61	.58	.56	.54	.53	.52	.52	.51
50	4.72	2.63	1.95	1.62	1.42	1.30	1.22	1.16	1.11	1.08	1.06	1.04	1.03	1.02
75	7.07	3.94	2.92	2.42	2.13	1.95	1.82	1.73	1.67	1.62	1.59	1.56	1.54	1.52
100	9.43	5.26	3.89	3.23	2.84	2.60	2.43	2.31	2.22	2.16	2.11	2.08	2.05	2.03
200	18.85	10.51	7.78	6.45	5.68	5.19	4.85	4.62	4.44	4.32	4.22	4.15	4.09	4.05
300	28.27	15.76	11.66	9.67	8.51	7.78	7.28	6.92	6.66	6.47	6.33	6.22	6.14	6.07
400	37.69	21.01	15.55	12.89	11.35	10.37	9.70	9.23	8.88	8.63	8.44	8.29	8.18	8.09
500	47.12	26.27	19.44	16.11	14.19	12.96	12.12	11.53	11.10	10.79	10.55	10.36	10.22	10.11
600	56.54	31.52	23.32	19.33	17.02	15.55	14.55	13.84	13.32	12.94	12.65	12.43	12.27	12.13
700	65.96	36.77	27.21	22.56	19.86	18.14	16.97	16.14	15.54	15.10	14.76	14.51	14.31	14.16
800	75.38	42.02	31.10	25.78	22.70	20.73	19.39	18.45	17.76	17.25	16.87	16.58	16.35	16.18
900	84.80	47.26	34.98	29.00	25.53	23.32	21.82	20.76	19.98	19.41	18.98	18.65	18.40	18.20
1000	94.23	52.53	38.87	32.22	28.37	25.91	24.24	23.06	22.20	21.57	21.09	20.72	20.44	20.22
2000	188.45	105.05	77.74	64.44	56.73	51.81	48.48	46.12	44.40	43.13	42.17	41.44	40.87	40.44
3000	282.67	157.57	116.60	96.65	85.09	77.72	72.71	69.17	66.60	64.69	63.25	62.15	61.31	60.65
4000	376.89	210.09	155.47	128.87	113.46	103.62	96.95	92.23	88.80	86.25	84.33	82.87	81.74	80.87
5000	471.11	262.62	194.34	161.09	141.82	129.52	121.18	115.28	111.00	107.81	105.41	103.58	102.18	101.08
6000	565.33	315.14	233.20	193.30	170.18	155.43	145.42	138.34	133.20	129.38	126.50	124.30	122.61	121.30
7000	659.55	367.66	272.07	225.52	198.55	181.33	169.65	161.40	155.39	150.94	147.58	145.02	143.04	141.52
8000	753.77	420.18	310.94	257.73	226.91	207.23	193.89	184.45	177.59	172.50	168.66	165.73	163.48	161.73
9000	848.00	472.71	349.80	289.95	255.27	233.14	218.12	207.51	199.79	194.06	189.74	186.45	183.91	181.95
10000	942.22	525.23	388.67	322.17	283.64	259.04	242.36	230.56	221.99	215.62	210.82	207.16	204.35	202.16
11000	1036.44	577.75	427.53	354.38	312.00	284.94	266.59	253.62	244.19	237.19	231.91	227.88	224.78	222.38
12000	1130.66	630.27	466.40	386.60	340.36	310.85	290.83	276.68	266.39	258.75	252.99	248.59	245.21	242.59
13000	1224.88	682.80	505.27	418.81	368.73	336.75	315.06	299.73	288.59	280.31	274.07	269.31	265.65	262.81
14000	1319.10	735.32	544.13	451.03	397.09	362.65	339.30	322.79	310.78	301.87	295.15	290.03	286.08	283.03
15000	1413.32	787.84	583.00	483.25	425.45	388.56	363.53	345.84	332.98	323.43	316.23	310.74	306.52	303.24
16000	1507.54	840.36	621.87	515.46	453.81	414.46	387.77	368.90	355.18	345.00	337.32	331.46	326.95	323.46
17000	1601.76	892.89	660.73	547.68	482.18	440.36	412.00	391.96	377.38	366.56	358.40	352.17	347.38	343.67
18000	1695.99	945.41	699.60	579.89	510.54	466.27	436.24	415.01	399.58	388.12	379.48	372.89	367.82	363.89
19000	1790.21	997.93	738.46	612.11	538.90	492.17	460.47	438.07	421.78	409.68	400.56	393.61	388.25	384.10
20000	1884.50	1050.45	777.33	644.33	567.27	518.08	484.71	461.12	443.98	431.24	421.64	414.32	408.69	404.32
21000	1978.65	1102.97	816.20	676.54	595.63	543.98	508.94	484.18	466.17	452.81	442.73	435.04	429.12	424.54
22000	2072.87	1155.50	855.06	708.76	623.99	569.88	533.18	507.24	488.37	474.37	463.81	455.75	449.55	444.75
23000	2167.09	1208.02	893.93	740.97	652.36	595.79	557.41	530.29	510.57	495.93	484.89	476.47	469.99	464.97
24000	2261.31	1260.54	932.80	773.19	680.72	621.69	581.65	553.35	532.77	517.49	505.97	497.18	490.42	485.18
25000	2355.53	1313.06	971.66	805.41	709.08	647.59	605.88	576.40	554.97	539.05	527.05	517.90	510.86	505.40
26000	2449.76	1365.59	1010.53	837.62	737.45	673.50	630.12	599.46	577.17	560.62	548.14	538.62	531.29	525.61
27000	2543.98	1418.11	1049.39	869.84	765.81	699.40	654.35	622.52	599.37	582.18	569.22	559.33	551.72	545.83
28000	2638.20	1470.63	1088.26	902.05	794.17	725.30	678.59	645.57	621.56	603.74	590.30	580.05	572.16	566.05
29000	2732.42	1523.15	1127.13	934.27	822.53	751.21	702.82	668.63	643.76	625.30	611.38	600.76	592.59	586.26
30000	2826.64	1575.68	1165.99	966.49	850.90	777.11	727.06	691.68	665.96	646.86	632.46	621.48	613.03	606.48
31000	2920.86	1628.20	1204.86	998.70	879.26	803.01	751.29	714.74	688.16	668.42	653.54	642.19	633.46	626.69
32000	3015.08	1680.72	1243.73	1030.92	907.62	828.92	775.53	737.80	710.36	689.99	674.63	662.91	653.89	646.91
33000	3109.30	1733.24	1282.59	1063.14	935.99	854.82	799.76	760.85	732.56	711.55	695.71	683.63	674.33	667.13
34000	3203.52	1785.77	1321.46	1095.35	964.35	880.72	824.00	783.91	754.76	733.11	716.79	704.34	694.76	687.34
35000	3297.75	1838.29	1360.32	1127.57	992.71	906.63	848.23	806.96	776.95	754.67	737.87	725.06	715.20	707.56
36000	3391.97	1890.81	1399.19	1159.78	1021.08	932.53	872.47	830.02	799.15	776.23	758.95	745.77	735.63	727.77
37000	3486.19	1943.33	1438.06	1192.00	1049.44	958.44	896.70	853.08	821.35	797.80	780.04	766.49	756.06	747.99
38000	3580.41	1995.85	1476.92	1224.22	1077.80	984.34	920.94	876.13	843.55	819.36	801.12	787.21	776.50	768.20
39000	3674.63	2048.38	1515.79	1256.43	1106.17	1010.24	945.17	899.19	865.75	840.92	822.20	807.92	796.93	788.42
40000	3768.85	2100.90	1554.65	1288.65	1134.53	1036.15	969.41	922.24	887.95	862.48	843.28	828.64	817.37	808.64
41000	3863.07	2153.42	1593.52	1320.86	1162.89	1062.05	993.64	945.30	910.15	884.04	864.36	849.35	837.80	828.85
42000	3957.29	2205.94	1632.39	1353.08	1191.26	1087.96	1017.88	968.36	932.34	905.61	885.45	870.07	858.24	849.07
43000	4051.52	2258.47	1671.25	1385.30	1219.62	1113.86	1042.11	991.41	954.54	927.17	906.53	890.78	878.67	869.28
44000	4145.74	2310.99	1710.12	1417.51	1247.98	1139.76	1066.35	1014.47	976.74	948.73	927.61	911.50	899.10	889.50
45000	4239.96	2363.51	1748.99	1449.73	1276.34	1165.66	1090.58	1037.52	998.94	970.29	948.69	932.22	919.54	909.71
46000	4334.18	2416.03	1787.85	1481.94	1304.71	1191.57	1114.82	1060.58	1021.14	991.85	969.77	952.93	939.97	929.93
47000	4428.40	2468.56	1826.72	1514.16	1333.07	1217.47	1139.05	1083.64	1043.34	1013.42	990.86	973.65	960.41	950.15
48000	4522.62	2521.08	1865.59	1546.38	1361.43	1243.37	1163.29	1106.69	1065.54	1034.98	1011.94	994.36	980.84	970.36
49000	4616.84	2573.60	1904.45	1578.59	1389.80	1269.28	1187.52	1129.75	1087.73	1056.54	1033.02	1015.08	1001.27	990.58
50000	4711.06	2626.12	1943.32	1610.81	1418.16	1295.18	1211.76	1152.80	1109.93	1078.10	1054.10	1035.79	1021.71	1010.79
55000	5182.17	2888.74	2137.65	1771.89	1559.98	1424.70	1332.93	1268.08	1220.92	1185.91	1159.51	1139.37	1123.88	1111.87
60000	5653.27	3151.35	2331.98	1932.97	1701.79	1554.22	1454.11	1383.36	1331.92	1293.72	1264.92	1242.95	1226.05	1212.95
65000	6124.38	3413.96	2526.31	2094.05	1843.61	1683.73	1575.28	1498.64	1442.91	1401.53	1370.33	1346.53	1328.22	1314.03
70000	6595.49	3676.57	2720.64	2255.13	1985.42	1813.25	1696.46	1613.92	1553.90	1509.34	1475.74	1450.11	1430.39	1415.11
75000	7066.59	3939.18	2914.97	2416.21	2127.24	1942.77	1817.63	1729.20	1664.90	1617.15	1581.15	1553.69	1532.56	1516.19
80000	7537.70	4201.79	3109.31	2577.29	2269.05	2072.29	1938.81	1844.48	1775.89	1724.96	1686.56	1657.27	1634.73	1617.27
85000	8008.80	4464.41	3303.64	2738.37	2410.87	2201.80	2059.98	1959.76	1886.88	1832.77	1791.97	1760.85	1736.90	1718.34
90000	8479.91	4727.02	3497.97	2899.45	2552.68	2331.32	2181.16	2075.04	1997.87	1940.58	1897.38	1864.43	1839.07	1819.42
95000	8951.02	4989.63	3692.30	3060.53	2694.50	2460.84	2302.33	2190.32	2108.87	2048.39	2002.79	1968.01	1941.24	1920.50
100000	9422.12	5252.24	3886.63	3221.61	2836.31	2590.36	2423.51	2305.60	2219.86	2156.20	2108.20	2071.58	2043.41	2021.58

TERM	15 Years	16 Years	17 Years	18 Years	19 Years	20 Years	21 Years	22 Years	23 Years	24 Years	25 Years	30 Years	35 Years	40 Years
AMOUNT														
5	.11	.10	.10	.10	.10	.10	.10	.10	.10	.10	.10	.10	.10	.10
10	.21	.20	.20	.20	.20	.20	.20	.20	.20	.20	.20	.20	.20	.20
15	.31	.30	.30	.30	.30	.30	.30	.30	.30	.30	.30	.30	.30	.30
25	.51	.50	.50	.50	.50	.50	.49	.49	.49	.49	.49	.49	.49	.49
50	1.01	1.00	1.00	.99	.99	.99	.98	.98	.98	.98	.98	.98	.98	.98
75	1.51	1.50	1.49	1.48	1.48	1.48	1.47	1.47	1.47	1.47	1.47	1.46	1.46	1.46
100	2.01	2.00	1.99	1.98	1.97	1.97	1.96	1.96	1.96	1.95	1.95	1.95	1.95	1.95
200	4.01	3.99	3.97	3.95	3.94	3.93	3.92	3.91	3.91	3.90	3.90	3.89	3.89	3.89
300	6.02	5.98	5.95	5.92	5.90	5.89	5.88	5.87	5.86	5.85	5.85	5.84	5.83	5.83
400	8.02	7.97	7.93	7.90	7.87	7.85	7.83	7.82	7.81	7.80	7.80	7.78	7.77	7.77
500	10.03	9.96	9.91	9.87	9.84	9.81	9.79	9.77	9.76	9.75	9.74	9.72	9.72	9.71
600	12.03	11.95	11.89	11.84	11.80	11.77	11.75	11.73	11.71	11.70	11.69	11.67	11.66	11.66
700	14.04	13.94	13.87	13.81	13.77	13.73	13.70	13.68	13.66	13.65	13.64	13.61	13.60	13.60
800	16.04	15.94	15.85	15.79	15.73	15.69	15.66	15.64	15.62	15.60	15.59	15.55	15.54	15.54
900	18.05	17.93	17.83	17.76	17.70	17.65	17.62	17.59	17.57	17.55	17.53	17.50	17.49	17.48
1000	20.05	19.92	19.81	19.73	19.67	19.62	19.58	19.54	19.52	19.50	19.48	19.44	19.43	19.42
2000	40.10	39.83	39.62	39.46	39.33	39.23	39.15	39.08	39.03	38.99	38.96	38.88	38.85	38.84
3000	60.14	59.74	59.43	59.18	58.99	58.84	58.72	58.62	58.54	58.48	58.44	58.31	58.27	58.26
4000	80.19	79.66	79.24	78.91	78.65	78.45	78.29	78.16	78.06	77.98	77.91	77.75	77.70	77.68
5000	100.23	99.57	99.05	98.64	98.31	98.06	97.86	97.70	97.57	97.47	97.39	97.18	97.12	97.10
6000	120.28	119.48	118.86	118.36	117.98	117.67	117.43	117.24	117.08	116.96	116.87	116.62	116.54	116.52
7000	140.33	139.39	138.66	138.09	137.64	137.28	137.00	136.78	136.60	136.46	136.35	136.06	135.96	135.93
8000	160.37	159.31	158.47	157.82	157.30	156.89	156.57	156.31	156.11	155.95	155.82	155.49	155.39	155.35
9000	180.42	179.22	178.28	177.54	176.96	176.50	176.14	175.85	175.62	175.44	175.30	174.93	174.81	174.77
10000	200.46	199.13	198.09	197.27	196.62	196.11	195.71	195.39	195.14	194.94	194.78	194.36	194.23	194.19
11000	220.51	219.05	217.90	217.00	216.28	215.72	215.28	214.93	214.65	214.43	214.26	213.80	213.65	213.61
12000	240.55	238.96	237.71	236.72	235.95	235.33	234.85	234.47	234.16	233.92	233.73	233.23	233.08	233.03
13000	260.60	258.87	257.52	256.45	255.61	254.95	254.42	254.01	253.68	253.42	253.21	252.67	252.50	252.45
14000	280.65	278.78	277.32	276.18	275.27	274.56	273.99	273.55	273.19	272.91	272.69	272.11	271.92	271.86
15000	300.69	298.70	297.13	295.90	294.93	294.17	293.56	293.08	292.70	292.40	292.17	291.54	291.35	291.28
16000	320.74	318.61	316.94	315.63	314.59	313.78	313.13	312.62	312.22	311.90	311.64	310.98	310.77	310.70
17000	340.78	338.52	336.75	335.35	334.26	333.39	332.70	332.16	331.73	331.39	331.12	330.41	330.19	330.12
18000	360.83	358.44	356.56	355.08	353.92	353.00	352.27	351.70	351.24	350.88	350.60	349.85	349.61	349.54
19000	380.87	378.35	376.37	374.81	373.58	372.61	371.84	371.24	370.76	370.38	370.08	369.29	369.04	368.96
20000	400.92	398.26	396.17	394.53	393.24	392.22	391.41	390.78	390.27	389.87	389.55	388.72	388.46	388.38
21000	420.97	418.17	415.98	414.26	412.90	411.83	410.98	410.32	409.78	409.36	409.03	408.16	407.88	407.79
22000	441.01	438.09	435.79	433.99	432.56	431.44	430.56	429.85	429.30	428.86	428.51	427.59	427.30	427.21
23000	461.06	458.00	455.60	453.71	452.23	451.05	450.13	449.39	448.81	448.35	447.99	447.03	446.73	446.63
24000	481.10	477.91	475.41	473.44	471.89	470.66	469.70	468.93	468.32	467.84	467.46	466.46	466.15	466.05
25000	501.15	497.83	495.22	493.17	491.55	490.27	489.27	488.47	487.84	487.34	486.94	485.90	485.57	485.47
26000	521.19	517.74	515.03	512.89	511.21	509.89	508.84	508.01	507.35	506.83	506.42	505.34	505.00	504.89
27000	541.24	537.65	534.83	532.62	530.87	529.50	528.41	527.55	526.86	526.32	525.90	524.77	524.42	524.31
28000	561.29	557.56	554.64	552.35	550.54	549.11	547.98	547.09	546.38	545.82	545.37	544.21	543.84	543.72
29000	581.33	577.48	574.45	572.07	570.20	568.72	567.55	566.62	565.89	565.31	564.85	563.64	563.26	563.14
30000	601.38	597.39	594.26	591.80	589.86	588.33	587.12	586.16	585.40	584.80	584.33	583.08	582.69	582.56
31000	621.42	617.30	614.07	611.53	609.52	607.94	606.69	605.70	604.92	604.30	603.81	602.52	602.11	601.98
32000	641.47	637.21	633.88	631.25	629.18	627.55	626.26	625.24	624.43	623.79	623.28	621.95	621.53	621.40
33000	661.51	657.13	653.69	650.98	648.84	647.16	645.83	644.78	643.94	643.28	642.76	641.39	640.95	640.82
34000	681.56	677.04	673.49	670.70	668.51	666.77	665.40	664.32	663.46	662.78	662.24	660.82	660.38	660.24
35000	701.61	696.95	693.30	690.43	688.17	686.38	684.97	683.86	682.97	682.27	681.72	680.26	679.80	679.65
36000	721.65	716.87	713.11	710.16	707.83	705.99	704.54	703.39	702.48	701.76	701.19	699.69	699.22	699.07
37000	741.70	736.78	732.92	729.88	727.49	725.60	724.11	722.93	722.00	721.26	720.67	719.13	718.64	718.49
38000	761.74	756.69	752.73	749.61	747.15	745.22	743.68	742.47	741.51	740.75	740.15	738.57	738.07	737.91
39000	781.79	776.60	772.54	769.34	766.82	764.83	763.25	762.01	761.02	760.24	759.63	758.00	757.49	757.33
40000	801.84	796.52	792.34	789.06	786.48	784.44	782.82	781.55	780.54	779.74	779.10	777.44	776.91	776.75
41000	821.88	816.43	812.15	808.79	806.14	804.05	802.39	801.09	800.05	799.23	798.58	796.87	796.34	796.17
42000	841.93	836.34	831.96	828.52	825.80	823.66	821.96	820.63	819.56	818.72	818.06	816.31	815.76	815.58
43000	861.97	856.26	851.77	848.24	845.46	843.27	841.54	840.16	839.08	838.22	837.54	835.74	835.19	835.00
44000	882.02	876.17	871.58	867.97	865.12	862.88	861.11	859.70	858.59	857.71	857.01	855.18	854.60	854.42
45000	902.06	896.08	891.39	887.70	884.79	882.49	880.68	879.24	878.10	877.20	876.49	874.62	874.03	873.84
46000	922.11	915.99	911.20	907.42	904.45	902.10	900.25	898.78	897.62	896.70	895.97	894.05	893.45	893.26
47000	942.16	935.91	931.00	927.15	924.11	921.71	919.82	918.32	917.13	916.19	915.45	913.49	912.87	912.68
48000	962.20	955.82	950.81	946.88	943.77	941.32	939.39	937.86	936.64	935.68	934.92	932.92	932.29	932.10
49000	982.25	975.73	970.62	966.60	963.43	960.93	958.96	957.40	956.16	955.18	954.40	952.36	951.72	951.51
50000	1002.29	995.65	990.43	986.33	983.10	980.54	978.53	976.93	975.67	974.67	973.88	971.80	971.14	970.93
55000	1102.52	1095.21	1089.47	1084.96	1081.40	1078.60	1076.38	1074.63	1073.24	1072.14	1071.27	1068.97	1068.25	1068.03
60000	1202.75	1194.77	1188.51	1183.59	1179.71	1176.65	1174.23	1172.32	1170.80	1169.60	1168.65	1166.15	1165.37	1165.12
65000	1302.98	1294.34	1287.56	1282.23	1278.02	1274.71	1272.09	1270.01	1268.37	1267.07	1266.04	1263.33	1262.48	1262.21
70000	1403.21	1393.90	1386.60	1380.86	1376.33	1372.76	1369.94	1367.71	1365.94	1364.54	1363.43	1360.51	1359.59	1359.30
75000	1503.44	1493.47	1485.64	1479.49	1474.64	1470.81	1467.79	1465.40	1463.50	1462.00	1460.82	1457.69	1456.71	1456.40
80000	1603.67	1593.03	1584.68	1578.12	1572.95	1568.87	1565.64	1563.09	1561.07	1559.47	1558.20	1554.87	1553.82	1553.49
85000	1703.89	1692.59	1683.73	1676.75	1671.26	1666.92	1663.49	1660.78	1658.64	1656.94	1655.59	1652.05	1650.93	1650.58
90000	1804.12	1792.16	1782.77	1775.39	1769.57	1764.98	1761.35	1758.20	1756.20	1754.40	1752.98	1749.23	1748.05	1747.68
95000	1904.35	1891.72	1881.81	1874.02	1867.88	1863.03	1859.20	1856.17	1853.77	1851.87	1850.37	1846.41	1845.16	1844.77
100000	2004.58	1991.29	1980.85	1972.65	1966.19	1961.08	1957.05	1953.86	1951.34	1949.34	1947.75	1943.59	1942.28	1941.86

MONTHLY PAYMENT
REQUIRED TO AMORTIZE A LOAN

TERM AMOUNT	1 Year	2 Years	3 Years	4 Years	5 Years	6 Years	7 Years	8 Years	9 Years	10 Years	11 Years	12 Years	13 Years	14 Years
5	.48	.27	.20	.17	.15	.13	.13	.12	.12	.11	.11	.11	.11	.11
10	.95	.53	.39	.33	.29	.26	.25	.24	.23	.22	.22	.21	.21	.21
15	1.42	.79	.59	.49	.43	.39	.37	.35	.34	.33	.32	.32	.31	.31
25	2.36	1.32	.98	.81	.72	.65	.61	.58	.56	.55	.53	.52	.52	.51
50	4.72	2.63	1.95	1.62	1.43	1.30	1.22	1.16	1.12	1.09	1.06	1.04	1.03	1.02
75	7.07	3.95	2.92	2.42	2.14	1.95	1.83	1.74	1.67	1.63	1.59	1.56	1.54	1.53
100	9.43	5.26	3.90	3.23	2.85	2.60	2.43	2.32	2.23	2.17	2.12	2.08	2.05	2.03
200	18.86	10.52	7.79	6.46	5.69	5.19	4.86	4.63	4.45	4.33	4.23	4.16	4.10	4.06
300	28.28	15.77	11.68	9.68	8.53	7.79	7.29	6.94	6.68	6.49	6.35	6.24	6.15	6.09
400	37.71	21.03	15.57	12.91	11.37	10.38	9.72	9.25	8.90	8.65	8.46	8.31	8.20	8.11
500	47.13	26.28	19.46	16.13	14.21	12.90	12.15	11.56	11.15	10.81	10.57	10.39	10.25	10.14
600	56.56	31.54	23.35	19.36	17.05	15.57	14.57	13.87	13.35	12.97	12.69	12.47	12.30	12.17
700	65.99	36.80	27.24	22.59	19.89	18.17	17.00	16.18	15.58	15.13	14.80	14.54	14.35	14.20
800	75.41	42.05	31.13	25.81	22.73	20.76	19.43	18.49	17.80	17.30	16.91	16.62	16.40	16.22
900	84.84	47.31	35.02	29.04	25.57	23.36	21.86	20.80	20.03	19.46	19.03	18.70	18.45	18.25
1000	94.26	52.56	38.91	32.26	28.41	25.95	24.29	23.11	22.25	21.62	21.14	20.78	20.49	20.28
2000	188.52	105.12	77.82	64.52	56.82	51.90	48.57	46.21	44.50	43.23	42.28	41.55	40.98	40.55
3000	282.78	157.68	116.72	96.78	85.22	77.85	72.85	69.32	66.75	64.85	63.41	62.32	61.47	60.82
4000	377.03	210.24	155.63	129.03	113.63	103.80	97.13	92.42	89.00	86.46	84.55	83.09	81.96	81.09
5000	471.29	262.80	194.53	161.29	142.04	129.75	121.42	115.53	111.25	108.07	105.68	103.86	102.45	101.37
6000	565.55	315.36	233.44	193.55	170.44	155.70	145.70	138.63	133.50	129.69	126.82	124.63	122.94	121.64
7000	659.81	367.92	272.34	225.81	198.85	181.65	169.98	161.74	155.75	151.30	147.95	145.40	143.43	141.91
8000	754.06	420.48	311.25	258.06	227.26	207.59	194.26	184.84	178.00	172.92	169.09	166.17	163.92	162.18
9000	848.32	473.04	350.15	290.32	255.66	233.54	218.54	207.95	200.25	194.53	190.22	186.94	184.41	182.46
10000	942.58	525.60	389.06	322.58	284.07	259.49	242.83	231.05	222.49	216.14	211.36	207.71	204.90	202.73
11000	1036.84	578.16	427.96	354.84	312.47	285.44	267.11	254.16	244.74	237.76	232.49	228.48	225.39	223.00
12000	1131.09	630.72	466.87	387.09	340.88	311.39	291.39	277.26	266.99	259.37	253.63	249.25	245.88	243.27
13000	1225.35	683.28	505.78	419.35	369.29	337.34	315.67	300.37	289.24	280.98	274.76	270.02	266.37	263.54
14000	1319.61	735.84	544.68	451.61	397.69	363.29	339.95	323.47	311.49	302.60	295.90	290.79	286.86	283.82
15000	1413.87	788.40	583.59	483.86	426.10	389.24	364.24	346.58	333.74	324.21	317.03	311.56	307.35	304.09
16000	1508.12	840.96	622.49	516.12	454.51	415.18	388.52	369.68	355.99	345.83	338.17	332.33	327.84	324.36
17000	1602.38	893.52	661.40	548.38	482.91	441.13	412.80	392.79	378.24	367.44	359.30	353.10	348.33	344.63
18000	1696.64	946.08	700.30	580.64	511.32	467.08	437.08	415.89	400.49	389.05	380.44	373.87	368.82	364.91
19000	1790.90	998.64	739.21	612.89	539.73	493.03	461.36	439.00	422.74	410.67	401.57	394.64	389.31	385.18
20000	1885.15	1051.20	778.11	645.15	568.13	518.98	485.65	462.10	444.98	432.28	422.71	415.41	409.80	405.45
21000	1979.41	1103.76	817.02	677.41	596.54	544.93	509.93	485.21	467.23	453.90	443.84	436.18	430.29	425.72
22000	2073.67	1156.32	855.92	709.67	624.94	570.88	534.21	508.31	489.48	475.51	464.98	456.95	450.78	446.00
23000	2167.93	1208.88	894.83	741.92	653.35	596.83	558.49	531.41	511.73	497.12	486.11	477.72	471.27	466.27
24000	2262.18	1261.44	933.74	774.18	681.76	622.77	582.77	554.52	533.98	518.74	507.25	498.49	491.76	486.54
25000	2356.44	1314.00	972.64	806.44	710.16	648.72	607.06	577.62	556.23	540.35	528.38	519.26	512.25	506.81
26000	2450.70	1366.56	1011.55	838.69	738.57	674.67	631.34	600.73	578.48	561.96	549.52	540.03	532.73	527.08
27000	2544.95	1419.12	1050.45	870.95	766.98	700.62	655.62	623.83	600.73	583.58	570.65	560.80	553.22	547.36
28000	2639.21	1471.68	1089.36	903.21	795.38	726.57	679.90	646.94	622.98	605.19	591.79	581.57	573.71	567.63
29000	2733.47	1524.24	1128.26	935.47	823.79	752.52	704.19	670.04	645.22	626.81	612.93	602.34	594.20	587.90
30000	2827.73	1576.80	1167.17	967.72	852.20	778.47	728.47	693.15	667.47	648.42	634.06	623.11	614.69	608.17
31000	2921.98	1629.35	1206.07	999.98	880.60	804.42	752.75	716.25	689.72	670.03	655.20	643.88	635.18	628.45
32000	3016.24	1681.91	1244.98	1032.24	909.01	830.36	777.03	739.36	711.97	691.65	676.33	664.65	655.67	648.72
33000	3110.50	1734.47	1283.88	1064.50	937.41	856.31	801.31	762.46	734.22	713.26	697.47	685.42	676.16	668.99
34000	3204.76	1787.03	1322.79	1096.75	965.82	882.26	825.60	785.57	756.47	734.88	718.60	706.19	696.65	689.26
35000	3299.01	1839.59	1361.70	1129.01	994.23	908.21	849.88	808.67	778.72	756.49	739.74	726.96	717.14	709.54
36000	3393.27	1892.15	1400.60	1161.27	1022.63	934.16	874.16	831.78	800.97	778.10	760.87	747.73	737.63	729.81
37000	3487.53	1944.71	1439.51	1193.52	1051.04	960.11	898.44	854.88	823.22	799.72	782.01	768.50	758.12	750.08
38000	3581.79	1997.27	1478.41	1225.78	1079.45	986.06	922.72	877.99	845.47	821.33	803.14	789.28	778.61	770.35
39000	3676.04	2049.83	1517.32	1258.04	1107.85	1012.01	947.01	901.09	867.71	842.94	824.28	810.05	799.10	790.62
40000	3770.30	2102.39	1556.22	1290.30	1136.26	1037.95	971.29	924.20	889.96	864.56	845.41	830.82	819.59	810.90
41000	3864.56	2154.95	1595.13	1322.55	1164.66	1063.90	995.57	947.30	912.21	886.17	866.55	851.59	840.08	831.17
42000	3958.82	2207.51	1634.03	1354.81	1193.07	1089.85	1019.85	970.41	934.46	907.79	887.68	872.36	860.57	851.44
43000	4053.07	2260.07	1672.94	1387.07	1221.48	1115.80	1044.13	993.51	956.71	929.40	908.82	893.13	881.06	871.71
44000	4147.33	2312.63	1711.84	1419.33	1249.88	1141.75	1068.42	1016.61	978.96	951.01	929.95	913.90	901.55	891.99
45000	4241.59	2365.19	1750.75	1451.58	1278.29	1167.70	1092.70	1039.72	1001.21	972.63	951.09	934.67	922.04	912.26
46000	4335.85	2417.75	1789.66	1483.84	1306.70	1193.65	1116.98	1062.82	1023.46	994.24	972.22	955.44	942.53	932.53
47000	4430.10	2470.31	1828.56	1516.10	1335.10	1219.59	1141.26	1085.93	1045.71	1015.85	993.36	976.21	963.02	952.80
48000	4524.36	2522.87	1867.47	1548.35	1363.51	1245.54	1165.54	1109.03	1067.96	1037.47	1014.49	996.98	983.51	973.07
49000	4618.62	2575.43	1906.37	1580.61	1391.92	1271.49	1189.83	1132.14	1090.20	1059.08	1035.63	1017.75	1004.00	993.35
50000	4712.87	2627.99	1945.28	1612.87	1420.32	1297.44	1214.11	1155.24	1112.45	1080.70	1056.76	1038.52	1024.49	1013.62
55000	5184.16	2890.79	2139.80	1774.16	1562.35	1427.18	1335.52	1270.77	1223.70	1188.77	1162.44	1142.37	1126.93	1114.98
60000	5655.45	3153.59	2334.33	1935.44	1704.39	1556.93	1456.93	1386.29	1334.94	1296.83	1268.12	1246.22	1229.38	1216.34
65000	6126.74	3416.38	2528.86	2096.73	1846.42	1686.67	1578.34	1501.81	1446.19	1404.90	1373.79	1350.07	1331.83	1317.70
70000	6598.02	3679.18	2723.39	2258.01	1988.45	1816.42	1699.75	1617.34	1557.43	1512.97	1479.47	1453.92	1434.28	1419.07
75000	7069.31	3941.98	2917.91	2419.30	2130.48	1946.16	1821.16	1732.86	1668.68	1621.04	1585.14	1557.77	1536.73	1520.43
80000	7540.60	4204.78	3112.44	2580.59	2272.51	2075.90	1942.57	1848.39	1779.92	1729.11	1690.82	1661.63	1639.17	1621.79
85000	8011.88	4467.58	3306.97	2741.87	2414.54	2205.65	2063.98	1963.91	1891.17	1837.18	1796.50	1765.48	1741.62	1723.15
90000	8483.17	4730.38	3501.50	2903.16	2556.58	2335.39	2185.39	2079.43	2002.41	1945.25	1902.17	1869.33	1844.07	1824.51
95000	8954.46	4993.17	3696.02	3064.45	2698.61	2465.13	2306.80	2194.96	2113.66	2053.32	2007.85	1973.18	1946.52	1925.87
100000	9425.74	5255.97	3890.55	3225.73	2840.64	2594.88	2428.21	2310.48	2224.90	2161.39	2113.52	2077.03	2048.97	2027.23

TERM	15 Years	16 Years	17 Years	18 Years	19 Years	20 Years	21 Years	22 Years	23 Years	24 Years	25 Years	30 Years	35 Years	40 Years
AMOUNT														
5	.11	.10	.10	.10	.10	.10	.10	.10	.10	.10	.10	.10	.10	.10
10	.21	.20	.20	.20	.20	.20	.20	.20	.20	.20	.20	.20	.20	.20
15	.31	.30	.30	.30	.30	.30	.30	.30	.30	.30	.30	.30	.30	.30
25	.51	.50	.50	.50	.50	.50	.50	.49	.49	.49	.49	.49	.49	.49
50	1.01	1.00	1.00	.99	.99	.99	.99	.98	.98	.98	.98	.98	.98	.98
75	1.51	1.50	1.50	1.49	1.48	1.48	1.48	1.47	1.47	1.47	1.47	1.47	1.47	1.47
100	2.02	2.00	1.99	1.98	1.98	1.97	1.97	1.96	1.96	1.96	1.96	1.95	1.95	1.95
200	4.03	4.00	3.98	3.96	3.95	3.94	3.93	3.92	3.92	3.92	3.91	3.90	3.90	3.90
300	6.04	6.00	5.97	5.94	5.92	5.91	5.89	5.88	5.88	5.87	5.87	5.85	5.85	5.85
400	8.05	7.99	7.95	7.92	7.89	7.87	7.86	7.84	7.83	7.83	7.82	7.80	7.80	7.80
500	10.06	9.99	9.94	9.90	9.87	9.84	9.82	9.80	9.79	9.78	9.77	9.75	9.75	9.75
600	12.07	11.99	11.93	11.88	11.84	11.81	11.78	11.76	11.75	11.74	11.73	11.70	11.70	11.69
700	14.08	13.98	13.91	13.86	13.81	13.77	13.75	13.72	13.71	13.69	13.68	13.65	13.64	13.64
800	16.09	15.98	15.90	15.83	15.78	15.74	15.71	15.68	15.66	15.65	15.64	15.60	15.59	15.59
900	18.10	17.98	17.89	17.81	17.75	17.71	17.67	17.64	17.62	17.60	17.59	17.55	17.54	17.54
1000	20.11	19.98	19.87	19.79	19.73	19.68	19.64	19.60	19.58	19.56	19.54	19.50	19.49	19.49
2000	40.21	39.95	39.74	39.58	39.45	39.35	39.27	39.20	39.15	39.11	39.08	39.00	38.98	38.97
3000	60.31	59.92	59.61	59.36	59.17	59.02	58.90	58.80	58.73	58.67	58.62	58.50	58.46	58.45
4000	80.42	79.89	79.47	79.15	78.89	78.69	78.53	78.40	78.30	78.22	78.16	78.00	77.95	77.93
5000	100.52	99.86	99.34	98.93	98.61	98.36	98.16	98.00	97.88	97.78	97.70	97.49	97.43	97.41
6000	120.62	119.83	119.21	118.72	118.33	118.03	117.79	117.60	117.45	117.33	117.24	116.99	116.92	116.89
7000	140.73	139.80	139.08	138.51	138.06	137.70	137.42	137.20	137.03	136.89	136.78	136.49	136.40	136.37
8000	160.83	159.77	158.94	158.29	157.78	157.37	157.05	156.80	156.60	156.44	156.32	155.99	155.89	155.85
9000	180.93	179.74	178.81	178.08	177.50	177.04	176.68	176.40	176.18	176.00	175.86	175.49	175.37	175.33
10000	201.04	199.71	198.68	197.86	197.22	196.72	196.32	196.00	195.75	195.55	195.40	194.98	194.86	194.82
11000	221.14	219.69	218.55	217.65	216.94	216.39	215.95	215.60	215.32	215.11	214.93	214.48	214.34	214.30
12000	241.24	239.66	238.41	237.43	236.66	236.06	235.58	235.20	234.90	234.66	234.47	233.98	233.83	233.78
13000	261.35	259.63	258.28	257.22	256.39	255.73	255.21	254.80	254.47	254.22	254.01	253.48	253.31	253.26
14000	281.45	279.60	278.15	277.01	276.11	275.40	274.84	274.40	274.05	273.77	273.55	272.98	272.80	272.74
15000	301.55	299.57	298.01	296.79	295.83	295.07	294.47	294.00	293.62	293.33	293.09	292.47	292.28	292.22
16000	321.66	319.54	317.88	316.58	315.55	314.74	314.10	313.60	313.20	312.88	312.63	311.97	311.77	311.70
17000	341.76	339.51	337.75	336.36	335.27	334.41	333.73	333.20	332.77	332.44	332.17	331.47	331.25	331.18
18000	361.86	359.48	357.62	356.15	354.99	354.08	353.36	352.80	352.35	351.99	351.71	350.97	350.74	350.66
19000	381.96	379.45	377.48	375.94	374.72	373.75	373.00	372.40	371.92	371.54	371.25	370.47	370.22	370.14
20000	402.07	399.42	397.35	395.72	394.44	393.43	392.63	391.99	391.50	391.10	390.79	389.96	389.71	389.63
21000	422.17	419.39	417.22	415.51	414.16	413.10	412.26	411.59	411.07	410.65	410.33	409.46	409.19	409.11
22000	442.27	439.37	437.09	435.29	433.88	432.77	431.89	431.19	430.64	430.21	429.86	428.96	428.68	428.59
23000	462.38	459.34	456.95	455.08	453.60	452.44	451.52	450.79	450.22	449.76	449.40	448.46	448.16	448.07
24000	482.48	479.31	476.82	474.86	473.32	472.11	471.15	470.39	469.79	469.32	468.94	467.96	467.65	467.55
25000	502.58	499.28	496.69	494.65	493.05	491.78	490.78	489.99	489.37	488.87	488.48	487.45	487.13	487.03
26000	522.69	519.25	516.55	514.44	512.77	511.45	510.41	509.59	508.94	508.43	508.02	506.95	506.62	506.51
27000	542.79	539.22	536.42	534.22	532.49	531.12	530.04	529.19	528.52	527.98	527.56	526.45	526.10	525.99
28000	562.89	559.19	556.29	554.01	552.21	550.79	549.68	548.79	548.09	547.54	547.10	545.95	545.59	545.47
29000	583.00	579.16	576.16	573.79	571.93	570.47	569.31	568.39	567.67	567.09	566.64	565.45	565.07	564.95
30000	603.10	599.13	596.02	593.58	591.65	590.14	588.94	587.99	587.24	586.65	586.18	584.94	584.56	584.44
31000	623.20	619.10	615.89	613.37	611.38	609.81	608.57	607.59	606.81	606.20	605.72	604.44	604.04	603.92
32000	643.31	639.07	635.76	633.15	631.10	629.48	628.20	627.19	626.39	625.76	625.26	623.94	623.53	623.40
33000	663.41	659.05	655.63	652.94	650.82	649.15	647.83	646.78	645.96	645.31	644.79	643.44	643.01	642.88
34000	683.51	679.02	675.49	672.72	670.54	668.82	667.46	666.39	665.54	664.87	664.33	662.94	662.50	662.36
35000	703.61	698.99	695.36	692.51	690.26	688.49	687.09	685.99	685.11	684.42	683.87	682.43	681.98	681.84
36000	723.72	718.96	715.23	712.29	709.98	708.16	706.72	705.59	704.69	703.98	703.41	701.93	701.47	701.32
37000	743.82	738.93	735.09	732.08	729.71	727.83	726.36	725.19	724.26	723.53	722.95	721.43	720.95	720.80
38000	763.92	758.90	754.96	751.87	749.43	747.50	745.99	744.79	743.84	743.08	742.49	740.93	740.44	740.28
39000	784.03	778.87	774.83	771.65	769.15	767.18	765.62	764.39	763.41	762.64	762.03	760.43	759.92	759.76
40000	804.13	798.84	794.70	791.44	788.87	786.85	785.25	783.98	782.99	782.19	781.57	779.92	779.41	779.25
41000	824.23	818.81	814.56	811.22	808.59	806.52	804.88	803.58	802.56	801.75	801.11	799.42	798.89	798.73
42000	844.34	838.78	834.43	831.01	828.31	826.19	824.51	823.18	822.13	821.30	820.65	818.92	818.38	818.21
43000	864.44	858.75	854.30	850.79	848.04	845.86	844.14	842.78	841.71	840.86	840.18	838.42	837.86	837.69
44000	884.54	878.73	874.17	870.58	867.76	865.53	863.77	862.38	861.28	860.41	859.72	857.91	857.35	857.17
45000	904.65	898.70	894.03	890.37	887.48	885.20	883.40	881.98	880.86	879.97	879.26	877.41	876.83	876.65
46000	924.75	918.67	913.90	910.15	907.20	904.87	903.03	901.58	900.43	899.52	898.80	896.91	896.32	896.13
47000	944.85	938.64	933.77	929.94	926.92	924.54	922.67	921.18	920.01	919.08	918.34	916.41	915.80	915.61
48000	964.96	958.61	953.63	949.72	946.64	944.22	942.30	940.78	939.58	938.63	937.88	935.91	935.29	935.09
49000	985.06	978.58	973.50	969.51	966.37	963.89	961.93	960.38	959.16	958.19	957.42	955.40	954.77	954.57
50000	1005.16	998.55	993.37	989.30	986.09	983.56	981.56	979.98	978.73	977.74	976.96	974.90	974.26	974.06
55000	1105.68	1098.41	1092.71	1088.22	1084.70	1081.91	1079.71	1077.98	1076.60	1075.51	1074.65	1072.39	1071.68	1071.46
60000	1206.19	1198.26	1192.04	1187.15	1183.30	1180.27	1177.87	1175.97	1174.48	1173.29	1172.35	1169.88	1169.11	1168.87
65000	1306.71	1298.12	1291.38	1286.08	1281.91	1278.62	1276.03	1273.97	1272.35	1271.06	1270.04	1267.37	1266.53	1266.27
70000	1407.22	1397.97	1390.71	1385.01	1380.52	1376.98	1374.18	1371.97	1370.22	1368.84	1367.74	1364.86	1363.96	1363.68
75000	1507.74	1497.82	1490.05	1483.94	1479.13	1475.33	1472.34	1469.97	1468.09	1466.61	1465.43	1462.35	1461.38	1461.08
80000	1608.26	1597.68	1589.39	1582.87	1577.74	1573.69	1570.49	1567.96	1565.97	1564.38	1563.13	1559.84	1558.81	1558.49
85000	1708.77	1697.53	1688.72	1681.80	1676.35	1672.04	1668.65	1665.96	1663.84	1662.16	1660.83	1657.33	1656.24	1655.89
90000	1809.29	1797.39	1788.06	1780.73	1774.95	1770.40	1766.80	1763.96	1761.71	1759.93	1758.52	1754.82	1753.66	1753.30
95000	1909.80	1897.24	1887.40	1879.66	1873.56	1868.75	1864.96	1861.96	1859.58	1857.70	1856.22	1852.31	1851.09	1850.70
100000	2010.32	1997.10	1986.73	1978.59	1972.17	1967.11	1963.11	1959.95	1957.46	1955.48	1953.91	1949.80	1948.51	1948.11

MONTHLY PAYMENT
REQUIRED TO AMORTIZE A LOAN

TERM AMOUNT	1 Year	2 Years	3 Years	4 Years	5 Years	6 Years	7 Years	8 Years	9 Years	10 Years	11 Years	12 Years	13 Years	14 Years
5	.48	.27	.20	.17	.15	.13	.13	.12	.12	.11	.11	.11	.11	.11
10	.95	.53	.39	.33	.29	.26	.25	.24	.23	.22	.22	.21	.21	.21
15	1.42	.79	.59	.49	.43	.39	.37	.35	.34	.33	.32	.32	.31	.31
25	2.36	1.32	.98	.81	.72	.65	.61	.58	.56	.55	.53	.52	.52	.51
50	4.72	2.63	1.95	1.62	1.43	1.30	1.22	1.16	1.12	1.09	1.06	1.04	1.03	1.02
75	7.08	3.95	2.92	2.43	2.14	1.95	1.83	1.74	1.67	1.63	1.59	1.56	1.54	1.53
100	9.43	5.26	3.90	3.23	2.85	2.60	2.43	2.32	2.23	2.17	2.12	2.08	2.06	2.03
200	18.86	10.52	7.79	6.46	5.69	5.20	4.86	4.63	4.46	4.33	4.24	4.16	4.11	4.06
300	28.29	15.78	11.68	9.69	8.53	7.79	7.29	6.94	6.68	6.49	6.35	6.24	6.16	6.09
400	37.71	21.03	15.57	12.91	11.37	10.39	9.72	9.25	8.91	8.66	8.47	8.32	8.21	8.12
500	47.14	28.29	19.48	16.14	14.22	12.99	12.15	11.57	11.14	10.82	10.58	10.40	10.26	10.15
600	56.57	31.55	23.36	19.37	17.06	15.58	14.58	13.88	13.36	12.98	12.70	12.48	12.31	12.18
700	65.99	36.81	27.25	22.59	19.90	18.18	17.01	16.19	15.59	15.15	14.81	14.56	14.36	14.21
800	75.42	42.06	31.14	25.82	22.74	20.78	19.44	18.50	17.82	17.31	16.93	16.64	16.41	16.24
900	84.85	47.32	35.03	29.05	25.58	23.37	21.87	20.81	20.04	19.47	19.04	18.71	18.46	18.27
1000	94.27	52.58	38.92	32.28	28.43	25.97	24.30	23.13	22.27	21.64	21.16	20.79	20.51	20.30
2000	188.54	105.15	77.84	64.55	56.85	51.93	48.60	46.25	44.54	43.27	42.31	41.58	41.02	40.59
3000	282.81	157.72	116.76	96.82	85.27	77.90	72.90	69.37	66.80	64.90	63.46	62.37	61.53	60.88
4000	377.08	210.29	155.68	129.09	113.69	103.86	97.20	92.49	89.07	86.53	84.62	83.16	82.04	81.17
5000	471.35	262.87	194.60	161.36	142.11	129.82	121.49	115.61	111.33	108.16	105.77	103.95	102.55	101.46
6000	565.62	315.44	233.52	193.63	170.53	155.79	145.79	138.73	133.60	129.79	126.92	124.74	123.05	121.75
7000	659.89	368.01	272.43	225.90	198.95	181.75	170.09	161.85	155.87	151.42	148.08	145.52	143.56	142.04
8000	754.16	420.58	311.35	258.17	227.37	207.72	194.39	184.97	178.13	173.05	169.23	166.31	164.07	162.33
9000	848.43	473.15	350.27	290.44	255.79	233.68	218.68	208.09	200.40	194.69	190.38	187.10	184.58	182.63
10000	942.70	525.73	389.19	322.72	284.21	259.64	242.98	231.22	222.66	216.32	211.53	207.89	205.09	202.92
11000	1036.97	578.30	428.11	354.99	312.63	285.61	267.28	254.34	244.93	237.95	232.69	228.68	225.59	223.21
12000	1131.24	630.87	467.03	387.26	341.05	311.57	291.58	277.46	267.19	259.58	253.84	249.47	246.10	243.50
13000	1225.51	683.44	505.95	419.53	369.47	337.53	315.88	300.58	289.46	281.21	274.99	270.25	266.61	263.79
14000	1319.78	736.01	544.86	451.80	397.90	363.50	340.17	323.70	311.73	302.84	296.15	291.04	287.12	284.08
15000	1414.05	788.59	583.78	484.07	426.32	389.46	364.47	346.82	333.99	324.47	317.30	311.83	307.63	304.37
16000	1508.32	841.16	622.70	516.34	454.74	415.43	388.77	369.94	356.26	346.10	338.45	332.62	328.14	324.66
17000	1602.59	893.73	661.62	548.61	483.16	441.39	413.07	393.06	378.52	367.73	359.60	353.41	348.64	344.95
18000	1696.86	946.30	700.54	580.88	511.58	467.35	437.36	416.18	400.79	389.37	380.76	374.20	369.15	365.25
19000	1791.13	998.88	739.46	613.15	540.00	493.32	461.66	439.30	423.05	411.00	401.91	394.99	389.66	385.54
20000	1885.39	1051.45	778.38	645.43	568.42	519.28	485.96	462.43	445.32	432.63	423.06	415.77	410.17	405.83
21000	1979.66	1104.02	817.29	677.70	596.84	545.24	510.26	485.55	467.59	454.26	444.22	436.56	430.68	426.12
22000	2073.93	1156.59	856.21	709.97	625.26	571.21	534.56	508.67	489.85	475.89	465.37	457.35	451.18	446.41
23000	2168.20	1209.16	895.13	742.24	653.68	597.17	558.85	531.79	512.12	497.52	486.52	478.14	471.69	466.70
24000	2262.47	1261.74	934.05	774.51	682.10	623.14	583.15	554.91	534.38	519.15	507.68	498.93	492.20	486.99
25000	2356.74	1314.31	972.97	806.78	710.52	649.10	607.45	578.03	556.65	540.78	528.83	519.72	512.71	507.28
26000	2451.01	1366.88	1011.89	839.05	738.94	675.06	631.75	601.15	578.92	562.41	549.98	540.50	533.22	527.57
27000	2545.28	1419.45	1050.80	871.32	767.37	701.03	656.04	624.27	601.18	584.05	571.13	561.29	553.72	547.87
28000	2639.55	1472.02	1089.72	903.59	795.79	726.99	680.34	647.39	623.45	605.68	592.29	582.08	574.23	568.16
29000	2733.82	1524.60	1128.64	935.86	824.21	752.96	704.64	670.52	645.71	627.31	613.44	602.87	594.74	588.45
30000	2828.09	1577.17	1167.56	968.14	852.63	778.92	728.94	693.64	667.98	648.94	634.59	623.66	615.25	608.74
31000	2922.36	1629.74	1206.48	1000.41	881.05	804.88	753.24	716.76	690.24	670.57	655.75	644.45	635.76	629.03
32000	3016.63	1682.31	1245.40	1032.68	909.47	830.85	777.53	739.88	712.51	692.20	676.90	665.23	656.27	649.32
33000	3110.90	1734.88	1284.32	1064.95	937.89	856.81	801.83	763.00	734.78	713.83	698.05	686.02	676.77	669.61
34000	3205.17	1787.46	1323.23	1097.22	966.31	882.77	826.13	786.12	757.04	735.46	719.20	706.81	697.28	689.90
35000	3299.44	1840.03	1362.15	1129.49	994.73	908.74	850.43	809.24	779.31	757.09	740.36	727.60	717.79	710.19
36000	3393.71	1892.60	1401.07	1161.76	1023.15	934.70	874.72	832.36	801.57	778.73	761.51	748.39	738.30	730.49
37000	3487.98	1945.17	1439.99	1194.03	1051.57	960.67	899.02	855.48	823.84	800.36	782.66	769.18	758.81	750.78
38000	3582.24	1997.75	1478.91	1226.30	1079.99	986.63	923.32	878.60	846.10	821.99	803.82	789.97	779.31	771.07
39000	3676.51	2050.32	1517.83	1258.57	1108.41	1012.59	947.62	901.73	868.37	843.62	824.97	810.75	799.82	791.36
40000	3770.78	2102.89	1556.75	1290.85	1136.84	1038.56	971.92	924.85	890.64	865.25	846.12	831.54	820.33	811.65
41000	3865.05	2155.46	1595.66	1323.12	1165.26	1064.52	996.21	947.97	912.90	886.88	867.28	852.33	840.84	831.94
42000	3959.32	2208.03	1634.58	1355.39	1193.68	1090.48	1020.51	971.09	935.17	908.51	888.43	873.12	861.35	852.23
43000	4053.59	2260.61	1673.50	1387.66	1222.10	1116.45	1044.81	994.21	957.43	930.14	909.58	893.91	881.85	872.52
44000	4147.86	2313.18	1712.42	1419.93	1250.52	1142.41	1069.11	1017.33	979.70	951.78	930.73	914.70	902.36	892.82
45000	4242.13	2365.75	1751.34	1452.20	1278.94	1168.38	1093.40	1040.45	1001.96	973.41	951.89	935.48	922.87	913.11
46000	4336.40	2418.32	1790.26	1484.47	1307.36	1194.34	1117.70	1063.57	1024.23	995.04	973.04	956.27	943.38	933.40
47000	4430.67	2470.89	1829.18	1516.74	1335.78	1220.30	1142.00	1086.69	1046.50	1016.67	994.19	977.06	963.89	953.69
48000	4524.94	2523.47	1868.09	1549.01	1364.20	1246.27	1166.30	1109.81	1068.76	1038.30	1015.35	997.85	984.40	973.98
49000	4619.21	2576.04	1907.01	1581.29	1392.62	1272.23	1190.60	1132.94	1091.03	1059.93	1036.50	1018.64	1004.90	994.27
50000	4713.48	2628.61	1945.93	1613.56	1421.04	1298.19	1214.89	1156.06	1113.29	1081.56	1057.65	1039.43	1025.41	1014.56
55000	5184.83	2891.47	2140.52	1774.91	1563.15	1428.01	1336.38	1271.66	1224.62	1189.72	1163.42	1143.37	1127.95	1116.02
60000	5656.17	3154.33	2335.12	1936.27	1705.25	1557.83	1457.87	1387.27	1335.95	1297.87	1269.18	1247.31	1230.49	1217.47
65000	6127.52	3417.19	2529.71	2097.62	1847.35	1687.65	1579.36	1502.87	1447.28	1406.03	1374.95	1351.25	1333.03	1318.93
70000	6598.87	3680.05	2724.30	2258.98	1989.46	1817.47	1700.85	1618.48	1558.61	1514.18	1480.71	1455.20	1435.57	1420.38
75000	7070.22	3942.91	2918.89	2420.33	2131.56	1947.29	1822.34	1734.08	1669.94	1622.34	1586.48	1559.14	1538.12	1521.84
80000	7541.56	4205.77	3113.49	2581.69	2273.67	2077.11	1943.83	1849.69	1781.27	1730.50	1692.24	1663.08	1640.66	1623.30
85000	8012.91	4468.63	3308.08	2743.04	2415.77	2206.93	2065.32	1965.29	1892.60	1838.65	1798.00	1767.02	1743.20	1724.75
90000	8484.26	4731.49	3502.67	2904.40	2557.87	2336.75	2186.80	2080.90	2003.92	1946.81	1903.77	1870.96	1845.74	1826.21
95000	8955.61	4994.36	3697.26	3065.75	2699.98	2466.57	2308.29	2196.50	2115.25	2054.96	2009.53	1974.91	1948.28	1927.66
100000	9426.95	5257.22	3891.86	3227.11	2842.08	2596.38	2429.78	2312.11	2226.58	2163.12	2115.30	2078.85	2050.82	2029.12

TERM	15 Years	16 Years	17 Years	18 Years	19 Years	20 Years	21 Years	22 Years	23 Years	24 Years	25 Years	30 Years	35 Years	40 Years
AMOUNT														
5	.11	.10	.10	.10	.10	.10	.10	.10	.10	.10	.10	.10	.10	.10
10	.21	.20	.20	.20	.20	.20	.20	.20	.20	.20	.20	.20	.20	.20
15	.31	.30	.30	.30	.30	.30	.30	.30	.30	.30	.30	.30	.30	.30
25	.51	.50	.50	.50	.50	.50	.50	.50	.49	.49	.49	.49	.49	.49
50	1.01	1.00	1.00	1.00	.99	.99	.99	.99	.98	.98	.98	.98	.98	.98
75	1.51	1.50	1.50	1.49	1.49	1.48	1.48	1.48	1.47	1.47	1.47	1.47	1.47	1.47
100	2.02	2.00	1.99	1.99	1.98	1.97	1.97	1.97	1.96	1.96	1.96	1.96	1.96	1.96
200	4.03	4.00	3.98	3.97	3.95	3.94	3.94	3.93	3.92	3.92	3.92	3.91	3.91	3.91
300	6.04	6.00	5.97	5.95	5.93	5.91	5.90	5.89	5.88	5.88	5.87	5.86	5.86	5.86
400	8.05	8.00	7.96	7.93	7.90	7.88	7.87	7.85	7.84	7.84	7.83	7.81	7.81	7.81
500	10.07	10.00	9.95	9.91	9.88	9.85	9.83	9.81	9.80	9.79	9.78	9.76	9.76	9.76
600	12.08	12.00	11.94	11.89	11.85	11.82	11.80	11.78	11.76	11.75	11.74	11.72	11.71	11.71
700	14.09	14.00	13.93	13.87	13.82	13.79	13.76	13.74	13.72	13.71	13.70	13.67	13.66	13.66
800	16.10	16.00	15.91	15.85	15.80	15.76	15.73	15.70	15.68	15.67	15.65	15.62	15.61	15.61
900	18.12	18.00	17.90	17.83	17.77	17.73	17.69	17.66	17.64	17.62	17.61	17.57	17.56	17.56
1000	20.13	20.00	19.89	19.81	19.75	19.70	19.66	19.62	19.60	19.58	19.56	19.52	19.51	19.51
2000	40.25	39.99	39.78	39.62	39.49	39.39	39.31	39.24	39.19	39.16	39.12	39.04	39.02	39.01
3000	60.37	59.98	59.67	59.42	59.23	59.08	58.96	58.86	58.79	58.73	58.68	58.56	58.52	58.51
4000	80.49	79.97	79.55	79.23	78.97	78.77	78.61	78.48	78.38	78.31	78.24	78.08	78.03	78.01
5000	100.62	99.96	99.44	99.03	98.71	98.46	98.26	98.10	97.98	97.88	97.80	97.60	97.53	97.51
6000	120.74	119.95	119.33	118.84	118.45	118.15	117.91	117.72	117.57	117.46	117.36	117.12	117.04	117.02
7000	140.86	139.94	139.21	138.64	138.20	137.84	137.56	137.34	137.17	137.03	136.92	136.64	136.55	136.52
8000	160.98	159.93	159.10	158.45	157.94	157.53	157.22	156.96	156.76	156.61	156.48	156.15	156.05	156.02
9000	181.11	179.92	178.99	178.26	177.68	177.23	176.87	176.58	176.36	176.18	176.04	175.67	175.56	175.52
10000	201.23	199.91	198.87	198.06	197.42	196.92	196.52	196.20	195.95	195.76	195.60	195.19	195.06	195.02
11000	221.35	219.90	218.76	217.87	217.16	216.61	216.17	215.82	215.55	215.33	215.16	214.71	214.57	214.53
12000	241.47	239.89	238.65	237.67	236.90	236.30	235.82	235.44	235.14	234.91	234.72	234.23	234.08	234.03
13000	261.59	259.88	258.53	257.48	256.65	255.99	255.47	255.06	254.74	254.48	254.28	253.75	253.58	253.53
14000	281.72	279.87	278.42	277.28	276.39	275.68	275.12	274.68	274.33	274.06	273.84	273.27	273.09	273.03
15000	301.84	299.86	298.31	297.09	296.13	295.37	294.77	294.30	293.93	293.63	293.40	292.78	292.59	292.53
16000	321.96	319.85	318.20	316.89	315.87	315.06	314.43	313.92	313.52	313.21	312.96	312.30	312.10	312.03
17000	342.08	339.84	338.08	336.70	335.61	334.75	334.08	333.54	333.12	332.78	332.52	331.82	331.60	331.54
18000	362.21	359.83	357.97	356.51	355.35	354.45	353.73	353.16	352.71	352.36	352.08	351.34	351.11	351.04
19000	382.33	379.82	377.86	376.31	375.10	374.14	373.38	372.78	372.31	371.93	371.64	370.86	370.62	370.54
20000	402.45	399.81	397.74	396.12	394.84	393.83	393.03	392.40	391.90	391.51	391.20	390.38	390.12	390.04
21000	422.57	419.80	417.63	415.92	414.58	413.52	412.68	412.02	411.50	411.08	410.76	409.90	409.63	409.54
22000	442.69	439.79	437.52	435.73	434.32	433.21	432.33	431.64	431.09	430.66	430.32	429.42	429.13	429.05
23000	462.82	459.78	457.40	455.53	454.06	452.90	451.98	451.26	450.69	450.23	449.88	448.93	448.64	448.55
24000	482.94	479.77	477.29	475.34	473.80	472.59	471.64	470.88	470.28	469.81	469.44	468.45	468.15	468.05
25000	503.06	499.76	497.18	495.14	493.54	492.28	491.29	490.50	489.88	489.38	488.99	487.97	487.65	487.55
26000	523.18	519.75	517.06	514.95	513.29	511.97	510.94	510.12	509.47	508.96	508.55	507.49	507.16	507.05
27000	543.31	539.74	536.95	534.76	533.03	531.67	530.59	529.74	529.07	528.54	528.11	527.01	526.66	526.55
28000	563.43	559.73	556.84	554.56	552.77	551.36	550.24	549.36	548.66	548.11	547.67	546.53	546.17	546.06
29000	583.55	579.72	576.72	574.37	572.51	571.05	569.89	568.98	568.26	567.69	567.23	566.05	565.67	565.56
30000	603.67	599.71	596.61	594.17	592.25	590.74	589.54	588.60	587.85	587.26	586.79	585.56	585.18	585.06
31000	623.80	619.70	616.50	613.98	611.99	610.43	609.19	608.22	607.45	606.84	606.35	605.08	604.69	604.56
32000	643.92	639.69	636.39	633.78	631.74	630.12	628.85	627.84	627.04	626.41	625.91	624.60	624.19	624.06
33000	664.04	659.69	656.27	653.59	651.48	649.81	648.50	647.46	646.64	645.99	645.47	644.12	643.70	643.57
34000	684.16	679.68	676.16	673.40	671.22	669.50	668.15	667.08	666.23	665.56	665.03	663.64	663.20	663.07
35000	704.28	699.67	696.05	693.20	690.96	689.19	687.80	686.70	685.83	685.14	684.59	683.16	682.71	682.57
36000	724.41	719.66	715.93	713.01	710.70	708.89	707.45	706.32	705.42	704.71	704.15	702.68	702.22	702.07
37000	744.53	739.65	735.82	732.81	730.44	728.58	727.10	725.94	725.02	724.29	723.71	722.20	721.72	721.57
38000	764.65	759.64	755.71	752.62	750.19	748.27	746.75	745.56	744.61	743.86	743.27	741.71	741.23	741.07
39000	784.77	779.63	775.59	772.42	769.93	767.96	766.41	765.18	764.21	763.44	762.83	761.23	760.73	760.58
40000	804.90	799.62	795.48	792.23	789.67	787.65	786.06	784.80	783.80	783.01	782.39	780.75	780.24	780.08
41000	825.02	819.61	815.37	812.03	809.41	807.34	805.71	804.42	803.40	802.59	801.95	800.27	799.75	799.58
42000	845.14	839.60	835.25	831.84	829.15	827.03	825.36	824.04	822.99	822.16	821.51	819.79	819.25	819.08
43000	865.26	859.59	855.14	851.65	848.89	846.72	845.01	843.66	842.59	841.74	841.07	839.31	838.76	838.58
44000	885.38	879.58	875.03	871.45	868.64	866.41	864.66	863.28	862.18	861.31	860.63	858.83	858.26	858.09
45000	905.51	899.57	894.91	891.26	888.38	886.11	884.31	882.90	881.78	880.89	880.19	878.34	877.77	877.59
46000	925.63	919.56	914.80	911.06	908.12	905.80	903.96	902.52	901.37	900.46	899.75	897.86	897.27	897.09
47000	945.75	939.55	934.69	930.87	927.86	925.49	923.62	922.14	920.97	920.04	919.31	917.38	916.78	916.59
48000	965.87	959.54	954.58	950.67	947.60	945.18	943.27	941.76	940.56	939.61	938.87	936.90	936.29	936.09
49000	986.00	979.53	974.46	970.48	967.34	964.87	962.92	961.38	960.16	959.19	958.43	956.42	955.79	955.60
50000	1006.12	999.52	994.35	990.28	987.08	984.56	982.57	981.00	979.75	978.76	977.98	975.94	975.30	975.10
55000	1106.73	1099.47	1093.78	1089.31	1085.79	1083.02	1080.83	1079.09	1077.72	1076.64	1075.78	1073.53	1072.83	1072.61
60000	1207.34	1199.42	1193.22	1188.34	1184.50	1181.47	1179.08	1177.19	1175.70	1174.52	1173.58	1171.12	1170.36	1170.12
65000	1307.95	1299.38	1292.65	1287.37	1283.21	1279.93	1277.34	1275.29	1273.67	1272.39	1271.38	1268.72	1267.89	1267.62
70000	1408.56	1399.33	1392.09	1386.40	1381.92	1378.38	1375.60	1373.39	1371.65	1370.27	1369.18	1366.31	1365.41	1365.13
75000	1509.17	1499.28	1491.52	1485.42	1480.62	1476.84	1473.85	1471.49	1469.62	1468.14	1466.97	1463.90	1462.94	1462.64
80000	1609.79	1599.23	1590.96	1584.45	1579.33	1575.30	1572.11	1569.59	1567.60	1566.02	1564.77	1561.50	1560.47	1560.15
85000	1710.40	1699.18	1690.39	1683.48	1678.04	1673.75	1670.36	1667.69	1665.57	1663.90	1662.57	1659.09	1658.00	1657.66
90000	1811.01	1799.13	1789.82	1782.51	1776.75	1772.21	1768.62	1765.79	1763.55	1761.77	1760.37	1756.68	1755.53	1755.17
95000	1911.62	1899.08	1889.26	1881.54	1875.46	1870.66	1866.88	1863.89	1861.52	1859.65	1858.17	1854.28	1853.06	1852.68
100000	2012.23	1999.04	1988.69	1980.56	1974.16	1969.12	1965.13	1961.99	1959.50	1957.52	1955.96	1951.87	1950.59	1950.19

MONTHLY PAYMENT
REQUIRED TO AMORTIZE A LOAN

TERM AMOUNT	1 Year	2 Years	3 Years	4 Years	5 Years	6 Years	7 Years	8 Years	9 Years	10 Years	11 Years	12 Years	13 Years	14 Years
5	.48	.27	.20	.17	.15	.14	.13	.12	.12	.11	.11	.11	.11	.11
10	.95	.53	.39	.33	.29	.27	.25	.24	.23	.22	.22	.21	.21	.21
15	1.42	.79	.59	.49	.43	.40	.37	.35	.34	.33	.32	.32	.31	.31
25	2.36	1.32	.98	.81	.72	.66	.61	.58	.56	.55	.54	.53	.52	.51
50	4.72	2.64	1.95	1.62	1.43	1.31	1.22	1.16	1.12	1.09	1.07	1.05	1.03	1.02
75	7.08	3.95	2.93	2.43	2.14	1.96	1.83	1.74	1.68	1.63	1.60	1.57	1.55	1.53
100	9.44	5.27	3.90	3.24	2.85	2.61	2.44	2.32	2.24	2.18	2.13	2.09	2.06	2.04
200	18.87	10.53	7.80	6.47	5.70	5.21	4.88	4.64	4.47	4.35	4.25	4.18	4.12	4.08
300	28.30	15.79	11.70	9.70	8.55	7.81	7.31	6.96	6.70	6.52	6.37	6.26	6.18	6.11
400	37.73	21.05	15.59	12.94	11.40	10.41	9.75	9.28	8.94	8.69	8.49	8.35	8.24	8.15
500	47.16	26.32	19.49	16.17	14.24	13.02	12.19	11.60	11.17	10.86	10.62	10.44	10.30	10.19
600	56.60	31.58	23.39	19.40	17.09	15.62	14.62	13.92	13.40	13.03	12.74	12.52	12.35	12.22
700	66.03	36.84	27.28	22.63	19.94	18.22	17.06	16.24	15.64	15.20	14.86	14.61	14.41	14.26
800	75.46	42.10	31.18	25.87	22.79	20.82	19.49	18.55	17.87	17.37	16.98	16.69	16.47	16.30
900	84.89	47.36	35.08	29.10	25.64	23.43	21.93	20.87	20.10	19.54	19.11	18.78	18.53	18.33
1000	94.32	52.63	38.98	32.33	28.48	26.03	24.37	23.19	22.34	21.71	21.23	20.87	20.59	20.37
2000	188.64	105.25	77.95	64.66	56.96	52.05	48.73	46.38	44.67	43.41	42.45	41.73	41.17	40.74
3000	282.96	157.87	116.92	96.98	85.44	78.08	73.09	69.56	67.00	65.11	63.68	62.59	61.75	61.10
4000	377.28	210.49	155.89	129.31	113.92	104.10	97.45	92.75	89.34	86.81	84.90	83.45	82.33	81.47
5000	471.59	263.11	194.86	161.64	142.40	130.13	121.81	115.94	111.67	108.51	106.13	104.31	102.92	101.84
6000	565.91	315.74	233.83	193.96	170.88	156.15	146.17	139.12	134.00	130.21	127.35	125.17	123.50	122.20
7000	660.23	368.36	272.80	226.29	199.35	182.17	170.53	162.31	156.34	151.91	148.57	146.03	144.08	142.57
8000	754.55	420.98	311.77	258.61	227.83	208.20	194.89	185.49	178.67	173.61	169.80	166.89	164.66	162.94
9000	848.87	473.60	350.74	290.94	256.31	234.22	219.25	208.68	201.00	195.31	191.02	187.76	185.25	183.30
10000	943.18	526.22	389.71	323.27	284.79	260.25	243.61	231.87	223.34	217.01	212.25	208.62	205.83	203.67
11000	1037.50	578.85	428.68	355.59	313.27	286.27	267.97	255.05	245.67	238.71	233.47	229.48	226.41	224.04
12000	1131.82	631.47	467.65	387.92	341.75	312.29	292.33	278.24	268.00	260.41	254.69	250.34	246.99	244.40
13000	1226.14	684.09	506.63	420.24	370.23	338.32	316.69	301.43	290.34	282.11	275.92	271.20	267.57	264.77
14000	1320.45	736.71	545.60	452.57	398.70	364.34	341.05	324.61	312.67	303.81	297.14	292.06	288.16	285.14
15000	1414.77	789.33	584.57	484.90	427.18	390.37	365.41	347.80	335.00	325.51	318.37	312.92	308.74	305.50
16000	1509.09	841.95	623.54	517.22	455.66	416.39	389.77	370.98	357.33	347.21	339.59	333.78	329.32	325.87
17000	1603.41	894.58	662.51	549.55	484.14	442.42	414.14	394.17	379.67	368.91	360.81	354.64	349.90	346.24
18000	1697.73	947.20	701.48	581.87	512.62	468.44	438.50	417.36	402.00	390.61	382.04	375.51	370.49	366.60
19000	1792.04	999.82	740.45	614.20	541.10	494.46	462.86	440.54	424.33	412.31	403.26	396.37	391.07	386.97
20000	1886.36	1052.44	779.42	646.53	569.57	520.49	487.22	463.73	446.67	434.01	424.49	417.23	411.65	407.34
21000	1980.68	1105.06	818.39	678.85	598.05	546.51	511.58	486.92	469.00	455.71	445.71	438.09	432.23	427.70
22000	2075.00	1157.69	857.36	711.18	626.53	572.54	535.94	510.10	491.33	477.41	466.93	458.95	452.82	448.07
23000	2169.31	1210.31	896.33	743.50	655.01	598.56	560.30	533.29	513.67	499.11	488.16	479.81	473.40	468.44
24000	2263.63	1262.93	935.30	775.83	683.49	624.58	584.66	556.47	536.00	520.82	509.38	500.67	493.98	488.80
25000	2357.95	1315.55	974.28	808.16	711.97	650.61	609.02	579.66	558.33	542.52	530.61	521.53	514.56	509.17
26000	2452.27	1368.17	1013.25	840.48	740.45	676.63	633.38	602.85	580.67	564.22	551.83	542.39	535.14	529.54
27000	2546.59	1420.80	1052.22	872.81	768.92	702.66	657.74	626.03	603.00	585.92	573.05	563.26	555.73	549.90
28000	2640.90	1473.42	1091.19	905.13	797.40	728.68	682.10	649.22	625.33	607.62	594.28	584.12	576.31	570.27
29000	2735.22	1526.04	1130.16	937.46	825.88	754.70	706.46	672.40	647.66	629.32	615.50	604.98	596.89	590.64
30000	2829.54	1578.66	1169.13	969.79	854.36	780.73	730.82	695.59	670.00	651.02	636.73	625.84	617.47	611.00
31000	2923.86	1631.28	1208.10	1002.11	882.84	806.75	755.18	718.78	692.33	672.72	657.95	646.70	638.06	631.37
32000	3018.17	1683.90	1247.07	1034.44	911.32	832.78	779.54	741.96	714.66	694.42	679.17	667.56	658.64	651.74
33000	3112.49	1736.53	1286.04	1066.76	939.79	858.80	803.90	765.15	737.00	716.12	700.40	688.42	679.22	672.10
34000	3206.81	1789.15	1325.01	1099.09	968.27	884.83	828.27	788.34	759.33	737.82	721.62	709.28	699.80	692.47
35000	3301.13	1841.77	1363.98	1131.42	996.75	910.85	852.63	811.52	781.66	759.52	742.85	730.14	720.39	712.84
36000	3395.45	1894.39	1402.95	1163.74	1025.23	936.87	876.99	834.71	804.00	781.22	764.07	751.01	740.97	733.20
37000	3489.76	1947.01	1441.92	1196.07	1053.71	962.90	901.35	857.89	826.33	802.92	785.29	771.87	761.55	753.57
38000	3584.08	1999.64	1480.90	1228.39	1082.19	988.92	925.71	881.08	848.66	824.62	806.52	792.73	782.13	773.94
39000	3678.40	2052.26	1519.87	1260.72	1110.67	1014.95	950.07	904.27	871.00	846.32	827.74	813.59	802.71	794.30
40000	3772.72	2104.88	1558.84	1293.05	1139.14	1040.97	974.43	927.45	893.33	868.02	848.97	834.45	823.30	814.67
41000	3867.03	2157.50	1597.81	1325.37	1167.62	1066.99	998.79	950.64	915.66	889.72	870.19	855.31	843.88	835.03
42000	3961.35	2210.12	1636.78	1357.70	1196.10	1093.02	1023.15	973.83	937.99	911.42	891.41	876.17	864.46	855.40
43000	4055.67	2262.75	1675.75	1390.02	1224.58	1119.04	1047.51	997.01	960.33	933.12	912.64	897.03	885.04	875.77
44000	4149.99	2315.37	1714.72	1422.35	1253.06	1145.07	1071.87	1020.20	982.66	954.82	933.86	917.90	905.63	896.13
45000	4244.31	2367.99	1753.69	1454.68	1281.54	1171.09	1096.23	1043.38	1004.99	976.52	955.09	938.76	926.21	916.50
46000	4338.62	2420.61	1792.66	1487.00	1310.02	1197.12	1120.59	1066.57	1027.33	998.22	976.31	959.62	946.79	936.87
47000	4432.94	2473.23	1831.63	1519.33	1338.49	1223.14	1144.95	1089.76	1049.66	1019.93	997.53	980.48	967.37	957.23
48000	4527.26	2525.85	1870.60	1551.65	1366.97	1249.16	1169.31	1112.94	1071.99	1041.63	1018.76	1001.34	987.96	977.60
49000	4621.58	2578.48	1909.57	1583.98	1395.45	1275.19	1193.67	1136.13	1094.33	1063.33	1039.98	1022.20	1008.54	997.97
50000	4715.89	2631.10	1948.55	1616.31	1423.93	1301.21	1218.03	1159.31	1116.66	1085.03	1061.21	1043.06	1029.12	1018.33
55000	5187.48	2894.21	2143.40	1777.94	1566.32	1431.33	1339.84	1275.25	1228.32	1193.53	1167.33	1147.37	1132.03	1120.17
60000	5659.07	3157.32	2338.25	1939.57	1708.71	1561.45	1461.64	1391.18	1339.99	1302.03	1273.45	1251.67	1234.94	1222.00
65000	6130.66	3420.43	2533.11	2101.20	1851.11	1691.57	1583.45	1507.11	1451.66	1410.53	1379.57	1355.98	1337.85	1323.83
70000	6602.25	3683.54	2727.96	2262.83	1993.50	1821.69	1705.25	1623.04	1563.32	1519.04	1485.69	1460.28	1440.77	1425.67
75000	7073.84	3946.65	2922.82	2424.46	2135.89	1951.82	1827.05	1738.97	1674.99	1627.54	1591.81	1564.59	1543.68	1527.50
80000	7545.43	4209.75	3117.67	2586.09	2278.28	2081.94	1948.85	1854.90	1786.65	1736.04	1697.93	1668.90	1646.59	1629.33
85000	8017.02	4472.86	3312.52	2747.72	2420.68	2212.06	2070.66	1970.83	1898.32	1844.54	1804.05	1773.20	1749.50	1731.16
90000	8488.61	4735.97	3507.38	2909.35	2563.07	2342.18	2192.46	2086.76	2009.98	1953.04	1910.17	1877.51	1852.41	1833.00
95000	8960.20	4999.08	3702.23	3070.98	2705.46	2472.30	2314.26	2202.69	2121.65	2061.55	2016.29	1981.81	1955.32	1934.83
100000	9431.78	5262.19	3897.09	3232.61	2847.85	2602.42	2436.06	2318.62	2233.31	2170.05	2122.41	2086.12	2058.23	2036.66

TERM	15 Years	16 Years	17 Years	18 Years	19 Years	20 Years	21 Years	22 Years	23 Years	24 Years	25 Years	30 Years	35 Years	40 Years
AMOUNT														
5	.11	.11	.10	.10	.10	.10	.10	.10	.10	.10	.10	.10	.10	.10
10	.21	.21	.20	.20	.20	.20	.20	.20	.20	.20	.20	.20	.20	.20
15	.31	.31	.30	.30	.30	.30	.30	.30	.30	.30	.30	.30	.30	.30
25	.51	.51	.50	.50	.50	.50	.50	.50	.50	.50	.50	.50	.49	.49
50	1.01	1.01	1.00	1.00	1.00	.99	.99	.99	.99	.99	.99	.99	.98	.98
75	1.52	1.51	1.50	1.50	1.49	1.49	1.48	1.48	1.48	1.48	1.48	1.48	1.47	1.47
100	2.02	2.01	2.00	1.99	1.99	1.98	1.98	1.98	1.97	1.97	1.97	1.97	1.96	1.96
200	4.04	4.02	4.00	3.98	3.97	3.96	3.95	3.95	3.94	3.94	3.93	3.93	3.92	3.92
300	6.06	6.03	5.99	5.97	5.95	5.94	5.92	5.92	5.91	5.90	5.90	5.89	5.88	5.88
400	8.08	8.03	7.99	7.96	7.93	7.91	7.90	7.89	7.88	7.87	7.86	7.85	7.84	7.84
500	10.10	10.04	9.99	9.95	9.92	9.89	9.87	9.86	9.84	9.83	9.83	9.81	9.80	9.80
600	12.12	12.05	11.98	11.94	11.90	11.87	11.84	11.83	11.81	11.80	11.79	11.77	11.76	11.76
700	14.14	14.05	13.98	13.92	13.88	13.85	13.82	13.80	13.78	13.76	13.75	13.73	13.72	13.71
800	16.16	16.06	15.98	15.91	15.86	15.82	15.79	15.77	15.75	15.73	15.72	15.69	15.68	15.67
900	18.18	18.07	17.97	17.90	17.84	17.80	17.76	17.74	17.71	17.70	17.68	17.65	17.64	17.63
1000	20.20	20.07	19.97	19.89	19.83	19.78	19.74	19.71	19.68	19.66	19.65	19.61	19.59	19.59
2000	40.40	40.14	39.94	39.77	39.65	39.55	39.47	39.41	39.36	39.32	39.29	39.21	39.18	39.18
3000	60.60	60.21	59.90	59.66	59.47	59.32	59.20	59.11	59.03	58.98	58.93	58.81	58.77	58.76
4000	80.80	80.28	79.87	79.54	79.29	79.09	78.93	78.81	78.71	78.63	78.57	78.41	78.36	78.35
5000	101.00	100.34	99.83	99.43	99.11	98.86	98.67	98.51	98.39	98.29	98.21	98.01	97.95	97.93
6000	121.20	120.41	119.80	119.31	118.93	118.63	118.40	118.21	118.06	117.95	117.86	117.61	117.54	117.52
7000	141.40	140.48	139.76	139.20	138.76	138.41	138.13	137.91	137.74	137.60	137.50	137.22	137.13	137.10
8000	161.60	160.55	159.73	159.08	158.58	158.18	157.86	157.61	157.42	157.26	157.14	156.82	156.72	156.69
9000	181.79	180.62	179.69	178.97	178.40	177.95	177.59	177.31	177.09	176.92	176.78	176.42	176.31	176.27
10000	201.99	200.68	199.66	198.85	198.22	197.72	197.33	197.02	196.77	196.58	196.42	196.02	195.90	195.86
11000	222.19	220.75	219.62	218.74	218.04	217.49	217.06	216.72	216.45	216.23	216.06	215.62	215.48	215.44
12000	242.39	240.82	239.59	238.62	237.86	237.26	236.79	236.42	236.12	235.89	235.71	235.22	235.07	235.03
13000	262.59	260.89	259.55	258.51	257.68	257.03	256.52	256.12	255.80	255.55	255.35	254.82	254.66	254.61
14000	282.79	280.96	279.52	278.39	277.51	276.81	276.26	275.82	275.48	275.20	274.99	274.43	274.25	274.20
15000	302.99	301.02	299.48	298.28	297.33	296.58	295.99	295.52	295.15	294.86	294.63	294.03	293.84	293.78
16000	323.19	321.09	319.45	318.16	317.15	316.35	315.72	315.22	314.83	314.52	314.27	313.63	313.43	313.37
17000	343.39	341.16	339.42	338.05	336.97	336.12	335.45	334.92	334.51	334.18	333.91	333.23	333.02	332.95
18000	363.58	361.23	359.38	357.93	356.79	355.89	355.18	354.62	354.18	353.83	353.56	352.83	352.61	352.54
19000	383.78	381.29	379.35	377.82	376.61	375.66	374.92	374.33	373.86	373.49	373.20	372.43	372.20	372.12
20000	403.98	401.36	399.31	397.70	396.43	395.44	394.65	394.03	393.54	393.15	392.84	392.04	391.79	391.71
21000	424.18	421.43	419.28	417.59	416.26	415.21	414.38	413.73	413.21	412.80	412.48	411.64	411.37	411.29
22000	444.38	441.50	439.24	437.47	436.00	434.90	434.11	433.43	432.89	432.46	432.12	431.24	430.96	430.88
23000	464.58	461.57	459.21	457.35	455.90	454.75	453.84	453.13	452.56	452.12	451.76	450.84	450.55	450.46
24000	484.78	481.63	479.17	477.24	475.72	474.52	473.58	472.83	472.24	471.78	471.41	470.44	470.14	470.05
25000	504.98	501.70	499.14	497.12	495.54	494.29	493.31	492.53	491.92	491.43	491.05	490.04	489.73	489.63
26000	525.17	521.77	519.10	517.01	515.36	514.06	513.04	512.23	511.59	511.09	510.69	509.64	509.32	509.22
27000	545.37	541.84	539.07	536.89	535.18	533.84	532.77	531.93	531.27	530.75	530.33	529.25	528.91	528.80
28000	565.57	561.91	559.03	556.78	555.01	553.61	552.51	551.63	550.95	550.40	549.97	548.85	548.50	548.39
29000	585.77	581.97	579.00	576.66	574.83	573.38	572.24	571.34	570.62	570.06	569.61	568.45	568.09	567.97
30000	605.97	602.04	598.96	596.55	594.65	593.15	591.97	591.04	590.30	589.72	589.26	588.05	587.68	587.56
31000	626.17	622.11	618.93	616.43	614.47	612.92	611.70	610.74	609.98	609.37	608.90	607.65	607.26	607.14
32000	646.37	642.18	638.90	636.32	634.29	632.69	631.43	630.44	629.65	629.03	628.54	627.25	626.85	626.73
33000	666.57	662.25	658.86	656.20	654.11	652.47	651.17	650.14	649.33	648.69	648.18	646.86	646.44	646.31
34000	686.77	682.31	678.83	676.09	673.93	672.24	670.90	669.84	669.01	668.35	667.82	666.46	666.03	665.90
35000	706.96	702.38	698.79	695.97	693.76	692.01	690.63	689.54	688.68	688.00	687.47	686.06	685.62	685.48
36000	727.16	722.45	718.76	715.86	713.58	711.78	710.36	709.24	708.36	707.66	707.11	705.66	705.21	705.07
37000	747.36	742.52	738.72	735.74	733.40	731.55	730.09	728.94	728.04	727.32	726.75	725.26	724.80	724.65
38000	767.56	762.58	758.69	755.63	753.22	751.32	749.83	748.65	747.71	746.97	746.39	744.86	744.39	744.24
39000	787.76	782.65	778.65	775.51	773.04	771.09	769.56	768.35	767.39	766.63	766.03	764.46	763.98	763.82
40000	807.96	802.72	798.62	795.40	792.86	790.87	789.29	788.05	787.07	786.29	785.67	784.07	783.57	783.41
41000	828.16	822.79	818.58	815.28	812.68	810.64	809.02	807.75	806.74	805.95	805.32	803.67	803.15	802.99
42000	848.36	842.86	838.55	835.17	832.51	830.41	828.76	827.45	826.42	825.60	824.96	823.27	822.74	822.58
43000	868.56	862.92	858.51	855.05	852.33	850.18	848.49	847.15	846.09	845.26	844.60	842.87	842.33	842.16
44000	888.75	882.99	878.48	874.94	872.15	869.95	868.22	866.85	865.77	864.92	864.24	862.47	861.92	861.75
45000	908.95	903.06	898.44	894.82	891.97	889.72	887.95	886.55	885.45	884.57	883.88	882.07	881.51	881.33
46000	929.15	923.13	918.41	914.70	911.79	909.49	907.68	906.25	905.12	904.23	903.52	901.68	901.10	900.92
47000	949.35	943.20	938.37	934.59	931.61	929.27	927.42	925.96	924.80	923.89	923.17	921.28	920.69	920.51
48000	969.55	963.26	958.34	954.47	951.43	949.04	947.15	945.66	944.48	943.55	942.81	940.88	940.28	940.09
49000	989.75	983.33	978.31	974.36	971.26	968.81	966.88	965.36	964.15	963.20	962.45	960.48	959.87	959.68
50000	1009.95	1003.40	998.27	994.24	991.08	988.58	986.61	985.06	983.83	982.86	982.09	980.08	979.46	979.26
55000	1110.94	1103.74	1098.10	1093.67	1090.18	1087.44	1085.27	1083.56	1082.21	1081.14	1080.30	1078.09	1077.40	1077.19
60000	1211.94	1204.08	1197.92	1193.09	1189.29	1186.30	1183.93	1182.07	1180.60	1179.43	1178.51	1176.10	1175.35	1175.11
65000	1312.93	1304.42	1297.75	1292.52	1288.40	1285.15	1282.59	1280.57	1278.98	1277.72	1276.72	1274.10	1273.29	1273.04
70000	1413.92	1404.76	1397.58	1391.94	1387.51	1384.01	1381.26	1379.08	1377.36	1376.00	1374.93	1372.11	1371.24	1370.96
75000	1514.92	1505.10	1497.40	1491.36	1486.61	1482.87	1479.92	1477.58	1475.74	1474.29	1473.13	1470.12	1469.18	1468.89
80000	1615.91	1605.44	1597.23	1590.79	1585.72	1581.73	1578.58	1576.09	1574.13	1572.57	1571.34	1568.13	1567.13	1566.81
85000	1716.91	1705.78	1697.06	1690.21	1684.83	1680.58	1677.24	1674.60	1672.51	1670.86	1669.55	1666.14	1665.07	1664.74
90000	1817.90	1806.11	1796.88	1789.64	1783.93	1779.44	1775.90	1773.10	1770.89	1769.14	1767.76	1764.14	1763.02	1762.66
95000	1918.90	1906.45	1896.71	1889.06	1883.04	1878.30	1874.56	1871.61	1869.27	1867.43	1865.97	1862.15	1860.96	1860.59
100000	2019.89	2006.79	1996.54	1988.48	1982.15	1977.16	1973.22	1970.11	1967.66	1965.71	1964.18	1960.16	1958.91	1958.52

MONTHLY PAYMENT
REQUIRED TO AMORTIZE A LOAN

TERM AMOUNT	1 Year	2 Years	3 Years	4 Years	5 Years	6 Years	7 Years	8 Years	9 Years	10 Years	11 Years	12 Years	13 Years	14 Years
5	.48	.27	.20	.17	.15	.14	.13	.12	.12	.11	.11	.11	.11	.11
10	.95	.53	.40	.33	.29	.27	.25	.24	.23	.22	.22	.21	.21	.21
15	1.42	.80	.59	.49	.43	.40	.37	.35	.34	.33	.32	.32	.31	.31
25	2.36	1.32	.98	.81	.72	.66	.62	.59	.57	.55	.54	.53	.52	.52
50	4.72	2.64	1.96	1.62	1.43	1.31	1.23	1.17	1.13	1.09	1.07	1.05	1.04	1.03
75	7.08	3.96	2.93	2.43	2.15	1.96	1.84	1.75	1.69	1.64	1.60	1.58	1.55	1.54
100	9.44	5.27	3.91	3.24	2.86	2.61	2.45	2.33	2.25	2.18	2.13	2.10	2.07	2.05
200	18.88	10.54	7.81	6.48	5.71	5.22	4.89	4.66	4.49	4.36	4.26	4.19	4.14	4.09
300	28.31	15.81	11.71	9.72	8.57	7.83	7.33	6.98	6.73	6.54	6.39	6.29	6.20	6.14
400	37.75	21.07	15.61	12.96	11.42	10.44	9.77	9.31	8.97	8.71	8.52	8.38	8.27	8.18
500	47.19	26.34	19.52	16.20	14.27	13.05	12.22	11.63	11.21	10.89	10.65	10.47	10.33	10.23
600	56.62	31.61	23.42	19.43	17.13	15.66	14.66	13.96	13.45	13.07	12.78	12.57	12.40	12.27
700	66.06	36.88	27.32	22.67	19.98	18.26	17.10	16.28	15.69	15.24	14.91	14.66	14.46	14.31
800	75.50	42.14	31.22	25.91	22.83	20.87	19.54	18.61	17.93	17.42	17.04	16.75	16.53	16.36
900	84.93	47.41	35.13	29.15	25.69	23.48	21.99	20.93	20.17	19.60	19.17	18.85	18.60	18.40
1000	94.37	52.68	39.03	32.39	28.54	26.09	24.43	23.26	22.41	21.77	21.30	20.94	20.66	20.45
2000	188.74	105.35	78.05	64.77	57.08	52.17	48.85	46.51	44.81	43.54	42.60	41.87	41.32	40.89
3000	283.10	158.02	117.07	97.15	85.61	78.26	73.28	69.76	67.21	65.31	63.89	62.81	61.97	61.33
4000	377.47	210.69	156.10	129.53	114.15	104.34	97.70	93.01	89.61	87.08	85.19	83.74	82.63	81.77
5000	471.84	263.36	195.12	161.91	142.69	130.43	122.12	116.26	112.01	108.85	106.48	104.67	103.29	102.22
6000	566.20	316.03	234.14	194.29	171.22	156.51	146.55	139.51	134.41	130.62	127.78	125.61	123.94	122.66
7000	660.57	368.71	273.17	226.67	199.76	182.60	170.97	162.77	156.81	152.39	149.07	146.54	144.60	143.10
8000	754.93	421.38	312.19	259.05	228.30	208.68	195.39	186.02	179.21	174.16	170.37	167.48	165.26	163.54
9000	849.30	474.05	351.21	291.43	256.83	234.77	219.82	209.27	201.61	195.93	191.66	188.41	185.91	183.98
10000	943.67	526.72	390.24	323.82	285.37	260.85	244.24	232.52	224.01	217.70	212.96	209.34	206.57	204.43
11000	1038.03	579.39	429.26	356.20	313.90	286.93	268.66	255.77	246.41	239.47	234.25	230.28	227.23	224.87
12000	1132.40	632.06	468.28	388.58	342.44	313.02	293.09	279.02	268.81	261.24	255.55	251.21	247.88	245.31
13000	1226.76	684.74	507.31	420.96	370.98	339.10	317.51	302.27	291.21	283.01	276.84	272.15	268.54	265.75
14000	1321.13	737.41	546.33	453.34	399.51	365.19	341.93	325.53	313.61	304.78	298.14	293.08	289.20	286.19
15000	1415.50	790.08	585.35	485.72	428.05	391.27	366.36	348.78	336.01	326.55	319.43	314.01	309.85	306.64
16000	1509.86	842.75	624.38	518.10	456.59	417.36	390.78	372.03	358.41	348.32	340.73	334.95	330.51	327.08
17000	1604.23	895.42	663.40	550.48	485.12	443.44	415.20	395.28	380.81	370.09	362.02	355.88	351.17	347.52
18000	1698.60	948.09	702.42	582.86	513.66	469.53	439.63	418.53	403.21	391.86	383.32	376.82	371.82	367.96
19000	1792.96	1000.77	741.44	615.25	542.19	495.61	464.05	441.78	425.61	413.63	404.61	397.75	392.48	388.40
20000	1887.33	1053.44	780.47	647.63	570.73	521.70	488.47	465.03	448.01	435.40	425.91	418.68	413.14	408.85
21000	1981.69	1106.11	819.49	680.01	599.27	547.78	512.90	488.29	470.42	457.17	447.20	439.62	433.79	429.29
22000	2076.06	1158.78	858.51	712.39	627.80	573.86	537.32	511.54	492.82	478.94	468.50	460.55	454.45	449.73
23000	2170.43	1211.45	897.54	744.77	656.34	599.95	561.75	534.79	515.22	500.71	489.79	481.49	475.11	470.17
24000	2264.79	1264.12	936.56	777.15	684.88	626.03	586.17	558.04	537.62	522.48	511.09	502.42	495.76	490.62
25000	2359.16	1316.80	975.58	809.53	713.41	652.12	610.59	581.29	560.02	544.25	532.38	523.35	516.42	511.06
26000	2453.52	1369.47	1014.61	841.91	741.95	678.20	635.02	604.54	582.42	566.02	553.68	544.29	537.07	531.50
27000	2547.89	1422.14	1053.63	874.29	770.48	704.29	659.44	627.79	604.82	587.79	574.98	565.22	557.73	551.94
28000	2642.26	1474.81	1092.65	906.68	799.02	730.37	683.86	651.04	627.22	609.56	596.27	586.16	578.39	572.38
29000	2736.62	1527.48	1131.68	939.06	827.56	756.46	708.29	674.30	649.62	631.33	617.57	607.09	599.04	592.83
30000	2830.99	1580.15	1170.70	971.44	856.09	782.54	732.71	697.55	672.02	653.10	638.86	628.02	619.70	613.27
31000	2925.35	1632.83	1209.72	1003.82	884.63	808.63	757.13	720.80	694.42	674.87	660.16	648.96	640.36	633.71
32000	3019.72	1685.50	1248.75	1036.20	913.17	834.71	781.56	744.05	716.82	696.64	681.45	669.89	661.01	654.15
33000	3114.09	1738.17	1287.77	1068.58	941.70	860.79	805.98	767.30	739.22	718.41	702.75	690.82	681.67	674.59
34000	3208.45	1790.84	1326.79	1100.96	970.24	886.88	830.40	790.55	761.62	740.18	724.04	711.76	702.33	695.04
35000	3302.82	1843.51	1365.81	1133.34	998.77	912.96	854.83	813.80	784.02	761.95	745.34	732.69	722.98	715.48
36000	3397.19	1896.18	1404.84	1165.72	1027.31	939.05	879.25	837.06	806.42	783.72	766.63	753.63	743.64	735.92
37000	3491.55	1948.86	1443.86	1198.11	1055.85	965.13	903.67	860.31	828.82	805.49	787.93	774.56	764.30	756.36
38000	3585.92	2001.53	1482.88	1230.49	1084.38	991.22	928.10	883.56	851.22	827.26	809.22	795.49	784.95	776.80
39000	3680.28	2054.20	1521.91	1262.87	1112.92	1017.30	952.52	906.81	873.62	849.03	830.52	816.43	805.61	797.25
40000	3774.65	2106.87	1560.93	1295.25	1141.46	1043.39	976.94	930.06	896.02	870.80	851.81	837.36	826.27	817.69
41000	3869.02	2159.54	1599.95	1327.63	1169.99	1069.47	1001.37	953.31	918.42	892.57	873.11	858.30	846.92	838.13
42000	3963.38	2212.21	1638.98	1360.01	1198.53	1095.56	1025.79	976.56	940.83	914.34	894.40	879.23	867.58	858.57
43000	4057.75	2264.89	1678.00	1392.39	1227.06	1121.64	1050.22	999.82	963.23	936.11	915.70	900.16	888.24	879.02
44000	4152.11	2317.56	1717.02	1424.77	1255.60	1147.72	1074.64	1023.07	985.63	957.88	936.99	921.10	908.89	899.46
45000	4246.48	2370.23	1756.05	1457.15	1284.14	1173.81	1099.06	1046.32	1008.03	979.65	958.29	942.03	929.55	919.90
46000	4340.85	2422.90	1795.07	1489.54	1312.67	1199.89	1123.49	1069.57	1030.43	1001.42	979.58	962.97	950.21	940.34
47000	4435.21	2475.57	1834.09	1521.92	1341.21	1225.98	1147.91	1092.82	1052.83	1023.19	1000.88	983.90	970.86	960.78
48000	4529.58	2528.24	1873.12	1554.30	1369.75	1252.06	1172.33	1116.07	1075.23	1044.96	1022.17	1004.83	991.52	981.23
49000	4623.95	2580.92	1912.14	1586.68	1398.28	1278.15	1196.76	1139.33	1097.63	1066.73	1043.47	1025.77	1012.17	1001.67
50000	4718.31	2633.59	1951.16	1619.06	1426.82	1304.23	1221.18	1162.58	1120.03	1088.50	1064.76	1046.70	1032.83	1022.11
55000	5190.14	2896.95	2146.28	1780.97	1569.50	1434.65	1343.30	1278.83	1232.03	1197.34	1171.24	1151.37	1136.11	1124.32
60000	5661.97	3160.30	2341.39	1942.87	1712.18	1565.08	1465.41	1395.09	1344.03	1306.19	1277.72	1256.04	1239.40	1226.53
65000	6133.80	3423.66	2536.51	2104.78	1854.86	1695.50	1587.53	1511.35	1456.04	1415.04	1384.19	1360.71	1342.68	1328.74
70000	6605.63	3687.02	2731.62	2266.68	1997.54	1825.92	1709.65	1627.61	1568.04	1523.89	1490.67	1465.38	1445.96	1430.95
75000	7077.46	3950.38	2926.74	2428.59	2140.22	1956.35	1831.77	1743.86	1680.04	1632.74	1597.14	1570.05	1549.24	1533.16
80000	7549.30	4213.74	3121.86	2590.49	2282.91	1953.88	1860.12	1792.04	1741.59	1703.62	1674.72	1652.53	1635.37	1635.37
85000	8021.13	4477.10	3316.97	2752.40	2425.59	2217.19	2076.00	1976.38	1904.05	1850.44	1810.10	1779.39	1755.81	1737.58
90000	8492.96	4740.45	3512.09	2914.30	2568.27	2347.61	2198.12	2092.63	2016.05	1959.29	1916.57	1884.06	1859.09	1839.79
95000	8964.79	5003.81	3707.20	3076.21	2710.95	2478.04	2320.24	2208.89	2128.05	2068.14	2023.05	1988.73	1962.38	1942.00
100000	9436.62	5267.17	3902.32	3238.11	2853.63	2608.46	2442.35	2325.15	2240.05	2176.99	2129.52	2093.40	2065.66	2044.21

MONTHLY PAYMENT
REQUIRED TO AMORTIZE A LOAN

23.600%

TERM / AMOUNT	15 Years	16 Years	17 Years	18 Years	19 Years	20 Years	21 Years	22 Years	23 Years	24 Years	25 Years	30 Years	35 Years	40 Years
5	.11	.11	.11	.10	.10	.10	.10	.10	.10	.10	.10	.10	.10	.10
10	.21	.21	.21	.20	.20	.20	.20	.20	.20	.20	.20	.20	.20	.20
15	.31	.31	.31	.30	.30	.30	.30	.30	.30	.30	.30	.30	.30	.30
25	.51	.51	.51	.50	.50	.50	.50	.50	.50	.50	.50	.50	.50	.50
50	1.02	1.01	1.01	1.00	1.00	1.00	1.00	.99	.99	.99	.99	.99	.99	.99
75	1.53	1.52	1.51	1.50	1.50	1.49	1.49	1.49	1.49	1.49	1.48	1.48	1.48	1.48
100	2.03	2.02	2.01	2.00	2.00	1.99	1.99	1.98	1.98	1.98	1.98	1.97	1.97	1.97
200	4.06	4.03	4.01	4.00	3.99	3.98	3.97	3.96	3.96	3.95	3.95	3.94	3.94	3.94
300	6.09	6.05	6.02	5.99	5.98	5.96	5.95	5.94	5.93	5.93	5.92	5.91	5.91	5.91
400	8.12	8.06	8.02	7.99	7.97	7.95	7.93	7.92	7.91	7.90	7.89	7.88	7.87	7.87
500	10.14	10.08	10.03	9.99	9.96	9.93	9.91	9.90	9.88	9.87	9.87	9.85	9.84	9.84
600	12.17	12.09	12.03	11.98	11.95	11.92	11.89	11.87	11.86	11.85	11.84	11.82	11.81	11.81
700	14.20	14.11	14.04	13.98	13.94	13.90	13.87	13.85	13.84	13.82	13.81	13.78	13.78	13.77
800	16.23	16.12	16.04	15.98	15.93	15.89	15.86	15.83	15.81	15.80	15.78	15.75	15.74	15.74
900	18.25	18.14	18.04	17.97	17.92	17.87	17.84	17.81	17.79	17.77	17.76	17.72	17.71	17.71
1000	20.28	20.15	20.05	19.97	19.91	19.86	19.82	19.79	19.76	19.74	19.73	19.69	19.68	19.67
2000	40.56	40.30	40.09	39.93	39.81	39.71	39.63	39.57	39.52	39.48	39.45	39.37	39.35	39.34
3000	60.83	60.44	60.14	59.90	59.71	59.56	59.44	59.35	59.28	59.22	59.18	59.06	59.02	59.01
4000	81.11	80.59	80.18	79.86	79.61	79.41	79.26	79.13	79.04	78.96	78.90	78.74	78.69	78.68
5000	101.38	100.73	100.22	99.83	99.51	99.26	99.07	98.92	98.80	98.70	98.62	98.43	98.37	98.35
6000	121.66	120.88	120.27	119.79	119.41	119.12	118.88	118.70	118.55	118.44	118.35	118.11	118.04	118.02
7000	141.93	141.02	140.31	139.75	139.31	138.97	138.70	138.48	138.31	138.18	138.07	137.80	137.71	137.68
8000	162.21	161.17	160.36	159.72	158.22	158.82	158.51	158.26	158.07	157.92	157.80	157.48	157.38	157.35
9000	182.48	181.31	180.40	179.68	179.12	178.67	178.32	178.05	177.83	177.66	177.52	177.16	177.05	177.02
10000	202.76	201.46	200.44	199.65	199.02	198.52	198.14	197.83	197.59	197.40	197.24	196.85	196.73	196.69
11000	223.04	221.61	220.49	219.61	218.92	218.38	217.95	217.61	217.34	217.13	216.97	216.53	216.40	216.36
12000	243.31	241.75	240.53	239.57	238.82	238.23	237.76	237.39	237.10	236.87	236.69	236.22	236.07	236.03
13000	263.59	261.90	260.57	259.54	258.72	258.08	257.57	257.18	256.86	256.61	256.42	255.90	255.74	255.69
14000	283.86	282.04	280.62	279.50	278.62	277.93	277.39	276.96	276.62	276.35	276.14	275.59	275.42	275.36
15000	304.14	302.19	300.66	299.47	298.52	297.78	297.20	296.74	296.38	296.09	295.86	295.27	295.09	295.03
16000	324.41	322.33	320.71	319.43	318.43	317.64	317.01	316.52	316.14	315.83	315.59	314.96	314.76	314.70
17000	344.69	342.48	340.75	339.39	338.33	337.49	336.83	336.31	335.89	335.57	335.31	334.64	334.43	334.37
18000	364.96	362.62	360.79	359.36	358.23	357.34	356.64	356.09	355.65	355.31	355.03	354.32	354.10	354.04
19000	385.24	382.77	380.84	379.32	378.13	377.19	376.45	375.87	375.41	375.05	374.76	374.01	373.78	373.70
20000	405.51	402.92	400.88	399.29	398.03	397.04	396.27	395.65	395.17	394.79	394.48	393.69	393.45	393.37
21000	425.79	423.06	420.92	419.25	417.93	416.90	416.08	415.43	414.93	414.52	414.21	413.38	413.12	413.04
22000	446.07	443.21	440.97	439.21	437.83	436.75	435.89	435.22	434.68	434.26	433.93	433.06	432.79	432.71
23000	466.34	463.35	461.01	459.18	457.74	456.60	455.71	455.00	454.44	454.00	453.65	452.75	452.47	452.38
24000	486.62	483.50	481.06	479.14	477.64	476.45	475.52	474.78	474.20	473.74	473.38	472.43	472.14	472.05
25000	506.89	503.64	501.10	499.11	497.54	496.30	495.33	494.56	493.96	493.48	493.10	492.12	491.81	491.71
26000	527.17	523.79	521.14	519.07	517.44	516.16	515.14	514.35	513.72	513.22	512.83	511.80	511.48	511.38
27000	547.44	543.93	541.19	539.03	537.34	536.01	534.96	534.13	533.47	532.96	532.55	531.48	531.15	531.05
28000	567.72	564.08	561.23	559.00	557.24	555.86	554.77	553.91	553.23	552.70	552.27	551.17	550.83	550.72
29000	587.99	584.22	581.28	578.96	577.14	575.71	574.58	573.69	572.99	572.44	572.00	570.85	570.50	570.39
30000	608.27	604.37	601.32	598.93	597.04	595.56	594.40	593.48	592.75	592.18	591.72	590.54	590.17	590.06
31000	628.55	624.52	621.36	618.89	616.95	615.42	614.21	613.26	612.51	611.91	611.45	610.22	609.84	609.72
32000	648.82	644.66	641.41	638.85	636.85	635.27	634.02	633.04	632.27	631.65	631.17	629.91	629.51	629.39
33000	669.10	664.81	661.45	658.82	656.75	655.12	653.84	652.82	652.02	651.39	650.89	649.59	649.19	649.06
34000	689.37	684.95	681.49	678.78	676.65	674.97	673.65	672.61	671.78	671.13	670.62	669.28	668.86	668.73
35000	709.65	705.10	701.54	698.75	696.55	694.82	693.46	692.39	691.54	690.87	690.34	688.96	688.53	688.40
36000	729.92	725.24	721.58	718.71	716.45	714.68	713.27	712.17	711.30	710.61	710.06	708.64	708.20	708.07
37000	750.20	745.39	741.63	738.67	736.35	734.53	733.09	731.95	731.06	730.35	729.79	728.33	727.88	727.74
38000	770.47	765.53	761.67	758.64	756.25	754.38	752.90	751.73	750.81	750.09	749.51	748.01	747.55	747.40
39000	790.75	785.68	781.71	778.60	776.16	774.23	772.71	771.52	770.57	769.83	769.24	767.70	767.22	767.07
40000	811.02	805.83	801.76	798.57	796.06	794.08	792.53	791.30	790.33	789.57	788.96	787.38	786.89	786.74
41000	831.30	825.97	821.80	818.53	815.96	813.93	812.34	811.08	810.09	809.30	808.68	807.07	806.56	806.41
42000	851.58	846.12	841.84	838.49	835.86	833.79	832.15	830.86	829.85	829.04	828.41	826.75	826.24	826.08
43000	871.85	866.26	861.89	858.46	855.76	853.64	851.97	850.65	849.60	848.78	848.13	846.43	845.91	845.75
44000	892.13	886.41	881.93	878.42	875.66	873.49	871.78	870.43	869.36	868.52	867.86	866.12	865.58	865.41
45000	912.40	906.55	901.98	898.39	895.56	893.34	891.59	890.21	889.12	888.26	887.58	885.80	885.25	885.08
46000	932.68	926.70	922.02	918.35	915.47	913.19	911.41	909.99	908.88	908.00	907.30	905.49	904.93	904.75
47000	952.95	946.84	942.06	938.31	935.37	933.05	931.22	929.78	928.64	927.73	927.03	925.17	924.60	924.42
48000	973.23	966.99	962.11	958.28	955.27	952.90	951.03	949.56	948.40	947.48	946.75	944.86	944.27	944.09
49000	993.50	987.14	982.15	978.24	975.17	972.75	970.84	969.34	968.15	967.22	966.48	964.54	963.94	963.76
50000	1013.78	1007.28	1002.20	998.21	995.07	992.60	990.66	989.12	987.91	986.96	986.20	984.23	983.61	983.42
55000	1115.16	1108.01	1102.41	1098.03	1094.58	1091.86	1089.72	1088.03	1086.70	1085.65	1084.82	1082.65	1081.97	1081.77
60000	1216.53	1208.74	1202.63	1197.85	1194.08	1191.12	1188.79	1186.95	1185.49	1184.35	1183.44	1181.07	1180.34	1180.11
65000	1317.91	1309.46	1302.85	1297.67	1293.59	1290.38	1287.85	1285.86	1284.28	1283.04	1282.06	1279.49	1278.70	1278.45
70000	1419.29	1410.19	1403.07	1397.49	1393.10	1389.64	1386.92	1384.77	1383.07	1381.74	1380.68	1377.91	1377.06	1376.79
75000	1520.67	1510.92	1503.29	1497.31	1492.60	1488.90	1485.98	1483.68	1481.87	1480.43	1479.30	1476.34	1475.42	1475.13
80000	1622.04	1611.65	1603.51	1597.13	1592.11	1588.16	1585.05	1582.59	1580.66	1579.13	1577.92	1574.76	1573.78	1573.48
85000	1723.42	1712.37	1703.73	1696.95	1691.62	1687.42	1684.11	1681.51	1679.45	1677.82	1676.54	1673.18	1672.14	1671.82
90000	1824.80	1813.10	1803.95	1796.77	1791.12	1786.68	1783.18	1780.42	1778.24	1776.52	1775.15	1771.60	1770.50	1770.16
95000	1926.18	1913.83	1904.17	1896.59	1890.63	1885.94	1882.24	1879.33	1877.03	1875.21	1873.77	1870.02	1868.86	1868.50
100000	2027.55	2014.56	2004.39	1996.41	1990.14	1985.20	1981.31	1978.24	1975.82	1973.91	1972.39	1968.45	1967.22	1966.84

MONTHLY PAYMENT
REQUIRED TO AMORTIZE A LOAN

TERM	1 Year	2 Years	3 Years	4 Years	5 Years	6 Years	7 Years	8 Years	9 Years	10 Years	11 Years	12 Years	13 Years	14 Years
AMOUNT														
5	.48	.27	.20	.17	.15	.14	.13	.12	.12	.11	.11	.11	.11	.11
10	.95	.53	.40	.33	.29	.27	.25	.24	.23	.22	.22	.21	.21	.21
15	1.42	.80	.59	.49	.43	.40	.37	.35	.34	.33	.32	.32	.32	.31
25	2.36	1.32	.98	.81	.72	.66	.62	.59	.57	.55	.54	.53	.52	.52
50	4.72	2.64	1.96	1.62	1.43	1.31	1.23	1.17	1.13	1.09	1.07	1.05	1.04	1.03
75	7.08	3.96	2.93	2.43	2.15	1.96	1.84	1.75	1.69	1.64	1.60	1.58	1.56	1.54
100	9.44	5.27	3.91	3.24	2.86	2.61	2.45	2.33	2.25	2.18	2.14	2.10	2.07	2.05
200	18.88	10.54	7.81	6.48	5.72	5.22	4.89	4.66	4.49	4.36	4.27	4.20	4.14	4.10
300	28.32	15.81	11.72	9.72	8.57	7.83	7.34	6.99	6.73	6.54	6.40	6.29	6.21	6.14
400	37.76	21.08	15.62	12.96	11.43	10.44	9.78	9.31	8.97	8.72	8.53	8.39	8.28	8.19
500	47.19	26.35	19.52	16.20	14.28	13.05	12.22	11.64	11.21	10.90	10.66	10.48	10.34	10.24
600	56.63	31.62	23.43	19.44	17.14	15.66	14.67	13.97	13.46	13.08	12.79	12.58	12.41	12.28
700	66.07	36.88	27.33	22.68	19.99	18.27	17.11	16.29	15.70	15.26	14.92	14.67	14.48	14.33
800	75.51	42.15	31.23	25.92	22.85	20.88	19.56	18.62	17.94	17.43	17.06	16.77	16.55	16.37
900	84.95	47.42	35.14	29.16	25.70	23.49	22.00	20.95	20.18	19.61	19.19	18.86	18.61	18.42
1000	94.38	52.69	39.04	32.40	28.56	26.10	24.44	23.27	22.42	21.79	21.32	20.96	20.68	20.47
2000	188.76	105.37	78.08	64.79	57.11	52.20	48.88	46.54	44.84	43.58	42.63	41.91	41.36	40.93
3000	283.14	158.06	117.11	97.19	85.66	78.30	73.32	69.81	67.26	65.37	63.94	62.86	62.03	61.39
4000	377.52	210.74	156.15	129.58	114.21	104.40	97.76	93.08	89.67	87.15	85.26	83.81	82.71	81.85
5000	471.90	263.43	195.19	161.98	142.76	130.50	122.20	116.34	112.09	108.94	106.57	104.77	103.38	102.31
6000	566.27	316.11	234.22	194.37	171.31	156.60	146.64	139.61	134.51	130.73	127.88	125.72	124.06	122.77
7000	660.65	368.79	273.26	226.77	199.86	182.70	171.08	162.88	156.93	152.52	149.20	146.67	144.73	143.23
8000	755.03	421.48	312.29	259.16	228.41	208.80	195.52	186.15	179.34	174.30	170.51	167.62	165.41	163.69
9000	849.41	474.16	351.33	291.56	256.96	234.90	219.96	209.41	201.76	196.09	191.82	188.57	186.08	184.15
10000	943.79	526.85	390.37	323.95	285.51	261.00	244.40	232.68	224.18	217.88	213.14	209.53	206.76	204.61
11000	1038.17	579.53	429.40	356.35	314.06	287.10	268.84	255.95	246.60	239.66	234.45	230.48	227.43	225.08
12000	1132.54	632.21	468.44	388.74	342.61	313.20	293.28	279.22	269.01	261.45	255.76	251.43	248.11	245.54
13000	1226.92	684.90	507.48	421.14	371.16	339.30	317.71	302.49	291.43	283.24	277.07	272.38	268.78	266.00
14000	1321.30	737.58	546.51	453.53	399.72	365.40	342.15	325.75	313.85	305.03	298.39	293.33	289.46	286.46
15000	1415.68	790.27	585.55	485.93	428.27	391.50	366.59	349.02	336.27	326.81	319.70	314.29	310.13	306.92
16000	1510.06	842.95	624.58	518.32	456.82	417.60	391.03	372.29	358.68	348.60	341.01	335.24	330.81	327.38
17000	1604.43	895.63	663.62	550.72	485.37	443.70	415.47	395.56	381.10	370.39	362.33	356.19	351.48	347.84
18000	1698.81	948.32	702.66	583.11	513.92	469.80	439.91	418.82	403.52	392.17	383.64	377.14	372.16	368.30
19000	1793.19	1001.00	741.69	615.51	542.47	495.90	464.35	442.09	425.93	413.96	404.95	398.10	392.83	388.76
20000	1887.57	1053.69	780.73	647.90	571.02	522.00	488.79	465.36	448.35	435.75	426.27	419.05	413.51	409.22
21000	1981.95	1106.37	819.77	680.30	599.57	548.10	513.23	488.63	470.77	457.54	447.58	440.00	434.18	429.69
22000	2076.33	1159.06	858.80	712.69	628.12	574.20	537.67	511.90	493.19	479.32	468.89	460.95	454.86	450.15
23000	2170.70	1211.74	897.84	745.09	656.67	600.30	562.11	535.16	515.60	501.11	490.20	481.90	475.53	470.61
24000	2265.08	1264.42	936.87	777.48	685.22	626.40	586.55	558.43	538.02	522.90	511.52	502.86	496.21	491.07
25000	2359.46	1317.11	975.91	809.88	713.77	652.50	610.99	581.70	560.44	544.68	532.83	523.81	516.88	511.53
26000	2453.84	1369.79	1014.95	842.27	742.32	678.60	635.42	604.97	582.86	566.47	554.14	544.76	537.56	531.99
27000	2548.22	1422.48	1053.98	874.67	770.87	704.70	659.86	628.23	605.27	588.26	575.46	565.71	558.23	552.45
28000	2642.59	1475.16	1093.02	907.06	799.43	730.80	684.30	651.50	627.69	610.05	596.77	586.66	578.91	572.91
29000	2736.97	1527.84	1132.06	939.46	827.98	756.89	708.74	674.77	650.11	631.83	618.08	607.62	599.58	593.37
30000	2831.35	1580.53	1171.09	971.85	856.53	782.99	733.18	698.04	672.53	653.62	639.40	628.57	620.26	613.83
31000	2925.73	1633.21	1210.13	1004.25	885.08	809.09	757.62	721.31	694.94	675.41	660.71	649.52	640.93	634.30
32000	3020.11	1685.90	1249.16	1036.64	913.63	835.19	782.06	744.57	717.36	697.19	682.02	670.47	661.61	654.76
33000	3114.49	1738.58	1288.20	1069.04	942.18	861.29	806.50	767.84	739.78	718.98	703.33	691.43	682.28	675.22
34000	3208.86	1791.27	1327.24	1101.43	970.73	887.39	830.94	791.11	762.19	740.77	724.65	712.38	702.96	695.68
35000	3303.24	1843.95	1366.27	1133.83	999.28	913.49	855.38	814.38	784.61	762.56	745.96	733.33	723.63	716.14
36000	3397.62	1896.63	1405.31	1166.22	1027.83	939.59	879.82	837.64	807.03	784.34	767.27	754.28	744.31	736.60
37000	3492.00	1949.32	1444.35	1198.62	1056.38	965.69	904.26	860.91	829.45	806.13	788.59	775.23	764.98	757.06
38000	3586.38	2002.00	1483.38	1231.01	1084.93	991.79	928.70	884.18	851.86	827.92	809.90	796.19	785.66	777.52
39000	3680.76	2054.69	1522.42	1263.40	1113.48	1017.89	953.13	907.45	874.28	849.70	831.21	817.14	806.33	797.98
40000	3775.13	2107.37	1561.45	1295.80	1142.03	1043.99	977.57	930.71	896.70	871.49	852.53	838.09	827.01	818.44
41000	3869.51	2160.05	1600.49	1328.19	1170.59	1070.09	1002.01	953.98	919.12	893.28	873.84	859.04	847.68	838.91
42000	3963.89	2212.74	1639.53	1360.59	1199.14	1096.19	1026.45	977.25	941.53	915.07	895.15	879.99	868.36	859.37
43000	4058.27	2265.42	1678.56	1392.98	1227.69	1122.29	1050.89	1000.52	963.95	936.85	916.46	900.95	889.03	879.83
44000	4152.65	2318.11	1717.60	1425.38	1256.24	1148.39	1075.33	1023.79	986.37	958.64	937.78	921.90	909.71	900.29
45000	4247.02	2370.79	1756.64	1457.77	1284.79	1174.49	1099.77	1047.05	1008.79	980.43	959.09	942.85	930.38	920.75
46000	4341.40	2423.47	1795.67	1490.17	1313.34	1200.59	1124.21	1070.32	1031.20	1002.21	980.40	963.80	951.06	941.21
47000	4435.78	2476.16	1834.71	1522.56	1341.89	1226.69	1148.65	1093.59	1053.62	1024.00	1001.72	984.76	971.73	961.67
48000	4530.16	2528.84	1873.74	1554.96	1370.44	1252.79	1173.09	1116.86	1076.04	1045.79	1023.03	1005.71	992.41	982.13
49000	4624.54	2581.53	1912.78	1587.35	1398.99	1278.89	1197.53	1140.12	1098.45	1067.58	1044.34	1026.66	1013.08	1002.59
50000	4718.92	2634.21	1951.82	1619.75	1427.54	1304.99	1221.97	1163.39	1120.87	1089.36	1065.66	1047.61	1033.76	1023.05
55000	5190.81	2897.63	2147.00	1781.72	1570.29	1435.49	1344.16	1279.73	1232.96	1198.30	1172.22	1152.37	1137.14	1125.36
60000	5662.70	3161.05	2342.18	1943.70	1713.05	1565.98	1466.36	1396.07	1345.05	1307.23	1278.79	1257.13	1240.51	1227.66
65000	6134.59	3424.47	2537.36	2105.67	1855.80	1696.48	1588.55	1512.41	1457.13	1416.17	1385.35	1361.89	1343.89	1329.97
70000	6606.48	3687.89	2732.54	2267.65	1998.56	1826.98	1710.75	1628.75	1569.22	1525.11	1491.92	1466.65	1447.26	1432.27
75000	7078.37	3951.31	2927.72	2429.62	2141.31	1957.48	1832.95	1745.09	1681.31	1634.04	1598.48	1571.42	1550.64	1534.58
80000	7550.26	4214.73	3122.90	2591.59	2284.06	2087.98	1955.14	1861.42	1793.39	1742.98	1705.05	1676.18	1654.01	1636.88
85000	8022.15	4478.15	3318.08	2753.57	2426.82	2218.48	2077.34	1977.76	1905.48	1851.91	1811.61	1780.94	1757.39	1739.19
90000	8494.04	4741.58	3513.27	2915.54	2569.57	2349.99	2199.54	2094.10	2017.57	1960.85	1918.18	1885.70	1860.76	1841.49
95000	8965.94	5005.00	3708.45	3077.52	2712.32	2479.47	2321.73	2210.44	2129.65	2069.79	2024.74	1990.46	1964.14	1943.80
100000	9437.83	5268.42	3903.63	3239.49	2855.08	2609.97	2443.93	2326.78	2241.74	2178.72	2131.31	2095.22	2067.51	2046.10

TERM	15 Years	16 Years	17 Years	18 Years	19 Years	20 Years	21 Years	22 Years	23 Years	24 Years	25 Years	30 Years	35 Years	40 Years
AMOUNT														
5	.11	.11	.11	.10	.10	.10	.10	.10	.10	.10	.10	.10	.10	.10
10	.21	.21	.21	.20	.20	.20	.20	.20	.20	.20	.20	.20	.20	.20
15	.31	.31	.31	.30	.30	.30	.30	.30	.30	.30	.30	.30	.30	.30
25	.51	.51	.51	.50	.50	.50	.50	.50	.50	.50	.50	.50	.50	.50
50	1.02	1.01	1.01	1.00	1.00	1.00	1.00	1.00	.99	.99	.99	.99	.99	.99
75	1.53	1.52	1.51	1.50	1.50	1.50	1.49	1.49	1.49	1.49	1.49	1.48	1.48	1.48
100	2.03	2.02	2.01	2.00	2.00	1.99	1.99	1.99	1.98	1.98	1.98	1.98	1.97	1.97
200	4.06	4.04	4.02	4.00	3.99	3.98	3.97	3.97	3.96	3.96	3.95	3.95	3.94	3.94
300	6.09	6.05	6.02	6.00	5.98	5.97	5.95	5.95	5.94	5.93	5.93	5.92	5.91	5.91
400	8.12	8.07	8.03	8.00	7.97	7.95	7.94	7.93	7.92	7.91	7.90	7.89	7.88	7.88
500	10.15	10.09	10.04	10.00	9.97	9.94	9.92	9.91	9.89	9.88	9.88	9.86	9.85	9.85
600	12.18	12.10	12.04	12.00	11.96	11.93	11.90	11.89	11.87	11.86	11.85	11.83	11.82	11.82
700	14.21	14.12	14.05	13.99	13.95	13.92	13.89	13.87	13.85	13.84	13.83	13.80	13.79	13.79
800	16.24	16.14	16.06	15.99	15.94	15.90	15.87	15.85	15.83	15.81	15.80	15.77	15.76	15.76
900	18.27	18.15	18.06	17.99	17.93	17.89	17.85	17.83	17.81	17.79	17.77	17.74	17.73	17.73
1000	20.30	20.17	20.07	19.99	19.93	19.88	19.84	19.81	19.78	19.76	19.75	19.71	19.70	19.69
2000	40.59	40.33	40.13	39.97	39.85	39.75	39.67	39.61	39.56	39.52	39.49	39.42	39.39	39.38
3000	60.89	60.50	60.20	59.96	59.77	59.62	59.50	59.41	59.34	59.28	59.24	59.12	59.08	59.07
4000	81.18	80.66	80.26	79.94	79.69	79.49	79.34	79.22	79.12	79.04	78.98	78.83	78.78	78.76
5000	101.48	100.83	100.32	99.92	99.61	99.37	99.17	99.02	98.90	98.80	98.73	98.53	98.47	98.45
6000	121.77	120.99	120.39	119.91	119.53	119.24	119.00	118.82	118.68	118.56	118.47	118.24	118.16	118.14
7000	142.07	141.16	140.45	139.89	139.45	139.11	138.84	138.62	138.45	138.32	138.22	137.94	137.86	137.83
8000	162.36	161.32	160.51	159.88	159.38	158.98	158.67	158.43	158.23	158.08	157.96	157.65	157.55	157.52
9000	182.66	181.49	180.58	179.86	179.30	178.85	178.50	178.23	178.01	177.84	177.70	177.35	177.24	177.21
10000	202.95	201.65	200.64	199.84	199.22	198.73	198.34	198.03	197.79	197.60	197.45	197.06	196.93	196.90
11000	223.25	221.82	220.70	219.83	219.14	218.60	218.17	217.83	217.57	217.36	217.19	216.76	216.63	216.59
12000	243.54	241.98	240.77	239.81	239.06	238.47	238.00	237.64	237.35	237.12	236.94	236.47	236.32	236.28
13000	263.04	262.15	260.83	259.79	258.98	258.34	257.84	257.44	257.13	256.88	256.68	256.17	256.01	255.96
14000	284.13	282.31	280.89	279.78	278.90	278.21	277.67	277.24	276.90	276.64	276.43	275.88	275.71	275.65
15000	304.42	302.48	300.96	299.76	298.82	298.09	297.50	297.05	296.68	296.40	296.17	295.58	295.40	295.34
16000	324.72	322.64	321.02	319.75	318.75	317.96	317.34	316.85	316.46	316.16	315.92	315.29	315.09	315.03
17000	345.01	342.81	341.08	339.73	338.67	337.83	337.17	336.65	336.24	335.92	335.66	334.99	334.79	334.72
18000	365.31	362.97	361.15	359.71	358.59	357.70	357.00	356.45	356.02	355.68	355.40	354.70	354.49	354.41
19000	385.60	383.14	381.21	379.70	378.51	377.57	376.84	376.26	375.80	375.44	375.15	374.40	374.17	374.10
20000	405.90	403.30	401.27	399.68	398.43	397.45	396.67	396.06	395.58	395.19	394.89	394.11	393.86	393.79
21000	426.19	423.47	421.34	419.67	418.35	417.32	416.50	415.86	415.35	414.95	414.64	413.81	413.56	413.48
22000	446.49	443.63	441.40	439.65	438.27	437.19	436.34	435.66	435.13	434.71	434.38	433.52	433.25	433.17
23000	466.78	463.80	461.46	459.63	458.19	457.06	456.17	455.47	454.91	454.47	454.13	453.22	452.94	452.86
24000	487.08	483.96	481.53	479.62	478.12	476.93	476.00	475.27	474.69	474.23	473.87	472.93	472.64	472.55
25000	507.37	504.13	501.59	499.60	498.04	496.81	495.84	495.07	494.47	493.99	493.62	492.63	492.33	492.23
26000	527.67	524.29	521.65	519.58	517.96	516.68	515.67	514.87	514.25	513.75	513.36	512.34	512.02	511.92
27000	547.96	544.46	541.72	539.57	537.88	536.55	535.50	534.68	534.03	533.51	533.10	532.04	531.72	531.61
28000	568.26	564.62	561.78	559.55	557.80	556.42	555.34	554.48	553.80	553.27	552.85	551.75	551.41	551.30
29000	588.55	584.79	581.84	579.54	577.72	576.29	575.17	574.28	573.58	573.03	572.59	571.45	571.10	570.99
30000	608.84	604.95	601.91	599.52	597.64	596.17	595.00	594.09	593.36	592.79	592.34	591.16	590.79	590.68
31000	629.14	625.12	621.97	619.50	617.56	616.04	614.84	613.89	613.14	612.55	612.08	610.86	610.49	610.37
32000	649.43	645.28	642.04	639.49	637.49	635.91	634.67	633.69	632.92	632.31	631.83	630.57	630.18	630.06
33000	669.73	665.45	662.10	659.47	657.41	655.78	654.50	653.49	652.70	652.07	651.57	650.27	649.87	649.75
34000	690.02	685.61	682.16	679.46	677.33	675.66	674.34	673.30	672.48	671.83	671.32	669.98	669.57	669.44
35000	710.32	705.78	702.23	699.44	697.25	695.53	694.17	693.10	692.25	691.59	691.06	689.68	689.26	689.13
36000	730.61	725.94	722.29	719.42	717.17	715.40	714.00	712.90	712.03	711.35	710.80	709.39	708.95	708.82
37000	750.91	746.11	742.35	739.41	737.09	735.27	733.84	732.70	731.81	731.11	730.55	729.10	728.64	728.51
38000	771.20	766.27	762.42	759.39	757.01	755.14	753.67	752.51	751.59	750.87	750.29	748.80	748.34	748.19
39000	791.50	786.44	782.48	779.37	776.94	775.02	773.50	772.31	771.37	770.62	770.04	768.51	768.03	767.88
40000	811.79	806.60	802.54	799.36	796.86	794.89	793.34	792.11	791.15	790.38	789.78	788.21	787.72	787.57
41000	832.09	826.77	822.61	819.34	816.78	814.76	813.17	811.92	810.93	810.14	809.53	807.92	807.42	807.26
42000	852.38	846.93	842.67	839.33	836.70	834.63	833.00	831.72	830.70	829.90	829.27	827.62	827.11	826.95
43000	872.68	867.10	862.73	859.31	856.62	854.50	852.84	851.52	850.48	849.66	849.02	847.33	846.80	846.64
44000	892.97	887.26	882.80	879.29	876.54	874.38	872.67	871.32	870.26	869.42	868.76	867.03	866.50	866.33
45000	913.26	907.43	902.86	899.28	896.46	894.25	892.50	891.13	890.04	889.18	888.50	886.74	886.19	886.02
46000	933.56	927.59	922.92	919.26	916.38	914.12	912.34	910.93	909.82	908.94	908.25	906.44	905.88	905.71
47000	953.85	947.76	942.99	939.25	936.31	933.99	932.17	930.73	929.60	928.70	927.99	926.15	925.57	925.40
48000	974.15	967.92	963.05	959.23	956.23	953.86	950.53	950.53	949.38	948.46	947.74	945.85	945.27	945.09
49000	994.44	988.09	983.11	979.21	976.15	973.74	971.84	970.34	969.15	968.22	967.48	965.56	964.96	964.78
50000	1014.74	1008.25	1003.18	999.20	996.07	993.61	991.67	990.14	988.93	987.98	987.23	985.26	984.65	984.46
55000	1116.21	1109.08	1103.49	1099.12	1095.68	1092.97	1090.84	1089.15	1087.83	1086.78	1085.95	1083.79	1083.12	1082.91
60000	1217.68	1209.90	1203.81	1199.04	1195.28	1192.33	1190.00	1188.17	1186.72	1185.57	1184.67	1182.31	1181.58	1181.36
65000	1319.16	1310.73	1304.13	1298.95	1294.89	1291.69	1289.17	1287.18	1285.61	1284.37	1283.39	1280.84	1280.05	1279.80
70000	1420.63	1411.55	1404.45	1398.87	1394.50	1391.05	1388.33	1386.19	1384.50	1383.17	1382.11	1379.36	1378.51	1378.25
75000	1522.10	1512.38	1504.76	1498.79	1494.10	1490.41	1487.50	1485.21	1483.40	1481.97	1480.84	1477.89	1476.98	1476.69
80000	1623.58	1613.20	1605.08	1598.71	1593.71	1589.77	1586.67	1584.22	1582.29	1580.76	1579.56	1576.42	1575.44	1575.14
85000	1725.05	1714.03	1705.40	1698.63	1693.31	1689.13	1685.83	1683.23	1681.18	1679.56	1678.28	1674.94	1673.91	1673.59
90000	1826.52	1814.85	1805.71	1798.55	1792.92	1788.49	1785.00	1782.25	1780.07	1778.36	1777.00	1773.47	1772.37	1772.03
95000	1928.00	1915.68	1906.03	1898.47	1892.53	1887.85	1884.17	1881.26	1878.97	1877.16	1875.73	1871.99	1870.84	1870.48
100000	2029.47	2016.50	2006.35	1998.39	1992.13	1987.21	1983.33	1980.27	1977.86	1975.95	1974.45	1970.52	1969.30	1968.92

MONTHLY PAYMENT
REQUIRED TO AMORTIZE A LOAN

TERM AMOUNT	1 Year	2 Years	3 Years	4 Years	5 Years	6 Years	7 Years	8 Years	9 Years	10 Years	11 Years	12 Years	13 Years	14 Years
5	.48	.27	.20	.17	.15	.14	.13	.12	.12	.11	.11	.11	.11	.11
10	.95	.53	.40	.33	.29	.27	.25	.24	.23	.22	.22	.22	.21	.21
15	1.42	.80	.59	.49	.43	.40	.37	.35	.34	.33	.33	.32	.32	.31
25	2.37	1.32	.98	.82	.72	.66	.62	.59	.57	.55	.54	.53	.52	.52
50	4.73	2.64	1.96	1.63	1.43	1.31	1.23	1.17	1.13	1.10	1.07	1.06	1.04	1.03
75	7.09	3.96	2.94	2.44	2.15	1.97	1.84	1.75	1.69	1.64	1.61	1.58	1.56	1.54
100	9.45	5.28	3.91	3.25	2.86	2.62	2.45	2.34	2.25	2.19	2.14	2.11	2.08	2.06
200	18.89	10.55	7.82	6.49	5.72	5.23	4.90	4.67	4.50	4.37	4.28	4.21	4.15	4.11
300	28.33	15.82	11.73	9.74	8.58	7.85	7.35	7.00	6.75	6.56	6.41	6.31	6.22	6.16
400	37.77	21.09	15.64	12.98	11.44	10.46	9.80	9.33	8.99	8.74	8.55	8.41	8.30	8.21
500	47.21	26.37	19.54	16.22	14.30	13.08	12.25	11.66	11.24	10.92	10.69	10.51	10.37	10.26
600	56.65	31.64	23.45	19.47	17.16	15.69	14.70	14.00	13.49	13.11	12.82	12.61	12.44	12.32
700	66.10	36.91	27.36	22.71	20.02	18.31	17.15	16.33	15.73	15.29	14.96	14.71	14.52	14.37
800	75.54	42.18	31.27	25.95	22.88	20.92	19.59	18.66	17.98	17.48	17.10	16.81	16.59	16.42
900	84.98	47.45	35.17	29.20	25.74	23.54	22.04	20.99	20.23	19.66	19.23	18.91	18.66	18.47
1000	94.42	52.73	39.08	32.44	28.60	26.15	24.49	23.32	22.47	21.84	21.37	21.01	20.74	20.52
2000	188.83	105.45	78.16	64.88	57.19	52.30	48.98	46.64	44.94	43.68	42.74	42.02	41.47	41.04
3000	283.25	158.17	117.23	97.31	85.79	78.44	73.46	69.96	67.41	65.52	64.10	63.03	62.20	61.56
4000	377.66	210.89	156.31	129.75	114.38	104.59	97.95	93.27	89.88	87.36	85.47	84.03	82.93	82.08
5000	472.08	263.61	195.38	162.19	142.98	130.73	122.44	116.59	112.34	109.20	106.84	105.04	103.66	102.59
6000	566.49	316.33	234.46	194.62	171.57	156.88	146.92	139.91	134.81	131.04	128.20	126.05	124.39	123.11
7000	660.91	369.06	273.53	227.06	200.16	183.02	171.41	163.22	157.28	152.88	149.57	147.05	145.12	143.63
8000	755.32	421.78	312.61	259.49	228.76	209.17	195.90	186.54	179.75	174.72	170.94	168.06	165.85	164.15
9000	849.74	474.50	351.68	291.93	257.35	235.31	220.38	209.86	202.22	196.56	192.30	189.07	186.58	184.66
10000	944.15	527.22	390.76	324.37	285.95	261.46	244.87	233.17	224.68	218.40	213.67	210.07	207.31	205.18
11000	1038.56	579.94	429.84	356.80	314.54	287.60	269.36	256.49	247.15	240.24	235.04	231.08	228.04	225.70
12000	1132.98	632.66	468.91	389.24	343.13	313.75	293.84	279.81	269.62	262.08	256.40	252.09	248.78	246.22
13000	1227.39	685.38	507.99	421.68	371.73	339.89	318.33	303.12	292.09	283.92	277.77	273.09	269.51	266.73
14000	1321.81	738.11	547.06	454.11	400.32	366.04	342.82	326.44	314.56	305.75	299.14	294.10	290.24	287.25
15000	1416.22	790.83	586.14	486.55	428.92	392.18	367.30	349.76	337.02	327.59	320.50	315.11	310.97	307.77
16000	1510.64	843.55	625.21	518.98	457.51	418.33	391.79	373.07	359.49	349.43	341.87	336.11	331.70	328.29
17000	1605.05	896.27	664.29	551.42	486.10	444.47	416.27	396.39	381.96	371.27	363.23	357.12	352.43	348.81
18000	1699.47	948.99	703.36	583.86	514.70	470.62	440.76	419.71	404.43	393.11	384.60	378.13	373.16	369.32
19000	1793.88	1001.71	742.44	616.29	543.29	496.76	465.25	443.02	426.90	414.95	405.97	399.13	393.89	389.84
20000	1888.29	1054.43	781.52	648.73	571.89	522.91	489.73	466.34	449.36	436.79	427.33	420.14	414.62	410.36
21000	1982.71	1107.16	820.59	681.17	600.48	549.05	514.22	489.66	471.83	458.63	448.70	441.15	435.35	430.88
22000	2077.12	1159.88	859.67	713.60	629.08	575.20	538.71	512.97	494.30	480.47	470.07	462.15	456.08	451.39
23000	2171.54	1212.60	898.74	746.04	657.67	601.34	563.19	536.29	516.77	502.31	491.43	483.16	476.81	471.91
24000	2265.95	1265.32	937.82	778.47	686.26	627.49	587.68	559.61	539.24	524.15	512.80	504.17	497.55	492.43
25000	2360.37	1318.04	976.89	810.91	714.86	653.63	612.17	582.92	561.70	545.99	534.17	525.17	518.28	512.95
26000	2454.78	1370.76	1015.97	843.35	743.45	679.78	636.65	606.24	584.17	567.83	555.53	546.18	539.01	533.46
27000	2549.20	1423.49	1055.04	875.78	772.05	705.92	661.14	629.56	606.64	589.66	576.90	567.19	559.74	553.98
28000	2643.61	1476.21	1094.12	908.22	800.64	732.07	685.63	652.87	629.11	611.50	598.27	588.20	580.47	574.50
29000	2738.02	1528.93	1133.19	940.66	829.23	758.21	710.11	676.19	651.58	633.34	619.63	609.20	601.20	595.02
30000	2832.44	1581.65	1172.27	973.09	857.83	784.36	734.60	699.51	674.04	655.18	641.00	630.21	621.93	615.54
31000	2926.85	1634.37	1211.35	1005.53	886.42	810.50	759.09	722.82	696.51	677.02	662.36	651.22	642.66	636.05
32000	3021.27	1687.09	1250.42	1037.96	915.02	836.65	783.57	746.14	718.98	698.86	683.73	672.22	663.39	656.57
33000	3115.68	1739.81	1289.50	1070.40	943.61	862.79	808.06	769.46	741.45	720.70	705.10	693.23	684.12	677.09
34000	3210.10	1792.54	1328.57	1102.84	972.20	888.94	832.54	792.77	763.92	742.54	726.46	714.24	704.85	697.61
35000	3304.51	1845.26	1367.65	1135.27	1000.80	915.08	857.03	816.09	786.38	764.38	747.83	735.24	725.58	718.12
36000	3398.93	1897.98	1406.72	1167.71	1029.39	941.23	881.52	839.41	808.85	786.22	769.20	756.25	746.32	738.64
37000	3493.34	1950.70	1445.80	1200.14	1057.99	967.37	906.00	862.72	831.32	808.06	790.56	777.26	767.05	759.16
38000	3587.76	2003.42	1484.87	1232.58	1086.58	993.52	930.49	886.04	853.79	829.90	811.93	798.26	787.78	779.68
39000	3682.17	2056.14	1523.95	1265.02	1115.17	1019.66	954.98	909.36	876.26	851.74	833.30	819.27	808.51	800.19
40000	3776.58	2108.86	1563.03	1297.45	1143.77	1045.81	979.46	932.67	898.72	873.58	854.66	840.28	829.24	820.71
41000	3871.00	2161.59	1602.10	1329.89	1172.36	1071.95	1003.95	955.99	921.19	895.41	876.03	861.28	849.97	841.23
42000	3965.41	2214.31	1641.18	1362.33	1200.96	1098.10	1028.44	979.31	943.66	917.25	897.40	882.29	870.70	861.75
43000	4059.83	2267.03	1680.25	1394.76	1229.55	1124.24	1052.92	1002.62	966.13	939.09	918.76	903.30	891.43	882.27
44000	4154.24	2319.75	1719.33	1427.20	1258.15	1150.39	1077.41	1025.94	988.60	960.93	940.13	924.30	912.16	902.78
45000	4248.66	2372.47	1758.40	1459.63	1286.74	1176.53	1101.90	1049.26	1011.06	982.77	961.50	945.31	932.89	923.30
46000	4343.07	2425.19	1797.48	1492.07	1315.33	1202.68	1126.38	1072.58	1033.53	1004.61	982.86	966.32	953.62	943.82
47000	4437.49	2477.91	1836.55	1524.51	1343.93	1228.82	1150.87	1095.89	1056.00	1026.45	1004.23	987.32	974.35	964.34
48000	4531.90	2530.64	1875.63	1556.94	1372.52	1254.97	1175.36	1119.21	1078.47	1048.29	1025.59	1008.33	995.09	984.85
49000	4626.31	2583.36	1914.70	1589.38	1401.12	1281.11	1199.84	1142.53	1100.93	1070.13	1046.96	1029.34	1015.82	1005.37
50000	4720.73	2636.08	1953.78	1621.82	1429.71	1307.26	1224.33	1165.84	1123.40	1091.97	1068.33	1050.34	1036.55	1025.89
55000	5192.80	2899.69	2149.16	1784.00	1572.68	1437.98	1346.76	1282.43	1235.74	1201.16	1175.16	1155.38	1140.20	1128.48
60000	5664.87	3163.29	2344.54	1946.18	1715.65	1568.71	1469.19	1399.01	1348.08	1310.36	1281.99	1260.41	1243.86	1231.07
65000	6136.95	3426.90	2539.91	2108.36	1858.62	1699.43	1591.63	1515.59	1460.42	1419.56	1388.82	1365.45	1347.51	1333.65
70000	6609.02	3690.51	2735.29	2270.54	2001.59	1830.16	1714.06	1632.18	1572.76	1528.75	1495.66	1470.48	1451.16	1436.24
75000	7081.09	3954.12	2930.67	2432.72	2144.56	1960.88	1836.49	1748.76	1685.10	1637.95	1602.49	1575.51	1554.82	1538.83
80000	7553.16	4217.72	3126.05	2594.90	2287.53	2091.61	1958.92	1865.34	1797.44	1747.15	1709.32	1680.55	1658.47	1641.42
85000	8025.24	4481.33	3321.42	2757.08	2430.50	2222.33	2081.35	1981.93	1909.78	1856.34	1816.15	1785.58	1762.13	1744.01
90000	8497.31	4744.94	3516.80	2919.26	2573.47	2353.06	2203.79	2098.51	2022.12	1965.54	1922.99	1890.62	1865.78	1846.60
95000	8969.38	5008.55	3712.18	3081.44	2716.44	2483.78	2326.22	2215.10	2134.46	2074.73	2029.82	1995.65	1969.43	1949.19
100000	9441.45	5272.15	3907.56	3243.63	2859.41	2614.51	2448.65	2331.68	2246.80	2183.93	2136.65	2100.68	2073.09	2051.77

TERM AMOUNT	15 Years	16 Years	17 Years	18 Years	19 Years	20 Years	21 Years	22 Years	23 Years	24 Years	25 Years	30 Years	35 Years	40 Years
5	.11	.11	.11	.11	.10	.10	.10	.10	.10	.10	.10	.10	.10	.10
10	.21	.21	.21	.21	.20	.20	.20	.20	.20	.20	.20	.20	.20	.20
15	.31	.31	.31	.31	.30	.30	.30	.30	.30	.30	.30	.30	.30	.30
25	.51	.51	.51	.51	.50	.50	.50	.50	.50	.50	.50	.50	.50	.50
50	1.02	1.02	1.01	1.01	1.00	1.00	1.00	1.00	1.00	1.00	1.00	.99	.99	.99
75	1.53	1.52	1.51	1.51	1.50	1.50	1.50	1.49	1.49	1.49	1.49	1.49	1.49	1.49
100	2.04	2.03	2.02	2.01	2.00	2.00	1.99	1.99	1.99	1.99	1.99	1.98	1.98	1.98
200	4.08	4.05	4.03	4.01	4.00	3.99	3.98	3.98	3.97	3.97	3.97	3.96	3.96	3.96
300	6.11	6.07	6.04	6.02	6.00	5.98	5.97	5.96	5.96	5.95	5.95	5.94	5.93	5.93
400	8.15	8.09	8.05	8.02	8.00	7.98	7.96	7.95	7.94	7.93	7.93	7.91	7.91	7.91
500	10.18	10.12	10.07	10.03	10.00	9.97	9.95	9.94	9.92	9.92	9.91	9.89	9.88	9.88
600	12.22	12.14	12.08	12.03	11.99	11.96	11.94	11.92	11.91	11.90	11.89	11.87	11.86	11.86
700	14.25	14.16	14.09	14.04	13.99	13.96	13.93	13.91	13.89	13.88	13.87	13.84	13.83	13.83
800	16.29	16.18	16.10	16.04	15.99	15.95	15.92	15.90	15.88	15.86	15.85	15.82	15.81	15.81
900	18.32	18.21	18.12	18.04	17.99	17.94	17.91	17.88	17.86	17.84	17.83	17.80	17.78	17.78
1000	20.36	20.23	20.13	20.05	19.99	19.94	19.90	19.87	19.84	19.83	19.81	19.77	19.76	19.76
2000	40.71	40.45	40.25	40.09	39.97	39.87	39.79	39.73	39.68	39.65	39.62	39.54	39.52	39.51
3000	61.06	60.67	60.37	60.13	59.95	59.80	59.69	59.60	59.52	59.47	59.42	59.31	59.27	59.26
4000	81.41	80.90	80.49	80.18	79.93	79.73	79.58	79.46	79.36	79.29	79.23	79.07	79.03	79.01
5000	101.77	101.12	100.62	100.22	99.91	99.67	99.47	99.32	99.20	99.11	99.04	98.84	98.78	98.76
6000	122.12	121.34	120.74	120.26	119.89	119.60	119.37	119.19	119.04	118.93	118.84	118.61	118.54	118.51
7000	142.47	141.57	140.86	140.31	139.87	139.53	139.26	139.05	138.88	138.75	138.65	138.38	138.29	138.27
8000	162.82	161.79	160.98	160.35	159.85	159.46	159.16	158.91	158.72	158.57	158.45	158.14	158.05	158.02
9000	183.17	182.01	181.11	160.39	179.84	179.40	179.05	178.78	178.56	178.39	178.26	177.91	177.80	177.77
10000	203.53	202.24	201.23	200.44	199.82	199.33	198.94	198.64	198.40	198.21	198.07	197.68	197.56	197.52
11000	223.88	222.46	221.35	220.48	219.80	219.26	218.84	218.51	218.24	218.04	217.87	217.45	217.31	217.27
12000	244.23	242.68	241.47	240.52	239.78	239.19	238.73	238.37	238.08	237.86	237.68	237.21	237.07	237.02
13000	264.58	262.91	261.60	260.57	259.76	259.13	258.63	258.23	257.92	257.68	257.48	256.98	256.82	256.78
14000	284.94	283.13	281.72	280.61	279.74	279.06	278.52	278.10	277.76	277.50	277.29	276.75	276.58	276.53
15000	305.29	303.35	301.84	300.65	299.72	298.99	298.41	297.96	297.60	297.32	297.10	296.51	296.34	296.28
16000	325.64	323.58	321.96	320.70	319.70	318.92	318.31	317.82	317.44	317.14	316.90	316.28	316.09	316.03
17000	345.99	343.80	342.09	340.74	339.69	338.86	338.20	337.69	337.28	336.96	336.71	336.05	335.85	335.78
18000	366.34	364.02	362.21	360.78	359.67	358.79	358.10	357.55	357.12	356.78	356.51	355.82	355.60	355.53
19000	386.70	384.25	382.33	380.83	379.65	378.72	377.99	377.42	376.96	376.60	376.32	375.58	375.36	375.29
20000	407.05	404.47	402.45	400.87	399.63	398.65	397.88	397.28	396.80	396.42	396.13	395.35	395.11	395.04
21000	427.40	424.69	422.57	420.91	419.61	418.59	417.78	417.14	416.64	416.24	415.93	415.12	414.87	414.79
22000	447.75	444.92	442.70	440.96	439.59	438.52	437.67	437.01	436.48	436.07	435.74	434.89	434.62	434.54
23000	468.11	465.14	462.82	461.00	459.57	458.45	457.57	456.87	456.32	455.89	455.54	454.65	454.38	454.29
24000	488.46	485.36	482.94	481.04	479.55	478.38	477.46	476.73	476.16	475.71	475.35	474.42	474.13	474.04
25000	508.81	505.59	503.06	501.09	499.54	498.32	497.35	496.60	496.00	495.53	495.16	494.19	493.89	493.80
26000	529.16	525.81	523.19	521.13	519.52	518.25	517.25	516.46	515.84	515.35	514.96	513.95	513.64	513.55
27000	549.51	546.03	543.31	541.17	539.50	538.18	537.14	536.32	535.68	535.17	534.77	533.72	533.40	533.30
28000	569.87	566.25	563.43	561.22	559.48	558.11	557.04	556.19	555.52	554.99	554.57	553.49	553.15	553.05
29000	590.22	586.48	583.55	581.26	579.46	578.05	576.93	576.05	575.36	574.81	574.38	573.26	572.91	572.80
30000	610.57	606.70	603.68	601.30	599.44	597.98	596.82	595.92	595.20	594.63	594.19	593.02	592.67	592.55
31000	630.92	626.92	623.80	621.35	619.42	617.91	616.72	615.78	615.04	614.45	613.99	612.79	612.42	612.31
32000	651.28	647.15	643.92	641.39	639.40	637.84	636.61	635.64	634.88	634.28	633.80	632.56	632.18	632.06
33000	671.63	667.37	664.04	661.43	659.39	657.77	656.51	655.51	654.72	654.10	653.61	652.33	651.93	651.81
34000	691.98	687.59	684.17	681.48	679.37	677.71	676.40	675.37	674.56	673.92	673.41	672.09	671.69	671.56
35000	712.33	707.82	704.29	701.52	699.35	697.64	696.29	695.23	694.40	693.74	693.22	691.86	691.44	691.31
36000	732.68	728.04	724.41	721.56	719.33	717.57	716.19	715.10	714.24	713.56	713.02	711.63	711.20	711.06
37000	753.04	748.26	744.53	741.61	739.31	737.50	736.08	734.96	734.08	733.38	732.83	731.40	730.95	730.82
38000	773.39	768.49	764.65	761.65	759.29	757.44	755.98	754.83	753.92	753.20	752.64	751.16	750.71	750.57
39000	793.74	788.71	784.78	781.69	779.27	777.37	775.87	774.69	773.76	773.02	772.44	770.93	770.46	770.32
40000	814.09	808.93	804.90	801.74	799.25	797.30	795.76	794.55	793.60	792.84	792.25	790.70	790.22	790.07
41000	834.45	829.16	825.02	821.78	819.24	817.23	815.66	814.42	813.44	812.66	812.05	810.46	809.97	809.82
42000	854.80	849.38	845.14	841.82	839.22	837.17	835.55	834.28	833.28	832.48	831.86	830.23	829.73	829.57
43000	875.15	869.60	865.27	861.87	859.20	857.10	855.45	854.14	853.12	852.31	851.67	850.00	849.49	849.33
44000	895.50	889.83	885.39	881.91	879.18	877.03	875.34	874.01	872.96	872.13	871.47	869.77	869.24	869.08
45000	915.85	910.05	905.51	901.95	899.16	896.96	895.23	893.87	892.80	891.95	891.28	889.53	889.00	888.83
46000	936.21	930.27	925.63	922.00	919.14	916.90	915.13	913.73	912.64	911.77	911.08	909.30	908.75	908.58
47000	956.56	950.50	945.76	942.04	939.12	936.83	935.02	933.60	932.48	931.59	930.89	929.07	928.51	928.33
48000	976.91	970.72	965.88	962.08	959.10	956.76	954.92	953.46	952.32	951.41	950.70	948.84	948.26	948.08
49000	997.26	990.94	986.00	982.13	979.09	976.69	974.81	973.33	972.16	971.23	970.50	968.60	968.02	967.84
50000	1017.62	1011.17	1006.12	1002.17	999.07	996.63	994.70	993.19	991.99	991.05	990.31	988.37	987.77	987.59
55000	1119.38	1112.28	1106.73	1102.39	1098.97	1096.29	1094.17	1092.51	1091.19	1090.16	1089.34	1087.21	1086.55	1086.35
60000	1221.14	1213.40	1207.35	1202.60	1198.88	1195.95	1193.64	1191.83	1190.39	1189.26	1188.37	1186.04	1185.33	1185.10
65000	1322.90	1314.51	1307.96	1302.82	1298.79	1295.61	1293.11	1291.14	1289.59	1288.37	1287.40	1284.88	1284.10	1283.86
70000	1424.66	1415.63	1408.57	1403.04	1398.69	1395.27	1392.58	1390.46	1388.79	1387.47	1386.43	1383.72	1382.88	1382.62
75000	1526.42	1516.75	1509.18	1503.25	1498.60	1494.94	1492.05	1489.78	1487.99	1486.58	1485.46	1482.55	1481.66	1481.38
80000	1628.18	1617.86	1609.79	1603.47	1598.50	1594.60	1591.52	1589.10	1587.19	1585.68	1584.49	1581.39	1580.43	1580.14
85000	1729.94	1718.98	1710.41	1703.68	1698.41	1694.26	1690.99	1688.42	1686.39	1684.79	1683.52	1680.23	1679.21	1678.90
90000	1831.70	1820.09	1811.02	1803.90	1798.32	1793.92	1790.46	1787.74	1785.59	1783.89	1782.55	1779.06	1777.99	1777.65
95000	1933.46	1921.21	1911.63	1904.12	1898.22	1893.58	1889.93	1887.06	1884.79	1883.00	1881.58	1877.90	1876.76	1876.41
100000	2035.23	2022.33	2012.24	2004.34	1998.13	1993.25	1989.40	1986.37	1983.98	1982.10	1980.61	1976.74	1975.54	1975.17

MONTHLY PAYMENT
REQUIRED TO AMORTIZE A LOAN

TERM AMOUNT	1 Year	2 Years	3 Years	4 Years	5 Years	6 Years	7 Years	8 Years	9 Years	10 Years	11 Years	12 Years	13 Years	14 Years
5	.48	.27	.20	.17	.15	.14	.13	.12	.12	.11	.11	.11	.11	.11
10	.95	.53	.40	.33	.29	.27	.25	.24	.23	.22	.22	.22	.21	.21
15	1.42	.80	.59	.49	.43	.40	.37	.36	.34	.33	.33	.32	.32	.31
25	2.37	1.32	.98	.82	.72	.66	.62	.59	.57	.55	.54	.53	.52	.52
50	4.73	2.64	1.96	1.63	1.44	1.31	1.23	1.17	1.13	1.10	1.08	1.06	1.04	1.03
75	7.09	3.96	2.94	2.44	2.15	1.97	1.84	1.76	1.69	1.65	1.61	1.58	1.56	1.55
100	9.45	5.28	3.92	3.25	2.87	2.62	2.46	2.34	2.26	2.19	2.15	2.11	2.08	2.06
200	18.89	10.55	7.83	6.50	5.73	5.24	4.91	4.67	4.51	4.38	4.29	4.21	4.16	4.12
300	28.34	15.83	11.74	9.74	8.59	7.86	7.36	7.01	6.76	6.57	6.43	6.32	6.24	6.17
400	37.78	21.10	15.65	12.99	11.45	10.48	9.81	9.34	9.01	8.75	8.57	8.42	9.31	8.23
500	47.22	26.38	19.56	16.24	14.32	13.09	12.26	11.68	11.26	10.94	10.71	10.53	10.39	10.28
600	56.67	31.65	23.47	19.48	17.18	15.71	14.72	14.01	13.51	13.13	12.85	12.63	12.47	12.34
700	66.11	36.93	27.38	22.73	20.04	18.33	17.17	16.35	15.76	15.32	14.99	14.74	14.54	14.39
800	75.56	42.20	31.29	25.98	22.90	20.95	19.62	18.68	18.01	17.50	17.13	16.84	16.62	16.45
900	85.00	47.48	35.20	29.22	25.77	23.56	22.07	21.02	20.26	19.69	19.27	18.94	18.70	18.50
1000	94.44	52.75	39.11	32.47	28.63	26.18	24.52	23.35	22.51	21.88	21.41	21.05	20.77	20.56
2000	188.88	105.50	78.21	64.93	57.25	52.36	49.04	46.70	45.01	43.75	42.81	42.09	41.54	41.12
3000	283.32	158.24	117.31	97.40	85.87	78.53	73.56	70.05	67.51	65.63	64.21	63.13	62.31	61.67
4000	377.76	210.99	156.41	129.86	114.50	104.71	98.08	93.40	90.01	87.50	85.61	84.18	83.08	82.23
5000	472.20	263.74	195.51	162.32	143.12	130.88	122.59	116.75	112.51	109.38	107.02	105.22	103.85	102.78
6000	566.64	316.48	234.62	194.79	171.74	157.06	147.11	140.10	135.02	131.25	128.42	126.26	124.61	123.34
7000	661.08	369.23	273.72	227.25	200.37	183.23	171.63	163.45	157.52	153.12	149.82	147.31	145.38	143.89
8000	755.51	421.98	312.82	259.72	228.99	209.41	196.15	186.80	180.02	175.00	171.22	168.35	166.15	164.45
9000	849.95	474.72	351.92	292.18	257.61	235.58	220.67	210.15	202.52	196.87	192.62	189.39	186.92	185.00
10000	944.39	527.47	391.02	324.64	286.24	261.76	245.18	233.50	225.02	218.75	214.03	210.44	207.69	205.56
11000	1038.83	580.22	430.12	357.11	314.86	287.93	269.70	256.85	247.52	240.62	235.43	231.48	228.45	226.12
12000	1133.27	632.96	469.23	389.57	343.48	314.11	294.22	280.20	270.03	262.49	256.83	252.52	249.22	246.67
13000	1227.71	685.71	508.33	422.03	372.10	340.28	318.74	303.55	292.53	284.37	278.23	273.57	269.99	267.23
14000	1322.15	738.45	547.43	454.50	400.73	366.46	343.26	326.90	315.03	306.24	299.63	294.61	290.76	287.78
15000	1416.58	791.20	586.53	486.96	429.35	392.63	367.77	350.25	337.53	328.12	321.04	315.65	311.53	308.34
16000	1511.02	843.95	625.63	519.43	457.97	418.81	392.29	373.60	360.03	349.99	342.44	336.70	332.29	328.89
17000	1605.46	896.69	664.73	551.89	486.60	444.98	416.81	396.95	382.53	371.86	363.84	357.74	353.06	349.45
18000	1699.90	949.44	703.84	584.35	515.22	471.16	441.33	420.29	405.04	393.74	385.24	378.78	373.83	370.00
19000	1794.34	1002.19	742.94	616.82	543.84	497.34	465.85	443.64	427.54	415.61	406.64	399.83	394.60	390.56
20000	1888.78	1054.93	782.04	649.28	572.47	523.51	490.36	466.99	450.04	437.49	428.05	420.87	415.37	411.12
21000	1983.22	1107.68	821.14	681.74	601.09	549.69	514.88	490.34	472.54	459.36	449.45	441.91	436.13	431.67
22000	2077.66	1160.43	860.24	714.21	629.71	575.86	539.40	513.69	495.04	481.23	470.85	462.96	456.90	452.23
23000	2172.09	1213.17	899.34	746.67	658.33	602.04	563.92	537.04	517.54	503.11	492.25	484.00	477.67	472.78
24000	2266.53	1265.92	938.45	779.14	686.96	628.21	588.44	560.39	540.05	524.98	513.66	505.04	498.44	493.34
25000	2360.97	1318.67	977.55	811.60	715.58	654.39	612.95	583.74	562.55	546.86	535.06	526.09	519.21	513.89
26000	2455.41	1371.41	1016.65	844.06	744.20	680.56	637.47	607.09	585.05	568.73	556.46	547.13	539.97	534.45
27000	2549.85	1424.16	1055.75	876.53	772.83	706.74	661.99	630.44	607.55	590.60	577.86	568.17	560.74	555.00
28000	2644.29	1476.90	1094.85	908.99	801.45	732.91	686.51	653.79	630.05	612.48	599.26	589.22	581.51	575.56
29000	2738.73	1529.65	1133.95	941.45	830.07	759.09	711.03	677.14	652.55	634.35	620.67	610.26	602.28	596.11
30000	2833.16	1582.40	1173.06	973.92	858.70	785.26	735.54	700.49	675.06	656.23	642.07	631.30	623.05	616.67
31000	2927.60	1635.14	1212.16	1006.38	887.32	811.44	760.06	723.84	697.56	678.10	663.47	652.35	643.81	637.23
32000	3022.04	1687.89	1251.26	1038.85	915.94	837.61	784.58	747.19	720.06	699.97	684.87	673.39	664.58	657.78
33000	3116.48	1740.64	1290.36	1071.31	944.57	863.79	809.10	770.54	742.56	721.85	706.27	694.43	685.35	678.34
34000	3210.92	1793.38	1329.46	1103.77	973.19	889.96	833.62	793.89	765.06	743.72	727.68	715.48	706.12	698.89
35000	3305.36	1846.13	1368.56	1136.24	1001.81	916.14	858.13	817.23	787.57	765.60	749.08	736.52	726.89	719.45
36000	3399.80	1898.88	1407.67	1168.70	1030.43	942.31	882.65	840.58	810.07	787.47	770.48	757.56	747.65	740.00
37000	3494.24	1951.62	1446.77	1201.16	1059.06	968.49	907.17	863.93	832.57	809.34	791.88	778.61	768.42	760.56
38000	3588.67	2004.37	1485.87	1233.63	1087.68	994.67	931.69	887.28	855.07	831.22	813.28	799.65	789.19	781.11
39000	3683.11	2057.11	1524.97	1266.09	1116.30	1020.84	956.21	910.63	877.57	853.09	834.69	820.69	809.96	801.67
40000	3777.55	2109.86	1564.07	1298.56	1144.93	1047.02	980.72	933.98	900.07	874.97	856.09	841.74	830.73	822.23
41000	3871.99	2162.61	1603.18	1331.02	1173.55	1073.19	1005.24	957.33	922.58	896.84	877.49	862.78	851.49	842.78
42000	3966.43	2215.35	1642.28	1363.48	1202.17	1099.37	1029.76	980.68	945.08	918.71	898.89	883.82	872.26	863.34
43000	4060.87	2268.10	1681.38	1395.95	1230.80	1125.54	1054.28	1004.03	967.58	940.59	920.30	904.87	893.03	883.89
44000	4155.31	2320.85	1720.48	1428.41	1259.42	1151.72	1078.80	1027.38	990.08	962.46	941.70	925.91	913.80	904.45
45000	4249.74	2373.59	1759.58	1460.88	1288.04	1177.89	1103.31	1050.73	1012.58	984.34	963.10	946.95	934.57	925.00
46000	4344.18	2426.34	1798.68	1493.34	1316.66	1204.07	1127.83	1074.08	1035.08	1006.21	984.50	967.99	955.33	945.56
47000	4438.62	2479.09	1837.79	1525.80	1345.29	1230.24	1152.35	1097.43	1057.59	1028.08	1005.90	989.04	976.10	966.11
48000	4533.06	2531.83	1876.89	1558.27	1373.91	1256.42	1176.87	1120.78	1080.09	1049.96	1027.31	1010.08	996.87	986.67
49000	4627.50	2584.58	1915.99	1590.73	1402.53	1282.59	1201.39	1144.13	1102.59	1071.83	1048.71	1031.12	1017.64	1007.22
50000	4721.94	2637.33	1955.09	1623.19	1431.16	1308.77	1225.90	1167.48	1125.09	1093.71	1070.11	1052.17	1038.41	1027.78
55000	5194.13	2901.06	2150.60	1785.51	1574.27	1439.65	1348.49	1284.22	1237.60	1203.08	1177.12	1157.38	1142.25	1130.56
60000	5666.32	3164.79	2346.11	1947.83	1717.39	1570.52	1471.08	1400.97	1350.11	1312.45	1284.13	1262.60	1246.09	1233.34
65000	6138.52	3428.52	2541.62	2110.15	1860.50	1701.40	1593.67	1517.72	1462.62	1421.82	1391.14	1367.82	1349.93	1336.11
70000	6610.71	3692.25	2737.12	2272.47	2003.62	1832.27	1716.26	1634.46	1575.13	1531.19	1498.15	1473.03	1453.77	1438.89
75000	7082.90	3955.99	2932.63	2434.79	2146.73	1963.15	1838.85	1751.21	1687.63	1640.56	1605.16	1578.25	1557.61	1541.67
80000	7555.10	4219.72	3128.14	2597.11	2289.85	2094.03	1961.44	1867.96	1800.14	1749.93	1712.17	1683.47	1661.45	1644.45
85000	8027.29	4483.45	3323.65	2759.43	2432.96	2224.90	2084.03	1984.71	1912.65	1859.30	1819.18	1788.68	1765.29	1747.22
90000	8499.48	4747.18	3519.16	2921.75	2576.08	2355.78	2206.62	2101.45	2025.16	1968.67	1926.19	1893.90	1869.13	1850.00
95000	8971.68	5010.91	3714.67	3084.06	2719.19	2486.66	2329.21	2218.20	2137.67	2078.04	2033.20	1999.11	1972.97	1952.78
100000	9443.87	5274.65	3910.18	3246.38	2862.31	2617.53	2451.80	2334.95	2250.18	2187.41	2140.22	2104.33	2076.81	2055.56

TERM	15 Years	16 Years	17 Years	18 Years	19 Years	20 Years	21 Years	22 Years	23 Years	24 Years	25 Years	30 Years	35 Years	40 Years
AMOUNT														
5	.11	.11	.11	.11	.11	.10	.10	.10	.10	.10	.10	.10	.10	.10
10	.21	.21	.21	.21	.21	.20	.20	.20	.20	.20	.20	.20	.20	.20
15	.31	.31	.31	.31	.31	.30	.30	.30	.30	.30	.30	.30	.30	.30
25	.51	.51	.51	.51	.51	.50	.50	.50	.50	.50	.50	.50	.50	.50
50	1.02	1.02	1.01	1.01	1.01	1.00	1.00	1.00	1.00	1.00	1.00	1.00	.99	.99
75	1.53	1.52	1.52	1.51	1.51	1.50	1.50	1.50	1.50	1.49	1.49	1.49	1.49	1.49
100	2.04	2.03	2.02	2.01	2.01	2.00	2.00	2.00	1.99	1.99	1.99	1.99	1.98	1.98
200	4.08	4.06	4.04	4.02	4.01	4.00	3.99	3.99	3.98	3.98	3.97	3.97	3.96	3.96
300	6.12	6.08	6.05	6.03	6.01	6.00	5.99	5.98	5.97	5.96	5.96	5.95	5.94	5.94
400	8.16	8.11	8.07	8.04	8.01	7.99	7.98	7.97	7.96	7.95	7.94	7.93	7.92	7.92
500	10.20	10.14	10.09	10.05	10.02	9.99	9.97	9.96	9.95	9.94	9.93	9.91	9.90	9.90
600	12.24	12.16	12.10	12.05	12.02	11.99	11.97	11.95	11.93	11.92	11.91	11.89	11.88	11.88
700	14.28	14.19	14.12	14.06	14.02	13.99	13.96	13.94	13.92	13.91	13.90	13.87	13.86	13.86
800	16.32	16.21	16.13	16.07	16.02	15.98	15.95	15.93	15.91	15.89	15.88	15.85	15.84	15.84
900	18.36	18.24	18.15	18.08	18.02	17.98	17.95	17.92	17.90	17.88	17.87	17.83	17.82	17.82
1000	20.40	20.27	20.17	20.09	20.03	19.98	19.94	19.91	19.89	19.87	19.85	19.81	19.80	19.80
2000	40.79	40.53	40.33	40.17	40.05	39.95	39.87	39.81	39.77	39.73	39.70	39.62	39.60	39.59
3000	61.18	60.79	60.49	60.25	60.07	59.92	59.81	59.72	59.65	59.59	59.55	59.43	59.40	59.38
4000	81.57	81.05	80.65	80.34	80.09	79.90	79.74	79.62	79.53	79.45	79.39	79.24	79.19	79.18
5000	101.96	101.32	100.81	100.42	100.11	99.87	99.68	99.53	99.41	99.31	99.24	99.05	98.99	98.97
6000	122.35	121.58	120.97	120.50	120.13	119.84	119.61	119.43	119.29	119.18	119.09	118.86	118.79	118.76
7000	142.74	141.84	141.14	140.59	140.15	139.81	139.55	139.34	139.17	139.04	138.94	138.67	138.58	138.56
8000	163.13	162.10	161.30	160.67	160.17	159.79	159.48	159.24	159.05	158.90	158.78	158.48	158.38	158.35
9000	183.52	182.36	181.46	180.75	180.20	179.76	179.42	179.14	178.93	178.76	178.63	178.28	178.18	178.14
10000	203.91	202.63	201.62	200.83	200.22	199.73	199.35	199.05	198.81	198.62	198.48	198.09	197.97	197.94
11000	224.30	222.89	221.78	220.92	220.24	219.70	219.28	218.95	218.69	218.49	218.32	217.90	217.77	217.73
12000	244.69	243.15	241.94	241.00	240.26	239.68	239.22	238.86	238.57	238.35	238.17	237.71	237.57	237.52
13000	265.08	263.41	262.11	261.08	260.28	259.65	259.15	258.76	258.45	258.21	258.02	257.52	257.37	257.32
14000	285.47	283.67	282.27	281.17	280.30	279.62	279.09	278.67	278.33	278.07	277.87	277.33	277.16	277.11
15000	305.86	303.94	302.43	301.25	300.32	299.60	299.02	298.57	298.21	297.93	297.71	297.14	296.96	296.90
16000	326.25	324.20	322.59	321.33	320.34	319.57	318.96	318.47	318.10	317.80	317.56	316.95	316.76	316.70
17000	346.64	344.46	342.75	341.42	340.37	339.54	338.89	338.38	337.98	337.66	337.41	336.75	336.55	336.49
18000	367.04	364.72	362.91	361.50	360.39	359.51	358.83	358.28	357.86	357.52	357.25	356.56	356.35	356.28
19000	387.43	384.98	383.08	381.58	380.41	379.49	378.76	378.19	377.74	377.38	377.10	376.37	376.15	376.08
20000	407.82	405.25	403.24	401.66	400.43	399.46	398.69	398.09	397.62	397.24	396.95	396.18	395.94	395.87
21000	428.21	425.51	423.40	421.75	420.45	419.43	418.63	418.00	417.50	417.11	416.80	415.99	415.74	415.66
22000	448.60	445.77	443.56	441.83	440.47	439.40	438.56	437.90	437.38	436.97	436.64	435.80	435.54	435.46
23000	468.99	466.03	463.72	461.91	460.49	459.38	458.50	457.81	457.26	456.83	456.49	455.61	455.33	455.25
24000	489.38	486.30	483.88	482.00	480.51	479.35	478.43	477.71	477.14	476.69	476.34	475.42	475.13	475.04
25000	509.77	506.56	504.05	502.08	500.54	499.32	498.37	497.61	497.02	496.55	496.18	495.22	494.93	494.84
26000	530.16	526.82	524.21	522.16	520.56	519.29	518.30	517.52	516.90	516.42	516.03	515.03	514.73	514.63
27000	550.55	547.08	544.37	542.25	540.58	539.27	538.24	537.42	536.78	536.28	535.88	534.84	534.52	534.42
28000	570.94	567.34	564.53	562.33	560.60	559.24	558.17	557.33	556.66	556.14	555.73	554.65	554.32	554.22
29000	591.33	587.61	584.69	582.41	580.62	579.21	578.10	577.23	576.54	576.00	575.57	574.46	574.12	574.01
30000	611.72	607.87	604.85	602.49	600.64	599.19	598.04	597.14	596.42	595.86	595.42	594.27	593.91	593.80
31000	632.11	628.13	625.02	622.58	620.66	619.16	617.97	617.04	616.30	615.72	615.27	614.00	613.71	613.60
32000	652.50	648.39	645.18	642.66	640.68	639.13	637.91	636.94	636.19	635.59	635.11	633.89	633.51	633.39
33000	672.89	668.65	665.34	662.74	660.71	659.10	657.84	656.85	656.07	655.45	654.96	653.69	653.30	653.18
34000	693.28	688.92	685.50	682.83	680.73	679.08	677.78	676.75	675.95	675.31	674.81	673.50	673.10	672.98
35000	713.68	709.18	705.66	702.91	700.75	699.05	697.71	696.66	695.83	695.17	694.66	693.31	692.90	692.77
36000	734.07	729.44	725.82	722.99	720.77	719.02	717.65	716.56	715.71	715.03	714.50	713.12	712.69	712.56
37000	754.46	749.70	745.99	743.08	740.79	738.99	737.58	736.47	735.59	734.90	734.35	732.93	732.49	732.36
38000	774.85	769.96	766.15	763.16	760.81	758.97	757.51	756.37	755.47	754.76	754.20	752.74	752.29	752.15
39000	795.24	790.23	786.31	783.24	780.83	778.94	777.45	776.28	775.35	774.62	774.04	772.55	772.09	771.94
40000	815.63	810.49	806.47	803.32	800.85	798.91	797.38	796.18	795.23	794.48	793.89	792.36	791.88	791.74
41000	836.02	830.75	826.63	823.41	820.87	818.88	817.32	816.08	815.11	814.34	813.74	812.16	811.68	811.53
42000	856.41	851.01	846.79	843.49	840.90	838.86	837.25	835.99	834.99	834.21	833.59	831.97	831.48	831.32
43000	876.80	871.27	866.96	863.57	860.92	858.83	857.19	855.89	854.87	854.07	853.43	851.78	851.27	851.12
44000	897.19	891.54	887.12	883.66	880.94	878.80	877.12	875.80	874.75	873.93	873.28	871.59	871.07	870.91
45000	917.58	911.80	907.28	903.74	900.96	898.78	897.06	895.70	894.63	893.79	893.13	891.40	890.87	890.70
46000	937.97	932.06	927.44	923.82	920.98	918.75	916.99	915.61	914.51	913.65	912.97	911.21	910.66	910.50
47000	958.36	952.32	947.60	943.90	941.00	938.72	936.92	935.51	934.40	933.52	932.82	931.02	930.46	930.29
48000	978.75	972.59	967.77	963.99	961.02	958.69	956.86	955.41	954.28	953.38	952.67	950.83	950.26	950.08
49000	999.14	992.85	987.93	984.07	981.04	978.67	976.79	975.32	974.16	973.24	972.52	970.63	970.05	969.88
50000	1019.53	1013.11	1008.09	1004.15	1001.07	998.64	996.73	995.22	994.04	993.10	992.36	990.44	989.85	989.67
55000	1121.49	1114.42	1108.90	1104.57	1101.17	1098.50	1096.40	1094.75	1093.44	1092.41	1091.60	1089.49	1088.84	1088.64
60000	1223.44	1215.73	1209.70	1204.98	1201.28	1198.37	1196.07	1194.27	1192.84	1191.72	1190.83	1188.53	1187.82	1187.60
65000	1325.39	1317.04	1310.51	1305.40	1301.38	1298.23	1295.75	1293.79	1292.25	1291.03	1290.07	1287.57	1286.81	1286.57
70000	1427.35	1418.35	1411.32	1405.81	1401.49	1398.09	1395.42	1393.31	1391.65	1390.34	1389.31	1386.62	1385.79	1385.54
75000	1529.30	1519.66	1512.13	1506.23	1501.60	1497.96	1495.09	1492.83	1491.05	1489.65	1488.54	1485.66	1484.78	1484.50
80000	1631.25	1620.97	1612.94	1606.64	1601.70	1597.82	1594.76	1592.35	1590.46	1588.96	1587.78	1584.71	1583.76	1583.47
85000	1733.20	1722.28	1713.75	1707.06	1701.81	1697.68	1694.43	1691.88	1689.86	1688.27	1687.01	1683.75	1682.74	1682.43
90000	1835.16	1823.59	1814.55	1807.47	1801.91	1797.55	1794.11	1791.40	1789.26	1787.58	1786.25	1782.79	1781.73	1781.40
95000	1937.11	1924.90	1915.36	1907.89	1902.02	1897.41	1893.78	1890.92	1888.67	1886.89	1885.49	1881.84	1880.71	1880.37
100000	2039.06	2026.21	2016.17	2008.30	2002.13	1997.27	1993.45	1990.44	1988.07	1986.20	1984.72	1980.88	1979.70	1979.33

MONTHLY PAYMENT
REQUIRED TO AMORTIZE A LOAN

TERM	1 Year	2 Years	3 Years	4 Years	5 Years	6 Years	7 Years	8 Years	9 Years	10 Years	11 Years	12 Years	13 Years	14 Years
AMOUNT														
5	.40	.27	.20	.17	.15	.14	.13	.12	.12	.11	.11	.11	.11	.11
10	.95	.53	.40	.33	.29	.27	.25	.24	.23	.22	.22	.22	.21	.21
15	1.42	.80	.59	.49	.43	.40	.37	.36	.34	.33	.33	.32	.32	.31
25	2.37	1.32	.98	.82	.72	.66	.62	.59	.57	.55	.54	.53	.53	.52
50	4.73	2.64	1.96	1.63	1.44	1.32	1.23	1.17	1.13	1.10	1.08	1.06	1.05	1.03
75	7.09	3.96	2.94	2.44	2.15	1.97	1.85	1.76	1.70	1.65	1.61	1.59	1.57	1.55
100	9.45	5.28	3.92	3.25	2.87	2.63	2.46	2.34	2.26	2.20	2.15	2.11	2.09	2.06
200	18.90	10.56	7.83	6.50	5.74	5.25	4.91	4.68	4.51	4.39	4.29	4.22	4.17	4.12
300	28.34	15.84	11.74	9.75	8.60	7.87	7.37	7.02	6.77	6.58	6.44	6.33	6.25	6.18
400	37.79	21.11	15.66	13.00	11.47	10.49	9.82	9.36	9.02	8.77	8.58	8.44	8.33	8.24
500	47.24	26.39	19.57	16.25	14.33	13.11	12.28	11.70	11.27	10.96	10.72	10.54	10.41	10.30
600	56.68	31.67	23.48	19.50	17.20	15.73	14.73	14.03	13.53	13.15	12.87	12.65	12.49	12.36
700	66.13	36.94	27.39	22.75	20.06	18.35	17.19	16.37	15.78	15.34	15.01	14.76	14.57	14.42
800	75.58	42.22	31.31	26.00	22.93	20.97	19.64	18.71	18.03	17.53	17.16	16.87	16.65	16.48
900	85.02	47.50	35.22	29.25	25.79	23.59	22.10	21.05	20.29	19.72	19.30	18.98	18.73	18.54
1000	94.47	52.78	39.13	32.50	28.66	26.21	24.55	23.39	22.54	21.91	21.44	21.08	20.81	20.60
2000	188.93	105.55	78.26	64.99	57.31	52.42	49.10	46.77	45.08	43.82	42.88	42.16	41.62	41.19
3000	283.39	158.32	117.39	97.48	85.96	78.62	73.65	70.15	67.61	65.73	64.32	63.24	62.42	61.79
4000	377.86	211.09	156.52	129.97	114.61	104.83	98.20	93.53	90.15	87.64	85.76	84.32	83.23	82.38
5000	472.32	263.86	195.64	162.46	143.26	131.03	122.75	116.92	112.68	109.55	107.19	105.40	104.03	102.97
6000	566.78	316.63	234.77	194.95	171.92	157.24	147.30	140.30	135.22	131.46	128.63	126.48	124.84	123.57
7000	661.24	369.40	273.90	227.44	200.57	183.44	171.85	163.68	157.75	153.37	150.07	147.56	145.64	144.16
8000	755.71	422.18	313.03	259.94	229.22	209.65	196.40	187.06	180.29	175.28	171.51	168.64	166.45	164.75
9000	850.17	474.95	352.16	292.43	257.87	235.85	220.95	210.44	202.82	197.18	192.95	189.72	187.25	185.35
10000	944.63	527.72	391.28	324.92	286.52	262.06	245.50	233.83	225.36	219.09	214.38	210.80	208.06	205.94
11000	1039.10	580.49	430.41	357.41	315.18	288.27	270.05	257.21	247.90	241.00	235.82	231.88	228.86	226.53
12000	1133.56	633.26	469.54	389.90	343.83	314.47	294.60	280.59	270.43	262.91	257.26	252.96	249.67	247.13
13000	1228.02	686.03	508.67	422.39	372.48	340.68	319.15	303.97	292.97	284.82	278.70	274.04	270.47	267.72
14000	1322.48	738.80	547.80	454.88	401.13	366.88	343.70	327.35	315.50	306.73	300.13	295.12	291.28	288.31
15000	1416.95	791.57	586.92	487.38	429.78	393.09	368.25	350.74	338.04	328.64	321.57	316.20	312.08	308.91
16000	1511.41	844.35	626.05	519.87	458.44	419.29	392.80	374.12	360.57	350.55	343.01	337.28	332.89	329.50
17000	1605.87	897.12	665.18	552.36	487.09	445.50	417.35	397.50	383.11	372.45	364.45	358.36	353.69	350.09
18000	1700.34	949.89	704.31	584.85	515.74	471.70	441.90	420.88	405.64	394.36	385.89	379.44	374.50	370.69
19000	1794.80	1002.66	743.44	617.34	544.39	497.91	466.45	444.27	428.18	416.27	407.32	400.52	395.30	391.28
20000	1889.26	1055.43	782.56	649.83	573.04	524.12	491.00	467.65	450.72	438.18	428.76	421.60	416.11	411.87
21000	1983.72	1108.20	821.69	682.32	601.70	550.32	515.54	491.03	473.25	460.09	450.20	442.68	436.91	432.47
22000	2078.19	1160.97	860.82	714.82	630.35	576.53	540.09	514.41	495.79	482.00	471.64	463.76	457.72	453.06
23000	2172.65	1213.75	899.95	747.31	659.00	602.73	564.64	537.79	518.32	503.91	493.07	484.84	478.53	473.65
24000	2267.11	1266.52	939.08	779.80	687.65	628.94	589.19	561.18	540.86	525.82	514.51	505.92	499.33	494.25
25000	2361.58	1319.29	978.20	812.29	716.30	655.14	613.74	584.56	563.39	547.72	535.95	527.00	520.14	514.84
26000	2456.04	1372.06	1017.33	844.78	744.96	681.35	638.29	607.94	585.93	569.63	557.39	548.08	540.94	535.43
27000	2550.50	1424.83	1056.46	877.27	773.61	707.55	662.84	631.32	608.46	591.54	578.83	569.16	561.75	556.03
28000	2644.96	1477.60	1095.59	909.76	802.26	733.76	687.39	654.70	631.00	613.45	600.26	590.24	582.55	576.62
29000	2739.43	1530.37	1134.71	942.25	830.91	759.97	711.94	678.09	653.53	635.36	621.70	611.32	603.36	597.21
30000	2833.89	1583.14	1173.84	974.75	859.56	786.17	736.49	701.47	676.07	657.27	643.14	632.40	624.16	617.81
31000	2928.35	1635.92	1212.97	1007.24	888.22	812.38	761.04	724.85	698.61	679.18	664.58	653.48	644.97	638.40
32000	3022.82	1688.69	1252.10	1039.73	916.87	838.58	785.59	748.23	721.14	701.09	686.01	674.56	665.77	658.99
33000	3117.28	1741.46	1291.23	1072.22	945.52	864.79	810.14	771.62	743.68	723.00	707.45	695.64	686.58	679.59
34000	3211.74	1794.23	1330.35	1104.71	974.17	890.99	834.69	795.00	766.21	744.90	728.89	716.72	707.38	700.18
35000	3306.20	1847.00	1369.48	1137.20	1002.82	917.20	859.24	818.38	788.75	766.81	750.33	737.80	728.19	720.77
36000	3400.67	1899.77	1408.61	1169.69	1031.48	943.40	883.79	841.76	811.28	788.72	771.77	758.88	748.99	741.37
37000	3495.13	1952.54	1447.74	1202.19	1060.13	969.61	908.34	865.14	833.82	810.63	793.20	779.96	769.80	761.96
38000	3589.59	2005.32	1486.87	1234.68	1088.78	995.82	932.89	888.53	856.35	832.54	814.64	801.04	790.60	782.55
39000	3684.06	2058.09	1525.99	1267.17	1117.43	1022.02	957.44	911.91	878.89	854.45	836.08	822.11	811.41	803.15
40000	3778.52	2110.86	1565.12	1299.66	1146.08	1048.23	981.99	935.29	901.43	876.36	857.52	843.19	832.21	823.74
41000	3872.98	2163.63	1604.25	1332.15	1174.74	1074.43	1006.53	958.67	923.96	898.27	878.95	864.27	853.02	844.33
42000	3967.44	2216.40	1643.38	1364.64	1203.39	1100.64	1031.08	982.05	946.50	920.17	900.39	885.35	873.82	864.93
43000	4061.91	2269.17	1682.51	1397.13	1232.04	1126.84	1055.63	1005.44	969.03	942.08	921.83	906.43	894.63	885.52
44000	4156.37	2321.94	1721.63	1429.63	1260.69	1153.05	1080.18	1028.82	991.57	963.99	943.27	927.51	915.43	906.11
45000	4250.83	2374.71	1760.76	1462.12	1289.34	1179.25	1104.73	1052.20	1014.10	985.90	964.71	948.59	936.24	926.71
46000	4345.30	2427.49	1799.89	1494.61	1318.00	1205.46	1129.28	1075.58	1036.64	1007.81	986.14	969.67	957.05	947.30
47000	4439.76	2480.26	1839.02	1527.10	1346.65	1231.67	1153.83	1098.96	1059.17	1029.72	1007.58	990.75	977.85	967.89
48000	4534.22	2533.03	1878.15	1559.59	1375.30	1257.87	1178.38	1122.35	1081.71	1051.63	1029.02	1011.83	998.66	988.49
49000	4628.68	2585.80	1917.27	1592.08	1403.95	1284.08	1202.93	1145.73	1104.24	1073.54	1050.46	1032.91	1019.46	1009.08
50000	4723.15	2638.57	1956.40	1624.57	1432.60	1310.28	1227.48	1169.11	1126.78	1095.44	1071.89	1053.99	1040.27	1029.67
55000	5195.46	2902.43	2152.04	1787.03	1575.86	1441.31	1350.23	1286.02	1239.46	1204.99	1179.08	1159.39	1144.29	1132.64
60000	5667.78	3166.28	2347.68	1949.49	1719.12	1572.34	1472.98	1402.93	1352.14	1314.53	1286.27	1264.79	1248.32	1235.61
65000	6140.09	3430.14	2543.32	2111.94	1862.38	1703.37	1595.72	1519.84	1464.81	1424.08	1393.46	1370.19	1352.34	1338.57
70000	6612.40	3694.00	2738.96	2274.40	2005.64	1834.39	1718.47	1636.75	1577.49	1533.62	1500.65	1475.59	1456.37	1441.54
75000	7084.72	3957.85	2934.60	2436.86	2148.90	1965.42	1841.22	1753.66	1690.17	1643.16	1607.84	1580.99	1560.40	1544.51
80000	7557.03	4221.71	3130.24	2599.31	2292.16	2096.45	1963.97	1870.58	1802.85	1752.71	1715.03	1686.38	1664.42	1647.47
85000	8029.35	4485.57	3325.88	2761.77	2435.42	2227.48	2086.71	1987.49	1915.52	1862.25	1822.22	1791.78	1768.45	1750.44
90000	8501.66	4749.42	3521.52	2924.23	2578.68	2358.50	2104.40	2028.20	1971.80	1929.41	1897.18	1872.48	1853.41	—
95000	8973.97	5013.28	3717.16	3086.68	2721.94	2489.53	2332.21	2221.31	2140.88	2081.34	2036.59	2002.58	1976.50	1956.37
100000	9446.29	5277.14	3912.80	3249.14	2865.20	2620.56	2454.96	2338.22	2253.56	2190.88	2143.78	2107.98	2080.53	2059.34

TERM	15 Years	16 Years	17 Years	18 Years	19 Years	20 Years	21 Years	22 Years	23 Years	24 Years	25 Years	30 Years	35 Years	40 Years
AMOUNT														
5	.11	.11	.11	.11	.11	.11	.10	.10	.10	.10	.10	.10	.10	.10
10	.21	.21	.21	.21	.21	.21	.20	.20	.20	.20	.20	.20	.20	.20
15	.31	.31	.31	.31	.31	.31	.30	.30	.30	.30	.30	.30	.30	.30
25	.52	.51	.51	.51	.51	.51	.50	.50	.50	.50	.50	.50	.50	.50
50	1.03	1.02	1.02	1.01	1.01	1.01	1.00	1.00	1.00	1.00	1.00	1.00	1.00	1.00
75	1.54	1.53	1.52	1.51	1.51	1.51	1.50	1.50	1.50	1.50	1.50	1.49	1.49	1.49
100	2.05	2.04	2.03	2.02	2.01	2.01	2.00	2.00	2.00	2.00	1.99	1.99	1.99	1.99
200	4.09	4.07	4.05	4.03	4.02	4.01	4.00	3.99	3.99	3.99	3.98	3.98	3.97	3.97
300	6.13	6.10	6.07	6.04	6.02	6.01	6.00	5.99	5.98	5.98	5.97	5.96	5.96	5.96
400	8.18	8.13	8.09	8.05	8.03	8.01	7.99	7.98	7.97	7.97	7.96	7.95	7.94	7.94
500	10.22	10.16	10.11	10.07	10.04	10.01	9.99	9.98	9.97	9.96	9.95	9.93	9.92	9.92
600	12.26	12.19	12.13	12.08	12.04	12.01	11.99	11.97	11.96	11.95	11.94	11.92	11.91	11.91
700	14.31	14.22	14.15	14.09	14.05	14.01	13.99	13.97	13.95	13.94	13.93	13.90	13.89	13.89
800	16.35	16.25	16.17	16.10	16.05	16.02	15.98	15.96	15.94	15.93	15.92	15.89	15.88	15.87
900	18.39	18.28	18.19	18.12	18.06	18.02	17.98	17.96	17.93	17.92	17.90	17.87	17.86	17.86
1000	20.43	20.31	20.21	20.13	20.07	20.02	19.98	19.95	19.93	19.91	19.89	19.86	19.84	19.84
2000	40.86	40.61	40.41	40.25	40.13	40.03	39.95	39.90	39.85	39.81	39.78	39.71	39.68	39.67
3000	61.29	60.91	60.61	60.37	60.19	60.04	59.93	59.84	59.77	59.71	59.67	59.56	59.52	59.51
4000	81.72	81.21	80.81	80.50	80.25	80.06	79.90	79.79	79.69	79.62	79.56	79.41	79.36	79.34
5000	102.15	101.51	101.01	100.62	100.31	100.07	99.88	99.73	99.61	99.52	99.45	99.26	99.20	99.18
6000	122.58	121.81	121.21	120.74	120.37	120.08	119.85	119.68	119.53	119.42	119.33	119.11	119.04	119.01
7000	143.01	142.11	141.41	140.86	140.43	140.10	139.83	139.62	139.46	139.33	139.22	138.96	138.87	138.85
8000	163.44	162.41	161.61	160.99	160.49	160.11	159.80	159.57	159.38	159.23	159.11	158.81	158.71	158.68
9000	183.87	182.71	181.81	181.11	180.56	180.12	179.78	179.51	179.30	179.13	179.00	178.66	178.55	178.52
10000	204.29	203.01	202.01	201.23	200.62	200.13	199.75	199.46	199.22	199.03	198.89	198.51	198.39	198.35
11000	224.72	223.32	222.22	221.35	220.68	220.15	219.73	219.40	219.14	218.94	218.78	218.36	218.23	218.19
12000	245.15	243.62	242.42	241.48	240.74	240.16	239.70	239.35	239.06	238.84	238.66	238.21	238.07	238.02
13000	265.58	263.92	262.62	261.60	260.80	260.17	259.68	259.29	258.98	258.74	258.55	258.06	257.91	257.86
14000	286.01	284.22	282.82	281.72	280.86	280.19	279.65	279.24	278.91	278.65	278.44	277.91	277.74	277.69
15000	306.44	304.52	303.02	301.84	300.92	300.20	299.63	299.18	298.83	298.55	298.33	297.76	297.58	297.53
16000	326.87	324.82	323.22	321.97	320.98	320.21	319.60	319.13	318.75	318.45	318.22	317.61	317.42	317.36
17000	347.30	345.12	343.42	342.09	341.05	340.22	339.58	339.07	338.67	338.35	338.11	337.46	337.26	337.20
18000	367.73	365.42	363.62	362.21	361.11	360.24	359.55	359.02	358.59	358.26	357.99	357.31	357.10	357.03
19000	388.16	385.72	383.82	382.34	381.17	380.25	379.53	378.96	378.51	378.16	377.88	377.16	376.94	376.87
20000	408.58	406.02	404.02	402.46	401.23	400.26	399.50	398.91	398.43	398.06	397.77	397.01	396.78	396.70
21000	429.01	426.33	424.23	422.58	421.29	420.28	419.48	418.85	418.36	417.97	417.66	416.86	416.61	416.54
22000	449.44	446.63	444.43	442.70	441.35	440.29	439.45	438.80	438.28	437.87	437.55	436.71	436.45	436.37
23000	469.87	466.93	464.63	462.83	461.41	460.30	459.43	458.74	458.20	457.77	457.44	456.56	456.29	456.21
24000	490.30	487.23	484.83	482.95	481.47	480.32	479.40	478.69	478.12	477.68	477.32	476.41	476.13	476.04
25000	510.73	507.53	505.03	503.07	501.54	500.33	499.38	498.63	498.04	497.58	497.21	496.26	495.97	495.88
26000	531.16	527.83	525.23	523.19	521.60	520.34	519.35	518.58	517.96	517.48	517.10	516.11	515.81	515.71
27000	551.59	548.13	545.43	543.32	541.66	540.35	539.33	538.52	537.89	537.38	536.99	535.96	535.65	535.55
28000	572.02	568.43	565.63	563.44	561.72	560.37	559.30	558.47	557.81	557.29	556.88	555.81	555.48	555.38
29000	592.45	588.73	585.83	583.56	581.78	580.38	579.28	578.41	577.73	577.19	576.76	575.66	575.32	575.22
30000	612.87	609.03	606.03	603.68	601.84	600.39	599.25	598.36	597.65	597.09	596.65	595.51	595.16	595.05
31000	633.30	629.34	626.23	623.81	621.90	620.41	619.23	618.30	617.57	617.00	616.54	615.36	615.00	614.89
32000	653.73	649.64	646.44	643.93	641.96	640.42	639.20	638.25	637.49	636.90	636.43	635.21	634.84	634.72
33000	674.16	669.94	666.64	664.05	662.02	660.43	659.18	658.19	657.41	656.80	656.32	655.06	654.68	654.56
34000	694.59	690.24	686.84	684.18	682.09	680.44	679.15	678.14	677.34	676.70	676.21	674.91	674.51	674.39
35000	715.02	710.54	707.04	704.30	702.15	700.46	699.13	698.08	697.26	696.61	696.09	694.76	694.35	694.23
36000	735.45	730.84	727.24	724.42	722.21	720.47	719.10	718.03	717.18	716.51	715.98	714.61	714.19	714.06
37000	755.88	751.14	747.44	744.54	742.27	740.48	739.08	737.97	737.10	736.41	735.87	734.46	734.03	733.90
38000	776.31	771.44	767.64	764.67	762.33	760.50	759.05	757.92	757.02	756.32	755.76	754.31	753.87	753.73
39000	796.74	791.74	787.84	784.79	782.39	780.51	779.03	777.86	776.94	776.22	775.65	774.16	773.71	773.57
40000	817.16	812.04	808.04	804.91	802.45	800.52	799.00	797.81	796.86	796.12	795.54	794.01	793.55	793.40
41000	837.59	832.34	828.24	825.03	822.51	820.54	818.98	817.75	816.79	816.02	815.42	813.86	813.38	813.24
42000	858.02	852.65	848.45	845.16	842.58	840.55	838.95	837.70	836.71	835.93	835.31	833.71	833.22	833.07
43000	878.45	872.95	868.65	865.28	862.64	860.56	858.93	857.64	856.63	855.83	855.20	853.56	853.06	852.91
44000	898.88	893.25	888.85	885.40	882.70	880.57	878.90	877.59	876.55	875.73	875.09	873.41	872.90	872.74
45000	919.31	913.55	909.05	905.52	902.76	900.59	898.88	897.53	896.47	895.64	894.98	893.26	892.74	892.58
46000	939.74	933.85	929.25	925.65	922.82	920.60	918.85	917.48	916.39	915.54	914.87	913.11	912.58	912.41
47000	960.17	954.15	949.45	945.77	942.88	940.61	938.83	937.42	936.32	935.44	934.75	932.96	932.42	932.25
48000	980.60	974.45	969.65	965.89	962.94	960.63	958.80	957.37	956.24	955.35	954.64	952.82	952.25	952.08
49000	1001.03	994.75	989.85	986.01	983.00	980.64	978.78	977.31	976.16	975.25	974.53	972.67	972.09	971.92
50000	1021.45	1015.05	1010.05	1006.14	1003.07	1000.65	998.75	997.26	996.08	995.15	994.42	992.52	991.93	991.75
55000	1123.60	1116.56	1111.06	1106.75	1103.37	1100.72	1098.63	1096.98	1095.69	1094.67	1093.86	1091.77	1091.12	1090.93
60000	1225.74	1218.06	1212.06	1207.36	1203.68	1200.78	1198.50	1196.71	1195.29	1194.18	1193.30	1191.02	1190.32	1190.10
65000	1327.89	1319.57	1313.07	1307.98	1303.98	1300.85	1298.38	1296.43	1294.90	1293.69	1292.74	1290.27	1289.51	1289.28
70000	1430.03	1421.07	1414.07	1408.59	1404.29	1400.91	1398.25	1396.16	1394.51	1393.21	1392.18	1389.52	1388.70	1388.45
75000	1532.18	1522.58	1515.08	1509.20	1504.60	1500.98	1498.13	1495.88	1494.12	1492.72	1491.63	1488.77	1487.89	1487.62
80000	1634.32	1624.08	1616.08	1609.82	1604.90	1601.04	1598.00	1595.61	1593.72	1592.24	1591.07	1588.02	1587.09	1586.80
85000	1736.47	1725.59	1717.09	1710.43	1705.21	1701.10	1697.88	1695.33	1693.33	1691.75	1690.51	1687.27	1686.28	1685.97
90000	1838.61	1827.09	1818.09	1811.04	1805.51	1801.17	1797.75	1795.06	1792.94	1791.27	1789.95	1786.52	1785.47	1785.15
95000	1940.76	1928.60	1919.10	1911.66	1905.82	1901.23	1897.63	1894.78	1892.55	1890.78	1889.39	1885.77	1884.66	1884.32
100000	2042.90	2030.10	2020.10	2012.27	2006.13	2001.30	1997.50	1994.51	1992.15	1990.30	1988.83	1985.03	1983.86	1983.50

MONTHLY PAYMENT
REQUIRED TO AMORTIZE A LOAN

TERM AMOUNT	1 Year	2 Years	3 Years	4 Years	5 Years	6 Years	7 Years	8 Years	9 Years	10 Years	11 Years	12 Years	13 Years	14 Years
5	.48	.27	.20	.17	.15	.14	.13	.12	.12	.11	.11	.11	.11	.11
10	.95	.53	.40	.33	.29	.27	.25	.24	.23	.22	.22	.22	.21	.21
15	1.42	.80	.59	.49	.44	.40	.37	.36	.34	.33	.33	.32	.32	.31
25	2.37	1.33	.98	.82	.72	.66	.62	.59	.57	.55	.54	.53	.53	.52
50	4.73	2.65	1.96	1.63	1.44	1.32	1.23	1.18	1.13	1.10	1.08	1.06	1.05	1.04
75	7.09	3.97	2.94	2.44	2.16	1.97	1.85	1.76	1.70	1.65	1.62	1.59	1.57	1.55
100	9.45	5.29	3.92	3.26	2.87	2.63	2.46	2.35	2.26	2.20	2.15	2.12	2.09	2.07
200	18.90	10.57	7.84	6.51	5.74	5.26	4.92	4.69	4.52	4.40	4.30	4.23	4.18	4.14
300	28.35	15.85	11.76	9.76	8.61	7.88	7.38	7.03	6.79	6.59	6.45	6.35	6.26	6.20
400	37.80	21.13	15.67	13.02	11.48	10.51	9.84	9.38	9.04	8.79	8.60	8.46	8.35	8.27
500	47.25	26.41	19.59	16.27	14.35	13.13	12.30	11.72	11.30	10.99	10.75	10.57	10.44	10.33
600	56.70	31.69	23.51	19.52	17.22	15.76	14.76	14.06	13.56	13.18	12.90	12.69	12.52	12.40
700	66.15	36.97	27.42	22.78	20.09	18.38	17.22	16.41	15.82	15.38	15.05	14.80	14.61	14.46
800	75.60	42.25	31.34	26.03	22.96	21.01	19.68	18.75	18.07	17.57	17.20	16.91	16.69	16.53
900	85.05	47.53	35.26	29.28	25.83	23.63	22.14	21.09	20.33	19.77	19.35	19.03	18.78	18.59
1000	94.50	52.81	39.17	32.54	28.70	26.26	24.60	23.44	22.59	21.97	21.50	21.14	20.87	20.66
2000	189.00	105.62	78.34	65.07	57.40	52.51	49.20	46.87	45.18	43.93	42.99	42.27	41.73	41.31
3000	283.50	158.43	117.51	97.60	86.09	78.76	73.80	70.30	67.76	65.89	64.48	63.41	62.59	61.96
4000	378.00	211.24	156.67	130.14	114.79	105.01	98.39	93.73	90.35	87.85	85.97	84.54	83.45	82.61
5000	472.50	264.05	195.84	162.67	143.48	131.26	122.99	117.16	112.94	109.81	107.46	105.68	104.31	103.26
6000	567.00	316.86	235.01	195.20	172.18	157.51	147.59	140.59	135.52	131.77	128.95	126.81	125.17	123.91
7000	661.50	369.67	274.18	227.73	200.87	183.76	172.18	164.02	158.11	153.73	150.44	147.95	146.03	144.56
8000	756.00	422.47	313.34	260.27	229.57	210.01	196.78	187.45	180.69	175.69	171.94	169.08	166.89	165.21
9000	850.50	475.28	352.51	292.80	258.26	236.26	221.38	210.89	203.28	197.65	193.43	190.22	187.75	185.86
10000	945.00	528.09	391.68	325.33	286.96	262.52	245.97	234.32	225.87	219.61	214.92	211.35	208.62	206.51
11000	1039.50	580.90	430.84	357.87	315.66	288.77	270.57	257.75	248.45	241.58	236.41	232.48	229.48	227.16
12000	1133.99	633.71	470.01	390.40	344.35	315.02	295.17	281.18	271.04	263.54	257.90	253.62	250.34	247.81
13000	1228.49	686.52	509.18	422.93	373.05	341.27	319.76	304.61	293.63	285.50	279.39	274.75	271.20	268.46
14000	1322.99	739.33	548.35	455.46	401.74	367.52	344.36	328.04	316.21	307.46	300.88	295.89	292.06	289.11
15000	1417.49	792.14	587.51	488.00	430.44	393.77	368.96	351.47	338.80	329.42	322.37	317.02	312.92	309.76
16000	1511.99	844.94	626.68	520.53	459.13	420.02	393.55	374.90	361.38	351.38	343.87	338.16	333.78	330.41
17000	1606.49	897.75	665.85	553.06	487.83	446.27	418.15	398.34	383.97	373.34	365.36	359.29	354.64	351.06
18000	1700.99	950.56	705.02	585.59	516.52	472.52	442.75	421.77	406.56	395.30	386.85	380.43	375.50	371.71
19000	1795.49	1003.37	744.18	618.13	545.22	498.77	467.34	445.20	429.14	417.26	408.34	401.56	396.37	392.36
20000	1889.99	1056.18	783.35	650.66	573.91	525.03	491.94	468.63	451.73	439.22	429.83	422.69	417.23	413.01
21000	1984.49	1108.99	822.52	683.19	602.61	551.28	516.54	492.06	474.32	461.19	451.32	443.83	438.09	433.66
22000	2078.99	1161.80	861.69	715.73	631.31	577.53	541.14	515.49	496.90	483.15	472.81	464.96	458.95	454.31
23000	2173.48	1214.61	900.85	748.26	660.00	603.78	565.73	538.92	519.49	505.11	494.31	486.10	479.81	474.96
24000	2267.98	1267.41	940.02	780.79	688.70	630.03	590.33	562.35	542.07	527.07	515.80	507.23	500.67	495.61
25000	2362.48	1320.22	979.19	813.32	717.39	656.28	614.93	585.79	564.66	549.03	537.29	528.37	521.53	516.26
26000	2456.98	1373.03	1018.35	845.86	746.09	682.53	639.52	609.22	587.25	570.99	558.78	549.50	542.39	536.91
27000	2551.48	1425.84	1057.52	878.39	774.78	708.78	664.12	632.65	609.83	592.95	580.27	570.64	563.25	557.56
28000	2645.98	1478.65	1096.69	910.92	803.48	735.03	688.72	656.08	632.42	614.91	601.76	591.77	584.11	578.21
29000	2740.48	1531.46	1135.86	943.46	832.17	761.28	713.31	679.51	655.01	636.87	623.25	612.91	604.98	598.86
30000	2834.98	1584.27	1175.02	975.99	860.87	787.54	737.91	702.94	677.59	658.83	644.74	634.04	625.84	619.51
31000	2929.48	1637.08	1214.19	1008.52	889.56	813.79	762.51	726.37	700.18	680.80	666.24	655.17	646.70	640.16
32000	3023.98	1689.88	1253.36	1041.05	918.26	840.04	787.10	749.80	722.76	702.76	687.73	676.31	667.56	660.81
33000	3118.48	1742.69	1292.52	1073.59	946.96	866.29	811.70	773.24	745.35	724.72	709.22	697.44	688.42	681.46
34000	3212.97	1795.50	1331.69	1106.12	975.65	892.54	836.30	796.67	767.94	746.68	730.71	718.58	709.28	702.11
35000	3307.47	1848.31	1370.86	1138.65	1004.35	918.79	860.89	820.10	790.52	768.64	752.20	739.71	730.14	722.76
36000	3401.97	1901.12	1410.03	1171.18	1033.04	945.04	885.49	843.53	813.11	790.60	773.69	760.85	751.00	743.41
37000	3496.47	1953.93	1449.19	1203.72	1061.74	971.29	910.09	866.96	835.70	812.56	795.18	781.98	771.86	764.06
38000	3590.97	2006.74	1488.36	1236.25	1090.43	997.54	934.68	890.39	858.28	834.52	816.68	803.12	792.73	784.71
39000	3685.47	2059.55	1527.53	1268.78	1119.13	1023.79	959.28	913.82	880.87	856.48	838.17	824.25	813.59	805.36
40000	3779.97	2112.35	1566.70	1301.32	1147.82	1050.05	983.88	937.25	903.45	878.44	859.66	845.38	834.45	826.01
41000	3874.47	2165.16	1605.86	1333.85	1176.52	1076.30	1008.48	960.68	926.04	900.41	881.15	866.52	855.31	846.66
42000	3968.97	2217.97	1645.03	1366.38	1205.21	1102.55	1033.07	984.12	948.63	922.37	902.64	887.65	876.17	867.31
43000	4063.47	2270.78	1684.20	1398.91	1233.91	1128.80	1057.67	1007.55	971.21	944.33	924.13	908.79	897.03	887.96
44000	4157.97	2323.59	1723.36	1431.45	1262.61	1155.05	1082.27	1030.98	993.80	966.29	945.62	929.92	917.89	908.61
45000	4252.47	2376.40	1762.53	1463.98	1291.30	1181.30	1106.86	1054.41	1016.39	988.25	967.11	951.06	938.75	929.26
46000	4346.96	2429.21	1801.70	1496.51	1320.00	1207.55	1131.46	1077.84	1038.97	1010.21	988.61	972.19	959.61	949.91
47000	4441.46	2482.02	1840.87	1529.05	1348.69	1233.80	1156.06	1101.27	1061.56	1032.17	1010.10	993.33	980.47	970.56
48000	4535.96	2534.82	1880.03	1561.58	1377.39	1260.05	1180.65	1124.70	1084.14	1054.13	1031.59	1014.46	1001.34	991.21
49000	4630.46	2587.63	1919.20	1594.11	1406.08	1286.30	1205.25	1148.13	1106.73	1076.09	1053.08	1035.60	1022.20	1011.86
50000	4724.96	2640.44	1958.37	1626.64	1434.78	1312.56	1229.85	1171.57	1129.32	1098.05	1074.57	1056.73	1043.06	1032.51
55000	5197.46	2904.49	2154.20	1789.31	1578.26	1443.81	1352.83	1288.72	1242.25	1207.86	1182.03	1162.40	1147.36	1135.76
60000	5669.95	3168.53	2350.04	1951.97	1721.73	1575.07	1475.82	1405.88	1355.18	1317.66	1289.48	1268.08	1251.67	1239.01
65000	6142.45	3432.57	2545.88	2114.64	1865.21	1706.32	1598.80	1523.03	1468.11	1427.47	1396.94	1373.75	1355.97	1342.26
70000	6614.94	3696.62	2741.71	2277.30	2008.69	1837.58	1721.78	1640.19	1581.04	1537.27	1504.40	1479.42	1460.28	1445.51
75000	7087.44	3960.66	2937.55	2439.96	2152.16	1968.83	1844.77	1757.35	1693.97	1647.08	1611.85	1585.09	1564.58	1548.77
80000	7559.93	4224.70	3133.39	2602.63	2295.64	2100.09	1967.75	1874.50	1806.90	1756.88	1719.31	1690.76	1668.89	1652.02
85000	8032.43	4488.75	3329.22	2765.29	2439.12	2231.34	2090.74	1991.66	1919.83	1866.69	1826.77	1796.44	1773.20	1755.27
90000	8504.93	4752.79	3525.06	2927.95	2582.60	2362.60	2213.72	2108.81	2032.77	1976.49	1934.22	1902.11	1877.50	1858.52
95000	8977.42	5016.83	3720.89	3090.62	2726.07	2493.85	2336.70	2225.97	2145.70	2086.30	2041.68	2007.78	1981.81	1961.77
100000	9449.92	5280.88	3916.73	3253.28	2869.55	2625.11	2459.69	2343.13	2258.63	2196.10	2149.14	2113.45	2086.11	2065.02

TERM	15 Years	16 Years	17 Years	18 Years	19 Years	20 Years	21 Years	22 Years	23 Years	24 Years	25 Years	30 Years	35 Years	40 Years
AMOUNT														
5	.11	.11	.11	.11	.11	.11	.11	.11	.10	.10	.10	.10	.10	.10
10	.21	.21	.21	.21	.21	.21	.21	.21	.20	.20	.20	.20	.20	.20
15	.31	.31	.31	.31	.31	.31	.31	.31	.30	.30	.30	.30	.30	.30
25	.52	.51	.51	.51	.51	.51	.51	.51	.50	.50	.50	.50	.50	.50
50	1.03	1.02	1.02	1.01	1.01	1.01	1.01	1.01	1.00	1.00	1.00	1.00	1.00	1.00
75	1.54	1.53	1.52	1.52	1.51	1.51	1.51	1.51	1.50	1.50	1.50	1.50	1.50	1.50
100	2.05	2.04	2.03	2.02	2.02	2.01	2.01	2.01	2.00	2.00	2.00	2.00	2.00	1.99
200	4.10	4.08	4.06	4.04	4.03	4.02	4.01	4.01	4.00	4.00	3.99	3.99	3.99	3.98
300	6.15	6.11	6.08	6.06	6.04	6.03	6.02	6.01	6.00	5.99	5.99	5.98	5.98	5.97
400	8.20	8.15	8.11	8.08	8.05	8.03	8.02	8.01	8.00	7.99	7.98	7.97	7.97	7.96
500	10.25	10.18	10.13	10.10	10.07	10.04	10.02	10.01	10.00	9.99	9.98	9.96	9.96	9.95
600	12.30	12.22	12.16	12.11	12.08	12.05	12.03	12.01	11.99	11.98	11.97	11.95	11.95	11.94
700	14.35	14.26	14.19	14.13	14.09	14.06	14.03	14.01	13.99	13.98	13.97	13.94	13.94	13.93
800	16.39	16.29	16.21	16.15	16.10	16.06	16.03	16.01	15.99	15.98	15.96	15.93	15.93	15.92
900	18.44	18.33	18.24	18.17	18.11	18.07	18.04	18.01	17.99	17.97	17.96	17.93	17.92	17.91
1000	20.49	20.36	20.26	20.19	20.13	20.08	20.04	20.01	19.99	19.97	19.95	19.92	19.91	19.90
2000	40.98	40.72	40.52	40.37	40.25	40.15	40.08	40.02	39.97	39.93	39.90	39.83	39.81	39.80
3000	61.46	61.08	60.78	60.55	60.37	60.23	60.11	60.02	59.95	59.90	59.85	59.74	59.71	59.70
4000	81.95	81.44	81.04	80.73	80.49	80.30	80.15	80.03	79.94	79.86	79.80	79.65	79.61	79.59
5000	102.44	101.80	101.30	100.92	100.61	100.37	100.18	100.04	99.92	99.83	99.75	99.57	99.51	99.49
6000	122.92	122.16	121.56	121.10	120.73	120.45	120.22	120.04	119.90	119.79	119.70	119.48	119.41	119.39
7000	143.41	142.52	141.82	141.28	140.85	140.52	140.25	140.05	139.88	139.76	139.65	139.39	139.31	139.29
8000	163.90	162.88	162.08	161.46	160.97	160.59	160.29	160.05	159.87	159.72	159.60	159.30	159.21	159.18
9000	184.38	183.24	182.34	181.64	181.10	180.67	180.33	180.06	179.85	179.68	179.55	179.22	179.11	179.08
10000	204.87	203.60	202.60	201.83	201.22	200.74	200.36	200.07	199.83	199.65	199.50	199.13	199.01	198.98
11000	225.36	223.96	222.86	222.01	221.34	220.81	220.40	220.07	219.82	219.61	219.45	219.04	218.91	218.88
12000	245.84	244.32	243.12	242.19	241.46	240.89	240.43	240.08	239.80	239.58	239.40	238.95	238.82	238.77
13000	266.33	264.68	263.38	262.37	261.58	260.96	260.47	260.08	259.78	259.54	259.35	258.87	258.72	258.67
14000	286.82	285.04	283.64	282.56	281.70	281.03	280.50	280.09	279.76	279.51	279.30	278.78	278.62	278.57
15000	307.30	305.39	303.90	302.74	301.82	301.11	300.54	300.10	299.75	299.47	299.25	298.69	298.52	298.47
16000	327.79	325.75	324.16	322.92	321.94	321.18	320.58	320.10	319.73	319.44	319.20	318.60	318.42	318.36
17000	348.28	346.11	344.42	343.10	342.07	341.25	340.61	340.11	339.71	339.40	339.15	338.52	338.32	338.26
18000	368.76	366.47	364.68	363.28	362.19	361.33	360.65	360.11	359.70	359.37	359.10	358.43	358.22	358.16
19000	389.25	386.83	384.94	383.47	382.31	381.40	380.68	380.12	379.68	379.33	379.05	378.34	378.12	378.06
20000	409.74	407.19	405.20	403.65	402.43	401.47	400.72	400.13	399.66	399.29	399.00	398.25	398.02	397.95
21000	430.22	427.55	425.46	423.83	422.55	421.55	420.75	420.13	419.64	419.26	418.95	418.17	417.92	417.85
22000	450.71	447.91	445.72	444.01	442.67	441.62	440.79	440.14	439.63	439.22	438.90	438.08	437.82	437.75
23000	471.20	468.27	465.98	464.20	462.79	461.69	460.83	460.15	459.61	459.19	458.85	457.99	457.72	457.64
24000	491.68	488.63	486.24	484.38	482.91	481.77	480.86	480.15	479.59	479.15	478.80	477.90	477.63	477.54
25000	512.17	508.99	506.50	504.56	503.04	501.84	500.90	500.16	499.57	499.12	498.75	497.81	497.53	497.44
26000	532.66	529.35	526.76	524.74	523.16	521.91	520.93	520.16	519.56	519.08	518.70	517.73	517.43	517.34
27000	553.14	549.71	547.02	544.92	543.28	541.99	540.97	540.17	539.54	539.04	538.65	537.64	537.33	537.23
28000	573.63	570.07	567.28	565.11	563.40	562.06	561.00	560.18	559.52	559.01	558.60	557.55	557.23	557.13
29000	594.12	590.43	587.54	585.29	583.52	582.13	581.04	580.18	579.51	578.97	578.55	577.46	577.13	577.03
30000	614.60	610.78	607.80	605.47	603.64	602.21	601.08	600.19	599.49	598.94	598.50	597.38	597.03	596.93
31000	635.09	631.14	628.06	625.65	623.76	622.28	621.11	620.19	619.47	618.90	618.45	617.29	616.93	616.82
32000	655.58	651.50	648.32	645.84	643.88	642.35	641.15	640.20	639.45	638.87	638.40	637.20	636.83	636.72
33000	676.06	671.86	668.58	666.02	664.01	662.43	661.18	660.21	659.44	658.83	658.35	657.11	656.73	656.62
34000	696.55	692.22	688.84	686.20	684.13	682.50	681.22	680.21	679.42	678.79	678.30	677.03	676.64	676.52
35000	717.04	712.58	709.10	706.38	704.25	702.57	701.25	700.22	699.40	698.76	698.25	696.94	696.54	696.41
36000	737.52	732.94	729.36	726.56	724.37	722.65	721.29	720.22	719.39	718.72	718.20	716.85	716.44	716.31
37000	758.01	753.30	749.62	746.75	744.49	742.72	741.33	740.23	739.37	738.69	738.15	736.76	736.34	736.21
38000	778.50	773.66	769.88	766.93	764.61	762.79	761.36	760.24	759.35	758.65	758.10	756.68	756.24	756.11
39000	798.98	794.02	790.14	787.11	784.73	782.87	781.40	780.24	779.33	778.62	778.05	776.59	776.14	776.00
40000	819.47	814.38	810.40	807.29	804.85	802.94	801.43	800.25	799.32	798.58	798.00	796.50	796.04	795.90
41000	839.96	834.74	830.66	827.47	824.98	823.01	821.47	820.25	819.30	818.55	817.95	816.41	815.94	815.80
42000	860.44	855.10	850.92	847.66	845.10	843.09	841.50	840.26	839.28	838.51	837.90	836.33	835.84	835.70
43000	880.93	875.46	871.18	867.84	865.22	863.16	861.54	860.27	859.26	858.47	857.85	856.24	855.74	855.59
44000	901.42	895.82	891.44	888.02	885.34	883.23	881.58	880.27	879.25	878.44	877.80	876.15	875.64	875.49
45000	921.90	916.17	911.70	908.20	905.46	903.31	901.61	900.28	899.23	898.40	897.75	896.06	895.55	895.39
46000	942.39	936.53	931.96	928.39	925.58	923.38	921.65	920.29	919.21	918.37	917.70	915.98	915.45	915.28
47000	962.88	956.89	952.22	948.57	945.70	943.45	941.68	940.29	939.20	938.33	937.65	935.89	935.35	935.18
48000	983.36	977.25	972.48	968.75	965.82	963.53	961.72	960.30	959.18	958.30	957.60	955.80	955.25	955.08
49000	1003.85	997.61	992.74	988.93	985.94	983.60	981.75	980.30	979.16	978.26	977.55	975.71	975.15	974.98
50000	1024.34	1017.97	1013.00	1009.11	1006.07	1003.67	1001.79	1000.31	999.14	998.23	997.50	995.62	995.05	994.87
55000	1126.77	1119.77	1114.30	1110.03	1106.67	1104.04	1101.97	1100.34	1099.06	1098.05	1097.25	1095.19	1094.55	1094.36
60000	1229.20	1221.56	1215.60	1210.94	1207.28	1204.41	1202.15	1200.37	1198.97	1197.87	1197.00	1194.75	1194.06	1193.85
65000	1331.63	1323.36	1316.90	1311.85	1307.88	1304.77	1302.33	1300.40	1298.89	1297.69	1296.75	1294.31	1293.56	1293.34
70000	1434.07	1425.16	1418.20	1412.76	1408.49	1405.14	1402.50	1400.43	1398.80	1397.51	1396.50	1393.87	1393.07	1392.82
75000	1536.50	1526.95	1519.50	1513.67	1509.10	1505.51	1502.68	1500.46	1498.71	1497.34	1496.25	1493.43	1492.57	1492.31
80000	1638.93	1628.75	1620.80	1614.58	1609.70	1605.87	1602.86	1600.49	1598.63	1597.16	1596.00	1593.00	1592.08	1591.80
85000	1741.37	1730.55	1722.10	1715.49	1710.31	1706.24	1703.04	1700.52	1698.54	1696.98	1695.75	1692.56	1691.58	1691.28
90000	1843.80	1832.34	1823.40	1816.40	1810.91	1806.61	1803.22	1800.55	1798.46	1796.80	1795.50	1792.12	1791.09	1790.77
95000	1946.23	1934.14	1924.70	1917.31	1911.52	1906.97	1903.40	1900.58	1898.37	1896.62	1895.25	1891.68	1890.59	1890.26
100000	2048.67	2035.94	2026.00	2018.22	2012.13	2007.34	2003.58	2000.61	1998.28	1996.45	1995.00	1991.24	1990.10	1989.74

MONTHLY PAYMENT
REQUIRED TO AMORTIZE A LOAN

TERM AMOUNT	1 Year	2 Years	3 Years	4 Years	5 Years	6 Years	7 Years	8 Years	9 Years	10 Years	11 Years	12 Years	13 Years	14 Years
5	.48	.27	.20	.17	.15	.14	.13	.12	.12	.11	.11	.11	.11	.11
10	.95	.53	.40	.33	.29	.27	.25	.24	.23	.22	.22	.22	.21	.21
15	1.42	.80	.59	.49	.44	.40	.37	.36	.34	.33	.33	.32	.32	.32
25	2.37	1.33	.98	.82	.72	.66	.62	.59	.57	.55	.54	.53	.53	.52
50	4.73	2.65	1.96	1.63	1.44	1.32	1.24	1.18	1.14	1.10	1.08	1.06	1.05	1.04
75	7.09	3.97	2.94	2.45	2.16	1.97	1.85	1.76	1.70	1.65	1.62	1.59	1.57	1.56
100	9.46	5.29	3.92	3.26	2.88	2.63	2.47	2.35	2.27	2.20	2.16	2.12	2.09	2.07
200	18.91	10.57	7.84	6.51	5.75	5.26	4.93	4.69	4.53	4.40	4.31	4.24	4.18	4.14
300	28.36	15.85	11.76	9.77	8.62	7.88	7.39	7.04	6.79	6.60	6.46	6.35	6.27	6.21
400	37.81	21.13	15.68	13.02	11.49	10.51	9.85	9.38	9.05	8.80	8.61	8.47	8.36	8.27
500	47.26	26.42	19.60	16.28	14.36	13.14	12.31	11.73	11.31	10.99	10.76	10.58	10.44	10.34
600	56.71	31.70	23.51	19.53	17.23	15.76	14.77	14.07	13.57	13.19	12.91	12.70	12.53	12.41
700	66.16	36.98	27.43	22.79	20.10	18.39	17.23	16.42	15.83	15.39	15.06	14.81	14.62	14.47
800	75.61	42.26	31.35	26.04	22.97	21.02	19.70	18.76	18.09	17.59	17.21	16.93	16.71	16.54
900	85.07	47.54	35.27	29.30	25.84	23.64	22.16	21.11	20.35	19.79	19.36	19.04	18.80	18.61
1000	94.52	52.83	39.19	32.55	28.71	26.27	24.62	23.45	22.61	21.98	21.51	21.16	20.88	20.67
2000	189.03	105.65	78.37	65.10	57.42	52.54	49.23	46.90	45.21	43.96	43.02	42.31	41.76	41.34
3000	283.54	158.47	117.55	97.64	86.13	78.80	73.84	70.35	67.81	65.94	64.53	63.46	62.64	62.01
4000	378.05	211.29	156.73	130.19	114.84	105.07	98.46	93.80	90.42	87.92	86.04	84.62	83.52	82.68
5000	472.56	264.11	195.91	162.74	143.55	131.34	123.07	117.24	113.02	109.90	107.55	105.77	104.40	103.35
6000	567.07	316.93	235.09	195.28	172.26	157.60	147.68	140.69	135.62	131.88	129.06	126.92	125.28	124.02
7000	661.58	369.75	274.27	227.83	200.97	183.87	172.29	164.14	158.23	153.85	150.57	148.07	146.16	144.69
8000	756.09	422.57	313.45	260.38	229.68	210.13	196.91	187.59	180.83	175.83	172.08	169.23	167.04	165.36
9000	850.61	475.40	352.63	292.92	258.39	236.40	221.52	211.03	203.43	197.81	193.59	190.38	187.92	186.03
10000	945.12	528.22	391.81	325.47	287.10	262.67	246.13	234.48	226.04	219.79	215.10	211.53	208.80	206.70
11000	1039.63	581.04	430.99	358.02	315.81	288.93	270.74	257.93	248.64	241.77	236.61	232.69	229.68	227.36
12000	1134.14	633.86	470.17	390.56	344.52	315.20	295.36	281.38	271.24	263.75	258.12	253.84	250.56	248.03
13000	1228.65	686.68	509.35	423.11	373.23	341.47	319.97	304.82	293.85	285.72	279.62	274.99	271.44	268.70
14000	1323.16	739.50	548.53	455.66	401.94	367.73	344.58	328.27	316.45	307.70	301.13	296.14	292.32	289.37
15000	1417.67	792.32	587.71	488.20	430.65	394.00	369.19	351.72	339.05	329.68	322.64	317.30	313.20	310.04
16000	1512.18	845.14	626.89	520.75	459.36	420.26	393.81	375.17	361.66	351.66	344.15	338.45	334.08	330.71
17000	1606.70	897.97	666.07	553.30	488.07	446.53	418.42	398.61	384.26	373.64	365.66	359.60	354.96	351.38
18000	1701.21	950.79	705.25	585.84	516.78	472.80	443.03	422.06	406.86	395.62	387.17	380.75	375.84	372.05
19000	1795.72	1003.61	744.43	618.39	545.49	499.06	467.64	445.51	429.46	417.59	408.68	401.91	396.72	392.72
20000	1890.23	1056.43	783.61	650.94	574.20	525.33	492.26	468.96	452.07	439.57	430.19	423.06	417.60	413.39
21000	1984.74	1109.25	822.79	683.48	602.91	551.59	516.87	492.40	474.67	461.55	451.70	444.21	438.48	434.06
22000	2079.25	1162.07	861.97	716.03	631.62	577.86	541.48	515.85	497.27	483.53	473.21	465.37	459.36	454.72
23000	2173.76	1214.89	901.15	748.58	660.33	604.13	566.10	539.30	519.88	505.51	494.72	486.52	480.24	475.39
24000	2268.27	1267.71	940.33	781.12	689.04	630.39	590.71	562.75	542.48	527.49	516.23	507.67	501.12	496.06
25000	2362.79	1320.54	979.51	813.67	717.75	656.66	615.32	586.19	565.08	549.47	537.73	528.82	522.00	516.73
26000	2457.30	1373.36	1018.69	846.22	746.46	682.93	639.93	609.64	587.69	571.44	559.24	549.98	542.88	537.40
27000	2551.81	1426.18	1057.87	878.76	775.17	709.19	664.55	633.09	610.29	593.42	580.75	571.13	563.76	558.07
28000	2646.32	1479.00	1097.06	911.31	803.88	735.46	689.16	656.54	632.89	615.40	602.26	592.28	584.64	578.74
29000	2740.83	1531.82	1136.24	943.86	832.59	761.72	713.77	679.99	655.50	637.38	623.77	613.44	605.52	599.41
30000	2835.34	1584.64	1175.42	976.40	861.30	787.99	738.38	703.43	678.10	659.36	645.28	634.59	626.40	620.08
31000	2929.85	1637.46	1214.60	1008.95	890.01	814.26	763.00	726.88	700.70	681.34	666.79	655.74	647.28	640.75
32000	3024.36	1690.28	1253.78	1041.50	918.72	840.52	787.61	750.33	723.31	703.31	688.30	676.89	668.15	661.42
33000	3118.87	1743.10	1292.96	1074.04	947.43	866.79	812.22	773.78	745.91	725.29	709.81	698.05	689.03	682.08
34000	3213.39	1795.93	1332.14	1106.59	976.14	893.05	836.83	797.22	768.51	747.27	731.32	719.20	709.91	702.75
35000	3307.90	1848.75	1371.32	1139.14	1004.85	919.32	861.45	820.67	791.11	769.25	752.83	740.35	730.79	723.42
36000	3402.41	1901.57	1410.50	1171.68	1033.56	945.59	886.06	844.12	813.72	791.23	774.34	761.50	751.67	744.09
37000	3496.92	1954.39	1449.68	1204.23	1062.27	971.85	910.67	867.57	836.32	813.21	795.84	782.66	772.55	764.76
38000	3591.43	2007.21	1488.86	1236.77	1090.98	998.12	935.28	891.01	858.92	835.18	817.35	803.81	793.43	785.43
39000	3685.94	2060.03	1528.04	1269.32	1119.69	1024.39	959.90	914.46	881.53	857.16	838.86	824.96	814.31	806.10
40000	3780.45	2112.85	1567.22	1301.87	1148.40	1050.65	984.51	937.91	904.13	879.14	860.37	846.12	835.19	826.77
41000	3874.96	2165.67	1606.40	1334.41	1177.11	1076.92	1009.12	961.36	926.73	901.12	881.88	867.27	856.07	847.44
42000	3969.48	2218.50	1645.58	1366.96	1205.82	1103.18	1033.74	984.80	949.34	923.10	903.39	888.42	876.95	868.11
43000	4063.99	2271.32	1684.76	1399.51	1234.53	1129.45	1058.35	1008.25	971.94	945.08	924.90	909.57	897.83	888.78
44000	4158.50	2324.14	1723.94	1432.05	1263.24	1155.72	1082.96	1031.70	994.54	967.05	946.41	930.73	918.71	909.44
45000	4253.01	2376.96	1763.12	1464.60	1291.95	1181.98	1107.57	1055.15	1017.15	989.03	967.92	951.88	939.59	930.11
46000	4347.52	2429.78	1802.30	1497.15	1320.66	1208.25	1132.19	1078.59	1039.75	1011.01	989.43	973.03	960.47	950.78
47000	4442.03	2482.60	1841.48	1529.69	1349.37	1234.51	1156.80	1102.04	1062.35	1032.99	1010.94	994.18	981.35	971.45
48000	4536.54	2535.42	1880.66	1562.24	1378.08	1260.78	1181.41	1125.49	1084.96	1054.97	1032.45	1015.34	1002.23	992.12
49000	4631.05	2588.24	1919.84	1594.79	1406.79	1287.05	1206.02	1148.94	1107.56	1076.95	1053.96	1036.49	1023.11	1012.79
50000	4725.57	2641.07	1959.02	1627.33	1435.50	1313.31	1230.64	1172.38	1130.16	1098.93	1075.46	1057.64	1043.99	1033.46
55000	5198.12	2905.17	2154.93	1790.07	1579.05	1444.64	1353.70	1289.62	1243.18	1208.82	1183.01	1163.41	1148.39	1136.80
60000	5670.68	3169.28	2350.83	1952.80	1722.60	1575.97	1476.76	1406.86	1356.19	1318.71	1290.56	1269.17	1252.79	1240.15
65000	6143.23	3433.38	2546.73	2115.53	1866.15	1707.31	1599.83	1524.10	1469.21	1428.60	1398.10	1374.93	1357.18	1343.49
70000	6615.79	3697.49	2742.63	2278.27	2009.70	1838.64	1722.89	1641.34	1582.22	1538.49	1505.65	1480.70	1461.58	1446.84
75000	7088.35	3961.59	2938.53	2441.00	2153.25	1969.97	1845.95	1758.57	1695.24	1648.39	1613.19	1586.46	1565.98	1550.19
80000	7560.90	4225.70	3134.43	2603.73	2296.80	2101.30	1969.01	1875.81	1808.26	1758.28	1720.74	1692.23	1670.38	1653.53
85000	8033.46	4489.81	3330.34	2766.46	2440.35	2232.63	2092.08	1993.05	1921.27	1868.17	1828.29	1797.99	1774.78	1756.88
90000	8506.01	4753.91	3526.24	2929.20	2583.90	2363.96	2215.14	2110.29	2034.29	1978.06	1935.83	1903.75	1879.18	1860.22
95000	8978.57	5018.02	3722.14	3091.93	2727.45	2495.29	2338.20	2227.53	2147.30	2087.95	2043.38	2009.52	1983.57	1963.57
100000	9451.13	5282.12	3918.04	3254.66	2871.00	2626.62	2461.27	2344.76	2260.32	2197.85	2150.92	2115.28	2087.97	2066.91

TERM	15 Years	16 Years	17 Years	18 Years	19 Years	20 Years	21 Years	22 Years	23 Years	24 Years	25 Years	30 Years	35 Years	40 Years
AMOUNT														
5	.11	.11	.11	.11	.11	.11	.11	.11	.11	.10	.10	.10	.10	.10
10	.21	.21	.21	.21	.21	.21	.21	.21	.21	.20	.20	.20	.20	.20
15	.31	.31	.31	.31	.31	.31	.31	.31	.31	.30	.30	.30	.30	.30
25	.52	.51	.51	.51	.51	.51	.51	.51	.51	.50	.50	.50	.50	.50
50	1.03	1.02	1.02	1.02	1.01	1.01	1.01	1.01	1.01	1.00	1.00	1.00	1.00	1.00
75	1.54	1.53	1.53	1.52	1.52	1.51	1.51	1.51	1.51	1.50	1.50	1.50	1.50	1.50
100	2.06	2.04	2.03	2.03	2.02	2.01	2.01	2.01	2.01	2.00	2.00	2.00	2.00	2.00
200	4.11	4.08	4.06	4.05	4.03	4.02	4.02	4.01	4.01	4.00	4.00	3.99	3.99	3.99
300	6.16	6.12	6.09	6.07	6.05	6.03	6.02	6.01	6.01	6.00	6.00	5.98	5.98	5.98
400	8.21	8.16	8.12	8.09	8.06	8.04	8.03	8.02	8.01	8.00	7.99	7.98	7.97	7.97
500	10.26	10.19	10.14	10.11	10.08	10.05	10.03	10.02	10.01	10.00	9.99	9.97	9.97	9.96
600	12.31	12.23	12.17	12.13	12.09	12.06	12.04	12.02	12.01	12.00	11.99	11.96	11.96	11.96
700	14.36	14.27	14.20	14.15	14.10	14.07	14.04	14.02	14.01	13.99	13.98	13.96	13.95	13.95
800	16.41	16.31	16.23	16.17	16.12	16.08	16.05	16.03	16.01	15.99	15.98	15.95	15.94	15.94
900	18.46	18.35	18.26	18.19	18.13	18.09	18.06	18.03	18.01	17.99	17.98	17.94	17.93	17.93
1000	20.51	20.38	20.28	20.21	20.15	20.10	20.06	20.03	20.01	19.99	19.98	19.94	19.93	19.92
2000	41.02	40.76	40.56	40.41	40.29	40.19	40.12	40.06	40.01	39.97	39.95	39.87	39.85	39.84
3000	61.52	61.14	60.84	60.61	60.43	60.29	60.17	60.08	60.01	59.96	59.92	59.80	59.77	59.76
4000	82.03	81.52	81.12	80.81	80.57	80.38	80.23	80.11	80.02	79.94	79.89	79.74	79.69	79.68
5000	102.53	101.90	101.40	101.02	100.71	100.47	100.28	100.14	100.02	99.93	99.86	99.67	99.61	99.60
6000	123.04	122.28	121.68	121.22	120.85	120.57	120.34	120.16	120.02	119.91	119.83	119.60	119.54	119.51
7000	143.55	142.66	141.96	141.42	140.99	140.66	140.40	140.19	140.03	139.90	139.80	139.54	139.46	139.43
8000	164.05	163.04	162.24	161.62	161.13	160.75	160.45	160.22	160.03	159.88	159.77	159.47	159.38	159.35
9000	184.56	183.41	182.52	181.82	181.28	180.85	180.51	180.24	180.03	179.87	179.74	179.40	179.30	179.27
10000	205.06	203.79	202.80	202.03	201.42	200.94	200.56	200.27	200.04	199.85	199.71	199.34	199.22	199.19
11000	225.57	224.17	223.08	222.23	221.56	221.03	220.62	220.30	220.04	219.84	219.68	219.27	219.14	219.11
12000	246.07	244.55	243.36	242.43	241.70	241.13	240.68	240.32	240.04	239.82	239.65	239.20	239.07	239.02
13000	266.58	264.93	263.64	262.63	261.84	261.22	260.73	260.35	260.05	259.81	259.62	259.14	258.99	258.94
14000	287.09	285.31	283.92	282.83	281.98	281.31	280.79	280.38	280.05	279.79	279.59	279.07	278.91	278.86
15000	307.59	305.69	304.20	303.04	302.12	301.41	300.84	300.40	300.05	299.78	299.56	299.00	298.83	298.78
16000	328.10	326.07	324.48	323.24	322.26	321.50	320.90	320.43	320.06	319.76	319.53	318.93	318.75	318.70
17000	348.60	346.44	344.76	343.44	342.41	341.59	340.96	340.45	340.06	339.75	339.50	338.87	338.67	338.61
18000	369.11	366.82	365.04	363.64	362.55	361.69	361.01	360.48	360.06	359.73	359.47	358.80	358.60	358.53
19000	389.62	387.20	385.32	383.84	382.69	381.78	381.07	380.51	380.07	379.72	379.44	378.73	378.52	378.45
20000	410.12	407.58	405.60	404.05	402.83	401.87	401.12	400.53	400.07	399.70	399.41	398.67	398.44	398.37
21000	430.63	427.96	425.88	424.25	422.97	421.97	421.18	420.56	420.07	419.69	419.39	418.60	418.36	418.29
22000	451.13	448.34	446.16	444.45	443.11	442.06	441.24	440.59	440.08	439.67	439.36	438.53	438.28	438.21
23000	471.64	468.72	466.44	464.65	463.25	462.16	461.29	460.61	460.08	459.66	459.33	458.47	458.20	458.12
24000	492.14	489.10	486.72	484.85	483.39	482.25	481.35	480.64	480.08	479.64	479.30	478.40	478.13	478.04
25000	512.65	509.47	507.00	505.06	503.54	502.34	501.40	500.67	500.09	499.63	499.27	498.33	498.05	497.96
26000	533.16	529.85	527.28	525.26	523.68	522.44	521.46	520.69	520.09	519.61	519.24	518.27	517.97	517.88
27000	553.66	550.23	547.56	545.46	543.82	542.53	541.52	540.72	540.09	539.60	539.21	538.20	537.89	537.80
28000	574.17	570.61	567.83	565.66	563.96	562.62	561.57	560.75	560.09	559.58	559.18	558.13	557.81	557.71
29000	594.67	590.99	588.11	585.86	584.10	582.72	581.63	580.77	580.10	579.57	579.15	578.07	577.73	577.63
30000	615.18	611.37	608.39	606.07	604.24	602.81	601.68	600.80	600.10	599.55	599.12	598.00	597.66	597.55
31000	635.69	631.75	628.67	626.27	624.38	622.90	621.74	620.82	620.10	619.54	619.09	617.93	617.58	617.47
32000	656.19	652.13	648.95	646.47	644.52	643.00	641.80	640.85	640.11	639.52	639.06	637.86	637.50	637.39
33000	676.70	672.51	669.23	666.67	664.67	663.09	661.85	660.88	660.11	659.51	659.03	657.80	657.42	657.31
34000	697.20	692.88	689.51	686.87	684.81	683.18	681.91	680.90	680.11	679.49	679.00	677.73	677.34	677.22
35000	717.71	713.26	709.79	707.08	704.95	703.28	701.96	700.93	700.12	699.48	698.97	697.66	697.26	697.14
36000	738.21	733.64	730.07	727.28	725.09	723.37	722.02	720.96	720.12	719.46	718.94	717.60	717.19	717.06
37000	758.72	754.02	750.35	747.48	745.23	743.46	742.08	740.98	740.12	739.45	738.91	737.53	737.11	736.98
38000	779.23	774.40	770.63	767.68	765.37	763.56	762.13	761.01	760.13	759.43	758.88	757.46	757.03	756.90
39000	799.73	794.78	790.91	787.88	785.51	783.65	782.19	781.04	780.13	779.42	778.85	777.40	776.95	776.82
40000	820.24	815.16	811.19	808.09	805.65	803.74	802.24	801.06	800.13	799.40	798.82	797.33	796.87	796.73
41000	840.74	835.54	831.47	828.29	825.80	823.84	822.30	821.09	820.14	819.39	818.80	817.26	816.79	816.65
42000	861.25	855.91	851.75	848.49	845.94	843.93	842.36	841.12	840.14	839.37	838.77	837.20	836.72	836.57
43000	881.76	876.29	872.03	868.69	866.08	864.02	862.41	861.14	860.14	859.36	858.74	857.13	856.64	856.49
44000	902.26	896.67	892.31	888.90	886.22	884.12	882.47	881.17	880.15	879.34	878.71	877.06	876.56	876.41
45000	922.77	917.05	912.59	909.10	906.36	904.21	902.52	901.20	900.15	899.33	898.68	897.00	896.48	896.32
46000	943.27	937.43	932.87	929.30	926.50	924.31	922.58	921.22	920.15	919.31	918.65	916.93	916.40	916.24
47000	963.78	957.81	953.15	949.50	946.64	944.40	942.64	941.25	940.16	939.30	938.62	936.86	936.33	936.16
48000	984.28	978.19	973.43	969.70	966.78	964.49	962.69	961.27	960.16	959.28	958.59	956.79	956.25	956.08
49000	1004.79	998.57	993.71	989.91	986.93	984.59	982.75	981.30	980.16	979.27	978.56	976.73	976.17	976.00
50000	1025.30	1018.94	1013.99	1010.11	1007.07	1004.68	1002.80	1001.33	1000.17	999.25	998.53	996.66	996.09	995.92
55000	1127.83	1120.84	1115.38	1111.12	1107.77	1105.15	1103.08	1101.46	1100.18	1099.18	1098.38	1096.33	1095.70	1095.51
60000	1230.35	1222.73	1216.78	1212.13	1208.48	1205.61	1203.36	1201.59	1200.20	1199.10	1198.23	1195.99	1195.31	1195.10
65000	1332.88	1324.63	1318.18	1313.14	1309.18	1306.08	1303.64	1301.72	1300.21	1299.02	1298.09	1295.66	1294.92	1294.69
70000	1435.41	1426.52	1419.58	1414.15	1409.89	1406.55	1403.92	1401.86	1400.23	1398.95	1397.94	1395.32	1394.52	1394.28
75000	1537.94	1528.41	1520.98	1515.16	1510.60	1507.02	1504.20	1501.99	1500.25	1498.87	1497.79	1494.99	1494.13	1493.87
80000	1640.47	1630.31	1622.38	1616.17	1611.30	1607.48	1604.48	1602.12	1600.26	1598.80	1597.64	1594.65	1593.74	1593.46
85000	1743.00	1732.20	1723.77	1717.18	1712.01	1707.95	1704.76	1702.25	1700.28	1698.72	1697.50	1694.32	1693.35	1693.05
90000	1845.53	1834.10	1825.17	1818.19	1812.72	1808.42	1805.04	1802.39	1800.29	1798.65	1797.35	1793.99	1792.96	1792.64
95000	1948.06	1935.99	1926.57	1919.20	1913.42	1908.89	1905.32	1902.52	1900.31	1898.57	1897.20	1893.65	1892.57	1892.23
100000	2050.59	2037.88	2027.97	2020.21	2014.13	2009.35	2005.60	2002.65	2000.33	1998.50	1997.05	1993.32	1992.18	1991.83

MONTHLY PAYMENT
REQUIRED TO AMORTIZE A LOAN

TERM AMOUNT	1 Year	2 Years	3 Years	4 Years	5 Years	6 Years	7 Years	8 Years	9 Years	10 Years	11 Years	12 Years	13 Years	14 Years
5	.48	.27	.20	.17	.15	.14	.13	.12	.12	.12	.11	.11	.11	.11
10	.95	.53	.40	.33	.29	.27	.25	.24	.23	.23	.22	.22	.21	.21
15	1.42	.80	.59	.49	.44	.40	.38	.36	.35	.34	.33	.32	.32	.32
25	2.37	1.33	.99	.82	.72	.66	.62	.59	.57	.56	.54	.54	.53	.52
50	4.73	2.65	1.97	1.64	1.44	1.32	1.24	1.18	1.14	1.11	1.08	1.07	1.05	1.04
75	7.10	3.97	2.95	2.45	2.16	1.98	1.86	1.77	1.71	1.66	1.62	1.60	1.58	1.56
100	9.46	5.29	3.93	3.27	2.88	2.64	2.47	2.36	2.27	2.21	2.16	2.13	2.10	2.08
200	18.92	10.58	7.85	6.53	5.76	5.27	4.94	4.71	4.54	4.41	4.32	4.25	4.20	4.15
300	28.37	15.87	11.77	9.79	8.64	7.90	7.41	7.06	6.81	6.62	6.48	6.37	6.29	6.23
400	37.83	21.15	15.70	13.05	11.51	10.54	9.88	9.41	9.07	8.82	8.64	8.50	8.39	8.30
500	47.28	26.44	19.62	16.31	14.39	13.17	12.34	11.76	11.34	11.03	10.80	10.62	10.48	10.38
600	56.74	31.73	23.54	19.57	17.27	15.80	14.81	14.11	13.61	13.23	12.95	12.74	12.58	12.45
700	66.20	37.01	27.47	22.83	20.14	18.43	17.28	16.46	15.87	15.44	15.11	14.86	14.67	14.53
800	75.65	42.30	31.39	26.09	23.02	21.07	19.75	18.82	18.14	17.64	17.27	16.99	16.77	16.60
900	85.11	47.59	35.31	29.35	25.90	23.70	22.21	21.17	20.41	19.85	19.43	19.11	18.86	18.68
1000	94.56	52.88	39.24	32.61	28.77	26.33	24.68	23.52	22.68	22.05	21.59	21.23	20.96	20.75
2000	189.12	105.75	78.47	65.21	57.54	52.66	49.36	47.03	45.35	44.10	43.17	42.46	41.91	41.49
3000	283.68	158.62	117.70	97.81	86.31	78.99	74.03	70.54	68.02	66.15	64.75	63.68	62.87	62.24
4000	378.24	211.49	156.94	130.41	115.08	105.31	98.71	94.06	90.69	88.20	86.33	84.91	83.82	82.98
5000	472.80	264.36	196.17	163.01	143.84	131.64	123.38	117.57	113.36	110.25	107.91	106.13	104.78	103.73
6000	567.36	317.23	235.40	195.62	172.61	157.97	148.06	141.08	136.03	132.29	129.49	127.36	125.73	124.47
7000	661.92	370.10	274.63	228.22	201.38	184.29	172.74	164.60	158.70	154.34	151.07	148.59	146.68	145.22
8000	756.48	422.97	313.87	260.82	230.15	210.62	197.41	188.11	181.37	176.39	172.65	169.81	167.64	165.96
9000	851.04	475.84	353.10	293.42	258.92	236.95	222.09	211.62	204.04	198.44	194.23	191.04	188.59	186.71
10000	945.60	528.72	392.33	326.02	287.68	263.27	246.76	235.14	226.71	220.49	215.81	212.26	209.55	207.45
11000	1040.16	581.59	431.57	358.63	316.45	289.60	271.44	258.65	249.38	242.53	237.39	233.49	230.50	228.20
12000	1134.72	634.46	470.80	391.23	345.22	315.93	296.11	282.16	272.06	264.58	258.97	254.72	251.46	248.94
13000	1229.28	687.33	510.03	423.83	373.99	342.25	320.79	305.68	294.73	286.63	280.55	275.94	272.41	269.69
14000	1323.84	740.20	549.26	456.43	402.76	368.58	345.47	329.19	317.40	308.68	302.13	297.17	293.36	290.43
15000	1418.40	793.07	588.50	489.03	431.52	394.91	370.14	352.70	340.07	330.73	323.72	318.39	314.32	311.18
16000	1512.96	845.94	627.73	521.63	460.29	421.23	394.82	376.22	362.74	352.77	345.30	339.62	335.27	331.92
17000	1607.52	898.81	666.96	554.24	489.06	447.56	419.49	399.73	385.41	374.82	366.88	360.84	356.23	352.67
18000	1702.08	951.68	706.20	586.84	517.83	473.89	444.17	423.24	408.08	396.87	388.46	382.07	377.18	373.41
19000	1796.64	1004.56	745.43	619.44	546.60	500.21	468.85	446.75	430.75	418.92	410.04	403.30	398.14	394.16
20000	1891.20	1057.43	784.66	652.04	575.36	526.54	493.52	470.27	453.42	440.97	431.62	424.52	419.09	414.90
21000	1985.76	1110.30	823.89	684.64	604.13	552.87	518.20	493.78	476.09	463.02	453.20	445.75	440.04	435.65
22000	2080.32	1163.17	863.13	717.25	632.90	579.20	542.87	517.29	498.76	485.06	474.78	466.97	461.00	456.39
23000	2174.88	1216.04	902.36	749.85	661.67	605.52	567.55	540.81	521.43	507.11	496.36	488.20	481.95	477.14
24000	2269.44	1268.91	941.59	782.45	690.44	631.85	592.22	564.32	544.11	529.16	517.94	509.43	502.90	497.88
25000	2363.99	1321.78	980.83	815.05	719.20	658.18	616.90	587.83	566.78	551.21	539.52	530.65	523.86	518.63
26000	2458.55	1374.65	1020.06	847.65	747.97	684.50	641.58	611.35	589.45	573.26	561.10	551.88	544.81	539.37
27000	2553.11	1427.52	1059.29	880.25	776.74	710.83	666.25	634.86	612.12	595.30	582.68	573.10	565.77	560.12
28000	2647.67	1480.40	1098.52	912.86	805.51	737.16	690.93	658.37	634.79	617.35	604.26	594.33	586.72	580.86
29000	2742.23	1533.27	1137.76	945.46	834.28	763.48	715.60	681.89	657.46	639.40	625.84	615.55	607.68	601.61
30000	2836.79	1586.14	1176.99	978.06	863.04	789.81	740.28	705.40	680.13	661.45	647.43	636.78	628.63	622.35
31000	2931.35	1639.01	1216.22	1010.66	891.81	816.14	764.96	728.91	702.80	683.50	669.01	658.01	649.59	643.10
32000	3025.91	1691.88	1255.46	1043.26	920.58	842.46	789.63	752.43	725.47	705.54	690.59	679.23	670.54	663.84
33000	3120.47	1744.75	1294.69	1075.87	949.35	868.79	814.31	775.94	748.14	727.59	712.17	700.46	691.49	684.59
34000	3215.03	1797.62	1333.92	1108.47	978.12	895.12	838.98	799.45	770.81	749.64	733.75	721.68	712.45	705.33
35000	3309.59	1850.49	1373.15	1141.07	1006.88	921.44	863.66	822.96	793.48	771.69	755.33	742.91	733.40	726.08
36000	3404.15	1903.36	1412.39	1173.67	1035.65	947.77	888.33	846.48	816.16	793.74	776.91	764.14	754.36	746.82
37000	3498.71	1956.24	1451.62	1206.27	1064.42	974.10	913.01	869.99	838.83	815.78	798.49	785.36	775.31	767.57
38000	3593.27	2009.11	1490.85	1238.87	1093.19	1000.42	937.69	893.50	861.50	837.83	820.07	806.59	796.27	788.31
39000	3687.83	2061.98	1530.09	1271.48	1121.96	1026.75	962.36	917.02	884.17	859.88	841.65	827.81	817.22	809.06
40000	3782.39	2114.85	1569.32	1304.08	1150.72	1053.08	987.04	940.53	906.84	881.93	863.23	849.04	838.17	829.80
41000	3876.95	2167.72	1608.55	1336.68	1179.49	1079.41	1011.71	964.04	929.51	903.98	884.81	870.27	859.13	850.54
42000	3971.51	2220.59	1647.78	1369.28	1208.26	1105.73	1036.39	987.56	952.18	926.03	906.39	891.49	880.08	871.29
43000	4066.07	2273.46	1687.02	1401.88	1237.03	1132.06	1061.06	1011.07	974.85	948.07	927.97	912.72	901.04	892.03
44000	4160.63	2326.33	1726.25	1434.49	1265.80	1158.39	1085.74	1034.58	997.52	970.12	949.55	933.94	921.99	912.78
45000	4255.19	2379.20	1765.48	1467.09	1294.56	1184.71	1110.42	1058.10	1020.19	992.17	971.14	955.17	942.94	933.52
46000	4349.75	2432.08	1804.72	1499.69	1323.33	1211.04	1135.09	1081.61	1042.86	1014.22	992.72	976.39	963.90	954.27
47000	4444.31	2484.95	1843.95	1532.29	1352.10	1237.37	1159.77	1105.12	1065.53	1036.27	1014.30	997.62	984.85	975.01
48000	4538.87	2537.82	1883.18	1564.89	1380.87	1263.69	1184.44	1128.64	1088.21	1058.31	1035.88	1018.85	1005.81	995.76
49000	4633.43	2590.69	1922.41	1597.49	1409.64	1290.02	1209.12	1152.15	1110.88	1080.36	1057.46	1040.07	1026.76	1016.50
50000	4727.98	2643.56	1961.65	1630.10	1438.40	1316.35	1233.80	1175.66	1133.55	1102.41	1079.04	1061.30	1047.72	1037.25
55000	5200.78	2907.92	2157.81	1793.11	1582.24	1447.98	1357.17	1293.23	1246.90	1212.65	1186.94	1167.43	1152.49	1140.97
60000	5673.58	3172.27	2353.98	1956.12	1726.08	1579.61	1480.55	1410.79	1360.26	1322.89	1294.85	1273.56	1257.26	1244.70
65000	6146.38	3436.63	2550.14	2119.12	1869.92	1711.25	1603.93	1528.36	1473.61	1433.13	1402.75	1379.69	1362.03	1348.42
70000	6619.18	3700.98	2746.30	2282.13	2013.76	1842.88	1727.31	1645.92	1586.96	1543.37	1510.65	1485.82	1466.80	1452.15
75000	7091.97	3965.34	2942.47	2445.14	2157.60	1974.52	1850.69	1763.49	1700.32	1653.61	1618.56	1591.94	1571.57	1555.87
80000	7564.77	4229.69	3138.63	2608.15	2301.44	2106.15	1974.07	1881.06	1813.67	1763.85	1726.46	1698.07	1676.34	1659.59
85000	8037.57	4494.05	3334.80	2771.16	2445.28	2237.79	2097.45	1998.62	1927.03	1874.09	1834.36	1804.20	1781.11	1763.32
90000	8510.37	4758.40	3530.96	2934.17	2589.12	2369.42	2220.83	2116.19	2040.38	1984.33	1942.27	1910.33	1885.88	1867.04
95000	8983.17	5022.76	3727.13	3097.18	2732.96	2501.05	2344.21	2233.75	2153.74	2094.57	2050.17	2016.46	1990.66	1970.77
100000	9455.97	5287.11	3923.29	3260.19	2876.80	2632.69	2467.59	2351.32	2267.09	2204.81	2158.07	2122.59	2095.43	2074.49

TERM AMOUNT	15 Years	16 Years	17 Years	18 Years	19 Years	20 Years	21 Years	22 Years	23 Years	24 Years	25 Years	30 Years	35 Years	40 Years
5	.11	.11	.11	.11	.11	.11	.11	.11	.11	.11	.11	.11	.11	.11
10	.21	.21	.21	.21	.21	.21	.21	.21	.21	.21	.21	.21	.21	.21
15	.31	.31	.31	.31	.31	.31	.31	.31	.31	.31	.31	.31	.31	.31
25	.52	.52	.51	.51	.51	.51	.51	.51	.51	.51	.51	.51	.51	.51
50	1.03	1.03	1.02	1.02	1.02	1.01	1.01	1.01	1.01	1.01	1.01	1.01	1.01	1.01
75	1.55	1.54	1.53	1.53	1.52	1.52	1.52	1.51	1.51	1.51	1.51	1.51	1.51	1.51
100	2.06	2.05	2.04	2.03	2.03	2.02	2.02	2.02	2.01	2.01	2.01	2.01	2.01	2.01
200	4.12	4.10	4.08	4.06	4.05	4.04	4.03	4.03	4.02	4.02	4.02	4.01	4.01	4.01
300	6.18	6.14	6.11	6.09	6.07	6.06	6.05	6.04	6.03	6.03	6.02	6.01	6.01	6.01
400	8.24	8.19	8.15	8.12	8.09	8.07	8.06	8.05	8.04	8.03	8.03	8.01	8.01	8.01
500	10.30	10.23	10.18	10.15	10.12	10.09	10.07	10.06	10.05	10.04	10.03	10.01	10.01	10.01
600	12.35	12.28	12.22	12.17	12.14	12.11	12.09	12.07	12.06	12.05	12.04	12.01	12.01	12.01
700	14.41	14.32	14.26	14.20	14.16	14.13	14.10	14.08	14.06	14.05	14.04	14.02	14.01	14.01
800	16.47	16.37	16.29	16.23	16.18	16.14	16.11	16.09	16.07	16.06	16.05	16.02	16.01	16.01
900	18.53	18.42	18.33	18.26	18.20	18.16	18.13	18.10	18.08	18.07	18.05	18.02	18.01	18.01
1000	20.59	20.46	20.36	20.29	20.23	20.18	20.14	20.11	20.09	20.07	20.06	20.02	20.01	20.01
2000	41.17	40.92	40.72	40.57	40.45	40.35	40.28	40.22	40.17	40.14	40.11	40.04	40.01	40.01
3000	61.75	61.38	61.08	60.85	60.67	60.53	60.42	60.33	60.26	60.21	60.16	60.05	60.02	60.01
4000	82.34	81.83	81.44	81.13	80.89	80.70	80.55	80.44	80.34	80.27	80.22	80.07	80.02	80.01
5000	102.92	102.29	101.80	101.41	101.11	100.88	100.69	100.54	100.43	100.34	100.27	100.09	100.03	100.01
6000	123.50	122.75	122.16	121.69	121.33	121.05	120.83	120.65	120.51	120.41	120.32	120.10	120.03	120.01
7000	144.08	143.20	142.51	141.98	141.55	141.22	140.96	140.76	140.60	140.47	140.37	140.12	140.04	140.02
8000	164.67	163.66	162.87	162.26	161.78	161.40	161.10	160.87	160.68	160.54	160.43	160.13	160.04	160.02
9000	185.25	184.12	183.23	182.54	182.00	181.57	181.23	180.98	180.77	180.61	180.48	180.15	180.05	180.02
10000	205.83	204.57	203.59	202.82	202.22	201.75	201.38	201.08	200.85	200.67	200.53	200.17	200.05	200.02
11000	226.42	225.03	223.95	223.10	222.44	221.92	221.51	221.19	220.94	220.74	220.59	220.18	220.06	220.02
12000	247.00	245.49	244.31	243.38	242.66	242.09	241.65	241.30	241.02	240.81	240.64	240.20	240.06	240.02
13000	267.58	265.94	264.66	263.66	262.88	262.27	261.79	261.41	261.11	260.88	260.69	260.21	260.07	260.02
14000	288.16	286.40	285.02	283.95	283.10	282.44	281.92	281.52	281.19	280.94	280.74	280.23	280.07	280.03
15000	308.75	306.86	305.38	304.23	303.32	302.62	302.06	301.62	301.28	301.01	300.80	300.25	300.08	300.03
16000	329.33	327.31	325.74	324.51	323.55	322.79	322.20	321.73	321.36	321.08	320.85	320.26	320.08	320.03
17000	349.91	347.77	346.10	344.79	343.77	342.96	342.33	341.84	341.45	341.14	340.90	340.28	340.09	340.03
18000	370.49	368.23	366.46	365.07	363.99	363.14	362.47	361.95	361.53	361.21	360.95	360.29	360.09	360.03
19000	391.08	388.68	386.81	385.35	384.21	383.31	382.61	382.05	381.62	381.28	381.01	380.31	380.10	380.03
20000	411.66	409.14	407.17	405.63	404.43	403.49	402.75	402.16	401.70	401.34	401.06	400.33	400.10	400.03
21000	432.24	429.60	427.53	425.92	424.65	423.66	422.88	422.27	421.79	421.41	421.11	420.34	420.11	420.04
22000	452.83	450.05	447.89	446.20	444.87	443.83	443.02	442.38	441.87	441.48	441.17	440.36	440.11	440.04
23000	473.41	470.51	468.25	466.48	465.09	464.01	463.16	462.49	461.96	461.54	461.22	460.37	460.12	460.04
24000	493.99	490.97	488.61	486.76	485.32	484.18	483.29	482.59	482.04	481.61	481.27	480.39	480.12	480.04
25000	514.57	511.42	508.96	507.04	505.54	504.36	503.43	502.70	502.13	501.68	501.32	500.41	500.13	500.04
26000	535.16	531.88	529.32	527.32	525.76	524.53	523.57	522.81	522.21	521.75	521.38	520.42	520.13	520.04
27000	555.74	552.34	549.68	547.61	545.98	544.71	543.70	542.92	542.30	541.81	541.43	540.44	540.14	540.05
28000	576.32	572.79	570.04	567.89	566.20	564.88	563.84	563.03	562.38	561.88	561.48	560.45	560.14	560.05
29000	596.90	593.25	590.40	588.17	586.42	585.05	583.98	583.13	582.47	581.95	581.53	580.47	580.15	580.05
30000	617.49	613.71	610.76	608.45	606.64	605.23	604.12	603.24	602.55	602.01	601.59	600.49	600.15	600.05
31000	638.07	634.16	631.11	628.73	626.87	625.40	624.25	623.35	622.64	622.08	621.64	620.50	620.16	620.05
32000	658.65	654.62	651.47	649.01	647.09	645.58	644.39	643.46	642.72	642.15	641.69	640.52	640.16	640.05
33000	679.24	675.08	671.83	669.29	667.31	665.75	664.53	663.56	662.81	662.21	661.75	660.53	660.17	660.05
34000	699.82	695.53	692.19	689.58	687.53	685.92	684.66	683.67	682.89	682.28	681.80	680.55	680.17	680.06
35000	720.40	715.99	712.55	709.86	707.75	706.10	704.80	703.78	702.98	702.35	701.85	700.57	700.18	700.06
36000	740.98	736.45	732.91	730.14	727.97	726.27	724.94	723.89	723.06	722.41	721.90	720.58	720.18	720.06
37000	761.57	756.90	753.26	750.42	748.19	746.45	745.07	744.00	743.15	742.48	741.96	740.60	740.19	740.06
38000	782.15	777.36	773.62	770.70	768.41	766.62	765.21	764.10	763.23	762.55	762.01	760.61	760.19	760.06
39000	802.73	797.82	793.98	790.98	788.64	786.79	785.35	784.21	783.32	782.62	782.06	780.63	780.20	780.06
40000	823.31	818.27	814.34	811.26	808.86	806.97	805.49	804.32	803.40	802.68	802.11	800.65	800.20	800.06
41000	843.90	838.73	834.70	831.55	829.08	827.14	825.62	824.43	823.49	822.75	822.17	820.66	820.21	820.07
42000	864.48	859.19	855.06	851.83	849.30	847.32	845.76	844.54	843.57	842.82	842.22	840.68	840.21	840.07
43000	885.06	879.64	875.41	872.11	869.52	867.49	865.90	864.64	863.66	862.88	862.27	860.69	860.22	860.07
44000	905.65	900.10	895.77	892.39	889.74	887.66	886.03	884.75	883.74	882.95	882.33	880.71	880.22	880.07
45000	926.23	920.56	916.13	912.67	909.96	907.84	906.17	904.86	903.83	903.02	902.38	900.73	900.22	900.07
46000	946.81	941.01	936.49	932.95	930.18	928.01	926.31	924.97	923.91	923.08	922.43	920.74	920.23	920.07
47000	967.39	961.47	956.85	953.24	950.41	948.19	946.44	945.08	944.00	943.15	942.48	940.76	940.23	940.07
48000	987.98	981.93	977.21	973.52	970.63	968.36	966.58	965.18	964.08	963.22	962.54	960.78	960.24	960.08
49000	1008.56	1002.38	997.56	993.80	990.85	988.53	986.72	985.29	984.17	983.28	982.59	980.79	980.24	980.08
50000	1029.14	1022.84	1017.92	1014.08	1011.07	1008.71	1006.86	1005.40	1004.25	1003.35	1002.64	1000.81	1000.25	1000.08
55000	1132.06	1125.12	1119.71	1115.49	1112.18	1109.58	1107.54	1105.94	1104.68	1103.69	1102.91	1100.89	1100.27	1100.09
60000	1234.97	1227.41	1221.51	1216.89	1213.28	1210.45	1208.23	1206.48	1205.10	1204.02	1203.17	1200.97	1200.30	1200.09
65000	1337.88	1329.69	1323.30	1318.30	1314.39	1311.32	1308.91	1307.02	1305.53	1304.36	1303.43	1301.05	1300.32	1300.10
70000	1440.80	1431.97	1425.09	1419.71	1415.50	1412.19	1409.60	1407.56	1405.95	1404.69	1403.70	1401.13	1400.35	1400.11
75000	1543.71	1534.26	1526.88	1521.12	1516.60	1513.06	1510.28	1508.10	1506.38	1505.02	1503.96	1501.21	1500.37	1500.12
80000	1646.62	1636.54	1628.67	1622.52	1617.71	1613.93	1610.97	1608.64	1606.80	1605.36	1604.22	1601.29	1600.40	1600.12
85000	1749.54	1738.82	1730.46	1723.93	1718.82	1714.80	1711.65	1709.17	1707.23	1705.69	1704.49	1701.37	1700.42	1700.13
90000	1852.45	1841.11	1832.26	1825.34	1819.92	1815.67	1812.34	1809.71	1807.65	1806.03	1804.75	1801.45	1800.44	1800.14
95000	1955.37	1943.39	1934.05	1926.75	1921.03	1916.54	1913.02	1910.25	1908.08	1906.36	1905.02	1901.53	1900.47	1900.15
100000	2058.28	2045.67	2035.84	2028.15	2022.13	2017.41	2013.71	2010.79	2008.50	2006.70	2005.28	2001.61	2000.49	2000.15

24%

MONTHLY PAYMENT
REQUIRED TO AMORTIZE A LOAN

TERM	1 Year	2 Years	3 Years	4 Years	5 Years	6 Years	7 Years	8 Years	9 Years	10 Years	11 Years	12 Years	13 Years	14 Years
AMOUNT														
5	.48	.27	.20	.17	.15	.14	.13	.12	.12	.12	.11	.11	.11	.11
10	.95	.53	.40	.33	.29	.27	.25	.24	.23	.23	.22	.22	.22	.21
15	1.42	.80	.59	.49	.44	.40	.38	.36	.35	.34	.33	.32	.32	.32
25	2.37	1.33	.99	.82	.73	.66	.62	.59	.57	.56	.55	.54	.53	.53
50	4.74	2.65	1.97	1.64	1.45	1.32	1.24	1.18	1.14	1.11	1.09	1.07	1.06	1.05
75	7.10	3.97	2.95	2.45	2.17	1.98	1.86	1.77	1.71	1.66	1.63	1.60	1.58	1.57
100	9.47	5.30	3.93	3.27	2.89	2.64	2.48	2.36	2.28	2.22	2.17	2.13	2.11	2.09
200	18.93	10.59	7.86	6.54	5.77	5.28	4.95	4.72	4.55	4.43	4.34	4.26	4.21	4.17
300	28.39	15.88	11.79	9.80	8.65	7.92	7.43	7.08	6.83	6.64	6.50	6.39	6.31	6.25
400	37.85	21.17	15.72	13.07	11.54	10.56	9.90	9.44	9.10	8.85	8.67	8.52	8.42	8.33
500	47.31	26.47	19.65	16.33	14.42	13.20	12.37	11.79	11.37	11.06	10.83	10.65	10.52	10.42
600	56.77	31.76	23.58	19.60	17.30	15.84	14.85	14.15	13.65	13.28	13.00	12.78	12.62	12.50
700	66.23	37.05	27.50	22.87	20.18	18.48	17.32	16.51	15.92	15.49	15.16	14.91	14.73	14.58
800	75.69	42.34	31.43	26.13	23.07	21.12	19.80	18.87	18.20	17.70	17.33	17.04	16.83	16.66
900	85.15	47.63	35.36	29.40	25.95	23.75	22.27	21.23	20.47	19.91	19.49	19.17	18.93	18.74
1000	94.61	52.93	39.29	32.66	28.83	26.39	24.74	23.58	22.74	22.12	21.66	21.30	21.03	20.83
2000	189.22	105.85	78.58	65.32	57.66	52.78	49.48	47.16	45.48	44.24	43.31	42.60	42.06	41.65
3000	283.83	158.77	117.86	97.98	86.48	79.17	74.22	70.74	68.22	66.36	64.96	63.90	63.09	62.47
4000	378.44	211.69	157.15	130.63	115.31	105.56	98.96	94.32	90.96	88.48	86.61	85.20	84.12	83.29
5000	473.04	264.61	196.43	163.29	144.14	131.94	123.70	117.90	113.70	110.59	108.27	106.50	105.15	104.11
6000	567.65	317.53	235.72	195.95	172.96	158.33	148.44	141.48	136.44	132.71	129.92	127.80	126.18	124.93
7000	662.26	370.45	275.00	228.61	201.79	184.72	173.18	165.06	159.18	154.83	151.57	149.10	147.21	145.75
8000	756.87	423.37	314.29	261.26	230.61	211.11	197.92	188.63	181.91	176.95	173.22	170.40	168.24	166.57
9000	851.48	476.29	353.57	293.92	259.44	237.49	222.66	212.21	204.65	199.07	194.88	191.70	189.26	187.39
10000	946.08	529.22	392.86	326.58	288.27	263.88	247.40	235.79	227.39	221.18	216.53	213.00	210.29	208.21
11000	1040.69	582.14	432.14	359.23	317.09	290.27	272.13	259.37	250.13	243.30	238.18	234.29	231.32	229.03
12000	1135.30	635.06	471.43	391.89	345.92	316.66	296.87	282.95	272.87	265.42	259.83	255.59	252.35	249.85
13000	1229.91	687.98	510.71	424.55	374.74	343.04	321.61	306.53	295.61	287.54	281.48	276.89	273.38	270.67
14000	1324.52	740.90	550.00	457.21	403.57	369.43	346.35	330.11	318.35	309.66	303.14	298.19	294.41	291.50
15000	1419.13	793.82	589.29	489.86	432.40	395.82	371.09	353.69	341.08	331.77	324.79	319.49	315.44	312.32
16000	1513.73	846.74	628.57	522.52	461.22	422.21	395.83	377.26	363.82	353.89	346.44	340.79	336.47	333.14
17000	1608.34	899.66	667.86	555.18	490.05	448.59	420.57	400.84	386.56	376.01	368.09	362.09	357.49	353.96
18000	1702.95	952.58	707.14	587.83	518.87	474.98	445.31	424.42	409.30	398.13	389.75	383.39	378.52	374.78
19000	1797.56	1005.50	746.43	620.49	547.70	501.37	470.05	448.00	432.04	420.24	411.40	404.69	399.55	395.60
20000	1892.16	1058.43	785.71	653.15	576.52	527.76	494.79	471.58	454.78	442.36	433.05	425.99	420.58	416.42
21000	1986.77	1111.35	825.00	685.81	605.35	554.14	519.53	495.16	477.52	464.48	454.70	447.28	441.61	437.24
22000	2081.38	1164.27	864.28	718.46	634.18	580.53	544.26	518.74	500.25	486.60	476.35	468.58	462.64	458.06
23000	2175.99	1217.19	903.57	751.12	663.00	606.92	569.00	542.32	522.99	508.72	498.01	489.88	483.67	478.88
24000	2270.60	1270.11	942.85	783.78	691.83	633.31	593.74	565.89	545.73	530.83	519.66	511.18	504.70	499.70
25000	2365.20	1323.03	982.14	816.43	720.66	659.69	618.48	589.47	568.47	552.95	541.31	532.48	525.73	520.52
26000	2459.81	1375.95	1021.42	849.09	749.48	686.08	643.22	613.05	591.21	575.07	562.96	553.78	546.75	541.34
27000	2554.42	1428.87	1060.71	881.75	778.31	712.47	667.96	636.63	613.95	597.19	584.62	575.08	567.78	562.16
28000	2649.03	1481.79	1100.00	914.41	807.13	738.86	692.70	660.21	636.69	619.31	606.27	596.38	588.81	582.99
29000	2743.64	1534.71	1139.28	947.06	835.96	765.24	717.44	683.79	659.43	641.42	627.92	617.68	609.84	603.81
30000	2838.24	1587.64	1178.57	979.72	864.79	791.63	742.18	707.37	682.16	663.54	649.57	638.98	630.87	624.63
31000	2932.85	1640.56	1217.85	1012.38	893.61	818.02	766.92	730.95	704.90	685.66	671.22	660.27	651.90	645.45
32000	3027.46	1693.48	1257.14	1045.03	922.44	844.41	791.66	754.52	727.64	707.78	692.88	681.57	672.93	666.27
33000	3122.07	1746.40	1296.42	1077.69	951.26	870.79	816.39	778.10	750.38	729.89	714.53	702.87	693.96	687.09
34000	3216.68	1799.32	1335.71	1110.35	980.09	897.18	841.13	801.68	773.12	752.01	736.18	724.17	714.98	707.91
35000	3311.28	1852.24	1374.99	1143.01	1008.92	923.57	865.87	825.26	795.86	774.13	757.83	745.47	736.01	728.73
36000	3405.89	1905.16	1414.28	1175.66	1037.74	949.96	890.61	848.84	818.60	796.25	779.49	766.77	757.04	749.55
37000	3500.50	1958.08	1453.56	1208.32	1066.57	976.35	915.35	872.42	841.33	818.37	801.14	788.07	778.07	770.37
38000	3595.11	2011.00	1492.85	1240.98	1095.39	1002.73	940.09	896.00	864.07	840.48	822.79	809.37	799.10	791.19
39000	3689.72	2063.92	1532.13	1273.63	1124.22	1029.12	964.83	919.58	886.81	862.60	844.44	830.67	820.13	812.01
40000	3784.32	2116.85	1571.42	1306.29	1153.05	1055.51	989.57	943.15	909.55	884.72	866.09	851.97	841.16	832.83
41000	3878.93	2169.77	1610.71	1338.95	1181.87	1081.90	1014.31	966.73	932.29	906.84	887.75	873.27	862.19	853.66
42000	3973.54	2222.69	1649.99	1371.61	1210.70	1108.28	1039.05	990.31	955.03	928.96	909.40	894.56	883.22	874.48
43000	4068.15	2275.61	1689.28	1404.26	1239.52	1134.67	1063.79	1013.89	977.77	951.07	931.05	915.86	904.24	895.30
44000	4162.76	2328.53	1728.56	1436.92	1268.35	1161.06	1088.52	1037.47	1000.50	973.19	952.70	937.16	925.27	916.12
45000	4257.36	2381.45	1767.85	1469.58	1297.18	1187.45	1113.26	1061.05	1023.24	995.31	974.35	958.46	946.30	936.94
46000	4351.97	2434.37	1807.13	1502.23	1326.00	1213.83	1138.00	1084.63	1045.98	1017.43	996.01	979.76	967.33	957.76
47000	4446.58	2487.29	1846.42	1534.89	1354.83	1240.22	1162.74	1108.21	1068.72	1039.54	1017.66	1001.06	988.36	978.58
48000	4541.19	2540.21	1885.70	1567.55	1383.65	1266.61	1187.48	1131.78	1091.46	1061.66	1039.31	1022.36	1009.39	999.40
49000	4635.80	2593.14	1924.99	1600.21	1412.48	1293.00	1212.22	1155.36	1114.20	1083.78	1060.96	1043.66	1030.42	1020.22
50000	4730.40	2646.06	1964.27	1632.86	1441.31	1319.38	1236.96	1178.94	1136.94	1105.90	1082.62	1064.96	1051.45	1041.04
55000	5203.44	2910.66	2160.70	1796.15	1585.44	1451.32	1360.65	1296.84	1250.63	1216.49	1190.88	1171.45	1156.59	1145.15
60000	5676.48	3175.27	2357.13	1959.43	1729.57	1583.26	1484.35	1414.73	1364.32	1327.08	1299.14	1277.95	1261.73	1249.25
65000	6149.52	3439.87	2553.55	2122.72	1873.70	1715.20	1608.04	1532.62	1478.02	1437.67	1407.40	1384.44	1366.88	1353.35
70000	6622.56	3704.48	2749.98	2286.01	2017.83	1847.13	1731.74	1650.52	1591.71	1548.26	1515.66	1490.94	1472.02	1457.46
75000	7095.60	3969.08	2946.41	2449.29	2161.96	1979.07	1855.44	1768.41	1705.40	1658.85	1623.92	1597.43	1577.17	1561.56
80000	7568.64	4233.69	3142.84	2612.58	2306.09	2111.01	1979.13	1886.30	1819.10	1769.43	1732.18	1703.93	1682.31	1665.66
85000	8041.68	4498.29	3339.26	2775.86	2450.22	2242.95	2102.83	2004.20	1932.79	1880.02	1840.45	1810.42	1787.45	1769.77
90000	8514.73	4762.90	3535.69	2939.15	2594.35	2374.89	2226.52	2122.09	2046.48	1990.61	1948.71	1916.92	1892.60	1873.87
95000	8987.77	5027.50	3732.12	3102.43	2738.48	2506.82	2350.22	2239.99	2160.18	2101.20	2056.97	2023.41	1997.74	1977.98
100000	9460.81	5292.11	3928.54	3265.72	2882.61	2638.76	2473.91	2357.88	2273.87	2211.79	2165.23	2129.91	2102.89	2082.08

TERM	15 Years	16 Years	17 Years	18 Years	19 Years	20 Years	21 Years	22 Years	23 Years	24 Years	25 Years	30 Years	35 Years	40 Years
AMOUNT														
5	.11	.11	.11	.11	.11	.11	.11	.11	.11	.11	.11	.11	.11	.11
10	.21	.21	.21	.21	.21	.21	.21	.21	.21	.21	.21	.21	.21	.21
15	.31	.31	.31	.31	.31	.31	.31	.31	.31	.31	.31	.31	.31	.31
25	.52	.52	.52	.51	.51	.51	.51	.51	.51	.51	.51	.51	.51	.51
50	1.04	1.03	1.03	1.02	1.02	1.02	1.02	1.01	1.01	1.01	1.01	1.01	1.01	1.01
75	1.55	1.55	1.54	1.53	1.53	1.52	1.52	1.52	1.52	1.52	1.52	1.51	1.51	1.51
100	2.07	2.06	2.05	2.04	2.04	2.03	2.03	2.02	2.02	2.02	2.02	2.01	2.01	2.01
200	4.14	4.11	4.09	4.08	4.07	4.06	4.05	4.04	4.04	4.03	4.03	4.02	4.02	4.02
300	6.20	6.17	6.14	6.11	6.10	6.08	6.07	6.06	6.06	6.05	6.05	6.03	6.03	6.03
400	8.27	8.22	8.18	8.15	8.13	8.11	8.09	8.08	8.07	8.06	8.06	8.04	8.04	8.04
500	10.33	10.27	10.22	10.19	10.16	10.13	10.11	10.10	10.09	10.08	10.07	10.05	10.05	10.05
600	12.40	12.33	12.27	12.22	12.19	12.16	12.14	12.12	12.11	12.09	12.09	12.06	12.06	12.06
700	14.47	14.38	14.31	14.26	14.22	14.18	14.16	14.14	14.12	14.11	14.10	14.07	14.07	14.06
800	16.53	16.43	16.35	16.29	16.25	16.21	16.18	16.16	16.14	16.12	16.11	16.08	16.08	16.07
900	18.60	18.49	18.40	18.33	18.28	18.23	18.20	18.18	18.16	18.14	18.13	18.09	18.08	18.08
1000	20.66	20.54	20.44	20.37	20.31	20.26	20.22	20.19	20.17	20.15	20.14	20.10	20.09	20.09
2000	41.32	41.07	40.88	40.73	40.61	40.51	40.44	40.38	40.34	40.30	40.28	40.20	40.18	40.17
3000	61.98	61.61	61.32	61.09	60.91	60.77	60.66	60.57	60.51	60.45	60.41	60.30	60.27	60.26
4000	82.64	82.14	81.75	81.45	81.21	81.02	80.88	80.76	80.67	80.60	80.55	80.40	80.36	80.34
5000	103.30	102.68	102.19	101.81	101.51	101.28	101.10	100.95	100.84	100.75	100.68	100.50	100.45	100.43
6000	123.96	123.21	122.63	122.17	121.81	121.53	121.31	121.14	121.01	120.90	120.82	120.60	120.53	120.51
7000	144.62	143.75	143.06	142.53	142.11	141.79	141.53	141.33	141.17	141.05	140.95	140.70	140.62	140.60
8000	165.28	164.28	163.50	162.89	162.42	162.04	161.75	161.52	161.34	161.20	161.09	160.80	160.71	160.68
9000	185.94	184.82	183.94	183.25	182.72	182.30	181.97	181.71	181.51	181.35	181.22	180.90	180.80	180.77
10000	206.60	205.35	204.38	203.61	203.02	202.55	202.19	201.90	201.67	201.49	201.36	200.99	200.89	200.85
11000	227.26	225.89	224.81	223.98	223.32	222.81	222.40	222.09	221.84	221.64	221.49	221.09	220.97	220.94
12000	247.92	246.42	245.25	244.34	243.62	243.06	242.62	242.28	242.01	241.79	241.63	241.19	241.06	241.02
13000	268.58	266.95	265.69	264.70	263.92	263.32	262.84	262.47	262.17	261.94	261.76	261.29	261.15	261.11
14000	289.24	287.49	286.12	285.06	284.22	283.57	283.06	282.66	282.34	282.09	281.90	281.39	281.24	281.19
15000	309.90	308.02	306.56	305.42	304.53	303.83	303.28	302.85	302.51	302.24	302.03	301.49	301.33	301.28
16000	330.56	328.66	327.00	325.78	324.83	324.08	323.49	323.03	322.67	322.39	322.17	321.59	321.41	321.36
17000	351.22	349.09	347.44	346.14	345.13	344.34	343.71	343.22	342.84	342.54	342.30	341.69	341.50	341.45
18000	371.00	369.63	367.87	366.50	365.43	364.59	363.93	363.41	363.01	362.69	362.44	361.79	361.59	361.53
19000	392.54	390.16	388.31	386.86	385.73	384.84	384.15	383.60	383.17	382.84	382.57	381.89	381.68	381.62
20000	413.20	410.70	408.75	407.22	406.03	405.10	404.37	403.79	403.34	402.98	402.71	401.98	401.77	401.70
21000	433.86	431.23	429.18	427.59	426.33	425.35	424.58	423.98	423.51	423.13	422.84	422.08	421.85	421.79
22000	454.52	451.77	449.62	447.95	446.64	445.61	444.80	444.17	443.67	443.28	442.98	442.18	441.94	441.87
23000	475.18	472.30	470.06	468.31	466.94	465.86	465.02	464.36	463.84	463.43	463.11	462.28	462.03	461.95
24000	495.84	492.84	490.50	488.67	487.24	486.12	485.24	484.55	484.01	483.58	483.25	482.38	482.12	482.04
25000	516.50	513.37	510.93	509.03	507.54	506.37	505.46	504.74	504.17	503.73	503.38	502.48	502.21	502.12
26000	537.16	533.90	531.37	529.39	527.84	526.63	525.68	524.93	524.34	523.88	523.52	522.58	522.29	522.21
27000	557.82	554.44	551.81	549.75	548.14	546.88	545.89	545.12	544.51	544.03	543.65	542.68	542.38	542.29
28000	578.48	574.97	572.24	570.11	568.44	567.14	566.11	565.31	564.67	564.18	563.79	562.78	562.47	562.38
29000	599.14	595.51	592.68	590.47	588.75	587.39	586.33	585.50	584.84	584.33	583.92	582.88	582.56	582.46
30000	619.80	616.04	613.12	610.83	609.05	607.65	606.55	605.69	605.01	604.47	604.06	602.97	602.65	602.55
31000	640.46	636.58	633.56	631.20	629.35	627.90	626.77	625.87	625.17	624.62	624.19	623.07	622.74	622.63
32000	661.12	657.11	653.99	651.56	649.65	648.16	646.98	646.06	645.34	644.77	644.33	643.17	642.82	642.72
33000	681.78	677.65	674.43	671.92	669.95	668.41	667.20	666.25	665.51	664.92	664.46	663.27	662.91	662.80
34000	702.44	698.18	694.87	692.28	690.25	688.67	687.42	686.44	685.67	685.07	684.60	683.37	683.00	682.89
35000	723.09	718.72	715.30	712.64	710.55	708.92	707.64	706.63	705.84	705.22	704.73	703.47	703.09	702.97
36000	743.75	739.25	735.74	733.00	730.86	729.17	727.86	726.82	726.01	725.37	724.87	723.57	723.18	723.06
37000	764.41	759.79	756.18	753.36	751.16	749.43	748.07	747.01	746.17	745.52	745.00	743.67	743.26	743.14
38000	785.07	780.32	776.62	773.72	771.46	769.68	768.29	767.20	766.34	765.67	765.14	763.77	763.35	763.23
39000	805.73	800.85	797.05	794.08	791.76	789.94	788.51	787.39	786.51	785.82	785.27	783.87	783.44	783.31
40000	826.39	821.39	817.49	814.44	812.06	810.19	808.73	807.58	806.67	805.96	805.41	803.96	803.53	803.40
41000	847.05	841.92	837.93	834.81	832.36	830.45	828.95	827.77	826.84	826.11	825.54	824.06	823.62	823.48
42000	867.71	862.46	858.36	855.17	852.66	850.70	849.16	847.96	847.01	846.26	845.68	844.16	843.70	843.57
43000	888.37	882.99	878.80	875.53	872.97	870.96	869.38	868.15	867.17	866.41	865.81	864.26	863.79	863.65
44000	909.03	903.53	899.24	895.89	893.27	891.21	889.60	888.34	887.34	886.56	885.95	884.36	883.88	883.73
45000	929.69	924.06	919.68	916.25	913.57	911.47	909.82	908.53	907.51	906.71	906.08	904.46	903.97	903.82
46000	950.35	944.60	940.11	936.61	933.87	931.72	930.04	928.71	927.68	926.86	926.22	924.56	924.06	923.90
47000	971.01	965.13	960.55	956.97	954.17	951.98	950.26	948.90	947.84	947.01	946.35	944.66	944.14	943.99
48000	991.67	985.67	980.99	977.33	974.47	972.23	970.47	969.09	968.01	967.16	966.49	964.76	964.23	964.07
49000	1012.33	1006.20	1001.42	997.69	994.77	992.49	990.69	989.28	988.18	987.30	986.62	984.85	984.32	984.16
50000	1032.99	1026.74	1021.86	1018.05	1015.08	1012.74	1010.91	1009.47	1008.34	1007.45	1006.76	1004.95	1004.41	1004.24
55000	1136.29	1129.41	1124.05	1119.86	1116.58	1114.01	1112.00	1110.42	1109.18	1108.20	1107.43	1105.45	1104.85	1104.67
60000	1239.59	1232.08	1226.23	1221.66	1218.09	1215.29	1211.09	1211.37	1210.01	1208.94	1208.11	1205.94	1205.29	1205.09
65000	1342.89	1334.75	1328.42	1323.47	1319.60	1316.56	1314.18	1312.31	1310.85	1309.69	1308.78	1306.44	1305.73	1305.52
70000	1446.18	1437.43	1430.60	1425.27	1421.10	1417.84	1415.27	1413.26	1411.68	1410.43	1409.46	1406.93	1406.17	1405.94
75000	1549.48	1540.10	1532.79	1527.08	1522.61	1519.11	1516.36	1514.21	1512.51	1511.18	1510.13	1507.43	1506.61	1506.36
80000	1652.78	1642.77	1634.97	1628.88	1624.12	1620.38	1617.45	1615.15	1613.34	1611.92	1610.81	1607.92	1607.05	1606.79
85000	1756.08	1745.45	1737.16	1730.69	1725.62	1721.66	1718.54	1716.10	1714.18	1712.67	1711.48	1708.42	1707.49	1707.21
90000	1859.38	1848.12	1839.35	1832.49	1827.13	1822.93	1819.63	1817.05	1815.01	1813.41	1812.16	1808.91	1807.93	1807.63
95000	1962.68	1950.79	1941.53	1934.30	1928.64	1924.20	1920.72	1917.99	1915.85	1914.16	1912.83	1909.41	1908.37	1908.06
100000	2065.98	2053.47	2043.72	2036.10	2030.15	2025.48	2021.81	2018.94	2016.68	2014.90	2013.51	2009.90	2008.81	2008.48

MONTHLY PAYMENT
REQUIRED TO AMORTIZE A LOAN

TERM	1 Year	2 Years	3 Years	4 Years	5 Years	6 Years	7 Years	8 Years	9 Years	10 Years	11 Years	12 Years	13 Years	14 Years
AMOUNT														
5	.48	.27	.20	.17	.15	.14	.13	.12	.12	.12	.11	.11	.11	.11
10	.95	.53	.40	.33	.29	.27	.25	.24	.23	.23	.22	.22	.22	.21
15	1.42	.80	.59	.50	.44	.40	.38	.36	.35	.34	.33	.32	.32	.32
25	2.37	1.33	.99	.82	.73	.67	.62	.59	.57	.56	.55	.54	.53	.53
50	4.74	2.65	1.97	1.64	1.45	1.33	1.24	1.18	1.14	1.11	1.09	1.07	1.06	1.05
75	7.10	3.98	2.95	2.46	2.17	1.99	1.86	1.77	1.71	1.67	1.63	1.60	1.58	1.57
100	9.47	5.30	3.93	3.27	2.89	2.65	2.48	2.36	2.28	2.22	2.17	2.14	2.11	2.09
200	18.93	10.59	7.86	6.54	5.77	5.29	4.96	4.72	4.56	4.43	4.34	4.27	4.21	4.17
300	28.39	15.89	11.79	9.81	8.66	7.93	7.43	7.08	6.83	6.65	6.51	6.40	6.32	6.26
400	37.85	21.18	15.72	13.07	11.54	10.57	9.91	9.44	9.11	8.86	8.67	8.53	8.42	8.34
500	47.31	26.47	19.65	16.34	14.43	13.21	12.38	11.80	11.38	11.07	10.84	10.66	10.53	10.42
600	56.78	31.77	23.58	19.61	17.31	15.85	14.86	14.16	13.66	13.29	13.01	12.80	12.63	12.51
700	66.24	37.06	27.51	22.87	20.19	18.49	17.33	16.52	15.93	15.50	15.17	14.93	14.74	14.59
800	75.70	42.35	31.44	26.14	23.08	21.13	19.81	18.88	18.21	17.71	17.34	17.06	16.84	16.68
900	85.16	47.65	35.37	29.41	25.96	23.77	22.28	21.24	20.49	19.93	19.51	19.19	18.95	18.76
1000	94.63	52.94	39.30	32.68	28.85	26.41	24.76	23.60	22.76	22.14	21.68	21.32	21.05	20.84
2000	189.25	105.87	78.60	65.35	57.69	52.81	49.51	47.20	45.52	44.28	43.35	42.64	42.10	41.68
3000	283.87	158.81	117.90	98.02	86.53	79.21	74.27	70.79	68.27	66.41	65.02	63.96	63.15	62.52
4000	378.49	211.74	157.20	130.69	115.37	105.62	99.02	94.39	91.03	88.55	86.69	85.27	84.19	83.36
5000	473.11	264.67	196.50	163.36	144.21	132.02	123.78	117.98	113.78	110.68	108.36	106.59	105.24	104.20
6000	567.73	317.61	235.80	196.03	173.05	158.42	148.53	141.58	136.54	132.82	130.03	127.91	126.29	125.04
7000	662.35	370.54	275.09	228.70	201.89	184.82	173.29	165.17	159.29	154.95	151.70	149.23	147.34	145.88
8000	756.97	423.47	314.39	261.37	230.73	211.23	198.04	188.77	182.05	177.09	173.37	170.54	168.38	166.72
9000	851.59	476.41	353.69	294.04	259.57	237.63	222.80	212.36	204.81	199.22	195.04	191.86	189.43	187.56
10000	946.21	529.34	392.99	326.71	288.41	264.03	247.55	235.96	227.56	221.36	216.71	213.18	210.48	208.40
11000	1040.83	582.27	432.29	359.39	317.25	290.44	272.31	259.55	250.32	243.49	238.38	234.50	231.53	229.24
12000	1135.45	635.21	471.59	392.06	346.09	316.84	297.06	283.15	273.07	265.63	260.05	255.81	252.57	250.08
13000	1230.07	688.14	510.89	424.73	374.93	343.24	321.82	306.74	295.83	287.76	281.72	277.13	273.62	270.92
14000	1324.69	741.07	550.18	457.40	403.77	369.64	346.57	330.34	318.58	309.90	303.39	298.45	294.67	291.76
15000	1419.31	794.01	589.48	490.07	432.61	396.05	371.33	353.93	341.34	332.03	325.06	319.77	315.72	312.60
16000	1513.93	846.94	628.78	522.74	461.45	422.45	396.08	377.53	364.09	354.17	346.73	341.08	336.76	333.44
17000	1608.55	899.87	668.08	555.41	490.29	448.85	420.84	401.12	386.85	376.31	368.40	362.40	357.81	354.28
18000	1703.17	952.81	707.38	588.08	519.14	475.25	445.59	424.72	409.61	398.44	390.07	383.72	378.86	375.12
19000	1797.79	1005.74	746.68	620.75	547.98	501.66	470.35	448.31	432.36	420.58	411.74	405.03	399.91	395.96
20000	1892.41	1058.68	785.98	653.42	576.82	528.06	495.10	471.91	455.12	442.71	433.41	426.35	420.95	416.80
21000	1987.03	1111.61	825.27	686.10	605.66	554.46	519.86	495.50	477.87	464.85	455.08	447.67	442.00	437.64
22000	2081.65	1164.54	864.57	718.77	634.50	580.87	544.61	519.10	500.63	486.98	476.75	468.99	463.05	458.48
23000	2176.27	1217.48	903.87	751.44	663.34	607.27	569.37	542.69	523.38	509.12	498.42	490.30	484.10	479.32
24000	2270.89	1270.41	943.17	784.11	692.18	633.67	594.12	566.29	546.14	531.25	520.09	511.62	505.14	500.16
25000	2365.51	1323.34	982.47	816.78	721.02	660.07	618.88	589.88	568.89	553.39	541.76	532.94	526.19	521.00
26000	2460.13	1376.28	1021.77	849.45	749.86	686.48	643.63	613.48	591.65	575.52	563.43	554.26	547.24	541.84
27000	2554.75	1429.21	1061.06	882.12	778.70	712.88	668.39	637.07	614.41	597.66	585.10	575.57	568.29	562.68
28000	2649.37	1482.14	1100.36	914.79	807.54	739.28	693.14	660.67	637.16	619.79	606.77	596.89	589.33	583.52
29000	2743.99	1535.08	1139.66	947.46	836.38	765.69	717.90	684.26	659.92	641.93	628.44	618.21	610.38	604.36
30000	2838.61	1588.01	1178.96	980.13	865.22	792.09	742.65	707.86	682.67	664.06	650.11	639.53	631.43	625.20
31000	2933.23	1640.94	1218.26	1012.81	894.06	818.49	767.41	731.45	705.43	686.20	671.78	660.84	652.48	646.04
32000	3027.85	1693.88	1257.56	1045.48	922.90	844.89	792.16	755.05	728.18	708.34	693.45	682.16	673.52	666.88
33000	3122.47	1746.81	1296.86	1078.15	951.74	871.30	816.92	778.65	750.94	730.47	715.12	703.48	694.57	687.72
34000	3217.09	1799.74	1336.15	1110.82	980.58	897.70	841.67	802.24	773.70	752.61	736.79	724.79	715.62	708.56
35000	3311.71	1852.68	1375.45	1143.49	1009.42	924.10	866.43	825.84	796.45	774.74	758.46	746.11	736.67	729.40
36000	3406.33	1905.61	1414.75	1176.16	1038.27	950.50	891.18	849.43	819.21	796.88	780.13	767.43	757.71	750.23
37000	3500.95	1958.54	1454.05	1208.83	1067.11	976.91	915.94	873.03	841.96	819.01	801.80	788.75	778.76	771.07
38000	3595.57	2011.48	1493.35	1241.50	1095.95	1003.31	940.69	896.62	864.72	841.15	823.47	810.06	799.81	791.91
39000	3690.19	2064.41	1532.65	1274.17	1124.79	1029.71	965.45	920.22	887.47	863.28	845.14	831.38	820.86	812.75
40000	3784.81	2117.35	1571.95	1306.84	1153.63	1056.12	990.20	943.81	910.23	885.42	866.81	852.70	841.90	833.59
41000	3879.43	2170.28	1611.24	1339.52	1182.47	1082.52	1014.96	967.41	932.98	907.55	888.48	874.02	862.95	854.43
42000	3974.05	2223.21	1650.54	1372.19	1211.31	1108.92	1039.71	991.00	955.74	929.69	910.15	895.33	884.00	875.27
43000	4068.67	2276.15	1689.84	1404.86	1240.15	1135.32	1064.47	1014.60	978.50	951.82	931.82	916.65	905.05	896.11
44000	4163.29	2329.08	1729.14	1437.53	1268.99	1161.73	1089.22	1038.19	1001.25	973.96	953.49	937.97	926.09	916.95
45000	4257.91	2382.01	1768.44	1470.20	1297.83	1188.13	1113.98	1061.79	1024.01	996.09	975.16	959.29	947.14	937.79
46000	4352.53	2434.95	1807.74	1502.87	1326.67	1214.53	1138.73	1085.38	1046.76	1018.23	996.83	980.60	968.19	958.63
47000	4447.15	2487.88	1847.04	1535.54	1355.51	1240.93	1163.49	1108.98	1069.52	1040.37	1018.50	1001.92	989.24	979.47
48000	4541.77	2540.81	1886.33	1568.21	1384.35	1267.34	1188.24	1132.57	1092.27	1062.50	1040.17	1023.24	1010.28	1000.31
49000	4636.39	2593.75	1925.63	1600.88	1413.19	1293.74	1213.00	1156.17	1115.03	1084.64	1061.84	1044.55	1031.33	1021.15
50000	4731.01	2646.68	1964.93	1633.55	1442.03	1320.14	1237.75	1179.76	1137.78	1106.77	1083.51	1065.87	1052.38	1041.99
55000	5204.11	2911.35	2161.42	1796.91	1586.24	1452.16	1361.52	1297.74	1251.56	1217.45	1191.86	1172.46	1157.62	1146.19
60000	5677.21	3176.02	2357.92	1960.26	1730.44	1584.17	1485.30	1415.71	1365.34	1328.12	1300.21	1279.05	1262.85	1250.39
65000	6150.31	3440.68	2554.41	2123.62	1874.64	1716.18	1609.07	1533.69	1479.12	1438.80	1408.56	1385.63	1368.09	1354.59
70000	6623.41	3705.35	2750.90	2286.97	2018.84	1848.20	1732.85	1651.67	1592.90	1549.48	1516.91	1492.22	1473.33	1458.79
75000	7096.51	3970.02	2947.39	2450.33	2163.05	1980.21	1856.62	1769.64	1706.67	1660.15	1625.27	1598.81	1578.57	1562.98
80000	7569.61	4234.69	3143.89	2613.68	2307.25	2112.23	1980.40	1887.62	1820.45	1770.83	1733.62	1705.39	1683.80	1667.18
85000	8042.71	4499.35	3340.38	2777.04	2451.45	2244.24	2104.17	2005.59	1934.23	1881.51	1841.97	1811.98	1789.04	1771.38
90000	8515.81	4764.02	3536.87	2940.39	2595.66	2376.25	2227.95	2123.57	2048.01	1992.18	1950.32	1918.57	1894.28	1875.58
95000	8988.91	5028.69	3733.36	3103.75	2739.86	2508.27	2351.72	2241.55	2161.79	2102.86	2058.67	2025.15	1999.52	1979.78
100000	9462.02	5293.36	3929.86	3267.10	2884.06	2640.28	2475.49	2359.52	2275.56	2213.54	2167.02	2131.74	2104.75	2083.98

MONTHLY PAYMENT
REQUIRED TO AMORTIZE A LOAN

TERM / AMOUNT	15 Years	16 Years	17 Years	18 Years	19 Years	20 Years	21 Years	22 Years	23 Years	24 Years	25 Years	30 Years	35 Years	40 Years
5	.11	.11	.11	.11	.11	.11	.11	.11	.11	.11	.11	.11	.11	.11
10	.21	.21	.21	.21	.21	.21	.21	.21	.21	.21	.21	.21	.21	.21
15	.32	.31	.31	.31	.31	.31	.31	.31	.31	.31	.31	.31	.31	.31
25	.52	.52	.52	.51	.51	.51	.51	.51	.51	.51	.51	.51	.51	.51
50	1.04	1.03	1.03	1.02	1.02	1.02	1.02	1.02	1.01	1.01	1.01	1.01	1.01	1.01
75	1.56	1.55	1.54	1.53	1.53	1.53	1.52	1.52	1.52	1.52	1.52	1.51	1.51	1.51
100	2.07	2.06	2.05	2.04	2.04	2.03	2.03	2.03	2.02	2.02	2.02	2.02	2.02	2.02
200	4.14	4.12	4.10	4.08	4.07	4.06	4.05	4.05	4.04	4.04	4.04	4.03	4.03	4.03
300	6.21	6.17	6.14	6.12	6.10	6.09	6.08	6.07	6.06	6.06	6.06	6.04	6.04	6.04
400	8.28	8.23	8.19	8.16	8.13	8.11	8.10	8.09	8.08	8.07	8.07	8.05	8.05	8.05
500	10.34	10.28	10.23	10.20	10.17	10.14	10.12	10.11	10.10	10.09	10.08	10.06	10.06	10.06
600	12.41	12.34	12.28	12.23	12.20	12.17	12.15	12.13	12.12	12.11	12.10	12.08	12.07	12.07
700	14.48	14.39	14.32	14.27	14.23	14.20	14.17	14.15	14.14	14.12	14.11	14.09	14.08	14.08
800	16.55	16.45	16.37	16.31	16.26	16.22	16.20	16.17	16.15	16.14	16.13	16.10	16.09	16.09
900	18.62	18.50	18.42	18.35	18.29	18.25	18.22	18.19	18.17	18.16	18.15	18.11	18.10	18.10
1000	20.68	20.56	20.46	20.39	20.33	20.28	20.24	20.21	20.19	20.17	20.16	20.12	20.11	20.11
2000	41.36	41.11	40.92	40.77	40.65	40.55	40.48	40.42	40.38	40.34	40.32	40.24	40.22	40.22
3000	62.04	61.67	61.38	61.15	60.97	60.83	60.72	60.63	60.57	60.51	60.47	60.36	60.33	60.32
4000	82.72	82.22	81.83	81.53	81.29	81.10	80.96	80.84	80.75	80.68	80.63	80.48	80.44	80.43
5000	103.40	102.78	102.29	101.91	101.61	101.38	101.20	101.05	100.94	100.85	100.78	100.60	100.55	100.53
6000	124.08	123.33	122.75	122.29	121.93	121.65	121.44	121.26	121.13	121.02	120.94	120.72	120.66	120.64
7000	144.76	143.88	143.20	142.67	142.26	141.93	141.67	141.47	141.32	141.19	141.09	140.84	140.77	140.74
8000	165.44	164.44	163.66	163.05	162.58	162.20	161.91	161.68	161.50	161.36	161.25	160.96	160.88	160.85
9000	186.12	184.99	184.12	183.43	182.90	182.48	182.15	181.89	181.69	181.53	181.41	181.08	180.98	180.96
10000	206.79	205.55	204.57	203.81	203.22	202.75	202.39	202.10	201.88	201.70	201.56	201.20	201.09	201.06
11000	227.47	226.10	225.03	224.19	223.54	223.03	222.63	222.31	222.06	221.87	221.72	221.32	221.20	221.17
12000	248.15	246.65	245.49	244.58	243.86	243.30	242.87	242.52	242.25	242.04	241.87	241.44	241.31	241.27
13000	268.83	267.21	265.94	264.96	264.18	263.58	263.10	262.73	262.44	262.21	262.03	261.56	261.42	261.38
14000	289.51	287.76	286.40	285.34	284.51	283.85	283.34	282.94	282.63	282.38	282.18	281.68	281.53	281.48
15000	310.19	308.32	306.86	305.72	304.83	304.13	303.58	303.15	302.81	302.55	302.34	301.80	301.64	301.59
16000	330.87	328.87	327.31	326.10	325.15	324.40	323.82	323.36	323.00	322.72	322.49	321.92	321.75	321.69
17000	351.55	349.42	347.77	346.48	345.47	344.68	344.06	343.57	343.19	342.89	342.65	342.04	341.86	341.80
18000	372.23	369.98	368.23	366.86	365.79	364.95	364.30	363.78	363.37	363.06	362.81	362.16	361.96	361.91
19000	392.91	390.53	388.68	387.24	386.11	385.23	384.53	383.99	383.56	383.23	382.96	382.28	382.07	382.01
20000	413.58	411.09	409.14	407.62	406.43	405.50	404.77	404.20	403.75	403.39	403.12	402.40	402.18	402.12
21000	434.26	431.64	429.60	428.00	426.76	425.78	425.01	424.41	423.94	423.56	423.27	422.52	422.29	422.22
22000	454.94	452.20	450.06	448.38	447.08	446.05	445.25	444.62	444.12	443.73	443.43	442.64	442.40	442.33
23000	475.62	472.75	470.51	468.76	467.40	466.33	465.49	464.83	464.31	463.90	463.58	462.76	462.51	462.43
24000	496.30	493.30	490.97	489.15	487.72	486.60	485.73	485.04	484.50	484.07	483.74	482.88	482.62	482.54
25000	516.98	513.86	511.43	509.53	508.04	506.88	505.96	505.25	504.68	504.24	503.89	503.00	502.73	502.64
26000	537.66	534.41	531.88	529.91	528.36	527.15	526.20	525.45	524.87	524.41	524.05	523.12	522.84	522.75
27000	558.34	554.97	552.34	550.29	548.68	547.43	546.44	545.67	545.06	544.58	544.21	543.24	542.94	542.86
28000	579.02	575.52	572.80	570.67	569.01	567.70	566.68	565.25	565.25	564.75	564.36	563.36	563.05	562.96
29000	599.69	596.07	593.25	591.05	589.33	587.98	586.92	586.09	585.43	584.92	584.52	583.48	583.16	583.07
30000	620.37	616.63	613.71	611.43	609.65	608.25	607.16	606.30	605.62	605.09	604.67	603.60	603.27	603.17
31000	641.05	637.18	634.17	631.81	629.97	628.53	627.39	626.51	625.81	625.26	624.83	623.72	623.38	623.28
32000	661.73	657.74	654.62	652.19	650.29	648.80	647.63	646.72	646.00	645.43	644.98	643.84	643.49	643.38
33000	682.41	678.29	675.08	672.57	670.61	669.08	667.87	666.93	666.18	665.60	665.14	663.96	663.60	663.49
34000	703.09	698.84	695.54	692.95	690.93	689.35	688.11	687.13	686.37	685.77	685.29	684.08	683.71	683.60
35000	723.77	719.40	715.99	713.34	711.26	709.63	708.35	707.34	706.56	705.94	705.45	704.19	703.82	703.70
36000	744.45	739.95	736.45	733.72	731.58	729.90	728.59	727.55	726.74	726.11	725.61	724.31	723.92	723.81
37000	765.13	760.51	756.91	754.10	751.90	750.18	748.82	747.76	746.93	746.28	745.76	744.43	744.03	743.91
38000	785.81	781.06	777.36	774.48	772.22	770.45	769.06	767.97	767.12	766.45	765.92	764.55	764.14	764.02
39000	806.48	801.61	797.82	794.86	792.54	790.73	789.30	788.18	787.31	786.62	786.07	784.67	784.25	784.12
40000	827.16	822.17	818.28	815.24	812.86	811.00	809.54	808.39	807.49	806.78	806.23	804.79	804.36	804.23
41000	847.84	842.72	838.73	835.62	833.18	831.28	829.78	828.60	827.68	826.95	826.38	824.91	824.47	824.33
42000	868.52	863.28	859.19	856.00	853.51	851.55	850.02	848.81	847.87	847.12	846.54	845.03	844.58	844.44
43000	889.20	883.83	879.65	876.38	873.83	871.82	870.25	869.02	868.05	867.29	866.69	865.15	864.69	864.55
44000	909.88	904.39	900.11	896.76	894.15	892.10	890.49	889.23	888.24	887.46	886.85	885.27	884.80	884.65
45000	930.56	924.94	920.56	917.14	914.47	912.37	910.73	909.44	908.43	907.63	907.01	905.39	904.90	904.76
46000	951.24	945.49	941.02	937.52	934.79	932.65	930.97	929.65	928.62	927.80	927.16	925.51	925.01	924.86
47000	971.92	966.05	961.48	957.91	955.11	952.92	951.21	949.86	948.80	947.97	947.32	945.63	945.12	944.97
48000	992.60	986.60	981.93	978.29	975.43	973.20	971.45	970.07	968.99	968.14	967.47	965.75	965.23	965.07
49000	1013.27	1007.16	1002.39	998.67	995.76	993.47	991.69	990.28	989.18	988.31	987.63	985.87	985.34	985.18
50000	1033.95	1027.71	1022.85	1019.05	1016.08	1013.75	1011.92	1010.49	1009.36	1008.48	1007.78	1005.99	1005.45	1005.28
55000	1137.35	1130.48	1125.13	1120.95	1117.68	1115.12	1113.12	1111.54	1110.30	1109.33	1108.56	1106.59	1105.99	1105.81
60000	1240.74	1233.25	1227.41	1222.86	1219.29	1216.50	1214.31	1212.59	1211.24	1210.17	1209.34	1207.19	1206.54	1206.34
65000	1344.14	1336.02	1329.70	1324.76	1320.90	1317.87	1315.50	1313.64	1312.17	1311.02	1310.12	1307.79	1307.09	1306.87
70000	1447.53	1438.79	1431.98	1426.67	1422.51	1419.25	1416.69	1414.68	1413.11	1411.87	1410.90	1408.38	1407.63	1407.40
75000	1550.93	1541.56	1534.27	1528.57	1524.11	1520.62	1517.88	1515.73	1514.04	1512.72	1511.67	1508.98	1508.17	1507.92
80000	1654.32	1644.33	1636.55	1630.47	1625.72	1622.00	1619.07	1616.78	1614.98	1613.56	1612.45	1609.58	1608.71	1608.45
85000	1757.72	1747.10	1738.84	1732.38	1727.33	1723.37	1720.27	1717.83	1715.92	1714.41	1713.23	1710.18	1709.26	1708.98
90000	1861.11	1849.87	1841.12	1834.28	1828.93	1824.74	1821.46	1818.88	1816.85	1815.26	1814.01	1810.78	1809.80	1809.51
95000	1964.51	1952.64	1943.40	1936.19	1930.54	1926.12	1922.65	1919.93	1917.79	1916.11	1914.78	1911.38	1910.35	1910.04
100000	2067.90	2055.42	2045.69	2038.09	2032.15	2027.49	2023.84	2020.98	2018.72	2016.95	2015.56	2011.98	2010.89	2010.56

TERM	1 Year	2 Years	3 Years	4 Years	5 Years	6 Years	7 Years	8 Years	9 Years	10 Years	11 Years	12 Years	13 Years	14 Years
AMOUNT
5	.48	.27	.20	.17	.15	.14	.13	.12	.12	.12	.11	.11	.11	.11
10	.95	.53	.40	.33	.29	.27	.25	.24	.23	.23	.22	.22	.22	.21
15	1.42	.80	.60	.50	.44	.40	.38	.36	.35	.34	.33	.33	.32	.32
25	2.37	1.33	.99	.82	.73	.63	.63	.60	.58	.56	.55	.54	.53	.53
50	4.74	2.65	1.97	1.64	1.45	1.33	1.25	1.19	1.15	1.11	1.09	1.07	1.06	1.05
75	7.10	3.98	2.96	2.46	2.17	1.99	1.87	1.78	1.72	1.67	1.63	1.61	1.59	1.57
100	9.47	5.30	3.94	3.28	2.89	2.65	2.49	2.37	2.29	2.22	2.18	2.14	2.12	2.09
200	18.94	10.60	7.87	6.55	5.76	5.29	4.97	4.73	4.57	4.44	4.35	4.28	4.23	4.18
300	28.40	15.90	11.81	9.82	8.67	7.94	7.45	7.10	6.85	6.66	6.52	6.42	6.34	6.27
400	37.87	21.19	16.75	13.09	11.56	10.58	9.93	9.46	9.13	8.88	8.69	8.55	8.45	8.36
500	47.33	26.49	19.67	16.36	14.45	13.23	12.41	11.83	11.41	11.10	10.87	10.69	10.56	10.45
600	56.80	31.79	23.61	19.63	17.34	15.87	14.89	14.19	13.69	13.32	13.04	12.83	12.67	12.54
700	66.26	37.08	27.54	22.90	20.22	18.52	17.37	16.56	15.97	15.54	15.21	14.97	14.78	14.63
800	75.73	42.38	31.48	26.18	23.11	21.16	19.85	18.92	18.25	17.76	17.38	17.10	16.89	16.72
900	85.20	47.68	35.41	29.45	26.00	23.81	22.33	21.28	20.53	19.97	19.56	19.24	19.00	18.81
1000	94.66	52.98	39.34	32.72	28.89	26.45	24.81	23.65	22.81	22.19	21.73	21.38	21.11	20.90
2000	189.32	105.95	78.68	65.43	57.77	52.90	49.61	47.29	45.62	44.38	43.45	42.75	42.21	41.80
3000	283.97	158.92	118.02	98.14	86.66	79.35	74.41	70.94	68.42	66.57	65.18	64.12	63.32	62.70
4000	378.63	211.89	157.36	130.86	115.54	105.80	99.21	94.58	91.23	88.76	86.90	85.49	84.42	83.59
5000	473.29	264.86	196.69	163.57	144.43	132.25	124.02	118.23	114.04	110.94	108.62	106.87	105.52	104.49
6000	567.94	317.83	236.03	196.28	173.31	158.70	148.82	141.87	136.84	133.13	130.35	128.24	126.63	125.39
7000	662.60	370.80	275.37	228.99	202.19	185.14	173.62	165.52	159.65	155.32	152.07	149.61	147.73	146.28
8000	757.26	423.77	314.71	261.71	231.08	211.59	198.42	189.16	182.46	177.51	173.80	170.98	168.83	167.18
9000	851.91	476.74	354.05	294.42	259.96	238.04	223.23	212.80	205.26	199.69	195.52	192.36	189.94	188.08
10000	946.57	529.71	393.38	327.13	288.85	264.49	248.03	236.45	228.07	221.88	217.24	213.73	211.04	208.97
11000	1041.23	582.69	432.72	359.84	317.73	290.94	272.83	260.09	250.88	244.07	238.97	235.10	232.14	229.87
12000	1135.88	635.66	472.06	392.56	346.62	317.39	297.63	283.74	273.68	266.26	260.69	256.47	253.25	250.77
13000	1230.54	688.63	511.40	425.27	375.50	343.83	322.44	307.38	296.49	288.45	282.42	277.84	274.35	271.66
14000	1325.19	741.60	550.74	457.98	404.38	370.28	347.24	331.03	319.30	310.63	304.14	299.22	295.45	292.56
15000	1419.85	794.57	590.07	490.69	433.27	396.73	372.04	354.67	342.10	332.82	325.86	320.59	316.56	313.46
16000	1514.51	847.54	629.41	523.41	462.15	423.18	396.84	378.32	364.91	355.01	347.59	341.96	337.66	334.35
17000	1609.16	900.51	668.75	556.12	491.04	449.63	421.65	401.96	387.72	377.20	369.31	363.33	358.76	355.25
18000	1703.82	953.48	708.09	588.83	519.92	476.08	446.45	425.60	410.52	399.38	391.03	384.71	379.87	376.15
19000	1798.48	1006.45	747.43	621.54	548.80	502.52	471.25	449.25	433.33	421.57	412.76	406.08	400.97	397.04
20000	1893.13	1059.42	786.76	654.26	577.69	528.97	496.05	472.89	456.14	443.76	434.48	427.45	422.07	417.94
21000	1987.79	1112.40	826.10	686.97	606.57	555.42	520.86	496.54	478.94	465.95	456.21	448.82	443.18	438.84
22000	2082.45	1165.37	865.44	719.68	635.46	581.87	545.66	520.18	501.75	488.13	477.93	470.20	464.28	459.73
23000	2177.10	1218.34	904.78	752.39	664.34	608.32	570.46	543.83	524.55	510.32	499.65	491.57	485.39	480.63
24000	2271.76	1271.31	944.12	785.11	693.23	634.77	595.26	567.47	547.36	532.51	521.38	512.94	506.49	501.53
25000	2366.42	1324.28	983.45	817.82	722.11	661.21	620.07	591.12	570.17	554.70	543.10	534.31	527.59	522.42
26000	2461.07	1377.25	1022.79	850.53	750.99	687.66	644.87	614.76	592.97	576.89	564.83	555.68	548.70	543.32
27000	2555.73	1430.22	1062.13	883.24	779.88	714.11	669.67	638.40	615.78	599.07	586.55	577.06	569.80	564.22
28000	2650.38	1483.19	1101.47	915.96	808.76	740.56	694.47	662.05	638.59	621.26	608.27	598.43	590.90	585.11
29000	2745.04	1536.16	1140.81	948.67	837.65	767.01	719.27	685.69	661.39	643.45	630.00	619.80	612.01	606.01
30000	2839.70	1589.13	1180.14	981.38	866.53	793.46	744.08	709.34	684.20	665.64	651.72	641.17	633.11	626.91
31000	2934.35	1642.11	1219.48	1014.09	895.41	819.90	768.88	732.98	707.01	687.82	673.45	662.55	654.21	647.80
32000	3029.01	1695.08	1258.82	1046.81	924.30	846.35	793.68	756.63	729.81	710.01	695.17	683.92	675.32	668.70
33000	3123.67	1748.05	1298.16	1079.52	953.18	872.80	818.48	780.27	752.62	732.20	716.89	705.29	696.42	689.60
34000	3218.32	1801.02	1337.50	1112.23	982.07	899.25	843.29	803.92	775.43	754.39	738.62	726.66	717.52	710.49
35000	3312.98	1853.99	1376.83	1144.94	1010.95	925.70	868.09	827.56	798.23	776.58	760.34	748.03	738.63	731.39
36000	3407.64	1906.96	1416.17	1177.66	1039.84	952.15	892.89	851.20	821.04	798.76	782.06	769.41	759.73	752.29
37000	3502.29	1959.93	1455.51	1210.37	1068.72	978.59	917.69	874.85	843.85	820.95	803.79	790.78	780.83	773.18
38000	3596.95	2012.90	1494.85	1243.08	1097.60	1005.04	942.50	898.49	866.65	843.14	825.51	812.15	801.94	794.08
39000	3691.61	2065.87	1534.18	1275.79	1126.49	1031.49	967.30	922.14	889.46	865.33	847.24	833.52	823.04	814.98
40000	3786.26	2118.84	1573.52	1308.51	1155.37	1057.94	992.10	945.78	912.27	887.51	868.96	854.90	844.14	835.87
41000	3880.92	2171.81	1612.86	1341.22	1184.26	1084.39	1016.90	969.43	935.07	909.70	890.68	876.27	865.25	856.77
42000	3975.57	2224.79	1652.20	1373.93	1213.14	1110.84	1041.71	993.07	957.88	931.89	912.41	897.64	886.35	877.67
43000	4070.23	2277.76	1691.54	1406.64	1242.02	1137.29	1066.51	1016.72	980.68	954.08	934.13	919.01	907.46	898.56
44000	4164.89	2330.73	1730.87	1439.36	1270.91	1163.73	1091.31	1040.36	1003.49	976.26	955.86	940.39	928.56	919.46
45000	4259.54	2383.70	1770.21	1472.07	1299.79	1190.18	1116.11	1064.00	1026.30	998.45	977.58	961.76	949.66	940.36
46000	4354.20	2436.67	1809.55	1504.78	1328.68	1216.63	1140.92	1087.65	1049.10	1020.64	999.30	983.13	970.77	961.25
47000	4448.86	2489.64	1848.89	1537.49	1357.56	1243.08	1165.72	1111.29	1071.91	1042.83	1021.03	1004.50	991.87	982.15
48000	4543.51	2542.61	1888.23	1570.21	1386.45	1269.53	1190.52	1134.94	1094.72	1065.02	1042.75	1025.87	1012.97	1003.05
49000	4638.17	2595.58	1927.56	1602.92	1415.33	1295.98	1215.32	1158.58	1117.52	1087.20	1064.48	1047.25	1034.08	1023.94
50000	4732.83	2648.55	1966.90	1635.63	1444.21	1322.42	1240.13	1182.23	1140.33	1109.39	1086.20	1068.62	1055.18	1044.84
55000	5206.11	2913.41	2163.59	1799.19	1588.63	1454.67	1364.14	1300.45	1254.36	1220.33	1194.82	1175.48	1160.70	1149.32
60000	5679.39	3178.26	2360.28	1962.76	1733.06	1586.91	1488.15	1418.67	1368.40	1331.27	1303.44	1282.34	1266.21	1253.81
65000	6152.67	3443.12	2556.97	2126.32	1877.48	1719.15	1612.16	1536.89	1482.43	1442.21	1412.06	1389.20	1371.73	1358.29
70000	6625.95	3707.97	2753.66	2289.88	2021.90	1851.39	1736.17	1655.12	1596.46	1553.15	1520.68	1496.06	1477.25	1462.77
75000	7099.24	3972.83	2950.35	2453.44	2166.32	1983.63	1860.19	1773.34	1710.49	1664.08	1629.30	1602.93	1582.77	1567.26
80000	7572.52	4237.68	3147.04	2617.01	2310.74	2115.87	1984.20	1891.56	1824.53	1775.02	1737.92	1709.79	1688.28	1671.74
85000	8045.80	4502.54	3343.73	2780.57	2455.16	2248.12	2108.21	2009.78	1938.56	1885.96	1846.53	1816.65	1793.80	1776.22
90000	8519.08	4767.39	3540.42	2944.13	2599.58	2380.36	2232.22	2128.00	2052.59	1996.90	1955.15	1923.51	1899.32	1880.71
95000	8992.36	5032.25	3737.11	3107.69	2744.00	2512.60	2356.23	2246.23	2166.62	2107.84	2063.77	2030.37	2004.84	1985.19
100000	9465.65	5297.10	3933.80	3271.26	2888.42	2644.84	2480.25	2364.45	2280.66	2218.78	2172.39	2137.23	2110.35	2089.67

MONTHLY PAYMENT
REQUIRED TO AMORTIZE A LOAN

24.200%

TERM	15 Years	16 Years	17 Years	18 Years	19 Years	20 Years	21 Years	22 Years	23 Years	24 Years	25 Years	30 Years	35 Years	40 Years
AMOUNT														
5	.11	.11	.11	.11	.11	.11	.11	.11	.11	.11	.11	.11	.11	.11
10	.21	.21	.21	.21	.21	.21	.21	.21	.21	.21	.21	.21	.21	.21
15	.32	.31	.31	.31	.31	.31	.31	.31	.31	.31	.31	.31	.31	.31
25	.52	.52	.52	.52	.51	.51	.51	.51	.51	.51	.51	.51	.51	.51
50	1.04	1.04	1.03	1.03	1.02	1.02	1.02	1.02	1.02	1.02	1.02	1.01	1.01	1.01
75	1.56	1.55	1.54	1.54	1.53	1.53	1.53	1.53	1.52	1.52	1.52	1.52	1.52	1.52
100	2.08	2.07	2.06	2.05	2.04	2.04	2.03	2.03	2.03	2.03	2.03	2.02	2.02	2.02
200	4.15	4.13	4.11	4.09	4.08	4.07	4.06	4.06	4.05	4.05	4.05	4.04	4.04	4.04
300	6.23	6.19	6.16	6.14	6.12	6.11	6.09	6.09	6.08	6.07	6.07	6.06	6.06	6.06
400	8.30	8.25	8.21	8.18	8.16	8.14	8.12	8.11	8.10	8.10	8.09	8.08	8.07	8.07
500	10.37	10.31	10.26	10.23	10.20	10.17	10.15	10.14	10.13	10.12	10.11	10.10	10.09	10.09
600	12.45	12.37	12.31	12.27	12.23	12.21	12.18	12.17	12.15	12.14	12.14	12.11	12.11	12.11
700	14.52	14.43	14.37	14.31	14.27	14.24	14.21	14.19	14.18	14.17	14.16	14.13	14.12	14.12
800	16.59	16.50	16.42	16.36	16.31	16.27	16.24	16.22	16.20	16.19	16.18	16.15	16.14	16.14
900	18.67	18.56	18.47	18.40	18.35	18.31	18.27	18.25	18.23	18.21	18.20	18.17	18.16	18.16
1000	20.74	20.62	20.52	20.45	20.39	20.34	20.30	20.28	20.25	20.24	20.22	20.19	20.18	20.17
2000	41.48	41.23	41.04	40.89	40.77	40.68	40.60	40.55	40.50	40.47	40.44	40.37	40.35	40.34
3000	62.22	61.84	61.55	61.33	61.15	61.01	60.90	60.82	60.75	60.70	60.66	60.55	60.52	60.51
4000	82.95	82.46	82.07	81.77	81.53	81.35	81.20	81.09	81.00	80.93	80.87	80.73	80.69	80.68
5000	103.69	103.07	102.58	102.21	101.91	101.68	101.50	101.36	101.25	101.16	101.09	100.91	100.86	100.85
6000	124.43	123.68	123.10	122.65	122.29	122.02	121.80	121.63	121.50	121.39	121.31	121.10	121.03	121.01
7000	145.16	144.29	143.62	143.09	142.68	142.35	142.10	141.90	141.74	141.62	141.53	141.28	141.20	141.18
8000	165.90	164.91	164.13	163.53	163.06	162.69	162.40	162.17	161.99	161.85	161.74	161.46	161.38	161.35
9000	186.64	185.52	184.65	183.97	183.44	183.02	182.70	182.44	182.24	182.08	181.96	181.64	181.55	181.52
10000	207.37	206.13	205.16	204.41	203.82	203.36	203.00	202.71	202.49	202.32	202.18	201.82	201.72	201.69
11000	228.11	226.74	225.68	224.85	224.20	223.69	223.30	222.98	222.74	222.55	222.40	222.01	221.89	221.85
12000	248.85	247.36	246.20	245.29	244.58	244.03	243.60	243.25	242.99	242.78	242.61	242.19	242.06	242.02
13000	269.58	267.97	266.71	265.73	264.97	264.37	263.89	263.53	263.24	263.01	262.83	262.37	262.23	262.19
14000	290.32	288.58	287.23	286.17	285.35	284.70	284.19	283.80	283.48	283.24	283.05	282.55	282.40	282.36
15000	311.06	309.19	307.74	306.61	305.73	305.04	304.49	304.07	303.73	303.47	303.26	302.73	302.57	302.53
16000	331.79	329.81	328.26	327.05	326.11	325.37	324.79	324.34	323.98	323.70	323.48	322.92	322.75	322.69
17000	352.53	350.42	348.70	347.49	346.49	345.71	345.09	344.61	344.23	343.93	343.70	343.10	342.92	342.86
18000	373.27	371.03	369.29	367.93	366.87	366.04	365.39	364.88	364.48	364.16	363.92	363.28	363.09	363.03
19000	394.00	391.64	389.81	388.38	387.25	386.38	385.69	385.15	384.73	384.39	384.13	383.46	383.26	383.20
20000	414.74	412.26	410.32	408.82	407.64	406.71	405.99	405.42	404.98	404.63	404.35	403.64	403.43	403.37
21000	435.48	432.87	430.84	429.26	428.02	427.05	426.29	425.69	425.22	424.86	424.57	423.83	423.60	423.53
22000	456.21	453.48	451.36	449.70	448.40	447.38	446.59	445.96	445.47	445.09	444.79	444.01	443.77	443.70
23000	476.95	474.09	471.87	470.14	468.78	467.72	466.89	466.23	465.72	465.32	465.00	464.19	463.94	463.87
24000	497.69	494.71	492.39	490.58	489.16	488.05	487.19	486.50	485.97	485.55	485.22	484.37	484.12	484.04
25000	518.42	515.32	512.90	511.02	509.54	508.39	507.49	506.78	506.22	505.78	505.44	504.55	504.29	504.21
26000	539.16	535.93	533.42	531.46	529.93	528.73	527.78	527.05	526.47	526.01	525.65	524.73	524.46	524.37
27000	559.90	556.55	553.94	551.90	550.31	549.06	548.08	547.32	546.72	546.24	545.87	544.92	544.63	544.54
28000	580.63	577.16	574.45	572.34	570.69	569.40	568.38	567.59	566.96	566.47	566.09	565.10	564.80	564.71
29000	601.37	597.77	594.97	592.78	591.07	589.73	588.68	587.86	587.21	586.71	586.31	585.28	584.97	584.88
30000	622.11	618.38	615.48	613.22	611.45	610.07	608.98	608.13	607.46	606.94	606.52	605.46	605.14	605.05
31000	642.84	639.00	636.00	633.66	631.83	630.40	629.28	628.40	627.71	627.17	626.74	625.64	625.31	625.21
32000	663.58	659.61	656.52	654.10	652.21	650.74	649.58	648.67	647.96	647.40	646.96	645.83	645.49	645.38
33000	684.32	680.22	677.03	674.54	672.60	671.07	669.88	668.94	668.21	667.63	667.18	666.01	665.66	665.55
34000	705.05	700.83	697.55	694.98	692.98	691.41	690.18	689.21	688.46	687.86	687.39	686.19	685.83	685.72
35000	725.79	721.45	718.06	715.42	713.36	711.74	710.48	709.48	708.70	708.09	707.61	706.37	706.00	705.89
36000	746.53	742.06	738.58	735.86	733.74	732.08	730.78	729.75	728.95	728.32	727.83	726.55	726.17	726.05
37000	767.26	762.67	759.10	756.30	754.12	752.41	751.08	750.03	749.20	748.55	748.04	746.74	746.34	746.22
38000	788.00	783.28	779.61	776.75	774.50	772.75	771.37	770.30	769.45	768.78	768.26	766.92	766.51	766.39
39000	808.74	803.90	800.13	797.19	794.89	793.09	791.67	790.57	789.70	789.02	788.48	787.10	786.68	786.56
40000	829.47	824.51	820.64	817.63	815.27	813.42	811.97	810.84	809.95	809.25	808.70	807.28	806.86	806.73
41000	850.21	845.12	841.16	838.07	835.65	833.76	832.27	831.11	830.20	829.48	828.91	827.46	827.03	826.90
42000	870.95	865.73	861.68	858.51	856.03	854.09	852.57	851.38	850.44	849.71	849.13	847.65	847.20	847.06
43000	891.69	886.35	882.19	878.95	876.41	874.43	872.87	871.65	870.69	869.94	869.35	867.83	867.37	867.23
44000	912.42	906.96	902.71	899.39	896.79	894.76	893.17	891.92	890.94	890.17	889.57	888.01	887.54	887.40
45000	933.16	927.57	923.22	919.83	917.18	915.10	913.47	912.19	911.19	910.40	909.78	908.19	907.71	907.57
46000	953.90	948.18	943.74	940.27	937.56	935.43	933.77	932.46	931.44	930.63	930.00	928.37	927.88	927.74
47000	974.63	968.80	964.25	960.71	957.94	955.77	954.07	952.73	951.69	950.86	950.22	948.56	948.05	947.90
48000	995.37	989.41	984.77	981.15	978.32	976.10	974.37	973.00	971.94	971.10	970.44	968.74	968.23	968.07
49000	1016.11	1010.02	1005.29	1001.59	998.70	996.44	994.67	993.28	992.18	991.33	990.65	988.92	988.40	988.24
50000	1036.84	1030.64	1025.80	1022.03	1019.08	1016.77	1014.97	1013.55	1012.43	1011.56	1010.87	1009.10	1008.57	1008.41
55000	1140.53	1133.70	1128.38	1124.23	1120.99	1118.45	1116.46	1114.90	1113.67	1112.71	1111.96	1110.01	1109.42	1109.25
60000	1244.21	1236.76	1230.96	1226.44	1222.90	1220.13	1217.96	1216.25	1214.92	1213.87	1213.04	1210.92	1210.28	1210.09
65000	1347.89	1339.82	1333.54	1328.64	1324.81	1321.81	1319.45	1317.61	1316.16	1315.02	1314.13	1311.83	1311.14	1310.93
70000	1451.58	1442.89	1436.12	1430.84	1426.71	1423.48	1420.95	1418.96	1417.40	1416.18	1415.22	1412.74	1411.99	1411.77
75000	1555.26	1545.95	1538.70	1533.04	1528.62	1525.16	1522.45	1520.32	1518.65	1517.33	1516.30	1513.65	1512.85	1512.61
80000	1658.94	1649.01	1641.28	1635.25	1630.53	1626.84	1623.94	1621.67	1619.89	1618.49	1617.39	1614.56	1613.71	1613.45
85000	1762.63	1752.08	1743.86	1737.45	1732.44	1728.51	1725.44	1723.03	1721.13	1719.64	1718.48	1715.47	1714.56	1714.29
90000	1866.31	1855.14	1846.44	1839.65	1834.35	1830.19	1826.93	1824.38	1822.37	1820.80	1819.56	1816.38	1815.42	1815.13
95000	1970.00	1958.20	1949.02	1941.86	1936.25	1931.87	1928.43	1925.73	1923.62	1921.95	1920.65	1917.29	1916.28	1915.97
100000	2073.68	2061.27	2051.60	2044.06	2038.16	2033.54	2029.93	2027.09	2024.86	2023.11	2021.73	2018.20	2017.13	2016.81

MONTHLY PAYMENT
REQUIRED TO AMORTIZE A LOAN

TERM	1 Year	2 Years	3 Years	4 Years	5 Years	6 Years	7 Years	8 Years	9 Years	10 Years	11 Years	12 Years	13 Years	14 Years
AMOUNT														
5	.48	.27	.20	.17	.15	.14	.13	.12	.12	.12	.11	.11	.11	.11
10	.95	.53	.40	.33	.29	.27	.25	.24	.23	.23	.22	.22	.22	.21
15	1.43	.80	.60	.50	.44	.40	.38	.36	.35	.34	.33	.33	.32	.32
25	2.37	1.33	.99	.82	.73	.67	.63	.60	.58	.56	.55	.54	.53	.53
50	4.74	2.65	1.97	1.64	1.45	1.33	1.25	1.19	1.15	1.12	1.09	1.08	1.06	1.05
75	7.11	3.98	2.96	2.46	2.17	1.99	1.87	1.78	1.72	1.67	1.64	1.61	1.59	1.58
100	9.47	5.30	3.94	3.28	2.90	2.65	2.49	2.37	2.29	2.23	2.18	2.15	2.12	2.10
200	18.94	10.60	7.88	6.55	5.79	5.30	4.97	4.74	4.57	4.45	4.36	4.29	4.23	4.19
300	28.41	15.90	11.81	9.83	8.68	7.95	7.46	7.11	6.86	6.67	6.53	6.43	6.35	6.29
400	37.88	21.20	15.75	13.10	11.57	10.60	9.94	9.48	9.14	8.89	8.71	8.57	8.46	8.38
500	47.35	26.50	19.69	16.38	14.46	13.24	12.42	11.84	11.43	11.12	10.88	10.71	10.58	10.47
600	56.81	31.80	23.62	19.65	17.35	15.89	14.91	14.21	13.71	13.34	13.06	12.85	12.69	12.57
700	66.28	37.10	27.56	22.92	20.24	18.54	17.39	16.58	15.99	15.56	15.24	14.99	14.80	14.66
800	75.75	42.40	31.50	26.20	23.14	21.19	19.87	18.95	18.28	17.78	17.41	17.13	16.92	16.75
900	85.22	47.70	35.43	29.47	26.03	23.84	22.36	21.31	20.56	20.01	19.59	19.27	19.03	18.85
1000	94.69	53.00	39.37	32.75	28.92	26.48	24.84	23.68	22.85	22.23	21.76	21.41	21.15	20.94
2000	189.37	106.00	78.73	65.49	57.83	52.96	49.67	47.36	45.69	44.45	43.52	42.82	42.29	41.87
3000	284.05	158.99	118.10	98.23	86.74	79.44	74.51	71.04	68.53	66.67	65.28	64.23	63.43	62.81
4000	378.73	211.99	157.46	130.97	115.66	105.92	99.34	94.71	91.37	88.90	87.04	85.64	84.57	83.74
5000	473.41	264.98	196.83	163.71	144.57	132.40	124.18	118.39	114.21	111.12	108.80	107.05	105.71	104.68
6000	568.09	317.98	236.19	196.45	173.48	158.88	149.01	142.07	137.05	133.34	130.56	128.46	126.85	125.61
7000	662.77	370.98	275.55	229.19	202.40	185.36	173.84	165.75	159.89	155.56	152.32	149.87	147.99	146.55
8000	757.45	423.97	314.92	261.93	231.31	211.84	198.68	189.42	182.73	177.79	174.08	171.28	169.13	167.48
9000	852.13	476.97	354.28	294.67	260.22	238.31	223.51	213.10	205.57	200.01	195.84	192.69	190.27	188.42
10000	946.81	529.96	393.65	327.41	289.14	264.79	248.35	236.78	228.41	222.23	217.60	214.09	211.41	209.35
11000	1041.49	582.96	433.01	360.15	318.05	291.27	273.18	260.46	251.25	244.45	239.36	235.50	232.55	230.29
12000	1136.17	635.96	472.38	392.89	346.96	317.75	296.01	284.13	274.09	266.68	261.12	256.91	253.70	251.22
13000	1230.85	688.95	511.74	425.63	375.88	344.23	322.85	307.81	296.93	288.90	282.88	278.32	274.84	272.16
14000	1325.53	741.95	551.10	458.37	404.79	370.71	347.68	331.49	319.77	311.12	304.64	299.73	295.98	293.09
15000	1420.21	794.94	590.47	491.11	433.70	397.19	372.52	355.16	342.61	333.35	326.40	321.14	317.12	314.03
16000	1514.90	847.94	629.83	523.85	462.62	423.67	397.35	378.84	365.45	355.57	348.16	342.55	338.26	334.96
17000	1609.58	900.94	669.20	556.59	491.53	450.14	422.18	402.52	388.29	377.79	369.92	363.96	359.40	355.89
18000	1704.26	953.93	708.56	589.33	520.44	476.62	447.02	426.20	411.13	400.01	391.68	385.37	380.54	376.83
19000	1798.94	1006.93	747.93	622.07	549.36	503.10	471.85	449.87	433.97	422.24	413.44	406.77	401.68	397.76
20000	1893.62	1059.92	787.29	654.81	578.27	529.58	496.69	473.55	456.81	444.46	435.20	428.18	422.82	418.70
21000	1988.30	1112.92	826.65	687.55	607.18	556.06	521.52	497.23	479.65	466.68	456.96	449.59	443.96	439.63
22000	2082.98	1165.92	866.02	720.29	636.10	582.54	546.36	520.91	502.50	488.90	478.72	471.00	465.10	460.57
23000	2177.66	1218.91	905.38	753.03	665.01	609.02	571.19	544.58	525.34	511.13	500.48	492.41	486.24	481.50
24000	2272.34	1271.91	944.75	785.77	693.92	635.50	596.02	568.26	548.18	533.35	522.24	513.82	507.39	502.44
25000	2367.02	1324.90	984.11	818.51	722.84	661.98	620.86	591.94	571.02	555.57	544.00	535.23	528.53	523.37
26000	2461.70	1377.90	1023.48	851.25	751.75	688.45	645.69	615.62	593.86	577.79	565.76	556.64	549.67	544.31
27000	2556.38	1430.90	1062.84	883.99	780.66	714.93	670.53	639.29	616.70	600.02	587.52	578.05	570.81	565.24
28000	2651.06	1483.89	1102.20	916.73	809.58	741.41	695.36	662.97	639.54	622.24	609.28	599.46	591.95	586.18
29000	2745.74	1536.89	1141.57	949.47	838.49	767.89	720.19	686.65	662.38	644.46	631.04	620.86	613.09	607.11
30000	2840.42	1589.88	1180.93	982.21	867.40	794.37	745.03	710.32	685.22	666.69	652.80	642.27	634.23	628.05
31000	2935.10	1642.88	1220.30	1014.95	896.32	820.85	769.86	734.00	708.06	688.91	674.56	663.68	655.37	648.98
32000	3029.78	1695.88	1259.66	1047.69	925.23	847.33	794.70	757.68	730.90	711.13	696.32	685.09	676.51	669.91
33000	3124.47	1748.87	1299.02	1080.43	954.14	873.81	819.53	781.36	753.74	733.35	718.08	706.50	697.65	690.85
34000	3219.15	1801.87	1338.39	1113.17	983.06	900.28	844.36	805.03	776.58	755.58	739.84	727.91	718.79	711.78
35000	3313.83	1854.86	1377.75	1145.91	1011.97	926.76	869.20	828.71	799.42	777.80	761.60	749.32	739.93	732.72
36000	3408.51	1907.86	1417.12	1178.65	1040.88	953.24	894.03	852.39	822.26	800.02	783.36	770.73	761.08	753.65
37000	3503.19	1960.86	1456.48	1211.39	1069.80	979.72	918.87	876.07	845.10	822.24	805.12	792.14	782.22	774.59
38000	3597.87	2013.85	1495.85	1244.13	1098.71	1006.20	943.70	899.74	867.94	844.47	826.87	813.54	803.36	795.52
39000	3692.55	2066.85	1535.21	1276.87	1127.62	1032.68	968.53	923.42	890.78	866.69	848.63	834.95	824.50	816.46
40000	3787.23	2119.84	1574.57	1309.61	1156.54	1059.16	993.37	947.10	913.62	888.91	870.39	856.36	845.64	837.39
41000	3881.91	2172.84	1613.94	1342.35	1185.45	1085.64	1018.20	970.77	936.46	911.13	892.15	877.77	866.78	858.33
42000	3976.59	2225.84	1653.30	1375.09	1214.36	1112.11	1043.04	994.45	959.30	933.36	913.91	899.18	887.92	879.26
43000	4071.27	2278.83	1692.67	1407.83	1243.28	1138.59	1067.87	1018.13	982.14	955.58	935.67	920.59	909.06	900.20
44000	4165.95	2331.83	1732.03	1440.57	1272.19	1165.07	1092.71	1041.81	1004.99	977.80	957.43	942.00	930.20	921.13
45000	4260.63	2384.82	1771.40	1473.31	1301.10	1191.55	1117.54	1065.48	1027.83	1000.03	979.19	963.41	951.34	942.07
46000	4355.31	2437.82	1810.76	1506.05	1330.01	1218.03	1142.37	1089.16	1050.67	1022.25	1000.95	984.82	972.48	963.00
47000	4449.99	2490.81	1850.12	1538.79	1358.93	1244.51	1167.21	1112.84	1073.51	1044.47	1022.71	1006.22	993.63	983.93
48000	4544.67	2543.81	1889.49	1571.53	1387.84	1270.99	1192.04	1136.52	1096.35	1066.69	1044.47	1027.63	1014.77	1004.87
49000	4639.36	2596.81	1928.85	1604.27	1416.75	1297.47	1216.88	1160.19	1119.19	1088.92	1066.23	1049.04	1035.91	1025.80
50000	4734.04	2649.80	1968.22	1637.01	1445.67	1323.95	1241.71	1183.87	1142.03	1111.14	1087.99	1070.45	1057.05	1046.74
55000	5207.44	2914.78	2165.04	1800.72	1590.23	1456.34	1365.88	1302.26	1256.23	1222.25	1196.79	1177.50	1162.75	1151.41
60000	5680.84	3179.76	2361.86	1964.42	1734.80	1588.73	1490.05	1420.64	1370.43	1333.37	1305.59	1284.54	1268.46	1256.09
65000	6154.25	3444.74	2558.68	2128.12	1879.37	1721.13	1614.22	1539.03	1484.64	1444.48	1414.39	1391.59	1374.16	1360.76
70000	6627.65	3709.72	2755.50	2291.82	2023.93	1853.52	1738.39	1657.42	1598.84	1555.59	1523.19	1498.63	1479.86	1465.43
75000	7101.05	3974.70	2952.32	2455.52	2168.50	1985.92	1862.56	1775.80	1713.04	1666.71	1631.98	1605.68	1585.57	1570.11
80000	7574.45	4239.68	3149.14	2619.22	2313.07	2118.31	1986.73	1894.19	1827.24	1777.82	1740.78	1712.72	1691.27	1674.78
85000	8047.86	4504.67	3345.97	2782.92	2457.63	2250.70	2110.90	2012.58	1941.44	1888.93	1849.58	1819.76	1796.98	1779.45
90000	8521.26	4769.64	3542.79	2946.62	2602.20	2383.10	2235.07	2130.97	2055.65	2000.05	1958.38	1926.81	1902.68	1884.13
95000	8994.66	5034.62	3739.61	3110.32	2746.76	2515.49	2359.24	2249.35	2169.85	2111.16	2067.18	2033.85	2008.39	1988.80
100000	9468.07	5299.60	3936.43	3274.02	2891.33	2647.89	2483.41	2367.74	2284.05	2222.27	2175.98	2140.90	2114.09	2093.47

TERM	15 Years	16 Years	17 Years	18 Years	19 Years	20 Years	21 Years	22 Years	23 Years	24 Years	25 Years	30 Years	35 Years	40 Years
AMOUNT														
5	.11	.11	.11	.11	.11	.11	.11	.11	.11	.11	.11	.11	.11	.11
10	.21	.21	.21	.21	.21	.21	.21	.21	.21	.21	.21	.21	.21	.21
15	.32	.31	.31	.31	.31	.31	.31	.31	.31	.31	.31	.31	.31	.31
25	.52	.52	.52	.52	.52	.51	.51	.51	.51	.51	.51	.51	.51	.51
50	1.04	1.04	1.03	1.03	1.03	1.02	1.02	1.02	1.02	1.02	1.02	1.02	1.02	1.02
75	1.56	1.55	1.55	1.54	1.54	1.53	1.53	1.53	1.53	1.53	1.52	1.52	1.52	1.52
100	2.08	2.07	2.06	2.05	2.05	2.04	2.04	2.04	2.03	2.03	2.03	2.03	2.03	2.03
200	4.16	4.14	4.12	4.10	4.09	4.08	4.07	4.07	4.06	4.06	4.06	4.05	4.05	4.05
300	6.24	6.20	6.17	6.15	6.13	6.12	6.11	6.10	6.09	6.09	6.08	6.07	6.07	6.07
400	8.32	8.27	8.23	8.20	8.17	8.16	8.14	8.13	8.12	8.11	8.11	8.09	8.09	8.09
500	10.39	10.33	10.28	10.25	10.22	10.19	10.17	10.16	10.15	10.14	10.13	10.12	10.11	10.11
600	12.47	12.40	12.34	12.29	12.26	12.23	12.21	12.19	12.18	12.17	12.16	12.14	12.13	12.13
700	14.55	14.46	14.39	14.34	14.30	14.27	14.24	14.22	14.21	14.20	14.19	14.16	14.15	14.15
800	16.63	16.53	16.45	16.39	16.34	16.31	16.28	16.25	16.24	16.22	16.21	16.18	16.18	16.17
900	18.70	18.59	18.50	18.44	18.38	18.34	18.31	18.29	18.27	18.25	18.24	18.21	18.20	18.19
1000	20.78	20.66	20.56	20.49	20.43	20.38	20.34	20.32	20.29	20.28	20.26	20.23	20.22	20.21
2000	41.56	41.31	41.12	40.97	40.85	40.76	40.68	40.63	40.58	40.55	40.52	40.45	40.43	40.42
3000	62.33	61.96	61.67	61.45	61.27	61.13	61.02	60.94	60.87	60.82	60.78	60.68	60.64	60.63
4000	83.11	82.61	82.23	81.93	81.69	81.51	81.36	81.25	81.16	81.09	81.04	80.90	80.86	80.84
5000	103.88	103.26	102.78	102.41	102.11	101.88	101.70	101.56	101.45	101.37	101.30	101.12	101.07	101.05
6000	124.66	123.91	123.34	122.89	122.53	122.26	122.04	121.87	121.74	121.64	121.56	121.35	121.28	121.26
7000	145.43	144.57	143.89	143.37	142.96	142.64	142.38	142.19	142.03	141.91	141.81	141.57	141.50	141.47
8000	166.21	165.22	164.45	163.85	163.38	163.01	162.72	162.50	162.32	162.18	162.07	161.79	161.71	161.68
9000	186.98	185.87	185.00	184.33	183.80	183.39	183.06	182.81	182.61	182.45	182.33	182.02	181.92	181.89
10000	207.76	206.52	205.56	204.81	204.22	203.76	203.40	203.12	202.90	202.73	202.59	202.24	202.13	202.10
11000	228.53	227.17	226.11	225.29	224.64	224.14	223.74	223.43	223.19	223.00	222.85	222.46	222.35	222.31
12000	249.31	247.82	246.67	245.77	245.06	244.51	244.08	243.74	243.48	243.27	243.11	242.69	242.56	242.52
13000	270.08	268.48	267.23	266.25	265.49	264.89	264.42	264.06	263.77	263.54	263.36	262.91	262.77	262.73
14000	290.86	289.13	287.78	286.73	285.91	285.27	284.76	284.37	284.06	283.81	283.62	283.13	282.99	282.94
15000	311.63	309.78	308.34	307.21	306.33	305.64	305.10	304.68	304.35	304.09	303.88	303.36	303.20	303.15
16000	332.41	330.43	328.89	327.69	326.75	326.02	325.44	324.99	324.64	324.36	324.14	323.58	323.41	323.36
17000	353.18	351.08	349.45	348.17	347.17	346.39	345.78	345.30	344.93	344.63	344.40	343.80	343.62	343.57
18000	373.96	371.73	370.00	368.65	367.59	366.77	366.12	365.61	365.22	364.90	364.66	364.03	363.84	363.78
19000	394.74	392.39	390.56	389.13	388.02	387.14	386.46	385.92	385.50	385.17	384.92	304.25	384.05	383.99
20000	415.51	413.04	411.11	409.61	408.44	407.52	406.80	406.24	405.79	405.45	405.17	405.17	404.26	404.20
21000	436.29	433.69	431.67	430.09	428.86	427.90	427.14	426.55	426.08	425.72	425.43	424.70	424.48	424.41
22000	457.06	454.34	452.22	450.57	449.28	448.27	447.48	446.86	446.37	445.99	445.69	444.92	444.69	444.62
23000	477.84	474.99	472.78	471.05	469.70	468.65	467.82	467.17	466.66	466.26	465.95	465.14	464.90	464.83
24000	498.61	495.64	493.33	491.53	490.12	489.02	488.16	487.48	486.95	486.54	486.21	485.37	485.11	485.04
25000	519.39	516.30	513.89	512.01	510.55	509.40	508.50	507.79	507.24	506.81	506.47	505.59	505.33	505.25
26000	540.16	536.95	534.45	532.49	530.97	529.77	528.84	528.11	527.53	527.08	526.72	525.81	525.54	525.46
27000	560.94	557.60	555.00	552.97	551.39	550.15	549.18	548.42	547.82	547.35	546.98	546.04	545.75	545.67
28000	581.71	578.25	575.56	573.45	571.81	570.53	569.52	568.73	568.11	567.62	567.24	566.26	565.97	565.88
29000	602.49	598.90	596.11	593.93	592.23	590.90	589.86	589.04	588.40	587.90	587.50	586.48	586.18	586.09
30000	623.26	619.55	616.67	614.41	612.65	611.28	610.20	609.35	608.69	608.17	607.76	606.71	606.39	606.30
31000	644.04	640.21	637.22	634.89	633.00	631.65	630.54	629.66	628.98	628.44	628.02	626.93	626.60	626.51
32000	664.81	660.86	657.78	655.38	653.50	652.03	650.88	649.90	649.27	648.71	648.28	647.15	646.82	646.72
33000	685.59	681.51	678.33	675.86	673.92	672.40	671.22	670.29	669.56	668.98	668.53	667.38	667.03	666.93
34000	706.36	702.16	698.89	696.34	694.34	692.78	691.56	690.60	689.85	689.26	688.79	687.60	687.24	687.13
35000	727.14	722.81	719.44	716.82	714.76	713.16	711.90	710.91	710.14	709.53	709.05	707.82	707.46	707.34
36000	747.92	743.46	740.00	737.30	735.18	733.53	732.24	731.22	730.43	729.80	729.31	728.05	727.67	727.55
37000	768.69	764.12	760.55	757.78	755.61	753.91	752.58	751.53	750.71	750.07	749.57	748.27	747.88	747.76
38000	789.47	784.77	781.11	778.26	776.03	774.28	772.92	771.85	771.00	770.34	769.83	768.49	768.09	767.97
39000	810.24	805.42	801.67	798.74	796.45	794.66	793.26	792.16	791.29	790.62	790.08	788.72	788.31	788.18
40000	831.02	826.07	822.22	819.22	816.87	815.03	813.60	812.47	811.58	810.89	810.34	808.94	808.52	808.39
41000	851.79	846.72	842.78	839.70	837.29	835.41	833.94	832.78	831.87	831.16	830.60	829.16	828.73	828.60
42000	872.57	867.37	863.33	860.18	857.71	855.79	854.28	853.09	852.16	851.43	850.86	849.39	848.95	848.81
43000	893.34	888.02	883.89	880.66	878.14	876.16	874.62	873.40	872.45	871.70	871.12	869.61	869.16	869.02
44000	914.12	908.68	904.44	901.14	898.56	896.54	894.96	893.71	892.74	891.98	891.38	889.83	889.37	889.23
45000	934.89	929.33	925.00	921.62	918.98	916.91	915.30	914.03	913.03	912.25	911.64	910.06	909.58	909.44
46000	955.67	949.98	945.55	942.10	939.40	937.29	935.63	934.34	933.32	932.52	931.89	930.28	929.80	929.65
47000	976.44	970.63	966.11	962.58	959.82	957.67	955.97	954.65	953.61	952.79	952.15	950.50	950.01	949.86
48000	997.22	991.28	986.66	983.06	980.24	978.04	976.31	974.96	973.90	973.07	972.41	970.73	970.22	970.07
49000	1017.99	1011.93	1007.22	1003.54	1000.67	998.42	996.65	995.27	994.19	993.34	992.67	990.95	990.44	990.28
50000	1038.77	1032.59	1027.77	1024.02	1021.09	1018.79	1016.99	1015.58	1014.48	1013.61	1012.93	1011.17	1010.65	1010.49
55000	1142.65	1135.84	1130.55	1126.42	1123.20	1120.67	1118.69	1117.14	1115.93	1114.97	1114.22	1112.29	1111.71	1111.54
60000	1246.52	1239.10	1233.33	1228.82	1225.30	1222.55	1220.39	1218.70	1217.37	1216.33	1215.51	1213.41	1212.78	1212.59
65000	1350.40	1342.36	1336.11	1331.23	1327.41	1324.43	1322.09	1320.26	1318.82	1317.69	1316.80	1314.53	1313.84	1313.64
70000	1454.28	1445.62	1438.88	1433.63	1429.52	1426.31	1423.79	1421.82	1420.27	1419.05	1418.10	1415.64	1414.91	1414.68
75000	1558.15	1548.88	1541.66	1536.03	1531.63	1528.19	1525.49	1523.37	1521.71	1520.41	1519.39	1516.76	1515.97	1515.73
80000	1662.03	1652.14	1644.44	1638.43	1633.74	1630.06	1627.19	1624.93	1623.16	1621.77	1620.68	1617.88	1617.03	1616.78
85000	1765.90	1755.39	1747.21	1740.83	1735.85	1731.94	1728.89	1726.49	1724.61	1723.13	1721.97	1718.99	1718.10	1717.83
90000	1869.78	1858.65	1849.99	1843.23	1837.95	1833.82	1830.59	1828.05	1826.06	1824.49	1823.27	1820.11	1819.16	1818.88
95000	1973.66	1961.91	1952.77	1945.64	1940.06	1935.70	1932.28	1929.61	1927.50	1925.85	1924.56	1921.23	1920.23	1919.93
100000	2077.53	2065.17	2055.54	2048.04	2042.17	2037.58	2033.98	2031.16	2028.95	2027.21	2025.85	2022.34	2021.29	2020.97

MONTHLY PAYMENT
REQUIRED TO AMORTIZE A LOAN

TERM	1 Year	2 Years	3 Years	4 Years	5 Years	6 Years	7 Years	8 Years	9 Years	10 Years	11 Years	12 Years	13 Years	14 Years
AMOUNT														
5	.48	.27	.20	.17	.15	.14	.13	.12	.12	.12	.11	.11	.11	.11
10	.95	.54	.40	.33	.29	.27	.25	.24	.23	.23	.22	.22	.22	.21
15	1.43	.80	.60	.50	.44	.40	.38	.36	.35	.34	.33	.33	.32	.32
25	2.37	1.33	.99	.82	.73	.67	.63	.60	.58	.56	.55	.54	.53	.53
50	4.74	2.66	1.97	1.64	1.45	1.33	1.25	1.19	1.15	1.12	1.09	1.08	1.06	1.05
75	7.11	3.98	2.96	2.46	2.18	1.99	1.87	1.78	1.72	1.67	1.64	1.61	1.59	1.58
100	9.48	5.31	3.94	3.28	2.90	2.66	2.49	2.38	2.29	2.23	2.18	2.15	2.12	2.10
200	18.95	10.61	7.88	6.56	5.79	5.31	4.98	4.75	4.58	4.46	4.36	4.29	4.24	4.20
300	28.42	15.91	11.82	9.84	8.69	7.96	7.46	7.12	6.87	6.68	6.54	6.44	6.36	6.30
400	37.89	21.21	15.76	13.11	11.58	10.61	9.95	9.49	9.15	8.91	8.72	8.58	8.48	8.39
500	47.36	26.52	19.70	16.39	14.48	13.26	12.44	11.86	11.44	11.13	10.90	10.73	10.59	10.49
600	56.83	31.82	23.64	19.67	17.37	15.91	14.92	14.23	13.73	13.36	13.08	12.87	12.71	12.59
700	66.30	37.12	27.58	22.94	20.26	18.56	17.41	16.60	16.02	15.59	15.26	15.02	14.83	14.69
800	75.77	42.42	31.52	26.22	23.16	21.21	19.90	18.97	18.30	17.81	17.44	17.16	16.95	16.78
900	85.24	47.72	35.46	29.50	26.05	23.86	22.38	21.34	20.59	20.04	19.62	19.31	19.07	18.88
1000	94.71	53.03	39.40	32.77	28.95	26.51	24.87	23.72	22.88	22.26	21.80	21.45	21.18	20.98
2000	189.41	106.05	78.79	65.54	57.89	53.02	49.74	47.43	45.75	44.52	43.60	42.90	42.36	41.95
3000	284.12	159.07	118.18	98.31	86.83	79.53	74.60	71.14	68.63	66.78	65.39	64.34	63.54	62.92
4000	378.82	212.09	157.57	131.08	115.77	106.04	99.47	94.85	91.50	89.04	87.19	85.79	84.72	83.90
5000	473.53	265.11	196.96	163.84	144.72	132.55	124.33	118.56	114.38	111.29	108.98	107.23	105.90	104.87
6000	568.23	318.13	236.35	196.61	173.66	159.06	149.20	142.27	137.25	133.55	130.78	128.68	127.07	125.84
7000	662.94	371.15	275.74	229.38	202.60	185.57	174.07	165.98	160.13	155.81	152.57	150.12	148.25	146.81
8000	757.64	424.17	315.13	262.15	231.54	212.08	198.93	189.69	183.00	178.07	174.37	171.57	169.43	167.79
9000	852.35	477.19	354.52	294.92	260.49	238.59	223.80	213.40	205.88	200.32	196.17	193.02	190.61	188.76
10000	947.05	530.21	393.91	327.68	289.43	265.10	248.66	237.11	228.75	222.58	217.96	214.46	211.79	209.73
11000	1041.76	583.24	433.30	360.45	318.37	291.61	273.53	260.82	251.62	244.84	239.76	235.91	232.97	230.70
12000	1136.46	636.26	472.69	393.22	347.31	318.12	298.39	284.53	274.50	267.10	261.55	257.35	254.14	251.68
13000	1231.17	689.28	512.08	425.99	376.26	344.63	323.26	308.24	297.37	289.35	283.35	278.80	275.32	272.65
14000	1325.87	742.30	551.47	458.76	405.20	371.13	348.13	331.95	320.25	311.61	305.14	300.24	296.50	293.62
15000	1420.58	795.32	590.86	491.52	434.14	397.64	372.99	355.66	343.12	333.87	326.94	321.69	317.68	314.60
16000	1515.28	848.34	630.25	524.29	463.08	424.15	397.86	379.37	366.00	356.13	348.73	343.13	338.86	335.57
17000	1609.99	901.36	669.64	557.06	492.03	450.66	422.72	403.08	388.87	378.38	370.53	364.58	360.04	356.54
18000	1704.69	954.38	709.03	589.83	520.97	477.17	447.59	426.79	411.75	400.64	392.33	386.03	381.21	377.51
19000	1799.40	1007.40	748.43	622.60	549.91	503.68	472.46	450.50	434.62	422.90	414.12	407.47	402.39	398.49
20000	1894.10	1060.42	787.82	655.36	578.85	530.19	497.32	474.21	457.49	445.16	435.92	428.92	423.57	419.46
21000	1988.81	1113.44	827.21	688.13	607.79	556.70	522.19	497.92	480.37	467.42	457.71	450.36	444.75	440.43
22000	2083.51	1166.47	866.60	720.90	636.74	583.21	547.05	521.63	503.24	489.67	479.51	471.81	465.93	461.40
23000	2178.22	1219.49	905.99	753.67	665.68	609.72	571.92	545.34	526.12	511.93	501.30	493.25	487.10	482.38
24000	2272.92	1272.51	945.38	786.43	694.62	636.23	596.78	569.05	548.99	534.19	523.10	514.70	508.28	503.35
25000	2367.63	1325.53	984.77	819.20	723.56	662.74	621.65	592.76	571.87	556.45	544.90	536.15	529.46	524.32
26000	2462.33	1378.55	1024.16	851.97	752.51	689.25	646.52	616.47	594.74	578.70	566.69	557.59	550.64	545.29
27000	2557.04	1431.57	1063.55	884.74	781.45	715.75	671.38	640.18	617.62	600.96	588.49	579.04	571.82	566.27
28000	2651.74	1484.59	1102.94	917.51	810.39	742.26	696.25	663.89	640.49	623.22	610.28	600.48	593.00	587.24
29000	2746.45	1537.61	1142.33	950.27	839.33	768.77	721.11	687.60	663.36	645.48	632.08	621.93	614.17	608.21
30000	2841.15	1590.63	1181.72	983.04	868.28	795.28	745.98	711.31	686.24	667.73	653.87	643.37	635.35	629.19
31000	2935.86	1643.65	1221.11	1015.81	897.22	821.79	770.85	735.02	709.11	689.99	675.67	664.82	656.53	650.16
32000	3030.56	1696.68	1260.50	1048.58	926.16	848.30	795.71	758.73	731.99	712.25	697.46	686.26	677.71	671.13
33000	3125.26	1749.70	1299.89	1081.35	955.10	874.81	820.58	782.44	754.86	734.51	719.26	707.71	698.89	692.10
34000	3219.97	1802.72	1339.28	1114.11	984.05	901.32	845.44	806.15	777.74	756.76	741.06	729.16	720.07	713.08
35000	3314.67	1855.74	1378.67	1146.88	1012.99	927.83	870.31	829.86	800.61	779.02	762.85	750.60	741.24	734.05
36000	3409.38	1908.76	1418.06	1179.65	1041.93	954.34	895.17	853.57	823.48	801.28	784.65	772.05	762.42	755.02
37000	3504.08	1961.78	1457.46	1212.42	1070.87	980.85	920.04	877.28	846.36	823.54	806.44	793.49	783.60	775.99
38000	3598.79	2014.80	1496.85	1245.19	1099.81	1007.36	944.91	900.99	869.23	845.80	828.24	814.94	804.78	796.97
39000	3693.49	2067.82	1536.24	1277.95	1128.76	1033.87	969.77	924.70	892.11	868.05	850.03	836.38	825.96	817.94
40000	3788.20	2120.84	1575.63	1310.72	1157.70	1060.37	994.64	948.41	914.98	890.31	871.83	857.83	847.13	838.91
41000	3882.90	2173.86	1615.02	1343.49	1186.64	1086.88	1019.50	972.12	937.86	912.57	893.62	879.27	868.31	859.88
42000	3977.61	2226.88	1654.41	1376.26	1215.58	1113.39	1044.37	995.83	960.73	934.83	915.42	900.72	889.49	880.86
43000	4072.31	2279.91	1693.80	1409.03	1244.53	1139.90	1069.23	1019.54	983.61	957.08	937.22	922.17	910.67	901.83
44000	4167.02	2332.93	1733.19	1441.79	1273.47	1166.41	1094.10	1043.25	1006.48	979.34	959.01	943.61	931.85	922.80
45000	4261.72	2385.95	1772.58	1474.56	1302.41	1192.92	1118.97	1066.96	1029.36	1001.60	980.81	965.06	953.03	943.78
46000	4356.43	2438.97	1811.97	1507.33	1331.35	1219.43	1143.83	1090.67	1052.23	1023.86	1002.60	986.50	974.20	964.75
47000	4451.13	2491.99	1851.36	1540.10	1360.30	1245.94	1168.70	1114.38	1075.10	1046.11	1024.40	1007.95	995.38	985.72
48000	4545.84	2545.01	1890.75	1572.86	1389.24	1272.45	1193.56	1138.09	1097.98	1068.37	1046.19	1029.39	1016.56	1006.69
49000	4640.54	2598.03	1930.14	1605.63	1418.18	1298.96	1218.43	1161.80	1120.85	1090.63	1067.99	1050.84	1037.74	1027.67
50000	4735.25	2651.05	1969.53	1638.40	1447.12	1325.47	1243.30	1185.52	1143.73	1112.89	1089.79	1072.29	1058.92	1048.64
55000	5208.77	2916.16	2166.48	1802.24	1591.83	1458.01	1367.62	1304.07	1258.10	1224.18	1198.76	1179.51	1164.81	1153.50
60000	5682.30	3181.26	2363.44	1966.08	1736.55	1590.56	1491.95	1422.62	1372.47	1335.46	1307.74	1286.74	1270.70	1258.37
65000	6155.82	3446.37	2560.39	2129.92	1881.26	1723.11	1616.28	1541.17	1486.84	1446.75	1416.72	1393.97	1376.59	1363.23
70000	6629.34	3711.47	2757.34	2293.76	2025.97	1855.65	1740.61	1659.72	1601.22	1558.04	1525.70	1501.20	1482.48	1468.09
75000	7102.87	3976.58	2954.30	2457.60	2170.68	1988.20	1864.94	1778.27	1715.59	1669.33	1634.68	1608.43	1588.37	1572.96
80000	7576.39	4241.68	3151.25	2621.44	2315.39	2120.74	1989.27	1896.82	1829.96	1780.62	1743.65	1715.65	1694.26	1677.82
85000	8049.92	4506.79	3348.20	2785.28	2460.11	2253.29	2113.60	2015.37	1944.33	1891.90	1852.63	1822.88	1800.16	1782.68
90000	8523.44	4771.89	3545.15	2949.12	2604.82	2385.84	2237.93	2133.92	2058.71	2003.19	1961.61	1930.11	1906.05	1887.55
95000	8996.97	5037.00	3742.11	3112.96	2749.53	2518.38	2362.26	2252.47	2173.08	2114.48	2070.59	2037.34	2011.94	1992.41
100000	9470.49	5302.10	3939.06	3276.80	2894.24	2650.93	2486.59	2371.03	2287.45	2225.77	2179.57	2144.57	2117.83	2097.27

TERM	15 Years	16 Years	17 Years	18 Years	19 Years	20 Years	21 Years	22 Years	23 Years	24 Years	25 Years	30 Years	35 Years	40 Years
AMOUNT														
5	.11	.11	.11	.11	.11	.11	.11	.11	.11	.11	.11	.11	.11	.11
10	.21	.21	.21	.21	.21	.21	.21	.21	.21	.21	.21	.21	.21	.21
15	.32	.32	.31	.31	.31	.31	.31	.31	.31	.31	.31	.31	.31	.31
25	.53	.52	.52	.52	.52	.52	.51	.51	.51	.51	.51	.51	.51	.51
50	1.05	1.04	1.03	1.03	1.03	1.03	1.02	1.02	1.02	1.02	1.02	1.02	1.02	1.02
75	1.57	1.56	1.55	1.54	1.54	1.54	1.53	1.53	1.53	1.53	1.53	1.52	1.52	1.52
100	2.09	2.07	2.06	2.06	2.05	2.05	2.04	2.04	2.04	2.04	2.03	2.03	2.03	2.03
200	4.17	4.14	4.12	4.11	4.10	4.09	4.08	4.08	4.07	4.07	4.06	4.06	4.06	4.06
300	6.25	6.21	6.18	6.16	6.14	6.13	6.12	6.11	6.10	6.10	6.09	6.08	6.08	6.08
400	8.33	8.28	8.24	8.21	8.19	8.17	8.16	8.15	8.14	8.13	8.12	8.11	8.11	8.11
500	10.41	10.35	10.30	10.27	10.24	10.21	10.20	10.18	10.17	10.16	10.15	10.14	10.13	10.13
600	12.49	12.42	12.36	12.32	12.28	12.25	12.23	12.22	12.20	12.19	12.18	12.16	12.16	12.16
700	14.57	14.49	14.42	14.37	14.33	14.30	14.27	14.25	14.24	14.22	14.21	14.19	14.18	14.18
800	16.66	16.56	16.48	16.42	16.37	16.34	16.31	16.29	16.27	16.26	16.24	16.22	16.21	16.21
900	18.74	18.63	18.54	18.47	18.42	18.38	18.35	18.32	18.30	18.29	18.27	18.24	18.23	18.23
1000	20.82	20.70	20.60	20.53	20.47	20.42	20.39	20.36	20.34	20.32	20.30	20.27	20.26	20.26
2000	41.63	41.39	41.19	41.05	40.93	40.84	40.77	40.71	40.67	40.63	40.60	40.53	40.51	40.51
3000	62.45	62.08	61.79	61.57	61.39	61.25	61.15	61.06	61.00	60.94	60.90	60.80	60.77	60.76
4000	83.26	82.77	82.38	82.09	81.85	81.67	81.53	81.41	81.33	81.26	81.20	81.06	81.02	81.01
5000	104.07	103.46	102.98	102.61	102.31	102.09	101.91	101.77	101.66	101.57	101.50	101.33	101.28	101.26
6000	124.89	124.15	123.57	123.13	122.78	122.50	122.29	122.12	121.99	121.88	121.80	121.59	121.53	121.51
7000	145.70	144.84	144.17	143.65	143.24	142.92	142.67	142.47	142.32	142.20	142.10	141.86	141.79	141.76
8000	166.52	165.53	164.76	164.17	163.70	163.33	163.05	162.82	162.65	162.51	162.40	162.12	162.04	162.02
9000	187.33	186.22	185.36	184.69	184.16	183.75	183.43	183.18	182.98	182.82	182.70	182.39	182.30	182.27
10000	208.14	206.91	205.95	205.21	204.62	204.17	203.81	203.53	203.31	203.14	203.00	202.65	202.55	202.52
11000	228.96	227.60	226.55	225.73	225.08	224.58	224.19	223.88	223.64	223.45	223.30	222.92	222.80	222.77
12000	249.77	248.29	247.14	246.25	245.55	245.00	244.57	244.23	243.97	243.76	243.60	243.18	243.06	243.02
13000	270.59	268.98	267.74	266.77	266.01	265.41	264.95	264.59	264.30	264.08	263.90	263.45	263.31	263.27
14000	291.40	289.67	288.33	287.29	286.47	285.83	285.33	284.94	284.63	284.39	284.20	283.71	283.57	283.52
15000	312.21	310.36	308.93	307.81	306.93	306.25	305.71	305.29	304.96	304.70	304.50	303.98	303.82	303.78
16000	333.03	331.06	329.52	328.33	327.39	326.66	326.09	325.64	325.29	325.02	324.80	324.24	324.08	324.03
17000	353.84	351.75	350.12	348.85	347.85	347.08	346.47	345.99	345.62	345.33	345.10	344.51	344.33	344.28
18000	374.65	372.44	370.71	369.37	368.32	367.49	366.85	366.35	365.95	365.64	365.40	364.77	364.59	364.53
19000	395.47	393.13	391.31	389.89	388.78	387.91	387.23	386.70	386.28	385.95	385.70	385.04	384.84	384.78
20000	416.28	413.82	411.90	410.41	409.24	408.33	407.61	407.05	406.61	406.27	406.00	405.30	405.09	405.03
21000	437.10	434.51	432.50	430.93	429.70	428.74	427.99	427.40	426.94	426.58	426.30	425.57	425.35	425.28
22000	457.91	455.20	453.09	451.45	450.16	449.16	448.37	447.76	447.27	446.89	446.60	445.83	445.60	445.53
23000	478.72	475.89	473.69	471.97	470.63	469.58	468.75	468.11	467.60	467.21	466.90	466.10	465.86	465.79
24000	499.54	496.58	494.28	492.49	491.09	489.99	489.13	488.46	487.93	487.52	487.20	486.36	486.11	486.04
25000	520.35	517.27	514.88	513.01	511.55	510.41	509.51	508.81	508.26	507.83	507.50	506.63	506.37	506.29
26000	541.17	537.96	535.47	533.53	532.01	530.82	529.89	529.17	528.59	528.15	527.79	526.89	526.62	526.54
27000	561.98	558.65	556.07	554.05	552.47	551.24	550.27	549.52	548.93	548.46	548.09	547.16	546.88	546.79
28000	582.79	579.34	576.66	574.57	572.93	571.66	570.66	569.87	569.26	568.77	568.39	567.42	567.13	567.04
29000	603.61	600.03	597.26	595.09	593.40	592.07	591.04	590.22	589.59	589.09	588.69	587.69	587.38	587.29
30000	624.42	620.72	617.85	615.61	613.86	612.49	611.42	610.58	609.92	609.40	608.99	607.95	607.64	607.55
31000	645.23	641.42	638.44	636.13	634.32	632.90	631.80	630.93	630.25	629.71	629.29	628.22	627.89	627.80
32000	666.05	662.11	659.04	656.65	654.78	653.32	652.18	651.28	650.58	650.03	649.59	648.48	648.15	648.05
33000	686.86	682.80	679.63	677.17	675.24	673.74	672.56	671.63	670.91	670.34	669.89	668.75	668.40	668.30
34000	707.68	703.49	700.23	697.69	695.70	694.15	692.94	691.98	691.24	690.65	690.19	689.01	688.66	688.55
35000	728.49	724.18	720.82	718.21	716.17	714.57	713.32	712.34	711.57	710.96	710.49	709.28	708.91	708.80
36000	749.30	744.87	741.42	738.73	736.63	734.98	733.70	732.69	731.90	731.28	730.79	729.54	729.17	729.05
37000	770.12	765.56	762.01	759.25	757.09	755.40	754.08	753.04	752.23	751.59	751.09	749.81	749.42	749.30
38000	790.93	786.25	782.61	779.77	777.55	775.82	774.46	773.39	772.56	771.90	771.39	770.07	769.67	769.56
39000	811.75	806.94	803.20	800.29	798.01	796.23	794.84	793.75	792.89	792.22	791.69	790.34	789.93	789.81
40000	832.56	827.63	823.80	820.81	818.48	816.65	815.22	814.10	813.22	812.53	811.99	810.60	810.18	810.06
41000	853.37	848.32	844.39	841.33	838.94	837.07	835.60	834.45	833.55	832.84	832.29	830.86	830.44	830.31
42000	874.19	869.01	864.99	861.85	859.40	857.48	855.98	854.80	853.88	853.16	852.59	851.13	850.69	850.56
43000	895.00	889.70	885.58	882.37	879.86	877.90	876.36	875.16	874.21	873.47	872.89	871.39	870.95	870.81
44000	915.81	910.39	906.18	902.89	900.32	898.31	896.74	895.51	894.54	893.78	893.19	891.66	891.20	891.06
45000	936.63	931.08	926.77	923.41	920.78	918.73	917.12	915.86	914.87	914.10	913.49	911.92	911.46	911.32
46000	957.44	951.78	947.37	943.93	941.25	939.15	937.50	936.21	935.20	934.41	933.79	932.19	931.71	931.57
47000	978.26	972.47	967.96	964.45	961.71	959.56	957.88	956.57	955.53	954.72	954.09	952.45	951.96	951.82
48000	999.07	993.16	988.56	984.97	982.17	979.98	978.26	976.92	975.86	975.04	974.39	972.72	972.22	972.07
49000	1019.88	1013.85	1009.15	1005.49	1002.63	1000.39	998.64	997.27	996.19	995.35	994.69	992.98	992.47	992.32
50000	1040.70	1034.54	1029.75	1026.01	1023.09	1020.81	1019.02	1017.62	1016.52	1015.66	1014.99	1013.25	1012.73	1012.57
55000	1144.77	1137.99	1132.72	1128.61	1125.40	1122.89	1120.92	1119.38	1118.18	1117.23	1116.48	1114.57	1114.00	1113.83
60000	1248.84	1241.44	1235.70	1231.21	1227.71	1224.97	1222.83	1221.15	1219.83	1218.79	1217.98	1215.90	1215.27	1215.09
65000	1352.91	1344.90	1338.67	1333.81	1330.02	1327.05	1324.73	1322.91	1321.48	1320.36	1319.48	1317.22	1316.55	1316.34
70000	1456.97	1448.35	1441.64	1436.41	1432.33	1429.13	1426.63	1424.67	1423.13	1421.92	1420.98	1418.55	1417.82	1417.60
75000	1561.04	1551.80	1544.62	1539.01	1534.64	1531.21	1528.53	1526.43	1524.78	1523.49	1522.48	1519.87	1519.09	1518.86
80000	1665.11	1655.26	1647.59	1641.61	1636.95	1633.29	1630.43	1628.19	1626.44	1625.06	1623.97	1621.19	1620.36	1620.11
85000	1769.18	1758.71	1750.57	1744.22	1739.25	1735.37	1732.34	1729.95	1728.09	1726.62	1725.47	1722.52	1721.63	1721.37
90000	1873.25	1862.16	1853.54	1846.82	1841.56	1837.45	1834.24	1831.72	1829.74	1828.19	1826.97	1823.84	1822.91	1822.63
95000	1977.32	1965.62	1956.51	1949.42	1943.87	1939.54	1936.14	1933.48	1931.39	1929.75	1928.47	1925.17	1924.18	1923.88
100000	2081.39	2069.07	2059.49	2052.02	2046.18	2041.62	2038.04	2035.24	2033.04	2031.32	2029.97	2026.49	2025.45	2025.14

24.375%

TERM AMOUNT	1 Year	2 Years	3 Years	4 Years	5 Years	6 Years	7 Years	8 Years	9 Years	10 Years	11 Years	12 Years	13 Years	14 Years
5	.48	.27	.20	.17	.15	.14	.13	.12	.12	.12	.11	.11	.11	.11
10	.95	.54	.40	.33	.29	.27	.25	.24	.23	.23	.22	.22	.22	.22
15	1.43	.80	.60	.50	.44	.40	.38	.36	.35	.34	.33	.33	.32	.32
25	2.37	1.33	.99	.83	.73	.67	.63	.60	.58	.56	.55	.54	.54	.53
50	4.74	2.66	1.98	1.65	1.45	1.33	1.25	1.19	1.15	1.12	1.10	1.08	1.07	1.06
75	7.11	3.98	2.96	2.47	2.18	2.00	1.87	1.79	1.72	1.68	1.64	1.62	1.60	1.58
100	9.48	5.31	3.95	3.29	2.90	2.66	2.50	2.38	2.30	2.24	2.19	2.16	2.13	2.11
200	18.95	10.62	7.89	6.57	5.80	5.32	4.99	4.76	4.59	4.47	4.37	4.31	4.25	4.21
300	28.43	15.92	11.83	9.85	8.70	7.97	7.48	7.13	6.88	6.70	6.56	6.46	6.38	6.31
400	37.90	21.23	15.78	13.13	11.60	10.63	9.97	9.51	9.18	8.93	8.74	8.61	8.50	8.42
500	47.38	26.53	19.72	16.41	14.50	13.28	12.46	11.88	11.47	11.16	10.93	10.76	10.62	10.52
600	56.85	31.84	23.66	19.69	17.40	15.94	14.95	14.26	13.76	13.39	13.11	12.91	12.75	12.62
700	66.32	37.15	27.61	22.97	20.30	18.59	17.44	16.64	16.05	15.62	15.30	15.06	14.87	14.73
800	75.80	42.45	31.55	26.25	23.19	21.25	19.94	19.01	18.35	17.85	17.48	17.21	16.99	16.83
900	85.27	47.76	35.49	29.53	26.09	23.90	22.43	21.39	20.64	20.08	19.67	19.36	19.12	18.93
1000	94.75	53.06	39.44	32.81	28.99	26.56	24.92	23.76	22.93	22.32	21.85	21.51	21.24	21.03
2000	189.49	106.12	78.87	65.62	57.98	53.11	49.83	47.52	45.86	44.63	43.70	43.01	42.47	42.06
3000	284.23	159.18	118.30	98.43	86.96	79.67	74.75	71.28	68.78	66.94	65.55	64.51	63.71	63.09
4000	378.97	212.24	157.73	131.24	115.95	106.22	99.66	95.04	91.71	89.25	87.40	86.01	84.94	84.12
5000	473.71	265.30	197.16	164.05	144.94	132.78	124.57	118.80	114.63	111.56	109.25	107.51	106.18	105.15
6000	568.45	318.36	236.59	196.86	173.92	159.33	149.49	142.56	137.56	133.87	131.10	129.01	127.41	126.18
7000	663.19	371.41	276.02	229.67	202.91	185.89	174.40	166.32	160.48	156.18	152.95	150.51	148.65	147.21
8000	757.93	424.47	315.45	262.48	231.89	212.44	199.31	190.08	183.41	178.49	174.80	172.01	169.88	168.24
9000	852.68	477.53	354.88	295.29	260.88	239.00	224.23	213.84	206.33	200.80	196.65	193.51	191.11	189.27
10000	947.42	530.59	394.31	328.10	289.87	265.55	249.14	237.60	229.26	223.11	218.50	215.01	212.35	210.30
11000	1042.16	583.65	433.74	360.91	318.85	292.11	274.05	261.36	252.18	245.42	240.35	236.51	233.58	231.33
12000	1136.90	636.71	473.17	393.72	347.84	318.66	298.97	285.12	275.11	267.73	262.20	258.01	254.82	252.36
13000	1231.64	689.76	512.60	426.53	376.82	345.22	323.88	308.88	298.04	290.04	284.05	279.51	276.05	273.39
14000	1326.38	742.82	552.03	459.34	405.81	371.77	348.79	332.64	320.96	312.35	305.90	301.01	297.29	294.42
15000	1421.12	795.88	591.46	492.15	434.80	398.33	373.71	356.40	343.89	334.66	327.75	322.51	318.52	315.45
16000	1515.86	848.94	630.89	524.96	463.78	424.88	398.62	380.16	366.81	356.97	349.60	344.02	339.75	336.48
17000	1610.60	902.00	670.32	557.77	492.77	451.44	423.53	403.92	389.74	379.28	371.45	365.52	360.99	357.51
18000	1705.35	955.06	709.75	590.58	521.75	477.99	448.45	427.68	412.66	401.59	393.29	387.02	382.22	378.54
19000	1800.09	1008.12	749.18	623.39	550.74	504.55	473.36	451.44	435.59	423.90	415.14	408.52	403.46	399.57
20000	1894.83	1061.17	788.61	656.19	579.73	531.10	498.27	475.20	458.51	446.21	436.99	430.02	424.69	420.60
21000	1989.57	1114.23	828.04	689.00	608.71	557.66	523.19	498.96	481.44	468.52	458.84	451.52	445.93	441.63
22000	2084.31	1167.29	867.47	721.81	637.70	584.21	548.10	522.72	504.36	490.83	480.69	473.02	467.16	462.66
23000	2179.05	1220.35	906.90	754.62	666.68	610.77	573.01	546.48	527.29	513.14	502.54	494.52	488.39	483.69
24000	2273.79	1273.41	946.33	787.43	695.67	637.32	597.93	570.23	550.22	535.45	524.39	516.02	509.63	504.72
25000	2368.53	1326.47	985.76	820.24	724.66	663.88	622.84	593.99	573.14	557.76	546.24	537.52	530.86	525.75
26000	2463.28	1379.52	1025.19	853.05	753.64	690.43	647.75	617.75	596.07	580.07	568.09	559.02	552.10	546.78
27000	2558.02	1432.58	1064.62	885.86	782.63	716.99	672.67	641.51	618.99	602.38	589.94	580.52	573.33	567.81
28000	2652.76	1485.64	1104.05	918.67	811.61	743.54	697.58	665.27	641.92	624.69	611.79	602.02	594.57	588.84
29000	2747.50	1538.70	1143.48	951.48	840.60	770.10	722.49	689.03	664.84	647.00	633.64	623.52	615.80	609.87
30000	2842.24	1591.76	1182.91	984.29	869.59	796.65	747.41	712.79	687.77	669.31	655.49	645.02	637.04	630.90
31000	2936.98	1644.82	1222.34	1017.10	898.57	823.21	772.32	736.55	710.69	691.62	677.34	666.53	658.27	651.93
32000	3031.72	1697.88	1261.77	1049.91	927.56	849.76	797.23	760.31	733.62	713.93	699.19	688.03	679.50	672.96
33000	3126.46	1750.93	1301.20	1082.72	956.54	876.32	822.15	784.07	756.54	736.24	721.04	709.53	700.74	693.99
34000	3221.20	1803.99	1340.63	1115.53	985.53	902.87	847.06	807.83	779.47	758.55	742.89	731.03	721.97	715.02
35000	3315.95	1857.05	1380.06	1148.34	1014.52	929.43	871.97	831.59	802.40	780.86	764.74	752.53	743.21	736.05
36000	3410.69	1910.11	1419.49	1181.15	1043.50	955.98	896.89	855.35	825.32	803.17	786.58	774.03	764.44	757.08
37000	3505.43	1963.17	1458.92	1213.96	1072.49	982.54	921.80	879.11	848.25	825.48	808.43	795.53	785.68	778.10
38000	3600.17	2016.23	1498.35	1246.77	1101.47	1009.09	946.71	902.87	871.17	847.79	830.28	817.03	806.91	799.13
39000	3694.91	2069.28	1537.78	1279.58	1130.46	1035.65	971.63	926.63	894.10	870.10	852.13	838.53	828.14	820.16
40000	3789.65	2122.34	1577.21	1312.38	1159.45	1062.20	996.54	950.39	917.02	892.41	873.98	860.03	849.38	841.19
41000	3884.39	2175.40	1616.64	1345.19	1188.43	1088.76	1021.45	974.15	939.95	914.72	895.83	881.53	870.61	862.22
42000	3979.13	2228.46	1656.07	1378.00	1217.42	1115.31	1046.37	997.91	962.87	937.03	917.68	903.03	891.85	883.25
43000	4073.88	2281.52	1695.50	1410.81	1246.40	1141.87	1071.28	1021.67	985.80	959.34	939.53	924.53	913.08	904.28
44000	4168.62	2334.58	1734.93	1443.62	1275.39	1168.42	1096.20	1045.43	1008.72	981.65	961.38	946.03	934.32	925.31
45000	4263.36	2387.64	1774.36	1476.43	1304.38	1194.98	1121.11	1069.19	1031.65	1003.96	983.23	967.53	955.55	946.34
46000	4358.10	2440.69	1813.79	1509.24	1333.36	1221.53	1146.02	1092.95	1054.58	1026.27	1005.08	989.03	976.78	967.37
47000	4452.84	2493.75	1853.22	1542.05	1362.35	1248.09	1170.94	1116.71	1077.50	1048.58	1026.93	1010.54	998.02	988.40
48000	4547.58	2546.81	1892.65	1574.86	1391.34	1274.64	1195.85	1140.46	1100.43	1070.89	1048.78	1032.04	1019.25	1009.43
49000	4642.32	2599.87	1932.08	1607.67	1420.32	1301.20	1220.76	1164.22	1123.35	1093.20	1070.63	1053.54	1040.49	1030.46
50000	4737.06	2652.93	1971.51	1640.48	1449.31	1327.75	1245.68	1187.98	1146.28	1115.51	1092.48	1075.04	1061.72	1051.49
55000	5210.77	2918.22	2168.66	1804.53	1594.24	1460.53	1370.24	1306.78	1260.90	1227.06	1201.72	1182.54	1167.89	1156.64
60000	5684.48	3183.51	2365.81	1968.57	1739.17	1593.30	1494.81	1425.58	1375.53	1338.61	1310.97	1290.04	1274.07	1261.79
65000	6158.18	3448.80	2562.96	2132.62	1884.10	1726.08	1619.38	1544.38	1490.16	1450.16	1420.22	1397.55	1380.24	1366.94
70000	6631.89	3714.10	2760.11	2296.67	2029.03	1858.85	1743.94	1663.18	1604.79	1561.71	1529.47	1505.05	1486.41	1472.09
75000	7105.59	3979.39	2957.26	2460.72	2173.96	1991.63	1868.51	1781.97	1719.41	1673.27	1638.71	1612.55	1592.58	1577.23
80000	7579.30	4244.68	3154.41	2624.76	2318.89	2124.40	1993.08	1900.77	1834.04	1784.82	1747.96	1720.06	1698.75	1682.38
85000	8053.00	4509.97	3351.56	2788.81	2463.82	2257.17	2117.64	2019.57	1948.67	1896.37	1857.21	1827.56	1804.92	1787.53
90000	8526.71	4775.27	3548.71	2952.86	2608.75	2389.95	2242.21	2138.37	2063.30	2007.92	1966.45	1935.06	1911.10	1892.68
95000	9000.42	5040.56	3745.86	3116.91	2753.68	2522.72	2366.78	2257.16	2177.92	2119.47	2075.70	2042.57	2017.27	1997.83
100000	9474.12	5305.85	3943.01	3280.95	2898.61	2655.50	2491.35	2375.96	2292.55	2231.02	2184.95	2150.07	2123.44	2102.98

TERM	15 Years	16 Years	17 Years	18 Years	19 Years	20 Years	21 Years	22 Years	23 Years	24 Years	25 Years	30 Years	35 Years	40 Years
AMOUNT														
5	.11	.11	.11	.11	.11	.11	.11	.11	.11	.11	.11	.11	.11	.11
10	.21	.21	.21	.21	.21	.21	.21	.21	.21	.21	.21	.21	.21	.21
15	.32	.32	.31	.31	.31	.31	.31	.31	.31	.31	.31	.31	.31	.31
25	.53	.52	.52	.52	.52	.52	.52	.52	.51	.51	.51	.51	.51	.51
50	1.05	1.04	1.04	1.03	1.03	1.03	1.03	1.03	1.02	1.02	1.02	1.02	1.02	1.02
75	1.57	1.56	1.55	1.55	1.54	1.54	1.54	1.54	1.53	1.53	1.53	1.53	1.53	1.53
100	2.09	2.08	2.07	2.06	2.06	2.05	2.05	2.05	2.04	2.04	2.04	2.04	2.04	2.04
200	4.18	4.15	4.14	4.12	4.11	4.10	4.09	4.09	4.08	4.08	4.08	4.07	4.07	4.07
300	6.27	6.23	6.20	6.18	6.16	6.15	6.14	6.13	6.12	6.12	6.11	6.10	6.10	6.10
400	8.35	8.30	8.27	8.24	8.21	8.20	8.18	8.17	8.16	8.15	8.15	8.14	8.13	8.13
500	10.44	10.38	10.33	10.29	10.27	10.24	10.23	10.21	10.20	10.19	10.19	10.17	10.16	10.16
600	12.53	12.45	12.40	12.35	12.32	12.29	12.27	12.25	12.24	12.23	12.22	12.20	12.20	12.19
700	14.62	14.53	14.46	14.41	14.37	14.34	14.31	14.29	14.28	14.27	14.26	14.23	14.23	14.22
800	16.70	16.60	16.53	16.47	16.42	16.39	16.36	16.34	16.32	16.30	16.29	16.27	16.26	16.26
900	18.79	18.68	18.59	18.53	18.47	18.43	18.40	18.38	18.36	18.34	18.33	18.30	18.29	18.29
1000	20.88	20.75	20.66	20.58	20.53	20.48	20.45	20.42	20.40	20.38	20.37	20.33	20.32	20.32
2000	41.75	41.50	41.31	41.16	41.05	40.96	40.89	40.83	40.79	40.75	40.73	40.66	40.64	40.63
3000	62.62	62.25	61.97	61.74	61.57	61.44	61.33	61.25	61.18	61.13	61.09	60.99	60.96	60.95
4000	83.49	83.00	82.62	82.32	82.09	81.91	81.77	81.66	81.57	81.50	81.45	81.31	81.27	81.26
5000	104.36	103.75	103.28	102.90	102.61	102.39	102.21	102.07	101.96	101.88	101.81	101.64	101.59	101.57
6000	125.24	124.50	123.93	123.48	123.14	122.87	122.65	122.49	122.36	122.25	122.17	121.97	121.91	121.89
7000	146.11	145.25	144.58	144.06	143.66	143.34	143.09	142.90	142.75	142.63	142.53	142.29	142.22	142.20
8000	166.98	166.00	165.24	164.64	164.18	163.82	163.53	163.31	163.14	163.00	162.90	162.62	162.54	162.52
9000	187.85	186.75	185.89	185.22	184.70	184.30	183.98	183.73	183.53	183.38	183.26	182.95	182.86	182.83
10000	208.72	207.50	206.55	205.80	205.22	204.77	204.42	204.14	203.92	203.75	203.62	203.28	203.17	203.14
11000	229.59	228.25	227.20	226.38	225.75	225.25	224.86	224.55	224.31	224.13	223.98	223.60	223.49	223.46
12000	250.47	249.00	247.85	246.96	246.27	245.73	245.30	244.97	244.71	244.50	244.34	243.93	243.81	243.77
13000	271.34	269.75	268.51	267.54	266.79	266.20	205.74	265.38	265.10	264.88	264.70	264.26	264.12	264.08
14000	292.21	290.49	289.16	288.12	287.31	286.68	286.18	285.79	285.49	285.25	285.06	284.58	284.44	284.40
15000	313.08	311.24	309.82	308.70	307.83	307.16	306.62	306.21	305.88	305.63	305.43	304.91	304.76	304.71
16000	333.95	331.99	330.47	329.28	328.36	327.63	327.06	326.62	326.27	326.00	325.79	325.24	325.07	325.03
17000	354.82	352.74	351.12	349.86	348.88	348.11	347.50	347.03	346.67	346.38	346.15	345.57	345.39	345.34
18000	375.70	373.49	371.78	370.44	369.40	368.59	367.95	367.45	367.06	366.75	366.51	365.89	365.71	365.65
19000	396.57	394.24	392.43	391.02	389.92	389.06	388.39	387.86	387.45	387.12	386.87	386.22	386.03	385.97
20000	417.44	414.99	413.09	411.60	410.44	409.54	408.83	408.28	407.84	407.50	407.23	406.55	406.34	406.28
21000	438.31	435.74	433.74	432.18	430.97	430.02	429.27	428.69	428.23	427.87	427.59	426.87	426.66	426.59
22000	459.18	456.49	454.39	452.76	451.49	450.49	449.71	449.10	448.62	448.25	447.95	447.20	446.98	446.91
23000	480.05	477.24	475.05	473.34	472.01	470.97	470.15	469.52	469.02	468.62	468.32	467.53	467.29	467.22
24000	500.93	497.99	495.70	493.92	492.53	491.45	490.59	489.93	489.41	489.00	488.68	487.86	487.61	487.54
25000	521.80	518.74	516.36	514.50	513.05	511.92	511.04	510.34	509.80	509.37	509.04	508.10	507.93	507.85
26000	542.67	539.49	537.01	535.08	533.58	532.40	531.48	530.76	530.19	529.75	529.40	528.51	528.24	528.16
27000	563.54	560.23	557.66	555.66	554.10	552.88	551.92	551.17	550.58	550.12	549.76	548.84	548.56	548.48
28000	584.41	580.98	578.32	576.24	574.62	573.35	572.36	571.58	570.97	570.50	570.12	569.16	568.88	568.79
29000	605.28	601.73	598.97	596.82	595.14	593.83	592.80	592.00	591.37	590.87	590.48	589.49	589.19	589.11
30000	626.16	622.48	619.63	617.40	615.66	614.31	613.24	612.41	611.76	611.25	610.85	609.82	609.51	609.42
31000	647.03	643.23	640.28	637.98	636.18	634.78	633.68	632.82	632.15	631.62	631.21	630.14	629.83	629.73
32000	667.90	663.98	660.93	658.56	656.71	655.26	654.12	653.24	652.54	652.00	651.57	650.47	650.14	650.05
33000	688.77	684.73	681.59	679.14	677.23	675.74	674.57	673.65	672.93	672.37	671.93	670.80	670.46	670.36
34000	709.64	705.48	702.24	699.72	697.75	696.21	695.01	694.06	693.33	692.75	692.29	691.13	690.78	690.67
35000	730.52	726.23	722.90	720.30	718.27	716.69	715.45	714.48	713.72	713.12	712.65	711.45	711.10	710.99
36000	751.39	746.98	743.55	740.88	738.79	737.17	735.89	734.89	734.11	733.49	733.01	731.78	731.41	731.30
37000	772.26	767.73	764.20	761.46	759.32	757.64	756.33	755.30	754.50	753.87	753.37	752.11	751.73	751.62
38000	793.13	788.48	784.86	782.04	779.84	778.12	776.77	775.72	774.89	774.24	773.74	772.43	772.05	771.93
39000	814.00	809.23	805.51	802.62	800.36	798.60	797.21	796.13	795.28	794.62	794.10	792.76	792.36	792.24
40000	834.87	829.97	826.17	823.20	820.88	819.07	817.65	816.55	815.68	814.99	814.46	813.09	812.68	812.56
41000	855.75	850.72	846.82	843.78	841.40	839.55	838.10	836.96	836.07	835.37	834.82	833.42	833.00	832.87
42000	876.62	871.47	867.47	864.36	861.93	860.03	858.54	857.37	856.46	855.74	855.18	853.74	853.31	853.18
43000	897.49	892.22	888.13	884.94	882.45	880.50	878.98	877.79	876.85	876.12	875.54	874.07	873.63	873.50
44000	918.36	912.97	908.78	905.52	902.97	900.98	899.42	898.20	897.24	896.49	895.90	894.40	893.95	893.81
45000	939.23	933.72	929.44	926.10	923.49	921.46	919.86	918.61	917.63	916.87	916.27	914.72	914.26	914.13
46000	960.10	954.47	950.09	946.68	944.01	941.93	940.30	939.03	938.03	937.24	936.63	935.05	934.58	934.44
47000	980.98	975.22	970.74	967.26	964.54	962.41	960.74	959.44	958.42	957.62	956.99	955.38	954.90	954.75
48000	1001.85	995.97	991.40	987.84	985.06	982.89	981.18	979.85	978.81	977.99	977.35	975.71	975.21	975.07
49000	1022.72	1016.72	1012.05	1008.42	1005.58	1003.36	1001.63	1000.27	999.20	998.37	997.71	996.03	995.53	995.38
50000	1043.59	1037.47	1032.71	1029.00	1026.10	1023.84	1022.07	1020.68	1019.59	1018.74	1018.07	1016.36	1015.85	1015.70
55000	1147.95	1141.21	1135.98	1131.90	1128.71	1126.22	1124.27	1122.75	1121.55	1120.61	1119.88	1118.00	1117.43	1117.26
60000	1252.31	1244.96	1239.25	1234.80	1231.32	1228.61	1226.48	1224.82	1223.51	1222.49	1221.69	1219.63	1219.02	1218.83
65000	1356.67	1348.71	1342.52	1337.69	1333.93	1330.99	1328.69	1326.88	1325.47	1324.36	1323.49	1321.27	1320.60	1320.40
70000	1461.03	1452.45	1445.79	1440.59	1436.54	1433.37	1430.89	1428.95	1427.43	1426.24	1425.30	1422.90	1422.19	1421.97
75000	1565.38	1556.20	1549.06	1543.49	1539.15	1535.76	1533.10	1531.02	1529.39	1528.11	1527.11	1524.54	1523.77	1523.54
80000	1669.74	1659.94	1652.33	1646.39	1641.76	1638.14	1635.30	1633.09	1631.35	1629.98	1628.91	1626.17	1625.35	1625.11
85000	1774.10	1763.69	1755.60	1749.29	1744.37	1740.52	1737.51	1735.15	1733.31	1731.86	1730.72	1727.81	1726.94	1726.68
90000	1878.46	1867.44	1858.87	1852.19	1846.98	1842.91	1839.72	1837.22	1835.26	1833.73	1832.53	1829.44	1828.52	1828.25
95000	1982.82	1971.18	1962.14	1955.09	1949.59	1945.29	1941.92	1939.29	1937.22	1935.60	1934.33	1931.08	1930.11	1929.82
100000	2087.18	2074.93	2065.41	2057.99	2052.20	2047.67	2044.13	2041.36	2039.18	2037.48	2036.14	2032.71	2031.69	2031.39

MONTHLY PAYMENT
REQUIRED TO AMORTIZE A LOAN

TERM AMOUNT	1 Year	2 Years	3 Years	4 Years	5 Years	6 Years	7 Years	8 Years	9 Years	10 Years	11 Years	12 Years	13 Years	14 Years
5	.48	.27	.20	.17	.15	.14	.13	.12	.12	.12	.11	.11	.11	.11
10	.95	.54	.40	.33	.30	.27	.25	.24	.23	.23	.22	.22	.22	.22
15	1.43	.80	.60	.50	.44	.40	.38	.36	.35	.34	.33	.33	.32	.32
25	2.37	1.33	.99	.83	.73	.67	.63	.60	.58	.56	.55	.54	.54	.53
50	4.74	2.66	1.98	1.65	1.46	1.33	1.25	1.19	1.15	1.12	1.10	1.08	1.07	1.06
75	7.11	3.99	2.96	2.47	2.18	2.00	1.87	1.79	1.73	1.68	1.65	1.62	1.60	1.58
100	9.48	5.31	3.95	3.29	2.91	2.66	2.50	2.38	2.30	2.24	2.19	2.16	2.13	2.11
200	18.96	10.62	7.89	6.57	5.81	5.32	4.99	4.76	4.59	4.47	4.38	4.31	4.26	4.21
300	28.43	15.93	11.84	9.85	8.71	7.98	7.48	7.14	6.89	6.70	6.57	6.46	6.38	6.32
400	37.91	21.23	15.78	13.13	11.61	10.63	9.98	9.52	9.18	8.94	8.75	8.61	8.51	8.42
500	47.38	26.54	19.73	16.42	14.51	13.29	12.47	11.89	11.48	11.17	10.94	10.76	10.63	10.53
600	56.86	31.85	23.67	19.70	17.41	15.95	14.96	14.27	13.77	13.40	13.13	12.92	12.76	12.63
700	66.33	37.15	27.62	22.98	20.31	18.60	17.46	16.65	16.06	15.63	15.31	15.07	14.88	14.74
800	75.81	42.46	31.56	26.26	23.21	21.26	19.95	19.03	18.36	17.87	17.50	17.22	17.01	16.84
900	85.28	47.77	35.50	29.55	26.11	23.92	22.44	21.40	20.65	20.10	19.69	19.37	19.13	18.95
1000	94.76	53.08	39.45	32.83	29.01	26.58	24.93	23.78	22.95	22.33	21.87	21.52	21.26	21.05
2000	189.51	106.15	78.89	65.65	58.01	53.15	49.86	47.56	45.89	44.66	43.74	43.04	42.51	42.10
3000	284.26	159.22	118.33	98.48	87.01	79.72	74.79	71.33	68.83	66.99	65.61	64.56	63.76	63.15
4000	379.02	212.29	157.78	131.30	116.01	106.29	99.72	95.11	91.77	89.32	87.47	86.08	85.02	84.20
5000	473.77	265.36	197.22	164.12	145.01	132.86	124.65	118.89	114.72	111.64	109.34	107.60	106.27	105.25
6000	568.52	318.43	236.66	196.95	174.01	159.43	149.58	142.66	137.66	133.97	131.21	129.12	127.52	126.30
7000	663.28	371.50	276.11	229.77	203.01	186.00	174.51	166.44	160.60	156.30	153.08	150.64	148.78	147.35
8000	758.03	424.57	315.55	262.59	232.01	212.57	199.44	190.21	183.54	178.63	174.94	172.16	170.03	168.39
9000	852.78	477.64	354.99	295.42	261.01	239.14	224.37	213.99	206.49	200.95	196.81	193.68	191.28	189.44
10000	947.54	530.71	394.44	328.24	290.01	265.71	249.30	237.77	229.43	223.28	218.68	215.20	212.54	210.49
11000	1042.29	583.79	433.88	361.06	319.01	292.28	274.23	261.54	252.37	245.61	240.55	236.71	233.79	231.54
12000	1137.04	636.86	473.32	393.89	348.01	318.85	299.16	285.32	275.31	267.94	262.41	258.23	255.04	252.59
13000	1231.80	689.93	512.77	426.71	377.01	345.42	324.09	309.09	298.26	290.26	284.28	279.75	276.29	273.64
14000	1326.55	743.00	552.21	459.53	406.01	371.99	349.02	332.87	321.20	312.59	306.15	301.27	297.55	294.69
15000	1421.30	796.07	591.65	492.36	435.01	398.56	373.94	356.65	344.14	334.92	328.02	322.79	318.80	315.74
16000	1516.06	849.14	631.10	525.18	464.01	425.13	398.87	380.42	367.08	357.25	349.88	344.31	340.05	336.78
17000	1610.81	902.21	670.54	558.00	493.02	451.70	423.80	404.20	390.03	379.58	371.75	365.83	361.31	357.83
18000	1705.56	955.28	709.98	590.83	522.02	478.27	448.73	427.97	412.97	401.90	393.62	387.35	382.56	378.88
19000	1800.32	1008.35	749.43	623.65	551.02	504.84	473.66	451.75	435.91	424.23	415.49	408.87	403.81	399.93
20000	1895.07	1061.42	788.87	656.47	580.02	531.41	498.59	475.53	458.85	446.56	437.35	430.39	425.07	420.98
21000	1989.82	1114.50	828.31	689.30	609.02	557.98	523.52	499.30	481.80	468.89	459.22	451.90	446.32	442.03
22000	2084.58	1167.57	867.76	722.12	638.02	584.55	548.45	523.08	504.74	491.21	481.09	473.42	467.57	463.08
23000	2179.33	1220.64	907.20	754.94	667.02	611.12	573.38	546.85	527.68	513.54	502.96	494.94	488.83	484.13
24000	2274.08	1273.71	946.64	787.77	696.02	637.69	598.31	570.63	550.62	535.87	524.82	516.46	510.08	505.17
25000	2368.84	1326.78	986.08	820.59	725.02	664.26	623.24	594.41	573.57	558.20	546.69	537.98	531.33	526.22
26000	2463.59	1379.85	1025.53	853.41	754.02	690.83	648.17	618.18	596.51	580.52	568.56	559.50	552.58	547.27
27000	2558.34	1432.92	1064.97	886.24	783.02	717.40	673.10	641.96	619.45	602.85	590.42	581.02	573.84	568.32
28000	2653.10	1485.99	1104.41	919.06	812.02	743.97	698.03	665.73	642.39	625.18	612.29	602.54	595.09	589.37
29000	2747.85	1539.06	1143.86	951.88	841.02	770.54	722.95	689.51	665.34	647.51	634.16	624.06	616.34	610.42
30000	2842.60	1592.13	1183.30	984.71	870.02	797.11	747.88	713.29	688.28	669.83	656.03	645.58	637.60	631.47
31000	2937.36	1645.20	1222.74	1017.53	899.02	823.68	772.81	737.06	711.22	692.16	677.89	667.09	658.85	652.52
32000	3032.11	1698.28	1262.19	1050.35	928.02	850.25	797.74	760.84	734.16	714.49	699.76	688.61	680.10	673.56
33000	3126.86	1751.35	1301.63	1083.18	957.03	876.82	822.67	784.61	757.11	736.82	721.63	710.13	701.36	694.61
34000	3221.62	1804.42	1341.07	1116.00	986.03	903.39	847.60	808.39	780.05	759.15	743.50	731.65	722.61	715.66
35000	3316.37	1857.49	1380.52	1148.82	1015.03	929.96	872.53	832.17	802.99	781.47	765.36	753.17	743.86	736.71
36000	3411.12	1910.56	1419.96	1181.65	1044.03	956.53	897.46	855.94	825.93	803.80	787.23	774.69	765.12	757.76
37000	3505.88	1963.63	1459.40	1214.47	1073.03	983.10	922.39	879.72	848.88	826.13	809.10	796.21	786.37	778.81
38000	3600.63	2016.70	1498.85	1247.29	1102.03	1009.67	947.32	903.49	871.82	848.46	830.97	817.73	807.62	799.86
39000	3695.38	2069.77	1538.29	1280.12	1131.03	1036.24	972.25	927.27	894.76	870.78	852.83	839.25	828.87	820.91
40000	3790.14	2122.84	1577.73	1312.94	1160.03	1062.81	997.18	951.05	917.70	893.11	874.70	860.77	850.13	841.95
41000	3884.89	2175.91	1617.18	1345.76	1189.03	1089.38	1022.11	974.82	940.65	915.44	896.57	882.28	871.38	863.00
42000	3979.64	2228.98	1656.62	1378.59	1218.03	1115.95	1047.04	998.60	963.59	937.77	918.44	903.80	892.63	884.05
43000	4074.40	2282.06	1696.06	1411.41	1247.03	1142.52	1071.96	1022.37	986.53	960.09	940.30	925.32	913.89	905.10
44000	4169.15	2335.13	1735.51	1444.23	1276.03	1169.09	1096.89	1046.15	1009.47	982.42	962.17	946.84	935.14	926.15
45000	4263.90	2388.20	1774.95	1477.06	1305.03	1195.66	1121.82	1069.93	1032.42	1004.75	984.04	968.36	956.39	947.20
46000	4358.66	2441.27	1814.39	1509.88	1334.03	1222.23	1146.75	1093.70	1055.36	1027.08	1005.91	989.88	977.65	968.25
47000	4453.41	2494.34	1853.83	1542.70	1363.03	1248.80	1171.68	1117.48	1078.30	1049.40	1027.77	1011.40	998.90	989.30
48000	4548.16	2547.41	1893.28	1575.53	1392.03	1275.37	1196.61	1141.26	1101.24	1071.73	1049.64	1032.92	1020.15	1010.34
49000	4642.92	2600.48	1932.72	1608.35	1421.03	1301.94	1221.54	1165.03	1124.19	1094.06	1071.51	1054.44	1041.40	1031.39
50000	4737.67	2653.55	1972.16	1641.17	1450.04	1328.51	1246.47	1188.81	1147.13	1116.39	1093.37	1075.96	1062.66	1052.44
55000	5211.44	2918.91	2169.38	1805.29	1595.04	1461.36	1371.12	1307.69	1261.84	1228.03	1202.71	1183.55	1168.92	1157.69
60000	5685.20	3184.26	2366.60	1969.41	1740.04	1594.22	1495.76	1426.57	1376.55	1339.66	1312.05	1291.15	1275.19	1262.93
65000	6158.97	3449.62	2563.81	2133.52	1885.04	1727.07	1620.41	1545.45	1491.27	1451.30	1421.39	1398.74	1381.45	1368.17
70000	6632.73	3714.97	2761.03	2297.64	2030.05	1859.92	1745.06	1664.33	1605.98	1562.94	1530.72	1506.34	1487.72	1473.42
75000	7106.50	3980.33	2958.24	2461.76	2175.05	1992.77	1869.70	1783.21	1720.69	1674.58	1640.06	1613.93	1593.98	1578.66
80000	7580.27	4245.68	3155.46	2625.87	2320.05	2125.62	1994.35	1902.09	1835.40	1786.22	1749.40	1721.53	1700.25	1683.90
85000	8054.03	4511.04	3352.68	2789.99	2465.06	2258.47	2118.99	2020.97	1950.11	1897.86	1858.73	1829.12	1806.51	1789.15
90000	8527.80	4776.39	3549.89	2954.11	2610.06	2391.32	2243.64	2139.85	2064.83	2009.49	1968.07	1936.72	1912.78	1894.39
95000	9001.57	5041.75	3747.11	3118.22	2755.06	2524.17	2368.29	2258.73	2179.54	2121.13	2077.41	2044.31	2019.05	1999.64
100000	9475.33	5307.10	3944.32	3282.34	2900.07	2657.02	2492.93	2377.61	2294.25	2232.77	2186.74	2151.91	2125.31	2104.88

MONTHLY PAYMENT
REQUIRED TO AMORTIZE A LOAN

24.400%

TERM	15 Years	16 Years	17 Years	18 Years	19 Years	20 Years	21 Years	22 Years	23 Years	24 Years	25 Years	30 Years	35 Years	40 Years
AMOUNT														
5	.11	.11	.11	.11	.11	.11	.11	.11	.11	.11	.11	.11	.11	.11
10	.21	.21	.21	.21	.21	.21	.21	.21	.21	.21	.21	.21	.21	.21
15	.32	.32	.32	.31	.31	.31	.31	.31	.31	.31	.31	.31	.31	.31
25	.53	.52	.52	.52	.52	.52	.52	.52	.52	.51	.51	.51	.51	.51
50	1.05	1.04	1.04	1.03	1.03	1.03	1.03	1.03	1.03	1.02	1.02	1.02	1.02	1.02
75	1.57	1.56	1.56	1.55	1.55	1.54	1.54	1.54	1.54	1.53	1.53	1.53	1.53	1.53
100	2.09	2.08	2.07	2.06	2.06	2.05	2.05	2.05	2.05	2.04	2.04	2.04	2.04	2.04
200	4.18	4.16	4.14	4.12	4.11	4.10	4.10	4.09	4.09	4.08	4.08	4.07	4.07	4.07
300	6.27	6.24	6.21	6.18	6.17	6.15	6.14	6.14	6.13	6.12	6.12	6.11	6.11	6.11
400	8.36	8.31	8.27	8.24	8.22	8.20	8.19	8.18	8.17	8.16	8.16	8.14	8.14	8.14
500	10.45	10.39	10.34	10.30	10.28	10.25	10.24	10.22	10.21	10.20	10.20	10.18	10.17	10.17
600	12.54	12.47	12.41	12.36	12.33	12.30	12.28	12.27	12.25	12.24	12.23	12.21	12.21	12.21
700	14.63	14.54	14.48	14.42	14.38	14.35	14.33	14.31	14.29	14.28	14.27	14.25	14.24	14.24
800	16.72	16.62	16.54	16.48	16.44	16.40	16.37	16.35	16.33	16.32	16.31	16.28	16.28	16.27
900	18.81	18.70	18.61	18.54	18.49	18.45	18.42	18.40	18.38	18.36	18.35	18.32	18.31	18.31
1000	20.90	20.77	20.68	20.60	20.55	20.50	20.47	20.44	20.42	20.40	20.39	20.35	20.34	20.34
2000	41.79	41.54	41.35	41.20	41.09	41.00	40.93	40.87	40.83	40.80	40.77	40.70	40.68	40.67
3000	62.68	62.31	62.03	61.80	61.63	61.50	61.39	61.31	61.24	61.19	61.15	61.05	61.02	61.01
4000	83.57	83.08	82.70	82.40	82.17	81.99	81.85	81.74	81.65	81.59	81.53	81.40	81.36	81.34
5000	104.46	103.85	103.37	103.00	102.71	102.49	102.31	102.17	102.07	101.98	101.91	101.74	101.69	101.68
6000	125.35	124.62	124.05	123.60	123.26	122.99	122.77	122.61	122.48	122.38	122.30	122.09	122.03	122.01
7000	146.24	145.39	144.72	144.20	143.80	143.48	143.24	143.04	142.89	142.77	142.68	142.44	142.37	142.35
8000	167.13	166.16	165.40	164.80	164.34	163.98	163.70	163.48	163.30	163.17	163.06	162.79	162.71	162.68
9000	188.02	186.92	186.07	185.40	184.88	184.48	184.16	183.91	183.72	183.56	183.44	183.14	183.04	183.02
10000	208.92	207.69	206.74	206.00	205.42	204.97	204.62	204.34	204.13	203.96	203.82	203.48	203.38	203.35
11000	229.81	228.46	227.42	226.60	225.97	225.47	225.08	224.78	224.54	224.35	224.21	223.83	223.72	223.69
12000	250.70	249.23	248.09	247.20	246.51	245.97	245.54	245.21	244.95	244.75	244.59	244.18	244.06	244.02
13000	271.59	270.00	268.76	267.80	267.05	266.46	266.01	265.65	265.36	265.14	264.97	264.53	264.39	264.36
14000	292.48	290.77	289.44	288.40	287.59	286.96	286.47	286.08	285.78	285.54	285.35	284.87	284.73	284.69
15000	313.37	311.54	310.11	309.00	308.13	307.46	306.93	306.51	306.19	305.93	305.73	305.22	305.07	305.02
16000	334.26	332.31	330.79	329.60	328.68	327.95	327.39	326.95	326.60	326.33	326.12	325.57	325.41	325.36
17000	355.15	353.07	351.46	350.20	349.22	348.45	347.85	347.38	347.01	346.72	346.50	345.92	345.75	345.69
18000	376.04	373.84	372.13	370.80	369.76	368.95	368.31	367.82	367.43	367.12	366.88	366.27	366.08	366.03
19000	396.93	394.61	392.81	391.40	390.30	389.45	388.77	388.25	387.84	387.51	387.26	386.61	386.42	386.36
20000	417.83	415.38	413.48	412.00	410.84	409.94	409.24	408.68	408.25	407.91	407.64	406.96	406.76	406.70
21000	438.72	436.15	434.15	432.60	431.39	430.44	429.70	429.12	428.66	428.31	428.03	427.31	427.10	427.03
22000	459.61	456.92	454.83	453.20	451.93	450.94	450.16	449.55	449.07	448.70	448.41	447.66	447.43	447.37
23000	480.50	477.69	475.50	473.80	472.47	471.43	470.62	469.98	469.49	469.10	468.79	468.01	467.77	467.70
24000	501.39	498.46	496.18	494.40	493.01	491.93	491.08	490.42	489.90	489.49	489.17	488.35	488.11	488.04
25000	522.28	519.22	516.85	515.00	513.55	512.43	511.54	510.85	510.31	509.89	509.55	508.70	508.45	508.37
26000	543.17	539.99	537.52	535.60	534.10	532.92	532.01	531.29	530.72	530.28	529.94	529.05	528.78	528.71
27000	564.06	560.76	558.20	556.20	554.64	553.42	552.47	551.72	551.14	550.68	550.32	549.40	549.12	549.04
28000	584.95	581.53	578.87	576.80	575.18	573.92	572.93	572.15	571.55	571.07	570.70	569.74	569.46	569.37
29000	605.84	602.30	599.54	597.40	595.72	594.41	593.39	592.59	591.96	591.47	591.08	590.09	589.80	589.71
30000	626.74	623.07	620.22	618.00	616.26	614.91	613.85	613.02	612.37	611.86	611.46	610.44	610.13	610.04
31000	647.63	643.84	640.89	638.60	636.81	635.41	634.31	633.46	632.78	632.26	631.84	630.79	630.47	630.38
32000	668.52	664.61	661.57	659.20	657.35	655.90	654.77	653.89	653.20	652.65	652.23	651.14	650.81	650.71
33000	689.41	685.37	682.24	679.80	677.89	676.40	675.24	674.32	673.61	673.05	672.61	671.48	671.15	671.05
34000	710.30	706.14	702.91	700.40	698.43	696.90	695.70	694.76	694.02	693.44	692.99	691.83	691.49	691.38
35000	731.19	726.91	723.59	721.00	718.97	717.40	716.16	715.19	714.43	713.84	713.37	712.18	711.82	711.72
36000	752.08	747.68	744.26	741.60	739.52	737.89	736.62	735.63	734.85	734.23	733.75	732.53	732.16	732.05
37000	772.97	768.45	764.93	762.20	760.06	758.39	757.08	756.06	755.26	754.63	754.14	752.87	752.50	752.39
38000	793.86	789.22	785.61	782.80	780.60	778.89	777.54	776.49	775.67	775.02	774.52	773.22	772.84	772.72
39000	814.75	809.99	806.28	803.40	801.14	799.38	798.01	796.93	796.08	795.42	794.90	793.57	793.17	793.06
40000	835.65	830.76	826.96	824.00	821.68	819.88	818.47	817.36	816.49	815.82	815.28	813.92	813.51	813.39
41000	856.54	851.52	847.63	844.60	842.23	840.38	838.93	837.79	836.91	836.21	835.66	834.27	833.85	833.72
42000	877.43	872.29	868.30	865.19	862.77	860.87	859.39	858.23	857.32	856.61	856.05	854.61	854.19	854.06
43000	898.32	893.06	888.98	885.79	883.31	881.37	879.85	878.66	877.73	877.00	876.43	874.96	874.52	874.39
44000	919.21	913.83	909.65	906.39	903.85	901.87	900.31	899.10	898.14	897.40	896.81	895.31	894.86	894.73
45000	940.10	934.60	930.32	926.99	924.39	922.36	920.77	919.53	918.56	917.79	917.19	915.66	915.20	915.06
46000	960.99	955.37	951.00	947.59	944.94	942.86	941.24	939.96	938.97	938.19	937.57	936.01	935.54	935.40
47000	981.88	976.14	971.67	968.19	965.48	963.36	961.70	960.40	959.38	958.58	957.96	956.35	955.88	955.73
48000	1002.77	996.91	992.35	988.79	986.02	983.85	982.16	980.83	979.79	978.98	978.34	976.70	976.21	976.07
49000	1023.66	1017.68	1013.02	1009.39	1006.56	1004.35	1002.62	1001.27	1000.20	999.37	998.72	997.05	996.55	996.40
50000	1044.56	1038.44	1033.69	1029.99	1027.10	1024.85	1023.08	1021.70	1020.62	1019.77	1019.10	1017.40	1016.89	1016.74
55000	1149.01	1142.29	1137.06	1132.99	1129.81	1127.33	1125.39	1123.87	1122.68	1121.74	1121.01	1119.14	1118.58	1118.41
60000	1253.47	1246.13	1240.43	1235.99	1232.52	1229.82	1227.70	1226.04	1224.74	1223.72	1222.92	1220.88	1220.26	1220.08
65000	1357.92	1349.98	1343.80	1338.99	1335.23	1332.30	1330.01	1328.21	1326.80	1325.70	1324.83	1322.61	1321.95	1321.76
70000	1462.38	1453.82	1447.17	1441.99	1437.94	1434.79	1432.31	1430.38	1428.86	1427.67	1426.74	1424.35	1423.64	1423.43
75000	1566.83	1557.66	1550.54	1544.99	1540.65	1537.27	1534.62	1532.55	1530.92	1529.65	1528.65	1526.09	1525.33	1525.10
80000	1671.29	1661.51	1653.91	1647.99	1643.36	1639.75	1636.93	1634.72	1632.98	1631.63	1630.56	1627.83	1627.02	1626.78
85000	1775.74	1765.35	1757.28	1750.98	1746.07	1742.24	1739.24	1736.89	1735.04	1733.60	1732.47	1729.57	1728.71	1728.45
90000	1880.20	1869.20	1860.64	1853.98	1848.78	1844.72	1841.54	1839.06	1837.11	1835.58	1834.38	1831.31	1830.39	1830.12
95000	1984.65	1973.04	1964.01	1956.98	1951.49	1947.21	1943.85	1941.23	1939.17	1937.55	1936.29	1933.05	1932.08	1931.79
100000	2089.11	2076.88	2067.38	2059.98	2054.20	2049.69	2046.16	2043.39	2041.23	2039.53	2038.20	2034.79	2033.77	2033.47

MONTHLY PAYMENT
REQUIRED TO AMORTIZE A LOAN

TERM AMOUNT	1 Year	2 Years	3 Years	4 Years	5 Years	6 Years	7 Years	8 Years	9 Years	10 Years	11 Years	12 Years	13 Years	14 Years
5	.48	.27	.20	.17	.15	.14	.13	.12	.12	.12	.11	.11	.11	.11
10	.95	.54	.40	.33	.30	.27	.25	.24	.24	.23	.22	.22	.22	.22
15	1.43	.80	.60	.50	.44	.40	.38	.36	.35	.34	.33	.33	.32	.32
25	2.38	1.33	.99	.83	.73	.67	.63	.60	.58	.56	.55	.54	.54	.53
50	4.75	2.66	1.98	1.65	1.46	1.34	1.25	1.20	1.16	1.12	1.10	1.08	1.07	1.06
75	7.12	3.99	2.97	2.47	2.18	2.00	1.88	1.79	1.73	1.68	1.65	1.62	1.60	1.59
100	9.49	5.32	3.95	3.29	2.91	2.67	2.50	2.39	2.31	2.24	2.20	2.16	2.14	2.12
200	18.97	10.63	7.90	6.58	5.82	5.33	5.00	4.77	4.61	4.48	4.39	4.32	4.27	4.23
300	28.45	15.94	11.85	9.87	8.72	7.99	7.50	7.16	6.91	6.72	6.59	6.48	6.40	6.34
400	37.93	21.25	15.80	13.16	11.63	10.66	10.00	9.54	9.21	8.96	8.78	8.64	8.54	8.45
500	47.41	26.57	19.75	16.44	14.53	13.32	12.50	11.93	11.51	11.20	10.97	10.80	10.67	10.57
600	56.89	31.88	23.70	19.73	17.44	15.98	15.00	14.31	13.81	13.44	13.17	12.96	12.80	12.68
700	66.37	37.19	27.65	23.02	20.35	18.65	17.50	16.69	16.11	15.68	15.36	15.12	14.93	14.79
800	75.85	42.50	31.60	26.31	23.25	21.31	20.00	19.08	18.41	17.92	17.56	17.28	17.07	16.90
900	85.33	47.81	35.55	29.60	26.16	23.97	22.50	21.46	20.71	20.16	19.75	19.44	19.20	19.02
1000	94.81	53.13	39.50	32.88	29.06	26.64	25.00	23.85	23.02	22.40	21.94	21.60	21.33	21.13
2000	189.61	106.25	79.00	65.76	58.12	53.27	49.99	47.69	46.03	44.80	43.88	43.19	42.66	42.25
3000	284.41	159.37	118.49	98.64	87.18	79.90	74.98	71.53	69.04	67.20	65.82	64.78	63.99	63.38
4000	379.21	212.49	157.99	131.52	116.24	106.53	99.98	95.37	92.05	89.60	87.76	86.37	85.32	84.50
5000	474.01	265.61	197.48	164.40	145.30	133.16	124.97	119.21	115.06	111.99	109.70	107.97	106.64	105.63
6000	568.82	318.73	236.98	197.28	174.36	159.79	149.96	143.06	138.07	134.39	131.64	129.56	127.97	126.75
7000	663.62	371.85	276.48	230.16	203.42	186.42	174.95	166.90	161.08	156.79	153.58	151.15	149.30	147.88
8000	758.42	424.97	315.97	263.04	232.48	213.05	199.95	190.74	184.09	179.19	175.52	172.74	170.63	169.00
9000	853.22	478.09	355.47	295.91	261.54	239.69	224.94	214.58	207.10	201.58	197.46	194.34	191.96	190.13
10000	948.02	531.21	394.96	328.79	290.59	266.32	249.93	238.42	230.11	223.98	219.40	215.93	213.28	211.25
11000	1042.82	584.34	434.46	361.67	319.65	292.95	274.93	262.27	253.12	246.38	241.34	237.52	234.61	232.38
12000	1137.63	637.46	473.96	394.55	348.71	319.58	299.92	286.11	276.13	268.78	263.28	259.11	255.94	253.50
13000	1232.43	690.58	513.45	427.43	377.77	346.21	324.91	309.95	299.14	291.18	285.22	280.71	277.27	274.63
14000	1327.23	743.70	552.95	460.31	406.83	372.84	349.90	333.79	322.15	313.57	307.15	302.30	298.60	295.75
15000	1422.03	796.82	592.44	493.19	435.89	399.47	374.90	357.63	345.16	335.97	329.09	323.89	319.92	316.88
16000	1516.83	849.94	631.94	526.07	464.95	426.10	399.89	381.48	368.17	358.37	351.03	345.48	341.25	338.00
17000	1611.63	903.06	671.43	558.95	494.01	452.74	424.88	405.32	391.18	380.77	372.97	367.08	362.58	359.13
18000	1706.44	956.18	710.93	591.82	523.07	479.37	449.88	429.16	414.20	403.16	394.91	388.67	383.91	380.25
19000	1801.24	1009.30	750.43	624.70	552.12	506.00	474.87	453.00	437.21	425.56	416.85	410.26	405.24	401.38
20000	1896.04	1062.42	789.92	657.58	581.18	532.63	499.86	476.84	460.22	447.96	438.79	431.85	426.56	422.50
21000	1990.84	1115.55	829.42	690.46	610.24	559.26	524.85	500.69	483.23	470.36	460.73	453.45	447.89	443.63
22000	2085.64	1168.67	868.91	723.34	639.30	585.89	549.85	524.53	506.24	492.76	482.67	475.04	469.22	464.75
23000	2180.44	1221.79	908.41	756.22	668.36	612.52	574.84	548.37	529.25	515.15	504.61	496.63	490.55	485.88
24000	2275.25	1274.91	947.91	789.10	697.42	639.15	599.83	572.21	552.26	537.55	526.55	518.22	511.88	507.00
25000	2370.05	1328.03	987.40	821.98	726.48	665.78	624.83	596.05	575.27	559.95	548.49	539.82	533.20	528.13
26000	2464.85	1381.15	1026.90	854.86	755.54	692.42	649.82	619.90	598.28	582.35	570.43	561.41	554.53	549.25
27000	2559.65	1434.27	1066.39	887.73	784.60	719.05	674.81	643.74	621.29	604.74	592.37	583.00	575.86	570.38
28000	2654.45	1487.39	1105.89	920.61	813.65	745.68	699.80	667.58	644.30	627.14	614.30	604.59	597.19	591.50
29000	2749.26	1540.51	1145.38	953.49	842.71	772.31	724.80	691.42	667.31	649.54	636.24	626.19	618.52	612.63
30000	2844.06	1593.63	1184.88	986.37	871.77	798.94	749.79	715.26	690.32	671.94	658.18	647.78	639.84	633.75
31000	2938.86	1646.76	1224.38	1019.25	900.83	825.57	774.78	739.11	713.33	694.33	680.12	669.37	661.17	654.88
32000	3033.66	1699.88	1263.87	1052.13	929.89	852.20	799.78	762.95	736.34	716.73	702.06	690.96	682.50	676.00
33000	3128.46	1753.00	1303.37	1085.01	958.95	878.83	824.77	786.79	759.35	739.13	724.00	712.56	703.83	697.13
34000	3223.26	1806.12	1342.86	1117.89	988.01	905.47	849.76	810.63	782.36	761.53	745.94	734.15	725.16	718.25
35000	3318.07	1859.24	1382.36	1150.77	1017.07	932.10	874.75	834.47	805.37	783.93	767.88	755.74	746.48	739.38
36000	3412.87	1912.36	1421.86	1183.64	1046.13	958.73	899.75	858.32	828.39	806.32	789.82	777.33	767.81	760.50
37000	3507.67	1965.48	1461.35	1216.52	1075.18	985.36	924.74	882.16	851.40	828.72	811.76	798.93	789.14	781.63
38000	3602.47	2018.60	1500.85	1249.40	1104.24	1011.99	949.73	906.00	874.41	851.12	833.70	820.52	810.47	802.75
39000	3697.27	2071.72	1540.34	1282.28	1133.30	1038.62	974.73	929.84	897.42	873.52	855.64	842.11	831.79	823.88
40000	3792.07	2124.84	1579.84	1315.16	1162.36	1065.25	999.72	953.68	920.43	895.91	877.58	863.70	853.12	845.00
41000	3886.88	2177.97	1619.34	1348.04	1191.42	1091.88	1024.71	977.53	943.44	918.31	899.52	885.30	874.45	866.13
42000	3981.68	2231.09	1658.83	1380.92	1220.48	1118.51	1049.70	1001.37	966.45	940.71	921.45	906.89	895.78	887.25
43000	4076.48	2284.21	1698.33	1413.80	1249.54	1145.15	1074.70	1025.21	989.46	963.11	943.39	928.48	917.11	908.38
44000	4171.28	2337.33	1737.82	1446.68	1278.60	1171.78	1099.69	1049.05	1012.47	985.51	965.33	950.07	938.43	929.50
45000	4266.08	2390.45	1777.32	1479.55	1307.66	1198.41	1124.68	1072.89	1035.48	1007.90	987.27	971.67	959.76	950.62
46000	4360.88	2443.57	1816.81	1512.43	1336.72	1225.04	1149.68	1096.74	1058.49	1030.30	1009.21	993.26	981.09	971.75
47000	4455.69	2496.69	1856.31	1545.31	1365.77	1251.67	1174.67	1120.58	1081.50	1052.70	1031.15	1014.85	1002.42	992.87
48000	4550.49	2549.81	1895.81	1578.19	1394.83	1278.30	1199.66	1144.42	1104.51	1075.10	1053.09	1036.44	1023.75	1014.00
49000	4645.29	2602.93	1935.30	1611.07	1423.89	1304.93	1224.65	1168.26	1127.52	1097.49	1075.03	1058.04	1045.07	1035.12
50000	4740.09	2656.05	1974.80	1643.95	1452.95	1331.56	1249.65	1192.10	1150.53	1119.89	1096.97	1079.63	1066.40	1056.25
55000	5214.10	2921.66	2172.28	1808.34	1598.25	1464.72	1374.61	1311.31	1265.59	1231.88	1206.66	1187.59	1173.04	1161.87
60000	5688.11	3187.26	2369.76	1972.74	1743.54	1597.88	1499.58	1430.52	1380.64	1343.87	1316.36	1295.55	1279.68	1267.50
65000	6162.12	3452.87	2567.24	2137.13	1888.83	1731.03	1624.54	1549.73	1495.69	1455.86	1426.06	1403.52	1386.32	1373.12
70000	6636.13	3718.47	2764.72	2301.53	2034.13	1864.19	1749.50	1668.94	1610.74	1567.85	1535.75	1511.48	1492.96	1478.75
75000	7110.14	3984.08	2962.19	2465.92	2179.42	1997.34	1874.47	1788.15	1725.80	1679.83	1645.45	1619.44	1599.60	1584.37
80000	7584.14	4249.68	3159.67	2630.31	2324.72	2130.50	1999.43	1907.36	1840.85	1791.82	1755.15	1727.40	1706.24	1690.00
85000	8058.15	4515.29	3357.15	2794.71	2470.01	2263.66	2124.40	2026.57	1955.90	1903.81	1864.84	1835.37	1812.88	1795.62
90000	8532.16	4780.89	3554.63	2959.10	2615.31	2396.81	2249.36	2145.78	2070.96	2015.80	1974.54	1943.33	1919.52	1901.24
95000	9006.17	5046.50	3752.11	3123.50	2760.60	2529.97	2374.32	2264.99	2186.01	2127.79	2084.24	2051.29	2026.16	2006.87
100000	9480.18	5312.10	3949.59	3287.89	2905.90	2663.12	2499.29	2384.20	2301.06	2239.78	2193.93	2159.25	2132.80	2112.49

TERM	15 Years	16 Years	17 Years	18 Years	19 Years	20 Years	21 Years	22 Years	23 Years	24 Years	25 Years	30 Years	35 Years	40 Years
AMOUNT														
5	.11	.11	.11	.11	.11	.11	.11	.11	.11	.11	.11	.11	.11	.11
10	.21	.21	.21	.21	.21	.21	.21	.21	.21	.21	.21	.21	.21	.21
15	.32	.32	.32	.32	.31	.31	.31	.31	.31	.31	.31	.31	.31	.31
25	.53	.53	.52	.52	.52	.52	.52	.52	.52	.52	.52	.52	.52	.52
50	1.05	1.05	1.04	1.04	1.04	1.03	1.03	1.03	1.03	1.03	1.03	1.03	1.03	1.03
75	1.58	1.57	1.56	1.56	1.55	1.55	1.55	1.54	1.54	1.54	1.54	1.54	1.54	1.54
100	2.10	2.09	2.08	2.07	2.07	2.06	2.06	2.06	2.05	2.05	2.05	2.05	2.05	2.05
200	4.20	4.17	4.16	4.14	4.13	4.12	4.11	4.11	4.10	4.10	4.10	4.09	4.09	4.09
300	6.30	6.26	6.23	6.21	6.19	6.18	6.17	6.16	6.15	6.15	6.14	6.13	6.13	6.13
400	8.39	8.34	8.31	8.28	8.25	8.24	8.22	8.21	8.20	8.20	8.19	8.18	8.17	8.17
500	10.49	10.43	10.38	10.34	10.32	10.29	10.28	10.26	10.25	10.24	10.24	10.22	10.22	10.21
600	12.59	12.51	12.46	12.41	12.38	12.35	12.33	12.31	12.30	12.29	12.28	12.26	12.26	12.26
700	14.68	14.60	14.53	14.48	14.44	14.41	14.38	14.37	14.35	14.34	14.33	14.31	14.30	14.30
800	16.78	16.68	16.61	16.55	16.50	16.47	16.44	16.42	16.40	16.39	16.38	16.35	16.34	16.34
900	18.88	18.77	18.68	18.62	18.57	18.52	18.49	18.47	18.45	18.43	18.42	18.39	18.38	18.38
1000	20.97	20.85	20.76	20.68	20.63	20.58	20.55	20.52	20.50	20.48	20.47	20.44	20.43	20.42
2000	41.94	41.70	41.51	41.36	41.25	41.16	41.09	41.04	40.99	40.96	40.93	40.87	40.85	40.84
3000	62.91	62.55	62.26	62.04	61.87	61.74	61.63	61.55	61.49	61.44	61.40	61.30	61.27	61.26
4000	83.88	83.39	83.02	82.72	82.49	82.32	82.18	82.07	81.98	81.91	81.86	81.73	81.69	81.68
5000	104.85	104.24	103.77	103.40	103.12	102.89	102.72	102.58	102.48	102.39	102.33	102.16	102.11	102.09
6000	125.81	125.09	124.52	124.08	123.74	123.47	123.26	123.10	122.97	122.87	122.79	122.59	122.53	122.51
7000	146.78	145.93	145.27	144.76	144.36	144.05	143.80	143.61	143.46	143.35	143.25	143.02	142.95	142.93
8000	167.75	166.78	166.03	165.44	164.98	164.63	164.34	164.13	163.96	163.82	163.72	163.45	163.37	163.35
9000	188.72	187.63	186.78	186.12	185.61	185.20	184.89	184.64	184.45	184.30	184.18	183.88	183.79	183.77
10000	209.69	208.47	207.53	206.80	206.23	205.78	205.43	205.16	204.95	204.78	204.65	204.31	204.21	204.18
11000	230.66	229.32	228.29	227.48	226.85	226.36	225.98	225.68	225.44	225.26	225.11	224.74	224.63	224.60
12000	251.62	250.17	249.04	248.16	247.47	246.94	246.52	246.19	245.93	245.73	245.58	245.17	245.06	245.02
13000	272.59	271.02	269.79	268.84	268.09	267.51	267.06	266.71	266.43	266.21	266.04	265.60	265.48	265.44
14000	293.56	291.86	290.54	289.52	288.72	288.09	287.60	287.22	286.92	286.69	286.50	286.04	285.90	285.86
15000	314.53	312.71	311.30	310.20	309.34	308.67	308.15	307.74	307.42	307.17	306.97	306.47	306.32	306.27
16000	335.50	333.56	332.05	330.88	329.96	329.25	328.69	328.25	327.91	327.64	327.43	326.90	326.74	326.69
17000	356.47	354.40	352.80	351.56	350.58	349.83	349.23	348.77	348.41	348.12	347.90	347.33	347.16	347.11
18000	377.43	375.25	373.55	372.24	371.21	370.40	369.77	369.28	368.90	368.60	368.36	367.76	367.58	367.53
19000	398.40	396.10	394.31	392.91	391.83	390.98	390.32	389.80	389.39	389.08	388.83	388.19	388.00	387.95
20000	419.37	416.94	415.06	413.59	412.45	411.56	410.86	410.31	409.89	409.55	409.29	408.62	408.42	408.36
21000	440.34	437.79	435.81	434.27	433.07	432.14	431.40	430.83	430.38	430.03	429.75	429.05	428.84	428.78
22000	461.31	458.64	456.57	454.95	453.70	452.71	451.95	451.35	450.88	450.51	450.22	449.48	449.26	449.20
23000	482.27	479.48	477.32	475.63	474.32	473.29	472.49	471.86	471.37	470.98	470.68	469.91	469.68	469.62
24000	503.24	500.33	498.07	496.31	494.94	493.87	493.03	492.38	491.86	491.46	491.15	490.34	490.11	490.04
25000	524.21	521.18	518.82	516.99	515.56	514.45	513.58	512.89	512.36	511.94	511.61	510.78	510.53	510.45
26000	545.18	542.03	539.58	537.67	536.18	535.02	534.12	533.41	532.85	532.42	532.08	531.21	530.95	530.87
27000	566.15	562.87	560.33	558.35	556.81	555.60	554.66	553.92	553.35	552.89	552.54	551.64	551.37	551.29
28000	587.12	583.72	581.08	579.03	577.43	576.18	575.20	574.44	573.84	573.37	573.00	572.07	571.79	571.71
29000	608.08	604.57	601.83	599.71	598.05	596.76	595.75	594.95	594.33	593.85	593.47	592.50	592.21	592.12
30000	629.05	625.41	622.59	620.39	618.67	617.33	616.29	615.47	614.83	614.33	613.93	612.93	612.63	612.54
31000	650.02	646.26	643.34	641.07	639.30	637.91	636.83	635.98	635.32	634.80	634.40	633.36	633.05	632.96
32000	670.99	667.11	664.09	661.75	659.92	658.49	657.37	656.50	655.82	655.28	654.86	653.79	653.47	653.38
33000	691.96	687.95	684.85	682.43	680.54	679.07	677.92	677.02	676.31	675.76	675.33	674.22	673.89	673.80
34000	712.93	708.80	705.60	703.11	701.16	699.65	698.46	697.53	696.81	696.24	695.79	694.65	694.31	694.21
35000	733.89	729.65	726.35	723.79	721.78	720.22	719.00	718.05	717.30	716.71	716.25	715.08	714.74	714.63
36000	754.86	750.50	747.10	744.47	742.41	740.80	739.54	738.56	737.79	737.19	736.72	735.51	735.16	735.05
37000	775.83	771.34	767.86	765.14	763.03	761.38	760.09	759.08	758.29	757.67	757.18	755.94	755.58	755.47
38000	796.80	792.19	788.61	785.82	783.65	781.96	780.63	779.59	778.78	778.15	777.65	776.38	776.00	775.89
39000	817.77	813.04	809.36	806.50	804.27	802.53	801.17	800.11	799.28	798.62	798.11	796.81	796.42	796.30
40000	838.73	833.88	830.12	827.18	824.90	823.11	821.72	820.62	819.77	819.10	818.58	817.24	816.84	816.72
41000	859.70	854.73	850.87	847.86	845.52	843.69	842.26	841.14	840.26	839.58	839.04	837.67	837.26	837.14
42000	880.67	875.58	871.62	868.54	866.14	864.27	862.80	861.66	860.76	860.06	859.50	858.10	857.68	857.56
43000	901.64	896.42	892.37	889.22	886.76	884.84	883.34	882.17	881.25	880.53	879.97	878.53	878.10	877.98
44000	922.61	917.27	913.13	909.90	907.39	905.42	903.89	902.69	901.75	901.01	900.43	898.96	898.52	898.39
45000	943.58	938.12	933.88	930.58	928.01	926.00	924.43	923.20	922.24	921.49	920.90	919.39	918.94	918.81
46000	964.54	958.96	954.63	951.26	948.63	946.58	944.97	943.72	942.73	941.96	941.36	939.82	939.36	939.23
47000	985.51	979.81	975.38	971.94	969.25	967.15	965.52	964.23	963.23	962.44	961.83	960.25	959.79	959.65
48000	1006.48	1000.66	996.14	992.62	989.87	987.73	986.06	984.75	983.72	982.92	982.29	980.68	980.21	980.06
49000	1027.45	1021.51	1016.89	1013.30	1010.50	1008.31	1006.60	1005.26	1004.22	1003.40	1002.75	1001.11	1000.63	1000.48
50000	1048.42	1042.35	1037.64	1033.98	1031.12	1028.89	1027.14	1025.78	1024.71	1023.87	1023.22	1021.55	1021.05	1020.90
55000	1153.26	1146.59	1141.41	1137.37	1134.23	1131.78	1129.86	1128.36	1127.18	1126.26	1125.54	1123.70	1123.15	1122.99
60000	1258.10	1250.82	1245.17	1240.77	1237.34	1234.66	1232.57	1230.93	1229.65	1228.65	1227.86	1225.85	1225.26	1225.08
65000	1362.94	1355.06	1348.93	1344.17	1340.45	1337.55	1335.28	1333.51	1332.12	1331.04	1330.18	1328.01	1327.36	1327.17
70000	1467.78	1459.29	1452.70	1447.57	1443.56	1440.44	1438.00	1436.09	1434.59	1433.42	1432.50	1430.16	1429.47	1429.26
75000	1572.62	1563.53	1556.46	1550.96	1546.68	1543.33	1540.71	1538.67	1537.06	1535.81	1534.83	1532.32	1531.57	1531.35
80000	1677.46	1667.76	1660.23	1654.36	1649.79	1646.22	1643.43	1641.24	1639.53	1638.20	1637.15	1634.47	1633.67	1633.44
85000	1782.31	1772.00	1763.99	1757.76	1752.90	1749.11	1746.14	1743.82	1742.01	1740.58	1739.47	1736.62	1735.78	1735.53
90000	1887.15	1876.23	1867.75	1861.16	1856.01	1851.99	1848.85	1846.40	1844.48	1842.97	1841.79	1838.78	1837.88	1837.62
95000	1991.99	1980.47	1971.52	1964.55	1959.12	1954.88	1951.57	1948.98	1946.95	1945.36	1944.11	1940.93	1939.99	1939.71
100000	2096.83	2084.70	2075.28	2067.95	2062.23	2057.77	2054.28	2051.55	2049.42	2047.74	2046.43	2043.09	2042.09	2041.80

MONTHLY PAYMENT
REQUIRED TO AMORTIZE A LOAN

TERM	1 Year	2 Years	3 Years	4 Years	5 Years	6 Years	7 Years	8 Years	9 Years	10 Years	11 Years	12 Years	13 Years	14 Years
AMOUNT														
5	.40	.21	.20	.17	.15	.14	.13	.12	.12	.12	.12	.11	.11	.11
10	.95	.54	.40	.33	.30	.27	.26	.24	.24	.23	.23	.22	.22	.22
15	1.43	.80	.60	.50	.44	.41	.38	.36	.35	.34	.34	.33	.33	.32
25	2.38	1.33	.99	.83	.73	.67	.63	.60	.58	.57	.56	.55	.54	.54
50	4.75	2.66	1.98	1.65	1.46	1.34	1.26	1.20	1.16	1.13	1.11	1.09	1.08	1.07
75	7.12	3.99	2.97	2.48	2.19	2.01	1.88	1.80	1.74	1.69	1.66	1.63	1.61	1.60
100	9.49	5.32	3.96	3.30	2.92	2.67	2.51	2.40	2.31	2.25	2.21	2.17	2.15	2.13
200	18.98	10.64	7.91	6.59	5.83	5.34	5.02	4.79	4.62	4.50	4.41	4.34	4.29	4.25
300	28.46	15.96	11.87	9.89	8.74	8.01	7.52	7.18	6.93	6.75	6.61	6.50	6.43	6.37
400	37.95	21.27	15.82	13.18	11.65	10.68	10.03	9.57	9.24	8.99	8.81	8.67	8.57	8.49
500	47.43	26.59	19.78	16.47	14.56	13.35	12.53	11.96	11.54	11.24	11.01	10.84	10.71	10.61
600	56.92	31.91	23.73	19.77	17.48	16.02	15.04	14.35	13.85	13.49	13.21	13.00	12.85	12.73
700	66.40	37.22	27.69	23.06	20.39	18.69	17.54	16.74	16.16	15.73	15.41	15.17	14.99	14.85
800	75.89	42.54	31.64	26.35	23.30	21.36	20.05	19.13	18.47	17.98	17.61	17.34	17.13	16.97
900	85.37	47.86	35.60	29.65	26.21	24.03	22.56	21.52	20.78	20.23	19.82	19.50	19.27	19.09
1000	94.86	53.18	39.55	32.94	29.12	26.70	25.06	23.91	23.08	22.47	22.02	21.67	21.41	21.21
2000	189.71	106.35	79.10	65.87	58.24	53.39	50.12	47.82	46.16	44.94	44.03	43.34	42.81	42.41
3000	284.56	159.52	118.65	98.81	87.36	80.08	75.17	71.73	69.24	67.41	66.04	65.00	64.21	63.61
4000	379.41	212.69	158.20	131.74	116.47	106.77	100.23	95.64	92.32	89.88	88.05	86.67	85.62	84.81
5000	474.26	265.86	197.75	164.68	145.59	133.47	125.29	119.54	115.40	112.34	110.06	108.34	107.02	106.01
6000	569.11	319.03	237.30	197.61	174.71	160.16	150.34	143.45	138.48	134.81	132.07	130.00	128.42	127.21
7000	663.96	372.20	276.85	230.55	203.83	186.85	175.40	167.36	161.56	157.28	154.08	151.67	149.83	148.41
8000	758.81	425.37	316.39	263.48	232.94	213.54	200.46	191.27	184.63	179.75	176.09	173.33	171.23	169.61
9000	853.66	478.54	355.94	296.41	262.06	240.24	225.51	215.18	207.71	202.22	198.11	195.00	192.63	190.81
10000	948.51	531.72	395.49	329.35	291.18	266.93	250.57	239.08	230.79	224.68	220.12	216.67	214.03	212.02
11000	1043.36	584.89	435.04	362.28	320.30	293.62	275.63	262.99	253.87	247.15	242.13	238.33	235.44	233.22
12000	1138.21	638.06	474.59	395.22	349.41	320.31	300.68	286.90	276.95	269.62	264.14	260.00	256.84	254.42
13000	1233.06	691.23	514.14	428.15	378.53	347.00	325.74	310.81	300.03	292.09	286.15	281.66	278.24	275.62
14000	1327.91	744.40	553.69	461.09	407.65	373.70	350.80	334.72	323.11	314.56	308.16	303.33	299.65	296.82
15000	1422.76	797.57	593.23	494.02	436.76	400.39	375.85	358.62	346.19	337.02	330.17	325.00	321.05	318.02
16000	1517.61	850.74	632.78	526.96	465.88	427.08	400.91	382.53	369.26	359.49	352.18	346.66	342.45	339.22
17000	1612.46	903.91	672.33	559.89	495.00	453.77	425.96	406.44	392.34	381.96	374.20	368.33	363.85	360.42
18000	1707.31	957.08	711.88	592.82	524.12	480.47	451.02	430.35	415.42	404.43	396.21	389.99	385.26	381.62
19000	1802.16	1010.25	751.43	625.76	553.23	507.16	476.08	454.26	438.50	426.89	418.22	411.66	406.66	402.83
20000	1897.01	1063.43	790.98	658.69	582.35	533.85	501.13	478.16	461.58	449.36	440.23	433.33	428.06	424.03
21000	1991.86	1116.60	830.53	691.63	611.47	560.54	526.19	502.07	484.66	471.83	462.24	454.99	449.47	445.23
22000	2086.71	1169.77	870.07	724.56	640.59	587.23	551.25	525.98	507.74	494.30	484.25	476.66	470.87	466.43
23000	2181.56	1222.94	909.62	757.50	669.70	613.93	576.30	549.89	530.82	516.77	506.26	498.32	492.27	487.63
24000	2276.41	1276.11	949.17	790.43	698.82	640.62	601.36	573.80	553.89	539.23	528.27	519.99	513.67	508.83
25000	2371.26	1329.28	988.72	823.37	727.94	667.31	626.42	597.70	576.97	561.70	550.29	541.66	535.08	530.03
26000	2466.11	1382.45	1028.27	856.30	757.05	694.00	651.47	621.61	600.05	584.17	572.30	563.32	556.48	551.23
27000	2560.96	1435.62	1067.82	889.23	786.17	720.70	676.53	645.52	623.13	606.64	594.31	584.99	577.88	572.43
28000	2655.81	1488.79	1107.37	922.17	815.29	747.39	701.59	669.43	646.21	629.11	616.32	606.65	599.29	593.64
29000	2750.66	1541.97	1146.91	955.10	844.41	774.08	726.64	693.34	669.29	651.57	638.33	628.32	620.69	614.84
30000	2845.51	1595.14	1186.46	988.04	873.52	800.77	751.70	717.24	692.37	674.04	660.34	649.99	642.09	636.04
31000	2940.36	1648.31	1226.01	1020.97	902.64	827.46	776.76	741.15	715.45	696.51	682.35	671.65	663.50	657.24
32000	3035.21	1701.48	1265.56	1053.91	931.76	854.16	801.81	765.06	738.52	718.98	704.36	693.32	684.90	678.44
33000	3130.06	1754.65	1305.11	1086.84	960.88	880.85	826.87	788.97	761.60	741.45	726.38	714.98	706.30	699.64
34000	3224.91	1807.82	1344.66	1119.78	989.99	907.54	851.92	812.88	784.68	763.91	748.39	736.65	727.70	720.84
35000	3319.76	1860.99	1384.21	1152.71	1019.11	934.23	876.98	836.78	807.76	786.38	770.40	758.32	749.11	742.04
36000	3414.61	1914.16	1423.75	1185.64	1048.23	960.93	902.04	860.69	830.84	808.85	792.41	779.98	770.51	763.24
37000	3509.46	1967.33	1463.30	1218.58	1077.34	987.62	927.09	884.60	853.92	831.32	814.42	801.65	791.91	784.45
38000	3604.31	2020.50	1502.85	1251.51	1106.46	1014.31	952.15	908.51	877.00	853.78	836.43	823.31	813.32	805.65
39000	3699.16	2073.68	1542.40	1284.45	1135.58	1041.00	977.21	932.42	900.08	876.25	858.44	844.98	834.72	826.85
40000	3794.01	2126.85	1581.95	1317.38	1164.70	1067.70	1002.26	956.32	923.15	898.72	880.45	866.65	856.12	848.05
41000	3888.86	2180.02	1621.50	1350.32	1193.81	1094.39	1027.32	980.23	946.23	921.19	902.46	888.31	877.52	869.25
42000	3983.71	2233.19	1661.05	1383.25	1222.93	1121.08	1052.38	1004.14	969.31	943.66	924.48	909.98	898.93	890.45
43000	4078.56	2286.36	1700.59	1416.19	1252.05	1147.77	1077.43	1028.05	992.39	966.12	946.49	931.64	920.33	911.65
44000	4173.41	2339.53	1740.14	1449.12	1281.17	1174.46	1102.49	1051.95	1015.47	988.59	968.50	953.31	941.73	932.85
45000	4268.26	2392.70	1779.69	1482.05	1310.28	1201.16	1127.55	1075.86	1038.55	1011.06	990.51	974.98	963.14	954.05
46000	4363.11	2445.87	1819.24	1514.99	1339.40	1227.85	1152.60	1099.77	1061.63	1033.53	1012.52	996.64	984.54	975.26
47000	4457.96	2499.04	1858.79	1547.92	1368.52	1254.54	1177.66	1123.68	1084.71	1056.00	1034.53	1018.31	1005.94	996.46
48000	4552.81	2552.21	1898.34	1580.86	1397.63	1281.23	1202.71	1147.59	1107.78	1078.46	1056.54	1039.97	1027.34	1017.66
49000	4647.66	2605.39	1937.89	1613.79	1426.75	1307.93	1227.77	1171.49	1130.86	1100.93	1078.55	1061.64	1048.75	1038.86
50000	4742.52	2658.56	1977.43	1646.73	1455.87	1334.62	1252.83	1195.40	1153.94	1123.40	1100.57	1083.31	1070.15	1060.06
55000	5216.77	2924.41	2175.18	1811.40	1601.46	1468.08	1378.11	1314.94	1269.34	1235.74	1210.62	1191.64	1177.16	1166.06
60000	5691.02	3190.27	2372.92	1976.07	1747.04	1601.54	1503.39	1434.48	1384.73	1348.08	1320.68	1299.97	1284.18	1272.07
65000	6165.27	3456.12	2570.66	2140.74	1892.63	1735.00	1628.67	1554.02	1500.12	1460.42	1430.73	1408.30	1391.19	1378.08
70000	6639.52	3721.98	2768.41	2305.41	2038.21	1868.46	1753.96	1673.56	1615.52	1572.76	1540.79	1516.63	1498.21	1484.08
75000	7113.77	3987.83	2966.15	2470.09	2183.80	2001.92	1879.24	1793.10	1730.91	1685.10	1650.85	1624.96	1605.22	1590.09
80000	7588.02	4253.69	3163.89	2634.76	2329.39	2135.39	2004.52	1912.64	1846.30	1797.44	1760.90	1733.29	1712.24	1696.09
85000	8062.27	4519.54	3361.63	2799.43	2474.97	2268.85	2129.80	2032.18	1961.70	1909.78	1870.96	1841.62	1819.25	1802.10
90000	8536.52	4785.40	3559.38	2964.10	2620.56	2402.31	2255.09	2151.72	2077.09	2022.12	1981.02	1949.95	1926.27	1908.10
95000	9010.77	5051.25	3757.12	3128.78	2766.15	2535.77	2380.37	2271.26	2192.49	2134.45	2091.07	2058.28	2033.28	2014.11
100000	9485.03	5317.11	3954.86	3293.45	2911.73	2669.23	2505.65	2390.80	2307.88	2246.79	2201.13	2166.61	2140.30	2120.11

MONTHLY PAYMENT
REQUIRED TO AMORTIZE A LOAN

24.600%

TERM AMOUNT	15 Years	16 Years	17 Years	18 Years	19 Years	20 Years	21 Years	22 Years	23 Years	24 Years	25 Years	30 Years	35 Years	40 Years
5	.11	.11	.11	.11	.11	.11	.11	.11	.11	.11	.11	.11	.11	.11
10	.22	.21	.21	.21	.21	.21	.21	.21	.21	.21	.21	.21	.21	.21
15	.32	.32	.32	.32	.32	.31	.31	.31	.31	.31	.31	.31	.31	.31
25	.53	.53	.53	.52	.52	.52	.52	.52	.52	.52	.52	.52	.52	.52
50	1.06	1.05	1.05	1.04	1.04	1.04	1.04	1.03	1.03	1.03	1.03	1.03	1.03	1.03
75	1.58	1.57	1.57	1.56	1.56	1.55	1.55	1.55	1.55	1.55	1.55	1.54	1.54	1.54
100	2.11	2.10	2.09	2.08	2.08	2.07	2.07	2.06	2.06	2.06	2.06	2.06	2.06	2.06
200	4.21	4.19	4.16	4.16	4.15	4.14	4.13	4.12	4.12	4.12	4.12	4.11	4.11	4.11
300	6.32	6.28	6.25	6.23	6.22	6.20	6.19	6.18	6.18	6.17	6.17	6.16	6.16	6.16
400	8.42	8.38	8.34	8.31	8.29	8.27	8.25	8.24	8.24	8.23	8.22	8.21	8.21	8.21
500	10.53	10.47	10.42	10.38	10.36	10.33	10.32	10.30	10.29	10.28	10.28	10.26	10.26	10.26
600	12.63	12.56	12.50	12.46	12.43	12.40	12.38	12.36	12.35	12.34	12.33	12.31	12.31	12.31
700	14.74	14.65	14.59	14.54	14.50	14.47	14.44	14.42	14.41	14.40	14.39	14.36	14.36	14.36
800	16.84	16.75	16.67	16.61	16.57	16.53	16.50	16.48	16.47	16.45	16.44	16.42	16.41	16.41
900	18.95	18.84	18.75	18.69	18.64	18.60	18.57	18.54	18.52	18.51	18.50	18.47	18.46	18.46
1000	21.05	20.93	20.84	20.76	20.71	20.66	20.63	20.60	20.58	20.56	20.55	20.52	20.51	20.51
2000	42.10	41.86	41.67	41.52	41.41	41.32	41.25	41.20	41.16	41.12	41.10	41.03	41.01	41.01
3000	63.14	62.78	62.50	62.28	62.11	61.98	61.88	61.80	61.73	61.68	61.64	61.55	61.52	61.51
4000	84.19	83.71	83.33	83.04	82.82	82.64	82.50	82.39	82.31	82.24	82.19	82.06	82.02	82.01
5000	105.23	104.63	104.16	103.80	103.52	103.30	103.13	102.99	102.89	102.80	102.74	102.57	102.53	102.51
6000	126.28	125.56	125.00	124.56	124.22	123.96	123.75	123.59	123.46	123.36	123.28	123.09	123.03	123.01
7000	147.32	146.48	145.83	145.32	144.92	144.61	144.37	144.18	144.04	143.92	143.83	143.60	143.53	143.51
8000	168.37	167.41	166.66	166.08	165.63	165.27	165.00	164.78	164.61	164.48	164.38	164.12	164.04	164.01
9000	189.41	188.33	187.49	186.84	186.33	185.93	185.62	185.38	185.19	185.04	184.92	184.63	184.54	184.52
10000	210.46	209.26	208.32	207.60	207.03	206.59	206.25	205.98	205.77	205.60	205.47	205.14	205.05	205.02
11000	231.51	230.18	229.15	228.36	227.73	227.25	226.87	226.57	226.34	226.16	226.02	225.66	225.55	225.52
12000	252.55	251.11	249.99	249.12	248.44	247.91	247.49	247.17	246.92	246.72	246.56	246.17	246.05	246.02
13000	273.60	272.03	270.82	269.87	269.14	268.57	268.12	267.77	267.49	267.28	267.11	266.68	266.56	266.52
14000	294.64	292.96	291.65	290.63	289.84	289.22	288.74	288.36	288.07	287.84	287.66	287.20	287.06	287.02
15000	315.69	313.88	312.48	311.39	310.54	309.88	309.37	308.96	308.65	308.40	308.20	307.71	307.57	307.52
16000	336.73	334.81	333.31	332.15	331.25	330.54	329.99	329.56	329.22	328.96	328.75	328.23	328.07	328.02
17000	357.78	355.73	354.15	352.91	351.95	351.20	350.61	350.16	349.80	349.52	349.30	348.74	348.57	348.53
18000	378.82	376.66	374.98	373.67	372.65	371.86	371.24	370.75	370.37	370.08	369.84	369.25	369.08	369.03
19000	399.87	397.58	395.81	394.43	393.35	392.52	391.86	391.35	390.95	390.64	390.39	389.77	389.58	389.53
20000	420.92	418.51	416.64	415.19	414.06	413.17	412.49	411.95	411.53	411.20	410.94	410.28	410.09	410.03
21000	441.96	439.43	437.47	435.95	434.76	433.83	433.11	432.54	432.10	431.76	431.48	430.79	430.59	430.53
22000	463.01	460.36	458.30	456.71	455.46	454.49	453.73	453.14	452.68	452.32	452.03	451.31	451.09	451.03
23000	484.05	481.28	479.14	477.47	476.17	475.15	474.36	473.74	473.25	472.87	472.58	471.82	471.60	471.53
24000	505.10	502.21	499.97	498.23	496.87	495.81	494.98	494.34	493.83	493.43	493.12	492.34	492.10	492.03
25000	526.14	523.13	520.80	518.98	517.57	516.47	515.61	514.93	514.41	513.99	513.67	512.85	512.61	512.54
26000	547.19	544.06	541.63	539.74	538.27	537.13	536.23	535.53	534.98	534.55	534.22	533.36	533.11	533.04
27000	568.23	564.98	562.46	560.50	558.98	557.78	556.85	556.13	555.56	555.11	554.76	553.88	553.62	553.54
28000	589.28	585.91	583.30	581.26	579.68	578.44	577.48	576.72	576.13	575.67	575.31	574.39	574.12	574.04
29000	610.33	606.84	604.13	602.02	600.38	599.10	598.10	597.32	596.71	596.23	595.86	594.90	594.62	594.54
30000	631.37	627.76	624.96	622.78	621.08	619.76	618.73	617.92	617.29	616.79	616.40	615.42	615.13	615.04
31000	652.42	648.69	645.79	643.54	641.79	640.42	639.35	638.51	637.86	637.35	636.95	635.93	635.63	635.54
32000	673.46	669.61	666.62	664.30	662.49	661.08	659.97	659.11	658.44	657.91	657.50	656.45	656.14	656.04
33000	694.51	690.54	687.45	685.06	683.19	681.73	680.60	679.71	679.01	678.47	678.04	676.96	676.64	676.54
34000	715.55	711.46	708.29	705.82	703.89	702.39	701.22	700.31	699.59	699.03	698.59	697.47	697.14	697.05
35000	736.60	732.39	729.12	726.58	724.60	723.05	721.85	720.90	720.17	719.59	719.14	717.99	717.65	717.55
36000	757.64	753.31	749.95	747.34	745.30	743.71	742.47	741.50	740.74	740.15	739.68	738.50	738.15	738.05
37000	778.69	774.24	770.78	768.09	766.00	764.37	763.09	762.10	761.32	760.71	760.23	759.01	758.66	758.55
38000	799.74	795.16	791.61	788.85	786.70	785.03	783.72	782.69	781.89	781.27	780.78	779.53	779.16	779.05
39000	820.78	816.09	812.45	809.61	807.41	805.69	804.34	803.29	802.47	801.83	801.32	800.04	799.66	799.55
40000	841.83	837.01	833.28	830.37	828.11	826.34	824.97	823.89	823.05	822.39	821.87	820.56	820.17	820.05
41000	862.87	857.94	854.11	851.13	848.81	847.00	845.59	844.49	843.62	842.95	842.42	841.07	840.67	840.55
42000	883.92	878.86	874.94	871.89	869.51	867.66	866.21	865.08	864.20	863.51	862.96	861.58	861.18	861.06
43000	904.96	899.79	895.77	892.65	890.22	888.32	886.84	885.68	884.77	884.07	883.51	882.10	881.68	881.56
44000	926.01	920.71	916.60	913.41	910.92	908.98	907.46	906.28	905.35	904.63	904.06	902.61	902.18	902.06
45000	947.05	941.64	937.44	934.17	931.62	929.64	928.09	926.87	925.93	925.18	924.60	923.13	922.69	922.56
46000	968.10	962.56	958.27	954.93	952.33	950.30	948.71	947.47	946.50	945.74	945.15	943.64	943.19	943.06
47000	989.14	983.49	979.10	975.69	973.03	970.95	969.33	968.07	967.08	966.30	965.70	964.15	963.70	963.56
48000	1010.19	1004.41	999.93	996.45	993.73	991.61	989.96	988.67	987.65	986.86	986.24	984.67	984.20	984.06
49000	1031.24	1025.34	1020.76	1017.20	1014.43	1012.27	1010.58	1009.26	1008.23	1007.42	1006.79	1005.18	1004.70	1004.56
50000	1052.28	1046.26	1041.59	1037.96	1035.14	1032.93	1031.21	1029.86	1028.81	1027.98	1027.34	1025.69	1025.21	1025.07
55000	1157.51	1150.89	1145.75	1141.76	1138.65	1136.22	1134.33	1132.84	1131.69	1130.78	1130.07	1128.26	1127.73	1127.57
60000	1262.74	1255.52	1249.91	1245.56	1242.16	1239.51	1237.45	1235.83	1234.57	1233.58	1232.80	1230.83	1230.25	1230.08
65000	1367.96	1360.14	1354.07	1349.35	1345.67	1342.81	1340.57	1338.82	1337.45	1336.38	1335.54	1333.40	1332.77	1332.58
70000	1473.19	1464.77	1458.23	1453.15	1449.19	1446.10	1443.69	1441.80	1440.33	1439.17	1438.27	1435.97	1435.29	1435.09
75000	1578.42	1569.39	1562.39	1556.94	1552.70	1549.39	1546.81	1544.79	1543.21	1541.97	1541.00	1538.54	1537.81	1537.60
80000	1683.65	1674.02	1666.55	1660.74	1656.21	1652.68	1649.93	1647.77	1646.09	1644.77	1643.74	1641.11	1640.33	1640.10
85000	1788.88	1778.65	1770.71	1764.54	1759.73	1755.98	1753.05	1750.76	1748.97	1747.57	1746.47	1743.68	1742.85	1742.61
90000	1894.10	1883.27	1874.87	1868.33	1863.24	1859.27	1856.17	1853.74	1851.85	1850.36	1849.20	1846.25	1845.37	1845.11
95000	1999.33	1987.90	1979.03	1972.13	1966.75	1962.56	1959.29	1956.73	1954.73	1953.16	1951.94	1948.81	1947.89	1947.62
100000	2104.56	2092.52	2083.18	2075.92	2070.27	2065.85	2062.41	2059.71	2057.61	2055.96	2054.67	2051.38	2050.41	2050.13

MONTHLY PAYMENT
REQUIRED TO AMORTIZE A LOAN

TERM AMOUNT	1 Year	2 Years	3 Years	4 Years	5 Years	6 Years	7 Years	8 Years	9 Years	10 Years	11 Years	12 Years	13 Years	14 Years
5	.48	.27	.20	.17	.15	.14	.13	.12	.12	.12	.12	.11	.11	.11
10	.95	.54	.40	.33	.30	.27	.26	.24	.24	.23	.23	.22	.22	.22
15	1.43	.80	.60	.50	.44	.41	.38	.36	.35	.34	.34	.33	.33	.32
25	2.38	1.33	.99	.83	.73	.67	.63	.60	.58	.57	.56	.55	.54	.54
50	4.75	2.66	1.98	1.65	1.46	1.34	1.26	1.20	1.16	1.13	1.11	1.09	1.08	1.07
75	7.12	3.99	2.97	2.48	2.19	2.01	1.89	1.80	1.74	1.69	1.66	1.63	1.61	1.60
100	9.49	5.32	3.96	3.30	2.92	2.68	2.51	2.40	2.31	2.25	2.21	2.17	2.15	2.13
200	18.98	10.64	7.92	6.59	5.83	5.35	5.02	4.79	4.62	4.50	4.41	4.33	4.23	4.25
300	28.46	15.96	11.87	9.89	8.74	8.03	7.53	7.18	6.93	6.75	6.61	6.51	6.43	6.37
400	37.95	21.28	15.83	13.18	11.66	10.69	10.03	9.57	9.24	9.00	8.82	8.68	8.57	8.49
500	47.44	26.60	19.79	16.48	14.57	13.36	12.54	11.97	11.55	11.25	11.02	10.85	10.72	10.62
600	56.92	31.92	23.74	19.77	17.48	16.03	15.05	14.36	13.86	13.50	13.22	13.02	12.86	12.74
700	66.41	37.23	27.70	23.07	20.40	18.70	17.56	16.75	16.17	15.74	15.43	15.18	15.00	14.86
800	75.89	42.55	31.65	26.36	23.31	21.37	20.06	19.14	18.48	17.99	17.63	17.35	17.14	16.98
900	85.38	47.87	35.61	29.66	26.22	24.04	22.57	21.54	20.79	20.24	19.83	19.52	19.28	19.10
1000	94.87	53.19	39.57	32.95	29.14	26.71	25.08	23.93	23.10	22.49	22.03	21.69	21.43	21.23
2000	189.73	106.37	79.13	65.90	58.27	53.42	50.15	47.85	46.20	44.98	44.06	43.37	42.85	42.45
3000	284.59	159.56	118.69	98.85	87.40	80.13	75.22	71.78	69.29	67.46	66.09	65.06	64.27	63.67
4000	379.45	212.74	158.25	131.80	116.53	106.84	100.29	95.70	92.39	89.95	88.12	86.74	85.69	84.89
5000	474.32	265.92	197.81	164.75	145.66	133.54	125.37	119.63	115.48	112.43	110.15	108.43	107.11	106.11
6000	569.18	319.11	237.38	197.69	174.80	160.25	150.44	143.55	138.58	134.92	132.18	130.11	128.53	127.33
7000	664.04	372.29	276.94	230.64	203.93	186.96	175.51	167.48	161.68	157.40	154.21	151.80	149.96	148.55
8000	758.90	425.47	316.50	263.59	233.06	213.67	200.58	191.40	184.77	179.89	176.24	173.48	171.38	169.77
9000	853.77	478.66	356.06	296.54	262.19	240.37	225.66	215.33	207.87	202.37	198.27	195.16	192.80	190.99
10000	948.63	531.84	395.62	329.49	291.32	267.08	250.73	239.25	230.96	224.86	220.30	216.85	214.22	212.21
11000	1043.49	585.02	435.18	362.44	320.46	293.79	275.80	263.17	254.06	247.34	242.33	238.53	235.64	233.43
12000	1138.35	638.21	474.75	395.38	349.59	320.50	300.87	287.10	277.15	269.83	264.36	260.22	257.06	254.65
13000	1233.22	691.39	514.31	428.33	378.72	347.20	325.95	311.02	300.25	292.32	286.38	281.90	278.49	275.87
14000	1328.08	744.57	553.87	461.28	407.85	373.91	351.02	334.95	323.35	314.80	308.41	303.59	299.91	297.09
15000	1422.94	797.76	593.43	494.23	436.98	400.62	376.09	358.87	346.44	337.29	330.44	325.27	321.33	318.31
16000	1517.80	850.94	632.99	527.18	466.12	427.33	401.16	382.80	369.54	359.77	352.47	346.96	342.75	339.53
17000	1612.66	904.13	672.55	560.13	495.25	454.03	426.24	406.72	392.63	382.26	374.50	368.64	364.17	360.75
18000	1707.53	957.31	712.12	593.07	524.38	480.74	451.31	430.65	415.73	404.74	396.53	390.32	385.59	381.97
19000	1802.39	1010.49	751.68	626.02	553.51	507.45	476.38	454.57	438.83	427.23	418.56	412.01	407.02	403.19
20000	1897.25	1063.68	791.24	658.97	582.64	534.16	501.45	478.49	461.92	449.71	440.59	433.69	428.44	424.41
21000	1992.11	1116.86	830.80	691.92	611.77	560.86	526.52	502.42	485.02	472.20	462.62	455.38	449.86	445.63
22000	2086.98	1170.04	870.36	724.87	640.91	587.57	551.60	526.34	508.11	494.68	484.65	477.06	471.28	466.85
23000	2181.84	1223.23	909.93	757.82	670.04	614.28	576.67	550.27	531.21	517.17	506.68	498.75	492.70	488.07
24000	2276.70	1276.41	949.49	790.76	699.17	640.99	601.74	574.19	554.30	539.66	528.71	520.43	514.12	509.29
25000	2371.56	1329.59	989.05	823.71	728.30	667.69	626.81	598.12	577.40	562.14	550.74	542.12	535.55	530.51
26000	2466.43	1382.78	1028.61	856.66	757.43	694.40	651.89	622.04	600.50	584.63	572.76	563.80	556.97	551.73
27000	2561.29	1435.96	1068.17	889.61	786.57	721.11	676.96	645.97	623.59	607.11	594.79	585.48	578.39	572.95
28000	2656.15	1489.14	1107.73	922.56	815.70	747.82	702.03	669.89	646.69	629.60	616.82	607.17	599.81	594.17
29000	2751.01	1542.33	1147.30	955.51	844.83	774.52	727.10	693.81	669.78	652.08	638.85	628.85	621.23	615.39
30000	2845.87	1595.51	1186.86	988.45	873.96	801.23	752.18	717.74	692.88	674.57	660.88	650.54	642.65	636.61
31000	2940.74	1648.70	1226.42	1021.40	903.09	827.94	777.25	741.66	715.97	697.05	682.91	672.22	664.08	657.83
32000	3035.60	1701.88	1265.98	1054.35	932.23	854.65	802.32	765.59	739.07	719.54	704.94	693.91	685.50	679.05
33000	3130.46	1755.06	1305.54	1087.30	961.36	881.35	827.39	789.51	762.17	742.02	726.97	715.59	706.92	700.27
34000	3225.32	1808.25	1345.10	1120.25	990.49	908.06	852.47	813.44	785.26	764.51	749.00	737.28	728.34	721.49
35000	3320.19	1861.43	1384.67	1153.20	1019.62	934.77	877.54	837.36	808.36	787.00	771.03	758.96	749.76	742.71
36000	3415.05	1914.61	1424.23	1186.14	1048.75	961.48	902.61	861.29	831.45	809.48	793.06	780.64	771.18	763.93
37000	3509.91	1967.80	1463.79	1219.09	1077.88	988.18	927.68	885.21	854.55	831.97	815.09	802.33	792.61	785.15
38000	3604.77	2020.98	1503.35	1252.04	1107.02	1014.89	952.75	909.13	877.65	854.45	837.12	824.01	814.03	806.37
39000	3699.64	2074.16	1542.91	1284.99	1136.15	1041.60	977.83	933.06	900.74	876.94	859.14	845.70	835.45	827.59
40000	3794.50	2127.35	1582.48	1317.94	1165.28	1068.31	1002.90	956.98	923.84	899.42	881.17	867.38	856.87	848.81
41000	3889.36	2180.53	1622.04	1350.89	1194.41	1095.01	1027.97	980.91	946.93	921.91	903.20	889.07	878.29	870.03
42000	3984.22	2233.71	1661.60	1383.83	1223.54	1121.72	1053.04	1004.83	970.03	944.39	925.23	910.75	899.71	891.25
43000	4079.08	2286.90	1701.16	1416.78	1252.68	1148.43	1078.12	1028.76	993.12	966.88	947.26	932.43	921.14	912.47
44000	4173.95	2340.08	1740.72	1449.73	1281.81	1175.14	1103.19	1052.68	1016.22	989.36	969.29	954.12	942.56	933.69
45000	4268.81	2393.26	1780.28	1482.68	1310.94	1201.84	1128.26	1076.61	1039.32	1011.85	991.32	975.80	963.98	954.91
46000	4363.67	2446.45	1819.85	1515.63	1340.07	1228.55	1153.33	1100.53	1062.41	1034.34	1013.35	997.49	985.40	976.13
47000	4458.53	2499.63	1859.41	1548.58	1369.20	1255.26	1178.41	1124.45	1085.51	1056.82	1035.38	1019.17	1006.82	997.35
48000	4553.40	2552.82	1898.97	1581.52	1398.34	1281.97	1203.48	1148.38	1108.60	1079.31	1057.41	1040.86	1028.24	1018.57
49000	4648.26	2606.00	1938.53	1614.47	1427.47	1308.67	1228.55	1172.30	1131.70	1101.79	1079.44	1062.54	1049.67	1039.79
50000	4743.12	2659.18	1978.09	1647.42	1456.60	1335.38	1253.62	1196.23	1154.79	1124.28	1101.47	1084.23	1071.09	1061.01
55000	5217.43	2925.10	2175.90	1812.16	1602.26	1468.92	1378.99	1315.85	1270.27	1236.70	1211.61	1192.65	1178.20	1167.11
60000	5691.74	3191.02	2373.71	1976.90	1747.92	1602.46	1504.35	1435.47	1385.75	1349.13	1321.76	1301.07	1285.30	1273.21
65000	6166.06	3456.94	2571.52	2141.65	1893.58	1735.99	1629.71	1555.10	1501.23	1461.56	1431.90	1409.49	1392.41	1379.31
70000	6640.37	3722.85	2769.33	2306.39	2039.24	1869.53	1755.07	1674.72	1616.71	1573.99	1542.05	1517.91	1499.52	1485.42
75000	7114.68	3988.77	2967.14	2471.13	2184.90	2003.07	1880.43	1794.34	1732.19	1686.41	1652.20	1626.34	1606.63	1591.52
80000	7588.99	4254.69	3164.95	2635.87	2330.56	2136.61	2005.79	1913.96	1847.67	1798.84	1762.34	1734.76	1713.74	1697.62
85000	8063.30	4520.61	3362.75	2800.61	2476.21	2270.14	2131.16	2033.58	1963.15	1911.27	1872.49	1843.18	1820.85	1803.72
90000	8537.61	4786.52	3560.56	2965.35	2621.87	2403.68	2256.52	2153.21	2078.63	2023.69	1982.63	1951.60	1927.95	1909.82
95000	9011.93	5052.44	3758.37	3130.10	2767.53	2537.22	2381.88	2272.83	2194.11	2136.12	2092.78	2060.02	2035.06	2015.92
100000	9486.24	5318.36	3956.18	3294.84	2913.19	2670.76	2507.24	2392.45	2309.58	2248.55	2202.93	2168.45	2142.17	2122.02

MONTHLY PAYMENT
REQUIRED TO AMORTIZE A LOAN
24.625%

TERM	15 Years	16 Years	17 Years	18 Years	19 Years	20 Years	21 Years	22 Years	23 Years	24 Years	25 Years	30 Years	35 Years	40 Years
AMOUNT														
5	.11	.11	.11	.11	.11	.11	.11	.11	.11	.11	.11	.11	.11	.11
10	.22	.21	.21	.21	.21	.21	.21	.21	.21	.21	.21	.21	.21	.21
15	.32	.32	.32	.32	.32	.32	.31	.31	.31	.31	.31	.31	.31	.31
25	.53	.53	.53	.52	.52	.52	.52	.52	.52	.52	.52	.52	.52	.52
50	1.06	1.05	1.05	1.04	1.04	1.04	1.04	1.04	1.03	1.03	1.03	1.03	1.03	1.03
75	1.58	1.58	1.57	1.56	1.56	1.56	1.55	1.55	1.55	1.55	1.55	1.55	1.54	1.54
100	2.11	2.10	2.09	2.08	2.08	2.07	2.07	2.07	2.06	2.06	2.06	2.06	2.06	2.06
200	4.22	4.19	4.18	4.16	4.15	4.14	4.13	4.13	4.12	4.12	4.12	4.11	4.11	4.11
300	6.32	6.29	6.26	6.24	6.22	6.21	6.20	6.19	6.18	6.18	6.18	6.17	6.16	6.16
400	8.43	8.38	8.35	8.32	8.29	8.28	8.26	8.25	8.24	8.24	8.23	8.22	8.21	8.21
500	10.54	10.48	10.43	10.39	10.37	10.34	10.33	10.31	10.30	10.30	10.29	10.27	10.27	10.27
600	12.64	12.57	12.52	12.47	12.44	12.41	12.39	12.38	12.36	12.35	12.35	12.33	12.32	12.32
700	14.75	14.67	14.60	14.55	14.51	14.48	14.46	14.44	14.42	14.41	14.40	14.38	14.37	14.37
800	16.86	16.76	16.69	16.63	16.58	16.55	16.52	16.50	16.48	16.47	16.46	16.43	16.42	16.42
900	18.96	18.86	18.77	18.71	18.66	18.62	18.58	18.56	18.54	18.53	18.52	18.49	18.48	18.47
1000	21.07	20.95	20.86	20.78	20.73	20.68	20.65	20.62	20.60	20.59	20.57	20.54	20.53	20.53
2000	42.13	41.89	41.71	41.56	41.45	41.36	41.29	41.24	41.20	41.17	41.14	41.07	41.05	41.05
3000	63.20	62.84	62.56	62.34	62.17	62.04	61.94	61.86	61.79	61.75	61.71	61.61	61.58	61.57
4000	84.26	83.78	83.41	83.12	82.90	82.72	82.58	82.47	82.39	82.33	82.27	82.14	82.10	82.09
5000	105.33	104.73	104.26	103.90	103.62	103.40	103.23	103.09	102.99	102.91	102.84	102.68	102.63	102.62
6000	126.39	125.67	125.11	124.68	124.34	124.08	123.87	123.71	123.58	123.49	123.41	123.21	123.15	123.14
7000	147.46	146.62	145.97	145.46	145.06	144.76	144.52	144.33	144.18	144.07	143.98	143.75	143.68	143.66
8000	168.52	167.56	166.82	166.24	165.79	165.43	165.16	164.94	164.78	164.65	164.54	164.28	164.20	164.18
9000	189.59	188.51	187.67	187.02	186.51	186.11	185.80	185.56	185.37	185.23	185.11	184.82	184.73	184.70
10000	210.65	209.45	208.52	207.80	207.23	206.79	206.45	206.18	205.97	205.81	205.68	205.35	205.25	205.23
11000	231.72	230.40	229.37	228.58	227.95	227.47	227.09	226.80	226.57	226.39	226.24	225.88	225.78	225.75
12000	252.78	251.34	250.22	249.35	248.68	248.15	247.74	247.41	247.16	246.97	246.81	246.42	246.30	246.27
13000	273.85	272.29	271.08	270.13	269.40	268.83	268.38	268.03	267.76	267.55	267.38	266.95	266.83	266.79
14000	294.91	293.23	291.93	290.91	290.12	289.51	289.03	288.65	288.36	288.13	287.95	287.49	287.35	287.31
15000	315.90	314.18	312.78	311.69	310.85	310.19	309.67	309.27	308.95	308.71	308.51	308.02	307.88	307.84
16000	337.04	335.12	333.63	332.47	331.57	330.86	330.31	329.88	329.55	329.29	329.08	328.56	328.40	328.36
17000	358.11	356.07	354.48	353.25	352.29	351.54	350.96	350.50	350.15	349.07	349.65	349.09	348.93	348.88
18000	379.17	377.01	375.33	374.03	373.01	372.22	371.60	371.12	370.74	370.45	370.22	369.63	369.45	369.40
19000	400.24	397.96	396.18	394.81	393.74	392.90	392.25	391.74	391.34	391.03	390.78	390.16	389.98	389.92
20000	421.30	418.90	417.04	415.59	414.46	413.58	412.89	412.35	411.94	411.61	411.35	410.70	410.50	410.45
21000	442.37	439.84	437.89	436.37	435.18	434.26	433.54	432.97	432.53	432.19	431.92	431.23	431.03	430.97
22000	463.43	460.79	458.74	457.15	455.90	454.94	454.18	453.59	453.13	452.77	452.48	451.76	451.55	451.49
23000	484.50	481.73	479.59	477.92	476.63	475.61	474.82	474.21	473.72	473.35	473.05	472.30	472.08	472.01
24000	505.56	502.68	500.44	498.70	497.35	496.29	495.47	494.82	494.32	493.93	493.62	492.83	492.60	492.53
25000	526.63	523.62	521.29	519.48	518.07	516.97	516.11	515.44	514.92	514.51	514.19	513.37	513.13	513.06
26000	547.69	544.57	542.15	540.26	538.80	537.65	536.76	536.06	535.51	535.09	534.75	533.90	533.65	533.58
27000	568.76	565.51	563.00	561.04	559.52	558.33	557.40	556.68	556.11	555.67	555.32	554.44	554.18	554.10
28000	589.82	586.46	583.85	581.82	580.24	579.01	578.05	577.29	576.71	576.25	575.89	574.97	574.70	574.62
29000	610.89	607.40	604.70	602.60	600.96	599.69	598.69	597.91	597.30	596.83	596.46	595.51	595.23	595.14
30000	631.95	628.35	625.55	623.38	621.69	620.37	619.34	618.53	617.90	617.41	617.02	616.04	615.75	615.67
31000	653.02	649.29	646.40	644.16	642.41	641.04	639.98	639.15	638.50	637.99	637.59	636.58	636.28	636.19
32000	674.08	670.24	667.26	664.94	663.13	661.72	660.62	659.76	659.09	658.57	658.16	657.11	656.80	656.71
33000	695.15	691.18	688.11	685.72	683.85	682.40	681.27	680.38	679.69	679.15	678.72	677.64	677.33	677.23
34000	716.21	712.13	708.96	706.50	704.58	703.08	701.91	701.00	700.29	699.73	699.29	698.18	697.85	697.75
35000	737.28	733.07	729.81	727.27	725.30	723.76	722.56	721.62	720.88	720.31	719.86	718.71	718.38	718.28
36000	758.34	754.02	750.66	748.05	746.02	744.44	743.20	742.23	741.48	740.89	740.43	739.25	738.90	738.80
37000	779.40	774.96	771.51	768.83	766.74	765.12	763.85	762.85	762.08	761.47	760.99	759.78	759.43	759.32
38000	800.47	795.91	792.36	789.61	787.47	785.80	784.49	783.47	782.67	782.05	781.56	780.32	779.95	779.84
39000	821.53	816.85	813.22	810.39	808.19	806.47	805.13	804.09	803.27	802.63	802.13	800.85	800.48	800.36
40000	842.60	837.79	834.07	831.17	828.91	827.15	825.78	824.70	823.87	823.21	822.69	821.39	821.00	820.89
41000	863.66	858.74	854.92	851.95	849.64	847.83	846.42	845.32	844.46	843.79	843.26	841.92	841.53	841.41
42000	884.73	879.68	875.77	872.73	870.36	868.51	867.07	865.94	865.06	864.37	863.83	862.46	862.05	861.93
43000	905.79	900.63	896.62	893.51	891.08	889.19	887.71	886.56	885.65	884.95	884.40	882.99	882.57	882.45
44000	926.86	921.57	917.47	914.29	911.80	909.87	908.36	907.17	906.25	905.53	904.96	903.52	903.10	902.97
45000	947.92	942.52	938.33	935.07	932.53	930.55	929.00	927.79	926.85	926.11	925.53	924.06	923.62	923.50
46000	968.99	963.46	959.18	955.84	953.25	951.22	949.64	948.41	947.44	946.69	946.10	944.59	944.15	944.02
47000	990.05	984.41	980.03	976.62	973.97	971.90	970.29	969.03	968.04	967.27	966.67	965.13	964.67	964.54
48000	1011.12	1005.35	1000.88	997.40	994.69	992.58	990.93	989.64	988.64	987.85	987.23	985.66	985.20	985.06
49000	1032.18	1026.30	1021.73	1018.18	1015.42	1013.26	1011.58	1010.26	1009.23	1008.43	1007.80	1006.20	1005.72	1005.58
50000	1053.25	1047.24	1042.58	1038.96	1036.14	1033.94	1032.22	1030.88	1029.83	1029.01	1028.37	1026.73	1026.25	1026.11
55000	1158.57	1151.97	1146.84	1142.86	1139.75	1137.33	1135.44	1133.97	1132.81	1131.91	1131.20	1129.40	1128.87	1128.72
60000	1263.90	1256.69	1251.10	1246.75	1243.37	1240.73	1238.67	1237.05	1235.80	1234.81	1234.04	1232.08	1231.50	1231.33
65000	1369.22	1361.41	1355.36	1350.65	1346.98	1344.12	1341.89	1340.14	1338.78	1337.71	1336.88	1334.75	1334.12	1333.94
70000	1474.55	1466.14	1459.61	1454.54	1450.59	1447.51	1445.11	1443.23	1441.76	1440.61	1439.71	1437.42	1436.75	1436.55
75000	1579.87	1570.86	1563.87	1558.44	1554.21	1550.91	1548.33	1546.32	1544.74	1543.51	1542.55	1540.09	1539.37	1539.16
80000	1685.19	1675.58	1668.13	1662.33	1657.82	1654.30	1651.55	1649.40	1647.73	1646.41	1645.38	1642.77	1642.00	1641.77
85000	1790.52	1780.31	1772.39	1766.23	1761.43	1757.69	1754.77	1752.49	1750.71	1749.31	1748.22	1745.44	1744.62	1744.38
90000	1895.84	1885.03	1876.65	1870.13	1865.05	1861.09	1858.00	1855.58	1853.69	1852.21	1851.06	1848.11	1847.24	1846.99
95000	2001.17	1989.76	1980.92	1974.02	1968.66	1964.49	1961.22	1958.67	1956.67	1955.11	1953.89	1950.79	1949.87	1949.60
100000	2106.49	2094.48	2085.16	2077.92	2072.27	2067.87	2064.44	2061.75	2059.66	2058.01	2056.73	2053.46	2052.49	2052.21

MONTHLY PAYMENT
REQUIRED TO AMORTIZE A LOAN

TERM	1 Year	2 Years	3 Years	4 Years	5 Years	6 Years	7 Years	8 Years	9 Years	10 Years	11 Years	12 Years	13 Years	14 Years
AMOUNT														
5	.48	.27	.20	.17	.15	.14	.13	.12	.12	.12	.12	.11	.11	.11
10	.95	.54	.40	.33	.30	.27	.26	.24	.24	.23	.23	.22	.22	.22
15	1.43	.80	.60	.50	.44	.41	.38	.36	.35	.34	.34	.33	.33	.32
25	2.38	1.34	1.00	.83	.73	.67	.63	.60	.58	.57	.56	.55	.54	.54
50	4.75	2.67	1.99	1.65	1.46	1.34	1.26	1.20	1.16	1.13	1.11	1.09	1.08	1.07
75	7.12	4.00	2.98	2.48	2.19	2.01	1.89	1.80	1.74	1.70	1.66	1.64	1.62	1.60
100	9.49	5.33	3.97	3.30	2.92	2.68	2.52	2.40	2.32	2.26	2.21	2.18	2.15	2.13
200	18.98	10.65	7.93	6.60	5.84	5.36	5.03	4.80	4.63	4.51	4.42	4.35	4.30	4.26
300	28.47	15.97	11.89	9.90	8.76	8.03	7.54	7.20	6.95	6.77	6.63	6.53	6.45	6.39
400	37.96	21.29	15.85	13.20	11.68	10.71	10.05	9.59	9.26	9.02	8.84	8.70	8.60	8.52
500	47.45	26.62	19.81	16.50	14.59	13.38	12.57	11.99	11.58	11.27	11.05	10.87	10.74	10.64
600	56.94	31.94	23.77	19.80	17.51	16.06	15.08	14.39	13.89	13.53	13.25	13.05	12.89	12.77
700	66.43	37.26	27.73	23.10	20.43	18.73	17.59	16.79	16.21	15.78	15.46	15.22	15.04	14.90
800	75.92	42.58	31.69	26.40	23.35	21.41	20.10	19.18	18.52	18.04	17.67	17.40	17.19	17.03
900	85.41	47.90	35.65	29.70	26.26	24.08	22.61	21.58	20.84	20.29	19.88	19.57	19.34	19.15
1000	94.90	53.23	39.61	33.00	29.18	26.76	25.13	23.98	23.15	22.54	22.09	21.74	21.48	21.28
2000	189.80	106.45	79.21	65.99	58.36	53.51	50.25	47.95	46.30	45.08	44.17	43.48	42.96	42.56
3000	284.70	159.67	118.81	98.98	87.53	80.27	75.37	71.93	69.45	67.62	66.25	65.22	64.44	63.84
4000	379.60	212.89	158.41	131.97	116.71	107.02	100.49	95.90	92.59	90.16	88.34	86.96	85.92	85.11
5000	474.50	266.11	198.01	164.96	145.88	133.77	125.61	119.88	115.74	112.70	110.42	108.70	107.39	106.39
6000	569.40	319.33	237.61	197.95	175.06	160.53	150.73	143.85	138.89	135.23	132.50	130.44	128.87	127.67
7000	664.30	372.55	277.21	230.94	204.23	187.28	175.85	167.82	162.03	157.77	154.59	152.18	150.35	148.95
8000	759.19	425.77	316.82	263.93	233.41	214.03	200.97	191.80	185.18	180.31	176.67	173.92	171.83	170.22
9000	854.09	479.00	356.42	296.92	262.59	240.79	226.09	215.77	208.33	202.85	198.75	195.66	193.31	191.50
10000	948.99	532.22	396.02	329.91	291.76	267.54	251.21	239.75	231.47	225.39	220.84	217.40	214.78	212.78
11000	1043.89	585.44	435.62	362.90	320.94	294.29	276.33	263.72	254.62	247.92	242.92	239.14	236.26	234.06
12000	1138.79	638.66	475.22	395.89	350.11	321.05	301.45	287.69	277.77	270.46	265.00	260.88	257.74	255.33
13000	1233.69	691.88	514.82	428.88	379.29	347.80	326.57	311.67	300.92	293.00	287.09	282.62	279.22	276.61
14000	1328.59	745.10	554.42	461.87	408.46	374.55	351.69	335.64	324.06	315.54	309.17	304.36	300.70	297.89
15000	1423.49	798.32	594.02	494.86	437.64	401.31	376.81	359.62	347.21	338.08	331.25	326.10	322.17	319.17
16000	1518.38	851.54	633.63	527.85	466.82	428.06	401.93	383.59	370.36	360.62	353.34	347.84	343.65	340.44
17000	1613.28	904.76	673.23	560.84	495.99	454.81	427.05	407.56	393.50	383.15	375.42	369.58	365.13	361.72
18000	1708.18	957.99	712.83	593.83	525.17	481.57	452.17	431.54	416.65	405.69	397.50	391.32	386.61	383.00
19000	1803.08	1011.21	752.43	626.82	554.34	508.32	477.29	455.51	439.80	428.23	419.59	413.06	408.09	404.27
20000	1897.98	1064.43	792.03	659.81	583.52	535.07	502.41	479.49	462.94	450.77	441.67	434.80	429.56	425.55
21000	1992.88	1117.65	831.63	692.80	612.69	561.83	527.53	503.46	486.09	473.31	463.75	456.54	451.04	446.83
22000	2087.78	1170.87	871.23	725.79	641.87	588.58	552.65	527.43	509.24	495.84	485.84	478.28	472.52	468.11
23000	2182.67	1224.09	910.84	758.78	671.05	615.33	577.77	551.41	532.39	518.38	507.92	500.02	494.00	489.38
24000	2277.57	1277.31	950.44	791.77	700.22	642.09	602.89	575.38	555.53	540.92	530.00	521.76	515.48	510.66
25000	2372.47	1330.53	990.04	824.76	729.40	668.84	628.01	599.36	578.68	563.46	552.09	543.50	536.95	531.94
26000	2467.37	1383.75	1029.64	857.75	758.57	695.59	653.13	623.33	601.83	586.00	574.17	565.24	558.43	553.22
27000	2562.27	1436.98	1069.24	890.74	787.75	722.35	678.25	647.30	624.97	608.53	596.25	586.98	579.91	574.49
28000	2657.17	1490.20	1108.84	923.73	816.92	749.10	703.37	671.28	648.12	631.07	618.34	608.71	601.39	595.77
29000	2752.07	1543.42	1148.44	956.72	846.10	775.85	728.49	695.25	671.27	653.61	640.42	630.45	622.87	617.05
30000	2846.97	1596.64	1188.04	989.71	875.28	802.61	753.61	719.23	694.41	676.15	662.50	652.19	644.34	638.33
31000	2941.86	1649.86	1227.65	1022.70	904.45	829.36	778.73	743.20	717.56	698.69	684.59	673.93	665.82	659.60
32000	3036.76	1703.08	1267.25	1055.69	933.63	856.11	803.85	767.17	740.71	721.23	706.67	695.67	687.30	680.88
33000	3131.66	1756.30	1306.85	1088.68	962.80	882.87	828.97	791.15	763.86	743.76	728.75	717.41	708.78	702.16
34000	3226.56	1809.52	1346.45	1121.67	991.98	909.62	854.09	815.12	787.00	766.30	750.84	739.15	730.25	723.44
35000	3321.46	1862.74	1386.05	1154.66	1021.15	936.37	879.21	839.10	810.15	788.84	772.92	760.89	751.73	744.71
36000	3416.36	1915.97	1425.65	1187.65	1050.33	963.13	904.33	863.07	833.30	811.38	795.00	782.63	773.21	765.99
37000	3511.26	1969.19	1465.25	1220.64	1079.51	989.88	929.45	887.04	856.44	833.92	817.08	804.37	794.69	787.27
38000	3606.15	2022.41	1504.86	1253.63	1108.68	1016.63	954.57	911.02	879.59	856.45	839.17	826.11	816.17	808.54
39000	3701.05	2075.63	1544.46	1286.62	1137.86	1043.39	979.69	934.99	902.74	878.99	861.25	847.85	837.64	829.82
40000	3795.95	2128.85	1584.06	1319.61	1167.03	1070.14	1004.81	958.97	925.88	901.53	883.33	869.59	859.12	851.10
41000	3890.85	2182.07	1623.66	1352.60	1196.21	1096.89	1029.93	982.94	949.03	924.07	905.42	891.33	880.60	872.38
42000	3985.75	2235.29	1663.26	1385.59	1225.38	1123.65	1055.05	1006.91	972.18	946.61	927.50	913.07	902.08	893.65
43000	4080.65	2288.51	1702.86	1418.58	1254.56	1150.40	1080.17	1030.89	995.33	969.14	949.58	934.81	923.56	914.93
44000	4175.55	2341.73	1742.46	1451.57	1283.74	1177.15	1105.29	1054.86	1018.47	991.68	971.67	956.55	945.03	936.21
45000	4270.45	2394.96	1782.06	1484.56	1312.91	1203.91	1130.41	1078.84	1041.62	1014.22	993.75	978.29	966.51	957.49
46000	4365.34	2448.18	1821.67	1517.55	1342.09	1230.66	1155.53	1102.81	1064.77	1036.76	1015.83	1000.03	987.99	978.76
47000	4460.24	2501.40	1861.27	1550.54	1371.26	1257.41	1180.65	1126.78	1087.91	1059.30	1037.92	1021.77	1009.47	1000.04
48000	4555.14	2554.62	1900.87	1583.53	1400.44	1284.17	1205.77	1150.76	1111.06	1081.84	1060.00	1043.51	1030.95	1021.32
49000	4650.04	2607.84	1940.47	1616.52	1429.61	1310.92	1230.89	1174.73	1134.21	1104.37	1082.08	1065.25	1052.42	1042.60
50000	4744.94	2661.06	1980.07	1649.51	1458.79	1337.67	1256.01	1198.71	1157.35	1126.91	1104.17	1086.99	1073.90	1063.87
55000	5219.43	2927.17	2178.08	1814.46	1604.67	1471.44	1381.61	1318.58	1273.09	1239.60	1214.58	1195.69	1181.29	1170.26
60000	5693.93	3193.27	2376.08	1979.41	1750.55	1605.21	1507.21	1438.45	1388.82	1352.29	1325.00	1304.38	1288.68	1276.65
65000	6168.42	3459.38	2574.09	2144.36	1896.43	1738.98	1632.81	1558.32	1504.56	1464.98	1435.42	1413.08	1396.07	1383.03
70000	6642.91	3725.48	2772.10	2309.31	2042.30	1872.74	1758.41	1678.19	1620.29	1577.67	1545.83	1521.78	1503.46	1489.42
75000	7117.41	3991.59	2970.10	2474.26	2188.18	2006.51	1884.02	1798.06	1736.03	1690.36	1656.25	1630.48	1610.85	1595.81
80000	7591.90	4257.69	3168.11	2639.21	2334.06	2140.28	2009.62	1917.93	1851.76	1803.06	1766.66	1739.18	1718.24	1702.19
85000	8066.39	4523.80	3366.12	2804.16	2479.94	2274.04	2135.22	2037.80	1967.50	1915.75	1877.08	1847.88	1825.63	1808.58
90000	8540.89	4789.91	3564.12	2969.11	2625.82	2407.81	2260.82	2157.67	2083.23	2028.44	1987.50	1956.57	1933.02	1914.97
95000	9015.38	5056.01	3762.13	3134.06	2771.70	2541.58	2386.42	2277.54	2198.97	2141.13	2097.91	2065.27	2040.41	2021.35
100000	9489.87	5322.12	3960.14	3299.01	2917.58	2675.34	2512.02	2397.41	2314.70	2253.82	2208.33	2173.97	2147.80	2127.74

TERM	15 Years	16 Years	17 Years	18 Years	19 Years	20 Years	21 Years	22 Years	23 Years	24 Years	25 Years	30 Years	35 Years	40 Years
AMOUNT														
5	.11	.11	.11	.11	.11	.11	.11	.11	.11	.11	.11	.11	.11	.11
10	.22	.22	.21	.21	.21	.21	.21	.21	.21	.21	.21	.21	.21	.21
15	.32	.32	.32	.32	.32	.32	.32	.32	.31	.31	.31	.31	.31	.31
25	.53	.53	.53	.53	.52	.52	.52	.52	.52	.52	.52	.52	.52	.52
50	1.06	1.06	1.05	1.05	1.04	1.04	1.04	1.04	1.04	1.04	1.04	1.03	1.03	1.03
75	1.59	1.58	1.57	1.57	1.56	1.56	1.56	1.56	1.55	1.55	1.55	1.55	1.55	1.55
100	2.12	2.11	2.10	2.09	2.08	2.08	2.08	2.07	2.07	2.07	2.07	2.06	2.06	2.06
200	4.23	4.21	4.19	4.17	4.16	4.15	4.15	4.14	4.14	4.13	4.13	4.12	4.12	4.12
300	6.34	6.31	6.28	6.26	6.24	6.23	6.22	6.21	6.20	6.20	6.19	6.18	6.18	6.18
400	8.45	8.41	8.37	8.34	8.32	8.30	8.29	8.28	8.27	8.26	8.26	8.24	8.24	8.24
500	10.57	10.51	10.46	10.42	10.40	10.37	10.36	10.34	10.33	10.33	10.32	10.30	10.30	10.30
600	12.68	12.61	12.55	12.51	12.47	12.45	12.43	12.41	12.40	12.39	12.38	12.36	12.36	12.36
700	14.79	14.71	14.64	14.59	14.55	14.52	14.50	14.48	14.47	14.45	14.45	14.42	14.42	14.41
800	16.90	16.81	16.73	16.68	16.63	16.60	16.57	16.55	16.53	16.52	16.51	16.48	16.47	16.47
900	19.02	18.91	18.82	18.76	18.71	18.67	18.64	18.62	18.60	18.58	18.57	18.54	18.53	18.53
1000	21.13	21.01	20.92	20.84	20.79	20.74	20.71	20.68	20.66	20.65	20.63	20.60	20.59	20.59
2000	42.25	42.01	41.83	41.68	41.57	41.48	41.42	41.36	41.32	41.29	41.26	41.20	41.18	41.17
3000	63.37	63.02	62.74	62.52	62.35	62.22	62.12	62.04	61.98	61.93	61.89	61.80	61.77	61.76
4000	84.50	84.02	83.65	83.36	83.14	82.96	82.83	82.72	82.64	82.57	82.52	82.39	82.35	82.34
5000	105.62	105.02	104.56	104.20	103.92	103.70	103.53	103.40	103.29	103.21	103.15	102.99	102.94	102.93
6000	126.74	126.03	125.47	125.04	124.70	124.44	124.24	124.08	123.95	123.86	123.78	123.59	123.53	123.51
7000	147.87	147.03	146.38	145.88	145.49	145.18	144.94	144.76	144.61	144.50	144.41	144.18	144.12	144.10
8000	168.99	168.03	167.29	166.72	166.27	165.92	165.65	165.43	165.27	165.14	165.04	164.78	164.70	164.68
9000	190.11	189.04	188.20	187.56	187.05	186.66	186.35	186.11	185.93	185.78	185.67	185.38	185.29	185.27
10000	211.23	210.04	209.11	208.39	207.83	207.40	207.06	206.79	206.58	206.42	206.30	205.97	205.88	205.85
11000	232.36	231.04	230.02	229.23	228.62	228.14	227.76	227.47	227.24	227.06	226.92	226.57	226.47	226.43
12000	253.48	252.05	250.94	250.07	249.40	248.88	248.47	248.15	247.90	247.71	247.55	247.17	247.05	247.02
13000	274.60	273.05	271.85	270.91	270.18	269.62	269.17	268.83	268.56	268.35	268.18	267.76	267.64	267.60
14000	295.73	294.05	292.76	291.75	290.97	290.36	289.88	289.51	289.22	288.99	288.81	288.36	288.23	288.19
15000	316.85	315.06	313.67	312.59	311.75	311.10	310.58	310.19	309.87	309.63	309.44	308.96	308.81	308.77
16000	337.97	336.06	334.58	333.43	332.53	331.83	331.29	330.86	330.53	330.27	330.07	329.55	329.40	329.36
17000	359.09	357.06	355.49	354.27	353.32	352.57	352.00	351.54	351.19	350.91	350.70	350.15	349.99	349.94
18000	380.22	378.07	376.40	375.11	374.10	373.31	372.70	372.22	371.85	371.56	371.33	370.75	370.58	370.53
19000	401.34	399.07	397.31	395.95	394.88	394.05	393.41	392.90	392.51	392.20	391.96	391.34	391.16	391.11
20000	422.46	420.07	418.22	416.78	415.66	414.79	414.11	413.58	413.16	412.84	412.59	411.94	411.75	411.69
21000	443.59	441.08	439.13	437.62	436.45	435.53	434.82	434.26	433.82	433.48	433.21	432.54	432.34	432.28
22000	464.71	462.08	460.04	458.46	457.23	456.27	455.52	454.94	454.48	454.12	453.84	453.13	452.93	452.86
23000	485.83	483.08	480.96	479.30	478.01	477.01	476.23	475.62	475.14	474.76	474.47	473.73	473.51	473.45
24000	506.95	504.09	501.87	500.14	498.80	497.75	496.93	496.29	495.80	495.41	495.10	494.33	494.10	494.03
25000	528.08	525.09	522.78	520.98	519.58	518.49	517.64	516.97	516.45	516.05	515.73	514.92	514.69	514.62
26000	549.20	546.10	543.69	541.82	540.36	539.23	538.34	537.65	537.11	536.69	536.36	535.52	535.27	535.20
27000	570.32	567.10	564.60	562.66	561.15	559.97	559.05	558.33	557.77	557.33	556.99	556.12	555.86	555.79
28000	591.45	588.10	585.51	583.50	581.93	580.71	579.75	579.01	578.43	577.97	577.62	576.71	576.45	576.37
29000	612.57	609.11	606.42	604.33	602.71	601.45	600.46	599.69	599.09	598.62	598.25	597.31	597.04	596.96
30000	633.69	630.11	627.33	625.17	623.49	622.19	621.16	620.37	619.74	619.26	618.88	617.91	617.62	617.54
31000	654.81	651.11	648.24	646.01	644.28	642.92	641.87	641.05	640.40	639.90	639.51	638.50	638.21	638.12
32000	675.94	672.12	669.15	666.85	665.06	663.66	662.57	661.72	661.06	660.54	660.13	659.10	658.80	658.71
33000	697.06	693.12	690.06	687.69	685.84	684.40	683.28	682.40	681.72	681.18	680.76	679.70	679.39	679.29
34000	718.18	714.12	710.98	708.53	706.63	705.14	703.99	703.08	702.38	701.82	701.39	700.30	699.97	699.88
35000	739.31	735.13	731.89	729.37	727.41	725.88	724.69	723.76	723.03	722.47	722.02	720.89	720.56	720.46
36000	760.43	756.13	752.80	750.21	748.19	746.62	745.40	744.44	743.69	743.11	742.65	741.49	741.15	741.05
37000	781.55	777.13	773.71	771.05	768.98	767.36	766.10	765.12	764.35	763.75	763.28	762.09	761.73	761.63
38000	802.67	798.14	794.62	791.89	789.76	788.10	786.81	785.80	785.01	784.39	783.91	782.68	782.32	782.22
39000	823.80	819.14	815.53	812.72	810.54	808.84	807.51	806.48	805.67	805.03	804.54	803.28	802.91	802.80
40000	844.92	840.14	836.44	833.56	831.32	829.58	828.22	827.15	826.32	825.67	825.17	823.88	823.50	823.38
41000	866.04	861.15	857.35	854.40	852.11	850.32	848.92	847.83	846.98	846.32	845.80	844.47	844.08	843.97
42000	887.17	882.15	878.26	875.24	872.89	871.06	869.63	868.51	867.64	866.96	866.42	865.07	864.67	864.55
43000	908.29	903.15	899.17	896.08	893.67	891.80	890.33	889.19	888.30	887.60	887.05	885.67	885.26	885.14
44000	929.41	924.16	920.09	916.92	914.46	912.54	911.04	909.87	908.96	908.24	907.68	906.26	905.85	905.72
45000	950.53	945.16	940.99	937.76	935.24	933.28	931.74	930.55	929.61	928.88	928.31	926.86	926.43	926.31
46000	971.66	966.16	961.91	958.60	956.02	954.01	952.45	951.23	950.27	949.52	948.94	947.46	947.02	946.89
47000	992.78	987.17	982.82	979.44	976.80	974.75	973.15	971.91	970.93	970.17	969.57	968.05	967.61	967.48
48000	1013.90	1008.17	1003.73	1000.28	997.59	995.49	993.86	992.58	991.59	990.81	990.20	988.65	988.19	988.06
49000	1035.03	1029.17	1024.64	1021.11	1018.37	1016.23	1014.57	1013.26	1012.25	1011.45	1010.83	1009.25	1008.78	1008.65
50000	1056.15	1050.18	1045.55	1041.95	1039.15	1036.97	1035.27	1033.94	1032.90	1032.09	1031.46	1029.84	1029.37	1029.23
55000	1161.76	1155.20	1150.10	1146.15	1143.07	1140.67	1138.80	1137.34	1136.19	1135.30	1134.60	1132.83	1132.31	1132.15
60000	1267.38	1260.21	1254.66	1250.34	1246.98	1244.37	1242.32	1240.73	1239.48	1238.51	1237.75	1235.81	1235.24	1235.07
65000	1372.99	1365.23	1359.21	1354.54	1350.90	1348.06	1345.85	1344.12	1342.77	1341.72	1340.89	1338.80	1338.18	1338.00
70000	1478.61	1470.25	1463.77	1458.73	1454.81	1451.76	1449.38	1447.52	1446.06	1444.93	1444.04	1441.78	1441.12	1440.92
75000	1584.22	1575.26	1568.32	1562.93	1558.73	1555.46	1552.90	1550.91	1549.35	1548.13	1547.18	1544.76	1544.05	1543.84
80000	1689.84	1680.28	1672.88	1667.12	1662.64	1659.15	1656.43	1654.30	1652.64	1651.34	1650.33	1647.75	1646.99	1646.76
85000	1795.45	1785.30	1777.43	1771.32	1766.56	1762.85	1759.96	1757.70	1755.93	1754.55	1753.47	1750.73	1749.92	1749.69
90000	1901.06	1890.32	1881.98	1875.51	1870.47	1866.55	1863.48	1861.09	1859.22	1857.76	1856.62	1853.71	1852.86	1852.61
95000	2006.68	1995.33	1986.54	1979.71	1974.39	1970.24	1967.01	1964.48	1962.51	1960.97	1959.76	1956.70	1955.80	1955.53
100000	2112.29	2100.35	2091.09	2083.90	2078.30	2073.94	2070.54	2067.88	2065.80	2064.18	2062.91	2059.68	2058.73	2058.45

MONTHLY PAYMENT
REQUIRED TO AMORTIZE A LOAN

TERM AMOUNT	1 Year	2 Years	3 Years	4 Years	5 Years	6 Years	7 Years	8 Years	9 Years	10 Years	11 Years	12 Years	13 Years	14 Years
5	.48	.27	.20	.17	.15	.14	.13	.13	.12	.12	.12	.11	.11	.11
10	.95	.54	.40	.34	.30	.27	.26	.25	.24	.23	.23	.22	.22	.22
15	1.43	.80	.60	.50	.44	.41	.38	.37	.35	.34	.34	.33	.33	.32
25	2.38	1.34	1.00	.83	.74	.67	.63	.61	.58	.57	.56	.55	.54	.54
50	4.75	2.67	1.99	1.66	1.47	1.34	1.26	1.21	1.16	1.13	1.11	1.09	1.08	1.07
75	7.12	4.00	2.98	2.48	2.20	2.01	1.89	1.81	1.74	1.70	1.66	1.64	1.62	1.60
100	9.50	5.33	3.97	3.31	2.93	2.68	2.52	2.41	2.32	2.26	2.22	2.18	2.16	2.14
200	18.99	10.65	7.93	6.61	5.85	5.36	5.04	4.81	4.64	4.52	4.43	4.36	4.31	4.27
300	28.48	15.98	11.89	9.91	8.77	8.04	7.55	7.21	6.96	6.78	6.64	6.54	6.46	6.40
400	37.97	21.30	15.86	13.21	11.69	10.72	10.07	9.61	9.28	9.03	8.85	8.72	8.61	8.53
500	47.47	26.63	19.82	16.51	14.61	13.40	12.58	12.01	11.60	11.29	11.06	10.89	10.76	10.66
600	56.96	31.95	23.78	19.82	17.53	16.08	15.10	14.41	13.91	13.55	13.28	13.07	12.91	12.79
700	66.45	37.28	27.74	23.12	20.45	18.75	17.61	16.81	16.23	15.81	15.49	15.25	15.07	14.93
800	75.94	42.60	31.71	26.42	23.37	21.43	20.13	19.21	18.55	18.06	17.70	17.43	17.22	17.06
900	85.44	47.93	35.67	29.72	26.29	24.11	22.64	21.61	20.87	20.32	19.91	19.60	19.37	19.19
1000	94.93	53.25	39.63	33.02	29.21	26.79	25.16	24.01	23.19	22.58	22.12	21.78	21.52	21.32
2000	189.85	106.50	79.26	66.04	58.41	53.57	50.31	48.02	46.37	45.15	44.24	43.56	43.04	42.64
3000	284.77	159.74	118.89	99.06	87.62	80.36	75.46	72.03	69.55	67.72	66.36	65.33	64.55	63.95
4000	379.70	212.99	158.52	132.08	116.82	107.14	100.61	96.03	92.73	90.30	88.48	87.11	86.07	85.27
5000	474.62	266.24	198.14	165.09	146.03	133.92	125.77	120.04	115.91	112.87	110.60	108.89	107.58	106.58
6000	569.54	319.48	237.77	198.11	175.23	160.71	150.92	144.05	139.09	135.44	132.72	130.66	129.10	127.90
7000	664.47	372.73	277.40	231.13	204.44	187.49	176.07	168.05	162.27	158.02	154.84	152.44	150.61	149.21
8000	759.39	425.97	317.03	264.15	214.28	214.28	201.22	192.06	185.45	180.59	176.96	174.22	172.13	170.53
9000	854.31	479.22	356.65	297.17	262.85	241.06	226.37	216.07	208.64	203.16	199.08	195.99	193.64	191.84
10000	949.23	532.47	396.28	330.18	292.05	267.84	251.53	240.08	231.82	225.74	221.20	217.77	215.16	213.16
11000	1044.16	585.71	435.91	363.20	321.26	294.63	276.68	264.08	255.00	248.31	243.32	239.55	236.68	234.48
12000	1139.08	638.96	475.54	396.22	350.46	321.41	301.83	288.09	278.18	270.88	265.44	261.32	258.19	255.79
13000	1234.00	692.21	515.17	429.24	379.67	348.20	326.98	312.10	301.36	293.46	287.56	283.10	279.71	277.11
14000	1328.93	745.45	554.79	462.25	408.87	374.98	352.13	336.10	324.54	316.03	309.67	304.88	301.22	298.42
15000	1423.85	798.70	594.42	495.27	438.08	401.76	377.29	360.11	347.72	338.60	331.79	326.65	322.74	319.74
16000	1518.77	851.94	634.05	528.29	467.28	428.55	402.44	384.12	370.90	361.18	353.91	348.43	344.25	341.05
17000	1613.69	905.19	673.68	561.31	496.49	455.33	427.59	408.13	394.08	383.75	376.03	370.21	365.77	362.37
18000	1708.62	958.44	713.30	594.33	525.69	482.12	452.74	432.13	417.27	406.32	398.15	391.98	387.28	383.68
19000	1803.54	1011.68	752.93	627.34	554.90	508.90	477.89	456.14	440.45	428.90	420.27	413.76	408.80	405.00
20000	1898.46	1064.93	792.56	660.36	584.10	535.68	503.05	480.15	463.63	451.47	442.39	435.53	430.31	426.32
21000	1993.39	1118.17	832.19	693.38	613.31	562.47	528.20	504.15	486.81	474.04	464.51	457.31	451.83	447.63
22000	2088.31	1171.42	871.81	726.40	642.51	589.25	553.35	528.16	509.99	496.62	486.63	479.09	473.35	468.95
23000	2183.23	1224.67	911.44	759.42	671.72	616.04	578.50	552.17	533.17	519.19	508.75	500.86	494.86	490.26
24000	2278.16	1277.91	951.07	792.43	700.92	642.82	603.65	576.17	556.35	541.76	530.87	522.64	516.38	511.58
25000	2373.08	1331.16	990.70	825.45	730.13	669.60	628.81	600.18	579.53	564.34	552.99	544.42	537.89	532.89
26000	2468.00	1384.41	1030.33	858.47	759.33	696.39	653.96	624.19	602.71	586.91	575.11	566.19	559.41	554.21
27000	2562.92	1437.65	1069.95	891.49	788.54	723.17	679.11	648.20	625.90	609.48	597.23	587.97	580.92	575.52
28000	2657.85	1490.90	1109.58	924.50	817.74	749.96	704.26	672.20	649.08	632.06	619.34	609.75	602.44	596.84
29000	2752.77	1544.14	1149.21	957.52	846.95	776.74	729.41	696.21	672.26	654.63	641.46	631.52	623.95	618.15
30000	2847.69	1597.39	1188.84	990.54	876.15	803.52	754.57	720.22	695.44	677.20	663.58	653.30	645.47	639.47
31000	2942.62	1650.64	1228.46	1023.56	905.36	830.31	779.72	744.22	718.62	699.78	685.70	675.08	666.98	660.79
32000	3037.54	1703.88	1268.09	1056.58	934.56	857.09	804.87	768.23	741.80	722.35	707.82	696.85	688.50	682.10
33000	3132.46	1757.13	1307.72	1089.59	963.77	883.88	830.02	792.24	764.98	744.92	729.94	718.63	710.02	703.42
34000	3227.38	1810.37	1347.35	1122.61	992.97	910.66	855.17	816.25	788.16	767.50	752.06	740.41	731.53	724.73
35000	3322.31	1863.62	1386.98	1155.63	1022.18	937.44	880.33	840.25	811.34	790.07	774.18	762.18	753.05	746.05
36000	3417.23	1916.87	1426.60	1188.65	1051.38	964.23	905.48	864.26	834.53	812.64	796.30	783.96	774.56	767.36
37000	3512.15	1970.11	1466.23	1221.67	1080.59	991.01	930.63	888.27	857.71	835.22	818.42	805.73	796.08	788.68
38000	3607.08	2023.36	1505.86	1254.68	1109.79	1017.80	955.78	912.27	880.89	857.79	840.54	827.51	817.59	809.99
39000	3702.00	2076.61	1545.49	1287.70	1139.00	1044.58	980.93	936.28	904.07	880.36	862.66	849.29	839.11	831.31
40000	3796.92	2129.85	1585.11	1320.72	1168.20	1071.36	1006.09	960.29	927.25	902.94	884.78	871.06	860.62	852.63
41000	3891.85	2183.10	1624.74	1353.74	1197.41	1098.15	1031.24	984.30	950.43	925.51	906.90	892.84	882.14	873.94
42000	3986.77	2236.34	1664.37	1386.75	1226.61	1124.93	1056.39	1008.30	973.61	948.08	929.01	914.62	903.66	895.26
43000	4081.69	2289.59	1704.00	1419.77	1255.82	1151.72	1081.54	1032.31	996.79	970.66	951.13	936.39	925.17	916.57
44000	4176.61	2342.84	1743.62	1452.79	1285.02	1178.50	1106.69	1056.32	1019.98	993.23	973.25	958.17	946.69	937.89
45000	4271.54	2396.08	1783.25	1485.81	1314.23	1205.28	1131.85	1080.32	1043.16	1015.80	995.37	979.95	968.20	959.20
46000	4366.46	2449.33	1822.88	1518.83	1343.43	1232.07	1157.00	1104.33	1066.34	1038.38	1017.49	1001.72	989.72	980.52
47000	4461.38	2502.57	1862.51	1551.84	1372.64	1258.85	1182.15	1128.34	1089.52	1060.95	1039.61	1023.50	1011.23	1001.83
48000	4556.31	2555.82	1902.14	1584.86	1401.84	1285.64	1207.30	1152.34	1112.70	1083.52	1061.73	1045.28	1032.75	1023.15
49000	4651.23	2609.07	1941.76	1617.88	1431.05	1312.42	1232.45	1176.35	1135.88	1106.10	1083.85	1067.05	1054.26	1044.47
50000	4746.15	2662.31	1981.39	1650.90	1460.25	1339.20	1257.61	1200.36	1159.06	1128.67	1105.97	1088.83	1075.78	1065.78
55000	5220.77	2928.54	2179.53	1815.99	1606.28	1473.12	1383.37	1320.39	1274.97	1241.54	1216.57	1197.71	1183.36	1172.36
60000	5695.38	3194.78	2377.67	1981.08	1752.30	1607.04	1509.13	1440.43	1390.87	1354.40	1327.16	1306.59	1290.93	1278.94
65000	6170.00	3461.01	2575.81	2146.16	1898.33	1740.96	1634.89	1560.47	1506.78	1467.27	1437.76	1415.48	1398.51	1385.51
70000	6644.61	3727.24	2773.95	2311.25	2044.35	1874.88	1760.65	1680.50	1622.69	1580.13	1548.35	1524.36	1506.09	1492.09
75000	7119.22	3993.47	2972.08	2476.34	2190.38	2008.80	1886.41	1800.54	1738.59	1693.00	1658.95	1633.24	1613.67	1598.67
80000	7593.84	4259.70	3170.22	2641.43	2336.40	2142.72	2012.17	1920.57	1854.50	1805.87	1769.55	1742.12	1721.24	1705.25
85000	8068.45	4525.93	3368.36	2806.52	2482.42	2276.64	2137.93	2040.61	1970.40	1918.73	1880.14	1851.01	1828.82	1811.82
90000	8543.07	4792.16	3566.50	2971.61	2628.45	2410.56	2263.69	2160.64	2086.31	2031.60	1990.74	1959.89	1936.40	1918.40
95000	9017.68	5058.39	3764.64	3136.70	2774.47	2544.48	2389.45	2280.68	2202.21	2144.47	2101.34	2068.77	2043.98	2024.98
100000	9492.30	5324.62	3962.78	3301.79	2920.50	2678.40	2515.21	2400.71	2318.12	2257.33	2211.93	2177.65	2151.55	2131.56

TERM	15 Years	16 Years	17 Years	18 Years	19 Years	20 Years	21 Years	22 Years	23 Years	24 Years	25 Years	30 Years	35 Years	40 Years
AMOUNT														
5	.11	.11	.11	.11	.11	.11	.11	.11	.11	.11	.11	.11	.11	.11
10	.22	.22	.21	.21	.21	.21	.21	.21	.21	.21	.21	.21	.21	.21
15	.32	.32	.32	.32	.32	.32	.32	.32	.32	.32	.32	.31	.31	.31
25	.53	.53	.53	.53	.53	.52	.52	.52	.52	.52	.52	.52	.52	.52
50	1.06	1.06	1.05	1.05	1.05	1.04	1.04	1.04	1.04	1.04	1.04	1.04	1.04	1.04
75	1.59	1.58	1.58	1.57	1.57	1.56	1.56	1.56	1.56	1.56	1.56	1.55	1.55	1.55
100	2.12	2.11	2.10	2.09	2.09	2.08	2.08	2.08	2.07	2.07	2.07	2.07	2.07	2.07
200	4.24	4.21	4.20	4.18	4.17	4.16	4.15	4.15	4.14	4.14	4.14	4.13	4.13	4.13
300	6.35	6.32	6.29	6.27	6.25	6.24	6.23	6.22	6.21	6.21	6.21	6.20	6.19	6.19
400	8.47	8.42	8.39	8.36	8.33	8.32	8.30	8.29	8.28	8.28	8.27	8.26	8.26	8.26
500	10.59	10.53	10.48	10.44	10.42	10.39	10.38	10.36	10.35	10.35	10.34	10.32	10.32	10.32
600	12.70	12.63	12.58	12.53	12.50	12.47	12.45	12.44	12.42	12.41	12.41	12.39	12.38	12.38
700	14.82	14.73	14.67	14.62	14.58	14.55	14.53	14.51	14.49	14.48	14.47	14.45	14.45	14.44
800	16.93	16.84	16.77	16.71	16.66	16.63	16.60	16.58	16.56	16.55	16.54	16.52	16.51	16.51
900	19.05	18.94	18.86	18.80	18.75	18.71	18.68	18.65	18.63	18.62	18.61	18.58	18.57	18.57
1000	21.17	21.05	20.96	20.88	20.83	20.78	20.75	20.72	20.70	20.69	20.68	20.64	20.63	20.63
2000	42.33	42.09	41.91	41.76	41.65	41.56	41.50	41.44	41.40	41.37	41.35	41.28	41.26	41.26
3000	63.49	63.13	62.86	62.64	62.47	62.34	62.24	62.16	62.10	62.05	62.02	61.92	61.89	61.88
4000	84.65	84.18	83.81	83.52	83.30	83.12	82.99	82.88	82.80	82.74	82.69	82.56	82.52	82.51
5000	105.81	105.22	104.76	104.40	104.12	103.90	103.73	103.60	103.50	103.42	103.36	103.20	103.15	103.14
6000	126.97	126.26	125.71	125.28	124.94	124.68	124.48	124.32	124.20	124.10	124.03	123.83	123.78	123.76
7000	148.14	147.30	146.66	146.16	145.77	145.46	145.23	145.04	144.90	144.78	144.70	144.47	144.41	144.39
8000	169.30	168.35	167.61	167.04	166.59	166.24	165.97	165.76	165.60	165.47	165.37	165.11	165.04	165.01
9000	190.46	189.39	188.56	187.91	187.41	187.02	186.72	186.48	186.30	186.15	186.04	185.75	185.67	185.64
10000	211.62	210.43	209.51	208.79	208.24	207.80	207.46	207.20	206.99	206.83	206.71	206.39	206.29	206.27
11000	232.78	231.47	230.46	229.67	229.06	228.58	228.21	227.92	227.69	227.52	227.38	227.03	226.92	226.89
12000	253.94	252.52	251.41	250.55	249.88	249.36	248.96	248.64	248.39	248.20	248.05	247.66	247.55	247.52
13000	275.11	273.56	272.36	271.43	270.71	270.14	269.70	269.36	269.09	268.88	268.72	268.30	268.18	268.14
14000	296.27	294.60	293.31	292.31	291.53	290.92	290.45	290.08	289.79	289.56	289.39	288.94	288.81	288.77
15000	317.43	315.64	314.26	313.19	312.35	311.70	311.19	310.80	310.49	310.25	310.06	309.58	309.44	309.40
16000	338.59	336.69	335.21	334.07	333.18	332.48	331.94	331.52	331.19	330.93	330.73	330.22	330.07	330.02
17000	359.75	357.73	356.16	354.95	354.00	353.26	352.69	352.24	351.89	351.61	351.40	350.86	350.70	350.65
18000	380.91	378.77	377.11	375.82	374.82	374.04	373.43	372.96	372.59	372.30	372.07	371.49	371.33	371.28
19000	402.07	399.81	398.06	396.70	395.65	394.82	394.18	393.68	393.28	392.98	392.74	392.13	391.95	391.90
20000	423.24	420.86	419.01	417.58	416.47	415.60	414.92	414.40	413.98	413.66	413.41	412.77	412.58	412.53
21000	444.40	441.90	439.96	438.46	437.29	436.38	435.67	435.12	434.68	434.34	434.08	433.41	433.21	433.15
22000	465.56	462.94	460.91	459.34	458.11	457.16	456.42	455.84	455.38	455.03	454.75	454.05	453.84	453.78
23000	486.72	483.99	481.87	480.22	478.94	477.94	477.16	476.55	476.08	475.71	475.42	474.69	474.47	474.41
24000	507.88	505.03	502.82	501.10	499.76	498.72	497.91	497.27	496.78	496.39	496.09	495.32	495.10	495.03
25000	529.04	526.07	523.77	521.98	520.58	519.50	518.65	517.99	517.48	517.08	516.76	515.96	515.73	515.66
26000	550.21	547.11	544.72	542.86	541.41	540.28	539.40	538.71	538.18	537.76	537.43	536.60	536.36	536.28
27000	571.37	568.16	565.67	563.73	562.23	561.06	560.15	559.43	558.88	558.44	558.10	557.24	556.99	556.91
28000	592.53	589.20	586.62	584.61	583.05	581.84	580.89	580.15	579.58	579.12	578.77	577.88	577.61	577.54
29000	613.69	610.24	607.57	605.49	603.88	602.62	601.64	600.87	600.27	599.81	599.44	598.51	598.24	598.16
30000	634.85	631.28	628.52	626.37	624.70	623.40	622.38	621.59	620.97	620.49	620.11	619.15	618.87	618.79
31000	656.01	652.33	649.47	647.25	645.52	644.18	643.13	642.31	641.67	641.17	640.78	639.79	639.50	639.42
32000	677.18	673.37	670.42	668.13	666.35	664.96	663.88	663.03	662.37	661.86	661.45	660.43	660.13	660.04
33000	698.34	694.41	691.37	689.01	687.17	685.74	684.62	683.75	683.07	682.54	682.12	681.07	680.76	680.67
34000	719.50	715.45	712.32	709.89	707.99	706.52	705.37	704.47	703.77	703.22	702.79	701.71	701.39	701.29
35000	740.66	736.50	733.27	730.77	728.82	727.30	726.11	725.19	724.47	723.90	723.46	722.34	722.02	721.92
36000	761.82	757.54	754.22	751.64	749.64	748.08	746.86	745.91	745.17	744.59	744.13	742.98	742.65	742.55
37000	782.98	778.58	775.17	772.52	770.46	768.86	767.61	766.63	765.87	765.27	764.80	763.62	763.27	763.17
38000	804.14	799.62	796.12	793.40	791.29	789.64	788.35	787.35	786.56	785.95	785.47	784.26	783.90	783.80
39000	825.31	820.67	817.07	814.28	812.11	810.42	809.10	808.07	807.26	806.64	806.14	804.90	804.53	804.42
40000	846.47	841.71	838.02	835.16	832.93	831.20	829.84	828.79	827.96	827.32	826.81	825.54	825.16	825.05
41000	867.63	862.75	858.97	856.04	853.76	851.98	850.59	849.51	848.66	848.00	847.48	846.17	845.79	845.68
42000	888.79	883.80	879.92	876.92	874.58	872.76	871.34	870.23	869.36	868.68	868.15	866.81	866.42	866.30
43000	909.95	904.84	900.87	897.80	895.40	893.54	892.08	890.95	890.06	889.37	888.83	887.45	887.05	886.93
44000	931.11	925.88	921.82	918.68	916.22	914.32	912.83	911.67	910.76	910.05	909.50	908.09	907.68	907.56
45000	952.28	946.92	942.78	939.55	937.05	935.10	933.57	932.39	931.46	930.73	930.17	928.73	928.31	928.18
46000	973.44	967.97	963.73	960.43	957.87	955.88	954.32	953.10	952.16	951.42	950.84	949.37	948.93	948.81
47000	994.60	989.01	984.68	981.31	978.69	976.66	975.07	973.82	972.86	972.10	971.51	970.00	969.56	969.43
48000	1015.76	1010.05	1005.63	1002.19	999.52	997.44	995.81	994.54	993.55	992.78	992.19	990.64	990.19	990.06
49000	1036.92	1031.09	1026.58	1023.07	1020.34	1018.21	1016.56	1015.26	1014.25	1013.46	1012.85	1011.28	1010.82	1010.69
50000	1058.08	1052.14	1047.53	1043.95	1041.16	1038.99	1037.30	1035.98	1034.95	1034.15	1033.52	1031.92	1031.45	1031.31
55000	1163.89	1157.35	1152.28	1148.34	1145.28	1142.89	1141.03	1139.58	1138.45	1137.56	1136.87	1135.11	1134.59	1134.44
60000	1269.70	1262.56	1257.03	1252.74	1249.40	1246.79	1244.76	1243.18	1241.94	1240.97	1240.22	1238.30	1237.74	1237.57
65000	1375.51	1367.78	1361.78	1357.13	1353.51	1350.69	1348.49	1346.78	1345.44	1344.39	1343.57	1341.49	1340.88	1340.70
70000	1481.32	1472.99	1466.54	1461.53	1457.63	1454.59	1452.22	1450.37	1448.93	1447.80	1446.92	1444.68	1444.03	1443.84
75000	1587.12	1578.20	1571.29	1565.92	1561.74	1558.49	1555.95	1553.97	1552.43	1551.22	1550.27	1547.88	1547.17	1546.97
80000	1692.93	1683.42	1676.04	1670.31	1665.86	1662.39	1659.68	1657.57	1655.92	1654.63	1653.62	1651.07	1650.32	1650.10
85000	1798.74	1788.63	1780.79	1774.71	1769.98	1766.29	1763.41	1761.17	1759.41	1758.05	1756.98	1754.26	1753.46	1753.23
90000	1904.55	1893.84	1885.55	1879.10	1874.09	1870.19	1867.14	1864.77	1862.91	1861.46	1860.33	1857.45	1856.61	1856.36
95000	2010.35	1999.05	1990.30	1983.50	1978.21	1974.09	1970.87	1968.36	1966.40	1964.87	1963.68	1960.64	1959.75	1959.49
100000	2116.16	2104.27	2095.05	2087.89	2082.32	2077.98	2074.60	2071.96	2069.90	2068.29	2067.03	2063.83	2062.89	2062.62

24.800%

TERM AMOUNT	1 Year	2 Years	3 Years	4 Years	5 Years	6 Years	7 Years	8 Years	9 Years	10 Years	11 Years	12 Years	13 Years	14 Years
5	.48	.27	.20	.17	.15	.14	.13	.13	.12	.12	.12	.11	.11	.11
10	.95	.54	.40	.34	.30	.27	.26	.25	.24	.23	.23	.22	.22	.22
15	1.43	.80	.60	.50	.44	.41	.38	.37	.35	.34	.34	.33	.33	.33
25	2.38	1.34	1.00	.83	.74	.68	.63	.61	.59	.57	.56	.55	.54	.54
50	4.75	2.67	1.99	1.66	1.47	1.35	1.26	1.21	1.17	1.14	1.11	1.10	1.08	1.07
75	7.13	4.00	2.98	2.48	2.20	2.02	1.89	1.81	1.75	1.70	1.67	1.64	1.62	1.61
100	9.50	5.33	3.97	3.31	2.93	2.69	2.52	2.41	2.33	2.27	2.22	2.19	2.16	2.14
200	18.99	10.66	7.94	6.61	5.85	5.37	5.04	4.81	4.65	4.53	4.44	4.37	4.32	4.28
300	28.49	15.99	11.90	9.92	8.78	8.05	7.56	7.22	6.97	6.79	6.65	6.55	6.47	6.41
400	37.98	21.31	15.87	13.22	11.70	10.73	10.08	9.62	9.29	9.05	8.87	8.73	8.63	8.55
500	47.48	26.64	19.83	16.53	14.62	13.41	12.60	12.03	11.61	11.31	11.08	10.91	10.78	10.68
600	56.97	31.97	23.80	19.83	17.55	16.09	15.12	14.43	13.93	13.57	13.30	13.09	12.94	12.82
700	66.47	37.29	27.76	23.14	20.47	18.78	17.63	16.83	16.26	15.83	15.51	15.27	15.09	14.95
800	75.96	42.62	31.73	26.44	23.39	21.46	20.15	19.24	18.58	18.09	17.73	17.46	17.25	17.09
900	85.46	47.95	35.69	29.75	26.32	24.14	22.67	21.64	20.90	20.35	19.94	19.64	19.40	19.22
1000	94.95	53.28	39.66	33.05	29.24	26.82	25.19	24.05	23.22	22.61	22.16	21.82	21.56	21.36
2000	189.90	106.55	79.31	66.10	58.47	53.63	50.37	48.09	46.44	45.22	44.32	43.63	43.11	42.71
3000	284.85	159.82	118.97	99.14	87.71	80.45	75.56	72.13	69.65	67.83	66.47	65.44	64.66	64.07
4000	379.79	213.09	158.62	132.19	116.94	107.26	100.74	96.17	92.87	90.44	88.63	87.26	86.22	85.42
5000	474.74	266.36	198.28	165.23	146.18	134.08	125.92	120.21	116.08	113.05	110.78	109.07	107.77	106.77
6000	569.69	319.63	237.93	198.28	175.41	160.89	151.11	144.25	139.30	135.66	132.94	130.88	129.32	128.13
7000	664.64	372.90	277.58	231.32	204.64	187.71	176.29	168.29	162.51	158.26	155.09	152.70	150.88	149.48
8000	759.58	426.17	317.24	264.37	233.88	214.52	201.48	192.33	185.73	180.87	177.25	174.51	172.43	170.83
9000	854.53	479.45	356.89	297.42	263.11	241.34	226.66	216.37	208.94	203.48	199.40	196.32	193.98	192.19
10000	949.48	532.72	396.55	330.46	292.35	268.15	251.84	240.41	232.16	226.09	221.56	218.14	215.54	213.54
11000	1044.42	585.99	436.20	363.51	321.58	294.97	277.03	264.45	255.37	248.70	243.71	239.95	237.09	234.90
12000	1139.37	639.26	475.85	396.55	350.82	321.78	302.21	288.49	278.59	271.31	265.87	261.76	258.64	256.25
13000	1234.32	692.53	515.51	429.60	380.05	348.59	327.40	312.53	301.80	293.91	288.02	283.58	280.19	277.60
14000	1329.27	745.80	555.16	462.64	409.28	375.41	352.58	336.57	325.02	316.52	310.18	305.39	301.75	298.96
15000	1424.21	799.07	594.82	495.69	438.52	402.22	377.76	360.61	348.23	339.13	332.34	327.20	323.30	320.31
16000	1519.16	852.34	634.47	528.74	467.75	429.04	402.95	384.65	371.45	361.74	354.49	349.02	344.85	341.66
17000	1614.11	905.62	674.13	561.78	496.99	455.85	428.13	408.69	394.67	384.35	376.65	370.83	366.41	363.02
18000	1709.05	958.89	713.78	594.83	526.22	482.67	453.32	432.73	417.88	406.96	398.80	392.64	387.96	384.37
19000	1804.00	1012.16	753.43	627.87	555.45	509.48	478.50	456.77	441.10	429.57	420.96	414.46	409.51	405.73
20000	1898.95	1065.43	793.09	660.92	584.69	536.30	503.68	480.81	464.31	452.17	443.11	436.27	431.07	427.08
21000	1993.90	1118.70	832.74	693.96	613.92	563.11	528.87	504.85	487.53	474.78	465.27	458.08	452.62	448.43
22000	2088.84	1171.97	872.40	727.01	643.16	589.93	554.05	528.89	510.74	497.39	487.42	479.90	474.17	469.79
23000	2183.79	1225.24	912.05	760.06	672.39	616.74	579.23	552.93	533.96	520.00	509.58	501.71	495.72	491.14
24000	2278.74	1278.51	951.70	793.10	701.63	643.56	604.42	576.97	557.17	542.61	531.73	523.52	517.28	512.49
25000	2373.68	1331.79	991.36	826.15	730.86	670.37	629.60	601.01	580.39	565.22	553.89	545.34	538.83	533.85
26000	2468.63	1385.06	1031.01	859.19	760.09	697.18	654.79	625.05	603.60	587.82	576.04	567.15	560.38	555.20
27000	2563.58	1438.33	1070.67	892.24	789.33	724.00	679.97	649.09	626.82	610.43	598.20	588.96	581.94	576.55
28000	2658.53	1491.60	1110.32	925.28	818.56	750.81	705.15	673.13	650.03	633.04	620.35	610.78	603.49	597.91
29000	2753.47	1544.87	1149.97	958.33	847.80	777.63	730.34	697.17	673.25	655.65	642.51	632.59	625.04	619.26
30000	2848.42	1598.14	1189.63	991.38	877.03	804.44	755.52	721.21	696.46	678.26	664.67	654.40	646.60	640.62
31000	2943.37	1651.41	1229.28	1024.42	906.26	831.26	780.71	745.25	719.68	700.87	686.82	676.22	668.15	661.97
32000	3038.31	1704.68	1268.94	1057.47	935.50	858.07	805.89	769.29	742.90	723.48	708.98	698.03	689.70	683.32
33000	3133.26	1757.96	1308.59	1090.51	964.73	884.89	831.07	793.33	766.11	746.08	731.13	719.84	711.26	704.68
34000	3228.21	1811.23	1348.25	1123.56	993.97	911.70	856.26	817.37	789.33	768.69	753.29	741.66	732.81	726.03
35000	3323.16	1864.50	1387.90	1156.60	1023.20	938.52	881.44	841.41	812.54	791.30	775.44	763.47	754.36	747.38
36000	3418.10	1917.77	1427.55	1189.65	1052.44	965.33	906.63	865.45	835.76	813.91	797.60	785.28	775.91	768.74
37000	3513.05	1971.04	1467.21	1081.67	992.14	931.81	889.49	858.97	836.52	819.75	807.10	797.47	790.09
38000	3608.00	2024.31	1506.86	1255.74	1110.90	1018.96	956.99	913.53	882.19	859.13	841.91	828.91	819.02	811.45
39000	3702.94	2077.58	1546.52	1288.79	1140.14	1045.77	982.18	937.57	905.40	881.73	864.06	850.72	840.57	832.80
40000	3797.89	2130.85	1586.17	1321.83	1169.37	1072.59	1007.36	961.61	928.62	904.34	886.22	872.54	862.13	854.15
41000	3892.84	2184.13	1625.82	1354.88	1198.61	1099.40	1032.55	985.65	951.83	926.95	908.37	894.35	883.68	875.51
42000	3987.79	2237.40	1665.48	1387.92	1227.84	1126.22	1057.73	1009.69	975.05	949.56	930.53	916.16	905.23	896.86
43000	4082.73	2290.67	1705.13	1420.97	1257.08	1153.03	1082.91	1033.73	998.26	972.17	952.68	937.98	926.79	918.21
44000	4177.68	2343.94	1744.79	1454.01	1286.31	1179.85	1108.10	1057.77	1021.48	994.78	974.84	959.79	948.34	939.57
45000	4272.63	2397.21	1784.44	1487.06	1315.54	1206.66	1133.28	1081.81	1044.69	1017.38	997.00	981.60	969.89	960.92
46000	4367.58	2450.48	1824.09	1520.11	1344.78	1233.48	1158.46	1105.85	1067.91	1039.99	1019.15	1003.42	991.44	982.27
47000	4462.52	2503.75	1863.75	1553.15	1374.01	1260.29	1183.65	1129.89	1091.12	1062.60	1041.31	1025.23	1013.00	1003.63
48000	4557.47	2557.02	1903.40	1586.20	1403.25	1287.11	1208.83	1153.93	1114.34	1085.21	1063.46	1047.04	1034.55	1024.98
49000	4652.42	2610.30	1943.06	1619.24	1432.48	1313.92	1234.02	1177.97	1137.56	1107.82	1085.62	1068.86	1056.10	1046.34
50000	4747.36	2663.57	1982.71	1652.29	1461.71	1340.73	1259.20	1202.01	1160.77	1130.43	1107.77	1090.67	1077.66	1067.69
55000	5222.10	2929.92	2180.98	1817.52	1607.89	1474.81	1385.12	1322.21	1276.85	1243.47	1218.55	1199.74	1185.42	1174.46
60000	5696.84	3196.28	2379.25	1982.75	1754.06	1608.88	1511.04	1442.41	1392.92	1356.51	1329.33	1308.80	1293.19	1281.23
65000	6171.57	3462.63	2577.52	2147.97	1900.23	1742.95	1636.96	1562.62	1509.00	1469.55	1440.10	1417.87	1400.95	1387.99
70000	6646.31	3728.99	2775.79	2313.20	2046.40	1877.03	1762.88	1682.82	1625.08	1582.60	1550.88	1526.94	1508.72	1494.76
75000	7121.04	3995.35	2974.06	2478.43	2192.57	2011.10	1888.80	1803.02	1741.15	1695.64	1661.66	1636.00	1616.48	1601.53
80000	7595.78	4261.70	3172.34	2643.66	2338.74	2145.17	2014.72	1923.22	1857.23	1808.68	1772.43	1745.07	1724.25	1708.30
85000	8070.51	4528.06	3370.61	2808.89	2484.91	2279.24	2140.64	2043.42	1973.31	1921.72	1883.21	1854.14	1832.01	1815.07
90000	8545.25	4794.42	3568.88	2974.12	2631.08	2413.32	2266.56	2163.62	2089.38	2034.76	1993.99	1963.20	1939.78	1921.84
95000	9019.99	5060.77	3767.15	3139.34	2777.25	2547.39	2392.48	2283.82	2205.46	2147.81	2104.76	2072.27	2047.54	2028.61
100000	9494.72	5327.13	3965.42	3304.57	2923.42	2681.46	2518.40	2404.02	2321.54	2260.85	2215.54	2181.34	2155.31	2135.37

TERM	15 Years	16 Years	17 Years	18 Years	19 Years	20 Years	21 Years	22 Years	23 Years	24 Years	25 Years	30 Years	35 Years	40 Years
AMOUNT														
5	.11	.11	.11	.11	.11	.11	.11	.11	.11	.11	.11	.11	.11	.11
10	.22	.22	.21	.21	.21	.21	.21	.21	.21	.21	.21	.21	.21	.21
15	.32	.32	.32	.32	.32	.32	.32	.32	.32	.32	.32	.32	.32	.32
25	.54	.53	.53	.53	.53	.53	.52	.52	.52	.52	.52	.52	.52	.52
50	1.07	1.06	1.05	1.05	1.05	1.05	1.04	1.04	1.04	1.04	1.04	1.04	1.04	1.04
75	1.60	1.59	1.58	1.57	1.57	1.57	1.56	1.56	1.56	1.56	1.56	1.56	1.56	1.56
100	2.13	2.11	2.10	2.10	2.09	2.09	2.08	2.08	2.08	2.08	2.08	2.07	2.07	2.07
200	4.25	4.22	4.20	4.19	4.18	4.17	4.16	4.16	4.15	4.15	4.15	4.14	4.14	4.14
300	6.37	6.33	6.30	6.28	6.26	6.25	6.24	6.23	6.23	6.22	6.22	6.21	6.21	6.21
400	8.49	8.44	8.40	8.37	8.35	8.33	8.32	8.31	8.30	8.29	8.29	8.28	8.27	8.27
500	10.61	10.55	10.50	10.46	10.44	10.42	10.40	10.39	10.37	10.37	10.36	10.34	10.34	10.34
600	12.73	12.65	12.60	12.56	12.52	12.50	12.48	12.46	12.45	12.44	12.43	12.41	12.41	12.41
700	14.85	14.76	14.70	14.65	14.61	14.58	14.56	14.54	14.52	14.51	14.50	14.48	14.47	14.47
800	16.97	16.87	16.80	16.74	16.70	16.66	16.63	16.61	16.60	16.58	16.57	16.55	16.54	16.54
900	19.09	18.98	18.90	18.83	18.78	18.74	18.71	18.69	18.67	18.66	18.65	18.62	18.61	18.61
1000	21.21	21.09	21.00	20.92	20.87	20.83	20.79	20.77	20.74	20.73	20.72	20.68	20.68	20.67
2000	42.41	42.17	41.99	41.84	41.73	41.65	41.58	41.53	41.48	41.45	41.43	41.36	41.35	41.34
3000	63.61	63.25	62.98	62.76	62.60	62.47	62.36	62.29	62.22	62.18	62.14	62.04	62.02	62.01
4000	84.81	84.33	83.97	83.68	83.46	83.29	83.15	83.05	82.96	82.90	82.85	82.72	82.69	82.68
5000	106.01	105.41	104.96	104.60	104.32	104.11	103.94	103.81	103.70	103.62	103.56	103.40	103.36	103.34
6000	127.21	126.50	125.95	125.52	125.19	124.93	124.72	124.57	124.44	124.35	124.27	124.08	124.03	124.01
7000	148.41	147.58	146.94	146.44	146.05	145.75	145.51	145.33	145.18	145.07	144.99	144.76	144.70	144.68
8000	169.61	168.66	167.93	167.36	166.91	166.57	166.30	166.09	165.92	165.80	165.70	165.44	165.37	165.35
9000	190.81	189.74	188.92	188.27	187.78	187.39	187.08	186.85	186.66	186.52	186.41	186.12	186.04	186.02
10000	212.01	210.82	209.91	209.19	208.64	208.21	207.87	207.61	207.40	207.24	207.12	206.80	206.71	206.68
11000	233.21	231.90	230.90	230.11	229.50	229.03	228.66	228.37	228.14	227.97	227.83	227.48	227.38	227.35
12000	254.41	252.99	251.89	251.03	250.37	249.85	249.44	249.13	248.88	248.69	248.54	248.16	248.05	248.02
13000	275.61	274.07	272.88	271.95	271.23	270.67	270.23	269.89	269.62	269.42	269.25	268.84	268.72	268.69
14000	296.81	295.15	293.87	292.87	292.09	291.49	291.02	290.65	290.36	290.14	289.97	289.52	289.39	289.35
15000	318.01	316.23	314.86	313.79	312.96	312.31	311.80	311.41	311.10	310.86	310.68	310.20	310.06	310.02
16000	339.21	337.31	335.85	334.71	333.82	333.13	332.59	332.17	331.84	331.59	331.39	330.88	330.73	330.69
17000	360.41	358.40	356.84	355.62	354.68	353.95	353.38	352.93	352.58	352.31	352.10	351.56	351.40	351.36
18000	381.61	379.48	377.83	376.54	375.55	374.77	374.16	373.69	373.32	373.04	372.81	372.24	372.07	372.03
19000	402.81	400.56	398.82	397.46	396.41	395.59	394.95	394.45	394.06	393.76	393.52	392.92	392.74	392.69
20000	424.01	421.64	419.81	418.38	417.27	416.41	415.74	415.21	414.80	414.48	414.23	413.60	413.42	413.36
21000	445.21	442.72	440.80	439.30	438.14	437.23	436.52	435.97	435.54	435.21	434.95	434.28	434.09	434.03
22000	466.41	463.80	461.79	460.22	459.00	458.05	457.31	456.73	456.28	455.93	455.66	454.96	454.76	454.70
23000	487.61	484.89	482.78	481.14	479.86	478.87	478.10	477.49	477.02	476.66	476.37	475.64	475.43	475.36
24000	508.81	505.97	503.77	502.06	500.73	499.69	498.88	498.25	497.76	497.38	497.08	496.32	496.10	496.03
25000	530.01	527.05	524.76	522.97	521.59	520.51	519.67	519.01	518.50	518.10	517.79	517.00	516.77	516.70
26000	551.21	548.13	545.75	543.89	542.45	541.33	540.46	539.78	539.24	538.83	538.50	537.68	537.44	537.37
27000	572.41	569.21	566.74	564.81	563.32	562.15	561.24	560.54	559.98	559.55	559.21	558.36	558.11	558.04
28000	593.61	590.30	587.73	585.73	584.18	582.97	582.03	581.30	580.72	580.28	579.93	579.04	578.78	578.70
29000	614.81	611.38	608.72	606.65	605.04	603.79	602.82	602.06	601.46	601.00	600.64	599.72	599.45	599.37
30000	636.01	632.46	629.71	627.57	625.91	624.61	623.60	622.82	622.20	621.72	621.35	620.40	620.12	620.04
31000	657.21	653.54	650.70	648.49	646.77	645.43	644.39	643.58	642.94	642.45	642.06	641.08	640.79	640.71
32000	678.41	674.62	671.69	669.41	667.63	666.25	665.18	664.34	663.68	663.17	662.77	661.76	661.46	661.37
33000	699.61	695.70	692.68	690.32	688.50	687.07	685.96	685.10	684.42	683.89	683.48	682.44	682.13	682.04
34000	720.81	716.79	713.67	711.24	709.36	707.89	706.75	705.86	705.16	704.62	704.19	703.12	702.80	702.71
35000	742.02	737.87	734.66	732.16	730.22	728.71	727.54	726.62	725.90	725.34	724.91	723.80	723.47	723.38
36000	763.22	758.95	755.65	753.08	751.09	749.53	748.32	747.38	746.64	746.07	745.62	744.48	744.14	744.05
37000	784.42	780.03	776.64	774.00	771.95	770.35	769.11	768.14	767.38	766.79	766.33	765.16	764.81	764.71
38000	805.62	801.11	797.63	794.92	792.81	791.17	789.90	788.90	788.12	787.51	787.04	785.84	785.48	785.38
39000	826.82	822.20	818.62	815.84	813.68	811.99	810.68	809.66	808.86	808.24	807.75	806.52	806.15	806.05
40000	848.02	843.28	839.61	836.76	834.54	832.81	831.47	830.42	829.60	828.96	828.46	827.20	826.83	826.72
41000	869.22	864.36	860.60	857.68	855.40	853.64	852.26	851.18	850.34	849.69	849.17	847.88	847.50	847.38
42000	890.42	885.44	881.59	878.59	876.27	874.46	873.04	871.94	871.08	870.41	869.89	868.56	868.17	868.05
43000	911.62	906.52	902.58	899.51	897.13	895.28	893.83	892.70	891.82	891.13	890.60	889.24	888.84	888.72
44000	932.82	927.60	923.57	920.43	917.99	916.10	914.62	913.46	912.56	911.86	911.31	909.91	909.51	909.39
45000	954.02	948.69	944.56	941.35	938.86	936.92	935.40	934.22	933.30	932.58	932.02	930.59	930.18	930.06
46000	975.22	969.77	965.55	962.27	959.72	957.74	956.19	954.98	954.04	953.31	952.73	951.27	950.85	950.72
47000	996.42	990.85	986.54	983.19	980.58	978.56	976.98	975.74	974.78	974.03	973.44	971.95	971.52	971.39
48000	1017.62	1011.93	1007.53	1004.11	1001.45	999.38	997.76	996.50	995.52	994.75	994.15	992.63	992.19	992.06
49000	1038.82	1033.01	1028.52	1025.03	1022.31	1020.20	1018.55	1017.26	1016.26	1015.48	1014.87	1013.31	1012.86	1012.73
50000	1060.02	1054.10	1049.51	1045.94	1043.17	1041.02	1039.34	1038.02	1037.00	1036.20	1035.58	1033.99	1033.53	1033.39
55000	1166.02	1159.50	1154.46	1150.54	1147.49	1145.12	1143.27	1141.83	1140.70	1139.82	1139.13	1137.39	1136.88	1136.73
60000	1272.02	1264.91	1259.41	1255.13	1251.81	1249.22	1247.20	1245.63	1244.40	1243.44	1242.69	1240.79	1240.24	1240.07
65000	1378.02	1370.32	1364.36	1359.73	1356.13	1353.32	1351.14	1349.43	1348.10	1347.06	1346.25	1344.19	1343.59	1343.41
70000	1484.03	1475.73	1469.31	1464.32	1460.44	1457.42	1455.07	1453.23	1451.80	1450.68	1449.81	1447.59	1446.94	1446.75
75000	1590.03	1581.14	1574.26	1568.91	1564.76	1561.52	1559.00	1557.03	1555.50	1554.30	1553.36	1550.99	1550.29	1550.09
80000	1696.03	1686.55	1679.21	1673.51	1669.08	1665.62	1662.94	1660.84	1659.20	1657.92	1656.92	1654.39	1653.65	1653.43
85000	1802.03	1791.96	1784.16	1778.10	1773.39	1769.73	1766.87	1764.64	1762.90	1761.54	1760.48	1757.79	1757.00	1756.77
90000	1908.03	1897.37	1889.11	1882.70	1877.71	1873.83	1870.80	1868.44	1866.60	1865.16	1864.03	1861.18	1860.35	1860.11
95000	2014.03	2002.78	1994.06	1987.29	1982.03	1977.93	1974.73	1972.24	1970.30	1968.78	1967.59	1964.58	1963.70	1963.45
100000	2120.03	2108.19	2099.01	2091.88	2086.34	2082.03	2078.67	2076.04	2074.00	2072.40	2071.15	2067.98	2067.06	2066.78

24.875%

MONTHLY PAYMENT
REQUIRED TO AMORTIZE A LOAN

TERM AMOUNT	1 Year	2 Years	3 Years	4 Years	5 Years	6 Years	7 Years	8 Years	9 Years	10 Years	11 Years	12 Years	13 Years	14 Years
5	.48	.27	.20	.17	.15	.14	.13	.13	.12	.12	.12	.11	.11	.11
10	.95	.54	.40	.34	.30	.27	.26	.25	.24	.23	.23	.22	.22	.22
15	1.43	.80	.60	.50	.44	.41	.38	.37	.35	.34	.34	.33	.33	.33
25	2.38	1.34	1.00	.83	.74	.68	.64	.61	.59	.57	.56	.55	.55	.54
50	4.75	2.67	1.99	1.66	1.47	1.35	1.27	1.21	1.17	1.14	1.12	1.10	1.09	1.08
75	7.13	4.00	2.98	2.49	2.20	2.02	1.90	1.81	1.75	1.70	1.67	1.65	1.63	1.61
100	9.50	5.34	3.97	3.31	2.93	2.69	2.53	2.41	2.33	2.27	2.23	2.19	2.17	2.15
200	19.00	10.67	7.94	6.62	5.86	5.38	5.05	4.82	4.66	4.54	4.45	4.38	4.33	4.29
300	28.50	16.00	11.91	9.93	8.79	8.06	7.57	7.23	6.98	6.80	6.67	6.57	6.49	6.43
400	38.00	21.33	15.88	13.24	11.72	10.75	10.10	9.64	9.31	9.07	8.89	8.76	8.65	8.57
500	47.50	26.66	19.85	16.55	14.64	13.44	12.62	12.05	11.64	11.34	11.11	10.94	10.81	10.71
600	57.00	31.99	23.82	19.86	17.57	16.12	15.14	14.46	13.96	13.60	13.33	13.13	12.97	12.85
700	66.49	37.32	27.79	23.17	20.50	18.81	17.67	16.87	16.29	15.87	15.55	15.31	15.13	14.99
800	75.99	42.65	31.76	26.47	23.43	21.49	20.19	19.28	18.62	18.13	17.77	17.50	17.29	17.13
900	85.49	47.98	35.73	29.78	26.36	24.18	22.71	21.69	20.94	20.40	19.99	19.69	19.45	19.27
1000	94.99	53.31	39.70	33.09	29.28	26.87	25.24	24.09	23.27	22.67	22.21	21.87	21.61	21.42
2000	189.97	106.62	79.39	66.18	58.56	53.73	50.47	48.18	46.54	45.33	44.42	43.74	43.22	42.83
3000	284.96	159.93	119.09	99.27	87.84	80.59	75.70	72.27	69.80	67.99	66.63	65.61	64.83	64.24
4000	379.94	213.24	158.78	132.35	117.12	107.45	100.93	96.36	93.07	90.65	88.84	87.48	86.44	85.65
5000	474.92	266.55	198.47	165.44	146.40	134.31	126.16	120.45	116.34	113.31	111.05	109.35	108.05	107.06
6000	569.91	319.86	238.17	198.53	175.67	161.17	151.40	144.54	139.60	135.97	133.26	131.22	129.66	128.47
7000	664.89	373.17	277.86	231.62	204.95	188.03	176.63	168.63	162.87	158.63	155.47	153.09	151.27	149.88
8000	759.87	426.48	317.55	264.70	234.23	214.89	201.86	192.72	186.14	181.29	177.68	174.95	172.88	171.29
9000	854.86	479.78	357.25	297.79	263.51	241.75	227.09	216.81	209.40	203.96	199.89	196.82	194.49	192.70
10000	949.84	533.09	396.94	330.88	292.79	268.61	252.32	240.90	232.67	226.62	222.10	218.69	216.10	214.11
11000	1044.82	586.40	436.64	363.97	322.06	295.47	277.55	264.99	255.94	249.28	244.31	240.56	237.71	235.53
12000	1139.81	639.71	476.33	397.05	351.34	322.33	302.79	289.08	279.20	271.94	266.52	262.43	259.32	256.94
13000	1234.79	693.02	516.02	430.14	380.62	349.19	328.02	313.17	302.47	294.60	288.73	284.30	280.93	278.35
14000	1329.77	746.33	555.72	463.23	409.90	376.05	353.25	337.26	325.74	317.26	310.94	306.17	302.54	299.76
15000	1424.76	799.64	595.41	496.32	439.18	402.91	378.48	361.35	349.00	339.92	333.15	328.03	324.15	321.17
16000	1519.74	852.95	635.10	529.40	468.45	429.77	403.71	385.44	372.27	362.58	355.36	349.90	345.76	342.58
17000	1614.73	906.26	674.80	562.49	497.73	456.63	428.95	409.53	395.54	385.25	377.57	371.77	367.36	363.99
18000	1709.71	959.56	714.49	595.58	527.01	483.49	454.18	433.62	418.80	407.91	399.78	393.64	388.97	385.40
19000	1804.69	1012.87	754.19	628.67	556.29	510.35	479.41	457.71	442.07	430.57	421.98	415.51	410.58	406.81
20000	1899.68	1066.18	793.88	661.75	585.57	537.22	504.64	481.80	465.34	453.23	444.19	437.38	432.19	428.22
21000	1994.66	1119.49	833.57	694.84	614.84	564.08	529.87	505.89	488.60	475.89	466.40	459.25	453.80	449.64
22000	2089.64	1172.80	873.27	727.93	644.12	590.94	555.10	529.98	511.87	498.55	488.61	481.12	475.41	471.05
23000	2184.63	1226.11	912.96	761.02	673.40	617.80	580.34	554.07	535.14	521.21	510.82	502.98	497.02	492.46
24000	2279.61	1279.42	952.65	794.10	702.68	644.66	605.57	578.16	558.40	543.87	533.03	524.85	518.63	513.87
25000	2374.59	1332.73	992.35	827.19	731.96	671.52	630.80	602.25	581.67	566.54	555.24	546.72	540.24	535.28
26000	2469.58	1386.03	1032.04	860.28	761.24	698.38	656.03	626.34	604.94	589.20	577.45	568.59	561.85	556.69
27000	2564.56	1439.34	1071.74	893.37	790.51	725.24	681.26	650.43	628.20	611.86	599.66	590.46	583.46	578.10
28000	2659.54	1492.65	1111.43	926.45	819.79	752.10	706.49	674.52	651.47	634.52	621.87	612.33	605.07	599.51
29000	2754.53	1545.96	1151.12	959.54	849.07	778.96	731.73	698.61	674.74	657.18	644.08	634.20	626.68	620.92
30000	2849.51	1599.27	1190.82	992.63	878.35	805.82	756.96	722.70	698.00	679.84	666.29	656.06	648.29	642.33
31000	2944.50	1652.58	1230.51	1025.72	907.63	832.68	782.19	746.79	721.27	702.50	688.50	677.93	669.90	663.75
32000	3039.48	1705.89	1270.20	1058.80	936.90	859.54	807.42	770.88	744.54	725.16	710.71	699.80	691.51	685.16
33000	3134.46	1759.20	1309.90	1091.89	966.18	886.40	832.65	794.97	767.80	747.83	732.92	721.67	713.12	706.57
34000	3229.45	1812.51	1349.59	1124.98	995.46	913.26	857.89	819.06	791.07	770.49	755.13	743.54	734.72	727.98
35000	3324.43	1865.81	1389.28	1158.07	1024.74	940.12	883.12	843.15	814.34	793.15	777.34	765.41	756.33	749.39
36000	3419.41	1919.12	1428.98	1191.15	1054.02	966.98	908.35	867.24	837.60	815.81	799.55	787.28	777.94	770.80
37000	3514.40	1972.43	1468.67	1224.24	1083.29	993.84	933.58	891.33	860.87	838.47	821.76	809.14	799.55	792.21
38000	3609.38	2025.74	1508.37	1257.33	1112.57	1020.70	958.81	915.42	884.14	861.13	843.96	831.01	821.16	813.62
39000	3704.36	2079.05	1548.06	1290.42	1141.85	1047.57	984.04	939.51	907.40	883.79	866.17	852.88	842.77	835.03
40000	3799.35	2132.36	1587.75	1323.50	1171.13	1074.43	1009.28	963.60	930.67	906.45	888.38	874.75	864.38	856.44
41000	3894.33	2185.67	1627.45	1356.59	1200.41	1101.29	1034.51	987.69	953.94	929.12	910.59	896.62	885.99	877.86
42000	3989.31	2238.98	1667.14	1389.68	1229.68	1128.15	1059.74	1011.78	977.20	951.78	932.80	918.49	907.60	899.27
43000	4084.30	2292.28	1706.84	1422.77	1258.96	1155.01	1084.97	1035.87	1000.47	974.44	955.01	940.36	929.21	920.68
44000	4179.28	2345.59	1746.53	1455.85	1288.24	1181.87	1110.20	1059.96	1023.74	997.10	977.22	962.23	950.82	942.09
45000	4274.27	2398.90	1786.22	1488.94	1317.52	1208.73	1135.43	1084.05	1047.00	1019.76	999.43	984.09	972.43	963.50
46000	4369.25	2452.21	1825.92	1522.03	1346.80	1235.59	1160.67	1108.14	1070.27	1042.42	1021.64	1005.96	994.04	984.91
47000	4464.23	2505.52	1865.61	1555.12	1376.08	1262.45	1185.90	1132.23	1093.54	1065.08	1043.85	1027.83	1015.65	1006.32
48000	4559.22	2558.83	1905.30	1588.20	1405.35	1289.31	1211.13	1156.32	1116.80	1087.74	1066.06	1049.70	1037.26	1027.73
49000	4654.20	2612.14	1945.00	1621.29	1434.63	1316.17	1236.36	1180.41	1140.07	1110.41	1088.27	1071.57	1058.87	1049.14
50000	4749.18	2665.45	1984.69	1654.38	1463.91	1343.03	1261.59	1204.50	1163.34	1133.07	1110.48	1093.44	1080.48	1070.55
55000	5224.10	2931.99	2183.16	1819.81	1610.30	1477.33	1387.75	1324.94	1279.67	1246.37	1221.53	1202.78	1188.52	1177.61
60000	5699.02	3198.53	2381.63	1985.25	1756.69	1611.64	1513.91	1445.39	1396.00	1359.68	1332.57	1312.12	1296.57	1284.66
65000	6173.94	3465.08	2580.10	2150.69	1903.08	1745.94	1640.07	1565.84	1512.33	1472.98	1443.62	1421.47	1404.62	1391.72
70000	6648.85	3731.62	2778.57	2316.13	2049.47	1880.24	1766.23	1686.29	1628.67	1586.29	1554.67	1530.81	1512.66	1498.77
75000	7123.77	3998.17	2977.04	2481.56	2195.86	2014.54	1892.39	1806.74	1745.00	1699.60	1665.71	1640.15	1620.71	1605.83
80000	7598.69	4264.71	3175.50	2647.00	2342.25	2148.85	2018.55	1927.19	1861.33	1812.90	1776.76	1749.50	1728.76	1712.88
85000	8073.61	4531.26	3373.97	2812.44	2488.64	2283.15	2144.71	2047.64	1977.67	1926.21	1887.81	1858.84	1836.80	1819.94
90000	8548.53	4797.80	3572.44	2977.88	2635.03	2417.45	2270.86	2168.09	2094.00	2039.52	1998.86	1968.18	1944.85	1926.99
95000	9023.44	5064.34	3770.91	3143.31	2781.42	2551.75	2397.02	2288.54	2210.33	2152.82	2109.90	2077.53	2052.90	2034.05
100000	9498.36	5330.89	3969.38	3308.75	2927.81	2686.06	2523.18	2408.99	2326.67	2266.13	2220.95	2186.87	2160.95	2141.10

MONTHLY PAYMENT
REQUIRED TO AMORTIZE A LOAN

24.875%

TERM	15 Years	16 Years	17 Years	18 Years	19 Years	20 Years	21 Years	22 Years	23 Years	24 Years	25 Years	30 Years	35 Years	40 Years
AMOUNT														
5	.11	.11	.11	.11	.11	.11	.11	.11	.11	.11	.11	.11	.11	.11
10	.22	.22	.22	.21	.21	.21	.21	.21	.21	.21	.21	.21	.21	.21
15	.32	.32	.32	.32	.32	.32	.32	.32	.32	.32	.32	.32	.32	.32
25	.54	.53	.53	.53	.53	.53	.53	.53	.53	.52	.52	.52	.52	.52
50	1.07	1.06	1.06	1.05	1.05	1.05	1.05	1.05	1.05	1.04	1.04	1.04	1.04	1.04
75	1.60	1.59	1.58	1.58	1.57	1.57	1.57	1.57	1.57	1.56	1.56	1.56	1.56	1.56
100	2.13	2.12	2.11	2.10	2.10	2.09	2.09	2.09	2.09	2.08	2.08	2.08	2.08	2.08
200	4.26	4.23	4.21	4.20	4.19	4.18	4.17	4.17	4.17	4.16	4.16	4.15	4.15	4.15
300	6.38	6.35	6.32	6.30	6.28	6.27	6.26	6.25	6.25	6.24	6.24	6.23	6.22	6.22
400	8.51	8.46	8.42	8.40	8.37	8.36	8.34	8.33	8.33	8.32	8.31	8.30	8.30	8.30
500	10.63	10.58	10.53	10.49	10.47	10.45	10.43	10.42	10.41	10.40	10.39	10.38	10.37	10.37
600	12.76	12.69	12.63	12.59	12.56	12.53	12.51	12.50	12.49	12.48	12.47	12.45	12.44	12.44
700	14.89	14.80	14.74	14.69	14.65	14.62	14.60	14.58	14.57	14.55	14.55	14.52	14.52	14.52
800	17.01	16.92	16.84	16.79	16.74	16.71	16.68	16.66	16.65	16.63	16.62	16.60	16.59	16.59
900	19.14	19.03	18.95	18.89	18.84	18.80	18.77	18.74	18.73	18.71	18.70	18.67	18.66	18.66
1000	21.26	21.15	21.05	20.98	20.93	20.89	20.85	20.83	20.81	20.79	20.78	20.75	20.74	20.74
2000	42.52	42.29	42.10	41.96	41.85	41.77	41.70	41.65	41.61	41.58	41.55	41.49	41.47	41.47
3000	63.78	63.43	63.15	62.94	62.78	62.65	62.55	62.47	62.41	62.36	62.32	62.23	62.20	62.20
4000	85.04	84.57	84.20	83.92	83.70	83.53	83.40	83.29	83.21	83.15	83.10	82.97	82.94	82.93
5000	106.30	105.71	105.25	104.90	104.62	104.41	104.24	104.11	104.01	103.93	103.87	103.72	103.67	103.66
6000	127.56	126.85	126.30	125.88	125.55	125.29	125.09	124.93	124.81	124.72	124.64	124.46	124.40	124.39
7000	148.81	147.99	147.35	146.86	146.47	146.17	145.94	145.76	145.61	145.50	145.42	145.20	145.14	145.12
8000	170.07	169.13	168.40	167.83	167.39	167.05	166.79	166.58	166.42	166.29	166.19	165.94	165.87	165.85
9000	191.33	190.27	189.45	188.81	188.32	187.93	187.63	187.40	187.22	187.08	186.96	186.68	186.60	186.58
10000	212.59	211.41	210.50	209.79	209.24	208.81	208.48	208.22	208.02	207.86	207.74	207.43	207.33	207.31
11000	233.85	232.55	231.55	230.77	230.17	229.70	229.33	229.04	228.82	228.65	228.51	228.17	228.07	228.04
12000	255.11	253.69	252.60	251.75	251.09	250.58	250.18	249.86	249.62	249.43	249.28	248.91	248.80	248.77
13000	276.36	274.83	273.65	272.73	272.01	271.46	271.02	270.69	270.42	270.22	270.06	269.65	269.53	269.50
14000	297.62	295.97	294.70	293.71	292.94	292.34	291.87	291.51	291.22	291.00	290.83	290.39	290.27	290.23
15000	318.88	317.11	315.75	314.69	313.86	313.22	312.72	312.33	312.03	311.79	311.60	311.14	311.00	310.96
16000	340.14	338.25	336.80	335.66	334.78	334.10	333.57	333.15	332.83	332.57	332.38	331.88	331.73	331.69
17000	361.40	359.40	357.85	356.64	355.71	354.98	354.41	353.97	353.63	353.36	353.15	352.62	352.46	352.42
18000	382.66	380.54	378.89	377.62	376.63	375.86	375.26	374.79	374.43	374.15	373.92	373.36	373.20	373.15
19000	403.91	401.68	399.94	398.60	397.56	396.74	396.11	395.62	395.23	394.93	394.70	394.10	393.93	393.88
20000	425.17	422.82	420.99	419.58	418.48	417.62	416.96	416.44	416.03	415.72	415.47	414.85	414.66	414.61
21000	446.43	443.96	442.04	440.56	439.40	438.50	437.81	437.26	436.83	436.50	436.24	435.59	435.40	435.34
22000	467.69	465.10	463.09	461.54	460.33	459.39	458.65	458.08	457.64	457.29	457.02	456.33	456.13	456.07
23000	488.95	486.24	484.14	482.51	481.25	480.27	479.50	478.90	478.44	478.07	477.79	477.07	476.86	476.80
24000	510.21	507.38	505.19	503.49	502.17	501.15	500.35	499.72	499.24	498.86	498.56	497.81	497.60	497.53
25000	531.46	528.52	526.24	524.47	523.10	522.03	521.20	520.55	520.04	519.64	519.34	518.56	518.33	518.26
26000	552.72	549.66	547.29	545.45	544.02	542.91	542.04	541.37	540.84	540.43	540.11	539.30	539.06	538.99
27000	573.98	570.80	568.34	566.43	564.95	563.79	562.89	562.19	561.64	561.22	560.88	560.04	559.79	559.72
28000	595.24	591.94	589.39	587.41	585.87	584.67	583.74	583.01	582.44	582.00	581.66	580.78	580.53	580.45
29000	616.50	613.08	610.44	608.39	606.79	605.55	604.59	603.83	603.25	602.79	602.43	601.52	601.26	601.18
30000	637.76	634.22	631.49	629.37	627.72	626.43	625.43	624.65	624.05	623.57	623.20	622.27	621.99	621.91
31000	659.01	655.36	652.54	650.34	648.64	647.31	646.28	645.48	644.85	644.36	643.98	643.01	642.73	642.64
32000	680.27	676.50	673.59	671.32	669.56	668.20	667.13	666.30	665.65	665.14	664.75	663.75	663.46	663.37
33000	701.53	697.64	694.64	692.30	690.49	689.08	687.98	687.12	686.45	685.93	685.52	684.49	684.19	684.10
34000	722.79	718.79	715.69	713.28	711.41	709.96	708.82	707.94	707.25	706.72	706.30	705.23	704.92	704.83
35000	744.05	739.93	736.73	734.26	732.34	730.84	729.67	728.76	728.05	727.50	727.07	725.98	725.66	725.56
36000	765.31	761.07	757.78	755.24	753.26	751.72	750.52	749.58	748.85	748.29	747.84	746.72	746.39	746.29
37000	786.57	782.21	778.83	776.22	774.18	772.60	771.37	770.41	769.66	769.07	768.62	767.46	767.12	767.02
38000	807.82	803.35	799.88	797.20	795.11	793.48	792.22	791.23	790.46	789.86	789.39	788.20	787.86	787.75
39000	829.08	824.49	820.93	818.17	816.03	814.36	813.06	812.05	811.26	810.64	810.16	808.94	808.59	808.49
40000	850.34	845.63	841.98	839.15	836.95	835.24	833.91	832.87	832.06	831.43	830.94	829.69	829.32	829.22
41000	871.60	866.77	863.03	860.13	857.88	856.12	854.76	853.69	852.86	852.21	851.71	850.43	850.05	849.95
42000	892.86	887.91	884.08	881.11	878.80	877.00	875.61	874.51	873.66	873.00	872.48	871.17	870.79	870.68
43000	914.12	909.05	905.13	902.09	899.72	897.89	896.45	895.34	894.47	893.79	893.26	891.91	891.52	891.41
44000	935.37	930.19	926.18	923.07	920.65	918.77	917.30	916.16	915.27	914.57	914.03	912.65	912.25	912.14
45000	956.63	951.33	947.23	944.05	941.57	939.65	938.15	936.98	936.07	935.36	934.80	933.40	932.99	932.87
46000	977.89	972.47	968.28	965.02	962.50	960.53	959.00	957.80	956.87	956.14	955.57	954.14	953.72	953.60
47000	999.15	993.61	989.33	986.00	983.42	981.41	979.84	978.62	977.67	976.93	976.35	974.88	974.45	974.33
48000	1020.41	1014.75	1010.38	1006.98	1004.34	1002.29	1000.69	999.44	998.47	997.71	997.12	995.62	995.19	995.06
49000	1041.67	1035.89	1031.43	1027.96	1025.27	1023.17	1021.54	1020.27	1019.27	1018.50	1017.89	1016.36	1015.92	1015.79
50000	1062.92	1057.03	1052.48	1048.94	1046.19	1044.05	1042.39	1041.09	1040.08	1039.29	1038.67	1037.11	1036.65	1036.52
55000	1169.22	1162.74	1157.72	1153.83	1150.81	1148.46	1146.63	1145.20	1144.08	1143.21	1142.53	1140.82	1140.32	1140.17
60000	1275.51	1268.44	1262.97	1258.73	1255.43	1252.86	1250.86	1249.30	1248.09	1247.14	1246.40	1244.53	1243.98	1243.82
65000	1381.80	1374.14	1368.22	1363.62	1360.05	1357.27	1355.10	1353.41	1352.10	1351.07	1350.27	1348.24	1347.64	1347.47
70000	1488.09	1479.85	1473.46	1468.51	1464.67	1461.67	1459.34	1457.52	1456.10	1455.00	1454.13	1451.95	1451.31	1451.12
75000	1594.38	1585.55	1578.71	1573.41	1569.28	1566.08	1563.58	1561.63	1560.11	1558.93	1558.00	1555.66	1554.97	1554.77
80000	1700.68	1691.25	1683.96	1678.30	1673.90	1670.48	1667.82	1665.74	1664.12	1662.85	1661.87	1659.37	1658.64	1658.43
85000	1806.97	1796.96	1789.21	1783.19	1778.52	1774.89	1772.05	1769.85	1768.12	1766.78	1765.73	1763.08	1762.30	1762.08
90000	1913.26	1902.66	1894.45	1888.09	1883.14	1879.29	1876.29	1873.95	1872.13	1870.71	1869.60	1866.79	1865.97	1865.73
95000	2019.55	2008.36	1999.70	1992.98	1987.76	1983.70	1980.53	1978.06	1976.14	1974.64	1973.46	1970.50	1969.63	1969.38
100000	2125.84	2114.06	2104.95	2097.87	2092.38	2088.10	2084.77	2082.17	2080.15	2078.56	2077.33	2074.21	2073.30	2073.03

MONTHLY PAYMENT
REQUIRED TO AMORTIZE A LOAN

TERM	1 Year	2 Years	3 Years	4 Years	5 Years	6 Years	7 Years	8 Years	9 Years	10 Years	11 Years	12 Years	13 Years	14 Years
AMOUNT														
5	.48	.27	.20	.17	.15	.14	.13	.13	.12	.12	.12	.11	.11	.11
10	.95	.54	.40	.34	.30	.27	.26	.25	.24	.23	.23	.22	.22	.22
15	1.43	.80	.60	.50	.44	.41	.38	.37	.35	.35	.34	.33	.33	.33
25	2.38	1.34	1.00	.83	.74	.68	.64	.61	.59	.57	.56	.55	.55	.54
50	4.75	2.67	1.99	1.66	1.47	1.35	1.27	1.21	1.17	1.14	1.12	1.10	1.09	1.08
75	7.13	4.00	2.98	2.49	2.20	2.02	1.90	1.81	1.75	1.71	1.67	1.65	1.63	1.61
100	9.50	5.34	3.98	3.32	2.93	2.69	2.53	2.42	2.33	2.27	2.23	2.19	2.17	2.15
200	19.00	10.67	7.95	6.63	5.84	5.38	5.05	4.83	4.66	4.54	4.45	4.38	4.33	4.29
300	28.50	16.00	11.92	9.94	8.79	8.07	7.58	7.24	6.99	6.81	6.67	6.57	6.49	6.43
400	38.00	21.33	15.89	13.25	11.72	10.76	10.10	9.65	9.32	9.08	8.90	8.76	8.66	8.58
500	47.50	26.67	19.86	16.56	14.65	13.44	12.63	12.06	11.65	11.34	11.12	10.95	10.82	10.72
600	57.00	32.00	23.83	19.87	17.58	16.13	15.15	14.47	13.98	13.61	13.34	13.14	12.98	12.86
700	66.50	37.33	27.80	23.18	20.51	18.82	17.68	16.88	16.30	15.88	15.56	15.33	15.14	15.01
800	76.00	42.66	31.77	26.49	23.44	21.51	20.20	19.29	18.63	18.15	17.79	17.51	17.31	17.15
900	85.50	47.99	35.74	29.80	26.37	24.19	22.73	21.70	20.96	20.42	20.01	19.70	19.47	19.29
1000	95.00	53.33	39.71	33.11	29.30	26.88	25.25	24.11	23.29	22.68	22.23	21.89	21.63	21.44
2000	190.00	106.65	79.42	66.21	58.59	53.76	50.50	48.22	46.57	45.36	44.46	43.78	43.26	42.87
3000	284.99	159.97	119.13	99.31	87.88	80.63	75.75	72.32	69.86	68.04	66.69	65.67	64.89	64.30
4000	379.99	213.29	158.83	132.41	117.18	107.51	101.00	96.43	93.14	90.72	88.92	87.55	86.52	85.73
5000	474.98	266.61	198.54	165.51	146.47	134.38	126.24	120.54	116.42	113.40	111.14	109.44	108.15	107.16
6000	569.98	319.93	238.25	198.61	175.76	161.26	151.49	144.64	139.71	136.08	133.37	131.33	129.77	128.59
7000	664.97	373.25	277.95	231.71	205.05	188.14	176.74	168.75	162.99	158.76	155.60	153.21	151.40	150.02
8000	759.97	426.58	317.66	264.82	234.35	215.01	201.99	192.86	186.27	181.44	177.83	175.10	173.03	171.45
9000	854.97	479.90	357.37	297.92	263.64	241.89	227.23	216.96	209.56	204.11	200.05	196.99	194.66	192.88
10000	949.96	533.22	397.07	331.02	292.93	268.76	252.48	241.07	232.84	226.79	222.28	218.88	216.29	214.31
11000	1044.96	586.54	436.78	364.12	322.22	295.64	277.73	265.18	256.13	249.47	244.51	240.76	237.92	235.74
12000	1139.95	639.86	476.49	397.22	351.52	322.52	302.98	289.28	279.41	272.15	266.74	262.65	259.54	257.17
13000	1234.95	693.18	516.20	430.32	380.81	349.39	328.23	313.39	302.69	294.83	288.96	284.54	281.17	278.60
14000	1329.94	746.50	555.90	463.42	410.10	376.27	353.47	337.49	325.98	317.51	311.19	306.42	302.80	300.03
15000	1424.94	799.83	595.61	496.53	439.40	403.14	378.72	361.60	349.26	340.19	333.42	328.31	324.43	321.46
16000	1519.94	853.15	635.32	529.63	468.69	430.02	403.97	385.71	372.54	362.87	355.65	350.20	346.06	342.89
17000	1614.93	906.47	675.02	562.73	497.98	456.89	429.22	409.81	395.83	385.55	377.87	372.09	367.68	364.32
18000	1709.93	959.79	714.73	595.83	527.27	483.77	454.46	433.92	419.11	408.22	400.10	393.97	389.31	385.75
19000	1804.92	1013.11	754.44	628.93	556.57	510.65	479.71	458.03	442.40	430.90	422.33	415.86	410.94	407.18
20000	1899.92	1066.43	794.14	662.03	585.86	537.52	504.96	482.13	465.68	453.58	444.56	437.75	432.57	428.61
21000	1994.91	1119.75	833.85	695.13	615.15	564.40	530.21	506.24	488.96	476.26	466.78	459.63	454.20	450.04
22000	2089.91	1173.07	873.56	728.24	644.44	591.27	555.46	530.35	512.25	498.94	489.01	481.52	475.83	471.47
23000	2184.91	1226.40	913.26	761.34	673.74	618.15	580.70	554.45	535.53	521.62	511.24	503.41	497.45	492.90
24000	2279.90	1279.72	952.97	794.44	703.03	645.03	605.95	578.56	558.81	544.30	533.47	525.30	519.08	514.33
25000	2374.90	1333.04	992.68	827.54	732.32	671.90	631.20	602.66	582.10	566.98	555.69	547.18	540.71	535.76
26000	2469.89	1386.36	1032.39	860.64	761.62	698.78	656.45	626.77	605.38	589.65	577.92	569.07	562.34	557.19
27000	2564.89	1439.68	1072.09	893.74	790.91	725.65	681.69	650.88	628.67	612.33	600.15	590.96	583.97	578.62
28000	2659.88	1493.00	1111.80	926.84	820.20	752.53	706.94	674.98	651.95	635.01	622.38	612.84	605.59	600.05
29000	2754.88	1546.32	1151.51	959.94	849.49	779.40	732.19	699.09	675.23	657.69	644.60	634.73	627.22	621.48
30000	2849.88	1599.65	1191.21	993.05	878.79	806.28	757.44	723.20	698.52	680.37	666.83	656.62	648.85	642.91
31000	2944.87	1652.97	1230.92	1026.15	908.08	833.16	782.68	747.30	721.80	703.05	689.06	678.50	670.48	664.34
32000	3039.87	1706.29	1270.63	1059.25	937.37	860.03	807.93	771.41	745.08	725.73	711.29	700.39	692.11	685.77
33000	3134.86	1759.61	1310.33	1092.35	966.66	886.91	833.18	795.52	768.37	748.41	733.51	722.28	713.74	707.20
34000	3229.86	1812.93	1350.04	1125.45	995.96	913.78	858.43	819.62	791.65	771.09	755.74	744.17	735.36	728.63
35000	3324.85	1866.25	1389.75	1158.55	1025.25	940.66	883.68	843.73	814.94	793.76	777.97	766.05	756.99	750.06
36000	3419.85	1919.57	1429.46	1191.65	1054.54	967.54	908.92	867.83	838.22	816.44	800.20	787.94	778.62	771.49
37000	3514.85	1972.90	1469.16	1224.76	1083.84	994.41	934.17	891.94	861.50	839.12	822.42	809.83	800.25	792.92
38000	3609.84	2026.22	1508.87	1257.86	1113.13	1021.29	959.42	916.05	884.79	861.80	844.65	831.71	821.88	814.35
39000	3704.84	2079.54	1548.58	1290.96	1142.42	1048.16	984.67	940.15	908.07	884.48	866.88	853.60	843.50	835.78
40000	3799.83	2132.86	1588.28	1324.06	1171.71	1075.04	1009.91	964.26	931.35	907.16	889.11	875.49	865.13	857.21
41000	3894.83	2186.18	1627.99	1357.16	1201.01	1101.91	1035.16	988.37	954.64	929.84	911.33	897.38	886.76	878.64
42000	3989.82	2239.50	1667.70	1390.26	1230.30	1128.79	1060.41	1012.47	977.92	952.52	933.56	919.26	908.39	900.07
43000	4084.82	2292.82	1707.40	1423.36	1259.59	1155.67	1085.66	1036.58	1001.20	975.19	955.79	941.15	930.02	921.50
44000	4179.82	2346.14	1747.11	1456.47	1288.88	1182.54	1110.91	1060.69	1024.49	997.87	978.02	963.04	951.65	942.93
45000	4274.81	2399.47	1786.82	1489.57	1318.18	1209.42	1136.15	1084.79	1047.77	1020.55	1000.24	984.92	973.27	964.36
46000	4369.81	2452.79	1826.53	1522.67	1347.47	1236.29	1161.40	1108.90	1071.06	1043.23	1022.47	1006.81	994.90	985.79
47000	4464.80	2506.11	1866.23	1555.77	1376.76	1263.17	1186.65	1133.00	1094.34	1065.91	1044.70	1028.70	1016.53	1007.22
48000	4559.80	2559.43	1905.94	1588.87	1406.06	1290.05	1211.90	1157.11	1117.62	1088.59	1066.93	1050.59	1038.16	1028.65
49000	4654.79	2612.75	1945.65	1621.97	1435.35	1316.92	1237.14	1181.22	1140.91	1111.27	1089.15	1072.47	1059.79	1050.08
50000	4749.79	2666.07	1985.35	1655.07	1464.64	1343.80	1262.39	1205.32	1164.19	1133.95	1111.38	1094.36	1081.42	1071.51
55000	5224.77	2932.68	2183.89	1820.58	1611.10	1478.18	1388.63	1325.86	1280.61	1247.34	1222.52	1203.80	1189.56	1178.66
60000	5699.75	3199.29	2382.42	1986.09	1757.57	1612.56	1514.87	1446.39	1397.03	1360.73	1333.66	1313.23	1297.70	1285.81
65000	6174.72	3465.89	2580.96	2151.59	1904.03	1746.94	1641.11	1566.92	1513.45	1474.13	1444.79	1422.67	1405.84	1392.96
70000	6649.70	3732.50	2779.49	2317.10	2050.50	1881.31	1767.35	1687.45	1629.87	1587.52	1555.93	1532.10	1513.98	1500.11
75000	7124.68	3999.11	2978.03	2482.61	2196.96	2015.69	1893.59	1807.98	1746.28	1700.92	1667.07	1641.54	1622.12	1607.26
80000	7599.66	4265.71	3176.56	2648.12	2343.42	2150.07	2019.82	1928.52	1862.70	1814.31	1778.21	1750.97	1730.26	1714.41
85000	8074.64	4532.32	3375.10	2813.62	2489.89	2284.45	2146.06	2049.05	1979.12	1927.71	1889.34	1860.41	1838.40	1821.56
90000	8549.62	4798.93	3573.63	2979.13	2636.35	2418.83	2272.30	2169.58	2095.54	2041.10	2000.48	1969.84	1946.54	1928.71
95000	9024.60	5065.53	3772.17	3144.64	2782.81	2553.21	2398.54	2290.11	2211.96	2154.49	2111.62	2079.28	2054.68	2035.86
100000	9499.57	5332.14	3970.70	3310.14	2929.28	2687.59	2524.78	2410.64	2328.38	2267.89	2222.76	2188.71	2162.83	2143.01

TERM	15 Years	16 Years	17 Years	18 Years	19 Years	20 Years	21 Years	22 Years	23 Years	24 Years	25 Years	30 Years	35 Years	40 Years
AMOUNT														
5	.11	.11	.11	.11	.11	.11	.11	.11	.11	.11	.11	.11	.11	.11
10	.22	.22	.22	.21	.21	.21	.21	.21	.21	.21	.21	.21	.21	.21
15	.32	.32	.32	.32	.32	.32	.32	.32	.32	.32	.32	.32	.32	.32
25	.54	.53	.53	.53	.53	.53	.53	.53	.53	.53	.52	.52	.52	.52
50	1.07	1.06	1.06	1.05	1.05	1.05	1.05	1.05	1.05	1.05	1.04	1.04	1.04	1.04
75	1.60	1.59	1.59	1.58	1.58	1.57	1.57	1.57	1.57	1.57	1.56	1.56	1.56	1.56
100	2.13	2.12	2.11	2.10	2.10	2.10	2.09	2.09	2.09	2.09	2.08	2.08	2.08	2.08
200	4.26	4.24	4.22	4.20	4.19	4.19	4.18	4.17	4.17	4.17	4.16	4.16	4.16	4.16
300	6.39	6.35	6.33	6.30	6.29	6.28	6.27	6.26	6.25	6.25	6.24	6.23	6.23	6.23
400	8.52	8.47	8.43	8.40	8.38	8.37	8.35	8.34	8.33	8.33	8.32	8.31	8.31	8.31
500	10.64	10.59	10.54	10.50	10.48	10.46	10.44	10.43	10.42	10.41	10.40	10.39	10.38	10.38
600	12.77	12.70	12.65	12.60	12.57	12.55	12.53	12.51	12.50	12.49	12.48	12.46	12.46	12.46
700	14.90	14.82	14.75	14.70	14.67	14.64	14.61	14.59	14.58	14.57	14.56	14.54	14.53	14.53
800	17.03	16.93	16.86	16.80	16.76	16.73	16.70	16.68	16.66	16.65	16.64	16.62	16.61	16.61
900	19.15	19.05	18.97	18.90	18.85	18.82	18.79	18.76	18.74	18.73	18.72	18.69	18.68	18.68
1000	21.28	21.17	21.07	21.00	20.95	20.91	20.87	20.85	20.83	20.81	20.80	20.77	20.76	20.76
2000	42.56	42.33	42.14	42.00	41.89	41.81	41.74	41.69	41.65	41.62	41.59	41.53	41.51	41.51
3000	63.84	63.49	63.21	63.00	62.84	62.71	62.61	62.53	62.47	62.42	62.39	62.29	62.27	62.26
4000	85.12	84.65	84.28	84.00	83.78	83.61	83.48	83.37	83.29	83.23	83.18	83.06	83.02	83.01
5000	106.39	105.81	105.35	105.00	104.72	104.51	104.34	104.22	104.11	104.04	103.97	103.82	103.77	103.76
6000	127.67	126.97	126.42	126.00	125.67	125.41	125.21	125.06	124.94	124.84	124.77	124.58	124.53	124.51
7000	148.95	148.13	147.49	147.00	146.61	146.31	146.08	145.90	145.76	145.65	145.56	145.34	145.28	145.26
8000	170.23	169.29	168.56	167.99	167.56	167.21	166.95	166.74	166.58	166.45	166.36	166.11	166.03	166.01
9000	191.50	190.45	189.63	188.99	188.50	188.12	187.82	187.58	187.40	187.26	187.15	186.87	186.79	186.76
10000	212.78	211.61	210.70	209.99	209.44	209.02	208.68	208.43	208.22	208.07	207.94	207.63	207.54	207.52
11000	234.06	232.77	231.77	230.99	230.39	229.92	229.55	229.27	229.05	228.87	228.74	228.40	228.30	228.27
12000	255.34	253.93	252.84	251.99	251.33	250.82	250.42	250.11	249.87	249.68	249.53	249.16	249.05	249.02
13000	276.62	275.09	273.90	272.99	272.27	271.72	271.29	270.95	270.69	270.49	270.33	269.92	269.80	269.77
14000	297.89	296.25	294.97	293.99	293.22	292.62	292.16	291.79	291.51	291.29	291.12	290.68	290.56	290.52
15000	319.17	317.41	316.04	314.98	314.16	313.52	313.02	312.64	312.33	312.10	311.91	311.45	311.31	311.27
16000	340.45	338.57	337.11	335.98	335.11	334.42	333.89	333.48	333.16	332.90	332.71	332.21	332.06	332.02
17000	361.73	359.73	358.18	356.98	356.05	355.33	354.76	354.32	353.98	353.71	353.50	352.97	352.82	352.77
18000	383.00	380.89	379.25	377.98	376.99	376.23	375.63	375.16	374.80	374.52	374.29	373.73	373.57	373.52
19000	404.28	402.05	400.32	398.98	397.94	397.13	396.50	396.00	395.62	395.32	395.09	394.50	394.33	394.28
20000	425.56	423.21	421.39	419.98	418.88	418.03	417.36	416.85	416.44	416.13	415.88	415.26	415.08	415.03
21000	446.84	444.37	442.46	440.98	439.83	438.93	438.23	437.69	437.27	436.93	436.68	436.02	435.83	435.78
22000	468.12	465.53	463.53	461.98	460.77	459.83	459.10	458.53	458.09	457.74	457.47	456.79	456.59	456.53
23000	489.39	486.69	484.60	482.97	481.71	480.73	479.97	479.37	478.91	478.55	478.26	477.55	477.34	477.28
24000	510.67	507.85	505.67	503.97	502.66	501.63	500.84	500.22	499.73	499.35	499.06	498.31	498.09	498.03
25000	531.95	529.01	526.74	524.97	523.60	522.53	521.70	521.06	520.55	520.16	519.85	519.07	518.85	518.78
26000	553.23	550.17	547.80	545.97	544.54	543.44	542.57	541.90	541.37	540.97	540.65	539.84	539.60	539.53
27000	574.50	571.33	568.87	566.97	565.49	564.34	563.44	562.74	562.20	561.77	561.44	560.60	560.36	560.28
28000	595.78	592.49	589.94	587.97	586.43	585.24	584.31	583.58	583.02	582.58	582.23	581.36	581.11	581.04
29000	617.06	613.65	611.01	608.97	607.38	606.14	605.18	604.43	603.84	603.38	603.03	602.13	601.86	601.79
30000	638.34	634.81	632.08	629.96	628.32	627.04	626.04	625.27	624.66	624.19	623.82	622.89	622.62	622.54
31000	659.62	655.97	653.15	650.96	649.26	647.94	646.91	646.11	645.48	645.00	644.61	643.65	643.37	643.29
32000	680.89	677.13	674.22	671.96	670.21	668.84	667.78	666.95	666.31	665.80	665.41	664.41	664.12	664.04
33000	702.17	698.29	695.29	692.96	691.15	689.74	688.65	687.79	687.13	686.61	686.20	685.18	684.88	684.79
34000	723.45	719.45	716.36	713.96	712.10	710.65	709.52	708.64	707.95	707.41	707.00	705.94	705.63	705.54
35000	744.73	740.61	737.43	734.96	733.04	731.55	730.38	729.48	728.77	728.22	727.79	726.70	726.39	726.29
36000	766.00	761.77	758.50	755.96	753.98	752.45	751.25	750.32	749.59	749.03	748.58	747.46	747.14	747.04
37000	787.28	782.93	779.57	776.96	774.93	773.35	772.12	771.16	770.42	769.83	769.38	768.23	767.89	767.80
38000	808.56	804.09	800.64	797.95	795.87	794.25	792.99	792.00	791.24	790.64	790.17	788.99	788.65	788.55
39000	829.84	825.25	821.70	818.95	816.81	815.15	813.86	812.85	812.06	811.45	810.97	809.75	809.40	809.30
40000	851.12	846.41	842.77	839.95	837.76	836.05	834.72	833.69	832.88	832.25	831.76	830.52	830.15	830.05
41000	872.39	867.57	863.84	860.95	858.70	856.95	855.59	854.53	853.70	853.06	852.55	851.28	850.91	850.80
42000	893.67	888.73	884.91	881.95	879.65	877.85	876.46	875.37	874.53	873.86	873.35	872.04	871.66	871.55
43000	914.95	909.89	905.98	902.95	900.59	898.76	897.33	896.21	895.35	894.67	894.14	892.80	892.42	892.30
44000	936.23	931.05	927.05	923.95	921.53	919.66	918.20	917.06	916.17	915.48	914.94	913.57	913.17	913.05
45000	957.50	952.21	948.12	944.94	942.48	940.56	939.06	937.90	936.99	936.28	935.73	934.33	933.92	933.80
46000	978.78	973.37	969.19	965.94	963.42	961.46	959.93	958.74	957.81	957.09	956.52	955.09	954.68	954.55
47000	1000.06	994.53	990.26	986.94	984.37	982.36	980.80	979.58	978.63	977.89	977.32	975.86	975.43	975.31
48000	1021.34	1015.69	1011.33	1007.94	1005.31	1003.26	1001.67	1000.43	999.46	998.70	998.11	996.62	996.18	996.06
49000	1042.62	1036.85	1032.40	1028.94	1026.25	1024.16	1022.54	1021.27	1020.28	1019.51	1018.90	1017.38	1016.94	1016.81
50000	1063.89	1058.02	1053.47	1049.94	1047.20	1045.06	1043.41	1042.11	1041.10	1040.31	1039.70	1038.14	1037.69	1037.56
55000	1170.28	1163.82	1158.81	1154.93	1151.92	1149.57	1147.74	1146.32	1145.21	1144.34	1143.67	1141.96	1141.46	1141.31
60000	1276.67	1269.62	1264.16	1259.92	1256.64	1254.08	1252.08	1250.53	1249.32	1248.37	1247.64	1245.77	1245.23	1245.07
65000	1383.06	1375.42	1369.50	1364.92	1361.35	1358.58	1356.42	1354.74	1353.43	1352.41	1351.61	1349.59	1349.00	1348.83
70000	1489.45	1481.22	1474.85	1469.91	1466.07	1463.09	1460.76	1458.95	1457.54	1456.44	1455.58	1453.40	1452.77	1452.58
75000	1595.84	1587.02	1580.20	1574.90	1570.79	1567.59	1565.10	1563.16	1561.65	1560.47	1559.54	1557.21	1556.53	1556.34
80000	1702.23	1692.82	1685.54	1679.90	1675.51	1672.10	1669.44	1667.37	1665.76	1664.50	1663.51	1661.03	1660.30	1660.09
85000	1808.61	1798.62	1790.89	1784.89	1780.23	1776.61	1773.78	1771.58	1769.87	1768.53	1767.48	1764.84	1764.07	1763.85
90000	1915.00	1904.42	1896.24	1889.88	1884.95	1881.11	1878.12	1875.79	1873.98	1872.56	1871.45	1868.65	1867.84	1867.60
95000	2021.39	2010.22	2001.58	1994.88	1989.67	1985.62	1982.46	1980.00	1978.09	1976.59	1975.42	1972.47	1971.61	1971.36
100000	2127.78	2116.03	2106.93	2099.87	2094.39	2090.12	2086.80	2084.21	2082.20	2080.62	2079.39	2076.28	2075.38	2075.11

MONTHLY PAYMENT
REQUIRED TO AMORTIZE A LOAN

TERM / AMOUNT	1 Year	2 Years	3 Years	4 Years	5 Years	6 Years	7 Years	8 Years	9 Years	10 Years	11 Years	12 Years	13 Years	14 Years
5	.48	.27	.20	.17	.15	.14	.13	.13	.12	.12	.12	.11	.11	.11
10	.96	.54	.40	.34	.30	.27	.26	.25	.24	.23	.23	.22	.22	.22
15	1.43	.81	.60	.50	.45	.41	.38	.37	.36	.35	.34	.33	.33	.33
25	2.38	1.34	1.00	.83	.74	.68	.64	.61	.59	.57	.56	.55	.55	.54
50	4.76	2.67	1.99	1.66	1.47	1.35	1.27	1.21	1.17	1.14	1.12	1.10	1.09	1.08
75	7.13	4.01	2.99	2.49	2.21	2.03	1.90	1.82	1.76	1.71	1.68	1.65	1.63	1.62
100	9.51	5.34	3.98	3.32	2.94	2.70	2.54	2.42	2.34	2.28	2.23	2.20	2.18	2.16
200	19.01	10.68	7.96	6.64	5.88	5.39	5.07	4.84	4.68	4.55	4.46	4.40	4.35	4.31
300	28.52	16.02	11.93	9.95	8.81	8.09	7.60	7.26	7.01	6.83	6.69	6.59	6.52	6.46
400	38.02	21.35	15.91	13.27	11.75	10.78	10.13	9.67	9.35	9.10	8.92	8.79	8.69	8.61
500	47.53	26.69	19.88	16.58	14.68	13.47	12.66	12.09	11.68	11.38	11.15	10.99	10.86	10.76
600	57.03	32.03	23.86	19.90	17.62	16.17	15.19	14.51	14.02	13.65	13.38	13.18	13.03	12.91
700	66.54	37.37	27.84	23.21	20.55	18.86	17.72	16.93	16.35	15.93	15.61	15.38	15.20	15.06
800	76.04	42.70	31.81	26.53	23.49	21.55	20.25	19.34	18.69	18.20	17.84	17.57	17.37	17.21
900	85.54	48.04	35.79	29.85	26.42	24.25	22.79	21.76	21.02	20.48	20.07	19.77	19.54	19.36
1000	95.05	53.38	39.76	33.16	29.36	26.94	25.32	24.18	23.36	22.75	22.30	21.97	21.71	21.51
2000	190.09	106.75	79.52	66.32	58.71	53.88	50.63	48.35	46.71	45.50	44.60	43.93	43.41	43.02
3000	285.14	160.12	119.28	99.48	88.06	80.82	75.94	72.52	70.06	68.25	66.90	65.89	65.12	64.52
4000	380.18	213.49	159.04	132.63	117.41	107.75	101.25	96.70	93.41	91.00	89.20	87.85	86.82	86.03
5000	475.23	266.86	198.80	165.79	146.76	134.69	126.56	120.87	116.77	113.75	111.50	109.81	108.52	107.54
6000	570.27	320.23	238.56	198.95	176.11	161.63	151.87	145.04	140.12	136.50	133.80	131.77	130.23	129.06
7000	665.31	373.61	278.32	232.10	205.46	188.57	177.19	169.21	163.47	159.25	156.10	153.73	151.93	150.55
8000	760.36	426.98	318.08	265.26	234.82	215.50	202.50	193.39	186.82	182.00	178.40	175.69	173.63	172.06
9000	855.40	480.35	357.84	298.42	264.17	242.44	227.81	217.56	210.17	204.75	200.70	197.65	195.34	193.56
10000	950.45	533.72	397.60	331.58	293.52	269.38	253.12	241.73	233.53	227.50	223.00	219.61	217.04	215.07
11000	1045.49	587.09	437.36	364.73	322.87	296.31	278.43	265.90	256.88	250.25	245.30	241.58	238.74	236.58
12000	1140.54	640.46	477.12	397.89	352.22	323.25	303.74	290.08	280.23	273.00	267.60	263.54	260.45	258.08
13000	1235.58	693.83	516.88	431.05	381.57	350.19	329.06	314.25	303.58	295.75	289.90	285.50	282.15	279.59
14000	1330.62	747.21	556.64	464.20	410.92	377.13	354.37	338.42	326.94	318.50	312.20	307.46	303.85	301.10
15000	1425.67	800.58	596.40	497.36	440.27	404.06	379.68	362.59	350.29	341.24	334.50	329.42	325.56	322.60
16000	1520.71	853.95	636.16	530.52	469.63	431.00	404.99	386.77	373.64	363.99	356.80	351.38	347.26	344.11
17000	1615.76	907.32	675.92	563.68	498.98	457.94	430.30	410.94	396.99	386.74	379.10	373.34	368.96	365.62
18000	1710.80	960.69	715.68	596.83	528.33	484.87	455.61	435.11	420.34	409.49	401.40	395.30	390.67	387.12
19000	1805.84	1014.06	755.44	629.99	557.68	511.81	480.93	459.29	443.70	432.24	423.70	417.26	412.37	408.63
20000	1900.89	1067.44	795.20	663.15	587.03	538.75	506.24	483.46	467.05	454.99	446.00	439.22	434.07	430.14
21000	1995.93	1120.81	834.96	696.30	616.38	565.69	531.55	507.63	490.40	477.74	468.30	461.18	455.78	451.64
22000	2090.98	1174.18	874.72	729.46	645.73	592.62	556.86	531.80	513.75	500.49	490.60	483.15	477.48	473.15
23000	2186.02	1227.55	914.48	762.62	675.09	619.56	582.17	555.98	537.11	523.24	512.90	505.11	499.18	494.66
24000	2281.07	1280.92	954.24	795.78	704.44	646.50	607.48	580.15	560.46	545.99	535.20	527.07	520.89	516.16
25000	2376.11	1334.29	994.00	828.93	733.79	673.43	632.80	604.32	583.81	568.74	557.50	549.03	542.59	537.67
26000	2471.15	1387.66	1033.76	862.09	763.14	700.37	658.11	628.49	607.16	591.49	579.80	570.99	564.29	559.18
27000	2566.20	1441.04	1073.52	895.25	792.49	727.31	683.42	652.67	630.51	614.24	602.10	592.95	586.00	580.68
28000	2661.24	1494.41	1113.28	928.40	821.84	754.25	708.73	676.84	653.87	636.99	624.40	614.91	607.70	602.19
29000	2756.29	1547.78	1153.04	961.56	851.19	781.18	734.04	701.01	677.22	659.73	646.70	636.87	629.40	623.70
30000	2851.33	1601.15	1192.80	994.72	880.54	808.12	759.35	725.18	700.57	682.48	669.00	658.83	651.11	645.20
31000	2946.38	1654.52	1232.56	1027.88	909.90	835.06	784.67	749.36	723.92	705.23	691.30	680.79	672.81	666.71
32000	3041.42	1707.89	1272.32	1061.03	939.25	861.99	809.98	773.53	747.28	727.98	713.60	702.75	694.52	688.21
33000	3136.46	1761.27	1312.08	1094.19	968.60	888.93	835.29	797.70	770.63	750.73	735.90	724.72	716.22	709.72
34000	3231.51	1814.64	1351.84	1127.35	997.95	915.87	860.60	821.88	793.98	773.48	758.20	746.68	737.92	731.23
35000	3326.55	1868.01	1391.60	1160.50	1027.30	942.81	885.91	846.05	817.33	796.23	780.50	768.64	759.63	752.73
36000	3421.60	1921.38	1431.36	1193.66	1056.65	969.74	911.22	870.22	840.68	818.98	802.80	790.60	781.33	774.24
37000	3516.64	1974.75	1471.12	1226.82	1086.00	996.68	936.54	894.39	864.04	841.73	825.10	812.56	803.03	795.75
38000	3611.68	2028.12	1510.88	1259.98	1115.36	1023.62	961.85	918.57	887.39	864.48	847.40	834.52	824.74	817.25
39000	3706.73	2081.49	1550.64	1293.13	1144.71	1050.55	987.16	942.74	910.74	887.23	869.70	856.48	846.44	838.76
40000	3801.77	2134.87	1590.40	1326.29	1174.06	1077.49	1012.47	966.91	934.09	909.98	892.00	878.44	868.14	860.27
41000	3896.82	2188.24	1630.16	1359.45	1203.41	1104.43	1037.78	991.08	957.45	932.73	914.30	900.40	889.85	881.77
42000	3991.86	2241.61	1669.92	1392.60	1232.76	1131.37	1063.09	1015.26	980.80	955.48	936.60	922.36	911.55	903.28
43000	4086.91	2294.98	1709.68	1425.76	1262.11	1158.30	1088.41	1039.43	1004.15	978.22	958.89	944.32	933.25	924.79
44000	4181.95	2348.35	1749.44	1458.92	1291.46	1185.24	1113.72	1063.60	1027.50	1000.97	981.19	966.29	954.96	946.29
45000	4276.99	2401.72	1789.20	1492.08	1320.81	1212.18	1139.03	1087.77	1050.85	1023.72	1003.49	988.25	976.66	967.80
46000	4372.04	2455.09	1828.96	1525.23	1350.17	1239.12	1164.34	1111.95	1074.21	1046.47	1025.79	1010.21	998.36	989.31
47000	4467.08	2508.47	1868.72	1558.39	1379.52	1266.05	1189.65	1136.12	1097.56	1069.22	1048.09	1032.17	1020.07	1010.81
48000	4562.13	2561.84	1908.48	1591.55	1408.87	1292.99	1214.96	1160.29	1120.91	1091.97	1070.39	1054.13	1041.77	1032.32
49000	4657.17	2615.21	1948.24	1624.70	1438.22	1319.93	1240.28	1184.47	1144.26	1114.72	1092.69	1076.09	1063.47	1053.83
50000	4752.22	2668.58	1988.00	1657.86	1467.57	1346.86	1265.59	1208.64	1167.61	1137.47	1114.99	1098.05	1085.18	1075.33
55000	5227.44	2935.44	2186.80	1823.65	1614.33	1481.55	1392.15	1329.50	1284.38	1251.22	1226.49	1207.86	1193.69	1182.87
60000	5702.66	3202.30	2385.59	1989.43	1761.08	1616.24	1518.70	1450.36	1401.14	1364.96	1337.99	1317.66	1302.21	1290.40
65000	6177.88	3469.15	2584.39	2155.22	1907.84	1750.92	1645.26	1571.23	1517.90	1478.71	1449.49	1427.47	1410.73	1397.93
70000	6653.10	3736.01	2783.19	2321.00	2054.60	1885.61	1771.82	1692.09	1634.66	1592.46	1560.99	1537.27	1519.25	1505.46
75000	7128.32	4002.87	2981.99	2486.79	2201.35	2020.29	1898.38	1812.95	1751.42	1706.20	1672.49	1647.07	1627.76	1613.00
80000	7603.54	4269.73	3180.79	2652.58	2348.11	2154.98	2024.94	1933.82	1868.18	1819.95	1783.99	1756.88	1736.28	1720.53
85000	8078.76	4536.58	3379.59	2818.36	2494.87	2289.67	2151.49	2054.68	1984.94	1933.70	1895.48	1866.68	1844.80	1828.06
90000	8553.98	4803.44	3578.39	2984.15	2641.62	2424.35	2278.05	2175.54	2101.70	2047.44	2006.98	1976.49	1953.31	1935.59
95000	9029.20	5070.30	3777.19	3149.93	2788.38	2559.04	2404.61	2296.41	2218.46	2161.19	2118.48	2086.29	2061.83	2043.13
100000	9504.43	5337.16	3975.99	3315.72	2935.14	2693.72	2531.17	2417.27	2335.22	2274.93	2229.98	2196.10	2170.35	2150.66

TERM AMOUNT	15 Years	16 Years	17 Years	18 Years	19 Years	20 Years	21 Years	22 Years	23 Years	24 Years	25 Years	30 Years	35 Years	40 Years
5	.11	.11	.11	.11	.11	.11	.11	.11	.11	.11	.11	.11	.11	.11
10	.22	.22	.22	.22	.22	.21	.21	.21	.21	.21	.21	.21	.21	.21
15	.33	.32	.32	.32	.32	.32	.32	.32	.32	.32	.32	.32	.32	.32
25	.54	.54	.53	.53	.53	.53	.53	.53	.53	.53	.53	.53	.53	.53
50	1.07	1.07	1.06	1.06	1.06	1.05	1.05	1.05	1.05	1.05	1.05	1.05	1.05	1.05
75	1.61	1.60	1.59	1.59	1.58	1.58	1.58	1.57	1.57	1.57	1.57	1.57	1.57	1.57
100	2.14	2.13	2.12	2.11	2.11	2.10	2.10	2.10	2.10	2.09	2.09	2.09	2.09	2.09
200	4.28	4.25	4.23	4.22	4.21	4.20	4.19	4.19	4.19	4.18	4.18	4.17	4.17	4.17
300	6.41	6.38	6.35	6.33	6.31	6.30	6.29	6.28	6.28	6.27	6.27	6.26	6.26	6.26
400	8.55	8.50	8.46	8.44	8.41	8.40	8.38	8.37	8.37	8.36	8.36	8.34	8.34	8.34
500	10.68	10.62	10.58	10.54	10.52	10.50	10.48	10.47	10.46	10.45	10.44	10.43	10.42	10.42
600	12.82	12.75	12.69	12.65	12.62	12.59	12.57	12.56	12.55	12.54	12.53	12.51	12.51	12.51
700	14.95	14.87	14.81	14.76	14.72	14.69	14.67	14.65	14.64	14.63	14.62	14.60	14.59	14.59
800	17.09	17.00	16.92	16.87	16.82	16.79	16.76	16.74	16.73	16.72	16.71	16.68	16.67	16.67
900	19.22	19.12	19.04	18.98	18.93	18.89	18.86	18.84	18.82	18.82	18.80	18.79	18.77	18.76
1000	21.36	21.24	21.15	21.08	21.03	20.99	20.95	20.93	20.91	20.89	20.88	20.85	20.84	20.84
2000	42.72	42.48	42.30	42.16	42.05	41.97	41.90	41.85	41.81	41.78	41.76	41.70	41.68	41.67
3000	64.07	63.72	63.45	63.24	63.08	62.95	62.85	62.78	62.72	62.67	62.63	62.54	62.52	62.51
4000	85.43	84.96	84.60	84.32	84.10	83.93	83.80	83.70	83.62	83.56	83.51	83.39	83.35	83.34
5000	106.78	106.20	105.75	105.40	105.13	104.92	104.75	104.62	104.52	104.45	104.39	104.23	104.19	104.18
6000	128.14	127.44	126.90	126.48	126.15	125.90	125.70	125.55	125.43	125.34	125.26	125.08	125.03	125.01
7000	149.49	148.68	148.04	147.56	147.18	146.88	146.65	146.47	146.33	146.22	146.14	145.93	145.86	145.85
8000	170.85	169.91	169.19	168.63	168.20	167.86	167.60	167.40	167.24	167.11	167.02	166.77	166.70	166.68
9000	192.20	191.15	190.34	189.71	189.22	188.84	188.55	188.32	188.14	188.00	187.89	187.62	187.54	187.51
10000	213.56	212.39	211.49	210.79	210.25	209.83	209.50	209.24	209.04	208.89	208.77	208.46	208.37	208.35
11000	234.91	233.63	232.64	231.87	231.27	230.81	230.45	230.17	229.95	229.78	229.64	229.31	229.21	229.18
12000	256.27	254.87	253.79	252.95	252.30	251.79	251.40	251.09	250.85	250.67	250.52	250.15	250.05	250.02
13000	277.62	276.11	274.94	274.03	273.32	272.77	272.35	272.01	271.76	271.55	271.40	271.00	270.89	270.85
14000	298.98	297.35	296.08	295.11	294.35	293.76	293.30	292.94	292.66	292.44	292.27	291.85	291.72	291.69
15000	320.33	318.58	317.23	316.18	315.37	314.74	314.25	313.86	313.56	313.33	313.15	312.69	312.56	312.52
16000	341.69	339.82	338.38	337.26	336.39	335.72	335.19	334.79	334.47	334.22	334.03	333.54	333.40	333.36
17000	363.04	361.06	359.53	358.34	357.42	356.70	356.14	355.71	355.37	355.11	354.90	354.38	354.23	354.19
18000	384.40	382.30	380.68	379.42	378.44	377.68	377.09	376.63	376.28	376.00	375.78	375.23	375.07	375.02
19000	405.76	403.54	401.83	400.50	399.47	398.67	398.04	397.56	397.18	396.88	396.65	396.07	395.91	395.86
20000	427.11	424.78	422.97	421.58	420.49	419.65	418.99	418.48	418.08	417.77	417.53	416.92	416.74	416.69
21000	448.47	446.02	444.12	442.66	441.52	440.63	439.94	439.41	438.99	438.66	438.41	437.77	437.58	437.53
22000	469.82	467.26	465.27	463.73	462.54	461.61	460.89	460.33	459.89	459.55	459.28	458.61	458.42	458.36
23000	491.18	488.49	486.42	484.81	483.56	482.59	481.84	481.25	480.80	480.44	480.16	479.46	479.25	479.20
24000	512.53	509.73	507.57	505.89	504.59	503.58	502.79	502.18	501.70	501.33	501.04	500.30	500.09	500.03
25000	533.89	530.97	528.72	526.97	525.61	524.56	523.74	523.10	522.60	522.22	521.91	521.15	520.93	520.86
26000	555.24	552.21	549.87	548.05	546.64	545.54	544.69	544.02	543.51	543.10	542.79	542.00	541.77	541.70
27000	576.60	573.45	571.01	569.13	567.66	566.52	565.64	564.95	564.41	563.99	563.67	562.84	562.60	562.53
28000	597.95	594.69	592.16	590.21	588.69	587.51	586.59	585.87	585.31	584.88	584.54	583.69	583.44	583.37
29000	619.31	615.93	613.31	611.28	609.71	608.49	607.54	606.80	606.22	605.77	605.42	604.53	604.28	604.20
30000	640.66	637.16	634.46	632.36	630.73	629.47	628.49	627.72	627.12	626.66	626.29	625.38	625.11	625.04
31000	662.02	658.40	655.61	653.44	651.76	650.45	649.44	648.64	648.03	647.55	647.17	646.22	645.95	645.87
32000	683.37	679.64	676.76	674.52	672.78	671.43	670.38	669.57	668.93	668.43	668.05	667.07	666.79	666.71
33000	704.73	700.88	697.90	695.60	693.81	692.42	691.33	690.49	689.83	689.32	688.92	687.92	687.62	687.54
34000	726.08	722.12	719.05	716.68	714.83	713.40	712.28	711.41	710.74	710.21	709.80	708.76	708.46	708.37
35000	747.44	743.36	740.20	737.76	735.86	734.38	733.23	732.34	731.64	731.10	730.68	729.61	729.30	729.21
36000	768.80	764.60	761.35	758.83	756.88	755.36	754.18	753.26	752.55	751.99	751.55	750.45	750.14	750.04
37000	790.15	785.84	782.50	779.91	777.91	776.35	775.13	774.19	773.45	772.88	772.43	771.30	770.97	770.88
38000	811.51	807.07	803.65	800.99	798.93	797.33	796.08	795.11	794.35	793.76	793.30	792.14	791.81	791.71
39000	832.86	828.31	824.80	822.07	819.95	818.31	817.03	816.03	815.26	814.65	814.18	812.99	812.65	812.55
40000	854.22	849.55	845.94	843.15	840.98	839.29	837.98	836.96	836.16	835.54	835.06	833.84	833.48	833.38
41000	875.57	870.79	867.09	864.23	862.00	860.27	858.93	857.88	857.07	856.43	855.93	854.68	854.32	854.21
42000	896.93	892.03	888.24	885.31	883.03	881.26	879.88	878.81	877.97	877.32	876.81	875.53	875.16	875.05
43000	918.28	913.27	909.39	906.38	904.05	902.24	900.83	899.73	898.87	898.21	897.69	896.37	895.99	895.88
44000	939.64	934.51	930.54	927.46	925.08	923.22	921.78	920.65	919.78	919.09	918.56	917.22	916.83	916.72
45000	960.99	955.74	951.69	948.54	946.10	944.20	942.73	941.58	940.68	939.98	939.44	938.07	937.67	937.55
46000	982.35	976.98	972.83	969.62	967.12	965.18	963.68	962.50	961.59	960.87	960.32	958.91	958.50	958.39
47000	1003.70	998.22	993.98	990.70	988.15	986.17	984.62	983.42	982.49	981.76	981.19	979.76	979.34	979.22
48000	1025.06	1019.46	1015.13	1011.78	1009.17	1007.15	1005.57	1004.35	1003.39	1002.65	1002.07	1000.60	1000.18	1000.06
49000	1046.41	1040.70	1036.28	1032.86	1030.20	1028.13	1026.52	1025.27	1024.30	1023.54	1022.94	1021.45	1021.02	1020.89
50000	1067.77	1061.94	1057.43	1053.93	1051.22	1049.11	1047.47	1046.20	1045.20	1044.43	1043.82	1042.29	1041.85	1041.72
55000	1174.55	1168.13	1163.17	1159.33	1156.34	1154.02	1152.22	1150.81	1149.72	1148.87	1148.20	1146.52	1146.04	1145.90
60000	1281.32	1274.32	1268.91	1264.72	1261.46	1258.93	1256.97	1255.43	1254.24	1253.31	1252.58	1250.75	1250.22	1250.07
65000	1388.10	1380.52	1374.66	1370.11	1366.59	1363.85	1361.71	1360.05	1358.76	1357.75	1356.96	1354.98	1354.41	1354.24
70000	1494.88	1486.71	1480.40	1475.51	1471.71	1468.76	1466.46	1464.67	1463.28	1462.19	1461.35	1459.21	1458.59	1458.41
75000	1601.65	1592.90	1586.14	1580.90	1576.83	1573.67	1571.21	1569.28	1567.80	1566.64	1565.73	1563.44	1562.78	1562.58
80000	1708.43	1699.10	1691.88	1686.29	1681.95	1678.58	1675.95	1673.91	1672.32	1671.08	1670.11	1667.67	1666.96	1666.76
85000	1815.20	1805.29	1797.62	1791.68	1787.07	1783.49	1780.70	1778.53	1776.84	1775.52	1774.49	1771.90	1771.15	1770.93
90000	1921.98	1911.48	1903.37	1897.08	1892.19	1888.40	1885.45	1883.15	1881.36	1879.96	1878.87	1876.13	1875.33	1875.10
95000	2028.76	2017.68	2009.11	2002.47	1997.32	1993.31	1990.19	1987.77	1985.88	1984.40	1983.25	1980.35	1979.51	1979.27
100000	2135.53	2123.87	2114.85	2107.86	2102.44	2098.22	2094.94	2092.39	2090.40	2088.85	2087.64	2084.58	2083.70	2083.44

25%

25.100%

TERM	1 Year	2 Years	3 Years	4 Years	5 Years	6 Years	7 Years	8 Years	9 Years	10 Years	11 Years	12 Years	13 Years	14 Years
AMOUNT														
5	.48	.27	.20	.17	.15	.14	.13	.13	.12	.12	.12	.12	.11	.11
10	.96	.54	.40	.34	.30	.27	.26	.25	.24	.23	.23	.23	.22	.22
15	1.43	.81	.60	.50	.45	.41	.39	.37	.36	.35	.34	.34	.33	.33
25	2.38	1.34	1.00	.84	.74	.68	.64	.61	.59	.58	.56	.56	.55	.54
50	4.76	2.68	2.00	1.67	1.48	1.35	1.27	1.22	1.18	1.15	1.12	1.11	1.09	1.08
75	7.14	4.01	2.99	2.50	2.21	2.03	1.91	1.82	1.76	1.72	1.68	1.66	1.64	1.62
100	9.51	5.35	3.99	3.33	2.95	2.70	2.54	2.43	2.35	2.29	2.24	2.21	2.18	2.16
200	19.02	10.69	7.97	6.65	5.89	5.40	5.08	4.85	4.69	4.57	4.48	4.41	4.36	4.32
300	28.53	16.03	11.95	9.97	8.83	8.10	7.62	7.28	7.03	6.85	6.72	6.62	6.54	6.48
400	38.04	21.37	15.93	13.29	11.77	10.80	10.16	9.70	9.37	9.13	8.95	8.82	8.72	8.64
500	47.55	26.72	19.91	16.61	14.71	13.50	12.69	12.12	11.72	11.41	11.19	11.02	10.89	10.80
600	57.06	32.06	23.89	19.93	17.65	16.20	15.23	14.55	14.06	13.70	13.43	13.23	13.07	12.95
700	66.57	37.40	27.87	23.25	20.59	18.90	17.77	16.97	16.40	15.98	15.67	15.43	15.25	15.11
800	76.08	42.74	31.86	26.58	23.53	21.60	20.31	19.40	18.74	18.26	17.90	17.63	17.43	17.27
900	85.59	48.08	35.84	29.90	26.47	24.30	22.84	21.82	21.08	20.54	20.14	19.84	19.61	19.43
1000	95.10	53.43	39.82	33.22	29.41	27.00	25.38	24.24	23.43	22.82	22.38	22.04	21.78	21.59
2000	190.19	106.85	79.63	66.43	58.82	54.00	50.76	48.48	46.85	45.64	44.75	44.07	43.56	43.17
3000	285.28	160.27	119.44	99.64	88.23	81.00	76.13	72.72	70.27	68.46	67.12	66.11	65.34	64.75
4000	380.38	213.69	159.26	132.86	117.64	108.00	101.51	96.96	93.69	91.28	89.49	88.14	87.12	86.34
5000	475.47	267.11	199.07	166.07	147.05	135.00	126.88	121.20	117.11	114.10	111.87	110.18	108.90	107.92
6000	570.56	320.54	238.88	199.28	176.46	162.00	152.26	145.44	140.53	136.92	134.24	132.21	130.68	129.50
7000	665.65	373.96	278.69	232.50	205.87	189.00	177.63	169.68	163.95	159.74	156.61	154.25	152.46	151.09
8000	760.75	427.38	318.51	265.71	235.28	215.99	203.01	193.92	187.37	182.56	178.98	176.28	174.23	172.67
9000	855.84	480.80	358.32	298.92	264.69	242.99	228.39	218.16	210.79	205.38	201.35	198.32	196.01	194.25
10000	950.93	534.22	398.13	332.13	294.10	269.99	253.76	242.40	234.21	228.20	223.73	220.35	217.79	215.84
11000	1046.03	587.64	437.95	365.35	323.51	296.99	279.14	266.63	257.63	251.02	246.10	242.39	239.57	237.42
12000	1141.12	641.07	477.76	398.56	352.92	323.99	304.51	290.87	281.05	273.84	268.47	264.42	261.35	259.00
13000	1236.21	694.49	517.57	431.77	382.33	350.99	329.89	315.11	304.47	296.66	290.84	286.46	283.13	280.59
14000	1331.30	747.91	557.38	464.99	411.74	377.99	355.26	339.35	327.90	319.48	313.21	308.49	304.91	302.17
15000	1426.40	801.33	597.20	498.20	441.15	404.98	380.64	363.59	351.32	342.30	335.59	330.53	326.69	323.75
16000	1521.49	854.75	637.01	531.41	470.56	431.98	406.01	387.83	374.74	365.12	357.96	352.56	348.46	345.33
17000	1616.58	908.17	676.82	564.62	499.97	458.98	431.39	412.07	398.16	387.94	380.33	374.60	370.24	366.92
18000	1711.67	961.60	716.63	597.84	529.38	485.98	456.77	436.31	421.58	410.76	402.70	396.63	392.02	388.50
19000	1806.77	1015.02	756.45	631.05	558.79	512.98	482.14	460.55	445.00	433.58	425.07	418.67	413.80	410.08
20000	1901.86	1068.44	796.26	664.26	588.20	539.98	507.52	484.79	468.42	456.40	447.45	440.70	435.58	431.67
21000	1996.95	1121.86	836.07	697.48	617.61	566.98	532.89	509.02	491.84	479.22	469.82	462.74	457.36	453.25
22000	2092.05	1175.28	875.89	730.69	647.02	593.97	558.27	533.26	515.26	502.04	492.19	484.77	479.14	474.83
23000	2187.14	1228.70	915.70	763.90	676.43	620.97	583.64	557.50	538.68	524.86	514.56	506.81	500.92	496.42
24000	2282.23	1282.13	955.51	797.12	705.84	647.97	609.02	581.74	562.10	547.68	536.94	528.84	522.69	518.00
25000	2377.32	1335.55	995.32	830.33	735.25	674.97	634.40	605.98	585.52	570.50	559.31	550.88	544.47	539.58
26000	2472.42	1388.97	1035.14	863.54	764.66	701.97	659.77	630.22	608.94	593.32	581.68	572.91	566.25	561.17
27000	2567.51	1442.39	1074.95	896.75	794.07	728.97	685.15	654.46	632.37	616.14	604.05	594.95	588.03	582.75
28000	2662.60	1495.81	1114.76	929.97	823.48	755.97	710.52	678.70	655.79	638.96	626.42	616.98	609.81	604.33
29000	2757.69	1549.23	1154.57	963.18	852.89	782.96	735.90	702.94	679.21	661.78	648.80	639.02	631.59	625.91
30000	2852.79	1602.66	1194.39	996.39	882.30	809.96	761.27	727.18	702.63	684.60	671.17	661.05	653.37	647.50
31000	2947.88	1656.08	1234.20	1029.61	911.71	836.96	786.65	751.41	726.05	707.42	693.54	683.08	675.15	669.08
32000	3042.97	1709.50	1274.01	1062.82	941.12	863.96	812.02	775.65	749.47	730.24	715.91	705.12	696.93	690.66
33000	3138.07	1762.92	1313.83	1096.03	970.53	890.96	837.40	799.89	772.89	753.06	738.28	727.15	718.70	712.25
34000	3233.16	1816.34	1353.64	1129.24	999.94	917.96	862.78	824.13	796.31	775.88	760.66	749.19	740.48	733.83
35000	3328.25	1869.76	1393.45	1162.46	1029.35	944.96	888.15	848.37	819.73	798.70	783.03	771.22	762.26	755.41
36000	3423.34	1923.19	1433.26	1195.67	1058.76	971.95	913.53	872.61	843.15	821.52	805.40	793.26	784.04	777.00
37000	3518.44	1976.61	1473.08	1228.88	1088.17	998.95	938.90	896.85	866.57	844.34	827.77	815.29	805.82	798.58
38000	3613.53	2030.03	1512.89	1262.10	1117.58	1025.95	964.28	921.09	889.99	867.16	850.14	837.33	827.60	820.16
39000	3708.62	2083.45	1552.70	1295.31	1146.99	1052.95	989.65	945.33	913.41	889.98	872.52	859.36	849.38	841.75
40000	3803.71	2136.87	1592.51	1328.52	1176.40	1079.95	1015.03	969.57	936.84	912.80	894.89	881.40	871.15	863.33
41000	3898.81	2190.30	1632.33	1361.74	1205.81	1106.95	1040.40	993.81	960.26	935.62	917.26	903.43	892.93	884.91
42000	3993.90	2243.72	1672.14	1394.95	1235.22	1133.95	1065.78	1018.04	983.68	958.44	939.63	925.47	914.71	906.49
43000	4088.99	2297.14	1711.95	1428.16	1264.63	1160.94	1091.16	1042.28	1007.10	981.26	962.00	947.50	936.49	928.08
44000	4184.09	2350.56	1751.77	1461.37	1294.04	1187.94	1116.53	1066.52	1030.52	1004.08	984.38	969.54	958.27	949.66
45000	4279.18	2403.98	1791.58	1494.59	1323.45	1214.94	1141.91	1090.76	1053.94	1026.90	1006.75	991.57	980.05	971.24
46000	4374.27	2457.40	1831.39	1527.80	1352.86	1241.94	1167.28	1115.00	1077.36	1049.72	1029.12	1013.61	1001.83	992.83
47000	4469.36	2510.83	1871.20	1561.01	1382.27	1268.94	1192.66	1139.24	1100.78	1072.54	1051.49	1035.64	1023.61	1014.41
48000	4564.46	2564.25	1911.02	1594.23	1411.68	1295.94	1218.03	1163.48	1124.20	1095.36	1073.87	1057.68	1045.38	1035.99
49000	4659.55	2617.67	1950.83	1627.44	1441.09	1322.94	1243.41	1187.72	1147.62	1118.18	1096.24	1079.71	1067.16	1057.58
50000	4754.64	2671.09	1990.64	1660.65	1470.50	1349.93	1268.79	1211.96	1171.04	1141.00	1118.61	1101.75	1088.94	1079.16
55000	5230.11	2938.20	2189.71	1826.72	1617.55	1484.93	1395.66	1333.15	1288.15	1255.10	1230.47	1211.92	1197.84	1187.07
60000	5705.57	3205.31	2388.77	1992.78	1764.60	1619.92	1522.54	1454.35	1405.24	1369.20	1342.33	1322.10	1306.73	1294.99
65000	6181.03	3472.42	2587.83	2158.85	1911.65	1754.91	1649.42	1575.54	1522.35	1483.29	1454.19	1432.27	1415.62	1402.91
70000	6656.50	3739.52	2786.90	2324.91	2058.70	1889.91	1776.30	1696.74	1639.46	1597.39	1566.05	1542.44	1524.52	1510.82
75000	7131.96	4006.63	2985.96	2490.97	2205.75	2024.90	1903.18	1817.93	1756.56	1711.49	1677.91	1652.62	1633.41	1618.74
80000	7607.42	4273.74	3185.02	2657.04	2352.80	2159.89	2030.05	1939.13	1873.67	1825.59	1789.77	1762.79	1742.30	1726.65
85000	8082.89	4540.85	3384.09	2823.10	2499.85	2294.88	2156.93	2060.32	1990.77	1939.69	1901.63	1872.97	1851.20	1834.57
90000	8558.35	4807.96	3583.15	2989.17	2646.90	2429.88	2283.81	2181.52	2107.87	2053.79	2013.49	1983.14	1960.09	1942.48
95000	9033.82	5075.07	3782.21	3155.23	2793.95	2564.87	2410.69	2302.71	2224.98	2167.89	2125.35	2093.32	2068.99	2050.40
100000	9509.28	5342.18	3981.28	3321.30	2941.00	2699.86	2537.57	2423.91	2342.08	2281.99	2237.21	2203.49	2177.88	2158.31

MONTHLY PAYMENT
REQUIRED TO AMORTIZE A LOAN

25.100%

TERM	15 Years	16 Years	17 Years	18 Years	19 Years	20 Years	21 Years	22 Years	23 Years	24 Years	25 Years	30 Years	35 Years	40 Years
AMOUNT														
5	.11	.11	.11	.11	.11	.11	.11	.11	.11	.11	.11	.11	.11	.11
10	.22	.22	.22	.22	.22	.22	.22	.22	.21	.21	.21	.21	.21	.21
15	.33	.32	.32	.32	.32	.32	.32	.32	.32	.32	.32	.32	.32	.32
25	.54	.54	.54	.53	.53	.53	.53	.53	.53	.53	.53	.53	.53	.53
50	1.08	1.07	1.07	1.06	1.06	1.06	1.06	1.06	1.05	1.05	1.05	1.05	1.05	1.05
75	1.61	1.60	1.60	1.59	1.59	1.58	1.58	1.58	1.58	1.58	1.58	1.57	1.57	1.57
100	2.15	2.14	2.13	2.12	2.12	2.11	2.11	2.11	2.10	2.10	2.10	2.10	2.10	2.10
200	4.29	4.27	4.25	4.24	4.23	4.22	4.21	4.21	4.20	4.20	4.20	4.19	4.19	4.19
300	6.43	6.40	6.37	6.35	6.34	6.32	6.31	6.31	6.30	6.30	6.29	6.28	6.28	6.28
400	8.58	8.53	8.50	8.47	8.45	8.43	8.42	8.41	8.40	8.39	8.39	8.38	8.37	8.37
500	10.72	10.66	10.62	10.58	10.56	10.54	10.52	10.51	10.50	10.49	10.48	10.47	10.47	10.46
600	12.86	12.80	12.74	12.70	12.67	12.64	12.62	12.61	12.60	12.59	12.58	12.56	12.56	12.56
700	15.01	14.93	14.86	14.82	14.78	14.75	14.73	14.71	14.70	14.68	14.68	14.66	14.65	14.65
800	17.15	17.06	16.99	16.93	16.89	16.86	16.83	16.81	16.79	16.78	16.77	16.75	16.74	16.74
900	19.29	19.19	19.11	19.05	19.00	18.96	18.93	18.91	18.89	18.88	18.87	18.84	18.83	18.83
1000	21.44	21.32	21.23	21.16	21.11	21.07	21.04	21.01	20.99	20.98	20.96	20.93	20.93	20.92
2000	42.87	42.64	42.46	42.32	42.21	42.13	42.07	42.02	41.98	41.95	41.92	41.86	41.85	41.84
3000	64.30	63.96	63.69	63.48	63.32	63.19	63.10	63.02	62.96	62.92	62.88	62.79	62.77	62.76
4000	85.74	85.27	84.92	84.64	84.42	84.26	84.13	84.03	83.95	83.89	83.84	83.72	83.69	83.68
5000	107.17	106.59	106.14	105.80	105.53	105.32	105.16	105.03	104.93	104.86	104.80	104.65	104.61	104.59
6000	128.60	127.91	127.37	126.96	126.63	126.38	126.19	126.04	125.92	125.83	125.76	125.58	125.53	125.51
7000	150.04	149.23	148.60	148.11	147.74	147.45	147.22	147.04	146.91	146.80	146.72	146.51	146.45	146.43
8000	171.47	170.54	169.83	169.27	168.84	168.51	168.25	168.05	167.89	167.77	167.68	167.44	167.37	167.35
9000	192.90	191.86	191.05	190.43	189.95	189.57	189.28	189.06	188.88	188.74	188.63	188.36	188.29	188.26
10000	214.33	213.18	212.28	211.59	211.05	210.64	210.31	210.06	209.86	209.71	209.59	209.29	209.21	209.18
11000	235.77	234.49	233.51	232.75	232.16	231.70	231.34	231.07	230.85	230.68	230.55	230.22	230.13	230.10
12000	257.20	255.81	254.74	253.91	253.26	252.76	252.37	252.07	251.84	251.65	251.51	251.15	251.06	251.02
13000	278.63	277.13	275.97	275.07	274.37	273.83	273.41	273.08	272.82	272.62	272.47	272.08	271.97	271.93
14000	300.07	298.45	297.19	296.22	295.47	294.89	294.44	294.08	293.81	293.59	293.43	293.01	292.89	292.85
15000	321.50	319.76	318.42	317.38	316.58	315.95	315.47	315.09	314.79	314.57	314.39	313.94	313.81	313.77
16000	342.93	341.08	339.65	338.54	337.68	337.02	336.50	336.09	335.78	335.54	335.35	334.87	334.73	334.69
17000	364.36	362.40	360.88	359.70	358.79	358.08	357.53	357.10	356.77	356.51	356.30	355.79	355.65	355.61
18000	385.80	383.71	382.10	380.86	379.89	379.14	378.56	378.11	377.75	377.48	377.26	376.72	376.57	376.52
19000	407.23	405.03	403.33	402.02	401.00	400.21	399.59	399.11	398.74	398.45	398.22	397.65	397.49	397.44
20000	428.66	426.35	424.56	423.18	422.10	421.27	420.62	420.12	419.72	419.42	419.18	418.58	418.41	418.36
21000	450.10	447.67	445.79	444.33	443.21	442.33	441.65	441.12	440.71	440.39	440.14	439.51	439.33	439.28
22000	471.53	468.98	467.02	465.49	464.31	463.39	462.68	462.13	461.70	461.36	461.10	460.44	460.25	460.19
23000	492.96	490.30	488.25	486.65	485.42	484.46	483.71	483.13	482.68	482.33	482.06	481.37	481.17	481.11
24000	514.39	511.62	509.47	507.81	506.52	505.52	504.74	504.14	503.67	503.30	503.02	502.30	502.09	502.03
25000	535.83	532.93	530.70	528.97	527.63	526.58	525.77	525.14	524.65	524.27	523.97	523.23	523.01	522.95
26000	557.26	554.25	551.93	550.13	548.73	547.65	546.81	546.15	545.64	545.24	544.93	544.15	543.93	543.86
27000	578.69	575.57	573.15	571.29	569.84	568.71	567.84	567.16	566.63	566.21	565.89	565.08	564.85	564.78
28000	600.13	596.89	594.38	592.44	590.94	589.77	588.87	588.16	587.61	587.18	586.85	586.01	585.77	585.70
29000	621.56	618.20	615.61	613.60	612.05	610.84	609.90	609.17	608.60	608.15	607.81	606.94	606.69	606.62
30000	642.99	639.52	636.84	634.76	633.15	631.90	630.93	630.17	629.58	629.13	628.77	627.87	627.61	627.54
31000	664.42	660.84	658.07	655.92	654.26	652.96	651.96	651.18	650.57	650.10	649.73	648.80	648.53	648.45
32000	685.86	682.15	679.29	677.08	675.36	674.03	672.99	672.18	671.56	671.07	670.69	669.73	669.45	669.37
33000	707.29	703.47	700.52	698.24	696.47	695.09	694.02	693.19	692.54	692.04	691.64	690.66	690.37	690.29
34000	728.72	724.79	721.75	719.40	717.57	716.15	715.05	714.19	713.53	713.01	712.60	711.58	711.29	711.21
35000	750.16	746.11	742.98	740.55	738.67	737.22	736.08	735.20	734.51	733.98	733.56	732.51	732.21	732.12
36000	771.59	767.42	764.20	761.71	759.78	758.28	757.11	756.21	755.50	754.95	754.52	753.44	753.13	753.04
37000	793.02	788.74	785.43	782.87	780.88	779.34	778.14	777.21	776.49	775.92	775.48	774.37	774.05	773.96
38000	814.45	810.06	806.66	804.03	801.99	800.41	799.17	798.22	797.47	796.89	796.44	795.30	794.97	794.88
39000	835.89	831.37	827.89	825.19	823.09	821.47	820.21	819.22	818.46	817.86	817.40	816.23	815.89	815.79
40000	857.32	852.69	849.12	846.35	844.20	842.53	841.24	840.23	839.44	838.83	838.36	837.16	836.81	836.71
41000	878.75	874.01	870.34	867.51	865.30	863.60	862.27	861.23	860.43	859.80	859.31	858.09	857.73	857.63
42000	900.19	895.33	891.57	888.66	886.41	884.66	883.30	882.24	881.41	880.77	880.27	879.01	878.65	878.55
43000	921.62	916.64	912.80	909.82	907.51	905.72	904.33	903.24	902.40	901.74	901.23	899.94	899.57	899.47
44000	943.05	937.96	934.03	930.98	928.62	926.78	925.36	924.25	923.39	922.71	922.19	920.87	920.49	920.38
45000	964.48	959.28	955.25	952.14	949.72	947.85	946.39	945.26	944.37	943.69	943.15	941.80	941.41	941.30
46000	985.92	980.59	976.48	973.30	970.83	968.91	967.42	966.26	965.36	964.66	964.11	962.73	962.33	962.22
47000	1007.35	1001.91	997.71	994.46	991.93	989.97	988.45	987.27	986.34	985.63	985.07	983.66	983.25	983.14
48000	1028.78	1023.23	1018.94	1015.61	1013.04	1011.04	1009.48	1008.27	1007.33	1006.60	1006.03	1004.59	1004.17	1004.05
49000	1050.22	1044.55	1040.17	1036.77	1034.14	1032.10	1030.51	1029.28	1028.32	1027.57	1026.98	1025.52	1025.09	1024.97
50000	1071.65	1065.86	1061.39	1057.93	1055.25	1053.16	1051.54	1050.28	1049.30	1048.54	1047.94	1046.45	1046.01	1045.89
55000	1178.81	1172.45	1167.53	1163.72	1160.77	1158.48	1156.70	1155.31	1154.23	1153.39	1152.74	1151.09	1150.61	1150.48
60000	1285.98	1279.03	1273.67	1269.52	1266.30	1263.80	1261.85	1260.34	1259.16	1258.25	1257.53	1255.73	1255.22	1255.07
65000	1393.14	1385.62	1379.81	1375.31	1371.82	1369.11	1367.01	1365.37	1364.09	1363.10	1362.32	1360.38	1359.82	1359.65
70000	1500.31	1492.21	1485.95	1481.10	1477.34	1474.43	1472.16	1470.39	1469.02	1467.95	1467.12	1465.02	1464.42	1464.24
75000	1607.47	1598.79	1592.09	1586.90	1582.87	1579.74	1577.31	1575.42	1573.95	1572.81	1571.91	1569.67	1569.02	1568.83
80000	1714.64	1705.38	1698.23	1692.69	1688.39	1685.06	1682.47	1680.45	1678.88	1677.66	1676.71	1674.31	1673.62	1673.42
85000	1821.80	1811.96	1804.36	1798.49	1793.92	1790.37	1787.62	1785.48	1783.81	1782.51	1781.50	1778.95	1778.22	1778.01
90000	1928.96	1918.55	1910.50	1904.28	1899.44	1895.69	1892.77	1890.51	1888.74	1887.37	1886.29	1883.60	1882.82	1882.60
95000	2036.13	2025.14	2016.64	2010.07	2004.97	2001.01	1997.93	1995.53	1993.67	1992.22	1991.09	1988.24	1987.42	1987.18
100000	2143.29	2131.72	2122.78	2115.86	2110.49	2106.32	2103.08	2100.56	2098.60	2097.07	2095.88	2092.89	2092.02	2091.77

MONTHLY PAYMENT
REQUIRED TO AMORTIZE A LOAN

TERM AMOUNT	1 Year	2 Years	3 Years	4 Years	5 Years	6 Years	7 Years	8 Years	9 Years	10 Years	11 Years	12 Years	13 Years	14 Years
5	.48	.27	.20	.17	.15	.14	.13	.13	.12	.12	.12	.12	.11	.11
10	.96	.54	.40	.34	.30	.28	.26	.25	.24	.23	.23	.23	.22	.22
15	1.43	.81	.60	.50	.45	.41	.39	.37	.36	.35	.34	.34	.33	.33
25	2.38	1.34	1.00	.84	.74	.68	.64	.61	.59	.58	.56	.56	.55	.55
50	4.76	2.68	2.00	1.67	1.48	1.36	1.27	1.22	1.18	1.15	1.12	1.11	1.09	1.09
75	7.14	4.01	2.99	2.50	2.21	2.03	1.91	1.82	1.76	1.72	1.68	1.66	1.64	1.63
100	9.52	5.35	3.99	3.33	2.95	2.71	2.54	2.43	2.35	2.29	2.24	2.21	2.18	2.17
200	19.03	10.69	7.97	6.65	5.89	5.41	5.08	4.86	4.69	4.57	4.48	4.42	4.36	4.33
300	28.54	16.04	11.95	9.97	8.83	8.11	7.62	7.28	7.04	6.86	6.72	6.62	6.54	6.49
400	38.05	21.38	15.94	13.30	11.77	10.81	10.16	9.71	9.38	9.14	8.96	8.83	8.72	8.65
500	47.56	26.72	19.92	16.62	14.72	13.51	12.70	12.13	11.72	11.42	11.20	11.03	10.90	10.81
600	57.07	32.07	23.90	19.94	17.66	16.21	15.24	14.56	14.07	13.71	13.44	13.24	13.08	12.97
700	66.58	37.41	27.88	23.26	20.60	18.91	17.78	16.98	16.41	15.99	15.68	15.44	15.26	15.13
800	76.09	42.75	31.87	26.59	23.54	21.62	20.32	19.41	18.76	18.27	17.92	17.65	17.44	17.29
900	85.60	48.10	35.85	29.91	26.49	24.32	22.86	21.84	21.10	20.56	20.16	19.85	19.62	19.45
1000	95.11	53.44	39.83	33.23	29.43	27.02	25.40	24.26	23.44	22.84	22.40	22.06	21.80	21.61
2000	190.21	106.87	79.66	66.46	58.85	54.03	50.79	48.52	46.88	45.68	44.79	44.11	43.60	43.21
3000	285.32	160.31	119.48	99.69	88.28	81.05	76.18	72.77	70.32	68.52	67.18	66.16	65.40	64.81
4000	380.42	213.74	159.31	132.91	117.70	108.06	101.57	97.03	93.76	91.35	89.57	88.22	87.20	86.41
5000	475.53	267.18	199.13	166.14	147.13	135.07	126.96	121.28	117.19	114.19	111.96	110.27	108.99	108.02
6000	570.63	320.61	238.96	199.37	176.55	162.09	152.35	145.54	140.63	137.03	134.35	132.32	130.79	129.62
7000	665.74	374.04	278.79	232.59	205.98	189.10	177.75	169.79	164.07	159.87	156.74	154.38	152.59	151.22
8000	760.84	427.48	318.61	265.82	235.40	216.12	203.14	194.05	187.51	182.70	179.13	176.43	174.39	172.82
9000	855.95	480.91	358.44	299.05	264.83	243.13	228.53	218.31	210.95	205.54	201.52	198.48	196.18	194.43
10000	951.05	534.35	398.26	332.27	294.25	270.14	253.92	242.56	234.38	228.38	223.91	220.54	217.98	216.03
11000	1046.16	587.78	438.09	365.50	323.68	297.16	279.31	266.82	257.82	251.22	246.30	242.59	239.78	237.63
12000	1141.26	641.22	477.92	398.73	353.10	324.17	304.70	291.07	281.26	274.05	268.69	264.64	261.58	259.23
13000	1236.37	694.65	517.74	431.95	382.53	351.19	330.10	315.33	304.70	296.89	291.08	286.70	283.37	280.83
14000	1331.47	748.08	557.57	465.18	411.95	378.20	355.49	339.58	328.14	319.73	313.47	308.75	305.17	302.44
15000	1426.58	801.52	597.39	498.41	441.37	405.21	380.88	363.84	351.57	342.57	335.86	330.80	326.97	324.04
16000	1521.68	854.95	637.22	531.64	470.80	432.23	406.27	388.10	375.01	365.40	358.25	352.86	348.77	345.64
17000	1616.79	908.39	677.05	564.86	500.22	459.24	431.66	412.35	398.45	388.24	380.64	374.91	370.56	367.24
18000	1711.89	961.82	716.87	598.09	529.65	486.26	457.05	436.61	421.89	411.08	403.03	396.96	392.36	388.85
19000	1807.00	1015.26	756.70	631.32	559.07	513.27	482.45	460.86	445.33	433.92	425.42	419.02	414.16	410.45
20000	1902.10	1068.69	796.52	664.54	588.50	540.28	507.84	485.12	468.76	456.75	447.81	441.07	435.96	432.05
21000	1997.21	1122.12	836.35	697.77	617.92	567.30	533.23	509.37	492.20	479.59	470.20	463.12	457.75	453.65
22000	2092.31	1175.56	876.18	731.00	647.35	594.31	558.62	533.63	515.64	502.43	492.59	485.18	479.55	475.25
23000	2187.42	1228.99	916.00	764.22	676.77	621.33	584.01	557.88	539.08	525.27	514.98	507.23	501.35	496.86
24000	2282.52	1282.43	955.83	797.45	706.20	648.34	609.40	582.14	562.51	548.10	537.37	529.28	523.15	518.46
25000	2377.63	1335.86	995.65	830.68	735.62	675.35	634.80	606.40	585.95	570.94	559.76	551.34	544.94	540.06
26000	2472.73	1389.30	1035.48	863.90	765.05	702.37	660.19	630.65	609.39	593.78	582.15	573.39	566.74	561.66
27000	2567.84	1442.73	1075.31	897.13	794.47	729.38	685.58	654.91	632.83	616.62	604.54	595.44	588.54	583.27
28000	2662.94	1496.16	1115.13	930.36	823.90	756.40	710.97	679.16	656.27	639.45	626.93	617.50	610.34	604.87
29000	2758.05	1549.60	1154.96	963.58	853.32	783.41	736.36	703.42	679.70	662.29	649.32	639.55	632.13	626.47
30000	2853.15	1603.03	1194.78	996.81	882.74	810.42	761.75	727.67	703.14	685.13	671.71	661.60	653.93	648.07
31000	2948.26	1656.47	1234.61	1030.04	912.17	837.44	787.14	751.93	726.58	707.97	694.10	683.66	675.73	669.67
32000	3043.36	1709.90	1274.44	1063.27	941.59	864.45	812.54	776.19	750.02	730.80	716.49	705.71	697.53	691.28
33000	3138.47	1763.34	1314.26	1096.49	971.02	891.46	837.93	800.44	773.46	753.64	738.88	727.76	719.33	712.88
34000	3233.57	1816.77	1354.09	1129.72	1000.44	918.48	863.32	824.70	796.89	776.48	761.27	749.82	741.12	734.48
35000	3328.68	1870.20	1393.91	1162.95	1029.87	945.49	888.71	848.95	820.33	799.32	783.66	771.87	762.92	756.08
36000	3423.78	1923.64	1433.74	1196.17	1059.29	972.51	914.10	873.21	843.77	822.15	806.05	793.92	784.72	777.69
37000	3518.89	1977.07	1473.57	1229.40	1088.72	999.52	939.49	897.46	867.21	844.99	828.44	815.98	806.52	799.29
38000	3613.99	2030.51	1513.39	1262.63	1118.14	1026.53	964.89	921.72	890.65	867.83	850.83	838.03	828.31	820.89
39000	3709.10	2083.94	1553.22	1295.85	1147.57	1053.55	990.28	945.97	914.09	890.67	873.22	860.08	850.11	842.49
40000	3804.20	2137.38	1593.04	1329.08	1176.99	1080.56	1015.67	970.23	937.52	913.50	895.61	882.14	871.91	864.09
41000	3899.30	2190.81	1632.87	1362.31	1206.42	1107.58	1041.06	994.49	960.96	936.34	918.00	904.19	893.71	885.70
42000	3994.41	2244.24	1672.70	1395.53	1235.84	1134.59	1066.45	1018.74	984.40	959.18	940.39	926.24	915.50	907.30
43000	4089.51	2297.68	1712.52	1428.76	1265.27	1161.60	1091.84	1043.00	1007.83	982.02	962.78	948.30	937.30	928.90
44000	4184.62	2351.11	1752.35	1461.99	1294.69	1188.62	1117.24	1067.25	1031.27	1004.85	985.17	970.35	959.10	950.50
45000	4279.72	2404.55	1792.17	1495.21	1324.11	1215.63	1142.63	1091.51	1054.71	1027.69	1007.56	992.40	980.90	972.11
46000	4374.83	2457.98	1832.00	1528.44	1353.54	1242.65	1168.02	1115.76	1078.15	1050.53	1029.95	1014.46	1002.69	993.71
47000	4469.93	2511.42	1871.83	1561.67	1382.96	1269.66	1193.41	1140.02	1101.59	1073.37	1052.34	1036.51	1024.49	1015.31
48000	4565.04	2564.85	1911.65	1594.90	1412.39	1296.67	1218.80	1164.28	1125.02	1096.20	1074.73	1058.56	1046.29	1036.91
49000	4660.14	2618.28	1951.48	1628.12	1441.81	1323.69	1244.19	1188.53	1148.46	1119.04	1097.12	1080.62	1068.09	1058.51
50000	4755.25	2671.72	1991.30	1661.35	1471.24	1350.70	1269.59	1212.79	1171.90	1141.88	1119.51	1102.67	1089.88	1080.12
55000	5230.77	2938.89	2190.43	1827.48	1618.36	1485.77	1396.54	1334.06	1289.09	1256.07	1231.46	1212.94	1198.87	1188.13
60000	5706.30	3206.06	2389.56	1993.62	1765.48	1620.84	1523.50	1455.34	1406.28	1370.25	1343.42	1323.20	1307.86	1296.14
65000	6181.82	3473.23	2588.69	2159.75	1912.61	1755.91	1650.46	1576.62	1523.47	1484.44	1455.37	1433.47	1416.85	1404.15
70000	6657.35	3740.40	2787.82	2325.89	2059.73	1890.98	1777.42	1697.90	1640.66	1598.63	1567.32	1543.74	1525.84	1512.16
75000	7132.87	4007.57	2986.95	2492.02	2206.85	2026.05	1904.38	1819.18	1757.85	1712.82	1679.27	1654.00	1634.82	1620.17
80000	7608.39	4274.75	3186.08	2658.16	2353.98	2161.12	2031.33	1940.46	1875.04	1827.00	1791.22	1764.27	1743.81	1728.18
85000	8083.92	4541.92	3385.21	2824.29	2501.10	2296.19	2158.29	2061.73	1992.23	1941.19	1903.17	1874.54	1852.80	1836.19
90000	8559.44	4809.09	3584.34	2990.42	2648.22	2431.26	2285.25	2183.01	2109.42	2055.38	2015.12	1984.80	1961.79	1944.21
95000	9034.97	5076.26	3783.47	3156.56	2795.35	2566.33	2412.21	2304.29	2226.61	2169.57	2127.07	2095.06	2070.78	2052.22
100000	9510.49	5343.43	3982.60	3322.69	2942.47	2701.40	2539.17	2425.57	2343.80	2283.75	2239.02	2205.34	2179.76	2160.23

TERM	15 Years	16 Years	17 Years	18 Years	19 Years	20 Years	21 Years	22 Years	23 Years	24 Years	25 Years	30 Years	35 Years	40 Years
AMOUNT														
5	.11	.11	.11	.11	.11	.11	.11	.11	.11	.11	.11	.11	.11	.11
10	.22	.22	.22	.22	.22	.22	.22	.22	.22	.21	.21	.21	.21	.21
15	.33	.33	.32	.32	.32	.32	.32	.32	.32	.32	.32	.32	.32	.32
25	.54	.54	.54	.53	.53	.53	.53	.53	.53	.53	.53	.53	.53	.53
50	1.08	1.07	1.07	1.06	1.06	1.06	1.06	1.06	1.06	1.05	1.05	1.05	1.05	1.05
75	1.61	1.61	1.60	1.59	1.59	1.59	1.58	1.58	1.58	1.58	1.58	1.58	1.58	1.58
100	2.15	2.14	2.13	2.12	2.12	2.11	2.11	2.11	2.11	2.10	2.10	2.10	2.10	2.10
200	4.30	4.27	4.25	4.24	4.23	4.22	4.22	4.21	4.21	4.20	4.20	4.19	4.19	4.19
300	6.44	6.41	6.38	6.36	6.34	6.33	6.32	6.31	6.31	6.30	6.30	6.29	6.29	6.29
400	8.59	8.54	8.50	8.48	8.45	8.44	8.43	8.42	8.41	8.40	8.40	8.38	8.38	8.38
500	10.73	10.67	10.63	10.59	10.57	10.55	10.53	10.52	10.51	10.50	10.49	10.48	10.48	10.47
600	12.88	12.81	12.75	12.71	12.68	12.66	12.64	12.62	12.61	12.60	12.59	12.57	12.57	12.57
700	15.02	14.94	14.88	14.83	14.79	14.76	14.74	14.72	14.71	14.70	14.69	14.67	14.66	14.66
800	17.17	17.07	17.00	16.95	16.90	16.87	16.85	16.83	16.81	16.80	16.79	16.76	16.76	16.76
900	19.31	19.21	19.13	19.07	19.02	18.98	18.95	18.93	18.91	18.90	18.89	18.86	18.85	18.85
1000	21.46	21.34	21.25	21.18	21.13	21.09	21.06	21.03	21.01	21.00	20.98	20.95	20.95	20.94
2000	42.91	42.68	42.50	42.36	42.25	42.17	42.11	42.06	42.02	41.99	41.96	41.90	41.89	41.88
3000	64.36	64.02	63.75	63.54	63.38	63.26	63.16	63.08	63.02	62.98	62.94	62.85	62.83	62.82
4000	85.81	85.35	85.00	84.72	84.50	84.34	84.21	84.11	84.03	83.97	83.92	83.80	83.77	83.76
5000	107.27	106.69	106.24	105.90	105.63	105.42	105.26	105.14	105.04	104.96	104.90	104.75	104.71	104.70
6000	128.72	128.03	127.49	127.08	126.75	126.51	126.31	126.16	126.04	125.95	125.88	125.70	125.65	125.64
7000	150.17	149.36	148.74	148.25	147.88	147.59	147.36	147.19	147.05	146.94	146.86	146.65	146.59	146.57
8000	171.62	170.70	169.99	169.43	169.00	168.67	168.41	168.21	168.06	167.93	167.84	167.60	167.53	167.51
9000	193.08	192.04	191.23	190.61	190.13	189.76	189.47	189.24	189.06	188.93	188.82	188.55	188.47	188.45
10000	214.53	213.37	212.48	211.79	211.25	210.84	210.52	210.27	210.07	209.92	209.80	209.50	209.41	209.39
11000	235.98	234.71	233.73	232.97	232.38	231.92	231.57	231.29	231.08	230.91	230.70	230.45	230.36	230.33
12000	257.43	256.05	254.98	254.15	253.50	253.01	252.62	252.32	252.08	251.90	251.76	251.40	251.30	251.27
13000	278.88	277.38	276.22	275.33	274.63	274.09	273.67	273.34	273.09	272.89	272.74	272.35	272.24	272.21
14000	300.34	298.72	297.47	296.50	295.75	295.17	294.72	294.37	294.10	293.88	293.72	293.30	293.18	293.14
15000	321.79	320.06	318.72	317.68	316.88	316.26	315.77	315.40	315.10	314.87	314.70	314.25	314.12	314.08
16000	343.24	341.39	339.97	338.86	338.00	337.34	336.82	336.42	336.11	335.86	335.68	335.20	335.06	335.02
17000	364.69	362.73	361.21	360.04	359.13	358.42	357.87	357.45	357.11	356.86	356.65	356.15	356.00	355.96
18000	386.15	384.07	382.46	381.22	380.25	379.51	378.93	378.47	378.12	377.85	377.63	377.10	376.94	376.90
19000	407.60	405.40	403.71	402.40	401.38	400.59	399.98	399.50	399.13	398.84	398.61	398.05	397.88	397.84
20000	429.05	426.74	424.96	423.58	422.50	421.67	421.03	420.53	420.13	419.83	419.59	419.00	418.82	418.78
21000	450.50	448.08	446.20	444.75	443.63	442.76	442.08	441.55	441.14	440.02	440.57	439.95	439.77	439.71
22000	471.96	469.41	467.45	465.93	464.75	463.84	463.13	462.58	462.15	461.81	461.55	460.90	460.71	460.65
23000	493.41	490.75	488.70	487.11	485.88	484.92	484.18	483.60	483.15	482.80	482.53	481.84	481.65	481.59
24000	514.86	512.09	509.95	508.29	507.00	506.01	505.23	504.63	504.16	503.79	503.51	502.79	502.59	502.53
25000	536.31	533.42	531.19	529.47	528.13	527.09	526.28	525.66	525.17	524.79	524.49	523.74	523.53	523.47
26000	557.76	554.76	552.44	550.65	549.25	548.17	547.33	546.68	546.17	545.78	545.47	544.69	544.47	544.41
27000	579.22	576.10	573.69	571.83	570.38	569.26	568.39	567.71	567.18	566.77	566.45	565.64	565.41	565.34
28000	600.67	597.44	594.94	593.00	591.50	590.34	589.44	588.73	588.19	587.76	587.43	586.59	586.35	586.28
29000	622.12	618.77	616.18	614.18	612.63	611.42	610.49	609.76	609.19	608.75	608.41	607.54	607.29	607.22
30000	643.57	640.11	637.43	635.36	633.75	632.51	631.54	630.79	630.20	629.74	629.39	628.49	628.23	628.16
31000	665.03	661.45	658.68	656.54	654.88	653.59	652.59	651.81	651.21	650.73	650.37	649.44	649.18	649.10
32000	686.48	682.78	679.93	677.72	676.00	674.67	673.64	672.84	672.21	671.72	671.35	670.39	670.12	670.04
33000	707.93	704.12	701.18	698.90	697.13	695.76	694.69	693.86	693.22	692.72	692.32	691.34	691.06	690.98
34000	729.38	725.46	722.42	720.08	718.25	716.84	715.74	714.89	714.22	713.71	713.30	712.29	712.00	711.91
35000	750.83	746.79	743.67	741.25	739.38	737.93	736.79	735.92	735.23	734.70	734.28	733.24	732.94	732.85
36000	772.29	768.13	764.92	762.43	760.50	759.01	757.85	756.94	756.24	755.69	755.26	754.19	753.88	753.79
37000	793.74	789.47	786.17	783.61	781.63	780.09	778.90	777.97	777.24	776.68	776.24	775.14	774.82	774.73
38000	815.19	810.80	807.41	804.79	802.75	801.18	799.95	798.99	798.25	797.67	797.22	796.09	795.76	795.67
39000	836.64	832.14	828.66	825.97	823.88	822.26	821.00	820.02	819.26	818.66	818.20	817.04	816.70	816.61
40000	858.10	853.48	849.91	847.15	845.00	843.34	842.05	841.05	840.26	839.65	839.18	837.99	837.64	837.55
41000	879.55	874.81	871.16	868.32	866.13	864.43	863.10	862.07	861.27	860.65	860.16	858.94	858.59	858.48
42000	901.00	896.15	892.40	889.50	887.25	885.51	884.15	883.10	882.28	881.64	881.14	879.89	879.53	879.42
43000	922.45	917.49	913.65	910.68	908.38	906.59	905.20	904.12	903.28	902.63	902.12	900.84	900.47	900.36
44000	943.91	938.82	934.90	931.86	929.50	927.68	926.25	925.15	924.29	923.62	923.10	921.79	921.41	921.30
45000	965.36	960.16	956.15	953.04	950.63	948.76	947.31	946.18	945.30	944.61	944.08	942.74	942.35	942.24
46000	986.81	981.50	977.39	974.22	971.75	969.84	968.36	967.20	966.30	965.60	965.06	963.68	963.29	963.18
47000	1008.26	1002.83	998.64	995.40	992.88	990.93	989.41	988.23	987.31	986.59	986.04	984.63	984.23	984.11
48000	1029.71	1024.17	1019.89	1016.57	1014.00	1012.01	1010.46	1009.25	1008.31	1007.58	1007.02	1005.58	1005.17	1005.05
49000	1051.17	1045.51	1041.14	1037.75	1035.13	1033.09	1031.51	1030.28	1029.32	1028.58	1027.99	1026.53	1026.11	1025.99
50000	1072.62	1066.84	1062.38	1058.93	1056.25	1054.18	1052.56	1051.31	1050.33	1049.57	1048.97	1047.48	1047.05	1046.93
55000	1179.88	1173.53	1168.62	1164.82	1161.88	1159.59	1157.82	1156.44	1155.36	1154.52	1153.87	1152.23	1151.76	1151.62
60000	1287.14	1280.21	1274.86	1270.72	1267.50	1265.01	1263.07	1261.57	1260.39	1259.48	1258.77	1256.98	1256.46	1256.32
65000	1394.40	1386.90	1381.10	1376.61	1373.13	1370.43	1368.33	1366.70	1365.42	1364.44	1363.66	1361.73	1361.17	1361.01
70000	1501.66	1493.58	1487.34	1482.50	1478.75	1475.85	1473.58	1471.83	1470.46	1469.39	1468.56	1466.47	1465.87	1465.70
75000	1608.93	1600.26	1593.57	1588.40	1584.38	1581.26	1578.84	1576.96	1575.49	1574.35	1573.46	1571.22	1570.58	1570.39
80000	1716.19	1706.95	1699.81	1694.29	1690.00	1686.68	1684.10	1682.09	1680.52	1679.30	1678.36	1675.97	1675.28	1675.09
85000	1823.45	1813.63	1806.05	1800.18	1795.63	1792.10	1789.35	1787.22	1785.55	1784.26	1783.25	1780.72	1779.99	1779.78
90000	1930.71	1920.32	1912.29	1906.07	1901.25	1897.51	1894.61	1892.35	1890.59	1889.22	1888.15	1885.47	1884.69	1884.47
95000	2037.97	2027.00	2018.53	2011.97	2006.88	2002.93	1999.86	1997.48	1995.62	1994.17	1993.05	1990.21	1989.40	1989.16
100000	2145.23	2133.68	2124.76	2117.86	2112.50	2108.35	2105.12	2102.61	2100.65	2099.13	2097.94	2094.96	2094.10	2093.86

MONTHLY PAYMENT
REQUIRED TO AMORTIZE A LOAN

TERM	1 Year	2 Years	3 Years	4 Years	5 Years	6 Years	7 Years	8 Years	9 Years	10 Years	11 Years	12 Years	13 Years	14 Years
AMOUNT														
5	.48	.27	.20	.17	.15	.14	.13	.13	.12	.12	.12	.12	.11	.11
10	.96	.54	.40	.34	.30	.28	.26	.25	.24	.23	.23	.23	.22	.22
15	1.43	.81	.60	.50	.45	.41	.39	.37	.36	.35	.34	.34	.33	.33
25	2.38	1.34	1.00	.84	.74	.68	.64	.61	.59	.58	.57	.56	.55	.55
50	4.76	2.68	2.00	1.67	1.48	1.36	1.28	1.22	1.18	1.15	1.13	1.11	1.10	1.09
75	7.14	4.02	2.99	2.50	2.22	2.03	1.91	1.83	1.77	1.72	1.69	1.66	1.64	1.63
100	9.52	5.35	3.99	3.33	2.95	2.71	2.55	2.44	2.35	2.29	2.25	2.22	2.19	2.17
200	19.03	10.70	7.98	6.66	5.90	5.42	5.09	4.87	4.70	4.58	4.49	4.43	4.38	4.34
300	28.55	16.05	11.96	9.99	8.85	8.12	7.64	7.30	7.05	6.87	6.74	6.64	6.56	6.50
400	38.06	21.39	15.95	13.31	11.79	10.83	10.18	9.73	9.40	9.16	8.98	8.85	8.75	8.67
500	47.58	26.74	19.94	16.64	14.74	13.54	12.72	12.16	11.75	11.45	11.23	11.06	10.93	10.83
600	57.09	32.09	23.92	19.97	17.69	16.24	15.27	14.59	14.10	13.74	13.47	13.27	13.12	13.00
700	66.60	37.44	27.91	23.29	20.63	18.95	17.81	17.02	16.45	16.03	15.72	15.48	15.30	15.17
800	76.12	42.78	31.90	26.62	23.58	21.65	20.36	19.45	18.80	18.32	17.96	17.69	17.49	17.33
900	85.63	48.13	35.88	29.95	26.53	24.36	22.90	21.88	21.15	20.61	20.21	19.90	19.67	19.50
1000	95.15	53.48	39.87	33.27	29.47	27.07	25.44	24.31	23.49	22.90	22.45	22.11	21.86	21.66
2000	190.29	106.95	79.74	66.54	58.94	54.13	50.88	48.62	46.98	45.79	44.89	44.22	43.71	43.32
3000	285.43	160.42	119.60	99.81	88.41	81.19	76.32	72.92	70.47	68.68	67.34	66.33	65.57	64.98
4000	380.57	213.89	159.47	133.08	117.88	108.25	101.76	97.23	93.96	91.57	89.78	88.44	87.42	86.64
5000	475.71	267.36	199.33	166.35	147.35	135.31	127.20	121.53	117.45	114.46	112.23	110.55	109.28	108.30
6000	570.85	320.84	239.20	199.62	176.82	162.37	152.64	145.84	140.94	137.35	134.67	132.66	131.13	129.96
7000	665.99	374.31	279.06	232.89	206.29	189.43	178.08	170.14	164.43	160.24	157.12	154.77	152.98	151.62
8000	761.14	427.78	318.93	266.16	235.75	216.49	203.52	194.45	187.92	183.13	179.56	176.88	174.84	173.28
9000	856.28	481.25	358.80	299.42	265.22	243.55	228.96	218.75	211.41	206.02	202.01	198.98	196.69	194.94
10000	951.42	534.72	398.66	332.69	294.69	270.61	254.40	243.06	234.90	228.91	224.45	221.09	218.55	216.60
11000	1046.56	588.20	438.53	365.96	324.16	297.67	279.84	267.37	258.39	251.80	246.89	243.20	240.40	238.26
12000	1141.70	641.67	478.39	399.23	353.63	324.73	305.28	291.67	281.88	274.69	269.34	265.31	262.25	259.92
13000	1236.84	695.14	518.26	432.50	383.10	351.79	330.72	315.98	305.37	297.58	291.78	287.42	284.11	281.58
14000	1331.98	748.61	558.12	465.77	412.57	378.85	356.16	340.28	328.86	320.47	314.23	309.53	305.96	303.24
15000	1427.12	802.08	597.99	499.04	442.04	405.91	381.60	364.59	352.35	343.36	336.67	331.64	327.82	324.90
16000	1522.27	855.56	637.86	532.31	471.50	432.97	407.04	388.89	375.84	366.25	359.12	353.75	349.67	346.56
17000	1617.41	909.03	677.72	565.57	500.97	460.03	432.48	413.20	399.32	389.14	381.56	375.86	371.52	368.22
18000	1712.55	962.50	717.59	598.84	530.44	487.09	457.92	437.50	422.81	412.03	404.01	397.96	393.38	389.88
19000	1807.69	1015.97	757.45	632.11	559.91	514.15	483.36	461.81	446.30	434.92	426.45	420.07	415.23	411.54
20000	1902.83	1069.44	797.32	665.38	589.38	541.21	508.80	486.11	469.79	457.81	448.89	442.18	437.09	433.20
21000	1997.97	1122.92	837.18	698.65	618.85	568.27	534.24	510.42	493.28	480.70	471.34	464.29	458.94	454.86
22000	2093.11	1176.39	877.05	731.92	648.32	595.33	559.68	534.73	516.77	503.59	493.78	486.40	480.80	476.52
23000	2188.25	1229.86	916.92	765.19	677.78	622.39	585.12	559.03	540.26	526.49	516.23	508.51	502.65	498.18
24000	2283.40	1283.33	956.78	798.46	707.25	649.45	610.56	583.34	563.75	549.38	538.67	530.62	524.50	519.84
25000	2378.54	1336.80	996.65	831.72	736.72	676.51	636.00	607.64	587.24	572.27	561.12	552.73	546.36	541.50
26000	2473.68	1390.27	1036.51	864.99	766.19	703.57	661.44	631.95	610.73	595.16	583.56	574.83	568.21	563.16
27000	2568.82	1443.75	1076.38	898.26	795.66	730.63	686.88	656.25	634.22	618.05	606.01	596.94	590.07	584.82
28000	2663.96	1497.22	1116.24	931.53	825.13	757.69	712.32	680.56	657.71	640.94	628.45	619.05	611.92	606.48
29000	2759.10	1550.69	1156.11	964.80	854.60	784.75	737.75	704.86	681.20	663.83	650.89	641.16	633.77	628.14
30000	2854.24	1604.16	1195.98	998.07	884.07	811.81	763.19	729.17	704.69	686.72	673.34	663.27	655.63	649.80
31000	2949.38	1657.63	1235.84	1031.34	913.53	838.87	788.63	753.47	728.18	709.61	695.78	685.38	677.48	671.45
32000	3044.53	1711.11	1275.71	1064.61	943.00	865.93	814.07	777.78	751.67	732.50	718.23	707.49	699.34	693.11
33000	3139.67	1764.58	1315.57	1097.87	972.47	892.99	839.51	802.09	775.15	755.39	740.67	729.60	721.19	714.77
34000	3234.81	1818.05	1355.44	1131.14	1001.94	920.05	864.95	826.39	798.64	778.28	763.12	751.70	743.04	736.43
35000	3329.95	1871.52	1395.30	1164.41	1031.41	947.11	890.39	850.70	822.13	801.17	785.56	773.81	764.90	758.09
36000	3425.09	1924.99	1435.17	1197.68	1060.86	974.17	915.83	875.00	845.62	824.06	808.01	795.92	786.75	779.75
37000	3520.23	1978.47	1475.04	1230.95	1090.35	1001.23	941.27	899.31	869.11	846.95	830.45	818.03	808.61	801.41
38000	3615.37	2031.94	1514.90	1264.22	1119.82	1028.29	966.71	923.61	892.60	869.84	852.90	840.14	830.46	823.07
39000	3710.52	2085.41	1554.77	1297.49	1149.28	1055.35	992.15	947.92	916.09	892.73	875.34	862.25	852.32	844.73
40000	3805.66	2138.88	1594.63	1330.76	1178.75	1082.41	1017.59	972.22	939.58	915.62	897.78	884.36	874.17	866.39
41000	3900.80	2192.35	1634.50	1364.02	1208.22	1109.47	1043.03	996.53	963.07	938.51	920.23	906.47	896.02	888.05
42000	3995.94	2245.83	1674.36	1397.29	1237.69	1136.53	1068.47	1020.83	986.56	961.40	942.67	928.58	917.88	909.71
43000	4091.08	2299.30	1714.23	1430.56	1267.16	1163.59	1093.91	1045.14	1010.05	984.29	965.12	950.68	939.73	931.37
44000	4186.22	2352.77	1754.09	1463.83	1296.63	1190.65	1119.35	1069.45	1033.54	1007.18	987.56	972.79	961.59	953.03
45000	4281.36	2406.24	1793.96	1497.10	1326.10	1217.71	1144.79	1093.75	1057.03	1030.08	1010.01	994.90	983.44	974.69
46000	4376.50	2459.71	1833.83	1530.37	1355.56	1244.77	1170.23	1118.06	1080.52	1052.97	1032.45	1017.01	1005.29	996.35
47000	4471.65	2513.19	1873.69	1563.64	1385.03	1271.83	1195.67	1142.36	1104.01	1075.86	1054.90	1039.12	1027.15	1018.01
48000	4566.79	2566.66	1913.56	1596.91	1414.50	1298.89	1221.11	1166.67	1127.50	1098.75	1077.34	1061.23	1049.00	1039.67
49000	4661.93	2620.13	1953.42	1630.17	1443.97	1325.95	1246.55	1190.97	1150.98	1121.64	1099.78	1083.34	1070.86	1061.33
50000	4757.07	2673.60	1993.29	1663.44	1473.44	1353.01	1271.99	1215.28	1174.47	1144.53	1122.23	1105.45	1092.71	1082.99
55000	5232.78	2940.96	2192.62	1829.79	1620.78	1488.31	1399.19	1336.81	1291.92	1258.98	1234.45	1215.99	1201.98	1191.29
60000	5708.48	3208.32	2391.95	1996.13	1768.13	1623.61	1526.38	1458.33	1409.37	1373.43	1346.67	1326.53	1311.25	1299.59
65000	6184.19	3475.68	2591.27	2162.48	1915.47	1758.91	1653.58	1579.86	1526.81	1487.88	1458.90	1437.08	1420.52	1407.88
70000	6659.89	3743.04	2790.60	2328.82	2062.81	1894.21	1780.78	1701.39	1644.26	1602.34	1571.12	1547.62	1529.79	1516.18
75000	7135.60	4010.40	2989.93	2495.16	2210.16	2029.51	1907.98	1822.91	1761.71	1716.79	1683.34	1658.17	1639.06	1624.48
80000	7611.31	4277.76	3189.26	2661.51	2357.50	2164.81	2035.18	1944.44	1879.16	1831.24	1795.56	1768.71	1748.33	1732.78
85000	8087.01	4545.12	3388.59	2827.85	2504.84	2300.11	2162.38	2065.97	1996.60	1945.69	1907.79	1879.25	1857.61	1841.08
90000	8562.72	4812.48	3587.92	2994.19	2652.19	2435.41	2289.57	2187.50	2114.05	2060.15	2020.01	1989.80	1966.88	1949.38
95000	9038.43	5079.84	3787.24	3160.54	2799.53	2570.71	2416.77	2309.02	2231.50	2174.60	2132.23	2100.34	2076.15	2057.67
100000	9514.13	5347.20	3986.57	3326.88	2946.87	2706.01	2543.97	2430.55	2348.94	2289.05	2244.45	2210.89	2185.42	2165.97

TERM	15 Years	16 Years	17 Years	18 Years	19 Years	20 Years	21 Years	22 Years	23 Years	24 Years	25 Years	30 Years	35 Years	40 Years
AMOUNT														
5	.11	.11	.11	.11	.11	.11	.11	.11	.11	.11	.11	.11	.11	.11
10	.22	.22	.22	.22	.22	.22	.22	.22	.22	.22	.22	.22	.22	.22
15	.33	.33	.32	.32	.32	.32	.32	.32	.32	.32	.32	.32	.32	.32
25	.54	.54	.54	.54	.53	.53	.53	.53	.53	.53	.53	.53	.53	.53
50	1.08	1.07	1.07	1.07	1.06	1.06	1.06	1.06	1.06	1.06	1.06	1.06	1.06	1.06
75	1.62	1.61	1.60	1.60	1.59	1.59	1.59	1.59	1.59	1.58	1.58	1.58	1.58	1.58
100	2.16	2.14	2.14	2.13	2.12	2.12	2.12	2.11	2.11	2.11	2.11	2.11	2.11	2.11
200	4.31	4.28	4.27	4.25	4.24	4.23	4.23	4.22	4.22	4.22	4.21	4.21	4.21	4.21
300	6.46	6.42	6.40	6.38	6.36	6.35	6.34	6.33	6.33	6.32	6.32	6.31	6.31	6.31
400	8.61	8.56	8.53	8.50	8.48	8.46	8.45	8.44	8.43	8.43	8.42	8.41	8.41	8.41
500	10.76	10.70	10.66	10.62	10.60	10.58	10.56	10.55	10.54	10.53	10.53	10.51	10.51	10.51
600	12.91	12.84	12.79	12.75	12.72	12.69	12.67	12.66	12.65	12.64	12.63	12.61	12.61	12.61
700	15.06	14.98	14.92	14.87	14.83	14.81	14.78	14.77	14.75	14.74	14.73	14.71	14.71	14.71
800	17.21	17.12	17.05	17.00	16.95	16.92	16.89	16.87	16.87	16.86	16.84	16.84	16.81	16.81
900	19.36	19.26	19.18	19.12	19.07	19.03	19.01	18.98	18.97	18.95	18.94	18.92	18.91	18.91
1000	21.52	21.40	21.31	21.24	21.19	21.15	21.12	21.09	21.07	21.06	21.05	21.02	21.01	21.01
2000	43.03	42.80	42.62	42.48	42.38	42.29	42.23	42.18	42.14	42.11	42.09	42.03	42.01	42.01
3000	64.54	64.19	63.93	63.72	63.56	63.44	63.34	63.27	63.21	63.16	63.13	63.04	63.02	63.01
4000	86.05	85.59	85.23	84.96	84.75	84.58	84.45	84.35	84.28	84.22	84.17	84.05	84.02	84.01
5000	107.56	106.98	106.54	106.20	105.93	105.73	105.57	105.44	105.35	105.27	105.21	105.06	105.02	105.01
6000	129.07	128.38	127.85	127.44	127.12	126.87	126.68	126.53	126.41	126.32	126.25	126.08	126.03	126.01
7000	150.58	149.78	149.15	148.67	148.30	148.01	147.79	147.62	147.48	147.38	147.29	147.09	147.03	147.01
8000	172.09	171.17	170.46	169.91	169.49	169.16	168.90	168.70	168.55	168.43	168.33	168.10	168.03	168.01
9000	193.60	192.57	191.77	191.15	190.67	190.30	190.01	189.79	189.62	189.48	189.38	189.11	189.04	189.01
10000	215.11	213.96	213.08	212.39	211.86	211.45	211.13	210.88	210.69	210.53	210.42	210.12	210.04	210.01
11000	236.62	235.36	234.38	233.63	233.04	232.59	232.24	231.97	231.75	231.59	231.46	231.14	231.04	231.02
12000	258.13	256.75	255.69	254.87	254.23	253.74	253.35	253.05	252.82	252.64	252.50	252.15	252.05	252.02
13000	279.64	278.15	277.00	276.11	275.42	274.88	274.46	274.14	273.89	273.69	273.54	273.16	273.05	273.02
14000	301.15	299.55	298.30	297.34	296.60	296.02	295.58	295.23	294.96	294.75	294.58	294.17	294.05	294.02
15000	322.66	320.94	319.61	318.58	317.79	317.17	316.69	316.32	316.03	315.80	315.62	315.18	315.06	315.02
16000	344.17	342.34	340.92	339.82	338.97	338.31	337.80	337.40	337.09	336.85	336.66	336.19	336.06	336.02
17000	365.68	363.73	362.23	361.06	360.16	359.46	358.91	358.49	358.16	357.91	357.71	357.21	357.06	357.02
18000	387.19	385.13	383.53	382.30	381.34	380.60	380.02	379.58	379.23	378.96	378.75	378.22	378.07	378.02
19000	408.70	406.52	404.84	403.54	402.53	401.75	401.14	400.66	400.30	400.01	399.79	399.23	399.07	399.02
20000	430.22	427.92	426.15	424.78	423.71	422.89	422.25	421.75	421.37	421.06	420.83	420.24	420.07	420.02
21000	451.73	449.32	447.45	446.01	444.90	444.03	443.36	442.84	442.43	442.12	441.87	441.25	441.08	441.03
22000	473.24	470.71	468.76	467.25	466.08	465.18	464.47	463.93	463.50	463.17	462.91	462.27	462.08	462.03
23000	494.75	492.11	490.07	488.49	487.27	486.32	485.59	485.01	484.57	484.22	483.95	483.28	483.08	483.03
24000	516.26	513.50	511.38	509.73	508.46	507.47	506.70	506.10	505.64	505.28	504.99	504.29	504.09	504.03
25000	537.77	534.90	532.68	530.97	529.64	528.61	527.81	527.19	526.71	526.33	526.04	525.30	525.09	525.03
26000	559.28	556.29	553.99	552.21	550.83	549.75	548.92	548.28	547.77	547.38	547.08	546.31	546.09	546.03
27000	580.79	577.69	575.30	573.45	572.01	570.90	570.03	569.36	568.84	568.43	568.12	567.32	567.10	567.03
28000	602.30	599.09	596.60	594.68	593.20	592.04	591.15	590.45	589.91	589.49	589.16	588.34	588.10	588.03
29000	623.81	620.48	617.91	615.92	614.38	613.19	612.26	611.54	610.98	610.54	610.20	609.35	609.10	609.03
30000	645.32	641.88	639.22	637.16	635.57	634.33	633.37	632.63	632.05	631.59	631.24	630.36	630.11	630.03
31000	666.83	663.27	660.52	658.40	656.75	655.48	654.48	653.71	653.11	652.65	652.28	651.37	651.11	651.04
32000	688.34	684.67	681.83	679.64	677.94	676.62	675.60	674.80	674.18	673.70	673.32	672.38	672.11	672.04
33000	709.85	706.06	703.14	700.88	699.12	697.76	696.71	695.89	695.25	694.75	694.37	693.40	693.12	693.04
34000	731.36	727.46	724.45	722.12	720.31	718.91	717.82	716.97	716.32	715.81	715.41	714.41	714.12	714.04
35000	752.87	748.86	745.75	743.35	741.49	740.05	738.93	738.06	737.39	736.86	736.45	735.42	735.12	735.04
36000	774.38	770.25	767.06	764.59	762.68	761.20	760.04	759.15	758.45	757.91	757.49	756.43	756.13	756.04
37000	795.89	791.65	788.37	785.83	783.87	782.34	781.16	780.24	779.52	778.96	778.53	777.44	777.13	777.04
38000	817.40	813.04	809.67	807.07	805.05	803.49	802.27	801.32	800.59	800.02	799.57	798.45	798.13	798.04
39000	838.92	834.44	830.98	828.31	826.24	824.63	823.38	822.41	821.66	821.07	820.61	819.47	819.14	819.04
40000	860.43	855.83	852.29	849.55	847.42	845.77	844.49	843.50	842.73	842.12	841.65	840.48	840.14	840.04
41000	881.94	877.23	873.60	870.79	868.61	866.92	865.61	864.59	863.79	863.18	862.70	861.49	861.14	861.05
42000	903.45	898.63	894.90	892.02	889.79	888.06	886.72	885.67	884.86	884.23	883.74	882.50	882.15	882.05
43000	924.96	920.02	916.21	913.26	910.98	909.21	907.83	906.76	905.93	905.28	904.78	903.51	903.15	903.05
44000	946.47	941.42	937.52	934.50	932.16	930.35	928.94	927.85	927.00	926.33	925.82	924.53	924.15	924.05
45000	967.98	962.81	958.82	955.74	953.35	951.49	950.05	948.94	948.07	947.39	946.86	945.54	945.16	945.05
46000	989.49	984.21	980.13	976.98	974.53	972.64	971.17	970.02	969.13	968.44	967.90	966.55	966.16	966.05
47000	1011.00	1005.60	1001.44	998.22	995.72	993.78	992.28	991.11	990.20	989.49	988.94	987.56	987.16	987.05
48000	1032.51	1027.00	1022.75	1019.46	1016.91	1014.93	1013.39	1012.20	1011.27	1010.55	1009.98	1008.57	1008.17	1008.05
49000	1054.02	1048.40	1044.05	1040.69	1038.09	1036.07	1034.50	1033.28	1032.34	1031.60	1031.03	1029.58	1029.17	1029.05
50000	1075.53	1069.79	1065.36	1061.93	1059.28	1057.22	1055.62	1054.37	1053.41	1052.65	1052.07	1050.60	1050.18	1050.05
55000	1183.08	1176.77	1171.90	1168.12	1165.20	1162.94	1161.18	1159.81	1158.75	1157.92	1157.27	1155.66	1155.19	1155.06
60000	1290.64	1283.75	1278.43	1274.32	1271.13	1268.66	1266.74	1265.25	1264.09	1263.18	1262.48	1260.72	1260.21	1260.06
65000	1398.19	1390.73	1384.97	1380.51	1377.06	1374.38	1372.30	1370.68	1369.43	1368.45	1367.69	1365.77	1365.23	1365.07
70000	1505.74	1497.71	1491.50	1486.70	1482.98	1480.10	1477.86	1476.12	1474.77	1473.71	1472.89	1470.83	1470.24	1470.07
75000	1613.29	1604.68	1598.04	1592.90	1588.91	1585.82	1583.42	1581.56	1580.11	1578.98	1578.10	1575.89	1575.26	1575.08
80000	1720.85	1711.66	1704.57	1699.09	1694.84	1691.54	1688.98	1686.99	1685.45	1684.24	1683.30	1680.95	1680.28	1680.08
85000	1828.40	1818.64	1811.11	1805.28	1800.77	1797.26	1794.54	1792.43	1790.79	1789.51	1788.51	1786.01	1785.29	1785.09
90000	1935.95	1925.62	1917.64	1911.47	1906.69	1902.98	1900.10	1897.87	1896.13	1894.77	1893.72	1891.07	1890.31	1890.09
95000	2043.50	2032.60	2024.18	2017.67	2012.62	2008.71	2005.67	2003.30	2001.47	2000.04	1998.92	1996.13	1995.33	1995.10
100000	2151.06	2139.58	2130.71	2123.86	2118.55	2114.43	2111.23	2108.74	2106.81	2105.30	2104.13	2101.19	2100.35	2100.10

MONTHLY PAYMENT
REQUIRED TO AMORTIZE A LOAN

TERM	1 Year	2 Years	3 Years	4 Years	5 Years	6 Years	7 Years	8 Years	9 Years	10 Years	11 Years	12 Years	13 Years	14 Years
AMOUNT														
5	.48	.27	.20	.17	.15	.14	.13	.13	.12	.12	.12	.12	.11	.11
10	.96	.54	.40	.34	.30	.28	.26	.25	.24	.23	.23	.23	.22	.22
15	1.43	.81	.60	.50	.45	.41	.39	.37	.36	.35	.34	.34	.33	.33
25	2.38	1.34	1.00	.84	.74	.68	.64	.61	.59	.58	.57	.56	.55	.55
50	4.76	2.68	2.00	1.67	1.48	1.36	1.28	1.22	1.18	1.15	1.13	1.11	1.10	1.09
75	7.14	4.02	3.00	2.50	2.22	2.04	1.92	1.83	1.77	1.72	1.69	1.67	1.65	1.63
100	9.52	5.35	3.99	3.33	2.95	2.71	2.55	2.44	2.36	2.30	2.25	2.22	2.19	2.17
200	19.04	10.70	7.70	6.66	5.90	5.42	5.10	4.87	4.71	4.59	4.50	4.43	4.38	4.34
300	28.55	16.05	11.97	9.99	8.85	8.13	7.65	7.31	7.06	6.88	6.75	6.65	6.57	6.51
400	38.07	21.40	15.96	13.32	11.80	10.84	10.19	9.74	9.41	9.18	9.00	8.86	8.76	8.68
500	47.59	26.75	19.95	16.65	14.75	13.55	12.74	12.17	11.77	11.47	11.25	11.08	10.95	10.85
600	57.10	32.10	23.94	19.98	17.70	16.26	15.29	14.61	14.12	13.76	13.49	13.29	13.14	13.02
700	66.62	37.45	27.93	23.31	20.65	18.97	17.84	17.04	16.47	16.05	15.74	15.51	15.33	15.19
800	76.14	42.80	31.92	26.64	23.60	21.68	20.38	19.48	18.82	18.35	17.99	17.72	17.52	17.36
900	85.65	48.15	35.91	29.97	26.55	24.39	22.93	21.91	21.18	20.64	20.24	19.94	19.71	19.53
1000	95.17	53.50	39.90	33.30	29.50	27.10	25.48	24.34	23.53	22.93	22.49	22.15	21.90	21.70
2000	190.34	107.00	79.79	66.60	59.00	54.19	50.95	48.68	47.05	45.86	44.97	44.30	43.79	43.40
3000	285.50	160.50	119.68	99.90	88.50	81.28	76.42	73.02	70.58	68.78	67.45	66.44	65.68	65.10
4000	380.67	213.99	159.57	133.19	118.00	108.37	101.89	97.36	94.10	91.71	89.93	88.59	87.57	86.80
5000	475.83	267.49	199.47	166.49	147.50	135.46	127.36	121.70	117.62	114.63	112.41	110.73	109.46	108.49
6000	571.00	320.99	239.36	199.79	176.99	162.55	152.84	146.04	141.15	137.56	134.89	132.88	131.36	130.19
7000	666.16	374.48	279.25	233.08	206.49	189.64	178.31	170.38	164.67	160.49	157.37	155.03	153.25	151.89
8000	761.33	427.98	319.14	266.38	235.99	216.73	203.78	194.71	188.19	183.41	179.85	177.17	175.14	173.59
9000	856.50	481.48	359.03	299.68	265.49	243.82	229.25	219.05	211.72	206.34	202.33	199.32	197.03	195.29
10000	951.66	534.98	398.93	332.97	294.99	270.91	254.72	243.39	235.24	229.26	224.81	221.46	218.92	216.98
11000	1046.83	588.47	438.82	366.27	324.48	298.00	280.19	267.73	258.77	252.19	247.29	243.61	240.82	238.68
12000	1141.99	641.97	478.71	399.57	353.98	325.09	305.67	292.07	282.29	275.11	269.77	265.75	262.71	260.38
13000	1237.16	695.47	518.60	432.86	383.48	352.19	331.14	316.41	305.81	298.04	292.25	287.90	284.60	282.08
14000	1332.32	748.96	558.50	466.16	412.98	379.28	356.61	340.75	329.34	320.97	314.73	310.05	306.49	303.78
15000	1427.49	802.46	598.39	499.46	442.48	406.37	382.08	365.09	352.86	343.89	337.22	332.19	328.38	325.47
16000	1522.65	855.96	638.28	532.75	471.97	433.46	407.55	389.42	376.38	366.82	359.70	354.34	350.27	347.17
17000	1617.82	909.45	678.17	566.05	501.47	460.55	433.02	413.76	399.91	389.74	382.18	376.48	372.17	368.87
18000	1712.99	962.95	718.06	599.35	530.97	487.64	458.50	438.10	423.43	412.67	404.66	398.63	394.06	390.57
19000	1808.15	1016.45	757.96	632.64	560.47	514.73	483.97	462.44	446.96	435.59	427.14	420.78	415.95	412.27
20000	1903.32	1069.95	797.85	665.94	589.97	541.82	509.44	486.78	470.48	458.52	449.62	442.92	437.84	433.96
21000	1998.48	1123.44	837.74	699.24	619.46	568.91	534.91	511.12	494.00	481.45	472.10	465.07	459.73	455.66
22000	2093.65	1176.94	877.63	732.53	648.96	596.00	560.38	535.46	517.53	504.37	494.58	487.21	481.63	477.36
23000	2188.81	1230.44	917.52	765.83	678.46	623.09	585.85	559.80	541.05	527.30	517.06	509.36	503.52	499.06
24000	2283.98	1283.93	957.42	799.13	707.96	650.18	611.33	584.13	564.57	550.22	539.54	531.50	525.41	520.76
25000	2379.14	1337.43	997.31	832.42	737.46	677.27	636.80	608.47	588.10	573.15	562.02	553.65	547.30	542.45
26000	2474.31	1390.93	1037.20	865.72	766.95	704.37	662.27	632.81	611.62	596.08	584.50	575.80	569.19	564.15
27000	2569.48	1444.43	1077.09	899.02	796.45	731.46	687.74	657.15	635.15	619.00	606.98	597.94	591.08	585.85
28000	2664.64	1497.92	1116.99	932.31	825.95	758.55	713.21	681.49	658.67	641.93	629.46	620.09	612.98	607.55
29000	2759.81	1551.42	1156.88	965.61	855.45	785.64	738.68	705.83	682.19	664.85	651.95	642.23	634.87	629.25
30000	2854.97	1604.92	1196.77	998.91	884.95	812.73	764.16	730.17	705.72	687.78	674.43	664.38	656.76	650.94
31000	2950.14	1658.41	1236.66	1032.20	914.45	839.82	789.63	754.51	729.24	710.70	696.91	686.53	678.65	672.64
32000	3045.30	1711.91	1276.55	1065.50	943.94	866.91	815.10	778.84	752.76	733.63	719.39	708.67	700.54	694.34
33000	3140.47	1765.41	1316.45	1098.80	973.44	894.00	840.57	803.18	776.29	756.56	741.87	730.82	722.44	716.04
34000	3235.63	1818.90	1356.34	1132.09	1002.94	921.09	866.04	827.52	799.81	779.48	764.35	752.96	744.33	737.74
35000	3330.80	1872.40	1396.23	1165.39	1032.44	948.18	891.51	851.86	823.34	802.41	786.83	775.11	766.22	759.43
36000	3425.97	1925.90	1436.12	1198.69	1061.94	975.27	916.99	876.20	846.86	825.33	809.31	797.25	788.11	781.13
37000	3521.13	1979.40	1476.02	1231.98	1091.43	1002.36	942.46	900.54	870.38	848.26	831.79	819.40	810.00	802.83
38000	3616.30	2032.89	1515.91	1265.28	1120.93	1029.45	967.93	924.88	893.91	871.18	854.27	841.55	831.89	824.53
39000	3711.46	2086.39	1555.80	1298.58	1150.43	1056.55	993.40	949.21	917.43	894.11	876.75	863.69	853.79	846.23
40000	3806.63	2139.89	1595.69	1331.87	1179.93	1083.64	1018.87	973.55	940.95	917.04	899.23	885.84	875.68	867.92
41000	3901.79	2193.38	1635.58	1365.17	1209.43	1110.73	1044.34	997.89	964.48	939.96	921.71	907.98	897.57	889.62
42000	3996.96	2246.88	1675.48	1398.47	1238.92	1137.82	1069.82	1022.23	988.00	962.89	944.19	930.13	919.46	911.32
43000	4092.12	2300.38	1715.37	1431.76	1268.42	1164.91	1095.29	1046.57	1011.53	985.81	966.68	952.28	941.35	933.02
44000	4187.29	2353.87	1755.26	1465.06	1297.92	1192.00	1120.76	1070.91	1035.05	1008.74	989.16	974.42	963.25	954.72
45000	4282.46	2407.37	1795.15	1498.36	1327.42	1219.09	1146.23	1095.25	1058.57	1031.67	1011.64	996.57	985.14	976.41
46000	4377.62	2460.87	1835.04	1531.65	1356.92	1246.18	1171.70	1119.59	1082.10	1054.59	1034.12	1018.71	1007.03	998.11
47000	4472.79	2514.37	1874.94	1564.95	1386.41	1273.27	1197.17	1143.92	1105.62	1077.52	1056.60	1040.86	1028.92	1019.81
48000	4567.95	2567.86	1914.83	1598.25	1415.91	1300.36	1222.65	1168.26	1129.14	1100.44	1079.08	1063.00	1050.81	1041.51
49000	4663.12	2621.36	1954.72	1631.54	1445.41	1327.45	1248.12	1192.60	1152.67	1123.37	1101.56	1085.15	1072.70	1063.21
50000	4758.28	2674.86	1994.61	1664.84	1474.91	1354.54	1273.59	1216.94	1176.19	1146.29	1124.04	1107.30	1094.60	1084.90
55000	5234.11	2942.34	2194.07	1831.32	1622.40	1490.00	1400.95	1338.63	1293.81	1260.92	1236.44	1218.03	1204.06	1193.39
60000	5709.94	3209.83	2393.54	1997.81	1769.89	1625.45	1528.31	1460.33	1411.43	1375.55	1348.85	1328.75	1313.51	1301.88
65000	6185.77	3477.31	2593.00	2164.29	1917.38	1760.91	1655.67	1582.02	1529.05	1490.18	1461.25	1439.48	1422.97	1410.37
70000	6661.59	3744.80	2792.46	2330.78	2064.87	1896.36	1783.02	1703.71	1646.67	1604.81	1573.65	1550.21	1532.43	1518.86
75000	7137.42	4012.28	2991.92	2497.26	2212.36	2031.81	1910.38	1825.41	1764.28	1719.44	1686.06	1660.94	1641.89	1627.35
80000	7613.25	4279.77	3191.38	2663.74	2359.85	2167.27	2037.74	1947.10	1881.90	1834.07	1798.46	1771.67	1751.35	1735.84
85000	8089.08	4547.25	3390.84	2830.23	2507.34	2302.72	2165.10	2068.80	1999.52	1948.70	1910.87	1882.40	1860.81	1844.33
90000	8564.91	4814.74	3590.30	2996.71	2654.83	2438.18	2292.46	2190.49	2117.14	2063.33	2023.27	1993.13	1970.27	1952.82
95000	9040.73	5082.22	3789.76	3163.19	2802.32	2573.63	2419.82	2312.18	2234.76	2177.95	2135.67	2103.86	2079.73	2061.31
100000	9516.56	5349.71	3989.22	3329.68	2949.81	2709.08	2547.17	2433.88	2352.38	2292.58	2248.08	2214.59	2189.19	2169.80

TERM	15 Years	16 Years	17 Years	18 Years	19 Years	20 Years	21 Years	22 Years	23 Years	24 Years	25 Years	30 Years	35 Years	40 Years
AMOUNT														
5	.11	.11	.11	.11	.11	.11	.11	.11	.11	.11	.11	.11	.11	.11
10	.22	.22	.22	.22	.22	.22	.22	.22	.22	.22	.22	.22	.22	.22
15	.33	.33	.33	.32	.32	.32	.32	.32	.32	.32	.32	.32	.32	.32
25	.54	.54	.54	.54	.54	.53	.53	.53	.53	.53	.53	.53	.53	.53
50	1.08	1.08	1.07	1.07	1.07	1.06	1.06	1.06	1.06	1.06	1.06	1.06	1.06	1.06
75	1.62	1.61	1.61	1.60	1.60	1.59	1.59	1.59	1.59	1.59	1.59	1.58	1.58	1.58
100	2.16	2.15	2.14	2.13	2.13	2.12	2.12	2.12	2.12	2.11	2.11	2.11	2.11	2.11
200	4.31	4.29	4.27	4.26	4.25	4.24	4.24	4.23	4.23	4.22	4.22	4.22	4.21	4.21
300	6.47	6.44	6.41	6.39	6.37	6.36	6.35	6.34	6.34	6.33	6.33	6.32	6.32	6.32
400	8.62	8.58	8.54	8.52	8.50	8.48	8.47	8.46	8.45	8.44	8.44	8.43	8.42	8.42
500	10.78	10.72	10.68	10.64	10.62	10.60	10.58	10.57	10.56	10.55	10.55	10.53	10.53	10.53
600	12.93	12.87	12.81	12.77	12.74	12.72	12.70	12.68	12.67	12.66	12.65	12.64	12.63	12.63
700	15.09	15.01	14.95	14.90	14.86	14.83	14.81	14.79	14.78	14.77	14.76	14.74	14.74	14.73
800	17.24	17.15	17.08	17.03	16.99	16.95	16.93	16.91	16.89	16.88	16.87	16.85	16.84	16.84
900	19.40	19.30	19.22	19.16	19.11	19.07	19.04	19.02	19.00	18.99	18.98	18.95	18.95	18.94
1000	21.55	21.44	21.35	21.28	21.23	21.19	21.16	21.13	21.11	21.10	21.09	21.06	21.05	21.05
2000	43.10	42.88	42.70	42.56	42.46	42.37	42.31	42.26	42.22	42.19	42.17	42.11	42.10	42.09
3000	64.65	64.31	64.05	63.84	63.68	63.56	63.46	63.39	63.33	63.29	63.25	63.17	63.14	63.13
4000	86.20	85.75	85.39	85.12	84.91	84.74	84.62	84.52	84.44	84.38	84.33	84.22	84.19	84.18
5000	107.75	107.18	106.74	106.40	106.13	105.93	105.77	105.65	105.55	105.48	105.42	105.27	105.23	105.22
6000	129.30	128.62	128.09	127.68	127.36	127.11	126.92	126.77	126.66	126.57	126.50	126.33	126.28	126.26
7000	150.85	150.05	149.43	148.95	148.59	148.30	148.08	147.90	147.77	147.66	147.58	147.38	147.32	147.30
8000	172.40	171.49	170.78	170.23	169.81	169.48	169.23	169.03	168.88	168.76	168.66	168.43	168.37	168.35
9000	193.95	192.92	192.13	191.51	191.04	190.67	190.38	190.16	189.99	189.85	189.75	189.49	189.41	189.39
10000	215.50	214.36	213.47	212.79	212.26	211.85	211.53	211.29	211.10	210.95	210.83	210.54	210.46	210.43
11000	237.05	235.79	234.82	234.07	233.49	233.04	232.69	232.42	232.20	232.04	231.91	231.59	231.50	231.47
12000	258.60	257.23	256.17	255.35	254.71	254.22	253.84	253.54	253.31	253.13	252.99	252.65	252.55	252.52
13000	280.15	278.66	277.51	276.63	275.94	275.41	274.99	274.67	274.42	274.23	274.08	273.70	273.59	273.56
14000	301.70	300.10	298.86	297.90	297.17	296.59	296.15	295.80	295.53	295.32	295.16	294.75	294.64	294.60
15000	323.25	321.53	320.21	319.18	318.39	317.78	317.30	316.93	316.64	316.42	316.24	315.81	315.68	315.64
16000	344.79	342.97	341.55	340.46	339.62	338.96	338.45	338.06	337.75	337.51	337.32	336.86	336.73	336.69
17000	366.34	364.40	362.90	361.74	360.84	360.15	359.61	359.19	358.86	358.60	358.41	357.91	357.77	357.73
18000	387.89	385.84	384.25	383.02	382.07	381.33	380.76	380.31	379.97	379.70	379.49	378.97	378.82	378.77
19000	409.44	407.27	405.59	404.30	403.29	402.52	401.91	401.44	401.08	400.79	400.57	400.02	399.86	399.81
20000	430.99	428.71	426.94	425.58	424.52	423.70	423.06	422.57	422.19	421.89	421.65	421.07	420.91	420.86
21000	452.54	450.14	448.29	446.85	445.75	444.88	444.22	443.70	443.29	442.98	442.74	442.12	441.95	441.90
22000	474.09	471.58	469.63	468.13	466.97	466.07	465.37	464.83	464.40	464.08	463.82	463.18	463.00	462.94
23000	495.64	493.01	490.98	489.41	488.20	487.25	486.52	485.95	485.51	485.17	484.90	484.23	484.04	483.99
24000	517.19	514.45	512.33	510.69	509.42	508.44	507.68	507.08	506.62	506.26	505.98	505.29	505.09	505.03
25000	530.74	535.88	533.67	531.97	530.65	529.62	528.83	528.21	527.73	527.36	527.07	526.34	526.13	526.07
26000	560.29	557.32	555.02	553.25	551.87	550.81	549.98	549.34	548.84	548.45	548.15	547.39	547.18	547.11
27000	581.84	578.75	576.37	574.53	573.10	571.99	571.13	570.47	569.95	569.55	569.23	568.45	568.22	568.16
28000	603.39	600.19	597.71	595.80	594.33	593.18	592.29	591.60	591.06	590.64	590.31	589.50	589.27	589.20
29000	624.94	621.62	619.06	617.08	615.55	614.36	613.44	612.72	612.17	611.73	611.40	610.55	610.31	610.24
30000	646.49	643.06	640.41	638.36	636.78	635.55	634.59	633.85	633.28	632.83	632.48	631.61	631.36	631.28
31000	668.04	664.49	661.76	659.64	658.00	656.73	655.75	654.98	654.39	653.92	653.56	652.66	652.40	652.33
32000	689.58	685.93	683.10	680.92	679.23	677.92	676.90	676.11	675.49	675.02	674.64	673.71	673.45	673.37
33000	711.13	707.36	704.45	702.20	700.45	699.10	698.05	697.24	696.60	696.11	695.73	694.77	694.49	694.41
34000	732.68	728.80	725.80	723.48	721.68	720.29	719.21	718.37	717.71	717.20	716.81	715.82	715.54	715.45
35000	754.23	750.23	747.14	744.75	742.91	741.47	740.36	739.49	738.82	738.30	737.89	736.87	736.58	736.50
36000	775.78	771.67	768.49	766.03	764.13	762.66	761.51	760.62	759.93	759.39	758.97	757.93	757.63	757.54
37000	797.33	793.10	789.84	787.31	785.36	783.84	782.66	781.75	781.04	780.49	780.06	778.98	778.67	778.58
38000	818.88	814.54	811.18	808.59	806.58	805.03	803.82	802.88	802.15	801.58	801.14	800.03	799.72	799.62
39000	840.43	835.97	832.53	829.87	827.81	826.21	824.97	824.01	823.26	822.68	822.22	821.09	820.76	820.67
40000	861.98	857.41	853.88	851.15	849.03	847.40	846.12	845.13	844.37	843.77	843.30	842.14	841.81	841.71
41000	883.53	878.84	875.22	872.43	870.26	868.58	867.28	866.26	865.48	864.86	864.39	863.19	862.85	862.75
42000	905.08	900.28	896.57	893.70	891.49	889.76	888.43	887.39	886.58	885.96	885.47	884.25	883.90	883.80
43000	926.63	921.71	917.92	914.98	912.71	910.95	909.58	908.52	907.69	907.05	906.55	905.30	904.94	904.84
44000	948.18	943.15	939.26	936.26	933.94	932.13	930.73	929.65	928.80	928.15	927.63	926.35	925.99	925.88
45000	969.73	964.58	960.61	957.54	955.16	953.32	951.89	950.78	949.91	949.24	948.72	947.41	947.03	946.92
46000	991.28	986.02	981.96	978.82	976.39	974.50	973.04	971.90	971.02	970.33	969.80	968.46	968.08	967.97
47000	1012.83	1007.45	1003.30	1000.10	997.61	995.69	994.19	993.03	992.13	991.43	990.88	989.51	989.12	989.01
48000	1034.37	1028.89	1024.65	1021.38	1018.84	1016.87	1015.35	1014.16	1013.24	1012.52	1011.96	1010.57	1010.17	1010.05
49000	1055.92	1050.32	1046.00	1042.65	1040.07	1038.06	1036.50	1035.29	1034.35	1033.62	1033.05	1031.62	1031.21	1031.09
50000	1077.47	1071.76	1067.34	1063.93	1061.29	1059.24	1057.65	1056.42	1055.46	1054.71	1054.13	1052.67	1052.26	1052.14
55000	1185.22	1178.93	1174.08	1170.33	1167.42	1165.17	1163.42	1162.06	1161.00	1160.18	1159.54	1157.94	1157.48	1157.35
60000	1292.97	1286.11	1280.81	1276.72	1273.55	1271.09	1269.18	1267.70	1266.55	1265.65	1264.95	1263.21	1262.71	1262.56
65000	1400.71	1393.28	1387.55	1383.11	1379.68	1377.01	1374.95	1373.34	1372.09	1371.12	1370.37	1368.47	1367.93	1367.78
70000	1508.46	1500.46	1494.28	1489.50	1485.81	1482.94	1480.71	1478.98	1477.64	1476.59	1475.78	1473.74	1473.16	1472.99
75000	1616.21	1607.63	1601.01	1595.90	1591.93	1588.86	1586.48	1584.62	1583.18	1582.06	1581.19	1579.01	1578.38	1578.20
80000	1723.95	1714.81	1707.75	1702.29	1698.06	1694.79	1692.24	1690.26	1688.73	1687.53	1686.60	1684.27	1683.61	1683.42
85000	1831.70	1821.98	1814.48	1808.68	1804.19	1800.71	1798.01	1795.91	1794.27	1793.00	1792.02	1789.54	1788.83	1788.63
90000	1939.45	1929.16	1921.22	1915.08	1910.32	1906.63	1903.77	1901.55	1899.82	1898.47	1897.43	1894.81	1894.06	1893.84
95000	2047.20	2036.33	2027.95	2021.47	2016.45	2012.56	2009.53	2007.19	2005.36	2003.94	2002.84	2000.07	1999.28	1999.05
100000	2154.94	2143.51	2134.68	2127.86	2122.58	2118.48	2115.30	2112.83	2110.91	2109.42	2108.25	2105.34	2104.51	2104.27

MONTHLY PAYMENT
REQUIRED TO AMORTIZE A LOAN

TERM	1 Year	2 Years	3 Years	4 Years	5 Years	6 Years	7 Years	8 Years	9 Years	10 Years	11 Years	12 Years	13 Years	14 Years
AMOUNT														
5	.48	.27	.20	.17	.15	.14	.13	.13	.12	.12	.12	.12	.11	.11
10	.96	.54	.40	.34	.30	.28	.26	.25	.24	.23	.23	.23	.22	.22
15	1.43	.81	.60	.50	.45	.41	.39	.37	.36	.35	.34	.34	.33	.33
25	2.38	1.34	1.00	.84	.74	.68	.64	.61	.59	.58	.57	.56	.55	.55
50	4.76	2.68	2.00	1.67	1.48	1.36	1.28	1.22	1.18	1.15	1.13	1.11	1.10	1.09
75	7.14	4.02	3.00	2.50	2.22	2.04	1.92	1.83	1.77	1.73	1.69	1.67	1.65	1.64
100	9.52	5.36	4.00	3.34	2.96	2.72	2.56	2.44	2.36	2.30	2.26	2.22	2.20	2.18
200	19.04	10.71	7.99	6.67	5.91	5.43	5.11	4.88	4.72	4.60	4.51	4.44	4.39	4.35
300	28.56	16.06	11.98	10.00	8.86	8.14	7.66	7.32	7.07	6.89	6.76	6.66	6.58	6.53
400	38.08	21.41	15.97	13.33	11.82	10.85	10.21	9.75	9.43	9.19	9.01	8.88	8.78	8.70
500	47.60	26.77	19.96	16.67	14.77	13.57	12.76	12.19	11.78	11.49	11.26	11.10	10.97	10.87
600	57.12	32.12	23.96	20.00	17.72	16.28	15.31	14.63	14.14	13.78	13.52	13.31	13.16	13.05
700	66.64	37.47	27.95	23.33	20.67	18.99	17.86	17.07	16.50	16.08	15.77	15.53	15.36	15.22
800	76.16	42.82	31.94	26.66	23.63	21.70	20.41	19.50	18.85	18.37	18.02	17.75	17.55	17.39
900	85.68	48.17	35.93	30.00	26.58	24.41	22.96	21.94	21.21	20.67	20.27	19.97	19.74	19.57
1000	95.19	53.53	39.92	33.33	29.53	27.13	25.51	24.38	23.56	22.97	22.52	22.19	21.93	21.74
2000	190.38	107.05	79.84	66.65	59.06	54.25	51.01	48.75	47.12	45.93	45.04	44.37	43.86	43.48
3000	285.57	160.57	119.76	99.98	88.59	81.37	76.52	73.12	70.68	68.89	67.56	66.55	65.79	65.21
4000	380.76	214.09	159.68	133.30	118.11	108.49	102.02	97.49	94.24	91.85	90.07	88.74	87.72	86.95
5000	475.95	267.62	199.60	166.63	147.64	135.61	127.52	121.86	117.80	114.81	112.59	110.92	109.65	108.69
6000	571.14	321.14	239.52	199.95	177.17	162.73	153.03	146.24	141.35	137.77	135.11	133.10	131.58	130.42
7000	666.33	374.66	279.44	233.28	206.70	189.86	178.53	170.61	164.91	160.73	157.62	155.29	153.51	152.16
8000	761.52	428.18	319.35	266.60	236.22	216.98	204.04	194.98	188.47	183.69	180.14	177.47	175.44	173.90
9000	856.71	481.70	359.27	299.93	265.75	244.10	229.54	219.35	212.03	206.66	202.66	199.65	197.37	195.63
10000	951.90	535.23	399.19	333.25	295.28	271.22	255.04	243.72	235.59	229.62	225.17	221.83	219.30	217.37
11000	1047.09	588.75	439.11	366.58	324.81	298.34	280.55	268.10	259.14	252.58	247.69	244.02	241.23	239.10
12000	1142.28	642.27	479.03	399.90	354.33	325.46	306.05	292.47	282.70	275.54	270.21	266.20	263.16	260.84
13000	1237.47	695.79	518.95	433.23	383.86	352.59	331.55	316.84	306.26	298.50	292.73	288.38	285.09	282.58
14000	1332.66	749.32	558.87	466.55	413.39	379.71	357.06	341.21	329.82	321.46	315.24	310.57	307.02	304.31
15000	1427.85	802.84	598.78	499.88	442.92	406.83	382.56	365.58	353.38	344.42	337.76	332.75	328.95	326.05
16000	1523.04	856.36	638.70	533.20	472.44	433.95	408.07	389.96	376.93	367.38	360.28	354.93	350.88	347.79
17000	1618.23	909.88	678.62	566.52	501.97	461.07	433.57	414.33	400.49	390.34	382.79	377.11	372.81	369.52
18000	1713.42	963.40	718.54	599.85	531.50	488.19	459.07	438.70	424.05	413.31	405.31	399.30	394.74	391.26
19000	1808.61	1016.93	758.46	633.17	561.03	515.31	484.58	463.07	447.61	436.27	427.83	421.48	416.67	413.00
20000	1903.80	1070.45	798.38	666.50	590.55	542.44	510.08	487.44	471.17	459.23	450.34	443.66	438.60	434.73
21000	1998.99	1123.97	838.30	699.82	620.08	569.56	535.58	511.82	494.72	482.19	472.86	465.85	460.53	456.47
22000	2094.18	1177.49	878.22	733.15	649.61	596.68	561.09	536.19	518.28	505.15	495.38	488.03	482.46	478.20
23000	2189.37	1231.01	918.13	766.47	679.14	623.80	586.59	560.56	541.84	528.11	517.89	510.21	504.38	499.94
24000	2284.56	1284.54	958.05	799.80	708.66	650.92	612.10	584.93	565.40	551.07	540.41	532.39	526.31	521.68
25000	2379.75	1338.06	997.97	833.12	738.19	678.04	637.60	609.30	588.96	574.03	562.93	554.58	548.24	543.41
26000	2474.94	1391.58	1037.89	866.45	767.72	705.17	663.11	633.68	612.52	596.99	585.45	576.76	570.17	565.15
27000	2570.13	1445.10	1077.81	899.77	797.25	732.29	688.61	658.05	636.07	619.96	607.96	598.94	592.10	586.89
28000	2665.32	1498.63	1117.73	933.10	826.77	759.41	714.11	682.42	659.63	642.92	630.48	621.13	614.03	608.62
29000	2760.51	1552.15	1157.65	966.42	856.30	786.53	739.61	706.79	683.19	665.88	653.00	643.31	635.96	630.36
30000	2855.70	1605.67	1197.56	999.75	885.83	813.65	765.12	731.16	706.75	688.84	675.51	665.49	657.89	652.09
31000	2950.89	1659.19	1237.48	1033.07	915.36	840.77	790.62	755.54	730.31	711.80	698.03	687.67	679.82	673.83
32000	3046.08	1712.71	1277.40	1066.39	944.88	867.89	816.13	779.91	753.86	734.76	720.55	709.86	701.75	695.57
33000	3141.27	1766.24	1317.32	1099.72	974.41	895.02	841.63	804.28	777.42	757.72	743.06	732.04	723.68	717.30
34000	3236.46	1819.76	1357.24	1133.04	1003.94	922.14	867.13	828.65	800.98	780.68	765.58	754.22	745.61	739.04
35000	3331.65	1873.28	1397.16	1166.37	1033.47	949.26	892.64	853.02	824.54	803.64	788.10	776.41	767.54	760.78
36000	3426.84	1926.80	1437.08	1199.69	1062.99	976.38	918.14	877.40	848.10	826.61	810.62	798.59	789.47	782.51
37000	3522.03	1980.32	1477.00	1233.02	1092.52	1003.50	943.64	901.77	871.65	849.57	833.13	820.77	811.40	804.25
38000	3617.22	2033.85	1516.91	1266.34	1122.05	1030.62	969.15	926.14	895.21	872.53	855.65	842.95	833.33	825.99
39000	3712.41	2087.37	1556.83	1299.67	1151.58	1057.75	994.65	950.51	918.77	895.49	878.17	865.14	855.26	847.72
40000	3807.60	2140.89	1596.75	1332.99	1181.10	1084.87	1020.16	974.88	942.33	918.45	900.68	887.32	877.19	869.46
41000	3902.79	2194.41	1636.67	1366.32	1210.63	1111.99	1045.66	999.26	965.89	941.41	923.20	909.50	899.12	891.19
42000	3997.98	2247.94	1676.59	1399.64	1240.16	1139.11	1071.16	1023.63	989.44	964.37	945.72	931.69	921.05	912.93
43000	4093.17	2301.46	1716.51	1432.97	1269.69	1166.23	1096.67	1048.00	1013.00	987.33	968.23	953.87	942.98	934.67
44000	4188.36	2354.98	1756.43	1466.29	1299.21	1193.35	1122.17	1072.37	1036.56	1010.30	990.75	976.05	964.91	956.40
45000	4283.55	2408.50	1796.34	1499.62	1328.74	1220.48	1147.67	1096.74	1060.12	1033.26	1013.27	998.23	986.84	978.14
46000	4378.74	2462.02	1836.26	1532.94	1358.27	1247.60	1173.18	1121.12	1083.68	1056.22	1035.78	1020.42	1008.76	999.88
47000	4473.93	2515.55	1876.18	1566.26	1387.80	1274.72	1198.68	1145.49	1107.24	1079.18	1058.30	1042.60	1030.69	1021.61
48000	4569.12	2569.07	1916.10	1599.59	1417.32	1301.84	1224.19	1169.86	1130.79	1102.14	1080.82	1064.78	1052.62	1043.35
49000	4664.31	2622.59	1956.02	1632.91	1446.85	1328.96	1249.69	1194.23	1154.35	1125.10	1103.34	1086.97	1074.55	1065.08
50000	4759.50	2676.11	1995.94	1666.24	1476.38	1356.08	1275.19	1218.60	1177.91	1148.06	1125.85	1109.15	1096.48	1086.82
55000	5235.45	2943.72	2195.53	1832.86	1624.02	1491.69	1402.71	1340.46	1295.70	1262.87	1238.44	1220.06	1206.13	1195.50
60000	5711.40	3211.33	2395.12	1999.49	1771.65	1627.30	1530.23	1462.32	1413.49	1377.67	1351.02	1330.98	1315.78	1304.18
65000	6187.34	3478.95	2594.72	2166.11	1919.29	1762.91	1657.75	1584.18	1531.28	1492.48	1463.61	1441.89	1425.43	1412.87
70000	6663.29	3746.56	2794.31	2332.73	2066.93	1898.51	1785.27	1706.04	1649.07	1607.28	1576.19	1552.81	1535.07	1521.55
75000	7139.24	4014.17	2993.90	2499.36	2214.56	2034.12	1912.79	1827.90	1766.86	1722.09	1688.78	1663.72	1644.72	1630.23
80000	7615.19	4281.78	3193.50	2665.98	2362.20	2169.73	2040.31	1949.76	1884.65	1836.90	1801.36	1774.63	1754.37	1738.91
85000	8091.14	4549.39	3393.09	2832.60	2509.84	2305.34	2167.82	2071.62	2002.44	1951.70	1913.95	1885.55	1864.02	1847.59
90000	8567.09	4817.00	3592.68	2999.23	2657.48	2440.95	2295.34	2193.48	2120.23	2066.51	2026.53	1996.46	1973.67	1956.27
95000	9043.04	5084.61	3792.28	3165.85	2805.11	2576.55	2422.86	2315.34	2238.02	2181.31	2139.12	2107.38	2083.31	2064.96
100000	9518.99	5352.22	3991.87	3332.47	2952.75	2712.16	2550.38	2437.20	2355.81	2296.12	2251.70	2218.29	2192.96	2173.64

TERM AMOUNT	15 Years	16 Years	17 Years	18 Years	19 Years	20 Years	21 Years	22 Years	23 Years	24 Years	25 Years	30 Years	35 Years	40 Years
5	.11	.11	.11	.11	.11	.11	.11	.11	.11	.11	.11	.11	.11	.11
10	.22	.22	.22	.22	.22	.22	.22	.22	.22	.22	.22	.22	.22	.22
15	.33	.33	.33	.32	.32	.32	.32	.32	.32	.32	.32	.32	.32	.32
25	.54	.54	.54	.54	.54	.54	.53	.53	.53	.53	.53	.53	.53	.53
50	1.08	1.08	1.07	1.07	1.07	1.07	1.06	1.06	1.06	1.06	1.06	1.06	1.06	1.06
75	1.62	1.62	1.61	1.60	1.60	1.60	1.59	1.59	1.59	1.59	1.59	1.59	1.59	1.59
100	2.16	2.15	2.14	2.14	2.13	2.13	2.12	2.12	2.12	2.12	2.12	2.11	2.11	2.11
200	4.32	4.30	4.28	4.27	4.26	4.25	4.24	4.24	4.24	4.23	4.23	4.22	4.22	4.22
300	6.48	6.45	6.42	6.40	6.38	6.37	6.36	6.36	6.35	6.35	6.34	6.33	6.33	6.33
400	8.64	8.59	8.56	8.53	8.51	8.50	8.48	8.47	8.47	8.46	8.45	8.44	8.44	8.44
500	10.80	10.74	10.70	10.66	10.64	10.62	10.60	10.59	10.58	10.57	10.57	10.55	10.55	10.55
600	12.96	12.89	12.84	12.80	12.76	12.74	12.72	12.71	12.70	12.69	12.68	12.66	12.66	12.66
700	15.12	15.04	14.98	14.93	14.89	14.86	14.84	14.82	14.81	14.80	14.79	14.77	14.77	14.76
800	17.28	17.18	17.11	17.06	17.02	16.99	16.96	16.94	16.93	16.91	16.90	16.88	16.87	16.87
900	19.43	19.33	19.25	19.19	19.14	19.11	19.08	19.06	19.04	19.03	19.02	18.99	18.98	18.98
1000	21.59	21.48	21.39	21.32	21.27	21.23	21.20	21.17	21.16	21.14	21.13	21.10	21.09	21.09
2000	43.18	42.95	42.78	42.64	42.54	42.46	42.39	42.34	42.31	42.28	42.25	42.19	42.18	42.17
3000	64.77	64.43	64.16	63.96	63.80	63.68	63.59	63.51	63.46	63.41	63.38	63.29	63.26	63.26
4000	86.36	85.90	85.55	85.28	85.07	84.91	84.78	84.68	84.61	84.55	84.50	84.38	84.35	84.34
5000	107.95	107.38	106.94	106.60	106.34	106.13	105.97	105.85	105.76	105.68	105.62	105.48	105.44	105.43
6000	129.53	128.85	128.32	127.92	127.60	127.36	127.17	127.02	126.91	126.82	126.75	126.57	126.52	126.51
7000	151.12	150.33	149.71	149.24	148.87	148.58	148.36	148.19	148.06	147.95	147.87	147.67	147.61	147.59
8000	172.71	171.80	171.10	170.55	170.13	169.81	169.55	169.36	169.21	169.09	168.99	168.76	168.70	168.68
9000	194.30	193.27	192.48	191.87	191.40	191.03	190.75	190.53	190.36	190.22	190.12	189.86	189.78	189.76
10000	215.89	214.75	213.87	213.19	212.67	212.26	211.94	211.70	211.51	211.36	211.24	210.95	210.87	210.85
11000	237.48	236.22	235.26	234.51	233.93	233.48	233.14	232.87	232.66	232.49	232.37	232.05	231.96	231.93
12000	259.06	257.70	256.64	255.83	255.20	254.71	254.33	254.03	253.81	253.63	253.49	253.14	253.04	253.02
13000	280.65	279.17	278.03	277.15	276.46	275.93	275.52	275.20	274.96	274.76	274.61	274.24	274.13	274.10
14000	302.24	300.65	299.42	298.47	297.73	297.16	296.72	296.37	296.11	295.90	295.74	295.33	295.22	295.18
15000	323.83	322.12	320.80	319.78	319.00	318.38	317.91	317.54	317.26	317.03	317.03	316.86	316.43	316.27
16000	345.42	343.59	342.19	341.10	340.26	339.61	339.10	338.71	338.41	338.17	337.98	337.52	337.39	337.35
17000	367.00	365.07	363.58	362.42	361.53	360.84	360.30	359.88	359.56	359.30	359.11	358.62	358.48	358.44
18000	388.59	386.54	384.96	383.74	382.79	382.06	381.49	381.05	380.71	380.44	380.23	379.71	379.56	379.52
19000	410.18	408.02	406.35	405.06	404.06	403.29	402.69	402.22	401.86	401.57	401.36	400.81	400.65	400.61
20000	431.77	429.49	427.73	426.38	425.33	424.51	423.89	423.39	423.01	422.71	422.48	421.90	421.74	421.69
21000	453.36	450.97	449.12	447.70	446.59	445.74	445.07	444.56	444.16	443.85	443.60	443.00	442.82	442.77
22000	474.95	472.44	470.51	469.01	467.86	466.96	466.27	465.73	465.31	464.98	464.73	464.09	463.91	463.86
23000	496.53	493.91	491.89	490.33	489.12	488.19	487.46	486.90	486.46	486.12	485.85	485.19	485.00	484.94
24000	518.12	515.39	513.28	511.65	510.39	509.41	508.65	508.06	507.61	507.25	506.97	506.28	506.08	506.03
25000	539.71	536.86	534.67	532.97	531.66	530.64	529.85	529.23	528.76	528.39	528.10	527.38	527.17	527.11
26000	561.30	558.34	556.05	554.29	552.92	551.86	551.04	550.40	549.91	549.52	549.22	548.47	548.26	548.20
27000	582.89	579.81	577.44	575.61	574.19	573.09	572.23	571.57	571.06	570.66	570.35	569.57	569.34	569.28
28000	604.48	601.29	598.83	596.93	595.45	594.31	593.43	592.74	592.21	591.79	591.47	590.66	590.43	590.36
29000	626.06	622.76	620.21	618.24	616.72	615.54	614.62	613.91	613.36	612.93	612.59	611.76	611.52	611.45
30000	647.65	644.23	641.60	639.56	637.99	636.76	635.82	635.08	634.51	634.06	633.72	632.85	632.60	632.53
31000	669.24	665.71	662.99	660.88	659.25	657.99	657.01	656.25	655.66	655.20	654.84	653.95	653.69	653.62
32000	690.83	687.18	684.37	682.20	680.52	679.21	678.20	677.42	676.81	676.33	675.96	675.04	674.78	674.70
33000	712.42	708.66	705.76	703.52	701.78	700.44	699.40	698.59	697.96	697.47	697.09	696.14	695.86	695.79
34000	734.00	730.13	727.15	724.84	723.05	721.67	720.59	719.76	719.11	718.60	718.21	717.23	716.95	716.87
35000	755.59	751.61	748.53	746.16	744.32	742.89	741.78	740.93	740.26	739.74	739.34	738.33	738.04	737.95
36000	777.18	773.08	769.92	767.47	765.58	764.12	762.98	762.09	761.41	760.87	760.46	759.42	759.12	759.04
37000	798.77	794.56	791.30	788.79	786.85	785.34	784.17	783.26	782.56	782.01	781.58	780.52	780.21	780.12
38000	820.36	816.03	812.69	810.11	808.11	806.57	805.37	804.43	803.71	803.14	802.71	801.61	801.30	801.21
39000	841.95	837.50	834.08	831.43	829.38	827.79	826.56	825.60	824.86	824.28	823.83	822.70	822.38	822.29
40000	863.53	858.98	855.46	852.75	850.65	849.02	847.75	846.77	846.01	845.42	844.95	843.80	843.47	843.38
41000	885.12	880.45	876.85	874.07	871.91	870.24	868.95	867.94	867.16	866.56	866.08	864.89	864.56	864.46
42000	906.71	901.93	898.24	895.39	893.18	891.47	890.14	889.11	888.31	887.69	887.20	885.99	885.64	885.54
43000	928.30	923.40	919.62	916.70	914.44	912.69	911.33	910.28	909.46	908.82	908.33	907.08	906.73	906.63
44000	949.89	944.88	941.01	938.02	935.71	933.92	932.53	931.45	930.61	929.96	929.45	928.18	927.82	927.71
45000	971.48	966.35	962.40	959.34	956.98	955.14	953.72	952.62	951.76	951.09	950.57	949.27	948.90	948.80
46000	993.06	987.82	983.78	980.66	978.24	976.37	974.91	973.79	972.91	972.23	971.70	970.37	969.99	969.88
47000	1014.65	1009.30	1005.17	1001.98	999.51	997.59	996.11	994.95	994.06	993.36	992.82	991.46	991.08	990.97
48000	1036.24	1030.77	1026.56	1023.30	1020.77	1018.82	1017.30	1016.12	1015.21	1014.50	1013.94	1012.56	1012.16	1012.05
49000	1057.83	1052.25	1047.94	1044.62	1042.04	1040.04	1038.50	1037.29	1036.36	1035.63	1035.07	1033.65	1033.25	1033.13
50000	1079.42	1073.72	1069.33	1065.93	1063.31	1061.27	1059.69	1058.46	1057.51	1056.77	1056.19	1054.75	1054.34	1054.22
55000	1187.36	1181.09	1176.26	1172.53	1169.64	1167.40	1165.66	1164.31	1163.26	1162.44	1161.81	1160.22	1159.77	1159.64
60000	1295.30	1288.46	1283.19	1279.12	1275.97	1273.52	1271.63	1270.15	1269.01	1268.12	1267.43	1265.70	1265.20	1265.06
65000	1403.24	1395.84	1390.13	1385.71	1382.30	1379.65	1377.59	1376.00	1374.76	1373.80	1373.05	1371.17	1370.64	1370.48
70000	1511.18	1503.21	1497.06	1492.31	1488.63	1485.78	1483.56	1481.85	1480.51	1479.47	1478.67	1476.65	1476.07	1475.90
75000	1619.12	1610.58	1603.99	1598.90	1594.96	1591.90	1589.53	1587.69	1586.26	1585.15	1584.29	1582.12	1581.50	1581.33
80000	1727.06	1717.95	1710.92	1705.49	1701.29	1698.03	1695.50	1693.54	1692.01	1690.83	1689.90	1687.59	1686.94	1686.75
85000	1835.00	1825.32	1817.86	1812.09	1807.62	1804.16	1801.47	1799.38	1797.76	1796.50	1795.52	1793.07	1792.37	1792.17
90000	1942.95	1932.69	1924.79	1918.68	1913.95	1910.28	1907.44	1905.23	1903.51	1902.18	1901.14	1898.54	1897.80	1897.59
95000	2050.89	2040.07	2031.72	2025.27	2020.28	2016.41	2013.41	2011.07	2009.26	2007.85	2006.76	2004.02	2003.24	2003.01
100000	2158.83	2147.44	2138.65	2131.86	2126.61	2122.53	2119.37	2116.92	2115.01	2113.53	2112.38	2109.49	2108.67	2108.43

MONTHLY PAYMENT
REQUIRED TO AMORTIZE A LOAN

TERM	1 Year	2 Years	3 Years	4 Years	5 Years	6 Years	7 Years	8 Years	9 Years	10 Years	11 Years	12 Years	13 Years	14 Years
AMOUNT														
5	.48	.27	.20	.17	.15	.14	.13	.13	.12	.12	.12	.12	.11	.11
10	.96	.54	.40	.34	.30	.28	.26	.25	.24	.24	.23	.23	.22	.22
15	1.43	.81	.60	.51	.45	.41	.39	.37	.36	.35	.34	.34	.33	.33
25	2.39	1.34	1.00	.84	.74	.68	.64	.62	.60	.58	.57	.56	.55	.55
50	4.77	2.68	2.00	1.67	1.48	1.36	1.28	1.23	1.19	1.16	1.13	1.12	1.10	1.09
75	7.15	4.02	3.00	2.51	2.22	2.04	1.92	1.84	1.78	1.73	1.70	1.67	1.65	1.64
100	9.53	5.36	4.00	3.34	2.96	2.72	2.56	2.45	2.37	2.31	2.26	2.23	2.20	2.18
200	19.05	10.72	8.00	6.68	5.92	5.44	5.12	4.89	4.73	4.61	4.52	4.45	4.40	4.36
300	28.57	16.07	11.99	10.01	8.88	8.16	7.67	7.33	7.09	6.91	6.78	6.68	6.60	6.54
400	38.10	21.43	15.99	13.35	11.83	10.87	10.23	9.77	9.45	9.21	9.03	8.90	8.80	8.72
500	47.62	26.78	19.98	16.69	14.79	13.59	12.78	12.22	11.81	11.51	11.29	11.12	11.00	10.90
600	57.14	32.14	23.98	20.02	17.75	16.31	15.34	14.66	14.17	13.81	13.55	13.35	13.20	13.08
700	66.66	37.50	27.98	23.36	20.71	19.02	17.89	17.10	16.53	16.11	15.80	15.57	15.40	15.26
800	76.19	42.85	31.97	26.70	23.66	21.74	20.45	19.54	18.89	18.42	18.06	17.80	17.59	17.44
900	85.71	48.21	35.97	30.03	26.62	24.46	23.00	21.98	21.25	20.72	20.32	20.02	19.79	19.62
1000	95.23	53.56	39.96	33.37	29.58	27.17	25.56	24.43	23.61	23.02	22.58	22.24	21.99	21.80
2000	190.46	107.12	79.92	66.74	59.15	54.34	51.11	48.85	47.22	46.03	45.15	44.48	43.98	43.59
3000	285.68	160.68	119.88	100.10	88.72	81.51	76.66	73.27	70.83	69.05	67.72	66.72	65.96	65.39
4000	380.91	214.24	159.84	133.47	118.29	108.68	102.21	97.69	94.44	92.06	90.29	88.96	87.95	87.18
5000	476.14	267.80	199.80	166.84	147.86	135.84	127.76	122.11	118.05	115.08	112.86	111.20	109.94	108.97
6000	571.36	321.36	239.76	200.20	177.43	163.01	153.32	146.54	141.66	138.09	135.43	133.44	131.92	130.77
7000	666.59	374.92	279.71	233.57	207.01	190.18	178.87	170.96	165.27	161.10	158.00	155.67	153.91	152.56
8000	761.82	428.48	319.67	266.94	236.58	217.35	204.42	195.38	188.88	184.12	180.58	177.91	175.89	174.36
9000	857.04	482.04	359.63	300.30	266.15	244.51	229.97	219.80	212.49	207.13	203.15	200.15	197.88	196.15
10000	952.27	535.60	399.59	333.67	295.72	271.68	255.52	244.22	236.10	230.15	225.72	222.39	219.87	217.94
11000	1047.49	589.16	439.55	367.04	325.29	298.85	281.08	268.65	259.71	253.16	248.29	244.63	241.85	239.74
12000	1142.72	642.72	479.51	400.40	354.86	326.02	306.63	293.07	283.32	276.18	270.86	266.87	263.84	261.53
13000	1237.95	696.28	519.46	433.77	384.44	353.19	332.18	317.49	306.93	299.19	293.43	289.10	285.83	283.33
14000	1333.17	749.84	559.42	467.14	414.01	380.35	357.73	341.91	330.54	322.20	316.00	311.34	307.81	305.12
15000	1428.40	803.40	599.38	500.50	443.58	407.52	383.28	366.33	354.15	345.22	338.58	333.58	329.80	326.91
16000	1523.63	856.96	639.34	533.87	473.15	434.69	408.84	390.76	377.76	368.23	361.15	355.82	351.78	348.71
17000	1618.85	910.52	679.30	567.24	502.72	461.86	434.39	415.18	401.37	391.25	383.72	378.06	373.77	370.50
18000	1714.08	964.08	719.26	600.60	532.29	489.02	459.94	439.60	424.98	414.26	406.29	400.30	395.76	392.29
19000	1809.30	1017.64	759.22	633.97	561.86	516.19	485.49	464.02	448.59	437.27	428.86	422.54	417.74	414.09
20000	1904.53	1071.20	799.17	667.34	591.44	543.36	511.04	488.44	472.20	460.29	451.43	444.77	439.73	435.88
21000	1999.76	1124.76	839.13	700.70	621.01	570.53	536.59	512.87	495.81	483.30	474.00	467.01	461.71	457.68
22000	2094.98	1178.32	879.09	734.07	650.58	597.70	562.15	537.29	519.42	506.32	496.57	489.25	483.70	479.47
23000	2190.21	1231.88	919.05	767.44	680.15	624.86	587.70	561.71	543.03	529.33	519.15	511.49	505.69	501.26
24000	2285.44	1285.44	959.01	800.80	709.72	652.03	613.25	586.13	566.64	552.35	541.72	533.73	527.67	523.06
25000	2380.66	1339.00	998.97	834.17	739.29	679.20	638.80	610.55	590.25	575.36	564.29	555.97	549.66	544.85
26000	2475.89	1392.56	1038.92	867.54	768.87	706.37	664.35	634.97	613.86	598.37	586.86	578.20	571.65	566.65
27000	2571.11	1446.12	1078.88	900.90	798.44	733.53	689.91	659.40	637.47	621.39	609.43	600.44	593.63	588.44
28000	2666.34	1499.68	1118.84	934.27	828.01	760.70	715.46	683.82	661.08	644.40	632.00	622.68	615.62	610.23
29000	2761.57	1553.24	1158.80	967.64	857.58	787.87	741.01	708.24	684.69	667.42	654.57	644.92	637.60	632.03
30000	2856.79	1606.80	1198.76	1001.00	887.15	815.04	766.56	732.66	708.29	690.43	677.15	667.16	659.59	653.82
31000	2952.02	1660.36	1238.72	1034.37	916.72	842.20	792.11	757.08	731.90	713.45	699.72	689.40	681.58	675.61
32000	3047.25	1713.92	1278.67	1067.74	946.30	869.37	817.67	781.51	755.51	736.46	722.29	711.64	703.56	697.41
33000	3142.47	1767.48	1318.63	1101.10	975.87	896.54	843.22	805.93	779.12	759.47	744.86	733.87	725.55	719.20
34000	3237.70	1821.04	1358.59	1134.47	1005.44	923.71	868.77	830.35	802.73	782.49	767.43	756.11	747.54	741.00
35000	3332.92	1874.60	1398.55	1167.84	1035.01	950.88	894.32	854.77	826.34	805.50	790.00	778.35	769.52	762.79
36000	3428.15	1928.16	1438.51	1201.20	1064.58	978.04	919.87	879.19	849.95	828.52	812.57	800.59	791.51	784.58
37000	3523.38	1981.72	1478.47	1234.57	1094.15	1005.21	945.43	903.62	873.56	851.53	835.14	822.83	813.49	806.38
38000	3618.60	2035.28	1518.43	1267.94	1123.73	1032.38	970.98	928.04	897.17	874.54	857.72	845.07	835.48	828.17
39000	3713.83	2088.84	1558.38	1301.30	1153.30	1059.55	996.53	952.46	920.78	897.56	880.29	867.30	857.47	849.97
40000	3809.06	2142.40	1598.34	1334.67	1182.87	1086.71	1022.08	976.88	944.39	920.57	902.86	889.54	879.45	871.76
41000	3904.28	2195.96	1638.30	1368.04	1212.44	1113.88	1047.63	1001.30	968.00	943.59	925.43	911.78	901.44	893.55
42000	3999.51	2249.52	1678.26	1401.40	1242.01	1141.05	1073.18	1025.73	991.61	966.60	948.00	934.02	923.42	915.35
43000	4094.73	2303.08	1718.22	1434.77	1271.58	1168.22	1098.74	1050.15	1015.22	989.62	970.57	956.26	945.41	937.14
44000	4189.96	2356.64	1758.18	1468.14	1301.15	1195.39	1124.29	1074.57	1038.83	1012.63	993.14	978.50	967.40	958.93
45000	4285.19	2410.20	1798.13	1501.50	1330.73	1222.55	1149.84	1098.99	1062.44	1035.64	1015.72	1000.73	989.38	980.73
46000	4380.41	2463.76	1838.09	1534.87	1360.30	1249.72	1175.39	1123.41	1086.05	1058.66	1038.29	1022.97	1011.37	1002.52
47000	4475.64	2517.32	1878.05	1568.24	1389.87	1276.89	1200.94	1147.83	1109.66	1081.67	1060.86	1045.21	1033.36	1024.32
48000	4570.87	2570.88	1918.01	1601.60	1419.44	1304.06	1226.50	1172.26	1133.27	1104.69	1083.43	1067.45	1055.34	1046.11
49000	4666.09	2624.44	1957.97	1634.97	1449.01	1331.22	1252.05	1196.68	1156.88	1127.70	1106.00	1089.69	1077.33	1067.90
50000	4761.32	2678.00	1997.93	1668.34	1478.58	1358.39	1277.60	1221.10	1180.49	1150.72	1128.57	1111.93	1099.31	1089.70
55000	5237.45	2945.80	2197.72	1835.17	1626.44	1494.23	1405.36	1343.21	1298.54	1265.79	1241.43	1223.12	1209.24	1198.67
60000	5713.58	3213.60	2397.51	2002.00	1774.30	1630.07	1533.12	1465.32	1416.58	1380.86	1354.29	1334.31	1319.18	1307.64
65000	6189.71	3481.40	2597.30	2168.84	1922.16	1765.91	1660.88	1587.43	1534.63	1495.93	1467.14	1445.50	1429.11	1416.61
70000	6665.84	3749.19	2797.09	2335.67	2070.02	1901.75	1788.64	1709.54	1652.68	1611.00	1580.00	1556.70	1539.04	1525.57
75000	7141.98	4016.99	2996.89	2502.50	2217.87	2037.59	1916.40	1831.65	1770.73	1726.07	1692.86	1667.89	1648.97	1634.54
80000	7618.11	4284.79	3196.68	2669.34	2365.73	2173.42	2044.16	1953.76	1888.78	1841.14	1805.71	1779.08	1758.90	1743.51
85000	8094.24	4552.59	3396.47	2836.17	2513.59	2309.26	2171.92	2075.87	2006.83	1956.21	1918.57	1890.27	1868.83	1852.48
90000	8570.37	4820.39	3596.26	3003.00	2661.45	2445.10	2299.68	2197.98	2124.87	2071.28	2031.43	2001.47	1978.76	1961.45
95000	9046.50	5088.19	3796.06	3169.83	2809.31	2580.94	2427.43	2320.09	2242.92	2186.35	2144.28	2112.66	2088.69	2070.42
100000	9522.63	5355.99	3995.85	3336.67	2957.16	2716.78	2555.19	2442.20	2360.97	2301.43	2257.14	2223.85	2198.62	2179.39

TERM	15 Years	16 Years	17 Years	18 Years	19 Years	20 Years	21 Years	22 Years	23 Years	24 Years	25 Years	30 Years	35 Years	40 Years
AMOUNT														
5	.11	.11	.11	.11	.11	.11	.11	.11	.11	.11	.11	.11	.11	.11
10	.22	.22	.22	.22	.22	.22	.22	.22	.22	.22	.22	.22	.22	.22
15	.33	.33	.33	.33	.32	.32	.32	.32	.32	.32	.32	.32	.32	.32
25	.55	.54	.54	.54	.54	.54	.54	.54	.54	.53	.53	.53	.53	.53
50	1.09	1.08	1.08	1.07	1.07	1.07	1.07	1.07	1.07	1.06	1.06	1.06	1.06	1.06
75	1.63	1.62	1.61	1.61	1.60	1.60	1.60	1.60	1.60	1.59	1.59	1.59	1.59	1.59
100	2.17	2.16	2.15	2.14	2.14	2.13	2.13	2.13	2.13	2.12	2.12	2.12	2.12	2.12
200	4.33	4.31	4.29	4.28	4.27	4.26	4.26	4.25	4.25	4.24	4.24	4.24	4.23	4.23
300	6.50	6.46	6.44	6.42	6.40	6.39	6.38	6.37	6.37	6.36	6.36	6.35	6.35	6.35
400	8.66	8.62	8.58	8.56	8.54	8.52	8.51	8.50	8.49	8.48	8.48	8.47	8.46	8.46
500	10.83	10.77	10.73	10.69	10.67	10.65	10.63	10.62	10.61	10.60	10.60	10.58	10.58	10.58
600	12.99	12.92	12.87	12.83	12.80	12.78	12.76	12.74	12.73	12.72	12.72	12.70	12.69	12.69
700	15.16	15.08	15.02	14.97	14.93	14.91	14.88	14.87	14.85	14.84	14.83	14.82	14.81	14.81
800	17.32	17.23	17.16	17.11	17.07	17.03	17.01	16.99	16.97	16.96	16.95	16.93	16.92	16.92
900	19.49	19.38	19.31	19.25	19.20	19.16	19.13	19.11	19.10	19.08	19.07	19.05	19.04	19.04
1000	21.65	21.54	21.45	21.38	21.33	21.29	21.26	21.24	21.22	21.20	21.19	21.16	21.15	21.15
2000	43.30	43.07	42.90	42.76	42.66	42.58	42.51	42.47	42.43	42.40	42.38	42.32	42.30	42.30
3000	64.94	64.60	64.34	64.14	63.98	63.86	63.77	63.70	63.64	63.60	63.56	63.48	63.45	63.45
4000	86.59	86.14	85.79	85.52	85.31	85.15	85.02	84.93	84.85	84.79	84.75	84.63	84.60	84.59
5000	108.24	107.67	107.24	106.90	106.64	106.44	106.28	106.16	106.06	105.99	105.93	105.79	105.75	105.74
6000	129.88	129.20	128.68	128.28	127.96	127.72	127.53	127.39	127.27	127.19	127.12	126.95	126.90	126.89
7000	151.53	150.74	150.13	149.66	149.29	149.01	148.79	148.62	148.49	148.38	148.30	148.11	148.05	148.03
8000	173.18	172.27	171.57	171.03	170.62	170.29	170.04	169.85	169.70	169.58	169.49	169.26	169.20	169.18
9000	194.82	193.80	193.02	192.41	191.94	191.58	191.30	191.08	190.91	190.78	190.68	190.42	190.35	190.33
10000	216.47	215.34	214.47	213.79	213.27	212.87	212.55	212.31	212.12	211.98	211.86	211.58	211.50	211.47
11000	238.12	236.87	235.91	235.17	234.60	234.15	233.81	233.54	233.33	233.17	233.05	232.73	232.64	232.62
12000	259.76	258.40	257.36	256.55	255.92	255.44	255.06	254.77	254.54	254.37	254.23	253.89	253.79	253.77
13000	281.41	279.94	278.80	277.93	277.25	276.72	276.32	276.00	275.76	275.57	275.42	275.05	274.94	274.91
14000	303.06	301.47	300.25	299.31	298.58	298.01	297.57	297.23	296.97	296.76	296.60	296.21	296.09	296.06
15000	324.70	323.00	321.70	320.68	319.90	319.30	318.83	318.46	318.18	317.96	317.79	317.36	317.24	317.21
16000	346.35	344.54	343.14	342.06	341.23	340.58	340.08	339.69	339.39	339.16	338.97	338.52	338.39	338.35
17000	368.00	366.07	364.59	363.44	362.56	361.87	361.34	360.92	360.60	360.35	360.16	359.68	359.54	359.50
18000	389.64	387.60	386.03	384.82	383.88	383.16	382.59	382.15	381.81	381.55	381.35	380.83	380.69	380.65
19000	411.29	409.14	407.48	406.20	405.21	404.44	403.85	403.38	403.03	402.75	402.53	401.99	401.84	401.79
20000	432.94	430.67	428.93	427.58	426.54	425.73	425.10	424.62	424.24	423.95	423.72	423.15	422.99	422.94
21000	454.58	452.20	450.37	448.96	447.86	447.01	446.36	445.85	445.45	445.14	444.90	444.31	444.14	444.09
22000	476.23	473.74	471.82	470.34	469.19	468.30	467.61	467.08	466.66	466.34	466.09	465.46	465.28	465.23
23000	497.88	495.27	493.26	491.71	490.51	489.59	488.87	488.31	487.87	487.54	487.27	486.62	486.43	486.38
24000	519.52	516.80	514.71	513.09	511.84	510.87	510.12	509.54	509.08	508.73	508.46	507.78	507.58	507.53
25000	541.17	538.34	536.16	534.47	533.17	532.16	531.38	530.77	530.30	529.93	529.65	528.93	528.73	528.67
26000	562.82	559.87	557.60	555.85	554.49	553.44	552.63	552.00	551.51	551.13	550.83	550.09	549.88	549.82
27000	584.46	581.40	579.05	577.23	575.82	574.73	573.88	573.23	572.72	572.32	572.02	571.25	571.03	570.97
28000	606.11	602.94	600.49	598.61	597.15	596.02	595.14	594.46	593.93	593.52	593.20	592.41	592.18	592.11
29000	627.75	624.47	621.94	619.99	618.47	617.30	616.39	615.69	615.14	614.72	614.39	613.56	613.33	613.26
30000	649.40	646.00	643.39	641.36	639.80	638.59	637.65	636.92	636.35	635.92	635.57	634.72	634.48	634.41
31000	671.05	667.54	664.83	662.74	661.13	659.87	658.90	658.15	657.57	657.11	656.76	655.88	655.63	655.55
32000	692.69	689.07	686.28	684.12	682.45	681.16	680.16	679.38	678.78	678.31	677.94	677.03	676.77	676.70
33000	714.34	710.60	707.72	705.50	703.78	702.45	701.41	700.61	699.99	699.51	699.13	698.19	697.92	697.85
34000	735.99	732.14	729.17	726.88	725.11	723.73	722.67	721.84	721.20	720.70	720.32	719.35	719.07	718.99
35000	757.63	753.67	750.62	748.26	746.43	745.02	743.92	743.07	742.41	741.90	741.50	740.51	740.22	740.14
36000	779.28	775.20	772.06	769.64	767.76	766.31	765.18	764.30	763.62	763.10	762.69	761.66	761.37	761.29
37000	800.93	796.74	793.51	791.02	789.09	787.59	786.43	785.53	784.84	784.29	783.87	782.82	782.52	782.43
38000	822.57	818.27	814.96	812.39	810.41	808.88	807.69	806.76	806.05	805.49	805.06	803.98	803.67	803.58
39000	844.22	839.80	836.40	833.77	831.74	830.16	828.94	828.00	827.26	826.69	826.24	825.13	824.82	824.73
40000	865.87	861.34	857.85	855.15	853.07	851.45	850.20	849.23	848.47	847.89	847.43	846.29	845.97	845.88
41000	887.51	882.87	879.29	876.53	874.39	872.74	871.45	870.46	869.68	869.08	868.62	867.45	867.12	867.02
42000	909.16	904.40	900.74	897.91	895.72	894.02	892.71	891.69	890.89	890.28	889.80	888.61	888.27	888.17
43000	930.81	925.94	922.19	919.29	917.05	915.31	913.96	912.92	912.11	911.48	910.99	909.76	909.41	909.32
44000	952.45	947.47	943.63	940.67	938.37	936.59	935.22	934.15	933.32	932.67	932.17	930.92	930.56	930.46
45000	974.10	969.00	965.08	962.04	959.70	957.88	956.47	955.38	954.53	953.87	953.36	952.08	951.71	951.61
46000	995.75	990.54	986.52	983.42	981.02	979.17	977.73	976.61	975.74	975.07	974.54	973.23	972.86	972.76
47000	1017.39	1012.07	1007.97	1004.80	1002.35	1000.45	998.98	997.84	996.96	996.26	995.73	994.39	994.01	993.90
48000	1039.04	1033.60	1029.42	1026.18	1023.68	1021.74	1020.24	1019.07	1018.16	1017.46	1016.91	1015.55	1015.16	1015.05
49000	1060.69	1055.14	1050.86	1047.56	1045.00	1043.03	1041.49	1040.30	1039.38	1038.66	1038.10	1036.71	1036.31	1036.20
50000	1082.33	1076.67	1072.31	1068.94	1066.33	1064.31	1062.75	1061.53	1060.59	1059.86	1059.29	1057.86	1057.46	1057.34
55000	1190.57	1184.34	1179.54	1175.83	1172.96	1170.74	1169.02	1167.68	1166.65	1165.84	1165.21	1163.65	1163.20	1163.08
60000	1298.80	1292.00	1286.77	1282.72	1279.60	1277.17	1275.29	1273.84	1272.70	1271.83	1271.14	1269.43	1268.95	1268.81
65000	1407.03	1399.67	1394.00	1389.62	1386.23	1383.60	1381.57	1379.99	1378.76	1377.81	1377.07	1375.22	1374.69	1374.54
70000	1515.26	1507.34	1501.23	1496.51	1492.86	1490.03	1487.84	1486.14	1484.82	1483.80	1483.00	1481.01	1480.44	1480.28
75000	1623.50	1615.00	1608.46	1603.40	1599.49	1596.46	1594.12	1592.29	1590.88	1589.78	1588.93	1586.79	1586.18	1586.01
80000	1731.73	1722.67	1715.69	1710.30	1706.13	1702.90	1700.39	1698.45	1696.94	1695.77	1694.85	1692.58	1691.93	1691.75
85000	1839.96	1830.34	1822.92	1817.19	1812.76	1809.33	1806.66	1804.60	1803.00	1801.75	1800.78	1798.36	1797.67	1797.48
90000	1948.19	1938.00	1930.15	1924.08	1919.39	1915.76	1912.94	1910.75	1909.05	1907.74	1906.71	1904.15	1903.42	1903.21
95000	2056.43	2045.67	2037.38	2030.98	2026.02	2022.19	2019.21	2016.90	2015.11	2013.72	2012.64	2009.93	2009.17	2008.95
100000	2164.66	2153.34	2144.61	2137.87	2132.66	2128.62	2125.49	2123.06	2121.17	2119.71	2118.57	2115.72	2114.91	2114.68

25.400%

TERM	1 Year	2 Years	3 Years	4 Years	5 Years	6 Years	7 Years	8 Years	9 Years	10 Years	11 Years	12 Years	13 Years	14 Years
AMOUNT														
5	.48	.27	.20	.17	.15	.14	.13	.13	.12	.12	.12	.12	.12	.11
10	.96	.54	.40	.34	.30	.28	.26	.25	.24	.24	.23	.23	.23	.22
15	1.43	.81	.60	.51	.45	.41	.39	.37	.36	.35	.34	.34	.34	.33
25	2.39	1.34	1.00	.84	.74	.68	.64	.62	.60	.58	.57	.56	.56	.55
50	4.77	2.68	2.00	1.67	1.48	1.36	1.28	1.23	1.19	1.16	1.13	1.12	1.11	1.10
75	7.15	4.02	3.00	2.51	2.22	2.04	1.92	1.84	1.78	1.73	1.70	1.67	1.66	1.64
100	9.53	5.36	4.00	3.34	2.96	2.72	2.56	2.45	2.37	2.31	2.26	2.23	2.21	2.19
200	19.05	10.72	8.00	6.68	5.92	5.44	5.12	4.89	4.73	4.61	4.52	4.46	4.41	4.37
300	28.58	16.08	12.00	10.02	8.88	8.16	7.68	7.34	7.09	6.91	6.78	6.68	6.61	6.55
400	38.10	21.43	15.99	13.36	11.84	10.88	10.23	9.78	9.46	9.22	9.04	8.91	8.81	8.73
500	47.62	26.79	19.99	16.70	14.80	13.60	12.79	12.22	11.82	11.52	11.30	11.13	11.01	10.91
600	57.15	32.15	23.99	20.03	17.76	16.31	15.35	14.67	14.18	13.82	13.56	13.36	13.21	13.09
700	66.67	37.51	27.99	23.37	20.72	19.03	17.90	17.11	16.54	16.13	15.82	15.58	15.41	15.27
800	76.20	42.86	31.98	26.71	23.67	21.75	20.46	19.56	18.91	18.43	18.08	17.81	17.61	17.46
900	85.72	48.22	35.98	30.05	26.63	24.47	23.02	22.00	21.27	20.73	20.34	20.04	19.81	19.64
1000	95.24	53.58	39.98	33.39	29.59	27.19	25.57	24.44	23.63	23.04	22.59	22.26	22.01	21.82
2000	190.48	107.15	79.95	66.77	59.18	54.37	51.14	48.88	47.26	46.07	45.18	44.52	44.02	43.63
3000	285.72	160.72	119.92	100.15	88.76	81.55	76.71	73.32	70.89	69.10	67.77	66.78	66.02	65.44
4000	380.96	214.29	159.89	133.53	118.35	108.74	102.28	97.76	94.51	92.13	90.36	89.03	88.03	87.26
5000	476.20	267.87	199.86	166.91	147.94	135.92	127.84	122.20	118.14	115.16	112.95	111.29	110.03	109.07
6000	571.44	321.44	239.84	200.29	177.52	163.10	153.41	146.64	141.77	138.20	135.54	133.55	132.04	130.88
7000	666.67	375.01	279.81	233.67	207.11	190.29	178.98	171.07	165.39	161.23	158.13	155.80	154.04	152.70
8000	761.91	428.58	319.78	267.05	236.70	217.47	204.55	195.51	189.02	184.26	180.72	178.06	176.05	174.51
9000	857.15	482.16	359.75	300.43	266.28	244.65	230.12	219.95	212.65	207.29	203.31	200.32	198.05	196.32
10000	952.39	535.73	399.72	333.81	295.87	271.84	255.68	244.39	236.27	230.32	225.90	222.57	220.06	218.14
11000	1047.63	589.30	439.69	367.19	325.45	299.02	281.25	268.83	259.90	253.36	248.49	244.83	242.06	239.95
12000	1142.87	642.87	479.67	400.57	355.04	326.20	306.82	293.27	283.53	276.39	271.08	267.09	264.07	261.76
13000	1238.10	696.45	519.64	433.95	384.63	353.39	332.39	317.71	307.15	299.42	293.67	289.35	286.07	283.57
14000	1333.34	750.02	559.61	467.33	414.21	380.57	357.96	342.14	330.78	322.45	316.26	311.60	308.08	305.39
15000	1428.58	803.59	599.58	500.71	443.80	407.75	383.52	366.58	354.41	345.48	338.85	333.86	330.08	327.20
16000	1523.82	857.16	639.55	534.09	473.39	434.94	409.09	391.02	378.03	368.52	361.44	356.12	352.09	349.01
17000	1619.06	910.74	679.52	567.48	502.97	462.12	434.66	415.46	401.66	391.55	384.03	378.37	374.09	370.83
18000	1714.30	964.31	719.50	600.86	532.56	489.30	460.23	439.90	425.29	414.58	406.62	400.63	396.10	392.64
19000	1809.53	1017.88	759.47	634.24	562.14	516.48	485.80	464.34	448.92	437.61	429.21	422.89	418.10	414.45
20000	1904.77	1071.45	799.44	667.62	591.73	543.67	511.36	488.78	472.54	460.64	451.79	445.14	440.11	436.27
21000	2000.01	1125.03	839.41	701.00	621.32	570.85	536.93	513.21	496.17	483.68	474.38	467.40	462.11	458.08
22000	2095.25	1178.60	879.38	734.38	650.90	598.03	562.50	537.65	519.80	506.71	496.97	489.66	484.12	479.89
23000	2190.49	1232.17	919.35	767.76	680.49	625.22	588.07	562.09	543.42	529.74	519.56	511.92	506.12	501.70
24000	2285.73	1285.74	959.33	801.14	710.08	652.40	613.64	586.53	567.05	552.77	542.15	534.17	528.13	523.52
25000	2380.97	1339.32	999.30	834.52	739.66	679.58	639.20	610.97	590.68	575.80	564.74	556.43	550.13	545.33
26000	2476.20	1392.89	1039.27	867.90	769.25	706.77	664.77	635.41	614.30	598.83	587.33	578.69	572.14	567.14
27000	2571.44	1446.46	1079.24	901.28	798.83	733.95	690.34	659.85	637.93	621.87	609.92	600.94	594.14	588.96
28000	2666.68	1500.03	1119.21	934.66	828.42	761.13	715.91	684.28	661.56	644.90	632.51	623.20	616.15	610.77
29000	2761.92	1553.61	1159.18	968.04	858.01	788.32	741.48	708.72	685.18	667.93	655.10	645.46	638.15	632.58
30000	2857.16	1607.18	1199.16	1001.42	887.59	815.50	767.04	733.16	708.81	690.96	677.69	667.71	660.16	654.40
31000	2952.40	1660.75	1239.13	1034.80	917.18	842.68	792.61	757.60	732.44	713.99	700.28	689.97	682.16	676.21
32000	3047.63	1714.32	1279.10	1068.18	946.77	869.87	818.18	782.04	756.06	737.03	722.87	712.23	704.17	698.02
33000	3142.87	1767.90	1319.07	1101.57	976.35	897.05	843.75	806.48	779.69	760.06	745.46	734.49	726.17	719.84
34000	3238.11	1821.47	1359.04	1134.95	1005.94	924.23	869.32	830.92	803.32	783.09	768.05	756.74	748.18	741.65
35000	3333.35	1875.04	1399.01	1168.33	1035.53	951.42	894.88	855.35	826.95	806.12	790.64	779.00	770.18	763.46
36000	3428.59	1928.61	1438.99	1201.71	1065.11	978.60	920.45	879.79	850.57	829.15	813.23	801.26	792.19	785.27
37000	3523.83	1982.18	1478.96	1235.09	1094.70	1005.78	946.02	904.23	874.20	852.19	835.82	823.51	814.19	807.09
38000	3619.06	2035.76	1518.93	1268.47	1124.28	1032.96	971.59	928.67	897.83	875.22	858.41	845.77	836.20	828.90
39000	3714.30	2089.33	1558.90	1301.85	1153.87	1060.15	997.15	953.11	921.45	898.25	881.00	868.03	858.20	850.71
40000	3809.54	2142.90	1598.87	1335.23	1183.46	1087.33	1022.72	977.55	945.08	921.28	903.58	890.28	880.21	872.53
41000	3904.78	2196.47	1638.84	1368.61	1213.04	1114.51	1048.29	1001.99	968.71	944.31	926.17	912.54	902.21	894.34
42000	4000.02	2250.05	1678.82	1401.99	1242.63	1141.70	1073.86	1026.42	992.33	967.34	948.76	934.80	924.22	916.15
43000	4095.26	2303.62	1718.79	1435.37	1272.22	1168.88	1099.43	1050.86	1015.96	990.38	971.35	957.06	946.22	937.97
44000	4190.50	2357.19	1758.76	1468.75	1301.80	1196.06	1124.99	1075.30	1039.59	1013.41	993.94	979.31	968.23	959.78
45000	4285.73	2410.76	1798.73	1502.13	1331.39	1223.25	1150.56	1099.74	1063.21	1036.44	1016.53	1001.57	990.23	981.59
46000	4380.97	2464.34	1838.70	1535.51	1360.97	1250.43	1176.13	1124.18	1086.84	1059.47	1039.12	1023.83	1012.24	1003.40
47000	4476.21	2517.91	1878.67	1568.89	1390.56	1277.61	1201.70	1148.62	1110.47	1082.50	1061.71	1046.08	1034.24	1025.22
48000	4571.45	2571.48	1918.65	1602.27	1420.15	1304.80	1227.27	1173.06	1134.09	1105.54	1084.30	1068.34	1056.25	1047.03
49000	4666.69	2625.05	1958.62	1635.66	1449.73	1331.98	1252.83	1197.49	1157.72	1128.57	1106.89	1090.60	1078.25	1068.84
50000	4761.93	2678.63	1998.59	1669.04	1479.32	1359.16	1278.40	1221.93	1181.35	1151.60	1129.48	1112.85	1100.26	1090.66
55000	5238.12	2946.49	2198.45	1835.94	1627.25	1495.08	1406.24	1344.13	1299.48	1266.76	1242.43	1224.14	1210.28	1199.72
60000	5714.31	3214.35	2398.31	2002.84	1775.18	1630.99	1534.08	1466.32	1417.62	1381.92	1355.37	1335.42	1320.31	1308.79
65000	6190.50	3482.21	2598.16	2169.75	1923.11	1766.91	1661.92	1588.51	1535.75	1497.08	1468.32	1446.71	1430.33	1417.85
70000	6666.69	3750.07	2798.02	2336.65	2071.05	1902.83	1789.76	1710.70	1653.89	1612.24	1581.27	1557.99	1540.36	1526.92
75000	7142.89	4017.94	2997.88	2503.55	2218.98	2038.74	1917.60	1832.90	1772.02	1727.40	1694.22	1669.28	1650.38	1635.98
80000	7619.08	4285.80	3197.74	2670.45	2366.91	2174.66	2045.44	1955.09	1890.15	1842.56	1807.16	1780.56	1760.41	1745.05
85000	8095.27	4553.66	3397.60	2837.36	2514.84	2310.57	2173.28	2077.28	2008.29	1957.72	1920.11	1891.85	1870.46	1854.11
90000	8571.46	4821.52	3597.46	3004.26	2662.77	2446.49	2301.12	2199.48	2126.42	2072.88	2033.06	2003.13	1980.46	1963.18
95000	9047.66	5089.39	3797.32	3171.16	2810.70	2582.40	2428.96	2321.67	2244.56	2188.04	2146.01	2114.42	2090.49	2072.24
100000	9523.85	5357.25	3997.17	3338.07	2958.63	2718.32	2556.80	2443.86	2362.69	2303.20	2258.95	2225.70	2200.51	2181.31

TERM	15 Years	16 Years	17 Years	18 Years	19 Years	20 Years	21 Years	22 Years	23 Years	24 Years	25 Years	30 Years	35 Years	40 Years
AMOUNT														
5	.11	.11	.11	.11	.11	.11	.11	.11	.11	.11	.11	.11	.11	.11
10	.22	.22	.22	.22	.22	.22	.22	.22	.22	.22	.22	.22	.22	.22
15	.33	.33	.33	.33	.33	.32	.32	.32	.32	.32	.32	.32	.32	.32
25	.55	.54	.54	.54	.54	.54	.54	.54	.54	.54	.54	.53	.53	.53
50	1.09	1.08	1.08	1.07	1.07	1.07	1.07	1.07	1.07	1.07	1.07	1.06	1.06	1.06
75	1.63	1.62	1.61	1.61	1.61	1.60	1.60	1.60	1.60	1.60	1.60	1.59	1.59	1.59
100	2.17	2.16	2.15	2.14	2.14	2.14	2.13	2.13	2.13	2.13	2.13	2.12	2.12	2.12
200	4.34	4.32	4.30	4.28	4.27	4.27	4.26	4.25	4.25	4.25	4.25	4.24	4.24	4.24
300	6.50	6.47	6.44	6.42	6.41	6.40	6.39	6.38	6.37	6.37	6.37	6.36	6.36	6.36
400	8.67	8.63	8.59	8.56	8.54	8.53	8.52	8.51	8.50	8.49	8.49	8.48	8.47	8.47
500	10.84	10.78	10.74	10.70	10.68	10.66	10.64	10.63	10.62	10.61	10.61	10.59	10.59	10.59
600	13.00	12.94	12.88	12.84	12.81	12.79	12.77	12.76	12.74	12.74	12.73	12.71	12.71	12.71
700	15.17	15.09	15.03	14.98	14.95	14.92	14.90	14.88	14.87	14.86	14.85	14.83	14.82	14.82
800	17.34	17.25	17.18	17.12	17.08	17.05	17.03	17.01	16.99	16.98	16.97	16.95	16.94	16.94
900	19.50	19.40	19.32	19.26	19.22	19.18	19.15	19.13	19.11	19.10	19.09	19.07	19.06	19.06
1000	21.67	21.56	21.47	21.40	21.35	21.31	21.28	21.26	21.24	21.22	21.21	21.18	21.17	21.17
2000	43.34	43.11	42.94	42.80	42.70	42.62	42.56	42.51	42.47	42.44	42.42	42.36	42.34	42.34
3000	65.00	64.66	64.40	64.20	64.05	63.92	63.83	63.76	63.70	63.66	63.62	63.54	63.51	63.51
4000	86.67	86.22	85.87	85.60	85.39	85.23	85.11	85.01	84.93	84.88	84.83	84.72	84.68	84.68
5000	108.33	107.77	107.33	107.00	106.74	106.54	106.38	106.26	106.17	106.09	106.04	105.89	105.85	105.84
6000	130.00	129.32	128.80	128.40	128.09	127.84	127.66	127.51	127.40	127.31	127.24	127.07	127.02	127.01
7000	151.67	150.88	150.27	149.80	149.43	149.15	148.93	148.76	148.63	148.53	148.45	148.25	148.19	148.18
8000	173.33	172.43	171.73	171.19	170.78	170.46	170.21	170.01	169.86	169.75	169.65	169.43	169.36	169.35
9000	195.00	193.98	193.20	192.59	192.13	191.77	191.48	191.26	191.09	190.96	190.86	190.61	190.53	190.51
10000	216.66	215.53	214.66	213.99	213.47	213.07	212.76	212.51	212.33	212.18	212.07	211.78	211.70	211.68
11000	238.33	237.09	236.13	235.39	234.82	234.38	234.03	233.77	233.56	233.40	233.27	232.96	232.87	232.85
12000	260.00	258.64	257.60	256.79	256.17	255.68	255.31	255.02	254.79	254.62	254.47	254.14	254.04	254.02
13000	281.66	280.19	279.06	278.19	277.51	276.99	276.58	276.27	276.02	275.83	275.69	275.32	275.21	275.18
14000	303.33	301.75	300.53	299.59	298.86	298.29	297.86	297.52	297.26	297.05	296.89	296.50	296.38	296.35
15000	324.99	323.30	321.99	320.99	320.21	319.60	319.13	318.77	318.49	318.27	318.10	317.67	317.55	317.52
16000	346.66	344.85	343.46	342.38	341.55	340.91	340.41	340.02	339.72	339.49	339.30	338.85	338.72	338.69
17000	368.33	366.41	364.93	363.78	362.90	362.21	361.68	361.27	360.95	360.70	360.51	360.03	359.89	359.86
18000	389.99	387.96	386.39	385.18	384.25	383.52	382.96	382.52	382.18	381.92	381.72	381.21	381.06	381.02
19000	411.66	409.51	407.86	406.58	405.59	404.83	404.23	403.77	403.42	403.14	402.92	402.39	402.23	402.19
20000	433.32	431.06	429.32	427.98	426.94	426.13	425.51	425.02	424.65	424.36	424.13	423.56	423.40	423.36
21000	454.99	452.62	450.79	449.38	448.29	447.44	446.78	446.28	445.88	445.57	445.34	444.74	444.57	444.52
22000	476.66	474.17	472.26	470.70	469.63	468.75	468.06	467.53	467.11	466.79	466.54	465.92	465.74	465.69
23000	498.32	495.72	493.72	492.17	490.98	490.05	489.33	488.78	488.35	488.01	487.75	487.10	486.91	486.86
24000	519.99	517.28	515.19	513.57	512.33	511.36	510.61	510.03	509.58	509.23	508.95	508.27	508.08	508.03
25000	541.65	538.83	536.65	534.97	533.67	532.67	531.88	531.28	530.81	530.44	530.16	529.45	529.25	529.19
26000	563.32	560.38	558.12	556.37	555.02	553.97	553.16	552.53	552.04	551.66	551.37	550.63	550.42	550.36
27000	584.99	581.94	579.58	577.77	576.37	575.28	574.44	573.78	573.27	572.88	572.57	571.81	571.59	571.53
28000	606.65	603.49	601.05	599.17	597.71	596.58	595.71	595.03	594.51	594.10	593.78	592.99	592.76	592.70
29000	628.32	625.04	622.52	620.57	619.06	617.89	616.99	616.28	615.74	615.31	614.99	614.16	613.93	613.86
30000	649.98	646.59	643.98	641.97	640.41	639.20	638.26	637.53	636.97	636.53	636.19	635.34	635.10	635.03
31000	671.65	668.15	665.45	663.36	661.75	660.50	659.54	658.79	658.20	657.75	657.40	656.52	656.27	656.20
32000	693.32	689.70	686.91	684.76	683.10	681.81	680.81	680.04	679.43	678.97	678.60	677.70	677.44	677.37
33000	714.98	711.25	708.38	706.16	704.45	703.12	702.09	701.29	700.67	700.19	699.81	698.88	698.61	698.54
34000	736.65	732.81	729.85	727.56	725.79	724.42	723.36	722.54	721.90	721.40	721.02	720.05	719.78	719.70
35000	758.31	754.36	751.31	748.96	747.14	745.73	744.64	743.79	743.13	742.62	742.22	741.23	740.95	740.87
36000	779.98	775.91	772.78	770.36	768.49	767.04	765.91	765.04	764.36	763.84	763.43	762.41	762.12	762.04
37000	801.65	797.47	794.24	791.76	789.83	788.34	787.19	786.29	785.60	785.06	784.64	783.59	783.29	783.21
38000	823.31	819.02	815.71	813.15	811.18	809.65	808.46	807.54	806.83	806.28	805.84	804.77	804.46	804.37
39000	844.98	840.57	837.18	834.55	832.53	830.95	829.74	828.79	828.06	827.49	827.05	825.94	825.63	825.54
40000	866.64	862.12	858.64	855.95	853.87	852.26	851.01	850.04	849.29	848.71	848.25	847.12	846.80	846.71
41000	888.31	883.68	880.11	877.35	875.22	873.57	872.29	871.29	870.52	869.93	869.46	868.30	867.97	867.88
42000	909.98	905.23	901.57	898.75	896.57	894.87	893.56	892.55	891.76	891.14	890.67	889.48	889.14	889.04
43000	931.64	926.78	923.04	920.15	917.91	916.18	914.84	913.80	912.99	912.36	911.87	910.66	910.31	910.21
44000	953.31	948.34	944.51	941.55	939.26	937.49	936.11	935.05	934.22	933.58	933.08	931.83	931.48	931.38
45000	974.97	969.89	965.97	962.95	960.61	958.79	957.39	956.30	955.45	954.80	954.29	953.01	952.65	952.55
46000	996.64	991.44	987.44	984.34	981.95	980.10	978.66	977.55	976.69	976.01	975.49	974.19	973.82	973.71
47000	1018.31	1013.00	1008.90	1005.74	1003.30	1001.41	999.94	998.80	997.92	997.23	996.70	995.37	994.99	994.88
48000	1039.97	1034.55	1030.37	1027.14	1024.65	1022.71	1021.21	1020.05	1019.15	1018.45	1017.90	1016.54	1016.16	1016.05
49000	1061.64	1056.10	1051.84	1048.54	1045.99	1044.02	1042.49	1041.30	1040.38	1039.67	1039.11	1037.72	1037.33	1037.22
50000	1083.30	1077.65	1073.30	1069.94	1067.34	1065.33	1063.76	1062.55	1061.61	1060.88	1060.32	1058.90	1058.50	1058.38
55000	1191.63	1185.42	1180.63	1176.93	1174.07	1171.86	1170.14	1168.81	1167.77	1166.97	1166.35	1164.79	1164.35	1164.22
60000	1299.96	1293.18	1287.96	1283.93	1280.81	1278.39	1276.52	1275.06	1273.94	1273.06	1272.38	1270.68	1270.20	1270.06
65000	1408.29	1400.95	1395.29	1390.92	1387.54	1384.92	1382.89	1381.32	1380.10	1379.15	1378.41	1376.57	1376.05	1375.90
70000	1516.62	1508.71	1502.62	1497.91	1494.27	1491.45	1489.27	1487.57	1486.26	1485.24	1484.44	1482.46	1481.90	1481.74
75000	1624.95	1616.48	1609.95	1604.91	1601.01	1597.99	1595.64	1593.83	1592.42	1591.32	1590.47	1588.35	1587.75	1587.57
80000	1733.28	1724.24	1717.28	1711.90	1707.74	1704.52	1702.02	1700.08	1698.58	1697.41	1696.50	1694.24	1693.59	1693.41
85000	1841.61	1832.01	1824.61	1818.89	1814.47	1811.05	1808.40	1806.34	1804.74	1803.50	1802.54	1800.13	1799.44	1799.25
90000	1949.94	1939.77	1931.94	1925.89	1921.21	1917.58	1914.77	1912.59	1910.90	1909.59	1908.57	1906.02	1905.29	1905.09
95000	2058.27	2047.54	2039.27	2032.88	2027.94	2024.11	2021.15	2018.85	2017.06	2015.68	2014.60	2011.91	2011.14	2010.92
100000	2166.60	2155.30	2146.60	2139.87	2134.67	2130.65	2127.52	2125.10	2123.22	2121.76	2120.63	2117.80	2116.99	2116.76

MONTHLY PAYMENT
REQUIRED TO AMORTIZE A LOAN

TERM	1 Year	2 Years	3 Years	4 Years	5 Years	6 Years	7 Years	8 Years	9 Years	10 Years	11 Years	12 Years	13 Years	14 Years
AMOUNT														
5	.48	.27	.21	.17	.15	.14	.13	.13	.12	.12	.12	.12	.12	.11
10	.96	.54	.41	.34	.30	.28	.26	.25	.24	.24	.23	.23	.23	.22
15	1.43	.81	.61	.51	.45	.41	.39	.37	.36	.35	.34	.34	.34	.33
25	2.39	1.35	1.01	.84	.75	.69	.65	.62	.60	.58	.57	.56	.56	.55
50	4.77	2.69	2.01	1.68	1.49	1.37	1.29	1.23	1.19	1.16	1.14	1.12	1.11	1.10
75	7.15	4.03	3.01	2.51	2.23	2.05	1.93	1.84	1.78	1.74	1.70	1.68	1.66	1.65
100	9.53	5.37	4.01	3.35	2.97	2.73	2.57	2.46	2.37	2.32	2.27	2.24	2.21	2.19
200	19.06	10.75	8.01	6.69	5.93	5.45	5.13	4.91	4.74	4.63	4.54	4.47	4.42	4.38
300	28.59	16.09	12.01	10.04	8.90	8.18	7.69	7.36	7.11	6.94	6.80	6.70	6.65	6.57
400	38.12	21.45	16.01	13.38	11.86	10.90	10.26	9.81	9.48	9.25	9.07	8.94	8.84	8.76
500	47.65	26.82	20.02	16.72	14.83	13.63	12.82	12.26	11.85	11.56	11.34	11.17	11.05	10.95
600	57.18	32.18	24.02	20.07	17.79	16.35	15.38	14.71	14.22	13.87	13.60	13.40	13.25	13.14
700	66.71	37.54	28.02	23.41	20.76	19.08	17.95	17.16	16.59	16.18	15.87	15.64	15.46	15.33
800	76.23	42.90	32.02	26.75	23.72	21.80	20.51	19.61	18.96	18.49	18.13	17.87	17.67	17.52
900	85.76	48.27	36.03	30.10	26.69	24.53	23.07	22.06	21.33	20.80	20.40	20.10	19.88	19.71
1000	95.29	53.63	40.03	33.44	29.65	27.25	25.64	24.51	23.70	23.11	22.67	22.34	22.09	21.89
2000	190.58	107.25	80.05	66.88	59.30	54.49	51.27	49.02	47.40	46.21	45.33	44.67	44.17	43.78
3000	285.87	160.87	120.08	100.31	88.94	81.74	76.90	73.52	71.09	69.31	67.99	67.00	66.25	65.67
4000	381.15	214.50	160.10	133.75	118.59	108.98	102.53	98.03	94.79	92.42	90.65	89.33	88.33	87.56
5000	476.44	268.12	200.13	167.19	148.23	136.23	128.17	122.53	118.48	115.52	113.32	111.66	110.41	109.45
6000	571.73	321.74	240.15	200.62	177.88	163.47	153.80	147.04	142.18	138.62	135.98	133.99	132.49	131.34
7000	667.01	375.36	280.18	234.06	207.52	190.72	179.43	171.54	165.88	161.72	158.64	156.32	154.57	153.23
8000	762.30	428.99	320.20	267.50	237.17	217.96	205.06	196.05	189.57	184.83	181.30	178.65	176.65	175.12
9000	857.59	482.61	360.23	300.93	266.81	245.21	230.69	220.55	213.27	207.93	203.96	200.99	198.73	197.01
10000	952.88	536.23	400.25	334.37	296.46	272.45	256.33	245.06	236.96	231.03	226.63	223.32	220.81	218.90
11000	1048.16	589.85	440.28	367.81	326.10	299.70	281.96	269.56	260.66	254.14	249.29	245.65	242.89	240.79
12000	1143.45	643.48	480.30	401.24	355.75	326.94	307.59	294.07	284.35	277.24	271.95	267.98	264.97	262.68
13000	1238.74	697.10	520.33	434.68	385.39	354.19	333.22	318.57	308.05	300.34	294.61	290.31	287.05	284.57
14000	1334.02	750.72	560.35	468.12	415.04	381.43	358.86	343.08	331.75	323.44	317.27	312.64	309.13	306.46
15000	1429.31	804.35	600.38	501.55	444.68	408.68	384.49	367.58	355.44	346.55	339.94	334.97	331.21	328.35
16000	1524.60	857.97	640.40	534.99	474.33	435.92	410.12	392.09	379.14	369.65	362.60	357.30	353.30	350.24
17000	1619.88	911.59	680.43	568.43	503.97	463.17	435.75	416.59	402.83	392.75	385.26	379.63	375.38	372.13
18000	1715.17	965.21	720.45	601.86	533.62	490.41	461.38	441.10	426.53	415.85	407.92	401.97	397.46	394.02
19000	1810.46	1018.84	760.48	635.30	563.26	517.66	487.02	465.60	450.22	438.96	430.59	424.30	419.54	415.91
20000	1905.75	1072.46	800.50	668.74	592.91	544.90	512.65	490.11	473.92	462.06	453.25	446.63	441.62	437.80
21000	2001.03	1126.08	840.52	702.17	622.55	572.15	538.28	514.61	497.62	485.16	475.91	468.96	463.70	459.69
22000	2096.32	1179.70	880.55	735.61	652.20	599.39	563.91	539.12	521.31	508.27	498.57	491.29	485.78	481.58
23000	2191.61	1233.33	920.57	769.05	681.84	626.64	589.55	563.62	545.01	531.37	521.23	513.62	507.86	503.47
24000	2286.89	1286.95	960.60	802.48	711.49	653.88	615.18	588.13	568.70	554.47	543.90	535.95	529.94	525.36
25000	2382.18	1340.57	1000.62	835.92	741.13	681.12	640.81	612.64	592.40	577.57	566.56	558.28	552.02	547.25
26000	2477.47	1394.20	1040.65	869.36	770.78	708.37	666.44	637.14	616.09	600.68	589.22	580.62	574.10	569.14
27000	2572.75	1447.82	1080.67	902.79	800.42	735.61	692.07	661.65	639.79	623.78	611.88	602.95	596.18	591.03
28000	2668.04	1501.44	1120.70	936.23	830.07	762.86	717.71	686.15	663.49	646.88	634.54	625.28	618.26	612.92
29000	2763.33	1555.06	1160.72	969.67	859.72	790.10	743.34	710.66	687.18	669.98	657.21	647.61	640.34	634.81
30000	2858.62	1608.69	1200.75	1003.10	889.36	817.35	768.97	735.16	710.88	693.09	679.87	669.94	662.42	656.70
31000	2953.90	1662.31	1240.77	1036.54	919.01	844.59	794.60	759.67	734.57	716.19	702.53	692.27	684.50	678.59
32000	3049.19	1715.93	1280.80	1069.98	948.65	871.84	820.24	784.17	758.27	739.29	725.19	714.60	706.59	700.48
33000	3144.48	1769.55	1320.82	1103.41	978.30	899.08	845.87	808.68	781.96	762.40	747.85	736.93	728.67	722.37
34000	3239.76	1823.18	1360.85	1136.85	1007.94	926.33	871.50	833.18	805.66	785.50	770.52	759.26	750.75	744.26
35000	3335.05	1876.80	1400.87	1170.29	1037.59	953.57	897.13	857.69	829.36	808.60	793.18	781.60	772.83	766.15
36000	3430.34	1930.42	1440.90	1203.72	1067.23	980.82	922.76	882.19	853.05	831.70	815.84	803.93	794.91	788.04
37000	3525.62	1984.05	1480.92	1237.16	1096.88	1008.06	948.40	906.70	876.75	854.81	838.50	826.26	816.99	809.93
38000	3620.91	2037.67	1520.95	1270.60	1126.52	1035.31	974.03	931.20	900.44	877.91	861.16	848.59	839.07	831.82
39000	3716.20	2091.29	1560.97	1304.03	1156.17	1062.55	999.66	955.71	924.14	901.01	883.83	870.92	861.15	853.71
40000	3811.49	2144.91	1600.99	1337.47	1185.81	1089.80	1025.29	980.21	947.83	924.11	906.49	893.25	883.23	875.60
41000	3906.77	2198.54	1641.02	1370.91	1215.46	1117.04	1050.93	1004.72	971.53	947.22	929.15	915.58	905.31	897.49
42000	4002.06	2252.16	1681.04	1404.34	1245.10	1144.29	1076.56	1029.22	995.23	970.32	951.81	937.91	927.39	919.38
43000	4097.35	2305.78	1721.07	1437.78	1274.75	1171.53	1102.19	1053.73	1018.92	993.42	974.48	960.25	949.47	941.27
44000	4192.63	2359.40	1761.09	1471.22	1304.39	1198.78	1127.82	1078.23	1042.62	1016.53	997.14	982.58	971.55	963.16
45000	4287.92	2413.03	1801.12	1504.65	1334.04	1226.02	1153.45	1102.74	1066.31	1039.63	1019.80	1004.91	993.63	985.05
46000	4383.21	2466.65	1841.14	1538.09	1363.68	1253.27	1179.09	1127.24	1090.01	1062.73	1042.46	1027.24	1015.71	1006.94
47000	4478.49	2520.27	1881.17	1571.53	1393.33	1280.51	1204.72	1151.75	1113.70	1085.83	1065.12	1049.57	1037.79	1028.83
48000	4573.78	2573.90	1921.19	1604.96	1422.97	1307.76	1230.35	1176.26	1137.40	1108.94	1087.79	1071.90	1059.88	1050.72
49000	4669.07	2627.52	1961.22	1638.40	1452.62	1335.00	1255.98	1200.76	1161.10	1132.04	1110.45	1094.23	1081.96	1072.61
50000	4764.36	2681.14	2001.24	1671.84	1482.26	1362.24	1281.61	1225.27	1184.79	1155.14	1133.11	1116.56	1104.04	1094.50
55000	5240.79	2949.25	2201.37	1839.02	1630.49	1498.47	1409.78	1347.79	1303.27	1270.66	1246.42	1228.22	1214.44	1203.94
60000	5717.23	3217.37	2401.49	2006.20	1778.72	1634.69	1537.94	1470.32	1421.75	1386.17	1359.73	1339.88	1324.84	1313.39
65000	6193.66	3485.48	2601.61	2173.38	1926.94	1770.92	1666.10	1592.84	1540.23	1501.68	1473.04	1451.53	1435.25	1422.84
70000	6670.10	3753.60	2801.74	2340.57	2075.17	1907.14	1794.25	1715.37	1658.71	1617.20	1586.35	1563.19	1545.65	1532.29
75000	7146.53	4021.71	3001.86	2507.75	2223.39	2043.36	1922.42	1837.90	1777.18	1732.71	1699.66	1674.84	1656.05	1641.74
80000	7622.97	4289.83	3201.98	2674.93	2371.62	2179.59	2050.58	1960.42	1895.66	1848.22	1812.97	1786.50	1766.46	1751.19
85000	8099.40	4557.94	3402.11	2842.12	2519.85	2315.81	2178.74	2082.95	2014.14	1963.74	1926.28	1898.15	1876.86	1860.64
90000	8575.84	4826.05	3602.23	3009.30	2668.07	2452.04	2306.90	2205.47	2132.62	2079.25	2039.59	2009.81	1987.26	1970.09
95000	9052.27	5094.16	3802.36	3176.48	2816.30	2588.26	2435.06	2328.00	2251.10	2194.77	2152.91	2121.47	2097.67	2079.54
100000	9528.71	5362.28	4002.48	3343.67	2964.52	2724.48	2563.22	2450.53	2369.58	2310.28	2266.22	2233.12	2208.07	2188.99

MONTHLY PAYMENT
REQUIRED TO AMORTIZE A LOAN

25.500%

TERM AMOUNT	15 Years	16 Years	17 Years	18 Years	19 Years	20 Years	21 Years	22 Years	23 Years	24 Years	25 Years	30 Years	35 Years	40 Years
5	.11	.11	.11	.11	.11	.11	.11	.11	.11	.11	.11	.11	.11	.11
10	.22	.22	.22	.22	.22	.22	.22	.22	.22	.22	.22	.22	.22	.22
15	.33	.33	.33	.33	.33	.33	.33	.32	.32	.32	.32	.32	.32	.32
25	.55	.55	.54	.54	.54	.54	.54	.54	.54	.54	.54	.54	.54	.54
50	1.09	1.09	1.08	1.08	1.08	1.07	1.07	1.07	1.07	1.07	1.07	1.07	1.07	1.07
75	1.64	1.63	1.62	1.62	1.61	1.61	1.61	1.60	1.60	1.60	1.60	1.60	1.60	1.60
100	2.18	2.17	2.16	2.15	2.15	2.14	2.14	2.14	2.14	2.13	2.13	2.13	2.13	2.13
200	4.35	4.33	4.31	4.30	4.29	4.28	4.28	4.27	4.27	4.26	4.26	4.26	4.26	4.26
300	6.53	6.49	6.47	6.45	6.43	6.42	6.41	6.40	6.40	6.39	6.39	6.38	6.38	6.38
400	8.70	8.66	8.62	8.60	8.58	8.56	8.55	8.54	8.53	8.52	8.52	8.51	8.51	8.51
500	10.88	10.82	10.78	10.74	10.72	10.70	10.68	10.67	10.66	10.65	10.65	10.64	10.63	10.63
600	13.05	12.98	12.93	12.89	12.86	12.84	12.82	12.80	12.79	12.78	12.78	12.76	12.76	12.76
700	15.23	15.15	15.09	15.04	15.00	14.98	14.95	14.94	14.93	14.91	14.91	14.89	14.88	14.88
800	17.40	17.31	17.24	17.19	17.15	17.12	17.09	17.07	17.06	17.04	17.04	17.01	17.01	17.01
900	19.57	19.47	19.40	19.34	19.29	19.25	19.23	19.20	19.19	19.17	19.16	19.14	19.13	19.13
1000	21.75	21.64	21.55	21.48	21.43	21.39	21.36	21.34	21.32	21.30	21.29	21.27	21.26	21.26
2000	43.49	43.27	43.10	42.96	42.86	42.78	42.72	42.67	42.63	42.60	42.58	42.53	42.51	42.51
3000	65.24	64.90	64.64	64.44	64.29	64.17	64.08	64.00	63.95	63.90	63.87	63.79	63.76	63.76
4000	86.98	86.53	86.19	85.92	85.71	85.56	85.43	85.34	85.26	85.20	85.16	85.05	85.02	85.01
5000	108.72	108.16	107.73	107.40	107.14	106.94	106.79	106.67	106.58	106.50	106.45	106.31	106.27	106.26
6000	130.47	129.80	129.28	128.88	128.57	128.33	128.15	128.00	127.89	127.80	127.74	127.57	127.52	127.51
7000	152.21	151.43	150.82	150.36	150.00	149.72	149.50	149.33	149.21	149.10	149.03	148.83	148.78	148.76
8000	173.96	173.06	172.37	171.84	171.42	171.11	170.86	170.67	170.52	170.40	170.32	170.09	170.03	170.01
9000	195.70	194.69	193.91	193.31	192.85	192.49	192.22	192.00	191.83	191.70	191.60	191.35	191.28	191.26
10000	217.44	216.32	215.46	214.79	214.28	213.88	213.57	213.33	213.15	213.00	212.89	212.61	212.54	212.51
11000	239.19	237.95	237.00	236.27	235.71	235.27	234.93	234.67	234.46	234.30	234.18	233.88	233.79	233.76
12000	260.93	259.59	258.55	257.75	257.13	256.66	256.29	256.00	255.78	255.60	255.47	255.14	255.04	255.02
13000	282.67	281.22	280.10	279.23	278.56	278.04	277.64	277.33	277.09	276.90	276.76	276.40	276.30	276.27
14000	304.42	302.85	301.64	300.71	299.99	299.43	299.00	298.66	298.41	298.20	298.05	297.66	297.55	297.52
15000	326.16	324.48	323.19	322.19	321.42	320.82	320.36	320.00	319.72	319.50	319.34	318.92	318.80	318.77
16000	347.91	346.11	344.73	343.67	342.84	342.21	341.71	341.33	341.03	340.80	340.63	340.18	340.05	340.02
17000	369.65	367.74	366.28	365.14	364.27	363.59	363.07	362.66	362.35	362.10	361.91	361.44	361.31	361.27
18000	391.39	389.38	387.82	386.62	385.70	384.98	384.43	384.00	383.66	383.40	383.20	382.70	382.56	382.52
19000	413.14	411.01	409.37	408.10	407.12	406.37	405.78	405.33	404.98	404.70	404.49	403.96	403.81	403.77
20000	434.88	432.64	430.91	429.58	428.55	427.76	427.14	426.66	426.29	426.00	425.78	425.22	425.07	425.02
21000	456.63	454.27	452.46	451.06	449.98	449.14	448.50	447.99	447.61	447.30	447.07	446.49	446.32	446.27
22000	478.37	475.90	474.00	472.54	471.41	470.53	469.85	469.33	468.92	468.60	468.36	467.75	467.57	467.52
23000	500.11	497.53	495.55	494.02	492.83	491.92	491.21	490.66	490.23	489.90	489.65	489.01	488.83	488.78
24000	521.86	519.17	517.09	515.50	514.26	513.31	512.57	511.99	511.55	511.20	510.94	510.27	510.08	510.03
25000	543.60	540.80	538.64	536.98	535.69	534.69	533.92	533.33	532.86	532.50	532.22	531.53	531.33	531.28
26000	565.34	562.43	560.19	558.45	557.12	556.08	555.28	554.66	554.18	553.80	553.51	552.79	552.59	552.53
27000	587.09	584.06	581.73	579.93	578.54	577.47	576.64	575.99	575.49	575.10	574.80	574.05	573.84	573.78
28000	608.83	605.69	603.28	601.41	599.97	598.86	597.99	597.32	596.80	596.40	596.09	595.31	595.09	595.03
29000	630.58	627.32	624.82	622.89	621.40	620.24	619.35	618.66	618.12	617.70	617.38	616.57	616.35	616.28
30000	652.32	648.96	646.37	644.37	642.83	641.63	640.71	639.99	639.43	639.00	638.67	637.83	637.60	637.53
31000	674.06	670.59	667.91	665.85	664.25	663.02	662.06	661.32	660.75	660.30	659.96	659.09	658.85	658.78
32000	695.81	692.22	689.46	687.33	685.68	684.41	683.42	682.66	682.06	681.60	681.25	680.36	680.10	680.03
33000	717.55	713.85	711.00	708.81	707.11	705.79	704.78	703.99	703.38	702.90	702.53	701.62	701.36	701.28
34000	739.29	735.48	732.55	730.28	728.54	727.18	726.13	725.32	724.69	724.20	723.82	722.88	722.61	722.53
35000	761.04	757.11	754.09	751.76	749.96	748.57	747.49	746.65	746.01	745.50	745.11	744.14	743.86	743.79
36000	782.78	778.75	775.64	773.24	771.39	769.96	768.85	767.99	767.32	766.80	766.40	765.40	765.12	765.04
37000	804.53	800.38	797.18	794.72	792.82	791.34	790.20	789.32	788.63	788.10	787.69	786.66	786.37	786.29
38000	826.27	822.01	818.73	816.20	814.24	812.73	811.56	810.65	809.95	809.40	808.98	807.92	807.62	807.54
39000	848.01	843.64	840.28	837.68	835.67	834.12	832.92	831.99	831.26	830.70	830.27	829.18	828.88	828.79
40000	869.76	865.27	861.82	859.16	857.10	855.51	854.27	853.32	852.58	852.00	851.56	850.44	850.13	850.04
41000	891.50	886.91	883.37	880.64	878.53	876.89	875.63	874.65	873.89	873.30	872.84	871.70	871.38	871.29
42000	913.25	908.54	904.91	902.12	899.95	898.28	896.99	895.98	895.21	894.60	894.13	892.97	892.64	892.54
43000	934.99	930.17	926.46	923.59	921.38	919.67	918.34	917.32	916.52	915.90	915.42	914.23	913.89	913.79
44000	956.73	951.80	948.00	945.07	942.81	941.06	939.70	938.65	937.83	937.20	936.71	935.49	935.14	935.04
45000	978.48	973.43	969.55	966.55	964.24	962.44	961.06	959.98	959.15	958.50	958.00	956.75	956.39	956.29
46000	1000.22	995.06	991.09	988.03	985.66	983.83	982.41	981.32	980.46	979.80	979.29	978.01	977.65	977.55
47000	1021.96	1016.70	1012.64	1009.51	1007.09	1005.22	1003.77	1002.65	1001.78	1001.10	1000.58	999.27	998.90	998.80
48000	1043.71	1038.33	1034.18	1030.99	1028.52	1026.61	1025.13	1023.98	1023.09	1022.40	1021.87	1020.53	1020.15	1020.05
49000	1065.45	1059.96	1055.73	1052.47	1049.95	1048.00	1046.48	1045.31	1044.41	1043.70	1043.15	1041.79	1041.41	1041.30
50000	1087.20	1081.59	1077.28	1073.95	1071.37	1069.38	1067.84	1066.65	1065.72	1065.00	1064.44	1063.05	1062.66	1062.55
55000	1195.91	1189.75	1185.00	1181.34	1178.51	1176.32	1174.62	1173.31	1172.29	1171.50	1170.89	1169.36	1168.93	1168.80
60000	1304.63	1297.91	1292.73	1288.73	1285.65	1283.26	1281.41	1279.97	1278.86	1278.00	1277.33	1275.66	1275.19	1275.06
65000	1413.35	1406.07	1400.46	1396.13	1392.78	1390.20	1388.19	1386.64	1385.43	1384.50	1383.78	1381.97	1381.46	1381.31
70000	1522.07	1514.22	1508.18	1503.52	1499.92	1497.13	1494.98	1493.30	1492.01	1491.00	1490.22	1488.27	1487.72	1487.57
75000	1630.79	1622.38	1615.91	1610.92	1607.06	1604.07	1601.76	1599.97	1598.58	1597.50	1596.66	1594.58	1593.99	1593.82
80000	1739.51	1730.54	1723.64	1718.31	1714.19	1711.01	1708.54	1706.63	1705.15	1704.00	1703.11	1700.88	1700.25	1700.08
85000	1848.23	1838.70	1831.36	1825.70	1821.33	1817.95	1815.33	1813.30	1811.72	1810.50	1809.55	1807.19	1806.52	1806.33
90000	1956.95	1946.86	1939.09	1933.10	1928.47	1924.88	1922.11	1919.96	1918.29	1917.00	1915.99	1913.49	1912.78	1912.58
95000	2065.67	2055.02	2046.82	2040.49	2035.60	2031.82	2028.89	2026.62	2024.86	2023.50	2022.44	2019.80	2019.05	2018.84
100000	2174.39	2163.18	2154.55	2147.89	2142.74	2138.76	2135.68	2133.29	2131.44	2130.00	2128.88	2126.10	2125.32	2125.09